Bartlett's
ROGET'S THESAURUS

Bartlett's
ROGET'S THESAURUS

LITTLE, BROWN AND COMPANY
Boston New York Toronto London

First Edition

Library of Congress Cataloging-in-Publication Data

Bartlett's Roget's thesaurus.
    p.   cm.
  Includes index.
  ISBN 0-316-10138-9
   1. English language — Synonyms and antonyms. I. Little, Brown and Company.
PE1591.B35 1996   96-18343
423' .1 — dc20

10 9 8 7 6 5 4 3 2 1

RM-KY

Designed by Caroline Hagen and Barbara Werden

Published simultaneously in Canada by Little, Brown & Company (Canada) Limited

PRINTED IN THE UNITED STATES OF AMERICA

Contents

ACKNOWLEDGMENTS

Chief Editor for *Bartlett's Roget's Thesaurus*
ELIZABETH WARD PITHA

Associate Editors
ANN GROMETSTEIN
PATRICIA BURKE HANSEN
KAY WYRTZEN MCMANUS
RANDALL GROMETSTEIN PUSTELL
SANDRA WRIGHT REINECKE
JEAN CROCKETT RITCHIE

At Little, Brown and Company
ROGER DONALD
CLIF GASKILL
CAROLINE HAGEN
TERESA LOCONTE
AMANDA MURRAY
DONNA PETERSON
BRYAN QUIBLE
MARY TONDORF-DICK

Typesetting by Market House Books
FRAN ALEXANDER
JOHN DAINTITH

The following experts, advisers, and consultants have been most generous in contributing to the book: Steve Bias, Carl Byington, Margaret Crockett Dickerman, William Hansen, Shirley Harwood, Daniel Harwood, Janice R. Herndon, Joseph Horner, Jennifer Jarvis, Justin Kaplan, Steven McManus, Sylvia Parker, Karen Patterson, Jacqueline Patterson, Carl Pitha, Robert Pitha, William Reinecke, Leland Nowell Ritchie, Alida Ward Schuchert, Douglass Shand-Tucci, Sheryl Silva, Dorothy Straight, David Travers, Harold N. Ward, Cecile Watters, Barbara Werden, Herman Wouk, and particularly Kathy Rooney of Bloomsbury Publishing Ltd.

Introduction

What Is a Thesaurus?

In 1852 Peter Mark Roget published a new type of reference book, which he called *A Thesaurus of English Words and Phrases, classified and arranged so as to facilitate the Expression of ideas and assist in Literary Composition.* What Roget had in mind was not a dictionary but a treasury of knowledge (the word *thesaurus* comes from the Greek word for treasure). A thesaurus came to mean a book that elaborated on variations of meanings, such as synonyms and almost-synonyms, in the English language.

Roget's work was immensely successful, and "Roget" has become a generic term for any book that supplies synonyms and antonyms, especially those in which the words are arranged thematically rather than in the A-to-Z form familiar from dictionaries and encyclopedias. More recently, *thesaurus* has been applied to any collection of words in a particular field, arranged or indexed for use in information processing. Many people use a thesaurus when writing in order to avoid Mark Twain's complaint "that the writer's balance at the vocabulary bank has run dry and he is too lazy to replenish it from the thesaurus."

Thesaurus versus Dictionary

The difference between a dictionary and a thesaurus is this: a dictionary provides information about a *word* by listing its meanings, whereas a thesaurus provides information about an *idea* by listing the range of words and phrases associated with it. A dictionary is organized alphabetically, and each entry is self-contained. A thesaurus, by contrast, generally is organized by subject or concept, and plentiful cross references help the user move from one topic to another. Thus the user may begin by searching for a synonym and end by exploring an entire range of related topics.

For example, the user might look up the entry "red" to be reminded of shades of red (crimson, scarlet, carnation, mauve), as well as of things that are typically red (blood, cherries, sunset, strawberries). Among the most useful features of a thesaurus are its functions as a guide to connotation and allusion and as an indicator of metaphors; it is interesting to note that a great many of our expressions in the English language are metaphorical. Thus a thesaurus extends not only one's vocabulary but also one's frame of reference and opens up networks that lead the user from synonyms for red through many types of red objects to figurative uses of red.

Our aim in producing a new thesaurus was to reflect the huge richness and variety of the English language today, as Roget did for his time. The classification system developed by Roget in the mid-nineteenth century was a magnificent creation, grouping words thematically into categories according to the ideas which they expressed. Roget's classification focused on abstract ideas, listing words under general headings such as "Relation," "Quantity," "Order." The world has changed since 1852, and Roget's abstract ideas are less relevant to the current *mise en scène.* Therefore, editors of later editions of Roget's thesaurus have created new categories to house the thousands of new words, objects, concepts, and phrases that have entered the language since then.

So the main motive behind the production of *Bartlett's Roget's Thesaurus* was to provide a thematic classification of the English language that would reflect today's proliferation of language and be as useful to modern-day readers as the original had been in the mid-nineteenth century.

Bartlett's Roget's Thesaurus

This new thesaurus was developed in Great Britain at Bloomsbury Publishing Ltd. There a team of expert lexicographers had the luxury of starting completely from scratch and working out the thematic organization. In contrast to Roget's intellectual abstractions, the categories and lists in *Bartlett's* reflect the world of computers, science, and technology, of television, new medicine, drugs, of fashion and postmodern culture. They represent as well the boom in sports and leisure activities, the worldwide spread of ethnic cuisines, the earth as a global village.

The editors in the United States refined the scope of the categories and the words and phrases to be included. Little, Brown determined that our edition would take into account the cultural and semantic differences between Great Britain and the United States and that *Bartlett's Roget's Thesaurus* would reflect more of our American English.

Given that we are surrounded by language, written and spoken — from hi-tech audio gizmos to TV advertising, from the proliferation of magazines to the latest paperback blockbuster, from junk mail to the Internet and on-line communication — it would not be practical, in a book of a useful size, to include every current word and phrase in the English language. So a selection was inevitable. It was based on usage, frequency of occurrence, and usefulness to the reader, focusing on contemporary English, including informal expressions and slang and occasionally the obsolete, obscure, and archaic. Since English is an international language, the book also contains many words and phrases from other parts of the English-speaking world, as well as foreign words and phrases that have become accepted in the language.

Organization

The thesaurus is divided into twenty-four general groups that follow a fairly logical order. Within each group there are categories that are related to the general group heading; see, for example, the group Foundations of Knowledge, which includes such categories as Anthropology, Sociology, History. Each category is divided according to the parts of speech — nouns, adjectives, verbs, adverbs, and occasionally interjections. These sections are subdivided into numbered paragraphs, headed by a keyword, corresponding to different aspects of the main idea. For example, at the noun section of the category Hope we have subdivided the noun into paragraphs introduced by the keywords **hope, expectation, aspiration, cheer,** and **hoper.** It is important for the user to know that all the words in each paragraph are not necessarily synonyms of the keyword, but they are all connected with it.

Within a paragraph words are, as far as possible, arranged in a logical order. We have not always given minor alternative spellings of a word, nor have we always provided the "-al" ending to adjectives that use that suffix, unless there is a significant difference in meaning, as, for example, "historic," "historical," "classic," "classical."

We have used many abbreviations in this book to help the reader know the terms that come from languages other than English, that are not formal, or that are archaic. (The list of abbreviations faces the first page of the text.) Terms that have come to be part of the English language, even though they are obviously not English in origin (for example, "amicus curiae," "au courant," "Doppelgänger"), are not labeled; those that appear in dictionaries in italics or in lists of foreign phrases are given in italics and labeled according to their origin. Some cultural terms are also so identified, as are archaic words.

Many words in the English language in common use are informal expressions, slang, vulgarisms, or outright obscenities. Censorship is long gone; words that no one would use in polite discourse or in writing were labeled as "taboo" in older thesauruses; and, of course, these words certainly were not included in Peter Roget's original book. We have felt compelled to include many of these terms, since they are encountered in current writing, television programs, and motion pictures, as well as in everyday speech. Slang is also a problem for the compilers of a thesaurus. Many slang terms are ephemeral; many endure. There are good compilations of American slang now available, but almost as soon as they appear they are, alas, out of date. We do not propose to house all the slang terms that have come into the language, but we have tried to include the more or less classic ones, as well as current informal terms that we think will endure.

To help the user of the thesaurus, we have labeled *all* informal expressions — slang, vulgarisms, and obscenities — with the appended abbreviation [Inf]. We have not labeled obscenities as such, but demeaning and offensive terms have the qualifying label [Off]. We acknowledge that these terms exist; we have reserved the right to make judgment calls in this area.

In many categories lists amplify the textual paragraphs. Here we have exercised a mini-encyclopedic purpose: to provide information that is not readily available in general reference books — for example, the French Republican Calendar at the category Timekeeping; the list of Children's Games and Party Games at the category Games, Pastimes, Amusements; the list of Imaginary Places at the category Imagination. There are many more. We hope the user will find these lists helpful, informative, and enlightening. Every term in the lists is indexed, and the lists are itemized by category beginning on page xxix.

Following many paragraphs are cross references to other categories; these are cited in book order with the category title and number. The user will find other related information at these entries.

Many categories are prefaced by quotations that illustrate one or more meanings of the words in the category. As Samuel Johnson said, "Every quotation contributes something to the stability or enlargement of the language"; and, as he might have noted, a certain juxtaposition of quotations can afford a great deal of amusement.

The Index

Roget said that most people who used his book start with the index. Unlike other thesauruses, which contain only selective indexes, *Bartlett's Roget's Thesaurus* indexes every occurrence of any word or phrase in the book, no matter how obscure the term or how long the phrase. Information on how to use both text and index follows this Introduction.

■

At the end of the twentieth century, there are many ways to deal with words and with language. The sturdy references for words, language, and knowledge — dictionaries, thesauruses, and encyclopedias — will endure, housed now on computer disks and in the ever-growing computer network as well as in books. We feel that the longest in durability will be the book, which one can hold, turn its pages, and examine the printed text. Our thesaurus has involved the compilation and classification of many thousands of words and the efforts of many people. We encourage you to browse through both the text and the index, on the premise that it not only will give you the information you require but also will provide you with a great deal of pleasure.

How to Use the Thesaurus

The Main Text

The text is divided into twenty-four large groups of related subjects: for example, Foundations of Knowledge; Living Things; Social Structure. Each group is divided into numbered main categories, and each category contains relevant words listed in order of part of speech: Nouns, Adjectives, Verbs, Adverbs (and occasionally Interjections). The categories are subdivided into numbered paragraphs, headed by a keyword or keywords in **boldface**, that group together words of similar meaning. Words that are related to the paragraph keyword but distinguish among various aspects of its meaning are separated within the paragraph by semicolons.

At the ends of many paragraphs you will find cross references to other categories that are related to the keyword or category you are consulting. These are introduced by an ornament and set in italics. The cross-referenced categories are arranged in the order in which they appear in the book. And at the beginning of many categories you will find quotations that illustrate some of the meanings of the words in the category.

Main category number and heading	**212 Sensation**
Quotation with author	*O for a Life of Sensations rather than of Thought!* — JOHN KEATS
Part of speech heading	**NOUNS**
Paragraph number and keyword	1 **sensation**, feeling, awareness, sentience, perception, experience,
Main paragraph text	· · ·
Cross reference	*Physical Pleasure 214*
Paragraph number and keyword	**2 sensitivity,** · · ·

A full list of the twenty-four groups and the categories in the order in which they appear begins on page xiii; an alphabetical list of the categories is given beginning on page xxi.

How to Use the Index

If you want to find a word or phrase, look for it first in the index. The order of words and phrases is strictly letter-by-letter, thus:

> **axed** [Inf]
> **Axel Heiberg Island**
> **axel jump**
> **axel lift**
> **axial**
> **axing**

Each word or phrase in the thesaurus text appears in the index and is set in **boldface**. All numbers in the index refer to category and paragraph. If an index entry is a keyword for a paragraph, it is followed by the particular category and paragraph number (or numbers) in boldface. Then the places where synonyms or other meanings of the keyword follow, given by category and paragraph number:

> *index entry, followed by category and paragraph*
> *numbers where the word is a keyword, followed by*
> *synonyms for the entry word*
> **absence 576.1, 718.6**; *invisibility* 245.1,
> *disappearance* 265.1, *desertion* 386.7

After this come phrases containing the keyword, with the category and paragraph numbers set in boldface when the phrase itself is a keyword, or with a synonym in italics and the category and paragraph number in roman:

> **absence of charge 497.6**
> **absence of dirt** *cleanliness* 111.1
> **absence of meaning** *lack of meaning* 362.1
> **absence of power** *powerlessness* 515.1
> **absence without leave (AWOL)** *desertion* 386.7

Every item in a list is indexed. The item is followed by the list name in roman type and the category number:

> **ablutophobia** Phobias 283
> **Abo** Nicknames for Inhabitants 61
> **Atlantic Ocean** Oceans and Seas 571

For phrases, especially adjectival and adverbial, you should look in the index at the article, preposition, or adverb that determines the phrase, not the noun. For example, the following phrases are indexed as shown:

> **as good as**
> **for heaven's sake**
> **in terms of**
> **in doubt**
> **my word**
> **not one's cup of tea**
> **so what**

We encourage you to scan the index thoroughly.

List of Categories

Power

Motivation 508
Operation 509
Counteraction 510
Instrumentality 511
Influence 512
Tendency 513
Power 514
Powerlessness 515
Strength 516
Weakness 517
Vigor 518
Inertness 519
Violence 520
Moderation 521
Production 522
Destruction 523

Material Characteristics

Material World 524
Nonmaterial World 525
Simplicity 526
Elegance 527
Inelegance 528
Beauty 529
Beautification 530
Ugliness 531
Decoration 532
Blemish 533
Refinement 534
Vulgarity 535
Fashion 536
Style 537
Heaviness 538
Lightness 539
Density 540
Sparseness 541
Hardness 542
Softness 543
Roughness 544
Smoothness 545
Elasticity 546
Toughness 547
Brittleness 548
Sharpness 549
Bluntness 550
Structure 551
Texture 552
Crumbliness, Powderiness 553

Friction 554
Fluid 555
Gas 556
Water 557
Air 558
Moisture 559
Dryness 560
Viscosity 561
Oiliness, Lubrication 562

Spatial Relations

Space 563
Region 564
Location 565
Country 566
Cities, Towns, and Villages 567
Lakes 568
Mountains and Hills 569
Rivers 570
Seas 571
Other Geographical Features 572
Situation 573
Displacement 574
Presence 575
Absence 576
Contents 577
Container 578
Size, Largeness 579
Littleness 580
Expansion 581
Contraction 582
Opening 583
Closure 584
Distance 585
Nearness 586
Interval 587
Layer 588
Measurement 589
Length 590
Shortness 591
Breadth 592
Narrowness 593
Thickness 594
Thinness 595
Height 596
Lowness 597
Depth 598

Shallowness 599
Summit 600
Base 601
Verticality 602
Horizontality 603
Suspension 604
Support 605
Parallelism 606
Obliqueness 607
Inversion 608
Interweaving 609
Exterior 610
Interior 611
Center 612
Covering 613
Uncovering 614
Surroundings 615
Interface 616
Outline 617
Edge 618
Enclosure 619
Limit 620
Front 621
Back 622
Side 623

Shape

Form 624
Shapelessness 625
Symmetry 626
Distortion 627
Angle 628
Curve 629
Straightness 630
Circularity 631
Convolution 632
Roundness 633
Convexity 634
Concavity 635
Notch 636
Fold 637
Furrow 638

Time

Time 639
Timelessness 640
Period 641
Duration 642
Transience 643

List of Categories

Alphabetical List of Categories

Alphabetical List of Categories

Alphabetical List of Categories

Directory of Lists

Bartlett's
ROGET'S THESAURUS

List of Abbreviations

Arch	Archaic
Aus	Australian
Brit	British
Can	Canadian
Chin	Chinese
Form	Formal
Fr	French
Ger	German
Gk	Greek
Heb	Hebrew
Inf	Informal (includes slang, obscenity)
Ir	Irish
Ital	Italian
L	Latin
Lit	Literary
Naut	Nautical
NZ	New Zealand
Off	Offensive
pl.	plural
Port	Portuguese
Russ	Russian
Scot	Scottish
S Afr	South African
Sp	Spanish
™	Trademark
US	United States

Foundations of Knowledge

1 Anthropology

Know then thyself, presume not God to scan / The proper study of Mankind is Man. — ALEXANDER POPE

NOUNS

1 **anthropology,** science of humankind, human studies, anthropogeny *or* anthropogenesis, anthropography, ethnology, ethnography, ethnogeny, ethnobotany, ethnomusicology, physical anthropology, somatology, biological anthropology, social anthropology, cultural anthropology, symbolic anthropology, economic anthropology, ethnoscientific studies, human geography, anthropogeography, demography, human ecology, behavioral science, anthropometry, craniometry, craniology
   ▶ *Sociology 2; Linguistics, Language 5; Life Science 13; Humankind 18; Economics 56; Psychology and Psychiatry 108*

2 **prehistoric anthropology,** paleoanthropology, archaeological anthropology, paleoanthropography, paleoethnography, paleoethnology, *etc.*
   ▶ *History 3; Humankind 18*

3 **anthropologist,** human scientist, ethnologist, ethnographer, ethnogenist, ethnomusicologist, anthropogeographer, demographer, human ecologist, behavioral scientist, anthropometrist, craniometrist, craniologer
   ▶ *Sociology 2; Linguistics, Language 5; Humankind 18; Psychology and Psychiatry 108*

4 **paleoanthropologist,** archaeological anthropologist, paleoethnographer, paleoethnologist, paleopsychologist, *etc.*; epigrapher, epigraphist
   ▶ *History 3; Humankind 18*

5 **race,** background, ethnic origin, color; Caucasoid race, Caucasian, White, Nordic type, Alpine type, Aryan, Latino; Negroid race, Negro, Black, Negrito, Negrillo, Nilotic type, Afro-Caribbean, African American, Afro-American, Anglo-African, Melanesian, Polynesian, Australasian; Mongoloid race, Oriental, Asian, Anglo-Indian; mixed race, mulatto, quadroon, octoroon, half-caste, half-breed; indigenous race, native, aborigine, Indian, Amerindian, Native American
   ▶ *Country 566*

6 **society,** people, nation, nationality, population, folk, tribe, clan, culture, community, race, ethnic group, strain, stock
   ▶ *Sociology 2; Humankind 18; Assembly 59; Country 566; Relatedness 727*

7 **tradition,** custom, habit, mores, praxis, ritual, rite, symbol, taboo, ancient wisdom, ways of the fathers, common law, immemorial wisdom, myth, archetypal myth, mythology, legend, lore, folklore, folk tale, folk motif, folk art, folk song, folk history, oral tradition, archetype, racial memory, tribal memory, collective unconscious
   ▶ *Burial 31; Marriage 64; Religion 81; Religious Ritual 85; Psychology and Psychiatry 108; Painting and Drawing 143; Memory 354; Habit, Custom 397; Celebration 405*

8 **physical type,** build, physique, phthisic build, linear build, apoplectic build, stocky build, somatotype, endomorphy, endomorph, mesomorphy, mesomorph, ectomorphy, ectomorph, brachycephaly, dolicocephaly

9 **measurement,** anthropometry, anthroscopy, biometrics, craniometry, osteology, osteometry, growth study, constitutional anthropology, height-weight ratio, Sheldon scale, skinfold, Bergmann's rule

ADJECTIVES

10 **anthropological,** anthropogenic, anthropographical, ethnological, ethnographic, ethnogenic, ethnoscientific, anthropogeographic, anthropogeographical, demographic, structuralist, functionalist, transactionalist, diffusionist, ecological, psychological, sociological, anatomical, anthropometric, anthropometrical, anthroposcopic, craniometric, craniometrical, craniological, osteometric

> *Sociology 2; Linguistics, Language 5; Humankind 18; Psychology and Psychiatry 108*

11 **paleoanthropological,** paleoanthropographic, paleoethnographic, paleoethnological, paleopsychological, epigraphic, epigraphical

> *History 3; Humankind 18*

12 **racial,** ethnic, Caucasian, Caucasoid, White, Nordic, Alpine, Aryan, Latino, Negroid, Black, Nilotic, Afro-Caribbean, Afro-American, Anglo-African, Melanesian, Polynesian, Australasian, Mongoloid, Oriental, Asian, Anglo-Indian, mixed, mulatto, quadroon, octoroon, indigenous, native, aboriginal, Indian, Amerindian, Native American

> *Country 566*

13 **societal,** communal, national, tribal, racial, ethnic, cultural, folk, established, time-honored, immemorial, traditional, customary, received, handed down, unwritten, oral, mythological, legendary, heroic, archetypal

14 **physical,** stocky, apoplectic, lightly built, phthisic, endomorphic, mesomorphic, ectomorphic, brachycephalic, dolicocephalic

ADVERBS

15 **anthropologically,** anthropographically, ethnologically, ethnographically, geographically, anthropogeographically, demographically, anthropometrically, craniometrically, craniologically

16 **paleoanthropologically,** paleoanthropographically, paleoethnographically, paleoethnologically, paleopsychologically, epigraphically

17 **societally,** nationally, communally, socially, tribally, racially, ethnically, culturally, traditionally, ritually, customarily, mythologically, mythically, archetypally, archetypically

2 Sociology

NOUNS

1 **sociology,** social science, behavioral science, social anthropology, rural sociology, urban sociology, sociobiology, political sociology, political behavior, social psychology, macrosociology, comparative macrosociology, social morphology, sociology of knowledge, comparative sociology, human ecology, cultural ecology, applied sociology, pragmatic sociology, demography

> *Anthropology 1; Psychology and Psychiatry 108; Knowledge 348*

2 **sociological research,** social survey, demography, demographic research, demographic survey, community study, population study, sociological theory, theory of social systems, role theory, locational theory, sociological method, sociometric technique, sociological model, sociological tool, questionnaire, survey, socio-

logical analysis, structural-functionalism, sociological perspective

3 **sociologist,** social scientist, empirical sociologist, sociobiologist, social psychologist, demographer, social worker, social reformer, economic determinist, Marxist

> *Philosophy 4; Economics 56*

4 **social environment,** society, social relations, interaction, social interaction, interpersonal relations, intercourse, human interaction, human communications, social contact, socialization, friendship, marriage, symbolic interaction, human social behavior, behavioral pattern, social trait, mores, values, value system, social role, sex role, social order, social differences

5 **social organization,** family, group, small group, primary group, family group, peer group, work group, ethnic group, racial group, age group, status group, group interaction, group behavior, group solidarity, community, clan, tribe, phyle, phratry, religious organization, political organization, industrial organization, social system, belief system, gemeinschaft, gesellschaft, society

> *Philosophy 4; Education 48; Government 49; Politics 50; Assembly 59; Friendship 62; Marriage 64; Family 65; Religion 81; Communications 169; Structure 551; Union 752; Order 765*

6 **society,** community, community relations, sense of community, social heterogeneity, homogeneity, collective adaptation, collectivity, mechanical solidarity, organic solidarity, rural sociology, rural society, folk society, rural sector, ruralism, rural-urban migration, urban society, urban sector, urban environment, urbanism, urbanization, suburbanization, urban planning, urban renewal, urban culture, industrialized society

> *Habitat 60; Inhabitant 61; Location 565*

7 **social stratification,** social pyramid, social hierarchy, pecking *or* peck order, hierarchy of authority, class boundary, social diversity, social status, prestige; economic status, economic power, educational status, employment status, earning status; class structure, social structure, social class, upper class, privileged class, ruling class, middle class, lower class, working class, underclass; class conflict, economic materialism, Marxism, social movement, mobility, social mobility, upward mobility, downward mobility

> *Economics 56; Power 514; Displacement 574; Changeableness 666; Class 777*

8 **social institution,** family, educational institution, school, religious institution, church, industrial institution, factory, political institution, political party, government institution, correctional institution

> *Education 48; Government 49; Politics 50; Labor Relations 57; Family 65; Religion 81; Punishment 454*

9 **social change,** social movement, social engineering,

social control, social planning, social transformation, human development, social progress, social obligation, social action, social policy, social benefit

10 **social services,** welfare, welfare organization, relief, social work, community service
> *Benevolence 305; Help 825*

ADJECTIVES

11 **sociological,** societal, social, behavioral, interactive, communal, communitywide, educational, religious, political, bureaucratic, military, environmental, sociobiological

12 **communal,** collective, organic, rural, rural-urban, urban, urbanized, urbanizing, industrial, industrialized, industrializing, governmental, correctional

13 **socioeconomic,** racial, occupational, economic, Marxist, privileged-class, ruling-class, upper-class, middle-class, lower-class, working-class, mobile, upward, downward, unequal, minority, communicative, productive, territorial, demographic(al), locational, structural-functional

VERBS

14 **socialize,** interact, communicate, contact, organize, form a community, have a sense of community, participate, mingle, intermingle, join in, live side by side, work together, employ, produce, improve living conditions, plan urban renewal, urbanize, industrialize, civilize, reform

ADVERBS

15 **sociologically,** socially, behaviorally, humanly, interactively, heterogeneously, collectively, symbolically, communally, educationally, religiously, politically, bureaucratically, governmentally, militarily, industrially, environmentally, sociobiologically, comparatively, culturally, pragmatically, ethnically, racially, economically, communicatively, socioeconomically, productively, territorially, demographically

3 History

The history of the world is but the biography of great men.
— THOMAS CARLYLE

History is more or less bunk. — HENRY FORD

History is past politics, and politics present history.
— JOHN ROBERT SEELEY

NOUNS

1 **history,** study of the past, record of the past; historiography, cliometrics, historical methodology, philosophy of history; chronicle, biography, archive, annals; past time, past age, epigraphy, archaeology
> *Past Time 651; Oldness 653*

2 **types of history,** social, economic, religious, political, constitutional, legal, local, revisionist, counterrevisionist; history of ideas, history of mathematics, history of science, historical materialism, Marxist history

3 **historian,** recorder, historiographer, cliometrician, chronicler, biographer, archivist, annalist, epigrapher, archaeologist

4 **chronicle,** history, account, record, recording, story, oral history; diary, journal, log, logbook, recollection; report, documentary, documentation, annals, archive; minutes, minute book, notes, case history; track record, file, dossier, background, summary; narrative, narration, description; tradition, legend, myth, folk tale, folk history

5 **biography,** biographical record, life story, autobiography, memoirs, memories, reminiscences, past, experiences; résumé, curriculum vitae *or* CV; obituary, necrology
> *Life 28; Information 170; Record 185; Memory 354*

6 **past time,** history, the past, yesterday, yesteryear, good old days, days of yore, days of old, olden days, old times, foretime, former times, bygone days, bygones, days gone by, long ago, auld lang syne, ancient history, ancient times, *ancien régime* [Fr], eld [Arch]; past age, dim and distant past, remote age, antiquity, time immemorial, way back when; prehistory, protohistory
> *Past Time 651; Oldness 653*

7 **historicism,** historical method, antiquarianism, medievalism; archaism; excavation, digging up the past, exhumation

8 **recollection,** remembering, remembrance, reminiscence, looking back, recalling, reviewing, harking back, nostalgia, flashback, déjà vu
> *Question 333; Memory 354*

9 **historicalness,** historicity, reality, realness, matter of fact, factualness, actuality, genuineness, authenticity, validity, fact, truth
> *Truth 721*

ADJECTIVES

10 **historical,** old, past, ancient, ancestral, archaeological, prehistoric, protohistoric, historic, historiographical, cliometric, diachronic, before the Flood, antediluvian; primordial, primal, aboriginal, antiquated, dated, archaic, former, prior, atavistic, vestigial, remaining, monumental; over, finished, bygone
> *Past Time 651; End 773*

11 **historic,** notable, famed, famous, renowned, memorable, classic
> *Importance 799*

12 **chronicled,** recorded, reported, logged, documented, archival, archived; minuted, filed; narrated, described, descriptive, related, told; traditional, legendary, mythical
> *Information 170; Evidence 339; Memory 354*

13 **biographical,** autobiographical; recollected, remembered, recalled

▶ *Memory 354*

14 **factual,** real, actual, authentic, genuine, valid, verifiable, true

▶ *Truth 721*

VERBS

15 **chronicle,** write history, record, keep a diary, log, register, report, document, minute, file, summarize; inform, tell, narrate, relate, describe

16 **recollect,** remember, recall, reminisce, review, hark back, call to mind; excavate, dig up the past, look back, trace back, exhume; turn back time, put the clock back, reconstruct, salvage

▶ *Memory 354; Uncovering 614; Past Time 651*

ADVERBS

17 **historically,** ancestrally, formerly; archaeologically, prehistorically, protohistorically, primordially, aboriginally, archaically, epigraphically; aforetime, hitherto, of old, of yore, ago, long ago, once, yesterday, yesteryear, in olden times, in the good old days, in the dim and distant past; from a historical perspective, retrospectively, until *or* till now

▶ *Memory 354; Time 639; Past Time 651; Originality 737; Precedence 769*

18 **biographically,** autobiographically, reminiscently, nostalgically; factually, authentically, really, actually, genuinely, validly, truly

▶ *Life 28; Information 170; Truth 721*

4 Philosophy

Philosophy . . . is our individual way of just seeing and feeling the total push and pressure of the cosmos.
— WILLIAM JAMES

Why is philosophy so complicated? It ought to be entirely simple. — LUDWIG WITTGENSTEIN

NOUNS

1 **philosophy,** viewpoint, point of view, outlook, attitude, opinion; doctrine, feeling, sentiment, idea, thought, notion, conclusion; judgment, tenet, dogma, principle; canon, maxim, axiom, aphorism, statement, assertion; proposition, premise, assumption, precept, presupposition, thesis, postulate, supposition, conjecture, speculation, philosophical speculation, hypothesis, philosophical theory; concept, explanation, theory of knowledge, rationalization, justification

▶ *Belief 87; Maxim 177; Feelings 266; Thought 317; Reason 319; Idea 327; Supposition 359*

2 **philosophical system,** belief system, set of beliefs *or* values, value system, value judgment, ethical system, ethos, morals, school of thought, code, moral code, code of practice, code of conduct, standards, principles, ideology, world view, *Weltanschauung* [Ger]; teaching, creed, credo, stance, position, manifesto

▶ *Religion 81; Belief 87; Feelings 266; Thought 317; Idea 327; Judgment 341; Supposition 359; Morality 431*

3 **philosophical attitude,** philosophicalness, detachment, disinterest, control, self-control, self-possession, self-restraint, dispassion, coolness, cool-headedness, calmness, imperturbability, composure, levelheadedness, reasonableness, common sense, rationality, lucidity, objectivity, equanimity, tolerance, balance, thoughtfulness, resignation

▶ *Indifference 289; Reason 319; Disinterestedness 443; Self-Restraint 455; Moderation 521*

4 **philosophical investigation,** inquiry *or* enquiry, examination, self-examination, introspection; analysis, consideration, scrutiny, investigation, search; survey, study, research, asking, challenge, questioning, speculation; reflection, reasoning, ratiocination, concentration, contemplation, cogitation, excogitation, heuristic; pondering, deliberation, musing, brainwork, conceptual thought, intuition, abstract thought, deduction, induction, inference

▶ *Wonder 294; Thought 317; Reason 319; Question 333; Supposition 359*

5 **philosophical argument,** discussion, dialogue, symposium, conversation, colloquy, debate, dialectic, syllogism, thesis, antithesis, synthesis, interlocution, disputation, argument, logomachy, polemic, eristic

▶ *Conversation 210; Argument 329; Sophistry 330*

6 **political and economic philosophy,** anarchism, Benthamism, capitalism, collectivism, communism, Hobbism, internationalism, isolationism, Keynesianism, Marxism, monetarism, nationalism, socialism, Spencerianism, syndicalism, utilitarianism, utopianism

▶ *Government 49; Politics 50*

7 **philosophical term,** analogy, antecedent, antithesis, argument ad hominem, argument a fortiori, argument a posteriori, argument a priori, argument from first principles, assertion sign, axiom, biconditional, bivalence, categorical proposition, conditional, conjunc-

---

BRANCHES OF PHILOSOPHY

aesthetics	philosophy of history
analytical philosophy	philosophy of language *or*
axiology	semantics
casuistry	philosophy of law
commonsense *or* naive	philosophy of mind
realism	philosophy of psychology
cosmology	philosophy of religion
deontology	philosophy of science
epistemology	philosophy of signs *or*
ethics *or* moral philosophy	semiotics
logic	political philosophy
metaphysics	sentential *or* propositional
natural philosophy	calculus
ontology	teleology
phenomenology	theology

tion, contingent truth, counterexample, counterfactual, deduction, dialectic, dichotomy, disjunction, elenchus, equivalence, function, gestalt, Hume's Law, hypothesis, identity, imperative, inference, Leibniz's Law, major premise *or* term, minor premise *or* term, modality, necessary truth, necessity, negation, non sequitur, noumenon, Ockham's *or* Occam's razor, operator, paradox, postulate, probability, quantifier, reductio ad absurdum, reference, salva veritate, sense, sense data, sensibilia, subaltern proposition, syllogism, synthesis, tautology, thesis, truth condition, truth function, truth table, truth value, utility principle, value judgment, verification principle

▶ *Mathematics 6*

8 **philosophical problem,** existence of God, a priori knowledge, nature of meaning, referential failure, (radical) indeterminacy of meaning, undistributed middle, antiprivate-language argument, speech-act theory, artificial intelligence, mental entities, mind-body problem, other minds, personal identity, free will, volition, predestination, categorical imperative, transcendental argument, weakness of will, moral relativism, contract theory of morality, primary quality, secondary quality, category mistake, causal theory of perception, first cause, cause and effect, possible worlds, nature of time, beginning of time, end of time, time-travel paradox, Barber paradox, paradox of the

PHILOSOPHICAL SCHOOLS OF THOUGHT AND THEIR FOLLOWERS

aestheticism; aesthete *or* aesthetic
agnosticism; agnostic
ahimsa
altruism; altruist
animism; animist
antirealism; antirealist
apriorism; apriorist
Aristotelian philosophy *or* Aristotelianism; Aristotelian
atomism; atomist
Augustinian philosophy *or* Augustinianism; Augustinian
Averroism; Averroist
Baconism; Baconian
Benthamism; Benthamite
Bergsonism; Bergsonian
Berkeleyism; Berkeleyan
Cartesianism; Cartesian
Comtism; Comtist
conceptualism; conceptualist
conceptual realism; conceptual realist
Confucianism; Confucian
consequentialism; consequentalist
contextualism; contextualist
Cynicism; cynic
Cyrenaic philosophy; Cyrenaic
deconstructionism; deconstructionist
deism; deist
descriptivism; descriptivist
determinism; determinist
dialectical materialism; dialectical materialist
dualism; dualist
dynamism; dynamist

egoism; egoist
Eleaticism; Eleaticist
emotivism; emotivist
empiricism; empiricist
Epicureanism; Epicurean
epiphenomenalism; epiphenomenalist
eristic school; eristic
essentialism; essentialist
eudemonism; eudemonist
euhemerism; euhemerist
existentialism; existentialist
fatalism; fatalist
Fichteanism; Fichtean
Fregeanism; Fregean
functionalism; functionalist
gnosticism; gnostic
hedonism; hedonist
Hegelianism; Hegelian
Heracliteanism; Heraclitean
Hobbism; Hobbesean
holism; holist
humanism; humanist
Humism; Humist
hylomorphism; hylomorphist
hylotheism; hylotheist
hylozoism; hylozoist
idealism; idealist
immaterialism; immaterialist
individualism; individualist
instrumentalism; instrumentalist
intuitionism; intuitionist
Kantianism; Kantian
Kierkegaardianism; Kierkegaardian
Leibnizianism; Leibnizian
linguistic analysis *or* ordinary-language philosophy *or* philosophical analysis; linguistic analyst

logical positivism *or* empiricism; logical positivist, empiricist
Lokayata; Lokayatika
materialism; materialist
mechanism; mechanist
mentalism; mentalist
Mimamsa; Mimamsan
Modernism; modernist
monism; monist
mysticism; mystic
naturalism; naturalist
Neoplatonism; Neoplatonist
Nietzscheism *or* Nietzscheanism; Nietzschean
nihilism; nihilist
nominalism; nominalist
noumenalism; noumenalist
Nyaya; Nyayan
objectivism; objectivist
occasionalism; occasionalist
ontologism; ontologist
optimism; optimist
organicism; organicist
panlogism; panlogist
pantheism; pantheist
Peripateticism *or* Aristotelianism; Peripatetic
personalism; personalist
pessimism; pessimist
phenomenalism; phenomenalist
phenomenology; phenomenologist
physicalism; physicalist
Platonism; Platonist
pluralism; pluralist
positivism; positivist
pragmatism; pragmatist
probabilism; probabilist

Pyrrhonism; Pyrrhonist
Pythagoreanism; Pythagorean
rationalism; rationalist
realism; realist
reductionism *or* reductivism; reductionist *or* reductivist
relativism; relativist
Sankhya *or* Samkhya; Sankhyan
Satyagraha; Satyagrahi
Schellingism; Schellingist
Scholasticism; Scholastic
Schopenhauerism; Schopenhauerean
Scotism; Scotist
secular humanism; secular humanist
sensationalism; sensationalist
skepticism; skeptic
Socratic philosophy; Socratic
solipsism; solipsist
Spinozism; Spinozist
Stoicism; Stoic
structuralism; structuralist
subjectivism; subjectivist
substantialism; substantialist
Taoism; Taoist
theism; theist
Thomism; Thomist
transcendentalism; transcendentalist
Vaisheshika; Vaisheshikan
vitalism; vitalist
Wittgensteinianism; Wittgensteinian
yoga; yogi

unexpected hanging, Zeno's paradoxes, Russell's paradox, Richard's paradox, Schrödinger's cat
> *Mathematics 6; Physics 10; Religion 81; Wonder 294; Thought 317; Idea 327; Question 333; Morality 431; Nonmaterial World 525; Existence 717*

9 **philosopher,** thinker, logician, dialectician, sophist, syllogist, metaphysician, cosmologist; moralist, theorist, theoretician, theorizer, speculator, hypothesizer, surmiser, investigator, inquirer, asker, seeker, searcher, dreamer, idealist, ideologue, visionary
> *Intellect 315; Reason 319; Question 333; Wisdom 352*

10 **political and economic philosopher,** anarchist, anarcho-syndicalist, capitalist, collectivist, communist, internationalist, isolationist, Keynesian, Marxist, monetarist, nationalist, pacifist, socialist, syndicalist, utilitarian, utopian
> *Government 49; Politics 50; Economics 56*

11 **sage,** wise man, wise woman, savant, academic, intellectual, highbrow, pundit, expert, genius, authority, consultant, counselor, adviser, mentor, teacher, tutor, guru, nobody's fool, Socrates, Nestor, Solon, Solomon
> *Authority 52; Intellect 315; Wisdom 352*

ADJECTIVES

12 **philosophical,** notional, abstract, esoteric, ideological, moral, ethical, normative, prescriptive, idiographic, nomothetic, descriptive, conceptual, conceptive, ideal, ideational, visionary, metaphysical, hypothetical, theoretical, conjectural, speculative, unapplied, impractical
> *Intellect 315; Thought 317; Idea 327; Supposition 359*

13 **of a philosophy,** aesthetic, agnostic, altruistic, animistic, *etc.*

14 **of a political philosophy,** anarchic, anarcho-syndicalist, capitalist, collectivistic, communist, Keynesian, Marxist, monetarist, nationalist, nationalistic, pacifist, socialist, socialistic, syndicalistic, utilitarian, utopian

15 **rational,** reasoned, reasonable, philosophical, logical, objective, impartial, sound, sensible, plausible, practical, pragmatic, down-to-earth, matter-of-fact, nononsense, commonsensical, realistic, ratiocinative, clearheaded, lucid, well-thought-out, well-reasoned, judicious, discriminating
> *Intellect 315; Reason 319; Discrimination 337; Judgment 341*

16 **dialectical,** cogent, analytic, deictic, apodeictic, aporetic, elenchic, a priori, a posteriori, a fortiori, synthetic, dyadic, monadic, polyadic, heuristic

17 **thoughtful,** attentive, studious, studying, concentrated, concentrating, thinking, meditative, cogitative, contemplative, reflective, in a brown study, ruminant, ruminative, deliberative, speculative, musing, pensive, absorbed, lost in thought, introspective, dreaming, brooding, preoccupied
> *Wonder 294; Intellect 315; Thought 317; Idea 327; Supposition 359*

18 **detached,** disinterested, unaffected, unemotional, unperturbed, imperturbable, undisturbed, unruffled, unshaken, unconcerned, dispassionate, unimpassioned, cool, cool-headed, pragmatic, sober, calm, collected, composed, levelheaded, equable, equanimous, tolerant, controlled, temperate, moderate, self-controlled, self-possessed, self-restrained, restrained, stoical, resigned, patient, enduring, steady, even-tempered, good-tempered, serene, tranquil, placid, pacific
> *Sobriety 120; Indifference 289; Inactivity 415; Disinterestedness 443; Self-Restraint 455; Moderation 521*

VERBS

19 **philosophize,** think about, speculate, conjecture, postulate, suppose, hypothesize, surmise, consider, conceptualize, visualize, contemplate, cogitate, excogitate, ratiocinate, reason, ruminate, reflect, deliberate, ponder, muse, wonder, challenge, analyze, examine, explore, look into, scrutinize, observe, survey, study, research, investigate, question, query, inquire *or* enquire, ask, seek, search, introspect
> *Intellect 315; Thought 317; Reason 319; Idea 327; Supposition 359*

20 **rationalize,** philosophize, reason, think through, think out, syllogize, intellectualize, interpret, construe, deduce, infer, work out, evaluate, unscramble, solve, resolve, figure out, calculate, compute, answer, fathom, understand, apprehend, realize, comprehend, follow, grasp, take to mean, take it that, read, define, expound, explicate, explain, elucidate, unfold, clarify, spell out, account for, clear up, make clear, illuminate, demonstrate, show, illustrate, exemplify, justify, vindicate, show sufficient grounds for
> *Thought 317; Answer 334; Judgment 341; Supposition 359; Meaning 361*

21 **propound a philosophy,** state, assert, put forward, propose, expound, aphorize, set forth, pose, posit, lay down; profess, pronounce, moralize, preach, sermonize, declare, proclaim; show, exhibit, demonstrate, espouse a theory; support, maintain, assume, presume, premise, suppose, postulate; judge, feel, conclude; deem, consider, tend to, be disposed to, opine, be of the opinion, hold an opinion; believe in, subscribe to, adhere to, follow, belong to a school of thought; view, take the attitude
> *Religion 81; Belief 87; Feelings 266; Thought 317; Reason 319; Demonstration 331; Judgment 341; Supposition 359*

22 **discuss,** debate, exchange ideas, colloquize, engage in dialectic, analyze, comment on, criticize, argue, logomachize, polemicize, contend, contest, dispute, dissent, refute, answer, respond, negate, contradict, deny, counter
> *Argument 329; Sophistry 330; Question 333; Judgment 341*

23 philosophically, intellectually, logically, analytically, deductively, dialectically, sophistically, metaphysically, argumentatively, polemically, rhetorically, epistemologically, axiologically, ontologically, phenomenologically, semantically, categorically

24 theoretically, notionally, ideally, academically, conceptually, abstractly, in the abstract, esoterically, idealistically, ideologically, morally, ethically, moralistically, proverbially, purportedly, as they say, supposedly, reputedly, seemingly, speculatively, hypothetically, ex hypothesi, assumptively, presumingly, presumptively, on the assumption that

25 rationally, philosophically, objectively, impartially, fairly, reasonably, logically, realistically, pragmatically, practically, sensibly, plausibly, lucidly, soundly, justifiably
◗ *Reason 319*

26 stoically, philosophically, dispassionately, imperturbably, restrainedly, moderately, temperately, soberly, coolly, calmly, composedly, unemotionally, equably, fairly, patiently, enduringly, resignedly, passively, quietly, serenely, placidly
◗ *Indifference 289; Moderation 521*

27 thoughtfully, studiously, attentively, carefully, meditatively, ruminatively, cogitatively, reflectively, contemplatively, deliberatively, introspectively, pensively

28 wisely, knowledgeably, expertly, authoritatively, advisably, advisedly, profoundly, deeply, inspirationally, inspiringly, discriminatingly, judiciously, judgmentally
◗ *Intellect 315; Wisdom 352*

5 Linguistics, Language

NOUNS

1 linguistics, linguistic science, science of language, glossology [Arch]

2 linguistic theory, Grimm's law, Verner's law; bow-wow theory, ding-dong theory, pooh-pooh theory, Sapir-Whorf hypothesis, Great Vowel Shift, transformational grammar, generative grammar

3 linguist, linguistic scholar, language student, linguistician, linguistic scientist, linguistic analyst; etymologist, grammarian, grammatist, phonetician, lexicographer, lexicologist, morphologist, orthographer, semanticist, paleographer, translator; bilingual, multilingual, polyglot; lover of language, philologist, logophile

4 language, tongue, phraseology, speech, use of words, locution, terminology, nomenclature, politically correct language; etymology, grammar, syntax, lexicography; spoken language, phonetics; written language, spelling, orthography; love of language, philology
◗ *Speech, Spoken Language 205*

5 native language, native tongue, mother tongue, par-

ent language, national language, regional language, dialect, patois, basic English

6 standard language, standard usage, official language, correct speech, formal language, written language, literary language; good English, queen's *or* king's English

7 nonstandard language, personal language, colloquial language, dialect, idiolect; body language, body English, gesture, signal, code, semiotics; baby talk, empty phrase, empty talk; substandard language, substandard usage, vulgarism, barbarism, obscenity, scatology; gobbledegook, babble, jabber, gibberish, glossolalia; slang, argot, lingo
◗ *Speech, Spoken Language 205; Curse 301; Lack of Meaning 362; Unintelligibility 364; Vulgarity 535*

8 international language, lingua franca, pidgin, Creole, koine, auxiliary language, diplomatic language, business language, trade language, Esperanto; language *or* linguistic universal

9 artificial language, sign language *or* sign, semaphore, code, Morse code, cryptography, cryptanalysis; computer language, data-processing language, assembly language; shorthand, phraseogram, phraseograph, stenography, stenotypy; American Sign Language *or* ASL *or* Ameslan
◗ *Computers 15; Sign 183; Deafness 229*

10 ancient language, archaism, archaic speech, classical language, dead language, lost language

11 language type, affixing, agglutinative, analytic, fusional, incorporative, inflectional, isolating, monosyllabic, polysyllabic, polysynthetic, polytonic, symbolic, synthetic, tonal

12 language family, language group, regional language;

LINGUISTIC STUDIES

anthropological linguistics	grammatology	orthoepy
applied linguistics	graphemics	paleography
comparative linguistics	historical *or* diachronic linguistics	philology
computational *or* mathematical linguistics	lexicography	phonemics
	lexicology	phonetics
	lexicostatistics	phonography
contrastive linguistics	linguistic analysis *or* ordinary-language philosophy *or* philosophical analysis	phonology
descriptive *or* synchronic linguistics		pragmatics
		psycholinguistics
dialect geography	morphology	semantics
dialectology	morphophonemics *or* morpho-phonology	semasiology
etymology		semiotics
general linguistics	nomenclature	sociolinguistics
general semantics	onomasiology	structuralism *or* structural linguistics
geolinguistics	onomastics *or* onomatology	stylistics
glossematics		syntactics
glottochronology		syntax
grammar		tagmemics
		typology

Indo-European: Indo-Iranian, Anatolian, Hellenic, Tocharian, Italic, Celtic, Germanic, Baltic, Slavic; Finno-Ugric; Afroasiatic *or* Hamito-Semitic; Sino-Tibetan; Austronesian

13 **language element,** letter, alphabet, word, phrase; grammar, part of speech, syntax; morpheme, phoneme, grapheme, sememe

14 **written letter,** writing, lexigraphy, lettering, print, printing, type, handwriting, cursive writing, penmanship, calligraphy; scribble, scrawl; symbol, character, written character, grapheme, digraph, phonetic symbol; sign, ideogram *or* ideograph, pictograph *or* pictogram, cuneiform, hieroglyphic *or* hieroglyph, rune, runic letter, Chinese character, kanji, Nagari; wynne *or* wen; initial, monogram
   ▶ *Information 170; Sign 183*

15 **spoken letter,** speech sound, phone, phonogram, phoneme, syllable, vowel, consonant, voiced consonant, guttural consonant, guttural, nasal, frictionless continuant, labial, labiodental, labionasal, liquid, spirant, sibilant, aspirate, glottal stop, fricative, sonant, polyphone, digraph, diphthong; stress, pitch, inflection
   ▶ *Emphasis 200; Speech, Spoken Language 205*

16 **alphabet,** ABC *or* ABCs; runic alphabet, futhark *or* futharc; ogham *or* ogam alphabet; phonetic alphabet, Initial Teaching Alphabet (i.t.a. *or* I.T.A.), International Phonetic Alphabet (IPA); syllabary; transliteration, pinyin, Wade-Giles

17 **word,** written unit, spoken unit, term, name; long word, polysyllable, sesquipedalian; short word, monosyllable, one-syllable word, easy word; rhyming word, echoic word, onomatopoeic word; hard word, difficult word, jawbreaker [Inf]; doublet, palindrome, pejorative, holophrase, intensive; synonym, cognate word, cognate, paronym, metonym, antonym; homonym, homograph, homophone; word meaning, definition, denotation, connotation; word formation, stem, root, etymon, prefix, suffix, proclitic, enclitic; back formation, clipped form *or* word; supply of words, vocabulary; word error: solecism, malapropism, spoonerism
   ▶ *Error 351; Meaning 361; Interpretation 365*

18 **new word,** new term, neologism *or* neology, coinage, unfamiliar word, newfangled expression, nonce word; loanword, loanshift, loan translation, calque, borrowed word, imported word; hybrid word *or* expression, hybrid, ghost word

19 **slang,** slang term *or* word, back slang [Brit], rhyming slang, dog Latin, pig Latin

20 **vulgarism,** swearword, taboo word, naughty word, bad word, rude word, obscenity, expletive, four-letter word; vulgar language, low language, obscene language, coprolalia, billingsgate, scatology *or* coprology
   ▶ *Curse 301; Vulgarity 535*

21 **jargon,** officialese, legalese, journalese, newspeak, telegraphese, technical word, technical term, technospeak, argot, cant, patter, lingo, psychobabble
   ▶ *Computers 15*

22 **catchword,** counterword, cliché, vogue word, catchphrase, portmanteau word, acronym; well-worn phrase, commonplace, hackneyed expression, maxim, adage, moral, proverb, quotation, slogan, motto, buzzword, quote, sound bite
   ▶ *Maxim 177*

23 **wordiness,** verbiage, verbosity, loquacity, pleonasm, tautology; equivocation, equivocalness, double-talk
   ▶ *Talkativeness 207; Sophistry 330; Equivocation 380*

24 **dialect,** idiom, patois, regionism, provincialism, vernacular
   ▶ *Speech, Spoken Language 205; Mixture 751*

25 **phrasing,** phraseology, choice of words, wording, structure, turn of phrase, well-turned phrase, choice of expression, turn of expression, fixed expression, set phrase, set terms; verbalism, locution, trope, metaphor, simile, complimentary phrase, elegant phrase, elegance, roundabout phrase, circumlocution, periphrasis, diffuseness, paraphrase, translation
   ▶ *Literature 139; Interpretation 365; Elegance 527*

26 **spelling,** orthography, orthographic convention; spelling game, spelling bee, crossword puzzle, anagram, anagrammatism, acrostic; spelling pronunciation, phonetic spelling; incorrect spelling, misspelling, cacography
   ▶ *Error 351; Right 429; Rule 780*

27 **word book,** dictionary, unabridged dictionary, lexicon; antonym dictionary, children's dictionary, concise *or* compact *or* abridged dictionary, concordance, desk dictionary, foreign language dictionary, general dictionary, reverse word dictionary, rhyming dictionary, school *or* college dictionary, slang dictionary, synonym dictionary, thesaurus; biographical dictionary, dictionary of names, dictionary of quotations, dictionary of dialects, glossary, gloss, gradus; storehouse *or* treasury of words; lexicography
   ▶ *Publication 173; Books 174*

28 **grammar,** sentence structure, rules of language; grammatical rules, grammaticalness, formal language, formal usage, structural linguistics; good grammar, good English, Standard English, correct English, traditional grammar, descriptive grammar, structural grammar, surface structure, shallow structure, deep structure, underlying structure; systemic grammar, case grammar, phrase-structure grammar, transformational grammar, transformation-generative grammar, bad grammar, incorrect usage
   ▶ *Error 351; Wrong 430*

29 **grammatical term,** number, singular, plural, collective; gender, masculine, feminine, neuter; inflection, declension, conjugation; case: nominative, vocative, genitive, possessive, dative, accusative, ablative, ob-

jective, locative; voice: active, middle, passive; mood: indicative, subjunctive, optative, imperative, jussive, infinitive; tense: present, present perfect, future, future perfect, past, imperfect, preterit, *passé composé* [Fr], past perfect, aorist, pluperfect, conditional, historical present, past historic; immediate constituent

30 part of speech, noun, common noun, proper noun, collective noun, substantive, gerund; pronoun; adjective; verb, predicate, reflexive verb, transitive verb, intransitive verb; participle, present participle, past participle, perfect participle; adverb, preposition, copula, conjunction, subordinating conjunction, coordinating conjunction, interjection, subject, object, direct object, indirect object; complement, modifier, article, definite article, indefinite article, particle, affix, prefix, infix, suffix, inflection, formative; semanteme, diminutive, intensive, augmentative, root, etymon, stem

31 clause, noun clause *or* phrase, verb clause *or* phrase, adverbial clause *or* phrase, adjectival clause *or* phrase, prepositional phrase *or* clause, conditional phrase *or* clause, ablative absolute; independent clause, coordinate clause, subordinate clause; indirect question; sentence, formula

32 syntax, word order, syntactic structure, syntactic meaning, syntactic analysis; agreement, paradigm, comparative grammar, grammatical studies, grammatical analysis, parsing, construing; punctuation, accentuation, gradation, attraction, assimilation, dissimilation, hypotaxis, parataxis, syndeton, asyndeton, ellipsis, apposition; faulty syntax
  ▶ *Accuracy 350; Structure 551*

33 language sign, accent, diacritical mark, punctuation mark, reference sign

ADJECTIVES

34 linguistic, lingual, bilingual, multilingual, polyglot, glossological [Arch]; applied, comparative, computational *or* mathematical, contrastive, descriptive *or* synchronic, *etc.*

35 of language, written, spoken, living, parent, native, mother, national, regional, educated, pure, correct, standard, official, formal, literary, politically correct; informal, common, vernacular, colloquial, conversational, childish, holophrastic, personal; dialectal; informal, slang, slangy, jargonistic, jargonal, jargonish; journalistic, jingoistic, everyday, idiomatic; nonstandard, low, rude, vulgar, scatological, blasphemous, four-letter, obscene, substandard, uneducated, illiterate; ancient, classical, artificial; inflected, affixing, analytic, agglutinative, polysynthetic, monosyllabic, polysyllabic, symbolic, tonal, polytonic

36 written, lettered, literal, graphical, printed, typed, handwritten; symbolical, alphabetical, phonogramic, phonographic, pictographic, ideographic, cuneiform, cuneal, hieroglyphical, transliterated
  ▶ *Publication 173; Interpretation 365*

37 voiced, spoken, pronounced, vocal, vocalic, consonantal, guttural, burring, frictionless, liquid, labial, nasal, spirant, sibilant, fricative, sonant, polyphonic, polyphonous, digraphic
  ▶ *Speech, Spoken Language 205*

38 worded, wording, verbal, vocabular, lexical, glossarial, named, synonymical, cognate, paronymic *or* paronymous, antonymous, homonymic *or* homonymous, homographic, homophonic, tautonymic *or* tautonymous; palindromic, root, back-formed; clipped, morphological, inflectional, meaningful, enclitic, pejorative, intensive, sesquipedalian; neologistical *or* neological, newfangled, coined; rhyming, echoic, onomatopoeic; argotic, canting, cant, portmanteau, cliché *or* clichéd, proverbial, commonplace, well-worn, hackneyed, redundant; vogue; pleonastic, wordy, verbose, loquacious, equivocal, pretentious; archaic, obsolete, barbarous *or* barbaric, corrupted, cacographical

39 phrased, phrasal, phrasing, phraseological, clausal, sentential, collocated, collocating, surface, deep, rounded, well-turned, well-rounded, fixed, set, locutionary; metaphorical, complimentary, elegant; roundabout, circumlocutory, periphrastic, diffuse, paraphrastic, paraphrased, paraphrasing, translated, translating, translatable, phraseographic, inscribed, lapidary, epitaphic

40 orthographic, spelled

41 of grammar, grammatical, structural, descriptive, systemic, transformational, transformational-generative, syntactic, diacritical, substantive, pronominal, adjecti-

---

PUNCTUATION MARKS

ampersand, **&**	guillemets, « »
angle brackets, <>	hyphen, -
apostrophe, '	parentheses *or* parens [Inf], ( )
brackets *or* square brackets, **[ ]**	period *or* point *or* decimal
colon, :	point *or* full stop [Brit], .
comma, ,	question mark *or* interrogation
curly braces, **{ }**	mark *or* point, ?
em dash, —	quotation marks *or* quotes, " "
en dash, –	semicolon, ;
ellipsis *or* suspension points, …	single quotation *or* quote
exclamation mark *or*	mark, ' '
exclamation point *or*	virgule *or* diagonal *or* slash *or*
screamer [Inf] *or* bang [Inf], !	solidus, /

COMMON ACCENTS AND DIACRITICAL MARKS

acute accent, é	ligature, æ
breve *or* caron, ĕ	macron, ū
cedilla, ç	rough breathing, 'o
circumflex, ô	schwa, ə
diaresis *or* umlaut, ü	slash, ø
grave accent, è	stroke, Ł
haček *or* wedge, š	tilde, ñ
krožek, å	

---

val, verbal, predicate, copular, reflexive, transitive, intransitive, regular, irregular; heteroclite *or* heteroclitic, participial, adverbial; prepositional, conjunctive, subordinating, coordinate; interjectional *or* interjectory; objective, subjective, direct, indirect, complementary, modifying; definite, indefinite; inflectional, inflected, formative, morphemic; diminutive, intensive, attributive, augmentative; comparative, superlative; masculine, feminine, neuter, singular, plural

VERBS

42 use language, communicate, write, speak, pronounce, utter, talk, state, verbalize, vocalize, voice, articulate, turn a sentence, rhyme, phrase, express, formulate, alphabetize; colloquialize, vernacularize, jargonize, cant, patter; be grammatical, grammaticize, parse; swear, blaspheme, curse

▶ *Literature 139; Communications 169; Publication 173; Speech, Spoken Language 205*

43 word, put into words, find words for, verbalize, define, syllabify, syllable; anagrammatize, neologize, coin a word; reword, rewrite, rephrase; write, letter, form letters, carve letters, handwrite, print; initial, inscribe, mark, sign, spell, spell out, misspell

ADVERBS

44 linguistically, grammatically, comparatively, descriptively, structurally, analytically, syntactically, orthographically, lexicographically, etymologically, semantically, philologically, bilingually, multilingually, literarily, literally, word for word, letter for letter, verbatim, hermeneutically, exegetically, epigraphically, graphically, alphabetically, hieroglyphically, symbolically, monosyllabically, polysyllabically, anagrammatically, vocally, polyphonically, polyphonously, tonally, phonetically

45 colloquially, verbally, conversationally, informally, journalistically, idiomatically, obscenely, blasphemously, scatologically, illiterately

46 lexically, glossarially, morphologically, inflectionally, meaningfully, pejoratively, intensively, pleonastically, wordily, verbosely, loquaciously, equivocally, pretentiously, neologistically *or* neologically, archaically, obsoletely

47 phraseologically, in set phrases, in set terms, in clauses, in sentences; metaphorically, proverbially, obsequiously, elegantly, periphrastically

48 grammatically, syntactically, correctly, formally, descriptively, transitively, intransitively, regularly, irregularly, participially, adverbially, prepositionally, conjunctively, subjunctively, objectively, subjectively, directly, indirectly, morphemically, attributively, comparatively, superlatively, singularly, plurally

6 Mathematics

As far as the laws of mathematics refer to reality, they are

not certain, and as far as they are certain, they do not refer to reality. — ALBERT EINSTEIN

Let no one ignorant of mathematics enter here.
— INSCRIPTION OVER PLATO'S ACADEMY

NOUNS

1 **mathematics,** math, maths [Brit]; pure mathematics, classical mathematics, new mathematics, higher mathematics, calculus, metamathematics, numeracy, calculation, computation, reckoning; numbers, figures, sums

2 **mathematician,** algebraist, geometrician *or* geometer, analyst, statistician, topologist

3 **applied mathematics,** mathematical biology, mathematical biophysics, mathematical computing, mathematical ecology, mathematical geography, mathematical physics, operations research

▶ *Physics 10; Engineering 14; Computers 15*

4 **number,** signed number, directed number, positive number, negative number, nonnegative number, even number, odd number, prime number *or* prime, composite number, perfect number; natural number, cardinal number, cardinal, ordinal number, ordinal, finite number, infinite number, transfinite number, random number

▶ *Number 783*

5 **real number,** real, imaginary number, rational number, rational, irrational number, irrational, integer, whole number, fraction, mixed number

6 **complex number,** real part, imaginary part, modulus, absolute value, argument, complex conjugate, algebraic number, transcendental number

7 **number system,** counting system, positional notation, place-value notation, decimal notation, decimal system, binary notation, binary system, octal notation, hexadecimal *or* hex notation, duodecimal notation, decimal number, binary number, base, radix point, decimal point, units place, tens place, hundreds

---

BRANCHES OF MATHEMATICS

algebra	control theory
commutative algebra	geometry
homological algebra	algebraic geometry
category theory	differential geometry
group theory	mathematical logic
analysis	number theory
Fourier analysis	numerical analysis
functional analysis	probability theory
harmonic analysis	set theory
measure theory	statistics
potential theory	systems theory
operational calculus	topology
arithmetic	algebraic topology
combinatorics	trigonometry

place, significant digits, significant figures, fixed-point notation, floating-point notation, precision, accuracy

8 **numeral,** Arabic numeral, Roman numeral, digit, figure, zero, one, two, three, four, five, six, seven, eight, nine, binary digit, bit, byte

▶ *Computers 15; One 788; Two 789; Three 790; Four 791; Five and Over 792; Plurality 793*

9 **absolutes,** zero, naught, nothing, nil, cipher; infinity, infinite number, transfinite number, infinitude

▶ *Zero 786; Infinity 798*

10 **numeration,** enumeration, quantification, numbering, counting, reckoning, figuring, quantifying, computation, calculation, mental arithmetic, measurement, count, census, tally, score, whole

11 **mathematical symbol,** plus sign, minus sign, multiplication sign, division sign, equal *or* equals sign, square root sign, radical sign, integral sign, implication sign, operator, operand, arithmetic operator, relational operator, logical operator, brackets, parentheses, square brackets, braces, angle brackets, vinculum

12 **operation,** arithmetic operation, algebraic operation, logical operation, associative operation *or* law, commutative operation *or* law, distributive operation *or* law, relation, relationship, formula, solution, result, results, value

13 **addition,** summation, sum, aggregate, total, addend

▶ *Addition 748*

14 **subtraction,** difference, subtrahend, minuend

▶ *Subtraction 749*

15 **multiplication,** product, multiplier, multiplicand, multiple, lowest *or* least common multiple (LCM), factor, submultiple, greatest common divisor (GCD), highest *or* greatest common factor (HCF, GCF [Brit]), prime factor, power, square, cube, fourth power, exponent, index, square root, cube root, surd, root mean square (rms), factorial, factorization, exponentiation, extraction of roots, multiplication tables

16 **division,** long division, short division, divisibility, quotient, ratio, proportion, percentage, quota, rate, reciprocal, inverse, dividend, divisor, aliquot part, remainder, residue, fraction, numerator, denominator, common denominator, decimal fraction, decimal, recurring decimal, repeated decimal, circular decimal, truncated decimal; vulgar fraction, simple fraction, proper fraction, common fraction, compound fraction, complex fraction, partial fraction, continued fraction; truncation, rounding up, rounding down, rounding off

17 **logarithm,** log, common logarithm, natural logarithm, base, mantissa, characteristic, antilogarithm, logarithmic scale, logarithm tables, log tables, Napierian logarithm, natural logarithm

18 **sequence,** progression, finite sequence, arithmetic progression, geometric progression, harmonic progression, series, convergent series, divergent series, arithmetic series, geometric series, binomial series, exponential series, logarithmic series, power series, Fourier series, Taylor series, Maclaurin series

19 **set,** finite set, infinite set, null set, empty set, universal set, complement, union, intersection, set difference, closure, disjoint sets, ordered set, n-tuple, subset, combination, unordered arrangement, permutation, ordered arrangement, element, member, identity element, identity, inverse, bound, upper bound, lower bound, class, group, ring, field, symmetric difference, partially ordered set (poset)

20 **matrix,** row, column, order, square matrix, diagonal matrix, identity matrix, null matrix, inverse, transpose, determinant

21 **algebra,** linear algebra, abstract algebra, algebra of propositions, Boolean algebra, ring, field

22 **evaluation,** simplification, manipulation, expansion, substitution, cross-multiplication, reduction, elimination, cancellation

23 **algebraic expression,** expression, binomial expression, binomial, polynomial expression, polynomial, multinomial, monomial term, variable, coefficient, numerical coefficient, constant, invariant, parameter

24 **equality,** inequality, identity, equivalence, congruence

25 **equation,** root, solution, solution set, degree, linear equation, quadratic equation, cubic equation, differential equation, integral equation, functional equation, simultaneous equations, system of equations

26 **algorithm,** recursive procedure, step-by-step procedure, effective procedure, iteration, recursion

27 **mathematical function,** function, mapping, transformation, domain, codomain, range, image, dependent variable, independent variable, argument, limit, continuous function, step function, inverse function, composite function, composition, trigonometric function, logarithmic function, exponential function, periodic function, gamma function, beta function, functional, kernel, cokernel, adjoint

28 **calculus,** infinitesimal calculus, differential calculus, integral calculus, calculus of variations, variational calculus, analysis, real analysis, complex analysis, functional analysis, vector analysis, tensor analysis

29 **differentiation,** integration, differential, increment, decrement, derivative, first derivative, second derivative, partial derivative, rate of change, fluxion, integral, indefinite integral, definite integral, limit, upper limit, lower limit, line integral, surface integral, volume integral, double integral, triple integral, convolution, differential equation, ordinary differential equation, partial differential equation, integral equation

30 **graph,** chart, plot, graphic representation, curve, bar graph, bar chart, histogram, pie chart, scatter diagram, scattergram, axis, x-axis, y-axis, z-axis, linear scale, logarithmic scale, origin, intercept

31 coordinates, coordinate system, Cartesian coordinates, polar coordinates, spherical coordinates, cylindrical coordinates, rectangular coordinates, x-coordinate, y-coordinate, z-coordinate, abscissa, ordinate, frame of reference
◗ *Measurement 589*

32 geometry, plane geometry, solid geometry, coordinate geometry, analytic geometry, algebraic geometry, projective geometry, differential geometry, spherical geometry, Euclidean geometry, non-Euclidean geometry, elliptic geometry, hyperbolic geometry, affine geometry

33 space, three-dimensional space, four-dimensional space, space-time continuum, n-space, n-dimensional space, hyperspace, hypercube, hypersphere, Euclidean space, Cartesian space, enclosed space, interior, inside, exterior, outside, spatial extension, extent, dimension, dimensions, size, area, volume capacity

34 point, fixed point, reference point, variable point, midpoint, set of points, coordinates (of a point), position, location, point of inflection, stationary point, fiducial point, point at infinity, locus (of a point), path

35 line, straight line, curved line, line segment, edge, side, boundary, curve, arc, contour, diagonal, diameter, chord, transversal *or* transverse, bisector, ray, tangent, asymptote, perpendicular, normal, binormal, geodesic, slope (of a line), gradient; parallel lines, intersecting lines, converging lines, diverging lines, skew lines, perpendicular lines, orientation, direction, linear measure, linear extent, length, width, breadth, height, depth, altitude, radius, perimeter, circumference, linearity

36 surface, flat surface, plane surface, plane, inclined plane, two-dimensional figure, curved surface, concave surface, convex surface, anticlastic surface, synclastic surface, closed surface, solid surface, lamina, face, side, surface measurement, surface area, superficial area, area, extent, flatness, curvature, concavity, convexity, sphericity

37 angle, vertex, apex, corner, cusp, node, plane angle, solid angle, dihedral angle, right angle, oblique angle, acute angle, obtuse angle, reflex angle, complementary angle, round angle *or* perigon, straight angle, interior angle, exterior angle, reentrant *or* reentering angle, salient angle; conjugate angles, supplementary angles, alternate angles, opposite angles, vertical angles, Euler angles; angle of elevation, angle of depression, angle subtended, angular measurement, angular distance, angular direction, bearing, bearings

38 curve, sine curve, sinusoid, spiral, Archimedes' spiral, logarithmic spiral, hyperbolic spiral, helix, catenary, cardioid, cissoid, cycloid, epicycloid, hypocycloid, folium, lemniscate, limaçon, logistic, trochoid, involute, evolute, trajectory, family (of curves), elliptic curve, fractal, witch of Agnesi; ellipse, oval, major axis,

minor axis, parabola, hyperbola, conic section *or* conic, focus, directrix, eccentricity; curvature, torsion
◗ *Curve 629*

39 geometric figure, figure, geometric shape, configuration, solid, bounded volume, closed figure, plane figure, solid figure, simplex, fractal, segment, sector, section, cross section, inscribed figure, circumscribed figure, escribed figure, symmetric(al) figure; symmetry, rotational symmetry, mirror symmetry, line *or* axis of symmetry, plane of symmetry, center of symmetry

40 circle, annulus, ring, disk, great circle, small circle, circumcircle, incircle, concentric circles, eccentric circles, semicircle, quadrant, sector, crescent, lune, meniscus, circumference, arc, radius, diameter, chord
◗ *Circularity 631*

41 triangle, right *or* right-angled triangle, acute *or* acute-angled triangle, obtuse *or* obtuse-angled triangle, equilateral triangle, isosceles triangle, scalene triangle, median triangle, circular triangle, spherical triangle; congruent triangles, similar triangles, equivalent triangles; adjacent, opposite, hypotenuse, base, altitude, median, centroid, orthocenter, incenter, circumcenter

42 polygon, triangle, square, rectangle, oblong, parallelogram, rhombus, rhomb, diamond, lozenge, rhomboid, quadrilateral, quadrangle, tetragon, trapezoid, trapezium, golden rectangle, pentagon, hexagon, heptagon, octagon, nonagon, decagon, regular polygon, star-shaped figure, pentagram, pentangle, pentacle, hexagram; golden mean, golden section

43 curved surface, closed surface, surface of revolution, solid of revolution, sphere, spheroid, ellipsoid, paraboloid, hyperboloid, cylinder, cone, truncated cone, frustum, torus, anchor ring, toroid, zone

44 polyhedron, tetrahedron, pentahedron, hexahedron, cube, cuboid, parallelepiped, octahedron, dodecahedron, icosahedron, pyramid, truncated pyramid, frustum, prism, wedge, prismatoid, prismoid, thombohedron, regular polyhedron, Platonic solid, irregular polyhedron, Archimedean solid

45 topology, algebraic topology, analysis situs [Arch], continuous distortion, stretching, knotting, knot, Möbius *or* Moebius strip, torus, Klein bottle, manifold

46 transformation, affine transformation, translation, reflection, rotation, glide reflection, dilation, dilatation, homothety, elation, homology, collineation, similitude, congruence, shear, projection, perspective projection, orthogonal projection, isometric projection, mirror image, enantiomorph

47 geometric construction, construction, configuration, drawing, geometric instrument, compass, compasses, pair of compasses, dividers, ruler, rule, straightedge, protractor, set square, T-square, squaring the circle

48 vector, vector quantity, scalar, scalar quantity, magnitude, direction, absolute value, unit vector, position vector, radius vector, component, resultant, parallelogram of forces, vector sum, scalar product, dot product, inner product, vector product, cross product, outer product, tensor product, exterior product, differential operator, nabla, del, gradient, divergence, curl, rot, tensor

49 trigonometry, trig [Inf], plane trigonometry, spherical trigonometry, triangulation, law of sines, law of cosines, law of tangents

50 trigonometric function, circular function, hyperbolic function, inverse trigonometric function, sine (sin), cosine (cos), tangent (tan), cotangent (cot *or* ctn), secant (sec), cosecant (cosec *or* csc), exsecant (exsec), versine (vers), coversine (covers), haversine (hav), hyperbolic sine (sinh), hyperbolic cosine (cosh), hyperbolic tangent (tanh), inverse sine (arcsine), inverse cosine (arccosine), inverse tangent (arctangent)

51 statistics, descriptive statistics, statistical inference, statistical analysis, probability theory, vital statistics, parametric statistics, nonparametric statistics

52 hypothesis testing, null hypothesis, alternative hypothesis, test statistic, significance level, significance test, one-tailed test, two-tailed test, goodness-of-fit test, chi-square test, f-test, t-test

53 statistical methods, analysis of variance, regression analysis, multivariate analysis, cluster analysis, factor analysis, principle component analysis

54 nonparametric methods, ordering, ranking, nominal scale, ordinal scale, interval scale, ratio scale, rank, order number

55 population, sample, random sample, biased sample, sample size, data collection, sampling, random sampling, systematic sampling, bias, crude data, data summarization, statistic, sample statistic, random variable, stochastic variable, stochastic process, Markov process

56 probability distribution, discrete distribution, continuous distribution, normal distribution, Gaussian distribution, binomial distribution, Poisson distribution, exponential distribution, gamma distribution, chi-square distribution, t-distribution, skew distribution, bimodal distribution, skewness, kurtosis, frequency function, probability density function, cumulative distribution function, frequency distribution, frequency, absolute frequency, relative frequency, histogram

57 parameter, characteristic, average, average value, typical value, expected value, mean, median, mode, arithmetic mean, geometric mean, weighted mean, weighting, variation, spread, dispersion, standard deviation, standard error, mean deviation, covariance, range, interquartile range, percentile, probable error, mean error, confidence level, confidence limits

58 correlation, positive correlation, negative correlation, association, correlation coefficient, significance

59 probability, chance, mathematical probability, empirical probability, conditional probability, certainty, impossibility, possible outcome, favorable outcome, likelihood, maximum likelihood, event, occurrence, particular instance, success, failure

▸ *Probability 838*

60 mathematical logic, symbolic logic, formal logic, propositional calculus, predicate calculus, functional calculus, logical proposition, proposition, statement, premise *or* premiss, assertion, affirmation, denial, logical expression, logical formula, well-formed formula (wff), logical operation, logical connective, operator, logical operator, negation, conjunction, logical product, disjunction, alternation, logical sum, implication, material implication, equivalence, conditional, relation, relationship, equivalence relation, ordering relation, transitive relation, reflexive relation, irreflexive relation, symmetric relation, antisymmetric relation, asymmetric relation, truth value, logical value, truth, falsity, truth table, universal quantifier, existential quantifier

61 reasoning, mathematical reasoning, logical reasoning, argument, inference, deduction, induction, derivation, rules of inference, valid argument, sound argument, invalid argument, unsound argument, conclusion, indication, heuristic solution, validation, verification, validity, soundness, rigor, correctness, truth, completeness, consistency, compatibility, sufficiency, invalidity, falsity, inconsistency, incompatibility, insufficiency, condition, restriction, contingency, necessary and sufficient condition, tautology, contradiction, converse, paradox, mathematical induction, transfinite induction, proof, rigorous proof, direct proof, indirect proof, Q.E.D. (quod erat demonstrandum), demonstration, test, procedure, method, evaluation, estimation, approximation, extrapolation, interpolation, error

62 theory, mathematical model, theoretical framework, simulation, generalization, abstraction, idealization, law, general principle, principle, criterion, rule, theorem, hypothesis, general proposition, proposition, lemma, corollary, formal expression, formula, equation, postulate, supposition, presupposition, premise *or* premiss, conjecture, axiom, first principles

63 combinatorics, discrete mathematics, graph, planar graph, graph coloring, four-coloring, four-color theorem, circuit, Eulerian circuit, Hamiltonian circuit, path, tree, network, matroid, permanent, poset, lattice, inclusion-exclusion (principle of), binomial coefficient, Stirling number (first and second kind), recursion, generating function, partition, Ferrers diagram, Latin square, Greco-Latin square, Hadamard matrix, design, block design, symmetric design, Steiner system, code, difference set

64 calculator, computer, adding machine, abacus, Napier's bones, tally stick, score card, cash register; rhabdology

MATHEMATICAL NAMED CONCEPTS, THEOREMS, LAWS

Abelian group	Cayley–Hamilton	Fermat prime	Julia set	Newton's method
Apollonius's theorem	theorem	Fermat's last theorem	Lagrange's theorem	Pascal's theorem
Archimedean axiom	Chebyshev's	French curve	Laplace or Laplacian	Pascal's triangle
Argand diagram	inequality	Fibonacci numbers	operator	Peano's axioms
Banach space	Chinese remainder	Fourier analysis	Lebesgue measure	Pell's equation
Bayes's theorem	theorem	Galois group	Legendre polynomials	Pythagorean theorem
Bernoulli trial	Cramer's rule	Gauss's lemma	Legendre symbol	Riemann hypothesis
Bessel functions	de Moivre–Laplace	Gauss's theorem	Leibniz's theorem	Riemannian geometry
Bolzano–Weierstrass	theorem	Gödel numbers	L'Hospital's rule	Riemann surface
theorem	de Moivre's formula	Goldbach conjecture	Lie group	Rolle's theorem
Brouwer fixed-point	de Morgan's rules	Green's theorem	Lobachevskian	Russell's paradox
theorem	Desargues's theorem	Gregory's series	geometry	Schur's lemma
Cantor set	Diophantine equation	Hamilton's principle	Maclaurin series	Simpson's rule
Cardano's formula	Dirichlet series	Hanoi, tower of	Mandelbrot set	Stokes's theorem
Cauchy–Schwarz	Eratosthenes, sieve of	Heron's or Hero's	Markov chain	Taylor series
inequality	Euclid's axioms	formula	Mersenne numbers	Venn diagram
Cauchy sequence	Euler's constant	Hilbert space	Mersenne prime	Zorn's lemma
Cavalieri's principle	Euler's formula	Hilbert's problems	Monte Carlo method	

▶ *Computers* 15; *Calculation* 784

ADJECTIVES

65 mathematical, arithmetical, algebraical, geometric, trigonometrical, analytical, topological, statistical, combinatorial

66 theoretical, abstract, analytical, formal, theorematic, theoremic, hypothetical, propositional, axiomatic, self-evident, obvious, empirical, observational, experiential, heuristic

67 universal, general, fundamental, basic, simple, standard, normal, canonical, uniform, continuous, discrete, noncontinuous, distinct, unique

68 numerical, signed, positive, negative, nonnegative, unsigned, even, odd, integral, whole, digital, fractional, decimal, denary, binary, ternary

69 complex, real, imaginary, rational, irrational, transcendental, infinitesimal, finite, infinite

70 numerable, enumerable, denumerable, countable, quantifiable, measurable, mensurable, calculable, computable, soluble, solvable, insoluble, insolvable, decidable, undecidable

71 divisible, indivisible, prime, composite, compound, reciprocal, inverse, in proportion, proportional, percentile, rational, commensurable, irrational, incommensurable

72 ranked, equal, identical, unequal, ordinal, ordered, partially ordered, cardinal, first, second, third, fourth, fifth, sixth, seventh, eighth, ninth, tenth, zeroth, maximal, greatest, largest, highest, minimal, least, lowest, smallest, upper, higher, greater, lower, lesser

73 functional, relational, exponential, logarithmic, linear, quadratic, cubic, binomial, trinomial, multinomial, polynomial, differential, integral, one-one, one-to-one, one-many, many-one, injective, surjective, bijective

74 given, assumed, known, stipulated, explicit, implicit, characteristic, dependent, variable, variate, independent, invariable, constant, parametric

75 pictorial, diagrammatic, graphic, tabular, schematic

76 spatial, flat, planar, plane, two-dimensional, coplanar, superficial, three-dimensional, solid, symmetrical, regular, asymmetrical, irregular, distorted

77 linear, lineal, straight, straight-lined, straight-edged, rectilinear, horizontal, flat, vertical, upright, oblique, sloping, slanted, at an angle, tangential, asymptotic, parallel, perpendicular, normal, orthogonal, orthographic, angular, angled, pointed, intersecting, convergent, divergent, skew, collinear, equidistant, equilateral

78 curvilinear, curved, arcuate, convex, concave, round, rounded, circular, annular, ringlike, ring-shaped, spiral, helical, semicircular, quadrantal, crescent-shaped, lunate, lenticular, elliptic(al), oval, parabolic, hyperbolic, central, focal, concentric, confocal, eccentric, radial, diametral, diametric, antipodal, fractal

79 polygonal, multiangular, triangular, wedge-shaped, three-sided, square, rectangular, oblong, rhombic, rhomboidal, diamond-shaped, quadrilateral, four-sided, tetragonal, pentagonal, five-sided, hexagonal, six-sided, heptagonal, seven-sided, octagonal, eight-sided

80 spherical, ellipsoidal, oval, ovoid, oblate, prolate, spheroidal, paraboloid(al), hyperboloid(al), cylindrical, disk-shaped, disklike, rod-shaped, conical, cone-shaped, toric, toroidal

81 cubic, cubiform, cuboid, oblong, hexahedral, octahedral, pyramidal, prismatic, wedge-shaped, polyhedral, multifacial

82 cyclic, periodic, harmonic, sinusoidal, recurrent

83 logical, deductive, inductive, inferential, valid, sound correct, true, invalid, unsound, incorrect, false, equivalent, complete, consistent, compatible, necessary, sufficient, inconsistent, incomplete, incompatible, contingent, conditional, tautological, contradictory, converse, paradoxical

VERBS

84 **theorize,** hypothesize, postulate, presuppose, assume, analyze, reason, deduce, infer, conclude, derive, generalize, prove, validate, demonstrate, satisfy, disprove, invalidate

85 **enumerate,** count, number, reckon up, quantify, measure, compute, calculate, determine, solve, evaluate, resolve

86 **add,** add up, sum, aggregate, subtract, take away, multiply, multiply out, cross multiply, times, raise to the power of, square, cube, extract a root, take the square root, factorize, borrow, carry, divide, subdivide, proportion, decimalize, truncate, round up, round down, round off

87 **manipulate,** simplify, expand, cancel, eliminate, substitute

88 **equate,** equalize, equal, approximate, estimate, sample, extrapolate, interpolate, correct for, correlate

89 **order,** rank, maximize, minimize, vary, approach a limit, tend to, vanish, standardize, normalize

90 **evaluate,** differentiate, integrate

91 **represent,** draw, configure, construct, generate, plot, graph, project, transform, translate, rotate, reflect

92 **align,** line up, extend, produce (a line), converge, diverge, intersect, disect, bisect, trisect, slope, curve, circle, encircle, circumscribe, inscribe

ADVERBS

93 **mathematically,** theoretically, analytically, generally, logically, fundamentally, basically, continuously, uniformly, discretely, numerically, positively, negatively, digitally, percent, infinitesimally, finitely, infinitely, equally, approximately, almost, about, unequally, functionally, exponentially, logarithmically, trigonometrically, spatially, linearly, spherically, evidently, obviously

7 Astronomy, Astronautics, and Rocketry

In my studies of astronomy and philosophy I hold this opinion about the universe, that the Sun remains fixed in the center of the circle of heavenly bodies, without changing its place; and the Earth, turning upon itself, moves round the sun. — GALILEO GALILEI

NOUNS

1 **astronomy,** stargazing, star watching, optical astronomy, observational astronomy, radio astronomy, infrared astronomy, X-ray astronomy, ultraviolet astronomy, gamma-ray astronomy, radar astronomy, astrophysics, cosmology, cosmogeny, uranography, uranology, astrometry, celestial mechanics, astrodynamics, stellar statistics, astrochemistry, cosmochemistry, astrobiology, exobiology, astrobotany, astrogeology, astrophotography

2 **astronomer,** observer, astrophysicist, cosmologist, cosmogenist, uranographer, cosmochemist, stargazer

3 **universe,** cosmos, macrocosm, totality, world, heavens, firmament, space, deep space, outer space, sky, empyrean, welkin, vault of heaven, creation; cosmological model, Ptolemaic universe, Copernican universe, Einsteinian universe, general relativity, steady-state universe, expanding universe, inflationary universe, oscillating universe, open universe, closed universe, flat universe; big bang, primordial fireball, cosmic background, microwave background, dark matter, gravitational force, gravitational constant

4 **celestial sphere,** celestial equator, celestial poles, ecliptic, horizon, meridian, zenith, nadir, galactic latitude, galactic longitude, celestial latitude, celestial longitude, right ascension, declination, hour angle, altitude, azimuth

5 **galaxy,** island universe, elliptical galaxy, spiral galaxy, barred spiral galaxy, irregular galaxy, lenticular galaxy, Hubble classification, supergiant elliptical, giant elliptical, giant spiral, dwarf elliptical, cluster, supercluster, active galaxy, radio galaxy, Seyfert galaxy, starburst galaxy, filament, void, galactic center, nucleus, disk, arm, halo, gravitational redshift, Hubble constant; the Local Group, Milky Way

6 **nebula,** interstellar cloud, nebulosity, emission nebula, reflection nebula, bright nebula, absorption nebula, dark nebula, gaseous nebula, diffuse nebula, planetary nebula, ring nebula, galactic nebula, anagalactic nebula; nebular hypothesis; Black Magellanic Cloud, Coalsack nebula, Crab nebula, Great Nebula in Orion

7 **interstellar matter,** cosmic dust, interstellar dust, interstellar gas, interstellar molecule, HI region, HII region, nebula; cosmic rays

8 **star,** luminary, orb, sphere, heavenly body; fixed star, circumpolar star, nebulous star, variable star, quasar, quasi-stellar radio source; double star, optical double, binary star, visual binary, eclipsing binary, spectroscopic binary, close binary, X-ray binary; multiple star, star cluster, open cluster, globular cluster; evening star, Hesperus, Vesper, morning star, Lucifer

9 **star catalog,** star chart, star atlas, sky survey, Messier Catalog, Dreyer's New General Catalog (NGC), ephemeris

10 **stellar evolution,** stellar birth, protostar, molecular cloud, main sequence, gravitational collapse, dying star, red giant, white dwarf; nova, supernova, supernova remnant, neutron star, pulsar, black hole, event horizon, singularity, white hole

11 **variable star,** Algol variable, pulsating variable, Cepheid variable, Mira variable, RR Lyrae star, cataclysmic variable, recurrent nova, flare star

12 **star luminosity,** magnitude, apparent magnitude, absolute magnitude; proper motion, radial velocity, parallax, precession, spectral type, luminosity class, supergiant, giant star, giant, subgiant, main-sequence star, Hertzsprung–Russell diagram

13 **constellation,** stellar group, configuration, stellar association, stellar population, asterism; zodiac, zodiacal constellation; star group, Great Square of Pegasus, Orion's Belt, Orion's Sword, Pleiades *or* Seven Sisters, Pointers (Ursa Major)

14 **solar system,** planetary system; Kepler's laws, interplanetary space, solar wind, zodiacal light, gegenschein, counterglow

15 **sun,** daystar; chromosphere, photosphere, corona, Baily's beads, solar flare, solar prominence, filament, sunspot, facula, granule; solar disk, limb; solar activity, active sun, quiet sun, solar cycle, sunspot cycle, 11-year cycle; solar eclipse, total eclipse, partial eclipse, annular eclipse; solar spectrum, Fraunhofer lines; Sol, Helios, Hyperion, Apollo, Ra, Amen-Ra

16 **planet,** major planet, Mercury, Venus, Earth, Mars (the Red Planet), Jupiter (the Jovian planet), Saturn, Uranus, Neptune, Pluto; inferior planet, wandering star, minor planet, asteroid, planetoid, asteroid belt; syzygy

17 **Earth,** third planet; earth light, earthshine, albedo; aurora, aurora borealis, northern lights, polar lights, Van Allen radiation belt

▶ *Geology 8*

18 **moon,** satellite, natural satellite; phase, new moon, full moon, harvest moon, hunter's moon, crescent moon, horned moon, first quarter, last quarter, half-moon, gibbous moon, waxing moon, waning moon, terminator, libration, lunar month, lunar eclipse; crater, mare (pl. maria), sea, basin, highlands, rill *or* rille, mascon; queen of the night, Sister Moon, Selene, Diana, Cynthia, Artemis, man in the moon

19 **satellite,** natural satellite, moon, Galilean satellite

20 **comet,** comet cloud, comet nucleus, coma, tail, Oort cloud; Halley's comet, Kohoutek, Shoemaker-Levy

21 **meteor,** shooting star, falling star, fireball, bolide, meteor shower, meteor swarm, radiant, meteorite, iron meteorite *or* iron, stony meteorite *or* stone, aerolite, siderite, siderolite, chondrite, carbonaceous chondrite, achondrite, find, fall, meteorite crater, tektite, meteoroid, micrometeorite

22 **orbit,** revolution, trajectory, orbital period, elliptical orbit, eccentricity, inclination, semimajor axis, perihelion, aphelion, parabolic orbit, hyperbolic orbit, ro-

---

CONSTELLATIONS*

Common Name (with technical name where different)

Air Pump or Pump (Antlia)
Altar (Ara)
Andromeda or Chained Lady (Andromeda)
Aquarius or Water Carrier (Aquarius)*
Archer (Sagittarius)*
Aries or Ram (Aries)*
Balance or Scales (Libra)*
Berenice's Hair (Coma Berenices)
Big Dipper
Bird of Paradise (Apus)
Bull (Taurus)*
Capricorn or Goat (Capricorn)*
Cassiopeia
Centaur (Centaurus)
Cepheus
Chained Lady or Andromeda
Chameleon (Chamaeleon)
Charioteer (Auriga)
Chisel (Caelum)
Clock (Horologium)
Compasses (Circinus)
Crab (Cancer)*
Crane (Grus)

Crow (Corvus)
Cup (Crater)
Dolphin (Delphinus)
Dove (Columba)
Dragon (Draco)
Eagle (Aquila)
Fishes (Pisces)*
Fly (Musca)
Flying Fish (Volans or Pisces Volans)
Furnace (Fornax)
Gemini or Twins (Gemini)*
Giraffe (Camelopardalis)
Goat or Capricorn*
Great Bear (Ursa Major)
Great Dog (Canis Major)
Hare (Lepus)
Hercules
Herdsman (Boötes)
Hunting Dogs (Canes Venatici)
Indian (Indus)
Keel (Carina)
Lion (Leo)*
Little Bear (Ursa Minor)
Little Dipper
Little Dog (Canis Minor)

Little Fox (Vulpecula)
Little Horse (Equuleus)
Little Lion (Leo Minor)
Lizard (Lacerta)
Lynx
Lyre (Lyra)
Maiden or Virgin (Virgo)*
Mariner's Compass (Pyxis)
Microscope (Microscopium)
Net (Reticulum)
Northern Crown (Corona Borealis)
Octant (Octans)
Orion
Painter (Pictor)
Peacock (Pavo)
Pegasus
Perseus
Phoenix
Pump or Air Pump (Antlia)
Ram or Aries*
River (Eridanus)
Rule (Norma)
Sails (Vela)
Scales or Balance (Libra)*
Scorpion (Scorpius or Scorpio)*

Sculptor
Serpent (Serpens)
Serpent Bearer (Ophiuchus)
Sextant (Sextans)
Shield (Scutum)
Southern Cross (Crux)
Southern Crown (Corona Australis)
Southern Fish (Piscis Austrinus)
Stern (Puppis)
Swan (Cygnus)
Swordfish (Dorado)
Table (Mensa)
Telescope (Telescopium)
Toucan (Tucana)
Triangle (Triangulum)
Twins or Gemini*
Unicorn (Monoceros)
Virgin or Maiden (Virgo)*
Water Carrier or Aquarius*
Water Snake (Hydrus)
Whale (Cetus)
Wolf (Lupus)

*Zodiac constellation

PLANETS AND THEIR SATELLITES

Mercury
Venus
Earth (Moon)
Mars (Phobos, Deimos)
Jupiter (Metis, Adrastea, Amalthea,
Thebe, Io, Europa, Ganymede,
Callisto, Leda, Himalia, Lysithea,
Elara, Ananke, Carme, Pasiphaë,
Sinope)
Saturn (Mimas, Enceladus, Tethys,
Telesto, Calypso, Dione, Rhea,
Helene, Titan, Hyperion, Iapetus,
Phoebe, Janus, Pan, Atlas, Prometheus,
Pandora, Epimetheus)

Uranus (Miranda, Ariel, Umbriel, Titania,
Oberon, Cordelia, Ophelia, Bianca,
Cressida, Desdemona, Juliet, Portia,
Rosalind, Belinda, Puck)
Neptune (Triton, Nereid, Naiad,
Thalassa, Despina, Galatea, Proteus)
Pluto (Charon)

Minor Planets or Asteroids
Achilles
Adonis
Amor
Apollo
Astraea
Aten

Ceres
Chiron
Eros
Eunomia
Euphrosyne
Hebe
Hermes
Hidalgo
Hygiea
Icarus
Iris
Juno
Pallas
Vesta

---

tation, rotational axis, rotational period, precession, eclipse, transit, occultation, twinkling, scintillation, zenith, nadir, fiducial point, reddening, redshift, blueshift

23 **astronomical unit,** light-year, parsec, solar mass

24 **observatory,** astronomical observatory, ground-based observatory, optical observatory, infrared observatory, dome, observation, seeing, light pollution, radio observatory; planetarium, planisphere, astrolabe, orrery

25 **telescope,** astronomical telescope, optical telescope, reflector *or* reflecting telescope; Hubble Space Telescope, Cassegrain telescope, Newtonian telescope, Schmidt telescope, refractor *or* refracting telescope, Galilean telescope, Keplerian telescope, infrared telescope, flux collector, solar telescope, heliostat

26 **radio telescope,** radio dish, antenna, receiver, array, radio interferometer, Very Large Array (VLA), aperture synthesis, very long baseline interferometry (VLBI), X-ray telescope, grazing-incidence telescope

27 **aerospace research,** astronautics, cosmonautics; space engineering, space technology, space science, space navigation, space exploration, space medicine; bioastronautics

28 **spacecraft,** space capsule, space probe, module, lunar module, space station *or* space platform; space shuttle, shuttle, space laboratory, Spacelab, spaceship

29 **space travel,** manned flight, spaceflight, space age, trip to the moon, astronaut, cosmonaut, spaceman, spacewoman, weightlessness, free fall, microgravity, spacesuit, space helmet, spacewalk, extravehicular activity (EVA), spaceport, lunar base, moon base

30 **artificial satellite,** satellite, earth satellite, unmanned satellite, research satellite, astronomical satellite, X-ray satellite, space observatory, orbiting observatory, geophysical satellite, communications satellite, geostationary orbit, geosynchronous orbit, meteorological satellite, weather satellite, navigational satellite, spy

satellite, solar cell, solar panel, telemetry, data transmission, satellite tracking, tracking station, relay station

31 **planetary probe,** orbiter, lander

32 **rocketry,** rocket propulsion, engine, booster, propellant, liquid fuel, solid fuel, burn, thrust, launch vehicle, launcher, multistage rocket, payload, retrorocket, solid rocket booster (SRB), escape velocity, orbit, earth orbit, perigee, apogee, parking orbit, transfer orbit, insertion, injection, trajectory, flyby, rendezvous, docking, reentry, splashdown, soft landing, hard landing

ADJECTIVES

33 **astronomical,** astrophysical, cosmological, uranographic(al), cosmic, celestial, heavenly, universal, infinite, boundless, galactic, intergalactic, extragalactic, interstellar, stellar, sidereal, starry, astral, star-studded, solar, heliacal, interplanetary, planetary, Mercurian, Venusian, Martian, Jovian, Saturnian, Neptunian, Uranian, Plutonian, extraterrestrial, extramundane, terrestrial, telluric, tellurian, synodic, lunar, asteroidal, cometary, meteoric, meteoritic, heliocentric, geocentric, telescopic, spectrometric, photometric, astronautic(al)

VERBS

34 **observe,** orbit, revolve, rotate, eclipse, transit, radiate, shine, twinkle, emit, absorb

35 **launch,** lift off, blast off, enter orbit, travel in space

ADVERBS

36 **astronomically,** astrophysically, cosmologically, cosmically, celestially, universally, infinitely, boundlessly, galactically, intergalactically, extragalactically, sidereally, extraterrestrially, terrestrially, meteorically, heliocentrically

8 Geology

NOUNS

1 **geology,** geoscience, earth science, physical geology, structural geology, mineralogy, crystallography, petrol-

ogy, hydrogeology, geochemistry, tectonics, volcanology *or* vulcanology, marine geology, glaciology, geomorphology, physiography, pedology, historical geology, stratigraphy, paleontology, paleogeography, paleoclimatology, geochronology, economic geology, geopolitics, planetology, astrogeology; geography, physical geography

2 **geophysics,** geodesy, geomagnetism, gravity geophysics, gravimetry, solid-earth geophysics, seismology, seismography, volcanology *or* vulcanology, plate tectonics, physical oceanography, climatology, meteorology

▶ *Meteorology and Climatology 9; Physics 10*

3 **geomagnetism,** terrestrial magnetism, geomagnetic field, geomagnetic pole, north magnetic pole, south magnetic pole, magnetic equator, aclinic line, agonic line, declination, dip, inclination, magnetic anomaly, magnetic storm; paleomagnetism, polarity reversal, magnetic reversal, polar wandering, magnetosphere

4 **geologist,** earth scientist, mineralogist, crystallographer, petrologist, hydrogeologist, geochemist, volcanologist *or* vulcanologist, glaciologist, geomorphologist, physiographer, pedologist, stratigrapher, paleogeographer, paleoclimatologist, paleontologist, geochronologist, planetologist

5 **geophysicist,** geodesist, geomagnetist, seismologist, volcanologist *or* vulcanologist, physical oceanographer, climatologist, meteorologist

6 **Earth,** planet Earth, world, globe; Mother Earth, Gaia, blue planet; atmosphere, hydrosphere, lithosphere, biosphere, ecosphere, geoid

▶ *Astronomy, Astronautics, and Rocketry 7*

7 **earth zone,** crust, plate, crustal plate; continental crust, oceanic crust, mantle, lithosphere, asthenosphere, outer core, inner core, discontinuity, Mohorovičić discontinuity (Moho)

8 **continent,** subcontinent, continental shelf, continental margin, continental slope, continental drift, land, mainland, landmass, ground, topography, relief, elevation, terrain, landscape

9 **landform,** surface feature, natural feature, geomorphic feature, physical geographical feature; basin, plain, coastal plain, flood plain; shield, valley, rift valley *or* graben, V-shaped valley, river valley, U-shaped valley, glacial valley, fjord, hanging valley, cirque, arrête, cwm, valley floor, canyon, gorge, ravine; hill, horst, plateau, mesa, butte, scarp *or* escarpment, mountain, volcano

▶ *Mountains and Hills 569; Other Geographical Features 572*

10 **running water,** drainage system, river, river network, stream channel, stream course, streambed, drainage pattern, drainage basin, catchment area, watershed, interstream divide, continental divide, meander, load, capacity, competence

▶ *Rivers 570*

11 **groundwater,** subsurface water, subterranean water, underground water, water table, zone of permeability, zone of saturation, aquifer, artesian basin, artesian spring, sinkhole; cave, stalactite, stalagmite

12 **water cycle,** hydrological cycle, evaporation, transpiration, precipitation, runoff, percolation

▶ *Water 557*

13 **coast,** coastline, shore, shoreline, littoral zone, seaside, cliff, stack, beach, shingle, sand dune, sand bar, spit, tombolo, sandbank, sand wave, barrier island, barrier reef, lagoon, peninsula

14 **ocean,** sea, ocean water, seawater, salinity, sea level; bathymetrics, coastal waters, bathyal waters, abyssal waters

▶ *Seas 571*

15 **ocean current,** surface current, wind-induced current, longshore current, tidal current, density current *or* subsurface current, circulation pattern, lateral movement, vertical movement, gyre, upwelling, downwelling

16 **wave,** sea wave, ocean wave, swell, roller, breaker, surf, spume, white horse, whitecap, white foam, storm wave, seiche, tsunami *or* seismic sea wave, tidal wave

17 **tide,** high tide, low tide, spring tide, neap tide, tidal range, intertidal zone

▶ *Seas 571*

18 **ocean floor,** seafloor, ocean basin, continental margin, continental shelf, continental slope, continental rise, submarine canyon, land bridge, abyssal plain, abyssal hill, midoceanic ridge, oceanic ridge, oceanic trench; volcanic island, seamount, guyot, atoll

19 **plate tectonics,** plate, lithospheric plate, plate margin, plate boundary, leading edge, trailing edge, divergence zone, convergence zone, subduction zone, island arc, midoceanic ridge, oceanic trench, transform fault, seafloor spreading, continental drift; Gondwana, Laurasia, Pangaea

20 **earth movement,** crustal movement, diastrophism, orogeny, epeirogeny, uplift, subsidence, tectonic forces, deformation, stress, strain, isostasy, isostatic anomaly, isostatic adjustment

21 **fault,** brittle deformation, fault system, fault scarp, fault zone, normal fault, reverse fault, thrust fault, block fault, basin and range, strike-slip fault, right lateral *or* left lateral detachment fault, fracture, slickensides

22 **fold,** plastic deformation, flexure, fold belt, mobile belt, geosyncline, anticline, syncline, symmetric *or* asymmetric fold, upright fold, inclined fold, overturned fold, recumbent fold, fold nappe

23 **mountain building,** orogenesis, orogeny, fold mountain, fold-belt mountain, alpine chain, fault-block mountain, basin and range, oceanic ridge, oceanic rise, volcanic mountain

24 seismic activity, earthquake, seismicity, seismic event, temblor, quake, macroseism, major earthquake, microseism, minor earthquake, earth tremor, shock, foreshock, main shock, aftershock, hypocenter (focus), epicenter; earthquake magnitude, Richter scale, intensity, earthquake zone, seismic belt, seismic swarm

25 seismic wave, body wave, primary *or* P wave, secondary *or* S wave, surface wave; seismograph, seismogram, seismic survey, seismic risk, seismic exploration (prospecting)

26 volcanic activity, volcanism *or* vulcanism, volcano, active volcano, inactive *or* dormant volcano, cinder cone, volcanic cone, shield volcano, composite volcano *or* stratovolcano, crater, caldera, vent, fissure, magma chamber, magma, melt

27 eruption, lava, ejecta, tephra, pyroclastic material, ash, pumice, volcanic gas, lava flow, aa *or* block lava, pahoehoe *or* ropy lava, pillow lava, fumarole, gas vent, geyser, hot spring, thermal spring

28 mass movement, landslide, slide, glide, slump, mudflow, debris flow, earthflow, lahar, creep, rock fall, avalanche

29 sediment, mud, sand, silt, clay, loess, rock, boulder, stone, gravel, granules, pebbles, shingle; deposit, organic sediment, inorganic sediment, oceanic sediment, pelagic ooze, ooze; alluvial deposit, delta, lake sediment; glacial deposit, eolian deposit

30 rock, mineral aggregate, stone, igneous rock, sedimentary rock, metamorphic rock; bedrock, rock formation, texture, composition, fabric, facies, rock-forming mineral, joint, cleavage, rock unit, formation, member

31 petrogenesis, rock cycle, lithification, sedimentation, deposition, consolidation, cementation, compaction, crystallization, magmatism (intrusion, extrusion), metamorphosis, recrystallization, foliation

32 igneous rock, magmatic rock, plutonic *or* intrusive rock, plutonic intrusion, hypabyssal intrusion, dike, sill, batholith, stock, laccolith, lopolith, pluton, volcanic rock, extrusive rock, acid rock, intermediate rock, basic rock, ultrabasic rock, mafic rock, ultramafic rock, felsic rock

33 types of igneous texture, aphanitic, phaneritic, porphyritic, pegmatitic, pyroclastic, glassy

34 sedimentary rock, lithified sediment, stratified rock, clastic rock, nonclastic rock, stratum (pl. strata), bed, bedding, bedding plane, ripple marks, desiccation cracks, fossils, sedimentary facies

35 metamorphism, regional metamorphism, contact metamorphism, thermal metamorphism, dynamic metamorphism, dislocation metamorphism, metamorphic grade, cataclasis, retrograde metamorphism, autometamorphism, metamorphic facies

36 metamorphic rock, parent rock, low-grade rock, high-grade rock, primary character, secondary character; foliated rock, schistosity, slaty cleavage, gneissic banding; nonfoliated rock

37 mineral, crystalline element *or* compound; cleavage, fracture, luster, mineraloid (amorphous); mineral resources

38 mineral types, inorganic, natural, rock-forming, silicate, carbonate, oxide, sulfide, sulfate (and other chemical groups)

39 crystal, external geometric form, microcrystal, macrocrystal, crystal growth, crystallization, crystal lattice, crystal system, isometric (cubic) crystal, tetragonal crystal, orthorhombic crystal, hexagonal crystal, monoclinic crystal, crystal axis, crystal symmetry

40 weathering, mechanical weathering, disintegration, chemical weathering, decomposition, exfoliation, frost and root wedging, oxidation, hydration, differential weathering

41 erosion, wearing away, denudation, abrasion, striation, scour, gouge, differential erosion; agents: running water, groundwater, glacial ice, waves, currents, wind

42 soil, earth, topsoil, subsoil, regolith, soil profile, soil horizon, A horizon, B horizon, C horizon, soil texture, gravel, sand, loam, silt, clay, soil structure, alluvium, pedalfer, podzol, pedocal, lateritic soil, soil erosion

43 dune, sand dune, coastal dune, desert dune, longitudinal dune, seif, crescent dune, barchan, transverse dune; dune face, dune field, migrating dune, stabilized dune

44 glacier, alpine glacier, valley glacier, cirque glacier, continental glacier, continental ice sheet, ice sheet, icecap, ice field, crevasse, icefall, sérac, ice shelf, ice tongue, snout, moraine, till, boulder clay, drift, erratic, meltwater, glacier milk; glacier flour, U-shaped valley, fjord, roche moutonnée, esker, drumlin, zone of accumulation, zone of melting, snowline

45 iceberg, berg, growler, calf, sea ice, ice floe, floe, pack ice, ice pack, ice raft

46 glaciation, glacial period, ice age, glacial advance, glacial surge, glacial maximum, stadial, interglacial, deglaciation, glacial recession *or* retreat, glacial budget

47 geological time, geological time scale, geological time unit, geochronological unit, eon, era, period, epoch, chronostratigraphic unit, time-rock unit, eonothem, erathem, system, series, stage zone, relative age, absolute age, uniformitarianism, catastrophism

48 dating, radioactive dating, radiometric dating, uranium-lead dating, potassium-argon dating, rubidium-strontium dating, radiocarbon dating, carbon-14 dating, parent-daughter relationship, half-life, dendrochronology

49 **fossil,** fossil record, index fossil, zone fossil, fossilization, permineralization, petrification (replacement), mold and cast, trace fossil
> *Animals (General) 34; Plants (General) 41*

ADJECTIVES

50 **geologic,** geological, mineralogical, petrological, hydrological, geochemical, volcanological, glaciological, geomorphological, pedological, geodetic, stratigraphical, paleontological, geochronological

51 **geophysical,** geomagnetic, paleomagnetic, gravimetric, seismological, seismographic, seismometric, oceanographic, bathymetric, hydrographic, climatological, meteorological
> *Meteorology and Climatology 9*

52 **terrestrial,** global, surficial, atmospheric, hydrospheric, geospheric, continental, topographic(al), subsurface, subterranean, underground

53 **oceanic,** deep-sea, marine, maritime, undersea, submarine, suboceanic, thalassic, pelagic, benthic, bathymal, abyssal, hadal, terrigenous
> *Seas 571*

54 **coastal,** littoral, neritic, tidal, intertidal, riverine, alluvial

55 **solid-earth,** crustal, lithospheric, sialic, isostatic

56 **tectonic,** deformational, diastrophic, orogenic, epeirogenic

57 **volcanic,** eruptive, seismic, pyroclastic, molten, laval

58 **petrographic,** petrographical, petrological, petrogenic, lithic, consolidated, unconsolidated, igneous, magmatic, volcanic, plutonic, pyroclastic, intrusive, extrusive, sedimentary, stratified, clastic, detrital, metamorphic, foliated

59 **chalky,** flinty, shaly, slaty, basaltic, granitic, gneissic, gneissoid, gneissose, schistose, calcareous

60 **earthy,** rocky, stony, gravelly, pebbly, sandy, loamy, silty, clayey

---

GEOLOGIC TIME INTERVALS IN CHRONOLOGICAL ORDER

Precambrian Era	Jurassic Period
Archaeozoic Period	Cretaceous Period
Proterozoic Period	
	Cenozoic Era
Paleozoic Era	Tertiary Period:
Cambrian Period	Paleocene Epoch
Ordovician Period	Eocene Epoch
Silurian Period	Oligocene Epoch
Devonian Period	Miocene Epoch
Carboniferous Period	Pliocene Epoch
Permian Period	Quaternary Period:
	Pleistocene Epoch
Mesozoic Era	Holocene *or* Recent Epoch
Triassic Period	

---

61 **weathered,** eroded, abraded, scoured, gouged, striated

62 **glaciated,** glacial, interglacial, postglacial, morainal, morainic

63 **fossilized,** petrified, mineralized, fossiliferous

VERBS

64 **drain,** ebb, flow, run off, percolate, well up, spring up, evaporate, transpire, precipitate, ooze, settle

65 **quake,** tremble, shake; erupt

66 **lithify,** petrify, crystallize, recrystallize, mineralize, fossilize, consolidate, cement

67 **erode,** denude, abrade, scour, gouge; weather, disintegrate, decompose

ADVERBS

68 **geologically,** geomorphologically, geodetically, paleogeologically, paleogeographically, *etc.*; topographically, seismologically, petrographically, petrologically, mineralogically, tidally, bathymetrically, hydrologically; geographically, meteorologically, continentally, volcanically, *etc.*

9 Meteorology and Climatology

Who has seen the wind? / Neither you nor I; / But when the trees bow down their heads, / The wind is passing by.
— CHRISTINA ROSSETTI

NOUNS

1 **meteorology,** weather science, synoptic meteorology, weather forecasting, aerology, micrometeorology, macrometeorology, mesometeorology, agricultural meteorology, aviation meteorology, maritime meteorology, mountain meteorology, numerical meteorology, atmospheric physics, hydrometeorology, hyetography, nephology, anemology, anemometry, climatology, planetary meteorology

2 **meteorologist,** climatologist, weather forecaster, weatherman, weatherwoman, weather observer, weather prophet

3 **weather,** weather situation, weather pattern, weather conditions, the elements, period, interval, spell, weather lore, dog days, halcyon days, blackthorn winter, Indian summer; climate

4 **weather forecast,** forecast, weather report, regional forecast, outlook, general outlook, travel report, road report, boating report, small craft advisory, short-term forecast, medium-term forecast, long-term forecast, long-range forecast, numerical forecast, shipping forecast, general synopsis; hurricane *or* storm *or* gale watch *or* warning, tornado watch *or* warning; weather map, synoptic map *or* chart, weather symbols, isobar, isotherm

5 **weather station,** land station, ground station, field station, coastal station, weather bureau, weather ship,

automatic buoy, weather satellite, weather balloon, radiosonde

6 **weather data,** elements, air pressure, pressure gradient, pressure tendency, rising pressure, falling pressure; air temperature, heat index, temperature-humidity index, dewpoint; humidity, relative humidity, absolute humidity, damp, dampness, moisture, precipitation; air density, air movement, wind speed, wind strength, chill factor, wind-chill factor, anemogram

7 **weather instrument,** barometer, aneroid barometer, barograph, mercury barometer, glass, weatherglass, storm glass, thermometer, thermograph, hygrometer, psychrometer, hygrograph, Stevenson screen, wind gauge, anemometer, anemograph, windsock, wind cone, wind sleeve, drogue, weather vane, weathercock, wind rose, rain gauge, pluviometer, udometer, weather radar, sunshine recorder
   ▶ *Physics 10*

8 **atmosphere,** air, atmospheric layer, troposphere, stratosphere, upper atmosphere, ionosphere, ozone layer, ozonosphere, exosphere, tropopause, stratopause, atmospheric water vapor; clean dry air, air mass, cold air, warm air, moist air, dry air, polar air, tropical air, condensation nuclei; atmospheric dust, pollution, pollutant, chlorofluorocarbon (CFC)
   ▶ *Physics 10; Air 558*

9 **atmospheric process,** radiation balance, energy balance, absorption, reflection, scattering, heat transfer, heat transport, convection, conduction, radiation, advection, adiabatic process, adiabatic cooling, adiabatic lapse rate, water balance, evaporation, condensation, sublimation, saturation, supercooling, Coriolis force, geostrophic force

10 **weather system,** pressure system, frontal system; low-pressure area, low, cyclone, depression, warm sector, trough *or* trough of low pressure; high-pressure area, high, anticyclone, ridge *or* ridge of high pressure

11 **air movement,** wind, air current, airflow, airstream, jet stream, atmospheric circulation; convection cell, thermal, downdraft, updraft; front, polar front, cold front, warm front, occluded front, occlusion, warm occlusion, cold occlusion

12 **wind,** surface wind, sea breeze, land breeze, onshore wind, offshore wind, local wind, katabatic wind, anabatic wind, mountain wind, valley wind, gust, squall, variable wind, wind storm, dust storm, sandstorm, upper wind, high-altitude wind, gradient wind, geostrophic wind; prevailing wind, headwind, crosswind, tailwind, following wind, favorable wind, wind shift, backing wind, veering wind, wind shear

13 **wind strength,** wind force, wind speed, Beaufort scale; calm, light air, puff *or* breath of wind, zephyr, breeze, light breeze, gentle breeze, moderate breeze, fresh breeze, strong breeze, fresh wind, brisk wind, high wind, strong wind, stiff wind, blow, blast, spanking wind, near gale, gale, strong gale, howling gale, half a gale, full gale, storm, violent storm, tempest

14 **wind vortex,** eddy, rotating air mass, tropical storm, cyclone, typhoon, hurricane, eye of the storm, waterspout, tornado, whirlwind, dust devil, sand column, twister [Inf]

15 **wind system,** polar easterlies, polar front, prevailing southwesterlies, prevailing northwesterlies, trade winds *or* trades, northeast trades, southeast trades, intertropical convergence zone (ITCZ), equatorial low *or* doldrums; horse latitudes, roaring forties, antitrade winds *or* antitrades

16 **wind god,** Aeolus, Boreas, Aquilo (north wind), Eurus (east wind), Notus, Auster (south wind), Zephyrus, Favonius (west wind); Argestes (northeast wind), Caurus *or* Caecias (northwest wind), Afer *or* Africus (southwest wind)

17 **cloud,** high cloud, low cloud, cloud base, ice cloud, water cloud, mixed cloud, cirrus, cirrocumulus, altostratus, cirrostratus, altocumulus, nimbostratus, stratocumulus *or* cumulostratus, stratus, cumulus, thunderhead, cumulonimbus, rain cloud, rain-bearing

---

NOTABLE WINDS

austru (Romania)
berg (South Africa)
bise (Switzerland, France, Italy)
bora (Adriatic coasts)
brickfielder (Australia)
buran (Central Asia)
Cape doctor (South Africa)
chinook *or* snow eater (Rocky
   Mountains)
etesian (Mediterranean)
foehn *or* föhn (Alps)
ghibli *or* gibli (North Africa)
gregale *or* Euroclydon (Mediterranean)
haboob (Sudan)

harmattan (West African coast)
khamsin *or* kamsin (Egypt)
levanter (Mediterranean)
libeccio *or* libecchio (Italy)
meltemi (Mediterranean)
mistral (southern France, Mediterranean
   coast)
monsoon (southern Asia)
nor'easter (New England, South Atlantic
   states)
nor'wester (New England, South Atlantic
   states; New Zealand)
pampero (Argentina)
papagayo (western Central America)

Santa Ana (southern California)
simoom *or* saniel (Arabia, North Africa)
sirocco (North Africa, southern Europe)
solano (Spain)
southerly buster (southeastern Australia)
Tehuantepec (southern Mexico)
tramontana (Italy and western
   Mediterranean)
tramontane (southern France)
wet chinook (Washington, Oregon
   coasts)
williwaw (United States, Canada)
willy-willy (Australia)
zonda (Argentina)

9 Meteorology and Climatology

cloud, nimbus, scud, storm cloud, thundercloud, anvil cloud, dark cloud, noctilucent cloud

18 **cloud cover,** cloudiness, thin cloud, patchy cloud, broken cloud, thick cloud, dense cloud, widespread cloud, low-level cloud, cloud ceiling; overcast sky, cloudless sky

19 **cloud appearance,** filamentary cloud, wispy cloud, billowy cloud, fleecy cloud, feathery cloud, cottony cloud, wisp *or* billow *or* patch of cloud, mare's-tail, heaped cloud, globular cloud, lumpy cloud, band of cloud, belt of cloud, bank of cloud, roll of cloud, sheet of cloud, layer cloud, veil of cloud, cloud tower, cloud street, lenticular cloud, lee-wave cloud, iridescent cloud, mackerel sky, buttermilk sky

20 **thunderstorm,** storm, thunder, thunderclap *or* clap of thunder, lightning, lightning flash *or* stroke, track, fork *or* forked lightning, sheet lightning, ball lightning, summer lightning, thunderbolt, bolt of lightning, fulguration; electric storm, lightning conductor

21 **sun,** sunshine, strong sun, weak sun, recorded sunshine, clear sky; solar radiation, sunlight, ultraviolet (UV) radiation, direct radiation, indirect radiation, solar power, solar energy

22 **hot weather,** heat, hot spell, dog days, heat wave, warm weather, warm spell, sunny weather, sunny period, sunny spell, summer, Indian summer; scorcher [Inf], sizzler [Inf]

23 **dryness,** drought, dry spell

24 **cold weather,** coolness, chill, chilliness, chill *or* nip in the air, cold, cold spell, cold snap, cold wave, winter, hard winter, wintriness; freezing weather, big freeze, hard freeze, freeze-up

25 **frost,** touch of frost, moderate frost, severe frost, hard frost, sharp frost, silver frost, glaze frost, glaze; ground frost, air frost, radiation frost, advection frost, hoar frost, hoar, white frost, rime, permafrost; ice, black ice; frost damage, frost heave

26 **precipitation,** rain, hail, sleet, freezing rain, snow, rainfall, snowfall; raindrop, hailstone, snowflake, ice crystal, hydrometeor

27 **rain,** rainfall, raininess, fine rain, drizzle, mizzle, light rain, shower, light shower, showeriness, occasional *or* intermittent showers *or* rain, scattered showers, April showers, thundershower, steady *or* persistent rain, rainstorm, torrential rain, driving rain, drenching rain, downfall, deluge, downpour, cloudburst, spate [Brit], gullywasher; pluviosity, wetness, rainy season, wet season, monsoon season, the rains; rain damage, flood, acid rain; rainmaking, cloud seeding, rain dance

28 **rainbow,** arc, double rainbow, primary rainbow, secondary rainbow, fogdog, fogbow *or* white rainbow *or* mistbow *or* seadog; rainbow's end

◗ *Color 251*

29 **hail,** hailstone, small hail, snow pellets *or* soft hail *or* graupel *or* tapioca snow

30 **snow,** snowfall, snow shower, flurry, snowstorm, blizzard; drifting snow, driven snow, whiteout; snow cover, mantle *or* blanket of snow, snowbank, snowdrift, snow bed; wet snow, corn snow, powdery snow *or* powder, granular snow, spindrift, consolidated snow *or* firn *or* névé; snowmelt, melt, meltwater, slush; snowslide, avalanche

◗ *Skiing, Ice Skating, Bobsledding 162*

31 **moisture,** humidity, humidness, fog, mist, dew

32 **fog,** ground fog, hill fog, lake fog, river fog, coastal fog, sea fog, radiation fog, freezing fog, fog drip, advection fog, dense fog, thick fog, fog bank, pea soup [Inf], pea-souper [Brit inf]; smog

33 **mist,** haze, heat haze, mountain mist, hill mist, thick mist, Scotch mist, brume

34 **dew,** condensation, dewdrop, dew point

35 **climate,** local climate, microclimate, regional climate, macroclimate; maritime *or* marine climate, Mediterranean climate, oceanic climate, continental climate, mountain climate, desert climate, tundra climate, rainforest climate, snow-forest climate, dry climate, arid climate, semiarid climate, humid climate, semihumid climate, hot climate, tropical climate, subtropical climate, temperate climate, moderate climate, cool climate, cold climate, polar climate *or* arctic climate; season

◗ *Season 654*

36 **climate zone,** tropics, equatorial rainy zone, tropical summer rainy zone *or* marginal tropics, subtropics, subtropical dry zone, subtropical winter rainy zone, temperate zone, continental zone, subpolar zone, polar zone, tundra

37 **climatic change,** climatic variation, climatic trend, ice age, glaciation, interglaciation, interglacial, postglaciation, global warming, greenhouse effect, desertification, climate modification

◗ *Geology 8; Physics 10*

ADJECTIVES

38 **meteorologic,** meteorological, synoptic, elemental, climatic, climatological, seasonal

◗ *Season 654*

39 **barometric,** barographic, isobaric, thermometric, thermographic, isothermal, hygrometric, hygrographic, psychrometric, anemometric, anemographic, pluviometric, udometric

40 **atmospheric,** tropospheric, stratospheric, ionospheric, geostrophic, radiative, thermal, convective, advective, adiabatic, isothermal, evaporated, condensed, sublimated, saturated, supercooled

41 **frontal,** cyclonic, anticyclonic

42 **windy,** breezy, blowy, cooling, windier, fresh, brisk, gusty, blustery, squally, keen, piercing, sharp, biting, cold, freezing, raw, bitter, icy, strong, high, gale-force, storm-force, hurricane-force; northerly, boreal, northeasterly, easterly, southeasterly, southerly, southwest-

erly, westerly, favonian, northwesterly, prevailing, aeolian, anemological

43 **fine,** fair, bright, sunny, solar, dry, rainless, calm, windless, clear, cloudless, brighter, sunnier, drier, settled, fresh, bracing, brisk, crisp, invigorating

44 **cloudy,** cloud-flecked, cloud-crossed, cloud-laden, cloud-covered, overcast, overclouded, cloud-capped, cloud-topped, dull, gloomy, dark, gray, heavy, cirrose *or* cirrous, cirriform, cumuliform, cumulous, cirrocumuliform, cirrocumulous, altocumuliform, altocumulous, stratous, stratiform, altostratous, cirrostratous, nimbostratous, cumulonimbiform, nephological

45 **stormy,** inclement, violent, rough, tempestuous, raging, foul, ugly, dirty, thundery

46 **warm,** mild, moderate, temperate, pleasant, balmy, milder, warmer, hotter

47 **hot,** sweltering, sweltry, blistering, torrid, boiling, sizzling [Inf]

48 **humid,** muggy, damp, close, heavy, oppressive, sticky, sweaty

49 **cool,** chilly, chill, coldish, nippy, cooler, colder, cold, bitterly cold, raw, frigid, frosty, frosted, frost-covered, freezing, icy, slushy, sludgy, below zero, snowy, snow-covered, snow-clad, sleety, bleak, arctic, Siberian, boreal, perishing

50 **rainy,** showery, wet, drizzly, drizzling, rainier, wetter, steady, persistent, heavy, torrential, driving, streaming, pouring, pelting, drumming, blinding, pluvial, pluvious *or* pluviose, hydrometeorologic(al), hyetographic(al); coming down in buckets *or* torrents *or* sheets; raining cats and dogs [Inf]

51 **foggy,** thick, fogbound, enshrouded, smoggy, misty, hazy, nebulous, dewy

VERBS

52 **forecast,** predict

53 **blow,** stir, sigh, sough, whisper, murmur, hum, freshen, blow up, get up, whistle, moan, gust, buffet, bluster, roar, howl, screech, wail, scream, shriek, back, veer

54 **cloud,** cloud over, darken, grow dark, roll, scud, break, thin

55 **storm,** gather, brew, set in, blow a gale, blow a hurricane, thunder, lightning

56 **shine,** radiate, glimmer, shimmer, blaze, burn, glare, shine brightly, brighten, lighten, clear

57 **rain,** precipitate, fall, shower, drizzle, patter, spatter, splatter, plash, pour, pelt, teem, stream, drum; spit, come down in buckets *or* torrents *or* sheets, rain cats and dogs [Inf]

58 **snow,** blizzard, sleet, hail, frost, ice, ice over, freeze, thaw, melt

59 **fog,** befog, enshroud, mist, bemist, enmist, haze

ADVERBS

60 **meteorologically,** synoptically, climatically, climatologically, windily, stormily, cloudily, warmly, mildly, hotly, swelteringly, humidly, wetly, moistly, coolingly, coldly, frostily, snowily, foggily, mistily, hazily

10 Physics

NOUNS

1 **physics,** physical science, exact science, natural science, natural philosophy; applied physics, theoretical physics

2 **classical physics,** dynamics, fluid dynamics, hydrodynamics, aerodynamics, statics, kinematics; mechanics, Newtonian mechanics, fluid mechanics; sound, acoustics; optics, geometric optics, physical optics; heat, thermodynamics; electricity, magnetism, magnetics, electrodynamics, electromagnetism

3 **theory,** kinetic theory, wave theory, electromagnetic theory, quantum theory, quantum field theory, special theory of relativity, general theory of relativity

4 **physical law,** principle, rule, criterion, equation, equation of state, effect, hypothesis, proposition, theorem, premise, thesis, statement, axiom; model, atmospheric model, cosmological model, mathematical model

5 **dimension,** space, position, space coordinates, coordinates, length, breadth, height, altitude; thickness, radius, diameter, area, volume, angle, plane angle, solid angle; free space, four-dimensional space, four-dimensional continuum, space-time, space-time continuum, space curvature

  ▶ *Mathematics 6*

6 **frequency,** period, interval, angular frequency, phase, motion; entropy, linear motion, circular motion, simple harmonic motion, turbulence

  ▶ *Time 639; Motion 677*

7 **speed,** velocity, relative velocity, angular velocity, ac-

---

FIELDS OF MODERN PHYSICS

astrophysics	nuclear physics
atomic physics	particle physics
biophysics	physical chemistry
chemical physics	plasma physics
cryogenics	quantum gravity
crystallography	quantum mechanics
electroacoustics	quantum statistics
electronics	quantum theory
electro-optics	radiation physics
electrothermodynamics	relativistic quantum mechanics
geophysics	relativity
high-energy physics	semiconductor physics
low-temperature physics	solid-state physics
magnetohydrodynamics	spectroscopy
mathematical physics	statistical mechanics
matrix mechanics	statistical physics
medical physics	theoretical physics
molecular physics	ultrasonics
nonlinear optics	wave mechanics

---

celeration, angular acceleration, acceleration due to gravity, free fall

▶ *Motion 677*

8 **mass,** density, relative density, specific gravity, momentum, angular momentum, inertia, moment of inertia, center of mass, center of gravity, conservation of mass, weight

9 **force,** gravitational force, centripetal force, centrifugal force, moment, torque, torsion, equilibrium, stable equilibrium, unstable equilibrium, metastable equilibrium, buoyancy, force field, flux, flux density, pressure, atmospheric pressure, vapor pressure, stress, strain, elasticity, viscosity; magnetic force, electrostatic force, nuclear force; friction, static friction, dynamic friction, rolling friction, osmosis, surface tension

10 **energy,** potential energy, kinetic energy, chemical energy, solar energy, electrical energy, nuclear energy, conservation of energy, conservation of mass and energy

▶ *Engineering 14; Power 514*

11 **wave,** vibration, oscillation, transient disturbance, undulation, wave motion, longitudinal wave, transverse wave, torsional wave, traveling wave, standing wave, surface wave, node, antinode, wave propagation, radiation; sound wave, acoustic wave, ultrasonic wave, water wave, ripple, tsunami *or* seismic sea wave, bow wave, shock wave, electrical oscillation, mechanical oscillation, vibration, oscillating current, vibrating string, forced vibration, resonance, resonant frequency

▶ *Oscillation 683*

12 **wave property,** transmission, attenuation, absorption, dissipation, aberration, deflection, diffusion, reflection, refraction, dispersion, scattering, interference, diffraction, polarization, plane polarization, circular polarization, elliptical polarization; wave velocity, phase velocity, speed of light, speed of sound

13 **wave form,** wave shape, sine wave, sinusoidal wave, nonsinusoidal wave, pulse, rectangular pulse, square wave, pulse train, wavelength, wave number, frequency, frequency band, frequency spectrum, amplitude, wave crest, wave trough

14 **electromagnetic radiation,** radio wave, microwave, radar, infrared (IR) radiation, near infrared, far infrared, light, visible radiation, ultraviolet (UV) radiation, near ultraviolet, far ultraviolet, UVA, UVB, X rays, gamma rays, electromagnetic spectrum, visible spectrum, radio spectrum

15 **sound,** noise, white noise, music, ultrasound, infrasound, audibility, inaudibility; acoustics, reverberation

▶ *Hearing 228; Sound 230*

16 **sounding,** echo sounding, depth sounding, sonar, ultrasonic imaging *or* ultrasonography, ultrasonic cleaning, ultrasonic welding

17 **light,** illuminance *or* illumination; brightness, clarity, contrast, luminance; light emission, incandescence, luminescence, bioluminescence, triboluminescence, chemiluminescence, thermoluminescence, fluores-

---

CLASSICAL PHYSICAL LAWS, EFFECTS, EQUATIONS

Ampère–Laplace law	de Broglie principle	Lambert's law	Newton's rings
Ampère's law	diesel cycle	laws of entropy	Ohm's law
Archimedes' principle	Dirac's equation	laws of motion	Otto cycle
Avogadro's hypothesis	Doppler effect	laws of reflection	Paschen series
Balmer series	Dulong and Petit's law	laws of refraction	Peltier effect
Barkhausen effect	Faraday effect	laws of thermodynamics	Planck's radiation law
Bell's inequality	Faraday's laws	Lenz's law	Poisson ratio
Bernoulli effect	Fermat's principle	Lorentz–Fitzgerald	Poynting vector
Biot–Savart law	fine-structure constant	contraction	Prévost's theory of
Bitter pattern	Fraunhofer diffraction	Lyman series	exchanges
Bloch wall	Fresnel diffraction	Mach number	Rayleigh scattering
Bohr atom	Gay-Lussac's law	Maxwell–Boltzmann	Reynolds number
Boltzmann constant	Gibbs function	statistics	Roentgen rays
Bose–Einstein statistics	Hall effect	Maxwell distribution	Rydberg constant
Boyle's law	Heisenberg uncertainty	Maxwell's equation	Schrödinger's cat
Bragg's law	principle	Meissner effect	Schrödinger's wave equation
Brewster angle	Helmholtz function	Michelson–Morley	Seebeck effect
Carnot cycle	Hooke's law	experiment	Stefan–Boltzmann constant
Charles's law	Joule–Kelvin *or*	Moseley's law	Stefan's law
Compton effect	Joule–Thomson effect	Néel temperature	Thomson effect
Coulomb's law	Joule's laws	Neumann's law	van der Waals equation
Curie's law	Kepler's laws	Newton's law of cooling	Wankel cycle
Curie–Weiss law	Kerr effect	Newton's law of gravitation	Wien's displacement law
Dalton's law	Kirchoff's laws	Newton's laws of motion	Young's experiment

cence, phosphorescence, radioluminescence; light beam, ray of light, pencil beam of light, luminous intensity, luminous flux, luminous efficiency, luminous efficacy

▶ *Vision 242; Light 246*

18 **laser (light amplification by stimulated emission of radiation),** gas laser, helium-neon laser, carbon dioxide laser, ruby laser, neodymium-glass laser, yttrium aluminum garnet (YAG) laser, semiconductor laser, tunable laser, dye laser, monochromatic radiation, coherent radiation, stimulated emission, population inversion, maser (microwave amplification by stimulated emission of radiation)

19 **polarized light,** plane-polarized light, circularly polarized light, elliptically polarized light, birefringence

▶ *Light 246; Color 251*

20 **optical element,** mirror, lens, spectacles, glasses, prism, diffraction grating, reflection grating, optical fiber; internal reflection, refraction, refractivity, refractive index, diffraction; hologram, holograph, holographic optical element, stereogram, kinogram, diffractive optical element

▶ *Vision 242*

21 **optical characteristic,** reflection, total internal reflection, refraction, refractivity, refractive index, diffraction, holography

22 **lens system,** compound lens, mirror system, catadioptric system, telecentric system, eyepiece, objective, condenser, camera lens, relay lens; focal length, focal plane, focal point, focus, principal plane, circle of least confusion, caustic, lens aperture, mirror aperture, depth of field, f-number *or* f number, relative aperture, object distance, image distance, real image, virtual image, optic axis, axial ray, paraxial ray

23 **photosensitivity,** photosensitive material, light-sensitive material, photoelectric effect, photoconductivity, photovoltaic effect, electro-optical effect, optical activity, optical rotation, optoelectronics, photorefractive effect

24 **photometry,** photography, photolithography, fiber optics, fiber-optics transmission

25 **heat,** quantity of heat, warmth, hotness, hot body, hot substance, heating device; combustion, burning, fuel

▶ *Fuel 106; Heat 217*

26 **cold,** cold body, cold substance, cooling system, refrigeration, freezing

▶ *Cold 218*

27 **heat flow,** heat transfer, conduction, convection, radiation, heat flow rate, heat exchange, thermal equilibrium, thermal conductivity, heat capacity, specific heat capacity, molar heat capacity

28 **heating effect,** incandescence, thermionic emission, thermoelectricity, thermoelectric effect, thermal radiation, blackbody radiation, blackbody *or* perfect radi-

ator; expansion, expansion coefficient, compression, compressibility, adiabatic change, isothermal change

29 **temperature,** temperature scale, phase change, transition, freezing, fusion, melting, boiling, ebullition, liquefaction, vaporization, evaporation, sublimation, transition temperature, freezing point, melting point, boiling point, sublimation point, triple point; thermometry, pyrometry, thermal imaging

▶ *Heat 217; Measurement 589*

30 **thermodynamics,** first law, second law, third law, thermodynamic temperature, absolute zero, triple point, volume, pressure, entropy, internal energy, enthalpy, work, external work, latent heat, specific latent heat, standard temperature and pressure (STP), normal temperature and pressure (NTP), standard atmosphere, equation of state, critical state, critical temperature

31 **electricity,** current electricity, static electricity, frictional electricity, atmospheric electricity, thermoelectricity, photoelectricity, bioelectricity

32 **photoelectricity,** photoemission, photoconduction; photoelectric device, photosensor, photometer, photoelectric cell, exposure meter, light-emitting diode (LED), liquid-crystal display (LCD)

33 **electrical conduction,** conductivity, conducting medium, conductor, metal conductor, liquid conductor, electrolytic conductor, semiconductor, insulator, electrolyte, electrode, anode, cathode, electrolysis, electrolytic cell, primary cell, secondary cell, battery, fuel cell

▶ *Chemistry 11*

34 **semiconductor,** n-type semiconductor, p-type semiconductor, charge carrier, electron, hole, electron conduction, hole conduction, n-type conductivity, p-type conductivity, p–n junction, energy band, conduction band, valence band, energy gap, impurity atom, acceptor impurity, donor impurity, doping, semiconductor device, diode, transistor band gap, integrated circuit, computer chip

35 **superconductivity,** superconductor, transition temperature, high-temperature superconductor, superconducting magnet

36 **insulation,** insulator, nonconductor, dielectric, dielectric constant, dielectric coefficient, dielectric polarization, breakdown voltage

37 **electromagnetic induction,** electrostatic induction, thermoelectric effect, photoelectric effect, photovoltaic effect, photoconductivity, piezoelectric effect, electrostriction

38 **electric charge,** quantity of electricity, charge, positive charge, negative charge, charged particle, electron, proton, ion, charged body, charged substance, charge attraction, charge repulsion, conservation of charge, dipole, dipole moment, quadrupole, charge density, electric constant

39 **electric current,** current, flow of electricity, direct

current (d.c.), alternating current (a.c.), transient current, pulse, frequency, phase, conduction current, displacement current, induced current, eddy current, current density, juice [Inf]

40 electric potential, potential, potential difference (pd), voltage, electromotive force (emf), back *or* counter emf, ground, earth, live, neutral

41 resistance, reactance, impedance, resistivity, conductivity, capacitance, inductance, mutual inductance, self-inductance, conductance, mutual conductance

42 electric field, electric field strength, electric flux, displacement, permittivity, relative permittivity

43 circuit, electronic circuit, electric circuit, network, interconnected circuits, circuit element, electronic component, electronic device, resistor, capacitor, inductor, diode, transistor, rectifier, amplifier, oscillator, filter, transformer, transducer

44 electrical energy, electric power, generator, electric motor, power station, power supply
  ◗ *Power 514*

45 magnetism, magnetic attraction, magnetic repulsion, electromagnetism, diamagnetism, paramagnetism; ferromagnetism, antiferromagnetism, ferrimagnetism

46 geomagnetism, terrestrial magnetism, earth's magnetism, magnetosphere, magnetic North, magnetic South, magnetic North Pole, magnetic South Pole, magnetic equator, magnetic meridian, magnetic declination *or* magnetic variation, magnetic dip *or* magnetic inclination, angle of dip, (geo)magnetic storm, paleomagnetism, magnetic reversal, magnetic epoch
  ◗ *Geology 8*

47 magnet, permanent magnet, bar magnet, horseshoe magnet, pot magnet, keeper, electromagnet, solenoid, magnetizing coil, coil, ferromagnetic core, superconducting magnet, magnetite, magnetic iron ore, lodestone, ferrite, magnetic monopole

48 magnetic quantity, magnetic variable, magnetomotive force, magnetic potential difference, magnetic field, magnetic field strength, magnetic flux, magnetic induction *or* magnetic flux density, magnetization, permeability, relative permeability, magnetic dipole moment, magnetic moment, magneton, magnetic constant

49 electromagnetic radiation, electromagnetic wave, electromagnetic spectrum

50 magnetic phenomenon, magnetic hysteresis, hysteresis, residual magnetization, remanence, electromagnetic induction, self-induction, mutual induction, magnetostriction, magneto-optical effect, magnetic damping, magnetic deflection, magnetic focusing, magnetic lens, magnetic mirror, magnetic levitation *or* maglev

51 magnetic recording, magnetic tape, videotape, magnetic track, magnetic storage, magnetic memory, magnetic disk, hard disk, floppy disk, magnetic ink char-

acter recognition (MICR), magnetic ink, magnetic card, magnetic stripe, magnetic resonance imaging (MRI)
  ◗ *Computers 15*

52 atom, atomic structure, nucleus, elementary particle, proton, neutron, nucleon, binding energy, electron, electron configuration, electron shell, subshell, s-electron, p-electron, d-electron, f-electron, atomic orbital, energy level

53 elementary particle, fundamental particle, subatomic particle, particle, lepton, electron, muon, tauon, neutrino, quark, quark flavor, quark color, hadron, baryon, meson, proton, neutron, nucleon, pion, pi meson, kaon, K meson, fermion, boson, antiparticle, antiproton, antineutron, positron, antielectron, antiquark

54 ion, positive ion, cation, negative ion, anion, charge number, ionization, ionization energy, ionization potential
  ◗ *Chemistry 11*

55 excited atom, excited state, ground state, metastable state, excitation, transition, quantum jump, excitation energy, quantum level

56 emission, absorption, emission spectrum, absorption spectrum, continuous spectrum, line spectrum, band spectrum, optical spectrum, infrared spectrum, ultraviolet spectrum, microwave spectrum, X-ray spectrum, gamma ray spectrum

57 isotope, nuclide, atomic mass, atomic mass constant, relative atomic mass, atomic weight, atomic number, proton number, mass number, nucleon number, neutron number

58 radioactivity, decay, radioactive decay, alpha decay, beta decay, radioactive substance, radioisotope, radionuclide, alpha emitter, beta emitter, parent nuclide, daughter nuclide, daughter product, alpha particle, beta particle, alpha rays, beta rays, gamma rays, radioactive series, half-life, mean life, decay constant, activity, energy imparted, absorbed dose, dose equivalent, ionizing radiation, high-energy radiation, X rays, particulate radiation, cosmic rays, radiometric dating, radiocarbon dating, potassium-argon dating, radiography, radiology, radiotherapy
  ◗ *Geology 8; Medicine 107*

59 nuclear reaction, disintegration, transmutation, collision, scattering, elastic scattering, inelastic scattering, cross section

60 nuclear fission, fission reaction, fission, chain reaction, splitting the atom, atom smashing, fissionable nuclide, fissile nuclide, fertile nuclide, fission product, critical mass

61 nuclear fusion, fusion reaction, fusion, thermonuclear fusion, controlled nuclear fusion, nuclear energy, atomic energy, nuclear power, nuclear engineering, nucleonics

62 nuclear problem, nuclear accident, meltdown, fall-

out, nuclear contamination, decontamination, radiation exposure; nuclear waste, radioactive waste, hazardous waste, high-level waste, low-level waste, intermediate-level waste, waste disposal, waste processing
▶ *Waste 96*

63 quantum, quantum of radiation, photon, phonon, quantized property, quantum number, charge, spin, isospin, parity, strangeness, charm, beauty

64 quantum theory, quantum mechanics, wave mechanics, matrix mechanics, Dirac notation, wave-particle duality, Copenhagen interpretation, quantum electrodynamics, quantum chromodynamics, quantum uncertainty, quantum jump

65 fundamental interaction, gravitational interaction, electromagnetic interaction, nuclear interaction, strong interaction, strong nuclear interaction, weak interaction, weak nuclear interaction, electroweak interaction, exchange force, unified field theory, string, superstring, grand unification theory

66 causality, cause and effect, causal law, deterministic law, determinism, unpredictability, chaos theory, probability, indeterminacy, uncertainty principle, Heisenberg uncertainty principle; butterfly effect, chaos

67 measurement, mensuration, metrology, telemetry; remote sensing, sensitivity, response, linear response, frequency response, calibration, accuracy, precision, error, systematic error, observational error, personal error, probable error, standard error, standard deviation, estimated value, computed value, specified value, root mean square (rms) value
▶ *Measurement 589*

68 microscopy, thermometry, pyrometry, spectrometry, spectroscopy, photometry, interferometry

69 fundamental constant, physical constant, universal constant, speed of light (in vacuum), gravitational constant, Planck constant, permeability of vacuum, magnetic constant, permittivity of vacuum, electric constant, elementary charge, electron mass, proton mass

ADJECTIVES

70 physical, classical, mechanical, dynamic, static, kinetic, kinematic; hydrodynamic, aerodynamic, acoustic, ultrasonic, subsonic, infrasonic, optic, optical, thermal, calorific, thermodynamic, cryogenic; electric, electrical, photoelectric, photoconductive, photoemissive; magnetic, electrodynamic, atomic, crystallographic, solid-state, spectroscopic, spectrometric, monochrome, polychrome, magnetohydrodynamic, nonclassical, quantum, quantum mechanical, quantized, statistical, relativistic

71 theoretical, hypothetical, mathematical, experimental, pure, applied

VERBS

72 experiment, observe, measure, calibrate, calculate, determine, compute, estimate, split the atom

▶ *Experiment 335*

73 interact, cause, effect, electrify, change, magnetize, crystallize, fuse, react, collide, conduct, induct, attract, absorb; resist, repel; transmute, disintegrate, scatter; accelerate, decelerate; pulse, phrase

74 heat, melt, boil, liquefy, vaporize, evaporate, sublime
▶ *Heat 217*

75 freeze, solidify

76 reflect, refract, diffract, polarize; luminesce, fluoresce, phosphoresce

77 wave, oscillate, vibrate, reverberate, resonate
▶ *Oscillation 683*

ADVERBS

78 physically, classically, mechanically, dynamically, statically, kinetically, kinematically, hydrodynamically, aerodynamically, acoustically, ultrasonically, subsonically, optically, thermally, calorifically, thermodynamically, cryogenically, electrically, magnetically, electrodynamically, crystallographically, spectroscopically, spectrometrically, magnetohydrodynamically, nonclassically, quantum mechanically, statistically, relativistically

11 Chemistry

NOUNS

1 chemistry, chemical science, science of substances; analysis, synthesis, kinetics
▶ *Biochemistry 12; Engineering 14*

2 chemist, chemical scientist; agricultural chemist, alchemist, analytical chemist, astrochemist, biochemist, inorganic chemist, organic chemist, physical chemist, physiochemist, theoretical chemist, *etc.*

3 chemical element, element, metal, nonmetal, semimetal, metalloid, heavy metal, alkali metal, noble metal, alkaline-earth element, transition element, noble gas, chalcogen, halogen, rare-earth element, inert gas, rare gas, lanthanide *or* lanthanon *or* lanthanoid, actinide *or* actinon *or* actinoid, transuranic element, supertransuranic element, superheavy element; period, short period, long period, family, group, s-block, p-block, d-block, f-block; periodic table of elements
▶ *Physics 10; Material World 524*

4 chemical compound, organic, inorganic, organometallic, covalent, electrovalent, univalent, monovalent, divalent, bivalent, trivalent, tervalent, tetravalent, quadrivalent, pentavalent, quinquevalent, hexavalent, sexivalent, heptavalent, septivalent, octavalent, ionic, coordination, interstitial, lamellar, intercalation, clathrate, eutectic, cryohydrate, intermetallic, stoichiometric, nonstoichiometric, polar, nonpolar, saturated, unsaturated, delocalized, electron-deficient, cyclic, acyclic, heterocyclic, homocyclic, carbocyclic, aromatic, aliphatic, alicyclic, pseudoaromatic, nonbenzenoid aromatic, binary, ternary, molecular, monatomic, diatomic, triatomic, polyatomic, complex, transient, metastable, chelate, sandwich; alloy, amalgam, ceramic, refractory, synthetic, biosynthetic, analog, by-product

5 **valence,** valency, valence-bond *or* VB theory, molecular-orbital *or* MO theory, crystal-field theory

6 **chemical bond,** valence bond, ionic bond, electrovalent bond, covalent bond, coordinate bond, ligand, dative bond, donor, acceptor, polar bond, heteropolar bond, homopolar bond, semipolar bond, intermediate bond, bond pair, lone pair, metallic bond, electron-deficient bond, multicenter bond, bent bond, banana bond, single bond, double bond, triple bond, dipole-dipole interaction, hydrogen bond; orbital, molecular orbital, bonding orbital, antibonding orbital, hybrid orbital; s-orbital, p-orbital, d-orbital, f-orbital, π-orbital, σ-orbital; dispersion force, van der Waals force, bond energy, bond strength, bond angle, dissociation energy; overlap integral, hybridization

7 **structure,** formula, structural formula, molecular formula, chemical formula, empirical formula, Lewis dot structure, stereochemistry, isomer, isomerism, structural isomer(ism), stereoisomer(ism), cis-trans isomer(ism), syn-anti isomer(ism); polarimetry: optical isomer(ism), epimer, epimerism, anomer, anomerism, asymmetric center, chiral center, chirality, optical activity, optical rotation, dextro form *or* d-form, levo form *or* l-form, meso form, racemate, racemic mixture, steric effect, steric hindrance, D-form, L-form, R-form, S-form, resolution, racemization, inversion, optical rotary dispersion (ORD)

8 **chemical reaction,** process, product, reactant, reagent, fast reaction, slow reaction, irreversible reaction, reversible reaction, equilibrium, equilibrium constant, main reaction, side reaction, fission reaction, heterolysis, heterolytic fission, ionization, homolytic fission, homolysis, addition, condensation, substitution, SN1, SN2, elimination, E1, E2, displacement, disproportionation, rearrangement, ring closure, cyclization, aromatization, ring opening, polymerization, pyrolysis, neutralization, electrophilic reaction, electrophile, nucleophilic reaction, nucleophilic substitution, nucleophile, kinetics, unimolecular reaction, bimolecular reaction, reaction order, mechanism, step, rate-determining step, absolute rate theory, collision theory, transition rate, activated complex, rate constant, activation energy, isotope effect, photochemical reaction, radiochemical reaction, chain reaction, synthesis

9 **polymer,** macromolecule, monomer; polymerization, chain, cross linking, addition polymer(ization), condensation polymer(ization), homopolymer(ization), copolymer(ization), stereospecific polymerization, stereoregular polymer, atactic polymer, isotactic polymer, syndiotactic polymer, polyvinyl chloride (PVC) *or* polychloroethene, ultrahard PVC (uPVC), polyethylene *or* polyethene *or* polythene, polypropylene *or* polypropene, polyester, nylon, polycarbonate, polyurethane, epoxide resin, polystyrene, expanded polystyrene, polytetrafluoroethylene (PTFE), Teflon™, polymethylmethacrylate, Plexiglas™, vulcanite, isoprene rubber, chloroprene rubber, resin, plasticizer, stabilizer, plastic, thermosetting plastic, thermoplastic material

10 **acid,** mineral acid, organic acid, carboxylic acid, protonic acid, Lewis acid, Lowry–Brønsted acid, strong acid, weak acid, monobasic acid, dibasic base, tribasic acid, amphoteric compound, pH

11 **base,** alkali, inorganic base, organic base, quaternary base, Lewis base, Lowry–Brønsted base, strong alkali, weak alkali, monoacidic base, diacidic base, triacidic base, amphoteric compound, pH

12 **salt,** acid salt, basic salt, double salt, alum, hydrate, hemihydrate, anhydride, anhydrous salt

13 **phase,** solid, liquid, gas, vapor, phase change, triple point, phase diagram, boiling, melting, freezing, evaporation, sublimation, condensation, solution, concentrated solution, dilute solution, saturated solution, unsaturated solution, supersaturated solution, solvent, solute, polar solvent, nonpolar solvent, precipitation, precipitate, flocculent precipitate, colloid, colloidal solution, disperse phase, continuous phase, stabilizer, destabilizer, sol, gel, emulsion, hydrosol, aerosol, mist, smoke, fog, thixotropy, colligative property, mixture, eutectic

14 **crystal,** single crystal, microcrystal, crystallite, crystal boundary, crystallization, supernatant liquid, growth, form, structure, habit, crystal system, lattice, glass, cubic crystal, liquid crystal, face-centered-cubic (f.c.c.) crystal, body-centered-cubic (b.c.c.) crystal, cubic close packing, tetragonal crystal, rhombic *or* orthorhombic crystal, hexagonal crystal, hexagonal close packing,

---

BRANCHES OF CHEMISTRY

agricultural chemistry	metallurgy
alchemy	natural product chemistry
analytical chemistry	nuclear chemistry
astrochemistry	organic chemistry
atomic chemistry	pharmaceutical chemistry
biochemistry	photochemistry
catalysis	physical chemistry
chemical engineering	polymer chemistry
chemical physics	quantum chemistry
chemurgy [Arch]	radiochemistry
crystallography	surface chemistry
electrochemistry	theoretical chemistry
geochemistry	thermochemistry
industrial chemistry	zoochemistry *or* zoochemy
inorganic chemistry	zymurgy

trigonal crystal, monoclinic crystal, triclinic crystal; crystallography, X-ray crystallography, Bragg's law

▶ *Geology 8*

15 process, precipitation, crystallization, fractional crystallization, filtration, vacuum filtration, separation, distillation, fractional distillation, refluxing, chromatography, saponification, sorption, adsorption, absorption, mixing synthesis, stoichiometric synthesis

16 catalysis, homogeneous catalysis, heterogeneous catalysis, acid-base catalysis, autocatalysis, deactivation; catalyst, accelerator, stabilizer, poison, substrate, inhibitor, platinum black, Raney nickel, enzyme

17 analysis, qualitative analysis, quantitative analysis, spectrographic analysis, spectrometry, spectrograph, spectrometer, spectrum, mass spectrometry, ultraviolet (UV) spectrometry, infrared (IR) spectrometry, X-ray spectroscopy, microwave spectroscopy, electron spectroscopy, photoelectron spectroscopy (PES), nuclear magnetic resonance (NMR), magnetic resonance imaging (MRI), electron spin resonance (ESR), electron nuclear double resonance (ENDOR), polarography, polarogram, chromatography, chromatograph, column chromatography, gas/solid chromatography (GSC), thin-layer chromatography (TLC), paper chromatog-

raphy, gel filtration, ion exchange chromatography, high-performance liquid chromatography (HPLC), electrophoresis, gel electrophoresis, electro-osmosis, dialysis, stationary phase, mobile phase, carrier, elution, eluant, solvent front, Rf value

18 gravimetric analysis, gravimetry, volumetric analysis, titration, titre, indicator, phenolphthalein, methyl orange, methyl red, mixed indicator, universal indicator, absorption indicator, conductiometric titration, equivalence point, end point, standard solution, standardization, gas analysis

19 electrochemistry, cell, anode, cathode, electrolyte, concentration cell, half cell, electrode potential (ΔE), resting potential, electromotive force (emf), electrochemical series, electromotive series, electrolysis, electrolytic cell, electrodeposition, electroplating, electrolytic refining, electrolytic forming, anode sludge, voltaic cell, battery, wet cell, dry cell, polarization, overpolarization, fuel cell, electrolytic corrosion, rusting, sacrificial anode, hydrogen electrode, glass electrode

20 surface chemistry, absorption, adsorption, chemisorption, physisorption, sorption, desorption, degassing, outgassing, flash desorption, field desorption,

---

CHEMICAL ELEMENTS AND COMMON ALLOTROPES (WITH SYMBOLS AND ATOMIC NUMBERS)

actinium (Ac) 89
aluminum (Al) 13
americium (Am) 95
antimony (Sb) 51
argon (Ar) 18
arsenic (As) 33
    gray arsenic
astatine (At) 85
barium (Ba) 56
berkelium (Bk) 97
beryllium (Bd) 4
bismuth (Bi) 83
boron (B) 5
bromine (Br) 35
cadmium (Cd) 48
calcium (Ca) 20
californium (Cf) 98
carbon (C) 6
    graphite
    diamond
cerium (Ce) 56
cesium (Cs) 55
chlorine (Cl) 17
chromium (Cr) 24
cobalt (Co) 27
copper (Cu) 29
curium (Cm) 96
dysprosium (Dy) 66
einsteinium (Es) 99
erbium (Er) 68

europium (Eu) 63
fermium (Fm) 100
fluorine (F) 9
francium (Fr) 87
gadolinium (Gd) 64
gallium (Ga) 31
germanium (Ge) 32
gold (Au) 79
hafnium (Hf) 72
helium (He) 2
holmium (Ho) 67
hydrogen (H) 1
    dihydrogen
    orthohydrogen
    nascent hydrogen
    parahydrogen
indium (In) 49
iodine (I) 53
iridium (Ir) 77
iron (Fe) 26
krypton (Kr) 36
lanthanum (La) 57
lawrencium (Lr) 103
lead (Pb) 82
lithium (Li) 3
lutetium (Lu) 71
magnesium (Mg) 12
manganese (Mn) 25
mendelevium (Md) 101
mercury (Hg) 80

molybdenum (Mo) 42
neodymium (Nd) 60
neon (Ne) 10
neptunium (Np) 93
nickel (Ni) 28
niobium (Nb) 41
nitrogen (N) 7
nobelium (Nb) 102
osmium (Os) 76
oxygen (O) 8
    dioxygen
    ozone
    trioxygen
palladium (Pd) 46
phosphorus (P) 15
    red phosphorus
    white phosphorus
platinum (Pt) 78
plutonium (Pu) 94
polonium (Po) 84
potassium (K) 19
praseodymium (Pr) 59
promethium (Pm) 61
protactinium (Pa) 91
radium (Ra) 88
radon (Rn) 86
rhenium (Re) 75
rhodium (Rh) 45
rubidium (Rb) 37
ruthenium (Ru) 44

samarium (Sm) 62
scandium (Sc) 21
selenium (Se) 34
silicon (Si) 14
silver (Ag) 47
sodium (Na) 11
strontium (Sr) 38
sulfur (S) 16
tantalum (Ta) 73
technetium (Tc) 43
tellurium (Te) 52
terbium (Tb) 65
thallium (Tl) 81
thorium (Th) 90
thulium (Tm) 69
tin (Sn) 50
titanium (Ti) 22
tungsten (W) 74
unnilhexium (Unh) 106
unnilpentium (Unp) 105
unnilquadrium (Unq) 104
uranium (U) 92
vanadium (V) 23
xenon (Xe) 54
ytterbium (Yb) 70
yttrium (Y) 39
zinc (Zn) 30
zirconium (Zr) 4

sputtering, gettering, vacuum, high vacuum, low vacuum, hard vacuum, soft vacuum, ultrahigh vacuum (UHV); vacuum pump, filter pump, rotary pump, diffusion pump, ion pump, sputter-ion pump, getter-ion pump, cryogenic pump, vacuum gauge, monometer, McLeod gauge, Pirani gauge, ionization gauge, Bayard-Alpert gauge, leak detector, residual gas analyzer (RGA), Tesla coil

21 **industrial chemistry,** chemical engineering, refining, oil refining, refinery, cracking, cat cracking, reforming, steam reforming, fractionation, fractional distillation, fraction; petrochemicals, plastics, fibers, dyestuffs, fertilizers, explosives, fine chemicals, pharmaceuticals, biotechnology, manufacturing
  ▶ *Engineering 14*

22 **metallurgy,** metal, metalloid, alloy, metallography, pyrometallurgy, powder metallurgy, eutectic, electrometallurgy, electrowinning, extractive metallurgy, production metallurgy, extraction, blast furnace, electrolytic extraction, refining, froth flotation, electrorefining, electroplating

23 **ore,** deposit, vein, lode, lodestuff, placer, gangue, mineral, metal, precious metal, gem
  ▶ *Geology 8*

ADJECTIVES

24 **chemical,** organic, inorganic, theoretical, thermodynamic, statistico-mechanical, quantum, analytical, crystallographic, synthetic, kinetic, catalytic, photochemical, radiochemical, biochemical, physicochemical, astrochemical, metallurgical, geologic, zymurgic, alchemical

25 **status adjectives,** solid, liquid, gaseous, vaporous, condensed, melted, molten, frozen, evaporated, sublimated, concentrated, dilute, saturated, unsaturated, supersaturated, precipitated, filtered, distilled, flocculent, colloidal, lyophobic, lyophilic, hydrophobic, hydrophilic, disperse, continuous, stabilized, destabilized, gelled, emulsoid, thiotropic, colligative, eutectic, pure, refined, crystalline, microcrystalline, crystallized, crystalloid, noncrystalline, amorphous, irregular, structural, cubic, tetragonal, rhombic, orthorhombic, hexagonal, trigonal, monoclinic, triclinic, face-centered, body-centered, close-packed, cubic close-packed, hexagonal close-packed

26 **elemental,** native, uncombined

27 **acid,** acidic, basic, alkaline, weak, strong, monobasic, dibasic, tribasic, monoacidic, diacidic, triacidic, protonic, amphoteric, neutral, saline, hydrated, anhydrous

28 **structural,** steric, conformational, isomeric, stereoisomeric, epimeric, anomeric, asymmetric, asymmetrical, chiral, racemized

29 **reactive,** unreactive, inactive, deactivated, passive, fast, slow, reversible, irreversible, equilibrated, homolytic, heterolytic, additive, substitutional, cyclic,

electrophilic, nucleophilic, polymeric, monomolecular, bimolecular, first-order, second-order, third-order

30 **catalytic,** autocatalytic, activated, activating, deactivated, poison, inhibiting

31 **synthetic,** synthesized, manufactured

32 **analytic,** quantitative, spectroscopic, spectrographic, polarographic, chromatographic, electrophoretic, stationary, mobile, reversed-phase, gravimetric, volumetric, standardized, neutralized, equivalent

33 **electrochemical,** electrolytic, electromotive, electrovoltaic, electrodeposited, electroplated, electroformed, anodic, cathodic

34 **absorbed,** adsorbed, physisorbed, chemisorbed, sorbed, desorbed, outgassed, degassed

35 **polymeric,** monomeric, copolymeric, stereospecific, stereoregular, atactic, tactic, isotactic, syndiotactic

36 **metallurgical,** metallurgic, extractive, alloyed

VERBS

37 **solidify,** crystallize, crystallize out, precipitate, seed, liquefy, vaporize, condense, evaporate, concentrate, melt, freeze, dilute, dissolve, saturate, supersaturate, disperse, stabilize, destabilize, flocculate, gel, emulsify, refine

38 **react,** bond, coordinate, add, substitute, condense, eliminate, transfer, rearrange, dissociate, ionize, heterolyze, neutralize, acidify, cyclize, pyrolyze, irradiate, polymerize, racemize, invert, catalyze, intercalate, inhibit, poison, activate, promote, reduce, saponify, solvate, ferment, acetylate, acylate, benzoylate, brominate, calcine, calcify, carbonate, carburize, chlorinate, deuterate, diazotize, esterify, fluorinate, fluoridate, halogenate, hydrate, hydrogenate, hydrolyze, nitrate, oxidize, ozonize, sulfonate, sulfurize, tritate, synthesize, degrade

39 **electrolyze,** electrodeposit, electroplate, electroform

40 **absorb,** adsorb, physisorb, chemisorb, sorb, desorb, degas, outgas, getter, sputter, field desorb, field ionize

41 **extract,** win, concentrate, purify, refine, sinter, alloy, anneal, case harden, work harden, temper, separate, filter, distill, steam distill, vacuum distill, fractionate

ADVERBS

42 **chemically,** practically, theoretically, thermodynamically, catalytically, photochemically, metallurgically, synthetically, analytically, colloidally, amorphously, covalently, ionically, electrovalently

12 Biochemistry

NOUNS

1 **biochemistry,** biosynthesis, bioenergetics, biochemical taxonomy, biotechnology, enzymology; cloning, gene therapy, Human Genome Project, pharmacology

2 **biochemist,** plant biochemist, enzymologist, biotechnologist, kineticist, pharmacologist

3 carbohydrate, sugar, saccharide, polysaccharide, starch, glycogen, cellulose, alcohol, ketone

4 saccharide, sugar, simple sugar, monosaccharide, triose, tetrose, pentose, hexose, heptose, octose, aldose, aldotriose, aldotetrose, aldopentose, aldohexose, aldoheptose, aldooctose, ketose, ketotriose, ketotetrose, ketopentose, ketohexose, ketoheptose, ketooctose, hemiacetal, pyranose, hemiketal, furanose; complex sugar, disaccharide, trisaccharide, tetrasaccharide, oligosaccharide, sugar alcohol, sorbitol, mannitol, aldaric acid, saccharic acid, uronic acid; sugar derivative, glycoside, glucoside

5 polysaccharide, glycan, homopolysaccharide, heteropolysaccharide, storage polysaccharide, starch, amylose, amylopectin, inulin, animal starch, glycogen, dextran, fructan, arabinan, xylon, mannan, structural polysaccharide, cellulose, hemicellulose, pectic substance, pectin, extensin, lignin, agar, gum arabic, chitin, mucopolysaccharide, glycosaminoglycan (GAG)

6 sugar test, alpha-naphthol test, Barfoed's test, Benedict's test, Fehling's test, Molisch's test, Schiff's reagent, Seliwanoff's test, Tollan's reagent

7 fat, oil, wax, lipid, fatty-acid ester, fatty acid, carboxylic acid, arachidonic acid, essential fatty acid, linoleate, linolenate, glyceride, acylglycerol, simple glyceride, mixed glyceride, monoglyceride, diglyceride, triglyceride, saturated fat, unsaturated fat, monounsaturated fat, polyunsaturated fat, complex lipid, saponifiable lipid, glycolipid, cerebroside, phospholipid, phosphoglyceride, phosphatide, glycerophosphatide, lecithin *or* phosphatidycholine, sphingolipid, sphingomyelin, cephalin *or* phosphatidylethanolamine, lipoprotein, simple lipid, nonsaponifiable lipid, terpene, steroid, sterol, cholesterol, bile acid, lipolysis

8 amino acid, essential amino acid, nonessential amino acid, imino acid, peptide, peptide bond, α amino group, α carboxyl group, dipeptide, tripeptide, oligopeptide, polypeptide, amino-acid residue, protein, D-isomer, L-isomer, optical activity, dipolar ions *or* zwitterions

9 protein, amino-acid chain, protein structure, primary structure, main chain, backbone, side chain, secondary structure, disulfide bonds, tertiary structure, quaternary structure, oligomeric protein, protomer, globular

COMMON SUGARS

arabinose	lactose *or* milk	ribose
dextrose *or* corn	sugar	sorbose
sugar *or* grape	maltose	sucrose *or* cane
sugar	mannose	sugar *or* beet
fructose *or*	pentose	sugar *or*
levulose *or* fruit	raffinose *or*	saccharose
sugar	gossypose *or*	xylose
fucose	melitose *or*	
galactose	melitriose	
glucose	rhamnose	

AMINO ACIDS

alanine	histidine*	threonine*
arginine*	isoleucine*	tryptophan*
asparagine	leucine*	tyrosine
aspartic acid	lycine*	valine*
citrulline	methionine*	
cysteine	ornithine	
glutamic acid	phenylalanine*	* indicates an
glutamine	proline	essential amino
glycine	serine	acid

protein, globulin, fibrous protein, alpha helix, conjugated protein, nucleoprotein, lipoprotein, glycoprotein, proteoglycan, mucoprotein, mucin, peptidoglycan, phosphoprotein, hemoprotein, flavoprotein, metalloprotein, scleroprotein, sclerotization, prosthetic group, biuret test, denaturization, albumin, casein, collagen, fibrin, gelatin, gluten, histone, immunoglobulin, interferon, keratin, myoglobin, hemoglobin

10 nucleotide, nitrogenous base, purine base, adenine, guanine, pyrimidine base, thymine, cytosine, uracil, nucleoside, deoxynucleotide, ribonucleotide, nucleic acid, deoxyribonucleic acid (DNA), copy DNA (cDNA), double helix, ribonucleic acid (RNA), messenger RNA (mRNA), transfer RNA (tRNA)

11 enzyme, substrate, active site, apoenzyme, cofactor, coenzyme, isoenzyme, prosthetic group, core enzyme, holoenzyme, inhibition, competitive inhibition, allosteric inhibition, feedback inhibition, enzyme class, oxidoreductase, transferase, hydrolase, lyase, isomerase, polymerase, ligase, amylase, diastase, dehydrogenase, lactase, lipase, lysozyme, papain, protease, peptidase, proteolytic enzyme, proteolysis, pepsin, trypsin, rennin, restriction enzyme, restriction endonuclease, transaminase, zymogen

12 coenzyme, coenzyme A (CoA), coenzyme Q (CoQ), nicotinamide adenine dinucleotide (NAD), nicotinamide adenine dinucleotide phosphate (NADP), flavin adenine dinucleotide (FAD), flavoprotein, thiamine, pyrophosphate, lipoamide, biocytin, pyridoxal phosphate

13 vitamin, coenzyme, cofactor; vitamin A (retinol); vitamin B complex, vitamin B_1 (thiamine), vitamin B_2 (riboflavin), vitamin B_6 (pyridoxine), vitamin B_{12} (cyanocobalamin), nicotinic acid, pantothenic acid, folic acid, biotin, lipoid acid, choline; vitamin C (ascorbic acid); vitamin D_2 (ergocalciferol *or* calciferol), vitamin D_3 (cholecalciferol); vitamin E (tocopherol); vitamin K (phylloquinone)
▶ *Food 90*

14 vitamin deficiency disease, avitaminosis; night blindness, xerophthalmia, beriberi, pellagra, pernicious anemia, scurvy, rickets, osteomalacia
▶ *Ill Health 114*

COMMON FATTY ACIDS

acetic	fumaric	oleic
acrylic	lactic	oxalic
butyric	lauric	palmitic
capric	linoleic	pelargonic
caproic	linolenic	propionic
caprylic	maleic	stearic
crotonic	malic	valeric
formic	myristic	

15 **essential element,** major element, macronutrient; carbon, hydrogen, oxygen, nitrogen, calcium, phosphorus, potassium, sodium, chlorine, sulfur, magnesium, trace element, micronutrient, iron, manganese, zinc, copper, iodine, cobalt, selenium, molybdenum, chromium, silicon

16 **hormone,** neurohormone, releasing hormone, catecholamine, dopamine, epinephrine, adrenaline, norepinephrine, steroid hormone, sex hormone, androgen, anabolic steroid, estrogen, oral contraceptive, corticosteroid, mineralocorticoid, glucocorticoid, gonadotrophin, gonadotropic hormone, externally acting hormone, ectohormone, pheromone, hormonelike substance, prostaglandin; chemical messenger

17 **plant hormone,** phytohormone, growth substance, auxin, giberellin, ethylene *or* ethene, abscisic acid, indoleacetic acid (IAA), 2,4-dichlorophenoxyacetic acid (2,4-D), 2,4,5-trichlorophenoxyacetic acid (2,4,5-T), cytokinin *or* kinin, zeatin

18 **pigment,** plant pigment, flavonoid, flavonol, flavone, anthocyanin, phytochrome, photosynthetic pigment, chlorophyll, phycobilin, carotenoid, carotene, xanthophyll, fucoxanthin, respiratory pigment, hemoglobin, bile pigment, bilirubin, biliverdin, melanin

19 **alkaloid,** morphine, cocaine, atropine, quinine, caffeine, aconite, papaverine, strychnine, coniine, colchicine

20 **terpene,** isoprene unit, monoterpene, sesquiterpene, diterpene, triterpene, tetraterpene, geraniol, limonene, menthol, pinene, camphor, carvone, farnesol, phytol, carotenoid, squalene; vitamin A, vitamin E, vitamin K

21 **metabolism,** catabolism, anabolism, metabolic pathway, metabolite

   ▶ *Life Science 13*

22 **photosynthesis,** light reaction, dark reaction, chlorophyll a, chlorophyll b, photophosphorylation, Calvin cycle

   ▶ *Plants (General) 41*

23 **bioenergetics,** adenosine triphosphate (ATP), adenosine diphosphate (ADP), adenosine monophosphate (AMP), cyclic adenosine monophosphate (cAMP), pyrophosphate (PP_i), phosphorylation, phosphate bond, energy-rich bond, phosphagen, creatine phosphate, ATP cycle, glycolysis, gluconeogenesis, citric acid cycle, tricarboxylic acid (TCA) cycle, Krebs cycle

24 **respiration,** aerobic respiration, anaerobic respiration, photorespiration, external respiration, internal respiration, cell respiration; hemoglobin, myoglobin, heme, glycolysis, Embden–Meyerhof pathway, Krebs cycle, citric acid cycle, tricarboxylic acid (TCA) cycle, respiratory chain, electron-transport chain

ADJECTIVES

25 **biochemical,** biosynthetic, biomolecular, enzymic, hormonal, metabolic, catabolic, anabolic, bioenergetic, photosynthetic, glycolytic, gluconeogenic

---

HUMAN HORMONES

adrenocorticoid	estradiol	melatonin
adrenocorticotropic hormone (ACTH) *or* adrenocorticotropin	estriol	oxytocin
	estrogen	pancreozymin *or* cholecystokinin *or* cholecystokinin-pancreozymin
aldosterone	estrone	
androgen	follicle-stimulating hormone (FSH)	parathyroid hormone *or* parathormone
androsterone	gastrin	progesterone
angiotensin	glucagon	progestin
antidiuretic hormone (ADH) *or* vasopressin	gonadotropin-releasing hormone	prolactin
	growth hormone *or* somatotropin	relaxin
calcitonin *or* thyrocalcitonin	hydrocortisone *or* cortisol	secretin
cholecystokinin (CCK) *or* cholecystokinin-pancreozymin *or* pancreozymin	insulin	somatostatin
	intermedin *or* melanocyte-stimulating hormone	somatotropin *or* growth hormone
corticoid		testosterone
corticosterone	interstitial-cell-stimulating hormone (ICSH)	thyrocalcitonin *or* calcitonin
cortisol *or* hydrocortisone	lipotropin	thyroid-stimulating hormone (TSH) *or* thyrotropin *or* thyrotropic hormone
cortisone	luteinizing hormone (LH)	
deoxycorticosterone	luteotropic hormone *or* luteotropin	thyroxine *or* thyroxin
enterogastrone	melanocyte-stimulating hormone (MSH) *or* intermedin	triiodothyronine
erythropoietin		vasotocin
		vasopressin *or* antidiuretic hormone

VERBS

26 **metabolize,** photosynthesize, synthesize, catalyze

ADVERBS

27 **biochemically,** biosynthetically, photosynthetically, enzymatically, hormonally, metabolically, catabolically, anabolically

13 Life Science

NOUNS

1 **life science,** natural history, biological science, anatomy, biochemistry, biology, embryology, paleontology, pathology; taxonomy, systematics
 ▶ *Anthropology 1; Biochemistry 12; Medicine 107*

2 **biology,** zoology, botany, ecology *or* bionomics, bioecology, biophysics, biometry *or* biometrics, marine biology, cryobiology, electrobiology, parasitology, sociobiology; microbiology, bacteriology, virology

3 **biochemistry,** enzymology, endocrinology, neuroscience, immunology

4 **histology,** cell biology, cytology, molecular biology, genetics, biogenetics, genetic engineering, biotechnology, bionics, cybernetics

5 **anatomy,** morphology, physiology

6 **developmental biology,** embryology, evolution

7 **botany,** algology, bryology, paleobotany, dendrology, pomology, phytochemistry, phytoecology, phytobiology, phytography, phytology, vegetable *or* plant pathology, vegetable *or* plant physiology

8 **space biology,** astrobiology *or* exobiology, xenobiology

9 **living world,** natural world, nature, plant life *or* flora, animal life *or* fauna, biota, biosphere, ecosphere
 ▶ *Life 28*

10 **living organism,** organism, being, living being, living thing, organic being, creature, entity, body, individual, animal, plant; cell, aerobe, anaerobe
 ▶ *Agriculture 16; Horticulture 17; Animals (General) 34; Plants (General) 41*

11 **microorganism,** animalcule, microphyte; protist, monad; microbe, germ, bacterium, coccus, bacillus, spirillum; rickettsia, mycoplasma; virus, filterable virus, bacteriophage, phage, retrovirus, virion
 ▶ *Animals (General) 34; Invertebrates 39; Plants (General) 41; Ill Health 114*

12 **anatomy,** form, structure, gross structure, morphology, comparative anatomy; dissection, zootomy, tissue structure
 ▶ *Structure 551; Fluid 555; Interior 611*

13 **physiology,** vital functions, nutrition, absorption, respiration; photosynthesis, metabolism, anabolism, catabolism; transpiration, guttation, osmoregulation, secretion, excretion; sensation, reproduction, growth, locomotion

 ▶ *Reproduction 21; Secretion 24; Excretion 25; Eating 92; Sensation 212; Air 558; Motion 677*

14 **cell biology,** cytology, cell structure, histology, cell physiology, ultrastructure; microscopical examination, light microscopy, electron microscopy, phase-contrast microscopy; fixation, sectioning, staining, counterstaining; cytochemistry, histochemistry, tissue culture; biochemistry, respiration, glycolysis, Krebs cycle
 ▶ *Biochemistry 12; Medicine 107*

15 **cell,** prokaryotic *or* procaryotic cell, eukaryotic *or* eucaryotic cell, plant cell, animal cell; protoplast, cellule; germ cell: germen, reproductive cell, gamete, spore; somatic cell: blood cell, corpuscle, muscle cell, bone cell, pigment cell
 ▶ *Reproduction 21*

16 **cell structure,** cell membrane *or* plasma membrane *or* plasmalemma, microvillus; cell wall, cellulose, lignin, cell plate, ectoplasm, endoplasm; cell cytoplasm *or* cytosome, cytosol, cytoskeleton, microfibril, microtubule, microsome, endoplasmic reticulum (ER), ribosome, polysome *or* polyribosome, tonoplast, vacuole, organelles: centrosome, Golgi body, lysosome, mitochondrion, plastid, chloroplast; cell nucleus, nuclear membrane *or* nuclear envelope, nucleoplasm *or* karyoplasm, nucleolus, chromonema, chromatin, karyosome, idioplasm *or* germ plasm, nucleoprotein, nucleic acid, deoxyribonucleic acid (DNA), ribonucleic acid (RNA), nucleotide, nucleosome

17 **cell division,** cell cycle, mitosis *or* karyokinesis: interphase, prophase, metaphase, anaphase, telophase, diaster, cytokinesis, spindle, centrosome, centromere, aster, spindle fibers; meiosis: reduction division, equational division, gametogenesis, equator, linkage, crossing over

18 **molecular biology,** macromolecular structure, protein structure, polypeptide chain, amino-acid sequence, nucleic-acid structure, DNA double helix; molecular genetics, gene structure, gene sequencing, gene mapping, recombinant DNA technology *or* gene splicing, biotechnology, genetic engineering, genetic *or* DNA fingerprinting, gene *or* DNA probe, restriction endonuclease, gene cloning, cloning vector, designer gene; genotype, phenotype
 ▶ *Biochemistry 12*

19 **genetics,** classical genetics, Mendelism *or* Mendelian genetics, Mendel's law; heredity, inheritance, hereditary character; factor, dominance, recessiveness, double recessiveness, genetic constitution, genotype, biotype, phenotype; population genetics, genecology, gene flow, gene frequency, gene pool, genetic drift, gene complex, cytogenetics, molecular genetics, biochemical genetics, microbial genetics, gene manipulation, eugenics
 ▶ *Medicine 107*

20 **genetic material,** DNA, RNA, genetic element, gene,

chromosome, genetic map, factor, allele; operon, structural gene, regulator gene, operator gene; gene complement, genome; genetic code, codon, anticodon, messenger RNA (mRNA), transfer RNA (tRNA), ribosomal RNA, exon, intron, gene splicing, protein synthesis, extrachromosomal genetic element; plasmagene, plasmid, transposon, gene mutation, gene sequence

21 **chromosome,** heterosome, autosome, heterochromosome, idiochromosome; sex chromosome, W chromosome, X chromosome, Y chromosome, Z chromosome, euchromosome, homologous chromosome, univalent chromosome, chromatid; chromosome mutation

22 **developmental biology,** embryology, ontogeny, embryogenesis, embryogeny; germination, cleavage, blastulation, gastrulation, induction, evocation; embryo, germ, primordium, rudiment, zygote; fetus, extraembryonic membrane, amnion, chorion, allantois; juvenile, larva, nymph, pupa, chrysalis, metamorphosis, pedogenesis, neoteny

   ▶ *Reptiles and Amphibians 37; Insects and Arachnids 40*

23 **evolution,** phylogeny, speciation; convergent evolution, parallel evolution; Darwinism, natural selection, survival of the fittest, Lamarckism, inheritance of acquired characteristics, neo-Darwinism, Weismannism, continuity of germ plasm, neo-Lamarckism, Lysenkoism; uniformitarianism, catastrophism, paleontology, fossil record, recapitulation

24 **taxonomy,** systematics, biological classification, classical taxonomy, cytotaxonomy, numerical taxonomy, experimental taxonomy, biosystematics, cladistics, cladism, clade, taxonomic group, taxon

   ▶ *Class 777*

25 **ecology,** synecology, autecology, plant ecology *or* phytoecology, animal ecology *or* zooecology; ecosystem, community, population, niche; ecophysiology, food chain, food web, food pyramid, producer, primary producer, consumer, primary consumer, secondary consumer; parasitism, parasite, host, mutualism, symbiosis, symbiont *or* symbiote, commensalism, commensal; competition, succession, sere

   ▶ *Animals (General) 34; Food 90*

26 **life scientist,** biologist, natural scientist, zoologist, botanist; microbiologist, bacteriologist, virologist, parasitologist; anatomist, morphologist, physiologist; biochemist, endocrinologist, immunologist, histologist, cell biologist, cytologist, molecular biologist; geneticist, developmental biologist, embryologist, paleontologist, evolutionist, Darwinist, neo-Darwinist, taxonomist, cladist; naturalist, marine biologist, ecologist; biophysicist, biometrist, cryobiologist; space biologist; ethnobiologist, sociobiologist

ADJECTIVES

27 **biological,** zoological, botanical; microbiological, bacteriological, virological, gnotobiotic, parasitological; anatomical, morphological, physiological; biochemical, endocrinological, endocrine, immunological, histological, cytological, genetic, biotechnological; embryological, evolutionary, paleontological, taxonomic, systematic, ecological, bionomic; biophysical, biometric, bionic, cryobiological; ethnobiological, sociobiological

28 **living,** live, alive, animate, vital, viable, organic, natural, biotic; plant, animal; microbial, bacterial, viral

   ▶ *Life 28*

29 **physiological,** metabolic, anabolic, catabolic; alimentary, respiratory, aerobic, anaerobic, photosynthetic, secretory, excretory; reproductive, locomotory

   ▶ *Reproduction 21; Secretion 24; Excretion 25; Eating 92; Sensation 212; Air 558; Motion 677*

30 **cellular,** cell, prokaryotic *or* procaryotic, eukaryotic *or* eucaryotic, multicellular, unicellular, single-celled, acellular; plasmic, protoplasmic, cytoplasmic, ectoplasmic, endoplasmic, reticular, coenocytic, syncytial, mitochondrial, ribosomal

31 **nuclear,** nucleal, nucleic, nucleate, uninucleate, multinucleate, nucleolar, nucleolate(d)

32 **genetic,** genotypic(al), genomic, gene, genic, factorial; hereditary, Mendelian, dominant, recessive, mutant, mutational; chromosomal, mitotic, meiotic

33 **developmental,** ontogenic *or* ontogenetic, developing, primordial, rudimentary, germ, germinal, germinating, germinant, germinative, budding, embryonic; fetal, amniotic, chorionic, allantoic; juvenile, larval, pupal, neotenous, pedogenetic *or* pedogenic

34 **evolutionary,** phylogenetic *or* phyletic, Darwinian, Lamarckian, neo-Darwinian, neo-Lamarckian, uniformitarian

35 **taxonomic,** systematic, biosystematic, cladistic; generic, specific, subspecific

ADVERBS

36 **biologically,** zoologically, botanically; anatomically, morphologically, physiologically; biochemically, immunologically, histologically, cytologically; genetically, embryologically; taxonomically, generically, systematically, specifically; ecologically

14 Engineering

NOUNS

1 **engineering,** mechanical engineering, civil engineering, chemical engineering, electrical engineering, mining and metallurgical engineering, industrial engineering

2 **engineer,** mechanical engineer, civil engineer, chemical engineer, electrical engineer, mining engineer, metallurgical engineer, industrial engineer; registered engineer

◗ *Geology 8; Physics 10; Chemistry 11; Transportation 686*

3 **mechanical engineering,** industrial engineering, automotive engineering, aerospace engineering, aeronautical engineering, astronautical engineering, marine engineering, agricultural engineering

◗ *Agriculture 16; Transportation 686; Aviation 689*

4 **mechanical engineer,** industrial engineer, automotive engineer, aerospace engineer, aeronautical engineer, astronautical engineer, marine engineer, agricultural engineer; mechanic, technician

5 **dynamic structure,** dynamic system, machinery, mechanical device, machine, engine, motor, mechanism, tool, servomechanism

6 **simple machine,** lever, wheel and axle, pulley, block and tackle, inclined plane, wedge, screw, gear, press

7 **gear,** spur gear, rack and pinion, helical gear, bevel gear, hypoid gear, skew gear, worm gear, gear train, internal gear, external gear, gear tooth, diametral pitch, pitch diameter

8 **machine element,** machine part, wheel, gear, gearwheel, pulley, shaft, crank, rod, axle, hub, cam belt, coupling, bearing, ball bearing, roller bearing, journal, bush, differential

9 **machine tool,** horizontal machine, vertical machine; drill, drilling machine, press drill, boring machine; lathe, engine lathe, turret lathe, capstan lathe; milling machine, broaching machine, facing machine, threading machine, tapping machine; grinder, planer, shaper, saw, circular saw, bandsaw, single-point tool, multipoint tool; speed, feed, cutting fluid, cooling fluid, coolant, high-speed steel

◗ *Tool 103*

10 **work,** useful work, efficiency, load, effort, mechanical advantage

11 **engine type,** internal-combustion, Wankel, external-combustion, reciprocating, steam, gasoline, diesel, jet, turboprop, turbojet, rocket, Stirling; automotive, aircraft, marine; engine part: piston, cylinder, crank, crankshaft, valve, compressor, turbine

◗ *Power 514; Propulsion 696*

12 **turbine type,** water, steam, gas, impulse, reaction, impulse-reaction

13 **engine cycle,** heat-engine cycle, four-stroke cycle, two-stroke cycle, Carnot cycle, Otto cycle, diesel cycle, Rankine cycle; thermal efficiency, thermodynamics

◗ *Physics 10; Chemistry 11; Power 514; Propulsion 696*

14 **load,** applied load, static load, dynamic load, live load, dead load, transverse load; stress, normal stress, shear stress, yield stress, ultimate stress, flow stress, tension, compression; strain, longitudinal strain, linear strain, volume strain, bulk strain, shear strain, elastic strain, inelastic strain, plastic strain; structural loading, forces, stability, center of gravity

15 **strength of materials,** cohesive strength, yield strength, ultimate tensile strength, resistance to compaction, resistance to sliding, stiffness, elasticity, modulus of elasticity, bending moment

16 **deformation,** distortion, elongation, compression, bending, sliding, angular deformation, torsion, plastic deformation, creep, instability, failure, rupture, fracture, metal fatigue, corrosion

◗ *Physics 10*

17 **civil engineering,** structural engineering, transportation engineering, hydraulic engineering; geotechnical engineering, rock mechanics, soil mechanics; construction engineering, construction; photogrammetry, surveying, topographic surveying, mapping, photoelastic modeling

18 **civil engineering tool,** theodolite, level, clinometer, alidade

19 **civil engineer,** structural engineer, transportation engineer, hydraulic engineer, geotechnical engineer, construction engineer; surveyor, contractor

20 **structure,** construction, building, superstructure, substructure

◗ *Power 514; Structure 551; Transportation 686*

21 **construction material,** structural material, building material; stone, brick; steel, rolled steel, sheet steel, plate steel, cast steel, stainless steel; cast iron, wrought iron, aluminum, magnesium alloy; concrete, reinforced concrete, prestressed concrete, precast concrete, cement, mortar; wood, timber, lumber, plywood, glue-laminated (glulam) lumber; plastic, fiberglass, Tarmac™, tarmacadam, asphalt, bitumen

◗ *Materials 104*

22 **masonry,** stonework, brickwork; building stone, stone, limestone, sandstone, granite, marble; brick, bricklaying, header, stretcher, bond, American bond, English bond, Flemish bond; cinder block, tile, slate, terra cotta, mortar, grout, plaster, cement, Portland cement, gravel, sand, clay, pavior

23 **construction equipment,** excavator, digger, trenching machine, trencher, power shovel, front-end loader, backhoe, dragline, clamshell, grab bucket, belt loader, dredge, dredger, bulldozer *or* dozer, scraper, hauler, earthmover, dump truck, rear-dump truck, pile driver, pile hammer, auger, compactor, hoist, crane, mobile crane, tower crane, derrick, guy derrick, cableway, elevator, conveyor

24 **chemical engineering,** chemical reaction engineering, materials engineering, polymer engineering, biochemical engineering, biomedical engineering, environmental engineering

◗ *Chemistry 11; Biochemistry 12*

25 **chemical engineer,** chemical reaction engineer, materials engineer, polymer engineer, biochemical engineer, biomedical engineer, environmental engineer; laboratory assistant, technician

26 **chemical process industries,** chemical manufactur-

ing, plastics manufacturing, pulp and paper manufacturing, petroleum refining, ceramics manufacturing, electronics industries, paint manufacturing, food processing, textile manufacturing, nuclear energy industries, biochemical industries, pharmaceutical industries; short fiber-reinforced polymers, long fiber-reinforced polymers, ceramics, ceramic composites, silicon wafers

27 industrial processes, process flow diagrams, material balances, thermodynamics, kinetics, transport processes, fluid mechanics, steady flow processes, heat engines, refrigeration cycles, separation processes, property estimation techniques; chemical manufacturing processes, rheology; purification, crystal growth, imaging processes, plasma and chemical etching

28 systems and process control, process simulation, batch processes, molecular design, process synthesis; catalysis, refining, impurities reduction; chemical reactor; feed-forward control, cascade loops, discrete representations of continuous systems, z-transform parametric models, state-space representation, decoupling of multiple control loops, controller tuning; sensors for pulp and paper processes, refiner control, continuous digester, kraft recovery cycle, washing and bleaching operations, mill-wide process control

▶ *Chemistry 11*

29 chemical reaction thermodynamics, kinetics, mass balances, energy balances, homogeneous reactors, heterogeneous reactors, catalytic reactions, noncatalytic reactions, multiphase reactions; pulp and paper processes, chemical pulping recovery; thermal plasmas, ionization, velocity distribution function, plasma parameters, collisions and diffusion, energy states, plasma generation

30 biochemical applications, membrane filtration, chromatography, centrifugation, electrochemical separation; neurotransmitter biochemistry, neurotransmitter pharmacology, cellular physiology

▶ *Biochemistry 12*

31 electrical engineering, electronic engineering, electrotechnology, electrotechnics

32 electrical engineer, electronic engineer, electrotechnician, electrician

33 electronics, microelectronics, computer electronics, optoelectronics, telecommunications

▶ *Computers 15; Communications 169; Power 514*

34 electricity, current electricity, static electricity; static electrical conduction, conduction, conductivity, conducting medium; conductor, metallic conductor, copper, aluminum; liquid conductor, electrolyte

▶ *Power 514*

35 nonconductor, insulator, dielectric, dielectric constant, insulating material, insulation

36 electric charge, charge, charge density, charge carrier

▶ *Physics 10; Power 514*

37 circuit, electronic circuit, electric circuit, network, printed circuit, printed circuit board *or* card, microcircuit, chip, microchip, silicon chip, integrated circuit, large-scale integration (LSI), very large-scale integration (VLSI); equivalent circuit, closed circuit, open circuit, short circuit *or* short, linear circuit, nonlinear circuit, digital circuit, logic circuit, gate, bistable circuit, flip-flop circuit, resonant circuit, tuned circuit, resonant frequency, coupling circuit, switching circuit, bridge, Wheatstone bridge; circuit diagram, circuit design, circuitry, electronics

38 circuit function, amplification, gain, feedback, negative feedback, oscillation, positive feedback, negative resistance, rectification, switching, filtering

39 circuit element, component, discrete component, electronic device, semiconductor device, solid-state device, series connection, parallel connection; resistor, rheostat, capacitor, inductor, diode, transistor

40 electron tube, gas-discharge tube, fluorescent lamp, mercury-vapor lamp, glow lamp, cathode-ray tube (CRT), television receiver, visual display unit (VDU), microwave generator, klystron, magnetron, vacuum tube, triode, tetrode, pentode, anode, cathode, grid, neon light

41 electrical instrument, ammeter, galvanometer, voltmeter, potentiometer, electrometer, wattmeter, oscilloscope

42 electron emission, thermionic emission, thermionic cathode, electron lens, electron gun, electron tube, electron multiplier, photoelectric effect, photoelectric emission, photoelectron, photocathode, photomultiplier; secondary emission, secondary electron, field emission

43 generator, alternating current (a.c.) generator, alternator, oscillator, dynamo, magneto, armature, windings, electrostatic generator, Van de Graaff generator, wind-driven generator, thermoelectric generator, direct current (d.c.) generator

ADJECTIVES

44 mechanical, dynamic, loaded, strong, deformed

45 structural, constructional, edificial, architectural, architectonic, skeletal, superstructural, substructural, foundational, fabricated, precast, prestressed

46 chemical, thermodynamic, kinetic, electrochemical, homogeneous, heterogeneous, catalytic, noncatalytic, multiphase, ceramic, polymeric, biochemical, biomedical, environmental

47 electric, electrical, electronic, photoelectric, thermoelectric, piezoelectric, hydroelectric, electrodynamic, electrolytic, electromagnetic(al), electromotive, electrostatic, negative, positive, neutral, live, resistive, capacitive, inductive, rechargeable, solid-state, amorphous, semicrystalline, textured, crystal-oriented

VERBS

48 engineer, construct, build, erect, plan, design, survey, map, excavate, dig, grade, dredge, drill, tunnel, blast, lay, pave, haul, hoist

49 load, stress, strain, deform, bend, slide, fail, fracture, rupture, shear

50 process, manufacture, simulate, control, generate; balance, measure, separate, centrifuge *or* centrifugalize; purify, refine, filter, synthesize

51 conduct, insulate, ground, charge, discharge, amplify, oscillate, connect, disconnect, switch *or* turn on *or* off, plug in, wire, fuse, input, output, electrocute, generate, transmit

ADVERBS

52 structurally, mechanically, architecturally, architectonically, constructionally

53 electrochemically, biochemically, biomedically, environmentally, thermodynamically, kinetically, catalytically, noncatalytically

54 electronically, electrically, photoelectrically, thermoelectrically, electrodynamically, electrolytically, electromagnetically, electromechanically, electrostatically, negatively, positively, in series, in parallel

15 Computers

To err is human but to really foul things up requires a computer. — FARMERS' ALMANAC 1978

I propose to consider the question, "Can machines think?" — ALAN TURING

NOUNS

1 computer, calculator, calculating machine, adding machine, abacus, Napier's bones, electronic brain, workstation, personal computer (PC), home computer, laptop computer, notebook computer, handheld computer, mainframe, supercomputer, minicomputer, microcomputer, parallel processor, personal organizer, personal digital assistant (PDA), hybrid computer
  ▸ *Calculation 784*

2 computing, computer science, systems analysis, programming, data processing (DP), electronic data processing (EDP), data entry, information technology (IT), desktop publishing (DTP), computer-integrated manufacture (CIM), computer-managed instruction (CMI), computer-aided design (CAD), computer-aided manufacturing (CAM), computer-aided testing (CAT), computer-assisted learning (CAL), computer-based learning (CBL), cybernetics, robotics, artificial intelligence, management information system (MIS), computer-aided molecular design (CAMD)

3 computer user, programmer, software engineer, computer engineer, computer scientist, DP manager, systems analyst, hacker [Inf], cracker, computer hobbyist, computer operator, system manager

4 computer part, central processing unit (CPU), processor, coprocessor, motherboard, bus, peripheral, chip, transistor, vacuum tube, LED, disk, memory, card, serial port, parallel port, small computer systems interface (SCSI) port, network adaptor, network controller, display, register, accumulator [Arch], cache

5 disk, hard disk, floppy disk, fixed disk, removable hard disk, optical disk, floptical disk, compact-disk read-only memory (CD-ROM), magneto-optical disk

6 memory, storage, main memory, primary memory, cache memory, semiconductor memory, magnetic core memory, solid-state memory, cryogenic memory, auxiliary *or* secondary memory, bulk memory, bubble memory, volatile memory, nonvolatile memory, dynamic memory, random-access memory (RAM), dynamic random-access memory (DRAM), read-only memory (ROM), programmable read-only memory (PROM), erasable programmable read-only memory (EPROM)

7 card, memory card, sound card, graphics card, graphics adaptor, controller card, communications adapter

8 peripheral, disk, display, hardcopy device, input device, magnetic tape drive, paper tape punch, paper tape reader, card punch, card reader, terminal

9 display, monitor, cathode-ray tube (CRT), video display unit (VDU), video display adaptor (VDA), liquid-crystal display (LCD), pixel, active matrix display, touchscreen

10 hardcopy device, printer, dot-matrix printer, ink-jet printer, laser printer, thermal printer, impact printer, line printer, band printer, belt printer, barrel printer, drum printer, chain printer, letter-quality printer, daisy-wheel printer, electrophotographic printer, electrostatic printer, bubble-jet printer, thermal ink-jet printer, ionographic printer, color printer, plotter, flat-bed plotter, x-y plotter

11 input device, keyboard, keypad, mouse, joystick, trackball, light pen, scanner, wand, bar-code reader, digitizer, data tablet, touchscreen

12 software, operating system (OS), program, system software, application software

13 system software, device driver, utility program, daemon, compiler, interpreter, linker, loader, filter, parser, analyzer, text editor, window manager, debugger [Inf]

14 application software, word processor, spelling checker, dictionary program, thesaurus, database program, spreadsheet program, desktop publishing (DTP) program, musical instrument digital interface (MIDI) program, screen saver, authoring tool, presentation software, communications software, computer game, office automation program

15 database, hierarchical database, relational database, network database, database management system (DBMS)

16 programming language, language, machine code, assembly code, high-level language, low-level language, compiled language, interpreted language, source code, object code, fourth-generation language, macro language, preprocessor language

17 computer information, data, bit, byte, nybble, half-word, word, quadword, character, binary, octal, decimal, hexadecimal

18 character, alphanumeric character, character set, American Standard Code for Information Interchange (ASCII), International Standards Organization 7-bit code (ISO-7), Extended Binary Coded Decimal Interchange Code (EBCDIC), printable character, nonprintable character, control character, escape character, escape sequence, control sequence, graphic character, carriage return (CR), newline (NL), linefeed (LF), backspace (BS), horizontal tab (HT), vertical tab (VT), null character (NC)

19 office automation tools, automatic calling unit (ACU), facsimile (fax) machine, electronic mail, e-mail, teleconferencing

20 character recognition, scanner, optical character recognition (OCR), intelligent character recognition (ICR), magnetic ink character recognition (MICR)

21 artificial intelligence, game theory, perceptual computing, natural-language processing, theorem roving, means-ends analysis, semantic net, expert system, rule-based system, cybernetics, robotics, neural net

22 computing terms, access, batch processing, bandwidth, baud rate, benchmark, bootstrap, channel, chip, clock, clock rate, command, compatibility, controller, counter, cursor, clock cycle, diagnostic, directory, display, download, downtime, emulator, floating-point operation (FLOP), icon, input, interface, job, leader, login, logon, logout, logoff, menu, million instructions per second (MIPS), multitasking, output, parity, pass-word, queue, raster, real time, sector, sprite, program suite, time-sharing, toolbox, Trojan horse, turnkey operation, virus, write ring, write-protect tab, WYSIWYG (what you see is what you get)

23 data-related concepts, address, archive, backup, binary tree, bit, bitmap, block, byte, data, direct access, directory, field, file, format, function key, gigabyte (gig), hash table, header, key, kilobyte (K), linked list, megabyte (meg *or* MB), random access, record, sequential access

24 programming concepts, software engineering, algorithm, bisectional search, sorting, branch, bug, crash, debugging [Inf], dump, goto, loop, nesting, patch, source code, beta test, user interface (UI), graphical user interface (GUI), parsing, linked list, hashing, data structure, object-oriented programming (OOP), graphics, structured programming

25 computer communications, general, electronic mail (e-mail), mailbox, World Wide Web (WWW), website, communications protocol, compression, encryption, telecommunications, electronic data interchange (EDI), packet, handshake, heartbeat, local area network (LAN), wide area network (WAN), token ring network, star network, file server, client, node, Ethernet, Euronet, ARPANET, BITNET (Because It's Time NETwork), Joint Academic Network (JANET), Social Security Network (SOSNET), USENET, Internet, FidoNet, information superhighway, cyberspace, multi-user dungeon (MUD)

▶ *Communications 169*

26 communications device, cable, multiplexer (mux), modulator-demodulator, modem, fax-modem, network, acoustic coupler, bridge, gateway, repeater, transceiver, router, packet switch

27 communications software, bulletin board system (BBS), electronic mail reader, e-mail reader, newsreader [Brit], World Wide Web (WWW) browser, file transfer protocol (ftp) program, telnet

ADJECTIVES

28 computerized, on-line, user-friendly, erasable, writable, read-only, write-enabled, automatic, off-line

VERBS

29 program, edit, save, run, disassemble, preprocess, test; abort, access, address, archive, back up, bootstrap, boot, boot up, branch, compile, copy, crash, debug [Inf], decode, decompile, delete, downgrade, download, dump, emulate, erase, format, hardwire, input, interface, load, log in, log on, log off, log out, loop, output, patch, read, scroll, spool, upgrade, write

16 Agriculture

NOUNS

1 agriculture, farming, husbandry; intensive farming, factory farming, mixed farming, crop farming, live-

---

PROGRAMMING LANGUAGES

Ada	Clear	IPL	Pascal
Algol	COBOL	JCL	PL/1 *or* PL/I
APL	COMAL	JOVIAL	POP
B	CORAL	LISP	POPLOG
Babbage	CPL	Logo	Prolog
BASIC	Forth	MIRANDA	SCHEME
BCPL	Fortran	ML	SIMULA
BLISS	HOPE	Modula	Smalltalk
C	IAL	MUMPS	SNOBOL
C++	ICON	OBERON	
CHILL	INTERCAL	PARLOG	

stock farming, organic farming, strip farming, share farming, subsistence farming, sharecropping; agrarianism, agrotechnology, agricultural science, agroscience *or* agriscience, geoponics, thremmatology; agronomy, agrology, agrobiology, agrogeology, agroforestry, agroecology, green revolution; agronomics, agrarian economics, agroindustry, rural economics, farm business, agribusiness *or* agrobusiness, agribiz [Inf]; agricultural sale, farmers' market

▶ *Horticulture 17*

2 **farm,** mixed farm, family farm, factory farm, organic farm; state farm, collective farm, kolkhoz, kibbutz;

BREEDS OF CATTLE

Aberdeen-Angus	Blacksided	Dutch Belted	Kalmyk	Polish Red-and-	Sokoto
Afrikander	Trondheim and	Dutch Black	Kankrej	White	South Anatolian
Ala-Tau	Nordland	Pied	Kazakh	Lowland	Red
Alambadi	Bleue du Nord	Eastern Red	Kazakh	Polish Simmental	South Devon
Albanian	Blonde	Pied	Whiteheaded	Polled Hereford	Spanish Pied
Alentejo	d'Aquitaine	Egyptian	Kenana	Polled Sinu	Sudanese Fulani
Amritmahal	Blue Albian	Estonian Red	Kerry	Pyrenean	Suksun
Anatolian Black	Bonsmara	Fighting Bull	Kholmogor	Rath	Suffolk
Andalusian	Braford	Finnish	Kostroma	Red Angus	Sussex
Andalusian Black	Brahlers	Finnish Ayrshire	Kyloe	Red Bororo	Swedish Friesian
Andalusian	Brahman	Flemish	Latvian Brown	Red Brangus	Swedish Jersey
Blond	Brangus	French Friesian	Lebedin	Red Butana	Swedish Polled
Angeln	Braunvieh	Fribourg	Limousin	Red Pied Friuli	Swedish Red-
Angoni	Brazilian Polled	Friesian	Lincoln Red	Red Poll	and-White
Ankole	Breton Black	Galician Blond	Lithuanian Red	Red Sindhi	Sychevka
Aosta	Pied	Galloway	Longhorn	Red Steppe	Tagil
Apulian	British Dane	Gaolao	Madurese	Reggio	Tambov Red
Aquitaine Blond	British Friesian	Garfagnana	Maine Anjou	Romagna	Tarentaise
Arouca	British White	Gascony	Malvi	Romagnola	Telemark
Asturian	Brown Swiss	Gelbvieh	Marche	Romanian	Texan Longhorn
Aubrac	Bulgarian Grey	German Black	Marchigiana	Brown	Tonga
Aulie-Ata	Bulgarian Red	Pied	Maremma	Romanian Red	Transylvanian
Australian	Busa	German Brown	Mashona	Romanian	Pinzgau
Illawarra	Campine Red	German Red	Meuse-Rhine-	Simmental	Tswana
Shorthorn	Pied	Pied	Yssel	Romanian	Tuareg
Austrian Brown	Canadian	German	Milking	Steppe	Tudanca
Austrian	Caracu	Simmental	Shorthorn	Rouge de	Tuli
Simmental	Cattalo	German Yellow	Modena	l'Ouest	Tunis
Austrian Tello	Caucasian	Gorbatov Red	Modica	Russian Black	Turino
Ayrshire	Brown	Groningen	Mongolian	Pied	Ukrainian Grey
Azouak	Central and	Whiteheaded	Murnau-	Russian Brown	Ukrainian
Bachaur	Upper Belgian	Guernsey	Werdenfels	Russian	Whiteheaded
Balinese	Charolais	Hereford	Murray Grey	Simmental	Villard-de-lans
Baltic Black Pied	Chiana	Herens	Nagori	Sahiwal	Vorderwald
Bambara	Chianina	Highland	N'Dama	Salers	Vosges
Baoule	Corriente	Holando-	Nellore	San Martin	Watusi
Bargur	Czech Pied	Argentina	Nguni	Santa Gertrudis	Welsh Black
Barotse	Dairy Shorthorn	Holstein-Friesian	Norfolk Red	Senegal Fulani	West Flemish
Barroso	Damascus	or Holstein	Polled	Scotch Highland	Red
Bazas	Damietta	Hungarian Pied	Normandy	Shahabadi	West Highland
Beefalo	Dangi	Hungarian	Norwegian Red	Shetland	White Caceres
Beef Friesian	Danish Black	Simmental	Oberinntal Grey	Shorthorn	White Fulani
Beefmaster	Pied	Icelandic	Ongole	Shuwa	White Park
Beef Shorthorn	Danish Red	Indo-Brazilian	Piedmontese	Siberian	White-Russian
Belgian Black	Danish Red Pied	Israeli Friesian	Pinzgauer	Simbrah	Red
Pied	Deoni	Istoben	Pisa	Simmental	Yaroslavl
Belgian Blue	Devon	Italian Brown	Plevna	Sinhala	Yugoslav Pied
Belted Galloway	Dexter	Italian Friesian	Polish Black-and-	Siri	Yurino
Bestuzhev	Dobrojea	Jamaica Hope	White	Slovakian Black	Zebu
Bhagnari	Drakensberger	Japanese	Lowland	Pied	
Black Angus	Droughtmaster	Jersey	Polish Red	Sofia Brown	

16 Agriculture

livestock farm, stock farm, dairy farm, poultry farm, chicken farm, beef farm, sheep farm, deer farm, mink farm, fish farm, trout farm, pig farm, piggery; ranch, rancho, spread, station [Aus], sheep ranch, cattle ranch, beef ranch, mink ranch; hacienda, hill farm, arable farm, grain farm, fruit farm, tree farm, mushroom farm, truck farm, market garden [Brit]; plantation, tea plantation, coffee plantation, estate, tea estate, coffee estate; farmstead, grange, homestead, steading [Brit], demesne, home farm, city farm, holding, small holding [Brit], croft [Brit]; farmland, cropland, grassland, pasture

3 farmland, arable land, arable, dairyland; Farm Belt, Corn Belt, Wheat Belt, Cotton Belt, Black Belt, Citrus Belt, Tobacco Belt; acreage; field, plot, piece, patch, parcel, paddock, strip, clearing, terrace, paddy, paddy field, rice paddy, potato field, cornfield, wheatfield, hayfield; grassland, meadow, mead [Arch], lea, pasture, grazing; enclosed land; headland; plowed land, cultivated land, furrow, drill, row, ridge, seedbed, swath or swathe, swale, windrow, haystack, haycock, hay, hayrick [Brit]; hedge, hedgerow, quick [Brit], quickset [Brit]

4 farm building, grange, farmhouse, barn, farmery [Brit]; dairy, milking parlor, granary, haybarn, smokehouse, oast-house [Brit], cowshed, farrowing house, byre [Brit], stable, fattening house, lambing house, tractor shed, workshop, farm office; chicken coop, hencoop, henhouse, hennery, hencote, broiler house; aviary; farmyard, barnyard, barnlot, feedlot, feedyard; box, stall, hutch, pen, loose box, pigsty, sty, farrowing crate, fold, sheepfold [Brit], pinfold, corral, chicken or hen run; silo, corncrib, grain bin, grain elevator, haymow, hayloft, hayrack; enclosure, fence, electric fence, barbed wire, hurdle [Brit]; post, stake, rail, gate; netting, wire netting, chicken wire

▶ *Enclosure 619*

5 farm tool, farm implement, farm machinery; tractor; drill, seed drill, harrow, disk harrow; cultivator, rototiller or rotary tiller, plow, subsoil plow, subsoiler, chisel, chisel plow; planter; harvester, combine; scythe, sickle; reaper, reaping machine; swather, binder, baler, bale sledge, bale carrier, bale wrapper; mower, mowing machine, rotary mower; thresher, flail; haymaker, hayfork, hay rake, tedder, hay wain, hay turner; front-end loader, front-loader, trailer; fertilizer spreader,

BREEDS OF SHEEP

Abyssinian	Baure-Campan	Campanian Barbary	Dartmoor	Grozny
Algarve Churro	Bellary	Campanica	Darvaz	Gujarati
Algerian Arab	Beni Ahsen	Canadian Corriedale	Debouillet	Gurez
Altai	Beni Guil	Castilian	Deccani	Hampshire
Altamura	Berber	Caucasian	Degeres	Hampshire Down
Amasya Herik	Bergamo	Central Pyrenean	Delaine Merino	Herdwick
American Merino	Bhadarwah	Chanothar	Derbyshire Gritstone	Hungarian Combing
American	Bhakarwal	Charmoise	Devon Closewool	Wool Merino
Rambouillet	Bibrik	Cher Berrichon	Devon Longwool	Hu-Yang
American Tunis	Biella	Cherkasy	Dorper	Icelandic
Apulian Merion	Bikaneri	Cheviot	Dorset	Ile-de-France
Arabi	Bizet	Chios	Dorset Down	Iraq Kurdi
Aragon	Blackface	Churro do Campo	Dorset Horn	Island Pramenka
Argentine Merino	Black-faced Highland	Chushka	Dubrovnik	Istrian Milk
Arles Merino	Blackhead Persian	Clun Forest Colbred	East Friesian	Jacob
Askanian	Black Merino	Columbia	Edilbaev	Jaidara
Ausimi	Black Welsh	Comiso	English Longwool	Karachaev
Australian Merino	Mountain	Common Albanian	Entre Minho e Douro	Karakachan
Avranchin	Blanc du Massif	Coopworth	Estonian Darkheaded	Karakul
Awassi	Central	Corriedale	Exmoor Horn	Karayaka
Azerbaijan Mountain	Bluefaced Leicester	Corsican	Finnish Landrace	Karnobat
Merino	Bluefaced Maine	Cotentin	Finnsheep	Kazakh Fat-rumped
Azov Tsigai	Border Leicester	Cotswold	Frabosa	Kazakh Finewool
Badano	Bosnian Mountain	Cyprus Fat-tailed	Fulani	Kerry Hill
Balbas	Boulonnais	Dagestan Mountain	Galway	Krasnoyarsk
Balkhi	Bozakh	Daglic	Garfagnana	Kuibyshev
Baluchi	Braganca Galician	Dala	German Blackheaded	Lacaune
Barbados	Brazilian Bergamo	Dalesbred	Mutton	Langhe
Barbados Blackbelly	Brazilian Somali	Dalmatian Karst	German Heath	Latvian Darkheaded
Bardoka	Buryat	Damani	German Mutton	Lecce
Barki	Calabrian	Danube Merino	Merino	Leicester

muckrake; shovel, pitchfork; sprayer, irrigator; hedge-cutter, plasher, electric fence, trough, feeder, drinker, water bowl, feedbin, milking machine, milk tank, bulk tank, churn; all-terrain vehicle (ATV)

6 **arable farming,** contour farming, crop farming, crop husbandry, boutique farming, dry farming, crop rotation, monoculture, monocropping, fen farming, fruit farming, grain farming, hydroponics, slash-and-burn, strip farming, strip cropping, strip planting, tree farming, forestry, truck farming, plant breeding, market gardening [Brit]
   ▶ *Horticulture 17; Trees 43*

7 **cultivation,** cultivating, culture, tillage, tilling, tilth; plowing, harrowing, furrowing; sowing, planting; hedging, pleaching, plashing; irrigation, watering; fertilizing, dunging, manuring, muckraking, muckspreading; weeding, pruning, thinning, hoeing; cropdusting, crop-spraying, insurance spraying; harvesting, hay-making, silaging
   ▶ *Horticulture 17; Trees 43*

8 **crop,** cash crop, catch crop, cover crop; wheat, winter wheat, barley, winter barley, oats, winter oats, rye, triticale, millet, timothy, corn, rice, sorghum, mustard,
clover, alfalfa, vetch, flax, fescue, ryegrass; root crop, fodder crop, fodderbeets, sugar beets, green manure; first early, second early, earlies; potatoes, turnips, rutabagas, swedes [Brit], peas, field peas, beans, soybeans, groundnuts, peanuts; okra, kale, cabbage, rape, linseed; tobacco; cotton; stubble, stalks

9 **fertilizer,** manure, muck, dung, muckheap, dunghill, midden, green manure, organic manure, compost; fish meal, bone meal, seaweed; sewage, effluent, sludge; nitrate, phosphate, potash, lime, limestone, quicklime, slaked lime, basic slag; granule, dust

10 **livestock farming,** animal *or* stock rearing *or* raising, ranching, animal husbandry, animal production; thremmatology, zootechnics, zooculture; animal breeding, artificial insemination; animal nutrition, animal health, gnotobiotics; dairy farming, dairying, beef farming, sheep farming, pig farming; poultry farming, chicken farming, fish farming, pisciculture, rabbit farming, mink farming, duck farming; herding, grazing, strip grazing, paddock grazing, zero grazing, folding
   ▶ *Animals (General) 34*

11 **livestock,** stock, beasts, fatstock [Brit]; cattle, cow, heifer, calf, stirk [Brit], fatling, veal calf, yearling,

BREEDS OF SHEEP

Limestone	Pleven Blackhead	Shetland	Swedish Landrace	Tunisian Barbary
Lincoln	Polish Merino	Shkodra	Swiss Black-Brown	Turcana
Lincoln Longwool	Polwarth	Shropshire	Mountain	Turkmen
Liski	Polypay	Shumen	Swiss Brownheaded	Fat-rumped
Lithuanian	Precoce	Sicilian	Mutton	Tushin
Blackheaded	Racka	Sicilian Barbary	Swiss White Alpine	Tyrol Mountain
Lohi	Rambouillet	Sinkiang Finewool	Swiss White	Valachian
Lonk	Red Karaman	Sjenica	Mountain	Valais Blacknose
Macina	Reshetilovka	Skopelos	Tadla	Varese
Mancha	Rhon	Sokolka	Tadmit	Velay Black
Mandya	Romanov	Solcava	Tajik	Voloshian
Massa	Romeldale	Sologne	Talavera	Vyatka
Merino	Romney	Somali	Tan-Yang	Waziri
Mongolian	Romney Marsh	Sopravissana	Tanganyika Long-	Welsh Hill
Montedale	Roscommon	South African	tailed	Welsh Mountain
Muzzafarnagri	Rough Fell	Merino	Targhee	Wensleydale
Navajo	Russian Long-tailed	South Devon	Teeswater	West African
Navajo-Churro	Russian Northern	Southdown	Telengit	Dwarf
Nejdi	Short-tailed	South Ural	Texel	White Dorper
Nellore	Ryeland	South Wales	Thal	White Face
New Zealand	Rygja	Mountain	Thibar	Dartmoor
Romney Marsh	Saloia	Soviet Merino	Thones-Marthod	White Karaman
North Caucasus	Salsk Finewood	Spanish Churro	Tibetan	White Klementina
Mutton-Wool	Santa Ines	Spanish Merino	Tirahi	White South
North Country	Sar Planina	Stavropol	Transbaikal	Bulgarian
Cheviot	Saraja	Steinschaf	Finewool	Wicklow Mountain
Ovce Polje	Sardinian	Stogos	Tsigai	Wiltshire Horn
Oxford Down	Savoy	Suffolk	Tuareg	Zante
Palas Merino	Scottish Blackface	Sumava	Tuj	Zemmour
Panama	Segura	Svishtov	Tung-Yang	Zeta Yellow
Penistone	Serra da Estrela	Swaledale	Tunis	

BREEDS OF FOWL

Chickens
Ameraucana
Ancona
Andalusian
Araucana
Australorp
Brahma
Buckeye
Buttercup
Campine
Catalanas
Chantecler
Cochin
Cornish
Crevecoeur
Cubalaya

Delaware
Dominique
Dorking
Faverolle
Fluer
Frizzle
Hamburg
Holland
Houdan
Ixworth
Java
Jersey Black Giant
La Fleche
Lakenvelder
Lamona
Langshan

Leghorn
Malay
Minorca
New Hampshire
Orpington
Phoenix
Plymouth Rock
Polish
Redcap
Rhode Island Red
Rock
Silkie
Spanish
Sultan
Sumatra
Sussex

Turken
Wyandotte

Geese
African
American Buff
Chinese
Embden
Roman
Sebastopol
Toulouse

Ducks
Aylesbury
Crested
Indian Runner

Khaki Campbell
Muscovy
White Pekin

Turkeys
Beltsville
Black
Bourbon Red
Broad-Breasted
  Bronze
Broad-Breasted
  White
Narragansett
Royal Palm
Slate
White Holland

milker, milk cow, milch cow, suckler cow, weaner, nurse cow, dry cow, barren cow, bull, steer, bullock, store, store cattle, cutter; sheep, ewe, lamb, teg, ram, wether, tup [Brit]; pig, hog, swine, sow, piglet, gilt, boar, porker, barrow; goat, nanny goat, billy goat, kid; poultry, chick, poult, pullet, bantam, chicken, hen, battery hen *or* chicken, free-range hen *or* chicken, fowl, laying hen, layer, broiler, roaster, cock, capon, rooster, goose, gander, gosling, duck, drake, duckling, turkey

▶ *Mammals 35; Birds 36*

12 **animal feed,** feedstuff, fodder, forage, provender, mash, meal; roughage, silage, ensilage, hay, haylage, dried grass, straw; clover, grass, timothy *or* timothy grass, wheatgrass; grain, corn, maize, oats, barley, wheat, bran, soybeans; sugar-beet pulp, fodderbeets, sainfoin, rape, mangel, molasses, malt culms, cotton *or* cottonseed cake, linseed cake *or* meal, fish meal, bone meal, chicken feed, scratch; slops, swill

13 **pest control,** extermination; rattrap, mousetrap; snare, scarecrow; sheep-dip, pesticide, rodenticide, rat poison, vermicide; insecticide, contact insecticide, residual insecticide, systemic insecticide; fungicide, weed-killer, herbicide, contact herbicide, systemic herbicide; spray, wetting agent, agrichemicals, agrochemicals, DDT, aldrin, dieldrin, parathion, warfarin, paraquat; fumigant, slug pellet, bug bomb

14 **agriculturist,** agriculturalist, agronomist, agrologist,

BREEDS OF PIGS

Alentejo
American Landrace
Andalusian Blond
Andalusian Spotted
Angeln Saddleback
Asturian
Belgian Landrace
Beltsville No. 1
Beltsville No. 2
Berkshire
Biasro
Black Iberian
Breitov
British Landrace
British Saddleback
Bulgarian White
Canastra
Canastrao
Caserta
Chester White
Conner Prairie

Czechoslovakian
  Improved White
Danish Landrace
Dermantsi Pied
Dorset
Duroc
Duroc Jersey
Dutch Landrace
Dutch Yorkshire
East Balkan
Estonian Bacon
Finnish Landrace
German Landrace
German Yorkshire
Gloucester Old
  Spots
Hampshire
Hereford
Hungarian White
Kemerovo
Lacombe

Landrace
Large Black
Large White
Livny
Managra
Mangalitsa
Middle White
Minnesota No. 1
Mirgorod
National Long White
  Lop-eared
Nilo
North Caucasus
North Siberian
Norwegian
  Landrace
Ohio Improved
  Chester
Piau
Pietrain
Poland China

Polish Large White
Polish White Lop-
  eared
Prestice
Pulawy
Romagna
Russian Large White
Russian Long-eared
  White
Russian Short-eared
  White
Siena Belted
Small White
South African
  Landrace
Spot
Swabian-Hall
Swedish Landrace
Swiss Improved
  Landrace
Swiss Yorkshire

Tamworth
Taoyuan
Tatu
Turopolje
Ukrainian Spotted
  Steppe
Ukrainian White
  Steppe
Urzhum
Vietnamese Pot-
  Bellied
Vitoria
Welsh
Wessex Saddleback
West French
  White
White-Russian Black
  Pied
Yorkshire

agrobiologist, agrogeologist, agroecologist, agrotechnician, rural economist; farmer, granger, husbandman, animal husbandman; tiller, tiller of the soil, yeoman [Brit], gentleman farmer, tenant farmer, peasant farmer, hill farmer, dirt farmer, sodbuster, small holder [Brit], crofter [Brit], kibbutznik, livestock farmer, stock farmer, dairy farmer, beef farmer, poultry farmer, pig farmer, sheep farmer, stock raiser, stockbreeder, breeder, cattle breeder, sheep breeder, pig breeder, cattleman, grazier [Brit]; rancher, ranchman, ranchero, arable farmer, grower, raiser, cultivator, sharecropper, tank farmer, truck farmer, fruit farmer, planter, tea planter, coffee planter

15 **farm worker,** farm manager, farm agent, bailiff [Brit], migrant worker, *campesino* [Sp], picker; farmhand, farmboy; stockman, stockperson, cowboy, cowgirl, cowhand, cowherd, cowpuncher, puncher, cowpoke, herder, herdsman, herd manager, drover; dairyman, dairymaid, dairywoman, dairyhand; swineherd, pigherd, pigman, hogherd; shepherd, shepherdess; goatherd; gooseboy, goosegirl; swanherd; broncobuster, buckaroo, gaucho, wrangler; groom, stableboy, stableman; tractor driver, plowman; crew

ADJECTIVES

16 **agricultural,** agrarian, agronomic, agrological, agroecological, agrobiological, thremmatological; geoponic, hydroponic, gnotobiotic, piscicultural; farm, farming, farmhouse; rustic, rural, pastoral, peasant, bucolic, agrestic, praedial *or* predial, georgic

17 **farmable,** arable, cultivable, plowable, tillable; fertile, productive, fruitful; farmed, cropped, plowed, broken down, tilled; grazed; fallow, undersown

18 **domesticated,** domestic, broken in, reared, raised, bred, milked, dry, far, purebred, crossbred, thoroughbred, inbred

VERBS

19 **farm,** work the land, cultivate, grow, sharecrop; till, till the soil, plow, rototill, dig, delve [Arch], spade, rake; plant, sow, harrow, drill, scatter seed, broadcast; topdress, fertilize, muck, dung; irrigate; spray; weed, hoe, mulch, mow; harvest, reap, glean, gather, swathe, turn, crop, bale
 ▸ *Horticulture 17*

20 **practice livestock farming,** ranch, raise, rear, grow, breed; feed, hand-feed, nurture, suckle, wean; fatten; run, graze; fodder, water, muck out, bed; drench, worm; groom, comb, rub down; castrate, dehorn, brand; milk, hand-milk, machine-milk; dry off, calve, lamb; harness, bridle, yoke, hitch, drive, herd, tend, drove, punch cattle, wrangle, round up, corral, shepherd, stable, pen

ADVERBS

21 **agriculturally,** hydroponically, pisciculturally, gnotobiotically, organically, ecologically, rurally, pastorally, rustically, bucolically, productively, fruitfully, down on the farm

17 Horticulture

1 **horticulture,** gardening, landscape gardening, groundskeeping, landscape architecture; floriculture, flower gardening, flower growing, rose growing; truck gardening, truck farming, market gardening [Brit], olericulture, vegetable growing, mushroom growing; fruit growing, citriculture, fruitage, viticulture, viniculture, pomology, arboriculture, silviculture; indoor gardening
 ▸ *Agriculture 16; Flowers 42; Trees 43; Fruits 44*

2 **garden,** flower garden, botanical garden, ornamental garden, formal garden, rock garden, alpine garden, herb garden, knot garden, parterre, Japanese garden, sunken garden, indoor garden, roof garden, winter garden, arboretum; bottle garden, hanging garden, bonsai; garden center, garden shop; vegetable garden, kitchen garden, victory garden, allotment [Brit]; cabbage patch, truck farm *or* garden, market garden [Brit]; fruit farm, orchard, lemon grove, olive grove, orange grove, citrus grove, vineyard, tea garden; civic garden, municipal garden, public garden, zoological garden; garden city, garden apartment; pleasure garden, garden of remembrance, garden of rest; Garden of Eden, Hanging Gardens of Babylon, Garden of the Hesperides
 ▸ *Agriculture 16; Trees 43*

3 **ornamental garden,** flower garden, flower bed, bed; rose bed, rosary, rosarium; border, herbaceous border; shrubbery, hedge, topiary; rock garden, rockery; lawn; pond, lily pond; fountain, garden gnome, birdbath; bench, garden seat, garden chair, sun lounger, patio set; fence, trellis, rustic fence, sunk fence, ha-ha; bower, arbor, grotto, sundial, summerhouse, gazebo, pergola, belvedere; garden path, paving, patio, terrace; hanging basket, window box

4 **nursery,** greenhouse, hothouse, conservatory, glasshouse [Brit], orangery; garden shed, potting shed, forcing house; forcing bed, hotbed, cold frame, propagator, cloche; compost pile *or* heap; flowerpot, planter, seed tray, jardiniere

5 **gardening,** growing plants; potting, repotting, transplanting; pruning, pinching back *or* out *or* off, cutting back, deadheading, hard pruning; feeding, watering, weeding, composting; aquiculture, hydroponics, propagation, planting, grafting, budding, layering, stooling

6 **plant breeding,** graft, rootstock, stock, scion, stool, heel, graft union, cutting, stem cutting, leaf cutting, offset, bud stick, whip, sucker, runner; variety, strain, cultivar, hybrid, diploid, triploid, polypoid, graft hybrid

7 **garden tool,** spade, shovel, fork, hoe, rake, lawn rake,

thatcher, trowel, dibble, drill, lopper, shears, hedge trimmer, pruner, pruning shears, pruning hook, secateurs [Brit]; edger, edging tool; lawn mower, power mower, rotary mower; cultivator, rototiller *or* rotary tiller; distributor, spreader; sprinkler, hose, sprayer, nozzle, trug, watering can, rose; leaf sweeper, leaf blower; wheelbarrow, bushel basket; stake, tie, rabbit guard, beanpole, smudge pot

8 fertilizer, manure, compost, mulch, peat, fish meal

9 pest killer, weed-killer, herbicide, moss killer, fungicide, systemic fungicide, Bordeaux mixture; pesticide, spray, insecticide, pyrethrum, derris, benzene hexachloride (BHC), dimethoate

10 garden plant, seedling, cutting, bulb, corm, rhizome, tuber, rock plant, alpine plant, bedding plant, annual, biennial, perennial, herb, flower, succulent, creeper, ground cover, turf, climber, climbing plant, rambler, woody plant, shrub, tree, specimen plant

▶ *Plants (General) 41; Flowers 42; Trees 43*

11 vegetable, green vegetable, brassica, salad vegetable, root vegetable, tuber, legume, bean, pulse, dried vegetable, herb, culinary herb, potherb, mushroom

▶ *Fungi, Algae, and Lichens 47; Food 90; Cooking 91*

12 pests and diseases, beetle, wireworm, Japanese beetle, asparagus beetle, flea beetle, Colorado potato beetle; thrips; weevil, boll weevil; scale insects, leafhopper, leaf miner, aphids, greenflies, whiteflies, sawflies, midges; caterpillars, cutworms, cabbageworms, codling moth, spider mites, mealy bug, slug, snail, earwig; clubroot, mildew, powdery mildew, downy mildew, false mildew; blight, brown rot, canker, damping-off, sooty mold, gray mold, leaf mold, botrytis, leaf curl, leaf spot, ring spot; rust, stem rust, crown rust, root rot; crown rot, stem rot, soft rot, bitter rot; wilt, spotted wilt, grown gall, fire blight, blackleg, chlorosis, scald, dieback, mosaic, yellow edge, crinkle leaf

▶ *Fungi, Algae, and Lichens 47*

13 horticulturist, gardener, green thumb; landscape gardener, landscape architect, topiarist; floriculturist, flower grower, rose grower, rosarian; seedman, nurseryman, nurserywoman, grower, fruiter, fruit farmer, pomologist, orchardist, vine grower, viniculturist; truck gardener, truck farmer, market gardener [Brit]; vegetable grower; picker; arborist, arboriculturist

▶ *Flowers 42; Trees 43*

ADJECTIVES

14 horticultural, floricultural, floral, flowery, florescent, efflorescent, in bloom, uniflorous, multiflorous; herbaceous, herbal; vegetable, vegetal, vegetative, leguminous, cereal, farinaceous; arboricultural, arboreal, arborous, foliar, dendroid, sylvan, silvicultural, pomological, viticultural, vinicultural; aquicultural, hydroponic

15 botanical, annual, biennial, perennial; hardy, half-hardy, winter-hardy; succulent, verdant, verdurous, mossy, grassy, bushy, fruity, woody, shrubby, scrubby; mildewy, rotten, moldy, blighted, wilting, weed-choked, bug-infested, gone to seed

16 herbicidal, pesticidal, fungicidal, insecticidal

17 ornamental, alpine, exotic, tropical, subtropical; landscaped; cultivated, cultured, forced; trained, pruned, grafted, cut; watered; hoed, raked

VERBS

18 garden, landscape, cultivate, grow fruit, grow vegetables, truck farm, market garden [Brit], have a green thumb

19 cultivate, plant, pot, sow, seed, put in, set, drill, heel in, dibble, puddle, puddle in, transplant, pot, prick out, plant out *or* off, bed, bed out; dig, double-dig, trench, delve [Arch], spade, fork, rototill, hoe, rake; weed, thin, thin out; train, tie up, stake, prune, cut, mow, crop, top, lop, deadhead, debud, deblossom; mulch, muck, dung, manure, straw, top-dress, fertilize, compost; sprinkle, water, spray, dust; propagate, breed, pollinate, graft, bud, take cuttings, layer

ADVERBS

20 horticulturally, hydroponically, pomologically, florally, botanically; annually, biennially, perennially; succulently, verdantly; ornamentally, exotically, tropically, subtropically

▶ *Flowers 42; Trees 43; Fruits 44*

Living Things

18 Humankind

I wish I loved the human race; / I wish I loved its silly face; / I wish I liked the way it walks; / I wish I liked the way it talks; / And when I'm introduced to one / I wish I thought, What jolly fun! — WALTER RALEIGH

NOUNS

1 **humankind,** mankind, womankind; humanity, human race, human species, *Homo sapiens*, hominid; man, generations of man, people, persons, peoples of the earth, mortals, earthlings, human family, family of man; the world, world population, society, the public, everyone, everybody, every living soul, the living, we, us, ourselves, generation of Adam, Adam's seed, image of God

2 **human fallibility,** human failing, human frailty, human weakness, mortality, flesh, human nature
  ▶ *Weakness 517*

3 **human ancestor,** anthropoid ape, ape-man *or* ape-woman, *Ramapithecus, Pithecanthropus, Homo erectus,* Java man, Peking man
  ▶ *History 3; Past Time 651*

4 **primitive humanity,** barbarians, savages, bushmen, aborigines; ancient man, early man, early humanity, primeval man, primeval humanity, caveman *or* cave-woman, cave dweller; early *Homo sapiens,* Swanscombe man, Steinheim man, *Homo neanderthalensis or* Neanderthal man; late *Homo sapiens,* Cro-Magnon man, Grimaldi man, Boskop man, Wadjak man
  ▶ *Past Time 651*

5 **civilized humanity,** civilized world, culture, civilization
  ▶ *Refinement 534; Improvement 807*

6 **study of humankind,** anthropology, sociology, psychology, humanitarianism, humanism, folklore, mythology

7 **studier of humankind,** anthropologist, sociologist, psychologist, humanist, folklorist, mythologist

  ▶ *Anthropology 1; Sociology 2*

8 **person,** individual, human being, human, being, man, woman, adult, girl, boy, teenager, adolescent, child, baby; Adamite, mortal, creature, fellow creature; body, soul, living soul, flesh and blood; the noble animal, the naked ape, earthling, tellurian; God's image, God's creation
  ▶ *Youth 26; Age 27*

9 **average person,** ordinary person, common man, everyman, everywoman, man *or* woman in the street, John Doe, Jane Doe, John Q. Public, hand; [Inf]: guy, chap, joe, Joe Blow, Joe Schmo, Joe Doakes
  ▶ *Commoner 71*

10 **someone,** I, one, somebody, individual, so-and-so, such a one, party, customer, character, type

11 **important person,** preeminent figure, personage, person of note, very important person (VIP) [Inf], head, man *or* woman at the top, celebrity, star
  ▶ *Aristocrat 70; Importance 799*

12 **humanlike machine,** robot, automaton, android, humanoid, cyborg, bionic man, bionic woman; thinking machine

13 **group,** all those concerned, cast, list of characters, dramatis personae, unit, element; family, clan, kinship group, brotherhood, fraternity, sisterhood, sorority, clique, set, social group, society, organized society, stratified society, class, social class; public, general public, general population, generality, populace, citizenry, inhabitants, the masses, commonality, plebs, hoi polloi, common people, common persons, people, folk, you and me; community at large, community, neighborhood, ghetto; ethnic minority, ethnic group, racial group *or* type, race; primitive society, tribe, tribalism; the human family, sociopolitical group, international society, community of nations
  ▶ *Sociology 2; Assembly 59; Inhabitant 61; Family 65; Aristocrat 70; Commoner 71; Country 566; Relatedness 727*

14 **nation,** people, country, realm, kingdom, national

entity, nationality, state, statehood, civil society, body politic, political entity, city-state, nation-state, multiracial state, melting pot; alliance of states, commonwealth, Commonwealth of Nations, the Commonwealth; polity; nationalism, national consciousness, ultranationalism

◗ *Government 49; Country 566*

ADJECTIVES

15 **human,** mortal, creaturely, earthborn, tellurian; frail, weak, fleshly, finite; anthropoid, humanoid, hominoid, humanlike, subhuman, civilized; anthropological, ethnographical, racial, ethnic, anthropocentric, anthropomorphic; personal, individual; humanistic, bionic

◗ *Anthropology 1*

16 **national,** state, civic, civil, public, general, communal, tribal, social, societal, governmental, democratic, republican, socialistic, communistic, totalitarian, oligarchical, dictatorial

◗ *Sociology 2; Government 49*

VERBS

17 **make human,** humanize, anthropomorphize, civilize

ADVERBS

18 **humanly,** mortally, anthropologically, ethnographically, racially, ethnically, individually, personally, humanistically, socially, nationally, internationally

19 Human Body

NOUNS

1 **body,** physique, physical self, physical organism, carcass, corporeal entity; flesh, flesh and blood, incarnation, embodiment, self, Brother Ass, bod [Inf]

2 **skeleton,** frame, framework, bones, structure
◗ *Structure 551*

3 **muscles,** musculature, cartilage, sinew, tendon, ligament; biceps, triceps, pectorals, laterals, abdominals

4 **body covering,** skin, integument, dermis, epidermis, epithelium, endothelium; nail, fingernail, toenail, cuticle; hair, head of hair, lock, tress; eyelashes, lashes, cilia; eyebrows, brows; mustache, beard, whiskers, sideburns, muttonchops, goatee, stubble, bristles, five o'clock shadow; membrane, pellicle, mucous membrane, dura mater, arachnoid, pia mater, eardrum, tympanic membrane, pleura, peritoneum, pericardium, hymen

◗ *Beautification 530; Covering 613*

5 **appendage,** external organ, member, limb; arm, forearm, elbow, wrist, hand, finger; first finger, thumb, forefinger, index finger, second finger, middle finger, third finger, ring finger, fourth finger, little finger, pinkie *or* pinky [Inf]; leg, thigh, knee, shin, calf, ankle, foot, toe, big toe, hallux, little toe

◗ *Part 760*

6 **head,** skull, scalp; face, nose, mouth, eyes, ears, eyebrows, cheeks, temples, chin, neck, nape; brain, cerebrum, cerebellum; [Inf]: noggin, bean, dome

7 **mouth,** oral cavity; lips, tongue, organ of taste, taste buds; mandible, jaw, upper jaw, lower jaw, gums, periodontal tissue, uvula, teeth

◗ *Speech, Spoken Language 205; Opening 583*

8 **teeth,** dentition; tooth, fang, tusk; incisor, front tooth, canine, eyetooth, premolar, carnassial, cuspid, bicuspid,

---

HUMAN BONES

alveolar arch *or* bone	femur *or* thighbone	lacrimal bone	phalanx, phalanges	sternum *or*
anklebone *or* talus	fibula	lunate bone	[pl]	breastbone
anvil *or* incus	floating rib	malar bone *or*	pterygoid	stirrup *or* stapes
astragalus	frontal bone	zygomatic bone	process	styloid process
backbone *or* spinal	funny bone *or* elbow	malleus *or* hammer	pubis	talus *or* anklebone
column *or* spine	*or* humerus	mandible *or* jawbone	rachis	tarsal *or* tarsus bones
breastbone *or*	hallux	mastoid bone	radius	temporal bone
sternum	hammer *or* malleus	maxilla	rib	thighbone *or* femur
calcaneus	haunch bone	metacarpal bones *or*	sacrum	tibia *or* shinbone
calf bone	heel bone	metacarpus	scaphoid bone *or*	trapezium
carpal bones *or*	hipbone	metatarsal bones *or*	navicular bone	trapezoid
carpus	humerus *or* funny	metatarsus	scapula *or* shoulder	ulna
cheekbone	bone	nasal bone	blade	vertebra
chinbone	hyoid bone	navicular bone *or*	shinbone *or* tibia	vertebral column *or*
clavicle *or* collarbone	ilium	scaphoid bone	shoulder blade *or*	spinal column
coccyx *or* tailbone	incus *or* anvil	occipital bone	scapula	vomer
collarbone *or* clavicle	innominate bone	palate bone	skull	zygomatic bone *or*
costa	ischium	parietal bone	sphenoid bone	malar bone
cranium	jawbone *or* mandible	patella *or*	spinal column *or*	
cuboid bone	kneecap *or* kneepan	kneecap	spine *or* backbone	
ethmoid bone	*or* patella	pelvis	stapes *or* stirrup	

---

molar, grinder, back tooth, wisdom tooth; bucktooth, snaggletooth; first tooth, milk tooth, baby tooth, deciduous tooth, permanent tooth; false tooth, denture, bridge, gold tooth, crown; set of teeth, ivories [Inf], pearly whites [Inf]

9 **eye,** visual organ, organ of sight, eyeball, orb; eyelid, eyelash, pupil, cornea, aqueous humor, vitreous humor, sclera, iris, conjunctiva, lens, vitreous humor, retina, rod, cone, optic nerve, blind spot; [Inf]: peepers, sparklers, baby blues
  ▹ *Sensation 212; Vision 242*

10 **ear,** hearing organ, auditory organ; outer ear, helix, auricle, pinna, earlobe, auditory *or* ear canal, concha; middle ear, tympanic cavity, tympanum, eardrum, tympanic membrane, malleus *or* hammer, incus *or* anvil, stapes *or* stirrup; mastoid process, Eustachian tube; inner ear, secondary eardrum, vestibule, semicircular canals, cochlea, auditory nerve
  ▹ *Sensation 212; Hearing 228*

11 **nose,** nasal organ; nostril, naris, nasal cavity, olfactory nerve, snout; [Inf]: schnoz *or* schnozzle, snoot, smeller, proboscis, beak, conk [Brit], hooter [Brit]
  ▹ *Odor 224; Fragrance 226*

12 **throat,** windpipe, trachea, larynx, voicebox, vocal cords, glottis, epiglottis
  ▹ *Speech, Spoken Language 205*

13 **internal organ,** viscera, vitals, insides, entrails, innards, guts; esophagus, pharynx, stomach, duodenum, bowels, intestines, small intestine, large intestine, colon, rectum, anus; lungs, bronchi, diaphragm; heart, atria, ventricles, aorta, pulmonary artery, blood vessels, arteries, veins, capillaries; liver, gallbladder, pancreas, spleen; kidneys, urethra; genitals, genitalia, sexual organs, reproductive organs, gonads; gland
  ▹ *Sex 20; Reproduction 21; Secretion 24*

14 **nervous system,** brain, cerebrum, cerebellum, neuron, axon, dendrite, myelin *or* medullary sheath, synapse, ganglion, nerves, central nervous system, spinal cord

15 **body process,** growth, metabolism, respiration, circulation, digestion, ingestion, secretion, excretion, reproduction
  ▹ *Biochemistry 12; Humankind 18; Reproduction 21; Fertility 22; Secretion 24; Excretion 25; Life 28; Male 32; Female 33; Medicine 107; Health 113; Ill Health 114*

16 **body fluid,** blood, lymph, plasma, saliva, chyle, rheum, mucus, phlegm, tears, ear wax, bile, perspiration, sweat, urine, semen, pus, milk, colostrum, hormone, humor [Arch]
  ▹ *Secretion 24; Fluid 555*

17 **bodily development,** growth, physical development; maturing, maturation, growing up; birth, infancy, childhood, adolescence, adulthood, full growth, middle age, senescence, old age, death

  ▹ *Humankind 18; Youth 26; Age 27; Beginning 771*

ADJECTIVES

18 **bodily,** physical, corporeal, fleshly; skeletal, bony, structural; muscular, cartilageous, sinewy

19 **skin,** cutaneous, skinlike, dermal, epidermal, subcutaneous

20 **hairy,** hirsute, tressed, shaggy, tonsorial; ciliary; bearded, whiskered, mustached, mustachioed

21 **toothed,** dental, dentoid

22 **sensory,** optic, sighted, visual, seeing, ophthalmic; hearing, aural, otic; tactile, touching, feeling
  ▹ *Sensation 212; Touch 216; Taste 219; Hearing 228; Vision 242*

23 **internal,** visceral; neural, nervous, cerebral, spinal, synaptic; membranous

24 **metabolic,** respiratory, breathing, tracheal, pulmonary, circulatory, circulating, digestive, gastric, secretive, excretive, reproductive, genital, generative

25 **fluid,** bloody, vascular, lymphatic, mucous, teary, lacrimal, perspiring, sweaty, urinary, seminal, pussy, hormonal
  ▹ *Secretion 24; Fluid 555*

20 Sex

NOUNS

1 **sex,** sexuality, gender; female, femaleness, femininity, womanhood; male, maleness, masculinity, manhood

2 **sexual organs,** genitals, genitalia, pudendum *or* pudenda, gonads, private parts, privates
  ▹ *Human Body 19; Reproduction 21; Male 32; Female 33*

3 **sexuality,** sexual nature, physical nature; sex life, love life, sexual activity; sensuality, voluptuousness, sexiness, sex appeal, sexual attraction *or* magnetism, animal magnetism; sexual urge *or* instinct, sexual drive, libido, carnality, flesh, fleshliness; mating instinct, potency

4 **sexual nature,** sexual orientation, sexual preference *or* persuasion *or* leaning; heterosexuality; bisexuality, bisexualism, ambisexuality, swinging *or* going both ways [Inf]; homosexuality, homoeroticism, homophilia, sexual inversion, the love that dare not speak its name; lesbianism, sapphism, tribadism *or* tribady, Boston marriage; transvestism, cross-dressing, eonism, transsexuality; androgyny, hermaphroditism, pseudohermaphrodism, gynandry, gynandromorphism; heterosexual, bisexual, homosexual, gay, lesbian, invert; transvestite, cross-dresser, transsexual; androgyne, hermaphrodite, pseudohermaphrodite, gynandromorph
  ▹ *Male 32; Female 33*

5 **sexual desire,** biological urge, heat, estrus, estrous cycle; bodily appetite, venereal appetite *or* desire, carnal *or* sensuous desire, desires of the flesh; chemistry, allure, allurement, fascination

▶ *Desire 288; Attraction 700*

6 sexual longing, lust, fleshly lust, desire, itch, weakness of the flesh, lusts of the flesh; passion, prurience *or* pruriency, concupiscence, hot blood, aphrodisia; lustfulness, goatishness, lasciviousness; [Inf]: letch, horniness, blue balls, the hots, hot pants *or* rocks *or* nuts

7 eroticism, erotism; erotomania, eromania; narcissism, narcissist, voyeurism; voyeur, Peeping Tom; aphrodisiac, love potion, love philter, cantharis, blister beetle, cantharides, Spanish fly

8 sex object, [Inf *and* Off]: piece, meat, piece of meat *or* ass; female [Inf *and* Off]: sex kitten, sex goddess, skirt, nooky *or* nookie, doll, chick, cupcake, mama, moll, cheesecake, broad, dame, baggage, tart, bint [Brit], bird [Brit], bit of fluff [Brit]; male [Inf *and* Off]: sex king, sex god, beefcake, hunk, stud

9 sexual intercourse, sex, sex act, safe sex, having sex, coupling, pairing, mating, intimacy, procreation; copulation, coition, coitus, venery [Arch]; sexual relations, relations, marital relations, marital act, consummation, sexual commerce, sexual congress, sexual union; sleeping together, sleeping with, going to bed with, act of love, making love, lovemaking; fornication, adultery, shacking up [Inf]; casual sex, one-night stand; wife swapping, husband swapping; [Inf]: screwing, balling, fucking, nooky *or* nookie, diddling, hankypanky, doing it, quickie, making it, making out, going all the way, rogering [Brit]

▶ *Love 299; Immorality 432*

10 sex act, foreplay, ejaculation, orgasm, climax; coitus interruptus, onanism; oral sex, oral-genital stimulation, fellatio *or* fellation, blow job [Inf]; cunnilingus, sixty-nine [Inf]; anal sex, anal intercourse, sodomy, buggery [Inf]; group sex, gangbang, serial sex, group grope [Inf]; sex shop, phone sex; masturbation, autoeroticism, manipulation, playing with oneself, self-abuse; [Inf]: jacking off, jerking off, hand job

11 sexual offense, sexual harassment, sex crime, unlawful sexual intercourse, rape, sexual abuse, molestation

▶ *Immorality 432*

12 sexual perversion, perversion, sexual deviation *or* deviance; satyrism, satyriasis, Don Juanism, nymphomania; paraphilia, sexual pathology, psychosexual disorder, sexual psychopathy; masochism, sadomasochism *or* s and m, bestiality, pederasty, pedophilia, incest, algolagnia, necrophilia, coprophilia; sexual pervert, sex fiend, sex criminal, deviant, deviate, pervert; satyr, Don Juan, nymphomaniac, nympho [Inf]; paraphiliac, sexual psychopath, masochist, sadomasochist, pederast

13 sexlessness, asexuality, impotency, frigidity, coldness; eunuch, castrato, neuter, spado, gelding, steer

14 sexology, sex study; sexual customs *or* mores *or* practices; sexual revolution, new morality, free love, sexual freedom *or* liberation; sexologist, sexual counselor, sexual surrogate

ADJECTIVES

15 sexual, sex, sexlike, gamic, genital; female, feminine, womanly, male, masculine, manly

▶ *Reproduction 21; Male 32; Female 33*

16 sensual, voluptuous, carnal, fleshly; sexy, appealing, attractive, magnetic, alluring, desirable

▶ *Desire 288*

17 of sexual nature, heterosexual, straight [Inf]; bisexual, ambisexual, epicene, AC/DC [Inf], ambisextrous [Inf]; homosexual, homoerotic, limp-wristed, gay, effeminate; lesbian, sapphic, tribadistic; [Inf *and* Off]: queer, faggoty, butch, dykey; transvestite, transsexual, androgynous, androgynal, hermaphrodite, hermaphroditic, pseudohermaphrodite, pseudohermaphroditic, gynandromorphic

18 desirous, amorous, driven, libidinous, lustful, lecherous; passionate, prurient, concupiscent, salacious; hot, hot-blooded, burning with desire, coital, steamy, goatish, randy; lewd, lickerish [Arch], lascivious; oversexed, excited, aroused; in heat, in rut, rutty, rutting, ruttish, estrous *or* estral; sex-starved, unsatisfied, frustrated; [Inf]: hot and bothered, hot to trot, horny, sexed-up

19 coupling, pairing, mating, intimate, procreating, copulating; potent, orgasmic, orgastic, ejaculatory

20 undersexed, sexless, unsexual, asexual; neuter, castrated, emasculated, eunuchized; frigid, impotent, cold

VERBS

21 have sex, have intercourse, couple, pair, mate, be intimate, procreate, copulate, have sexual relations, have marital relations, consummate; sleep together, sleep with, go to bed with, lie with, perform the act of love, make love; cover, mount, serve, service; commit adultery, fornicate; [Inf]: go all the way, shack up with, lay, get laid, screw, ball, fuck, diddle, do it, make it, make out, roger [Brit]

22 stimulate, have foreplay, masturbate, abuse oneself, ejaculate, achieve *or* reach orgasm, climax; fellate, sodomize; [Inf]: come, get off, suck *or* suck off, go down on, give head; bugger; play with oneself, jack off, whack off

ADVERBS

23 sexily, sexually, sensually, erotically, erogenously

24 lustfully, passionately, amorously, desirously, with longing; wantonly, lasciviously, libidinously, licentiously, lewdly, lecherously

21 Reproduction

NOUNS

1 reproduction, multiplication, proliferation, repetition, replication, duplication, reduplication, copy,

photocopy, Xerox™, photostat, stat [Inf], photoreproduction, reprography; thermography, xerography, microfilming, scanned image; printing, lithography, publishing, mass production
- *Photography 132; Publication 173; Sameness 730; Imitation 736; Plurality 793*

2 restoration, reconstruction, renovation, renewal, replica
- *Repair 809*

3 reprint, print, offprint, duplicate, facsimile, edition, new edition, revised edition, clone, replica, copy, carbon copy, repro [Inf]
- *Publication 173; Books 174*

4 propagation, reproduction, generation, procreation; sex, sexual intercourse, copulation, coition; breeding, spawning, engendering, fathering, siring
- *Sex 20*

5 genesis, biogenesis, abiogenesis; autogenesis, spontaneous generation, parthenogenesis, virgin birth; conception, pregnancy, gestation, incubation, hatching, birth, childbirth, parturition, nativity, blessed event; birthrate, natality
- *Medicine 107*

6 fertilization, pollination, fecundation, germination, fructification, fruition, florescence, efflorescence, flowering; impregnation, insemination; artificial insemination, in vitro fertilization (IVF)
- *Fertility 22; Beginning 771*

7 propagator, pollinator, fertilizer, cultivator, procreator, begetter, inseminator, impregnator; parent, father, mother, sire, dam

8 progeny, offspring, child, children, baby, young, chick, kid [Inf], litter; fruit, seed
- *Mammals 35; Family 65*

9 organs of reproduction, reproductive organs, genitalia, genitals, pudenda, private parts, privates; female sex organs: vulva, clitoris, labia majora, labia minora, vagina, uterus, womb, cervix, neck of the womb, ovary, Fallopian tubes, ovum, egg, ovipositor; male sex organs: penis, phallus, intromittent organ, male member, privy member, glans penis, foreskin, testicles, testes, scrotum, prostate, prostate gland, vas deferens, semen, seminal fluid, sperm, spermatozoa; plant reproductive organs: stigma, style, stamen, anther, gynoecium, pollen, seed, fruit; [Inf]: cunt, pussy, twat, slit; cock, prick, dick, tool, pecker, balls, rocks, nuts

ADJECTIVES

10 reproduced, multiplied, proliferated, repeated, duplicated, copied, photocopied, scanned, printed, reprinted; restored, reconstructed, renovated, renewed, replicated

11 reproductive, generative, procreative, procreant, lifegiving, originative, germinal, genetic; sexual, genital, vulvar, clitoral, vaginal, cervical, ovarian; penile, phal-

lic, scrotal; in season, in heat, breeding, broody, fecundative

12 pregnant, impregnated, enceinte, with child, big with, heavy with, gravid, expecting, expectant, expecting a baby, expecting a blessed event, in the family way, in an interesting condition, in a delicate condition, eating for two; about to give birth, parturient, in labor, antenatal, perinatal, postnatal, puerperal; live-bearing, viviparous, oviparous, parthenogenetic

VERBS

13 reproduce, repeat, echo, duplicate, replicate, clone, copy, make a copy of, photocopy, Xerox™, microfilm, photostat, scan; mass-produce; print, reprint; restore, reconstruct, renovate, renew

14 reproduce oneself, inseminate, impregnate; germinate, sprout, bloom, flower; conceive, get pregnant, become pregnant

15 propagate, generate, produce, procreate, breed, produce offspring, bring into existence, bring *or* call into being, bring into the world, give life to, beget, spawn, engender, father, sire, carry on the line; make pregnant, impregnate, inseminate, knock up [Inf]; fertilize, fecundate, pollinate; hatch, incubate, raise from seed, bud, graft, take cuttings, layer, air layer

16 have young, give birth, bring to birth, bring forth, bear, be brought to bed of [Arch], have a baby, have children, have progeny, have offspring, lay eggs, spawn, hatch, drop, foal, lamb, farrow, pup, whelp, calve, cub, kitten, litter; fruit, bear fruit, fructify
- *Fertility 22; Mammals 35; Medicine 107; Plurality 793*

ADVERBS

17 reproductively, procreatively, genetically, sexually

18 repeatedly, again

22 Fertility

NOUNS

1 fertility, fecundity, fruitfulness, prolificness, prolificity, prolificacy, exuberance, luxuriance, lushness, richness, abundance, plenty, cornucopia, horn of plenty, plenitude, plentifulness, wealth, riot, profusion, rich harvest, bounty, bountifulness; overabundance, embarrassment of riches, *embarras de richesses* [Fr], superabundance, superfluity, glut
- *Sufficiency 97; Excess 99*

2 fertile land, rich soil, land of milk and honey, hotbed, seedbed
- *Prosperity 847*

3 productiveness, productivity, high productivity, prosperity, mass production, boom, economic boom, economic upturn; high birthrate, population explosion, baby boom, biotic potential
- *Economics 56; Excess 99; Production 522*

4 procreation, reproduction, propagation, fructification, fecundation, pullulation; fertilization, insemination, impregnation, pollination

> *Reproduction 21*

5 **enrichment,** resourcefulness, inventiveness, imagination, imaginativeness, creativity

> *Imagination 360*

6 **fertilizer,** enricher, procreator, propagator; gamete, seed, semen, sperm, fertility drug; manure, dung, guano, compost, bone meal, fish meal, leaf mold, peat moss, humus, mulch, phosphate, nitrogen, nitrate, potash, ammonium salts, sulfate, lime, marl, dressing, top dressing

> *Agriculture 16; Reproduction 21*

7 **fertility cult,** fertility rite, fertility symbol

> *Deity 82; Occultism 86*

ADJECTIVES

8 **fertile,** fecund, fruitful, fructiferous, fruit-bearing; prolific, exuberant, luxuriant, lush, rich, abundant, copious, plentiful, plenteous, wealthy, profuse, profusive, bountiful, bounteous; overabundant, superabundant; verdant, rife, thriving, flourishing

9 **productive,** profitable, prosperous, booming, paying, lucrative, high-yielding, teeming, streaming

10 **procreative,** procreant, propagatory, fecund, regenerative, seminal, pregnant

11 **enriching,** resourceful, inventive, imaginative, creative

VERBS

12 **fertilize,** make fertile, fecundate, fructify, enrich, richen, inseminate, impregnate, pollinate, germinate, seed; compost, feed, mulch, marl, dress, top-dress

13 **be fertile,** thrive, flourish, burgeon, bloom, blossom, fructify; produce, be productive, prosper, boom, mass-produce

14 **procreate,** reproduce, propagate, generate, engender, beget, conceive, give birth, bear, teem, swarm, pullulate, proliferate, mushroom, multiply, populate

> *Reproduction 21; Prosperity 847*

ADVERBS

15 **fruitfully,** productively, profitably, prolifically, abundantly, resourcefully, creatively, inventively

23   Infertility

NOUNS

1 **infertility,** infecundity, fruitlessness, unproductiveness, unproductivity, barrenness, sterility, impotence, childlessness; fallowness, aridity, aridness, dryness

2 **infertile land,** drought-stricken land, desert, dust bowl, desert island, waste, wasteland, lunar landscape, Arctic waste, Antarctic waste, barren waste, wild, wilderness, desolation; desertification, soil erosion, deforestation, defoliation, scorched-earth policy

3 **infertile state,** menopause, change of life, abortion, spontaneous abortion, miscarriage; falling birth rate,

low birth rate, zero population growth, dying race; economic decline, recession, stagnation, economic stagnation, slump, depression, unprofitableness, unprofitability, poor return, low yield; dearth, famine, waste

> *Waste 96; Insufficiency 98; Loss 468; Destruction 523; Dryness 560; Decrease 747; Uselessness 802*

4 **that which makes infertile,** sterilization, tube tying, hysterectomy, vasectomy, castration, neutering, spaying, gelding

5 **birth control,** abstinence, celibacy, contraception, prophylactic, planned parenthood, family planning, rhythm method, coitus interruptus

6 **contraceptive,** barrier contraceptive, diaphragm, Dutch cap, condom, sheath, French letter [Inf], rubber [Inf], female condom, femidom, contraceptive sponge; chemical contraceptive, contraceptive foam, spermicide, oral contraceptive, the pill, minipill, morning-after pill, male pill, contraceptive injection; intrauterine device (IUD), coil, loop

ADJECTIVES

7 **infertile,** infecund, fruitless, unfruitful, unproductive, unprolific, barren, sterile, impotent, childless; fallow, arid, dry, drought-stricken, desert, empty, treeless, gaunt, bleak, stark, bare, sparse, uncultivated, stony, shallow, eroded, withered, shriveled, dead, blasted, waste, desolate; stagnating, stagnant, recessionary, unprofitable, depressed, low-yield

VERBS

8 **be infertile,** lie fallow, stagnate, rust, rot, run to seed; prove infertile, fail, come to nothing, come to naught, abort, miscarry, lose the baby, have no issue, have no offspring, die without issue *or* offspring, be childless; hide one's abilities, bury one's talents, hide one's light under a bushel, hang fire [Inf]

> *Uselessness 802; Deterioration 808; Failure 846*

9 **make infertile,** sterilize, vasectomize, unman, emasculate, castrate, geld, spay, neuter

10 **practice birth control,** abstain, use a contraceptive, plan one's family, take precautions

11 **waste,** lay waste, desolate, deforest, defoliate, overgraze

> *Waste 96; Hygiene 116; Destruction 523*

ADVERBS

12 **unproductively,** fruitlessly, impotently, unprofitably; without issue, without offspring

24   Secretion

NOUNS

1 **secretion,** exudation, emission, transudation, excretion, discharge, release, voidance, ejection, emanation, lactation, lacrimation, crying, weeping, guttation, salivation, sweating, perspiration; eccrine secretion, apocrine secretion, holocrine secretion

2 secreted substance, secretion; hormone, chalone, digestive juice, gastric juice, pancreatic juice, bile, gall, mucus; phlegm, sputum, saliva, tears, rheum, seminal fluid, semen, milk, colostrum, sweat; sebum, musk, pheromone, ectohormone, honeydew; nectar, latex, resin, tannin, gum

▶ *Biochemistry 12; Excretion 25; Trees 43; Fluid 555; Viscosity 561*

3 secretory mechanism, gland, endocrine gland, ductless gland, exocrine gland, eccrine gland, apocrine gland, holocrine gland, intestinal gland, sweat gland, mammary gland, lacrimal *or* lachrymal gland, scent gland; plant gland, oil gland, uropygeal gland, salt gland; nectary, laticifer, hydathode

ADJECTIVES

4 secretory, secretionary, secretive, exudative, transudatory, emissive, excretory, emanative, emanatory, emanational, glandular, eccrine, apocrine, holocrine, secreting, lactating, lactational, lactescent, lactiferous, laticiferous, lacrimatory, crying, weeping, sebaceous, sebiferous, sweating, sweaty, sudatory, salivating

5 of a secretion, glandular, glandulous, hormonal, endocrine, adrenal, ovarian, testicular, seminal, pineal, pituitary, placental, luteal, thyroidal, exocrine, eccrine, lacrimal *or* lachrymal, lacrimatory, mammary, lacteal, lacteous [Arch], mucous *or* mucose, mucoid, sudoral, sebaceous, salivary, parotid, sialoid, gastric, pyloric, pancreatic, prostatic

6 inducing secretion, lactogenic, sialogogic, lacrimatory, sudatory, sudorific, cholagogic

VERBS

7 secrete, exude, transude, produce, emit, excrete, discharge, release, liberate, void, eject, give up, give off, emanate, produce secretion, lactate; cry, weep, tear, lacrimate; salivate, sweat, perspire

▶ *Excretion 25; Expulsion 709*

ADVERBS

8 glandularly, glandulously, lactationally, lacteally, weepily, tearfully, sweatily

25 Excretion

NOUNS

1 excretion, egestion, elimination, expulsion, discharge, ejection, extrusion, emission, emanation, secretion, transudation, exudation, extravasation, flux, flow, expectoration, ejaculation, ecchymosis, effusion; call of nature [Inf]

▶ *Secretion 24; Expulsion 709*

2 excrement, excreta, egesta, ejecta, ejectamenta, waste, waste matter, dejection, dejecture, dejecta, exudation, exudate, transudate, extravasate, effluent, sewage, sewerage

3 defecation, evacuation, voidance, dejection, purge, purgation, catharsis, clearance; bowel movement (BM), movement, diarrhea, loose bowels, tourista *or* turista; flux, bloody flux, dysentery, lientery; constipation; [Inf]: the runs, the trots, the shits, Delhi belly, GI's, Montezuma's revenge, Aztec two-step, squits [Brit]

▶ *Medicine 107; Ill Health 114; Remedy 115*

4 urination, micturation, incontinence, weak bladder, enuresis, bed-wetting, nocturnal enuresis; urinalysis, urinometer; [Inf]: piss, piddling, leak, call of nature

5 feces, stool, movement, feculence, ordure, night soil, dung, muck; manure, cow pat, cow flop, cow chip, buffalo chip, guano, dirt, droppings, coprolite; [Inf]: shit, crap, poop, poo-poo, ca-ca, number two, dingleberry, turd

6 urine, water, urea, uric acid; [Inf]: pee, peepee, wee-wee, piss, leak, piddle, number one

7 pus, discharge, matter, ichor, sanies, purulence, pussiness, suppuration, festering, mattering, running, weeping, rankling, gleet, leukorrhea

8 sweat, perspiration, sudor, sweating, perspiring, sudation, sudoresis, diaphoresis, exudation, exudate, beads of sweat, induced sweat; honest sweat, cold sweat, sweat of one's brow

9 saliva, spit, spittle, salivation, salivary gland, ptyalism, sialorrhea, dribble, drivel, slaver, slobber, slabber, drool, froth, foam; cough, coughing, expectoration, spitting, phlegm, catarrh, mucus, rheum, snot [Inf]

10 bleeding, extravasation of blood, nosebleeds, ecchymosis, petechia, bruising, bruise, hemorrhage, hemorrhea, hematemesis, hemoptysis, hematuria, hemophilia; menstruation, menses, menstrual flow *or* flux *or* discharge, monthly discharge, catamenia, catamenial discharge, period, courses, time of the month, flowers [Arch]; menarche, menopause, amenorrhea, dysmenorrhea, epimenorrhea, hypomenorrhea, menorrhagia, oligomenorrhea; [Inf]: the curse, one's friend, the curse of Eve, monthlies

11 place for excretion, lavatory, bathroom, washroom, toilet, convenience, public convenience, water closet (WC), latrine, head, rest room, comfort station, ladies' room, women's room, little girls' room, powder room, men's room, little boys' room, privy, stool, outhouse, backhouse, earth closet; commode, urinal, chamber pot, potty, potty-chair, closestool, bedpan, chemical toilet; [Inf]: john, can, crapper, shithouse, the ladies', the gents', loo [Brit], bog [Brit]; throne, jerry [Brit], pisspot, thundermug

ADJECTIVES

12 excretory, excretive, excretionary, egestive, eliminative, eliminant, ejective, exudative, transudative, secretory

13 excremental, excrementary; incontinent, continent;

---

toilet-trained, potty-trained, housebroken, house-trained [Brit]

14 **fecal,** feculent, scatologic(al), stercoral, stercorous, stercoraceous, dungy, cathartic, purgative, laxative, aperient; shitty [Inf], crappy [Inf]

15 **urinary,** urinative, diuretic, enuretic

16 **purulent,** suppurative, festering, pussy, mattering, running

17 **sweaty,** sudatory, sudoric, sudorific, diaphoretic, sweating, perspiring, bathed in sweat, drenched with sweat, wet with sweat, clammy, sticky, wilting, glowing

18 **salivating,** spitting, coughing, spluttering, slobbering, slavering, dribbling, drooling, frothing, foaming, rheumy, watery, expectorant

19 **bleeding,** hemorrhaging, blood-soaked, bloody, ecchymosed; menstrual, catamenial, monthly, menopausal, menstruating; on the rag [Inf]

VERBS

20 **excrete,** egest, eliminate, pass, expel, discharge, eject, extrude, emit, give off, secrete, transude, exude, extravasate, weep, expectorate, ejaculate, relieve *or* ease oneself, go to the bathroom *or* toilet; [Inf]: go, answer the call of nature, pay a call, make a pit stop
▸ *Expulsion 709*

21 **defecate,** have a bowel movement (BM), move one's bowels, move, pass, evacuate, void, purge, foul, soil; [Inf]: shit, have *or* take a shit, shit oneself, crap, poop, make poo-poo, ca-ca, do number two, have the runs *or* trots *or* shits *or* squits [Brit]

22 **urinate,** micturate, pass *or* make water, wet, wet oneself, wet the bed; stale; [Inf]: piss, pee, peepee, weewee, piddle, tinkle, do number one, take a leak

23 **fester,** suppurate, run, weep, rankle, matter, come to a head

24 **sweat,** perspire, exude, break out in a sweat, sweat like a trooper *or* horse *or* pig, swelter, wilt, steam, glow
▸ *Heat 217*

25 **salivate,** water at the mouth, spit, splutter, slobber, slabber, slaver, dribble, drivel, drool, froth *or* foam at the mouth, cough, cough up, expectorate, hawk, clear one's throat, blow one's nose

26 **bleed,** spill *or* lose blood, bloody, ecchymose, extravasate, hemorrhage; menstruate, bleed, have one's period; [Inf]: have the curse, have one's friend, fall off the roof, be on the rag

ADVERBS

27 **excrementally,** fecally, sweatily, bloodily; scatologically; shittily [Inf], crappily [Inf]

26 Youth

Better is a poor and a wise child than an old and foolish king. — BIBLE: ECCLESIASTES

Youth is a malady of which one becomes cured a little every day. — BENITO MUSSOLINI

My salad days, when I was green in judgment. — WILLIAM SHAKESPEARE

NOUNS

1 **youth,** babyhood, infancy, childhood, girlhood, boyhood, preteens, puberty, pubescence, age of puberty, adolescence, teens; young days, younger days, school days, student days, college days, pupilage, apprenticeship, wardship; early life, springtime of life, bloom of youth, tender age, awkward age, immaturity, puerility, nonage, minority; happiest days of one's life, prime of life, salad days, heyday
▸ *Newness 652; Beginning 771*

2 **youthfulness,** youngness, childishness, boyishness, girlishness, maidenliness, juvenescence, juvenility, juvenilia; young blood, vigor, freshness, sappiness, juiciness, growing pains

3 **immaturity,** inexperience, undevelopment, greenness, rawness, naiveté, ingenuousness, awkwardness, callowness, unreadiness, unpreparedness
▸ *Lack of Preparation 389*

4 **young animal,** young, yearling, fawn, kitten, puppy, pup, kid, lamb, lambkin, cub, whelp, piglet, shoat; duckling, cygnet, chick; fry, fledgling, nestling, calf, colt, foal, filly; larva, grub, nymph, pupa, chrysalis, cocoon, caterpillar; tadpole, polliwog; brood, clutch, spawn, farrow, litter

5 **young plant,** sprout, seedling, set, shoot, offshoot, sucker, twig, spring, scion, sapling

6 **child,** baby, babe, bouncing baby, nursling, bundle of joy, babe in arms, infant, tot, tyke, mite, toddler; little one, darling, little angel, little monkey, little cherub, little imp; youngster, moppet, brat, boy, lad, girl, lass; [Inf]: kid, kiddie, peewee, nipper, rug rat

7 **young person,** youngster, youth, minor, adolescent, teenager, young adult, juvenile, junior, young hopeful, youngling; [Inf]: kid, young un, teenybopper

8 **young man,** youth, boy, lad, laddie, stripling, schoolboy, urchin, street urchin, cub; [Inf]: kid, shaver, little shaver, pup, young pup, squirt

9 **young woman,** girl, young lady, miss, lass, lassie, chit, slip (of a girl), schoolgirl, maid, maiden, virgin; tomboy, hoyden, minx, hussy, wench; nymph, nymphet; [Inf]: missy, baggage, chick, babe, baby, bird [Brit]

10 **the young,** young people, youth, young blood, children, schoolchildren, kids [Inf]; younger generation, new generation; baby boomers, twenty somethings

ADJECTIVES

11 **young,** youthful, juvenile, juvenescent; infant, infantile, baby, babyish, unfledged, fledgling, new-fledged, in the cradle, at the breast, in diapers; childlike, child-

ish, knee-high, boylike, boyish, beardless, girl-like, girlish, maidenly, virginal, innocent; underage, underaged, undeveloped, minor, preschool, school-age, junior; teenage, teenaged, sweet sixteen, adolescent, pubescent, in one's teens, in the flower of youth

▶ *Age 27*

12 immature, inexperienced, undeveloped, green, raw, naive, ingenuous, awkward, callow, unready, unprepared

VERBS

13 be young, bloom, stay young; make young, rejuvenate, reinvigorate

ADVERBS

14 youthfully, babyishly, childishly, boyishly, girlishly, virginally, innocently, juvenilely; immaturely, greenly, rawly, awkwardly, unreadily, unpreparedly

27 Age

Therefore I summon age to grant youth's heritage.
— ROBERT BROWNING

But at my back I always hear / Time's wingèd chariot hurrying near. — ANDREW MARVELL

How soon hath Time, the subtle thief of youth, / Stol'n on his wing my three-and-twentieth year. — JOHN MILTON

NOUNS

1 age, lifetime, life span, timespan, years, one's age, one's time of life, longevity; seven ages of man: infancy, childhood, youth, adolescence, adulthood, middle age, maturity, old age, senility

▶ *Youth 26; Time 639; Period 641; Duration 642*

2 adulthood, adultness, maturity, maturation, full growth, manhood, womanhood, matronliness, middle age, seniority, oldness, old age, ripeness

▶ *Oldness 653*

3 maturity, matureness, experience, professionalism, confidence, readiness, preparedness, leadership, mellowness, ripeness

4 middle age, middle life, middle years, riper years, years of discretion, one's prime, prime of life; change of life, menopause, climacteric, male menopause, midlife crisis, dangerous age, wrong side of forty

5 old age, elderliness, agedness, senescence, seniority; retirement age, pensionable age, ripe old age, golden years, advanced years, allotted span, threescore years and ten; declining years, decline, hoariness, grayness, frailty, infirmity, anility, senility, second childhood, dotage, anecdotage; evening of one's life, autumn of one's life, winter of one's life

▶ *Weakness 517; Oldness 653*

6 gerontology, geriatric medicine; gerontologist, geriatrician

▶ *Medicine 107*

7 older person, adult, grownup, elder, senior, sage, doyen *or* doyenne, retired person, pensioner, old person, golden ager, mentor, retiree, senior citizen, veteran, geriatric; sexagenarian, septuagenarian, octogenarian, nonagenarian, centenarian, Methuselah; old fogy, dotard, Gray Panther, oldster, dodderer, no spring chicken [Inf]

▶ *Oldness 653*

8 man, husband, father, grandfather, patron, patriarch, widower; old bachelor, man of the world, older man, old man, old boy, old codger, veteran, graybeard, pantaloon; [Inf]: old dog, old guy, old-timer, old geezer

▶ *Male 32*

9 woman, wife, mother, grandmother, matron, matriarch, widow, spinster; older woman, woman of the world; old woman, granny, old witch; [Inf *and* Off]: old gal, old bag, old bat

▶ *Female 33*

10 old people, the old, the elderly, older generation, seniors, retirees, over-the-hill gang [Inf]

ADJECTIVES

11 adult, mature, grown-up, full-grown, experienced, confident, ready, prepared, developed, mellow, ripe, ripened, wise

12 maturing, growing, developing, ripening, rounding out

13 aging, growing old, getting old, senescent, getting on *or* along in years, gaining wisdom, going gray, graying, getting crow's feet, getting a middle-aged spread, slowing down, declining, weakening, waning, on the wane, running *or* going to seed, sinking, moribund

14 middle-aged, mature, of mature years, fatherly, motherly, matronly, wise, menopausal, climacteric, overblown, gone to pot, not as young as one was, long in the tooth, thirty-something, forty-something

15 aged, old, elderly, venerable, grown old, patriarchal, matriarchal, geriatric, gerontologic(al), ageist; advanced in years, past one's prime, well-preserved, in possession of one's faculties, gray-haired, white-haired, old and gray, hoary, wrinkled, wizened, shriveled, lined, decrepit, failing, anile, senile; over the hill, burdened with age, stricken in years, moribund, living on borrowed time, not long for this world, with one foot in the grave; ancient, old as the hills, old as Methuselah, doddering, too old to cut the mustard [Inf], gaga [Inf]

VERBS

16 age, grow, bud, flower, get *or* become older, grow up; be (some) years old; grow old, get old, pass one's prime, get on, get on in years, get a middle-aged spread, get crow's feet, show one's years, go gray, gray, turn white, wrinkle, wizen, shrivel; live to a ripe old age, become long in the tooth, go to seed, go to pot, decline, dodder, sink, weaken, deteriorate, have one foot in the grave

17 **mature,** develop, come of age, leave the nest, attain *or* reach one's majority, reach manhood *or* womanhood, reach the prime of one's life, mellow, ripen

ADVERBS

18 **maturely,** preparedly, ripely, in full bloom, in one's prime, venerably, patriarchally, matriarchally, climacterically, agedly, hoarily, anilely, senilely, moribundly

28 Life

Life is an incurable disease. — ABRAHAM COWLEY

Lift not the painted veil which those who live / Call Life.
— PERCY BYSSHE SHELLEY

NOUNS

1 **life,** living, being alive, having life, being, existing, existence, subsistence; animate existence, animation, animal kingdom, animal life, human existence, human life, humankind, mankind, vegetable life, plant life; creation, evolution
 ◗ *Humankind 18; Animals (General) 34; Plants (General) 41; Existence 717*

2 **life force,** vital force, vital spark, vital flame, élan vital, consciousness, seat of life, beating heart; soul, spirit
 ◗ *Power 514; Strength 516; Vigor 518; Essence 723*

3 **living being,** human being, living person, person, individual, entity, survivor; living soul, living thing, life on earth, the living, the living and breathing, the quick
 ◗ *Humankind 18*

4 **living matter,** protoplasm, bioplasm, tissue, living tissue, macromolecule, bioplast, cell, gene, organism
 ◗ *Biochemistry 12; Life Science 13*

5 **life requirement,** vital necessity, sustenance; nourishment, food, daily bread, manna, water, oxygen, air, breath of life, blood, lifeblood
 ◗ *Biochemistry 12; Food 90; Air 558*

6 **life function,** biological function, life activity, life process; birth, growth, ingestion, excretion, reproduction, propagation, procreation, death; life senses: sight, hearing, touch, taste, smell; breathing, respiration, exhalation
 ◗ *Life Science 13; Reproduction 21; Fertility 22; Death 29; Sensation 212; Beginning 771*

7 **life cycle,** lifetime, life span, allotted span, life expectancy, threescore years and ten, one's born days; biological clock, biorhythm, biometry, longevity, survival, survivability, capacity for life, hold on life, will to live
 ◗ *Age 27; Time 639*

8 **new life,** new birth, rebirth, renaissance, revivification, revival, reanimation, reincarnation, resurrection;

life after death, life to come, immortal life, immortality, eternal life
 ◗ *Death 29; Religion 81; Eternity 644; Beginning 771*

9 **study of life,** life science: anthropology, anatomy, biochemistry, biology, botany, ecology, embryology, genetics, pathology, zoology; sociology, psychology, humanities
 ◗ *Anthropology 1; Sociology 2; Biochemistry 12; Life Science 13; Animals (General) 34; Plants (General) 41; Psychology and Psychiatry 108*

10 **classification of life,** taxonomy, systematics, cladistics
 ◗ *Life Science 13; Class 777*

11 **life story,** history, biography, autobiography, memoirs; lifestyle, way of life
 ◗ *History 3; Literature 139; Record 185; Description 202; Habit, Custom 397; Conduct 399; Way 691*

12 **liveliness,** vivacity, energy, sprightliness, vitality, vitalization, vivification, animation, quickening, sensation, sentience, sensibility, ginger [Inf]
 ◗ *Power 514; Strength 516; Vigor 518; Essence 723*

ADJECTIVES

13 **alive,** live, living, alive and kicking, animate, conscious, breathing, in life, in the flesh, incarnate; born, existing, extant, surviving, ongoing, in the land of the living, still with us, still breathing, quick [Arch], above ground, on this side of the grave; capable of life, viable, vital, vivifying, life-giving; vivified, enlivened, Promethean

14 **pertaining to life,** biologic(al), biotic, biogenetic, protoplasmic; living, eating, breathing, reproducing, propagating, procreating, surviving; long-lived, lasting, lifelong

15 **given new life,** reborn, revived, quickened, restored, reanimated, reincarnated, resurrected

16 **lively,** animated, vivacious, spirited, energetic, vigorous, dynamic, active, sprightly, gingery [Inf]

VERBS

17 **live,** be alive, have life, be, be born, have being, exist, subsist; draw breath, breathe, respire; walk the earth, live one's life; come to life, quicken, come to, come around, regain consciousness, revive; not die, be spared, survive, endure, come through, carry on, continue, last, persist, cheat death, have nine lives, be reborn
 ◗ *Existence 717; Repair 809*

18 **be born,** come to life, come into the world, come into existence, see the light of day, begin, draw breath, sprout
 ◗ *Beginning 771*

19 **give birth to,** give life to, create life, impart life; conceive, beget, breed, spawn, procreate, reproduce, fructify

20 **bring back to life,** raise up, revive, bring around, re-

store to consciousness, quicken, resurrect, raise from the dead

21 **support life,** feed, nourish, provide for, provide a living for, keep alive, save the life of; keep body and soul together
> *Provision 89; Food 90; Help 825*

22 **invigorate,** vivify, revitalize, revive, put new life into, rejuvenate, enliven, liven up, energize, animate, quicken, give a shot in the arm, put a new lease on life, reanimate, restore

ADVERBS

23 **vitally,** viably, biologically, biotically; lively, animatedly, vivaciously

29   Death

Any man's death diminishes me, because I am involved in Mankind; And therefore never send to know for whom the bell tolls; it tolls for thee. — JOHN DONNE

Death's a debt; his mandamus binds all alike — no bail, no demurrer. — RICHARD BRINSLEY SHERIDAN

O Death, where is thy sting-a-ling-a-ling, / O Grave, thy victoree? / The bells of hell go ting-a-ling-a-ling / For you but not for me. — ANONYMOUS

NOUNS

1 **death,** decease, demise, loss of life, no life, expiry, expiration [Arch]; exit, departure, end of life, ending, end, quietus, grave; sleep, release, eternal rest, reward, just reward; the beyond, the other side, the Great Divide; doom, crack of doom, knell, death knell; curtains [Inf], last roundup [Inf]

2 **mortality,** perishability, extinction, dissolution, abiosis; biological death, clinical death, brain death, cerebral death

3 **dying,** act of dying, process of death, moribundity, perishing, making an end, departing, passing, passing away, passing over, crossing over, crossing the bar, crossing the Styx *or* Lethe *or* Jordan; dying day, deathbed, deathwatch, death struggle, death throes, throes of death, last hour, last breath, dying breath, last gasp, last agony, death rattle; deathbed repentance, deathbed confession, final words, last words, swan song; near-death experience; extreme unction, last rites

4 **personifications and symbols,** Grim Reaper, great leveler, thief in the night, Last Summoner, Azrael, angel of death, death's bright angel, pale horse, pale rider, shadow of death, hand of death, cold fingers of death, jaws of death, dance of death, valley of the shadow of death; skull, skull and crossbones, death's-head, sickle, scythe, memento mori

5 **way of dying,** natural death, death from old age,

easy death, quiet end *or* death, peaceful death, welcome release, euthanasia, stillbirth; suicide, violent death, murder, assassination, sudden death, untimely end, accidental death, fatal accident, death in action, death by misadventure; fatality, drowning, starvation, fatal *or* mortal *or* terminal illness *or* disease; martyrdom, capital punishment, execution
> *Killing 30; War 76; Ill Health 114; Punishment 454; End 773*

6 **dying person,** dying *or* terminal patient, hopeless case, condemned man *or* woman, the condemned; [Inf]: dead duck, dead pigeon, goner

7 **dead person,** dead body, body, corpse, cadaver, carcass, fatality, casualty, victim, stillbirth, the deceased, the dear departed, the defunct, the late lamented; mummy, embalmed body, remains, mortal remains, relic, ashes, carrion, stiff [Inf]; the dead, ancestors, forefathers

8 **person dealing with the dead,** doctor, pathologist, coroner, police, undertaker, mortician, funeral director, embalmer
> *Burial 31*

9 **after death,** death certificate, rigor mortis, postmortem, autopsy, necropsy, inquest, embalming; mortuary, morgue, charnel house; passing bell, wake, funeral home, funeral, funeral rites, obsequies; next world, afterlife, hereafter, heaven, purgatory, hell, Elysian fields, happy hunting ground, Abraham's bosom, paradise
> *Burial 31; Religion 81; Deity 82; Nonmaterial World 525*

10 **death count,** mortality rate, death rate, mortality table, death register, death roll, death toll, fatality list, casualty list, body count; martyrology, necrology; death column, obituary *or* obit, death notice, death record

ADJECTIVES

11 **dead,** deceased, defunct, demised, lifeless, breathless, still, inanimate, exanimate, cold, extinct, finished, stone-dead; bereft of life, no more, passed, passed away, passed over, crossed over, released, departed, gone, gone before, gone to join one's ancestors, long gone, gone but not forgotten; late, lamented, late lamented; born dead, stillborn, dead on arrival (DOA); dead as a doornail; launched into eternity, on the other side, taken *or* called by God, called to eternal rest, gathered to one's fathers, in Abraham's bosom, asleep in Jesus, in Paradise, at the Pearly Gates; [Inf]: done for, deep-sixed, six feet under

12 **dying,** expiring, deathlike, moribund, perishing; on the danger list, in a critical condition, fatally *or* mortally *or* terminally ill, sick unto death; hopeless, doomed *or* fated to die; condemned to die, sentenced to death; half-dead, on one's deathbed, at the point of death, *in extremis* [L], slipping away, sinking, fading, hanging by

a thread, struggling for breath, not long for this world, going, about gone, far gone

 ▶ *Ill Health 114; Punishment 454; End 773*

13 **killed,** murdered, assassinated, slaughtered, massacred, sacrificed, martyred

 ▶ *Killing 30; Punishment 454*

14 **deadly,** mortal, fatal, terminal, lethal, murderous, life-threatening

15 **deathly,** deathlike, corpselike, morbid, cadaverous, ghastly, livid, pallid

16 **posthumous,** postmortem, post-obit, funereal, embalmed, mummified, fossilized

VERBS

17 **die,** decease, be dead, lose one's life, succumb, expire, perish, depart, end; pass, pass away, pass over, cross over, cross the bar, cross the Styx *or* Lethe *or* Jordan; meet one's maker *or* death *or* end *or* fate; be no more, cease to be *or* live, be gone, stop breathing, breathe one's last, give up the ghost, bite the dust, come *or* turn to dust; [Inf]: go west, turn up one's toes, push up daisies, kick the bucket, buy the farm, cash in one's chips, pop off, go belly up

 ▶ *Cessation 668; Nonexistence 718; End 773*

ADVERBS

18 **fatally,** terminally, mortally, moribundly, lifelessly, inanimately, postmortem; after death, posthumously

30 Killing

Killing/ Is the ultimate simplification of life.
— HUGH MACDIARMID

Yet each man kills the thing he loves, / By each let this be heard, / Some do it with a bitter look, / Some with a flattering word. / The coward does it with a kiss, / The brave man with a sword! — OSCAR WILDE

NOUNS

1 **killing,** slaying, murder, manslaughter; destruction, destruction of life, taking life, causing death, dealing death, execution, bloodshedding, bloodletting; ritual killing, accidental killing, mercy killing, euthanasia

 ▶ *Death 29; Destruction 523*

2 **murder,** first-degree murder, second-degree murder, premeditated murder, capital murder, assassination, contract murder, mass murder, gang murder, terrorist killing, brutal murder, murder most foul, classic murder, crime of passion, manslaughter; unlawful killing, thuggery, shooting, knifing, poisoning, suffocation, asphyxiation, strangulation, garroting, hanging, drowning, bludgeoning; [Inf]: bumping off, rubbing out, blowing away, wasting

3 **murder weapon,** gun, knife, blunt instrument, rope, garrote, bomb, poison

4 **homicide,** regicide, tyrannicide, parricide, patricide, matricide, uxoricide, fratricide, sororicide, infanticide, infant exposure

5 **slaughter,** massacre, war, battle, bloodbath, carnage, gladiatorial combat, duel; butchery, wholesale murder, high casualties, great bloodshed, noyade, battue, holocaust, pogrom, purge, annihilation, liquidation, decimation, extermination, destruction, genocide, ethnic cleansing; the Holocaust, Final Solution, Custer's Last Stand, Roman holiday, Massacre of the Innocents, Sicilian Vespers, St. Bartholomew's Day Massacre, Night of the Long Knives

 ▶ *War 76; Destruction 523*

6 **execution,** capital punishment, death penalty, legalized killing, judicial murder, auto-da-fé, hanging, electrocution, shooting, firing squad, lethal injection, gas chamber, beheading, burning alive, stoning; extrajudicial execution, lynching; dispatch, deathblow, *coup de grâce* [Fr], final stroke, quietus

 ▶ *Punishment 454*

7 **ritual killing,** sacrifice, religious sacrifice, martyrdom, martyrization, immolation, crucifixion

 ▶ *Religion 81*

8 **suicide,** self-destruction, self-slaughter, killing oneself, doing away with oneself, dying by one's own hand, felo-de-se, slashing one's wrists, jumping from a high place, hanging oneself, shooting oneself, taking an overdose, starving oneself, gassing oneself; ritual suicide, self-immolation, suttee, hara-kiri *or* seppuku, kamikaze; mass suicide, suicide pact

9 **accidental killing,** manslaughter, violent death, fatal accident, traffic death, fatal car *or* train *or* plane crash, accidental shooting, drive-by shooting; death by misadventure

 ▶ *Death 29*

10 **animal killing,** blood sport, cockfighting, bullfighting; hunting, shooting, wildfowling, chase, trapping; selective killing, cull, extermination, slaughtering, butchering, knackery [Brit]; vivisection, animal suicide, beaching

11 **killer,** slayer, murderer, man of blood, soldier, combatant, guerrilla, urban guerrilla, terrorist, lyncher, slaughterer, butcher, executioner, hangman, punisher, tribal killer, headhunter, cannibal; mercy killer, euthanasiast

 ▶ *Combatant 77; Punishment 454*

12 **murderer,** murderess, cold-blooded murderer, killer, assassin, hired killer, contract killer, professional killer, mass murderer, serial killer, psychopathic killer, psychopath, pathological killer, homicidal maniac; terrorist, bomber, poisoner, strangler, garroter, ax murderer, hatchet man, gangster, gang member, gunman, hired gun, bravo, desperado, cutthroat, thug, ruffian, hit man [Inf]

13 executioner, hangman, firing squad member, electrocutioner, axman

14 animal killer, hunter, huntsman, trapper; butcher, slaughterman, knacker [Brit], bullfighter, matador, toreador, picador, pest exterminator, rat-catcher, mole-catcher; vivisectionist; predator, bird of prey, beast of prey

15 killing agent, poison, pesticide, insecticide, ratsbane, rodenticide, vermicide, germicide; plant killer, weed-killer, herbicide, fungicide, algicide
> *Agriculture 16*

16 slaughterhouse, abattoir, knacker's yard [Brit], shambles, bullring, arena, battleground, field of battle, battlefield, killing field, gas chamber, death camp

ADJECTIVES

17 killing, deadly, lethal, mortal, fatal, deathly, fell, life-threatening, capital, death-bringing, malignant, poisonous, toxic, asphyxiant, suffocating, stifling, unhealthy, miasmic, insalubrious, inoperable, incurable, terminal
> *Death 29; Ill Health 114*

18 murderous, homicidal, psychopathic, pathological, genocidal, internecine, slaughterous, death-dealing, destructive, cold-blooded, sanguinary, ensanguined, bloody, gory, bloodstained, red-handed, bloodthirsty, thirsting for blood, cruel, savage, brutal, headhunting, lynching, man-eating, cannibalistic, suicidal, self-destructive, trigger-happy [Inf]
> *Malevolence 306; Destruction 523*

VERBS

19 kill, slay, murder, take life, deprive of life, rob of life, shorten someone's life, hasten someone's end, end someone's life, dispatch, destroy, do away with, make away with, get rid of, cut off, put down, put to sleep, exterminate, drive to death, work to death, send out of the world, send to one's account, send to one's Maker, launch into eternity, put out of one's misery, snuff out [Inf]
> *Death 29*

20 murder, commit murder, assassinate, poison, stab, stab to death, knife, saber, spear, put to the sword, lance, bayonet, run through, shoot, shoot down, gun down, pick off, pistol, blow out the brains of; bomb, strangle, wring the neck of, garrote, choke, smother, burke, suffocate, asphyxiate, stifle, drown, wall up, bury alive; strike, smite, brain, spill the brains of, poleax, sandbag, beat to death; burn, burn alive, roast alive, gas, electrocute, starve to death; arrange a fatal accident, eliminate; [Inf]: waste, blow away, do in, bump off, rub out, take for a ride, deep-six

21 slaughter, butcher, poleax, cut the throat of, drain the lifeblood of, massacre, slay en masse, smite hip and thigh, put to the sword, cut to pieces, cut to ribbons, cut down, decimate, mow down, shoot down, gun down, steep one's hands in blood, wade in blood, give no quarter, spare none, take no prisoners, destroy, wipe out, wipe off the face of the earth, annihilate, exterminate, liquidate, purge, send to the gas chamber, commit genocide
> *Destruction 523*

22 execute, condemn, put to death, hang, send to the scaffold, send to the gallows, electrocute, gas, give a lethal injection, shoot, behead, guillotine, send to the stake, burn alive, stone to death, lynch, garrote, deal a deathblow, string up [Inf]
> *Punishment 454*

23 kill ritually, sacrifice, offer up, martyr, martyrize, crucify, immolate
> *Religion 81*

24 commit suicide, kill oneself, take one's own life, put an end to one's life, do away with oneself, die by one's own hand, make away with oneself, commit hara-kiri *or* seppuku, commit suttee, hang oneself, shoot oneself, blow out one's brains, cut one's throat, slash one's wrists, fall on one's sword, die Roman fashion, put one's head in the oven, gas oneself, starve oneself, take poison, overdose, jump from a high place, jump overboard, drown oneself, get oneself killed, request euthanasia, do oneself in [Inf], off oneself [Inf]

25 kill animals, hunt, shoot, trap, fish, angle, poison, cull, exterminate, put to sleep, put down, experiment on, vivisect

ADVERBS

26 deadly, lethally, mortally, fatally, malignantly, terminally, murderously, homicidally, bloodthirstily, suicidally

31 Burial

NOUNS

1 burial, burying, disposal of the dead, interment, inhumation, entombment; sepulture, urn burial, mass burial, burial at sea, military burial, full military rites, embalmment, embalming, mummification

2 cremation, incineration, crematorium, pyre, scattering of the ashes

3 mortuary, funeral home *or* house, morgue, charnel house
> *Death 29*

4 funeral, funeral rites, funeral ceremony, funeral service, burial service, graveside service, memorial service; requiem, obsequies, exequies, obituary; mourning, weeping and wailing, keen, lamentation, wake, Irish wake, lying-in-state, viewing the body, receiving family friends, funeral procession, cortege, dead march, knell, passing bell, muffled drum, last post, taps; funeral hymn, *Dies Irae* [L], funeral oration, funeral sermon, eulogy, elegy, dirge, lament, lowering the body, closing the grave

▶ *Death 29; Lamentation 280*

5 **funeral person,** funeral director, undertaker, mortician, pallbearer, gravedigger; sexton, priest, minister, mourner, weeper, keener, hired mourner, mute; embalmer, monument mason, eulogist, eulogizer, elegist, epitaphist, obituary writer, obituarist, necrologist

▶ *Religion 81; Lamentation 280*

6 **funeral object,** hearse, coffin, casket, shell, cist, bier, pall, urn, cinerary urn, funeral urn, bone urn, ossuary, canopic urn *or* jar *or* vase; inscription, epitaph, monument, tombstone, gravestone, headstone, footstone, brass, hatchment, cross, memorial, war memorial, cenotaph; burial clothes, grave clothes, cerements, cerecloth, shroud, winding sheet, mummy wrapping, flowers, wreath; Rest in Peace (RIP), here lies, *hic jacet* [L]

▶ *Memory 354*

7 **burial place,** cemetery, grave, tomb, mausoleum, vault, crypt, burial chamber, sepulcher, catafalque; grave pit, plague pit, common grave, mass grave, open grave; mummy chamber, pyramid, mastaba, dakhma *or* fogou, tower of silence; long home, beehive tomb, shaft tomb, barrow, mound, tumulus, cromlech, dolmen, menhir, cairn, shrine, memorial, cenotaph; graveyard, churchyard, burial ground, plot, family plot, final resting place, God's acre; catacomb, columbarium, cinerarium, necropolis, city of the dead, golgotha, chapel of remembrance, garden of remembrance, garden of rest, military cemetery, pet cemetery, boneyard [Inf]

ADJECTIVES

8 **buried,** interred, inhumed, laid to rest, entombed, coffined, urned, cremated; embalmed, mummified, in the grave, below ground, six feet under [Inf], pushing up daisies [Inf]

▶ *Death 29*

9 **funeral,** burial, funerary, funereal, somber, black, dark, sad, mournful, mourning, lamenting, dirgelike, dirgeful, mortuary, cinerary, crematory, crematorial, sepulchral, memorial, obsequial, eulogistic, eulogistical, elegiac, elegiacal, obituary, necrological, lapidary, epitaphic

▶ *Darkness 247; Blackness 254; Sorrow 270; Lamentation 280*

VERBS

10 **bury,** inter, inhume, lay to rest, lay in the grave, consign to earth, lower the body, lay out; prepare for burial, close the eyes, embalm, mummify, coffin, encoffin, entomb, ensepulcher, plant [Inf]

11 **cremate,** incinerate, burn on the pyre

12 **pay one's last respects,** wake, hold a wake, go to a funeral, toll the knell, sing a requiem, sound the last post, mourn, keen, lament

▶ *Death 29; Lamentation 280*

ADVERBS

13 **funereally,** somberly, sepulchrally, eulogistically, elegiacally, in memoriam

32 Male

NOUNS

1 **male,** male person, man, gentleman, old man, young man, youth, boy, little boy, lad, fellow, he, him, himself, Adam, blade, swain, codger; [Inf]: gent, guy, Joe, chap, buck, stud, dude, bozo, prick, joker, card, gay dog, geezer, gaffer, duffer

2 **maleness,** masculine gender, manhood, paternity, fatherhood, masculinity, manliness, mannishness, virility, virilism, potency, machismo, male chauvinism, male-dominated society, patriarchy

▶ *Sex 20; Youth 26; Age 27; Power 514*

3 **male title of address,** Mr., mister, Sir *or* sir, esquire *or* Esq., Father, master, Lord *or* lord, my good man, my dear man *or* sir, gentleman, goodman [Arch]; monsieur [Fr], Herr [Ger], signorino, signor, signore [Ital], Don, señor [Sp], Dom, senhor [Port], sahib [India], sri [Hindu], babu [Hindu], *tovarishch* [Russ] *or* tovarich *or* comrade; boy, son, sonny, lad; [Inf]: man, fellow, mac, mate, pal, buddy, bud, buster, sport, squire [Brit], Jack, pop, old man, gramps, Mister Charlie

▶ *Friendship 62; Title 72*

4 **boyfriend,** boy, suitor, beau, escort, engaged man, fiancé, bridegroom, groom, Adonis, lover boy; [Inf]: sugar daddy

▶ *Love 299*

5 **single man,** unmarried man, bachelor, available man, unattached male, divorcé, ex-husband, widower

6 **macho man,** muscleman, he-man, hunk, beefcake, jock, caveman, male chauvinist pig [Inf *and* Off]

▶ *Sex 20*

7 **libertine,** rake, cad, bounder, philanderer, heartbreaker, satyr; Casanova, Don Juan, Lothario; man of the world, worldly man, gigolo, ladies' man, male prostitute; stud [Inf], buck [Inf]

▶ *Immorality 432; Nonconformity 782*

8 **effeminate male,** mollycoddle, mother's boy, mama's boy, Lord Fauntleroy, goody-goody, sissy, pantywaist [Inf]

9 **homosexual,** gay, Uranian, invert; [Inf *and* Off]: fairy, homo, queer, queen, faggot, fag, pansy

▶ *Sex 20*

10 **bisexual,** transsexual, transvestite, cross-dresser, AC/DC guy [Inf], bi-guy [Inf]

11 **eunuch,** castrate, castrato, gelding

▶ *Weakness 517*

12 **man in the family,** family man, married man, husband, live-in lover, widower, househusband, man about the house, father, papa [Inf], patriarch, paterfamilias, son, brother, uncle, nephew, godfather, godson,

grandfather, grandson; [Inf]: old man, grandpa, gramps, daddy, dad, pop, pa, pater [Brit]

▸ *Marriage 64; Family 65; Relatedness 727*

13 **liberated man,** new man, male feminist, sensitive man, caring father

14 **menfolk,** men, the boys, spear side, stag party, the lads [Inf]

15 **male animal,** lion, tiger, bull, bullock, ox, steer, stallion, studhorse, stud, entire horse, colt, stag, buck, hart, boar, hog, ram, billy goat, dog, dog fox, tomcat, jack, cock, cockerel, rooster, drake, gander, tom, drone

▸ *Mammals 35; Birds 36; Insects and Arachnids 40*

ADJECTIVES

16 **male,** masculine, manly, macho, virile, muscular, gentlemanly, chivalrous, mannish, manlike; unmanly, effeminate, gay, homosexual, bisexual, transvestite, castrated

33 Female

NOUNS

1 **female,** female person, woman, lady, old woman, matron, dowager, maid, maiden, young woman, girl, little girl, lass, lassie, minx, wench; she, her, herself; Eve, nymph, damsel [Arch]; [Inf]: gal, missy, sister, babe, toots, skirt, jane

▸ *Youth 26; Age 27*

2 **femaleness,** feminine gender, womanhood, maternity, motherhood, femininity, feminineness, feminacy, femineity, womanliness, womanishness, girlishness; feminism, matriarchy, gynarchy, effeminacy; gynecology, obstetrics

▸ *Sex 20; Medicine 107; Liberation 831*

3 **female title of address,** Miss *or* miss, Mrs., Ms., Madam *or* madam, ma'am, marm, missus, mistress, goody [Arch], goodwife [Arch]; Dame, Lady [Brit]; lady, milady, my good lady, my dear woman *or* lady; mademoiselle, madame [Fr]; Fraulein, Frau [Ger]; signorina, Donna, signora [Ital]; señorita, señora [Sp]; senhorita, senhora [Port]; memsahib [India]

▸ *Friendship 62; Title 72*

4 **girlfriend,** girl, sweetheart, engaged woman, betrothed, fiancée, bride, mistress, concubine, kept woman, hetaera *or* hetaira, geisha

▸ *Love 299*

5 **single woman,** single girl, unmarried woman, virgin, maiden, single mother, bachelor girl, spinster, old maid [Off], unattached female, divorcée, ex-wife, widow

6 **loose woman,** nymphet, hussy, siren, seductress, vamp, femme fatale, nymphomaniac, nympho [Inf]; prostitute, whore, lady of the evening, call girl, harlot, strumpet, tart [Inf]

▸ *Immorality 432*

7 **unpleasant woman,** jade, shrew, minx, virago, scold,

harpy, nag, Xanthippe, witch; [Inf *and* Off]: bitch, cow, (old) bag

8 **woman considered as a sex object [Inf *and* Off],** skirt, doll, bird [Brit], chick, honey, cupcake, baby, babe, little mama, moll, cheesecake, bit of fluff, broad, dame, baggage, tart, cunt

9 **mannish female,** amazon, tomboy, hoyden, androgyne

10 **homosexual,** gay, lesbian, Sapphic, invert, tribade; [Inf *and* Off]: lesbo, lez, dyke, butch, bull-dyke

11 **bisexual,** transsexual, female transvestite; AC/DC gal [Inf], bi-gal [Inf]

▸ *Sex 20; Love 299; Nonconformity 782*

12 **liberated woman,** modern woman, career woman, working woman, working wife *or* mother, superwoman; suffragette, feminist, sister, (women's) libber [Inf], bra-burner [Inf]

▸ *Work 122; Liberation 831*

13 **woman in the family,** married woman, wife, spouse, live-in lover, widow, housewife, mother, matriarch, materfamilias, daughter, sister, aunt, niece, godmother, goddaughter, grandmother, granddaughter; [Inf]: mummy, mum, mom, mama, ma, mater [Brit], sis, auntie, grandma, grandmama, old lady, old woman

▸ *Marriage 64; Family 65*

14 **womenfolk,** women, sisterhood, matronage, distaff side, women's quarters, harem *or* seraglio, zenana, purdah; [Inf]: hen party, the girls, the gals, second *or* weaker sex [Off]

15 **female animal,** lioness, tigress, cow, heifer, mare, filly, hind, doe, vixen, sow, gilt, ewe, ewe lamb, nanny goat, jenny, bitch, hen, pen, queen bee

▸ *Mammals 35; Birds 36; Insects and Arachnids 40*

ADJECTIVES

16 **female,** feminine, womanly, womanish, anile, effeminate, ladylike, girlish, maidenly, matronly, child-bearing, feminist, feministic; unfeminine, amazonian, tomboyish, hoydenish, lesbian, butch [Inf *and* Off], dykey [Inf *and* Off]

34 Animals (General)

And God said, Let the earth bring forth the living creature after his kind, cattle, and creeping thing, and beast of the earth. — BIBLE: GENESIS

There are two things for which animals are to be envied: they know nothing of future evils or of what people say about them. — VOLTAIRE

NOUNS

1 **animal,** creature, brute, beast, living thing, living being, creeping thing; dumb animal, furry friend, four-legged friend, varmint [Inf], critter [Inf]; insect, worm, bird, fish, mollusk

2 **animals,** animal life, animal kingdom, fauna; the beasts of the field, the fowl of the air, the fish of the sea; Animalia

3 **domestic animal,** pet, house pet, tame animal; farm animal, stock, livestock, cattle; circus animal, trained animal

▶ *Agriculture 16*

4 **wild animal,** untamed animal, wildlife, game, small game, big game

5 **type of animal,** invertebrate, animalcule, zooid, protist, protozoan; worm, mollusk, gastropod, arthropod, insect, arachnid; vertebrate, chordate; fish, amphibian, reptile, bird, mammal; biped, quadruped; herbivore, grazer, scavenger, carnivore, flesh-eater, meat-eater, insectivore, predator, omnivore; parasite, bloodsucker; ungulate, ruminant, marsupial, canine, feline, rodent, primate

6 **animal science,** biology, ecology, embryology, entomology, ethology, helminthology, herpetology, ichthyology, malacology, mammalogy, ornithology, paleontology, primatology, taxonomy, thremmatology, zoology

7 **animal scientist,** biologist, ecologist, embryologist, entomologist, ethologist, helminthologist, herpetologist, ichthyologist, malacologist, mammalogist, ornithologist, paleontologist, primatologist, taxonomist, thremmatologist, zoologist

8 **animal welfare,** animal health, veterinary science, animal conservation, animal protection; zoo, zoological garden, safari park, wildlife park, game reserve, animal shelter, pound, aquarium, bird sanctuary; animal rights movement, antivivisection

9 **animal welfarist,** veterinarian, vet [Inf], caretaker, dog *or* cat sitter, conservationist, zookeeper, game warden; zoophile, animal lover, pet owner, dog *or* cat lover, animal rights activist, antivivisectionist

10 **animal disease,** mange, rabies, distemper, canine distemper, hard pad, equine distemper, strangles, bovine spongiform encephalopathy (BSE), mad cow disease, scrapie, foot-and-mouth disease, hoof-and-mouth disease, hog cholera, swinepox, variola porcina, myxomatosis, rinderpest, murrain, anthrax, blackleg, sheeprot, bloat, liver fluke, worms, megrims, staggers, glanders, farcy, sweeny, spavin, thrush, parrot fever, psittacosis

11 **feeling for animals,** love of animals, zoophilia, animality, animalism; fear of animals, zoophobia

ADJECTIVES

12 **animalian,** animal, animalic, animalistic; brutish, bestial, beastly, beastlike, animal-like, subhuman, dumb, brutal; theriomorphic *or* theriomorphous, zoomorphic

13 **of animals,** invertebrate, animalcular, zooidal, chordate, vertebrate, bipedal, quadrupedal; domesticated, tame; feral, wild; solitary, social, colonial, terrestrial, arboreal, aquatic, marine, pelagic; diurnal, nocturnal; carnivorous, herbivorous, insectivorous, omnivorous; predacious, predatory, parasitic, symbiotic; zoological, zoographic(al), paleozoological; embryological, ethological; zoophilic, zoophobic

35 Mammals

NOUNS

1 **mammal,** warm-blooded animal, homoiotherm *or* homeotherm, Mammalia

2 **mammalogist,** primatologist, zoologist

▶ *Animals (General) 34*

3 **mammalian characteristic,** mammary gland, mammilla, mamma, udder, dug, nipple, teat, pap, papilla, milk, colostrum, beestings *or* beastings, sweat gland, sebaceous gland, scent gland, musk gland, hair, spine, bristle, whisker, vibrissa, wool, fur, pelage

4 **egg-laying mammal,** prototherian, Prototheria, monotreme, Monotremata; platypus *or* duck-billed platypus *or* duckbill, echidna *or* spiny anteater

5 **pouched mammal,** metatherian, Metatheria, marsupial, Marsupialia (kangaroo, opossum, bandicoot, wombat); marsupial characteristic, marsupium, pouch

6 **placental mammal,** eutherian, Eutheria; eutherian characteristic, placenta, uterus

7 **insect-eating mammal,** insectivore, Insectivora (hedgehog, shrew, mole); anteater, scaly anteater, pangolin, pholidote, echidna *or* spiny anteater, ant bear, aardvark, tubulidentate

8 **flying mammal,** chiropteran *or* chiropter, Chiroptera (bat); dermopteran, Dermoptera (flying lemur)

BREEDS AND VARIETIES OF CATS

Abyssinian	Cornish rex	oriental
American bobtail	cymric	shorthair
American curl	Egyptian mau	peke-faced Persian
American	exotic shorthair	Persian
shorthair	Havana brown	ragdoll
American wirehair	Himalayan	rex
Angora *or* Turkish	colorpoint	Russian blue
angora	Himalayan hybrids	Scottish fold
Balinese	Japanese bobtail	longhair
Bengal	Javanese	Selkirk rex
Birman	Kashmir	Siamese
Bombay	Korat	Siberian
British shorthair	Maine coon	Singapura
Burmese	Maltese	snowshoe
Burmilla	Manx	Somali
calico *or*	munchkin	sphynx
tortoiseshell	nebelung	tabby
California spangled	Norwegian	Tonkinese
colorpoint	forest	Turkish van
shorthair	ocicat	

9 flesh-eating mammal, carnivore, Carnivora; canine, canid, Canidae (dog, wolf, fox, jackal); ursid, Ursidae (bear); mustelid, Mustelidae (weasel, otter, badger); procyonid, Procyonidae (raccoon); viverrid, Viverridae (mongoose, civet); hyaenid, Hyaenidae (hyena *or* hyaena); feline, felid, Felidae (cat)

10 dog, canine, bitch, whelp, pup, puppy, puppy dog, mongrel, crossbreed, lurcher, cur, tyke, pariah dog, pye-dog, dingo; hound, hunting dog, gundog; working dog, guard dog, watchdog, police dog, tracker dog, sniffer dog, guide dog, sheepdog; show dog, toy dog, lap dog, man's best friend; [Inf]: bowwow, mutt, pooch

11 cat, feline, wild cat, big cat, domestic cat, mouser, ratter, house cat, tomcat *or* tom, gib, queen, grimalkin, kitten; kitty *or* kit, puss *or* pussy *or* pussycat

12 marine mammal, cetacean, Cetacea (whale, dolphin, porpoise); pinniped, Pinnipedia (seal, phocid, sea lion, walrus); sirenian, Sirenia (dugong, sea cow, manatee)

13 gnawing mammal, rodent, Rodentia; sciuromorph (beaver, squirrel, chipmunk); myomorph (murid, rat, mouse, lemming, gerbil, vole); histricomorph (porcupine, cavy); lagomorph, Lagomorpha (pika *or* cony, leporid, rabbit, hare)

14 toothless mammal, edentate, Edentata (anteater, sloth, armadillo)

15 pachyderm, subungulate, proboscidean, Proboscidea

BREEDS OF DOGS

Aberdeen *or* Scottish terrier
Abruzzi sheepdog
affenpinscher *or* monkey pinscher *or* monkey dog
Afghan hound
Airedale terrier
Akita
Alaskan malamute *or* malamute
Alsatian *or* German shepherd *or* police dog
American cocker spaniel
American foxhound
American Staffordshire terrier
American water spaniel
Australian cattle dog
Australian heeler
Australian kelpie
Australian shepherd
Australian terrier
Basenji
basset hound
beagle
Bedlington terrier
Belgian griffon
Belgian shepherd dog *or* Belgian sheepdog
Bernese mountain dog
Bichon Frise
black Labrador
Blenheim spaniel
bloodhound
bluetick coonhound
Border collie
Border terrier

borzoi
Boston terrier
Bouvier des Flandres
boxer
Briard
Brittany spaniel
Brussels griffon
bulldog
bull mastiff
bull terrier
cairn terrier
carriage *or* coach dog
Chesapeake Bay retriever
Chihuahua
Chinese crested
chow chow *or* chow
clumber spaniel
cocker spaniel
collie
coonhound
corgi
curly-coated retriever
dachshund
Dalmatian
Dandie Dinmont
deerhound
Doberman pinscher
elkhound
English cocker spaniel
English foxhound
English setter
English springer spaniel
English toy spaniel
Eskimo dog *or* husky
field spaniel
foxhound
fox terrier
French bulldog

gazehound
gazelle hound
German shepherd
German shorthaired pointer
German wirehaired pointer
giant schnauzer
golden retriever
Gordon setter
Great Dane
Great Pyrenees
greyhound
griffon
Groenendael
harrier
Hungarian pointer
husky
Ibizan hound
Irish setter
Irish terrier
Irish water spaniel
Irish wolfhound
Italian greyhound
Jack Russell terrier
Japanese Chin *or* Japanese spaniel
keeshond
kelpie
Kerry blue terrier
King Charles spaniel
Komondor
kuvasz
Labrador retriever
Lakeland terrier
Lhasa apso
malamute
Maltese
Manchester terrier
mastiff
Mexican hairless
miniature pinscher

miniature poodle
miniature schnauzer
Newfoundland
Norfolk terrier
Norwegian elkhound
Norwich terrier
Old English sheepdog
otterhound
papillon
Pekingese
pharaoh hound
pit bull terrier
Plott hound
pointer
police dog
Pomeranian
poodle
Portuguese water dog
pug
puli
retriever
Rhodesian ridgeback *or* African lion hound
Rottweiler
St. Bernard
Saluki
Samoyed
schipperke
schnauzer
Scottish terrier
Scottish deerhound
Sealyham terrier
setter
Shar-Pei
Shetland sheepdog *or* sheltie
Shih Tzu
Siberian husky
sighthound

silky terrier
Skye terrier
soft-coated wheaten terrier
spaniel
spitz
springer spaniel
Staffordshire bull terrier
staghound
Sussex spaniel
terrier
toy poodle
toy spaniel
toy terrier
vizsla
Weimaraner
Welsh corgi
Welsh sheepdog
Welsh springer spaniel
Welsh terrier
West Highland white terrier
whippet
wirehaired dachshund
wirehaired pointing griffon
wirehair fox terrier *or* wirehaired terrier
yellow Labrador
Yorkshire terrier

(elephant, mastodon, mammoth); rhinoceros, hippopotamus, river horse

16 **hoofed mammal,** ungulate, ungulant; odd-toed ungulate, perissodactyl, Perissodactyla (equine, equid, horse, tapir, rhinoceros); even-toed ungulate, artiodactyl, Artiodactyla; suid, Suidae (pig, hog, swine); hippopotamus, ruminant, cud-chewer; Ruminantia, camelid, Camelidae (camel, llama); cervid, Cervidae (deer); giraffe, camelopard [Arch], okapi; bovid, bovine, Bovidae (cattle, antelope, gazelle, goat, ovine, sheep), hyracoid, Hyracoidea (hyrax or cony)
> *Agriculture 16; Horses, Horseback Riding, Horse Racing 159*

17 **primate,** Primate, prosimian (lemur, loris, bush baby, tarsier), anthropoid, monkey, New World monkey (capuchin, howler, marmoset, tamarin), Old World monkey (macaque, baboon), ape, anthropoid ape, pongid, Pongidae (gibbon, great ape, orangutan, chimpanzee, gorilla), hominid, Hominidae (man, *Homo sapiens*, human, human being)
> *Humankind 18*

18 **male mammal,** dog, buck, stag, hart, stallion, colt, bull, boar, ram, tom, lion, tiger, leopard, billy goat, roebuck, jackass, jack

19 **female mammal,** bitch, doe, hind, mare, filly, cow, heifer, sow, gilt, ewe, vixen, tigress, leopardess, lioness, nanny goat, jenny, queen, jill

20 **young mammal,** kitten, kit, pup *or* puppy, whelp, cub, calf, dogie, weaner, foal, colt, filly, piglet *or* shoat *or* farrow *or* suckling, lamb *or* lambkin, kid, yearling, fawn, leveret, joey

21 **mammal dwelling,** lair, den, covert, form, burrow, earth, sett *or* set, lodge, couch, run, drey, sty, pen, pound, cage, corral, stable, stall, hutch

22 **assemblage of mammals,** pack, herd, drove, train, troop, team, flock, school, bevy, leap, pride
> *Assembly 59*

ADJECTIVES

23 **mammalian,** mammal-like, warm-blooded, homoiothermic, prototherian, monotrematous, metatherian, marsupial, eutherian, placental *or* placentate

24 **insectivorous,** anteating, pholidote, tubulidentate, edentate, toothless

25 **chiropteran,** dermopteran, winged, flying

26 **carnivorous,** flesh-eating, clawed, unguiculate, canine, doglike, doggy, doggish, puppyish, foxy, foxlike, vulpine, vulpecular, wolflike, wolfish, lupine, bearish, bearlike, ursine, weaselly, musteline, viverrine, feline, catlike, cattish, catty, kittenish, leonine, lionlike, tigerish, tigerlike

27 **cetacean,** cetaceous, whalelike, pinniped, pinnipedian, seal-like, sirenian

28 **rodentlike,** rodentian, gnawing, murine, ratlike, rattish, ratty, mouselike, mousy *or* mousey, squirrel-like, sciurine

29 **rabbitlike,** rabbity, harelike, lagomorphic, lagomorphous, leporid, leporine

30 **elephantlike,** pachydermatous, subungulate, proboscidean *or* proboscidian, elephantine, elephantoid, rhinocerotic

31 **ungulate,** hoofed, unguligrade, cloven-hoofed, perissodactyl, odd-toed, equine, horselike, horsy *or* horsey, asinine, mulish, artiodactyl, artiodactylous, even-toed, piglike, piggy, piggish, porcine, hoggish, swinish, ruminant, cud-chewing, camel-like, camelid, deerlike, cervid, cervine, oxlike, bovid, bovine, cowlike, cowish, bull-like, bullish, taurine, sheeplike, ovine, goatlike, caprine, hircine, cavicorn, hyraxlike, hyracoid

32 **primate,** primatial, prosimian, anthropoid, simian, simious, pongid, hominid

VERBS

33 **give birth,** drop, farrow, lamb, foal, calve, cub, pup, whelp, kitten, litter, kindle
> *Reproduction 21*

34 **lactate,** milk, nurse, suckle, breast-feed

35 **graze,** ruminate, chew the cud, browse, grass

36 Birds

NOUNS

1 **birds,** birdlife, avifauna, Aves, wildfowl, fowl of the air, fowl, feathered friend, bird of peace, dove, bird of passage, migratory bird, migrant; birdie

2 **ornithology,** bird watching, ringing, bird banding, aviculture

3 **ornithologist,** aviculturist, fancier, pigeon fancier, ringer, bird watcher, birder, twitcher [Inf]

4 **dwelling,** aviary, swannery, bird sanctuary, bird re-

ENDANGERED BIRDS (CONTINENTAL UNITED STATES)

bobwhite, masked	rail, California clapper
caracara, Audubon's crested	rail, light-footed clapper
condor, California	rail, Yuma clapper
crane, Mississippi sandhill	shrike, San Clemente
crane, whooping	loggerhead
eagle, bald	sparrow, Cape Sable seaside
falcon, American peregrine	sparrow, Florida grasshopper
falcon, Arctic peregrine	sparrow, San Clemente sage
falcon, northern aplomado	stork, wood
goose, Aleutian Canada	tern, least
jay, Florida scrub	tern, roseate
kite, Everglade snail	towhee, Inyo California
murrelet, marbled	(brown)
owl, Mexican spotted	vireo, black-capped
owl, northern spotted	vireo, least Bell's
pelican, brown	warbler, Bachman's
plover, piping	warbler, golden-cheeked
plover, western snowy	warbler, Kirtland's
prairie-chicken, Attwater's	woodpecker, ivory-billed
greater	woodpecker, red-cockaded

serve, birdhouse, birdcage, dovecote, pigeon loft, columbarium, hatchery; nest, perch, roost, aerie *or* eyrie, rookery, covert, mew, lek, nest site; nest building, nidification

5 eggs, hatch, clutch, egg, shell, eggshell, white, yolk, vitelline membrane, chalaza

6 avian characteristic, bill, beak, feathers, wings, talons, syrinx, carina, keel, wishbone, crop, gizzard, webbed feet

7 plumage, feathers, ruff, crest, plume, frill, feather, contour feather, quill, vane, rachis, barbule, barbicel, aftershaft, down feathers, plumulae, down, eiderdown, swansdown, flight feather, wing feather, primary, secondary, tail feather, rectrix (pl. rectrices), remex (pl. remiges), alula, bastard wing, filoplume, covert, tectrix (pl. tectrices), pteryla, apterium

8 flightless bird, ratite, ostrich, rhea, cassowary, emu, kiwi, notornis *or* takahe, penguin

9 water bird, seabird, oceanic bird, gull, seagull, shag, tern, skua, puffin, auk, albatross, petrel, fulmar, shearwater, frigate bird, jaeger, gannet, cormorant, fishing bird, pelican, kingfisher, diving bird, diver, loon, grebe, wading bird, wader, marsh bird, mud hen, shore bird, plover, sandpiper, lapwing, curlew, snipe, avocet, oystercatcher, crane, rail, crake, coot, heron, bittern, stork, flamingo, spoonbill, ibis, waterfowl, duck, dabbling duck, diving duck, perching duck, whistling duck, sea duck, swan, goose

10 table bird, gamebird, game fowl, chicken, pheasant, partridge, grouse, quail, snipe, woodcock, guinea fowl, pigeon, turkey, domestic fowl
▶ *Agriculture 16; Food 90*

11 bird of prey, raptor, falcon, hawk, goshawk, eagle, osprey, kestrel, harrier, kite, vulture, condor, buzzard, owl, barn owl, screech owl, hoot owl, horned owl

12 songbird, passerine bird, oscine bird, perching bird, lark, wren, warbler, flycatcher, thrush, tit, shrike, wagtail, pipit, bunting, finch, Darwin's *or* Galapagos finch, weaverbird, sparrow, starling, oriole, crow, magpie, jackdaw, rook, raven, nightingale

13 cage bird, cageling; canary, songster, talking bird, parrot, parakeet, budgerigar *or* budgie, myna *or* mynah, cockatoo

14 extinct bird, fossil bird, Archaeopteryx, Aepyornis, elephant bird, moa, dodo, great auk, passenger pigeon

15 male bird, cock, cockerel, chanticleer, rooster, tom turkey, turkey cock, gobbler [Inf], peacock, guinea cock, drake, gander, cob, blackcock, heath cock, cock-sparrow, cock-robin

16 female bird, hen, peahen, pen, grayhen, heath hen, goose, duck

17 young bird, chick, poult, pullet, eaglet, owlet, cygnet, duckling, gosling, eyas, squab, nestling, fledgling, cockerel; clutch, hatch, brood

18 assemblage of birds, flock, flight, gaggle, skein, covey, covert, wing
▶ *Assembly 59*

ADJECTIVES

19 avian, birdlike, birdy; flightless, ratite, ostrichlike, struthious; gooselike, goosy, anserine *or* anserous, anseriform; fowl-like, gallinaceous, galliform, rasorial; dovelike, pigeonlike, columbine, columbiform; parrotlike, psittacine, psittaciform; cuckoolike, cuculiform; raptorial, predatory, hawkish, aquiline, vulturine, owllike, owlish, strigiform; swallowlike, hirundine, perching, passerine, passeriform; singing, oscine; finchlike, fringilline *or* fringillid; thrushlike, turdine; crowlike, corvine

20 newly hatched, unfledged, altricial, newly fledged, precocial, nidicolous, nidifugous

21 ornithological, avicultural

VERBS

22 nest, nidify, brood, hatch, perch, peck, preen

23 fly, take wing, wing, soar, hover

37 Reptiles and Amphibians

A narrow Fellow in the Grass / Occasionally rides . . . / But never met this Fellow / Attended or alone / Without a tighter breathing / And Zero at the Bone.
— EMILY DICKINSON

NOUNS

1 reptile, reptilian, cold-blooded animal, poikilotherm, Reptilia, Squamata (lizards, snakes), Rhynchocephalia (tuatara), Crocodilia (crocodilians)

2 herpetology, ophiology

3 herpetologist, ophiologist

4 reptile dwelling, reptile house, reptilarium, reptiliary

5 lizard, saurian, Sauria, lacertilian *or* lacertian, Lacertilia; iguana, chameleon, gecko, skink, monitor, glass snake, Komodo dragon, basilisk, slow worm, tuatara, rhynchocephalian; lizardlike reptile

6 snake, serpent, Serpentes, ophidian, Ophidia; nonvenomous snake, constrictor, boa, python, anaconda; venomous snake, viper, asp, cobra, mamba, rattlesnake *or* rattler

7 turtle, chelonian, chelonid, tortoise, terrapin

8 crocodile, crocodilian, alligator, cayman, croc [Inf], gator [Inf]

9 extinct reptile, fossil reptile, giant reptile, terrestrial reptile, dinosaur, ornithischian, ornithopod, saurischian, sauropod, marine reptile, ichthyopterygian, ichthyosaur, sauropterygian, plesiosaur, nothosaur, mosasaur, flying reptile, pterosaur, mammal-like reptile, therapsid

10 amphibian, batrachian, Amphibia, limbless amphibian, caecilian, apodan, Apoda *or* Gymnophiona, tailed amphibian, urodele, caudate, Urodela *or* Caudata (salamander, newt); tailless amphibian, salientian, anuran, Salienta *or* Anura (frog, toad), paddock [Arch]

11 **young amphibian,** frogspawn, tadpole, polliwog, froglet, toadlet, immature amphibian, neotenous amphibian, axolotl

ADJECTIVES

12 **reptilian,** reptilelike, reptiliform, reptiloid, apodal *or* apodous, cold-blooded, poikilothermic, creeping, slithering, reptant, lizardlike, saurian, lacertilian, snakelike, ophidian, turtlelike, chelonian, crocodilian, scaly, squamous

13 **snakelike,** snaky, serpentine, serpentiform, sinuous, twisting, ophidian, ophiomorphic, colubrine, colubriform, anguine, viperlike, viperish, viperous *or* viperine, hissing

14 **amphibian,** batrachian, apodan, salamandrian, newtlike, caudate, neotenous, froglike, froggy, toadlike, toadish, anuran, salientian

15 **herpetological,** ophiological

38 Fishes

NOUNS

1 **fishes,** fish, Pisces, saltwater fishes, marine fishes, freshwater fishes; shoal, school

2 **study of fish,** ichthyology, fish breeding

3 **ichthyologist,** aquarist, fish lover, ichthyophile

4 **dwelling,** fish farm, aquarium, fishpond; fishtank, fishbowl

5 **fish,** jawless fish, cyclostome, cartilaginous fish, Chondrichthyes, elasmobranch, selachian, holocephalan, bony fish, lobe-finned fish, crossopterygian, dipnoan, ray-finned fish, teleost fish, flying fish, mouthbreeder, flatfish, food fish, game fish, aquarium fish, tropical fish

6 **young fish,** fry, elver, alevin, fingerling, parr, smolt, grilse

7 **fossil fish,** placoderm, arthrodire, ostracoderm, Pteraspis, crossopterygian, Osteolepis, living fossil, coelacanth, ichthyolite

8 **fish characteristic,** fin, pectoral fin, pelvic fin, dorsal fin, anal fin, caudal fin, tail fin, scale, placoid scale, ganoid scale, cosmoid scale, gill, gill cover, operculum, gill slit, spiracle, swim bladder, air bladder, lateral line, roe, soft roe, hard roe

9 **fish product,** fish roe, herring roe, caviar, fish-liver oil, cod-liver oil, fishmeal, fish glue, isinglass

ADJECTIVES

10 **fishlike,** fishy, cold-blooded, poikilothermic, piscine, pisciform, piscatorial *or* piscatory, ichthyic, ichthyoid(al), ichthyomorphic; sharklike, sharkish, selachian; herringlike, clupeoid; codlike, gadid *or* gadoid; perchlike, percoid; carplike, cyprinoid; eel-like, anguilliform

11 **ichthyological,** piscicultural, piscatorial *or* piscatory, scaly, squamous

39 Invertebrates

NOUNS

1 **invertebrate,** lower animal, invertebrate chordate, protochordate, many-celled invertebrate, metazoan, Metazoa, nonchordate invertebrate, mesozoan, parazoan, single-celled invertebrate, protozoan, protist

2 **invertebrate zoology,** arachnology, entomology, malacology, conchology, helminthology, protozoology, parasitology
  ‣ *Insects and Arachnids 40*

3 **invertebrate zoologist,** arachnologist, entomologist, malacologist, conchologist, helminthologist, protozoologist, parasitologist
  ‣ *Insects and Arachnids 40*

4 **protochordate,** hemichordate, Hemichordata, acorn worm, chordate, Chordata, urochordate, Urochordata, tunicate, ascidian, sea squirt, salp, cephalochordate, Cephalochordata *or* Acrania, lancelet, amphioxus, craniate, Craniata (vertebrates)

5 **echinoderm,** Echinodermata; crinoid, sea lily, feather star; asteroid *or* asteroidean, starfish, crown-of-thorns, sea star; ophiuroid, brittle star; echinoid, sea urchin, heart urchin, sand dollar, sea biscuit; holothurian, sea cucumber, trepang, bêche-de-mer

6 **arthropod,** Arthropoda (insects, spiders and arachnids, crustaceans, myriapods)

7 **extinct arthropod,** trilobite, eurypterid, living fossil, horseshoe *or* king crab, limulus

8 **arachnid,** Arachnida (scorpion, spider, tick, mite)

9 **insect,** Insecta, pycnogonid, Pycnogonida (sea spider)

10 **crustacean,** Crustacea, branchiopod, fairy shrimp, brine shrimp, tadpole shrimp, water flea, daphnia, ostracod, mussel shrimp, seed shrimp; copepod, cyclops, branchiuran, fish louse, cirripede, barnacle, acorn barnacle, stalked barnacle, goose barnacle, malacostracan, amphipod, mantis shrimp, Tasmanian shrimp, opossum shrimp; sand hopper *or* beach flea, skeleton shrimp, whale louse, isopod, water louse, woodlouse, pill bug, sow bug, slater [Aus], gribble, shrimp, prawn, crab, hermit crab, robber *or* coconut crab, fiddler crab, pea crab, spider crab, land crab, lobster, crayfish, spiny lobster, crawfish, shellfish

11 **myriapod,** Myriapoda, diplopod, Diplopoda (millipede); chilopod, Chilopoda (centipede), pauropod, symphylan

12 **arthropodlike invertebrate,** tardigrade, water bear, Tardigrada, pentastomid, Pentastomida, onychophoran, Onychophora
  ‣ *Insects and Arachnids 40*

13 **mollusk,** Mollusca, amphineuran, Amphineura (chiton), gastropod *or* gasteropod, Gastropoda (limpet, snail, slug); bivalve, lamellibranch, Bivalvia *or* Lamellibranchia (shellfish, clam, mussel, scallop, oyster),

scaphopod, Scaphopoda (tusk shell); cephalopod, Cephalopoda (cuttlefish, squid, octopod, octopus), mollusklike invertebrate, lampshell, brachiopod, Brachiopoda

14 worm, parasitic worm, helminth, flatworm, platyhelminth, Platyhelminthes; glowworm, bookworm, insect larva, woodworm, wireworm, caterpillar, silkworm

▶ *Insects and Arachnids 40*

15 coelenterate, cnidarian, Cnidaria, polyp, medusa, hydrozoan, Hydrozoa (sea fir, hydra, Portuguese man-of-war); scyphozoan, Scyphozoa (jellyfish, box jellyfish, sea wasp); anthozoan, Anthozoa (coral, organ-pipe coral, dead-man's fingers, sea fan, sea pen, sea pansy, sea anemone); ctenophore *or* ctenophoran, comb jelly, Ctenophora (sea gooseberry, Venus's girdle); polypoid invertebrate, bryozoan, Bryozoa, ectoproct, Ectoprocta (sea mats, moss animals), entoproct, Entoprocta

16 sponge, bath sponge, Venus's flower basket, poriferan, Porifera, parazoan, Parazoa

17 protozoan *or* **protozoon,** Protozoa, flagellate protozoan, flagellate, mastigophoran, Mastigophora (*Euglena, Chlamydomonas,* volvox, dinoflagellate, trypanosome, trichomonad); amoeboid protozoan, Sarcodina (amoeba, foraminiferan, radiolarian, heliozoan); spore-producing protozoan, sporozoan, Sporozoa (malaria parasite, plasmodium); ciliate protozoan, ciliate, Ciliata (paramecium)

18 parasite, fish louse, whale louse, sand hopper *or* beach flea, helminth, fluke, blood fluke, liver fluke, tapeworm, pinworm, guinea worm, hookworm, protozoan, entameba, trypanosome, piroplasm, leishmania, giardia, toxoplasma, bloodsucker, leech

▶ *Ill Health 114*

19 invertebrate larva, tornaria, nauplius, trochophore, veliger, microfilaria, redia, cercaria, miracidium, hydatid, cysticercus, caenurus, onchosphere, hexacanth

▶ *Insects and Arachnids 40*

ADJECTIVES

20 invertebrate, protochordate, hemichordate, urochordate, cephalochordate, acraniate, coelomate, pseudocoelomate, acoelomate, metazoan, mesozoan, protozoan

21 echinodermal, echinodermatous, crinoidal, asteroidal, ophiuroid, echinoid, holothurian, holothurioid

22 arthropodal, arthropodan *or* arthropodous, jointed; chelicerate, arachnidan, arachnoid, spiderlike, spidery; insectlike, insectile; crustacean, crustaceous; chitinous, chitinoid; shrimplike, crablike; arachnological, entomological

▶ *Insects and Arachnids 40*

23 molluskan, gastropodous, snail-like, univalved *or* univalvular, sluglike; bivalved *or* bivalvular, clamlike, oysterlike; cephalopodic, cephalopodous, cephalopodan, octopod; malacological, conchological

24 wormlike, vermicular, vermiform, helminthic, helminthoid, platyhelminthic, fluky, cestoid, annelid, annelidan, segmented, polychaetous, oligochaetous, lumbricoid, hirudinean, leechlike, helminthologic(al)

25 coelenterate, cnidarian, hydroid, polypoid, medusoid, hydrozoan, scyphozoan, anthozoan, coralline, coralloid, ctenophoran

26 spongelike, poriferan, poriferous, spongy, fibrous, calcareous

27 protozoan, protozoic, amoebic, amoeboid, flagellate, ciliate, sporozoan, protozoological

40 Insects and Arachnids

If insects were to vanish, the environment would collapse into chaos. — EDWARD O. WILSON

NOUNS

1 insect, Insecta, Hexapoda; winged insect, fly, gnat, midge, mosquito, cranefly, dragonfly, caddis fly, butterfly, moth, bee, wasp; ant, beetle, cockroach *or* roach, earwig, stick insect, mantis, hopper, grasshopper, locust, leafhopper, creepy-crawly [Inf], skeeter [Inf]

2 study of insects, entomology; beekeeping; sericulture; lepidopterology, arachnology, acarology

3 entomologist, beekeeper, apiarist; sericulturist; lepidopterist, arachnologist, acarologist; bug hunter

4 arachnid, Arachnida, scorpion, pseudoscorpion, false scorpion, spider, black widow, tarantula, phalangid, opilionid, daddy-longlegs *or* harvestman, acarid *or* acarine, mite, tick, hard tick, soft tick

5 pest, parasite, vermin, cockroach, weevil, borer, woodworm, bookworm, wireworm, chafer, scale, locust, bug, louse, nit, flea, chigger, mite, bedbug, tick, mosquito, midge, cootie [Inf]

6 social insect, bee, honeybee, wasp, yellow jacket, ant, pismire, termite, queen, queen bee, drone, king (termite), worker, soldier, soldier ant

7 dwelling, nest, nidus; hive, beehive, apiary, beeswax, honey; wasps' nest, vespiary; anthill, antheap; termite colony, termitarium; swarm, army, plague

▶ *Assembly 59*

8 insect metamorphal stage, egg, larva, cocoon, chrysalis, imago

9 larva, grub, maggot, nymph, pupa; spiderling *or* spiderlet; caterpillar, woolly bear, looper, armyworm, bagworm, silkworm, cutworm, ant lion, doodlebug, leatherjacket, caddisworm, bloodworm, glowworm, mealworm, wireworm, screwworm

▶ *Invertebrates 39*

10 spinner, spider, silkworm, silk, silk gland, spinneret, cocoon, web, spider web, cobweb

11 **insectile,** insectiform, insectlike, thysanuran, dipluran, collembolan, proturan, ephemeropteran, plecopteran, orthopteran *or* orthopterous, phasmid, dermapteran, embiopteran, dictyopteran, isopteran, psocopteran, mallophagan, anopluran, hemipteran *or* hemipterous, homopteran, heteropteran, thysanopteran, grylloblatodean, zorapteran, neuropteran *or* neuropterous, megalopteran, mecopteran, lepidopteran *or* lepidopterous, trichopteran, dipteran *or* dipterous, siphonapteran, hymenopteran *or* hymenopterous, coleopteran *or* coleopterous, strepsipteran

12 **arachnidan,** spiderlike, spidery, arachnoid, mitelike, ticklike, acarid *or* acarine, acaroid

13 **verminous,** infested, buggy, weevily, maggoty, grubby, lousy, flea-bitten, mothy, moth-eaten, flyblown
  ▶ *Dirtiness 112*

14 **immature,** larval, pupal, chrysalid

15 **entomological,** apiarian, sericultural, lepidopterological

16 **arachnological,** acarological

VERBS

17 **infest,** invade, swarm, buzz, drone, plague, sting, bite, parasitize, swarm with, crawl with, teem with, contaminate, flyblow
  ▶ *Dirtiness 112; Attack 418*

18 **develop,** hatch, pupate, metamorphose

41 Plants (General)

Annihilating all that's made / To a green thought in a green shade. — ANDREW MARVELL

NOUNS

1 **plants,** plant life, flora, plant kingdom, Plantae; vegetable kingdom, vegetable life, vegetation, green plants; growth, herbage, flowerage, verdure, greenery, forest, jungle, grassland, savanna *or* savannah, steppe, scrub, chaparral, pampas, veld *or* veldt
  ▶ *Trees 43; Grasses 45; Greenness 260*

2 **plant,** green plant, vascular plant, herbaceous plant; seedling, herb, flower, wildflower, weed, escape; cultivated plant, garden plant, houseplant, pot plant, greenhouse plant, hothouse plant, exotic; food plant, cereal, vegetable, potherb, culinary herb; medicinal plant, medicinal herb, wort, succulent, cactus, xerophyte, aquatic plant, hydrophyte; air plant, epiphyte, parasite; ephemeral, annual, biennial, triennial, perennial, herbaceous perennial, woody perennial; woody plant, tree, sapling, shrub, bush, evergreen; climber, twiner, vine, liana *or* liane
  ▶ *Horticulture 17; Flowers 42; Trees 43*

3 **seed plant,** spermatophyte, Spermatophyta; phanerogam, Phanerogamia; gymnosperm, Gymnospermae (conifers, softwoods, cycads); flowering plant,

angiosperm, Angiospermae; monocotyledon *or* monocot *or* monocotyl, Monocotyledonae: palms, grasses, cereals, reeds (Gramineae *or* Poaceae); sedge family (Cyperaceae); rush family (Juncaceae); orchids (Orchidaceae); lily family (Liliaceae); pineapple family (Bromeliaceae, bromeliads); dicotyledon *or* dicot *or* dicotyl, Dicotyledonae: rose family (Rosaceae); daisy and sunflower families (Compositae, composites); buttercup family (Ranunculaceae); mustard family (Cruciferae, Brassicaceae, crucifers, brassicas); parsley *or* carrot family (Umbelliferae, umbellifers); nettle *or* mint family (Labiatae, labiates); pea family (Leguminosae, legumes); goosefoot family (Chenopodiaceae, chenopods)
  ▶ *Flowers 42; Trees 43; Grasses 45*

4 **lower plant,** nonseed-bearing plant, cryptogam, pteridophyte, Pteridophyta (ferns, horsetails, club mosses), bryophyte, Bryophyta (mosses, liverworts); thallus, thallophyte, Thallophyta (algae, mushrooms); fungus, saprophyte, parasite, lichen, alga, seaweed
  ▶ *Ferns and Mosses 46; Fungi, Algae, and Lichens 47*

5 **stem,** axis, caudex, trunk, shoot, sprout, plumule, internode, node, axil, offshoot, scion, branch, twig, spray, stalk, stipe, seta, leafstalk, petiole, rachis *or* rhachis, rachilla *or* rhachilla; flower stalk, peduncle, pedicel; seed stalk, funicle *or* funiculus; underground stem *or* shoot, rhizome, runner, stolon, sucker; rootstock, stock, corm, bulb, tuber, stem tuber, stem tissue, epidermis, cortex, pith, medulla, cambium, vascular bundle, xylem, phloem
  ▶ *Trees 43; Grasses 45*

6 **leaf,** leaflet, needle, frond, leaf blade, lamina, vein, leafstalk, petiole, leaves, foliage, greenery, leaflike part, bract, bracteole, bractlet, cladode, cladophyll, phylloclade, phyllode, involucre, involucel, scale leaf, scaler, bud scale, ligule, stipule, modified leaf, tendril, spine, floral leaf, petal, sepal, calyx, seed leaf, cotyledon, leaf tissue, palisade, mesophyll, stoma (pl. stomata), guard cell, abscission
  ▶ *Flowers 42; Grasses 45; Greenness 260*

7 **root,** radix, rootlet, radicle; taproot, lateral root, fibrous root, prop root, brace root, buttress root, stilt root, adventitious root, aerial root, tuberous root, root tuber, tuber, rootcap, calyptra, root hair, root nodule, rootlike part, rootstock, rhizoid, rhizomorph

8 **bud,** burgeon, leaf bud, foliage bud, flower bud, apical bud, terminal bud, axillary bud, lateral bud, adventitious bud, winter bud, resting bud, dormancy, gemma, gemmule, budding, gemmation, gemmulation
  ▶ *Reproduction 21; Fertility 22*

9 **seed,** grain, kernel, berry, stone, pit, nut, pip; seedcase, seed capsule, seed vessel, pericarp, seed pod, seed coat, testa, micropyle, hilum, seed stalk, funicle *or* funiculus, seed leaf, cotyledon, embryo, ovule, endosperm,

germinating seed, germination, seedling, shoot, plumule, acrospire, coleoptile, radicle, coleorhiza; hull, husk

▸ *Reproduction 21; Fertility 22; Fruits 44*

10 **plant science,** botany, phytology, plant taxonomy, phytography, plant biochemistry, phytochemistry, phytogenesis, plant anatomy, phytotomy, plant physiology, plant cytology, plant ecology, phytoecology, phytosociology, plant geography, phytogeography, plant pathology, phytopathology, paleobotany, palynology, pollen analysis, ethnobotany, pteridology, bryology, mycology, phycology, algology, lichenology, fungology, dendrology, economic botany; arboriculture, silviculture, horticulture, forestry, pomology, crop husbandry, agrobiology, floriculture, seed biology

▸ *Agriculture 16; Horticulture 17; Flowers 42; Trees 43; Fungi, Algae, and Lichens 47*

11 **plant scientist,** botanist, plant hunter, herbalist, naturalist, phytologist, phytographer, phytochemist, phytogeneticist, phytogeographer, phytopathologist, ethnobotanist, phytosociologist, paleobotanist, agrobiologist, dendrologist, pomologist, pteridologist, bryologist, mycologist, phycologist, algologist, lichenologist, fungologist, dendrologist, economic biologist

12 **herbarium,** hortus siccus, botanical garden, seed bank, flora, herbal

▸ *Horticulture 17*

ADJECTIVES

13 **plantlike,** vegetable, vegetal, vegetative; herbal, herbaceous, green; grassy, leafy, verdant, flourishing, planted, plant-covered, wooded, forested, growing, luxuriant, lush; dense, overgrown; rank, weedy, unweeded, weed-choked, gone to seed

▸ *Trees 43; Grasses 45*

14 **of plants,** green, herbaceous; ephemeral, annual, biennial, triennial, perennial; bulbous, cormous, tuberous, woody; deciduous, evergreen, leafy, foliate, branched; succulent, xerophytic, aquatic, hydrophytic; terrestrial, land; creeping, prostrate, erect, twining, climbing, epiphytic, parasitic, saprophytic, insectivorous, carnivorous, photosynthetic

15 **wild,** native, indigenous, cultivated, alien, exotic, introduced, escaped, naturalized, hardy, half-hardy

16 **taxonomic,** vascular, seed-bearing, phanerogamic, cone-bearing, coniferous, flowering, monocotyledonous, cyperaceous, juncaceous, orchidaceous, liliaceous, bromeliaceous, dicotyledonous, rosaceous, composite, ranunculaceous, cruciferous, brassicaceous, umbelliferous, labiate, leguminous, chenopodiaceous, nonseed-bearing, cryptogamic, thallophytic

17 **of stems,** axial, cauline, rachial *or* rachidial, axillary

18 **of leaves,** simple, entire, ovate, lanceolate, linear, orbicular, cordate, lobed, toothed, serrate, dentate, crenate, hastate, sagittate, stalked, unstalked, sessile,

peltate, compound, trifoliate, palmate, pinnate, bipinnate

19 **of roots,** radical, radicular, rooted, fibrous-rooted, tuberous-rooted, rootlike, rhizoid

20 **botanical,** plant, phytological, phytographic(al), phytochemical, phytogeographic(al), phytopathological, ethnobotanical, phytosociological

▸ *Agriculture 16; Horticulture 17; Flowers 42; Trees 43; Ferns and Mosses 46; Fungi, Algae, and Lichens 47*

VERBS

21 **vegetate,** grow, germinate, pullulate, root, take root, sprout, sprout up, shoot, shoot up; bud, gemmate, unfold, leaf, flower, blossom, bloom; flourish, riot, burgeon, overgrow, overrun; run to seed, shed seeds, dehisce, photosynthesize

▸ *Increase 746*

22 **be dormant,** shed leaves, abscise; wilt, wither, suspend growth, overwinter, perennate, survive, exist, rest, vegetate

23 **study plants,** collect plants, botanize, be a botanist

ADVERBS

24 **herbaceously,** exotically, succulently, ephemerally, annually, biennially, triennially, perennially, xerophytically, epiphytically, saprophytically, photosynthetically

25 **botanically,** phytologically, horticulturally, ecologically, phytogenetically, phytosociologically, algologically, dendrologically

42 Flowers

And I will make thee beds of roses / And a thousand fragrant posies. — CHRISTOPHER MARLOWE

NOUNS

1 **flower,** floweret, floret, flowerlet, bloom, blossom, blow; wildflower, garden flower, pot plant; flower arrangement, spray, festoon, cut flowers, posy, bouquet, garland, lei, chaplet, wreath, corsage, nosegay, daisy chain, boutonniere *or* buttonhole [Brit]; dried flower, everlasting flower, strawflower, pressed flower

▸ *Decoration 532*

2 **flowering plant,** flowerer, bloomer, annual, biennial, triennial, ephemeral, perennial, bulb, corm, angiosperm

▸ *Plants (General) 41*

3 **flower part,** sepal, calyx, petal, nectary, corolla, perianth, floral envelope, epicalyx, involucre *or* involucrum, bract, whorl, spathe, stamen, filament, anther, androecium, pollen, pollen grain, pollen sac, pollen tube, stigma, style, ovary, carpel, gynoecium, pistil, ovule, micropyle, receptacle

▸ *Plants (General) 41; Fruits 44*

4 **flower head,** flower cluster, inflorescence, racemose

inflorescence, raceme, panicle, corymb, spadix, spike, spikelet, catkin, ament, umbel, capitulum, ray flower *or* floret, disk flower *or* floret, cyme, cymose inflorescence, monochasium, monochasial cyme, dichasium, dichasial cyme, thyrse *or* thyrsus, verticillaster

5 **flowering,** florescence, efflorescence, blossoming, blooming, flowerage, unfolding, anthesis, blowing, blow, full blow, full bloom

6 **pollination,** cross-pollination, self-pollination

7 **flower culture,** floriculture, flower growing, flower selling, floristics; floriculturist, flower grower, florist, flower seller

▹ *Horticulture 17*

8 **figurative usage,** flower child, flower power, daisy-

cutter, daisy wheel, primrose path, rose window, rosette, Sunflower State, bed of roses, shrinking violet, wallflower

ADJECTIVES

9 **floral,** flowered, flowery, bloomy, floristic, flowerlike, fragrant, florid, ornate, floreate, floriate *or* floriated

▹ *Fragrance 226; Decoration 532*

10 **flowering,** in flower, in bloom, in full bloom, in full blow, in blossom, blossoming, blooming, abloom, flourishing, florescent, inflorescent, efflorescent

▹ *Prosperity 847*

11 **of flowers,** staminate, male, pistillate, female, imperfect, perfect, monoecious, dioecious, regular, irregular, synsepalous, aposepalous, hypogynous, epigynous,

---

FLOWERS AND FLOWERING PLANTS

Aaron's-beard *or* rose of Sharon	bellflower	century plant	dandelion	germander
acacia	bergenia	chamomile *or* camomile	datura	ghostweed
acanthus	billbergia		daylily	gillyflower
aconite	bindweed	China rose *or* rose of China	delphinium	gladiolus *or* gladiola
Adam's-needle	bird-of-paradise		dianthus	globeflower
aechmea	bittersweet	Chinese lantern	dogbane	globe thistle
African violet	black-eyed Susan	Christmas cactus	dog rose	gloxinia
agapanthus	bladderwort	chrysanthemum	dogtooth violet	goatsbeard
agave	blanket-flower	cineraria	dog violet	gold dust
ageratum	bleeding heart	cinquefoil	Dutchman's breeches	golden bell
agrimony	bluebell	clarkia	dyer's-broom *or* woadwaxen	goldenrod
allamanda	bluet *or* bluets	cleavers *or* clivers		goldflower
allium	bougainvillea	clematis	Easter lily	granadilla
althaea	bridal wreath	clianthus	edelweiss	grape hyacinth
alyssum	broom	clivia	eglantine	grass of Parnassus
amaranthus	browallia	clover	English daisy	guelder rose
amaryllis	bryony	cockscomb	epiphyllum	gypsophila
Amazon lily	buddleia	coleus	eucharis	harebell
anchusa	bugloss	columbine	euphorbia	hawkweed
anemone	burning bush	coneflower	exacum	heather
arum lily	butterbur	convolvulus	farewell-to-spring	hedgehog cactus
asphodel	buttercup	coreopsis	firethorn	heliotrope
aster	butterfly flower	cornflower	flag	hellebore
astilbe	cactus	corydalis	fleabane	herb Robert
aubrietia	calceolaria	cosmos	fleur-de-lis	hibiscus
auricula	calendula	cowbell	flowering quince	hollyhock
autumn crocus	calla lily	cowslip	forget-me-not	honesty
avens	camellia	cranesbill	forsythia	honeysuckle
azalea	campanula	creamcups	four-o'clock	hoya
baby's-breath	campion	creeping Jenny	foxglove	hyacinth
bachelor's button	candytuft	crocus	frangipani	hydrangea
balloon flower	canna	crowfoot	freesia	hypericum
basket flower	Canterbury bell	crown of thorns	fritillary	hyssop
basket-of-gold	cardinal flower	cuckoo flower	fuchsia	impatiens
beautybush	carnation	cuckoopint	gaillardia	Indian paintbrush
bedstraw	catchfly	cyclamen	gardenia	iris
bee balm	cattleya orchid	cymbidium	gazania	jack-in-the-pulpit
begonia	ceanothus	daffodil	gentian	japonica
belladonna	celandine	dahlia	geranium	jonquil
	celosia	daisy	gerbera daisy	kalanchoe

perigynous, racemose, cymose, corymbose, umbelliferous

▶ *Plants (General) 41*

VERBS

12 **flower,** bud, bloom, blossom, blow [Arch], be in flower, be in bloom, effloresce, flourish, burgeon

ADVERBS

13 **florally,** floristically, floridly, fragrantly

43 Trees

I think that I shall never see / a poem lovely as a tree. — JOYCE KILMER

I think that I shall never see / A billboard lovely as a tree. /

Indeed, unless the billboards fall, / I'll never see a tree at all. — OGDEN NASH

NOUNS

1 **tree,** timber, shrub, bush, sapling; shade tree, timber tree, fruit tree; coniferous tree, conifer, evergreen (tree), deciduous tree, broad-leaved tree, palm tree; softwood (tree), hardwood (tree), tropical hardwood; ornamental tree, Christmas tree, bonsai; dwarf tree, hedgerow tree, specimen tree, standard, pollard

2 **tree part,** trunk, bole, gnarl, knot, burl, burr, crutch, fork, crown, limb, branch, bough, twig, switch, sprig, spur, leader, leaf, palm leaf, palm frond, needle, pine needle, cone, pine cone, fir cone, tree stump, stump, snag, stool, root, base; annual *or* growth *or* tree ring

---

FLOWERS AND FLOWERING PLANTS

knapweed	mock orange	pimpernel	shrimp plant	thunbergia
laburnum	moneywort	pincushion flower *or*	slipper flower	tiger lily
lady's-slipper	monkey flower	scabious	slipperwort	toad lily
larkspur	monkshood	pink	snake's-head	tormentil
lavender	montbretia	plantain	snapdragon	touch-me-not
leopard lily	moonflower	plumbago	snowdrop	tradescantia
lilac	morning glory	poinsettia	snow-on-the-	traveler's-joy
lily-of-the-Nile	moschatel	polyanthus	mountain	trillium
lily of the valley	moss pink	poppy	soapwort	trumpet creeper
lipstick plant	moss rose	portulaca	Solomon's seal	trumpet flower
lobelia	mullein	potentilla	sowbread	tuberose
lords-and-ladies	musk rose	pot marigold	speedwell	tulip
lotus	narcissus	prickly poppy	spider flower	Turk's-cap lily *or*
love-in-a-mist	nasturtium	primrose	spirea	Martagon lily
love-lies-bleeding	nemesia	primula	spurge	valerian
lungwort	nicotiana	Queen Anne's lace	spurry	verbena
lupine	nierembergia	ragged robin	squill	veronica
Madonna lily	old-man cactus	ragwort	star of Bethlehem	vervain
magnolia	old-man's-beard	ranunculus	statice	viburnum
mallow	oleander	red-hot poker	stephanotis	vinca
Maltese cross	opium poppy	rhododendron	stitchwort	viola
marguerite	opuntia	rock cress	St. John's wort	violet
marigold	orchid	rock jasmine	stock	wallflower
marsh mallow	organ-pipe cactus	rock rose	strawflower	water lily
marsh marigold	oxalis	rose	strelitzia	windflower
Martagon lily *or*	oxeye daisy	rose of China *or*	streptocarpus	winter aconite
Turk's-cap lily	oxlip	China rose	sunflower	winter jasmine
marvel-of-Peru	painted tongue	rose of Sharon *or*	sun rose	wisteria
mayflower	pansy	Aaron's-beard	sweet alyssum	woadwaxen *or* dyer's
meadow saffron	paper-white	rudbeckia	sweetbrier	broom
meadow rue	narcissus	safflower	sweet pea	wolfsbane
meadowsweet	paphiopedilum	sainfoin	sweet william	wood sorrel
mecanopsis	pansy	salpiglossis	syringa	woolflower
merrybells	passionflower	salvia	tansy	wormwood
Michaelmas daisy	pelargonium	saxifrage	tassel flower	woundwort
mignonette	pennyroyal	scabious *or*	tea rose	yarrow
milfoil	peony	pincushion flower	teasel	yucca
milkwort	periwinkle	sea lavender	thistle	zinnia
mimosa	petunia	sedum	thorn apple	
moccasin flower	phlox	shooting star	thrift	

3 timber, wood, lumber, cordwood, cord, cordage, log, pole, flitch, faggot, brushwood, driftwood, dead wood, firewood, kindling, pulpwood, sapwood, alburnum, heartwood, duramen, reaction wood, tension wood, compression wood, springwood, summerwood, early wood, late wood, woody tissue, bark, cork, phellem, lignin, cellulose, phloem, xylem

▶ *Hardness 542*

4 trees, tree line *or* zone, timberline, forest, rainforest, tropical forest, jungle, wildwood, gallery forest, fringing forest, virgin forest, primeval forest, coniferous forest; taiga, woodland, woods, ancient woodland, chaparral, scrub, scrubland; brush, bocage, wood, greenwood, copse *or* coppice, spinney [Brit], thicket, clearing, glade, bower, arbor, grove, motte; under-wood, undergrowth, tree litter, leaf litter, leaf mold, beech mast, brake, covert, bosket *or* bosquet, bosk, holt [Arch]; plantation, stand, timberland, wood lot *or* woodlot, bush lot [Can], tree farm, arboretum, pinetum, pinery, tree nursery, orchard, orangery, bush; national forest, state forest, conservation land

▶ *Horticulture 17*

5 forestry, tree farming, agroforestry, tree planting, afforestation, reforestation, deforestation, conservation, dendrology, dendrochronology, arboriculture, silviculture

▶ *Agriculture 16*

6 tree management, beating up, brashing, thinning, pruning, lopping, topping, drop-crotching, coppicing, pollarding, tree surgery, tapping, felling, logging, lumbering

---

TREES AND SHRUBS

Conifers and Related Trees
alerce
araucaria
arborvitae
bald cypress
balsam fir
bead tree
big tree
black pine
black spruce
blue spruce
bristlecone pine
bunya-bunya
cade
cedar
cedar of Lebanon
celery pine
Chilean pine
cryptomeria
cypress
cypress pine
dawn redwood
deodar
Douglas fir
fir
gingko
hemlock *or* hemlock spruce
hoop pine
Huon pine
incense cedar
jack pine
Japanese cedar
juniper
kahika
kauri *or* kauri pine
larch
lignum vitae

loblolly pine
longleaf pine
maidenhair tree
monkey puzzle
Norfolk Island pine
Norway spruce
nut pine
Paraná pine
pencil cedar
pinyon pine
podocarpus
red cedar
red fir
red pine
redwood
sandarac
savin
Scotch *or* Scots pine
sequoia
silver fir
Sitka spruce
southern cypress
spruce
spruce pine
stone pine
sugar pine
swamp cypress
tamarack
thuja
umbrella pine
wellingtonia
western hemlock
western red cedar
white cedar
white pine
white spruce
yew

Palms
areca palm
babassu
betel palm
cabbage palm
coco de mer
coconut palm
coquito
date palm
doum palm
funeral palm
gomuti
gru-gru palm
ivory palm
nikau *or* nikau palm
nipa
oil palm
palmyra
parlor palm
queen palm
sago palm
sugar palm
talipot *or* talipot palm
Washington palm
wax palm
wine palm

Hardwoods, Ornamentals, and Others
acacia
acer
ailanthus *or* tree of heaven
alder
almond
ambatch
apple
apple box

arbutus
ash
aspen
assegai
bael tree
balata
balsa
balsam poplar
banksia
banyan
baobab
basswood
bayberry
bay rum tree
bay *or* bay tree
bean tree
bebeeru
beech
beefwood
bela *or* belah tree
birch
black bean
blackjack
blackthorn
black walnut
blackwood
bladdernut
blue gum
bo *or* bodhi tree
bottlebrush
bottle tree
box *or* boxwood
box elder
bully *or* bullet tree
buckeye
butcher's broom
butternut
buttonball
buttonwood

cabbage tree
cacao
calabash
camphor tree
camwood
candleberry
candlenut tree
candlewood
carapa
cassia
casuarina
catalpa
champac *or* champaca
chaste tree
chaulmoogra
chestnut
chinaberry *or* China tree
chittamwood
cockspur
coffee tree
coolabah
coral tree
cork oak
corkwood
cornel
cottonwood
crabwood
croton
cucumber tree
daphne
devil tree
divi-divi
dogwood
dragon tree
durmast *or* durmast oak
Dutch elm
ebony

7 forester, forest manager, ranger, forest ranger, verderer, woodlander, woodcutter, lumberjack, timberman, woodsman, woodman, logger, lumberer, tapper, tree farmer, tree surgeon, arboriculturist, arborist, silviculturist, dendrologist

8 tree disease, defoliation, mosaic, ring spot, leaf curl, dieback, witches'-broom, wilt, canker, rot, blight, mildew, rust, crown gall, oak apple, oak gall, Dutch elm disease

▸ *Horticulture 17; Fungi, Algae, and Lichens 47*

9 figurative usage, family tree, genealogical tree, shoetree, axletree, manteltree, rooftree, ridgetree, summertree, saddletree, swingletree, swiveltree, whippletree *or* whiffletree, crosstree, trestletree, olive branch; tree of knowledge, tree of life, tree of Jesse, Yggdrasil

or Ygdrasil; wood nymph, tree nymph, dryad, hamadryad, Daphne

ADJECTIVES

10 treelike, arboreal, arboraceous, arborescent, dendritic, dendroid *or* dendroidal, dendriform, palmate, palmaceous, branching, slender, willowy, shrubby, bushy, gnarled, deciduous, coniferous, evergreen, piny *or* piney, resinous

11 woody, wood, ligneous, ligniform, hardwood, softwood, hard-grained, soft-grained, wooden

12 wooded, forested, forestal, timbered, afforested, reforested, planted, tree-covered, arboreous, woodland, sylvan *or* silvan, sylvatic, shaded, shady, bosky, copsy, braky, woodsy

13 arboricultural, silvicultural, silvical, dendrologic(al), dendrologous, dendrochronological

---

TREES AND SHRUBS

elder	jojoba	neem	sassafras	tamarisk
elm	Joshua tree	Norway maple	sasswood *or*	teak
eucalyptus	Judas tree	nux vomica	sassywood *or* sassy	tea tree
eucryphia	juneberry	oak	*or* sassy bark	terebinth
euonymus	kalmia	ocotillo	satinwood	thorn tree
false acacia	karri tree	osier	screw pine	toon
fever tree	kingwood	pagoda tree	seringa	toothache tree
flame-of-the-forest	koa	paper mulberry	serviceberry	tree of heaven *or*
flame tree	kowhai	paulownia	service tree	ailanthus
flowering ash	kurrajong	pepper tree	shadbush *or* shadblow	tulip tree
fringe tree	lacquer tree	pipal *or* peepul	shagbark	tupelo
gaboon	lancewood	plane tree	shea	Turkey oak
gean	laurel	poinciana	silk-cotton tree	turpentine tree
greasewood	lemon	poison oak	silk oak *or* silky oak	umbrella tree
greenheart	lilly-pilly	poison sumac	silk tree	upas
guaiacum	lime	poplar	silver birch	varnish tree
guayule	linden	prickly ash	silver maple	wahoo
gum *or* gum tree	liquidambar	privet	simarouba	walnut
haematoxylon	locust	puriri	slippery elm	wandoo
hakea	logwood	pussy willow	smoke tree	wattle
hawthorn	madrone	quassia	snowdrop tree	wax tree
hazel	mahogany	quebracho	soapbark	wayfaring tree
Hercules-club	mallee tree	rain tree	sorb *or* sorb apple	weeping willow
hevea	manchineel	redbud	sorrel tree	whitebeam
hickory	mangrove	red gum	sour gum	white oak
holly	manuka	red oak	sourwood	white poplar
holm oak *or* holly oak	maple	ribbonwood	Spanish cedar	willow
honey locust	marblewood	roble	spindle tree	witch hazel
hoptree	marmalade tree	rosewood	strawberry bush	wych elm
hornbeam	maté	rowan	strawberry tree	yarran
horse chestnut	may tree [Brit]	royal poinciana	sugar gum	yaupon
horseradish tree	mazzard	rubber plant	sugar maple	yellow poplar
Indian mulberry	melaleuca	rubber tree	sumac	yellowwood
inkberry	mesquite	sallow	sweet bay	ylang-ylang
ironwood	monkey-bread tree	sandalwood	sweet gum	yucca
jacaranda	monkeypod	sandbox tree	sycamine	zebrawood
Japanese maple	mountain ash	sapele	sycamore	
jarrah	myrtle	sappanwood	tallow wood	
jelutong	needle-flower tree	saskatoon	tamarind	

TREE PRODUCTS

acaroid resin *or* accroides gum	dragon's blood	pereira bark
animé	frankincense	pine tar
annatto	fruit	rauwolfia
araroba	fustic	resin
balm-of-Gilead *or* Mecca balsam	gamboge	rubber
balsam	Goa powder	sassafras
benzoin	gutta-percha	sassafras oil
borneol	hematoxylin	senna pods
cajeput	henna	storax
calisaya	kapok	tacamahac
camphor	kermes	tolu
canella	kino gum	tragacanth
carnauba	latex	tung oil
cascara	maple sugar	turpentine
cassia bark	mastic	wax
catechu	methyl *or* wood alcohol	wood coal
chicle	myrrh	wood pitch
cinchona	nuts	wood sugar
copaiba	olive oil	wood tar
copal	ouabain	wood vinegar *or* pyroligneous acid
	palm oil	yohimbine

VERBS

14 manage trees, practice forestry, thin, prune, grub, lop, top, pollard, coppice, tap, cut timber, fell, clear, log, lumber

15 grow, spread, bloom, flower, leaf out, lose *or* drop *or* shed leaves, branch out; shade, fruit, whisper, weep, change color

ADVERBS

16 arboriculturally, silviculturally, dendrologically, dendrochronologically

44 Fruits

NOUNS

1 fruits, fruits of the earth, produce, crop, yield, soft

fruit, stone fruit, citrus fruit, dried fruit, nuts, kernels, grain, seeds, pulses, vegetables, legumes, root vegetables, roots, tubers, green vegetables, salad vegetables

▶ *Agriculture 16; Horticulture 17; Fertility 22; Grasses 45; Food 90*

2 botanical fruit, simple fruit, true fruit, composite fruit, aggregate fruit, multiple fruit, false fruit, succulent fruit, citrus fruit, drupe, berry, pome, pepo, sorosis, syconium, hesperidium, dry fruit, dehiscent fruit, legume, pod, capsule, follicle, siliqua, silicula, silicle, pyxidium, indehiscent fruit, nut, achene *or* akene, samara, caryopsis, cypsela, schizocarpic fruit, schizocarp, cremocarp, loment, regma, fruiting body

▶ *Plants (General) 41*

3 fruit structure, fruit wall, pericarp, exocarp *or* epicarp, skin, rind, peel, shell, shuck, husk, seed pod, seed capsule, mesocarp, endocarp, flesh, pulp, meat, pith, stone, pit, nutlet, seed, pip, kernel, grain

▶ *Reproduction 21; Plants (General) 41*

4 figurative usage, forbidden fruit, apple of one's eye, Adam's apple, apple of discord, apple-pie order, lotus-eater, cherry picker, strawberry mark, banana republic [Off]; [Inf]: grapevine, raspberry, peanuts, bananas, top banana, lemon, melon, limey, applesauce, apple polisher, cherry

ADJECTIVES

5 fruiting, fruit-bearing, fructiferous, pomiferous, leguminous, fructuous, fruitful, productive, fertile

▶ *Fertility 22*

6 fruitlike, fruity, citrus, citrous, citric, citrine

7 fruit-eating, herbivorous, frugivorous, vegetarian

8 of a fruit, fleshy, succulent, ripe, unripe, indehiscent, dehiscent, monocarpellary, bicarpellary, polycarpellary, syncarpous, apocarpous, monocarpic, schizocarpic, parthenocarpic

VERBS

9 fruit, bear fruit, fructify, ripen, be fruitful, yield, release seeds, dehisce

▶ *Reproduction 21; Fertility 22; Prosperity 847*

VARIETIES OF APPLES

Anna	Earliblaze	Jonathan	Prima	Spartan
Arkansas Black	Ein Shemer	Liberty	Priscilla	Starkrimson
Baldwin	Empire	Lodi	Red Delicious	Starr
Blue Permain	Freedom	Macoun	Redfree	Stayman
Braeburn	Gala	McIntosh	Red Rome	Twenty Ounce
Bramley	Golden Delicious	Monroe	Rhode Island Greening	Tydeman's Red
Cortland	Granny Smith	Mutsu	Rome	Wealthy
Cox's Orange Pippin	Gravenstein	Newton Pippin	Rome Beauty	Winesap
Criterion	Grimes Golden	Northern Spy	Roxbury Russet	Winter Banana
Delicious	Idared	Ortley	Russet	Yellow Transparent
Dorset Golden	Jerseymac	Permain	Sir Prize	York Imperial
	Jonared	Pippin		

10 **fructiferously,** fruitily, fructuously, succulently, fruit-fully, productively

45 Grasses

NOUNS

1 **grass,** grass family, Gramineae or Poaceae, graminaceous plant; ornamental grass, mowing grass, lawn grass, fodder grass, meadow grass, pasture grass, ley grass, cereal grass; grasslike plant: rush, sedge, reed, cane, bamboo, papyrus

2 **grassland,** meadow, field, meadowland, lea or ley, mead [Arch]; pastureland, pasturage, herbage, verdure, grazing, plain, range; prairie, pampas, savanna or savannah, llano, campo, veld or veldt, steppe, champaign, campagna; common, moor, moorland, heath, downs, downland, wold; park, parkland, lawn, green, sward, greensward; turf, grass, sod, divot, clump, tussock, tuft, hassock
   ▶ *Agriculture 16; Greenness 260*

3 **grass plant,** stem, culm, haulm, cane, reed, straw, spear, spire, blade, blade of grass, leaf, sheath, ligule, auricle, grass flower, spike, panicle, spikelet, glume, rachilla, lemma, palea, awn, lodicule, tassel

4 **cereal grass,** cereal, grain, ear, cob, corncob, husk, bran, chaff, stubble, straw; wheat, buckwheat, rye, corn, maize, oats, rice, barley, millet
   ▶ *Agriculture 16; Fruits 44; Food 90*

5 **grasscutter,** lawn mower, mowing machine, scythe, reed cutter, thatcher
   ▶ *Agriculture 16; Horticulture 17*

6 **grass eater,** grazer, browser, graminivore, herbivore

ADJECTIVES

7 **grasslike,** gramineous, graminaceous, poaceous, graminiferous, farinaceous

8 **grassy,** verdant, green, grass-green, grass-covered, verdured, meadowy, swardy, turfy, reedy, rushy, sedgy
   ▶ *Plants (General) 41; Greenness 260*

9 **grass-eating,** grazing, browsing, graminivorous, herbivorous

VERBS

10 **manage grassland,** cut, mow, scythe, grass, grass over, turf, sod, seed, sow seed, fertilize, feed, water, weed, spray, roll, thatch

11 **eat grass,** graze, browse, crop, forage, pasture, ruminate, chew the cud, put out to grass or pasture, fodder

ADVERBS

12 **herbivorously,** verdantly

46 Ferns and Mosses

NOUNS

1 **fern,** true fern, pteridophyte, Filicinae; bracken, brake,

tropical fern, tree fern, fern ally, sphenopsid, horsetail, equisetum, Dutch rush, scouring rush, calamite, lycopsid, club moss, Lycopodium, lycopod, ground pine, quillwort; fernlike plant, asparagus fern, seed fern, pteridosperm, cycad, cycad fern
   ▶ *Plants (General) 41*

2 **fern plant,** stem, rootstock, stalk, rachis, leaf, frond, leaflet, pinna, pinnule, plant body, sporophyte, fern seed, spore, spore case, sporangium, sorus, fruit dot, indusium, prothallium, reproductive organ; archegonium, antheridium

3 **study of ferns,** pteridology; pteridologist

4 **moss,** true moss, bryophyte, Musci, Bryopsida, bryopsid, peat moss, bog moss, sphagnum; moss ally, liverwort, Hepaticae, Hepaticopsida, leafy liverwort, hornwort; mosslike plant, lichen, Spanish moss, long moss, reindeer moss, oakmoss, alga, Irish moss, carrageen
   ▶ *Fungi, Algae, and Lichens 47*

5 **moss plant,** plant body, gametophyte, root, rhizoid, spore capsule, seta, stalk, calyptra, cap, elater, foot, propagation, gemma, gemma cup; reproductive organ: archegonium, antheridium, venter; study of mosses, bryology, bryologist

ADJECTIVES

6 **fernlike,** ferny, pteridophyte, pteridophytic, pteridophytous, pteridological, pinnatifid

7 **mosslike,** mossy, moss-covered, moss-grown, bryophyte, bryophytic, hepatic, bryological

47 Fungi, Algae, and Lichens

NOUNS

1 **fungus,** fungosity, mold, must, mildew, rot, dry rot, wet rot, blight, canker
   ▶ *Affliction 117*

2 **mushroom,** toadstool, champignon, cultivated mushroom, button mushroom, wild mushroom, field mushroom, meadow mushroom [Brit], fairy ring
   ▶ *Horticulture 17; Food 90*

3 **fungi,** Fungi or Mycota, true fungi, Eumycota, basidiomycetes, Basidiomycota, agarics, bracket fungi, pore fungi, tooth fungi, club fungi, skin fungi, jelly fungi, rusts, smuts, ascomycetes, Ascomycota, sac fungi, cup fungi, flask fungi, deuteromycetes, imperfect fungi, Deuteromycota or Fungi Imperfecta, phycomycetes, Mastigomycotina, Zygomycota, myxomycetes, Myxomycota, slime molds, cellular slime molds

4 **fungal body,** thallus, mycelium, hypha, haustorium, rhizoid, rhizomorph, plasmodium, reproductive body, carpophore, fruiting body, mushroom, cap, pileus, gill, lamella, stalk, stipe, veil, volva, annulus, bracket, conk, sporophore, basidiocarp, basidium, hymenium, sterigma, ascocarp, ascus, spore, basidiospore, ascospore, conidium

5 **fungal association,** symbiosis, mycorrhiza, ectotrophic mycorrhiza, endotrophic mycorrhiza, fungus root, lichen, symbiotic fungus, mycobiont, parasitism, parasitic fungus, parasite, dermatophyte, saprophyte, saprobe

6 **fungal disease,** mycosis, dermatophytosis, ringworm, tinea, athlete's foot, dhobi itch, favus, thrush, candidiasis, moniliasis, phycomycosis, aspergillosis, ergotism, histoplasmosis, farmer's lung, mycetoma, Madura foot, blastomycosis, coccidioidomycosis, plant disease, damping-off, dieback, Dutch elm disease
  ◗ *Agriculture 16; Horticulture 17; Trees 43; Ill Health 114*

7 **fungal antibiotic,** penicillin, streptomycin, actinomycin, neomycin, chloramphenicol

8 **antifungal agent,** fungicide, fungistat, antimycotic, mycostat
  ◗ *Remedy 115*

9 **study of fungi,** mycology; mycologist, mushroom grower, mushroom farmer, mushroom farm, truffle hunter; mushroom eating, mycophagy; mycophagist

10 **alga,** thallophyte, seaweed, wrack, kelp, phytoplankton, algal bloom, eutrophication, red tide, mat, pond scum, frog spit, symbiotic alga, phycobiont, lichen

11 **algae,** blue-green algae, cyanobacteria, Cyanophyta, golden-brown algae, Chrysophyta, chrysophyte, yellow-green algae, Xanthophyta, xanthophyte, green algae, Chlorophyta, chlorophyte, isokont, brown algae *or* seaweeds, Phaeophyta, phaeophyte, red algae *or* seaweeds, Rhodophyta, rhodophyte

12 **study of algae,** algology, phycology; algologist, phycologist

13 **plant body,** thallus, frond, holdfast, hapteron, stem, stipe, branch, branchlet, lamina, blade, float, air bladder, thread, rhizoid, protonema, frustule, theca, epitheca, hypotheca, algal pigment, chlorophyll, carotene, xanthophyll, phycocyanin, phycoerythrin, eyespot, stigma, food store, pyrenoid, starch

14 **reproductive body,** zoospore, aplanospore, akinete, hypnospore, autospore, cyst, propagule, coenobium, sexual reproduction, isogamy, anisogamy, oogamy, gamete, spermatozoid, antherozoid, oosphere, gonidium, antheridium, oogonium, manubrium, conceptacle, spermatium, carpogonium, carpospore

15 **algal product,** agar, algin, alginate, laver, miru [Jap], kombu [Jap], fossil algae, diatomaceous earth, stromatolite

16 **lichen,** reindeer moss, rock tripe *or* tripe-de-roche, oakmoss, Spanish moss, crustose lichen, foliose lichen, fruticose lichen, symbiosis, fungal constituent, mycobiont, algal constituent, phycobiont, root, propagation, podetium, isidium, soredium

17 **study of lichens,** lichenology, lichenometry; lichenologist
  ◗ *Ferns and Mosses 46*

ADJECTIVES

18 **fungal,** fungous, fungoid, fungiform, moldy, mildewed, mildewy, musty, rotten, blighted, cankered, yeasty, fermented

19 **of fungi,** saprophytic, parasitic, homothallic, heterothallic, basidomycetous, mycelial, hyphal, ascogenous, mycotic, mycological, coprophilous, decurrent, epigeal, deliquescent, adnate, adnexed, alveolate, amyloid, bulbous, cespitose, fusiform, reticulate, sessile

20 **algal,** algoid, diatomaceous, conferval, confervoid, fucoid, unicellular, colonial, coenobial, filamentous, thalloid, siphonaceous, palmelloid, dendroid, sessile, motile, symbiotic, epiphytic, epilithic, flagellate, uniflagellate, biflagellate, multiflagellate, parenchymatous, pseudoparenchymatous, algological, phycological

21 **lichenoid,** lichenous, lichenose, lichened, lichenized, licheniform, crustose, foliose, fruticose, corticolous, saxicolous, lichenological

VERBS

22 **mold,** molder, mildew, rot, putrefy, decompose, ferment, deliquesce
  ◗ *Deterioration 808*

23 **mushroom,** germinate, spring up, flourish, burgeon, proliferate, multiply
  ◗ *Size, Largeness 579; Increase 746*

ADVERBS

24 **saprophytically,** parasitically, symbiotically

25 **algologically,** colonially, epiphytically, symbiotically

48 Education

Education is simply the soul of a society as it passes from one generation to another. — G. K. CHESTERTON

Education made us what we are.
— CLAUDE-ADRIEN HELVÉTIUS

He who can, does. He who cannot, teaches.
— GEORGE BERNARD SHAW

NOUNS

1 **education,** teaching, schooling, scholarship, pedagogy, tuition, direction, coaching, guidance, catechization, tutoring, tutelage, training, instruction, drilling, indoctrination, preparation, advice; illumination, enlightenment, edification, betterment, progress, amelioration, melioration, advancement, development, cultivation, civilization, rearing, raising, upbringing, nurture
   ▶ *Advice 176; Preparation 388; Raising 715; Improvement 807*

2 **educational system,** nursery education, preschool education, primary education, special education, Froebel system, Montessori system, Waldorf system, home schooling, secondary education, tertiary education, higher education, adult education, moral education, remedial education, vocational training, job training, employment training, on-the-job training, in-service training; self-education, correspondence course, autodidactics, recreational education, teacher training

3 **subject,** discipline, field, area, major, minor, concentration, specialty, province, domain, branch, realm, bailiwick, sphere, department; curriculum, syllabus, course, module, timetable, core curriculum; science subject, technical subject, language, humanities, liberal arts, general studies, civics; religious education, religious instruction, catechism, scholasticate; physical

education (PE), sex education, interdisciplinary education
   ▶ *Qualification 340*

4 **educator,** teacher, head teacher, headmaster, headmistress, principal, vice-principal; chancellor, vice-chancellor, dean, don, professor, professor emeritus, doctor, lecturer, fellow, intern, reader, academic, preceptor, tutor, instructor, governess, schoolman, schoolma'am *or* schoolmarm, schoolteacher, schoolmistress, schoolmaster, master, mistress, form teacher [Brit], student teacher; home tutor, private tutor, pedagogue, coach, trainer, mentor, adviser, authority, expert, pundit *or* pandit, guru, mullah, maestro, docent, preacher, rabbi, homilist, educationalist, educationist, educational psychologist, truant officer, guidance counselor; staff, department, faculty, school board, trustee
   ▶ *Authority 52; Master 68; Wisdom 352*

5 **instructorship,** tutorship, tutorage, tutelage, chair, professorship, professorate, readership, lectureship, fellowship, research fellowship, assistantship
   ▶ *Authority 52; Master 68*

6 **learner,** student, pupil, apprentice, novice, tyro, beginner, recruit, initiate, rookie; neophyte, abecedarian, schoolchild, schoolboy, schoolgirl, schooler, classmate; freshman, sophomore, junior, senior, underclassman, undergraduate, fellow student, scholar, bookworm, researcher; postgraduate, alumnus, alumna; autodidact; undergrad [Inf]
   ▶ *Friendship 62; Intellect 315; Newness 652; Beginning 771*

7 **learning,** study, erudition, acquisition of knowledge, scholarship, extensive study, storing *or* stocking the mind, broadening *or* expanding the mind, brainwork, absorption, assimilation, contemplation, perusal, review, reading; cramming [Inf], boning up [Inf]
   ▶ *Intellect 315; Thought 317; Knowledge 348*

8 **learnedness,** studiousness, scholarliness, scholarship, intellectuality, literacy, bookishness, polymathy, erudition, expertise, nous, savvy [Inf]

9 educatability, educability, aptitude, intelligence, aptness, quickness, quick study, cleverness, brightness, readiness, willingness to learn, teachability, plasticity, motivation, receptivity, curiosity, inquisitiveness, susceptibility, malleability, pliability, docility

> *Intellect 315; Curiosity 321; Willingness 373; Motivation 508*

10 refinement, education, taste, discernment, finesse, connoisseurship, discrimination, judgment, perception, perceptiveness, insight, acumen, sensitivity, sensibility, cultivation, sophistication, urbanity, suavity, elegance, breeding, background, savoir-faire

> *Taste 219; Sensitivity 267; Intellect 315; Intuition 320; Discrimination 337; Judgment 341; Elegance 527; Refinement 534*

11 school, educational institution, nursery school, playgroup, day-care center, crèche [Brit], play school, preschool, kindergarten, primary school, grade school, grammar school, middle school, secondary school, junior high, high school, senior high, preparatory school, prep school, college, graduate school

12 type of school, public school, private school, lyceum, *lycée* [Fr], day school, boarding school, state school, comprehensive school, single-sex school, denominational school, special school, special needs school, open classroom school, summer school, night school, community college, junior college, adult-education center, institute, academy, finishing school, conservatory, choir school, music school, ballet school, art college, drama college, riding school, military academy, officer-training school, graduate school, law school, medical school, library school, design school, film school, business school, secretarial school

13 religious school, Bible school, Sunday school, parochial school, catholic school, schola cantorum, convent school, seminary, scholasticate, Hebrew school, Talmud Torah, yeshiva, madrasah

14 university, college, women's college, institute of higher learning, degree-granting institution, polytechnic institute, polytechnic, halls of Ivy, Oxbridge [Brit], redbrick university [Brit inf]

> *Class 777*

15 schoolbook, textbook, reader, grammar, grammar book, primer, abecedarium, crib, answer book, Cliffs Notes™, Monarch Notes™; dictionary, source book, lexicon, encyclopedia, thesaurus, atlas, reference; notebook, copybook, case book, exercise book, workbook, scratch pad, manual, handbook, database, exam book, blue book, bibliography

> *Information 170; Publication 173*

16 school place, school, schoolroom, classroom, hall, lecture hall, assembly hall, auditorium, library, laboratory, language laboratory, workshop, music room, art room, dining room, cafeteria, cafetorium, common room, sick room, infirmary; schoolyard, playground, gymnasium, sports field, playing field, dormitory, dorm [Inf], residence hall, fraternity house, frat house [Inf], sorority house, schoolhouse, quadrangle, quad [Inf], campus, yard

> *Workplace 124; Form 624; Class 777*

ADJECTIVES

17 educational, educatory, educative, instructive, instructional, informative, informational, revealing, illuminating, enlightening, edifying, improving, remedial, bettering, progressive, revelatory, eye-opening, communicative, helpful, guiding, advisory, authoritative, expert, academic, scholastic, pedagogical, didactic, preachy

> *Authority 52; Communications 169; Information 170; Wisdom 352; Improvement 807*

18 educatable, educable, teachable, trainable, schoolable, instructable, bright, clever, intelligent, quick, apt, willing, motivated, ready, receptive, hungry *or* thirsty for knowledge, curious, inquisitive, susceptible, impressionable, malleable, pliable, docile

> *Curiosity 321; Question 333; Willingness 373; Obedience 426; Motivation 508*

19 educated, learned, knowledgeable, erudite, literate, literary, numerate, well-read, versed, skilled, academic, highbrow, intellectual, sagacious, wise, scholarly, scholastic, gnostic, book-wise, bookish, bibliographic, polymathic, autodidactic, self-taught, studious, absorbed, contemplative, clever, brainy [Inf]; prepared, primed, briefed, cognizant, familiar, in the know, conversant with, *au fait* [Fr], at home with, strong in, experienced, practiced, accomplished, qualified, enlightened, in touch, up to date, au courant, clued-in, streetwise, street-smart; with it [Inf], hip [Inf]

> *Master 68; Skillfulness 127; Information 170; Intellect 315; Thought 317; Knowledge 348; Wisdom 352; Preparation 388*

20 refined, educated, cultivated, cultured, civilized, discerning, critical, sensitive, sensible, discriminating, judicious, perceptive, insightful, shrewd, astute, sharp, polished, sophisticated, urbane, suave, soigné *or* soignée, tasteful

> *Taste 219; Sensitivity 267; Discrimination 337; Judgment 341; Elegance 527; Refinement 534; Sharpness 549*

21 curricular, intramural, extramural, extracurricular, doctoral, graduate, postgraduate, collegiate, varsity, canonical, doctrinal, specialized, technical, classical, liberal

VERBS

22 educate, teach, tutor, train, instruct, school, direct, coach, drill, discipline, indoctrinate, instill, inculcate, make ready, prepare, equip, brief, prime, ground, verse, acquaint, inform, tell, apprise, notify, impart, disclose, divulge, reveal, report, communicate, tip off, guide, advise, illuminate, enlighten, improve, further, promote, develop, cultivate, civilize, refine, advance, encourage, mold, shape, form, foster, nurture, rear, raise, bring up

▶ *Communications 169; Information 170; Advice 176; Knowledge 348; Preparation 388; Raising 715*

23 **learn,** study, attend classes, go to school, take lessons, practice, train, go into training, take part in a training program, serve an apprenticeship, apprentice, be taught, be instructed, acquire knowledge, discover, research, find out, ascertain, become aware of, contemplate, broaden the mind, store *or* stock the mind, peruse, read, major *or* minor in, concentrate, focus, con, read up on, brush up on, study up on, polish up; [Inf]: bone up, cram, pull an all-nighter, rub up [Brit]

▶ *Information 170; Curiosity 321; Discovery 345; Knowledge 348; Memory 354*

24 **know,** be informed, be up on, be grounded in, know by heart, know like a book, know backward and forward, know inside out, know the ropes, know the score, know what's what, know like the back of one's hand; understand, comprehend, command, master, realize, fathom, be proficient in, perceive, sense, judge, discern, discriminate, recognize, catch on, get the hang of, make out, get a fix on, latch onto [Inf], see the light, make heads or tails of

▶ *Authority 52; Skillfulness 127; Sensitivity 267; Discrimination 337; Judgment 341; Knowledge 348; Wisdom 352*

ADVERBS

25 **educationally,** instructively, pedagogically, informatively, informedly, canonically, authoritatively, wisely, sagaciously, expertly, helpfully, advisedly, illuminatingly, revealingly, edifyingly, improvingly, remedially, progressively, encouragingly

▶ *Authority 52; Skillfulness 127; Information 170; Advice 176; Wisdom 352; Improvement 807*

26 **studiously,** academically, scholastically, brainily, bookishly, thoughtfully, contemplatively, intellectually, intelligently, aptly, quickly, cleverly, skillfully, technically, receptively, susceptibly, malleably, pliably, docilely

▶ *Skillfulness 127; Intellect 315; Thought 317; Attention 323*

27 **discerningly,** tastefully, discriminatingly, judiciously, judgmentally, insightfully, perceptively, sensitively, sophisticatedly, urbanely, suavely, elegantly

▶ *Taste 219; Sensitivity 267; Discrimination 337; Judgment 341; Elegance 527; Refinement 534*

49 Government

The right of governing was not property but a trust.
— CHARLES JAMES FOX

Every country has the government it deserves.
— JOSEPH DE MAISTRE

NOUNS

1 **government,** governance, discipline, regulation, direction, management, supervision, administration; form of government, political system, political organization, polity, social order, civil government; local government, state government, national government, international government, world government

▶ *Politics 50; Management 126*

2 **tribalism,** clan system, patriarchy

3 **government by women,** matriarchy, gynarchy, gynecocracy

4 **theocracy,** thearchy, priestly government, hierocracy, hierarchy, clericalism, ecclesiasticism, church government, papal rule

5 **feudalism,** feudality, physiocracy, government by estates, squirearchy; suzerainty

6 **monarchy,** monarchical government, kingship, queenship, absolute monarchy, constitutional monarchy

7 **federal government,** federalism, federation

8 **constitutional government,** republicanism, democracy, representative democracy, parliamentary democracy, majority rule; republic, commonwealth

9 **self-government,** autocracy, autarchy, self-rule, self-determination, home rule

10 **oligarchy,** aristocracy, elitism, plutocracy, minority rule; dyarchy, duumvirate, triarchy, triumvirate; meritocracy, gerontocracy

11 **isocracy,** egalitarianism

12 **mob rule,** ochlocracy, mobocracy, anarchy

13 **totalitarianism,** totalitarian government, police state; fascism, communism, demagogy; dictatorship, tyranny, despotism, benevolent despotism, dictatorship of the proletariat

14 **caretaker government,** regency, interregnum, provisional government, coalition government

15 **colonial government,** colonialism, neocolonialism

16 **military government,** army rule, martial law, stratocracy

17 **world government,** supranational government, World Federalism, League of Nations, United Nations

18 **governance,** rule, direction, governmental power, reins of government, command, sway, control; empire, empery, dominion, imperialism, sovereignty, raj, overlordship; reign, regnancy, regency, dynasty; regime, regimen

19 **governing body,** the government, authorities, powers that be, government circles; city council, board of aldermen, town meeting

20 **officialdom,** officialism, bureaucracy, apparat, civil service, petty officialdom, beadledom

21 **United States government,** federal government;

executive branch, president, cabinet; legislative branch, legislature, Congress, Senate, Upper House, House of Representatives, House, Lower House; judicial branch, judiciary, Supreme Court

22 British government, monarchy, prime minister, cabinet; legislature, House of Lords, House of Peers, Upper House, Upper Chamber, House of Commons, Lower House, Lower Chamber, Mother of Parliaments; Scottish Grand Committee, Welsh Grand Committee

23 governor, executive, ruler, administrator, director, controller, leader; president, vice president, prime minister, premier, mayor; statesman, stateswoman

ADJECTIVES

24 governmental, administrative, democratic, republican, independent, constitutional, federal, state, local; public, civil, civic, executive, presidential, gubernatorial, ministerial, legislative, senatorial, congressional, parliamentary; official, bureaucratic, centralized, technocratic; tribal, matriarchal, patriarchal, theocratic, feudal, monarchical, aristocratic, meritocratic, oligarchic, plutocratic, dictatorial, totalitarian, fascist, fascistic, communist, communistic; popular, classless, self-governing, self-ruling, autonomous, autarchic, anarchic
  ❯ *Politics 50; Anarchy 51; Authority 52; Management 126; Freedom 829*

25 governing, ruling, directing, managing, leading, commanding, controlling, dictating, acting, titular; presiding, reigning, regnant, regnal, sovereign, royal, regal, monarchical, kinglike, kingly, queenlike, queenly, princely, lordly, dynastic, imperial, magisterial, colonial, neocolonial
  ❯ *Politics 50; Authority 52; Master 68; Management 126*

VERBS

26 govern, rule, direct, regulate, administer, manage, command, control, supervise, lead, be in charge, hold sway, hold the reins, hold office, preside over, reign, sit on the throne, wear the crown, wield the scepter; occupy a post, be in power, have power, have authority, tyrannize, oppress, dictate, lay down the law
  ❯ *Politics 50; Authority 52; Law 53; Management 126; Command 425; Power 514*

ADVERBS

27 governmentally, administratively, presidentially, democratically, constitutionally, ministerially, bureaucratically, dictatorially, communistically, by law, by authority

50 Politics

Man is by nature a political animal. — ARISTOTLE

Politics is the art of the possible. — OTTO VON BISMARCK

NOUNS

1 politics, polity, public affairs, civic affairs; statecraft, statesmanship, diplomacy; foreign policy, foreign affairs; party *or* partisan politics, politicking, gerrymandering, redistricting

2 political science, politics, government, civics, political philosophy, political theory, international relations, political geography, geopolitics, poli-sci [Inf]

3 body politic, political organization, country, state, nation-state, nation, republic, commonwealth, county, region, district, province; realm, kingdom, city-state, city, free city, polis, municipality, town; federation, confederation, principality, duchy, archduchy, dukedom, palatinate; empire, dominion, colony, dependency, protectorate, territory, mandated territory, buffer state, corporative state, social state, welfare state, banana republic [Off]; superpower
  ❯ *Government 49; Law 53; Region 564; Superiority 744; Inferiority 745*

4 political organization, political party, political convention, caucus; lobby, political action committee (PAC)

5 political party, major party, minor party, third party, splinter party; right, left, center, popular front, bloc, coalition

6 political party member, party member, party leader, party boss, party hack, political worker, committeeman, committeewoman, precinct captain, precinct leader, party chairperson, state chairperson, national

---

POLITICAL PARTIES

American Labor party	Progressive Conservative
Bull Moose party	party (Canada)
Citizens party (US)	Progressive Democrat party
Communist party	(Ireland)
Conservative party (Britain;	Republican party, Grand Old
Canada)	Party *or* GOP (US)
Conservative Union party	Scottish National party
(Canada)	(Scotland)
Democratic party (US)	Sinn Fein (Northern Ireland)
Federalist party (US)	Social and Liberal Democratic
Fianna Fáil (Ireland)	party (Britain)
Fine Gael (Ireland)	Social Democratic and Labour
Green party	party (Northern Ireland)
Labour party (Britain)	Social Democratic party (US;
Liberal Democrat party	Britain)
(Britain)	Socialist Labor party (US)
Liberal party (Britain, Canada)	Socialist party (US)
Libertarian party (US)	Socialist Workers party (US)
National Front (Britain)	States' Rights Democratic
New Alliance party (US)	party *or* Dixiecrats (US)
New Democratic party	Tory party (Britain)
(Canada)	Ulster Democratic Unionist
Plaid Cymru (Wales)	party (Northern Ireland)
Populist/America First party	US Labor party
(US)	Whig party (Britain)

chairperson; rightist, right-winger, reactionary, hard-liner; leftist, left-winger, Red; dry, wet; [Inf]: lefty *or* leftie, pinko, commie

7 **politician,** politico, political leader, professional politician, pol [Inf]; strategist, machinator, logroller, power-broker, wheeler-dealer [Inf]; diplomat, advocate, cabinet member, secretary, undersecretary, cabinet minister, minister, junior minister

▶ *Master 68; Management 126*

8 **elected official,** officeholder, public servant, public official, politician; member of Congress, congressman, congresswoman, representative, senator; Senate majority leader, Senate minority leader, House majority leader, House minority leader, majority whip, minority whip; member of Parliament (MP), parliamentarian, backbencher, peer, leader of the House of Commons, leader of the opposition, party manager, whip, chief whip

▶ *Government 49; Selection 382*

ADJECTIVES

9 **political,** politic, governmental, civic; partisan, bipartisan, nonpartisan; geopolitical, statesmanlike, diplomatic, influential, public

VERBS

10 **run for office,** go into politics, run, electioneer, campaign, stump, make a speech; be elected, be voted in; hold office, be in office; influence, promote, seek power, politick, lobby, gerrymander

▶ *Selection 382*

ADVERBS

11 **politically,** governmentally, civically, partisanly, geopolitically, diplomatically, publicly

51 Anarchy

NOUNS

1 **anarchy,** anarchism, confusion, lawlessness, arrogation, defiance of authority, lack of authority, breakdown of authority, breakdown of law and order; subversion, sedition, revolution, revolt; unrestraint, indiscipline, disobedience, insubordination; breakdown of government, overthrow, coup, coup d'état

▶ *Disobedience 427; Powerlessness 515; Disorder 766*

2 **confusion,** disorder, unruliness, disorderliness, disruption, disorganization, turmoil, chaos, riot, tohubohu

▶ *Disorder 766*

3 **anarchism,** nihilism, antinomianism, syndicalism, anarcho-syndicalism, ochlocracy, mobocracy; mob rule, reign of terror, law of the jungle, every man for himself, dog eat dog

4 **anarchist,** nihilist, antinomian, syndicalist, anarcho-syndicalist; revolutionary, rebel, subversive, seditionary, anarch [Arch]

▶ *War 76; Resistance 417; Disobedience 427*

ADJECTIVES

5 **anarchic,** anarchical, confused, lawless, arrogating, defiant; subversive, seditious, revolutionary, rebellious; unrestrained, undisciplined, disobedient, insubordinate, ungoverned

6 **disorderly,** unruly, disruptive, disorganized, disordered, in turmoil, chaotic, wild, riotous; wildcat, uncontrolled, unrestrained, unbridled, unreined, rampant

7 **anarchistic,** nihilistic, antinomian, syndicalistic, ochlocratic, mobocratic

VERBS

8 **be anarchic,** cause anarchy, confuse, instigate lawlessness, usurp, usurp power *or* authority, undermine, arrogate, reject *or* defy authority, break down authority; subvert, revolt, rebel, resist control; disobey, overthrow, depose, topple (a government)

9 **cause confusion,** cause disorder, be unruly, be disorderly, disrupt, cause disarray, cause *or* throw into turmoil, reduce to chaos, riot

ADVERBS

10 **anarchically,** confusedly, lawlessly, without authority; subversively, seditiously, rebelliously; disobediently, insubordinately

11 **confusedly,** disruptively, in turmoil, chaotically, wildly, uncontrollably, unrestrainedly, rampantly, riotously

52 Authority

NOUNS

1 **authority,** rule, command, leadership, direction, governance; authoritativeness, sway, control, influence, dominance, domination, predominance, overbearance; imperiousness, lordliness, preeminence; power, might, strength, potency *or* potence; ascendancy, hegemony, mastery, magisterialness, magistrality, superiority, supremacy, seniority; manipulation, influence, pressure, patronage, puissance; hidden power, power behind the throne, string pulling, wire pulling; upper hand, whip hand, financial control, purse strings, clout [Inf]

▶ *Money 484; Power 514; Superiority 744*

2 **legal power,** legitimacy, legal *or* lawful authority, legality, law; eminent domain, right, rightful authority, divine right, prerogative, constituted *or* invested authority, delegated authority, derived authority, inherent authority; trueness, authenticity, genuineness, reliability, conclusiveness, certainty, positiveness, surety

▶ *Law 53; Right 429*

3 **authorization,** permission, approval, allowance, sanction, justification; permit, warrant, license, charter, visa, credential, reference, avowal; testimonial, testimony, declaration, evidence; say, say-so, rubber stamp

> *Evidence 339; Permission 502*

4 position of authority, office of power, high office, chair, chairmanship, directorship; chieftainship, presidency, premiership, secretariat, superintendency, inspectorship, judgeship, police rank, military rank; government post, federal post, seat of government, cabinet seat, congressional seat, Senate seat, House seat; governorship, mayoralty, consulate, proconsulate, prefecture, magistracy

> *Government 49; Law 53; Management 126*

5 acquisition of authority *or* **power,** empowerment, election, mandate, popular authority *or* mandate, people's *or* electoral mandate; selection, delegation, deputation, appointment, authorization, grant; succession, legitimate *or* royal succession, accession, coronation, anointment, consecration; seizure of power, usurpation, arrogation, assumption, takeover, coup d'état, coup, revolution, overthrowing, taking over

> *Government 49; Politics 50; Precedence 769*

6 governance, government, politics, administration, management, bureaucracy, red tape, officialism, beadledom; jurisdiction, faculty, competence *or* competency, direction, hold, grip, claws, clutches, talons, iron hand; reign, sovereignty, suzerainty, dominion, officialdom; governmental authority, big government, authorities, ruling class, the power structure; the system, the powers that be, the Establishment, Big Brother, the man [Inf], the top, the high command, the inner circle, the board, the directorship, higher-ups [Inf]

> *Government 49; Management 126*

7 person in authority, leader, director, executive, manager, superior, head, chief, boss; string puller, wire puller, tin god; ruler, autocrat, tyrant, dictator, despot, sovereign, monarch, king, queen, emperor, empress; pope, cardinal, primate, archbishop, bishop, dean, archdeacon, rabbi, swami; president, prime minister, premier, minister of state [Brit], senator, congressman, congresswoman, representative, Speaker of the House, president pro tempore of the Senate, majority leader, minority leader, House whip, Senate whip; Member of Parliament (MP) [Brit], cabinet member; governor, military governor, consul, proconsul, consul general, mayor; judge, magistrate, sheriff, constable, marshal, justice of the peace (JP), official, party official, commissioner, police officer; commander in chief, commanding officer, commander, military officer; executive officer, educator, principal, headmaster, headmistress, chancellor, vice chancellor, provost

> *Education 48; Government 49; Law 53; Military Affairs 58; Master 68; Aristocrat 70; Clergy 84; Management 126*

8 expert, master, specialist, pundit, scholar, teacher, professor, don, genius, intellectual, mentor; wise man, wise woman, sage, guru, ace, wizard *or* whiz *or* wiz; walking encyclopedia, maestro, virtuoso, connoisseur; practitioner, consultant, guide, professional; old master, old hand; [Inf]: whiz kid, pro, dab hand *or* dab, boffin [Brit]

> *Skillfulness 127; Intellect 315; Knowledge 348; Wisdom 352*

ADJECTIVES

9 authoritative, ruling, commanding, leading, governing, directing; administrative, managerial, bureaucratic, high-handed, officious, authoritarian, controlling; influential, dominant, domineering, predominant, overbearing, bossy; imperative, imperious, lordly, absolute, preeminent, peremptory, overruling; powerful, empowered, mighty, strong, potent; ascendant, hegemonic, hegemonistic, masterful, superior, supreme, senior; manipulating, high-pressure

> *Management 126; Power 514*

10 legitimate, legal, legalized, lawful, definitive, eminent, rightful, constituted, delegated; true, authentic, authenticated, official, genuine, reliable, conclusive, certain, positive, sure

> *Law 53; Right 429*

11 authorized, permitted, approved, allowed, sanctioned, justified, cleared, OK'd; warranted, licensed, chartered, accredited, avowed; testified, declared, evidentiary; empowered, elected, mandated, selected, chosen, delegated, deputized, appointed, granted; successional, accessional, crowned, ordained, coronated, anointed, consecrated

> *Power 514*

12 expert, masterly, specialized, scholarly, tutored, intellectual; knowledgeable, skilled, accomplished, professional

VERBS

13 have authority, rule, command, lead, direct, govern; be authoritarian, hold sway, control, influence, dominate, domineer, predominate, have under one's thumb, bend to one's will; be in charge, act imperiously, lord over; possess *or* exercise power, be mighty, show strength, be potent; ascend, aggress, expand, reign supreme; manipulate, pressure, patronize; pull strings, pull wires; wear the pants *or* the trousers, crack the whip, hold in the palm of one's hand, have the sayso, have over a barrel [Inf], have clout [Inf]

14 authorize, legitimize, legalize, make legal, grant lawful *or* legal authority; bestow rights, invest authority, delegate authority; grant *or* give permission, approve, allow, sanction, justify; permit, warrant, license, charter, accredit, give a referral, avow; testify, declare, present evidence

> *Law 53*

15 gain authority, empower, power, elect, mandate, select, delegate, deputize, appoint, grant; succeed to, accede, crown, coronate, ordain, anoint, consecrate; take *or* assume authority, seize power, usurp, arrogate, take over, lead a coup d'état, overthrow; mount the throne, take office, take *or* assume command, take the helm, take over the reins, gain the upper hand, get the whip hand

16 **wield authority,** rule, govern, hold the reins of government, administer, administrate, manage, officialize, legislate; hold jurisdiction over, preside over, direct; hold office, reign, sit on the throne, wear the crown, wield the scepter; rule the roost, keep order, police, lay down the law, rule with an iron hand; control the purse strings, call the shots [Inf], call the tune, throw one's weight around

17 **be an authority on,** be an expert on, master, specialize in, have expertise, be up on; know inside out, know back to front, know one's stuff, have the know-how

ADVERBS

18 **authoritatively,** with *or* by authority, powerfully, with *or* by power, ex cathedra, in the name of, by warrant of, in *or* by virtue of one's authority; dominantly, mightily, strongly, potently; commandingly, high-handedly, arrogantly, with an air of superiority, supremely

19 **legitimately,** lawfully, rightfully; truly, authentically, officially, genuinely, reliably, conclusively, certainly, positively, surely; with authorization *or* permission *or* approval; with authority, politically, administratively, managerially

20 **in authority,** in charge, in control, in command; in the driver's seat, at the wheel, at the helm, at the reins, in the saddle

21 **expertly,** in an expert manner, masterfully, masterly, ingeniously, intellectually; knowledgeably, skillfully, with skill, professionally

53 Law

Law, says the judge as he looks down his nose, / Speaking clearly and most severely, / Law is as I've told you before, / Law is as you know I suppose, / Law is but let me explain it once more, / Law is the Law. — W. H. AUDEN

NOUNS

1 **law,** the law, body of law, corpus juris, set of principles; law, bylaw, statute, decree, mandate, manifesto, ordinance, edict, order, standing order, canon, rule, rescript, precept; law and equity, constitution, written constitution, unwritten constitution, charter, institution, codification, codified law, legal code, pandect, penal code, civil code, written law, lex scripta, statute law, common law, unwritten law, private law; international law, law of nations, jus gentium, jus civile; military law, law of the sea, law of the air, law of commerce, commercial law, business law, lex mer-

catoria, contracts law, criminal law, civil law, constitutional law, law of the land, long arm of the law; canon law, ecclesiastical law, encyclical, bull

> *Litigation 54; Military Affairs 58*

2 **the Law,** Constitution of the United States of America, Bill of Rights, Corpus Juris Civilis, Codex Juris Canonici, Digest *or* Pandects of Justinian, Law of Moses, Ten Commandments, Pentateuch, Torah *or* Tora, Code of Hammurabi, Koran *or* Qur'an, Twelve Tables, Bible, Magna Carta, Napoleonic Code

> *Government 49; Religion 81*

3 **jurisdiction,** judicature, magistracy, mandate, authority, legal authority

> *Litigation 54*

4 **legal justice,** good judgment, justice served, rightfulness, lawfulness, justness, legitimacy, legality; equity, ruling, verdict, sentence, award, finding, adjudication; righteousness, unprejudiceness, fairness, fair play, impartiality

5 **legal injustice,** bad judgment, misjudgment, miscarriage of justice, false arrest, wrong verdict, wrong conviction, wrongful execution; bad law, legal flaw, loophole, let-out [Brit], contradictory law, antinomy, error of law, mistake of law, overruled verdict, overturned verdict; prejudice, malice

6 **law officer,** legal administrator, public prosecutor, judge advocate, lawyer, solicitor, district attorney (DA), officer of the court, Attorney General, federal marshal, state attorney general, prosecuting attorney, judge, sheriff, justice of the peace (JP), Crown attorney [Can], Solicitor General [Brit]

> *Litigation 54*

7 **law enforcement agency,** police force, police, the force, law enforcement agency, forces of law and order, long arm of the law, constabulary, narcotics officer, military police (MP), shore patrol (SP), airport police, mounted police, state police *or* troopers, highway patrol, special weapons and tactics (SWAT) team, Federal Bureau of Investigation (FBI), Central Intelligence Agency (CIA), Justice Department; Home Office [Brit], Royal Canadian Mounted Police, gendarmerie, international police, Interpol; [Inf]: pigs, fuzz, feds, heat

8 **law enforcement officer,** police officer, policeman *or* policewoman, law enforcer, state police, state trooper; patrolman *or* patrolwoman, traffic cop, police sergeant, desk sergeant, police lieutenant, police detective, plainclothes officer, police inspector, police superintendent, chief of police, police chief, commissioner of police, police commissioner, coroner, constable [Brit], chief constable [Brit], gendarme; provost marshal, provost guard, provost sergeant; watch, neighborhood watch, posse, posse comitatus, private detective *or* investigator (PI), detective, private police, security officer, bodyguard; [Inf]: cop, copper, flatfoot, bull, pig, smokey *or*

Smokey Bear, Mountie, dick, fly dick, private eye, narc; [Brit inf]: bobby, rozzer

▶ *Safety 810*

9 **legality,** lawfulness, licitness, legitimacy, legitimateness, validity, justice, right, keeping within the law, adherence to the law, adherence to the letter of the law, legalism, respect for the law, respect for legal principles; legalization, legitimization, decriminalization, authorization, sanction, permission, authority, license, warrant; rightfulness, genuineness, authenticity

▶ *Right 429; Permission 502*

10 **illegality,** illegitimacy, illicitness, unlawfulness, ban, proscription, veto, prohibition, impermissibility, unauthorization, irregularity

▶ *Disobedience 427; Stealing 479*

11 **lawmaking,** legislating, legislation, nomology, lawgiving, becoming law, passing into law, codification, ratification, enactment, enacting, validation, confirmation, affirmation, regulation, regulation by law, regulation by statute, constitutionality

12 **lawmaker,** legislator *or* legislatrix, legislature, lawgiver, solon

13 **jurisprudence,** nomology, science of law, knowledge of law, legal learning, law consultancy, legal advice, constitutionalism, penology *or* poenology; form of law, form, formula, legal formality, formality, rite, procedure, workings of the law, letter of the law, four corners of the law

▶ *Judgment 341*

14 **lawbreaking,** crime, trespass, offense, transgression, violation, infringement, infraction, breach, nonfeasance, encroachment, contravention, overstepping; sin, vice, fraud, wickedness, villainy, guilt, culpability, criminality, delinquency, dishonesty, improbity; crookedness, shadiness

15 **lawbreaker,** criminal, felon, offender, wrongdoer, miscreant, malefactor, villain, delinquent, culprit, convict, recidivist, thief, car thief, robber, bank robber, burglar, housebreaker, rapist, murderer; crook, mugger, jailbird; con [Inf], lag [Brit inf]

▶ *Malevolence 306; Wrong 430*

ADJECTIVES

16 **legal,** lawful, licit, legitimate, valid, just, right, proper, within the law, sanctioned; allowable, permissible, permitted, authorized, licensed, warranted, legalized, legitimized, decriminalized, according to law, by right, de jure, legit [Inf]

▶ *Right 429; Permission 502*

17 **legislative,** lawmaking, lawgiving, legislatorial, legislational, decretal, nomothetic, nomological, jurisprudential

18 **jurisdictional,** jurisdictive, judicatory, judicatorial, justiciary, regional, judiciary, juridical, justiciable, subject to jurisdiction, liable to the law

▶ *Litigation 54; Management 126*

19 **judiciary,** judicatory, judicial, judicative, inquisitional; Rhadamanthine, tribunal, magisterial, judicious

▶ *Litigation 54*

20 **law-abiding,** honest, upright, obedient, authorized, licensed, competent

▶ *Obedience 426*

21 **legitimate,** rightful, genuine, authentic, real, true

22 **legalistic,** litigious, disputatious, sententious, quibbling

23 **unlawful,** illegal, unauthorized, without authority, unlicensed, unofficial, informal, irregular, unconstitutional, instatutory, unwarranted, injudicial, extrajudicial, not covered by law, without legal backing, having no legal protection

24 **unjust,** unwarrantable, wrongful, wrong, tortuous, justiciable, cognizable, triable, actionable, accusable, punishable

▶ *Wrong 430; Accusation 442; Evil 446*

25 **offending,** breaking the law, trespassing, transgressing, violating, breaching, infringing, encroaching, sinning, bad, wicked, nefarious, heinous, villainous, guilty, culpable, criminal, felonious, dishonest, fraudulent, corrupt, crooked, shady, bent [Brit inf]

▶ *Wickedness 448; Guilt 450; Overstepping 712*

26 **lawless,** without the law, anarchic, antinomian, chaotic, every man for himself, ungovernable, licentious, riotous, rebellious, seditious, mutinous, insurgent, violent; above the law, acting as a law unto oneself, despotic, tyrannical, dictatorial, oppressive, overmighty

▶ *Anarchy 51; Insolence 400; Severity 424; Disobedience 427*

VERBS

27 **make legal,** legalize, legitimize, legitimatize, decriminalize, bring within the law; validate, sanction, allow, permit, authorize, license, warrant

28 **be legal,** come within the law, stand up in court; follow the law, abide by the law, respect the law, follow the letter of the law, keep within the law, stay on the right side of the law

29 **make illegal,** outlaw, criminalize, illegalize, ban, proscribe, veto, prohibit, forbid, punish, bastardize, illegitimize

▶ *Punishment 454; Prohibition 503*

30 **be illegal,** break the law, violate the law, circumvent the law, bend the law, twist the law, torture the law, defy the law, do wrong, offend, commit a crime; be lawless, have no law, know no law, take the law into one's own hands, please oneself, exceed one's authority, stand above the law, stand outside the law

▶ *Anarchy 51; Wrong 430*

31 **legislate,** make laws, give laws, enact, decree, ordain,

order, codify; ratify, pass, vote, confirm, affirm, formalize, endorse, vest, establish

32 **judge,** administer justice, exercise judgment, decide, pass sentence, pronounce, decree
> *Litigation 54*

33 **legally,** lawfully, judicially, jurisdictionally, jurisprudentially, juristically; within the law, by order, through the legislative process, through the courts, in court, before the bench *or* bar *or* court, in the eyes of the law; licitly, legitimately, validly, justly, rightly, properly

34 **illegally,** illicitly, unlawfully, criminally, wrongly, against the law, contrary to law, without authority, without legal backing

35 **lawlessly,** anarchically, riotously, rebelliously, violently

36 **summarily,** arbitrarily, despotically, tyrannically, dictatorially

37 **forgivingly,** mercifully, leniently, freely, guiltlessly, innocently, pardonably

38 **guiltily,** culpably, wickedly, illegally, unlawfully, against the law

54 Litigation

NOUNS

1 **litigation,** legal action, case, legal case, legal dispute, legal issue, legal remedy, action, cause of action; dispute, quarrel, issue, contest; lawsuit, suit at law, suit, countersuit, claim, counterclaim; seeking legal protection, seeking a verdict, seeking justice, going to law, matter for judgment, case for decision, test case; one's day in court
> *Disagreement 463*

2 **jurisdiction,** legal authority, dominion, mandate, cognizance; original *or* appellate jurisdiction; exclusive *or* concurrent jurisdiction; common-law *or* equitable jurisdiction; in rem jurisdiction, in personam jurisdiction, subject-matter jurisdiction, territorial jurisdiction
> *Authority 52; Region 564; Commission 833*

3 **legal process,** proceedings, legal proceedings, legal procedure, due process, course of law, (long) arm of the law; trial, inquest, hearing; legal trial, fair trial, justice seen to be done, trial by law, trial by jury, civil trial, criminal trial, trial by one's peers, trial at the bar, bench trial, assize, court sessions, sessions, court sitting; writ, stay, order, certiorari, mandamus, nisi prius

4 **litigant,** party, party to a suit, suitor; plaintiff, petitioner, claimant, libelant, pursuer, appellant; defendant, codefendant, respondent, corespondent, libelee, appellee; intervenor; accused, accused person, prisoner before the court, prisoner at the bar
> *Information 170; Accusation 442*

5 **lawyer,** attorney, attorney-at-law, counselor, counselor-at-law, legal counsel, counsel, Juris Doctor *or*

Jur. D. (J.D.), legal practitioner, member of the bar, solicitor [Brit], barrister [Brit]; jurist, agent, adviser, advocate; pettifogger, Philadelphia lawyer, ambulance chaser; [Inf]: shyster, mouthpiece, legal eagle, fixer

6 **tribunal,** seat of justice, judgment seat, inquisition
> *Judgment 341*

7 **court officer,** attorney, prosecutor, judge, clerk of the court, bailiff, summoner, process server, sheriff, court reporter

8 **law court,** court, open court, court of law, court of justice, high court; court of original jurisdiction, trial court, appellate court; court of general jurisdiction, court of limited jurisdiction; court of record; superior court, inferior court; equity court; court of sessions, criminal court; civil court

9 **type of court,** state court, federal court, county court, municipal court; police court, probate court, family court, juvenile court, night court, land court, small claims court, coroner's court, tax court, admiralty court, bankruptcy court, military court, court-martial; district court, superior court, court of appeals, state supreme court; federal district court, circuit court of appeals, United States Supreme Court

10 **judge,** justice, your honor, his *or* her honor, court, justiciar, presiding officer, hearing officer, military judge, judge advocate general; chief justice, associate justice, trial judge; magistrate, district magistrate, city magistrate, police magistrate, justice of the peace (JP); bench, judiciary, magistracy, arbiter, arbitrator, umpire, referee, assessor, estimator; Solomon, Rhadamanthys, Daniel, hanging judge
> *Judgment 341*

11 **jury,** jury panel, jury list, juror, juryman *or* jurywoman, foreman *or* foreperson of the jury; venireman, venire facias, jury of one's peers, twelve good men and true, twelve just men, twelve men in a box; grand jury, petit jury, common jury, special jury *or* struck jury, trial jury, coroner's jury, sheriff's jury

12 **courtroom,** court, courthouse, law court, bench, bar, jury box, dock, witness stand

13 **pretrial proceedings,** pleadings, complaint, summons and complaint, writ, service of process, answer, jurisdiction, citation; motion for summary judgment, demurrer; grand jury, indictment, true bill, no bill; warrant, search warrant, bench warrant, affidavit; apprehension, arrest, recitation of rights, detention, questioning, arraignment, hearing, prosecution, appointment of counsel, committal, restraint, bail, habeas corpus, surety, security, recognizance, personal recognizance; discovery, written interrogatories, deposition on oral *or* written questions, production of documents *or* things, permission to enter upon land or other property, physical and mental examination, request for admission, bill of particulars; fishing trip *or* expedition [Inf]; subpoena, witness list; plea bargaining

14 jury selection, jury service, questioning of potential jurors, voir dire, peremptory challenge, challenge for cause, impaneling a jury, sequestration, alternate jurors

15 evidence, prima facie evidence, circumstantial evidence, insufficient evidence, hearsay evidence; taking of evidence, recording of evidence; counterevidence, counterargument, rebutter, rebuttal, rejoinder, proof, demonstration, disproof

▶ *Evidence 339*

16 witness, expert witness, swearing in, oath; testimony, examination, direct examination, cross-examination, reexamination, objection sustained, objection overruled; perjury

17 closing arguments, summation; charge to the jury, instructions to the jury, jury instructions

▶ *Argument 329; Evidence 339*

18 verdict, judgment, adjudication; majority verdict, general verdict, special verdict, directed verdict, verdict contrary to law, sealed verdict; finding, finding of fact

▶ *Judgment 341*

19 favorable verdict, award of damages; acquittal, verdict of not guilty, verdict of not proven, proven innocent; successful defense, defeat of the prosecution, nonsuit, case dismissed *or* thrown out of court, dismissal for lack of evidence, no case, charge withdrawn; benefit of the doubt, innocence, clearance, exoneration, exculpation, absolution, discharge, release, liberation, deliverance, freedom, justification, compurgation, vindication, quashing, quietus; reprieve, pardon, stay, forgiveness, nonprosecution, exemption, impunity, thumbs up

▶ *Forgiveness 312; Exemption 434; Vindication 441; Innocence 449*

20 unfavorable verdict, losing the case, payment of damages, filing an appeal; conviction, condemnation, verdict of guilty, hostile verdict, hostile jury, unsuccessful defense, successful prosecution, judgment; sentence, punishment, fine, court costs, prison sentence, thumbs down

▶ *Guilt 450; Punishment 454*

ADJECTIVES

21 litigating, litigant, suing, accusing, bringing legal action against, appearing in court, appearing before the judge; claiming, contesting, objecting, disputing, arguing, quarreling, litigious, quarrelsome, argumentative

▶ *Argument 329; Accusation 442; Disagreement 463*

22 litigated, on trial, up for trial, brought before the court *or* judge, *coram judice* [L]; argued, disputed, contested, claimed, submitted for judgment, offered for arbitration, sub judice; litigable, actionable, justiciable, disputable, arguable, suable, accusable

▶ *Wrong 430*

23 jurisdictional, jurisdictive, justiciable, subject to jurisdiction, liable to the law

24 judicatory, judicatorial, judicial, judicative, jural, jurisprudential, justiciary; inquisitional, forensic; Rhadamanthine, magisterial

25 acquitted, not guilty, not proven, guiltless, innocent, clear, cleared, in the clear, exonerated, exculpated, absolved, vindicated, without a stain on one's character; uncondemned, unpunished, unchastised, let off, let go, let off the hook; discharged, released, liberated, freed, reprieved, pardoned, forgiven, recommended for leniency, recommended for mercy; immune, exempted, exempt, nonliable

26 convicted, condemned, guilty, blameworthy, liable, confessing; without a case, having no case, without a leg to stand on, nonsuited; sentenced

▶ *Guilt 450; Punishment 454*

VERBS

27 litigate, sue, bring legal action, start an action, bring a lawsuit, bring a suit, bring suit against, implead; seek legal protection, seek a verdict, seek justice, go to the law, appeal to law, set the law in motion, institute legal proceedings, petition, request, prepare a case, prepare a brief, file a brief, claim, file a claim, take to court, bring before the court *or* judge, have *or* haul before the court *or* judge; arraign, impeach, accuse, charge, prefer charges, press charges, indict, cite, summon, serve notice on; prosecute, try, put on trial, bring to trial, bring to justice, bring to the bar, interplead; argue one's case (before a jury), take the stand, swear in, testify, advocate, plead, argue

▶ *Argument 329; Accusation 442*

28 try a case, take cognizance, put down for hearing, commit for trial, impanel a jury, question potential jurors; hear a case, call witnesses, subpoena witnesses, examine, direct-examine, cross-examine, object, take statements; sit in judgment, rule, find, decide, adjudicate, judge, close the proceedings, sum up, charge the jury, sequester the jury; bring in a verdict, have the verdict read, pronounce sentence

29 stand trial, come before the court, come up for trial, be on trial, stand in the dock; plead guilty, plead not guilty, plead nolo contendere, plead to the charge, defend an action, put in one's defense, make one's defense, maintain one's innocence; submit to judgment

30 have jurisdiction over, have authority over; have power over; be in one's bailiwick, be within one's sphere

31 judge, hold court, administer justice, sit on the bench, sit in judgment, judge, hear a complaint, hear a cause of action, hear a case, try a case, take cognizance, take judicial notice, return a verdict, pass judgment, decide, pass sentence, pronounce, decree

▶ *Judgment 341*

32 acquit, find *or* pronounce not guilty, find for, prove innocent, find the case not proven, give the benefit of the doubt, find a lack of evidence, find no case to answer, clear, exonerate, exculpate, absolve, vindicate; discharge, dismiss charges, release, liberate, free, reprieve, respite, grant a respite, pardon, forgive, not press charges, not prosecute; set aside the sentence, quash, quash the conviction, remit the penalty, reduce the fine, recommend for leniency, recommend for mercy, justify, allow a dismissal, allow an appeal, abrogate, make immune, exempt, make exempt; let off, let go, let off the hook; be acquitted, get off, beat the rap [Inf]

▶ *Forgiveness 312; Exemption 434; Vindication 441; Liberation 831*

33 convict, condemn, find guilty, pronounce guilty, find against, bring in an unfavorable verdict, reject one's defense, prove guilty, find liable, sentence, reject one's appeal, reject, attaint; convict oneself, confess, sign a confession, plead guilty, stand condemned

▶ *Rejection 383; Punishment 454*

ADVERBS

34 in litigation, at law, in the matter of *or* in re, in court, before the judge, *coram judice* [L], pendente lite, litigiously

55 Prison

NOUNS

1 prison, prison house, correctional institution, minimum- *or* maximum-security facility, penitentiary, penal institution; federal prison, state prison, county jail, city jail; jail, jailhouse, lockup, compound, pound, bridewell [Brit], gaol [Brit], tolbooth [Scot]; bastille, dungeon, oubliette, hole, black hole; prison camp, concentration camp, labor camp, gulag, prison farm, prison colony, debtor's colony *or* prison; house of detention *or* correction, halfway house, reformatory, reform school, detention home, borstal *or* borstal institution [Brit]; military prison, guardhouse, brig, stockade; detention center *or* camp, internment camp, prisoner-of-war *or* POW camp

2 the inside [Inf]: pen, clink, cooler, coop, stir, slammer, joint, jug, can, tank, hoosegow *or* hoosgow, poky *or* pokey, booby hatch, big house; [Brit]: glasshouse, quod, choky *or* chokey

3 prison cell, detention cell, holding cell, cellblock, cellhouse; confinement, solitary confinement, death cell, death row; jail cell, lockup; [Inf]: solitary, bull pen, icebox, drunk tank *or* tank

4 imprisonment, confinement, restraint, incarceration, durance, durance vile, detention, detainment, internment, immurement *or* immuration; minimum- *or* maximum-security imprisonment, lockdown, solitary confinement, seclusion, corrective training, forced labor

5 arrest, capture, seizure, apprehension, house arrest, protective *or* preventive custody; captivity, entrap-

ment, restraint, constraint, astriction; binding, tying, caging, cooping, penning in, shutting in; collar [Inf]

6 prison sentence, jail sentence, period of detention, maximum *or* minimum sentence, suspended sentence, life sentence, death sentence; [Inf]: time, stretch, lag [Brit]

7 prisoner, captive, hostage, detainee, internee, prisoner of war (POW), prisoner of conscience, political prisoner; condemned prisoner, convict, inmate, chain-gang member; jailbird, trusty *or* trustee; [Inf]: lifer, con, yardbird, collar, gaolbird [Brit], lag *or* lagger [Brit]

8 prison officer, jailer, gaoler [Brit], warden, warder [Brit], superintendent, guardian, prison guard, corrections officer; caretaker, keeper, turnkey, screw [Inf]

ADJECTIVES

9 imprisoned, incarcerated, interned, immured, buried; serving a sentence; confined, held, restrained, detained, in detention; captive, in captivity, entrapped, constrained, astricted; bound, tied, caged, cooped up, penned in, shut in; [Inf]: doing time, on the inside, in the cooler, on ice, up the river, in the big house, in solitary

10 arrested, captured, remanded to custody, on remand; seized, apprehended

VERBS

11 imprison, put under security, jail, lock up, put *or* throw in jail, put behind bars, put away, pronounce a sentence; incarcerate, intern, immure, put in solitary confinement; confine, hold, restrain, detain, hold in detention; [Inf]: put in solitary, throw in the tank, throw in the cooler, jug, send up the river, send to the big house

12 arrest, put under arrest, capture, take prisoner, remand to custody, hold against one's will, hold captive *or* hostage; entrap, constrain, astrict; bind, tie, cage, coop up, pen in, shut in; seize, apprehend, impound; [Inf]: nab, collar, nick [Brit]

13 be in prison, serve a sentence, join the chain gang; [Inf]: do time, land in the cooler, serve a stretch, lag [Brit]

ADVERBS

14 in prison, under maximum *or* minimum security, in jail, under lock and key, behind bars, on death row, on the inside [Inf], on ice [Inf]

56 Economics

The Dismal Science. — THOMAS CARLYLE

NOUNS

1 economics, economic policy, fiscal policy, monetary policy, economic growth, microeconomics, macroeconomics; economic system, mixed economy, centrally planned economy, welfare economics, private enterprise, privatization, public enterprise, nationalization, denationalization, public ownership, state-owned industry, bimetallism, autarky; economic theory, classical economics, Keynesian economics, capitalism, capitalist system, communism, socialism, socialist system, supply-side economics, trickle-down theory, laissez faire, invisible hand, physiocratic school

2 **home economics,** thrifty management, husbandry, conservation; economizing, home management, budgeting, keeping to one's budget, conserving, saving, thriftiness; cutting corners, tightening one's belt, making ends meet

> ◗ *Finance 457*

3 **economy,** market, free-market economy, national economy, national income *or* earnings; economic sector, financial sector, private sector, personal sector, corporate sector, public sector, foreign sector; healthy *or* sound economy, weak economy

> ◗ *Finance 457; Trade 480; Sale 482; Price 494; Production 522*

4 **economic indicator,** economic statistics, economic analysis, financial analysis, econometrics, regression analysis; gross national product (GNP), price index, consumer price index (CPI), retail price index (RPI), unemployment rate, cost-of-living index; economic productivity, prices, vital statistics, national debt, budget deficit; exchange rate, exchange rate mechanism (ERM)

5 **economic development,** economic growth, industrialization, developed country, undeveloped country; capital accumulation, capital investment, public debt, improved technology, research and development (R and D), improved productivity, restructuring of industry, demographic transition, population growth, market expansion

> ◗ *Finance 457; Improvement 807*

6 **economic organization,** International Finance Corporation (IFC), International Development Association, International Bank for Reconstruction and Development (IBRD) *or* World Bank, International Monetary Fund (IMF); trade organization, North American Free Trade Association (NAFTA), European Free Trade Association (EFTA), European Union (EU), Organization of Petroleum-Exporting Countries (OPEC), Benelux, Council for Mutual Economic Assistance (COMECON), Group of Seven (G7), Caribbean Community and Common Market (CARICOM), Latin American Integration Association (LAIA), Organization of African Unity (OAU), Organization of American States (OAS), Organization for Economic Cooperation and Development (OECD)

7 **international trade,** free trade, free-trade zone, economic zone, commerce, restraint of trade, economic union, trade integration, visible trade, invisible trade, balance of trade, balance of payments; trade agreement, restrictive trade agreement, General Agreement

on Tariffs and Trade (GATT); foreign market, Pacific Rim, Third World; import, export, duty, tariff, trade barrier, customs barrier, tariff barrier, protection quota, intervention; free goods, free port

> ◗ *Agreement 462; Trade 480*

8 **economic factor,** economic force, capital market, buyer's market, seller's market, supply and demand, competition, monopoly, cartel, revenue, sales revenue, pricing, profit, profit motive, profit margin, technology, automation, productivity, production, production costs, production efficiency, distribution, price controls, fiscal policy; public expenditure, employment rate, unemployment rate, disposable income, consumer spending, consumer savings, purchasing power, wages, real wages, pay increases; business cycle, price-wage spiral, tax increase, tax decrease, tax bracket, interest rates, balance of payments, money supply, exchange rate, standard of living, income, gross income, net income; economic upturn, boom, boom/bust cycle, economic downturn, recession, depression, slump, stagflation, inflation, inflationary spiral, deflation, disinflation, stagnation, deficit financing, deficit spending

> ◗ *Government 49; Politics 50; Management 126; Finance 457; Market 483; Production 522*

9 **economist,** economic expert, political economist, economic analyst, financial analyst, business analyst

> ◗ *Management 126*

ADJECTIVES

10 **economic,** fiscal, monetary, pecuniary, financial, budgetary, inflationary, deflationary; mercantile, commercial, commercialistic, export, import, nationalized, privatized

VERBS

11 **economize,** conserve, save, use sparingly, manage, husband, budget; nationalize, privatize

12 **trade,** trade with, open a trade, traffic in, export, import; negotiate, barter, market, merchandise

ADVERBS

13 **economically,** fiscally, financially, commercially, profitably

57 Labor Relations

NOUNS

1 **labor relations,** industrial relations, management-employee relations, labor-management relations, union-management relations, work relations, workforce relations; employee relations, employer–employee relations, on-the-job relations, employment relations; social charter, employee rights, employer rights, employee jurisdiction, employer jurisdiction, employers' organization *or* association

2 **work** *or* **working practices,** custom and practice, terms and conditions, employment laws, employment contract, employment rules, workplace rules, joint

regulations; industrial unionism, unionism; unfair labor practices, featherbedding

3 employer, manager, boss, employment manager; director, managing director, executive, overseer, supervisor, head of the department *or* department head; training officer, personnel manager, personnel office; arbitrator, mediator, counselor, conciliator
▸ *Master 68; Management 126*

4 employee, worker, wage earner, wageworker, staff member; white-collar worker, nonmanual worker, skilled worker, semiskilled worker, unskilled worker, blue-collar worker, manual worker, laborer; part-time worker, freelance worker, hourly worker
▸ *Worker 123*

5 organized labor, labor union, trade union, international union organization, World Federation of Trade Unions (WFTU), International Confederation of Free Trade Unions (ICFTU), International Federation of Christian Trade Unions (IFCTU); national union organization, American Federation of Labor–Congress of Industrial Organizations (AFL–CIO), Trades Union Congress (TUC) [Brit]; independent union, general union, craft union, guild, industrial union, in-company union, white-collar union, blue-collar union, public sector union, union shop, union branch, union demands, union dues, union subscriptions, closed shop, open shop

6 union member, unioned employee; organizer, union organizer, labor organizer; shop steward, councilor, convenor; labor union official, national official, district official, elected representative, health and safety representative, staff representative, workplace representative

7 industrial dispute, labor dispute, industrial conflict, industrial strife, strike; employee claim, claim, grievance, complaint, whipsaw tactics, political action, work-to-rule

8 strike, striking, walkout, work stoppage, union strike, strike notice, called strike, organized strike, general strike, mass strike, industry-wide strike, official strike, approved strike, sympathy strike, unofficial strike, wildcat strike, spontaneous strike, sit-down strike, sit-in, stay-in strike, lightning strike [Brit]; slowdown, work-in, ca'canny [Brit inf]; organized boycott, boycott; picketing, picket line, secondary picketing, flying picket; striker, picket; strikebreaking, overtime ban, management lock-out, sympathy lock-out, crossing the picket lines; strikebreaker, scab, rat [Inf], goon [Inf]; strike settlement, pattern settlement, disputes procedure, grievance procedure, joint consultation; negotiations, breakdown in negotiations, arbitration, arbitration of rights, arbitration of interests, voluntary arbitration, compulsory arbitration, arbitration tribunal, arbitration court, arbitration award; me-

diation, conciliation; Taft–Hartley Act, eighty-day injunction
▸ *Persuasion 178; Conversation 210; Cessation 668*

9 bargaining, collective bargaining, company-wide bargaining, association bargaining, salary negotiations, industrial tribunal, collective agreement; employee negotiations, negotiating, negotiations, labor negotiations; negotiating rights, negotiated points; common rule, no strike–no lockout agreement, multiemployer agreement, piecemeal agreement; management practices, employee practices, management demands, employee demands, labor-management body, works council, labor force, work group
▸ *Work 122; Command 425; Agreement 462; Trade 480; Accord 735*

10 bargaining terms, negotiation points; nonwage demands, union recognition, employment standards, conditions of employment, employer's liability; modernization, automation, computerization; compensation, employee compensation, pay differential, wage rates, minimum wages, sliding-scale rates, cost-of-living adjustment, systematic wage structure, method of payment, bonuses, disability, sick leave, maternity leave, paternity leave; training and education, induction training, on-the-job *or* in-service training; hours worked, working hours, minimum hours, make-work rules, overtime work, night-shift work; work measurement, work efficiency, work achievement, employee incentive programs; seniority, promotion, hiring practices, probationary period, contractual obligations, violation of contract, disciplinary procedure, discipline, transfers, retraining, grounds for dismissal, laying off, layoff, firing, redundancy [Brit], excessing, sacking [Inf]; worker participation, work demarcation, allocation of work, job description, job flexibility; safety and health, accident prevention, guaranteed wage *or* payments, workman's compensation, retirement, voluntary retirement, early retirement
▸ *Ill Health 114; Money 484; Payment 489; Absence 576; Time 639; Newness 652; Safety 810; Ease 819*

11 benefits, fringe benefits; health insurance, life insurance, disability insurance; profit-sharing, holidays, vacation time, flextime *or* flexitime; employer contributions, pension program
▸ *Health 113; Finance 457; Safety 810*

12 labor law, industrial law, uniform labor law policy, right-to-work law, National Labor Relations Act (NLRA)
▸ *Law 53*

ADJECTIVES

13 industrial, employer, employee, labor, work, employment, employed, employing, employable, contractual, contracting, contracted, regulatory, collective, piecemeal, managerial, managed, managing, supervised, supervising, working, worked, wage-earning, staff, manual, nonmanual, skilled, semiskilled, un-skilled

14 **unionized,** union, organized, independent, in-company, public-sector, white-collar, blue-collar, closed, open

15 **disputed,** argued, negotiated, bargained; work-to-rule, slow-down, sit-in, sit-down, stay-in, work-in; picketed, picketing, striking, industry-wide, official, unofficial, wildcat, spontaneous; boycotted, boycotting; strikebreaking, arbitrated, arbitrating, mediated, conciliatory, injunctive

16 **negotiated,** negotiating, negotiable; sliding-scale, cost-of-living, systematic, profit-sharing, fringe; featherbedded, featherbedding, overtime, night-shift

17 **hired,** hiring, probationary, promoted, retraining, retrained, modernized, modernizing, automated, computerized; disciplinary, disciplining, disciplined, dismissed, laid off, fired, excessed, sacked [Inf]

VERBS

18 **employ,** hire, give a job to, offer employment, train, provide on-the-job or in-service training; retrain, promote; conduct employee relations, meet contractual obligations; modernize, automate, computerize; discipline, demote, dismiss, fire, lay off, excess, sack [Inf]

19 **be employed,** gain employment, work, work overtime, work the night shift, work on flexitime or flextime, contract for employment, take on a job; resign, quit, walk out

20 **have an industrial dispute,** complain, take action, work to rule; slow down, stop work, walk out, sit in, sit down; strike, call a strike, call out, boycott; lock out, cross picket lines; settle a strike, negotiate, arbitrate, mediate

21 **unionize,** organize, bargain, bargain collectively, negotiate, negotiate a contract, approve a contract

ADVERBS

22 **industrially,** contractually, under contract, collectively, together, managerially, under supervision, with supervision, manually, with one's hands, through negotiations, on the job, independently, officially, unofficially, spontaneously, through arbitration, conciliatorily

58 Military Affairs

War is much too serious a matter to be entrusted to the military. — CHARLES MAURICE DE TALLEYRAND-PÉRIGORD

NOUNS

1 **military affairs,** military science, military strategy, grand strategy, general policy, war, war plans, art of war, strategic objectives, military tactics, military operations, logistics, battle plan, campaign; command of the sea, command of the air; mobilization, military service, recruiting, compulsory service, conscription,

conscripting, the draft, impressment; military installations, headquarters (HQ), base, camp, barracks, billet, military equipment
▶ *War 76; Plan 387; Preparation 388*

2 **the military,** armed forces, military forces, the service, army, National Guard, air force, navy, marines; active forces or standing army, ready reserves, standby reserves, retired reserves; volunteer army; mercenary forces, Territorial Army [Brit], militia, citizen's army; military branch, branch of service, Pentagon
▶ *Combatant 77; Security 464*

3 **military training,** boot camp, maneuvers, officer training, National War College, United States Military Academy (West Point), United States Naval Academy (Annapolis), United States Air Force Academy, Reserve Officers Training Corps (ROTC); [Brit]: Imperial Defence College, Royal Military College (Sandhurst), Royal Naval College (Dartmouth), Royal Air Force Academy (Cranwell), Royal Military College of Canada; *École Spéciale Militaire* [Fr]
▶ *Education 48*

4 **military organization,** Department of Defense, Joint Chiefs of Staff, theater of operations command, operational command; field army, army group, army corps, rank, division, brigade, regiment, battalion, squadron, troop, company, battery, platoon, section, squad, detail, party, band, unit, detachment, combat team; combat unit, commando unit, support unit, administrative unit; flight, wing, division, command; fleet, operational fleet, task group, amphibious force squadron, flotilla, destroyer flotilla, support fleet, auxiliary fleet, reserve fleet, outfit

5 **military staff,** general staff, Joint Chiefs of Staff, Supreme Headquarters Allied Powers, Europe (SHAPE), Defence Council [Brit]; army staff, air force staff, navy staff, military headquarters staff; commander, chief of staff, deputy chief of staff, staff officers, plans and operations staff, training staff, supply staff, personnel staff, intelligence staff, military intelligence

6 **military position,** commanding officer, general officer, flag officer, field grade officer, company grade of-

ficer, junior officer, noncommissioned officer (NCO); field army commander, task force commander
  ▶ *Combatant 77*

7 **military law,** Uniform Code of Military Justice; court-martial, general court-martial, special court-martial
  ▶ *Law 53*

8 **military custom,** militarism, military tradition, military bearing, military salute, military band, military music, military honors, military spirit, morale

9 **military honor,** honors, honorable discharge, knight, knighthood, decoration, medal; title, spurs, badge, pips, stripes, star, gold star, garter, order; military dishonor, military disgrace, dishonorable discharge, disgrace to one's uniform, conduct unbecoming an officer

ADJECTIVES

10 **military,** martial, militant, army, naval, air force, marine, service, fighting, soldierly, gladiatorial; strategic, tactical, offensive, defensive, preemptive; aggressive, pugnacious, combative, bellicose, warlike, belligerent, gung-ho [Inf]

  ▶ *Combatant 77*

11 **enlisted,** volunteer, conscripted, drafted, commissioned, noncommissioned, regular, irregular, reserve, combatant, noncombatant

12 **honored,** decorated, knighted, honorable; dishonored, disgraced; dishonorable, disgraceful

VERBS

13 **enlist,** join up, join the service; call to the colors, recruit, conscript, draft, impress, mobilize

14 **honor,** decorate, knight, wreath, crown; dishonor, disgrace

ADVERBS

15 **militarily,** martially, strategically, tactically, offensively, defensively, preemptively

16 **with honor,** honorably, with distinction; dishonorably, disgracedly, disgracefully

59 Assembly

NOUNS

1 **assembly,** assemblage, group, party, herd, audience, congregation

UNITED STATES MILITARY RANKS

ARMY	NAVY	AIR FORCE	MARINE CORPS
Officers	**Officers**	**Officers**	**Officers**
General of the Army	Fleet Admiral	General of the Air Force	General
General	Admiral	General	Lieutenant General
Lieutenant General	Vice Admiral	Lieutenant General	Major General
Major General	Rear Admiral (upper half)	Major General	Brigadier General
Brigadier General	Commodore (wartime only)	Brigadier General	Colonel
Colonel	Rear Admiral (lower half)	Colonel	Lieutenant Colonel
Lieutenant Colonel	Captain	Lieutenant Colonel	Major
Major	Commander	Major	Captain
Captain	Lieutenant Commander	Captain	First Lieutenant
First Lieutenant	Lieutenant	First Lieutenant	Second Lieutenant
Second Lieutenant	Lieutenant (junior grade)	Second Lieutenant	
	Ensign		**Warrant Officers**
Warrant Officers		**Warrant Officers**	[same as Army]
Chief Warrant Officer (W-4)	**Warrant Officers**	[same as Army]	
Chief Warrant Officer (W-3)	[same as Army]		**Enlisted Personnel**
Chief Warrant Officer (W-2)		**Enlisted Personnel**	Sergeant Major of the
Warrant Officer (W-1)	**Enlisted Personnel**	Chief Master Sergeant of the	Marine Corps (only one)
	Master Chief Petty Officer of	Air Force (only one)	Sergeant Major or Master
	the Navy (only one)	Chief Master Sergeant	Gunnery Sergeant
Enlisted Personnel	Master Chief Petty Officer	Senior Master Sergeant	First Sergeant or Master
Sergeant Major of the Army	Senior Chief Petty Officer	Master Sergeant	Sergeant
(only one)	Chief Petty Officer	Technical Sergeant	Gunnery Sergeant
Command Sergeant Major	Petty Officer First Class	Staff Sergeant	Staff Sergeant
or Sergeant Major	Petty Officer Second Class	Sergeant or Senior Airman	Sergeant
First Sergeant or Master	Petty Officer Third Class	Airman First Class	Corporal
Sergeant	Seaman	Airman	Lance Corporal
Sergeant First Class	Seaman Apprentice	Airman Basic	Private First Class
Staff Sergeant/Specialist 6	Seaman Recruit		Private
Sergeant/Specialist 5			
Corporal/Specialist 4			
Private First Class			
Private			

2 collection, gathering, collecting, ingathering, forgathering, grouping; mobilization, muster, rally, call-up; combination, joining together, bringing together, coming together, junction, collocation, colligation

◗ *Union 752; Connection 754; Combination 757*

3 party, group, body, band, company, set, bunch, gang; cabal, alliance, federation, faction, wing; mob, outfit, force, side, league, ring, camp; committee, working committee, council, commission, panel, board, council, cabinet; sect, denomination, church, fellowship

◗ *Politics 50; Relatedness 727; Part 760; Cooperation 827*

4 association, organization, society, club, lodge, secret society, order, house; union, trade union, guild, syndicate, fellowship, brotherhood, fraternity, confraternity, fraternal order, fraternal society, sisterhood, sorority; labor union, trade union, cooperative

◗ *Labor Relations 57; Sociability 408; Union 752*

5 conference, symposium, convention, convocation, colloquium, congress, caucus, synod, diet, council, legislature, conclave; meeting, assembly, gathering, meet; sitting, session, board meeting, business meeting, discussion group; concourse, turnout

◗ *Government 49; Politics 50*

6 rally, mass meeting, demonstration, protest meeting, sit-in, demo [Inf]

◗ *Demonstration 331; Protest 507*

7 social gathering, get-together, reunion, gathering of the clans; party, celebration, festival, fiesta, festivity, social, fete; reception, breakfast, lunch, dinner, function, dance, ball; stag party, hen party [Inf], open house, at-

---

COLLECTIVE NAMES FOR CREATURES

army: ants, caterpillars, frogs, herring
bale: turtles
band: jays
barrel: monkeys
barren: mules
bask: crocodiles
bevy: larks, pheasants, quails, roebucks, roe deer
bloat: hippopotami
brace: greyhounds
brood: chickens, pheasants
building: rooks
bury: rabbits
business: ferrets, flies
cast: hawks
catch: fish
cete: badgers
charm: finches, hummingbirds
chattering: choughs, starlings
clew: worms
cloud: grasshoppers
clowder: cats
cluster: cats
clutter: cats
colony: ants, frogs, penguins, rabbits
company: parrots
congregation: plovers
convocation: eagles
couple: spaniels
cover: coots
covey: grouse, partridges, quails
crash: rhinoceros, seals
deceit: lapwings
descent: woodpeckers
desert: lapwings

destruction: wildcats
dissimulation: birds
dopping: sheldrakes
dout: wildcats
down: hares
doylt: swine
dray: squirrels
drift: hogs, swans
drove: asses, bullocks, cattle, hares, horses, ponies
dule: doves
earth: foxes
exaltation: larks
fall: woodcocks
field: racehorses
flight: goshawks, hawks, swallows
flock: chickens, goats, lice, lions, parrots, sheep
fluther: jellyfish
gaggle: geese
gam: whales
gang: elks
glean: herring
gulp: swallows
harras: horses
herd: antelope, asses, bison, buffaloes, cattle, cranes, curlews, deer, elephants, giraffes, goats, horses, pigs, seals, swans, wolves, wrens, zebras
hill: ruffs
hive: bees
host: sparrows
hover: trout
husk: hares
kennel: dogs
kindle: kittens

knot: toads
labor: moles
leap: leopards
leash: greyhounds, merlins
litter: kittens, pigs, puppies
mob: kangaroos, whales
murder: crows
murmuration: starlings
muster: peacocks, penguins
mustering: storks
mutation: thrushes
mute: hares, hounds
nest: vipers
nye: pheasants
obstinacy: buffaloes
ostentation: peacocks
pace: asses
pack: dogs, grouse, hounds, wolves
paddling: ducks
pandemonium: parrots
parade: elephants
parcel: penguins
parliament: owls
party: jays
pass: asses
peep: chickens
plague: locusts
pod: seals, whales
pride: lions
quantity: smelt
rafter: turkeys
rag: colts
rake: mules
richness: martens
rookery: rooks, seals
rout: wolves
route: wolves
run: fish, poultry, whales

safe: ducks
sawt: lions
school: fish, mackerel, porpoises, whales
serge: herons
shoal: bass, fish, herring, mackerel
shrewdness: apes
siege: herons
singular: boars
skein: geese
skulk: foxes
sleuth: bears, hounds
sloth: bears
smack: jellyfish
sorde: mallards
sounder: boars, swine
sowse: lions
span: mules
spring: teals
stare: owls
string: ponies
stud: mares
swarm: bees, eels, locusts
team: ducks, oxen
tidings: magpies
tittering: magpies
trace: hares
tribe: goats, monkeys
trip: goats
troop: kangaroos, monkeys
true love: turtledoves
turmoil: porpoises
turn: turtles
unkindness: ravens
walk: snipe
watch: nightingales
wedge: swans
zeal: zebras

home, soirée, housewarming, do [Brit]; shindig *or* shindy [Inf], bash [Inf]

> ◗ *Celebration 405; Sociability 408*

8 **group,** grouping, party, company, body, band, gang, pack, ring, circle, posse, bevy, crowd, bunch; peer group, age group, cohort, compeers, social group; clique, set, coterie, cadre, in-crowd, in-group; family, household, community, class, clan, tribe, people

> ◗ *Sociology 2; Class 777*

9 **team,** squad, crew, outfit, complement, corps; troupe, cast, company; orchestra, band, rock group, pop group, combo [Inf]

> ◗ *Drama and Theater 136; Music 140*

10 **force,** armed force, army, troop, squadron, squad, platoon, unit, regiment, corps, battalion, division, brigade, legion, fleet; work force, workers, staff, personnel, manpower, crew, factory floor, shop floor

> ◗ *Military Affairs 58; Combatant 77; Worker 123*

11 **crowd,** mob, mass, throng, multitude, horde, host, swarm, all and then some; flood, deluge, spate, surge, stream, storm, crush, squeeze, press

> ◗ *Humankind 18; Excess 99; Generality 778; Multitude 795*

12 **assembling,** herd, roundup, shepherding, driving, corraling, marshaling, rodeo

13 **assemblage,** collection, set, batch; accumulation, congeries, agglomeration, conglomeration, aggregation, hoard, store, stockpile; mass, heap, pile, stack, mound; bundle, wad, clump, cluster; arrangement, bunch, bouquet, nosegay, posy, spray

> ◗ *Excess 99; Store 105; Combination 757*

14 **compilation,** collection, corpus, compendium, anthology, chrestomathy, composition; exhibition, show, display

> ◗ *Mixture 751*

15 **miscellany,** miscellanea, variety, collectanea; medley, assortment, mixture, mixed bag, mixed lot; potpourri, smorgasbord, jumble, hodgepodge; sundries, oddments, bits and pieces, odds and ends

> ◗ *Mixture 751; Part 760*

COLLECTIVE NAMES BY CREATURE

antelopes: herd
ants: army, colony
apes: shrewdness
asses: drove, herd, pace, pass
badgers: cete
bass: shoal
bears: sleuth, sloth
bees: hive, swarm
birds: dissimulation
bison: herd
boar: singular, sounder
buffaloes: herd, obstinacy
bullocks: drove
caterpillars: army
cats: clowder, cluster, clutter
cattle: drove, herd
chickens: brood, flock, peep
choughs: chattering
colts: rag
coots: cover
cranes: herd
crocodiles: bask
crows: murder
curlews: herd
deer: herd
dogs: kennel, pack
doves: dule
ducks: paddling, safe, team
eagles: convocation
eels: swarm
elephants: herd, parade
elks: gang
ferrets: business

finches: charm
fish: catch, run, school, shoal
flies: business
foxes: earth, skulk
frogs: army, colony
geese: gaggle, skein
giraffes: herd
goats: flock, herd, tribe, trip
goshawks: flight
grasshoppers: cloud
greyhounds: brace, leash
grouse: covey, pack
hares: down, drove, husk, mute, trace
hawks: cast, flight
herons: serge, siege
herring: army, glean, shoal
hippopotami: bloat
hogs: drift
horses: drove, harras, herd
hounds: mute, pack, sleuth
hummingbirds: charm
jays: band, party
jellyfish: fluther, smack
kangaroos: mob, troop
kittens: kindle, litter
lapwings: deceit, desert
larks: bevy, exaltation
leopards: leap
lice: flock
lions: flock, pride, sawt, sowse, troop
locusts: plague, swarm
mackerel: school, shoal

magpies: tidings, tittering
mallards: sorde
mares: stud
martens: richness
merlins: leash
moles: labor
monkeys: barrel, tribe, troop
mules: barren, rake, span
nightingales: watch
owls: parliament, stare
oxen: team
parrots: company, flock, pandemonium
partridges: covey
peacocks: muster, ostentation
penguins: colony, muster, parcel
pheasants: brood, bevy, nye
pigs: herd, litter
plovers: congregation
ponies: drove, string
porpoises: school, turmoil
poultry: run
puppies: litter
quails: bevy, covey
rabbits: bury, colony
racehorses: field
ravens: unkindness
rhinoceros: crash
roebucks: bevy
roe deer: bevy
rooks: building, rookery

ruffs: hill
seals: crash, herd, pod, rookery
sheep: flock
sheldrakes: dopping
smelt: quantity
snipes: walk
spaniels: couple
sparrows: host
squirrels: dray
starlings: chattering, murmuration
storks: mustering
swallows: flight, gulp
swans: drift, herd, wedge
swine: sounder, doylt
teals: spring
thrushes: mutation
toads: knot
trout: hover
turkeys: rafter
turtledoves: true love
turtles: bale, turn
vipers: nest
whales: gam, mob, pod, run, school
wildcats: destruction, dout
wolves: herd, pack, rout, route
woodcocks: fall
woodpeckers: descent
worms: clew
wrens: herd
zebras: herd, zeal

16 **construction,** assembly, assemblage, collage, montage, construction, erection, connection; fitting *or* joining *or* piecing *or* putting together; manufacture, fabrication, assembly line, production line, assembly plant
> *Production 522; Connection 754*

17 **collector,** accumulator, assembler, gatherer, gleaner, fancier, enthusiast, connoisseur; beachcomber, harvester, reaper; hoarder, pack rat
> *Agriculture 16; Store 105; Payment 489*

ADJECTIVES

18 **assembled,** gathered, congregate, congregated, convened, summoned, mobilized, called-up, herded, mustered, shepherded, rounded up

19 **collected,** amassed, massed, accumulated, hoarded, stockpiled, heaped, piled, stacked, put together

20 **cumulate,** glomerate, conglomerate, agglomerate, aggregate, convergent, confluent, collective, combined, joined, united, connected

21 **grouped,** clumped, clustered, bunched, arranged; bundled, packaged, parceled, baled, trussed, wrapped, wrapped up, fasciculate; congressional, congregational, factional, cabalistic

22 **crowded,** packed, jam-packed, crammed, chockablock, dense, close, serried; seething, teeming, swarming, bristling, milling, crawling

VERBS

23 **assemble,** collect, gather, bring together, draw together, group, group together; accumulate, agglomerate, aggregate, mass, amass; hoard, store, stockpile, heap, pile, stack, build up, bank
> *Store 105*

24 **group,** batch, clump, cluster, bunch, bundle, parcel, package, wrap, bale, truss, bind

25 **come together,** collect, gather, forgather, meet, rendezvous; congregate, group, flock; gather around, rally around, huddle, cluster, bunch

26 **crowd,** mass, throng, pack, cram, mill, mill around; seethe, teem, crawl, swarm, horde, troop, flood, stream, pour, surge, sweep, flow, rush
> *Multitude 795*

27 **band together,** get together, join forces, unite, team up, join up, link up, gang up, fall in, swell the ranks
> *Cooperation 827*

28 **call together,** convene, convoke, summon, call a meeting, hold a meeting, muster, marshal, rally, mobilize, call up

29 **herd,** shepherd, round up, corral, drive, drive together, whip in, call in

30 **put together,** compose, compile, colligate, connect, join, unite, combine, fit *or* join *or* piece together, construct, erect, fabricate, manufacture, make; reassemble, rejoin, put back together
> *Production 522; Union 752; Connection 754; Combination 757*

ADVERBS

31 **together,** unitedly, collectively, all together, en masse, in a mass, in a body, as one

32 **cliquishly,** exclusively, denominationally, communally, as one, fraternally, confraternally, sisterly; cooperatively, jointly, conjointly, in partnership, in association, societally; institutionally, as an institution, corporately, monopolistically; racially, tribally, clannishly

60 Habitat

NOUNS

1 **habitat,** environment, surroundings; microhabitat, ecosystem; territory, range, domain, element, terrain; locality, locale, environs, haunt, purlieu, home ground, base, bailiwick, own backyard, neighborhood, stamping ground, hangout [Inf]
> *Geology 8; Region 564; Location 565; Situation 573; Surroundings 615; Circumstances 726*

2 **habitation,** abode, dwelling, dwelling place, residence, place of residence, domicile, place, place where one lives *or* resides, home, house, roof over one's head, accommodations, quarters, living quarters, lodgings, lodging, billet, rooms; [Inf]: crash pad, digs, crib
> *Inhabitant 61; Address 209*

3 **home,** domicile, homestead, home sweet home, household, hearth and home, hearth, fireside, inglenook, base, nest, place where one hangs one's hat; hometown, birthplace, cradle, homeland, native land, motherland, fatherland
> *Base 601*

4 **house,** town house, semidetached house, duplex, detached house, row house, split-level house; prefabricated house, prefab, modular house; ranch house, farmhouse, country house, vacation home; lodge, bungalow, cottage, cabin, log cabin; wigwam, tepee *or* tipi, hogan, igloo
> *Architecture 134; Property 470*

5 **mansion,** stately home, estate, ancestral hall *or* seat, manor house; palace, castle; château, villa; grange, hacienda, plantation

6 **official residence,** presidential palace, governor's mansion; embassy, consulate; vicarage, rectory, parsonage, deanery, manse

7 **apartment,** room, rooms, pied-à-terre; suite; penthouse, studio, duplex, maisonette; flat [Brit], bed-sitter [Brit]

8 **apartment house,** tower block, apartment complex, tenement, high-rise apartments *or* flats [Brit]; cooperative apartment house *or* co-op; condominium *or* condo [Inf]
> *Structure 551; Space 563; Container 578*

9 **room,** chamber; entryway, entrance hall, vestibule, foyer, lobby, anteroom; hall, hallway, corridor, breeze-

way; reception room, waiting room, drawing room, salon, front room, parlor; living room, sitting room, lounge; dining room, dining hall, dinette, breakfast room, breakfast nook, canteen, mess hall, messroom; kitchen, kitchenette, galley; pantry, larder, scullery, stillroom; utility room, laundry room, sewing room, closet, cloakroom, checkroom, dressing room; den, family room, snug *or* snuggery [Brit]; recreation room *or* rec room [Inf], game room, rumpus room, playroom; study, library, studio, workroom, office; bedroom, bedchamber, boudoir, master bedroom, nursery, dormitory *or* dorm room [Inf]; bathroom, washroom, rest room, lavatory, toilet, water closet (WC), comfort station, lav [Inf], loo [Brit inf]; storeroom, storage room, junk room, box room [Brit]; cellar, basement, subbasement, glory hole, bunker; loft, attic, garret; conservatory, solarium; porch, portico, sun porch, sunroom, sun lounge, sleeping porch

▶ *Architecture 134*

10 **shack,** shed, hut, lean-to, hutch, shanty, hovel, tumbledown shack, squat, outhouse, booth, slum; hole, rathole, pigsty, pigpen, dump [Inf]

▶ *Poverty 486*

11 **mobile home,** trailer, motor home, recreational vehicle (RV), camper, camper truck, caravan [Brit]; houseboat, yacht; tent, tepee *or* tipi, wigwam

12 **hotel,** hostelry, inn, motel, motor inn *or* lodge, lodge, guesthouse, bed-and-breakfast (B and B), bed and lodging, youth hostel, bed and board, boardinghouse, rooming house, flophouse, dormitory, pension; [Inf]: dorm, fleabag, dive, joint

13 **retreat,** haven, refuge, sanctuary, hideaway, halfway house, sheltered housing *or* shelter, hospice

▶ *Refuge 812*

14 **zoo,** zoological garden, menagerie, marine park, sea zoo; vivarium, terrarium; animal shelter

15 **cage,** hutch, cote, run; barn, stable, stall; cowshed, byre [Brit]; fold; sty, pigsty, pigpen; kennel, pound; dog pound, doghouse; cattery; coop, chicken coop, henhouse, hencoop, hennery, brooder; birdhouse, aviary, birdcage, dovecote, pigeon loft, columbary, roost; aquarium, fishtank

▶ *Mammals 35; Birds 36; Fishes 38; Enclosure 619*

16 **natural habitat,** lair, den, cave, couch, lodge; hole, covert, burrow, warren, tunnel, earth; nest, aerie *or* eyrie, perch, roost; beehive, apiary, hornet's nest, wasp's nest, vespiary; anthill

▶ *Mammals 35; Birds 36; Insects and Arachnids 40*

ADJECTIVES

17 **environmental,** surrounding, neighborhood, territorial, local, urban, suburban, built-up, metropolitan, inner-city

▶ *Region 564; Cities, Towns, and Villages 567*

18 **inhabiting,** abiding, residing, residential, residentiary, resident, in residence, at home, dwelling, living, stay-

ing, domiciled, housed, roofed, lodged, billeted, sheltered

19 **fit for habitation,** inhabitable, livable; homelike, homey *or* homy, comfortable, cozy; homely, plain, simple, unpretentious

20 **domestic,** household, home, domiciliary

21 **manorial,** palatial, grand, stately, presidential; detached, semidetached, duplex, back to back, split-level, single-story, multistory, high-rise

VERBS

22 **inhabit,** dwell, reside, live, live in, abide in, occupy

23 **housekeep,** keep house, run *or* maintain a household

24 **take up residence,** move in, hang up one's hat, make one's nest, nest, nestle, perch, roost, burrow, stable, pitch one's tent, camp, encamp, bivouac, quarter, room, board, lodge, put up at; crash [Inf], park one's carcass [Inf]

25 **frequent,** haunt, visit, hang out at [Inf]

ADVERBS

26 **environmentally,** territorially, locally, around, in the vicinity, in the neighborhood

61 Inhabitant

NOUNS

1 **inhabitant,** habitant, inhabiter, native, national; abo-

NICKNAMES FOR INHABITANTS*

Abo: Aborigine	Jap: Japanese
Anglo: white American of non-Hispanic descent	Jerry: German
	Jock: Scot
Argie: Argentine	kipper: Aborigine
Aussie: Australian	Kraut: German
Balt: Estonian, Latvian, Lithuanian	limey: British
	Mick: Irish
Binghi: Aborigine	Newfie: Newfoundlander
Boche: German	Nip: Japanese
bogtrotter: Irish	Paddy: Irish
bohunk: Eastern European	Paki: Pakistani
Canuck: French Canadian	Pepsi: French Canadian
Chink: Chinese	Polack: Pole
coolie *or* cooly: Chinese, Indian	pommy: British
dago: Italian, Spanish	Russki *or* Russkie *or* Russky: Russian
Eyetie: Italian	
Frog: French	spic: Spanish American
gook: Far Easterner	squarehead: German, Dutch, Scandinavian
greaseball: Mediterranean, Latin American	
	Taffy: Welsh
greaser: Mexican	WASP: white Anglo-Saxon Protestant
gringo: one of US or British descent	
	wetback: Mexican
guinea: Italian	wop: Italian
gyppo: Egyptian	Yank *or* Yankee: American
Hun: German	
Hunky *or* Hunkie: Hungarian, Slav	*These terms are informal and generally considered offensive.

rigine, autochthon, indigene, earliest inhabitant, first comer, local; occupant, occupier, dweller, settler, resident, resider, residentiary, denizen, indweller, inmate

▶ *Humankind 18; Habitat 60*

2 **inhabitants,** population, native population, populace, people, people at large, public, general public, citizenry; colony, commune, community, neighborhood, dwellers, residents; household, family, ménage, tribe, clan

▶ *Anthropology 1; Humankind 18; Commoner 71*

3 **national,** subject, citizen, naturalized citizen, citizen by adoption, compatriot, fellow countryman *or* countrywoman, fellow citizen, citizen of the world; nationality, nativeness, indigenousness *or* indigeneity, citizenship, dual citizenship *or* nationality

4 **settler,** pioneer, precursor, incomer, immigrant, colonist, colonizer, colonial, homesteader, squatter

▶ *Originality 737; Precedence 769*

5 **householder,** homeowner, head of the household, occupier, owner-occupier, addressee, proprietor, freeholder

6 **resident,** tenant, renter, leaser, lessee, leaseholder, time-sharer, lodger, roomer, paying guest, boarder, roommate, flatmate [Brit]; guest, visitor

▶ *Address 209; Possession 469; Property 470*

7 **townsperson,** townsman, townswoman, burgess, burgher, oppidan; city dweller, city person, metropolitan, urbanite, suburbanite; city slicker, townie *or* towny [Inf]

8 **countryman,** countrywoman, country gentleman, country dweller, ruralist, provincial, rustic, peasant, villager; country cousin, country bumpkin, hayseed, hick, yokel; farmer, planter; frontiersman, backwoodsman; hillbilly [Off], cracker [Inf *and* Off], redneck [Inf *and* Off]; [Brit]: cottager, smallholder, crofter

9 **illegal occupant,** illegal immigrant, uninvited guest, gate-crasher [Inf], crasher [Inf]

ADJECTIVES

10 **inhabited,** populated, residential, lived in; occupied, indwelt, tenanted, rented, leased, let; squatted, communal, settled, domiciled, colonized

11 **resident,** residing, living in, freehold, dwelling, naturalized, immigrant

12 **native,** indigenous, aboriginal, autochthonous *or* autochthonic *or* autochthonal, ethnic, tribal; local, metropolitan, urban, suburban, rural, rustic, provincial

VERBS

13 **inhabit,** dwell, reside, live in, abide in, occupy; lease, rent, lodge, board, take rooms; stay, sojourn, visit

▶ *Habitat 60*

14 **settle,** pioneer, immigrate, colonize, people, populate, squat; move in, set up house, domicile, crash [Inf]

Human Relations

62 Friendship

Two may talk together under the same roof for many years, yet never really meet; and two others at first speech are old friends. — MARY CATHERWOOD

NOUNS

1 **friendship,** companionship, friendliness, amicableness, amicability, amiableness, amity, congeniality, affection, peaceableness, fraternization, fellowship; comradeship, camaraderie, colleagueship; acquaintanceship, togetherness, bonding, solidarity, cooperation, concord, harmony, sociability, neighborliness; goodwill, benevolence, philanthropy, kindness, kindliness; hospitality, warmth, warm-heartedness, warmness, cordiality, courtesy, regard; heartiness, bonhomie, geniality; fraternalism, fraternity, confraternity, brotherhood, brotherly interest; sodality, sorority, sisterhood; partiality, prejudice, favoritism, partisanship, support; chumminess [Inf], mateyness [Brit inf]

> *Benevolence 305; Philanthropy 307; Sociability 408; Courtesy 410; Agreement 462; Cooperation 827*

2 **friend,** comrade, companion, girlfriend, boyfriend, colleague, fellow, amigo, chum, crony, sidekick, mutual friend; acquaintance, mate, shipmate, messmate, playmate, roommate, classmate, schoolmate, schoolfellow, circle of friends; close friend, bosom friend, best friend, boon companion, intimate, confidant *or* confidante, familiar; alter ego, another self, shadow, inseparable; [Inf]: pal, buddy, bosom buddy, goombah, my man

3 **friendly relations,** familiarity, compatibility, harmony, rapport, sympathy, agreement, accord, understanding, rapprochement, fellow feeling, community of interest, esprit de corps, mutual support *or* respect *or* regard *or* goodwill; entente, entente cordiale, good terms, two minds with but a single thought, hands across the sea

4 **intimacy,** warm *or* fast *or* close friendship, passionate friendship; closeness, nearness, inseparability, affinity, devotion, devotedness, dedication, steadfastness, commitment, constancy, trueness

ADJECTIVES

5 **friendly,** friendlike, cordial, courteous, amicable, amiable, kindly, kind, peaceable, unhostile; sociable, affectionate, gracious, harmonious, pleasant, congenial, compatible, cooperative, agreeable, favorable, hospitable; demonstrative, effusive, backslapping, ardent, warm; warm-hearted, genial, well-meaning, well-disposed, well-intended, generous, benevolent, philanthropic; companionable, fraternal, confraternal, brotherly, sisterly, neighborly; welcoming, receptive, hearty, sympathetic, understanding, comradely, simpatico; [Inf]: chummy, matey [Brit], pally, palsy-walsy, buddy-buddy

6 **friendly with,** friends with, acquainted with, at home with, in favor, on good terms, on a good footing, on the right side of, in the good grace of, in the good books of, regarded highly by, familiar, on a first-name basis with, in with

> *Sociability 408*

7 **intimate,** confidential, on intimate terms, favorite, close, near, inseparable, devoted, dedicated, supportive, loyal, true, faithful, steadfast, constant, committed, firm, fast, staunch, trustful, trusty, trustworthy

---

NOTABLE FRIENDSHIPS

Achilles and Patroclus	Lone Ranger and Tonto
Callimachus and Heraclitus	Nisus and Euryalus
Castor and Pollux	Pylades and Orestes
Robinson Crusoe and Friday	Don Quixote and Sancho Panza
Damon and Pythias	Ruth and Naomi
David and Jonathan	Tom Sawyer and Huckleberry Finn
Diomedes and Sthenelus	Gertrude Stein and Alice B. Toklas
Epaminondas and Pelopidas	
Harmodius and Aristogiton	Theseus and Pirithoüs
Hercules and Iolaus	Three Musketeers, the
Jesus and the beloved disciple	

8 favorable, beneficial, helpful, promising, auspicious, propitious, advantageous, useful, profitable

VERBS

9 be friends, have friends, be long acquainted, go way back, be old friends, be friends of long standing; fraternize, hobnob with

10 befriend, be friendly with, make *or* win friends, strike up a friendship *or* an acquaintance, gain the friendship of, cultivate a friendship, enjoy friendship with; get to know, get acquainted, break the ice, shake hands with, make overtures, win friends, win friends and influence people, warm to; show benevolence, have dealings with, keep company with, go around with, become inseparable, be best friends with

11 seek friendship, make friendly overtures to, extend the hand of friendship, seek the company of; make advances, court, pay court, woo, run after, date, take out, go out with; [Inf]: make up to, play up to, cotton to *or* on to, suck up to
▶ *Love 299*

12 be favorable, provide a benefit, help, promise, seem propitious, serve a use, profit

ADVERBS

13 amicably, amiably, friendly, friendlily, in a friendly way *or* spirit, as friends, cordially, courteously, sociably, affectionately, with affection; graciously, harmoniously, pleasantly, compatibly, cooperatively, agreeably, kindly, hospitably; effusively, ardently, warmly, warm-heartedly, heartily; genially, generously, benevolently, fraternally, receptively, with open arms, sympathetically

14 intimately, familiarly, closely, in an intimate fashion, inseparably, arm in arm, hand in hand, hand in glove; devotedly, supportively, with devotion, in support, loyally, truly, faithfully, steadfastly, constantly, committedly, firmly, fastly, staunchly, trustfully

15 favorably, beneficially, helpfully, with a helping hand, promisingly, with promise, auspiciously, propitiously, advantageously, usefully, profitably

63 Hostility

We have met the enemy and he is us. — WALT KELLY

NOUNS

1 hostility, unfriendliness, inimicality, uncordiality, coolness, iciness, coldness, chilliness, frostiness, unamiability, ungeniality, disaffection; enmity, disaffinity, animosity, antipathy, animus, opposition, aggression, bellicosity, antagonism; conflict, contention, collision, clash, clashing, friction, quarreling, quarrelsomeness, dissension, belligerence, bad blood, a bone to pick; dislike, spite, spitefulness, despitefulness; intolerance, bigotry, prejudice, persecution, racism, color bar, segregation

▶ *Dislike 291; Hate 300; Malevolence 306; Discrimination 337; Unsociability 409; Attack 418; Contention 422; Opposition 828*

2 personal conflict, strain, tension; envy, jealousy, the green-eyed monster; incompatibility, estrangement, alienation, separation; disloyalty, unfaithfulness, breach, breach of friendship; divorce
▶ *Divorce and Widowhood 66; Envy 314*

3 ill feeling, ill will, acrimony, sourness, bitterness, rancor, soreness, resentment, hard feelings, bad blood, no love lost, grudge, peevishness
▶ *Resentment, Anger 302*

4 act of hostility, war, declaration of war, state of war, conflict, hostilities, vendetta, feud, blood feud, casus belli

5 hostile person, enemy, sworn enemy, archenemy, no friend, foe, adversary, opponent; rival, competitor, contender, antagonist; traitor, public enemy (number one); combatant, aggressor, invader; troublemaker, ill-wisher, secret enemy, viper in one's bosom; xenophobe, racist, bigot
▶ *Dislike 291; Discrimination 337*

ADJECTIVES

6 hostile, unfriendly, inimical, uncordial, cool, icy, cold, chilly, frosty, aloof; inhospitable, unsociable, antisocial, unsympathetic, unamicable, ungenial; discordant, strained, tense, unharmonious; ill-disposed, acrimonious, bitter, rancorous, sour, sore, resentful, grudging, peevish; envious, jealous, green-eyed, green with envy; malevolent, full of hate
▶ *Hate 300; Resentment, Anger 302; Envy 314; Unsociability 409*

7 intolerant, persecuting, oppressive, racist *or* racialist, prejudiced, bigoted, xenophobic, anti-Semitic

8 estranged, alienated, separated, irreconcilable, distant; disloyal, unfaithful, disaffected, disinclined, not well inclined, at variance, divided, disunited, torn; on bad terms, not on speaking terms, in someone's bad books, in someone's black book, in bad with [Inf]

9 aggressive, antagonistic, conflicting, contentious, clashing, opposing, opposed, quarrelsome, dissenting, belligerent, bellicose, at war, militant, at loggerheads, at odds, at each other's throats, at cross-purposes, at sixes and sevens

VERBS

10 be hostile, bear ill will, bear malice, bear a grudge, hold it against; resent, grudge, take offense, take umbrage; harden one's heart, hate, scorn

11 oppose, oppress, persecute, hound, hunt down, clash, collide, conflict, quarrel, dissent, differ, fall out; come to blows, fight, feud, make war on, wage war, battle

12 antagonize, make enemies, set against, provoke, estrange, cause offense, irritate; infuriate, madden, divide, disunite, alienate, set at each other's throats; aggravate, heat up, embitter, set at odds

13 **hostilely,** with enmity, inimically, uncordially, coolly, coldly, frostily, unsympathetically, without sympathy, unkindly, inhospitably, unsociably, antisocially, alone, unamiably, ungenially, discordantly, unharmoniously, unfaithfully, disloyally, disaffectedly, acrimoniously, sourly, resentfully, unsympathetically, grudgingly, peevishly, enviously, with envy, jealously, intolerantly, oppressively

14 **aggressively,** antagonistically, with antagonism, contentiously, hatefully, spitefully, in a spiteful way

64 Marriage

If ever two were one, then surely we. / If ever man were loved by wife, then thee; / If ever wife was happy in a man, / Compare with me ye women if you can.
— ANNE BRADSTREET

I'm gettin' married in the mornin'! / Ding, dong! the bells are gonna chime! / Pull out the stopper, / Let's have a whopper, / But get me to the church on time!
— ALAN JAY LERNER

NOUNS

1 **marriage,** matrimony, holy matrimony, wedlock, holy wedlock, conjugality, union, sacrament of marriage, match, one flesh, alliance; married status *or* state, wedded status *or* state, state of matrimony; wedding *or* nuptial *or* conjugal bond, marriage tie; wedded bliss, conjugal bliss, weddedness; wifehood, husbandhood, spousehood, coverture [Form]; bridal bed, marriage bed, bridebed; cohabitation, living as man and wife; [Inf]: tying the knot, getting hitched, getting spliced
▶ *Religion 81; Joy, Cheerfulness 269; Love 299; Union 752*

2 **alliance,** merger, union, link, connection, consolidation, association, amalgamation, meld, partnership, tie-up, hookup [Inf]

3 **type of marriage,** monogamy, monogyny, monandry, polygamy, Mormonism, polygyny, polyandry, bigamy; second marriage, remarriage, digamy, deuterogamy, trigamy; marriage of convenience, *mariage de convenance* [Fr]; love match, levirate, morganatic marriage, left-handed marriage, companionate marriage; trial marriage, common-law marriage, picture marriage; interfaith marriage, mixed marriage, intermarriage, interracial marriage, intercaste marriage, miscegenation, exogamy, endogamy; misalliance, mésalliance; spiritual marriage, compulsory marriage, arranged marriage, marriage by proxy; concubinage; homosexual marriage, lesbian marriage

4 **marriageability,** marriageableness, nubility, marriageable age, age of consent, ripeness, fitness for marriage; dowry, bride price; good match, proper match, suitable match, suitable party, eligible party, eligible bachelor

5 **wedding,** church wedding, civil wedding, civil ceremony, courthouse wedding, marriage by a justice of the peace; spousal *or* spousals, wedding ceremony, wedding service, white wedding, nuptial mass, nuptial benediction, marriage vows, nuptial vows, nuptials, hymeneal rites; solemn wedding, quiet wedding; elopement, Gretna Green wedding *or* marriage [Brit inf], forced wedding, shotgun wedding

6 **general wedding terms,** marriage license, wedding announcement, bridal shower, wedding invitation, wedding banns, wedding rehearsal, rehearsal dinner, stag *or* bachelor party, wedding day, wedding morning; wedding bells, ring, wedding ring, wedding canopy, wedding processional, wedding march, wedding music, wedding song, marriage song, nuptial song, nuptial ode, hymeneal, prothalamion, epithalamion, marriage procession, wedding recessional; wedding dress, bridal veil, saffron veil, saffron robe; wedding reception, wedding present *or* gift, bridal bouquet, wedding cake, wedding breakfast, marriage feast, marriage toast, wedding photographs; honeymoon, bridal chamber, honeymoon suite, bridal suite
▶ *Celebration 405*

7 **wedding party,** bride, bridal attendant, bridesmaid, maid *or* matron of honor, attendant, flower girl, mother of the bride, father of the bride, train bearer; bridegroom, groom, best man, groomsman, usher, page, pageboy, ring bearer, mother of the groom, father of the groom

8 **spouse,** espouser, espoused, bride, blushing bride, war bride, GI bride; bridegroom, groom; one's promised, one's betrothed, soul mate, helpmate, helpmeet, marriage partner, partner, faithful spouse, better half, consort

9 **married couple,** happy couple, bridal pair, newlyweds, honeymooners, man and wife, husband and wife, *vir et uxor* [L], one flesh, Mr. and Mrs.

10 **married man,** husband, househusband, benedict *or* Benedick, monogamist, monogynist; henpecked husband, injured husband, cuckold, second husband; much-married man, bigamist, polygamist, polygynist, Mormon, Bluebeard; goodman [Arch], lord and master [Arch]; old man [Inf], hubby [Inf]

11 **married woman,** wife, housewife, lady, good lady, matron, feme covert [Form]; second wife, wife in name only, wife in all but name, common-law wife, concubine; [Arch]: goodwife, goody, missis *or* missus; [Inf]: old lady, trouble and strife [Brit], squaw [Off]

12 **common-law wife** *or* **husband,** partner, cohabitant, live-in lover, POSSLQ (person of opposite sex sharing living quarters)

13 **matchmaker,** marriage broker, *shadchan* [Yiddish], matrimonial agent, go-between, marriage adviser, mar-

riage guidance counselor, mediator; marriage bureau, dating agency, lonely hearts club, lonely hearts column, dating service, computer dating
  ▶ *Mediation 75*

14 gods and goddesses of marriage, Hymen, Hera, Juno, Teleia, Pronuba, Frigg

ADJECTIVES

15 matrimonial, marital, conjugal, connubial, nuptial, hymeneal, spousal, premarital, concubinal, concubinary, matronly, wifely, bridal, husbandly

16 married, wedded, united, espoused, partnered, joined, paired, coupled, mated, newlywed, matched, ill-matched, made man and wife, one, made one, one bone and one flesh, in double harness, remarried; [Inf]: hitched, spliced, hooked

17 marriageable, nubile, eligible, suitable, fit for marriage, ripe for marriage, of marriageable age; betrothed, engaged, promised, affianced, plighted, spoken for

18 monogamous, bigamous, digamous, deuterogamous, polygamous, polygynous, polyandrous, morganatic, miscegenetic

VERBS

19 marry, get married, wed, say "I do," take a wife, take a husband, wive, couple, become one, take for better or for worse, quit the single state, elope, run away; make an honest woman of, lead to the altar; engage, affiance, betroth, espouse, publish the banns, ask for someone's hand, bestow one's hand upon, accept a proposal, plight one's troth; contract matrimony, live as man and wife, share one's bed and board, set up house together; honeymoon, go on a honeymoon, consummate one's marriage; marry well, marry into money, make a good match; mismarry, make a bad match, marry in haste; remarry, rewed, commit bigamy; intermarry, miscegenate; [Inf]: get spliced, tie the knot, get hitched

20 join in marriage, join in holy wedlock, join, unite, unite in marriage *or* holy matrimony, celebrate a marriage, conduct the ceremony, conduct the wedding, read the wedding vows, read the wedding service, make one, pronounce man and wife; give in marriage, give away, marry off, bestow in marriage

21 merge, ally, unite, link, connect, consolidate, associate, amalgamate, form a partnership, tie up with, hook up with [Inf]

22 matchmake, make a match, match, mate, find a mate for, find a husband *or* wife for, arrange a marriage
  ▶ *Mediation 75*

ADVERBS

23 matrimonially, maritally, conjugally, connubially, nuptially, in double harness, as one, in the way of marriage, in holy wedlock, like man and wife, monogamously, bigamously, with two wives, polygamously, morganatically

65 Family

My family history begins with me, but yours ends with you.
— IPHICRATES

I am my own ancestor. — ANDOCHE JUNOT

NOUNS

1 family, household, ménage, kin, brood, relatives, relations, next of kin, sib, kinship group; unit, ensemble, set, category; social group, peer group, community, class, clan, tribe, people
  ▶ *Sociology 2; Mathematics 6; Life Science 13; Assembly 59; Love 299; Whole 759; Arrangement 767*

2 family member, wife, husband, spouse; parent, mother, father, materfamilias, paterfamilias; child, daughter, son, offspring; illegitimate child, bastard; brother, sister, sibling, half sister, half brother; grandparent, grandmother, grandfather, grandsire; grandchild, granddaughter, grandson; great-grandparent, great-grandmother, great-grandfather; great-grandchild, great-granddaughter, great-grandson; aunt, uncle; grandaunt *or* great-aunt, granduncle *or* great-uncle; niece, nephew; grandniece, grandnephew; cousin, cousin-german, first cousin, second cousin, *etc.*; cousin once removed, cousin twice removed, *etc.*; mother-in-law, father-in-law, daughter-in-law, son-in-law, sister-in-law, brother-in-law; stepparent, stepmother, stepfather, stepchild, stepdaughter, stepson, stepsister, stepbrother; foster child, foster sister, foster brother; in-laws; head of the family *or* house, lady of the house, man of the house; [Inf]: mom, mommy, mama, ma; dad, daddy, papa, pa; kid, kids; bro, bud, buddy, sis; grandma, grandmommy, nana, grandpa, granddad, granddaddy; auntie, unc, coz
  ▶ *Life Science 13; Male 32; Female 33; Assembly 59; Relatedness 727*

3 family tree, descent, lineage, line, bloodline, ancestry; scion, progeny; house, breed, blood, pedigree, dynasty, genealogy, tribe, race, ilk; approved lineage, good family [Brit]
  ▶ *Class 777*

4 family circle, brood, immediate family, nuclear family, extended family; godparent, godmother, godfather, goddaughter, godson; the folks [Inf]

5 human family, family of humankind, family of nations, people, humanity, human race, humankind, mankind
  ▶ *Humankind 18*

ADJECTIVES

6 family, familial, related, kindred, akin, consanguineous; parental, motherly, maternal, fatherly, paternal; sisterly, brotherly, sororial, fraternal; categorical; lineal, clannish, tribal, dynastic, genealogical

66 Divorce and Widowhood

NOUNS

1 **divorce,** divorcement, dissolution of marriage; divorce decree, decree nisi, decree absolute; annulment, decree of nullity, no marriage, nonconsummation of marriage; breakdown of marriage, broken marriage, broken home, breakup, split-up, split, marriage on the rocks [Inf]; grass widowhood, grass widowerhood
   ▶ *Separation 753*

2 **separation,** legal separation, judicial separation, estrangement, living apart, desertion, impediment [Form]

3 **divorce court,** divorce case, matrimonial cause; grounds for divorce: no-fault, incompatibility, abandonment, desertion, cruelty, mental cruelty, adultery; divorce settlement: maintenance, alimony, child support, custody of children, visiting rights; party in divorce case, corespondent
   ▶ *Malevolence 306; Immorality 432; Money 484*

4 **divorced person,** divorcer, divorced woman, divorcée, grass widow, divorced man, divorcé, grass widower

5 **widowhood,** viduity, widowerhood; weeds, widow's weeds
   ▶ *Death 29; Clothing 100*

6 **surviving spouse,** survivor, widow, dowager, dowager queen, war widow, grass widow, merry widow, widow woman [Arch], relict [Arch]; widower, grass widower, widowman [Arch]

ADJECTIVES

7 **divorced,** dissolved, separated, legally separated, split, estranged, living apart, deserted, abandoned, on the rocks [Inf]

8 **widowed,** husbandless; widowered, wifeless; widowly, widowish, widowlike

VERBS

9 **divorce,** obtain a divorce, get divorced, dissolve one's marriage, unmarry, untie the knot [Inf]; sue for divorce, file (suit) for divorce; break up, split up, split, sever, sunder, come to a parting of the ways, be granted a final decree; be granted an annulment, be granted a decree of nullity, have one's marriage annulled; put asunder, put away, revert to the single state, revert to bachelorhood, regain one's freedom

10 **separate,** live separately, live apart, part, be estranged

11 **desert,** abandon, leave, walk out

12 **widow,** die before one's spouse, bereave, make a widow, make a widower, leave one's wife a widow, leave one's husband a widower

13 **be widowed,** be bereaved, outlive one's spouse, survive one's spouse, lose one's husband *or* wife, put on widow's weeds

ADVERBS

14 **without one's spouse,** without one's husband, without one's wife, by decree nisi *or* absolute, by decree of nullity, by annulment, in estrangement, apart

67 Celibacy

NOUNS

1 **celibacy,** single *or* unmarried *or* unwed condition *or* state, singleness, single blessedness; bachelorhood, spinsterhood; sexual abstinence *or* abstention, continence, self-restraint, self-denial, misogamy
   ▶ *Dislike 291; Self-Restraint 455*

2 **virginity,** maidenhood, maidenhead, chastity, chasteness

3 **monasticism,** reclusive life, solitary state, spiritual marriage; monastic order, celibate order, holy orders, the veil; monastery, convent, nunnery
   ▶ *Religion 81*

4 **celibate,** celibate person, monk, monastic, priest, nun, cenobite, eremite; recluse, hermit, virgin, virgo intacta, vestal virgin, vestal

5 **single person,** single man *or* woman, unmarried man *or* woman, unwed man *or* woman, unattached man, unattached woman; single, bachelor, confirmed bachelor, spinster, maid, maiden, maiden lady, single girl, bachelor girl, lone woman, maiden aunt, old maid [Off]; enemy *or* hater of marriage, misogamist; (old) bach [Inf]

ADJECTIVES

6 **celibate,** celibatic, single, unmarried, unwed, unwedded, sole [Arch], spouseless, wifeless, husbandless, unpartnered, unmated, mateless; bachelorly, bachelorlike; spinsterly, spinsterlike, maiden, maidenly, old-maidish; unwooed, unasked, independent, unattached, free, fancy-free; abstinent, continent, self-restrained; agamous, misogamic; on the shelf [Inf]

7 **virginal,** virgin, chaste, pure, virtuous, innocent, maidenly, intact

8 **monastic,** monachal, monkish, cenobitic, nunnish, priestly

VERBS

9 **be celibate,** practice celibacy, remain unmarried, stay single, live alone, live in single blessedness, have no offers, receive no proposals, sit on the shelf [Inf], bach (it) [Inf]

10 **be continent,** be abstinent, be chaste, remain a virgin, stay pure, abstain, have no sex, forgo sex

11 **be monastic,** live like a monk *or* nun, take holy orders, take the veil, live like a hermit

ADVERBS

12 **celibately,** singly, solitarily, by oneself, independently, freely, without obligations; continently, abstinently, virginally, chastely, purely, like a monk, like a nun

68 Master

NOUNS

1 **master,** mistress, lord, lord and master, lord paramount, overlord, liege lord, liege; lord of the manor, lady of the manor, master of the house, paterfamilias, mistress of the house, materfamilias; man of the house, husband, lady of the house, wife, matron; patriarch, matriarch, chatelaine, dowager; owner, property owner, landowner, squire, laird [Scot], landlord, landlady, proprietor, governor, guv [Brit inf]; sahib [India], bwana [Africa], seigneur
   ▶ *Male 32; Female 33; Aristocrat 70; Title 72; Possession 469*

2 **sovereign,** crowned head, monarch, absolute monarch, king, rex, queen, regina, queen regent, emperor, empress; Caesar, kaiser, rajah, rani *or* ranee, czar *or* tsar, czarina *or* tsarina, Pharaoh, shah, khan, mikado, Mogul, Great Mogul, maharajah, maharani *or* maharanee, nabob, sultan, caliph, Dalai Lama
   ▶ *Authority 52; Superiority 744; Importance 799*

3 **leader,** head of state, chief of state, chief executive, ruler, potentate, protector, chief, chieftain, headman, sheik, mandarin; president, prime minister, premier, chancellor; cabinet secretary, secretary of state; governor, lieutenant governor, mayor, mayoress; [Brit]: minister of state, governor general, high commissioner, Lord Mayor, Lady Mayor; commissioner, military governor, pasha, suzerain, viceroy, proconsul, consul general, consul

4 **judge,** Supreme Court justice, associate justice, chief justice; chief magistrate, magistrate, sheriff, constable, marshal, justice of the peace, justice, bailie [Scot], bailiff [Brit]
   ▶ *Litigation 54; Judgment 341*

5 **party official,** Senate president, Speaker of the House, majority *or* minority leader, whip, Democratic whip, Republican whip, chief whip [Brit]

6 **official,** officer, functionary, dignitary, person in office, person in authority
   ▶ *Government 49; Politics 50; Authority 52*

7 **absolute ruler,** autocrat, tyrant, dictator, despot, duce, *Führer* [Ger], satrap, warlord, shogun, oppressor, captor, martinet, tin god, petty tyrant, gauleiter

8 **company leader,** company official, superior, senior, chief executive officer (CEO), chief financial officer (CFO), executive, director, chairman of the board, board member, chairman, chairwoman, chair, chairperson, manager, controller; plutocrat, oligarch, tycoon, captain of industry; boss, head, chief, employer, doyen, doyenne, queen bee, cock of the walk, top dog; [Inf]: kingpin, bigwig, big gun, big shot, big wheel, big cheese, head honcho, kingfish, big enchilada, very important person (VIP)

▶ *Management 126; Superiority 744; Importance 799*

9 **religious leader,** pope, pontiff, cardinal, dean, archbishop, bishop, provost, high priest, ecclesiarch; abbot, abbess, mother superior; rabbi, ayatollah, imam, guru
   ▶ *Religion 81; Clergy 84*

10 **military leader,** military officer, commissioned officer, commander in chief, commanding officer, commander, commandant, general, generalissimo, field marshal [Brit], air marshal [Brit], admiral, fleet admiral, executive officer; [Inf]: exec, the Old Man, brass hat
   ▶ *Military Affairs 58; Combatant 77*

11 **educational leader,** scholar, intellectual, thinker, highbrow, philosopher, sage, wise man, mentor, guru, swami; trustee, regent, college president, university president, chancellor, vice chancellor, provost, dean, professor, instructor, don [Brit], fellow, reader, lecturer; governor, head, master, headmaster, headmistress, principal, department head, department chairman *or* chairwoman *or* chair; schoolmaster, schoolmistress, teacher, pedagogue, tutor, housemaster, housemother, schoolma'am *or* schoolmarm
   ▶ *Education 48*

12 **the power structure,** the ruling class *or* classes, ruling party, the Establishment, authorities, officialdom, principalities and powers, powers that be, Big Brother; the government, Washington, the White House, the Hill, the Capitol, Capitol Hill, Pentagon; [Brit]: Whitehall, Downing Street, Westminster; the Kremlin, the (Russian) White House; the board, the directorship, the top, corridors of power, inner circle, in-group, top brass [Inf], higher-ups [Inf]
   ▶ *Authority 52; Management 126*

13 **expert,** grand master, master, champion, genius; maestro, virtuoso; specialist, past master, adept, ace, practitioner, graduate, consultant, guide, professional, skilled worker, right person for the job, old hand, walking encyclopedia; [Inf]: champ, pro, dab hand *or* dab
   ▶ *Authority 52*

14 **masterpiece,** masterwork, chef-d'oeuvre, tour de force, magnum opus, classic, treasure, work of art, epic, perfection, crème de la crème
   ▶ *Literature 139; Painting and Drawing 143*

ADJECTIVES

15 **masterful,** magistral, lordly, noble, aristocratic, magisterial; matronly, patriarchal, matriarchal, elder; sovereign, majestic, crowned, absolute, divine, royal; head, chief, principal, main, major, great, leading, controlling; autocratic, authoritarian, dominating, domineering, coercive, imperious, dictatorial, despotic, oppressive; executive, managerial, capitalistic, plutocratic, oligarchic; papal, pontifical, cardinal, rabbinical; commissioned, commanding, able; powerful, established
   ▶ *Authority 52; Power 514*

16 **excellent,** expert, master, champion, specialist, professional; masterly, skilled, skillful, adept, proficient,

first-rate, supreme, consummate, polished, finished, competent, good at, experienced, qualified, ace [Inf]

VERBS

17 **master,** rule, lead, govern, dictate, oppress, lord it over; win, conquer, vanquish, defeat, beat, overpower, overcome, crush, quell, subdue, subjugate, dominate, control; command, direct, manage, boss, head; operate in the corridors of power, sit on the board, hold a directorship, reach the top; head an institution, head a school, teach, instruct, tutor, specialize

18 **learn,** master, understand, comprehend, apprehend, grasp, acquire, become proficient, retain, remember, know how to, assimilate, learn by heart, memorize, specialize in, know all the answers, ace [Inf]

ADVERBS

19 **masterfully,** nobly, in a noble manner, aristocratically, absolutely, royally; autocratically, dominatingly, domineeringly, imperiously, dictatorially, oppressively, in order to oppress; executively, managerially; excellently, expertly, with expertise, professionally; skillfully, adeptly, proficiently; supremely, consummately, competently

69 Servant

NOUNS

1 **servant,** paid helper, help, retainer, household servant, domestic, worker, hired hand, farmhand, laborer, handyman, odd-job man, factotum; employee, assistant, subordinate, subaltern, attendant, servitor, orderly, humble servant, follower, henchman, liegeman; occasional help, hired help; menial, underling, hireling, inferior, minion, flunky, lackey, drudge, Mister Fix-it
 ▶ *Worker 123; Obedience 426; Inferiority 745; Usefulness 801; Help 825*

2 **servitude,** service, slavery, serfdom, thralldom

3 **public servant,** public official, civil servant, politician, public office holder
 ▶ *Politics 50*

4 **attendant,** usher, server, maid, valet, butler, batman [Brit]; airline hostess, airline attendant, flight attendant, cabin crew; maître d'hôtel, maître d', hostess, head waiter, waiter, waitress, steward, stewardess, wine steward, sommelier, busboy, carhop, bartender, barkeeper *or* barkeep, barmaid, soda jerk [Inf]; page, bellboy, bellhop, porter, redcap, skycap, caddie, hatcheck girl, cloakroom attendant; counterman, salesclerk *or* clerk, salesperson, shop assistant [Brit]; shoeshine boy, bootblack, shoeblack; caretaker, concierge, custodian, janitor
 ▶ *Activity 414; Sale 482*

5 **personal attendant,** personal servant, companion, confidant *or* confidante, nurse; nursemaid, au pair, governess, nanny, ayah, amah, chaperon, tutor, driver,

chauffeur; bodyguard, henchman; barber, hairdresser, masseur, masseuse

6 **office assistant,** assistant, administrative assistant, secretary, stenographer, clerk, data-entry clerk, right-hand man *or* woman, girl *or* man Friday, copy aide, messenger, runner, courier; employee, office worker, staff member, peon, gofer [Inf], dogsbody [Brit inf]
 ▶ *Worker 123; Management 126*

7 **domestic servant,** domestic, steward, house steward, bailiff [Brit], housekeeper, chamberlain, butler, major-domo, houseman, boy, houseboy; cook, maid, maidservant, live-in maid, housemaid, parlormaid, chambermaid, servant girl, wench; handmaid, handmaiden, lady's maid, maid-in-waiting, lady-in-waiting, lord-in-waiting, lady of the bedchamber, lord of the bedchamber, gentleman's gentleman, gentleman, man, manservant, serving man, serving maid, kitchen maid, dishwasher, kitchen boy, laundry maid, cleaning woman, daily help, daily [Brit], charwoman *or* char [Brit]; footman, stableman, stableboy, groom, gardener, groundskeeper, tweeny [Brit inf]
 ▶ *Cleanliness 111; Worker 123*

8 **serf,** bond servant, bondman, bondmaid, thrall, vassal, slave, galley slave, captive

ADJECTIVES

9 **serving,** attending, attendant, helping, ministering, aiding, waiting on, working

10 **obedient,** menial, subject, servile, at someone's beck and call, unfree

VERBS

11 **serve,** be in service, do service, work for, care for, take care of, help, tend, look after, wait upon, attend upon, live in, make oneself useful, minister to, administer to, assist, do housework, do chores, clean for, accompany, follow, oblige, obey, pander to, wait on hand and foot, dance attendance on, char [Brit], do for [Brit]

ADVERBS

12 **obediently,** menially, servilely; in (domestic) service, in employment, in someone's employ, on the staff, on the payroll, in someone's pay; in servitude, in slavery, in captivity, in bonds

70 Aristocrat

The Stately Homes of England / How beautiful they stand, / To prove the upper classes / Have still the upper hand.
— NOËL COWARD

NOUNS

1 **nobleman,** noblewoman, noble, lord, lady; peer, life peer, grand duke, duke, duchess, marquis, marquise, margrave, margravine, count, countess, earl, viscount, viscountess, baron, baronet, knight, dame; gentleman, gentlewoman, titled person, blue blood,

Brahmin, jet-setter, patrician; [Inf]: gent, nob [Brit], toff [Brit]

▶ *Master 68; Title 72*

2 **aristocracy,** royalty, nobility, *ancien régime* [Fr]; peerage, lordship, dukedom, earldom, viscountcy, barony, baronetcy; gentry, landed gentry, ruling class, upper class, gentlefolk, elite, high society, Social Register™, beau monde, jet set

3 **nobleness,** nobility, kingliness, quality, virtue, distinction; lineage, pedigree, gentility, noble family, dynasty, good breeding, line, ancestry

ADJECTIVES

4 **aristocratic,** noble, blue-blooded, thoroughbred, ennobled, titled, high-class, upper-class, socially prominent; gentlemanly, ladylike, baronial, ducal, lordly, princely, kingly, well-born, high-born, well-bred, patrician, high-caste, first-class, top-drawer, of good family, Brahminic, classy [Inf], U [Inf]

VERBS

5 **make noble,** ennoble, raise to the peerage, knight

ADVERBS

6 **aristocratically,** nobly, kingly, regally, royally, lordly; with distinction, honorably, notably, eminently, illustriously, prominently

71 Commoner

The masters have been done away with; the morality of the common man has triumphed. — FRIEDRICH NIETZSCHE

NOUNS

1 **commoner,** plebeian, pleb, proletarian, man-in-the-street, regular guy, everyman, common man, little man, underling, Mr. Nobody, bourgeois; peasant, rustic, serf, villein, churl; hick, yokel, bumpkin, country bumpkin, country cousin, hillbilly [Off]; prole [Inf], Joe Blow *or* Doakes [Inf]

2 **common people,** commonalty, the people, the masses, proletariat, plebeians, plebs, rank and file, grass roots, working classes, bourgeoisie; hoi polloi, lower orders, second-class citizens, vulgar masses, great unwashed, the have-nots; peasantry, serfdom, villeinage; Tom, Dick, and Harry

ADJECTIVES

3 **common,** plebeian, rank-and-file, provincial, of the people, titleless, lowly, second-class, lowborn, lower-class, proletarian, of humble birth; parvenu, vulgar, uncultured, churlish, infra dig, non-U [Inf]

ADVERBS

4 **commonly,** humbly, plainly, simply, popularly

5 **vulgarly,** rudely, coarsely, rustically, churlishly

▶ *Vulgarity 535*

72 Title

NOUNS

1 **title,** name, appellation, appellative, heading, designation, denomination, term, calling; honorific, reward, award; entitlement, due, expectation, duty, merit

▶ *Literature 139; Books 174; Address 209; Duty 433; Reward 453; Property 470*

2 **claim,** pretension, right, privilege, prerogative, birthright; reason, ground, argument, proof

3 **honor,** prize, accolade, championship, trophy, reward; honors, laurels, palm, palms, crown, medal, ribbon, decoration

▶ *Reward 453*

4 **titleholder,** possessor, holder, owner, landowner, landlord, landlady; champion, winner, prizewinner

▶ *Sports 145; Property 470*

5 **honorific,** Your *or* His *or* Her Majesty, Your *or* His *or* Her Highness *or* Royal Highness, Your *or* His *or* Her Excellency *or* Excellence, Your *or* His *or* Her Honor; Your *or* His Lordship, Your *or* Her Ladyship; Sir, Lady, Dame, Squire

6 **professional title** *or* **honorific,** Reverend, Your *or* His *or* Her Reverence, Your *or* His *or* Her Grace; Right Reverend, Monsignor, Holiness, His Holiness; Bishop, Abbot, Dom, Brother, Sister, Father, Mother, Rabbi, *Reb* [Yiddish]; Professor, Doctor, Esquire

7 **title of respect** *or* **address,** sir, madam, madame, mistress, Mr., Mrs., Ms., Miss

▶ *Address 209*

8 **military title,** General, Major General, Brigadier General, Major, Captain, Lieutenant, Sergeant, Corporal, Private; Admiral, Commodore, Commander, Ensign

▶ *Military Affairs 58*

ADJECTIVES

9 **titled,** named, appellative, headed, designated, denominated, termed, called

10 **titular,** titulary, honorary

11 **honored,** entitled, worthy, deserving, meritorious, decorated, prizewinning

VERBS

12 **have a title,** be called, be named, be designated, be termed

13 **be entitled to,** earn, deserve, be worthy of, merit, claim, expect, inherit

ADVERBS

14 **worthily,** honorarily, deservingly, meritoriously

73 Peace

NOUNS

1 **peace,** freedom from war, peacetime, state of peace; peaceable kingdom, peace that passeth all understanding, quiet life; line of least resistance, no hassle;

peacefulness, peace and quiet, quiescence, rest, stillness; peace of mind, harmony, concord; lasting peace, universal peace; Pax Romana, Pax Britannica, imposed peace; law and order, order

▸ *Pacification 74; Cessation 668; Ease 819*

2 truce, temporary truce, uneasy truce, lull in hostilities, armistice; cessation, end of war, end of hostilities, cease-fire; conquest, surrender; demobilization, military discharge

3 coexistence, armed neutrality, neutrality, nonalignment, nonaligned nations, noninvolvement; indifference, nonintervention, avoidance; peaceableness, nonaggression, cordial relations, amity, friendship

4 pacifism, pacification, peace movement, ahimsa

▸ *Pacification 74*

5 peace treaty, peace agreement, nonaggression pact, disarmament treaty; burying the hatchet, amnesty, pardon, forgiveness

▸ *Friendship 62; Mediation 75; War 76; Forgiveness 312; Agreement 462; Cessation 668; Accord 735; Ease 819*

6 symbol of peace, dove, lamb, olive branch, flag of truce, white flag, peace sign, peace pipe, golden age

▸ *Pacification 74*

7 pacifier, man *or* woman of peace, peace lover, pacifist; peacemaker, peace negotiator, mediator, intermediary; peacekeeper, United Nations peacekeeping force

▸ *Pacification 74; Mediation 75*

ADJECTIVES

8 peaceful, quiet, quiet as a lamb, quiescent, tranquil, serene, still, calm, halcyon; bloodless, harmonious, peacelike, dovelike

▸ *Silence 231; Lack of Motion 678*

9 harmless, inoffensive, innocent, mild, mild-mannered, easygoing, good-natured, agreeable, amiable, friendly, tolerant, uncompetitive, uncontentious, peaceable; without enemies, at peace, not at war; prewar, antebellum, postwar, postbellum, peacetime

▸ *Friendship 62; Pacification 74; Mediation 75; War 76; Submission 421; Agreement 462; Accord 735; Ease 819*

VERBS

10 be at peace, enjoy peace, stay at peace; observe neutrality, keep the peace, keep out of war; make love not war, jaw jaw not war war; avoid bloodshed, keep out of trouble, mean no harm

11 make peace, pacify; mediate, settle one's differences; disarm, lay down one's arms, put down one's gun, sheathe the sword, put up one's sword, beat swords into plowshares; sign *or* make *or* call a truce, suspend hostilities, demilitarize, demobilize; leash the dogs of war, make the world a safer place, make the lion lie down with the lamb; conquer, surrender, sue for peace; end hostilities, call a truce, forget one's differences, bury the hatchet, smoke the peace pipe

▸ *Pacification 74; Mediation 75*

ADVERBS

12 peacefully, peaceably, pacifically, without violence, without fear, bloodlessly, safely; quietly, softly, tranquilly, serenely; in peace, in a peaceful way, at peace

INTERJECTIONS

13 peace!, keep the peace!, God's peace!, peace be with you!

74 Pacification

NOUNS

1 pacification, pacifying, peacemaking, irenics, nonviolence; conciliation, propitiation, appeasement, peace at any price; mollification, soothing, moderation, reconciliation, reconcilement, improved relations, détente, rapprochement, accommodation, adjustment, agreement, compromise, settlement of differences *or* a dispute; mediation, arbitration, good offices; convention, entente, understanding

2 treaty, peace treaty, imposed peace, forced reconciliation, cease-fire, compulsive cease-fire, truce

▸ *Peace 73*

3 disarmament, unilateral disarmament, defense cuts, arms cuts, arms reduction, arms control; Strategic Arms Limitation Talks (SALT), SALT I Treaty, Strategic Arms Reduction Talks (START), START 2; moratorium, moratorium on nuclear testing, ban on testing, test ban, comprehensive test ban; reduction of nuclear stockpiles, destruction of weapons, deescalation

▸ *Agreement 462*

4 peace movement, antiwar movement, anti–Vietnam War movement, ban-the-bomb movement; peace process, demobilization, disbanding; nuclear-free zone, freedom from war; peace party, peace camp, peacemaking, irenics

▸ *Peace 73; Mediation 75; Compulsion 428; Contract 459; Compromise 461; Agreement 462; Moderation 521; Cessation 668*

5 peace offering, olive branch, peace offer, peace overture; peaceful approach, friendly approach, hand of friendship, outstretched hand, friendliness; flag of truce, white flag; peace pipe, calumet; compensation, reparation, atonement, restitution, wergild; fair offer, easy terms; amnesty, pardon, full pardon; mercy, forgiveness, leniency, clemency

▸ *Peace 73; Forgiveness 312; Atonement 313; Moderation 521*

6 pacifist, passive resister, conscientious objector (CO), Quaker; dove, noncombatant, nonbelligerent; peacenik [Inf]

▸ *Peace 73; Mediation 75*

ADJECTIVES

7 pacific, law-abiding, peace-loving, unmilitary, unwarlike, unmilitant; nonaggressive, unaggressive, pacifist, nonviolent, unresisting, passive, submissive, submitting; unarmed, noncombatant, civilian, neutral, nonaligned

8 **pacificatory,** pacifying, conciliatory, placatory, propitiatory, appeasing, irenic *or* irenical, peacemaking; peace-loving, dovelike; friendly, disarming, satisfying, calming, soothing, emollient, lenitive; mediatory, negotiated, pacifiable, pacified, satisfied, happy, content
   ▶ *Peace 73; Mediation 75; Moderation 521*

VERBS

9 **pacify,** make peace, live in peace, enjoy peace, keep the peace, stay at peace; avoid war, avoid strife; impose peace, give peace to; halt the arms race; hold out the olive branch, hold out the peace pipe, hold out one's hand, return a soft answer, turn the other cheek

10 **conciliate,** propitiate, disarm; reconcile, placate, appease, satisfy, content, make happy; pour oil on troubled waters, put out the fire, douse the flames; allay, ease, alleviate, soothe, take the sting out of, tranquilize, mollify, assuage, calm down, cool one's temper, quell, subdue, smooth over, smooth one's ruffled feathers, compose; pour balm into *or* on one's wounds, restore, make well, heal, cure; restore peace, restore harmony, harmonize; win over, bring to terms, resolve problems, settle differences, accommodate, adjust, bridge over, bring together, mediate; show (tender) mercy, grant clemency, grant a truce, grant an armistice, grant peace, give terms
   ▶ *Peace 73; Mediation 75; Satisfaction 273; Forgiveness 312; Agreement 462; Moderation 521; Repair 809*

11 **pacify,** make peace, sue for peace, stop fighting, halt hostilities, call it quits, cry quits, break it up, bury the hatchet, let bygones be bygones, forgive and forget, forget grievances, pretend it never happened; make friends, shake hands, shake on it; make it up, kiss and make up, patch up a quarrel, come to an understanding, make a deal, get together, learn to live together; settle differences *or* a dispute, compromise, meet halfway, agree, agree to differ, agree to disagree
   ▶ *Forgiveness 312; Contract 459; Compromise 461; Agreement 462; Cessation 668*

ADVERBS

12 **pacifically,** peacefully, irenically, moderately, mediatorially; accommodatingly, leniently, mercifully, forgivingly, clemently, soothingly, agreeably, in agreement, together
   ▶ *Mediation 75; Agreement 462; Accord 735*

75 Mediation

NOUNS

1 **mediation,** intermediation, negotiation, give and take, conciliation, reconciliation, diplomacy, statesmanship; arbitration, judgment, umpirage; pacification, propitiation, moderation; intervention, interposition, intercession, stepping in, troubleshooting, good offices
   ▶ *Pacification 74; Advice 176; Judgment 341; Activity 414; Negotiation 460; Moderation 521*

2 **mediator,** intermediary, intermediator, intercessor, interceder, negotiator; arbiter, arbitrator, referee, umpire, judge; diplomat, diplomatist, statesman; pacifier, propitiator, peacemaker, dove, appeaser, conciliator; moderator, moderating influence, troubleshooter, common friend, middleman, go-between, liaison, third party; matchmaker, marriage broker; adviser, counselor; marriage adviser, marriage counselor, marriage guidance counselor
   ▶ *Judgment 341; Activity 414; Negotiation 460; Moderation 521; Interface 616*

3 **representative,** rep [Inf], delegate, spokesman, spokeswoman, spokesperson, mouthpiece; agent, publicist, public relations (PR) person, press agent, ombudsman; attorney, accountant, consultant, adviser, counselor; pleader, propitiator, peacemaker
   ▶ *Deputy 80; Advice 176*

4 **conference,** peace conference, parley, talks
   ▶ *Conversation 210*

ADJECTIVES

5 **mediatory,** mediatorial, arbitral, arbitrational; diplomatic, intercessory, intercessional; pacificatory, propitiatory, conciliatory; advisory
   ▶ *Pacification 74; Advice 176; Judgment 341; Interface 616*

VERBS

6 **mediate,** intermediate, negotiate; arbitrate, referee, umpire, judge, officiate; find agreement, settle differences, reconcile, conciliate; pacify, propitiate, moderate; intercede, be a go-between, put oneself between, jump in the middle, intervene, interpose, step in; bring together, bring to the table; act as agent for, run messages for, offer one's intercession, proffer one's good offices
   ▶ *Pacification 74; Advice 176; Judgment 341; Activity 414; Moderation 521; Interface 616*

ADVERBS

7 **mediatorially,** mediately, intermediately; conciliatorily, diplomatically; judgmentally

76 War

NOUNS

1 **war,** conflict, armed conflict, military conflict, intervention, armed intervention, arms, the sword; quarrel, struggle, warpath; real war, hot war, aggressive war; fortunes of war, wager of battle, arbitrament of war; war of conquest, war of expansion, imperialist war; limited war, war of containment, localized war; war on all fronts, triphibious war, all-out war, major war, general war; *ultima ratio regum* [L]

2 world war, global war, total war; World War I, war to end all wars, the Great War, World War II, Armageddon

3 warfare, war, warring, waging war, making war, declaring war, open war; military operation; atomic war, nuclear war, total destruction; modern warfare, push-button war, high-tech war, computer war; desert warfare, mountain warfare, jungle warfare; battles, skirmishes, sieges; bloodshed, deeds of blood, violence, fighting, campaigning, soldiering; truceless war, war to the knife, war to the end *or* the death, no prisoners taken, no holds barred

4 atomic warfare, nuclear warfare, strategic nuclear warfare, theater nuclear warfare, tactical nuclear warfare, limited nuclear warfare, Mutual Assured Destruction (MAD)

5 chemical warfare, gas warfare, biological warfare, bacteriological warfare, germ warfare; poison gas, nerve gas; defoliant, Agent Orange

6 civil war, brother war, internecine war

7 economic warfare, sanctions, economic sanctions, arms sanctions, trade sanctions, military sanctions, blockade, attrition, scorched-earth policy

8 holy war, religious war, crusade, jihad

9 war of independence, revolt, revolution, ideological war, war of liberation

10 naval warfare, submarine warfare, undersea warfare, amphibious warfare, sea battle, sea bombardment, sea raiding, fleet blockade

11 offensive warfare, attack, campaign, expedition, mission, operation; operations, land operations, sea operations, naval operations, air operations, amphibious operations, combined operation, allied operation, joint operation; invasion, incursion, raid; mobile warfare, blitz *or* blitzkrieg; static warfare, trench warfare; guerrilla warfare, sniping

12 preventive warfare, defense, Strategic Defense Initiative (SDI) *or* Star Wars

13 psychological warfare, wartime propaganda, wartime censorship; paper war, war of words, war of attrition, polemic, war of nerves, saber-rattling, gunboat diplomacy, intimidation, undeclared war; uneasy peace, cold war

14 belligerency, militancy, militarism, military tradition; hostilities; state of war, state of siege; resort to arms, declaration of war, outbreak of war; wartime, wartime conditions, time of war, the war years

15 bellicosity, pugnacity, pugnaciousness, combativeness; war fever, love of war, warlike habits, military spirit, fighting spirit; aggressiveness, aggression, expansionism; hawkishness, saber-rattling, might is right; patriotism, fervent patriotism, jingoism, chauvinism, my country right or wrong

 ▶ *Argument 329; Misjudgment 342; Contention 422; Disagreement 463*

16 art of war, tactics of war, war strategy, war skills, grand strategy; warcraft, siegecraft, fortification; military leadership, generalship, soldiership, seamanship, airmanship; staffwork, logistics, planning; plan, plan of battle, battle plan, campaign plan; military evolutions, maneuvers, tactics, strategy; war games, military experience, battlefield knowledge, knowledge of the enemy

 ▶ *Military Affairs 58; Skillfulness 127; Knowledge 348; Plan 387*

17 glory of war, pomp and circumstance of war, panoply of war, triumphal procession; chivalry, shining armor; martial music, military band, drums, bugle, trumpet; bugle call, battle call; battle cry, battle yell, rallying cry, rebel yell, war cry, war whoop; war song, war dance

18 war measures, war policy, war footing, war readiness, war preparations; war effort, war work, arming, appeal to arms; call to arms, clarion call, call, rally; call-up, mobilization, recruitment, conscription, the draft, national service, military duty; enlisting, volunteering,

---

MAJOR WARS AND CONFLICTS

American Civil War *or* War Between the States (1861–65)

American Revolution *or* War of Independence *or* Revolutionary War (1775–83)

Boer Wars (1880–81; 1899–1902)

Crimean War (1853–56)

Crusades (11th–13th centuries)

English Civil War (1642–46)

Falklands War (1982)

Franco-Prussian War (1870–71)

French and Indian War (1754–63)

French Revolution (1789–99)

Hundred Years War (1337–1453)

Iran-Iraq War (1980–88)

Korean War (1950–53)

Mexican Civil War (1910–20)

Mexican War (1846–48)

Napoleonic Wars (1796–1815)

Opium Wars (1839–42; 1856–60)

Peloponnesian Wars (431–404 B.C.)

Persian Gulf War (1991)

Punic Wars (264–146 B.C.)

Russian Revolution (1918–20)

Russo-Japanese War (1904–05)

Samnite Wars (350–200 B.C.)

Seven Years War (1756–63)

Sino-Japanese Wars (1894–95; 1937–45)

Six-Day War (1967)

Spanish-American War (1898)

Spanish Civil War (1936–39)

Taiping Rebellion (1850–64)

Thirty Years War (1618–48)

Vietnam War (1957–75)

War of 1812 (1812–15)

War of the Austrian Succession (1740–48)

War of the Spanish Succession (1701–13)

Wars of the Roses (1455–85)

Winter War *or* Russo-Finnish War (1939–40)

World War I (1914–18)

World War II (1939–45)

Yom Kippur War (1973)

joining up, doing one's duty for God and country; rationing, blackout, civilian evacuation, victory gardens, censorship, propaganda; internment
> *Sign 183; Preparation 388*

19 **military training,** military academy, war college, staff college; training, drill, march, obstacle course; ballistics, gunnery, rifle practice, musketry practice

20 **word of command,** order, military orders, battle orders, command; password, watchword
> *Combatant 77; Weapon 78; Attack 418; Defense 419; Contention 422*

21 **bombing,** strategic bombing, tactical bombing, bombardment, saturation bombing, carpet bombing

22 **blockading,** besieging; investment, enclosure, artillery warfare, aerial warfare

23 **battle,** pitched battle, battle royal; armed conflict, action, fight, skirmish, brush, collision, clash, shootout, scrap [Inf]; offensive, blitz, attack; defense, defensive battle, stand; engagement, infantry engagement, naval engagement, sea fight, air fight, dogfight; line of battle, order of battle

24 **battleground,** battlefield, field of battle, field of conflict, killing field; battle zone, war zone, theater of war, combat zone; area of hostilities, front line, front, firing line, beachhead, bridgehead; sector, salient, bulge, pocket, field of blood, Aceldama
> *Attack 418; Defense 419; Contention 422*

25 **warrior,** fighter, serviceman *or* servicewoman, soldier, sailor, pilot, marine
> *Combatant 77*

ADJECTIVES

26 **warring,** fighting, battling, contending, campaigning; at war, waging war, engaged in war, on the warpath, in a state of war; belligerent, aggressive, bellicose, militant; on active duty, mobilized, called, called-up, drafted, conscripted; armed, uniformed, in the army *or* the military; arrayed, embattled, up in arms, sword in hand; at the front, in battle, engaged, at grips; on the offensive, attacking, on the defensive, defending; at loggerheads
> *Preparation 388; Attack 418; Defense 419; Contention 422; Disagreement 463*

27 **warlike,** militaristic, bellicose, hawkish, unpacific, militant, aggressive, belligerent, pugnacious, pugilistic, combative, gung-ho [Inf]; war-loving, warmongering, bloodthirsty, battle-hungry, war-fevered; fierce, tough, cruel, ass-kicking [Inf]
> *Violence 520*

28 **military,** paramilitary, mercenary, martial, exercised in arms, bearing arms; veteran, battle-scarred, shell-shocked; knightly, chivalrous, soldierly, soldierlike, naval; operational, strategic, tactical

VERBS

29 **go to war,** declare war, resort to arms, choose the military solution, open hostilities; call to arms, appeal

to arms, take to arms, fly to arms; unleash the dogs of war, unsheathe the sword, throw away the scabbard, whet the sword; take up the cause, take up the cudgels for, fight; rise, rebel, revolt, overthrow

30 **arm,** militarize, mobilize, prepare for war, put on a war footing; rally, call up, call to the colors

31 **join the army,** join up, enlist, enroll, volunteer, answer the call, get one's call-up papers, receive a letter from Uncle Sam; recruit, conscript, draft, put on a uniform; commission, give *or* take a commission, serve one's country
> *Military Affairs 58; Contention 422*

32 **be at war,** make war, wage war, engage in war *or* hostilities, march to war, go on the warpath; war, war against, war upon; go on active service, ship out, shoulder a musket, smell powder, taste battle, flesh one's sword, open a campaign, campaign, soldier, take the field; take the offensive, invade, attack, raid, ambush, cut down; keep the field, hold one's ground, resist incursions, stand firm; defend, act on the defensive; counterattack, counter, maneuver, march, countermarch; blockade, cut off, beleaguer, besiege, starve out, invest, surround; shed blood, bloody, put to the sword, slaughter, mow down, slay, kill, ravage, rape, burn, scorch, lay waste, destroy, demolish; press the button, drop the bomb, nuke [Inf]; kick ass [Inf]
> *Killing 30; Attack 418; Defense 419; Contention 422; Destruction 523*

33 **battle,** do battle, give battle, offer battle, accept battle; cross swords with, take issue with, contest, dispute, resist; make *or* take a stand, stand, take a position, choose one's ground, dig in; sound the charge, beat the drum, go over the top, charge, engage, provoke an engagement, call for a showdown, confront; join in battle, meet on the battlefield, open fire, fire at, shoot at, stage a shootout, skirmish, brush with, contend, combat; fight, fight it out, fight to the finish, fight to the last man, fight the good fight; close the ranks, rally
> *Defiance 416; Resistance 417; Contention 422*

ADVERBS

34 **at war,** at arms; at the front, in the thick of the fray, at swords' points, at the point of a bayonet, in the cannon's mouth, in the face of death; belligerently, militantly, militarily, militaristically

77 Combatant

NOUNS

1 **combatant,** fighter, battler, struggler, contender, adversary, opponent; agonist, aggressor, assailant, assaulter; attacker, besieger, stormer, escalader; fighting man, belligerent, militarist, man-at-arms, warrior, brave; dueler, duelist; swordsman, blade, knight, paladin; gunman, assassin, killer, bravo; strong-arm man, bully, rowdy, tough, ruffian, fire-eater, swashbuckler

swaggerer, hooligan; thug, gangster, hoodlum, bully-boy, rough; skinhead [Inf], hit man [Inf]

> *Killing 30; Combat Sports 152; Attack 418; Contention 422; Violence 520*

2 defender, protector, policeman, sheriff; bodyguard, security guard, secret service member; vigilante, bouncer

> *Defense 419; Safety 810*

3 militarist, warmonger, hawk, militant, hard-liner; jingoist, chauvinist; imperialist, expansionist; crusader, warrior for God, conquistador; professional soldier, janissary, mercenary, soldier of fortune, adventurer, condottiere; privateer, pirate, buccaneer, freebooter, marauder, raider, plunderer

> *Military Affairs 58; War 76; Stealing 479*

4 soldier, serviceman, servicewoman, military man, fighting man, professional soldier, warrior; officer, standard-bearer, colorbearer, private soldier, common soldier, rookie, GI, Tommy [Brit inf]; recruit, volunteer, conscript, enlisted man, draftee, pressed man, effective; man-at-arms, redcoat [Brit], tribal warrior, brave; long-term soldier, trooper, regular, campaigner, reservist, militiaman, irregular; [Inf]: grunt, Yank, doughboy; weekend warrior

5 former soldier, ex-serviceman, ex-servicewoman, old soldier, old trooper, old campaigner, veteran, vet [Inf], Veterans of Foreign Wars (VFW) member, American Legion member

6 former servicewoman; member of: Women's Army Corps (WAC), Women in the Air Force (WAF), Women Accepted for Voluntary Emergency Service (WAVES); female warrior, battlemaid, amazon

7 guerrilla, freedom fighter, resistance fighter, underground fighter, partisan, terrorist, raider, fedayeen

> *War 76; Resistance 417; Contention 422*

8 historical soldier, archer, bowman, crossbowman, arbalester; spearman, pikeman, halberdier, lancer, cataphract; harquebusier, matchlockman, musketeer, fusilier, rifleman, pistoleer, carabineer, grenadier; cannoneer, miner; legion, cohort, century, decury, maniple

9 armed forces, military forces, services: US Army, US Air Force, US Navy, US Marines, US Coast Guard; professional forces, standing forces, regular forces, veteran forces, reserve forces, volunteer forces, conscript forces; militia, mercenary forces; fighting forces, combat troops, support troops, combat-ready forces, reserve forces, allied forces, enemy forces

10 armed force, spearhead, advance party, reconnaissance party, landing force, expeditionary force, striking force, flying column, elite troops, assault troops, commandos; task force, raiding party, field army; line, front line, first echelon, wing, van, vanguard, second echelon, center, main body, staff, rear, base, rear guard, reserve troops, garrison, base troops

11 reinforcements, ready reserves, standby reserves, National Guard; recruits, replacements, conscripts, draftees, auxiliaries, militia

> *Fear 283; Resistance 417; Defense 419; Safety 810*

12 army, US Army, US Army Reserve, active *or* standing army, regular army, veteran army, reserve army; volunteer army, conscript army, militia, mercenary army; National Guard

13 army commands, forces, US European Command, US Forces Korea, US Forces Japan, US Pacific Command, training and doctrine, matériel, information systems, health services, intelligence and security, management, military District of Washington, criminal investigation, corps of engineers, special operations

14 army unit, army group, army, corps, division, brigade, regiment, battalion; squadron, troop, company, battery, platoon, section, squad; detail, party, band, unit, detachment

> *War 76*

15 army formation, array, column, file, rank

16 army combat specialist, artilleryman, infantryman, cavalryman, tanker, paratrooper, signalman, machine gunner, mortarman

17 army person, army officer, warrant officer, enlisted person; common soldier, infantryman, foot soldier, foot, footslogger; man-at-arms, the ranks, rank and file, cannon fodder, food for powder, gallant company, merry men, peon

18 navy, US Navy (USN), US Coast Guard (USCG), US Naval Reserve (USNR), merchant marine; admiralty, senior service, silent service, naval armament, sea power; gunboat diplomacy, sail, wooden walls, mothball fleet

19 naval commands, operating forces: manpower and training, submarine warfare, surface warfare, logistics, air warfare, plans and operations; matériel, medicine and surgery, education and training, personnel, air systems, electronic systems, facilities, engineering, sea systems, supply systems

20 naval unit, fleet, task force, division, flotilla, squadron, convoy, armada, argosy

21 warship, war vessel, man-of-war, flagship, command ship, flotilla leader, capital ship; aircraft carrier, flattop [Inf], escort carrier, nuclear carrier, battleship, pocket battleship, battle cruiser, cruiser, heavy cruiser, light cruiser, destroyer, destroyer escort, corvette, cutter, patrol boat *or* PT boat *or* motor torpedo boat, gunboat; submarine, U-boat [Ger], nuclear submarine, ballistic missile submarine *or* boomer [Inf], attack submarine; submarine chaser; minelayer, minesweeper, blockship, Q-ship; landing craft, amphibious truck *or* duck, amphibian *or* amtrac; fleet auxiliary vessels: transport ship, troopship, tender, repair ship, store ship, depot ship, ammunition ship, supply ship, fuel ship, tanker, hospital ship, icebreaker

▶ *Water Transportation* 690

22 historical warships, longship; war galley, bireme, trireme, quinquereme, galleon, galleass; ship of the line, frigate, sloop, bomb ship, fire ship; ironclad, dreadnought

23 naval mine, torpedo, depth charge

24 navy specialties, marine engineering, weapons control, data systems, construction, health care, logistics, cryptology, communications, intelligence, aviation-sensor operations, ship maintenance

25 naval person, naval officer, warrant officer, enlisted person; sailor, bluejacket, coastguardsman, submariner, naval airman, Seabee; [Inf]: gob, swabby, limey [Brit]
▶ *Military Affairs* 58

26 marines, US Marines, marine; [Inf]: leatherneck, gyrene, jarhead

27 air force, US Air Force (USAF), US Air Force Reserves, Air National Guard

28 air force commands, air combat, air mobility, matériel, space, education and training, intelligence, special operations; planning, Pacific Air Forces, US Air Forces Europe

29 air force unit, air force, air division, group, wing, squadron, flight, element

30 military aircraft, aircraft, plane, airplane, warplane, battle plane, bomber, fighter-bomber, heavy bomber, medium bomber, strategic bomber, light bomber, attack bomber, fighter, pursuit fighter, night fighter, interceptor, antisubmarine plane, ground-attack aircraft; reconnaissance fighter *or* bomber, spy plane, airborne warning and control systems (AWACS) plane, patrol plane, scout; transport plane, troop carrier; amphibian, flying boat; helicopter, helicopter gunship, transport helicopter; trainer; zeppelin, blimp
▶ *Transportation* 686; *Aviation* 689

31 air force person, air force officer, warrant officer, enlisted man; aircraft commander, fighter pilot, bomber pilot, transport pilot, reconnaissance pilot, copilot, navigator, gunner, bombardier, observer, radioman, radarman, technician, specialist, instructor, air crew, crew chief, engineer, ground crew, medic, cook
▶ *Military Affairs* 58

ADJECTIVES

32 combative, aggressive, hostile, adversarial, opposing, agonistic; bellicose, belligerent, pugnacious; militant, militaristic, warlike; hard-line, crusading; buccaneering, piratical, bloodthirsty; rowdy, rough, tough, thuggish; trigger-happy [Inf], gung-ho [Inf]
▶ *Military Affairs* 58; *War* 76; *Attack* 418

33 martial, pugilistic; mercenary, auxiliary; soldierly, soldierlike; brave, heroic; armed, armored; enlisted, drafted, conscripted, recruited, signed up
▶ *Military Affairs* 58; *War* 76

VERBS

34 combat, make trouble, rabble-rouse; warmonger, crusade; break cease-fire, shatter the peace; declare war,

wage a campaign; send (in) the marines, attack, assault, assail, storm, besiege, lay siege to
▶ *War* 76; *Attack* 418; *Contention* 422

35 fight, shoot, fire, pull the trigger, gun down, bomb, blast; charge, strike, spear, lance, joust, tilt, fence; spar, put on one's boxing gloves, box, punch, hit, wrestle, grapple
▶ *Military Affairs* 58; *War* 76; *Sports* 145

36 conquer, win, subdue, quell, overcome; storm, take over, invade; maraud, raid, plunder, rob; kill, assassinate, massacre; terrorize
▶ *Killing* 30; *Taking* 477

37 defend, protect; police, guard; resist, oppose
▶ *Resistance* 417; *Defense* 419; *Protest* 507; *Opposition* 828

ADVERBS

38 aggressively, inimically, agonistically, antagonistically, belligerently, pugnaciously; militantly, militaristically; bloodthirstily, rowdily, litigiously, combatively

39 martially, pugilistically; bravely, heroically; at war, up in arms, under fire, under siege; on the front line, in the cannon's mouth, in the thick of the fray

78 Weapon

NOUNS

1 weapon, arm; natural weapon: teeth, fist, claws, nails; man-powered weapon: sword, lance, catapult; conventional *or* machine weapon: rifle, cannon, warplane; chemical weapon, bacteriological weapon; nuclear weapon: strategic nuclear weapon, theater nuclear weapon, tactical nuclear weapon; secret weapon, death ray
▶ *War* 76; *Affliction* 117; *Attack* 418; *Defense* 419; *Sharpness* 549

2 arms race, defense, arms traffic, (nuclear) proliferation, arms trade, gunrunning
▶ *Defense* 419

3 arsenal, armory, arms depot, arms cache; ammunition ship, powder magazine, ammunition dump, ammunition train, ammunition room, ammunition chest, caisson; gun room, powder barrel *or* keg, bomb bay, bomb rack, ammo dump [Inf]
▶ *Store* 105; *Container* 578

4 modern missile weapon, missile, ballistic missile, intercontinental ballistic missile (ICBM), multiple independently targetable reentry vehicle (MIRV); missile site, launching pad, silo, ballistic missile submarine; theater ballistic missile, tactical ballistic missile, guided missile, surface-to-air missile (SAM), cruise missile, surface-to-surface missile; defensive missile, antimissile missile, antiballistic missile (ABM); artillery missile, antitank missile, bazooka; rocket launcher, rocket, rocket site; V-1, V-2

5 blunt weapon, blunt instrument; club, bludgeon, sandbag, blackjack, truncheon, billy, baton, cudgel, shillelagh, lathi; pole hammer, tomahawk, hammer, mace; staff, stave, weighted walking stick, knobkerrie, stick, switch, quarterstaff; battering ram, ram, rifle butt; knuckle-duster *or* brass knuckles; bicycle chain, rock, stone, slingshot, bottle, baseball bat, pipe, whip, flail, cosh

▶ *Impulsion 695*

6 **sharp weapon,** lance, javelin, harpoon, pike, assegai, partisan, guisarme, pigsticker; arrow, bow and arrow; gaff, bill, halberd; ax, broadax, battle-ax, poleax, hatchet; sword, blade, broadsword, cutlass, glaive [Arch], bilbo [Arch], claymore, short sword, falchion, hanger, scimitar, cavalry sword, saber, yataghan; rapier, tuck [Arch], fencing sword, foil, épée; bayonet, dagger, poniard, snickersnee, dirk, skean, skean dhu, dudgeon, misericord *or* misericorde, stylet, stiletto; machete, kukri, creese, parang, panga; knife, bowie knife, switchblade (knife)

▶ *Sharpness 549*

7 **firearm,** small arms, gun, handgun, revolver, pistol, piece, derringer, six-shooter, zip gun; shotgun, fowling piece, sporting gun, sawed-off shotgun, smoothbore, rifle bore; breechloader, bolt-action firearm, pump-action firearm, gas-operated firearm, recoil-operated firearm; automatic, semiautomatic, single-shot repeater; rifle, magazine-fed rifle, clip-fed rifle, repeating rifle, grenade launcher; machine gun, light machine gun, carbine, submachine gun, *mitrailleuse* [Fr], flamethrower; [Inf]: rod, Saturday night special, gat, shooting iron, equalizer

8 **historical handgun,** harquebus *or* hackbut *or* hagbut, matchlock, wheel lock, flintlock, fusil, musket, blunderbuss, muzzleloader, chassepot; dueling pistol, horse pistol; petronel

9 **guns,** ordnance, cannonry, artillery, light artillery, medium artillery, heavy artillery, self-propelled artillery, mountain artillery, coast artillery; battery, broadside, artillery park, gun park, gun emplacement; field piece, field gun, howitzer, trench mortar; antiaircraft gun, antiaircraft artillery, pompom; bazooka; guncarriage, limber, caisson

10 **historical gun,** bombard, swivel, culverin; mortar, cannon, brass cannon, horse artillery

11 **ammunition,** round, live ammunition; armor-piercing ammunition, tracer ammunition, explosive ammunition, fléchette ammunition, illuminating ammunition, white phosphorus ammunition, fragmentation ammunition, incendiary ammunition, training ammunition; powder, shot, buckshot, ball; bullet, expanding *or* soft-nosed *or* dumdum bullet, rubber bullet, plastic bullet; slug, pellet; projectile, missile; shell, shrapnel, flak, ack-ack [Inf]; ammunition box, clip, magazine, cartridge, cartridge belt, cartridge case, bandoleer; sheath, holster

12 **historical ammunition,** round shot *or* cannonball, canister (shot), case shot, grapeshot, chain shot, buckshot, ball; heated shot, explosive shot; bullet pouch, powder flask, powder horn, wad, cartouche; arrow case, quiver; scabbard

▶ *Propulsion 696*

13 **explosive,** high explosive, dynamite, gelignite, trinitrotoluene (TNT), nitroglycerine, lyddite, melinite, cordite, plastic explosive, semtex; cap, detonator, fuse, priming, charge; warhead, atomic warhead, fissionable material

14 **propellant,** powder, gunpowder, saltpeter, guncotton; fireworks, Greek fire

15 **bomb,** explosive device, shell, bombshell; grenade, hand grenade, Molotov cocktail, pineapple [Inf]; megaton bomb, atom bomb *or* A-bomb, nuclear bomb, hydrogen bomb *or* H-bomb, neutron bomb, enhanced radiation bomb; cluster bomb, fragmentation bomb, nail bomb, firebomb, incendiary bomb, napalm bomb, blockbuster; mine, landmine, magnetic mine, acoustic mine, limpet mine; letter bomb, mail bomb, car bomb, time bomb, booby trap, infernal machine; depth charge, torpedo, tin fish; flying bomb, rocket bomb, V-1, V-2

ADJECTIVES

16 **strategic,** theater, tactical; ballistic, intercontinental, guided, surface-to-air, surface-to-surface, defensive; antimissile, antiballistic, antitank

17 **bolt-action,** pump-action, gas-operated, recoil-operated, magazine-fed, clip-fed, repeating

18 **armor-piercing,** tracer, explosive, illuminating, fragmentation, incendiary, training; expanding, soft-nosed, dumdum, rubber, plastic

79 Delegate

An ambassador is an honest man sent to lie abroad for the commonwealth. — SIR HENRY WOTTON

NOUNS

1 **delegate,** elected person, appointed person, appointee, envoy, emissary; elected representative, offi-

---

HISTORICAL MISSILE WEAPONS

arbalest	brick	javelin	stick
arrow	brickbat	longbow	stone
atlatl	cannon	mangonel	throwing
ball	catapult	mounted	club
ballista	chakram	crossbow	throwing
barb	crossbow	onager	knife
blowgun	dart	quarrel	throwing
blowpipe	firearm	shot	stick
bola	fléchette	sling	tomahawk
bolt	gun	spear	torpedo
boomerang	hand grenade	spear-	trebuchet
bow	harpoon	thrower	woomera

cial representative, political representative, congressman, congresswoman, representative, senator, member of Parliament (MP) [Brit], parliamentarian [Brit]; cabinet member, secretary, minister; diplomat, diplomatic officer, ambassador, attaché, legate, commissioner, chargé d'affaires, consul; nuncio, negotiator; legislator, councilor or councillor; convention or conference or workshop delegate

2 **representative body,** delegation, legation, foreign service, diplomatic corps; embassy, consulate, mission, trade delegation; legislature, Congress, House of Representatives, Senate, parliament; town meeting, council, city council, town council, board of aldermen, aldermanic board, county board; official body, negotiating body, committee, forum, round table; workshop, convention, conference, conclave
   ▶ *Government 49; Politics 50; Deputy 80*

3 **delegation,** authorization, appointment, nomination, assignment, election; delegation of work, delegation of power; shared responsibility, decentralization, devolution, devolvement, job sharing; deputation, deputizing, deputing, assignment of work, consignation
   ▶ *Transfer 685; Commission 833*

ADJECTIVES

4 **delegated,** delegable, elected, appointed; legislative, representative, congressional, senatorial, parliamentary; ministerial, diplomatic, ambassadorial, legatine, legationary, plenipotentiary, consular, proconsular; intermediary, deputy

5 **decentralized,** devolved, shared; deputed, assigned, consigned

VERBS

6 **delegate,** depute, deputize; assign, consign; appoint, elect; authorize, commission, empower, entrust; spread the load, share the work; devolve, decentralize; transfer, turn over to

7 **represent,** act for, stand for, speak for, substitute for; represent the interests of, serve as a representative, act as proxy; attend a council meeting or convention or conference, serve on a working party
   ▶ *Deputy 80; Commission 833*

ADVERBS

8 **representatively,** congressionally, senatorially, parliamentarily; ministerially, diplomatically

80 Deputy

NOUNS

1 **deputy,** vicegerent, assistant, right hand, second-in-command, number two; aide, lieutenant; deputy sheriff, vice-regent, vice president, undersecretary, vice-chairman, vice-chancellor, vice-admiral, viceroy, vice-consul, proconsul, vicar, vicar-general; administrative assistant, secretary, girl or man Friday; auxiliary, relief worker, temporary worker, temp [Inf]; spokesperson, spokesman, spokeswoman, public relations (PR) person; power behind the throne, gray eminence or éminence grise
   ▶ *Management 126; News 171; Persuasion 178; Help 825*

2 **alternative,** alternate, surrogate, proxy; substitute, sub [Inf], scrub, replacement, pinch hitter, reserve; understudy, double, stand-in, backup, stunt man or woman; ghost writer
   ▶ *Drama and Theater 136; Literature 139; Baseball 147; Football 155; Substitution 672*

3 **agent,** go-between, representative, delegate, intermediary, middleman, messenger; trustee, broker, literary agent, contact; negotiator, arbitrator, mediator; lawyer, solicitor, attorney, barrister [Brit]; diplomatic agent, emissary, envoy, plenipotentiary, consular agent; matchmaker; pander or panderer, pimp
   ▶ *Government 49; Law 53; Delegate 79; Negotiation 460; Interface 616; Cooperation 827*

ADJECTIVES

4 **deputizing,** deputative, representing, acting, standing in, stand-in, substituting, substitute; intermediary, provisional, temporary; imitative, imitation, ersatz, second-best

VERBS

5 **substitute for,** act for, act on behalf of, act instead of, do duty for, (temporarily) replace; appear for, negotiate for; understudy, double for, back up; stand in for, stand in the stead of; ghostwrite or ghost, act as proxy, front for, pinch-hit for [Inf]

6 **represent,** negotiate, arbitrate, mediate; assist, help, aid; speak for, act as a mouthpiece for, act as broker for, act as a go-between; hold in trust, manage the business of, manage the interests of, manage

7 **deputize,** depute, authorize, empower, charge, designate, nominate
   ▶ *Delegate 79*

ADVERBS

8 **indirectly,** in or on behalf of, for, by proxy; diplomatically, imitatively
   ▶ *Delegate 79*

81 Religion

Religion is love; in no case is it logic. — BEATRICE WEBB

NOUNS

1 **religion,** faith, belief, belief system, set of beliefs, creed, credo, dogma, doctrine, persuasion, conviction; way of life, attitude, outlook, morals, ethics, moral code, philosophy of life, point of view, perspective, theology
   ▶ *Philosophy 4; Belief 87; Persuasion 178; Thought 317; Certainty 840*

2 **religiousness,** piety, piousness, reverence, honor, veneration, observance, strictness, faithfulness, ritualism; deism, theism, mysticism, spirituality; prayerfulness, communion with God, trust in God, self-surrender,

self-sacrifice, fear of God, theopathy; humility, prostration, dedication, devotion, adoration, unction, zeal, enthusiasm, fervor, speaking in tongues, glossolalia; sanctimony, sanctimoniousness, religiosity, preachiness, churchiness, unctuousness; Bible worship, Biblicism, bibliolatry, literalness, fundamentalism, salvationism, religionism
   ▶ *Religious Ritual 85; Submission 421; Obedience 426*

3 **religious studies,** religious education, religious instruction
   ▶ *Philosophy 4; Education 48*

4 **religious group,** religious movement, denomination, church, school, branch, movement, order, sect, cult, faction, chapter, congregation, meeting
   ▶ *Worship 83; Religious Ritual 85*

5 **Christianity,** Christendom, Western Christianity, Eastern Christianity; Roman Catholicism, Catholicism, Catholic Church, papalism, papism [Off]; Anglo-Catholicism, Anglicanism, High Church, Low Church, Broad Church, Church of England; Protestantism, Reform, Evangelicalism; Christian Science, Mormonism; trinitarianism, unitarianism, fundamentalism

6 **Judaism,** Hebraism, Orthodox Judaism, Conservative Judaism, Reform Judaism, Hasidism

7 **Islam,** Muslimism, Muhammadanism *or* Mohammedanism, Sufism, Shi'ism, Druzism, Black Muslimism, Muslim fundamentalism

8 **other religions,** Buddhism, Zen Buddhism, Hinduism, Sikhism, Shintoism, Jainism, Baha'ism, Rastafarianism, Zoroastrianism, Confucianism

9 **religious person,** believer, religious, pietist, worshiper, man *or* woman of prayer, monk, nun, priest, rabbi, votary, convert, devotee, disciple, missionary, evangelist, salvationist; child of God, saint, marabout, Bodhisattva, martyr, pilgrim, palmer, hajji, mystic, charismatic, holy man, sadhu, sannyasi, bhikshu, fakir, neophyte, catechumen, acolyte
   ▶ *Clergy 84; Belief 87*

10 **Christian,** practicing Christian, communicant, con-

CHRISTIAN GROUPS

Adventist churches	Evangelicalism
African Methodist Episcopal churches	Friends *or* Quakers
	Grace Gospel Fellowship
African Methodist Episcopal Zion churches	Jehovah's Witnesses
	Latter-Day Saints *or* Mormonism
Anglicanism	Lutheranism
Anglo-Catholicism	Mennonite churches
Antinomianism	Methodism
Assemblies of God	Moral Rearmament
Baptist churches	Moravianism
Calvinism	Pentecostal churches
Christian Science *or* Church of Christ, Scientist	Presbyterianism
	Reformed churches
Churches of Christ	Roman Catholicism
Churches of God	Russian Orthodoxy
Churches of the Brethren	Salvation Army
Churches of the Nazarene	Swedenborgianism
Congregationalism	Unification Church
Coptic Church	Unitarian Universalism
Eastern Orthodoxy	Wesleyanism
Episcopalianism	

---

formist, Catholic, Roman Catholic, papist [Off]; Anglo-Catholic, Anglican, Episcopalian, Protestant, Unitarian, Trinitarian, Evangelical, born-again Christian, Nonconformist, Moonie

11 **Jew,** Orthodox Jew, Conservative Jew, Reform Jew, Hasid, Zionist; Essene, Pharisee, Sadducee

12 **Muslim,** Muhammadan *or* Mohammedan, Mussulman [Arch], Sufi, Shi'ite, Sunnite, Druze, Wahhabi, Black Muslim, Muslim fundamentalist

13 **other religious member,** Hindu, Buddhist, Zen Buddhist, Sikh, Jain *or* Jaina *or* Jainist, Baha'i, Rastafarian, Zoroastrian, Parsee *or* Parsi, Confucian

14 **religionist,** zealot, iconoclast, formalist, precisian, inerrantist, Sabbatarian, bibliolater, preacher, pulpiteer, sermonizer, salvationist, missionary, fanatic, cultist; evangelist, TV evangelist *or* televangelist, fundamentalist, militant Christian, revivalist; [Inf]: Jesus freak, Bible-thumper, Holy Roller [Off]

15 **religious text,** sacred text, scripture, sacred writings; word of God, canonical writings, canon

16 **Christian text,** Bible, Holy Bible, the Book, the Good Book, the Word, King James Version, Authorized Version, Revised Version, New English Bible, Geneva Bible, Douay Bible, Jerusalem Bible; Vulgate, Septuagint; Old Testament, New Testament, Gospels, Synoptic Gospels, Epistles; Apocrypha; Christian Science text, *Science and Health with Key to the Scriptures*; Mormon text, Book of Mormon

17 **Jewish text,** Torah, Targum, Talmud, Mishnah, Gemara, Masorah, Bahir, Midrash

18 **Islamic text,** Koran *or* Qur'an, the Glorious Koran, Hadith, Sunna

19 **other text,** Ancient Egyptian text, Book of the Dead; Buddhist text, Pitaka, Tripitaka, Theravada, Dhamma, Dhammapada, Jataka, Apadana, Avadana, Lotus of the True Law, Nikaya, Dipavamsa, Mahavastu, Pali Canon, sutras; Confucian text, I Ching, Shih Ching, Shu Ching, Li Chi, Yueh Ching, Ch'un Chiu; Hindu text, Smriti, sruti, shastra, Upanishad, Bhagavad-Gita,

Purana, Veda, Rigveda, Yajurveda, Samaveda, Atharvaveda, Aranyaka, Granth; Jainist text, Agama; Shinto text, Nihongi, Yengishiki; Zoroastrian text, Avesta, Zend-Avesta

◗ *Religious Ritual 85*

20 **theologian,** theologist, theologician, theologizer, theologer, theologue, divine, scholastic, theology *or* divinity student

◗ *Philosophy 4; Interpretation 365*

ADJECTIVES

21 **religious,** pious, devout, holy, godly, saintly, spiritual, mystic, otherworldly, transcendent, churchgoing, practicing; strict, faithful, believing, holding *or* keeping the faith, orthodox, pure, reverent, worshipful, prayerful, devoted, devotional, reverential, solemn, dedicated; born-again, God-fearing, theopathic, self-surrendering, humble, prostrate, self-sacrificing, monastic, anchoretic, ascetic, hermitlike

22 **zealous,** ardent, unctuous, overreligious, priest-ridden, formalistic, pharisaic, overstrict, ritualistic, churchy, overdevout, overrighteous, holier-than-thou, self-righteous, sanctimonious, fervent, preachy, canting, Bible-worshiping, fundamentalist, evangelical, crusading, militant, missionary, fanatical, witch-hunting, Bible-thumping [Inf]

◗ *Belief 87*

23 **denominational,** sectarian, fundamentalist, Christian, Catholic, Roman, Roman Catholic, RC, popish, papish, papist [Off], Protestant, Anglican, Church of England, C of E, High-Church, Low-Church, Episcopalian, Nonconformist; Orthodox, Judaeo-Christian, Jewish, Judaic *or* Judaical, Hebrew, Reform, Conservative, Hasidic, Sephardic; Islamic, Muslim, Hindu, Buddhist, Taoist

24 **theological,** religious, divine, patristic, physicotheological, ontotheological, hierological, hierographical, hagiological, hagiographical, soteriological, Christological, eschatological, doctrinal, ecclesiological, canonical, scriptural, metaphysical

◗ *Philosophy 4; Meaning 361; Interpretation 365*

VERBS

25 **be religious,** get religion, meet God, receive Christ, accept the Lord, enter the church, hold *or* keep the faith, believe, have faith, recite the creed, go to church, receive communion, support the church

26 **revere,** venerate, honor, observe, trust in God, worship, adore, obey, devote oneself, prostrate oneself, humble oneself, surrender oneself, fear God, feel the spirit, be possessed by the spirit, go on a pilgrimage, perform the hajj

27 **recant,** repent, turn, convert, be converted, be saved, have a crisis of faith, be born again

◗ *Religious Ritual 85; Belief 87; Humility 298; Conversion 670*

28 **theologize,** study theology, interpret the scriptures,

THEOLOGIES

angelology	hermeneutics	philosophical
apologetics	hierography,	theology
Buddhology	hierology	physicotheology
crisis theology	liberation	process theology
dialogical theology	theology	rationalism
doctrinal theology	Mariology	scholastic
dogmatic theology	natural theology	theology
ecclesiology	ontotheology	secularism
eschatology	pastoral	soteriology or
existential	theology	Christology
theology	patristic theology,	systematic
feminist theology	patristics	theology
hagiography,	phenomenological	theological
hagiology	theology	metaphysics

study the Bible, ponder the nature of God, philosophize

◗ *Philosophy 4; Meaning 361; Interpretation 365*

ADVERBS

29 **religiously,** piously, spiritually, devoutly, strictly, worshipfully, faithfully, humbly, reverentially, solemnly, ardently; zealously, fanatically, theologically, doctrinally, denominationally, canonically, ecclesiastically, by the book

◗ *Accuracy 350*

82 Deity

The Lord God is subtle but malicious he is not.
— ALBERT EINSTEIN

The world is charged with the grandeur of God.
— GERARD MANLEY HOPKINS

Beloved Pan, and all ye other gods who haunt this place,
  give me beauty in the inward soul; and may the outward
  and inward man be at one. — PLATO

NOUNS

1 **deity,** divinity, supernatural being, immortal; godhead, divineness, divine essence, divine principle, Shekhinah; god, goddess, Olympian, Aesir

◗ *Religion 81*

2 **minor deity,** demigod, spirit, guiding spirit, numen, daemon, genius, inspiration; fertility god, corn god, rain god, earth goddess, moon goddess; household god, Lares, Penates; Muse, Fate, Norn; animistic spirit, mana, nagual, deva; faun, satyr, nymph, dryad, hamadryad, oread, naiad, sea nymph, undine, Nereid; object of worship, idol, fetish, totem

◗ *Worship 83; Religious Ritual 85; Occultism 86*

3 **world soul,** world spirit, *anima mundi* [L], oversoul, life force; the Mother, Great Mother, Mother Nature; celestial, celestial being, angel

4 **divine attribute,** divine nature, perfection, sanctitude, sanctity, holiness, hallowedness, sacredness, sacrosanctity, transcendence, enlightenment; eternity, infinity, immortality, truth, love, mercy, salvation, wisdom, power, supremacy, sovereignty, majesty, omnipresence, omniscience, omnipotence, almightiness

◗ *Authority 52; Good 445; Power 514; Timelessness 640; Eternity 644; Perfection 805*

5 **divine manifestation,** epiphany, avatar, materialization, incarnation, embodiment, appearance, ap-

DEITIES

Greek		Roman	Norse and	Egyptian
Aphrodite	Hephaestus	**Roman**	**Germanic**	Amen
Apollo	Hera	Apollo	Balder	Amen-Ra
Ares	Hermes	Aurora	Brag	Anubis
Artemis	Hestia	Bacchus	Eir	Atmu
Asclepius *or*	Horae, the: Dike,	Bellona	Eostre *or* Estre	Aton *or* Aten
Aesculapius	Eirene, Eunomia	Ceres	Forseti	Bast
Athena *or* Athene	Hyperion	Cupid *or* Amor	Freya *or* Freyja	Chnoumis
Castor	Hypnus	Cybele	Frey *or* Freyr	Geb
Cronus *or* Cronos	Irene	Diana	Frigg	Hathor
Demeter	Iris	Faunus	Gerda	Horus
Dionysus	Muses, the: Calliope,	Fortuna	Heimdall	Isis
Eos	Clio, Erato,	Juno	Hel	Khnemu *or* Khnum
Eris	Euterpe,	Jupiter *or* Jove	Hermoder	Maat
Eros	Melpomene,	Juventas	Hoder	Meshkenit
Fates, the: Atropos,	Polyhymnia,	Mars	Hoenir	Min
Clotho, Lachesis	Terpsichore, Thalia,	Mercury	Loki	Munt *or* Ont
Furies *or* Erinyes *or*	Urania	Minerva	Nanna	Neneh
Eumenides *or*	Nemesis	Mors	Njord *or* Njorth	Nephthys
Kindly Ones, the:	Nike	Neptune	Norns, the: Skuld,	Nut
Alecto, Megaera,	Pan	Pluto	Urd, Verdandi	Osiris
Tisiphone	Persephone *or* Kore	Proserpina	Odmir	Ptah
Gaea *or* Ge	Plutus	Saturn	Thor	Ra *or* Re
Graces, the: Aglaia,	Pollux	Sol	Tiu *or* Tiw *or* Tyr	Rehpet
Euphrosyne, Thalia	Poseidon	Uranus	Vali	Seb
Hades *or* Pluto	Rhea	Venus	Valkyries	Sekhmet
Harpies, the	Selene	Vesta	Vidar	Set *or* Seth
Hebe	Thanatos	Vulcan	Woden *or* Odin *or*	Thoth
Hecate	Tuche		Wotan	
Helios	Uranus			
	Zeus			

parition, visitation, vision, theophany, revelation, mystical experience, meeting with God, mystical intuition, divination, clairvoyance

6 **God,** Lord, Maker, Creator, Supreme Being, Almighty God, the Almighty, King of Kings, Lord of Lords, the Eternal, First Cause, Prime Mover, *primum mobile* [L], Providence; Jehovah, Yahweh, Adonai, Elohim, Hashem; Allah, Great Spirit; Supreme Soul, Atman, Universal Self, Blessed One, Om, Brahma the Creator, Vishnu the Preserver, Siva the Destroyer; Buddha, Blessed One, Teacher, Bodhisattva; Ahura Mazda, Ormazd, Lord of Wisdom, Wise Lord, King of Light; demiurge, Demiourgos, manitou; the Mind, Divine Mind, Father/Mother God
  ◗ *Authority 52; Religion 81; Good 445; Power 514; Eternity 644; Cause 675; Infinity 798*

7 **trinitarian god,** Holy Trinity, Three in One, God the Father, God the Son, God the Holy Ghost *or* Holy Spirit; Trimurti

8 **God the Father,** Father Almighty, Everlasting Father, Maker of all things, Judge of all men

9 **God the Son,** Jesus Christ, Christ, Christ Jesus, Son of God, Emmanuel, Savior, Redeemer, Messiah, Anointed One, Lamb of God, Son of Man, Good Shepherd, Prince of Peace; the Way, the Truth, and the Life, Light of the World, the Word, Logos, the Word Made Flesh, God Incarnate, the Incarnation, King of the Jews

10 **God the Holy Ghost,** Holy Spirit, Spirit of God, Lord and Giver of Life, Paraclete, Comforter, Counselor, Dove

11 **angel,** celestial, heavenly being, archangel, seraph, cherub, guardian angel, ministering spirit, messenger of God; heavenly host, angelic host, choir invisible; Gabriel, Michael, Raphael, Uriel; fallen angel, Lucifer; Azrael, angel of death, death's bright angel; angelology
  ◗ *Good 445; Evil 446; Help 825*

12 **angelic order (highest to lowest),** seraphim, cherubim, thrones, dominations, virtues, powers, principalities, archangels, angels

13 **deification,** divinization, immortalization, idolization, apotheosis, canonization, beatification, sanctification, consecration, enshrinement, exaltation, glorification, elevation
  ◗ *Religion 81; Worship 83; Religious Ritual 85*

14 **deified person,** saint, beatified soul, canonized person; Blessed Virgin Mary, Virgin, Virgin Mother, Madonna, Our Lady, Mother of God, Holy Mary, Queen of Heaven, Queen of Angels; hagiography, hagiolatry, hagiology, Mariology, Mariolatry

15 **heaven,** paradise, sky, firmament, empyrean, celestial kingdom, Kingdom of God; Holy City, Zion, New Jerusalem, Celestial City, City of God, *civitas Dei* [L]; throne of God; Alfardaws, Assuma, Falak al Aflak; nirvana, devaloka, land of the gods; Olympus, Mount Olympus, Elysium, Elysian fields; Islands of the Blessed, Abode of the Gods, Valhalla, Asgard, Fensalir; Avalon, Hesperides, Tir-na-n'Og; happy hunting ground, happy land, Land o' the Leal [Scot], kingdom come
  ◗ *Death 29; Good 445; Nonmaterial World 525; Eternity 644*

ADJECTIVES

16 **divine,** godly, godlike, supernatural, immortal, eternal, infinite, sublime, perfect, supreme, sovereign, majestic, providential, omnipresent, ubiquitous, all-seeing, prescient, all-knowing, omniscient, oracular, all-powerful, omnipotent, almighty, absolute, immeasurable, ineffable, mystical
  ◗ *Authority 52; Power 514; Timelessness 640; Eternity 644; Infinity 798; Perfection 805*

17 **Jehovan,** Yahwistic *or* Jahwistic *or* Yavistic, Elohistic

18 **Christlike,** Christly, messianic, incarnate, theomorphic, epiphanic

19 **holy,** hallowed, sacred, sacrosanct, numinous, transcendent, transcendental, enlightened

20 **deified,** immortalized, canonized, beatified, sanctified, haloed, consecrated, enshrined, elevated, magnified, exalted, glorified, idolized, blessed

21 **angelic,** angelical, archangelic, seraphic, cherubic, saintly, full of grace

22 **heavenly,** celestial, empyrean, empyreal, on high, paradisaical, paradisiacal, paradisiac, paradisal, supernal, ethereal

VERBS

23 **deify,** divinize, immortalize, apotheosize, canonize, bless, beatify, sanctify, angelize, consecrate, hallow, enshrine, elevate, magnify, exalt, glorify, idolize
  ◗ *Religion 81; Worship 83; Religious Ritual 85*

ADVERBS

24 **divinely,** numinously, perfectly, sacredly, transcendentally, sublimely, supremely, majestically, providentially, ineffably, infinitely, absolutely, ubiquitously, omnisciently, almightily, omnipotently, eternally, supernaturally, spiritually, mystically, gracefully; messianically, angelically, seraphically, cherubically; by God's will, *Deo volente* [L], by divine right

83 Worship

NOUNS

1 **worship,** honor, homage, reverence, devotion, devotedness, dedication, veneration, adoration, adulation, esteem, idolatry, bhakti; dignification, glorification, exaltation, magnification, laudation, praise, extolment, puja

2 **act of worship,** celebration, thanksgiving, ritual, blessing, hymn singing, psalm singing; supplication, petition, prayer, praying, kneeling, genuflection, prostration, offering, oblation, sacrifice, penitence; contemplation, meditation, communion, asceticism, fasting; pilgrimage, hajj

> Religion 81; Deity 82; Religious Ritual 85; Music 140; Humility 298; Gratitude 310; Celebration 405; Submission 421; Penitence 451; Offer 504; Request 505

3 **public worship,** church service, divine service, divine office, form of worship, liturgy; prayer meeting, call to prayer, azan, muezzin's cry; morning service, morning prayer, matins, lauds; prime, tierce, sext, nones; evening service, evening prayer, evensong, vespers, compline; *Musaf, Shaharith, Minhah* or *Minchah, Maariv,* Kaddish, Yahrzeit [all Hebrew]

4 **idolatry,** idolism, idolization, iconolatry; cult, cultism, totemism, fetishism or fetichism, phallicism, obeah; animism, animatism, anthropolatry; animal worship, zoolatry, zoomorphism, theriolatry, snake worship, ophiolatry, sun worship, heliolatry, star worship, Sabaism, fire worship, pyrolatry, tree worship, dendrolatry, devil worship, diabolism, demonism, Satanism; ancestor worship, necrolatry, hero worship

> Religion 81; Deity 82; Religious Ritual 85; Occultism 86

5 **idol,** image, graven image, effigy, golden calf, god, deity, icon, totem, fetish, symbol; hero, heroine, celebrity, superstar, megastar, darling, pet, favorite

> Occultism 86; Approval 437; Success 845

6 **worshiper,** venerator, adorer, adulator, praise singer, hymn singer; celebrant; churchgoer, parishioner, chapelgoer, communicant, supplicant, petitioner, penitent, votary, follower; worshipers, fold, flock, congregation, sheep, assembly, gathering, concourse, *minyan* [Hebrew]

> Assembly 59; Religion 81

7 **idolater,** idolizer, iconolater, cultist, totemist, fetishist, phallicist, animist, animatist, anthropolater, animal worshiper, zoolater, theriolater, zoomorphist, snake worshiper, ophiolater, sun worshiper, heliolater, star worshiper, Sabaist, fire worshiper, pyrolater, tree worshiper, dendrolater, devil worshiper, diabolist, Satanist, ancestor worshiper, necrolater; admirer, lionizer, devotee, aficionado, hero-worshiper, fan, groupie [Inf]

> Religion 81; Occultism 86

8 **place of worship,** church, kirk, mission, meeting house, conventicle, house of God, house of prayer, house of worship, bethel, kirk [Scot]; chapel, Lady chapel, chapel of rest, chantry, oratory; abbey, cathedral, minster, basilica, duomo [Ital]; temple, tabernacle, synagogue, *shul* [Yiddish]; mosque, *masjid* [Arabic]; wat, ziggurat, pagoda, pantheon, fane [Arch]; shrine, cell, monastery, convent

> Religion 81

9 **church interior,** altar, sanctuary, pulpit, lectern, choir, nave, transept, aisle, pew, stall, font, rood screen, sacristy, presbytery, vestry, narthex

> Architecture 134

10 **shrine,** holy place, sacred place, sanctum sanctorum, holy of holies, sacrarium, reliquary; cella, naos, delubrum, dagoba, stupa, tope

11 **sacred object,** cross, crucifix, rood, chalice, monstrance, ostensory or ostensorium, pyx, ciborium, relic; holy water, aspergillum, aspersorium, incense, thurible, censer, chrism, urceole; veronica, icon, bambino [Ital], rosary beads, chaplet; candle, votive candle, paschal candle, vigil light; sanctus bell; tabernacle, Torah, Holy Ark, *Aron Kodesh* [Hebrew], phylactery, tefillin, mezuzah, menorah; bo or bodhi tree, prayer wheel, prayer rug; totem, totem pole, talisman, charm, amulet, fetish, juju

ADJECTIVES

12 **worshipful,** worshiping, honoring, reverent, reverential, religious, devout, pious, devoted, devotional, dedicated, venerational, adoring, adulating, esteeming, dignifying, glorifying, exultant, lauding, praising, extolling, celebrating, blessing; supplicating, supplicatory, supplicant, suppliant, praying, prayerful, penitent, sacrificial; contemplative, meditative, ascetic, fasting

13 **idolatrous,** idolizing, iconolatrous, cultish, totemic, totemistic, fetishistic, animistic, zoolatrous, zoomorphic, theriolatrous, ophiolatrous, heliolatrous, star-worshiping, pyrolatrous, dendrolatrous, diabolic, demonic, Satanic; ancestor-worshiping, necrolatrous, hero-worshiping, lionizing

14 **worshiped,** honored, revered, venerated, adored, adulated, esteemed, glorified, exalted, magnified, lauded, praised, extolled, lionized, idolized

VERBS

15 **worship,** honor, respect, revere, reverence, be devoted to, dedicate oneself to, venerate, adore, adulate, esteem, dignify, glorify, exalt, magnify, laud, praise, extol; celebrate, acclaim, give thanks, sing praises; pray, say prayers, petition, kneel, genuflect, prostrate oneself, humble oneself, obey, propitiate, offer, sacrifice, atone; contemplate, meditate, commune, take communion, fast, make or go on a pilgrimage

16 **idolize,** idolatrize, worship idols, make an idol of, fetishize, totemize, put on a pedestal, idealize, lionize, admire, look up to, hero-worship, deify

ADVERBS

17 **worshipfully,** honorifically, honorably, reverentially, devotedly, devotionally, adoringly; humbly, ascetically, penitentially, sacrificially, contemplatively, meditatively; idolatrously

INTERJECTIONS

18 **hallelujah!,** alleluia!, hosanna!, amen!, praise the Lord!, glory to God in the highest!, God bless!, God save!

84 Clergy

NOUNS

1 **clergy,** ministry, the cloth, priesthood, holy orders

2 **priesthood,** hierocracy, ecclesiasticism, clericalism, sacerdotalism; ministry, pastorate, pastorage, pastoral care, the Church; rabbinate, pontificate, papacy, popedom, cardinalship, primacy, prelature, abbacy, bishopric, bishopdom, episcopate, deanery, deanship, curacy, rectorship, rectorate, vicarship, vicariate, pastorship, deaconry, deaconship, chaplaincy, chaplainship

3 **ordination,** ordainment, election, nomination, appointment, induction, institution, investiture, conferment, preferment

4 **clerical venue,** diocese, see, archdiocese, bishopric, archbishopric, province, parish
   ◗ *Religious Ritual 85*

5 **member of the clergy,** clergyman, clergywoman, person of the cloth, person in holy orders, cleric, minister, pastor, deacon, deaconess, ordinand, dean, canon, monsignor, parson, vicar, rector, curate, elder, father, confessor, chaplain, padre; Holy Joe [Inf], sky pilot [Inf]

6 **rabbi** , rebbe, Cohen *or* Kohen, maggid; cantor, *hazan*, Levite, scribe, *maftir*

7 **imam,** ayatollah, muezzin, mullah, qadi; sheikh, qasisha, mujtahid, darshan, rishi, dhammaduta, zen-ji, lama, poonghie, houngan, mamaloi, papaloi, haruspex, augur, precentor, succentor, mukdam

8 **priest,** priestess, high priest, pope, pontiff, pontifex maximus; chief rabbi, hakham; Grand Lama, Dalai Lama, Panchen Lama, Dastur, Kalif *or* Caliph, hierophant, flamen, Brahman, Gosain, guru, pundit, purohita; cardinal, bishop, archbishop, primate, patriarch, hierarch, diocesan, suffragan, prelate, divine, rector, ecclesiastic, ecclesiarch, churchman
   ◗ *Authority 52; Master 68*

9 **religious,** monk, nun, prior, prioress, abbot, abbess, mother superior, reverend father, superioress, reverend mother, canoness, monastic, sister, brother; kalogeros, trapa, talapoin, bo-san, shonin; bhikshu *or* bhikku, bhikshuni *or* bhikkuni, bonze; fakir, dervish, caloyer; cenobite, conventual, hieromonach, mendicant, friar, pilgrim, palmer, stylite, pillarist, beadsman, hermit, abbacomes, anchorite, ascetic, novice, postulant, lay disciple, upasaka, upasika, koji, chela

10 **clerical dwelling,** vicarage, parsonage, rectory, deanery, manse, presbytery, archdeaconry, bishop's palace, Lambeth Palace, Vatican; ashram, retreat, hermitage, priory, friary, cloister, chapterhouse, monastery, convent, nunnery, lamasery
   ◗ *Architecture 134*

11 **vestment,** canonicals, regalia, habit, veil, robes, cloth, vesture, liturgical garment, ceremonial attire, pontificals, pontificalia, episcopal vestment, frock, mantle, gown, cloak, surplice, scapular, cassock, cope, pallium, amice, chasuble, alb, tunicle, tallith, ephod, apron, soutane, hood, capuche, clerical collar, fanon, head-dress, wimple, cardinal's hat, miter, tiara, triple crown, priest's cap, biretta, prayer cap, skullcap, yarmulke, turban, calotte, zucchetto, Salvation Army bonnet, stole, tippet, cingulum, maniple, crosier, crook, staff, episcopal ring, orphrey, clericals [Inf], dog collar [Inf]
   ◗ *Religious Ritual 85; Clothing 100; Habit, Custom 397*

ADJECTIVES

12 **priestly,** ecclesiastic(al), sacerdotal, hierarchical, hieratic, clerical, ministerial, churchly, pastoral, canonical; papal, pontifical, episcopal; prelatic, presbyterial, hierophantic, hierocratic, parochial, diocesan; ordained; rabbinical
   ◗ *Authority 52; Master 68*

13 **monastic,** monachal, monkish, conventual

VERBS

14 **preach,** spread the Word, spread the good news, save, redeem, fight the good fight, speak in tongues, sermonize

15 **proselytize,** evangelize, convert, convince, win for Christ, receive into the church, baptize, Christianize, Islamize, Judaize, depaganize, crusade; preachify, Bible-thump [Inf]
   ◗ *Persuasion 178*

16 **ordain,** consecrate, elect, nominate, appoint, invest, frock, anoint, call, confer holy orders on; be ordained, take holy orders, take vows, take the veil, wear the cloth

ADVERBS

17 **clerically,** ecclesiastically, sacerdotally, ministerially; pontifically, hierophantically, hierocratically, parochially, rabbinically

85 Religious Ritual

NOUNS

1 **ritual,** rite, ritual act, ceremony, ceremonial, liturgy, sacrament, ordinance; form, formula, formulary, duty, order, observance; office, service, order of worship
   ◗ *Religion 81; Worship 83; Habit, Custom 397; Ceremony 405; Formality 406; Observance 465*

2 **ritualism,** rituality, ritualization, ceremonialism, liturgics, liturgiology

---

STATIONS OF THE CROSS

1. Condemnation of Jesus by Pilate	8. Jesus' encounter with the women of Jerusalem
2. Jesus' acceptance of the cross	9. Jesus' third fall
3. Jesus' first fall	10. Jesus being stripped of his garments
4. The encounter with his mother	11. The crucifixion
5. Simon of Cyrene helping Jesus	12. Jesus' death
6. Veronica wiping Jesus' face	13. Jesus' removal from the cross
7. Jesus' second fall	14. Burial of Jesus

---

3 sacramentalism, sacramentarianism, formalism, solemnization, symbolism

4 symbolics, cult, cultism, sabbatism, Sabbatarianism
▶ *Worship 83; Occultism 86*

5 Christian rite, holy rite, sacrament; ablution, anointing of the sick, Asperges, cleansing, confession, absolution, kiss of peace, last rites, laying on of hands, lustration, penitence, purification, sprinkling, thurification, viaticum; sign of the cross, Stations of the Cross, novena, paternoster, Our Father; denunciation, excommunication, exorcism; seven sacraments: baptism, confirmation, Eucharist, matrimony, penance *or* reconciliation, holy orders, extreme unction

6 baptism, baptizement, christening; affusion, immersion, total immersion; baptistery *or* baptistry

7 Eucharist, Communion, Holy Communion, Lord's Supper, Sacrament, Liturgy, Mass, High Mass, *Missa solemnis* [L], Low Mass; intinction, consubstantiation, transubstantiation, real presence, impanation; order of the Mass: introit, Kyrie, Gloria, collect(s), Lesson(s), Epistle, Gradual, Gospel, sermon, creed *or* credo, kiss of peace, general confession, offertory, oblation, lavabo, biddings, Sursum Corda, consecration, consecrated elements, bread and wine, body and blood of Christ, Host, elevation of the Host, thanksgiving, blessing, dismissal

8 non-Christian ritual, initiation, rite of passage; circumcision, *Brith* or *Bris*, bar mitzvah, bat *or* bas mitzvah, *mikvah*, Kaddish, shivah [all Hebrew]; female circumcision, clitoridectomy, couvade, circumambulation, ritual cleansing, ritual bathing, fertility rite, ghost dance, sun dance, potlatch, rain dance, war dance, witches' Sabbath, Black Mass, hara-kiri
▶ *Occultism 86*

9 ritual music, hymn, hymn singing, psalm, psalm

singing, psalmody, psalter; chant, Gregorian chant, Anglican chant, Ambrosian chant, Milanese chant, plainsong, plainchant; anthem, carol, exultet, cantata, motet, canticle, kontakion; doxology, antiphon, response, gradual; paean, gospel song; hymnal, hymnology, hymnography
▶ *Music 140*

10 prayer, orison, devotion, petition, request, impetration, petitionary prayer, bidding prayer, invocation, intercession *or* intercessory prayer, suffrage; prayer for the dead, anamnesis, vigil; special prayer, supplication, confession, rogation; eulogia, blessing, benediction, grace, thanks, thanksgiving, benison; litany, collect; mantra, *berakhah* [Hebrew], Om, *Om mani padme hum* [Buddhism]; Christian prayers: Angelus, Introit, Miserere, Gloria *or* Gloria Patri, Te Deum, Gloria in excelsis *or* Doxology, Lord's Prayer, Paternoster, Our Father, Ave, Ave Maria, Hail Mary, Magnificat, Kyrie Eleison, Pax, Agnus Dei, Nunc Dimittis, Sursum Corda, Benedicite

11 **ritual manual,** prayer book, Book of Common Prayer, breviary, missal, book of hours, lectionary, pontifical, psalter, psalmbook, church book, mass book; *mahzor, siddur* [Hebrew]; rubric

12 **holy day,** holiday, feast, feast day, fast day; Sabbath, Sunday, Lord's day; saint's day

13 **religious festival,** festival, fiesta, carnival, celebration, agape, encaenia; Ramadan, Bairam, Muharram; Chinese New Year; Beltane, Samhain; Diwali, Festival of Lights, Holi, Dasehra *or* Durga-puja; Saturnalia, Lupercalia, Panathenaea, Dionysia, Anthesteria
 ▶ *Rejoicing 279; Gratitude 310; Memory 354; Celebration 405*

14 **ritualist,** priest, minister, pastor, clergyperson, rabbi, celebrant, ceremonialist, liturgist; crucifer, thurifer, acolyte; hierophant
 ▶ *Religion 81; Clergy 84*

ADJECTIVES

15 **ritualistic,** ceremonial, liturgical, sacramental, formulaic, official, solemn, ordained; festive, festal, celebratory, laudatory, glorified, glorious, extolled; baptismal, confirmational, sacrificial, oblational, libational, eucharistic, consecrated, consubstantial, transubstantial, matrimonial, nuptial, penitential, funereal; comminatory, exorcised, excommunicated, cursed; symbolic, totemistic, fetishistic
 ▶ *Burial 31; Religion 81; Occultism 86; Lamentation 280; Celebration 405; Observance 465*

16 **singing,** hymn-singing, psalm-singing, chanting, antiphonal, hymnological, hymnographical

17 **prayerful,** praying, impetrational, petitionary, invocational, supplicatory, confessional; devotional, dutiful, observant, faithful

VERBS

18 **perform rites,** ritualize, celebrate, solemnize, minister, officiate, anoint, confirm, bless, baptize, christen, marry, sprinkle, asperse, hear one's confession, shrive, absolve; denounce, excommunicate, exorcise, curse

19 **follow rites,** observe, obey, kneel, genuflect, bow, cross oneself, make the sign of the cross, confess, receive the sacrament, commune, receive the sacrament, receive extreme unction; give thanks, sing hymns, chant, intone

20 **pray,** say one's prayers, offer a prayer, request, invoke, impetrate, petition, intercede, supplicate, implore, beseech, confess; say the Lord's Prayer *or* Our Father, say grace, bless, invoke a blessing, recite the rosary, count *or* tell *or* say one's beads
 ▶ *Respect 435; Approval 437; Request 505; Repetition 797*

ADVERBS

21 **ritually,** ritualistically, ceremonially, liturgically, sacra-

mentally, observantly, officially, solemnly, dutifully, devoutly, worshipfully, prayerfully, festally, communally, penitentially, symbolically

86 Occultism

From ghoulies and ghosties and long-leggety beasties / And things that go bump in the night / Good Lord, deliver us!
— CORNISH PRAYER

NOUNS

1 **occultism,** esoterica, esotericism; mystery, mystification, mysticism, shamanism, spiritism, animism, Rosicrucianism; hermetics, hermeticism, alchemy; symbolics, symbolism, anagoge; cabalism; voodooism, witchcraft, magic, reincarnationism, spiritualism, mediumism, poltergeistism, mesmerism, hypnotism, autohypnotism, faith healing; astral projection; pyramidology, ufology, phrenology
 ▶ *Philosophy 4*

2 **the occult,** the paranormal, the supernatural, the supersensible, supernature, supranature, spirit world, astral plane; esoterica, enigma, arcanum, cabala, sealed book, code, cipher; occultness, obscurity, secrecy, mystery, mysteriousness, miraculousness, supernaturalness, supernaturality, supernormalness, supersensitiveness, superphysicalness, superhumanity, unearthliness, unworldliness, otherworldliness, spirituality, eeriness, ghostliness, numinousness
 ▶ *Concealment 181; Secrecy 182; Obscurity 197; Power 514; Nonmaterial World 525; Latency 844*

3 **supernaturalism,** supranaturalism, preternaturalism, metaphysics, hyperphysics, transphysical science, psychic research, metapsychology, parapsychology, psychosophy, theosophy, anthroposophy, scientology, pseudopsychology

4 **psychic power,** sixth sense, inner sense, extrasensory perception (ESP), intuition, mind reading, feyness, second sight, psi faculty, third eye, precognition, premonition, clairvoyance, clairaudience, clairsentience; insight, foresight, crystal vision, psychometry, telepathy, cosmic consciousness; telepathic transmission, telergy, telesthesia, thought transference
 ▶ *Secrecy 182; Vision 242; Intuition 320; Knowledge 348; Foresight 357; Prediction 358; Power 514; Nonmaterial World 525*

5 **divination,** divining, prophecy, soothsaying, clairvoyance, prediction, premonition, precognition; forecasting, fortunetelling, tea-leaf reading, tarot reading, dowsing, water-divining, divining rods, dowsing rods, rhabdomancy, hydromancy, augury, sortilege, haruspicy *or* haruspication; ichthyomancy, ophiomancy, pythonism; palmistry, palm reading, chiromancy; crystal-gazing, crystal ball; astrology, horoscopy, sideromancy, astromancy, horoscope, star chart, birth *or*

natal chart; numerology, arithmancy *or* arithmomancy, bibliomancy, logomancy; dream interpretation, oneiromancy, psephomancy, pyromancy, geomancy, necromancy, psychomancy; sibylline books, I Ching, tarot

   ▶ *Intuition 320; Foresight 357; Prediction 358*

6 witchcraft, witchery, bewitchery, witchwork, sorcery, wicca, wizardry, necromancy, spellcraft, spellbinding, spellcasting, enchantment; bedevilment, possession, voodooism, voodoo, hoodoo, wanga, jujuism, obeah, totemism, fetishism *or* fetichism, vampirism; magic, sortilege, theurgy, thaumaturgy, thaumaturgia, thaumaturgics, alchemy, natural magic, sympathetic magic, white magic, chaos magic, black magic, black art, diablerie, demonology, Satanism; coven, Sabbat *or* witches' Sabbath, Black Mass, witching hour, Walpurgis Night, Halloween

   ▶ *Religion 81; Worship 83; Evil 446; Influence 512; Power 514*

7 occult and psychic phenomena, automatic writing, spirit writing, psychography, Kirlian photography, trance speaking, glossolalia, automatism; spirit manifestation, spirit rapping, table tapping, psychokinesis *or* telekinesis, fork bending, teleportation, levitation; illusion, hallucination, telepathic hallucination, déjà vu, telepathic dream, premonition, maya, trance, samadhi; hypnosis, hypnotic trance, mediumistic trance; spirit raising, séance, sitting, Ouija™ (board), planchette, ectoplasm, bioplasma, exteriorized protoplasm, aura, emanation, ectoplasy, effluvium, biofeedback, cosmic vibration, synchronicity, out-of-body experience, crop circle, UFO sighting, alien encounter

   ▶ *Possession 469; Nonmaterial World 525*

8 spell, magic spell, charm, potion, philter, rune, glamour; wanga, evil eye, hex, jinx, whammy [Inf]; conjuration, evocation, invocation, incantation, chant, magic words, hocus-pocus, mumbo jumbo, abraxas, pentagram *or* pentacle; abracadabra, paternoster, open sesame

   ▶ *Obscurity 197; Curse 301; Unintelligibility 364; Power 514*

9 talisman, charm, mascot, amulet, periapt, phylactery; fetish, totem, juju, obeah *or* obi, mojo, tiki; medallion, relic, symbol, emblem, mandala, ankh, scarab *or* scarabaeus, swastika, fylfot, gammadion, lucky charm, good-luck charm, luck piece, lucky bean, four-leaf clover, shamrock, horseshoe, rabbit's foot, antidote, garlic, silver bullet; bell, book, and candle; witch's broomstick, wizard's cap, familiar, familiar spirit, black cat; magic circle, magic ring, ring of invisibility, magic belt, magic sword, magic carpet, seven-league boots, cap of darkness, wishbone, wishing well, wishing stone, fairy ring

   ▶ *Religious Ritual 85; Secrecy 182; Sign 183*

10 spirit, soul, geist, atman, mind, inner mind, inner being, psyche, pneuma, animus, anima, third eye, astral body, design body, bliss body, Buddhic body, karmic body, kamarupa, mental body, causal body, subtle body, vital body, spiritual body, etheric body, soul body

   ▶ *Life 28; Nonmaterial World 525; Latency 844*

11 ghost, spirit, ghoul, phantom, apparition, manifestation, materialization, poltergeist, shade, manes, lemures, specter, spook [Inf], phantasm, wraith, presence, undead, vampire, zombie, fetch, demon, lamia, jinn *or* djin, genie

12 sprite, familiar, elemental spirit, will-o'-the-wisp, fairy, fay, sylph, genius, elf, alfar, pixie, brownie, gnome, dwarf, troll, kobold; goblin, imp, hobgoblin, leprechaun, cluricaune; monster, orc, werewolf, werecat; gremlin, little green men, alien, extraterrestrial (ET), Martian; Mab, Titania, Befana, Puck

   ▶ *Appearance 264; Imagination 360; Presence 575*

13 occultist, psychic, esoteric, mystic, mystagogue, cabalist, Rosicrucian, druid, druidess, houngan, supernaturalist, telepathist, mind reader, thought reader; telekinetic, fork bender, telesthetic, panpsychist, metaphysician, metaphysicist, metapsychist; spiritualist, spiritist, medium, ecstatic, automatist, psychographist; alchemist, hypnotist, faith healer, psychometer, psychometrist; anthroposophist, theosophist, parapsychologist, pyramidologist, ufologist, phrenologist; adept, mahatma, fakir, exorcist, exorciser, unspeller, spirit rapper, table tapper

   ▶ *Religion 81; Concealment 181; Secrecy 182; Intuition 320; Nonmaterial World 525*

14 diviner, dowser, predictor, foreteller, forecaster, psychic, clairvoyant, clairaudient, clairsentient, seer, prophet, soothsayer, *vates* [L], augur, auspex, haruspex, weather prophet, astrologer, fortuneteller, tea-leaf reader, tarot reader, crystal gazer, palmist, palm reader, chiromancer, Gypsy, Romany; wise woman, sibyl, pythoness, oracle, Delphic oracle, Pythia, Pythian oracle; geomancer, necromancer, psychomancer, icthyomancer, ophiomancer, pythonist, sideromancer, astromancer, numerologist, dream interpreter, oneiromancer, pyromancer, capnomancer, psephomancer, hieromancer, theomancer, Nostradamus

   ▶ *Sign 183; Intuition 320; Knowledge 348; Wisdom 352; Foresight 357; Prediction 358*

15 witch, witchwoman, witchman, witch master, witch doctor, conjure man, obeah doctor, voodooist, wangateur, medicine man, medicine woman; isangoma, mundunugu, shaman, shamanist, sorcerer, sorceress, magician, magus, mage [Arch], necromancer, wizard, warlock, theurgist, thaumaturge, thaumaturgist; bewitcher, charmer, enchanter, enchantress, spellbinder, conjurator, siren, mermaid, Lorelei, water witch, white witch, weird sister; Merlin, Witch of Endor, Hecate, Circe, Medusa, Medea

   ▶ *Religion 81; Wisdom 352; Influence 512; Power 514*

ADJECTIVES

16 occult, esoteric, recondite, obscure, secret, mysterious, cryptic, enigmatic, arcane; paranormal, supersensible, superphysical; supernatural, supranatural, supernormal, preternatural, hermetic, symbolic, anagogical, cabalistic, runic, Rosicrucian; latent, covert, encoded

▶ *Concealment 181; Secrecy 182; Obscurity 197; Interpretation 365; Latency 844*

17 **psychic,** psychical, unconscious, subconscious, cosmic, telepathic, telekinetic, psychokinetic, telergic, telesthetic, extrasensory, spiritualistic, mediumistic, transphysical, hyperphysical, metapsychic, metapsychical, panpsychic, parapsychological, theosophical, anthroposophical, scientological, pseudopsychological

▶ *Influence 512; Power 514*

18 **divinatory,** prophetic, clairvoyant, clairaudient, clairsentient, predictive, predictable, predicted, premonitory, precognitive, augural, mantic, haruspical, sibylline, oracular, astrological

▶ *Intuition 320; Foresight 357; Prediction 358*

19 **witchlike,** wizardlike, wizardly, sorcerous, necromantic, alchemical, alchemistic, druidic, shamanic, talismanic, Circean, bewitching; magical, theurgic, enchanting, charming, spellbinding, entrancing, fascinating; invocational, conjural, incantational, incantatory, hypnotic, autohypnotic, voodooistic, totemistic, totemic, fetishistic *or* fetichistic; diabolic, diabolical, demonic, demonical, fiendish, devilish, Satanic, hellish, undead, vampiric, vampirish

▶ *Deity 82; Wonder 294; Curse 301; Evil 446; Power 514*

20 **spiritual,** immaterial, nonmaterial, incorporeal, insubstantial, intangible, disembodied, unphysical, nonphysical, ethereal, airy, elemental, fairy, fey, ghostly, spectral, shadowy, phantom, phantasmic, phantasmal, wraithlike, unearthly, otherworldly, astral, alien, extraterrestrial, ufological, extramundane, supramundane, transmundane, unworldly, eerie, weird, eldritch, uncanny, strange, creepy, spooky [Inf]

▶ *Death 29; Invisibility 245; Transparency 249*

21 **bewitched,** enchanted, charmed, spellbound, entranced, fascinated, hypnotized, mesmerized, hagridden, obsessed, possessed, bedeviled, cursed, hexed, jinxed, haunted, ghostridden, spooked [Inf]

▶ *Curse 301; Possession 469*

VERBS

22 **occult,** hide, obscure, veil, cloak, mystify, symbolize, encode, spiritualize, dematerialize, immaterialize, etherealize

▶ *Concealment 181; Secrecy 182; Sign 183; Obscurity 197; Invisibility 245; Dimness 248; Nonmaterial World 525; Latency 844*

23 **experience psychic phenomena,** see signs, see auras, sense vibrations, hallucinate, transmit thoughts, transfer thoughts, read minds, bend forks, leave one's body, astral-project, travel in the astral plane, levitate, teleport, go into a trance, see the little people, communicate with aliens, encounter aliens

▶ *Imagination 360; Nonmaterial World 525*

24 **divine,** prophesy, soothsay, predict, forecast, foretell, foresee, intuit, tell fortunes, read tea leaves, read *or* consult the tarot, read palms, crystal-gaze, cast nativities, draw up birth *or* natal charts, plot horoscopes, cast the I Ching, interpret dreams, dowse, water-divine, read signs

▶ *Card Playing 168; Sensitivity 267; Intuition 320; Foresight 357; Prediction 358; Power 514*

25 **bewitch,** enchant, incant, charm, mesmerize, hypnotize, practice witchcraft, cast spells, spellbind, say magic words, wave a wand, ride a broomstick, put the evil eye on, hex, jinx, curse, sorcerize, theurgize, thaumaturgize, shamanize, diabolize, demonize, bedevil, possess

▶ *Religious Ritual 85; Curse 301; Influence 512; Power 514*

26 **conjure,** conjure up, invoke, evoke, raise ghosts, wake the dead, practice spiritualism, call up spirits, summon spirits, hold a séance *or* sitting

ADVERBS

27 **occultly,** obscurely, mystically, mysteriously, secretly, secretively, enigmatically, arcanely, cabalistically, esoterically, metaphysically, spiritually, supernaturally, paranormally, psychically, parapsychologically, telepathically, mesmerically, hypnotically, prophetically, clairvoyantly, astrologically, consciously, subconsciously

28 **magically,** eerily, spookily, weirdly [Inf], ghoulishly, necromantically, thaumaturgically, theurgically, superstitiously, diabolically, demonically

87 Belief

NOUNS

1 **belief,** opinion, view, point of view, viewpoint, angle, stand, standpoint, position, attitude, stance; impression, feeling, sentiment, intuition, thought, idea, notion, premise, principle; proposition, theory, thesis, hypothesis, judgment, conjecture, supposition, surmise, speculation; popular belief, climate of opinion, persuasion; conviction, certainty

▶ *Feelings 266; Thought 317; Intuition 320; Idea 327; Judgment 341; Supposition 359; Certainty 840*

2 **believing,** faith, trust, confidence, assurance, reliance, dependence, credence, credit, credulity, credulousness; gullibility, blind faith, suspension of disbelief; expectation, hope, acceptance, pledge, word of honor

▶ *Hope 281; Expectation 356*

3 **belief system,** religion, faith, piety, religious belief, religious feeling, persuasion; creed, credo, dogma, canon, principle, tenet, articles of faith, declaration of faith, statement of belief, catechism; manifesto, doctrine, school, cult, philosophy, ideology

▶ *Philosophy 4; Religion 81*

4 **believability,** credibility, plausibility, trustworthiness, reliability

5 **believer,** true believer, truster, faithful, conformer,

conformist; trusting person, innocent, naïf; lamb to the slaughter, sucker [Inf]

ADJECTIVES

6 believing, assured, confident, convinced, sure, certain, positive, opinionated, dogmatic; faithful, conformist, orthodox, converted, born-again; trusting, trustful, unhesitating, unquestioning, undoubting, unsuspecting, credulous; gullible, innocent, naive, green, wet behind the ears
  ◗ *Religion 81; Naïveté 821; Certainty 840*

7 believable, credible, creditable, tenable, plausible, reasonable, realistic, possible, probable, likely, convincing, persuasive, impressive, commanding, reliable, trustworthy
  ◗ *Possibility 836; Probability 838*

8 believed, undisputed, unquestioned, authoritative, accredited, doctrinal, creedal, received, accepted, maintained; putative, supposed, alleged, hypothetical

VERBS

9 believe, have faith in, put one's faith in, have no doubts about, credit, accept, be led to believe, take someone's word for, accept on faith, take on trust, trust, swallow; confide in, rely on, depend on, count on, bank on, swear by, take for granted, rest assured, know, maintain, hold, declare, affirm, profess, confess; [Inf]: fall for, buy, swallow *or* fall for hook, line, and sinker
  ◗ *Affirmation 189; Knowledge 348*

10 be of the opinion, opine, presume, assume, surmise, guess, suppose, think, suspect, understand, be under the impression, get it into one's head, have in mind, have the opinion, imagine, fancy, regard, consider, deem, esteem
  ◗ *Thought 317; Supposition 359*

11 make someone believe, assure, convince, persuade, influence, convert, win over, evangelize, proselytize, propagandize, spread the word, indoctrinate, brainwash, deceive, dupe, take in
  ◗ *Religion 81; Deception 193; Influence 512*

ADVERBS

12 believingly, confidently, positively, dogmatically, trustfully, unhesitatingly, unsuspectingly, faithfully, credulously, gullibly, naively

13 believably, credibly, plausibly, reasonably, convincingly, persuasively, supposedly, allegedly, hypothetically

88 Disbelief

NOUNS

1 disbelief, doubt, doubtfulness, dubiousness, dubiety, uncertainty, hesitancy, hesitation, distrust, mistrust, misgiving, qualm, scruple, reservation, skepticism, scorn, suspiciousness, suspicion; disagreement, dissent, demur, demurral
  ◗ *Dissent 347; Derision 369; Disagreement 463; Uncertainty 841*

2 unbelievability, incredibility, impossibility, improbability, implausibility, untenability
  ◗ *Impossibility 837; Improbability 839*

3 incredulity, amazement, bewilderment, bafflement, perplexity, nonbelief, discredit, rejection, denial
  ◗ *Negation 190; Surprise 292*

4 unbelief, agnosticism, atheism, irreligion, loss of faith; infidelity, paganism, heathenism, misbelief
  ◗ *Religion 81*

5 disbeliever, unbeliever, nonbeliever, heretic, pagan, heathen, infidel, agnostic, atheist; doubter, doubting Thomas, apostate, dissenter, dissident, nonconformist, skeptic, mocker, detractor, irreligionist, secularist, rationalist, freethinker, materialist
  ◗ *Religion 81; Freedom 829*

ADJECTIVES

6 disbelieving, unbelieving, incredulous, skeptical, scornful, doubtful, doubting, dubious, demurring; uncertain, hesitant, distrustful, mistrustful, suspicious, dissenting; agnostic, atheistic, irreligious, faithless, unfaithful; pagan, heathen, misbelieving
  ◗ *Religion 81; Dissent 347; Uncertainty 841*

7 disbelieved, unbelieved, discredited, exploded, unbelievable, incredible, beyond belief, impossible, improbable, implausible, untenable, hard to believe, farfetched, unreliable, suspect, suspected, suspicious, so-called, self-styled, questionable, disputable
  ◗ *Ridiculousness 368; Impossibility 837; Improbability 839*

VERBS

8 disbelieve, refuse to believe, dissent, disagree, scorn, ridicule, mock, scoff at, deny, negate; challenge, dispute, discredit, question, doubt, have doubts about, hesitate, waver, half-believe, have reservations, distrust, mistrust, suspect, smell a rat, take with a pinch *or* grain of salt, apostatize, lapse
  ◗ *Negation 190; Question 333; Dissent 347; Derision 369*

9 cause disbelief, cast doubt, call into question, discredit, raise suspicions, amaze, stagger
  ◗ *Surprise 292; Question 333*

ADVERBS

10 disbelievingly, unbelievingly, incredulously, skeptically, doubtfully, dubiously, uncertainly, hesitantly, distrustfully, mistrustfully, suspiciously

11 unbelievably, incredibly, implausibly, unreliably, questionably, disputably

89 Provision

NOUNS

1 **provision,** supply, equipment, accouterment, purveyance, provender, stock, service, care, investment, endowment; condition, stipulation, proviso
▶ *Food 90; Tool 103; Store 105; Qualification 340; Preparation 388; Giving 472; Help 825*

2 **provisioning,** providing, supplying, catering, equipping, furnishing, outfitting, purveying, procuring

3 **provisions,** food, provender, sustenance, rations, victuals; clothing, furniture, accommodations, facilities, lodgings; services, support, supplies, stores, reserves, replenishment
▶ *Habitat 60; Food 90; Clothing 100; Furniture 101*

4 **provisioner,** supplier, provider, donor, giver, caterer; shopkeeper, grocer, vintner, merchant, wholesaler, retailer; lender, creditor, bursar, treasurer; commissary, quartermaster, storekeeper; procurer, pander *or* panderer, pimp
▶ *Food 90; Immorality 432; Giving 472; Lending 475; Trade 480; Money 484*

5 **caterer,** purveyor, hotelier, hotel manager, innkeeper, restaurateur, waiter, waitress, steward, butler; cook, chef
▶ *Cooking 91*

ADJECTIVES

6 **provisioning,** supplying, providing, furnishing, equipping, catering, commissarial, servicing, sufficing, available, in stock, on the menu

7 **supplied,** provided, furnished, equipped, catered, victualed, supported, given, donated, prepared, stocked, replenished
▶ *Preparation 388; Giving 472*

8 **provisional,** conditional, provisory, restricted, limited, qualified
▶ *Qualification 340*

VERBS

9 **provision,** supply, provide, furnish, equip, outfit, purvey; feed, cater, serve, cook for, entertain; clothe, accommodate, board; service, maintain, sell, deliver, bring in, distribute, hand out; support, assist, afford, offer, lend, contribute, give, donate, endow; procure, pander, pimp

10 **replenish,** resupply, reinforce, fill, refill, restock, refuel
▶ *Completeness 761*

11 **stipulate,** restrict, limit, qualify

ADVERBS

12 **provisionally,** conditionally, provisorily

90 Food

Food is an important part of a balanced diet.
— FRAN LEBOWITZ

NOUNS

1 **food,** sustenance, nourishment, aliment, alimentation, nutrition, nutriment, pabulum, nurture, provender, diet; foodstuffs, edibles, eatables, viands, comestibles, victuals, fare, tack, rations; provisions, groceries, stores, supplies; bread, daily bread, staff of life, fuel; meat, staple food; baby food, pap; rich food, heavy food, bulk, stodge; packaged food, vacuum-packed food, canned food, frozen food, freezer stock, freeze-dried food, dried food, dehydrated food; processed food, convenience food, junk food, fast food, short-order food; healthy food, health food, organic food, hydroponic food, homegrown food, high-fiber food, low-fat food, low-salt *or* low-sodium food, kosher food; creature comforts, cheer *or* good cheer; food of the gods, manna, ambrosia; soul food, vittles; [Inf]: eats, grub, nosh, chow, chuck, peckings, tuck [Brit], tucker [Aus]
▶ *Provision 89; Eating 92; Drinking 93*

2 **animal food,** pet food, dog food, cat food, birdseed, fish food, feed, chicken feed, provender, fodder, pasture, pasturage, forage, corn, oats, barley, grain, hay,

grass, clover, alfalfa; dry feed, pig swill, cattle cake, winter feed, silage, salt lick

> *Agriculture 16; Provision 89*

3 **food content,** carbohydrates, starch, sugar, glucose, sucrose, lactose, fructose; protein, amino acid; fat, oil, saturated fat, polyunsaturates; vitamins, water, minerals, salt, calcium, iron; fiber, roughage, bulk, calories; (food) additive, preservative, flavor enhancer, artificial flavoring, artificial coloring, artificial sweetener, emulsifier; food chain, food pyramid

> *Biochemistry 12; Eating 92; Taste 219; Addition 748*

4 **plenty,** cornucopia, food mountain, milk and honey, groaning board, loaded table, festal cheer, festive board, oversupply

> *Sufficiency 97; Excess 99*

5 **scarcity,** lack of food, insufficient food, meager diet, poor table, bare cupboard, starvation diet, short rations, famine

> *Insufficiency 98; Ill Health 114*

6 **food provider,** grocer, grocery store, market, supermarket; fisherman, fish store, fishmonger [Brit]; baker, bakery, bakeshop; butcher, butcher shop, meat market; farmers' market, greengrocer [Brit]; health food shop, natural food store, organic food store; candy store, confectioner's, sweet-shop [Brit]; commissary, commissariat; farmer, rancher; restaurant, restaurateur, café, delicatessen, deli [Inf], fast-food place, chef, cook, caterer

> *Provision 89; Cooking 91*

7 **dish,** course, menu, serving; hors d'oeuvre, savory, first course, starter, soup, fish course, entrée, main course, main dish, side dish, salad, cheese, fruit, entremets, dessert, sweet [Brit]; special, dish of the day, soup of the day; specialty, specialty of the house, *spécialité de la maison* [Fr]; culinary masterpiece, dish fit for a king *or* queen

> *Eating 92*

8 **snack,** nibbles, tidbits, potato chips, crisps [Brit], nuts, pretzels, popcorn, fruit, crackers, cheese, munchies [Inf], nosh [Inf]

9 **sandwich,** club sandwich, double-decker, finger sandwich, open sandwich, hero, hoagie, submarine, sub [Inf], grinder, poor boy, hamburger, cheeseburger, hot dog, toasted sandwich, Dagwood sandwich, French dip sandwich

10 **bread,** dough, crust, crumb; white bread, French bread; brown bread, whole-wheat bread, rye bread, pumpernickel; corn bread, corn pone, hush puppy, johnnycake; raisin bread, nut bread; loaf, baguette; toast, rusk, crouton, breadstick; English muffin, tortilla, pita, focaccia, chapati; bun, roll, bagel, crumpet, muffin, popover; sweet roll, coffeecake; biscuit, cracker, graham cracker, soda cracker

11 **pancake,** griddlecake, hot cake, flapjack, crêpe, waffle, blintz

12 **cereal,** cornflakes, bran, bran flakes, wheat germ, muesli, oatmeal, porridge, gruel, mush, polenta

13 **hors d'oeuvre,** appetizer, antipasto, smorgasbord, canapé, starter [Brit]; delicacies, dainties, nibbles, tidbits, crackers and cheese, dip, pâté, shrimp cocktail, tapa, dim sum, crudités, potato skins

14 **soup,** cream soup, clear soup, broth, consommé, stock, bouillon, potage, bisque, borscht, gumbo, fish soup, bouillabaisse, chowder

15 **side dish,** salad, vegetables, condiments, dressing, stuffing, pickles, olives, relishes, chutney, sauce, gravy

16 **salad,** tossed salad, greens, chef's salad, Caesar salad, fruit salad, Waldorf salad, pasta salad, potato salad, molded salad, aspic, coleslaw, tabbouleh

17 **sauce,** tomato sauce, ketchup *or* catsup; brown sauce, Worcestershire sauce, soy sauce, Bordelaise; Tabasco™ sauce, barbecue sauce, tartar sauce, horseradish; salsa, guacamole, pesto; cranberry sauce, applesauce, mint sauce; mayonnaise, salad dressing, vinaigrette, aioli; white sauce, roux, velouté, Béarnaise, hollandaise, béchamel

18 **egg dish,** omelette *or* omelet, frittata, soufflé, custard, quiche; hard-boiled *or* soft-boiled egg, three-minute egg; fried egg, scrambled egg, poached egg, eggs Benedict, coddled egg, dropped egg, shirred egg; deviled egg, egg salad

19 **fish dish,** fried fish, boiled fish, broiled fish, poached fish, fish cake *or* fish ball, fish finger, fish stick, rollmop, fish pie, scrod *or* schrod, gefilte fish, fish and chips [Brit]; roe, caviar; jellied eel, smoked fish, cured fish, lox, gravlax *or* gravlaks, kippered fish; rissole, quenelle

20 **food fish and shellfish,** albacore, anchovy, arctic char, bass, bluefish, carp, catfish, coalfish, cod, cusk, dogfish, eel, flatfish, flounder, grayling, haddock, hake, halibut, herring, kingfish, mackerel, mahi-mahi, mako, monkfish, mullet, orange roughy, perch, pike, pilchard, plaice, pollack, red snapper, salmon, sardine, skate, sole, sprat, swordfish, trout, tuna, turbot, whiting; octopus, squid, calamari; oyster, scallop, clam, mussel, winkle, whelk, shrimp, prawn, crab, lobster, spiny lobster, *langouste* [Fr], crayfish, crawfish *or* crawdad; snail, *escargot* [Fr]

21 **meat dish,** roast, pot roast, chop, cutlet, grill, mixed grill, stew, casserole, goulash, pie, pasty [Brit], hash, fricassee, rissole

---

VARIETIES OF BEANS

black	French	pinto	stringless
broad	green	pole	wax
bush	horsebean	Scotch	Windsor
butter	horticultural	shell	yellow wax
civit	lima	snap	
fava	mung	soy	
flageolet	navy	string	

---

22 meat, flesh, red meat, white meat; beef, veal, pork, lamb, mutton; poultry, chicken, turkey, goose, duck; game, rabbit, hare, venison, pheasant, grouse, partridge, pigeon, quail

23 meat substitute, tofu, bean curd, textured vegetable protein (TVP)™

24 beef, chuck, rib roast, short loin, tenderloin, sirloin, steak, round, boneless rump, shank, short plate, brisket; corned beef, dried beef, chipped beef, pastrami; ground beef, hamburger, ground round

25 veal, shoulder, rib roast, chops, loin, rump, shank, leg, cutlet, escallop, breast, neck

26 pork, loin, tenderloin, rib roast, chop, butt, shoulder, picnic, hock, fresh ham, cured ham, boiled ham; bacon, smoked bacon, Canadian bacon, gammon

27 lamb, shoulder roast, neck slice, rib, loin, chop, leg, breast, rack, saddle

28 poultry, white meat, dark meat, breast, leg, thigh, drumstick, wing, wishbone, pope's *or* parson's nose [Inf]

29 sausage, pork sausage, beef sausage, banger [Brit], sausage meat, cocktail sausage, frankfurter, wiener, weenie [Inf]; wienerwurst, Vienna sausage, liver sausage, herb sausage, garlic sausage, saveloy [Brit], salami, bologna, polony [Brit]; knackwurst *or* knockwurst, bratwurst, kielbasa; black pudding, blood sausage, blood pudding, haggis [Scot]; pâté, *pâté de foie gras* [Fr]

30 variety meat, organ meat, offal; liver, kidney, heart, tongue, ox cheek, pig's head, calf's head, brains, chitterlings, sweetbread, pig's feet, pig's knuckles, trotters, tripe, prairie *or* mountain oyster

31 pasta, noodles, spaghetti, linguine, fettuccine, macaroni, ravioli, ramen; dumpling, kreplach, spaetzle

32 rice, white rice, long-grain rice, brown rice, wild rice, arborio, basmati; pilaf, jambalaya, risotto

33 vegetable, produce, leafy vegetable, stem vegetable, root vegetable, tuber, flower vegetable, seed vegetable, legume, pulse, veggie [Inf]; mushroom; vegetable dish, vegetable plate, mixed vegetables, vegetable casserole, ratatouille, sauerkraut; potatoes, baked potatoes, mashed potatoes, whipped potatoes, fried potatoes, French fries, hash browns
> *Plants (General) 41; Fungi, Algae, and Lichens 47*

34 fruit, produce, stone fruit, drupe, citrus fruit, berry, pome; fruit dish, fruit cocktail, fruit cup, fruit compote, fruit salad, stewed fruit
> *Fruits 44; Sweetness 222*

35 dessert, cake, pie, cobbler, turnover, pudding, custard, mousse, flan, gelatin, Jell-O™; ice cream, ice-cream cone, frozen yogurt, sundae, sherbet, sorbet, bombe, ice, gelato, tortoni; cheese

36 cake, layer cake, devil's food cake, angel cake *or* angel food cake, Bundt cake, pound cake, sponge cake, gâteau [Brit, Fr], upside-down cake, fruitcake, trifle,

gingerbread, seedcake, cheesecake, shortcake, torte; cupcake, brownie, petit four, madeleine, doughnut, sinker [Inf]; cookie, wafer, biscuit [Brit]

37 pastry, flake pastry, puff pastry, phyllo *or* filo; Danish pastry, croissant, brioche, éclair, cream puff, baklava, shortbread, scone

38 pie, single-crust pie, double-crust pie, deep-dish pie, fruit pie, custard pie, meringue pie, tart, strudel

39 sweets, candy, sweetmeat, bonbon, confectionery, toffee, butterscotch, caramel, chocolate, fudge, gumdrop, jelly bean, hard candy, lollipop, sourball; marshmallow, marzipan, peppermint, praline, candied fruit; preserves, jam, jelly, marmalade, conserve, dried fruit

40 notable international dishes, couscous, harissa [North Africa]; cock-a-leekie, Yorkshire pudding, ploughman's lunch [Britain]; Peking duck, fried rice, stir fry [China]; coq au vin, boeuf bourguignon, bouillabaisse, quiche Lorraine [France]; Wiener schnitzel, sauerbraten, apfelstrudel [Germany]; moussaka, taramasalata, baklava [Greece]; tandoori chicken, basmati rice, raita [India]; pizza, calzone, tiramisu [Italy]; sushi, teriyaki, sukiyaki, miso soup [Japan]; enchilada, mole poblano, refried beans, tostada [Mexico]; hummus, falafel, baba ghanouj, stuffed grape leaves, shish kebab [Middle East]; kasha, borscht, beef stroganoff, shashlik [Russia]; Southern fried chicken, succotash, roast turkey, apple pie [United States]

VERBS

41 feed, provide food, give to eat, nourish, nurture, sustain, aliment, take care of, board; cater, purvey, provision; have to dinner, cook for, wine and dine, feast, fete, regale; nurse, breast-feed, suckle, give suck; force-feed, drip-feed; graze, pasture, put out to pasture, fatten, fatten up, stuff
> *Provision 89; Cooking 91; Eating 92; Sociability 408*

91 Cooking

Kissing don't last; cookery do! — GEORGE MEREDITH

NOUNS

1 cooking, food preparation, food processing, cookery, culinary art, style of cooking, cuisine, haute cuisine, *nouvelle cuisine* [Fr], catering, provisioning; home economics, domestic science, gastronomy, nutrition; recipe, receipt [Arch], cookbook, cookery book [Brit]
> *Provision 89; Food 90; Eating 92; Refreshment 94*

2 cooking technique, baking, barbecuing, boiling, parboiling, braising, stewing, broiling, pan-broiling, charbroiling, casseroling, coddling, curing, frying, deep-fat frying, pan-frying, stir-frying, grilling, microwave cooking, pickling, poaching, pressure-cooking, rendering, roasting, oven-roasting, spit-roasting, pot-roasting, sautéing, smoking, steaming, toasting, canning, preserving

▶ *Preservation 815*

3 cook, cooker, chef, sous-chef, apprentice chef, cordon bleu chef, pastry chef, chuck-wagon cook, fast-food cook, ranch-house cook, short-order cook; baker, *cuisinier* [Fr], *cuisinière* [Fr], culinary artist; caterer

4 cooking place, kitchen, kitchenette; bakehouse, bakery, barbecue, cookhouse, cookroom, cookery, galley, scullery; buttery, cellar, larder, pantry

5 cooker, stove, range, broiler, grill, griddle, hot plate, oven, microwave oven, toaster, toaster oven, barbecue, spit, hibachi

6 cooking equipment, pan, saucepan, frying pan, frypan, skillet, griddle, frier, deep-fat frier, roasting pan, omelette pan, wok, pressure cooker; hot plate, kettle, toaster, waffle iron, sandwich maker, crêpe pan, flan ring; pot, Dutch oven, casserole, Crockpot™, cocotte; chopping bowl, cutting board; pie plate, springform pan, cake tin, muffin pan *or* tin, baking dish, Bundt™ pan, tube pan, mold, soufflé dish; skimmer, steamer, poacher, pudding basin, bain-marie, double boiler; mixing bowl, measuring cup, measuring spoon, scales, rolling pin, pastry bag, flour sifter, cookie cutter, cookie press, cookie sheet; chopping board, trussing needle, larding needle; vegetable peeler, grater, zester; colander, strainer, sieve; whisk, beater, hand beater, rotary beater, eggbeater, electric mixer, food processor, blender, bread machine, liquidizer, juicer, grinder, coffee grinder, mincer, garlic press, vegetable mill; spatula, wooden spoon, ladle, baster, funnel, tongs, can opener, lemon squeezer; meat thermometer, candy thermometer; coffeepot, teapot; wax paper, aluminum foil, shrink-wrap, plastic wrap; hot pad, oven glove, oven mitt, potholder, trivet

7 kitchen container, bowl, bread bin, cabinet, cake tin, canister, jar, cookie jar, biscuit barrel [Brit]; larder, pantry; refrigerator, fridge [Inf], icebox, meat compartment, vegetable compartment; freezer, deep freezer
▶ *Store 105; Container 578*

8 basic cooking ingredient, flour, meal, cornmeal, bread crumbs, cornstarch; baking powder, yeast, baking soda, leavening agent; fat, butter, margarine, shortening, lard, suet, grease, drippings; oil, vegetable oil, olive oil, corn oil, canola oil, safflower oil; eggs; sugar, granulated sugar, caster sugar, confectioner's sugar, powdered sugar, brown sugar, demerara sugar, molasses; milk, cream; salt, table salt, sea salt, kosher salt, pepper; vinegar, malt vinegar, wine vinegar, balsamic vinegar; herbs, spices, bouquet garni
▶ *Sweetness 222; Oiliness, Lubrication 562; Mixture 751*

ADJECTIVES

9 culinary, gastronomic, epicurean, mealtime, mensal; preprandial, postprandial, after-dinner; dressed, stuffed, oven-ready, prepared, precooked, made-up, ready-to-serve, cooked, done, well-done; underdone, undercooked, red, raw, rare; medium, al dente; overcooked, burned; roasted, browned, seared, blackened; smoked, toasted, broiled, barbecued, deviled, curried, fried, deep-fried, sautéed, stir-fried; scrambled, coddled, boiled, steamed, poached, stewed, braised, beaten, chopped, ground, minced, au gratin, au naturel, à la mode, à la carte, table d'hôte
▶ *Preparation 388; Lack of Preparation 389*

VERBS

10 cook, prepare a meal, bake, microwave, pressure-cook, heat, heat up, warm, reheat; roast, spit-roast, pot-roast; brown, toast, broil, charbroil, barbecue, spatchcock, griddle, devil, curry; fry, sauté, deep-fry, pan-fry, stir-fry, refry; scramble, coddle; boil, parboil, blanch, scald, seethe, simmer, steam, poach; stew, braise; baste, lard; stir, flip, whip, whisk, beat, blend, knead, mix, fold in, liquidize; draw, gut, bone, fillet, stuff, dress, garnish; peel, pare, core, cut, chop, dice, shred, grind, mince, grate, julienne; flavor, spice, season, salt; whip something up [Inf], throw something together [Inf]

ADVERBS

11 culinarily, gastronomically, nutritiously, palatably, succulently, flavorfully

---

CULINARY HERBS AND SPICES

allspice	cayenne pepper	costmary	lavender	paprika, hot *or*	sage
angelica	celery salt,	cumin	lemon mint	sweet	salad burnet
anise	celery seed	curry powder	lemon verbena	parsley	savory
arugula	chamomile *or*	dill, dill seed	licorice root	peppercorns	sesame seed
barberry	camomile	elecampane	lovage	peppermint	sorrel
basil	chervil	fennel	mace	pimiento *or*	spearmint
bay leaf	chicory	fenugreek	marjoram	pimento	star anise
black pepper	chili powder	garlic, garlic salt	mint	plantain	tansy
borage	chives	ginger	mustard,	pokeweed	tarragon
capers	cilantro	ginseng	mustard seed	poppy seed	thyme
capsicum	cinnamon	horehound	nutmeg	potherb	turmeric
caraway seed	clove	horseradish	onion, onion	rosemary	vanilla bean
cardamon	comfrey	hyssop	flakes, onion salt	safflower	white pepper
cassia	coriander	juniper berries	oregano	saffron	wintergreen

92 Eating

The United States has thirty-two religions but only one dish. — CHARLES MAURICE DE TALLEYRAND-PÉRIGORD

Appetite comes with eating — FRANÇOIS RABELAIS

NOUNS

1 **eating,** consuming, consumption, feeding, taking in food, ingesting, ingestion, ingurgitation; chewing, mastication, munching, manduction [Arch], biting, gnashing, champing, chomping; swallowing, deglutition, downing, getting down, gulping, slurping; digestion, absorption; gastronomy

2 **appetite,** hunger, craving; voracity, voraciousness, wolfishness; overeating, gluttony, greed, gormandizing, gourmandism, devouring, engorgement, gobbling, bolting, guzzling; overindulgence; feasting, gorging, stuffing oneself, excessive consumption, compulsive eating, bulimia; [Inf]: pig-out, binging, binge
   ▶ *Gluttony 119; Desire 288; Self-Indulgence 456*

3 **delicate eating,** tasting, relishing, savoring, palate-tickling; refined palate, educated palate, gourmet eating, epicureanism, dainty palate, nibbling, licking, pecking; lack of appetite, picking at *or* playing with *or* toying with one's food; dieting, fasting, anorexia nervosa
   ▶ *Food 90; Fasting 118; Thinness 595*

4 **eating meals,** dining, lunching, breakfasting, supping, having tea; snacking, eating on the run, eating in bed, breakfasting in bed, eating alone, brown-bagging, eating out, dining out; communal eating, eating together, messing, partaking; formal dining, feasting, banqueting, regalement, hospitality, entertainment; noshing [Inf], grazing [Inf]
   ▶ *Food 90; Refreshment 94; Habit, Custom 397; Sociability 408*

5 **diet,** nutrition, dietetics, healthy eating, proper eating, balanced diet, recommended diet; special diet, macrobiotic diet, vegetarian diet, lactovegetarian diet, vegan diet, protein diet, carbohydrate diet, fruit diet, salt-free diet, low-fat diet, fat-free diet, low-cholesterol diet, diabetic diet, sugar-free diet, calorie-controlled diet, weight-loss diet, crash diet, liquid diet, food-combining diet; food pyramid
   ▶ *Biochemistry 12*

6 **dieting,** weight-watching, losing weight, reducing, slimming, regulated diet, diet regimen *or* regime, course, dietary plan, dietary, diet sheet, calorie counter

7 **eating habit,** meat eating, flesh eating, carnivorousness; omophagia, creophagy, ichthyophagy, insectivorousness; anthropophagy, man eating, cannibalism; vegetarianism, veganism, herbivority, phytophagy; rumination, chewing the cud, pasturing, cropping, graminivorousness, frugivorousness, omnivorousness, grazing [Inf]

8 **meal,** repast, refection, refreshment, collation, informal meal, light meal, stand-up meal, buffet, snack, bite to eat, take-out meal, chance meal, potluck; full meal, square meal, three-course meal, formal meal, sit-down meal, family meal; breakfast, American breakfast, English breakfast, continental breakfast, *petit déjeuner* [Fr], brunch, Sunday brunch, elevenses [Brit]; lunch, luncheon, tiffin [Brit inf], light lunch, box lunch, packed lunch, brown-bag lunch; tea, afternoon tea, cream tea [Brit], high tea [Brit], tea for two; evening meal, dinner, supper, TV dinner, midnight supper *or* snack

9 **feast,** banquet, regale; harvest supper, harvest home; formal dinner, formal occasion; dinner, dinner party, dinner dance; Thanksgiving dinner, Christmas dinner, festive gathering, party; picnic, *fête champêtre* [Fr], tailgate picnic, barbecue, cookout, clambake, wiener roast; junket, orgy, Roman orgy, bacchanalia, Lucullan banquet, feeding frenzy; [Inf]: weenie roast; feed; spread
   ▶ *Celebration 405; Sociability 408*

10 **bite,** taste, nibble, piece, morsel, chew, mouthful, bolus, gobbet, slice, sliver; appetizer, hors d'oeuvre, tidbit

11 **helping,** serving, portion, second helping, seconds

12 **course,** dish, first course, starter, soup, fish course, entrée, main course, side dish, entremets, dessert, sweets
   ▶ *Food 90*

13 **tableware,** knife, carving knife, fish knife, fruit knife, steak knife, butter knife, fork, fish fork, oyster fork, salad fork, fruit fork, fondue fork, spoon, teaspoon, tablespoon, soup spoon, dessert spoon, coffee spoon, ladle; chopsticks; dish, plate, cup, saucer, bowl, gravy boat, platter; flatware, silverware, stainless-steel ware, cutlery, dishware, china, glassware; table linen, tablecloth, place mat, napkin, table pad, napery
   ▶ *Container 578*

14 **eating organ,** teeth, jaws, mandibles, mouth, tongue, throat, gullet, esophagus, stomach, belly, paunch, crop, maw, intestines, bowels, guts

15 **eater,** feeder, consumer, partaker, luncher, diner, picnicker; big eater, hearty eater, heavy eater, devourer, feaster, banqueter, glutton, overeater, gourmand, bon vivant, trencherman, trencherwoman, Lucullus, bulimic; boarder, messmate; small eater, light eater, dainty eater, gourmet, gastronome, epicure, connoisseur, taster, nibbler; dieter, weight-watcher, slimmer, anorexic; meat-eater, flesh-eater, carnivore, man-eater, cannibal, anthropophagite, insectivore, omnivore; vegetarian, lactovegetarian, vegan, plant-eater, frugivore, herbivore, phytophage; gobbler, pig, hog, wolf;

fussy eater, picky eater, pecker; foodie [Inf], veggie [Inf]

> *Gluttony 119; Discrimination 337; Sociability 408*

16 **dietitian,** dietician, dietary expert, nutritionist, nutrition expert

17 **eating place,** kitchen, breakfast nook, dining room, dinette, dining hall, banquet *or* banqueting hall, refectory, lunchroom; canteen, mess hall, mess; restaurant, health food restaurant, wholefood restaurant [Brit], fast-food restaurant, hamburger place, café, cafeteria, self-service restaurant, Automat™; diner, luncheonette, crêperie, trattoria, spaghetti house, pizzeria, bistro, delicatessen, brasserie, steakhouse, chophouse, grill, carvery, coffeehouse, coffee shop, espresso café, coffee bar [Brit], milk bar [Brit], ice-cream parlor, soda fountain, drugstore counter, lunch counter, fast-food counter, snack bar, sandwich bar; sushi bar, juice bar, teahouse, tea shop, tearoom, pancake house, waffle house; drive-in, hot dog stand, highway restaurant, roadside café, buffet, dining car, diner, vending machine; [Inf]: takeout, eatery, greasy spoon, beanery

ADJECTIVES

18 **eating,** feeding, dining, grazing; meat-eating, flesh-eating, carnivorous, creophagous, man-eating, cannibalistic, omophagic, omophagous, insectivorous; herbivorous, graminivorous, frugivorous, vegetarian, vegan, omnivorous; greedy, gluttonous, hungry, ravenous, voracious, devouring, guzzling, bulimic, wolfish; well-fed, well-nourished, full, bloated, full-up, stuffed, sated

> *Fasting 118; Gluttony 119; Desire 288*

19 **chewing,** masticating, masticatory; biting, tasting, nibbling, licking

20 **edible,** eatable, consumable, esculent, comestible, digestible, predigested; nourishing, nutritious, nutritive, nutritional, feeding, sustaining, alimental, alimentary; dietary, kosher, dietetic, slimming, low-calorie, low-fat, wholesome, good, appetizing, palate-tickling, palatable, mouth-watering, dainty, tasty, savory, sweet; calorific, high-calorie, fattening, bodybuilding, protein-rich, rich; succulent, delicious, scrumptious, finger-licking

> *Health 113; Taste 219*

VERBS

21 **eat,** take nourishment, subsist, fare, consume, feed, ingest, ingurgitate, engulf, take in food; swallow, gulp, gulp down, slurp, suck, devour, take down, get down, digest, absorb; graze, browse, pasture, crop

22 **chew,** chew up, munch, crunch, scrunch, masticate, manducate [Arch], gnash, champ, chomp, mouth, worry, gnaw, grind, bite, nibble, peck, tear, rend, ruminate, chew the cud

23 **eat well,** have a good appetite, be well-nourished; hunger, hunger for, water at the mouth, drool, salivate,

fall to, set to, tuck into, get one's teeth into, sink one's teeth into, devour, gobble, snap up, dispatch, bolt, wolf (down); overeat, overindulge, gorge oneself, engorge, stuff oneself, fork in, shovel in, fill one's stomach, sate, guzzle, gormandize, gluttonize, eat like a pig, take every course, eat everything in sight, eat up, clean one's plate, lick the platter clean; put away, polish off, do justice to, make short work of, ask for seconds, ask for more, fatten on, batten on, prey on; [Inf]: pitch in, lay into, put on the feedbag, lay it on [Brit], get the hungries, have the munchies, binge, feed one's face, pig out, scarf up *or* down, scoff

24 **taste,** relish, savor, nibble, lick, sample, peck at, pick at *or* play with *or* toy with one's food, have a poor appetite, sniff at, eat less, diet, count calories

> *Thinness 595*

25 **have a meal,** board, mess, partake, have a feed, break bread, break one's fast, breakfast, brunch, lunch, brown-bag, have *or* take tea, dine, sup, snack, eat between meals; eat out, dine out, feast, banquet, regale; nosh [Inf], graze [Inf]

> *Provision 89; Food 90; Cooking 91; Sociability 408*

ADVERBS

26 **edibly,** eatably, consumably, digestibly, nutritiously, calorifically, succulently, tastily, deliciously

27 **carnivorously,** creophagously, cannibalistically, omophagically, omophagously, insectivorously, herbivorously, omnivorously, gluttonously, hungrily, ravenously, voraciously, greedily

INTERJECTIONS

28 **come and get it!,** soup's on!, grub's on!, eat up!, chow down!, *bon appétit!* [Fr]

93 Drinking

NOUNS

1 **drinking,** imbibing, imbibition, fluid intake, potation; lapping, sipping, sucking, tasting, nipping, supping, gulping, swallowing; swilling, quaffing, toping; wine-tasting, winebibbing; swigging [Inf], soaking [Inf]

> *Ill Health 114; Substance Abuse 121; Celebration 405; Sociability 408*

2 **drink,** beverage, potation, libation, oblation, thirst-quencher; chaser, stirrup cup, doch-an-dorrach; toast, health; mixed drink, cocktail, nightcap [Inf]; concoction, potion, decoction, infusion; drink of the gods, nectar

> *Refreshment 94; Remedy 115; Mixture 751*

3 **size of drink,** long drink, tall drink, bumper, stiff one, two fingers, short drink, short one, quick one, nip, noggin, shot, dram, jigger, heeltap, tot [Brit]; draft, gulp, swallow, sip, glass, glassful, cup, cupful, can, bottleful, pint, half [Brit], gill [Brit]; [Inf]: quickie, slug, swig, snort, snifter, pick-me-up

4 **water,** drinking water, tap water, ice water, filtered

water, spring water, mineral water, sparkling water, carbonated water, seltzer water, fizzwater, soda water

> *Water 557*

5 **milk,** cow's milk, goat's milk, mare's milk, kumiss *or* koumis, camel's milk, fresh milk, pasteurized milk, homogenized milk, low-fat milk, skim milk; mother's milk, breast milk, beestings *or* beastings; dried milk, powdered milk, condensed milk, evaporated milk; ice milk, milkshake, frappe *or* frappé, malted milk, chocolate milk, hot chocolate, cocoa; top of the milk, cream

6 **coffee,** black coffee, coffee with cream, coffee with milk, café au lait, white coffee [Brit]; cappuccino, espresso; arabica *or* Arabian coffee; Brazilian coffee, Colombian coffee, French coffee, Irish coffee, robusta coffee, Turkish coffee, flavored coffee; iced coffee, instant coffee, decaffeinated coffee, decaf [Inf], java [Inf]

7 **tea,** green tea, black tea, pekoe, orange pekoe; herbal tea, lemon tea, jasmine tea, chamomile tea, peppermint tea; Ceylon tea, China tea, Indian tea, Russian tea; maté, tisane

8 **soft drink,** nonalcoholic beverage, mixer, fizz; soda, root beer, ginger ale, cola, Coca-Cola™, Coke™, Pepsi™; fruit juice, orangeade, lemonade, vegetable juice, tomato juice, coconut milk; ice-cream soda, black cow, float; pop [Inf], tonic [Inf]

9 **alcoholic drink,** alcohol, liquor, fermented drink, distilled liquor, spirits; beer, ale, stout, hard cider, mead, wine, gin, rum, whiskey, brandy, vodka, cognac, liqueur, cordial, ouzo, absinthe, punch; [Inf]: firewater, hard stuff, booze, juice, sauce, poison, hooch *or* hootch, rotgut, moonshine

> *Substance Abuse 121*

10 **beer,** lager, draft beer, home-brew; [Inf]: brew, brewskie, suds

11 **wine,** the grape, juice of the grape; red wine, white wine, rosé wine, vin rosé, dry wine, sweet wine, fortified wine, sparkling wine, champagne; [Inf]: vino, bubbly, plonk [Brit]

12 **mixed drink,** highball, cocktail, julep; mixer, juice, soda, tonic water, vermouth, angostura bitters, Worcestershire sauce, Tabasco™

13 **drink container,** glass, shot glass, tumbler, mug, cup, coffee cup, teacup, goblet, wineglass, flute, loving cup, can, bottle, flask, hip flask, thermos bottle, jug, canteen, decanter, bowl, punch bowl

> *Container 578*

14 **drink occasion,** coffee break, coffee hour, morning coffee; tea, afternoon tea, tea party; cocktail hour, cocktail party, happy hour

15 **drink provider,** water fountain, bubbler; soda fountain, drinking place, coffee shop, coffeehouse, tea shop, bar, wine bar, bistro, cocktail lounge, saloon, tavern, nightclub, cabaret, taproom, alehouse; public house [Brit], pub, local [Brit inf]; drink seller, bartender, barman, barmaid, alewife, publican [Brit]; wine merchant, vintner, liquor store, package store; distillery, brewery, winery

16 **drinker,** light drinker, social drinker, sipper, winetaster, imbiber, winebibber, heavy drinker, hard drinker, guzzler, bibber, swiller, quaffer, tippler

> *Substance Abuse 121*

ADJECTIVES

17 **drinking,** imbibing, swilling, tippling, bibulous; drunken, off the wagon [Inf], boozing [Inf]

> *Sobriety 120; Substance Abuse 121*

18 **drinkable,** potable, milky, lactic, white, diluted, weak, brewed, steeped, strong, undiluted, black, nonalcoholic, soft, fizzy, alcoholic, fermented, distilled, spirituous, hard, vinous, sparkling, still, sweet, dry, light, full-bodied, vintage

VERBS

19 **drink,** imbibe, suck, lap up, sip, taste, nip, quench *or* slake one's thirst, have a drink, drink up, quaff, gulp, gulp down, swallow, sup, drain, down, swill, drink one's fill, drink like a fish, tipple, tope; [Inf]: knock back, chug-a-lug, swig, booze, get pissed, wet one's whistle

> *Substance Abuse 121*

20 **drink to,** toast, drink the health of, raise a *or* one's glass, pledge, salute

> *Celebration 405*

21 **provide drink,** water, breast-feed, nurse, suckle, give suck; wine, give one a refill, freshen, sweeten; brew, steep, distill

INTERJECTIONS

22 **cheers!,** to your health!, to us!, here's to you!, here's looking at you!, here's mud in your eye!, bottoms up!, down the hatch!, absent friends!; prosit!, skoal!, *à votre santé!* [Fr], *salud!* [Sp], *cincin!* [Ital], *l'chaim!* [Hebrew], *sláinte!* [Irish]

94 Refreshment

NOUNS

1 **refreshment,** freshness, freshening up, invigoration, vitalization, animation, exhilaration, stimulation, perking up; reinvigoration, rejuvenation, revitalization, reanimation, renewal, recruitment, rest, recreation, rest and recreation (R and R), recovery, recuperation, revival, resuscitation; restoration, renovation, repair; ease, relief, repose; ventilation, aeration, air conditioning, fan, shade, coolness, cooling off, cooling down, refrigeration

> *Cleanliness 111; Cold 218; Relief 275; Vigor 518; Air 558; Repair 809*

2 **refresher,** reviver, restorative, stimulant, tonic, air, breath of air, breath of fresh air, breather, breeze, cool breeze, oxygen, shower, cold shower, wash, wash and

brush up; rest, repose, break, vacation, holiday, change of scene, recess

3 **refreshments,** refection, food, drink, one for the road, sustenance, snack; [Inf]: pick-me-up, quickie, nineteenth hole
  ▶ *Food 90; Drinking 93; Cold 218; Air 558; Ease 819*

ADJECTIVES

4 **refreshing,** invigorating, exhilarating, stimulating, bracing, reinvigorating, rejuvenating, revitalizing, fortifying, recreative, recreational, reviving, restorative, tonic, relieving, comforting; fresh, cool, cooling, cold

5 **refreshed,** freshened up, invigorated, enlivened, exhilarated, stimulated, braced, perked up, reinvigorated, rejuvenated, revitalized, fortified, renewed, rested, revived, restored, ready for more, ready for another round; cool, cooled off, chilled, refrigerated
  ▶ *Cold 218; Repair 809*

VERBS

6 **refresh,** freshen, freshen up, invigorate, enliven, vitalize, animate, exhilarate, stimulate, brace; reinvigorate, rejuvenate, revitalize, reanimate, strengthen, fortify, renew, recruit, recreate, rest, relax, revive, resuscitate, breathe new life into; restore, renovate, repair, retouch; ease, relieve, dispel, give a break, feed, give food and drink, cheer, give a breather [Inf]

7 **air,** ventilate, aerate, air-condition, provide oxygen, open windows, fan; shade, cool, cool off, cool down, chill, refrigerate

8 **be refreshed,** feel refreshed, refresh oneself, be restored, recover, recuperate, be revived, renew oneself, breathe deeply, draw breath, get one's breath back, regain *or* recover one's breath, take a deep breath, fill one's lungs, take in oxygen, respire, clear one's head, come to, get one's second wind, perk up, feel like a new person, feel oneself again, feel like a kid again; stretch one's legs, take *or* have a break, take a recess, be rested, have a rest, sleep it off, be changed, have a change of pace, go on leave; cool off; clear the cobwebs out, snap out of it, come around; take a breather, take five or ten [Inf], sack out [Inf]
  ▶ *Repair 809; Ease 819*

ADVERBS

9 **refreshingly,** invigoratingly, exhilaratingly, freshly, restoratively, restfully, coolly

95 Necessity

NOUNS

1 **necessity,** essential, fundamental, must, necessary, requirement, requisite, precondition, imperative, need, want, sine qua non, desideratum, necessariness, necessitude [Arch], urgency, exigency, matter of life and death

  ▶ *Qualification 340; Importance 799*

2 **indispensability,** indispensableness, essentialness, needfulness

3 **neediness,** poverty, penury, want, hardship, indigence, privation, destitution
  ▶ *Poverty 486*

4 **need,** want, lack, insufficiency, shortage, shortfall, slippage, gap, lacuna; gap in the market, demand, consumer demand, call, call for
  ▶ *Insufficiency 98; Market 483; Debt 488; Absence 576*

5 **necessitation,** lack of choice, obligation, constraint, duty, compulsion, coercion, Hobson's choice

6 **inevitability,** certainty, unavoidability, inexorability, ineluctability; what must be, one's lot, destiny, fate, nemesis, doom, karma, God's will, will of Allah, sword of Damocles
  ▶ *Certainty 840*

7 **necessitarianism,** determinism, fatalism, predetermination, predestination, circumstances beyond one's control, force of circumstance, act of God
  ▶ *Predetermination 384*

8 **necessitarian,** determinist, fatalist, predeterminist

9 **involuntariness,** compulsion, instinctiveness, reflex, reflex action, Pavlovian reaction, impulse, knee-jerk reaction [Inf]

ADJECTIVES

10 **necessary,** essential, required, requisite, indispensable, fundamental, needed, imperative, urgent, vital, exigent, demanded, called for
  ▶ *Essence 723*

11 **necessitative,** obligatory, compulsory, de rigueur, mandatory, binding, imperative

12 **needy,** needful, necessitous, needing, wanting, lacking, poor, destitute, indigent, poverty-stricken, deprived; broke, dead broke, stone-broke, flat broke, in hock ; hard up [Inf], busted [Inf]
  ▶ *Insufficiency 98; Desire 288; Poverty 486*

13 **demanding,** crying out for, calling for, exacting, crying, pressing, squeezing, pinching

14 **inevitable,** certain, inescapable, unavoidable, inexorable, ineluctable; preordained, ordained, fated, doomed, karmic, predestined, destined, necessitarian, deterministic

15 **involuntary,** compulsory, impulsive, automatic, instinctive, mechanical, autonomic, reflex

VERBS

16 **need,** want, lack, desiderate, require, must have, demand, call for

17 **necessitate,** oblige, compel, coerce, impel, force, mandate, impose, leave no choice *or* alternative
  ▶ *Qualification 340; Command 425; Compulsion 428; Request 505*

18 **be needy,** be poor, live in poverty, live on a pittance, live from hand to mouth, be broke

▶ *Poverty 486*

19 make a virtue out of necessity, make the best of it

ADVERBS

20 with need, essentially, fundamentally, indispensably, urgently, vitally

21 in need, in want, needfully, necessitously, in a pinch

22 necessarily, by necessity, of necessity, imperatively; inevitably, certainly, surely, unavoidably, inexorably, ineluctably; fatedly, come what may, by force of circumstance, perforce, whether willing or not, willy-nilly, *nolens volens* [L]

23 involuntarily, impulsively, automatically, instinctively, mechanically, autonomically

96 Waste

NOUNS

1 waste, wastage, wastefulness; squandering, frittering away, extravagance, overspending, thriftlessness, improvidence, useless expenditure, prodigality, lavishness, splurge, spree; dissipation, dispersion; overwork, overproduction
▶ *Excess 99; Misuse 395; Expenditure 491; Extravagance 500*

2 neglect, nonutilization, waste of opportunity
▶ *Nonuse 394*

3 erosion, wear and tear, damage
▶ *Deterioration 808*

4 wasting away, emaciation, atrophy, decay, decline, deterioration; diminution, decrease, leakage, ebb, outflow, loss
▶ *Decrease 747; Deterioration 808*

5 devastation, wreck, ruin, havoc, disaster area
▶ *Destruction 523*

6 desert, wilderness, wasteland

7 waste product, litter, refuse, rubbish, trash, garbage, leftovers, scraps, atomic waste, toxic waste; effluvia, excrement, feces, urine, sewage, sewerage
▶ *Dirtiness 112; Remainder 750; Uselessness 802*

8 waster, squanderer, wastrel, spendthrift, prodigal, big spender, last of the big spenders
▶ *Expenditure 491; Extravagance 500*

ADJECTIVES

9 wasteful, extravagant, unnecessary, uneconomic, uneconomical, improvident, thriftless, prodigal, lavish, spendthrift, penny wise and pound foolish
▶ *Expenditure 491; Extravagance 500*

10 waste, superfluous, extra, surplus, excess, unused, leftover; useless, worthless, throwaway
▶ *Excess 99; Uselessness 802*

11 consumed, exhausted, depleted, drained, debilitated

12 devastated, ravaged, ruined, ghostly
▶ *Destruction 523*

13 desolate, barren, wild, uninhabited, desert

14 wasted, drunk, intoxicated, high [Inf], buzzed [Inf]
▶ *Substance Abuse 121*

VERBS

15 waste, squander, fritter away, overspend, run through, lavish, splurge, throw away, pour down the drain; dissipate, scatter, disperse, throw to the four winds, blow [Inf]
▶ *Expenditure 491; Extravagance 500*

16 expend, use up, exhaust, deplete, drain, suck dry, empty; misuse, abuse, overwork, overcrop, overfish, overgraze, impoverish, milk dry
▶ *Insufficiency 98; Use 393; Misuse 395; Expenditure 491; Uselessness 802*

17 misspend, misapply, cast pearls before swine, waste effort, labor in vain
▶ *Misuse 395*

18 not use, make no use of, waste an opportunity
▶ *Nonuse 394*

19 erode, wear away, wear out
▶ *Deterioration 808*

20 waste away, emaciate, decline, perish, wane, decay, deteriorate, weaken, wither, wilt, shrivel; decrease, diminish, dwindle, fade, leak, ebb away, flow out, run low, dry up, melt, melt away
▶ *Weakness 517; Decrease 747; Deterioration 808*

21 lay waste, devastate, ravage, ruin
▶ *Destruction 523*

22 be wasted, go to waste, go down the drain, run to waste, run to seed, go to ruin, go to pot

ADVERBS

23 wastefully, extravagantly, unnecessarily, uneconomically, improvidently, thriftlessly, prodigally, lavishly, superfluously, uselessly

24 devastatingly, damagingly

97 Sufficiency

NOUNS

1 sufficiency, adequacy, satisfactoriness, acceptability, suitability, right qualities, assets, qualification, requirement, competence, pass, pass mark, passing grade; enough, adequate amount, satisfactory amount; right amount, exact amount, no surplus, full measure, required number, quorum; adequate income, living wage, enough to live on, enough to get by, enough to keep body and soul together; minimum, bare minimum, no less, least one can do, minimum requirement; satisfaction, contentment, content, completion, fulfillment, the possible, all that is possible, all that could be desired; self-sufficiency
▶ *Satisfaction 273; Completeness 761; Possibility 836*

2 plenty, plentifulness, plenteousness, God's plenty, seven years of plenty, horn of plenty, cornucopia, plenitude, amplitude, bounty, abundance, copiousness, profusion, great quantity, lots, galore, oodles [Inf], lashings [Brit inf], bountiful supply, more where it came from; more than enough, fullness, repletion, one's fill

▶ *Excess 99; Store 105*

ADJECTIVES

3 **sufficient,** adequate, satisfactory, acceptable, sufficing, all-sufficing, suitable, fitting, competent, up to the mark, up to snuff [Inf]; enough, enough to go around; equal, equal to, commensurate, measured, just right, not too much, not too little; barely sufficient, only just enough, hand-to-mouth, makeshift, provisional; satisfying, contenting, complete, fulfilled; self-sufficient

▶ *Provision 89; Insufficiency 98; Satisfaction 273; Substitution 672; Equality 740; Completeness 761*

4 **plentiful,** plenteous, plenitudinous, ample, abundant, bountiful, copious; enough and to spare, more than enough, beyond expectations; openhanded, generous, lavish, liberal; wholesale, unsparing, unmeasured; great, luxuriant, luxuriating, lush, fat, fertile, prolific, profuse

▶ *Fertility 22; Excess 99; Wealth 485; Generosity 498; Extravagance 500*

5 **filled,** well-filled, filled to the brim, full, full-up, chock-full, chockablock, flush; replete, sated; satisfied, contented, content; well-provided, well-provisioned, well-stocked, well-furnished

▶ *Provision 89; Satisfaction 273; Completeness 761*

VERBS

6 **suffice,** be enough, prove adequate, prove acceptable, satisfy, content, do, answer, quench, just do, do and no more, get the job done, get one by, serve, serve as a makeshift, qualify, reach, make the grade, pass, pass muster, measure up to, meet requirements, withstand testing, do all that is possible, rise to the occasion, stand, stand up to, take the strain, support, do what is required, fulfill, carry out; fill, refill, replenish; fill up, fill the bill

▶ *Support 605; Success 845*

7 **have enough,** eat one's fill, drink one's fill; have more than enough; be fed up, have had it up to here; afford, have the means

▶ *Eating 92; Satisfaction 273; Dissatisfaction 274; Wealth 485*

8 **abound,** be plentiful, proliferate, teem, swarm, bristle with, crawl with, wallow in, swim in, luxuriate, grow in profusion, pour, flow, stream, shower, rain, snow, brim, overflow, flow with milk and honey; [Inf]: rain cats and dogs, roll in, stink of

▶ *Fertility 22; Excess 99; Wealth 485; Multitude 795*

ADVERBS

9 **sufficiently,** adequately, satisfactorily, acceptably, tolerably

10 **enough,** just enough, exactly enough, on the nose [Inf]; more than enough, to the full, to one's heart's content, without stint, ad libitum, ad lib, on tap [Inf], on demand

11 **plentifully,** plenteously, amply, abundantly, copiously, profusely, luxuriantly, prolifically

98 Insufficiency

NOUNS

1 **insufficiency,** inadequacy, unsatisfactoriness, nonsatisfaction, disappointment, discontent, nonfulfillment; deficiency, deficit, shortfall, slippage, noncompletion; inferiority, incompetence, imperfection, defect, weakness, tinkering, failure

▶ *Dissatisfaction 274; Disappointment 293; Incompleteness 762; Imperfection 806*

2 **incompleteness,** no quorum, not a full team, not a full deck; small amount, small quantity, little, few, drop in the bucket, drop in the ocean, spit in the ocean, skimpiness, scantiness, scantness, meagerness, stinginess, meanness, parsimony; bankruptcy, insolvency, bare subsistence, subsistence level, poverty level, low pay, minimum wage, pittance, dole [Brit], mite, minimum allowance; austerity, belt-tightening, iron rations, starvation rations, half rations, Lenten fare, Spartan fare, starvation diet, bread and water, fast, asceticism

▶ *Fasting 118; Poverty 486; Nonpayment 490; Meanness 501; Incompleteness 762; Few 796*

3 **scarcity,** scarceness, paucity, dearth, shortage, leanness, want, lack, nothing *or* none to spare, short supply, seller's market, bear market; rarity, infrequency; seven lean years, drought, famine, starvation, infertility, unproductiveness, power cut, energy crisis

▶ *Infertility 23; Necessity 95; Poverty 486; Few 796*

ADJECTIVES

4 **insufficient,** not sufficient, inadequate, unsatisfactory, unsatisfying, disappointing, unacceptable; deficient, incomplete, lacking, light on, low on, wanting, found wanting, poor, inferior, incompetent, incapable, unequal to, not up to it, not up to snuff [Inf], weak, thin, watery

▶ *Unskillfulness 128; Dissatisfaction 274; Disappointment 293; Weakness 517; Unreality 720; Inferiority 745; Incompleteness 762*

5 **not enough,** too little, too few; insubstantial, too small, limited, sketchy, cramped, skimpy, scanty, scant, meager, stingy, miserly, niggardly, mean, parsimonious, hard to find, out of stock

▶ *Meanness 501*

6 **unprovided,** unsupplied, unfurnished, unequipped, ill-supplied, ill-furnished, ill-equipped, unprovided for, unaccommodated, unstocked, unfilled, unreplenished, absent, vacant, bare, empty, empty-handed, with empty pockets; unsuccessful, unsatisfied, discontented, unfulfilled, insatiable, greedy; unsated, stinted, ra-

tioned, skimped, starved of; lacking, needing, hindered, scraping by, poor, undercapitalized, underfinanced, underfunded, underpaid, understaffed, undermanned, short-handed, hard up [Inf]

> *Provision 89; Dissatisfaction 274; Desire 288; Poverty 486; Absence 576; Hindrance 826; Failure 846*

7 underfed, half-fed, half-starved, undernourished, jejune, starveling, scurvy; unfed, fasting, anorectic, famine-stricken, starved; hungry, hungry as a bear, famished, starving, voracious, ravenous, ravening; emaciated, macerated, thin, thin as a rail, lean, spare, skinny, gaunt, scrawny, scraggy, stunted

> *Fasting 118; Thinness 595*

8 scarce, rare, uncommon, infrequent, sparse, few, few and far between, short, unavailable, unobtainable, unprocurable, nonexistent

> *Infrequency 662; Few 796*

VERBS

9 be insufficient, not suffice, not meet requirements, not meet expectations, disappoint; lack, need, want, require; fail, fall below, fall short, come short, default, run out, dry up, take half measures, tinker, leave a gap, paper over the cracks; cramp one's style [Inf], hinder, restrain, restrict, limit

> *Necessity 95; Dissatisfaction 274; Disappointment 293; Incompleteness 762; Imperfection 806; Restraint 830*

10 be unsatisfied, feel unfulfilled, miss, feel the lack, stand in need of, feel something is missing; feel dissatisfied, feel cheated, increase one's demands, reject an offer, laugh at an offer; want, desire, desiderate, long for, yearn for; ask for more, beg for more, come back, come again, take a second helping, still feel hungry

> *Necessity 95; Fasting 118; Gluttony 119; Dissatisfaction 274; Desire 288; Rejection 383*

ADVERBS

11 insufficiently, inadequately, unsatisfactorily, disappointingly, unacceptably; incompetently, poorly

12 not enough, less than somewhat; insubstantially, skimpily, scantily, scantly, sketchily, meagerly, stingily, parsimoniously; scarcely, sparsely, rarely, infrequently

99 Excess

NOUNS

1 excess, overspill, overflow, inundation, stream, steady stream, flood, outflow, deluge; abundance, superabundance, glut, surfeit, exuberance, luxuriance, riot, profusion, plenty, richness, *embarras de richesses* [Fr]; more than is fair, lion's share, most, main part; increase, upsurge, uprush, avalanche, spate; great quantity, too many, plethora; congestion, mob, crowd, overpopulation; saturation, supersaturation, saturation point, all the market can bear; plenitude, waste, excessiveness, overabundance, nimiety; exorbitance, out-

rageousness, unreasonableness, extremes, too much, exaggeration, fulsomeness

> *Waste 96; Sufficiency 97; Store 105; Exaggeration 194; Exit 707; Increase 746; Completeness 761*

2 immoderation, intemperance, overindulgence, overfulfillment, overkill, too much of a good thing, overeating, overfeeding, gluttony, overdrinking, drunkenness, engorgement, satiety, more than enough, one too many, bellyful, fat, fattiness, obesity, overdose, OD

> *Gluttony 119; Substance Abuse 121; Self-Indulgence 456*

3 overdoing it, overextension, overexpansion, overstretching oneself, too much on one's plate, too many irons in the fire, overactivity, overexertion, overwork, overachievement; overexpression, overreaction, overemphasis, officiousness, overkill, overpraise, overpoliteness, effusiveness, overoptimism, overestimation, overpayment, overload, burden, last straw, overtaxation, bureaucracy, red tape

> *Sufficiency 97; Overestimation 343; Activity 414*

4 superfluity, superfluousness, more than is needed, redundancy, redundance, duplication, overlap; surplus, overplus, leftovers, overstock, overage, overrun, overmeasurement, oversupply; margin, remainder, balance; luxury, luxuriousness, extravagance, nonessential, extra, frill, perquisite, bonus, lagniappe, spare cash, money to burn; accessory, spare tire, fifth wheel, excrescence, parasite, uselessness, inutility; expletive, padding, filling, pleonasm, prolixity, rambling speech, wordiness, diffuseness, tautology

> *Diffuseness 199; Remainder 750; Uselessness 802*

ADJECTIVES

5 excessive, overflowing, filled to overflowing, brimming over, running over, full, overfull, fulsome, streaming, flooding, flowing, overwhelming, overwhelmed; abundant, superabundant, exuberant, luxuriant, riotous, profuse, plentiful; too many, plethoric, overpopulated, bristling, teeming, swarming, crawling, congested, outnumbered; saturated, supersaturated, drenched, soaked; too much, overmuch, exorbitant, extreme, inordinate, disproportionate, unreasonable

> *Sufficiency 97; Moisture 559; Multitude 795*

6 immoderate, overindulgent, overfulfilled, cloyed, satiated, sated, replete, overfed, gorged, crammed, stuffed, bloated, ready to burst, bursting; overfulfilling, cloying, satiating, nauseating, sickening

> *Gluttony 119; Self-Indulgence 456*

7 overdone, overextended, overstretched, overactive, overworked; overplayed, overacted, exaggerated; overpolite, effusive, gushing, overexcited, overoptimistic, over the moon [Inf]; overburdened, overloaded, overcharged, overtaxed; bureaucratic

> *Exaggeration 194*

8 superfluous, supererogatory, redundant, duplicative,

unnecessary, needless, otiose; excess, extra, spare, surplus, leftover, remaining; nonessential, luxury, extravagant; useless; diffuse, rambling, circuitous, tautologous, tautological, pleonastic, prolix

▶ *Necessity 95; Diffuseness 199; Remainder 750; Uselessness 802*

VERBS

9 **be excessive,** have an excess of, overspill, overflow, brim over, well over, inundate, stream, flood, engulf, flow, flow out, deluge, overwhelm, burst at the seams, ooze at every pore; abound, superabound, luxuriate, riot, run riot; overproduce, overpopulate, bristle with, teem with, swarm with, crawl with, outnumber, meet one at every turn, extend, know no bounds, spread far and wide, reach to the far ends of the earth, reach to the four corners of the earth; soak, saturate, drench, stuff, cram, fill, congest, choke, suffocate

10 **overindulge,** overfulfill, oversatisfy, pamper, overeat, overfeed, gorge, overdrink, glut, cloy, surfeit, satiate, sate, sicken, overdose, OD

▶ *Gluttony 119; Self-Indulgence 456*

11 **overdo,** do more than enough, go overboard, overextend, overexpand, have too much on one's plate, have too many irons in the fire, bite off more than one can chew, overexert, overwork, overachieve; overplay, overact, overpraise, overstep the mark, talk too much, lay it on thick, exaggerate; overload, overburden, overcharge, surcharge, overtax; overspend, oversubscribe, lavish, lavish upon, spoil; oversell, flood the market, dump on the market

▶ *Fertility 22; Sufficiency 97; Exaggeration 194; Generosity 498; Extravagance 500; Moisture 559; Space 563; Overstepping 712; Completeness 761; Multitude 795*

12 **be superfluous,** duplicate, do twice over, paint *or* gild the lily, bring coals to Newcastle, teach one's grandmother to suck eggs, labor the obvious, flog a dead horse; exceed requirements, have no use; make superfluous, overstock, oversupply, overrun

▶ *Inactivity 415; Remainder 750; Uselessness 802*

ADVERBS

13 **excessively,** overwhelmingly; abundantly, enough and to spare, superabundantly, beyond measure, exuberantly, profusely; over and above, in excess of requirements, above expectations; overly, too much, overmuch, exorbitantly, extremely, inordinately, disproportionately, unreasonably, fulsomely

14 **immoderately,** to excess, overindulgently

15 **superfluously,** redundantly, unnecessarily, needlessly; uselessly; diffusely, circuitously

100 Clothing

NOUNS

1 **clothing,** clothes, apparel, wear, attire, habiliments, accouterment, dress, togs, garb, raiment, robes; linens; outfit, wardrobe; garment, article of clothing, vestment; men's clothing, men's wear; women's clothing, women's wear, trousseau, wedding clothes, bridal outfit, maternity clothes; unisex clothes; [Inf]: toggery, duds, threads, number

▶ *Decoration 532; Covering 613*

2 **dressing,** covering, investiture, investment, vesture [Arch], toilet, toilette; turnout, dressing up; overdressing, foppishness; casualness, informal dress, underdressing; dishabille, careless dress, negligent dress; fashion, the latest fashion, the latest style, the fashion world, fashion designing, Paris fashion, high fashion, haute couture

▶ *Negligence 326; Showiness 404; Informality 407; Elegance 527; Decoration 532; Fashion 536; Covering 613*

3 **store-bought clothes,** ready-to-wear clothes, off-the-rack clothes, wash-and-wear clothes, dry goods

4 **tailor-made clothes,** custom-made clothes, made-to-order clothes, bespoke clothes [Brit]

5 **formal clothes,** best clothes, Sunday best, best bib and tucker; formal, morning dress, morning coat, full dress, dress suit, tail coat *or* swallow-tailed coat, tails, white tie and tails, evening dress, evening gown; semiformal dress, tuxedo *or* dinner jacket, black tie, bow tie, cummerbund, dinner dress *or* gown, party dress; academic dress, academic costume, academicals, academic robe, academic gown, mortarboard, cap and gown, hood; [Inf]: Sunday-go-to-meeting clothes, soup-and-fish, tux

▶ *Formality 406*

6 **finery,** regalia, caparison, panoply, array, frippery, ostrich feathers, fig *or* full fig; glad rags [Inf]

▶ *Showiness 404*

7 **informal clothes,** casual clothes, casual wear, leisurewear, plain clothes; slacks, slack suit, pants, pantsuit, blazer, sports jacket, sport shirt, T-shirt; denims, jeans, blue jeans, work *or* working clothes; sportswear, activewear, track suit, sweat suit, sweatpants, sweatshirt; loungewear, smoking jacket, bed jacket, lounging robe, lounging pajamas, slippers; mufti, civilian clothes, civvies

▶ *Leisure 125; Sports 145*

8 **old clothes,** worn clothes, castoffs, tatters, slops, secondhand clothes, seconds; hand-me-downs, rags

9 **uniform,** military uniform, dress uniform, full-dress uniform, blues, dress blues, whites, dress whites, uniform slops, battle dress, khaki uniform, khakis, olive-drabs, regimentals, fatigues, sailor suit; school uniform; clerical dress, clerical garb, vestments, canonicals, nun's habit; nurse's uniform; police officer's uniform, firefighter's uniform; servant's uniform, livery; riding habit; sports team uniform

▶ *Clergy 84; Identification 184*

10 **costume,** costumery, fancy dress, masquerade, bedizenment; character dress, gear, outfit, getup [Inf]; dis-

guise, camouflage, mask; motley, silks, colors, cap and bells; buskin, cothurnus, sock and buskin; makeup, greasepaint, powder, lipstick, wig, beard

▶ *Drama and Theater 136; Concealment 181*

11 **dress,** frock, housedress, sundress, backless dress, strapless dress, tube dress, party dress, cocktail dress, dinner dress *or* gown, gown, tea gown, evening gown, ball gown, wedding gown *or* dress, maternity dress, maxidress *or* maxi, minidress *or* mini, shirtwaist *or* shirt-dress, sheath, sweater dress, jumper, pinafore, overdress, mantua, Mother Hubbard, sack *or* sacque, sari, muumuu, cheongsam

12 **skirt,** maxiskirt *or* maxi, midiskirt *or* midi, miniskirt *or* mini, microskirt *or* micro, straight skirt, full skirt, flared skirt, A-line skirt, gored skirt, gathered skirt, dirndl, pleated skirt, kilt, tartan, filibeg *or* philibeg, peasant skirt, tight skirt, hobble skirt, slit skirt, split skirt, culottes; sarong, overskirt, farthingale, hoop skirt, crinoline, grass skirt, sports skirt, riding skirt, tennis skirt, ballet skirt, tutu

▶ *Dance and Ballet 135*

13 **shirt,** long-sleeved shirt, button-down shirt, dress shirt, evening shirt, short-sleeved shirt, sport shirt, polo shirt, workshirt, blouse, shell, peasant blouse, overblouse, blouson, dashiki; middy blouse, top, tank top, halter, tube top, crop top, bustier; body shirt, bodysuit, T-shirt, sweatshirt, dickey, doublet [Arch]

14 **pants,** trousers, slacks, long pants, corduroys *or* cords, flannels, ducks, pinstripes, bell-bottoms, hiphuggers, Capri pants *or* Capris, pegged pants *or* trousers, toreador pants, pedal pushers, leggings, jeans, blue jeans, dungarees, denims, overalls, knickers *or* knickerbockers, plus fours, breeches *or* knee breeches, britches, galligaskins, buckskins, riding breeches, riding pants, jodhpurs, lederhosen, bloomers, pantaloons, jogging pants, sweatpants

15 **shorts,** short pants, Bermuda shorts, Jamaica shorts, hot pants, short shorts, cycling shorts, gym shorts

16 **suit,** outfit, costume, ensemble, coordinates, separates; dress suit, monkey suit [Inf], one-piece suit, two-piece suit, three-piece suit, business suit, single-breasted suit, double-breasted suit, pinstripe suit, tailored suit, tweed suit, leisure suit, slack suit, zoot suit, pantsuit, bodysuit, sunsuit, rompers, coveralls, jumpsuit, track suit, jogging suit, sweat suit, wet suit, ski suit, snowsuit, flight suit, anti-G suit *or* G-suit, spacesuit

17 **sweater,** jersey, cardigan, pullover, slipover, pull-on sweater, jumper [Brit], poor boy sweater, cashmere sweater, knitted sweater, knit, hand-knit *or* hand-knitted sweater, V-neck sweater, crew-neck sweater, turtle-neck sweater, ski sweater, fisherman sweater, cable-stitched sweater, guernsey, sloppy joe, twin sweater set *or* twin set

18 **jacket,** cutaway, morning *or* tail *or* swallow-tailed coat, dress coat, tails, dinner jacket, Eton jacket, mess jacket, shell jacket; vest; sports jacket, blazer, cardigan *or* cardigan jacket; Norfolk jacket; sack coat, Mackinaw coat, lumberjacket *or* lumber jack; denim jacket; leather jacket, bomber jacket, battle jacket *or* Eisenhower jacket; parka, ski jacket, anorak, Windbreaker™, loden jacket; dolman jacket; shirt jacket; Nehru jacket, Mao jacket; jerkin, spencer, bolero, tunic, tabard; monkey jacket, claw hammer [Inf]

19 **coat,** overcoat, topcoat, topper, surcoat, greatcoat [Brit], frock coat *or* frock, Prince Albert, surtout, chesterfield, raglan, ulster, midicoat, car coat, peacoat *or* pea jacket, reefer, redingote, paletot, duster, fur coat, cashmere coat, wool coat, tweed coat, down coat, storm coat, duffel *or* duffle coat, fearnought *or* fearnaught, gabardine *or* gaberdine coat, raincoat, mackintosh, trench coat, oilskins, slicker, sou'wester; cloak, capote, cape, mantle, shawl, wrap, poncho, serape, rebozo

▶ *Covering 613*

20 **robe,** bathrobe, dressing gown, *robe-de-chambre* [Fr], peignoir, negligee, housecoat, wrapper, caftan *or* kaftan, kimono; jubbah, burka *or* bourkha *or* burkha; toga, toga virilis, tunic, djellabah, chiton, himation [Arch]; clerical robe, cassock, surplice, choir robe

▶ *Religion 81; Religious Ritual 85*

21 **nightwear,** nightclothes, sleepwear, nightdress; nightgown, nightie [Inf], negligee, nightshirt; pajamas, p.j.'s *or* P.J.'s [Inf], baby doll pajamas; bed jacket, nightcap

▶ *Inactivity 415*

22 **underwear,** underclothes, underclothing, undergarments, underthings, lingerie, intimate apparel, unmentionables, undies; thermal underwear, long underwear, union suit, long johns [Inf]; underpants, panties, scanties, pantalets *or* pantalettes, bloomers, knickers [Brit], camiknickers [Brit], step-ins; briefs, drawers *or* underdrawers, shorts *or* undershorts, boxer shorts; brassiere, bra, falsies [Inf]; undershirt, T-shirt, skivvy *or* skivvy shirt [Inf], skivvies [Inf]; camisole, chemise, shift; teddy; slip, full slip, half-slip, underskirt, petticoat, crinoline, Balmoral; body stocking; foundation garment, girdle, panty girdle, corset, stays, supporter, jockstrap *or* athletic supporter; garter, garter belt; bustle, hoop, farthingale, pannier; loincloth, waistcloth, G-string

▶ *Heat 217; Support 605*

23 **beachwear,** swimwear, swimsuit, bathing suit; one-piece suit, tank suit, maillot, monokini, two-piece suit, bikini, string bikini, thong; trunks *or* swimming trunks; coverup

▶ *Swimming 164*

24 **baby clothes,** layette, infants' wear, swaddling clothes, creeper, rompers, playsuit, sunsuit, sleeper; diaper, booties, bib

25 graveclothes, cerements, shroud, winding sheet; mourning clothes, black, widow's weeds
▶ *Burial 31*

26 legwear, hosiery, hose; stockings, sheer stockings, seamless stockings, seamed stockings, silk stockings, rayon stockings, lisle stockings, nylons, pantyhose; tights, fishnet tights, leotard; socks, anklets, ankle socks, bobbysocks, argyles, crew socks, knee-socks, athletic socks, sweat socks, tube socks; leg warmers, galligaskins, chaps, leggings, gaiters, spats, puttees, spatterdashes

27 part of garment, neck, yolk, collar; top, bodice, bosom, corsage, bib, stomacher, shirt front; waistline, empire waist, peplum; train; crotch, codpiece; arm, armhole, sleeve, short sleeve, long sleeve, dolman sleeve, raglan sleeve, puff sleeve, leg-of-mutton sleeve; flap, coattail, placket, opening, pocket, patch pocket; gusset, gore, pleat, kick pleat; lapel, fold, cuff, hemline, edging, garniture, trim button; fly, zipper, hook and eye, Velcro™; décolletage, plunging neckline
▶ *Beautification 530; Edge 618; Fold 637; Union 752; Connection 754*

28 accessory, accouterment, paraphernalia; muff; earmuffs; scarf, lungi, apron, pinafore; armlet, armband; shoulder pads; belt, cincture, bandoleer, baldric, sash, obi; glove, gauntlet, mitten, mitt; wristband; handkerchief; sunglasses, shades [Inf]; jewelry
▶ *Decoration 532; Part 760*

29 neckwear, tie, necktie, cravat, bow tie, Windsor tie, four-in-hand, string tie; scarf, muffler, comforter, neckpiece, neckerchief, bandanna *or* bandana, kerchief, fichu, shawl, tallith, stole, boa, tippet, jabot, tucker, chemisette, guimpe; ascot, neckcloth; necklace, neckband, band, choker, stock, collar, starched collar, stiff collar, rabato, high collar, Vandyke collar, Peter Pan collar, bertha collar, Eton collar, mandarin collar, stand-up collar, button-down collar, shawl collar, clerical collar *or* Roman collar *or* reversed collar, dog collar [Inf]; ruff; dickey

30 shoes, footwear, footgear; leather shoes, patent leather shoes, oxfords *or* Oxford shoes, saddle shoes, buckled shoes; square-toed shoes, pointed shoes; flat shoes *or* flats; pumps, espadrilles, sling-backs; high heels, spike *or* stiletto heels, platform heels, Cuban heels, French heels, Spanish heels, wedge heels *or* wedgies; canvas shoes, sneakers, tennis shoes, gym shoes, running shoes, walking shoes, golf shoes, spikes, cleats; wing tips, brogues, penny loafers, moccasins, slip-ons; rubber-soled shoes, crepe-soled *or* crepe rubber-soled shoes; sandals, flip-flops *or* thongs, zoris; wooden shoes, clogs, sabots, pattens; ballet shoes *or* slippers; slippers, mules, scuffs; buskins *or* cothurnuses; work shoes, clodhoppers

31 boots, walking boots, hiking boots, wafflestompers; riding boots, cowboy boots; hip boots, waders; combat boots, paratrooper boots, jackboots; stogies, hobnail boots; ski boots, snowshoes, overshoes, galoshes, rubbers, gumshoes, moon boots; lace-ups, buskins, chukka boots; fashion boots, high boots, top boots, thigh boots, go-go boots [Inf], shitkickers [Inf]

32 hat, headgear, millinery, chapeau, lid [Inf]; bonnet, Easter bonnet, poke *or* poke bonnet, sunbonnet, sun hat, picture hat; pillbox, toque, cloche; top hat, topper [Inf], high hat, opera hat, silk hat, stovepipe hat [Inf], plug *or* plug hat; felt hat, derby, bowler, homburg, fedora, porkpie, Tyrolean hat; straw hat, boater, Panama hat *or* Panama, coolie hat; cowboy hat, Stetson™, ten-gallon hat, sombrero, slouch hat; rain hat, sou'wester *or* southwester; woolly hat, bobble hat, fur hat; clerical hat, biretta *or* berretta *or* birretta, shovel hat; witch's hat, wizard's hat; cocked hat, bicorne *or* bicorn, tricorn *or* tricorne

33 cap, stocking cap, balaclava, tuque [Can]; baseball cap, jockey cap; surgeon's cap, nurse's cap; mortarboard; skullcap, beanie, coif, Juliet cap; mobcap; beret; tam-o'-shanter *or* tam, glengarry, balmoral; beaver, coonskin cap *or* hat, deerstalker *or* fore-and-after; military cap, kepi, shako; fez; dunce cap *or* dunce's cap *or* fool's cap, cockscomb
▶ *Combatant 77; Baseball 147*

34 helmet, hard hat, safety hat, crash helmet, tin hat [Inf]; kettle hat *or* chapel de fer; topee *or* topi, pith helmet
▶ *Combatant 77; Worker 123*

35 headdress, head scarf, mantilla, veil, yashmak, kaffiyeh *or* keffiyeh, headcloth, turban, wimple, hood, cowl; crown, coronet, tiara; ribbon, headband, sweatband, fillet, snood, hair net

36 the clothing business, tailoring, dressmaking, garment-making, habilimentation, rag trade [Inf], Garment District, Garment Center; hosiery, millinery, hatmaking, hatting, shoemaking, cobbling, bootmaking
▶ *Trade 480; Fashion 536*

37 clothier, outfitter, couturier *or* couturière, fashion designer; dressmaker, tailor, busheler; modiste, haberdasher; costumer, costumier, costume designer; milliner, hatter; furrier; fabric dealer, dry-goods dealer, cutter, needleworker, seamstress, sewer, stitcher, finisher, fitter; hosier; shoemaker, cobbler, cordwainer [Arch], bootmaker
▶ *Materials 104; Fabrics and Fabric Handling 130; Trade 480; Production 522; Decoration 532; Fashion 536*

ADJECTIVES

38 dressed, clothed, clad, attired, appareled, garbed, bedecked, arrayed, vested, invested, habited, habilimented, frocked, wrapped, draped, robed, mantled, cloaked, gowned, decked out, bedighted [Arch]; turned out, costumed, uniformed, liveried; hatted, coifed, capped, bonneted, hooded, bewigged, gloved, shod, shoed, booted

▶ *Concealment 181*

39 **dressed up,** well-dressed, fashionable, modish, à la mode, chic, dapper, spruce, groomed, bedizened; dressy; overdressed; natty, dressed to kill, dressed to the nines, in fine feather, togged, spruced up; [Inf]: gussied up, dolled up, spiffed up

▶ *Elegance 527; Fashion 536*

40 **in dishabille,** carelessly dressed, negligently dressed; underdressed, underclothed; half-dressed, half-clothed; informally dressed, casually dressed, in one's shirt-sleeves

▶ *Negligence 326; Informality 407*

41 **tailored,** sartorial, tailor-made, custom-made, made-to-order, bespoke [Brit], styled, designer; store-bought, ready-made, ready-to-wear, off-the-rack; single-breasted, double-breasted, one-piece, two-piece, unisex

42 **stylish,** smart, well-cut, matching, color-coordinated, classic; dressy; casual, informal, sporty; baggy, sloppy; skintight, décolleté, low-necked, low-cut, off-the-shoulder, strapless; tattered, threadbare; slinky, natty, snazzy

VERBS

43 **clothe,** dress, garment, attire, apparel, accouter, robe, enrobe, gown, drape, cloak, mantle, garb, enfold, envelop, wrap, bundle up, swaddle, swathe, shroud, sheathe, cover, vest, invest, cap, coif, hood, glove, shoe

44 **make clothing,** outfit, tailor, tailor-make, custom-make, make to order, design, costume, accouter, uniform; cobble, measure, adjust, gather, fold, blouse, seam, sew, stitch, pleat, hem, finish, fit, bushel

▶ *Fabrics and Fabric Handling 130*

45 **dress up,** bedeck, deck out, turn out, array, titivate, groom, primp, prink, bedizen, bedight [Arch]; dress to kill, dress to the nines, dress in one's best bib and tucker, spruce up; [Inf]: gussy up, doll up, spiff up

46 **wear,** dress in, have on, don, get dressed, put on, pull on, slip on, slip *or* get into, step in; change one's clothes, get changed, change, try on; button, zip, snap, lace, tie

ADVERBS

47 **dressily,** fashionably, stylishly, modishly, in vogue, chicly, elegantly, smartly, nattily, glamorously; casually, informally, sportily; carelessly, negligently

▶ *Fashion 536*

101 Furniture

NOUNS

1 **furniture,** furnishing, house *or* home furnishings, household goods, household effects, suite, set of furniture; office furniture, school furniture, church furniture, library furniture; piece of furniture, chair, table, desk, couch, sofa, cabinet, bed, mirror, clock, screen

2 **type of furniture,** wood, soft, upholstered, leather, plastic, metal, painted, refinished, laminated, veneer, lacquered, japanned, inlaid, marquetried, built-in, unit

3 **furniture making,** furniture designing, upholstering, cabinetmaking, crafting, inlaying, finishing; furniture factory, furniture shop *or* store; furniture maker, upholsterer, cabinetmaker, inlayer, finisher

▶ *Materials 104; Workplace 124; Woodworking 131; Property 470; Decoration 532; Layer 588; Covering 613*

4 **type of chair,** armchair, barrel, bentwood, Brewster, camp, cane, captain's, carver, club, deck, dining, director's, easy, folding, highchair, ladder-back, leather, lounge, panel-back, recliner *or* reclining, rocker *or* rocking, straight, side, swivel, upholstered, wheel-back, Windsor, wing, wooden; bench, pew, settle, stall; stool, barstool, milking stool

▶ *Support 605*

5 **type of table,** bedside, board, card, coffee, console, dining, dressing, drop-leaf, end, gaming, gate-leg, kitchen, library, night, nightstand, pedestal, picnic, pier, refectory, rent, side, tea, work, writing

6 **type of desk,** bombé, davenport [Brit], escritoire, Governor Winthrop, knee-hole, lectern, reading, roll-top, secretary *or* secretaire, slant- *or* slope-top

7 **couch,** sofa, camelback couch, chaise longue, chesterfield couch, convertible couch, sofa bed, davenport, divan, Grecian couch, love seat, méridienne, pull-out couch, settee, studio couch

8 **cabinet,** bureau, dresser, Welsh dresser, double *or* triple dresser, chest, chest of drawers, hope chest, cassone, commode; highboy, lowboy, tallboy, wardrobe,

---

STYLES AND PERIODS OF FURNITURE

Adam	early American	mannerist
Adirondack	Egyptian	modernist
art deco	Elizabethan	Morris
art nouveau	Empire	neoclassical
Arts and Crafts	Federal	Palladian
baroque	French Provincial	Pennsylvania
Bauhaus	French	Dutch
Biedermeier	Renaissance	Queen Anne
boule *or*	Georgian	Regency
boulework	Gothic	rococo
Byzantine	Hepplewhite	Scandinavian
Chinese	International	modern
Chippendale	Gothic *or*	Shaker
chinoiserie	International	Sheraton
Chippendale	Italian Renaissance	Spanish
colonial	Jacobean	Renaissance
contemporary	Japanese	Stuart
de Stijl	Louis Quatorze	Tudor
Directoire	Louis Quinze	Victorian
Duncan Phyfe	Louis Seize	William and Mary

armoire; canterbury, magazine stand, china cabinet, curio cabinet, whatnot, hutch, sideboard, liquor cabinet, drinks cabinet; file cabinet, bookcase, console, entertainment center

▶ *Container 578*

9 **type of bed,** single, twin, double, queen-size, king-size, four-poster, paneled, canopied, bunk, feather, water, sleigh *or* boat, adjustable, daybed, sofa, convertible sofa, sofa bed; futon, divan, foldaway, Murphy, truckle *or* trundle; cot, camp; cradle, crib, bassinet; hammock, berth; bedstead, headboard, footboard

▶ *Support 605*

102 Means

Let us all be happy and live within our means, even if we have to borrow the money to do it with.
— ARTEMUS WARD

NOUNS

1 **means,** way, manner, mode, modality; method, measures, steps, course, system; ways and means, resources, wherewithal; power, capacity, ability, capability; strong hand, trump, trump card, ace; conveniences, facilities, appliances, tools, tools of the trade, tricks of the trade, bag of tricks; technology, high technology, high tech, knowledge, technique, knack, skill, know-how; process, approach, resort, recourse, expedient, device, contrivance, makeshift, ad hoc measure, substitute; means of escape, remedy, cure, desperate remedy, last resort, last hope, last gasp, last throw, alternative, choice, freedom of choice

▶ *Tool 103; Remedy 115; Skillfulness 127; Knowledge 348; Selection 382; Plan 387; Power 514; Way 691; Escape 816; Chance 842*

2 **instrumentality,** instrument, means, vehicle, medium, agency, tool, mechanism

3 **supplies,** basic *or* vital supplies, basics; provisions, stock, materials, equipment, machinery, munitions, ammunition; resources, natural resources, raw material, nuts and bolts

▶ *Provision 89; Materials 104*

4 **resources,** labor resources, labor pool, work force, manpower, personnel, staff, workers; financial resources, finances, funds, wealth, money, substance, liquidity, cash; capital, start-up capital, investment capital, working capital; assets, stock in trade, premises, property, stocks and shares, stocks and bonds, investments, investment portfolio, revenue, income, receipts; credit, overdraft, borrowing capacity, credit limit, line of credit, credit rating, creditworthiness; backing, support, sponsorship, subsidy

▶ *Worker 123; Property 470; Money 484; Wealth 485; Credit 487; Receipt 492; Support 605*

5 **reserves,** store, something in reserve, backup, emer-gency funds, nest egg, standby, safeguard, ace *or* card up one's sleeve

▶ *Store 105; Safety 810*

VERBS

6 **find means,** find a way, develop a method, provide the wherewithal, enable, facilitate, secure the basics; find, supply, furnish, provide, equip, buy supplies, fit out, make ready, prepare; hire personnel, staff; finance, fund, raise money, promote, sponsor, float, subsidize; have the means, be able, plan, contrive, think laterally, get by any means; beg, borrow, or steal; get by hook or by crook, get by fair means or foul, acquire

▶ *Provision 89; Plan 387; Preparation 388; Gain 467; Power 514*

ADVERBS

7 **by means of,** with, wherewith, by, by use of, using, through, with the aid of, by resorting to, with recourse to, by dint of, by hook or by crook, by fair means or foul, how, somehow

103 Tool

Paintbrushes are ancient tools, as are eyes, fingers, and neurons. Finding new uses for reliable tools is part of the artist's job. — MARY JANE KENTON

NOUNS

1 **tool,** implement, instrument, utensil; agricultural tool, precision tool, machine tool, hand tool, garden tool, kitchen tool; contraption, gadget, contrivance, widget; [Inf]: gismo *or* gizmo, doodad, thingamabob *or* thingumabob, thingamajig *or* thingumajig, thingummy, doohickey, whatsis *or* whatsit

▶ *Physics 10; Chemistry 11; Engineering 14; Agriculture 16; Horticulture 17; Cooking 91; Instrumentality 511*

2 **apparatus,** equipment, appliance, machine, device, mechanical device, mechanical aid

3 **hand tool,** screwdriver, hammer, ram, drill, electric drill, punch, awl; wrench, monkey wrench, pipe wrench, Stillson™ wrench, torque wrench, spanner [Brit]; pliers, pincers, tweezers, nippers; clamp, vise; chisel, wedge, edged tool, ax, knife; saw, jigsaw, fret saw, chain saw, saber saw, spokeshave; rope, cable, peg; hanger, hook, support; prop, lever, shim, jimmy; crowbar, handspike, jack, pivot, grip, lug, handle, pulley, sheave, wheel, switch, stopcock; trigger, pedal, pole

4 **garden tool,** spade, shovel, trowel, fork, pitchfork, pickax, sickle, scythe; billhook, rake, hoe, cultivator, tiller, plow; mattock, dibble *or* dibber, riddle; roller, edging iron *or* knife, pruning saw, hedge clipper *or* trimmer, lopper, shears, secateurs [Brit]; lawn mower

▶ *Horticulture 17; Grasses 45*

5 **machinery,** mechanical device, machine, mechanism;

works, clockwork, wheelwork, wheels within wheels, nuts and bolts; part, component, servomechanism, servomotor, robot, automaton
▶ *Power 514; Part 760*

6 equipment, tools, utensils, appointments, fittings, fixtures, adjunct, upholstery, furnishing, trappings, accouterments, dress, outfit, kit, gear, tackle, harness, paraphernalia

ADJECTIVES

7 mechanical, mechanized, mechanistic, motorized, technological, hydraulic, electronic, powered, power-driven, labor-saving, robotic, automatic, automated, machine-minded, tool-using, instrumental

VERBS

8 use tools, mechanize

ADVERBS

9 instrumentally, mechanically, automatically, hydraulically, electronically, cybernetically, technologically

104 Materials

NOUNS

1 materials, material, stuff, substance, matter, staple, stock, grist, apparatus, supply; raw materials, basic materials, essentials, basics, tools, equipment; resources, natural resources, elements, components, constituents, ideas; mineral, ore, fuel; building materials; fiber, fabric, paper, plastics, leather
▶ *Geology 8; Chemistry 11; Provision 89; Food 90; Means 102; Tool 103; Fuel 106; Literature 139*

2 building materials, wood, clay, adobe, concrete, cement, glass, steel, block, cinder block, brick, stone, sandstone, marble, granite, ashlar, masonry, mortar, plaster, lath, tile; slate, shingle, thatch; paving, flagstone, cobble, tar, tarmacadam, macadam, asphalt, blacktop, Tarmac™; gravel, soil, dirt
▶ *Trees 43*

3 fiber, filament, thread, yarn, rope, fiberglass

4 fabric, cloth, material, yard goods, textiles
▶ *Fabrics and Fabric Handling 130*

5 paper, sheet, writing paper, stationery, notepaper, typing paper, onionskin, foolscap, yellow paper, newsprint, computer paper; cotton paper, rag paper, Bible paper, India paper, fiber paper, bond paper, rice paper, watermarked paper; wrapping paper, tissue paper; tracing paper, carbon paper; greaseproof paper, wax paper, waterproof paper; laminated paper, glossy paper, art paper, crepe paper; toilet paper, paper towel; cardboard, pasteboard, Bristol board, posterboard, matboard, fiberboard; papier-mâché; quire, ream

6 plastics, polymers, synthetic resin, thermoplastics, celluloid, polyethylene, polyvinyl chloride (PVC), acrylic, nylon, rayon, polyester, polyurethane, epoxy, latex

▶ *Chemistry 11*

7 leather, hide, skin, rawhide, parchment, vellum, chamois, cowhide, sheepskin, horsehide, goatskin, pigskin, doeskin
▶ *Covering 613*

ADJECTIVES

8 material, basic, essential, elemental, constituent, structural

VERBS

9 procure, supply, provide, store, stock, equip
▶ *Provision 89; Store 105*

ADVERBS

10 materially, provisionally

105 Store

NOUNS

1 store, stock, supply, provision; collection, accumulation, stockpile, buildup, backlog, reserve, hoard; crop, harvest, vintage; mass, heap, load, stack, pile
▶ *Assembly 59; Provision 89; Market 483*

2 stock in trade, merchandise, inventory; property, assets, matériel, capital, holdings, investment, fund, community chest
▶ *Gain 467; Market 483*

3 reserve, reserves, emergency reserves, reserve fund, unexpended balance, savings, savings account, nest egg, kitty, deposit; hope chest, trousseau; treasure, buried treasure, cache
▶ *Provision 89; Finance 457*

4 source of supply, source, resource, fund, pool, reservoir, pipeline, tap, well, natural resources, deposit, quarry, mine, lode, vein, gas field, oil field; fountain, fount, spring, wellspring; bonanza, strike, discovery
▶ *Provision 89; Sufficiency 97*

5 quantity, abundance, plenty, cornucopia; amount, aggregate, bundle
▶ *Sufficiency 97; Excess 99; Container 578; Quantity 738*

6 storage, stowage, gathering, garnering, accumulation, conservation, preservation, safekeeping, protection, warehousing, stabling; cold storage, cold store; silage, ensilage, bottling, canning, freezing; custody, escrow
▶ *Assembly 59; Space 563; Safety 810; Preservation 815*

7 storeroom, stockroom, box room [Brit], attic, loft, hold, bunker, basement, cellar, root cellar, wine cellar, pantry, larder, buttery

8 storehouse, warehouse, depository, supply base, depot, entrepôt, shed, stable, garage; dock, wharf; magazine, arsenal, armory, gun room; chamber; treasure house, treasury, coffers, exchequer, strongroom, bank; granary, garner, grain elevator, grain bin, barn, silo, mow; water tower, reservoir, cistern, tank; gas tank, gasometer [Brit], gas pump, gas station, filling station

9 vault, safe, coffer, money box, moneybag, till, money drawer, strongbox, safe-deposit box, night safe, blood bank, sperm bank, data bank, memory; storage battery

> *Computers 15; Memory 354; Container 578*

10 refrigerator, fridge [Inf], icebox, freezer, deep freezer

11 receptacle, container, holder, vessel, box, crate, carton, bag, bucket, bottle, can; suitcase, carryall, portmanteau [Brit], chest, trunk, foot locker, packing case, luggage, baggage; cupboard, cabinet, shelf, bookshelf, bookcase, drawer, chest of drawers, bureau, dresser, hutch, closet, locker

> *Furniture 101; Container 578*

12 collection, accumulation, set, inventory, archive, archives, record, file, folder, bundle, portfolio; yearbook, diary, journal, almanac, encyclopedia, dictionary, thesaurus, ana; art collection, stamp collection, coin collection, *etc.*; repertory, repertoire, bag of tricks

> *Assembly 59; Books 174; Record 185; Display 843*

13 repository, museum, art museum, gallery, art gallery, exhibit, exhibition; waxworks; library; zoo, menagerie, aquarium

> *Display 843*

ADJECTIVES

14 stored, stocked, supplied, provided; collected, accumulated; stockpiled, hoarded; heaped, amassed, loaded, stacked, piled, piled up, bundled, packaged

> *Assembly 59; Provision 89*

15 saved, kept, retained, held; filed, recorded, archived; reserved, put aside, set aside; in reserve, unused, unspent, unexpended, banked, funded, in escrow, invested; in storage, conserved, preserved, protected, warehoused, stowed away, packed away, mothballed, in mothballs; bottled, pickled, canned, refrigerated, frozen

> *Nonuse 394; Preservation 815*

16 available, in stock, spare; abundant, plentiful

VERBS

17 store, stock, supply, provision, provide; collect, accumulate, garner, gather, harvest, reap, mow, pick, glean; stockpile, hoard, bunker, build up, stock up, build up one's stocks, increase, augment

> *Assembly 59; Provision 89; Increase 746*

18 store fuel, take on, take in, fill, fill up, fuel, fuel up, top up, refill, refuel, replenish

19 heap, amass, load, stack, pile, pile up, bundle, package

20 save, keep, retain, keep on hand, hang on to, hold on to; file, record, archive, back up; leave, set aside, put aside, reserve, put in escrow, put in the hope chest, lay away, salt away, sock away [Inf]; put into storage, conserve, preserve, protect, warehouse, stable, stow, stow away, pack, pack away, put away, put in mothballs, mothball, lay up, fold up, roll up; bottle, can, pickle, refrigerate, freeze

> *Preservation 815*

21 deposit, bank, invest, treasure; economize, husband,

save up, make a nest egg, prepare for a rainy day; fund, pool, put in the kitty, share, communalize

> *Preparation 388; Thrift 499*

22 bury, hide, conceal, secrete, cache, stash away, squirrel away

> *Concealment 181*

106 Fuel

NOUNS

1 fuel, energy source, heat source, renewable energy source, nonrenewable energy source, fossil fuel, solid fuel

2 fuels, alcohol, benzine, charcoal, coal, coke, diesel fuel *or* oil, electricity, ethane, ethanol, gas, gasoline, heptane, hexane, jet fuel, kerosene, methanol, oil, peat, pentane, turf, wood; nuclear *or* atomic power; solar energy; windpower; food

> *Food 90; Power 514*

3 fuel starter, lighter, igniter, sparker, fire lighter, tinder, tinderbox, kindling, firewood, log, fagot, brushwood, spunk, punk, touchwood, touch paper, spill; match, matchstick, friction match, lucifer, vesta [Brit], safety match; wick; spark, scintilla; flint; burning glass *or* sunglass; torch, firebrand; ignition system, spark plug, cap, percussion cap, detonator, fuse

> *Heat 217*

4 coal, black diamonds; anthracite *or* hard coal, bituminous *or* soft coal, cannel coal, coke, lignite *or* brown coal; charcoal, briquette *or* briquet, coal dust, slack; coal bed, coal seam, coal measures, coal field, coal mine, coal pit, coal bunker, coalbin, coal scuttle, coal hod; coaling station

> *Geology 8*

5 electricity, electric charge, hydroelectricity; generating station, power station; generator, turbine, power pack, magneto *or* magnetoelectric generator *or* magnetogenerator, dynamo, converter; electric motor; electricity supply, electric current, national grid, pylon, underground cable, power cable, electric lead, cord, power point, socket, electric switch, light switch, fuel cell, electric battery, battery; electricity meter; power cut, power outage, blackout, brownout; electrification, electrocution, electric chair

> *Engineering 14; Power 514*

6 gas, natural gas, coal gas, producer *or* air gas, propane, butane, methane, rocket fuel, propellant, liquid oxygen *or* lox *or* LOX; gas field, gasworks, gasometer, gas tank, gas main, gas pipe, gas meter, gas burner, gas turbine; octane number *or* rating; gas station *or* filling station, gas pump, gas can

> *Fluid 555; Gas 556; Transportation 686; Propulsion 696*

7 oil, petroleum, crude oil *or* crude *or* crude petroleum, mineral oil, gasoline *or* gas, petrol [Brit], unleaded gas, diesel fuel *or* oil, motor oil, aviation fuel, kerosene, coal oil, naphtha; oil reserves, oil field, oil well, oil derrick, oil rig *or* drill rig, offshore rig, oil refinery; refining, fractionation, distillation, cracking; oil pipeline, oil tanker, oil drum, oilcan; oil shale, oil slick; fuel injection

▶ *Geology 8; Oiliness, Lubrication 562; Mixture 751*

8 **nuclear power,** atomic power, nuclear energy *or* atomic energy; nuclear generating station; nuclear reactor *or* nuclear pile; nuclear fuel, core, fuel rod, uranium, enriched uranium, plutonium; nuclear fission, nuclear fusion

▶ *Physics 10; Power 514*

9 **renewable energy,** soft energy; solar power, solar energy, solar battery, solar cell, photovoltaic cell; wind power, windmill, wind pump, wind generator, wind turbine; geothermal energy; water power, water mill, water turbine; hydroelectric power, wave power, tidal power, tidal energy; biomass

▶ *Power 514*

10 **power worker,** stoker, coal miner, coal heaver, coal merchant, charcoal burner; gas fitter, gasman, boilermaker, meter reader; electrician; oil worker, oilman; lumberjack, woodcutter; peat cutter

ADJECTIVES

11 **fueled,** fueled up, stoked, refueled; fuel-efficient

12 **combustible,** inflammable, flammable, explosive, incendiary; woody, ligneous; wood-burning

13 **fired,** coal-fired, gas-fired, oil-fired, *etc.*; powered, coal-powered, gas-powered, oil-powered, nuclear-powered, solar-powered, wind-powered, *etc.*; driven, wind-driven, water-driven, *etc.*; charged, electrified

14 **gas,** gaseous; electric, hydroelectric, electrical, magnetoelectric, electrifying; coaly, bituminous, lignitic, carbonaceous, carboniferous; oil, petroleous, diesel, kerosene, crude, raw, refined; gasolinic, high-octane, unleaded, gas-guzzling [Inf]; nuclear, atomic, thermonuclear, thermal

15 **renewable,** solar, geothermal *or* geothermic, steam-operated; nonrenewable

VERBS

16 **fuel,** fuel up, stoke, fill up, top off, refuel, add fuel; light, ignite, kindle, fire up, fire, strike, put a match to; burn coal, burn gas; detonate, set off, touch off, trigger, explode

17 **power,** charge, recharge; electrify, plug in, switch on

18 **mine coal,** dig coal; strike oil, pump oil, refine oil; pump gas

ADVERBS

19 **powerfully,** at full power, at full steam; combustibly, explosively; electrically, hydroelectrically; thermally

Health and Well-being

107 Medicine

NOUNS

1 medicine, medical practice, medical profession, medical care, health care, primary care; orthodox medicine, allopathic medicine, conventional medicine, osteopathic medicine, general medicine, internal medicine, preventive medicine; community medicine, industrial medicine, occupational medicine, public-health medicine, tropical medicine

2 medical ethics, medical jurisprudence, Hippocratic oath

3 medical practice, general practice, group practice, private practice; health maintenance organization (HMO), National Health Service [Brit]; medical insurance, Medicare, Medicaid

▶ *Psychology and Psychiatry 108; Ill Health 114*

4 alternative medicine, natural medicine, traditional medicine, holistic medicine; complementary medicine, supplementary medicine; chiropractic, acupuncture, acupressure, shiatsu; unorthodox medicine, unconventional medicine, fringe medicine; herbalism, folk medicine, old wives' medicine; faith healing; homeopathy, naturopathy, aromatherapy, reflexology, Ayurvedic medicine [Hindu]

▶ *Remedy 115*

5 medical science, immunology, endocrinology, biochemistry, genetics, eugenics; bacteriology, microbiology, molecular biology, virology, parasitology, toxicology; pharmacology, biomedicine, epidemiology, nosology, etiology, symptomatology, semiology; pathology, forensic medicine, space medicine

▶ *Life Science 13; Law 53; Psychology and Psychiatry 108*

6 dentistry, dental surgery, oral surgery, exodontics, endodontics, orthodontics, prosthetic dentistry, prosthodontics, periodontics, periodontology; oral pathology, fillings, root canal work, crowning, capping, scaling, polishing, extraction, fissure sealing; preventative dentistry, fluoride treatment

7 health care, health promotion, health education, community medicine, public-health medicine; preventive medicine, prophylaxis, immunization, vaccination, fluoridation, nutrition, dietetics, hygiene, genetic counseling, midwifery; medical home visit, medical history, case history, medical examination, medical, checkup, physical examination, physical, internal examination; second opinion, referral, consultation, consult; prognosis, follow-up

▶ *Biochemistry 12; Health 113; Remedy 115; Hygiene 116*

8 diagnosis, diagnostics, differential diagnosis, workup, treatment options, risk, risk-benefit ratio; prognosis; diagnostic test, test, study, medical test, laboratory test, screening test, screening, mass screening

9 prenatal diagnosis, amniocentesis, chorionic villus sampling (CVS), fetoscopy, screening ultrasonography,

---

MEDICAL SPECIALTIES

anesthesiology	maternal/fetal medicine
critical care medicine	reproductive medicine
emergency medicine	endocrinology
family practice	ophthalmology
internal medicine	pathology
cardiology	pediatrics
dermatology	neonatology
endocrinology	adolescence medicine
gastroenterology	psychiatry
geriatrics	radiology
hematology	surgery
immunology	cardiac surgery
nephrology	neurosurgery
neurology	orthopedics
oncology	otolaryngology
pulmonology	pediatric surgery
rheumatology	plastic surgery
obstetrics and gynecology	urology
(ob-gyn)	

---

biophysical profile, fetal heart rate monitor, nonstress test, stress test

10 **test** *or* **study,** vision test, hearing test; blood test, serotest, sputum test, skin test; samples of: blood, stool, urine, semen, cerebral spinal fluid (CSF), tissue

11 **diagnostic procedure,** electrocardiography, electrocardiogram (EKG), electroencephalogy, electroencephalogram (EEG), electromyography, electromyogram (EMG); pregnancy test; pap smear *or* cervical smear; tap; biopsy, needle aspirate, lumbar puncture; cultures of: blood, CSF, stool, urine; ova and parasite screen, toxicology screen; endoscopy, bronchoscopy, laparoscopy, gastroscopy, colposcopy, urethroscopy, cystoscopy

12 **diagnostic radiology,** scanning, scan, radiography, radiograph, X ray, mass X ray, chest X ray, skeletal survey; arteriography, angiography, angiogram, lymphography, lymphogram, venography, venogram; thermography, mammothermography, mammography, mammogram; pyelography, pyelogram, intravenous (IV) pyelogram, barium swallow, barium enema, upper gastrointestinal (GI) series; ultrasound scan, body scan, Grain scan; tomography, tomogram, computerized axial tomography (CAT *or* CT) scan, positron emission tomography (PET) scan, thallium scan, magnetic resonance imaging (MRI), nuclear magnetic resonance (NMR) scan

13 **diagnostic instrument,** thermometer, sphygmomanometer, reflex hammer, tuning fork, stethoscope, ophthalmoscope, auriscope, otoscope, endoscope, fiberscope, fetoscope, bronchoscope, gastroscope, laparoscope, colposcope, urethroscope, cystoscope, hysteroscope, resectoscope; bitewing, pick

14 **treatment,** therapy, therapeutics, medical treatment, medical care, intensive therapy *or* care; nursing care, nursing; medical intervention, clinical treatment, allopathy, conservative treatment, palliative treatment, radical treatment, active treatment; drug treatment, medication, prescription, hormone replacement therapy (HRT), chemotherapy, immunotherapy, radiotherapy, therapeutic radiology; gene therapy, gene replacement therapy, dialysis; surgical treatment, surgery; naturopathy, homeopathy, herbalism, osteopathy, chiropractic, acupuncture; manipulative treatment, physical therapy, speech therapy, occupational therapy; rehabilitation, aftercare
  ◗ *Remedy 115*

15 **surgery,** surgical treatment, surgical intervention; major surgery, minor surgery, laser surgery, surgical operation, operation, op.; premedication, sedation, induction, anesthesia; incision, section, resection, division, excision, amputation, advancement, transplantation, grafting; transfusion, perfusion; suture
  ◗ *Psychology and Psychiatry 108; Remedy 115*

16 **hospital,** general hospital, teaching hospital, univer-

sity hospital; women's hospital, maternity hospital, children's hospital; day hospital, community hospital, county hospital, cooperative hospital, private hospital, municipal hospital, city hospital, health center; infirmary, sanitarium; hospital ward, ward, isolation ward; operating room, intensive care unit (ICU), critical care unit (CCU); dispensary, inpatient pharmacy; clinic, outpatient clinic, private office, surgery [Brit], consulting room
  ◗ *Remedy 115*

17 **postmortem (examination) (PM),** autopsy, pathologic specimen, surgical specimen, pathology report

18 **nursing home,** convalescent home, geriatric center, rest home, hospice

19 **doctor,** physician, medical doctor (M.D.), medical practitioner, leech [Arch]; surgeon, general practitioner (G.P.), family doctor, family practitioner; medical student, medic, hospital doctor, intern, resident, consultant; Medical Officer (M.O.); health officer, community physician, public-health physician; [Inf]: doc, medico, sawbones
  ◗ *Psychology and Psychiatry 108; Remedy 115*

20 **medical specialist,** consultant, clinician, diagnostician; family practitioner, internist, obstetrician, gynecologist, surgeon, ophthalmologist, radiologist, anesthesiologist, pediatrician, pathologist, psychiatrist, emergency practitioner; immunologist, endocrinologist, microbiologist, virologist, parasitologist, toxicologist, epidemiologist, posologist; medical examiner

21 **dentist,** dental surgeon, oral surgeon, children's dentist; exodontist, endodontist, orthodontist, prosthodontist, periodontist, periodontologist, oral pathologist

22 **healer,** faith healer, Christian Science practitioner, herbalist; alternative practitioner, homeopathist, naturopath, osteopath, chiropractor, acupuncturist, aromatherapist, bonesetter, hakim, reflexologist

23 **nurse,** caregiver, student nurse, trainee nurse, probationer; staff nurse, head nurse, charge nurse, scrub nurse, sister [Brit], clinical educator; nurse practitioner, registered nurse (R.N.); private nurse, visiting nurse, licensed practical nurse (LPN), special nurse, children's nurse, school nurse, day nurse, night nurse, district nurse, home nurse, nurse practitioner; midwife; Florence Nightingale, lady with the lamp, ministering angel, angel of mercy

24 **paramedic,** emergency medical technician (EMT); physical therapist, occupational therapist, speech therapist; dietician, nutritionist; medical attendant, stretcher-bearer; medical assistant, surgical assistant; medical auxiliary, nursing auxiliary; orderly, ward orderly; hospital social worker, hospital administrator; dental surgery assistant; dental auxiliary; dental technician, hygienist, dental *or* oral hygienist

▶ *Remedy 115*

25 **patient,** sick person, inpatient, outpatient, client, case, invalid

▶ *Ill Health 114*

26 **veterinary medicine,** veterinary practice, small-animal practice, large-animal practice, veterinary clinic, veterinary surgery; animal welfare

▶ *Agriculture 16; Animals (General) 34*

27 **veterinarian,** veterinary, veterinary practitioner, veterinary surgeon, veterinary student, veterinary nurse, veterinary technician, animal doctor, vet [Inf]

ADJECTIVES

28 **medical,** iatric, Hippocratic, clinical; surgical, internal, obstetric, gynecological, pediatric, ophthalmological, radiological, pathological; epidemiological; forensic; allopathic, homeopathic, osteopathic; veterinary

▶ *Remedy 115*

29 **diagnostic,** symptomatological, symptomatic, prognostic, indicative

30 **therapeutic,** medicinal, preventive *or* preventative; prophylactic, remedial, curative, healing; nursing, tending

▶ *Remedy 115; Relief 275*

31 **dental,** oral, orthodontic, exodontic, endodontic, prosthodontic, periodontic, periodontal

VERBS

32 **practice medicine,** hold surgery; attend, advise, examine; refer, seek a second opinion, consult; diagnose, prognosticate; immunize, vaccinate; test, screen (for), scan; treat, doctor, prescribe, medicate, administer, inject; care for, look after, minister to, nurse, tend, support; relieve, ease, palliate; restore, cure, heal; rehabilitate, follow up; make a house call, be on call

▶ *Remedy 115; Hygiene 116; Relief 275*

33 **practice surgery,** prepare for surgery, prep, operate, make an incision, incise, divide, excise, suture, amputate, transplant, perfuse, dialyse, transfuse; sedate, anesthetize; induce, maintain

▶ *Remedy 115*

34 **practice dentistry,** treat teeth, descale, clean teeth, polish, drill, fill, stop, crown, extract, pull

ADVERBS

35 **medically,** clinically, surgically, diagnostically, therapeutically, pathologically, neurologically; dentally

108 Psychology and Psychiatry

NOUNS

1 **psychology,** science of the mind, science of human and animal behavior, mental state, mental processes, mental chemistry

2 **psychiatry,** neuropsychiatry, medicopsychology, prophylactic psychiatry, psychodiagnostics, psychodiagnosis, orthopsychiatry; psychological medicine, psychosocial medicine, psychosomatic medicine

▶ *Medicine 107*

3 **psychiatric treatment,** psychiatric care; antipsychotic, drug treatment, psychotropic drug; psychosurgery, prefrontal lobotomy; shock treatment, shock therapy, convulsive therapy, Metrazol™ shock therapy, insulin shock therapy, electroconvulsive therapy (ECT), electroconvulsive shock therapy (EST), nonconvulsive electric treatment

▶ *Medicine 107; Remedy 115*

4 **psychotherapy,** psychoanalysis, analysis, ego analysis; psychoanalytic method, transactional analysis (TA), counseling; behavior therapy, behavior modification, biofeedback, client-centered therapy, group psychotherapy, family therapy, conjoint therapy, modeling, nondirective therapy, role-playing, supportive therapy, suggestion therapy, hypnotherapy, transcendental meditation; the couch [Inf]

5 **psychometrics,** psychometry, intelligence testing, mental test, psychological screening, psychography; lie detector, polygraph, psychogalvanometer, psychogalvanic skin response

6 **personality type,** personality tendency, humor, complexion [Arch]; introversion, introvertedness, ingoingness, introvert; extroversion, extrovertedness, outgoingness, extrovert; other-directedness, syntony, ambiversion, ambivert; choleric, melancholic, sanguine, phlegmatic; cyclothyme, cycloid; ectomorphy, ectomorphism, ectomorph; endomorphy, endomorphism, endomorph; mesomorphism, mesomorphy, mesomorph

7 **personality disorder,** long-duration disordered personality, early-onset personality dysfunction; paranoid personality disorder, schizoid personality disorder, schizotypal personality disorder, antisocial personality disorder, borderline personality disorder, histrionic personality disorder, narcissistic personality disorder, avoidant personality disorder, dependent personality disorder, obsessive-compulsive personality disorder, mental retardation; neurotic personality, emotionally disturbed person

8 **mental disorder,** neurosis, psychosis, insanity, mental illness, clinical disorder; cognitive disorders, delirium, dementia, amnesic disorder; substance-related disorders; psychotic disorders, mood disorders, anxiety disorders, somatoform disorders, factitious disorders, dissociative disorders, sexual and gender disorders, eating disorders, sleep disorders, impulse-control disorders, adjustment disorders, breakdown, nervous breakdown; sociopath, psychopathic personality, psychotic, psychotic personality

▶ *Insanity 110; Substance Abuse 121*

9 **neurosis,** psychoneurosis, neuroticism, neurotic disorder; anxiety reaction, neurotic-depressive reaction, dissociation reaction, flight reaction, obsessional neu-

rosis, obsessive-compulsive neurosis *or* reaction, affective disorder, depression, mania, eating disorder
> *Fear 283*

10 **psychosis,** insanity, mental illness, psychopathy; schizophrenia, paranoid-type schizophrenia, disorganized-type schizophrenia, catatonic-type schizophrenia, residual-type schizophrenia; schizophreniform disorder; schizoaffective disorder; delusional disorder, erotomanic-type delusional disorder, grandiose-type delusional disorder, jealous-type delusional disorder, persecutory-type delusional disorder, somatic-type delusional disorder
> *Insanity 110*

11 **anxiety disorder,** panic attack, agoraphobia, specific phobia, social phobia *or* social anxiety disorder, obsessive-compulsive disorder, posttraumatic stress disorder, acute stress disorder, generalized anxiety disorder; psychological stress, emotional strain *or* tension; frustration, conflict, ambivalence (of impulse), trauma, traumatism, mental *or* emotional shock, decompensation; stress reaction: premenstrual syndrome (PMS), anxiety, psychalgia, hysteria, anxiety hysteria, nervous tic
> *Fear 283*

12 **mood disorder,** affective disorder: major depressive disorder, dysthymic disorder, bipolar disorder *or* manic-depressive psychosis, cyclothymic disorder; mood episodes: major depressive episode, manic episode, mixed episode, hypomanic episode; depression, clinical depression, endogenous depression *or* melancholia, involutional melancholia, seasonal affective disorder (SAD) syndrome, postpartum depression; dejection, detachment, alienation, withdrawal; abstraction, preoccupation, apathy, lethargy; insomnia, somnolence; indifference, unresponsiveness, insensibility, stupor, catatonic stupor
> *Sorrow 270*

13 **compulsion,** urge, craving, dipsomania, passion, obsession, impulsion, craze; mania, megalomania, monomania, egomania, paranoia, nymphomania, satyriasis; death instinct, death wish, thanatos, suicidalism
> *Insanity 110; Habit, Custom 397*

14 **sexual disorder,** sexual dysfunction; paraphilias: exhibitionism, fetishism, frotteurism, pedophilia, sexual masochism, sexual sadism, transvestic fetishism, voyeurism; gender identity disorder

15 **eating disorder,** anorexia nervosa, bulimia nervosa

16 **impulse-control disorder,** intermittent explosive disorder, kleptomania, pyromania, pathological gambling, trichotillomania

17 **dissociative disorder,** dissociative amnesia, dissociative fugue *or* psychogenic fugue, dissociative identity disorder *or* multiple personality disorder, depersonalization disorder; dissociation, disconnection, disintegration of personality, schizoidism, schizoid personality, split personality, schizothymia, schizophrenia; paranoia, paranoid personality

18 **trance,** stupor, daze, hypnotic trance, catatonic trance, hysterical trance, trance state, catalepsy; cataplexy; dream state, reverie, daydreaming; fugue, fugue state, amnesia; meditation, religious ecstasy; aphasia

19 **somatoform disorder,** somatization disorder *or* hysteria *or* Briquet's syndrome, conversion disorder, pain disorder, hypochondriasis, body dysmorphic disorder

20 **sleep disorder,** dyssomnia, primary insomnia, primary hypersomnia, narcolepsy, breathing-related sleep

---

PSYCHOLOGICAL THEORIES, SCHOOLS, AND DISCIPLINES

abnormal psychology	educational psychology	metapsychology	psychometrics
academic psychology	empirical psychology	morbid psychology	psychoneurosis
Adlerian psychology	existential psychology	neuropsychology	psychopathology
analytical psychology	experimental psychology	objective psychology	psychopharmacology
animal psychology	faculty psychology	parapsychology	psychophysics
applied psychology	folk *or* ethnic psychology	Pavlovian psychology	psychophysiology
association psychology	Freudian psychology	phenomenological	psychosexuality
behavioral psychology,	functional psychology	psychology	psychosociology
behaviorism	genetic psychology	physiological psychology	psychosomatics
child psychology	Gestalt psychology *or*	popular psychology	psychotechnology
clinical psychology	configurationism	psychic determinism	psychotherapy
cognitive psychology	group psychology	psychoacoustics	race psychology
comparative psychology	hormic psychology	psychobiochemistry	rational psychology
constitutional psychology	Horneyan psychology	psychobiology	Reichian psychology
criminal psychology	humanistic psychology	psychodynamics	self psychology
depth psychology	individual psychology	psychoendocrinology	Skinnerian psychology
developmental psychology	industrial psychology	psychogenesis	social psychology
differential psychology	introspection psychology	psychogeriatrics	structural psychology
dynamic psychology	Jungian psychology	psychographics	Watsonian psychology
ecological psychology	Lacanian psychology	psycholinguistics	

PSYCHOLOGICAL TESTS

association test
Bernreuter personality
 inventory
Brown personality inventory
controlled-association test
free-association test
frustration test
Gesell's development schedule
graduated reciprocation in
 tension reduction
group test
Holtzman inkblot technique
House-Tree-Person (HTP)
 Projective Test
inkblot test
Lüscher color test
Minnesota Multiphasic
 Personality Inventory
 (MMPI)

Oseretsky test
personality test
personality adjustment
 test
personality inventory
personality research form
projective test
Rogers's process scale
Rorschach test
Rotter incomplete sentences
 blank
scientific aptitude test
strong vocational interest
 test
Szondi test
Thematic Apperception Test
 (TAT)
word association test

---

disorder, circadian rhythm sleep disorder; parasomnia, nightmare disorder *or* dream anxiety disorder, sleep terror disorder; sleepwalking disorder, somnambulism

21 **fixation,** libido fixation; libido arrest, arrested development; fixation of affect, infantile fixation, Freudian fixation, parent fixation, mother fixation, father fixation

22 **type of complex,** inferiority, superiority, parent, Oedipus, mother, Electra, father, Diana, persecution, castration, compulsion

23 **defense mechanism,** defense reaction, censor, repression, suppression, inhibition; block, blocking, blockage, resistance, avoidance, denial, negation, rejection; reaction formation, splitting, rigid control, suppressed desire, sublimation, regression, reversion, projection, identification; fantasy, escapism, flight, withdrawal, isolation; negativism, alienation; dreamlike thinking, wishful thinking; autism, dereism; compensation, overcompensation, decompensation; substitution, blame-shifting, displacement, rationalization

24 **conditioning,** Pavlovian conditioning, classical conditioning, operant conditioning, psychagogy, reeducation, reorientation; conditioned reflex, reinforcement, positive reinforcement, negative reinforcement; counterconditioning, avoidance conditioning; simple reflex, unconditioned reflex, reflex, suggestion

25 **psyche,** psychic apparatus, self, ego, conscious mind, conscious self, id, superego, ethical self, ego ideal; ego-id conflict; psychological me, mind, pneuma, soul, personality; preconscious, foreconscious, stream of consciousness, unconscious *or* subconscious, subliminal, subliminal self, unconscious mind; primitive self,

anima, animus, persona; collective unconscious, racial unconscious

26 **libido,** id, sex(ual) drive, life instinct, Eros, vital force, motive force, psychic energy; sex instinct, libidinal energy, libidinal *or* libido object, libido analog; erotic desire, eroticism, pleasure principle

27 **memory,** recall, reproduction, recognition, recollection, retention; engram, memory trace, unconscious memory, forgetting
 ▶ *Memory 354*

28 **symbol,** universal symbol, father symbol, mother symbol, phallic symbol, fertility symbol; dream-symbol interpretation, imago, image, archetype, archetypal image *or* symbol, father *or* mother *or* child image; symbolism, symbolization

29 **surrogate,** substitute, father figure *or* image *or* surrogate, mother figure *or* image *or* surrogate

30 **perceptual concept,** gestalt, pattern, figure, form, configuration, sensory pattern, figure-ground

31 **association of ideas,** association, linking, reinforcement, controlled association, free association, association by contiguity, word association, association by sound, clang association, stream of consciousness; transference, negative transference, synesthesia

32 **cathexis,** cathection, desire concentration, charge, energy charge, cathectic energy; anticathexis, countercathexis, counterinvestment; hypercathexis, overcharge

33 **psychologist,** psychologue, clinical psychologist, clinician, psychotherapist, therapist, counselor, psychoanalyst, analyst, child psychologist, psychopathologist; psychotechnologist, hypnotherapist, narcotherapist, dramatherapist, behavior therapist, industrial psychologist, psychobiologist, psychophysicist, psychographer, psychosociologist; psychiatric social worker; notable psychologists: Jung, Horney, James, Pavlov, Reich, Skinner, Watson, Kleine, Piaget

34 **psychiatrist,** medical specialist, mental disorders specialist, neuropsychiatrist; analyst, psychoanalyzer, psychotherapist, psychotherapeutist; psychophysiologist,

---

INTELLIGENCE TESTS

Allport-Vernon draw-a-person
 test
Allport-Vernon study of
 values
alpha test
Army General Classification
 Test (AGCT)
Babcock-Levy test
beta test
Binet *or* Binet-Simon test
Cattell's Infant Intelligence
 Scale
intelligence quotient (IQ) test

General Aptitude Test Battery
 (GATB)
Goldstein-Sheerer test
Kent mental test
Minnesota Preschool Scale
Stanford-Binet Intelligence
 Scale
Wechsler Adult Intelligence
 Scale (WAIS)
Wechsler-Bellevue Intelligence
 Test
Wechsler Intelligence Scale for
 Children (WISC)

psychochemist, psychopharmacologist; notable psychiatrists: Adler, Freud, Laing; shrink [Inf], headshrinker [Inf]

) *Insanity 110*

35 psychiatric hospital, psychiatric unit, psychiatric ward; special hospital, mental hospital

) *Insanity 110; Remedy 115*

ADJECTIVES

36 psychological, psychiatric, neuropsychiatric, psychotherapeutic, psychoanalytical, psychodiagnostic, psychopathological, psychopharmacological; psychobiological, psychogenetic, psychogenic, psychogeriatric, psychometric, psychoneurological, psychophysical, psychosexual, psychosocial, psychosomatic, psychotechnical; hypnotherapeutic

37 introverted, introvert, introversive, ingoing, inner-directed, withdrawn, isolated

38 extroverted, extrovert, extroversive, outgoing, outer-directed

39 psychologically disturbed, neurotic, psychotic, sociopathic, psychopathic, traumatized, delirious, demented, deluded, schizoid, schizophrenic, hypochondriacal, paranoid, dissociated, disconnected, depressed, maniacal

40 unconscious, subliminal, subconscious; repressed, suppressed, inhibited, restrained, blocked, controlled

VERBS

41 psychologize, psychoanalyze, analyze, counsel, condition

ADVERBS

42 psychologically, psychiatrically, unconsciously, subconsciously, subliminally; neurotically, hysterically, inhibitedly, depressively

109 Sanity

NOUNS

1 sanity, saneness, sound mind, soundness of mind, *mens sana* [L], stability, balanced mind, mental equilibrium, mental health, normality, sobriety

) *Sobriety 120*

2 rationality, reasonableness, reason, intelligibility, lucidity, coherence, good sense, common sense, wits, intelligence

) *Wisdom 352; Intelligibility 363*

ADJECTIVES

3 sane, not mad, *compos mentis* [L], in one's right mind, in full possession of one's faculties, of sound mind, mentally sound, normal, sober; [Inf]: all there, together, with both oars in the water, right in the head, playing with a full deck

) *Sobriety 120*

4 rational, reasonable, coherent, intelligible, lucid, clearheaded, balanced, well-balanced, levelheaded, stable,

steady, sound, sensible, commonsensical, intelligent, cool-headed

) *Wisdom 352; Intelligibility 363*

VERBS

5 be sane, have one's wits about one, become sane, come to one's senses, sober up, make sane, restore to sanity, play with a full deck [Inf]

ADVERBS

6 sanely, soberly, rationally, reasonably, coherently, lucidly

110 Insanity

NOUNS

1 insanity, madness, lunacy, irrationality, unsound mind, sick mind, mental illness *or* disorder, (mental) derangement, mental instability, unbalanced mind, balance of mind disturbed; criminal insanity, M'Naghten rule, Durham Rule, irresistible impulse, diminished responsibility, insanity defense; abnormality, aberration, incoherence, eccentricity, oddness, freakishness, craziness; nuttiness [Inf], battiness [Inf]

) *Law 53; Psychology and Psychiatry 108; Folly 353; Nonconformity 782*

2 delusion, illusion, hallucination, paraphrenia, shared delusions, communicated insanity, folie à deux, paranoia, monomania, obsessive behavior, hypochondria, obsession, complex, phobia, persecution mania, fixation, compulsion, urge, craving, craze, passion, elation, ecstasy, hypomania, mania, frenzy, hysteria, ravings, delirium, delirium tremens *or* d.t.'s, megalomania, delusions of grandeur, theomania, religious mania, necromania, fetishism

) *Psychology and Psychiatry 108; Fear 283; Imagination 360; Immorality 432; Unreality 720*

3 psychosis, psychopathy, schizophrenia *or* dementia praecox, split personality, schizoid personality, hebephrenia, catatonia, bipolar disorder *or* manic-depressive illness *or* manic-depression, cyclothymia, alcoholic psychosis, Korsakoff's psychosis *or* syndrome

) *Psychology and Psychiatry 108*

4 mental breakdown, nervous breakdown, crackup, brainstorm; neurosis, psychoneurosis, neuroticism, neurasthenia, anxiety, (personal) crisis, depression, clinical depression, endogenous depression *or* melancholia, hysteria, conversion disorder, battle fatigue *or* shell shock; attack of nerves

) *Psychology and Psychiatry 108; Sorrow 270; Fear 283; Agitation 684*

5 insane person, madman, madwoman, lunatic, mental case, maniac, manic-depressive, megalomaniac, monomaniac, hypomaniac; psychopath, psychotic, paranoid *or* paranoiac, obsessive, hysteric, neurotic, hypochondriac, schizoid, schizophrenic, melancholic, depressive; [Inf]: kook, crackpot, headcase, nut, nut case, screwball, fruitcake, loony, loony tune, loon, psycho, sickie *or* sicko, space cadet

6 **mental hospital,** mental institution, mental home, lunatic asylum, insane asylum, madhouse, bedlam, psychiatric hospital, special hospital, psychiatric unit, psychiatric ward, padded cell; [Inf]: loony bin, nut house *or* nuthouse, funny farm, bughouse, booby hatch
  ▸ *Psychology and Psychiatry 108*

7 **treatment,** psychiatric care, psychoanalysis, analysis, psychotherapy, counseling, electroconvulsive therapy (ECT), shock therapy *or* treatment, electroshock

8 **psychiatrist,** psychoanalyst, psychotherapist; headshrinker [Inf], shrink [Inf]
  ▸ *Psychology and Psychiatry 108; Remedy 115*

ADJECTIVES

9 **insane,** mad, crazy, of unsound mind, *non compos mentis* [L], deranged, demented, abnormal, disturbed, unbalanced, daft, unhinged, alienated, weird, peculiar, odd, out of one's mind *or* senses, raving mad, stark raving *or* staring mad, mad as a march hare *or* as a hatter; out of one's head; [Inf]: mental, certifiable, wacky, screwy, queer in the head, touched in the head, crackbrained, cuckoo, bonkers, nuts, nutty, nutty as a fruitcake, balmy, bananas, bats, batty, dotty, dippy, loco, loopy, a few bricks short of a full load, off one's nut *or* noodle *or* onion *or* rocker, off the wall, out of one's skull, meshuga [Yiddish]

10 **manic,** ranting, raving, frenzied, frenetic, frantic, hysterical, demented, rabid, foaming at the mouth, wild, berserk, delirious, deluded, hallucinating

11 **mentally ill,** disturbed, sick, abnormal, neurotic, depressed, depressive, melancholic, paranoid *or* paranoiac, fixated, psychotic, schizophrenic, schizoid, catatonic, psychopathic, certified, schizo [Inf]
  ▸ *Psychology and Psychiatry 108; Ill Health 114*

VERBS

12 **become insane,** go mad, lose one's wits, be insane, rave, run amuck *or* amok, take leave of one's senses; [Inf]: have a screw loose, have bats in one's belfry, lose one's marbles, go off one's head

13 **make insane,** madden, drive mad, derange, dement, unbalance, unhinge, confuse, drive crazy; [Inf]: drive up the wall, drive round the bend, send over the edge

14 **certify,** commit, put away

ADVERBS

15 **insanely,** madly, dementedly, psychotically, abnormally, neurotically, crazily

111 Cleanliness

NOUNS

1 **cleanliness,** cleanness, keeping clean, freedom from dirt, absence of dirt; immaculateness, spotlessness; freshness, dewiness; purity, whiteness; shine, polish; daintiness, fastidiousness, spit and polish

2 **cleaning,** spring-cleaning, housecleaning, cleaning up, cleanup, clearing up, tidying; dishwashing, wiping up, mopping up, scrubbing, dusting, sweeping, vacuuming, polishing; washing, laundry, dry cleaning; washing out, flushing out, dialysis; cleansing, purification, edulcoration, purging, purgation; freshening, ventilation, airing; deodorization, fumigation, desalination, decontamination, disinfestation, delousing, disinfection; sterilization, antisepsis, asepsis; chlorination, pasteurization; refining, distillation, clarification, filtration, percolation; hygiene, sanitation, drainage, plumbing, sewerage
  ▸ *Excretion 25; Dirtiness 112; Hygiene 116*

3 **religious cleansing,** purification, baptism, Asperges, sprinkling of water, *mikvah* [Hebrew], lustration, purgation, purgatory
  ▸ *Religious Ritual 85*

4 **ablutions,** washing, wash, toilet; hygiene, oral hygiene; lavage, lavation, bathing; dipping, dip, rinsing, soaking, soaping, lathering, shampoo

5 **censorship,** expurgation, bowdlerization, blue-penciling, editing

6 **bath,** hot bath, hot tub, cold bath, bubble bath, steam bath, vapor bath, Turkish bath, sauna, sponge bath, footbath; shower, hot shower, cold shower, douche; bathtub, tub, bidet, basin, washbasin, washbowl, washstand, basin and pitcher, basin and ewer, bathroom, washroom; baths, public baths, Turkish baths, thermae, sudatorium *or* sudatory

7 **washer,** washing machine, washer-dryer, washtub, washboard, boiler, Laundromat™, launderette, dishwasher, car wash

8 **laundry,** wash, washing, dirty clothes, dirty linen, dirty dishes, washing up

9 **cleaning agent,** cleansing agent, cleaner, cleanser, purifier; antiseptic, disinfectant, carbolic acid, phenol, bleach; purgative, laxative, enema, aperient; freshener, air freshener, room freshener, baking soda, deodorant; soda, washing soda, detergent, washing powder; soap, scented soap, toilet soap, guest soap; soap flakes, soap powder, dishwashing liquid; soap and water, water, hot water; shampoo, bubble bath, shower gel; cleansing cream, face cream, cold cream; mouthwash, gargle, toothpaste, dentifrice, dental powder; abrasive, pumice, pumice stone, hearthstone, holystone, scouring powder, scouring pad, soap pad; polish, furniture polish, floor polish, shoe polish, boot polish, blacking, whiting; wax, varnish, whitewash, paint

10 **cleaning tool,** broom, besom, mop, sponge, swab, scourer; strigil, loofah *or* luffa; dust cloth, dishcloth, feather duster, whisk broom; brush, scrub brush, shoe brush, clothes brush, lint remover; nailbrush, tooth-

brush, toothpick, dental floss; hairbrush, comb, pocket comb; dog brush; dustpan and brush, carpet sweeper, vacuum cleaner; streetsweeper, snowplow; wastepaper basket, wastebasket, trash can, waste can, litter basket; garbage disposal unit, trash compactor, pooper-scooper *or* poop scooper; doormat, boot-scraper; squeegee *or* squilgee, pipe cleaner, reamer; windshield wiper; screen, sieve, riddle, strainer, filter; air filter, oil filter, fuel filter, water filter; blotter, eraser, rubber; rake, hoe; sprinkler, waterworks; sewer, drainpipe, wastepipe

11 **cleaning cloth,** dust cloth; dishcloth, dishrag, dish towel; chamois *or* chammy *or* shammy, leather; washcloth, washrag, towel, bath towel, hand towel; handkerchief, paper handkerchief, tissue; toilet paper, toilet tissue, toilet roll

12 **cleaner,** cleanser, launderer, laundryman, laundrywoman, washerman, washerwoman, washwoman; dry cleaner; scrubber, swabber, washer-up, dishwasher, scullion [Arch]; charwoman, housecleaner, housemaid, maid; scavenger, street cleaner, sweeper, garbage collector, trash collector, dustman [Brit]; men's *or* ladies' room attendant, janitor, sanitary engineer; chimney sweep, window cleaner; bootblack, shoeshiner, shoeshine boy, barber, hairdresser, beautician; gleaner, picker, beachcomber

▶ *Beautification 530*

ADJECTIVES

13 **clean,** dirt-free, unsoiled, unsullied, undefiled, virginal, untainted, unmuddied, untarnished, unstained; immaculate, spotless, stainless; blank, perfect; cleanly, dainty, nice, fastidious, fresh, dewy; pure, unmixed, unadulterated, unpolluted, uncontaminated; hygienic, sanitary, sterile, aseptic, antiseptic, salubrious; spruce, dapper, well-groomed, neat, tidy, spick-and-span, orderly; bright, shining, white, snowy; kosher, ritually clean, ritually prepared; untouched; clean as a whistle, fresh as a daisy, bright as a new pin, bright as silver, white as snow, natty, squeaky-clean [Inf]

▶ *Hygiene 116; Light 246; Whiteness 253; Perfection 805*

14 **cleaned,** freshened, disinfected, cleaned up, cleaned out; trimmed, shaven, washed; scrubbed, scoured, swept, brushed; polished, whitened, bleached, laundered, starched, ironed; cleansed, purified, purged; decontaminated, sterilized, pasteurized, refined, distilled, filtered

15 **expurgated,** bowdlerized, blue-penciled, edited, cleaned up

16 **cleansing,** lustral, purificatory; disinfectant, hygienic, sanitary, purgative; purgatory; cleaning, detergent, abstergent, ablutionary, balneal

VERBS

17 **clean,** make clean, keep clean, remove the dirt, make immaculate, make fresh, freshen, freshen up; disinfect, phenolate, carbolize; spring-clean, clean up, clean out,

clear, clear up, clear out; spruce, spruce up, groom, valet, make neat, neaten, tidy, make tidy, trim, shave; wash, wash clean, wash up, wash off, wash out, wash down; wipe, wipe clean, wipe up, wipe off *or* away; sponge, sponge off, mop, mop up, swab, scrub, scour, do the cleaning, dust, whisk, sweep, sweep up, beat, vacuum; brush, brush up, brush off, comb; polish, shine, buff; whiten, whitewash, bleach, launder, do the washing, do the laundry, starch, iron, dry-clean; erase, rub out, obliterate; strip, strip clean, pick clean; rake out, muck out, make a clean sweep; flush, flush out; sandblast, holystone, scrape, rub; dry, drip-dry, tumble-dry, wring, wring out

▶ *Obliteration 186; Light 246; Whiteness 253; Arrangement 767*

18 **bathe,** take *or* have a bath, dip, dunk, rinse, soak, steep, soap, lather, shampoo, shower, take *or* have a shower, douche, sluice, swill (out), drench

▶ *Water 557; Moisture 559*

19 **purify,** purge, censor, expurgate, bowdlerize, bluepencil, edit out, clean up; sublimate, cleanse; wash, lave, lustrate, purify oneself; freshen, ventilate, air, fan, deodorize, fumigate; edulcorate, desalt, desalinate, desalinize; decontaminate, disinfect, sterilize, antisepticize, chlorinate, pasteurize, sanitize; free from impurities, depurate, refine, distill, clarify, rack, skim, scum, decarbonize, elutriate, decant, strain, filter, percolate; lixiviate, leach; sift, sieve, eliminate, sort out, weed out, flush out; dialyze, catheterize; clean out, wash out, drain

▶ *Hygiene 116*

ADVERBS

20 **cleanly,** spotlessly, hygienically, neatly, tidily, purely

21 **clean [Inf],** altogether, wholly, entirely, totally, completely, utterly, absolutely, quite

112 Dirtiness

NOUNS

1 **dirtiness,** uncleanness, soiling, defilement; muckiness, grubbiness, griminess, filthiness, pollution; foulness, squalor, squalidity, squalidness; sleaziness, slumminess, untidiness, slovenliness, sluttishness; blackness, dinginess; messiness, muddiness, sliminess, miriness, encrustation; turbidity, cloudiness; mustiness, moldiness

2 **uncleanness,** unholiness, profanity, corruption, impurity; coarseness; sepsis, infection; contamination, foulness, abomination; stink, stench, fetor; excretion; dirty habits, beastliness; scruffiness, shabbiness, pediculosis, phthiriasis; rot, decomposition, putrefaction, putrescence, taint

▶ *Excretion 25; Stench 227*

3 **lack of hygiene,** uncleanliness, lack of sanitation, unsanitariness, insanitation; verminousness, infesta-

tion, dirtiness, filth; insalubrity, unhealthiness, unwholesomeness; unhealthy conditions, unwholesome surroundings, condemned housing, slum, squalor; mephitis, poisonous fumes, unhealthy climate, bad air, pollution, miasma, greenhouse effect, smoke, smog, fug; radioactivity, fallout, deadliness, poisonousness, bane; infectiousness, contagiousness; sepsis, purulence, suppuration; decay, mold, stagnant water, bad drains, open sewer

▸ *Affliction 117*

4 **obscenity,** rudeness, indecency, ribaldry; smuttiness, scatology, pornography; dirty joke, dirty book, dirty magazine, dirty film; salaciousness, prurience; lewdness, lasciviousness, licentiousness, porn [Inf]

▸ *Immorality 432*

5 **dirt,** muck, grime, filth; stain, mark, patch, spot, blot, smudge, smear; mud, mire, quagmire, bog, soil, earth, clay, loam; dung, manure, ordure, feces, excrement, stool, night soil, droppings, guano; mucus, nasal mucus, snot [Inf]; pus, matter; dust, mote, smut, soot, smoke; grounds, grouts, dregs, lees, draff, sweepings, scourings, offscourings, shavings, leavings, leftovers, residue, residuum; sediment, sedimentation, deposit, sludge; slime, ooze; precipitate, scum, froth, dross, scoria, ash, cinder, clinker, slag, castoff, castoff skin, exuviae, slough, dandruff, scurf, scales; tartar, plaque; feculence, litter, rubbish, garbage, trash, refuse; rot, dry rot, wet rot, rust, mildew, mold, fungus, decay; carrion, offal; vermin, flea, nit, louse, cobweb; [Inf]: goo, shit, crap, crud, gunk, grunge, dreck

▸ *Excretion 25; Waste 96; Viscosity 561*

6 **swill,** pigswill, slops, hogwash; bilge water, bilge, dishwater, ditchwater, stagnant water, dirty water; sewage, sewerage, drainage; wallow, hog wallow, slough

ADJECTIVES

7 **dirty,** unclean, uncleaned, soiled, defiled; mucky, grubby, grimy, filthy, dusty, sooty, smoky, polluted; unwashed, unwiped, unscrubbed, unscoured, unrinsed, unswept, littered; foul, fouled, befouled; squalid, sleazy, slummy; untidy, unkempt, bedraggled, frowzy, slatternly, slovenly, sluttish; black, dingy, unpolished, unburnished, tarnished; stained, spotted, smudged, besmirched, besmeared; messy, greasy, oily, muddy, slimy, miry, begrimed, clotted, caked, matted, encrusted, dirt-encrusted, mud-dried; thick, turbid, cloudy, murky, clogged, scummy; musty, moldy, fusty, cobwebby

8 **unclean,** unhallowed, unholy, profane, corrupt, impure; coarse, unrefined, unpurified; septic, festering; poisonous, toxic; unsterilized, nonsterile, unsanitary, unhygienic, infectious, contaminated, insalubrious, unhealthy; offensive, foul, nasty, abominable, disgusting, repulsive, noisome, nauseous, nauseating, malodorous, stinking, stinky, fetid; uncleanly, unfas-

tidious; beastly, hoggish; sordid, squalid, scruffy, shabby; scurfy, leprous, scabby, mangy, pediculous, crawling; fecal, dungy, stercoraceous, excrementitious *or* excremental; carious, rotting, rotted; tainted, flyblown, flea-bitten, lousy, maggoty, yucky *or* yecchy, grotty [Inf]

▸ *Excretion 25; Stench 227*

9 **obscene,** dirty, filthy, rude, indecent, risqué, ribald, smutty, scatological, pornographic, blue, adult, off-color, salacious, prurient, lewd, lascivious, licentious, scabrous

▸ *Immorality 432*

VERBS

10 **be dirty,** get dirty, collect dust; foul up, clog, rust; mildew, molder; fester, have gangrene, gangrene, mortify, putrefy, decay, rot, go bad; go off, addle; grow rank, smell, stink; wallow, roll in the dirt *or* mud

11 **dirty,** make dirty, make unclean, soil, muck; defile, foul, befoul, grime, begrime, cover with dust; stain, spot, patch, maculate [Arch], blot, sully, tarnish, blacken; untidy, make a mess (of), mess up; daub, smear, besmear, smirch, besmirch, smudge, blur, streak; grease, cake, clot, clog, muddy, bemire, beslime; roil, rile; draggle, bedraggle, drabble, spatter, bespatter, splash; slobber, slaver; poison, taint, corrupt, pollute, contaminate, infect; profane, desecrate, unhallow

ADVERBS

12 **dirtily,** grubbily, untidily, sluttishly, messily, mustily, uncleanly; coarsely, offensively, sordidly, obscenely, rudely; indecently, salaciously, pruriently, lewdly, lasciviously

113 Health

NOUNS

1 **health,** good health, glowing health, robust health, rude health, healthiness; fitness, well-being, physical well-being, soundness, trim, form, condition, good condition, tiptop condition, pink of condition; heartiness, constitution, good constitution, iron constitution; strength, vigor, health and strength, energy, vitality, robustness; bloom, ruddy complexion, rosiness, rosy cheeks, apple cheeks; eupepsia, haleness, *mens sana in corpore sano* [L]; incorruption, incorruptibility; long life, longevity, ripe old age; shape, tone, fettle, state, healthy state, clean bill of health; recuperation, convalescence

▸ *Remedy 115; Strength 516; Vigor 518; Repair 809*

2 **healthfulness,** wholesomeness, goodness, nutritiousness, hygiene, salubriousness, salubrity

▸ *Hygiene 116*

3 **health improvement,** keeping healthy, keeping fit, exercise, physical training (P.T.), work-out, aerobics, isometrics, calisthenics; sports, swimming, running, jogging, walking, constitutional, cycling, gymnastics,

---

weightlifting, yoga; hygienics; sanitarium *or* sanatorium, health spa, spa, hot springs, thermae, health resort, health farm, health club; good diet, balanced diet, good nutrition

▶ *Food 90; Sports 145; Improvement 807*

4 **healthy,** fit, well, fine, sound, in health, in good health, bursting with health, fighting fit, eupeptic; fresh, thriving, flourishing, blooming, glowing; ruddy, rosy, rosy-cheeked, florid; hale, hearty, hale and hearty; bouncing, bonny, lusty, energetic, full of vitality, vigorous; fit and ready, in condition, in good condition, in good shape, in good heart, in peak condition, in A one *or* A number one *or* A 1 condition [Inf], in fine fettle, in fine form, in trim, in fine trim, in fine *or* high feather; [Inf]: in tiptop condition, in the pink, full of beans, full of steam, all steamed up

5 **of good constitution,** never ill; strapping, robust, hardy, sturdy, stalwart; strong, strong as a horse *or* an ox

▶ *Strength 516*

6 **health-giving,** salutary, what the doctor ordered, beneficial; wholesome, nutritious, nourishing, high-fiber, low-fat, low-salt; bodybuilding; noninjurious, harmless, benign, nonmalignant, uninfectious, noninfectious, innoxious, innocuous; immune, immunized, vaccinated, inoculated, protected; invulnerable

7 **healthful,** health-giving, wholesome, good for one, nutritious, nourishing, tonic, bracing, invigorating; hygienic, sanitary, salubrious, salutary, beneficial

8 **feeling well,** feeling fine, feeling good, feeling great, feeling like a million dollars; fit as a fiddle, sound in wind and limb, sound as a bell, the picture of health, fresh as a daisy

9 **getting well,** convalescent, on the mend, on the upgrade, on one's legs, up and about, cured, healed, restored to health; pretty good, not bad, in fair health, fair to middling, no worse, comfortable, holding one's own, as well as can be expected; safe and sound, unharmed

▶ *Remedy 115; Strength 516; Vigor 518; Repair 809*

10 **keeping fit,** exercising, practicing; gymnastic, athletic

11 **be healthy,** mind one's health, look after oneself, take care of oneself; feel well, feel fine, feel good, feel great, feel like a million dollars, have never felt better; look young, wear well, be well-preserved; bloom, thrive, flourish; have a clean bill of health, enjoy good health, brim with good health, keep (up) one's health, keep fit, exercise, warm up, limber up, run, jog, cycle, walk, swim, work out; keep well, be in the pink [Inf]

12 **get healthy,** get well, recover, recover one's health, return to health, recuperate, feel *or* look like oneself again, get the color back in one's cheeks, respond to

treatment, mend, convalesce, become convalescent, get back on one's feet, take a fresh *or* new lease on life, become a new man *or* woman, bounce back

▶ *Improvement 807*

13 **make healthy,** make well, treat, cure, heal, revive, restore, restore to health, put the color back in one's cheeks

▶ *Medicine 107; Remedy 115; Repair 809*

14 **healthily,** heartily, healthfully, nutritiously, hygienically, salubriously

114   Ill Health

1 **ill health,** bad health, poor health, delicate health, failing health, unhealthiness; delicacy, weak constitution, lack of fitness, lack of strength, weakness, weakliness, infirmity, debility, diathesis, sickliness, loss of condition; morbidity, illness, sickness, indisposition, chronic illness, chronic complaint, chronic ill health, allergy; invalidism, valetudinarianism, hypochondria, nerves, neurosis, seediness

▶ *Insanity 110; Weakness 517; Deterioration 808; Fatigue 820*

2 **illness,** disease, disorder, sickness, ailment, indisposition, malady, distemper, affliction, complaint; disability, handicap, infirmity; weakness, condition, history of illness; bout of sickness, visitation, attack, acute attack; spasm, stroke, seizure, apoplexy, fit, shock; poisoning; complication; terminal illness, terminal disease, fatal illness, coma, death

▶ *Death 29*

3 **symptom,** sign, sign of illness, indication, syndrome; rash, spot, sore, blister, discharge; congestion, breathing difficulty, hoarseness, sore throat, cough; lack of appetite, weight loss; weakness, fatigue, malaise, depression, numbness; diarrhea, nausea, queasiness, queasy stomach, vomiting; inflammation, swelling, dropsy, lump; temperature, high temperature, feverishness, fever, calenture, pyrexia, hyperpyrexia, hyperthermia, delirium, ague; chill, hypothermia, shivers, shakes [Inf]; spasm, pain; headache, splitting headache, migraine; seizure; dizziness, fainting, loss of consciousness; breakdown, collapse, unconsciousness, insensibility, prostration; stiffness, paralysis; bleeding, internal bleeding, hemorrhage, high blood pressure, hypertension, low blood pressure, hypotension

▶ *Insensibility 213; Physical Pain 215; Fatigue 820*

4 **disease,** brain disease; cardiopulmonary disease, cardiovascular disease, circulatory disease; communicable disease; congenital disease; contagion, contagious disease; deficiency disease; degenerative disease; dermatological disease; endemic disease; endocrine disease; epidemic disease; febrile disease; functional disease;

gastrointestinal disease; heart disease; hematopoietic disease; infection, infectious disease; mental disorder; musculoskeletal disease; neoplastic disease; neurological disease; notifiable disease; occupational disease; organic disease; respiratory disease; sexually transmitted disease (STD) *or* venereal disease (VD); substance abuse; traumatic disease; tropical disease; urogenital disease; wasting disease; the crud [Inf]

5 disease-causing agent, pathogen, virus, lentivirus, retrovirus; bacterium, germ, microbe, bacillus, contagium, microorganism; parasite, worm, helminth, insect; protozoan; vector, host, carrier; bug [Inf]

6 plague, pest, scourge, bane, pestilence, infection, contagion, epidemic, pandemic; pneumonic plague, bubonic plague, Black Death

▶ *Affliction 117*

7 infection, contagion, virulence, miasma, affliction, blight; infectiousness, contagiousness; plague spot, trouble spot, hotbed; sepsis, purulence, suppuration, festering, toxemia, septicemia, pyemia, gangrene; infectious hepatitis, measles, German measles, rubella, rubeola, roseola, whooping cough, pertussis, mumps, chickenpox, smallpox, variola, scarlet fever, scarlatina; typhus, trench fever, typhoid, paratyphoid, glandular fever; infectious mononucleosis *or* mono; poliomyelitis *or* polio *or* infantile paralysis; meningitis; tetanus *or* lockjaw; rabies *or* hydrophobia; kissing disease [Inf]

8 poisoning, toxicity, toxin, poisonousness, poison; blood poisoning, food poisoning, ptomaine poisoning, botulism

9 infectious person, ill person, sick person, invalid, convalescent; patient, case; carrier, symptomless carrier, germ-carrier, HIV-carrier, syphilitic, gonorrheic; Typhoid Mary

10 tropical disease, fever, malarial fever, malaria, ague, cholera, Asiatic cholera; yellow fever, blackwater fever, miliary fever *or* sweating sickness, breakbone fever *or* dengue, Lassa fever, green monkey disease *or* Marburg-Ebola disease; kala-azar *or* visceral leishmaniasis; trypanosomiasis, (South) American trypanosomiasis *or* Chagas' disease; sleeping sickness *or* encephalitis lethargica; schistosomiasis *or* bilharziasis; ascariasis, ancylostomiasis *or* hookworm disease; trachoma, glaucoma, onchocerciasis *or* river blindness; frambesia *or* yaws; dhobie itch *or* tinea cruris; leprosy *or* Hansen's disease; beriberi, kwashiorkor

11 gastroenterological disease, upset stomach, stomachache, cramps, colic, gripes; acidity, hyperacidity, acidosis, heartburn, pyrosis, gastralgia; cardialgia, dyspepsia, liverishness, biliousness; nausea, vomiting, retching, stomach flu; stomach ulcer, peptic ulcer, gastric ulcer, duodenal ulcer; stomach cancer; gastritis, gastroenteritis, enteritis, regional enteritis *or* Crohn's disease, colitis, duodenitis; dysentery, cholera; food poisoning, ptomaine poisoning, botulism, salmonel-losis, listeriosis; flatulence, flatus, gas, wind, diarrhea, constipation; [Inf]: bellyache, butterflies, the trots, the runs, Montezuma's revenge

▶ *Excretion 25; Expulsion 709*

12 respiratory disease, cough, cold, common cold, head cold, runny nose, watering eyes, catarrh, coryza, rhinitis, rhinorrhea, sinusitis; influenza, flu; sore throat, swollen adenoids, tonsillitis, pharyngitis, laryngitis, tracheitis; croup, bronchitis, asthma, emphysema, pleurisy, pneumonia, bronchopneumonia, legionnaire's disease, diphtheria, whooping cough, pertussis, lung cancer; pneumoconiosis, asbestosis, silicosis, anthracosis *or* black lung disease; cystic fibrosis, tuberculosis (TB) *or* phthisis *or* consumption

13 cardiovascular disease, heart disease, heart condition, heart trouble, bad heart, weak heart; coronary heart disease, rheumatic heart disease, cardiac disease; carditis (endocarditis, myocarditis, pericarditis), angina pectoris, angina, chest pain, chest spasm, breast pang; brachycardia, tachycardia, galloping *or* gallop rhythm, palpitation, dyspnea; valvulitis, valvular lesion, mitral stenosis, cardiac hypertrophy, enlarged heart, athlete's heart, fatty degeneration of the heart; cardiac arrest, heart attack, heart failure, coronary thrombosis, coronary, myocardial infarction (MI), stroke; high blood pressure, hypertension, low blood pressure, hypotension; vascular disease, atheroma, aneurysm *or* aneurism, hardening of the arteries, arteriosclerosis, arteritis; phlebitis, thrombosis, clot, blood clot, embolism, infarction

14 blood disease, anemia, aplastic anemia, hemolytic anemia, hemorrhagic anemia, pernicious anemia, sickle cell anemia; leukemia, lymphoma, Hodgkin's disease; blood poisoning, toxemia, septicemia; hemophilia

15 cancer, neoplasm, growth, cancerous growth, primary growth, secondary growth; tumor, benign tumor, innocent tumor, malignant tumor, cancerous tumor, carcinoma, sarcoma; epithelioma, melanoma, skin cancer, breast cancer, throat cancer, lung cancer, stomach cancer, bone cancer, brain cancer, cervical cancer, prostate cancer, pancreatic cancer, leukemia; the big C [Inf]

16 skin disease, dermatitis, cutaneous disease, skin lesion; scabies, erythema, leucoderma, vitiligo, albinism, lupus, frambesia *or* yaws, leprosy *or* Hansen's disease, eczema, mange, miliaria; heat rash, prickly heat; erysipelas *or* St. Anthony's fire, impetigo, herpes, herpes zoster *or* shingles, serpigo *or* ringworm; prurigo, pruritus, itch, dhobie itch *or* tinea cruris, athlete's foot, formication, urticaria, hives, nettle rash; rash, eruption, breaking out, acne, spot, pimple, blackhead, pustule, cyst, blister; wart, verruca, swelling, blemish, macula, mole, freckle, birthmark, pockmark; smallpox, variola, chickenpox; melanoma, skin cancer; tetter

> *Touch 216; Blemish 533; Convexity 634*

17 **sexually transmitted disease (STD)** *or* **venereal disease (VD),** sexual disease, social disease; acquired immune deficiency syndrome (AIDS), AIDS-related complex, syphilis, gonorrhea, nonspecific urethritis (NSU), chlamydia *or* lymphogranuloma venereum, pelvic inflammatory disease (PID), herpes, herpes simplex, crabs; venereal ulcer, chancre, syphilitic sore; [Inf]: French disease, clap, dose

18 **ulcer,** ulceration, gathering, fester, purulence, inflammation, sore, abscess, boil *or* furuncle, carbuncle; fistula, cyst, blain, chilblain *or* kibe [Arch], swelling; corn, hard corn, soft corn; gangrene, rot, decay, discharge, pus, matter

> *Disintegration 758*

19 **joint disease,** rheumatism, rheumatic fever, muscular rheumatism *or* myalgia *or* fibrositis; tendonitis, tennis elbow, bursitis, frozen shoulder, prepatellar bursitis *or* housemaid's knee, repetitive strain injury (RSI); arthritis, rheumatoid arthritis, gout, osteoarthritis, degenerative joint disease; lumbago; slipped disk, pulled muscle

20 **neurological disease,** neuralgia, sciatica, neurilemmitis; meningitis; paralysis, general paralysis, quadriplegia, tetraplegia, hemiplegia, diplegia, bilateral paralysis, paraplegia, atrophy, numbness, insensibility, partial paralysis, general paresis, paresis, palsy, cerebral palsy; tic, tic douloureux *or* trigeminal neuralgia, twitch, tremor, spasm; epilepsy *or* falling sickness, petit mal, grand mal; poliomyelitis *or* polio *or* infantile paralysis; spina bifida; parkinsonism *or* Parkinson's disease; Alzheimer's disease; amyotrophic lateral sclerosis *or* Lou Gehrig's disease; chorea *or* Huntington's chorea *or* St. Vitus's dance; multiple sclerosis (MS), disseminated sclerosis, muscular dystrophy, myasthenia gravis, myasthenia, motor neuron disease

> *Insensibility 213; Agitation 684*

21 **psychiatric disease,** affective disorder, depression, mania, schizophrenia, personality-type disorder, eating disorder, substance abuse, alcoholism; neurasthenia

> *Psychology and Psychiatry 108; Substance Abuse 121*

22 **sick person,** invalid, patient, hospital patient, nursing home patient, pediatric patient, geriatric patient; inpatient, outpatient, shut-in, sufferer, case, stretcher case, hospital case, mental case; chronic invalid, valetudinarian, hypochondriac, malingerer, martyr to ill health, weakling; consumptive, asthmatic, bronchitic, dyspeptic, diabetic, hemophiliac, bleeder, insomniac; neuropath, addict, drug addict, alcoholic, spastic, arthritic, paralytic, paraplegic, quadriplegic, hemiplegic, disabled person, cripple

> *Insanity 110; Weakness 517*

ADJECTIVES

23 **unhealthy,** ill, unfit, unsound, sickly, infirm, decrepit, weakly, weak; tired, fatigued, exhausted, run down; delicate, of weak constitution, prone to sickness, liable to illness; chronically ill, chronically sick, always ill; invalid, valetudinarian, hypochondriac; undernourished, underfed, anorectic, malnourished, emaciated; sallow, wan, pale, white, pale as a ghost, white as a sheet; peaked, peaky, anemic, colorless; jaundiced, yellow, bilious, green

> *Weakness 517; Fatigue 820*

24 **sick,** ill, unwell, not well, not in good health, in bad health, in poor health, in poor condition, in poor shape, in a bad way, bad; poorly, peaky, below par, indisposed, out of sorts, out of kilter, off-color, drooping, under the weather, seedy; flagging, pining, languishing, wasting away, in a decline; squeamish, queer, queasy, nauseated; ailing, showing signs of, showing symptoms of, coming down with; off one's food, refusing to eat; feverish, headachy; confined, quarantined; shut in, bedridden, (flat) on one's back, prostrate, in bed; diseased, infected, contaminated, tainted, affected, stricken, plague-stricken; in the hospital, hospitalized, on the sick list; invalided, taken ill, taken bad, collapsed; comatose, in a coma; on the danger list, in intensive care, in ICU, not allowed visitors; serious, critical, chronic; incurable, terminal, inoperable, mortally ill, dying, near death, moribund; [Inf]: crummy, shitty, like death warmed over, green around the gills, laid up

25 **of disease,** pathological, pathogenic, morbid, morbific, insalubrious, unhygienic; iatrogenic, psychosomatic; vitiated; rotten, rotting, gangrenous, decaying, decomposed; infectious, festering, purulent; degenerative; consumptive, phthisic, tuberculous, tubercular; diabetic; hydrocephalic, hydrocephalous; anemic, bloodless; leukemic, hemophilic; arthritic, rheumatic, rheumatoid; rickety; palsied, paralyzed, paralytic, spastic; epileptic; leprous; carcinomatous, carcinomatoid, cancerous, oncogenic, oncogenous, carcinogenic; syphilitic, venereal; swollen, edematous *or* edematose, dropsical; gouty; bronchial, bronchitic; throaty, croupy, sniffly, snuffly; asthmatic, allergic; pyretic, febrile, fevered, feverish, delirious; shivering, aguish; sore, tender, painful; ulcerous, ulcerated; inflamed, rashy, spotty, erysipelatous

> *Physical Pain 215; Disintegration 758*

26 **contagious,** infectious, catching, catchable, communicable, infective, morbific, pathogenic, germ-carrying, zymotic, pestiferous, pestilent, plague-stricken; epidemic, pandemic, endemic, epizootic, enzootic, sporadic; unsterilized, nonsterile; infected, septic, contaminated, dirty

> *Dirtiness 112*

27 **unhygienic,** unhealthy, detrimental to health, unwholesome, unsanitary, insanitary, insalubrious; verminous, dirty, filthy, unclean, squalid, sordid, bad,

nasty, noxious, miasmal, dangerous, injurious, harmful, corrupting, polluting, deadly; infested, undrained, marshy, stagnant, foul; polluted, undrinkable, inedible, indigestible, unnutritious; unsound, not fresh, stale, gone bad, off, rotten, decayed, moldy; unventilated, windowless, airless, sealed off, musty, fusty, smoke-filled, smoky, humid, stuffy, muggy, overheated, steaming, underheated, freezing

▶ *Dirtiness 112; Closure 584; Deterioration 808*

28 toxic, poisonous, mephitic, pestilent, pestilential, germ-laden; venomous, envenomed, poisoned; gathering, festering, septic, pussy, purulent, suppurating; lethal, deadly

VERBS

29 be unhealthy, be ill, be sick, be in poor health, ail; suffer from, undergo treatment for, complain of, have a complaint, have an affliction; not feel well, feel ill, feel bad, feel rotten, feel sick, sicken, fall sick, fall ill; catch something, catch an infection, contract a disease, come down with, break out with, have an attack; vomit; have a heart attack, have a stroke, collapse, faint, have a seizure; take to one's bed, go to the hospital, be hospitalized, become a patient, become an inpatient, become an outpatient; languish, pine, peak, droop, go into a decline, lose strength, weaken, grow weak, fail, flag, drop, sink, fade away, deteriorate, get worse; be laid up, waste away, feel like hell [Inf]

▶ *Weakness 517; Expulsion 709; Deterioration 808*

30 cause ill health, infect, transmit, carry; be contagious, be pestilential; poison

▶ *Dirtiness 112; Deterioration 808*

ADVERBS

31 unhealthily, weakly, chronically, morbidly, pathologically; in the hospital, under a doctor's care, under doctor's orders, in the doctor's hands, under treatment, on the sick list

32 unhygienically, uncleanly, insalubriously, unhealthily, unwholesomely; dirtily, filthily, squalidly; noxiously, venomously, poisonously, septically, pestilentially, morbidly, contagiously, infectiously

115 Remedy

NOUNS

1 remedy, cure, antidote, help, aid, succor, relief, oil on troubled waters, remedial measure; corrective, correction, amendment, redress, amends, restitution; expiation, atonement; certain cure, recuperation, recovery; medicinal value, healing quality *or* property, healing gift, sovereign remedy, specific remedy, specific; answer, solution; prescribed remedy, prescription, recipe, formula; quack remedy, nostrum, patent medicine; panacea, heal-all, cure-all, catholicon, elixir, philosophers' stone

▶ *Relief 275; Answer 334; Giving Back 478; Moderation 521; Improvement 807; Repair 809; Help 825*

2 medicine, remedy, pharmaceutical, drug, prescription drug; tonic, physic, materia medica, pharmacopoeia, pharmacognosy; herbal remedy, vegetable remedy, galenical, herb, medicinal herb, simple, balm, balsam; medication, medicament, over-the-counter medication, patent medicine, proprietary drug, generic drug, ethical drug; antibody, antiserum; mithridate, theriac *or* theriaca; antipyretic, febrifuge; vermifuge, anthelmintic; antigen, interferon, antibiosis, antibiotic, immunosuppressive, antispasmodic, anticonvulsant, anticoagulant; sedative, muscle relaxant; placebo

3 dose of medicine, dosage; pill, bolus, tablet, capsule, timed-release Caplet™, lozenge, dragée, troche, pastille; draft, dose, gel, drops, inhalant, douche; drip, injection, shot; infusion, potion, elixir, decoction, preparation, mixture, powder, lincture *or* linctus; ointment, salve, cream, balm, balsam, lotion, unguent, paint, poultice, unction, oil, emollient

▶ *Medicine 107*

4 prophylaxis, prophylactic, preventive, preventative, contraception; sanitation, sanitary precaution, quarantine, isolation, cordon sanitaire, hygiene; immunization, inoculation, vaccination, vaccine, triple vaccine; antisepsis, disinfection, sterilization; vasectomy, tubal ligation; antiseptic, disinfectant, iodine, carbolic, boric acid, boracic acid, bactericide, germicide; insecticide, poison, fumigant; dentifrice, toothpaste, tooth powder, dental floss, mouthwash, gargle, fluoride; hydrogen peroxide

▶ *Infertility 23; Cleanliness 111; Health 113; Hygiene 116; Affliction 117; Avoidance 386*

5 antidote, countermeasure; antitoxin, counterirritant, antihistamine

▶ *Counteraction 510*

6 analgesic, painkiller, anodyne, analgesia, pain relief; nepenthe, palliative, paregoric; balm, salve, demulcent, arnica; aspirin, acetaminophen, ibuprofen, naproxen sodium, nonsteroidal anti-inflammatory drug (NSAID); codeine, meperidine; morphine, morphia, laudanum; anesthetic, local anesthetic, general anesthetic, nitrous oxide, laughing gas, anesthesia, local anesthesia, general anesthesia; acupuncture, hypnosis, mind over matter

▶ *Physical Pain 215*

7 purgative, purge, cathartic, laxative, aperient; castor oil, Epsom salt *or* salts, health salts, senna pods, cascara, milk of magnesia; diuretic, expectorant, emetic, nauseant, antacid, ipecac, carminative, digestive, douche, enema

8 tonic, restorative, roborant, cordial; tonic water *or* quinine water; reviver, refresher, stimulant, amphetamine, caffeine; smelling salts, sal volatile, hartshorn;

infusion, tisane, herb tea, ginseng, royal jelly, vitamin, iron, pep pill, pick-me-up [Inf]

> *Refreshment 94; Vigor 518*

9 **drug,** wonder drug, miracle drug, synthetic drug, designer drug, orphan drug, over-the-counter drug, prescription drug; intoxicating drug, illegal drug, controlled substance, street drug, narcotic; [Inf]: dope, upper, downer

> *Substance Abuse 121*

10 **druggist,** pharmacist, apothecary, chemist [Brit], dispenser, posologist, pharmacologist; drugstore, pharmacy

11 **balm,** balsam, oil, soothing syrup, emollient, liniment, lotion, embrocation; salve, ointment, unguent, cerate; cream, face cream, moisturizer; petrolatum, petroleum jelly, lotion; wash, collyrium *or* eyewash

> *Beautification 530*

12 **therapy,** therapeutics, medical care, healing art, treatment, hospitalization; medical treatment, clinical treatment, nursing, bedside manner, first aid, aftercare; course, cure, faith cure, nature cure, cold-water cure, hydrotherapy, regimen, diet; chiropractic, bonesetting, manipulation, massage, orthopedics, osteopathy; hypnotherapy; hormone therapy, hormone replacement therapy (HRT), immunotherapy, chemotherapy, physiotherapy, occupational therapy, radiotherapy, phototherapy, heat treatment, electrotherapy; shock treatment, electroconvulsive therapy (ECT), mental treatment; clinical psychology, child psychology, psychotherapy, psychiatry, psychoanalysis; group therapy; acupuncture, acupressure, catheterization, intravenous injection, drip, drip-feed; surgery, dental surgery; physical therapy, occupational therapy, speech therapy

> *Medicine 107; Psychology and Psychiatry 108*

13 **healing art,** therapeutics, healing, art of healing, gift of healing, healing touch, recuperation, medicine; allopathy, homeopathy, naturopathy, nature cure, acupuncture, alternative medicine, holistic medicine, folk medicine; faith healing, laying on of hands

> *Medicine 107; Ill Health 114; Repair 809*

ADJECTIVES

14 **remedial,** corrective, therapeutic, medicinal, analeptic, curative, first-aid, restorative, helpful, beneficial, healing, curing, vulnerary, hygienic, sanitary, salutary, salubrious, salutiferous; antidotal, counteractant, theriacal; disinfectant, antiseptic; antipyretic, febrifugal; tonic, stimulative, stimulating

> *Health 113; Hygiene 116; Insensibility 213; Counteraction 510; Moderation 521; Repair 809*

15 **medicinal,** specific, sovereign, panacean, soothing, balsamic, demulcent, emollient, lenitive; narcotic, hypnotic; peptic, digestive, purging, cleansing, cathartic, emetic, vomitory, laxative, purgative; prophylactic,

preventive, preventative; analgesic, pain-relieving, anodyne, palliative, anesthetic, paregoric [Arch]

> *Cleanliness 111*

VERBS

16 **remedy,** make better, correct, restore, fix, mend, put right, help, aid, succor, apply a remedy, treat, heal, cure, work a cure, palliate, alleviate, soothe, neutralize, relieve, ease

> *Relief 275; Improvement 807; Repair 809; Help 825*

17 **treat,** remedy, heal, prescribe, advise, attend, minister to, tend, nurse, give first aid, give the kiss of life, revive, hospitalize, put on the sick list, put to bed; dress, bind, swathe, bandage; stop the bleeding, apply a tourniquet, staunch; set, put in splints, put a cast on; bleed, phlebotomize, transfuse, perfuse; massage, rub, manipulate; draw, extract, pull, fill, crown; immunize, vaccinate, inoculate; sterilize, antisepticize, disinfect, sanitate

> *Medicine 107; Hygiene 116*

18 **medicate,** prescribe medication, treat; physic, prescribe, dose, purge, inject, give a shot, give a pill, apply a compress, dress; drug, dope [Inf], anesthetize

ADVERBS

19 **remedially,** curatively, correctively; healthfully, salutarily

20 **medically,** therapeutically, pathologically, surgically, clinically

21 **medicinally,** pharmaceutically, effectively

116 Hygiene

NOUNS

1 **hygiene,** public health, sanitation, cleanliness, cleanness; asepsis, antisepsis, disinfection, sterilization, chlorination, pasteurization; preventive medicine, prophylaxis, prophylactic; quarantine, isolation, cordon sanitaire, protection; immunity, immunization, inoculation, vaccination, disease prevention; fumigation, decontamination; purification

> *Medicine 107; Cleanliness 111; Remedy 115; Safety 810*

2 **hygienist,** sanitarian, health inspector, public health inspector, sanitary engineer, medical officer, nutritionist, dietitian *or* dietician, fresh-air fiend [Inf]

ADJECTIVES

3 **hygienic,** sanitary; disinfected, chlorinated, pasteurized; sterilized, sterile, clean, pure, aseptic, antiseptic, germ-free; sanative, curative, sanatory, prophylactic; immunizing, protective, remedial; salubrious, healthy, healthful, health-giving; ventilated, well-ventilated; refreshing, restorative

VERBS

4 **practice hygiene,** make hygienic, prevent disease; sanitate, sanitize; disinfect, chlorinate, pasteurize, boil, sterilize, antisepticize; immunize, inoculate, vaccinate; quarantine, put in quarantine, isolate; ventilate, aer-

ate, freshen; fumigate, decontaminate; purify, cleanse, clean; drain, dry; conserve, preserve
> *Cleanliness 111; Preservation 815*

ADVERBS

5 **hygienically,** sanitarily, antiseptically, aseptically, salubriously, healthily, healthfully, wholesomely
> *Health 113*

117 Affliction

NOUNS

1 **affliction,** evil, harm, curse; illness, malady, disease, plague, infestation, pestilence, pest, scourge, blight; distress, ruin, bane, visitation; addiction
> *Ill Health 114*

2 **adversity,** trouble, calamity, disaster; woe, grief, misery, sorrow, cross to bear, cross, trial; bugbear, bugaboo, bogey *or* bogy, bête noire
> *Adversity 848*

3 **burden,** imposition, charge, duty, white elephant, albatross, millstone, thorn in one's flesh *or* side

4 **strain,** stress, fear, pressure, worry, anxiety, angst, torment, bitterness, sourness, acid, gall, wormwood

5 **pain,** hurt, agony, ache, pang, twinge, soreness, tenderness
> *Ill Health 114; Physical Pain 215; Sorrow 270; Adversity 848*

6 **poisoning,** poisonousness, toxicity, venomousness
> *Ill Health 114*

7 **poison,** toxin, venom; hemlock, arsenic, arsenic oxide, prussic acid, hydrogen cyanide, sodium cyanide, cyanide, strychnine, rat poison, ratsbane, rodenticide, warfarin; insecticide, rotenone, herbicide, weed-killer, paraquat; carcinogen

8 **pollution,** pollutant; smoke, tar, smog, effluvium, miasma, mephitis, secondhand smoke, acid rain; sulfur dioxide, sulfuric acid, leaching, carbon dioxide, halon, chlorofluorocarbon (CFC), hydrochlorofluorocarbon (HCFC), contamination, contaminant, dioxin, tetrachlorodibenzodioxin (TCDD), polychlorinated biphenyl (PCB), phosphate; carbon monoxide, exhaust fumes; ozone depletion, oxygen depletion, greenhouse effect
> *Ill Health 114*

9 **chemical warfare,** chemical weapon, asphyxiant, tear gas, Mace™, poison gas
> *War 76*

10 **addictive drug,** intoxicant, narcotic, cannabis, tranquilizer, sleeping pill; amphetamine; nicotine, alcohol, caffeine; dope [Inf], upper [Inf]
> *Substance Abuse 121*

ADJECTIVES

11 **afflicting,** blighting; evil, harmful, cursed; pestilent; blighted; distressed, ruined

> *Evil 446*

12 **miserable,** afflicted, sorrowful, troubled, pained, hurt, agonized, sore, tender; painful

13 **strained,** stressed, pressured, worried, anxious, tormented, bitter, sour

14 **poisonous,** venomous, envenomed, toxic, baneful, malevolent, noxious, noisome

15 **polluting,** polluted, pestilent, unclean, impure, contaminated
> *Dirtiness 112*

VERBS

16 **afflict,** harm, curse, strike down, plague, infest, visit, blight; blast, wither, shrivel, decay, rot, mildew, mold, rust; mar, burden, strain, worry, pressure, torment, bite, sting

17 **be miserable,** be sorrowful, be troubled, be afflicted

18 **poison,** drug, pollute, taint, contaminate; infect, spoil
> *Dirtiness 112; Ill Health 114*

ADVERBS

19 **banefully,** balefully, harmfully, virulently, malevolently, noxiously

118 Fasting

NOUNS

1 **fasting,** fast, abstinence from food, abstinence, abstemiousness, austerity, atrophy, religious fasting; hunger strike

2 **dieting,** diet, prescribed diet, health diet, crash diet, starvation diet, slimming diet, liquid diet; weight loss, slimming, reducing, weight-watching, losing weight; counting calories; anorexia nervosa

3 **short rations,** military rations, K rations, asceticism, Spartan fare, Lenten fare, prison fare, diet of bread and water; hunger striking, bare subsistence, bare cupboard, insufficient diet, hunger, starvation
> *Insufficiency 98; Ill Health 114; Self-Restraint 455; Cessation 668*

4 **fast,** fast day, day of abstinence, meatless day, fish day, Lent, Friday, Good Friday, Yom Kippur, Tishah b'Av, Ramadan
> *Religious Ritual 85*

ADJECTIVES

5 **fasting,** abstinent, abstemious; not eating, without food, off food; unfed, going without, with an empty stomach, empty; keeping one's fast, keeping Lent, Lenten; keeping a Spartan regimen, Spartan; austere, ascetic

6 **on a diet,** slimming, reducing; on a crash diet, on a starvation diet, on a liquid diet; on meager rations, on a hunger strike, on bread and water

7 **underfed,** poorly fed, thin; half-starved, starving, starved; famishing, famished; ravenous, hungry, dying for food, wasting away, hungry enough to eat a horse

VERBS

8 fast, abstain, eat nothing, have nothing to eat, live on air, go hungry, hunger, go without food, go without; avoid food, have an empty stomach, suffer from anorexia nervosa, give up eating, refuse food, go on a hunger strike; eat sparingly, eat like a bird; eat no meat; follow a Spartan regimen, live on bread and water, live on rations

9 eat less, control one's appetite, lose weight, take off weight; diet, go on a diet, go on a crash diet, go on a starvation diet, go on a liquid diet; slim, reduce; count calories, half starve

10 starve, famish, die for food, tighten one's belt, make a little go a long way

ADVERBS

11 abstemiously, Spartanly, on bread and water, without food, ravenously, hungrily

119 Gluttony

NOUNS

1 gluttony, greediness, greed, overeating; big appetite, wolfishness, piggishness, hoggishness; self-indulgence, overindulgence, overindulging; intemperance, insatiability; voraciousness, voracity, ravenousness, rapacity, edacity, polyphagia; bulimia, bulimarexia, binge-purge syndrome, bulimia nervosa, binging [Inf]
  ▶ *Eating 92; Desire 288; Self-Indulgence 456*

2 glutton, greedy person, good eater, big eater, hearty eater, heavy eater, omnivore; guzzler, gorger, binger [Inf], bulimic; trencherman, trencherwoman; bacchanal, bon vivant, foodaholic; wolf, gobbler, pig, hog

ADJECTIVES

3 gluttonous, greedy, esurient, voracious, ravenous, rapacious, insatiable, never full; intemperate, hedonistic, overeating, self-indulgent, overindulgent; edacious, polyphagous, omnivorous; devouring, all-devouring; stuffing, stuffed, cramming, bolting; gobbling, gulping, glutting, gluttonizing; gorging, gorged, overgorging, overgorged, engorged; bulimic, guzzling, wolfing, wolfish, piggish, hoggish, binging [Inf]

VERBS

4 be greedy, gluttonize, gormandize, hedonize, overeat; self-indulge, overindulge, indulge one's appetite, indulge oneself, tuck into; have a big appetite, love food, love to eat, live to eat; eat up, set to, wipe the plate clean; devour, bolt, guzzle, gobble, gulp, snap up, wolf; make a pig *or* hog of oneself, fill oneself, stuff oneself, stuff, cram; glut oneself, glut, gorge, engorge; have eyes bigger than one's stomach, eat like a horse, eat one's head off, eat out of house and home, have a hollow leg; [Inf]: binge, go on a binge; pig, pig out

ADVERBS

5 gluttonously, greedily, self-indulgently, hungrily; with one bite, at a gulp, voraciously, ravenously, out of

house and home, edaciously; like a horse, wolfishly, like a wolf, piggishly, like a pig, hoggishly, like a hog

120 Sobriety

NOUNS

1 sobriety, soberness, abstinence; abstemiousness, temperance, teetotalism; state of sobriety, clear head, no hangover
  ▶ *Avoidance 386; Self-Restraint 455; Moderation 521*

2 prohibition of alcohol, Prohibition, Volstead Act, Eighteenth Amendment, the noble experiment; dry county, dry state

3 temperance society, Women's Christian Temperance Union (WCTU), Alcoholics Anonymous (AA)

4 sober person, nondrinker, nonalcoholic, nonaddict; moderate drinker, social drinker; abstainer, teetotaler, prohibitionist

ADJECTIVES

5 sober, not drunk, unintoxicated; clearheaded, with a clear head, without a hangover, sobered up, unfuddled; abstinent, not indulging; abstemious, temperate; teetotal, prohibitionist, nondrinking; off drink, off the hard stuff, off the bottle; dry, drying out; sober as a judge; stone-cold sober [Inf], on the wagon [Inf]
  ▶ *Avoidance 386; Self-Restraint 455; Moderation 521*

VERBS

6 give up alcohol, give up drinking, teetotal, become a teetotaler, kick the habit; turn prohibitionist, sign the pledge, be dry, go on the wagon [Inf]

7 sober up, clear one's head, sleep it off, get rid of a hangover, detoxify, dry out, get the fumes out of one's brain

8 be sober, stay sober, keep *or* have a clear head; not drink, not imbibe, not indulge, abstain, avoid alcohol, keep off liquor, stay away from the hard stuff; never touch a drop, never let liquor pass one's lips; drink water, prefer soft drinks; drink moderately, drink sociably, hold *or* carry one's liquor

ADVERBS

9 soberly, abstemiously, temperately, with a clear head

121 Substance Abuse

NOUNS

1 substance abuse, drinking, alcohol abuse, alcoholism, dipsomania, hitting the bottle [Inf]; drug taking, drug abuse; smoking, use of tobacco

2 drinking, excessive drinking, hard drinking, getting drunk, intemperance, bibulousness, winebibbing, tippling, toping, swilling, compotation; weakness for liquor, fondness for the bottle, Dutch courage, soaking [Inf]
  ▶ *Drinking 93*

3 drunkenness, inebriation, intoxication, inebriety, insobriety, tipsiness, sottishness, drunken *or* alcoholic stupor, being under the influence of alcohol, wooziness, befuddlement, blind staggers [Inf]; crapulence, crapulousness

4 **drunken behavior,** stimulation, exhilaration, elevation, excitation; hiccups, slurred speech, thick speech, stuttering, stammering, seeing double, dizziness, staggering, reeling, blackout; hangover, queasiness, thick head, fuzzy tongue, nausea, vomiting; tremors, delirium tremens *or* d.t.'s, seeing pink elephants; [Inf]: jim-jams, horrors, heebie-jeebies

5 **alcohol,** drink, alcoholic drink, liquor, alcoholic liquor, hard liquor, intoxicating liquor, hard drink, strong drink, potation, libation, grog, wine, beer, spirits, aqua vitae, John Barleycorn; bootleg, home-brew; [Inf]: booze, juice, vino, hooch *or* hootch, moonshine, rotgut
▶ *Drinking 93*

6 **drink,** beverage, potation, libation, libation to Bacchus, flowing bowl, cup that cheers, tipple, nip, dram, drop, chaser, shot, finger, round, round of drinks, one for the road; cocktail, tall *or* long drink, highball; [Inf]: snort, snifter, hair of the dog
▶ *Drinking 93*

7 **drinking bout,** spree, orgy of drinking, bacchanalia, revel, jag, pub crawl; [Inf]: binge, lush, blind, bender, booze-up

8 **drunkard,** drunk, inebriate, intoxicated person, habitual drunkard, sot, alcoholic, dipsomaniac, slave to drink; drinker, hard drinker, problem drinker, secret drinker, bibber, winebibber, tippler, swiller, toper, tosspot, thirsty soul, devotee of Bacchus, bacchanal *or* bacchant, maenad, Silenus, carouser, reveler, pub-crawler; [Inf]: wino, boozer, boozehound, lush, soaker, (old) soak, souse, sponge, barfly

9 **drug use,** drug addiction, drug abuse, drug dependence, habit, jones [Inf]; smoking, sniffing, glue sniffing, injecting; [Inf]: snorting, freebasing, hitting up, shooting up, skin-popping, mainlining, pill-popping, banging, blowing, cocktailing; buzz, trip, acid trip, bad trip; tracks, needle marks, shooting gallery

10 **drug pushing,** drug peddling, drug trafficking, possessing narcotics with intent to sell, holding [Inf]

11 **withdrawal,** withdrawal symptoms, withdrawal sickness; cold turkey [Inf], bogue [Inf]

12 **drug taker,** drug user, drug addict; [Inf]: druggie, junkie, dope fiend, drug scorer, freak, head, acid-head, hophead, chippy, cokehead, mainliner, hype, pillhead, pill popper

13 **drug pusher,** pusher, drug peddler, drug dealer; [Inf]: connection, candy man, reefer man

14 **drug,** drugs, narcotic, narcotics; hard drug, soft drug, designer drug, illegal drug, controlled substance, street drug; dope [Inf]

15 **drug dose,** [Inf]: fix, hit, bhang, shot, spliff, snort, blockbuster, toke, blast, shoot-up, hype, roach, reefer, joint, dime bag, hot shot

16 **hemp derivatives,** marijuana, cannabis, hashish, ganja, hemp, kef *or* keef; [Inf]: Mary Ann, Mary Jane, Mary Warner, grass, weed, rope, pot, Acapulco gold, tea, stick, hash

17 **opiates,** opium, [Inf]: brown stuff, black stuff; morphine, [Inf]: morph, M; heroin, [Inf]: horse, junk, smack, H, jones, scag *or* skag, boy, white stuff, shmee

18 **stimulants,** cocaine, [Inf]: coke, candy, snow, crack *or* rock, crack cocaine, C, white stuff, H and C *or* speedball, Peruvian marching powder, nose candy, girl, flake; amphetamine, pep pill, [Inf]: dex, dexie, dexo, upper, speed, ecstasy, greenie

19 **sedatives,** barbiturates, [Inf]: barb, downer, black beauty, purple heart, yellow jacket, blue heaven *or* angel *or* devil, nimby *or* goofball

20 **hallucinogens,** lysergic acid diethylamide (LSD), [Inf]: acid, big D, blue cheer, yellow sunshine, orange sunshine; mescaline; peyote; psilocybin, magic mushroom, STP

21 **tranquilizers,** tranks [Inf]; phenylcyclidine (PCP), angel dust [Inf]

22 **smoking,** draw, puff, drag; chain-smoking, passive smoking, secondhand smoke; smoking area, smoking compartment, smoker; smoke-free area, nonsmoker; tobacco dealer, tobacconist; smoker's cough, bronchitis, emphysema, lung cancer
▶ *Ill Health 114*

23 **tobacco,** Virginia tobacco, Turkish tobacco; nicotine, tar; cigar, Havana, corona, panatella, cheroot, cigarillo; cigarette, filter tip, cork tip, king-size, 100s, high tar, low tar, menthol; cigarette end, stub, butt; cigarette paper, roll-your-own, rolling tobacco; snuff, snuffbox, pinch of snuff; oral tobacco, chewing tobacco, plug, quid; tobacco sachet, pipe tobacco, shag; [Inf]: the weed, fag, butt, cancer stick, coffin nail

24 **tobacco implements,** humidor, cigarette case, cigarette lighter, cigarette holder, packet, carton, box; cigarette machine, ashtray; pipe, brier *or* briar, clay pipe, meerschaum, churchwarden; tobacco pouch; water pipe, hubble-bubble, narghile, hookah; pipe of peace, calumet

ADJECTIVES

25 **drunk,** inebriated, intoxicated, under the influence, having had (a drop) too much, having had one too many, in liquor, the worse for liquor; comfortably drunk, gloriously drunk, roaring drunk, fighting drunk, pot-valiant, drunk and disorderly; drunken, drunk as a lord, drunk as a fiddler, drunk as a skunk, drunk as an owl, in one's cups, hung over, crapulous, crapulent; [Inf]: tight, half-seas over, three sheets in *or* to the wind, boozed-up, ginned up, liquored up, lit up, high, tanked up, well-oiled, well-lubricated, soused, pickled, potted, canned, stewed, fried

26 **slightly drunk,** tipsy, maudlin; seeing double, woozy, dizzy, giddy, reeling, staggering, hiccupping; fuddled, muddled, flustered; [Inf]: pie-eyed, half-bagged, half-shot, boozy

27 **dead drunk,** stupefied, in a drunken stupor, under the table; [Inf]: stinking, stinko, blind drunk, blinded, blotto, stoned, smashed, sloshed, sozzled, soused, soaked, juiced, lushed, loaded, plastered, bagged, plotzed, shitfaced, gone, shot, blitzed, bombed, zonked (out), zonkers, wiped out, stiff, out of it, out cold, snockered, paralyzed

28 **drunken,** inebriate, intemperate, alcoholic, dipsomaniacal, with a drink problem, addicted to alcohol, given to drink; on the bottle, sottish, sodden, gin-sodden; smelling of drink, stinking of liquor; fond of a drink, thirsty, bibulous, bibbing, winebibbing, tippling, toping, swilling, guzzling, hard-drinking, carousing, wassailing; [Inf]: swigging, boozy, boozing

29 **intoxicating,** intoxicant, inebriating, inebriant, stimulant, exhilarating, exciting, going to the head, heady; winy, vinous, beery, spiritous, alcoholic, hard; potent, strong, double-strength; proof, overproof; straight, neat, unmixed, undiluted; addictive, habit-forming

30 **drugged,** incapacitated, insensible; [Inf]: high, doped, stoned, zonked (out), zonkers, spaced out, freaked out, loaded, turned-on, bogue, high as a kite, bombed, zoned out, twisted, wasted, strung-out

31 **addicted,** drug-dependent, hooked [Inf]

32 **addictive,** habit-forming; narcotic, hallucinogenic, psychedelic, mind-blowing [Inf]

33 **tobacco,** smoking, smoke-free, smoking-related; filter-tip, cork-tip, king-size, high-tar, low-tar, menthol, roll-your-own

VERBS

34 **be drunk,** have had (a drop) too much, have had one too many, not hold one's liquor; hiccup, slur one's words, stutter, stammer, see double, see pink elephants, not walk straight, lurch, stagger, reel, succumb, pass out

35 **get drunk,** have (a drop) too much, have one too many, drink, drink deep, drink hard, drink like a fish, tipple, tope, guzzle, swill, quaff, chug-a-lug, crack a bottle, hit the bottle, go on a spree, pub-carouse, wassail, fuddle, pub-crawl, drown one's sorrows; [Inf]: booze, swig, souse, soak, lush, liquor up, tank up, bend one's elbow, knock back a few, go on a blind, go on a bender, barhop

36 **be intoxicating,** inebriate, make drunk, stupefy; stimulate, exhilarate, elevate, excite, go to one's head, make one's head swim, fuddle, befuddle, put one under the table

37 **drug oneself,** take drugs, smoke, inject oneself, possess narcotics, traffic in drugs, have withdrawal symptoms, dry out; [Inf]: snort, drop, drop acid, freebase, shoot up, mainline, turn on, trip out, take a trip, blow one's mind, freak out, bang, blow, blow smoke, chippy, score, hold, go cold turkey

38 **smoke,** smoke cigarettes, smoke cigars, smoke a pipe, draw, puff, drag, inhale, chain-smoke, roll, chew

ADVERBS

39 **drunkenly,** under the influence, tipsily, in a drunken stupor, crapulously, crapulently

40 **in a trance,** insensibly, dopily [Inf], psychedelically, narcotically, habitually, dependently

Occupations and Crafts

122 Work

Work keeps us from three great evils, boredom, vice, and poverty. — VOLTAIRE

NOUNS

1 **work,** labor, toil, industry; assigned work, assignment; easy work, labor of love; hard work, moil, heavy work, uphill work, long haul, warm work, exhausting work, punishing work, backbreaking work; spadework, legwork, donkey work [Inf]; manual work, manual labor, getting one's hands dirty, sweat of one's brow, sweat; everyday work, school work, daily grind, chores; housework, kitchen work; garden work, fieldwork, farmwork; work without pay, slavery; travail, thankless task, drudgery, grind, strain, dreary routine, treadmill, grindstone, hack work; penal work, hard labor, penalty, forced labor, corvée, compulsion; fatigue *or* fatigue duty, spell of duty, duty; piecework, taskwork, take-home work, homework, journeywork
▶ *Compulsion 428; Punishment 454*

2 **task,** chore, job, operation, exercise, assignment, project, commission; deed, feat, trick; shift, stint, stretch, bout, spell of work, period of work; extra work, overtime; working life, working week, working day, man-hours
▶ *Undertaking 391; Action 412; Duty 433; Production 522; Period 641*

3 **job,** occupation, employment, profession, trade, métier, business, line of work, line of business, career, vocation; calling, mission, craft; racket [Inf], game [Inf]

4 **exertion,** effort, attempt, endeavor; struggle, straining, strain, stress, might and main; tug, squeeze, pull, push, stretch, rub, scrub, heave, lift, throw; drive, force, pressure, full pressure, maximum pressure, unbearable pressure; energy, applied energy, directed energy; power, manpower, horsepower, ergonomics; mighty effort, impressive effort; the hard way, muscle, muscle

power, elbow grease, sweat of one's brow; pains, taking pains, operoseness, assiduity, elaboration; overwork, overexertion, overactivity, overdoing it, working oneself to death; battle, campaign, fray; ado, hassle, trouble, toil and trouble
▶ *Attempt 390; Activity 414; Power 514*

5 **training,** practice, regular practice, exercise, drill, preparation
▶ *Health 113; Preparation 388; Activity 414*

ADJECTIVES

6 **working,** laboring, busy, industrious, employed; born to toil, horny-handed, drudging, sweating, grinding, slogging; hardworking, plodding, persevering; tireless, energetic, active; attentive, diligent, assiduous; on the go, hard at it
▶ *Attention 323; Perseverance 377; Activity 414*

7 **laborious,** strenuous, full of labor, involving effort, requiring great effort; grueling, punishing, unremitting; toilsome, troublesome, weary, wearisome, tiring, very tiring, exhausting; backbreaking, crushing, killing, painful; burdensome, heroic, herculean, arduous, hard, heavy, uphill, difficult, hard-fought, hard-won; thorough, painstaking; labored, elaborate, detailed; fiddling, fussy, nitpicking
▶ *Difficulty 824*

VERBS

8 **work,** labor, be busy, do easy work, do hard work, work at home, freelance, work in the field; toil, drudge, fag, grind, slog, peg away, moil, sweat, work up a sweat, work up a lather; clean, scrub, rub; lift, heave, pull, haul, tug, push, shove, dig, spade; do the work, soil one's hands, get one's hands dirty, spit on one's palms; clock in, punch in, begin, get down to it, set about, set to, take one's coat off, roll up one's sleeves; finish the job, quit work, clock out, punch out; earn a wage, be a breadwinner; make short work of, make up for lost time; continue working, keep at it, ply with the oars, plod, persevere, work hard; work all day, work all week, work a forty-hour week, work overtime, work

double time, do two jobs, moonlight, work double; work shifts, work day shifts, work night shifts; [Inf]: hump, get on the gravy train, do a nine-to-five

9 overwork, work all hours, work night and day, burn the midnight oil, burn the candle at both ends; slave, slave away, work one's fingers to the bone, work like a demon *or* galley slave *or* horse *or* Trojan; work oneself to death *or* into the grave, overdo it, overwork, sweat blood [Inf], bust one's ass [Inf]

▶ *Perseverance 377; Action 412; Activity 414; Operation 509; Beginning 771*

10 work for, serve, minister to; put to work, employ; task, tax, fatigue

▶ *Fatigue 820; Help 825*

11 exert oneself, strive, strain, struggle; apply oneself to, put one's best foot forward, make an effort, try, attempt, endeavor; travail, bestir oneself, spare no effort, do one's utmost, try one's best, bend over backward, put oneself out, trouble oneself; leave no stone unturned, turn every stone, use one's best endeavors, do all one can, go all out, go to any lengths, move heaven and earth, pull out all the stops, put one's heart and soul into it; put one's back into it, strain to the utmost, strain every nerve, use every muscle, give one's all; love one's job, have one's heart in one's work; force one's way, elbow one's way, drive through, wade through; persevere, hammer at, slog at, battle, campaign, take action

▶ *Willingness 373; Perseverance 377; Attempt 390; Action 412; Activity 414*

12 train, practice, drill, exercise, prepare, work out

▶ *Preparation 388*

ADVERBS

13 laboriously, arduously, strenuously; energetically, lustily, heartily; the hard way, manually, by hand, by the sweat of one's brow, on the treadmill; with heart and soul, with might and main, with all one's might; on all cylinders, tooth and nail, hammer and tongs, for all one is worth, to one's utmost; on overtime, on double time

123 Worker

Try first thyself, and after call in God; / For to the worker God himself lends aid. — EURIPIDES

NOUNS

1 worker, employee, employee at will, hand, operative, working man, working woman; toiler, moiler, drudge, factotum; busy person, Stakhanovite, jack-of-all-trades; [Inf]: gofer, beaver, bee, busy bee, ant

▶ *Activity 414*

2 breadwinner, person who brings home the bacon, earner, salary earner, salaried worker, wage earner, wage slave

3 independent worker, freelance, freelancer, self-employed person; voluntary worker, charity worker, volunteer, philanthropist, consultant, independent contractor

4 domestic worker, housewife, hausfrau, housekeeper, chief cook and bottlewasher; baby-sitter, childcare worker, au pair, nanny; domestic servant, domestic, butler, valet, maid, cook, chauffeur, gardener, cleaner, charwoman, help, home help; stay-at-home dad [Inf], Mr. Mom [Inf]; servant, flunky, menial

5 clerical worker, office worker, desk worker, white-collar worker, pink-collar worker; administrative assistant, personal assistant, girl *or* man Friday; secretary, typist, clerk-typist, stenographer, receptionist, telephone *or* switchboard operator

6 sales worker, sales representative *or* rep [Inf], salesman *or* saleswoman; salesclerk, inside sales worker, outside sales worker; manufacturer's representative *or* rep [Inf]; independent distributor

▶ *Sale 482*

7 service worker, waitress, waiter, busboy, dishwasher, attendant, porter

8 repair worker, repairman, serviceman, servicewoman; tinker, cobbler, handyman, Mister Fixit

▶ *Activity 414*

9 laborer, unskilled laborer, casual laborer, day laborer, coolie *or* cooly [Off]; workman, manual worker, pieceworker, blue-collar worker, factory worker, factory hand; miner, coal miner, collier; steelworker, foundry worker; construction worker, excavator, sandhog, road worker, trackman; docker, stevedore; packer, meat packer, butcher; garbageman, janitor, sanitation worker, sanitary engineer

10 agricultural laborer, farm worker, migrant worker, picker, farm hand, farmer, gardener

▶ *Agriculture 16; Horticulture 17*

11 professional worker, businessman, businesswoman, career woman, executive; intellectual, professor, teacher, scientist; architect, engineer, civil engineer, mining engineer, mechanical engineer, electrical engineer, radio engineer, television engineer; computer programmer; editor, publisher, journalist, reporter, newsman, newswoman, newscaster, anchorman, anchorwoman; aviator, pilot; doctor, physician, nurse, psychiatrist; social worker; lawyer, member of the clergy

12 artistic worker, artist, producer, director, writer, performer, player, actor, actress, dancer, singer, musician, orchestra conductor, orchestra director, concertmaster, executant

13 artisan, artificer, skilled worker, master, technician; semiskilled worker, tradesman, journeyman, apprentice, learner; craftsman, craftswoman, handicraftsman, handicraftswoman; carpenter, joiner, carver, woodworker, cabinetmaker, turner, sawyer, cooper; wright, wheelwright, wainwright, coach builder; shipwright, shipbuilder, boatbuilder; builder, master mason, mason, bricklayer, plasterer, tiler, roofer; painter, decorator; metalworker, forger, smith, blacksmith, tinsmith, goldsmith, silversmith; gunsmith, locksmith; weaver, spinner, tailor, cutter, needlewoman, clothier; watchmaker, clockmaker, jeweler, glassblower; mechanic, automobile *or* car mechanic, aircraft mechanic; machinist, fitter; computer repairman; power-plant worker; gasman, plumber, welder, electrician; grease monkey [Inf]

▶ *Skillfulness 127*

14 **technical worker,** technician, laboratory technician, X-ray technician, paraprofessional, nursing assistant, nurse's aide, teacher's aide, computer technician

15 **agent,** operator, doer, practitioner, participator, perpetrator, minister, officer, functionary, instrument, tool; representative, rep [Inf], distributor, middleman; delegate, convention delegate, official, spokesman, spokeswoman, spokesperson, mediator, diplomat, go-between, troubleshooter; deputy, proxy, substitute, executor, executrix; fiduciary

▶ *Delegate 79; Deputy 80; Substitution 672*

16 **personnel,** employees, workers, workpeople, staff, work force, labor force, company, organization; team, gang, squad, crew, complement, cadre, retinue, nucleus, band, cast, hands, men, women; payroll, labor, casual labor, labor pool, manpower; working classes, proletariat

▶ *Assembly 59; Drama and Theater 136; Class 777*

17 **coworker,** partner, associate, fellow worker, colleague, fellow servant

▶ *Help 825; Cooperation 827*

124 Workplace

NOUNS

1 **workplace,** workshop, workroom, place of work, work area, workspace, work station; company, firm, concern, agency

2 **office,** main office, head office, branch office, subsidiary office, executive office, bureau, business house; company headquarters

3 **home workplace,** kitchen, laundry room, sewing room, shop, office, den, study

4 **store,** department store, grocery store, supermarket, shop, showroom

5 **service workplace,** restaurant, hotel, motel; hospital, nursing home, rest home; gas station

6 **studio,** atelier, loft; library

7 **plant,** installation, establishment, industrial park, research park; laboratory, research laboratory, lab

8 **factory,** manufacturing plant, yard; sweatshop, mill, cotton mill, sawmill, paper mill; shop floor, bench, assembly line, production line

9 **works,** foundry, metalworks, steelyard, steelworks, smelter, refinery, furnace, blast furnace, forge, smithy, stithy; brickworks, quarry, mine, colliery, coal mine, pit, tin mine; mint

10 **construction workplace,** construction site, building site, excavation site; dockyard, shipyard, slips, wharf, dock

11 **farm,** dairy, creamery, stock farm, ranch; nursery, tree farm, garden

▶ *Agriculture 16; Horticulture 17*

12 **power station,** power plant, powerhouse; gasworks, waterworks; arsenal, armory

▶ *Power 514*

13 **government office,** congressional offices, parliamentary offices [Brit], secretariat; embassy

14 **industrial area,** industrial town, manufacturing town, hive of industry

125 Leisure

The wisdom of a learned man cometh by opportunity of leisure; and he that hath little business shall become wise.
— BIBLE: ECCLESIASTICUS

NOUNS

1 **leisure,** free time, spare time, spare hours, free moments, vacant moments, idle moments, odd moments; time to oneself, time for oneself, time one can call one's own, time on one's hands, time to kill; downtime, breathing space *or* room; freedom, liberty, opportunity, convenience; no work, not enough work, sinecure, idleness, *dolce far niente* [Ital], inactivity; rest, repose, ease, relaxation; no hurry, time to spare, ample time, all the time in the world

▶ *Inactivity 415; Ease 819*

2 **time off,** holiday, vacation, day off, half-holiday; leave, sabbatical, furlough; break, recess, time-out; respite, relief, peace, quiet, recreation, breather; unemployment

▶ *Interval 587; Resignation 835*

ADJECTIVES

3 **leisure,** free, spare, unoccupied, recreational

4 **leisurely,** unhurried, slow, deliberate, relaxed, laid-back [Inf]; easy, laborsaving; idle, inactive, resting, reposeful, leisured, at leisure; unoccupied, free, available; disengaged, at loose ends; at ease, off-duty, on holiday, on vacation, on leave, on furlough, on sabbatical; unemployed, retired, in retirement

▶ *Inactivity 415; Slowness 693; Ease 819; Resignation 835*

VERBS

5 **have leisure time,** have free time, have spare time, find time for, have plenty of time, have all the time in the world, have time on one's hands, be master of one's time; take one's ease, see no cause for haste, be

in no hurry, take one's own good time, take time to smell the flowers *or* roses; move slowly, spend, pass, while away; want something to do, have no work, find time hangs heavy on one's hands; take a holiday, take a vacation, take a break, take time-out, take leave, take a sabbatical, go on a furlough; rest, repose; resign, give up work, retire, go into retirement, take early retirement

> *Inactivity 415; Slowness 693; Ease 819; Resignation 835*

ADVERBS

6 **leisurely,** unhurriedly; conveniently, at one's convenience, at one's leisure, in one's own time; at any odd moment, in one's spare time

126 Management

NOUNS

1 **management,** managing, administration, organization, orchestration, control, conduct of affairs; business management, decision making; manipulation, direction, running, handling, managership, stewardship, proctorship; agency, commission, power, governance, authority, supervision, superintendence; overview, surveillance, care, charge, patronage, protection; home economics, household management, housekeeping, housewifery, husbandry; regulation, legislation, lawmaking

> *Government 49; Politics 50; Authority 52; Economics 56; Finance 457; Commission 833*

2 **management board,** managers, executives, employers, bosses, owners, directors, controllers, upper echelon, council, board, board of directors, directorate; management team, governing board, board of governors, governing body, controlling body, supervisory body; administration, committee, steering committee, standing committee, select committee, cabinet, inner cabinet, quango [Brit], higher-ups, high-muck-a-mucks; [Inf]: brass, top brass

3 **management system,** management information system (MIS); organizational management, administrative management, office management, retail management, marketing management, inventory management, financial management; management study, policy management, management theory, management by objectives (MBO), decentralization, centralization, environments matrix, existence/relatedness/growth (ERG) theory, expectant theory, Maslow's Hierarchy of Needs, matrix structure, total quality management (TQM)

4 **personnel management,** employee management, employee relations, human resources, personnel, staff management, line management; art of management, tact, way with, judgment, skill, employee planning;

motivation, incentive, goal setting, organizational management, organizational behavior

> *Labor Relations 57*

5 **directorship,** direction, directing, responsibility, command, control, administrative control, managerial control; dictatorship, leadership, premiership, chairmanship, captaincy *or* captainship; guidance, steering, pilotage

> *Command 425; Superiority 744*

6 **guide,** direction, controls, reins, helm, wheel, joystick, automatic pilot *or* autopilot, compass, radar, lighthouse, signpost, arrows, remote control *or* remote

7 **manager,** director, boss, responsible person, person in charge, key person, kingpin, top dog, administrator, executive; chief executive officer (CEO), chief operating officer (COO), president, vice president (VP), company director, director, chairperson, chairman *or* chairwoman, chair, managing director; master, mastermind, power behind the throne, Rasputin; employer, store manager, office manager, sales manager; superintendent, supervisor, inspector, overseer, foreman, forewoman, charge hand, warden, proctor, disciplinarian; executor, doer, procurator, agent, factor, consignee; major-domo, seneschal, steward; [Brit]: ganger, gaffer, bailiff, reeve; [Inf]: bigwig, big shot, very important person (VIP), big cheese, head honcho, top banana, old man

> *Government 49; Politics 50; Delegate 79; Action 412; Importance 799*

8 **leader,** motivator, influence, speaker, captain, team captain, quarterback (QB), skipper, navigator, pilot, guide; conductor, master of ceremonies *or* emcee *or* M.C.; pacesetter, bellwether, standard-bearer; protector, custodian, caretaker, curator, keeper; charismatic leader, ringmaster, high priest, mystagogue, ringleader, demagogue, rabble-rouser, agitator, autocrat, dictator

> *Government 49; Master 68; Superiority 744*

ADJECTIVES

9 **managerial,** administrative, executive, organizational; directorial, directing, leading, heading up, hegemonic, directional, guiding, steering, navigational, governing; controlling, in control, official, in charge, at the helm, holding the reins, in the driver's seat, at the wheel, chairing; authoritative, authoritarian, officious, dictatorial, despotic, tyrannical, supervisory, managing, nomothetic *or* nomothetical; high level, top level, important

VERBS

10 **manage,** administer, organize, orchestrate, mastermind, carry out goals, govern, rule, regulate, control, control results, influence; supervise, supervise staff, watch over, superintend, motivate, direct, lead, oversee, have charge of; have the measure of, know, handle, conduct, run, carry on, minister, prescribe, invigilate, proctor, nurse, look after, take care of, hold the

purse strings, control the finances, hold the reins, manipulate, maneuver, pull strings, keep order, police, sway, have a way with, be the boss; work out, accomplish, achieve, effect, realize, attain, polish off; step up to the plate, take *or* grab the wheel

> *Authority 52; Provision 89; Persuasion 178; Carefulness 325; Knowledge 348; Influence 512; Success 845*

11 **direct,** command, be in charge, boss, dictate, wear the trousers, hold power, hold office, have command, hold *or* have a responsible position, have responsibility, have overall responsibility; incur a duty, preside, take the chair, be in the chair, chair; point, point to, show, show the way, indicate, advise, counsel, shepherd, guide, conduct, accompany, channel, canalize, funnel, route; train, introduce, compère [Brit]; crack the whip, call the shots [Inf]

> *Advice 176; Identification 184; Command 425; Duty 433; Direction 697; Precedence 769; Accompaniment 794*

12 **lead,** lead the way, lead over, lead through, lead on, escort; pioneer, precede, come before; head, head up, captain, skipper, pilot, stroke, cox, steer, navigate; assume command, assume responsibility, take the helm, hold the tiller, hold the reins; host, act as a master of ceremonies, emcee

ADVERBS

13 **managerially,** administratively, officially, politically, economically, authoritatively, in control, in charge, in command; at the helm, at the wheel, in the driver's seat, in the saddle, in the chair, at the head, ex officio, on the cutting edge, in the hot seat [Inf]

127 Skillfulness

Skill without imagination is craftsmanship and gives us many useful objects such as wickerwork picnic baskets. Imagination without skill gives us modern art.
— TOM STOPPARD

NOUNS

1 **skill,** skillfulness, ability, proficiency, competence, efficiency, faculty, special faculty, capability, capacity; many-sidedness, all-around capacity, ingenuity, resourcefulness, versatility, adaptability, amphibiousness; grip, control, mastery, mastership, command, wizardry, virtuosity; goodness, excellence, prowess, expertise, expertness, technical knowledge, professionalism, professional skill; forte, strength, strong point, strong card, specialty; specialism, major subject, major, métier; technical skill, accomplishment, attainment, acquirement, experience, knowledge, major suit

> *Discrimination 337; Knowledge 348; Wisdom 352; Plan 387; Conduct 399; Power 514*

2 **manual skill,** practical ability, practical knowledge, everyday knowledge; adroitness, dexterity, dexter-

ousness, handiness, deftness, adeptness, cleverness, address, ease, facility; ambidexterity, ambidextrousness, flexibility, suppleness, touch, clever hands, deft fingers; craftsmanship, delicacy, fine workmanship, technique, execution, finish, perfection; craft, craftiness, cunning, cleverness, sharpness

> *Use 393; Perfection 805; Cunning 822; Easiness 823*

3 **social skill,** common sense, worldly wisdom, sophistication, sagacity, savoir-faire, savoir-vivre, finesse, tact, discretion, discrimination; grace, style, elegance, neatness; savvy [Inf]; gimmick, dodge, contrivance, trick; stratagem, tactics, use; exploitation

> *Deception 193; Wisdom 352; Elegance 527*

4 **aptitude,** talent, innate ability, inborn aptitude, inherent ability, feeling for, eye for, ear for; propensity, inclination, tendency, bent, natural bent, natural talent, faculty, endowment, instinct, gift, flair, knack, turn, genius; aptness, fitness, qualification, good head for, know-how, right stuff [Inf]

> *Tendency 513*

5 **masterpiece,** art, artistry, work of art, creation of genius, creation, chef-d'oeuvre; masterwork, *pièce de résistance* [Fr], great work, epic work, magnum opus; stroke of genius, masterstroke, *coup de maître* [Fr], tour de force, brilliance, bravura, fireworks

6 **workmanlike job,** coup, exploit, feat, feat of skill, stunt, sporting feat, clincher; collector's piece *or* item, classic; hit, smash hit

> *Action 412*

7 **skilled person,** skillful person, proficient person, expert, adept; all-rounder, jack-of-all-trades, journeyman, handyman; paragon, Renaissance man *or* woman, person of many parts; master, past master, graduate, intellectual; mastermind, sage, genius, wizard; gifted child, prodigy, wunderkind; maestro, virtuoso, bravura player, musician, first chair, prima donna, diva, prima ballerina, star

8 **prizewinner,** victor, champion, medalist, cordon bleu, blue-ribbon winner, titleholder, cupholder; belt holder, black belt, brown belt, dan; ace, top selection, picked man, lettered player, varsity player, first-stringer, first-string player; all-pro, all-American, star player, Most Valuable Player (MVP), seeded player, seed, top seed; crack shot, dead shot

> *Sports 145; Strength 516; Perfection 805*

9 **expert,** professional, practitioner, specialist, authority, doyen, learned person, intellectual, professor, teacher, scholar, pundit, guru, savant, polymath, scientist; veteran, old hand, old stager, old soldier, sea dog, shellback, practiced hand, practiced eye, knowing person; tactician, strategist; diplomat; artist, artisan, craftsman, craftswoman; technician, skilled worker, experienced hand; right person for the job, key man; consultant, adviser, planner; connoisseur, cognoscente, fancier; walk-

ing encyclopedia, smart customer, smart cookie; [Inf]: pro, brain, egghead, whiz kid

▶ *Worker 123; Advice 176; Knowledge 348; Plan 387; Cunning 822*

ADJECTIVES

10 **skillful,** skilled, able, proficient, competent, efficient, talented, gifted, good, good at; excellent, superb, top-notch, top-flight, top-level; apt, handy, adroit, dexterous, ambidextrous, deft, adept, slick, neat; agile, spry, surefooted, sure-handed, nimble, nimble-fingered; clever, quick, quick-witted, shrewd, cunning, crafty; smart, intelligent; politic, diplomatic, statesmanlike, wise, sagacious; many-sided, versatile, adaptable, flexible, ingenious, resourceful; ready, ready for anything, sound, competitive, masterful; masterly, magisterial, expert, highly qualified, accomplished, finished, perfect, first-rate, ace, crack; A one *or* A number one *or* A 1 [Inf]

▶ *Wisdom 352; Importance 799; Perfection 805*

11 **gifted,** talented, blessed with talent, of many parts, endowed, well-endowed; born for, suited for, cut out for

12 **expert,** skilled, experienced, accomplished; tried, seasoned, veteran, versed in, *au fait* [Fr]; instructed, trained, practiced, well-practiced, well-prepared; finished, passed; qualified, highly qualified, specialized, matured, proficient, up on, well up on; competent, efficient, professional, businesslike

▶ *Knowledge 348; Preparation 388*

13 **well-made,** expertly made, well-crafted, professional, workmanlike, shipshape, finished; stylish, elegant; artistic, artificial, daedal, cunning, clever, craftily contrived; deep-laid

▶ *Elegance 527*

VERBS

14 **be skillful,** excel, do well, shine, have a flair for, have a knack for, have the knack, have a gift for, show a talent for, show aptitude, have the trick of, have (just) the right touch, have an eye for, have an ear for, have one's hand in; play one's cards well, not put a foot wrong, know what one is about, know just when to stop; use skillfully, exploit, take advantage of, squeeze the last ounce out of, make hay while the sun shines, profit by; live by one's wits, get around, know all the answers, have a good head for, have one's wits about one, be wise, exercise discretion, discriminate, know what's what [Inf]

▶ *Discrimination 337; Wisdom 352; Use 393; Timeliness 659; Superiority 744*

15 **be expert,** be professional, know, know backward, know backward and forward, know all the ins and outs, have the knowledge, have experience; display one's skill, demonstrate, have the know-how; [Inf]: know one's stuff, know the ropes, know one's onions

▶ *Education 48; Knowledge 348; Showiness 404*

16 **skillfully,** ably, adroitly, dexterously, proficiently, capably, competently, efficiently; well, with skill, without fault, with aplomb, like an expert, like a master, with genius; handily, deftly, adeptly; neatly, stylishly, artistically; ingeniously, resourcefully; cleverly, shrewdly; intelligently, knowledgeably, expertly, professionally, scientifically; without fault, like a machine; naturally, as to the manner born, swimmingly

128 Unskillfulness

NOUNS

1 **unskillfulness,** lack of skill, want of skill, lack of ability, lack of proficiency; lack of professionalism, amateurism; lack of talent, no gift for, ineptitude, ineptness, inaptness, inability, impotence, incompetence, inexpertness, inefficiency, ineffectuality; lack of practice, rustiness, nonuse; ignorance, inexperience, immaturity, unreadiness, rawness, greenness, unripeness, underdevelopment; incapacity, disqualification, unfitness; pretension, quackery, charlatanism; clumsiness, awkwardness, ham-handedness, gaucherie, lubberliness, unhandiness, heavy-handedness; backwardness, slowness, unintelligence, booby prize

▶ *Ignorance 349; Folly 353; Affectation 367; Lack of Preparation 389; Nonuse 394; Powerlessness 515*

2 **bungling,** botching, bumbling, tinkering, half measures, pale imitation, travesty, noncompletion, bungle, botch, mess, shambles; bad day, off day, one of those days; poor performance, poor show *or* showing, bad job, unsatisfactory work, fluff, failure, flop, missed chance, untimeliness; dropped catch, fumble, foozle, muff, flub, miss, misfire, mishit, slice, misthrow, overthrow, bobble, mistake, error; thoughtlessness, inattention, tactlessness, indiscretion, infelicity, gaffe, faux pas; mishandling, mismanagement, misapplication, misuse, too many cooks, too many chiefs and not enough Indians; misrule, misgovernment, maladministration; misjudgment, misperception; misconduct, antics; foul-up [Inf], ballup [Inf]

▶ *Sports 145; Inattention 324; Misjudgment 342; Error 351; Misuse 395; Untimeliness 660; Incompleteness 762; Uselessness 802; Failure 846*

3 **unskilled person,** learner, apprentice, trainee, student, probationer; beginner, novice, greenhorn, tyro, raw recruit, colt, rookie, stooge, amateur, dabbler, tinker; bungler, failure, loser, bad learner, one's despair, incompetent, botcher, muffer, muff, bumbler, blunderer, blunderbuss, bungling idiot, marplot, mismanager; fumbler, lump, hulk, lubber, lout, clumsy lout, oaf, clumsy oaf, butterfingers, bull in a china shop, dolt, ass, fool, nitwit, booby, looby, slob; clown, buffoon, joke, butt, bumpkin, country bumpkin, hick, clod; scribbler, hack, ham, dauber; bad hand, poor hand; bad

shot, poor shot, no marksman; landlubber, fair-weather sailor, freshwater sailor, horse marine; imposter, quack, charlatan, mountebank; [Inf]: cowboy, nerd, dipstick, boob, swab, stumblebum, duffer, galoot, bozo, jerk, rube

> *Folly 353; Untruth 722; Disorder 766; Failure 846*

ADJECTIVES

4 **unskillful,** ungifted, untalented, talentless, unendowed, unaccomplished, unremarkable, unimpressive, unpromising, unversatile; unqualified, disqualified, unfit, inept; inapt, unable, incapable, impotent, undependable; untrained, uninstructed, unenlightened, unequipped; incompetent, inefficient, ineffectual, not up to scratch; unpractical, unadapted, like a fish out of water, unadventurous; unbusinesslike, unprofessional; unstatesmanlike, undiplomatic; impolitic, ill-considered, uninformed; stupid, dumb, silly, foolish, unwise, thoughtless, inattentive, undiscerning; wild, giddy, impulsive, scatterbrained, carefree, easygoing, happy-go-lucky, light-minded; feckless, futile, failed, unsuccessful, unacclaimed; inadequate, insufficient; dimwitted [Inf]

> *Insufficiency 98; Inattention 324; Folly 353; Inactivity 415; Disagreement 463; Powerlessness 515; Failure 846*

5 **unskilled,** raw, green, unripe, undeveloped, young, callow, not dry behind the ears, immature; inexperienced, uninitiated, wet behind the ears, in training, apprenticed, half-skilled, semiskilled; unseasoned, unprepared, unqualified, inexpert; ignorant, unversed, unconversant, untrained, uninstructed, uneducated, untaught, untutored; uneducable, unteachable, unfinished; unprofessional, nonspecialist, lay, amateurish, amateur, self-taught, self-made, autodidactic; unscientific, unsound; charlatan, quack, quackish, specious; pretentious, affected

> *Ignorance 349; Affectation 367; Lack of Preparation 389*

6 **clumsy,** awkward, gauche, gawky, gawkish, ungainly; uneasy, uncertain; boorish, churlish, discourteous, uncouth, unrefined, ill-mannered, rude, surly; stuttering, stammering, babbling, driveling; tactless, indiscreet, indiscriminating; bumbling, bungling, lubberly, maladroit, ham-handed, butterfingered, unhandy, all thumbs, one-handed, heavy-handed, heavy-footed; unsteady, unbalanced, lumbering, hulking, gangling, stumbling, shambling, wobbly-legged; stiff, rusty, unused, on the shelf [Inf]; unaccustomed, unhabituated, unpracticed, out of practice, out of training, out of kilter, off one's timing, off one's stride, off form; out of touch, losing one's touch, losing one's feet, losing it, slipping; careless, hasty, haphazard, slapdash, negligent; fumbling, groping, tentative, experimental; ungraceful, graceless, inelegant, clownish; top-heavy, lopsided, unequal, cumbersome, ponderous, clumsily

built; unmanageable, unsteerable, unwieldy; inexact, unadjusted; out of sync [Inf]

> *Speech, Spoken Language 205; Negligence 326; Experiment 335; Error 351; Nonuse 394; Unaccustomedness 398; Discourtesy 411; Inelegance 528; Size, Largeness 579; Inequality 741*

7 **bungled,** badly done, botched, messed up, foozled; mismanaged, mishandled, maladministered, misapplied; botchy, messy, faulty, imperfect; misguided, ill-advised, ill-judged, ill-timed; unhappy, infelicitous; unplanned, unprepared, ill-contrived, ill-considered, ill-devised, ill-defined, ill-prepared, half-baked, thrown together, cobbled together; crude, unpolished, rough-and-ready; inartistic, amateurish, amateur, jerry-built, homemade, do-it-yourself, artless, slapdash, superficial, perfunctory; neglected, uncompleted; [Inf]: screwed up, fouled up, fucked up, half-assed

> *Negligence 326; Lack of Preparation 389; Incompleteness 762; Imperfection 806; Naiveté 821*

VERBS

8 **be unskillful,** lack skill, lack talent, not have the skills; not know how, not know, show one's ignorance, not have a clue [Inf], go about it the wrong way, start at the wrong end, do things backward; do things halfway, do things by halves, not complete, not finish the job, tinker, paper over the cracks; burn one's fingers, put one's foot in it, catch a Tartar; mishandle, mismanage, maladminister, misconduct, misrule, misgovern, misapply, misuse, misdirect; blunder, err, make a mistake, miss one's cue, forget one's words, fluff one's lines; overact, ham it up, underact; lose one's touch, lose one's feel, lose one's cunning, lose one's skill, lose one's nerves, lose it; go rusty, get out of practice, disaccustom; fail, lose out, face disaster, come unstuck, come a cropper [Inf]

> *Fear 283; Surprise 292; Ignorance 349; Error 351; Forgetfulness 355; Unaccustomedness 398; Incompleteness 762; Failure 846*

9 **be clumsy,** blunder, fumble, bumble, flounder, stumble, trip, trip over, not look where one is going, grope; lumber, hulk, galumph; get in the way, stand in the light; stutter, stammer, muff, fluff; foozle, pull, slice, mishit, misthrow, overthrow, overshoot, overstep, play into the hands of, spill, drop, drop a catch, drop a pop-up, bobble, let fall; make a faux pas, do a bad job, do badly, bungle, botch, mess up, make a mess of, make a hash of; spoil, mar, blot, fool with, impair, meddle, miscarry, fail; [Inf]: foul up, louse up, goof *or* goof up, blow, put one's foot in it, put one's foot in one's mouth, get egg on one's face

> *Inattention 324; Experiment 335; Error 351; Activity 414; Overstepping 712; Lowering 716; Deterioration 808; Failure 846*

10 **act foolishly,** make a fool of oneself, make an ass of oneself, lose face; not know what one is about, not

know one's own business; blunder, labor in vain, waste effort, attempt the impossible; be one's own worst enemy, act in one's own worst interests, stand in one's own light, self-destruct, fall in one's own trap

11 **figurative expressions,** knock one's head against a brick wall, cut one's own throat, cut off one's nose to spite one's face, paint oneself into a corner, throw the baby out with the bathwater; quarrel with one's bread and butter, bite the hand that feeds one, kill the goose that lays the golden eggs, saw off the limb one sits on, shoot oneself in the foot; put the cart before the horse, be penny wise and pound foolish, put all one's eggs in one basket, bite off more than one can chew, have too many irons in the fire; try to put a square peg in a round hole, put new wine into old bottles; go on a fool's errand, go on a wild-goose chase, lean on a broken reed; have egg on one's face [Inf]

❯ *Folly 353; Uselessness 802; Impossibility 837*

ADVERBS

12 **unskillfully,** ineptly, incompetently, inefficiently; unprofessionally, undiplomatically; foolishly, unsuccessfully; inexpertly, amateurishly; clumsily, awkwardly; carelessly, negligently, badly, imperfectly

129 Ceramics

NOUNS

1 **ceramics,** ceramic ware, ornamental ware; pottery, art pottery, porous pottery, coarse pottery; ware, marbled ware, earthenware, creamware, blue and white ware, tin-enameled ware; translucent ceramics, porcelain, porcelain enamel; china, chinaware, crockery; glass, decorative glass, art glass, brown glass, bottle glass, lead crystal, photochromic glass

❯ *Sculpture and Engraving 144; Sign 183; Decoration 532; Hardness 542; Softness 543; Container 578*

2 **material,** clay, potter's clay *or* earth, argil, adobe, terra cotta, porcelain clay, refractory clay, lean clay, fat clay, pipe clay, marl, kaolin, china clay *or* stone, pegmatite, calcareous clay, slip, engobe, china stone, petuntze *or* petuntse, ball clay, blue ball clay; feldspar, silica, Cornish stone, flint, flint pebbles, gypsum, bone ash; grout, tile, tessera

3 **glaze,** transparent glaze, opaque white glaze, eggshell glaze, smear glaze, soft glaze, matte *or* matt glaze, semiopaque glaze, raw glaze, fritted glaze, salt glaze, colored glaze, underglaze, underglaze decoration, overglaze, overglaze decoration, hare's fur glaze; crackle, crazing, slip, body slip

4 **decoration,** transfer printing, decalcomania, handpainted decoration, gold decoration, gilded decoration; porcelain mark, earthenware mark, factory mark, monogram, seal, trademark

5 **ceramic process,** grinding, plastic mixing, blunging, ball milling, pugging, screening, magnetic separating, filter pressing, de-airing, wedging, throwing, wheel throwing, slip casting, luting, collaring, steaming, smoking, drying, glazing, firing, glaze firing, hard fir-

CERAMICS

agateware	Coalport	ironstone *or*	ovenware	slipware
Albion ware	Crabstock ware	ironstone china	Palissy ware	soft-paste
Alcora ware	crackleware	istoriato ware	Parian porcelain	porcelain
Aller Vale pottery	crouchware	Jackfield ware	Pennsylvania Dutch	Spode
Arita ware	Crown Derby	jasper *or* jasperware	or German ware	spongeware
Arretine ware *or*	porcelain	Kakiemon ware	porcelain	Staffordshire ware
terra sigillata	Dedham pottery	Kinkozan ware	queen's ware	Steingut
basaltware *or* basalts	delft *or* delftware	Kubachi ware	redware	stoneware
Belleek ware	Derby porcelain	Kutani porcelain	refractory ware	Sung ware
Berlin ware	Doulton ware	Leeds pottery	Rockingham	Talavera ware
biscuit *or* bisque ware	Dresden china	Limoges *or* Limoges	ware	T'ang ware
blackware *or* black	earthenware	ware	Rookwood pottery	terra sigillata *or*
stoneware	eggshell porcelain	Lowestoft ware	Royal Copenhagen	Arretine ware
bone china	enamel *or*	lusterware	porcelain	Tiffany glass
Bonnin and Morris	enamelware	majolica	Royal Doulton	Tiger ware
porcelain	faience	Meissen ware	porcelain	ting ware
Castleford ware	glassware	Mennecy ware	Royal Worcester	Toft ware
Castor ware	glazed ware	mezza-majolica	porcelain	Tucker porcelain
champlevé	gombroon	Ming ware	Rozane art ware	tulip ware
Chantilly ware	hard paste porcelain	Nabeshima ware	salt-glazed ware	Vincennes ware
Chelsea porcelain	Hirado ware	Nanking ware	Samian ware	Wedgwood *or*
china *or* chinaware	Hispano-Moresque	Nautilus ware	Satsuma porcelain	Wedgwood ware
Ch'ing porcelain	ware	Neideviller ware	Seto ware	whiteware
clayware	Hizen porcelain	Old Worcester	Sèvres *or* Sèvres	Worcester
cloisonné	Imari ware	ware	porcelain	porcelain

ing, soft firing, biscuit *or* bisque firing, ghost firing, raku firing, soaking, fettling, slab method, glassworking, glassblowing

6 **industrial ceramics,** porcelain insulation, electrical porcelain; brick, sun-dried brick, adobe, firebrick, refractory brick, mud brick; cement, natural cement, Portland cement, hydraulic cement, concrete; drain tile, hollow tile, architectural tile, quarry tile, roofing tile, pantile, wall tile, floor tile; china plumbing ware, chemical porcelain; glass, crystallized glass, devitrified glass, structural glass, window glass, plate glass, safety glass, laminated glass, optical glass, photosensitive glass, glass fiber, foam glass, light bulb, fluorescent tube, electronic tube, lens

7 **ceramist** *or* **ceramicist,** potter, turner, firer, glazer, pyroglazer, china decorator, china painter, tiler, tile painter, majolica painter, enameler *or* enamelist, glassworker, glassblower

8 **ceramic workshop and tools,** potter's workplace, pottery, pottery factory; wheel, potter's wheel, slow wheel, hand-turned wheel, kick wheel, pedal wheel, power wheel, electrical wheel; jigger, blunger, dolly *or* dolly peg, pug, pug mill; kiln, glaze kiln, acid kiln, brick kiln, cement kiln, enamel kiln, muffle kiln, limekiln, bottle kiln, beehive kiln, tunnel kiln, downdrawn kiln, raku kiln, reverberatory, reverberatory kiln; kiln furniture: ribs, oven, stove, furnace, open hearth, converter, smelter, ore roaster, pyrometer, pyrometric cone, Seger cone, mixing tank, filter press, filter cloth
▶ *Workplace 124*

ADJECTIVES

9 **ceramic,** enameled, enameling, tin-enameled, stanniferous, ornamental, glazed, unglazed, underglazed, overglazed, translucent, fired, soft-paste, soft, hardpaste, hard, fine, encaustic, refractory, transparent, opaque, matte *or* matt, semiopaque, hand-painted, gilded, blunged, pugging, screened, hand-turned, wedged, thrown, down-drawn, reverberatory, pyrometric(al), industrial, bricking, sun-dried, crystallized, devitrified, optical, photosensitive, electronic

VERBS

10 **make ceramics,** pot, mold, mold clay, grind, mix, blunge, pug, screen filter, de-air, lute, shape, cast, wedge, throw, throw a pot, turn a pot, hand-turn, jigger, roll a slab, dry, fire, bake glaze, pyroglaze, glaze-fire, hard-fire, soft-fire, ghost-fire, draw a kiln, underglaze, overglaze, tin-glaze, fettle, enamel, tin-enamel, decorate, paint, hand-paint, gild, transfer a decal, mark, monogram, seal, tile, insulate, brick, cement, concrete, glass, devitrify, crystallize, laminate

ADVERBS

11 **ornamentally,** translucently, encaustically, refractorily, transparently, opaquely, semiopaquely, by hand, pyrometrically, optically

130 Fabrics and Fabric Handling

NOUNS

1 **fabric,** cloth, woven cloth, textile, material, drapery, rag; natural fabric, synthetic fabric, synthetic; woven fabric *or* cloth, knitted fabric, soft furnishing, print, screen print; carpet, carpeting, broadcloth, broadloom; tartan, suiting, crepe, crepon, voile, jersey, taffeta, lace, tissue, dotted swiss
▶ *Materials 104*

2 **fiber,** thread, filament, yarn, worsted, lisle, crewel, denier; natural fiber, synthetic fiber, braided fiber, monofilament, modacrylic, polyester, rayon, ramie, spandex, nylon, olefin, viscose, acetate, acrylic fiber; Acrilan™, Dacron™, Orlon™

3 **dry goods,** soft goods, textiles, fabric, linens, napery, knitwear, clothing; men's wear, ladies' wear, children's wear, infants' wear, outerwear, sportswear, leatherware; sporting goods, leather goods

4 **spinning,** twining, intertwining, braiding, interbraiding, braid, plaiting, plait, extrusion, webbing

5 **sewing,** mending, basting, darning, seaming, hemming, tailoring; needlework, smocking, gathering, quilting, stitching, stitchery, fancywork, embroidery, crewelwork, cross-stitching, tatting, lacemaking, lacework; suture, knotting
▶ *Union 752*

6 **weaving,** weave, plain weave, twill weave, leno weave, weft, warp, woof [Brit], selvage *or* selvedge, brocade; web, webbing, lace, lacing, crisscross, wreathing, rug braiding, hooking, pleaching *or* plashing, texture, nap, pattern, knit, tatting, macramé, knot, twist; interlacing, interweaving
▶ *Interweaving 609*

7 **knitting,** knit, stitch; plain stitch, purl stitch, garter stitch, stockinette *or* stockinette stitch, cable stitch, moss stitch, seed stitch, ribbing, interlock stitch, crochet, chain stitch, machine knitting
▶ *Clothing 100; Fashion 536*

8 **dye,** colorant, dyestuff, natural dye, vegetable dye, mineral dye, synthetic dye, chemical dye, acid dye, basic dye, vat dye, direct dye; tint, shade, stain; mordant

9 **dyeing,** coloring, staining, patterning, printing, screen printing, tie-dyeing, batik, ikat

10 **fabric treatment,** cleaning, washing, laundering, dry cleaning, ironing, pressing, stain removal, bleaching; flameproofing, preshrinking, wrinkleproofing, waterproofing, mothproofing

11 **fabric handler,** spinner, sewer, needleworker, seamstress, dressmaker, tailor, clothing maker, garment-maker, embroiderer, lace maker, weaver; launderer, laundress, dry cleaner

12 **fabric-handling tool,** needle, thimble, threader,

pin, spool, gauge, sewing machine, pattern, frame, embroidery hoop; knitting needle, knitting machine, stitch holder, crochet hook; loom, Jacquard loom, hand loom, machine loom, latchet hook; extruder, shuttle, bobbin, spinning wheel, spinning mule, spinning jenny, spinner, spinerette; dyestuff, dyewood; washer, washing machine, dryer, iron, flatiron, press, mangle

ADJECTIVES

13 **spun,** twisted, braided, twined, plaited, extrudable, extruded

14 **sewn,** stitched, tailored, embroidered, smocked, laced, knotted

15 **woven,** knitted, hooked, braided; cloth, fabric, fine, sheer, coarse, netted, fine-weave, open-weave, ikat-weave; twill, felted, brushed, napped, looped, uncut, cut

16 **treated,** washed, prewashed, stonewashed, bleached, dry-cleaned; dyed, colored, dyed-in-the-wool, dyed-in-the-yarn, tie-dyed; coated, flameproof, preshrunk, waterproof *or* waterproofed, showerproof *or* shower-

proofed, mothproof *or* mothproofed, drip-dry, crease-resistant

VERBS

17 **spin,** twist, braid, extrude

18 **sew,** stitch, mend, tailor, crochet, baste, darn, embroider, lace, knot

19 **knit,** purl, crochet, hook, tat

20 **weave,** plait, felt, mat, brush, nap, interweave, lace

21 **treat,** wash, bleach, stonewash, dry-clean, dye, tinge, tie-dye, flameproof, preshrink, waterproof, shower-proof, mothproof

131 Woodworking

NOUNS

1 **woodworking,** woodwork, carpentry, joinery, cabinetmaking, cabinetry; timberwork, woodcraft, carving, woodcarving, whittling, wood sculpting, wood sculpture, wood turning; treen, treenware, woodenware; lignography, wood burning, pyrography, pyrograph, pyrogravure, xylopyrography, xylography, xy-

---

FABRICS AND FIBERS

alpaca	chintz	Georgette crepe	mackinaw	plaid	suede *or* suede
angora	cord	gingham	mackintosh	plush	leather
astrakhan	corduroy	gossamer	madras	pongee	surah
baize	cotton	grenadine	malines *or*	poplin	swansdown
balbriggan	crash	grogram	maline	prunella	swanskin
barathea	crepe de Chine	grosgrain	marquisette	Qiana™	tabaret
batiste	cretonne	gunny	marseilles	rep	tabby
brocade	crinoline	haircloth	matting	russet	tapestry
brocatel *or*	damask	Harris tweed	melton	sackcloth	tarpaulin
brocatelle	denim	herringbone	merino	sacking	terry
buckram	dimity	hessian	messaline	samite	ticking *or* tick
bunting	doeskin	homespun	mohair	sarcenet *or*	toile
burlap	Donegal tweed	honan	moiré	sarsenet *or*	toweling
calico	drill	hopsack	moleskin	sarsnet	tricot
cambric	drugget	horsehair	moquette	sateen	tricotine
camel hair *or*	duck	huckaback *or*	*mousseline de*	satin	tulle
camel's hair	duffel	huck	*laine* [Fr]	say	tussah *or* tussore
Canton crepe	dungaree	jacquard *or*	*mousseline de*	scrim	tweed
canvas	duvetyn *or*	jacquard	*soie* [Fr]	seersucker	twill
cashmere *or*	duvetyne *or*	weave	muslin	serge	velour *or* velours
Kashmir	duvetine	jean	nainsook	shalloon	velure
cassimere *or*	faille	jersey	nankeen	shantung	velvet
casimere *or*	felt	jute	net	sharkskin	velveteen
casimire	flannel	khaddar *or* khadi	netting	sheer	vicuna
castor	flannelet *or*	khaki	oilskin	shoddy	vinyon
challis	flannelette	lamé	organdy *or*	shot silk	webbing
chambray	fleece	lawn	organdie	silk	wool
cheesecloth	foulard	leatherette	organza	silkaline *or*	worsted wool
chenille	frieze	leno	paisley	silkoline *or*	
cheviot	fustian	linen	panne velvet	silkolene	
chiffon	gabardine *or*	linsey-woolsey	percale	stamin	
chinchilla	gaberdine	loden	percaline	stockinette *or*	
chino	gauze	longcloth	piqué	stockinet	

---

lograph, woodcut, cut, woodcut illustration, woodblock, woodblock printing, woodprint, relief printing, wood engraving

> *Furniture 101; Painting and Drawing 143; Sculpture and Engraving 144*

2 **decorative woodwork,** wood inlay, certosina work, intarsia, horn inlay, mother-of-pearl inlay, tortoiseshell inlay, brass inlay, metal inlay, silver inlay, goodsheet inlay, true inlay, buhl *or* boule *or* boulle, boulework; marquetry, floral marquetry, seaweed marquetry, oysterwood marquetry, oyster pieces, brass on shell, première partie, shell on brass, contre-partie, parquetry

> *Decoration 532; Nearness 586; Notch 636; Furrow 638*

3 **wood,** timber, lumber, softwood, hardwood, heartwood, sapwood; beam, rafter, joist, board, boarding, plank, planking, deal, two-by-four, slab, puncheon, slat, splat, stick, stave, pole, post, lath, lathing, lathwork, timbering, timberwood, logging; sheeting, paneling, panelboard, panelwork, plywood, sheathing, sheathing board; siding, weatherboard, clapboard, hardboard, blockboard, chipboard, shingle, shake, log, cordwood; woodgrain, wood texture, end-grain wood

> *Trees 43; Texture 552; Breadth 592*

4 **woodworker,** carpenter, joiner, cabinetmaker, timberjack, lumberjack, logger, sawyer, cooper, woodcrafter, carver, woodcarver, wood sculptor, turner, woodturner, pyrographer, xylopyrographer, xylographer, woodcutter, wood engraver, form engraver, marquetry worker

> *Worker 123; Sculpture and Engraving 144*

5 **carpenter's term,** bevel, joint, miter, miter joint, timber joint, housed joint, lap joint, fish joint, scarf joint, flitched joint, tusk tenon joint, bird's-mouth joint, tenon, mortise, mortise and tenon, dovetailing, cogging, trimming, framing, joist, trimmed joist, strut, strutting, herringbone strutting, truss, king-post truss, queen-post truss, lath, stud

> *Structure 551; Union 752; Adhesion 755*

6 **woodworking tool,** lathe, saw, tenon saw, ripsaw, crosscut saw, panel saw, bandsaw, jigsaw, circular saw, power-driven saw, radial-arm saw; plane, smoothing plane, jack plane, planer *or* surfacer; drawknife *or* drawshave, spokeshave, adz, jointer, shaper, router; sander, belt sander, disk sander, spindle sander; mortiser, hollow-chisel mortiser, chainsaw mortiser; tenoner, single tenoner, double tenoner, boring machine, borer, drill, wood-engraving tool, chisel, burin, graver, tint tool, velo, lamina, sandpaper

> *Tool 103*

ADJECTIVES

7 **woodcrafted,** carved, woodcarved, whittled, woodsculpted, wood-turned, wood-burned, xylographic(al), xylopyrographic(al), pyrographic(al), woodcut, woodblocked, woodprinted, wood-engraved

8 **joined,** built, jointed, mitered, timbered, logged, housed, flitched, mortised, dovetailed, cogged, trimmed, framed, joisted, herringbone, beamed, boarded, two-by-four, slatted

VERBS

9 **work wood,** woodwork, laminate, veneer, lacquer, paint, inlay, carve, whittle, sculpt wood, turn wood, engrave wood

10 **carpenter,** miter, mortise, dovetail, cog, trim, frame, joist, strut, truss, lathe, saw, cut, crosscut, rip, drill, screw, plane, shape, sand tenon, bore, chisel, fit a beam, raise a rafter, board, plank, post, slat, lath, timber, sheet, panel, shingle

132 Photography

NOUNS

1 **photography,** picture taking, color photography, black-and-white photography

2 **photographic specialties,** aerial photography, astrophotography, landscape photography, architectural photography, underwater photography, wildlife photography, documentary photography; photojournalism, sports photography, fashion photography, studio photography, portraiture, still-life photography; time-lapse photography, telephotography, macrophotography, microphotography, flash photography, infrared photography; cinematography, motion-picture photography; stereophotography, holography, phototopography, radiography

3 **photograph,** photo, picture, image, snapshot, snap, shot, candid, take; black and white, monotone, halftone; color photograph, transparency, slide, positive reproduction; picture story, photonovel, photo biography; radiograph, X ray, shadowgraph; photograph album, Polaroid™

4 **older photograph,** daguerreotype, ferrotype *or* tintype, ambrotype, calotype *or* Talbotype, collotype *or* albertype *or* artotype *or* heliotype

5 **portrait,** closeup, pinup, glossy; group photograph, group shot, team photo, class photo, rogues' gallery; landscape, cloudscape, seascape; silhouette, action shot, studio photograph, still life, abstract; split image, multiple image, action sequence, photomontage, photomural; [Inf]: mug shot, beefcake, cheesecake

6 **photoreproduction,** photocopying, Xerography, photogrammetry, photogravure, photolithography, photointaglio; photocopy, photostat, stat [Inf]; microfilm, microfiche, microphotograph, microcopy

> *Reproduction 21; Imitation 736*

7 **stereoscopic image,** holographic image, hologram *or* holograph, color hologram, reflection hologram

8 **film,** roll film, black-and-white film, color film, panchromatic film, chromogenic film, Polaroid™ film; photographic plate, negative, color negative; movie

film, Super-8, videotape; X-ray film, infrared film; film plane, film advance, film rewind, spool, take-up spool *or* reel, reel, cassette, cartridge

9 emulsion, silver halide, gelatin, backing, latent image

10 camera, single-lens reflex (SLR), twin-lens reflex (TLR), large-format camera, 35mm camera; automatic camera, compact camera, miniature camera, disposable camera, photo booth, Instamatic™, Polaroid™; plate camera, camera obscura, pinhole camera; video camera, camcorder, TV camera, security camera, motion-picture camera, movie camera; camera equipment, camera case, film case, camera strap, tripod, flash attachment

11 lens, lens system, standard *or* normal lens; fixed-focus lens, autofocus lens, long-focus lens, telephoto lens, mirror lens, reflex lens, zoom lens, short- *or* wide-angle zoom, mid-range zoom, telephoto zoom, wide-angle lens, ultrawide lens, shift lens, fisheye lens, macro lens; prism, pentaprism; lens mount, lens attachment, lens filter, lens cap, lens cover, lens hood

12 exposure equipment, shutter, shutter release, cable release, shutter speed, B setting, self-timer, motor drive; aperture, diaphragm, iris diaphragm, aperture setting, f-stop *or* f stop, f-number *or* f number; viewfinder, range finder; light meter, through-the-lens (TTL) meter, CdS meter, selenium meter, spot meter; focusing screen, depth of focus; autoexposure, aperture priority, shutter priority

13 flash, flashtube, flashbulb, flashcube, electronic flash; synchronized flash, flashgun, hot shoe, slave unit

14 filter, lens filter, color-balancing filter, color-correcting *or* compensating filter, UV *or* haze filter, skylight filter, polarizing (PL) filter, neutral-density (ND) filter, diffusing filter

15 exposure, fine grain, coarse grain, graininess; film speed, fast film, slow film, sensitivity, photosensitivity, ISO rating, ASA number, DIN number, DX code; hypersensitization, photographic density, transmission density, opacity, characteristic curve, Hurter-Driffield (H-D) curve, dynamic range; gamma, reciprocity failure, saturation level, fog level

16 lighting, light source, daylight, natural light, ambient light, white light, soft light, hard light, backlighting, frontlighting, textured lighting, artificial lighting, tungsten lighting, studio lighting; studio flash, spotlight *or* spot [Inf], photoflood, floodlight, bounced light, fill-in light; diffuser, reflector; color temperature, guide number

17 composition, framing, perspective, color balance, contrast; shadows, highlights, lowlights, gray scale, tonal range, high key, low key; angle of view, sharpness, focus, depth of field, focal length, focal point, hyperfocal distance, infinity, vanishing point; image blur, acutance, overexposure, underexposure, color cast, flare, fog, red-eye; closeup shot, medium shot, long shot

18 framing, cropping, bracketing, soft focusing, differential focusing, controlled blur; panning, pulling, pushing *or* uprating, solarization

19 development, processing, film processing, color processing, developing

20 printing, enlarging; print, color print, contact print, contact sheet, enlargement, blowup, reprint; photographic paper, bromide paper; diapositive, sepia print, lantern slide, silver print, gum print, sun print, enprint; printing paper, gloss finish, matte *or* matt finish, semimatte *or* semimatt finish

21 darkroom equipment, enlarger, negative carrier, safelight, timer, spool, reel, tub, sink, tray, thermometer, dryer; solution, developer, acid stop, stop bath *or* shortstop bath, clearing agent, hypo, fixing solution, fixer, photoflo

22 viewer, slide viewer, projector, slide projector, overhead projector, magic lantern, slide carrier, screen, stereopticon

23 photographer, daguerreotypist, photojournalist, press photographer, paparazzo; cameraperson, cameraman, camerawoman, cinematographer; [Inf]: lensman, shooter, shutterbug, photog

▶ *Motion Pictures 137*

ADJECTIVES

24 photographic, photogenic, picturesome; camera-shy, photosensitive

25 exposed, overexposed, underexposed, dark, light; grainy, flat, contrasty, saturated

VERBS

26 photograph, shoot, take a photograph *or* photo *or* picture, snap a picture; film, video

27 compose a photograph, focus, stop down, open up, zoom in, zoom out, pan, expose, light

28 develop, process, print, enlarge, blow up, reduce, project

ADVERBS

29 photographically, photogenically

The Arts

133 Art

NOUNS

1 **visual arts,** art, the arts, fine arts, applied arts,
beaux arts, graphic arts, decorative arts, decoration,
design, arts of design, plastic art, commercial art, industrial design, industrial art, kinetic art

2 **craft,** handicraft, arts and crafts, painting, drawing, illustration, sculpture, engraving, etching, calligraphy,
batik, printmaking, screen printing, silkscreening, embroidery, tapestry, woodcarving, metalwork, enameling, ceramics, mosaics, glassmaking, stained glass, photography, lithography
 ▶ *Ceramics 129; Fabrics and Fabric Handling 130; Photography 132; Painting and Drawing 143; Sculpture
and Engraving 144*

3 **artistry,** art, artistic skill, artistic flair, talent, genius,
mastery, invention, artistic invention, artistic technique, artistic quality, artistic taste, virtu, connoisseurship, craftsmanship, artisanship, artistic temperament; [Inf]: artiness, artsy-craftiness, artsy-fartsiness
 ▶ *Skillfulness 127; Idea 327; Discrimination 337; Refinement 534; Originality 737*

4 **work of art,** artwork, work, objet d'art, art object,
artistic production *or* creation, composition, design,
study, piece, masterpiece, masterwork, chef-d'oeuvre,
article *or* object *or* piece of virtu, museum piece, old
master

5 **picture,** likeness, image, representation, illustration,
painting, drawing, photograph, engraving, miniature,
tableau, illumination, mosaic, tapestry, stained-glass
window; reproduction, copy; plate, print, color print,
block print, photoprint, photogravure; woodcut,
aquatint, poster, picture postcard, montage, photomontage, collage, brass-rubbing, frottage
 ▶ *Photography 132; Painting and Drawing 143; Sculpture and Engraving 144; Representation 187; Imitation
736*

6 **visual artist,** artist, graphic artist, designer, commercial artist, industrial artist, industrial designer, craftsman, craftswoman, artisan, painter, colorist, dauber;
drawer, draftsman, draftswoman, sketcher, limner, delineator, illustrator, copyist, illuminator, miniaturist,
poster artist, cartoonist, political cartoonist, caricaturist, animator, comic-strip artist, doodler; enameler,
enamelist, ceramist, potter, photographer, sculptor,
lithographer; fashion artist, architectural artist; master,
old master, modern master, academician
 ▶ *Ceramics 129; Painting and Drawing 143; Sculpture
and Engraving 144; Imagination 360; Fashion 536;
Originality 737*

ADJECTIVES

7 **artistic,** painterly, imaginative, creative, illustrative,
stylized, decorative, ornamental, picturesque, aesthetic,
tasteful, beautiful, scenic, statuesque; well-arranged,
well-composed; art-minded, art-conscious; [Inf]: arty,
artsy-craftsy, artsy-fartsy
 ▶ *Imagination 360; Beauty 529*

8 **pictorial,** graphic, pictographic, calligraphic, geometric, linear, foreshortened, optical, illusionistic, atmospheric, photographic, iconic, mosaic

VERBS

9 **design,** create, visualize, put on paper, lay out, compose, plan, arrange, group, balance, foreshorten; paint,
draw, sculpt, engrave, silkscreen, photograph
 ▶ *Painting and Drawing 143; Sculpture and Engraving
144; Vision 242; Plan 387; Symmetry 626; Originality
737; Arrangement 767*

ADVERBS

10 **artistically,** imaginatively, creatively, conceptually, il-

abstract expressionism
Abstraction-Création
academic art
action painting
Aegean art
aesthetic movement
Alexandrian school
American scene painting
analytic cubism
Ancients
anti-art
archaicism or retardataire
art brut
art deco
arte povera
arte informel
art nouveau
Arts and Crafts movement
Ashcan school
automatism
avant-garde
Bambocciade
barbaric art
Barbizon school
baroque
Bauhaus
Biedermeier
Blaue Reiter
body art
Brücke
Byzantine art
Carolingian art
Celtic art
classicism

Cobra group
color-field painting
conceptual art
concrete art
constructivism or Tatlinism
Coptic art
cubism
Dada
de Stijl
divisionism
early Christian art
earth art
eclecticism
Eight, the
environment art
Etruscan art
expressionism
Fascist aesthetic movement
fauvism or Les Fauves
figurative art
fin-de-siècle art
Florentine school
fluxus
folk art
funk art
futurism
genre painting
geometric art
Germanic art
Gesamtkunstwerke
Glasgow school
Gothic art
graffiti art
grand style or grand manner

Groupe de Recherche d'Art Visuel (GRAV)
Group Zero
Gutai group
Harlem Renaissance
Hellenistic art
Hispano-Moresque art
history painting
Hudson River school
impressionism
International Gothic or International style
intimism
Jugendstil
junk art
kinetic art
kitsch
lettrism
luminism
lyrical abstraction
magic realism
mannerism
media art
metaphysical art
minimal art
modernism
mosan
Nabis
naive art
narrative art
naturalism
Nazarenes
neoclassicism
neoexpressionism
neoimpressionism

neoplasticism
neoromanticism
Neue Sachlichkeit
new objectivity
new realism or nouveau realisme
New York school
nonobjective art
nonrepresentational art
Northern Renaissance art
Novembergruppe
op art
orphism or Orphic cubism or Section d'Or
"outsider" art
Painters Eleven
Paris, school of
perceptual abstraction
performance art
photorealism
Plasticiens
pleinairism
pointillism
pop art
postimpressionism
postmodernism
post-painterly abstraction
precise realism
precisionism
pre-Columbian art
prehistorical art
Pre-Raphaelite Brotherhood

primitive art
primitivism
process art
purism
rayonism
realism
regionalism
representational art
Rocky Mountain school
rococo art
Romanesque art
romanticism
Ruralists, Brotherhood of
Scottish Colorists
serial art
Seven, Group of
situationism
socialist realism
social realism
soft style
superrealism
suprematism
surrealism
symbolism
synchromism
synthetic cubism
synthetism
systemic painting
tachisme
tenebrists
Unit One
Vingt, Les
vorticism
Wanderers
World of Art group

---

lustratively, decoratively, picturesquely, aesthetically, scenically, atmospherically

11 **pictorially,** visually, graphically, optically, sculpturally, photographically, geometrically, figuratively, symbolically

134 Architecture

No person who is not a great sculptor or painter can be an architect. If he is not a sculptor or painter, he can only be a builder. — JOHN RUSKIN

I call architecture frozen music.
— JOHANN WOLFGANG VON GOETHE

NOUNS

1 **architecture,** building design, building style, archi-

tectonics, tectonics, architectural engineering; rendering, drawing, perspective

2 **architectural types,** civic, domestic, governmental, industrial, landscape, military, recreational, religious
❯ *Horticulture 17; Worship 83*

3 **architect,** building designer, architectural engineer, master builder; civil architect, domestic architect, industrial architect, *etc.*

4 **architectural structure,** building, structure, erection, edifice, pile; cottage, house, church, cathedral, synagogue, mosque, temple, castle, apartment house, condominium, high-rise, skyscraper; architectural monstrosity, eyesore
❯ *Habitat 60; Structure 551*

5 **arch,** arcade, arcuation; arch types: basket, catenary, centered, corbel, crocket, depressed, Dutch, elliptical, false, hanse *or* haunch, horseshoe, inverted, lancet,

Norman, ogee, ogive, parabolic, raking, rampant, rounded, rowlock, segmental, semicircular, shouldered, skew, stilted, strainer

6 **column,** support, pillar, post, pier, pilaster; column types *or* orders: Doric, Tuscan, Ionic, Corinthian, Composite; columniation, intercolumniation, colonnade, peristyle

7 **roof,** covering, shelter, top of the house; roof types: barrel, flat, gable, gambrel, geodesic *or* geodesic dome, hammer-beam, hip *or* hipped, imbricated *or* imbricate, lean-to, mansard, pendentive *or* pendentive dome,

pitched *or* pitch, saddle, saucer dome

8 **vault,** vaulting; vault types: barrel *or* tunnel, conical, domical, fan, groin, intersecting, lierne, parabolic, pendant, rib, quadripartite, segmental, shell, wagon

9 **wall,** divider, separator, support, screen; wall types: curtain, cheek, load-bearing, nonbearing

▶ *Support 605*

10 **window,** casement, sash, opening, glass, outlook, fenestration; window types: bay, dormer, French, lancet, lunette, oriel, Palladian, picture, transom

▶ *Vision 242; Transparency 249*

ARCHITECTURAL ELEMENTS, FEATURES, DECORATIONS

abacus	blind arcade	diaper	gorgerin	patera	skylight
abutment	blindstory	die	groin	patio	spandrel
acanthus	boss	dogtooth	guilloche	patio door	splay
accolade	buttress	ornament	gutta	pavilion	springer
acroterium	calotte	dome	half round	peardrop	squinch
ancon	canephora *or*	door	headwork	pearl molding	staircase
annulet	canephoros	drip	helix	pediment	strigil
anta	cantilever	dripstone	hood mold	pendant	string *or* stringer
antefix	capital	drop	hypophyge	peristyle	stringcourse
anthemion	capstone	drop ornament	imbrex	perron	stucco
apophyge	cartouche	Dutch door	impost	pier	table
apron	caryatid	echinus	intrados	pilaster	tablet flower
arabesque	cavetto	egg and dart *or*	jamb	podium	taenia *or* tenia
arcade	ceiling	egg and tongue	joist	poppyhead	tailpiece
arch	cella *or* naos	*or* egg and	keel	porch	talon molding
architrave	chamfer	anchor	key banding	portico	tambour *or*
archivolt	chaplet	entablature	keystone	propylaeum	drum
astragal	chevron	epistyle	label	prostyle	telamon
atlas (pl.	Christian door	extrados	lantern	pulvinatus	term *or* terminal
atlantes)	coffering	fanlight *or*	leaf	putto (pl. putti)	*or* terminus
attic	colonette	sunburst	lierne rib	quadriga	tooth ornament
baguette *or*	column	fantail	linenfold	quarter round	torus
bagnette	conch *or* concha	fanwork	lintel	quatrefoil	tower
balconet	congé *or* congee	fascia	list, listel	quirk	transom
balcony	coping stone *or*	fenestra	loggia	quirk bead *or*	trefoil
baldachin	copestone	festoon *or* swag	louver	flush bead	triglyph
ballflower	corbel	fillet	lozenge	quoin *or* coign	trumeau
baluster	cordon	finial	lunette	rafter	truss
balustrade	cornerstone	fleur-de-lis	medallion	reed, reeding	tympanum *or*
band	cornice	floor	metope	reglet	tympan
bandelet *or*	corona	flute, fluting	modillion	regula	verge
bandlet	cove	flying buttress	module	relief	vestibule
banderole *or*	crenelation	foil	molding	repoussé	vignette
bannerol	crest, cresting	foliation	mullion	respond	Vitruvian scroll
bargeboard *or*	crocket	French door	mutule	reveal	*or* running dog
vergeboard	crown	fret	nailhead	rib	volute
bas-relief *or*	cupola	frieze	nebulé *or* nebuly	rinceau	voussoir
basso-relievo	cusp	frontispiece	molding	roof	wall
bay leaf garland	cyma	gable	neck, necking	rosette	wave molding
bead	cyma recta,	gableboard	ogee	rotunda	window
bead and reel	cyma reversa	gadroon *or*	ogive	rustic work	wreath
beakhead	cymatium	godroon	ovolo	scallop	zigzag molding
bezant *or* besant	dado	gargoyle	pace	scotia	
or byzant	dentil	garland	parapet	scrollwork	
billet	diamond fret	gazebo	parquetry	shafting	

Anglo-Saxon architecture
art deco
art nouveau
baroque
Bauhaus
Beaux-Arts architecture
brutalism
Byzantine architecture
Byzantine Revival
Carolingian architecture
Chicago School
Chinese architecture
churrigueresque architecture
cinquecento architecture
classical architecture
Classical Revival
colonial architecture
Colonial Revival
Cyclopean construction
Decorated style
de Stijl
early American architecture
early Christian architecture
early English style
Edwardian style
Egyptian architecture
Elizabethan architecture
Empire style
English architecture

Etruscan architecture
flamboyant style
folk Victorian style
François Premier style
Frankish style
French architecture
French colonial style
functionalism
Georgian architecture
German architecture
gingerbread style
Gothic architecture
Gothic Revival
Greek architecture
Henri Deux style
Henri Quatre style
High Renaissance style
Hispano-Moresque
    architecture
Hittite architecture
Incan architecture
Indian architecture
International Gothic or
    International style
Islamic architecture
Italian architecture
Italianate architecture
Italian Renaissance style
Jacobean architecture

Japanese architecture
Jugendstil
Louis Quatorze style
Louis Quinze style
Louis Seize style
Louis Treize style
mannerism
Mayan architecture
medieval architecture
Mesopotamian architecture
Minoan architecture
mission architecture
modernism
Moorish architecture
Mozarabic style
Mudéjar style
Muslim or Saracenic
    architecture
Mycenaean architecture
neoclassicism
Neo-Gothic architecture
New Brutalism
New England colonial
    architecture
Norman architecture
octagon style
Ottonian architecture
Palladianism
Palladian Revival

Parthian architecture
perpendicular or rectilinear
    style
Persian architecture
postmodernism
Prairie style
Pueblo Revival
quattrocento architecture
Queen Anne style
Régence style
Regency style
Renaissance architecture
Richardsonian Romanesque
    style
rococo
Roman architecture
Romanesque architecture
Romanesque Revival
Sassanian architecture
Shingle style
Southern colonial style
Spanish architecture
Stick style
Stuart architecture
transitional style
Tudor architecture
vernacular architecture
Victorian architecture

11 **church architecture,** cruciform church, cuneiform church, basilica, hall church, Greek cross plan, Latin cross plan; aisle, ambulatory, apse, baptistery or baptistry, chancel, chapel, chevet, choir, clerestory or clearstory, conch, confessional, crossing, crypt, dome, flèche, galilee porch, Lady chapel, liturgical east end, narthex, nave, pew, rood screen, rose window, sanctuary, sedilia, spire, squint, steeple, tower, transept, tribune, triforium, vestibule, westwork
▶ *Worship 83; Decoration 532*

ADJECTIVES

12 **architectural,** architectonic, tectonic, designed, edificial; arched, arcuated, arcuate, rounded; columned, columnated, columnar, supported, pillared, buttressed; roofed, covered, sheltered; structured, formed, erected, built; decorated, ornamented, ornamental

VERBS

13 **be an architect,** design, draw blueprints, render; build, construct, structure, erect, fabricate, package; select materials, decorate, ornament
▶ *Representation 187; Decoration 532; Structure 551*

ADVERBS

14 **architecturally,** architectonically, tectonically, constructionally, structurally, by design, ornamentally, decoratively

135   Dance and Ballet

On with the dance! let joy be unconfined; / No sleep till morn, when Youth and Pleasure meet / To chase the glowing Hours with flying feet. — LORD BYRON

NOUNS

1 **dance,** dancing, promenade, formal dance, cotillion or cotillon; ball, masked ball, masquerade, costume ball, fancy-dress ball; tea dance [Brit], dinner dance; mixer, disco dance; barn dance, square dance, country dance, hoedown, eurhythmics; ballet, modern dance; dance drama; prom, formal; [Inf]: hop, shindig, knees-up [Brit]
▶ *Drama and Theater 136*

2 **ballet,** ballet dancing, classical ballet, modern ballet, Russian ballet, romantic ballet, toe dance; choreography

3 **dance hall,** ballroom, discotheque, disco, dance floor, casino, nightclub; dance band, big band, combo [Inf]

4 **dancer,** classical dancer, soft-shoe dancer, tap-dancer, clog dancer, disco dancer, go-go dancer, can-can dancer, high-kicker, waltzer, foxtrotter, shuffler, jiver, jitterbug, *etc.*; hoofer, chorus boy, chorus girl, chorine,

aerobic dancing	folk dancing	round dancing
ballet dancing	go-go dancing	shuffle dancing
ballroom dancing	interpretive	slam dancing
belly dancing	dancing	soft-shoe
break dancing	jazz dancing	dancing
clog dancing	jitterbugging	square dancing
country dancing	line dancing	stepdancing
dirty dancing	marathon dancing	sword dancing
disco dancing	modern dancing	tap-dancing
fan dancing	morris dancing	taxi dancing
flamenco	ritual dancing	

chorus line; taxi dancer, fan dancer, topless dancer, stripteaser; nautch dancer, bayadere; choreographer

▶ *Light Entertainment 138*

5 **ballet dancer,** danseur, danseuse, ballerina, prima ballerina, corps de ballet; modern dancer

ADJECTIVES

6 **dancing,** terpsichorean, balletic, choreographic, dance

VERBS

7 **dance,** go dancing, trip, trip the light fantastic, gambol, prance, caper, jig, jig about, cavort, frolic, bob up and down, shuffle, tread a measure, skip, hop, leap; fox-trot, jitterbug, tap-dance, waltz, *etc.*; hoof [Inf], hoof it [Inf]; choreograph

ADVERBS

8 **dancingly,** trippingly, balletically, gracefully, prancingly, rhythmically, choreographically

DANCES

allemande	fox trot	paso doble
beguine	galliard	pavane
Big Apple	galop	polka
bolero	gavotte	polonaise
bossanova	gigue	quadrille
cakewalk	gopak *or* hopak	quickstep
can-can	habanera	reel
carioca	Highland fling	rigadoon
Castle walk	hora	rumba
cha-cha	hornpipe	samba
Charleston	hula-hula *or* hula	saraband
conga	Irish jig	schottische
contredanse *or*	jig	Sir Roger de
contradance	Lambeth walk	Coverley
cooch *or* hootchy-	lancers	strathspey
kootchy	lindy *or* Lindy	tango
courante	Hop	tarantella
czardas	mambo	twist
Duke of Perth	mazurka	two-step
écossaise	minuet	Virginia reel
fandango	nautch	waltz
farandole	one-step	

136 Drama and Theater

NOUNS

1 **drama,** the drama, theater, the theater, the stage, the play, scenes, traffic of the stage, dramatic entertainment; the footlights, the boards; dramatics, amateur dramatics; theatrics, theatricals, amateur theatricals; histrionics, dramatic *or* histrionic *or* thespian art; theater world, stage world, stageland, stagedom, playland, Broadway, off Broadway, off off Broadway, West End [Brit]; the Fringe, fringe theater, repertory, live theater, legitimate theater, straight drama, alternative theater, street theater, dinner theater, summer theater, strawhat theater, summer stock, pub theatre [Brit], experimental theater; legit [Inf], rep [Inf]; American Theatre Wing, Tony awards

▶ *Light Entertainment 138; Literature 139; Demonstration 331; Display 843*

2 **play,** stage play, drama, dramatic representation, dramatic recital, show, work, piece, vehicle; monologue, dramatic monologue, monodrama, one-person show, duologue, duodrama, two-hander, dialogue, skit, sketch, playlet, divertissement, divertimento, burlesque, double bill; one-act play, five-act play, trilogy, tetralogy, dramatic cycle

3 **dramatic style,** Greek drama, *fabula* [L], Nō play, kyogen, kabuki, mystery play, morality play, miracle play, liturgical drama, passion play, Oberammergau; folk play, mummers' play, sword play, commedia dell'arte, farce, interlude, harlequinade, pantomime, mime, dumb show, masque, antimasque, pastoral; verse drama, poetic drama, closet drama, melodrama, heroic drama, Grand Guignol, drama of suspense, problem play, sociodrama, psychodrama, slice of life, kitchen-sink drama, community drama, collective creation, improvised drama, improvisation, happening

4 **broadcast drama,** radio drama, radio play, television drama, television play, teleplay, serial, series, soap opera, soap [Inf]

▶ *Motion Pictures 137; Radio and Television 172*

5 **musical drama,** music drama, opera, operetta, musical, Broadway musical, show, musical comedy, comic opera, opera buffa, opera seria, ballad opera, singspiel, rock opera, ballet, cabaret

▶ *Dance and Ballet 135; Light Entertainment 138; Music 140*

6 **dramaturgy,** dramatic art, dramatic structure, dramatic form, play construction, the well-made play, stagecraft, theater craft; theatrical convention, dramatic convention, dramatic unities, the unities, dramatic irony, dramatic conflict, agon, dramatic tension, alienation effect, a-effect; playwriting, scriptwriting, plot, subplot, characterization, story, dialogue, mono-

logue, soliloquy, stichomythia; staging, choreography, action, movement, gesture, business, theatricality, theatrics, dramatics, melodramatics, histrionics, sensationalism, blood and thunder, dramatic coup, dramatic stroke, *coup de théâtre* [Fr], spectacle

> *Skillfulness 127; Literature 139; Sensation 212; Vision 242; Topic 328; Showiness 404*

7 **script,** playbook, text, lines, book, book of words, libretto, promptbook

8 **play part,** act, scene, speech, monologue, soliloquy, episode, item, piece, turn; bill, top of the bill, bottom of the bill; curtain music, overture, curtain-raiser, curtain-lifter; prologue, introduction, opening scene, expository scene, chorus, intermission, interval [Brit], break, entr'acte, intermezzo, interlude, climax, catastrophe, denouement, resolution; exposure scene, recognition scene, deus ex machina, battle scene, alarums and excursions, love scene, sex scene, transformation scene, set piece; finale, curtain, drop of the curtain, final curtain, curtain call, blackout, epilogue, encore, exodus, afterpiece; applause, ovation, standing ovation, chaser [Brit]

9 **theater movements,** activism, *Aktie Tomaat* [Dutch], Angry Young Men theater, community theater, constructivism, *Décentralisation Dramatique* [Fr], documentary theater, epic theater, expressionism, feminist theater, formalism, kitchen-sink drama, naturalism, New Drama, realism, ritual drama, Sturm und Drang, theater of the absurd, theater of cruelty, theater of fact, theater of silence, *théâtre du quotidien* [Fr], total theater, verismo, *Vormingstoneel* [Dutch]

10 **tragedy,** tragic drama, high tragedy, classical tragedy, Greek tragedy, Aeschylean tragedy, Euripidean tragedy, Sophoclean tragedy, Senecan tragedy, Renaissance tragedy, Shakespearean tragedy, Elizabethan tragedy, Jacobean tragedy, revenge tragedy, domestic tragedy, drama of fate, romantic tragedy, melodrama, tragicomedy; cothurnus, buskin; hubris, catharsis, tragic flaw, hamartia

11 **comedy,** high comedy, low comedy, broad comedy, light comedy, romantic comedy, sentimental comedy, *comédie larmoyante* [Fr], comedy of manners, comedy of ideas, comedy of humors, comedy of intrigue, comedy of morals, comedy of character, sex comedy, realistic comedy, black comedy, dark comedy, bitter comedy, *comédie rosse* [Fr], tragicomedy, satire, satirical comedy, knockabout *or* knockabout comedy; farce, bedroom farce, French farce; slapstick comedy, burlesque, burletta, camp, high camp, low camp, alternative comedy; comic business, comic relief, light relief

> *Light Entertainment 138; Humor 277*

12 **historic comedy,** satyr play, Aristophanean comedy, Old Comedy, Middle Comedy, New Comedy, Roman comedy, commedia dell'arte, interlude, Shakespearean comedy, Jonsonian comedy, Restoration comedy, drawing-room comedy

13 **theatrical performance,** performance, show, production, presentation, stage presentation, presentment, exhibition, bill, preview, first performance, premiere, first night, opening night, gala night, debut, farewell performance, command performance, bespeak performance [Arch], benefit performance, benefit, charity performance, charity gala, matinée, first house, second house; successful production, success, critical success, sellout, full house, hit, box-office hit, smash hit, long run; failure, flop, short run, bomb [Inf], turkey [Inf]

> *Display 843; Success 845; Failure 846*

14 **production,** direction, staging, mounting, putting on, stage management, audition, casting, read-through, walk-through, run-through, blocking; rehearsal, dress rehearsal, technical rehearsal; new production, revival, modern production, modern-dress production

> *Preparation 388; Production 522*

15 **engagement,** theatrical engagement, playing engagement, booking, date, stand, one-night stand, run, tour, circuit, barnstorming, variety circuit, club circuit, pub circuit [Brit], vaudeville circuit, repertory circuit, strawhat circuit, gig [Inf]

16 **theater,** playhouse, house, hall, hippodrome, auditorium, arena, amphitheater, stadium, circus, Greek theater, odeum, odeon, Elizabethan theater, spectacle theater, open-air theater, outdoor theater, theater-in-the-round, circle theater, arena theater, little theater, showboat, toy theater, fleapit [Brit inf]

17 **auditorium,** seating, parterre, parquet circle, stalls [Brit], pit [Brit], front rows, loge, box, box seat, stage box, royal box, circle, upper circle, orchestra circle, dress circle, balcony, gallery, peanut gallery [Inf], the gods, mezzanine, standing room, front of house; foyer, box office

18 **stage,** performing area, acting area, playing area, the boards; proscenium, proscenium arch, bridge, picture-frame stage, apron stage, apron, forestage, thrust stage, segment stage, wagon stage, slip stage, revolving stage, trap, stage left, stage right, upstage, downstage, center stage, front stage, above, below; orchestra pit, orchestra, pit, bandstand, podium, rostrum, dais, soapbox; wings, backstage, dressing room, greenroom, stage door, flies, fly floor *or* gallery, gridiron, grid, lightboard, switchboard, board, sound desk, prompter's box, scene dock

19 **stage set,** stage setting, setting, set, box set, scenery, scene, *mise en scène* [Fr], decor, flat, side scene, cyclorama, stage screw, wing, wing flat, border, tormentor, teaser, flipper, batten, drop, drop curtain, drop scene, cloth, backdrop, backcloth [Brit], hanging, gauze, scrim, transparency, transformation scene, curtain, drape, house curtain, tableau curtain, act curtain, act drop, tabs, safety *or* fire curtain

20 stage lighting, lights, footlights *or* foots, limelight, floodlight, flood, spotlight, arc light, arc, bunch light, battens, houselights, klieg light, color filter, color wheel, medium, gelatin *or* gel, diaphragm, iris diaphragm, iris, projector, stroboscope *or* strobe *or* strobe light, lightboard, spot [Inf], following spot [Inf]
▸ *Light 246; Color 251*

21 stage requisite, stage property, properties *or* props, handprop; costume, wardrobe; theatrical makeup, theatrical cosmetics, greasepaint, spirit gum
▸ *Decoration 532; Fashion 536*

22 acting, performing, playacting, playing, role-playing, taking a role *or* part, creating a role *or* part; impersonation, personation, portrayal, representation, characterization, interpretation, projection, performance, enactment; mimesis, mimicry, mimicking, miming, pantomiming, mummery; character acting, Method acting; improvisation, improvising; histrionics, overacting, ham acting *or* hamming *or* hamming it up, camping it up; stage business, business, byplay, stage whisper, aside; entrance, exit, cue, theatrical technique, stage presence; stage fever, first-night nerves *or* jitters, stage fright, butterflies [Inf]
▸ *Representation 187; Exaggeration 194; Appearance 264; Fear 283; Interpretation 365; Showiness 404; Imitation 736; Display 843*

23 role, part, character, person, personage; title role *or* part, name part, starring role, leading role, lead role, lead, chief part, good part, top billing; principal character, hero, heroine, antihero, villain, protagonist, jeune premier, jeune première; [Inf]: fat part, juicy part, heavy, bad guy; supporting role, supporting part, supporting character, antagonist, deuteragonist; minor role, bit part *or* bit, speaking part, walk-on part, walking part, straight part, straight man, cameo, vignette, feed *or* feeder [Inf]; chorus, Greek chorus

24 stock part, stock character, stereotype; ingenue, soubrette, juvenile lead, principal boy, principal girl, love interest, confidant *or* confidante, merry widow, injured husband, breeches part, stage villain, heavy, stage Irishman, stage drunk, buffoon, fool; Harlequin, Columbine, Pantaloon *or* Pantalone, Pierrot, Scaramouch *or* Scaramouche
▸ *Light Entertainment 138*

25 actor, actress, playactor, player, stage player, thespian, trouper, stage performer, Roscius [Arch], repertory player, barnstormer, actor-manager; tragedian, tragedienne, comedian, comedienne, comedy actor, comedy actress, light comedian, low comedian, farceur, character actor, character actress, Method actor, Method actress, improviser, ad-libber, pantomimist, mime, mummer; star of stage and screen, leading man, leading lady, lead, juvenile lead, jeune premier, jeune première, supporting actor *or* actress, support; understudy, standby, substitute; extra, bit player, walk-on, spear

carrier, supernumerary, super [Inf]; opera singer, diva, prima donna; prologue, presenter, narrator, speaker; ham, scene-stealer
▸ *Motion Pictures 137; Music 140*

26 cast, characters, actors, dramatis personae, persons of the drama, chorus, ladies and gentlemen of the chorus, supporting cast, cast of thousands; ensemble, company, repertory company, stock company, touring company, outfit, troupe
▸ *Assembly 59; Light Entertainment 138*

27 dramatist, dramaturge, playwright, play doctor, librettist, radio dramatist, television dramatist, farceur, farceuse, joke writer, gagman, gag writer, tragedian, comedian, melodramatist
▸ *Literature 139; Radio and Television 172; Imagination 360; Originality 737*

28 producer, director, stage director, stage manager, manager, actor-manager, impresario; choreographer, régisseur, choragus *or* choregus; designer, set designer, costume designer, costumer, costumier *or* costumière; business manager, publicity manager, press officer, press agent, advance man, agent, booking agent, ten percenter [Inf], play agent *or* playbroker; patron, backer, promoter, angel [Inf]
▸ *Authority 52; Production 522; Help 825*

29 stagehand, stage technician, flyman, stage crew, electrician, sound man, scene master, scene painter, stage carpenter; dresser, wardrobe mistress, makeup artist, wigmaker; callboy, prompter; ticket collector, program seller, usher, doorkeeper, box-office staff

30 theatergoer, playgoer, operagoer, opera buff; audience, house, full house, packed house, thin house; spectator, groundling, standee, fan; claque, claqueur, plant; critic, reviewer, talent scout, firstnighter, stagedoor Johnny, deadhead [Inf]

ADJECTIVES

31 dramatic, dramaturgic, thespian, theatrical *or* theatric, stagy, spectacular, sensational, melodramatic, histrionic; tragic, buskined, tragicomic *or* tragicomical, comic, burlesque, farcical, romantic, cathartic; mimetic, musical, operatic, choral, choreographic, terpsichorean

32 dramatized, produced, directed, scripted, cast, rehearsed, staged, choreographed, stage-managed, prompted, enacted, performed, interpreted, characterized, improvised, ad-libbed; overacted, overplayed, hammed-up, hammy, campy; underacted, underplayed; stereotypical, stereotyped, typecast, miscast

VERBS

33 dramatize, melodramatize, theatricalize, adapt for the stage, write, script, produce, put on, direct; stage-manage, cue, prompt; cast, bill, star, feature, typecast, miscast; present, release, preview, premiere, open, raise the curtain

---

▸ *Authority 52; Literature 139; Production 522; Opening 583; Originality 737*

34 act, play, playact, role-play, portray, perform, enact, project, interpret; mimic, imitate, impersonate, personify, represent; improvise, ad-lib, wing it [Inf]; take a role *or* part, create a role *or* part, play the lead, star, costar, support, appear, understudy; enter, make an entrance, take the stage, tread the boards; exit, take a bow
▸ *Lack of Preparation 389; Entry 706; Exit 707; Imitation 736; Display 843*

35 overact, overplay, ham, ham *or* camp it up, mug up, chew the scenery, rant, roar, play to the gallery, milk it; upstage, steal the show
▸ *Excess 99; Exaggeration 194; Showiness 404*

36 underact, underplay; walk on, have a cameo role; miss one's cue, fluff, dry up, forget one's lines, go blank
▸ *Understatement 195; Error 351*

37 rehearse, practice, run through, read through, walk through, block; learn one's lines, memorize, con, recite; interpret the part, get into character
▸ *Preparation 388*

ADVERBS

38 dramatically, dramaturgically, theatrically, spectacularly, sensationally, melodramatically, histrionically; tragically, tragicomically, comically, romantically, cathartically; mimetically, musically, operatically, chorally, choreographically

39 onstage, in the spotlight *or* limelight, stage left, stage right, upstage, downstage, center stage, front stage, offstage, in the wings, backstage, behind the scenes

137 Motion Pictures

NOUNS

1 motion pictures, movies, the movies, cinema, the films, the big screen, the silver screen, the flicks [Inf]; motion-picture industry, moviedom, filmdom, screenland, movieland, Hollywood; Academy of Motion Picture Arts and Sciences, Academy Award, Oscar

2 motion picture, movie, film, picture, picture show, flick [Inf]

3 movie type, feature film, drama, comedy, musical, love story, mystery, thriller, adventure, romance, Western, historical film, epic film, futuristic film, science-fiction film, sci-fi film [Inf], foreign *or* foreign-language film, film noir; documentary film, cinéma vérité, docudrama; cartoon, animated movie, claymation, live animation; silent movie, sound motion picture *or* sound film, talking picture *or* talkie, made-for-television *or* -TV movie, cable movie, series movie, miniseries; preview, sneak preview, short, short movie; B-movie, low-budget picture, underground movie, cult movie, snuff film [Inf]; educational film, training film; videocassette movie, rental movie, pay-per-view movie, interactive film, virtual reality

▸ *Radio and Television 172*

4 film-rating system, G (general audience), PG (parental guidance suggested), PG-13 (parents strongly cautioned), R (restricted; children under 17 require accompanying parent or guardian), NC-17 *or* X (no children under 17 admitted)

5 script, screenplay, original screenplay, screen adaptation; scriptwriting, screenwriting; shooting script, scenario, storyboard; plot, subplot, story, characterization, dialogue, book, lines

6 production, casting, screen test, direction, rehearsal, run-through, read-through, walk-through; lighting, sound recording, special effects, visual effects, sound effects, musical score
▸ *Drama and Theater 136*

7 motion-picture studio, movie studio, film studio, motion-picture company, film company, production company, dream factory [Inf]; lot, back lot, sound stage, set, location; setting, locale, scene, scenery, *mise en scène* [Fr]; properties *or* props, costumes

8 motion-picture editing, film editing, arranging, cutting, slicing, synchronizing; transition, fade, fade-in, fade-out, dissolve, lap dissolve *or* cross-dissolve

9 motion-picture photography, cinematography, cinematics, camera work, camera angle, camera position; shot, take, retake, footage; color photography, black-and-white photography, colorization; Technicolor™; CinemaScope™

10 motion-picture theater, movie theater, cinema, movie house, picture house, drive-in *or* drive-in theater, fleapit [Brit inf]

11 box-office hit, smash hit, critical success, popular success

12 acting, role. *See* Drama and Theater.

13 actor, actress, film actor *or* actress, cinemactor *or* cinemactress, character actor *or* actress, featured player, Method actor *or* actress; star, film star, superstar, starlet, star of stage and screen, matinée idol, idol, icon; lead actor *or* actress, leading man *or* lady, supporting actor *or* actress; extra, walk-on, bit player, cameo; lookalike, double, stand-in, substitute; stunt person, stunt man *or* woman
▸ *Drama and Theater 136*

14 filmmaker, moviemaker, auteur; producer, executive producer, director, executive director, first assistant director, second assistant director; screenwriter, scriptwriter, scenario writer, scenarist; casting director, central casting; production designer, production manager, production coordinator, production assistant; cinematographer, director of photography, camera operator, cameraperson, cameraman *or* camerawoman, camera *or* film crew; art director, music director, composer; recordist *or* sound recordist, sound engineer, mixer, sound mixer, re-recording mixer, sound editor, sound man, boom operator; film editor, assistant editor; set designer, set decorator, set dresser, property master, construction coordinator, key grip, second grip, dolly grip, gaffer, best boy [Inf]; costume designer, costumer, makeup artist, hair stylist

ADJECTIVES

15 **motion-picture,** movie, film, cinematic, filmic; color, black-and-white, colorized; animated

16 **dramatic,** comic, melodramatic, romantic, historical, futuristic, science-fiction, sci-fi [Inf], epic, musical, made-for-television or -TV; documentary, serial, short, low-budget; educational, training

17 **produced,** directed, written, scripted, cast, filmed, edited

18 **starring,** costarring, featuring, introducing

VERBS

19 **film,** shoot, reshoot, photograph, test, take, edit, screen

20 **act,** perform, play, portray; appear, face the cameras, star, play the lead, support, costar, have a cameo role; rehearse, learn one's lines, con, memorize, run through, read through, walk through, have a screen test

21 **produce,** make a film, cinematize, adapt, script; screen-test, cast, direct, feature, introduce, edit; score, compose

138 Light Entertainment

NOUNS

1 **show business,** entertainment, entertainment industry, showmanship, show biz [Inf]; variety, vaudeville, burlesque, music hall, song and dance, improvisation, stand-up comedy, slapstick
  ▶ *Drama and Theater 136; Motion Pictures 137; Radio and Television 172; Humor 277*

2 **circus,** traveling circus, the big top, the ring, three-ring circus, circus troupe, flying circus; carnival, fair, sideshow; rodeo or rodeo show, ice show, pageant

3 **magic,** conjuring, art of illusion, sleight of hand, legerdemain, prestidigitation, magic show; escapology [Brit]; hypnotism, mind reading
  ▶ *Deception 193*

4 **show,** spectacle, extravaganza, stage show, live show, variety show, variety, vaudeville show, vaudeville, comedy show, song-and-dance show, minstrel show, floor show, cabaret, revue or review, follies, burlesque show, burlesque; strip show, striptease show, hootchy-kootchy show, girlie show [Inf], nudie show [Inf], peep show, raree show; road show, street theater, medicine show; marionette show, puppet show, puppetry, puppet theater, Punch-and-Judy show, shadow play or shadow show or shadow theater; slide show, light show, laser show, sound-and-light show, *son et lumière* [Fr]

▶ *Drama and Theater 136; Motion Pictures 137; Radio and Television 172; Humor 277; Demonstration 331; Display 843*

5 **number,** performance, routine, act, skit, sketch, charade

6 **engagement,** booking, date, stand, one-night stand, run, tour; circuit, variety circuit, vaudeville circuit, club circuit, borscht circuit or belt, pub circuit [Brit], gig [Inf]

7 **club,** nightclub, nightspot, cabaret, supper club, boîte, *boîte de nuit* [Fr], striptease or strip club, topless bar; vaudeville or variety theater, music hall, hall, house, pavilion, fleabag [Inf]

8 **entertainer,** public entertainer, artiste, artist, performer; showman, presenter, master of ceremonies or emcee or M.C.; variety artist, vaudeville artist, vaudevillian, song-and-dance man; show girl, chorus girl, chorus boy; improviser, comedian, comedienne, comic, stand-up comic, humorist, straight man, foil, stooge, feed or feeder [Inf], second banana [Inf]; puppeteer, ventriloquist; impressionist, mimic, impersonator, female impersonator, drag artist; burlesque queen, stripper or stripteaser, striptease artist, ecdysiast, exotic dancer; minstrel, troubadour, jongleur, juggler, street performer
  ▶ *Imitation 736; Display 843*

9 **circus performer,** ringmaster, circus clown, tightrope walker, ropedancer or ropewalker, slack-rope artist, high-wire artist, equilibrist, trapeze artist, acrobat, tumbler, contortionist, juggler, strongman, human cannonball, fire-eater, snake charmer, lion tamer, bareback rider, equestrian director, barker, spieler

10 **clown,** fool, zany, joker, jester, buffoon, merry-andrew; comic performer, buffo, slapstick comedian; fool's cap, cap and bells, motley, slapstick, bladder; Punch, Punchinello, Harlequin, Columbine, Pantaloon or Pantalone, Pierrot, Scaramouch or Scaramouche
  ▶ *Humor 277; Ridiculousness 368*

11 **magician,** conjuror, illusionist, sleight-of-hand artist, legerdemainist, prestidigitator; escape artist, escapologist [Brit]; hypnotist, mind reader
  ▶ *Deception 193*

ADJECTIVES

12 **entertaining,** artistic, showy, spectacular, extravagant, stagy or staged, live, traveling, road-show
  ▶ *Showiness 404*

13 **variety,** vaudeville, vaudevillian, cabaret, burlesque, song-and-dance, improvisatory, comic or comical, stand-up, slapstick, farcical, knockabout
  ▶ *Humor 277*

14 **clownish,** zany, buffoonish, foolish

15 **magical,** conjuring, prestidigitatory or prestidigitatorial, mind-reading

VERBS

16 **entertain,** put on a show, present, emcee; perform,

sing, dance, tell jokes, play the straight man, play second banana [Inf]; impersonate, do impressions, mimic, imitate, improvise, clown, joke, jest, juggle; strip, striptease; perform magic, conjure, hypnotize, read minds; go on tour, go on the road

⦿ *Humor 277; Imitation 736; Display 843*

ADVERBS

17 **entertainingly,** artistically, showily, spectacularly, extravagantly; improvisatorily, comically, farcically, clownishly

139 Literature

The proper study of mankind is books. — ALDOUS HUXLEY

Literature and butterflies are the two sweetest passions known to man. — VLADIMIR NABOKOV

NOUNS

1 **literature,** writing(s), letters, belles-lettres, litterae humaniores, republic of letters; serious literature, popular literature, underground literature, folk literature, oral history; the classics, the arts, the humanities, learning, erudition, culture, lore

⦿ *Knowledge 348*

2 **fiction,** prose fiction, narrative fiction, pulp fiction, novel, short story; drama

⦿ *Drama and Theater 136*

3 **novel,** novella, novelette, *roman* [Fr], *nouvelle* [Fr]; antinovel, autobiographical novel, Bildungsroman, bodice ripper [Inf], cliff-hanger, dystopian novel, epic novel, epistolary novel, erotic novel, fantasy novel,

---

POEM OR VERSE FORMS

alba	epode	psalm
aubade	free verse *or* vers	reverdie
ballad	libre	rondeau
ballade	georgic	rondel *or* roundel
cento *or* pastiche	haiku	roundelay
chanson	hymn	saga
cinquain	idyll	satire
clerihew	jingle	sestina
complaint	lay	song
conversation poem	limerick	sonnet: Petrarchan,
dirge	lyric	Shakespearean,
dithyramb	macaronic	Spenserian
ditty	madrigal	sonnet sequence
double dactyl	monody	tanka
dramatic	narrative poem	threnody
monologue	nursery rhyme	triolet
eclogue	ode: choric,	troubadour
elegiac poem	Horatian,	poem
elegy	Pindaric, Sapphic	verse epistle
epic poem	palinode	villanelle
epigram	pastoral *or* bucolic	virelay
epithalamion	prothalamion	

---

fictional biography, gothic novel, historical novel, novel of sensibility *or* sentimental novel, novel of ideas, penny dreadful [Brit], picaresque novel, pornographic novel, psychological thriller, psychological novel, regional novel, *roman à clef* [Fr], romance, *roman-fleuve* [Fr], science fiction *or* sci-fi novel [Inf], social novel, stream-of-consciousness novel, thesis novel, thriller, utopian novel, Victorian novel, Western

4 **story,** short story, vignette, sketch; adventure story, crime story, detective story, ghost story, horror story, love story, mystery story, spy story; supernatural tale, fairy tale, *Märchen* [Ger], legend, myth, folk tale, folk story, fable, fabliau, beast fable; parable, *conte* [Fr], gest *or* geste

5 **aspect of fiction,** story, storyline, narrative, plot, subplot; scenario, argument, plan, scheme, subject; theme, motif, leitmotiv *or* leitmotif; development, structure, architecture, continuity, action; incident, episode, complication, turning point, denouement, recognition, device, contrivance, coincidence; atmosphere, tone, mood, background, description, symbolism; local color, characterization; dramatic irony, comic relief, catharsis; stream of consciousness, digression, interior monologue, metanarrative; point of view, narrative voice, first-person narrative, third-person narrative, omniscient narrator

6 **nonfiction,** descriptive writing, history, annals, chronicle, record; life story, biography, profile, biographical sketch, autobiography, journal, diary, memoir, confessions, kiss-and-tell confession; hagiography, historiography; travel writing, travelogue *or* travelog; treatise, discourse, thesis, dissertation, essay, study, commentary, critique, criticism, review

⦿ *History 3; Dissertation 203*

7 **prose,** prose fiction, expository prose; prose poem, poetic prose, polyphonic prose

8 **poetry,** poesy, poem, verse, rhyme, song, balladry, versification, poetics, doggerel, numbers [Arch]; blank verse, comic poetry, concrete poetry, confessional poetry, didactic poetry, dramatic poetry, elegiac poetry, epic poetry *or* epos, erotic poetry, folk poetry, free verse, heroic poetry, Hudibrastic verse, light verse, lyric poetry, metaphysical poetry, mock-heroic poetry, narrative poetry, nonsense poetry *or* verse, occasional verse, pastoral poetry, pattern poetry, performance poetry, runic verse, satirical poetry, topographical poetry

9 **part of poem,** verse, stanza, stave, measure, strain, strophe, antistrophe, epode; line, half line, foot; hemistich, monostich, distich, tristich, tetrastich, pentastich, hexastich, heptastich, octastich; couplet, rhyming couplet, closed couplet, triplet, tercet, quatrain, sestet, septet, octet, octave, verse paragraph, refrain, chorus, envoy *or* envoi, burden, book, canto, fit

10 meter, metrics, measure, rhythm, scansion, prosody, quantitative meter, syllabic meter, accentual meter, accentual-syllabic meter, duple meter, triple meter, accent, accentuation, stress, beat, emphasis, quantity; metrical unit, foot, dipody, iamb, spondee, trochee, bacchius, dactyl, anapest *or* anapaest, pyrrhic *or* dibrach, tribrach, amphibrach, amphimacer, cretic, ionic, paeon, choriamb; monometer, dimeter, trimeter, tetrameter, pentameter, hexameter, heptameter, octameter; iambic pentameter, elegiac pentameter; Alexandrine, dactylic hexameter; heroic couplet, elegiac couplet, elegiac distich; sprung rhythm, counterpoint, anacrusis, catalexis, caesura

11 rhyme, masculine rhyme, feminine rhyme, single rhyme, double rhyme, end rhyme, tail rhyme, eye rhyme, broken rhyme, half rhyme, near rhyme, pararhyme, internal rhyme, initial rhyme; rhyme scheme, terza rima, ottava rima, rhyme royal, rime riche

12 literary device, poetic language, poetic diction, poeticism, archaism, decorum, the grand style, aureate diction, alliteration, repetition; anaphora, epistrophe, assonance, consonance, onomatopoeia, euphony, elision, inversion, chiasmus, periphrasis; figurative language, imagery, conceit, trope, metaphor, simile, Homeric simile, epic simile; Homeric epithet, compound epithet, transferred epithet, kenning, personification, prosopopoeia, apostrophe; metonymy, synecdoche; antonomasia, paronomasia, parallelism, synesthesia, pathetic fallacy, poetic license, pseudostatement, irony, pun; peripeteia, anagnorisis, deus ex machina

13 author, writer, narrator, fiction writer, storyteller, novelist, short-story writer, crime writer, fabler, fabulist, teller of tales, mythologist, allegorist, romancer, novelettist, chronicler, historian, historiographer; biographer, autobiographer, diarist, essayist, annalist, expository writer; poet, poetess, major poet, minor poet, poet laureate, minnesinger, Meistersinger, rhapsodist, dithyrambist, elegist, satirist, sonneteer, symbolist, lyric poet, epic poet, pastoral poet, metaphysical poet, Lake poet, romantic poet, modern poet, modernist, beat poet, librettist, lyricist, vers-librist; rhymer, rhymester, versemonger, versifier, versesmith, versemaker, poetaster, balladeer, ballad monger, ballad maker, bard, minstrel, jongleur, trouvère, troubadour, scop, skald, comic poet, tragic poet, dramatic poet, playwright, dramatist, dramaturge, screenwriter; wordsmith, penman, scribe

▶ *Drama and Theater 136; Description 202*

14 literary person, woman *or* man of letters, belletrist, literary scholar, educator, student of literature, literary critic, book reviewer, cultural commentator; the clerisy, literati

▶ *Education 48; Books 174*

ADJECTIVES

15 literary, written, humanistic, belletristic, polished, learned, lettered, formal, scholarly, erudite, well-read, critical, interpretive, classical, romantic, surrealistic, realistic, futuristic, decadent, neoclassical, naturalistic, metaphysical

16 fictional, fictionalized, mythical, mythological, legendary, fabulous, allegorical, romantic, Victorian

17 descriptive, well-drawn, graphic, depictive, expressive

18 narrative, storified, biographical, autobiographical, historiographical, prosaic, storied

19 poetic, poetical, Parnassian, Homeric, Dantesque, Miltonic, Pindaric, Sapphic, Horatian, Virgilian, Augustan, Shakespearean, Petrarchan, Spenserian; dramatic, epic, heroic, mock-heroic, elegiac, lyrical, pastoral, bucolic, idyllic, rhapsodic, tragic, comic, doggerel

20 metrical, rhythmical, measured, accentual, scanning, scanned, octosyllabic, hendecasyllabic, iambic, trochaic,

---

WESTERN LITERARY GROUPS, MOVEMENTS, AND ASSOCIATIONS

absurdism	euphuism	Liverpool poets	Pléiade, la	sentimentalism
acmeism	existentialism	magic realism	postmodernism	socialist realism
aestheticism	expressionism	medievalism	poststructuralism	social realism
Angry Young Men	futurism	Metaphysical poets	Pre-Raphaelite	spasmodic school
Augustans	Georgian poetry	modernism	Brotherhood	structuralism
beat poets	Goliardic verse	modernismo	preromanticism	Sturm und Drang
Bloomsbury group	Gongorism	naturalism	primitivism	surrealism
Cavalier poets	graveyard school	neoclassicism	realism	symbolism
Celtic twilight	Group 47	neorealism	regionalism	Transcendentalism
classicism	Harlem Renaissance	New Criticism	Renaissance	tremendismo
Crepuscolari	Hermeticism	new humanism	humanism	verismo
Dadaism	imagism	New Wave	Restoration comedy	Victorian novelists
Decadence	Jugendstil	nouveau roman	romanticism	vorticism
deconstruction	Kailyard school	nouvelle vague	Russian formalists	Wertherism
Elizabethan poets	kitchen-sink drama	Parnassians	Scottish Chaucerians	
Encyclopédistes	Lake poets	philosophes	Scottish Renaissance	

181

spondaic, dactylic, anapestic, catalectic, rhyming, assonant, alliterative, onomatopoeic

VERBS

21 **write,** narrate, recount, tell, compose, pen; write a novel, dramatize, write a play; ghostwrite, freelance; prose, describe, portray, represent, express, delineate, characterize; write a poem, poetize, versify, elegize, rhyme, write *or* compose poetry

ADVERBS

22 **narratively,** prosaically

23 **poetically,** lyrically, rhythmically, metrically

24 **descriptively,** expressively, vividly, dramatically

140 Music

There's sure no passion in the human soul, / But finds its food in music. — GEORGE LILLO

Music, when soft voices die, / Vibrates in the memory. — PERCY BYSSHE SHELLEY

NOUNS

1 **music,** harmony, melody, tunefulness, melodiousness, musicalness, musicality

2 **classical music,** concert music, serious music, symphonic music; chamber music, impressionist music, operatic music, bel canto, ballet, orchestral music, organ music, romantic music, modern music; absolute *or* abstract music, program music

3 **sacred music,** church music, liturgical music, chant, Gregorian chant, Anglican chant, plainsong, hymn, psalm, chorale, anthem, motet, oratorio, passion, mass, requiem mass, requiem, cantata; doxology, introit, canticle, recessional, paean; spiritual, gospel music; hymnody, hymnology, psalmody

▶ *Religious Ritual 85*

4 **popular music,** pop music, pop, popular song, pop

song, light music, hit, hit tune, ballad, torch song, ragtime, doo-wop, karaoke; dance music, ballet music, ballroom music, modern dance music, disco, swing, pops

▶ *Dance and Ballet 135*

5 **jazz,** mainstream jazz, modern jazz, progressive jazz, avant-garde jazz, third-stream jazz, cool jazz, acid jazz, traditional jazz; blues, syncopation, swing, jive, bebop, bop, boogie-woogie, scat singing, skiffle; Dixieland jazz, Basin Street jazz, New Orleans jazz, Chicago jazz

6 **rock music,** rock and roll *or* rock-'n'-roll, hard rock, soft rock, acid rock, folk rock, country rock, rockabilly, rhythm-and-blues (R and B); hard core, heavy metal, thrash metal, punk rock, New Wave, rap, jazzfunk, fusion, electro, hip-hop, grunge

7 **folk music,** folk song, folk ballad, folk rock, country music, country-and-western, bluegrass, hillbilly music; ethnic music, soul, reggae, merengue, ska, calypso, raga

8 **opera,** grand opera, musical drama, operetta, light opera, comic opera, musical

▶ *Drama and Theater 136*

9 **musical composition,** opus, piece, arrangement, adaptation, setting, transcription, accompaniment

10 **melody,** tune, air, strain, song, aria; measure, theme, subject, motif, leitmotiv *or* leitmotif; line, melodic line, cantus *or* cantus firmus, canto, refrain, reprise, descant; theme song, signature tune, Broadway melody, simple melody, popular melody, lost melody

11 **song,** lied, chanson, aubade, serenade, lullaby, cradle song, berceuse, barcarole, part song, round, madrigal, folk song, glee, lay, roundelay, lilt, chantey *or* chanty *or* shantey, yodel; chorus, solo; popular song, calypso, cavatina, spiritual, love song, torch song; chant, plainsong *or* plainchant, canticle, chorale, carol, Christmas carol, hymn, psalm, anthem

▶ *Musician 141*

12 **melodiousness,** musicality, musicalness, musical quality, musical texture, euphony, euphoniousness, harmoniousness, harmony, chime, concord, consonance, attunement, consent [Arch]

13 **harmonics,** harmony, harmonization, harmonic progression, orchestration, instrumentation, arrangement, setting, accompaniment; music theory, musicography, musicology

14 **harmonic element,** homophony, monophony, monody; counterpoint, polyphony, heterophony; tonality, resolution, cadence, perfect cadence, fauxbourdon *or* faburden, thorough bass, basso continuo, continuo, figured bass, ground bass, walking bass; phrasing, phrase, passage, figure, sequence, tonal sequence; musica ficta *or* musica falsa

15 **musical note,** natural, sharp, flat, double flat, double sharp, accidental, semitone, keynote, overtone, harmonic; leading tone, tonic, subtonic, supertonic, mediant, submediant, dominant, subdominant

---

MUSICAL FORMS

adagio	étude	motet	rondo
allemande	fanfare	nocturne	sarabande
anthem	fantasy	opera	scherzo
arabesque	fugue	operetta	serenade
berceuse	galliard	oratorio	sonata
canon	gavotte	overture	sonatina
cantata	gigue	partita	string
canticle	humoresque	passacaglia	quartet
canzone	hymn	passion	suite
chaconne	impromptu	pavane	symphony
chorale	intermezzo	piano	Te Deum
concerto	lied	quintet	theme and
concerto	madrigal	polonaise	variations
grosso	Magnificat	prelude	toccata
courante	march	requiem	tone poem
divertimento	mass	romance	waltz
elegy	minuet	rondino	

---

16 scale, gamut, tonic sol-fa, solfeggio, solfège, solmization; major scale, minor scale, harmonic minor scale, diatonic scale, modal scale, chromatic scale, harmonic scale, melodic scale, enharmonic scale, twelve-tone scale, series, tone row

17 mode, Greek mode, Dorian mode, hypodorian mode, Phrygian mode, hypophrygian mode, Locrian mode, Lydian mode, hypolydian mode, mixolydian mode, hypomixolydian mode, Aeolian mode, hypoaeolian mode, Ionian mode, hypoionian mode, church *or* Gregorian mode; authentic mode, plagal mode; Indian mode

18 chord, common chord, primary chord, secondary chord, second, tertiary chord, triad, third, tetrachord,

fourth, fifth, sixth, seventh, diminished seventh, octave, ninth; interval, major *or* minor interval

19 musical ornament, arpeggio, grace note, crush note, appoggiatura, acciaccatura, mordent, turn, shake, trill, tremolo, broken chord, cadenza

20 notation, breve, whole note *or* semibreve, half note *or* minim, quarter note *or* crotchet, eighth note *or* quaver, sixteenth note *or* semiquaver, thirty-second note *or* demisemiquaver, sixty-fourth note *or* hemidemisemiquaver

21 written music, sheet music, score, notation, proportional notation, chart [Inf], paper [Inf]; signature, time signature, key signature, clef, C clef, treble clef *or* G clef,

---

MUSICAL TERMS AND EXPRESSION MARKS

a battuta, return to strict time
a bene placito, as you please
a cappella, unaccompanied *or* chapel style
accelerando, accelerating
adagietto, slow
adagio, quite slow
adagissimo, extremely slow
ad libitum, at will
a due, by two
affannato, affannoso, excited, hurried, agitated
affettuoso, tender
affrettando, hurrying
agevole, easy, smooth
agiatamente, with ease
agilmente, nimbly, with agility
al fine, to the end
alla breve, cut time
allargando, broadening; more dignified
allegretto, light, lively, brisk
allegro, lively, brisk
al segno, to the sign
amorevole, con amore, amiable, with love
andante, moderately slow
animato, spirited
aperto, open
a piacere, as you please
assai, very
a tempo, return to normal tempo
attacca, continue without a pause
bassa, low
bewegt, animated, with motion
bis, repeat
calando, gradually diminishing
cantabile, in a singing fashion
chiaramente, clearly, distinctly

col arco, with the bow
col legno, strike strings with the wood of the bow
con abbandano, unrestrained
con brio, with vigor
con fuoco, fiery, vigorous
crescendo, cresc., growing louder
da capo, D.C., from the beginning
dal segno, repeat from the sign
decrescendo, decr., decresc., growing softer
dehors, emphasized
diminuendo, dim., becoming softer
divisi, divided
dolce, sweetly, softly
dolente, doloroso, sorrowful
doppio, double
estinto, barely audible
fastoso, pompous
fioritura, embellishment
forte, f, loud
forte-piano, fp, loud followed by soft
fortissimo, ff, very loud
giocoso, merry, playful
glissando, rapid notes produced by sliding movement
grave, solemnly
in modo di, in the manner of
larghetto, slow
largo, very slow
legato, smoothly, with no breaks between notes
leggiero, light, nimble
lento, slow
maestoso, majestic
marcando, marcato, marked, stressed

marcia, march
meno, less
meno mosso, less quickly
mesto, sad, mournful
mezza voce, "half voice"; in restrained tones
mezzo, half
mezzoforte, mf, moderately loud
minacciando, menacing
moderato, moderately
molto, very
morbido, soft, delicate
mosso, moved, agitated
moto, motion
niente, nothing
nobile, noble
nobilmente, nobly
obbligato, not to be omitted
ossia, or, or else
parlando, as if spoken
perdendo, dying away
pesante, weightily, importantly
pianissimo, pp, very softly
piano, p, soft
più, more
pizzicato, plucked
prestissimo, as fast as possible
presto, very fast
quasi, as if
rallentando, rall., slowing down
rattenando, rattenuto, holding back
ravvivando, quickening
retenu, held back
rinforzando, rf, rfz, rinf., accentuated; sudden accent
ritardando, rit., ritardo, slowing down

ritenuto, immediate reduction of speed
scherzando, playful
schleppend, dragging, heavy
schnell, fast
scorrevole, scorrendo, gliding; fluent
segno, sign
senza, without
sfoggiando, ostentatiously
sforzando, sforzato, sf, sfz, forcing
sin' al fin, until the end
sin' al segno, until the sign
sino, up to, until
slentando, slowing down
soave, sweet, gentle
sostenuto, sustained tone
sotto voce, quiet, subdued tone
sourd, muffled, muted
spiccato, separated; staccato bowing
staccato, detached, shortened
stark, strong, loud
stringendo, hastening, intensifying
subito, suddenly
tace, tacet, instrument is silent
tanto, much
tardo, tardamente, slow
tenuto, ten., held, sustained
tief, deep, low
tutti, all
veloce, fast
via, away
vibrato, vibrated, pulsing
vif, lively
vivace, quick, lively
vivement, lively
zart, tender, soft

bass clef *or* F clef, tenor clef, alto clef; measure, bar, phrase, staff, stave, line, ledger *or* leger line, space, brace, rest, pause, fermata, interval

22 **tempo,** time, beat, rhythm, measure, pulse, meter, timing, syncopation, counterpoint rhythm, upbeat, downbeat, short note, suspension, suspended note, long note, prolonged note, backbeat [Inf]

23 **key,** tonality, major key, minor key; temperament, even temperament

24 **tone,** register, pitch, concert pitch, high pitch, low pitch, absolute pitch, perfect pitch, high note, stridor, low note, resonance, undertone, overtone, harmonic, upper partial, sustained note, monotone, drone, key center

ADJECTIVES

25 **musical,** harmonic, melodic, tuneful, philharmonic, classical, serious, romantic, sacred, operatic, popular, light, ragtime, jazz, syncopated, avant-garde, cool, mainstream, traditional, Dixieland, bluesy, pop, swinging, punk; folk, folksy, country, soul

26 **melodious,** tuneful, attuned, in tune, tonal, symphonic, symphonious, synchronous, homophonic, harmonious, melodic, mellifluent, mellifluous, mellow, lyric *or* lyrical, dulcet, singable, catchy

27 **harmonic,** homophonic, monophonic, polyphonic, contrapuntal; cadenced, phrased, sequenced; major, minor, twelve-tone; modal; timed, rhythmic, syncopated; even-tempered, well-tempered; tuned, pitched
  ▶ *Agreement 462; Accord 735*

VERBS

28 **harmonize,** melodize, be melodic, attune, assonate, tune, pitch, be in tune, accord, symphonize, chime, blend, segue

29 **beat time,** keep time, keep tempo; syncopate, swing, jam [Inf], riff [Inf], rock
  ▶ *Musician 141*

ADVERBS

30 **tunefully,** harmonically, melodiously, melodically, mellifluously, euphoniously, resonantly; harmoniously, in harmony, in tune, on pitch, in key, in time, in tempo; rhythmically, syncopatedly, jazzily

141 Musician

A wandering minstrel I — / A thing of shreds and patches, / Of ballads, songs and snatches, / And dreamy lullaby!
— W. S. GILBERT

NOUNS

1 **musician,** music maker, player, performer, artist, artiste, singer, soloist, virtuoso, street musician, busker [Brit]

2 **player,** instrumentalist, orchestra player; accompanist *or* accompanyist; wind player, horn player, flutist *or* flautist, oboist, clarinettist, bassoonist, saxophonist,

trombonist, trumpeter; string musician, violinist, fiddler, violist, cellist, bassist, bass player; harpist, banjo player, guitarist, lutenist; piano player, pianist, harpsichordist, clavichordist; organ player, organist; drummer, percussionist, timpanist, kettledrummer, triangle player, cymbalist, bell ringer, campanologist
  ▶ *Music 140; Musical Instruments 142*

3 **instrumental group,** duet, trio, quartet, string quartet, quintet, sextet, septet, octet, nonet, ensemble; chamber group, chamber orchestra; sinfonietta, orchestra, symphony orchestra, philharmonic orchestra; band, marching band, military band, jazz band, ragtime band, brass band, skiffle group, steel band, rock band *or* group, punk rock band *or* group; one-man band; folk group

4 **singer,** songster, voice, vocalist, lead vocalist, backing *or* backup vocalist; cantor, chanter, precentor; soloist, opera singer, diva, prima donna; bard, minstrel, troubadour, minnesinger, Meistersinger, ballad singer, balladeer, crooner, warbler, hummer, yodeler; chanteuse, blues singer, scat singer, torch singer, belter [Inf], songbird [Inf]; folk singer, folk-rock singer, country-and-western singer

5 **voice,** soprano, lyric soprano, coloratura soprano, dramatic soprano, boy soprano; mezzo-soprano, alto, contralto; tenor, lyric tenor, operatic tenor, countertenor *or* male alto; baritone, bass, basso, basso cantante, basso profundo; treble, falsetto, castrato

6 **singing group,** chorus, choir, chorale, choral group; men's *or* women's chorus, mixed group, glee club, barbershop quartet

7 **musical director,** conductor, maestro, concertmaster; Kapellmeister, choirmaster, chorus master, bandmaster, répétiteur, music teacher, music master

8 **performance,** concert, symphony concert, opera, chamber concert, popular concert *or* pops, band concert, recital, show, jam session, gig [Inf]; concert hall, opera house, music hall, salon, auditorium

9 **composer,** writer, scorer, arranger, adapter, orchestrator, improviser; songwriter, librettist, lyricist, balladeer, hymn writer, psalmist; syncopator, jazzman, cat [Inf], bluesman [Inf]

10 **music lover,** musicophile, concertgoer, operagoer, opera lover

ADJECTIVES

11 **musical,** music-making, performing, playing, singing; instrumental, vocal, choral, operatic

12 **directed,** conducted, performed

13 **composed,** written, scored, arranged, adapted, orchestrated, improvised

VERBS

14 **play,** make music, perform, render, interpret, play by ear, improvise, syncopate, swing, jam

15 **sound,** blow, toot, whistle; lip, tongue, double-tongue, triple-tongue, trumpet; bow, fiddle; pluck, strum, pick,

twang; beat, hammer, ring, clash; pull out the stops, pedal, tickle the ivories [Inf]

16 **sing,** break *or* burst into song, vocalize, carol, warble, quaver, trill, intone, chant, hum, yodel, croon, belt out [Inf]; sing together, chorus, harmonize

17 **conduct,** direct, lead, wield the baton

18 **compose,** write, score, arrange, adapt, orchestrate, improvise

19 **enjoy music,** love music, listen, go to a concert *or* the opera, attend a symphony

ADVERBS

20 **musically,** interpretively, instrumentally

142 Musical Instruments

Blow, bugle, blow, set the wild echoes flying, / Blow, bugle; answer, echoes dying, dying, dying.
— ALFRED, LORD TENNYSON

NOUNS

1 **musical instrument,** aerophone, idiophone, membranophone, chordophone, electrophone; stringed instrument, plucked string instrument, bowed string instrument, brass, woodwind, percussion instrument, keyboard instrument

2 **part of stringed instrument,** string, bow, fiddlestick, bridge, sound hole, tuning peg, scroll, fingerboard, fret, plectrum; G string, D string, A string, E string

3 **brass instrument,** brass wind instrument, horn; part of brass instrument: mouthpiece, embouchure, slide, crook, bell, valve, pipe

4 **woodwind,** woodwind instrument, reed instrument; part of woodwind instrument: key, reed, double reed, bellows, chanter, drone

5 **percussion instrument,** drum, bell, cymbal; bells, carillon, chimes, hand bells, bell ringing, change ringing, peal, change; campanology; part of percussion instrument: drumhead, drumstick, whisk, whip, brush, wire brush

6 **part of keyboard instrument,** keys, piano keys, keyboard, clavier, console, black notes, white notes, ivories [Inf], eighty-eights [Inf]; string, hammer, jack; manual, stop, rank, register, pedal

7 **instrumental aid,** metronome, tuning fork, pitch pipe, mute, resin; music stand; baton; case

MUSICAL INSTRUMENTS

Brass Winds and Horns
alphorn *or* alpenhorn
althorn *or* alto horn
baritone
bass horn
bombardon
buccina
bugle
buisine
clarion
cornet
cornett
cornu
euphonium
flügelhorn
French horn
hand horn
helicon
horn
Kent bugle
lituus
lur
mellophone
natural trumpet
oliphant
ophicleide
sackbut
saxhorn
saxophone
saxotromba
saxtuba
serpent
shofar
slide trumpet
sousaphone
tenor horn
tromba
trombone
trumpet
tuba

Bowed String Instruments
arpeggione
baryton
bass viol *or* viola da gamba
cello *or* violoncello
contrabass
crwth
double bass *or* violone *or* bass fiddle
gusla *or* gusle
kit
lira da braccio
lira da gamba
lyra viol
nail harmonica *or* nail fiddle
nyckelharpa
octo-basse
pochette
rebab
rebec
rotta *or* rote
sarangi
sarod
tromba marina
vielle
viol
viola
viola da braccio
viola da gamba *or* bass viol
viola d'amore
viola pomposa
violin
violoncello *or* cello
violone

Mechanical and Electric Instruments
barrel organ
calliope
electric guitar
electric organ
geigenwerk
hurdy-gurdy
hydraulis *or* hydraulos
music box
ondes martenot
player piano *or* pianola
neo-Bechstein piano
synthesizer
theremin

Percussion Instruments and Drums
anklung
anvil
bass drum
bata
bells
bones
bongo drums
bull roarer *or* thunder stick
carillon
castanets
celesta
chimes
cimbalom *or* cymbalom
clappers
claves
conga drums
cowbell
cymbals
glass harmonica *or* musical glasses
glockenspiel
gong
hackbrett
hand bells
high-hat cymbals
Jew's harp
jingling Johnny *or* Turkish crescent
kazoo
kettledrums *or* timpani
lithophone
maracas
marimba
metallophone
mirliton
musical glasses *or* glass harmonica
musical saw
rattle
santir
side *or* snare drum
sistrum
sleigh bells
slit-drum
snare *or* side drum
spoons
tabla

tabor	banjolin	samisen	harpsichord	flageolet
tambourin	bouzouki *or*	sitar	piano *or* pianoforte	flute
tambourine	buzuki	steel guitar *or*	spinet	hautboy *or* hautbois
tam-tam	chitarra	Hawaiian guitar	square piano	*or* oboe
tenor drum	chitarra battente	tambura *or*	upright piano	heckelclarina
thumb piano	chittarone	tamboura	virginal	heckelphone *or* bass
timbale	cithara *or* kithara	theorbo		oboe
timbrel	cittern	ukulele *or* uke [Inf]	**Woodwinds**	musette
timpani *or*	classical guitar	vihuela	aulos	oboe *or* hautboy *or*
kettledrums	colascione	vina	bagpipe	hautbois
tom-tom	dital harp	zither	bassanello	oboe da caccia
triangle	gekkin		bass clarinet	oboe d'amore
tubular bells	gittern	**Reed Organs**	basset horn	ocarina *or* sweet
Turkish crescent *or*	guitar	accordion	bass oboe *or*	potato
jingling Johnny	gusli	bandoneon	heckelphone	panpipe
vibraphone *or*	harp	concertina	bassoon	penny whistle
vibraharp *or* vibes	Hawaiian guitar *or*	harmonica	bombarde	pibcorn
[Inf]	steel guitar	harmonium	chalumeau	piccolo
woodblock	kantele	melodeon	clarinet	pipe
xylophone	kithara *or* cithara	melodia	contrabassoon	pommer
xylorimba	koto	mouth organ	cor anglais *or* English	racket
	lute	organ	horn	recorder
Plucked String	lyre	reed organ	cornemuse	sarrusophone
Instruments	mando-bass	regal	crumhorn	shakuhachi
acoustic guitar	mando-cello		curtal	shawm
angelica *or* angel lute	mandola	**Stringed**	doodlesack *or*	syrinx
Appalachian dulcimer	mandolin	**Keyboards**	dudelsack	tenoroon
Autoharp™	orpharion	clavicembalo	double bassoon	tin whistle
balalaika	oud	clavichord	English horn *or* cor	whistle
bandore	pandora	clavicytherium	anglais	
bandurria	penorcon	fortepiano	fife	
banjo	psaltery	grand piano	fipple flute	

ADJECTIVES

8 **instrumental,** bowed, tuned, blown, struck

VERBS

9 **play an instrument,** bow, fiddle, pluck, blow, finger, strike, set *or* pull a stop, set a register, pitch, use a mute, time, tune

143 Painting and Drawing

My business is to paint not what I know, but what I see.
— JOSEPH M. W. TURNER

I have a predilection for painting that lends joyousness to a wall. — PIERRE AUGUSTE RENOIR

NOUNS

1 **(act of) painting,** coloring, colorizing, daubing, washing, underpainting, overpainting, tinting, touching up, illumination, composition, brush

2 **(act of) drawing,** sketching, drafting, delineating, delineation, limning, outlining, rendering, illustrating, draftsmanship, tracing, copying, cartooning, doodling, penciling

▶ *Representation 187; Outline 617*

3 **painting,** oil, airbrush, acrylic, watercolor, easel, cabinet, portrait, miniature; wall, fresco, mural; religious icon, altarpiece, diptych, triptych; cave, rock, prehistoric; action, spray-can, finger; canvas, daub; gouache, aquarelle, wash, tempera, grisaille, monochrome, polychrome, sand, encaustic

▶ *Religion 81; Architecture 134*

4 **drawing,** line drawing, delineation, black-and-white, illustration; sketch, thumbnail sketch, lightning sketch; draft, outline; study, design, rendering, vignette; silhouette; caricature, cartoon, comic, comic strip, animated cartoon, animation; pen-and-ink, pencil drawing, charcoal drawing, crayon drawing, pastel drawing, silverpoint drawing; diagram, graph, mechanical drawing, tracing, doodle, scribble, graffito

▶ *Architecture 134; Representation 187; Preparation 388; Outline 617*

5 type of painting, portrait, profile, head, full-face portrait, full-length portrait, half-length portrait, three-quarter-length portrait, primitive, nude; landscape, seascape, marine painting, riverscape, skyscape, cloudscape, townscape; scene, prospect, panorama, bird's-eye view, pastoral, nocturne, interior, exterior, historical event, battle painting, genre painting, *fête galante* [Fr], conversation piece, animal painting, equestrian painting, still life, flower painting, fruit painting; religious, annunciation, nativity, crucifixion, Pietà

6 treatment, technique, draftsmanship, brushwork, painterliness, painterly values, tactile values, significant form; tone, value, form, color, local color, shadow, shading, sfumato, chiaroscuro, scumbling, marbling; ambience, atmosphere, line, composition, balance, arrangement, grouping, design; golden section, golden mean, foreshortening, illusionism, trompe l'oeil, vanishing point; perspective, aerial perspective, geometric perspective, linear perspective, optical perspective, Renaissance perspective, scientific perspective

▶ *Skillfulness 127; Light 246; Color 251; Plan 387; Style 537; Structure 551; Texture 552; Form 624; Symmetry 626; Arrangement 767*

7 painter, artist, limner, easel painter, action painter, oil painter, mural painter, icon painter, portrait painter, portraitist, landscape painter, marine painter, historical painter, genre painter, still-life painter, flower painter, fruit painter, animal painter, equestrian painter, religious painter, scene painter, sign painter, finger painter, aquarellist, pastelist, watercolorist

8 drawer, drafter, sketcher, limner, delineator, outliner, designer, renderer, cartoonist, animator, doodler, scribbler

9 material *or* **tool,** paints, pigments, oil paint, oils, acrylics, watercolors, gouache, gesso, tempera, distemper; paintbrush, paint tube, palette, palette knife, spatula, mahlstick *or* maulstick, spray gun, airbrush; ground, medium, solvent, thinner, turpentine, siccative, fixative, size, varnish; canvas, easel, stretcher; pen, pencil, drawing pencil, ink, chalk, charcoal, crayon, pastel; paper, art paper, drawing paper, sketchpad, scratch pad, sketchbook, drawing frame; camera obscura, camera lucida; studio, atelier; model, sitter, subject; picture frame, retable, picture gallery, salon, art museum

▶ *Tool 103; Materials 104; Color 251*

ADJECTIVES

10 painted, colored, colorized, tinted, coated, brushed, shaded, washed, daubed, illuminated

11 drawn, sketched, drafted, delineated, outlined, designed, rendered, inked, traced, copied, caricatured, cartooned

VERBS

12 paint, color, colorize, tint, coat, brush, tone, overpaint, underpaint, scumble, wash, shade, daub, illuminate, ink in, touch up

▶ *Color 251; Decoration 532*

13 draw, sketch, draft, delineate, outline, illustrate, render, pencil, chalk, limn, represent, portray, depict, trace, copy, cartoon, caricature, stencil, silhouette, hatch, cross-hatch, doodle

▶ *Outline 617; Imitation 736; Representation 187*

144 Sculpture and Engraving

NOUNS

1 sculpture, sculpturing, figuring, modeling, plastic art; carving, stone carving, direct carving, pointing, stonecutting; statuary, monumental sculpture, architectural sculpture, statue, statuette, figure, figurine, bust, head, torso, group, caryatid, telamon, atlas (pl. atlantes), herm; garden sculpture, portrait sculpture, funerary sculpture, abstract sculpture; stone sculpture, metal sculpture, wire sculpture, paper sculpture, glass sculpture, clay sculpture; earth art, mobile, stabile, kinetic sculpture, minimal sculpture; collage, assemblage, found object, *objet trouvé* [Fr], ready-made object; marble, bronze, terra cotta, woodcarving, whittling, ivory carving, bone carving, scrimshaw, rock carving, petroglyph, wax modeling, model, maquette, molding, ceroplastics, casting, sand casting, plaster casting, cast, plaster cast, lost-wax casting, cire perdue, waxwork

▶ *Woodworking 131; Architecture 134*

2 relief carving, relief, relievo, low relief, bas-relief, basso-relievo, half relief, mezzo-relievo, high relief, alto-relievo; intaglio, glyph, anaglyph, anaglyphy; cameo, medallion, medal, embossment, boss, embossing, engraving, chasing

3 engraving, etching, woodcut, line cut, line engraving, plate engraving; drypoint, metal engraving, steel engraving, copper engraving, brass engraving, chalcography, zincography; wood engraving, xylography, lignography; linoleum block, linocut; lithograph; cerography, gem engraving, glyptography, glyptics, chasing, aquatint, mezzotint

▶ *Woodworking 131*

4 sculptor, carver, stone carver, monumental sculptor, architectural sculptor, figurist, modeler, wax modeler, molder, caster, metal sculptor, abstract sculptor

▶ *Architecture 134*

5 engraver, etcher, metal engraver, wood engraver, gem engraver, aquatinter, chaser, lapidary, type cutter, typographer, printer

▶ *Publication 173*

6 material *or* **tool,** mallet, chisel, claw chisel, burin, gouge, graver, needle, style, etching point; modeling tool, point, spatula, drill, punch, pointing machine;

welding torch, cutting torch, soldering iron, armature; modeling clay, wax, sculptor's wax, plaster, solder, etchant; marble, granite, bronze, terra cotta, stucco, plaster of Paris, papier-mâché, stone, block, woodblock, linoleum block, plate, steel plate, copper plate

ADJECTIVES

7 **sculptural,** molded, monumental, marmoreal, ceramic, tactile, plastic, glyptic, anaglyptic, ceroplastic, toreutic

8 **sculpted,** sculptured, carved, modeled, molded, cast, embossed

9 **engraved,** etched, chased, carved, incised, impressed, printed

VERBS

10 **sculpt,** carve, cut, chisel, chip, whittle, emboss, shape, cast, model, mold, form

11 **engrave,** grave, incise, etch, chase, scrape, bite, impress, aquatint, print

Sports and Enjoyments

145 Sports

NOUNS

1 **sports,** sport, athletics, game, contest, competition, match, event, meet, meeting, bout, round, set, tournament

2 **sports ground,** stadium, arena, venue, field, track, ground, ballpark, park, course, links, court, gymnasium, gym, rink, ring, green, alley

3 **sporting activity,** indoor sport, outdoor sport, participator sport, spectator sport, contact sport, blood sport

4 **sportsman,** sportswoman, athlete, player, contender, defender, challenger, opponent, team member, sporty type, jock [Inf]; sportsmen, sportswomen, players, team, lineup, side, squad, league, division

▶ *Combatant 77; Pursuit 385; Side 623*

ADJECTIVES

5 **sporting,** sportive, sporty, athletic, gymnastic, acrobatic, sportsmanlike; competitive, agonistic

VERBS

6 **participate,** take part, play, join in, enter; compete, vie, challenge, contend, contest

ADVERBS

7 **sportingly,** athletically, gymnastically, acrobatically, competitively, agonistically

---

SPORTING ACTIVITIES

Air Sports
aerobatics
air racing
ballooning
freefalling
gliding
hang gliding
kiting
parachuting
paragliding
parascending
skydiving

Animal Sports
bullfighting
cockfighting
dressage
falconry
greyhound racing
gymkhana
harness (horse)
  racing
horseback riding
horse racing

hunting
pato
pigeon racing
point-to-point
polo
rodeo
show jumping
sled dog racing
steeplechasing
three-day eventing
trotting

Combat Sports
aikido
arm or wrist
  wrestling
boxing
fencing
haphido
judo
jujitsu
karate
kendo
kenipo

kick boxing
kung fu
martial arts
tae kwon do
tang soo do
Thai boxing
wrestling

Court Games
badminton
court tennis
handball
jai alai or pelota
racquetball
squash
table tennis or Ping-
  Pong™
tennis

Fishing
big-game fishing
coarse fishing
deep-sea fishing
fly-fishing

freshwater fishing
game fishing
ice fishing
match fishing
saltwater fishing

Gymnastics
asymmetric (uneven)
  bars
balance beam
floor exercises
horizontal bar (high
  bar)
parallel bars
pommel or side horse
rhythmic gymnastics
rings
sports aerobics
trampolining
tumbling
vaulting

Target Ball Games
boccie or bocci

bowling
Canadian 5-pin
  bowling
candlepins
carom billiards
croquet
curling
duckpins
golf
green bowling
pool
skittles [Brit]
snooker
tenpins

Target Sports
air-gun shooting
archery
clay pigeon shooting
crossbow archery
darts
down-the-line
  shooting
field archery

horseshoe pitching
pistol shooting
rifle shooting
rough shooting
running-game target
  shooting
sharpshooting
skeet *or* skeet shooting
trapshooting

Team Games
Australian rules
  football
bandy
baseball
basketball
beach volleyball
Canadian football
cricket [Brit]
curling
field hockey
football
French cricket
Gaelic football
hurling
ice hockey
lacrosse
netball
roller hockey
rounders [Brit]
rugby
soccer *or* association
  football [Brit]

softball
speedball
team handball
volleyball

**Track and Field
Events**
cross-country
  running
decathlon
discus throwing
fitness walking
hammer throwing
heptathlon
high jumping
hurdling
javelin throwing
long-distance
  running
long jumping
marathon running
middle-distance
  running
modern pentathlon
mountain running
pole vault
race walking
relay racing
shot put
sprinting
steeplechasing
triathlon
triple jump *or* jumping

tug of war

Water Sports
Canadian canoe
  racing
canoe polo
canoe sailing
canoe slalom racing
canoe sprint racing
diving
jet skiing
kayaking
laser sailing
offshore yacht racing
powerboat racing
punting
rafting
rowing
sailboarding
sailing
sailplaning
scuba diving
sculling
skin diving *or* free
  diving [Brit]
snorkeling
surfboarding
swimming
synchronized
  swimming
underwater diving
water polo
water skiing

whitewater canoeing
whitewater rafting
wild-water racing
windsurfing
yacht racing

Wheel Sports
autocross
automobile racing
bicycling
cycle racing
drag racing
in-line skating
karting *or* go-karting
motorcycle racing
motor racing
mountain biking
rally cross
roller derby
roller hockey
roller skating
sidecar racing
skateboarding
stock-car racing

Winter Sports
Alpine combined
  event
Alpine skiing
biathlon
bobsledding
cross-country *or*
  Nordic skiing

downhill racing
figure skating
freestyle skiing
giant slalom
iceboating
ice dancing
luge
Nordic combined
  event
off-piste skiing
short-track speed
  skating
skibob racing
ski jumping
ski mountaineering
slalom
snowboarding
speed skating
tobogganing

Other
Alpine climbing
backpacking
bungee jumping
camping
Frisbee™
hiking
ice climbing
mountaineering
orienteering
rock climbing
spelunking
weightlifting

146 Automobile Racing

NOUNS

1 **automobile racing,** auto racing, car racing, motor racing, international racing, endurance racing, speedway racing; production car racing, Indy Car racing, Formula car racing, stock-car racing, drag racing, midget-car racing, hot-rod racing, vintage-car racing, grasstrack racing, autocross; automobile rally, rallying, hill climbing, karting *or* go-karting; endurance event, maximum-speed event, maximum-acceleration event, sprint, reliability trial

2 **racing automobile,** racing car, formula car, stock car, Indy Car, sports car, touring car, production car; supercharger, turbocharger, carburetor; chassis, frame, body, nose, wings, diffuser, air box, spoiler, roll bar, roll cage, skirt; wheels, racing tires, slicks, rain tires; gear box, clutch, suspension

3 **automobile racing terms,** track, grid, oval, circuit, banked circuit, road circuit, straight, straightaway, corner, banked corner, turn, curve, bend, S-bend, switch-

back, hairpin, sweeper, chicane, safety barrier, Armco™, pit, pit lane, pit wall; double-clutching, gearing, clutch-slip, changing down; warm-up lap, start, Le Mans start, grid start, paced start, flying start, restart, pole position, lap, tucking in, slipstreaming, groove, peeling off, spoiling, outbreaking, drift, sliding off, spinning out, spin-out, black flag, white flag, checkered flag

▶ *Circularity 631; Beginning 771*

4 **races,** Formula 1 (F1) races, Formula 1 World Championship races, Grand Prix (GP) races, Indy Car races, Formula Super Vee races, Formula 2 (F2) races, Formula 2000 races, Formula 3 (F3) races, Formula 3000 races, touring car races, sports car races; Indianapolis 500 race, Le Mans 24-hour race, Monza 1000-kilometer race, Sebring 12-hour race, Targa Florio, Daytona 500 race, Winston Cup race

5 **Formula 1 World Championship races,** Grand Prix (GP), United States GP at Phoenix, Brazilian GP at Interlagos, San Marino GP at San Marino, Monaco GP at Monte Carlo, Mexican GP at Mexico City, Canadian GP

at Montreal, French GP at Bandol, British GP at Silverstone, German GP at Hockenheim, Hungarian GP at Hungaroring, Belgian GP at Spa Francorchamps, Italian GP at Monza, Portuguese GP at Estoril, Spanish GP at Jerez, Japanese GP at Suzuka, Australian GP at Adelaide

6 **automobile rallies,** Acropolis, Alpine, East African Safari, Monte Carlo, Netherlands Tulip Rally, San Remo Rally of the Flowers, Swedish Midnight Sun

> ◗ *Contention 422; Motion 677*

7 **racing governing bodies,** Fédération Internationale de l'Automobile (FIA), United States Automobile Club (USAC), National Association for Stock Car Auto Racing (NASCAR), National Hot Rod Association (NHRA), Sports Car Club of America (SCCA), Indy Racing League (IRL), Indianapolis Motor Speedway Association (IMSA), Vintage Automobile Racing Association (VARA), World Sports Car (WSC), Canadian Auto Sports Club (CASC), Royal Automobile Club (RAC) [Brit], British Racing Drivers' Club (BRDC)

8 **driver,** number-one driver, number-two driver; racer, Grand Prix racer, Formula 1 racer, Indy Car racer, Formula car racer, automobile racer, sports car racer, production car racer, vintage car racer, drag racer; pit mechanic, marshal

ADJECTIVES

9 **racing,** automobile *or* auto, endurance, maximum-acceleration, maximum-speed, speedway, international, Grand Prix, Formula 1, Formula 2, stock-car, go-kart, grasstrack, dirt-track, banked, mountain, lapped, lapping, spun-out, six-gear, off-camber, right-hand, left-hand

VERBS

10 **race,** auto race, race sports cars, road-race, race internationally, do Formula 1 racing, race stock cars, drag-race, race midget cars, race hot-rods, do grasstrack racing, do dirt-track racing, scramble

11 **be on the track,** have the pole position, go to the starting grid, get the green light, start, restart, hold position, scramble, set up, slipstream, slide off, clip the apex, clip, gear, double-clutch, use the bottom gear, clutch-slip, change down, crank over, peel off, tuck in, spin out, spoil, straight-line, out brake, sweep, funnel, have ground clearance, have G-force loading, lap, pit, make a pit stop, fuel, make a fuel stop, change the tires, hit a straight, run the chicane, hit the groove, turn a corner, get the checkered flag, over-rev [Inf], blow the engine

147 Baseball

It's done / on a diamond, / and for fun. / It's about / home, and it's about run. — MAY SWENSON

NOUNS

1 **baseball,** ball game, the great American game, America's national sport, America's pastime; professional baseball, major league baseball, minor league baseball, college baseball, National Collegiate Athletic Association (NCAA) baseball, Little League baseball, hardball, softball; National Baseball Hall of Fame and Museum

2 **baseball team,** team, nine, roster, squad, club, the boys of summer; baseball player, ballplayer, battery; pitcher, relief pitcher, catcher, fielder, infielder, first baseman, second baseman, third baseman, shortstop; outfielder, left fielder, center fielder, right fielder; lineup, starting lineup, batter, hitter, home-run hitter, power hitter, designated hitter, pinch hitter, right-handed hitter, left-handed hitter, lefty [Inf], southpaw [Inf], slugger, leadoff man, cleanup man, closer; runner, base runner, designated runner, starter, substitute; batting champion, home-run leader, runs-batted-in (RBI) leader, earned-run-average (ERA) leader, all-star, all-American, Rookie of the Year, Most Valuable Player (MVP); manager, pitching coach, batting coach, umpire, first-base umpire, second-base umpire, third-base umpire, official scorer; scout, talent scout

3 **baseball field,** ballpark, ball field, baseball stadium; stands, grandstand, bleachers; diamond, infield, batter's box, catcher's box, pitcher's mound; home plate, first base, second base, third base, foul line; outfield, left field, center field, right field, outfield fence, fair territory, foul territory; dugout, bull pen, on-deck circle

4 **baseball equipment,** baseball *or* ball, bat; baseball uniform, stockings, baseball shoes, cleats, cap, sliding pads; catcher's mitt, batting glove, catcher's mask, umpire's mask, birdcage mask, chest protector, shin guards, shin pads, batting helmet; [Inf]: pill, apple, Louisville slugger, horsehide, lumber

5 **pitching terms,** catcher's sign, strike zone, strike, ball, windup, hard pitch, soft pitch, curve ball, reverse curve, fast ball, knuckle ball, change-up, change of pace, slider, breaker, fadeaway, screwball, spit ball; brush-off, brushing *or* dusting off the batter, dust-off, strikeout, wild pitch, balk, intentional walk *or* pass, base on balls, loading the bases, walking a man, forcing a run, shutout; perfect game, earned-run average (ERA), win, save

6 **batting terms,** hit, single, line drive, pop single; double, triple, home run, inside-the-park home run, grand-slam home run, grand-slammer; hat trick; fair ball, foul ball, foul tip, ground ball, up-the-middle hit, grounder, hopper, dribbler, fly ball, fly, pop fly, pop-up, bunt; squeeze play, suicide squeeze, sacrifice, sacrifice fly, perfect sacrifice; hit-and-run play, interference, being hit by a pitch; runs batted in (RBI), batting average; one you can hang the wash on [Inf], Texas leaguer [Inf]

7 other game terms, inning, seventh inning stretch, extra inning; doubleheader; double play, triple play, out, put-out, throw-out, force play, rundown, tag-out, forced out; infield fly, infield fly rule, stolen base, pickup, fly-out, hot corner, shoestring catch

8 baseball leagues and championship games, National League, American League, World Series, all-star game; pennant winner, world champions; Triple-A league, Double-A league, farm club, the minors, bush leagues; Little League, Little League World Series

VERBS

9 play baseball, take the field, come to bat; pitch, throw a fast ball, throw a curve, throw a slider, throw a wild pitch, balk, brush off the batter, hit the batter, load the bases, walk, pitch a shutout, pitch a perfect game, be relieved, call for a relief pitcher; swing, strike out, foul off, foul, hit, hit a line drive, hit a fly, hit a grounder, single, hit a single, double, hit a double, triple, hit a triple, hit a home run *or* homer, hit a grand-slam home run, hit a grand-slammer, ground, hit into a double play, force out, fly out, pop up, bunt, sacrifice, squeeze; be thrown out, be intentionally walked, be hit by a pitch, be brushed off, drive in a run, leave a runner stranded, run the bases, slide home, steal a base, score a run, score; catch a fly, throw out, make a double play; make an error, be caught in a rundown, take a trip to the showers [Inf]

148 Basketball

NOUNS

1 basketball, basketball game, professional basketball, college basketball, Basketball Hall of Fame; quarter, half, halftime, overtime

2 basketball team, team, roster, five; center, forward, power forward, small forward, guard, point guard, shooting guard, swingman, sixth man, pivot man, shooter, foul shooter, scorer, passer, blocker, rebounder; all-American, all-star; varsity player, first-team player, captain, rookie, veteran, draft, draft pick, substitute, sub [Inf], NBA Most Valuable Player, NBA Rookie of the Year; coach, head coach, assistant coach, official, referee, ref [Inf], timer

3 basketball court, court, center court, backcourt, front court, 10-second line, halfcourt line, sideline, baseline, 3-point line, key, foul line *or* free throw line, free throw lane; basket, net, rim, backboard; scorer's table, shot-clock; uniform, jersey, shorts, gym shoes, sneakers, knee guard

4 playing terms, dribbling, shooting, dunking, passing, holding, rebounding, pivoting, screening, blocking, guarding; 1-pointer, 2-pointer, 3-pointer; foul, personal foul, technical foul, double foul, offensive foul; free throw, foul shot, penalty shot, hook shot, jump shot, bank shot, lay-up, dunk, slam dunk, 1-hand shot,

2-hand shot, set shot, field goal, tip-in; pass, bounce pass, hook pass, behind-the-back pass, rebound; loose ball, live ball, held ball, dead ball, jump ball; possession, fast break offense, running offense, shoot-and-run offense, ball-control offense, high post, low post, man-to-man defense, zone defense, pressing defense; [Inf]: air ball, hanger, swish

5 violations, running with the ball, traveling, walking, double-dribbling, kicking the ball, tripping, hacking, 3-second lane violation, 10-second backcourt violation, goaltending, stepping over foul line during a free throw, stepping over end line on a throw-in, technical foul

6 basketball associations and tournaments, National Basketball Association (NBA), NBA Playoffs, NBA Championship; National Collegiate Athletic Association (NCAA), NCAA Championship; National Invitational Tournament (NIT); National Association of Intercollegiate Athletics (NAIA) Tournament

VERBS

7 play basketball, dribble, shoot, use the backboard, hit a shot, make a bank shot, make a jump shot, make a hook shot, tip in, dunk, slam dunk, make a free throw; pass, make a bounce pass; hold the ball, rebound, pivot, screen, block, guard, drive, cut, foul, foul out; travel, walk, double-dribble, kick the ball, trip, hack, goaltend, draw a personal foul, draw a technical foul, take a foul shot, shoot a free throw, play run-and-shoot, play man-to-man, press; [Inf]: can a shot, knock the bottom out, shoot an air ball

149 Billiards, Pool, Snooker

NOUNS

1 billiards, pool, pocket billiards, snooker; English billiards, French billiards; billiard table, center spot, cushion, pocket, billiard cloth, baize, pool table; billiard ball, pool ball, numbered ball, white cue ball, rack, triangle; cue *or* cue stick, cue rest *or* bridge, chalk; billiards club, billiards saloon [Brit], pool hall

2 billiards play, run-through, safety, scratch, inning, break, bank shot, carom, dead ball, English, massé shot *or* massé, frozen ball, full-ball aim, spot stroke, half-ball stroke, screw, hazard, long loser, long on-off, stun and stab, miscue, miss, pocketing the ball

3 pool, pocket billiards, open table, pool table, lineup, eightball; bumper pool *or* bumpers, breaking violation, lag, scratch

4 snooker, volunteer snooker, frame, snooker table, pocket billiard table, balk, spot, D area, cushion, pocket, free ball, nominated ball, cue ball

5 player, billiards player, pool player, snooker player, striker, referee, marker

ADJECTIVES

6 billiard, numbered, cue, cued, miscued, missed,

stroked, spotted, pocketed, foul, played; free, nominated, called, snookered, crotched, in balk, full-ball, half-ball

7 **play,** play billiards, play pool, play snooker; take a turn at the table, break, make a break, chalk a stick, make a bank shot, carom, put English on the ball, drive out of balk, take a shot, take a stroke, miscue, miss, pocket the ball

150 Boating Sports

NOUNS

1 **boating sports,** sailing, canoeing, rowing, sculling, punting, windsurfing, sailboarding, rafting

2 **sailing,** yachting, cruising, day sailing, ocean sailing, international sailing, competitive sailing, passage

3 **sailboat,** sailing dinghy, day sailor, coastal cruiser, coastal racer, offshore boat, ocean cruiser, ocean racer, one-design boat, vessel, yacht; catboat, sloop, cutter, yawl, ketch, schooner, double-ender, keel, fin keel, centerboard, daggerboard, leeboard, catamaran, trimaran, stiff boat, tender boat, Marconi-rigged sailboat, gaff-rigged sailboat, square-rigged sailboat

 ◗ *Water Transportation 690*

4 **sailboat parts and accessories,** hull, beam, draft, freeboard, headroom, bow, stem, pulpit, amidships, quarter, stern, transom, deck, coaming, scuppers, cockpit, companionway, hatch, cabin, bulkhead, bilge, wood hull, aluminum hull, ferroconcrete hull, fiberglass hull; spars, mast, mainmast, mizzen mast, foremast, deck-stepped mast, keel-stepped mast; yards, boom, gaff; keel, ballast, helm, tiller, wheel, rudder, rudderpost, lifelines, ratline, winch, coffee grinder; rigging, standing rigging, shrouds, forestay, backstay, spreaders, tang, chain plates, turnbuckle; running rigging, halyard, sheet, traveler, boom vang, lazy jacks, Cunningham tackle, outhaul, downhaul, topping lift, fairlead, gooseneck, chock, cleat, jam cleat, bitt, block, snatch block, reef point; sails, mainsail, trysail, headsail, jib, Genoa, reaching jib, spinnaker, gaffsail, staysail, loose-footed sail, battens; lines: anchor rode, painter, mooring line, spring, heaving line; fenders, fender board, flag, ensign, pennant, burgee, bosun's chair

 ◗ *Water Transportation 690*

5 **sailing terms,** starboard tack, port tack, heading up, luffing, wearing, bearing off, coming about, jibe, slam jibe, close reaching, beam reaching, broad reaching, running, wing and wing, close hauling, sheeting in, sheeting out; true wind, apparent wind, sea breeze, land breeze; course, wake course, lee helm, weather helm, balance, rounding up

6 **competitive sailing,** regatta, yacht racing, handicap racing, one-design racing, Olympic-class racing, Performance Racing Handicap Factor (PRHF) racing, International Measurement System (IMS) racing, Midget Ocean Racing Club (MORC) racing, tall-ship racing, single-handed racing, offshore racing, ocean racing, transatlantic racing, around-the-world racing, sailing trophy, America's Cup race

7 **yacht racing associations,** International Yacht Racing Union (IYRU), Intercollegiate Yacht Racing Association (IYRA), United States Yacht Racing Union (USYRU), Royal Yachting Association (RYA) [Brit]

8 **canoeing,** paddling, double-paddle canoeing, recreational canoeing, whitewater canoeing

9 **canoe,** birchbark canoe, dugout canoe, open canoe, Canadian canoe, paddling canoe, racing canoe, cruising canoe, sailing canoe, international 10-square-meter canoe, war canoe, folding canoe, foldboat, faltboat; outrigger, catamaran, V-bottom; kayak, decked kayak

10 **canoe parts,** bow, stern, keel, gunwale *or* gunnel, seat, thwart, sliding outrigger seat, deck well, cockpit, paddle, single-bladed paddle, double-bladed paddle, double-ended paddle

11 **canoeing techniques,** stroke, cruising stroke, bow stroke, J stroke, draw stroke, turning stroke, pushover stroke, sweep stroke, jamming stroke, stopping stroke, cruising hook, locking, Eskimo roll, shaking out

12 **canoe racing,** slalom racing, Olympic canoeing; canoe race, one-man (C-1) canoe race; two-man (C-2) canoe race; single kayak (K-1) race, double kayak (K-2) race, four-man kayak (K-4) race, single-blade race, double-blade race, tandem race, open cruising race, decked-canoe race; water course, gate

13 **canoe associations,** International Canoe Federation (ICF), American Canoe Association (ACA), British Canoe Union; International Challenge Cup

14 **rowing,** amateur rowing, single-oar rowing, fixed-seat rowing, sweep rowing, double-oar rowing; sculling, single sculling, double sculling, quadruple sculling; competitive rowing, racing, scull racing, skiff racing, Olympic rowing, Olympic regatta; intercollegiate rowing

15 **rowboat parts,** seat, sliding seat, fixed seat, stroke side, bow side, oar, racing oar, spade oar, spoon oar, scull, handle, blade, loom, collar, button, rowlock, notch, tholepin, gunwale *or* gunnel, swivel, thwart, stretcher

16 **rowing techniques,** catch, stroke, American stroke, English stroke, recovery, feathering, finish, squaring balance, diving, striking, paddling, blade slip, catching a crab [Inf]

17 **rowing associations,** American Rowing Association, Fédération Internationale Sociétés d'Aviron (FISA)

18 **rowing competitions,** Harvard–Yale race, Oxford–Cambridge race, Henley Royal Regatta, Royal Canadian Henley Olympic rowing, Olympic regatta, World Championship

19 windsurfing, sailboarding, boardsurfing, sailing, freestyle sailing, displacement sailing; windsurf racing, slalom racing, one-design racing, open-class racing, ins-and-outs, wave sailing, wave riding, wave jumping, ice surfing

20 sailboard parts, board, custom board, customs, glass-reinforced plastic (GRP) board, flatboard, displacement board, roundboard, pop-out board, funboard, gun, floater, sinker, marginal, tandem, tridem, rail, fin, skeg, wing, sail, funboard storm sail, rotational sail, rotating asymmetric foil (RAF), powerhead, fathead, universal joint, boom, wishbone boom, footstrap, harness, harness line, ding, hull, V-shape hull, daggerboard, bowline, bumper, rocker, downhaul line, camber inducer, cleat, clew

21 windsurfing terms, center of effort (CE), center of lateral resistance (CLR), cavatation, railing, spin-out, wipe-out, Le Mans start, water start, foot steering, planing, pumping, off-the-lip turn

22 windsurfing classes, Division I, Division II, Division III, slalom course

23 rafting, whitewater rafting, wild-water racing

24 boating person, sailor, canoeist, rower, punter, sculler, windsurfer, sailboarder; mariner, boater; captain, skipper, navigator, helmsman; coxswain; yachtsman, yachtswoman, paddler, oarsman *or* oar

▶ *Water Transportation 690*

ADJECTIVES

25 sailing, yachting, planing, cruising, ocean-cruising, ocean-racing, offshore, transatlantic, multihull, single-handed, Marconi, gaff, Olympic, one-design, square-rigged, Marconi-rigged, gaff-rigged, fiberglass, fore-and-aft, forward, aft, deck-stepped, keel-stepped, underway, abeam, adrift, aloft, aweigh, close-hauled, roller-reefed, head-to-wind, luffing, in irons, stop, off-wind, slam, quartering, stiff, tender, heaving, mooring, anchor, foul, clear, Cunningham, goosenecked, jam

26 canoeing, canoe, paddling, paddled, wild-water, whitewater, birchbark, dugout, open, Canadian, V-bottom, war, decked, folding, cruising, sailing, single-paddle, double-paddle, single-bladed, double-bladed, double-ended, softwood, hardwood, bow, forward bow, J, turning, pushover, sweep, jamming, stopping; kayaking

27 rowing, single-oar, single, fixed-seat, sweep, double-oar, double, quadruple, scull, skiff, intercollegiate, coxed, coxswainless, stroke, bow, spade, spoon, recovering, feathering, finished, squared, squaring, balanced, balancing, diving, striking, paddling; punting; rafting

28 windsurfing, sailboarding, boardsurfing, freestyle, displacement, pop-out, floater, sinker, marginal, tandem, tridem, rotational, universal, wishbone, V-shape, downhaul, planing, subplaning, hooked-in, pumping, off-the-lip

VERBS

29 sail, launch, make way, cast off, slip anchor; captain, skipper, crew, steer, navigate; sail close-hauled, sail close to the wind, sail starboard tack, sail port tack, head up, fall off, luff, reach, close reach, beam reach, broad reach, bear off, run, come about, tack, beat, jibe, maintain course, go astern, stand on, heel, fetch, broach, pitchpole, heave to, ride out the storm

30 handle sailboat equipment, rig, jury-rig; loose, hoist, make sail; bend, hank, furl, roll, reef, back a sail; sheet in, sheet out, heave, harden, snub, ease, pay, let fly, loose a line, wear, drop anchor, sound the depth, splice ropes, bend lines, lay up a sailboat

31 canoe, paddle, go whitewater canoeing, shoot the rapids, race, sail, use a J stroke, use a turning stroke, lock the blade, shake out

32 row, scull, race, cox, skiff-race, stroke, catch, feather, recover, finish, square, balance, dive, strike, paddle, swing, slide, lift an oar, drop and oar, cover a blade, run level, clear the water, lurch, steer, catch a crab [Inf]

33 windsurf, sailboard, boardsurf, go freestyle sailing, go displacement sailing, wave sail, ride a wave, jump a wave, cavatate, rail, spin out, wipe out, plane, sub-plane, pump, hook in, make an off-the-lip turn, tip the board

34 raft, go rafting, wild-water race

ADVERBS

35 offshore, onshore, on the rail, on the nose, on the tail, on the quarter, broadside, to windward, to weather, to leeward, to starboard, to port, about, astern, athwart, ahull, aback, abaft, abeam, adrift, aloft, inboard, outboard

151 Bowling

NOUNS

1 bowling, tenpin bowling *or* tenpins, duckpins, candlepins, green bowling; ninepins, skittles [Brit]; bowling alley, bowling lane, foul line, gutter, rear cushion, pit, 1-3-strike pocket, ball return, automatic pinsetter, range finder; bowling ball, pin *or* bowling pin, tenpin, candlepin, duckpin; bowling shoes, bowling bag; frame

2 bowling delivery, 4-step delivery, straight-line delivery, hook, curve, backup, follow-through, strike, spare, split, converted split, triple, turkey, error, gutter shot, gutter ball

3 green bowling, lawn bowling, bowls, level-green bowls, crown-green bowls, bowls match, singles match *or* singles, pairs match *or* pairs, triples match *or* triples, 3-on-a-side match, fours match *or* fours; end, green, bowling green, slow green, fast green, bowling rink, boundary, backboard, ditch, bank, wood, bowl, bias, jack, kitty, mat, bowling side, rank

4 grip, forehand grip, backhand grip, the claw, the palm, aiming point, delivery, smooth delivery, wobble, head, plant, weight, whip, shot, path, grass, green; backhand shot, controlled shot, yard-on, running shot, reaching shot, wrestling shot, upshot, onshot, run-through shot, trail shot, block shot, draw shot *or* draw, drive, firing shot; cant, tilt, follow-through, front bowls, shot bowl, dead bowl, live bowl, dead jack, live jack, backwood bowl, backest bowl, toucher, wrestling toucher, chalk mark, hit, direct hit, burnt end, shots up, shots down, foot fault

5 **bowler,** tenpin bowler, duckpin bowler, candlepin bowler, professional bowler; bowls player, leader, second, third *or* vice-skip, skip *or* captain, marker, measurer, umpire

ADJECTIVES

6 **bowling,** tenpin, duckpin, candlepin; foul, head, split, gutter, converted, 4-step, straight-line, hooked, curved, backup, follow-through

7 **bowls,** level-green, crown-green, singles, pairs, triples, 3-on-a-side, fours, slow fast, forehand, backhand, aiming, smooth, controlled, yard-on, running, reaching, wrestling, run-through, block, draw, firing, follow-through, front, dead, live, backest, jack-high, draw-weight, rolling the jack

VERBS

8 **bowl,** play a frame, release the ball, bowl a hook ball, knock down pins, make *or* score a strike, score a spare, split, score a perfect game, score 300; roll the jack, fire a shot, draw a shot, draw close to jack, go for the jack, go short and wide, lay a block, tilt the bowl, drive with the bowl, take more grass, take out

152 Combat Sports

Not only do I knock 'em out, I pick the round.
— MUHAMMAD ALI

NOUNS

1 **combat sport,** combative sport, fighting sport, fighting skill; fighting, boxing, professional boxing, wrestling, professional wrestling; martial art, self-defense, judo, jujitsu, karate, tae kwon do, aikido
▶ *Combatant 77; Contention 422*

2 **boxing,** fighting, prizefighting, pugilism, noble art of self-defense, shadowboxing, fisticuffs, sparring, jabbing, socking, slugging, pummeling; boxing match, prizefight, fight, championship fight, fixed fight, haymaker [Inf]

3 **boxing terms,** boxing purse, receipts, boxing rules, Marquess of Queensberry rules, point system, boxing ring, corner, ropes, bell, round, boxing scorecard, decision

4 **boxing equipment,** boxing gloves, boxing shorts, mouthpiece, sparring helmet

5 **boxing techniques,** stance, footwork, dance, bob, feint, parry, block, boxing punch, left jab, left hook, right hook, right cross, straight punch, straight left, left uppercut, right uppercut, swing, knockdown punch, knockdown, knockout punch, knockout, count, technical knockout (TKO), foul, hitting below the belt, butt, rabbit punch

6 **boxing weight divisions,** light-flyweight, flyweight, bantamweight, super bantamweight, featherweight, junior lightweight, lightweight, light welterweight, welterweight, light middleweight, middleweight, light heavyweight, cruiserweight, heavyweight, super heavyweight

7 **boxing associations,** International Boxing Federation, World Boxing Association (WBA), European Boxing Union, British Boxing Board of Control (BBBC); Amateur Athletic Union (AAU), Gold Gloves, International Amateur Boxing Association (IABA), Olympic Games

8 **boxer,** professional boxer, amateur boxer, Olympic boxer, fighter, prizefighter, pugilist, slugger, puncher, jabber, sparring partner, champion, heavyweight champion, world champion, titleholder, challenger, second; manager, trainer, referee, champ; [Inf]: southpaw, pug

9 **type of wrestling,** professional, amateur, Olympic, Greco-Roman, freestyle, catch-as-catch-can, no-holds-barred, tag-team, mud, sumo

10 **wrestling terms,** wrestling match, round, wrestling ring, corner, rope; wrestling hold, full nelson, half nelson, flying mare, headlock, body slam, fall, pin; illegal hold, choke, strangling, stranglehold, kick, gouge, hair-pulling

11 **wrestling weight divisions,** 106 pounds, 115 pounds, 126 pounds, 137 pounds, 150 pounds, 163 pounds, 181 pounds, 198 pounds, 220 pounds, 286 pounds

12 **wrestler,** professional wrestler, amateur wrestler, Olympic wrestler, Greco-Roman wrestler, freestyle wrestler, National Collegiate Athletic Association (NCAA) wrestler, grappler, referee, grunt-and-groaner [Inf]

13 **judo,** the way of gentleness, women's judo, junior judo, judo kata; judo grade, brown belt, dan grade, black belt; judo mat, judo club, dojo (practice hall); judoist, judoka (judo player), *tori* (attacker), *uka* (defender); judo match, competition judo; judo referee, corner judge, timekeeper, recorder

14 **karate,** the way of the empty hand, sport karate, recreational karate; karate grade, dan grade, red belt, white belt, yellow belt, orange belt, green belt, brown belt, black belt; karate mat, karate club, dojo (practice hall); karate expert, karate combatant, karate referee, judge, arbitrator, timekeeper, scorekeeper

15 **tae kwon do,** the way of the foot and fist, tae kwon do combinations, tae kwon do patterns, competitive tae kwon do; tae kwon do grade, white belt, yellow

belt, green belt, blue belt, red belt, black belt; competitor, referee, judge, jury

16 **aikido,** the way of harmony of the spirit, competition aikido; aikido grade, yellow belt, orange belt, green belt, blue belt, brown belt; *tori* (thrower), *uke* (attacker)

ADJECTIVES

17 **combat,** combative, fighting, professional, amateur, pugilistic, self-defensive, sparring, jabbed, jabbing, slugged, slugging, hit, hitting, on the ropes, knocked out, in the corner, dancing, bobbing, feinting, parrying, blocking, mixing it up [Inf], left, right, straight, knockdown, knockout; light-flyweight, flyweight, bantamweight, super-bantamweight, featherweight, junior-lightweight, lightweight, light-welterweight, welterweight, light-middleweight, middleweight, light-heavyweight, cruiserweight, heavyweight, super-heavyweight; Olympic, champion, world champion

18 **wrestling,** Greco-Roman, freestyle, catch-as-catch-can, no-holds-barred, tag-team, grunt-and-groan [Inf]; judo, all-red, red-and-white, black, throwing; karate, sport, recreational, punching, kicking, blocking; tae kwon do, lunge, flying, crescent, competitive; aikido, immobilized, wooden

VERBS

19 **box,** fight, spar, prizefight, practice self-defense, shadow box, engage in fisticuffs, fight as a heavyweight, land a blow, jab, sock, slug, stun, pummel, hold a boxing match, have a prizefight, fix a fight, throw a fight, enter the ring, go to one's corner, have someone on the ropes, save by the bell, box a round, dance about, bob, feint, parry, block, jab, throw a left hook, swing, knock down, knock out, win by a TKO, foul, hit below the belt, butt, land a rabbit punch

20 **wrestle,** wrestle freestyle, grapple, hold a wrestling match, last a round, have a full nelson on, secure a fall, pin, choke, strangle, kick, gouge, pull hair

21 **do martial arts,** practice judo, earn a black belt, become a karate expert, practice tae kwon do, use aikido techniques, immobilize

ADVERBS

22 **professionally,** as an amateur, competitively, in the ring, in self-defense, with footwork, by feinting, below the belt, squarely, on the nose, on the chin, for the count, freestyle, evasively, by deflection

153 Fencing

NOUNS

1 **fencing,** foil fencing, épée fencing, saber fencing, fencing bout, fencing assault, swordplay, *escrime* [Fr], *scherma* [Ital], dueling, historic fencing, singlestick, quarterstaff, cane, kendo, *Schläger-Mensur* [Ger], bayonet fencing; fencing area, piste

▶ *Contention 422*

2 **fencing equipment,** fencing weapon, foil, electric foil, foil button, foil guard, foil grip; dueling sword, épée, electric épée, épée prongs; saber, blade; fencing clothes: wire-mesh mask, chest protector, sailcloth jacket, padded glove, elbow guard, body cord

▶ *Weapon 78*

3 **fencing movements,** on guard, en garde, attack, composite attack, straight thrust *or* cut, lunge, bind, envelopment, jump, march, running attack, flèche, glide, cutover, coupé, line of attack, high-outside, high-inside, low-outside, low-inside; parry, composite parry, redoublement, disengage, false attack, feint, counter *or* circular parry, semicircle, *mezzocerchio* [Ital]; beat, counterattack, riposte *or* ripost, counter-riposte *or* counter-ripost, stop thrust, remise, time thrust *or* cut; closing in, *corps à corps* [Fr], clinch, guard; pronation, supination, hit, touch

▶ *Attack 418; Defense 419; Retaliation 420*

4 **fencing associations,** Fédération Internationale d'Escrime (FIE) [Fr], United States Fencing Association (USFA)

5 **fencer,** foilsman, épéeist, dueler *or* duelist

ADJECTIVES

6 **fencing,** foil, épée, saber, electric, padded, wire-mesh, attacking, lunging, running, cutover, high-outside, high-inside, low-outside, low-inside, parried, parrying, disengaged, false, feinting, countered, countering, composite, counterattacking, pronated, supinated

VERBS

7 **fence,** duel, foil-fence, épée-fence, saber-fence, bayonet-fence, have a fencing bout, be on guard, attack, thrust, lunge, recover, make a false attack, use footwork, jump forward, march, make a running attack, glide, parry, avoid a parry, block an attack, feint, counterattack, disengage, riposte *or* ripost, clinch, guard, hit, touch, pronate, supinate

ADVERBS

8 **on guard,** with swordplay, with footwork, by parrying, by counterattacking, high-outside, high-inside, low-outside, low-inside

154 Fishing

I have laid aside business, and gone a-fishing.
— IZAAK WALTON

NOUNS

1 **fishing,** angling, game fishing, still fishing, bait fishing, freshwater bait fishing, trolling, float fishing, trotting, ledgering, coarse *or* bottom fishing, casting, bait casting, fly casting, spinning, spin-casting

2 **fly-fishing,** dapping, natural fly-fishing, artificial fly-fishing, wet fly-fishing, dry fly-fishing, fishing the water, fishing to the rise

3 **saltwater fishing,** saltwater bait fishing, surf fishing, beach-casting, saltwater trolling, deep-sea fishing,

deep-sea trolling, strip-casting, mooching, big-game fishing

4 **ice fishing,** ice hole, ice bar, ice spoon

5 **competitive fishing,** competitive casting, tournament casting, distance event, accuracy event

6 **bait,** worm, insect, minnow, maggot, bread, ground bait, chum; fly, natural fly, artificial fly, lure, artificial lure, tied fly, dressed fly, jig, streamer, plug, surface plug, floating plug, floating diver, popper, underwater plug, sinking plug, deep diver, jointed plugs, spoon, fly spoon, barspoon, spinner, wagtail, mackerel spinner, artificial minnow

7 **fishing tackle,** fishing rod *or* rod, double-handed rod, single-handed rod, telescopic rod, float rod, ledger rod, spinning rod, fishing pole *or* pole, bamboo pole, fly rod, casting rod, handgrip, butt guide, ferrule, tiptop, reel, center-pin reel, single-action reel, multiplier reel, fixed-spool *or* spinning reel, closed-face *or* spin-casting reel, open-face reel, float tackle, float, line, nylon line, sunk line, bobber, sinker, lead sinker, lead, coffin lead, barleycorn lead, plummet lead, fishhook *or* hook, eye, shank, bend, point, double hook, treble hook, shot, split-shot, gaff, cork, bobbin, keepnet, forcep, disgorger

8 **fighting chair,** turntable chair, chair socket, harness, throwout level, braided line, sea swivel

9 **catch,** bite, strike, take

10 **game fish,** salmon, trout, rainbow trout, bass, perch, pike, muskellunge, walleye, arctic char, sailfish, marlin, swordfish, tuna, tarpon, bonefish, bluefish, yellowtail, snook, bonito, flounder, barracuda, snapper, shark, mackerel, Spanish mackerel

11 **fishing associations,** American Casting Association, International Casting Federation

12 **fisherman,** fisher, angler, fly-fisher, saltwater fisherman, freshwater fisherman, sea angler, deep-sea fisherman, big-game fisherman, trawlerman *or* trawler

ADJECTIVES

13 **fishing,** angling, fished, piscatorial *or* piscatory, saltwater, freshwater, deep-sea, coarse, bottom, wet-fly, dry-fly, ground, baited, baiting, casting, cast, trolling, trolled, tied, dressed, artificial, natural, floating, surface, underwater, sinking, jointed, double-handed, single-handed, single-action, fixed-spool, center-pin, spinning, closed-face, open-face

VERBS

14 **fish,** angle, cast, spin-cast, fish the water, fish with bait, fish to the rise, catch fish, trawl, fly-fish; saltwater fish, freshwater fish, deep-sea fish, big-game fish, ice fish; entangle one's line, bait the hook, anchor bait, cast bait, cast a lure, cock the float, pump a fish, watch the float, have a bite, hook, reel in, haul in, net, tie a fly, dress a fly, troll

ADVERBS

15 **on the water,** on the surface, by casting, by trolling,

underwater, naturally, artificially, piscatorially, competitively

155 Football

NOUNS

1 **football,** football game; professional football, exhibition game, playoff game, Super Bowl, Pro Bowl; college football, National Collegiate Athletic Association (NCAA) football, bowl game, Rose Bowl, Sugar Bowl, Cotton Bowl, Fiesta Bowl, Gator Bowl, Orange Bowl; high school football, touch football, tag football; ball, pigskin [Inf]

2 **football uniform,** jersey, helmet, flak jacket, facemask, mouthguard, pads, shoulder pads, cleats

3 **stadium,** bowl, field, Astroturf™, artificial grass, rug [Inf], carpet [Inf], gridiron, goalposts, crossbar, uprights, press box, scoreboard, clock, midfield stripe, goal line, end line, end zone, sideline, restraining line, hash mark, yard marker, chains

4 **game time,** quarter, half, halftime, time-out, official's time-out, television *or* commercial time-out, 2-minute warning, overtime, sudden death

5 **scoring,** touchdown, extra point, point after touchdown (PAT), conversion, 2-point conversion, field goal, safety

6 **offense,** offensive team, offensive drive, possession, forward progress, 2-minute offense, 2-minute drill, hurry-up offense, run-and-shoot offense; offensive formation, I-formation, T-formation, shotgun formation, spread formation, slot formation, single-wing formation, double-wing formation; strong side, weak side, balanced line, unbalanced line; offensive backfield, offensive back, quarterback, signal-caller [Inf], field general [Inf], passer, fullback, halfback, running back, runner, up back, wingback, blocker; offensive line, offensive lineman, center, guard, tackle, receiver, wide receiver, flanker, tight end

7 **huddle,** set, shift, signals, line call, read, audible, snap count, quick count, snap

8 **play,** ground game, running game, run, quarterback sneak, option run, block, cross block, lead block, scissors block, isolation block, pulling linemen, pitchout, bootleg, keeper, lateral, draw, cutback, sweep, power sweep, rollout, reverse, end around, inside run, outside run, misdirection, trap, hand-off, play-action pass, play fake, trick play, gadget play, fumble, turnover, passing game, pass, complete pass, pass reception, incomplete pass, intercepted pass, interception, pocket, protection, option pass, screen pass, flare pass, spot pass, square-out pass, square-in pass, hook pass, curl pass, slant-in pass, fly pattern, bomb, hail-Mary, flea-flicker, post pattern, Z pattern

9 **defense,** defensive team, defensive formation, zone defense, nickel defense, dime defense, flex defense,

4-3 defense, 3-4 defense, prevent defense, man-to-man defense, single coverage, double coverage, zone coverage, overshift, undershift, slant, stunt, pinch, penetration, defensive backfield, defensive backs, secondary, cornerback, safety, strong safety, linebacker, defensive line, defensive lineman, defensive end, defensive tackle, nose guard, the front four

10 **defensive huddle,** pass rush, rush, blitz, dog, sack, bump and run

11 **special team,** specialty team, kicking team, receiving team, kicker, field-goal kicker, place-kicker, drop-kicker, punter, quick-kicker, holder, long snapper

12 **kick,** kicking tee, kickoff, onside kick, squib kick, place kick, drop kick, punt, quick kick, free kick, fake kick; hang time, catch, fair catch, touchback, run back, return

13 **penalty,** 5-yard penalty, 10-yard penalty, 15-yard penalty, penalty marker, penalty flag, offensive foul, defensive foul, dead-ball foul, spot of enforcement, delay of game, offside, encroachment, holding, faceguarding, facemask, clipping, crackback block, illegal motion, false start, personal foul, unsportsmanlike conduct, ineligible receiver, pass interference, intentional grounding, illegal use of hands, roughing the passer, roughing the kicker, late hit [Inf]

14 **football associations,** National Football League (NFL), American Football Conference (AFC), National Football Conference (NFC)

15 **football player,** all-pro, all-American, varsity player, junior varsity player, captain, redshirt, rookie, draft pick, free agent, substitute, sub [Inf]; coach, head coach, assistant coach, offensive coordinator, defensive coordinator; referee, umpire, head linesman, field judge, back judge, line judge, side judge, sideline crew, zebra [Inf], chain gang [Inf]

16 **miscellaneous terms,** cheerleader, coin-toss, game plan, pep rally, pep squad, spike, training camp, transfer, yardage, waiver

ADJECTIVES

17 **varsity,** collegiate, professional, offensive, defensive, specialist, kicking

VERBS

18 **play offense,** run the hurry-up offense, call the plays, be in the shotgun, pass, have possession, lateral, fake, sweep, sneak, run the quarterback sneak, call an audible, read the defense, throw a completion, hit a receiver, throw a pass, stick to the ground game, trap, hand off, option, pitch out, bootleg, keep, roll out, leave the pocket, get sacked, score, convert, run a pattern, protect, block, cross block, lead block, center, cutback, run the power sweep

19 **play defense,** cover, overshift, undershift, slant, stunt, pinch, penetrate, rush the passer, red-dog, pass rush, rush, blitz, dog, sack, bump and run, play back

20 **kick,** place-kick, drop-kick, punt, kick a field goal, quick-kick, split the uprights, hit the crossbar, kick off, have good hang time, call for a fair catch, make a fair catch, have a touchback, run back, return, be on the special team

21 **exhibit penalty behavior,** be penalized, be offside, encroach, hold, faceguard, clip, throw a crackback block, move illegally, false-start, draw a personal foul, behave in an unsportsmanlike way, throw to an ineligible receiver, interfere, ground intentionally, rough the passer, rough the kicker, pile on, use hands illegally, facemask, take too much time, illegally ground the ball

156 Golf

NOUNS

1 **golf,** golfing, golf game, game of golf, round, golf match; stroke play, medal play, match play, best-ball match; single, twosome, 2-ball match, threesome, 3-ball match, foursome, 4-ball match, mixed foursome

2 **golf course,** 9-hole course, 18-hole course, links; tee, teeing ground, fairway, green, putting green, approach; loose impediments, obstruction, bunker, hazard, water hazard, trap, sand trap, rough, blind, bent grass, ground under repair; hole, dogleg hole; cup, flag, flagstick, pin; out of bounds

3 **golfing terms,** lie of the ball, hole-high ball, hanging ball, rub of the green, divot; score, par, bogey, double bogey, birdie, eagle, double eagle, hole in one, ace; score card, Nassau scoring, defaulted match, odd, gross score, net score, handicap, handicap score, sudden death; halved hole, conceded hole, stroke play, like stroke, square match, all-square match, up side, down side, dormie side, bye holes; golf rules, honor system, nineteenth hole [Inf]

4 **golf shots,** teeing off, drive, putt; wood shot, iron shot, approaching shot, sand shot, lofted shot, recovery shot, bunker shot, dubbed shot; backswing, downswing, follow-through; honors, pivot, stance, stroke, carry, line, penalty stroke, handicap stroke, bisque, long game, gobble, pull, slice, fade, hook, draw, sclaff, chip, backspin, sidespin, ace, hole in one, hole out

5 **golf equipment,** golf ball, ball, feather ball *or* feathery, special, gutta-percha ball *or* guttie, rubber-core ball; club, golf club, driver, putter, Texas wedge, wood, iron, wedge; baffy, brassie, cleek, mashie, mashie niblick, niblick, sand iron, spade mashie, spoon, track iron; golf club part: cap, plug, grip, shaft, socket, hosel, neck, face, head, heel, sole, soleplate, toe; golf glove, tee, golf bag, club cover

6 **golfing associations and tournaments,** golf club, Professional Golfers' Association (PGA), Ladies' Professional Golfers' Association (LPGA), United States Golf Association (USGA), Royal and Ancient Golf Club; Australian Masters, British Open, Curtis Cup, Grand

Slam, LPGA Championship, Masters Golf Tournament, PGA Championship, Ryder Cup, US Open, USGA National Amateur, Walker Cup, World Amateur Team Championship, World Cup

7 **golfer,** player, linksman, putter, scratch player; caddie, outside agency, referee, marker, forecaddie, observer; [Inf]: duffer, dub, hacker

VERBS

8 **play,** play golf, tee up *or* off, drive, hit, pitch, putt, use backspin, pull, slice, fade, hook, chip, sclaff, top, loft, sky, dunk, recover, shoot par, birdie, bogey, eagle, hole, make a hole in one, ace; take a penalty stroke, concede a hole

INTERJECTION

9 **Fore!**

157 Gymnastics

NOUNS

1 **gymnastics,** free exercises, strength exercises, balancing exercises, rhythmic gymnastics, artistic gymnastics, Swedish gymnastics, German gymnastics; competitive gymnastics, Olympic gymnastics; floor exercise, jumping, tumbling, vaulting, trampolining; prescribed *or* compulsory exercise, optional exercise, gymnastics routine, gymnastic scoring; fluency, correctness, execution, difficulty, originality
   ▶ *Contention 422; Strength 516; Motion 677*

2 **gymnastics equipment,** leotard, gym suit, track suit, wrist bandage, handstrap, gym shoes, sneakers, rosin; mat, balance beam, horizontal bar, parallel bars, uneven parallel bars, pommel *or* side horse, stationary rings, trampoline, springboard

3 **balance beam,** vaulting, jump, jumping, turning, sitting, lying, steps, running, held position, scale, front scale, horizontal scale

4 **floor exercise,** calisthenics, movement, tumbling, handspring, cartwheel, somersault, forward somersault, backward somersault, flip-flop, backflip, half-turn, round-off, aerial, jump, jumping, holding splits, backbend; balance, rhythm, harmony

5 **horizontal bar,** steel poles, guy wires; balance, swinging, vaulting, turn, pirouette, upstart, back and front, giant circles, handstand, grip, straddle, somersault, landing, finish

6 **uneven parallel bars,** swinging, balance movement, cross handstand

7 **pommel** *or* **side horse,** pommel, saddle, neck, croup; circle, scissors, turn; vaulting *or* long horse, vault, elastic board, run, rebound, vault, handspring, pivot cartwheel

8 **stationary rings,** strap, handstand, lever; upstart, uprise, cross, hand, L position, circle

9 **gymnastics organizations,** gymnastics club, gymnastics association, Amateur Athletic Union of the United States (AAU), British Amateur Gymnastics Association, Fédération Internationale de Gymnastique

10 **gymnast,** athlete, exerciser, somersaulter, vaulter, jumper, swinger, tumbler; gymnastics judge, gymnastics coach

ADJECTIVES

11 **gymnastic,** free, balancing, vaulting, tumbling, agile, rhythmic, artistic, competitive, prescribed, optional, Olympic

VERBS

12 **exercise,** compete in gymnastics, do a prescribed *or* an optional exercise, mount, dismount, swing, pirouette, tumble, do a handstand, do a handspring, do the splits, somersault, vault, jump, turn, rebound, sit, lie, hold a position, hang, hold, stick a landing

ADVERBS

13 **gymnastically,** competitively, rhythmically, artistically, correctly, with balance

158 Hockey

NOUNS

1 **hockey,** ice hockey, field hockey, professional hockey, amateur hockey, Olympic hockey, hurling [Brit]

2 **hockey areas,** ice rink, rink, barrier board, sideboards, endboards, red goal line, goal crease, blue line, center line, center spot, face-off circle, red face-off spot, zone, defense zone, neutral zone, center zone, attacking zone, slot, point, goal, net, cage; field, pitch, goal line, goalpost, striking circle, shooting circle, penalty spot

3 **hockey equipment,** ice hockey stick, left stick, right stick, neutral stick, goalkeeper's *or* goalie stick, puck; hockey stick, ball, hockey ball

4 **ice hockey tactics,** face-off, stickhandling, carrying the puck, rushing the puck, puck possession, stealing the puck, triangular offense, 3-man combination attack, 2-1-2 system, power play, check, assist, pass, drop pass, headmanning the puck, draw, fake, deke, backcheck, backhand shot, breakout play, peel-off, give and go, man-to-man assignment, 1-on-1 assignment, screening, dribble, playing short-handed, dead puck, goal, garbage goal, pulling the goalie; penalty plays: offsides, offside pass, icing, charging, body-checking, boarding, crosschecking, kneeing, elbowing, highsticking, holding, roughing, hooking, tripping, spearing, slashing, butt-ending, interference, fighting; penalty award, 5-minute penalty, penalty shot, misconduct penalty, 10-minute penalty, penalty box

5 **field hockey tactics,** stroke, push stroke, push, flick stroke, scoop, pass, clearing, dribble, strike, push-in, hit-in, hitting, pass-back; penalty plays: hook, hold, interference, highsticking, tripping, charging, penalty award, penalty corner, penalty stroke, free hit

6 **hockey clothing,** hockey skates, knee pad, elbow pad, shin guard, protective shoulder pads, helmet, gloves; goalkeeper's protective clothing: catching glove, stick glove, facemask, leather leg guard, shoulder guard, arm guard, chest protector, abdominal protector

7 **hockey organizations,** International Ice Hockey Federation, National Hockey League (NHL), Stanley Cup, Olympics, all-star game; Fédération Internationale de Hockey (FIH), International Hockey Board, All England Women's Hockey Association (AEWHA)

8 **hockey player,** forward, center, winger, left wing, right wing, defender, left defense, right defense, linesman, forechecker, backchecker, puck carrier, goalminder, goalkeeper, goaltender, goalie; center forward, halfback, center half, wing half, fullback; hockey team, squad, referee, umpire, timekeeper

VERBS

9 **play ice hockey,** skate, play, face off, hit, steal, puckhandle, rag, deke, check, give-and-go, break out, pass, shoot, score, ice the puck, make a hat trick

10 **play field hockey,** play, stroke, stickhandle, push, flick, scoop, pass, dribble, strike, hook, hold, interfere, highstick, trip, charge

159 Horses, Horseback Riding, Horse Racing

The horse, the horse! The symbol of surging potency and power of movement, of action, in man.
— D. H. LAWRENCE

NOUNS

1 **horse,** equine, quadruped, horseflesh, dobbin, pony, mount, steed; stallion, sire, studhorse, stud, gelding; mare, broodmare, dam; foal, colt, filly, yearling; wild horse, untamed horse, bronco, outlaw, trail horse, range horse, rogue, unbreakable *or* untrainable horse; stable horse, circus horse, hunter; Indian pony, cayuse, mustang; purebred, bloodstock, Thoroughbred, blood horse; old horse, nag, jade, hack, plug [Inf]

2 **racehorse,** racer, pacer, stepper, high-stepper, trotter, goer, stayer, turf horse, sprinter, speeder, steeplechaser, chaser, bangtail [Inf]

3 **workhorse,** draft horse, packhorse, plow horse, cart horse, dray horse, shaft horse, wheel horse, trace horse, carriage horse, coach horse, post horse, hackney, cow pony, beast of burden

4 **war-horse,** cavalry horse, charger, courser, steed, remount, destrier [Arch]

5 **saddle horse,** riding horse, mount, hack, steed, roadster, ambler, palfrey, livery horse

6 **pony,** Shetland, Fell pony, dell pony, polo pony, riding pony, Galloway, cob

7 **horse by color,** roan, strawberry roan, gray, dapple-

gray, bay, blood bay, chestnut, liver chestnut, sorrel, black, piebald, skewbald, pinto, dun, palomino, buckskin, seal brown

8 **equestrianism,** horsemanship, horsewomanship, horseback riding, riding school, equitation, classical riding, manège, dressage, haute école, Spanish Riding School; horse show, horse trials, combined training, show jumping, eventing, gymkhana, hunter trials, hunter pace, long-distance riding, competitive trail riding, ride and tie, polo, rodeo

9 **riding equipment,** tack, harness, reins, checkrein, cribbing strap, crupper strap, bit, blinkers, halter, bridle, headstall, hackamore, bosal, noseband, cavesson, browband, neckstrap, martingale, breastplate; whip, crop, riding crop; saddle, English saddle, Western saddle, racing saddle, sidesaddle, girth, cinch, saddle pad, saddlecloth, saddle blanket, stirrup, stirrup leather, stirrup iron; hoofpick, tail guard, sweat scraper, currycomb, grooming kit; livery, stable, farriery

10 **horse racing,** racing, sport of kings, the turf, race meeting, meet, mixed meeting; horse race, flat race, harness race, trotting, pacing; steeplechase, hurdle race, point-to-point race, match race, walkover, maiden race; post, start, finish, racing form, handicap, penalty; weight allowance, weight cloth, weights, weigh-in; the field, entry, runner, scratch, favorite,

NOTABLE HORSES OF FACT, FICTION, AND LEGEND

Affirmed (racehorse)
Al Borak (Muhammad's winged horse)
Assault (racehorse)
Bayard (legend)
Black Beauty (story by Anna Sewell)
Black Bess (Dick Turpin's horse)
Blaze (stories by C. W. Anderson)
Bucephalus (Alexander the Great's horse)
Buttermilk (Dale Evans's horse)
Champion (Gene Autry's horse)
Citation (racehorse)
Copenhagen (Duke of Wellington's horse)
Count Fleet (racehorse)
Flicka (stories by Mary O'Hara)
Forego (racehorse)
Gallant Fox (racehorse)
Grani (Siegfried's horse)
Incitatus (Caligula's horse)
Kelso (racehorse)

Man o' War (racehorse)
Marengo (Napoleon's horse)
Misty of Chincoteague (story by Marguerite Henry)
Nashua (racehorse)
Native Dancer (racehorse)
Omaha (racehorse)
Pegasus (winged horse of myth)
Rosinante (Don Quixote's horse)
Ruffian (racehorse)
Seabiscuit (racehorse)
Seattle Slew (racehorse)
Scout (Tonto's horse)
Secretariat (racehorse)
Sir Barton (racehorse)
Sleipnir (Odin's eight-legged horse)
Silver (Lone Ranger's horse)
Tony (Tom Mix's horse)
Traveller (Robert E. Lee's horse)
Trigger (Roy Rogers's horse)
Velvet (story by Enid Bagnold)
War Admiral (racehorse)
Whirlaway (racehorse)

HORSE AND PONY BREEDS AND VARIETIES

Akhal Teké
Albino
Alter-Réal
American Quarter
  Horse or Quarter
  Horse
American Saddle
  Horse or American
  Saddlebred or
  Saddlebred
American Shetland
  pony
American
  Standardbred or
  Standardbred
American Welsh
  pony
Andalusian
Andalusian-
  Carthusian or
  Carthusian
Anglo-Arab
Anglo-Norman
Appaloosa
Arab
Ardennais
Assateague pony
Australian pony
Australian Stock
  Horse
Auxois
Avelignese pony
Balearic pony
Bali pony
Barb
Bashkirsky pony
Basque pony
Basuto pony
Batak or Deli pony
Bavarian Warmblood
Beberbeck
Belgian Ardennes
Belgian Heavy
  Draught or Brabant
Bhutia pony
Bosnian pony
Boulonnais
Brabant or Belgian
  Heavy Draught
Breton
Breton Heavy
  Draught
Brumby
Budyonny
Burma or Shan
  pony
Calabrese
Camargue pony

Campolino
Canadian Cutting
  Horse
Carthusian or
  Andalusian-
  Carthusian
Caspian pony
Charollais Half-bred
Chincoteague pony
Cleveland Bay
Clydesdale
Cob
Comtois
Connemara pony
Corlay
Criollo
Dales pony
Danubian
Darashomi or
  Slurazi
Darashouri
Dartmoor pony
Deli or Batak pony
Demi-Sang or French
  Trotter
Don
Døole
  Gudbrandshal
Døole Trotter
Dülmen pony
Dutch Draught
East Bulgarian
East Friesian
Einsiedler
Exmoor pony
Falabella pony
Faxaflói pony
Fell pony
Finnish
Fjord or Westlands
  pony
Frederiksborg
Freiberger Saddle
  Horse
French Saddle Horse
  or Selle Français
French Trotter or
  Demi-Sang
Friesian
Furioso
Galiceño
Galloway
Garrano or Minho
  pony
Gayoe pony
Gelderland
German Trotter
Gidran

Gotland pony
Groningen
Hackney
Hackney pony
Haflinger pony
Hanoverian
Highland pony
Hispano Arab or
  Spanish Anglo-
  Arab
Holstein
Huçul pony
Iceland pony
Iomud
Irish Cob
Irish Draught
Irish Hunter
Italian Heavy
  Draught
Jaf
Java pony
Jutland
Kabardin
Karabair
Karabakh
Karacabey
Karadagh
Kathiawari pony
Kazakh pony
Kladruber
Knabstrup
Konik pony
Kustanair
Landais pony
Latvian Harness
  Horse
Libyan Barb
Limousin
  Half-bred
Lippizaner
Lithuanian Heavy
  Draught
Lokai
Lusitano
Malapolski
Mangalarga
Manipur pony
Maremmana or
  Maremma
Marwari pony
Masuren
Mecklenburg
Mérens pony
Merlin or Welsh
  pony
Métis Trotter
Minho or Garrano
  pony

Missouri Fox Trotter
Mongolian Wild
  Horse or
  Przewalski's Horse
  (pony)
Morgan
Muraköz
Murgese
Mustang
Nanfan or Tibetan
  pony
Native Mexican
Native Turkish
  pony
New Forest pony
New Kirgiz or
  Novokirghiz
Nonius
Norfolk Trotter
Norman
North Swedish
North Swedish
  Trotter
Norwegian Racing
  Trotter
Novokirghiz or New
  Kirgiz
Oldenburg
Orlov Trotter
Pahlavan
Palomino
Paso Fino
Peneia pony
Percheron
Peruvian Stepping
  Horse or Peruvian
  Paso
Pindos pony
Pinto
Pinzgauer Noriker
Plateau Persian
Pleven
Poitevin
Pony of the
  Americas
Postier
Przewalski's Horse or
  Mongolian Wild
  Horse (pony)
Quarter Horse or
  American Quarter
  Horse
Rhineland Heavy
  Draught
Rottaler
Russian Heavy
  Draught
Sable Island pony

Saddlebred or
  American
  Saddlebred or
  American Saddle
  Horse
Salerno
Sandalwood pony
Sardinian
Schleswig Heavy
  Draught
Shagya Arab
Shan or Burma pony
Shetland pony
Shire
Skyros pony
Slurazi or Darashomi
Sokólsky
Sorraia pony
Spanish Anglo-
  Arab or Hispano
  Arab
Spiti pony
Standardbred or
  American
  Standardbred
Suffolk Punch
Sumba pony
Sumbawa pony
Swedish Half-bred or
  Swedish
  Warmblood
Tarpan pony
Tartar pony
Tchenaran
Tennessee Walking
  Horse
Tersky
Thoroughbred
Tibetan or Nanfan
  pony
Timor pony
Toric
Trait du Nord
Trakehner
Turkoman
Viatka pony
Vladimir Heavy
  Draught
Waler
Welsh Cob (pony)
Welsh Mountain
  pony
Welsh or Merlin pony
Westlands or Fjord
  pony
Wielkopolski
Württemberg
Zemaituka pony

co-favorite, stablemate, odds-on bet, certainty, dark horse, ringer [Inf], outsider, maiden, sprinter, stayer, rabbit, mudder, pacemaker, also-ran, starter's orders, dead heat, photo finish, objection, weigh-out

11 **horse-racing betting terms,** betting, odds, even money, price, bet, parimutuel, perfecta, exacta, win, place, show, all-way bet, daily double, payoff, winning ticket

12 **racetrack,** racecourse, racing track, dirt track, bush track, turf, paddock, post, start, oval, course, strip, rail, infield, post, backstretch, home stretch, finish, winner's circle

13 **famous horse races,** Triple Crown, Kentucky Derby, Preakness, Belmont Stakes; Travers, Wood, Breeders' Cup, Maryland Hunt Cup; [Brit]: English Classics, Epsom Derby, Oaks, 1000 Guineas, 2000 Guineas, St. Leger, National Hunt, Grand National, Ascot, Aintree

14 **horse person,** breeder, owner, rider, horse rider, horseman, horsewoman, equestrian, equestrienne, postilion, postboy; courier, mounted police, mounted troops, mounted rifles, cavalry, light-horse cavalry, horse artillery, horse soldier, cavalryman, light-horseman, yeoman, trooper, sowar, hussar, lancer, dragoon, Ironsides, Cossack; cavalier, knight; racing steward, jockey, jump jockey [Brit], steeplechase rider; bookmaker, bookie [Inf], tipster, bettor; show-jumper, eventer; trainer, breaker, roughrider, bareback rider, broncobuster, buckaroo, cowboy, cowgirl, cowpuncher, gaucho, rodeo rider; saddler, harness maker, lorimer, bootmaker, blacksmith, farrier; veterinarian, vet [Inf], horse doctor; hostler, groom, stableboy, lad [Brit inf]

ADJECTIVES

15 **equine,** equestrian, riding, horseback-riding, racing, horse-racing, jumping, show-jumping, eventing, cross-country, mounted, purebred, warm-blooded

VERBS

16 **ride,** walk, trot, jog, canter, lope, gallop, hack, trail-ride, ride bareback, ride sidesaddle, drive; saddle, bridle, mount; halter-break, break, train, race, steeplechase, hunt, jump, groom, curry

160 Hunting and Shooting

NOUNS

1 **target shooting,** pistol shooting, revolver shooting, shotgun shooting, air-rifle shooting, rifle shooting, small-bore rifle shooting; Olympic target shooting: prone position, sitting position, kneeling position, standing position; skeet or skeet shooting, trapshooting, moving target shooting; slow fire, timed fire, rapid fire; marksmanship

2 **hunting,** game shooting, shoot, field sports, gunning, hunt, venery [Arch]; small-game hunting, big-game hunting, trapping, snaring; coursing, field trial, fal-

conry; tracking, stalking, woodland stalking, still hunting; killing, culling; driving, beating, dogging; sitting, calling, sighting-in

▶ *Pursuit 385*

3 **game laws,** hunting season, open season, closed season, hunting limit, bag limit, hunting license, game license

▶ *Killing 30; Pursuit 385*

4 **hunting equipment,** firearms; hunting rifle: single-shot rifle, pump rifle, bolt-action rifle, automatic rifle; air rifle, high-powered rifle, sporting rifle [Brit]; single-barreled single-shot shotgun, side-by-side double-barreled shotgun, over-and-under double-barreled shotgun, bolt-action shotgun, pump-action shotgun, automatic shotgun; bow and arrow, boomerang, sling; trap, snare; ammunition round, ammunition, pellet, shot, slug, bullet

▶ *Weapon 78*

5 **hunting accessories,** decoy, shooting kit [Brit]; telescopic sight, scope sight; shooting stick, stalking stick; binoculars, rifle sling; hunting clothes, hunting jacket, Day-Glo™ vest, hunting boots

▶ *Clothing 100*

6 **game,** quarry, prey; small-game birds: quail, duck, partridge, grouse, pheasant, goose, turkey; small-game animals: rabbit, hare, woodchuck, squirrel; big-game animals: fox, deer, moose, mountain lion, wild boar, wild goat, bear, elk, caribou, reindeer, wolf; antelope, gazelle, zebra, tiger, leopard, lion, giraffe, rhinoceros, elephant

7 **hunting dog,** sporting dog, gun dog, courser; hound, setter, pointer, spaniel, retriever

8 **hunting associations,** National Rifle Association (NRA), United States Revolver Association, International Shooting Union (ISU); hunting party, hunting lodge

9 **hunter,** small-game hunter, big-game hunter; trapper, snarer; courser; falconer; stalker, tracker, beater; poacher; Diana, Nimrod

10 **shooter,** skeet shooter, trapshooter; marksman or markswoman, sharpshooter, expert, master

ADJECTIVES

11 **hunting,** shooting, small-game, big-game, stalking; killed, culled; open, closed; single-shot, pump-action, bolt-action, automatic; small-bore, high-powered; single-barreled, single-shot, side by side, double-barreled, over-and-under; prone, sitting, kneeling, standing; slow, timed, rapid; open-field, woodland

VERBS

12 **hunt,** go hunting, shoot, go shooting, shoot game, shoot fowl, hunt for, go small-game or big-game hunting; trap, snare, course, falcon; stalk, track, trail, follow the scent, scent out, dog; kill, cull; drive, beat, flush; poach; join a hunting party, sight quarry, scent game;

point, retrieve, aim at, draw a bead on, sight in, zero (a rifle), fire at, pull *or* squeeze the trigger

ADVERBS

13 **on the trail,** on the track, on the scent, hot on the trail, in hot pursuit

161 Mountaineering

Why do I want to climb Mount Everest? Because it is there.
— GEORGE LEIGH MALLORY

NOUNS

1 **mountaineering,** climbing, mountain climbing, rock climbing, bouldering, free climbing, clean climbing, aid climbing, big wall climbing; snow climbing, ice climbing, alpinism, Alpine-style climbing

2 **climbing expedition,** camp, base camp, advance camp, bivouac; route, bolt route, classic route, artificial route, aid route

3 **climbing techniques,** chimneying, liebacking *or* laybacking, balance climbing, smearing, jamming, crack climbing, face climbing, stemming, mantel move, edging, leading, cleaning, top roping, yoyoing, soloing, moving together, pendulum, traverse, Tyrolean traverse, prusiking, jumaring; ascent, ascending, descent, descending, downclimbing, rappel, rappelling, abseil; belaying, body belay, mechanical belay, dynamic belay, self-belay, snow bollard belay, boot–ice ax belay, carabiner–ice ax belay, glissading, front-pointing, flat-footing, step-cutting, stepkicking, plunge-stepping, self-arrest, roped travel (glacier), route-finding

4 **climbing equipment,** boots, climbing boots, climbing shoes, helmet, climbing gear, rack *or* equipment rack, harness, waist *or* swami belt, body harness, chalk, chalk bag, carabiner, locking carabiner, camming device, chock, hexentric nut (hex), nut, wedge, bong, bolt, bolt hammer *or* drill, piton, realized ultimate reality piton (RURP), skyhook, runners; nylon webbing, sling, gear sling, rappel ring, belay device, cleaning tool, rappelling device, Sticht plate, ascenders, jumars, prusiks, rope, kernmantel rope, ice ax, crampons, ice screws, snow fluke, deadman, snow wands; tent, sleeping bag, backpack, daypack *or* rucksack, map, compass, guidebook, barometer/altimeter, sunglasses *or* goggles, mittens, parka, gaiters

5 **climbing dangers,** storms, weather, lightning, loose *or* falling rocks, avalanche, ice, hidden crevasse; frostbite, hypothermia, cerebral edema, pulmonary edema, altitude sickness, mountain sickness, snow blindness, sunburn

6 **rock face,** wall, crag, ridge, rib, slab, outcrop, nose, pillar, pitch, route, ledge, ramp, hold, foothold, handhold, corner, open book, dihedral, crack, finger crack, offwidth crack, chimney, chockstone, flake, mantel, shelf, roof, prow, care, amphitheater, knife edge, bulge, over-

hand, gully, couloir, col, buttress, cirque, arête, glacier, firn, crevasse, cornice, bergschrund, moat, serac, sun-cup, névé, bollard, mountaintop, peak, pinnacle, summit

◗ *Summit 600*

7 **mountaineering associations,** American Alpine Club (AAC), The Mountaineers, Appalachian Mountain Club (AMC), Union Internationale des Associations d'Alpinisme (UIAA)

8 **mountaineer,** climber, rock climber, mountain climber, alpinist, sport climber; guide, Sherpa guide, porter

ADJECTIVES

9 **mountaineering,** climbing, alpine, rock, snow, ice, bold, classic, extreme, exposed, multipitch, high-altitude, traditional, sport, mixed, free, clean, aid, fixed, artificial, natural, solo, body, mechanical, bombproof, belay, belaying, offwidth, flared, loose, falling, protected

VERBS

10 **mountaineer,** climb, go mountaineering, climb a mountain, mountain-climb, rock-climb, climb a rock, boulder, scale a peak, peakbag, ascend, scramble, mantel, jam, smear, edge, chimney, lieback *or* layback, stem, lead, clean, belay, anchor, top-rope, solo, pendulum, traverse, descend, downclimb, lower off, rappel, abseil, haul, prusik, jumar, kick *or* cut steps, crampon, flatfoot, front-point, glissade, arrest, bivouac, navigate; reach the top, summit

162 Skiing, Ice Skating, Bobsledding

NOUNS

1 **skiing,** Alpine skiing, downhill skiing, recreational skiing; competitive skiing, Olympic skiing, freestyle skiing, ballet skiing, mogul skiing, acrobatic skiing, stunt skiing, hotdogging, somersaulting, helicopter skiing *or* heli-skiing, off-trail skiing, skiing on ice, mountain skiing; cross-country skiing, Nordic skiing, snowboarding, touring, biathlon; ski jumping, jump, ski jump, acrobatic jump; ski mountaineering, speed-skiing, grass-skiing; ski teaching method, graduated length method (GLM)

2 **ski run,** downhill ski run, ski trail, marked trail, moguled trail, ski slope, artificial slope, beginner's slope, run, novice *or* green run, intermediate *or* blue run, advanced *or* black run, expert *or* double-black run, straight run, schuss; fall line, wall; ski tow, lift, ski lift, rope tow, T-bar, poma, chairlift, high-speed chairlift, cable car, tramway, funicular

3 **skiing snow,** powder snow, packed-powder snow, machine-groomed snow, soft damp snow, heavy wet snow, spring skiing, slush, hard-packed snow, breakable crust, wind crust, windslab, ice, frozen corn snow, bump, mogul, rut, ridge, washboard, ledge

4 ski race, race, Alpine race, downhill race, super giant slalom race *or* super G race, giant slalom race, slalom race; slalom pole, rapid slalom pole, gate, open gate, vertical gate, flush gate, diagonal gate, hairpin, closed gate; National Standard Race (NASTAR), (ski) skating, single-sided skating, double-sided skating, ski orienteering *or* Ski-O

5 skiing techniques, compensation technique, skiing posture, side step, edge, climb, herringbone, snowplow *or* wedge, traverse, step turn, kick turn, pole plant, sideslip, ski turn, snowplow turn, stem, stem turn, christie, stem christie, uphill christie, parallel christie, carved turn, short swing, parallel swing, wedeln, racing-step turn, jet turn, rotation turn, tuck, schuss, jump turn, hockey stop

6 Alpine ski championships, World Championship, World Cup, Winter Olympics

7 cross-country skiing, Nordic skiing, ski touring, mountain ski touring, off-track touring, ski rambling; biathlon race, biathlon relay race, sprinting race, marathon, American Birkebeiner, Canadian Coureur des Bois

8 cross-country techniques, two-phase walk, star turn, kick turn, side step, stepping a curve, diagonal side step, double-pole, double-pole with leg kick, swing, herringbone, direct descent, traverse downhill, snowplow glide, snowplow turn, stem turn, parallel turn, telemark, tacking, two-phase uphill, swing to the hill, snowplow brake

9 cross-country skiing championships, World Grand Prix of Cross-Country Skiers, Winter Olympics, Giant's Ridge International Classic Marathon, Internationaler Deutscher Skimarathon in Hirschau

10 ski equipment, ski, downhill ski, Alpine ski, shovel, waist, sidecut, heel, stiffness, softness, twist; recreational ski, short ski, soft ski, all-terrain ski, racing ski, long ski, stiff ski, slalom ski, giant slalom ski, RS-ski; wooden ski, metal ski, fiberglass ski, laminated ski; safety strap, ski pole, basket, boot, binding, antifriction pad, ski brake, ski wax, ski tuning; slipper pad, toe piece, klister wax; ski clothing, ski suit, racing suit, ski pants, bib pants, ski jacket, ski parka, anorak, ski hat, ski mask, gloves, gaiters, sunglasses, goggles

11 snowboarding, balancing, sideslipping, heelside turn, toeside turn, linked turn, carving, skidding, snowboard racing

12 snowboarding equipment, Alpine snowboard, freestyle snowboard, free-riding snowboard, snowboard edge, twin tip, soft snowboard boots, hard snowboard boots, snowboard freestyle bindings, snowboard plate bindings

13 skiing associations, United States Skiing Association (USSA), United States Olympic Committee (USOC), Canadian Ski Association (CSA), International Ski Federation (ISF)

14 skier, recreational skier, downhill skier, ski racer, slalom racer, giant slalom racer, downhill racer, mogul racer; freestyle skier, snowboarder, cross-country skier, touring skier

15 ice skating, figure skating, free skating, pair skating, pairs, shadow skating, competitive ice skating, Olympic skating

16 ice-skating techniques, compulsory figure, three, paragraph double three, loop, change loop, paragraph loop, bracket, paragraph bracket, rocker, counter, free-skating movement; jump, loop jump, salchow jump, axel jump, double axel, triple axel, toe jump, split jump; spin, camel spin, lay-back spin, one-foot upright spin, sit spin, cross-foot spin; pair-skating movement, death spiral, pairs sit spin, catch-waist camel spin, lift, axel lift, lasso lift, split lutz lift, twist lift; flying axel, throw axel, double throw axel, throw salchow

17 skating equipment, skate, skating boot, blade

18 ice dancing, dancing on ice, competitive ice dancing, Olympic ice dancing, compulsory dancing, set pattern dancing, free dancing

19 ice-dancing move, dance step, arabesque, pivot, pirouette, hold, killian hold, reverse killian hold, waltz hold, turn, three turn, dropped three, dropped mohawk, dance lift; ice-dance music, Viennese waltz, Yankee polka, the blues, Westminster waltz, paso doble, rumba, starlight waltz, killian, tango romantica, Ravensburger waltz, quickstep, Argentine tango; competitive scoring, originality, variety, difficulty, timing, selection of music

20 speed skating, sprint skating, long-distance racing, middle-distance racing, short-distance racing, short-track racing, speed-skating race, 500-meter race, 1500-meter race, 5000-meter race, 10,000-meter race, speed-skating circuit, speed-skating track

21 ice-skating association, International Skating Union

22 ice skater, figure skater, ice dancer, speed skater

23 bobsledding, bobsled, bob, two-man bobsled, four-man bobsled, luge, one-seater toboggan, two-seater toboggan, skeleton

24 toboggan parts, hood, runner, axle, cable, brake, cowling

25 toboggan race, luge race, lugeing, competitive lugeing, Olympic lugeing; luge techniques, steering, lifting, dragging, run, bobrun, toboggan chute, toboggan run

26 bobsledder, tobogganist, bobsled captain

ADJECTIVES

27 ski, skiing, Alpine, downhill, Nordic, Olympic, freestyle, acrobatic, ballet, stunt, mogul, moguled, hot dogging, somersaulting, off-trail, mountain, aerial, speed, artificial, beginner's, green *or* novice, blue *or* intermediate, black *or* advanced, double-black *or* expert

28 snow, hard-packed, breakable, powder, packed-powder, corn, machine-groomed, rutted, ridged, ledged

29 snowplow, stem, christie, parallel, mogul; single-sided, double-sided, open, vertical, flush, hairpin, closed; compensation, schussing, tucked, tucking, unweighting, jet, rotation, jump, kick, carved, sideslipping, sidestepping, traversing, climbing; short, soft, long, stiff, wooden, metal, plastic, fiberglass, laminated

30 snowboarding, balancing, turning, carving, skidding

31 cross-country, touring, off-track, biathlon, sprinting, two-phase, diagonal, double-pole, direct, step, star, scissors, pressure, compression; safety, antifriction, klister

32 ice-skating, figure-skating, free, free-skating, pair, pair-skating, shadow, compulsory, change, paragraph, catch-waist, lifted, lifting, twist, flying, ice-dance, dropped, killian, original, varied, difficult, timed, selected

33 speed-skating, sprint, long-distance, middle-distance, short-distance, short-track

34 bobsledding, lugeing, steering, lifting, dragging

VERBS

35 ski, snow ski, Alpine ski, downhill ski, ski competitively, ski freestyle, do stunt-skiing, hot dog, somersault, ski on ice, ski-jump, do speed-skiing, make a downhill run, take a ski lift, snowplow, turn, parallel turn, race on skis, Alpine race, win a downhill race, hit a slalom pole, schuss, use the tuck position, do a christie, sideslip, traverse, climb, make a hockey stop; snowboard, carve, jib, bonk, railslide, race; ski cross-country, use a diagonal stride, double-pole, tack, swing to the hill, corner, stem, swing, telemark, make a scissors turn; wax a ski, tune a ski

36 ice-skate, figure-skate, free-skate, shadow-skate, do compulsory figures, jump, spin, dance on ice, do set pattern dancing, pivot, pirouette

37 speed-skate, sprint-skate

38 bobsled, luge, toboggan, steer, lift, drag, make a run

INTERJECTIONS

39 danger!, look out!, on your right!, on your left!, ice!, avalanche!

163 Soccer

NOUNS

1 **soccer,** football, soccer football, association football [Brit]; soccer game *or* match; soccer club, soccer team

2 **stadium,** field, pitch, goal, goal area, goalpost, crossbar, net, stanchion, scoreboard, perimeter, touchline *or* by-line, penalty area, penalty spot, 6-yard box, 18-yard box, halfway line, center circle, goal line, corner area, corner flag

3 **soccer uniform,** shorts, boots, knee-socks, soccer shoes, shin pads, gloves

4 **soccer participant,** team, squad; soccer player, footballer [Brit], captain, goalkeeper *or* goalie, defender, fullback, center back, center half, center forward, wing

half, right half, left half, outside left, outside right, inside left, inside right, winger, striker, midfield striker, sweeper, stopper, offensive halfback, defensive halfback, substitute, sub [Inf], reserve; manager, coach, trainer, referee, linesman, fan

5 **soccer play,** start, restart, kickoff, kick, kicking, pass, passing, back pass, head, header, heading, foul, fouling, advantage, trip, shoot, shooting, save, miss, layoff, through ball, long pass, slide tackle, tackle, tackling, dribbling, trapping, parrying, handball, throw-in, punt, goal kick, corner kick *or* corner, drop ball, scoring, score; penalty, handling, kicking, tripping, pushing, charging, violent charging, serious foul play, striking, holding offside, onside, free kick, direct free kick, indirect free kick, penalty kick, obstruction, yellow card, red card, ejection, send-off

6 **soccer associations and awards,** US Soccer Federation, Fédération Internationale de Football Association (FIFA); Intercollegiate Soccer Football Association of America, National Collegiate Athletic Association (NCAA); soccer championship, World Cup, European Cup, European Cup Winners' Cup; NCAA Championship

ADJECTIVES

7 **soccer,** football, professional, collegiate, international; 6-yard, 18-yard, halfway, kicked, kicking, passed, passing, headed, heading, fouled, fouling, tripped, tripping, shooting, missed, tackled, tackling, dribbled, dribbling, trapped, trapping, corner, scored, handled, deliberate, pushed, pushing, held, holding, offside, onside, direct, indirect, free; outside, inside, right, left, midfield

VERBS

8 **play soccer,** kick off, kick, pass, make a pass, make a back pass, head, throw in, throw, shoot, save, miss, tackle, score, foul, trip, push, hold, go offside, go onside, have a free shot, have a free kick, have a goal kick, take a corner, trap, dive, strike, parry, flick, stab, smother, chip, lay off, make a hat trick

164 Swimming

NOUNS

1 **swimming,** natation; recreational swimming, skinny-dipping [Inf]; competitive swimming, open-water swimming, long-distance swimming, swimming the English Channel, synchronized swimming; underwater swimming, subaqueous swimming; diving, skin diving, scuba (self-contained underwater breathing apparatus) diving, snorkeling

2 **swimming techniques,** float, tuck float, prone *or* face float, dead-man's float, supine *or* back float; sculling, bobbing, treading water; stroke, kick, stretch, recover, breath control, alternate breathing; swimming strokes: crawl *or* American crawl *or* Australian

crawl, elementary backstroke, back crawl, sidestroke, breaststroke, butterfly stroke, inverted breaststroke; kicks: flutter kick, scissors kick, back kick, wedge kick, frog kick, whip kick, dolphin kick

3 **competitive swimming,** swim team, racing, Olympic swimming; individual events: sprint freestyle race, distance freestyle race, back crawl race, breaststroke race, butterfly race, individual medley race; relay events: freestyle relay race, medley relay race; racing dive, back crawl start, grab turn, touch turn, flip turn

▸ *Skillfulness 127*

4 **survival swimming,** drown-proofing, dog-paddling; survival devices: floating device, float, inner tube, water wings, armband, life ring, life preserver, life belt, life jacket, life vest, Mae West, life buoy

5 **swimming rescue,** lifeguarding, lifesaving, sidestroke, swim-and-tow, artificial respiration, mouth-to-mouth resuscitation, kiss of life

▸ *Safety 810; Help 825*

6 **diving,** recreational diving, surface diving, competitive diving; dives: tuck surface dive, pike surface dive, foot-first surface dive, swim-down surface dive; jumps: plain jump, tuck *or* cannonball jump; deck dives: kneeling dive, standing dive; springboard dives: spring dive, running spring dive; platform dive, high dive; swan dive, belly flop *or* belly bust *or* belly whop

7 **competitive diving,** springboard diving, walking steps, hurdle; dive categories: forward dive, backward dive, inward *or* cutaway dive, reverse dive, twisting dive; dive positions: tuck, pike *or* jackknife, layout *or* straight body; dive difficulty: handstand, somersault, somersault with twist, double somersault, triple somersault; competitive diving marks: form, approach and hurdle, height, technique and control, entry, difficulty; 1-meter springboard diving, 3-meter springboard diving, 10-meter platform diving

▸ *Descent 714*

8 **swimming equipment,** goggles, underwater mask, underwater breathing tube, snorkel, fin, flipper, hand paddle, flutter board; starting block, touch pad, electronic timer, springboard *or* diving board, bathhouse; swimwear: bathing suit, swimsuit, one-piece swimsuit, racing suit, monokini; two-piece swimsuit, bikini; swimming trunks, trunks, racing trunks; bathing cap

▸ *Clothing 100*

9 **swimming place,** swimming pool, outdoor *or* indoor pool, natatorium, short-course pool, long-course pool, Olympic-size(d) pool; wading pool, children's swimming pool; swimming area, swimming hole, lake, pond, river, beach; leisure pool, wave pool, heated pool

10 **swimming associations,** International Swimming Federation, National Collegiate Athletic Association (NCAA) swimming, Amateur Athletic Association (AAA) swimming, United States Swimming Association (USSA)

11 **swimmer,** competitive swimmer, sprint swimmer, distance swimmer, long-distance swimmer, underwater swimmer, skin diver, scuba diver, snorkeler; lifeguard, lifesaver; diver, competitive diver

ADJECTIVES

12 **swimming,** swim, bathing [Brit], natatory *or* natatorial, natational, recreational, skinny-dipping [Inf], competitive, freestyle, medley, relay, racing, flip; open-water, long-distance, cross-Channel, synchronized; floated, floating, subaqueous, underwater; flutter, scissors, back, wedge, frog, whip, dolphin; survival, dog-paddling, drown-proofed, drown-proofing, mouth-to-mouth; outdoor, indoor, short-course, long-course, sprint, distance, Olympic-size(d), wading; one-piece, two-piece

13 **diving,** forward, backward, inward, reverse, twisting, tuck, pike, layout, plain, handstand, somersault; surface, deck, spring, platform; swan, cannonball

VERBS

14 **swim,** float, scull, bob, tread water, crawl, pull, push, glide, kick, dog-paddle, swim under water, snorkel, scuba, skinny-dip [Inf]

15 **dive,** plunge, skin-dive, scuba-dive, cannonball, belly-flop *or* belly-bust *or* belly-whop, jump in

165   Tennis, Squash, Badminton

NOUNS

1 **tennis,** lawn tennis, outdoor tennis, indoor tennis, court *or* royal tennis; table tennis, Ping-Pong™

2 **tennis strokes,** service *or* serve, flat service, slice service, American twist service, reverse twist; ground stroke, swing, backswing, follow-through, forehand drive, forehand, backhand drive, backhand, ground drive; approach shot, rally, volley, half volley, overhead smash *or* smash, lob, chop, topspin, drop shot, slice

3 **tennis court,** court, singles sideline, doubles sideline, alley, baseline, center mark, service line, midline, backcourt, forecourt, midcourt, ad court, deuce court; net, strap, band, post; grass court, clay court, hard court

4 **tennis player equipment,** tennis racket *or* racquet, tennis ball, tennis shoes

5 **tennis terms,** singles, doubles, partner, net position; foot fault, fault, netball, let, in, out; score, point, ace, love, deuce, advantage *or* ad, game point, service break, break point, set point, match point; game, set, match

6 **tennis participant,** singles player, doubles player, net player, server, receiver, volleyer; umpire, linesman, ball boy

7 **tennis organizations,** International Tennis Federation (ITF), United States Tennis Association (USTA),

World Team Tennis (WTT)

8 **notable tennis competitions,** Australian Open, British Open *or* Wimbledon, French Open, Italian Open, US Open, Masters Tournament, Davis Cup *or* International Lawn Tennis Challenge Trophy, Wightman Cup, Olympic Games

9 **squash,** squash racquets, squash tennis

10 **squash terms,** racket *or* racquet, squash ball, board, telltale, back wall, service line, service court line, squash court, doubles court; service box, hand in, hand out, in-play wall, out-of-play wall, eight all, set two, sudden death

11 **badminton terms,** shuttlecock, battledore, shuttle, plastic shuttle, bird, feathers, racket *or* racquet; badminton court, net posts, short service line, side boundary line, back boundary line, center line; shot, clear shot, smash, drop shot, drive, in side, out side, server, receiver, fault, let

ADJECTIVES

12 **forehand,** backhand, overhand, singles, doubles

VERBS

13 **play tennis,** serve, return, rally, drive, volley, smash, lob, chop, slice, fault, footfault, score, make a point; play squash, play badminton

166 Track and Field Events

NOUNS

1 **track event,** race *or* racing, run *or* running, heat, preliminary race, semifinal race, final; starting position, set position, start, false start; disqualification, acceleration, curve running, full stride, finishing, finish tape, lane, leg

2 **sprint racing,** sprint *or* sprinting, sprint race, 50-yard dash, 50-meter race, 100-meter race, 200-meter race

3 **middle-distance running,** middle-distance racing, 400-meter race, 800-meter race, 1500-meter race, 1-mile race; women's 3000-meter race, 5000-meter race

4 **long-distance running,** long-distance racing, marathon, marathon racing

5 **relay racing,** relay race, 400-meter relay race, 1600-meter relay race, medley relay race; baton, baton change *or* changing, changeover, upsweep method, downsweep method, takeover zone, relay box

6 **hurdles,** 80-meter hurdles race, 100-meter hurdles race, 110-meter hurdles race, 200-meter hurdles race, 400-meter hurdles race; hurdle, barrier, obstacle

7 **steeplechase,** 3000-meter steeplechase, water jump

8 **cross-country racing,** 10,000-meter race

9 **race walking,** walking race, walk *or* walking, 20-kilometer walk, 50-kilometer walk
   ▶ *Motion 677; Impulsion 695*

10 **field event,** jumping, pole vault, shot put, discus throwing, hammer throwing, javelin throwing, multi-event contest

11 **jumping,** jump, high jump *or* jumping, back-layout style, straddle style, scissors style, Eastern cutoff style, Western roll style, flop; long jump, broad jump, scratch line, runup, approach, 8-step approach; plant, takeoff, takeoff point, clearance, landing, landing area, sandpit; hitchkick technique, hand technique; triple jump *or* jumping; hop, step, and jump; 10-step approach, bounding, hopping, running hop

12 **shot put,** shot, 16-pound shot put, shot velocity

13 **discus throwing,** discus, discus throw, preliminary swing, transition, swingback, turn, release, drive-foot landing

14 **hammer throwing,** hammer, hammer throw, hammer glove, circle, lift, single-support phase, rotation, acceleration path

15 **javelin throwing,** javelin, javelin throw, javelin carrying

16 **multi-event contest,** biathlon, triathlon, pentathlon, heptathlon, decathlon
   ▶ *Distance 585; Length 590; Height 596; Propulsion 696; Ascent 713*

17 **sports equipment,** running shoes, spiked shoes *or* spikes, starting blocks, starting pistol, running shorts, running vest, track suit, jogging suit, shell suit, jockstrap, athletic supporter, sport bra

18 **competition,** games, World Games, European Games, Pan-American Games, Commonwealth Games, Olympic Games; record, title, medal, gold medal, silver medal, bronze medal; drug test, anabolic steroid test, sex test

19 **track and field eventer,** athlete, competitor, runner, marathoner, sprinter, racer, hurdler, steeplechaser, race walker; jumper, pole-vaulter, shot-putter, thrower; coach, judge

ADJECTIVES

20 **track and field,** track, field, athletic [Brit]; running, racing, sprinting, hurdling, steeplechasing, race-walking, walking, jumping, pole-vaulting, shot-putting, throwing; competitive, Olympic, gold, silver, bronze

VERBS

21 **compete in track and field,** compete, contest, contend, vie, come in first, win, set *or* break a record; coach, train, judge

22 **participate,** race, start, run, sprint, accelerate, finish, hand over the baton, hurdle, race-walk, walk; throw, swing, release; jump, leap, spring, bound, pole-vault, land

ADVERBS

23 **fast,** at full stride, with a sprint, at a good pace, with velocity, speedily; far, high

aerobics
appliquéing
autograph collecting
backpacking
basket making,
    basketry
batik
beachcombing
beekeeping
beer making
bicycle riding
bird watching
bookbinding
brass-rubbing
butterfly collecting
    (lepidoptery)
calligraphy
candle making

caning
choral, instrumental
    music making
coin collecting
    (numismatics)
collage
collecting
computer games
computer network
    surfing
cooking
crocheting
crossword puzzles
découpage
dramatics
dressmaking
embroidering
enameling

exercising
flower arranging
flower pressing
folk dancing, square
    dancing
fossil hunting
gardening
genealogy
glass engraving
greenhouse gardening
hiking
jigsaw puzzles
keeping fit
kiteflying
knitting
lacemaking
lampshade making
macramé

marquetry
model making
model railroading
mosaics
museum going
origami
painting
patchworking
photography
pottery making
quilting
raffia work
reading
rug making
shell collecting
singing
spelunking (cave
    exploring)

spinning
stamp collecting
    (philately)
stenciling
stonecutting,
    engraving
tapestry making
tatting
tie-dyeing
topiary
traveling
upholstering
walking
weaving
whitewater rafting
winemaking
woodworking

167 Games, Pastimes, Amusements

NOUNS

1 **game,** pastime, recreation, amusement, sport, play, entertainment, diversion
   ▶ *Sports 145*
2 **type of game,** ball game, board game, card game, children's game, computer game, darts game, dice game, gambling game, indoor game, outdoor game, table game, video game, war game, word game

▶ *Sports 145; Card Playing 168*

3 **board game,** chess, chessboard, chessman, chess piece, pawn, rook *or* castle, knight, bishop, king, queen; opening, gambit, fork, pin, castling, capture, end game, check, checkmate, mate; checkers, checkerboard, checker, capture, crowning, king; Chinese checkers
4 **gambling,** playing, betting, bet, wager, stake, kitty; poker bet, dice bet, craps bet, roulette bet; odds, short odds, long odds; dice, die, spots, throw, double, snake eyes, craps

CHILDREN'S GAMES AND PARTY GAMES

alphabet game
anagrams
apple bob
authors
beanbag toss
biography
blind man's buff *or*
    bluff
button button
buzz
capture the flag
card toss
catch
cat's cradle
charades
chew the string
circle chat
concentration
consequences
cowboys and Indians
cracker race

crambo
cross-out fortunes
cup and ball
dodge ball
dreidel game
duck duck goose
dumb crambo
egg and spoon race
egg carry race
follow the leader
freeze tag
frog in the middle
geography
ghost
gossip
grandmother's tea
hangman
hidden treasure
hide-and-seek
hide in sight
hide the thimble

hopscotch
horseshoes
hot or cold
hot potato
I spy
jacks
jackstraws
jump rope
kickball
kick the can
leapfrog
London Bridge
mailman
marbles
memory game
minister's cat
Mother, may I?
mumbledypeg
murder
musical chairs
observation

pantomime
paper-clip fishing
paper-plate throw
pick-up-sticks
piñata
pin the tail on the
    donkey
post-mortem
post office
potato-sack race
prisoner's base
red rover
relay race
ringtoss
roadside alphabet
rock paper scissors
rumor
sack race
sardines
scavenger hunt
seek, don't speak

signboard
    alphabet
Simon says
spin the bottle
statue tag
stoop tag
tag
telegrams
telephone
three-legged race
tic-tac-toe
tiddly-winks
tip-cat
tug of war
TV tag
twenty questions
what am I?
wheelbarrow race
who am I?
wink
wonder ball

BOARD AND TABLE GAMES

backgammon	draughts	reversi
Battleship™	fox and geese	roulette
billiards	go	Scrabble™
bingo	goose	shut the box
caroms	halma	snakes and
checkers	lotto	ladders
chess	mah-jongg	snooker
Chinese checkers	mancala	table hockey
Chinese chess	Monopoly™	table tennis or
craps	Ouija™	Ping-Pong™
dice	Parcheesi™	Trivial Pursuit™
dominoes	pool	

▶ *Horses, Horseback Riding, Horse Racing 159; Card Playing 168; Chance 842*

5 **gambling house,** casino, gaming house, betting house, betting parlor, gambling den; [Inf]: crib, dive, joint

6 **gambler,** player, gamester, sport, speculator, bettor, wagerer, punter, high roller, sharp, cardsharp, shark, card shark, crapshooter

▶ *Horses, Horseback Riding, Horse Racing 159; Card Playing 168*

7 **amusement,** merrymaking, revelry, festivity, entertainment; fair, carnival, amusement park, theme park, playground; hobby, avocation, sideline, diversion, toy

▶ *Light Entertainment 138*

8 **amusement park and playground equipment,** ride, roller coaster, Ferris wheel, chute-the-chute, merry-go-round, carousel, tether ball; sandbox, slide, seesaw or teetertotter, junglegym or monkey bars, swing, trapeze; funhouse, arcade

▶ *Joy, Cheerfulness 269; Celebration 405*

9 **toy,** plaything, bauble; doll, dollhouse, doll carriage, paper doll, rocking horse, teddy bear, stuffed animal, puppet, marionette, tin or wooden soldier, ball, hoop, top, blocks, building blocks

ADJECTIVES

10 **recreational,** amusing, playing, playful, sporting, sportive, entertaining, avocational, diverting

11 **gambling,** risking, risky, staking, betting

VERBS

12 **play,** play games, sport; play chess, open, move, castle, queen, capture, mate, checkmate; play checkers, crown, king

13 **make merry,** revel, party, be festive; have a hobby, have an avocation

14 **gamble,** ante, stake, call, raise, throw the dice, throw in, fold

ADVERBS

15 **recreationally,** amusingly, entertainingly

168 Card Playing

Let spades be trumps! she said, and trumps they were.
— ALEXANDER POPE

NOUNS

1 **card playing,** card game, shuffling, cutting, cut, dealing, deal, misdealing, misdeal; gambling, gambling game

2 **cards,** playing cards, deck, pack, bezique pack, canasta pack, pinochle pack, piquet pack, tarot deck; suit, clubs, diamonds, hearts, spades; picture card, face card, court card, king, queen, jack, knave; ace, two, deuce, two-spot, three, trey, three-spot, four, four-spot, five, five-spot; wild card, joker, greater trumps; hand

CARD GAMES

all fours or high-low-jack	briscola	Earl of Coventry	knock rummy	pontoon	solitaire
American whist	canasta	écarté	loo	Pope Joan	solo
animals	casino	eights	matrimony	primero	speculation
auction bridge	chemin de fer	enflé	mau-mau	quadrille	strip poker
authors	Chicago	euchre	memory	quince	stud poker
baccarat	Chinese fan-tan	fan-tan	Michigan	ramino	tarok
banker and broker	cinch	faro	monte	red dog	thirty-one
bezique	club	fish	napoleon or nap	rouge et noir	three-card monte
blackjack or twenty-one or vingt et un	concentration	five hundred	Newmarket	rummy	tonk
black maria	contract bridge	frog	old maid	Russian whist	trente et quarante
blackout	cooncan or conquian	frog in the pond	old man's bundle	samba	war
boodle	cornet	German solo	old sledge	Saratoga	whist
Boston	crazy eights	gin rummy	ombre	sevens	ziginette
bridge	cribbage	go fish	patience	seven-up	
	dig	hearts	pinochle	skat	
	donkey	I doubt it	piquet	slap jack	
	draw poker	klondike	pitch	snip-snap-snorem	
		knock poker	poker		

3 cardplayer, dealer, cutter, bidder

4 bridge, auction bridge, contract bridge, rubber bridge, duplicate bridge, tournament bridge; bridge player, partner, North, South, East, West, bidder, declarer, dummy; major suit, minor suit, trump suit *or* trumps, honors *or* honor cards, yarborough; bid, opening bid, no-trump bid, demand bid, double, pass, underbid, renege, bidding convention; play, lead, trick, finesse, ruff, crossruff; score, small slam, grand slam, game, rubber, premium, set

5 poker, draw poker, stud poker, five-card stud, six-card stud, seven-card stud, eight-card stud, strip poker; betting, pot, jackpot, pool, ante, chip, stake, call, checking, raise, wild card; poker hand, five of a kind, straight flush, royal flush, four of a kind, full house, flush, straight, three of a kind, two pairs, one pair

ADJECTIVES

6 card-playing, shuffling, cutting, dealing; bidding, raising, opening, leading, ruffing, winning, scoring

VERBS

7 play cards, shuffle, cut, deal, misdeal; bid, renege, double, pass, ruff, crossruff, take a trick, finesse; play poker, gamble, ante, stake, call, raise, see, fade, fold

Communications

169 Communications

NOUNS

1 **communications,** means of communication, speech, talking, writing, correspondence, long-distance communication, electronic communication, telecommunication, telegraph, signaling, telephone, radio communication, broadcasting; mass communications, communications medium, mass media, radio, television, the press
  ▶ *Information 170; News 171; Radio and Television 172; Publication 173; Books 174; Periodicals 175; Speech, Spoken Language 205*

2 **correspondence,** letter writing, personal correspondence, business correspondence; letter, epistle, message, note; card, postcard, postal card; envelope, name, address, zip code, postal code [Brit]

3 **correspondent,** letter writer, note writer, pen pal

4 **postal communication,** mail, post, junk mail, direct mail, fan mail, registered letter, dead letter, money order, package, parcel; postage, stamp, postage stamp, postmark, cancellation, frank; mailbox, post office box, pigeonhole, mailbag, mail pouch; diplomatic pouch, dispatch box, postage *or* postal meter

5 **postal service,** United States Postal Service, post office, sorting office, dead-letter office; domestic mail, general delivery, forwarded mail, international mail, overseas mail, airmail, surface mail, express mail, priority mail, special handling, special delivery; first- *or* second- *or* third- *or* fourth-class mail; sea mail, parcel post, cash *or* collect on delivery (C.O.D.); registered mail, certified mail, insured mail, metered mail; penny post [Arch], Pony Express [Arch]

6 **postal worker,** postmaster general, postmaster, postmistress, mail carrier, letter carrier, mailman, mailwoman, postman, postwoman, sorter, messenger, special-delivery messenger, courier

7 **telecommunication,** transmission, propagation, two-way communication, one-way communication; tele-

phony, radiotelephony, telegraphy, radiotelegraphy; communications engineering, radio engineering, telephone engineering; communications system, network, computer networking, Internet, communication channel, communications link; communications line, transmission line, cable, coaxial cable *or* coax, fiber cable, fiberoptic cable; satellite communication
  ▶ *Engineering 14; Computers 15*

8 **data transmission,** telegraph, telegram, Mailgram™, radiotelegraph, cablegram, cable, wire, telex, teleprinter, teletypewriter, facsimile transmission, fax, modem; electronic mail, e-mail, cybernetics; Morse code
  ▶ *Computers 15*

9 **signaling,** signal, semaphore, flag signals, Morse code, railroad signals, smoke signals, radio signaling
  ▶ *Radio and Television 172; Sign 183*

10 **telephone,** phone, telephone set, handset, receiver, earpiece, mouthpiece, horn [Inf]; dial *or* rotary telephone, push-button telephone, cordless phone, mobile phone, car phone, cellular phone, radiotelephone *or* radiophone, ship-to-shore telephone, speakerphone, videophone; public telephone, pay phone, telephone booth *or* phone booth, call box [Brit], telephone kiosk [Brit]; public telephone system, party line, trunk line, hot line

11 **telephone call,** call, phone call, local call, long-distance call, toll call, toll-free call, overseas call, collect call, person-to-person call, personal call, business call, conference call, station-to-station call, crank call, nuisance call, ring; voice mail, phonemail, telemarketing; [Inf]: ringy-dingy, jingle, tinkle

12 **dial,** push button, button, headset, headphone, extension, intercom, answering machine, beeper; telephone number, dialing code, area code, telephone book, phone book, directory; dial tone, busy signal, reorder signal; dialing, direct distance dialing, speed calling, call waiting, call forwarding, Touch-Tone™ service, redialing

13 telephone exchange, telephone office, central [Arch]; switchboard, private exchange, private branch exchange (PBX)

14 telephone personnel, caller, phoner, subscriber, party; telephone operator *or* operator, switchboard operator, telephone mechanic, telephone engineer, lineman *or* linewoman

ADJECTIVES

15 communicated, told, spoken, written, posted, sent, signaled, transmitted, relayed, announced, advertised, radioed, televised; received, read, seen, heard
 ▶ *Radio and Television 172; Publication 173*

16 communicative, talkative, conversational, gossipy, newsy [Inf], open, candid, accessible
 ▶ *Talkativeness 207; Conversation 210*

17 communicational, communicating, oral, verbal, epistolary, postal, telecommunicational, telephonic, telegraphic; communicable, impartable, transmittable
 ▶ *Transfer 685*

VERBS

18 communicate, communicate with, be *or* get in touch, impart, tell, inform, speak to, talk to, write to, signal, send, relay, transmit, telegraph, cable, wire, telex, fax, network, broadcast
 ▶ *Information 170; News 171; Radio and Television 172; Publication 173; Speech, Spoken Language 205*

19 correspond, write to, correspond with, exchange letters, send *or* mail a letter, drop a line *or* card *or* note, reply, respond, answer, acknowledge; address, stamp, frank, mail, post [Brit], airmail, forward; dispatch, sort, deliver

20 telephone, call *or* call up, phone, ring (up), make a call, give someone a call *or* ring; [Inf]: give someone a buzz *or* tinkle *or* jingle

170 Information

There are three kinds of lies: lies, damned lies and statistics.
— BENJAMIN DISRAELI

There are two kinds of statistics, the kind you look up and the kind you make up. — REX STOUT

NOUNS

1 information, data, facts, facts and figures, knowledge, intelligence, news, tidings, word, acquaintance, order, briefing, instruction, advice; [Inf]: info, the know, the gen [Brit]

2 communication, transmission, notification, announcement, dissemination, presentation; document, report, account, word, message; dispatch, communiqué, bulletin, wire, telephone call, telegram, telex, cable, cablegram, fax, e-mail
 ▶ *Communications 169*

3 document, paper, certificate, record, report, review,·

compte rendu [Fr], statement, estimate, specification; financial statement, bank statement, tax return; file, dossier

4 inside information, advice, word, word to the wise, word of mouth, hint, clue, whisper, aside, suggestion, tip, inference, intimation, insinuation, pointer; rumor, leak, gossip; gesture, prompt, reminder, signal, nod, wink, look, nudge; caution, warning; privileged information, classified information; [Inf]: hot tip, tip-off, scuttlebutt, scoop, dope, dirt, lowdown
 ▶ *Advice 176; Disclosure 180; Secrecy 182*

5 public information, public knowledge, common knowledge, open information; news, advertisement, dissemination, broadside
 ▶ *News 171; Periodicals 175*

6 information source, source, authority, reference, reference book, library, information center, news agency, directory; grapevine, hot line, channel
 ▶ *News 171; Books 174; Periodicals 175*

7 information technology (IT), computerized information, data communications, information retrieval, database, viewdata, data processing (DP), information processing, information theory, statistics
 ▶ *Computers 15*

8 informer, informant, adviser, messenger, herald, teller, witness, announcer, teacher, instructor, communicator, correspondent; contact, source, tipster, gossip, talebearer, telltale, tattler, tattletale; newsmonger, inside agent, betrayer, fifth columnist, accuser, mole, whistleblower; [Inf]: stool pigeon *or* stoolie *or* stooly, snitch, fink, squealer, squeaker, blabber, nark [Brit]
 ▶ *Education 48; Communications 169; News 171*

ADJECTIVES

9 informed, enlightened, notified, educated, advised, briefed, posted, told, in touch, au courant, up-to-date; in the know, in on, clued in, wised up [Inf], genned up [Brit inf]

10 informative, informational, informatory, revealing, illuminating, enlightening, educational, instructive, instructional, advisory; cautionary, monitory; indicating, insinuating, suggesting; candid, explicit, clear, definite, plain-spoken; communicative, overcommunicative, indiscreet, telltale, loquacious, talkative, chatty, gossipy, bigmouthed
 ▶ *Disclosure 180; Talkativeness 207*

VERBS

11 inform, tell, apprise, advise, acquaint, clue in, confide, notify, certify, testify, brief, instruct, teach, enlighten, educate; point out, correct, put right, disabuse, undeceive, disillusion, let know, keep posted; [Inf]: put in the picture, fill in, wise up, tip off

12 communicate, make known, impart, transmit, disseminate, convey, recount, narrate, describe; publicize, break the news, broadcast, announce, televise, publish, report, correspond, document, post, wire, cable, telegraph, telex, telephone, fax

◣ *Communications 169; Publication 173; Periodicals 175*

13 inform on *or* **against,** betray, denounce, accuse, turn state's evidence, tell on, let the cat out of the bag, blow the whistle on; [Inf]: blab, spill the beans, stool, sell down the river, sing, snitch, squeal, rat, grass [Brit], shop [Brit]

◣ *Disclosure 180*

14 tip, hint, breathe, whisper, indicate, nudge, signal, suggest, imply, intimate, insinuate, tip off [Inf]

15 be informed, know, come to know, be told, be taught, learn, realize, understand, discover, be in the know; infer, get wind of, scent, hear, overhear, be a fly on the wall, have it from, have it on good authority, be told by a little bird [Inf]

ADVERBS

16 reportedly, as stated, on information given, straight from the horse's mouth; as it is said, from the grapevine, by word of mouth, apparently; from what one can gather, if one can trust one's ears

171 News

NOUNS

1 news, tidings, intelligence, information, facts, happenings, current affairs, hot news, hard news, front-page news; good news, glad tidings, good word, evangel, bad news; journalism, print journalism, broadcast journalism, television journalism; news media, newspaper, newsletter, newsmagazine, radio, television, the fourth estate

◣ *Communications 169; Information 170; Radio and Television 172; Publication 173; Books 174; Periodicals 175*

2 news event, news happening, breaking news, bulletin, flash; message, dispatch, word, communication, communiqué, press release, press conference, news conference, photo opportunity, outtake, sound bite

3 news story, news item, news article, news report, account, eyewitness account, article, story, piece, close-up; lead story, running story, feature story, feature article; editorial, letter to the editor, sidebar, column, opinion column, Op-Ed page, gossip column, advice column, humor column, sports column; births, marriages, obituaries, personals; scoop, exclusive, extra, news dispatch, interview, news release, press release, press notice, handout [Inf]; news analysis, journalese, media hype [Inf]

◣ *Radio and Television 172; Periodicals 175*

4 news source, informer, contact, adviser, tipster, newsmonger; tip, advice, word, word in the ear, lead, rumor, leak, gossip, scuttlebutt [Inf]; press office, news agency, news syndicate, press service, wire service

5 news reporting, reporting, news gathering, coverage, live coverage, journalism; news reporter, reporter,

journalist, correspondent, dispatcher, interviewer, writer, announcer, broadcaster, anchorman, anchorwoman

6 broadcast news, newscast, news program, news report, news update, news brief, news flash, news bulletin, live coverage, sportscast; radio news, television news; documentary, newsreel

◣ *Radio and Television 172*

7 print news, news story, news article, headline

◣ *Periodicals 175*

ADJECTIVES

8 newsworthy, newsy [Inf], informative, eyewitness, live; reportorial, reported, journalistic, reportable, front-page, exclusive, up-to-date, hot off the press; gossipy, alleged, rumored, whispered, in the news, in circulation, in the air, going the rounds

VERBS

9 report, give a report, give an account of, tell, relate, inform, interview, editorialize, write, broadcast, telecast; gather the news, break the news, give tidings of, announce, transmit, document, disclose, issue, dispatch, scoop, publish, publicize, gossip, dig up the dirt [Inf]

◣ *Information 170; Radio and Television 172; Publication 173; Periodicals 175*

ADVERBS

10 newsworthily, journalistically, reportedly, informatively, editorially, allegedly

172 Radio and Television

NOUNS

1 radio, wireless communication, radiotelephony, radiotelegraphy, telecommunication, wireless [Brit]; radio set, console, radio cabinet, crystal set, clock radio, car radio, portable radio, mobile radio, battery radio, transistor radio, shortwave radio, ship-to-shore radio, walkie-talkie, Walkman™, stereo, boom box [Inf], ghetto blaster [Inf]; pager, beeper

◣ *Communications 169*

2 radio reception, radio receiver, receiver, receiving antenna, amplifier, booster, audiofrequency, speaker, woofer, tweeter, tuner; volume control, tone control, fine-tuning, stereo system, hi-fi system; reception, fade *or* fading, drift, creeping, crawling, distortion, interference, noise, static, white noise, hum, hiss

◣ *Loudness 232*

3 radio transmission, broadcasting, radio signal, radio wave, long wave, medium wave, shortwave, radio spectrum, microwave, radio frequency, frequency band, wave band, frequency modulation (FM), amplitude modulation (AM), phase modulation (PM); radio signaling, radio navigation, radiobeacon; radio transmitter, microphone, transmitting antenna

◣ *Communications 169*

4 radio broadcasting, radio station, broadcasting station, FM station, AM station, studio, shortwave station; public radio, commercial radio, local radio, college radio, satellite radio, Citizens Band (CB), amateur radio, ham radio; relay station, booster station, radio mast, radio tower, mobile radio station, mobile unit, radio car, radiomobile; station identification, call letters, call sign

5 **television (TV),** video, black-and-white television, monochrome television, color television, portable television, broadcast television, network television, local television, closed-circuit television, high-definition television (HDTV), cable television, pay *or* subscription television

6 **television set,** TV set, screen, receiver, controls, volume, color, contrast, preset tuning, remote control, small screen, large screen; television *or* picture tube, cathode-ray tube (CRT), video signal, audio signal, sequential scanning, interlaced scanning, line, field, frame; [Inf]: idiot box, boob tube, telly [Brit], the box [Brit]

7 **television recording,** tape recording, tape deck, video recording, videocassette, videocassette recorder (VCR), videotape; video game, TV game; television camera, telecamera, video camera, mobile camera, camcorder, tape recorder

8 **television broadcasting,** transmission, broadcasting station, television channel; television station, relay station, booster station, television mast, television tower, mobile station, satellite transmission

9 **broadcast material,** broadcast, transmission, telecast, simulcast, on-site broadcast, relay, live relay, live coverage; recording, repeat, rerun, transcription; commercial, commercial break, station break, public service announcement, teletext, viewdata; educational broadcasting, religious broadcasting

10 **program,** radio program, TV program, prime-time program, syndicated program, series, miniseries, serial, drama series, costume drama, saga, docudrama, faction; radio drama, radio play, soap opera, soap [Inf], daytime drama, situation comedy, sitcom [Inf], variety show, quiz show, game show, panel show, talk show, chat show [Brit], made-for-television *or* -TV movie, audience participation, telethon, phone-in
▶ *Drama and Theater 136; Light Entertainment 138*

11 **broadcasting personnel,** radio broadcaster, television broadcaster, announcer, commentator, talking head [Inf], master of ceremonies *or* emcee *or* M.C., host, talk show host, game show host, quiz show host, quizmaster, disc jockey *or* deejay *or* D.J., televangelist, media personality; newscaster, anchorman, anchorwoman, television reporter, newsreader [Brit], investigative reporter, news commentator, news crew, news cameraman *or* camerawoman, news camera crew, sportscaster, weather forecaster, weatherman, weatherwoman; voiceover

12 **broadcast,** transmitted, sent, announced, advertised, radioed, televised, amplified, modulated, repeated, received, seen, heard, read, transcribed, recorded, photographed, taped, videotaped, rerun, rebroadcast

13 **broadcast,** report, transmit, radio, televise, telecast, program, simulcast, put on the air, put on the airwaves, announce, inform, document, cover

14 **tune,** adjust, change the station *or* channel, channel-surf [Inf]

15 **record,** tape-record, tape, video, videotape, audiotape

173 Publication

1 **publication,** book, periodical, newsletter, announcement, declaration, proclamation, notice, notification, pronouncement, speech, statement, sermon; report, news, communiqué, bulletin, manifesto, pronunciamento, edict, decree, encyclical, ukase, ban
▶ *Communications 169; News 171; Books 174; Periodicals 175*

2 **publishing,** dissemination, circulation, ventilation, divulgence *or* divulgement, disclosure, promulgation, printing; public address system, spreading the word, broadcasting, broadcast, unconfirmed report, rumor, hearsay, gossip, trial balloon
▶ *Communications 169; Information 170; Disclosure 180; Speech, Spoken Language 205*

3 **printing,** typesetting, composition, reproduction, photographic reproduction, letterpress typography, lithography, offset lithography, offset, photo-offset, web-offset; color printing, chromolithography, chromotypography, two- *or* three- *or* four-color printing; presswork, make-ready; press, printing press, web press; print, imprint, stamp, impression; reprint, reissue, offprint
▶ *Reproduction 21*

4 **typesetting,** composing, hot-metal typesetting, cold-type typesetting, computer composition, computerized typesetting, photocomposition; imposition, justification; typesetting machine, Linotype™; kerning, line of type, slug, furniture

5 **type,** type style, typeface *or* face, font, fount [Brit], type size; roman type, italic type, cursive type, boldface *or* bold type, lightface type, sans serif type, Gothic type, Old English type; capital letter, capital, cap, upper case, majuscule, uncial; small letter, lower case, minuscule; type body, shank, stem, kern, ascender, descender, serif

6 **publication media,** mass media, the media, communication, mass communication; telecommunication, television, radio, broadcasting, the press, journalism, periodical, newspaper, magazine, journal, book

◗ *Communications 169; News 171; Books 174; Periodicals 175*

7 publicity, limelight, spotlight, coverage, public recognition, public eye; fame, famousness, renown, notoriety, infamy; exposure, common knowledge, public knowledge, openness, currency, circulation, wide currency, wide *or* countrywide *or* nationwide circulation; public discussion, conference, public forum, pulpit, platform, soapbox, rostrum, hustings

8 public relations (PR), press notice, press release, press announcement, press conference, news conference; promotion, advertising, propaganda, media event, staged event, exhibition, photocall, photo opportunity; display, top billing, medicine show, showmanship, ostentation, sensationalism, exaggeration, puff, ballyhoo, buildup, flackery, name in bright lights, letters a foot high; [Inf]: promo, plug, hype, hoopla

9 advertisement, commercial, notice, announcement, message; trailer, poster, flier, insert *or* insertion, leaflet, pamphlet, brochure, blurb, circular, handbill, broadside, bill, billboard, placard, banner, sandwich board, display board, bulletin board; classified advertisement, commercial listing; [Inf]: ad, classified ad, want ad, blad, handout, teaser, spiel, words from the sponsor, infomercial

10 printer, compositor, typesetter, typographer, lithographer, linotyper, pressman

11 publicizer, publicist, promoter, propagandist, publicity agent, press agent, imagemaker, publisher; advertiser, advertising agent, advertising account executive, persuader; copywriter, blurb writer, public relations (PR) person; notifier, announcer, messenger, proclaimer, crier, huckster, herald, flack, barker, spieler, pamphleteer, billposter *or* billsticker, sandwich man; [Inf]: spin doctor, shill, tout

◗ *Books 174; Periodicals 175*

ADJECTIVES

12 published, in print, printed, in circulation, circulating, circulated, in the air, current, in the news, in the open, open, public, made public, revealed, reported, disclosed, exposed, announced, declared, proclaimed, issued, on press, hot off the press; ventilated, communicated, disseminated, distributed, circularized, spread around *or* about, broadcast, aired, televised

◗ *Communications 169; Disclosure 180*

13 printed, composed, typeset; typographic, typographical; roman, italic, cursive, boldface, lightface, capital, uppercase, small, lowercase

14 publicized, well-known, celebrated, advertised, renowned, famed, famous, popular, widely known, in the headlines, headlined, in the public eye, on everyone's lips, manifest; infamous, notorious, flagrant, blatant, glaring, sensational

VERBS

15 publish, put out, put about, release, circulate, promulgate, propagate, inform, make *or* go public, bring to public notice, bring into the open, tell the world, let it be known, make known, divulge, reveal, disclose, disseminate, expose, ventilate, air, communicate, relay, televise, broadcast, transmit, spread, spread the word, print; rumor, spread a rumor, launch a trial balloon, bruit about, noise, bring up, mention, talk about, gossip, retail, pass around, bandy about, hawk, buzz

◗ *Communications 169; Information 170; Books 174; Periodicals 175*

16 proclaim, announce, notify, pronounce, declare, declaim, herald, trumpet, blast, blazon, blaze, cry, shout, shout from the rooftops, scream, thunder, beat the big drum, raise a hue and cry, raise the roof [Inf]

17 print, issue, imprint, stamp, impress; reprint, reissue; compose, set, typeset, impose, justify, kern

18 publicize, promote, boost, build up, push, feature, highlight, spotlight, pinpoint, headline, put in the headlines, make famous, put on the map, make one's name (known), make someone; extol, glorify, rave about; advertise, advertise for, place an advertisement, sell, puff, ballyhoo, bill, post bills, pamphlet, placard, propagandize; [Inf]: plug, hype, shill, tout

19 be published, become public knowledge, come out, see oneself *or* one's name in print, appear, break, hit the news, hit the streets, be in the limelight; be sold, circulate, spread, pass around, go the rounds, get around *or* about, sell well, sell like hot cakes; be famous, be in the news, get into the papers, be hot off the press, hit the headlines, make *or* be on the front page, make it to the top, become known from coast to coast

ADVERBS

20 publicly, openly, blatantly, out in the open, out front, in open court, with open doors, in full view, on stage, in the public eye, in the spotlight *or* limelight, for all to see

174 Books

NOUNS

1 book, publication, volume, tome, work, opus, title, writing, literary composition, literary work, work of literature; classic, bestseller, rare book; hardcover, paperback, softcover; edition, printing, print run

◗ *Literature 139*

2 rare book, first edition, signed edition, manuscript, codex, scroll, incunabulum

3 type of book, textbook, schoolbook, primer, grammar, reader; children's book, picture book, coloring book, storybook; trade book, coffee-table book; reference book, encyclopedia, almanac, dictionary, lexicon, concordance, thesaurus, directory, index, guidebook, Baedeker, travelogue *or* travelog, field guide, sports book, handbook, cookbook, manual, vade mecum, how-to book, atlas, gazetteer, nautical almanac, astronomical almanac, ephemeris, catalog, telephone directory *or* book

4 compilation, anthology, ana, collection, quotation book, festschrift, series, serialization, yearbook; collected works, complete works, *oeuvres* [Fr]

5 book part, front matter *or* preliminaries *or* prelims [Inf], half title *or* bastard title, imprimatur, frontispiece, title page, copyright page *or* copyright notice, publishing history, Cataloging in Publication (CIP) data, International Standard Book Number (ISBN), permissions notice, dedication, epigraph, table of contents, list of illustrations, list of tables, preface, acknowledgments, introduction; text, part, chapter, page, right-hand page, recto, left-hand page, verso; back matter *or* end matter, appendix, notes, glossary, bibliography, index, colophon; main head, subhead, running head *or* foot, page number *or* folio

6 book publishing, publishing, book trade, bookmaking, book manufacturing, book production

7 stage of book production, manuscript preparation, substantive editing, mechanical editing, copyediting, production editing; design, keymarking *or* coding, typesetting, layout, proof, dummy, proofreading, printing, binding

8 design and makeup, trim size, type page, type specifications *or* specs [Inf], type size *or* point size, type font *or* typeface, leading, castoff, sample pages

▸ *Publication 173*

9 stage of proof, galley proof, page proof, confirmational proof; mechanical, camera-ready copy, reproduction proof *or* repro, foundry proof; film proof, blueproof, blueline, blueprint, blues, Vandyke *or* brownprint; color proof; folded and gathered sheets (F and Gs)

10 book printing, letterpress printing, hot-metal printing, offset printing, offset lithography; web-fed printing, sheet-fed printing, two-color printing, four-color process printing

11 bookbinding, case binding, paper binding, mechanical binding, spiral binding, library binding; Smyth sewing *or* stitching, side sewing *or* side wiring, saddle-stitching *or* saddle wiring, perfect binding; book jacket, dust jacket, dust cover, slipcase; flyleaf, end paper, end leaf, end sheet, signature

12 book publishing personnel, publisher, book publisher, publishing house, publishing company; author, writer, novelist, ghost writer; literary agent, agent; editor, managing editor, editor in chief, manuscript editor, fiction editor, reference editor, production editor, copyeditor, fact checker, designer; proofreader, printer, typesetter, compositor, comp [Inf]; bookbinder

▸ *Literature 139; Description 202*

13 book review, review, criticism, critique; book reviewer, reviewer, literary critic, critic, textual critic

▸ *Interpretation 365*

14 library, book depository, learning center, information center; public library, municipal library, county library, state library, national library; special library, circulating library, lending library [Brit], rental library, private library; book wagon, bookmobile; athenaeum, reading room; library science, librarianship; librarian

15 bookshop, bookstore, bookstall, bookstand, book club; bookseller, book dealer, publisher's agent, book salesman, bibliopole

16 booklover, bibliophile, bibliophage, book collector, bookworm

ADJECTIVES

17 bookloving, bibliophilic, bibliopolic, bibliophagic

18 published, written, edited, designed, printed, in print, in circulation, circulating, issued, produced, bound, distributed, sold

▸ *Literature 139*

VERBS

19 publish, prepare for publication, edit, copyedit, design, typeset, proofread, paginate, print, bind, manufacture, issue, bring out, put out, distribute, sell

175 Periodicals

NOUNS

1 periodical, newspaper, magazine, serial, journal, gazette; daybook, diary

2 newspaper, paper, local paper, national paper, international paper; morning paper, evening paper, daily paper, daily, weekly paper, Sunday paper; giveaway, throwaway, sheet, flier, broadside; tabloid, scandal sheet, rag [Inf]; edition, early edition, late edition, stop-press edition, extra edition *or* extra, late extra, special edition, sports edition; magazine section, comics, supplement, color supplement, trade supplement, feuilleton; want-ad section, agony column, personal section

3 magazine, periodical, journal; newsmagazine, glossy magazine, picture magazine, women's magazine, men's magazine, fashion magazine, business magazine, sports magazine, literary magazine, comic magazine, comic book; pulp magazine, in-flight magazine; serial, series, edition, issue; daily, weekly, biweekly, fortnightly, semimonthly, monthly, quarterly, seasonal, annual; specialist publication, academic journal, professional journal, trade journal, trade paper, organ, house organ, house magazine; newsletter, pamphlet

4 print journalism, reportage, news reporting, news gathering, coverage, blanket coverage, investigative reporting, in-depth reporting, political reporting, interpretive reporting, analytical journalism, objective reporting, photojournalism, legwork, muckraking; the press, the fourth estate, print medium, serious press, yellow press, underground press, Fleet Street, newspaper publishing, magazine publishing

> *Communications 169; News 171; Publication 173*

5 **print journalist,** reporter, news reporter, cub reporter, newspaperman, newspaperwoman, newsman, newswoman, newshawk [Inf], newshound [Inf], news photographer, photojournalist, paparazzo; correspondent, foreign correspondent, special correspondent, war correspondent; investigative journalist, feature writer, sports reporter, fashion reporter, freelance reporter, freelance writer, stringer; columnist, critic, gossip columnist, hack, scandalmonger, muckraker; news bureau chief, managing editor, editor, city editor, features editor, sports editor, copyeditor, subeditor, copyreader; press baron, press corps

ADJECTIVES

6 **periodical,** serial, magazinish, magaziny, newspaperish, newspapery

7 **newsworthy,** front-page, lead, headline, newsy [Inf]; journalistic, reportorial, reportable, editorial, informative, reported

> *News 171*

8 **published,** printed, in print, in circulation, circulating, in the news, made public, public, disseminated, issued

> *Publication 173*

VERBS

9 **report,** write, write up, cover, interview, investigate, break a story, scoop; edit, copyedit, subedit; publish, prepare for publication, typeset, print, go to press, issue, serialize, distribute, circulate, deliver

ADVERBS

10 **journalistically,** reportorially, reportedly, editorially, informatively, as reported

176 Advice

NOUNS

1 **advice,** counsel, guidance, recommendation, communication, consultation; word of advice, piece of advice, words of wisdom, pearls of wisdom, maxim; caution, warning, admonition, caveat; counseling, advising, therapy, rede [Brit]; didacticism, moralizing, preaching, sermonizing, precept

> *Remedy 115; Wisdom 352; Warning 814*

2 **recommendation,** suggestion, submission, proposition, proposal, motion, urging, exhortation; opinion, view, estimate, judgment, criticism, constructive criticism

> *Judgment 341*

3 **communication,** information, intelligence, news, word; advisory, notice, notification, communiqué; tip, hint, word in the ear, word to the wise, flea in the ear, verbum sap; instruction, briefing, charge, charge to the jury, advice for, persuasion, advice against, dissuasion

> *Litigation 54; Communications 169; Information 170; Persuasion 178; Dissuasion 179*

4 **consultation,** counsel, conference, deliberation, discussion, tête-à-tête, parley, negotiation, negotiations, round table, exchange of views, open exchange, reference, taking counsel, seeking advice; advisement

> *Management 126; Conversation 210; Negotiation 460*

5 **adviser,** counselor, consultant, professional consultant, expert, management consultant, financial consultant *or* adviser, legal adviser, medical adviser; prescriber, recommender, suggester, advocate; troubleshooter, arbitrator, arbiter, judge, referee, umpire; psychologist, therapist, psychotherapist, psychiatrist, psychoanalyst, analyst, marriage counselor, social worker; teacher, tutor, professor, guidance counselor, mentor, coach; personal adviser, confidant *or* confidante, friend, aide, guide; monitor, watchdog, admonisher, reminder, remembrancer, Dutch uncle; meddler, backseat driver, kibitzer, busybody, gossip, yenta [Inf], buttinsky [Inf]

6 **advisory body,** consultative body, council, board, board of advisers, governmental committee, congressional committee, parliamentary committee [Brit], select *or* special committee; huddle, powwow [Inf]

ADJECTIVES

7 **advisory,** advising, counseling, guiding, therapeutic; consultative, consultatory, deliberative; recommending, recommendatory, encouraging, persuasive, hortatory *or* hortative, urging, exhorting, exhortative; informative, instructive, prescriptive; didactic, preachy, moral, moralizing; dissuasive, critical, admonishing, admonitory *or* monitory, warning, cautionary

> *Persuasion 178; Dissuasion 179; Warning 814*

8 **advisable,** recommendable, prudent, wise, judicious, politic, sensible, practical, expedient

> *Wisdom 352; Convenience 803*

VERBS

9 **advise,** give advice, offer advice, counsel, give counsel, offer counsel; guide, teach, coach; advocate, recommend, commend, suggest, propose, move, put to, submit, propound; encourage, prompt, press, urge, exhort, persuade; advise against, dissuade, admonish, warn, caution; criticize, moralize; judge, arbitrate, rule, regulate

> *Persuasion 178; Dissuasion 179; Supposition 359; Warning 814*

10 **communicate,** inform, notify, give notice, apprise; hint, tip, give a word to the wise; instruct, brief, charge a jury

> *Information 170*

11 **consult,** seek *or* solicit advice, ask for advice, seek an opinion, seek a second opinion, refer to, refer to arbitration; confide in, have at one's elbow, accept advice, take advice, follow advice, take one's cue from; confer, deliberate, discuss, have a tête-à-tête with, parley, ne-

gotiate, iron out problems, exchange views, swap ideas, put heads together, huddle, have a powwow with [Inf]

ADVERBS

12 **advisorily,** consultatively, deliberatively; persuasively, encouragingly, hortatorily; informatively, instructively, prescriptively, preceptively, commandingly, mandatorially; didactically, preachily, morally; dissuasively, critically, admonishingly, admonitorily or monitorily

13 **advisably,** recommendably, prudently, wisely, judiciously, sensibly, expediently

177 Maxim

NOUNS

1 **maxim,** saying, proverb, adage, aphorism, apothegm or apophthegm, words of wisdom, saw, gnome, gnomic formula, oracle, mot, witticism, epigram, epigraph, motto, slogan, catchphrase, catchword, watchword, byword, epithet, tag, moral, axiom, truth, truism, banality, cliché, platitude, commonplace, bromide, hackneyed phrase, stock phrase, precept, order, dictum, formula, mantra, theorem, rule, law, observation, principle, chestnut

> ❱ *Advice 176; Conciseness 198; Humor 277; Wisdom 352*

ADJECTIVES

2 **proverbial,** aphoristic, gnomic, epigrammatic, axiomatic, banal, clichéd, platitudinous, commonplace, trite, hackneyed, stock, stereotyped, sententious, moralistic, moralizing, preceptive, witty, pithy, enigmatic, oracular

VERBS

3 **aphorize,** epigrammatize, coin a phrase, proverb, moralize, pronounce, utter, theorize, formulate, observe, propose, remark

ADVERBS

4 **proverbially,** aphoristically, epigrammatically, axiomatically, platitudinously; as they say, as the saying goes, to coin a phrase, in a nutshell

178 Persuasion

NOUNS

1 **persuasion,** influence, suasion, advice, counseling, inducement, sway; cajolery, coaxing, wheedling, flattery, inveiglement, blandishment, honeyed words, persuasiveness, suasiveness, convincingness, cogency, forcefulness, insistence, pressure, lobbying; soft soap [Inf], sweet talking [Inf]

> ❱ *Advice 176; Motivation 508; Influence 512*

2 **exhortation,** entreaty, pleading, advocacy, solicitation, importunity, urging, incitement, encouragement; pep talk, pep rally, rallying cry, clarion call, trumpet call

3 **enticement,** allurement, attraction, invitation, temptation, tantalization, lure, seduction or seducement,

siren song, come-on [Inf]; allure, appeal, attractiveness, fascination, charm, winning ways, charisma, magnetism, witchery, bewitchment, seductiveness, sex appeal, turnon [Inf], it [Inf]; decoy, decoy duck, trap, bait, baited trap; special offer, sale of the century, loss leader

> ❱ *Attraction 700; Trap 813*

4 **incentive,** inducement, motivator, motivation, incitement, stimulus, provocation, carrot, carrot and stick, spur, fillip; goad, nudge, prod, slap, whip, crack of the whip; big stick, threat; intimidation, browbeating, bullying, coercion, muscle; bribe, kickback, slush fund, sop, greased palm, offer one cannot refuse; [Inf]: payoff, payola, pork barrel, backhander [Brit]

> ❱ *Offer 504*

5 **motive,** reason, cause, cause of action, rationale, reasoning, justification, ground or grounds, basis; motivation, driving force, impetus, mainspring, causation, impulse, ulterior motive; intention, objective, purpose, end, aim, goal, aspiration, ambition; ideal, guiding principle, words to live by, guiding light, direction

> ❱ *Hope 281; Improvisation 396; Duty 433; Selfishness 444; Motivation 508; Cause 675*

6 **calling,** call, vocation, conscience, dictate of conscience, honor, duty, personal reasons, conviction, belief; sect, group, faction

> ❱ *Assembly 59; Religion 81; Belief 87*

7 **publicity,** public relations (PR), advertising, direct marketing, advertisement, promotion, flackery, sales promotion, promotional literature, direct mail; salesmanship, soft selling, soft sell, hard selling, hard sell, sales talk, ballyhoo, Madison Avenue; propagandizing, propaganda, pamphleteering, agitprop, indoctrination, brainwashing; [Inf]: sales pitch, hoopla, hype

> ❱ *Publication 173*

8 **persuadability,** persuasibility, convincibility, receptiveness, willingness, tractability, teachableness, malleability, pliability, pliancy, impressionability, impressibility, susceptibility or susceptivity, suggestibility, credulity, credulousness; putty in one's hands

9 **persuader,** convincer, influencer, swayer; cajoler, coaxer, wheedler, flatterer, inveigler; pleader, advocate, solicitor, orator, rhetor, rhetorician, lecturer; public relations (PR) person, spin doctor [Inf], publicist, publicizer, press agent, promoter, advertiser, adman, direct-mailer, salesperson, salesman or saleswoman; propagandist, agitpropist, indoctrinator, brainwasher

> ❱ *Publication 173; Speech, Spoken Language 205; Flattery 439*

10 **tempter,** tantalizer, lurer, charmer; seducer, Romeo, Casanova, rake; temptress, Eve, seductress, vamp, femme fatale, siren, Circe, Lorelei; Satan, the devil

11 **motivator,** inspirer, influence, counselor, adviser, manager, agent, teacher, coach; suggester, prompter, stimulator, instigator; tactician, strategist, planner, mover, prime mover, maneuverer, manipulator, wire-

puller, mover and shaker [Inf]; abettor, aider and abettor, agent provocateur, ringleader, firebrand, rabble-rouser, demagogue, agitator, seditionary *or* seditionist, activist; lobbyist, lobbyer; lobby, pressure group, special-interest group, watchdog group

▶ *Management 126; Advice 176; Plan 387; Influence 512; Help 825*

ADJECTIVES

12 **persuasive,** influential, suasive, impressive, convincing, cogent, compelling, forceful, effective; prompting, inducing, inciting, motivating, incentive, stimulating, provocative; encouraging, exhorting, hortatory *or* hortative, pleading; didactic, insisting; promotional, hard-selling, propagandistic

▶ *Belief 87; Influence 512*

13 **enticing,** alluring, attractive, appealing, inviting, tempting, tantalizing, fascinating, charming, winning, charismatic, magnetic, bewitching, seductive, sexy, irresistible, habit-forming, addictive

▶ *Habit, Custom 397; Attraction 700*

14 **persuadable,** persuasible, convincible, swayable, impressionable, impressible, susceptible, suggestible, open to suggestion, receptive, willing, tractable, teachable, malleable, pliable, pliant, credulous, soft [Inf]; inducible, incitable; persuaded, convinced, impressed, inspired, motivated, induced, incited, egged on, encouraged, urged

VERBS

15 **persuade,** influence, advise, counsel, prevail upon, compel, induce; impress, convince, bring around, talk around; sway, talk into, win over; cajole, coax, wheedle, inveigle, flatter, blandish, lay it on thick, exhort, entreat, plead, advocate, urge, encourage; impel, insist, pressure, lobby; soft-soap [Inf], sweet-talk [Inf]

▶ *Belief 87; Flattery 439; Influence 512*

16 **entice,** allure, attract, invite, tempt, lead into temptation, tantalize, lure, seduce, dangle before one's eyes, hold out a carrot, turn on [Inf], sweeten the pot; fascinate, charm, charismatize, bewitch; decoy, trap, bait

▶ *Attraction 700; Trap 813*

17 **motivate,** inspire, move, prompt, incite, stimulate, spur, instigate, bring about, cause, provoke; reason with, rationalize, justify, satisfy; goad, nudge, prod, slap, whip; push into, drive into, nag into, bully into, wear down, browbeat, intimidate, force, coerce, threaten, twist one's arm, put the screws on

▶ *Reason 319; Conversion 670*

18 **bribe,** offer a bribe, offer an inducement, pay under the table, buy off, grease the palm, oil, suborn, corrupt; give a sop to Cerberus, reward; [Inf]: pay off, grease, square

▶ *Reward 453; Offer 504*

19 **publicize,** promote, advertise, sell, hard-sell, soft-sell, pitch [Inf], hype [Inf]; propagandize, pamphleteer, indoctrinate, convert, enlist, brainwash

20 **be persuaded,** agree, consent, come around, believe, buy [Inf], yield, succumb, submit, give up, concede; come *or* fall under the influence of, feel the urge, hear the call, follow one's conscience

▶ *Agreement 462*

ADVERBS

21 **persuasively,** influentially, suasively, impressively, convincingly, cogently, forcefully, effectively

22 **enticingly,** alluringly, attractively, appealingly, charmingly, temptingly, tantalizingly, seductively, sexily, irresistibly

179 Dissuasion

Let's find out what everyone is doing, and then stop everyone from doing it. — A. P. HERBERT

NOUNS

1 **dissuasion,** discouragement, caution, warning, contrary advice, contraindication; expostulation, remonstration, objection, protest, resistance, opposition; reproof, reproach, rebuke, admonition

▶ *Resistance 417; Warning 814; Opposition 828*

2 **deterrence,** deterrent, disincentive, chilling effect, restraint, hindrance; deflection, roadblock, red light, closed door, setback; intimidation, terrorism

▶ *Fear 283; Deviation 698; Hindrance 826; Restraint 830*

3 **disaffection,** alienation, unwillingness, disinclination; disheartenment, dejection, disillusionment, disenchantment; damper, wet blanket

▶ *Dislike 291*

ADJECTIVES

4 **dissuasive,** dissuading, discouraging, cautionary, warning, admonitory *or* monitory; contrary, contradictory, opposing; expostulatory, remonstrant; deterrent, preventive, deflective, chilling; off-putting, repellent, disgusting; daunting, intimidating, threatening; disheartening, depressing, disenchanting

5 **dissuaded,** discouraged, persuaded against; deterred, restrained, hindered, hampered; deflected, steered away from; daunted, intimidated, threatened, terrorized; unnerved, rattled, shaken, shaken up; put off, alienated, disinclined, indisposed, unwilling, disaffected, repelled, disgusted

▶ *Unwillingness 375*

6 **discouraged,** disheartened, dispirited, dejected, depressed, disillusioned, disenchanted; deadened, dampened, cooled, chilled

VERBS

7 **dissuade,** discourage, caution, warn, advise against, contraindicate, convince to the contrary, convince otherwise, talk out of; confute, argue against, expostulate, remonstrate, dispute, protest against, resist; castigate, reprove, admonish

> *Refutation 332; Disapproval 438; Protest 507; Warning 814*

8 deter, discourage, restrain, hold back, keep back, crush, nip in the bud, quench, squelch; stop, prevent, check, avert; deflect, head off, halt one's progress, steer one away from

> *Deviation 698; Restraint 830*

9 daunt, cow, intimidate, threaten, terrorize, frighten off, frighten away; unnerve, rattle, shake, shake up, stagger, make one stop in one's tracks, make one pause

> *Fear 283*

10 put off, alienate, disincline, indispose, disaffect, set against, turn against, repel, disgust

> *Dislike 291*

11 discourage, dishearten, dispirit, deject, depress, disillusion, disenchant; throw cold water on, extinguish, deaden, dull, blunt, dampen, cool, chill, be a wet blanket, wet-blanket

> *Sorrow 270; Moderation 521*

ADVERBS

12 dissuasively, discouragingly, admonishingly, admonitorily *or* monitorily; expostulatingly, remonstrantly; as a deterrent, preventively; dauntingly, intimidatingly, threateningly; unwillingly, disaffectedly, repellently, disgustedly

13 dishearteningly, depressingly, disenchantingly; dispiritedly, dejectedly

180 Disclosure

NOUNS

1 disclosure, exposure, revelation, uncovering, unveiling, manifestation, epiphany, apocalypse; discovery, diagnosis, denouement, resolution, explanation, showdown, catastrophe

> *Discovery 345*

2 divulgence *or* **divulgement,** announcement, declaration, communication, publication, broadcast, full report, exposé; betrayal, leak, hint, telltale sign, indiscretion, giveaway, state's evidence, queen's *or* king's evidence, admission, acknowledgment, avowal, affirmation, confession

> *Communications 169; Periodicals 175*

3 openness, candor, frankness, directness, forthrightness, downrightness, forthcomingness, unreservedness, outspokenness, truth, honesty, *glasnost* [Russ]

> *Truthfulness 191; Talkativeness 207*

4 discloser, revealer, exposer, announcer, communicator, discoverer, researcher, investigator, investigative journalist, reporter, publicizer, broadcaster; confessor, informant, informer, betrayer, talebearer, tattletale, whistle-blower; [Inf]: squealer, snitch, blab *or* blabber

> *Information 170; Publication 173; Periodicals 175*

ADJECTIVES

5 disclosed, revealed, exposed, shown; showing, visible, clear, obvious, transparent, open, manifest; laid bare, leaked, uncovered, unearthed, unmasked; confessed, admitted, avowed, acknowledged

6 disclosing, revealing, divulging, open, candid, frank, direct, plain-spoken, forthright, downright, forthcoming, informative, communicative, talkative; unreserved, outspoken, indiscreet

> *Talkativeness 207*

7 revelatory, expository, explicatory, explanatory, interpretive, epiphanic, apocalyptic

VERBS

8 disclose, reveal, expose, make known, show, manifest, bring to light, bring into the open; discover, diagnose, take the lid off; let out, unleash, unkennel, hold up to view, take the wraps off, uncloak, bare, lay *or* strip bare, denude; unfold, unroll, unfurl, unpack, unwrap, uncover, unshroud; unveil, lift the veil, raise the curtain, shine some light on, let in daylight, let some light in; unclose, unseal, break the seal, break the wax, open, lay open, open up, dig up, disinter, show up, unmask, tear off the mask, let slip, show for what it is, show one's true colors

9 divulge, announce, declare, communicate, publicize, publish, broadcast, inform, educate, break the news, break it to, give out, vent, give vent to, ventilate, air, speak out, come out with, tell all, come out of the closet, go public; let on, tell, talk, speak, utter, breathe; hint, confide, leak, let one in on, let drop, let fall; let out, open the books, set straight *or* right, set the record straight, straighten the record, show one's hand, show one's cards, put one's cards on the table, talk straight; [Inf]: talk turkey, blow the lid off, let it all hang out

> *Communications 169; Publication 173; Periodicals 175*

10 tell on, betray, give away, inform on, accuse, name names, turn state's evidence, turn queen's *or* king's evidence; blurt out, talk out of turn, blow the whistle on, blow someone's cover, tell tales out of school, let the cat out of the bag; [Inf]: spill the beans, give the game away, shoot off one's mouth, blab, sing, snitch, squeal, rat on

11 admit, allow, acknowledge, concede, grant, assent, affirm, avow, own, confess, own up, plead guilty, come clean, make a clean breast of it, get it off one's chest, open one's heart to, unbosom oneself, unburden oneself, bare one's soul

12 be disclosed, become known, appear, stand revealed, emerge, transpire, leak out, come to light, come out, break, get out, become public knowledge, break through the clouds, show one's face, show one's true colors

ADVERBS

13 openly, unreservedly, in the open, with no holds barred, outright, freely, frankly, plainly, candidly, directly, forthrightly, forthcomingly, indiscreetly

181 Concealment

NOUNS

1 **concealment,** hiding, cover, invisibility, disappearance, eclipse, occultation, reconditeness; silence, evasion, disguise, privacy

2 **hiding place,** hideout, hideaway, hidey-hole [Inf], cache, stash; foxhole, dugout, trench, bolt-hole; shelter, bomb shelter, refuge, sanctuary, asylum, safe house; recess, cave, nook, cranny, niche, cubbyhole, pigeonhole, closet, cellar, doormat, mattress, secret compartment, secret panel, secret passage, hollow tree, mother's skirts; safe, safe-deposit box, bank vault
  ▶ *Secrecy 182*

3 **verbal concealment,** whisper, silence, taciturnity, reserve, closeness, discretion, confidentiality, privacy, private conversation; censorship, suppression; security, national security, classified information
  ▶ *Secrecy 182*

4 **cover,** mask, screen, veil, purdah, camouflage, wraps, cover-up, smoke screen; anonymity, disguise, costume, costume party, masked ball, *bal masqué* [Fr]; ambush, trap, blind
  ▶ *Covering 613; Latency 844*

5 **evasion,** evasiveness, avoidance, dodging, escape, equivocation, quibbling, vagueness, obscurity, mystification, obfuscation, deception, misinformation; lie, alibi, prevarication, dishonesty, cover-up, false evidence, perjury, deceitfulness, dissimulation, duplicity, trickery, subterfuge
  ▶ *Untruthfulness, Falsehood 192; Deception 193*

6 **privacy,** seclusion, isolation, retreat, sanctum, confessional, monastery, convent, nunnery, closed order; private garden, private club, lair, den, library, closet, boudoir, bedroom, bath, toilet; outpost, desert island, mountaintop, ivory tower

7 **one who conceals,** concealer, hider, hermit, recluse, lone wolf, power behind the throne, gray eminence *or* éminence grise, undercover agent, face in the crowd, dissembler, masquerader, evader, deceiver, disguiser, conspirator
  ▶ *Secrecy 182*

ADJECTIVES

8 **concealed,** hidden, unseen, secluded, sequestered, screened, hooded, recondite, veiled, covered, overprinted, eclipsed, obscured, blotted out, under wraps [Inf], blind, smothered, stifled, censored, suppressed

9 **disguised,** camouflaged, costumed, masked; unrecognized, unrecognizable, incognito, anonymous, cryptic, secret, covert, occult, latent, coded, codified, cryptographic

10 **silent,** taciturn, reticent, reserved, withdrawn, aloof, reclusive, incommunicado, out of touch, private, unsociable; noncommittal, uncommunicative, uninforma-tive, vague, evasive, close, discreet, secretive, cagey, buttoned-up [Inf]

11 **noncommittal,** uncommunicative, vague, evasive, uninformative, clamlike, tight-lipped, poker-faced, close, discreet

VERBS

12 **conceal,** hide, hide away, secrete, ensconce; cover, cover up, wrap up, disguise, paper over, whitewash, gloss over, overlay, paint over, varnish; bury, inter, confine, seclude; stow away, lock up, seal up, wall up, bottle up, store, stash away, sweep under the rug *or* carpet *or* mat; smother, stifle, censor, suppress; screen, cloak, shroud, curtain, blanket, veil, draw a veil over, keep under wraps, muffle; ambush, waylay, set a trap for
  ▶ *Covering 613*

13 **disguise,** camouflage, mask, obscure, eclipse, darken, fog, befog, cloud, becloud, muddle, obfuscate, dim, muddy the waters, encode

14 **deceive,** mislead, confuse, cozen, dupe, fool, hoodwink, trick, defraud, dissemble, masquerade, blindfold, pull the wool over someone's eyes, bamboozle

15 **conceal oneself,** hide, hide out, retreat into one's shell, keep *or* fade *or* stay in the background, keep a low profile, stay out of the limelight, stay in the shadows; dodge, shun, evade, elude, avoid, play hide-and-seek, steal away, slip by; slink, glide, creep, tiptoe, lurk, sneak, skulk, pussyfoot, leave no address, cover one's tracks, lay a false scent *or* trail, take cover, go to earth, go underground, lie low, be on the run, take to the hills; vanish, vanish into thin air, disappear, exit; [Inf]: skip town, hit the road, go on the lam, lie doggo

16 **be silent,** keep still, say nothing, keep one's mouth shut, hold one's tongue, look blank, keep a straight face, keep mum, act dumb, shut one's trap *or* face [Inf]; zip *or* button one's lips *or* mouth [Inf]
  ▶ *Secrecy 182; Silence 231*

17 **evade,** prevaricate, equivocate, hedge, fence, stonewall, beat about the bush
  ▶ *Untruthfulness, Falsehood 192*

ADVERBS

18 **privately,** secretly, in private, in secret, behind closed doors; reclusively, silently, noncommittally, vaguely, evasively
  ▶ *Secrecy 182*

182 Secrecy

NOUNS

1 **secrecy,** confidentiality, privacy, hiding, silence; concealment, secretiveness, evasiveness, subterfuge; censorship, suppression
  ▶ *Concealment 181*

2 **secret,** confidence, confession, seal *or* secret of the

confessional; family secret, skeleton in the closet; confidential information, privileged information, sealed orders, state secret, classified information, top-secret file; secret meeting, private meeting, closed session, executive session

3 **secretiveness,** stealth, stealthiness, furtiveness, clandestineness, hugger-mugger, covertness, espionage, spying, counterintelligence, underhandedness; intrigue, plot, conspiracy, cabal; secret service, intelligence service, Central Intelligence Agency (CIA)

4 **mystery,** enigma, problem, poser, conundrum, magic, mystification, puzzle; esotericism, esoterica, curiosa, secrecy, obscurity, occultism, gnosis, cabalism, cabala, arcanum, secret society, secret lore, secret art, alchemy
▶ *Occultism 86; Latency 844*

5 **puzzle,** riddle, brainteaser, brain twister, charade, Chinese puzzle, tangram, maze, labyrinth, word puzzle, crossword puzzle, acrostic, rebus; cipher, code, cryptogram, cryptography, hieroglyphics; problem, knotty *or* difficult problem, hard nut to crack, Gordian knot, squaring the circle, riddle of the Sphinx

6 **secret person,** confidant *or* confidante, undercover agent, spy, double agent, mole; cryptographer, decoder, magician, alchemist, wizard

7 **anonymity,** unknown quantity, unknown person, mysterious stranger, no-name, invisible man *or* woman, Unknown Soldier; namelessness, code name, X, Anon., assumed name, stage name, pen name, pseudonym, nom de plume, alias, incognito; unknown country, terra incognita; [Inf]: what's-his-name, what's-her-name, what's-its-name, what-d'ya-call-it, whatchamacallit, whatzit

ADJECTIVES

8 **secret,** confidential, private, intimate, privy, closed, secluded, sealed, isolated, unrevealed, undisclosed, undivulged, unspoken, untold; top-secret, classified, restricted, censored, suppressed, off-the-record, hush-hush, hugger-mugger

9 **secretive,** silent, close, close-mouthed, stealthy, furtive, covert, sly, clandestine, undercover, underhand, conspiratory, cabalistic, cloak-and-dagger [Inf]

10 **mysterious,** enigmatic, inscrutable, unknowable, esoteric, arcane, occult, abstruse, mystifying; confusing, bewildering, puzzling, perplexing, unresolved, unintelligible; problematic, complex, intricate, labyrinthine, difficult, knotty; cryptic, hidden, coded, concealed, camouflaged, disguised, incognito, unknown, anonymous, no-name

VERBS

11 **keep secret,** conceal, hide, withhold, veil, suppress, stifle, seal, ban, restrict; classify, censor, keep close, keep under wraps, keep under one's hat, give nothing away, keep one's mouth shut, hold one's tongue, not breathe a word, not tell, keep mum, keep one's counsel, make no sign, neither confirm nor deny, make no

comment, let (it) go no further, hush up, cover up; [Inf]: clam up, put *or* keep the lid on, black out
▶ *Concealment 181*

12 **mystify,** puzzle, baffle, perplex, bewilder, confuse, deceive, keep (someone) in the dark, stump

13 **make mysterious,** obscure, obfuscate, code, encode, cipher, encipher

ADVERBS

14 **secretly,** in secret, privately, behind closed doors, in camera, sub rosa; confidentially, in confidence, just *or* strictly between ourselves, entre nous, off the record, for your ears only, between you, me, and the lamppost *or* gatepost, sotto voce, in a whisper; anonymously, incognito, with nobody the wiser

15 **stealthily,** furtively, covertly, clandestinely, surreptitiously, conspiratorially, like a thief in the night, under a cloak of darkness, behind someone's back, invisibly; on the sly, on the quiet, on the q.t. [Inf]

183 Sign

If only God would give me some clear sign! Like making a large deposit in my name at a Swiss bank.
— WOODY ALLEN

I have only one eye; I have a right to be blind sometimes. . . I really did not see the signal. — LORD NELSON

NOUNS

1 **sign,** symbol, signification, meaning, connotation, representation; signal, indicator, indication, pointing out, identification sign; signature, autograph, mark, X, fingerprint, name tag; directional sign, signpost, road sign, highway sign; banner, poster, advertisement, billboard, signboard, trade sign; placard; rallying symbol, political symbol, emblem; religious symbol, sacred symbol, magic symbol, talisman; conventional symbol, image, token, letter; evidence, telltale sign, omen, sure sign, sign of the times; identifying sign, brand, trademark, hallmark, insignia; imprint, track, trail, piste, contrail *or* condensation trail *or* vapor trail
▶ *Religion 81; Information 170; Publication 173; Secrecy 182; Identification 184; Representation 187; Interpretation 365; Display 843*

2 **signs,** traces, scent, clue, cue, key, lead, marker; sign of illness, symptom, syndrome; warning sign, danger sign
▶ *Ill Health 114; Information 170; Record 185*

3 **symbol,** secret symbol, secret sign, shibboleth, high sign, countersign, password, cipher, code; picture writing, hieroglyphic *or* hieroglyph, rune, Gypsy sign, scout sign; musical notation; mathematical notation, plus sign, minus sign, multiplication sign, division sign, equal *or* equals sign, decimal point; symbol list, reference sign

▶ *Linguistics, Language 5; Mathematics 6; Occultism 86; Music 140; List 785*

4 symbolism, symbology, symbolization, semiotics, pragmatics, syntactics, semiology, symptomatology, iconology, iconography

5 gesture, gesticulation, body language, kinesics; sign language, signing, dactylology; demeanor, look, twinkle, glance, smile, blush, ogle, leer, wink, raised eyebrows, tic, twitch, frown, scowl, pout, moue, pursed lips, grimace, clenched jaw *or* teeth, arms akimbo, stuck-out tongue, nod of the head, shake of the head; laugh, cheer, hiss, sigh, moan, hoot, boo, whistle, catcall; hand signal, fist, clenched fist, wringing of hands, hands on hips, hands in pockets, folded hands; tearing one's hair, pointing, point, wave, wagging forefinger, drumming fingers, clapping, applause; touch, handshake, grip, clasp, pat, pinch, poke, hug, nudge, push, shove, slap, tap, stamp, kick; crossed legs, folded arms; lewd *or* rude gesture

▶ *Deafness 229; Joy, Cheerfulness 269; Sorrow 270; Rejoicing 279; Irascibility 303; Disrespect 436; Disapproval 438; Motion 677; Impulsion 695*

6 signal, message, sign; signal lamp, fire, watch fire, smoke signal; danger signal, warning signal, warning flag, red flag; signal lamp *or* light; traffic light *or* signal; warning light, beacon, flashing light, lighthouse beacon, railway signal; distress signal, SOS, rocket, signal rocket, flare, Very lights; minute gun, warning sound, horn, car horn, foghorn, starter's gun; whistle, referee's whistle, police whistle; alarm, fire alarm, burglar alarm, car alarm; siren, police siren, ambulance siren, fire-engine siren, air-raid siren, all-clear siren; telephone ring, beep, beeper; door buzzer, door knocker, doorbell, bell, church bell, Angelus bell, dinner bell, dinner gong; knell, muffled drum; manifestation, signaling, alarum [Arch]

▶ *Communications 169; Light 246; Danger 811*

7 indicator, guide, index, gauge, measuring instrument; thermometer, barometer, speedometer, odometer; cynosure, pointer, finger, index finger, forefinger, arm, needle, arrow, cursor; time indicator, timekeeper, clock, alarm clock, watch, stopwatch, hour hand, minute hand, second hand; direction indicator, turn signal, blinker; compass, compass needle, magnetic needle, radar; weather vane, weathercock, windsock *or* air sleeve; white line, signpost, road sign, highway sign, guidepost, crossroad sign, finger post; milepost, milestone, landmark, bench mark, cairn, monument; seamark, lighthouse, lightship, buoy; star, guiding star, lodestar; depth indicator, water line, watermark, tidemark, load line, Plimsoll line, triangulation point

▶ *Measurement 589; Timekeeping 646; Water Transportation 690*

8 proclamation, publication, announcement; marriage banns, invitation, summons; catchword, slogan, watchword; call, shout, hail; hue and cry, call to prayer, muezzin's call; cry for help, distress call, SOS, Mayday

▶ *News 171; Publication 173; Loudness 232; Help 825*

9 military call, command, word of command, rallying cry, war cry, battle cry, rebel yell, call to arms, bugle call, trumpet call, fanfare, sennet, flourish, reveille, assemble, charge, advance, rally, tattoo, retreat, lights out, taps, drumbeat

▶ *War 76*

10 linguistic sign, punctuation mark, accent, diacritical mark, reference sign

▶ *Linguistics, Language 5*

ADJECTIVES

11 signifying, indicative, indicatory, significative, identifying, directional, pointing, connotative, denotative, signalizing, disclosing, revealing, explanatory, betraying, giving away, telltale, signaling

12 symbolic, symbolical, symbolistic, symbological, semiotic, semiological; symptomatic, symptomatological, diagnostic, expressive, implicative, demonstrative, meaningful, suggestive, suggesting, evidential, representative, representing, nominal, diagrammatic, typical, characteristic, individual, special, interpretive, prophetic, presaging, ominous

13 gestural, gesticulative, dactylographic, pantomimic, signing, thumbing, looking, glancing, smiling, winking, grimacing, laughing, sighing, moaning, whistling, clapping, patting, pushing, slapping, stamping

14 signaling, telegraphic, heliographic, semaphoric, flashing, warning, summoning, ringing, bell ringing, beeping, shouting, hailing, proclaiming, publishing, announcing, inviting, calling, commanding

15 punctuated, hyphenated, referenced, cross-referenced, accented, abbreviated, indented, paragraphed, underlined, italicized

VERBS

16 signify, represent, symbolize, stand for, mean, denote, connote, imply, indicate, suggest, intimate, hint at, give evidence of, show signs of, characterize, bear the marks of, bear the stamp of, smack of, smell of, witness to, bear witness to, typify, betoken, disclose, reveal, signalize, emphasize, highlight, blazon

17 gesture, motion, gesticulate, attract, use body language; notice, pantomime, mime, mimic, imitate; use

---

REFERENCE SIGNS

asterisk, *	leaders, ...
asterism, *** *or* ***	obelus, ÷
bullet *or* centered dot, ·	paragraph, ¶
caret, ʌ	parallels, ‖
dagger *or* obelisk, †	prime, ′
ditto mark, "	section, §
double prime, ″	swung dash, ~
index *or* fist, ☞	

---

sign language, sign; suit the action to the word, give a look, shrug, nod *or* shake one's head; beckon, gaze, glance, look, look *or* speak volumes, ogle, leer, look daggers at; wink, raise one's eyebrows, frown, scowl, pout, moue, purse one's lips, grimace; show anger, curl one's lip, snap, bite, clench one's jaw, clench *or* grit *or* gnash one's teeth; stick out one's tongue, pull faces, twinkle, smile; laugh, hiss, sigh, moan, hoot, boo, whistle, catcall; clench one's fist, wring one's hands, raise one's hand, wave, chop the air, flag down, wave to *or* on *or* by *or* through, tear one's hair, point, point one's finger, point at *or* to, drum one's fingers; clap, applaud; hold out one's hand, salute, greet, squeeze someone's hand; clasp, clap, pinch, poke, hug, nudge, pat, stroke, caress, jog, elbow, push, shove, prod, slap, tap, stamp, stomp, kick; shuffle, scrape one's feet, paw the ground, cross one's legs, fold one's arms, make a lewd *or* rude gesture

18 **signal,** send a signal, semaphore, flag, wigwag, send smoke signals, give a hand signal; communicate, publish, inform, announce, declare, herald, hail, proclaim; call, cry, shout, summon, command, call to prayer, send a message, tap out a message, use Morse code; call for help, send out a distress call, send an SOS, warn, fire a warning shot, alert, honk, whistle, set off an alarm, raise the alarm, ring the church bells, sound the trumpets, beat the drum, beat a retreat
  ◗ *Communications 169; Publication 173*

19 **sign,** sign one's name, put one's signature to, sign on the dotted line, autograph, initial, countersign; use symbols; signal, gesture, indicate, point to, point out, signpost, mark, mark the way, point the way, show the way, direct, guide, blaze, demarcate, mark out, chalk out, lay out, delineate, fingerprint; give someone a secret sign, give a password, code, put the finger on [Inf], finger [Inf]
  ◗ *Identification 184*

20 **punctuate,** abbreviate, accent, indent, parenthesize, underline *or* underscore, italicize, stress, emphasize, dot, dash, hyphenate, cross, cross out, dot one's i's and cross one's t's, put in quotes

ADVERBS

21 **indicatively,** revealingly, symptomatically, diagnostically, expressively, demonstratively, meaningfully, significantly, suggestive, evidentially, by this token, in token of, representatively, symbolically, semiologically, typically, characteristically, individually, specially; interpretively, prophetically, as a sign, ominously, telegraphically, semaphorically

184 Identification

NOUNS

1 **identification,** recognition, detection, distinguishing, differentiation, diagnosis, indicating, indication, pointing out, pinpointing, designation, naming, labeling, characterization; characteristic, form, shape, outline, size, color, coloring, mannerism, trait, denomination, classifying, classification, categorization, cataloging, analysis, establishing, establishment, authentication, verification, substantiation, corroboration
  ◗ *Medicine 107; Sign 183; Representation 187; Affirmation 189; Description 202; Outline 617; Form 624; Number 783*

2 **identity,** particularity, individuality, distinctiveness, uniqueness, personality, self
  ◗ *Essence 723*

3 **means of identification,** ID, fingerprint, thumbprint, footprint, dental record, genetic fingerprinting, DNA; fingerprinting, photograph, Identikit™; International Standard Book Number (ISBN); call sign, call letters; secret word, password, open sesame, watchword, token, countersign, shibboleth, secret signal; trademark, brand, brand name, trade name, model, copyright, logo *or* logotype; hallmark, cachet, official stamp, seal, great seal, privy seal, signet, sigil; superscription, impress *or* impression, imprint, watermark, letterhead, masthead, colophon, bookplate, ex libris; tally, earmark; label, sticker, badge, emblem, plate, brass plate, card, sign, certificate; ticket, airline ticket, train ticket, bus ticket, theater ticket, movie ticket, raffle ticket, ticket stub, chit; docket, invoice, bill, bill of lading, waybill; copy, duplicate; dog tag [Inf]
  ◗ *Title 72; Radio and Television 172; Secrecy 182; Sign 183*

4 **personal identification,** name, title, letters after one's name, name, name and address, signature, autograph, paraph, initials, mark, X, monogram, identification papers, identity *or* ID card, passport, visa, letter of introduction, permit, credentials, endorsement, passport photograph; personal identification number *or* PIN, Social Security number, student number, military service number, driver's license number, bank-account number, telephone number, credit-card number, license plate number, vanity license plate; label, luggage label, tie-on label, clothes marking, clothes label, tag; name badge, name tape, nameplate, visiting card, business card, place card; birth certificate, marriage certificate, death certificate; caste mark, tattoo, birthmark, strawberry mark, blemish, scar, stigma
  ◗ *Record 185; Address 209*

5 **insignia,** badge, markings; throne, scepter, orb, crown, regalia, robes of office, badge of office, chain of office, mark of authority, sword of state, gavel, mace, staff, pastoral staff, wand, baton, keys; military insignia, badge of rank, spread eagle, star, bar, stripe, chevron, wings, epaulet *or* epaulette, brassard *or* brassart, aiguillette, cockade, sash, medal, ribbon, decoration, cross, badge of merit, victory laurels, garland, wreath, bays, chaplet, trophy, gold medal, silver medal, bronze

medal, silver cup, silver plate, rosette, blue ribbon, school letter; emblem, crest, armory, blazon, coat of arms; heraldic sign, heraldry; [Inf]: pip, hash mark, Hershey bar

▶ *Military Affairs 58; Title 72; Reward 453*

6 clothing, uniform, military uniform, regimentals; school uniform, sports uniform, sports outfit, nurse's uniform, Boy Scout uniform, chauffeur's uniform, livery; stable colors, jockey's colors; prison clothes, mourning clothes, widow's weeds, crepe, black dress, black armband; ecclesiastical vestments; dunce cap, cap and gown, mortarboard, tie, club tie, old school tie [Brit]; school ring, class ring, signet ring, lapel pin; sphragistics

▶ *Clergy 84; Clothing 100*

7 national emblem, national device; American eagle, British lion and unicorn, English rose, Scottish thistle, Welsh leek, Welsh daffodil, Irish shamrock, Canadian maple leaf, French fleur-de-lis, Russian bear, Soviet hammer and sickle, Japanese rising sun, Turkish crescent and star, Swiss cross, Nazi swastika, Roman eagle

▶ *Country 566*

8 flag, standard, banner, ensign, bunting, colors, national colors, national flag; American Stars and Stripes, Old Glory, Star-Spangled Banner, red, white, and blue, Confederate flag, Stars and Bars; British Union Jack, Union flag; French tricolor; red flag; military flag, regimental colors; ship's colors, pilot jack, merchant jack, blue peter, flag of convenience; pirate flag, skull and crossbones, black flag, Jolly Roger; vexillum, labarum, gonfalon, guidon, oriflamme, banneret *or* bannerette, streamer, pennon, banderole, pennant, swallowtail; burgee, quarantine flag, yellow flag; flag of truce, flag of surrender, white flag; flagpole, flagstaff, hoist, fly, grommet, halyard, heading, sleeve, truck, clip; vexillology

ADJECTIVES

9 identified, recognized, established, authenticated, verified, substantiated, corroborated; identifiable, recognizable, shown; known, known by, known as, designated, denoted, named; labeled, tagged, marked, hallmarked, trademarked, earmarked, characterized, classified, categorized, referenced, cataloged, indexed, lettered, numbered, patterned, signed, signatory, symbolic, sigillary, titled, imprinted, fingerprinted, photographed, pictured, stigmatized, scarred, branded, tattooed

10 heraldic, emblematic, crested, armorial, blazoned, emblazoned

VERBS

11 identify, recognize, detect, distinguish, differentiate, diagnose, analyze; indicate, show, exhibit, point out, pinpoint; establish, authenticate, verify, substantiate, corroborate; designate, name, give a name to, specify, characterize; hallmark, earmark, label, docket, tag, tab, keep tabs on; classify, categorize, catalog, reference, number, letter, page, paginate; record, photograph, picture, fingerprint, register, ticket, delimit, limit; note, annotate, mark, put a mark on, underline, underscore, check, tick off, check off, mark off; etch, engrave, imprint, tattoo, pierce, notch, chalk, scar, disfigure, blaze, brand, burn in; stamp, seal, punch, impress, emboss, overprint; emblazon, blazon, impale, dimidiate, quarter, difference, marshal, charge

12 identify oneself, sign, ratify, countersign, endorse, autograph, write one's signature, write one's name, inscribe, put one's hand to, subscribe, undersign, initial,

---

HERALDIC TERMS

achievement	blazon	dexter	fur	martlet	regardant
animal charge	blazonry	difference	fusil	metal	rustre
annulet	bordure	differencing,	gardant	motto	sable
antelope	canton	dimidiation	garland	mullet	saltire
argent	chaplet	displayed	griffin	murrey	sejant
armorial	charge	eagle	gules	nombril point	seme
bearings	chevron	erased	gyron	or	shield
armory	chief	ermine	hatchment	ordinary	sinister
arms	cinquefoil	erminois	helmet	pale	statant
azure	coat of arms	escutcheon *or*	heraldic tincture	passant	supporters
badge	cockatrice	scutcheon	honor point	pean	tenne
bandeau	coronet	falcon	impalement	pile	torse
bar	couchant	fesse point	impaling	pomme	trefoil
bar sinister	couped	field	label	portcullis	tresure
base	crescent	flanch	lambrequin	potent	unicorn
baton	crest	fleur-de-lis	lioncel	purpure	vair
bearing	cross	fleury	lozenge	quartering	vert
bend	crown	floral charge	mantling	rampant	wreath
bend sinister	device	fret	marshaling	rebus	

paraph, put one's mark on, put one's cross on; be identified, be conspicuous, stand out, stick out

▶ *Sign 183*

ADVERBS

13 **identifiably,** indicatively, symbolically, emblematically, heraldically

185 Record

NOUNS

1 **record,** recording, documentation, document, form, documents, papers, recorded material; chronicle, history, historical record, historical documents, annals, archives; account, narrative, memoir, autobiography, biography, biographical record, case history, obituary, personal history, curriculum vitae (CV), vita, résumé; correspondence, memorabilia, clipping, press clipping; visual record, photograph, picture, snapshot, portrait, sketch; representation, list, inventory, file, dossier, portfolio, personal file, public record, public file, police record, criminal record; official record, official publication, Congressional Record, government papers; recorded proceedings, transactions, minutes, report, official report, company report, annual report, school report, report card; office memorandum, memo, reminder, note, entry, item, return, income tax return, invoice, bill, check, statement, bank statement, receipt, voucher, docket, stub, check stub, check register; tally, scoresheet, scoreboard

▶ *History 3; Information 170; Identification 184; Representation 187; Description 202; Evidence 339; Memory 354; Security 464; List 785*

2 **certificate,** credential, charter, authorization, birth certificate, marriage certificate, death certificate, passport, identification (ID), diploma, muniments, deed, title, title deed, ownership papers, car papers, registration document, insurance papers, insurance certificate, ticket, warranty, testimonial, sworn statement, affidavit, notarized statement, deposition, daybook

▶ *Identification 184*

3 **notes,** school notes, annotation, marginal notes, marginalia, jottings, writing

▶ *Interpretation 365*

4 **inscription,** personal note, signature, autograph, initials, legend, wall writing, graffiti, epitaph; epigraphy

5 **record book,** notebook, scrapbook, album, commonplace book; minute book, registry, register, chartulary *or* cartulary; roll, roll book, directory; address book, logbook, log, diary, journal, daybook, datebook, calendar; tablet, table, notepad, memo pad, scratch pad, jotter; ledger, cashbook, account book, checkbook, catalog, index, card, index card; microfilm, microfiche, microcard, tape, magnetic tape, computer file, disk, database

▶ *Computers 15; Accounting 493; Calculation 784*

6 **recording,** phonograph record, gramophone record, record, LP (long-playing record), single, EP (extended-play record), compact disk *or* CD, laser disk; pressing, cassette tape, cassette, tape, magnetic tape, film, motion-picture film, videotape; CD-ROM (compact disk read-only memory), laser disk, optical disk, videodisk; copy, photocopy, carbon copy, duplicate

▶ *Reproduction 21; Motion Pictures 137; Radio and Television 172*

7 **recordkeeping,** registration, registry, recording, writing, printing, inscribing, engraving, enrollment, enlistment, empanelment, booking, reservation; bookkeeping, entry, double-entry bookkeeping, accounting, accounts, filing, indexing, cataloging, listing, data processing (DP)

▶ *Accounting 493*

8 **record keeper,** recorder, registrar, chronicler, annalist, archivist, historian, archaeologist, antiquarian, diarist, columnist, journalist, reporter, press photographer, writer, biographer, autobiographer, amanuensis, notary, stenographer, typist, computer operator, keyboarder, scribe, secretary, receptionist, clerk, file clerk, bookkeeper, accountant, petitioner, artist, engraver, photographer, cameraman, scorekeeper, timekeeper

▶ *History 3; Photography 132; News 171*

9 **recording instrument,** photocopier, camera, video camera, camcorder, recorder, tape recorder, tape machine, cassette recorder, electronic listening device, wiretap, bug [Inf]; answering machine, computer, videotape, videocassette recorder (VCR), Dictaphone™, cash register, seismograph, speedometer, gauge, flight recorder, black box, stopwatch

▶ *Photography 132; Communications 169; Measurement 589; Timekeeping 646*

10 **monument,** memorial, war memorial, memorial arch, victory arch, column, pillar, national monument, tomb of an unknown soldier, tomb, mausoleum, pyramid, shrine, statue, bust, plaque, tablet, slab, memorial inscription, gravestone, tombstone; ancient monument, monolith, obelisk, megalith, dolmen, menhir, cromlech, cairn, barrow, earthwork, mound; testimonial, cup, trophy, prize, ribbon, medal, decoration, memento, souvenir

▶ *Burial 31; Memory 354; Past Time 651*

11 **vestige,** trace, track, trail, piste, scent, spoor, mark, print, footprint, footstep, fingerprint, tire mark, tidemark, stain, relic, remains

▶ *Sign 183; Evidence 339; Blemish 533; Unimportance 800*

ADJECTIVES

12 **recorded,** documented, chronicled, archived; logged, noted, inscribed, written down, on paper, in black and white; printed, entered, registered, enrolled, filed, in-

dexed, listed; taped, videotaped, filmed, copied, photocopied; official, documentary
▶ *Information 170; List 785*

VERBS

13 **record,** document, chronicle, log, put *or* place on record, put in the minutes, inscribe, register, enroll, file, index, catalog, tabulate, list, empanel; copy, photocopy, print; store in a database, input, tape, tape-record, videotape, film, photograph, take a picture, capture on film, preserve for posterity, archive, store in the archives, paint, represent, relate, narrate, recount, recite
▶ *History 3; Information 170; Representation 187; Description 202*

14 **inscribe,** transcribe, write, write down, commit to writing, put on paper, put *or* set down, set down in black and white, enter in a book, take minutes; make notes, note, note down, take down, mark down, jot, jot down; engrave, cut, incise, etch, carve
▶ *Linguistics, Language 5; Literature 139*

15 **register,** enter, docket, enter names, check off names, put on the list, enroll, enlist, empanel, book, reserve, list, itemize, tabulate, score, tally, notch
▶ *List 785*

ADVERBS

16 **on record,** in the minutes, in black and white, on paper, on the books, in the book, in the file, in the index, on the list, on the waiting list, in the database, on tape, on film; officially

186 Obliteration

NOUNS

1 **obliteration,** erasure, erasing, expunction, elimination, deletion, dele, removal, effacement, defacement, writing over, printing over, overprinting, painting over, illegibility, covering up, cover, concealment, crossing out, rubbing out; cancellation, annulment, abrogation, cessation, amnesty, editorial change, editing, blue pencil, censorship; palimpsest, clean slate, tabula rasa

2 **destruction,** eradication, extirpation, annihilation, demolition, liquidation, extermination, purge, interment, burial, oblivion

3 **forgetfulness,** forgetting, amnesia, loss of memory, memory gap, absent-mindedness, mental block, repression, suppression
▶ *Memory 354; Forgetfulness 355*

ADJECTIVES

4 **obliterated,** erased, expunged, eliminated, deleted, effaced, illegible, scribbled out, covered, concealed, crossed out, rubbed out; abrogated, canceled, edited, censored, out of print

5 **destroyed,** eradicated, annihilated, demolished, razed to the ground, vaporized, liquidated, extirpated, exterminated, buried

6 **forgotten,** unremembered, unrecorded, unregistered, unwritten, intestate
▶ *Concealment 181; Destruction 523; Covering 613; Cancellation 834*

7 **forgetful,** inclined to forget, unremembering, absent-minded, oblivious
▶ *Memory 354; Forgetfulness 355*

VERBS

8 **obliterate,** eliminate, delete, dele, take out, remove, efface, deface, write over, print over, overprint, paint over, make illegible, scribble out, cover up, cover, conceal, remove any trace; cancel, annul, abrogate, edit out, blue-pencil, censor, take out of print, leave on the cutting-room floor

9 **erase,** expunge, scratch out, scratch through, score out, score through, strike out, strike through, cross out, cross through, rule out, rub out, rub off, sponge off, sponge out, wash out, wash off, wipe out, wipe off, blot, blot out, black out, white out, brush off

10 **destroy,** eradicate, extirpate, annihilate, demolish, raze, burn to the ground, liquidate, exterminate, purge, leave no survivors, leave no trace, vaporize, wipe off the map, bury, force into oblivion, submerge, sink without a trace, drown, silence, scrub [Inf]
▶ *Killing 30; Burial 31; Cleanliness 111; Concealment 181; Silence 231; Disappearance 265; Destruction 523; Friction 554; Covering 613; Cancellation 834*

11 **forget,** misremember, have a mental block, block out, repress, suppress
▶ *Memory 354*

ADVERBS

12 **forgetfully,** obliviously, illegibly, unmindfully

187 Representation

NOUNS

1 **representation,** depiction, delineation, portrayal, rendering; embodiment, personification, incarnation, realization, typification, epitome; quintessence, type, figuration, symbolization, indication; conventional representation, manifestation, evocation, presentation, presentment; imitation, impression, similarity, semblance, outline, description, writing, picture writing, pictogram, hieroglyphic *or* hieroglyph, rune; notation, mathematical notation, musical notation, dance notation, choreography
▶ *Linguistics, Language 5; Mathematics 6; Dance and Ballet 135; Music 140; Identification 184; Description 202; Outline 617; Imitation 736; Display 843*

2 **illustration,** photograph, carbon copy, photocopy, reproduction; print, graphics, etching, engraving, lithograph, collotype; blueprint, diagram, map, chart, graph, plan, draft, sketch, cartoon, caricature; picture, book illustration, tracing, drawing, isometric drawing, axiometric drawing, technical drawing, mechanical draw-

ing; artwork, painting, oil painting, oil, watercolor, portraiture, portrait, fine art, illumination; visual, visual aid, X ray

> *Reproduction 21; Photography 132; Painting and Drawing 143; Plan 387; Decoration 532; Form 624*

3 **image,** symbol, likeness, very image, clear image, exact image, very picture, exact picture; duplicate, eidetic image, look-alike, exact likeness, twin, double, copy, clone, replica, facsimile; mental image, idea, thought, afterthought, afterimage; reflected image, reflection, mirror image, projection, hologram, shadow figure; silhouette, painted image, icon, idol, graven image, effigy, gargoyle, sculpture, statue, statuette; dead ringer [Inf], spitting image [Inf]

> *Painting and Drawing 143; Sculpture and Engraving 144*

4 **figure,** figurine, wax figure, waxwork, model, working model, replica, manikin, dummy, tailor's dummy; doll, china doll, rag doll, stuffed animal, teddy bear; puppet, marionette, finger puppet, glove puppet; snowman, snowwoman, gingerbread woman, gingerbread man, scarecrow, robot, automaton

> *Sign 183; Appearance 264*

5 **map,** world map, county map, city map, town plan, plat, road map, relief map, survey map, sketch map, elevation, topographical map; projection, azimuthal equidistant projection, orthographic *or* orthogonal projection, conic projection, isometric projection; chart, diagram; scale, legend, inset; cartogram, statistics; atlas, world atlas, globe; map of the heavens, star map; treasure map, political map, historical map, genetic map; mapping, cartography, chorography, topography, photogrammetry, phototopography

> *Plan 387; Outline 617*

6 **acting,** portraying, portrayal, playing, playing a character, playing the part of, impersonating, impersonation, posing, characterizing, characterization, performing, performance, enactment, role-playing, mimicry, charade, mime, dumb show, masquerade

> *Drama and Theater 136; Activity 414; Production 522; Imitation 736*

7 **representative,** example, exemplar, exponent, sample, specimen, cross section; agent, agency, proxy, substitute, replacement, stand-in; deputy, delegate, ambassador, envoy, spokesman *or* spokeswoman, spokesperson, congressman, congresswoman

> *Politics 50; Delegate 79; Deputy 80; Substitution 672*

ADJECTIVES

8 **representational,** representing, representative, depictive, delineatory, portraying, symbolic, emblematic, figurative, typical, quintessential, archetypal, characteristic, exemplary, evocative, descriptive, illustrative, graphic, pictorial, hieroglyphic, reflecting, similar, like, imitative, iconic, diagrammatic, vivid, realistic, eidetic,

naturalistic, true to life, artistic, painterly, paintable, photogenic, photographic

> *Photography 132; Painting and Drawing 143; Sculpture and Engraving 144; Sign 183; Description 202; Plan 387; Similarity 733; Imitation 736*

9 **acting,** portraying, playing, impersonating, performing

VERBS

10 **represent,** depict, delineate, portray, render, embody, personify, incarnate, realize, typify, symbolize, epitomize, manifest, evoke, present; imitate, impersonate, personate, pretend to be; resemble, look like, copy, duplicate, reproduce, reflect, mirror, image, catch, capture, catch exactly, catch a likeness; register, record, photograph, film, snap, shoot, take a picture, scan, X-ray, process, print, enlarge, blow up, project

> *Photography 132; Identification 184; Record 185; Deception 193; Similarity 733; Imitation 736*

11 **illustrate,** draw, sketch, paint, caricature, picture; draft, sketch out, rough out, block out, plan, diagram, make a diagram, draw a blueprint; design, outline, describe, trace, shape, form, mold, carve, sculpt, cast, cut, engrave, etch, print

> *Painting and Drawing 143; Description 202; Plan 387; Outline 617; Form 624*

12 **map,** plot, plat, survey, project, outline, chart, diagram, draw to scale

> *Plan 387; Outline 617*

13 **act,** portray, present, dramatize, play, play a character, play *or* act the part of, assume the role of, role-play, characterize, perform, enact, impersonate, take off, pose as, go as, mimic, mime, masquerade

> *Drama and Theater 136; Imitation 736*

14 **stand for,** mean, denote, exemplify, show, pass for, pass as, replace, substitute for, stand in for, act for

> *Deputy 80; Meaning 361; Substitution 672; Display 843*

ADVERBS

15 **representationally,** representatively, symbolically, emblematically, figuratively, typically, characteristically, descriptively, illustratively, graphically, pictorially, vividly, realistically

188 Misrepresentation

NOUNS

1 **misrepresentation,** distortion, deformation, twist; perversion, falsification, lie, fib, falsehood, deception; untrue picture, false depiction, false impression, false light, bad likeness, poor likeness; exaggeration, grotesquerie, coloring, overemphasis, overdramatization; caricature, travesty, parody, burlesque, ridicule, flattering, flattery; nonrealism, bad art, daubing, botch, anamorphosis, false image, distorted image

⟩ *Untruthfulness, Falsehood 192; Deception 193; Exaggeration 194; Distortion 627*

2 **adulteration,** counterfeiting, forgery, fraudulent alteration

⟩ *Wrong 430*

3 **misinformation,** disinformation, false information, misstatement, misteaching, misdirection, misguidance; wrong instruction, wrong explanation, false sense, false idea; misuse of words, abuse of language; circumlocution, misquotation, garbling; misevaluation, overestimation, underestimation, exaggeration; traducement, defamation, libel, slander

⟩ *Deception 193; Misinterpretation 366; Wrong 430*

ADJECTIVES

4 **misrepresented,** misrepresenting, distorted, deformed, twisted, perverted, false, untrue; wrong, incorrect, inaccurate, dissimilar, unlike, biased, slanted, not representative, unrepresentative, unfair, unjust; exaggerated, caricatured, parodied, grotesque; nonrepresentational, cardboard

⟩ *Untruthfulness, Falsehood 192; Deception 193; Exaggeration 194; Derision 369; Wrong 430; Distortion 627; Dissimilarity 734*

5 **misinformed,** mistaught, misinterpreted, garbled, misstated, misquoted

⟩ *Deception 193; Misinterpretation 366; Wrong 430*

VERBS

6 **misrepresent,** distort, deform, twist, make dissimilar, pervert, falsify, slant, put in a false light, lie, belie; represent unfairly, make a poor likeness, make a false image, exaggerate, color, overemphasize, overdramatize; caricature, parody, travesty, burlesque; overdraw, daub, botch

⟩ *Painting and Drawing 143; Sculpture and Engraving 144; Untruthfulness, Falsehood 192; Exaggeration 194; Derision 369; Wrong 430; Distortion 627; Dissimilarity 734*

7 **misinform,** give false information, disinform, misteach, misevaluate, misinterpret, garble, misstate, misquote

⟩ *Information 170; Misinterpretation 366*

ADVERBS

8 **unrepresentatively,** falsely, wrongly, incorrectly, inaccurately, unfairly, unjustly, in a false light

189 Affirmation

NOUNS

1 **affirmation,** affirmance, statement, positive statement, affirmative, assertion, averment, asseveration, declaration, dictum, *ipse dixit* [L]; announcement, annunciation, enunciation, pronouncement, proclamation, predication, manifesto, position paper; emphasis, stress, stressed point, overstatement

⟩ *Publication 173; Emphasis 200; Speech, Spoken Language 205*

2 **attestation,** certification, authentication, validation, verification, establishment, vouch [Arch]; corroboration, substantiation, proof, evidence; testimony, sworn testimony *or* statement, statement under *or* on oath, deposition, affidavit

⟩ *Litigation 54; Evidence 339*

3 **vow,** pledge, promise, guarantee, assurance, commitment, word, solemn word, word of honor; oath, solemn oath, ironclad oath, judicial oath, extrajudicial oath, oath of office, oath of allegiance, loyalty oath

⟩ *Promise 458*

4 **contention,** claim, allegation; postulation, submission, proposal, proposition, theory, thesis, hypothesis, supposition

⟩ *Supposition 359; Accusation 442*

5 **confirmation,** ratification, approval, assent, agreement; endorsement, support, backing, defense

⟩ *Approval 437; Agreement 462; Support 605*

6 **definiteness,** positiveness, absoluteness, categoricalness, unequivocalness, certainty, unquestionableness, indubitability *or* indubitableness, indisputability *or* indisputableness

⟩ *Certainty 840*

7 **avowal,** profession, acknowledgment, avouchment, admission, confession, disclosure, deposition

⟩ *Disclosure 180*

8 **assertiveness,** forcefulness, self-assurance, decisiveness, incisiveness, pointedness, explicitness, outspokenness, bluntness, plainness

9 **affirmer,** affirmant, declarer, declarant, asserter; announcer, annunciator, enunciator, proclaimer; attestant, attester, attestor, attestator, voucher, certifier, authenticator, validator, verifier, corroborator; testifier, witness, eyewitness; vower, pledger, guarantor, swearer; confirmer, ratifier, upholder, approver, assenter, endorser, seconder, supporter, backer, advocate, defender; avower, avoucher, professor, confessor, discloser

ADJECTIVES

10 **affirmative,** affirmatory, assertional, assertory, asseverative, declarative, declaratory; annunciative, annunciatory, enunciative *or* enunciatory, predicational *or* predicative

⟩ *Publication 173; Speech, Spoken Language 205*

11 **affirmed,** stated, asserted, averred, asseverated, declared, announced, annunciated, enunciated, pronounced, proclaimed; emphasized, stressed, strongly worded, emphatic, pointed, underscored, overstated

⟩ *Publication 173; Emphasis 200; Speech, Spoken Language 205*

12 **attestive,** certificatory, certifying, authenticating, validatory, validating, verifying; corroborative *or* corrob-

oratory or corroborating, substantiative or substantiating

> *Evidence 339*

13 **attested,** certified, authentic, authenticated, validated, verified, established; corroborated, substantiated, proved, proven

> *Evidence 339*

14 **vowed,** pledged, promised, guaranteed, assured, committed, vouched for, sworn, sworn to

> *Promise 458*

15 **contended,** claimed, alleged, maintained; postulated, submitted, proposed, theorized, hypothesized, supposed; postulational, propositional, theoretical, hypothetical, suppositional

> *Supposition 359; Accusation 442*

16 **confirming,** affirming, assenting, assentive, agreeing, agreeable, consenting, supportive, endorsive

> *Agreement 462; Support 605*

17 **confirmed,** ratified, approved, agreed; endorsed, supported, backed, defended

> *Approval 437; Agreement 462; Support 605*

18 **definite,** positive, absolute, categorical, unequivocal, certain, unquestionable, indubitable, indisputable

> *Certainty 840*

19 **avowed,** acknowledged, professed, owned, admitted, confessed, self-confessed, disclosed, deposed

> *Disclosure 180*

20 **assertive,** forceful, self-assured, decisive, incisive, pointed, explicit, outspoken, blunt, plain

VERBS

21 **affirm,** state positively, assert, aver, asseverate, declare, announce, annunciate, enunciate, pronounce, proclaim, predicate; emphasize, stress, stress a point, underscore, overstate

> *Publication 173; Emphasis 200; Speech, Spoken Language 205*

22 **attest,** vouch for, certify, authenticate, validate, verify, establish, declare as true; corroborate, substantiate, prove, show evidence; bear witness to, testify, give sworn testimony, depose, state under or on oath, give a sworn statement, make a deposition, sign an affidavit; administer an oath, place or put under oath, swear in, charge, adjure

> *Litigation 54; Evidence 339*

23 **vow,** pledge, promise, guarantee, assure, commit oneself, swear to, give one's (solemn) word or oath, give one's word of honor, swear on the Bible, kiss the Book, swear to God, swear by all that is holy, cross one's heart (and hope to die)

> *Promise 458*

24 **contend,** claim, allege, maintain; postulate, submit, propose, put forward, theorize, hypothesize, suppose

> *Supposition 359; Accusation 442*

25 **confirm,** ratify, uphold, approve, give approval to,

give assent to, yes, endorse, second, support, back, back up, defend

> *Approval 437; Support 605*

26 **be definite,** be positive, mean what one says, not equivocate, not question, not doubt, not dispute

> *Certainty 840*

27 **avow,** acknowledge, avouch, profess, own, own up to, admit, confess, disclose

> *Disclosure 180*

28 **be assertive,** assure, act forcefully, act decisively, speak out or up, have one's say, say so, have the last word, put it bluntly, insist

ADVERBS

29 **affirmatively,** assertorily, asseveratively, declaratively, enunciatively; assertedly, with emphasis, emphatically, pointedly

30 **assuredly,** with assurance, without fear of contradiction; with commitment, in earnest, with a promise; truthfully, in truth, truly, verily, indeed, yes, yea; in all conscience, upon one's word, upon's one honor, in sworn testimony, under or on oath, on the Bible

31 **allegedly,** as claimed, supposedly; propositionally, theoretically, hypothetically, suppositionally

> *Supposition 359; Accusation 442*

32 **confirmingly,** affirmingly, assentingly, agreeingly, agreeably, consentingly, approvingly, supportively, endorsingly

> *Approval 437; Agreement 462; Support 605*

33 **definitely,** positively, absolutely, categorically, unequivocally, certainly, unquestionably, indubitably, undoubtedly, indisputably

> *Certainty 840*

34 **avowedly,** with acknowledgment, professedly, by open declaration, declaredly, admittedly

35 **assertively,** forcefully, confidently, decisively, pointedly, explicitly, outspokenly, bluntly, plainly

INTERJECTIONS

36 **yes!,** all right!, OK! or O.K.! or okay!, sure!, certainly!, affirmative!, roger! [Inf]; as God is my witness!, honest to God!, on my word of honor!, as I stand here!, cross my heart and hope to die!, scout's honor!

190 Negation

NOUNS

1 **negation,** denial, flat denial, emphatic denial; negative statement, contrary assertion, disaffirmation or disaffirmance, contradiction, flat or absolute contradiction, refutation, disproof, confutation, rebuttal, rejoinder, retortion, retort; objection, demurral, demur, dissent, disagreement, opposition, contravention, protest, defiance, challenge, impugnment

> *Dissent 347; Defiance 416; Protest 507*

2 **refusal,** lack of consent, denial, rejection, veto, disallowance, prohibition, recusancy, no, negative, nay

▶ *Refusal 506*

3 disavowal, disclaimer, disclamation, dissociation, disassociation, repudiation, rejection, disowning, disownment; relinquishment, abnegation, renunciation, abjuration, forswearing; recantation, retraction, withdrawal; nullification, invalidation, annulment, void, cancellation, countermand, rescindment, rescission, abrogation, revocation, repeal

▶ *Rejection 383; Relinquishment 392; Cancellation 834*

4 unacceptance, skepticism, doubtfulness, questioning, agnosticism, unbelief, disbelief, atheism; nonobservance, apostasy, disobedience

▶ *Religion 81; Disbelief 88; Disobedience 427; Nonobservance 466*

5 nonentity, nothing, vacuum, void, nix [Inf]; nonexistence, nothingness, nullity, invalidity, vacuity, emptiness

▶ *Nonexistence 718*

6 oppositeness, contrariness, reversal, about-face; antithesis, opposite, contrary, reverse

▶ *Oppositeness 731*

7 negativism, negativeness, negativity, negative attitude, pessimism, defeatism, despondence *or* despondency

▶ *Hopelessness 282*

8 negator, negationist, contradictor, rebutter, gainsayer; objector, dissenter, opposer, protester, protestant, challenger; refuser, prohibiter, vetoer, rejecter; relinquisher, abnegator, renouncer, recanter, retractor; nullifier, nullificationist *or* nullificator, invalidator, rescinder, repealer, revoker; skeptic, doubter, doubting Thomas, questioner, agnostic, disbeliever, atheist, apostate; nonentity, cipher, nullity, nobody, zero [Inf]; naysayer, pessimist, defeatist

ADJECTIVES

9 negational, negative, negatory, denying; contrary, counter, opposite, contradictive *or* contradictory, refuting; dissenting, disagreeing, opposing, protestive, protestant, defiant, obstructive, impugning

▶ *Dissent 347; Defiance 416; Protest 507*

10 negated, denied, contradicted, disproved, refuted, confuted, rebutted, rejoined; objected to, opposed, contested, disputed, protested, defied, challenged, impugned

▶ *Dissent 347; Defiance 416; Protest 507*

11 disagreeing, denying, recusant, negative, naysaying, prohibitory; denied, rejected, vetoed, nixed [Inf]; disallowed, prohibited

▶ *Refusal 506*

12 disavowing, disclamatory, dissociative, repudiative *or* repudiatory, renunciative *or* renunciatory, rejective, abjuratory, forswearing; negating, negational, nullifying, invalidating, abrogative, revocative *or* revocatory; disavowed, disclaimed, dissociated, disassociated, repudiated, renounced, rejected, disowned; negated,

nullified, invalidated, annulled, countermanded, voided, canceled, revoked, repealed, rescinded, retracted, recanted

▶ *Rejection 383; Relinquishment 392; Cancellation 834*

13 unaccepting, skeptical, doubtful, doubting, questioning, agnostic, unbelieving, disbelieving, atheistic, unobservant, disobedient; doubted, questioned, disbelieved, disobeyed

▶ *Religion 81; Disbelief 88; Disobedience 427; Nonobservance 466*

14 nonexistent, unexistent, nonexisting, unexisting, negational, null, void, null and void; vacuous, vacant, empty

▶ *Nonexistence 718*

15 negative, unoptimistic, pessimistic, defeatist, despairing, despondent

▶ *Hopelessness 282*

VERBS

16 negate, deny, emphatically deny, issue a flat denial; disaffirm, affirm the contrary, disprove, counter, go counter to, contradict, belie, give the lie to, gainsay, refute, confute, rebut, rejoin, retort; object, take issue with, demur, dissent, disagree, oppose, contest, dispute, contravene, controvert, deprecate, protest, defy, challenge, impugn

▶ *Dissent 347; Defiance 416; Protest 507*

17 refuse, refuse assent *or* consent, deny, reject, veto, disallow, prohibit, say no, no, naysay, shake one's head, nix [Inf]

▶ *Refusal 506*

18 disavow, disclaim, dissociate oneself, disassociate oneself, repudiate, reject, disown, cast off; relinquish, abnegate, renounce, abjure, forswear, swear off; withdraw, recant, retract, take back, eat one's words; nullify, render void *or* inoperative, invalidate, annul, void, cancel, countermand, rescind, abrogate, revoke, repeal

▶ *Rejection 383; Relinquishment 392; Cancellation 834*

19 not accept, refuse to accept, deny, disbelieve; be skeptical, doubt, express doubts, call into question, question, be agnostic; not observe, apostasize, disobey

▶ *Religion 81; Disbelief 88; Disobedience 427; Nonobservance 466*

20 be nothing, have no existence, not exist, not be, be null and void

▶ *Nonexistence 718*

21 be negative, be pessimistic, have a bad attitude, have a bleak outlook, despair

▶ *Hopelessness 282*

ADVERBS

22 negatively, in the negative, not at all, in no way; contrarily, counter, oppositely, in contradiction, contradictively *or* contradictorily; dissentingly, in opposition, opposingly, protestingly, defiantly, obstructively

23 denyingly, prohibitorily, negatively, in the negative, negative, no; [Inf]: nix, no way or noways, nowise

24 retractively, recantingly, with a disclaimer, revokingly; disavowedly

25 nonacceptantly, skeptically, doubtfully, doubtingly, questioningly, agnostically, disbelievingly, atheistically, unobservantly, apostatically, disobediently

26 pessimistically, negatively, unoptimistically, with a bad attitude, despairingly, despondently

27 to the contrary, not so, not really, *au contraire* [Fr], quite the contrary, nothing of the kind, nothing of the sort, not at all, not in the least, not by a long shot, far from it

INTERJECTIONS

28 no!, nay!, *non!* [Fr], *nein!* [Ger], *nyet!* [Russ]; certainly not!, absolutely not!, a thousand times no!, out of the question!, forget it!, I think not!, not if I can help it!, not for the world!, not for love nor money!, not for the life of me!, over my dead body!, never!, anything but!; [Inf]: no way!, no way José!, no sir!, no sirree!, no sirree Bob!, nothing doing!, nope!, nix!

191 Truthfulness

NOUNS

1 truthfulness, trueness, veraciousness, veridicality, lack of exaggeration, lack of bias or prejudice, objectivity; genuineness, sincerity, honesty, veracity, credibility, honorableness, integrity, uprightness; trustworthiness, loyalty, faithfulness, fidelity, steadfastness, firmness, staunchness, constancy, steadiness, true-heartedness

▶ *Respect 435; Disinterestedness 443; Truth 721*

2 candor, candidness, frankness, directness, bluntness, forthrightness, straightforwardness, baldness, downrightness, lack of disguise; openness, open-heartedness, outspokenness, plain speech; lack of reserve, lack of restraint, freedom, boldness

▶ *Disclosure 180; Bluntness 550*

3 ingenuousness, naiveté, naiveness, innocence, artlessness, guilelessness, simpleness, simplicity, plainness, unpretentiousness, unassumingness, unaffectedness

▶ *Innocence 449; Simplicity 526; Naiveté 821*

ADJECTIVES

4 truthful, true, veracious, veridical, unexaggerated, unbiased, objective; genuine, sincere, unfeigned, honest, honorable, upright, all wool and a yard wide; trustworthy, loyal, faithful, steadfast, firm, staunch, constant, steady, unwavering, true-blue, truehearted

▶ *Respect 435; Disinterestedness 443; Truth 721*

5 candid, frank, direct, blunt, forthright, straightforward, straight-from-the-shoulder, aboveboard, undisguised, bald, downright; open, open-hearted, outspoken, unreserved, unrestrained, free, bold, uninhibited

▶ *Disclosure 180; Bluntness 550*

6 ingenuous, naive, innocent, artless, guileless, simple, plain, unpretending, unpretentious, unassuming, unaffected

▶ *Innocence 449; Simplicity 526; Naiveté 821*

VERBS

7 be truthful, tell the truth, speak the truth, give the true story, stick to the facts; be objective, lack bias or prejudice

▶ *Disinterestedness 443; Truth 721*

8 be sincere, be honest, be true, be faithful, be loyal; be open, open up, open one's heart, confess the truth, make a clean breast of it; be frank, not mince words or matters, make no bones about it, call a spade a spade, play it straight [Inf], shoot from the hip [Inf]

▶ *Disclosure 180; Respect 435; Bluntness 550*

ADVERBS

9 truthfully, truly, veraciously, veridically, without exaggeration, objectively, without bias; genuinely, sincerely, honestly, honorably; loyally, faithfully, steadfastly, firmly, staunchly, unwaveringly

10 candidly, frankly, directly, bluntly, forthrightly, straightforwardly; openly, open-heartedly, outspokenly, freely, boldly, uninhibitedly

11 ingenuously, naively, innocently, artlessly, guilelessly, simply, plainly, unpretentiously, unassumingly, unaffectedly

192 Untruthfulness, Falsehood

Tell a tale of cock and bull, / Of convincing detail full; / Tale tremendous, / Heaven defend us! / What a tale of cock and bull! — W. S. GILBERT

NOUNS

1 untruthfulness, dishonesty, mendacity, mendaciousness, unveraciousness, lack of veracity, inveracity, untrueness

▶ *Deception 193; Untruth 722*

2 ungenuineness, disingenuousness, insincerity, false-heartedness, hollowness, emptiness, falseness, fakery, artificiality, affectation, pretentiousness, mockery, meretriciousness; hypocrisy, hypocriticalness, pretense, dissimulation, dissemblance, cant, mealy-mouthedness; two-facedness, sycophancy; sanctimoniousness, sanctimony, false piety, religionism, religiosity, unctuousness; tokenism, empty gesture, lip service, cupboard love, crocodile tears, snow job [Inf]; veneer, facade or façade, front, show, mask, guise, false face, false colors

▶ *Concealment 181; Misrepresentation 188; Deception 193; Servility 401; Flattery 439; Exterior 610*

3 dishonorableness, lack of integrity, lack of probity,

lack of scruples, unscrupulousness, crookedness; bad faith, perfidy, disloyalty, treachery, treacherousness, betrayal, double cross, unfaithfulness, infidelity, adultery, cheating; breach of promise, broken promise, broken word, broken vows, breach of confidence, breach of faith; treason, subversion, subversivism, subversiveness, sedition

> *Deception 193; Immorality 432; Disrespect 436; Protest 507*

4 **lack of candor,** uncandidness, unfrankness, indirectness; reserve, restraint, inhibition, reticence; evasiveness, equivocation, ambiguousness, fencing, fudging *or* dodging the issue; evasion, double-talk *or* doubletalk, equivoke, ambiguity; sophistry, casuistry, jesuitism *or* jesuitry

> *Concealment 181; Sophistry 330; Equivocation 380*

5 **lying,** untruthfulness, fibbing; pathological lying, habitual lying, shameless lying, barefaced lying, pseudology, mythomania; falsification, perjury, false oath, false plea; libel, slander, slanderousness, vilification, defamation, calumny, calumniation

> *Deception 193; Disparagement 440; Untruth 722*

6 **falsehood,** false statement, untruth, intentional untruth, prevarication, misstatement, trumped-up story, cock-and-bull story; lie, downright lie, shameless lie, monstrous lie, barefaced lie, dirty lie, big lie, pack of lies, tissue of lies; fib, white lie *or* little white lie; fabrication, concoction, invention, fiction, story, romanticized version, tale, yarn, fable, tall story, tall tale, old wives' tale, myth, legend; [Inf]: taradiddle *or* tarradiddle, unfact, whopper, bullshit, load of crap

> *Deception 193; Exaggeration 194; Untruth 722*

7 **partial truth,** half-truth, economy with the truth, distorted truth, propaganda, rumor, false rumor, gossip, empty gossip *or* talk, canard; distortion, slant, understatement, less than the truth, overstatement, more than the truth, exaggeration, elaboration, embroidery, embellishment; fictionalization, propagandism

> *Misrepresentation 188; Exaggeration 194; Distortion 627*

8 **nonsense,** nonsensical talk, senseless talk, drivel, prattle, moonshine, twaddle, balderdash, rubbish, rot, bosh, poppycock, hogwash, claptrap, bunkum *or* buncombe, hokum, humbug; [Inf]: bunk, hooey, baloney, eyewash, applesauce, guff, crap *or* crapola, bull, bullshit

> *Lack of Meaning 362*

9 **hypocrite,** pharisee, dissembler, dissimulator, canter, pretender, poseur, poser; cupboard lover, fair-weather friend, false friend, snake, snake in the grass, serpent, sneak, adulterer, cheater; betrayer, double-crosser, traitor, Judas, Brutus, Benedict Arnold; double agent, informer; turncoat, renegade, subversive, quisling, fifth columnist; [Inf]: pseud, two-timer, rat, stool pigeon *or* stoolie *or* stooly

10 **liar,** fibber, fibster, prevaricator; consummate liar, pathological liar, confirmed liar, habitual liar, shameless liar, barefaced liar, dirty liar, pseudologist, mythomane; evader, equivocator, double-talker; falsifier, perjurer, false witness; slanderer, maligner, libeler, libelant, vilifier, defamer, calumniator; fabricator, faker, storyteller; bullshitter [Inf]

> *Deception 193; Equivocation 380*

11 **gossip,** gossiper, gossipmonger, rumormonger, talebearer, propagandist; exaggerator, elaborator, embroiderer, embellisher; yenta [Inf]

ADJECTIVES

12 **untruthful,** dishonest, mendacious, unveracious, untrue, bad-faith, not trustworthy; exaggerative *or* exaggeratory, elaborative, propagandistic

> *Deception 193; Exaggeration 194; Untruth 722*

13 **ungenuine,** disingenuous, insincere, false-hearted, hollow, empty, tongue-in-cheek, feigned, contrived, false, pseudo, artificial, phony *or* phoney, affected, pretentious, mocking, meretricious; sanctimonious, religiose, unctuous, pharisaic; hypocritical, pretending, dissimulating, dissembling, timeserving, fair-weather, mealy-mouthed, double-tongued, two-faced; masked, veiled, disguised, incognito *or* incognita, concealed

> *Concealment 181; Misrepresentation 188; Deception 193; Flattery 439; Exterior 610*

14 **dishonorable,** lacking integrity, unscrupulous, knavish, crooked; perfidious, disloyal, unfaithful, adulterous, cheating, two-timing [Inf]; treacherous, traitorous, treasonable, treasonous, renegade, subversive, seditious

> *Deception 193; Immorality 432; Disrespect 436; Protest 507*

15 **uncandid,** unfrank, indirect, evasive, equivocal, ambiguous; reserved, restrained, inhibited, reticent, closemouthed, tight-lipped

> *Concealment 181; Sophistry 330; Equivocation 380*

16 **lying,** fibbing, prevaricative, prevaricatory, mythomaniac, pathological; falsifying, perjurious; libelous, slanderous, maligning, vilifying, defamatory, calumnious, calumniatory

> *Deception 193; Disparagement 440; Untruth 722*

17 **fabricated,** concocted, trumped-up, made-up, invented, fictionalized, romanticized, mythicized, mythologized; fictional, romantic, fabled, legendary, mythical, mythological

> *Deception 193; Exaggeration 194; Imagination 360; Untruth 722*

18 **partially true,** half-true, falsely colored, distorted, warped, slanted, twisted, garbled, understated, overstated, exaggerated, stretched, elaborated, embroidered, embellished

> *Exaggeration 194; Untruth 722*

19 **nonsensical,** driveling, prating, prattling, babbling

VERBS

20 be untruthful, not tell the truth, be dishonest; be false, be insincere, give a false impression, affect, posture, pose, pretend, feign, pay lip service to, shed crocodile tears; be hypocritical, dissimulate, dissemble, cant, speak with a forked tongue; mask, veil, conceal, disguise, put on a false face, put on a front, sail under false colors; assume the guise of, impersonate, pose as, pass oneself off as

▶ *Deception 193; Exterior 610; Untruth 722*

21 be dishonorable, lack integrity, lack scruples, show bad faith, break one's promise, go against one's word, break one's vows; be disloyal, betray, double-cross, inform; be untrue, be unfaithful, commit adultery, cheat, sneak around; lead a double life, play a double role; [Inf]: rat, play around, two-time, cheat on

▶ *Concealment 181; Immorality 432*

22 lack candor, not be frank, be indirect, be reserved, be inhibited, show restraint, refrain from talking, keep under one's hat, seal one's lips, clam up [Inf]; evade, equivocate, fence, fudge *or* dodge the issue, dance around the issue, double-talk *or* doubletalk; run with the hare and hunt with the hounds

▶ *Concealment 181; Equivocation 380*

23 lie, tell a lie, tell a white lie *or* a little white lie, fib, tell a fib, prevaricate, misstate, trump up, lie in one's throat *or* teeth, lie through one's teeth, pathologically lie, habitually lie; falsify, perjure, bear false witness; libel, slander, malign, vilify, revile, defame, calumniate; bullshit [Inf]

▶ *Deception 193; Disparagement 440; Untruth 722*

24 fabricate, concoct, make up, invent, fictionalize, romanticize, tell a tale *or* story, spin a yarn, fable, mythicize, mythologize; yarn [Inf]

▶ *Exaggeration 194; Imagination 360; Untruth 722*

25 distort the truth, slant, warp, twist, garble, understate, overstate, exaggerate, stretch the truth, elaborate, embroider, embellish, falsely color; propagandize, spread rumors, spread gossip, gossip

▶ *News 171; Exaggeration 194; Distortion 627*

26 talk nonsense, twaddle, prate, prattle, drivel, babble, hoke

▶ *Talkativeness 207; Lack of Meaning 362*

ADVERBS

27 untruthfully, dishonestly, mendaciously, unveraciously; exaggeratively, exaggeratingly, elaboratively, propagandistically; ungenuinely, disingenuously, insincerely, false-heartedly, with tongue in cheek, falsely, artificially, pretentiously, mockingly, meretriciously; sanctimoniously, unctuously, pharisaically; hypocritically, dissemblingly, mealy-mouthedly, two-facedly

▶ *Deception 193; Exaggeration 194; Untruth 722*

28 dishonorably, without integrity, unscrupulously, knavishly, crookedly; disloyally, unfaithfully, adulterously; treacherously, subversively, seditiously

▶ *Deception 193; Immorality 432; Protest 507*

29 uncandidly, unfrankly, indirectly, evasively, equivocally, ambiguously; with reserve, with restraint, inhibitedly, reticently

▶ *Equivocation 380*

30 nonsensically, pratingly, prattlingly, drivelingly

193 Deception

NOUNS

1 deception, deceptiveness, deceit, deceitfulness, delusion, delusiveness, misleadingness, duplicity, doubleness, double-dealing, sharp practice, cozenage, cheating, beguilement, trickery, dodgery, chicanery, chicane, knavery; fraud, fraudulence *or* fraudulency, humbuggery, fakery, charlatanism *or* charlatanry, quackery, quackishness, mountebankery, imposture, illegitimacy

▶ *Untruthfulness, Falsehood 192; Trap 813*

2 self-deception, self-deceit, self-delusion, delusiveness, wishful thinking, living in cloud-cuckoo-land, living in a fool's paradise, living in one's own little world, living in an ivory tower; delusion, chimera, fond illusion, confabulation

▶ *Folly 353; Imagination 360*

3 guile, artfulness, craftiness, slyness, cunning, insidiousness, deviousness, Machiavellianism; sneakiness, surreptitiousness, furtiveness, underhandedness, shiftiness, elusiveness; circumvention, escape, elusion

▶ *Cunning 822*

4 misrepresentation, distortion, perversion, false pretenses, falsification, counterfeiting, forgery; misinformation, disinformation, misdirection, misguidance; concealment, cover-up, whitewash

▶ *Concealment 181; Misrepresentation 188; Untruth 722*

5 artifice, fraud, subterfuge, intrigue, machination, machinations, sleight, stratagem, ruse, scheme, plot, conspiracy, ploy, wile, maneuver, wangle, gambit, expedient, contrivance, gimmick, wrinkle [Inf]; trick, bag of tricks, dirty trick, joker, dodge, shift, fetch; diversion, red herring, smoke screen, blind, feint, bluff

▶ *Cunning 822*

6 foul play, skulduggery, monkey business; swindle, scam, confidence game, shell game, gyp *or* gip, bamboozlement, underhanded deal, insider dealing *or* trading; [Inf]: con, sting, ripoff, bunko *or* bunco, flam, flimflam; fix, shenanigan *or* shenanigans, hanky-panky, jiggery-pokery [Brit]

▶ *Trap 813; Cunning 822*

7 hoax, deception, fraud, fake, imposture, humbug, sham; spoof, joke, put-on [Inf]

▶ *Humor 277; Derision 369*

8 deceiver, deluder, duper, double-dealer, Machiavellian, cozener, cheater, cheat, beguiler, trickster, dodger, knave; fraud, humbug, malingerer, fake, charlatan, quack, mountebank, wolf in sheep's clothing, shyster [Inf]

9 **one who misrepresents,** misrepresenter, distorter, perverter, falsifier, counterfeiter, forger; misinformer, disinformer, misguider, misleader, manipulator

▶ *Misrepresentation 188*

10 **schemer,** machinator, plotter, conspirer, conspirator, intrigant *or* intriguant, intriguer, maneuverer, wangler; swindler, defrauder, bilker, fleecer, sharper *or* sharpie, confidence man, scammer, gypper *or* gypster, crook, bamboozler, chiseler, bluffer; [Inf]: con man, con artist, flammer, flimflammer, flimflam man, bunko steerer, goldbricker

11 **hoaxer,** fraud, fake, faker, impostor *or* imposter, impersonator, phony *or* phoney, humbugger, sham, shammer

ADJECTIVES

12 **deceptive,** deceitful, deceiving, delusive *or* delusory, misleading, duplicitous, double-dealing, treacherous, cheating, beguiling, knavish, conniving; fraudulent, fake, impostrous *or* imposturous, malingering, quackish, illegitimate; self-deceptive, self-deceiving, self-deluding, delusional *or* delusionary, chimerical, confabulatory

▶ *Untruthfulness, Falsehood 192; Folly 353; Imagination 360; Trap 813*

13 **artful,** guileful, crafty, wily, sly, cunning, insidious, devious, tricky, Machiavellian; calculating, scheming, plotting, conspiratorial, maneuvering, wangling; sneaky, surreptitious, furtive, underhanded, shifty, elusive *or* elusory, slippery, smooth, slick; flamming [Inf], flimflamming [Inf]

▶ *Concealment 181; Cunning 822*

14 **misrepresentative,** distortive, perversive, manipulative, manipulating; misrepresented, distorted, perverted, twisted, falsified, manipulated, adulterated, altered, tampered with, doctored, faked, fake, counterfeited, forged; misinformed, disinformed, misdirected, misguided

▶ *Misrepresentation 188; Distortion 627*

15 **deceived,** deluded, misled, duped, victimized, fooled, befooled, hoodwinked, beguiled, cheated, tricked

▶ *Folly 353; Trap 813*

VERBS

16 **deceive,** delude, mislead, lead on, lead up *or* down the garden path, cozen, dupe, fool, befool, gull, hoodwink, beguile, cheat, welsh [Inf *and* Off], double-deal; humbug, malinger, trick, dodge, chicane, pull the wool over someone's eyes, string along [Inf]; elude, avoid, escape, circumvent, outwit, outsmart, outmaneuver; deceive oneself, delude, confabulate, indulge in wishful thinking, have fond illusions, live in cloud-cuckooland, live in a fool's paradise, live in one's own little world, live in an ivory tower

▶ *Untruthfulness, Falsehood 192; Folly 353; Imagination 360; Trap 813; Escape 816*

17 **misrepresent,** distort, pervert, falsify, counterfeit, forge; misinform, disinform, misdirect, misguide; conceal, cover up, whitewash

▶ *Concealment 181; Misrepresentation 188; Untruth 722*

18 **scheme,** plot, strategize, machinate, connive, conspire, collude, maneuver, wangle, contrive; trick, dodge, shift, fetch

▶ *Trap 813; Cunning 822*

19 **swindle,** defraud, scam, gyp *or* gip, bamboozle, chisel, bilk, fleece, sell someone a bill of goods, take in; [Inf]: con, rip off, do out of, flam, flimflam, pull a fast one, take for a ride, fake someone out, diddle, hornswoggle

▶ *Trap 813; Cunning 822*

20 **hoax,** deceive, fake, humbug, sham, victimize, spoof, pull someone's leg, kid [Inf], play a joke on

▶ *Humor 277; Folly 353; Derision 369*

ADVERBS

21 **deceptively,** deceitfully, delusively, duplicitously, treacherously, manipulatively, under false pretenses; fraudulently, quackishly, cheatingly, illegitimately; artfully, guilefully, craftily, slyly, deviously; sneakily, surreptitiously, furtively, underhandedly, shiftily, elusively

▶ *Untruthfulness, Falsehood 192; Cunning 822; Concealment 181*

194 Exaggeration

Camp . . . is the love of the exaggerated, the "off," of things-being-what-they-are-not. — SUSAN SONTAG

NOUNS

1 **exaggeration,** exaggerating, overemphasis, overstress, overstatement; excessiveness, excess, extremism, extremes, exorbitance, overkill; overexposure; hyperbolism, hyperbole, superlative; sensationalism, sensation, overdoing, excitement, overselling, fulsomeness; embellishment, enhancement, embroidery, touching up, painting *or* gilding the lily, varnish, overcoloring; prodigality, overreaction, fuss, uproar, commotion; overestimation, overvaluation, exaggerated lengths, overcompensation; overacting, histrionics, hamming, overdrawing, overwriting; melodrama, burlesque, travesty, caricature; making a mountain out of a molehill, tempest in a teapot *or* teacup; ballyhoo, puffery; [Inf]: to-do, hype, hoopla

▶ *Aggravation 276; Misjudgment 342; Overestimation 343; Imagination 360; Derision 369; Decoration 532; Distortion 627; Agitation 684; Untruth 722*

2 **enlargement,** magnification, amplification, dilation *or* dilatation; maximization, inflation, expansion, aggrandizement, heightening; blowing up, puffing up

▶ *Expansion 581; Addition 748*

3 **extravagance,** excessiveness, flamboyance, ostentation, outrageousness, profuseness, profusion, lavishness, overindulgence; overspending, intemperance; going to extremes, running riot, overdoing it, carrying too far, going too far, overshooting, overstepping the mark

▶ *Self-Indulgence 456*

4 **bombast,** pomposity, inflatedness, magniloquence, grandiloquence, boasting, boast, bragging, self-glorification; ranting, raving; huckstering, talking in superlatives, overpraise, flattery, overrating, glowing terms, purple prose, making much of, hot air [Inf]

▶ *Diffuseness 199; Flattery 439*

5 **tall story,** traveler's tale, fisherman's *or* angler's tale, flight of fancy, stretch of the imagination, yarn, fish story [Inf]

6 **exaggerator,** boaster, braggart, braggadocio, blusterer, hector, fanfaron, panjandrum, sensationalist, liar, fanatic, windbag [Inf], bullshitter *or* bullshit artist [Inf]

ADJECTIVES

7 **exaggerated,** overemphasized, overstressed, overstated, overdone; sensationalized, inflated, puffed, overrated, overpraised, oversold, fulsome; flattered, embellished, embroidered, touched up, varnished; highly colored, overcolored, overdrawn, far-fetched; excessive, hyperbolic; overexposed, exorbitant, extreme, inordinate, superlative, prodigious; overestimated, overvalued; enhanced, overwritten, overacted, histrionic, melodramatic, ballyhooed, hyped [Inf]

8 **enlarged,** magnified, amplified, dilated, maximized, inflated, expanded, aggrandized, heightened, blown up, puffed up

9 **extravagant,** excessive, flamboyant, ostentatious, outrageous, profuse, lavish, grandiose, overindulgent; overspending, pound-foolish, intemperate, inordinate, exorbitant; overdone, overshot, overstepping

10 **bombastic,** boasting, bragging, raving, inflating, self-glorifying, magniloquent, grandiloquent, pompous, fustian, hyping [Inf]

VERBS

11 **exaggerate,** overemphasize, overstate, overstress, hyperbolize, sensationalize, overdo; embellish, embroider, touch up, enhance, paint *or* gild the lily, varnish, color highly, overcolor; overexpose, overkill, overreact, make a commotion, go to exaggerated lengths; overestimate, overvalue; overact, have histrionics, ham, ham it up, chew the scenery; overdraw, overwrite; burlesque, travesty, caricature; make a mountain out of a molehill, create a tempest in a teapot *or* teacup, ballyhoo, hype [Inf], make a to-do [Inf]

12 **enlarge,** magnify, amplify, dilate, maximize, inflate, expand, distend, aggrandize, heighten, blow up, puff up

13 **be extravagant,** overdo, overdo it, lavish, over-

indulge, overspend, run riot, go to extremes, carry too far, go too far, overshoot, overstep the mark, not know when to stop

14 **boast,** brag, bombast, rant, rave, huckster, talk in superlatives, blow up (out of all proportion), oversell, overrate, overpraise, flatter, inflate, depict in glowing terms, make much of, self-glorify, out-Herod Herod, lay it on, lay it on thick, lay it on with a trowel

15 **tell a tall story,** have a flight of fancy, stretch the imagination, spin a yarn

ADVERBS

16 **exaggeratedly,** hyperbolically, superlatively, overenthusiastically, overemphatically, excitedly, sensationally, histrionically, melodramatically, magniloquently, grandiloquently, bombastically, fulsomely, pompously

17 **excessively,** extremely, outrageously, extravagantly, exorbitantly, inordinately, prodigiously, flamboyantly, ostentatiously, lavishly, profusely, intemperately, too much

195 Understatement

NOUNS

1 **understatement,** underemphasis, minimization, underestimation, undervaluation, conservative estimate, underreckoning; litotes

▶ *Underestimation 344*

2 **disparagement,** detraction, belittlement, faint praise, two cheers

3 **subtlety,** delicacy, restraint, restrainedness, elegance, refinement, good taste, finesse, discrimination, fastidiousness

▶ *Discrimination 337; Refinement 534*

4 **simplicity,** simpleness, plainness, modesty, Spartan simplicity, bareness, austerity, austereness, starkness, unelaborateness, unfussiness, minimalism, unpretentiousness, unostentatiousness, unaffectedness

▶ *Simplicity 526*

5 **reserve,** reticence, restraint, constraint, diffidence, modesty, quietness, subduedness, retiring disposition

▶ *Modesty 403; Restraint 830*

6 **downplaying,** de-emphasis, dilution, watering down, diminishment, curtailment, moderation, restraint, constraint, disregard, playing down, underplaying, making light of, shrugging off, paring down, cutting down to size

▶ *Lack of Emphasis 201*

7 **deflation,** puncturing, depreciation, cutting down, cutting back

ADJECTIVES

8 **understated,** underemphasized, conservative, minimized, underestimated, undervalued, underreckoned, underrated, low-key

9 **subtle,** delicate, restrained, elegant, refined, tasteful, discriminating, fastidious, pastel

10 simple, plain, modest, bare, austere, stark, unelaborate, unfussy, unpretentious, unostentatious, unadorned, unaffected, minimal

11 reserved, reticent, restrained, constrained, diffident, modest, quiet, subdued, retiring, unassuming, low-profile

12 deflated, punctured, depreciated, cut down, cut back

13 downplayed, played down, underplayed, toned down, moderated, de-emphasized, diluted, watered down, reduced, diminished, curtailed, restrained, constrained, disregarded, pared, pared down

VERBS

14 understate, underemphasize, underreckon, minimize, underplay, underestimate, undervalue, underrate, sell short

15 disparage, detract from, underpraise, belittle, damn with faint praise, give two cheers

16 deflate, puncture, depreciate, cut back, bring down to earth, cut down, cut down to size, let the air out of, take the wind out of someone's sails

17 play down, downplay, underplay, tone down, moderate, de-emphasize, deprecate, dilute, water down, reduce, diminish, curtail, restrain, constrain, disregard, make light of, set no store by, shrug off, pare, pare down, spare one's blushes

▶ *Lack of Emphasis 201*

ADVERBS

18 understatedly, moderately, restrainedly, in a low-key manner

19 simply, plainly, austerely, starkly, unelaborately, unfussily, unpretentiously, unostentatiously, minimally

20 reservedly, reticently, diffidently, modestly, quietly, unassumingly

196 Clarity

The chief merit of language is clearness.
— GALEN

The great enemy of clear language is insincerity.
— GEORGE ORWELL

NOUNS

1 clarity, clearness, lucidity, pellucidity *or* pellucidness, perspicuity, perspicuousness; transparency, purity, limpidity; coherence, intelligibility, comprehensibility; plainness, simplicity, austerity, starkness, straightforwardness, directness, unambiguity, unambiguousness; explicitness, definition, definiteness, distinctness, obviousness, exactness, accuracy

▶ *Visibility 244; Light 246; Transparency 249; Accuracy 350; Intelligibility 363; Simplicity 526*

ADJECTIVES

2 clear, lucid, pellucid, perspicuous; limpid, transparent, pure; coherent, intelligible, comprehensible; plain, unadorned, simple, austere, stark; straightforward, direct, unambiguous; explicit, clear-cut, definite, distinct, obvious, exact, accurate, uninvolved

▶ *Visibility 244; Light 246; Transparency 249; Accuracy 350; Intelligibility 363; Simplicity 526*

VERBS

3 clarify, make clear, disambiguate; define, demonstrate, explicate; interpret, decipher; elucidate, illuminate, enlighten, fill in

ADVERBS

4 clearly, lucidly, pellucidly, perspicuously; limpidly, transparently, purely; coherently, intelligibly, comprehensibly; plainly, simply, straightforwardly, directly, unambiguously; explicitly, distinctly, obviously, exactly, accurately

197 Obscurity

I'm afraid of losing my obscurity. Genuineness only thrives in the dark. Like celery. — ALDOUS HUXLEY

NOUNS

1 obscurity, obscuration, lack of clarity, obfuscation, unintelligibility, incomprehensibility; opacity, lack of transparency, cloudiness, fogginess, fuzziness, murkiness, muddiness; difficult language, hard words, Johnsonese, overornamentation, purple prose, tortuousness, involved style, euphuism, complexity; muddle, gobbledegook, confusion; indistinctness, vagueness, uncertainty, imprecision, impreciseness, inexactness, inaccuracy, indefiniteness; abstraction, indirectness, allusion; ambiguity, equivocation, equivocalness, shapelessness, amorphousness, convolution; mysteriousness, enigma, riddle; abstruseness, profundity, depth; overcompression, ellipsis; flood of words, verbiage, diffuseness, gibberish, mumbo jumbo

▶ *Linguistics, Language 5; Concealment 181; Diffuseness 199; Darkness 247; Dimness 248; Opaqueness 250; Unintelligibility 364; Depth 598; Disorder 766; Unimportance 800; Difficulty 824; Uncertainty 841; Latency 844*

ADJECTIVES

2 obscure, unclear, obfuscatory, unintelligible, incomprehensible; opaque, not transparent, cloudy, foggy, fuzzy, murky, muddy, clear as mud; hard, difficult, full of difficult words, Johnsonian, overornamented, purple, tortuous, convoluted, involved, euphuistic, complex; confused, muddled, indistinct, vague, uncertain; imprecise, inexact, inaccurate; indefinite, abstract, indirect, allusive, ambiguous, equivocal, shapeless, amorphous; cabalistic, mysterious, enigmatic, cryptic; abstruse, esoteric, arcane, recondite, profound, deep; overcompressed, elliptical; diffuse, gibbering

▶ *Concealment 181; Diffuseness 199; Darkness 247; Dimness 248; Opaqueness 250; Unintelligibility 364; Decoration 532; Depth 598; Disorder 766; Unimportance 800; Difficulty 824; Uncertainty 841; Latency 844*

VERBS

3 **make obscure,** obscure, obfuscate, make abstruse, complicate, confound, muddy, confuse, muddle, mix up, garble

▶ *Lack of Meaning 362*

ADVERBS

4 **obscurely,** unintelligibly, incomprehensibly; fuzzily, murkily; overornamentally, tortuously; indistinctly, vaguely, imprecisely, inexactly, inaccurately, indefinitely; indirectly, allusively, ambiguously, equivocally; mysteriously, enigmatically, cryptically; abstrusely, profoundly; elliptically

198 Conciseness

Brevity is the soul of wit. — WILLIAM SHAKESPEARE

Brevity is the soul of lingerie. — DOROTHY PARKER

NOUNS

1 **conciseness,** concision, brevity, briefness, shortness; laconism *or* laconicism, succinctness, pithiness, crispness, compactness; terseness, curtness, brusqueness, briskness; taciturnity, monosyllabism, words of one syllable; exactness, incisiveness, pointedness; the long and the short of it, heart of the matter; brachylogy, concise style, economy of words, no words wasted, few words; clipped form *or* word, portmanteau word, compression, telegraphese; ellipsis, elision, syncope, apocope, abbreviation, contraction; truncation, shortening, compendiousness, sententiousness, abridgment

▶ *Taciturnity 208; Discourtesy 411; Shortness 591*

2 **outline,** summary, abstract, synopsis, précis, résumé, brief sketch, compendium, condensation, abridgment

▶ *Summary 204*

3 **pithy saying,** epitome, maxim, aphorism, epigram, proverb

▶ *Maxim 177*

ADJECTIVES

4 **concise,** brief, short; laconic, succinct, pithy, crisp, compact; terse, curt, brusque, brisk; taciturn, monosyllabic, sparing of words; exact, incisive, trenchant, pointed; to the point, short and sweet; brachylogous, concisely styled, economically worded, tight-knit; portmanteau, clipped, compressed, telegraphic; elliptic, syncopic *or* syncopal, abbreviated, contracted; truncated, shortened, compendious; epitomical, aphoristic, epigrammatic, sententious; outlined, summarized,

summary; condensed, abridged, cut; not long in the telling

▶ *Taciturnity 208; Discourtesy 411; Shortness 591*

VERBS

5 **be concise,** waste no words; need few words, put in a nutshell, express pithily, cut a long story short; put it bluntly, not beat about the bush, come (straight) to the point; telescope, compress, compact, condense, abridge, cut, abbreviate, truncate, clip, shorten, contract; outline, sketch, epitomize, synopsize, sum up, summarize, abstract, précis; cut short, cut off; epigrammatize; get down to the nuts and bolts; [Inf]: pull no punches, talk turkey, get down to brass tacks, get down to the nitty-gritty, cut the cackle, tell it straight, tell it like it is

▶ *Summary 204; Shortness 591*

ADVERBS

6 **concisely,** briefly; laconically, succinctly, pithily, crisply, compactly; tersely, curtly, brusquely, briskly; exactly, incisively, trenchantly, pointedly; telegraphically, elliptically; compendiously, sententiously, summarily; with few words, without wasting words, in brief, in short, in a word, in a nutshell, to the point; in outline, to sum up, to put it succinctly; to cut a long story short, in words of one syllable

199 Diffuseness

NOUNS

1 **diffuseness,** diffusion, diffusiveness; profuseness, copiousness, abundance, superabundance; amplitude, amplification, elaboration, expansion, extension, protraction, enlargement, expatiation; filler, expletive, padding, extra; circumstantiality, minuteness, detail, detailed account, blow-by-blow account; superfluity, repetitiveness, repetition, reiterativeness, reiteration, twice-told tale, redundancy, tautology, pleonasm, excess; flow, outpouring, exuberance, gush, effusiveness, effusion; verboseness, verbosity, loquacity, talkativeness, nonstop talking, wordiness, verbiage, long-windedness; prolixity, cloud of words, epic length, tedium, rigmarole *or* rigamarole, empty talk; rhetoric, bombast, logorrhea, verbal diarrhea [Inf], blah-blah-blah [Inf]

▶ *Excess 99; Exaggeration 194; Speech, Spoken Language 205; Talkativeness 207; Lack of Meaning 362; Expansion 581; Duration 642; Repetition 797*

2 **circumlocution,** circuitous writing, periphrasis, ambages [Arch], ambagiousness, roundabout phrase; digression, deviation, discursion, excursion, excursus, rambling, wandering, indirectness; irrelevance, pointlessness, aimlessness; sidetrack, departure, beating around the bush, equivocation, equivocalness

▶ *Equivocation 380; Deviation 698; Unrelatedness 728; Addition 748; Disorder 766*

3 **diffuse,** diffusive; profuse, prolific, copious, abundant, superabundant; detailed, minute; amplified, expanded, extended, protracted, long-drawn-out *or* drawn-out, spun out, padded; long, loose-knit, lengthy, never-ending, nonstop, going on and on; repetitive, reiterative, repeated, tautologous *or* tautological, redundant, pleonastic, superfluous, excessive; talkative, verbose, loquacious, fluent, gushing, effuse, effusive, wordy, exuberant, flowing, overflowing; polysyllabic, sesquipedalian; prosy, prolix, long-winded, windy, flatulent, pretentious, empty, incoherent; ornate, rhetorical, magniloquent, fustian, bombastic, turgid; voluminous, tedious, boring

> *Fertility 22; Excess 99; Speech, Spoken Language 205; Talkativeness 207; Lack of Meaning 362; Expansion 581; Length 590; Duration 642; Repetition 797*

4 **circumlocutory,** circuitous, periphrastic, ambagious, roundabout; deviating, digressive, discursive, excursive, rambling, wandering; oblique, indirect; irrelevant, pointless, aimless, sidetracked

> *Deviation 698; Unrelatedness 728; Addition 748; Disorder 766*

VERBS

5 **be diffuse,** amplify, enlarge upon, expatiate, dilate, expand; extend, lengthen, protract, draw out, spin out, pad; repeat, repeat oneself, reiterate, tautologize; gush, flow, overflow, pour out, let oneself go, wax eloquent; elaborate, particularize, detail, go into detail; go on and on, never end, discourse at length, harangue, rant, rant and rave; use long words, bore, spin a long tale, ramble on, blather on

> *Talkativeness 207; Boredom 296; Expansion 581; Length 590; Repetition 797*

6 **be circuitous,** digress, diverge, deviate, ramble, maunder, wander; make no point, not come to the point, beat around the bush; get sidetracked, get off the subject, go off on *or* at a tangent

> *Deviation 698; Unrelatedness 728*

ADVERBS

7 **diffusely,** diffusively; profusely, prolifically, copiously, abundantly; minutely, in detail; repetitively, tautologously *or* tautologically; verbosely, loquaciously, effusively, in full, long-windedly; bombastically, turgidly, with many words, in love with one's own voice, at length, at great length, on and on, ad nauseam, *in extenso* [L]

8 **circuitously,** periphrastically, in a roundabout way, digressively, discursively; obliquely, indirectly, on *or* at a tangent

200 Emphasis

NOUNS

1 **emphasis,** stress, accent, accentuation; underlining, underscoring, italics; vehemence, insistence, urgency, priority; iteration, reiteration, repetition; enthusiasm, fervor, passion, feeling, ardor, fire; warmth, glow, spirit, inspiration; vigor, vigorousness, vim, gusto, zest, verve; boldness, dash, raciness, sparkle, panache, liveliness, vitality, vivaciousness, vivacity, vividness; positive outlook, affirmation; piquancy, poignancy, bite, sharpness, mordancy, pungency; penetration, asperity, acuity, intensity, incisiveness, keenness, trenchancy; strength, strong language, power, force, forcefulness, energy, drive, punch, oomph [Inf]

> *Affirmation 189; Exaggeration 194; Piquancy 221; Power 514; Strength 516; Vigor 518; Sharpness 549; Repetition 797*

2 **seriousness,** solemnity, gravity, weight, importance, significance; attention, prominence; impressiveness, loftiness, elevation, sublimity; eloquence, grandeur, grandiloquence, magniloquence

> *Attention 323; Importance 799*

ADJECTIVES

3 **emphatic,** vehement, earnest, insistent, urgent; firm, uncompromising, dogmatic; iterative, reiterative, repetitive; enthusiastic, fervent, passionate, impassioned, ardent, fiery, glowing; warm, spirited, inspired; vigorous, zestful, bold, dashing, racy, sparkling, lively, vivacious; positive, affirmative, categorical, unequivocal, definite, sure, certain; incisive, cutting, slashing, pulling no punches, penetrating, keen, trenchant, pointed; sententious, pithy, meaty, thought-provoking; pungent, sharp, mordant, piquant, poignant; vivid, graphic, strong, strongly worded; eloquent, compelling, convincing, effective, cogent; forceful, powerful, strenuous, energetic, brisk, zingy, peppy [Inf], punchy [Inf]

> *Piquancy 221; Sensitivity 267; Compulsion 428; Power 514; Strength 516; Vigor 518; Sharpness 549; Repetition 797; Certainty 840*

4 **emphasized,** stressed, accentuated; highlighted, enhanced, underlined, in italics; pointed out, marked, pronounced

> *Affirmation 189*

5 **serious,** solemn, grave, weighty; important, significant, heavy, intense, solid, impressive; lofty, elevated, sublime, grand, grandiloquent, majestic, magniloquent

> *Importance 799*

VERBS

6 **emphasize,** stress, accent, accentuate; highlight, enhance, spotlight, feature, underline, underscore, italicize, put in italics; point out, call *or* draw attention to; insist, urge; reaffirm, reassert, reiterate, repeat, dwell on, plug [Inf]; raise one's voice, shout, roar, thunder, bellow; glow, dash, sparkle; penetrate, provoke thought, convince; impress on, press home, drive home, din in, hammer home, rub it in [Inf], pull no punches [Inf]

> *Affirmation 189; Exaggeration 194; Speech, Spoken Language 205; Attention 323; Repetition 797; Importance 799*

ADVERBS

7 **emphatically,** vehemently, earnestly, insistently, urgently; dogmatically; enthusiastically, fervently, passionately, ardently, positively; incisively, strongly, forcefully, vigorously, energetically, strenuously; solemnly, gravely; with conviction, in no uncertain terms; with eloquence, in glowing terms, grandiloquently, magniloquently, majestically

201   Lack of Emphasis

NOUNS

1 **lack of emphasis,** lack of passion, lack of spirit, lack of force, lack of inspiration, lack of sparkle, lack of style; tameness, emptiness, pointlessness, lameness; boredom, monotony, sameness, staleness, prosiness, plainness, commonplace, platitude, cliché, convention, insipidity, wanness, dullness, vapidity, flatness, thinness, wateriness; carelessness, inexactitude; flatulence, disconnection, garble; looseness, limpness, sloppiness, ineffectiveness; feebleness, weakness, weak style, enervation, enervated style, anticlimax, meagerness, flaccidity, exhaustion

> *Understatement 195; Diffuseness 199; Tastelessness 220; Boredom 296; Weakness 517; Simplicity 526*

ADJECTIVES

2 **unemphatic,** unimpassioned, unspirited, unexciting, uninspiring, tame, undramatic; inane, empty, pointless, lame, uninspired; boring, monotonous, stale, prosaic, prosy, commonplace, platitudinous, hackneyed, cliché-ridden, clichéd, conventional, insipid, wan, colorless, dull, dry, vapid, flat, thin, watery; poorly done, careless, inexact, slovenly, slipshod; rambling, prolix, flatulent, disjointed, disconnected, garbled, amorphous, shapeless; loose, limp, sloppy, wishy-washy, unconvincing, ineffective, feeble, weak, meager, languid, flaccid, exhausted, spent

> *Understatement 195; Diffuseness 199; Tastelessness 220; Boredom 296; Sophistry 330; Weakness 517; Simplicity 526; Vulgarity 535*

VERBS

3 **de-emphasize,** reduce, weaken, enervate; lack passion, lack spirit

ADVERBS

4 **unemphatically,** uninspiringly, tamely; lamely, prosaically, platitudinously, conventionally, sentimentally, tastelessly; plainly, colorlessly, vapidly; carelessly, inexactly, loosely; unconvincingly, feebly, weakly

202   Description

NOUNS

1 **description,** account, detailed description *or* account, statement, statement of fact, details, particulars, inventory, background; specification, report, record, delineation; depiction, picture, portrait, portrayal, characterization, profile, character sketch, case history, version, explanation; sort

> *Information 170; Record 185*

2 **brief description,** caption, legend, indication, heading, subtitle, word portrait, thumbnail sketch, summary, outline, précis, cameo, vignette, exposé

> *Summary 204; Outline 617*

3 **narration,** narrative, narrative writing, account, essay, story, anecdote

> *Literature 139*

4 **factual account,** nonfiction, documentary, documentary account, report, play-by-play *or* blow-by-blow account; journalism, biography, autobiography, life story

> *Record 185; Dissertation 203*

5 **fictional account,** descriptive writing, creative writing, creative composition; faction [Inf]

> *Literature 139*

6 **sort,** kind, type, genre, variety, breed, species, nature, character, ilk, kidney

> *Class 777*

7 **nomenclature,** naming, addressing, calling, roll call, appellation, denomination, terminology; taxonomy, classification, designation; description, identification, indication, antonomasia; naming ceremony, christening, baptizing, baptism, nicknaming; study of names, eponymy, onomastics, onomatology, orismology; study of place names, toponymy; misnaming, pseudonymity

> *Identification 184; Class 777*

8 **name,** nomen, noun, proper noun, appellation, appellative, full name; first name, forename, praenomen, Christian name, baptismal name, given name, confirmation name; middle name, second name, agnomen; last name, married name, surname, family name; patronymic, matronymic, cognomen, maiden name; pet name, diminutive, sweetheart name, familiar name; pen name, nom de plume, false name, alias, assumed name, pseudonym, allonym, stage name; sobriquet, nickname, namesake; epithet, title, autograph, signature, label, tag, term, technical term, password, place name, eponym, toponym, tautonym, trademark, tradename, hallmark, markings, moniker *or* monicker [Inf], handle [Inf]

> *Title 72; Religious Ritual 85; Identification 184; Address 209; Love 299*

9 **representation,** imitation, likeness, impression; picture, true picture, portrait; sketch, drawing, mechan-

ical drawing, freehand drawing, technical drawing; duplicate, double, spitting image [Inf], facsimile, tracing, photocopy, lithograph

 ▶ *Painting and Drawing 143; Representation 187; Sameness 730*

10 descriptive writer, creative writer, wordsmith, literary person, man *or* woman of letters, writer, author; novelist, fiction writer, fictionist, crime writer, essayist; poet, playwright, dramatist, librettist, scriptwriter; fabulist, teller of tales, storyteller, raconteur, anecdotist; biographer, hagiographer, diarist, historian, chronicler, annalist, recorder, historiographer; journalist, reporter, correspondent, special correspondent, war correspondent, sports correspondent, columnist; scribbler, ghost writer, hack, pen *or* pencil pusher [Inf]

 ▶ *Literature 139; News 171; Publication 173*

ADJECTIVES

11 descriptive, representational, graphic, vivid, detailed, full, informative, illustrative, explicatory, explanatory, elucidatory, illuminating, expository, expositive, interpretive, amplifying; well-drawn, true to life, real-life, realistic, naturalistic, photographic, eidetic, convincing; picturesque, expressive, impressionistic, suggestive, evocative, moving, poignant, thrilling, exciting, striking, highly colored, forceful

 ▶ *Information 170*

12 narrative, factual, documentary, biographical, autobiographical; fictional, imaginative, mythological, epic, heroic, romantic, picaresque, anecdotal

 ▶ *Literature 139*

13 named, naming, called, described, identified, nicknamed

14 representing, representative, iconic, pictorial, emblematic, symbolic, figurative, diagrammatic, representational, photographic, artistic, primitive, naive, impressionistic, surrealistic, surreal, abstract

 ▶ *Photography 132; Painting and Drawing 143*

VERBS

15 describe, delineate, draw, sketch, picture, depict, portray, limn, paint, represent, illustrate, characterize, form, shape, fashion, design, draft, sketch out, adumbrate, rough out, outline, make a diagram of, do a portrait, catch a likeness, capture an expression, doodle, scribble

16 recount, relate, tell, retell, narrate; tell a story, tell a tale, spin a yarn, reminisce, evoke, bring to life; characterize, detail, recapitulate, review, record, chronicle; repeat, recite, rehearse, pass on the information; communicate, report, cover, submit a report, make a statement, testify, keep posted, correspond; write an account of, write a story about, fictionalize, dramatize, romanticize, mythologize, imagine

 ▶ *Communications 169; Information 170; Imagination 360*

17 name, define, specify, mention, detail, particularize, itemize, inventory, explain, interpret

ADVERBS

18 descriptively, graphically, vividly, realistically, illustratively, imaginatively

203 Dissertation

NOUNS

1 dissertation, discourse, disquisition, treatise, tract, tractate, exposition, summary, theme, argument, thesis, essay, composition; study, lucubration, examination, survey, inquiry, discussion, symposium; paper, research paper, term paper, position paper, monograph; memoir, screed, harangue, homily, sermon, oration, peroration, tirade, lecture, lesson, prolegomenon, exegesis, interpretation, explanation, gloss, annotation, comment, descant, commentary

 ▶ *Summary 204; Speech, Spoken Language 205; Argument 329*

2 article, lead article, leader, editorial comment, editorial, Op-Ed column; review, notice, critique, criticism

 ▶ *News 171; Publication 173*

3 dissertator, essayist, pamphleteer, propagandist, preacher, orator, speaker, lecturer, teacher, writer, author, editorialist, contributor, reviewer, critic, commentator, exponent, expounder, expositor, exegete, glossarist, annotator; scholar, doctoral *or* Ph.D. candidate

ADJECTIVES

4 dissertational, discursive, disquisitional, critical, interpretive *or* interpretative, expository, exegetical, illuminating, editorial, glossarial, annotative

VERBS

5 dissertate, discourse, speak, write, put forward an argument, argue, develop a thesis, go into, deal with in depth, do *or* write a paper, write a thesis *or* treatise; hold a symposium, inquire into, survey, discuss, comment on, descant, criticize, commentate, gloss, annotate, interpret, explain, elucidate, define, expound, orate, perorate, sermonize, preach, pontificate

 ▶ *Speech, Spoken Language 205; Argument 329; Interpretation 365*

ADVERBS

6 discursively, critically, interpretively *or* interpretatively, explanatorily, expositorily, expositively, exegetically, illuminatingly, editorially

204 Summary

NOUNS

1 summary, synopsis, précis, *aperçu* [Fr], digest, epitome, abstract, review, recapitulation, gist, drift, conspectus, survey, bird's-eye view, overview, rundown, sketch, thumbnail sketch; résumé, curriculum vitae (CV), recap

2 **outline,** skeleton, plan, blueprint, syllabus, prospectus, brochure, abridgment, concise version, potted version [Brit], abbreviation, shortening, diminution, contraction, truncation, pruning, compression
  ▸ *Conciseness 198; Plan 387; Contraction 582; List 785*

3 **compendium,** anthology, treasury, collection, compilation, corpus, chrestomathy, miscellany, miscellanea, album, scrapbook, ephemera, cuttings, extracts, excerpts, selections
  ▸ *Assembly 59; Selection 382*

4 **summariness,** briefness, brevity, shortness, terseness, brusqueness, conciseness, pithiness, succinctness, compactness, pointedness, compendiousness, laconism *or* laconicism
  ▸ *Conciseness 198; Shortness 591*

ADJECTIVES

5 **summary,** brief, short, short and sweet, curt, brusque, terse, concise, pithy, compendious, succinct, compact, pointed, epigrammatic, epigrammatical, laconic, irreducible
  ▸ *Conciseness 198; Shortness 591; Haste 818*

6 **summarized,** synopsized, abstracted, clipped, shortened, abbreviated, abridged, pruned, docked, truncated, cut, cut short, contracted, compacted, collected
  ▸ *Contraction 582; Shortness 591*

VERBS

7 **summarize,** précis, write a résumé, synopsize, write a synopsis, abstract; condense, digest, epitomize, encapsulate, reduce, shorten, abbreviate, abridge, contract, truncate, cut short, give an outline of, outline, sketch, sketch out, boil down, sum up, recapitulate, epigrammatize, recap
  ▸ *Conciseness 198; Contraction 582; Shortness 591*

8 **compile,** consolidate, collect together, anthologize, excerpt, select
  ▸ *Assembly 59; Selection 382*

9 **be brief,** come to the point, cut a long story short

ADVERBS

10 **summarily,** briefly, shortly, brusquely, tersely, crisply, laconically, concisely, pithily, succintly, pointedly; in short, without wasting words, in a word, in a nutshell, in a few words, to the point, epigrammatically

205 Speech, Spoken Language

NOUNS

1 **speech,** spoken language, oral communication, talk, talking, speaking, verbal intercourse; dialogue, conversation, colloquy, discourse; [Inf]: yak *or* yack *or* yackety-yak, chinwag, spiel, rap
  ▸ *Linguistics, Language 5; Communications 169*

2 **spoken language,** speech, tongue, talk, vocalism, parlance; living language, mother tongue, native tongue; natural language, informal language *or* speech, common speech, English as it is spoken; vernacular, colloquialism; phonetics
  ▸ *Linguistics, Language 5*

3 **phonetics,** pronunciation, phonology, phonography, phonemics, orthoepy, morphophonemics, morphology, morphophonology
  ▸ *Linguistics, Language 5*

4 **speech organ,** voice, mouth, tongue, teeth, lips; vocal organs, vocal cords, vocal folds; voicebox, larynx, Adam's apple; glottis, epiglottis, hard palate, alveolar palate, soft palate, uvula, nasal cavity, oral cavity, pharynx, throat

5 **power of speech,** articulation, articulateness, articulacy, eloquence, fluency, command of language, way with words, word power; style, rich vocabulary, grandiloquence, magniloquence, orotundity; purple passage, flowery speech, talkativeness, volubility, loquacity; glossolalia, speaking in tongues; prolixity, logorrhea, verbosity, verbiage, wordiness, long-windedness, repetitiveness; blarney, gift of the gab [Inf], verbal diarrhea [Inf]
  ▸ *Diffuseness 199; Talkativeness 207; Style 537; Repetition 797*

6 **mode of speech,** tone, tone of voice, voice, speaking voice, voice quality, cadence, timbre, intonation, pitch, modulation, inflection, stress, emphasis; pronunciation, accent, regional accent, native accent, foreign accent, broad accent, brogue, twang, burr, trill, drawl, whine, nasality, stridor; speech impediment, speech defect, lisping, stammer, stutter, mispronunciation; ventriloquism

7 **regional** *or* **local pronunciation,** argot, patois, localism, accent, guttural accent, clipped accent, brogue, burr, twang; Africanism, Afro-Americanism, American accent, Southern accent, Boston accent, Brooklyn accent, Midwestern accent, New England accent, Cajun dialect, Texas accent, Mid-Atlantic accent; British accent, Oxford accent, Cornish accent, Welsh accent, Scottish accent, Irish accent, cockney accent; Briticism, Anglicism, Irishism, Hibernicism, Teutonism, Gallicism; hybrid language, broken English, pidgin English, Canadian French, Pennsylvania Dutch *or* German, Australian English, strine, Franglais; dialectology, speech community, isogloss

8 **vernacular,** vulgar tongue, colloquial speech, idiomatic speech, idiom, dialect, patois, *parole* [Fr]; parlance, private language, code, idiolect, slang, cant, jargon, gobbledegook, computerese, technobabble, newspeak, patter, chat, natter, chatter, psychobabble, lingo
  ▸ *Linguistics, Language 5; Communications 169; Address 209; Conversation 210*

9 **articulation,** diction, elocution, enunciation, phonation, vocalization, voicing, utterance, delivery, attack;

sign language, meaningful look, gesticulation, gesture, body language

▶ *Sign 183*

10 utterance, vocalization, spoken word, word of mouth, word, phrase, sentence, expression, locution, syllable, remark, observation, comment, dictum, statement, affirmation, assertion, averment, declaration, pronouncement, allegation, thought, reflection, interjection, exclamation, ejaculation, gasp, mutter, murmur, whisper, aside, question, answer, reply, response, address, greeting, opinion, two cents worth, contribution, say; crack [Inf]

▶ *Affirmation 189*

11 public speaking, speech, oration, address, welcoming address, panegyric, eulogy, encomium, farewell oration, farewell address; valedictory, obsequies, after-dinner speech, vote of thanks; reading, recital, declaration, broadcast; sermon, exhortation, homily; harangue, mouthful, earful, tirade, diatribe, invective, obloquy, flea in one's ear, lecture, dissertation, peroration; preamble, proem, prologue, foreword; monologue, soliloquy; oratory, stump oratory, rhetoric, speechmaking, speechifying, tub-thumping, declamation, ranting, rant, soapbox oratory

▶ *Dissertation 203; Address 209; Soliloquy 211*

12 speaker, utterer, talker, sayer, chatterer, prattler, gossip, gossiper, yenta [Inf]; communicator, conversationalist, interlocutor; monologist, soliloquizer, soliloquist; public speaker, after-dinner speaker, speech-maker, speechifier, orator, rhetorician; ranter, soapbox orator, tub-thumper, haranguer, demagogue; preacher, sermonizer, lecturer; presenter, announcer, broadcaster; actor, narrator, chorus; spokesperson, spokesman, spokeswoman, delegate; advocate, mediator, intermediary; salesperson, salesman, saleswoman, representative, rep [Inf]; smooth-talker, bigmouth, blabbermouth [Inf]

▶ *Drama and Theater 136; Radio and Television 172; Conversation 210; Soliloquy 211; Display 843*

ADJECTIVES

13 spoken, oral, uttered, said, articulated, voiced, vocalized, pronounced, enunciated, spoken aloud; unwritten, nuncupative, lingual, linguistic, vocal; viva voce, parol

14 phonetic, phonic, tonic, tonal, pitched, accented, stressed, unstressed, unaccented, nasal, twangy, throaty, guttural, aspirated, aspirate, voiced, voiceless

▶ *Linguistics, Language 5*

15 speaking, talking, able to speak, with a tongue in one's head; talkative, loquacious, voluble, free-speaking, plain-spoken, outspoken; loud-spoken, soft-spoken, quietly spoken, well-spoken; wordy, prolix; monolingual, unilingual, bilingual, trilingual, multilingual, polyglottic, monoglottic

▶ *Talkativeness 207*

16 articulate, eloquent, fluent, silver-tongued, smooth-talking, rhetorical, grandiloquent, magniloquent, tub-thumping, ranting, declamatory, bombastic, dithyrambic

VERBS

17 speak, talk, say, utter, declare, proclaim, state, aver, assert, affirm, allege, tell, relate, recite, quote, cite, give utterance to, enunciate, voice, express, verbalize, put into words, find words for, find words to express, formulate, convey, impart, communicate, disclose, blurt out, interject, exclaim, ejaculate, interrupt, have one's say, answer, reply, respond, call attention to, refer to, allude to, mention

▶ *Disclosure 180; Affirmation 189*

18 speak in a particular way, breathe, whisper, murmur, mutter, mumble; sigh, gasp, pant, pipe, flute, warble, coo; speak loudly, speak up, shout, yell, cry, bawl, roar, boom, thunder, trumpet, blare, scream, shriek, screech, exclaim; sing out, chant, cackle, crow, bark, yelp, growl, snap, snarl, squeak, whine, sob, wail, drawl, sibilate

▶ *Loudness 232; Harsh Sound 238; Human Cry 239*

19 speak to, address, talk to, apostrophize, discourse, lecture, sermonize, preach, hold forth, orate, deliver a speech, make speeches, speechify, take the floor, perorate, rant, tub-thump, rail, harangue, invoke, appeal to

▶ *Talkativeness 207; Address 209; Conversation 210; Improvisation 396; Flattery 439*

20 talk to oneself, soliloquize

▶ *Soliloquy 211*

ADVERBS

21 orally, vocally, verbally, viva voce, by word of mouth, phonetically, linguistically, eloquently, articulately, rhetorically, grandiloquently, magniloquently

206 Speech Difficulty

NOUNS

1 speech difficulty, voicelessness, loss of voice, no voice, aphonia, dysphonia; inarticulation, inarticulateness, difficulty in speaking, speech defect; hoarseness, huskiness, croakiness; changing voice, breaking voice; thickness of voice, raucousness, harsh voice; unmusicality, tuneless voice

▶ *Harsh Sound 238*

2 speech defect, speech impediment, aphasia, dysphasia; dysphemia, stammer, stammering, stutter, stuttering, lisp, lisping, sibilation, lallation; unintelligible speech, babbling

▶ *Hissing Sound 237; Lack of Meaning 362; Unintelligibility 364*

3 mutism, deaf-mutism, muteness, dumbness, speechlessness

▶ *Taciturnity 208; Deafness 229; Silence 231*

4 **voiceless speech,** sign language, American Sign Language *or* ASL *or* Ameslan; sign, gesture, gesticulation, signal, meaningful look

▶ *Sign 183; Deafness 229*

ADJECTIVES

5 **voiceless,** unvoiced, aphonic, dysphonic; inarticulate, inaudible; breaking, cracked, hoarse, husky, croaking, with a frog in one's throat

▶ *Silence 231; Faintness of Sound 233*

6 **inarticulate,** aphasic, dysphasic; dysphemic, stammering, stuttering, lisping, sibilant, hissing; unintelligible, babbling

▶ *Unintelligibility 364*

7 **speechless,** mute, dumb, tongue-tied; silenced, gagged, choked; dumbfounded, struck dumb

▶ *Taciturnity 208; Silence 231; Surprise 292*

VERBS

8 **be voiceless,** not speak, be silent, keep quiet, keep mum, hold one's tongue, not breathe a word, button one's lip

9 **have difficulty speaking,** stammer, stutter, lisp, hiss; lose one's voice, be struck dumb, lose one's powers of speech, lose one's tongue; use sign language, sign, gesture, gesticulate; babble

▶ *Sign 183*

10 **strike dumb,** make mute, dumbfound, take one's breath away; muffle, mute, deaden, silence, hush, gag, suppress, reduce to silence

▶ *Silence 231*

ADVERBS

11 **voicelessly,** silently, hoarsely, huskily

207 Talkativeness

Revolutions are always verbose. — LEON TROTSKY

NOUNS

1 **talkativeness,** loquacity, loquaciousness, volubility, garrulousness, garrulity; verbosity, wordiness; prolixity, logorrhea, logomania, runaway tongue, long-windedness, windiness; fluency, glibness, fluent tongue, eloquence; flow of words, chattiness, bigmouth, gabbiness; [Inf]: gassiness, verbal diarrhea, gift of the gab, spiel

▶ *Diffuseness 199; Speech, Spoken Language 205*

2 **effusiveness,** effusion, gushiness, gush; candor, openness, frankness; communicativeness, sociability

▶ *Sociability 408*

3 **talk,** small talk, chat, chatter, chattering; empty talk, babble, gabble, jabber, jabbering, prattle, prating, palaver; gossip, idle gossip, tittle-tattle; [Inf]: rap, gab, blab, chinwag, gas, hot air, yak *or* yack *or* yackety-yak, jaw, guff, blah-blah-blah

▶ *Speech, Spoken Language 205; Conversation 210; Lack of Meaning 362*

4 **talker,** speaker, nonstop talker, chatterer, chatterbox, babbler, jabberer; informer, gossip, tattler, tittle-tattler, driveler; ranter, bigmouth; magpie, jay; [Inf]: blabber, blabbermouth, gabber, gasser, gasbag, windbag, motor-mouth

ADJECTIVES

5 **talkative,** loquacious, voluble, garrulous; verbose, wordy, prolix, long-winded, windy; chattering, babbling, gabbling, jabbering, gibbering, running on; fluent, glib, eloquent; gassy [Inf], gabby [Inf]

▶ *Diffuseness 199; Speech, Spoken Language 205*

6 **effusive,** gushing, expansive; candid, frank; communicative, sociable, chatty, conversational; gossipy, tattling; prattling, prating, bigmouthed, all mouth, mouthy; [Inf]: blabbing, yakking, lippy, flip

▶ *Conversation 210; Sociability 408*

VERBS

7 **be talkative,** talk, chat, chatter, talk at length, go on and on; babble, gabble, jabber, gibber, prate, natter, prattle on, rattle on, ramble on, talk too much; spin out, expatiate; gush, hold forth; drone on, bore, buttonhole, monopolize the conversation, not let anyone get a word in edgeways; like the sound of one's own voice, talk nineteen to the dozen, talk one's head off; oil one's tongue, have a big mouth, talk until one is blue in the face; [Inf]: gab, blab, blah, jaw, gas, run off at the mouth, spout

8 **outtalk,** shout down, bamboozle; filibuster, stonewall

▶ *Sophistry 330*

ADVERBS

9 **talkatively,** loquaciously; volubly, garrulously; fluently, glibly, eloquently

10 **effusively,** gushingly, expansively; candidly, frankly; sociably, communicatively, chattily

208 Taciturnity

The most precious things in speech are pauses.
— RALPH RICHARDSON

NOUNS

1 **taciturnity,** quietness, reticence, reserve; diffidence, shyness, incommunicativeness, uncommunicativeness; shortness, brevity, brusqueness, curtness

▶ *Secrecy 182*

2 **silence,** muteness, dumbness, voicelessness; speechlessness, inarticulateness

▶ *Speech Difficulty 206; Silence 231*

3 **guarded speech,** laconism *or* laconicism, conciseness, succinctness, terseness

▶ *Conciseness 198*

ADJECTIVES

4 **taciturn,** quiet, reticent, reserved, diffident, with-

drawn, shy; incommunicative, uncommunicative, unforthcoming; not to be drawn out, mum, tight-lipped; antisocial, unsociable, self-contained

▶ *Unsociability 409*

5 **silent,** mute, dumb, voiceless; speechless, inarticulate

▶ *Speech Difficulty 206; Silence 231*

6 **sparing with words,** short, brief, saying little, laconic, terse, succinct, concise, monosyllabic; guarded, cautious, playing one's cards close to one's chest, secretive, with sealed lips; uninformative, vague, evasive, cagey; brusque, gruff, curt

▶ *Secrecy 182; Caution 287*

VERBS

7 **be taciturn,** spare one's words, use few words, have little to say; stay silent, keep quiet, say nothing, make no answer, keep one's counsel; refuse to comment, neither confirm nor deny; hold one's tongue, keep one's mouth shut, keep to oneself, keep one's trap shut [Inf]

8 **lapse into silence,** have the words taken out of one's mouth, lose one's voice, dry up; not mention, leave out, pass over; waste no words over, save one's breath, pipe down [Inf]

ADVERBS

9 **taciturnly,** quietly, reticently, incommunicatively, uncommunicatively; silently, voicelessly, without speaking, without a word

209 Address

Addresses are given to us to conceal our whereabouts.
— SAKI [H. H. MUNRO]

NOUNS

1 **address,** lecture, discourse; recitation, recital, reading, talk, presentation; speech, oration, public speech, formal speech, set speech, prepared speech, allocution, apostrophe; disquisition, declamation; tirade, diatribe, earful, invective, harangue, rant, screed, philippic; rodomontade; jeremiad; sermon, homily; mouthful [Inf]

▶ *Literature 139; Speech, Spoken Language 205*

2 **salutation,** greeting, salaam, hail; salutatory address, address of welcome, valedictory address, valedictory, valediction, inaugural address; pep talk, exhortation, peroration, appeal, invocation, interpellation; interjection

▶ *Courtesy 410; Request 505*

3 **approach,** method, way, mode, line, attack

▶ *Means 102; Way 691*

4 **place of residence,** residence, domicile, habitation, abode, home, house, habitat; location, whereabouts, house number, number, road *or* street name, district, zip code

▶ *Habitat 60; Location 565*

5 **public speaker,** speechmaker, lecturer, discourser, reader; orator, rhetorician, silver-tongued orator, soapbox orator, stump orator; spokesperson, spokesman, spokeswoman; declaimer, ranter, tub-thumper, rabble-rouser, demagogue; pulpiteer, preacher, sermonizer; pontificator, expositor, expounder

ADJECTIVES

6 **addressing,** oratorical, speech-making, rhetorical, silver-tongued; declamatory, ranting, tub-thumping; demagogic, demagogical; preaching, sermonizing, pontificating

7 **salutatory,** greeting, hailing, welcoming; exhorting, appealing, invocating; vocative, invocatory, valedictory

VERBS

8 **address,** speak, talk, lecture, apostrophize; take the floor, give a talk, make a speech *or* presentation, deliver an address; discourse, speechify, hold forth; declaim, orate, perorate, pontificate; harangue, rant, tub-thump, rabble-rouse; sermonize, preach

▶ *Speech, Spoken Language 205*

9 **appeal to,** address, invoke, pray to, apply to, find a way to; entreat, petition, go cap in hand to

▶ *Request 505*

10 **approach,** accost, buttonhole; call to, salute, hail, greet, say good morning to; pass the time of day with, parley with, converse with

▶ *Conversation 210; Courtesy 410*

11 **send,** direct, address; consign, transmit, dispatch; post, mail; seal, stamp, frank; send on, forward, redirect, readdress

▶ *Communications 169*

12 **title,** entitle; style, term, call sir *or* madam

▶ *Title 72; Courtesy 410*

13 **address oneself to,** go in for, take up, undertake, engage in; apply oneself to, devote oneself to

▶ *Undertaking 391*

ADVERBS

14 **oratorically,** rhetorically; demagogically, exhortingly, exhortatively; sermonically

210 Conversation

There is no such thing as conversation. There are intersecting monologues, that is all. — REBECCA WEST

NOUNS

1 **conversation,** talk, chat, dialogue, duologue, interlocution, colloquy, discourse; intercourse, verbal intercourse, social intercourse, communication, intercommunication; communion

▶ *Communications 169; Address 209*

2 **chat,** natter, small talk, table talk; friendly talk, tête-à-tête, fireside chat, cozy chat, causerie; idle talk, prat-

tle, tattle; tittle-tattle, gossip, idle gossip, chitchat; repartee, banter, confabulation; [Inf]: confab, heart-to-heart, backchat

▶ *Talkativeness 207*

3 debate, debating, exchange of views, discussion, colloquium, consultation; polemics, dialectic, talks, high-level talks, summit talks; negotiations, bargaining, treaty making

▶ *Negotiation 460*

4 interview, audience, audition; interrogation, interlocution, examination; question-and-answer session

▶ *Question 333; Answer 334*

5 place for conversation, social gathering, social, party, soirée; conference, parley, congress, conclave, meeting, gathering, assembly, convention; forum, open forum, symposium, seminar, council, round-table conference; huddle, putting heads together; summit, summit meeting; powwow [Inf]

▶ *Assembly 59; Sociability 408*

6 conversationalist, converser, talker, discourser, confabulator, colloquist, interlocutor; interviewer, examiner, cross-examiner, interrogator, interpellator; inquirer, respondent

7 chatterer, natterer, gossip, tittle-tattler; [Inf]: gasser, gasbag, windbag

ADJECTIVES

8 conversing, talking, chatting; interlocutory, confabulatory; talkative, loquacious, communicative, unreserved

▶ *Talkativeness 207*

9 discussing, conferring, conferential; in conference, in committee; consultative *or* consultatory, advisory

10 conversational, chatty, colloquial, informal, gossipy; informative, newsy [Inf]

VERBS

11 converse, discourse, talk together, talk, speak, parley, communicate, commune, confabulate; have a talk, hold a conversation, engage in conversation, carry on a conversation; have a word with, have a quick word with; exchange words, exchange pleasantries, pass the time of day; chew the fat [Inf]

12 chat, natter, chatter, prattle, prate, gossip, have a chat,

talk tête-à-tête, go into a huddle, put heads together, talk privately, whisper together, have a heart-to-heart [Inf]

13 confer, hold a conference, parley, sit down together, meet around a conference table, gather around the table; talk over, thrash out, debate, discuss, exchange views; sit in council, sit in committee, consider the pros and cons, deliberate, analyze; canvass, consult, refer to; negotiate, bargain; hold talks, hold a summit; hold a council; powwow [Inf]

ADVERBS

14 conversationally, colloquially, informally, tête-à-tête; loquaciously, communicatively, unreservedly; off the record

211 Soliloquy

soliloquy, n. *An utterance or discourse by a person who is talking to himself or herself or who is disregardful of or oblivious to any hearers present.*

— RANDOM HOUSE DICTIONARY OF THE ENGLISH LANGUAGE

NOUNS

1 soliloquy, monologue, monology, monody, monodrama, interior monologue, stream of consciousness, apostrophe, aside, one-man *or* one-woman show

▶ *One 788*

2 soliloquist, soliloquizer, monologist, monodist

ADJECTIVES

3 soliloquizing, monologic, monological, apostrophic, monodramatic, soloistic, thinking aloud, talking to oneself

VERBS

4 soliloquize, monologize, talk to oneself, talk to the wall, have an audience of one, say to oneself, tell oneself, think aloud; apostrophize

5 monopolize the conversation, do all the talking, hold forth without interruption

▶ *Talkativeness 207*

ADVERBS

6 soliloquizingly, monodically, monologically

The Senses

212 Sensation

O for a Life of Sensations rather than of Thoughts!
— JOHN KEATS

NOUNS

1 sensation, feeling, awareness, sentience, perception, experience, sense perception; impression, sense datum, sensum; response, reaction, receptivity, receptiveness; consciousness, emotion, sentiment; the senses, sight, hearing, touch, taste, smell; sixth sense, second sight, extrasensory perception (ESP), telepathy, clairvoyance; agitation, excitement, thrill, esthesia, esthesis
  ‣ *Physical Pleasure 214*

2 sensitivity, feelings, susceptibility; irritability, tenderness, thin skin, vulnerability, soft underbelly; hyperesthesia, prickliness, ticklishness, touchiness, delicacy; sensuousness, sensuality; warm-bloodedness, oversensitivity, allergy; threshold *or* limen
  ‣ *Physical Pain 215*

3 stimulus, goad, prick, stimulant, heightener, thrill; stimulus response, throb, prickle, tingle, frisson, fluttering, buzz, kick, tickle, itch, horripilation, goose pimples, goose flesh, shivers, formication; pins and needles, sore spot, titillation, stimulation, the creeps [Inf], heebie-jeebies [Inf]

4 sense organ, eye, ear, nose, tongue, hand, finger, fingertip, skin; feeler, toucher, whisker, antenna, proboscis, tentacle, paw, flipper; sensorium, nervous system, nerve, nerve fiber, raw nerve, nerve end *or* nerve ending, nerve cell, neuron, nerve center
  ‣ *Human Body 19*

ADJECTIVES

5 sensate, perceptible, audible, visible, tactile, palpable, tangible, noticeable; sensory, sensorial
  ‣ *Touch 216; Hearing 228; Vision 242*

6 sensible, sensitive, aware, aware of, alive to, sentient, sensuous, feeling, percipient; conscious, awake, wide awake; clued in

7 susceptible, impressionable, perceptive, responsive, oversensitive, allergic; thin-skinned, delicate, tender; touchy, irritable, tetchy, jumpy, excited, temperamental, agitated, irritated; stimulated, thrilled, hot-blooded, stirred, overexcited, hyperactive, hyped-up [Inf]

8 exciting, sensational, titillating, thrilling, stimulating, keen, breathtaking, impressive, stirring, emotive, poignant, striking, electric, electrifying, hair-raising, itchy, prickly, tingly, tickly

VERBS

9 sense, perceive, see, hear, touch, taste, smell, feel, realize, experience; be sensitive, be alive to, respond, react, tingle, prickle, tickle, itch, be itchy, be irritated, be irritable; shiver, have goose flesh *or* goose pimples, horripilate; be aware, be aware of, detect

10 awake, wake up, wake, waken, regain consciousness, come to one's senses, be on a high, have one's wits about one, be on the ball, stretch one's nerves

11 arouse sensation, enliven, activate, galvanize, stir, quicken, disturb, agitate, impress, invigorate, animate; stimulate, titillate, whet, cause a sensation, thrill, excite, arouse; touch a raw nerve, heighten awareness, raise one's consciousness
  ‣ *Physical Pleasure 214*

ADVERBS

12 sensationally, feelingly, emotionally, thrillingly, excitingly

213 Insensibility

NOUNS

1 insensibility, lack of feeling, lack of awareness, lack of sensation, analgesia, paralysis, anesthesia; clumsiness, heavy-handedness, dullness, insensitiveness, apathy
  ‣ *Insensitivity 268*

2 desensitization, narcotization, stupefaction, hypnosis, numbness, paralysis; unconsciousness, faint, swoon, sleep, doze, snooze, nap, catnap; sleepiness, somnolence; coma, torpor, stupor, trance, suspended animation

3 **anesthetic,** anesthesia, painkiller, analgesic, narcotic, opium, laudanum, dope [Inf], drug, ether, novocaine, cocaine, pethidine, barbiturate, halothane, lignocaine, acupuncture, hypnosis, sleeping pill, somnifacient, sleeping draught, knockout drops, tranquilizer; Mickey or Mickey Finn [Inf]

▶ *Medicine 107; Remedy 115; Substance Abuse 121*

ADJECTIVES

4 **insensible,** unfeeling, blind, deaf, insentient, nerveless, senseless, insensitive; clumsy, heavy-handed, unresponsive, impassive, cold-blooded, apathetic, oblivious, unmindful, forgetful, unwary, impervious, unemotional, hardened, stolid

5 **desensitized,** unconscious, stunned, concussed, comatose, asleep, out cold [Inf], catatonic, out for the count, dead to the world, knocked out; anesthetized, etherized, torpid, drugged, frozen, paralyzed, hypnotized, insensible, numb, inert, deadened; zonked [Inf]

6 **anesthetic,** analgesic, deadening, numbing, hypnotic; narcotic, soporific, somnific, somniferous, sleepy, somnolent, dopey [Inf], drowsy, fuzzy, woozy

VERBS

7 **be insensible,** be unfeeling, be impassive, be apathetic, be oblivious; be unconscious; drowse, doze, sleep, sleepwalk, somnambulate, fall asleep, go to sleep, nod off, drop off, faint, pass out, black out, shut off, shut oneself off, switch off, ignore

8 **anesthetize,** render insensible, etherize, put to sleep, put under, desensitize, deaden, blunt, benumb, freeze, hypnotize, mesmerize, narcotize, stun, stupefy, knock out, brain, render unconscious, concuss

ADVERBS

9 **insensibly,** unfeelingly, bluntly, insensitively, sleepily, drowsily, somnolently, unconsciously, obliviously, imperceptibly

214 Physical Pleasure

All the things I really like to do are either immoral, illegal, or fattening. — ALEXANDER WOOLLCOTT

NOUNS

1 **physical pleasure,** sensual pleasure, sensualism, hedonism, pleasure principle; dissipation, carnality, voluptuousness, sexual pleasure, eroticism, titillation, sexual intercourse, arousal, satisfaction, gratification, orgasm, climax, masturbation; sensuousness, loveliness, softness, smoothness, tastiness, sweetness, fragrance, melodiousness

▶ *Sex 20; Music 140; Touch 216; Taste 219; Sweetness 222; Fragrance 226*

2 **pleasure,** pleasant sensation, good feeling, well-being, ease, contentment, comfort, pleasantness, coziness, enjoyment, conviviality; fun, zest, *joie de vivre* [Fr], happiness, felicity, delight, bliss, euphoria; indulgence, the good life, luxury, opulence; self-indulgence, self-gratification, profligacy, gourmandizing, epicureanism, kick [Inf]

▶ *Pleasantness 271; Self-Indulgence 456; Ease 819*

3 **good time,** happy hour, fun time, whale of a time; wine, women, and song; bread and circuses, *la dolce vita* [Ital]; [Inf]: life of Riley, just what the doctor ordered, just the ticket

▶ *Pleasantness 271; Wealth 485; Softness 543; Ease 819; Prosperity 847*

4 **pleasure-seeker,** jet-setter, connoisseur, bon vivant, epicure, epicurean, gourmet, gourmand; lotus-eater, sybarite, sensualist, hedonist, voluptuary

▶ *Desire 288*

5 **idealized pleasure,** easy street, bed of roses, land of milk and honey, Elysium, Elysian fields, heaven, heaven on earth, earthly paradise

ADJECTIVES

6 **pleasurable,** sensual, titillating, seductive, sexy, erotic, carnal, voluptuous; tasty, palatable, appetizing, delicious, flavorful, mouth-watering, ambrosial, sweet, succulent, sweet-scented, perfumed, fragrant; euphonious, dulcet, mellifluous

▶ *Taste 219; Fragrance 226*

7 **pleasant,** comfortable, easeful, restful, relaxing, soothing, comforting, warm, congenial, agreeable, likable, nice; pleasing, pleasurable, satisfying, gratifying, attractive, refreshing, enjoyable, convivial; delectable, charming, delightful

8 **luscious,** opulent, luxuriant, luxurious, exquisite, sumptuous, de luxe, lush; lovely, silken, smooth, fun, welcome, inviting, snug, cozy, soft, cuddly, cuddlesome, lovable, blissful; scrumptious, cushy [Inf]

9 **pleased,** relaxed, comfortable, warm, snug, content, contented, at ease, delighted; gratified, satisfied, coddled, mollycoddled, cosseted, pampered, merry, euphoric; [Inf]: tickled pink, snug as a bug in a rug, high, turned-on, on a high

10 **pleasure-seeking,** hedonistic, fun-loving, wanton, sybaritic, aroused, excited, licentious; sensual, self-indulgent, profligate, voluptuous

11 **idyllic,** Elysian, paradisiacal *or* paradisiac, heavenly, divine

VERBS

12 **feel pleasure,** feel good, enjoy, relish, revel in, take pleasure in, enjoy oneself, please oneself, have fun, bask, bask in, indulge oneself; savor, gourmandize, splurge, luxuriate, wallow, purr, nestle; enjoy sex, climax; have a ball [Inf], get a kick out of [Inf]

13 **give pleasure,** please, cheer, gladden, delight, charm, gratify, indulge, entertain, amuse, treat, regale; cuddle,

hug, fondle, pet, stimulate, arouse, tickle, titillate, thrill, excite; satisfy, sate, satiate, warm the cockles of one's heart, take one's fancy, tickle pink [Inf]

14 **comfort,** ease, relieve, slake, alleviate, appease, salve, soothe, soften, sympathize with, offer sympathy to, refresh, content, hug, cuddle, warm, mother, pet, make comfortable, coddle, mollycoddle, cosset, pamper, spoil

ADVERBS

15 **pleasingly,** sensually, satisfyingly, luxuriously, indulgently, enjoyably, comfortably, happily, painlessly, warmly, cozily, blissfully, with pleasure, for kicks

215 Physical Pain

There was a faith-healer of Deal, / Who said, "Although pain isn't real, / If I sit on a pin / And it punctures my skin, / I dislike what I fancy I feel." — ANONYMOUS

NOUNS

1 **pain,** hurt, painfulness, hurtfulness, soreness, suffering, dolor [Form], malaise, affliction, discomfort, distress; irritation, tenderness, sore spot; pinprick, pins and needles, twinge, pang, pangs; smarting, throes, cramp, spasm, stitch, stab, grip, lancination; ache, aches and pains, throb, throbbing; agony, anguish, ordeal, torment, hell on earth, martyrdom; punishment, physical punishment, torture
 ◗ *Unpleasantness 272; Punishment 454*

2 **painful condition,** headache, toothache, earache, sore throat, ulcer, hunger pain *or* pang, stomachache, backache, lumbago, sciatica, rheumatism, arthritis, charley horse; heart pain; cramps, dysmenorrhea, labor pain, afterpain

3 **painful injury,** wound, lesion, trauma, scratch, scrape, graze, abrasion, bruise, contusion, bump, hit, sprain, burn, scald, cut, stab, puncture, jab, tear, slash, gash, laceration, bite; fracture, broken bone, bloody nose, black eye; [Inf]: bellyache, tummy ache, shiner
 ◗ *Ill Health 114; Sensitivity 267*

ADJECTIVES

4 **painful,** sore, hurting, uncomfortable, distressing, miserable; chronic, acute, stinging, tingling, smarting, cramping, aching; tender, raw, throbbing, biting, gnawing, gripping; stabbing, shooting, grinding, splitting, pounding; agonizing, exquisite, racking, harrowing, burning, searing, scalding, traumatic, extreme, unbearable, intolerable

5 **injured,** wounded, bruised, grazed, cut, punctured, scraped, sprained, lacerated, torn, fractured, broken, blackened

6 **feeling pain,** pained, suffering, hurting, distressed, sore, hurt, aching, achy, aching all over; anguished, in agony, agonized, convulsed, wincing, writhing, tormented, tortured, afflicted; raw, black-and-blue, bleeding, blistered, traumatized

7 **inflicting pain,** painful, hurtful, hurting, torturing, tormenting, brutal, cruel, sadistic

VERBS

8 **feel pain,** suffer, hurt, ache, agonize, be afflicted, smart, wince, flinch, twitch, chafe, writhe, squirm, go through hell, be a martyr, endure
 ◗ *Courage 284*

9 **be painful,** hurt, sting, tingle, smart, cramp, ache, throb, bite, gnaw, grip, stab, shoot, grind, pound, burn, sear

10 **inflict pain,** pain, hurt, injure, wound, hit, scratch, scrape, graze, prick, pinch, nip, tweak, sting, bruise, contuse, bump, sprain, burn, scald, jab, cut, tear, slash, gash, draw blood, bloody, puncture, run through, impale, fracture, punish, shoot, maul, mangle, savage, bite, claw, knife, stab, beat, beat up, beat black and blue, batter, smash, flog, thrash, convulse, traumatize, excruciate, wring, harrow, torment, torture, rack, martyr, crucify, touch a raw nerve, cut to the quick, give someone a bad time

11 **express pain,** cry, sob, wail, moan, gasp, whimper, groan, squeal, squawk, yelp, scream, shriek, screech, howl, yowl, yell
 ◗ *Human Cry 239*

ADVERBS

12 **painfully,** throbbingly, achingly, excruciatingly, hurtfully, to the quick

216 Touch

NOUNS

1 **touch,** sense of touch, feeling, tactile sensation, impression, sense perception; sensitivity, tactility, tangibility, solidity, concreteness, reality, palpability, texture, consistency, feel, vibration
 ◗ *Sensation 212; Texture 552*

2 **touching,** physical contact, handling, fingering, palpating, manipulating, applying pressure, massaging, stroking, rubbing, holding, grasping, gripping, clutching; laying on of hands, osteopathy, chiropractic, fondling, caressing; [Inf]: petting, groping, goosing

3 **type of touch,** brush, graze, skim, flick, tickle, pinch, nip, tweak, twitch, press, pull, tug, yank, dab, blow, hit, knock, strike, jab, bump, elbow, push, slap, punch, bop, smash, kick, nudge, poke, prod; caress, kiss, fondle, rub, stroke, nuzzle, maul, paw, pet [Inf], grope [Inf]

4 **contiguity,** convergence, confluence, conjunction, meeting, abutment, junction, tangency
 ◗ *Nearness 586; Interface 616; Adhesion 755*

ADJECTIVES

5 **touchable,** palpable, tangible, solid, concrete, material, real, substantial, perceptible, attainable, at hand,

handy, reachable; sensory, tactual, tactile, sensuous, sensitive to touch, sensitive, tender

6 **touching,** brushing, grazing, skimming, flicking, tickling, *etc.*

7 **handling,** light-handed, neat, delicate; heavy-handed, clumsy; manual, hand-operated, touch-operated, hands-on

8 **contiguous,** converging, conjoining, meeting, touching; adjacent, adjoining, bordering, abutting, intersecting, glancing, colliding, crashing, overlapping, interfacing, connecting; hand in hand, hand-in-glove, tangent, tangential

▶ *Nearness 586; Interface 616*

VERBS

9 **touch,** contact, feel, finger, handle, palpate, manipulate, maneuver, press; massage, rub, rub noses, nuzzle, knead, caress, kiss, stroke; fumble, fondle, maul, paw, grope; graze, skim, shave, brush; flick, tickle, nip, pinch, stick, tweak, twitch; pull, pluck, tug, yank; hit, strike, pat, tap, dab, knock, slap, bat, punch, smash, kick; jab, poke, prod, nudge, elbow; play with, tamper with, tinker, tinker with, toy with, fiddle, fiddle with; buttonhole, pick up, seize, catch, hold, hold fast, hold on; lay hands on, grab, snatch, clutch, grasp, grip; [Inf]: pet, feel up, grope, goose

10 **be touched by,** feel, be sensitive, tingle, itch

▶ *Sensation 212*

11 **adjoin,** touch, meet, be contiguous, border, abut, intersect, verge on, contact, come into contact, overlap, interface, connect

ADVERBS

12 **palpably,** tangibly, solidly, substantially

13 **manually,** by hand, hand to hand

217 Heat

NOUNS

1 **heat,** hotness, warmness, warmth; lukewarmness, tepidity, tepidness, temperature, room temperature; radiant heat, body heat, blood heat, warm-bloodedness; raised temperature, calescence, high temperature; fever, pyrexia, feverishness, inflammation, flush, hot flush, blush; stuffiness, fug; steam, steaminess, overheating, sweatiness, sweat, perspiration; white heat, incandescence, flash point, melting point, boiling point; burn, first-degree burn, second-degree burn, third-degree burn

▶ *Fuel 106; Medicine 107*

2 **heat measurement,** temperature, calorific value, joule, calorie, kilocalorie, heat unit, British thermal unit (BTU), therm; calorimeter, thermometer, clinical thermometer, thermograph, thermostat; Fahrenheit scale, Celsius scale, centigrade scale, Réaumur scale, specific heat, latent heat

▶ *Measurement 589*

3 **heater,** warmer, heating element, space heater, space heating, fan heater, convection heater, gas heater, central heating, radiator, furnace, hot-water tank, hot-water pipe, boiler, immersion heater, geyser [Brit]; underfloor heating, hypocaust, hot-air vent *or* duct; solar heating, solar panel, antifreeze, ethylene glycol, deicer; double glazing, lagging, insulation, polystyrene; sunlamp, foot warmer, poultice, fomentation, warming pan, hot-water bottle, electric blanket; iron, mangle, branding iron, soldering iron, crucible, thermos

4 **burner,** stove, cooker, kitchen range; hot plate, grill, griddle, toaster, waffle iron, sandwich maker, barbecue pit, spit; oven, toaster oven, microwave oven, Dutch oven

▶ *Cooking 91*

5 **hot place,** tropics, equator, Torrid Zone, Africa, South Pacific, Amazon Basin, desert, Sahara, Kalahari, Gobi, Death Valley; sun deck, solarium, sauna, steam bath; furnace, oven; hell

6 **hot weather,** summer, warm spell, hot spell, long hot summer, midday sun, warm front; heat wave, tropical heat, sultriness; thaw, melting, global warming, greenhouse effect, warming of the earth's atmosphere; hot day, sizzler [Inf], scorcher [Inf]

▶ *Meteorology and Climatology 9; Light 246; Season 654*

7 **effects of hot weather,** sunbathing, sunbath, suntan, tan, tanning, browning, bronzing, sunburn, peeling, redness, blister, heat rash, sunstroke, heat exhaustion, heatstroke

8 **fire,** combustion, flame, flames, blaze, glow, conflagration, holocaust, fireball, smoke; bonfire, beacon fire, forest fire, house fire; sheet of fire, sea of flames, towering inferno; flammability, inflammability, combustibility, spontaneous combustion, ignition

▶ *Fuel 106; Light 246*

9 **place for fire,** fireplace, hearth, chimney corner, inglenook, grate, hearthstone, flue, chimney, brazier, kiln, furnace, smelter, forge, oast-house *or* oast [Brit]; pyre, funeral pyre, coal fire, open fire, wood fire, campfire, wood stove, firebox, gas fire, gas jet, pilot light, gas oven, kerosene stove, Bunsen burner, electric fire, heat lamp; stake, crematorium

10 **cause of fire,** match, lighter, incinerator, firebrand, torch, blowtorch, flamethrower, oxyacetylene torch; arson, pyromania, firebomb, incendiary bomb, Greek fire, wildfire, firestorm; arsonist, pyromaniac, incendiary, firebomber, firebug [Inf]

ADJECTIVES

11 **hot,** thermal, thermic; warm, mild, tepid, lukewarm, room-temperature, snug; stuffy, fuggy; blistering, scorching, sizzling [Inf], sweltering; red-hot, white-hot, incandescent, candent, molten, glowing; hot as hell, hot enough to fry an egg on

12 **heating,** warming, calefacient, calorific; overheated,

suffocating, piping hot, baking hot, fiery, fierce, scalding, searing, scorching, cauterizing, roasting, boiling, on the boil; simmering, steaming, smoking, smoldering

13 **warm,** balmy, temperate, springlike, mild, fair, clement, summery, sunny; sunbaked, humid, muggy, close, steamy, sticky, stifling, sultry, subtropical, tropical, equatorial; warm as toast

14 **warm-blooded,** mammalian, homoiothermal
   ▸ *Mammals 35; Sensitivity 267; Pity 308*

15 **heated,** warmed up, warmed through, defrosted, heated up, preheated, baked, roasted, boiled, toasted, reheated, burned, fired, burned-out, burned down, singed, scorched, molten; insulated, lined, padded, double-glazed, lagged, centrally heated, coal-fired, coal-burning, wood-burning, gas-fired, oil-fired

16 **on fire,** alight, flaming, in flames, burning, ablaze, flaring, burned to a crisp, burned to a cinder; burnable, inflammable, flammable, combustible, incendiary; igneous, caustic, thermonuclear, volcanic, pyrogenic

VERBS

17 **heat,** heat up, glow, heat through, defrost, thaw, melt, de-ice; warm, warm up, reheat, cook, roast, toast, simmer, boil, scald, parboil, steam, bake, stew, braise, broil, fry; parch, wither, shrivel up, melt down, smelt, solder, weld, fuse, lag, insulate, line, pad; rub, chafe, take the chill off, stamp one's feet

18 **burn,** set fire to, set on fire, fire, set alight, torch, kindle, ignite, put a match to, catch fire, be on fire; flame, flare, blaze, crackle, smoke, fume, smolder, burn up, burn down, burn out, singe, scorch, sear, calcine, char, carbonize; cremate, incinerate; vaporize, cauterize, brand, reduce to ashes, burn to a cinder, burn at the stake, burn to the ground, burst into flames, go up in flames

19 **feel hot,** be hot, keep warm, dress warmly; get overheated, blush, flush, sweat, perspire; run a temperature, be feverish; swelter, bask, sunbathe, sun oneself, suntan, tan, get a tan, brown, burn, peel, blister, sizzle [Inf]

ADVERBS

20 **warmly,** hotly, ardently, fierily, feverishly, to the boiling point, to a cinder

218 Cold

*Cold dark deep and absolutely clear / element bearable to
no mortal, / to fish and to seals . . .* — ELIZABETH BISHOP

NOUNS

1 **cold,** coldness, lack of heat, chill, chilliness, coolness, chilling, cooling, low temperature; freshness, nippiness; cryogenics

2 **freezing,** frost, freezing cold, icing, iciness, frigidity, gelidity, algidity, sub-zero temperature, absolute zero; cryonics

   ▸ *Physics 10*

3 **chills,** shivers, cold in the head; chilblain, frostbite, shakes [Inf]

4 **cooler,** air conditioner, fan, punkah, refrigerator, fridge [Inf], icebox, ice bag, ice bucket, ice pack, ice house, ice machine, freezer, deep freezer, refrigerator-freezer, cooling tower; refrigerant, coolant, liquid oxygen, lox *or* LOX, cryogen, cryostat

   ▸ *Physics 10; Cooking 91*

5 **ice,** ice cube, cracked ice, frosting, glaze, dry ice, glacier, ice sheet, pack ice, icecap, ice field, ice floe; frost, frostiness, hoar frost, white frost, rime, freeze-up, black frost, hard frost, black ice, icicle; frozen rain, sleet, Jack Frost

6 **snow,** snow flurry, snowfall, snowstorm, blizzard, whiteout; snowflake, snow crystal, wet snow, slush, powder snow, granular snow, dry snow, driven snow, snowdrift, avalanche, hail, hailstorm, hailstone, snowman, snowball

   ▸ *Skiing, Ice Skating, Bobsledding 162*

7 **cold place,** Alaska, Arctic, Arctic Circle, North Pole, Iceland, Greenland, Siberia; Tierra del Fuego, Antarctica, Antarctic Circle, South Pole; ocean depths, snow house, igloo, freezer

8 **cold weather,** cold spell, cold snap, nippiness, severe weather, nip in the air, cold season, inclemency, cold front; chill factor, wind-chill factor, ice age, winter, wintriness, arctic conditions, dead *or* depths of winter

   ▸ *Meteorology and Climatology 9*

ADJECTIVES

9 **cold,** raw, chill, chilly, cool, coolish, unheated, chilled; fresh, bracing, nippy, invigorating; sharp, inclement, breezy, shivery, pinched, biting, bitter, bleak, wintry, severe; snowy, sleety, frosty, icy, snowbound, snowed in, iced up, icebound; blue with cold, stiff with cold, chilled to the bone *or* marrow; ice-cold, algid, glacial, frigid, freezing

10 **frozen,** gelid, frostbitten, frozen solid *or* stiff, unmelted, quick-frozen, freeze-dried; frosted, hoar, frappé; iced, glazed, on ice, on the rocks; polar, Arctic, Siberian; cold as the grave *or* marble *or* charity

11 **cooled,** air-conditioned, air-cooled, water-cooled, chilled, refrigerated, insulated, refrigerant, frigorific, freezable, freezing, cryogenic, cryonic

12 **cold-blooded,** reptilian, poikilothermal
   ▸ *Reptiles and Amphibians 37; Indifference 289; Pitilessness 309*

VERBS

13 **be cold,** shiver, tremble, shudder, quiver, freeze, have goose flesh *or* goose pimples; catch cold, take a chill, have the shivers

14 **become cold,** cool down, lose heat, cool off, freeze, freeze over, congeal; ice over, ice up; be snowed in, be snowed under, freeze to death, get frostbite, be so cold one's toes *or* fingers drop off *or* one's teeth chatter

15 make cold, chill, freshen, sharpen, air-condition, ventilate, fan, benumb, freeze, refrigerate, glaciate, freeze-dry

ADVERBS

16 coldly, coolly, wintrily, frigidly, icily, bitterly, frostily

219 Taste

NOUNS

1 **taste,** sense of taste, palate, tastiness; pleasant taste, sapidity, deliciousness, palatability; unpleasant taste, unpalatability; sharp taste, acid taste, tart taste, salty taste, spicy taste, sweet taste, sour taste, bitter taste, pungent taste, aftertaste; tongue, taste bud, nose; appetite, taste test, taste treat, tasting cup, tester

  ◗ *Piquancy 221; Sweetness 222; Sourness 223*

2 **appetizer,** hors d'oeuvre, canapé, apéritif, starter [Brit]; tidbit, *bonne bouche* [Fr]; delicacy, dainty, sample, sampler, tapas; drop, morsel, snippet, mouthful, nibble, nip, soupçon, tasting, sampling, gustation, degustation

3 **flavor,** gusto, relish, savor, richness, sweetness, saltiness, sourness, bitterness, strong flavor, delicate flavor, flavoring, seasoning, flavor enhancer

  ◗ *Piquancy 221*

ADJECTIVES

4 **tasty,** palatable, delicious; tastable, edible *or* eatable, esculent, comestible, sapid; tasteful, savorous, savory, appetizing, inviting, relishable, delectable, dainty, epicurean, flavorful *or* flavorsome, ambrosial, potable, drinkable, toothsome, mouth-watering, succulent; sharp, unpleasant, unpalatable, acid, spicy, sweet, sour, tart, bitter, pungent, salty, scrumptious, yummy

  ◗ *Refinement 534*

VERBS

5 **taste,** try, sample, bite, eat, nibble, drink, test, experience, savor, degust, snack; enjoy, appreciate, relish, tickle one's palate, tickle one's fancy

6 **make taste,** add taste to, enhance, flavor, dress, garnish, spice, sauce

  ◗ *Cooking 91*

ADVERBS

7 **tastily,** deliciously, full of flavor, palatably, succulently, sweetly, bitterly, pungently, scrumptiously, mouth-wateringly, tastefully, elegantly

220 Tastelessness

NOUNS

1 **tastelessness,** blandness, mildness, insipidity, insipidness, plainness, unsavoriness, tameness, dullness, vapidness, vapidity, weakness, weakening, thinness, feebleness, adulteration, dilution

2 **dilution,** wateriness, watering, watering down, staleness, flatness, banality, triteness, lifelessness, dryness,

aridity, monotony, boredom, wishy-washiness, jejuneness, dissatisfaction, indifference

  ◗ *Dissatisfaction 274; Indifference 289; Boredom 296; Weakness 517; Oldness 653*

3 **bad taste,** tastelessness, rancidity, nasty taste, rankness, unpalatability

ADJECTIVES

4 **tasteless,** bland, mild, insipid, plain, tame, dull; weak, thin, feeble, flat, stale; dry, arid, humdrum, monotonous, nondescript, unexciting, uninviting, lifeless; flavorless, unflavored, unsalted, unseasoned; watered, watered down, diluted, adulterated, dilute, milk-and-water, unappetizing; banal, trite, uninspired, boring, jejune, unsatisfying; indifferent, characterless, dull as ditchwater *or* dishwater, dry-as-dust, wishy-washy

5 **unpalatable,** unpleasant, rancid, nasty, rank

VERBS

6 **be tasteless,** have no taste, lack flavor, taste stale, taste flat, lose taste, be unappetizing

7 **dilute,** water down, thin, weaken, adulterate

ADVERBS

8 **without taste,** blandly, insipidly, mildly, dully, weakly, flatly, dryly, aridly

221 Piquancy

NOUNS

1 **piquancy,** pungency, strong flavor, spiciness, sting, sharpness, tang, tanginess, smokiness, tartness, bite, kick; sourness, bitterness, gaminess, raciness; poignancy, aroma

  ◗ *Cooking 91; Taste 219; Sourness 223*

2 **seasoning,** flavoring, condiment, salt, sea salt, pepper, black pepper, white pepper, peppercorn, herb, spice

  ◗ *Cooking 91*

3 **curing,** smoking

4 **stimulation,** titillation, liveliness, spirit, zest, archness, harshness, roughness, poignancy

5 **stimulant,** reviver, restorative, tonic, medicinal drink, cordial, nip, toddy, smelling salts, sal volatile, pick-me-up [Inf]

ADJECTIVES

6 **piquant,** pungent, aromatic, flavorful; appetizing, stinging, biting, hot, peppery; seasoned, spiced, herby, savory, tangy, tart, sharp, sour; bitter, minty, highly flavored, highly seasoned, spicy, salty, strong; smoky, smoked, cured; kippered, pickled, soused, gamy, racy

7 **stimulating,** interesting, intriguing, titillating, exciting, lively, restorative, medicinal, provocative, spirited, poignant, arch

VERBS

8 **season,** flavor, salt, pepper, marinate, souse, smoke, kipper, cure, dry, pickle, spice, curry

9 **be piquant,** sting, bite, pique, goad, interest, stimu-

late; revive, restore; titillate, intrigue, excite, provoke, stir

ADVERBS

10 **piquantly,** pungently, aromatically, tartly, sharply, bitterly, medicinally

11 **stimulatingly,** interestingly, intriguingly, provocatively, spiritedly, poignantly

222 Sweetness

NOUNS

1 **sweetness,** sugariness, syrupiness, saccharinity, sweet tooth, fragrance, pleasantness, melodiousness, freshness, smoothness; oversweetness, sickly sweetness
  ▶ *Cooking 91; Fragrance 226; Pleasantness 271; Liking 290; Smoothness 545*

2 **sweetener,** sweetening, sugar, cane sugar, beet sugar, sugar lump, sugar loaf, caster sugar, granulated sugar, powdered sugar, icing sugar, refined sugar, unrefined sugar, brown sugar, demerara sugar; syrup, maple syrup, molasses, treacle [Brit], glycerol; artificial sweetener, saccharine, aspartame, cyclamate; honey, honeycomb, honeydew, jam, jelly, preserve, conserve, marmalade, nectar, delicacy, sweetmeat; fruit, candied fruit, glacé fruit, ambrosia; a spoonful of sugar, sugar and spice and all things nice

3 **confectionery,** candy, sweets, sweeties [Brit], dessert, cookies, cake, pie, pastry, tart, frosting, icing, baked goods, ice cream, sherbet *or* sorbet; candy store, confectioner's, sweet-shop [Brit], bakery, pastry shop
  ▶ *Food 90*

4 **sweet drink,** cocoa, hot chocolate, cordial, fruit juice, squash [Brit], fruit crush, lemonade, orangeade, soft drink, cream soda, ice-cream soda, sherbet [Brit], mead, sweet wine, dessert wine, hot toddy, fruit cup, punch, liqueur
  ▶ *Food 90; Drinking 93*

ADJECTIVES

5 **sweet,** sweetish, sweetened, saccharine, cloying, sickly, sickly-sweet; honeyed, mellifluous, mellifluent, melliferous, sugared, sugary, sugar-coated, treacly, syrupy, ambrosial, nectared, nectarous; candied, crystallized, glazed, iced, frosted; bittersweet, sweet-and-sour, sweet as sugar *or* honey *or* a nut, dulcet [Arch]

6 **pleasant,** fresh, smooth, fragrant, melodious
  ▶ *Physical Pleasure 214*

VERBS

7 **sweeten,** sugar, sugar-coat, candy; honey, ice, frost, glaze, mull, make pleasant, make fragrant, sugar the pill, dulcify, saccharify

ADVERBS

8 **sweetly,** pleasantly, freshly, smoothly, fragrantly, melodiously

223 Sourness

NOUNS

1 **sourness,** sour taste, tartness, bitterness, sharp flavor, sharpness, dryness, acerbity, acidity, astringency, acidulousness, subacidity, vinegariness, unripeness, greenness

2 **unpalatability,** bitterness, gall, acridity, bile, nasty taste, foul taste, staleness, rancidity, mold, rottenness, unwholesomeness, rankness, brackishness, dankness
  ▶ *Tastelessness 220*

3 **sour *or* bitter thing,** crab apple, green apple, lemon, lime, aloes, sloe, vinegar, vinaigrette, bitters, angostura bitters, wormwood, sour milk, sour cream, sloe gin, whiskey sour, dry wine, sour wine, tartaric acid, acetic acid, bile, gall, gall and wormwood

4 **spleen,** rancor, bile, biliousness, crabbedness, moroseness, sullenness, bitterness, sour grapes

ADJECTIVES

5 **acid,** acidic, sharp, sour, tangy, tart, pungent, acerbic, acidulous, lemony, vinegary, acidulated, subacid, unripe, green, immature, hard, unsweetened, dry, acrid, biting, bitter

6 **unpalatable,** unappetizing, uninviting, unsavory, unpleasant, disagreeable, nasty, disgusting, foul-tasting, nauseating, uneatable, inedible, dank, brackish, undrinkable, corked, harsh, stale, rough, rancid, overripe, moldy, rotten, high, bad, off [Brit], curdled, fermented, on the turn, turned, unwholesome, contaminated

7 **splenetic,** rancorous, bilious, sarcastic, harsh, crabbed, crabby, bitter, morose, sullen, grumpy

VERBS

8 **sour,** be sour, go sour, turn sour, acidify, sharpen, taste bad, taste foul, curdle, spoil, turn, ferment, go off, go bad, go moldy, molder, set one's teeth on edge

ADVERBS

9 **sourly,** bitterly, tartly, sharply, drily, pungently, harshly, unpleasantly, inedibly, nauseatingly

10 **splenetically,** rancorously, biliously, harshly, sarcastically, morosely, sullenly, grumpily, bitterly, crabbily

224 Odor

NOUNS

1 **odor,** smell, smelliness, odorousness; scent, sweet smell, fragrance, perfume; unpleasant smell, stench, stink, pong [Brit inf]; slight smell, faint smell; aroma, aromaticity, bouquet, nose; savor, breath; air, suggestion, whiff, waft; smoke, vapor, exhalation, emanation; heady scent, redolence, strong smell, fruitiness, pungency, fresh smell; olfactology, olfactologist, olfactronics, odorimetry, olfactometry
  ▶ *Fragrance 226; Stench 227; Gas 556; Essence 723*

2 **sense of smell,** smelling, act of smelling, olfaction, in-

halation, sniff, sniffing, sniffle, nosing; nose, nostril, naris, nasal cavity, olfactory nerve
  ▶ *Human Body 19*

3 **scent,** trail, scent gland, pheromone
  ▶ *Record 185; Pursuit 385*

4 **reputation,** repute, regard, aura, tone, character, savor, emanation, good odor, bad odor, odor of sanctity, smell of success

ADJECTIVES

5 **odorous,** odoriferous, smelling, olent, redolent, pungent, heady, fragrant, perfumed, scented; smelly, stinking, noisome, noxious; aromatic, savorous, herby, spicy, downwind of, emanative, pheromonal, keen-scented, sharp-nosed
  ▶ *Fragrance 226; Stench 227; Discrimination 337*

6 **olfactory,** olfactive, nasal, rhinological

VERBS

7 **smell,** breathe, breathe in, inhale, sniff, nose, sniff at, smell at, snuff, snuffle, sniffle, sniff out, smell out, nose out, catch a whiff of, get wind of, follow the scent, follow one's nose
  ▶ *Pursuit 385; Air 558*

8 **have odor,** smell, smell of, emanate, exhale, stink, reek, pong [Brit inf]
  ▶ *Stench 227*

9 **impart odor to,** perfume, scent, aromatize
  ▶ *Fragrance 226*

ADVERBS

10 **odorously,** odoriferously, olfactorily, nasally, aromatically, headily, pungently

225 Odorlessness

NOUNS

1 **odorlessness,** inodorousness, lack of smell, scentlessness; deodorization, fumigation, freshness, cleanness, fresh air, ventilation; breath of fresh air, smoke-free zone *or* area, smokeless zone, no-smoking area

2 **lack of sense of smell,** anosmia, bad nose, nasal congestion, blocked nose, cold in the nose *or* head, head cold
  ▶ *Cleanliness 111; Insensibility 213; Air 558; Absence 576; Nonexistence 718*

3 **deodorant,** antiperspirant, mouthwash, breath-freshener, breath-sweetener, cachou; deodorizer, fumigator, ventilator, air filter, air purifier, air freshener; disinfectant, drain cleaner
  ▶ *Hygiene 116; Fragrance 226*

ADJECTIVES

4 **odorless,** inodorous, scentless, unperfumed, unscented, fragrance-free, odor-free, smoke-free, smokeless; deodorized, disinfected, fumigated, clean, fresh, ventilated, upwind of, in the fresh air

  ▶ *Cleanliness 111; Hygiene 116; Air 558*

5 **deodorizing,** deodorant, cleansing, freshening, disinfectant

VERBS

6 **deodorize,** disinfect, fumigate, ventilate, freshen, clean, cleanse, clear the air, open a window, put off the scent

7 **have no smell,** lose one's sense of smell, have a cold in the nose, hold one's nose, be upwind of, lose the scent

ADVERBS

8 **odorlessly,** cleanly, freshly, upwind, in the fresh air

226 Fragrance

You may break, you may shatter the vase, if you will, / But the scent of the roses will hang round it still.
— THOMAS MOORE

NOUNS

1 **fragrance,** fragrancy, sweet smell, bouquet, aroma, scent, perfume, *parfum* [Fr], musk, muskiness, spice, spiciness, balm, balminess; perfume dynamics, aromatherapy, aromatherapist
  ▶ *Cleanliness 111; Sweetness 222; Odor 224*

2 **source of fragrance,** bakery, coffee grinder, sea air, new-mown lawn *or* field, flower, flower garden, herb, spice, soap, cologne, perfume, aftershave, sachet, pomander ball, potpourri, incense
  ▶ *Flowers 42; Physical Pleasure 214; Pleasantness 271; Beauty 529; Beautification 530; Essence 723*

3 **incense,** frangipani, resin, olibanum, frankincense, myrrh, camphor, eucalyptus, spikenard, musk, civet, attar *or* ottar *or* otto, ambergris, patchouli, sandalwood, vetiver, chypre; censer, thurible, thurifer, joss stick
  ▶ *Religion 81*

ADJECTIVES

4 **fragrant,** sweet-smelling, scented, sweet-scented, perfumed, aromatic; flowery, floral, spicy, musky, fruity, pungent; heady, camphorated, balmy, ambrosial, aromatherapeutic
  ▶ *Piquancy 221; Sweetness 222; Odor 224; Pleasantness 271*

VERBS

5 **be fragrant,** smell sweet, smell like a flower garden
  ▶ *Sweetness 222; Odor 224*

6 **perfume,** scent, aromatize, spray, burn incense, cense, thurify, embalm, lay up in lavender
  ▶ *Religion 81*

ADVERBS

7 **fragrantly,** aromatically, florally, spicily, muskily, pungently

227 Stench

NOUNS

1 **stench,** stink, unpleasant smell, bad odor, malodor, malodorousness, smelliness, fetor *or* foetor, fetidness *or* foetidness, mephitis, miasma, gas, effluvium, reek, exhalation, osmidrosis, sweatiness, fug, staleness, mustiness, frowstiness, frowziness, fustiness, fust, lack of ventilation, whiff, pong [Brit inf]
   ▶ *Odor 224; Unpleasantness 272*

2 **unpleasant-smelling thing,** drain, sewer, sewer gas, cesspit, cesspool, latrine; exhaust fumes, air pollution, smog, cigarette smoke; boiled cabbage, spoiled vegetables, sour milk, strong cheese; stinker, stink bomb, hydrogen sulfide, sulfur dioxide, bad egg, rotten egg; body odor *or* BO, sweat, halitosis, bad breath, dog's breath; ammonia, urine, excrement, sewage, dung; farmyard; breaking wind, flatus, fart [Inf]; skunk, polecat, billy goat; stinkard, stinkhorn, asafetida *or* asafoetida, putrefaction, putrescence, decomposition, decay, rancidity, gaminess, corruption
   ▶ *Chemistry 11; Agriculture 16; Excretion 25; Dirtiness 112; Sourness 223; Gas 556; Deterioration 808*

ADJECTIVES

3 **stinking,** smelly, reeking, noisome, offensive, malodorous, foul-smelling, evil-smelling, mephitic, miasmic, miasmal, overpowering; unwholesome, sweaty, unwashed, fetid *or* foetid; frowsty, frowzy, musty, unventilated, fusty, fuggy, stale, rank, gassy, asphyxiating, sulfurous, ammoniacal, pong [Brit inf]
   ▶ *Dirtiness 112; Odor 224; Oldness 653*

4 **putrid,** putrescent, decaying, rotting, rotten, decomposed, high, off, gamy, rancid, sour, tainted
   ▶ *Sourness 223; Deterioration 808*

VERBS

5 **stink,** smell, smell bad, smell foul, reek, stink out, have bad breath, have halitosis, have body odor *or* BO, stink to high heaven, smell like a drain, smell like a midden, smell of rotten eggs, pong [Brit inf]
   ▶ *Excretion 25; Dirtiness 112; Odor 224*

ADVERBS

6 **stinkingly,** smellily, malodorously, sourly, mustily, fustily, rankly

228 Hearing

NOUNS

1 **hearing,** sense of hearing, audition, ear; earshot, hearing distance, auditory range, audibility; listening, attention, heed, heeding, mind, auscultation, listening in, eavesdropping, overhearing; sharp ear, good ear, musical ear, musicality, perfect pitch, absolute pitch; bad ear, poor ear, tin ear
   ▶ *Physics 10; Music 140; Loudness 232; Intelligibility 363*

2 **ear,** hearing organ; outer ear, earlobe, earhole; middle ear, tympanic cavity, eardrum, tympanum, tympanic membrane, auditory ossicle, incus, anvil, malleus, hammer, stapes, stirrup, Eustachian tube; inner ear, labyrinth, cochlea, cochlear nerve, semicircular canals; ear shape, cauliflower ear, jug ear, bat ear
   ▶ *Human Body 19*

3 **study of hearing,** otology, otolaryngology, otorhinolaryngology; ear, nose, and throat (ENT); audiology, otoscopy; auriscope, auscultator, stethoscope, audiometer

4 **ear problem,** ear wax, ear drops, earache, otalgia, otitis, labyrinthitis, otosclerosis, tinnitus, ringing in the ears, Menière's syndrome *or* disease

5 **ear doctor,** otologist, otolaryngologist, otorhinolaryngologist, ENT specialist, audiologist, aurist, hearing specialist

6 **audition,** hearing, tryout, audience, interview; oral examination

7 **hearer,** listener, auditor, auditioner, hearkener, earwitness; audience, congregation, house; eavesdropper, telephone tapper, monitor, networker

ADJECTIVES

8 **aural,** auricular, audial, auditory, auditive, acoustic, otic

9 **hearing,** listening, attentive, sharp-eared, musical, all ears [Inf]; tin-eared
   ▶ *Music 140; Deafness 229; Attention 323; Discrimination 337*

10 **eared,** having ears, auricular, auriculate, ear-shaped, earlike, auriform, big-eared, long-eared, jug-eared, cauliflower-eared, lop-eared, crop-eared

11 **otological,** audiological, otolaryngological, otorhinolaryngological; ear, nose, and throat (ENT); otalgic, otoscopic

12 **hearable,** audible, reachable, within range, within earshot, loud, soft, resonant, sonorous, echoing, echoic, carrying, listenable, easy-listening, easy on the ear, harsh, ear-splitting, loud enough to wake the dead
   ▶ *Loudness 232; Faintness of Sound 233; Resonance 236; Harsh Sound 238*

VERBS

13 **hear,** hear things, hear voices, perceive, catch; hear of, hear tell, hear on the grapevine, hear from, be in touch with; listen, give ear, lend an ear, hearken, hark, listen to, give a hearing, hear out, attend, pay attention, concentrate, heed, mind, learn, gather, auscultate, sound, listen in, tune in, pick up, overhear, eavesdrop, get an earful; prick up one's ears, keep one's ear to the ground, keep one's ears open, have long ears, make someone's ears burn, have someone's ear, hang on someone's words *or* lips, be all ears [Inf]

◗ *Communications 169; Attention 323*

14 have an ear for, have a good ear, have perfect *or* absolute pitch, have a poor ear, have a tin ear

15 be heard, fall on the ear, reach, carry, come within earshot, sound, resound, reverberate, echo; audition, try out, be interviewed

◗ *Resonance 236*

ADVERBS

16 aurally, auricularly, within earshot, within range, within hearing, within call, hearably, audibly, aloud, out loud, attentively, auscultatorily, by ear, at first hearing

229 Deafness

NOUNS

1 deafness, hearing loss, hearing impairment, partial deafness, total deafness, deaf-mutism, poor hearing, defective hearing, failure to hear; tone deafness, unmusicalness

2 inattention, lack of attention, daydreaming, indifference, heedlessness, oblivion, insensitivity, deaf ears

◗ *Insensitivity 268; Indifference 289*

3 aid to the deaf, lipreading, sign language, American Sign Language *or* ASL *or* Ameslan, signing, dactylology, finger alphabet, smoke signal, semaphore, hearing aid, deaf aid, ear trumpet

◗ *Medicine 107; Communications 169; Sign 183; Hearing 228; Silence 231*

ADJECTIVES

4 deaf, unhearing, without hearing, hard of hearing, hearing-impaired, partially deaf, totally deaf, stone deaf, deaf as a post, deaf-mute, deaf-and-dumb [Off], tone-deaf, unmusical, earless; deafened, stunned

◗ *Medicine 107; Hearing 228*

5 unhearing, unaware, oblivious, deaf to, heedless, unheeding, unconcerned, indifferent, insensitive, inattentive, dead to the world

◗ *Insensitivity 268; Indifference 289; Inattention 324*

6 deafening, ear-splitting, piercing, ear-shattering

◗ *Loudness 232*

7 unheard, inaudible, toneless, faint, difficult to hear, muted, soundproof, ultrasonic, out of range, out of earshot, off-air, off the air, turned off, switched off

◗ *Silence 231; Faintness of Sound 233; Indifference 289*

VERBS

8 be deaf, go deaf, lose one's hearing; lipread, use sign language, sign

9 fail to hear, miss, ignore, turn a deaf ear, close one's ears, not listen, tune out, have no ear for

◗ *Inattention 324*

10 deafen, make deaf, burst the eardrums, stun

◗ *Loudness 232*

11 muffle, mute, baffle, deaden, silence, soundproof, in-

sulate, jam, drown out, use earplugs, put one's fingers in one's ears, turn the sound down *or* off

◗ *Silence 231*

12 be unheard, fall on deaf ears, go in one ear and out the other, go off the air

ADVERBS

13 deafly, deafeningly, inaudibly, tonelessly, out of earshot, out of range

230 Sound

NOUNS

1 sound, noise, tone, voice, sonance, auditory phenomenon, acoustic phenomenon; pitch, timbre, loudness, softness; white noise, music, ultrasound, infrasound; acoustics; unit of sound, decibel, bel, phon

◗ *Loudness 232; Faintness of Sound 233*

2 tone, pitch, overtone, undertone, harmonic; sonics, sonar, resonance, frequency, vibration, sounding, radiophonics

◗ *Music 140*

3 sound propagation, speed of sound, subsonic speed, supersonic speed, sonic boom; sound *or* sonic barrier, audiofrequency, ultrasonic frequency, infrasonic frequency, sound level, sound-pressure level, sound-power level, loudness level; ultrasound scanner, echolocation, radar, sonar, asdic, sonic depth finder, sonobuoy

4 sound quality, monophonic sound, stereophonic sound, quadraphonic sound, listenability, reception; amplitude, tone control, graphic equalizer, equalization, bias, phase, bass, treble, range, level; reverberation, echo

5 sound amplifier, earphone, amplifier, speaker, loudspeaker, megaphone, loud-hailer [Brit], bullhorn, sound truck, public address system; volume control, broadcasting device, pickup, microphone

◗ *Loudness 232*

6 sound reproduction, sound system, high-fidelity *or* hi-fi system, stereo system; record, recording, tape, disk, compact disk *or* CD; radio, record player, phonograph, tape recorder, tape deck, cassette, cassette recorder; audio-cassette player, compact disk *or* CD player

◗ *Radio and Television 172*

ADJECTIVES

7 sounding, noisy, tonal, sonorous, voiced, sonic, acoustic; pitched, monotonic, stereophonic; subsonic, ultrasonic; audible, heard, hearable; high-fidelity *or* hi-fi

◗ *Radio and Television 172*

VERBS

8 sound, make a noise, speak, resound, reverberate, echo; broadcast, amplify

9 record, tape, tape-record

231 Silence

When you have nothing to say, say nothing.
— CHARLES CALEB COLTON

NOUNS

1 **silence,** quiet, quietness, inaudibility, noiselessness, soundlessness; taciturnity, muteness, dumbness, voicelessness, aphonia, laryngitis, speechlessness, wordlessness; hush, stillness, lull, rest, calm, peace, quietude, quiescence; softness, faintness, mutedness; solemn silence, awful silence, dead silence, deathlike silence, deathly hush, uncanny silence, perfect silence, total silence, not a sound, not a squeak
  ▶ *Peace 73; Taciturnity 208; Faintness of Sound 233; Lack of Motion 678*

ADJECTIVES

2 **silent,** quiet, inaudible, noiseless, soundless; taciturn, mute, mum, tight-lipped, dumb, voiceless, aphonic, aphasic, tongueless, speechless, dumbfounded, wordless; hushed, still, stilly, calm, peaceful, quiescent; soft, faint, muted, soundproof, unsounded, unuttered, unspoken, tacit; solemn, awful, deathlike, quiet as a mouse, quiet as a lamb, silent as the grave, silent as the tomb, so quiet one could hear a pin drop, clammed up [Inf]
  ▶ *Peace 73; Taciturnity 208; Faintness of Sound 233*

VERBS

3 **be silent,** be quiet, keep silent, keep quiet, keep mum, not speak, not say a word, not open one's mouth, hold one's tongue, clench one's teeth, hold one's breath, make no noise, not make a sound, not make a peep, not utter a squeak, become silent, fall silent, stop talking, lose one's voice, get laryngitis, be struck dumb; [Inf]: clam up, pipe down, knock it off
  ▶ *Taciturnity 208; Faintness of Sound 233*

4 **silence,** quiet, quieten, hush, still, lull, quell, subdue; mute, stifle, smother, muffle, muzzle, gag, stop, stop someone's mouth, put to silence, soft-pedal, play down, dumbfound; can it [Inf], put the lid on [Inf]
  ▶ *Speech Difficulty 206*

ADVERBS

5 **silently,** in silence, quietly, inaudibly, noiselessly, soundlessly, mutedly, dumbly; calmly, peacefully, softly, faintly

INTERJECTIONS

6 **hush!,** sh!, silence!, quiet!, shut up!, that's enough!, peace!, soft!, mum's the word!, whist!, hold your tongue!, keep still!, keep quiet!, keep your mouth shut!; [Inf]: keep your trap shut!, dry up!, pipe down!, stow it!, can it!, knock it off!

232 Loudness

Loudly let the trumpets bray / Tantantara!
— W. S. GILBERT

NOUNS

1 **loudness,** noisiness, high volume, noise, loud noise, ear-splitting noise; racket, clamor, outcry, uproar, din; shattered silence

2 **loud sound,** reverberation; bray, loud laughter, cachinnation; loud breathing, stertor, stertorousness, snoring; rumble, roll, rattle, thunder, thunderstorm, thunderbolts of Thor, war in heaven; blitz; stridency, stridor, brassiness, shrillness, blare

3 **loud tone,** clang, clangor, plangency, ringing tone, bells, peal, chimes; diapason, swell, surge; crescendo, forte, fortissimo, tutti, full blast, full chorus
  ▶ *Resonance 236*

4 **burst of sound,** report, loud report, explosion, bang, blast, boom, sonic boom, burst, shell burst, slam, clap, thunderclap; alarm, siren, honk, toot; retort, fire, gunfire, artillery, bombardment; fanfare, flourish, trumpet blast, clarion call, call
  ▶ *Sudden Sound 234*

5 **tumult,** shouting, vociferation, ballyhoo; screaming, roaring, bawling, yelling, hooting, chanting; shout, scream, shriek, cry, roar, whoop, howl, ululation; slamming, banging, stamping, crash, clash, clatter, row, deafening row, rumpus, shindy [Inf]; bedlam, pandemonium, hubbub, hullabaloo, turmoil; all hell let loose, enough noise to wake the dead
  ▶ *Human Cry 239; Animal Sound 240; Violence 520; Disorder 766*

ADJECTIVES

6 **loud,** noisy, full of noise, at full volume, at full pitch, full; stentorian *or* stentorious, booming, ringing, carrying, deafening, ear-splitting, ear-rending; thundering, thunderous, rattling, crashing, pealing; clangorous, dinning, rackety; shrill, piercing, high-sounding, strident; braying, blaring, brassy; swelling, crescendo, forte, fortissimo

7 **shouting,** yelling, whooping, screaming, bellowing, crying; bigmouthed, loudmouthed, lusty, powerful, full-throated, brazen-mouthed, trumpet-tongued; uproarious, rowdy, rambunctious, boisterous, disorderly; many-tongued, vociferous, clamorous, clamant
  ▶ *Harsh Sound 238; Human Cry 239; Animal Sound 240; Dissonance 241; Disorder 766*

VERBS

8 **be loud,** be noisy, split the ears, make a racket; reverberate, bray, cachinnate, snore; sound, speak up, raise *or* strain *or* crack one's voice; shout, yell, roar, bawl, bellow, call, catcall, caterwaul, yowl, howl, ululate, shriek, shrill, cry, scream, squawk, vociferate;

trumpet, bugle, blare, whistle; resound, ring, peal, clang; rattle, thunder, storm; clash, crash, clatter, slam, bang; blast

9 **burst,** boom, explode, detonate, fulminate, go off; knock, knock hard, hammer, drill, din

10 **shatter the peace,** stun, deafen, rend the eardrums, shatter the eardrums; swell, fill the air, rend the skies, make the welkin ring [Arch], rattle the windows, bring the house down, awake the echoes, wake the dead; make a devil of a row, raise all hell, rampage, go on a rampage; [Inf]: raise the roof, kick up a row *or* rumpus *or* shindy, raise Cain
   ▶ *Sudden Sound 234; Resonance 236; Harsh Sound 238; Human Cry 239; Rejoicing 279; Disorder 766*

ADVERBS
ADVERBS

11 **loudly,** noisily, stridently, stertorously, uproariously; vociferously, lustily, at the top of one's voice *or* lungs, in full cry; full blast, full chorus, tutti, forte, fortissimo, crescendo; with a deafening roar, like all hell let loose, enough to wake the dead

233 Faintness of Sound

O hark, O hear! how thin and clear . . . / The horns of Elfland faintly blowing! — ALFRED, LORD TENNYSON

NOUNS

1 **faintness of sound,** faintness, softness, soft sound, faint sound; less sound, low volume, sound reduction, noise abatement, muffled sound, muted sound, mutedness; distant sound; indistinctness, inaudibility

2 **dull sound,** heavy sound, thud, clunk, thump, bump, plump, plunk, plonk, plop

3 **undercurrent of sound,** nonresonance, voicelessness; hoarseness, whisper, whispering, susurration, breath, bated breath; soft voice, quiet tone, muffled tone *or* voice, hushed tone, low voice, undertone, aside, mumble, mutter, murmur, murmuration, purl, hum, sixty-cycle hum; white noise *or* sound, drone, roll, sigh, sough, moan, purr
   ▶ *Speech Difficulty 206; Dimness 248*

4 **small sound,** scratch, squeak, creak, pop, tick, click, tinkle, clink, chink, buzz, whir; ripple, plash, plop; babble, burble, gurgle; rustle, swoosh, swish, froufrou; squish, squash; patter, pitter-patter, pitapat, soft footfall, pad
   ▶ *Repeated Sound 235*

5 **sound reducer,** baffle, silencer, muffler; soft pedal, mute, mute button, sordino, sourdine, damper, dampener, filter; cork, double glazing, soundproofing; rubber heel, rubber sole; grease, oil, lubricant; earplugs, gag
   ▶ *Music 140*

ADJECTIVES

6 **faint,** soft, quiet, low, gentle, distant; indistinct, unclear, barely audible; just caught, just heard, half-heard, barely heard, weak, feeble, trembling in the air, dying away; unemphatic, unstressed, unaccented; piano, pianissimo, hushed

7 **nonresonant,** dead, deadened, damped, dampened, muted, muffled, stifled, smothered, soundproofed; dull, heavy, flat, dead, soft-pedaled, subdued, suppressed, bated; whispered, muttered, mumbled, whispering, muted; muttering, mumbling; faint, low; hoarse, husky, wheezy, rasping, gravelly; murmured, murmuring, humming, sighing; purring, gurgling, rustling, pattering
   ▶ *Silence 231; Harsh Sound 238*

VERBS

8 **sound faint,** speak low, speak softly, speak under one's breath, speak in muted tones, speak *or* say sotto voce, drop *or* lower one's voice, breathe, whisper, murmur, mutter, mumble, hum, croon, sing low, sing softly; drone, moan, sigh, sough; purl, ripple, plash, splash, lap, plop, babble, burble, gurgle, flow, patter; squeak, creak, tick, click, tinkle, clink, chink; purr, buzz, whir, wheeze, blow, rustle, swish, swoosh, squish, squash; float *or* steal *or* melt on the air, die in the ear, die away, fade away, sink into silence
   ▶ *Silence 231; Water 557; Air 558*

9 **mute,** soften, dull, deaden, dampen, damp down, play piano, soft-pedal, subdue, turn down *or* lower the volume; soundproof, muffle, stifle, hush, quiet, still, silence, stop
   ▶ *Silence 231*

10 **be nonresonant,** sound dead, fall dead on the ear, arouse no echoes; thud, clunk, thump, plump, plunk, plonk, plop

ADVERBS

11 **faintly,** softly, quietly, low, indistinctly, in a whisper, in an undertone, sotto voce, aside, under one's breath, with bated breath, between the teeth; distantly, out of earshot; piano, pianissimo

234 Sudden Sound

NOUNS

1 **bang,** slam, wham, whack, clash, thump, thud; blast, report, discharge, explosion, detonation, burst, volley, round, salvo, shot; blowout, backfire; boom, sonic boom; peal, thunderclap, clap of thunder, crash
   ▶ *Loudness 232*

2 **crack,** crackle, crackling, crepitation; click, snap, slap, smack, clap, tap, rap, ratatat, knock; pop, plop, plunk
   ▶ *Repeated Sound 235; Hissing Sound 237*

3 **banger,** cracker, firecracker, squib; explosive, bomb, grenade; firearm, gun, shotgun, popgun, rifle, air rifle, air gun

▶ *Weapon 78*

ADJECTIVES

4 **banging,** crashing, slamming; bursting, exploding, explosive; booming, thundering, thunderous
▶ *Loudness 232*

5 **crackling,** crepitant; clicking, rattling, popping

VERBS

6 **bang,** slam, wham, clash, blast, burst, burst on the ear; discharge, explode, blow up, detonate, backfire; boom, thunder, rumble, peal, crash; resound, echo

7 **crack,** crackle, crepitate, spit, effervesce; click, clunk, clatter, rattle; snap, clap, rap, tap, slap, smack; pop, plop, plonk, plunk

ADVERBS

8 **explosively,** bang; abruptly, suddenly
▶ *Surprise 292*

INTERJECTIONS

9 **bang!,** kaboom!, kapow!

235 Repeated Sound

NOUNS

1 **drumming,** thrumming, roll, rumble, rumbling, grumble, grumbling; reverberation, echo; vibration, pulsation, palpitation, throbbing, pounding, beat, pulse; beating, drumbeat, rub-a-dub, rataplan, drum-roll, thrum, tattoo, tom-tom
▶ *Loudness 232; Resonance 236; Repetition 797*

2 **humming,** whirring, buzzing; hum, whir, buzz, purr, drone, bombination; mutter, murmur

3 **rattle,** clatter, chatter, babble; clack, racket

4 **knock,** knocking, ratatat, pitter-patter, pitapat, tick, ticktock *or* tictoc, drip, dripping

5 **ringing,** ring, ping, pinging, ding, ding-dong; chiming, pealing

ADJECTIVES

6 **drumming,** rolling, thrumming, reverberant, reverberative, resonant; throbbing, pounding, beating, pulsing; insistent, persistent, incessant, repeated
▶ *Repetition 797*

7 **humming,** whirring, buzzing, droning; monotonous, repetitive, unvaried

8 **rattling,** clattering, chattering, sputtering, clicking, ticking, knocking

9 **pealing,** chiming, repeating

VERBS

10 **drum,** thrum, roll, rumble, grumble, boom; reverberate, resound, resonate, echo, reecho; vibrate, pulse, pulsate; throb, pound, beat, rataplan, beat *or* sound a tattoo, tattoo

11 **hum,** whir, buzz, purr, drone, bombinate; mutter, murmur

12 **rattle,** clatter, clack, chatter, babble, sputter; chug, chuff

13 **knock,** tap, tick, ticktock, patter, drip

14 **ring,** ping, clang, chime, peal, toll

ADVERBS

15 **repeatedly,** resonantly, rhythmically; over and over, insistently, persistently, repetitively, monotonously, incessantly

236 Resonance

NOUNS

1 **resonance,** resonation, reverberation, hollowness; resounding, rebounding, echo, reecho, lingering note, reflection, recurrence; vibration, whirring, humming, buzzing, oscillation; sympathetic vibration
▶ *Repeated Sound 235; Oscillation 683*

2 **ringing,** bell ringing, tintinnabulation, campanology; peal, toll, knell, chime; tinkle, jingle, chink, clink, ping, ting-a-ling; clang, clangor; sounding brass, brass, blare, flourish, fanfare, tucket
▶ *Loudness 232*

3 **deepness,** lowness, booming, thundering, fullness, richness, sonorousness, sonority, plangency; deep note, low note, bass note, grave note, pedal note; low voice: bass, basso, basso profundo, baritone, bass-baritone, contralto

4 **source of resonance,** tube, tunnel; bell, hand bell, church bell, carillon, chimes, doorbell, telephone bell, fire bell; cowbell, clapper; gong, triangle, trumpet, horn, stringed instrument
▶ *Musical Instruments 142*

5 **resonator,** sounding board, sound box, resonating chamber *or* cavity, echo chamber, sustaining *or* sostenuto pedal

ADJECTIVES

6 **resonant,** resonating, reverberating, reverberative, reboant, stentorian, resounding, rebounding; hollow, echoing, reechoing, vibrating, pulsating, carrying, echoic, lingering, persisting, persistent; humming, whirring, buzzing

7 **ringing,** tintinnabular *or* tintinnabulary, campanological; pealing, tolling, sounding, chiming

8 **deep,** deep-toned, deep-pitched, deep-sounding, deep-voiced, low, sepulchral; sonorous, vibrant, booming, thundering, plangent; full, rich, mellow, rounded, orotund
▶ *Music 140*

VERBS

9 **resonate,** reverberate, boom; resound, rebound, echo, reecho, be repeated, be reflected, recur; vibrate, pulse, oscillate, hum, whir, buzz

10 **ring,** ring in the ear, tintinnabulate, peal, toll, sound, knell, chime

ADVERBS

11 **resonantly,** reverberantly; resoundingly, reflectively, recurrently; deeply, richly, vibrantly, sonorously, plangently

237 Hissing Sound

NOUNS

1 **hiss,** hissing, sibilation, sibilance *or* sibilancy, assibilation; lisp, lisping, whisper, whispering, stage whisper, susurration; shush, hush; rustle, rustling, swish, swoosh, froufrou; sputter, splutter, splash, plash; wheeze, wheezing, rhonchus, sneeze, sneezing; fizz, sizzle, sizzling, effervescence; whiz

ADJECTIVES

2 **hissing,** sibilant, catcalling; rustling; whispering; sneezing, wheezy, asthmatic; fizzy, sizzling, fizzling, effervescent

VERBS

3 **hiss,** sibilate, assibilate, lisp, whisper, susurrate; shush, hush; rustle, swish, swoosh; sputter, splutter, splash, plash; wheeze, rasp, snuffle, sneeze; fizz, fizzle, sizzle, effervesce; whiz

ADVERBS

4 **sibilantly,** swishingly; squashily; effervescently; asthmatically, wheezily

238 Harsh Sound

NOUNS

1 **harsh sound,** stridency *or* stridence, harshness, stridulousness, discord, discordance, clamor; stridor, cacophony, raucousness, dissonance; squawk, yawp, yaup, yelp, yell, howl, bawl, wail, ululation, bray; brassiness, brass, blare, blast, tantara, skirl [Scot]
 ▶ *Loudness 232; Dissonance 241*

2 **hoarseness,** roughness, huskiness, gruffness; lowness, gutturalness, throatiness; guttural sound, rasping sound; caw, croak, grunt, snort, snore, stertor, cough, belch; cracked voice, frog in the throat, rustiness; nasality, nasal tone, twang; friction, scrape, scratch

3 **shrillness,** high pitch, shriek, scream, squeal, screech, squeak; piping, whistling; catcall, whistle, wolf whistle, penny whistle, tin whistle; bleep, bleeper; high note, falsetto; squeakiness, creakiness, creak

ADJECTIVES

4 **strident,** stridulous *or* stridulant, harsh, raucous, discordant, grating, jarring; flat, inharmonious, unmelodious, unmusical; metallic, twangy; penetrating, loud, clamorous, cacophonous, dissonant, ear-splitting; squawky, squawking, howling, ululant; brassy, brazen, braying, blaring

5 **hoarse,** husky, rough, gruff; low, guttural, throaty, gravelly, rasping; cawing, croaky, croaking, grunting, snorting, snoring, stertorous, cracked; nonresonant, dry, rusty, unoiled, grating, scraping, scratchy; clanking, clinking

6 **shrill,** high, high-pitched, piercing, ear-piercing; squeaky, squeaking, creaky, creaking; tinny, reedy, piping, whistling; bleeping

VERBS

7 **be strident,** jar, clash, discord, jangle; grate on one's ears, set one's teeth on edge, go right through one; squawk, yawp, yaup, yelp, yowl, yawl [Brit], yell, howl, bawl, wail, ululate, bray; blare, skirl [Scot], blast; raise the roof [Inf]

8 **sound hoarse,** rasp, grate, grind, crunch, scrunch, gutturalize; caw, croak, grunt, snort; snore, cough, hawk, clear one's throat, belch, choke, gasp; crack one's voice, have a frog in one's throat; scrape, saw, scratch, clank, twang

9 **be shrill,** shriek, scream, screech, squeal; squeak, creak; pipe, whistle, wolf-whistle, catcall

ADVERBS

10 **stridently,** stridulously, loudly, harshly, discordantly; raspingly, gutturally, shrilly

239 Human Cry

NOUNS

1 **cry,** call, loud cry, outcry, exclamation, ejaculation, outburst; battle cry, war cry, rallying cry; vociferation, clamor, uproar, hullabaloo, hubbub; scream, screech, shriek; shout, yell, holler, roar, bellow, howl, bawl, yowl, yawl [Brit], squall, caterwaul
 ▶ *Loudness 232*

2 **cry of amusement,** laugh, laughter; chortle, chuckle, giggle, titter, snicker *or* snigger; cachinnation, horse-laugh, guffaw, whoop, bray
 ▶ *Joy, Cheerfulness 269; Humor 277*

3 **cry of praise,** acclamation, paean; hallelujah, alleluia, hosanna; applause, cheer, whoop; bravo, hurrah, hooray, hoorah, huzzah; hip, hip, hooray
 ▶ *Rejoicing 279; Approval 437*

4 **cry of greeting,** hello, hi, yo, hail, greetings, salutations
 ▶ *Sociability 408; Courtesy 410*

5 **cry of pain,** scream, shriek, yipe, squeal; gasp, whine, whimper, groan, moan; ouch, ow

6 **cry of sorrow,** crying, weeping, weeping and wailing, keening, ululation, lamentation; cry, wail, howl, bawl, blubber, sob, sigh, boohoo [Inf]
 ▶ *Sorrow 270; Lamentation 280*

7 **cry of disapproval,** hoot, jeer, boo, hiss, catcall, curse, razz, Bronx cheer *or* raspberry [Inf], bird [Inf]
 ▶ *Curse 301; Disapproval 438*

8 **crier,** town crier, barker, street trader, hawker; shouter, screamer, yeller, bawler; hooter, booer, jeerer; cheerer, cheerleader, rooter

ADJECTIVES

9 **vociferous,** noisy, loud, loudmouthed, vocal, exclamatory, ejaculatory, stentorian; thundering, thunderous, booming, blasting, deafening; shouting,

screaming, yelling, bellowing, roaring; uproarious, clamorous

10 **cheering,** rousing, whooping; laughing, chuckling, giggling

11 **crying,** sobbing; sighing, groaning, moaning, whimpering; weeping, lamenting, wailing, blubbering; howling, ululant

12 **hissing,** hooting, booing, jeering, cursing, razzing

VERBS

13 **cry out,** call, call out, exclaim, ejaculate, vociferate, raise a cry, raise one's voice, strain one's lungs *or* voice *or* vocal cords; shout, shout out, shout oneself hoarse, shout at the top of one's voice *or* lungs; burst out, blast out, thunder out, explode; scream, shriek, yell, holler, roar, bellow, yawp, bawl, howl, yowl, yawl [Brit], squall, caterwaul, scream *or* yell bloody murder

14 **laugh,** chortle, chuckle, giggle, titter, snicker *or* snigger; cachinnate, guffaw, whoop, split one's sides
 ◗ *Humor 277*

15 **cheer,** cheer for, give three cheers, hurrah, hooray, hoorah; sing the praises of, acclaim; huzzah, shout for, root for

16 **cry,** sob, sigh, groan, moan; whine, whimper, mewl, pule, yammer [Inf]; gasp, fret; lament, weep, wail, keen, ululate, howl, bawl, blubber, boohoo [Inf]

17 **hiss,** hoot, boo, jeer, razz; catcall, curse, swear at, shout down, tell off [Inf], bawl out [Inf]

ADVERBS

18 **vociferously,** noisily, loudly, vocally; thunderously, deafeningly; uproariously, clamorously, obstreperously, at the top of one's voice *or* lungs

240 Animal Sound

NOUNS

1 **animal sound,** warning cry, call, wailing, ululation; bark, bay, howl, yelp, yap, yowl, snap, snarl, growl, roar, woof, whine; hiss, meow *or* miaow, mew, purr; bell, bleat, baa; moo, low, lowing, bellow; oink, squeal, grunt; neigh, whinny, whicker, nicker, bray, hee-haw

2 **bird sound,** bird song, call, note, chirp, cheep, peep, tweet, chirrup, chatter, pipe, twitter, warble, squeak; cuckoo, hoot, tu-whit tu-whoo, whoop, crow, cock-a-doodle-doo, croak, caw, coo, honk, hiss, quack, cluck; squawk, screech

3 **insect sound,** buzz, chirr, hum, drone, whine, stridulation, bombination

ADJECTIVES

4 **ululant,** howling, yowling, barking, whining, snarling, growling; purring, meowing, hissing; bellowing, lowing, mooing; neighing, whinnying, braying; grunting

5 **singing,** chirping, cheeping, peeping, tweeting, twittering, warbling, twittery, chattering

6 **humming,** buzzing, chirring, droning, stridulous *or* stridulant

VERBS

7 **make an animal sound,** cry, call, ululate, give tongue, bay, howl, bell, throat, yowl, yawl [Brit], caterwaul; bark, yelp, yap, whine, snap, snarl, growl; meow *or* miaow, purr, mew, mewl, pule, hiss; bleat, baa; moo, low, bellow, roar; trumpet; neigh, bray, whinny, whicker, nicker; oink, grunt, snort, squeal; croak, squeak

8 **make a bird sound,** sing, sing like a bird, warble, carol, whistle, chirp, chirrup, cheep, peep, pipe, tweet, twitter, chatter; caw, coo, hoot, screech, hiss, honk, quack, cluck, clack, cackle, crow, chuckle, gobble, squawk

9 **make an insect sound,** buzz, hum, chirr, drone, whine, stridulate, grate, rasp, bombinate

241 Dissonance

NOUNS

1 **dissonance,** discord, discordance, disharmony, harshness, stridency, hoarseness; jangle, clash, cacophony, babel; cat's concert, caterwauling, yowling; row, din, noise, clamor, uproar, racket, hullabaloo, hubbub, pandemonium, bedlam, tumult, turmoil
 ◗ *Loudness 232; Harsh Sound 238*

2 **musical dissonance,** discord, tunelessness, unmelodiousness, flatness, sharpness, dissonant chord, wrong note, false note, sour note, off note, clinker [Inf]; atonality, twelve-note *or* twelve-tone composition, twelve-note *or* twelve-tone scale, dodecaphonism *or* dodecaphony, tone *or* note row, series, serialism
 ◗ *Music 140*

3 **broadcast dissonance,** static, wow, flutter, hiss, white noise, interference
 ◗ *Radio and Television 172*

ADJECTIVES

4 **dissonant,** discordant, inharmonious, harsh, strident, shrill, hoarse; jangling, jarring, clashing, grating, scraping, rasping, raucous, cacophonous

5 **unmelodious,** unmusical, unharmonized, untuneful, tuneless, droning, singsong; untuned, cracked, off-pitch, off-key, off, out of tune, sharp, flat, toneless, atonal, twelve-toned

VERBS

6 **be dissonant,** lack harmony; jangle, jar, grate, clash, crash, saw, scrape, rasp; drone, whine; thrum, play sharp, play flat, hurt the ears, hit a wrong *or* sour note *or* clinker [Inf]

ADVERBS

7 **dissonantly,** discordantly, disharmoniously, harshly, stridently, shrilly; janglingly, jarringly, raucously, hoarsely, raspingly; unmelodiously, cacophonously, tunelessly, atonally

NOUNS

1 **vision,** sense of sight, faculty of sight, power of seeing, sight, eyesight, seeing, visual sense

2 **visual acuity,** normal vision, normal sight, good eyesight, perfect vision, 20/20 vision; night vision, scotopia; farsightedness, nearsightedness, astigmatism
> *Faulty Vision 243*

3 **eye,** orb, optic, eyeball, eyesocket, orbit; white of the eye, sclera, conjunctiva, cornea, iris, pupil, lens, aqueous humor, vitreous humor, retina, light-sensitive cell, cone, rod, blind spot, optic nerve, eye muscle; eyelid, eyelash, cilia; eyebrow; [Inf]: peepers, sparklers, baby blues
> *Human Body 19*

4 **sharp eye,** keen eye, penetrating eye, gimlet eye, X-ray eye, eagle eye; Argus

5 **observation,** examination, scanning, inspection, supervision, perusal, scrutiny, scan, study, survey; watching, watchfulness, surveillance, espionage, spying, peering, prying, voyeurism, reconnaissance; [Inf]: look-see, once-over, recce [Brit]

6 **visualization,** consideration, contemplation, imagination, mind's eye; insight, anticipation, foresight, farsightedness, discernment, perception, awareness, perspicacity
> *Clarity 196; Foresight 357; Imagination 360*

7 **look,** glance, glimpse, *coup d'oeil* [Fr], peep, peek, squint, sideways look, sidelong look; gaze, stare, gape; grimace, black look, glare, glower, scowl, evil eye; dirty look, leer, ogle; roving eye, come-hither look, sheep's eyes, melting look; glad eye [Inf], gander [Inf]

8 **view,** sight, aspect, vista, panorama, prospect, outlook; scene, scenery, landscape, townscape, cityscape, seascape; show, peep show, spectacle, pageant, display, tableau, spectator sport, performance; exhibition, showing, picture, painting, drawing, photograph, motion picture, snapshot, slide; eyesore, blemish, blot on the landscape, fright; eyeful, eyeopener, sight for sore eyes

9 **reflection,** image, mirror image, likeness, representation

10 **reflector,** mirror, glass, looking glass, hand mirror, magnifying mirror, shaving mirror, dressing-table mirror, full-length mirror, cheval glass, pier glass; wing mirror, rearview mirror, distorting mirror; road reflector, cat's-eye, speculum

11 **imaging device,** camera, movie camera, camcorder, videorecorder; projector, magic lantern, stereopticon; computer scanner, CAT scanner
> *Medicine 107; Photography 132*

12 **viewpoint,** perspective, scope, range, eyeshot, field of vision; standpoint, point of view, bird's-eye view, worm's-eye view

13 **place for viewing,** peephole, sight hole, peep sight, spyhole; window, windscreen, picture window, store window; squint *or* hagioscope, belvedere, mirador, gazebo; watchtower, observation point, conning tower, bridge, crow's nest; observatory, planetarium, observation car; theater, stalls [Brit], pit, dress circle, circle, gallery, gods; cinema, stadium, amphitheater, arena; ringside seat, terrace, stands, grandstand, bleachers

14 **visual aid,** eyeglass, reading glass, spectacles, pair of spectacles, specs [Inf], glasses, frames, lenses; gold-rimmed *or* steel-rimmed *or* horn-rimmed glasses; reading glasses, pebble glasses, granny glasses, bifocals, half-moon glasses, trifocals, monocle, lorgnette, pince-nez; contact lenses, hard *or* soft *or* gas-permeable lenses, disposable lenses, contacts; eyeshade, sightscreen; sunglasses, dark glasses, tinted glasses, Polaroid™ glasses, shades [Inf]; night glasses; protective glasses, goggles; magnifier, magnifying glass, loupe; microfilm reader, microreader; opera glasses, binoculars, field glasses, optical instrument; telephoto lens, zoom lens, wide-angle lens, fisheye lens; spyglass, telescope, telescopic sight; gun sight, foresight, backsight, cross hairs; microscope, optics, magnification, microscopy, telescopy, stereoscopy, spectroscopy
> *Physics 10; Faulty Vision 243*

15 **observer,** spectator, audience, sightseer, tourist, beholder, viewer, looker; onlooker, looker-on, witness, eyewitness, bystander; watcher, bird watcher, spotter, lookout, sentry, sentinel, scout; watchman, night watchman, caretaker, guard, watchdog, vigilante; patrolman, security man *or* woman; inspector, supervisor, overseer, monitor, scanner, invigilator, scrutinizer, scrutator, scrutineer [Brit]; gazer, stargazer, crystal gazer, clairvoyant, seer, seeress, visionary; starer, gaper, gawper, peerer, prier, Peeping Tom, voyeur, Nosy Parker [Inf], rubbernecker [Inf]

ADJECTIVES

16 **visual,** optical, optic, ophthalmic, eyelike, ocular, binocular; mirrorlike, reflecting; two-dimensional, telescopic, microscopic, stereoscopic; three-dimensional, panoramic, scenic

17 **seeing,** sighted; eyed, sharp-eyed, eagle-eyed, hawk-eyed, gimlet-eyed, Argus-eyed; staring, glaring; goggle-eyed, popeyed; noticing, watching, looking, on the lookout, observant, watchful, vigilant, aware, perceptive; clear-sighted, clear-eyed, farseeing

18 **bespectacled,** wearing glasses, four-eyed [Inf]
> *Faulty Vision 243*

19 **visible,** perceivable, in view, before one's eyes, perceptible, discernible, detectable, recognizable, apparent, observable; distinct, clear, clear-cut, evident, manifest, plain, obvious, patent, conspicuous, noticeable; watch-

able, viewable, worth watching, easy on the eye, eye-catching, eye-opening, spectacular

VERBS

20 **see,** use one's eyes, behold, sight, catch sight of, glimpse, catch a glimpse of, espy, spy, notice, witness; perceive, discern, be aware of, distinguish, descry, make out, spot, recognize, pick out, discover; sightsee, spectate, see the sights, rubberneck [Inf]; see with the naked eye, see with half an eye, have X-ray eyes, have eyes in the back of one's head, see through a brick wall, see around corners, lay *or* clap *or* set eyes on [Inf]

21 **look,** look at, regard, focus on, look straight at, look someone in the face *or* eye; feast one's eyes, devour with one's eyes, gaze, stare, gape, gawk, gawp [Dial], goggle, be all eyes; look sideways, glance, steal a glance, peep, peek, squint; grimace, give someone a black *or* dirty look, glare, glower, scowl, look daggers at; look down one's nose at, look askance; leer, ogle, eye; flutter one's eyelashes at, make (sheep's) eyes at, give someone the (glad *or* evil) eye [Inf]

22 **inspect,** examine, view; reconnoiter, scout; look closely at, scrutinize, study, pore over; look over, survey, scan, peruse, read, cast *or* run one's eye(s) over, have *or* take a look at; [Inf]: give someone *or* something the once-over, have a look-see, take *or* have a gander (at), eyeball

23 **watch,** observe, keep under observation, keep one's eyes *or* an eye on, monitor, survey, watch over, oversee, invigilate, supervise; watch out for, keep a lookout for, keep an eye out for *or* open for, spy on, watch like a hawk, keep one's eyes skinned *or* peeled

24 **visualize,** picture, imagine, see in the mind's eye, consider, contemplate, take stock of, anticipate, foresee, plan, perceive, discern, be aware of, understand

25 **make visible,** reveal, reflect, mirror; show, display, exhibit, bring to light, demonstrate; point out, uncover, unmask, expose
  ◗ *Disclosure 180*

26 **be visible,** appear, come into view, come to light, emerge; catch the eye, loom up, loom large; show, show through, stand out
  ◗ *Visibility 244*

ADVERBS

27 **visually,** optically, by eye, by sight, in sight, within sight, at sight, at first sight, prima facie

28 **visibly,** perceptibly, recognizably, apparently, observably; distinctly, clearly, at a glance, evidently, manifestly, plainly, obviously, patently, conspicuously, noticeably

29 **watchfully,** observantly, vigilantly; sideways, sidelong, glancingly, out of the corner of one's eye

243 Faulty Vision

Eyeless in Gaza at the mill with slaves. — JOHN MILTON

NOUNS

1 **faulty vision,** failing sight, visual handicap, poor sight, impaired vision; day blindness *or* hemeralopia, night blindness *or* nyctalopia, color blindness, daltonism, protanopia, deuteranopia, tritanopia; poor vision, amblyopia, dim sight, snow blindness, sandblindness, purblindness; squint, strabismus, wandering eye, cast, cockeye; walleye, divergent strabismus, exotropia; crossed eyes *or* cross-eye, convergent strabismus, esotropia; nystagmus, winking, blinking, nictitation, (eye) tic; bloodshot eyes, red eyes

2 **sight defect,** far sight, farsightedness, hyperopia, presbyopia; short sight, near sight, nearsightedness, shortsightedness, myopia; astigmatism; tunnel vision, detached retina; eyestrain, double vision, diplopia, seeing double; blurred vision, bleariness

3 **blindness,** sightlessness, eyelessness, lack of sight, stoneblindness, loss of vision, amaurosis; glaucoma, onchocerciasis *or* river blindness, trachoma, cataract, going blind; darkness, whiteout, blackout

4 **eye disease,** ophthalmia *or* ophthalmitis, retinopathy, diabetic retinopathy, conjunctivitis, pink eye, sty *or* stye

5 **aid for poor sight,** eye hospital, eye clinic, ophthalmology, ophthalmologist; eyewash, eye drops; optometry, optometrist, optician; large-print book, spectacles, glasses; contact lenses, contacts; Braille, talking book, guide dog, white stick *or* cane
  ◗ *Vision 242*

6 **visual distortion,** prism, refraction, reflection; optical illusion, distorting mirror, hall of mirrors
  ◗ *Distortion 627*

7 **blinder,** blindfold, blinders, eyepatch, patch; cover, covering, cloak, screen, smoke, smoke screen; curtain, blind; eclipse; camouflage, facade *or* façade
  ◗ *Covering 613*

8 **figurative blindness,** lack of perception, inability to see, blind side, blind flying; unawareness, unconcern, disregard, obliviousness, unconsciousness, blind eye, thoughtlessness, lack of consideration; ignorance, prejudice, unenlightenment, lack of enlightenment, blind spot, lack of discernment, benightedness
  ◗ *Inattention 324; Ignorance 349*

ADJECTIVES

9 **visually impaired,** having poor sight *or* vision, visually handicapped, partially sighted, one-eyed; day-blind *or* hemeralopic, nightblind *or* nyctalopic, colorblind, protanopic, deuteranopic, tritanopic; amblyopic, dim-sighted, purblind, sand-blind; squinting, strabis-

mic, walleyed, cross-eyed, cockeyed, boss-eyed [Brit inf]

10 **weak-sighted,** farsighted, hyperopic, presbyopic, shortsighted, nearsighted, myopic; astigmatic; blinking, winking, nystagmatic; bleary, bleary-eyed; bloodshot, red-eyed; blurry, watery-eyed, seeing double

11 **blind,** lacking sight, sightless, unsighted, deprived of vision, unseeing, eyeless, amaurotic; glaucomatous, legally blind, visionless, snow-blind; blind as a bat *or* mole

12 **blinded,** snow-blind, sand-blind, dazzled; blindfold, blinkered

13 **blinding,** dazzling, bedazzling, stunning; darkening; obscuring, hiding, masking; deceptive, misleading
 ▶ *Deception 193*

14 **blind to,** imperceptive, unaware of, unconcerned, oblivious, unconscious; thoughtless, inconsiderate; unobservant, unmindful, ignorant, in the dark, unenlightened, blinkered, undiscerning, benighted

15 **hidden,** dark, obscure, indistinct; camouflaged; invisible, unseen
 ▶ *Concealment 181*

VERBS

16 **see badly,** have defective sight, be nearsighted, be farsighted; squint, blink, wink, screw up one's eyes; see double, have something in one's eye, have spots in front of one's eyes, be unable to see straight

17 **blind,** deprive of sight, make blind, strike blind, put *or* gouge someone's eyes out; darken, obscure, blur, eclipse; dazzle, bedazzle; blindfold, blinker; camouflage, mask, screen; deceive, hoodwink

18 **be blind,** not see, go blind, lose one's sight, black out

19 **be blind to,** ignore, disregard, overlook; look away, look the other way, drop one's eyes, avert one's gaze *or* eyes; shut one's eyes to, turn a blind eye to, take no notice of; wink at, blink at; be unable to see something under one's nose *or* in front of one's eyes, be unable to see the forest *or* wood for the trees, have a blind spot

ADVERBS

20 **blindly,** without looking, by touch, by feel, by ear

21 **blindingly,** dazzlingly

244 Visibility

NOUNS

1 **visibility,** visibleness, eyesight, eyeshot, naked eye, range, horizon, visible horizon, skyline, sightline, line of sight; observability, discernibility, perceptibility, perceivability, detectability; identifiability, recognizability; distinctness, conspicuousness, overtness, evidence; availability, presence, tangibility; lack of concealment, revelation; field of vision
 ▶ *Disclosure 180; Identification 184; Vision 242; Appearance 264; Presence 575; Uncovering 614*

2 **clarity,** clearness, plainness, brightness, brilliance; definition, focus, sharpness, ease of viewing; publicity, exposure, high profile, prominence, starkness; obviousness, blatancy, showiness, vividness
 ▶ *Clarity 196; Showiness 404*

3 **manifestation,** display, demonstration, exposition, exhibition, show, performance, exposure; attraction, cynosure
 ▶ *Showiness 404; Display 843*

4 **that which makes visible,** visual aid, light, illumination, spotlight; highlighter, underlining; pointer, sign, signpost; high relief, bold relief; fluorescent paint *or* clothing; reflector; shop window, showcase; range finder; optical instrument, spectacles, telescope, microscope; X ray, tomography
 ▶ *Medicine 107; Emphasis 200; Vision 242; Light 246; Expansion 581*

ADJECTIVES

5 **visible,** seeable, in sight, viewable, in view, in full view; observable, distinguishable, discernible, perceptible, perceivable, discoverable, detectable; above the horizon, noticeable, conspicuous, clear, open, overt, plain, evident, manifest, obvious, patent; unhidden, unconcealed, undisguised; exposed, showing, apparent, distinct, easily distinguished; identifiable, recognizable, unmistakable; public, available, present; concrete, material, tangible, palpable; external, outward, superficial, surface; in focus, visible to the naked eye
 ▶ *Disclosure 180; Identification 184; Clarity 196; Vision 242; Appearance 264; Material World 524; Presence 575; Exterior 610; Uncovering 614*

6 **clear,** plain, easy to see, bright, light; signed, signposted; clear-cut, distinct, defined; in focus, sharp, high-definition; open, exposed, exposed to view, uncovered, naked; showy, garish, gaudy, lurid, vivid, brilliant, spectacular, glitzy [Inf]; glaring, unmissable, eye-catching, remarkable, outstanding, striking, blatant, salient, prominent; stark, crystal-clear, lucid, visual; lit up, well-lit, highlighted, spotlighted, illuminated, picked out; in high relief, in bold relief, on show, on display, high-profile; as clear as day, in front of one's face *or* eyes, staring one in the face, under one's nose, plain to see, plain as the nose on one's face; open to view, open to the public, in the public eye, for all to see
 ▶ *Disclosure 180; Clarity 196; Emphasis 200; Light 246; Showiness 404; Uncovering 614; Display 843*

VERBS

7 **be visible,** be seen; show, stand out, stick out, be obvious, have a high profile; hit *or* strike one in the eye, stare *or* strike one in the face, stick out like a sore thumb [Inf]
 ▶ *Vision 242; Showiness 404*

8 **appear,** materialize, become visible, be manifest; come to light, crop up, open out, show up, turn up; show through, shine through; come to the surface, loom, heave in sight, come over the horizon; come into focus,

come out from the woodwork, make an entrance, put in an appearance, pop in [Inf]

▶ *Disclosure 180; Appearance 264; Arrival 704; Entry 706*

9 **make visible,** focus, focus on, show, reveal, disclose, demonstrate, manifest; display, put on view *or* display, exhibit; signal, indicate, sign, signpost, point out; open up, bring to light, uncover, unwrap, expose, illuminate, light up, spotlight; unmask, lay bare, raise the curtain, take the lid off; highlight, underline; clarify, elucidate, illustrate; keep sight of, keep in sight, keep in view, not let out of one's sight

▶ *Disclosure 180; Identification 184; Clarity 196; Light 246; Uncovering 614*

ADVERBS

10 **visibly,** in sight, in view, into sight, into view, out of hiding; outwards, outwardly, externally, superficially, on the surface, apparently, ostensibly, to all appearances, evidently, seemingly; in public, openly, in plain view, clearly, plainly, distinctly; obviously, patently, blatantly, manifestly, conspicuously, noticeably, perceptibly, discernibly

245   Invisibility

NOUNS

1 **invisibility,** disappearance, vanishing, nonappearance, nonpresence, absence; transparency, insubstantiality; darkness, blackness, obscurity; poor visibility, bad visibility, haze, haziness, mist, mistiness, fog, fogginess; fuzziness, indistinctness, faintness, paleness, low definition, poor definition; imperceptibility, indistinguishability, indiscernibility; undetectability, zero visibility, low profile, latency; concealment, hiding, secrecy, privacy

▶ *Concealment 181; Secrecy 182; Dimness 248; Opaqueness 250; Disappearance 265; Absence 576*

2 **that which makes invisible,** darkness, night; mist, film, fog, pea soup [Inf], haze, smoke, smoke screen, muddy waters; black light; correction fluid, masking tape; eclipse, distance, remoteness, horizon, edge of sight, vanishing point; veil, yashmak *or* yashmac, purdah, mask, domino, disguise; front, camouflage, protective coloring; shroud, curtain, blind, shade, shutter, screen, partition, brick wall, blank wall, plain wrapper; hunting blind, hiding place, hidey-hole [Inf]; interference, jamming, snow

▶ *Concealment 181; Obliteration 186; Darkness 247; Dimness 248; Opaqueness 250; Covering 613*

ADJECTIVES

3 **invisible,** unable to be seen, unseeable, out of sight, unperceivable; indistinguishable, indiscernible, unnoticeable, undetectable; unmarked, not signposted; not apparent, unapparent, imperceptible, inappreciable; immaterial, insubstantial, unsubstantial, transparent; unseen, unsighted, unobserved, unwitnessed, unnoticed, unperceived; eclipsed, latent, buried, submerged; lurking, in ambush; over the horizon, below the horizon, out of range

▶ *Transparency 249; Nonmaterial World 525; Distance 585; Latency 844*

4 **difficult to see,** partly visible, half-seen, inconspicuous, low-profile; very small, infinitesimal, microscopic, subliminal; distant, remote, lost in the distance; dark, darkened, faint, pale; indefinite, unclear, indistinct, unfocused, undefined, blurred, blurry, bleared, bleary; hazy, misty, foggy, filmy, shadowy, obscured, dim, low-definition; out-of-focus, ill-defined, fuzzy

▶ *Obscurity 197; Darkness 247; Dimness 248; Opaqueness 250*

5 **private,** internal, inward; hidden, concealed, covert, secret, clandestine; disguised, camouflaged, screened, masked, covered, veiled; under wraps, dark, blacked out, recondite, obscure, obscured, obstructed; behind the scenes, backstage, in camera

▶ *Concealment 181; Secrecy 182; Obscurity 197; Darkness 247; Covering 613*

VERBS

6 **become invisible,** disappear, vanish; fade, fade away, blur, dim, darken; escape notice, hide, retreat, go into purdah, go into hiding, play hide-and-seek, lurk; lie low, keep one's head down, keep a low profile, blend into the background, sink without a trace

▶ *Concealment 181; Dimness 248; Disappearance 265*

7 **make invisible,** put out of sight, hide, hide away, bury, conceal; mask, screen, cloak, veil, eclipse, cover (up), put under wraps, obscure, disguise; white out, black out; blur, dim, darken; put a lid on, hide under a bushel, sweep under the carpet

▶ *Concealment 181; Obliteration 186; Obscurity 197; Darkness 247; Covering 613*

ADVERBS

8 **invisibly,** out of view, out of sight, out of range; imperceptibly, indistinguishably, indiscernibly, unnoticeably, unrecognizably, unidentifiably; sight unseen, under plain cover, in hiding, behind the scenes, backstage; in camera, in private, secretly, under cover; internally, inwardly, inward, underneath; indistinctly, dimly, indefinitely, hazily; on the blind side

246   Light

And God said, Let there be light, and there was light.
— BIBLE: GENESIS

We all know what light is, but it is not easy to tell what it is. — SAMUEL JOHNSON

NOUNS

1 **light,** luminance *or* luminosity, luminousness; lu-

cency, phosphorescence, fluorescence, luminescence; illumination, candescence, incandescence; luster, radiance, radiation, refulgence, splendor, resplendence, brightness, brilliance, vividness; luminous *or* radiant energy, visible radiation, light wave, light ray, beam, rays of the sun; electromagnetic radiation, ultraviolet light, infrared radiation, photon; monochromatic light, coherent light, visible spectrum

▶ *Physics 10; Vision 242; Visibility 244*

2 **quality of light,** soft light, glow, shimmer, shimmering, gleam, glint, glister, sheen, gloss, patina, polish, luster, iridescence, opalescence; shine, shininess, glassiness, glistening, shining, beam; bright light, brightness, effulgence, glare, dazzle, flare, brilliance, sparkle, twinkle, twinkling, scintillation, glitter; spark, flash, coruscation, flashing, flicker, flickering

▶ *Showiness 404*

3 **lightening,** illumination, making light; giving light, shedding light; brightening, bleaching, peroxide; overexposure

4 **natural light,** daylight, sun, sunlight, sunshine, sunbeam; moon, moonlight, moonshine, moonbeam, moonrise, full moon, harvest moon; star, starlight, starshine, Milky Way, nova, supernova; meteor, shooting star; comet; northern lights, aurora borealis, southern lights, aurora australis; streamers, gegenschein *or* counterglow, zodiacal light, earthshine; lightning, sheet *or* forked *or* ball lightning, heat *or* summer lightning, flash, thunderbolt, streak

▶ *Astronomy, Astronautics, and Rocketry 7; Geology 8; Meteorology and Climatology 9; Daytime 655*

5 **incandescent light,** light source, lighting, lamplight; combustion light, fire, flames; candle, candlelight, tallow candle, wax candle; rush candle *or* light, torch, torchlight, link, flambeau, brand; lamp, oil lamp, paraffin lamp, alcohol lamp, kerosene lamp, acetylene lamp; gas lamp, gaslight, gas mantle, gas jet; filament lamp

▶ *Physics 10*

6 **electric light,** artificial light, light bulb, bulb, frosted bulb, clear bulb; ceiling light, wall light, sconce; standard lamp, table lamp, bedside lamp, reading lamp, desk lamp; strip light, fluorescent light, halogen light, quartz-iodine light; streetlight, streetlamp, mercury-vapor lamp, sodium-vapor lamp; sunlamp, sunray lamp; stroboscopic lamp, strobe light; searchlight, floodlight; spotlight, limelight, klieg light, footlights, house lights; neon light, neon lighting, illuminated sign; flash lamp, flashgun, flashbulb, photoflood lamp, arc lamp; fairy lights, Christmas tree lights

7 **safety light,** headlight, fog light, high-beam *or* low-beam headlight, dimmed headlights, parking light, taillight, brake light, backup light, directional signal light, interior light, courtesy light; traffic light *or* signal, red light, amber light, green light, stop light, pedestrian light; beacon, lighthouse, pharos, flashing light, oc-

culting light, lightship, light buoy, navigation lights; running lights, masthead light, stern light, sidelight, anchor light, riding lights; aviation beacon, flare path, approach light, runway lights; light signal, warning light, blinker

▶ *Physics 10; Transportation 686; Warning 814*

8 **lantern,** dark lantern, flashlight, Chinese *or* Japanese lantern, night-light; miner's lamp, safety lamp, Davy lamp

9 **fire,** flame, firelight, embers, glow, red glow, red heat, white heat; blaze, conflagration, brush fire, wildfire; bonfire, watch fire, balefire, signal fire, beacon; Very lights, flare; spill, match, friction match *or* lucifer, safety match, taper, fire lighter, lighter, spark, scintilla, igniter, pyrophoric alloy; fireworks, pyrotechnics, sparkler, Roman candle, Catherine wheel, pinwheel, banger, rocket

▶ *Fuel 106; Heat 217*

10 **flickering light,** firefly, glowworm; corona discharge *or* St. Elmo's fire, ignis fatuus *or* will-o'-the-wisp *or* friar's lantern, jack-o'-lantern, candle flame

11 **photoemission,** light-emitting diode (LED), liquid-crystal display (LCD), light pen, solar energy

12 **highlight,** downlight, uplighting, reflection, chiaroscuro; light show, sound-and-light show, *son et lumière* [Fr]; laser, laser show; holography, hologram, halo, aureole, gloriole, nimbus; corona, rainbow, spectrum

▶ *Painting and Drawing 143; Color 251; Colorlessness 252*

ADJECTIVES

13 **lucent,** luminous, radiant, refulgent, glowing, lambent, glimmering; burning, candescent, incandescent, aglow; phosphorescent, fluorescent, luminescent; photoemissive; flickering, flickery, blinking, winking, flashing, occulting, stroboscopic; lighting, lightening, illuminating, shedding light on, brightening, beaming

▶ *Vision 242; Visibility 244*

14 **bright,** brilliant, effulgent, resplendent, shining, dazzling, blinding, glaring; flashing, sparking, coruscating, glinting, sparkling, scintillating, twinkling, glittering, glittery, tinselly, spangly; fiery, flaming, aflame, alight, blazing, ablaze, flaring

▶ *Heat 217; Visibility 244; Showiness 404*

15 **lustrous,** glossy, gleaming, shiny, polished, burnished, glacé, glassy, glistening; shimmering, shimmery, opalescent, iridescent, pearly, pearlized, haloed

16 **lit,** illuminated, lightened, brightened; luminiferous, lit up, well-lit, light; lamplit, candlelit, torchlit, firelit, spotlit, floodlit, flashlit, highlighted; sunlit, starlit, moonlit

17 **sunny,** daylight, light as day, sunshiny, cloudless, unclouded, clear

18 **starry,** starbright, star-spangled, star-studded

VERBS

19 **light,** give light, illuminate, illumine, light up, lighten;

switch *or* turn *or* put on a light; strike a light, strike; ignite, set alight, kindle, fire, set fire to; floodlight, spotlight, highlight, irradiate, dazzle, bedazzle, blind
  ▶ *Heat 217*

20 **light up,** gleam, glint, glance, glisten, glimmer; blink, wink, flicker, twinkle, sparkle, spark, flash, coruscate, scintillate, glitter, spangle; shine, glow; glare, flare, flare up, flame, blaze, burn, incandesce; radiate, radiate light, beam; luminesce, fluoresce, phosphoresce, iridesce

21 **grow light,** get light, dawn, break, lighten

22 **glaze,** polish, burnish, rub up; take a shine, shine like a new pin, reflect, refract

ADVERBS

23 **lightly,** brightly, radiantly, incandescently; twinklingly, scintillatingly; glowingly, gleamingly, luminously, illuminatingly; dazzlingly, brilliantly, at first light, by day, by daylight; by artificial light

247 Darkness

Hello darkness my old friend / I've come to talk with you again. — PAUL SIMON

NOUNS

1 **darkness,** dark, lack of light, sunlessness, dimness; shadow, shadows, shade; gloom, gloominess, murk, murkiness; lividness, leadenness; somberness, drabness, obscurity, bad light, poor light, twilight, dusk; blindness, blackout; eclipse, total eclipse, eclipse of the sun, solar eclipse, eclipse of the moon, lunar eclipse; blackness, pitch-darkness, Stygian gloom, night blindness, darkest hour
  ▶ *Concealment 181; Obscurity 197; Faulty Vision 243; Invisibility 245; Light 246; Dimness 248; Blackness 254; Covering 613; Nighttime 656*

2 **darkening,** dimming, turning the lights down *or* off *or* out, switching the lights off *or* out, extinguishment, obscuration, obfuscation, occultation, underexposure, blackening, blackout, dim-out, eclipse, fadeout; lights out, power cut, dimmer switch, cutout; shading, hatching, cross-hatching, Ben Day process
  ▶ *Painting and Drawing 143; Light 246*

3 **dark thing,** dark glasses, dark lantern; cloud, thundercloud; soot, smut; ink, jet, obsidian, pitch, coal, raven, ebony; darkroom, dungeon, cellar; dark clothes: business suit, man's evening dress, little black dress, mourning clothes; silhouette, shadow; dark star, dark matter, black hole
  ▶ *Clothing 100; Photography 132; Blackness 254*

4 **shade maker,** parasol, beach umbrella, sunshade, awning; smoked glass, dark glasses, sunglasses; eyeshade, sun visor, sun hat; shutters, drape, blind, roller blind, Venetian blind, festoon blind, blackout; blindfold, hood, shroud, cover, lid; shades [Inf]

  ▶ *Opaqueness 250; Covering 613; Safety 810*

ADJECTIVES

5 **dark,** unlit, unlighted, unilluminated; darkish, dim, badly lit, ill-lit, darkling, underexposed; lightproof, lighttight [Brit]; lightless, sunless, moonless, starless, pitch-dark; shady, shaded, umbrageous; overcast, cloudy, stormy, thundery, lowering *or* louring; dusky, gloomy, dingy, murky, tenebrous; black, Stygian, Cimmerian, nocturnal
  ▶ *Light 246; Dimness 248; Opaqueness 250*

6 **darkening,** extinguishing, dimming; shading, shadowing, screening, obscuring; casting a shadow
  ▶ *Concealment 181; Covering 613*

7 **dark-colored,** dark, deep-colored, subfuscous *or* subfusc; dark-haired, dark-skinned, swarthy, swart, black, melanistic; livid, leaden; drab, funereal
  ▶ *Blackness 254*

VERBS

8 **be dark,** lack light; lurk in the shadows; wear mourning

9 **become dark,** darken, darkle, deepen, blacken; grow dark, cloud over, look like rain, lower *or* lour; dim, be extinguished, go out; night falls, sun sets *or* goes down, light fails
  ▶ *Dimness 248; Blackness 254*

10 **make dark,** darken, turn the lights down *or* out *or* off, switch the lights off *or* out, extinguish, douse, quench, snuff, snuff out, blow out the candle, dim; shade, shadow, adumbrate, overshadow, cast a shadow, put in the shade, occult, eclipse, blot out; shutter, close the shutters, draw the curtains, pull down the blind, keep dark, black out, block out light, underexpose; blindfold, hood, cover (over), veil, shroud, silhouette; shade in, hatch, cross-hatch
  ▶ *Painting and Drawing 143; Concealment 181; Secrecy 182; Obscurity 197; Dimness 248; Blackness 254; Covering 613*

ADVERBS

11 **darkly,** dimly, obscurely, blackly; at nightfall, by night, in the night, at midnight, nocturnally, in the dark; in the shade, shadily, gloomily

248 Dimness

NOUNS

1 **dimness,** faintness, paleness, half-light, semidarkness; twilight, gloaming, evening light, late evening, dusk, duskiness; first light, early morning; thick cloud; waning of the moon, penumbra, partial eclipse; oblique light, bad light, poor light; shadiness, shade, shadow; dim lighting, romantic lighting, dimmed lights
  ▶ *Light 246; Darkness 247; Daytime 655; Nighttime 656*

2 **murk,** murkiness, fog, fogginess, dense fog, pea soup [Inf], smog; mist, mistiness, sea mist, haar [Scot], con-

densation, steam, miasma, exhalation, smoke, cloudiness, haze, haziness; dusty air, sandstorm; low visibility, poor visibility, impaired visibility, obscurity; distance, remoteness; vagueness, indistinctness, low definition; soft focus, blur, blurriness, fuzziness, bleariness; poor sight, cataract; dullness, matt finish, tarnish; grayness, dinginess, drabness; opaqueness, semitransparency, smoked glass, frosted glass, film, filminess, veil

▶ *Obscurity 197; Vision 242; Faulty Vision 243; Visibility 244; Invisibility 245; Opaqueness 250; Grayness 255*

3 **dimming,** making dim, becoming dim; clouding over, shading, shadowing, overshadowing, blackening

ADJECTIVES

4 **dim,** half-lit, half-dark, semidark; twilit, crepuscular, waning; dimly lit, ill-lit; dark, darkish, somber, livid, leaden, dusky, gray, dull; overcast, cloudy, lowering *or* louring, stormy; sunless, shady, shadowy, tenebrous

▶ *Darkness 247; Grayness 255*

5 **murky,** foggy, smoggy, smog-laden, thick, dusty, smoky, smoke-laden, smoke-filled; misty, steamy, steamed up, miasmal, miasmic, cloudy, nebulous, hazy; distant, remote, vague, indistinct, unclear; low-definition, soft-focus, blurred, blurry, fuzzy, blear, bleary, bleared; opaque, smoked, frosted, milky; veiled, filmy, obscured, obscure, shadowy, ill-defined, indistinguishable, faint, feeble, weak, muted, diffused

▶ *Obscurity 197; Opaqueness 250*

6 **dimmed,** clouded, dull, dulled, faded; drab, dingy, gloomy; lackluster, lusterless, matt, unpolished; tarnished, rusty, dusty, dirty

▶ *Dirtiness 112*

VERBS

7 **be dim,** become dim, grow dim, darken; cloud over, film over, glaze over, mist over, steam up; lower *or* lour, pale, grow pale *or* faint, wane, fade, fade out, gutter

▶ *Darkness 247; Opaqueness 250; Grayness 255*

8 **make dim,** bedim, fade, cloud, becloud, fog, befog, mist; blur, blear, film, smear, glaze; darken, lower the lights, turn the lights down; shade, shadow, cast a shadow, obscure, obfuscate; veil, shroud

▶ *Concealment 181; Obscurity 197; Opaqueness 250*

9 **tarnish,** rust, dull, lose its shine; deaden, tone down; dirty, sully, muddy

▶ *Dirtiness 112*

ADVERBS

10 **dimly,** cloudily, hazily, foggily, mistily, blearily; obscurely, darkly, vaguely, indistinctly, faintly, dingily, drably; in the twilight, in the gloaming, through a glass darkly

249 Transparency

NOUNS

1 **transparency,** clarity, clearness, limpidity, limpidness,

pellucidity, pellucidness, colorlessness; glassiness, vitreousness, vitreosity, crystallinity; wateriness; purity, cleanness; unobstructed view; cloudlessness

▶ *Cleanliness 111; Invisibility 245; Water 557*

2 **translucency,** translucence; diaphanousness, gauziness, open texture, sheerness, thinness; flimsiness, filminess, fineness, insubstantiality, vaporousness

▶ *Thinness 595*

3 **semitransparency,** translucency, milkiness; mistiness, smokiness; pearliness, opalescence

▶ *Opaqueness 250*

4 **transparent thing,** water, ice, vapor, air; glass, window, showcase, greenhouse, conservatory; lens, eyeglass, spectacles, glasses; crystal, hyalite, hyaline, clear varnish; cellophane, plastic wrap, bubble pack, blister pack, window envelope; slide, transparency, negative, film; gossamer, sheer fabric, scrim, gauze, chiffon, organdy, organza, tiffany, voile, net, lace, smoke, mist, haze

▶ *Vision 242; Opaqueness 250; Opening 583*

5 **glass,** clear glass, crystal, crystal glass, rock crystal, lead glass, lead crystal; bottle glass, crown glass, flint glass, plate glass, sheet glass, window glass; bulletproof glass, laminated glass, safety glass, toughened glass, reinforced glass; opal glass, frosted glass, ground glass, stained glass; quartz glass, glassware; window, windowpane, pane; windshield; two-way mirror

▶ *Light 246; Opening 583*

6 **openness,** apparentness, obviousness; plainness, lucidity, guilelessness, ingenuousness, straightforwardness, forthrightness, frankness, open-heartedness

▶ *Disclosure 180; Clarity 196; Visibility 244; Intelligibility 363*

ADJECTIVES

7 **transparent,** clear, limpid, pellucid, colorless; crystal, crystalline, crystal-clear, glassy, vitreous, glasslike, hyaline; transpicuous, dioptric, refractive, nonreflective; watery, liquid, clarified; pure, cloudless, unclouded, unobstructed; clear as crystal, clear as air

▶ *Cleanliness 111; Invisibility 245; Light 246; Colorlessness 252; Water 557; Air 558*

8 **translucent,** see-through, revealing, diaphanous, lucent; gauzy, open-textured, sheer, thin; flimsy, filmy, fine, insubstantial, vaporous

▶ *Thinness 595; Nonexistence 718*

9 **semitransparent,** translucent, milky; misty, smoky, smoked; tinted, stained, frosted; pearly, opalescent, opaline, semiopaque

▶ *Opaqueness 250*

10 **easily seen through,** open, guileless, ingenuous; direct, forthright, straightforward, frank, candid, open-hearted, undisguised; evident, obvious, patent, easily detected, manifest, plain, unambiguous, lucid

▶ *Disclosure 180; Clarity 196; Visibility 244; Intelligibility 363*

VERBS

11 **be transparent,** reveal, show through, shine through, transmit light; become transparent, crystallize, liquefy, vaporize

12 **make transparent,** crystallize; purify, clarify, refine, brighten; wipe, clean, cleanse; open, open out, demist, uncloud

ADVERBS

13 **transparently,** clearly, limpidly, pellucidly; translucently, diaphanously, flimsily, insubstantially, mistily, smokily; openly, directly, obviously, plainly

250 Opaqueness

NOUNS

1 **opaqueness,** opacity, density, thickness, solidity, impenetrability, impermeability, imperviousness; darkness, obscurity, blackness, murkiness, dullness; muddiness, turbidity, cloudiness; fuzziness, dimness, haziness, fogginess, obfuscation
   ▶ *Darkness 247; Dimness 248; Transparency 249; Blackness 254; Density 540; Thickness 594*

2 **obscurity,** inscrutability, abstruseness, ambiguity, unclearness, unintelligibility, opacity
   ▶ *Obscurity 197; Unintelligibility 364*

ADJECTIVES

3 **opaque,** nontransparent, nontranslucent; dense, thick; solid, impenetrable, impermeable, impervious; lightproof, lighttight [Brit]; dark, black; windowless, blank, covered, coated
   ▶ *Darkness 247; Blackness 254; Density 540; Thickness 594; Covering 613*

4 **shady,** obscure, dark; murky, dirty, grimy, dusty; dull, lusterless, matt; muddy, muddied, turbid, cloudy, milky; fuzzy, blurred, vague, dim; hazy, smoky, foggy, misty, misted, steamed up, clouded, obfuscated; opaline, frosted, smoked, filmy; semiopaque
   ▶ *Obscurity 197; Darkness 247; Dimness 248; Transparency 249*

5 **inscrutable,** baffling, mystifying, cryptic, enigmatic, arcane, recondite; unclear, ambiguous, indefinite; unknowable, unfathomable, unintelligible; clear as mud
   ▶ *Concealment 181; Secrecy 182; Unintelligibility 364*

VERBS

6 **be opaque,** become opaque; cloud over, steam up, mist, fog, thicken

7 **opaque,** thicken, muddy, roil, stir up; cloud, darken, dim, frost, smoke; devitrify; screen, cover, coat; obfuscate, obscure
   ▶ *Darkness 247; Dimness 248; Thickness 594; Covering 613*

8 **obscure,** mystify, puzzle, baffle, perplex
   ▶ *Obscurity 197; Unintelligibility 364*

ADVERBS

9 **opaquely,** densely, solidly, impenetrably, impermeably, imperviously; obscurely, cloudily, foggily, mistily; inscrutably, cryptically, ambiguously, unfathomably, unintelligibly

251 Color

The purest and most thoughtful minds are those which love colour the most. — JOHN RUSKIN

Artists can color the sky red because they know it's blue. Those of us who aren't artists must color things the way they are or people might think we're stupid.
— JULES FEIFFER

NOUNS

1 **color,** coloring, coloration, hue, pigmentation; monochrome, spectral color, primary color, secondary color, tertiary color; natural color, complementary color, neutral color; heraldic color, grain [Arch]
   ▶ *Whiteness 253; Blackness 254; Grayness 255; Brownness 256; Redness 257; Orangeness 258; Yellowness 259; Greenness 260; Blueness 261; Purpleness 262*

2 **chromaticism,** chromatism, chromatic aberration, color vision, color perception, color blindness

3 **spectrum,** spectrum color: red, orange, yellow, green, blue, indigo, violet; rainbow; refracted color, range of color, colorfulness, variegation, multicolor, polychrome, polychromatism, riot or splash of color; color disk, color wheel, color circle, color scheme, color harmony, color coordination, color chart, pigment chart, color code, colorcast
   ▶ *Variegation 263*

4 **hue,** color temperature, warm hue, cool hue, chroma, chromaticity, saturation, purity; color quality, tone, value, tint, tincture, tinge, shade, cast; darkness, loudness, intensity, brilliance, luminosity, softness, warmth, dullness, deadness, paleness, faded hue, discoloration, patina, halftone, half-light, mezzotint
   ▶ *Light 246*

5 **coloring agent,** pigment, colorant, staining pigment, organic pigment, inorganic pigment, opaque pigment, semitransparent pigment, transparent pigment, metallic pigment; coloring, coloring matter, additive color, subtractive color; artificial coloring, dye, dyestuff, stain, fast dye, natural dye, vegetable dye, artificial dye, synthetic dye, aniline, madder; tint, paint, enamel, glaze, wash, colorwash, whitewash, distemper, mordant, colorfastness

6 **paint,** medium, emulsion paint, undercoat, primer, oil paint, acrylic paint, gouache, poster paint, watercolor, watercolor pigment; artist's colors, palette; colored pencil, colored crayon, colored chalk, colored paper

▸ *Art 133; Painting and Drawing 143*

7 **color image,** color painting, chromatic painting, color-field painting; color photography, color film, color slides, color transparency, color negative, color print, color printing, color reproduction, color filter, colorization, chromolithography; Technicolor™, color television

▸ *Photography 132; Painting and Drawing 143*

8 **chromatics,** chromatology, science of color, color theory, colorimetry, spectrum analysis, spectrography, spectrophotometry, spectroscope, chromascope, colorimeter, spectrometer, tintometer, spectrophotometer, spectrograph, chromaticity chart, chromaticity diagram

9 **face color,** complexion, natural color, healthy hue, flush, blush, glow, rosy cheeks, ruddiness, sickly hue, paleness, pallor; cosmetics, makeup

▸ *Health 113; Ill Health 114; Whiteness 253; Redness 257; Beautification 530*

ADJECTIVES

10 **colored,** hued, pigmented, stained, dyed, tinted, tinct, tinged, toned, shaded; painted, technicolored, colorized; multicolored, many-colored, polychrome, polychromatic, variegated, kaleidoscopic; prismatic, spectroscopic, chromatic, monochromatic, colorable, colorific, tinctorial, colorfast, fast, unfading, constant

▸ *Variegation 263*

11 **colorful,** full-colored, uniform, matching, agreeing, harmonious; toning, intense, strong, emphatic, florid, high-colored, deep, deep-colored, rich, warm, glowing, bright, bright-colored, brilliant, vivid, gay

▸ *Light 246; Accord 735*

12 **gaudy,** garish, tawdry, overstated, showy, flashy, lurid, loud, glaring, flaring, flaunting, spectacular, clashing, disagreeing, discordant, screaming, shrieking, harsh, stark, raw, crude

▸ *Dissonance 241; Showiness 404*

13 **soft-hued,** soft, quiet, understated, mellow, delicate, refined, discreet; whitish, pearly, creamy, light, pale, pastel; muted, flat, matte *or* matt, simple, plain, sober, somber, discolored, patinated, weathered

▸ *Darkness 247; Colorlessness 252; Whiteness 253*

14 **chromolithographic,** colorimetric, spectrophotometric, spectrographic, chromatological, photochromic, calorochromic

15 **off-color,** discordant, inharmonious, discolored, harsh, clashing, conflicting

VERBS

16 **color,** color in, paint, watercolor, crayon, color-print, colorize, variegate, pigment, stain, dye, tie-dye, imbrue, imbue, tint, tincture, tinge, tone, shade, wash, colorwash, distemper, lacquer, enamel, coat, discolor, fade, weather, mellow, tone down, whiten, whitewash, silver, yellow, gild, make up, tan, darken; brighten, illuminate, emblazon; color-code

▸ *Painting and Drawing 143; Beautification 530*

17 **colorcast,** transmit color

18 **be off-color,** clash, conflict, fight

ADVERBS

19 **colorfully,** coloristically, brightly, brilliantly, gaudily, garishly, polychromatically, in Technicolor™

252 Colorlessness

NOUNS

1 **colorlessness,** lack *or* absence of color, achromatism, achromaticity, neutral hue, decoloration, decolorization, etiolation, bleaching, blanching, fading, weathering, neutral tint

▸ *Whiteness 253*

2 **paleness,** pallor, pallidity, lightness, faintness; anemia, bloodlessness, whitening, whiteness, albinism, pigment deficiency

▸ *Whiteness 253*

3 **pen-and-ink sketch,** black-and-white drawing *or* photograph *or* print, overexposure, overexposed photograph *or* negative, underexposure, underexposed photograph *or* negative

▸ *Photography 132*

4 **color remover,** bleach, bleaching powder, bleacher, blancher, whitener, decolorant, color remover, hydrogen peroxide, peroxide, lime, chloride of lime, chlorinated lime

ADJECTIVES

5 **colorless,** hueless, toneless, neutral, uncolored, achromatic, decolored, discolored, bleached, etiolated; overexposed, underexposed, weathered, faint, faded, fading, washed-out, washy, unpigmented, whitish, yellowish, lusterless, mousy, dingy, milky, dull, leaden, gray, lackluster, without gloss, dim

6 **drained of color,** white-skinned, light-skinned, white, faint-colored, bloodless, anemic, albinotic, peaked, peaky, pale, pallid, mousy, ashy, ashen, ashen-hued, livid, tallow-faced, pasty, doughy, mealy, sallow, sickly, unhealthy, blank, glassy, lackluster, insipid, lurid, ghastly, wan, deathly, deathlike

▸ *Whiteness 253; Grayness 255*

VERBS

7 **lose color,** pale, fade, run, bleach, blanch, whiten, come out in the wash, turn pale, change countenance

8 **decolor,** decolorize, achromatize, fade, etiolate, bleach, blanch, peroxide, whiten, drain of color, wash out, tone down, deaden, weaken, pale, dim, bedim, dull, tarnish, discolor

ADVERBS

9 **colorlessly,** tonelessly, achromatically, neutrally, faintly, dimly, dully, dingily, blankly

253 Whiteness

NOUNS

1 **whiteness,** snowiness, milkiness, lactescence, whitishness, albescence, off-whiteness, pearliness, chalkiness, creaminess, silveriness, fairness, canescence, hoariness; colorlessness, achromatism, semitransparency, paleness, pallor, sallowness, albinism, lack of pigment, leukoderma
   ◗ *Colorlessness 252*

2 **whitening,** whitewashing, bleaching, blanching, etiolation

3 **whitener,** bleach, whiting, white alkali, white arsenic, white lead, pipe clay, whitewash, calcimine, white paint, Chinese white, Luma white, Paris white, flake white, zinc white, titanium white

4 **white thing,** alabaster, chalk, frost, hoar, ivory, lily, marble, milk, pearl, platinum, silver, snow, swan, teeth, white ant, whitebait, white blood cell, white bread, whitecap, white clover, white coffee [Brit], white dwarf, whitefish, white flag, white flour, whitefly, white gold, white goods, white heat, white horse, white keys, white light, white meat, white metal, white oak, white paper, white pepper, white poplar, white rose, white sale, white sauce, white shark, white spruce, white-tailed deer *or* whitetail, white tie, whitethorn [Brit], whitethroat, whitewall tire, white water, white whale, white wine; White Cliffs of Dover, the White House

5 **figurative usage,** white alert, white-collar worker, white elephant, white feather, white hat, white hope, white knight, white lie, white lightning [Inf], white stuff [Inf], whited sepulcher; White Friar, White Nile, White Mountains, White Russia, White Sea, White Volta

6 **purity,** chastity, cleanness, spotlessness
   ◗ *Cleanliness 111*

ADJECTIVES

7 **white,** pure-white, snow-white, snowy, lily-white, milk-white, milky, whitish, albescent, off-white, half-white, oyster-white, pearly, ivory, alabaster, marble, chalky, creamy, ecru, undyed, greige, mushroom, beige, silver, silvery, silvered, argent [Heraldic], argentine, argental; white as the driven snow *or* a ghost *or* a lily *or* milk *or* marble *or* ivory *or* a sheet; fair-skinned, light-complexioned, albinic, albinistic

8 **whitened,** bleached, blanched, decolorized, faded, colorless, achromatic, etiolated, semitransparent, whitewashed, snow-capped, hoary, frosty, frosted, foam-flecked, foaming, spumy, soapy, lathery, white with dust, dusty, white-hot
   ◗ *Heat 217; Colorlessness 252*

9 **white-haired,** fair-haired, fair, blond *or* blonde, ash-blond, platinum-blond, flaxen-haired, tow-headed; peroxide blond
   ◗ *Yellowness 259; Beautification 530*

10 **pale,** pallid, sallow, waxen, ashen, ashy, livid, ghastly
   ◗ *Colorlessness 252*

11 **pure,** chaste, virginal, clean, spotless, immaculate
   ◗ *Cleanliness 111*

VERBS

12 **whiten,** white, bleach, blanch, pipe-clay, whitewash, calcimine, wash, clean, pale, blench, fade, decolorize, etiolate, frost, silver, grizzle

ADVERBS

13 **whitely,** palely, pallidly, achromatically, lightly, chalkily, creamily

254 Blackness

NOUNS

1 **blackness,** inkiness, blackishness, nigrescence, nigritude, darkness, dark, night, dark color, dark coloring, deep tone, black and white, chiaroscuro, blackening, darkening, obscuration; melanism, melanosis, swarthiness, swartness, duskiness
   ◗ *Darkness 247*

2 **black pigment,** melanin, blacking, lampblack, black-lead, ivory black, blue-black, nigrosine, japan, niello, burnt cork, India ink, China ink, printer's ink, newsprint ink, indelible ink

3 **black thing,** black Angus, black bass, black bear, black belt, blackberry, blackbird, blackboard, black card, black checker, black coffee, black currant, black eye, black-eyed Susan, blackface, blackfish, black flag, black fly, black grouse, black hat, blackhead, black hole, blacking, black keys, black light, black nightshade, black olive, blackout, black pepper, black pudding, blacksnake, black spruce, black swan, blacktail deer, blackthorn, black tie, blacktop, black widow, bruise, charcoal, coal, crepe, crow, ebony, ink, jet, mourning clothes, obsidian, pitch, raven, sable, shadow, silhouette, sloe, smut, soot, tar; Black and Tan [Brit], Black Shirt, Black Watch [Brit]

4 **figurative usage,** black art, blackball, black book, black bottom, black-bottom pie, black box, black diamonds, black economy, black gold, blackguard, black humor, black ice, blackjack, blacklist, black look, black magic, blackmail, black market, black mood, black sheep, black spot [Brit]; the Black Country, Black Death, Black Friar, Black Forest, Black Hills, Black Maria, Black Mass, Black Panthers, Black Prince, Black Sea

ADJECTIVES

5 **black,** raven, ebon, ebony, jet, jet-black, jetty, pitch-black, pitchy, inky, sooty, fuliginous, coal-black, sloe-black, sable [Heraldic]; blackish, nigrescent, blue-black, gray-black, brown-black; black as coal *or* soot *or* jet *or*

pitch *or* night *or* midnight *or* ink *or* thunder *or* hell *or* one's hat [Brit]

6 **dark,** deep, of the deepest dye, achromatic, low-toned, low in tone, dim, dingy, murky, smudgy, smoky, dusky, swarthy, swart; pigmented, melanistic, dark-complexioned
   ▶ *Darkness 247; Appearance 264*

7 **blackened,** singed, charred, tanned, suntanned, sunburned, black-and-blue
   ▶ *Heat 217; Brownness 256*

8 **black-haired,** black-locked, raven-haired, dark-haired, dark-headed, brunet *or* brunette; black-eyed, sloe-eyed

9 **black-hearted,** evil, wicked, nefarious, heinous, villainous, blackguardly
   ▶ *Evil 446*

10 **sad,** somber, gloomy, depressed, depressing, mournful, mourning, funereal
   ▶ *Burial 31; Sorrow 270; Lamentation 280*

VERBS

11 **blacken,** black, blacklead, japan, niello, ink, ink in, dirty, blot, smudge, smirch, sully, darken, deepen, singe, char, burn, tan, suntan; blackball, blacklist, boycott

ADVERBS

12 **blackly,** darkly, deeply, inkily, duskily, swarthily, obscurely, gloomily

255 Grayness

NOUNS

1 **grayness,** gray color, grayishness, canescence, neutral tint, grisaille, oyster, taupe, greige

2 **gray pigment,** Payne's gray

3 **gray thing,** ash, gray hair, gray hen, greyhound, graylag, gray squirrel, graywacke, gray whale, gray wolf, gunmetal, iron, lead, pewter, silver, slate, steel, thundercloud

4 **figurative usage,** gray area, graybeard, gray eminence *or* éminence gris, gray knight, gray market, gray matter, gray population; Gray Friar, Gray Lady, Gray Panther

5 **dullness,** drabness, dreariness, gloominess, darkness, cloudiness, murk

ADJECTIVES

6 **gray,** grayish, canescent, griseous, silver-gray, silver, silvery, silvered, light-gray, pale-gray, powder-gray, dove-gray, pearl-gray, pearly, mouse-colored, mousy, taupe, dun, brown-gray, donkey-gray, steel-gray, steely, iron-gray, leaden, charcoal-gray, dark-gray, blue-gray, slate-gray, slate-colored, ash-gray, ashen, ashy, cinereous, smoky, fuliginous, dapple-gray, neutral, unbleached, undyed, greige, ecru

▶ *Whiteness 253*

7 **gray-haired,** gray, gray-headed, grizzled, grizzly, pepper-and-salt, hoary, hoar, graying
   ▶ *Age 27; Whiteness 253*

8 **dull,** drab, dreary, gloomy, somber, dark, leaden, overcast, cloudy, murky, misty, foggy

VERBS

9 **gray,** turn gray, go gray, silver, frost

ADVERBS

10 **grayly,** dully, drably, drearily, gloomily, somberly, cloudily, mistily, murkily, foggily, smokily

256 Brownness

NOUNS

1 **brownness,** brown color, brown pigmentation, melanin, mole, freckle, suntan, sunburn, dark skin, dark complexion
   ▶ *Humankind 18*

2 **brown pigment,** bistre *or* bister, ocher *or* ochre, sepia, raw sienna, burnt sienna, raw umber, burnt umber, Vandyke brown, brown dye, Bismarck brown

3 **brown thing,** brown algae, brown bat, brown bear, brown belt, brown betty, brown bread, brown coal, brown fat, brownie (small cake), brown-lung disease, brown paper bag, brown recluse spider, brown rice, brown rot, brownstone, brown sugar, Brown Swiss cattle, brown-tail moth, brown trout, Burmese cat, burnt almond, butterscotch, caramel, chocolate, chocolate-point Siamese cat, cinnamon, coffee, dead leaf, demerara, lignite, molasses, muscovado, pumpernickel, seal-point Siamese cat, tobacco leaf, toffee, whole-wheat bread

4 **figurative usage,** brown-bagger, brownie (elf), Brownie point [Inf], brown-nose *or* brown-noser [Inf], brownout, brown study; Brownie Girl Scout, Brownie Guide [Brit], Brown Shirt

ADJECTIVES

5 **brown,** pale-brown, oatmeal, beige, buff, fawn, biscuit, mushroom, café-au-lait, ecru, snuff-colored, yellow-brown, dun, khaki, hazel, walnut, orange-brown, amber, bronze, tawny, fulvous, sorrel, reddish-brown, nutbrown, tan, foxy, bay, roan, chestnut, auburn, mahogany, copper, coppery, copper-colored, cupreous, russet, rust-colored, rusty, rubiginous, ferruginous, liver-colored, maroon, purple-brown, puce, dark brown, peat-brown, mocha, chocolate, coffee, coffee-colored, fuscous

6 **browned,** bronzed, dark, brunet *or* brunette, tanned, suntanned, sunburned, toasted, grilled, charred, singed; brown as a berry *or* nut

VERBS

7 **brown,** embrown, tan, suntan, bronze, sunburn, burn, singe, char, grill, sauté, toast, rust; brown-bag, brown-nose [Inf]

257 Redness

NOUNS

1 **redness,** red color, reddening, rubescence, rubefaction, rubefacient, rufescence; red complexion, blush, flush, hectic flush; red rash, erythema; glow, warmth, rosiness, bloom, high color, ruddiness, floridness, floridity, rubicundity

2 **red pigment,** red dye, cadmium red, cadmium scarlet, Windsor red, Grumbacher red, Thalo red, Indian red, murex, cochineal, carmine, kermes, dragon's blood, cinnabar, vermilion, minium, red lead, ruddle, madder lake, rose madder, alizarin, alizarin crimson, crimson lake, Venetian red, rosaniline, solferino, red ocher, light red oxide; red cosmetic, henna, rouge, blusher, lipstick, nail polish

3 **red thing,** apple, beet, blood, brick, burgundy, cardinal, carnation, carnelian, carrot-top [Inf], cherry, claret, danger signal, dawn, fire, fire engine, garnet, geranium, gore, ketchup *or* catsup, mulberry, peach, peony, pillar box [Brit], plum, poppy, port, raspberry, red admiral, red blood cell *or* corpuscle, redbug, red card, red checker, red cheeks, red clover, red currant, red deer, red dwarf, red fox, red giant, red grouse, red hair, redhead, red ink, red light, red meat, red pencil, red pepper, red planet (Mars), red salmon, red snapper, red squirrel, red stuff, red wine, redwing, redwood, robin, rose, ruby, rust, salsa, scarlet tanager, strawberry, strawberry mark, sunset, tomato

4 **figurative usage,** red alert, red carpet, red cent [Inf], redcoat [Brit], red-eye *or* red-eye special [Inf], red herring, red-letter day, red-light district, redneck [Inf], red tape, scarlet fever; Red (communist), Red Crescent, Red Cross, Red Sea

ADJECTIVES

5 **red,** cherry, cherry-red, cerise, bright red, blood-red, carmine, crimson, cramoisy [Arch], scarlet, cardinal red, Turkey red, vermilion, vermeil, gules [Heraldic], brick-red, fire-engine red, pillar-box red [Brit]; pink, coral, coral-pink, orange-pink, shell-pink, flesh-pink, flesh-colored, peach-colored, salmon-pink, shocking pink, rose-pink, damask, carnation, rosy, roseate, rose-colored, rose-red; flame-colored, deep red, ruby, wine-colored, purple-red, beet-red, fuchsia, cyclamen, magenta, maroon, murrey [Arch], brownish-red, oxblood, rust-colored, rufous, rufescent, russet

▶ *Brownness 256; Purpleness 262*

6 **red-faced,** red-cheeked, apple-cheeked, rosy-cheeked, cherry-lipped; rosy, glowing, blooming, flushing, blushing, rubescent; ruddy, sanguine, rubicund, florid, blowzy, rouged, reddened, flushed, red as a beet *or* a lobster, sunburned, hectic, fevered, feverish, fiery, red-hot

▶ *Ill Health 114; Heat 217*

7 **red-haired,** ginger-haired, carroty, sandy, Titian, auburn, chestnut

8 **bloody,** bloodstained, bloodshot, gory, sanguineous, sanguinary, ensanguined, incarnadine

VERBS

9 **redden,** crimson, make red, rubefy, ruddle, rouge, raddle, rubricate, mantle, incarnadine; flush, blush, glow, color, color up; red-ink, red-pencil, redline

ADVERBS

10 **ruddily,** rosily, blushingly, in the pink, floridly, sanguineously, sanguinarily, warmly

258 Orangeness

NOUNS

1 **orangeness,** orange color

2 **orange pigment,** ocher, raw sienna, Mars orange, cadmium orange, henna, carotene

3 **orange thing,** apricot, brass, cantaloupe, carrot, clementine, copper, goldfish, mandarin orange, marigold, nectarine, orange, orangeade, orange hawkweed, orange juice, orange marmalade, orange squash [Brit], peach, pomelo, pumpkin, saffron, sand, tangerine, tequila sunrise cocktail

4 **figurative usage,** orange blossom cocktail, orange flower oil *or* neroli oil, orangery, orange pekoe, orange stick, orangewood; Orange Free State, Orangeman, Orangeman's Day

ADJECTIVES

5 **orange,** reddish-yellow, yellowish-red, ochreous, saffron, apricot, peach, golden, old-gold, or [Heraldic]; carroty, Titian, ginger, tan, bronze, brassy, flame-colored, coppery

▶ *Brownness 256; Redness 257; Yellowness 259*

259 Yellowness

NOUNS

1 **yellowness,** yellow color, yellowishness, goldenness

2 **yellow pigment,** cadmium yellow, cadmium lemon, gamboge, chrome yellow, Windsor yellow, Indian yellow, Naples yellow, lemon yellow, orpiment, yellow ocher, Claude tint, massicot, weld, luteolin, xanthene, xanthophyll

3 **yellow skin,** jaundice, icterus, yellow fever, biliousness

4 **yellow thing,** amber, banana, brimstone, butter, buttercup, citron, cowslip, crocus, daffodil, dandelion, gold, golden hair, honey, lemon, mustard, old ivory, primrose, quarantine flag *or* yellow jack [Inf], sulfur, topaz, urine, winter jasmine, yellowhammer, yellow jacket, yellow light, Yellow Pages, yellow rain, yellow spot (macula lutea), yellowtail, yellowthroat

5 **figurative usage,** yellow alert, yellowbelly [Inf], yel-

low-dog contract, yellow journalism, yellow peril [Off], yellow press, yellow streak [Inf], Yellow Sea, Yellowstone National Park

6 **yellow streak [Inf],** cowardice, cravenness, spinelessness, timidity
  ◗ *Cowardice 285*

ADJECTIVES

7 **yellow,** bright yellow, canary-yellow, sunshine-yellow, gold, golden, golden-yellow, gilt, gilded, aureate, or [Heraldic]; pale-yellow, cream-colored, creamy, beige, honey-colored, straw-colored, fallow, champagne; greenish-yellow, citron, chartreuse, primrose-yellow, lemon-yellow, citrine, amber, brownish-yellow, old-gold, mustard-yellow, mustard, buff, tawny

8 **yellowish,** xanthous, luteous, fulvous, flavescent, sulfurous

9 **yellow-haired,** golden-haired, blond, strawberry-blond, honey-blond

10 **yellow-faced,** yellow-complexioned, sallow, jaundiced, bilious

11 **chicken-hearted [Inf],** yellow [Inf], chicken [Inf]

VERBS

12 **make** *or* **become yellow,** yellow, gild

ADVERBS

13 **yellowly,** goldenly, creamily; sallowly, biliously

260 Greenness

NOUNS

1 **greenness,** green color, viridity, viridescence, virescence, verdancy, verdure

2 **green place,** woodland, greenery, greenwood, turf, sward, grassland, farmland, pasture, common, greenbelt, park, lawn, green, village green, bowling green, greenskeeper *or* greenkeeper

3 **green pigment,** chlorophyll, terre verte, celadonite, viridian, verditer, Paris green, Windsor green, Thalo yellow green, Hooker's green, phthalocyanine green

4 **green thing,** aquamarine, avocado, beryl, bowling green, broccoli, cabbage, chrysoprase, emerald, evergreen, foliage, grass, green bean, green card, greenfinch, green flash, greenfly, greengage plum, greenheart, green leaf, green light, green olive, green pea, green pepper, green porphyry, greens, greensand, green snake, greenstone, green turtle, holly, ivy, jade, lettuce, lime, malachite, moss, olivine, parsley, patina, putting green, spinach, verd antique, verdigris; Green Paper [Brit], greenie [Inf]

5 **figurative usage,** greenback, green-eyed monster, greenhorn, greenhouse, greenhouse effect, greenmail, green pound [Brit], greenroom, greenstick fracture, green stuff [Inf], green tea, green thumb, little green men; Green Bay, Green Berets, Greenland, Greenland Sea, Green Mountains, Green River ordinance

6 **green politics,** Green party, Greens, environmental-ism, preservationism, conservationism, Greenpeace, Friends of the Earth [Brit]

ADJECTIVES

7 **green,** emerald, jade, vert [Heraldic]; grass-green, leaf-green, pea-green, leek-green; greenish, virescent, viridescent; yellow-green, lime-green, chartreuse; Lincoln green, olive-green, sage-green, avocado, celadon, gray-green, reseda, mignonette, blue-green, glaucous, sea-green, Nile green, loden green, aquamarine, dull-green, dark-green, bottle-green, jungle-green, forest-green; patinous
  ◗ *Yellowness 259; Blueness 261*

8 **verdant,** grassy, leafy, green, fresh

9 **raw,** green, unripe, unseasoned, immature, callow, inexperienced, unskilled, inexpert, untrained, untried, untested, unsophisticated, naive, ingenuous, artless, innocent, credulous, gullible, gauche, awkward, wet behind the ears
  ◗ *Youth 26; Ignorance 349*

10 **fresh,** new, young, youthful, evergreen, sappy, springlike, vernal, vigorous, flourishing, blooming
  ◗ *Youth 26*

11 **green-eyed,** jealous, envious, green with envy, covetous, resentful
  ◗ *Envy 314*

12 **sick,** nauseated, green, bilious, greensick, green around the gills [Inf]
  ◗ *Ill Health 114*

13 **environmental,** green, conservationist, preservationist

VERBS

14 **green,** become green, make green; patinate, patine; nauseate

ADVERBS

15 **greenly,** verdantly, freshly, youthfully; rawly, immaturely; sickly

261 Blueness

NOUNS

1 **blueness,** blue color, azure, cyan, indigo; lividness, lividity, cyanosis, bruising

2 **blue pigment,** blue dye, Prussian blue, ultramarine, cobalt blue, cerulean blue, Antwerp blue, phthalocyanine blue, zaffer, smalt, methylene blue, gentian blue, woad

3 **blue thing,** aquamarine, beryl, blue baby, bluebell, blueberry, bluebill, bluebird, bluebonnet, blue book, blue cheese, blue crab, bluefish, blue fox, bluegill, bluegrass, blue heron, blue ice, blue jay, blue jeans, blue mold, blue pencil, blue peter, blue-point Siamese cat, blueprint, blue racer, blue ribbon, blue sea, blue sky, bluestone, blue tit, blue whale, bruise, cornflower, forget-me-not, lapis lazuli, sapphire, turquoise

4 **figurative usage,** blue alert, blue blood, blue chip,

blue-collar worker, blue devils, blue-eyed boy [Brit], blue flu, blue funk [Inf], bluegrass [Music], bluejacket, blue language, blue law, blue moon, blue movie, blue murder, blue note, blue pencil, blue-plate special, blue-point oyster, blueprint, blues or the blues, blue-sky law, bluestocking, blue streak, the blue; [Inf]: blue balls, blue blazes, blue cheer, blue heaven or angel or devil, blue velvet; Bluebeard, Blue Cross, Blue Mountains, Blue Nile, Blue Ridge Mountains, Blue Shield

ADJECTIVES

5 **blue,** light-blue, sky-blue, pale-blue, ice-blue, powder-blue, Wedgwood-blue, gray-blue, slate-blue, smoke-blue, steel-blue, green-blue, robin's-egg blue, aquamarine, turquoise, peacock-blue, kingfisher-blue, cobalt-blue, cyan, cyanic, bright-blue, cerulean, sapphire, air force blue, electric-blue, ultramarine, deep-blue, royal-blue, dark-blue, midnight-blue, navy-blue, navy, perse, purplish-blue, azure [Heraldic], indigo, hyacinthine
▶ *Greenness 260; Purpleness 262*

6 **bluish,** black-and-blue, livid, cyanotic, cyanosed, bruised, cesious, blue with cold, freezing, blue in the face

7 **depressed,** dejected, downcast, despondent, blue, unhappy, sad, melancholy, glum, gloomy

8 **indecent,** smutty, risqué, bawdy, blue, coarse, obscene
▶ *Immorality 432*

VERBS

9 **blue,** turn blue, dye blue, azure

10 **blue-pencil,** edit

ADVERBS

11 **bluely,** lividly, cyanotically; dejectedly, despondently, gloomily; indecently, smuttily, bawdily

262 Purpleness

NOUNS

1 **purpleness,** purple color, purplishness, lavender, lilac, violet, magenta, mauve; mourning color, funeral color

2 **purple pigment,** purple dye, Tyrian purple, gentian violet, Parma violet, cobalt violet, methyl violet, amaranth, permanent magenta, Windsor violet, Thalo purple, Thio violet

3 **purple thing,** amethyst, clematis, damson plum, eggplant, heather, heliotrope, hyancinth, lavender, lilac, pansy, plum, purple foxglove, purple-fringed orchid, purple gallinule, purple grackle, purpleheart, purple loosestrife, purple martin, purple passion, violet; Purple Heart

4 **figurative usage,** bishop's purple, born to the purple, imperial purple, purple passage, purple patch [Brit], purple prose

5 **lividness,** lividity, bruising, bruise

ADJECTIVES

6 **purple,** purplish, purply, purpled, pale-purple, lavender, lilac, violet, magenta, mauve, purple-red; fuchsia, plum, plum-colored, damson-colored, puce, amaranthine, hyacinthine, heliotrope, violet, violaceous, amethystine, deep purple, dark purple, aubergine, orchid, mulberry, murrey [Arch], purpure [Heraldic], purple-blue, indigo
▶ *Redness 257; Blueness 261*

VERBS

7 **empurple,** purple, make purple

263 Variegation

Variety's the very spice of life / That gives it all its flavour.
— WILLIAM COWPER

NOUNS

1 **variegation,** variety, difference, diversification, diversity, diversity of colors, motley, medley or mixture of colors, riot of color, spectrum, rainbow, play of color; iridescence, opalescence, pearliness, chatoyancy, moiré; dichroism, dichromatism, trichroism, trichromatism, polychromatism, polychrome

2 **check,** checker, hound's tooth or hound's tooth check, plaid, tartan, mosaic, patch, patchiness, patchwork, inlay, damascene, marquetry, parquetry, tessellation, tessera

3 **stripe,** striping, striation, stria, band, bar, line, streak, streakiness, marbling, crack, craze, crackle, reticulation

4 **maculation,** mottling, mottle, mottlement, dappling, brindling, stippling, pointillism, freckling, spottiness, patchiness; patch, speck, speckle, spot, sunspot, dot, polka dot, macula, foxing, brindle, fleck, freckle, pimple, blotch, splotch, birthmark, strawberry mark, splodge, splash
▶ *Blemish 533*

5 **variegated thing,** agate, bar code, buttermilk sky, calico cat, chameleon, checkerboard, chessboard, collage, confetti, cracked glass, crazy paving [Brit], Dalmatian, dancing light, dapple horse, dragonfly, enamelwork, glancing light, Harlequin, jaguar, jasper, Joseph's coat, kaleidoscope, leopard, mackerel sky, marbled paper, moiré, mother-of-pearl, motley, nacre, opal, parquet, patchwork quilt, peacock's tail, piebald, rainbow, sequin, serpentine, shot silk, spangle, spectrum, stained glass, tabby cat, tapestry, tartan, tiger, tiger's-eye, tortoiseshell, tortoiseshell butterfly, tortoiseshell cat, tricolor, watered silk, zebra

ADJECTIVES

6 **variegated,** bicolor or bicolored, dichroic, dichromatic, trichroic, trichromatic, polychrome or polychromatic, multicolored, parti-colored, pied, varicolored, versicolor, many-colored, many-hued, rainbowed, motley, kaleidoscopic, spectral, prismatic, colorful, florid,

ornamental, patterned, embroidered, worked, chameleonic, changeable

7 **iridescent,** opalescent, opaline, nacreous, pearly, semitransparent, shot, shot through with, pavonine, moiré, watered, chatoyant

8 **checked,** checkered, plaid, tartan, tortoiseshell, inlaid, tessellated, patched, patchy, pied, black-and-white, piebald, pinto, skewbald, fasciate, stripy

9 **striped,** stripy, striate or striated, banded, barred, lined, streaked, marbled, marbly, veined, jaspé, reticulate, paneled, paned

10 **mottled,** dappled, brindled, tabby, grizzled, pepper-and-salt, roan, spotted, maculate, macular, foxed, dotted, studded, peppered, sprinkled, powdered, dusted, dusty, cloudy, hazy, blemished, fly-spotted, speckled, freckled, spotty, pimply, pocked, pockmarked

VERBS

11 **variegate,** diversify, pattern, checker, check, patch, spangle, damascene, inlay, enamel, tessellate, mottle, dapple, brindle, stipple, grizzle, spot, maculate, dot, stud, pepper, sprinkle, powder, dust, speckle, freckle, stripe, striate, band, bar, streak, marble, vein, craze, crack, cloud, stain, blot, discolor, fox

ADVERBS

12 **variedly,** diversely, polychromatically, kaleidoscopically, floridly, ornamentally, iridescently, nacreously, patchily, fasciately, reticulately

264 Appearance

Gentlemen always seem to remember blondes.
— ANITA LOOS

Cleopatra's nose, had it been shorter, the whole face of the world would have been changed. — BLAISE PASCAL

NOUNS

1 **appearance,** arrival, appearing, coming, coming into view, showing up; being, materialization, manifestation, embodiment, incarnation, realization, image

2 **birth,** emergence, onset, arising, rise, coming, coming into being, advent, arrival, debut, entrance, introduction, presentation

3 **first appearance,** publication, issue, launch, release; preview, opening, premiere; opening up, unfolding, blooming, waxing; disclosure, revelation, exposure
▶ *Publication 173; Disclosure 180; Opening 583; Arrival 704; Beginning 771*

4 **visibility,** presence, attendance; existence, being, being there, occurrence, happening, phenomenon, performance, show, parade, display, exhibition
▶ *Drama and Theater 136; Visibility 244; Showiness 404; Presence 575; Existence 717; Display 843*

5 **external appearance,** demeanor, look, outward form or appearance, superficies, surface; form, shape, format, dimensions, outline, contour, silhouette, relief, elevation, section, aspect, side, facet, angle, point of view; facies, outside, exterior, externals, front, facade or façade, facing, covering, veneer; dress, clothes, clothing, garb, fashion, cut, style; demeanor, manner, mien, bearing, posture, carriage, deportment, air, feature, characteristic, marking, trait; figure, body, body type, physical type, face, physiognomy, visage, countenance, lineaments, features; expression, facial expression, body language, skin, skin color, complexion, looks
▶ *Human Body 19; Clothing 100; Fashion 536; Exterior 610; Covering 613; Front 621; Form 624*

6 **spectacle,** sight, revelation, apocalypse, theophany, epiphany, miracle, marvel, prodigy, apparition, ghost, specter, phantom, emanation, ectoplasm, illusion, hallucination, vision, dream, chimera, image, afterimage, mirage, hologram, seeming, semblance, pretense, pose, guise, disguise
▶ *Vision 242; Nonmaterial World 525; Unreality 720*

7 **impression,** effect, first impression, impact, visual appeal; face value, public persona, public image, reflection, mirror image, likeness, similarity, match, lookalike, double, copy, clone, imitation, ringer, representation, picture, photograph, model, replica
▶ *Reproduction 21; Similarity 733; Imitation 736*

8 **reappearance,** return, reissue, republication, second showing, repeat, recurrence, second coming, déjà vu
▶ *Repetition 797*

ADJECTIVES

9 **appearing,** apparent, coming into sight, coming into view, coming into being; material, embodied, incarnate, realized; present, obvious, evident, patent, manifest, showing, visible, in sight; on show, on view, exposed, displayed, revealed, epiphanic, theophanic, salient, prominent, conspicuous, jutting, impressive, effective, spectacular, phenomenal, apocalyptic; beginning, coming, arriving, entering, coming on the scene, emergent, arising, developing, unfolding, waxing, recurring, repeated
▶ *Visibility 244; Presence 575; Arrival 704; Beginning 771*

10 **outer,** outward, ostensible, evident, superficial, surface, external, exterior; visual, reflected, mirrored, reflecting, mirroring, visible

11 **seeming,** appearing, deceptive, specious, illusory, visionary, dreamlike, chimerical, imaginary, hallucinatory
▶ *Deception 193; Nonmaterial World 525; Unreality 720*

VERBS

12 **appear,** show, show up, be present, attend, be at, be there, be; look, seem, appear like, look like, seem like, seem to be, look to be, appear to be, have a look of, have the appearance of; take the shape of, take the guise of, disguise oneself as, dress up as, imitate, copy; reflect, mirror, match, resemble

▶ *Visibility 244; Presence 575; Similarity 733; Imitation 736*

13 become visible, materialize, appear, come to light, see the light; begin, dawn, come forth, come forward, come out, emerge, issue, rise, arise; surface, come to the surface, come up, crop up, show, show up, show oneself, turn up, come, arrive, enter, present itself *or* oneself, make *or* put in an appearance; come into the picture, come on the scene, reveal itself, be manifest; peep, peep out, crawl out of the woodwork, come over the horizon, loom, wax, fade in, heave in sight, come in sight, rear its *or* one's head, pop up, flash

▶ *Visibility 244; Material World 524; Arrival 704; Beginning 771*

14 occur, happen, perform, play, act, appear in, act in, star in, appear on stage, come on the stage, appear on film *or* screen, be published; come out, become available; appear, recur, reappear, come around again

▶ *Drama and Theater 136; Motion Pictures 137; Publication 173*

15 present, put forward, make apparent, realize, show, show up; reveal, disclose, expose, display, exhibit, expose oneself; publish, issue, launch, release, screen, point out, point up, highlight, silhouette, outline

▶ *Publication 173; Disclosure 180; Beautification 530; Display 843*

ADVERBS

16 apparently, evidently, obviously, plainly, clearly, manifestly, to all appearances; seemingly, ostensibly, on the face of it, on the surface, superficially, outwardly, externally, facially, for the sake of appearances, at face value; at sight, at first sight, at first blush, on sight, in outline

265 Disappearance

NOUNS

1 disappearance, vanishing, disappearing, cessation, end, extinction, dying out, death, dying, passing, passing away; wane, ebb, dematerialization, disembodiment; vaporization, evaporation, dissolution; evanescence, melting, fading, fading away, fading out, dwindling; erosion, wearing away, dispersal, dispersion, dissipation, scattering, departure, exit, going, going away; escape, running away, flight, withdrawal, retreat, desertion, truancy, nonappearance; staying away, absence, nonexistence, invisibility, vanishing trick, fade-out, blackout, vanishing point, horizon, disappearing act

▶ *Death 29; Absence 576; Cessation 668; Departure 705; Exit 707; Nonexistence 718; End 773*

2 blacking out, occultation, eclipse, obscuring, obscu-ration, hiding, concealment, burial, erasure, obliteration, cancellation, elimination, annihilation, destruction, loss

▶ *Concealment 181; Darkness 247; Cancellation 834*

ADJECTIVES

3 disappearing, vanishing, evanescent, fugitive, going, departing, escaping, transient, fleeting, passing, fading, waning, dying, dissolving, evaporating, hiding, obsolescent, here today gone tomorrow, now you see it now you don't

▶ *Transience 643*

4 disappeared, vanished, absent, not present, gone, gone away, away, missing, lost, dead, extinct, obsolete, past, past and gone, nonexistent, invisible, eclipsed, occulted, hidden, gone to ground, concealed, buried, dispersed, dissipated, worn away, eroded, out of the picture, out of sight, lost to sight, out of range

▶ *Concealment 181; Invisibility 245; Absence 576; Departure 705; Nonexistence 718*

VERBS

5 disappear, vanish, cease, end, cease to be, cease to exist, become extinct, die out, die, expire, perish, pass away, pass; wane, ebb, recede, dematerialize, become invisible, evanesce, evaporate, dissolve, melt, fade, fade away, fade out, dwindle, dwindle away, peter out; hide, lie low, go to ground, lurk, disappear into thin air; blend into the background, sink below the horizon, sink without a trace; go out of use, become obsolete, cease publication, go out of print, go off the air, close, close down

▶ *Death 29; Concealment 181; Invisibility 245; Cessation 668; Nonexistence 718; Decrease 747; End 773*

6 depart, decamp, go, go away, escape, run, run away, flee, fly, withdraw, retire, go into retirement, retreat, go into retreat, melt away, absent oneself, go AWOL, take French leave, play truant, not appear, fail to appear, stay away, play hooky, scarper [Brit], vamoose [Inf]

▶ *Absence 576; Departure 705; Exit 707*

7 cause to disappear, vaporize, liquidate, disembody, destroy, annihilate, waste, disperse, dissipate, dispel, scatter, dismiss, send away, expel, hide, conceal, obscure, bury, disguise, camouflage, erase, blot out, obliterate, rub, rub out, wipe, wipe out, scrub, cancel, get rid of, eliminate, remove, take away, spirit away

▶ *Burial 31; Concealment 181; Obliteration 186; Destruction 523; Expulsion 709; Cancellation 834*

ADVERBS

8 fleetingly, transiently, fugitively, evanescently, away, invisibly, inwardly, below the surface, below the horizon, in hiding, underground

266 Feelings

NOUNS

1 **feelings,** sensations, perception, sense, awareness, consciousness, realization, understanding, knowledge, experience, reaction, attitude; sentiments, sensibilities, susceptibilities, affections, sympathies, finer feelings, beliefs, opinion, view, viewpoint
  ▶ *Sensation 212; Sensitivity 267; Knowledge 348*

2 **impression,** idea, notion, belief, fancy, inkling; intimation, suggestion, hint, nuance, undercurrent; instinctive feeling, intuition, sixth sense, insight, extrasensory perception (ESP), clairvoyance, presentiment, divination; instinct, impulse, reflex, hunch, gut reaction [Inf], vibes [Inf]
  ▶ *Occultism 86; Intuition 320*

3 **emotion,** feeling, sentiment; mood, attitude, frame *or* state of mind; strong feeling, passion, ardor, fervor, fire, heat, verve, ecstasy, rapture, zeal, intensity, vehemence, obsession, fanaticism, mania
  ▶ *Excess 99; Joy, Cheerfulness 269; Hate 300*

4 **good feeling,** fellow feeling, tender feeling, fondness, sympathy, empathy, cordiality, warmth, friendliness, amicability, responsiveness, involvement, liking, love, devotion
  ▶ *Sensitivity 267; Love 299*

5 **bad feeling,** hard feelings, animosity, resentment, bitterness, ill will, offense, dislike, intolerance, spite, jealously, grudge, envy, hatred, fury, rage; bad atmosphere, bad vibes [Inf]
  ▶ *Dislike 291; Envy 314*

6 **emotionalism,** emotionality, emotiveness, nostalgia, romanticism, sentimentality, mawkishness, bathos, overemotionalism, excitability, emotional instability

7 **seat of feelings,** core of one's being, deepest feelings, secret places, heart, bosom, soul, spirit, bottom of one's heart, cockles of one's heart, pit of one's stomach, bones, guts

8 **feeling person,** sensitive person, emotional person; sympathizer, friend, carer; bundle of nerves, hothead, hater, wild boy *or* man, virago, shrew, spitfire
  ▶ *Excess 99; Sensitivity 267; Love 299; Hate 300*

ADJECTIVES

9 **feeling,** sensing, sentient, sensible, perceptive, aware, conscious, knowing, realizing, understanding, responsible; sensitive, impressionable, susceptible
  ▶ *Sensation 212; Sensitivity 267*

10 **intuitive,** instinctive, impulsive, inspirational, clairvoyant, fey, gut [Inf]

11 **sensitive,** sympathetic, empathetic, feeling, caring, involved with, emotional, jittery
  ▶ *Sensitivity 267*

12 **passionate,** impassioned, intense, effusive, ardent, fervent, zealous, vehement, rapturous, ecstatic, fiery, heated, inflamed, excitable, impetuous, hotheaded, temperamental, touchy, volatile, mercurial, unstable, melodramatic, hysterical, obsessed, jealous, envious, fanatical, manic
  ▶ *Excess 99; Joy, Cheerfulness 269; Hate 300; Envy 314*

13 **emotive,** affecting, touching, moving, deeply felt, heartfelt, overwhelming

VERBS

14 **feel,** sense, experience, perceive, be aware of, realize, understand, go through, live through, undergo; believe, think, opine, maintain, hold; show emotion

15 **feel instinctively,** feel in one's bones *or* guts, sense, intuit, know by instinct, guess at, have a hunch
  ▶ *Intuition 320*

16 **feel deeply,** take to heart, get agitated about, have hysterics, throw a tantrum, go mad, throw a fit, run amuck *or* amok, explode; [Inf]: hit the roof *or* ceiling, see red, freak out

17 **feel for,** empathize, relate to, enter into the spirit of, sympathize, commiserate, pity, be sorry for, grieve for, bleed for
  ▶ *Sensitivity 267; Pity 308*

ADVERBS

18 **with feeling,** feelingly, affectingly, touchingly,

warmly, with all one's heart, from the bottom of one's heart; emotionally, sentimentally, mawkishly; passionately, ardently, fervently, intensely, zealously, vehemently, rapturously, ecstatically, hysterically

267 Sensitivity

NOUNS

1 **sensitivity,** sensitiveness, sensibility, responsiveness, receptivity, aesthesia, awareness, perceptiveness, sentience; susceptibility, impressionability, suggestibility, affectability; delicacy, finer feelings, tenderness, empathy, tact, sympathy, commiseration, compassion, pity, sentimentality
   ⟩ *Sensation 212; Feelings 266*

2 **oversensitivity,** hypersensitivity, touchiness, prickliness, irritability, irascibility, raw feelings, thin skin, soreness, sore point
   ⟩ *Sensation 212; Physical Pain 215; Feelings 266*

ADJECTIVES

3 **sensitive,** sensible, responsive, receptive, aware, perceptive, sentient; susceptible, affectable, feeling; delicate, sympathetic, empathetic, tactful; fond, cordial, friendly, amicable, warm, compassionate, caring, warm-hearted, tender, tender-hearted, soft-hearted; romantic, emotional, sentimental, bathetic, maudlin, mawkish, sloppy

4 **oversensitive,** hypersensitive, touchy, prickly, irritable, irascible, thin-skinned, highly strung, temperamental, nervy, jumpy, jittery; overemotional, tearful, overcome, overwhelmed, overwrought
   ⟩ *Feelings 266*

VERBS

5 **be sensitive,** feel for, pity, sympathize, empathize, be tactful, commiserate, show feelings, feel deeply, take to heart, be all heart; overreact, become irritable, have the jitters; be overcome, be overwhelmed

ADVERBS

6 **sensitively,** emotionally, feelingly, with feeling, perceptively, tactfully, delicately, sympathetically, compassionately, caringly, tenderly

7 **oversensitively,** overemotionally, irritably, temperamentally

268 Insensitivity

NOUNS

1 **insensitivity,** insensitiveness, insensibility, unresponsiveness, unawareness, unperceptiveness; unsusceptibility, standoffishness, apathy; lack of feeling, coldness, tactlessness, bluntness, dullness, philistinism, heedlessness
   ⟩ *Insensibility 213; Distance 585*

2 **heedlessness,** impassivity, indifference, hardness, cal-

lousness, hardheartedness, cold-heartedness, heartlessness, thick skin

3 **insensitive person,** cold heart, icicle, stoic, philistine; [Inf]: cold fish, iceberg, ice queen

ADJECTIVES

4 **insensitive,** insensible, unresponsive, unemotional, stoic, unaware, unconscious, imperceptive, impercipient; unsusceptible, immune, unimpressionable, unimpressible, unaffected, uncaring; indifferent, apathetic, impassive, unfeeling, thick-skinned, impervious; tactless, blunt, dull; cold, frigid, tough, hardened

5 **heedless,** unmindful, impassive, cold-blooded, cold-hearted, heartless

VERBS

6 **be insensitive,** be unresponsive, be cold, be unemotional, be thick-skinned, couldn't care less

ADVERBS

7 **insensitively,** unfeelingly, indifferently, apathetically, unemotionally, unsympathetically, coldly, heartlessly, callously, tactlessly, bluntly

269 Joy, Cheerfulness

One joy scatters a hundred griefs. — CHINESE PROVERB

I have tried too in my time to be a philosopher; but I don't know how, cheerfulness was always breaking in.
   — OLIVER EDWARDS

NOUNS

1 **joy,** joyfulness, joyousness; happiness, contentment, felicity, gladness, heaven, bliss; *joie de vivre* [Fr], gusto, zest, high spirits, exuberance, ebullience, exaltation, exhilaration, euphoria, rapture, elation, enchantment
   ⟩ *Rejoicing 279*

2 **cheerfulness,** cheer, cheeriness, sunniness, light-heartedness, optimism; geniality, sociability, conviviality; good spirits, good cheer, good humor

3 **gaiety,** glee, gleefulness, jollity, joviality, levity, mirth, laughter, delight, pleasure, enjoyment, merriment, merrymaking, fun; vivacity, jauntiness, liveliness, animation

4 **fun,** good time, enjoyment, entertainment, playfulness, amusement, merriment, pleasure, play, lark, sport, thrill; kick [Inf], buzz [Inf]
   ⟩ *Humor 277; Celebration 405; Sociability 408*

5 **joyful person,** merrymaker, reveler, partygoer, rejoicer; cheerful person, smiler, grinner, optimist; life of the party, ray of sunshine, spark plug [Inf]
   ⟩ *Rejoicing 279*

ADJECTIVES

6 **joyful,** joyous, happy, contented, elated, delighted, pleased, captivated, enchanted; glad, gladsome, blissful; exuberant, ebullient, exhilarated, euphoric; cele-

bratory, jubilant, overjoyed, thrilled; pleased as Punch, in seventh heaven, tickled to death; [Inf]: over the moon, on cloud nine, tickled pink, high as a kite

7 **cheerful,** cheery, radiant, sunny, lighthearted, optimistic, carefree; smiling, grinning, beaming, laughing; genial, sociable, convivial, good-natured, good-humored; gay, blithe, gleeful, jolly, jovial, merry; vivacious, jaunty, lively, animated, buoyant, perky, chirpy, bouncy, bouncing, bonhomous, high [Inf], up [Inf]

8 **cheering,** encouraging, heart-warming, reviving, uplifting, amusing, diverting, entertaining, wacky [Inf]

VERBS

9 **enjoy,** have fun, celebrate, relish, delight in, take pleasure in, have a good time; eat, drink, and be merry; kick up one's heels

10 **show joy,** be cheerful, smile, grin, beam, sparkle, laugh, chuckle, giggle, sing, purr, rejoice
▶ *Humor 277; Rejoicing 279*

11 **cause joy,** gladden, please, thrill, delight, charm, enchant, enrapture, enthrall, captivate, send [Inf]

12 **bring cheer,** cheer, cheer up, revive the spirits, brighten, lighten, hearten, enliven, uplift, animate, perk up, buck up, sparkplug [Inf]

ADVERBS

13 **joyfully,** joyously, happily, contentedly, gladly, blissfully

14 **cheerfully,** cheerily, with good cheer, radiantly, lightheartedly, optimistically, genially, good-naturedly, good-humoredly, gaily, blithely, gleefully, merrily, jauntily, perkily, buoyantly, with *or* in high spirits

270 Sorrow

Do you hear the children weeping, O my brothers, / Ere the sorrow comes with years?
— ELIZABETH BARRETT BROWNING

When sorrows come, they come not single spies, / But in battalions. — WILLIAM SHAKESPEARE

NOUNS

1 **sorrow,** sadness, regret, remorse, unhappiness, sorrowfulness, heartache, sadheartedness, downheartedness, heavy-heartedness; wretchedness, misery, desolation, heartbreak, suffering, distress, anguish, languishment, agony, pain, torment; woe, grief, dolor, mourning, weeping and wailing and gnashing of teeth
▶ *Lamentation 280; Adversity 848*

2 **depression,** melancholy, joylessness, cheerlessness, low spirits, lowness, glumness, dejection, dejectedness, despondency, despair, Slough of Despond, gloom, gloominess, doldrums, malaise, funk, droopiness, dreariness, dispiritedness, death wish, the blues

▶ *Psychology and Psychiatry 108; Hopelessness 282*

3 **sad person,** sorrower, mourner; depressed person, depressive, melancholic, moper, whiner, complainer, killjoy, spoilsport, Eeyore, wet blanket, sourpuss [Inf]

ADJECTIVES

4 **sorrowful,** sad, unhappy, crestfallen, saddened, sadhearted, downhearted, heavy-hearted, disheartened, distressed, miserable, wretched, forlorn, languishing, woebegone, tearful, doleful, dolorous, mournful, pining, heartbroken, brokenhearted, disconsolate, inconsolable, desolate, grief-stricken, mourning, ululant, cut up

5 **depressed,** melancholic, downcast, low, joyless, dejected, dispirited, despondent, in the doldrums, droopy, dreary, lackluster, listless, lugubrious, gloomy, morose, atrabilious, glum, dismal, long-faced, moping, suicidal; down, down in the dumps, Eeyorish, blue

6 **distressing,** depressing, dispiriting, sorry, lamentable, heartbreaking, harrowing, painful, tragic, grievous

VERBS

7 **grieve,** sorrow, be saddened, languish, pine, mourn, sigh, lament, cry, weep, sob, moan, howl, wail, ululate; eat one's heart out, be cut up

8 **despair,** despond, lose heart, lose hope, droop, mope, wilt, flag, brood, hit bottom

9 **cause sorrow,** depress, sadden, bring down, dishearten, dispirit, dampen, dampen the spirits, put a wet blanket on, throw cold water on

ADVERBS

10 **sorrowfully,** sadly, unhappily, miserably, mournfully, dolefully; joylessly, gloomily, glumly, drearily, listlessly, dismally, lugubriously

271 Pleasantness

NOUNS

1 **pleasantness,** pleasure, niceness, agreeableness, amiability, charm, appeal; sweetness, delight, delightfulness, felicitousness, loveliness, heaven, bliss
▶ *Joy, Cheerfulness 269*

2 **pleasure,** enjoyment, gratification, satisfaction; ease, comfort, luxury; self-indulgence, hedonism; entertainment, amusement, diversion
▶ *Physical Pleasure 214; Self-Indulgence 456*

3 **amiability,** affability, friendliness, warmth, compatibility, congeniality, geniality, good company; attractiveness, kindliness, cordiality, courtesy, politeness

4 **pleasant thing,** treat, present, gift, holiday, honeymoon, pleasantry, compliment, praise, tribute, honor, flattery; pleasant person, charmer, delight, pleasure, joy
▶ *Flattery 439*

ADJECTIVES

5 **pleasant,** pleasing, nice, likable, enjoyable, pleasurable, agreeable, comfortable; gratifying, satisfying, tasteful, inviting, welcome; charming, appealing,

sweet, lovely, delightful; idyllic, heavenly, divine, Elysian, sublime, blissful, out of this world

6 **likable,** amiable, affable, friendly, warm, compatible, congenial, genial, engaging, good-natured, easygoing, amusing, bright, sunny, attractive, kind, kindly, cordial, courteous, polite, well-mannered

7 **delightful,** lovely, wonderful, marvelous, heavenly, enchanting, gorgeous, entrancing, charming, enthralling, captivating

8 **comfortable,** soothing, relaxing, restful, dulcet, mellow, easy, cozy, snug, comfy [Inf]

9 **pleasure-loving,** pleasure-seeking, self-indulgent, hedonic, hedonistic
> *Physical Pleasure 214; Self-Indulgence 456*

VERBS

10 **make pleasant,** give pleasure, please, gratify, satisfy, comfort, soothe; agree with, charm, delight, brighten one's day

11 **take pleasure in,** like, appreciate, delight in, enjoy, relish, savor

ADVERBS

12 **pleasantly,** nicely, agreeably, with pleasure, with good grace, warmly, genially, cordially, politely

272 Unpleasantness

NOUNS

1 **unpleasantness,** disagreeableness, discomfort, pain, annoyance, umbrage; distastefulness, unpalatability; nastiness, repulsiveness
> *Physical Pain 215*

2 **objectionability,** unacceptability, offensiveness, ungraciousness, impoliteness, incivility, discourtesy, unkindness, impertinence, rudeness, bad manners, boorishness, meanness, cantankerousness, aggressiveness, beastliness

3 **dissension,** disagreement, disharmony, friction, disunity, discord, discordance, aggravation, antagonism, squabbling, quarreling, fighting, bickering
> *Aggravation 276; Attack 418; Disagreement 463*

4 **quarrel,** argument, difference of opinion, altercation, conflict, strife; squabble, scuffle, clash, scrap, wrangle, brawl, row, fisticuffs, feud, vendetta; set-to, tiff, aggro [Brit *and* Aus inf]

5 **unpleasant person,** pest, nuisance, boor, oaf, lout, cad, shrew, troublemaker, mischief-maker, quarreler, wrangler, aggressor, fighter, hooligan, beast; [Inf]: pain, pain in the neck *or* ass, shit

ADJECTIVES

6 **unpleasant,** displeasing, unpleasing, disagreeable; uncomfortable, painful; discordant, unharmonious, trying, annoying, rebarbative, irksome; unwelcome, uninviting, disliked; distasteful, unpalatable, unsavory; nasty, horrible, invidious, hateful, horrid, disgusting,

odious, repulsive, loathsome, revolting, sickening, nauseating
> *Dissonance 241; Hate 300; Repulsion 701*

7 **objectionable,** unacceptable, offensive; ungracious, discomforting, impolite, uncivil, discourteous, unchivalrous; unkind, uncouth, impertinent, rude, boorish, mean, cantankerous, obnoxious, dissentious, quarrelsome, quarreling, crabbed, aggressive, bellicose, bloody-minded; crabby [Inf], beastly [Inf]
> *Aggravation 276; Argument 329; Attack 418*

VERBS

8 **displease,** make unpleasant, offend, annoy, disturb, put off, discomfort, enrage, repel, appall, horrify, sicken, disgust, revolt, nauseate, stick in one's throat

9 **quarrel,** disagree, dissent, argue, have differences with, nag, take umbrage, insult, offend, squabble, wrangle, scrap, bicker, brawl, fight, cross swords with, clash, conflict, feud

ADVERBS

10 **unpleasantly,** disagreeably, discourteously, nastily, distastefully, offensively, aggressively, repulsively

273 Satisfaction

NOUNS

1 **satisfaction,** fulfillment, gratification; contentedness, contentment, content, peace of mind, serenity, equanimity; happiness, pleasure, enjoyment, comfort, ease; satiation, satiety; self-satisfaction, smugness, complacency
> *Physical Pleasure 214; Joy, Cheerfulness 269; Pleasantness 271; Relief 275*

2 **reparation,** recompense, compensation, atonement, amends, apology, indemnity, expiation, reconciliation, appeasement, propitiation
> *Atonement 313*

3 **satisfactoriness,** sufficiency, competency, adequacy, tolerability

ADJECTIVES

4 **satisfied,** fulfilled, gratified; content, contented, serene, uncomplaining, undemanding; happy, pleased, comfortable, secure, safe; satiated, full, full-up, self-satisfied, smug, complacent

5 **satisfying,** fulfilling, gratifying, pleasing; pacifying, comforting; satiating, filling, ample

6 **satisfactory,** sufficient, sufficing, enough, competent, adequate, acceptable, passable, tolerable, all right, not bad, good enough, fair; OK, so-so

VERBS

7 **satisfy,** fulfill, gratify, content, please, indulge, satiate, sate, fill, quench, slake

8 **be satisfied,** have nothing to complain about, have nothing to grumble about, be at ease, delight in, have one's heart's desire, have all one could ask for, purr

9 **comfort,** pacify, placate, appease, lull, reassure, assure,

convince, persuade, put someone's mind at rest, set at ease

10 **suffice,** serve, do, answer, settle, meet, meet the needs of

11 **recompense,** compensate, atone, make amends, apologize, indemnify, expiate, reconcile, propitiate

ADVERBS

12 **satisfactorily,** sufficiently, competently, adequately, enough

13 **with satisfaction,** contentedly, serenely, happily

274 Dissatisfaction

NOUNS

1 **dissatisfaction,** displeasure, disgruntlement, discontent, discontentment; disappointment, disillusionment, consternation; disapprobation, disapproval, rejection, reprobation, censure; dislike, derision, deprecation, disgust, contempt, contemptuousness, scorn

2 **expression of dissatisfaction,** complaint, criticism, boo, hiss, Bronx cheer, whistle, snub, reprimand, remonstration, black mark, rebuke, reproof; [Inf]: gripe, grouse, telling off, raspberry

3 **dissatisfied person,** dissatisfied customer, reprover, complainer, grumbler, carper, moaner, whiner, bleater, spoilsport, malcontent, moper, sulker, brooder, angry young man; [Inf]: bellyacher, griper, grouser, kvetch

ADJECTIVES

4 **dissatisfied,** displeased, disgruntled, discontented, discontent, malcontent, malcontented, sulking, sulky, brooding, disaffected, complaining, disappointed, disillusioned, disapproving, unapproving; unimpressed, critical of, pejorative, disgusted, contemptuous, scornful, derisive, derisory

5 **unsatisfactory,** dissatisfactory, disappointing, substandard, unapproved, unpopular, rejected, not up to snuff [Inf]

VERBS

6 **dissatisfy,** displease, disgruntle, disappoint, disillusion; disgust, revolt, sicken

7 **be dissatisfied,** disapprove, not hold with, not think much of, dislike, resent, disfavor, criticize, slate, find fault with, pick holes in, look askance at, tut-tut at, object to, cavil; grumble, carp, complain, whine, moan, sulk, brood, run down, belittle, deride, deprecate, deplore, reprove, rebuke, condemn, reject, abhor, scorn, defame, revile, vilify, boo, hiss; [Inf]: bellyache, gripe, grouse, kvetch

ADVERBS

8 **discontentedly,** disapprovingly, disgustedly, contemptuously, scornfully

275 Relief

NOUNS

1 **ease,** comfort, solace, consolation, reassurance; mitigation, assuagement, alleviation, palliation, mollification, appeasement, relaxation, abatement, remission, respite, lull; anesthetization, tranquilization, sedation; load off one's mind or shoulders [Inf]

2 **aid,** assistance, help, succor, support, helping hand, rescue, deliverance, liberation, release, emancipation, salvation, salvage

3 **charity,** alms, almsgiving, poor relief, benefaction, gift, donation, relief, aid, emergency aid, disaster relief, famine relief

4 **reliever,** comforter, consoler, mollifier, palliative; remedy, cure, balm; anodyne, analgesic, painkiller, emollient, soother, anesthetic, tranquilizer, sedative, opiate, soporific, hypnotic, sleeping pill, sleeping draft, ray of sunshine

▶ *Remedy 115*

5 **helper,** assistant, auxiliary, deputy, helpmate, helpmeet, right-hand man or woman, secretary, girl or man Friday, aide, aide-de-camp; medic, paramedic, doctor, nurse; understudy, substitute, replacement, stand-in; reserve, stopgap, backup, supporter, right hand, locum, locum tenens [Brit]

ADJECTIVES

6 **relieved,** calmed, restored, refreshed; eased, comforted, soothed, consoled, reassured; assuaged, mollified, appeased; relaxed, sedated, cured

7 **relieving,** helping, helpful, refreshing, restorative; comforting, soothing, consoling, reassuring; relaxing, easing, calming, balsamic, curative, remedial, assuaging, palliative, sedative, hypnotic

VERBS

8 **relieve,** ease, comfort, solace, pacify, soothe, calm, quiet, console, reassure, allay; mitigate, assuage, alleviate, palliate, mollify, appease; moderate, temper, abate, diminish, lessen, soften, relax, tranquilize, sedate, anesthetize, take the sting out of

9 **save,** rescue, throw a lifeline to, come to the rescue of, reprieve, deliver, free, set free, liberate, emancipate, release, rid

10 **aid,** assist, help, deputize for, stand in for, do duty for, substitute for, understudy for, step into the shoes of, take over from, replace, succeed

11 **relieve from duty,** dismiss, fire, let go, lay off; [Inf]: sack, ax, can

12 **relieve oneself,** urinate, defecate

▶ *Excretion 25*

13 **take away,** confiscate, disencumber, sequestrate, commandeer, dispossess, snatch, steal, rob, mug, run away with

14 **comfortingly,** reassuringly, refreshingly, soothingly, helpfully

276 Aggravation

NOUNS

1 **aggravation,** exacerbation, worsening, deterioration, intensification, heightening, deepening, magnification, augmentation, enhancement, exaggeration
  ▶ *Increase 746; Deterioration 808*
2 **annoyance,** irritation, exasperation, vexation, provocation, anger, nuisance, bother, trouble, harassment, hassle [Inf], aggro [Brit *and* Aus inf]
  ▶ *Unpleasantness 272; Attack 418*

ADJECTIVES

3 **aggravated,** exacerbated, worsened, intensified, heightened, deepened, increased, magnified, enhanced, enlarged
4 **aggravating,** annoying, irritating, exasperating, provoking, vexing, vexatious

VERBS

5 **aggravate,** exacerbate, make worse, worsen, inflame, intensify, heighten, deepen, increase, augment, magnify, enhance, exaggerate, rub salt in the wound, bring to a head; rub it in [Inf], rub one's nose in it [Inf]
6 **become aggravated,** get worse, worsen, build up, go from bad to worse, deteriorate, degenerate, decline
7 **annoy,** irritate, exasperate, goad, provoke, antagonize, anger, vex, tease, peeve, hassle [Inf]

ADVERBS

8 **from bad to worse,** out of the frying pan into the fire
9 **annoyingly,** irritatingly, vexatiously

277 Humor

True wit is nature to advantage dress'd; / What oft was thought, but ne'er so well express'd. — ALEXANDER POPE

NOUNS

1 **humor,** humorousness, wit, wittiness, funniness, jokiness, drollery, dry humor, facetiousness, flippancy, waggishness, waggery
2 **amusement,** entertainment, enjoyment, diversion, fun, merriment, mirth, laughter, hilarity; joking, jesting, joshing, teasing, kidding, japery; clowning, buffoonery
  ▶ *Light Entertainment 138; Rejoicing 279*
3 **wit,** ready wit, dry wit, witticism, quip, bon mot, play on words, wordplay, banter, badinage, repartee, sarcasm, irony
4 **entertainment,** comedy, satire, parody, caricature, send-up, takeoff, spoof, farce, lampoon, burlesque, slapstick; cartoon, comic strip, funny paper, the funnies

  ▶ *Light Entertainment 138; Deception 193*
5 **sense of humor,** risibility, funny bone
6 **joke,** jest, jape, gag, one-liner, quip, pun, witticism, pleasantry, funny story, yarn, old chestnut, shaggy-dog story, tall story, blue joke, double entendre, dirty story; prank, lark, leg-pull, caper, trick, practical joke; [Inf]: wisecrack, funny, laugh, belly laugh, hoot, scream
  ▶ *Deception 193*
7 **humorist,** wit, wag, joke, jester, funnyman, quipster, tease, teaser, gagster, gag writer, wisecracker [Inf], jokesmith; ironist, satirist, lampooner, caricaturist, cartoonist; comic, comedian, straight man, clown, buffoon
  ▶ *Light Entertainment 138; Lack of Meaning 362*
8 **laughter,** giggle, titter, chuckle, chortle, snigger, guffaw, hilarity

ADJECTIVES

9 **humorous,** funny, amusing, diverting, entertaining, laughable, risible, hilarious, uproarious, side-splitting, hysterical; jocular, jocose, joking, slapstick, waggish; comic, comical, droll, whimsical, quirky, zany, merry, facetious; farcical, sarcastic, ironic, satirical; flippant, teasing, jokey, corny [Inf]
10 **witty,** clever, nimble-witted, quick-witted, dry-witted, smart

VERBS

11 **be humorous,** entertain, amuse, regale, divert; joke, crack a joke, josh, jest; banter, pun, quip, wisecrack [Inf]; clown, play the fool; make fun of, poke fun at, play a joke on, tease, rag, twit, kid, rib, scoff, mock, pull someone's leg, satirize, parody, send up, take off, lampoon, caricature
12 **laugh,** laugh at, giggle, get the giggles, snigger, snicker, titter, chuckle, chortle, guffaw, howl, roar, slap one's thighs, split one's sides, roll in the aisles, laugh till one cries, laugh one's head off

ADVERBS

13 **humorously,** amusingly, funnily, laughably, hilariously, wittily; comically, drolly, whimsically, dryly, facetiously, farcically, sarcastically, ironically, satirically; jokingly, as a joke, for *or* in fun, with tongue in cheek

278 Seriousness

NOUNS

1 **seriousness,** solemnity, gravity, severity, staidness, sternness, grimness, thoughtfulness, humorlessness, dourness, sullenness, gloom; earnestness, importance
2 **earnestness,** sincerity, resolution, determination, dedication, commitment, eagerness
  ▶ *Willingness 373*
3 **importance,** import, significance, consequence, weightiness, momentousness, moment, gravity, severity

▶ *Importance 799*

ADJECTIVES

4 **serious,** solemn, grave, thoughtful, pensive, sedate, staid, sober, sober as a judge, stern, severe, unsmiling, straight-faced, grim, poker-faced, stony-faced, deadpan, humorless, somber, dour, sullen, glum, long-faced, frowning; earnest, important

5 **earnest,** sincere, genuine, resolute, determined, purposeful, intent, dedicated, committed, eager

6 **important,** significant, of consequence, serious, weighty, momentous, crucial, vital, life-and-death, critical

VERBS

7 **be serious,** be solemn, look serious, keep a straight face, keep from laughing, wipe the smile off one's face, pull *or* make a long face, frown, glare, glower

8 **take seriously,** be in earnest, consider *or* regard as important

ADVERBS

9 **solemnly,** gravely, seriously, thoughtfully, pensively, soberly, with a straight face, sternly, severely, sullenly, glumly

10 **earnestly,** sincerely, genuinely, resolutely, purposefully, really, actually, truly, honestly, in all seriousness; indeed, certainly, seriously, in all conscience, absolutely, definitely, importantly, unquestionably, undeniably

279 Rejoicing

To rejoice in life, to find the world beautiful and delightful to live in, was a mark of the Greek spirit which distinguished it from all that had gone before. It is a vital distinction. — EDITH HAMILTON

NOUNS

1 **rejoicing,** celebrating, jubilation, exultation, triumph; happiness, joyfulness, joy, delight, jolliness, merriment, roistering, merrymaking; festivity, celebration, special day, holiday, festival, anniversary, jubilee, party, revel, revelry, great day, feast, feast day, banquet, rave [Brit inf]
▶ *Food 90; Joy, Cheerfulness 269; Celebration 405*

2 **applause,** fanfare, salute, ovation, cry, shout, yell, cheer, three cheers, high-five, hurrah, huzzah; hosanna, hallelujah, hymn, praise, laud, glory, thanksgiving, congratulations
▶ *Religion 81; Loudness 232; Approval 437*

3 **rejoicer,** celebrator, celebrant, reveler, merrymaker, roisterer, partyer, cheerer, lauder, raver [Brit inf]

ADJECTIVES

4 **rejoicing,** celebratory, jubilant, exultant, triumphant, glorious, ecstatic, euphoric, happy, joyful, cheerful, cheery, merry, jolly, reveling, applauding, cheering, high

▶ *Joy, Cheerfulness 269; Celebration 405; Approval 437*

VERBS

5 **rejoice,** celebrate, jubilate, exult, triumph, glory, jump for joy, make merry, throw a party, have a party, roister, revel, carouse, dance, feast, banquet, go into ecstasies; [Inf]: party, make whoopee, paint the town red, go on a binge, whoop it up, have a ball, rave [Brit]
▶ *Joy, Cheerfulness 269; Celebration 405*

6 **fete,** honor, praise, laud, congratulate, lionize, sing the praises of, pay respects to, salute, high-five, kill the fatted calf for
▶ *Approval 437*

ADVERBS

7 **rejoicingly,** jubilantly, triumphantly, ecstatically, euphorically, joyfully, merrily

INTERJECTIONS

8 **hurrah!,** hip, hip, hooray!, cheers!, hosanna!, hallelujah!, yippee!

280 Lamentation

NOUNS

1 **lamentation,** lamenting, grieving, mourning; crying, sobbing, bawling, weeping, wailing; weeping and wailing and gnashing of teeth; keening; dolefulness, tearfulness, weepiness, sadness, sorrow, sorrowfulness, grief, mournfulness, plangency, wretchedness, misery, woe, distress; last rites, wake, funeral
▶ *Burial 31; Human Cry 239; Sorrow 270*

2 **lament,** lamentation, requiem, obsequy, dirge, elegy, threnody, coronach [Scot, Irish], knell, eulogy, thanatopsis, taps; keen, howl, ululation, cry, sob, whimper, moan, groan, sigh; sob story, tale of woe, complaint
▶ *Music 140; Sorrow 270; Dissatisfaction 274*

3 **lamenter,** griever, mourner, elegist, threnodist; weeper, wailer, keener, blubberer, crybaby, sniveler, moaner, groaner, complainer
▶ *Sullenness 304*

ADJECTIVES

4 **lamenting,** grieving, mourning; crying, weeping, wailing, keening; mournful, tearful, lachrymose, miserable, doleful, wretched, woebegone, disconsolate, unhappy, sad, sorrowful, wet-eyed, red-eyed; plaintive, plangent, dirgelike, elegiac, threnodic; depressed, down
▶ *Sorrow 270*

5 **lamented,** mourned, grieved for, elegized, eulogized

6 **lamentable,** regrettable, deplorable, unfortunate, pitiful, pitiable, heartbreaking, distressing, depressing, tearjerking [Inf]

VERBS

7 **lament,** grieve, mourn, mourn for, go into mourning, sorrow, elegize; weep for, wail, keen, beat one's breast, bewail, sing the blues; bemoan, complain; deplore, regret, rue

> *Burial 31; Sorrow 270; Dissatisfaction 274; Sullenness 304*

8 **weep,** cry, sob, wail, shed tears, weep over, cry one's eyes out, bawl, howl, ululate, blubber, whimper, snivel
> *Human Cry 239*

ADVERBS

9 **lamentingly,** mournfully, tearfully, dolefully, sorrowfully, sadly, plaintively, plangently; in mourning, in black, in sackcloth and ashes, at half-mast

10 **lamentably,** regretfully, deplorably, ruefully, unfortunately, pitifully

281 Hope

NOUNS

1 **hope,** hoping, hopefulness, optimism, positive thinking, cheerfulness, buoyancy; bright side, silver lining; rose-colored glasses, rose-tinted view, wishful thinking, false hope; hope and a prayer, faint hope, ray of hope, glimmer of hope, last hope
> *Joy, Cheerfulness 269*

2 **expectation,** expectations, expectancy, anticipation; assumption, presumption, trust, confidence, faith, belief, conviction
> *Belief 87; Expectation 356*

3 **aspiration,** ambition, dream, vision, high hopes, great expectations, aim, goal, objective, intention; wish, desire, longing, yearning, craving; pipe dream, fantasy, castles in the air *or* in Spain; dream world, fool's paradise, promised land, cloud-cuckoo-land, Utopia, Erewhon
> *Desire 288; Overestimation 343; Unreality 720; Improbability 839*

4 **cheer,** encouragement, support, comfort, solace, reassurance, security; promise, auspiciousness, propitiousness, prospects
> *Prediction 358; Promise 458*

5 **hoper,** optimist, aspirant, aspirer, hopeful; dreamer, visionary, idealist, utopian, Pollyanna

ADJECTIVES

6 **hopeful,** hoping, full of hope, optimistic, bullish, sanguine, cheerful, buoyant, positive, upbeat, up [Inf]; idealistic, starry-eyed
> *Joy, Cheerfulness 269*

7 **expectant,** expecting, anticipating; confident, assured
> *Belief 87; Expectation 356*

8 **aspiring,** aspirant, ambitious; dreaming, visionary, wishful, desirous, longing, yearning, craving
> *Desire 288*

9 **cheering,** heartening, comforting, reassuring, encouraging; promising, auspicious, propitious, favorable, bright, sunny, golden, rosy, rose-colored
> *Promise 458*

VERBS

10 **hope,** be optimistic, be sanguine, hope for the best, think positively, look on the bright side, look for the silver lining, make the best of it; look *or* see through rose-colored glasses; live in hope, cling to hope, hope against hope, hope and pray, hope to God; pin one's hopes on, count on, rely on, bank on

11 **be hopeful,** cross one's fingers, keep one's fingers crossed, knock on *or* touch wood; take heart, cheer up, buck up, get *or* keep one's hopes *or* spirits up, keep smiling, see light at the end of the tunnel

12 **expect,** look forward to, await, anticipate; assume, presume, trust, believe, have faith, feel confident, rest assured
> *Belief 87; Expectation 356*

13 **aspire,** aim, dream, have high hopes; wish, desire, long for, yearn for, crave; pipe-dream, fantasize, build castles in the air *or* in Spain
> *Desire 288*

14 **inspire hope,** cheer, cheer up, encourage, support, comfort, console, reassure; raise one's hopes, hold out hope, promise, augur well, bid fair *or* well
> *Joy, Cheerfulness 269; Prediction 358; Promise 458; Possibility 836*

ADVERBS

15 **hopefully,** hopingly, with hope, optimistically, sanguinely, positively, cheerfully, buoyantly

16 **expectantly,** presumably, confidently; ambitiously

17 **comfortingly,** encouragingly, reassuringly; promisingly, auspiciously, propitiously

INTERJECTIONS

18 **never despair!,** *nil desperandum!* [L], never say die!, where there's life, there's hope!

282 Hopelessness

All hope abandon, ye who enter here. — DANTE

NOUNS

1 **hopelessness,** no hope, remedilessness, irreparability, irredeemability, irretrievability, irrecoverableness, incurability; irrevocability, irreversibility; incorrigibility, irreformability
> *Death 29*

2 **lack of hope,** loss of hope, despair, despond, despondency, dejection, disconsolation, cheerlessness, unhopefulness, forlornness, gloom, gloominess, gloom and doom, bleakness, depression, melancholy, desolation; discouragement, disappointment, dashed hopes, letdown, desperation; defeatism, doubt, self-doubt, negativism, pessimism, cynicism; inauspiciousness, unpropitiousness, bad omen, doom
> *Sorrow 270; Disappointment 293*

3 **futility,** uselessness, worthlessness, fruitlessness, pointlessness, impossibility; hopeless situation, hope-

less case, lost cause, not a ghost of a chance, fool's errand, wild-goose chase, Catch-22, no way out, predicament, plight, quandary, dilemma; write-off [Inf], downer [Inf]

▶ *Uselessness 802; Difficulty 824; Impossibility 837*

4 **lack of skill,** incompetence, ineptitude, inadequacy, inferiority, hopelessness

▶ *Unskillfulness 128*

5 **hopeless person,** loser, born loser, failure; melancholic, moper, defeatist, negativist, pessimist, worrywart, killjoy, Eeyore; cynic, prophet of doom, Cassandra, Job's comforter; [Inf]: drag, goner, dead duck

▶ *Failure 846*

ADJECTIVES

6 **hopeless,** beyond hope, past hope, abject, irremediable, remediless, irreparable, irredeemable, irretrievable, unsalvageable, irrecoverable, inoperable, incurable, terminal; irrevocable, irreversible, beyond recall; incorrigible, irreformable

7 **without hope,** despairing, despondent, dejected, disconsolate, inconsolable, cheerless, unhopeful, comfortless, forlorn, gloomy, bleak, depressed, melancholic, desolate, blue, disheartened, downhearted, downcast, down, down in the dumps, down in the mouth, in the doldrums; discouraged, defeated, desperate, suicidal; defeatist, negative, negativistic, pessimistic, cynical

▶ *Sorrow 270*

8 **inauspicious,** unpropitious, unpromising, unfavorable, ill-omened, ominous, doomed

9 **futile,** useless, worthless, fruitless, pointless, vain, impossible, unsolvable, unresolvable

▶ *Uselessness 802; Impossibility 837*

10 **without skill,** incompetent, inept, inadequate, inferior, no good, bad, poor, awful, terrible, hopeless, pathetic

▶ *Unskillfulness 128*

VERBS

11 **be hopeless,** have no remedy, have no cure, be irreparable; lack hope, lose hope, give up hope, give up, despair, lose heart, doubt, think negatively, think the worst, write off

12 **disappoint,** crush, shatter one's hopes, burst one's bubble, dash the cup from one's lips, drive to despair

▶ *Disappointment 293*

ADVERBS

13 **hopelessly,** irreparably, irredeemably, irretrievably, irrecoverably, incurably, terminally; irrevocably, irreversibly; incorrigibly

14 **unhopefully,** despairingly, despondently, dejectedly, disconsolately, inconsolably, cheerlessly, forlornly, gloomily, bleakly, desperately; negatively, pessimistically, cynically

15 **inauspiciously,** unpropitiously, unfavorably, ominously

16 **futilely,** uselessly, worthlessly, fruitlessly, pointlessly, in vain, impossibly

17 **unskillfully,** incompetently, ineptly, inadequately, badly, poorly, awfully, terribly, hopelessly, pathetically

283 Fear

Fear has many eyes and can see things underground.
— MIGUEL DE CERVANTES

The only thing we have to fear is fear itself.
— FRANKLIN D. ROOSEVELT

NOUNS

1 **fear,** terror, horror, fright, scare, affright [Arch], funk, consternation, dismay, alarm, panic, dread, awe; phobia, aversion; mortal fear, fear and trembling, unholy terror, fit of terror, blind panic

2 **fearfulness,** apprehension, apprehensiveness, trepidation, timorousness, timidity, anxiety, nervousness, jumpiness, skittishness, foreboding, tension, uneasiness, unease, perturbation, disquiet, disquietude, agitation, misgiving, qualm

▶ *Cowardice 285*

PHOBIAS BY NAME

ablutophobia: washing *or* bathing
acarophobia: mites, small objects
acerophobia *or* acerbophobia: sourness
acousticophobia: sound
acrophobia *or* altophobia *or* hypsophobia
  or hypsiphobia: heights
aeroacrophobia: open, high places
aeronausiphobia: airsickness
aerophagiaphobia: swallowing air
aerophobia: drafts, air, gases
agoraphobia: open places, crowds
agrizoophobia: wild animals
agyiophobia: being in streets
agyrophobia: crossing streets

aichurophobia: points, pointed objects
ailurophobia *or* aelurophobia: cats
albuminurophobia: kidney disease
alektorophobia: chickens
alliumphobia: garlic
allodoxaphobia: opinions
amathophobia *or* koniophobia: dust
amaxophobia: being in vehicles
amychophobia: scratches
ancraophobia *or* anemophobia:
  wind
androphobia: men
anginophobia: narrowness; heart
  problems

Anglophobia: England, the English
ankylophobia: joint immobility
anthophobia: flowers
anthropophobia: people
antlophobia: floods
anuptaphobia: staying single
apeirophobia: infinity
apiphobia: bees
arachnophobia: spiders
arithmophobia *or* numerophobia:
  numbers
asthenophobia: weakness; fainting
astraphobia *or* astrapophobia: thunder
  and lightning

---

ataxiophobia: disorder
atelophobia: imperfection
atephobia: ruin; ruins
aulophobia: flutes
aurophobia: gold
auroraphobia: aurora
automysophobia: being dirty
autophobia *or* monophobia *or*
    eremitophobia: loneliness
aviatophobia: flying
bacteriophobia: bacteria
ballistophobia: bullets; missiles
barophobia: gravity
basiphobia: walking
bathophobia: depth
batophobia: high buildings
batrachophobia: frogs; reptiles
belonophobia: needles
bibliophobia: books
blennophobia *or* myxophobia: slime
botanophobia: plants
bromidrophobia *or* bromidrosiphobia:
    body odor
brontophobia *or* keraunophobia *or*
    tonitrophobia: thunder
cainophobia *or* cainotophobia *or*
    centophobia: newness; novelty
cancerphobia *or* cancerophobia *or*
    carcinophobia: cancer
cardiophobia: heart disease
carnophobia: meat
catagelophobia: ridicule
cathisophobia: sitting
catoptrophobia *or* eisoptrophobia:
    mirrors
cenophobia: empty rooms; open
    places
chaetophobia *or* trichophobia: hair
cheimaphobia *or* cheimatophobia *or*
    psychrophobia: cold
cherophobia: happiness; gaiety
chionophobia: snow
cholerophobia: cholera
chorophobia: dancing
chrematophobia: money
chromophobia *or* chromatophobia:
    color
chronophobia: duration of time
cibophobia *or* sitophobia: food
claustrophobia: enclosed places
climacophobia: stairs
clinophobia: beds
cnidophobia: insect stings
coimetrophobia: cemeteries
coitophobia: coitus
cometophobia: comets
contrectophobia: sexual abuse
coprophobia *or* scatophobia: feces

coprostasophobia: constipation
cremnophobia: precipices
cryophobia *or* pagophobia: ice, frost
crystallophobia: crystals, glass
cyberphobia: computers
cyclophobia: bicycles
cymophobia: waves
cynophobia: dogs
cyprianophobia: prostitutes
decidophobia: decisions
deipnophobia: dining
demonophobia: demons
demophobia: crowds
dendrophobia: trees
dentophobia: dentists
dermatopathophobia: skin disease
dermatosiophobia: skin
dextrophobia: the right
diabetophobia: diabetes
didaskaleinophobia *or* scolionophobia:
    school
dikephobia: justice
dinophobia: dizziness; whirlpools
dipsophobia: drinking
doraphobia: animal skin, fur
dromophobia: motion; crossing
    streets
dystychiphobia: accidents
ecclesiophobia: church
ecophobia *or* oikophobia: home
    surroundings
electrophobia: electricity
eleutherophobia: freedom
emetophobia: vomiting
enetophobia: pins
entomophobia: insects
eosophobia: dawn
epistaxiophobia: nosebleeds
eremophobia *or* eremiophobia: being by
    oneself
ergophobia: work
erotophobia: sexual love
erythrophobia: blushing; color red
esodophobia: virginity
euphobia: good news
febriphobia *or* pyrexiophobia: fever
feminophobia *or* gynephobia: women
Francophobia: France, the French
frigophobia: cold things
gametophobia *or* gamophobia: marriage
geliophobia: laughter
geniophobia: chins
genophobia: sexual intercourse
genuphobia: knees
gephyrophobia: bridges
gerascophobia: growing old
Germanophobia: Germans
gerontophobia: old people

geumatophobia *or* geumaphobia *or*
    geumophobia: taste
graphophobia: writing
gymnophobia *or* nudophobia: nudity
hadephobia *or* stygiophobia: hell
hagiophobia: holy things; saints
hamartophobia: sin; error
haptophobia *or* hapnophobia: touch
harpaxophobia: robbers
hedonophobia: pleasure
heliophobia: sunlight
Hellenologophobia: Greek terms
helminthophobia *or* scoleciphobia *or*
    vermiphobia: worms
hematophobia *or* hemophobia *or*
    hemaphobia: blood
herpetophobia: reptiles; snakes
hierophobia: priests; religious
    objects
hippophobia: horses
hodophobia: travel
homichlophobia *or* nebulaphobia: fog
homilophobia: sermons
homophobia: homosexuality
hormephobia: shock
hyalophobia *or* hyelophobia *or*
    nelophobia: glass
hydrophobia *or* aquaphobia: water
hydrophobophobia: rabies
hygrophobia: dampness
hypegiaphobia: responsibility
hypnophobia: hypnosis
iatrophobia: doctors, hospitals
ichthyophobia: fish
ideophobia: ideas
ilingophobia: vertigo
iophobia: poisons; rust
isolophobia: solitude
isopterophobia: termites
kakorraphiophobia *or* atychiphobia:
    failure
kinetophobia: motion
kleptophobia: stealing
koinoniphobia: room
kopophobia: fatigue
lachanophobia: vegetables
lalophobia *or* laliophobia *or* glossophobia
    or phonophobia: speech
leprophobia *or* lepraphobia: leprosy
leukophobia: color white
levophobia: left side
ligyrophobia: noise
lilapsophobia: hurricanes
limnophobia: lakes
linonophobia: string
litigaphobia: litigation; lawsuits
logophobia: words
lygophobia: dark *or* gloomy places

lyssophobia *or* maniaphobia *or* dementophobia: insanity

macrophobia: long waits

malaxophobia: love play

mastigophobia: beating

mechanophobia: machinery

megalophobia: large objects

melissophobia: bees; insects

meningitophobia: meningitis

menophobia: menstruation

metallophobia: metal

meteorphobia: meteors

methyphobia: alcohol

metrophobia: poetry

microbiophobia *or* bacillophobia: microbes; germs

microphobia: small things

mnemophobia: memories

monophobia: one thing

myrmecophobia: ants

mysophobia: dirt

mythophobia: false statements

necrophobia: corpses

neophobia: new things

nephophobia: clouds

nosemaphobia *or* nosophobia: illness

nosocomephobia: hospitals

nostophobia: returning home

nucleomitophobia: nuclear weapons

nyctophobia *or* achluophobia *or* scotophobia: darkness, night

obesophobia *or* pocrescophobia: gaining weight

ochlophobia: mobs

ochophobia: moving vehicles

odontophobia: teeth

odynesphobia *or* odynephobia *or* odynophobia *or* algophobia: pain

oenophobia: wine

olfactophobia *or* osmophobia *or* ophresiophobia: smell

ommataphobia: eyes

oneirophobia: dreams

onomatophobia: names

ophidiophobia *or* ophiophobia: snakes, reptiles

optophobia: opening eyes

ornithophobia: birds

orthophobia: propriety

ostraconophobia: shellfish

panphobia: everything

papyrophobia: paper

paraphobia: sexual perversion

parasitophobia: parasites

parthenophobia: young girls; virgins

pathophobia: disease

patriophobia: heredity

peccatiphobia: sin

pediaphobia: dolls *or* small figures

pedophobia: children

peniaphobia: poverty

pentheraphobia: mother-in-law

phagophobia: swallowing *or* eating

phalacrophobia: baldness

pharmacophobia: drugs

phasmophobia *or* spectrophobia: ghosts

phengophobia: daylight *or* sunlight

philemaphobia *or* philematophobia: kissing

philophobia: love

philosophobia: philosophy

phobophobia: fear

phonophobia: noise; telephones

photoalgiaphobia: eye pain

photoaugiaphobia: glaring lights

photophobia: light

phronemophobia: thinking

phthiriophobia *or* pediculophobia: lice, parasites

phthisiophobia: tuberculosis

placophobia: tombstones

pluviophobia *or* ombrophobia: rain

pneumatophobia: spirits

pnigophobia *or* pnigerophobia: smothering; choking

pogonophobia: beards

poinephobia: punishment

politicophobia: politics

polyphobia: many things

ponophobia: work; fatigue

porphyrophobia: color purple

potamophobia: rivers

potophobia: drink

prosophobia: progress

psellismophobia: stuttering

psychophobia: the mind

pteronophobia: feathers

pyrophobia: fire

radiophobia: radiation

rectophobia *or* proctophobia: rectal diseases

rhabdophobia: rods

rhytiphobia: wrinkles

rypophobia: soiling

Satanophobia: Satan

scabiophobia: scabies

scelerophobia: attack by the wicked

sciaphobia *or* sciophobia: shadows

scopophobia *or* scoptophobia: being stared at

selaphobia: flashing lights

selenophobia: moon

seplophobia: decaying matter

sexophobia *or* heterophobia: opposite sex

siderodromophobia: railroads; trains

siderophobia: stars

sinistrophobia: the left

Sinophobia: Chinese

soceraphobia: parents-in-law

sociophobia: society

sophophobia: learning

spheksophobia: wasps

stasiphobia: standing

staurophobia: crucifixes

suriphobia *or* murophobia *or* musophobia: mice

symbolophobia: symbolism

symmetrophobia: symmetry

syngenesophobia: relatives

syphilophobia: syphilis

tachophobia: speed

taphophobia: being buried alive

technophobia: technology

telephonophobia: telephone

teletophobia: religious ceremony

teratophobia: monsters

textophobia: fabric

thalassophobia: sea

thanatophobia: death

theatrophobia: theaters

theologicophobia: theology

theophobia: God

thermophobia: heat

tocophobia: childbirth

tomophobia: surgery

topophobia: certain places; being onstage

toxiphobia *or* toxicophobia: poison

traumatophobia: injury

tremophobia: trembling

trichopathophobia: hair disease

triskaidekaphobia: thirteen

tropophobia: moving; change

tuberculophobia: tuberculosis

tyrannophobia: tyrants

uranophobia: heaven

urophobia: urine; urination

vacciniophobia *or* trypanophobia: inoculation

venereophobia *or* cypridophobia: venereal disease

venustaphobia: beautiful women

vestiphobia: clothing

virgivitiphobia: rape

vitricophobia: stepfather

xenophobia: foreigners *or* strangers

xerophobia: dryness

xylophobia: forests

zelophobia: jealousy

zoophobia: animals

accidents: dystychiphobia
airsickness: aeronausiphobia
alcohol: methyphobia
animal skin, fur: doraphobia
animals: zoophobia
ants: myrmecophobia
attack by the wicked: scelerophobia
aurora: auroraphobia
bacteria: bacteriophobia
baldness: phalacrophobia
beards: pogonophobia
beating: mastigophobia
beautiful women: venustaphobia
beds: clinophobia
bees: apiphobia
bees; insects: melissophobia
being buried alive: taphophobia
being by oneself: eremophobia *or* eremiophobia
being dirty: automysophobia
being in streets: agyiophobia
being in vehicles: amaxophobia
being stared at: scopophobia *or* scoptophobia
bicycles: cyclophobia
birds: ornithophobia
blood: hematophobia *or* hemophobia *or* hemaphobia
blushing; color red: erythrophobia
body odor: bromidrophobia *or* bromidrosiphobia
books: bibliophobia
bridges: gephyrophobia
bullets; missiles: ballistophobia
cancer: cancerphobia *or* cancerophobia *or* carcinophobia
cats: ailurophobia *or* aelurophobia
cemeteries: coimetrophobia
certain places; being onstage: topophobia
chickens: alektorophobia
childbirth: tocophobia
children: pedophobia
Chinese: Sinophobia
chins: geniophobia
cholera: cholerophobia
church: ecclesiophobia
clothing: vestiphobia
clouds: nephophobia
coitus: coitophobia
cold: cheimaphobia *or* cheimatophobia *or* psychrophobia
cold things: frigophobia
color: chromophobia *or* chromatophobia
color purple: porphyrophobia
color white: leukophobia
comets: cometophobia
computers: cyberphobia

constipation: coprostasophobia
corpses: necrophobia
crossing streets: agyrophobia
crowds: demophobia
crucifixes: staurophobia
crystals, glass: crystallophobia
dampness: hygrophobia
dancing: chorophobia
dark *or* gloomy places: lygophobia
darkness, night: nyctophobia *or* achluophobia *or* scotophobia
dawn: eosophobia
daylight *or* sunlight: phengophobia
death: thanatophobia
decaying matter: seplophobia
decisions: decidophobia
demons: demonophobia
dentists: dentophobia
depth: bathophobia
diabetes: diabetophobia
dining: deipnophobia
dirt: mysophobia
disease: pathophobia
disorder: ataxiophobia
dizziness; whirlpools: dinophobia
doctors, hospitals: iatrophobia
dogs: cynophobia
dolls *or* small figures: pediaphobia
drafts, air, gases: aerophobia
dreams: oneirophobia
drink: potophobia
drinking: dipsophobia
drugs: pharmacophobia
dryness: xerophobia
duration of time: chronophobia
dust: amathophobia *or* koniophobia
electricity: electrophobia
empty rooms; open places: cenophobia
enclosed places: claustrophobia
England, the English: Anglophobia
everything: panphobia
eye pain: photoalgiaphobia
eyes: ommataphobia
fabric: textophobia
failure: kakorraphiophobia *or* atychiphobia
false statements: mythophobia
fatigue: kopophobia
fear: phobophobia
feathers: pteronophobia
feces: coprophobia *or* scatophobia
fever: febriphobia *or* pyrexiophobia
fire: pyrophobia
fish: ichthyophobia
flashing lights: selaphobia
floods: antlophobia
flowers: anthophobia
flutes: aulophobia

flying: aviatophobia
fog: homichlophobia *or* nebulaphobia
food: cibophobia *or* sitophobia
foreigners *or* strangers: xenophobia
forests: xylophobia
France, the French: Francophobia
freedom: eleutherophobia
frogs; reptiles: batrachophobia
gaining weight: obesophobia *or* pocrescophobia
garlic: alliumphobia
Germans: Germanophobia
ghosts: phasmophobia *or* spectrophobia
glaring lights: photoaugiaphobia
glass: hyalophobia *or* hyelophobia *or* nelophobia
God: theophobia
gold: aurophobia
good news: euphobia
gravity: barophobia
Greek terms: Hellenologophobia
growing old: gerascophobia
hair: chaetophobia *or* trichophobia
hair disease: trichopathophobia
happiness; gaiety: cherophobia
heart disease: cardiophobia
heat: thermophobia
heaven: uranophobia
heights: acrophobia *or* altophobia *or* hypsophobia *or* hypsiphobia
hell: hadephobia *or* stygiophobia
heredity: patriophobia
high buildings: batophobia
holy things; saints: hagiophobia
home surroundings: ecophobia *or* oikophobia
homosexuality: homophobia
horses: hippophobia
hospitals: nosocomephobia
hurricanes: lilapsophobia
hypnosis: hypnophobia
ice, frost: cryophobia *or* pagophobia
ideas: ideophobia
illness: nosemaphobia *or* nosophobia
imperfection: atelophobia
infinity: apeirophobia
injury: traumatophobia
inoculation: vacciniophobia *or* trypanophobia
insanity: lyssophobia *or* maniaphobia *or* dementophobia
insects: entomophobia
insect stings: cnidophobia
jealousy: zelophobia
joint immobility: ankylophobia
justice: dikephobia
kidney disease: albuminurophobia

kissing: philemaphobia *or* philematophobia

knees: genuphobia

lakes: limnophobia

large objects: megalophobia

laughter: geliophobia

learning: sophophobia

left side: levophobia

left, the: sinistrophobia

leprosy: leprophobia *or* lepraphobia

lice; parasites: phthiriophobia *or* pediculophobia

light: photophobia

litigation; lawsuits: litigaphobia

loneliness: autophobia *or* monophobia *or* eremitophobia

long waits: macrophobia

love: philophobia

love play: malaxophobia

machinery: mechanophobia

many things: polyphobia

marriage: gametophobia *or* gamophobia

meat: carnophobia

memories: mnemophobia

men: androphobia

meningitis: meningitophobia

menstruation: menophobia

metal: metallophobia

meteors: meteorphobia

mice: suriphobia *or* murophobia *or* musophobia

microbes; germs: microbiophobia *or* bacillophobia

mind, the: psychophobia

mirrors: catoptrophobia *or* eisoptrophobia

mites; small objects: acarophobia

mobs: ochlophobia

money: chrematophobia

monsters: teratophobia

moon: selenophobia

mother-in-law: pentheraphobia

motion: kinetophobia

motion; crossing streets: dromophobia

moving; change: tropophobia

moving vehicles: ochophobia

music: melophobia *or* musicophobia

names: onomatophobia

narrowness; heart problems: anginophobia

needles: belonophobia

newness; novelty: cainophobia *or* cainotophobia *or* centophobia

new things: neophobia

noise: ligyrophobia

noise; telephones: phonophobia

nosebleeds: epistaxiophobia

nuclear weapons: nucleomitophobia

nudity: gymnophobia *or* nudophobia

numbers: arithmophobia *or* numerophobia

old people: gerontophobia

one thing: monophobia

open, high places: aeroacrophobia

opening eyes: optophobia

open places, crowds: agoraphobia

opinions: allodoxaphobia

opposite sex: sexophobia *or* heterophobia

pain: odynesphobia *or* odynephobia *or* odynophobia *or* algophobia

paper: papyrophobia

parasites: parasitophobia

parents-in-law: soceraphobia

people: anthropophobia

philosophy: philosophobia

pins: enetophobia

plants: botanophobia

pleasure: hedonophobia

poetry: metrophobia

points, pointed objects: aichurophobia

poison: toxiphobia *or* toxicophobia

poisons; rust: iophobia

politics: politicophobia

poverty: peniaphobia

precipices: cremnophobia

priests; religious objects: hierophobia

progress: prosophobia

propriety: orthophobia

prostitutes: cyprianophobia

punishment: poinephobia

rabies: hydrophobophobia

radiation: radiophobia

railroads; trains: siderodromophobia

rain: pluviophobia *or* ombrophobia

rape: virgivitiphobia

rectal diseases: rectophobia *or* proctophobia

relatives: syngenesophobia

religious ceremony: teletophobia

reptiles; snakes: herpetophobia

responsibility: hypegiaphobia

returning home: nostophobia

ridicule: catagelophobia

right, the: dextrophobia

rivers: potamophobia

robbers: harpaxophobia

rods; rhabdophobia

room: koinoniphobia

ruin; ruins: atephobia

Satan: Satanophobia

scabies: scabiophobia

school: didaskaleinophobia *or* scolionophobia

scratches: amychophobia

sea: thalassophobia

sermons: homilophobia

sexual abuse: contrectophobia

sexual intercourse: genophobia

sexual love: erotophobia

sexual perversion: paraphobia

shadows: sciaphobia *or* sciophobia

shellfish: ostraconophobia

shock: hormephobia

sin: peccatiphobia

sin; error: hamartophobia

sitting: cathisophobia

skin: dermatosiophobia

skin disease: dermatopathophobia

slime: blennophobia *or* myxophobia

small things: microphobia

smell: olfactophobia *or* osmophobia *or* ophresiophobia

smothering; choking: pnigophobia *or* pnigerophobia

snakes, reptiles: ophidiophobia *or* ophiophobia

snow: chionophobia

society: sociophobia

soiling: rypophobia

solitude: isolophobia

sound: acousticophobia

sourness: acerophobia *or* acerbophobia

speech: lalophobia *or* laliophobia *or* glossophobia *or* phonophobia

speed: tachophobia

spiders: arachnophobia

spirits: pneumatophobia

stairs: climacophobia

standing: stasiphobia

stars: siderophobia

staying single: anuptaphobia

stealing: kleptophobia

stepfather: vitricophobia

string: linonophobia

stuttering: psellismophobia

sunlight: heliophobia

surgery: tomophobia

swallowing air: aerophagiaphobia

swallowing *or* eating: phagophobia

symbolism: symbolophobia

symmetry: symmetrophobia

syphilis: syphilophobia

taste: geumatophobia *or* geumaphobia *or* geumophobia

technology: technophobia

teeth: odontophobia

telephone: telephonophobia

termites: isopterophobia

theaters: theatrophobia

theology: theologicophobia

thinking: phronemophobia

thirteen: triskaidekaphobia

thunder: brontophobia *or* keraunophobia *or* tonitrophobia

thunder and lightning: astraphobia *or* astrapophobia

tombstones: placophobia

touch: haptophobia *or* hapnophobia

travel: hodophobia

trees: dendrophobia

trembling: tremophobia

tuberculosis: phthisiophobia *or* tuberculophobia

tyrants: tyrannophobia

urine; urination: urophobia

vegetables: lachanophobia

venereal disease: venereophobia *or* cypridophobia

vertigo: ilingophobia

virginity: esodophobia

vomiting: emetophobia

walking: basiphobia

washing *or* bathing: ablutophobia

wasps: spheksophobia

water: hydrophobia *or* aquaphobia

waves: cymophobia

weakness; fainting: asthenophobia

wild animals: agrizoophobia

wind: ancraophobia *or* anemophobia

wine: oenophobia

women: feminophobia *or* gynephobia

words: logophobia

work: ergophobia

work; fatigue: ponophobia

worms: helminthophobia *or* scoleciphobia *or* vermiphobia

wrinkles: rhytiphobia

writing: graphophobia

young girls; virgins: parthenophobia

---

3 symptoms of fear, cold sweat, blood running cold, hair standing on end, chattering teeth, knocking knees, nerves, palpitations, shivers, trembling, shaking, quaking, goose bumps, goose pimples, goose flesh, butterflies in one's stomach, sinking stomach, stage fright, shivers up and down one's spine, jitters; [Inf]: cold feet, willies, heebie-jeebies, the creeps, jumps, jimjams, collywobbles

4 worry, anxiety, uneasiness, angst, fretting, concern
▶ *Attention 323; Disturbance 768*

5 terrorization, terrorism, horrification, rule by terror, reign of terror, scare tactics, scariness, sword of Damocles

6 intimidation, threat, cowing, browbeating, bulldozing, bullying, hectoring; demoralization, psychological warfare, war of nerves
▶ *Aggravation 276; Attack 418*

7 frightener, scarer, terrorizer, terrorist, intimidator, bully; alarmist, scaremonger, doomsayer; bogeyman *or* bogyman, bogey *or* bogy, hobgoblin, scarecrow, bugbear, ogre, monster, vampire, werewolf, ghoul; witch, goblin; specter, ghost, phantom, apparition; nightmare
▶ *Occultism 86; Attack 418; Evil 446*

8 frightened person, mouse, nervous person, bundle of nerves, nervous wreck, blencher, milquetoast; [Inf]: nervous Nellie, fraidy-cat, scaredy-cat, chicken
▶ *Cowardice 285*

ADJECTIVES

9 frightened, afraid, scared, fear-stricken, terrified, terror-struck, horrified, horror-struck, aghast, petrified, panic-stricken, alarmed, phobic; in mortal fear, in fear and trembling, paralyzed with fear, rooted to the spot, scared *or* frightened *or* terrified out of one's wits, scared *or* frightened to death, white as a sheet, pale *or* white as a ghost, blanched, ashen-faced, in a cold sweat, in a funk; [Inf]: spooked, scared stiff, scared shitless
▶ *Cowardice 285*

10 fearful, apprehensive, timorous, timid, tremulous,

anxious, panicky, nervous, uneasy, disquieted, agitated, perturbed, distressed, tense, strained, highly strung, edgy, on edge, jittery, jumpy, skittish, uptight [Inf]; trembling, quaking, quivering, shaky, shaking, shaking like a leaf, afraid of one's shadow; in suspense, on pins and needles, on tenterhooks, on the edge of a cliff, waiting for the bomb to drop

11 worried, fretting, anxious for *or* about, concerned, solicitous, caring; troubled, disturbed, tormented, plagued, haunted, harassed

12 frightening, scary, terrifying, horrifying, petrifying, bloodcurdling, hair-raising, alarming, dismaying, shocking, startling, unnerving, creepy, spooky [Inf]; frightful, fearful, dreadful, dire, grim, terrible, awful, horrible, horrific, horrendous, horrid, hideous, appalling, ghastly, grisly, gruesome, revolting, ghoulish, macabre

13 fearsome, awesome, daunting, formidable, menacing, threatening, intimidating, demoralizing

VERBS

14 be afraid, be afraid of, be frightened *or* terrified *or* horrified, fear, funk, dread, take fright, affright [Arch], panic; show fear, flinch, shrink, draw back, recoil, quail, cringe, wince, blench, jump out of one's skin, turn pale *or* white, look as if one had seen a ghost; be petrified, be paralyzed with fear, freeze with horror, be rooted to the spot, have one's heart stand still, have one's heart skip *or* miss a beat

15 be fearful, apprehend, be anxious, be nervous, be on edge, have one's heart in one's mouth, have misgivings, have qualms, think twice, get cold feet [Inf]; palpitate, flutter, twitch, shiver, shudder, tremble, quiver, shake, shake like a leaf, quake, quake in one's boots, sweat, break out in a cold sweat, sweat bullets [Inf]

16 worry, fret, be worried about *or* for, fear for, be fearful for, be anxious for *or* about, agonize over, bite *or* chew one's nails, sweat blood [Inf]; be troubled, be concerned, be disquieted, be disturbed, be tormented, be plagued, be haunted, be harassed

17 frighten, scare, terrify, terrorize, horrify, appall, petrify, fright, affright [Arch], alarm, panic, dismay, shock, startle, unnerve, spook [Inf], give someone a fright, put the fear of God into, scare someone half to death, scare *or* frighten someone to death, scare *or* frighten someone out of his *or* her wits, scare the living daylights out of, scare the pants off, scare the shit out of [Inf]

18 intimidate, overawe, daunt, menace, threaten, cow, browbeat, bulldoze, bully, hector, demoralize

ADVERBS

19 fearfully, in fear of, apprehensively, timorously, timidly, tremulously, anxiously, nervously, uneasily, with fear and trembling, with one's heart in one's mouth

20 frighteningly, terrifyingly, horrifyingly, alarmingly, spookily [Inf]; frightfully, dreadfully, terribly, awfully, horribly, horrifically, horrendously, hideously

21 fearsomely, awesomely, dauntingly, formidably, menacingly, threateningly, intimidatingly

284 Courage

And as she looked about, she did behold, / How over that same door was likewise writ, / Be bold, be bold, and everywhere Be bold. — EDMUND SPENSER

Two o'clock in the morning courage: I mean unprepared courage. — NAPOLEON I

NOUNS

1 courage, bravery, courageousness, braveness, fearlessness, dauntlessness, intrepidity, lionheartedness; mettle, spirit, fighting spirit, pluck, spunk, nerve, daring, derring-do, boldness, hardihood, hardiness, audacity, audaciousness, nerves of steel; [Inf]: guts, gutsiness
  ▶ *Strength 516*

2 heroism, valor, valiancy *or* valiance, prowess, knightliness, gallantry, chivalry; manliness, manfulness, masculinity, virility, machismo; aggressiveness, bellicosity, militancy
  ▶ *War 76; Courtesy 410*

3 steadfastness, resoluteness, resolution, stout-heartedness, doughtiness, determination, perseverance, tenacity, endurance, stamina, fortitude, backbone, grit, true grit, stiff upper lip; confidence, sureness, surety, security, self-confidence, self-assurance, self-reliance
  ▶ *Resolution 376; Perseverance 377*

4 adventurousness, gameness; temerity, foolhardiness, recklessness, impetuousness, rashness
  ▶ *Rashness 286*

5 bold front, bold façade, brave *or* bold face, bravado, Dutch courage

6 encouragement, assurance, reassurance, incitement, inspiration, exhortation, bucking up

  ▶ *Motivation 508*

7 courageous act, act of courage, feat, exploit, deed, prowess, derring-do, bravura, gallantry, chivalry [Arch], heroics
  ▶ *Action 412*

8 courageous person, brave person, brave, hero, heroine, knight, knight in shining armor, warrior, he-man, daredevil, stunt person, stunt man *or* woman, tiger, lion
  ▶ *Combatant 77*

ADJECTIVES

9 courageous, brave, fearless, dauntless, undaunted, intrepid, lionhearted; mettlesome, spirited, plucky, spunky, daring, bold, hardy, nervy, audacious; gutsy [Inf], ballsy [Inf]
  ▶ *Strength 516*

10 heroic, valorous, valiant, knightly, gallant, chivalrous; manly, manful, masculine, virile, macho; aggressive, bellicose, militant, soldierly, martial, warlike
  ▶ *War 76; Courtesy 410*

11 steadfast, resolute, stout-hearted, doughty, determined, persevering, dogged, tenacious, enduring, unflinching, unshrinking, unshakable, unbowed, indomitable; confident, sure, secure, unafraid, unfearing, self-confident, self-assured, self-reliant
  ▶ *Resolution 376; Perseverance 377*

12 adventurous, venturesome, game; foolhardy, danger-loving, reckless, impetuous, rash
  ▶ *Rashness 286*

13 encouraging, assuring, reassuring, heartening, inciting, inspiring

VERBS

14 be courageous, dare, venture, hazard, brave, face, confront, show one's mettle, bell the cat, take the plunge, take the bull by the horns; defy, outbrave, beard, outface, face down, stare down, stand up to, brazen out *or* through; have the courage of one's convictions, stick to one's guns, face the music; court disaster, laugh at danger; have guts [Inf], have balls [Inf]
  ▶ *Rashness 286; Undertaking 391; Defiance 416; Contention 422*

15 take courage, take heart, put on a brave *or* bold face, dare, steel oneself, pluck up courage, muster *or* summon up courage, screw up one's courage, screw your courage to the sticking place; endure, keep a stiff upper lip, keep one's chin up, bite the bullet, grin and bear it, stick it out, hang in there [Inf]; persevere, persist, hang tough [Inf]
  ▶ *Perseverance 377*

16 give courage, encourage, hearten, assure, reassure, embolden, bolster, inspirit, inspire, incite, exhort, buck up
  ▶ *Motivation 508*

17 courageously, bravely, fearlessly, dauntlessly, intrepidly, boldly, defiantly, audaciously

18 heroically, valiantly, gallantly, chivalrously; manfully, masculinely; aggressively, bellicosely, militantly

19 steadfastly, resolutely, stout-heartedly, doughtily, tenaciously, doggedly, indomitably; confidently, surely, securely, self-confidently

20 adventurously, venturesomely, gamely; foolhardily, recklessly, impetuously, rashly

21 encouragingly, assuringly, reassuringly, hearteningly

285 Cowardice

NOUNS

1 cowardice, cowardliness, lack of courage, pusillanimity, faintheartedness, fearfulness, weak knees, timidity, timorousness, overcaution, white feather [Brit]; lack of spirit, defeatism; [Inf]: gutlessness, chicken-heartedness, yellowness, yellow streak, cold feet
 ▶ *Fear 283; Caution 287*

2 dastardliness, cravenness, poltroonery, abjectness; weakness, baseness, lack of moral fiber, treachery, desertion

3 coward, faintheart, sissy, baby, mouse, milksop, milquetoast, namby-pamby; dastard, poltroon, craven, recreant, deserter; [Inf]: yellowbelly, chicken, fraidy-cat, scaredy-cat, wimp, jellyfish, rat
 ▶ *Fear 283; Weakness 517*

ADJECTIVES

4 cowardly, coward, uncourageous, pusillanimous, lily-livered, white-livered, sissy, fainthearted, fearful, timid, timorous, shy, overcautious; unspirited, defeatist; unheroic, unvaliant, unvalorous, undaring, unable to say "boo" to a goose; afraid, scared, daunted, cowed; cowering, quailing, cringing, shrinking; [Inf]: gutless, yellow, yellow-bellied, chicken, chicken-hearted, chicken-livered
 ▶ *Fear 283*

5 spineless, weak, irresolute, unsteadfast, unstaunch, indecisive, milksoppy, milksopping, namby-pamby, weak-kneed, wimpy [Inf]
 ▶ *Weakness 517*

6 dastardly, dastard, craven, recreant, poltroonish, poltroon, base, base-spirited, despicable, abject; sneaking, skulking, slinking, sneaky, slinky

VERBS

7 be a coward, lack courage, lose one's nerve, back out, cry craven, show the white feather [Brit]; cower, quail, cringe, shrink, recoil, have no stomach for; [Inf]: have no guts, chicken out, wimp out, get cold feet
 ▶ *Fear 283; Weakness 517*

8 retreat, desert, run away, turn tail, flee, beat a hasty retreat, scuttle, cut and run, rat [Inf]; sneak, skulk, slink

ADVERBS

9 cowardly, uncourageously, pusillanimously, faint-heartedly, fearfully, timidly, timorously, shyly, over-cautiously; unheroically, unvaliantly; spinelessly, weakly, irresolutely; cravenly, poltroonishly, despicably, sneakily; gutlessly [Inf], chicken-heartedly [Inf]

286 Rashness

NOUNS

1 rashness, impetuousness, impetuosity, hotheadedness, impulsiveness, precipitancy *or* precipitance, precipitateness, hastiness, haste, overhastiness
 ▶ *Haste 818*

2 recklessness, heedlessness, daring, adventurousness, brinkmanship, boldness, overboldness, audacity, audaciousness, temerity, presumption, presumptuousness, overconfidence, brashness; wildness, foolhardiness, folly, daredeviltry *or* daredevilry, playing with fire, courting disaster, flirting with death; overenthusiasm, overzealousness, impatience, desperation, desperateness
 ▶ *Courage 284; Folly 353; Insolence 400; Danger 811*

3 imprudence, injudiciousness, improvidence, indiscretion, indiscreetness, unwariness, incautiousness, riskiness, foolishness; inconsideration, thoughtlessness, inattention, negligence, neglect, carelessness, regardlessness, irresponsibility; capriciousness, caprice, frivolity, flippancy
 ▶ *Inattention 324; Negligence 326; Folly 353; Danger 811*

4 rash move, risk, needless risk, dangerous game, leap in the dark, gamble; rash person, hothead, adventurer, brinkman, madcap, gambler, daredevil, desperado, risktaker
 ▶ *Danger 811; Chance 842*

ADJECTIVES

5 rash, impetuous, hotheaded, impulsive, precipitant, precipitate, hasty, overhasty, headlong, breakneck
 ▶ *Haste 818*

6 reckless, heedless, daring, adventurous, venturesome, bold, overbold, audacious, presumptuous, overconfident, brash; harebrained, madcap, wild, foolhardy, trigger-happy [Inf], daredevil, death-defying, danger-loving, risk-taking, asking for trouble, asking for it; overenthusiastic, overzealous, impatient, frantic, desperate, do-or-die
 ▶ *Courage 284; Folly 353; Danger 811*

7 imprudent, injudicious, improvident, indiscreet, incautious, risky, uncircumspect, unwary, ill-advised, unwise, foolish; ill-considered, inconsiderate, thoughtless, inattentive, remiss, negligent, neglectful, offhand, slapdash, hit-or-miss, careless, regardless, irresponsible;

capricious, frivolous, flippant, couldn't-care-less, devil-may-care, free and easy, happy-go-lucky

▸ *Inattention 324; Negligence 326; Folly 353*

VERBS

8 **be rash,** rush into, rush in where angels fear to tread, throw caution to the wind, go to sea in a sieve, ignore the consequences, carry on regardless; bell the cat, take risks, gamble, stick one's neck out [Inf], go out on a limb, take a leap in the dark, buy a pig in a poke, count one's chickens before they are hatched; play with fire, court disaster, tempt fate *or* providence, defy danger, play Russian roulette, flirt with death, ask for trouble, ask for it

▸ *Courage 284; Danger 811; Haste 818; Chance 842*

ADVERBS

9 **rashly,** impetuously, impulsively, precipitantly, precipitately, hastily, overhastily, headlong, headfirst

10 **recklessly,** heedlessly, daringly, adventurously, boldly, overboldly, audaciously, presumptuously, overconfidently, brashly; wildly, foolhardily; overenthusiastically, overzealously, impatiently, frantically, desperately

11 **imprudently,** injudiciously, indiscreetly, incautiously, riskily, unwarily, unwisely, foolishly; inconsiderately, thoughtlessly, inattentively, negligently, neglectfully, slapdash, carelessly, irresponsibly; capriciously, frivolously, flippantly

287 Caution

NOUNS

1 **caution,** carefulness, care, wariness, chariness, caginess, shrewdness, watchfulness, vigilance, alertness, guardedness

▸ *Carefulness 325*

2 **prudence,** wisdom, judiciousness, deliberation, careful consideration, discretion *or* discreetness, circumspection, caginess, wait-and-see policy; heed, heedfulness, mindfulness, attentiveness, awareness, thoughtfulness

▸ *Thought 317; Attention 323; Wisdom 352*

3 **reticence,** reservedness, restraint, uncommunicativeness, secretiveness; skepticism, suspicion, doubt, reservation, second thoughts, hesitance, hesitancy, tentativeness, reluctance, slowness; overcaution, overcautiousness, unadventurousness

▸ *Secrecy 182*

4 **precaution,** foresight, forethought, anticipation, prevention, protection, security; preventive measure *or* step, safeguard, safety net, insurance, insurance policy, rainy-day policy, savings, nest egg; providence, provision, thrift, thriftiness, frugality, canniness

▸ *Provision 89; Foresight 357; Thrift 499; Safety 810*

5 **warning,** forewarning, notice, admonition, advice, counsel

▸ *Warning 814*

ADJECTIVES

6 **cautious,** careful, wary, chary, watchful, vigilant, alert, guarded, on guard

▸ *Carefulness 325*

7 **prudent,** wise, judicious, well-considered, discreet, circumspect, politic, cagey, on the safe side; heedful, mindful, attentive, aware, thoughtful, regardful

▸ *Thought 317; Attention 323; Wisdom 352*

8 **reticent,** reserved, restrained, uncommunicative, secretive; skeptical, suspicious, leery, doubtful, hesitant, tentative, reluctant, slow, gingerly; overcautious, unadventurous

▸ *Secrecy 182*

9 **precautionary,** precautious, precautional, foresighted, forethoughtful, anticipatory, preventive, preemptive, prophylactic; provident, provisional, thrifty, economical, frugal, canny

▸ *Provision 89; Foresight 357; Thrift 499; Safety 810*

10 **warning,** admonitory, advisable, advisory

VERBS

11 **be cautious,** be careful, take care, take heed; be aware, beware, watch out, look out, be on the lookout, be on one's guard, look sharp, keep one's eyes open, keep an eye on, keep tabs on [Inf]

12 **proceed with caution,** watch one's step, tread warily, take tentative steps, take it one step *or* day at a time, take it slowly, take it easy, put a toe in the water; see how the land lies, get the lay of the land, see how the wind blows, look before one leaps; take no risks, play it safe; cover oneself, hedge, hedge one's bets; pussyfoot, tiptoe, walk on eggshells, walk on thin ice

13 **doubt,** suspect, have reservations, have second thoughts, think twice, hesitate, hang back; hold back, restrain oneself, draw *or* pull in one's horns, hold one's tongue

14 **take precautions,** anticipate, prevent, protect, safeguard, secure, leave nothing to chance, leave no room *or* margin for error; take preventive measures *or* steps, insure, take out insurance, provide for, save, economize

15 **caution,** warn, forewarn, give notice, put on guard, admonish, advise, counsel

▸ *Warning 814*

ADVERBS

16 **cautiously,** with caution, carefully, warily, charily, watchfully, vigilantly, alertly, guardedly

17 **prudently,** wisely, judiciously, discreetly, circumspectly, on the safe side; heedfully, mindfully, attentively, thoughtfully

18 **reticently,** reservedly, uncommunicatively, secretively; skeptically, suspiciously, askance *or* askant, leerily, doubtfully, hesitantly, tentatively, reluctantly, slowly, gingerly; overcautiously, unadventurously

19 **precautiously,** precautionally, preventively, preemp-

tively, prophylactically; providently, provisionally, thriftily, economically, frugally, cannily

20 be careful!, take care!, beware!, look out!, watch out!, watch your step!; [Inf]: take it easy!, easy does it!, go easy!

288 Desire

Suddenly, like a thing that leaped to him across infinite distances with the speed of light, desire (salt, black, ravenous, unanswerable desire) took him by the throat.
— C. S. LEWIS

NOUNS

1 **desire,** craving, longing, yearning, hankering, appetite, appetence, lust, passion, urge, yen [Inf]; pining, wistfulness, nostalgia, homesickness

2 **wish,** want, need, requirement, demand, command; aspiration, ambition, aim, goal, objective, dream, hope
 ▶ *Necessity 95; Hope 281; Intention 374*

3 **eagerness,** avidity *or* avidness, voracity, zeal, fervor, passion, ardor; fascination, curiosity
 ▶ *Curiosity 321; Willingness 373*

4 **covetousness,** possessiveness, greed, greediness, cupidity, avarice
 ▶ *Envy 314; Selfishness 444; Taking 477*

5 **sexual desire,** carnal desire, concupiscence, lust, passion, sexual appetite, sexual urge, sexual drive, libido; libidinousness, lustfulness, randiness, lechery, lecherousness, lewdness, lasciviousness, nymphomania, Don Juanism, satyriasis; [Inf]: horniness, the hots, hot pants
 ▶ *Sex 20; Love 299; Immorality 432*

6 **appetite,** hunger, hungriness, thirst, thirstiness, dryness, craving
 ▶ *Eating 92; Drinking 93*

7 **desirability,** desirableness, appeal, attraction, draw, lure, allure, seductiveness, temptation; agreeability, meritoriousness, creditability, praiseworthiness, worthiness; expediency, convenience, advisability, suitability, acceptability
 ▶ *Liking 290; Attraction 700*

8 **object of desire,** wish, want, desideratum, desirable, heart's desire, hope, weakness, temptation; requirement, request; catch, prize, trophy, brass ring [Inf]; ideal, the unattainable, forbidden fruit
 ▶ *Reward 453; Request 505*

9 **desirer,** craver, yearner, hankerer, wisher, piner; wanter, fancier, aspirant, hoper, dreamer, would-be; worshiper, devotee, votary, zealot; coveter, envier, freak [Inf]; glutton, addict, greedy pig; lover, lecher, letch, libertine, Don Juan, satyr, satyromaniac, nymphomaniac, nympho [Inf]
 ▶ *Gluttony 119; Envy 314*

ADJECTIVES

10 **desired,** craved, longed for, yearned, wished, wanted; needed, necessary, required, requested, demanded; coveted, envied; sought-after, in demand, popular
 ▶ *Necessity 95; Envy 314; Request 505*

11 **desirable,** pleasing, pleasant, pleasurable, likable, appealing, attractive; preferable, favorable; inviting, tempting, appetizing, mouth-watering; admirable, creditable, laudable, praiseworthy, worthy, meritorious, deserving, worthwhile, good, beneficial, advantageous, profitable; alluring, concupiscible, sexually desirable, sexy, seductive, provocative, titillating
 ▶ *Pleasantness 271; Good 445; Gain 467*

12 **expedient,** convenient, advisable, recommendable; acceptable, suitable, fitting, apt, appropriate, proper
 ▶ *Convenience 803*

13 **desirous,** craving, longing, yearning, pining, hankering, partial to, fond of; wistful, nostalgic, homesick; wishful, wanting, needing, demanding; aspiring, ambitious, hopeful, hoping, would-be; eager, enthusiastic, avid, zealous, passionate, ardent, fervent, dying for, freaking out [Inf]
 ▶ *Hope 281*

14 **covetous,** coveting, possessive, acquisitive, envious; greedy, voracious, gluttonous, insatiable
 ▶ *Gluttony 119; Envy 314*

15 **lustful,** concupiscent, passionate, libidinous, randy, lecherous, lewd, lascivious, nymphomaniacal, satyrical, horny [Inf], hot for [Inf]
 ▶ *Immorality 432*

16 **hungry,** ravenous, famished, starving, starved, half-starved, empty, peckish [Brit inf], thirsty, parched, dry, dehydrated

VERBS

17 **desire,** crave, long for, yearn for, pray for, itch for, pine for, die for; want, need, require, command, demand; like, fancy, favor, prefer, love; cry out for, ask for, request, call, summon, welcome
 ▶ *Necessity 95; Liking 290; Command 425; Request 505*

18 **covet,** envy, have one's eye on, set one's heart on
 ▶ *Envy 314*

19 **aspire to,** aim for, set one's sights on, dream of, hope for; hunger for, thirst for

20 **lust after,** want, desire, pant for, be turned on by [Inf], have the hots for [Inf]; woo, court, chase, pursue
 ▶ *Love 299; Pursuit 385; Immorality 432*

21 **be hungry,** hunger, raven, be thirsty, thirst, lick one's lips, salivate, starve, be starving, be famished, be parched

22 **cause desire,** awaken desire, fill with longing, tempt, tantalize, attract, allure, lure, draw; fill with desire, excite, titillate, arouse, stimulate, turn on [Inf]; whet one's appetite, make one's mouth water

▶ *Attraction 700*

23 be desirable, suit, befit, answer the problem, serve the purpose, fill the bill

▶ *Usefulness 801*

ADVERBS

24 desirably, pleasingly, pleasantly, pleasurably, appealingly, attractively; preferably, favorably; invitingly, temptingly, appetizingly; admirably, creditably, laudably, meritoriously, deservingly, beneficially, advantageously, profitably; sexily, seductively, provocatively, titillatingly

25 expediently, conveniently, advisably, recommendably; acceptably, suitably, fittingly, aptly, appropriately, properly

26 desirously, wishfully, longingly, wistfully, nostalgically; aspiringly, ambitiously, hopefully, hopingly

27 eagerly, avidly, zealously, passionately, ardently, fervently; hungrily, ravenously, thirstily

28 covetously, covetingly, possessively, acquisitively, enviously; greedily, voraciously, gluttonously, insatiably

29 lustfully, passionately, libidinously, lecherously, lewdly, lasciviously, hornily [Inf]

289 Indifference

NOUNS

1 indifference, unconcern, apathy, lack of interest, uninterestedness, disinterest, incuriosity; aloofness, detachment, dispassion, noninvolvement; inertia, inactivity, passivity *or* passiveness; nonchalance, insouciance, inexcitability, calmness, ataraxia; lack of desire, inappetence *or* inappetency, lack of appetite; phlegmaticalness *or* phlegmaticness, phlegm, lethargy, lackadaisicalness, listlessness, spiritlessness, sluggishness, dullness, the blahs [Inf]; halfheartedness, lukewarmness, perfunctoriness, coolness, cold shoulder, coldness, cold-heartedness, cold-bloodedness; insensibility, insensitivity, numbness; systematic indifference, indifferentism, adiaphorism

> ▶ *Insensitivity 268; Lack of Wonder 295; Incuriosity 322; Unwillingness 375; Inactivity 415*

2 carelessness, disregard, inattention, oscitancy *or* oscitance, laxity, negligence, neglect, heedlessness, recklessness, rashness; promiscuousness, amorality

> ▶ *Rashness 286; Inattention 324; Negligence 326; Lack of Discrimination 338*

3 impartiality, indiscrimination, disinterestedness, objectivity, unbiased attitude, open mind, neutrality, fairness, justice

> ▶ *Judgment 341; Right 429*

4 insignificance, unimportance, triviality, irrelevance, inconsequence, immateriality

> ▶ *Unimportance 800*

5 mediocrity, averageness, ordinariness, passableness, tolerability

▶ *Conformity 781*

6 indifferent person, neutral, neutralist, fence-sitter; indifferent, indifferentist, Laodicean, wet blanket; slacker, laggard, pococurante, cold fish [Inf]

ADJECTIVES

7 indifferent, unconcerned, uncaring, apathetic, incurious, uninquisitive, uninterested, disinterested; detached, dispassionate, uninvolved, withdrawn, aloof, cool, impersonal, matter of fact; inert, inactive, listless, spiritless, sluggish, dull, blah [Inf]; phlegmatic *or* phlegmatical, impassive, lethargic, lackadaisical; insouciant, nonchalant, pococurante, ataractic, calm, inexcitable, unruffled; passionless, unaffectionate, undesirous, inappetent; lukewarm, halfhearted, perfunctory, blasé, unimpressed; unaffected, unfeeling, untouched, unemotional, unmoved, cold, frigid, frosty, cold-hearted, cold-blooded; insensible, numb, benumbed, unresponsive, insensitive, thick-skinned; unaware, oblivious, insensible to, blind to, deaf to, unconscious, comatose

8 careless, disregarding, inattentive, oscitant, lax, negligent, neglectful, heedless, reckless, rash, devil-may-care; promiscuous, amoral

9 impartial, disinterested, objective, unbiased, unprejudiced, indiscriminative, open-minded, neutral, fair, just

10 insignificant, unimportant, trivial, irrelevant, inconsequential, immaterial

11 mediocre, average, middling, ordinary, commonplace, unexceptional, unremarkable, unnotable, undistinguished, uninspired, fair, passable, tolerable, all right, so-so, no great shakes [Inf]

VERBS

12 be indifferent, show no concern for, not care, not mind, care nothing for, couldn't care less, not care a straw about, not give a fig, not give a hoot [Inf], not give a damn [Inf]; take no interest, be incurious, not wonder; detach oneself, withdraw, stay in one's shell, become aloof; dismiss, shrug off, not think twice about, not lose any sleep over; close one's eyes to, look the other way, mind one's own business; not have one's heart in it; fail to act, not respond, not be affected by, remain unmoved, have a heart of stone, harden, harden one's heart, have a thick skin; show no excitement, not turn a hair, show no surprise, see nothing wonderful; have no desires, have no passion, fall out of love, lose interest

13 make indifferent, lose someone's attention, fail to move, fail to inspire, make no impact on; make insensitive, dull, blunt, desensitize, numb, benumb, deaden, bore, turn off [Inf]

14 be careless, disregard, neglect, act negligently, fail to heed, act recklessly, have no morals

15 be impartial, be objective, be unbiased, have no prejudice, be nonpartisan, remain neutral, not take sides, take neither side, sit on the fence

16 be mediocre, have no aspirations, get by, pass, not set the world on fire, sit and watch the world go by

ADVERBS

17 indifferently, uncaringly, apathetically, incuriously, uninquisitively, uninterestedly, disinterestedly, with no interest; dispassionately, aloofly, coolly, impersonally, matter-of-factly; obliviously, unconsciously; inertly, inactively, listlessly, spiritlessly, sluggishly, phlegmatically, impassively, lethargically, lackadaisically; nonchalantly, insouciantly, inexcitably, calmly; lukewarmly, halfheartedly, perfunctorily; unfeelingly, without feelings, unemotionally, coldly, cold-heartedly, cold-bloodedly, in cold blood; insensibly, numbly, unresponsively, insensitively

18 carelessly, without a worry, inattentively, negligently, neglectfully, heedlessly, recklessly, rashly; promiscuously, amorally, without morals

19 impartially, disinterestedly, objectively, unbiasedly, open-mindedly, with an open mind, neutrally, fairly, justly

20 unexceptionally, unremarkably, unnotably, undistinguishedly, uninspiredly, averagely, middlingly, fairly, passably, tolerably, so-so; insignificantly, without significance, unimportantly, trivially, irrelevantly, inconsequentially, immaterially

INTERJECTIONS

21 who cares?, so what?, what does it matter?; what's the difference?, what's the dif? [Inf], it's all the same to me!, never mind!, forget it!

290 Liking

NOUNS

1 liking, fondness, fond feeling, affection, tenderness, tender feeling; friendship, friendliness, affinity, mutual affinity, attachment, sentimental attachment, devotion, loyal devotion, intimacy, empathy, sympathy; approval, favorable attitude, appreciation, admiration, esteem, regard, respect; love, mutual love, adoration; fascination, captivation, infatuation, attraction, titillation, allurement, temptation; desire, wishing, longing, yearning, hankering; passion, zest, fervor, appetite
  ▶ *Friendship 62; Desire 288; Love 299; Sociability 408*

2 inclination, leaning, tendency, bent, predisposition, disposition, propensity, proclivity, penchant, weakness, preference, favor, predilection, partiality, prejudice, bias; intention, readiness, willingness, eagerness, mind, cast of mind
  ▶ *Persuasion 178; Intention 374; Selection 382; Predetermination 384*

3 likes, liking, hobby, fancy, pleasure, enjoyment, delight, relish, taste, soft spot; selection, choice; wish,

craving, infatuation; trend, mode, vogue, craze, mania, rage, fad, crush [Inf]
  ▶ *Desire 288; Selection 382; Fashion 536*

ADJECTIVES

4 liking, fond of, admiring, adoring, loving, affectionate, appreciative, respectful; devoted, loyal, intimate, empathetic, sympathetic; fascinated, captivated, attracted, infatuated, titillated, tempted; passionate, zestful; desirous, wishing, longing, yearning, hankering

5 inclined toward, leaning, bending, predisposed, disposed, prejudiced, biased, favoring, favorable toward, preferring, partial to; ready, willing, eager

6 liked, favored, approved, admired, esteemed, respected; cherished, treasured, prized, appreciated; desired, wished for, yearned for, longed for; popular, in vogue, in style, all the rage
  ▶ *Desire 288; Respect 435*

7 likable, amicable, friendly, genial, congenial, winsome, engaging, appealing, adorable, lovable, lovely, attractive, pleasing, endearing; fascinating, captivating, infatuating, titillating, tempting, alluring
  ▶ *Pleasantness 271*

VERBS

8 like, be fond of, care for, have an affinity for, have an attachment to, empathize with, sympathize with; approve, admire, think the world of, have high regard for, esteem, respect; cherish, hold dear, treasure, prize, appreciate; love, adore, be infatuated with; desire, wish for, set one's heart on, have designs on, long for, yearn for, hanker after, be sweet on [Inf], have a crush on [Inf]
  ▶ *Friendship 62; Desire 288; Love 299*

9 enjoy, delight in, take a fancy to, take to, fancy, relish, savor, have a passion for; like to, want to, wish to, love to, dearly love to, long to, choose to

10 be inclined toward, lean toward, bend, predispose oneself, have a propensity for, have a penchant for, have a weakness for, prefer, have a preference for, favor, be partial to; intend, be ready, be willing, have a cast of mind
  ▶ *Intention 374*

ADVERBS

11 admiringly, with great admiration, favorably, approvingly, appreciatively, respectfully; adoringly, lovingly, with love, affectionately, with affection; devotedly, loyally, intimately, empathetically, sympathetically; zestfully, passionately, desirously, longingly; readily, willingly, eagerly

12 likably, amicably, genially, congenially, winsomely, appealingly, adorably, lovably, attractively, pleasingly, endearingly; popularly, fascinatingly, captivatingly, titillatingly, temptingly, alluringly

NOUNS

1 **dislike,** distaste, aversion, allergy [Inf]; disrelish, displeasure, discontent, dissatisfaction; disfavor, unfavorable regard, disesteem, disrespect, prejudice, bias, instinctive dislike, instant dislike, scunner; disapproval, disapprobation, condemnation, rejection
   ▶ *Dissatisfaction 274; Rejection 383; Disrespect 436; Disapproval 438*

2 **antipathy,** disgust, repulsion, detestation, loathing, abhorrence, abomination; unpleasantness, disagreeableness, unfriendliness, hostility, ill will, disaffection, animosity, animus, bad blood, enmity, antagonism, hatred, hate; resentment, bitterness, sourness, gall and wormwood; horror, fear, phobia, xenophobia
   ▶ *Hostility 63; Unpleasantness 272; Fear 283; Hate 300; Resentment, Anger 302; Dissent 347; Repulsion 701*

3 **disinclination,** reluctance, resistance, unwillingness, no inclination for, no stomach for
   ▶ *Unwillingness 375*

4 **misanthropy,** hatred of humankind, dislike *or* distrust of humankind; misandry, misogyny, male chauvinism; cynicism, antisociability, unsociability; inhumanity, malevolence; selfishness, egotism, egoism, self-centeredness
   ▶ *Hostility 63; Unsociability 409; Selfishness 444*

5 **misanthrope,** misanthropist, hater of humankind, misandrist, misogynist, antifeminist, male chauvinist, male chauvinist pig [Inf *and* Off]; solitary, cynic, egotist, egoist

ADJECTIVES

6 **displeased,** discontent, disaffected, dissatisfied, disillusioned, disenchanted, not charmed, unsympathetic, fed up, sick of, sick and tired of; disapproving, intolerant, judgmental, prejudiced against, biased against

7 **antipathetic,** unpleasant, disagreeable, unfriendly, hostile, inimical, antagonistic; resentful, hateful, bitter, sour; repelled, put off, disgusted, repulsed, revolted, nauseated, sickened; fearful, fearing, phobic, xenophobic

8 **misanthropic,** antisocial, unsocial, cynical; egoistic, egotistical, selfish, self-centered; misandrous, man-hating, misogynous, woman-hating, sexist

9 **disinclined,** reluctant, resistant, averse, unwilling, loath to

10 **disliked,** dislikable, unlikable, misliked [Arch], disrelished, unrelished, distasteful, not to one's taste, unsavory, not one's cup of tea, yucky [Inf]; displeasing, dissatisfying, annoying, irritating, irksome, grating, repellent, rebarbative; unprepossessing, unpopular, unappreciated, uncared for, unwanted, unloved, undesired, undesirous, unwelcome; out of favor, disfavored, disesteemed, disrespected; disapproved, condemned, unchosen, rejected, spurned, jilted, thrown over
   ▶ *Unpleasantness 272; Dissatisfaction 274; Sullenness 304; Rejection 383; Disapproval 438*

11 **detested,** despised, loathed, abhorred, hated; detestable, despicable, objectionable, offensive, repugnant, loathsome, intolerable, insufferable, disgusting, repulsive, abhorrent, abominable, revolting, foul, stinking, nauseating, sickening, fulsome; feared, fearsome, frightening

VERBS

12 **dislike,** disrelish, not care for, find not to one's taste, have an aversion to, take a dislike to, not like the look of, mislike [Arch]; disfavor, hold in low regard, disesteem, disrespect; disapprove, take a dim view of, look down on, look down one's nose at, condemn, reject, spurn, jilt, throw over
   ▶ *Hostility 63*

13 **detest,** despise, loathe, abhor, abominate, execrate, can't stand, can't bear, hate, resent, have a grudge against; hate the world, lose faith in human nature; fear, feel fear
   ▶ *Fear 283; Hate 300*

14 **be disinclined,** prefer not to, be reluctant, resist; have no inclination for, have no desire for, have no use for, have no time for, have no stomach for

15 **react against,** disagree, dissent, object to, mind, take offense at; shun, not choose, turn away, turn up one's nose at; look askance, grimace, frown, scowl, make a face, sneer at; yell *or* scream at, fight, hit, strike out, attack; recoil, shrink from, shudder, feel sick
   ▶ *Sullenness 304; Disagreement 463*

16 **cause dislike,** displease, dissatisfy, upset; annoy, irritate, grate, irk, rile, rub the wrong way, disincline, put off, get on one's nerves, bug; offend, repel, disgust, revolt, nauseate, sicken, gross out [Inf]; antagonize, provoke, set against, put one's back up, press one's buttons, get one's goat [Inf]; anger, inflame, madden, incense, infuriate, enrage; turn one against, make bad blood, incur blame; frighten, horrify, shock
   ▶ *Unpleasantness 272; Resentment, Anger 302; Repulsion 701*

ADVERBS

17 **discontentedly,** unsympathetically, unwillingly, under duress, reluctantly, with misgivings; unpleasantly, disagreeably, hostilely, antagonistically; resentfully, hatefully, bitterly

18 **misanthropically,** antisocially, unsocially, cynically; egotistically, egoistically, selfishly

19 **distastefully,** displeasingly, annoyingly, irritatingly, rebarbatively, offensively, intolerably, insufferably, disgustingly, repugnantly, repulsively, abhorrently, abominably, sickeningly, fulsomely

292 Surprise

NOUNS

1 **surprise,** surprisal, unexpectedness, suddenness, unpreparedness, unreadiness
  ▶ *Lack of Preparation 389*

2 **astonishment,** wonder, amazement, astoundment, speechlessness, stupefaction, shock, incredulity, disconcertion *or* disconcertment, bewilderment
  ▶ *Disbelief 88; Wonder 294*

3 **shock,** start, jolt, jar, jump, fright; bolt from *or* out of the blue, thunderbolt, bomb *or* bombshell
  ▶ *Fear 283*

4 **ambush,** attack, entrapment, capture
  ▶ *Trap 813*

ADJECTIVES

5 **surprised,** taken aback, caught unawares, caught napping; off guard, unprepared, unready; startled, jarred, jolted, frightened; ambushed, attacked, ensnared, trapped, captured, blindsided [Inf]
  ▶ *Fear 283; Discovery 345; Lack of Preparation 389; Trap 813*

6 **astonished,** awed, awe-struck *or* awestruck, awe-stricken *or* awestricken, amazed, astounded, flabbergasted, thunderstruck, staggered, bowled over, dumbfounded, struck dumb, speechless, stupefied, stunned, shocked, incredulous, disconcerted, bewildered
  ▶ *Disbelief 88; Wonder 294*

7 **surprising,** unexpected, sudden, unforeseen, unanticipated, unpredicted; startling, jarring, jolting, shocking, frightening
  ▶ *Fear 283; Lack of Preparation 389*

8 **astonishing,** amazing, astounding, stupefying, staggering, boggling, shocking, disconcerting, bewildering
  ▶ *Wonder 294*

VERBS

9 **surprise,** take by surprise, take *or* catch unawares, catch napping, catch off guard, discover, catch red-handed, catch out [Brit]; startle, jar, jolt, drop a bomb *or* bombshell, frighten, shock, give someone a fright, make someone jump
  ▶ *Fear 283; Discovery 345; Lack of Preparation 389*

10 **astonish,** amaze, astound, flabbergast, bowl over, nonplus, floor, dumbfound, strike dumb, leave speechless, stupefy, stagger, boggle, stun, shock, disconcert, bewilder; come as a surprise, come out of the blue, come out of nowhere, throw *or* knock for a loop [Inf]
  ▶ *Wonder 294; Lack of Preparation 389*

11 **ambush,** bushwhack, ensnare, trap, entrap; creep up on, pounce on, spring on, capture, blindside [Inf]
  ▶ *Trap 813*

12 **be surprised,** not expect, be taken by surprise, be taken aback; start, shy, jump, jump out of one's skin

  ▶ *Fear 283; Lack of Preparation 389*

ADVERBS

13 **with surprise,** with astonishment, astonishedly, speechlessly, incredulously, disconcertedly, bewilderedly
  ▶ *Disbelief 88; Wonder 294*

14 **surprisingly,** by surprise, unawares, unexpectedly, suddenly, without warning, out of the blue, like a bolt from *or* out of the blue; to one's surprise, astonishingly, amazingly, astoundingly, stupefyingly, shockingly, startlingly, incredulously, disconcertingly, bewilderingly
  ▶ *Disbelief 88; Wonder 294; Lack of Preparation 389*

INTERJECTIONS

15 **good heavens!,** great Scott!, you don't say!, I don't believe it!, you could have knocked me over with a feather!, marry! [Arch]
  ▶ *Wonder 294*

293 Disappointment

NOUNS

1 **disappointment,** letdown, unfulfilled expectations, nonfulfillment, noncompletion, dissatisfaction, discontent, disillusionment, disenchantment, sourness, chagrin, regret; discouragement, disheartenment, dejection, depression, sadness, despair, hopelessness
  ▶ *Sorrow 270; Dissatisfaction 274; Hopelessness 282*

2 **frustration,** bafflement, tantalization, false hopes, vain expectation, hopes unrealized, blighted hopes, dashed hopes, betrayed hopes; hindrance, obstruction, impediment, obstacle, hitch; denial, refusal, rejection
  ▶ *Rejection 383; Hindrance 826*

3 **bad outcome,** bad result, not what one had expected *or* hoped for; bad news, shock, blow, setback; misfortune, disaster, fiasco; failure, defeat, devastation, bummer [Inf]
  ▶ *Dissatisfaction 274; Surprise 292; Failure 846*

ADJECTIVES

4 **disappointed,** let down, badly served, unfulfilled, unsatisfied, dissatisfied, discontented, disillusioned, disenchanted, soured, chagrined, regretful; discouraged, disheartened, dispirited, dejected, depressed, saddened, crestfallen, heartbroken, hopeless; crushed, defeated, devastated
  ▶ *Sorrow 270; Dissatisfaction 274; Hopelessness 282*

5 **frustrated,** thwarted, baffled, hindered, obstructed, hampered, balked, bilked, foiled; denied, refused, rejected, turned away, jilted
  ▶ *Rejection 383; Hindrance 826*

6 **disappointing,** falling short, not up to expectations, less than one's hopes, not up to scratch, second-best, second-rate, insufficient, inadequate, poor, inferior; unfulfilling, unsatisfying, dissatisfying, discontenting;

disillusioning, disenchanting, discouraging, disheartening, depressing, sad

▶ *Insufficiency 98; Dissatisfaction 274; Hopelessness 282*

7 **frustrating,** tantalizing, baffling, hindering, hampering; miscarried, abortive, unsuccessful

▶ *Hindrance 826; Failure 846*

VERBS

8 **be disappointed,** be let down, not realize one's expectations, expect more *or* better, have hoped for better, have one's plans ruined, have a bad outcome *or* result, regret; be crestfallen, be heartbroken, be depressed, lose hope, despair

▶ *Sorrow 270; Hopelessness 282*

9 **disappoint,** fall short, let down, fail, fail to deliver, not meet expectations, dissatisfy, discontent, belie one's expectations, disillusion, disenchant, leave in the lurch, go wrong, turn sour; discourage, dishearten, dispirit, deject, depress, sadden, sour, burst someone's bubble; crush, defeat, devastate

▶ *Sorrow 270; Dissatisfaction 274; Hopelessness 282*

10 **thwart,** frustrate, tantalize, baffle, hinder, obstruct, hamper, balk, bilk, foil; dash *or* crush someone's hopes, dash the cup from one's lips, betray someone's hopes; deny, refuse, reject, turn away, jilt

▶ *Rejection 383; Hindrance 826*

ADVERBS

11 **disappointedly,** dissatisfiedly, discontentedly, disenchantedly, dispiritedly, dejectedly, hopelessly, defeatedly

12 **disappointingly,** unsatisfactorily, insufficiently, inadequately, poorly; frustratingly, tantalizingly, so near and yet so far, unsuccessfully; discouragingly, depressingly

294 Wonder

Two things fill the mind with ever-increasing wonder and awe: . . . the starry heavens above me and the moral law within me. — IMMANUEL KANT

All things bright and beautiful, / All creatures great and small, / All things wise and wonderful, / The Lord God made them all.
— CECIL FRANCES ALEXANDER

NOUNS

1 **wonder,** sense of wonder, state of wonder, wonderment, awe, veneration, admiration, fascination, enchantment, raptness, hero worship; surprise, astonishment, amazement, astoundment, shock, stupefaction, dumbfoundment

▶ *Surprise 292; Unintelligibility 364*

2 **speculation,** conjecture, doubt, question, puzzle, bafflement, puzzlement, bewilderment; consternation, fear

3 **marvel,** cause of wonder, phenomenon, wonder, wonderment, object of wonder, object of admiration, admiration, spectacle, sight, eye-popper [Inf]; surprise, astonishment, shock; one for the book *or* books, one in a thousand *or* million, rarity, exception; miracle, wonderwork, portent; masterpiece *or* masterwork, chefd'oeuvre, masterstroke; sensation, drama, cause célèbre, nine days' wonder; *annus mirabilis* [L]; fantasy, fantasyland, cloud-cuckoo-land, Utopia, wonderland, fairyland

▶ *Drama and Theater 136; Imagination 360*

4 **cause of wonder,** wonder working, miracle working, thaumaturgy, magic, wizardry, sorcery; stroke of genius, feat, exploit, deed

▶ *Religion 81; Occultism 86; Skillfulness 127*

5 **wonderfulness,** wondrousness, marvelousness, awesomeness, miraculousness, remarkableness, extraordinariness, mysteriousness

6 **wonderful person,** wonder, marvel, phenomenon, rara avis, portent, prodigy, child prodigy, wonder child, wunderkind, genius, wonder boy *or* girl; wonderworker, miracle worker, thaumaturge, magician, sorcerer *or* sorceress, wizard, witch, fairy godmother; paragon, nonpareil, nonesuch, hero, heroine, star, idol, superman, superwoman; puzzle, enigma; curiosity, idiot savant, oddity, freak, monster, monstrosity; [Inf]: knockout, stunner, whiz kid

▶ *Occultism 86; Surprise 292; Intellect 315*

ADJECTIVES

7 **wondering,** marveling, rapt in wonder, lost in wonder, wonder-stricken *or* wonderstruck, admiring, impressed, awed, awe-struck *or* awestruck, awe-stricken *or* awestricken, dazzled; fascinated, spellbound, enchanted, entranced, bewitched; surprised, astonished, amazed, astounded, flabbergasted, thunderstruck, bowled over; shocked, aghast, stupefied, dazed, stunned, petrified, dumbfounded; agog, all agog, breathless, gasping, popeyed, wide-eyed, openmouthed, agape, gaping, gazing, dumb, dumbstruck, inarticulate, speechless, wordless, left without words, silenced, silent, transfixed, rooted to the spot; baffled, bewildered, confounded, nonplussed, perplexed, puzzled; fearful, frightened

---

SEVEN WONDERS OF THE ANCIENT WORLD

Pyramids of Egypt (at Giza)
Hanging Gardens of Babylon
Colossus of Rhodes
Mausoleum at Halicarnassus
Pharos (lighthouse) at Alexandria
Statue of Zeus at Olympia
Temple of Artemis (Diana) at Ephesus

▶ *Fear 283; Surprise 292*

8 speculative, speculating, conjecturing, questioning, doubting, wondering

▶ *Question 333; Uncertainty 841*

9 wondrous, wonderful, marvelous, prodigious, phenomenal, sensational, spectacular, awesome, awe-inspiring, miraculous, admirable, impressive, breathtaking, exquisite, dazzling, striking, dramatic, electrifying; fascinating, captivating, spellbinding, enchanting, bewitching; great, excellent, fantastic, fantabulous [Inf]; stupendous, remarkable, notable, noteworthy, extraordinary, unusual, rare, exceptional, singular, unique; unprecedented, unheard-of, record-breaking, best

10 astonishing, surprising, amazing, astounding, staggering, overwhelming, shocking, stupefying, petrifying; baffling, bewildering, perplexing, puzzling, boggling; unaccountable, mysterious, enigmatic, peculiar, curious, strange, odd, exotic, outlandish, bizarre, outré, weird, grotesque, monstrous, freakish; fearsome, frightening; unbelievable, beyond belief, incredible, inconceivable, unimaginable; indescribable, ineffable, inexpressible, unspeakable, unutterable; [Inf]: mind-boggling, mind-blowing, freaky

11 wonder-working, miracle-working, thaumaturgic *or* thaumaturgical, magic *or* magical, sorcerous

VERBS

12 wonder, marvel, admire, venerate, revere, hero-worship, idolize; show wonder, stand in amazement, gasp, stare, gaze, goggle at, gawk, gape, gawp, drop one's jaw, not believe one's eyes *or* ears, have no words to express, not know what to say, fear

13 speculate, wonder, conjecture, suspect, have a suspicion, suppose, guess, guess at, hazard, hazard a guess; ponder, meditate, muse, think, question, query, ask oneself, doubt

▶ *Thought 317; Question 333; Uncertainty 841*

14 be wondrous, be wonderful, be marvelous, awe, inspire awe, take one's breath away, impress, dazzle, electrify; fascinate, spellbind, enchant, entrance, bewitch; surprise, astonish, amaze, astound, flabbergast, bowl over, stagger, shock, stupefy, daze, stun, petrify, dumbfound, strike dumb; baffle, bewilder, confound, nonplus, perplex, puzzle, consternate, boggle, boggle the mind, make one's head swim; beggar *or* baffle description, stagger belief; [Inf]: blow one's mind, blow away, knock one's socks off

15 do wonders, work wonders, work miracles, achieve marvels, perform magic

ADVERBS

16 wonderingly, admiringly, in awe, enchantedly; astonishedly, in amazement, in a daze

17 speculatively, conjecturally, doubtfully, bewilderedly, confoundedly, perplexedly, puzzledly; breathlessly, dumbly, wordlessly, silently

18 wondrously, in wonder, wonderfully, marvelously, prodigiously, miraculously, phenomenally, sensationally, spectacularly, awesomely, admirably, impressively, breathtakingly; fascinatingly, captivatingly, enchantingly, bewitchingly, magically; fantastically, stupendously, remarkably, notably, extraordinarily, unusually, rarely, exceptionally, singularly, uniquely

19 astonishingly, surprisingly, to one's surprise, amazingly, to one's amazement, astoundingly, shockingly, stupefyingly; bewilderingly, bafflingly, perplexingly, puzzlingly; unaccountably, mysteriously, enigmatically, peculiarly, curiously, strange to say, marvelous to relate, *mirabile dictu* [L]; strangely, oddly, exotically, outlandishly, weirdly, grotesquely, freakishly, monstrously; unbelievably, incredibly, inconceivably, unimaginably; indescribably, ineffably, inexpressibly, unspeakably

INTERJECTIONS

20 wonderful!, marvelous!, great!, amazing!, fantastic!, fabulous!, smashing!; my gosh!, wow!, my goodness!, goodness gracious!, good heavens!, bless my soul!, bless my heart!, my stars!, my word!, I declare!, how about that!, what do you know!, imagine that!, fancy that!, what do you know about that!, who would have thought it!, can you beat that!, will wonders never cease!, whatever next!; I don't believe it!, really!, what!, what on earth!, what in the world!, go on!, you don't say!, did you ever!, never!, well I never!; [Inf]: gee!, awesome!, fab!, cool!, wicked!, holy cow!, holy mackerel!, holy moly!, holy Moses!, holy smoke!, holy shit!

295 Lack of Wonder

NOUNS

1 lack of wonder, lack of awe, lack of admiration, refusal to be impressed, irreverence; lack of astonishment, expectedness, lack of amazement, unamazedness; calm, calmness, coolness, cool, collectedness, composure, inexcitability, imperturbability, serenity, tranquillity, acceptance; indifference, blankness, nonchalance, insouciance, disinterest, lack of interest, unconcern, incuriosity, unimaginativeness, dullness, impassivity, apathy, phlegmaticalness *or* phlegmaticness, failure to arouse, lack of spirit

▶ *Insensitivity 268; Indifference 289; Expectation 356*

2 predictability, lack of surprise, unimpressiveness, unimpressionability, customariness, ordinariness, commonness, usualness, plainness

▶ *Habit, Custom 397; Conformity 781; Probability 838*

ADJECTIVES

3 wonderless, unmoved, unawed, aweless, uninspired, unimpressed, blasé, unimpressionable, unadmiring, irreverent; unsurprised, unamazed, calm, cool, cool as a cucumber, collected, composed, unexcited, inexcitable, imperturbable, serene, tranquil; indifferent, blank, deaf to, blind to, dead to, nonchalant, insouciant, disinterested, uninterested, unconcerned, incurious, unquestioning, unimaginative, unenthusiastic, dull, impassive, sanguine, apathetic, phlegmatical *or* phlegmatic, unaroused, unspirited, spiritless

4 **predictable,** unsurprising, unimpressive, customary, expected, ordinary, routine, everyday, run-of-the-mill, commonplace, common, usual, plain, plain as day, just as *or* what one thought, nothing to it, nothing to wonder about, nothing to write home about, all in a day's work

VERBS

5 **not wonder about,** not admire, refuse to be impressed, show irreverence; lack amazement, show no excitement, not raise an eyebrow, not turn a hair, not blink an eye, take in stride, expect, see it coming, know it all; calm *or* collect *or* compose oneself, keep a stiff upper lip, keep one's cool

6 **understand,** have no questions *or* doubts about, accept, have seen it all before, be in the know, catch on; [Inf]: know the score, get wise to, wise up

▶ *Answer 334*

7 **not cause wonder,** not interest, unimpress, uninspire, not arouse, fail to amaze; be predictable, offer no surprises, appear straightforward, have nothing to it

▶ *Indifference 289*

ADVERBS

8 **without wonder,** awelessly, uninspiredly, unimpressionably, without admiration, unadmiringly, irreverently; unamazedly, without turning a hair, calmly, coolly, collectedly, unexcitedly, inexcitably, imperturbably, serenely, tranquilly; indifferently, blankly, nonchalantly, insouciantly, disinterestedly, uninterestedly, apathetically, without concern, incuriously, unquestioningly, unimaginatively, unenthusiastically, dully, impassively, sanguinely, phlegmatically

9 **predictably,** unsurprisingly, unimpressively, customarily, expectedly, ordinarily, routinely, commonly, usually, plainly

INTERJECTIONS

10 **naturally!,** of course!, nothing to it!; big deal!, so what?, so?, why not?

296 Boredom

I wanted to be bored to death, as good a way to go as any.
— PETER DE VRIES

NOUNS

1 **boredom,** tedium, ennui, weariness, languor, listlessness, uninterestedness, indifference; melancholy, *taedium vitae* [L], world-weariness, *Weltschmerz* [Ger]; dissatisfaction, dislike, lack of enjoyment; satiation, satiety, jadedness

▶ *Dissatisfaction 274; Indifference 289; Dislike 291*

2 **boringness,** tediousness, tiresomeness, irksomeness; dullness, dreariness, humdrumness, slowness; monotony, monotonousness, sameness, uniformity, lack of variation, singsong; plainness, tastelessness, insipidity, flatness, staleness, dryness, aridity; stodginess, stuffiness, heaviness, ponderousness; repetitiousness, repetitiveness, long-windedness, prolixity; banality, triteness, prosaicness, prosiness, commonplaceness

▶ *Tastelessness 220; Sameness 730; Repetition 797*

3 **boring thing,** bore, utter bore, same old thing *or* story, same damn thing, more of the same, broken record; too much of a good thing; time to kill, time on one's hands, leaden hours; twice-told tale, dull speech, longueur; bromide, platitude, chestnut, stale joke; beaten track, rut, grindstone, treadmill, drag [Inf]

▶ *Repetition 797*

4 **boring person,** bore, utter *or* frightful *or* crashing bore, bromide; stick-in-the-mud, old fogy; long-winded person, egoist, egotist; buttonholer, pest, nuisance; [Inf]: drag, drip, nerd, pain, pain in the neck *or* ass

ADJECTIVES

5 **bored,** bored to death, bored to tears, bored stiff, bored to distraction, bored out of one's mind; uninterested, indifferent, listless, languid, weary, wearied, fatigued, tired, good and tired [Inf]; melancholy, world-weary, tired of living; jaded, satiated, sated, sick of, tired of, sick and tired of, fed up, dissatisfied, irked

▶ *Unpleasantness 272*

6 **boring,** boresome, tedious, wearisome, wearying, fatiguing, tiresome, wearing, irksome; dull, uninteresting, dry-as-dust, drab, dreary, humdrum, ho-hum, slow, deadly; monotonous, uniform, unvarying, singsong; plain, tasteless, insipid, flat, stale, dry, arid; stodgy, stuffy, heavy, ponderous, leaden; repetitious, repetitive, long-winded, prolix, overlong, prolonged, protracted; banal, trite, platitudinous, prosaic, prosy, pedestrian, commonplace, blah [Inf]

VERBS

7 **be bored,** suffer boredom, lack interest; lead a boring life, have a monotonous job, have *or* keep one's nose to the grindstone, do the same old thing, be in a rut; have time to kill, have time on one's hands, twiddle one's thumbs

8 **bore,** be boring, bore to death, bore to tears, bore stiff, bore to distraction, bore the pants off, be tedious, fail to interest, make one yawn, weary, fatigue, put one to sleep, tire; irk, wear, wear on, annoy, pester, buttonhole; repeat oneself, sound like a broken record, lack variation, draw out, go on forever, go on and on, drone on, never end, talk too long; stay too long, wear out *or* outstay one's welcome; provide no enjoyment, dissatisfy; sate, satiate, jade, cloy, pall, glut

9 **in a bored manner,** uninterestedly, indifferently, listlessly, languorously, languidly, wearily, tiredly, jadedly

10 **boringly,** tediously, wearisomely, wearyingly, tiresomely, irksomely, in a boring manner; dully, uninterestingly, drably, drearily, slowly; monotonously, uniformly, unvaryingly, without variety, with no frills, without a change of scenery or pace, in a rut, on a treadmill; plainly, tastelessly, insipidly, flatly, stalely, dryly; stodgily, stuffily, heavily, ponderously; repetitiously, repetitively, to death, ad nauseam, long-windedly; banally, tritely, platitudinously, prosaically, prosily, commonplacely

297 Pride

Pride goeth before destruction, and an haughty spirit before a fall. — BIBLE: PROVERBS

NOUNS

1 **pride,** pridefulness, conceit, vanity, self-admiration, egotism, egoism, overconfidence, overweening pride, hubris, self-importance, vainglory, boastfulness, self-praise, self-glorification, bigheadedness [Inf]
▶ *Vanity 402; Selfishness 444*

2 **arrogance,** haughtiness, hauteur, loftiness, insolence, disdain, condescension; false pride, pretention, pretentiousness, affectation, airs, uppityness, snobbery, snobbishness; grandiosity, pompousness, ostentation, ostentatiousness, pomp, pomp and circumstance, showiness; stiff-necked pride, stiff-neckedness, obstinacy
▶ *Affectation 367; Obstinacy 379; Insolence 400; Showiness 404; Disrespect 436*

3 **proudness,** self-esteem, self-regard, self-respect, *amour propre* [Fr], proud bearing, dignity; self-confidence, self-sufficiency, self-reliance, independence, courage, spirit, mettle; fulfillment, satisfaction, contentment, enjoyment
▶ *Satisfaction 273; Courage 284; Freedom 829*

4 **dignity,** honor, nobility, worthiness, venerability; prestige, reputation, repute, distinction, esteem; solemnity, sobriety, gravity, sedateness
▶ *Repute 370; Formality 406; Respect 435*

5 **majesty,** stateliness, augustness, grandeur, magnificence, regality, lordliness, princeliness
▶ *Showiness 404; Elegance 527*

6 **object of pride,** pride and joy, favorite, jewel in the crown, pick of the bunch; source of pride, boast, pride of place

7 **proud person,** vain person, egotist, egoist, boaster, bragger, braggart, show-off, flaunter, swaggerer, blusterer, peacock, popinjay, cock of the walk, prima donna, snob, high-hatter, aristocrat, grande dame; his or her nibs [Inf]

▶ *Aristocrat 70; Vanity 402; Superiority 744*

ADJECTIVES

8 **prideful,** conceited, vain, self-admiring, egotistical, self-satisfied, smug, pleased with oneself, flushed with pride, puffed up, bloated, bursting or swollen with pride, swellheaded or swelled-headed, bigheaded [Inf]; overconfident, hubristic, self-important, holier-than-thou; vainglorious, boastful, self-praising, self-glorifying, swaggering, strutting
▶ *Vanity 402; Selfishness 444*

9 **arrogant,** haughty, high-and-mighty, lofty, overbearing, insolent, brazen, cocky, bumptious, disdainful, condescending, patronizing, imperious, magisterial, presumptuous, high-handed; supercilious, proud as a peacock; pretentious, affected, uppity, hoity-toity, snobbish, grandiose, pompous, ostentatious, swanky, showy, flaunty, purse-proud, house-proud; highflying, high-flown, erect, stiff-necked, obstinate; [Inf]: snooty, stuck-up, highfalutin or hifalutin, toffee-nosed [Brit]
▶ *Affectation 367; Obstinacy 379; Insolence 400; Showiness 404; Disrespect 436*

10 **proud,** proudhearted, self-regarding, self-respecting; self-confident, self-sufficient, self-reliant, independent, courageous, spirited, high-spirited, mettlesome; fulfilled, satisfied, contented
▶ *Satisfaction 273; Freedom 829*

11 **dignified,** honorable, noble, worthy, venerable, high-minded, exalted, elevated; prestigious, distinguished, esteemed; solemn, somber, grave, sedate
▶ *Formality 406*

12 **majestic,** stately, aristocratic, august, imposing, grand, magnificent, regal, lordly, princely, kingly, queenly
▶ *Showiness 404; Elegance 527*

VERBS

13 **pride oneself,** preen oneself, congratulate oneself, pat oneself on the back, burst or swell with pride; be prideful, be too proud, be vain, think too much of oneself, flatter oneself, overween [Arch], be on an ego trip [Inf]; boast, brag, swagger, strut
▶ *Vanity 402*

14 **disdain,** despise, scorn, be on one's high horse, condescend, patronize, think it beneath one, look down on, look down one's nose at, turn up one's nose at; pull rank, throw one's weight around, lord it over, queen it over, put on airs, affect, pretend; be ostentatious, show off, swank, flaunt
▶ *Affectation 367; Showiness 404*

15 **be proud,** have one's pride, have one's self-respect, hold one's head high, stand erect, stand up straight, stand on one's dignity; look one in the face or eye; be proud of, take pride or glory in, exult in

16 **guard one's pride,** preserve one's dignity or honor, keep one's reputation intact, be jealous of one's good name, save face, do one proud

17 **pridefully,** conceitedly, vainly, egotistically, smugly; overconfidently, self-importantly; vaingloriously, boastfully

18 **arrogantly,** haughtily, loftily, overbearingly, insolently, brazenly, cockily, bumptiously, disdainfully, condescendingly, patronizingly, imperiously, magisterially, presumptuously, high-handedly, superciliously; pretentiously, affectedly, snobbishly, snootily [Inf]; grandiosely, pompously, ostentatiously, swankily, flauntingly; stiff-neckedly, obstinately

19 **proudly,** with pride, with head held high; self-confidently, self-sufficiently, self-reliantly, independently, courageously, with spirit

20 **with dignity,** honorably, nobly, worthily, venerably, high-mindedly, exaltedly; prestigiously, with distinction; solemnly, somberly, gravely, sedately

21 **majestically,** augustly, aristocratically, imposingly, grandly, magnificently, regally, royally, like a lord

298 Humility

It is difficult to be humble. Even if you aim at humility, there is no guarantee that when you have attained the state you will not be proud of the feat.
— BONAMY DOBRÉE

NOUNS

1 **humility,** humbleness, modesty, unpretentiousness, unassumingness, meekness, harmlessness; simplicity, plainness, homeliness
▶ *Modesty 403; Simplicity 526*

2 **lowliness,** poorness, meanness, smallness, commonness, working class
▶ *Commoner 71; Inferiority 745*

3 **submissiveness,** compliance, acquiescence, resignation, subservience, obedience, obsequiousness; deference, respect, politeness, courtesy; genuflection, bow, curtsy, scrape
▶ *Servility 401; Courtesy 410; Submission 421; Obedience 426*

4 **self-abasement,** self-abnegation, self-sacrifice, unselfishness, disinterestedness; self-deprecation, self-depreciation, self-effacement, self-doubt
▶ *Modesty 403; Disinterestedness 443*

5 **humiliation,** mortification, shame, disgrace, indignity, abashment, chagrin, embarrassment, wounded *or* injured *or* hurt pride, egg on one's face [Inf]; comedown, descent, deflation, climb-down; hangdog look *or* expression, shamefacedness, shamefastness [Arch]
▶ *Disrespect 436*

6 **abasement,** debasement, degradation, disparagement, deprecation, belittlement, diminishment, dishonor, disrepute, disfavor, slap in the face, put-down [Inf]

▶ *Disrepute 371; Disrespect 436; Disparagement 440; Lowering 716*

7 **humble person,** mouse, shrinking violet, wimp [Inf]; servant, sycophant, toady, spaniel, flatterer, groveler, Uriah Heep
▶ *Modesty 403; Submission 421; Flattery 439*

ADJECTIVES

8 **humble,** not proud, modest, unpretentious, unpretending, without airs, unassuming; meek, mouselike, harmless, inoffensive; simple, plain, homely, undistinguished, unimportant
▶ *Modesty 403; Simplicity 526*

9 **lowly,** low, poor, mean, small, common, lowborn, plebeian, working-class
▶ *Commoner 71; Inferiority 745*

10 **submissive,** compliant, acquiescent, resigned, subservient, obedient, obsequious; deferent, respectful, polite, courteous
▶ *Servility 401; Submission 421; Obedience 426; Respect 435*

11 **self-abasing,** self-abnegating, self-sacrificing, unselfish, disinterested; self-deprecating, self-depreciating, self-effacing, self-doubting
▶ *Modesty 403; Disinterestedness 443*

12 **humiliated,** humbled, mortified, ashamed, shamed, disgraced, abashed, chagrined, embarrassed, disconcerted, out of countenance; diminished, reduced, deflated, wounded, dispirited, crestfallen, hangdog, shamefaced
▶ *Disrespect 436*

13 **abased,** debased, degraded, lowered, brought down, taken down a peg or two, cut down to size, disparaged, belittled, chastened; crushed, defeated, slapped in the face, debunked
▶ *Disrespect 436; Disapproval 438; Disparagement 440; Lowering 716*

14 **humiliating,** humbling, humilatory, humilative, mortifying, embarrassing, wounding, disconcerting, discomfiting

15 **debasing,** degrading, abject, demeaning, disparaging, belittling
▶ *Disparagement 440; Lowering 716*

VERBS

16 **be humble,** be modest, stay in the background, put others first, take a backseat, play second fiddle, have no sense of pride
▶ *Modesty 403*

17 **submit,** defer, yield, knuckle under, acquiesce, resign, comply, accede, capitulate, agree, obey; genuflect, bow, curtsy, scrape, tip one's hat
▶ *Servility 401; Courtesy 410; Submission 421; Obedience 426*

18 **humble oneself,** abase oneself, demean oneself, lower oneself, stoop, swallow one's pride, put one's pride in one's pocket, drink the cup of humiliation, set

one's dignity aside; come on bended knee, come hat in hand, grovel, crawl, lick the dust, eat humble pie, eat one's words, eat crow *or* dirt [Inf]; climb down, get down from one's high horse, draw *or* pull in one's horns

19 **humiliate,** humble, mortify, shame, put to shame, disgrace, make a fool of, abash, embarrass, disconcert, discomfit, put out, put out of countenance; diminish, reduce, deflate, wound, dispirit, make one feel small *or* this high

▶ *Disrespect 436*

20 **abase,** debase, degrade, lower, bring down, take down, take down a peg or two, cut down to size, put someone in his *or* her place, demean, disparage, deprecate, belittle; crush, defeat, slap in the face, debunk, put down [Inf]

▶ *Disrespect 436; Disparagement 440; Lowering 716*

21 **rebuke,** reproof, reproach, reprimand, disapprove, chasten

▶ *Disapproval 438*

ADVERBS

22 **humbly,** modestly, unpretentiously, unassumingly, meekly, inoffensively; simply, plainly

23 **submissively,** compliantly, acquiescently, subserviently, obediently, obsequiously; deferentially, with due deference, respectfully, politely, courteously, with hat in hand, on bended knee

24 **embarrassedly,** with one's tail between one's legs, shamefacedly

25 **humiliatingly,** mortifyingly, embarrassingly, disconcertingly; degradingly, abjectly, disparagingly, deprecatingly

299 Love

Love, all alike, no season knows, nor clime, / Nor hours, days, months, which are the rags of time.
— JOHN DONNE

Set me as a seal upon thine heart, as a seal upon thine arm; for love is strong as death; jealousy is cruel as the grave. Many waters cannot quench love, neither can the floods drown it. — BIBLE: SONG OF SOLOMON

NOUNS

1 **love,** affection, fondness, endearment, tenderness, attachment, devotion, loyalty; parental love, filial love, maternal love, paternal love; brotherly love, Christian love, Christian charity, charity, agape, fellow feeling; spiritual love, Platonic love, friendship, amity, compatibility, understanding; liking, partiality, regard, esteem, admiration, respect, reverence, veneration; adoration, adulation, worship, hero worship, idolization, idolatry; self-love, narcissism, egotism; love of one's country, patriotism, nationalism

▶ *Friendship 62; Feelings 266; Sensitivity 267; Liking 290; Benevolence 305; Philanthropy 307; Respect 435*

2 **romantic love,** romance, passion, ardor, transport of love, bewitchment, enchantment, fascination; falling in love, truelove, the real thing; first love, young love, puppy love *or* calf love, infatuation, fancy, passing fancy, crush [Inf]

▶ *Liking 290*

3 **sexual love,** physical love, passion, amorousness, flames of love, desire, yearning, longing, lust, aphrodisia, desires of the flesh, eroticism, erotomania; sexual drive, sexual urge, libido, mating instinct; lustfulness, wantonness, lasciviousness, licentiousness, lewdness, libertinism, prurience, randiness, horniness [Inf], venery [Arch]; lovemaking, making love, intimacy

▶ *Sex 20; Desire 288*

4 **lovingness,** amorousness, amativeness, affectionateness, demonstrativeness, tenderness, kindness; romanticism, susceptibility; lovesickness, languishment, lovelornness

5 **lovability,** lovableness, endearing qualities, likability, amiability, agreeability; sweetness, charm, charms, winsomeness, winning ways; attractiveness, beauty, appeal, allurement, adorability, desirability, sex appeal, sexiness

▶ *Desire 288; Beauty 529*

6 **communication of love,** loving words, endearments, billing and cooing, sweet nothings, pet names, sweet talk [Inf]; loving looks, sheep's eyes, coquettish glance, ogle, wink, come-hither look, goo-goo eyes [Inf]; loving touch, pat, love tap, pinch, hug, bear hug, embrace, squeeze, caress, stroke; kiss, soul kiss *or* French kiss, smack, smack on the lips, osculation, peck, peck on the cheek; cuddling, tickling, snuggling, kissing, petting, fooling around, hugging, embracing, nuzzling, squeezing, caressing, fondling; [Inf]: necking, lallygagging *or* lollygagging, making out, smooching, spooning, groping, making whoopee

▶ *Touch 216*

7 **term of endearment,** angel, darling, dear, dear heart, lamb, lambkin, love, lover, pet, poppet [Brit], precious, sweetheart, sugar; [Inf]: babe, baby, baby doll, cookie, deary *or* dearie, doll, ducky *or* ducks [Brit], hon, honey, honey bun, honeybunch, honey child, lovey [Brit], sweetie, sweetie pie, sweets

8 **love token,** pin, ring, engagement ring, wedding ring; love letter, billet-doux, valentine, love poem, love sonnet, love lyric; love song, serenade, aubade; flowers, red roses, chocolates, candy, sweets

9 **love affair,** romance, affair of the heart, amour, *affaire d'amour* [Fr], *affaire de coeur* [Fr], relationship, romantic tie, entanglement, involvement, flirtation; liaison,

intrigue, forbidden love, affair, adultery, infidelity, unfaithfulness, cuckoldry

> *Sex 20; Immorality 432*

10 **courtship,** courting, wooing, lovemaking, suit, suing, pursuit, addresses, walking out with [Brit]; taking out, dating, getting pinned; flirtation, coquetry, dalliance, dallying, toying; offer of one's hand in marriage, proposal, bestowal of love, betrothal, engagement, marriage, love match, espousal; [Inf]: going together, going with *or* going out with, going steady

> *Marriage 64; Pursuit 385*

11 **lover,** adorer, amorist, wooer, suitor, pursuer, paramour, gallant, swain, Romeo; date, escort, squire, cavalier, *cavalier servente* [Ital]; ladylove, mistress, the other woman, kept woman; flirt, coquette, seductress, temptress, vamp, siren, femme fatale; gigolo, cicisbeo, seducer, ladies' man, heartbreaker, philanderer, womanizer, woman-chaser, lecher, libertine, rake, Casanova, Don Juan, Lothario; conquest, catch; [Inf]: sugar daddy, lady-killer, sheik, skirt chaser, wolf, masher, gold digger

> *Male 32; Female 33; Desire 288*

12 **lovers,** soul mates, loving couple, sweethearts, turtledoves, lovebirds, newlyweds, honeymooners; star-crossed lovers

13 **loved one,** love, beloved, dearly beloved, object of one's affections, apple of one's eye, light of one's life; truelove, soul mate, sweetheart, valentine, turtledove, heartthrob, significant other, inamorata *or* inamorato, gill, jo [Scot]; girl, girlfriend, lass, dulcinea; boyfriend, beau; betrothed, fiancée *or* fiancé, intended [Inf]; wife, husband, spouse; child, offspring, son, daughter, sister, brother, parent, mother, father; [Inf]: sweetie, steady, main squeeze, flame, new flame, old flame, old lady; fellow *or* fella, old man

> *Male 32; Female 33; Marriage 64; Family 65*

14 **goddesses and gods of love,** Venus, Aphrodite, Astarte, Freya; Cupid, Amor, Eros, Kama

ADJECTIVES

15 **loving,** affectionate, fond, endearing, attached, devoted, loyal; motherly, maternal, fatherly, paternal, fraternal, Platonic, spiritual, Christian, brotherly, charitable; friendly, amicable, compatible, understanding, sympathetic; admiring, respectful, reverent, adoring, worshipful, idolizing; doting, uxorious; self-loving, narcissistic, egotistical; patriotic, nationalist *or* nationalistic

> *Friendship 62; Feelings 266; Liking 290; Respect 435*

16 **in love,** head over heels in love, in love with, infatuated with, enamored of *or* with, smitten with, taken with, besotted with, mad about; [Inf]: crazy about, wild about, sweet on, stuck on, gone on

17 **enamored,** attracted, charmed, becharmed, captivated, fascinated, bewitched, enchanted, enraptured, enthralled, transported

18 **amorous,** amative, amatory, gallant, affectionate, demonstrative, tender, soft, lovey-dovey [Inf]; feeling, emotional, passionate, ardent, romantic, sentimental, susceptible, mushy, melting, lovesick, languishing, moping, mooning, lovelorn; flirtatious, flirty, coquettish, coy

19 **beloved,** loved, dearly loved, darling, dear, dear to one's heart, cherished, treasured, prized, valued; liked, well-liked, esteemed, admired, respected, revered, adored, worshiped, idolized; pampered, spoon-fed, coddled, spoiled

> *Liking 290; Respect 435*

20 **lovable,** lovesome, adorable, endearing, amiable, congenial, compatible, agreeable, pleasing; sweet, charming, winsome, winning, engaging; captivating, fascinating, bewitching, enchanting; attractive, beautiful, lovely, appealing, alluring, seductive, desirable, sexy; kissable, cuddly *or* cuddlesome, huggable, caressable

> *Desire 288; Beauty 529*

VERBS

21 **love,** show affection, show endearment, attach oneself to, dearly love, hold dear, cherish, treasure, prize, value; like, esteem, have high regard for, think the world of, admire, respect, revere, venerate, adore, adulate, worship, hero-worship, idolize; dote on, mother,

---

FAMOUS LOVERS OF FACT AND FICTION

Antony and Cleopatra	Harlequin and Columbine	Paris and Helen
Aucassin and Nicolette	Heathcliff and Cathy	Charles Parnell and Kitty O'Shea
Beatrice and Benedick	Héloïse and Abélard	Pelléas and Mélisande
Elizabeth Bennet and Fitzwilliam Darcy	Hero and Leander	Petrarch and Laura
Dante and Beatrice	Anna Karenina and Aleksei Vronski	Pygmalion and Galatea
Daphnis and Chloë	Lancelot and Guinevere	Pyramus and Thisbe
David and Bathsheba	Napoleon and Joséphine	Romeo and Juliet
Edward VIII and Wallis Simpson	Lord Nelson and Lady Hamilton	Rosalind and Orlando
Eros and Psyche	Scarlett O'Hara and Rhett Butler	Tristan and Isolde
Jane Eyre and Edward Rochester	Paolo and Francesca	Troilus and Cressida

pamper, spoon-feed, coddle, dandle, cosset, spoil; sympathize, feel for

22 like, fancy, prefer, be partial to, be fond of, have a fondness for, have a weakness for; take a liking to, take a fancy to, take to, cotton to *or* onto [Inf]; take pleasure in, appreciate, relish, delight in, enjoy
  ▸ *Liking 290*

23 be in love, fall in love, fall head over heels in love, lose one's heart, become enamored with, love to distraction, be crazy about, have it bad, be infatuated with; [Inf]: fall for, be sweet on, have a crush on

24 desire, yearn for, long for, burn with passion, lust after, make advances, make overtures, seduce, vamp, make a pass [Inf]
  ▸ *Sex 20; Desire 288*

25 communicate love, declare one's love, bill and coo, whisper endearments *or* sweet nothings, sweet-talk [Inf]; make eyes at, wink, ogle, drool over; touch, pat, pat on the head, chuck under the chin, brush the cheek, stroke, hold hands, cuddle, tickle, snuggle, nuzzle, nestle, hug, embrace, take into one's arms, hold in one's arms, throw one's arms around, squeeze, caress, fondle, pet, kiss, blow a kiss, soul-kiss *or* French-kiss, smack, buss, osculate; [Inf]: neck, make out, lallygag *or* lollygag; smooch, spoon, grope, play footsie with, make whoopee
  ▸ *Touch 216*

26 court, go courting, pay court to, woo, sue, walk out with [Brit]; pursue, chase, set one's cap for, make addresses; take out, date, escort, squire, get pinned; flirt, tease, dally, toy, trifle, lead on, coquet, philander, womanize; [Inf]: romance, go together, go with *or* go out with, go steady

27 win the love of, win the heart of, enamor, attract, appeal, allure, charm, becharm, captivate, fascinate, enrapture, enthrall, bewitch, enchant, sweep off one's feet

28 propose (marriage), offer *or* request *or* ask for one's hand, go down on bended knee, pop the question [Inf], become engaged, announce one's engagement, publish the banns; marry, get married, wed, plight one's troth, lead to the altar, walk down the aisle
  ▸ *Marriage 64*

ADVERBS

29 lovingly, with love, with all one's love, affectionately, with affection, in an affectionate way, fondly, endearingly, tenderly, dearly, devotedly, loyally; Platonically, spiritually, charitably, understandingly, sympathetically; admiringly, respectfully, reverently, adoringly, worshipfully; patriotically

30 amorously, amatively, amatorily, gallantly, affectionately, demonstratively, tenderly, softly; emotionally, passionately, ardently, romantically, sentimentally; flirtatiously, flirtingly, coquettishly, coyly

31 lovably, adorably, endearingly, amiably, congenially,

amicably, compatibly, agreeably, pleasingly; sweetly, charmingly, winsomely, engagingly; captivatingly, fascinatingly, bewitchingly, enchantingly; attractively, beautifully, appealingly, alluringly, seductively, desirably, sexily

300 Hate

I am free of all prejudice. I hate everyone equally.
— W. C. FIELDS

NOUNS

1 hate, hatred, odium, detestation, loathing, abhorrence, execration, abomination; antagonism, hostility, animosity, animus, ill will, enmity, bad blood; resentment, envy, jealousy, bitterness, hard feelings, gall, spite, spitefulness, acrimony, malice, malice aforethought, spleen, malevolence, malignity, rancor, venom, virulence, grudge; contempt, disdain, scorn, rejection; racism, bigotry
  ▸ *Hostility 63; Resentment, Anger 302; Envy 314*

2 dislike, disrelish, distaste, displeasure, disfavor, aversion, objection, repugnance, antipathy; revulsion, repulsion, disgust; disapproval, disapprobation, censure, condemnation; disaffection, alienation, estrangement
  ▸ *Dislike 291; Curse 301; Resentment, Anger 302; Malevolence 306; Disapproval 438; Disagreement 463*

3 misanthropy, misogyny, misandry, misogamy, misopedia, misoneism, misology
  ▸ *Dislike 291*

4 hatefulness, odiousness, detestability, loathsomeness, abominableness, invidiousness, offensiveness, obnoxiousness, despicability, contemptibility, beastliness [Inf]
  ▸ *Disrespect 436*

5 hated thing, anathema, abomination, detestation, abhorrence, execration; antipathy, aversion, pet aversion, pet hate, peeve, pet peeve, bugbear, bête noire, bane, bitter pill; phobia, fear
  ▸ *Fear 283*

6 hater, detester, loather, abhorrer; misanthrope *or* misanthropist, misogynist, woman-hater, misandrist, man-hater, misogamist, misopedist, misoneist, misologist; phobic, xenophobic, racist, bigot
  ▸ *Fear 283; Dislike 291*

ADJECTIVES

7 hating, full of hate, hateful, execrative; antipathetic, averse to, antagonistic, hostile; resentful, envious, jealous, green-eyed, begrudging, bitter, spiteful, vindictive, acrimonious, malicious, vicious, spleenful, malevolent, malign, malignant, rancorous, venomous, virulent; contemptuous, disdainful, scornful; revolted, repelled, disgusted; racist, bigoted, prejudiced

> *Hostility 63; Resentment, Anger 302; Malevolence 306; Envy 314*

8 **misanthropic,** misogynic *or* misogynous *or* misogynistic, misogamic, misoneistic
> *Dislike 291*

9 **hated,** detested, loathed, abhorred, execrated; resented, envied, begrudged; despised, held in contempt, scorned; disliked, disrelished; disapproved, censured, condemned; unpopular, disaffected, alienated, estranged
> *Dislike 291; Envy 314; Disapproval 438*

10 **hateful,** hateable, odious, detestable, loathsome, abhorrent, execrable, abominable, invidious, offensive, obnoxious, unlikable; contemptible, despicable, beastly [Inf]; aversive, objectionable, repugnant, antipathetic, revolting, repulsive, disgusting, vile
> *Dislike 291*

VERBS

11 **hate,** detest, utterly detest, loathe, abhor, execrate, abominate, hate someone's guts [Inf]; despise, hold in contempt, disdain, contemn, scorn, spit on; spurn, reject, refuse, not choose, object to; dislike, disrelish, have no love for, take an aversion to, show displeasure, resent, envy, begrudge, hold a grudge; bear malice toward, curse, have it in for, bare one's fangs; disapprove, deplore, censure, condemn, denounce; shudder at, turn away from, recoil at, shrink from
> *Hostility 63; Fear 283; Dislike 291; Resentment, Anger 302; Envy 314; Disapproval 438*

12 **cause hate,** excite hate, antagonize, aggravate, alienate, estrange; embitter, sour, envenom, poison; incense, enrage, infuriate, anger, madden, provoke; displease, vex, irritate, exasperate; disgust, repel, revolt, nauseate; make enemies, sow dissension, create bad blood, destroy goodwill
> *Resentment, Anger 302; Malevolence 306*

ADVERBS

13 **with hate,** loathingly, execratively; antipathetically, aversely, antagonistically, hostilely; resentfully, enviously, jealously, begrudgingly, bitterly, spitefully, vindictively, acrimoniously, maliciously, with malice, viciously, spleenfully, malevolently, malignly, malignantly, rancorously, venomously, virulently; contemptuously, disdainfully, scornfully

14 **hatefully,** odiously, detestably, loathsomely, abhorrently, execrably, abominably, invidiously, offensively, obnoxiously; contemptibly, despicably; aversively, repugnantly, antipathetically, revoltingly, repulsively, disgustingly, vilely

301 Curse

NOUNS

1 **curse,** imprecation, execration, malediction, ill wishes, malison [Arch]; spell, evil spell, voodoo spell, hex, charm, evil eye, jinx, whammy *or* double whammy [Inf]; damnation, ban, excommunication, anathema, proscription, commination
> *Religion 81; Dislike 291*

2 **vilification,** vituperation, verbal abuse, volley of abuse, revilement, scurrility, invective, thundering, tongue-lashing, billingsgate; denunciation, denouncement, fulmination, condemnation, censure, reproach, obloquy, opprobrium, disparagement, aspersion, defamation, calumny, slander, libel; threat, onslaught, attack, assault, slanging match [Inf]
> *Disrespect 436; Disapproval 438; Disparagement 440; Accusation 442*

3 **profanity,** profanation, blasphemy, sacrilege; obscenity, indecency, scurrility, ribaldry, scatology *or* coprology, bawdiness; bawdy verse, dirty joke, blue joke; cursing, swearing; filth, foul mouth; [Inf]: dirty mouth, dirty talk, talking dirty
> *Vulgarity 535*

4 **curse word,** oath, profanity, swearword, bad word, naughty word, dirty word, four-letter word, expletive, unrepeatable expression, obscenity, vulgarity, dysphemism, cuss *or* cussword [Inf]
> *Vulgarity 535*

5 **offensive language,** indelicate language, bad language, profane language, blue language, colorful language, strong language, obscene language, foul language, vile language, filthy language, Anglo-Saxon
> *Vulgarity 535*

6 **misfortune,** calamity, trouble; bane, scourge, plague, affliction, torment
> *Affliction 117; Evil 446*

ADJECTIVES

7 **cursing,** imprecatory, execrative *or* execratory, maledictive *or* maledictory; damning, comminatory *or* comminative
> *Dislike 291*

8 **cursed,** imprecated, execrated; accursed, hexed, jinxed, under a spell; damned, condemned, unblessed *or* unblest, banned, excommunicated, proscribed
> *Religion 81; Dislike 291*

9 **vilifying,** vituperative, abusive, reviling, vitriolic, invective, thundering, blasting; denunciatory *or* denunciative, denouncing, fulminatory, condemning, reproachful, opprobrious, ignominious, disparaging, defamatory, calumnious, slanderous, libelous; threatening, attacking, assaulting, slanging [Inf]
> *Disrespect 436; Disparagement 440*

10 **profane,** profaning, profanatory, blasphemous, sacrilegious; obscene, vulgar, bad, indecent, scurrilous, ribald, scatological, offensive, dysphemistic, indelicate, colorful, risqué, bawdy, Rabelaisian, raw, Anglo-Saxon, dirty, blue, filthy, vile, foul; cursing, swearing, foulmouthed

▶ *Vulgarity 535*

11 afflicted, plagued, scourged, vexed, tormented, tortured, doomed
▶ *Affliction 117; Evil 446*

12 miscellaneous euphemisms, blasted, confounded, dad-blamed, dad-blasted, dad-burned, dad-gummed, dang *or* danged, deuced [Brit]; [Inf]: blamed, blankety-blank, blessed *or* blest, darn *or* darned, doggone *or* doggoned, durn *or* durned, goldarn *or* goldarned, ruddy [Brit]

VERBS

13 curse, imprecate, execrate, wish ill, maledict [Arch]; put a curse *or* spell *or* hex on, hex, charm, give the evil eye to, jinx, put a whammy *or* double whammy on [Inf]; damn, ban, excommunicate, anathematize, proscribe, comminate
▶ *Religion 81; Dislike 291*

14 blaspheme, use profanity, profane, commit a sacrilege, take the Lord's name in vain; curse, swear, use obscene *or* bad language, use expletives, swear like a trooper, tell a dirty joke; cuss [Inf], talk dirty [Inf]
▶ *Linguistics, Language 5; Vulgarity 535*

15 vilify, vituperate, abuse, heap abuse on, hurl a volley of abuse at, revile, blackguard, rail against, inveigh against, thunder, blast, tongue-lash, slang, pour vitriol on; denounce, denunciate, fulminate, condemn, damn, censure, reproach; disparage, call names, disgrace, malign, asperse, cast aspersions on, calumniate, defame, slander, libel; threaten, attack, assault
▶ *Disrespect 436; Disapproval 438; Disparagement 440; Accusation 442*

16 afflict, plague, scourge, vex, torment, torture, doom
▶ *Affliction 117; Evil 446*

ADVERBS

17 execratively, damningly, as a curse, accursedly, bewitchingly

18 vilifyingly, vituperatively, abusively, revilingly, invectively, thunderingly; denunciatively, condemningly, reproachfully, opprobriously, ignominiously, disparagingly, defamingly, calumniously, slanderously, libelously; threateningly
▶ *Disparagement 440*

19 profanely, swearingly, blasphemously, sacrilegiously; obscenely, vulgarly, indecently, scurrilously, ribaldly, offensively, indelicately, colorfully, bawdily, filthily, vilely
▶ *Vulgarity 535*

INTERJECTIONS

20 miscellaneous swearwords, Christ!, Christ Almighty!, damn!, damnation!, damn it!, God!, God Almighty!, God in Heaven!, good God!, good God Almighty!, hell!, Jesus!, Jesus Christ!, Mother of God!; [Inf]: balls!, fuck!, fuck it!, fuck me!, fuck off!, fuck you!, goddamn it! *or* goddammit!, go to blazes!, go

to hell!, piss off!, shit!, bugger it! [Brit], bugger off! [Brit]

21 miscellaneous euphemisms, crikey!, cripes!, dash! [Brit], goodness!, goodness gracious!, gosh!, heck!, jeepers *or* jeepers creepers!; [Inf]: darn!, gee!, gee whillikers!, gee whiz!, golly!, golly gee!

302 Resentment, Anger

NOUNS

1 resentment, bitterness, bitter resentment, burning resentment, resentfulness, jealousy, envy, green-eyed monster; acrimony, asperity, animosity, hard feelings, ill feelings, rancor, gall, gall and wormwood, spleen, ill humor, peevishness, acidity, acidulousness, ill will, virulence, spite, spitefulness, grudge, malice; dudgeon, high dudgeon, indignation, umbrage, pique; irritation, aggravation, annoyance, vexation, exasperation, heartburning, miff; displeasure, discontent, dissatisfaction, disapproval, disapprobation; slow burn [Inf]
▶ *Unpleasantness 272; Dissatisfaction 274; Dislike 291; Hate 300; Envy 314; Agitation 684*

2 offense, indignity, affront, insult, hurt, wrong, outrage
▶ *Insolence 400; Disrespect 436*

3 provocation, red rag, red flag, irritation, pinprick, last straw, raw nerve, tender subject, dangerous subject, sore point

4 anger, wrath, wrathfulness, ire, rage, blind rage, fury, blind fury, choler; aggression, belligerence *or* belligerency, bellicosity, pugnacity *or* pugnaciousness, aggro [Brit *and* Aus inf]; vehemence, violence, heat, hotheadedness, passion, temper, bad temper, short temper, quick temper, dander [Inf]
▶ *Dislike 291; Hate 300; Irascibility 303; Sullenness 304; Violence 520*

5 irritableness, irritability, irascibility, choler, crossness, snappishness, biliousness, sullenness, soreness [Inf]
▶ *Irascibility 303; Sullenness 304*

6 burst of anger, fit of anger, huff, fit, fit of temper, conniption *or* conniption fit [Inf], tantrum, temper tantrum, outburst, eruption, explosion, blowup, flareup, paroxysm, frenzy, madness, rage, tearing rage; convulsion, commotion, ferment, storm, scene; going on a rampage, raging, shouting, roaring, stamping one's foot, gnashing one's teeth
▶ *Loudness 232; Violence 520*

7 quarrel, tiff, falling-out, argument, dispute, altercation, fight
▶ *Argument 329; Contention 422; Disagreement 463*

ADJECTIVES

8 resentful, bitter, embittered, jealous, envious, green-eyed, green with envy; acrimonious, rancorous, spleenful, splenetic, ill-humored, peevish, acid, acidulous, acerbic, caustic, virulent, spiteful, grudging, malicious; provoked, riled, worked-up, wrought-up; irritated, aggravated, annoyed, vexed, exasperated, nettled, huffed, miffed, peeved, put out, in a snit, browned off [Inf], fit to be tied [Inf]; disapproving, displeased, discontented, dissatisfied

> *Unpleasantness 272; Dissatisfaction 274; Dislike 291; Hate 300; Envy 314; Agitation 684*

9 **offended,** indignant, piqued, stung, hurt, pained, insulted, affronted, wronged, outraged, in high dudgeon, up in arms

> *Insolence 400; Disrespect 436*

10 **irritable,** irascible, choleric, cross, short-tempered, hotheaded, snappish, bilious, sullen, sore [Inf]

> *Irascibility 303; Sullenness 304*

11 **angry,** angered, wrathful, ireful, mad, maddish, maddened, enraged, irate, furious, infuriated, incensed, inflamed, livid, flushed with rage, foaming at the mouth, boiling, boiling mad, fuming, burning, smoldering; vehement, fierce, violent, explosive, paroxysmic, frenzied, heated, sulphurous, passionate, fighting mad, hopping mad, mad as a hornet, convulsive, apoplectic, storming, raging, in a rage, in a huff, ranting, raving, beside oneself, rabid, berserk; aggressive, belligerent, bellicose, pugnacious; [Inf]: het up, sizzling, hot under the collar, pissed *or* pissed off *or* p.o.'d, ticked *or* ticked off

> *Dislike 291; Hate 300; Violence 520*

12 **maddening,** enraging, infuriating; provoking, irritating, aggravating, annoying, vexing, exasperating; displeasing, dissatisfying; offensive, stinging, insulting, affronting, outraging

VERBS

13 **resent,** be resentful, feel resentment, nurse *or* harbor resentment, bear *or* hold a grudge, bear malice

14 **be offended,** take offense, take amiss, take exception to, take umbrage, get huffy, be *or* get miffed, not take a joke, get one's back up [Inf]; feel offended, feel piqued, feel hurt, feel insulted, have one's nose out of joint

15 **offend,** insult, affront, wound, hurt, grieve, aggrieve, step *or* tread on someone's toes, give umbrage, put someone's nose out of joint, miff, huff, outrage

> *Insolence 400; Disrespect 436*

16 **irritate,** aggravate, annoy, vex, exasperate, put out, nettle, fret, pique, chafe, rankle, rub the wrong way, ruffle, ruffle one's feathers, get on one's nerves, stick in one's throat; bother, harass, pester, tease, bait, taunt, torment, needle [Inf], drive up the wall [Inf]

> *Irascibility 303*

17 **quarrel,** have a tiff, have a falling-out, argue, dispute, fight

> *Argument 329; Contention 422; Disagreement 463*

18 **make angry,** anger, madden, enrage, infuriate, incense, inflame, provoke, arouse, rile, work up, stir up, goad, sting, envenom, embitter, make one's blood boil, make one's gorge rise, raise one's hackles, put

into a rage, drive into a frenzy, piss off [Inf], tick off [Inf]

19 **be angry,** rage, rave, rant, rant and rave, burn, fume, seethe, simmer, smolder, boil, foam at the mouth, breathe fire, be pissed *or* pissed off [Inf], be ticked *or* ticked off [Inf]; show anger, frown, scowl, lower, glower, glare, look daggers at; growl, snarl, bark, bite, snap

20 **become angry,** get angry, anger, get mad, lose one's temper, lose patience, bridle, bristle, reach the boiling point, explode, blow up, flare up, go into a frenzy, go *or* fly into a rage, go berserk, storm, rampage, create *or* make a scene, have *or* throw a fit, have *or* throw a temper tantrum; [Inf]: get hot under the collar, do a slow burn, get sore, see red, get one's dander up, get one's Irish up, fly off the handle, hit the roof *or* ceiling, flip one's lid, blow one's stack *or* top *or* lid, blow a fuse *or* gasket, blow one's cool, have *or* throw a conniption fit

> *Violence 520*

21 **vent one's anger,** snap at, bite *or* take someone's head off, stamp one's foot, gnash one's teeth, shout, roar, go on a rampage, raise the devil; [Inf]: jump down someone's throat, take it out on someone, blow *or* let off steam, raise hell, raise Cain

> *Loudness 232*

ADVERBS

22 **resentfully,** bitterly, jealously, enviously; acrimoniously, rancorously, spleenfully, splenetically, peevishly, acidly, caustically, virulently, spitefully, maliciously, with malice

23 **irritably,** irascibly, crossly, hotheadedly, snappishly, biliously, sullenly; indignantly, with indignation

24 **angrily,** with anger, in anger, wrathfully, irefully, madly, irately, furiously, lividly; vehemently, fiercely, violently, explosively, paroxysmally, heatedly, sulfurously, passionately, in the heat of the moment; aggressively, belligerently, bellicosely, pugnaciously

25 **maddeningly,** infuriatingly; provokingly, irritatingly, aggravatingly, annoyingly, exasperatingly; displeasingly, dissatisfyingly; offensively, insultingly

303 Irascibility

NOUNS

1 **irascibility,** irascibleness, irritability, impatience, fretfulness, petulance, peevishness, cantankerousness, querulousness, testiness, pepperiness, choler, hotheadedness

> *Rashness 286; Resentment, Anger 302*

2 **ill nature,** ill temper, ill-naturedness, ill-temperedness, churlishness, orneriness, gruffness, crustiness, meanness, shrewishness, bitchiness [Inf]; sharpness, tartness, acerbity, sourness, acidity; disagreeableness, fractiousness, quarrelsomeness, contentiousness, dis-

putatiousness, argumentativeness, belligerence, bellicosity

> *Unsociability 409; Disagreement 463*

3 touchiness, tetchiness, prickliness, huffiness, oversensitivity, hypersensitivity; excitability, hot-bloodedness

> *Sensitivity 267*

4 crossness, snappishness, snappiness, shortness, ill-humoredness, sullenness, biliousness, grumpiness, grouchiness, crotchetiness, crankiness, crabbedness, resentfulness, waspishness, angriness; [Inf]: crabbiness, bearishness, soreness

> *Resentment, Anger 302; Sullenness 304*

5 short temper, quick temper, hot temper, bad temper, short fuse [Inf]; ill temper, ill humor; sharp tongue

> *Resentment, Anger 302*

6 sign of irascibility, black look, frown, lower *or* lour, scowl, glower, glare, grimace; growl, snarl, snap

> *Sullenness 304*

7 irascible person, tartar, grump, grouch; fishwife, nag, harridan, scold, spitfire, shrew, vixen, virago, termagant, witch, she-devil; tiger, tigress, hothead, bear; [Inf]: crab, crank, crosspatch, sorehead, battle-ax, bitch

> *Resentment, Anger 302; Sullenness 304*

ADJECTIVES

8 irascible, irritable, short-tempered, quick-tempered, hot-tempered, hotheaded, choleric, peppery, impatient, fretful *or* fretsome, petulant, peevish, cantankerous, querulous, testy

> *Rashness 286; Resentment, Anger 302*

9 ill-natured, ill-tempered, bad-tempered, churlish, ornery, gruff, crusty, mean, shrewish, vixenish, bitchy [Inf]; sharp-tongued, sharp, tart, acerbic, sour, acid; disagreeable, fractious, quarrelsome, contentious, disputatious, argumentative, belligerent, bellicose

> *Unsociability 409; Disagreement 463*

10 touchy, tetchy *or* techy, prickly, huffy, thin-skinned, oversensitive, hypersensitive; temperamental, high-strung, excitable, hot-blooded, uptight [Inf]

11 cross, snappish, snappy, short, ill-humored, sullen, dyspeptic, bilious, grumpy, grouchy, crotchety, cranky, crabbed; irritated, annoyed, riled, vexed, nettled, offended; resentful, waspish, angry; [Inf]: crabby, bearish, sore

> *Resentment, Anger 302; Sullenness 304*

12 frowning, lowering *or* louring, scowling, glowering, grimacing, pouting, growling, snarling, snapping

> *Sullenness 304*

VERBS

13 be irascible, have a short *or* quick temper, have a short fuse [Inf], have no patience, fret, get up on the wrong side of the bed; have a temper, have a bad temper, have an uncontrollable temper, act like a vixen, act

like a bitch [Inf], have a sharp tongue; disagree, quarrel, dispute, argue

> *Resentment, Anger 302; Disagreement 463*

14 show impatience, snap at, bite someone's head off, become annoyed, resent, get angry, get sore [Inf], jump down someone's throat [Inf]

> *Resentment, Anger 302*

15 frown, lower *or* lour, scowl, glower, glare, grimace; growl, snarl, snap

> *Sullenness 304*

16 make irascible, irritate, annoy, peeve, bother, test someone's patience; rouse, rile, vex, nettle, offend, make angry, anger

> *Resentment, Anger 302*

ADVERBS

17 irascibly, irritably, impatiently, fretfully, petulantly, peevishly, cantankerously, querulously, testily, cholerically, hotheadedly

> *Rashness 286; Resentment, Anger 302*

18 ill-naturedly, churlishly, gruffly, crustily, meanly, shrewishly, bitchily [Inf]; with a sharp tongue, in a sharp tone, sharply, tartly, acerbically, sourly, acidly; disagreeably, fractiously, quarrelsomely, contentiously, disputatiously, argumentatively, belligerently, bellicosely

> *Unsociability 409; Disagreement 463*

19 touchily, tetchily, huffily, oversensitively, hypersensitively; temperamentally, excitably

> *Sensitivity 267*

20 crossly, snappishly, snappily; ill-humoredly, sullenly, dyspeptically, biliously, grumpily, grouchily, resentfully, waspishly, angrily; with a frown *or* scowl *or* grimace; [Inf]: crabbily, bearishly, sorely

> *Sullenness 304; Resentment, Anger 302*

304 Sullenness

NOUNS

1 sullenness, sulkiness, mopiness, glumness, grumness, gloominess, moroseness, atrabiliousness, moodiness; dejection, mopishness, disheartenment, downheartedness, dispiritedness, depression, melancholy, cheerlessness, despondency; grimness, sternness, dourness, saturnineness *or* saturninity, seriousness, somberness

> *Sorrow 270; Seriousness 278; Hopelessness 282*

2 sign of sullenness, sullen look, hangdog look, long face, pout, moue, sigh, moan; the blues, blue devils, the mopes, the dumps, the sulks, fit of the sulks

> *Sorrow 270*

3 irritableness, irritability, ill humor, ill-humoredness, discontent, discontentedness, dissatisfaction; sourness, surliness, irascibility, unsociability, disagreeableness, quarrelsomeness, cantankerousness, biliousness, crossness, peevishness, snappishness, abruptness, brusqueness, gruffness, grouchiness, grumpiness or grumpishness, whininess, crankiness, crabbiness [Inf]; ill nature, ill-naturedness, bile, ill temper, ill-temperedness, churlishness, shrewishness, bitchiness [Inf]

> *Sourness 223; Dissatisfaction 274; Irascibility 303; Unsociability 409; Discourtesy 411*

4 **sign of irritability,** frown, lower or lour, scowl, glower, black look, glare, grimace, wry face, mow [Arch]; growl, snarl, snort; bad mood, peeve, mulligrubs; bad temper, short or quick temper, short fuse [Inf], the grumps [Inf]

> *Resentment, Anger 302; Irascibility 303*

5 **complaint,** grumble, whine, moan, carp; [Inf]: grouse, bellyache, beef, bitch

> *Dissatisfaction 274; Irascibility 303*

6 **overcast,** cloudiness, gloominess, dismalness, dullness, sulkiness

7 **sullen person,** sulker, pouter, moper, brooder; complainer, grumbler, whiner; grouch, grump, bear, curmudgeon, churl; [Inf]: sourpuss, grouser, bellyacher, whinger [Aus], crank, crosspatch, crab, sorehead, bitch

> *Resentment, Anger 302; Irascibility 303; Unsociability 409*

ADJECTIVES

8 **sullen,** sulky, mopey or mopy, pouty, long-faced, glum, grum, gloomy, morose, atrabilious, moody, brooding; dejected, mopish, downcast, disheartened, downhearted, dispirited, depressed, out of sorts, blue, melancholy, melancholic, cheerless, despondent; grim, stern, dour, saturnine, serious, somber, black

> *Sorrow 270; Seriousness 278; Hopelessness 282*

9 **irritable,** ill-humored, out of humor, in a bad humor, in a bad mood, discontented, dissatisfied, sour, surly, irascible, unsociable, disagreeable, quarrelsome, cantankerous, curmudgeonly, bilious, dyspeptic, cross, peevish, snappish, snappy, abrupt, brusque, gruff, grouchy, grumpy or grumpish, grumbly, whiny, cranky, growly, snarly, crabby [Inf]; ill-natured, ill-tempered, bad-tempered, churlish, shrewish, vixenish, bitchy [Inf]

> *Dissatisfaction 274; Irascibility 303; Unsociability 409; Discourtesy 411*

10 **frowning,** unsmiling, lowering or louring, scowling, glowering, glaring; growling, snarling, snapping

> *Irascibility 303*

11 **overcast,** cloudy, clouded, gloomy, depressing, dismal, dull, sulky, somber; sunless, dark, menacing, threatening, lowering or louring, glowering

VERBS

12 **be sullen,** sulk, get oneself into a sulk, mope, mump, pout, make a lip, hang one's lip, brood, fret, moan, sigh; have a long face, have the blues, be down in the dumps, be out of sorts

> *Sorrow 270; Dissatisfaction 274*

13 **make sullen,** deject, mope, dishearten, dispirit, depress, give someone the blues, put someone in a melancholy mood

> *Sorrow 270*

14 **be irritable,** be in a peeve, be annoyed, be in a bad mood, get up on the wrong side of the bed; show irritation, frown, lower or lour, scowl, glower, glare, knit one's brow, grimace, make a wry face, mow [Arch]; growl, snarl, snap at, snort, bare one's teeth or fangs, spit; complain, grumble, mutter, grump, grouch, whine, moan, carp; [Inf]: grouse, bellyache, beef, bitch, crab

> *Dissatisfaction 274; Resentment, Anger 302; Irascibility 303*

15 **make irritable,** irritate, annoy, peeve, rub the wrong way, offend, exasperate, put someone in a bad mood; acerbate, exacerbate, sour, make bitter, embitter, envenom; displease, discontent, dissatisfy

> *Dissatisfaction 274; Resentment, Anger 302; Irascibility 303*

ADVERBS

16 **sullenly,** sulkily, poutingly, glumly, grumly, gloomily, morosely, moodily, broodingly; dejectedly, mopishly, downheartedly, cheerlessly, despondently; grimly, sternly, dourly, saturninely, seriously, somberly

> *Sorrow 270; Seriousness 278; Hopelessness 282*

17 **irritably,** ill-humoredly, in an ill humor, discontently, sourly, surlily, irascibly, unsociably, disagreeably, quarrelsomely, cantankerously, biliously, dyspeptically, crossly, peevishly, snappishly, snappily, abruptly, brusquely, gruffly, grouchily, grumpily or grumpishly, grumblingly, whiningly, whinily, crankily, crabbily [Inf]; ill-naturedly, ill-temperedly, churlishly, shrewishly, bitchily [Inf]

> *Dissatisfaction 274; Irascibility 303; Unsociability 409; Discourtesy 411*

18 **frowningly,** unsmilingly, scowlingly, glaringly, gloweringly; growlingly, snarlingly

> *Irascibility 303*

19 **dismally,** gloomily, depressingly, sulkily; darkly, under a black cloud, blackly, menacingly, threateningly

305 Benevolence

Benevolence is the tranquil habitation of man, and righteousness is his straight path. — MENCIUS

NOUNS

1 **benevolence,** kindness, kindliness, loving-kindness, milk of human kindness, niceness; goodness, goodwill, benignity; benevolent disposition, kindly disposition, well-disposedness, good nature, open-heartedness, kindheartedness, largeheartedness, big-heartedness, heart of gold, friendship; cordiality, courteousness, ge-

niality, affability, graciousness, amiability, sociability, bonhomie

- *Friendship 62; Sociability 408; Courtesy 410; Good 445*

2 **compassion,** tolerance, toleration, consideration; tenderness, tender-heartedness, condolence, sympathy, empathy; pity, mercy, goodness and mercy, forgiveness, clemency; helpfulness, thoughtfulness, attentiveness, mindfulness; fellowship, humanness, humanity, humanitarianism, love of mankind *or* humankind, brotherly *or* sisterly love

- *Love 299; Pity 308; Forgiveness 312; Leniency 423; Help 825; Cooperation 827*

3 **charity,** charitableness, beneficence, hospitality, good works, Christian charity, generosity, generousness, bountifulness, munificence, liberality, patronage, philanthropy, magnanimity, altruism, unselfishness, selflessness, openhandedness

4 **charitable organization,** local aid society, food bank, meals on wheels, home, shelter, homeless shelter; food drive, fund-raising, fund-raiser, fund drive, bake sale, charity raffle, walkathon, March of Dimes, Walk for Hunger, bikeathon, danceathon; relief organization: International Red Cross, Oxfam, Salvation Army, United Way, Amnesty International, UNICEF (United Nations Children's Fund *or* International Children's Emergency Fund), St. Vincent de Paul Society, Catholic Charities

- *Philanthropy 307; Giving 472; Generosity 498*

5 **benevolent act,** kind act, kindness, helpful act, act of grace, charitable act *or* deed, act of charity, labor of love, kind deed, good deed, good turn, good work, *mitzvah* or *mitsvah* [Hebrew]; favor, rescue, courtesy, service, benefit, relief, loan, present, gift, largess, bestowal, benefaction; contribution, offering, donation, alms, almsgiving

6 **benevolent person,** kind person, good Samaritan, Christian, good neighbor, sympathizer, well-wisher, altruist, welfarist, humanitarian, welfare worker, social worker, reformer, liberal; patron, philanthropist, contributor, almsgiver, almoner; bleeding heart, do-gooder

- *Good 445*

ADJECTIVES

7 **benevolent,** kind, kindly, full of the milk of human kindness, loving, affectionate, nice; good, goodwilled, benign; kindly disposed, well-disposed, good-natured, open-hearted, kindhearted, largehearted, big-hearted, friendly; cordial, courteous, congenial, genial, affable, gracious, amiable, sociable, bonhomous

8 **compassionate,** tolerant, considerate; tender, tender-hearted, condolent, sympathetic, empathetic; pitying, merciful, forgiving; helpful, thoughtful, attentive, solicitous, mindful; good-fellowed, humane, brotherly, sisterly

9 **charitable,** beneficent, hospitable, Christian, gener-

ous, bountiful, magnanimous, liberal, philanthropic, altruistic, unselfish, selfless, openhanded; giving, almsgiving; well-meant, well-meaning, well-intentioned, with the best of intentions

VERBS

10 **be benevolent,** be kind, do a kindness, love, be nice; show consideration, show concern, have regard for, remember, return good for evil, do as one would be done by, practice the golden rule, have a heart of gold, have a generous *or* a big heart, have one's heart in the right place, reform, oblige, respect, wish well, wish the best for, give one's blessing, support, encourage, look favorably on

11 **be compassionate,** show compassion, understand, tolerate, accommodate; pity, show mercy, forgive, grant clemency; help, aid, provide aid, mind, comfort, relieve, mother, nurse, condole, sympathize, empathize

12 **be charitable,** be benevolent, benefit, do good works, act like a Christian, do a favor, treat well, mean well, have the best intentions; practice philanthropy, give freely, provide needed funds, give financial support, raise money

ADVERBS

13 **benevolently,** kindly, with kindness, out of kindness, with loving kindness, lovingly, with love, with tender loving care, affectionately, nicely, benignly; cordially, good-naturedly, courteously, genially, congenially, affably, graciously; kindheartedly, big-heartedly; amiably, sociably, friendly *or* friendlily

14 **compassionately,** tolerantly, considerately; tenderly, tender-heartedly, sympathetically, empathetically; with consideration, with mercy, forgivingly, with clemency; helpfully, in a helpful way, thoughtfully, attentively, solicitously, mindfully; in good fellowship, humanely, brotherly, sisterly

15 **charitably,** through charity, beneficently, hospitably, generously, bountifully, liberally, philanthropically, magnanimously, altruistically, unselfishly, openhandedly, with open hands

306 Malevolence

Evil communications corrupt good manners.
— BIBLE: I CORINTHIANS

NOUNS

1 **malevolence,** evilness, badness, hate, malice; evil will, bad will, hatred, ill will; evil disposition, bad nature, bad blood, bad temper, hatefulness, ill disposition, ill nature; loathing, fury, blind fury, smoldering fury

- *Hate 300; Evil 446*

2 **malice,** maliciousness, malice aforethought *or* prepense, maleficence; balefulness, banefulness, malignity, malignancy *or* malignance, harmfulness, evil in-

tent, bad intent *or* intention, worst intention; abhorrence, enmity, hostility, animosity, antagonism, vengefulness; revengefulness, mercilessness, pitilessness, ruthlessness; wickedness, perniciousness, balefulness, invidiousness, iniquitousness; meanness, cattiness, nastiness, beastliness, snideness; gloating, unholy joy, schadenfreude, bitchiness [Inf]

> *Hostility 63; Wickedness 448*

3 **bitterness,** acrimony, asperity, astringency, acerbity, tartness, sourness, acidity, mordacity, mordancy, causticity, causticness; sharpness, keenness, incisiveness, piercingness, trenchancy; caustic reply, sharp tongue, biting comment *or* tongue; spite, spitefulness, despitefulness, waspishness, rancor; gall, gall and wormwood, spleen, bile, virulence, venom, venomousness, vitriol; vindictiveness, resentment, grudge

> *Hostility 63*

4 **cruelty,** cruelness, sadistic *or* insensate *or* wanton cruelty; inhumanity, inhumaneness, crime against humanity, torture, barbarism, barbarity, brutality, brutalness, brutishness, savagery, savageness, truculence; bestiality, animality, viciousness, ferocity, ferociousness, harshness, roughness, severity, ruthlessness; atrociousness, atrocity, violence, vandalism, terrorism, sadism, heinousness, fiendishness, monstrousness; bloodthirstiness, bloodthirst, bloodlust, cannibalism, cold-bloodedness; heartlessness, coldheartedness

> *Killing 30; Pitilessness 309; Danger 811*

5 **malignity,** act of malevolence, bad deed, bad turn, harm, hurt, disservice, ill service, ill turn; crime, threat, menace, foul play, outrage, evil act; reign of terror, bloodshed, murder, killing, mass murder, massacre, slaughter, serial killing, homicide; intimidation, assault, sexual assault, rape, abuse, sexual abuse, child abuse, physical *or* verbal abuse, battery; personal violence, ill-treatment, misuse, maltreatment; intolerance, persecution, blackmail, intimidation, victimization; tyrannization, bullying, harassment, sexual harassment, racial harassment, racial hatred, racism, racialism

> *Killing 30; Hostility 63; Discrimination 337; Severity 424*

6 **malefactor,** bad person, malfeasor, malfeasant, evildoer; miscreant, scoundrel, vandal, bad egg, villain, blackguard, rogue; ruffian, bully, bullyboy, thug, lout, ugly customer, nasty piece of work, criminal, offender, racist, anarchist, nihilist, terrorist, tyrant; traitor, betrayer, backstabber, double-crosser, Judas; fiend, vulture, predator, snake, viper; murderer, killer, butcher, cutthroat; [Inf]: terror, holy terror, punk, bruiser, skinhead

> *Irascibility 303; Evil 446; Wickedness 448; Destruction 523*

ADJECTIVES

7 **malevolent,** evil, bad, hateful, malicious; evil-willed, bad-willed, hating, ill-willed, ill-wishing; evil-minded, bad-natured, bad-tempered, hate-filled, ill-disposed, ill-natured; loathing, full of loathing, furious, smoldering

8 **malicious,** maleficent, malefic; baneful, malign, malignant, meaning harm, intending evil *or* harm, bad-intentioned, ill-intentioned; abhorrent, hostile, antagonistic, vengeful; revengeful, merciless, pitiless, ruthless; wicked, pernicious, baleful, invidious, iniquitous, mean, catty, nasty, beastly, snide, bitchy [Inf]

> *Evil 446; Wickedness 448*

9 **bitter,** bitter and twisted, acrimonious, astringent, acerbic, tart, sour, acidic, acid, acrid, mordacious, mordant, caustic; sharp, keen, incisive, piercing, trenchant; sharp-tongued, cutting, biting, stinging, stabbing; spiteful, despiteful, despiteous [Arch], waspish, rancorous; splenetic *or* splenetical, spleenful, virulent, venomous, envenomed, vitriolic; vindictive, resentful, grudging; indignant, piqued, furious, raging, choleric

10 **cruel,** cruelhearted, sadistic, insensate, wanton; inhuman, inhumane, subhuman, dehumanized, torturous, barbaric, brutal, brutish, savage, truculent; bestial, beastly, animal, animal-like, vicious, ferocious, harsh, rough, severe, ruthless; atrocious, violent, vandalous, terrorist, terrorful, terroristic, sadist, heinous, fiendish, fiendlike, monstrous; bloodthirsty, bloody, cannibalistic; gloating, heartless, cold-hearted

> *Severity 424; Wickedness 448*

11 **malign,** harmful, hurtful, injurious; criminal, threatening, menacing; murderous, homicidal; intimidating, assault, assaulting, abusive, sexually abusive, physically *or* verbally abusive; intolerant, persecuting, intimidating, victimizing; tyrannical, bullying, harassing, racist

VERBS

12 **be malevolent,** hate, bear malice, malign, show ill will, bear ill will; do one a bad turn, be cruel; loathe, rage against, spite, wreak one's spite, abhor, show animosity; exact revenge, take one's revenge, show no mercy *or* pity; resent, grudge, bear a grudge, cherish a grudge, have it in for

13 **harm,** hurt, injure, torment, torture, attack; savage, vandalize, terrorize, cannibalize, thirst for blood; hound, harry, threaten, menace; murder, kill, kill in cold blood, massacre, slaughter; assault, sexually assault, molest, rape, abuse, physically *or* verbally abuse, beat, beat up, batter, bash, cut up; violate, ill-treat, misuse, mistreat, maltreat; oppress, persecute, blackmail, demand, frighten, scare, intimidate, victimize; tyrannize, bully, bullyrag, harass, sexually harass, racially harass; work over [Inf]

> *Affliction 117; Misuse 395; Deterioration 808*

14 **malevolently,** evilly, hatefully, with hate, with *or* bearing ill will; loathingly, furiously; resentfully, grudgingly

15 **maliciously,** with malice aforethought *or* prepense; banefully, with evil intent, with the worst intentions; abhorrently, hostilely, antagonistically, vengefully; revengefully, mercilessly, ruthlessly; wickedly, perniciously, balefully, invidiously, iniquitously, meanly, cattily, nastily, snidely

16 **bitterly,** acrimoniously, acerbically, tartly, mordaciously, caustically; sharply, keenly, incisively, piercingly; spitefully, out of spite, in spite, despitefully, waspishly, rancorously, virulently, venomously; vindictively, resentfully, grudgingly; indignantly, ragingly

17 **cruelly,** sadistically, wantonly; inhumanly, criminally, torturously, tormentingly, barbarically, brutally, brutishly, savagely, truculently; viciously, ferociously, harshly, roughly, severely, ruthlessly; atrociously, violently, terrifyingly, heinously, fiendishly, monstrously; heartlessly, cold-heartedly

18 **malignly,** harmfully, criminally, threateningly, menacingly, outrageously; murderously, abusively, injuriously; intolerantly, tyrannically, prejudicially

307 Philanthropy

NOUNS

1 **philanthropy,** humanitarianism, altruism, unselfishness, benevolence, benevolentness, brotherly love, goodwill, grace, kindheartedness, kindliness, kindness, benignity, humaneness, humanity, compassion, compassionateness, beneficence, charity, benefaction, helpfulness, Samaritanism, do-goodism *or* do-gooderism; welfare, social welfare; charitableness, generosity, openhandedness, munificence, munificentness, bountifulness, bounty, liberality
  ◗ *Love 299; Benevolence 305; Pity 308; Willingness 373; Virtue 447; Giving 472; Help 825*

2 **public-spiritedness,** public spirit, social conscience, social consciousness, citizenship, good citizenship, civism; utilitarianism, Benthamism, humanitarianism, universal benevolence, reformism
  ◗ *Virtue 447; Improvement 807*

3 **charity,** good works, beneficence, benefaction; donation, gift, alms, aid, assistance, helping hand, relief, disaster relief; worthy cause, charitable foundation, fund, community chest; charity event, fund-raising, fundraiser, telethon; handout [Inf]
  ◗ *Giving 472; Help 825*

4 **social welfare,** welfare state, welfare statism, welfarism; child welfare, social services, Social Security; poor relief, assistance, food stamps, Aid to Families

with Dependent Children (AFDC), unemployment benefit, the dole

5 **philanthropist,** humanitarian, altruist, benefactor, benefactress *or* benefactrix, bleeding heart; good citizen, good neighbor, good Samaritan, helper, do-gooder; welfarist, welfare worker, social worker, caseworker, community service worker, charity worker, volunteer, almoner, almsgiver; Robin Hood, Lady Bountiful; utilitarian, Benthamite, internationalist, reformer
  ◗ *Love 299; Benevolence 305; Pity 308; Virtue 447; Giving 472; Help 825*

ADJECTIVES

6 **philanthropic,** philanthropical, humanitarian, altruistic, unselfish, benevolent, gracious, kindhearted, kindly, kind, benign, humane, compassionate, beneficent, helpful; welfarist, welfaristic; charitable, almsgiving, eleemosynary, generous, openhanded, munificent, bountiful, liberal
  ◗ *Love 299; Benevolence 305; Pity 308; Willingness 373; Virtue 447; Giving 472; Help 825*

7 **public-spirited,** civic-minded, socially conscious; utilitarian, Benthamic, humanitarian, reformist
  ◗ *Virtue 447; Improvement 807*

VERBS

8 **philanthropize,** show benevolence, be charitable, do good, do a good turn, do a good deed; help, render assistance, aid, give a helping hand, benefit, give relief, relieve, donate, give, give alms, fund; be public-spirited, have a social conscience, be a good citizen
  ◗ *Benevolence 305; Giving 472; Help 825*

ADVERBS

9 **philanthropically,** altruistically, unselfishly, benevolently, with goodwill, graciously, kindheartedly, kindly, benignly, humanely, compassionately, beneficently, helpfully; charitably, generously, openhandedly, munificently, bountifully
  ◗ *Benevolence 305; Pity 308; Willingness 373; Virtue 447; Giving 472; Help 825*

10 **for the public good,** civic-mindedly, *pro bono publico* [L]
  ◗ *Improvement 807*

308 Pity

For Mercy has a human heart, / Pity, a human face.
— WILLIAM BLAKE

NOUNS

1 **pity,** sympathy, commiseration, compassion, compassionateness, feeling, fellow feeling, empathy, pathos; mercy, mercifulness, charity, humanity, benevolence, kindness, tenderness, gentleness, soft-heartedness, tender-heartedness, warm-heartedness; self-pity, tears of self-pity, tears for oneself

▶ *Sorrow 270; Disappointment 293; Benevolence 305; Leniency 423*

2 condolence, condolences, sympathy, tears of sympathy, shared grief *or* sorrow *or* suffering, commiseration; comfort, balm, consolation; mourning, lament, lamentation, keen, wake

▶ *Sorrow 270; Lamentation 280*

3 mercy, compassion, ruth, forgiveness, forbearance, indulgence, quarter; mercifulness, forgivingness, grace, clemency, leniency; lenity, favor, relief, mitigation, second chance, reprieve, pardon, acquittal

▶ *Forgiveness 312; Punishment 454*

ADJECTIVES

4 pitying, sorry for, sympathizing, sympathetic, commiserating, commiserative, compassionate, ruthful, caring, empathetic, understanding; condolent, comforting, consoling, soothing; merciful, forgiving, forbearing, indulgent, gracious, clement, lenient; charitable, humane, benevolent, kind, tender, gentle, kind-hearted, soft-hearted, tender-hearted, warm-hearted; self-pitying, self-pitiful, sorry for oneself

▶ *Sorrow 270; Disappointment 293; Benevolence 305; Forgiveness 312; Leniency 423*

5 pitiful, pitiable, piteous, commiserable, pathetic, sad, distressing, grievous; heartrending, heartbreaking, touching, moving, affecting, tearjerking [Inf]

▶ *Sorrow 270*

VERBS

6 pity, feel pity, have pity for, feel sorry for, feel sorrow for, feel for, bleed, bleed for; commiserate, sympathize, sympathize with, empathize, empathize with, understand

▶ *Sorrow 270*

7 grieve, grieve for, sorrow, mourn, mourn for, lament, weep for; share grief, share sorrow, condole with, commiserate, weep with; comfort, console, soothe, wipe away one's tears; express sympathy for, send one's condolences, pay one's respects

▶ *Sorrow 270; Lamentation 280*

8 show pity, have pity, take pity on, show mercy, have mercy on, relent, relax, give quarter, spare, go easy on, give respite, be lenient, forgive, forbear, indulge, favor, relieve, mitigate, give a second *or* last chance to, reprieve, pardon, grant a pardon, absolve, acquit, put out of one's misery; give (someone) a break [Inf]

▶ *Forgiveness 312; Punishment 454*

9 move to compassion, melt, melt the heart, thaw, soften, move, touch, affect, reach, move to tears, disarm

10 ask for mercy, ask for pity, plead *or* beg for mercy, plead with, plead *or* beg for one's life, ask for quarter, fall on one's knees, throw oneself at someone's mercy, plead *or* beg for forgiveness

▶ *Forgiveness 312*

ADVERBS

11 pityingly, sympathizingly, sympathetically, in sympathy, commiseratively, compassionately, with compassion, ruthfully, empathetically, understandingly; comfortingly, consolingly, soothingly; mercifully, with mercy, forgivingly, forbearingly, indulgently, graciously, clemently, leniently; charitably, humanely, for humane reasons, benevolently, kindly, tenderly, gently, kind-heartedly, soft-heartedly, tender-heartedly, warm-heartedly

▶ *Sorrow 270; Benevolence 305; Forgiveness 312; Leniency 423*

12 pitifully, pitiably, piteously, pathetically, sadly; heartrendingly, heartbreakingly, touchingly, movingly

▶ *Sorrow 270*

INTERJECTIONS

13 have pity!, have mercy!, take pity!, have a heart!, for pity's sake!, for mercy's sake!, for the love of God!

309 Pitilessness

NOUNS

1 pitilessness, lack of pity, lack of sympathy *or* compassion, uncompassion, unfeelingness, unresponsiveness, callousness, coldness, cold-heartedness, cold-bloodedness, hardheartedness, heartlessness, heart of stone; unkindness, hardness, harshness, severity, ruthlessness, cruelness, cruelty, brutality, barbarousness, inhumanity, remorselessness; mercilessness, unmercifulness, inclemency, unforgivingness; vindictiveness, vengefulness, revengefulness

▶ *Insensitivity 268; Dislike 291; Severity 424; Hardness 542*

2 relentlessness, unrelentingness, mercilessness, unyieldingness, flintiness, obdurateness, implacability, inexorability, intractability, inflexibility, unbendingness

▶ *Obstinacy 379*

ADJECTIVES

3 pitiless, unpitying, unsympathizing, unsympathetic, uncommiserating, uncommiserative, without compassion, uncompassionate, uncaring; unfeeling, unresponsive, callous, cold, cold-hearted, cold-blooded, hardhearted, stony-hearted, heartless; unkind, hard, harsh, severe, ruthless, cruelhearted, malevolent, cruel, brutal, inhumane, remorseless, unremorseful; merciless, unmerciful, inclement, unforgiving; vindictive, vengeful, revengeful

▶ *Insensitivity 268; Dislike 291; Severity 424; Hardness 542*

4 relentless, unrelenting, merciless, unyielding, flinty, obdurate, implacable, inexorable, intractable, inflexible, unbending

▶ *Obstinacy 379*

VERBS

5 be pitiless, feel *or* show no pity, be unsympathetic, lack compassion; be unfeeling, have no heart
▶ *Insensitivity 268*

6 have *or* **show no mercy,** show no leniency, give no quarter, turn a deaf ear, be unmoved; insist on *or* claim one's pound of flesh, stand by *or* on the letter of the law, go by the rule book, show no flexibility

ADVERBS

7 pitilessly, without pity, unsympathizingly, unsympathetically, uncommiseratively, without compassion, uncompassionately; unfeelingly, unresponsively, callously, coldly, cold-heartedly, cold-bloodedly, in cold blood, hardheartedly, heartlessly; harshly, severely, ruthlessly, malevolently, cruelly, brutally, sadistically, barbarously, inhumanely, remorselessly; mercilessly, unmercifully, inclemently; vindictively, vengefully, revengefully
▶ *Insensitivity 268; Dislike 291; Severity 424; Hardness 542*

8 relentlessly, unrelentingly, mercilessly, unyieldingly, obdurately, implacably, inexorably, intractably, inflexibly
▶ *Obstinacy 379*

310 Gratitude

NOUNS

1 gratitude, thanks, appreciation, gratefulness, thankfulness, appreciativeness; indebtedness, obligation, sense *or* feeling of obligation *or* indebtedness
▶ *Approval 437; Motivation 508*

2 thanks, thank-you, grateful thanks, hearty thanks, sincere thanks; thanksgiving, eucharist, blessing, benediction; prayer, prayer of thanks, grace, grace before meals; praise, hymn, hymn of thanks, paean
▶ *Worship 83; Religious Ritual 85; Celebration 405; Approval 437*

3 acknowledgment, recognition, credit, acknowledgments, credits, credit line, byline; thank-you letter *or* note *or* card, bread-and-butter letter; thank offering, thank-you gift *or* present, token of one's gratitude, reward, bonus, tip, gratuity, recognition of one's services, parting gift, retirement gift, gold watch, golden handshake; vote of thanks, praise, applause, round of applause, standing ovation, tribute, testimonial
▶ *Reward 453*

ADJECTIVES

4 grateful, thankful, appreciative, appreciatory; indebted, beholden, obliged, much obliged, obligated, under obligation

5 thanking, acknowledging, crediting, giving credit, bread-and-butter, praising, blessing

VERBS

6 be grateful, be thankful, be thankful for small mercies, appreciate, be obliged to, be obligated *or* indebted, feel *or* have an obligation; express gratitude, thank, say thank you, extend gratitude *or* thanks, render thanks, return thanks; acknowledge, recognize, credit, give credit to, attribute; show gratitude, show appreciation, reward, give a bonus, tip; praise, applaud, give a hand *or* big hand, give three cheers, pay tribute
▶ *Approval 437; Reward 453*

7 give thanks, say grace, bless, say a prayer of thanks, thank God, praise heaven; thank *or* bless one's lucky stars, count one's blessings

ADVERBS

8 gratefully, with gratitude, thankfully, with thanks *or* special thanks, appreciatively, appreciatorily; as a token of one's gratitude, in recognition of one's services

INTERJECTIONS

9 thank you!, thank you very much!, *merci!* [Fr], *¡gracias!* [Sp], bless you!, much obliged!; thank goodness!, thank God!, thank heavens!; [Inf]: thanks!, many thanks!, thanks a lot!, ta! [Brit]

311 Ingratitude

How sharper than a serpent's tooth it is / To have a thankless child. — WILLIAM SHAKESPEARE

NOUNS

1 ingratitude, lack of gratitude, ungratefulness, unthankfulness, thanklessness, lack of appreciation, unappreciation, unappreciativeness; ungraciousness, discourteousness, rudeness, thoughtlessness, forgetfulness, inconsiderateness, selfishness; nonrecognition, no reward, no thanks, grudging *or* halfhearted thanks; ingrate
▶ *Insensitivity 268; Discourtesy 411; Selfishness 444*

ADJECTIVES

2 ungrateful, unthankful, unappreciative; ungracious, ill-mannered, discourteous, rude, thoughtless, heedless, forgetful, unmindful, inconsiderate, selfish
▶ *Insensitivity 268; Discourtesy 411; Selfishness 444*

3 unthanked, unrecognized, unacknowledged, uncredited, unrewarded, forgotten, neglected, ignored, unrequited

4 thankless, unappreciated, unrewarding, unprofitable, vain, useless, fruitless

VERBS

5 be ungrateful, be unappreciative, fail to appreciate, see no reason to thank, feel no obligation, give no credit; be thoughtless, be forgetful of, forget, neglect, ignore; look a gift horse in the mouth, bite the hand that feeds one

ADVERBS

6 ungratefully, unthankfully, unappreciatively, without appreciation; ungraciously, discourteously, rudely, thoughtlessly, heedlessly, forgetfully, unmindfully, inconsiderately, selfishly

▸ *Insensitivity 268; Discourtesy 411; Selfishness 444*

7 **thanklessly,** without thanks, without acknowledgment; unprofitably, vainly, uselessly, fruitlessly

312 Forgiveness

NOUNS

1 **forgiveness,** pardon, excuse, indulgence, amnesty, reprieve; indemnity, exemption, immunity, grace; dispensation, remission *or* forgiveness of sin, absolution, shrift [Arch]

▸ *Religion 81; Pity 308; Atonement 313; Leniency 423*

2 **absolution,** acquittal, discharge, dismissal, release, freeing, deliverance; exoneration, exculpation, vindication, justification

▸ *Vindication 441*

3 **forgivingness,** forgiving nature, placability *or* placableness, magnanimity, unresentfulness, unvindictiveness; mercifulness, clemency, lenity, compassion, compassionateness, kindness, benevolence; overlooking, connivery, disregard, condonation *or* condonance, tolerance, toleration, indulgence, forbearance, patience, endurance, longanimity, long-suffering, sufferance, stoicism

▸ *Benevolence 305; Pity 308; Leniency 423*

ADJECTIVES

4 **forgiving,** placable, magnanimous, unresenting, unresentful, unvindictive; merciful, clement, lenient, compassionate, kind, benevolent; condoning, tolerant, indulgent, overlooking, conniving, forbearing, patient, longanimous, long-suffering, stoic

▸ *Benevolence 305; Pity 308; Leniency 423*

5 **forgiven,** pardoned, excused, let off, granted amnesty, reprieved, spared, exempted; absolved, shriven, acquitted, discharged, dismissed, released, freed, delivered; exonerated, exculpated, vindicated, justified; wiped away, swept clean, removed *or* erased *or* expunged from the record

▸ *Vindication 441*

6 **overlooked,** ignored, disregarded, not held against one; tolerated, endured, indulged, condoned

7 **forgivable,** pardonable, venial, excusable, easily excused, remittable; exculpable, justifiable; disregardable, tolerable, endurable, brookable, bearable, condonable

VERBS

8 **forgive,** give *or* grant forgiveness, pardon, excuse, indulge, grant amnesty, reprieve, spare; indemnify, exempt, grant immunity; remit, forgive one's sins, absolve, grant absolution, shrive

▸ *Religion 81; Pity 308; Leniency 423*

9 **forgive and forget,** forget, let bygones be bygones,

reconcile, become reconciled, make up, bury the hatchet, make peace, smoke the peace pipe, shake hands, kiss and make up

10 **absolve,** acquit, discharge, dismiss, let off, release, free, set free, liberate, deliver; exonerate, clear one's name, wipe the slate clean, remove *or* erase *or* expunge from the record, exculpate, vindicate, justify

▸ *Vindication 441*

11 **show mercy,** be merciful, show compassion, be lenient; not hold against one, bear no malice, take no offense, turn the other cheek, pocket the affront; tolerate, endure, brook, put up with, be patient with, bear with, indulge, make allowances for, give one the benefit of the doubt; overlook, connive, wink at, turn a blind eye to, ignore, disregard, condone, let pass

▸ *Pity 308; Leniency 423*

12 **ask forgiveness,** beg *or* plead for forgiveness, beg one's pardon, offer one's apologies, ask for absolution, ask *or* beg for mercy

ADVERBS

13 **forgivingly,** magnanimously, unresentfully, without bearing a grudge, unvindictively; mercifully, clemently, leniently, compassionately, kindly, benevolently; tolerantly, indulgently, forbearingly, patiently, with patience, long-sufferingly, stoically

▸ *Benevolence 305; Pity 308; Leniency 423*

14 **forgivably,** pardonably, venially, excusably, justifiably; tolerably, endurably, bearably

313 Atonement

NOUNS

1 **atonement,** amends, satisfaction, expiation, reparation, redress, restitution, restoration, redemption, remedy, rectification; compensation, indemnity, indemnification, payment, remuneration, recompense, requital, quittance, reimbursement, repayment; blood money, wergild, eye for an eye, measure for measure; propitiation, appeasement, pacification, conciliation, reconciliation

▸ *Pacification 74; Compromise 461; Giving Back 478*

2 **apology,** abject apology, expression of regret, acknowledgment, acknowledgment of guilt, *mea culpa* [L], admission, confession, shrift [Arch]; regrets, excuse, explanation, justification

3 **penitence,** repentance, contrition, contriteness, regret, remorse, compunction; penance, breast-beating, expiatory offering, offering, oblation, sacrifice, burnt offering, piaculum, peace offering, votive offering; penitential act *or* exercise, lustration, cleansing, purifying, purgation, purgatory, fasting, flagellation, mortification, self-mortification, austerities, asceticism; sackcloth and ashes, hair shirt; Yom Kippur *or* Day of Atonement, Lent

> *Religion 81; Cleanliness 111; Penitence 451; Punishment 454*

4 **atoner,** amender, expiator, redresser, rectifier; compensator, indemnifier, recompenser, requiter; propitiator, appeaser, pacifier, conciliator, reconciler, apologizer; penitent, repenter, flagellant, ascetic

ADJECTIVES

5 **atoning,** expiatory, expiational, reparative *or* reparatory, piacular, restitutive *or* restitutory, redeeming, remedial, rectifying; compensatory *or* compensative, compensational, indemnificatory; propitiatory *or* propitiative, appeasing, pacifying, conciliatory *or* conciliative, reconciliatory
> *Pacification 74; Compromise 461; Giving Back 478*

6 **apologetic,** regretful, sorry; penitent, penitential, repentant, repenting, contrite, remorseful; oblatory, oblational, sacrificial; lustral, lustrative, cleansing, purifying, purgative, purgatorial, mortifying, ascetic
> *Cleanliness 111; Penitence 451*

VERBS

7 **atone,** atone for, make amends, make amends for, satisfy, give satisfaction, expiate, make reparation, repair, redress, make restitution, restitute, restore, make good, make up for, redeem, remedy, rectify, make right, square things, clear the air; compensate, indemnify, pay, remunerate, recompense, requite, quit, reimburse, repay, pay back, square; propitiate, appease, pacify, conciliate, reconcile, pour oil on troubled waters
> *Pacification 74; Compromise 461; Giving Back 478*

8 **apologize,** make *or* offer one's apologies, say one is sorry, beg one's pardon *or* forgiveness, come cap in hand, get down on one's knees, express regret, acknowledge, acknowledge guilt, admit, confess; send regrets, offer an excuse *or* explanation, justify
> *Forgiveness 312*

9 **repent,** be penitent, be contrite, regret, show remorse *or* compunction; do penance, beat one's breast, make an offering, offer a sacrifice; lustrate, cleanse oneself of sin *or* guilt, purify oneself, suffer purgatory, fast, flagellate oneself, mortify oneself, practice ascetism
> *Religion 81; Cleanliness 111; Penitence 451; Punishment 454*

ADVERBS

10 **atoningly,** remedially; propitiatorily, propitiatingly, appeasingly, pacifyingly, conciliatorily, conciliatingly, reconcilingly, piacularly
> *Pacification 74; Compromise 461; Giving Back 478*

11 **apologetically,** regretfully, sorrily; penitently, penitentially, repentantly, in repentance, contritely, remorsefully; as penance, sacrificially; purgatively, mortifyingly, ascetically
> *Penitence 451*

314 Envy

> *From envy, hatred, and malice, and all uncharitableness, Good Lord, deliver us.* — BOOK OF COMMON PRAYER

NOUNS

1 **envy,** enviousness, jealousy, invidiousness, emulousness [Arch]; covetousness, desire, want, wanting, yen, longing *or* wishing for; discontent *or* discontentment, malcontentedness, dissatisfaction, meanspiritedness
> *Dissatisfaction 274; Desire 288; Resentment, Anger 302*

2 **jealousy,** jealousness, resentment, resentfulness, ill will, spite, bitterness, hostility; grudge, grudgingness, begrudgingness; greed, cupidity, possessiveness; rivalry, competition, competitiveness, competitive spirit; eternal triangle, heartburning, heartburn, jaundice, jaundiced eye *or* view *or* look, green-eyed monster
> *Hostility 63; Love 299; Hate 300; Resentment, Anger 302; Contention 422*

3 **suspicion,** suspiciousness, distrust, distrustfulness, mistrust, mistrustfulness, lack of confidence, doubt, misdoubt, wariness; watchfulness, guardedness, vigilance; defensiveness, insecurity, paranoia, anxiety, apprehension *or* apprehensiveness
> *Disbelief 88; Uncertainty 841*

ADJECTIVES

4 **envious,** envying, jealous, invidious, emulous, emulative; covetous, desirous, desiring, longing, wishful; discontented, malcontented, dissatisfied, meanspirited; green with envy

5 **jealous,** resentful, ill-willed, spiteful, bitter, sour, hostile; grudging, begrudging, greedy, cupidinous, possessive, overpossessive; rival, competitive, competing; devoured *or* consumed *or* obsessed *or* eaten up with jealousy; jaundiced, green, green-eyed, yellow, yellow-eyed, lynx-eyed

6 **suspicious,** distrustful, mistrustful, unconfident, doubtful, misdoubtful, wary; watchful, guarded, vigilant, Argus-eyed; defensive, insecure, paranoid, anxious, apprehensive

VERBS

7 **envy,** be envious of, covet, be covetous of, desire, desire for oneself, cast envious eyes, want, long for, lust, crave, hanker; turn green with envy

8 **be jealous,** view with jealousy, resent, spite; grudge, begrudge; rival, compete; view with a jaundiced eye, suffer pangs of jealousy, eat one's heart out, brook no rival; be possessive, be overpossessive, strive to keep for oneself

9 **suspect,** distrust, mistrust, doubt, misdoubt, be wary; watch, guard, not allow out of one's sight

10 **arouse jealousy,** make jealous, create resentment, give someone an inferiority complex, put someone's nose out of joint

ADVERBS

11 **enviously,** with envy, jealously, invidiously, emulously; covetously, desirously, wantingly, longingly, discontentedly

12 **jealously,** with a jealous heart, resentfully, spitefully, bitterly, hostilely; grudgingly, begrudgingly; greedily; competitively

13 **suspiciously,** distrustfully, mistrustfully, doubtfully, misdoubtfully, warily; watchfully, guardedly, vigilantly, possessively; defensively, insecurely, anxiously, apprehensively

The Intellect and Ideas

315 Intellect

We should take care not to make the intellect our god; it has, of course, powerful muscles, but no personality.
— ALBERT EINSTEIN

The voice of the intellect is a soft one, but it does not rest till it has gained a hearing. — SIGMUND FREUD

The highest intellects, like the tops of mountains, are the first to catch and to reflect the dawn.
— THOMAS BABINGTON MACAULAY

NOUNS

1 **intellect,** mind, mentality, rationality, conception, intellectualism, intellectuality; intelligence, cognition, knowledge, perception, perceptiveness, percipience
   ▶ *Psychology and Psychiatry 108; Thought 317; Knowledge 348*

2 **intelligence,** intellect, understanding, comprehension, apperception, sense, judgment, mentality, mind, brain *or* brains, wit *or* wits, reason, nous; intelligence quotient (IQ)

3 **cleverness,** flair, brains, smartness, wit, wisdom, sagacity, sapience, erudition, knowledgeableness; brightness, incisiveness, shrewdness, astuteness, aptitude, brilliance, genius; alertness, sharpness, acuity, acuteness, quickness, quick-wittedness, keen-wittedness, canniness, subtlety, braininess [Inf]
   ▶ *Knowledge 348; Wisdom 352*

4 **common sense,** sense, sensibleness, sound judgment, discernment, clear thinking, horse sense, native wit, mother wit; [Inf]: savvy, smarts, nous [Brit]

5 **thought,** thinking, thoughtfulness, judiciousness, consideration, reflection, reflectiveness, circumspection, profundity, profoundness, depth
   ▶ *Thought 317*

6 **brain,** head, cerebrum, gray matter, seat of thought

▶ *Human Body 19*

7 **intellectual,** thinker, scholar, student, academic, academician, professor; wise man, wise woman, sage, savant, intellect, master; guru, elder statesman, oracle, pundit, philosopher, polymath, Renaissance man *or* woman, littérateur, bluestocking, highbrow, genius, walking encyclopedia, illuminati; [Inf]: egghead, brain, know-it-all *or* knowall

ADJECTIVES

8 **intellectual,** rational, reasoning, thinking, conceptual, conceptive, cerebral, noetic, phrenic, logical, deductive, inductive

9 **intelligent,** understanding, clever, learned, erudite, knowledgeable, wise, sage, sagacious, bright, smart, shrewd, astute, brilliant, alert, sharp, acute, quick-witted, keen-witted, gifted, brainy [Inf]

10 **thoughtful,** judicious, reflective, circumspect, sapient, profound, sensible, reasonable, sound, deep

VERBS

11 **be intelligent,** use one's head *or* wits, be clever, be sharp, be smart, have one's head screwed on the right way [Inf], have one's wits about one, have a good head on one's shoulders [Inf], know what's what [Inf]

12 **think,** reason, rationalize, ratiocinate, perceive, conceptualize, apperceive, ideate, deduce, induce
   ▶ *Thought 317*

ADVERBS

13 **mentally,** intellectually, cerebrally, conceptually, instinctively

14 **intelligently,** sensibly, reasonably, rationally, logically, knowledgeably, wisely, cleverly, sagaciously, profoundly, reflectively, judiciously, thoughtfully, shrewdly, astutely, alertly, acutely, smartly

316 Lack of Intellect

"Is it weakness of intellect, birdie?" I cried, / "Or a rather tough worm in your little inside?" — W. S. GILBERT

NOUNS

1 **lack** *or* **absence of intellect,** unintelligence, intellectual weakness, mental weakness, stupidity, lack of brains, low mental age *or* IQ, simplemindedness, backwardness, slowness, imbecility, idiocy, mindlessness, senselessness, brainlessness, vacancy, vacuity

2 **mental deficiency,** mental retardation, mental handicap, feeble-mindedness, brain damage

3 **ignorance,** lack of knowledge, lack of wisdom, foolishness, folly, thoughtlessness, illogicality, empty-headedness, inanity, fatuity, puerility, childishness, immaturity, lack of understanding, incomprehension, unperceptiveness *or* imperceptiveness, obtuseness, stolidity, thickheadedness, hebetude, oafishness, boorishness, lack of wit, witlessness, dimwittedness, dimness

▸ *Unskillfulness 128; Lack of Thought 318; Inattention 324; Ignorance 349; Folly 353; Simplicity 526; Naiveté 821*

4 **unintelligent person,** ignoramus, fool, dunce, simpleton, Simple Simon, idiot, imbecile, moron, cretin, dolt, dullard, blockhead, thickhead, clod, oaf, boor, numskull *or* numbskull, dumbbell, half-wit, dunderhead, ninny, nitwit, nincompoop, silly, scatterbrain; [Inf]: dummy, dimwit, dope, lamebrain, pinhead, peabrain, birdbrain, vegetable, dim-bulb, dum-dum, klutz

ADJECTIVES

5 **lacking intellect,** intellectually weak, mentally weak, simple, simpleminded, slow, backward, dull, vacuous, vacant, mindless, senseless, brainless

6 **unintelligent,** ignorant, stupid, dense, silly, thick, dumb, daft, foolish, thoughtless, unthinking, illogical, inane, fatuous, empty-headed, puerile, childish, childlike, infantile, immature, unwise, unperceptive *or* imperceptive, obtuse, stolid, thickheaded, blockheaded, half-witted, oafish, boorish, doltish, witless; [Inf]: dimwitted, dim, dopey, klutzy, soft in the head, not sixteen ounces to the pound, not playing with a full deck, out to lunch, not all there, three bricks shy of a load

▸ *Ignorance 349*

7 **intellectually subnormal,** mentally deficient, mentally subnormal, subnormal, mentally handicapped, retarded, backward, simple, simpleminded, feeble-minded, imbecilic, idiotic, moronic, cretinous, brain-damaged

VERBS

8 **lack intellect,** have a low IQ (intelligence quotient), lack reason, show ignorance, be unintelligent, be stupid, fail to see, not see beyond one's nose, fail to comprehend; [Inf]: not have *or* lose one's marbles, not have brains enough to come in out of the rain, not find one's way to first base, be not all there

ADVERBS

9 **unintelligently,** without intelligence, unthinkingly, without thinking, empty-headedly, absently, vacantly, vacuously, inanely, fatuously, ignorantly, stupidly, mindlessly, senselessly, brainlessly, feeble-mindedly, simplemindedly, idiotically, moronically, irrationally, illogically, unwisely, foolishly, imperceptively, obtusely

317 Thought

I think, therefore I am. — RENÉ DESCARTES

There is nothing either good or bad, but thinking makes it so. — WILLIAM SHAKESPEARE

NOUNS

1 **thought,** thinking, reasoning, reason, cogitation, mental process, thought process, mental activity, cerebration, deduction, ratiocination, rumination, workings of the mind; deep thinking, hard thinking, profound thought, headwork, brainwork, ideation; train of thought, stream of consciousness

▸ *Reason 319; Idea 327*

2 **thoughtfulness,** concentration, contemplation, reflection, consideration, speculation, retrospection, pensiveness, reverie, study, brown study, thinking cap; introspection, musing, daydreaming, meditation, meditativeness, innermost thought; deliberation, pondering, abstract thought, abstractedness, profundity; courteousness, courtesy

▸ *Supposition 359; Courtesy 410*

3 **creative thought,** inventiveness, originality, inventive power, inspiration, flash of inspiration, idea, flow of ideas, imagination, novel idea, crazy idea, good idea, quantum leap, brainstorm, brain wave [Inf]

▸ *Intellect 315; Attention 323; Idea 327; Wisdom 352; Memory 354; Imagination 360*

4 **way of thinking,** logic, formal reasoning, deduction, induction, reasoning, rationale, ratiocination; insight, acumen, inspiration, intuition

▸ *Philosophy 4; Reason 319; Intuition 320*

ADJECTIVES

5 **thoughtful,** thinking, reasoning, mental, intellectual, cognitive, cerebral, ruminative, philosophical; considerate, courteous

▸ *Philosophy 4; Courtesy 410*

6 **reasoning,** intelligent, rational, ratiocinative, logical, intellectual, philosophical, professorial, scholarly, ideological, Socratic

7 **concentrating,** contemplative, pensive, reflective, absorbed, lost in thought

8 **speculative,** introspective, meditative, profound, deliberative, pondered, pondering, musing, inventive, dreamy, notional, conceptual, fanciful, theoretical, conjectural, suppositional, in a brown study, in a world of one's own, miles away

VERBS

9 **think,** reason, cogitate, ruminate, ponder, consider, meditate, exercise one's intellect, cerebrate, ratiocinate, think deeply, think hard, think profoundly, use one's head, use one's brain, rack one's brains, speculate, imagine; philosophize, intellectualize, internalize, introspect; think about, work out, weigh up, take stock of, deliberate; be thoughtful, be considerate, be courteous

10 **concentrate,** contemplate, mull over, reflect, reflect upon, study, apply one's mind

11 **have second thoughts,** think over, rethink, reconsider, think again, sleep on it

12 **have an idea,** conceive of, premise, theorize, conjecture, ideate, hypothesize, deduce, infer, speculate, suppose, surmise, conclude, have *or* hold a point of view, defend one's attitude, originate, invent, imagine, have a good idea, brainstorm; have a brainstorm *or* brain wave [Inf]
　▶ *Idea 327*

ADVERBS

13 **thoughtfully,** reflectively, philosophically, contemplatively, on reconsideration, on second thought, rationally, logically, intuitively, introspectively, creatively, inventively, imaginatively; considerately, courteously

318 Lack of Thought

NOUNS

1 **lack of thought,** thoughtlessness, mindlessness, vacancy, inanity, fatuity, vacuity, blankness, empty-headedness, empty head, blank mind; absent-mindedness, folly, head in the clouds, fallow mind, tranquillity, calm, oblivion
　▶ *Inattention 324*

2 **ignorance,** unintelligence, unawareness, nescience, stupidity
　▶ *Lack of Intellect 316; Inattention 324; Ignorance 349; Absence 576*

3 **instinct,** instinctiveness, intuition, impulse, conditioned reflex, Pavlovian reaction, knee-jerk response [Inf], gut reaction [Inf]
　▶ *Intuition 320*

4 **inconsideration,** thoughtlessness, discourtesy, insensitivity, insensitiveness, inattention, neglect, selfishness, unkindness, tactlessness
　▶ *Discourtesy 411; Selfishness 444*

5 **mental block,** blank spot, blind spot, amnesia, lack of memory

6 **impulsiveness,** impetuosity, precipitance, recklessness, rashness, foolhardiness

ADJECTIVES

7 **thoughtless,** mindless, unthinking, incapable of thought, unreflective, inane, fatuous, vacuous, vacant, blank, empty-headed, absent-minded, abstracted, fal-

low, oblivious, ignorant, foolish, carefree, easygoing, happy-go-lucky, devil-may-care

8 **instinctive,** intuitive, automatic, involuntary, reflex, knee-jerk [Inf]

9 **inconsiderate,** thoughtless, insensitive, heedless, inattentive, neglectful, uncaring, selfish, oblivious, unkind, tactless, pestering, bothering, discourteous, rude
　▶ *Discourtesy 411; Selfishness 444*

10 **unthought-of,** unconsidered, unconceived, unimagined, undreamed-of

11 **impulsive,** impetuous, precipitant, reckless, rash, foolhardy

VERBS

12 **lack thought,** forget, act without thinking, speak without thinking, not stop and think, be absent-minded, have one's head in the clouds, hit a mental block, blank out, daydream, suffer from amnesia, lose one's memory, ignore the consequences, rush in where angels fear to tread

13 **be inconsiderate,** pester, bother, be rude, be discourteous

14 **act impulsively,** be precipitous

ADVERBS

15 **thoughtlessly,** instinctively, insensitively, mindlessly, obliviously, with one's head in the clouds, without a care in the world; selfishly, discourteously, rudely

16 **impulsively,** impetuously, precipitously, recklessly, rashly, headlong

319 Reason

Reason is itself a matter of faith. It is an act of faith to assert that our thoughts have any relation to reality at all.
— G. K. CHESTERTON

NOUNS

1 **reason,** mind, intellect, power of reason, rationality, intelligence, understanding, perception, judgment, wisdom, sense, sanity, saneness, power of conception
　▶ *Sanity 109; Intellect 315; Thought 317; Discrimination 337; Knowledge 348*

2 **reasoning,** rationalizing, rationalism, rationality, rationalization, logical process, logical thought, logic, ratiocination; generalization, inference, deductive reasoning, deduction, inductive reasoning, induction, a priori reasoning, a posteriori reasoning, syllogism, analysis, discursive reasoning
　▶ *Mathematics 6; Thought 317*

3 **debate,** polemics, dialectics, dialecticism, apologetics, argumentation, argument, formal argument, legal argument, dissent, dispute, disputation, litigation
　▶ *Litigation 54; Dissent 347; Disagreement 463*

4 **explanation,** cause, motive, grounds, premise, pre-

text, theory, basis, assumption, justification, defense, speculation, hypothesis, valid point, excuse

◗ *Supposition 359; Cause 675; Uncertainty 841*

5 **reasoner,** thinker, intellectual, academic, philosopher, logician, rationalist, apologist, dialectician, syllogist

6 **arguer,** debater, litigator, disputant, plaintiff, defendant, jurist, polemicist *or* polemist, casuist, proponent, wrangler, lawyer

◗ *Litigation 54; Argument 329*

ADJECTIVES

7 **reasoning,** reasonable, rational, thinking, intellectual, intelligent, understanding, perceptive, knowledgeable, judgmental, wise, sensible, sane

8 **rational,** rationalistic, logical, ratiocinative, analytical, inferential, deductive, inductive, a priori, a posteriori

9 **causal,** theoretical, assumptive, valid, explanatory, justified, defended, defensive, excused

10 **argumentative,** dissenting, disputing, litigious, polemic *or* polemical, dialectical

VERBS

11 **reason,** rationalize, analyze, think, think logically, logicize, understand, perceive, judge, ratiocinate, generalize, synthesize, infer, deduce, induce

12 **be reasonable,** show wisdom, make sense, hold water

13 **debate,** argue, dissent, dispute, litigate, enter into argument, exchange opinions

14 **premise,** theorize, postulate, philosophize, assume, explain, justify, defend, excuse

ADVERBS

15 **reasonably,** rationally, logically, sensibly, sanely, within bounds, as far as possible

320 Intuition

NOUNS

1 **intuition,** intuitiveness, intuitive reasoning, feminine intuition, feeling, insight, perception, inspiration, gut feeling *or* reaction [Inf]

2 **precognition,** a priori knowledge, sixth sense, second sight, clairvoyance, divination, telepathy, extrasensory perception (ESP), presentiment

◗ *Feelings 266; Intellect 315; Improvisation 396*

3 **insight,** foreboding, impression, feeling, impulse, hunch, flash

4 **instinct,** innate reaction, proclivity, subconscious, unconscious, automatic reaction, Pavlovian response, knee-jerk response [Inf], gut reaction [Inf]

5 **intuitive person,** clairvoyant, medium, seer, prophet, diviner, sibyl

ADJECTIVES

6 **intuitive,** insightful, perceptive, sensitive, sensing, inspired

7 **precognitive,** a priori, unmediated, second-sighted, clairvoyant, divinatory, telepathic, extrasensory, presentient

8 **instinctive,** instinctual, automatic, spontaneous, reflex, innate, Pavlovian, knee-jerk [Inf]

VERBS

9 **be intuitive,** intuit, feel, have a feeling about, go on one's feelings, perceive, divine, have a hunch, follow one's hunch, feel it in one's bones, have a funny feeling about, have a gut feeling *or* reaction [Inf], just know

10 **be instinctive,** react automatically, have a knee-jerk reaction [Inf]

ADVERBS

11 **intuitively,** instinctively, by *or* on instinct, automatically, spontaneously

321 Curiosity

Curiosity killed the cat. — PROVERB

NOUNS

1 **curiosity,** curiousness, inquisitiveness, questioning, interest, inquisition, inquiry *or* enquiry, desire *or* thirst for knowledge, inquiring mind, alertness, watchfulness

2 **prying,** nosiness, meddling, officiousness, gossip, tittle-tattle, morbid curiosity, prurience, voyeurism, rubbernecking [Inf], snooping [Inf]

◗ *News 171; Attention 323; Question 333; Activity 414*

3 **curious person,** inquirer *or* enquirer, inquisitor, investigator, examiner, questioner, detective, lawyer, teacher, explorer, adventurer, sightseer, tourist, spectator, traveler, journalist, rubbernecker [Inf]

4 **meddler,** gossip, gossipmonger, scandalmonger, stirrer, prier, spy, mole, tittle-tattler, eavesdropper, voyeur, Peeping Tom, quidnunc, kibitzer, Paul Pry, busybody; [Inf]: snoop, Nosy Parker, yenta

ADJECTIVES

5 **curious,** inquisitive, inquiring, inquisitorial, questioning, quizzical, interested, keen, adventurous, alert, watchful, sightseeing, rubbernecking [Inf]

6 **prying,** officious, meddlesome, meddling, prurient, gossipy, nosy, snooping *or* snoopy [Inf]

VERBS

7 **be curious,** inquire *or* enquire, inquire *or* enquire after, question, quiz, interrogate, investigate, search for, show interest, desire knowledge, thirst for knowledge, want to know, seek out, feel concern for, show interest in, sightsee, rubberneck [Inf]

8 **meddle,** gossip, tittle-tattle, eavesdrop, pry, prick up one's ears, sniff out, nose, snoop [Inf], poke one's nose in [Inf]

ADVERBS

9 **curiously,** inquisitively, inquisitorially, questioningly, keenly, adventurously, alertly, watchfully

10 **officiously,** pruriently, nosily

322 Incuriosity

NOUNS

1 **incuriosity,** lack of curiosity, lack of interest, uninterest, disinterest, unconcern, boredom, complacency, insouciance, detachment, indifference, impassivity, imperturbability, uninvolvement, aloofness; credulity, gullibility, blind faith
   ▶ *Inattention 324*
2 **apathy,** numbness, stupor, insensibility, inactivity, stagnation, idleness, sluggishness, slowness, mental inertia, nonchalance, pococurantism
   ▶ *Insensitivity 268; Indifference 289; Lack of Wonder 295; Boredom 296*

ADJECTIVES

3 **incurious,** uninterested, disinterested, unconcerned, bored, complacent, insouciant, detached, indifferent, impassive, imperturbable, uninvolved, uninquisitive, unquestioning, unthinking, heedless, nonchalant; credulous, trusting, gullible
4 **apathetic,** numb, stuporous, insensible, inactive, stagnated, phlegmatic, unmoved, distant, disengaged, unenthusiastic, unstirred, idle, sluggish, slow, deadpan, lackadaisical, dull, unresponsive, aloof

VERBS

5 **be incurious,** disregard, take *or* show no interest in, feel no concern for, not care, could not care less, disengage, detach oneself, not mind, be easy about, be able to take it *or* leave it, be neutral about, be cold, not trouble oneself, mind one's own business, live in an ivory tower; not ask, not question, take on trust, believe, be taken in

ADVERBS

6 **incuriously,** uninterestedly, disinterestedly, uninquisitively, unquestioningly, credulously, trustingly, gullibly
7 **apathetically,** numbly, unconcernedly, heedlessly, indifferently, impassively, imperturbably, insensitively, inertly, stagnantly, phlegmatically, unenthusiastically, lackadaisically, idly, dully, complacently, aloofly

323 Attention

NOUNS

1 **attention,** attentiveness, notice, regard, concern, consideration, mindfulness
2 **close attention,** undivided attention, attention to detail, close observance, scrutiny, close examination, watchfulness, alertness
   ▶ *Curiosity 321*
3 **carefulness,** meticulousness, fastidiousness, finickiness, nitpicking, sedulousness, circumspection, surveillance, vigilance, wariness, heed, concentration, application, assiduousness

▶ *Caution 287; Carefulness 325*
4 **diligence,** studiousness, single-mindedness, fixation, pedantry, purism, obsession, preoccupation, hang-up [Inf]
5 **solicitude,** care, consideration, protection, indulgence, attendance, courtesy, gallantry, spoiling, fussing over

ADJECTIVES

6 **watchful,** alert, attentive, observant, sharp-eyed, vigilant, on guard, careful, wary, circumspect, scrutinizing, surveying, heedful, curious
7 **diligent,** studious, painstaking, meticulous, fastidious, sedulous, assiduous, undistracted, single-minded, rapt, all eyes, engrossed, obsessed, fixated, pedantic, purist, preoccupied; hung-up [Inf], all ears [Inf]
8 **solicitous,** caring, concerned, protective, considerate, mindful, indulgent, attentive, courteous, gallant, fussy

VERBS

9 **be attentive,** regard, consider, notice, note, pay attention, pay heed, dance attendance on, attend, care for
10 **take note of,** register, mark, keep an eye on, give undivided attention to, watch, observe, examine, miss nothing, stay alert, guard against, prick up one's ears
11 **scrutinize,** survey, heed, study, fix upon, nitpick
12 **attract attention,** draw attention, excite the attention of, be the center of attention, catch the eye, act as a magnet
13 **be solicitous,** indulge, pay attention to, show consideration, shower attention on, hover over, court, spoil, flirt, grovel, toady, fawn over, crawl, fuss over, suck up to [Inf], brown-nose [Inf]

ADVERBS

14 **attentively,** mindfully, observantly, watchfully, alertly, heedfully, carefully, meticulously, fastidiously, sedulously, circumspectly, vigilantly, warily, assiduously, diligently, studiously, pedantically

324 Inattention

NOUNS

1 **inattention,** inattentiveness, incuriosity, thoughtlessness, unmindfulness, forgetfulness, aberration, heedlessness, unconcern, detachment, obliviousness, apathy, disregard, distraction, nonobservance, carelessness, negligence, rashness, desultoriness, superficiality, indifference
   ▶ *Indifference 289; Lack of Thought 318; Incuriosity 322*
2 **absent-mindedness,** daydreaming, dizziness, frivolity, flightiness, woolgathering, stargazing, head in the clouds
   ▶ *Lack of Thought 318; Incuriosity 322; Shallowness 599*
3 **thoughtlessness,** inconsideration, disregard, indifference, ignoring, insensitivity, selfishness

▶ *Lack of Thought 318; Selfishness 444*

4 **negligence,** oversight, lapse, slip, error, mistake, blunder, mishap, slip-up
    ▶ *Negligence 326; Error 351*

ADJECTIVES

5 **inattentive,** thoughtless, unthinking, not concentrating, incurious, unmindful, forgetful, heedless, unheeding, unconcerned, detached, oblivious, apathetic, listless, disregarding, distracted, unobservant

6 **absent-minded,** lost in thought, daydreaming, woolgathering, stargazing, in a brown study, in a world of one's own, out to lunch [Inf], not with it [Inf]

7 **thoughtless,** inconsiderate, uncaring, selfish, insensitive, unthinking

8 **careless,** negligent, neglectful, slack, remiss, sloppy, slapdash, slipshod, hit-or-miss, dizzy, flighty, rash, scatterbrained
    ▶ *Lack of Thought 318*

9 **perfunctory,** casual, lackadaisical, desultory, superficial

VERBS

10 **be inattentive,** show unconcern, disregard, ignore, not notice, not listen, pay no attention, take no notice of, pay no heed to, overlook, put out of mind, allow one's mind to wander, daydream, stargaze, woolgather, be elsewhere, build castles in the air *or* in Spain

11 **be thoughtless,** be inattentive, show inconsideration for, disregard, ignore, slight, turn one's back on
    ▶ *Indifference 289*

ADVERBS

12 **inattentively,** incuriously, thoughtlessly, unmindfully, forgetfully, heedlessly, selfishly, inconsiderately, indifferently, obliviously, apathetically, carelessly, negligently, rashly, impetuously, recklessly

325 Carefulness

NOUNS

1 **carefulness,** care, caution, attentiveness, attention, mindfulness, conscientiousness, diligence, heed, assiduity, thoroughness, exactness, precision, meticulousness
    ▶ *Attention 323; Accuracy 350; Preparation 388; Order 765*

2 **consideration,** solicitude, concern, thoughtfulness, compassion, mindfulness, caregiving, care, loving care, tender loving care (TLC)
    ▶ *Attention 323; Courtesy 410*

3 **circumspection,** watchfulness, alertness, vigilance, readiness, preparation, prudence, scruples, scrupulousness

4 **fastidiousness,** particularity, exactitude, perfectionism, orderliness, tidiness, neatness, perfection, painstakingness, attention to detail, niceness, pedantry, finickiness, persnicketiness [Inf]

▶ *Caution 287; Foresight 357; Preparation 388; Order 765*

5 **watchfulness,** surveillance, vigilance, wariness, guard, guarding, guardedness, watching, watch, lookout, inspection, vigil, guard duty
    ▶ *Safety 810*

ADJECTIVES

6 **careful,** cautious, attentive, mindful, diligent, heedful, assiduous, thorough, meticulous

7 **considerate,** solicitous, mindful, caring, caregiving, loving

8 **circumspect,** chary, watchful, observant, wide-awake, alert, vigilant, ready, prepared, prudent, scrupulous

9 **fastidious,** particular, exact, perfectionistic, orderly, tidy, neat, painstaking, precise, nice, pedantic, finicky, persnickety [Inf]

10 **watchful,** surveillant, vigilant, wary, guarding, watching, on guard

VERBS

11 **be careful,** mind, heed, watch, prepare, be vigilant, be cautious, tread carefully, pay attention to, tread warily, walk on eggshells

12 **care for,** take charge of, safeguard, guard, stand guard, look out for, survey, check, inspect, watch over, keep an eye on, attend to, take care of

ADVERBS

13 **carefully,** with care, cautiously, gingerly, charily; diligently, with precision, in detail, with exactitude, thoroughly, precisely, perfectly, alertly, warily

14 **caringly,** tenderly, solicitously, compassionately, mindfully

326 Negligence

NOUNS

1 **negligence,** carelessness, inattention, thoughtlessness, unmindfulness, nonchalance, unconcern, omission, oblivion, insouciance, disregard, neglectfulness, dereliction, forgetfulness, heedlessness, remissness, oversight
    ▶ *Incuriosity 322; Inattention 324*

2 **indifference,** informality, casualness, inexactitude, unscrupulousness, superficiality, shallowness, offhandedness, slackness, shoddiness, laziness, untidiness, messiness, slovenliness, sloppiness, sluttishness, procrastination, avoidance, delay
    ▶ *Indifference 289; Inattention 324*

3 **neglector,** ignorer, procrastinator, idler, slacker, shirker, malingerer, goldbrick [Inf], sloven, slut, slob

ADJECTIVES

4 **negligent,** neglectful, careless, inattentive, thoughtless, unmindful, nonchalant, unconcerned, uncaring, oblivious, insouciant, disregardful, forgetful, heedless, remiss

5 indifferent, informal, casual, lackadaisical, inexact, unscrupulous, superficial, shallow, offhanded, procrastinating, avoiding, shirking, malingering, delaying; slack, lax, slipshod, slapdash, incomplete, shoddy, lazy, untidy, dirty, messy, slovenly, sluttish, sloppy

6 neglected, untended, disregarded, overlooked, missed, ignored, unheeded, undone, half-done, incomplete

VERBS

7 be neglectful, neglect, be negligent, disregard, take no notice of, not care for, ignore, turn a blind eye to, forget, not heed, procrastinate, take things slowly, put off till tomorrow, take it easy, put one's feet up; avoid, shirk, malinger, delay, leave undone, leave half-done, not complete, give a lick and a promise

ADVERBS

8 negligently, neglectfully, carelessly, cursorily, remissly, laxly, incompletely, shoddily, lazily, untidily, messily, sluttishly, sloppily, any which *or* old way [Inf]

327 Idea

A stand can be made against invasion by an army; no stand can be made against invasion by an idea.
— VICTOR HUGO

An idea isn't responsible for the people who believe in it.
— DON MARQUIS

Man's mind, once stretched by a new idea, never regains its original dimensions. — OLIVER WENDELL HOLMES

NOUNS

1 idea, notion, abstraction, thought, thinking, concept, conception, observation, perception, understanding, awareness, apprehension, reflection, assumption, presumption, reaction, estimation, feeling, sentiment, memory; construct, mental picture, mental image, mental object; imago, ideatum, noumenon, essence, Platonic idea, absolute idea
▶ *Philosophy 4; Sensitivity 267; Intellect 315; Thought 317; Intuition 320; Memory 354; Supposition 359; Nonmaterial World 525*

2 theory, idea, hypothesis, suggestion, conjecture, surmise, speculation, supposition, suspicion, indication; fancy, clue, hint, guess, feeling, intuition, hunch, inkling, thesis, premise, conjecture; opinion, view, viewpoint, stand, stance, position
▶ *Philosophy 4; Supposition 359*

3 plan, intention, scheme, project, proposal, invention, bright idea, good idea, brainstorm, brainchild, brain wave [Inf]; crazy idea, absurd idea
▶ *Intention 374; Plan 387; Originality 737*

4 purpose, plan, aim, design, function, goal, object, objective, target, end, point, reason, significance, meaning
▶ *Reason 319; Meaning 361; Will 372; Intention 374; Plan 387; Motivation 508; End 773*

5 ideology, philosophy, belief, principle, creed, credo, teaching, tenet; ideals, morals, standards, prejudices; world view
▶ *Philosophy 4; Religion 81; Belief 87*

6 ideal, model, example, exemplar, paragon, paradigm, standard, pattern, quintessence, epitome, prototype, archetype, vision, dream, Utopia
▶ *Hope 281; Imagination 360; Perfection 805*

7 idealism, idealization, optimism, utopianism, romanticism, daydreaming, wishful thinking, impracticality, ideality, idealness
▶ *Philosophy 4; Hope 281; Perfection 805*

8 imagination, imaginativeness, inventiveness, originality, creativity, ingenuity, inspiration, perception, visualization, conceptualization
▶ *Sensitivity 267; Wonder 294; Imagination 360; Originality 737*

ADJECTIVES

9 ideational, mental, cerebral, intellectual, in the mind, in the mind's eye, in one's head, imagined, visualized, conceived, conceptualized, inspired; aware, reflective, imaginative, inventive, creative, original, ingenious, fanciful

10 theoretical, notional, abstract, putative, conceptual, perceptual, philosophical, hypothetical, conjectural, speculative, suppositional, propositional, suggestive, indicative, suspected, assumed, presumed, estimated, guesstimated [Inf]

11 purposive, functional, goal-directed, teleological, aiming, functioning, targeting, intentional, proposed, aimed, targeted, schematic, designed, planned, reasoned, well-reasoned, reasonable, significant, meaningful
▶ *Cause 675*

12 ideal, model, exemplary, paradigmatic *or* paradigmatical, epitomical, quintessential, prototypical, archetypal, visionary, fantastic, idealistic, idealized, optimistic, utopian, romantic, sentimental, dreamy, impractical, ideological
▶ *Philosophy 4; Hope 281; Perfection 805*

VERBS

13 have an idea, come to mind, enter one's head, cross one's mind, suggest itself, dawn upon, realize, perceive, remember, come to one, occur to one, hit one, strike one, be struck by, deduce, understand, apprehend, intuit, see, grasp, pop into one's head, grab one [Inf], get [Inf]
▶ *Answer 334*

14 imagine, ideate, think, reflect, deliberate, feel, conceive, visualize, conceptualize, picture, envision, envisage, formulate, create, invent, originate, think up,

conjure up, dream up, dream, fancy, fantasize, idealize, romanticize, daydream, pipe-dream, see through rose-colored glasses, build castles in the air *or* in Spain
▸ *Intellect 315; Thought 317; Imagination 360*

15 **inspire,** inspirit, fire one's imagination, animate, exhilarate, enliven

16 **theorize,** hypothesize, conjecture, suggest, suspect, guess, reckon, estimate, suppose, opine, believe, assume, presume, have a hunch, guesstimate [Inf]
▸ *Philosophy 4; Thought 317*

17 **aim,** plan, plot, scheme, design, propose, intend, target, point to, head for, get ideas, set one's sights on, aspire, aim high, overreach, overstep oneself, have thoughts above one's station, go all out for
▸ *Will 372; Intention 374; Plan 387; Motivation 508*

18 **epitomize,** exemplify, set an example, model, pattern, indicate, represent, signify, mean

ADVERBS

19 **theoretically,** notionally, in theory, abstractly, abstractedly, putatively, philosophically, thoughtfully, conceptually, hypothetically, conjecturally, reflectively, mentally, in the mind, in the mind's eye, in one's head, upstairs [Inf]

20 **purposively,** intentionally, schematically, indicatively, functionally, significantly, meaningfully, reasonably, to the point, with an aim in mind, with a view to, on purpose, deliberately

21 **imaginatively,** originally, inventively, creatively, ingeniously, perceptively, inspirationally, optimistically, romantically, sentimentally, impractically, dreamily, fantastically, idealistically, through rose-colored glasses

22 **ideally,** perfectly, under the best circumstances, in a perfect world, at best, all things being equal

23 **ideologically,** standardly, archetypally, paradigmatically, so it seems, as one sees it, to one's way of thinking, in one's opinion

328 Topic

NOUNS

1 **topic,** subject, contents, text, subject matter, matter; theme, plot, angle, interest, concern, point, motif, leitmotiv; program, statement, message, argument; thesis, theorem, proposition, supposition, heart of the matter, main point, keynote, essence, idea, gist, drift, pith, meat, basis, foundation; category, rubric, topic sentence
▸ *Dissertation 203; Summary 204; Idea 327; Meaning 361; Contents 577; Angle 628; Essence 723*

2 **issue,** point at issue, concern, focus, question, topic, problem, bone of contention, moot point, matter for discussion, case, point, item, motion, agenda, business at hand
▸ *Argument 329; Question 333; Contention 422; Negotiation 460; Disagreement 463*

3 **matter of interest,** topic for discussion, events, news, happenings, rumor, gossip, story, affair, business, proceedings, goings-on [Inf]
▸ *Information 170; News 171*

4 **educational topic,** subject, field, branch, discipline, course, project, class project, individual project, special topic
▸ *Education 48; Dissertation 203*

ADJECTIVES

5 **topical,** thematic; in the news, current, present, immediate, contemporary, up-to-date, up-to-the-minute, hot off the press, straight from the horse's mouth, timely, happening
▸ *News 171*

6 **focused,** subjective, angled, pointed, founded, based, concerned with, dealing with, supposed, proposed, programmed, thematic, central, basic

7 **problematic,** moot, mooted, undecided, questioned, challenged, challenging, curious, interesting, thought-provoking, debatable, worthy of discussion, on the agenda

8 **local,** familiar, domestic, nearby, local-interest, gossipy, telltale

VERBS

9 **focus on,** concentrate on, center on, point to, be concerned with, contain, include, state, argue, propose, suppose
▸ *Essence 723; Inclusion 763*

10 **raise the point,** raise the issue, point out, make a point, put on the agenda, put forward (a suggestion), deal with, discuss, debate, contend, question, inquire, study, get to the heart of the matter, do a project on
▸ *Argument 329; Negotiation 460; Disagreement 463*

ADVERBS

11 **topically,** locally, domestically, currently, in the news, as it happens, up to date, up to the minute, in the mind, on the brain, in one's thoughts
▸ *Location 565; Surroundings 615; Time 639*

12 **problematically,** curiously, interestingly, challengingly, questionably, debatably, in question, under consideration, under discussion, afoot, on the agenda, on the table, before the house, before the committee
▸ *Negotiation 460*

13 **thematically,** essentially, basically, centrally, supposedly, pointedly, to the point, in essence, in short
▸ *Summary 204; Essence 723*

329 Argument

NOUNS

1 **argument,** disagreement, dispute, quarrel, contention, controversy, discord; misunderstanding, quibble, difference, altercation, wrangle, squabble, bicker; tiff,

spat, row, set-to, falling-out; name-calling, argy-bargy [Brit]; [Inf]: scrap, to-do, slanging match

◗ *Hostility 63; Dissent 347; Attack 418; Disagreement 463; Friction 554; Exchange 673; Disturbance 768*

2 logical argument, reasoning, argumentum; debate, discussion, disputation, dialogue, dialectic, polemic, heuristic, elenchus; logic, sophistry, argumentation, discourse, reasoning, ratiocination, deliberation, deduction, induction, consideration, reflection, thought, challenge; questioning, inquiry, doubt; teleological argument, argument from design; art of dispute, eristic, polemics

◗ *Philosophy 4; Conversation 210; Thought 317; Reason 319; Sophistry 330; Question 333; Negotiation 460*

3 line of argument, line of reasoning, rationale, topic, issue, thesis, hypothesis, postulate, proposition, premise, pretext, point, case, claim, assertion, statement, affirmation, attestation, testimony, position, opinion, stance, grounds, evidence

◗ *Idea 327; Topic 328; Evidence 339; Supposition 359; Contention 422; Certainty 840*

4 gist, outline, summary, essence, theme, subject, topic, idea, point, nub, argument, issue, plot, subplot, scenario, setting, moral

◗ *Topic 328; Meaning 361; Essence 723*

5 plea, pleading, argument, request, entreaty, cry, suit, consideration, excuse, answer, apology, apologia, defense, claim, justification, explanation, rationalization, vindication, cause

◗ *Litigation 54; Answer 334; Vindication 441; Request 505; Cause 675*

ADJECTIVES

6 arguing, disagreeing, disputing, quibbling, quarreling, wrangling, squabbling, bickering; different, diverse, discordant, incompatible, dissenting, dissentient, rowing

◗ *Dissent 347; Diversity 732; Disturbance 768*

7 argumentative, quarrelsome, disagreeable, disputatious, litigious, dissentious, factious, querulous, peevish, irritable, contrary, testy, petulant, fractious, choleric, cross, irascible, cantankerous, grouchy; at odds, at cross-purposes, at loggerheads, competitive, scrappy [Inf]

◗ *Aggravation 276; Irascibility 303; Obstinacy 379*

8 arguable, debatable, disputable, contentious, topical, controversial, questionable, doubtful, dubious, challenging, problematic, refutable, open to question, in question, moot, unsettled, undecided, misunderstood

9 logical, dialectical, discussable, hypothetical, propositional, proposed, postulated, claimed, asserted, stated, affirmed, attested; heuristic, maieutic, hermeneutic; sophistic *or* sophistical

◗ *Philosophy 4*

10 apologetic, in defense, defensive, pleading, justifi-

able, explicable, vindicated, justified, rational, explained, causal, caused

VERBS

11 argue, disagree, bicker, wrangle, quarrel, have words, quibble, squabble; remonstrate, altercate, gainsay, contradict, polemicize, oppose, dissent, differ, dispute, contest, have a set-to, clash, conflict

◗ *Negation 190; Disagreement 463*

12 discuss, debate, exchange opinions, reason, ratiocinate, logicize, logomachize, deliberate, consider, weigh up, reflect, doubt, question, inquire, challenge, moot, deduce, induce, cavil, argue the toss

◗ *Sophistry 330; Negotiation 460; Exchange 673*

13 state, argue, maintain, say, affirm, attest, hold, claim, hypothesize, propose, postulate, suggest, imply, indicate, signify, betoken, denote, show, demonstrate, establish, evince, prove

◗ *Supposition 359; Certainty 840*

14 plead, argue, request, entreat, prevail upon, persuade, canvass, put one's case, apologize, defend, claim, answer, justify, explain, rationalize, vindicate

◗ *Vindication 441; Request 505*

ADVERBS

15 argumentatively, disagreeably, irritably, petulantly, crossly, discordantly, incompatibly, diversely, differently, polemically, antagonistically, provocatively, inimically, in conflict

16 arguably, disputedly, topically, controversially, contrarily, on the contrary, on the other hand, at issue, under investigation, in question, doubtfully, hypothetically, plausibly

17 logically, dialectically, deductively, inductively, reflectively, thoughtfully, deliberately

18 apologetically, in defense, as a defense, in answer, in response, justifiably, explicably, rationally, reasonably, causally

330 Sophistry

Universities incline wits to sophistry and affectation.
— FRANCIS BACON

NOUNS

1 sophistry, casuistry, philosophism, Jesuitism *or* Jesuitry; false *or* specious reasoning, choplogic, faulty logic, illogicality, illogicalness; fallaciousness, fallacy, speciousness, invalidity, untenableness, unsoundness; irrationality, inconsistency, circularity, equivocation, subterfuge, sleight, distortion, misapplication, solecism, mere rhetoric, empty words, moonshine

◗ *Philosophy 4; Misrepresentation 188; Argument 329; Lack of Meaning 362; Equivocation 380; Distortion 627; Circularity 631; Untruth 722*

2 sophism, paralogism, pseudosyllogism, solecism; flawed argument, circular argument, argument ad hominem, non sequitur, paradox, contradiction in terms, antilogy, reductio ad absurdum, fallacy; dodge, trick, ruse, shuffle, quibble, quip, quirk, cavil, contrivance, stratagem, subterfuge; red herring, scheme, misinformation, disinformation

> *Untruthfulness, Falsehood 192; Deception 193; Obscurity 197; Argument 329; Plan 387*

3 **cunning,** sophistication, craftiness, artfulness, art, artifice, slyness, foxiness, slipperiness, shiftiness, trickiness, sneakiness, insidiousness, machination, manipulation, demagoguery, pulling the wool over someone's eyes, mystification, obfuscation

> *Skillfulness 127; Persuasion 178; Deception 193; Obscurity 197; Influence 512; Cunning 822*

4 **quibbling,** captiousness, hairsplitting, nitpicking, caviling, subtlety, oversubtlety, paltering, evasion, equivocation, hedging, shuffling, beating around the bush, pettifoggery, pussyfooting

> *Litigation 54; Lack of Meaning 362; Equivocation 380*

5 **hypocrisy,** deceit, deception, duplicity, pretense, humbug, double-dealing, insincerity, disingenuousness, guile, evasion, mendacity, fakery, chicanery, quackery, charlatanism, mountebankery, pharisaism, Tartuffery

> *Untruthfulness, Falsehood 192; Deception 193; Shallowness 599; Untruth 722*

6 **sophist,** sophister, sophisticator, paralogist, philosophist, casuist, Jesuit, solecist, logic chopper, equivocator, prevaricator, caviler, quibbler, nitpicker, hairsplitter, pussyfooter, pettifogger, waffler [Inf]

> *Philosophy 4; Litigation 54; Deception 193*

ADJECTIVES

7 **sophistic,** sophistical, casuistical, Jesuitical, solecistical, rhetorical, logic-chopping, paralogistic, pseudosyllogistic; specious, fallacious, spurious, faulty, flawed, inconsistent; circular, equivocal, erroneous, illogical, paradoxical, contradictory, unreasonable, irrational, unfounded, baseless, groundless, invalid, untenable, unsound, distorted, misapplied, contrived, tortuous, misleading, inconsequential, dubious, fictitious, illusory, superficial, misinformed

> *Misrepresentation 188; Lack of Meaning 362; Wrong 430; Nonconformity 782*

8 **cunning,** sophisticated, crafty, artful, sly, foxy, sneaky, shifty, dodgy, tricky, insidious, underhand, perfidious, evasive, elusive, manipulating, demagogic, mystifying, obfuscated

> *Skillfulness 127; Persuasion 178; Deception 193; Obscurity 197; Influence 512; Cunning 822*

9 **quibbling,** caviling, captious, hairsplitting, nitpicking, shuffling, hedging, equivocal, equivocating, prevaricating, pettifogging, pussyfooting

10 **hypocritical,** deceptive, deceitful, pretended, feigning, dissembling, dissimulating, double-dealing, unreliable, insincere, disingenuous, tongue-in-cheek, fraudulent, dishonest, lying, mendacious, false, bogus, sham, counterfeit, fake, faking, pharisaic *or* pharisaical

> *Untruthfulness, Falsehood 192; Untruth 722*

VERBS

11 **practice sophistry,** chop logic, misapply, misconstrue, misrepresent, misquote, contradict oneself, falsify, distort, strain, warp, slant, twist, gild, gloss, whitewash, dress up, embroider, disguise, camouflage, mask, juggle, rig, contrive, scheme, manipulate, machinate, propagandize, sway the crowd, misinform, mislead, pull the wool over someone's eyes, mystify, obfuscate, fudge

> *Misrepresentation 188*

12 **deceive,** dissimulate, dissemble, pretend, feign, bluff, masquerade, put on an act, put up a front, lie, fake, dodge, trick, elude, evade

> *Concealment 181; Secrecy 182; Deception 193*

13 **quibble,** cavil, split hairs, nitpick, palter, bandy words, hedge, shuffle, pettifog, equivocate, beg the question, prevaricate, beat around the bush, avoid the issue, filibuster, pussyfoot

> *Argument 329; Equivocation 380; Convolution 632*

ADVERBS

14 **sophistically,** casuistically, jesuitically, solecistically, speciously, falsely, fallaciously, illogically, irrationally, unsoundly, inconsistently, paradoxically, erroneously, groundlessly, circularly, equivocally, captiously, subtly, dubiously, spuriously, rhetorically

15 **hypocritically,** deceitfully, deceptively, dishonestly, insincerely, disingenuously, with tongue in cheek, unreliably, dodgily, sneakily, craftily, artfully, slyly, on the sly, cunningly, insidiously, perfidiously, evasively, elusively, strategically, demagogically, pharisaically

331 Demonstration

NOUNS

1 **demonstration,** display, manifestation, showing, show, exhibition, exposition, presentation, disclosure, revelation, presentment, publication, performance, expo

> *Publication 173; Disclosure 180; Appearance 264; Uncovering 614; Display 843*

2 **demonstrativeness,** openness, frankness, candor, emotionality, affection, effusiveness, expansiveness, ostentation, showiness, flashiness, flamboyance, exhibitionism, showing off, dramatics, theatrics, staginess, emotionalism, overemotionalism, histrionics

> *Display 843*

3 **explanation,** demonstration, clarification, elucidation, exposition, indication, illustration, description, depiction, delineation, illumination, exemplification, expounding, exegesis, briefing, instructions, lecture, talk, discourse, example, model, sample, specimen

■ *Education 48; Information 170; Description 202; Dissertation 203*

4 proof, demonstration, evidence, substantiation, confirmation, verification, determination, ascertainment, settlement, ratification, corroboration, bearing out, justification, affirmation, attestation, testimonial
■ *Litigation 54; Affirmation 189; Verification 336; Evidence 339*

5 demonstrability, demonstrableness, provability, verifiability, confirmability, accountability, certainty; likelihood, probability
■ *Verification 336; Probability 838; Certainty 840*

6 demonstrator, explainer, explicator, clarifier, exponent, expositor, expounder, exegete *or* exegetist, illustrator, instructor, lecturer, experimenter; displayer, producer, presenter, performer, showman, show-off, exhibitionist
■ *Education 48; Drama and Theater 136; Experiment 335*

7 mass demonstration, parade, pageant, spectacle, march, protest march, rally, protest, picket, strike, industrial action, boycott, occupation, takeover, sit-in, demo [Inf]
■ *Assembly 59; Protest 507; Disturbance 768*

8 protester, dissenter, dissident, objector, demonstrator, political activist, agitator, minority voice, voice of opposition, picket, striker
■ *Dissent 347; Defiance 416; Resistance 417; Protest 507; Agitation 684; Opposition 828*

ADJECTIVES

9 demonstrated, shown, displayed; obvious, manifest, plain, clear, express, explicit, exhibited, disclosed, exposed, revealed, made public, published, publicized, expository, expositional, exhibitional, revelatory, apodictic
■ *Publication 173; Disclosure 180; Visibility 244; Display 843*

10 demonstrative, open, unrestrained, frank, candid, warm, affectionate, effusive, expansive, ostentatious, showy, flashy, flamboyant, dramatic, stagy, theatrical, exhibitionist, emotional, exhibitionistic, emotionalistic, histrionic

11 explanatory, explicatory, illustrative, indicative, descriptive, representative, exemplificatory, exemplifying, illuminating, exegetic; explained, demonstrated, clarified, cleared up, elucidated, illustrated, described, depicted, delineated, illuminated, exemplified, expounded
■ *Description 202*

12 demonstrable, provable, confirmable, attestable, verifiable, evident, self-evident, obvious, undeniable, apparent, perspicuous, distinct, indisputable, unquestionable, positive, certain, conclusive, clear-cut
■ *Visibility 244; Evidence 339; Certainty 840*

13 proven, proved, demonstrated, shown, substantiated, confirmed, verified, determined, ascertained, settled, ratified, corroborated, borne out, justified, affirmed, attested, evidential, probative, probatory, corroborative, relevant; Q.E.D. (quod erat demonstrandum)
■ *Affirmation 189; Verification 336*

14 demonstrating, protesting, objecting, opposing, dissenting, agitating, rallying, marching, parading, on parade, striking, picketing, boycotting
■ *Assembly 59; Dissent 347; Protest 507; Opposition 828*

VERBS

15 demonstrate, show, display, exhibit, manifest, disclose, expose, point out, bring out, roll out, reveal, produce, air, put forward, publish, perform, flaunt, brandish, flourish
■ *Publication 173; Disclosure 180; Display 843*

16 explain, expound, show how, elucidate, express, indicate, unfold, make clear, clarify, illuminate, exemplify, illustrate, quote, cite, itemize, particularize, give instances, delineate, depict, describe, brief, instruct, lecture
■ *Education 48; Description 202*

17 prove, evince, substantiate, establish, evidence, validate, ratify, verify, corroborate, support, bear out, circumstantiate, justify, determine, ascertain, fix, settle, confirm, affirm, attest, prove one's point, remove all doubt, clinch
■ *Affirmation 189; Verification 336; Evidence 339*

18 appear, materialize, come forth, take a stand, stand up and be counted, speak out, raise one's voice, speak one's mind, assert oneself, draw attention to oneself, play to the gallery, perform, show off, dramatize, emotionalize
■ *Appearance 264*

19 protest, dissent, object, complain about, oppose, agitate, demonstrate, rally, march, parade, strike, picket, boycott, occupy, take over, stage a sit-in, sit in, stage a demo [Inf]
■ *Protest 507; Opposition 828*

ADVERBS

20 manifestly, obviously, plainly, clearly, publicly, in public, for all to see, in broad daylight, under one's nose, to one's face, as plain as the nose on one's face

21 demonstratively, openly, frankly, candidly, emotionally, expressively, affectionately, warmly, effusively, expansively, ostentatiously, flamboyantly, dramatically, theatrically, histrionically

22 demonstrably, verifiably, justifiably, accountably, certainly, likely, probably, in all likelihood, illuminatingly, illustratively, indicatively, descriptively, exegetically, as an example, in proof, as proof, as evidence, in evidence, in other words, that is, *id est* [L] *or* i.e., that is to say

23 protestingly, in protest, in opposition

332 Refutation

NOUNS

1 **refutation,** disproof, disproval, invalidation, negation, negativity, naysaying, nullification, annulment, disaffirmation, disconfirmation, confounding, discrediting, abrogation, disallowal, dismissal, reversal, undermining, subversion, overthrow; elenchus, conclusive argument, knockdown argument, clincher, floorer [Inf]

> *Dissuasion 179; Negation 190; Argument 329; Derision 369; Accusation 442; Disagreement 463; Prohibition 503; Cancellation 834*

2 **denial,** refutation, rebuttal, contradiction, confutation, contravention, contention, negation, disaffirmation, rejection, repudiation, renunciation, abnegation, recantation, recusancy, withdrawal, reversal, disclaimer, disavowal, disownment, apostasy

> *Negation 190; Rejection 383; Attack 418; Contention 422; Reversion 671*

3 **countercharge,** refutation, counterclaim, counteraccusation, counterstatement, counterblast, counteraction, comeback, counterargument, rebuttal, rejoinder, reply, answer, response, retort, riposte, retaliation, objection, defense, statement of defense, demurrer, demurral

> *Law 53; Litigation 54; Answer 334; Dissent 347; Defense 419; Retaliation 420; Refusal 506; Counteraction 510; Compensation 743; Opposition 828*

4 **refutability,** confutability, disprovability, defeasibility

ADJECTIVES

5 **refutable,** confutable, disprovable, defeasible

6 **refuting,** confuting, confounding, confutative, refutative, refutatory, contradictory, contrary, counteractive, retaliatory, answering, responding, contravening, rebutting, repudiating, renouncing, abnegating, disclaiming, disowning, discrediting, exploding, disproving, negating, invalidating, overturning

> *Negation 190; Disrepute 371; Refusal 506; Opposition 828*

VERBS

7 **refute,** confute, confound, disprove, prove the contrary, invalidate, nullify, annul, negate, disallow, forbid, dismiss, abrogate, dispose of, disconfirm, discredit, expose, show up, belie, deflate, undermine, overturn, overthrow, defeat, outsmart, outwit, demolish, destroy, explode, crush, squash, quash, floor, silence, have the last word, argue into a corner, argue down, knock down, shout down, not leave a leg to stand on, score points against, force to step down, show what's what

> *Obliteration 186; Derision 369; Disrepute 371; Submission 421; Destruction 523*

8 **deny,** refute, contradict, gainsay, naysay, argue against, argue with, raise doubts about, question, dispute, oppose, controvert, contravene, disaffirm, reject, repudiate, renounce, abnegate, recant, reverse, withdraw, disclaim, disavow, disown, repugn

> *Argument 329; Question 333; Uncertainty 841*

9 **countercharge,** counter, counterclaim, counterblast, rebut, parry, retaliate, retort, answer, answer back, reply, rejoin, respond, object, offer in defense, demur

> *Litigation 54; Counteraction 510*

ADVERBS

10 **in reply,** in response, in answer, as an answer, as a defense, in defense, defensively, dismissively, negatively, destructively, conclusively

11 **refutably,** confutably, disprovably, defeasibly, disputedly

333 Question

What is the answer? [Silence] In that case, what is the question? — GERTRUDE STEIN

NOUNS

1 **question,** query, doubt, uncertainty, reservation, problem, difficulty, confusion, puzzle, challenge, objection, issue, point, proposition, request, inquiry, entreaty, plea

> *Disbelief 88; Idea 327; Topic 328; Ignorance 349; Request 505; Difficulty 824; Uncertainty 841*

2 **questioning,** inquiry *or* enquiry, querying, interrogation, interpellation, inquisition, cross-questioning, cross-examination, challenge, philosophical inquiry; argument, investigation, analysis, inspection, scrutiny, survey, review, study, probe; inquest, criminal investigation, scientific investigation, research, poll, consumer *or* market research, search, quest, pumping, grilling, third degree

> *Philosophy 4; Law 53; Litigation 54; Argument 329; Experiment 335*

3 **questionnaire,** quiz, examination, test, poll, census, checklist, trial, catechism, oral examination, viva voce examination [Brit]; hearing, audition, question-time, question-and-answer session, interview

> *Sociology 2; Education 48; Religion 81; Answer 334; Qualification 340; Judgment 341*

4 **difficult question,** awkward question, personal question, burning question, sixty-four-(thousand)-dollar question, leading question; bone of contention, controversy, moot point, catch, trick question; knotty problem, poser, stumper, mystery, tough nut to crack, brainteaser, conundrum, riddle, enigma; dilemma, moral dilemma, crux, crisis, Hobson's choice, Catch-22, mind-boggler [Inf]

> *Obscurity 197; Argument 329; Unintelligibility 364; Morality 431; Disagreement 463; Trap 813; Difficulty 824*

5 easy question, silly question, stupid question, rhetorical question, formality, trivia quiz, child's play; [Inf]: cinch, breeze, pushover, piece of cake
  ◗ *Formality 406; Unimportance 800; Ease 819; Easiness 823*

6 uncertainty, questioning, doubt, doubtfulness, skepticism, Pyrrhonism, agnosticism, misgiving, mistrust, distrust, hesitation, conjecture, guesswork, anybody's guess
  ◗ *Philosophy 4; Disbelief 88; Ignorance 349; Supposition 359; Vacillation 378; Uncertainty 841*

7 questionableness, dubiousness, doubtfulness, implausibility, unlikelihood, improbability, uncertainty, wild chance, faint hope, risk, riskiness, unreliability, untrustworthiness, deceptiveness, deceitfulness, ambiguity
  ◗ *Deception 193; Obscurity 197; Sophistry 330; Equivocation 380; Improbability 839; Uncertainty 841*

8 curiosity, inquisitiveness, inquiring *or* enquiring mind, insatiable curiosity, desire *or* thirst for knowledge, wonder, puzzlement, soul-searching, probing, prying
  ◗ *Wonder 294; Curiosity 321*

9 questioner, asker, inquirer, interrogator, interpellator, investigator, journalist, interviewer, talk- *or* game-show host, quizmaster; prober, examiner, inquisitor, cross-examiner, interlocutor, lawyer, coroner, detective, inspector, scrutineer [Brit]; student, researcher, tester, experimenter, scientist, surveyor, reviewer, analyst, pollster, canvasser, consumer *or* market researcher, seeker; doubter, philosopher, skeptic, doubting Thomas, agnostic, dissenter, detractor
  ◗ *Education 48; Litigation 54; Radio and Television 172; Publication 173; Wonder 294; Thought 317; Idea 327; Experiment 335; Protest 507; Opposition 828*

10 person questioned, interviewee, talk- *or* game-show guest, examinee, candidate, defendant, suspect, witness, testifier, plaintiff

ADJECTIVES

11 questioning, requesting, pleading, inquiring, interrogative, curious, inquisitive, investigative, examining, fact-finding, knowledge-seeking, exploratory, analytic, interpellant, probing, searching, researching, questing, prying, introspective, wondering, doubting
  ◗ *Information 170; Curiosity 321; Experiment 335*

12 problematic, difficult, confusing, confused, puzzling, challenging, quizzical, tricky, sticky, knotty, tough, mysterious, riddling, enigmatic, crucial, examinational, catechismic
  ◗ *Obscurity 197; Morality 431; Difficulty 824*

13 questionable, doubtful, uncertain, moot, at issue, open to question, in question, in doubt, open to debate, debatable, under discussion, controversial, borderline, arguable, disputable, equivocal, suspicious, dubious, implausible, unlikely, improbable, chancy,

risky, unreliable, unverifiable, untrustworthy, deceptive, deceitful, ambiguous, shady, spurious
  ◗ *Deception 193; Argument 329; Sophistry 330; Equivocation 380; Improbability 839; Chance 842*

14 skeptical, doubting, Pyrrhonist, agnostic, distrustful, journalistic, scientific, criminal, philosophical, legal, experimental, conjectural, guessing, hesitating
  ◗ *Philosophy 4; Disbelief 88; Experiment 335*

15 questioned, asked, interrogated, cross-examined, cross-questioned, quizzed, examined, analyzed, researched, challenged, investigated, inspected, scrutinized, reviewed, surveyed, studied, probed, polled, canvassed, sought, grilled, pumped, given the third degree
  ◗ *Sociology 2; Litigation 54; Request 505*

VERBS

16 question, inquire *or* enquire, ask, quiz, query, plead, entreat, request, appeal, interpellate; examine, test, try, check, catechize; hear, audition, interview, sound out, pick the brains of; investigate, analyze, conduct an inquiry, inspect, scrutinize, survey, scan, review, study, fact-find, hunt the facts, probe, research, poll, canvass; search, wonder, introspect, soul-search, pry, hunt, pursue, search out, seek, quest
  ◗ *Information 170; Experiment 335; Request 505*

17 interrogate, question, examine, cross-question, cross-examine, hold for questioning, pump, grill, third-degree, run *or* put through the mill [Inf]
  ◗ *Litigation 54*

18 be questioned, be asked *or* examined *or* tested; be heard *or* auditioned *or* interviewed; be investigated *or* analyzed *or* interrogated
  ◗ *Litigation 54*

19 doubt, question, have one's doubts, have misgivings, mistrust, distrust, suspect, disbelieve, cast doubt, call into question, moot, raise the issue, make the point, propose, debate, discuss, dispute, contest, impugn, refute, confute, disagree, dissent, object, hesitate, conjecture, guess, risk, chance
  ◗ *Argument 329; Disagreement 463; Protest 507; Opposition 828; Uncertainty 841; Chance 842*

20 confuse, challenge, puzzle, pose, set a riddle, boggle, mystify, stump, trick, deceive; be confused *or* challenged *or* puzzled *or* mystified
  ◗ *Deception 193; Difficulty 824*

ADVERBS

21 questioningly, curiously, quizzically, inquisitively, probingly, searchingly, on a quest, on a mission, on a fact-finding mission; analytically, investigatively, scientifically, experimentally, agnostically, skeptically, philosophically, introspectively

22 questionably, hesitatingly, doubtfully, in doubt, dubiously, challengingly, puzzlingly, arguably, debatably, disputably, in question, under discussion, in a dilemma *or* on the horns of a dilemma, on the borderline, controversially, conjecturally, riskily, suspiciously, equivocally, unreliably, problematically, trickily, enigmatically, deceptively, deceitfully, ambiguously, implausibly, improbably

334 Answer

The answer, my friend, is blowin' in the wind.
— BOB DYLAN

NOUNS

1 **answer,** reply, response, rejoinder, responsion, respondence, replication, retort, riposte, comeback, repartee, witty repartee, short answer, snappy answer, back talk, insolence, backchat [Inf]
 ▶ *Speech, Spoken Language 205; Conversation 210; Intellect 315; Insolence 400; Discourtesy 411*

2 **acknowledgment,** answer, written reply, official reply, rescript, receipt, confirmation, RSVP
 ▶ *Communications 169; Affirmation 189; Receiving 473; Receipt 492*

3 **question and answer,** dialogue, interchange, interlocution, interview, exchange, interaction
 ▶ *Conversation 210; Argument 329; Question 333; Exchange 673; Reciprocity 729*

4 **response,** reaction, answer, retroaction, recoil, reflex, return, reflux, rebuff, backlash, kickback, recalcitration, bounceback, repercussion, reverberation, echo; responsory, antiphon, antiphonal chant, antistrophe
 ▶ *Religious Ritual 85; Music 140; Repeated Sound 235; Repetition 797*

5 **counterstatement,** answer, countercharge, counterblast, retaliation, defense, plea, argument, refutation, rebuttal, contradiction, objection, vindication, last word, parting shot, interjection
 ▶ *Litigation 54; Argument 329; Refutation 332; Retaliation 420; Vindication 441; Compensation 743*

6 **solution,** answer, result, issue, outcome, upshot, denouement, resolution, conclusion, discovery; resolving, working out, unscrambling, clearing up, sorting out, decoding; interpretation, explanation, reason, resource, contrivance, measure, plan, remedy, antidote
 ▶ *Remedy 115; Reason 319; Discovery 345; Interpretation 365; Resolution 376; Plan 387; Effect 676*

7 **numerical answer,** sum, total, difference, remainder, product, quotient
 ▶ *Mathematics 6; Completeness 761; Number 783; Calculation 784*

8 **correspondence,** answerableness, correlation, parallelism, symmetry, equivalence, congruence, conformity; twin, match, tally, agreement, aptness, fitness, suitability, relevance, usefulness
 ▶ *Sufficiency 97; Agreement 462; Parallelism 606; Sameness 730; Accord 735; Conformity 781; Usefulness 801*

9 **answerability,** responsibility, liability, accountability, obligation, duty, requirement
 ▶ *Duty 433*

10 **answerer,** respondent, replier, correspondent, interlocutor, dialectician; talker, chatterer, conversationalist; addressee, interviewee, objector, defendant; solver, planner, decoder, mathematician
 ▶ *Philosophy 4; Law 53; Litigation 54; Talkativeness 207; Question 333; Sociability 408*

ADJECTIVES

11 **answering,** replying, responsive, responding, respondent, retorting; acknowledging, confirming; backchatting, insolent; acknowledged, confirmed, returned
 ▶ *Insolence 400*

12 **reactive,** interlocutory, interactive, retroactive, recoiling, reflexive, returning, refluent, rebuffed, recalcitrant, repercussive, reverberatory, echoing, antiphonal, antithetical

13 **retaliatory,** counterstated, countercharged, counterblasted, defensive, pleading, argumentative, refutative, refutatory, rebutted, objectionable, objecting, vindicating, vindicated, interjecting, interjected
 ▶ *Argument 329; Refutation 332; Retaliation 420; Vindication 441*

14 **solvable,** soluble, resolvable, capable of *or* open to solution, answerable, decipherable

15 **solved,** answered, resolved, concluded, discovered, worked out, unscrambled, cleared up, sorted out, decoded, interpreted, interpretational, explanatory, explained, reasoned, contrived, measured, planned, remedial, antidotal
 ▶ *Remedy 115; Discovery 345; Resolution 376; Plan 387*

16 **correspondent,** corresponding, correlative, parallel, reciprocal, symmetrical, equivalent, congruent, conforming, twin, matching, tallying, agreeing, apt, fitting, suitable, relevant, useful
 ▶ *Parallelism 606; Reciprocity 729; Sameness 730; Usefulness 801*

17 **answerable,** responsible, liable, accountable, required, obliged, obligatory, under obligation, duty-bound, beholden, dutiful
 ▶ *Duty 433*

VERBS

18 **answer,** reply, respond, rejoin, riposte, retort, return, acknowledge, confirm, come back

19 **answer back,** talk back, contradict, confute, counterstate, countercharge, counterblast, refute, rebut, defend, vindicate, plead, argue, object, butt in, interject, insult, taunt, provoke, have the last word, fire the parting shot, have the final say, lip off [Inf], backchat [Inf]
 ▶ *Refutation 332; Insolence 400; Discourtesy 411*

20 **react,** exchange, interact, converse, interview, interlocute, interchange, retroact, recoil, return, rebuff, kick back, recalcitrate, bounce back, reverberate, echo

▶ *Resonance 236; Compensation 743*

21 solve, sum, score, equate, total, resolve, conclude, discover, work out, unscramble, clear up, sort out, decode, interpret, explain, reason, contrive, measure, plan, remedy

▶ *Reason 319; Discovery 345; Interpretation 365; Resolution 376; Plan 387; Calculation 784*

22 answer to, correspond, correlate, parallel, reciprocate, conform, twin, match, tally, agree, oblige, require

▶ *Agreement 462; Parallelism 606; Reciprocity 729; Sameness 730; Accord 735; Conformity 781*

23 be the answer, pertain, fit, suit, fulfill expectations, rise to the occasion, be just the thing, do the trick

▶ *Sufficiency 97; Satisfaction 273; Hope 281*

24 answer for, be responsible, act on behalf of, represent, speak for, appear for, replace, stand in for, deputize, understudy

▶ *Delegate 79; Deputy 80; Representation 187; Undertaking 391; Duty 433*

ADVERBS

25 in answer, in reply, in response, responsively, reflexively, reactively, retroactively, interactively, interchangeably, reciprocally, exchangeably, conversationally, dialectically, in conversation; argumentatively, insolently, defensively, in defense, recalcitrantly, antithetically, reverberantly, echoingly, on the rebound, on the bounce

26 conclusively, in conclusion, in the end, as it turns out, solubly

27 correspondingly, answerably, correlatively, in parallel, symmetrically, equivalently, congruently, conformingly, agreeably, aptly, fittingly, suitably, relevantly, usefully, remedially, reasonably

28 answerably, responsibly, representatively, accountably, dutifully; instead, in lieu, in place, as a replacement

335 Experiment

NOUNS

1 experiment, investigation, probe, analysis, diagnosis, assay, essay; test, acid test, trial, inquiry *or* enquiry, probation; sounding out, feeler, check, venture, bid, endeavor, effort, gambit, risk, try, trial and error, shot, go, fling, stab, crack [Inf], whack [Inf]

▶ *Judgment 341; Discovery 345; Perseverance 377; Attempt 390; Observance 465; Operation 509*

2 rehearsal, testing, trying, practice, audition, tryout, hearing, model, mock-up, rough draft, sketch, trial, trial run, single-blind experiment *or* trial, double-blind experiment *or* trial, dummy run, practice run, pilot run, dry run, road test, flight test, test flight, trial balloon; sample, control

3 experimentation, experimentalism, empiricism,

pragmatism, instrumentalism, research, research and development (R and D), investigation, examination, exploration, verification, determination, ascertainment; speculation, conjecture, guesswork, estimation, rule of thumb

▶ *Identification 184; Wonder 294; Demonstration 331; Question 333; Verification 336; Evidence 339; Prediction 358; Measurement 589; Effect 676*

4 originality, experimentation, inventiveness, creativity; daring, recklessness

▶ *Imagination 360; Newness 652; Originality 737*

5 experimenter, experimentalist, empiricist, investigator, scientist, researcher, research scientist, research worker, vivisectionist, R and D worker, analyst, assayer, quester, striver, inquirer *or* enquirer, trier, tester, test driver, test pilot, speculator, inventor, innovator, creator

6 place of experimentation, laboratory, lab, research facility *or* center *or* establishment *or* institute, field station, proving ground, think tank *or* factory, workshop, studio

7 experimental subject, testee, patient, subject, experimentee, guinea pig, laboratory animal, lab rat

ADJECTIVES

8 experimental, empirical, pragmatic, scientific, analytic, instrumental, probational, probationary, exploratory, investigative; experimenting, inquiring, trying, testing, researching; verifying, verifiable, determining, determinable; speculative, conjectural, tentative, provisional, mock, rough, trial, test, cut-and-try, dummy, practice, model, simulated

9 original, experimental, inventive; daring, enterprising, reckless, risky, chancy

▶ *Imagination 360; Newness 652; Originality 737*

10 tested, experimented upon, tried, researched, determined, verified, checked, essayed, ventured, estimated, risked, chanced

VERBS

11 experiment, experimentalize, conduct *or* run an experiment, test, try, essay, assay, try out, put on trial, put to the test *or* proof; research, sound out, test the water, explore, analyze, feel the pulse, test the depth, investigate, probe, sample, examine, inquire *or* enquire; verify, substantiate, confirm, check, check out, determine, prove, ascertain, speculate, prospect, conjecture, guess, estimate, have *or* give it a go, make a stab at, take a crack *or* whack at [Inf]

▶ *Question 333; Measurement 589*

12 rehearse, practice, audition, mock up, sketch, try out, road-test, flight-test, simulate, model

13 invent, create, innovate, dare, risk, chance, take chances, gamble, try one's luck, try one's hand, try one's strength, venture, attempt, endeavor, try, undertake

▸ *Imagination 360; Attempt 390; Originality 737; Chance 842*

ADVERBS

14 **experimentally,** empirically, scientifically, analytically, investigatively, provisionally, conjecturally, speculatively, on spec, by rule of thumb, by trial and error, by hit and miss, by guess and by gosh, on trial, on probation, under examination

15 **inventively,** experimentally, creatively, innovatively, daringly, recklessly, riskily, for the first time, as never before

336   Verification

You will find it a very good practice always to verify your references. — MARTIN JOSEPH ROUTH

NOUNS

1 **verification,** validation, confirmation, ratification, authentication, certification, documentation, seal, signature, documentation, documents, ticket, passport, visa, permit; assurance, surety, check, double check, crosscheck, collation
   ▸ *Identification 184; Affirmation 189; Qualification 340; Accuracy 350; Vindication 441; Security 464; Truth 721; Certainty 840*

2 **proof,** proving, demonstration, illustration, clarification, corroboration, support, substantiation, circumstantiation, determination, ascertainment, establishment
   ▸ *Argument 329; Demonstration 331; Experiment 335; Discovery 345*

3 **evidence,** confirmation, statement, credential, testimonial, reference, recommendation; attestation, affirmation, avouchment, avowal, averment, counterevidence
   ▸ *Information 170; Evidence 339; Qualification 340*

4 **verifier,** testifier, voucher, swearer, attestant, signatory, witness, eyewitness, spectator, bystander, passerby, informant, informer, rat [Inf], squealer [Inf]
   ▸ *Information 170; Observance 465*

ADJECTIVES

5 **verifiable,** certifiable, documented, authentic, recorded, seconded, proved, witnessed
   ▸ *History 3; Description 202; Truth 721*

6 **verificatory,** verificative, demonstrative, illustrative, evidential, determining, validating, assuring, establishing, confirming, testificatory, ratificatory, prima facie, corroborative, supportive, substantial, circumstantial, probative, collative, checking, cross-checking, double-checking

7 **verified,** validated, confirmed, ratified, authenticated, certified, documented, attested, affirmed, avouched, avowed, averred, assured, sure, certain, checked, double-checked, cross-checked, collated

VERBS

8 **verify,** validate, confirm, ratify, authenticate, certify, record, document; assure, guarantee, warrant, second, support, sign, countersign, endorse; vindicate, make certain, remove doubt, make good, ensure, check, double-check, crosscheck, recheck, collate
   ▸ *Vindication 441; Security 464*

9 **prove,** demonstrate, illustrate, clarify, clear up, show, evince, corroborate, sustain, bear out, support, substantiate, circumstantiate, determine, ascertain, establish, witness
   ▸ *Demonstration 331*

10 **testify,** attest, affirm, state, assert, avow, avouch, aver, give evidence, turn state's evidence, witness, inform; [Inf]: rat, squeal, sing, grass [Brit]
   ▸ *Litigation 54; Affirmation 189; Evidence 339; Observance 465*

ADVERBS

11 **verifiably,** certifiably, demonstratively, illustratively, corroboratively, supportively, circumstantially, authentically, genuinely, with appropriate papers, with all documents
   ▸ *Reality 719*

12 **assuredly,** certainly, surely, indisputably, really, for certain, for sure, in truth, most certainly, indeed, to be sure, sure enough, beyond question, no two ways about it
   ▸ *Knowledge 348; Truth 721; Certainty 840*

337   Discrimination

NOUNS

1 **discrimination,** selection, selectivity, selectiveness, distinction, differentiation; appraisal, sorting, graduation, separation, demarcation, division, segregation, exclusion; diagnosis, interpretation
   ▸ *Interpretation 365; Selection 382; Measurement 589; Separation 753; Exclusion 764; Arrangement 767*

2 **judiciousness,** judgment, discrimination, discretion, taste, good taste, sensitivity, sensibility, discernment, criticism, appreciation, feel, perception, insight, acumen, flair, connoisseurship, palate, refined palate, refinement, delicacy, finesse, fastidiousness, meticulousness, perfectionism; quibbling, hairsplitting
   ▸ *Taste 219; Sensitivity 267; Judgment 341; Perfection 805*

3 **prejudice,** discrimination, bias, bigotry, narrow-mindedness, narrowness, tunnel vision, small-mindedness, close-mindedness, pettiness, intolerance, insularism, parochialism, one-sidedness, partisanship, jaundice, prejudgment, inequity, unfairness
   ▸ *Obstinacy 379; Inequality 741*

4 **social discrimination,** sexual discrimination, sexism, male chauvinism, misogyny, misandry, homophobia; racial discrimination, racism, racialism, race

hatred, anti-Semitism, apartheid, segregation, ghettoization, xenophobia; ethnocentricity, ethnic cleansing, pogrom; political persecution, McCarthyism; elitism, class prejudice, class discrimination, classism, class war; fascism, jingoism, chauvinism, ultranationalism, superpatriotism; religious persecution, fanaticism, witch-hunting, heresy-hunting; age discrimination, ageism

▸ *Hate 300; Misuse 395; Attack 418; Violence 520; Exclusion 764; Class 777*

5 **favoritism,** nepotism, partisanship, positive discrimination, preferential treatment

6 **discriminator,** critic, selector, judge, connoisseur, gourmet, epicure, idealist, purist, pedant, perfectionist, quibbler, hairsplitter

7 **bigot,** dogmatist, partisan, elitist, fanatic, persecutor; sexist, chauvinist, misogynist, misandrist, homophobe; racist, racialist, anti-Semite, xenophobe; fascist, jingo, jingoist, ultranationalist, superpatriot; ageist; witch hunter; [Inf *and* Off]: male chauvinist pig, pig, redneck

▸ *Obstinacy 379*

8 **victim of discrimination,** victim of oppression, sufferer, prey, martyr, minority-group member, unfortunate, scapegoat, the persecuted, the exploited, the oppressed, slave, underdog

▸ *Adversity 848*

ADJECTIVES

9 **discriminating,** judicious, selective, tasteful, sensitive, differential, separating, discerning, divisional, critical, diagnostic, interpretational, appreciative, epicurean, perceptive, insightful, refined, delicate, fastidious, meticulous, perfectionist, pedantic, quibbling, hairsplitting, choosy, picky, finicky

▸ *Carefulness 325; Sophistry 330; Selection 382; Separation 753*

10 **judged,** selected, distinct, discrete, diagnosed, interpreted, differentiated, sorted, graded, graduated, separated, excluded, demarcated, divided; segregated, discriminated against, persecuted, exploited, oppressed

▸ *Judgment 341; Exclusion 764*

11 **discriminatory,** prejudicial, one-sided, partisan, jaundiced, inequitable, unfair, partial, preferential, nepotistic; prejudiced, biased, bigoted, narrow-minded, blinkered, small-minded, close-minded, petty, intolerant, dogmatic, insular, parochial; elitist, classist, ageist, sexist, misogynist, misogynous, misandrist, misandrous, homophobic, racist, racialist, anti-Semitic, xenophobic, jingoistic, ethnocentric, fascist, ultranationalistic, superpatriotic, chauvinistic, fanatical

VERBS

12 **discriminate,** select, choose, favor, prefer, judge, distinguish, differentiate, discern, pick, pick out, pick and choose, compare and contrast, sort, analyze; grade, graduate, separate, demarcate, divide, segregate, exclude; diagnose, interpret; quibble, split hairs, separate

the sheep from the goats, separate the wheat from the chaff

▸ *Judgment 341; Selection 382*

13 **prejudge,** forjudge, precondemn, bias, prejudice, warp, not see beyond one's nose, put on blinkers, blind oneself, close one's mind, have tunnel vision, listen with deaf ears

▸ *Ignorance 349; Influence 512; Distortion 627*

14 **discriminate against,** criticize, persecute, harass, treat unfairly, oppress, exploit, witch-hunt, pick on [Inf]

ADVERBS

15 **discriminatingly,** selectively, distinctly, separately, differentially, divisively, diagnostically

16 **judiciously,** judgmentally, with discretion, tastefully, sensitively, discerningly, critically, analytically, appreciatively, perceptively, insightfully, delicately, fastidiously, meticulously, pedantically

17 **prejudicially,** preferentially, dogmatically, inequitably, unfairly, narrow-mindedly, close-mindedly, small-mindedly; intolerantly, parochially, fanatically, homophobically, racially, xenophobically, ethnocentrically, chauvinistically, jingoistically, ultranationalistically, superpatriotically

338 Lack of Discrimination

NOUNS

1 **lack of discrimination,** indiscrimination, unselectiveness, catholicity, catholic tastes, uncriticalness, indifference; color blindness, tone-deafness

2 **impartiality,** equanimity, fairness, justice, neutrality, nonalignment, mugwumpism, disinterestedness, tolerance, fair-mindedness, broad-mindedness; antidiscrimination, political correctness

▸ *Disinterestedness 443; Equality 740; Freedom 829*

3 **tastelessness,** bad taste, insensitivity, indelicacy, vulgarity, promiscuity, lack of restraint, negligence, thoughtlessness, indiscretion, carelessness, inaccuracy

▸ *Insensitivity 268; Immorality 432; Self-Indulgence 456; Vulgarity 535*

4 **indiscrimination,** randomness, generality, universality, vagueness, inexactitude, confusion, muddle, jumble, mixture, heap

▸ *Mixture 751; Inclusion 763; Generality 778*

ADJECTIVES

5 **undiscriminating,** unselective, catholic, omnivorous, undiscerning, undifferentiating, uncritical, indifferent, color-blind, tone-deaf; unfussy, unfastidious

▸ *Indifference 289*

6 **impartial,** equanimous, fair, fair-minded, neutral, nonaligned, nonpartisan, mugwumpish; disinterested, unbiased, unprejudiced, nonjudgmental, uncriticizing, tolerant, liberal, broad-minded; antidiscriminatory, politically correct

▸ *Morality 431; Disinterestedness 443; Moderation 521*

7 unrefined, tasteless, indelicate, insensitive, coarse, vulgar, promiscuous, unrestrained, lax, loose, sloppy, casual, negligent, thoughtless, indiscreet, slipshod, careless, unmeticulous, inaccurate, cursory, perfunctory
▸ *Negligence 326; Immorality 432; Self-Indulgence 456; Vulgarity 535*

8 indiscriminate, random, haphazard, unsystematic, mixed, assorted, unsorted, unselected, miscellaneous, motley; unorganized, disorganized, confused, jumbled, muddled, intermingled, disordered, mixed up, chaotic, scrambled, higgledy-piggledy
▸ *Mixture 751; Disorder 766*

9 vague, indistinct, indistinctive, inexact, desultory, undefined, ill-defined, undifferentiated, undistinguished, undistinguishable, interchangeable, standard, average, alike
▸ *Average 742; Generality 778*

VERBS

10 be indiscriminate, not discriminate, see no difference between, make no distinction; disregard, generalize, universalize; swallow *or* fall for hook, line, and sinker [Inf]; take as one, roll into one, muddle, confound, jumble, mix, heap, lump together, smooth over the differences, average out
▸ *Mixture 751; Whole 759; Inclusion 763*

11 be impartial, remain neutral, sit on the fence, refuse to judge *or* take sides, keep an open mind, see both sides, tolerate, live with, accept; be politically correct
▸ *Moderation 521; Equality 740; Middle 772*

ADVERBS

12 unselectively, indifferently, imperceptively, uncritically, insensitively

13 impartially, fairly, neutrally, equanimously, tolerantly, disinterestedly

14 tastelessly, coarsely, indelicately, promiscuously

15 indiscriminately, vaguely, universally, generally, commonly, indistinguishably, haphazardly, inexactly, randomly, inaccurately, in a muddle, in a mess, in a heap, all mixed up together

339 Evidence

Some circumstantial evidence is very strong, as when you find a trout in the milk. — HENRY DAVID THOREAU

NOUNS

1 evidence, grounds, reason, premise, basis for belief; data, information, facts, relevant facts, record, reference, report, intelligence, lowdown [Inf]
▸ *Information 170; Description 202; Reason 319; Knowledge 348*

2 proof, verification, demonstration, corroboration, substantiation, confirmation, certainty, smoking gun

▸ *Demonstration 331; Verification 336; Certainty 840*

3 indication, indicator, pointer, sign, token, symptom, clue, remains, mark, track, trail, footprint, wake, vapor trail, spoor, scent; evidence, manifestation, obviousness, appearance, self-evidence, visibility, prominence
▸ *Sign 183; Visibility 244; Appearance 264; Discovery 345; Pursuit 385*

4 legal evidence, testimony, statement, declaration, admission, deposition; documentary evidence, exhibit, confession, affidavit; circumstantial evidence, hearsay evidence, incriminating evidence, inadmissible evidence
▸ *Litigation 54*

5 counterevidence, answer, defense, rebuttal, surrebuttal, rejoinder, surrejoinder; retaliation, contradiction, confutation, refutation, denial, demurral; comeback, contraindication, counterstatement, countercharge, counterblast, counterreply, counterclaim

6 documentation, document, authority, papers, case history, record, testimonial, recommendation, character reference, reference, credential; curriculum vitae (CV), résumé, warrant, warranty, ticket, chit, receipt, voucher, passport, identity card, ID, visa, permit, pass
▸ *Authority 52; Identification 184; Record 185; Qualification 340*

7 witness, testifier, attestant, attester, attestor, attestator; defendant, plaintiff, deponent; spectator, eyewitness, bystander, passerby, informer, informant
▸ *Litigation 54*

ADJECTIVES

8 evidential, evidentiary, significant, factual, relevant, informed, witnessed, attested; circumstantial, direct, documented, documentary, recorded, reported; corroborative, probative, constructive, indicative, pointing, demonstrative, telltale, authentic, empirical, verified, confirmed, proved, certain

9 evident, apparent, manifest, obvious, self-evident, visible, prominent, ostensible, clear
▸ *Appearance 264*

10 counterevident, countering, answering, defending, rebutting, denying, contradictory

VERBS

11 make evident, show, evince, show signs of, represent, speak for itself, suggest, indicate, imply

12 give evidence, witness, testify, swear, take the oath, attest, depose, affirm, assert, declare, state, bear witness to, swear to, allege; turn state's evidence, inform

13 counter, answer, retort, rebut, rejoin, retaliate, contradict, deny, demur, counterstate, countercharge, counterblast, counterreply, counterclaim

14 prove, verify, validate, corroborate, support, sustain, back up, circumstantiate, authenticate, confirm, certify, countersign, endorse; document, record, warrant, vouch for

15 as evidence, in evidence, in proof, certainly, factually, authentically, relevantly, significantly, circumstantially, indicatively, demonstratively, reportedly, with reason, on good grounds

16 evidently, manifestly, obviously, apparently, self-evidently, visibly, ostensibly, clearly, prominently, on display, for all to see, in broad daylight

17 to the contrary, on the contrary, contrarily, *au contraire* [Fr], on the other hand

340 Qualification

NOUNS

1 qualification, qualifiedness, eligibility, suitability, suitableness, suitedness, acceptability, appropriateness, propriety; fitness, fittedness, preparedness, readiness; adequacy, sufficiency, efficacy, appositeness, relevance, applicability; aptness, aptitude, ability, ableness, capability, capableness, worthiness, deservedness, dueness, entitlement; competence, efficiency, proficiency, potentiality, equipment
> *Skillfulness 127; Preparation 388; Usefulness 801*

2 ability, facility, faculty, capability, capacity, quality, mastery, attribute, tendency, endowment, natural power, innate ability, talent, skill, genius, flair, gift, bent, knack, what it takes, know-how, green thumb
> *Skillfulness 127; Information 170; Knowledge 348; Wisdom 352*

3 permission, authorization, empowerment, enablement, investment, endowment, equipment
> *Authority 52; Approval 437; Permission 502*

4 authorization, permit, license, documentation, certification, certificate, diploma, degree, licentiate, baccalaureate, examination *or* test results, skills, expertise, experience, record, background, history, references, credentials, testimonial
> *Education 48; Authority 52; Skillfulness 127; Permission 502*

5 modification, qualification, adjustment, adaptation, alteration, change, variation, modulation, coordination, regulation, attunement, improvement, reconciliation, palliation, mitigation, softening, allowance, extenuating circumstances
> *Refinement 534; Accord 735; Compensation 743; Improvement 807*

6 specification, qualification, frame of reference, terms of reference, definition, determination, limitation, restriction, circumscription, bounding, confinement, control, check, demarcation, delimitation, prescription, proscription, mandate, bounds; conditions, criteria, grounds, reservations, parameters; stipulation, obligation, requisite, prerequisite, provision, proviso, limiting condition, boundary condition, escape clause, saving clause, small print

> *Provision 89; Contract 459; Enclosure 619; Limit 620*

ADJECTIVES

7 qualified, eligible, suitable, suited, well-adapted, acceptable, appropriate; fit, fitting, fitted, prepared, ready; adequate, sufficient, efficacious, apposite, relevant; apt, able, capable, worthy, deserved, due, entitled, merited; competent, efficient, proficient, professional, businesslike, equipped, endowed, talented, gifted, masterful, expert, skilled, skillful, experienced, practiced, versed, tried and tested, cut out for

8 authorized, certified, empowered, enabled, permitted, licensed, entitled, allowed, documented

9 modified, qualified, adjusted, adapted, altered, changed, varied, variational, modulated, coordinated, conditioned, regulated, attuned, improved, reconciled, palliative, palliated, mitigatory, mitigated, softened, moderated

10 conditional, qualificatory, reserved, stipulatory, stipulated, parametric, obligatory, requisitional, provisional, provisory, specified, defined, definitional, mandatory, determined, limiting, limited, restricted, restrictive, circumscribed, contingent, bound, confined, controlled, checked, curbed, demarcated, delimited, prescribed, prescriptive, proscribed, proscriptive

VERBS

11 qualify, be qualified, be eligible, suit, fit, suffice, apply, deserve, merit; be able, know how, know one's job, have the knack, be trained (in), pass, get into the final, get through

12 permit, authorize, empower, enable, invest, endow, equip, license, certify

13 modify, qualify, adjust, adapt, alter, change, vary, color, modulate, coordinate, regulate, attune, improve, reconcile, temper, palliate, tone down, mitigate, moderate, soften, allow, extenuate, make allowances, make exception, set apart, split hairs

14 specify, qualify, frame, define, determine, limit, restrain, restrict, circumscribe, bind, confine, control, check, demarcate, delimit, prescribe, proscribe, stipulate, reserve, oblige, require, state terms, propose conditions, set criteria

ADVERBS

15 capably, ably, masterfully, competently, efficiently, proficiently, professionally, skillfully, acceptably, aptly, appropriately, properly, fittingly, readily, worthily, deservedly

16 conditionally, with qualifications, provisionally, contingently, restrictively, proscriptively, prescriptively, with the proviso, with strings attached

341 Judgment

And why beholdest thou the mote that is in thy brother's eye, but considerest not the beam that is in thine own eye? — BIBLE: MATTHEW

NOUNS

1 **judgment,** discrimination, discernment; distinction, differentiation, selection, choice; discretion, taste, wisdom, sense; judging, adjudication, arbitration, umpirage; faculty of judgment, reasoning, ratiocination; deduction, inference; dissertation, corollary, consideration, view, belief, opinion; assessment, evaluation, speculation, conjecture, surmise, sensibleness, guesswork, guess, estimate, estimation, calculation; rating, valuation, appraisal, appreciation; survey, inspection, report, review, notice, remark, comment; critique, criticism, constructive criticism, censure, value judgment, second opinion; public opinion, vox populi, vote, referendum, plebiscite
   ▶ *Belief 87; Reason 319; Discrimination 337; Wisdom 352; Selection 382; Approval 437; Disapproval 438; Calculation 784*

2 **verdict,** judgment, adjudication, summing up, recapitulation, decision, conclusion, ruling, finding, award, sentence, pronouncement, order, edict, decree, decree nisi, decree absolute, acquittal, condemnation, execution of judgment
   ▶ *Litigation 54; Summary 204; Command 425*

3 **place of judgment,** tribunal, seat of justice, judgment seat, inquisition, Inquisition, Areopagus, the throne; bar of justice, court of conscience, confessional, Judgment Day; forum, board, curia, council; public opinion, vox populi, electorate, judiciary, bench; bench of judges, panel of judges, judge and jury, judicial assembly; woolsack [Brit]

4 **judgment day,** day of judgment, Last Judgment, Last Day, Doomsday, millennium, resurrection day, afterlife, hereafter
   ▶ *Religion 81*

5 **judge,** adjudicator, jurist, chief justice, justice; arbiter, umpire, referee, mediator, arbitrator; assessor, valuer, appraiser; surveyor, inspector, examiner, tester, reporter, commentator, censor, editor, critic, reviewer; expert, connoisseur, adviser, counselor
   ▶ *Litigation 54; Mediation 75; Advice 176; Discrimination 337*

6 **jury,** juror, foreman *or* foreperson of the jury, grand jury, petty *or* petit jury, coroner's jury, trial jury
   ▶ *Litigation 54*

ADJECTIVES

7 **judging,** discriminating, discerning; selecting, selective; criticizing, critical, judgmental, inquisitional; moralistic, sententious; approving, appreciative; disapproving, condemnatory, censorious
   ▶ *Discrimination 337; Selection 382; Approval 437; Disapproval 438*

8 **judicious,** discerning, discriminating; sensitive, accurate; right, just, fair, unbiased, dispassionate; wise, shrewd; judicial, judicatory, juridical

▶ *Discrimination 337; Wisdom 352; Right 429; Disinterestedness 443*

9 **judged,** submitted for judgment, under consideration, on trial, up for trial, sub judice, before the bar

VERBS

10 **judge,** umpire, referee; sit in judgment, arbitrate, hear, hear the case, commit for trial, try; sum up, award, decree, adjudge, adjudicate, decide, conclude, find, find for, find against, determine, settle, settle the matter, rule, pronounce sentence, pass judgment, charge the jury, bring a verdict, acquit, find guilty; condemn, censure, censor, criticize, disapprove of, approve of
    ▶ *Litigation 54; Approval 437; Disapproval 438*

11 **estimate,** judge, gauge, calculate, reckon, size up, evaluate, assess, value, appraise, rate; regard, deem, esteem, think, believe; guess, surmise, conjecture, judge by eye, weigh, ponder over, consider, reason, deduce, infer, examine, investigate, inspect, survey; vet [Inf], make a report on, review, criticize, comment on, scan, check, check out
    ▶ *Reason 319; Calculation 784*

ADVERBS

12 **judicially,** judiciously, selectively, critically, approvingly, disapprovingly; discerningly, discriminatingly; judgmentally, moralistically; rightly, justly, fairly, dispassionately; wisely, shrewdly

13 **considering,** taking into account, all things considered, everything being equal, all things being equal

342 Misjudgment

"No, no!" said the Queen. "Sentence first — verdict afterwards." — LEWIS CARROLL

NOUNS

1 **misjudgment,** poor judgment; miscalculation, misconception, misconstruction, misinterpretation; wrong impression; misunderstanding, cross-purposes; inexactness, underestimation, overestimation, undervaluation, overvaluation; false reading, distortion, deception, fallacy, fallibility; gullibility, self-deception, fool's paradise, wrong end of the stick
   ▶ *Deception 193; Lack of Discrimination 338; Overestimation 343; Underestimation 344*

2 **mistake,** error, blunder, howler, bungling, botch, bloomer, faux pas, slip; misbelief, miscalculation, misconception, misconstruction, miscarriage, misdiagnosis, misinterpretation, misimpression, misinformation, misprision; [Inf]: blooper, boo-boo, miscue
   ▶ *Error 351*

3 **injustice,** miscarriage of justice, mistrial, packed jury; lynch law, kangaroo court; partiality, partisanship, one-sidedness; preferential treatment, favoritism, nepotism; intolerance, discrimination, unfairness, inequality

▶ *Inequality 741*

4 **unfair treatment,** bias, prejudice, prejudicial treatment, chauvinism, sectarianism, provincialism, parochialism, insularity, xenophobia, racism, racialism, racial prejudice, racial intolerance, apartheid, segregation, anti-Semitism, sexism, ageism, homophobia; bigotry, fanaticism, narrow-mindedness, tunnel vision, narrow mind, closed mind, jaundiced eye, foul play

> ▶ *Hate 300; Discrimination 337*

5 **prejudgment,** preconception, preconceived idea, *parti pris* [Fr], mind made up, fixed idea, *idée fixe* [Fr], fixation, obsession, predetermination, foregone conclusion, presupposition

> ▶ *Predetermination 384*

ADJECTIVES

6 **misjudging,** in error, mistaken, wrong, wrongheaded, muddled, fallible, gullible, misguided, misled, deluded, deceived

> ▶ *Deception 193; Error 351*

7 **unjust,** unfair, discriminatory, prejudicial; partial, partisan, subjective, one-sided, predisposed, preferential; intolerant, biased, prejudiced; jaundiced, warped, twisted, chauvinistic, sectarian, provincial, parochial, insular, xenophobic, racist, anti-Semitic, sexist, ageist, homophobic; snobbish, bigoted, fanatical, narrow-minded, narrow, hidebound, prejudged, preconceived, fixed

> ▶ *Discrimination 337; Predetermination 384; Distortion 627*

8 **misjudged,** misunderstood, wrongly accused, unfairly treated, misconstrued, misinterpreted; underestimated, overestimated, undervalued, overvalued, underrated, overrated, wrong, mistaken, ill-timed, untimely, inconvenient, ill-advised, foolish

> ▶ *Overestimation 343; Underestimation 344; Error 351; Folly 353; Untimeliness 660; Inconvenience 804*

VERBS

9 **misjudge,** miscalculate, misreckon, misinterpret, misconstrue, misunderstand, misconceive, misread, misdiagnose, misdo, get wrong, mistake, twist, distort, let slip, waste an opportunity, miss, trip, slip, stumble, blunder, bungle; time badly, mistime, overestimate, underestimate, misestimate, overvalue, undervalue, overrate, underrate; be unable to see the forest *or* woods for the trees, get hold of the wrong end of the stick

> ▶ *Overestimation 343; Underestimation 344; Error 351; Distortion 627*

10 **be unjust,** treat unfairly, discriminate against, take sides, prejudge, preconceive

> ▶ *Discrimination 337*

11 **bias,** prejudice, jaundice, warp, twist, predispose

> ▶ *Distortion 627*

ADVERBS

12 **misguidedly,** mistakenly, in error, wrongly, fallibly, gullibly, foolishly

13 **unjustly,** unfairly, discriminatorily; partially, subjectively, preferentially, intolerantly, chauvinistically, parochially, fanatically, narrow-mindedly

343 Overestimation

NOUNS

1 **overestimation,** overvaluation, overrating; misjudgment, miscalculation; overconfidence, rashness, overoptimism, idealism; overweening pride, conceit, hubris, arrogance, egomania; exaggeration, overstatement, hyperbole, hype [Inf]; megalomania, vanity, showing off, blowing one's own horn [Inf]

> ▶ *Exaggeration 194; Rashness 286; Misjudgment 342; Vanity 402; Showiness 404*

2 **overestimator,** optimist, hopeful, idealist; megalomaniac, panjandrum; exaggerator, promoter

3 **figurative overestimation,** much ado about nothing, tempest *or* storm in a teacup, pipe dream, castles in the air *or* in Spain, fool's paradise; fuss, hot air [Inf], big deal [Inf]

ADJECTIVES

4 **overestimating,** overconfident, rash; overoptimistic, overenthusiastic; hubristic, arrogant

> ▶ *Hope 281; Rashness 286*

5 **overestimated,** overvalued, overrated; overpriced, dear, expensive; misjudged, exaggerated, overpraised; not all it's cracked up to be [Inf]

> ▶ *Exaggeration 194*

VERBS

6 **overestimate,** overvalue, overrate, overprize; overprice, price oneself out of the market, overcharge, misjudge, miscalculate; exaggerate, overstate, make a mountain out of a molehill, make a fuss about; maximize, make the most of; be too good to be true; overpraise, hype [Inf]

> ▶ *Exaggeration 194; Misjudgment 342; Costliness 496*

ADVERBS

7 **overoptimistically,** idealistically; overenthusiastically, hyperbolically, overconfidently; rashly, arrogantly, vainly

344 Underestimation

NOUNS

1 **underestimation,** undervaluation, underrating, misjudgment, miscalculation; underestimate, conservative estimate, minimization; deprecation, self-deprecation, depreciation, self-depreciation, detraction, understatement, litotes; self-effacement, humility, modesty; pessimism, defeatism, negative outlook, cynicism

▶ *Understatement 195; Hopelessness 282; Humility 298; Misjudgment 342; Affectation 367; Modesty 403; Disparagement 440*

2 underestimator, pessimist, defeatist, cynic; minimizer, detractor

ADJECTIVES

3 underestimating, deprecating, depreciatory, detracting, disparaging, scornful, minimizing; conservative, moderate; pessimistic, defeatist; modest, humble

▶ *Hopelessness 282; Humility 298; Modesty 403; Disparagement 440*

4 underestimated, undervalued, underrated; misjudged, miscalculated; underpriced, cheap

▶ *Misjudgment 342; Cheapness 497*

VERBS

5 underestimate, undervalue, underrate, misprize, misjudge, miscalculate; underprice, hold cheap, scorn, set no store by, not do justice to; minimize, play down, understate; make little of, make light of, shrug off, soft-pedal [Inf]; pooh-pooh, belittle, disparage, underpraise

▶ *Understatement 195; Misjudgment 342; Derision 369; Disparagement 440; Cheapness 497*

ADVERBS

6 pessimistically, cynically, scornfully, disparagingly; conservatively, moderately, modestly, humbly

345 Discovery

NOUNS

1 discovery, finding, location; accidental discovery, serendipity; encounter, meeting; spotting, perception, sight, sighting, glimpse; observation, recognition, identification

▶ *Identification 184; Vision 242; Location 565*

2 detection, ferreting out, tracking down, digging up; catching, catch; excavation, archaeology; uncovering, exposure, unveiling, unmasking, disclosure, eyeopener

▶ *Disclosure 180; Question 333; Uncovering 614*

3 finding out, learning, ascertaining; realization, understanding, enlightenment, illumination; heuristic

▶ *Information 170; Knowledge 348; Intelligibility 363*

4 invention, designing, design, device, contrivance; idea, inspiration, origination, creation, pioneering; exploration, experiment; rediscovery

▶ *Experiment 335; Production 522; Beginning 771*

5 find, discovery, lucky find, treasure-trove, strike

6 detector, metal detector, lie detector, polygraph; sonar, radar, probe, sensor; divining rod *or* dowsing rod

7 discoverer, finder, spotter, scout, observer; dowser, water diviner; prospector; archaeologist; detective, private detective, spy, mole; inventor, designer, author, founder, originator; forerunner, herald, pioneer, pathfinder, explorer, traveler; private eye [Inf], gumshoe [Inf]

ADJECTIVES

8 discovering, finding; on the trail, on the right track, warm; revelatory, revealing, serendipitous; inventive, pioneering; exploratory, experimental

▶ *Disclosure 180; Experiment 335*

9 discovered, found, located, seen, spotted; unearthed, uncovered, exposed; unmasked, revealed

▶ *Vision 242; Location 565; Uncovering 614*

10 discoverable, findable; recognizable, identifiable; perceptible, detectable; heuristic

VERBS

11 discover, find, locate, place; come across, come upon, happen upon, stumble upon *or* on, hit upon, encounter, meet with, meet; see, spy, espy, spot, descry, perceive, sight, glimpse, catch a glimpse of, set eyes on; notice, observe, watch; recognize, identify

▶ *Identification 184; Vision 242; Location 565*

12 detect, ferret out, worm out; track down, run down, run to earth, smell out, sniff out, get wind of; get warm, find a clue; ensnare, catch, catch red-handed, catch in the act; acquire, unearth, disinter, dig up, uncover, bring to light, expose, lay bare; unveil, lift the veil, unmask; disclose, reveal, divulge, betray, spill the beans [Inf]; show up, show one's true colors

▶ *Disclosure 180; Question 333; Pursuit 385; Uncovering 614*

13 find out, find out about, learn, ascertain, determine; realize, understand, catch on, see the light, get it [Inf]

▶ *Information 170; Knowledge 348; Intelligibility 363*

14 invent, design, devise, contrive; have an idea, originate, create, pioneer; herald, be in the vanguard, lead the way, explore, rediscover

▶ *Idea 327; Experiment 335; Production 522; Beginning 771*

15 be discovered, be unmasked, come to light; appear, show up, turn up

▶ *Appearance 264*

ADVERBS

16 originally, experimentally, inventively; at first sight, at a glance, apparently; identifiably, recognizably; obviously, manifestly, revealingly

346 Assent

NOUNS

1 assent, agreement, corroboration, confirmation, affirmation, consent; acquiescence, acceptance, approval, approbation; admission, acknowledgment, recognition, confession; sanction, permission; concordance, harmony, accord, concurrence, consensus; unanimity, single voice

▶ *Affirmation 189; Willingness 373; Approval 437; Agreement 462; Permission 502; Similarity 733; Accord 735*

2 yes, affirmative; ratification, validation, certification; endorsement, nod of approval, seal of approval, rub-

ber stamp, green light, thumbs up, aye, yea, OK, amen; yeah [Inf], the nod [Inf]
> *Affirmation 189; Approval 437; Permission 502*

3 **assenter,** conformist, fellow traveler, ally, collaborator, sympathizer; supporter, subscriber, endorser, seconder, signatory, underwriter, consenter; yes-man, flatterer, sycophant, toady, fawner, back scratcher; hypocrite, fair-weather friend
> *Servility 401; Flattery 439; Support 605; Conformity 781; Cooperation 827*

ADJECTIVES

4 **assenting,** agreeing, in agreement, concurring, concordant; unanimous, solid, like-minded; confirmative, affirmative, approving, consenting, supportive, sympathetic, cooperative, collaborating; willing, acquiescent, compliant

5 **agreed,** carried; signed, sealed, ratified, validated; countersigned, underwritten

VERBS

6 **assent,** agree, concur, see eye to eye, agree with, go along with, agree in principle; like the idea, welcome, jump at the chance, go all the way with; echo, say the same as, chime in, rubber-stamp, corroborate, confirm; affirm, approve, say yes, nod, consent to, give the green light, give the OK *or* O.K. *or* okay, give thumbs up; sanction, authorize, permit, allow; concede, give in, grant, admit, acknowledge, recognize, confess; support, subscribe to, second, vote for, endorse, authenticate, ratify; validate, countersign, underwrite
> *Affirmation 189; Approval 437; Agreement 462; Permission 502; Support 605; Accord 735*

7 **assent to,** acquiesce, accede, comply, accept; tolerate, bear, put up with; submit, yield, defer, let the ayes have it, sign on the dotted line; conform, jump on the bandwagon, follow the crowd
> *Submission 421; Conformity 781*

ADVERBS

8 **unanimously,** with one voice, as one, to a man, with one accord; affirmatively, in the affirmative, willingly, acquiescently, compliantly

347 Dissent

NOUNS

1 **dissent,** difference of opinion, variance, difference, differences, conflict, friction, disagreement; dispute, controversy, quarrel, altercation, feud
> *Contention 422; Disagreement 463; Disturbance 768*

2 **disapproval,** disapprobation, rejection, refusal, denial, negation; no, nay, negative, red light, objection, thumbs down; demur, demurral, protest, complaint, dissatisfaction
> *Negation 190; Dissatisfaction 274; Rejection 383; Disapproval 438; Prohibition 503; Refusal 506*

3 **dissentience,** dissenting, quarrelsomeness, dissidence, dissension, discordance, discord, disharmony, disunion, intolerance; recrimination, unpleasantness, disobedience, noncooperation, opposition, rebellion, sedition, strike, walkout; nonconformity, nonconformism, unorthodoxy, counterculture, sectarianism, separatism, factionalism; disaffection, secession, withdrawal
> *Disobedience 427; Disagreement 463; Separation 753; Nonconformity 782; Opposition 828*

4 **faction,** split, schism, separation, parting of the ways, rift, breach, rupture, severance of relations, division
> *Separation 753*

5 **dissenter,** dissident, dissentient, nonconformist, protestant, recusant; sectarian, partisan, separatist, schismatic, factionalist; malcontent, protester, caviler, critic, detractor; conscientious objector, passive resister; opponent, disputer, heckler, scold, shrew; odd man out, unconventionalist, angry young man, bohemian, hippie, dropout

6 **dissenters,** the opposition, the noes, the nays; splinter group, breakaway group, dissidents, separatists, faction, minority
> *Disobedience 427; Separation 753; Opposition 828*

ADJECTIVES

7 **dissenting,** dissentient, differing, of another opinion, at odds; opposing, conflicting, heterodox, unorthodox, heretical; skeptical, unconvinced, dissatisfied; protesting, unwilling, resistant; intolerant, dissident, seditious, divisive, separatist, schismatic; party-minded, partisan, clannish, sectarian; nonconformist, schismatical, secessionist, seceding, breakaway, rebel, recusant, rebellious; protestant, quarreling, arguing, contentious, disputatious
> *Unwillingness 375; Contention 422; Disagreement 463; Separation 753; Nonconformity 782*

VERBS

8 **dissent,** disagree, differ, beg to differ; take issue, quarrel, clash, conflict, dispute, confute; be at odds with, fall out with, have differences with *or* a difference of opinion with, argue with; schismatize, separate, divide, secede, break away from, rebel
> *Defiance 416; Contention 422; Disagreement 463; Protest 507; Divergence 703; Separation 753*

9 **refuse,** say no, shake one's head; disapprove, object, demur, protest, complain; oppose, contradict, negate, deny, reject, give the red light, give thumbs down
> *Negation 190; Dissatisfaction 274; Argument 329; Rejection 383; Resistance 417; Disapproval 438; Prohibition 503; Refusal 506; Opposition 828*

ADVERBS

10 **dissentiently,** dissentingly, protestingly, in protest, unwillingly; divisively, rebelliously, contentiously

348 Knowledge

I have taken all knowledge to be my province.
— FRANCIS BACON

NOUNS

1 **knowledge,** knowing, ken, cognition, cognizance, gnosis, realization, perception, understanding, comprehension, apprehension, grasp, mastery; awareness, consciousness, acquaintance, familiarity, illumination, enlightenment; foresight, foreknowledge, intuition, discernment, savoir-faire, *Aufklärung* [Ger], savvy [Inf]
   ◗ *Intuition 320; Foresight 357; Intelligibility 363*

2 **information,** data, common knowledge, general knowledge, facts; know-how, expertise, skill, aptitude, forte, métier; touch, technique, accomplishment; partial knowledge, smattering, inkling, intimation, suspicion
   ◗ *Skillfulness 127; Information 170; Ignorance 349*

3 **learning,** lore, erudition, sagacity, wisdom; scholarship, letters, omniscience, polymathy; proficiency, mastery, craftsmanship, literacy, numeracy; acquired knowledge, book learning, bookishness, education, schooling, instruction, teaching; culture, cultivation, civilization; science, arts, humanities; self-education, self-instruction; accomplishments, acquirements; attainment, experience, practical experience, practice
   ◗ *Wisdom 352*

4 **intellect,** mind, brain, intelligence, wit, faculty, brains, brain power, smarts [Inf], street smarts [Inf]
   ◗ *Intellect 315*

5 **knowledgeable person,** mastermind, genius, sage, wise man, savant; mine of information, walking encyclopedia, polymath; expert, authority; scholar, don, academic, pedant, teacher, scientist; intellectual, highbrow, bluestocking, autodidact, egghead [Inf]
   ◗ *Intellect 315; Wisdom 352*

6 **academia,** groves of academe, intelligentsia, literati, illuminati

ADJECTIVES

7 **knowledgeable,** knowing, well-informed, learned, erudite; all-knowing, omniscient, polymathic, encyclopedic; sagacious, wise, enlightened, informed, instructed, trained, cognizant, qualified; experienced, practiced, versed, competent, skilled, proficient, efficient, expert, well-versed, good at; aware, conscious, mindful, attentive; acquainted with, no stranger to, familiar with, conversant with, briefed, primed, *au fait* [Fr], au courant, in the know, in the picture; shrewd, astute, perceptive, smart, street-smart, streetwise; brainy [Inf], wise to [Inf]
   ◗ *Skillfulness 127; Information 170; Intellect 315; Wisdom 352*

8 **literate,** numerate, schooled, educated, well-educated; scholarly, donnish, academic, pedantic, intellectual, highbrow
   ◗ *Education 48; Intellect 315*

9 **known,** verified, proved, true, certain; discovered, explored; recognized, perceived, seen, knowable, heard of; well-known, famous, infamous, notorious, celebrated, renowned; common, public, no secret
   ◗ *Evidence 339; Truth 721; Certainty 840*

VERBS

10 **know,** understand, comprehend, apprehend, realize, conceive, appreciate; recognize, identify, distinguish, discern, catch on, perceive, see, master, retain; savvy [Inf]
   ◗ *Identification 184; Intellect 315; Intelligibility 363*

11 **know by heart,** know inside out *or* backward *or* backward and forward; learn by rote, memorize; know all the answers, know from A to Z, know full well; [Inf]: know one's stuff, know the ropes, know like the back of one's hand
   ◗ *Memory 354*

12 **get to know,** acquaint oneself with, familiarize oneself with, experience; study, con, learn, discover, find out; take in, grasp, get wise to [Inf]
   ◗ *Discovery 345*

13 **cause to know,** tell, inform, brief, prime; teach, instruct, school, educate, train, coach
   ◗ *Education 48; Information 170*

ADVERBS

14 **knowledgeably,** knowingly, proficiently, consciously; intellectually, academically, pedantically, cognitively; as far as one knows, as every schoolchild knows

349 Ignorance

Where ignorance is bliss, / 'Tis folly to be wise.
— THOMAS GRAY

I count religion but a childish toy, / And hold there is no sin but ignorance. — CHRISTOPHER MARLOWE

NOUNS

1 **ignorance,** lack of knowledge, nescience, incognizance; incomprehension, unawareness, insensibility, unconsciousness, blankness, nonrecognition, unfamiliarity; awkwardness, gaucherie, backwardness, uncertainty; illiteracy, unenlightenment; unskillfulness, artlessness, naiveté, innocence; empty-headedness, folly
   ◗ *Unskillfulness 128; Insensibility 213; Folly 353; Naiveté 821*

2 **lack of knowledge,** inexperience, inexpertness, amateurism, amateurishness; semiliteracy, smattering of knowledge; dabbling, superficiality, sciolism, dilettantism

3 unknown thing, unknown quantity; mystery, enigma, riddle, secret, anonymity; the unknown, unknown territory, terra incognita; guesswork, anybody's guess, complete blank, closed *or* sealed book, all Greek [Inf]
▶ *Secrecy 182; Unintelligibility 364*

4 ignorant person, ignoramus, simpleton, fool, bungler; amateur, dilettante, dabbler, layperson; philistine, illiterate, dunce; novice, tyro, greenhorn, beginner, duffer [Inf]

ADJECTIVES

5 ignorant, unknowing, nescient, incognizant, unwitting, unaware, oblivious, unconscious, blank; uninformed, in the dark, misinformed, misled; unskilled, uninitiated, green, naive, simple, innocent, gauche, awkward, backward, unenlightened; illiterate, unlettered, unschooled, untutored, uneducated, untaught, uninstructed, unscholarly, lowbrow, philistine, emptyheaded, clueless [Inf]
▶ *Unskillfulness 128; Naiveté 821*

6 semiskilled, semiliterate; lay, amateur, amateurish; inexperienced, inexpert, unqualified; shallow, superficial, dilettante, half-baked

7 unknown, mysterious, strange, unfamiliar, unrecognized; unnamed, anonymous, unidentified, secret; obscure, unbeknown, unperceived, unseen, unheard-of; unspoken, ineffable, untold; unrealized, unexplored, uncharted; unknowable, beyond the frontiers of knowledge
▶ *Secrecy 182; Unintelligibility 364*

VERBS

8 be ignorant, not know, know nothing, wallow in ignorance, be in the dark; lack information, have nothing to go on, have a lot to learn; be stumped, give up; not have the foggiest idea, shrug one's shoulders, not have a clue [Inf]

9 know little, have a smattering of knowledge, dabble in

10 make ignorant, keep in the dark, mystify; mislead, misinform

ADVERBS

11 ignorantly, unknowingly, unwittingly, unconsciously, obliviously, in ignorance

350 Accuracy

NOUNS

1 accuracy, precision, preciseness, exactness, exactitude; meticulousness, fastidiousness, scrupulousness; subtlety, nicety, refinement; strictness, rigidity, pedantry, rigor, rigorousness, acuity; attention to detail, hairsplitting, pinpoint accuracy; mathematical precision, clockwork precision, perfect pitch, finetuning

▶ *Sensitivity 267; Carefulness 325; Truth 721*

2 correctness, attention to fact, factualness, factualism; truth, literalness, literalism, the literal truth; faithfulness, fidelity, realism
▶ *Reality 719; Truth 721*

ADJECTIVES

3 accurate, correct, precise, exact, perfect, pinpoint; detailed, meticulous, scrupulous; rigorous, strict, rigid, pedantic; hairsplitting; subtle, nice; dead-right, on the button [Inf]

4 correct, factual, truthful, literal; true to the letter, letter-perfect, unerring, verbatim; true to life, faithful, lifelike, realistic, photographic

VERBS

5 be accurate, correct, edit, emend; go into details, go into particulars, particularize; refine, fine-tune, hone, split hairs; stick to the facts, stick to the letter, go by the book, dot one's i's and cross one's t's, hit the nail on the head, score a bull's-eye [Inf]

ADVERBS

6 accurately, precisely, exactly, just, just so, dead, squarely, on the mark, plumb, plumb on, to a hair, to a T; right, to a nicety, correctly, by the book, (according) to the letter, to the nth degree; literally, faithfully, verbatim, word for word, letter by letter

351 Error

I beseech you, in the bowels of Christ, think it possible you may be mistaken. — OLIVER CROMWELL

The physician can bury his mistakes, but the architect can only advise his client to plant vines.
— FRANK LLOYD WRIGHT

NOUNS

1 error, mistake, fault, miscalculation, misconstruction, misconception, misinterpretation, misjudgment, misapprehension, misunderstanding, false conclusion; wrong turning, false move, bad move, false step

2 erroneousness, wrongness, untrueness; untruth, falsity, falseness, incorrectness, fallaciousness

3 inaccuracy, imprecision, inexactness, inexactitude, looseness, sloppiness, carelessness, laxity, negligence; approximation, guesswork, speculation, generalization; randomness, haphazardness, hit or miss, shooting in the dark
▶ *Untruthfulness, Falsehood 192; Deception 193*

4 faulty reasoning, fallacy, sophistry, illogic, choplogic, flawed logic; circular argument, inconsistency, self-contradiction, sloppy thinking
▶ *Philosophy 4; Sophistry 330*

5 misrepresentation, distortion, falsification; misquotation, misstatement; travesty

6 fallibility, human error; subjectivity, prejudice, bias, superstition; self-deception, wishful thinking; delusion, illusion, hallucination; false impression, popular misconception, old wives' tale

> *Belief 87*

7 errancy, wrongdoing, culpability, guiltiness; aberrancy, deviancy, perversion, heresy, heterodoxy, unorthodoxy; moral error, sin, transgression, misdeed, offense, crime

> *Religion 81; Wrong 430; Immorality 432; Guilt 450*

8 trivial error, slip, slip-up, lapse, oversight, omission; slip of the tongue, *lapsus linguae* [L]; slip of the pen, *lapsus calami* [L]; Freudian slip, miscue [Inf]

9 blunder, bungle, gaffe, faux pas, glaring error, bloomer, boner, howler, muff, fluff, botch, snafu; [Inf]: blooper, boo-boo, ballup, goof, foul-up, louse up, fuckup, screwup

> *Misjudgment 342*

10 language error, spelling mistake, misspelling; mispronunciation, cacology; grammatical error, solecism, bad grammar, incorrect usage, faulty syntax, misusage; abuse of language, abuse of terms, barbarism; spoonerism, malapropism, Goldwynism, ambiguity, tautology, double negative, split infinitive, dangling participle, mixed metaphor, catachresis; folk etymology, anacoluthia [Form], murder of the queen's *or* king's English [Inf]

> *Linguistics, Language 5*

ADJECTIVES

11 erroneous, wrong, untrue, incorrect, false, fallacious; illogical, faulty, flawed, falsified, inaccurate, inexact, loose; inconsistent, self-contradictory, distorted

12 errant, erring, fallible; culpable, guilty, sinful; aberrant, deviant, perverse, perverted, heretical, unorthodox

13 mistaken, in error, at fault, wrong, all wrong, self-contradicting; prejudiced, biased; deluded; wide of *or* way off the mark

VERBS

14 err, make a mistake, miscalculate, misconstrue, misinterpret, misjudge; misrepresent, distort, falsify; misstate, misquote, overlook, omit; misspell, mispronounce, misprint; slip, slip up, lapse, bungle, blunder, muff, botch up; [Inf]: ball up, foul up, louse up, screw up, fuck up

15 be in error, misunderstand, misapprehend, get it wrong, labor under a false impression, bark up the wrong tree, back the wrong horse

16 transgress, err, sin, deviate, lapse, fall

ADVERBS

17 erroneously, in error, mistakenly, by mistake

18 wrongly, incorrectly, badly, faultily; awry, amiss; inaccurately; approximately, imprecisely, out of true, inexactly; loosely, carelessly, without thinking

352 Wisdom

The price of wisdom is above rubies. — BIBLE: JOB

It is the province of knowledge to speak and it is the privilege of wisdom to listen.
— OLIVER WENDELL HOLMES

NOUNS

1 wisdom, sagacity, sagaciousness, sapience, reason, judgment; discretion, discernment, discrimination, perspicacity, penetration, perception, insight; intuition, understanding, comprehension, breadth of vision, profundity; knowledge, erudition, learning, experience, enlightenment; objectivity, soundness of mind; shrewdness, acumen, astuteness, tact; levelheadedness, prudence, thoughtfulness, judiciousness; farsightedness, foresight, forethought

> *Caution 287; Discrimination 337; Judgment 341; Knowledge 348; Foresight 357*

2 intelligence, intellect, mind; understanding, quick-wittedness, cleverness, smartness, brightness, brilliance, intellectualism; aptitude, talent, genius, high IQ (intelligence quotient); inspiration, bright idea, brainstorm, brain wave [Inf]; wit, wits, mother wit, sense, common sense, horse sense, good sense, brain *or* brains, gray matter [Inf]

> *Intellect 315*

3 wise person, wise man, wise woman, sage, guru; witch, shaman, sibyl, oracle, seer, prophet; thinker, philosopher; Solomon; intellectual, scholar

> *Philosophy 4; Intellect 315; Knowledge 348; Prediction 358*

ADJECTIVES

4 wise, sagacious, sapient, thoughtful, thinking, reflecting, reasoning, rational, sensible; profound, deep, intellectual, highbrow; knowledgeable, knowing, erudite, learned; perspicacious, perceptive, oracular; levelheaded, prudent, judicious, balanced, objective, impartial, just, fair-minded; broad-minded, unprejudiced; circumspect, statesmanlike, diplomatic, discreet, tactful, politic, well-advised

> *Sanity 109; Caution 287; Judgment 341; Foresight 357; Disinterestedness 443*

5 intelligent, clever, smart, bright, brilliant; talented, on the ball, gifted; capable, able, skillful, skilled; quick, quick-witted, sharp, sharp-witted, alert, astute, shrewd, street-smart *or* streetwise, canny; farsighted, clearheaded; brainy [Inf], all there [Inf]

> *Skillfulness 127; Intellect 315; Cunning 822*

VERBS

6 be wise, understand, grasp, fathom, discern, see through; distinguish, discriminate, judge; intuit, use one's head, use one's intelligence, have one's wits about one, know the score [Inf], know what's what [Inf]

▶ *Discrimination 337; Judgment 341; Intelligibility 363*

7 **be intelligent,** have brains, be smart, know; shine, scintillate, have one's head screwed on the right way [Inf]

▶ *Intellect 315; Knowledge 348*

ADVERBS

8 **wisely,** sagaciously, thoughtfully, rationally, sensibly; perspicaciously; prudently, judiciously; objectively; diplomatically, discreetly

9 **intelligently,** cleverly, brilliantly; astutely, shrewdly

353 Folly

Wisdom, and Wit are little seen, / But Folly's at full length.
— JANE BRERETON

NOUNS

1 **folly,** foolishness, ineptitude, inanity; rashness, recklessness, madness, senselessness; silliness, absurdity, ridiculousness, ludicrousness, asininity; childishness, puerility; fatuousness, pointlessness, extravagance, frivolity, flippancy, giddiness; thoughtlessness, irresponsibility, injudiciousness, imprudence, indiscretion; conceit, heedlessness, eccentricity, insanity, madness, lunacy, dotage, craziness, daftness, idiocy

▶ *Rashness 286; Ignorance 349; Ridiculousness 368*

2 **act of folly,** foolery, tomfoolery; mistake, error, misjudgment; gaffe, blunder, blooper [Inf]

▶ *Misjudgment 342; Error 351; Lack of Meaning 362*

3 **foolish person,** fool, simpleton, idiot, ass, jackass, dolt, blockhead, dunce, dotard, noodle, nincompoop, ninny, nitwit; [Inf]: birdbrain, dope, twit, dingbat, pinhead, meathead, jerk, sucker

▶ *Ignorance 349*

4 **rash person,** hothead, daredevil; adventurer, madcap, eccentric

ADJECTIVES

5 **foolish,** stupid, inept, inane, idiotic, mad; ill-advised, ill-considered, unwise, imprudent, injudicious, uncircumspect, incautious; rash, reckless, daft, crazy, foolhardy, harebrained, heedless, inattentive; hotheaded, hellbent, headstrong, wild, prodigal, devil-may-care, daredevil, madcap, eccentric; frivolous, flippant, silly, asinine, anserine, lunatic; senseless, brainless, emptyheaded, simple, slow, doltish, dull; fatuous, pointless, absurd, ludicrous, ridiculous, nonsensical, preposterous; childish, puerile, senile, eccentric; [Inf]: birdbrained, dimwitted, nutty, balmy, spaced-out, potty [Brit], gaga

▶ *Rashness 286; Lack of Intellect 316; Ridiculousness 368*

VERBS

6 **be foolish,** take leave of one's senses, go mad, lose

one's head; throw caution to the wind, take a leap in the dark; play with fire, have no thought for the consequences; ask for trouble, tempt fate, never learn, not have the sense one was born with, buy a pig in a poke, stick one's neck out [Inf]

▶ *Rashness 286*

7 **play the fool,** act the fool, make a fool of oneself, clown, clown around, horse around [Inf]

▶ *Ridiculousness 368*

ADVERBS

8 **foolishly,** stupidly, unwisely, imprudently, rashly, recklessly; idiotically, senselessly, brainlessly, unintelligently; absurdly, ludicrously, ridiculously, nonsensically

354 Memory

The sound of hunting horns, when it dies, / On the wind, is like our memories. — GUILLAUME APPOLLINAIRE

NOUNS

1 **memory,** recollection, remembrance, remembering, recall; total recall, good memory, photographic memory; retention, retentiveness; memorization, learning by heart, learning by rote; reminiscence, anamnesis, retrospection, reflection, hindsight, evocation, mind's eye, nostalgia; recognition, identification; collective memory, racial memory

▶ *Identification 184; Knowledge 348*

2 **retrospect,** retrospective, review, flashback, déjà vu; history, memoirs, autobiography, anecdote

▶ *History 3; Record 185*

3 **memento,** souvenir, token, keepsake, memorabilia, trophy, relic; commemoration, memorial, monument, statue, plaque, tribute

4 **reminder,** memorandum, memo, note; engagement calendar, scheduler; album, photograph album, scrapbook, diary, record; mnemonic, aide-mémoire, cue, prompt, prompter

▶ *Information 170; Record 185*

5 **day to remember,** birthday, anniversary; centennial, centenary, bicentennial, bicentenary, tercentennial, tercentenary; memorable date, date in history, place in history; holiday, celebration

▶ *Celebration 405*

6 **artificial memory,** computer memory, random-access memory (RAM), read-only memory (ROM)

▶ *Computers 15*

ADJECTIVES

7 **memorable,** unforgettable, notable, noteworthy; remembered, unforgotten; indelible, stamped on one's memory, forever in one's memory; haunting, evocative, reminiscent, nostalgic; reminding, mnemonic

◗ *Importance 799*

8 **remembering,** bearing *or* keeping in mind, unable to forget, retrospective, mindful

9 **memorized,** learned by heart, learned by rote, committed to memory, retained

10 **memorial,** commemorative, celebratory

VERBS

11 **memorize,** learn, learn by heart, learn by rote, commit to memory; remember, retain, fix in one's mind, hold in one's mind, bear *or* keep in mind, store in one's heart
◗ *Knowledge 348*

12 **remember,** recall, call to mind, recollect, think of, call up, summon up, conjure up; recognize, identify, know again; review, retrace, recapture; hark back, look back, think back, reminisce, reflect; rake up the past, write one's memoirs
◗ *Identification 184*

13 **remind,** bring to mind, bring back, take back; jog one's memory, ring a bell, refresh one's memory; brush up, recapitulate, review; haunt, not allow to forget; prompt, remind oneself, tie a knot in one's handkerchief, make a note
◗ *Record 185; Repetition 797*

14 **commemorate,** memorialize, remember, honor, pay tribute, toast, observe, celebrate, mark the occasion
◗ *Celebration 405*

15 **be remembered,** make history, live on, make an impression, stick in the mind, be engraved on one's memory, recur, come back, be unforgotten

ADVERBS

16 **memorably,** unforgettably, reminiscently, mnemonically, retrospectively, commemoratively, in memory of, in memoriam; by heart, by rote

355 Forgetfulness

Better by far you should forget and smile / Than that you should remember and be sad. — CHRISTINA ROSSETTI

NOUNS

1 **forgetfulness,** loss of memory, amnesia, total blank, mental block, blackout; blankness, vacancy, vacuity, emptiness of mind, empty-headedness, absent-mindedness
◗ *Inattention 324*

2 **poor memory,** dim memory, hazy recollection, lapse of memory; mind *or* brain like a sieve

3 **unthinkingness,** thoughtlessness, unmindfulness, heedlessness, inattention, disregard, neglect, carelessness; selfishness, ingratitude, indifference
◗ *Ingratitude 311; Selfishness 444*

4 **oblivion,** obliviousness, abstractedness, detachment, ataraxia, withdrawal; absorption, self-absorption, introspection; self-loss, depersonalization, catatonia;

senselessness, insensibility, unconsciousness, coma, stupor, narcosis; trance, meditative trance, yoga trance; rapture, ecstasy, hypnosis
◗ *Insensibility 213; Inattention 324*

5 **amnesty,** pardon, forgiveness, absolution
◗ *Forgiveness 312*

ADJECTIVES

6 **forgetful,** blank, vacant, vacuous, empty-headed; absent-minded, forgetting, amnesiac *or* amnesic

7 **forgotten,** not remembered, not missed; forgettable, unmemorable; best forgotten; out of sight, out of mind; dead and buried; past, gone, lost, beyond recall; half-remembered, on the tip of one's tongue

8 **unthinking,** thoughtless, unmindful; heedless, inattentive, disregarding; neglectful, negligent; careless, selfish; ungrateful, indifferent

9 **oblivious,** abstracted; detached, withdrawn, (self-)absorbed, introspective, head in the clouds, wandering; distracted, preoccupied, otherwise engaged, miles away; blind, deaf, unaware, in a world of one's own; depersonalized, catatonic, senseless, insensible, unconscious; rapturous, ecstatic, in a trance, hypnotized; spaced-out [Inf], out to lunch [Inf]
◗ *Inattention 324; Negligence 326*

VERBS

10 **forget,** have no recollection of, not remember; overlook, neglect, omit; think no more of, not give another thought to; erase *or* efface from one's memory, unlearn, leave behind, break with the past, consign to oblivion; clean forget [Inf]
◗ *Obliteration 186; Inattention 324*

11 **be forgetful,** be oblivious, have a mind *or* brain like a sieve, have a short memory; misremember, remember wrongly; forget *or* fluff one's lines, dry up

12 **be forgotten,** slip one's mind, fade from one's memory; sink into oblivion, sink without a trace, drop from view; miss, go in one ear and out the other

13 **forgive,** forgive and forget, let bygones be bygones, bury the hatchet
◗ *Forgiveness 312*

ADVERBS

14 **forgetfully,** absent-mindedly, abstractedly, distractedly; negligently, inattentively, unthinkingly, thoughtlessly; heedlessly, carelessly, indifferently; obliviously, unconsciously, senselessly; blankly, vacantly, vacuously; ecstatically, in a dream, in a trance, hypnotically

356 Expectation

NOUNS

1 **expectation,** anticipation, expectancy *or* expectance, contemplation, prospect; hope, hopefulness, eagerness, optimism; presumption, assumption, confidence, assurance, reliance, trust, belief; waiting, suspense,

apprehension, apprehensiveness; pessimism, dread, fear, foreboding, anxiety, uncertainty; possibility, probability, likelihood, certainty

♦ *Belief 87; Hope 281; Fear 283; Possibility 836; Probability 838; Certainty 840; Uncertainty 841*

2 **expectations,** demands, desires; hopes, prospects, outlook; forecast, prognosis, prediction; accountability, responsibility; contingency, possibility; dream, aspiration, ambition; omen, portent, augury

♦ *Hope 281; Prediction 358; Future Time 650*

3 **expected thing,** the done thing, the usual, the normal, standard; normal behavior, custom, tradition, habit, practice; just what one would have expected

♦ *Habit, Custom 397*

ADJECTIVES

4 **expecting,** expectant, in expectation, in high hopes, full of hope, hopeful; confident, sanguine, optimistic; desiring, wanting; sure, certain; anticipating, anticipant, anticipative, anticipatory, pregnant, atiptoe; prepared, ready, waiting, on the waiting list, on standby; forewarned, forearmed, unsurprised; on the lookout, vigilant, watchful; on tenterhooks, in suspense; excited, eager, agog; prognostic; apprehensive, dreading, pessimistic, anxious

♦ *Reproduction 21; Hope 281; Fear 283; Desire 288; Preparation 388; Certainty 840*

5 **expected,** predicted, foreseen, unsurprising; designated, chosen, promised; due, anticipated; probable, likely; apparent, predictable, foreseeable, sure, certain, long-awaited; future, prospective, contemplated, impending, imminent, in *or* on the cards; hoped for, desired; feared, dreaded

♦ *Fear 283; Desire 288; Prediction 358; Selection 382; Future Time 650*

VERBS

6 **expect,** anticipate, look forward to, look for, see coming; look at, contemplate, face; have in prospect, intend, plan, envisage; hope, hope for; apprehend, dread, fear, expect the worst

♦ *Hope 281; Fear 283; Intention 374; Plan 387*

7 **predict,** foresee, forecast; think, believe, estimate, reckon, calculate, bargain for; count on, bank on, take for granted, assume, presume, count one's chickens before they are hatched

♦ *Belief 87; Hope 281; Judgment 341; Prediction 358*

8 **wait,** bide one's time, wait for, await, be on the waiting list; line up for, stand by, be on standby, be on call; look out for, watch out for

9 **demand,** insist on, call for; require, need; want, wish

♦ *Necessity 95; Desire 288*

ADVERBS

10 **expectantly,** hopefully; confidently, optimistically, eagerly, anticipatively, anticipatorily; apprehensively, pessimistically, anxiously; in suspense, on tenterhooks, with bated breath

11 **expectedly,** unsurprisingly, predictably, foreseeably

12 **demandingly,** insistently

357 Foresight

NOUNS

1 **foresight,** prudence, caution, care, circumspection, wisdom, sagacity, forethought, precaution; farsightedness, long-sightedness, providence, provision, readiness, preparation, planning, consideration, contemplation, intelligent anticipation; perspicacity, discernment, awareness, understanding, insight, vision, futurology; premeditation, predetermination, predestination

♦ *Caution 287; Carefulness 325; Wisdom 352; Predetermination 384; Preparation 388*

2 **plan,** long-range plan, emergency plan, contingency plan, forward planning; program, prospectus, schedule, itinerary; appointments calendar, calendar of events, almanac

♦ *Prediction 358; Plan 387*

3 **prediction,** expectation, precognition, foreknowledge, premonition, divination

♦ *Occultism 86; Expectation 356; Prediction 358; Certainty 840*

4 **predictor,** forecaster, prophet, prognosticator; diviner, clairvoyant; visionary, planner, preparer, futurologist

♦ *Prediction 358*

ADJECTIVES

5 **foreseeing,** foresighted, planning ahead, looking ahead, expectant, anticipant, anticipatory; prudent, provident, cautious, careful, aware, perceptive, circumspect; wise, sagacious, discerning, farseeing, perspicacious; predictive, prognostic, precognitive, prospective; clairvoyant, intuitive, telepathic; secondsighted, prescient, farsighted, long-sighted, weatherwise

♦ *Caution 287; Wisdom 352; Expectation 356; Prediction 358*

6 **foresighted,** planning, planning ahead

7 **foreseeable,** predictable, probable; predicted, forecast

♦ *Prediction 358*

VERBS

8 **have foresight,** be cautious, keep a sharp lookout, guard against, take precautions, feel one's way; look ahead, consider, contemplate, take stock of; plan ahead, plan, prepare, prepare for the future, provide against, make provisions, lay up for a rainy day, look to the future, have an eye to the future *or* the main chance; test the waters, send up a trial balloon, see which way the wind blows, see the lay of the land, look before one leaps

♦ *Provision 89; Caution 287; Attention 323; Wisdom 352; Plan 387; Preparation 388; Future Time 650*

9 **foresee,** see ahead, know in advance, foreknow, have

advance knowledge, have prior information; predict, forewarn, warn; look for, expect, envisage, envision; be prepared, anticipate, forestall; surmise, make a good guess, suppose, presume; forejudge, portend, foreshadow, forebode, promise, presage, foretell; see *or* peep *or* pry into the future, read the future; have second sight, have clairvoyance, be clairvoyant, feel *or* see it coming, feel it in one's bones, scent, scent from afar; predetermine, predestine

> *Information 170; Knowledge 348; Expectation 356; Prediction 358; Supposition 359; Predetermination 384; Preparation 388; Earliness 657; Warning 814*

ADVERBS

10 **foresightedly,** with foresight, prophetically, clairvoyantly, in one's crystal ball, telepathically; farsightedly, long-sightedly, expectantly; prudently, perceptively, providently; cautiously, discerningly, wisely, for a rainy day

358 Prediction

NOUNS

1 **prediction,** forecast; forecasting, foretelling, forewarning, prophecy, apocalypse, revelation; prognosis, prognostication, syndrome, symptom; presentiment, premonition, hunch, feeling, foreboding; foresight, prevision, prescience, certainty, foretaste, second sight, prefiguration, prefigurement, prior consideration; expectation, prospect, weather forecast; horoscope, fortune

> *Expectation 356; Foresight 357; Future Time 650*

2 **divination,** extrasensory perception (ESP), telepathy, clairvoyance; augury, taking the auspices, soothsaying, haruspicy, vaticination; astrology, horoscopy; physiognomy, phrenology; graphology; casting nativities, fortunetelling, occultism; dowsing; discovery, guesswork, speculation

> *Occultism 86*

3 **notice,** advance notice, preview, announcement, publication, prepublication; warning, preliminary warning, warning sign, warning shot, danger signal; hint, suggestion, intimation

> *Publication 173; Warning 814*

4 **model,** working model, test model, test design, prototype; shape of things to come

5 **omen,** good omen, bad omen; sign, indication, portent, presage, augury, auspices, writing on the wall; prognostic, caution, warning, forewarning, harbinger, precursor, forerunner; herald, messenger, prefigurement, foretoken, type; ominousness, portentousness, sign of the times

> *News 171; Identification 184; Precedence 769; Danger 811; Warning 814*

6 **good-luck sign,** good-luck charm, talisman, mascot, horseshoe, four-leaf clover, rabbit's foot, St. Christopher's medal; shooting star, finding a penny, knocking on wood

> *Chance 842*

7 **bad-luck sign,** broken mirror, stopped clock, spilled salt, walking under a ladder, opening an umbrella indoors, stepping on a crack, telling one's dream before breakfast, black cat crossing one's path, rocking an empty rocking chair

> *Chance 842*

8 **oracle,** sage, prophet, prophetess, sibyl; prophet of doom, doomsayer, doomster, doom watcher, warner; seer, visionary, vaticinator, soothsayer, clairvoyant

> *Occultism 86; Judgment 341; Warning 814*

9 **forecaster,** consultant; weather forecaster, meteorologist, weatherman *or* weatherwoman; financial forecaster, sports forecaster, racing forecaster, oddsmaker, tipster; gambler, speculator; prognosticator, futurologist, diviner, dowser, astrologer, fortuneteller, interpreter of dreams

> *Occultism 86; Foresight 357*

10 **means of prediction,** cards, tarot cards, Ouija™ board; runes, dice, lot; tripod; crystal ball, mirror, tea leaves; palm, head; entrails; texts, Bible

ADJECTIVES

11 **predicting,** predictive, foretelling, forewarning; presentient, prescient, foreseeing, clairvoyant, fortunetelling, weather-wise, prophetic, oracular, mantic, vatic, fatidic *or* fatidical, apocalyptic, sibylline, sibyllic; monitory, premonitory, foreboding, cautionary; heralding, prefiguring, precursory; signifying, indicative, symptomatic

> *Foresight 357; Precedence 769; Warning 814*

12 **predicted,** foretold, forecast; predictable, foreseeable

> *Foresight 357*

13 **presageful,** portentous, significant, fateful, augural, auspicial, haruspical; of good omen, auspicious, propitious, promising, fortunate, favorable, prosperous; ill-omened, ominous, ill-starred, big with fate, pregnant with doom, inauspicious, sinister, adverse, unfavorable

> *Chance 842; Prosperity 847; Adversity 848*

VERBS

14 **predict,** foresee, forecast, foretell, prophesy, reveal, make a prediction; make an educated guess, guess, guesstimate [Inf], speculate; prognosticate, make a prognosis, vaticinate, forebode, bode, augur, foretoken, presage, portend, foreshow, foreshadow, prefigure; forerun, herald, harbinger, usher in, go before, come before; point to, indicate, signify, betoken, represent, typify, hint, suggest; announce, give notice, notify, advertise, forewarn, warn, give warning; promise, augur well, bid fair, give hope, hold out *or* build up hopes, raise *or* excite expectations; look black, look ominous, lower *or* lour, menace, threaten, depress

> *Publication 173; Identification 184; Hope 281; Foresight 357; Precedence 769; Warning 814*

15 divine, have extrasensory perception (ESP), soothsay, augur, take *or* read the auspices, take *or* read the omens, interpret dreams, vaticinate, cast a horoscope; cast lots, gamble; tell fortunes, read the future *or* the signs, gaze into a crystal ball, read the stars *or* cards *or* runes *or* entrails *or* tea leaves, read palms

  ▶ *Occultism 86*

ADVERBS

16 predictively, prophetically; predictably, foreseeably; portentously, significantly, fatefully; auspiciously, promisingly; inauspiciously, ominously

359 Supposition

It is a good morning exercise for a research scientist to discard a pet hypothesis every day before breakfast. It keeps him young. — KONRAD LORENZ

NOUNS

1 supposition, assumption, presumption; notion, idea, the idea of, fancy, conceit, ideality; pretense, pretending, affectation; presupposition, condition, stipulation; proposal, proposition, offer, submission; argument, hypothetical argument, postulation, postulate, premise, theory, hypothesis, working hypothesis; explanation, tentative explanation, model, theorem, mathematical theorem, topic, thesis; position, stand, attitude, orientation, point of view, standpoint; opinion, suggestion

  ▶ *Belief 87; Information 170; Idea 327; Topic 328; Argument 329; Imagination 360; Affectation 367; Negotiation 460; Offer 504*

2 basis of supposition, hint, clue, evidence, data, research data, datum; deduction, induction, inference; suspicion, sneaking suspicion, hunch, inkling, intimation, intuition, instinct; thought, thinking, lateral thinking, association of ideas, causal relationship; probability, possibility

  ▶ *Thought 317; Intuition 320; Evidence 339; Possibility 836; Probability 838*

3 conjecture, speculation, suspicion; guess, surmise, mere notion; gamble, try, shot, shot in the dark; gambling, guessing, guesswork, rough guess, crude estimate; shrewd idea, intuition; construction, reconstruction; guesstimate [Inf]

  ▶ *Intuition 320; Judgment 341*

4 theorist, theorizer, theoretician, hypothesist, thinker, philosopher; academic, researcher, research worker, academic researcher, scientific researcher, theory builder; experimenter, experimental scientist, scientist, model builder; supposer, surmiser, guesser, critic; doctrinaire; speculator; gambler; planner

  ▶ *Thought 317; Plan 387; Certainty 840*

ADJECTIVES

5 suppositional, suppositive, supposing, assumptive,

presumptive; notional, conjectural, guessing, intuitive; propositional, hypothetical, theoretical, postulatory, supposititious, supposititious; unverified, moot, armchair, speculative, wildly speculative, blue-sky, gratuitous; suggestive, hinting, allusive, hard to pin down; stimulating, thought-provoking, of academic interest, academic; guesstimating [Inf]

  ▶ *Belief 87; Intuition 320*

6 supposed, assumed, presumed, premised, a priori, postulated, surmised, conjectured, guessed, hypothesized; understood, taken, taken as read, taken for granted; proposed, suggested, mooted, topical, given, granted, granted for the sake of argument, assented; inferred, deduced, pretended, alleged, reputed, putative, so-called, titular, quasi; not real, unreal; abstract, fanciful, fancied, imagined, imaginary, fabled, untrue; supposable, assumable, presumable, surmisable, imaginable

  ▶ *Topic 328; Assent 346; Imagination 360; Nonexistence 718; Untruth 722*

7 meant, intended, designed, expected; obliged, required

  ▶ *Intention 374*

VERBS

8 suppose, assume, presume; have a notion, have an idea, imagine, pretend, fancy, dream; think, conceive, draw a mental picture, take *or* get into one's head, opine; divine, suspect, have a hunch, have an inkling, guess, hazard *or* make a guess, guesstimate [Inf], suppose so, daresay; intuit, infer, deduce, conclude, surmise, conjecture; convince oneself, persuade oneself, believe, understand, gather, presuppose, presurmise; premise, posit, postulate, lay down, assert, affirm; predicate, take for granted, take, take it; reason, speculate, form a hypothesis, hypothesize, have a theory, theorize, let; sketch, draft, outline, plan; rely on supposition, gamble

  ▶ *Belief 87; Affirmation 189; Thought 317; Reason 319; Intuition 320; Argument 329; Imagination 360; Plan 387*

9 propound, propose, suggest, make a suggestion, mean seriously, offer, put on the agenda; moot, move, propose a motion, bring up for debate, request, put a case, submit, make one's submission; argue, plead *or* put a case, put forth *or* forward, advance; venture to say, make a point, throw out an idea; advise, outline, adumbrate; allude, hint, put an idea into someone's head; persuade, urge, motivate, influence

  ▶ *Information 170; Advice 176; Persuasion 178; Reason 319; Offer 504; Request 505*

ADVERBS

10 supposedly, allegedly, reputedly, as rumor has it, seemingly, possibly; conjecturally, hypothetically, theoretically, if, speculatively; in theory, as it were, at a guess

360 Imagination

Nor till the poets among us can be / "literalists of the imagination" / and can present / for inspection, ... "imaginary gardens with real toads in them," / shall we have it.
— MARIANNE MOORE

How reconcile this world of fact with the bright world of my imagining? — HELEN KELLER

NOUNS

1 **imagination,** imaginativeness, vision, perception, creativity, creativeness, invention, inventiveness; originality, ingenuity, resourcefulness, enterprise, skill; fancy, fancifulness, fantasy, fantasticality *or* fantasticalness; mind's eye, visualization, objectification, conceptualization; imagery, image-building, word-painting, artistry, creative thought, creative work, creative force

 ▶ *Skillfulness 127; Originality 737*

2 **inspiration,** stimulus, incitement; Muse, inspiration from the Muse, afflatus, divine afflatus; frenzy, poetic frenzy, ecstasy; genius

3 **insight,** understanding, empathy, sympathy; moral sensibility, sensitivity

 ▶ *Sensitivity 267*

4 **conception,** concept, thought, ideation, mental image, mental picture, impression; ideality, idealization, ideal, appearance, image, picture, projection, fancy, conceit; brainchild, notion, idea; whim, maggot [Arch], vagary, caprice, whimsy *or* whimsey, whimsical notion, figment, figment of the imagination; fiction, work of fiction, creative writing, story, novel, romance, science fiction, fantasy, fairy tale, imaginary world; poetry; imaginative exercise, creative exercise, flight of fancy, play of fancy, daydream; uncontrolled imagination, extravaganza, rhapsody, exaggeration, absurdity, unreality, falsehood, poetic license; quixotism, knight-errantry, tilting at windmills, shadowboxing, sciamachy

 ▶ *Literature 139; Untruthfulness, Falsehood 192; Deception 193; Exaggeration 194; Description 202; Appearance 264; Thought 317; Idea 327; Caprice 381; Unreality 720*

5 **fantasy,** fabrication, improvisation, make-believe, vision, wildest dreams; dream, bad dream, nightmare; bogey *or* bogy, phantom, ghost, apparition, specter, shadow, vapor [Arch]; dimness, mirage, visual fallacy, fancy, illusion, optical illusion, trompe l'oeil, delusion, hallucination, chimera, error

 ▶ *Vision 242; Dimness 248; Error 351; Nonconformity 782*

6 **reverie,** daydream, brown study, abstractedness, abstraction, head in the clouds; trance, insensibility; delirium, frenzy; subjectivism; autosuggestion; wishful thinking, window-shopping, golden dream, pipe dream, fantasia, wish, desire; romance, stardust, romanticism, escapism

 ▶ *Insensibility 213; Desire 288; Inattention 324*

7 **idealism,** utopianism, castles in the air *or* in Spain, pie

---

NOTABLE IMAGINARY PLACES (with comments and authors)

Asgard (dwelling of the Aesir; Scandinavian mythology)

Atlantis (submerged continent in Atlantic Ocean; Plato)

Avalon (King Arthur's last retreat; Sir Thomas Malory)

Brobdingnag (peninsula on California coast; inhabitants are as tall as church steeples; Jonathan Swift)

Camelot (King Arthur's court; Sir Thomas Malory)

Cloud-cuckoo-land (city built on air above plain of Phlegra, Greece; Aristophanes)

Cockaigne (a happy place; of unknown location and author)

Dracula's Castle (in Carpathian Mountains; Bram Stoker)

El Dorado (somewhere between the Amazon and Peru; Sir Walter Ralegh)

Emerald City (capital of Oz; L. Frank Baum)

Erewhon (probably in central or northern Australia; Samuel Butler)

Flatland (two-dimensional land; Edwin A. Abbott)

Fortunate Isles (in Atlantic Ocean, just outside entrance to Mediterranean; Homer)

Fountain of Youth (Bahamas or Florida; sought by Ponce de Leon)

Garden of Eden (first paradise; Genesis)

Houyhnhnm Land (chief citizens are horses; Jonathan Swift)

Islandia (Austin Tappan Wright)

Laputa (floating island; Jonathan Swift)

Lilliput (southwest of Sumatra; inhabitants are six inches high; Jonathan Swift)

Looking-Glass Land (inhabited by chessmen and others; Lewis Carroll)

Lyonnesse (birthplace of Tristan; Sir Thomas Malory)

Middle-Earth (dwelling of hobbits and others; J.R.R. Tolkien)

Narnia (created by Aslan; C. S. Lewis)

Neverland (abode of Peter Pan; Sir James M. Barrie)

Olympus (mountain in Greece, dwelling of the gods; Greek mythology)

Oz (somewhere over the rainbow; L. Frank Baum)

Pern (planet world; Anne McCaffrey)

Ruritania (European kingdom reached by train from Dresden; Anthony Hope)

Shangri-la (Paradise in Tibet; James Hilton)

Treasure Island (off the coast of Mexico; Robert Louis Stevenson)

Utopia (the ideal place, an island off the coast of South America; Sir Thomas More)

Valhalla (palace of Odin; Scandinavian mythology)

Wonderland (reached by falling down a rabbit hole; Lewis Carroll)

Zanth (land of magic adjacent to all known countries; Piers Anthony)

---

in the sky, end of the rainbow, good times coming, millennium; idle fancy, myth, fable

> *Desire 288; Future Time 650*

8 **dreamland,** dream world, fantasyland, promised land, fairyland, land of milk and honey, Happy Valley, Arcadia, end of the rainbow

> *Nonmaterial World 525*

9 **visionary,** seer, diviner, dreamer, daydreamer, fantast, idealist, utopian; escapist, ostrich, avoider, lotus-eater; wishful thinker, romantic, romancer, romanticist, mythmaker, rhapsodist, enthusiast; knight-errant, Don Quixote, eccentric, crank; fantasist, creative worker, composer, artist, poet

> *Inattention 324; Prediction 358; Avoidance 386*

ADJECTIVES

10 **imaginative,** creative, inventive, innovative, original, ingenious; resourceful, enterprising, skillful, clever; eidetic, visualizing, perceptive; fertile, fecund, productive; inspired, romancing, romantic, high-flown, rhapsodic *or* rhapsodical, enthusiastic, carried away, exaggerated; lively, vivid, bold, visual, poetic, fictional; utopian, idealistic; dreamy, dreaming, daydreaming, in a brown study, in a trance

> *Fertility 22; Skillfulness 127; Exaggeration 194; Inattention 324*

11 **fantastic,** fantastical, unreal, bizarre, grotesque, extravagant; whimsical, fanciful, airy-fairy [Inf]; preposterous, absurd, outlandish, impractical; visional, visionary, otherworldly, starry-eyed, quixotic

> *Lack of Meaning 362; Unreality 720*

12 **imaginary,** imagined, unreal, abstract, illusory *or* illusive; fanciful, fancied, chimerical, ethereal, unsubstantial, insubstantial, lacking substance; subjective, hypothetical, suppositional, conceptual, notional, ideal; dreamy, dreamlike, visionary, not of this world, of another world; cloudy, vaporous, shadowy; fictitious, fictional, fictive, storybook, make-believe, thought-up, dreamed-up, created, invented, fabricated, contrived, devised; pretend, not real, simulated, imitated; nonexistent, untrue, illusionary, unhistorical, mythical *or* mythic, mythological, legendary, fabulous, fabled

> *Error 351; Supposition 359; Nonmaterial World 525; Unreality 720; Untruth 722*

13 **imaginable,** conceivable, thinkable

> *Idea 327*

VERBS

14 **imagine,** perceive, conceive, create, invent, think, consider, contemplate, suppose; think of *or* up, conjure up, fancy, dream, dream up, make up; devise, concoct, coin, hatch, produce, fabricate, originate, excogitate, improvise; have an inspiration, visualize, envisage, envision, see in the mind's eye, see, picture, conceptualize; conjure up a vision, form an image of, get a mental picture of, picture to oneself, represent to oneself; represent, paint, write, compose, paint in words, write a portrait of; realize, objectify, capture, recapture; call to mind, call up, summon up; use one's imagination, give rein to one's imagination, let one's imagination run riot, exaggerate, play with one's thoughts; pretend, make believe; hallucinate

> *Representation 187; Vision 242; Thought 317; Supposition 359; Improvisation 396; Production 522*

15 **fantasize,** live in a dream world, build utopias, build castles in the air *or* in Spain; see visions, dream of other worlds, dream dreams; daydream, muse, go into a brown study; idealize, see through rose-colored glasses; romanticize, poeticize, fictionalize; rhapsodize, exaggerate

> *Exaggeration 194; Inattention 324*

16 **have insight,** have understanding, understand, empathize, sympathize

> *Sensitivity 267; Intelligibility 363*

ADVERBS

17 **imaginatively,** creatively, inventively, ingeniously, resourcefully; with imagination, in a flight of fancy; in the mind's eye; with one's head in the clouds, fancifully, romantically, idealistically

---

LEGENDARY CREATURES

Abominable Snowman *or* yeti	chimera	golem	jinn	Midgard serpent	snark
	cockatrice	Gorgon	kelpie	Minotaur	sphinx
	Cyclops	gremlin	King Kong	oni	thunderbird
amphisbaena	Dracula	griffin *or* griffon *or* gryphon	kobold	orc	troll
banshee	dragon		kraken	Pegasus	unicorn
basilisk	drake [Arch]	Harpy	lamia	phoenix	vampire
behemoth	firedrake	hippogriff *or* hippogryph	leprechaun	roc	Wendigo
Bigfoot	Fomorian		Leviathan	Sasquatch	werewolf
Blob, the	Frankenstein's monster	hobbit	Loch Ness monster	satyr	wyvern
bogeyman *or* bogyman	garuda	Houynhnhnm	manticore	Scylla	Yahoo
bunyip	ghoul	humanoid	Medusa	sea serpent	yeti *or* Abominable Snowman
centaur	giant	hydra	mermaid	senmurv	
Cerberus	Godzilla	Iblis	merman	simurg	zombie
		Iceman		siren	

" Then you should say what you mean," the March Hare went on. "I do," Alice hastily replied; "at least — at least I mean what I say — that's the same thing, you know." "Not the same thing a bit!" said the Hatter. "Why, you might just as well say that 'I see what I eat' is the same as 'I eat what I see!'" — LEWIS CARROLL

NOUNS

1 **meaning,** signification, sense, message, idea, message *or* idea conveyed; denotation, substance, essence, spirit, sum, sum and substance, gist, pith, core, nuts and bolts; contents, text, matter, subject matter, topic; semantic content, deep structure, value, drift, tenor, purport, import, implication, connotation, coloring; effect, force, relevance, bearing, scope, context, meaningfulness; semantic flow, expression, mode of expression, diction, style; semantics, general semantics, semasiology, semiotics, semiology, linguistics; nitty-gritty [Inf]
 ▶ *Linguistics, Language 5; Sign 183; Topic 328; Style 537*

2 **significance,** seriousness, importance, import
 ▶ *Importance 799*

3 **comprehensibility,** clarity, plainness, explicitness, clear message, single meaning, univocal, monosemy, unambiguity, unambiguousness, unambiguous passage
 ▶ *Intelligibility 363; Equivocation 380; Simplicity 526*

4 **type of meaning,** level of meaning; denotation, literal meaning, plainness, literality; connotation, interpretation, explanation, definition; reference, application, construction, context, intention, intelligibility, meaningfulness, semantic field; original meaning, derivation, etymology, chief meaning, main meaning, leading sense, received meaning, accepted meaning, allegorical meaning; usage, practice, lexical meaning, grammatical meaning; technical meaning, specialized meaning, special meaning, jargon, argot, idiom; same meaning, equivalent meaning, equivalence, synonym, synonymousness, synonymity, synonymy, identity; opposite meaning, contradictory meaning, opposite, antonym; changed meaning, semantic shift; figurative meaning, paraphrase, metaphorical meaning, metaphor, image, trope; hidden meaning, latent meaning, tropical meaning, latency, esoteric sense, implied sense
 ▶ *Intelligibility 363; Interpretation 365; Habit, Custom 397; Simplicity 526; Cause 675; Specialty 779; Latency 844*

5 **point,** purpose, aim, object, end; idea, plan, design, intention, intent; value, worth, use
 ▶ *Intention 374; Plan 387; Usefulness 801*

ADJECTIVES

6 **meaningful,** comprehensible, intelligible, telling, eloquent, unambiguous, clear, plain, lucid, perspicuous; literal, express, explicit, pointed, declaratory, straight-from-the-shoulder; full of meaning, pregnant, significant, multivocal

7 **similar,** repeated, tautological *or* tautologous, identical; synonymous, equivalent, paraphrastic, tantamount; connotative, implied, implicit, inferred, tacit, suggestive

8 **symbolic,** figurative, metaphorical, allegorical; idiomatic; significative, importing, purporting, indicating, telltale; evocative, expressive, interpretive *or* interpretative, allusive

9 **linguistic,** etymological, denotative, univocal, monosemous, affirmative, indicative, antonymous, homonymous, extended, transferred; multivocal, polysemous; semantic, semasiological, semiotic, semiological; philological, lexical
 ▶ *Linguistics, Language 5*

10 **technical,** professional, special, specialized, jargonistic, argotic

11 **significant,** consequential, serious, important; weighty, substantial, pithy, meaty, of moment
 ▶ *Importance 799*

12 **meant,** implied, intended, deliberate, designed, planned; destined, predestined
 ▶ *Intention 374; Predetermination 384*

VERBS

13 **mean,** signify, have a meaning, have a sense, mean something; convey a meaning *or* a message *or* an idea, get across, communicate; denote, say clearly, say plainly, use plain words, say directly, spell out; declare, assert, affirm, express, inform, tell; connote, imply, indicate, symbolize, stand for, represent, betoken, designate; import, purport, intend, point to, add up to, boil down to, spell; convey, bespeak, tell of, speak of, breathe of, savor of, speak volumes, evidence; mean to say, try to say, be getting at, be driving at, really mean, have in mind, contemplate; allude to, refer to, hint at, suggest, intimate; say in other words, put another way, rephrase, paraphrase; repeat, tautologize; have the same meaning, agree in meaning, mean the same thing, coincide, accord; conflict in meaning, mean something else, mean the opposite, mean the reverse, contradict, disagree; talk turkey [Inf]
 ▶ *Information 170; Identification 184; Representation 187; Affirmation 189; Evidence 339; Intelligibility 363; Dissimilarity 734; Accord 735; Repetition 797; Latency 844*

14 **infer,** draw a meaning, deduce; understand, understand by
 ▶ *Supposition 359*

15 **intend,** aim, purpose, plan, design, destine, predestine; cause, result in, bring about, entail, involve; portend, presage, augur

▸ *Prediction 358; Intention 374; Predetermination 384; Plan 387; Cause 675*

ADVERBS

16 **meaningfully,** meaningly, with meaning, significantly, intelligibly; clearly, directly, explicitly, plainly, unambiguously, in plain words; to the effect that, in the sense that *or* of, in a sense, in some sense; as meant, as intended, as understood, according to the book, from the context; literally, verbatim, word for word; in other words, so to speak; figuratively, metaphorically, symbolically

▸ *Interpretation 365*

362 Lack of Meaning

Colorless green ideas sleep furiously. — NOAM CHOMSKY

NOUNS

1 **lack of meaning,** meaninglessness, absence of meaning, no meaning; no context, no bearing, irrelevance, nonsignificance, insignificance, unimportance

▸ *Unrelatedness 728; Unimportance 800*

2 **nonsense,** nonsensicality, nonsensical writing *or* verse, amphigory *or* amphigouri, absurdity, senselessness, inanity, vacuity, emptiness; bombast, triteness, truism, platitude, commonplace, cliché; mere words, empty words, verbalism; unreason, lack of reason, illogicality, sophistry; invalidity, dead letter, nullity, ineffectuality, illegibility, scribble, doodle, scribbling, scrawl, daub, misrepresentation; empty sound, meaningless noise, strumming, sounding brass, tinkling cymbal, loudness; jargon, abracadabra, hocus-pocus, mumbo jumbo; unintelligibility, incoherence, raving, delirium, frenzy

▸ *Insanity 110; Misrepresentation 188; Sophistry 330; Unintelligibility 364; Powerlessness 515*

3 **aimlessness,** purposelessness, lack of purpose, pointlessness, futility, worthlessness, ineffectuality

▸ *Uselessness 802*

4 **senseless talk,** foolish talk, silly talk, empty talk; nonsense, utter nonsense, absurdity, stuff, stuff and nonsense, balderdash, gibberish, gobbledegook, rigmarole *or* rigamarole, double-talk, doublespeak, babel, trash, rubbish, rot, tommyrot, bosh, blah, hokum, poppycock, drivel, twaddle; [Inf]: Greek, bunk, tripe, eyewash, piffle, bilge water *or* bilge, bull, bullshit, crap, yak *or* yack *or* yackety-yak

5 **empty talk,** empty chatter, idle speech, verbiage, diffuseness; jabber, jaw, babble, gabble, prattle, prate, psychobabble; sweet nothings, endearments, flattery, blarney; flummery, trumpery; bunkum *or* buncombe, moonshine, humbug, claptrap, wind, vaporing, galimatias, fable, falsehood, exaggeration, blather *or* blether; sales talk, sales blandishment, sales patter, patter, glib talk; [Inf]: spiel, gas, line, hot air, spouting,

yammer, blah-blah-blah, flapdoodle, jazz, jive, junk, guff, malarkey *or* malarky, baloney, hooey, flimflam

▸ *Untruthfulness, Falsehood 192; Diffuseness 199; Talkativeness 207; Flattery 439; Untruth 722*

6 **aimlessness,** purposelessness, lack of purpose, pointlessness, futility

▸ *Uselessness 802*

ADJECTIVES

7 **meaningless,** senseless, unmeaning, without meaning; irrelevant, nonsignificant, insignificant, unimportant; trite, commonplace, platitudinous, hackneyed, clichéd, banal, trivial, trifling; nonsense, nonsensical, amphigoric, absurd, inane, foolish, silly, fatuous, illogical, sophistic *or* sophistical; incoherent, unintelligible, illegible, mystifying, without rhyme or reason; piffling, ineffectual, ineffective; invalid, null, empty, vacuous, hollow; unexpressive, unidiomatic, unapt, rubbishy, trashy; ridiculous, ludicrous, asinine, anserine, preposterous, idiotic, mad, crazy, delirious; frenzied, ranting, raving; prattling, gibbering, blithering, windy, exaggerated, Pickwickian

▸ *Insanity 110; Exaggeration 194; Folly 353; Ridiculousness 368; Dissimilarity 734; Unimportance 800*

8 **aimless,** purposeless, pointless, futile, vain, worthless, inconsequential, ineffectual

▸ *Uselessness 802*

9 **unmeant,** unintentional, unintended, involuntary, unimplied; misunderstood, misread, mistranslated, misinterpreted; misrepresented, mistaken; insincere, flattering, tongue-in-cheek

▸ *Misrepresentation 188; Misinterpretation 366; Flattery 439*

VERBS

10 **mean nothing,** have no meaning, have no bearing, make no sense, be nonsense, make nonsense of; act aimlessly, scribble, daub, fiddle, tap, drum, strum, scratch

▸ *Unimportance 800*

11 **not understand,** misinterpret, miss the meaning of, miss the point of, have no meaning for, pass over one's head; puzzle, confuse, be Greek to [Inf]

▸ *Unintelligibility 364; Uncertainty 841*

12 **talk nonsense,** not mean what one says, talk rubbish, talk bunkum; talk like an idiot, rant, rave, rant and rave; twaddle, jabber, jaw, babble, gabble, blather *or* blether, garble, psychobabble, vapor, prattle, prate, gibber, talk gibberish, drivel, double-talk, flatter, blarney, gush; [Inf]: yak *or* yack *or* yackety-yak, spread the bull, bullshit, spiel, yammer

▸ *Exaggeration 194; Talkativeness 207; Folly 353; Unintelligibility 364; Misinterpretation 366; Flattery 439; Uncertainty 841*

ADVERBS

13 **meaninglessly,** senselessly, irrelevantly, insignifi-

cantly, nonsensically, foolishly, absurdly, ridiculously; illogically, unintelligibly, aimlessly, purposelessly

INTERJECTIONS

14 **nonsense!,** bunk!, humbug!, rubbish!, poppycock!, rot!, what rot!, stuff and nonsense!, baloney! [Inf], hooey! [Inf]

363 Intelligibility

Unless one is a genius, it is best to aim at being intelligible.
— ANTHONY HOPE

NOUNS

1 **intelligibility,** comprehensibility, understandability, knowability, apprehensibility; fathomableness, penetrability, scrutability, interpretability, explicability, teachability; coherence, unambiguity, unambivalence; precision, preciseness, definiteness, positiveness, certainty; sense, meaningfulness, informativeness; vividness, graphicness, descriptiveness
> *Knowledge 348; Meaning 361*

2 **clarity,** simplicity, clearness, plainness, plain speaking, plain speech; explicitness, articulateness, articulacy, distinctness, directness, straightforwardness, downrightness, forthrightness; uninvolvement, unadornment, unadorned style, simple eloquence; readability, legibility, decipherability, clear handwriting, clear printing; decoding, easiness, facility, obviousness, self-evidence; explanation, amplification, interpretation; simplification, popularization, lowest common denominator; short words, words of one syllable, plain words, simple language, plain English, mother tongue; limpidity, transparency, lucidity, pellucidity, perspicuity
> *Clarity 196; Transparency 249; Interpretation 365; Simplicity 526; Easiness 823*

3 **recognizability,** cognizability; distinguishability, distinctiveness, distinction; definiteness, definition
> *Certainty 840*

4 **understanding,** comprehension, realization, apprehension; mastery, grasp; learning, knowledge; perception, recognition
> *Identification 184; Knowledge 348*

ADJECTIVES

5 **intelligible,** comprehensible, understandable, knowable; apprehensible, fathomable, penetrable, scrutable, interpretable, realizable, coherent, sensible, making sense, sane; audible, coming through loud and clear, visible, luminous; unambiguous, unambivalent, unequivocal, univocal; meaningful, explicable, teachable; unblurred, focused, clear-cut, precise, definite, certain, positive; telling, striking; vivid, graphic, highly colored; descriptive, illustrative, explanatory, explicatory; interpretive *or* interpretative, informative

> *Sanity 109; Description 202; Visibility 244; Knowledge 348; Meaning 361*

6 **simple,** clear, crystal-clear, plain; plainly stated, explicit, articulate, well-spoken, distinct; direct, straightforward, straight-from-the-shoulder, unevasive, unadorned, downright, forthright; uninvolved, uncomplicated, obvious, self-explanatory, self-evident, easy, easily understood, easy to comprehend, easy to follow, easy to grasp, made easy, made simple, clear to anyone; easy to read, readable, legible, decipherable, clearly handwritten, clearly printed; uncoded, decoded, explained, interpreted, simplified; popularized, popular, exoteric, for everyone, for the layman, for the general public, reaching a mass audience, aiming for the lowest common denominator, available to all; apodictic; using short words, using simple language, limpid, transparent, lucid, pellucid, perspicuous, easy as pie, as clear as day, as plain as the nose on one's face
> *Clarity 196; Transparency 249; Interpretation 365; Simplicity 526; Easiness 823*

7 **recognizable,** distinguishable, identifiable, distinct, defined, well-defined; standing out, definite, unmistakable, knowable
> *Specialty 779; Certainty 840*

VERBS

8 **make comprehensible,** simplify, make clear, make crystal-clear, make plain; state plainly, speak clearly, articulate, repeat, recapitulate; make easy, predigest, make easily understood; popularize, write for the layperson, address the general public, reach a mass audience; aim for the lowest common denominator, make available to all; spell out, put in plain words, state in plain English; use short words, use simple language, avoid gobbledegook, offer an easy read; facilitate, explain, explicate, interpret, elucidate; clarify, clear up, belabor the obvious, emphasize, get *or* put across
> *Clarity 196; Interpretation 365; Simplicity 526; Repetition 797; Easiness 823*

9 **understand,** comprehend, know, realize, apprehend, fathom, penetrate; master, learn, have, hold, retain, remember, have understanding, get to the bottom of, grasp, grasp the meaning; get the gist of, get the idea, catch on, get the picture, see the lay of the land, catch the drift of, get hold of, seize, be on to, take in, follow, get, begin to understand, come to understand; have insight, have one's eyes opened, see the light, see through, see it all, be undeceived, get to know, be told, be informed; [Inf]: be with it, latch onto, get wise to, get the hang of, tumble to, dig, savvy
> *Information 170; Vision 242; Discovery 345; Knowledge 348; Wisdom 352; Memory 354*

10 **be intelligible,** make sense, come through loud and clear; come alive, take on depth; offer readability, read easily; add up, speak to one's understanding, tell its own tale, speak for itself, speak volumes; have no se-

crets, become apparent, get across, sink in, penetrate, dawn on, register, open one's eyes

> *Visibility 244; Argument 329; Evidence 339*

11 recognize, detect, identify, spot, descry, distinguish, discern, make out, perceive, conceive; see at a glance, see with half an eye, see, make no mistake

> *Identification 184; Affirmation 189; Vision 242; Certainty 840*

12 be recognizable, have a distinctive appearance, stand out, leap out

ADVERBS

13 intelligibly, comprehensibly, understandably, coherently, articulately, expressively; simply, clearly, lucidly, plainly, distinctly; unmistakably, explicitly, concisely, in words of one syllable; with clarity, in a clear style, in plain terms, in no uncertain terms, unambiguously, in plain English; for the layperson, for the general public

364 Unintelligibility

NOUNS

1 unintelligibility, incomprehensibility, inapprehensibility, meaninglessness, lack of meaning, lack of sense, nonsense, so much nonsense; unclearness, lack of clarity, obscurity, uncertainty, ambiguity, equivocation; esotericism, difficulty, perplexity, bafflement, confusion, mystification; impenetrability, inscrutability, the unknown, inconceivability, lack of understanding, inexplicability, unaccountability; impossibility of discovery, secrecy; babbling, mumbling, stuttering, stammering; blankness, lack of expression, impassivity; inaudibility, faintness, muteness; illegibility, unreadability, invisibility; privacy, arcaneness, mystery; profoundness, deepness, occultism, mysticism; inexpressibility, unspeakableness, ineffability, incommunicability, indefinableness

> *Occultism 86; Speech, Spoken Language 205; Faintness of Sound 233; Lack of Meaning 362; Uncertainty 841*

2 lack of clarity, confused message, double meaning, extended meaning, ambiguity, ambiguousness, equivocation

3 unintelligible thing, obscure point, perplexing question, puzzle, puzzler, problem, conundrum, knotty problem, hard *or* tough nut to crack, baffling attitude, poker face; mysterious message, secret, secret book, code, cipher, secret language; gibberish, scrawl, scribble; mystery, enigma, riddle, paradox

> *Secrecy 182; Obscurity 197; Uncertainty 841*

ADJECTIVES

4 unintelligible, incomprehensible, meaningless; unclear, obscure, inconceivable, not understandable; impossible to explain, inexplicable, unexplainable, unaccountable; nonsensical, gibbering, incoherent, rambling, inarticulate; unknown, undiscoverable, unfathomable, inapprehensible, unbridgeable, impenetrable, unsearchable, inscrutable; blank, expressionless, deadpan, impassive, poker-faced; inaudible, muted; scrambled, garbled, scrawly, scribbled, cramped, crabbed, encoded; hard to decode, undecipherable, unreadable, illegible; undiscernible, unseen, invisible, hidden, unknowable; private, arcane, cryptic, mysterious, shrouded in mystery, enigmatic; esoteric, gnostic, oracular, profound, deep, occult, mystic, mystical; inexpressible, unspeakable, unpronounceable, unutterable, ineffable, incommunicable, untranslatable; indefinable

> *Religion 81; Concealment 181; Obscurity 197; Taciturnity 208; Lack of Meaning 362; Depth 598*

5 unclear, obscure, confused, ambiguous, equivocal

6 unexplained, never solved, without a solution, without a clue, unsolvable, insoluble; unsolved, unresolved, uncertain, shrouded in mystery

7 unrecognizable, incognizable, indistinguishable, unidentifiable; indistinct, undefined, poorly defined, hidden; indefinite, easily mistaken; unknowable

> *Faintness of Sound 233; Insensitivity 268; Ignorance 349*

8 difficult, confusing, puzzling, baffling, perplexing, hard to understand; complex, complicated, beyond one's comprehension, defying comprehension, beyond one, over one's head; recondite, abstruse, elusive, amorphous, shadowy, obscure; enigmatic, inscrutable, mysterious, occult; nebulous, vague, murky, muddy, misty, foggy, hazy, fuzzy, dim; clear as mud, unclear; ambiguous, equivocal, paradoxical, of doubtful meaning, oracular

> *Obscurity 197; Dimness 248; Equivocation 380; Difficulty 824; Latency 844*

9 strange, odd, weird, abnormal, unexpected, bizarre; quaint, eccentric, oddball [Inf]

> *Surprise 292; Nonconformity 782; Uncertainty 841*

10 confused, puzzled, baffled, perplexed, mystified; unable to understand, wondering, bewildered, stumped, confounded, nonplussed; out of one's depth; [Inf]: out of it, not getting it, flummoxed

VERBS

11 be unintelligible, defy comprehension, not make sense, elude one, escape one, lose one, make one's head swim *or* ache; need an interpreter, present a puzzle, keep one guessing, talk in riddles; speak in tongues, talk nonsense, gibber, ramble, mean nothing; speak badly, speak gobbledegook, talk like an idiot, babble; look blank, look expressionless, look deadpan; go over one's head, be beyond one's reach

> *Disbelief 88; Lack of Meaning 362; Disturbance 768; Uncertainty 841*

12 puzzle, cause doubt, baffle, perplex, mystify, bewilder;

confound, stump; confuse, bedevil, entangle, flummox [Inf]

13 **make unintelligible,** scribble, scrawl, doodle; scramble, garble, encode, encipher; shroud in mystery, obscure, complicate, confuse

14 **find unintelligible,** not understand, find hard to understand, find too difficult; misjudge, misunderstand, get wrong, get the wrong idea, not know, not register, have a blind spot; have no grasp of, not have the slightest idea, not make out, not grasp it, not know what to make of, make neither head nor tail of, make nothing of, throw up one's hands; puzzle, wonder, rack one's brains; be out of one's depth, not know what one is about, be lost, be at sea, be on a different wavelength; not get it [Inf]

> *Unskillfulness 128; Faulty Vision 243; Inattention 324; Evidence 339; Misjudgment 342; Error 351*

15 **be unexplained,** require explanation, remain unsolved, be unanswered, have no solution, give no clue

ADVERBS

16 **unintelligibly,** incomprehensibly, meaninglessly, inconceivably; inexplicably, unaccountably, incoherently, inarticulately; unfathomably, impenetrably; inscrutably, expressionlessly, blankly, impassively; inaudibly; unreadably, illegibly; ambiguously, cryptically, esoterically, mysteriously, enigmatically

365 Interpretation

NOUNS

1 **interpretation,** construction, rendering, way of putting; explanation, definition, description, explication; emendation, amendment, editing, simplification; exposition, biblical interpretation, exegesis, hermeneutics, epexegesis, eisegesis; judgment, estimate, personal feeling; understanding, insight, enlightenment, light, clarification, elucidation, illumination; illustration, exemplification, demonstration, example; resolution, solution, answer, key; clue, the secret, decipherment, decoding, code cracking, analysis; application, particular interpretation, twist, turn, reading, lection, meaning, subaudition, connotation; euhemerism, demythologization, allegorization, metaphor; accepted reading, usual text, vulgate; edited text, alternative reading, variant reading, rendition, conflation; version, edition, critical edition, variorum

> *Linguistics, Language 5; Literature 139; Clarity 196; Answer 334; Discovery 345; Meaning 361; Intelligibility 363; Simplicity 526; Improvement 807*

2 **annotation,** gloss, footnote, textual note, marginalia, scholium; note, note of explanation, legend, appendix; explanatory remark, word of explanation, inscription, comment, editorial comment, commentary, apparatus criticus

> *Judgment 341; Addition 748*

3 **criticism,** critique, review, notice; theater *or* art *or* music *or* book *or* film *or* television review; rave review, puff, favorable review, good review; negative review, bad review, panning; biblical criticism, higher criticism, lower criticism *or* textual criticism; form criticism, new criticism, deconstruction

> *Literature 139; Advice 176; Dissertation 203*

4 **translation,** transcription, literary conversion, rendering, literal translation, word-for-word translation, verbal translation; loose translation, free translation; bilingual text; version, edition, redaction, epitome; rewording, paraphrase, adaptation, simplification, amplification, transliteration; decoding, unscrambling, decipherment; lipreading, key; [Inf]: crib, pony, trot

> *Representation 187; Summary 204; Accuracy 350; Intelligibility 363*

5 **science of interpretation,** exegetics, hermeneutics, tropology; epigraphy, cryptology, cryptography, cryptanalysis, paleography, semiology; lexicography; linguistics; diagnostics, symptomatology; oneirocriticism

> *Linguistics, Language 5; Meaning 361*

6 **interpreter,** explainer, clarifier, paraphraser, paraphrast, simplifier, popularizer; translator, linguist; lexicographer, definer; teacher, expounder, exponent, reviewer, critic, textual critic, literary critic; editor, copyeditor, emender, emendator; annotator, glossator, glossarist, scholiast, commentator; exegete, exegetist; euhemerist, demythologizer; epigraphist, paleographer, cryptographer, cryptologist, cryptanalyst, decoder, decipherer, lipreader; oneirocritic, medium, spiritualist, diviner

> *Education 48; Religion 81; Literature 139; Knowledge 348; Prediction 358*

7 **news interpreter,** journalist, reporter, columnist, commentator, editorial writer; news source, specialist source; public relations (PR) person, PR representative *or* officer, press officer, press agent, flack, public information officer, publicizer; spokesperson, mouthpiece, spin doctor [Inf]

> *Communications 169; Information 170; News 171; Publication 173*

ADJECTIVES

8 **interpretive,** interpretative, interpretational, constructive; explanatory, explicative *or* explicatory, explaining, descriptive, expository *or* expositive; insightful; illustrative, demonstrative, definitional, definitive, defining, exemplary; exegetic *or* exegetical, hermeneutic; clarifying, elucidative, illuminating; semiological, euhemeristic, demythologizing; divining, oneirocritical

> *Clarity 196; Meaning 361; Simplicity 526*

9 **interpreted,** glossed, explained, defined; illustrated, elucidated, clarified, simplified; annotated, commented on; edited, emended, amended, conflated; translated,

rendered, deciphered, decoded, unscrambled, cracked, unlocked

 ▶ *Intelligibility 363*

10 **annotative,** glossarial, scholiastic, explanatory; critical, editorial, commentarial

 ▶ *Addition 748*

11 **translational,** paraphrastic, metaphrastic; polyglot, multilingual, bilingual; synonymous, equivalent, literal, word-for-word, verbatim, faithful; free, loose

 ▶ *Linguistics, Language 5*

VERBS

12 **interpret,** construe, put a construction on, render, put; explain, explicate, inform, expound, comment on, give a sense to, ascribe a meaning to, make sense of; understand, take to mean, read, read into, read between the lines, deduce, infer, reason; define, describe, emend, amend, twist, turn; conflate, edit, copyedit; simplify, spell out, popularize; facilitate, judge, estimate; give insight, give enlightenment, clarify, make clear, disambiguate, analyze, elucidate, illuminate, throw *or* shed light on; illustrate, exemplify, give an example, demonstrate, show, act as guide

 ▶ *Clarity 196; Judgment 341; Discovery 345; Meaning 361; Intelligibility 363; Simplicity 526; Improvement 807*

13 **decipher,** crack, crack a code *or* cipher, unlock a code; decode, unscramble, find the meaning; read hieroglyphics, read, spell out, puzzle out, make out, work out, sort out; piece together, find the sense of, find the key to, solve, resolve, find a solution *or* resolution, enucleate [Arch]; unravel, unriddle, demystify, disentangle

 ▶ *Answer 334; Intelligibility 363*

14 **annotate,** gloss, footnote, add commentary, add explanation, write notes for, inscribe, comment on

 ▶ *Addition 748*

15 **criticize,** review, critique, evaluate, give *or* offer criticism, slate; give *or* offer constructive criticism, puff, pan [Inf]

 ▶ *Literature 139; Advice 176*

16 **translate,** transcribe, transliterate, render; paraphrase, rephrase, reword, restate, rehash; make a new version, put into, turn into, adapt, simplify, amplify; decipher, read sign language, read lips, lipread; interpret, act as interpreter, offer an interpretation; [Inf]: use a crib *or* pony *or* trot

 ▶ *Representation 187; Summary 204*

17 **interpret news,** report, cover, write a column, slant, comment on, write an editorial; do public relations, serve as press officer for, act as spokesperson for, spin [Inf], give a spin to [Inf]

 ▶ *Communications 169; Information 170; News 171; Publication 173; Periodicals 175*

ADVERBS

18 **in other words,** in words to that effect, that is to say,

that is, i.e., namely, *videlicet* [L] *or* viz., to wit, to put it another way; plainly, in plain words, in plain English; to be clear, to explain, in explanation, interpretively, interpretatively, illustratively, exegetically

366 Misinterpretation

NOUNS

1 **misinterpretation,** wrong interpretation, misunderstanding, misapprehension; mistake, error; mistranslation, translator's error, misreading, false reading, wrong words; misconstruction, false construction, misapplication, misconception, misjudgment; misdiagnosis, miscomputation, miscalculation

 ▶ *Misjudgment 342; Error 351*

2 **misrepresentation,** distortion, lying, perversion, coloring the truth; overestimation, underestimation, exaggeration; wrong explanation, false depiction *or* impression

 ▶ *Misrepresentation 188; Deception 193; Exaggeration 194; Overestimation 343; Underestimation 344; Distortion 627*

ADJECTIVES

3 **misinterpreted,** misunderstood, mistranslated, misread, misconstrued, misconceived; misquoted, garbled, falsified, distorted, exaggerated, inflated, misrepresented

VERBS

4 **misinterpret,** misunderstand, misapprehend; mistranslate, render incorrectly, garble; misread, misconstrue, put a wrong construction on, get wrong, get one wrong, take wrong, misconceive, misjudge; miscompute, misdiagnose, mistake; err, blunder

5 **misrepresent,** distort, lie, pervert; overestimate, underestimate, exaggerate; explain wrongly, give a false idea, give a false depiction *or* impression

 ▶ *Misrepresentation 188; Exaggeration 194; Overestimation 343; Underestimation 344; Distortion 627*

ADVERBS

6 **mistakenly,** erroneously, in error, wrongly, falsely

 ▶ *Error 351*

7 **misrepresentedly,** distortedly, exaggeratedly

367 Affectation

NOUNS

1 **affectation,** affectedness, pretentiousness, artifice, histrionics, theatricality, showmanship, exhibition; sanctimoniousness, sanctimony; irony, speciosity, speciousness, deceptiveness; pretension, pretense, pompousness, euphuism; falsity, false display, false front, posture, pose, sophistry; putting on airs

 ▶ *Untruthfulness, Falsehood 192*

2 **pretender,** humbug, actor, bluffer, deceiver; poseur,

poser, fraud, charlatan, attitudinizer, ironist, hypocrite, exhibitionist

ADJECTIVES

3 **affected,** pretentious, mannered, artificial, histrionic, theatrical, stagy, showy; sanctimonious; ironic, ironical, specious, deceptive; precious, euphuistic; false, posturing, posing, self-conscious, conceited, unnatural, stilted, meretricious, pompous, puffed up, boastful, chichi

VERBS

4 **be affected,** affect, attitudinize, pose, put on airs, pretend, assume, posture, bluff, show off, playact, play to the gallery

ADVERBS

5 **affectedly,** pretentiously, artificially; pompously, stuffily, self-consciously, unnaturally, sanctimoniously; ironically, speciously, with tongue in cheek

6 **showily,** for effect, meretriciously, insincerely, theatrically, stagily, flashily, histrionically, boastfully

368   Ridiculousness

Now is not this ridiculous — and is not this preposterous? / A thorough-paced absurdity — explain it if you can.
— W. S. GILBERT

NOUNS

1 **ridiculousness,** ludicrousness, absurdity, laughableness, pricelessness, foolishness; comicality, drollery; daftness, eccentricity, whimsicality; clowning, buffoonery, zaniness, bizarreness, bathos, folly, senselessness, fatuity, fatuousness, nuttiness [Inf]
   ▶ *Lack of Meaning 362*

2 **comedy,** farce, burlesque, slapstick, knockabout
   ▶ *Light Entertainment 138; Humor 277*

3 **object of ridicule,** laughingstock, idiot, fool, clown, eccentric, buffoon, butt, figure of fun, nut [Inf]
   ▶ *Derision 369*

4 **joke,** gag, jape, quip, howler, blunder, boo-boo [Inf]; wisecrack, jest, gibe, ridicule, derision, teasing, mockery
   ▶ *Humor 277; Derision 369*

ADJECTIVES

5 **ridiculous,** ludicrous, absurd, laughable, preposterous, priceless, foolish; funny, comical, comic, droll, daft, eccentric, whimsical; clownish, zany, bizarre, bathetic, asinine, humorous, risible, hilarious, fatuous, derisory; comic, farcical, burlesque, slapstick, knockabout; rib-tickling, side-splitting; nutty [Inf]

VERBS

6 **be ridiculous,** play the fool, go from the sublime to the ridiculous, clown

7 **make someone laugh,** have them rolling in the aisles, be funny, be hilarious; tickle, amuse, give one the giggles

▶ *Humor 277*

ADVERBS

8 **ridiculously,** ludicrously, foolishly, stupidly, sillily, idiotically, daftly, absurdly, senselessly, fatuously

9 **eccentrically,** whimsically, bizarrely, quaintly

10 **funnily,** wittily, comically, hilariously

369   Derision

NOUNS

1 **derision,** mockery, derisiveness, ridicule, banter, badinage, sarcasm, scoffing

2 **form of derision,** satire, parody, caricature, cartoon, burlesque, lampoon, joke, denunciation, mockery; takeoff, put-down [Inf]
   ▶ *Ridiculousness 368*

3 **derider,** satirist, lampooner *or* lampoonist, joker, mimic, caricaturist, cartoonist

4 **laughingstock,** butt, target, goat, dupe, fool, figure of fun, stooge, fall guy [Inf]

ADJECTIVES

5 **derisive,** mocking, ridiculing, bantering, sarcastic, scoffing

6 **satirical,** sardonic, quizzical, caustic

VERBS

7 **deride,** mock, laugh at, snigger about, poke fun at, send up, scoff at, jeer at, put down, make a mockery of; pillory, satirize, lampoon, caricature, denounce, debunk, deflate, guy

ADVERBS

8 **derisively,** mockingly, jokingly, jeeringly, banteringly, contemputously, sarcastically, scoffingly

9 **satirically,** sardonically, quizzically, cynically, caustically

370   Repute

Reputation is an idle and most false imposition; oft got without merit, and lost without deserving.
— WILLIAM SHAKESPEARE

NOUNS

1 **repute,** estimation, reputation, report, good report, reference, good reference; respect, regard, esteem, favor, good color, cachet; approval, approbation, distinction, eminence, mark, prestige, credit, credibility, claim to fame
   ▶ *Respect 435; Approval 437; Importance 799*

2 **person of repute,** man *or* woman of honor, pillar of the community, man *or* woman of high standing, notable, eminence; somebody, celebrity, star, megastar, favorite; [Inf]: big shot, fat cat, very important person (VIP)
   ▶ *Importance 799*

3 **reputable,** of repute, creditworthy, creditable, respected, respectable, regarded, esteemed, favored, well-thought-of, highly thought of, honored, honorable, distinguished, notable, eminent, approved; renowned, famous, fabled, popular, in favor

4 **reputed,** alleged, supposed

VERBS

5 **have a good reputation,** be respected, be esteemed, be famous, be well thought of, be highly thought of, make a name for oneself

ADVERBS

6 **reputably,** estimably, creditably, respectably, honorably

7 **eminently,** prestigiously, prominently, famously, notably, notedly, nobly, illustriously, outstandingly, conspicuously, distinctively, notoriously, popularly, celebratedly

8 **reputedly,** allegedly, supposedly

371 Disrepute

NOUNS

1 **disrepute,** disrespect, notoriety, bad name, shady past; bad reputation, bad odor, bad light, infamy, ill repute, disreputability; unseemliness, disfavor, discredit, dishonor, slur, ignominy, degradation, disgrace, shame, scandal
▶ *Disrespect 436*

2 **disreputable character,** rogue, blackguard, undesirable, ugly customer, scoundrel, bad lot, bad egg, bad influence, black sheep, ne'er-do-well, cad, bounder, talk of the town
▶ *Disobedience 427; Immorality 432*

3 **disreputable action,** foul play, dirty trick, skulduggery, fraud, swindle, scam, petty crime, sharp practice; con trick *or* con [Inf], hanky-panky [Inf]
▶ *Disobedience 427; Immorality 432*

ADJECTIVES

4 **disreputable,** notorious, ignominious, disgraced; degrading, infamous, nefarious, debased; shady, questionable, scandalous, dishonorable, shameless, immoral, underhand, fraudulent, devious, suspicious, dodgy; iffy [Inf], not on the level [Inf]
▶ *Immorality 432*

VERBS

5 **be disreputable,** lose repute, be shamed, fall from grace *or* favor, disgrace oneself, lower oneself, demean oneself, degrade oneself; show oneself up, humiliate oneself, forfeit one's reputation

6 **bring into disrepute,** shame, put to shame, bring shame upon; desecrate, defile, dishonor, discredit, debase, cast a slur, malign

ADVERBS

7 **disreputably,** dishonorably, discreditably, ignobly, ignominiously, infamously, notoriously, nefariously, unseemly, unrespectably

8 **disgracefully,** shamefully, shockingly, heinously, atrociously, scandalously, outrageously, contemptibly, despicably, abominably, execrably, deplorably

9 **deviously,** suspiciously, shabbily, shoddily, basely, meanly

Will and Behavior

372 Will

NOUNS

1 **will,** willing, volition, conation, intention, intent, purpose, wish; liking, desire, choice, option, preference, pleasure, fancy; inclination, disposition, notion, mind, half a mind; discretion, determination, decision
▶ *Desire 288*

2 **willpower,** strength of will *or* mind *or* purpose, firmness of purpose, iron will, fortitude, moral fiber, determination, steadfastness, resoluteness; resolution, resolve, tenacity, mind over matter, self-control

3 **willfulness,** self-will, one's own sweet will, mind *or* will of one's own, single-mindedness; waywardness, obstinacy, obduracy, doggedness, intransigence; stubbornness, pigheadedness, hardheadedness, mulishness, bloody-mindedness [Brit]
▶ *Perseverance 377; Selfishness 444*

4 **free will,** independence, self-determination, autonomy, freedom of choice, personal freedom, discretion, free hand, free spirit

5 **final will** *or* **wishes,** last will and testament, testament; legacy, bequest
▶ *Law 53*

ADJECTIVES

6 **willed,** volitional, volitive, conative, intentional, purposeful, deliberate; desired, chosen, opted for, preferred; willing, inclined, disposed, with a mind to; at will, discretionary, determining, determined, decided
▶ *Willingness 373*

7 **iron-willed,** strong-willed, purposeful, firm, determined, steadfast, resolute, adamant, unyielding; resolved, tenacious, self-controlled

8 **willful,** self-willed, single-minded, headstrong; wayward, obstinate, obdurate, dogged, intransigent; stubborn, pigheaded, hardheaded, bullheaded, mulish, bloody-minded [Brit]

9 **free-willed,** independent, autonomous, self-determined

10 **bequeathed,** willed, passed on, handed down, left, conferred

VERBS

11 **will,** intend, propose, wish, want; like, desire, choose, opt for, plump for, prefer, fancy, favor; determine, decide, think best, see fit

12 **cause,** bring about, effect, be bent *or* hellbent on

13 **follow one's own will,** do as one likes *or* chooses *or* pleases, please oneself, go one's own way, know one's own mind, have a mind of one's own, be one's own man *or* woman

14 **impose one's will,** assert oneself; command, demand, order, ordain, decree; dominate, have one's own way, have it all one's own way; force, trample over, bulldoze, bully

15 **bequeath,** will, impart, bestow, pass on, hand down, leave, confer

ADVERBS

16 **at will,** as one pleases *or* wishes, when and how one pleases, at one's pleasure; as one thinks fit *or* best, ad libitum, ad lib

373 Willingness

NOUNS

1 **willingness,** readiness, preparedness, promptness; gameness, quickness, receptiveness, receptivity, responsiveness; compliance, cooperativeness, cooperation, consent; contentedness, favorableness
▶ *Cooperation 827*

2 **eagerness,** enthusiasm, keenness, avidity; alacrity, ardor, fervor, fervidity, zeal, zealousness
▶ *Desire 288*

3 **acquiescence,** agreeability, amenability, compliance, pliancy, pliability, tractability, persuadability, docility, obedience
▶ *Obedience 426*

4 **goodwill,** benevolence, graciousness, cordiality, helpfulness, collaboration, right mood

▶ *Benevolence 305; Help 825*

5 voluntary work, voluntary service, voluntary aid, unpaid work, self-appointed task, labor of love, charitable work, community work; volunteering, volunteerism, voluntarism
▶ *Relief 275*

6 willing worker, willing hand, helping hand, volunteer, unpaid worker, aid worker, charity worker, eager beaver

ADJECTIVES

7 willing, ready, prepared, prompt; game, receptive, responsive; compliant, cooperative, consenting, assenting; content, disposed, prone, agreeable, in favor

8 eager, ready and willing, willing and able, enthusiastic, keen, avid; alacritous, arduous, fervent, zealous, champing at the bit; [Inf]: raring to go, spoiling for, gung-ho

9 acquiescent, amenable, pliant, pliable, tractable, persuadable, docile, obedient

10 goodwilled, benevolent, gracious, cordial, helpful, cooperative, collaborative
▶ *Benevolence 305; Philanthropy 307*

11 voluntary, unprompted, spontaneous, offered, unbidden, unpaid, offering, self-appointed

VERBS

12 be willing, be ready, comply, cooperate, consent, assent, agree, have a good mind to; acquiesce, obey, abide by, accept, go along with

13 be eager, show enthusiasm, go off like a shot, go off at the drop of a hat, jump at, leap at, catch at, go out of one's way to, bend over *or* lean over backward; help, collaborate, aid, assist, lend a hand
▶ *Help 825*

14 volunteer, offer, put forward, put oneself in the firing line, sacrifice oneself

ADVERBS

15 willingly, with a will, without demur, cheerfully, readily, agreeably, gladly, with gusto, with good grace, with all one's heart, with open arms

16 eagerly, enthusiastically, keenly, ardently, avidly, zealously

17 voluntarily, spontaneously, at the drop of a hat, without hesitation, like a shot, of one's own free will, on one's own, without prompting, of one's own accord, on one's own initiative *or* volition

374 Intention

NOUNS

1 intention, purpose, set purpose, settled purpose, intent, intendment; meaning, tenor, gist; motive, mens rea *or* criminal intent; good intention, benevolence; ulterior motive, ax to grind
▶ *Benevolence 305; Malevolence 306; Meaning 361; Motivation 508*

2 intentionality, deliberateness, calculation, calculated risk, predetermination, premeditation; determination, resolve, resolution, decision, judgment, final decision, final word; ultimatum, threat, promise, engagement, bid, attempt
▶ *Judgment 341; Resolution 376; Predetermination 384; Attempt 390; Promise 458; Calculation 784*

3 future intention, prospect, view, purview, plan, proposal, design; project, enterprise, undertaking, pursuit, study, occupation, preoccupation; aspiration, aim, goal, objective
▶ *Desire 288; Undertaking 391; Future Time 650*

4 final intention, overall design, ultimate purpose, the grand scheme, the big picture; final cause, last things; raison d'être, be-all and end-all; trend, tendency, intentional bias, tendentiousness
▶ *Cause 675; End 773*

5 objective, final objective, end, destination, end in view, aim, hope, object, goal; mark, target, butt, stationary target, moving target, target area, bull's-eye; prey, quarry, game; finish line, finish tape, winning post; prize, cup, trophy, crown, wreath, laurels; dream, lifelong dream, vision, heart's desire, Promised Land, land of milk and honey, Mecca, El Dorado, Shangri-la, Fountain of Youth, philosophers' stone, Holy Grail, pot of gold
▶ *Desire 288; Pursuit 385; Reward 453; End 773*

ADJECTIVES

6 intending, prospective, aspiring, ambitious, would-be, hopeful; serious, serious-minded, purposive; intent on, determined, resolved, resolute, set, out to, out for, bent, hellbent; inclined, disposed, so minded, so inclined
▶ *Desire 288; Resolution 376*

7 intentional, intended, meant, designed, planned, deliberate, purposed, purposeful, for a purpose, for a reason; voluntary, volitional, willful; calculated, studied, premeditated, aforethought, predetermined
▶ *Will 372; Predetermination 384; Plan 387*

VERBS

8 intend, mean, purpose, design, propose, have in mind, have in view, have an eye to, harbor a design; contemplate, think of, ponder, meditate, calculate, reckon; plan, plan for, prepare for, look for, expect, foresee
▶ *Expectation 356; Foresight 357; Plan 387*

9 resolve, determine, determine to, mean to, have a mind to, have every intention, promise, threaten; premeditate, predetermine, have a purpose, have a motive; undertake, engage, take on oneself, shoulder
▶ *Resolution 376; Undertaking 391; Promise 458; Warning 814*

10 aim, aim at, go for, try for, bid for; aspire to, dream of, envision, strive for, work for, have designs on, set one's sights on, focus on, go for broke, go for it [Inf]

> *Attempt 390; Direction 697*

11 **intend for,** destine for, predestine; earmark, put aside for, hold for, keep for, reserve for, put on layaway

ADVERBS

12 **prospectively,** aspiringly, ambitiously, hopefully; seriously, serious-mindedly, purposively; determinedly, resolutely

13 **intentionally,** purposefully, purposely, on purpose, deliberately; voluntarily, volitionally, willfully, wittingly; by design, according to plan, as planned, as arranged; with meditation, with forethought, with malice aforethought

14 **with the intention of,** for a purpose, in order to, with the object of, with an eye to, pursuant to

375 Unwillingness

NOUNS

1 **unwillingness,** loathness, reluctance, indisposedness, disinclination, indisposition, dislike; grudgingness, grudging consent
> *Disagreement 463; Protest 507*

2 **opposition,** resistance, renitency, recalcitrance, unhelpfulness, noncooperation; disagreement, demur, refusal, rejection; hindrance, objection, protest, filibuster, balking; rebuff, turndown, dissent
> *Refusal 506; Hindrance 826; Opposition 828*

3 **unenthusiasm,** lack of enthusiasm *or* zeal, halfheartedness, dragging of the feet *or* foot-dragging; apathy, indifference, lifelessness, faintheartedness, want of alacrity, backwardness, slowness, hesitation, wariness
> *Slowness 693*

4 **dissociation,** nonassociation, abstention, antipathy; repugnance, abhorrence, recoil, aversion, averseness, no stomach for; scruple, qualm, doubt, shrinking, shyness, bashfulness, modesty
> *Indifference 289; Avoidance 386; Modesty 403*

5 **disobedience,** nonobservance, noncompliance; indocility, refractoriness, fractiousness, sulkiness, sullenness, grudging service, perfunctoriness; dereliction, neglect, negligence, remissness
> *Sullenness 304; Negligence 326; Disobedience 427*

6 **delay,** procrastination, postponement, putting on the back burner, putting off (till tomorrow), hangfire, shelving; sluggishness, laziness
> *Inactivity 415*

7 **reluctant person,** objector, resister, protester; abstainer, dropout, nonactivist; procrastinator, shirker, sulker, lazybones [Inf]

ADJECTIVES

8 **unwilling,** disinclined, indisposed, loath, reluctant, demurring, averse, not prepared, not so minded, not in the mood, not feeling like, not ready

9 **refusing,** recalcitrant, renitent, unconsenting, unreconciled, unconvinced, dissenting, dissident, adverse,

opposing, opposed, opting out, disagreeing, antipathetic, digging in one's toes *or* heels

10 **unenthusiastic,** cautious, wary, chary, hesitant, shy, bashful, modest, shrinking, shirking, unzealous, unsympathetic, halfhearted, foot-dragging, lukewarm, backward, unhelpful, uncooperative, apathetic; reluctant, resistant, protesting, sulky, sullen
> *Sullenness 304*

11 **procrastinating,** postponing, delaying, sluggish, lazy, neglectful, negligent, remiss

VERBS

12 **be unwilling,** loath, dislike; not have the heart to, have no stomach for, stickle, stick, have scruples, boggle at
> *Dissent 347; Rejection 383; Disagreement 463; Protest 507*

13 **oppose,** resist, refuse, reject; disagree, demur, dissent; hinder, object, protest, filibuster, stonewall, balk; opt out, rebuff, turn down; blench, flinch, fight, shy away
> *Refusal 506*

14 **dissociate,** abstain, abhor, recoil, avert, turn away, back away, edge away, not face; shrink from, duck, jib, shirk, elude; turn one's back, drop out; disobey, not cooperate, obstruct, not do one's part, not pull one's weight, not play, not play ball, neglect, have no truck with [Inf]

15 **grudge,** begrudge, turn up one's nose, show one's distaste; force oneself, make oneself, do with a heavy heart, sulk

16 **delay,** procrastinate, postpone, put on the back burner, put off, shelve; hold back, hang back, drag one's feet, sit back, sit tight, hesitate, tread warily, put off (till tomorrow), hang fire

ADVERBS

17 **unwillingly,** reluctantly, under protest, under duress, under pressure, in spite of oneself, against one's will, against the grain; regretfully, with regret, grudgingly, begrudgingly, without enthusiasm, unenthusiastically; halfheartedly, with dragging feet, with a heavy heart, with a long face, hesitantly, warily; sulkily, sullenly

376 Resolution

NOUNS

1 **resolution,** resolve, resolvedness, fixed *or* firm resolve, determination, grim determination; resoluteness, determinedness, doggedness, decidedness, decisiveness, deliberateness, purposefulness; firmness, firmness of purpose, firmness of mind *or* spirit, fixity of purpose, single-mindedness

2 **declaration,** decree, judgment, proclamation, statement; formal intention *or* opinion, concurrent resolution, joint resolution; mind made up, intention, intent, aim, decision; objective, plan, purpose

Intention 374

3 seriousness, earnestness, sincerity, commitment, total commitment, devotion, utter devotion, self-devotion, devotedness; staunchness, settledness, steadiness, stability, constancy, steadfastness, unshakableness; dedication, zeal, ardor, eagerness, drive, vigor

▸ *Activity 414; Vigor 518; Stability 674*

4 tenacity, persistence, perseverance; stubbornness, obstinacy, relentlessness, ruthlessness, inexorability, implacability, sternness; flintiness, hardness, steeliness, inflexibility, rigidity; doggedness, insistence, force; strength, fortitude, endurance; heroism, courage, courageousness; dauntlessness, undauntedness, fearlessness

▸ *Courage 284; Perseverance 377; Obstinacy 379; Compulsion 428*

5 will, iron will, willpower, strength of character, self-control, self-restraint, self-mastery, self-command, self-possession; fortitude, spirit, grit, backbone, mettle; courage, pluck, dash, aplomb, moral fiber, stiff upper lip; gritted teeth, clenched teeth, clenched jaw, backbone of steel, heart of oak, bulldoggedness

▸ *Courage 284; Will 372; Perseverance 377; Self-Restraint 455*

6 solution, answer, finding; outcome, upshot, end, result, end result; explanation, explication, reason; unraveling, disentanglement, unscrambling, sorting out

ADJECTIVES

7 resolute, resolved, determined, decided, decisive, deliberate, purposeful; firm, firm-minded, single-minded; intent upon, dead set upon, bent upon, hellbent, obsessed

▸ *Intention 374; Perseverance 377*

8 steady, stable, constant, reliable, dependable; staunch, steadfast, unshakable, solid, like the rock of Gibraltar; dedicated, zealous, eager, driven; serious, earnest, sincere, committed, totally committed, devoted, utterly devoted

▸ *Self-Restraint 455; Stability 674*

9 tenacious, persistent, persevering, stubborn, obstinate, immovable, unchangeable; relentless, ruthless, inexorable, implacable, stern; flinty, hard, steeled, armored, inflexible, rigid; dogged, insistent, pressing, driving, forceful; strong, fortified, enduring; heroic, courageous, unfearing, fearless; unshrinking, unflinching, unwavering, unhesitant, dauntless, undaunted; hard-hitting, stopping at nothing, all out, all-consuming, whole-hearted

▸ *Courage 284; Attention 323; Perseverance 377; Vigor 518*

10 strong-willed, iron-willed, strong-minded; self-controlled, self-restrained, self-mastered, self-possessed; uncompromising, unbending, inflexible, unyielding, intransigent; adamant, obstinate, stubborn, relentless, ruthless, inexorable, implacable, stern, grim, unfeeling,

stony, icy; rock-hard, hard as iron, iron, cast-iron, steely, tough as steel

▸ *Pitilessness 309; Obstinacy 379; Hardness 542; Toughness 547*

VERBS

11 be resolute, be determined, know one's own mind, mean business; stop at nothing, stick at nothing, go through fire and water, go to all lengths, go to any length, push to extremes; see through, carry through, go the whole hog

▸ *Completeness 761*

12 resolve, make up one's mind, decide, determine, determine once and for all, purpose, intend, will; make a resolution, settle, settle on, fix, seal; conclude, come to a conclusion *or* decision *or* determination

▸ *Will 372; Intention 374; End 773*

13 brace oneself, steel oneself, clench one's teeth, grit one's teeth, face, face the issue, face the odds, rise to the occasion; dare, defy, take on all comers, take what comes, bell the cat, outface, stare down; take the bull by the horns, take the bit between one's teeth, bite the bullet, take the plunge, cross the Rubicon; show one's colors, nail one's colors to the mast, set one's face, go for broke, go for it [Inf]

▸ *Defiance 416; Danger 811*

14 insist, urge, press, make something happen, not take no for an answer, put one's foot down, stand no nonsense; stand firm *or* fast, take one's stand, dig in, dig in one's toes *or* heels, hold *or* stand one's ground; stay put, not budge, not yield, not compromise, not give an inch, hold fast, stick fast, adhere; persist, stick it out, stick to one's guns, stick with it, hold out *or* fast; [Inf]: hang in, hang in there, hang tough

▸ *Perseverance 377*

ADVERBS

15 resolutely, decisively, purposefully, deliberately, single-mindedly, intently, seriously

16 earnestly, in earnest, with body and soul, with tooth and nail, with might and main, at all costs, at any price, come what may, come rain or shine, come hell or high water [Inf]

17 persistently, doggedly, manfully, like a man, once and for all

INTERJECTIONS

18 here goes!, go for it! [Inf], once more unto the breach!, damn the torpedoes — full speed ahead!

377 Perseverance

NOUNS

1 perseverance, persistence, doggedness, tenacity; determination, resolve, resolution, unremittance; pertinacity, pertinaciousness, stubbornness, obstinacy, insistence

---

▶ *Resolution 376; Obstinacy 379*

2 commitment, total commitment, single-mindedness, singleness of purpose, concentration, attention, application, sedulity, sedulousness, assiduity, assiduousness, abidingness; sleeplessness, vigilance, tirelessness, indefatigability; industriousness, effort, exertion, hard work, repeated efforts, unflagging efforts, stick-to-itiveness [Inf]

▶ *Work 122; Attention 323; Activity 414*

3 constancy, steadfastness, fidelity, staunchness, maintenance, continuance; plodding, pursuance, ceaselessness, patience, diligence, permanence; iteration, reiteration, repetition

▶ *Permanence 667; Continuity, Continuation 669; Repetition 797*

4 stamina, endurance, staying power, fortitude, intestinal fortitude, strength, inner strength; courage, grit, true grit, backbone, gameness, pluck, mettle; [Inf]: guts, gutsiness, moxie, sand

▶ *Courage 284; Strength 516*

5 tenacious person, die-hard, loyal supporter, hardcore supporter; intransigent, irreconcilable, resister; willing worker, workaholic, workhorse; bitterender

ADJECTIVES

6 persevering, persistent, dogged, tenacious; determined, resolved, resolute, unremitting, indomitable, unyielding; pertinacious, stubborn, obstinate, insistent

7 committed, single-minded, concentrated, attentive, applying, sedulous, assiduous, abiding; unsleeping, sleepless, vigilant, tireless, untiring, undrooping, unwearied, indefatigable; industrious, unflagging, trying hard, strenuous, stick-to-it-ive [Inf]

▶ *Work 122; Resolution 376; Obstinacy 379; Attempt 390; Activity 414*

8 constant, steadfast, steady, faithful, staunch, maintaining, unceasing, continuing; unfaltering, unwavering, unflagging, unfailing; plodding, slogging away, ceaseless, patient, diligent, permanent; renewed, iterated, reiterated, repeated

▶ *Continuity, Continuation 669; Repetition 797*

9 enduring, undaunted, undiscouraged, undeterred, strong; courageous, gritty, game, plucky; hanging in there, going down fighting, going down with guns blazing, true to the bitter end, gutsy [Inf]

▶ *Courage 284; Success 845*

VERBS

10 persevere, persist, continue, keep on *or* at; perseverate, try and try again, repeat, iterate, reiterate, renew one's efforts, double one's efforts; strive, labor, struggle, toil, moil, grub, grind, drudge, plod, plug away, slog away, peg away, hammer away; work unflaggingly, work day and night, work around the clock, work one's fingers to the bone, work till one drops, work one's ass *or* butt *or* tail off [Inf]

▶ *Work 122; Attempt 390*

11 pursue, chase down, follow up; go to any lengths, go the limit, go the whole hog, stop at nothing, move heaven and earth

12 maintain, sustain, keep up, follow through, see through; continue, carry on, keep on keeping on, go on, keep going, keep the ball rolling

▶ *Continuity, Continuation 669*

13 hold out, hold out for, not take "no" for an answer, stand firm, maintain one's ground, not budge, dig in one's toes *or* heels, grit one's teeth; hold out to the last, die at one's post, go down with one's ship; never despair, never say quit, never say die, never give up hope; hang on, not let go, hold fast, maintain one's grip, cling, stick like glue, hang on by one's teeth, hang on for dear life, hang on like grim death; stick to one's guns, sink or swim

▶ *Hope 281; Resolution 376; Retention 471*

14 endure, remain undaunted, be strong, remain, survive; have what it takes, stick it out, see it through, stay till the bitter end, come up *or* back for more; carry through, complete

▶ *Completeness 761*

15 bolster, sustain, uphold, support; prop, brace, buttress, underpin; shoulder, hold up, shore up, bear up

▶ *Support 605; Help 825*

ADVERBS

16 perseveringly, persistently, doggedly, tenaciously, resolutely, patiently; for better or for worse, through thick and thin, through fire and water, to the last man, to the bitter end

17 continually, repeatedly, unendingly, ceaselessly, till the cows come home

378 Vacillation

NOUNS

1 vacillation, irresolution, irresoluteness, unsettledness, ambivalence, double-mindedness, mixed feelings; indecision, uncertainty, incertitude, unsureness, wavering, hesitation, hesitancy, faltering; doubt, infirmity of purpose; equivocation, tergiversation, lack of resolution, lack of commitment, nonperseverance, broken resolve, broken promise

▶ *Equivocation 380; Uncertainty 841*

2 inconstancy, fluctuation, changeableness, variability, going back and forth, varying, oscillation, erraticism; blowing hot and cold, fickleness, levity, whimsicality, capriciousness, irresponsibility; shilly-shally, shilly-shallying, fence-sitting, fence-straddling, wishy-washiness

▶ *Caprice 381; Weakness 517; Changeableness 666*

3 vacillator, wobbler, waverer, ditherer, butterfly, chameleon, yo-yo [Inf]; don't-know, uncommitted voter, floating voter [Brit]

▶ *Equivocation 380*

4 swaying, moving back and forth, rise and fall, rising and falling, ebb and flow, flux and reflux; unsteady movement, rocking, reeling, staggering, tottering, wavering, wobbling
▶ *Oscillation 683*

ADJECTIVES

5 vacillating, irresolute, unsettled, ambivalent, double-minded, mixed-up; indecisive, undecided, uncertain, undetermined, unsure, wavering, hesitant, faltering, doubtful; infirm, equivocal, tergiversating, unresolved, uncommitted, noncommittal; of *or* in two minds, unable to make up one's mind, yo-yo [Inf]

6 inconstant, fluctuating, changeable, variable, varying, oscillating, erratic; not to be pinned down, without ballast, fickle, whimsical, capricious, irresponsible, shilly-shallying; unstable, unreliable, unstaunch, unsteadfast, unpersevering; temperamental, featherbrained, light-minded, as changeable as a weathercock *or* the weather *or* the moon
▶ *Equivocation 380; Uncertainty 841*

7 unsteady, swaying, dithering, wobbling, wobbly, boggling, shifty, teetering, tottering; flexible, pliant, putty-like
▶ *Caprice 381; Changeableness 666*

VERBS

8 vacillate, waver, falter, doubt; equivocate, tergiversate, lack resolve *or* commitment; fluctuate, change, vary, go back and forth, go to-and-fro, oscillate; blow hot and cold, yo-yo [Inf]

9 be irresolute, be of *or* in two minds, sit on the fence, go where the wind blows, go around in circles; put off a decision, delay, put off till tomorrow, procrastinate, dally, dilly-dally, leave undecided, leave in suspense; change sides, go over, apostatize, cross the floor, shift one's ground
▶ *Lateness 658; Uncertainty 841*

10 hesitate, have second thoughts, change one's mind, back away, balk, shy, jib, shirk, evade, avoid
▶ *Avoidance 386*

11 balance, weigh up the pros and cons, discuss, debate, argue, hem and haw, will and will not
▶ *Argument 329*

12 sway, seesaw, wobble, teeter, boggle, dither, quibble, shuffle, shilly-shally
▶ *Equivocation 380; Changeableness 666; Oscillation 683*

ADVERBS

13 irresolutely, indecisively, equivocally, noncommittally; from pillar to post

14 ambivalently, uncertainly, unsurely, hesitantly, falteringly, doubtfully

379 Obstinacy

NOUNS

1 obstinacy, stubbornness, obduracy, obdurateness, adamancy *or* adamance, bullheadedness, pigheadedness, muleheadedness, mulishness, orneriness; pertinaciousness, pertinacity, self-will, mind of one's own; perversity, perverseness, contrariness, contumacy, disobedience, resistance; intractability, incorrigibility, stiff neck, wrongheadedness, dourness, indocility, feistiness; cussedness [Inf], bloody-mindedness [Brit]
▶ *Sullenness 304; Will 372; Resistance 417; Disobedience 427*

2 determination, resolution, will, willfulness, single-mindedness; grimness, doggedness, tenacity, tenaciousness, bulldoggedness, perseverance, persistence, stubborn persistence; inelasticity, inflexibility, immovability, intransigence, intractability, irreversibility; imperviousness, impenetrableness, toughness, hardness, hard line, no compromise, fixity
▶ *Resolution 376; Perseverance 377; Hardness 542*

3 opinionatedness, dogmatism, rigorism, intolerance, prejudice, bias, bigotry; zealotry, fanaticism, ruling passion, obsession, *idée fixe* [Fr]; blind side, blindness, deafness, closed mind, narrow-mindedness; illiberality, obscurantism, strait-lacedness
▶ *Misjudgment 342; Ignorance 349; Certainty 840*

4 obstinate person, hard-liner, hardhead, rigorist; stickler, purist, pedant, dogmatist, fanatic, zealot, bigot, old fogy, conservative, intransigent, maverick, obscurantist, reactionary; bullethead, dog in the manger, diehard, donkey, stick-in-the-mud, last-ditcher, bitterender; [Inf]: mule, hard-nose, hard-ass

ADJECTIVES

5 obstinate, stubborn, hardheaded, obdurate, adamant, adamantine, headstrong, bullheaded, pigheaded, muleheaded, mulish, stubborn as a mule, ornery; pertinacious, willful, self-willed, froward; perverse, contrary, contumacious, disobedient, resistant; intractable, incorrigible, stiff-necked, wrongheaded, dour, indocile, feisty; cussed [Inf], bloody-minded [Brit]

6 refractory, recalcitrant, wayward, arbitrary, perverse, contrary, contumacious; disobedient, unruly, restive, unmanageable, uncontrollable, ungovernable, unpersuadable, incorrigible, irrepressible; stiff-necked, hard-mouthed, cross-grained, crotchety, irascible
▶ *Irascibility 303; Sullenness 304; Defiance 416; Resistance 417; Disobedience 427; Impenitence 452*

7 determined, resolved, resolute, strong-willed, single-minded; grim, dogged, tenacious, bulldogged, persevering, persistent; immovable, intransigent, irreversible, irremovable; wooden, tough, hard, hardened, casehardened, hard-line, hard-shell, hard-core, hard *or* tough as nails

▶ *Resolution 376; Perseverance 377*

8 unyielding, firm, fixed, tenacious; inelastic, inflexible, stiff, rigid, unbending, hidebound; impervious, impenetrable, uncompromising, unmoved, uninfluenced; unrelenting, inexorable, unappeasable, implacable; merciless, incurable, chronic

▶ *Pitilessness 309; Hardness 542; Permanence 667*

9 opinionated, dogmatic, rigorous, intolerant, prejudiced, biased, bigoted; zealous, fanatical, ruled by passions, obsessed, blind, blinded, deaf, closed-minded, narrow-minded; illiberal, old-school, strait-laced, set, set in one's ways

▶ *Misjudgment 342*

VERBS

10 be obstinate, persist, persevere, brazen it out, stick to one's guns; dig in one's toes *or* heels, not budge, sit tight, stay put, stand firm, insist, brook no denial, not take "no" for an answer; want one's own way, dogmatize, have a closed mind, stay in a rut, cling to custom, not listen, turn a deaf ear, take no advice

▶ *Rashness 286; Resolution 376; Perseverance 377; Habit, Custom 397; Resistance 417; Selfishness 444; Impenitence 452; Certainty 840*

ADVERBS

11 obstinately, stubbornly, obdurately, pigheadedly, mulishly, like a mule; willfully, doggedly, tenaciously; in an uncompromising way, intransigently, inexorably

380 Equivocation

NOUNS

1 equivocation, equivocalness, ambiguity, ambivalence, indefiniteness, vagueness, uncertainty; balancing act, sophistry, two voices; double meaning, double entendre, amphiboly, wordplay, play on words, pun, paronomasia; equivoque, newspeak, Pentagonese, double-talk, gobbledegook; circumlocution, fallacy, conundrum, enigma, riddle, oracle, parable, polysemy

▶ *Linguistics, Language 5; Concealment 181; Humor 277; Sophistry 330; Meaning 361; Lack of Meaning 362; Unintelligibility 364; Avoidance 386; Untruth 722; Uncertainty 841*

2 evasion, elusion, avoidance, shuffling, shifting, hedging, beating around the bush; concealment, prevarication, speciousness, lie, white lie, falsehood, untruth; dodge, quibble, quibbling

▶ *Untruthfulness, Falsehood 192*

3 vacillation, tergiversation, change of mind, better thoughts, afterthought, second thoughts; change of purpose, alteration of plan, change of direction; inconsistency, irresolution, deviation, shifting one's ground; reversal, back-pedaling, about-face, U-turn, volte-face, withdrawal; versatility, change of mood, caprice

▶ *Vacillation 378; Caprice 381; Relinquishment 392; Penitence 451; Change 665; Deviation 698*

4 equivocator, tergiversator, prevaricator, liar, quibbler, sophist; opportunist, double-dealer, double-talker, weasel, two-faced person, Janus; recanter, forswearer, recreant, apostate; traitor, Judas, betrayer, disloyal *or* fair-weather friend, slippery customer [Inf], rat [Inf]

▶ *Deception 193; Avoidance 386; Changeableness 666; Cooperation 827*

ADJECTIVES

5 equivocal, equivocating, ambiguous, ambivalent, prevaricatory, ambivalent, indefinite, vague, uncertain; double-tongued, two-edged, facing both ways, left-handed, backhanded; roundabout, circumlocutory, fallacious; oracular, amphibolous, homonymous, anagrammatic; evasive, eluding, misleading, avoiding, shuffling, shifting, concealing, prevaricating, specious, false

▶ *Circularity 631*

6 equivocating, tergiversating, vacillating, slippery; inconsistent, irresolute, deviating; reversible, back-pedaling, going back; double-dealing, double-talking, two-faced, Janus-faced; apostate, lying, traitorous, betraying, disloyal

▶ *Untruthfulness, Falsehood 192; Vacillation 378; Caprice 381*

VERBS

7 be equivocal, equivocate, be ambiguous, prevaricate, be ambivalent; cut both ways, play on words, pun, have two meanings, have a double meaning, have a second meaning, speak with two voices, double-talk; say in a roundabout way, mince words, speak oracles; fudge, hedge, beat around the bush, fence, sit on the fence, straddle; quibble, dissemble, deceive, mislead, lie; avoid, evade, dodge, sidestep, pussyfoot; waffle [Inf], speak with a forked tongue, weasel out

▶ *Untruthfulness, Falsehood 192; Deception 193; Sophistry 330; Meaning 361; Avoidance 386*

8 equivocate, tergiversate, change one's mind, vacillate, think again, think better of it, have second thoughts; change one's tune, shift one's ground, shift gears, shuffle, shift, deviate; back-pedal, about-face, do a U-turn, withdraw; change moods, be capricious; face both ways, be two-faced, run with the hare and hunt with the hounds

▶ *Vacillation 378; Caprice 381; Change 665*

ADVERBS

9 equivocally, ambiguously, ambivalently, evasively, amphibolously; elusively, speciously, falsely, untruthfully

381 Caprice

NOUNS

1 caprice, change, vagary, notion, impulse, crank; erraticism, turn, twist, fit; whim, whimsy, megrim, idea, fancy, passing fancy, change of mind, flip-flop [Inf], vagary, maggot [Arch]; outlandish notion, crotchet, humor, mood, temperament; peculiarity, idiosyncrasy, idiocrasy, eccentricity, quirk, kink, oddity; fad, craze, freak, escapade, prank, wild-goose chase; coquetry, flirtation; brainstorm

> *Insanity 110; Folly 353; Imagination 360; Improvisation 396*

2 **capriciousness,** arbitrariness, fitfulness, uncertainty; flightiness, unpredictability, inconsistency, inconstancy, changeableness, changeability, variability; instability, unreliability, fickleness, fecklessness, irresponsibility; coquettishness, flirtatiousness, frivolousness, frivolity, giddiness, levity, light-mindedness, whimsicality; eccentricity, crankiness, freakishness, quirkiness, fretfulness, pettishness; irascibility, playfulness, mischief, waywardness; motivelessness, purposelessness, faddishness, faddism, flakiness [Inf]

3 **capricious person,** man *or* woman of impulse, flirt, coquette, tease, trifler, prankster; featherbrain, butterfly, fair-weather friend; eccentric, freak, crank; imp, monkey, oddball [Inf], flake [Inf]

ADJECTIVES

4 **capricious,** changeable, vague, impulsive; turning, twisting, fitful; whimsical, fanciful, fickle, feckless, flighty, faddish, frivolous; coquettish, flirtatious, skittish, giddy, featherbrained, light-minded, playful, mischievous; peculiar, idiosyncratic, eccentric, quirky, kinky, odd, oddball [Inf]; fantastic, offbeat, freakish, prankish, flaky [Inf]

> *Insanity 110; Surprise 292; Inattention 324; Changeableness 666; Uncertainty 841*

5 **erratic,** arbitrary, fitful, uncertain; unpredictable, inconsistent, inconstant, variable; volatile, unexpected, mercurial, unstable, unreliable, irresponsible; irascible, temperamental, moody, crotchety; wayward, undisciplined, wanton, motiveless, purposeless

> *Vacillation 378; Uncertainty 841*

VERBS

6 **be capricious,** submit to a whim, take it into one's head, take *or* have a flight of fancy; chop and change, blow hot and cold, flip-flop [Inf], vary, change, vacillate, fluctuate; trifle with, tease, flirt, coquet

> *Folly 353; Vacillation 378; Changeableness 666*

ADVERBS

7 **capriciously,** frivolously, fancifully, on impulse, as the mood takes one, as the fancy takes one, from one extreme to the other, at the drop of a hat, at one's own sweet will

8 **erratically,** arbitrarily, fitfully, by fits and starts, uncertainly; unpredictably, inconsistently, variably

> *Vacillation 378; Uncertainty 841*

382 Selection

NOUNS

1 **selection,** choice, decision, determination, judgment, discretion, discrimination, eclecticism; selectivity, pickiness, finickiness, fastidiousness; adoption, cooption, cooptation; nomination, appointment, commission, designation, vote, election; pick, variety, assortment, collection, anthology, gathering; range, range of choice, list, short list, *embarras de richesses* [Fr], *embarras de choix* [Fr]

> *Discrimination 337; Judgment 341; Will 372; Offer 504*

2 **preference,** predilection, partiality, inclination, leaning, tendency; prejudice, bias, favoritism; taste, liking, favor, fancy, preferability, desirability

> *Liking 290*

3 **choice,** option, alternative, decision, volition; limited choice, limited options, only choice, no real alternative, no choice, zero option, Hobson's choice; difficult choice, tough decision, dilemma, unlucky choice, bad bargain; best option, better choice, greater good, lesser evil, lesser of two evils

4 **selecting,** choosing, picking, picking and choosing, picking out, picking over, handpicking, singling out, setting apart *or* aside, separating, separation; deciding on, making up one's mind, settling on, opting for *or* against; sifting out, weeding out, screening out, sorting out *or* through

5 **electing,** vote, voting, representation, say, voice; voice vote, yeas and nays, aye, yea, counting heads, counting hands, counting noses; positive vote, vote of confidence, majority vote, deciding vote, absentee vote, absentee ballot; ballot, secret ballot, open vote, show of hands; poll, public opinion poll, straw poll, jury poll, direct vote, plebiscite, referendum; psephology

6 **election,** general election, national election, federal election, state election, local election, midterm election, by-election [Brit]; caucus, primary election, primary, direct primary, open primary, closed primary; election day, polling place, polls, polling, ballot, ballot box, voting booth, voting machine; election returns, vote counting, tabulation of ballots, evaluation of returns

> *Politics 50*

7 **electorate,** voter, registered voter, voters, absentee voter, constituent, elector, balloter; electoral college

8 **chosen thing** *or* **person,** selection, pick, pick of the crop, pickings, gleanings, first choice, excerpt; nominee, candidate, elected official, winner, victorious candidate; the best, the cream, crème de la crème, the chosen, chosen people, elite

> *Superiority 744*

9 **selecting,** choosing, deciding, decisive, determining; discretionary *or* discretional, discriminating, discerning, eclectic; selective, choosy, picky, finicky, fastidious, fussy, particular

▶ *Liking 290; Discrimination 337; Will 372; Approval 437*

10 **preferential,** showing preference, partial, inclined, tending toward, opting; prejudiced, biased, favoring; preferable, better, desirable, advisable, preferred, special, favorite, fancy, pet, by appointment, not to be sniffed *or* sneezed at [Inf]

11 **selected,** chosen, opted for, optional, decided upon, volitive, volitionary; designate, elected, adopted, voted in; picked, sorted, assorted, seeded, appointed; well-chosen, worth choosing, jumped at; select, choice, recherché, handpicked, elite, elect

▶ *Liking 290; Superiority 744*

VERBS

12 **select,** choose, make a choice, decide, decide on, determine, make up one's mind; judge best, exercise one's discretion, discriminate, pick and choose; take up an option, take up, pick out, settle on, accept, approve, pass, adopt, coopt; recommend, nominate, second, appoint, put up, propose, commission, designate, delegate; collect, gather, anthologize

▶ *Judgment 341; Will 372; Approval 437*

13 **prefer,** have a preference, like better, like best, incline, lean, have a bias, tend; would like, would rather, favor, fancy, desire; might as well, might do worse, see fit, think fit, think it best to

▶ *Liking 290; Approval 437*

14 **choose,** opt, opt for, eliminate the alternatives; pick, pick out, handpick, single out, detail, highlight, mark out, mark down; preselect, earmark, reserve, set aside, set apart; distinguish, identify, separate, isolate, abstract, excerpt, cull, glean, winnow, sift; skim, skim off, cream, skim off the cream, pick the best; take one's pick, indulge one's fancy

▶ *Identification 184; Discrimination 337; Separation 753; Commission 833*

15 **side with,** take sides, back, support, plump for, endorse, come out for, come out on one side; embrace, espouse, cast *or* throw in one's lot with, commit oneself, take for better or for worse

▶ *Marriage 64; Resolution 376; Help 825*

16 **vote,** vote for, vote in, elect, reelect, return; choose by ballot, go to the polls; cast a vote, register one's vote, cast one's ballot, be counted, raise one's hand

▶ *Government 49; Politics 50; Rejection 383*

ADVERBS

17 **selectively,** decidedly, with discretion, discriminatingly, eclectically

18 **by choice,** optionally, alternatively, preferentially, preferably, rather, sooner

383 Rejection

NOUNS

1 **rejection,** declination, nonacceptance, refusal, nonapproval, disapproval; veto, negative vote, no, nay, vote of no confidence, blackball vote; repulse, repulsion, repellence; denial, turndown, renouncement; forbiddance, disallowance, interdiction, proscription, negation; exclusion, exception, exemption, avoidance, disregard; slight, snub, rebuff, cold shoulder, cold reception, cool welcome, brush-off; bum's rush [Inf], heave-ho [Inf]

▶ *Unsociability 409; Disapproval 438; Refusal 506; Exclusion 764*

2 **rejecting,** declining, refusing, disapproving, repelling; blackballing, slighting, snubbing, spurning, shunning, avoiding, ignoring, neglecting, eschewing

3 **discarding,** disuse, nonuse, abandonment, elimination, ejection, expulsion; dismissal, the door, ouster, unemployment, disemployment, firing, layoff, redundancy [Brit], gate [Inf]; defeat, electoral defeat, nonelection, lost election

▶ *Nonuse 394; Expulsion 709; Failure 846*

4 **renunciation,** disclamation, disclaimer, disclaiming, retraction, recantation, apostasy; abrogation, cancellation, abnegation, abjuration, repudiation, denial, disavowal, disaffirmation; disproving, exploding, negating, denying, contradiction, contradicting; disowning, disinheriting, disinheritance

▶ *Negation 190; Equivocation 380; Cancellation 834*

5 **rejection notice,** rejection slip, rejection letter, Dear John *or* Jane letter, blue slip, pink slip, layoff notice

ADJECTIVES

6 **rejected,** declined, refused, vetoed, not accepted; repulsed, repelled, denied, turned down, forbidden, disallowed, negated; excluded, excepted, exempted, avoided, disregarded; slighted, snubbed, rebuffed, blackballed, spurned, shunned, eschewed; [Inf]: kicked out, given the bum's rush, given the heave-ho

7 **unselected,** unchosen, ineligible, unqualified, unsuitable, unacceptable; unaccepted, unrequited, returned, sent back; unusable, unfit for human consumption, unfit for consideration, not to be thought of, out of the question, unwanted

8 **discarded,** disused, abandoned, eliminated, ejected, expelled, thrown away; cast out, dismissed, ousted, unemployed, disemployed, fired, laid off, redundant, shown the door; defeated, impeached, thrown out of office

9 **renounced,** disclaimed, retracted, apostatized; abrogated, canceled, abjuratory, repudiated, denied, disavowed; disproven, exploded, negated, contradicted; disowned, disinherited

10 **reject,** decline, refuse, disapprove, renounce; rebuff, repulse, repel, deny, turn down, forbid, disallow, draw the line at, interdict, proscribe, negate, veto; not select, not consider, pass over; dismiss out of hand, return, send back, look a gift horse in the mouth

> *Negligence 326; Disapproval 438; Refusal 506*

11 **exclude,** except, exempt, count out, not count, avoid, disregard, turn one's back on; blackball, slight, snub, rebuff, spurn, shun, eschew; give the bum's rush to [Inf], brush off, freeze out, cold-shoulder, give a cold reception to, give a cool welcome to, make unwelcome; not cater to *or* for, not want, turn up one's nose at, sniff at, scorn, pan, disdain, mock, deride, laugh at, ridicule, sneeze at [Inf]

> *Derision 369; Unsociability 409; Discourtesy 411; Exclusion 764*

12 **discard,** disuse, abandon, eliminate, get rid of, kick upstairs, throw out, cast out, jettison, eject, expel; throw away, scrap, ditch, junk, sling out, throw aside, lay aside, set aside, give up; depose, dismiss, oust, fire, lay off, show the door; defeat, vote against, cast a negative vote; [Inf]: kick out, boot out, give the heave-ho, chuck out

> *Nonuse 394; Expulsion 709*

13 **renounce,** disclaim, retract, recant, apostatize, revoke; abrogate, cancel, abnegate, abjure, repudiate, deny, disavow; disprove, explode, negate, contradict; disown, disinherit

> *Negation 190; Equivocation 380; Cancellation 834*

384 Predetermination

NOUNS

1 **predetermination,** early settlement *or* decision *or* resolution, resolve; preconception, preconceived notion *or* opinion, closed mind, presettlement, prearrangement, arrangement; plan, project, intention, preparation, order of the day, agenda, plot, *parti pris* [Fr]; foregone conclusion, agreed result, ready-made verdict, closed book, open-and-shut case; premeditation, predeliberation, early agreement; packed jury, primed witness, stacked deck, loaded dice; [Inf]: frame-up, put-up job, setup

> *Intention 374; Plan 387; Preparation 388*

2 **predestination,** destination, appointment, foreordination, preordination, destiny, intention; fate, doom, lot, karma, kismet, will, decree

> *Necessity 95; Will 372*

3 **direction,** compelling force, drive, urge, obligation

ADJECTIVES

4 **predetermined,** settled *or* decided *or* resolved beforehand; preconceived, presettled, prearranged, arranged; projected, intended, prepared; concluded, open-and-shut; primed, packed, stacked, loaded, in

the cards, cut-and-dried; [Inf]: fixed up, framed, put-up

> *Necessity 95; Future Time 650*

5 **deliberate,** intentional, willed, premeditated, predeliberated, prepense, with a motive; preset, set, pre-established, fixed, controlled, planned, preplanned; considered, studied, measured, weighed, calculated, designed, advised, devised, contrived

> *Intention 374; Plan 387; Arrangement 767*

6 **predestined,** destined, appointed, foreordained, preordained, ordained, intended; fated, doomed, willed, decreed

7 **directed,** compelled, impelled, driven, urged, obliged

VERBS

8 **predetermine,** settle *or* decide *or* resolve beforehand; preconceive, preset, prearrange, arrange; plan, project, prepare, intend; premeditate, contrive, agree beforehand, preconcert; effect *or* ensure a result, pack a jury, prime a witness, stack the deck, load the dice; [Inf]: set up, fix, fix up, frame

> *Untruthfulness, Falsehood 192; Plan 387; Cause 675; Arrangement 767*

9 **predestine,** destine, predestinate, appoint, foreordain, preordain, decree, intend

> *Necessity 95; Intention 374; Future Time 650*

10 **direct,** impel, compel, drive, urge, oblige

ADVERBS

11 **predeterminately,** preconceivedly, preparedly, premeditatedly, predeliberately, with forethought

385 Pursuit

We seek him here, we seek him there. / Those Frenchies seek him everywhere. / Is he in heaven? Is he in hell? / That demmed, elusive Pimpernel! — BARONESS ORCZY

NOUNS

1 **pursuit,** pursuing, pursuance, going after, seeking, looking for; search, quest, hunting, tracking, tracking down, trailing, shadowing, tailing [Inf]; stalking, following, following up, dogging, hounding, persisting, persistence, persevering, perseverance; manhunt, dragnet, all points bulletin (APB); persecution, witch hunt, McCarthyism

> *Question 333; Perseverance 377; Sequence 770*

2 **chase,** chasing, pursuit, hot pursuit, run, paper chase; steeplechase, race, racing

> *Horses, Horseback Riding, Horse Racing 159*

3 **hunt,** hunting, spooring, casting; hue and cry, beat, drive, battue, beating, shooting, gunning; hunting and shooting, fishing; blood sport, venery [Arch]

> *Killing 30; Fishing 154; Hunting and Shooting 160; Contention 422; Gain 467*

4 **activity,** work, business, occupation, career, vocation;

leisure pursuit, hobby, pastime, interest, recreation, avocation

> *Work 122; Games, Pastimes, Amusements 167*

5 **pursuer,** seeker, searcher, pursuant, quester; search party member, vigilante committee member; follower, dogger, shadow, sleuth, tail [Inf]; recruiter, headhunter

6 **hunter,** huntsman, huntress, tracker, trailer, stalker, trapper, poacher; bloodhound, Nimrod, Diana; whipper-in, beater; marksman, markswoman, sniper, shot, good shot, gun; big-game hunter, safari hunter, shikari [India]; fisher, fisherman, angler, piscator, guddler [Scot]

> *Fishing 154; Hunting and Shooting 160*

7 **the hunted,** prey, quarry, game, big game, kill, beast of venery [Arch]; victim, fugitive, escapee, deserter, missing person, lost child; suspect, lead, criminal, person on the lam [Inf]

> *Escape 816*

ADJECTIVES

8 **pursuing,** pursuant, seeking, searching, questing, in quest of; following, chasing, trailing; tailing [Inf]

9 **hunting,** shooting, fishing, piscatory, piscatorial

10 **pursued,** sought, followed, chased, hounded, hunted, trailed

VERBS

11 **pursue,** go after, seek, look, search, cast about, hunt, hound, persist, persevere, fish for, dig for; organize a search party, organize a vigilante committee, organize a dragnet, send out a search party; be gunning for, be in hot pursuit, witch-hunt; persecute, oppress, harass, chevy [Brit]

> *Question 333; Perseverance 377*

12 **follow,** track, track down, trail, stalk, prowl after, sneak after; dog, shadow, sleuth, dog one's footsteps, stick like glue; follow the scent, follow the trail, scent out, sniff out, run to ground; tail [Inf], stay on one's tail [Inf]

> *Discovery 345; Sequence 770*

13 **chase,** give chase, run after, make after; whoop, halloo, hark, raise the hunt, raise the hue and cry; run down, ride down, rush at, charge at, tilt at, ride full tilt at; leap at, jump at, grab away, snatch at, grab the brass ring [Inf]

> *Attack 418; Taking 477*

14 **hunt,** go hunting, hunt down, poach, shoot, go shooting, bag; join the chase, follow the hounds, ride to hounds, course; fish, cast one's net, angle, guddle [Scot], trap, ensnare, lay traps, set snares; beat, thrush, play cat and mouse

> *Killing 30; Trap 813*

15 **aim at,** be after, mark as one's prey, make one's quarry, set one's course for, steer for; woo, court, throw oneself at, mob, swarm over; strive for *or* after, make it one's business to, pursue one's goals, pursue one's ends, pursue one's interest; set one's cap for

> *Intention 374; Direction 697*

16 **follow up,** contact again, press on, progress, push one's way, elbow one's way, force one's way, fight one's way; carry on, continue, execute, perform, undertake

> *Undertaking 391; Action 412; Forward Motion 679*

ADVERBS

17 **pursuant to,** in pursuance of, in search of, in quest of, on the lookout for; after, in pursuit, in hot pursuit

18 **on the trail,** on the track, on the scent, hot on the trail, in full cry

INTERJECTIONS

19 **after him!,** stop thief!, follow that car!, shoot!, fire!, halloo!; view halloo!, yoicks!, tallyho!

386 Avoidance

Beware the Jubjub bird, and shun / The frumious Bandersnatch! — LEWIS CARROLL

NOUNS

1 **avoidance,** bypassing, circumvention; averting, prevention, obstruction, hindrance; distance, safe distance, wide berth; shunning, aloofness, cold shoulder, snub

> *Rejection 383; Unsociability 409; Distance 585; Deviation 698*

2 **abstinence,** abstention, forswearing, self-denial, refraining, forbearance, temperance, moderation

> *Sobriety 120; Self-Restraint 455; Moderation 521*

3 **shyness,** shrinking, unwillingness, reluctance, refusal, revulsion; recoil, retreat, withdrawal, retirement; neutrality, noninvolvement, nonintervention, isolationism

> *Fear 283; Indifference 289; Unwillingness 375; Inactivity 415; Refusal 506*

4 **shirking,** slacking, inaction, apathy, inactivity, passivity, malingering, passing the buck; [Inf]: cop-out, goldbricking, goofing off

> *Negligence 326; Inactivity 415*

5 **evasion,** elusion, deflection, parry, dodge, duck; defense mechanism, defensive reaction, escape; cowering, hiding

> *Concealment 181; Defense 419; Escape 816*

6 **evasiveness,** elusiveness, avoiding the issue, sidestepping, pussyfooting; equivocation, prevarication, procrastination, delaying action, noncooperation; escapism, denial, repression, suppression, waffle [Inf]

> *Negation 190; Equivocation 380; Lateness 658*

7 **desertion,** truancy, French leave, elopement; absence, departure, flight, hooky *or* hookey, absence without leave (AWOL), making a run for it, bugging out [Inf], flit [Brit]

> *Absence 576; Departure 705; Escape 816*

8 **avoider,** abstainer, nondrinker, teetotaler; dodger,

sidestepper, evader, coward; quitter, shirker, malingerer, slacker, idler; draft dodger, truant, deserter, absentee, runaway; refugee, displaced person (DP), boat person, escapee, escaper, fugitive; nonrealist, escapist, dreamer, visionary, ostrich; [Inf]: wetback, goldbricker, goof-off, bugout

 ▶ *Sobriety 120; Cowardice 285; Imagination 360; Inactivity 415; Self-Restraint 455; Escape 816*

ADJECTIVES

9 **avoiding,** evasive, equivocal, elusive, slippery, hard to catch, shy, shrinking; unwilling, reluctant, uncooperative, noncommittal, unforthcoming, taciturn, passive, inert; inactive, not involved, apathetic, uncommitted, neutral, centrifugal

10 **fugitive,** escaped, runaway, hunted, hiding, hidden, cowering; latent, repressive, suppressive, escapist; aversive, obstructive, hindering, preventive; on the lam [Inf]

 ▶ *Taciturnity 208; Fear 283; Unwillingness 375; Equivocation 380; Latency 844*

11 **abstaining,** abstinent, ascetic, dry, shunning, going *or* doing without, temperate, moderate, on the wagon [Inf]

12 **avoidable,** avertable, preventable, evadable, escapable, eludable

VERBS

13 **avoid,** keep away from, keep from, stay away from; bypass, circumvent, steer clear, keep clear, stand clear, get out of the way; make way for, stand back, hold off, keep one's distance, keep at arm's length, give a wide berth to

14 **shun,** eschew, leave, let alone, have nothing to do with, keep out of, not touch with a ten-foot pole; stand aloof, stand apart, keep oneself to oneself, have no hand in, play no part in, keep one's hands clean; turn away, turn aside, look the other way, turn a blind eye, ignore; cold-shoulder, snub, not give the time of day, cut, give the go-by [Inf]

 ▶ *Rejection 383; Unsociability 409; Distance 585; Deviation 698*

15 **avert,** prevent, foil, obstruct, hinder

 ▶ *Hindrance 826*

16 **abstain,** forswear, deny oneself, go *or* do without, pass up, not indulge, not touch, refrain, forbear, spare, hold back; kick the habit [Inf], go on the wagon [Inf]

 ▶ *Sobriety 120; Self-Restraint 455; Moderation 521*

17 **shy,** shrink; fight shy, balk at, refuse, demur; give a miss, not try, not attempt, back away, back off, shy away; draw back, retreat, hang back, drag one's feet, turn tail

 ▶ *Fear 283; Unwillingness 375; Refusal 506*

18 **shirk,** get out of, make excuses, malinger, pass the buck, cop out [Inf], goldbrick [Inf]

 ▶ *Negligence 326; Inactivity 415*

19 **evade,** take evasive action, dodge, duck, deflect, ward off, parry, escape, elude, give one the slip, cower, hide; send on a wild goose chase, lead on a dance, throw off the scent

 ▶ *Concealment 181; Defense 419; Escape 816*

20 **be evasive,** avoid the issue, duck the issue, sidestep, pussyfoot, skirt, talk around; equivocate, hedge, fence, fudge, prevaricate; procrastinate, delay, postpone, shelve, table; deny, disown, bury one's head in the sand, repress, suppress; beat around the bush, waffle [Inf]

 ▶ *Negation 190; Equivocation 380; Lateness 658*

21 **run away,** run off, escape, desert, jump bail, take French leave, be absent without leave (AWOL); play truant, truant, play hooky *or* hookey; abscond, elope, flit [Brit], absent oneself, decamp, depart, leave, quit; [Inf]: scram, scat, cut out, bug off, go on the lam, slope off [Brit]

22 **retreat,** beat a retreat, withdraw, turn one's back, turn tail; flee, fly, take flight, be off, make off, bolt, run, run for it, run for one's life, take to one's heels, cut and run, make oneself scarce, scoot; part company, break away, slip the cable, shake the dust from one's feet; steal away, sneak off, slink off, shuffle off, creep off; [Inf]: make tracks, skedaddle, bug out, beat it

 ▶ *Absence 576; Backward Motion 680; Departure 705; Escape 816; Haste 818*

ADVERBS

23 **away,** clear, aloof, apart, distantly, abstinently, temperately, moderately

24 **evasively,** equivocally, elusively, avoidably, avertably, preventably, preventively, obstructively

25 **shyly,** reluctantly, unwillingly, hesitantly, apathetically, passively

INTERJECTIONS

26 **hands off!,** keep off!, keep your distance!, run for it!, run for your life!, beware!, forbear!, beat it! [Inf], scram! [Inf]

387 Plan

A man, a plan, a canal — Panama!
 — TRADITIONAL PALINDROME

NOUNS

1 **plan,** scheme, design, method, program, project; proposal, proposition, suggestion, resolution; intention, proposed action, proposed line of action, scenario, game plan; master plan, overall plan, corporate plan, management by objectives, financial plan, budget, national planning, five-year plan, long-term *or* long-range plan; schedule, schedule of events, timetable, agenda, order of the day

 ▶ *Intention 374*

2 **procedure,** policy, mandate, formula, rule, working plan, company policy; system, strategy, plan *or* course

of action, modus operandi; contingency plan, emergency plan, emergency procedure; tactics, preventive action, forethought, foresight; way, approach, address, attack, steps, measures, countermeasures

3 **prospectus,** brochure, manifesto, platform, party ticket, ticket, slate, party line
> *Politics 50; Means 102; Foresight 357; Prediction 358; Action 412; Way 691; Rule 780*

4 **method,** device, gimmick, trick, stratagem, artifice, ruse, dodge, evasion, ploy, shift, fiddle, swindle, knack, stunt, feat; masterstroke, tour de force, bold move, inspiration, brainstorm, ingenious plan; bright idea, idea, right idea, notion, thought, invention; ad hoc measure, improvisation, makeshift, stopgap, wangle, brain wave [Inf]
> *Skillfulness 127; Idea 327; Improvisation 396*

5 **expedient,** expedient plan, contrivance, resource, resort, last resort, *pis aller* [Fr], eleventh-hour rescue, last-minute rescue; recipe, nostrum, antidote, remedy, answer; loophole, way out, technicality, flag of convenience; winning card, trump card, card up one's sleeve, ace in the hole
> *Means 102; Remedy 115; Escape 816; Cunning 822*

6 **plot,** secret plan, scheme, intrigue, web of intrigue, web; cabal, conspiracy, inside job, secret influence, secrecy, latency, counterplot, countermine; racket, game, manipulation, machination, maneuvering, put-up job [Inf]
> *Secrecy 182; Defense 419; Latency 844*

7 **map,** plan, layout, plat, town plan, street map, road map, atlas; ground plan, floor plan, sketch, rough draft, drawing, scale drawing, blueprint; outline, summary, skeleton, model, pattern; diagram, flow diagram, chart, flow chart, graph, bar graph, pie chart, pie graph
> *Representation 187; Summary 204; Outline 617*

8 **planning,** scheming, contrivance, organization, order, systematization, rationalization, centralization; operational research, management review, drawing board; planning office, back room, operations room
> *Management 126; Order 765*

9 **planner,** organizer, manager, deviser, contriver, framer; inventor, originator, hatcher, proposer, enterpriser, promoter, projector, founder; designer, architect, town planner; systematizer, systems analyst, strategist, tactician, maneuverer; mastermind, Machiavelli, schemer, plotter, intriguer, intrigant, plot-spinner, cabalist, conspirator; mapper; brains [Inf], wheeler-dealer [Inf]

ADJECTIVES

10 **planned,** intended, intentional, rational, meant, premeditated; contrived, designed, organized, rational, schematic, systematic, orderly, methodical; worked out, prepared, arranged, prearranged, strategic, tactical; drawn up, sketched out, charted, mapped

11 **planning,** scheming, cunning, contriving, calculat-

ing, designing; resourceful, ingenious, purposeful, up to something; plotting, conspiratorial, Machiavellian

VERBS

12 **plan,** design, organize, systematize, methodize, rationalize, centralize, order; program, propose, suggest, project, make a plan, conceive *or* form a plan; concoct, formulate, think up, contrive, devise, engineer, rig
> *Discovery 345; Imagination 360; Intention 374; Order 765*

13 **plan ahead,** prepare, arrange, prearrange, predetermine; think ahead, look ahead, forecast, predict, foresee, envisage, expect; follow a plan, have a policy, work to a schedule, budget
> *Expectation 356; Foresight 357; Prediction 358; Predetermination 384; Preparation 388; Arrangement 767*

14 **plan out,** draw up, draft, frame, shape, form, work out; map, plot, plat, chart, lay out, sketch, sketch out, chalk out; design, draw up a design *or* plan, design a prototype, construct a model, program *or* draw up a program; lay the foundation, lay the cornerstone, map *or* mark out *or* shape a course; schedule, draw up a schedule, set a timetable
> *Representation 187; Form 624*

15 **plot,** scheme, have designs, be up to something, conspire, connive, collude; machinate, maneuver, finesse, cabal, concoct; brew *or* hatch a plot, undermine, countermine, counterplot, set *or* lay a trap for; plot against, work against; wheel and deal [Inf], cook up [Inf]
> *Deception 193; Influence 512; Trap 813; Cunning 822*

ADVERBS

16 **as planned,** intentionally, purposefully, according to schedule, schematically, methodically, systematically, strategically, tactically

17 **under discussion,** under consideration, at the planning stage, in the works, on the drawing board, in draft

18 **conspiratorially,** cunningly, intriguingly, resourcefully, ingeniously

388 Preparation

Semper paratus. — MOTTO OF THE US COAST GUARD

NOUNS

1 **preparation,** preparing, readying, getting ready, making ready; taking steps, taking measures; pioneering, scouting, trailblazing; mobilization, battening down the hatches, tuning, priming, loading, cocking; planning, organization, prearrangement, premeditation, predetermination, consultation, preconsultation; forethought, anticipation, foresight
> *Advice 176; Foresight 357; Predetermination 384; Plan 387; Precedence 769*

2 **preparations,** preliminaries, measures, steps, preliminary step, preliminary course, preparatory work,

study, homework; trial run, trial, practice, rehearsal, dress rehearsal; groundwork, spadework, foundation, basis, framework, frame, scaffold, scaffolding; sketch, draft, outline, map, plan, blueprint, model, prototype; arrangement, arrangements; savings, reserves, store, hope chest, nest egg

▶ *Store 105; Work 122; Plan 387; Base 601; Support 605; Arrangement 767; Beginning 771*

3 **fitting out,** provisioning, furnishing, supply; equipment, provisions, kit, gear, outfit, armament, arms; marshaling, array, commission

4 **briefing,** instruction, education; training, drill, exercise, practice; apprenticeship, novitiate, probationary period

5 **preparedness,** readiness, maturity, fitness; prime condition, top condition, shipshape condition

▶ *Age 27; Perfection 805*

6 **preparer,** teacher, tutor, coach, trainer, drillmaster, drill sergeant; torchbearer, trailblazer, pioneer, paver *or* pavior; fitter, equipper, provisioner, provider; cultivator, plowman, sower, planter

ADJECTIVES

7 **preparatory,** preparative, preparing, preliminary, introductory, prerequisite

▶ *Improvisation 396; Precedence 769; Beginning 771*

8 **in preparation,** afoot, on foot, on the stocks, on the anvil, on the drawing board; in the offing, forthcoming, impending, planned, being discussed, under consideration; learning, training

▶ *Future Time 650*

9 **prepared,** ready, alert, vigilant, made ready, readied, in readiness, at the ready; mobilized, standing by, on call, set, all set, ready to go; teed up, keyed up; trained, fully trained, qualified, well-prepared, practiced, rehearsed, well-rehearsed; tuned, primed, on one's marks, briefed, instructed, tutored, warned, forewarned, forearmed; [Inf]: psyched up, raring to go, spoiling for

10 **equipped,** furnished, fully furnished, rigged, rigged out; saddled, in the saddle, in harness, armed, in armor, fully armed, armed to the teeth, armed at all points, dressed for battle; well-appointed, groomed, accoutered, dressed, fully dressed, in one's best bib and tucker; in full war paint [Inf]

11 **in hand,** in store, ready to hand, ready for use, ready for anything, fit for use, in working order, operational

12 **treated,** pretreated, processed, predigested; cured, tanned, tawed; fitted, adapted, adjusted, suited, tailored

13 **ready-made,** ready-mixed, cut-and-dried, ready to use, ready-to-wear, off-the-rack; ready-formed, prefabricated; convenience, convenient, oven-ready, ready-to-cook, precooked, ready-to-serve, instant

VERBS

14 **prepare,** make preparations, prep, do the prep work; get ready, make ready, make provision, take steps, take measures

15 **prepare the way,** pave the way, lead the way, show the way, go before, pioneer, scout the territory, see the lay of the land; smooth the way, build a bridge, make contact; do the groundwork, provide the basis, prepare the ground, sow the seeds

▶ *Precedence 769*

16 **lay the foundations,** found, establish; set the stage, predispose, incline, soften up; plan, organize, plot, contrive, concert, prearrange, predetermine, make basic plans; gather notes, outline, draft, sketch, make a rough sketch, cut out, block out, rough-hew

▶ *Predetermination 384; Plan 387; Beginning 771*

17 **be prepared,** be ready, stand ready, be on standby, be on call, hold oneself in readiness; prepare for, forearm, guard against, insure, ensure, take precautions, anticipate, look for, wait for, expect; save, put something aside

▶ *Provision 89; Expectation 356; Thrift 499; Safety 810*

18 **prepare for action,** ready, make ready, finish one's preparations, have ready, set in order, put in readiness, mobilize, put on alert; make operational, commission, put in commission, put into working order, fix, adjust, focus, tune, tune up; array, order, put together, assemble; count down, prepare for blastoff, prepare for takeoff, fasten *or* buckle one's seatbelt, buckle up, batten down the hatches; tee up, set the alarm, whet the knife, load the gun, prime, cock; raise steam, heat the boiler, stoke up, warm up, crank, crank up, get into gear, gear up, wind, wind up, screw up, rev up [Inf]

▶ *Store 105; Order 765; Arrangement 767; Repair 809*

19 **equip,** fit, fit out, outfit, furnish, provide, supply; crew, man, rig out, dress, arm, provide with arms, provide firepower

▶ *Provision 89*

20 **brief,** inform, bring up-to-date, instruct, teach, educate; train, coach, groom, drill, exercise, rehearse

▶ *Education 48; Information 170*

21 **prepare oneself,** ready oneself, get ready, get set, compose oneself, brace oneself, study, do one's homework; serve an apprenticeship, train, exercise, rehearse, practice; limber up, warm up, gear oneself up, gird up one's loins, roll up one's sleeves, flex one's muscles; buckle on one's armor, take sword in hand, shoulder arms, get ready for action; order one's life, put one's house in order, keep one's powder dry, psych oneself up [Inf]

ADVERBS

22 **in preparation,** in hand, under way, under construction, on the stocks; under consideration, in anticipation; vigilantly, in readiness, readily, willingly

23 **preparatorily,** preparatively, preliminarily, introductorily, provisionally

389 Lack of Preparation

NOUNS

1 **lack of preparation,** unpreparedness, nonpreparation, unreadiness, disorganization; belatedness, lateness; lack of training, want of practice, rustiness, unfitness

2 **unpremeditation,** thoughtlessness, improvidence, nonprovision; rashness, hastiness, impetuousness, precipitance; spontaneity, improvisation, extemporization, surprise, impromptu, snap answer, ad lib
  ◗ *Unskillfulness 128; Rashness 286; Surprise 292; Improvisation 396; Haste 818*

3 **immaturity,** unripeness, prematurity, greenness, youth, childishness; newness, undevelopment, underdevelopment, imperfection, incompleteness; rawness, unrefinement, rudeness, roughness, crudity, crudeness, coarseness
  ◗ *Youth 26; Newness 652; Earliness 657; Incompleteness 762; Imperfection 806*

4 **natural state,** state of nature, native state; virginity, virgin soil, untilled ground; raw material, diamond in the rough

ADJECTIVES

5 **unprepared,** unready, not ready, disorganized, unorganized, unarranged, in all directions, at sixes and sevens; backward, behind, behindhand, behind time, late; surprised, caught unawares, caught napping, taken off guard, inexpectant; unguarded, exposed, vulnerable; with one's pants down [Inf]
  ◗ *Surprise 292; Lateness 658; Disorder 766*

6 **spontaneous,** ad hoc, extemporized, improvised, impromptu, ad-lib, unrehearsed; on the spur of the moment, snap, uncontrived, unstudied, off-the-cuff, off the top of one's head [Inf]
  ◗ *Improvisation 396*

7 **unpremeditated,** thoughtless, with little or no thought, reckless, careless; inadequate, negligent, rushed, makeshift, jerry-built; precipitant, precipitous, improvident, rash, hasty; unplanned, without planning, poorly planned, carefree, easygoing; half-baked
  ◗ *Joy, Cheerfulness 269; Rashness 286; Inattention 324; Negligence 326; Extravagance 500; Haste 818*

8 **untrained,** untaught, untutored, uninstructed, ignorant; undrilled, unexercised, unpracticed, rusty, unfit; inexperienced, unskilled, apprentice, scratch [Inf]
  ◗ *Ignorance 349; Naïveté 821*

9 **immature,** half-grown, green, unripe, unripened, underripe, half-ripe, unmellowed, unseasoned; unfledged, callow, childlike, childish, puerile; undeveloped, half-developed, underdeveloped, inchoate [Brit], embryonic, rudimentary, elementary; premature, forced, abortive, half-cocked, wet behind the ears
  ◗ *Youth 26; Incompleteness 762; Imperfection 806*

10 **unprocessed,** natural, in a natural state, uncultivated, unworked, unrefined; untilled, fallow, virgin, unused; simple, unsophisticated, artless
  ◗ *Unskillfulness 128; Nonuse 394*

11 **unformed,** half-formed, unfashioned, unhewn, unwrought, unworked, uncut; rough-hewn, rough, unpolished, imperfect, unfinished, half-finished; unlicked, crude, coarse, boorish, rude, savage, uncivilized
  ◗ *Discourtesy 411; Earliness 657*

12 **uncooked,** raw, underdone, half-cooked, half-baked; unprepared, undressed, ungarnished
  ◗ *Cooking 91; Toughness 547*

13 **unequipped,** untrimmed, unrigged, dismasted, dismantled, undressed, uncovered; unfurnished, half-furnished, ill-provided, deficient
  ◗ *Insufficiency 98; Uncovering 614*

VERBS

14 **be unprepared,** lack preparation, make no preparations, lack planning, have no plans, go off half-cocked, take no precautions; want practice, need training, rust; live from day to day, let tomorrow take care of itself; drop one's guard, catch unawares, surprise
  ◗ *Surprise 292; Inattention 324; Negligence 326; Improvisation 396; Earliness 657; Incompleteness 762; Deterioration 808*

15 **improvise,** extemporize, ad-lib, make it up as one goes along; talk off the top of one's head [Inf], wing it [Inf]

ADVERBS

16 **unreadily,** without preparation, unpreparedly; unpremeditatedly, thoughtlessly, unskillfully, improvidently; rashly, hastily, impetuously

17 **spontaneously,** surprisingly, extempore, impromptu, ad hoc, offhand, on the spur of the moment, off the cuff
  ◗ *Improvisation 396*

18 **immaturely,** childishly, embryonically, prematurely; incompletely, imperfectly, crudely, coarsely

390 Attempt

'Tis a lesson you should heed, / Try, try again.
— THOMAS H. PALMER

NOUNS

1 **attempt,** try, essay, assay; bid, move, step, gambit; endeavor, effort, struggle, strain, tackle; good try, stout try, brave try, valiant effort, best one can do, best effort, one's level best; determined effort, old college try; half-hearted attempt, first attempt, debut, first go, final attempt, last try, swan song, last bid, last challenge, last shot; go, run, leap, shot, best shot, stab, whirl, fling; crack [Inf], whack [Inf]

▶ *Resolution 376; Beginning 771; End 773*

2   venture, speculation, trial run, experiment; operation, exercise, undertaking; aim, goal, objective, intention; worthy aim, high endeavor, quest, adventure

▶ *Experiment 335; Intention 374; Undertaking 391; Perfection 805*

3   attempter, trier, essayer, bidder, volunteer, tackler; tester, experimenter, researcher, searcher, inquirer; striver, struggler, contestant, contender, fighter, challenger; idealist, activist, reformer; undertaker, contractor, entrepreneur; adventurer, adventurous person, quester

▶ *Question 333; Contention 422; Perfection 805; Improvement 807*

ADJECTIVES

4   attempting, trying, essaying; striving, doing one's best; game, nothing daunted, daring, venturesome, ambitious, enterprising

5   tentative, experimental, trial, pilot, testing; searching, inquiring; probationary, on approval

▶ *Willingness 373; Resolution 376*

VERBS

6   attempt, make an attempt, essay, assay, seek to, aim to, make it one's aim; bid, make a bid, offer, make shift to, do something about, make the effort; not just stand there, not let grass grow under one's feet; try, try one's hand at, have a go, give it a try *or* go *or* whirl, take a stab at, take a shot at; take a crack *or* whack at [Inf]

▶ *Question 333; Intention 374*

7   try hard, endeavor, struggle, strive, give it one's all, try and try again, do one's best, double *or* redouble one's efforts, go all out; exert oneself, work, labor, pull hard, push hard, strain, sweat; give it one's best shot, go for broke, do one's damnedest [Inf], go flat out [Inf]

▶ *Work 122; Resolution 376*

8   tackle, take on, undertake, get down to, take the bull by the horns, die in the attempt; take a chance, try one's luck, tempt providence, tempt fate; venture, speculate, gamble

▶ *Undertaking 391; Chance 842; Failure 846*

9   test, experiment, put out a feeler, dip a toe in the water, hold a finger to the wind; make a trial of, launch a trial balloon, fly a kite, run it up the flagpole [Inf]

▶ *Caution 287; Experiment 335*

ADVERBS

10   ambitiously, out for *or* to, as far as one can, with all one's might; experimentally, tentatively, speculatively; valiantly, adventurously; on the make [Inf]

INTERJECTIONS

11   here goes!, give it your best shot!, have a go!, go for it! [Inf], nothing ventured, nothing gained!

391   Undertaking

NOUNS

1   undertaking, engagement, inquiry, venture, affair, business, occupation, matter at hand; job, task, self-imposed task, work, assignment, project, campaign; effort, enterprise, struggle, labor of love, mission, pilgrimage; endeavor, quest, adventure, emprise, search; operation, exercise, program, plan, design, planned event; big undertaking, tall order, feat, a lot to ask, hard task; try, attempt, speculation, gamble

▶ *Work 122; Question 333; Willingness 373; Plan 387; Attempt 390; Action 412; Difficulty 824*

2   contract, agreement, signed agreement, gentleman's agreement; promise, pledge, vow, assurance, guarantee; obligation, engagement, commitment

▶ *Promise 458; Contract 459*

3   person who undertakes, adventurer, speculator, innovator, pioneer; volunteer, hard worker, workaholic, entrepreneur, enterprising businessman *or* businesswoman, go-getter [Inf]

ADJECTIVES

4   undertaken, done, executed, incurred, assumed, accepted, self-imposed, assigned; promised, with obligations, contractual

5   enterprising, resourceful, innovative, pioneering; adventurous, venturesome, speculative, daring, courageous; progressive, opportunistic, alive to opportunity, with an eye to the main chance, ambitious; responsible, managerial, taking on responsibility, shouldering responsibility

▶ *Courage 284; Desire 288; Newness 652*

6   overambitious, rash, overloaded, overextended, snowed under

▶ *Rashness 286*

VERBS

7   undertake, do, engage in, devote oneself to, apply oneself to, address oneself to, get one's mind into, take up, go in for; venture on, tackle, confront, try, attempt, endeavor, go about, take in hand, turn *or* put *or* set one's hand to; get going, get about, start, launch, initiate, begin, set about, embark on, launch into, plunge into, proceed to, get down to; set to, buckle down, get one's head down, put one's best foot forward, set one's shoulder to the wheel, set one's hand to the plow, get one's teeth into; come to grips with, take the bull by the horns, grasp the nettle [Aus]; assume, take on, assume *or* accept responsibility; show enterprise, pioneer, venture, adventure, dare, challenge, take a shot at; apprentice oneself, prepare oneself, take a crack *or* whack at [Inf]

▶ *Courage 284; Attempt 390; Action 412; Beginning 771*

8   take charge of, direct, manage, execute, carry out; have fish to fry, have irons in the fire; shoulder, take on one's shoulders, take upon oneself, assume an obligation, volunteer, sign up, get involved; agree, promise, contract, pledge, vow, engage, commit oneself, let oneself in for

> *Management 126; Willingness 373; Preparation 388; Activity 414; Duty 433; Promise 458; Completeness 761*

9 **take on too much,** bite off more than one can chew, have too many irons in the fire, have too much on one's plate

ADVERBS

10 **responsibly,** under obligation, contractually, as agreed

11 **enterprisingly,** innovatively, ambitiously, progressively; adventurously, daringly, as never before

12 **rashly,** overambitiously

392 Relinquishment

NOUNS

1 **relinquishment,** release, giving up, letting go, disposal, surrender; resignation, retirement, abdication; yielding, waiving, waiver, forgoing, transfer, cession, forfeit, sacrifice; rejection, abjuration, abnegation, renunciation, recantation, retraction; abandonment, desertion, evacuation, dereliction, defection, withdrawal, secession; abstinence, avoidance, disuse, nonuse, discontinuance, desuetude, cancellation

> *Rejection 383; Avoidance 386; Nonuse 394; Unsociability 409; Cessation 668; Departure 705; Cancellation 834; Resignation 835*

ADJECTIVES

2 **relinquished,** released, given up, let go, disposed of, surrendered; resigned, retired, abdicated; dropped, waived, forgone, avoided, scrapped, jettisoned, castoff, castaway, forsaken, forfeited, sacrificed; rejected, abjured, abnegated, renounced, recanted, retracted; apostate, abandoned, derelict, deserted, defected; discontinued, canceled

VERBS

3 **relinquish,** release, give up, let go, dispose of, surrender, render up; loosen one's grip, quit one's hold, unclench, leave, drop; back down, lower one's sights, yield; waive, forgo, cede, transfer, hand over, assign, forfeit, sacrifice; pack it in, cough up [Inf]

> *Humility 298; Equivocation 380; Loss 468*

4 **renounce,** swear off, abnegate, abjure, recant, change one's mind, tergiversate; drop *or* give up the idea, forget it, drop it; wean oneself, disaccustom, forswear, deny oneself, abstain; avoid, shed, slough, slough off, cast off; discard, get rid of, tear up, shred, jettison, throw away, scrap, junk, stop using; lose interest, have other *or* bigger fish to fry; ditch [Inf]

> *Indifference 289; Avoidance 386; Nonuse 394*

5 **withdraw,** decline, remove one's name from, scratch, retire, abdicate, resign, stand down, drop out, throw in

the sponge *or* towel, throw in one's hand, give up, give in, lose; quit, vacate, evacuate, move out, abandon; forsake one's duties, quit one's post; walk out, secede, divide, apostatize; break off (a relationship), end an affair, go back on one's word, jilt; seek seclusion, turn one's back on the world

> *Equivocation 380; Absence 576; Lateness 658; Departure 705; Cancellation 834; Resignation 835*

ADVERBS

6 **resignedly,** absently, distantly, apostatically, delinquently; indifferently, apathetically

393 Use

NOUNS

1 **use,** utilization, making use of, employment, employ; usage, practice, exercise, application, appliance, deployment; disposal, enjoyment, right of use, usufruct, possession; resort, recourse, control, management; treatment, handling, normal use, good use, proper treatment, carefulness; hard use, wrong use, misuse, abuse; effect of use, depreciation, wear, wear and tear, dilapidation, exhaustion, consumption, conspicuous consumption, waste

> *Waste 96; Carefulness 325; Misuse 395; Possession 469; Deterioration 808*

2 **usefulness,** advantage, benefit, good, profit; service, serviceability, practicality, convertibility, applicability; utility, function, purpose, point, avail, functioning, power; end use, immediate purpose, ultimate purpose

> *Usefulness 801*

3 **reuse,** conversion, recycling, reclamation, recyclable product *or* substance, recyclable [Inf]

4 **user,** customer, shopper, client, enjoyer, frequenter; driver, operator; consumer, owner, exploiter, abuser

> *Substance Abuse 121; Purchase 481*

ADJECTIVES

5 **used,** put to use, utilized, employed, occupied, exercised; exploited, subservient, instrumental, like putty in one's hands; used up, exhausted, consumed, spent, worn, worn out, threadbare, shabby, down-at-heel, dilapidated; secondhand, previously owned, preowned; reused, recycled, reclaimed, hand-me-down; well-used, well-thumbed, dog-eared, well-worn

> *Usefulness 801; Convenience 803; Deterioration 808*

6 **usable,** of use, utilizable, employable, exploitable, applicable; available, at one's service *or* disposal, disposable, convenient, accessible, handy, on hand, on deck, on tap [Inf]; functioning, working, in operation

7 **useful,** profitable, advantageous, to one's profit *or* advantage, beneficial; utilitarian, practical, functional, pragmatic, banausic; consumable, reusable, recyclable

> *Usefulness 801*

8 **in use,** in practice, in effect, in force; in service, open

for use *or* service, in operation, in commission, in constant use, in everyday use

VERBS

9 **use,** make use of, put to use, utilize, employ; exercise, practice, put into practice, put into operation, take up, adopt, apply, try out, try; work, drive, manipulate, maneuver, operate, wield, ply, brandish; prepare for use, work on, work up
▶ *Touch 216; Habit, Custom 397; Form 624*

10 **frequent,** be a regular customer of, shop at, use the services of, avail oneself of
▶ *Purchase 481; Frequency 661*

11 **exploit,** make the most of, use to the full *or* fullest, maximize, milk, drain, extract; convert, reuse, recycle, reclaim; find useful, put to good use, turn to account, capitalize on, use to advantage, make hay of, profit by; take advantage of, make play with, play on, trade on, cash in on, play off against; abuse, misuse, exhaust the possibilities of; use people, make a tool *or* handle of, make a pawn of, make a cat's-paw of, befool, make a fool of; make a patsy of [Inf]
▶ *Substance Abuse 121; Deception 193; Misuse 395; Gain 467; Extraction 711; Usefulness 801*

12 **use up,** exhaust, wear out, wear; go through, spend, expend; absorb, consume, waste, squander; handle, finger, touch, tread on; overwork, tax, task, fatigue; get mileage out of, get the best out of, get one's money's worth, run into the ground
▶ *Waste 96; Work 122*

13 **resort to,** have recourse to, fall back on, rely on; run to, turn to, draw on, impose on, presume on; ask favors of, press into service, enlist in one's service, pick someone's brains

14 **have at one's disposal,** control, command, have at one's command, do what one likes with; assign, allot, allocate, apportion, requisition; call into play, call in, set in motion, set in action, set going, deploy, motivate; enjoy, have the use of; make do with, make shift with, get by on, do what one can with, make the most *or* best of; be of use
▶ *Persuasion 178; Possession 469; Allocation 474*

ADVERBS

15 **usefully,** usably, practically, pragmatically, instrumentally, conveniently; profitably, advantageously, beneficially, powerfully, convertibly, reusably

394 Nonuse

NOUNS

1 **nonuse,** lack of use, abeyance, suspension; abstinence, forbearance, avoidance; neglect, negligence, underuse, underutilization, superfluity; unemployment, underemployment; reserve, store, storage
▶ *Store 105; Negligence 326; Rejection 383; Avoidance 386*

2 **newness,** cleanness, blankness, purity, freshness, virginity, mint condition
▶ *Youth 26; Newness 652; Originality 737*

3 **disuse,** desuetude, dereliction, abandonment, rejection; limbo, inactivity, idleness, disposal, discarding, dumping, scrapping; dismissal, discharge, resignation, retirement, superannuation, redundancy [Brit]; obsolescence, obsoleteness
▶ *Expulsion 709; Deterioration 808; Resignation 835*

4 **unused thing,** spare, extra; store, savings, stockpile; remainder, remains, reject, castoff, discard
▶ *Store 105; Rejection 383; Remainder 750*

ADJECTIVES

5 **unused,** not used, not utilized, not activated, out of order, out of service, inoperational; not available, absent, unusable; useless, unemployable, impractical, lacking application, unapplied, unconverted, nonconvertible; in reserve, reserved, saved, stored; spare, extra, unspent, unconsumed, preserved
▶ *Store 105; Absence 576; Uselessness 802; Inconvenience 804; Preservation 815*

6 **idle,** fallow, untried, unessayed, unexercised, in abeyance; suspended, deferred, pigeonholed, left to rot, wasted
▶ *Waste 96*

7 **new,** clean, blank, pure, fresh, unopened; untilled, virgin, unexploited, untapped; undeveloped, untrodden, unbeaten, untouched, unhandled
▶ *Lack of Preparation 389; Newness 652*

8 **disused,** derelict, abandoned, discarded, castoff, jettisoned, scrapped, laid up, mothballed; out of commission, decommissioned, frozen, rusting, in limbo, neglected; underused, underutilized; done with, retired, out of use, discontinued, discredited, junked; supplanted, superseded, superannuated; obsolete, old-fashioned, antiquated, archaic; written off [Inf], on the shelf [Inf]
▶ *Negligence 326; Deterioration 808*

VERBS

9 **not use,** not utilize, have no use for, not activate, hold in abeyance, not touch, leave alone; abstain, forbear, hold off, do without, avoid, waive, not proceed with, not accept, decline, refuse, reject; overlook, disregard, ignore, neglect; underuse, underutilize, waste, fail to take advantage of; keep, spare, save, reserve, store, stockpile, squirrel away, have *or* keep in reserve, have on the side, keep in hand
▶ *Store 105; Negligence 326; Rejection 383; Avoidance 386; Relinquishment 392*

10 **stop using,** disuse, turn off, leave off, ban, stop, cease, leave; lay up, put in mothballs, put out of commission, decommission, freeze; be finished with, have done with, lay aside, put aside, set aside, put on the shelf, pack away, hang up; discard, dump, ditch, scrap, jettison, throw away, throw overboard, eject, slough, cast

off, doff, take off, give up, relinquish; put in limbo, suspend, withdraw, cancel, abrogate, drop; supersede, replace, substitute; write off

> *Store 105; Relinquishment 392; Uncovering 614; Cessation 668; Substitution 672; Expulsion 709; Uselessness 802; Deterioration 808; Cancellation 834*

11 **be unused,** lie idle, lie fallow, deteriorate

12 **stop work,** quit work, resign, retire, take a pension; be dismissed *or* discharged *or* laid off; hang it up [Inf], hang up one's spikes [Inf]

> *Work 122; Expulsion 709; Resignation 835*

ADVERBS

13 **out of use,** idly, out of operation; unusably, uselessly, impractically; superfluously, redundantly, obsolescently, obsoletely

14 **newly,** cleanly, blankly, purely, freshly

395 Misuse

NOUNS

1 **misuse,** abuse, wrong use, misemployment, bad use; manipulation, misdirection, diversion; misappropriation, embezzlement, peculation, fraud; violation, desecration, profanation, defilement, impiety, prostitution, perversion, distortion; environmental abuse, pollution; misrule, mismanagement, maladministration, malpractice; mishandling, bungling, misuse of words, misusage; extravagance, waste, misapplication; misjudgment, overreaction, wasted effort

> *Linguistics, Language 5; Waste 96; Dirtiness 112; Error 351; Disparagement 440; Stealing 479; Deterioration 808*

2 **ill-use,** ill-treatment, mistreatment, maltreatment; molestation, violence, harm, injury, beating, battery, assault, force; exploitation, misuse *or* abuse of power, oppression, persecution; overuse, overwork, fatigue, damage; substance abuse

> *Substance Abuse 121; Severity 424; Immorality 432; Evil 446; Violence 520*

ADJECTIVES

3 **misused,** abused, misemployed; manipulated, misdirected, diverted; misappropriated, embezzled; violated, desecrated, profaned, defiled, perverted, distorted; polluted, spoilt, made unclean

> *Dirtiness 112; Distortion 627*

4 **ill-used,** ill-treated, mistreated, maltreated, beaten, battered; exploited, used, oppressed; mishandled, bungled, solecistic; wasted

> *Waste 96; Use 393; Violence 520*

5 **abusive,** violent, harmful, injurious, forceful, offensive; damaging, exploitative, oppressive; fraudulent, extravagant, wasteful; outrageous, impious, profane

> *Immorality 432; Evil 446*

VERBS

6 **misuse,** abuse, use wrongly, misemploy, put to bad

use; misdirect, divert, misappropriate, expropriate, embezzle, defraud; violate, desecrate, defile, take in vain, profane, prostitute, pervert, distort; pollute, spoil, make unclean; misgovern, misrule, mismanage, maladminister; mishandle, bungle, misuse words; squander, fritter, waste, misapply; misjudge, overreact, use a sledgehammer to crack a nut, waste effort

7 **ill-use,** ill-treat, maltreat, mistreat; molest, do violence to, harm, injure, manhandle, beat, batter, knock about, attack, force, strain; take advantage of, exploit, misuse *or* abuse power, oppress; overuse, overwork, overtask, overtax, fatigue, work hard, wear out, impair, damage

> *Use 393; Violence 520*

ADVERBS

8 **abusively,** badly, wrongly, evilly; profanely, impiously, outrageously, pervertedly, distortedly; extravagantly, wastefully

9 **offensively,** forcefully, violently, harmfully, injuriously, exploitatively, oppressively, fraudulently

396 Improvisation

NOUNS

1 **improvisation,** ad hoc measure, unpremeditation, offhandedness; invention, extemporization, jam session, cadenza, ad lib, impromptu talk; ad-libbing, extemporizing, making the best of it, thinking on one's feet, making do, jury-rigging

2 **spontaneity,** impulse, impetuosity, natural *or* blind impulse, instinct, intuition, hunch; sudden thought, idea, flash, inspiration, snap decision; involuntariness, urge, tendency; spontaneousness, impulsiveness, impetuousness, naturalness, instinctiveness, intuitiveness

> *Intuition 320; Idea 327*

3 **improviser,** innovator, inventor, extemporizer, ad-libber, *improvvisatore* [Ital], creature of impulse, spontaneous person

ADJECTIVES

4 **improvised,** ad hoc, unpremeditated, offhand, offhanded; inventive, extemporized, extemporaneous, extemporary, extempore, ad-lib, impromptu, unrehearsed, unprompted, unprepared; makeshift, jury-rigged, strung *or* thrown together, catch-as-catch-can, potluck, off-the-cuff

5 **spontaneous,** impulsive, impetuous, natural, instinctive, intuitive, on a hunch; unguarded, incautious, rash, emotional, blind; inspired, snap, sudden, spur-of-the-moment, last-minute; unthinking, involuntary; unmotivated, unprovoked, untaught

> *Feelings 266; Rashness 286; Intuition 320; Willingness 373; Naïveté 821*

VERBS

6 **improvise,** invent, extemporize, devise, contrive,

come up with, think up, dream up; ad-lib, make the best of it, vamp, play by ear, jam, think on one's feet; make do, jury-rig, string *or* throw together, rise to the occasion; act impulsively, do what comes naturally, act on the spur of the moment; come out with, blurt, say whatever comes into one's mind, say whatever pops into one's head, have a brainstorm *or* have a brain wave [Inf]

ADVERBS

7 extempore, extemporaneously, impromptu, ad hoc, ad-lib, offhand, offhandedly; off the top of one's head, out of thin air, off-the-cuff

8 spontaneously, impulsively, impetuously, naturally, instinctively, intuitively; involuntarily, suddenly, on the spur of the moment, on the run

397 Habit, Custom

Curious things, habits. People themselves never knew they had them. — AGATHA CHRISTIE

NOUNS

1 habit, good habit, bad habit, confirmed habit, long habit; habitual action, force of habit, second nature, matter of course; conditioned reflex, reflex, knee-jerk reaction [Inf]; pattern, custom, practice, regularity, familiarity, inveteracy; addiction, dependence, compulsion, urge, cacoëthes, mania, obsession, fixation, complex
  ▶ *Substance Abuse 121; Regularity 663*

2 tendency, habitude, leaning, bent, inclination, predisposition, propensity, proclivity, proneness; penchant, trait, idiosyncrasy, mannerism
  ▶ *Tendency 513*

3 way, ways, established ways, fixed ways, lifestyle, way of life; daily habit, constitutional, routine, run, round, daily round, work habit; groove, rut, beaten track, treadmill

4 custom, usage, use, wont, standard usage, praxis, established custom, standing custom; native custom, the old way, tradition, folkways, folklore, lore, native fashion; social custom, social usage, mores, manners and customs, behavior patterns, fashion; institution, ritual, rite, ceremony, observance, religious observance
  ▶ *Religious Ritual 85; Fashion 536; Duration 642; Continuity, Continuation 669*

5 tradition, time-honored practice, consuetude, law, prescription, legal precedent, rules, rules and regulations; house rules, rules of business, social convention, convention, protocol, unwritten law, order of the day; formality, form, etiquette, conduct, manners, social manners, table manners, eating habits
  ▶ *Law 53; Conduct 399; Formality 406; Rule 780*

6 standard procedure, official procedure, recognized procedure, general procedure, procedure; usual policy, policy, practice, standard practice, common practice, convention; routine, routine practice, system, drill
  ▶ *Order 765; Conformity 781*

7 habituation, systemization, institutionalization, indoctrination, brainwashing, inurement, memorization, rote; naturalization, acclimatization, adaptation, orientation, conditioning, association; training, drilling, hardening, seasoning, maturing
  ▶ *Memory 354; Preparation 388*

8 creature of habit, habitué, conservative, old guard, traditionalist, conventionalist, old fogy, stick-in-the-mud, dodo; regular, regular customer, frequent patron, frequenter, longstanding client; addict, drug addict, alcoholic, substance abuser
  ▶ *Substance Abuse 121; Purchase 481; Conformity 781*

ADJECTIVES

9 habitual, customary, accustomed, wonted, predictable, invariable; usual, regular, routine, everyday, workaday; daily, quotidian, weekly, monthly, annual, seasonal; frequent, recurrent, constant, perpetual, cyclic, successive, repeating
  ▶ *Time 639; Frequency 661; Regularity 663; Stability 674; Repetition 797*

10 familiar, known, well-known, household, ordinary, common, commonplace, garden-variety, unexceptional, unoriginal; stock, trite, banal, hackneyed, clichéd, well-worn, trodden, beaten; current, prevalent, widespread, obtaining, universal
  ▶ *Generality 778*

11 customary, normal, normative, natural, in character, typical, stereotyped; reflex, knee-jerk [Inf]; conventional, orthodox, traditional *or* traditionary *or* traditive, ritual; permanent, lasting, time-honored, old, old-fashioned, old-world, old-line
  ▶ *Permanence 667; Conformity 781*

12 established, set, prescribed, prescriptive, standard; standardized, uniform, regulation, approved, accepted, socially accepted; recognized, understood, accredited, instituted, institutionalized; hallowed by custom, fashionable, in fashion, in vogue; official, de rigueur, done, practiced
  ▶ *Compulsion 428; Approval 437; Fashion 536*

13 fixed, set in one's ways, ingrained, implanted, rooted, deep-rooted, deep-seated; dyed-in-the-wool, imbued, permeated, soaked, dyed
  ▶ *Essence 723*

14 habituated, in the habit, used, accustomed, familiar, at home, orientated *or* oriented; familiarized, acclimated *or* acclimatized, naturalized; conversant, *au fait* [Fr], practiced, trained, conditioned; inured, seasoned, hardened, casehardened, tamed, broken in; confirmed, chronic, inveterate, addicted, given
  ▶ *Knowledge 348; Preparation 388; Frequency 661; Continuity, Continuation 669*

15 habit-forming, addictive, obsessive, haunting, besetting, clinging

▶ *Persuasion 178*

VERBS

16 have a habit, have the habit of, be known to, have a tendency, do regularly, go regularly, haunt, frequent; habituate, make a habit of, take up, go in for; never vary, observe routine, be in a rut, be stuck in a groove, tread the beaten path *or* track, cling to custom, observe tradition

17 become a habit, become acceptable, become fixed, catch on, grow on one, take hold of one, take one over, become part of one; stick, cling, adhere, settle, take root; be the rule, obtain, prevail, come into use *or* fashion, acquire the force of habit *or* custom

18 accustom, familiarize, orient *or* orientate, acclimate *or* acclimatize, naturalize, adapt, condition; inure, season, harden, caseharden, teach, train, domesticate, tame, break in; implant, ingraft, imbue, indoctrinate, brainwash

19 accustom oneself, get used to, get the feel of, get the knack of, warm up, get into one's stride, take to, take to like a duck to water; keep one's hand in, practice, get the hang of [Inf]; acquire the habit, learn a habit, develop a habit, cultivate a habit, fall into a habit, get into a habit; be slave to a habit, become addicted, catch oneself doing

▶ *Influence 512*

ADVERBS

20 habitually, by force of habit, by tradition, by custom, customarily, wontedly, traditionally, conventionally

21 regularly, with regularity, as usual, usually, as always, invariably, as is one's wont

22 systematically, mechanically, automatically, without thinking, in one's stride

398 Unaccustomedness

NOUNS

1 unaccustomedness, disusage, disuse, discomfort, discontinuance, nonobservance, unfamiliarity, unwontedness; inexperience, ignorance, unskillfulness; innocence, unacquaintance, unconversance, naiveté, freshness, rawness, callowness; deterioration, staleness, lack of practice, rustiness, shakiness; unconventionality, nonconformity

2 beginner, newcomer, rookie, tyro, novice, neophyte; tenderfoot, cub; apprentice, trainee, greenhorn

▶ *Newness 652; Beginning 771*

ADJECTIVES

3 unaccustomed, not used to, unused to, uncomfortable with, not in the habit of, nonobservant, unfamiliar, not customary, unwonted; unhabituated, untaught, uninstructed, untrained, uneducated, inexperienced, unpracticed, ignorant of; innocent,

naive, new to, new, fresh, raw, callow, green, tyronic, unskillful; disaccustomed, out of the habit, rusty, shaky; unseasoned, unripe, immature, unweaned, undomesticated, untamed, unbroken, not broken, wild, still wet behind the ears

▶ *Youth 26; Unskillfulness 128; Ignorance 349; Lack of Preparation 389; Naiveté 821*

4 uncustomary, not done, not customarily done, out of the ordinary, unusual, uncommon, nonprevalent; bad form, tactless, without manners, gauche, vulgar; not current, out of step *or* fashion, out of touch, unfashionable, antiquated, old-fashioned, old hat, stale, defunct, past, outgrown, discarded; unconventional, nonconformist, unsanctified by custom, untraditional, unprecedented; unhackneyed, avant-garde, original, experimental, odd, strange, offbeat; [Inf]: way-out, far-out, non-U

▶ *Tastelessness 220; Discourtesy 411; Diversity 732; Nonconformity 782*

VERBS

5 be unaccustomed, not be used to, be unused to, be uncomfortable with; slip, lapse, fall into disuse, grow rusty, deteriorate

6 disaccustom, wean from, rid oneself of, break with *or* away *or* off *or* from, swear off, stop, give up; break *or* drop a habit, kick a habit [Inf]; cure, reform, shake off, throw off, slough off, shed

▶ *Substance Abuse 121; Rejection 383*

ADVERBS

7 unaccustomedly, uncomfortably, ignorantly, innocently, naively, immaturely

8 unskillfully, inexpertly, incapably, inadequately, incompetently

9 unusually, uncommonly, oddly, strangely, unconventionally, eccentrically, originally, experimentally

399 Conduct

NOUNS

1 conduct, behavior, deportment, bearing; personal bearing, comportment, carriage, posture, port [Arch]; demeanor, mien, attitude; mental attitude, aspect, outlook, mood, opinion, feeling; look, look in one's eyes, appearance; tone, tone of voice, voice, delivery; motion, action, actions, gesticulation, gesture; proposed conduct, intentions, good intentions; past behavior, known attitudes, record, track record, history

▶ *Identification 184; Appearance 264; Feelings 266*

2 mode of behavior, manners, manner, style, fashion, guise, air; pose, affectation, role-playing; role model, example; democratic behavior, gesture of equality, common touch; reward of conduct, reciprocal manners, deserts, dueness

▶ *Belief 87; Affectation 367*

3 study of conduct, psychology, behaviorism

4 line of action, policy, course, race, walk [Arch]; vocation, career; observance, rules, rules of life, golden rule, rules of business, rules of the road
> *Plan 387*

5 good conduct, good behavior, goodness, virtue; breeding, poise, dignity, presence, savoir-faire; etiquette, protocol, good manners, gracious manners, graciousness, courtesy, politeness, gentlemanly *or* ladylike behavior
> *Refreshment 94; Courtesy 410; Good 445; Virtue 447*

6 well-behaved person, well-mannered person, gentleman, lady, gracious host *or* hostess, polite listener; good child, law-abiding citizen, saint, moralist
> *Courtesy 410; Obedience 426; Good 445; Virtue 447*

7 bad conduct, misconduct, bad behavior, misbehavior; mischief, naughtiness; badness, vice, wickedness, crime; ill-breeding, bad manners, ungraciousness, boorishness; rudeness, discourtesy
> *Discourtesy 411; Disobedience 427; Wickedness 448*

8 badly behaved person, ill-mannered person, rude person, obnoxious person; boor, lout, cad, bounder; naughty child; criminal; egomaniac; amoralist
> *Discourtesy 411; Disobedience 427; Wickedness 448*

9 way of life, lifestyle; ethos, morals, principles, ideals; customs, traditions, conventions, mores, praxis, modus vivendi, manners, habits
> *Philosophy 4; Religion 81; Habit, Custom 397*

10 way, proven way, new way, method, method of operating, modus operandi; tried-and-true method, experimental method; practice, everyday practice, routine, procedure, routine procedure, process
> *Way 691*

11 treatment, handling, manipulation, control, discipline, regulation, direction; management, administration, operation, organization, orchestration, masterminding, leadership, command, guidance, supervision; dealings, actions, transactions, affairs, deeds; gentle handling, tact, diplomacy; leniency, kid gloves, velvet glove; rough handling, severity, iron hand, boot, jackboot, kick in the pants, kick in the ass [Inf]
> *Management 126; Leniency 423; Severity 424; Reward 453; Punishment 454; Direction 697*

12 tactics, strategy, campaign, plan, plan of campaign, plan of attack, game plan, logistics, program; policy, line, party line, rules of the game, game rules; political science, politics; art of the possible, opportunism, realpolitik; diplomacy, statesmanship; governance; lifemanship, gamesmanship, cunning, brinkmanship; generalship, seamanship, skill, maneuvers, maneuvering; outflanking, jockeying, jockeying for position, one-upmanship; advantage, tactical advantage, built-in advantage, vantage, vantage ground, starting ahead of the game; stalling for time, playing for time, delay; maneuver, move, gambit, deed, game, little game, tactic, strata-

gem, trick, shift, contrivance; wheeling and dealing [Inf]
> *Authority 52; Skillfulness 127; Plan 387; Action 412; Lateness 658; Superiority 744; Cunning 822*

13 conductor, guide, leader, director; escort, usher; carrier, driver, pilot

ADJECTIVES

14 behaving, behavioral, behavioristic, ethological; tactical, strategical; political, statesmanlike, governmental, businesslike

15 well-behaved, on one's best behavior; well-bred, gentlemanly, ladylike, dignified, well-mannered, gracious, courteous, polite; good, ethical, virtuous, law-abiding
> *Courtesy 410; Good 445; Virtue 447*

16 badly behaved, ill-bred, mischievous, naughty, bad, wicked; ill-mannered, ungracious, boorish, rude, discourteous, impolite; selfish, inconsiderate, obnoxious, bad news [Inf]
> *Discourtesy 411; Evil 446; Wickedness 448*

VERBS

17 conduct oneself, behave, carry oneself, bear oneself, deport oneself, comport oneself, acquit oneself; act, do, set an example, provide a role model, gesture, gesticulate, posture, pose, affect, indulge in, play one's part; participate, pursue, follow a course, follow one's career, shape one's career, steer one's career, steer for, conduct one's affairs, busy oneself; be master of one's own ship, shift for oneself; employ tactics, maneuver, manipulate, mastermind, jockey, twist, turn, take advantage of, use; paddle one's own canoe [Inf]
> *Identification 184; Affectation 367; Action 412; Activity 414; Direction 697; Freedom 829*

18 behave well, behave oneself, behave, be good, keep out of mischief; conduct oneself properly, comport oneself well, lead a good life, set a good example, mind one's p's and q's; abide by the rules, play the game, deserve well of
> *Good 445; Virtue 447*

19 behave badly, misbehave, demean oneself, lead a bad life, set a bad example; break the rules, carry on, deserve ill of
> *Discourtesy 411; Evil 446; Wickedness 448*

20 behave toward, treat, deal with, handle, do, see to; put on one's calendar, have in one's book, have on one's plate, have to do with; conduct, operate, carry on, run, direct, manage, cope with, manipulate, control, organize, orchestrate, mastermind, lead; act, transact, enact, execute, dispatch, carry out, carry through; put into practice, put into effect, initiate; plan, work out, program, work at, think through, work through, wade through, go through, read, study, research
> *Work 122; Management 126; Plan 387; Action 412; Completeness 761*

21 conduct, guide, lead, direct; navigate, steer, pilot; escort, usher; carry, transmit, convey

▶ *Transfer 685; Direction 697*

ADVERBS

22 **well,** in a gentlemanly *or* ladylike manner, properly, with propriety, politely, graciously, courteously; virtuously, ethically

23 **badly,** in an ungentlemanly *or* unladylike manner, wickedly, naughtily, ungraciously, rudely, discourteously, impolitely; selfishly, inconsiderately, obnoxiously

400   Insolence

NOUNS

1 **insolence,** impertinence, effrontery, impudence, brashness, brazenness, shamelessness
▶ *Pride 297; Disrespect 436*

2 **rudeness,** incivility, impoliteness, discourtesy, disrespect, disrespectfulness; flippancy, pertness, smartness, sauciness, back talk, mouth; [Inf]: sauce, backchat, sass, lip
▶ *Answer 334; Discourtesy 411; Disrespect 436*

3 **audacity,** boldness, defiance, presumption, presumptuousness, assurance, nerve, gall, brass, cheek, cheekiness, face; bumptiousness, forwardness, obtrusiveness; [Inf]: pushiness, freshness, chutzpa *or* hutzpa, crust
▶ *Vanity 402; Defiance 416; Front 621*

4 **arrogance,** cockiness, haughtiness, loftiness, contempt, contumely, scorn, disdain; uppishness [Inf], uppityness [Inf]
▶ *Pride 297; Vanity 402; Disrespect 436*

5 **derision,** ridicule, taunt, snook, sneer, sneering, disparagement, scoff, gibe, jeer
▶ *Disrespect 436; Disparagement 440*

6 **insult,** affront, contumely, offense, outrage, slight
▶ *Answer 334; Discourtesy 411*

7 **insolent person,** insolent, impertinence, *chutzpadik* [Yiddish], saucebox [Inf], malapert [Arch]; upstart, whippersnapper, puppy; smart aleck, smarty, smarty-pants, know-it-all; swaggerer, blusterer, bragger, braggart, braggadocio, boaster; tin god, cockalorum, cock of the walk; minx, hussy, baggage [Off], madam; [Inf]: wise guy *or* wiseacre, wisenheimer, wise-ass, smart-ass
▶ *Pride 297; Vanity 402*

ADJECTIVES

8 **insolent,** impertinent, impudent, brash, brazen, brazen-faced, bold-faced, barefaced, shameless, unabashed, unblushing
▶ *Pride 297; Disrespect 436*

9 **rude,** incivil, uncivil, impolite, discourteous, disrespectful; flippant, pert, mouthy, saucy, smart, malapert [Arch], smart-alecky; [Inf]: flip, sassy, wise-guy, wise-ass, smart-ass
▶ *Answer 334; Discourtesy 411; Disrespect 436*

10 **audacious,** bold, defiant, presumptuous, overween-

ing, assured, nervy, cheeky, brassy; bumptious, forward, obtrusive; pushy [Inf], fresh [Inf]
▶ *Vanity 402; Defiance 416; Front 621*

11 **arrogant,** cocky, haughty, lofty, contemptuous, contumelious, scornful, disdainful; uppish [Inf], uppity [Inf]
▶ *Pride 297; Vanity 402; Disrespect 436*

12 **derisive,** ridiculing, taunting, sneering, disparaging, derogatory, scoffing, gibing, jeering; insulting, offensive, outrageous, slighting, affrontive [Arch]
▶ *Humility 298; Disrespect 436; Disparagement 440*

13 **swaggering,** blustering, bragging, boasting

VERBS

14 **be insolent,** be rude, disrespect; answer back, retort, talk back, back-talk, get smart; [Inf]: sass, mouth off, lip off
▶ *Answer 334; Discourtesy 411; Disrespect 436*

15 **have the audacity,** have the nerve *or* gall *or* cheek; make bold, brazen it out, dare, presume, take liberties, make free with, get fresh [Inf]
▶ *Vanity 402; Defiance 416; Front 621*

16 **disdain,** contemn, hold in contempt, despise, scorn, spurn; deride, ridicule, mock, make fun of, laugh at, laugh out of court, scoff at, jeer at, guy, disparage, demean, taunt, gibe, thumb one's nose, stick out one's tongue, snort, sneer; insult, affront, offend, slight, give a Bronx cheer, blow a raspberry [Inf]
▶ *Humility 298; Disrespect 436; Disparagement 440*

17 **brag,** boast, swagger, bluster, swank, show off, swell
▶ *Pride 297*

ADVERBS

18 **insolently,** impertinently, impudently, brashly, brazenly, brazen-facedly, barefacedly, shamelessly, unabashedly, unblushingly
▶ *Pride 297; Disrespect 436*

19 **rudely,** uncivilly, impolitely, discourteously, disrespectfully; flippantly, pertly, saucily, smartly, malapertly [Arch]
▶ *Discourtesy 411; Disrespect 436*

20 **audaciously,** boldly, defiantly, presumptuously, overweeningly, assuredly, nervily, cheekily, brassily; bumptiously, forwardly, obtrusively; pushily [Inf], freshly [Inf]
▶ *Vanity 402; Defiance 416; Front 621*

21 **arrogantly,** cockily, haughtily, loftily, contemptuously, contumeliously, scornfully, disdainfully, uppishly [Inf]
▶ *Pride 297; Vanity 402; Disrespect 436*

22 **derisively,** tauntingly, sneeringly, disparagingly, derogatorily, scoffingly, gibingly, jeeringly; insultingly, offensively, outrageously, slightingly
▶ *Disrespect 436; Disparagement 440*

401 Servility

NOUNS

1 **servility,** slavishness, deference, compliance, pliancy, subservience; abjectness, submission, submissiveness, slavery, serfdom, helotism, peonage
 ▶ *Submission 421*

2 **sycophancy,** obsequiousness, fawning, toadying, groveling, flattery; sponging, parasitism, cringing, bootlicking, back scratching, timeserving; obeisance, prostration, crawling, bowing and scraping; ingratiation, truckling; [Inf]: soft-soaping, ass-kissing, brown-nosing, apple-polishing
 ▶ *Flattery 439*

3 **sycophant,** toady, toad, flatterer; timeserver, crawler, bootlicker, groveler, lickspittle, yes-man, lap dog, spaniel, jackal, creature; cat's-paw, dupe, stooge, footstool, doormat, instrument, tool, puppet; minion, lackey, kowtower, ass-kisser [Inf], brown-nose *or* brown-noser [Inf]
 ▶ *Flattery 439*

4 **sponger,** parasite, leech, sponge, barnacle, deadbeat, gigolo, freeloader [Inf]

5 **adherent,** hanger-on, follower, appendage, satellite, dangler, dependent, shadow, collaborator, retainer, servant, man
 ▶ *Servant 69*

ADJECTIVES

6 **servile,** slavish, deferential, ingratiating, compliant, pliant, subservient, menial, abject, submissive, not free, dependent, under one's thumb

7 **sycophantic,** obsequious, flattering, fawning, groveling, toadying, sponging, parasitic, cringing, bootlicking, back-scratching, timeserving; obeisant, prostrate, mealymouthed, ingratiating, truckling, smarmy, whining, cringing, cowering, sniveling; beggarly, hangdog, on one's knees, on bended knee, bowed, stooping, kowtowing, bowing, scraping, crawling; unctuous, soapy, oily, slimy, overattentive; [Inf]: ass-kissing, brown-nosing, freeloading, soft-soaping, apple-polishing

VERBS

8 **be servile,** defer, comply, be subservient; be abject, submit, let oneself be walked all over

9 **fawn,** toady, ingratiate oneself, insinuate oneself, flatter, truckle, crawl, grovel, curry favor, bootlick, lick the feet of, lick the shoes *or* boots of, pay court to, worm one's way, play up to, polish the apple, get into the good graces of, get on the right side of; [Inf]: suck up to, make up to, soft-soap, kiss ass, brown-nose

10 **knuckle under,** demean oneself, cower, cringe, crouch, kneel, make obeisance, stoop, bend the knee, fall on one's knees, prostrate oneself, throw oneself at the feet of, defer to, bow, kowtow, bow and scrape,

fetch and carry, be the tool of, lick the dust, agree to anything
 ▶ *Humility 298; Courtesy 410*

11 **pander to,** wait on *or* upon, wait on hand and foot, cater to, fetch and carry, do service, serve, jump at the bidding of, do the dirty work of, stooge for, squire, dance attendance on, fall at a person's feet, do the bidding of, run after

12 **beg,** beg for favors, wheedle, whine, beg for crumbs

13 **sponge,** sponge on, feed on, live off, parasitize, fatten on, use, make use of, use as a meal ticket

14 **follow,** batten on, hang on, adhere to, follow the crowd, swim with the tide, latch onto [Inf], hang on the skirts *or* sleeve of, jump on the bandwagon, go with the flow [Inf]

ADVERBS

15 **servilely,** slavishly, subserviently, abjectly, menially, submissively, with cap in hand

16 **sycophantically,** obsequiously, ingratiatingly, fawningly, grovelingly, on one's knees

17 **parasitically,** like a leech

402 Vanity

Vanity of vanities, saith the Preacher, vanity of vanities: all is vanity. — BIBLE: ECCLESIASTES

We are so vain that we even care for the opinion of those we don't care for. — MARIE EBNER VON ESCHENBACH

NOUNS

1 **vanity,** vainness, immodesty, vain pride, empty pride, conceit, conceitedness, self-importance, swelledheadedness *or* swellheadedness, egomania, megalomania; vainglory, bigheadedness [Inf]

2 **self-satisfaction,** self-congratulation, self-assurance, self-content, self-approbation, smugness, complacency, solipsism

3 **cockiness,** bumptiousness, pertness, aggressiveness, obtrusiveness, self-confidence, self-assertiveness, airs and graces, pomposity *or* pompousness

4 **self-admiration,** self-esteem, self-praise, self-applause, self-flattery, self-worship, self-love, self-endearment, *amour propre* [Fr], self-infatuation, narcissism
 ▶ *Pride 297*

5 **selfishness,** self-interest, egotism, egoism, self-centeredness, self-gratification, ego trip [Inf]
 ▶ *Selfishness 444*

6 **boastfulness,** pride, conceit, arrogance, showing off, exhibitionism, self-display, ostentation, affectation, hubris
 ▶ *Affectation 367*

7 **vain person,** egotist, egoist, show-off, self-admirer, exhibitionist, peacock, turkey cock, Narcissus, brag-

gart, know-all or know-it-all, swelled head, smarty-pants, stuffed shirt, empty head, fop, smart aleck; [Inf]: pompous twit, wise guy or wiseacre, wise-ass, smart-ass

ADJECTIVES

8 **vain,** immodest, overproud, conceited, self-important, swelled-headed or swellheaded, egomaniac, megalomaniac; [Inf]: bigheaded, snooty, stuck-up

9 **self-satisfied,** self-congratulatory, self-assured, self-contented, complacent, contented, smug

10 **self-admiring,** self-worshiping, self-loving, self-endearing, self-infatuated, narcissistic, self-glorifying, smug, supercilious, vainglorious, self-approving, impressed or pleased with oneself, all wrapped up in oneself, stuck on oneself [Inf]

11 **cocky,** pert, bumptious, aggressive, self-confident, self-assertive, foppish, obtrusive, full of oneself, too clever by half, too smart for one's own good; puffed up, swaggering, pompous, pretentious, putting on airs, affected, smart-alecky, smart-ass [Inf]

12 **selfish,** self-interested, selfish, egotistical, egocentric, solipsistic, self-centered
   ▶ *Selfishness 444*

13 **boastful,** proud, prideful, arrogant, exhibitionistic, conceited, ostentatious, opinionated, too big for one's boots, peacockish, know-it-all, hubristic

VERBS

14 **be vain,** be conceited, have a high opinion of oneself, be stuck on oneself, be impressed with oneself, think a lot of oneself, flatter oneself, be puffed up, think one knows it all; fish for compliments, be pleased with oneself, be full of oneself, be wrapped up in oneself, set a high value on oneself, think oneself God Almighty, think oneself God's gift to mankind, think well of oneself, think one is it, have no self-doubt, love the sound of one's own voice, give oneself airs, get above oneself, give oneself a pat on the back, think oneself the cat's pajamas or the cat's meow [Inf]

15 **show off,** feel pride, boast, hug oneself, strut, put on airs, talk big, talk for effect, preen oneself, push oneself forward, blow or toot one's own horn [Inf]

16 **become conceited,** inflate, puff up, have one's head turned

ADVERBS

17 **vainly,** immodestly, conceitedly, vaingloriously, self-importantly

18 **smugly,** complacently, self-assuredly, self-congratulatory, self-contentedly, egocentrically, solipsistically

19 **cockily,** pertly, bumptiously, pompously, aggressively, obtrusively, self-confidently, self-assertively, pretentiously, affectedly, foppishly, superciliously

20 **selfishly,** egotistically, egocentrically

21 **boastfully,** proudly, arrogantly, conceitedly, ostentatiously

---

403 Modesty

I have often wished I had time to cultivate modesty. . . . But I am too busy thinking about myself. — EDITH SITWELL

NOUNS

1 **modesty,** meekness, humility, unpretentiousness, unassumingness, unassuming nature, unostentatiousness, lack of ostentation, unobtrusiveness, privacy
   ▶ *Humility 298*

2 **blushing,** blush, flushing, flush, coloring, reddening, crimsoning, red face
   ▶ *Redness 257*

3 **shyness,** timidity, timidness, diffidence, self-consciousness, retiring disposition, timorousness, embarrassment, stage fright; bashfulness, coyness, prudishness, demureness, shamefacedness, shamefastness [Arch], skittishness

4 **self-deprecation,** self-effacement, self-distrust, self-doubt, lack of self-confidence, weak ego

5 **reserve,** restraint, reticence, constraint, backwardness, reluctance
   ▶ *Restraint 830*

ADJECTIVES

6 **modest,** meek, humble, unpretentious, unpretending, unassuming, unostentatious, unobtrusive, unboastful, unimposing, unimpressive, unaspiring, private
   ▶ *Humility 298*

7 **blushing,** flushed, red, ruddy, reddening, crimsoning

8 **shy,** timid, diffident, self-conscious, timorous, embarrassed, frightened, mousy, shrinking, unsure of oneself, inarticulate; bashful, coy, prudish, shockable, demure, shamefaced, shamefast [Arch], confused

9 **self-deprecating,** self-effacing, self-doubting, unambitious, self-distrustful

10 **reserved,** restrained, reticent, constrained, backward, reluctant, unseen, unheard, quiet

VERBS

11 **be modest,** show moderation, ration oneself, be temperate, not push oneself forward, yield to others, play second fiddle, know one's place, not look for praise, not blow or toot one's own horn [Inf]

12 **blush,** flush, crimson, color up, turn red

13 **be shy,** be self-conscious, squirm, die of embarrassment, feel shame, die of shame

14 **escape notice,** avoid, hide one's light under a bushel, take a backseat, keep a low profile, keep in or merge into or stay in the background, shun the limelight, hang back, shrink back, hesitate, crawl or creep into one's shell, shrink from public gaze, retire; be private

ADVERBS

15 **modestly,** quietly, demurely, meekly, humbly, un-

pretentiously, unobtrusively, without ceremony, without fuss or frills, privately

16 **shyly,** timidly, bashfully, diffidently, timorously, coyly, shamefacedly, shamefastly [Arch], sheepishly; blushingly, with downcast eyes

404 Showiness

NOUNS

1 **showiness,** ostentation, ostentatiousness, pretension, pretentiousness, showmanship, razzle-dazzle [Inf]

2 **airs,** airs and graces, loftiness, high-and-mightiness, delusions of grandeur, highfalutin ways [Inf]

3 **dramatics,** histrionics, theater, theatricality, sensationalism, camp
   ▶ *Drama and Theater 136*

4 **flashiness,** gaudiness, loudness, extravagance, bombast, flamboyance, panache, dash, splash, splurge, garishness, glitter, tinsel, tawdriness, meretriciousness, colorfulness, dazzle, razzmatazz [Inf]
   ▶ *Vulgarity 535; Display 843*

5 **pomposity,** pompousness, pontification, stuffiness, self-importance, grandiloquence, turgidity, bombast, magniloquence
   ▶ *Vanity 402*

6 **blatancy,** flagrancy, shamelessness, brazenness, luridness, extravagance, sensationalism, obtrusiveness, crudeness, self-importance, fuss

7 **pomp,** majesty, pageantry, parade, circumstance, state, stateliness; pride, formality, solemnity, stiffness, starchiness

8 **bravado,** brag, bluster, bombast, braggadocio, fanfaronade

9 **exhibitionism,** showing off, vanity, boasting, flaunting, swaggering, strutting, swashbuckling, peacockery, window dressing, fuss and feathers
   ▶ *Vanity 402*

10 **grandeur,** grandness, grandiosity, splendor, splendiferousness, magnificence, gorgeousness, resplendence, brilliance, glory, sumptuousness, lavishness, luxuriousness, elegance, elaborateness, luxury, poshness, plushness, swankiness, ritziness [Inf]

11 **ceremonial,** state occasion, function, procession, review, grand parade; flourish, trumpet fanfare, drumming, red carpet; ceremony, rite, formalities; solemnity, convention, ceremoniousness, punctilio
   ▶ *Formality 406*

12 **show,** display, demonstration, manifestation, exhibition, parade, pageant, fete, gala, tournament, tattoo [Brit], spectacle, tableau, set piece, display, sound-and-light show, *son et lumière* [Fr], stunt, pyrotechnics, fireworks, carnival; stage show, play, act, scene, grand finale, concert, opera, ballet, mime, circus, big top, theater, burlesque, vaudeville

   ▶ *Drama and Theater 136; Light Entertainment 138*

13 **show-off,** exhibitionist, swashbuckler, peacock, grandstander, hot shot [Inf]

ADJECTIVES

14 **showy,** ostentatious, pretentious, shameless

15 **lofty,** high-and-mighty, prestigious, swanky, highfalutin [Inf]

16 **dramatic,** histrionic, theatrical, sensational, daring, stagy

17 **flashy,** gaudy, loud, extravagant, flamboyant, exhibitionistic, bombastic, garish, frothy, frilly, glittering, tinselly, tawdry, meretricious, colorful, dazzling, painted, foppish, snazzy, rakish, gay, jaunty, sporty, dressed to kill, dressed to the nines; tarted up [Inf], dolled up [Inf]

18 **pompous,** stuffy, self-important, grandiloquent, bombastic, turgid, pontificating, windy, long-drawn-out

19 **blatant,** flagrant, shameless, brazen, lurid, extravagant, sensational, obtrusive, vulgar, crude, fussy, public, screaming, camp

20 **swaggering,** swashbuckling, strutting; heroic, macho, dashing, gallant

21 **majestic,** stately, royal, proud, formal, princely, solemn, stiff, starchy, dignified, grand, fine, ceremonious, palatial

22 **grand,** grandiose, awe-inspiring, imposing, splendid, spectacular, scenic, magnificent, gorgeous, resplendent, brilliant, glorious, sumptuous, lavish, luxurious, elegant, elaborate, luxuriant, de luxe, superb, diamond-studded, costly, expensive, impressive, plush, swanky, posh, ritzy [Inf], glitzy [Inf]

23 **ceremonious,** smart, correct, formal, ceremonial, standing on ceremony, punctilious, ritualistic, celebratory

VERBS

24 **show,** exhibit, display, demonstrate, manifest, parade, present, perform, act, act the showman, stage-manage, march, promenade, march past, sport, advertise

25 **flourish,** brandish, wave, wave banners, trumpet, emblazon, dangle before one's eyes, beat the big drum, proclaim, vaunt, flash

26 **show off,** play to the gallery, grab or hog the limelight, attract notice, put oneself forward, advertise oneself, dramatize oneself, fish for compliments, cut a dash, flaunt oneself, prance, promenade, peacock, strut, swagger, make a public exhibition of oneself, make people stare, do for effect, take center stage, upstage, make oneself conspicuous, ham it up

27 **put on airs,** give oneself airs, put (it) on, put up a front, look big, act the grand seigneur or grande dame, pontificate, exaggerate, swank, put on the ritz [Inf]

28 **put on a show,** make a show, cut a dash or swath or figure, make a splash, splurge on, do for effect, observe the formalities, stand on ceremony, glitter, dazzle, sensationalize, camp up, talk for effect, paper over the

cracks, pull out all the stops, step to the front, parade one's wares

ADVERBS

29 **showily,** ostentatiously, pretentiously, shamelessly, with a flourish, with flying colors

30 **loftily,** swankily, prestigiously

31 **dramatically,** histrionically, theatrically, sensationally, daringly, stagily

32 **flashily,** gaudily, loudly, extravagantly, flamboyantly, bombastically, garishly, glitteringly, meretriciously, colorfully, dazzlingly, foppishly, rakishly, jauntily, sportily, snazzily

33 **pompously,** stuffily, self-importantly, grandiloquently, turgidly, pontificatingly, windily, bombastically, magniloquently

34 **blatantly,** flagrantly, shamelessly, brazenly, luridly, extravagantly, sensationally, obtrusively, vulgarly, crudely, fussily, publicly, screamingly

35 **swaggeringly,** struttingly, heroically, gallantly, dashingly

36 **majestically,** stately, royally, proudly, formally, solemnly, stiffly, starchily, grandly, ceremoniously

37 **grandly,** grandiosely, splendidly, magnificently, spectacularly, resplendently, brilliantly, gloriously, sumptuously, lavishly, luxuriously, elegantly, elaborately, luxuriantly, swankily, superbly, expensively, ritzily [Inf], glitzily [Inf]

38 **ceremoniously,** ritualistically, correctly, formally, ceremonially, punctiliously

405 Celebration

And pomp, and feast, and revelry, / With mask, and antique pageantry, / Such sights as youthful poets dream / On summer eves by haunted stream. — JOHN MILTON

NOUNS

1 **celebration,** observance, festival, festivity *or* festivities, festive occasion; fete, fiesta, festa, field day, function; picnic, party, feast, banquet; celebrating, rejoicing, revel, revelry, revels, carousal, orgy, debauch, drinking bout, saturnalia; performance, occasion, jubilation, jubilee, merrymaking, merriment, gaiety, jollity, jollification, conviviality, skylarking, holiday, gala, jamboree, high jinks; fair, carnival; [Inf]: binge, bender, blowout, making whoopee
  ▶ *Drinking 93*

2 **commemoration,** memorialization, honoring, remembrance, memory, observance, ceremonial, solemnization, marking the occasion, jubilee, memorial service, remembrance service, anniversary

3 **ceremony,** ceremonial function, function, ritual, service, office, state occasion, solemn observance, ritual observance, rite, liturgy; ovation, coronation, enthronement, triumph; rite of passage, bar mitzvah, bat

or bas mitzvah, confirmation, convocation, graduation, marriage, christening, baptism; inauguration, initiation, debut; mummery
  ▶ *Religious Ritual 85; Formality 406*

4 **reception,** hero's welcome, parade, ticker-tape parade, red-carpet treatment

5 **anniversary,** special day, day to remember, great day, feast day, fast day, red-letter day, holy day, saint's day; birthday, name day, wedding anniversary, silver wedding anniversary, golden wedding anniversary, diamond wedding anniversary; centennial, bicentennial, tricentennial, sesquicentennial; jubilee, silver jubilee, golden jubilee, diamond jubilee
  ▶ *Memory 354; Regularity 663*

6 **tribute,** testimonial, testimonial banquet *or* dinner, toast, health, congratulations, cheering, applause, ovation, standing ovation, flag waving

7 **salute,** salvo, fanfare, march-past, drumroll, tattoo; dressing ship, flags, banners, waving, bunting, streamers, ticker tape, decorations, Chinese lanterns, illuminations, fireworks, bonfire

8 **rejoicing,** jubilation, exultation, hosanna, hallelujah

ADJECTIVES

9 **celebrative,** celebratory, festive, festal, jubilatory, joyous; merry, gay, convivial, gala; commemorative, ceremonial, solemn, memorial, honorable; ritual, triumphal, crowning; congratulatory, welcoming, complimentary, auspicious

VERBS

10 **celebrate,** rejoice, jubilate, revel, make merry; fete, party, junket, feast; carouse, debauch, drink, get drunk, binge [Inf], make whoopee [Inf]
  ▶ *Drinking 93*

11 **commemorate,** honor, keep, mark, remember, memorialize, solemnize, observe, hallow, keep holy, perform, sanctify, mark the occasion, pay one's respects

12 **congratulate,** felicitate, toast, drink the health of, drink to, raise *or* fill one's glass, praise, pay tribute, sing the praises of, reward, drain a bumper, sing Happy Birthday

13 **salute,** welcome, cheer, applaud, roll out the red carpet, kill the fatted calf, fete, lionize, hang out the flags *or* bunting, dress ship, garland; throw a party, make much of, do one proud, carry shoulder high, mob, deck *or* wreathe with flowers, fling wide the gates, beat a tattoo, blow the trumpets, fire a salvo
  ▶ *Courtesy 410*

14 **launch,** enthrone, crown, inaugurate, induct, install; initiate, present, auspicate; debut, make one's debut, come out, graduate

ADVERBS

15 **in honor of,** in memory of, in commemoration of, on the occasion of, in remembrance of

406 Formality

NOUNS

1 **formality,** form, good form, right form, formalness, state, stateliness; dignity, ceremoniousness; stiffness, sedateness, staidness, starchiness, solemnity, solemnness; etiquette, correct behavior, protocol, the thing to do, doing the right thing; smartness, spit and polish, red carpet; correctness, correctitude, fastidiousness; decorum, decorousness, strait-lacedness, hideboundness, stuffiness, preciseness, conventionality, propriety, best behavior, stylization, primness, rigidness, pomp, circumstance, pride, gravity, weightiness

2 **formalism,** ritualism, ceremonialism, pedantry, preciseness, precision, preciousness, preciosity, punctiliousness, scrupulousness, conventionalism, conventionality; overrefinement, overpreciseness

3 **etiquette,** rules of conduct, social code, formalities, prescribed form, set form, social procedures, social graces, social conduct, social convention, social image, custom, good manners, politeness, politesse, natural politeness, civilities, comity, decencies, elegancies, mores, proprieties, decorum, good form, right form, protocol, diplomatic code, punctilio, point of etiquette, convention
   ‣ *Courtesy 410*

4 **formal occasion,** ceremony, ceremonial, celebration, ball; procedure, ritual, drill; spectacle, set piece, tableau, scene, show, review, parade, pageant, fete, gala, gala performance; rite, religious ceremony; coronation, inauguration, graduation, wedding, funeral; rite of passage
   ‣ *Dance and Ballet 135; Showiness 404; Celebration 405*

5 **formal clothing,** formal attire, full dress, court dress, robes, regalia, finery; tails, black tie, white tie, white tie and tails, cutaway, dinner jacket, dress suit, tuxedo, tux [Inf]; morning dress, cocktail dress, evening dress, evening gown, ball gown, long dress, formal; best bib and tucker, Sunday best; academic dress, cap and gown; mourning wear, widow's weeds; uniform, regimentals, livery, dress uniform, mess kit, battle dress, school uniform; vestments, clerical dress
   ‣ *Clergy 84; Clothing 100; Identification 184*

ADJECTIVES

6 **formal,** formalistic, legalistic, pedantic, stately, dignified, ceremonious, ceremonial; stiff, refined, starchy, sedate, staid, stilted, rigid, solemn, royal; correct, smart; conventional, ritual, procedural, standing on ceremony, official, stylized; prim, punctilious, precise; scrupulous, fastidious, precious, puristic; exact, meticulous, orderly, methodical; elegant, decorous, strait-laced, proud, grave, pompous, weighty

‣ *Conformity 781*

7 **ceremonious,** ceremonial, ritual, ritualistic, solemn, pompous, liturgical, stately

8 **formally dressed,** dressed up, in full dress; black-tie, white-tie, in white tie and tails, in one's Sunday best, in one's best bib and tucker, in fine feather, well turned out, dressed to kill, dressed to the nines; uniformed; [Inf]: spiffed up, slicked up, dolled up

VERBS

9 **formalize,** ritualize, solemnize, conventionalize, stylize

10 **celebrate,** dignify
   ‣ *Celebration 405*

11 **be formal,** observe the formalities, stand on ceremony, do things by the book, follow protocol, mind one's manners, mind one's p's and q's, conform; dress formally, dress up
   ‣ *Conformity 781*

ADVERBS

12 **formally,** in due form, in set form, pro forma, as a matter of form, precisely, smartly, officially, starchily, stiffly, stiltedly, rigidly, primly, solemnly, procedurally, conventionally, ritually, royally, correctly, ceremoniously, ceremonially

407 Informality

NOUNS

1 **informality,** informalness, lack of formality, lack of ceremony, unceremoniousness, lack of convention, indifference, nonconformity, casualness, offhandedness
   ‣ *Indifference 289; Nonconformity 782*

2 **sociability,** affability, graciousness, cordiality, relaxedness
   ‣ *Sociability 408*

3 **familiarity,** naturalness, simplicity, plainness, homeliness, homeyness, folksiness, common touch, unaffectedness
   ‣ *Simplicity 526*

4 **freedom,** license, indulgence, toleration, free speech, free will, free thought; free hand, leeway, margin, unconstraint, latitude, independence; freedom of action, laxity, permissiveness, relaxation, forbearance, ease, easygoingness, leave, looseness, irregularity, permissive society, bohemianism
   ‣ *Easiness 823; Freedom 829; Liberation 831*

5 **informal clothing,** casual clothing *or* casual clothes, sportswear, leisurewear, loungewear; mufti, civvies [Inf]
   ‣ *Clothing 100*

ADJECTIVES

6 **informal,** unceremonious, unconventional, unofficial, indifferent, nonconformist, casual, offhand, unstuffy, unaffected, unassuming

7 **sociable,** affable, gracious, cordial, relaxed

8 **familiar,** natural, simple, plain, unpretentious, homely, folksy, common, unaffected

9 **free,** indulgent, tolerant, unconstrained, independent, freethinking; lax, permissive, easygoing, free and easy, loose, irregular, bohemian

VERBS

10 **be informal,** not stand on ceremony, be oneself, be natural, relax, feel at home, make oneself at home, not insist, waive the rules, come as you are, let one's hair down [Inf]

ADVERBS

11 **informally,** unceremoniously, without ceremony; casually, offhand, offhandedly, relaxedly, familiarly; naturally, simply, plainly; unaffectedly, unassumingly, unconstrainedly, unofficially, *en famille* [Fr]

12 **freely,** indulgently, tolerantly, unconstrainedly, permissively, loosely, irregularly

408 Sociability

NOUNS

1 **sociability,** sociableness, socialness, sociality, affability, amicability, amiability, friendliness, neighborliness, kindness, gregariousness, warmth; fondness for company, geniality, congeniality, cordiality, conviviality; enjoyment, joviality, jollity, revelry, festivity, merriment, merrymaking, gaiety, cheer, good cheer, hospitality, companionability, compatibility; clubbishness, fraternization; participation, membership, cooperation, sharing, partaking, hobnobbing; conversation, communicativeness, communication, intercommunication, communion, intercommunion; social skill, social ability, social relations, social intercourse, social activity; group activity, association, consociation, affiliation, familiarity, intimacy, consorting
  ▶ *Assembly 59; Communications 169; Conversation 210; Joy, Cheerfulness 269; Celebration 405; Informality 407; Courtesy 410; Generosity 498; Cooperation 827*

2 **social ambition,** ambition, social climbing, status-seeking, upward mobility, keeping up with the Joneses

3 **social success,** popularity, social graces, good manners, savoir-vivre, refinement, breeding, courtesy, easy manner, savoir-faire, ability to mix, affability, conversableness, social demand
  ▶ *Conduct 399; Courtesy 410; Success 845*

4 **social gathering,** meeting, appointment, engagement, rendezvous, assignation, date, double date; social, social affair, gathering, at-home, meeting one's friends, tête-à-tête, soirée, party; coffee, tea, afternoon tea, high tea; reception, wedding reception, entertainment; seeing one's family, family reunion, class reunion; visiting, visit, formal visit, official visit, visitation, interview, call, social call, courtesy call, stay; social round,

round of visits, social whirl, tryst, get-together, drop-in [Inf]
  ▶ *Celebration 405*

5 **meeting place,** stadium, public hall, restaurant, salon, drawing room, love nest

6 **party,** entertainment, festivity, feast; banquet, dinner, dinner party, supper party, tea party, house party, weekend party; open house, at-home, housewarming, surprise party, garden party, lawn party, *fête champêtre* [Fr]; costume party, fancy-dress party, masked ball, masquerade, masque *or* mask; cocktail party, sherry party, beer party, smoker, mixed party; birthday party, coming-out party, coming-out, debut, presentation; stag party, wedding reception; dance, ball, barn dance, square dance, hoedown; potluck *or* potluck dinner, barbecue, cookout, picnic, wiener roast, gala, ice-cream social; [Inf]: shindig, shindy, weenie roast, hen party, hop, blowout, bash, thrash [Brit], beanfeast [Brit]
  ▶ *Eating 92; Dance and Ballet 135; Celebration 405*

7 **social person,** convivial person, social butterfly, good host *or* hostess, socialite, debutante, good neighbor, good fellow, charming fellow, conversationalist, friend, visitor, guest, welcome guest, one of the family, good company, good companion, bon vivant, playboy, man about town, social lion, habitué, clubman *or* clubwoman, active member, backslapper; host, hostess, mine host [Arch]; chum, mate, mixer, good mixer, joiner, life and soul of the party, pal [Inf]
  ▶ *Friendship 62*

8 **society,** social group, social circle, social set; high society, beau monde; peer group, the crowd, family, family circle, home circle, friends and relations, friends and acquaintances
  ▶ *Sociology 2; Friendship 62; Family 65; Conformity 781*

9 **good company,** company, comradeship, friendship, fellowship, good fellowship, fraternity, camaraderie, togetherness, bonhomie, cordiality, hospitality
  ▶ *Friendship 62*

10 **welcome,** welcoming, hearty welcome, cordial welcome, warm welcome, warmth, warm reception, smiling reception, greeting, handshake, handclasp, embrace, welcoming embrace, kiss, hug, peck on the cheek, backslapping
  ▶ *Arrival 704*

ADJECTIVES

11 **sociable,** social, communal, collective, common, public, civic; companionable, amicable, amiable, affable, clubby, communicative, friendly, fond of company, courteous, civil, urbane, easy, easygoing, free and easy; party-minded, cordial, genial, witty, amusing, charming, charismatic, extroverted, gregarious, outgoing, hearty, lively, hail-fellow well met, convivial, jolly, jovial, merry, cheerful, smiling, welcoming, warm, af-

fectionate, hospitable, neighborly, inviting, pally [Inf], matey [Brit inf]

12 **popular,** liked, sought-after, welcome, welcomed with open arms, socially accepted, accepted as one of the family, made to feel at home, socially successful, entertained, feted, dined, wined and dined

13 **festive,** carnival-like, entertaining, fun, joyous

VERBS

14 **be sociable,** be social, enjoy company, love company, entertain, invite, be hospitable, give *or* throw a party; host, act as host *or* hostess, receive; hold an open house, welcome, bid welcome, make welcome, welcome with open arms, put out the welcome mat, hug, embrace, do the honors, preside

15 **participate,** mix with, mingle with, get together, join in, be a good mixer, know how to mix; get about *or* around, go out, dine out; go to parties, fish for invitations, accept invitations, share, eat off the same platter, crack a bottle with, toast, drink to, pledge; love a party, go partying, go nightclubbing, go out on the town, pub-crawl; go on a spree, kill the fatted calf, associate with, consort with, rub shoulders *or* elbows with, go Dutch, treat; take potluck, keep up with the Joneses, paint the town red [Inf], freeload [Inf]

16 **visit,** call, call on, pay a visit, look up, see, stop off, stop over, make oneself welcome, make oneself at home, make oneself one of the family, unbend, relax, leave one's card; sojourn, stay, weekend, keep up *or* in touch with, be on visiting terms, drop in, drop by

17 **fraternize,** have friends, make friends, have fun with, introduce oneself, get along with, get on well with, keep company with, walk hand in hand with, club together, date, make a date, seek *or* make acquaintance with; [Inf]: pal around with, hang around *or* out with, hook up with
  ◗ *Friendship 62*

18 **welcome,** greet, shake hands with, embrace, kiss, hug, backslap, glad-hand [Inf]

ADVERBS

19 **sociably,** socially, affably, amicably, amiably, convivially, family-oriented, *en famille* [Fr]; genially, in friendship, in a friendly fashion, like friends, companionably, arm in arm, hand in hand; affectionately, with love; communicatively, courteously, civilly, easily, cordially, hospitably; wittily, amusingly, charmingly, with great charm, gregariously, heartily; with open arms, warmly, merrily, cheerfully, with good cheer, joyously, festively, entertainingly

409 Unsociability

NOUNS

1 **unsociability,** unsociableness, dissociability, unsocial habits, antisocial habits; ungregariousness, uncongeniality, incompatibility; unfriendliness, sullenness,

mopishness, moroseness; taciturnity, reticence, uncommunicativeness; standoffishness, haughtiness, lonely pride, reserve, aloofness, remoteness, detachment, indifference, apartness, distance, maintaining one's distance; reclusiveness, coolness, coldness, frigidity, chill, chilliness, iciness, frostiness, inhospitality, unreceptiveness; ungraciousness, discourtesy, avoidance, withdrawal, refusal to mix, cutting; keeping one's own company, keeping to oneself, seclusiveness, self-containment, retirement, singleness, celibacy, unapproachability, inaccessibility, exclusivity, privacy, private world
  ◗ *Taciturnity 208; Pride 297; Sullenness 304; Avoidance 386; Discourtesy 411; Exclusion 764*

2 **shyness,** bashfulness, timidity, diffidence, modesty, introversion, agoraphobia
  ◗ *Fear 283; Modesty 403*

3 **separation,** seclusion, isolation, splendid isolation, solitariness, solitude, loneliness; exclusion, retreat, rejection, exile; banishment, deportation, expulsion, segregation, apartheid; blacklist, blackball, ostracism, boycott, quarantine, concealment, purdah, balkanization
  ◗ *Concealment 181; Rejection 383; Expulsion 709; Separation 753*

4 **solitary place,** retreat, sanctuary, sanctum, den, study, cloister, cell, cave; sequestered nook, ivory tower, private quarters, secret garden; backwater, desert island, hiding place, hideout, godforsaken hole
  ◗ *Refuge 812*

5 **unsocial person,** solitary person, stay-at-home, recluse, hermit, anchorite, ascetic, cave dweller, cenobite; marabout, sannyasi, eremite, monk, outsider; oddity, eccentric, misfit, marooned person, castaway; loner, homebody, troglodyte, iceberg [Inf], lone wolf [Inf]
  ◗ *Extraneousness 724; Nonadhesion 756*

ADJECTIVES

6 **unsociable,** unsocial, dissociable, dissocial, antisocial; ungregarious, uncompanionable, uncongenial; uncommunicative, reclusive, reticent; silent, sullen, mopy, morose, private, close; autistic, unforthcoming, unapproachable, withdrawn, in one's shell; domestic, seclusive, retiring, shy; standoffish, aloof, haughty, remote, removed, distant, apart; detached, indifferent, Olympian, inaccessible, exclusive, self-sufficient, self-contained; forbidding, discourteous; unfriendly, cool, cold, chilly, icy, frigid, frosty, unneighborly, unwelcoming
  ◗ *Sullenness 304; Avoidance 386; Discourtesy 411*

7 **shy,** bashful, timid, taciturn, silent, introverted, afraid, afraid of company
  ◗ *Fear 283; Modesty 403*

8 **lonely,** lonesome, alone, on one's own, solitary, isolated, secluded, stay-at-home; unpopular, friendless, boycotted, shunned, banned; desolate, lorn, forlorn,

godforsaken, uninvited, deserted; avoided, rejected, ostracized, exiled, banished, deported, expelled, displaced, disbarred, cold-shouldered

9 **secluded,** private, isolated, quiet, off the beaten track, out-of-the-way, remote, deserted, desolate, hidden, screened, cloistered, sequestered, unvisited

VERBS

10 **be unsocial,** keep to oneself, keep one's distance, shun company, stand aloof; seclude oneself, go into seclusion, retire, go into retirement, retire from the world, give up one's friends, give up one's social life; stay at home, shut oneself up, withdraw, see no one, bury oneself; creep into a corner, stay in one's shell, abandon the world, take the veil, lead a cloistered life

11 **ignore,** not acknowledge, avoid, have nothing to do with, shun, snub; cold-shoulder, cut

12 **exclude,** ban, shut *or* close the door on, segregate, blacklist, blackball; treat as a leper, treat as an outsider, keep at arm's length; repel, act rude, rebuff, frown on, turn one's back on; isolate, ostracize, freeze out, cut off, shut out; reject, boycott, prohibit, outlaw, turn out, displace; exile, banish, deport, expel, cast out, disbar; conceal, keep private, keep in purdah, confine, shut up, quarantine, seclude, sequester, imprison, jail

ADVERBS

13 **unsocially,** antisocially, inhospitably, incompatibly; taciturnly, reticently, quietly, silently, without a word; sullenly, morosely; privately, in private, at home, domestically; aloofly, haughtily, disdainfully, remotely, distantly, indifferently; inaccessibly, behind closed doors, exclusively, self-sufficiently, without assistance; forbiddingly, discourteously, impolitely, uncivilly, ungraciously, rudely, disrespectfully; coolly, coldly, icily, frigidly; shyly, in a shy manner, bashfully, timidly

410 Courtesy

Call him bounteous Buckingham, / The mirror of all courtesy. — WILLIAM SHAKESPEARE

NOUNS

1 **courtesy,** courteousness, common courtesy, politeness, civility, comity; kindness, kindliness, amiability, sweetness, niceness, amenity; agreeableness, affability, graciousness, humility; consideration, thoughtfulness, solicitousness, solicitude, decency; tact, tactfulness, discretion; charity, generosity, benevolence, help; friendliness, sociability, gallantry, chivalry, chivalrousness, courtliness, noblesse oblige; gracefulness, suavity, suaveness, blandness, smoothness, flattery; easy temper, even temper, good humor, gentleness, mildness, mild manner, mansuetude, obligingness, common touch

▶ *Friendship 62; Persuasion 178; Humility 298; Benevolence 305; Sociability 408; Flattery 439; Help 825*

2 **good manners,** etiquette, mannerliness, good behavior; breeding, good breeding, good deportment; refinement, polish, culture, gentility, genteelness; sophistication, elegance, urbanity, savoir-vivre, savoir-faire; gentlemanliness, ladylikeness; formality, correctness, convention, protocol, custom, diplomacy

▶ *Sociability 408; Refinement 534; Fashion 536*

3 **courtesies,** social courtesies, civilities, urbanities, amenities, graces, gentilities, pleasantries, compliments, compliments of the season, regards, best regards, best wishes, best respects; love, kind remembrances, elegancies, dignities; respect, respectfulness, formalities

▶ *Attention 323; Celebration 405; Formality 406; Respect 435; Departure 705*

4 **deference,** obeisance, compliance; complaisance, condescension, glibness, sycophancy, ingratiation; doffing one's cap, touching one's cap, kissing someone's hand, bowing, nodding, kowtowing, salaaming, laying it on

▶ *Servility 401; Obedience 426; Lowering 716*

5 **sign of courtesy,** act of kindness, salutation, salute, greeting, handshake, handclasp, hug, kiss, embrace, smile, wave, graceful gesture, bow, curtsy

▶ *Sign 183*

ADJECTIVES

6 **courteous,** polite, civil, urbane, agreeable, affable, genial, amiable, gracious; humble, fair, considerate, thoughtful, solicitous; decent, tactful, discreet, generous, benevolent, charitable, accommodating, lenient; even-tempered, gentle, mild, mild-mannered, good-humored, obliging, amenable; sociable, friendly, kind, kindly, sweet, nice, welcoming, gallant, chivalrous, courtly, graceful, old-fashioned, old-world

7 **good-mannered,** well-behaved, well-bred, well-spoken, refined, cultured, cultivated, genteel; gentlemanly, ladylike, correct, urbane, polished, elegant, conventional, suave, bland, smooth, flattering, formal, de rigueur, ceremonious, diplomatic, respectful, sweet-talking [Inf]

8 **deferential,** obeisant, compliant, condescending, complaisant, glib, sycophantic, ingratiating, bowing, nodding, kowtowing

▶ *Servility 401*

VERBS

9 **be courteous,** be polite, be civil, be considerate, care, take care; be tactful, use tact; give one's best regards *or* best wishes

10 **have good manners,** mind one's manners, behave well, behave properly, be on one's best behavior, treat with politeness, observe etiquette, mind one's p's and q's, have good breeding, show refinement, act like a

lady *or* gentleman, observe protocol, follow custom, use diplomacy

▶ *Formality 406*

11 **greet,** welcome, welcome home, welcome with open arms, advance to meet, salute, hail, wave, smile, hug, squeeze, embrace, kiss, blow a kiss; say hello, bid good day, raise one's hat *or* cap, shake hands, clasp hands, squeeze one's hand, pump one's hand; honor, fire a salute, parade, present arms, turn out, give a hero's welcome, crown, wreathe, garland, fete, celebrate

▶ *Celebration 405; Arrival 704*

12 **defer to,** treat with deference, send one's respects, give *or* pay respects, pay homage, make obeisance, comply, condescend, ingratiate oneself, act sycophantic, bow, curtsy, doff one's hat, touch one's cap, kiss someone's hand, kneel, kowtow, salaam, prostrate oneself, toady to, fawn on, lay it on

▶ *Servility 401*

ADVERBS

13 **courteously,** with courtesy, politely, in a polite manner, civilly; agreeably, affably, amiably, graciously, humbly; considerately, thoughtfully, solicitously, decently, tactfully, discreetly; generously, benevolently, charitably, accommodatingly, leniently; gently, mildly, good-humoredly; obligingly, amenably, sociably, kindly, with kindness, sweetly, nicely, gallantly, chivalrously, courtly, knightly, like a knight in shining armor, gracefully, with good grace, old-worldly

14 **genteelly,** correctly, urbanely, elegantly, conventionally; suavely, blandly, smoothly, politely, respectfully, with respect; considerately, thoughtfully, as a thoughtful gesture, generously, benevolently, solicitously, decently, tactfully, discreetly, charitably, accommodatingly, formally, with dignity, ceremoniously, diplomatically

15 **deferentially,** with deference, obeisantly, compliantly, complaisantly, glibly, sycophantically, ingratiatingly

411 Discourtesy

NOUNS

1 **discourtesy,** rudeness, discourteousness, impoliteness, incivility, inurbanity; disagreeableness, ungraciousness, ungallantness, uncourtliness, ungentlemanliness; thoughtlessness, shortness, inconsideration, lack of consideration, unsolicitousness; tactlessness, insensitivity, inattention; sullenness, excessive frankness, bluntness, acerbity, sharpness, tartness, asperity, gruffness, bluffness, roughness, harshness, severity, brusqueness, ungentleness; unfriendliness, unpleasantness, surliness, crustiness, nastiness; ridicule, derision, mockery, raillery, scoffing, jeering

▶ *Conciseness 198; Resentment, Anger 302; Sullenness 304; Inattention 324; Derision 369; Severity 424; Disrespect 436*

2 **bad manners,** no manners, lack of manners, unmannerliness, want of chivalry, lack of politeness; scant courtesy, rudeness, insolence, impudence, truculence, churlishness, impatience, interruption, vulgarity, offensiveness, coarseness, boorishness, caddishness, grossness, gross behavior, crudeness, loutishness, misconduct, bad behavior, conduct unbecoming, cheek; [Inf]: sauce, lip, sass

▶ *Dissatisfaction 274; Irascibility 303; Insolence 400; Vulgarity 535*

3 **act of discourtesy,** short answer, angry reply, rebuff, insult, jeer, snub, abuse, rude *or* lewd gesture, black look, sour look, scowl, frown, bad language, rude *or* bad words, dirty joke, cold shoulder

4 **discourteous person,** rude person, insolent person, faultfinder, boor, lout, brute, Yahoo, savage, barbarian, no shining knight, no gentleman, no lady, curmudgeon, bear, sulker, grouch, loudmouth; [Inf]: grouser, crosspatch, bellyacher

ADJECTIVES

5 **discourteous,** impolite, uncivil, disagreeable, inurbane; ungracious, ungallant, uncourtly, ungentlemanly, ungentlemanlike, unladylike; unpleasant, surly, sullen, crusty, nasty, unkind, thoughtless, inconsiderate, unsolicitous, tactless; insensitive, inattentive, cavalier, abusive, vituperative, not anxious to please, unsmiling, grim, unneighborly, unsociable, unfriendly; uncomplimentary, unflattering, disrespectful, familiar, gruff, blunt, overfrank; harsh, severe, ungentle, rough, rugged, brutal, brusque, curt, short, abrupt; impatient, discontented, peevish, testy, acerbic, sharp, sharp-tongued, tart, snappy, biting, growling, acrimonious, aggressive, bearish [Inf]

6 **bad-mannered,** rude, ill-mannered, unmannerly, unchivalrous; badly behaved, insolent, impudent, impertinent, saucy, churlish, truculent; abusive, cursing, obstreperous, forward, irascible, difficult; vulgar, offensive, injurious, coarse, foul-mouthed, boorish, caddish, gross, crude, loutish; ill-bred, unrefined, uncouth, uncultured, barbarian, savage, growling, grumbling, swearing, cheeky, sassy [Inf], lippy [Inf]

VERBS

7 **be discourteous,** not respect, ruffle feelings, show no regard for someone's feelings, abuse, affront, outrage; take liberties, make free with, make bold; treat rudely, have no manners, display bad manners, flout etiquette, cause offense, insult; stare, ogle, gaze, ignore, interrupt, cut, snub; look right through, have no time for, turn one's back on, make unwelcome, show the door, behave badly, cut dead, cold-shoulder, give someone lip [Inf], sass [Inf]

8 discourteously, rudely, impolitely, uncivilly, uncourtly, ungallantly; ungraciously, ungentlemanly, charmlessly, without charm, disagreeably, unchivalrously, unpleasantly, sullenly, sulkily; nastily, unkindly, thoughtlessly, offhandedly, inconsiderately; tactlessly, insensitively, inattentively; abusively, vituperatively, grimly, unsociably; impatiently, discontentedly, peevishly; gruffly, bluntly, harshly, severely, ungently, roughly, brutally, brusquely, curtly, abruptly, tartly, sharply, crossly, acrimoniously, aggressively

9 rudely, disrespectfully, without respect, insolently, impudently, impertinently, saucily, churlishly, abusively, with a volley of abuse, obstreperously, irascibly, vulgarly, offensively, coarsely, boorishly, caddishly; loutishly, grossly, crudely, uncouthly, savagely, derisively, mockingly, scoffingly, jeeringly, cheekily

412 Action

Easier said than done. — PROVERB

Suit the action to the word, the word to the action; with this special observance, that you o'erstep not the modesty of nature. — WILLIAM SHAKESPEARE

NOUNS

1 action, doing, happening, performance, execution, steps, measures; move, enactment, policy, transaction, commission, perpetration, dispatch; accomplishment, achievement, effectuation, completion; proceeding, process, procedure, routine, custom, praxis, practice, behavior, conduct; movement, play, swing, motion; operation, functioning, working; interaction, evolution, agency; force, pressure, sway, control, influence, effect; power, work, labor; exertion, effort, attempt, endeavor; campaign, program, activism, crusade; battle, war, militancy; activeness, activity, occupation, business, manufacture, production, employment; use, implementation, putting into effect; administration, handling, management, direction; legal action, legal proceeding, lawsuit
  ▶ *War 76; Work 122; Management 126; Plan 387; Attempt 390; Use 393; Habit, Custom 397; Activity 414; Influence 512; Power 514; Production 522; Motion 677; Completeness 761*

2 deed, act, overt act, action, exploit, feat; achievement, accomplishment; gesture, *beau geste* [Fr]; wrongdoing, criminal act, crime, foul play; stunt; tour de force, special effort, stroke of genius; pretense, dissimulation, posture, affectation, gesticulation; measure, step, move, policy, maneuver, evolution, tactics; sudden action, stroke, blow, coup, *coup de main* [Fr], *coup de grâce* [Fr], coup d'état, overthrow; job, task, work, operation, exercise; undertaking, proceeding, transaction, deal, doings, actions, dealings, affairs
  ▶ *Skillfulness 127; Deception 193; Description 202; Courage 284; Plan 387; Undertaking 391*

3 doer, man *or* woman of action, self-starter, busy person; practical person, practitioner, executant, perpetrator, committer, realist, street fighter; finisher, achiever, high achiever; highflier; hero, heroine, good role model; benefactor; [Inf]: go-getter, live wire, whiz kid, mover and shaker

4 activist, political activist, lobbyist; active supporter, campaigner, canvasser; crusader, militant
  ▶ *Skillfulness 127; Courage 284; Activity 414*

5 performer, player, actor, actress, stunt man *or* woman; creative person, creative worker, artistic person, artist
  ▶ *Drama and Theater 136; Painting and Drawing 143*

6 evildoer, offender, criminal, gangster, malefactor
  ▶ *Malevolence 306*

7 operator, agent, contractor; undertaker, entrepreneur, executor; executive, chief executive, administrator, manager, general manager, managing director, director, controller; manipulator, motivator
  ▶ *Management 126*

8 worker, hand, manual worker, workman, operative; craftsman *or* craftswoman, handicraftsman *or* handicraftswoman, handicraft worker, artisan
  ▶ *Worker 123*

ADJECTIVES

9 acting, doing, happening, performing, enacting; working, at work, occupational; in action, red-handed; in operation, in harness, operative, up and doing; industrious, busy, active, interactive; creative, artistic, dramatic; militant, crusading; brave, heroic
  ▶ *Work 122; Activity 414*

10 effective, forceful, powerful; productive, useful; direct, influential; functional, operational, procedural; professional, managerial, executive, administrative; tactical
  ▶ *Work 122; Power 514; Effect 676*

VERBS

11 act, do, happen; perform, carry out, execute; take action, take steps, take measures; enact, legislate, commission, dispatch; accomplish, achieve, complete, carry through; get in on the act, be in on the action; take effect, come into operation; operate, function
  ▶ *Completeness 761*

12 motivate, militate for, militate against, act upon, sway, influence; use tactics, manipulate, move; work for, strike a blow for; help, aid, canvass, campaign; twist, turn, maneuver
  ▶ *Persuasion 178; Influence 512*

13 do something, proceed, proceed with, get on with, push on with, get going, get cracking [Inf]; make an *or* the effort, lift a finger, raise a finger, try, attempt; tackle, take on, shoulder, undertake; do the deed, perpetrate, commit; do what is required *or* needed, do the needful, take care of; implement, fulfill, put into practice, put into use; solemnize, observe

14 **do great deeds,** make history, win renown, become celebrated, become famous, acquire a reputation; stunt, perform a stunt, show off; pretend, feign, dissemble

▶ *Attempt 390; Undertaking 391; Activity 414; Operation 509*

15 **occupy oneself,** busy oneself, do business, practice, exercise, carry on, discharge, prosecute, pursue; ply, ply one's trade, work, labor, sweat, employ oneself; transact, deal, conduct oneself, indulge in, behave; play about, frolic about, lark around, skylark, fool around

16 **direct,** be in charge, administer, administrate, manage, officiate, control; use, exploit, take advantage of, make the most of

17 **be active in,** have a hand in, take part in; have to do with, deal with; play a role *or* part in, have a finger in, participate; interfere, intervene, come between; deal in, get mixed up in, meddle

▶ *Cunning 822*

ADVERBS

18 **actively,** overtly, in the act, red-handed, flagrante delicto; in the midst of, in the thick of; by enactment, by custom, with a stroke

19 **effectively,** forcefully, powerfully; productively, usefully; directly, influentially; functionally

413 Inaction

NOUNS

1 **inaction,** lack of action, nonaction, nothing happening; inertia, inertness; inability to act, impotence; refusal to act, failure to act, neglect, negligence, abstinence from action, laissez *or* laisser faire, abstention, refraining; avoidance, passive resistance, suspension, abeyance, dormancy, inactivity, nonuse; deadlock, stalemate, logjam; stop, standstill, lack of progress, bogging down

▶ *Negligence 326; Avoidance 386; Inactivity 415; Inertness 519; Lack of Motion 678*

2 **immobility,** motionlessness, paralysis, impassivity, insensibility; passivity, apathy, stagnation, vegetation, doldrums

3 **stillness,** quiet, quietness, calm, calmness, tranquillity, quiescence

4 **leisure,** time to kill, idle hours, *dolce far niente* [Ital], rest, repose, relaxing, relaxation; lack of ambition, laziness, loafing, idleness, indolence; watching *or* letting the world go by, twiddling one's thumbs; all the time in the world, time on one's hands

▶ *Insensibility 213; Indifference 289; Ease 819*

5 **unemployment,** nonemployment, underemployment, joblessness, no work; easy work, sinecure

6 **do-nothingism,** delay, putting off till tomorrow, procrastination; noninterference, nonintervention, hands off

7 **defeatism,** pessimism, nihilism, hopelessness; no courage, cowardice; indifference; head in the sand

▶ *Cowardice 285; Nonuse 394; Powerlessness 515; Lateness 658; Cessation 668*

8 **inactive person,** idler, idle rich, leisured classes; loafer, layabout, shirker; sleeper, dreamer, daydreamer; waverer, ditherer, hesitator; nihilist, solipsist, pessimist, fatalist, defeatist; noninterventionist, abstainer; killjoy, wallflower, party pooper [Inf]; coward, chicken [Inf]

ADJECTIVES

9 **inactive,** nonactive, inert; unable to act, impotent, powerless; negligent, neglectful; abstaining, abstentious; suspended, in abeyance, dormant, inoperative; deadlocked, stalemated, at a standstill, stationary, immobile, motionless; still, calm, becalmed, tranquil, quiet, quiescent, stagnant, not stirring; hardly breathing, half-dead, half-gone, without a sign of life; gone, dead, extinct; benumbed, cold, frozen, paralyzed; impassive, insensible, passive, apathetic, phlegmatic, dull, sluggish; leisured, leisurely, relaxed; lazy, indolent, idle, fallow, unoccupied, doing nothing; do-nothing, wait-and-see, unprogressive, ostrichlike; refraining, delaying, procrastinating, cunctative; defeatist, cowardly, hopeless; indifferent, neutral, hands-off, tolerant; unseeing, unhearing, blind, deaf

▶ *Death 29; Leisure 125; Insensibility 213; Indifference 289; Negligence 326; Inactivity 415; Powerlessness 515; Inertness 519; Lateness 658; Lack of Motion 678; Ease 819*

10 **unemployed,** without employment, underemployed; laid off, jobless, without a job, out of work, collecting unemployment, on the dole

VERBS

11 **not act,** do nothing, fail to act, refuse to act, be inactive, be inert, suffer from inertia, stay still; refrain, avoid, abstain; stop, pause, desist, quit, cease; have no life, be lifeless, lie dead, die; pass up, stand by, look on, watch; show no sign of life, not raise *or* lift a finger, stagnate, vegetate; rest on one's laurels, rest on one's oars, relax one's efforts; drift, glide, slide, coast, freewheel, tread water [Inf]

▶ *Death 29; Inertness 519; Lateness 658*

12 **procrastinate,** watch and wait, wait and see, bide one's time, wait, sit tight; delay, hang fire, put off (till tomorrow), defer

▶ *Inactivity 415*

13 **leave alone,** live and let live, let things take their course, let things take care of themselves, let alone, let sleeping dogs lie, let well enough alone; hold no brief for, wash one's hands of, pass the buck; keep out of, stay neutral, sit on the fence; tolerate

14 **ignore,** pretend not to see, neglect, disregard; let pass,

not react; keep quiet, keep mum, button one's lip [Inf]; not move, not budge, not stir, not bat an eye

> *Indifference 289*

15 **have free time,** have nothing to do, kill time, twiddle one's thumbs, loaf, idle, watch the world go by, let the world go by, look out the window, sit on one's hands, rust, gather dust; sit back, relax, unwind, rest, repose; have no function, be superfluous, be useless; lie idle, lie fallow; stay on the shelf, stay packed away; be unemployed

> *Leisure 125; Cessation 668; Uselessness 802; Ease 819*

ADVERBS

16 **inactively,** without action, without movement, inertly; with one's hands in one's pockets, with folded arms; powerlessly; negligently; impassively, apathetically, indifferently; lazily, idly; calmly, quietly, tranquilly, at rest

414 Activity

NOUNS

1 **activity,** action, activeness, movement, motion, life, stirring, stir; agitation, excitation, stimulation; ado, much ado, great doings, drama; commotion, racket, disturbance, row, quarrel, squabble, brawl, fray, tumult, turmoil, frenzy, whirl; maelstrom, vortex, midst of things, thick of things, thick of the action; [Inf]: to-do, kick, buzz

> *Argument 329; Action 412; Motion 677; Rotation 682; Agitation 684; Disorder 766*

2 **social activity,** group activity, interaction, person-to-person interaction; participation, active participation; volunteering; sociability, mingling, mixing; interest, special interest, active interest; hobby, pastime, pursuit, occupation, enterprise, undertaking, venture

> *Work 122; Leisure 125; Undertaking 391; Sociability 408; Action 412; Possession 469*

3 **alacrity,** nimbleness, briskness, promptitude, willingness, readiness, punctuality; quickness, speed, velocity, haste, dispatch, expedition; scramble, mad scramble, race, mad race, dash, mad dash, wild dash, burst, spurt; fit, spasm, overhastiness, frantic haste; hurry, flurry, hurry-scurry, hustle, bustle, hustle and bustle; fuss, bother, fuss and bother, nuisance, botheration, hassle [Inf], rat race [Inf]

> *Willingness 373; Earliness 657; Haste 818*

4 **energy,** ceaseless energy, dynamic energy, dynamism, vigor, vigorousness, abandon, frenzy; vitality, vivacity, vivaciousness, life; liveliness, animation, spirit, high spirits; eagerness, enthusiasm; ardor, fervor, vehemence, strong feeling, warm feeling; activation, motive, reason, cause; aggressiveness, enterprise, initiative, drive, push, ambition, go, get-up-and-go, moxie [Inf], pep [Inf]

5 **activism,** political activism; militancy, militant scene;

mass movement, popular movement, political movement; uprising, sedition

> *Feelings 266; Vigor 518*

6 **business,** industry; call on one's time, imposition on one's time; press of business, pressure of work, several *or* many irons in the fire, pressure of deadlines; no sinecure, plenty to do, busyness, no break, no rest for the wicked; hive of activity, hive of industry, hive, beehive; main street, marketplace, workshop; hum of activity, hum; press, crush, jostling crowd, seething mob, hoi polloi, madding crowd

> *Work 122; Workplace 124*

7 **restlessness,** aimlessness, aimless activity, randomness, desultoriness; lack of concentration, inattention; dawdling, puttering, pottering [Brit], fiddling; fidgetiness, the fidgets, wanderlust, itchy foot, unrest, unease, unquietness, unquiet; jumpiness, nervousness, nerves, agitation, excitability, fever, fret; sleeplessness, insomnia, wakefulness, watchfulness

> *Inattention 324; Carefulness 325*

8 **assiduity,** application, concentration, intentness, attention, diligence, sedulity; industriousness, industry, hard work, labor, laboriousness; monotonous work, drudgery; determination, resolution, earnestness; tirelessness, indefatigability, perseverance, stamina, stickability; studiousness, painstaking, perfectionism, attention to detail; devotedness, wholeheartedness, gung-ho attitude [Inf], stick-to-it-iveness [Inf]

> *Work 122; Attention 323; Resolution 376; Perseverance 377*

9 **overactivity,** hyperactivity; overextension, overexpansion, overdiversification, overambition; oversupply, excess, redundancy; Parkinson's law, displacement activity; useless work, futile activity, wild goose chase, chasing one's own tail, lost labor, wasted effort, useless exercise; hyperthyroidism, overexertion; petty officialdom, petty bureaucracy, red tape, officiousness, beadledom; meddlesomeness, interference, intrusiveness, interruption, meddling, interfering, sticking one's nose in, a finger in every pie, tampering; intrigue, conspiracy, secret plot, plot

> *Excess 99; Plan 387; Agitation 684; Uselessness 802*

10 **busy person,** active person, fully occupied person; socially active person, socialite, jet-setter; energetic person, bustler, hustler; someone in a hurry; fidget, hyperactive child; person of active habits, man *or* woman of action, activist, militant, zealot, fanatic, enthusiast, devotee; doer, participator, volunteer; sharp guy, sharpie, dynamo, human dynamo, pusher, thruster, yuppie; [Inf]: no slouch, wheeler-dealer, live wire

11 **hard worker,** toiler, slogger, careerist; eager beaver, tireless worker, fanatical worker, high-pressure worker, Stakhanovite, demon for work, glutton for work *or* punishment, workaholic; worker, factotum, handyman, jack-of-all-trades, drudge, fag, slave, galley slave,

workhorse, Trojan, powerhouse, buff; [Inf]: whiz kid, whiz, go-getter, gofer, beaver, busy bee

◗ *Worker 123; Obstinacy 379; Action 412*

12 meddler, meddling person, prying person, busybody, interferer, intermeddler, dabbler, stirrer, troublemaker, spoilsport, officious person, inquisitive person, tamperer, intriguer, planner, adviser, nuisance, fussbudget, fusspot, backseat driver, Nosy Parker [Inf], kibitzer [Inf]

◗ *Advice 176; Curiosity 321; Plan 387*

ADJECTIVES

13 active, interactive, sociable, activated, moving, going, running, working, operative, in action; incessant, unceasing; expeditious, quick, fast, speedy, brisk, spry, nimble, agile, light-footed, lightsome, tripping; smart, keen; able, able-bodied, strong, vigorous, strenuous, energetic, forceful; dynamic, thrustful, thrusting, stirring, pushing, up-and-coming, enterprising; lively, sprightly, frisky, coltish, dashing, spirited, mettlesome; live, alive, alive and kicking, full of vitality, animated, vivacious; eager, ardent, fervent, perfervid; fierce, desperate; resolute, determined, enthusiastic, fanatical, zealous; prompt, instant; ready, willing; alert, on one's toes, awake, wakeful, watchful, careful, on the alert, on the qui vive, vigilant; involved, actively involved, deeply involved, engagé, aggressive, militant; go-getting [Inf], full of beans [Inf]

◗ *Carefulness 325; Willingness 373; Resolution 376; Undertaking 391; Action 412; Strength 516; Vigor 518; Continuity, Continuation 669; Motion 677; Haste 818*

14 fidgety, sleepless, restless, feverish, fretful, tossing; dancing, nervous, nervy, jumpy, agitated, tense, fussy, like a cat on a hot tin roof; frenzied, frenetic, frantic, manic, demonic; hyperactive, overactive, overwrought, excitable, hyper [Inf]

◗ *Feelings 266; Agitation 684*

15 busy, active, bustling, hustling, hectic, humming, lively, eventful, in full swing; coming and going, rushing to and fro; puttering, doing chores; up and doing, stirring, astir, afoot, on the move, on the go; employed, in harness, at work, at one's desk, engaged, occupied, fully occupied, fully engaged; hard at work, hard at it, slogging; overworked, overemployed, rushed off one's feet, working oneself into the grave; fussing like a hen with chickens, busy as a bee, busy as a beaver, on the trot; on the make [Inf], up to one's neck *or* eyes *or* ears *or* elbows [Inf]

16 industrious, sedulous, diligent, assiduous, studious, persevering, hardworking, workaholic; plodding, slogging, laboring, laborious; unflagging, unwearied, tireless, indefatigable, full of stamina, energetic; unsleeping, keeping long hours, burning the midnight oil, burning the candle at both ends; efficient, workmanlike, businesslike, professional; stick-to-it-ive [Inf]

◗ *Work 122; Perseverance 377*

17 meddling, overbusy, officious, interfering, meddlesome, intrusive, nosy, prying; irritating, annoying, troublesome, tyrannical; intriguing, dabbling, fiddling; participating, taking part, in the business; pushy [Inf]

◗ *Curiosity 321; Entry 706*

VERBS

18 be active, act, do; wake up, rouse oneself, bestir oneself, rub the sleep from one's eyes, rise and shine, rise, get up, be up and doing, move, stir; agitate, squabble, start a row, roar, rage, bluster; run riot, rampage, have one's fling, blow, explode, burst; spurt, flow, surge; rush, dash, race, fly, run, move fast, hasten, hurry, scurry, scramble, have no time to lose, make the dust fly, go at it nineteen to the dozen; come and go, rush to and fro, hustle, bustle; fuss, bother, fret, fume, drum one's fingers, stamp with impatience; have other things to do, have other fish to fry; [Inf]: stir one's stumps, get the lead out, get one's ass in gear, kick up a shindy

◗ *Action 412; Violence 520; Motion 677; Agitation 684; Disorder 766; Haste 818*

19 be busy, busy oneself, keep busy, hum; prosper, thrive, make progress, progress; keep moving, keep on the go, keep on, have several irons in the fire, have one's hands full, spread oneself thin; not have a moment to spare *or* to call one's own, live in a whirl, not know which way to turn, run around in circles, chase one's tail, not know which way is up, waste effort; rise early, go to bed late, burn the midnight oil; burn the candle at both ends, make hay while the sun shines, not let grass grow under one's feet, keep the pot boiling; have one's plate full [Inf], join the rat race [Inf]

◗ *Forward Motion 679; Uselessness 802; Success 845*

20 push, shove, thrust, drive, impel; elbow one's way, thrust oneself forward, assert oneself; seize the opportunity, take one's chance, take the bull by the horns, profit by; protest, demonstrate, defy, react, react sharply, show fight, be up in arms, not take it lying down; be willing, show willingness, jump to it, show zeal, burn with zeal; not sleep, wake, watch; be on one's toes, be alert, respond, anticipate

◗ *Willingness 373; Defiance 416; Protest 507; Vigor 518; Impulsion 695*

21 try, attempt, try hard, take pains, make an effort, exert oneself, strain oneself, do one's best, rise to the occasion; dispatch, make short work of, work wonders; concentrate, put one's mind to, buckle down, put one's shoulder to the wheel, put one's hand to the tiller, persist, persevere; work, slave, slog, overwork, overdo it, make work, never stop, plug away; go the whole hog, make things hum, make the sparks fly; do one's damnedest [Inf], polish off [Inf]

◗ *Work 122; Attention 323; Perseverance 377; Attempt 390*

22 be sociable, interact, mingle, circulate, mix, join in;

participate actively, participate, volunteer, have an active interest, show interest, interest oneself in, get a piece of the action [Inf]

> *Sociability 408; Possession 469*

23 meddle, intermeddle, interpose, intervene, interfere, be officious, have a finger in every pie, not mind one's own business; pry, pry into, spy; put one's oar in, put one's two cents in, butt in, interrupt, intrude; pester, bother, dun, importune; annoy, irritate, trouble, harass, persecute; boss, boss around, bully; tyrannize, oppress; tinker, tamper, fiddle, touch, impair; poke one's nose in [Inf], hassle [Inf]

> *Unpleasantness 272; Curiosity 321; Severity 424; Entry 706*

ADVERBS

24 actively, fast, nimbly; vigorously, forcefully; eagerly, enthusiastically, promptly; restlessly; busily, industriously; on the go, on one's toes, full tilt, on all cylinders, with haste; with might and main, for all one is worth, for dear life, as if one's life depended on it

415 Inactivity

We would all be idle if we could. — SAMUEL JOHNSON

NOUNS

1 inactivity, quiescence, stillness, quietness, quiet, silence; immobility, inaction, inertia, passivity, inertness; lull, suspension, cessation; extinction, lifelessness

> *Inaction 413; Inertness 519*

2 unemployment, shutdown, layoff; slump, recession, depression

3 idleness, laziness, indolence, sloth, slothfulness; absenteeism; slowness, slow progress, dawdling, delay, procrastination; sluggishness, lethargy, languor, dullness, listlessness, torpor, apathy, indifference, phlegm, impassivity

4 nonworker, idler, shirker, slacker, dawdler, sluggard, fainéant, clock watcher; passenger, dummy, sinecurist, silent partner, absentee landlord; *rentier* [Fr], idle rich, leisured classes, dreamer, lotus-eater; drifter, vagrant, tramp, hobo; beggar, drone, leech, parasite, cadger, sponger, scrounger; layabout, *flâneur* [Fr], loafer, lounger, bum; [Inf]: freeloader, free rider, couch potato

> *Leisure 125*

5 sleep, sleepiness, somnolence, doziness, drowsiness, heaviness, oscitancy; slumber, rest, repose, land of Nod, Morpheus, dreamland, sandman; heavy sleep, dormancy, hibernation, estivation; unconsciousness, coma, stupor, trance, catalepsy, hypnosis, oblivion, insensibility; light sleep, nap, catnap, snooze, doze, siesta; [Inf]: forty winks, shuteye, bye-byes

6 soporific, somnifacient, sleeping pill *or* draught, seda-

tive, barbiturate; narcotic, opiate, poppy, opium, morphine, nepenthe, nightcap [Inf]; anesthetic

7 sleeper, slumberer, dozer, drowser, lie-abed, sleepyhead; hibernator, Rip van Winkle, Sleeping Beauty

ADJECTIVES

8 inactive, quiescent, still, quiet; motionless, immobile, stationary, static; sedentary, stagnant, inert, passive; supine, bedridden, disabled, on one's back; extinct, lifeless, inanimate

> *Silence 231; Inaction 413; Inertness 519; Lack of Motion 678*

9 housebound, stay-at-home, untraveled, shut-in, home-loving, domesticated

10 not working *or* **operating,** unemployed, idle, unengaged, laid off, on strike, out, out of work, between jobs, jobless, off work, off-duty, resting, free, available, at a loose end; laid up, out of action, out of commission, off; at a standstill, broken down, unused, fallow, idle, disengaged; unoccupied, vacant, empty

11 not participating, lazy, idle, indolent, slothful, bone idle, loafing, lolling, parasitic, slack, lax; slow, dilatory, dawdling, tardy, procrastinating, laggard; sluggish, lethargic, languid, dull, listless, torpid; apathetic, indifferent, uninterested, phlegmatic, impassive

12 not awake, somnolent, drowsy, dozy, sleepy, soporific, heavy-eyed, slumberous, nodding off, yawning, dozing, resting, half-asleep; drugged, sedated, narcotized, anesthetized, hypnotized; dormant, torpid, hibernating, estivating; sleeping, asleep, dreaming, fast asleep, sound asleep, dead to the world; unconscious, insensible, comatose; [Inf]: out cold, dopey, doped, flaked out

VERBS

13 be inactive, stagnate, vegetate, do nothing; idle, laze, loaf, lounge; cadge, sponge, mooch; kill time, waste time, lie around, kick around [Inf], hang around *or* about [Inf]; delay, procrastinate, dawdle; drift

14 sleep, snooze, doze, drowse, yawn, nod off, nap, catnap, rest, slumber, retire, go to bed, sleep like a log *or* top; lie dormant, hibernate, estivate; take forty winks [Inf]

15 pause, rest, tarry, relax, rest on one's oars; tread water [Inf], coast; cease, stop, halt, stop short, stop in one's tracks; slow down, decelerate; pull up, check, brake, come to a standstill, come to a halt, come to journey's end; stand fast, stick fast; remain at anchor; subside, settle, settle down, die down, come to rest; stay at home, stay indoors, not go out; take a breather

16 make inactive, inactivate, deactivate, dismantle; defuse, neutralize, extinguish; shut down, suspend, lay up; lay off, dismiss, fire, sack, demobilize; immobilize, incapacitate, disable; deaden, drug, sedate, narcotize, knock out, anesthetize; hypnotize, dope [Inf]

17 inactively, motionlessly, statically; at a standstill, at rest; inertly, passively; lifelessly, inanimately

18 impassively, indifferently, apathetically, listlessly, dully, languidly, lethargically, sluggishly; slothfully, indolently, lazily

19 sleepily, somnolently, soporifically, dozily, dopily [Inf], drowsily; insensibly, unconsciously

416 Defiance

NOUNS

1 defiance, defying, audacity, nerve, impertinence, pertness, impudence, insolence, belligerence; courage, boldness, bold front, brave face, bravura, daringness, daring; presumption, temerity, self-assertion, assurance, self-assurance, arrogance; bluster, bravado, bumptiousness; shamelessness, contrariness, cockiness, brashness, brazenness, rashness, effrontery, barefaced effrontery, provocativeness, sauce, sauciness, cheekiness, cheek, nerviness; brass, brassiness; [Inf]: cussedness, chutzpa *or* hutzpa, lip, sass

  ▶ *Courage 284; Rashness 286; Pride 297; Insolence 400; Showiness 404*

2 disobedience, insubordination, resistance, opposition, dissent, disagreement; confrontation, challenge, rebelliousness, rebellion, refusal, contumacy; contemptuousness, contempt, derision, disdain, disregard

  ▶ *Dissent 347; Disobedience 427; Disagreement 463; Opposition 828*

3 act of defiance, challenge, dare, threat, taunt, insult, rude remark, contumely, answering back, back talk, impudent talk; opposition rally, demonstration, sit-in, march; treason, insurrection, revolution, declaration of war, battle cry, rebel yell

  ▶ *War 76; Disrespect 436*

4 defiant person, challenger, opponent, usurper, militant, protester, rebel, leader of the opposition; demonstrator, marcher, activist; martyr, nonconformist, conscientious objector; devil's advocate

ADJECTIVES

5 defiant, outspoken, assertive, emphatic, assured, self-assured, unabashed, audacious, bold; arrogant, presumptuous, stubborn, obstinate, stiff-necked, bumptious, offensive, impudent, impertinent, pert, insolent, insulting, contemptuous, disdainful, derisive; shameless, brash, brazen, bold as brass, brassy; courageous, daring; reckless, saucy, cocky, cheeky, nervy, sassy [Inf]

6 defying, challenging, disagreeing, disobedient; recalcitrant, refractory, obstinate; antagonistic, belligerent, bellicose, provocative, aggressive, rebellious, militant, warlike

VERBS

7 defy, challenge, oppose, protest, bid defiance to, hurl defiance at; flout, show insolence, show courage, face danger, dare, brave, bare one's teeth; fly in the face of, stand up to, withstand, refuse to bow to, call one's bluff, run the gauntlet, take one up on, present a bold front, present a brave face, outstare, brazen it out; presume, bluster, crow over, provoke, affront, have temerity, have (a) nerve, have barefaced cheek, have cheek, get on one's high horse; [Inf]: have chutzpa *or* hutzpa, give someone some lip, sass

8 be insubordinate, show contempt, scorn, spurn, slight, disregard, ignore; resist, refuse, confront, disobey, disagree, threaten, challenge, oppose, dissent; throw down the gauntlet, throw one's hat in the ring; dare, taunt, act insolent, snap one's fingers at, laugh in someone's face, insult, make a rude remark, answer back, play the devil's advocate; demonstrate, hold a demonstration, stage *or* hold a sit-in, march; rebel, usurp, declare war, give the battle cry, give a rebel yell

ADVERBS

9 defiantly, assertively, emphatically, with emphasis; courageously, in a courageous way, in the face of, in the teeth of, assuredly, self-assuredly, unabashedly, audaciously, boldly, to one's face; daringly, as a dare, arrogantly, presumptuously, stubbornly, obstinately, bumptiously; offensively, impudently, impertinently, pertly, insolently, insultingly, contemptuously, disdainfully, derisively; shamelessly, without shame, without embarrassment; brashly, with a lot of nerve, brazenly, under the very nose of, courageously; recklessly, saucily, cockily, cheekily, nervily

10 in defiance, challengingly, as a challenge, disobediently; obstinately, antagonistically, with antagonism, belligerently, in a belligerent way, bellicosely, provocatively; aggressively, rebelliously, in open rebellion, militantly

417 Resistance

NOUNS

1 resistance, refusal, unwillingness, noncooperation, uncooperativeness, opposition; objection, challenge, stand, brave front; refusal to work, strike, walkout; deprecation, protest, dissent, defiance, repulse, repulsion, repellence, rebuff, reluctance, renitency, negativeness

  ▶ *Unwillingness 375; Defiance 416; Refusal 506; Protest 507; Repulsion 701; Opposition 828*

2 obstinacy, intractability, refractoriness, recalcitrance, stubbornness, hardheadedness, obduracy; firmness, hardness, toughness, callousness; stiffness, starchiness, rigidity, inflexibility, inelasticity, not bending, not yielding

  ▶ *Obstinacy 379; Hardness 542*

3 resistance movement, self-defense, withstanding, nonviolent resistance, passive resistance, civil disobedience; mutiny, uprising, insurgence, insurrection, revolution, revolt, guerrilla warfare, terrorism

◗ *War 76; Defiance 416; Defense 419; Contention 422*

4 **desisting,** desistance, denial, self-denial, self-restraint, denying oneself, refusal, refusing oneself, refraining; abstaining, forbearance, forbearing, doing without, not touching

◗ *Self-Restraint 455*

5 **resister,** defender, repeller, opponent, opposer, revolutionary, freedom fighter, resistance fighter, maquis; reactionary, terrorist, anarchist; die-hard, traditionalist, reactionary, conservative, hard-liner, stick-in-the-mud; conscientious objector, pacifist; refrainer, abstainer, forbearer

◗ *Government 49; Politics 50*

ADJECTIVES

6 **resistant,** resisting, renitent, withstanding; reluctant, negative, refusing, striking, unwilling, noncooperative, uncooperative, opposing, opposed, objecting, challenging, challenged; deprecative, deprecating, protesting, dissenting, defiant, rebuffing, repulsing, repellent, repelling, obstructive; hardheaded, hard-shell, hard-core, hard-nosed [Inf]

7 **obstinate,** intractable, refractory, recalcitrant; callous, hard, rigid, firm, standing firm, tough, stiff, starchy; stubborn, obdurate, inflexible, unbending, unyielding, unmalleable; die-hard, hard-line, traditional, conservative

8 **resisting,** unsubmissive, up in arms, undefeated, unsubdued, unbowed, unquelled; unbeatable, invincible; bulletproof, self-defensive; revolutionary, rebellious, mutinous, insurgent, reactionary

9 **desisting,** denying, self-denying, refraining, abstaining, abstemious, forbearing

VERBS

10 **resist,** offer resistance, withstand, endure, make a stand, stand against, put up a brave front, not give way; show reluctance, refuse, strike, walk out, not cooperate, not be tempted by; oppose, object to, confront, contend with, obstruct, hinder, challenge; deprecate, protest, dissent, defy, refuse to bow down; repulse, repel, rebuff, hold off, keep at arm's length, keep at bay

11 **be obstinate,** stand firm, stand rigid, show no flexibility, not bend, not yield, stick to one's guns, dig in one's heels, refuse to budge

12 **revolt,** mutiny, rise up, not take it lying down, fight off, defend oneself

13 **desist,** deny oneself, refuse oneself, restrain from, refrain from; abstain, forbear, do without, not touch

ADVERBS

14 **resistingly,** resistantly; reluctantly, negatively, unwillingly; noncooperatively, challengingly, deprecatingly, protestingly, under protest, dissentingly, repellently; hardheadedly, obstinately, intractably, traditionally, conservatively; callously, firmly, rigidly,

toughly, stiffly, inflexibly, unbendingly, invincibly, defiantly, unsubmissively; mutinously, rebelliously

15 **abstemiously,** abstinently, forbearingly, with forbearance, through self-denial

INTERJECTIONS

16 **fight on!,** no surrender!, rise up!, resist!, we shall overcome!

418 Attack

NOUNS

1 **attack,** assault, aggression, aggressiveness, pugnacity, belligerence, combativeness, bellicosity; hostility, intimidation, harassment, diatribe

2 **military attack,** hostile attack, offensive, offensive operations, offensive campaign; strike, preemptive strike, onslaught, onset; charge, drive, push, thrust, rush, run, dead set, shock; raid, foray, search-and-destroy mission, surprise attack, blind attack, night attack, surprise offensive, surprise blow, shock tactics, *coup de main* [Fr]; siege, blockade, encirclement, encroachment, infringement, inroad, investment; counterattack, counteroffensive, retaliation, rebellion; sally, sortie, breakout; breakthrough, taking by storm, storm, escalade, irruption; overrunning, ingress, invasion, incursion, occupation, subjection; bloodbath, slaughter, devastation, laying waste; dragonnade, pillage, havoc

◗ *War 76*

3 **land attack,** armored attack, ground-force attack, infantry assault, tank assault; blitzkrieg, pincer movement, flanking attack, enfilade

4 **air attack,** air campaign, air strike, air raid, aerial bombardment; bomb dropping, bomb run; bombing, strategic bombing, tactical bombing, precision bombing, dive bombing, surgical air strike, saturation bombing, carpet bombing, indiscriminate bombing, kamikaze bombing, suicide bombing, high-level bombing, low-level bombing; missile strike, laser targeting; strafe, strafing

5 **combined attack,** sea attack, boarding, torpedoing; bombardment, heavy bombardment, artillery bombardment, barrage, mortar attack, cannonade; concentrated attack, blitz, massed attack, relentless attack, day-and-night attack

◗ *War 76*

6 **firing,** fire, shooting, musketry, gunnery, gunfire; broadside, shot across the bows; volley, salvo, burst, spray, strafe, fusillade, rapid fire; cross fire, plunging fire, raking fire; sharpshooting, sniping

◗ *Weapon 78*

7 **terrorist attack,** terror tactics, hostage taking, kidnapping, assassination, bombing, letter *or* mail *or* car bombing, guerrilla attack, sniping, war of attrition

8 **personal attack,** physical attack, physical violence, mugging, armed robbery, assault and battery; rape,

date rape, indecent *or* sexual assault; foul play, stab in the back, injustice; verbal attack, criticism, censure, aspersion, disparagement, denigration, decrial, denunciation; slander, defamation, libel, calumny, slur, smear, abuse, vilification, revilement
  ▶ *Aggravation 276; Disapproval 438; Disparagement 440; Violence 520*

9 **hit,** blow, punch, knock, swipe, kick, stab, jab, cut; stabbing, knifing, bayoneting; impalement, goring; stoning, lapidation

10 **attacker,** assailant, aggressor, warrior, crusader, holy warrior; attacking force, spearhead, strike force; fighter pilot, air ace, top gun, bomber, dive bomber, bombardier; sharpshooter, snipe; terrorist; guerrilla; besieger, blockader, raider, invader, stormer, escalader; mugger, rapist, murderer, assassin, killer
  ▶ *Combatant 77; Violence 520*

11 **seizure,** bout, spell, spasm, fit, paroxysm
  ▶ *Ill Health 114*

ADJECTIVES

12 **aggressive,** antagonistic, pugnacious, truculent, threatening; provocative, quarrelsome, contentious, disputatious, litigious

13 **militant,** combative, hawkish, warlike, warring; offensive, on the offensive; on the warpath, spoiling for a fight [Inf]
  ▶ *War 76*

14 **attacking,** assaulting, invading, storming, charging, boarding; fighting, striking, harrying, kicking, punching, flailing; cutting, slashing; destructive, violent, bloody; bloodthirsty, brutish, cruel; uncontrollable, overpowering, overwhelming; frenzied, raging, berserk
  ▶ *Violence 520*

15 **counterattacking,** resisting, opposing, retaliatory; challenging, defiant, rebellious
  ▶ *Resistance 417; Opposition 828*

16 **critical,** censorious; disparaging, denigrating, maligning, decrying, denunciatory; defamatory, slanderous, libelous, vituperative, abusive
  ▶ *Curse 301; Disparagement 440*

VERBS

17 **attack,** launch an attack, break the peace, start a fight; take the offensive, assume the offensive, go onto the offensive, go on the attack, engage, strike first, strike the first blow, fire the first shot; sound the charge, advance, advance against, march against, ride against, drive against, sail against, fly against; go over the top, escalade, storm, bear down on, board, lay aboard, charge, charge against; rush, rush at, run at, dash at, gallop at, go full belt at, tilt at, ride full tilt at; go for, make a dead set at; drive, thrust, push, raid, foray, strike, burst in, grapple; pound, assault, blitz, bombard; assail, harry, hunt; ram, collide with; ambush, surprise

18 **fire,** fire on, open fire (on), fire at; level, draw a bead on, aim, find *or* get in the cross hairs, pull *or* squeeze the trigger; take a potshot, pop at, snipe at, pick off; shoot, shoot at, let fly, volley, blast, pour a broadside into, shoot down, bring down, torpedo, strafe, cannonade, shell, bombard; fusillade, pepper, rake, enfilade

19 **bomb,** throw bombs, drop bombs, carpet-bomb, drop the payload, hit the target, make the rubble bounce, blitz; [Inf]: nuke, lay eggs, plaster

20 **besiege,** lay siege to, starve out, surround, enclose, encircle, encroach, infringe, blockade, hem in, beset, beleaguer, invest

21 **strike,** hit, go for, set on, have a fling at, pounce upon, fall upon, jump, sail into, launch out at, lash out at, let someone have it, tear into, lace into, round on, strike at; raise one's hand against, grapple with, close with, fetch a blow, lay about one, swipe (at); flail, hammer, punch, butt, push, poke (at), kick; knock down, bring down, lay low; beat up, mug, attack tooth and nail, go berserk, run amuck *or* amok, savage, maul; [Inf]: kick ass, pitch into, lay into
  ▶ *Violence 520*

22 **stab,** make a pass at, have a cut at, lunge, thrust, thrust at; pierce, cut, slash, impale, run through, cut down; knife, spear, lance, bayonet

23 **stone,** throw a stone, heave a brick, lapidate; sling, pelt, shy, throw at, hurl at, chuck

24 **counterattack,** fight back, retaliate, oppose, rebel against, confront, defy, challenge, take on, stand against, take a stand against; strike back at, return blow for blow, break out, sally, make a sortie
  ▶ *Defiance 416; Resistance 417; Retaliation 420*

25 **attack successfully,** break through, breach, take over, take by storm, carry, invade; incur upon, capture, overrun, overcome, overmaster, overwhelm, overpower, ride down, run down, trample, beat, corner, bring to bay; go on the rampage, slaughter, kill, ravage, rape, terrorize, torture, wreak havoc, scorch, burn, lay waste
  ▶ *Subjection 832*

26 **criticize,** censure, cast aspersions on, inveigh against, disparage, denigrate, malign; decry, denounce, condemn; slander, defame, libel, slur, smear; berate, vituperate, abuse, vilify, revile
  ▶ *Disapproval 438; Disparagement 440*

ADVERBS

27 **aggressively,** forcefully, assertively, with hostility; offensively, on the offensive, on the attack, on the warpath, in combat

419 Defense

NOUNS

1 **defense,** defensive move, defensive tactic, the defensive; resistance, passive resistance, active resistance,

parry, warding off; safeguarding, safekeeping, preserving, preservation

2 **safeguard,** protection, buffer, screen, rampart, bulwark

3 **counter,** counterforce, counteraction, counterstroke
▶ Retaliation 420

4 **defensiveness,** defense mechanism, camouflage, protective coloring, elusiveness; shyness, nervousness

5 **self-defense,** boxing, martial arts, judo, karate; security, surveillance, burglar alarm, car alarm, personal alarm, whistle, Mace™, pepper spray, guard dog

6 **protective clothing,** helmet, crash helmet, head guard, goggles, visor; body padding, shoulder pads, shin pads, gloves, gauntlets, protective belt, body belt; fireproof clothing, bulletproof vest, gas mask, breathing apparatus; camouflage clothing, Day-Glo™ clothing, reflective clothing

7 **modern armor,** steel-plate armor, armor plate; rolled homogeneous armor, ceramic armor, reactive armor; steel helmet, Kevlar™ helmet, plastic helmet, visor, shield, facemask; gas mask, respirator; body armor, bulletproof vest, flack suit, flack vest; heat-resistant or Nomex™ suit, fire-resistant suit, tin hat [Inf]

8 **historic armor,** jousting armor, full armor, mail, chain mail, chain armor, scale armor, fluted armor, splint armor, breastplate, backplate, cuirass, harness, lance rest, lorica, plastron, hauberk, habergeon, brigandine, coat of mail, corselet or corslet; helmet, helm, coif, gorget, casque, basinet, sallet, morion, siege cap, bowl, skull, visor, vambrace, brassard, cubitiere, elbow-cop, gauntlet, cuisse, greave; shield, buckler, scutum, target, pavis, mantelet, testudo

9 **military defenses,** defensive line, fortified line, entrenchment, fixed position; fieldwork, breastwork, parados, earthwork; embankment, mound, sandbag, moat, ditch, fosse, trench, dugout, foxhole; trip wire, trap, mine; antiaircraft fire, antiaircraft artillery, ack-ack [Inf], tracer flare; Strategic Defense Initiative (SDI) or Star Wars

10 **barrier,** barricade, blockade, boom, fence, wall, roadblock; stakes, pales, paling, abatis, palisade, stockade, zareba, defensive circle, circle of wagons; entanglements, razor wire, concertina wire, electric fence, spike, chevaux-de-frise, caltrop

11 **shelter,** air-raid shelter, fallout shelter, concrete shelter, underground shelter, bunker, blockhouse; blackout, smoke screen

12 **fortification,** stronghold, fastness, wall, town wall, buttress, abutment; emplacement, gun emplacement; stockade, pillbox, blockhouse, strong point; circumvallation, outwork; gabion

13 **fort,** fortress, fortalice, bastion, demibastion, demilune, rampart, earthwork, bulwark, parapet, scarp, escarp, counterscarp, glacis; tower, turret, curtain; battlement,

merlon, crenel, loophole, embrasure, casemate, banquette, bartizan, barbette, ravelin; barbican; dungeon; portcullis, drawbridge, moat, gate, gatehouse, machicolation, postern, sally port; castle, keep, bailey, ward, citadel, acropolis, refuge

14 **defender,** champion, patron, aider, supporter, henchman, angel [Inf]; knight, knight-errant, white knight, paladin

15 **guard,** bodyguard; lifeguard; watch, sentry, sentinel, picket, armed guard, vanguard, rear guard, patrol, patrolman, patrolwoman; security guard, watchman, night watchman, night watch; doorman, bouncer, escort

16 **protector,** guardian, warden, custodian, warder, keeper, park keeper, gamekeeper; goalkeeper

ADJECTIVES

17 **defending,** defensive, on the defensive, on guard, resisting; extenuating, excusing, vindicating; challenged; protective, tutelary, responsible

18 **defended,** protected, secured; armored, armor-plated, heavy-armed, accoutered, prepared, barricaded, fortified, entrenched, dug in

19 **invulnerable,** bombproof, bulletproof, unconquerable

VERBS

20 **defend,** guard, protect, secure, keep, watch; safeguard, lock up, ward

21 **fence,** wall, hedge, moat, circumscribe, enclose; barricade, palisade; block, obstruct, booby-trap, mine

22 **buffer,** cushion, pad, shield; camouflage, curtain, cover, screen, cloak, conceal

23 **reinforce,** armor, fortify, strengthen, beef up

24 **entrench,** dig in, make a stand, stand firm, stand in front; stand by, stand ready, garrison, man the fort; man the guns, man the defenses; man the breach, plug the gap, stop the gap

25 **plead for,** hold a brief for, argue for; take up the cause of, protect the interests of, support, champion, vindicate; fight for, take up arms for, take up the cudgels for

26 **rescue,** come to the rescue, save, deliver

27 **parry,** counter, riposte, fence; fend off, throw back, ward off, hold off, keep off, fight off, stave off; hold or keep at bay, keep at arm's length, avoid, turn, avert, deflect

28 **stall,** beat about the bush, quibble, vacillate, blow hot and cold; stonewall, block, obstruct, delay

29 **act on the defensive,** fight a defensive battle, take evasive action, play for a draw, stalemate

30 **retaliate,** fight back, come back, show fight, show one's mettle, give a warm reception to; resist, repulse, repel, butt away

31 **survive,** escape, withstand, bear the brunt, hold one's own; fall back on, beat a strategic retreat, get out while the going is good, retire, turn back; scrape through, live to fight another day

32 **defensively,** protectively, on the defensive, on guard; at bay, in defense, self-defensively, in self-defense

420 Retaliation

NOUNS

1 **retaliation,** reprisal, revenge, just revenge, vengeance; redress, desert, deserts, just deserts, dueness, justice; retribution, reparation, repayment, nemesis; comeuppance [Inf], punishment; backlash, counter, counterpunch, counterstroke, counterblast, counterplot, countermine, counteraction, countersuit; answering back, comeback, riposte, retort, rejoinder, heaping coals of fire; reciprocation, talion, like for like, tit for tat, quid pro quo, measure for measure, blow for blow, an eye for an eye and a tooth for a tooth; taste of one's own medicine, game at which two can play

  ▶ *Counteraction 510*

2 **revenger,** avenger, vigilante, guerrilla, saboteur; member of the resistance, member of the underground

ADJECTIVES

3 **retaliatory,** in retaliation, in reprisal, in self-defense; retaliative, retributive, punitive, recriminatory, like for like, reciprocal; revengeful, vindictive, vengeful; rightly served

VERBS

4 **retaliate,** take reprisals, get satisfaction, exact compensation, recoup, repay, redress, redress the balance; inflict punishment, avenge, take vengeance, punish, revenge, make good; counter, riposte, parry, pay one back, shoot back; pay off old scores, wipe out a score, square the account, be quits, get even with, get one's own back; reciprocate, give and take, fight fire with fire, return like for like, return the compliment, give as good as one got, pay one in his own coin, give a quid pro quo; return, retort, cap, answer back, answer, countersue, countercharge; round on, kick back, hit back; not take it lying down, resist, requite

5 **serve one right,** be rightly served, be one's own fault, make one's bed and lie in it, be taught a lesson, have had one's lesson; restitute, pay off; find one's match, meet one's match; get what one deserves, get one's deserts, get what was due, get what was coming, get a dose of one's own medicine, be hoist with one's own petard; be chastised, be punished

ADVERBS

6 **with vengeance,** by way of return, in requital, tit for tat

INTERJECTIONS

7 **revenge!,** it serves you right!, take that!, see how it feels!, put that in your pipe and smoke it!, the joke's *or* laugh's on you!

421 Submission

NOUNS

1 **submission,** submissiveness, appeasement, deference, obedience, tameness, submitting, succumbing, subservience, slavishness, servitude; collaboration, acquiescence, compliance, consent, concession, assent, agreeing; nonresistance, passivity, passiveness, docility, peace at any price, line of least resistance; resignation, fatalism; supineness, lethargy, apathy, inactivity, surrender, yielding, giving way, giving in, giving up the fort, cave-in, caving in [Inf], the white flag, capitulation, unconditional surrender; cession, abandonment, relinquishment, abdication, resignation; deference, abject loyalty, homage, bow, curtsy, humble submission; humility, kneeling, genuflection, kowtow, prostration, groveling, obeisance; sexual submission, passive sex; masochism

  ▶ *Humility 298; Inactivity 415; Obedience 426; Agreement 462*

2 **submitter,** appeaser, defeatist, quitter; mouse, doormat, coward; sycophant, groveler, toady; servant, menial; slave; masochist; [Inf]: pushover, wimp, brownnose *or* brown-noser, grunt, gofer

  ▶ *Servant 69; Cowardice 285*

ADJECTIVES

3 **submitting,** surrendering; quiet, meek, humble, tame, docile, unresisting, nonresisting; law-abiding, peaceful, submissive; subservient, servile, menial, lowly, low, abject, obedient, slavish; unconcerned, fatalistic, resigned, subdued; acquiescent, concessionary, assenting, pliant, accommodating, malleable, biddable, tractable, amenable, agreeable; soft, weak-kneed, bending, crouching, crawling, cringing, lying down, supine, prostrate; bootlicking, bowing and scraping, kneeling, on bended knee, sycophantic, toadying; masochistic

  ▶ *Assent 346; Servility 401; Obedience 426; Agreement 462*

VERBS

4 **submit,** yield, obey, give in, not resist, not insist; make no waves, keep quiet, pussyfoot (around), defer to, bow to; accept, face reality, face the facts, resign oneself, be resigned, make a virtue of necessity; appease, collaborate with, yield with a good grace, admit defeat, yield the palm; play it low-key, take things easy, condone, comply, consent, assent, relent, abide; [Inf]: take the heat, cool it, buy

  ▶ *Resignation 835*

5 **acquiesce,** go along with, play along with, grant, concede; shrug one's shoulders, be indifferent, turn a blind eye toward, show apathy for, avoid responsibility for; withdraw, retreat, retire, hang it up [Inf], fade into the background, leave, step aside, make way for, turn

back; not contest, let judgment go by default, pass up, pull out, be inactive

◗ *Indifference 289*

6 **capitulate,** surrender, be defeated; cease resistance, stop fighting, sue for peace, subdue oneself, call it a day, have no fight left, have all the fight knocked out of one; give up, give way, cry quits, cry uncle [Inf], have had enough, abandon one's cause, relinquish, throw in the sponge *or* towel; hold up one's hands, show the white flag, ask for terms, haul down the flag, strike colors, ask for mercy, give oneself up, yield oneself, lay down one's arms, hand over one's sword; abdicate, renounce authority, resign, stand down

◗ *Failure 846*

7 **succumb,** knuckle under, break under pressure, yield to the pressure, be out for the count; collapse, sag, wilt, tire, faint, drop, show no fight; take the line of least resistance, bow before the inevitable, bow before the storm, be swept aside, be submissive; submit, learn obedience, keep in one's place, know one's place; do homage, bow, curtsy; swallow the pill, bite the bullet; apologize, eat humble pie; be humble, take it, take it from one, take it lying down, pocket the insult, grin and bear it, bear; suffer in patience, endure, digest, stomach, put up with, suffer; bend, kneel, kowtow, toady, crouch, cringe, crawl, bow and scrape, stoop; grovel, lick the dust, kiss the rod; [Inf]: cave in, eat crow, lump it, take one's lumps, brown-nose, take it on the chin, eat dirt

◗ *Subjection 832*

ADVERBS

8 **with humility,** humbly, meekly, obediently, without resistance

INTERJECTIONS

9 **I/we surrender!,** enough!, mercy!, uncle! [Inf]

422 Contention

NOUNS

1 **contention,** conflict, struggle, fight, clash, tussle, strife; military conflict, combat, fighting, battle, pitched battle, running battle; skirmish, engagement, encounter, firefight; fight to the death, fight to the last man; ding-dong battle, knock-down-drag-out fight; debate, dispute, dissent, dissension, controversy, polemics, paper warfare; words, war of words, mudslinging, argument, quarrel, open quarrel, squabble, spat, hassle, wrangle, altercation; cold war

◗ *War 76; Argument 329*

2 **rivalry,** competition, emulation, jealousy, competitiveness, gamesmanship; survival of the fittest, cutthroat competition, dog-eat-dog competition; stakes, bone of contention, root of dissension, area of disagreement, provocation, casus belli; rat race [Inf], rhubarb [Inf]

3 **sports,** sport, team sports, field sports, games, athletic competition, athletics

4 **contest,** trial, trial of strength, test of endurance; tussle, struggle, effort, essay, exertion; bitter struggle, grudge match, revenge match; equal contest, even match, close fight; close finish, photo finish, neck-and-neck finish; competition, tournament, championship, ball-buster [Inf]

5 **prize competition,** open competition, pro-am, knockout competition; stakes, trophy; game, set, rubber, match, exhibition game; meet, event, rally, handicap, heat, round, runoff, quarterfinal, semifinal, final; World Series, Super Bowl, Olympic Games, Olympics, Summer Olympics, Winter Olympics, Special Olympics

6 **sporting event,** sport, amusement, field day, gymkhana; automobile rally; horse show, show jumping, rodeo; orienteering; tug of war, sack race, egg and spoon race, pancake race

7 **athletics,** track event, track and field meet; gymnastics; swimming; karate; professional athletics, basketball, baseball, football, golf, hockey, soccer, tennis; boxing, prizefighting; wrestling

8 **race,** racing, speed contest, speeding; running, races, foot race; Alpine ski racing, cross-country ski racing; horse racing, dog racing, greyhound racing; automobile racing; motorcycle racing, bicycle racing; boat racing, yacht racing

◗ *Sports 145; Automobile Racing 146; Boating Sports 150; Combat Sports 152; Horses, Horseback Riding, Horse Racing 159; Skiing, Ice Skating, Bobsledding 162; Track and Field Events 166; Attempt 390*

9 **fight,** free fight, free-for-all, showdown, rough-and-tumble, scuffle, brawl, broil, upheaval, affray, tussle, scrap, brush, scrimmage, scramble, dogfight, melee, fracas, riot, uproar; gang warfare, street fight, blows, hard knocks, give and take, running fight; close fighting, close grips, close quarters, infighting, punch-up *or* punch-out [Inf]

◗ *Disagreement 463; Violence 520*

10 **warfare,** war, belligerency, blowup; appeal to arms, war of attrition; deed of arms, feat of arms, passage of arms; combat, fray, clash, military conflict, skirmish, engagement, encounter, military encounter, military action, stand-up fight, firefight, shootout; battle, battle royal, pitched battle, campaign; struggle, death struggle, death grapple, war to the knife, final battle

11 **field of battle,** battlefield, battleground, battlefront, killing fields

◗ *War 76; Argument 329; Disorder 766*

12 **duel,** dueling, duel to the death, affair of honor, pistols for two and coffee for one, seconds out; single combat, gladiatorial combat, one-on-one, mano a mano, head-to-head contest, hand-to-hand fight, nose-to-nose confrontation; close grips, close quarters; jousting, joust, tilting, tilt, tournament, tourney;

fencing, swordplay, singlestick, quarterstaff, kendo; bullfight, tauromachy, bloodless bullfight, dogfight, cockfight

▶ *Combatant 77; Fencing 153*

13 **contender,** combatant, challenger, contestant, player, participant, competitor, pothunter; rival, emulator, opponent, adversary

14 **fighter,** soldier, striver, struggler, tussler; gamecock, fighting cock; gladiator, bullfighter; scrapper [Inf]

15 **athlete,** boxer, prizefighter, wrestler; fencer; runner, racer, gymnast, swimmer, jockey; game participant, professional athlete, pro [Inf]

16 **finalist,** semifinalist, front runner; favorite, odds-on favorite, the pick, the choice; seed, top seed; starter; runner-up, also-ran; the field, all comers

17 **debater,** quarreler, mudslinger

▶ *Argument 329*

18 **candidate,** applicant, hopeful, entrant, examinee

▶ *Combatant 77; Selection 382*

ADJECTIVES

19 **contending,** battling, fighting, grappling, struggling; competing, contesting, challenging, racing, rival, rivaling, vying; outdoing, surpassing, agonistic; athletic, sporting; starting, running, in the running, in with a chance

20 **contentious,** argumentative, quarrelsome, quarreling, irritable, irascible; aggressive, combative, fight-hungry, pugilistic, gladiatorial, pugnacious, bellicose, warmongering, warlike, hawkish; at loggerheads, at odds, at war, belligerent, warring; head to head, hand to hand, mano a mano, nose to nose, close, at close quarters, at close grips, at close range, spoiling for a fight [Inf]

▶ *War 76; Argument 329*

21 **competitive,** keen, cutthroat, dog-eat-dog; hotly contested, ding-dong, close-run, cliff-hanging, well-fought; fought to the finish, fought to the death

VERBS

22 **contend,** combat, battle, fight, tussle, wrestle, grapple, tackle; attempt, try, venture, essay, strive, struggle, try and try again; oppose, resist, withstand, struggle against, make a stand, put up a fight; argue for, hold out for, make a point (of), insist on, emphasize; contest, compete, enter, enter for, challenge, take on; stake, wager, bet, play, play against; race, run a race, match oneself, vie with, emulate, rival, outrival, outdo; enter the lists, descend into the arena, take up the challenge, give it a try, pick up the gauntlet; close with, grapple with; engage with, lock horns with, strike at, cross swords with, tilt with, joust with, break a lance with, slug it out with; try a fall, try conclusions with, have a go at; stonewall, do a job on [Inf]

▶ *Combatant 77; Attempt 390; Opposition 828*

23 **fight,** have a fight, scuffle, row, scrimmage, scrap; set to, go for, take on, engage, wade in, have at, sail into, assail, lay on, strike at; lay about one, join in the melee, come to blows, exchange blows, give hard knocks, give and take, give as good as one gets, kick, scratch, bite; fall foul of, call out, answer for, give satisfaction; meet, encounter, have a brush with, scrap with, grapple, lock horns, come to grips, come to close quarters, fight hand-to-hand; [Inf]: pitch into, have a punch-up, mix it up, give one a knuckle sandwich

24 **duel,** fence; box, engage in fisticuffs

25 **declare war,** go to war, raise one's banner; combat, attack, campaign, wage war; open fire, skirmish, exchange shots, fight a pitched battle, give battle; fight the good fight, shed blood, fight hard, shoot to kill, fight like devils *or* fiends; fight it out, fight to the finish, fight to the last man

▶ *War 76; Attack 418; Violence 520; Disorder 766*

26 **conflict,** differ, disagree, dissent, dispute, join issue with, debate; quarrel, row, squabble, argue; affirm, aver, maintain

▶ *Affirmation 189; Argument 329; Dissimilarity 734*

ADVERBS

27 **contentiously,** argumentatively, irritably, irascibly; aggressively, pugnaciously, belligerently

423 Leniency

To Mercy, Pity, Peace, and Love / All pray in their distress; / And to these virtues of delight / Return their thankfulness. — WILLIAM BLAKE

NOUNS

1 **leniency,** lenience, lenity, laxity, easiness, mildness, moderation; gentleness, softness, tenderness; patience, tolerance, toleration, forbearance; compassion, pity, mercifulness, mercy, quarter; forgiveness, pardon, amnesty, clemency; reasonableness, humanity, humaneness, benevolence, kindness, kindliness, graciousness; charitableness, charity, magnanimity, generousness; favor, concession, sop, humoring, consideration; leave, allowance, permission, permissiveness, indulgence, laissez faire, spoiling, gratification; light rein, light hand, velvet glove, kid gloves, kid-glove treatment

▶ *Benevolence 305; Pity 308; Forgiveness 312; Permission 502; Moderation 521*

2 **lenient person,** indulger, permitter, permissive parent, philanthropist, latitudinarian, liberal, wet, old softy [Inf]

ADJECTIVES

3 **lenient,** lax, easy, easygoing, mild, moderate, clement, gentle, soft, tender; patient, tolerant, forbearing, long-suffering; compassionate, pitying, merciful, forgiving; reasonable, considerate, humane, benevolent, kind, kindly, gracious; charitable, accepting, magnanimous,

accommodating, generous; permissive, indulgent, spoiling

▶ *Benevolence 305*

4 **given consideration,** given permission, allowed, permitted; granted amnesty, pardoned, forgiven; pitied; indulged, gratified, spoiled, spoiled rotten

▶ *Forgiveness 312; Permission 502*

VERBS

5 **be lenient,** show leniency, go easy on, moderate, treat kindly; treat lightly, make no demands, make few demands, deal gently, handle tenderly; tolerate, forbear, not press, bear with; stretch a point, bend a rule, give quarter; have compassion, have pity, pity, show mercy; forgive, forget, pardon, spare, grant amnesty, favor, concede, humor, show consideration; allow, permit, indulge, oblige, gratify; spare the rod, handle with kid or velvet gloves, keep or use a light rein, let off the hook, use a light hand, live and let live, pull one's punches [Inf]

ADVERBS

6 **leniently,** easily, mildly, moderately, gently, softly, tenderly, patiently; with kid gloves, with a light rein, with a light hand; tolerantly, compassionately, mercifully, reasonably, considerately; humanely, benevolently, kindly, with kindness, graciously, in a gracious manner, charitably, magnanimously, accommodatingly, generously; permissively, indulgently, gratifyingly

424 Severity

And he shall rule them with a rod of iron.
— BIBLE: REVELATIONS

NOUNS

1 **severity,** strictness, fastidiousness, pedantry, meticulousness, stringency, sternness; ruggedness, toughness, harshness, hardness; intolerance, no compromise, uncharitableness; rigorousness, rigor, fundamentalism, Draconian measures, rigidity, formality, orthodoxy; firmness, firm hand, strong hand, hard hand, firm control, tight rein, restraint, tight ship; inflexibility, stubbornness, obstinacy, bigotry; regimentation, discipline, strict discipline, clampdown, martial law, letter of the law; authority, power, arbitrary power, no appeal; inclemency, lack of mercy, harsh treatment, asperity, callousness, pitilessness, pound of flesh; inhumanity, cruelty, bullying, outrage

▶ *Authority 52; Pitilessness 309; Obstinacy 379; Power 514; Hardness 542*

2 **suppression,** oppression, repression, subjugation, subjection; persecution, coercion, harassment, victimization, extortion, exploitation, inquisition; censorship, expurgation, blue laws; absolutism, authoritarianism, autocracy, totalitarianism, militarism, dictatorship,

despotism, tyranny, fascism, Nazism, Stalinism; brute force, naked force, show of force, iron rule, iron hand, mailed fist, jackboot; atrocity, torture, execution

▶ *Wrong 430; Immorality 432; Wickedness 448; Punishment 454; Violence 520; Restraint 830; Subjection 832*

3 **unadornment,** plainness, simplicity, austerity, Spartanism; asceticism, askesis or ascesis, restraint, self-restraint, self-denial, self-mortification; prudery, puritanism

▶ *Self-Restraint 455; Sparseness 541*

4 **strict person,** Spartan, puritan, prude, purist, pedant, stickler, Dutch uncle, bureaucrat, disciplinarian; martinet, petty tyrant, militarist, sergeant major; hanging judge, oppressive person, oppressor; Big Brother, authoritarian, despot, dictator, autocrat, inquisitor, persecutor, bully; hard master, taskmaster, taskmistress, slave driver; prohibitionist, dry; hard-liner, hawk [Inf]

▶ *Master 68*

ADJECTIVES

5 **severe,** strict, rigorous, harsh, hard, uncompromising, unbending, stubborn, obstinate, hardheaded, stern, rigid, firm, inflexible, uncharitable, Draconian; exacting, exact, pedantic, formal, orthodox, fundamental, fastidious, meticulous, stringent, censorious, censorial; regimented, disciplined, rugged, tough, hardhearted; intolerant, inquisitorial, bigoted, inclement, callous; pitiless, merciless, unsparing, unforgiving; inhumane, cruel, brutal; coercive, oppressive, repressive, exploitative; undemocratic, militaristic, authoritarian, totalitarian, despotic, dictatorial, autocratic, fascist, tyrannical; domineering, dominating, highhanded, overbearing, heavy-handed, bossy

6 **suppressed,** oppressed, repressed, subjugated, subjected; persecuted, coerced, harassed; censored, expurgated; exploited, victimized, tyrannized; tortured, executed

7 **unadorned,** plain, simple, purist, restrained, self-restrained, austere, ascetic, Spartan; prudish, puritanical, strait-laced

VERBS

8 **be severe,** restrain, regiment, discipline, chastise, punish; wield power, exert authority, maintain firm control, put one's foot down, run a tight ship, keep a tight rein; take Draconian measures, get tough, deal harshly with, come down on, intimidate, frighten, take the heart out of; clamp down on, put a stop to, not tolerate, squeeze, crush; impose martial law, allow no appeal, give no quarter, offer no compromise; lack mercy, show no mercy, show no pity; shove around, boss around, wave the big stick, bully, bait, hassle; stick to the letter of the law, have one's pound of flesh

▶ *Pitilessness 309; Hardness 542*

9 **suppress,** oppress, repress, subjugate, subject, persecute, hunt down, coerce, harass, abuse; abuse one's authority, misgovern, misrule, mishandle, victimize, ex-

tort, exploit, enslave; censor, expurgate; tyrannize, use brute force, have a show of force, treat rough, get tough with, ride roughshod over, put the screws on, stamp on, tread on, tread under foot, walk over; torment, terrorize, rule with an iron hand, torture, commit an atrocity; execute, shed blood, put to the sword, pull no punches [Inf]

▶ *Punishment 454; Restraint 830; Subjection 832*

10 **be unadorned,** be simple, restrain oneself, show self-restraint, live a Spartan life, be austere

▶ *Self-Restraint 455; Sparseness 541*

ADVERBS

11 **severely,** strictly, under strict regulations, rigorously, harshly; stubbornly, obstinately, sternly, rigidly, firmly, inflexibly, stringently, uncharitably; exactingly, pedantically, formally, fundamentally, fastidiously, meticulously; uncompromisingly, without compromise, unsparingly, relentlessly, unrelentingly, intolerantly, callously, hardheartedly; inhumanely, cruelly, toughly, unyieldingly, mercilessly, brutally; high-handedly, in a high-handed manner, arbitrarily; heavy-handedly, with a heavy hand, with an iron hand, oppressively, repressively, dictatorially, autocratically, tyrannically

12 **plainly,** simply, without adornment, austerely, ascetically; prudishly, puritanically

425 Command

Whoe'er she be, / That not impossible she / That shall command my heart and me. — RICHARD CRASHAW

NOUNS

1 **command,** commandment, order, direct order; instruction, direction, ruling, rule, regulation, directive, word, sign, signal; law, act, enactment, legislation, manifesto, prescription, precept, charge, behest, dictate, ordinance, edict, fiat; canon, bull, encyclical, papal decree; decree, ukase, prescript; order of the day, marching orders; statement, pronouncement, proclamation, declaration, dictum, royal command; negative command, prohibition, proscription, countermand, interdict, veto, ban, embargo

▶ *Government 49; Information 170; Sign 183; Affirmation 189; Compulsion 428; Prohibition 503*

2 **demand,** claim, requisition, warning notice; final warning, final demand, ultimatum, legal order, tax demand, levy; warrant, bench warrant, warrant of arrest, search warrant, mittimus [Form]; writ, process, summons, writ of summons, subpoena, citation, habeas corpus, injunction, interdict *or* interdiction; bidding, beck, call, beck and call; threat, extortion, blackmail

▶ *Litigation 54; Request 505*

3 **authority,** rule, control; government; power, sway, mastery; sovereignty, suzerainty, dominion, domina-

tion; self-assurance, self-confidence, presence, look of power

▶ *Authority 52*

4 **authorization,** commission, charge; written authority, permit, letters patent [Form], patronage, appointment; mandate, electoral mandate

▶ *Authority 52; Selection 382; Permission 502; Commission 833*

5 **person in command,** chief executive, chief executive officer (CEO); head of state, president, prime minister, premier, chancellor; judge, policeman, jailer; commander, commander in chief, commanding officer (CO), commandant, general, admiral

▶ *Government 49; Law 53; Military Affairs 58*

6 **overview,** survey, ballpark view, summary, the big picture; vantage point, observation post, watchtower, crow's nest, bridge, cockpit

ADJECTIVES

7 **commanding,** ordering, imperative, directive, compelling; ruling, regulatory, enacted, legislative, prescriptive; encyclical, papal, pontifical; authoritative, governmental, mandatory, obligatory, compulsory, dictatorial; prohibitive, proscriptive, injunctive; countermanded, interdicted, vetoed, banned, embargoed

8 **authoritative,** controlling, domineering; superior, lordly; powerful, autocratic, imperious, high-handed, bossy; self-assured, self-confident

9 **authorized,** commissioned, appointed, mandated, commanded

VERBS

10 **command,** order, give an order, issue a command, direct, instruct, rule, regulate, signal; enact, legislate, make law, lay down the law, issue a manifesto, promulgate, prescribe; give a direction, give a mandate, charge, call upon, dictate, decree; sign a decree, pass a decree, issue an edict, issue a statement; pronounce, pontificate, proclaim, declare, say so, invite; prohibit, proscribe, countermand, interdict, veto, ban, impose a ban, embargo, impose an embargo

▶ *Government 49; Prohibition 503*

11 **demand,** make demands, ask for, call for, insist on; lay upon, require, impose, make obligatory; claim, make claims upon, requisition; warn, issue a warning, give final notice, present with an ultimatum, take a strong line, put one's foot down; demand payment, levy, exact; warrant, issue a warrant, subpoena, issue an injunction, interdict; threaten, extort, blackmail

12 **have authority over,** have power *or* sway *or* rule over, rule, govern, control; compel, impose, dominate, dictate to; judge, pass judgment, give a ruling; show authority, have the look of power; call the signals, call the shots [Inf]

13 **be available to one,** have at one's command, have at one's disposal, have at one's beck and call

14 authorize, commission, charge; permit; appoint; mandate

ADVERBS

15 commandingly, by command, at the word of command; by order, as ordered, as required, imperatively, compellingly, prescriptively, to order; authoritatively, governmentally, obligatorily, dictatorially; prohibitively, proscriptively; self-assuredly, self-confidently, with confidence; domineeringly, superiorly, powerfully, autocratically, imperiously, high-handedly

426 Obedience

Go tell the Spartans, thou who passest by, / That here, obedient to their laws, we lie. — SIMONIDES

NOUNS

1 obedience, compliance, complaisance, acquiescence, deference, obsequiousness; dutifulness, duty, abiding by the law, goodness, observance, conformity, willingness, readiness; nonresistance, meekness, submissiveness, submission; passivity, passiveness, yielding, docility, subservience, servility, slavishness; tractability, pliancy, malleability, softness, tameness; inactivity
  ◗ *Peace 73; Pacification 74; Willingness 373; Servility 401; Inactivity 415; Submission 421; Duty 433; Observance 465; Softness 543; Conformity 781*

2 loyalty, fidelity, fealty, allegiance, devotion, service, faithfulness, good faith, good behavior; constancy, comity, steadfastness, staunchness

3 obeisance, homage, worship, reverence, kneeling, humility; respect, courtesy, bow, curtsy, genuflection, salaam; prostration, groveling, kowtow
  ◗ *Worship 83; Servility 401; Courtesy 410*

ADJECTIVES

4 obedient, compliant, complying, complaisant, acquiescent, deferential, obsequious; dutiful, duteous, conforming, law-abiding, observant, good; willing, ready, nonresisting, unresisting, meek, sheeplike, submitting, submissive, passive, yielding, docile, resigned; disciplined, well-behaved, well-trained, biddable, under control; at one's beck and call, at one's command, at one's pleasure, at one's disposal; subservient, servile, slavish; tractable, amenable, pliant, inactive, manageable, malleable, soft, tame; trained, regimented; under one's thumb, like putty in one's hands, like a puppet on a string, on a leash *or* lead
  ◗ *Willingness 373; Submission 421; Conformity 781*

5 loyal, faithful, devoted, devoted to, dedicated to, sworn to; constant, steadfast, staunch, true, sycophantic, true-blue

6 obeisant, offering homage, worshiping, reverential; kneeling, humble, respectful, courteous

VERBS

7 obey, comply, comply with, acquiesce, consent, assent, defer, defer to, yield to; do one's duty, show good faith, behave well, show devotion to, abide by the law, keep the law, observe the rules, follow the book, conform, not resist; obey orders, take orders, follow orders, follow like sheep, wait for the command, do as one is told, do the will of; carry out orders, discharge, perform, heed, mind, come to heel, toe the line, stay in line, submit, yield; bear allegiance, give allegiance to, go along with, follow the party line; serve, do service, put oneself at someone's service, do someone's bidding, come at someone's call, wait upon, minister to, follow to the ends of the earth
  ◗ *Duty 433; Observance 465; Conformity 781*

8 show obeisance to, pay homage, offer homage, keep the faith, worship; kneel, show humility; show respect, pay tribute, show courtesy, bow, curtsy, bend, stoop, genuflect, salaam; prostrate oneself, grovel, scrape, kowtow
  ◗ *Servility 401; Courtesy 410*

ADVERBS

9 obediently, in obedience to, compliantly, in compliance with; under orders, to order, as ordered; complaisantly, acquiescently, deferentially, obsequiously; dutifully, conformingly, in conformity with, observantly; willingly, readily, unresistingly, meekly, submissively, passively, docilely; subserviently, servilely, slavishly, tractably, pliantly, inactively, softly, tamely; loyally, faithfully, devotedly; steadfastly, staunchly, constantly; reverentially, respectfully, courteously

427 Disobedience

Why do you have to be a nonconformist like everybody else? — JAMES THURBER

NOUNS

1 disobedience, noncompliance, noncooperation, uncooperativeness, nonconformity, nonobservance, undutifulness, unwillingness, opposition; recalcitrance, refractoriness, obstinacy, stubbornness, intractability; obstructionism, obstreperousness, indiscipline; restlessness, restiveness, wildness, delinquency, unruliness; dissension, defiance, defiance of orders, refusal to obey orders, violation of orders; disloyalty, perfidiousness, perfidy, unfaithfulness, faithlessness; defection, desertion, absence without leave (AWOL), French leave; tergiversation, insubordination, strike, mutinousness, mutineering, mutiny; civil disobedience, passive resistance, resistance, conscientious objection, religious disobedience; immorality, wickedness, sin, sinfulness; misbehavior, mischief-making, naughtiness, orneriness

Unwillingness 375; Defiance 416; Wickedness 448; Nonobservance 466; Violence 520; Destruction 523; Agitation 684; Disorder 766; Nonconformity 782; Opposition 828

2 **violation of the law,** infraction, infringement, transgression; felony, trespass, extortion; breach of the peace, civil disturbance, disorder, riot, street riot, rioting, street fight, tumult, turmoil, gang warfare; lawlessness, lawbreaking, criminality; crime, vandalism, robbery; murder, regicide, tyrannicide, homicide

▶ *Killing 30; Immorality 432; Stealing 479*

3 **subversion,** subversiveness, underground activities, agitprop, agitation, sedition, seditiousness; conspiracy, intrigue, plot; cabal, faction, secret society; infiltration, spying, espionage, fifth columnism, fifth column; sabotage, terrorism, anarchy; treasonable activities, treason, high treason, lese majesty

▶ *Plan 387; Resistance 417*

4 **revolution,** rebellion, rebelliousness, sans-culottism, mutinousness; uprising, mutiny, revolt, coup d'état, coup, putsch; breakaway, schism, secession; sedition, insurrection, insurgence, insurgency, resistance movement, resistance; terrorism, guerrilla warfare, civil war, war

▶ *War 76; Resistance 417; Protest 507*

5 **troublemaker,** mischief-maker, naughty child, scamp, rascal, scalawag *or* scallywag, imp, little monkey; nonconformist, protestant, deviationist; radical, Jacobin; maverick, opponent, malcontent, frondeur; protester, suffragist, suffragette, demonstrator, marcher; dissident, recusant, recalcitrant, striker, picketer; agitator, agent provocateur, ringleader, rabble-rouser; [Inf]: handful, pain in the neck *or* ass; women's libber

6 **criminal,** lawbreaker, robber, mugger, bandit, thief, burglar, housebreaker, arsonist; kidnapper, extortionist; murderer, assassin, killer; rapist, sexual abuser, batterer; gang member, gangster, Mafia member, mafioso, mobster; petty criminal, brawler, rowdy, ruffian, hoodlum, hooligan, hood [Inf]

7 **seditionist,** seditionary, subversive, conspirator; traitor, collaborator, quisling, tergiversator; extremist, insurrectionist, insurgent, infiltrator, fifth columnist, anarchist; rioter, terrorist, guerrilla, urban guerrilla, partisan, saboteur

8 **rebel,** revolutionary, revolutionist, sans-culotte, revolter, mutineer, secessionist, seceder; contra, Bolshevist, Trotskyite *or* Trotskyist, Red

9 **reactionary,** counterrevolutionary, conservative, monarchist, White Russian, counterterrorist; nonstriker, strikebreaker, scab

ADJECTIVES

10 **disobedient,** noncompliant, uncomplying, noncooperative, uncooperative, nonobservant, undutiful; unwilling, opposing, recalcitrant, obstinate, stubborn, intractable, ornery; obstructive, insubordinate, ob-

streperous; undisciplined, poorly disciplined, transgressing; restless, restive; wild, out of control, unmanageable; disobeying, misbehaved, mischief-making, naughty, delinquent; disorderly, riotous, tumultuous, unruly; dissenting, defiant, recusant, disloyal, perfidious, deserting, tergiversatory; mutinous, lawless, lawbreaking, criminal; immoral, wicked, sinning

11 **subversive,** seditious, conspiratorial, factional, anarchic, anarchical; treasonable, revolutionary, rebellious, in rebellion, mutinous, insurgent, insurrectional, insurrectionary; breakaway, schismatic

VERBS

12 **disobey,** be disobedient, not listen to, pay no heed to, ignore instructions, not do as one is told; refuse to cooperate, not cooperate, not comply with, not conform; oppose, hinder, obstruct; misbehave, make mischief, get into mischief; dissent, flout authority, show insubordination, defy, refuse to obey orders, violate orders; defect, desert, go absent without leave (AWOL), take French leave, tergiversate, strike; break the law, violate the law, commit a crime; infringe, transgress, breach the peace, trespass; riot, vandalize, rob, murder; sin; snap one's fingers at, thumb one's nose at

13 **subvert,** be subversive, conspire, plot, betray, infiltrate, spy; agitate, sabotage, terrorize, create anarchy, lead a rebellion; uprise, rise in arms, mount the barricades, mutiny, revolt, stage a revolt, rebel, fight; overthrow, lead a coup, kick over the traces

ADVERBS

14 **disobediently,** contrary to orders; unwillingly; obstinately, stubbornly, intractably; insubordinately, obstreperously, restlessly, restively; wildly, naughtily, delinquently, riotously, tumultuously; dissentingly, defiantly, as a protest; disloyally, perfidiously; mutinously, lawlessly, criminally; immorally, without regard to morality, wickedly, in a wicked way

15 **subversively,** seditiously, conspiratorially; rebelliously, mutinously; schismatically

428 Compulsion

I have with me two gods, Persuasion and Compulsion.
— THEMISTOCLES

NOUNS

1 **compulsion,** compulsiveness, irresistibility, irresistible force; obsessiveness, obsessive need, obsession, preoccupation; need, urge, drive, essential, necessity; obligation, requirement, prerequisite; zero options, no choice, Hobson's choice, a must

▶ *Necessity 95; Duty 433*

2 **coercion,** pressure, order, command, mandate, forcing, force, legal force, enforcement; main force, phys-

ical force, duress; restraint, constraint; intimidation, bullying, browbeating, threat; violence, brute force

> *Command 425; Power 514; Violence 520; Restraint 830; Subjection 832*

3 **coercive method,** blackmail, extortion; bribery; carrot and stick; big stick, bludgeon, strong-arm tactics, arm-twisting, force-feeding; kidnapping, forced labor, labor camp, slavery, impressment, press gang; sanctions; conscription, call-up, draft; penalty clause, fine, jail; torture

> *War 76; Severity 424; Punishment 454; Subjection 832*

4 **coercer,** forcer, forceful person, steamroller, bulldozer, bully; briber, robber, blackmailer, extortionist; mugger, kidnapper, hijacker, gunman, terrorist, torturer

5 **compulsive person,** addict; monomaniac: compulsive eater *or* gambler *or* talker *or* liar *or* shopper; shoplifter, kleptomaniac; obsessive dieter, anorexic, bulimic; alcoholic, smoker, workaholic; megalomaniac

> *Substance Abuse 121*

ADJECTIVES

6 **compelling,** compulsive, coercive; involuntary; unavoidable, inevitable, necessary, of necessity; commanding, imperative, urgent, overriding, pressing, driving, high-pressure; oppressive, dictatorial; enforcing, binding, restraining, constraining; steamroller, steamrolling; forceful, forcible, violent, bludgeoning, strong-arm, bulldozing; irresistible, hypnotic, mesmeric; cogent, convincing; inspiring, influential, persuasive

> *Severity 424; Command 425*

7 **compulsory,** mandatory, necessary, unavoidable, ineluctable; obligatory, required, requisite, prerequisite

> *Necessity 95*

VERBS

8 **compel,** coerce, urge, oblige, make, insist on, insist, make a point of, emphasize, not take no for an answer; pressure, bring pressure to bear, put pressure on, apply pressure, bear down on, press, put under duress, squeeze; impel, drive, force someone's hand, twist one's arm; leave no choice *or* alternative, leave no option, leave no escape; pin down, tie down, bind, constrain, restrain, hold back, oppress; necessitate, require, command, demand, dictate, mandate, order; regiment, discipline, impose, impose a duty, enforce, lean on [Inf]

> *Command 425*

9 **be irresistible,** hypnotize, mesmerize; compel, convince, inspire, influence, persuade

10 **force,** intimidate, threaten; force upon, force to accept, force-feed, foist on, fob off on; take, take by force, requisition, commandeer; constrain, extort, blackmail, kidnap, hold to ransom; exact, wring from, drag from; use force against, bring legal force to bear; conscript, call up, draft, impress, dragoon; use physical force, inflict, bully, bully into, browbeat, steamroller, blud-

geon, press-gang, use violence, ram down one's throat, stampede, strong-arm, bulldoze, put the screws on, turn on the heat [Inf]

11 **be compelled,** be coerced, yield to pressure; have no choice, have no option, must, should, have to, cannot help but, cannot do otherwise, cannot be helped

ADVERBS

12 **compellingly,** compulsively, on compulsion, coercively; involuntarily, unavoidably, inevitably, willynilly, necessarily, of necessity, perforce, obligatorily; imperatively, urgently, oppressively, under pressure to, under duress, commandingly; violently, forcefully, forcibly, by force; by main force, by force of arms, at swords' points, at the point of a gun, at gunpoint, at knifepoint; irresistibly, hypnotically; cogently, convincingly, influentially, persuasively

429 Right

NOUNS

1 **rightfulness,** rightness, goodness, properness, justice; fairness, fair-mindedness, impartiality, equity, equitableness, equality; righteousness, virtuousness; uprightness, nobility, integrity, probity, truth, honesty; morality, moral fiber *or* rectitude, integrity, honor; godliness, cleanliness, purity, scrupulousness

> *Judgment 341; Morality 431; Good 445; Virtue 447*

2 **right,** correctness, accurateness, accuracy; authenticity, genuineness, validity, validness, legitimacy, trueness, veracity, verity, veritableness; absoluteness, certainty, sureness, positivity, definiteness, fixedness; exactness, exactitude, precision, preciseness; fact, factuality, actuality; unerringness, inerrancy, faultlessness, infallibility, flawlessness, perfection

> *Carefulness 325; Truth 721*

3 **claim,** right, right of, legal right, prerogative, privilege, power, authority, perquisite; title, entitlement, entitledness, appanage, divine right; due, merit, deservedness, desert; holding, possession, ownership, equity, interest, portion, concern; financial right *or* rights, share, part, stake

> *Law 53; Litigation 54; Title 72*

4 **rights,** birthright, inalienable rights, legal rights, civil rights, human rights, women's rights, children's rights, gay rights, animal rights; right to vote, right to representation, equal rights, reproductive rights, right to life, right to die, right to know, right to work; constitutional rights, rights of man, Bill of Rights, Constitution, Magna Carta

> *Freedom 829; Liberation 831*

5 **properness,** correctness, correctitude, decency, decorum, propriety, seemliness; etiquette, fittingness, fitness, appropriateness, suitability, what is right; what is done

◗ *Morality 431; Good 445; Refinement 534*

6 righting wrong, setting to rights, reform, reformation, rectification, regeneration, transformation; improvement, correction, revision, revisal, repair, revampment

◗ *Change 665; Improvement 807; Repair 809*

ADJECTIVES

7 right, good, proper, just; fair, impartial, equitable, equal; righteous, virtuous; upright, upstanding, noble, sterling, truthful, honest, straight; moral, moralistic, ethical, high-principled, honorable; godly, clean, pure, scrupulous

◗ *Religion 81; Judgment 341; Morality 431*

8 correct, accurate, unerring, infallible; authentic, genuine, valid, legitimate, true, veracious; absolute, certain, sure, provable, positive, definite, fixed; straightforward, exact, precise, dead, dead-right; factual, actual, inerrant, flawless, faultless, perfect, just right; [Inf]: dead-on, right-on, bang on [Brit]

◗ *Carefulness 325; Truth 721*

9 rightful, legitimate, lawful, legal, licit, qualified, worthy; entitled, privileged, empowered, authorized; deserved, fit, due, condign, warranted, justified, just; inviolable, inalienable, admitted, permitted, allowed, sanctioned

◗ *Permission 502*

10 proper, correct, decent, decorous, seemly; fitting, appropriate, apt, suitable; ethical, principled; as it should be, all right, fine, well, balanced, OK, up to par, according to Hoyle, *comme il faut* [Fr]

◗ *Health 113; Virtue 447*

11 in the right, rightful, fair, equitable; justified, justifiable, supportable, well-founded, well-grounded; excusable, forgivable, defensible, unimpeachable, unchallengeable; right-minded, decent, law-abiding, sporting, sportsmanlike, on the side of the angels, squeaky-clean [Inf], straight-arrow [Inf]

VERBS

12 be right, be in the right, have right on one's side, have grounds for, be correct; be fair, see justice done, play fair, do the right thing, play the game, hear both sides, judge fairly, arbitrate, give the devil his due

◗ *Judgment 341*

13 have rights, have the right, claim, lay claim to, have a rightful claim to, be within one's rights, be justified, be entitled to; deserve, merit, be qualified for, be worthy of; warrant, justify, have coming; exercise one's rights *or* prerogative, stake a claim, demand one's rights, stand up for one's rights, insist on one's rights; have equity *or* interest *or* a stake in

14 put right, right, put *or* set right, set to rights, square, make good *or* right; correct, redress, rectify, mend, emend, amend, reform, right a wrong; compensate, renumerate, requite, restitute, recompense, make reparation, pay reparations, give satisfaction; remedy,

fix, repair, cure, heal; sort out, straighten out, bring into line

ADVERBS

15 right, rightly, rightfully, properly, justly, deservedly; fairly, squarely, impartially, equitably, equally; in fairness, without bias, without distinction, without fear *or* favor; righteously, uprightly, nobly, truthfully, honestly, morally, honorably

16 correctly, accurately, aright; authentically, genuinely, validly, legitimately, truly; absolutely, certainly, assuredly, positively, definitely, decidedly; exactly, precisely, factually, unerringly, infallibly, flawlessly, perfectly, on the nose [Inf], on the button [Inf]

17 by rights, within one's rights, in the right

18 properly, fittingly, as is fitting, as is befitting, appropriately, aptly, befittingly, satisfactorily, suitably, duly

19 all right, advantageously, favorably, well

20 right away, right off, straightaway, straight, directly, immediately, instantly, instantaneously, forthwith, at once, anon [Arch]; completely, quite, all the way

430 Wrong

A child becomes an adult when he realizes that he has a right not only to be right but also to be wrong.
— THOMAS SZASZ

NOUNS

1 wrong, wrongfulness, badness, evil, evilness, wickedness, iniquity, immorality, unrighteousness; unfairness, injustice, inequity, discrimination, bias, unevenness, partiality, prejudice, partisanship

◗ *Discrimination 337; Misjudgment 342; Immorality 432; Evil 446; Wickedness 448*

2 fault, complaint, grievance, injury, injustice, tort, foul play; [Inf]: raw deal, grouse, gripe

3 incorrectness, mistake, falseness, error, wrong, imprecision, impreciseness, inexactitude; untruthfulness, inaccuracy, fallaciousness, erroneousness, unsoundness, invalidity, mistakenness, misinformation

◗ *Error 351; Untruth 722*

4 abnormality, irregularity, oddity, oddness, queerness, aberrance, aberration, deviation, perversion

◗ *Irregularity 664; Nonconformity 782*

5 impropriety, unseemliness, indecorum, indecorousness, vulgarity, vulgarness, bad taste; inappropriateness, inaptness, incongruity, misstep, bad move, wrong turn; dishonor, disgrace, scandal; shame, crying shame, slur, stain, stigma, blot

◗ *Tastelessness 220; Evil 446; Vulgarity 535*

6 unlawfulness, lawlessness, illegality, illegitimacy, illicitness, delinquency, criminality, foul play

7 wrongdoing, wrong, sin, vice, guilty act, bad deed, evil deed, misdeed; abomination, crime, offense, misdoing, malfeasance, trespass, transgression, infraction, infringement, violation; injury, harm, hurt, abuse, mischief

> *Error 351; Conduct 399; Wickedness 448*

8 **wrongdoer,** sinner, offender, culprit, criminal, felon, lawbreaker, delinquent, juvenile delinquent, trespasser, transgressor, infractor, miscreant, villain, malefactor, crook

> *Immorality 432; Evil 446; Wickedness 448*

9 **failure,** breakdown, collapse, wreck, defect, malfunction, dysfunction; nonsuccess, downfall, frustration, breakup, debacle, washout [Inf]

ADJECTIVES

10 **wrongful,** bad, evil, wicked, iniquitous, reprehensible, immoral, unrighteous; unfair, unjust, inequitable, discriminatory, biased, uneven, unbalanced, weighted, one-sided, leaning to one side, favoring, partial, prejudiced, partisan; unsportsmanlike; below the belt, not cricket, out of line, not playing the game [Inf]

> *Misjudgment 342*

11 **immoral,** amoral, corrupt, vicious, abominable; unprincipled, unethical, dishonest, dishonorable; disgraceful, shameful, shamefaced, shameless, scandalous, infamous; in the wrong, guilty, at fault, blameworthy, to be blamed, sinful, culpable

> *Immorality 432*

12 **wrong,** dead-wrong, mistaken, misinformed, incorrect, imprecise, not right, false; untrue, untruthful, inaccurate, fallacious, erroneous, unsound, invalid; at fault, off course, off target, wide of the mark; off the beam [Inf], off-base [Inf]

> *Error 351; Untruth 722*

13 **abnormal,** irregular, odd, queer, aberrant, perverted, deviant, unsound, unhinged, wrong in the head

> *Insanity 110; Irregularity 664; Nonconformity 782*

14 **improper,** unseemly, indecorous, vulgar, tasteless, off-color; unsuitable, unfit, unfitting, unbefitting, inappropriate, inapt, incongruous; all wrong, not done

> *Tastelessness 220*

15 **unlawful,** lawless, illegal, illegitimate, illicit, delinquent, criminal, crooked, felonious, malfeasant; transgressive, infringing, violative, offensive, abusive, injurious, hurtful, harmful, mischievous

> *Guilt 450*

16 **unforgivable,** unpardonable, unjustifiable, unexculpable, inexcusable; uncondonable, irremissible, unexpiable, unatonable; blameworthy, reprehensible, deplorable, contemptible, despicable, objectionable, condemnable, censurable

17 **gone wrong,** failed, not working, broken, broken down; out of commission, out of order, in need of repair, on the blink; defective, malfunctioning, awry, askew; [Inf]: conked out, kaput, buggered up [Brit]

> *Failure 846*

VERBS

18 **be wrong,** make a mistake, give the wrong answer,

err; mistake, confuse, confound; blunder, flounder, stumble, slip, slip up, mess up; miscalculate, misjudge, misreckon, miscount; fail, miss, miscarry, miss the mark; botch *or* botch up, make a bloomer, flub; [Inf]: screw up, goof *or* goof up, blow

> *Error 351*

19 **wrong,** hurt, harm, injure, abuse, misuse, ill-use; maltreat, mistreat, ill-treat, aggrieve; oppress, persecute; exploit, use, take advantage of, walk all over, impose upon; cheat, defraud, shaft [Inf]; offend, desecrate, profane, defile, malign, defame, dishonor, slur; denigrate, belittle, disparage, minimize, insult, mock, scorn, ridicule

> *Disparagement 440*

20 **do wrong,** break the law, commit a crime, commit an offense, offend, trespass, transgress, infringe, violate, cheat, not play by *or* break the rules, commit a foul, hit below the belt, not play the game [Inf]

21 **discriminate,** discriminate against, be biased, show partiality, show favoritism, favor, lean toward, lean to one side; prejudge, presuppose, presume

> *Misjudgment 342*

22 **sin,** sin against, fall from grace, err, fault, lapse, trip; misbehave, go astray, stray from the straight and narrow, go to the bad; go to hell, go to hell in a handbasket, go to the dogs [Inf]

> *Religion 81; Error 351; Immorality 432*

23 **go wrong,** fail, break, break down, go out of commission, be out of order, go on the blink, need repair; malfunction, go awry, go askew; [Inf]: conk out, go kaput

ADVERBS

24 **wrongly,** badly, wickedly, iniquitously, immorally, unrighteously, unfairly, unjustly, inequitably, indiscriminately, unevenly, one-sidedly, with prejudice

25 **wrongfully,** mistakenly, incorrectly, imprecisely, falsely; untruthfully, inaccurately, erroneously, unsoundly, invalidly; confusedly, confoundedly

26 **improperly,** unsuitably, inappropriately, indecorously, vulgarly; disgracefully, scandalously, shamefully, shamedly, infamously

27 **immorally,** viciously, unethically, dishonestly, dishonorably; sinfully, wickedly, unlawfully, illicitly

431 Morality

NOUNS

1 **morality,** goodness, rectitude, moral fiber, moral strength, moral tone; moral behavior *or* conduct, ethics, ethicality, ethicalness, scruples, good conscience; ethos, moral climate, moral standards

2 **morals,** ethics, principles, values, standards, ideals, customs, rules, mores, manners; goodness, integrity, honesty, propriety, probity, decency, virtue, honor, character, respectability, nobility, responsibility; cor-

rectness, rectitude, uprightness, righteousness, right, sense of right and wrong, conscience, voice of conscience; equity, justice, justness, fairness, fair play, scrupulousness; faithfulness, good faith, fidelity, trustworthiness, constancy, loyalty

▶ *Habit, Custom 397; Right 429; Virtue 447; Refinement 534*

3 **chastity,** innocence, modesty; continence, abstinence, nonindulgence, self-restraint, self-control, reserve, self-discipline, temperance, moderation

▶ *Celibacy 67; Virtue 447*

4 **purity,** wholesomeness, freshness, faultlessness, perfection, sinlessness; cleanliness, refinement, unsulliedness, unaffectedness, unadulteratedness

5 **moral,** lesson, teaching, message, point, precept, homily, maxim, apothegm *or* apophthegm, adage, proverb, saying, saw, epigram, motto

▶ *Advice 176; Maxim 177*

6 **chaste person,** pure person, virgin, maiden, vestal, vestal virgin, virgo intacta; celibate, monk, nun, saint; Encratite, Sir Galahad, the Virgin Mary

▶ *Celibacy 67; Virtue 447*

7 **self-righteousness,** narrow-mindedness, mealy-mouthedness, prudery, prudishness; Grundyism, priggishness, primness, smugness, snobbery, sanctimony, sanctimoniousness, Tartuffery; pietism, puritanism, gravity, graveness, seriousness, sternness; censorship, expurgation, bowdlerization, expunction; shockability, squeamishness, overmodesty, false modesty, false shame, *mauvaise honte* [Fr], nice-nellyism

▶ *Affectation 367; Severity 424*

8 **moralist,** puritan, Victorian, prig, prude, Mrs. Grundy, wowser [Aus *and* NZ inf]; prohibitionist, teetotaler, Carry Nation; watchdog, censor, guardian of morality, fundamentalist, Bible-thumper [Inf]

ADJECTIVES

9 **moral,** ethical, strong, well-behaved, principled, value-laden, mannered, high-minded; good, honest, decent, virtuous, honorable, respectable, noble, responsible; correct, upright, righteous, right, right-minded, proper, conscionable, of good conscience; equitable, just, fair, scrupulous; faithful, trustworthy, constant, loyal; spiritual, pious, saintly

10 **chaste,** innocent, modest, blushing; continent, abstinent, abstemious, platonic, nonindulgent, self-restrained, self-controlled, reserved, self-disciplined, temperate, moderate, refraining, forbearing, desisting; unfallen, virgin, virginal, maidenly *or* maidenish, vestal; celibate, sexless

11 **pure,** wholesome, fresh, faultless, perfect, sinless; spotless, clean, pristine, immaculate, unsoiled, unsullied; untouched, unused, undefiled, uncorrupted, unaffected, unadulterated; purified, refined, sublimated; snowy, white, pure as the driven snow

12 **moralistic,** moralizing, self-righteous, narrow-minded, mealy-mouthed, prude, prudish; priggish, prim, old-maidish, holier-than-thou, smug, snobbish, sanctimonious; pious, grave, serious, severe, stern, censorious; censored, expurgated, bowdlerized, expunged; shockable, squeamish, overmodest, falsely modest, nice-nellyish; puritan, Victorian, strait-laced

VERBS

13 **be moral,** be good, do no wrong, fight the good fight, follow *or* keep to the straight and narrow, obey the law; abstain, wait, forgo sex, practice abstinence, be celibate, remain a virgin, be pure

▶ *Good 445; Virtue 447*

14 **moralize,** sermonize, preach, pontificate, homilize, evangelize; harangue, hold forth, go on about, point a moral, have a moral attitude; lecture, explain, teach, instruct, enlighten, inculcate; censor, expurgate, bowdlerize, expunge

ADVERBS

15 **morally,** ethically, in good conscience, with integrity, honestly, decently, virtuously, honorably, respectably, nobly, responsibly; correctly, with moral rectitude, uprightly, righteously, rightly, lawfully; equitably, justly, fairly, scrupulously; faithfully, with constancy, loyally; spiritually, piously, chastely, purely

16 **moralistically,** self-righteously, narrow-mindedly, prohibitively; prudishly, priggishly, primly, smugly, sanctimoniously; gravely, seriously, severely, sternly, censoriously, squeamishly, modestly, puritanically

432 Immorality

NOUNS

1 **immorality,** moral badness, bad morals, moral delinquency, moral turpitude, decadence; amorality, amoralism, no morals, lack of morals, unmorality, lack of principles, unethicalness, unscrupulousness, moral abandonment; badness, evilness, wickedness, dissoluteness, profligacy, dissipation; indecency, defilement, uncleanness, vulgarity, nastiness, naughtiness, ribaldry, raunchiness, bawdiness, bawdry [Arch]; vice, fault, frailty, shortcoming, moral weakness, wrongdoing, delinquency, crime, criminality, dishonesty; baseness, vileness, filthiness, filth, dirt, smut, corruption, moral corruption; graft, greed, avarice, avidity, cupidity

▶ *Untruthfulness, Falsehood 192; Deception 193; Error 351; Wrong 430; Disrespect 436; Evil 446; Wickedness 448; Guilt 450; Impenitence 452; Stealing 479; Untruth 722*

2 **sexual immorality,** promiscuity, unchastity, easy virtue, laxity, shamelessness, immodesty, wantonness, loose *or* weak morals, morals of an alley cat; impure thoughts, roving eye, incontinence, libido, lust, lustfulness, prurience, pruriency, concupiscence, lecherousness, lechery; lasciviousness, lewdness, lubricity,

obscenity, salaciousness, salacity, lickerishness [Arch]; carnality, fleshliness, degeneracy, sexual deviance, debauchery, depravity, sexual license, libertinism *or* libertinage, venery [Arch]; seduction, defloration, womanizing; satyriasis, Don Juanism, nymphomania, priapism

▶ *Physical Pleasure 214; Vanity 402; Self-Indulgence 456*

3 **fornication,** liaison, illicit love, intrigue, amour, concubinage; forbidden love *or* fruit, guilty love, unlawful desires, unlawful carnal knowledge, irregular union, ménage à trois; adultery, criminal conversation, infidelity, extramarital relations, unfaithfulness, bed-hopping, running around, fooling around; cuckoldry, cuckolding; permissive society, free love, wife swapping, sexual delinquency; [Inf]: cheating, sleeping around, screwing around, fucking around, letching *or* leching

▶ *Marriage 64; Love 299; Disobedience 427*

4 **prostitution,** harlotry, soliciting, importuning, whoredom, whorishness; streetwalking, harlot's trade, oldest profession, Mrs. Warren's profession; living on immoral earnings, brothel keeping, white slave trade *or* traffic; whoremongering *or* whoremastery, pimping, pandering, procuring; whoring, wenching [Arch]

5 **brothel,** bordello, bagnio, whorehouse, bawdyhouse, house of ill repute *or* ill fame *or* assignation, sporting house, massage parlor, crib, juke house, cathouse [Inf]; red-light district, street of fallen women

6 **sexual offense,** offensive *or* lewd talk, filthy mouth *or* language *or* talk; dirty joke *or* story, blue joke, smoking-room story, double entendre; sexual assault, sexual perversion, sexual deviancy, incest, sodomy, bestiality, sadism, sadomasochism *or* S and M; sexual abuse, pederasty, indecent assault, rape, ravishment, violation, gang rape, date rape, gross indecency, indecent exposure, exposing oneself; [Inf]: gangbang, flashing, mooning, buggery

▶ *Sex 20; War 76; Hate 300; Attack 418*

7 **pornography,** soft-core pornography, hard-core pornography, child pornography; sexploitation [Inf]; X-rated movie *or* film, blue movie, stag movie, peep show, dirty magazine, dirty pictures; erotica, eroticism, erotism, voyeurism; voyeur, pornographer, pornographic model, stripper, male stripper, exotic dancer, ecdysiast, topless performer *or* dancer; striptease *or* strip club, topless bar; [Inf]: porn, soft porn, hard porn, child porn, porn *or* skin flick, snuff film, porn house, porn hall; porno star, porn queen

8 **sexually immoral person,** sex offender *or* fiend *or* criminal; rapist, sadist, child abuser *or* molester, pedophile, pederast; catamite, pervert, male prostitute, pornographer; adulterer, rake, rakehell, libertine, lecher, degenerate, debauchee, roué, satyr, womanizer, philanderer, playboy, gigolo, Cyprian, Casanova, Don Juan; fallen woman, adulteress, loose woman, scarlet woman, hussy, slut, nymphet, nymphomaniac; cour-

tesan, concubine, kept woman, prostitute, whore, harlot, strumpet, streetwalker, call girl, quean; madam, whoremonger *or* whoremaster, pimp, pander; [Inf]: hooker, tart, roundheels, nympho, chippy, floozy; flasher, hustler; dirty old man, rent boy [Brit]

ADJECTIVES

9 **immoral,** decadent, amoral, morally bad, lacking in morals, unmoral, unprincipled, unethical, unscrupulous; bad, wicked, evil, licentious, dissolute, profligate, dissipated; indecent, defiling, defiled, unclean, scrofulous; faulted, frail, wrong, morally wrong, delinquent, criminal, illegal, dishonest; base, vile, filthy, dirty, smutty, stinking, rank, corrupt, morally corrupt

10 **unchaste,** promiscuous, wild, rakish, easy, unvirtuous, lax, shameless, immodest, unblushing; impure, incontinent, libidinous, lustful, prurient, concupiscent, lecherous, lascivious, randy, goatish; lewd, lubricious, salacious, wanton, loose, ruttish, lickerish [Arch]; carnal, fleshly, degenerate, debauched, depraved, libertine, licentious; seduced, deflowered, fallen, adulterous, unfaithful; prostituted, scarlet, whorish, meretricious, whoremongering; [Inf]: horny, turned-on, round-heeled, tarty

11 **offensive,** obscene, scabrous, pornographic, shocking, uncensored, unexpurgated, unmentionable, unquotable, unprintable; provocative, risqué, racy, suggestive, titillating, arousing, voluptuous, erotic, naughty, blue, coarse, vulgar, nasty, naughty, ribald, raunchy, bawdy, strong

12 **perverted,** abnormal, deviant, incestuous, sadistic, sadomasochistic, bestial, animalistic; nymphomaniac, priapic, kinky [Inf]

VERBS

13 **be immoral,** have no morals, err, sin, do wrong; go wrong, stray, go astray, fall, fall from grace, lapse; sink, degenerate, go to the bad, go to rack and ruin, go to pot, go to the dogs [Inf]

14 **fornicate,** have a liaison, commit adultery, be unfaithful, cuckold, philander; womanize, bed-hop, run around, fool around; [Inf]: cheat, sleep around, screw around, fuck around, letch *or* lech

15 **demoralize,** debase, defile, humiliate, smirch, sully, soil; debauch, deprave, vitiate, pervert, corrupt; lead astray, ruin, wreck, disgrace, shame, dishonor; offend, shock

16 **seduce,** take advantage of, have one's way with, take one's pleasure with, deflower; ravish, rape, force, violate, sexually assault, indecently assault, abuse, sexually abuse, interfere with [Brit]

17 **prostitute,** solicit, importune, whore, streetwalk, live on immoral earnings, pimp, pander, procure; hook [Inf], hustle [Inf]

ADVERBS

18 **immorally,** without morals, amorally, unmorally, unethically, unscrupulously, badly, evilly, wickedly, sin-

fully, dissolutely, dissipatedly; indecently, vulgarly, nastily, naughtily, raunchily, bawdily; wrongly, delinquently, criminally, dishonestly, corruptly, greedily, with avarice

19 **promiscuously,** shamelessly, immodestly, wantonly; adulterously, suggestively, impurely, libidinously, lustfully, pruriently, lecherously, lasciviously, lewdly, obscenely, salaciously; carnally, degeneratively; deviantly, debauchedly

433 Duty

Stern daughter of the voice of God!
— WILLIAM WORDSWORTH

NOUNS

1 **duty,** obligation, moral obligation, legal obligation, moral imperative, legal imperative; one's duty, the right thing, the proper thing, bounden duty, devoir; contract, tie, bond, covenant, assurance, understanding, gentleman's agreement; commitment, promise, pledge, vow, oath, word, word of honor
  ▶ *Promise 458; Contract 459*

2 **sense of duty,** duteousness, devotion *or* dedication to duty; moral sense, conscience, claims of conscience, inner voice; code of duty *or* honor, unwritten code; responsibility, liability, incumbency, accountability, amenability, answerability
  ▶ *Maxim 177; Willingness 373; Morality 431; Rule 780*

3 **line of duty,** trust, care, charge, shift, watch; task, chore, job, function, work, service, office, station, place, calling; engagement, commission, mission, assignment; province, affair, concern, occupation, business, profession, line of work
  ▶ *Work 122*

4 **deference,** loyalty, fealty, faithfulness; homage, devotion, dedication, allegiance, respect, reverence, rite; willingness, obedience, compliance, comity, submission, docility
  ▶ *Religious Ritual 85; Submission 421; Obedience 426; Respect 435*

5 **payment,** tax, levy, tariff, charge, excise, customs, impost, dues, fee, toll, rate

ADJECTIVES

6 **dutiful,** obligatory, morally right, legally right; right, proper; contracted, engaged, tied, bound, beholden; committed, promised, pledged, sworn

7 **duteous,** moral, conscientious, scrupulous, punctilious; responsible, liable, incumbent, accountable, amenable, answerable
  ▶ *Willingness 373; Morality 431; Good 445; Virtue 447*

8 **duty-bound,** entrusted, charged, obliged, obligated; engaged, commissioned, assigned, saddled; mandatory, compulsory, de rigueur, binding; incumbent on,

inescapable, unavoidable, unconditional, categorical, peremptory, imperative
  ▶ *Compulsion 428*

9 **deferential,** loyal, faithful; dedicated, respectful, reverent, reverential; willing, obedient, compliant, submissive, docile, tractable
  ▶ *Submission 421; Obedience 426; Respect 435*

10 **on-duty,** engaged, occupied, on the job, busy, at work, tied up, on call

11 **off-duty,** at liberty, unoccupied, off work, off, on vacation

VERBS

12 **be dutiful,** fulfill an obligation, do one's duty, do the right *or* proper thing; fulfill a contract, keep a covenant, offer assurance *or* understanding, keep to an agreement, fulfill a commitment *or* promise, keep a pledge *or* vow *or* oath, keep one's word

13 **have a sense of duty,** be duteous, have a moral sense *or* conscience, fulfill a code of duty *or* honor; be responsible, be liable (for), be incumbent upon, be accountable, account for, be answerable, answer for

14 **impose a duty,** entrust, charge, oblige, put under an obligation, obligate; engage, commission, assign, saddle, contract, tie, bind, commit, promise, pledge; make mandatory, make compulsory, require, order, command, decree, call upon, enjoin, expect, expect it of, look to; tax, levy
  ▶ *Command 425*

15 **incur a duty,** make it one's duty, incur a responsibility, take on the responsibility, accept the responsibility, take upon one's shoulders, make oneself liable; be entrusted, be charged, take on a job, accept an office, answer the call; become engaged, engage oneself, pledge oneself, commit oneself, accept a commission *or* appointment, accept an assignment; take on a concern

16 **be the duty of,** fall to, fall to the lot of, rest with, rest on the shoulders of, devolve upon, belong to, lie at the door of, be up to; behoove, become, befit, must, should, ought to, had better, had best
  ▶ *Compulsion 428*

17 **do one's duty,** discharge one's duty, carry out *or* perform *or* fulfill one's duty, do what one has to do, shoulder one's responsibilities; obey, acquit, do the needful, do what is necessary, do what is expected, do one's bit, act *or* play one's part, stay at one's post, go down with one's ship
  ▶ *Obedience 426*

18 **pay duty on,** declare, be taxed

ADVERBS

19 **dutifully,** duteously, with a sense of duty, morally, legally, rightly, properly, ethically; responsibly, conscientiously, accountably, professionally, in the line of duty; loyally, devotedly, honorably, respectfully

434 Exemption

NOUNS

1 **exemption,** immunity, impunity, nonliability; non-responsibility, dispensation, special treatment, privilege; exception, exclusion, diplomatic immunity
   ◗ *Exclusion 764*

2 **acquittal,** absolution, pardon, exoneration, excuse; discharge, release, liberation; freedom, liberty, independence
   ◗ *Forgiveness 312; Freedom 829; Liberation 831*

3 **self-exemption,** escapism, evasion of responsibility, dereliction of duty, passing of the buck, washing of one's hands

4 **license,** permission, permit; certificate of exemption, charter, franchise, patent, privilege; leave, compassionate leave, leave of absence
   ◗ *Permission 502*

ADJECTIVES

5 **exempt,** exempted, immune, not subject to, nonliable, not liable; not responsible, unaccountable, not accountable, unanswerable, not answerable; dispensed, privileged, excepted, excluded, shielded, protected, unpunishable
   ◗ *Exclusion 764; Safety 810*

6 **acquitted,** absolved, pardoned, exonerated, excused, let off; spared, clear, free, freed from blame; discharged, released, liberated, off the hook

7 **independent,** free, unrestricted, unbound, unconstrained, uncontrolled

8 **tax-free,** tax-exempt, duty-free, franked

VERBS

9 **exempt,** exclude, except, frank, leave out, set apart; dispense, privilege, grant immunity *or* impunity

10 **acquit,** exonerate, exculpate, absolve, grant absolution, pardon, excuse, let off, let off scot-free, spare; show mercy, forgive, grant amnesty to; dismiss, discharge, release, liberate, free, set free, set at liberty, let go
   ◗ *Forgiveness 312; Liberation 831*

11 **be exempt,** have no liability, have no responsibility, have immunity, have diplomatic immunity

12 **exempt oneself,** excuse oneself, go on leave, take compassionate leave; escape, evade one's responsibilities, fail in one's duty, admit no responsibility, evade liability; shift *or* transfer responsibility, shift the blame, pass the buck, shrug off, wash one's hands of; get off scot-free, get away with, get away with murder [Inf]

ADVERBS

13 **with impunity,** freely, tax-free, duty-free

435 Respect

We owe respect to the living; to the dead we owe only truth.
— VOLTAIRE

NOUNS

1 **respect,** regard, esteem; consideration, attention; honor, favor, approbation, approval, appreciation; repute, recognition, good opinion, high opinion; high standing, prestige, authority
   ◗ *Authority 52; Approval 437*

2 **admiration,** adoration, adulation; worship, hero-worship, idolization, veneration, awe; reverence, homage, fealty, obeisance; great respect, high regard
   ◗ *Worship 83; Wonder 294*

3 **respectfulness,** due respect, deference; humbleness, humility, devotion, loyalty; courtesy, comity, polite regard, attentions
   ◗ *Humility 298; Courtesy 410; Obedience 426*

4 **mark of respect,** show of respect, salute, nod, inclination; bend, bending, bow, bowing and scraping, stooping, curtsy, bob, bending the knee, genuflection, kneeling; prostration, kissing the hem, salaam, kowtow, obeisance; presenting arms, standing at *or* to attention, dipping the colors; guard of honor, parade of honor, red carpet, ticker-tape parade *or* reception
   ◗ *Obedience 426*

5 **greeting,** welcome, salutation, salute, obeisance; respects, regards, kind regards, kindest regards; greetings, salutations; compliments, devoirs, good wishes, best wishes
   ◗ *Courtesy 410*

ADJECTIVES

6 **respectful,** regardful, considerate, attentive, honorific, ceremonious, appreciative

7 **showing respect,** deferential, courteous, polite, gracious; standing, on one's feet, upstanding, rising; kneeling, on bended knee, on one's knees; prostrate, saluting, cap in hand, bareheaded; nodding, bending, bowing; curtsying, bobbing, bowing and scraping, stooping; dutiful, obeisant, humble, knowing one's place, conscious of one's place; submissive, submitting, compliant; obsequious, servile, ingratiating, fawning, kowtowing, bootlicking
   ◗ *Humility 298; Servility 401; Courtesy 410; Duty 433*

8 **greeting,** welcoming, saluting, complimenting

9 **reverent,** reverential, venerative, venerational; admiring, adoring, worshiping, worshipful, adulatory; deifying, hero-worshiping, idolizing; awe-struck *or* awestruck, awe-stricken *or* awestricken, in awe, wondering

10 **respected,** held in respect, well-respected, highly regarded, esteemed; honored, revered, reverenced, admired, well-thought-of, highly thought of, highly con-

sidered; appreciated, valued, prized, time-honored, prestigious

11 **respectable,** reputable, upright, worthy, venerable, estimable, praiseworthy, laudable
  ▶ *Good 445*

12 **awe-inspiring,** imposing, impressive, important, authoritative, august, sage, wise
  ▶ *Authority 52; Wisdom 352; Importance 799*

13 **respect,** regard, esteem, have respect for; think well of, think highly of, regard highly, hold in high regard; hold in high esteem, have *or* hold a high opinion of, look up to, rank high *or* highly; hold dear, value, admire; prize, treasure, favor, appreciate, set store by
  ▶ *Approval 437*

14 **revere,** reverence, hold in reverence, venerate; honor, admire, adore, cherish, think the world of, look up to; worship, lionize, hero-worship, put on a pedestal, worship the ground one walks on, idolize, deify, apotheosize
  ▶ *Worship 83*

15 **praise,** exalt, extol, acclaim, glorify, laud, sing the praises of

16 **show respect,** accord respect to, defer to, heed, obey, consider; do *or* pay homage, pay one's respects, pay tribute; acknowledge, do the honors; take off one's hat, uncover one's head, doff one's cap, tug one's forelock; rise, stand, rise to one's feet; nod, incline *or* bow one's head, bow, bow and scrape, bow down; bend, stoop, salaam, curtsy, bob, bob down; genuflect, bend the knee, kneel, get down on one's knees, fall on one's knees; fall down before, fall at the feet of, prostrate oneself; kiss the hem of someone's garment, kiss the ring of; make obeisance, grovel, kowtow
  ▶ *Humility 298; Servility 401*

17 **salute,** present arms, fire a salute; turn out the guard, roll out the red carpet, put out the bunting, raise the flag; greet, welcome, address
  ▶ *Address 209*

18 **command respect,** compel *or* inspire respect; impose, impress, rank high, stand high; awe, overawe, overwhelm
  ▶ *Importance 799*

19 **respectfully,** deferentially, courteously, politely, graciously; with all due respect; reverentially, reverently, worshipfully; humbly, obsequiously

436 Disrespect

1 **disrespect,** rudeness, discourtesy, impoliteness, unmannerliness, incivility; impertinence, impudence, insolence, irreverence, lack of veneration; blasphemy, scurrility, defamation, obloquy, opprobrium; disrespectfulness, lack of respect, want of respect
  ▶ *Insolence 400; Discourtesy 411; Disparagement 440*

2 **disesteem,** undervaluation, underestimation; disregard, neglect, dishonor, disrepute, disfavor, disapprobation, disapproval
  ▶ *Negligence 326; Underestimation 344; Disapproval 438*

3 **contempt,** contemptuousness, scorn, scornfulness, disdain, disdainfulness; superciliousness, superiority, loftiness; contumely, despite, low opinion, low esteem

4 **ridicule,** mockery, derision, sarcasm, irony, satire; imitation, impersonation, burlesque; caricature, lampoon, parody, takeoff, send-up
  ▶ *Derision 369; Imitation 736*

5 **insult,** aspersion, affront, snub, slight; rebuff, repulse, spurn, spurning, cold shoulder, slap in the face; backhanded compliment, left-handed compliment; cut, cutting remark, unkindest cut of all; put-down [Inf], go-by [Inf]

6 **taunt,** jeer, mock, scoff, gibe *or* jibe, dig, barb; sneer, snort, sniff, hiss, boo, catcall, hoot; brickbat, banter, chaff, teasing
  ▶ *Disapproval 438*

7 **indignity,** humiliation, degradation; mortification, chagrin, embarrassment; lewd gesture, rude gesture; loss of face, egg on one's face [Inf]
  ▶ *Humility 298*

8 **butt,** dupe, target, victim, game, fair game, fool, jest, joke, figure of fun, laughingstock; monkey, stooge; easy mark [Inf], fall guy [Inf]
  ▶ *Derision 369*

9 **disrespectful,** wanting in respect, irreverent; blasphemous, scurrilous, rude, discourteous; impolite, unmannered, uncivil; impertinent, cheeky, saucy, pert; impudent, insolent, insubordinate; brazen, brazen-faced, bold; audacious, forward, familiar; [Inf]: sassy, fresh, lippy
  ▶ *Insolence 400; Discourtesy 411*

10 **insulting,** abusive, offensive, pejorative; defamatory, opprobrious, contumacious, outrageous; snubbing, slighting, rebuffing, repulsing, spurning; backhanded, left-handed, cutting
  ▶ *Disparagement 440*

11 **disregardful,** neglectful, negligent, dishonorable, disreputable; contemptible, despicable, worthless; shameful, base, low
  ▶ *Negligence 326; Disrepute 371*

12 **contemptuous,** scornful, disdainful, pejorative; supercilious, lofty, haughty; arrogant, snobbish, contumelious, snotty [Inf], snooty [Inf]

13 **ridiculing,** mocking, derisive, derisory; sarcastic, ironic, satirical; imitating, burlesque, caricatural, parodic

▶ *Derision 369*

14 **taunting,** jeering, mocking, flouting; scoffing, scorning, gibing *or* jibing; sneering, hissing, booing; catcalling, hooting, chaffing, teasing

15 **humiliating,** degrading, mortifying, embarrassing
▶ *Humility 298; Modesty 403*

16 **disrespected,** unrespected, unrevered, unreverenced, unvenerated; held in low esteem, trivialized, of no value, of no account
▶ *Disrespect 436*

17 **undervalued,** underestimated, underrated; disparaged, belittled, denigrated; ignored, disregarded, unregarded, neglected
▶ *Negligence 326; Underestimation 344*

VERBS

18 **disrespect,** have no respect *or* regard for; have a low opinion of, hold in low esteem; hold in contempt, have no time for, rank low; hold cheap, underrate, underestimate, undervalue; misprize; show disrespect, show no respect, be rude, lack courtesy, turn one's back on; tread on someone's toes, ride roughshod over; brush aside, shove aside, elbow aside; crowd, jostle, remain seated, keep one's hat on
▶ *Underestimation 344; Insolence 400; Discourtesy 411*

19 **scorn,** disdain, despise, asperse, look down on, hold in contempt; disparage, belittle, trivialize; denigrate, depreciate, run down, defame, look down one's nose at
▶ *Disparagement 440*

20 **dishonor,** disregard, disgrace, shame, put to shame, drag in the mud [Inf]; disregard, ignore, neglect

21 **insult,** offend, affront, snub, slight, rebuff, repulse; spurn, give the cold shoulder, cold-shoulder; cut dead; slap in the face, add insult to injury; [Inf]: give the go-by, dump on, put down

22 **ridicule,** mock, deride, make fun of; satirize, imitate, caricature, send up; make a laughingstock of, poke fun at, tease, take off, pull someone's leg; roast [Inf], rag [Inf]
▶ *Derision 369*

23 **taunt,** jeer, mock, scoff, gibe *or* jibe, dig at; sneer, snort, sniff, hiss, boo; catcall, hoot; heckle, rail at, laugh at; call names, twit, thumb one's nose, stick out one's tongue, make faces at, spit at, moon [Inf]
▶ *Insolence 400*

24 **desecrate,** despoil, defile, profane, commit sacrilege; cheapen, lower, degrade; humiliate, treat like dirt, treat like shit [Inf]
▶ *Disapproval 438*

ADVERBS

25 **disrespectfully,** irreverently, rudely, discourteously; impertinently, impudently, insolently, sassily [Inf]

26 **mockingly,** derisively, sarcastically, satirically

27 **contemptuously,** scornfully, disdainfully, superciliously

437 Approval

NOUNS

1 **approval,** approbation, satisfaction, acceptance, adoption, sanction, formal sanction, countenance; permission, authorization, assent, consent, blessing, leave; vote, imprimatur, favor, endorsement, support, backing, advocacy, championship, patronage, recommendation; agreement, formal agreement, concurrence, acquiescence; ratification, mandate, license, certification, validation; rubber stamp, stamp *or* seal of approval, nod of approval, nod, wink, the OK *or* O.K. *or* okay, go-ahead, green light, thumbs up
▶ *Authority 52; Satisfaction 273; Assent 346; Agreement 462; Permission 502; Help 825; Cooperation 827*

2 **admiration,** respect, regard, esteem; credit, acknowledgment, recognition, appreciation; honor, good opinion, good books, good graces, popularity, prestige, liking, affection
▶ *Liking 290; Respect 435*

3 **praise,** word of praise, honor, laud, laudation, glory, glorification, extolment, exaltation; overpraise, overestimation, adulation, idolatry, idolizing, deification, apotheosis, lionization, hero worship; eulogy, encomium, panegyric, tribute, homage, meed of praise
▶ *Overestimation 343; Flattery 439*

4 **compliment,** complimentary *or* flattering remark, flattery, congratulation, felicitation; pat on the back, good word, commendation, citation, honorable mention, accolade, kudos; glowing terms, favorable review, rave review, good notice, good press; bouquet, posy, paean, stroke, trade-last [Arch inf]

5 **acclaim,** acclamation, éclat, plaudit; applause, round *or* burst of applause, thunderous applause, clap, clapping, handclap, handclapping, hand, big hand, ovation, standing ovation, curtain call, encore; cheer, cheering, three cheers, huzzah, whistling, stamping

6 **recommendation,** testimonial, reference, character reference, credential, letter of introduction

7 **approver,** admirer, follower, advocate, supporter, backer, patron, champion, sponsor, recommender, favorable critic; hero-worshiper, praiser, commender, laudator, eulogist, eulogizer, panegyrist, extoller; applauder, clapper, claqueur, claque, fan, fan club
▶ *Support 605*

ADJECTIVES

8 **approved,** approbated, satisfied, passed, content, accepted, sanctioned; permitted, authorized, assented to, consented to, given a blessing, given leave; voted in, favored, endorsed, supported, backed, advocated, championed, patronized, recommended; agreed, concurred, acquiesced; ratified, adopted, mandated, licensed, certified, validated

9 **approving,** approbative *or* approbatory, admiring, re-

spectful; acknowledging, appreciative, appreciatory; laudatory, acclamatory, overpraising, overestimating, adulatory, overappreciative; eulogistic, encomiastic, panegyric, tributive, lionizing, hero-worshiping; complimentary, flattering, well-inclined, favorable, congratulatory, felicitous, commending *or* commendatory

▶ *Satisfaction 273; Liking 290; Gratitude 310; Flattery 439*

10 **acclamatory,** applauding, clapping, cheering

11 **recommending,** supporting, supportive, backing, advocating, championing, in favor, for, pro

▶ *Help 825*

12 **praiseworthy,** laudable, commendable, worthy, estimable, creditable, meritorious, deserving, well-deserving, admirable; admired, respected, well-thought-of, popular, in demand, in good odor, in high esteem

▶ *Respect 435*

13 **approvable,** satisfactory, acceptable, passable, permissible, worthwhile

VERBS

14 **approve,** approve of, show satisfaction, accept, sanction, give formal sanction, countenance; permit, authorize, assent, consent, condone, bless, give one's blessing, give leave; vote for, favor, endorse, support, back, advocate, champion, patronize, recommend; agree, concur, acquiesce, hold with; ratify, adopt, pass, mandate, license, certify, validate; give the stamp *or* seal *or* nod of approval, rubber-stamp; nod, wink, tip the wink, OK *or* O.K. *or* okay, give the OK *or* O.K. *or* okay, give the go-ahead, give the green light, give thumbs up

▶ *Assent 346; Agreement 462; Permission 502*

15 **admire,** respect, regard highly, hold in high regard, esteem; credit, acknowledge, recognize, appreciate, value, prize; honor, like, think well of, think highly of, think the best of, have no fault to find, find no fault

▶ *Liking 290; Respect 435*

16 **praise,** honor, laud, glorify, extol, exalt; magnify, overpraise, overestimate, adulate, idolize, deify, apotheosize, lionize, hero-worship; eulogize, panegyrize, pay tribute, pay homage, sing the praises of, trumpet, praise to the skies, wax lyrical

▶ *Overestimation 343; Flattery 439*

17 **compliment,** pay a compliment, flatter, congratulate; pat on the back, give a good word to, commend, give a bouquet *or* posy, take one's hat off to, doff one's hat to, hand it to; cry up, boost, puff up, rave about, hype [Inf]

18 **acclaim,** hail, applaud, clap, clap one's hands, put one's hands together, give a big hand; give a standing ovation; cheer, give three cheers, huzzah, whistle, stamp; shout bravo, roar one's approval, encore, shout for more, bring the house down, throw flowers, raise the roof [Inf]

19 **recommend,** give a reference for, speak well of, speak highly of, speak up for, put in a good word for

20 **meet with approval,** meet with approbation, win praise, redound to the honor of, ring with the praises of, find favor with, gain credit, do credit to; satisfy, pass muster, pass the test, come up to scratch, gain one's spurs

▶ *Satisfaction 273; Success 845*

ADVERBS

21 **approvingly,** admiringly, with compliments, with praise

22 **approvably,** satisfactorily, acceptably, passably, to approval, to satisfaction

INTERJECTIONS

23 **bravo!,** encore!, more!, *bis!* [Fr], well done!, hear hear!, hurrah!, hurray!, olé!

438 Disapproval

NOUNS

1 **disapproval,** disapprobation, disfavor, disrespect, disesteem; low *or* poor opinion, dim view, low estimation, low rating; dissatisfaction, discontent, discontentment, discontentedness, unhappiness, displeasure, disgruntlement, indignation, distaste, dislike; nonapproval, nonacceptance, rejection, refusal, veto, red light; exclusion, ostracism, blackballing, blackball, ban, bar, cold shoulder; thumbs down

▶ *Negation 190; Sorrow 270; Dissatisfaction 274; Dislike 291; Rejection 383; Refusal 506; Exclusion 764*

2 **condemnation,** denouncement, impeachment, castigation, chastisement, damnation, fulmination, anathema; flaying, fustigation, excoriation; reproof, reproval, reprimand, rebuke, reproach, upbraiding, objurgation, scolding, chiding, earful, admonishment, admonition, warning, lesson, lecture, sermon, talking-to, taking to task, dressing-down, raking *or* hauling *or* dragging over the coals, home truth, rap on the knuckles, flea in one's ear, black mark; [Inf]: skinning alive, piece of one's mind, telling off, wigging [Brit], carpeting [Brit]

▶ *Punishment 454; Warning 814*

3 **censure,** reprehension, stricture, reprobation, denunciation, denouncement, obloquy; blame, accusation, recrimination, complaint, charge; disagreement, dissension, opposition, hostility, objection, complaint, exception, contradiction, cavil

▶ *Dissent 347; Accusation 442; Disagreement 463; Opposition 828*

4 **criticism,** hostile *or* harsh criticism, adverse *or* negative criticism; dispraise, critical remarks, critical review, unfavorable review, bad press, bad notice, flak, slating, panning, brickbat, animadversion, aspersion; faultfinding, taking exception, carping, caviling, pettifoggery, captiousness; niggling, quibbling, fastidiousness, fussing, pestering, nitpicking, nagging; overcrit-

icalness, hypercriticism, hypercriticalness, censoriousness; [Inf]: roasting, rap, knock, slam, crabbing

⟩ *Disparagement 440*

5 **berating,** rating, lambasting, railing, abuse, tirade, diatribe, onslaught, attack; decrying, verbal attack, harsh words, hard *or* cutting *or* bitter words, rough edge of one's tongue, tongue-lashing; vituperation, execration, revilement, invective, vilification; [Inf]: laying into, bawling out, pitching into, roasting

⟩ *Hate 300; Attack 418*

6 **show** *or* **display of disapproval,** hiss, boo, catcall, taunt, jeer, sneer; derision, ridicule, protest, clamor, outcry; dirty *or* nasty look, black look, reproving look *or* glance, raised eyebrow, glare, silent reproach, frown, scowl; Bronx cheer *or* raspberry [Inf]

⟩ *Derision 369; Disrespect 436; Protest 507*

7 **disapprover,** objector, opposer, opponent, attacker; censor, censurer, castigator; critic, criticizer, faultfinder, pettifogger, quibbler, nitpicker

ADJECTIVES

8 **disapproving,** disapprobatory, disfavorable, disrespectful; unapproving, dissatisfied, discontented, unhappy, displeased, disgruntled, disappointed, indignant, disliking; nonapproving, nonaccepting, rejecting, refusing; excluding, displeased, disgruntled, indignant, disrespectful

⟩ *Sorrow 270; Dissatisfaction 274; Dislike 291; Disrespect 436*

9 **disapproved,** disfavored, unapproved, unaccepted, rejected, refused, vetoed, excluded, ostracized, blackballed, blacklisted, banned, barred

⟩ *Rejection 383; Prohibition 503; Refusal 506; Exclusion 764*

10 **condemning,** denouncing, impeaching, castigating, chastising, damning, fulminatory, excoriating; rebuking, reproaching, upbraiding, objurgatory, objurgative, scolding, chiding, admonishing

11 **condemned,** denounced, impeached, castigated, chastised, damned; reproved, reprimanded, rebuked, reproached, upbraided, admonished; taken to task, dressed down; blamed, accused, recriminated, charged

⟩ *Accusation 442*

12 **censuring,** castigatory, chastising, reprimanding, rebuking, reproaching, reproachful, upbraiding, chiding, scolding, admonitory *or* monitory, stern, obloquial; disagreeing, dissenting, opposing, hostile, objecting, contradicting, contradictory, against, agin [Inf]; censured, reprobated, denounced, decried

⟩ *Dissent 347; Disagreement 463*

13 **critical,** harsh, adverse, negative; dispraising, abusive, execratory, vituperative, disparaging, deprecatory, belittling, damaging, defamatory, derogatory; unfavorable, poor, uncomplimentary; faultfinding, captious, carping, caviling, pettifogging; niggling, quibbling, fastidious, fussy, pestering, nagging; overcritical, hyper-

critical, ultracritical, censorious, nitpicking, crabbing [Inf]

⟩ *Disparagement 440*

14 **criticized,** dispraised, uncommended, run down, given a bad press; hissed, booed, taunted, jeered, sneered at, derided, ridiculed, slated; berated, lambasted, abused, attacked, assailed; given the rough edge of one's tongue; [Inf]: laid into, bawled out, skinned alive, panned, roasted

⟩ *Attack 418*

15 **unsatisfactory,** unacceptable, unpraiseworthy, uncommendable, not to be recommended, found wanting, not good enough, inadequate, insufficient; blameworthy, blamable, to blame, responsible, culpable, criminal, guilty, open to criticism, reprehensible, objectionable, impeachable

⟩ *Insufficiency 98; Dissatisfaction 274*

VERBS

16 **disapprove,** disapprove of, not approve, express disapproval, express disapprobation, disfavor, have no respect for, have no regard for, hold in low esteem; view with disfavor, have a low *or* poor opinion of, take a dim view of, hold in low estimation, think little of, give a low rating; hold in contempt, think ill of, dislike, have a disliking for; not admire, discountenance, look down on, frown on, look down one's nose at, turn up one's nose at

⟩ *Dislike 291; Disrespect 436*

17 **withhold approval,** say no, not hear of, turn down, reject, refuse, disallow, veto, give the red light; exclude, ostracize, blackball, blacklist, ban, bar; cold-shoulder, send to Coventry; give *or* turn thumbs down, nix [Inf]

⟩ *Rejection 383; Refusal 506; Exclusion 764*

18 **condemn,** denounce, impeach, chastise, damn, fulminate; castigate, flay, fustigate, excoriate; reproof, reprove, reprimand, rebuke, reproach, upbraid, objurgate, scold, chide, read the riot act to; censure, reprehend, admonish, set down, take to task, dress down, give a talking-to, rake *or* haul *or* drag over the coals, rap on the knuckles, blacken; [Inf]: skin alive, give a piece of one's mind, put a flea in one's ear, tell off, wig [Brit], carpet [Brit]

19 **criticize,** dispraise, disparage, deprecate, depreciate, belittle, damage, defame; find fault, fault, take exception, carp, carp at, cavil, niggle, quibble, fuss, pester, pick to pieces, nitpick, derogate

20 **berate,** lambaste *or* lambast, rail, rage against, abuse, assail, attack, denigrate, slate, decry, cry down, run down, tear apart, hand out brickbats, snipe, give the rough edge of one's tongue, lash, give a tongue lashing, give one what for; vituperate, execrate, revile, vilify; [Inf]: rap, knock, slam, lay into, bawl out, pitch into, roast, pan

> *Disparagement 440*

21 **show disapproval,** frown, scowl, raise one's eyebrows, hiss, boo, catcall, jeer, heckle, shout down, throw stones, pelt with rotten eggs, deride, ridicule, throw mud [Inf]

> *Derision 369; Disrespect 436*

22 **be open to criticism,** get a bad press, meet with disapproval, get a bad name, take the blame, take the rap [Inf], carry the can [Brit inf]

ADVERBS

23 **disapprovingly,** critically, censoriously, reproachfully

439 Flattery

The world is a king, and, like a king, desires flattery in return for favor; but true art is selfish and perverse — it will not submit to the mold of flattery.
— LUDWIG VAN BEETHOVEN

NOUNS

1 **flattery,** adulation, compliments, praise, overpraise, excessive praise, overlaudation, hagiography, panegyric, insincere praise, insincerity, hypocrisy, eyewash [Inf], hype [Inf]

> *Deception 193; Exaggeration 194; Approval 437*

2 **blarney,** honeyed words, honeyed phrases; salve, bunkum *or* buncombe, sweet talk [Inf], soft soap [Inf]

3 **cajolery,** wheedling, inveiglement; blandishment *or* blandishments, ingratiation

> *Persuasion 178*

4 **unctuousness,** unctuosity, oiliness, sliminess

5 **sycophancy,** servility, obsequiousness, toadyism, fawning, bootlicking, back scratching

> *Servility 401*

6 **flatterer,** adulator, charmer, smooth talker; cajoler, wheedler, inveigler; sycophant, toady, fawner; yesman, bootlicker, back scratcher, hanger-on; [Inf]: brown-nose *or* brown-noser, ass-kisser

ADJECTIVES

7 **flattering,** adulatory, complimentary, laudatory, praising; insincere, hypocritical, tongue-in-cheek

> *Deception 193; Approval 437*

8 **honeyed,** sugary, saccharine; blarneying, honey-tongued, smooth-tongued, smooth-spoken, buttery; sweet-talking [Inf], soft-soaping [Inf]

9 **cajoling,** wheedling, inveigling, blandishing, coaxing, ingratiating

10 **unctuous,** oily, smarmy, slimy, greasy

11 **sycophantic,** servile, obsequious, toadyish, fawning; creeping, crawling, bootlicking, back scratching, brown-nosing [Inf], ass-kissing [Inf]

> *Servility 401*

VERBS

12 **flatter,** adulate, compliment, praise; overpraise, overcommend, overesteem; overestimate, puff; overdo it,

lay it on, lay it on thick, lay it on with a trowel, hype [Inf]

> *Exaggeration 194; Overestimation 343; Approval 437*

13 **blarney,** sugar, charm; oil, oil the tongue, flatter to deceive, soften up; [Inf]: sweet-talk, soft-soap, butter up

14 **cajole,** wheedle, inveigle, blandish, coax; court, ingratiate oneself, curry favor; suck up to [Inf], make up to [Inf]

15 **be sycophantic,** insinuate oneself, toady, fawn, fawn on; creep, crawl, bootlick, back scratch, brown-nose [Inf]

> *Servility 401*

ADVERBS

16 **flatteringly,** with honeyed words, unctuously, smarmily, sycophantically, obsequiously

440 Disparagement

NOUNS

1 **disparagement,** deprecation, depreciation; decrial, detraction, derogation, denigration; belittlement, slighting, crying down; underestimation, understatement, faint praise, lukewarm support; faultfinding, nitpicking; running down, putting down [Inf]

> *Underestimation 344*

2 **criticism,** hostile criticism, animadversion; bad review, bad press, flak *or* flack, slating, panning, brickbat, hatchet job; knocking [Inf], slam [Inf]

> *Disrespect 436; Disapproval 438*

3 **defamation,** defamation of character, character assassination; slander, libel, traducement, calumny, obloquy; smear campaign, muckraking, mudslinging; scandal, gossip, malicious gossip, backbiting

> *Misrepresentation 188; Attack 418*

4 **aspersion,** insinuation, innuendo, slur, smear; disparaging remark, defamatory remark, slighting remark; poison-pen letter

> *Disrepute 371; Accusation 442; Untruth 722*

5 **scorn,** contempt, disdain, derision; revilement, vilification, abuse; insult, degradation, debasement, scurrility; defilement, blackening, tarnishing

> *Derision 369; Disrespect 436*

6 **ridicule,** lampoon, satire, pasquinade; burlesque, take-off, send-up, skit; squib, caricature

> *Derision 369; Disrespect 436*

7 **disparager,** depreciator, decrier, detractor; derogator, belittler; faultfinder, nitpicker; critic, hostile critic, animadverter; defamer, slanderer, libeler, muckraker, mudslinger; backbiter, smircher, smearer; gossiper *or* gossip, scandalmonger, gossip columnist; ridiculer, lampooner, lampoonist, satirist, caricaturist, mocker; hatchet man, knocker [Inf]

ADJECTIVES

8 **disparaging,** deprecatory, depreciatory, decrying, detractory; derogatory, pejorative, denigratory; belittling,

slighting, minimizing; critical, nitpicking, knocking [Inf]

> *Disapproval 438*

9 **defamatory,** slanderous, libelous, calumnious, calumniatory; scandalous, scurrilous, abusive, insulting, aspersive, insinuating, gossiping, whispering, catty; mudslinging, smearing, besmirching, blackening, tarnishing; damaging, injurious, destructive; venomous, caustic, bitter, backbiting, snide, bitchy [Inf]

> *Disrepute 371; Disrespect 436*

10 **scornful,** contemptuous, contumelious, sarcastic; ridiculing, mocking, scoffing, sneering, derisive

> *Derision 369; Disrespect 436*

VERBS

11 **disparage,** deprecate, depreciate, decry, detract; derogate, denigrate, belittle, slight; cry down, minimize, play down; underestimate, underrate, undervalue, understate; run down, sell short, put down [Inf]

> *Underestimation 344; Lowering 716*

12 **criticize,** find fault, dispraise, animadvert, nitpick, slate, pull apart, tear down; [Inf]: knock, pan, slam

> *Disapproval 438*

13 **defame,** slander, libel, traduce, calumniate, malign, damage, compromise, discredit, dishonor, bring into disrepute; blacken, tarnish, sully, soil, smear, besmear, smirch, besmirch, bespatter; drag through the gutter, muckrake, backbite, stab in the back; [Inf]: bad-mouth, drag through the mud, throw mud, sling mud

> *Disrepute 371*

14 **vilify,** revile, abuse, degrade, debase, defile, asperse, cast aspersions on, insinuate, slur, cast a slur, whisper, gossip, talk about, talk about behind one's back, speak ill of

15 **ridicule,** lampoon, satirize, caricature, make fun of; poke fun at, mock, guy; scoff, sneer, deride, scorn, send up, take off

> *Derision 369; Disrespect 436*

ADVERBS

16 **disparagingly,** derogatorily, pejoratively, slightingly, critically, slanderously, libelously, scornfully, contemptuously, derisively

441 Vindication

NOUNS

1 **vindication,** exoneration, exculpation, compurgation, absolution, remission, remittal; acquittal, verdict of acquittal; verdict of innocence, verdict of not guilty, quashing of the charge; discharge, dismissal, release, pardon, clearance; clearing from guilt, clearing of one's name; purging, purgation; reinstatement, restitution, restoration, rehabilitation; triumph of justice, assertion of truth, the OK *or* O.K. *or* okay, green light

> *Litigation 54; Judgment 341; Innocence 449*

2 **defense,** legal defense, successful defense, reply for the defense; rebuttal, refutation, rejoinder; retort, recrimination, *tu quoque* [L]; counterargument, argument, plea; justification, explanation, grounds, good grounds; truth, reason, good reason; excuse, good excuse, alibi; cause, just cause; supportive evidence, corroboration, partial excuse; extenuation, extenuating circumstances; mitigation, mitigating circumstances; palliation, qualification, allowance, out

> *Answer 334; Qualification 340; Accuracy 350; Defense 419; Truth 721*

3 **cover-up,** whitewash, whitewashing, cop-out [Inf]

4 **revenge,** vengeance, reprisal, requital; retribution, fitting retribution; punishment, just punishment; poetic justice

> *Retaliation 420; Punishment 454*

5 **vindicator,** justifier, defender, pleader; advocate, proponent; apologist, excuser, champion, palliator; whitewasher

6 **avenger,** vindicator, retaliator, punisher, Nemesis

ADJECTIVES

7 **vindicatory,** vindicating, exculpatory, exculpating, exonerative, exonerating, justifying; defensive, defending; argumentative, refuting, rejoining, retorting, rebutting; explanatory, excusatory, excusing; supportive, corroborative, apologetic; extenuating, extenuatory; mitigative, mitigating; qualifying, palliative; remissive, justifying

8 **vindicated,** innocent, not guilty, acquitted, dismissed; discharged, released; pardoned, cleared, restored; rehabilitated

> *Innocence 449*

9 **vindicable,** justifiable, defensible, arguable, refutable, rebuttable; warrantable, admissible, allowable, reasonable; explainable, excusable, having an excuse; pardonable, remissible, forgivable; condonable, venial, exemptible, dispensable

10 **vindictive,** vengeful, revengeful; avenging, requiting, retributive; unforgiving, spiteful, venomous; malicious, malevolent; punitive, punishing

> *Malevolence 306; Punishment 454*

VERBS

11 **vindicate,** exonerate, exculpate, absolve, remit, grant remission; allow for, make allowances for, excuse, pardon; clear, put in the clear, clear one's name; free from blame, withdraw the charge, acquit; discharge, dismiss; release, liberate, free, set free, purge; reinstate, restore, rehabilitate; make good, assert the truth, do justice to; set right, give the OK *or* O.K. *or* okay, give the green light

12 **justify,** defend, make a legal defense; rebut the charge, rebut, refute; rejoin, retort, recriminate; argue, argue for; plead, plead one's own cause; attest to, warrant, explain, show good grounds; prove the truth of, prove, demonstrate; corroborate, substantiate, give supportive evidence; give a good reason, furnish a good ex-

cuse, make excuses for, alibi; speak up for, champion, uphold, stand up for; extenuate, mitigate, palliate; soften, ease, qualify, find an out, stick up for

13 **cover up,** whitewash, cop out

14 **avenge,** revenge, requite, give fitting retribution, punish

ADVERBS

15 **justifyingly,** defensively; argumentatively, in vindication, in explanation, as an excuse; supportively, in support; apologetically, extenuatingly, with qualifications; palliatively, remissively, justifyingly, with justification; forgivably, venially

16 **vindictively,** vengefully, revengefully, retributively, unforgivably; spitefully, in a spiteful manner, venomously; maliciously, with malice, malevolently; punitively, punishingly, as punishment

442 Accusation

NOUNS

1 **accusation,** complaint, accusing, bringing of charges, charge, countercharge, blame; insinuation, implication, reproach; denunciation, denouncement; allegation, imputation; plaint, suit, lawsuit, action, litigation; citation, summons, arrest, booking, prosecution; impeachment, indictment, true bill, gravamen, incrimination, recrimination; count, case, court case, case for the prosecution; evidence

   ▶ *Litigation 54; Argument 329; Evidence 339; Defiance 416; Disapproval 438; Disparagement 440*

2 **false accusation,** false charge, false evidence, fake confession, perjured testimony, perjury; libel, slander, calumny, scandal, defamation, misrepresentation; trumped-up charge; [Inf]: plant, cooked-up charge; put-up job, frame-up, frame

3 **accuser,** denouncer, incriminator, charger, petitioner, plaintiff, complainant, claimant, litigant, appellant, party to a suit, witness for the prosecution, hostile witness, indicter; prosecutor, public prosecutor, district attorney (DA); impeacher, false witness, perjurer, libeler, libelant; whistle-blower, informer; [Inf]: stool pigeon *or* stoolie *or* stooly, squealer, fink, snitch *or* snitcher, canary

4 **accused person,** the accused, defendant; respondent, corespondent; culprit, suspect, prisoner; guilty party, marked man

ADJECTIVES

5 **accused,** charged, countercharged, blamed, implicated, denunciated, denounced; under suspicion, cited, summoned, arrested, booked; awaiting trial, liable to prosecution; prosecuted, impeached, indicted, incriminated, recriminated; hauled up

6 **accusatory,** accusing, imputative, pointing to; denunciatory, alleging, litigious; impeachable, indictable, incriminatory, recriminatory

7 **perjurious,** perjured; libelous *or* libellous, libeled; slanderous, slandered; defamatory, defamed; misrepresented, calumnious; trumped-up; [Inf]: planted, cooked-up, put-up, framed

VERBS

8 **accuse,** blame, lay the blame on, charge; complain, bring charges, countercharge; insinuate, implicate, impute, reproach, denunciate, denounce, allegate; sue, litigate; serve a citation, serve a summons, summon, serve with a writ, cite, prosecute, impeach, indict, swear *or* bring an indictment, inculpate, incriminate, recriminate; arrest, arraign, book, haul up; hold a court case, put on trial, hold a trial, try, send before the judge, put in the dock; bring evidence against, witness, bear witness, lodge a complaint; inform against *or* on, point the finger, blow the whistle; [Inf]: throw the book at, stool, put the finger on, squeal, fink, snitch, sing

   ▶ *Litigation 54*

9 **accuse falsely,** give false evidence, bear false witness; fake the evidence, fake a confession, commit perjury, perjure oneself; libel, slander, defame, misrepresent, calumniate; trump up a charge, plant evidence; [Inf]: frame, cook up a charge; cook the evidence

10 **be accused,** stand accused, receive a summons, have charges brought against one; await trial, go on trial, stand before the judge, stand in the dock; defend oneself, offer a defense

ADVERBS

11 **accusingly,** in accusation, allegedly, before the judge, litigiously, perjuriously; libelously, slanderously, defamatorily

443 Disinterestedness

NOUNS

1 **disinterestedness,** disinterest, detachment, indifference; ataraxia; impartiality, lack of bias, lack of prejudice, objectivity; equitableness, fairness; fair-mindedness, open-mindedness; justice, neutrality, nonalignment, noninvolvement; lack of emotion, self-control, self-restraint, dispassion; stoicism, keeping a stiff upper lip, keeping cool

   ▶ *Indifference 289; Right 429; Self-Restraint 455*

2 **unselfishness,** selflessness, altruism; thought for others, considerateness, consideration; kindness, compassion; sympathy, pity; humility, modesty; self-denial, self-effacement, self-abnegation, self-sacrifice, martyrdom; idealism, high-mindedness, honesty, honorableness; sublimity, loftiness, magnanimity, nobleness; munificence, benevolence, charity, generosity, openhandedness, big-heartedness

3 **impartial person,** judge, jury member; arbitrator, moderator, referee, umpire

ADJECTIVES

4 **disinterested,** detached, impersonal, indifferent; impartial, unbiased, unprejudiced, objective, equitable, nonpartisan; fair, fair-minded, open-minded, open, just; neutral, nonaligned, uninvolved; not bothered, cool, self-controlled, dispassionate, self-restrained, stoic

5 **unselfish,** selfless, altruistic; considerate, kind, compassionate, sympathetic; humble, modest; self-denying, self-effacing, self-abnegating, self-sacrificing, ready to die for, martyred; idealistic, high-minded; honest, honorable, sublime; lofty, magnanimous, noble; munificent, benevolent, charitable, generous, openhanded, big-hearted

VERBS

6 **be disinterested,** lack bias, lack prejudice, keep an open mind, open one's mind to, do the fair thing; show *or* take no interest in, be indifferent; lack emotion, demonstrate self-control, keep a stiff upper lip, keep cool; mind one's own business, live and let live

7 **be unselfish,** think of others first, put oneself last; sacrifice oneself, make a sacrifice, sacrifice; rise above oneself, do the right thing by; show compassion, sympathize with, pity; give generously, have a big heart; take a backseat, bend *or* lean *or* fall over backward

ADVERBS

8 **disinterestedly,** impersonally; impartially, objectively, without bias, without prejudice, equitably, fairly; open-mindedly, with an open mind; openly, justly, neutrally; indifferently, dispassionately, with a stiff upper lip, coolly

9 **unselfishly,** selflessly, altruistically; with others in mind, for the sake of others; considerately, kindly, compassionately, sympathetically; humbly, in a humble manner, modestly, with modesty; idealistically, high-mindedly, honestly, honorably, sublimely; loftily, magnanimously, nobly, with noble intentions; munificently, benevolently, charitably; generously, openhandedly, big-heartedly

444 Selfishness

I have been a selfish being all my life, in practice, though not in principle. — JANE AUSTEN

NOUNS

1 **selfishness,** self-interest, self-concern, self-pity; self-preservation, self-consideration, self-indulgence, self-pleasing, self-seeking; personal desires, personal aims; possessiveness, keeping for oneself, covetousness; jealousy, envy, avarice, acquisitiveness, greed, opportunism, individualism; stinginess, miserliness, niggardliness, littleness; mean-mindedness, meanspiritedness, meanness, parsimony; charity that begins at home, looking out for number one

▶ *Desire 288; Envy 314; Self-Indulgence 456; Possession 469; Retention 471; Meanness 501*

2 **egotism,** egoism, ego; conceit, vanity; self-love, self-devotion, narcissism, self-absorption; self-centeredness, no thought for others, egocentrism, egocentricity; self-praise, ego trip [Inf]

▶ *Vanity 402*

3 **selfish person,** egotist, egoist, egomaniac; narcissist, self-seeker, self-pleaser, self-server; opportunist, monopolist, dog in the manger, hog, moneygrubber [Inf]

ADJECTIVES

4 **selfish,** self-concerned, self-indulgent, self-interested, self-seeking, self-serving; possessive, covetous, jealous, envious, avaricious; acquisitive, greedy, monopolistic, opportunistic, individualistic; ungenerous, uncharitable, stingy, miserly, niggardly; mean, meanspirited; parsimonious, cold-hearted, hoggish, moneygrubbing [Inf]

5 **egotistic,** egotistical, egoistic, egoistical; conceited, vain, boastful, narcissistic, self-loving; self-absorbed, self-centered, egocentric, wrapped up in oneself, looking out for number one, stuck on oneself [Inf]

▶ *Vanity 402*

VERBS

6 **be selfish,** indulge oneself, spoil oneself, please oneself; put oneself first, think only of oneself; pursue one's interests, advance one's own interests, sacrifice the interests of others, have personal motives; covet, envy; monopolize, be greedy, hog; possess, keep for oneself, hang on to; feather one's nest, have an ax to grind

7 **be egotistic,** be egoistic, love oneself, have no thought for others; praise oneself, brag, boast; take care of *or* look out for number one, ego-trip [Inf]

ADVERBS

8 **selfishly,** only for oneself, for one's own sake, self-indulgently; possessively, covetously, jealously, enviously, avariciously, acquisitively; from personal motives, for private ends, greedily, individualistically; ungenerously, uncharitably; stingily, meanly, parsimoniously, cold-heartedly

9 **egoistically,** egotistically, egocentrically, conceitedly, vainly; self-lovingly, with no thought for others, on an ego trip [Inf]

445 Good

NOUNS

1 **good,** goodness, moral excellence, morality, righteousness, rectitude, virtue, ideal; benefit, profit, profitability, gain, boon, gift, merit, worth, worthiness, praiseworthiness, value; soundness, healthiness, favorableness, auspiciousness, suitableness, appropriateness, aptness, rightness

▶ *Health 113; Right 429; Morality 431*

2 **welfare,** general welfare, well-being, public weal, common good; interest, behalf, guidance, edification; betterment, improvement, happiness, blessing, benediction, prosperity; use, usefulness, favor, advantage

3 **kindness,** kindliness, goodliness, niceness, good-naturedness, friendliness, graciousness, grace, benignity; benevolence, beneficence, altruism, generosity, charity, goodwill, thoughtfulness, helpfulness; humanity, sympathy, compassion, tenderness; good-heartedness, kindheartedness, soft-heartedness, warm-heartedness; kind act, good turn; good behavior, good manners, obedience, willingness, dutifulness
 ▶ *Benevolence 305; Willingness 373; Obedience 426; Duty 433; Virtue 447; Giving 472; Conformity 781; Cooperation 827*

4 **excellence,** quality, good *or* high quality, superiority, supremacy, eminence, preeminence, superbness, splendidness, distinction, greatness, wonderfulness, magnificence, exquisiteness, perfection; best, very best, best ever, tops, essence, quintessence; choice, pick, elite, cream, cream *or* pick of the crop, flower, paragon, nonpareil, gem of the first water, jewel in the crown, top mark *or* grade, grade A, head of the class, first class, finest class; goodliness, largeness, substantiality
 ▶ *Size, Largeness 579; Superiority 744*

5 **proficiency,** efficiency, competence, ability, talent, gift; masterfulness, masterliness, expertise, skill, skillfulness; deftness, dexterousness, adroitness, handiness

6 **good person,** person of goodwill, saint, angel, angel of mercy, good Samaritan, white knight, rescuer; friend, good neighbor, well-wisher, helper; humanitarian, altruist, philanthropist
 ▶ *Benevolence 305*

7 **superior person,** superlative, acme, champion, superman, superwoman, *übermensch* [Ger]; prodigy, genius, wonder, virtuoso; star, superstar, ace, highflier, pick of the bunch, nonesuch *or* nonsuch, first-rater, number one, numero uno, topnotcher; [Inf]: whiz kid, whiz, crackerjack *or* crackajack, the cat's pajamas *or* meow
 ▶ *Wonder 294*

8 **goody-goody,** goody two shoes, bleeding heart, brown-nose *or* brown-noser [Inf], ass-kisser [Inf]

9 **good thing,** the very thing, just the thing, treasure, gem, jewel, prize, find; good luck, good fortune, fortune, favor, blessing, godsend, windfall, halcyon days, happy days *or* ending; winner, record-setter, masterstroke, pride, pride and joy; tour de force, chef-d'oeuvre, work of art, masterpiece, collector's item; record-breaker, bestseller; hit, smash hit, [Inf]: smash, dandy, jim-dandy, peach, plum, knockout, humdinger, corker, doozie *or* doozy, killer, killer-diller, dilly, beaut, lollapalooza

ADJECTIVES

10 **good,** goodly, moral, excellent, righteous, virtuous, idealized; beneficial, profitable, gainful, having merits, worthy, praiseworthy, admirable, valuable; sound, healthy, favorable, auspicious, suitable, appropriate, apt, right

11 **beneficial,** good for, helpful, serviceable, availing; in the best interest of, on behalf of, edifying, bettering, improving, prosperous; useful, favoring, advantageous
 ▶ *Benevolence 305; Giving 472*

12 **kind,** nice, goodly, good-natured, friendly, gracious, graceful, benign; benevolent, altruistic, generous, charitable, thoughtful, well-wishing, helpful; humane, sympathetic, compassionate, tender; good-hearted, kindhearted, soft-hearted, warm-hearted; well-behaved, well-mannered, obedient, willing, dutiful
 ▶ *Submission 421; Virtue 447; Cooperation 827*

13 **excellent,** superior, supreme, eminent, preeminent, superlative, superb, splendid, distinct, great, wonderful, magnificent, exquisite, perfect, flawless; better, best, very best, best ever, top, essential, quintessential; choice, elite, unequaled, nonpareil, peerless, matchless, record-breaking, top mark, grade A, first-class, high-class, first-rate; fine, superfine, terrific, impressive

14 **great,** goodly, large, substantial; heaven-sent, lucky; topnotch, smashing, crack; [Inf]: fabulous, fine and dandy, super, crackerjack *or* crackajack, A-OK *or* A-Okay, dandy, jim-dandy; cool, hunky-dory, radical, rad, swell, spiffy, corking, copacetic; bad, wicked
 ▶ *Wealth 485; Size, Largeness 579; Superiority 744; Prosperity 847*

15 **proficient,** efficient, competent, able, accomplished, talented, gifted; masterful, masterly, expert, skilled, skillful; deft, dexterous, adroit, handy
 ▶ *Skillfulness 127; Perfection 805*

VERBS

16 **be good,** be moral, do the right thing, be virtuous; do well, benefit, profit, gain, get better, increase worth *or* value; thrive, flourish, prosper, succeed, turn to good account; make money, get rich, be on top of the world, be on the crest of a wave

17 **better,** make better, benefit, serve, avail, edify, improve, advance, promote, bring prosperity; do good, do a world of good, show kindness, befriend, help, do a good turn, favor, bless; behave well, show *or* have good manners, obey

18 **be good at,** do well at, have the knack *or* gift for, master, excel, transcend, perform skillfully, exploit, play one's card's right

ADVERBS

19 **well,** morally, rightly, virtuously, ideally; beneficially, profitably, worthily; soundly, healthily, favorably, auspiciously, suitably, appropriately, aptly; advantageously, usefully

20 **kindly,** nicely, good-naturedly, graciously; benevo-

lently, altruistically, generously, charitably, thoughtfully, helpfully; humanely, sympathetically, compassionately, tenderly, kindheartedly, warm-heartedly; obediently, willingly, dutifully

21 **excellently,** supremely, eminently, preeminently, superbly, splendidly, distinctly, greatly, wonderfully, magnificently, exquisitely, perfectly, peerlessly, fabulously [Inf]

22 **proficiently,** efficiently, competently, ably, masterfully, expertly, skillfully; deftly, dexterously, adroitly, handily

23 **for good,** for good and all, permanently, forever, eternally, always

INTERJECTIONS

24 **good!,** great!; [Inf]: super!, fab!, right on!, bad!, wizard! [Brit]

446 Evil

NOUNS

1 **evil,** evilness, bad, badness, wickedness, meanness, wrongness, wrong; sin, peccancy, sacrilege, unholiness, ungodliness, deadliness; malevolence, maleficence, malignity, malice, viciousness, hatefulness, ill will, vindictiveness, revengefulness; heinousness, flagitiousness, nefariousness, iniquity, vice, immorality; corruption, defilement, depravity, foulness, vileness, baseness, nastiness, noxiousness, wretchedness, rottenness; terribleness, dreadfulness, horribleness, awfulness, atrociousness, deadliness; mischievousness, mischief, deviltry or devilry

▶ *Malevolence 306; Wrong 430; Immorality 432*

2 **evil thing,** evil plight, evil wish, evil power, power of darkness; bane, poison, pollution, pollutant, bad influence, malign influence; malediction, curse, plague, pestilence, blight, ruin, scourge; abomination, atrocity, horror, crime, murder, foul play; skeleton in the closet, Pandora's Box; bad spell, evil spell, evil eye, evil star, ill wind

▶ *Death 29; Affliction 117; Curse 301; Adversity 848*

3 **evil person,** bane, evil genius, evildoer, wrongdoer, malefactor, malfeasor, sinner, transgressor, culprit; mischief-maker, snake in the grass, villain, blackguard, scoundrel, reprobate, miscreant, wretch, caitiff [Arch]; fiend, hellhound, criminal, baddie or baddy, outlaw, felon, gangster, gang member, crook, abuser, murderer, terrorist, poisoner, traitor, assassin, cutthroat, holy terror [Inf]

▶ *Wickedness 448*

4 **evil spirit,** ghost, goblin, gnome, gremlin, ghoul, ogre; fiend, imp, lost soul; fallen angel, rebel angel, demon, devil, she-devil, dickens, deuce, wicked jinn or djinn, dybbuk or dibbuk, incubus, succubus, afreet or afrit; lamia, harpy, werewolf, witch; Namtar, Azazel, Asmodeus, Set, Loki, Baba Yaga

▶ *Occultism 86; Fear 283*

5 **devil,** Satan, Lucifer, Evil One, Enemy, Common Enemy, Prince of Darkness, His Satanic Majesty, Monarch of Hell, Lord of the Flies, Serpent, Devil Incarnate, Archfiend, Foul Fiend, Antichrist, Tempter; Diabolus, Belial, Beelzebub, Mephisto, Mephistopheles, Ash-Shaytan or Shaitan, Iblis or Eblis, Apollyon, Abaddon, Angra Mainyu or Ahriman, Sammael, Mara, Typhon; Old Clootie [Brit], deil [Scot], *diable* [Fr], *diavolo* [Ital], *diablo* [Sp], *Teufel* [Ger], Old Harry [Arch]; [Inf]: Old Nick, Old Scratch, Old Horny

6 **evil place,** hell, place of the dead, limbo, purgatory, inferno, Pandemonium, abyss, bottomless pit, lake of fire and brimstone, perdition, eternal damnation; Sheol, Abaddon, Tophet, Gehenna; lower world, underworld, nether world, Hades, Dis, Tartarus, Avernus, Erebus, Orcus, realm of Pluto; Hel, Niflheim, Arallu, Naraka; rivers of Hades: Styx, Stygian creek, Stygian shores; Acheron, River of Woe; Cocytus, River of Wailing; Phlegethon or Pyriphlegethon, River of Fire; Lethe, River of Forgetfulness

▶ *Death 29; Punishment 454*

ADJECTIVES

7 **evil,** bad, wicked, mean, wrong, sinful, sinister, peccant, sacrilegious, unholy, ungodly; malevolent, maleficent, malefic, malignant, malicious, vicious, hateful, odious; ill-willed, vindictive, revengeful; heinous, flagitious, nefarious, iniquitous, immoral; corrupt, depraved, deplorable, foul, vile, base, nasty, noxious, wretched, rotten; despicable, detestable, contemptible, reprehensible; terrible, dreadful, dreaded, horrible, awful, atrocious; mischievous, devilish

▶ *Wrong 430; Wickedness 448*

8 **detrimental,** damaging, destructive, deleterious, harmful, injurious, painful, hurtful, abusive; baleful, baneful, pernicious, toxic, corruptive, corrosive, malignant; ruinous, tragic, calamitous, disastrous, catastrophic, dire, fatal, mortal, deadly

9 **demonic,** demonical, demoniac, demoniacal; evil, diabolic, diabolical, fiendish, fiendlike; hellish, infernal, abysmal, sulphurous, chthonian or chthonic, pandemonic, pandemoniacal, Plutonian, Avernal, Tartarean; Satanic, devilish, devil-like, Mephistophelean; fallen, damned, hellborn

VERBS

10 **be evil,** do evil, work evil, do wrong, sin, do mischief, do ill; wrong, distress, depress, aggrieve, bestow sorrow, afflict, plague, torment, hurt, harm, injure, wound; harass, persecute, condemn, seek revenge, threaten, menace, wreak havoc; mistreat, maltreat, abuse, molest; defile, violate, ruin, despoil, lay a hand on, befoul, foul, corrupt, pervert; damage, impair, blight, pollute, poison; destroy, doom, kill

▶ *Wrong 430; Wickedness 448*

11 **make evil,** demonize, devilize, diabolize, bedevil, pos-

sess; damn, condemn, curse, jinx, hex, put the whammy or double whammy on [Inf]

▶ *Occultism 86; Curse 301*

ADVERBS

12 **evilly,** badly, ill, wickedly, meanly, wrongly, wrong, all wrong, sinfully, sinisterly, peccantly; malevolently, maliciously, with malice, viciously, hatefully, with hate, odiously; vindictively, in a vindictive way, revengefully, for revenge, heinously, flagitiously, nefariously, iniquitously, immorally; corruptly, deplorably, nastily, noxiously, wretchedly; terribly, dreadfully, horribly, awfully, atrociously, reprehensibly; mischievously

13 **destructively,** depressingly, distressingly, miserably, grievously, sorrowfully, to one's sorrow, woefully, sadly; balefully, perniciously, harmfully, hurtfully, maliciously, deleteriously; painfully, tragically, disastrously, fatally, mortally

▶ *Malevolence 306*

14 **devilishly,** satanically, diabolically, demonically, fiendishly; infernally, hellishly, in hell, in hellfire, in torment

▶ *Death 29; Wickedness 448; Punishment 454; Occultism 86*

447 Virtue

NOUNS

1 **virtue,** virtuousness, moral excellence, goodness, goodliness, probity, perfection; righteousness, uprightness, ethicalness, irreproachability, impeccability, guiltlessness, innocence, honor, personal honor, integrity, respectability; sinlessness, saintliness, sanctity, piety, godliness, holiness, spirituality; magnanimity, philanthropy, benevolence, generosity, altruism, unselfishness, idealism; upstandingness, nobility, decency, chivalry, properness, good conscience, clear conscience, the straight and narrow

▶ *Religion 81; Benevolence 305; Right 429; Morality 431; Good 445; Innocence 449; Perfection 805*

2 **virtues,** principles, high principles, morals, mores, ethics, ideals, moral laws; love, chastity, purity, virginity, soberness, self-control, character, honesty, duty, fidelity, trustworthiness; obedience, good behavior, virtuous conduct, Christian conduct; grace, saving grace, qualities, fine or saving qualities; heroic qualities, heroism, valor; cardinal virtues: justice, prudence, temperance, fortitude; theological or natural or supernatural virtues: faith, hope, charity; fairness, love

▶ *Law 53; Morality 431; Approval 437; Self-Restraint 455*

3 **worth,** worthiness, excellence, credit, merit, quality, desert

▶ *Approval 437*

4 **power,** effect, effectiveness, effectuality, efficacy, effi-

caciousness; energy, potency, strength, cogency, dint, productivity

ADJECTIVES

5 **virtuous,** moral, good, goodly, good as gold, perfect; righteous, upright, ethical, irreproachable, above reproach, impeccable, unerring, guiltless, innocent, honorable, respectable, above temptation; sinless, immaculate, saintly, seraphic, angelic, sanctified, pious, godly, holy, spiritual, Christian; magnanimous, philanthropic, benevolent, generous, altruistic, unselfish, idealistic; upstanding, noble, decent, chivalrous, proper, conscionable; on the side of the angels, pure as the driven snow

6 **principled,** high-principled, ethical, moral; chaste, pure, virginal, sober, self-controlled; honest, dutiful; obedient, behaved, well-behaved; graceful, fine, heroic, valorous; just, fair, prudent, temperate, strong; faithful, hopeful, charitable, loving

7 **worthy,** praiseworthy, excellent, creditable, commendable, meritorious, exemplary

VERBS

8 **be virtuous,** be moral, be good, do good, love good, do no evil, hate evil, hear or see or speak no evil; practice virtue, have all the virtues, resist temptation, rise above temptation, control one's passions, control oneself; discharge one's obligations, do one's duty, set a good example, be a shining example or light, fight the good fight; follow one's conscience, keep or go straight, keep to or on the straight and narrow, fly right; walk (humbly) with one's God, shame the devil; behave, obey, be on one's good or best behavior; have saving graces, have fine qualities

ADVERBS

9 **virtuously,** morally, in goodness, with good or the best of intentions, perfectly; righteously, uprightly, ethically, irreproachable, impeccably, guiltlessly, innocently, in all innocence, honorably, with honor, respectably; sinlessly, without sin, spiritually, angelically, immaculately; magnanimously, benevolently, generously, altruistically, unselfishly, for the benefit of others, idealistically; upstandingly, nobly, for noble reasons, decently, chivalrously, properly, conscientiously, unselfishly

10 **ethically,** morally; chastely, purely, virginally, soberly, with self-restraint or control; honestly, with honesty, dutifully, obediently; finely, heroically, justly, fairly, prudently, temperately; faithfully, hopefully, charitably, lovingly, with a loving heart

11 **worthily,** excellently, in an excellent manner, creditably, commendably, meritoriously

12 **by virtue of,** by reason of, because of, on account of, in view of, due to, thanks to, owing to, by dint of, as a result of

NOUNS

1 **wickedness,** badness, unrighteousness, sin, sinfulness, evilness, wrong; wicked *or* bad behavior, evildoing, wrongdoing; wicked *or* bad ways, bad character, sinful *or* immoral *or* evil ways; rankness, foulness, nefariousness, shamefulness, flagitiousness, infamousness; villainousness, fiendishness, delinquency, criminality, villainy, knavery, roguery; malevolence, enormity, atrociousness, heinousness, viciousness, cruelness, inhumanity; notoriety, notoriousness, scandalousness, infamy, flagrancy
   ▶ *Malevolence 306; Wrong 430; Evil 446*

2 **depravity,** unvirtuousness, impurity, corruption, vitiation, loss of innocence; vice, obscenity, indecency, lust, vulgarity, carnality, debauchery, vileness, baseness; degradation, perversion, degeneration, degeneracy; disrepute, fallen nature, recidivism, backsliding, deterioration; profligacy, turpitude, moral turpitude, shamelessness; immorality, amorality, amoralism, no morals, loose morals, moral weakness, weakness of the flesh; weak point, laxity, lack of principle
   ▶ *Disrepute 371; Immorality 432; Deterioration 808*

3 **iniquity,** wicked deed, peccability, transgression, trespass, improbity, dishonesty; flaw, fatal flaw, failing, frailty, infirmity, fault, defect, demerit; sin, venial sin, original sin, capital sin, carnal sin, mortal sin, deadly sin; seven deadly sins: pride, covetousness *or* avarice, lust, anger, gluttony, envy, sloth
   ▶ *Religion 81; Desire 288; Pride 297; Envy 314; Immorality 432; Weakness 517*

4 **impiety,** ungodliness, godlessness, blasphemy, sacrilege, desecration, profaneness, profanity, idolatry, deviltry, devil worship, Satanism, diabolism, witchcraft, sorcery
   ▶ *Occultism 86; Evil 446*

5 **villain,** blackguard, criminal, lawbreaker, crook, malefactor, outlaw, desperado, culprit, offender, roughneck, hooligan, hoodlum; felon, cheat, thief, robber, tough, mugger; rapist, child abuser, pedophile; drug peddler *or* dealer, racketeer, gangster, mobster, mafioso; killer, murderer, hired killer, assassin, hatchet man, terrorist, bomber, suicide bomber; wrongdoer, evildoer, transgressor, sinner, black sheep; traitor, betrayer, quisling, Judas, snake, snake in the grass, swine, swindler; pimp, nasty type, thug, bully, brute, savage, sadist, ogre; scum, scum of the earth, dregs of society; criminal world, underworld, gangland, organized crime, syndicate, Mafia, the Mob, Cosa Nostra, Black Hand; [Inf]: the rackets, hood, con man, hit man
   ▶ *Malevolence 306; Immorality 432; Evil 446*

6 **miscreant,** renegade, recreant, troublemaker, good-for-nothing, ne'er-do-well; scamp, rake, knave, rogue, rascal, scoundrel, rapscallion, reprobate, wastrel, profligate, degenerate, lecher, pervert; ugly customer, bad egg, baddie *or* baddy, bad lot, lowlife; [Inf]: bad *or* rotten apple, bastard, rat, skunk, polecat, bitch, stinker, wrong'un, son of a bitch *or* S.O.B., bad news, louse, rotter [Brit]

7 **wicked act,** criminal act, criminal offense, punishable offense, hanging offense, guilty act, foul play; unlawful act, lawbreaking, misdemeanor, shoplifting, delinquency, juvenile delinquency; crime, white-collar crime, felony, drug peddling *or* dealing, racketeering; robbery, rape, assault, assault and battery, assault with a deadly weapon; murder, assassination, terrorism, bombing, capital crime, deadly crime, career of crime
   ▶ *Killing 30; Substance Abuse 121; Guilt 450*

8 **wicked place,** sewer, gutter, pit, sink, sink of corruption, sinkhole, hole; den, den of iniquity *or* vice, fleshpot, brothel, bordello, house of prostitution, cathouse [Inf]; drug house, opium den, gambling den; road to hell, hell, hellhole
   ▶ *Substance Abuse 121; Immorality 432*

ADJECTIVES

9 **wicked,** bad, unrighteous, sinful, sinning, evil; behaving badly, evildoing, wrong, wrongdoing; rank, foul, arrant, nefarious, disreputable, disgraceful, shameful, flagitious, infamous; fiendish, delinquent, criminal, villainous, knavish, roguish; malevolent, atrocious, heinous, vicious, cruel, inhuman; notorious, scandalous, flagrant

10 **depraved,** unvirtuous, virtueless, scarlet, impure, unchaste, corrupt, debased; rotten, rotten to the core, steeped in vice, obscene, indecent, lustful, vulgar, carnal, debauched, vile, base; degrading, degraded, perverting, perverted, perverse, degenerate, degenerating, degenerative, profligate; disreputed, fallen, recidivistic, recidivous, slipping, sliding, backsliding, deteriorating, deteriorated; shameless; without morals, immoral, amoral, morally weak, lax, unprincipled
   ▶ *Immorality 432*

11 **impious,** irreligious, ungodly, godless, godforsaken, blasphemous, sacrilegious, desecrating, profane, devilish, Satanic, diabolic; flawed, failing, frail, infirm, faulted, defected; proud, covetous, avaricious, lustful, angry, gluttonous, envious, shiftless, lazy
   ▶ *Evil 446*

12 **villainous,** illegal, unlawful, lawbreaking, outlaw, desperate, offensive; culpable, accusable, blameworthy, guilty; felonious, cheating, thieving, abusive; murderous, terrorist; traitorous, Judas-like, snakelike, recreant; troublesome, scampish, rascally, lowdown [Inf], crooked, stinking, rotten

VERBS

13 **be wicked,** act wickedly, be bad, stray, stray from the path of righteousness, sin, commit sin, wrong, do wrong, fall from grace; have one's foibles, have one's

weak side; transgress, trespass, offend, cheat, thieve, betray, swindle, rob, rape, abuse, brutalize, savage; kill, murder, assassinate, terrorize; shock, scoff at virtue, blaspheme, profane; corrupt, become corrupt, go to the bad, fall into evil ways, shame oneself, disgrace oneself, ruin one's name; lapse, relapse, backslide, deviate from the path of virtue, stray from the straight and narrow, go to the dogs [Inf]

14 **deprave,** make wicked, corrupt, distort, vitiate; lust after, seduce, debauch, degrade, pervert, degenerate; set a bad example, mislead, lead astray, teach wickedness, tempt, diabolize; demoralize, shame, dehumanize

ADVERBS

15 **wickedly,** badly, unrighteously, sinfully, evilly, with evil intentions, wrongly; foully, arrantly, nefariously, disgracefully, shamefully, flagitiously, infamously; villainously, fiendishly, delinquently, criminally, knavishly; malevolently, atrociously, heinously, viciously, cruelly, inhumanely; notoriously, scandalously, flagrantly

16 **unvirtuously,** impurely, corruptly, obscenely, in an obscene manner, indecently, lustfully, vulgarly, carnally, vilely, basely; degradingly, to one's discredit, pervertly, degeneratively; disreputably, recidivatingly; shamelessly, immorally, amorally, without morals; iniquitously, dishonestly, unscrupulously

17 **impiously,** ungodly, irreligiously, blasphemously, sacrilegiously, profanely, devilishly, diabolically, satanically

18 **villainously,** criminally, illegally, unlawfully, culpably, offensively, with offense, feloniously, guiltily, murderously

449 Innocence

No, it is not only our fate but our business to lose innocence, and once we have lost that, it is futile to attempt a picnic in Eden. — ELIZABETH BOWEN

NOUNS

1 **innocence,** virtue, goodness; morality, uprightness, probity; purity, virginity, chastity; purity of heart, saintliness, state of grace, perfection; immaculacy, cleanness, cleanliness, spotlessness, stainlessness, whiteness; playfulness, harmlessness, inoffensiveness
  ▶ *Cleanliness 111; Modesty 403; Virtue 447*

2 **incorruption,** incorruptibility, incorruptedness, sinlessness; freedom from sin, guiltlessness, inculpability, clear conscience, clean hands, faultlessness, impeccability; blamelessness, freedom from blame, irreproachability, nothing to confess, nothing to declare; innocent intentions, pure motives
  ▶ *Cleanliness 111; Morality 431*

3 **legal innocence,** verdict of innocence, finding of in-nocence; acquittal, exoneration, exculpation, absolution
  ▶ *Law 53; Litigation 54*

4 **naiveté,** ingenuousness, guilelessness, artlessness; unsophistication, inexperience, immaturity; callowness, greenness, unworldliness; naturalness, simplicity, credulousness; childhood, days of innocence, golden age, salad days
  ▶ *Youth 26; Ignorance 349; Naiveté 821*

5 **innocent person,** innocent party, innocent; beginner, ingenue, virgin, newcomer, greenhorn, tenderfoot; infant, child, babe, newborn babe, babe in the woods *or* wood; good person, saint, lamb, dove, angel; goody two shoes, goody-goody

ADJECTIVES

6 **innocent,** virtuous, good, upright; pure, virginal, chaste; pure of heart, saintly, perfect, angelic; immaculate, unblemished, untainted; stainless, spotless, unspotted; unsullied, undefiled, unsoiled; clean, pristine, white; prelapsarian, untouched by evil, unerring, innocent as a lamb, lamblike, innocent as a dove, dovelike, gentle; inoffensive, harmless, innocuous, safe; playful, holier than thou, goody-goody

7 **incorrupt,** incorruptible, sinless, free from sin; guiltless, inculpable, faultless, impeccable; blameless, unblamable, unblameworthy; irreprehensible, reproachless, irreproachable, above suspicion; not guilty, cleared, in the clear; with clean hands, clean-handed; uncorrupt, uncorruptible, uncorrupted

8 **declared innocent,** found innocent, found not guilty; cleared, acquitted, exonerated, exculpated, absolved

9 **naive,** ingenuous, guileless, artless; unsophisticated, credulous; inexperienced, immature, callow, green; unworldly, natural, simple; knowing no wrong, knowing no better; prelapsarian, childlike; innocent as a child, innocent as a newborn babe

VERBS

10 **be innocent,** have no guilt, stand above suspicion, wrong no one; have clean hands, have a clear conscience, have nothing to be ashamed of, have nothing to hide, have nothing to declare, have nothing to confess; live in a state of grace, not fall from grace; mean no harm, have the best intentions, salve one's conscience

11 **declare innocent,** find innocent, find not guilty; clear, acquit, exonerate, exculpate, absolve

12 **be naive,** have no guile, lack sophistication, lack experience, lack maturity; know no wrong, know no better; have the innocence of a child, be childlike

ADVERBS

13 **innocently,** in all innocence, with clean hands, with a clear conscience, with an easy conscience; virtuously, uprightly, purely, with pure intentions; virginally, chastely; perfectly, to perfection, in a perfect way, angelically; immaculately, spotlessly, unerringly;

inoffensively, harmlessly, in a harmless way, innocuously; with the best of intentions, unknowingly, unconsciously, unawares; playfully

14 **faultlessly,** impeccably, guiltlessly, with no guilt; blamelessly, irreproachably

15 **naively,** ingenuously, guilelessly, artlessly; without affectation, credulously; immaturely, naturally, simply

450 Guilt

All the perfumes of Arabia will not sweeten this little hand.
— WILLIAM SHAKESPEARE

NOUNS

1 **guilt,** guiltiness, culpability, liability, one's fault, bloodguilt, red-handedness; delinquency, illegality, criminality; implication, complicity, aiding and abetting; responsibility, reproach, reproachfulness; censure, blame, peccancy, inculpation; reprehensibility, blameworthiness, impeachability, indictability; accusation of guilt, accusation; conviction of guilt, conviction
   ◗ *Litigation 54; Disclosure 180; Accusation 442; Wickedness 448*

2 **sign of guilt,** burden of guilt, onus of guilt; guilt complex, guilty feelings, guilty conscience; bad conscience, twinge of conscience, qualms; remorse, shame, contrition, regret; self-reproach, self-accusation, penitence; guilty behavior, blush, stammer, embarrassment; dirty hands, bloody hands, red hands
   ◗ *Penitence 451*

3 **sin,** sinfulness, sinning; deadly sin, mortal sin, venial sin, original sin; vice, iniquity, wickedness; guilty act, wrongdoing, misconduct, misdoing, misdeed, misbehavior; lapse, slip, faux pas, blunder, mistake; fault, failure, dereliction of duty; injury, wrong, sin of omission, negligence, culpable omission; unprofessional conduct, indiscretion, impropriety, peccadillo; naughtiness, wicked deed, transgression, trespass, injustice
   ◗ *Malevolence 306; Negligence 326; Error 351; Wrong 430; Immorality 432*

4 **illegality,** crime, criminal offense, offense, misdemeanor, tort; white-collar crime, malpractice, felony; atrocity, outrage, enormity
   ◗ *Wrong 430; Immorality 432*

5 **guilty person,** guilty party, offender, culprit, wrongdoer; reprobate, recidivist, malefactor, delinquent, accomplice; criminal, confessed criminal, convicted criminal; felon, convict, prisoner, prison inmate, jailbird

ADJECTIVES

6 **guilty,** bloodguilty, responsible, reprehensible, reprehensive, censurable; inexcusable, without excuse; unjustifiable, unpardonable, unforgivable; reproachable, reproachful, reprovable; in the wrong, at fault, to

blame, culpable; inculpated, caught, caught in the act *or* red-handed *or* with one's pants down [Inf]; impeachable, chargeable, accusable, blameworthy, blameful, blamed, implicated, censured, peccant; condemned, convicted, found guilty, proved guilty

7 **appearing guilty,** looking guilty, shamefaced, shameful, ashamed; sheepish, blushing, stammering, hangdog, red-handed; feeling guilty, contrite, conscience-stricken; remorseful, regretful, sorry

8 **sinful,** wicked, illegal, criminal; trespassing, transgressing, heinous; mortal, deadly, murderous

VERBS

9 **be guilty,** be at fault, have no excuse, have no alibi, have nothing to say for oneself; get caught, get caught in the act *or* red-handed *or* with one's pants down [Inf]; have crimes to answer for, have blood on one's hands; acknowledge one's guilt, acknowledge one's sins, bear the blame, plead guilty, confess; stand condemned

10 **appear guilty,** look guilty, seem guilty, look ashamed; look embarrassed, look sheepish, blush, stammer; feel guilty, have a bad conscience; accuse oneself, torture oneself, punish oneself, wear a hair shirt

11 **sin,** trespass, transgress; commit a crime, commit a white-collar crime, commit a misdemeanor, commit a felony; rob, steal; kidnap, murder, assassinate

ADVERBS

12 **guiltily,** reprehensibly, reprehensively; inexcusably, without excuse; unjustifiably, unpardonably, unforgivably; reproachfully, with reproach, blamefully; criminally, red-handed, red-handedly, in the (very) act, flagrante delicto; shamefacedly, shamefully, ashamedly; sheepishly, blushingly; contritely, remorsefully, regretfully, sorrily, with sorrow; with a guilty conscience

451 Penitence

NOUNS

1 **penitence,** repentance, contrition, remorsefulness, remorse, self-reproach; regretfulness, regret, regretting, sorriness; shamefulness, shame; scruples, qualms, soul-searching, compunction; guilt, guilt feelings, self-accusation, self-condemnation; guilty conscience, bad conscience, uneasy conscience, twinge of conscience, pangs of conscience, pangs, pricking of conscience, voice of one's conscience, weight on one's mind

2 **confession,** humble confession, recantation; apology, heartfelt apology, humble apology, abject apology, grudging apology; deathbed repentance, deathbed confession; reformation, conversion, change of heart
   ◗ *Religion 81; Disclosure 180; Lamentation 280; Guilt 450; Conversion 670; Improvement 807*

3 **type of penance,** atonement, act of contrition, reparation; mortification, mortification of the flesh, breast-beating; sackcloth and ashes, wearing a sackcloth,

wearing a hair shirt; flagellation, self-flagellation, self-scourging; prostration, self-punishment, self-humiliation; purification, purgation

> *Humility 298; Atonement 313; Submission 421*

4 penitent person, penitent, confessor; flagellant, ascetic; prodigal son, prodigal returned; contrite sinner, born-again Christian, reformed character; sadder but wiser man *or* woman

ADJECTIVES

5 penitent, repentant, repenting, contrite; remorseful, full of remorse; regretful, full of regrets, regretting; lamenting, sorry, apologetic; sorrowful, rueful, ashamed, shamefaced, shamefast [Arch]; self-reproachful, self-reproaching, self-accusing, self-condemning, compunctious; guilty, full of guilt, conscience-stricken, pricked by conscience, plagued by conscience; confessing, confessed; reformed, regenerate, reclaimed, converted, born-again

6 penitential, penitentiary, doing penance; atoning, atoned, self-punishing; humiliating, humiliated

> *Atonement 313*

VERBS

7 be penitent, do penance, repent, feel contrite, feel remorse; blame oneself, reprove oneself, accuse oneself, reproach oneself; search one's soul, rue the day, wish undone, regret, have regrets, express regrets; feel sorry, say one is sorry, apologize; feel shame, hang one's head in shame, show compunction; feel guilty, have guilt feelings; condemn oneself, bewail one's sins

8 confess, confess one's sins, go to confession; acknowledge one's sins, acknowledge one's faults; recant one's errors, recant; think again, have second thoughts, think better of; learn one's lesson, learn from (bitter) experience, see the error of one's ways, see the light; reform, make a fresh start, turn from sin, return to the straight and narrow, become a born-again Christian, turn over a new leaf, wipe the slate clean

9 do penance, atone for, make amends, salve one's conscience; mortify one's flesh, beat one's breast; repent in sackcloth and ashes, wear a hair shirt, flagellate oneself, scourge oneself; prostrate oneself, punish oneself, humiliate oneself

ADVERBS

10 penitently, repentantly, with repentance; contritely, remorsefully, regretfully, with regret; apologetically, to apologize; sorrowfully, ruefully; shamefacedly; self-accusingly, in self-reproach, self-reproachingly; compunctiously, guiltily, with a guilty conscience; penitentially, like a penitent; in sackcloth and ashes, humiliatingly

452 Impenitence

NOUNS

1 impenitence, impenitentness, nonrepentance, lack

of contrition, refusal to recant, lack of confession; incorrigibility, obstinacy, stubbornness, obduracy; hardness, hardness of heart, cold-heartedness, hardheartedness, heart of stone; callousness, induration, remorselessness, pitilessness, shamelessness, seared conscience; no apologies, no regrets, no remorse, no going back

> *Pitilessness 309; Perseverance 377; Obstinacy 379; Hardness 542*

ADJECTIVES

2 impenitent, unrepentant, unrepenting; incorrigible, inveterate, obdurate, obstinate; brazen, shameless, unreformed; not sorry, unapologetic, uncontrite; unmoved, unashamed, unblushing; unremorseful, without remorse, remorseless; unsorrowful, unregretful, without regrets, having no regrets, regretless, unregretting, without a pang of regret; without compunction; without a conscience, conscienceless; heartless, cold-hearted, hardhearted; hardened, hard, callous, indurative, untouched; hopeless, lost, irreclaimable; irredeemable, not redeemable, not redeemed, unredeemed; unreconciled, unreformed, unregenerated, unchastened, unrecanting, unshriven, not confessing; rotten to the core

3 unatoned, unrepented, unregretted, unapologized for

VERBS

4 be impenitent, remain unrepentant, not reform; have no regrets, have no remorse, have no conscience, feel nothing; remain obstinate, refuse to recant, make no confession, not confess, offer no apologies, want no forgiveness; feel no remorse, harden one's heart, steel oneself, indurate, refuse to see the error of one's ways

ADVERBS

5 impenitently, unregretfully, with no regrets, without regret; unremorsefully, remorselessly, with no remorse, without remorse, without compunction; unashamedly, shamelessly, unblushingly; cold-heartedly, hardheartedly; without qualms, without scruples, without looking back, without seeing the error of one's ways

453 Reward

NOUNS

1 reward, financial reward, remuneration, recompense; deserved reward, deserts, just deserts; justice, guerdon, meed [Arch]; satisfaction, job satisfaction, personal reward; recognition, public recognition, due recognition; credit, due credit; acknowledgment, thanks, gratitude, favor; tribute, deserved tribute, proof of regard; acclaim, acclamation; bouquet, praise, honor, honors, decoration; title, honorary degree, honorary title

> *Title 72; Satisfaction 273; Gratitude 310; Approval 437*

2 prize, award, crown, trophy, cup; pot, shield, certificate, medal, blue ribbon, kewpie doll; consolation prize, second prize, runner-up prize, booby prize, wooden spoon; cash prize, prize money, jackpot, kitty

3 **prizes,** Nobel Prize, Pulitzer Prize, Booker Prize [Brit], Academy Award, Oscar, Emmy, Tony, Obie, Man/Woman of the Year, Olympic Gold *or* Silver *or* Bronze Medal, America's Cup

4 **grant,** aid, assistance, subsidy, subvention, fellowship, scholarship, stipend, allowance

5 **reward for service,** remuneration, fee, retainer, honorarium; emolument, payment, payment in kind, payoff, promotion; pension, retirement benefits; pay, wages, salary, basic salary, take-home pay, compensation; severance pay, golden handshake, golden parachute; income, earnings; wage *or* salary scale, raise, increment, overtime pay, commission, bonus; incentive, inducement, enticement, offer, tempting offer; bait, lure, perquisite, fringe benefits, hidden income, expense account, perk [Inf]
   ▶ *Payment 489; Offer 504*

6 **return,** profitable return, gain; profit, gross profit, net profit, pretax profit, profit after tax; profit margin, margin of profit, bottom line
   ▶ *Gain 467*

7 **compensation,** indemnification, indemnity, satisfaction, consideration, solatium, damages; quid pro quo, requital, retaliation, reparation, amends, restitution; comeuppance [Inf]
   ▶ *Retaliation 420; Giving Back 478*

8 **bounty,** premium, gift, gratuity, tip, baksheesh
   ▶ *Giving 472*

ADJECTIVES

9 **rewarding,** financially rewarding, satisfying, paying; profitable, moneymaking, lucrative, remunerative, gainful
   ▶ *Gain 467; Payment 489*

10 **rewarded,** recognized, credited, acknowledged, acclaimed, praised

11 **compensatory,** indemnificatory, reparatory
   ▶ *Compensation 743*

12 **giving,** generous, openhanded, liberal, offering
   ▶ *Giving 472; Generosity 498; Offer 504*

VERBS

13 **reward,** offer *or* give a reward, remunerate, recompense; give financial reward, give a deserved reward, guerdon; promote, satisfy, give job satisfaction, give personal reward; recognize, credit, acknowledge, thank, show one's gratitude; pay tribute, pat on the back, acclaim, praise; hand out bouquets, award, present, offer *or* give a prize, honor, decorate, bestow a medal, bestow an honorary degree, honor with a title
   ▶ *Title 72; Gratitude 310; Repute 370; Approval 437; Decoration 532*

14 **grant,** aid, assist, subsidize, award a fellowship, give a scholarship

15 **pay,** remunerate, give, tip, tip well, pay off; repay, give what is due, settle up, compensate, indemnify
   ▶ *Giving 472; Payment 489*

16 **be rewarded,** get a reward, gain a reward, have one's reward; get one's deserts, receive one's due, get what is coming to one; receive a promotion, get job satisfaction; win a prize, get a medal, receive an honorary degree, receive a title, get one's comeuppance [Inf]

17 **get paid,** draw a salary, earn an income, have a gainful occupation, accept payment, accept a gratification
   ▶ *Receiving 473*

18 **gain,** reap, reap a profit, reap the fruits
   ▶ *Gain 467*

ADVERBS

19 **rewardingly,** satisfyingly, as a reward, as a prize, for one's service, in compensation

20 **profitably,** lucratively, remuneratively, gainfully

454 Punishment

My object all sublime / I shall achieve in time — / To let the punishment fit the crime. — W. S. GILBERT

NOUNS

1 **punishment,** penalization, discipline, disciplinary action; chastisement, chastening, chiding, correction, lesson; castigation, admonition, dressing-down, reprimand, reproof, rebuke; scolding, rap on the knuckles, slap on the wrist; persecution, victimization, example, shame; tarring and feathering, tossing in a blanket, ducking, keelhauling, walking the plank, binding over; demotion, degrading, downgrading, unfrocking, suspension; *peine forte et dure* [Fr]; [Inf]: telling off, chewing out, kicking ass, grounding
   ▶ *Severity 424*

2 **imprisonment,** incarceration, confinement, internment, prison *or* jail sentence, debt to society, penal servitude; prison, hard labor, chain gang, labor camp, penal colony, Gulag; house arrest, detention
   ▶ *Prison 55*

3 **exile,** deportation, expulsion, banishment, ostracism, blackballing, outlawing, proscription, banning

4 **confiscation,** deprivation; forfeit, forfeiture; escheat, expropriation, sequestration

5 **penalty,** official punishment, legal punishment, prescribed punishment; pains and penalties, condemnation; sentence, sentencing, execution of sentence; execution of justice, exaction of penalty

6 **liability,** court award, damages, costs, compensation, restoration, restitution; payment, court payment, compulsory payment, compensatory payment; ransom, fine, fining, court fine, amercement, mulct

7 **retribution,** just *or* fitting retribution, Nemesis; deserts, just deserts, meet reward; justice, poetic justice, divine justice, retributive justice

8 reckoning, doom, doomsday; judgment, day of judgment, day of reckoning, what is coming, reward; retaliation, reprisal, requital, repayment, revenge, getting even; what for, hell *or* the devil to pay, comeuppance [Inf]

▶ *Retaliation 420*

9 affliction, infliction, visitation, imposition, trial, task, punishing experience; dose, hard dose, pill, bitter pill; hard *or* tough row (to hoe), adversity, suffering; damage, loss, injury

▶ *Affliction 117; Adversity 848*

10 self-punishment, penance, atonement, self-mortification, self-discipline, asceticism; hara-kiri, seppuki, felo-de-se, suicide

11 corporal punishment, chastisement of the flesh, bodily chastisement; hitting, striking, spanking, smacking; slapping, paddling, drubbing, trouncing; beating, caning, birching, thrashing, thrashing of a lifetime; flogging, whipping, horsewhipping, scourging, flagellation, running the gauntlet; hit, spank, smack, slap, slap on the wrist; rap, rap on the knuckles, box on the ear; blow, buffet, cuff, clout, stroke, stripe; torture, third degree; racking, breaking on the wheel, hanging by the wrists, strappado, bastinado, death by a thousand cuts, dusting, hiding [Inf]

▶ *Physical Pain 215*

12 capital punishment, execution, legalized killing, judicial murder; extreme penalty, death sentence, death penalty, death warrant; traitor's death; electrocution; hanging, drawing, and quartering; gas, poison, injection, shooting; guillotining, beheading, decapitation; decollation, strangulation, garrote; stoning, lapidation; impalement, crucifixion; flaying alive; burning, burning at the stake, auto-da-fé; drowning, noyade; massacre, mass murder, mass execution, purge, genocide, slaughter; martyrdom, martyrization, persecution to the death; illegal execution, lynching

▶ *Killing 30*

13 instrument of punishment, pillory, stocks; ducking stool, cucking stool; stool of repentance, corner, dunce's cap; open hand, hairbrush, belt, strap, thong, quirt, lash; whip, horsewhip, cowhide, knout, scourge, cat-o'-nine-tails, cat, rope's end; whipping post, ruler, ferule, stick, birch, switch, big stick, rattan, cane, rod, cudgel, cosh, club, rubber hose, bicycle chain, sandbag; chain, irons, bilboes, fetters; cell, jail, prison, prison house

▶ *Prison 55; Restraint 830*

14 instrument of torture, rack, thumbscrew, iron boot, pilliwinks, triangle, wheel, treadmill, tightened headband, weights; spiked device, iron maiden; crushing device, scavenger's daughter; torture chamber, Inquisition, Star Chamber

15 instrument of execution, electric chair, the chair, hot seat [Inf]; hanging rope, rope, noose, halter; hempen collar; gas, hemlock, poison, lethal injection; bullet, firing squad; ax, headsman's ax, block, guillotine; garrote, bowstring; cross, stake

16 punisher, discipliner, chastiser, chastener, corrector, castigator; persecutor, tyrant; vindicator, revenger, avenger, retaliator; sentencer, magistrate, judge; caner, whipper, flogger, flagellator, scourger; torturer, inquisitor, witch hunter; executioner, high executioner, hangman, hanging judge, headsman; garrotter, bowstringer, lyncher; assassin, murderer, hatchet man, hit man [Inf]

▶ *Litigation 54*

17 penology, penal code, penologist

ADJECTIVES

18 punitive, punitory, punishing, penalizing, penal, penological; capital, corporal; disciplinary, corrective, correctional; instructive, castigatory, admonitory *or* monitory; vindictive, retributive, revengeful, retaliatory

19 punished, disciplined, castigated; imprisoned, in confinement, under house arrest; fined, beaten, tortured, executed, grounded [Inf]

20 punishing, hard, arduous, strenuous, exhausting, grueling, laborious, backbreaking, demanding, taxing; torturous, painful

21 punishable, liable, deserving punishment; condemned, awaiting execution; amerceable, mulctable

VERBS

22 punish, inflict punishment, discipline, take disciplinary action; give *or* teach a lesson, chastise, chasten, correct, administer correction; castigate, admonish, reprimand, have *or* call on the carpet, dress down, give a dressing-down, reprove, rebuke, chide, scold, take to task; rap on the knuckles, slap the wrist, have one's head for, hurt, inflict pain; afflict, inflict, visit, impose; persecute, victimize; make an example of, shame, pillory, put in the stocks; tar and feather, duck; masthead, keelhaul, picket; demote, degrade, downgrade, unfrock, reduce to the ranks; suspend, strafe [Inf], tell off [Inf]

23 imprison, jail, incarcerate, intern, lock up; transport, condemn to the galleys; put in detention, keep in; put away, send down *or* up, ground

24 exile, expel, cashier, drum out; ban, proscribe; banish, deport; ostracize, blackball, outlaw

▶ *Unsociability 409; Separation 753; Exclusion 764*

25 confiscate, take away, deprive, forfeit, escheat, sequestrate, fine, amerce, mulct

▶ *Severity 424*

26 penalize, come down on, come down hard on; impose a penalty, exact a penalty; condemn, sentence, execute *or* carry out a sentence, execute justice

27 exact retribution, settle, fix, bring to book, give what is coming to him *or* her, give one what for; retaliate, settle with, get even with, pay back, avenge, revenge oneself; [Inf]: throw the book at, give his *or* her comeuppance

▶ *Retaliation 420*

28 **hit,** strike, smack, slap, slap on the wrist; lambaste, paddle, spank, slipper, put across one's knee; cuff, clout, box one's ears, rap on the knuckles, dust off; drub, trounce, beat, beat black and blue, beat the living daylights out of; belt, strap, leather, larrup, wallop, welt, tan, tan one's hide; cane, birch, switch; whack, thwack, thrash, flog; whip, horsewhip; lash, lay on the lash; scourge, give stripes, give strokes; flay, flay one's back, lay one's back open, flail, flagellate; bastinado, cudgel, belabor, fustigate, [Inf]: give a hiding, hide, lather

29 **torture,** put to torture, torment, inflict pain, give the third degree; thumbscrew, rack, put on the rack, break on the wheel; press, mutilate, kneecap; persecute, martyr, martyrize, work over, give the works [Inf]

▶ *Physical Pain 215*

30 **execute,** put to death, punish with death, condemn to death, sentence to death, kill, lynch; electrocute, send to the chair; hang, hang by the neck, send to the gallows, send to the scaffold, gibbet; hang, draw, and quarter; gas, put in the gas chamber, give a lethal injection; shoot, put in front of a firing squad, stand against a wall; guillotine, behead, cut off one's head, decapitate, decollate, send to the block; strangle, garrote, bowstring; burn, burn alive, burn at the stake; flay, flay alive; stone, stone to death, lapidate; dismember, tear limb from limb; impale, crucify; hold mass executions, commit genocide, purge, massacre, decimate, slaughter, murder, butcher; send to the hot seat [Inf], string up [Inf]

▶ *Killing 30*

31 **be punished,** suffer punishment, take the consequences, face the music, take one's medicine; have it coming to one, get what one is asking for, get one's deserts; regret it; go to prison *or* jail, be incarcerated; be fined, pay a penalty; [Inf]: get one's comeuppance, catch it, take the rap, take the fall

32 **be executed,** be hanged, face the firing squad, pay for it with one's head, lay one's head on the block, go to the gallows; pay the ultimate price

ADVERBS

33 **punitively,** penally, penologically, vindictively, retributively, punishingly, punishably

455 Self-Restraint

NOUNS

1 **self-restraint,** self-control, self-discipline, self-denial, self-abnegation, self-mastery; restraint, constraint, restriction, repression; avoidance, eschewal, forbearance; renunciation, relinquishment, refrainment; abstaining, abstinence, abstention, abstemiousness; asceti-

cism, Spartanism, frugality, parsimony, economy, simple life, plain living, plainness, passing up

▶ *Avoidance 386; Relinquishment 392; Morality 431; Disinterestedness 443; Thrift 499*

2 **abstinence,** sexual abstinence, askesis *or* ascesis, celibacy, chastity; purity, puritanism, continence; soberness, sobriety, total abstinence, teetotalism; dieting, weight-watching, vegetarianism, veganism, fast, fasting

▶ *Celibacy 67; Fasting 118; Sobriety 120*

3 **moderation,** moderateness, prudence, reasonableness, temperance, temperateness, nothing in excess; middle way, happy medium, golden mean

▶ *Moderation 521*

4 **calmness,** composure, lack of emotion, stoicism, keeping a stiff upper lip, sang-froid

▶ *Insensibility 213; Hindrance 826*

5 **self-restrained person,** sober person, abstainer, total abstainer, teetotaler, prohibitionist, dry, nonsmoker; vegetarian, vegan, ascetic, dieter, faster; puritan, Spartan, sobersides [Inf], tight-ass [Inf]

ADJECTIVES

6 **self-restrained,** self-controlled, self-disciplined, self-denying; restrictive, restricted, strict; repressive, repressed, prohibited, renunciative, relinquished, restrained, anal-retentive; refraining, forbearing, abstaining, abstemious, abstinent; costive, frugal, economical, parsimonious, ascetic, plain; Spartan, stinting, sparing, tight-assed [Inf], uptight [Inf]

7 **abstinent,** sexually abstinent, celibate, continent, chaste; pure, puritanical, strait-laced; sober, teetotal, dry, sworn off, on the wagon [Inf]; dieting, vegetarian, vegan, fasting

8 **temperate,** tempered, not excessive, not overdoing; moderate, prudent, reasonable, measured, within bounds, circumscribed, confined, within reasonable limits, limiting, limited, under control

9 **calm,** composed, lacking emotion, stoic, keeping a stiff upper lip

VERBS

10 **be self-restrained,** restrain oneself, control oneself, exercise self-control, discipline oneself, restrict oneself, limit oneself, deny oneself, do without, never touch, constrain oneself, ration oneself; refrain, repress, retard, hold back, rein in; avoid excess, avoid, eschew, forbear; renounce, relinquish, put a stop to, swear off, give up, forgo, ban, curb, brake, veto; know when to stop, know when one has had enough, temper; economize, live plainly, live simply, live frugally, tighten one's belt, pass up

11 **abstain,** abstain from sex, control one's lusts, repress one's desires, mortify the flesh; shun alcohol, prohibit drinking, renounce drinking, take *or* sign the pledge, be dry, go on the wagon [Inf]; diet, go on a diet, lose weight, control one's appetite, eat sparingly, eat in

---

moderation; eat to live, not live to eat; half starve, starve, fast

12 **be moderate,** be temperate, do nothing in excess, keep within bounds, circumscribe, confine, observe a limit; keep to the middle way, keep a happy medium, keep the golden mean

13 **be calm,** be composed, lack emotion, keep a stiff upper lip

ADVERBS

14 **with self-restraint,** with self-control, restrictively, strictly, repressively, forbearingly; abstemiously, chastely, purely, puritanically; temperately, teetotally, without excess, without overdoing it; ascetically, Spartanly, plainly, frugally, economically, parsimoniously, stintingly, sparingly

15 **moderately,** with moderation; prudently, with prudence; reasonably, within reason, within bounds, within reasonable limits; under control

16 **calmly,** without emotion, stoically, with a stiff upper lip

456 Self-Indulgence

NOUNS

1 **self-indulgence,** self-gratification, pleasure seeking, highlife, hedonism, sybaritism, epicureanism, luxury, sensuality, voluptuousness, carnality
▶ *Physical Pleasure 214*

2 **dissipation,** riotous living, dissoluteness, licentiousness, debauchery, profligacy, carousal, orgy, saturnalia, fast lane [Inf]

3 **overindulgence,** immoderation, uncontrol, unrestraint; abandon, undiscipline, inordinateness; overdoing, excess, excessiveness, incontinence, concupiscence; intemperance, drunkenness, crapulence; addiction; overeating, greed, gluttony, gormandizing; extravagance, wastefulness, prodigality
▶ *Excess 99; Gluttony 119; Substance Abuse 121; Extravagance 500*

4 **self-absorption,** self-obsession, self-devotion, self-worship, self-love, narcissism, vanity, self-centeredness, egotism, egoism, selfishness
▶ *Vanity 402; Selfishness 444*

5 **self-indulgent person,** pleasure-seeker, free liver, hedonist, sybarite; epicure, bon vivant, gourmet, gourmand, glutton; toper, voluptuary, sensualist, debauchee; narcissist, egotist, egoist, high liver [Inf]
▶ *Physical Pleasure 214*

ADJECTIVES

6 **self-indulgent,** self-gratifying, pleasure-seeking, high-living, pleasure-bound, hedonistic, sybaritic, epicurean, sensual, voluptuous, carnal

7 **dissipated,** dissipating, dissolute, riotous; fast-living, free-living; licentious, debauched, debauching, profligate

8 **overindulgent,** immoderate, uncontrolled, unrestrained, undisciplined, abandoned; inordinate, excessive, incontinent, concupiscent, intemperate, drunk; crapulent, addicted; greedy, gluttonous, gormandizing; extravagant, wasteful, prodigal

9 **self-absorbed,** self-obsessed, self-devoted, self-worshiping, self-loving, narcissistic; vain, self-centered, egotistic, egoistic, selfish

VERBS

10 **indulge oneself,** indulge in, luxuriate in, wallow in; deny oneself nothing, put oneself first, look out for number one; live high off *or* on the hog, live it up [Inf]

11 **overindulge,** overdo, waste, squander, dissipate; gorge, debauch, carouse; not know when to stop, burn the candle at both ends; sow one's wild oats; have a fling; binge [Inf], go on a bender [Inf]

ADVERBS

12 **self-indulgently,** intemperately, incontinently, immoderately; excessively, in *or* to excess, beyond all bounds; in the fast lane [Inf]

Negotiations and Fiscal Relations

457 Finance

NOUNS

1 **finance,** world of finance, high finance, financial control, money power, purse strings, power of the purse, money dealings, cash transaction, financial affairs, budget, money management, financial management, deficit finance, investment, investment strength, money market, mutual fund; banking, prime rate, prime lending rate, interest rate, bank rate, minimum lending rate, effective rate; accounting, financial accounting, managerial accounting, financial year, fiscal year; arbitrage, sinking fund, equalization fund, revolving fund

▶ *Economics 56; Money 484; Expenditure 491; Accounting 493; Improvement 807; Deterioration 808*

2 **international finance,** foreign market, foreign currency reserves; exchange rate, exchange premium, parity, par, agio, agiotage, floating currency, devaluation, depreciation, falling exchange rate, deterioration, rising exchange rate, strong currency, rallying, improvement; bimetallism, gold standard, managed currency

▶ *Economics 56; Trade 480*

3 **stock exchange,** exchange, stock market, bull market, bear market, market, Wall Street, Big Board [Inf]; Dow Jones Industrial Index *or* Dow Industrials *or* the Dow, American Express Industrial Index *or* AMEX Index, Standard and Poore Index *or* S & P Index, National Association of Securities Dealers Automated Quotation System *or* NASDAQ system, British Market, Nikkei Market; bond market, currency market, commodities exchange; issue, issue price, bid price, dividends, earnings per share, blue chips, preferred issue, common stock

▶ *Market 483*

4 **financial adviser,** accountant, business manager, investment specialist, portfolio manager; financier, banker, investor, bidder, backer, stockbroker, broker,

specialist, penny broker, bond broker, commodities broker, exchange broker, trader, futures trader, speculator, arbitrager *or* arbitrageur

▶ *Money 484; Payment 489*

5 **personal finance,** savings, budget, keeping to a budget; deposit, bank account, savings account, checking account, Christmas account; pension, 401(k) fund, Individual Retirement Account (IRA), Keogh plan, something for a rainy day

▶ *Money 484; Wealth 485; Credit 487*

ADJECTIVES

6 **financial,** monetary, fiscal, pecuniary, economic; rising, bull, falling, bear; devaluated, depreciated, devalued; inflationary, deflationary, disinflationary, reflationary, managed

▶ *Economics 56*

VERBS

7 **finance,** invest, venture, risk, speculate, put one's money to work, sink one's capital in, invest in, fund finance, hold the purse strings, act as a white knight [Inf], finance, underwrite, bankroll [Inf]; go into stocks *or* bonds, play the big board, play the stock exchange, float, buy stocks, trade, arbitrage, be long *or* short in; play the futures market, deal in futures; bid, buy, sell, sell short, sell long

▶ *Payment 489*

8 **trade in,** trade with, open a trade, traffic in, export, import, market, merchandise, offer for sale, have on offer; profit, sell at a profit, make a profit, realize one's capital, commercialize, corner the market, monopolize

▶ *Trade 480; Sale 482; Market 483*

9 **deal,** negotiate, barter, bargain, drive a hard bargain, make a bid, raise the bid; take over, hostile takeover, friendly takeover, merge

▶ *Economics 56*

10 **budget,** save, plan, economize, deposit, open an account; allow, allocate, ration

11 **financially,** monetarily, fiscally, economically, pecuniarily

458 Promise

Promises and pie-crust are made to be broken.
— JONATHAN SWIFT

NOUNS

1 **promise,** solemn promise, commitment, voluntary commitment, pledge, vow, oath, one's word, swearing on the Bible, swearing, affirmation; firm date, delivery date; assurance, profession, obligation, declaration, promise-making, gentleman's agreement, mutual pledge, unwritten agreement, handshake; covenant, bond, compact, contract, debt of honor
▶ *Affirmation 189; Contract 459; Agreement 462; Borrowing 476; Debt 488; Truth 721*

2 **betrothal,** intention, declaration of intent, banns, engagement, marriage contract, exchange of vows; prenuptial agreement *or* contract
▶ *Marriage 64; Intention 374*

3 **guarantee,** security, warrant, warranty, entitlement, promissory note, contract, IOU, voucher, pawn ticket, chit
▶ *Security 464*

4 **potential,** possibilities, capacity, capability, ability; good things to come, good omen, favorable auspices, good prospects, bright prospects

5 **promised land,** land of promise, land of milk and honey, Canaan, Israel
▶ *Imagination 360; Nonmaterial World 525*

6 **promise maker,** promiser, promisor, guarantor, party, surety, signatory, signer, signee, cosignatory, cosigner, bondsman, obligor, swearer

7 **someone promised,** betrothed, fiancé, fiancée, affianced, engaged person, lucky man, bride-to-be, intended [Inf]; promisee, assignee

ADJECTIVES

8 **promised,** pledged, bound, committed, sworn, on *or* under oath, on one's word, under hand and seal, avowed, votive, assured, professed; engaged, betrothed, spoken for, plighted, affianced

9 **guaranteeing,** guaranteed, authenticating, authenticated, certified, assured, attested; certain, warranted, underwritten; signed, cosigned, securing, secured, pledging, pledged, committed, bound, obligated, promissory, contracted

10 **auspicious,** promising, propitious, full of promise; full of potential, likely, fortunate, favorable, optimistic, good, bright; eventual, potential, prospective, probable, possible, anticipated, predicted, predictable, foreseeable, sure, certain, destined, fated

VERBS

11 **promise,** make *or* give a promise, solemnly promise, pledge, pledge one's word *or* oneself *or* one's honor, give one's word, vow, swear, swear on *or* under oath, swear on the Holy Bible *or* on one's mother's life *or* head, cross one's heart (and hope to die); commit oneself, take responsibility for, confirm, assure, say yes, say one will; enter into an agreement, give a firm date, make a gentleman's agreement, shake on it, sign on the dotted line, covenant, contract

12 **get engaged to,** become engaged, become betrothed, plight one's troth, exchange vows, espouse, ask for someone's hand, accept a proposal, post *or* put up the banns, read *or* publish the banns, say "I do"

13 **guarantee,** warrant, certify, assure, answer for, vouch for, attest; commit oneself, make it one's duty, take on, accept responsibility, accept obligation; accept liability, secure, insure, underwrite, stand bail, go bond for; give a written guarantee, sign a promissory note, cosign a note, make a contract, promise to pay, give one's IOU; receive a voucher, receive a pawn ticket

14 **show potential,** show promise, have possibilities, hope, receive a good omen, have good prospects, have a bright future, get better, improve, develop, evolve, prove fruitful; be auspicious, be likely, promise to, promise well, augur well, hold out hopes for, build up hope, bid fair

15 **promise oneself,** look forward to, set one's heart on, have designs on

ADVERBS

16 **as promised,** as agreed, upon one's word, on *or* under oath, under hand and seal, votively, assuredly, with assurance, certainly, solemnly

17 **auspiciously,** propitiously, promisingly, with promise, fortunately, favorably, optimistically, in an optimistic way; potentially, eventually, prospectively, probably, predictably, surely, certainly

459 Contract

NOUNS

1 **contract,** formal contract, obligation, commitment, promise, compact, undertaking; escrow, security, deed; arrangement, understanding, cooperation, accord, agreement, mise; bond, union, betrothal, vow; alliance, partnership, covenant, pact, treaty; deal, settlement, (assassination) contract [Inf]
▶ *Marriage 64; Undertaking 391; Promise 458; Negotiation 460; Agreement 462; Security 464; Accord 735; Cooperation 827*

2 **agreements,** mutual, legal, binding, formal, informal, gentleman's, prenuptial
▶ *Promise 458; Agreement 462; Accord 735*

3 **purchase contract,** building contract, service contract, rental contract, leasing contract, lease, employ-

ment contract, teaching contract, publishing contract, insurance policy; promissory note, IOU, debenture, debenture bond, mortgage, trust deed *or* deed of trust
> *Money 484; Credit 487; Debt 488*

4 ratification, completion, confirmation, consent, assent, seal, signet, signature, cosignature, countersignature, execution, discharge, fulfillment

5 alliance, league, cartel, consortium, trust, entente, entente cordiale, protocol, international agreement, international pact, trade agreement, convention; treaty, peace treaty, nonaggression pact, concordat, mutual defense treaty, arms control agreement
> *Government 49; Politics 50; Pacification 74; Trade 480*

6 contractor, contracting party, signatory, signer, cosigner, countersigner, the undersigned, endorser, ratifier; covenanter, consenting party, assenter; jobber, entrepreneur, dealer

ADJECTIVES

7 contractual, contracted, obligated, obligatory, committed, promised, deeded, covenantal, covenanted; arranged, agreeable, agreed, sworn, consensual, assenting, ratifying; bilateral, multilateral; signed on the dotted line, cosigned, countersigned; signed, sealed and delivered; under one's hand and seal, ratified, assigned; matrimonial, nuptial, conjugal; allied, united

VERBS

8 contract, enter into a contract, execute a contract; make a compact, sign a pact, commit oneself, bind oneself; contract a marriage, betroth, marry, wed; sign on the dotted line, cosign, countersign, seal; subscribe to, underwrite, endorse, ratify, attest, confirm; covenant, sign a treaty, enter into an alliance, ally, join a consortium, league with, go into league with, form a cartel; bargain, strike a bargain, settle, make terms, agree, come to an agreement, come to terms; transfer, convey, deed; go into a partnership, form a partnership; deal, make *or* close a deal; [Inf]: cut a deal, put out a contract on, tie the knot

ADVERBS

9 contractually, as contracted for, according to the contract, covenantally, as agreed upon, as promised, according to the agreement, consensually, with consent; bilaterally, multilaterally; matrimonially, nuptially, conjugally; conspiratorially

460 Negotiation

NOUNS

1 negotiation, negotiations, mediation, arbitration, conciliation; exchange, discussion, bargaining, collective bargaining, hard bargaining; barter, bartering, compromising, compromise, horse trading, trade-off, give-and-take, haggling, wrangling, making terms; treaty making, diplomacy, communication, intercommunication, transaction; deal, offer one cannot refuse
> *Communications 169; Compromise 461; Trade 480*

2 basis for negotiations, frame of reference, contract, terms, written terms, set of terms, conditions, part of the bargain, offer, trade-off, provision, article, articles of agreement; requirement, qualification, clause, essential clause, sine qua non; escape clause, proviso, stipulation, concession, reservation, strings, small print
> *Qualification 340; Contract 459; Offer 504*

3 discussion, round-table discussion, conference, teleconference, videoconference, bargaining session, debate, high-level talks, summit meeting, summit conference, summit, cabinet meeting, exchange of views, powwow [Inf]
> *Advice 176; Conversation 210; Disagreement 463*

4 negotiator, mediator, arbitrator, intermediary, intercessor, moderator, referee, umpire, go-between; treaty maker, peacemaker, diplomat *or* diplomatist, ambassador, chargé d'affaires; matchmaker, broker, lawyer, solicitor, middleman, stockbroker; American Arbitration Association, Advisory Conciliation and Arbitration Service (ACAS) [Brit]
> *Government 49; Politics 50; Law 53; Sports 145*

ADJECTIVES

5 negotiated, mediated, arbitrated, negotiable, negotiating; practicable, practical, feasible, workable, pragmatic; transferable, conveyable, exchangeable; subject to terms, conditional, provisional, provisory, stipulatory; concessionary, conciliatory, compromising, collective, haggling, wrangling; treaty-making, diplomatic; communicative, intercommunicative

VERBS

6 negotiate, mediate, arbitrate, seek agreement, settle, conciliate, cooperate, compromise; exchange, exchange views, discuss, communicate, intercommunicate; bargain, hard bargain, collective bargain, barter, trade, horse-trade, trade off, haggle, wrangle, come to terms; use diplomacy, treat, make a treaty; hold a conference, attend a conference; have a summit meeting, hold a summit; confer, hold talks, deliberate, have a discussion, put heads together; transact, do business, reach an agreement, make overtures, test the ground, offer a solution, work out a formula, work something out, get something through, deal, make *or* do a deal, powwow [Inf]

7 make conditions, impose conditions, make terms *or* proposals *or* a bid *or* demands *or* concessions, stipulate, put in clauses, add strings, leave a loophole, add an escape clause, leave the options open, hedge one's bets, read the small print

8 act as a go-between, broker, matchmake, act as a middleman, stand in for, replace, proxy

ADVERBS

9 feasibly, pragmatically, conditionally, under certain

conditions, provisionally, with provisions; conciliatorily, compromisingly, as a compromise, as a trade-off; collectively, diplomatically, in diplomatic language, like a diplomat, communicatively

461 Compromise

All government — indeed, every human benefit and enjoyment, every virtue, and every prudent act — is founded on compromise and barter. — EDMUND BURKE

NOUNS

1 **compromise,** adaptation, adaptability, accommodation, sharing, cooperation, agreement, arrangement, working arrangement, modus vivendi, understanding; concession, mutual concession, give-and-take, adjustment, settlement, negotiation, negotiability, arbitration; middle way, middle course, middle ground, halfway, happy medium, balance, balancing act, central position, meeting halfway, splitting the difference, equal swap, trade-off, bargain, deal
   ◗ *Mediation 75; Contract 459; Negotiation 460; Trade 480; Accord 735; Average 742; Cooperation 827*

2 **half-measure,** stopgap, temporary substitute, second best
   ◗ *Substitution 672*

3 **irresolution,** hesitation, vacillation, lack of resolution, lack of conviction, lack of commitment, fence-sitting, lukewarmness, neutrality; evasion of responsibility, desertion of principles, dishonor, shame, cop-out [Inf]
   ◗ *Disrepute 371; Vacillation 378*

ADJECTIVES

4 **compromising,** accommodating, adjusted, negotiable, adaptable, conceding, agreeing, agreed, arranged, settled, give-and-take, averaging out, averaged out, halfway, balancing, balanced, neither one nor the other

5 **half-measure,** stopgap, temporary, second-best

6 **irresolute,** noncommittal, lukewarm, neutral, evasive; discredited, dishonorable, dishonored, damaging

VERBS

7 **compromise,** reach *or* make a compromise, settle, accommodate, cooperate, make adjustments, adjust, readjust, adapt, concede; negotiate, go to arbitration, arbitrate, plea-bargain; make mutual concessions, give and take, average out, split the difference, agree to some of it, agree to half of it, strike a balance, meet halfway, steer a middle course, strike an average, go half and half, stretch a point; play politics; go so far but no further; take what's offered, take the good with the bad, make the best of a bad job, make a virtue of necessity, make a deal, go fifty-fifty

8 **be irresolute,** lack resolution, sit on the fence, lack conviction, desert one's principles, evade one's responsibilities, duck responsibility, sidestep, cop out [Inf]

ADVERBS

9 **compromisingly,** accommodatingly, in an accommodating manner, by negotiating, agreeably, under an agreement, under an arrangement; halfway, as a half-measure, in equal measure, in equal parts; in a temporary manner

10 **irresolutely,** without resolution, noncommittally, without commitment, lukewarmly, neutrally; evasively, in an evasive manner, dishonorably, without honor, as a cop-out [Inf]

462 Agreement

NOUNS

1 **agreement,** concord, concordance, accord, accordance, concurrence; approval, thumbs up, the OK *or* O.K. *or* okay, assent, consent, general consent, affirmation, affirmative, confirmation, blessing, approbation, permission; willingness, consensus, cooperation, working together, comity; acquiescence, acceptance, toleration, compliance; unity, unanimity, unison; understanding, mutual understanding, mutual support; attunement, congeniality, harmony, harmonization, sympathy, empathy, reciprocity, amity; cordiality, rapport, friendship, fellowship, fellow feeling, feeling of identity, like-mindedness; kinship, family feeling, affinity; reconciliation, detente, rapprochement, coexistence; goodwill, peace, love and peace, honeymoon period; [Inf]: the nod, good vibrations, good vibes
   ◗ *Friendship 62; Peace 73; Love 299; Assent 346; Approval 437; Relatedness 727; Accord 735; Cooperation 827*

2 **contract,** pact, compact, covenant, settlement, gentleman's agreement, undertaking, transaction, bargain, deal; obligation, promise, pledge, IOU, bond; sanction, international agreement, concordat, treaty, peace treaty, surrender treaty, entente, entente cordiale; ratification, endorsement, authentication, seal, mark, stamp, indenture, title deed
   ◗ *Pacification 74; Accuracy 350; Promise 458; Contract 459; Debt 488*

3 **compatibility,** conformation, conformity, correspondence, congruity, consistency, uniformity, synchronization, timeliness; equality, parallelism, similarity, coinciding, good fit, perfect fit
   ◗ *Sameness 730; Similarity 733; Conformity 781*

4 **suitability,** fitness, aptness; relevance, relevancy, pertinence; the very thing

5 **assenter,** cooperator, surrenderer; conformist, follower, yes man, sycophant, traditionalist; authenticator, endorser, ratifier, covenanter, pledger, contractor, contracting party, treaty maker, peacemaker; sympathizer; perfect candidate, right person for the job, right man *or* woman in the right place

ADJECTIVES

6 agreeing, agreed, agreeable, concordant, accordant, concurrent, concurring, approving, approved; voted in, carried, consenting, affirmative, confirmative, blessed; willing, acquiescent, acquiescing, accepting, compliant; united, unanimous, in unison, in chorus, with one voice, of one mind; unopposed, uncontradicted, unchallenged, undisputed, uncontested, uncontroversial; attuned, in tune, congenial, harmonious, in step, sympathetic, empathetic, en rapport, in rapport with, in keeping with, in accord with, reciprocal; cooperative, cordial, on good terms, cooperating, coexistent, coexisting, friendly, like-minded, of like mind, reconciliatory, reconcilable, peaceful, at peace

7 contractual, contracting, contracted, obligatory, promised, pledged; ratified, endorsed, authentic, signed (on the dotted line), signed, sealed, and delivered

8 compatible, conforming, corresponding, coinciding, congruent, congruous, consistent; matching, equal, uniform, synchronized, parallel, similar

9 suitable, fit, fitting, apt, appropriate, relevant, pertinent

VERBS

10 agree with, agree, concur, acquiesce, approve, assent, consent, say yes, give the OK or O.K. or okay, give the green light, give thumbs up, respond favorably; vote in the affirmative, affirm, confirm, bless, give one's blessing to, give permission; show willingness, comply with, not oppose, not mind, have no objection to, accept; tolerate, concede, put up with, fall in with, arrive at a consensus, subscribe to; like the idea, welcome, unite, reach a unanimous decision, understand, support, echo, ditto, rubber-stamp; harmonize, sympathize, empathize, cooperate, reciprocate; act friendly, show friendship for, feel kinship for; see eye to eye, talk the same language, be on the same wavelength, have an affinity for, reach an accord, work together, pull together, reconcile, have a honeymoon period; [Inf]: hit it off, have good vibrations, have good vibes, give the nod to

11 contract, sign a pact, sign on the dotted line, make a compact, covenant, make terms, settle, reach a gentleman's agreement; undertake, transact, bargain, strike a bargain; obligate, promise, pledge, give one's IOU; sanction, reach an international agreement, sign a treaty, ratify, endorse, second, attest, authenticate, seal, mark, stamp, indenture; deal, make or sign or do a deal, shake on it

12 be compatible, be uniform, conform, match, tally, correspond, synchronize, coincide, equal, run parallel, have conformity, maintain consistency

13 be suitable, be fit for, fit well, fit perfectly, have relevance, have pertinence, find the very thing

ADVERBS

14 agreeably, with agreement, as agreed, concordantly, accordantly, concurrently, concurringly; approvingly, with approval, under official sanction, affirmatively; willingly, without hesitation, acquiescently, compliantly, as ordered, unanimously, with one voice; congenially, harmoniously, in harmony, sympathetically, with sympathy, empathetically, with empathy, eye to eye, on the same wavelength, reciprocally, cooperatively, with cooperation, cordially, on good terms; like-mindedly, with a single mind, with one thought; reconcilably, peacefully, in a peaceful manner

15 contractually, under contract, by a contract, obligatorily, as an obligation, authentically, with authenticity

16 compatibly, conformingly, to order, correspondingly, together, in the same way, at the same time, congruently; consistently, with consistency, equally, in equal portions, uniformly; similarly

17 suitably, aptly, appropriately, relevantly, with relevance, pertinently

463 Disagreement

NOUNS

1 disagreement, difference of opinion, difference; argument, altercation, contention, contentiousness, dissension, dissent, dissidence, criticism, disaccord, discordance; disharmony, unharmoniousness, dissonance, friction, noncooperation, unpleasantness, controversy; confrontation, difficulty, misunderstanding, disunity; breach of friendship, parting of the ways, estrangement; uptightness [Inf]

2 divisiveness, division, polarization, incompatibility, irreconcilability; enmity, irascibility, provocativeness, cantankerousness, prickliness, quarrelsomeness, bickering, wrangling; hostility, bellicosity, combativeness, aggressiveness, belligerence, strife, fighting, infighting, clashing; area of disagreement, disputed area, sore point, ticklish issue, contention, bone to pick, casus belli, house divided against itself

   ❯ *Hostility 63; Dissonance 241; Dissent 347; Contention 422; Diversity 732; Separation 753; Opposition 828*

3 dispute, argument, debate, polemic, quarrel, row, spat, tiff, fuss, discord; split, rift, breach, cleft, rupture, schism; struggle, scrimmage, squabble, wrangle, rumpus, tussle; brawl, fight, fisticuffs, donnybrook, fracas, clash, conflict, open conflict; feud, blood feud; falling-out, set-to, run-in, dustup, ruckus, ruction, knockdown-drag-out fight; [Inf]: hassle, flap, shindy, scrap, rhubarb, rumble

   ❯ *Argument 329; Defiance 416; Contention 422*

4 difference, dissimilarity, nonconformity, deviation, divergence, variance, disparity, discord, discrepancy, incompatibility, incongruity, inequality, ambiguity, ambivalence, inconsistency, credibility gap; bad match, bad fit, misfitting, mismatching, misaligning, mistiming

> *Distortion 627; Untimeliness 660; Dissimilarity 734; Inequality 741; Nonconformity 782*

5 dissenter, dissident, dissentient, protester, objector, disputer, critic; quarreler, troublemaker, intruder, noncooperator; scab, outsider, misfit; gate-crasher [Inf]

> *Deception 193*

ADJECTIVES

6 disagreeing, differing, argumentative, polemic *or* polemical, contentious, dissenting, dissident, dissentient, discordant; disharmonious, unharmonious, dissonant, noncooperative, unpleasant, controversial; confrontational, disputing, disputatious, factious, quarrelsome, quarreling, at odds, at variance, at cross-purposes, at loggerheads, criticizing, bickering, wrangling; divisive, polarizing, schismatic, incompatible, irreconcilable; irascible, provocative, cantankerous, prickly, hostile, inimical, bellicose, combative, aggressive, militant, antagonistic, belligerent; fighting, squabbling, brawling, at strife, up in arms, like cats and dogs, knock-down-drag-out

7 different, differing, dissimilar, deviating, divergent, variant, odd, alien, unsuitable, discordant, discrepant, incompatible, incongruous, unequal, ambiguous, ambivalent, inconsistent, misfitting

VERBS

8 disagree, differ, differ with, agree to differ, have differences with, hold opposite views; not get along, contend, dissent, object to, not cooperate, not play ball, have nothing to do with; confront, quarrel, criticize, bicker, wrangle; misunderstand, divide, polarize; sever relations, part company with, come to a parting of the ways, fall out, have a falling-out, split up, break away from; provoke, show hostility, fight, fight like cats and dogs, clash, have a bone to pick

9 dispute, debate, quarrel, altercate, row, argue, spat, tiff, fuss, struggle, squabble, wrangle, tussle, clash, conflict, lock horns, split up, rupture, go to court; brawl, engage in fisticuffs, have a donnybrook, feud, fight, carry on a vendetta, have a set-to, have a run-in, have a dustup, have a knock-down-drag-out fight; [Inf]: scrap, hassle, kick up a shindy

10 pick a fight, pick a quarrel; sow dissension, divide, provoke, set at odds; stir up trouble, make trouble, look for trouble, go looking for trouble, look for a disagreement; spoil for a fight, challenge, intrude, pick a bone with, have a bone to pick, rub the wrong way, have a chip on one's shoulder, go on the warpath

11 be different, be at variance, vary, deviate, diverge, have a credibility gap; match poorly, fit badly, not fit in with, misfit, go against the grain, march to a different drummer

ADVERBS

12 in disagreement, disputatiously, argumentatively, contentiously, dissentingly, discordantly; in defiance of, in contempt of, disharmoniously, without harmony, dissonantly, uncooperatively, without cooperation, despite, in spite of; unpleasantly, controversially, in a controversial way; divisively, schismatically, incompatibly, at odds, irreconcilably, irascibly, provocatively, in order to provoke, cantankerously, hostilely, with hostility, inimically, bellicosely, combatively, aggressively, antagonistically, belligerently

13 differently, in a different way, dissimilarly, without similarity, divergently; unsuitably, discordantly, discrepantly, incompatibly, incongruously, unequally; ambiguously, ambivalently, in more than one way, inconsistently, without consistency

464 Security

NOUNS

1 security, safety, safeness, safekeeping, invulnerability, impregnability, immunity, secure position; protection, asylum, sanctuary, shelter, refuge, cover; mainstay, anchor, support, hope, pillar of strength; defense, safeguard, shield; security system, alarm system, deterrent; sense of security, reliance, faith, confidence, courage; health insurance, Medicare, unemployment benefits, Social Security, welfare, retirement benefits, relief, dole

> *Courage 284; Caution 287; Carefulness 325; Defense 419; Safety 810; Preservation 815*

2 promise, pledge, word, word of honor, assurance, insurance, credit; recognizance, warrant, warranty, escrow, surety, bail; obligation, guarantee, underwriting, certificate, bond, coupon, gilt-edged security, stocks, share, debenture, title deed, deed, mortgage, collateral, indemnity, covenant, IOU; stub, check stub, counterfoil [Brit], ticket stub, acquittance, quittance; ticket, pawn ticket, receipt, proof of purchase; authentication, verification, passport, visa, permit, authority, authorization, endorsement, stamp, seal, signature, insurance policy, will, last will and testament

> *Record 185; Evidence 339; Promise 458; Contract 459; Lending 475; Payment 489*

3 security force, national defense, armed forces, army, navy, air force, marines, National Guard, police force, private security company; security officer, protector, sentinel, sentry, watchman, night watchman, watch, bodyguard, lifeguard, policeman, policewoman, police officer

> *Law 53; Defense 419*

4 safe, wall safe, lockbox, coffer, strongbox, safe-deposit box, vault, bank vault

ADJECTIVES

5 secure, safe, sure, without risk, safe and sound, protected, sheltered, invulnerable, impregnable; protective, locked away, locked up, immune, safeguarded, shielded; deterrent

6 guaranteed, warranted, under warranty, certified, authenticated; assured, certain, reliant, unshaken, gilt-edged; covered, insured, mortgaged, on mortgage, guaranteed, covenanted; pledged, promised, pawned, in hock, hocked

7 secured, accomplished, done, won, completed; [Inf]: sewn up, under one's belt, in the bag
   ◗ *Success 845*

8 fast, fixed, sound, steadfast, stable, steady; immovable, irremovable
   ◗ *Stability 674; Union 752*

VERBS

9 secure, make safe, protect, keep order, police, patrol, guard; safekeep, keep safe and sound, lock away, lock up, keep under lock and key; shelter, offer refuge *or* shelter; anchor, tie up; support, defend, safeguard, shield, give a sense of security

10 promise, pledge, give one's word, give one's IOU, assure, insure, ensure, give personal recognizance, warrant, guarantee, act as guarantor, act as security, stand surety, stand bail, vouch for, endorse; seal, stamp, countersign, indemnify, underwrite; safeguard, make certain

11 certify, authenticate, cover, insure, mortgage, pledge, promise, verify, offer collateral, give security

12 secure one's objective, accomplish, reach one's goal, win through, win, succeed, complete, bring it off; [Inf]: sew up, have under one's belt, have in the bag

13 make fast, make firm, fortify, stabilize, steady, strengthen, make sound, make steadfast, fix to, secure to, nail down, screw down, make immovable

14 reserve, make a reservation, book, order, pay in advance, leave *or* make a deposit
   ◗ *Record 185*

ADVERBS

15 surely, safely, in a safe manner, without risk, safe and sound, protectively, invulnerably, impregnably, reliably, assuredly, verifiably, with assurance

16 fastly, fixedly, in a fixed position, soundly, steadfastly, immovably, without moving

465 Observance

You know my method. It is founded upon the observance of trifles. — ARTHUR CONAN DOYLE

NOUNS

1 observance, observation, compliance, recognition, adherence; following, heeding, heed, heedfulness, regard, caring, care, keeping, acknowledgment, attention to, attending to, vigilance, diligence, conscientiousness; conformity, conformance, accordance, regularity, dependability, reliability, accuracy; attachment, faith-

fulness, faith, fidelity, loyalty, obedience, duty; respect, paying respect to, sense of responsibility, obeying the law, keeping on the right side of the law
   ◗ *Attention 323; Accuracy 350; Obedience 426; Duty 433; Conformity 781*

2 performance, practice, procedure, convention, custom, usage, routine, rule of business; discharge, execution, acquittal, carrying out, fulfillment, satisfaction, sufficiency; ritual, ceremony, ceremonial, rite, religious observance
   ◗ *Religious Ritual 85; Sufficiency 97; Celebration 405; Action 412; Completeness 761*

ADJECTIVES

3 observant, observing, heeding, heeded, heedful, watchful, regarding, regardful, attentive; careful of, conscientious, diligent, meticulous, scrupulous, fastidious, punctual, punctilious, literal, pedantic, exact, accurate; reliable, responsible, dependable, dutiful, duteous, constant, compliant, conforming, conformable, obedient; adherent to, adhering to, sticking to; faithful, devout, religious, orthodox, traditional, conventional, loyal, true, honorable, as good as one's word

VERBS

4 observe, comply with, recognize, adhere to, stick to, cling to, heed; regard, have regard for, care, keep, follow, hold to *or* by, abide by, acknowledge, give attention to, attend to; show diligence, keep the proper observance, keep a full observance, keep to the spirit of, conform to, be faithful to, keep faith with; show respect, pay one's respects, pay homage, have a sense of loyalty, have a sense of responsibility, obey the law

5 perform, practice, observe a practice, follow a procedure, keep a routine, observe the rule of business, discharge, discharge one's responsibility *or* function, execute, do, do one's duty, acquit, carry out, carry out to the letter, fulfill; meet, satisfy, suffice, make good, make good one's word *or* promise, keep one's promise, redeem one's pledge, honor one's obligations; observe a ceremony *or* ritual, perform rites

ADVERBS

6 observantly, heedfully, watchfully, while keeping watch, attentively; conscientiously, diligently, meticulously, scrupulously, fastidiously, punctually, punctiliously, literally, pedantically, exactly, to the letter; reliably, responsibly, dependably; dutifully, duteously, constantly, compliantly, conformingly, conformably, obediently; faithfully, devoutly, religiously, orthodoxly, traditionally, conventionally; loyally, truly, honorably

466 Nonobservance

NOUNS

1 nonobservance, inobservance, unobservance, non-adherence, lack of ceremony, nonconformity, disconformity, nonconformance, noncompliance, noncooperation; rejection, indifference, inattention, avoidance; disregard, heedlessness, unmindfulness, obliviousness, oversight, overlooking, forgetfulness, carelessness, remissness, sloppiness, negligence, neglectfulness, neglect, laches [Form]; thoughtlessness, slight, casualness, procrastination, laxity, informality, superficiality, perfunctoriness, breach, breach of promise *or* trust *or* contract *or* faith, repudiation, disdain, discourtesy, bad faith, contempt

> ◗ *Negligence 326; Rejection 383; Avoidance 386; Disrespect 436; Nonconformity 782*

2 **nonperformance,** nonpractice, noncompletion, nonfulfillment, nonfeasance, dereliction of duty, undutifulness; omission, failure, default, shortcoming, insufficiency, defect

> ◗ *Insufficiency 98; Inactivity 415; Incompleteness 762; Cancellation 834*

3 **defiance,** disregard of orders, insubordination, disobedience, disrespect; disloyalty, dissidence, mutinousness, mutiny, defection, desertion, treachery, treason

> ◗ *Disobedience 427; Protest 507*

4 **infraction,** violation, breaking, infringement, unlawfulness, illegality; transgression, trespass, delinquency, contravention, offense, breach of the peace; disorder, anarchy

> ◗ *Anarchy 51; Immorality 432; Violence 520*

ADJECTIVES

5 **nonobservant,** inobservant, unobservant, nonadherent, lacking ceremony, nonconformant, nonconforming, noncompliant, nonconformist, independent, nonpracticing; nonbelieving, disbelieving, rejecting, heretical, skeptical, atheist, atheistic, agnostic, unconverted; inattentive, unmindful, regardless, disregardful, disregarding, avoiding, heedless, thoughtless, oblivious, overlooking, overlooked, forgetful, careless, remissive, remiss, negligent, neglectful, casual, procrastinating, lax, unprofessional, informal, superficial, unthorough, perfunctory; repudiating, dissident, unconventional, bohemian; noncooperative, indifferent, disdainful, discourteous, contemptuous, sloppy

> ◗ *Disbelief 88; Negligence 326; Nonconformity 782*

6 **nonperforming,** nonpracticing, nonfulfilling, undutiful; omissive, insufficient; failing, failed, defective, defaulting, defaulted, evading, dodging; truant, dropout, runaway, deserting

7 **defiant,** noncompliant, insubordinate, disobedient, disrespectful, disloyal, unloyal, untrue, unfaithful, dissident; mutinous, renegade, defecting, deserting, treacherous, treasonous

8 **violating,** violated, breaking, broken, infringing, infringed, unlawful, illegal, against the rules, transgressive, transgressing, transgressed, trespassing, delinquent, contravening, breaching, disorderly, anarchic

VERBS

9 **not observe,** not adhere, not follow, not conform, stand out, not cooperate, not comply; not believe, disbelieve, reject, remain skeptical, disregard, avoid, ignore, have an oversight, overlook, pay no regard to, pay no heed to, pass over, skip, wink at, neglect, slight, procrastinate; repudiate, not accept; breach *or* break faith, break one's promise *or* word, neglect one's vows, neglect one's obligations, renege, go back on, back out, retract; dissent, rebel, live a bohemian life, do one's own thing [Inf], show disdain, snap one's fingers at

10 **not perform,** not practice, not complete, not fulfill, fail, prove unreliable, let someone down, omit, default, have a shortcoming; evade, avoid, elude, shirk, drop out, dodge, run away, desert

11 **defy,** disregard orders, violate orders, disobey, flout, not do as one is told, fail in duty; show disrespect *or* no respect, show disloyalty; mutiny, defect, desert, show treachery, act treasonously

12 **violate the law,** break, infringe on, transgress, trespass, contravene, offend, ride roughshod over, trample on, trample underfoot, breach, breach the peace, lack order, cause anarchy, take the law into one's own hands

ADVERBS

13 **inattentively,** heedlessly, unmindfully, obliviously, forgetfully, carelessly, thoughtlessly, casually, informally, superficially, insufficiently, negligently, defectively, sloppily

14 **defiantly,** disobediently, disloyally, discourteously, disrespectfully, heretically, skeptically, independently, anarchically, unlawfully, illegally, treacherously, mutinously

467 Gain

NOUNS

1 **gain,** acquisition, acquirement, obtainment, attainment, attainability; gaining, getting, receiving, taking, winning; advantage, unfair advantage, benefit, personal benefit, coming by, gathering in, bringing in; securement, procurement, procural, procurance, procuration, earnings, moneymaking, breadwinning; profitableness, profitability, profit making, profit taking; lucrative deal, successful speculation; realization, gainfulness, remuneration, fund-raising; profiteering, usury, greed; grist to one's mill, getting ahead, raking it in, pulling down [Inf], moneygrubbing [Inf]

> ◗ *Selfishness 444; Receiving 473; Taking 477; Money 484*

2 **augmentation,** increase, gain in value, appreciation, price increase; pay increase, raise, increment, development, growth, expansion; broadening, widening, spreading, spread, escalation; inflation, dilation

3 **advance,** approach, headway, gaining ground, ground gained, improvement; performance gain, betterment,

higher jump, faster race, farther throw, longer endurance; gaining on, overtaking, leaving behind; gaining time

▶ *Track and Field Events 166; Sale 482; Earliness 657; Increase 746*

4 acquisition, collection, gathering, gleaning, bringing together, assembly, assembling, assemblage, accumulation, cumulation, amassment, accretion; catch, hoard, store, heap, stack, pile, cache, stock, stockpile, mountain, pool, haul, bundle [Inf]

▶ *Assembly 59; Store 105*

5 earnings, income, private *or* corporate *or* earned *or* unearned income, advance earnings, advance, royalty, revenue; wages, salary, pay, pay packet, paycheck; takings, receipts, gross receipts, net receipts; gross revenue, turnover, net revenue, return, gross return, net return, returns, proceeds; gate money *or* winnings, pickings, gleanings; retirement pay, Social Security payments, pension, stipend, annuity, tontine; maintenance, alimony, palimony, fee, remuneration, take [Inf]; gross national product (GNP), privy purse [Brit]

▶ *Government 49; Politics 50; Marriage 64; Payment 489; Receipt 492*

6 profit, gain, gains, capital gains, clear profit, profits, gross profit *or* gross, net profit *or* net, emolument, interest, compound interest, simple interest, percentage, dividends; inheritance, bequest, legacy, endowment, dowry; grant, subsidy, compensation, honorarium, fellowship, scholarship; benefit, fringe benefit, extra, bonus, perquisite, commission, expense account, golden handshake, golden parachute; reward, allowance, pocket money, pin money, extra money; lucre, filthy lucre; pelf, killing; [Inf]: plum, cleanup, gravy, boodle, perk

7 windfall, trophy, prize, jackpot; spoils, spoils of war; something for nothing, gift, free gift, giveaway; find, finding, discovery, trove, treasure-trove, buried treasure, piece of luck; easy money, freebie [Inf]

8 yield, output, production, proceeds, produce, product; crop, vintage crop, bumper crop, cash crop, second crop; gleanings, harvest; fruit, vintage

▶ *Agriculture 16; Production 522*

9 gainer, winner, moneymaker, breadwinner, wealthy *or* rich person, billionaire, millionaire; parvenu, capitalist, tycoon, magnate; heir, heiress, beneficiary; procurer, earner, fund-raiser, profiteer, usurer, collector, gatherer, gleaner, hoarder; wage earner, wage worker, saver; thief, robber, briber, plunderer; [Inf]: moneygrubber, gold digger, fat cat

▶ *Wealth 485*

ADJECTIVES

10 gainful, beneficial, acquiring, acquired, obtainable, attainable, available, procurable; inheriting, beneficiary; compensatory, fund-raising, moneymaking, capitalistic, profitable, profit-making, profit-taking, gross,

net, on the credit side; gratuitous, giveaway, windfall; financially worthwhile, useful; paid, paying, well-paying, lucrative, remunerative, rewarding

11 gain-seeking, greedy, avaricious, acquisitive, grasping, grabby; moneygrubbing [Inf], gold-digging [Inf]

12 well-off, well-to-do, in the black, comfortably off, doing fine, doing very nicely *or* great, solvent, well-provided for; affluent, prosperous, rich, filthy rich, wealthy, worth millions, rich as Croesus, flush; [Inf]: well-heeled, rolling in it, loaded

▶ *Wealth 485*

13 acquisitive, acquisitional, collective, accumulative, cumulative; mountainous, augmentative, augmented, expansive, gaining, ahead of time, ahead of schedule, widening, inflationary, improvable, improved

14 yielding, productive, fruitful, fertile, prolific, bumper, harvested

VERBS

15 gain, get, win, have success; acquire, obtain, make one's own, appropriate, annex, attain; have an advantage, benefit, receive a benefit; come by, gather in, bring in; secure, procure, earn, make, make money, profit, make a profit, realize; raise funds, collect funds, launch an appeal; beg, borrow, or steal; profiteer, lay hands on, get one's fingers on, get hold of; pull down [Inf], glom onto [Inf]

16 augment, escalate, gain in value, appreciate, rise in price; receive a pay increase *or* a raise, reach a crescendo

17 increase, grow, gain height, put on weight, gain weight, get fatter; develop, proliferate, mushroom, flower, expand, snowball, broaden, widen, spread, become larger, inflate, dilate

18 improve, advance, advance on, approach, get nearer, reach, get to, make headway, make rapid strides, cover the ground, gain ground; perform better, jump higher, run faster, throw farther, endure longer; gain on, gain time, recover lost ground, overtake, outstrip, leave behind

19 acquire, collect, gather together; gather in, have a bumper crop, glean, harvest; assemble, accumulate, cumulate, accrete, amass, save up, save; bring together, get together, scrape together *or* up, round up, dig up; cache, hoard, store away; heap, stack, pile up, pile, stockpile, stock up, pool together, pool, bunch, scare up [Inf]

20 earn, earn a living, be gainfully employed, receive a stipend, have an income, make money; get *or* receive an advance, get *or* receive royalties; have regular wages, get paid, draw a salary, draw a pay check, bring home the bacon; credit to one's account, have money coming in, have wealth; draw retirement pay, get Social Security payments, be on a pension, receive maintenance, receive alimony, receive palimony

21 be profitable, be financially worthwhile, offer a good living, show a profit, pay, pay well, yield, produce, net, bring in a return; pay interest, pay a dividend, accrue; roll in [Inf]

22 **profit,** make a profit, make a net profit, clear, take a profit, reap a profit, turn to profit, sell at profit; capitalize on, make capital out of, have capital gains; cash in on, make a good living, make a fortune, have the Midas touch, prosper; draw interest, take a percentage, earn a dividend, pay dividends; inherit, succeed to, come into money, fall heir to, receive a bequest *or a* legacy; compensate, receive a scholarship, receive a fringe benefit, receive a bonus, have an expense account, draw an allowance; have extra money, save; make a killing, line one's pockets, laugh all the way to the bank, rake it in, clean up [Inf], make one's pile [Inf]

23 **win an award,** receive a tip, get a medal, win a trophy, win a prize; break the bank, win the lottery, win the pools [Brit], find the pot of gold, get something for nothing, receive a free gift; discover a treasure trove, come across, light upon, have a piece of luck, receive a windfall profit, receive a golden handshake, hit the jackpot [Inf]

ADVERBS

24 **gainfully,** beneficially, for money *or* profit *or* gain, advantageously, acquisitively, profitably, at a profit; gratuitously, lucratively, remuneratively; greedily, avariciously; affluently, prosperously, richly, wealthily; collectively, accumulatively, cumulatively; expansively, productively, fruitfully, fertilely, prolifically, in the black

468 Loss

Where have all the flowers gone? / The girls have picked them every one. / Oh, when will they ever learn?
— PETE SEEGER

To lose one parent, Mr. Worthing, may be regarded as a misfortune; to lose both looks like carelessness.
— OSCAR WILDE

NOUNS

1 **loss,** losing, misplacing, mislaying, taking away; nonrestoration; decrease, decrement, subtraction, deprivation, privation; losing streak, hopeless loss, dead loss, total loss, utter loss, irreparable loss, irretrievable loss; dispossession, eviction, expropriation, divestment, robbery, stripping; detriment, disadvantage, setback, check, reverse, reversal; sabotage, harm, injury, impairment, damage, failure, defeat
▶ *Disappearance 265; Absence 576; Decrease 747; Subtraction 749*

2 **forfeiture,** forfeit, penalty; loss of freedom, loss of rights; disentitlement, disenfranchisement *or* disfranchisement, disqualification; loss of consciousness,

coma, death; bereavement; spiritual loss, perdition; sacrifice, denial
▶ *Death 29; Law 53; Punishment 454*

3 **loss of weight,** weight loss, dieting, fasting, weight-watching, figure-watching, anorexia nervosa
▶ *Eating 92; Fasting 118; Thinness 595*

4 **financial loss,** loss of profit, lack of profit, loss of earnings, poor return; cut price, cut rate, discount, loss leader; diminishing returns, losses, losings, deficit, deficiency, insufficiency, shortfall, overspending, overdraft, debit; insolvency, bankruptcy, going to the wall, going belly up [Inf]
▶ *Money 484; Poverty 486; Credit 487; Debt 488; Discount 495*

5 **waste,** wastefulness, wastage; squandering, dissipation, misuse; losing battle, wasted effort, loss of interest, unproductiveness, fruitlessness; waste of breath, waste of time, vain labor, labor of Sisyphus, fool's errand, wild-goose chase
▶ *Waste 96; Uselessness 802*

6 **lessening,** dwindling, falling off, waning, wasting away, fading out, dimming; wearing, wearing away, erosion, wear and tear; exhaustion, depletion, shrinkage, depreciation, diminution; outflow, draining, drain, dribbling away, seeping away, leakage, hemorrhage; evaporation; impoverishment, deterioration
▶ *Deterioration 808*

7 **destruction,** denudation, spoiling, despoilment, spoliation, willful destruction, ruin; ablation
▶ *Destruction 523*

8 **loser,** born loser, failure, reject; disqualified athlete, unsuccessful candidate, lame duck; black sheep, lost sheep, lost soul, damned soul, fallen angel, sinner, dissipated person, good-for-nothing, ne'er-do-well; scapegoat, victim, dupe, prey; bungler, incompetent; star-crossed lover, social outcast, down-and-outer, wasteful person, waster, squanderer, overspender, polluter; defaulter, bankrupt; wallflower, no-good, flop, fall guy [Inf]; dieter, weight-watcher, faster, anorexic

ADJECTIVES

9 **losing,** lost, missing, misplaced, mislaid, gone missing, astray; without, lacking, out of sight, out of view, lost from view, fallen by the wayside, nowhere to be found; long-lost, gone forever, gone for good, gone by the board, forgotten, out of mind; dead and buried, lost at sea, sunk, irrecoverable, irretrievable; incorrigible, irredeemable, hopeless, depriving, deprived, failing, failed; squandered, depleted, stripped of, shorn of, bereft, spent; destroyed, ruined, irreclaimable, unsalvageable; the worse for wear, nonrecyclable, gone down the drain

10 **unprofitable,** profitless, nonprofit-making, cut-price, cut-rate, loss-leading, loss-making; out-of-pocket, out, unsuccessful, deficient, insufficient, poor, cash-poor, in the red, broke; prodigal, wasteful, squandering; over-

spent, overextended, overdrawn, nonpaying; insolvent, impoverished, ruined, ruinous, bankrupt, bust [Inf], belly up [Inf]

11 **at a loss,** out of place, off course, off familiar territory; lost in thought, disoriented, confused, bewildered; lost in amazement, astonished, dumbstruck; astray, floundering, out of one's element, out of one's depth, all at sea

VERBS

12 **lose,** suffer *or* incur *or* meet with a loss; have no more, not find, lose sight of, not be able to find, look in vain for, misplace, mislay; miss, lose track of, lose contact with; lose one's memory, forget; take away, decrease, subtract, consume; deprive, dispossess, evict, expropriate, divest, rob, strip; have a setback, have a reversal, fail; lose a chance, miss an opportunity, say goodbye to, kiss off [Inf]; face defeat, lose out, lose the battle, lose the election, lose the day, lose the game; almost win, lose by a whisker

13 **forfeit,** incur a penalty, sacrifice, relinquish; lose one's freedom, become a prisoner, lose one's rights; become disenfranchised *or* disfranchised, face disqualification; face a total loss, lose consciousness, faint, collapse, die

14 **lose weight,** diet, slim down, fast, starve oneself, refuse food, go on a hunger strike, become anorectic

15 **lose money,** have a financial loss, incur losses, sell at a loss, lose profits, lose earnings, have a poor return, cut prices, have diminishing returns, suffer a setback, have losses; operate at a loss, run at a loss, make no profit, not make ends meet, run a deficit, fall short, have nothing to show for, go in the red, overspend, throw good money after bad; overdraw, run up an overdraft; become insolvent, face bankruptcy, go to the wall, go broke, go bust [Inf], go belly up [Inf]

16 **be wasteful,** waste, squander, dissipate, throw away, fritter away, pour down the drain, let slip through one's fingers; waste one's efforts, waste one's breath, waste one's time, labor in vain; draw a blank, go on a fool's errand, go on a wild-goose chase

17 **lessen,** dwindle, wane, fade out, dim; deplete, depreciate, diminish, deteriorate; waste away, wear, wear away, erode; drain, dribble away, leak, hemorrhage, seep away, evaporate, shrink; impoverish, become impoverished, undergo privation; lose the battle, lose interest in

18 **destroy,** misuse, despoil, spoliate, spoil, denude; willfully destroy, sabotage, harm, injure, impair, damage, ruin, ablate

19 **go to waste,** come to nothing, come to naught, go *or* run to seed, go to pot; dissipate, scatter to the winds, go up *or* end up in smoke, go down the drain, go down the tube [Inf], go to the dogs [Inf]

20 **lose someone,** give someone the slip, avoid, evade, elude, dodge, escape; outrun, outstrip, leave behind, shake off

ADVERBS

21 **irrecoverably,** irretrievably, irredeemably, irreclaimably, hopelessly

22 **at a loss,** at a cut price, at a cut rate, out-of-pocket; unsuccessfully, deficiently, insufficiently; prodigally, wastefully, in the red

469 Possession

NOUNS

1 **possession,** possessing, owning, ownership, proprietorship; right of possession, possessorship; lawful *or* legal *or* rightful possession; enjoyment, property rights, proprietary rights; lordship, dominion, sovereignty, holding; hold, grasp, grip, retention; nine tenths of the law, nine points of the law, bird in the hand
   ▶ *Economics 56; Title 72; Use 393; Finance 457; Property 470; Taking 477*

2 **claiming,** laying claim to, making one's own, taking, taking possession, appropriating, appropriation; control, marking one's territory, occupying, occupancy, occupation, squatting, squatterdom, squatter's right, hoisting one's flag over

3 **possession of property,** landownership, landowning, landholding, land tenure, custody, title, lease, leasehold, freehold, tenure, tenancy, tenantry, sublease; owned property, estate, landed estate, plantation, colony, dependency, protectorate, dominion; personal property, effects, belongings, accouterments, appurtenances, bag and baggage, stuff, gear, things, chattel, goods and chattels
   ▶ *History 3; Property 470*

4 **monopoly,** exclusive *or* sole possession, monopolization; corner, cornering of the market, engrossment, forestallment

5 **inheritance,** heirship, heirdom, heritage, patrimony

6 **joint possession,** possession in common, having a part, having a share, joint tenancy, tenancy in common, joint ownership, common ownership, shared ownership; time-sharing, time-share apartment; condominium, part ownership, partnership, copartnership; public corporation, public company, common stock, share; joint bank account, pool, kitty, tontine, common supplies, store, common property, common land, common

7 **public ownership,** nationalization, public domain, state ownership
   ▶ *Government 49; Property 470; Money 484; Inclusion 763; Cooperation 827*

8 **legal ownership,** preemption, de facto possession, de jure possession; prescription, fee simple, seizin, uti possidetis, chose in possession, dominium

9 **medieval ownership,** villeinage, socage, villein socage, free socage, burgage [Arch], frankalmoign [Arch], fee *or* feud, fief, feudality

10 possessor, owner, monopolizer, buyer, purchaser; holder, landowner, property owner; lord, overlord, master, mistress, squire, thane, man *or* woman of property; leaseholder, lessee, householder, occupant, occupier, owner-occupier, mortgagee, proprietor, proprietress, landlord, landlady, resident, tenant, co-tenant, fellow tenant, joint owner, time-share owner, condominium owner, partner, copartner, shareholder; rent-payer, lodger, boarder, paying guest, squatter

  ◗ *Inhabitant 61; Master 68; Arrival 704; Subjection 832*

ADJECTIVES

11 possessing, in possession, having possessions, possessory; owning, landowning, landed, property-owning, propertied; having, having and holding, holding, enjoying, proprietorial; occupying, squatting; exclusive, unshared, monopolistic

12 jointly possessing, jointly possessed, joint, corporate, profit-sharing, time-sharing, house-sharing, apartment-sharing

13 possessed, owned, owned by, in *or* under the ownership of, one's own; possessed of, in the possession of, in the hands of, in one's hands, in one's grasp, held; belonging to, in one's name, at one's disposal, at one's command, on hand, in store, in the bank; exclusive, unshared, monopolized by

VERBS

14 possess, own, have in one's possession, have in hand, have in one's grip *or* one's grasp; command, have at one's disposal; take up residence in, occupy, dwell in, move into; take out a tenancy, take out a mortgage, buy, become the owner of, have, have title to, have the deed for, have tenure of, have in one's name, have and hold, hold; number among one's possessions, call one's own, enjoy, monopolize, have all to oneself, keep for oneself, have exclusive possession of, have exclusive rights to, forestall, engross, tie up, corner, get a corner on, corner the market, hog; rent, let; claim, squat, squat on, claim squatter's rights

15 have joint possession, hold in common, take a share, have a stake in

ADVERBS

16 possessively, in the possession of, in one's name, at one's disposal, at one's command, monopolistically, exclusively

17 in common, commonly, together, jointly

470 Property

NOUNS

1 property, possession, realty, real estate, real property; freehold, leasehold, tenure, appanage, estate, legal estate, praediality; title, right, copyright, patent; receipt, claim; domain, building, public property, common property, church property; benefice, living; holding, small holding [Brit], homestead, farm, cottage, bungalow, house, ranch, hacienda, chalet, villa, manor, mansion, castle; tenement, flat [Brit], apartment, condominium, penthouse; plantation, land, lands, acres, broad acres, acreage, tract; grounds, lot, plot, parcel, allotment [Brit]; demesne, landed estate, landed property; common land, common; political possession, territory, dependency, dominion; attribute, characteristic, quality

  ◗ *Authority 52; Habitat 60; Title 72; Publication 173; Possession 469*

2 legal property terms, personalty, domain, chose, chose in possession, chose in action, messuage, tenement, hereditament, fee simple, fee tail, mortmain *or* dead hand, immovables, movables, jointure, entail, remainder, reversion, limitation

3 historical property terms, toft [Brit], allodium, frankalmoign [Arch], fee *or* feud, fief, fiefdom, feudality, villeinage, socage, villein socage, free socage, burgage [Arch], copyhold [Brit], seigneury

4 transfer of property, transfer, transference, change of ownership, transmission, transmittal; deeding, conveyancing, conveyance, consignment, delivery, handover, change of hands; lease, let, rental, hire, buying, sale, trade, trade-off, barter; conversion, exchange, interchange, nationalization, privatization, takeover, takeover bid; delegation, devolution, settlement, marriage *or* divorce settlement, settling, vesting, conferment, conferral, assignment, disposal, gift, dowry, disposition, bequeathal, bequest, heritability, succession, reversion, inheritance; leaseback *or* sale and leaseback

  ◗ *Divorce and Widowhood 66; Giving 472; Lending 475; Trade 480; Sale 482; Wealth 485; Substitution 672; Exchange 673*

5 possessions, personal property, effects, belongings, gear, stuff, things, material things, chattel, goods, worldly goods, trappings, temporalities, paraphernalia, accouterments, duffel, accessories; impedimenta, luggage, baggage, bag and baggage; furniture, fixtures, fittings, bits and pieces, what one can call one's own, what one has to one's name, one's all

  ◗ *Possession 469; Contents 577*

6 personal estate, worth, net worth, circumstances, state; assessed valuation, assets, resources, collateral, valuables; one's money, one's fortune, wealth; inheritance, legacy, heirloom, funds, income, capital, revenue, means, substance, securities, stocks, shares, bonds, portfolio; tangible assets, tangibles, intangible assets, intangibles, fixed assets, frozen assets, liquid assets, net assets, current assets stock, merchandise, stock in trade, wares, goods, contents, plant

  ◗ *Means 102; Giving 472; Wealth 485*

7 property owner, man *or* woman of property, man *or* lady of the house, lord *or* lady of the manor [Brit]; freeholder, owner, landowner, holder, householder, lease-holder, lessee, tenant

▶ *Master 68*

8 **person transferring property,** conveyancer, seller, buyer, renter, hirer, pawnbroker; real-estate agent, Realtor™, dealer in real estate, estate agent [Brit]; speculator, investor, stockholder, shareholder, developer

ADJECTIVES

9 **propertied,** proprietary, possessing, possessed, free-hold, leasehold, copyhold [Brit]; movable, immovable, real; allotted, territorial, landed, praedial, manorial, seignorial, feudal, feudatory, allodial, patrimonial; hereditary, heritable, testamentary, limited; assessed, collateral, secured; tangible, intangible, fixed, frozen, liquid, net; endowed, dowered, established; copyrighted, patented

10 **transferring property,** transferred, transferable, devisable [Form], exchangeable; conveyed, conveyable, deeded over, made over, assigned, assignable, consignable; bequeathing, bequeathed, bequeathable, bestowable, giveable, inheritable

VERBS

11 **own property,** possess, inherit, buy property, have an estate, occupy a freehold, rule a territory; own personal effects, have belongings, have to one's name; own assets, have resources, put up collateral, have substance, own shares of stocks, own bonds, have a portfolio; put in possession, endow, dower, possess with, bless with, give, devise, bequeath, grant, allot, assign

12 **transfer property,** transfer ownership, transfer, convey, deliver, deed, deed over, confer ownership upon, put in possession; lease, lend, let, rent, hire; buy, sell, trade, make a trade-off, barter; convert, exchange, interchange, nationalize, privatize; consign, give delivery, hand over, cede, make over, sign over, sign away, change hands; take over, make a takeover bid; delegate, devolve, settle, vest, confer, assign, dispose, make a disposition, make a bequest, bequeath, put in one's will, hand down, hand on, pass on, inherit

13 **be transferred,** change ownership, change hands, come into the hands of, pass from hand to hand, pass to another; devolve, pass on, descend

ADVERBS

14 **proprietarily,** hereditarily, heritably, with a dowry, patrimonially, collaterally, territorially

15 **by transfer,** by conveyance, by deed, in exchange, under the terms of one's will, as a bequest

471 Retention

NOUNS

1 **retention,** retainment, keeping, holding on, grabbing, prehension, prehensility; adhesion, stickiness, viscidity; hanging on, clinging on *or* to; tenaciousness, tenac-

ity, persistence; handhold, foothold, footing, toehold; clutch, clamp, clinch, clench, grasp, hug, bear hug, embrace, clasp, cuddle, squeeze, compression; hold, firm hold, seizure, grip, tight grip, iron grip, grip of steel, viselike grip, death grip; stranglehold, lock, headlock, hammerlock, full nelson, half nelson

▶ *Combat Sports 152; Touch 216; Contraction 582; Support 605; Union 752; Connection 754; Adhesion 755; Restraint 830*

2 **detention,** suppression, repression, containment, envelopment, enclosing, pincer movement; keeping in, imprisoning, holding in, bottling up, plug, stop, stopper, cork, locking in, holding back; saving, cherishing, maintenance, preservation

▶ *Store 105; Concealment 181; Refusal 506; Closure 584; Preservation 815; Hindrance 826*

3 **retainer,** pliers, wrench, tongs, tweezers, forceps, pincers, nippers; vise, clamp, grip; grapnel, grappling iron, hook, anchor; fastener, staple, glue, gum, paste, adhesive; clasp, clip, paper clip, tie clasp *or* clip; finger, fingers, fist, clenched fist, hand, paw; claw, talon, fingernails, nails; tooth, teeth, fangs; tentacle, tendril, feeler; wall, fence, buttress, bulwark, embankment, levee; [Inf]: dukes, hooks, meat hooks, mitts

▶ *Tool 103; Enclosure 619*

4 **retentiveness,** retention, constipation; remembrance, memory, recall, recalling, recollection, memorizing, memorization

▶ *Memory 354*

ADJECTIVES

5 **retentive,** retaining, tenacious, cohesive, adhesive, costive, constipated, clogged, indissoluble, firm; sticky, viscid, gluelike, gluey, gummy, gooey; prehensile; tight-fisted, parsimonious; grasping, gripping, clinging, clasping, viselike, strangling, throttling, restraining

6 **retained,** stuck firm *or* fast, fast, held, bound, glued, gummed, grasped, gripped, in the grip of, clasped, clutched, pinioned, pinned, stapled, strangled; detained, imprisoned, penned, kept in, held in, walled in, fenced in, contained, circumscribed; saved, kept (back), withheld, refused; preserved, memorized

VERBS

7 **retain,** keep, hold on, take hold of, buttonhole, get a firm hold, maintain one's hold, hold tight *or* fast, cleave to, not let go, grab, stick to, adhere to, agglutinate, hang on to; staple, glue, gum, paste; fasten on, cling on *or* to; get a foothold, get one's footing, get a toehold; clutch, clamp, clinch, clench, grasp, hug, bear-hug, embrace, grapple, clasp, cuddle, squeeze, compress, seize, grip, get a tight grip; get a stranglehold on, get a half nelson on, have by the throat, throttle, strangle; lock, get a headlock on, tighten one's grip, fix one's teeth into, dig in one's toes *or* heels

8 **show tenaciousness,** have tenacity, have persistence; have an iron grip, have a grip of iron, have a grip of

steel, have a viselike grip; never let go, hang on with all one's might, hang on for dear life, hold on like a bulldog, hold on like a snapping turtle *or* snapper, stick like a leech, gripe

9 **detain,** suppress, repress, restrain, imprison, hold *or* pin down, get *or* keep a firm hold on, catch; steady, support; contain, draw the line, envelop, enclose, keep in, hold in, wall in, fence in, bottle up, plug, stop, cork, clog, constipate, lock in; keep secret, keep *or* hold back, hold up, keep to one side, keep to oneself, keep in one's own hands, keep in hand, keep, have in hand, hold on to, keep a tight hold *or* rein on, retain, withhold, refuse, monopolize; save, maintain, preserve, cherish, take to one's bosom, not part with, not dispose of, store

10 **remember,** recall, recollect, memorize, hold in one's mind, not forget

ADVERBS

11 **tenaciously,** with resolution, cohesively, adhesively, like glue, indissolubly, stickily; parsimoniously, with a tight fist; firmly, in a firm grip, like a vise; for keeps, to keep, for good, for good and all, forever, for always

472 Giving

NOUNS

1 **giving,** donation, bestowal, charity, almsgiving, benevolence, benefaction, philanthropy, subvention, subsidization; generosity, generous giving, generous nature, liberality, largess, bounty; contributing, contribution, offering, tithing, subscription; prize-giving, presentation, presentment, awarding; service, commitment, labor of love, voluntary work, charity work; consignment, conveyance, imparting, impartation, delivery, supplying, transfer, provision, concession, surrender, surrendering; endowing, endowment, settlement, dowry, grant, granting, conferral, conferment, investment, investiture, enfeoffment; bequeathal, leaving, will-making, will, testament, last will and testament; gifting, bribing

  ▸ *Law 53; Marriage 64; Benevolence 305; Philanthropy 307; Property 470; Money 484; Generosity 498*

2 **gift,** present, birthday present, anniversary present, Christmas present, Christmas box [Brit]; souvenir, memento, keepsake, a little something, token, token of esteem, gift token, gift voucher; tip, gratuity, lagniappe, baksheesh, cumshaw, *pourboire* [Fr], *Trinkgeld* [Ger]; fee, honorarium, tribute, incentive pay; subsidy, subvention, support; sweetener, price support, tax benefit, tax write-off; grant, grant-in-aid; allowance, pocket money, stipend, allotment; aid, financial assistance, sensitive payment, help, scholarship, fellowship; alimony, palimony; bequest, legacy, inheritance

3 **bribe,** kickback, douceur, slush fund, inducement,

conscience money; hush money, schmear [Inf], grease [Inf]

4 **reward,** prize, award, presentation, trophy, bonus, bonanza, something extra, expense account, benefit, blessing, boon, grace, favor, golden handshake, perquisite, perk [Inf]

5 **giveaway,** free gift, outright gift, ex gratia payment, piece of luck, windfall, (unsolicited) repayment, handsel; gravy [Inf], freebie [Inf]

6 **offering,** dedication, consecration, votive offering, peace offering, thanksgiving offering; offertory, collection; sacrifice, self-sacrifice, oblation, Easter offering, Peter's pence *or* Peter pence, tithe, widow's mite; contribution, subscription, tag day, appeal, benefit, charity game, benefit performance; alms, dole, food aid, food parcel, food stamps, meal ticket, free meal; bounty, manna, largess; donation, donative, handout [Inf]

7 **giver,** good giver, cheerful giver, generous giver, philanthropist, provider, benefactor, donator, donor, blood donor, organ donor; bestower, rewarder, tipper, briber, grantor, conferrer, awarder, imparter, presenter, prizegiver; subscriber, contributor, sacrificer, worshiper, tributary, tribute-payer, subject, almoner, almsgiver; saint, good Samaritan, kind person, helper, savior; supporter, backer, financier, funder, patron, patroness, distributor of largesse; [Form]: settlor, testator *or* testatrix, legator, devisor; bequeather; rich uncle, fairy godmother, Lady Bountiful, Santa Claus, Father Christmas, angel [Inf], sugar daddy [Inf]

  ▸ *Willingness 373; Generosity 498*

ADJECTIVES

8 **given,** givable, bestowable, impartable, available; saleable, for sale; subventionary, bequeathed, willed, bequeathable, transferable, granted, accorded, bestowed, bonus; giveaway, given away, gratis, free (of charge), uncharged, for nothing, costing nothing, for the asking, voluntary, gratuitous, complimentary, courtesy; sacrificial, votive, oblatory, God-given; donative, contributory, tributary; [Form]: testate, testamentary, testamental; endowed, subsidized, dowered, stipendiary, pensionary, insurable

9 **giving,** bestowing, imparting, granting, transferring; almsgiving, charitable, benevolent, philanthropic; generous, openhanded, bountiful, liberal

  ▸ *Philanthropy 307; Willingness 373; Generosity 498*

VERBS

10 **give,** make a gift, make a present of, give a present, give a gift, gift; give away, give free, not charge, treat, entertain; have a generous nature, pour out, lavish upon, shower upon, enrich, spare no expense, subscribe to; present, make a presentation, transmit; impart, convey, deliver, supply, consign, lend, render, provide; honor with, favor with, show favor; make *or* leave time for, grant, vouchsafe, bestow upon, confer upon, award, reward, accord, give a prize, tender, put

into the hands of, lay at the feet of; transfer, turn over, hand over, give over, make over

11 will, give by will, will to, make a will, draw up a will, execute a will, make a bequest, bequeath, leave, provide for, endow, dower

12 give out, deal out, measure out, mete out, dole out, share out, share, share with, dispense, part with, come across with, accommodate with; delegate, allot, commission, dispatch, send, give up, cede, yield, entrust, vest, invest with, stand, sweeten the kitty, put something in the pot, chip in; [Inf]: dish out, shell out, fork out *or* over *or* up

13 give praise to, dedicate, devote, consecrate; vow, offer, offer up, sacrifice

14 tip, give a gratuity, cross someone's palm (with silver); bribe, slip money to

15 fund, finance, subsidize, pay, pay for, help, help with money; pay one's share, commit oneself, pass around the hat

16 give to charity, philanthropize, donate, tithe, contribute to, commit money; commit time, volunteer; give alms, bestow alms; give freely, give generously, open one's purse, put one's hand in one's pocket
▸ *Philanthropy 307; Generosity 498*

ADVERBS

17 as a gift, gratuitously, gratis, free (of charge), for free, without payment, on the house, on one; charitably, with charity, benevolently; generously, bountifully, liberally, sacrificially, votively, oblatorily

473 Receiving

Freely ye have received, freely give. — BIBLE: MATTHEW

NOUNS

1 receiving, recipience, reception, getting, taking, accepting, acceptance, acquisition, collection, collecting, collectorship, receivership; inheritance, heritage, patrimony, legacy, bequest, bequeathal, birthright, heirship, succession, line of succession, primogeniture, hereditament, heirloom
▸ *Possession 469; Taking 477*

2 something received, gift, token, tribute, prize, trophy; money received: earnings, profits, income, salary, pay, take-home pay, revenue, net receipts, gross receipts, proceeds, receipts, returns, box-office returns, gate money, the gate, takings, credits, dividend; bursary [Brit], stipend, scholarship, fellowship; maintenance, annuity, tontine; allowance, pin money, pocket money; alimony, palimony; pension, compensation, bonus, commission, perquisite, perk [Inf], fringe benefit; winnings, ill-gotten gains
▸ *Giving 472; Money 484*

3 acknowledgment of payment, receipt, voucher, ticket, ticket stub, check stub, counterfoil [Brit]

4 reception, admitting, admission, admittance, greeting, welcoming, entertaining, welcoming ceremony; baptism, christening, confirmation; initiation, debut; reception room
▸ *Sociability 408; Admittance 708*

5 recipient, receiver, getter, taker, accepter, acceptor; buyer, purchaser, customer; acquirer, obtainer, procurer; holder, payee, endorsee, consignee, donee [Form], grantee [Form], trustee, allottee, lessee, licensee; earner, wage earner, pensioner, annuitant, dependent; receiver of honors, scholarship winner, fellowship winner, fellow, valedictorian, prizewinner; message receiver, addressee, reader, listener, hearer, viewer, spectator, beholder, audience; one at the receiving end, object of charity, charity case, beggar, sufferer, scapegoat, victim, butt, panhandler [Inf]; receiver of stolen property, fence [Inf]
▸ *Relief 275; Reward 453; Punishment 454*

6 beneficiary, heir, heiress, legal heir, heritor, heir apparent, heir presumptive, heir-at-law, inheritor, inheritress *or* inheritrix, successor, coheir, joint heir, next in line; fiduciary, legatee, assignee, assign, devisee
▸ *Property 470*

7 collector, tax collector, customs officer, excise officer, exciseman; bill collector, debt collector, rent collector, *rentier* [Fr]; bailiff, confiscator, sequestrator, receiver, official receiver, liquidator, administrative receiver
▸ *Debt 488*

8 receiver, radio receiver, radar receiver, telephone receiver; headset, headphones, earphones; antenna
▸ *Communications 169*

ADJECTIVES

9 receiving, recipient, receptive, taking, accepting, acceptant; wage-earning, salaried, paid, compensated, pensioned, pensioned-off; awarded, rewarded, given, allotted, on the receiving end

10 receptive, welcoming, open, open-minded, generous-hearted

11 received, accepted, taken, taken over, acquired, gained, collected, secured, inherited; admitted, taken in; heard, read, seen, acknowledged; well-received, welcomed, entertained, received into the church

12 receivable, takable, gettable, collectable; compensatory, compensative, pensionary; hereditary, primogenitary

VERBS

13 receive, be given, have from, get, take, take in, take up, accept, acquire, gain, collect, obtain, secure, come by, come to hand; earn, have an income, gross, net, clear, bring in, take home, pocket; draw a pension, receive Social Security; inherit, become an heir *or* heiress, receive a bequest, succeed to, come to one, come into, come in for, pass into one's hand, fall into one's hands; fall to one's lot, fall to one's share, step into the shoes of, take over, take off someone's hands; acknowledge, receipt, give a receipt, credit; accept stolen property, fence [Inf]

14 **receive someone,** admit, greet, welcome, make welcome; shake hands with, hold out one's hand to, advance to meet; receive guests, usher in, entertain, host, act as host *or* hostess, be at home to, open one's doors to, keep open house; receive into the church

 ‣ *Sociability 408*

ADVERBS

15 **receptively,** in a receptive way, as a wage earner, hereditarily, with a warm welcome, as a new member, as a convert; with openness, with an open mind, in an open-minded way, with a generous heart, in a generous-hearted manner

474 Allocation

NOUNS

1 **allocation,** allotting, allotment, assignment, appointment; apportionment, apportioning, appropriation, earmarking, tagging, setting aside; division, subdivision, partition, delimitation, demarcation; sharing, distribution, sharing out, parceling out, doling out, dealing out, dispensing, dispensation, divvying [Inf]

 ‣ *Possession 469; Part 760*

2 **portion,** share, dividend, allocation, allotment; lot, plot, strip of land; proportion, ratio, quota; dole, pittance, allowance, ration; dose, dosage, measure, dollop, helping, slice, slice of the cake, piece of the pie, piece of the action [Inf]

 ‣ *Limit 620; Degree 739*

3 **allotted task,** assigned task *or* job, chore, stint, shift, stretch, bout, period, spell of work

ADJECTIVES

4 **allocated,** allotted, assigned, apportioned, divided; shared out, distributed; dividable, divisible, divvied [Inf]

VERBS

5 **allocate,** allot, assign, appoint, detail; apportion, appropriate, earmark, tag, demarcate, delimit, limit; divide, divide proportionately, split down the middle, prorate, divide up, subdivide, carve up, bisect, split, cut; share, share out, distribute, spread around, dispense, deal out, deal; portion out, dole out, parcel out, mete out, measure, ration, dose, divvy [Inf], dish out [Inf]

6 **get one's allotment,** get one's share, get a share, take a share, be cut in, go halves, get a piece of the action [Inf], take one's cut

ADVERBS

7 **proportionately,** respectively, pro rata, per head, per capita

475 Lending

NOUNS

1 **lending,** loaning, giving temporarily, giving, lending money, moneylending; advancing, advancing on salary, advancing on royalties, advance, advancement, accommodation, grant; giving credit, lending at interest, lending on security, lending on collateral, pawnbroking, hocking; loansharking, usury, extortion

 ‣ *Credit 487*

2 **loan,** unsecured loan, secured loan, collateral loan, long-term loan, short-term loan, student loan, installment loan, bank loan, personal loan, business loan, international loan, foreign loan, lend-lease

3 **lender,** loaner, creditor, moneylender, money broker, banker, bank manager, loan officer, financier, mortgagee, mortgage holder; usurer, loan shark, Shylock; pawnbroker, uncle [Inf]

4 **lending institution,** financial institution, savings and loan association, building society [Brit], credit company, credit-card company, finance company *or* corporation, loan office, mortgage company, bank, credit union; International Monetary Fund (IMF), World Bank, European Bank; *mont-de-piété* [Fr]; pawnbroker's shop, hockshop, uncle's [Inf]

ADJECTIVES

5 **loaned,** on loan, lending, accommodative; secured, on collateral, unsecured; usurious, extortionate, on credit

VERBS

6 **lend,** loan, give temporarily, give one a loan, negotiate a loan, float a loan, lend money; make an unsecured loan, make a secured loan, lend on security, lend on collateral; give a long-term loan, give a short-term loan, advance, accommodate, grant, allow credit, give credit, lend at interest; practice usury, extort

ADVERBS

7 **on loan,** on security, on collateral, on *or* in advance, on credit

476 Borrowing

NOUNS

1 **borrowing,** request for money, advance; request for credit, loan application, loan transaction, loan agreement; buying on credit, installment buying, repayment plan; taking out a loan: financing, mortgaging, pledging, pawning, hocking; begging, touching (up) [Inf], hitting up [Inf]

 ‣ *Receiving 473; Lending 475; Taking 477; Request 505*

2 **adoption,** adoptability, appropriation, assumption, using as one's own; adaptation

 ‣ *Use 393*

3 **illegal borrowing,** unauthorized borrowing, misappropriation, infringement of copyright, plagiarism, pla-

giarizing, copying, piracy, pirating; imitating, imitation, fake, pastiche *or* pasticcio, stealing, joyriding; cribbing [Inf], lifting [Inf]

▸ *Literature 139; Music 140; Deception 193; Stealing 479; Imitation 736*

4 **credit,** credit account, credit facility; credit card, charge card; installment buying, installment plan, hire-purchase [Brit], plastic

▸ *Purchase 481; Credit 487*

5 **loan,** bank loan, personal loan, business loan; secured loan, mortgage; overdraft, debt, repayable amount, outstanding balance, IOU

▸ *Debt 488*

6 **mortgage,** adjustable-rate mortgage, balloon mortgage, blanket mortgage, chattel mortgage, closed mortgage, fixed-rate mortgage; first mortgage, second mortgage

7 **borrower,** debtor, ower, mortgagor *or* mortgager, credit user, credit-card holder, pawner, pledger; sponger, cadger; plagiarist, pirate, imitator

ADJECTIVES

8 **borrowed,** loaned, mortgaged, secured, securing, borrowing; repayable, outstanding, credit-card, plastic, installment, pawned; adopted, appropriated, infringed, copied, plagiarized, pirated, imitated, fake, ersatz; stolen

9 **adoptive,** adopting, adopted, adoptable, appropriating, appropriated, appropriable, capable of being used

VERBS

10 **borrow,** request money, take a salary advance, take an advance on royalties; request credit, make a loan application, sign a loan agreement, take out *or* negotiate *or* float *or* secure a loan, secure a personal loan, take out a business loan, provide collateral, finance a purchase, give one's IOU, mortgage one's house, take out a (second) mortgage, have an overdraft, pledge; pawn, hock, beg, scrounge, cadge, sponge; [Inf]: touch someone (up), hit someone up, bum

11 **adopt,** appropriate, take on, avail oneself of, assume, use as one's own; adapt, parody

12 **borrow illegally,** borrow without permission *or* authorization, infringe a copyright, plagiarize, copy, pirate, imitate, fake, steal, joyride; crib [Inf], lift [Inf]

▸ *Stealing 479*

13 **buy on credit,** open a credit account, use a credit card, get on credit, run up an account, run up a debt, incur liabilities, buy in installments, buy on the installment plan, put on the cuff [Inf]

ADVERBS

14 **on loan,** as an advance, by credit, with a credit card, on one's credit account, in installments

477 Taking

NOUNS

1 **taking,** capture, seizure, obtaining, snatching, grabbing, clutching, grasping; grasping nature, avarice, greed, rapacity; taking in, consumption; taking on, employment, engagement, taking in hand, taking hold; possession, taking possession, assuming ownership, inheritance; getting, profit taking, winning; cadging, scrounging; [Inf]: touching (up), hitting up, bumming, mooching

2 **sexual possession,** sexual assault, rape, ravishment, violation, deflowerment

▸ *Immorality 432*

3 **taking over,** takeover, takeover bid, buyout, buyup, merger; appropriation, infringement of copyright, plagiarism; arrogation, annexation, colonization, subjection, subjugation, subduing, conquering, confiscation, nationalization, assumption; requisition, acquisition; usurpation, seizure of power, coup, coup d'état

▸ *Malevolence 306; Attack 418; Borrowing 476; Possession 469*

4 **taking back,** recovery, retrieval, recoupment, regaining, recapturing, recapture, reclaiming, foreclosing, foreclosure; eviction, seizure, confiscation, taxing, levying, dispossession, distraint, repossession, annexation, impounding, sequestration, expropriation; disinheritance, deprivation, divestment; withdrawing, retracting, recanting, backtracking, reversal, making a U-turn

5 **taking away,** removal, eradication, deletion, erasure, blotting out, rubbing out; subtraction, extraction, deduction, cut, taking out, borrowing; plagiarism, imitation, purloining, stealing, thieving, theft; taking money away: extorting, extortion, swindle, embezzlement, blackmail, shakedown; [Inf]: pinch, ripoff, heist

6 **conquest,** raiding, plundering, despoiling; capturing, arresting, apprehending, taking a prisoner; abduction, kidnapping

▸ *Law 53; War 76; Immorality 432; Stealing 479*

7 **taking in,** welcoming, opening one's doors, granting a visa; hospitality, access, shelter, sanctuary, asylum

▸ *Benevolence 305; Sociability 408*

8 **takings,** take, catch, capture, tax, levy; ill-gotten gains; pickings, rich pickings, gleanings; revenue, receipts, proceeds, turnover, earnings, winnings, savings; spoils, spoils of war, booty, plunder, prize, haul; [Inf]: plum, swag, boodle, hot goods, hot property

▸ *Gain 467; Receiving 473; Money 484*

9 **taker,** usurper, seizer, remover, snatcher, bag snatcher, grabber, cadger, appropriator, confiscator, sequestrator, receiver, expropriator; infringer, plagiarist, spoiler

10 **raider,** pillager, marauder, sacker, ransacker, looter, despoiler; embezzler, robber, crook, mugger, rapist; cap-

tor, abductor, kidnapper, hijacker, skyjacker, extortionist, extortioner, blackmailer, racketeer

11 **greedy person,** leech, parasite, vampire, locust, predator, vulture, wolf, shark, shakedown artist
   ▶ *Stealing 479*

ADJECTIVES

12 **taking,** avaricious, greedy, grasping, rapacious, predatory, possessive; assaulted, raped; acquisitive, acquiring, merged, takeover, inheriting; appropriated, requisitionary, acquisitional, retrievable, taxable, expropriatory, confiscatory, commandeering, annexed; deductive; plundering, plundered, extortionate, thieving, ripoff [Inf]

13 **attractive,** captivating, winning, pleasing
   ▶ *Attraction 700*

VERBS

14 **take,** capture, seize, obtain, snatch, grab, clutch at, grasp; have a grasping nature, show greed; take in, accept, consume; take on, employ, engage, take in hand; inherit, take hold of, get hold of, lay one's hands on, stake one's claim to, possess, take possession of, squat; get, take profits, win, scrounge; [Inf]: touch up, hit up, bum, mooch

15 **ravish,** take sexual possession of, assault sexually, rape, violate, deflower

16 **take over,** buy out, buy up, merge; take for oneself, appropriate, infringe a copyright, plagiarize; annex, colonize, conquer, subject, subjugate, subdue, overrun, swarm over; earmark, confiscate, nationalize, communalize, assume, assume ownership; requisition, acquire; usurp, seize power, lead a coup

17 **take back,** recover, retrieve, recoup, recover one's costs, recover one's losses; recapture, regain, reclaim, foreclose; evict, seize, confiscate, tax, overtax, levy, dispossess, repossess, distrain, annex, impound, sequester, expropriate; disinherit, cut someone out of one's will, deprive, divest; withdraw, retract, recant, backtrack, make a U-turn, eat one's words, eat humble pie

18 **take away,** remove, eradicate, delete, erase, blot out, rub out, subtract, extract, deduct, take off, cut; mine, tap, milk; take out, borrow; plagiarize, imitate, purloin, steal, thieve, pilfer, shoplift; help oneself to, run away with, carry off, run off with, elope with

19 **take away forcefully,** conquer, raid, plunder, pillage, sack, loot, despoil, grab, take into custody, take captive, capture, make a prisoner, press-gang, trap, ensnare, hold, arrest, apprehend, nab [Inf], pinch [Inf]; abduct, kidnap, run in, take hostage, enslave, shanghai; hijack, skyjack

20 **take money away,** extort, extort protection money, swindle, embezzle, fleece, blackmail; [Inf]: take to the cleaners, take for a ride, run a protection racket, rip off, shake down, heist
   ▶ *Stealing 479*

21 **be hospitable,** take in, take on board, invite, allow in, give access to, ask in, give shelter to, shelter; give sanctuary to, give asylum to, grant a visa to, open one's doors to

ADVERBS

22 **avariciously,** with avarice, greedily, in a greedy fashion, graspingly, rapaciously, predatorily, like a predator, possessively, acquisitively, retrievably, deductively, extortionately

23 **takingly,** captivatingly, winningly, pleasingly

478 Giving Back

NOUNS

1 **giving back,** returning, return, handing back, sending back, extradition; restitution, reversion; bringing back, repatriation, reinstatement, reappointment, reenthronement; reestablishment, restoration, restoring; recycling, retrocession, reinvestment, rehabilitation, replacement, redemption, ransom, rescue
   ▶ *Repair 809; Deliverance 817*

2 **compensation,** repayment, recoupment, refund, reimbursement; indemnification, indemnity; damages, penalty; amends, making amends, making good; reparation, recompense, paying back, squaring, conscience money
   ▶ *Punishment 454; Payment 489*

3 **returner,** compensator, restorer, reinstator; redeemer, refunder, recycler

ADJECTIVES

4 **restoring,** restored, restitutive, restitutory, restorable, redemptive, redemptional, redeeming, redeemed, refunding, refunded, compensatory, indemnificatory, indemnifying, reparative, reparatory

VERBS

5 **give back,** return, hand back, send back, extradite; make restitution, bring back, repatriate, reinstate, reappoint, reenthrone, restore one to favor, give back one's position; reestablish, restore; recycle, retrocede, reinvest, rehabilitate, replace; redeem, deliver, requite, ransom, rescue

6 **compensate,** repay, refund, reimburse, give one's money back; indemnify, pay indemnity, pay damages, make redress, make amends for; make good, render good, make reparations, recompense, square; pay back, pay back taxes, pay off a loan, pay conscience money

ADVERBS

7 **redemptively,** in redemption, in recompense, in restitution, in compensation, in amends, in requital

479 Stealing

NOUNS

1 **stealing,** thieving, filching, scrounging, taking, pilfering, purloining, shoplifting, robbing, robbing the till; mugging, snatching, purse snatching, grabbing, pick-

pocketing; burglarizing, housebreaking, breaking and entering; safecracking; hijacking, skyjacking; raiding, rustling, cattle rustling, poaching; [Inf]: lifting, pinching, snitching, swiping, boosting, hustling

2 **theft,** thievery, thievishness, petty theft, grand theft, pilferage, larceny, petty larceny, grand larceny; robbery, armed robbery, snatch; burglary, aggravated burglary, break-in, unlawful entry; piracy, kleptomania, light-fingeredness; [Inf]: sticky fingers, job, steal, lift, heist, caper, stickup, bag job, pinch

> *Attack 418; Immorality 432; Taking 477*

3 **kidnapping,** abduction, shanghaiing, impressment, crimping; dognapping

4 **stolen goods,** ill-gotten gains; spoils, spoils of war, pillage, booty, loot, plunder, prize; pickings, rich pickings, haul, stealings, gleanings, graft, spoils of office; [Inf]: take, steal, swag, boodle, ripoff, hot goods, hot property

5 **plundering,** plunder, pillaging, pillage, foray, looting, sacking, sack, ransacking; privateering, buccaneering, brigandism, brigandage, banditry, outlawry, freebooting; despoliation, despoiling, despoilment, spoliation, depredation; graverobbing, body snatching; ravaging, raping, rape, ravishment

> *War 76; Immorality 432*

6 **infringement,** illegal borrowing, unauthorized borrowing, misappropriation; infringement of copyright, plagiarism, plagiarizing; cheating, piracy, pirating, bootlegging; copying, imitating, imitation, fake, cribbing [Inf], lifting [Inf]

> *Literature 139; Untruthfulness, Falsehood 192; Borrowing 476; Taking 477; Imitation 736*

7 **dishonesty,** cheating, deception; misappropriation of funds, embezzlement, fraud, forgery, counterfeiting, graft, extortion, blackmail; tax evasion, computer crime, hacking; insider trading, insider dealing; swindle, confidence game, tricky business, shady business, skin game, scam, crookedness; [Inf]: protection racket, con game, flimflam, sting, ripoff

> *Computers 15; Immorality 432; Money 484*

8 **thief,** stealer, robber, bank robber, train robber, highway robber, highwayman, bushranger [Aus], mugger; purloiner, taker, scrounger, pickpocket, kleptomaniac, shoplifter, pilferer, filcher, petty thief, sneak thief; prowler, larcenist, purse snatcher, burglar, cat burglar, housebreaker; safecracker, picklock; hijacker, skyjacker; terrorist, kidnapper, abductor, shanghaier, crimp; rustler, cattle rustler, poacher, dognapper; cutpurse [Arch]; [Inf]: lifter, dip, cracksman, yegg *or* yeggman, peterman, booster

> *Taking 477*

9 **plunderer,** pillager, sacker, ransacker, brigand, bandit, mosstrooper [Arch], marauder; slave raider, buccaneer, privateer, corsair, freebooter; ravager, ravisher, rapist; spoiler, despoiler, depredator, wrecker; grave-robber, body snatcher

10 **infringer,** plagiarist, cheat, pirate, record pirate, video pirate, bootlegger; copier, imitator, cribber [Inf]

11 **dishonest person,** criminal, confidence man, trickster; receiver of stolen property; cheat, forger, counterfeiter; white-collar criminal, computer criminal; tax evader, creative accountant, defrauder, embezzler, peculator; swindler, sharper, shark; outlaw, thug, crook, gangster, gang member, mob member, mobster, hoodlum, racketeer; gunman, holdup man; [Inf]: fence, hacker, flimflam man, con man, stickup man, ganef

ADJECTIVES

12 **stolen,** purloined, pilfered, thieving, thievish, light-fingered, burglarious, brigandish, kleptomaniac, larcenous, ill-gotten; kidnapped, kidnapping, hijacked, hijacking, skyjacking; poaching, predatory, predacious; buccaneering, privateering, piratelike, plunderous, plundering, looting, pillaging, marauding, ravaging; graverobbing, body snatching; [Inf]: sticky-fingered, hot, ripoff

13 **fraudulent,** dishonest, cheating, cheated, deceptive; infringed, pirated, piratic(al), plagiarized, misappropriated, unauthorized; blackmailed, blackmailing; swindled, crooked, scrounging

VERBS

14 **steal,** thieve, pilfer, filch, appropriate, purloin, rob, commit robbery; rob the till, borrow, make off with, sneak off with, walk off with; pull off a robbery, mug, hold someone up, snatch a purse, pick someone's pocket, pickpocket, relieve one of; burglarize, burgle, commit burglary, break into a house, housebreak, make an unlawful entry; crack a safe; hijack, skyjack; rustle cattle, dognap, poach; shoplift, snatch, scrounge; [Inf]: lift, pinch, have sticky fingers, do a job, snitch, swipe, stick someone up, knock off, boost, hustle, heist

15 **kidnap,** abduct, hold for ransom, shanghai, spirit away, carry off *or* away; impress, crimp

16 **plunder,** pillage, raid, prey upon, foray, loot, sack, ransack; freeboot, despoil, spoliate, depredate; rob a grave; ravage, rape, ravish

17 **infringe,** plagiarize, pirate, copy, imitate; crib [Inf], lift [Inf]

18 **act dishonestly,** cheat, defraud, forge, counterfeit, deceive, bilk, dupe, embezzle, misappropriate, do insider trading, do insider dealing, swindle, fleece, extort, chisel, cook the books [Inf]

ADVERBS

19 **thievishly,** larcenously, with light fingers; predatorily; fraudulently, dishonestly, in a dishonest way, deceptively, with deception; piratically; with sticky fingers [Inf]

No nation was ever ruined by trade.
— BENJAMIN FRANKLIN

NOUNS

1 **trade,** commerce, business; exchange, fair exchange, trade-off, barter, truck, swap, exchange of goods, payment in kind; transaction, commercial transaction, deal, business deal, trading, dealing, doing business, merchandising, buying and selling, trafficking, traffic; factorage, factorship, brokerage, brokering, jobbing, agiotage, arbitrage; drug traffic, prostitution, white slave traffic, slave trade, smuggling, black market, black economy, racketeering, profiteering

2 **commercial trade,** commercial intercourse, export and import, exporting and importing; visible trade, visible goods, visible earnings, visibles; invisible trade, invisible goods, invisible earnings, invisibles; foreign trade, international trade, home trade, domestic trade

3 **protectionism,** protection, protective tariff, protective duty, protective quota; customs barrier, tariff barrier, trade barrier, trade restriction; intervention, interventionism

4 **economic zone,** open market, free-trade, economic integration, chamber of commerce, junior chamber of commerce (Jaycees), international economic cooperation agreements
▶ *Economics 56; Agreement 462*

5 **capitalism,** free trade, free enterprise, free economy, laissez faire, free-market economy, boom and bust, fluctuation

6 **business,** venture, undertaking, enterprise, industry; profession, vocation, calling, craft, métier, job, occupation, line of work
▶ *Work 122; Undertaking 391*

7 **company,** firm, concern; private company: sole proprietor, partnership, limited partnership; public company: corporation, conglomerate, international corporation, multinational corporation, incorporated company (Inc.), limited company (Ltd); holding company

8 **association,** party, partnership, institution, institute, establishment, enterprise, foundation, corporation, conglomerate, syndicate, consortium, cartel, monopoly, trust

9 **speculation,** investment, playing the stock market; gambling

10 **bargaining,** negotiation, haggling, higgling, hard bargaining, horse-trading; tender, offer, bid; takeover, (leveraged) buyout, merger; greenmail; bargain, deal, agreement, contract, trade agreement
▶ *Negotiation 460*

11 **trader,** businessman, businesswoman, merchant, white knight [Inf]; dealer, wholesaler, jobber, retailer, vendor, seller, marketer; buyer, purchaser; exporter, importer, merchandiser, distributor, broker; stockbroker, speculator; negotiator, barterer, haggler, horse trader; profiteer, racketeer, smuggler, fence [Inf]
▶ *Purchase 481; Sale 482*

12 **custom,** customers, clientele, clients, patronage, patrons

ADJECTIVES

13 **mercantile,** merchantlike, trading; exchanging, exchangeable, swapping; commercial, commercialistic, wholesale, retail, marketable, merchantable, saleable

14 **economic,** monetary, financial, fiscal

15 **professional,** vocational, occupational, industrial

16 **contractual,** tendered, negotiated, leveraged

17 **corporate,** incorporated, limited, public, nationalized; private, sole, privatized, merged, parent, holding, international, multinational

VERBS

18 **trade,** exchange, barter, truck, swap, do a swap, transact, deal, trade off; do business, merchandise, market, buy and sell, export and import, open a trade, drive a trade; sell, peddle, push, promote, traffic, buy cheap and sell dear, trade in, deal in, handle, traffic in; smuggle, operate on the black market, deal in the black market, racketeer, fence [Inf], profiteer; turn over, turn over one's stock; nationalize, privatize, commercialize; put on a business footing, intervene, raise trade barriers, float, incorporate; trade with, do business with, deal with, have dealings with, open an account with, sell to, buy from, solicit business, go out for trade; turn ideas into profits, have an eye for *or* to business
▶ *Purchase 481; Sale 482; Exchange 673*

19 **speculate,** venture, risk, gamble; invest, sink one's capital in, put one's money to work, make one's money work for one; go on the stock exchange, play the stock market, play the futures market, deal in futures, dabble in stocks, operate; bull, bear, rig the market, manipulate market prices, make a killing, go bust [Inf]

20 **bargain,** negotiate, deal, haggle, chaffer [Arch], huckster, higgle, dicker, push up, beat down; offer, make an offer, tender, bid, make a bid, outbid, overbid, underbid; make a takeover bid, propose a merger, initiate a (leveraged) buyout; resort to greenmail, act as a white knight [Inf], preempt a takeover; stickle, drive a hard bargain, state one's terms, ask for, stick out for, hold out for, charge; settle for, take, agree to, shake hands, shake on it, sign on the dotted line, contract, make *or* do a deal
▶ *Contract 459; Negotiation 460*

21 **federate,** form a partnership, incorporate, syndicate, collaborate, cooperate

22 **in trade,** in commerce, in business, in the market-place, across the counter, under the counter

▶ *Gain 467; Loss 468; Cooperation 827*

481 Purchase

NOUNS

1 **purchase,** buy, acquisition, purchases, shopping; good buy, bargain, find, one's money's worth; bad buy, ripoff [Inf]

2 **purchasing,** buying, outright purchase, on-the-spot purchase, cash purchase; deferred payment, credit *or* charge-card purchase, purchase on account *or* on credit *or* on the installment plan; buying up, takeover, cornering, (leveraged) buyout, bid, takeover bid, offer; management buyout, greenmail, preemption, forestalling, buyback; first refusal, right of purchase

▶ *Payment 489; Offer 504*

3 **shopping,** shopping spree, mail-order shopping, catalog shopping, teleshopping; window-shopping, shopping around, comparison shopping; spending, expenditure, requirements, shopping list

▶ *Expenditure 491*

4 **repurchase,** redemption, ransom

5 **bribery,** subornment, corruption

6 **custom,** patronage, demand, consumer demand

7 **purchaser,** buyer, emptor, customer, patron, client, clientele; consumer, shopper, spender; bargain hunter, bargainer, haggler; investor, speculator, stock buyer, bull; vendee, transferee, consignee; offerer, bidder, highest bidder, taker, acceptor; hoarder, preemptor, redeemer, ransomer, briber

ADJECTIVES

8 **bought,** purchased, paid for, charged, purchasable, worth buying; ransomed, redeemed, bribed, bribable

9 **buying,** purchasing, shopping, marketing, teleshopping; cash-and-carry, cash *or* collect on delivery (C.O.D); cut price, for a song; bidding, bargaining, haggling; investing, speculative, bullish, preemptive, redemptive, acquisitive

▶ *Discount 495; Costliness 496; Cheapness 497*

VERBS

10 **purchase,** buy, get, obtain, come by, procure, acquire, make a purchase; pay for, buy outright, buy over the counter, buy on the spot, snap up, pay cash for, pay on the spot, complete a purchase

11 **buy cheaply,** buy for a song, buy at a cut price, make a find, make a good buy, get a bargain, get one's money's worth

12 **buy on credit,** purchase by mail order, order, order through a catalog, order by telephone, teleshop, buy on approval, buy on the installment plan, buy on account, pay by credit *or* charge card, pay by check

13 **buy in,** hoard, buy up, buy up the shop, preempt, corner, make a corner in, corner the market, monopolize, engross; buy out, make a (leveraged) buyout; buy oneself in, buy a piece of, invest in, sink one's money in, buy stocks

14 **bargain,** barter, bid, bid for, bid up, offer, make an offer, speculate, make a buy

▶ *Receiving 473; Borrowing 476; Credit 487; Payment 489; Offer 504*

15 **shop,** market, go shopping, shop till one drops; spend, expend; window-shop, comparison-shop, shop for, have a shopping list, require, hit the shops [Inf]

▶ *Expenditure 491; Extravagance 500*

16 **buy back,** repurchase, redeem, ransom

17 **buy off,** bribe, suborn, corrupt, pay off [Inf]

18 **defray,** pay for, square, bear the cost, finance, bankroll [Inf]

ADVERBS

19 **cheaply,** inexpensively

20 **expensively,** dearly

21 **acquisitively,** preemptively, redemptively, profitably

INTERJECTIONS

22 **buyer beware!,** caveat emptor!

482 Sale

NOUNS

1 **selling,** mail-order selling, catalog selling, television selling; sale, vending, vendition, disposal, transfer, conveyance, transaction, distribution, sales coverage; promotion, advertisement, traffic, trafficking, trade, trading, marketing, merchandising, deal, dealing, barter, exchange, peddling, canvassing, soliciting; auction, wholesale, retail, simony; private sale, exclusive sale, monopoly, oligopoly

▶ *Trade 480; Purchase 481*

2 **sale,** sellout, bargain sale, grand opening sale, sale of the century, spring sale, summer sale, autumn sale, winter sale, holiday sale, January sale; stock-taking sale, clearance sale, clearance, closing-down sale, going-out-of-business sale, fire sale, white sale; rummage sale *or* jumble sale [Brit], garage sale, yard sale; charity sale, bazaar, church bazaar, charity bazaar, second-hand sale, junk sale; public sale, auction, silent auction, Dutch auction, vendue

▶ *Market 483*

3 **sales,** good sales, boom; bad sales, recession, depression

▶ *Prosperity 847; Adversity 848*

4 **salesmanship,** service, sales talk, pitch, sales patter, spiel [Inf], hard sell, soft sell; sales conference, sales forecasting

5 **market,** market research, consumer questionnaire, product testing, marketability, salability, vendibility

▶ *Market 483*

6 **merchandise,** product, article, article for sale,

vendible, article of commerce, line, range, repertoire, store, selling line; bestseller, loss leader, staple, commodity, salable commodity, stock, stock in trade, supplies, wares, goods; goods on approval, goods on assignment, consignment goods; capital goods, shop goods, consumer goods, consumer durables, durables, perishable goods, perishables, canned goods, dry goods, white goods, sundries; freight, load, cargo

> *Store 105; Contents 577*

7 **seller,** vendor, consignor, transferor; stock seller, bear; auctioneer

8 **salesperson,** salesman, saleswoman, salesgirl, salesclerk, clerk, floorwalker, sales representative, representative, rep [Inf], agent; door-to-door salesman, traveler, commercial traveler, traveling salesman *or* saleswoman; sales force

9 **peddler,** seller, junkman *or* junk dealer, rag-and-bone man *or* ragman; street seller, street vendor, hawker, tinker, gypsy, traveler, huckster, colporteur, bagman [Brit], chapman [Arch], cheap-jack, costermonger *or* coster [Brit], market trader, stall keeper, sutler [Arch], *vivandière* [Fr]

10 **merchant,** marketer, merchandiser, wholesaler, wholesale merchant, merchant prince, merchant venturer, speculator, operator; monopolist, oligopolist; importer, exporter, dealer, middleman, broker; stockbroker, share pusher, financier, company promoter; banker, lender, moneylender, moneychanger, foreign exchange dealer, cambist; procurer, trafficker, canvasser; agent, Realtor™, real-estate agent; ticket agent, booking clerk, fence [Inf], tout [Inf]

11 **retailer,** middleman, regrater, shopkeeper, storekeeper, shop owner, store owner; dealer, merchant, trader, tradesman, florist, milliner, tailor, textile merchant, haberdasher, shoe seller, fishmonger [Brit], ironmonger [Brit]; grocer, groceryman, greengrocer [Brit], provision merchant, provisioner, butcher, baker; tobacconist, newsdealer

> *Market 483*

ADJECTIVES

12 **selling,** marketing, vending; wholesale, retail

13 **salable,** vendible, marketable, merchandisable, merchantable, available, profitable

14 **sold,** sold out, in demand, popular, sought-after, called for

VERBS

15 **sell,** vend, dispose of, transfer, convey, market, merchandise; put on sale, put up for sale, offer for sale, have for sale, bring to market; have on offer, make a sale, deal, trade, barter, exchange; unload on the market, unload, dump, get rid of; hawk, peddle, traffic in, push, promote, canvass, solicit, cater to *or* for, tout [Inf]

16 **auction,** auction off, put to auction, sell by auction,

bring under the hammer, put to *or* on the block, sell to the highest bidder, knock down to

17 **merchandise,** wholesale, retail, handle, carry, stock, deal in, sell over the counter, turn over one's stock, realize, sell under the counter, black-market, black-marketeer

18 **sell at a profit,** make a profit, make a killing, gain
> *Gain 467*

19 **sell at a loss,** sell at a sacrifice, lose money on, lose, undercut, have a price war, reduce

20 **sell off,** remainder, clear stock, hold *or* have a sale, hold a clearance sale, hold a going-out-of-business sale, hold a fire sale, sell up, sell out, wind up, sell short

21 **sell again,** resell, sell forward
> *Gain 467; Loss 468; Trade 480*

22 **be sold,** change hands, be on sale, come under the hammer, go to *or* on the block, fetch a good price, go for a good price; sell, have a buyer, have a market, meet a demand, be in demand, sell well, sell like hot cakes, sell out, boom, be a bestseller; sell badly, stay on the shelf, gather dust, flop

ADVERBS

23 **marketably,** salably, commercially, profitably, speculatively, unprofitably

24 **on sale,** for sale, on the shelves, in the shops *or* stores, in stock, on the market, up for sale, up for grabs, at auction, under the hammer, on the block

483 Market

NOUNS

1 **market,** daily market, weekly market, weekend market; farmers' market, mart, open market, street market; salesroom, produce market, vegetable market, flower market, livestock market, meat market, fish market; auction room, saleroom [Brit]; exchange, corn exchange, corn market, wheat pit, custom house, horse fair, goose fair

2 **fair,** world fair, international fair, trade fair, industries fair; show, trade show, motor show, boat show; exhibition, exposition

3 **seller's market,** buyer's market, bear market, bull market, over-the-counter market, curb market; black market, black economy, underground economy, gray market
> *Sale 482*

4 **free market,** free-trade zone, open market, single market, international market, multinational market; economic zone, economic integration, open-door policy
> *Agreement 462; Trade 480*

5 **market sector,** private sector, private enterprise, privatization; public sector, state enterprise, nationalization

6 **stock market,** stock exchange, securities market, un-

listed securities market, bourse, Wall Street, the City [Brit], bucket shop, commodity market, commodity exchange, pit

7 **marketplace,** market town [Brit], forum, agora; emporium, general market, covered market, arcade, shopping mall, mall, pedestrian precinct, shopping center, trading center, trading post; free port, entrepôt, depot, warehouse, wharf, quay

> ▶ *Store 105*

8 **store,** shop, retail outlet, retailer's, department store, specialty store, discount store, chain store, multiple store *or* shop, boutique, bargain basement; corner store, neighborhood store, convenience store, mom-and-pop store; grocery store, supermarket, superstore, warehouse store, cash and carry; concern, firm, establishment, trading company, trading house, house

9 **stall,** booth, stand, newsstand, kiosk, pushcart, roadside stand, barrow [Brit], vending machine, counter; store window, shop window, window display

10 **bazaar,** flea market, rummage sale *or* jumble sale [Brit], garage sale, yard sale, trunk sale

> ▶ *Sale 482*

484 Money

The love of money is the root of all evil.
— BIBLE: I TIMOTHY

Lack of money is the root of all evil.
— GEORGE BERNARD SHAW

NOUNS

1 **money,** legal tender, medium of exchange, specie, coinage, circulating medium; monetary unit, monetary denomination, currency, decimal currency, managed currency, fluctuating currency, hard currency, soft currency, sound currency, honest money, money of account; dollar, sterling [Brit], pound sterling [Brit]; precious metal, gold, ringing gold, clinking gold, silver, bullion; coin, paper money, shell money, cowrie, wampum [Inf]

2 **cash,** paper money, coinage, hard cash, petty cash, ready money; pelf, mammon, lucre, filthy lucre; [Inf]: the ready, spot cash, shekels, dough, bread, bucks, jack, dibs, moola *or* moolah, spondulicks, coin, brass [Brit], loot, swag, boodle, do-re-mi, wampum, gelt, green stuff, green, cabbage *or* lettuce *or* kale, folding money, folding green, sugar, gravy, palm oil, palm grease, mad money

> ▶ *Gain 467*

3 **change,** small change, coins, silver, coppers; pin money, allowance, pocket money, spending money; paltry sum, pittance, chicken feed [Inf], peanuts [Inf]

4 **fortune,** wealth, riches, millions, billions, grand [Inf]

> ▶ *Wealth 485*

5 **sum,** sum of money, round sum, lump sum, figure, ballpark figure [Inf]

6 **funds,** cash supplies, monies, treasure, purse, store, provision; liquidity, hot money, liquid assets, money in the bank, account, bank account, checking account, deposit account, savings account, certificate of deposit account, bank annuities; wherewithal, means, ready money, capital, funds in hand, funds for investment; reserves, capital reserves, dollar reserves, gold reserves, reserve liability; balances, sterling balances; finances, financial provision, cash flow; remittance, payment

7 **finance,** International Monetary Fund (IMF), World Bank, European Bank, International Finance Corporation (IFC); financial control, power of the purse, almighty dollar, cash transaction

> ▶ *Finance 457*

8 **currency market,** exchange rate, floating exchange rate, free exchange rate, exchange rate parity, parity, valuta, agio, agiotage, par; exchange control, managed currency, bank rate, prime lending rate; devaluation, depreciation, falling exchange rate, rising exchange rate; bimetallism, gold and silver standard, monometallism, gold standard

9 **inflation,** inflationary spiral, stagflation, stagnation, reflation, disinflation, deflation

> ▶ *Finance 457; Market 483*

10 **US coinage,** mill, penny, cent, one cent, nickel, five cents, dime, ten cents, quarter, twenty-five cents, half-dollar, fifty cents, dollar, silver dollar, Susan B. Anthony dollar, two-and-a-half-dollar gold piece [Arch], American eagle silver *or* gold bullion coin, eagle; US paper money: one-dollar bill, greenback, two-dollar bill, five-dollar bill, ten-dollar bill, twenty-dollar bill, fifty-dollar bill, 100-dollar bill; [Inf]: red cent, two bits, four bits, shinplaster [Arch], buck, smacker, fiver, fin, tenner, sawbuck, century, C-note, grand

11 **national coins,** new penny, pence, pound; franc, new franc, centime; mark, Deutschmark, pfennig; schilling, groschen; guilder, krona, krone, markka, drachma, lira, peseta, escudo; peso, centavo, centesimo; cruzado, rupee; ruble, kopek; yuan, yen, won, kip, dinar, zloty, lek, riyal, paisa, piaster, dirham, rand

12 **ancient coins,** shekel, talent, denarius, obolus, soldo, ducat, sou, bezant, pistole, piece of eight

13 **coinage,** coins, minting, issue, specie, metallic currency, fractional currency; stamped coinage, minted coinage, gold coinage, silver coinage, electrum coinage, copper coinage, nickel coinage, billon coinage, bronze coinage; coin, piece, coin of the realm; coin collecting, numismatics, numismatology

14 **paper money,** note, bill, fiat money, fiduciary currency, assignat [Arch], banknote; bill of exchange, negotiable instrument, draft, order, money order, postal order, check, cashier's check, certified check, traveler's

check, letter of credit, certificate; debenture, promissory note, IOU, note of hand, commercial paper, coupon, warrant, scrip, scrip certificate; Treasury bill, Treasury note, Treasury certificate, Treasury bond, bond, bearer bond, corporate bond, convertible bond, zero coupon bond, savings bond, Treasuries [Inf]

15 **false money,** bad money, counterfeit money, base coin, forgery, forged note, kite; clipped coinage, demonetized coinage, withdrawn coinage, obsolete coinage, depreciated currency, devalued currency; bad check, rubber check, bounced check; funny money [Inf], bum check [Inf]

▶ *Nonpayment 490*

16 **bullion,** bar, gold bar, ingot, nugget, gold, solid gold, silver, solid silver, precious metal, yellow metal, platinum, electrum, billon, white gold; false gold, fool's gold

17 **financier,** moneyman, moneyer [Arch], minter, mint master, coiner, forger; money dealer, moneychanger, cambist; moneylender, usurer; capitalist, tycoon, magnate; coin collector, numismatist

18 **treasurer,** honorary treasurer, keeper of the purse, cashier, teller, payer, paymaster, bursar, almoner, purser, depositary; stakeholder, trustee, steward, consignee; bookkeeper, accountant, banker, financier, controller *or* comptroller, Treasurer of the US, chairman of the Federal Reserve System

19 **treasury,** treasure house, governmental funds, public money, public purse, Treasury [US], exchequer [Brit], reserves, fund, store, counting house, custom *or* customs house, bursary, almonry, bank, Bank of England [Brit], Federal Reserve System, clearinghouse; commercial bank, financial company, savings bank, savings and loan association, building and loan association, mortgage company, credit union

20 **money storage,** coffer, chest, box, treasure chest; depository, federal depository, Fort Knox; strongroom, strongbox, safe, wall safe, safe-deposit box; cash box, money box, moneybag, piggy bank; money belt, pocket, wallet, billfold, change purse, purse, pocketbook, handbag; stocking, mattress

21 **till,** cash register, cash desk, slot machine, cash dispenser, automated teller machine (ATM), personal identification number *or* PIN

▶ *Store 105; Container 578*

ADJECTIVES

22 **monetary,** pecuniary, financial, fiscal, numismatic, budgetary, sumptuary; coined, stamped, minted, issued, nummular, nummary; fiduciary, gold-based, sterling-based, inflationary, deflationary, floating; clipped, devalued, depreciated, withdrawn, demonetized; decimal

23 **solvent,** sound, rich, wealthy

▶ *Wealth 485*

VERBS

24 **monetize,** mint, coin, print, stamp, issue, circulate; counterfeit, forge, pass, utter, pass a bad check, kite a check

25 **demonetize,** withdraw, withdraw from circulation, call in, debase, clip, devalue, depreciate, inflate

26 **bank,** save, deposit, draw, withdraw, cash, realize, liquidate; write a check, cash a check, endorse a check; pay, change, exchange

ADVERBS

27 **monetarily,** financially, fiscally, numismatically, pecuniously, solvently

485 Wealth

It is the wretchedness of being rich that you have to live with rich people. — LOGAN PEARSALL SMITH

NOUNS

1 **wealth,** richness, affluence, prosperity, financial power, fortune, handsome fortune, substantial resources, limitless resources, substantial capital; high income, high tax bracket, surtax bracket, moneymaking; savings, nest egg, savings account, investments, investment account; large inheritance, generous endowment, estate, money, property, possessions; well-lined purse, bottomless purse; bonanza, mine, gold mine, cash cow [Inf]; El Dorado, golconda, pot of gold, philosophers' stone, golden goose, golden touch, Midas touch

▶ *Excess 99; Finance 457; Gain 467; Receiving 473; Thrift 499; Prosperity 847*

2 **money,** riches, cash, old money, new money, mint, mountain of money, tidy sum, king's ransom; [Inf]: pots of money, heaps of money, scads of money, pile, wad, bundle, cool million, zillions, megabucks, big bucks, long bread, long green

▶ *Money 484*

3 **opulence,** luxury, lavishness, sumptuousness; comfort, comfortable circumstances, ease, easy circumstances, the good life, good times; plenty, abundance, bounty, profusion, superfluity, cornucopia, fat of the land, fleshpot, plushness; easy street, life of Riley [Inf]

4 **solvency,** financial stability, financial soundness, soundness, solidity, substance; credit, creditworthiness, fiscal competence; independence, self-sufficiency

▶ *Credit 487*

5 **plutocracy,** timocracy, capitalism

6 **wealthy person,** rich person, millionaire, millionairess, multimillionaire, billionaire; moneymaker, big earner, tycoon, magnate, baron, self-made man *or* woman, man *or* woman of means, Croesus, Midas, Dives, Rockefeller, capitalist, plutocrat, parvenu, heir, beneficiary, heir to a fortune, heiress, moneybags, moneymaker, nabob, fat cat [Inf]

7 the rich, the well-off, the well-to-do, the haves, the privileged, privileged class, moneyed class, propertied class, leisure class, the upper classes, the cream of society, the county set [Brit], the country-club set, the well-heeled [Inf], jet set, glitterati, beau monde, beautiful people, *jeunesse dorée* [Fr], the newly rich, nouveaux riches

▶ *Gain 467; Prosperity 847*

ADJECTIVES

8 wealthy, rich, affluent, well-off, prosperous, well-to-do, in the money, moneyed, propertied; worth a lot, worth a mint, worth millions, rolling in money [Inf], dripping with wealth, filthy rich, made of money; well-situated, well-provided for, well-endowed, well-housed, comfortably off, comfortable, in easy circumstances, flush, in clover, on easy street, raking it in, doing nicely thank you; rich as Croesus, rich as Rockefeller, born with a silver spoon in one's mouth, born in *or* to the purple, blessed with this world's goods; [Inf]: stinking rich, rolling in it, rolling, loaded, well-heeled, worth a bundle, worth a packet, lousy with money, in the chips, in the gravy, in the dough

▶ *Money 484; Prosperity 847*

9 solvent, financially stable, financially sound, sound, solid, taken care of; in the black, in funds, in cash, out of debt, creditworthy, good credit risk, able to pay, good for it

▶ *Credit 487; Payment 489*

10 opulent, luxurious, lavish, sumptuous, palatial, splendid, first-class, deluxe; expensive, dear, costly; richly furnished, elegantly upholstered, diamond-studded, gilded, glittering, plush; [Inf]: plushy, ritzy, glitzy

▶ *Showiness 404*

11 lush, fat, fertile, fecund, productive, prolific; abundant, plentiful, plenteous, bountiful, flowing with milk and honey

▶ *Fertility 22; Production 522*

VERBS

12 be rich, have wealth, have money, have money to burn, draw a large income; command capital, have the golden touch, turn all to gold; drip with wealth, wallow in riches, rake it in, sit on a gold mine, live on easy street; [Inf]: have money coming out of one's ears, stink of money, roll in money, live the life of Riley

13 get rich, prosper, enrich oneself, make money, mint money, coin money, spin money, attract money; come into money, inherit; gain, make a profit, make one's fortune, make a mint; rake in the cash, feather one's nest, line one's pocket, strike it rich, win the pools [Brit], win the lottery *or* sweepstakes, have one's ship come in *or* home, find the philosophers' stone, find one's El Dorado, find the pot of gold at the end of the rainbow, rake it in, make a killing; [Inf]: make it, make a bundle, make a pile, hit the jackpot, clean up

▶ *Gain 467; Receiving 473; Prosperity 847*

14 seek riches, chase fame and fortune, worship the almighty dollar, worship the golden calf, pay tribute to mammon

15 make rich, enrich, provide money, bequeath, endow, enhance, improve

ADVERBS

16 wealthily, richly, affluently, prosperously, well; comfortably, opulently, bountifully, luxuriously, lavishly; in clover, high off *or* on the hog, on the gravy train [Inf]

486 Poverty

I want there to be no peasant in my realm so poor that he will not have a chicken in his pot every Sunday.
— HENRI IV

The rich rob the poor and the poor rob one another.
— SOJOURNER TRUTH

NOUNS

1 poverty, poorness, impecuniousness, impecuniosity, pennilessness, penury, impoverishment, destitution, pauperism; deprivation, privation, hardship, need, neediness, necessity, dire necessity, necessitousness; indigence, want, lack, distress, difficulties, dire straits; reduced circumstances, straitened circumstances, hand-to-mouth existence, mere existence; low pay, low income, insufficient income, slender means, narrow means, meager resources, subsistence level; bread line, poverty line, poverty trap, wolf at the door

▶ *Necessity 95; Nonpayment 490; Difficulty 824*

2 insolvency, debt, indebtedness, dependence; unsoundness, financial unsoundness, fiscal incompetence; bankruptcy, ruin, financial ruin, financial collapse, financial embarrassment, loss of fortune; dispossession, disinheritance; hard times, bad times, depression, recession, slump, belt-tightening, shortage of cash, shortage of funds, insufficient funds; light pocket, empty purse, bare cupboard, empty pantry, pinch, Queer Street

3 beggary, beggardom, beggarliness, mendicancy; homelessness; hunger, fasting, famine; raggedness, rags, tatters, shabbiness, scruffiness; meanness, seediness; squalor, dilapidation, slum, substandard housing, workhouse, poorhouse, rattrap

▶ *Dirtiness 112; Meanness 501*

4 renunciation of wealth, voluntary poverty, vow of poverty, asceticism

5 inadequacy, insufficiency, deficiency, lack, shortage, dearth, scarcity, paucity, meagerness, scantness, scantiness, skimpiness

▶ *Insufficiency 98*

6 poor person, needy person, pauper, indigent, down-and-outer, bankrupt, insolvent, broken man *or*

woman, beggar, mendicant; mendicant friar, lazar, monk, nun, Job, Lazarus, Cinderella, poor relation; vagrant, bag lady, tramp, hobo, homeless person, squatter, slumdweller, ghetto resident, ragpicker, bum, freeloader [Inf]

7 **the poor,** the needy, the have-nots, the underprivileged, underprivileged class, the disadvantaged, the deprived, the lower classes, the underclass, the newly poor; depressed population, underprivileged nation, Third World

ADJECTIVES

8 **poor,** impecunious, penniless, moneyless, penurious, poverty-stricken; badly off, poorly off, unprovided for, low-paid, underpaid; underprivileged, deprived, needy, in need, indigent, wanting, in want, in distress; in reduced circumstances, straitened, hand-to-mouth, destitute, necessitous; on the breadline, below the poverty line, in the poverty trap; on the dole, on welfare; without prospects, with nothing to hope for, poor as dirt, poor as a church mouse, poor as Lazarus, poor as Job, poor as Mother Hubbard; unable to keep the wolf from the door, not blessed with this world's goods, hard up [Inf]

▶ *Necessity 95; Nonpayment 490; Difficulty 824*

9 **indebted,** in debt, owing; bankrupt, ruined, financially ruined; financially embarrassed, in the red, in hock

10 **insolvent,** short, short of cash, short of funds, down to one's last penny, without a cent, in difficulties; not knowing which way to turn, up against it, broke, stone-broke, strapped, hurting, pinched *or* pushed *or* pressed (for money), in Queer Street, hard-pressed, dead broke, hard put to it; [Inf]: stony-broke, flat broke, flat, hard up, on one's uppers, on one's beamends, without a bean [Brit], skint [Brit]

11 **impoverished,** pauperized, reduced to poverty *or* beggary; broken, dispossessed, stripped; fleeced, robbed; disinherited, dowerless, portionless; out-of-pocket, cleaned out, wiped out; [Inf]: bust, busted, belly up

12 **beggarly,** mendicant, down-and-out, on the street, homeless, shelterless; hungry, underfed, starving; barefoot, in rags, ragged, tattered, tatty, patched, threadbare, shabby, scruffy, down-at-heel, out at (the) elbows; mean, seedy, squalid, dirty, slummy, dilapidated, gone to ruin, gone to pot

13 **inadequate,** insufficient, deficient, lacking; scarce, meager, scant, scanty, skimpy

VERBS

14 **be poor,** live poorly, live in poverty; need, want, lack, be broke, not have a penny, not have two pennies to rub together, earn little *or* nothing, live on a pittance, eke out a livelihood, scratch (out) a living, feel the pinch, pinch pennies, pinch, live from hand to mouth, watch the pennies, tighten one's belt; fall below the poverty line, be caught in the poverty trap, go on re-

lief, go on welfare, use food stamps, receive unemployment compensation; beg for one's bread, sing for one's supper; starve, have no prospects

15 **lose one's money,** lose everything, go to pot, go to ruin, go bankrupt; fall on hard times, decline in fortune, come down in the world, sell the family silver, go into debt, be deeply in debt, declare Chapter 11, go to the wall, go broke; [Inf]: go bust, go busted, go belly up

16 **impoverish,** make poor, reduce to poverty, beggar, pauperize, leave destitute, ruin, bankrupt, dispossess, disinherit, disendow, cut off without a penny, deprive, strip; fleece, rob

ADVERBS

17 **poorly,** impecuniously, penuriously; in need, in reduced circumstances; on the breadline, on the poverty line, in the poverty trap, on welfare, on the dole, on the street, on the rocks [Inf], on one's uppers [Inf]

18 **meanly,** shabbily, scruffily, seedily

19 **inadequately,** insufficiently, meagerly, scantly, scantily, skimpily

487 Credit

NOUNS

1 **credit,** customer credit, banker's credit; creditworthiness, sound proposition, good credit risk, solvency; credit rating, borrowing capacity, credit limit, line of credit, credit control, liquidity ratio; overdraft, the red; loan, mortgage; debt, account, charge account, credit account, department store account, customer account; budget account, deferred payment, installment plan, installment buying, paying off; score, tally, bill; accounts payable, unpaid bill; overdue account, outstanding balance

▶ *Lending 475; Borrowing 476; Debt 488; Accounting 493*

2 **credit card,** bank card, charge card, plastic money, plastic, phonecard; credit note, letter of credit

▶ *Borrowing 476*

3 **deposit,** bank deposit, building society deposit [Brit], checking account deposit, savings account deposit, credit account, certificate of deposit account; credit, balance, credit balance, right-hand entry, receipt

▶ *Receipt 492*

4 **bank,** commercial bank, finance company, savings bank, savings and loan association, building and loan association, credit union, credit bureau

▶ *Finance 457*

5 **lender,** loan maker, mortgagee, pledgee, pawnbroker, usurer, loan shark, extortionist; debt collector, (debt) collection agency, dun

▶ *Lending 475*

6 **depositor,** investor, saver

7 **repute,** reputation, standing, prestige; trust, confidence, reliability, probity

▶ *Belief 87; Respect 435*

ADJECTIVES

8 **in credit,** in the black, creditworthy, solvent

9 **charged,** deferred; overdrawn, in the red

VERBS

10 **credit,** give *or* furnish credit, extend credit, lend, loan, grant a loan, grant, arrange a mortgage, sell on credit; await payment, seek payment, dun

▶ *Lending 475; Debt 488*

11 **acquire credit,** take out credit, open a charge *or* credit account, have an account with; charge, charge to one's account, run up an account, run up a bill; defer payment, forgo repayment; buy on the installment plan, buy on time, put on layaway; borrow, take out a loan, mortgage; overdraw, go into the red

▶ *Borrowing 476*

12 **deposit,** make a deposit, credit one's account, place in one's account, place to one's credit, stay in the black

13 **recognize,** give recognition, ascribe, attribute, give credit where credit is due

ADVERBS

14 **on credit,** on account, by deferred payment, by installments, on the cuff [Inf]

15 **in the black,** out of the red; in the red, out of the black

488 Debt

NOUNS

1 **debt,** indebtedness, owing, liability, obligation, commitment, encumbrance, accountability, responsibility; secured debt, unsecured debt, debt of honor, good debt, bad debt, short-term debt, floating debt, promise to pay; something owing, what one owes, bills, debit, charge; overdraft, the red; charge account, credit account; charge card, credit card, bank card

▶ *Credit 487*

2 **national debt,** national credit, government debt, federal debt, funded debt, trade deficit, trade gap, negative balance of payments, public sector borrowing

3 **loan,** bank loan, business loan, leverage; personal loan, secured loan, guaranteed loan, mortgage, second mortgage, remortgage, guaranty, collateral security, unsecured loan; sum entrusted, loan capital, debt capital; loan repayment, mortgage repayment; lending, borrowing

▶ *Lending 475; Borrowing 476*

4 **interest,** prime (lending) rate, premium, rate of interest, annual percentage rate (APR), bank rate; simple interest, compound interest; high interest, excessive interest, usury, pound of flesh

5 **amount owing,** unpaid amount, deficit; bill, account, tally, score, balance to pay; accounts receivable, receivables, overdue amount, overdue payment, arrears, accumulated arrears; back pay, back rent, foreclosure, repossession; inability to pay, insufficient funds, over-

draft, defaulting; write-off, bad debt, bounced check; payment refused, frozen balance, blocked account, frozen assets, lien

▶ *Loss 468; Nonpayment 490*

6 **debtor,** credit buyer, cardholder, borrower, personal borrower, business borrower, loanee; guarantor, cosigner, obligor, drawee, mortgagor, pledgor; bad debtor, defaulter, nonpayer, bilker, insolvent, bankrupt

ADJECTIVES

7 **indebted,** pledged, bound, obliged, committed, encumbered, mortgaged, liable, responsible, accountable, answerable, beholden, borrowing, owing, in debt, in hock, unpaid, due; overdrawn, in the red, minus; in difficulties, in dire straits, deep in debt, burdened with debt, up to one's ears in debt, over one's head in debt, mortgaged to the hilt

8 **unable to pay,** insolvent, nonpaying, defaulting, at the mercy of one's creditors; in the hands of the receiver, foreclosed, repossessed

VERBS

9 **be in debt,** owe, owe money, borrow money, have to repay, have bills to pay, run up a bill, run up an account, run *or* get into debt; overspend, overdraw, go into the red; pay interest, accept a charge, get credit, have an account with, live on credit, buy on credit, buy on the installment plan, charge, charge to one's account; back another's credit, cosign a loan, make oneself responsible, go bail for

▶ *Borrowing 476; Credit 487*

10 **not pay,** default, reschedule one's debts, leave one's bills unpaid; cheat one's creditors, bilk, outrun the constable, welsh [Inf *and* Off]

▶ *Nonpayment 490*

ADVERBS

11 **insolvently,** in debt, in over one's head, in the red, in arrears, on loan, on credit, on the cuff [Inf]

489 Payment

He who pays the piper calls the tune. — PROVERB

NOUNS

1 **payment,** paying, paying out, payout, disbursement, remittance, expenditure, outlay; paying for, meeting the cost, bearing the cost, defrayment, defrayal, defraying; paying off, payoff, discharge, written discharge, quittance, acquittance, release, satisfaction, full satisfaction, liquidation, clearance, settlement, full settlement, settlement on account; accounts receivable, receivables

2 **receipt,** receipted payment, receipt for payment, receipt in full

▶ *Receipt 492*

3 **type of payment,** cash payment, money, ready cash,

payment in kind, advance payment, due payment, overdue payment, first payment, partial payment; down payment, deposit, earnest money, earnest, handsel; installment, premium, regular payments; deferred payment, charge account payment, installment plan payment, collect *or* cash on delivery (COD)

4 **voluntary payment,** donation, contribution, offering, appeal, collection
   ▶ *Expenditure 491; Receipt 492*

5 **repayment,** reimbursement, refund, compensation, recompense, indemnity, restitution; payment in lieu, substitution, composition

6 **pay,** remuneration, salary, wages, stipend, emolument, honorarium, fee, commission, royalty, advance; payroll, payout, pay envelope, pay slip, pay check, take-home pay, income, earnings; reward, tip, gratuity; pension, annuity, retirement pay; back pay, retroactive pay, ex gratia payment, payment in lieu, overtime pay; severance pay, payoff, golden handshake, golden parachute
   ▶ *Reward 453*

7 **grant,** grant-in-aid, subsidy, subvention; voluntary payment, donation, contribution, offering, tribute, appeal, collection
   ▶ *Giving 472*

8 **damages,** indemnity, penalty; tax; ransom, payoff, bribe, sweetener, payola [Inf]

9 **payer,** paymaster, bursar, purser, cashier, treasurer; disburser, spender, expender, taxpayer
   ▶ *Purchase 481; Price 494*

ADJECTIVES

10 **paying,** disbursing, expending, spending

11 **paid,** paid in full, out of debt, liquidated, in the black, out of the red, owing nothing, debt-free; cleared, settled, discharged

12 **payable,** payable on demand, due, owed, owing; remittable, refundable, redeemable

13 **profitable,** worthwhile, advantageous, lucrative, remunerative, rewarding, moneymaking

14 **receiving pay,** earning, salaried, wage-earning, waged, hired; prepaid, paid in advance, postpaid

15 **paying in return,** compensatory, retributive, redemptive

VERBS

16 **pay,** pay out, disburse, remit, expend, spend, subscribe; make a payment, pay for, pay cash, pay by check, pay by cashier's check, pay by standing order *or* direct debit, pay in kind; trade, negotiate a trade-off, barter; make a down payment, put down; pay in advance, put money up front; pay on sight, pay on call, pay on delivery, pay on demand, pay on the dot; pay dearly, pay an exorbitant price, pay through the nose; unloose the purse strings, open one's wallet *or* purse, empty one's pocket; [Inf]: lay out, shell out, fork out

or over *or* up, ante up, cough up, come across, do the needful
   ▶ *Expenditure 491*

17 **pay off,** discharge, satisfy, redeem, meet, liquidate, clear; settle, settle an account, honor, honor a bill, clear *or* square accounts with, pay up, pay in full

18 **defray,** defray the cost, pay for, meet the cost, bear the cost, stand the cost, stand; treat, give, donate, contribute, fund, finance, put up money; pick up the bill *or* tab, pay the piper, foot the bill, pay the freight [Inf]

19 **pay one's way,** pay one's share, share expenses, go Dutch; buy a round, stand a round

20 **pay back,** repay, reimburse, refund; compensate, recompense, indemnify, restitute

21 **remunerate,** pay wages, pay a salary, pay commission; distribute, reward, sweeten the pot, provide a sweetener, tip; dole out, dish out [Inf]; tickle *or* grease one's palm, cross one's palm with silver, bribe, pay off [Inf]
   ▶ *Reward 453*

22 **be profitable,** yield a return, benefit, avail
   ▶ *Gain 467*

23 **retaliate,** avenge oneself, revenge oneself; reciprocate, requite, pay back; pay off, pay off old scores, take an eye for an eye, give tit for tat, settle a score, get even, get one's own back
   ▶ *Retaliation 420*

24 **atone,** make amends, suffer, answer

ADVERBS

25 **cash down,** in advance, collect *or* cash on delivery (COD), in installments, by check, on demand

490 Nonpayment

NOUNS

1 **nonpayment,** default, refusal to pay, avoiding financial obligations; tax avoidance, tax evasion, creative accounting; embezzlement, defalcation [Form]; swindling, defrauding, scam; protest (by creditor), repudiation of debts, forgiveness of debts, cancellation of debts
   ▶ *Avoidance 386*

2 **stoppage,** deduction, moratorium, embargo, freeze

3 **bad payment,** bad check, dishonored check, bogus check, bounced check, rubber check, bum check [Inf]; protested bill
   ▶ *Money 484*

4 **depreciation,** devaluation, devalued currency; counterfeit money
   ▶ *Economics 56; Finance 457; Money 484*

5 **insolvency,** inability to pay, debt, insurmountable debt, unpayable debt; failure to meet one's obligations, nothing in the kitty, overdrawn account, overdraft, cash-flow crisis, financial crisis; crash, collapse, failure, ruin, financial ruin, bank failure, failure of credit;

lien, bankruptcy, bankruptcy court, bankruptcy proceedings, Chapter 11

⟩ *Debt 488*

6 **nonpayer,** miser, skinflint; defaulter, bankrupt, discharged bankrupt, undischarged bankrupt; debtor, insolvent debtor; embezzler, defalcator, defrauder, tax dodger, tax evader, bilker, absconder, welsher [Inf *and* Off]

ADJECTIVES

7 **nonpaying,** miserly, mean, measly, skinflint; defaulting, behindhand, in arrears, in the red, in hock; unable to pay, insolvent, bankrupt, indebted, up to one's ears in debt, over one's head in debt; poor, beggared, ruined

⟩ *Poverty 486; Debt 488*

8 **unpaid,** unrewarded, unremunerated, uncompensated, unrecompensed, unpayable, irredeemable

VERBS

9 **not pay,** default, refuse to pay, avoid financial obligations, practice tax evasion, evade taxes; divert, embezzle, defalcate [Form], swindle, defraud, bilk; evade one's creditors, outrun the constable, abscond, decamp, welsh [Inf *and* Off]

10 **stop payment,** withhold payment, refuse payment, disallow payment, freeze, block, dishonor a check; protest a bill, repudiate

11 **be unable to pay,** have no ready cash, get into debt, fall into arrears, get behindhand, become insolvent, have a cash-flow crisis; go bankrupt, go through the bankruptcy court; go to the wall, sink, fail, break, crash, collapse, wind up, go into liquidation, go belly up [Inf], go bust [Inf]

⟩ *Poverty 486; Debt 488*

12 **forgive a debt,** cancel a debt, wipe the slate clean, discharge a bankrupt, write off

13 **be parsimonious,** keep one's wallet *or* purse shut, economize, scrimp, scrape and save, make ends meet

⟩ *Thrift 499; Meanness 501*

14 **devalue the currency,** depreciate the currency, lower the official rate of exchange, go off the gold standard, demonetize

⟩ *Money 484*

ADVERBS

15 **without paying,** in arrears, in the red, in debt, insolvently

491 Expenditure

Annual income twenty pounds, annual expenditure nineteen nineteen six, result happiness. Annual income twenty pounds, annual expenditure twenty pounds ought and six, result misery. — CHARLES DICKENS

NOUNS

1 **expenditure,** spending, disbursement, payment; buying, buy, purchase

⟩ *Purchase 481; Payment 489*

2 **expense,** expenses, expense account, miscellaneous expenses, out-of-pocket expenses, extras; fee, charge, price, rate; investment; tax

3 **cost(s),** buying price, purchase price, outlay, expenses, expenditure; monthly bills, cost of living; cost-of-living index, inflation; hidden cost(s), damages [Inf]

4 **business expenses,** start-up costs, running costs, overhead, purchase *or* rental of premises, office supplies, postage, utilities; wages, wage bill, salary bill, legal costs; transportation charges, freight charges, freightage, wharfage, lighterage; damages, salvage

5 **extravagance,** prodigality, spree, splurge

⟩ *Extravagance 500*

6 **donation,** giving, contribution; support, backing, finance; generosity, liberality

⟩ *Giving 472; Generosity 498*

7 **spender,** buyer, purchaser, shopper; investor; spendthrift, profligate, squanderer, wastrel

⟩ *Purchase 481; Extravagance 500*

ADJECTIVES

8 **expending,** spending, sumptuary; out-of-pocket, lighter in one's purse; generous, liberal; spendthrift, extravagant, profligate, prodigal, spending money like water *or* as if it grows on trees; living on *or* off capital

9 **expended,** spent, disbursed, paid, paid out; invested, contributed; at one's expense, laid out [Inf], blown [Inf]

10 **used,** used up, exhausted, depleted

VERBS

11 **expend,** spend, disburse, pay, pay out; buy, purchase; incur costs, incur expenses; invest, sink money; afford, meet the cost; run down one's account, use up one's credit; live on *or* off capital, dip into capital, draw on one's savings, dissave, disinvest; untie the purse strings, empty *or* open one's pocket, spare no expense, spend lavishly, splurge, overspend, be out of pocket; squander, fritter away, throw away, dissipate; go on a spending spree, shop till one drops, fling money around, throw money at, spend money like water *or* as if it grows on trees; [Inf]: lay out, fork out, shell out, blow, blow one's cash, blow a fortune

⟩ *Purchase 481; Payment 489; Extravagance 500*

12 **consume,** use; use up, exhaust, deplete; go through, run through, get through; waste

⟩ *Waste 96; Use 393*

13 **donate,** give, give money, give to charity, contribute; support, back, finance, pay for; defray, bear the cost, treat, stand, bankroll [Inf]

⟩ *Giving 472; Generosity 498*

ADVERBS

14 **generously,** liberally, extravagantly, profligately, prodigally

492 Receipt

NOUNS

1 receipt, voucher, ticket, stub, check stub, counterfoil [Brit], proof of purchase, written acknowledgment of payment; bank statement, canceled check
▶ *Accounting 493*

2 money received, receipts, gross receipts, net receipts, box-office receipts, gate money, gate, revenue, sales revenue, proceeds, return; royalty, royalties, money coming in, incomings, credits, profits, gross profits, net profits, mesne profits; interest, gain, capital gains; bonus, premium; tax, taxes, direct tax, indirect tax, duty, customs, tariff; rent, rent-roll; dues; takings, returns, take [Inf]
▶ *Gain 467; Receiving 473; Price 494*

3 income, national income, business income, private income; emolument, regular income, earnings, remuneration, salary, wages, pay, half pay, freelance pay; fees; pension, pension fund, retirement benefits, annuity, tontine; grant, allowance, draw, spending money, pin money, pocket money, money for a rainy day; financial support, scholarship, fellowship, work-study grant; maintenance, aliment, alimony, child support, palimony
▶ *Reward 453; Payment 489*

4 legacy, inheritance, dower, bequest, heritage, birthright, patrimony

5 winnings, prize, lucky draw, raffle, lottery, grab bag, rake-off, cut [Inf]
▶ *Discount 495*

ADJECTIVES

6 received, paid, credited; gained, gotten, accepted, taken; receipted, acknowledged, acknowledged with thanks; inherited, bequeathed, hereditary, patrimonial; granted, salaried, waged; profitable, gainful

VERBS

7 receive, get, gain, take, acquire, accept; admit, receipt, acknowledge, mark paid; earn, gross, net; come into, inherit, fall to one; accrue, yield, credit
▶ *Receiving 473*

ADVERBS

8 profitably, gainfully, in profit; in receipt, at a premium, remuneratively, with interest; patrimonially; supportively, financially

493 Accounting

NOUNS

1 accounting, reckoning; calculation, computation, enumeration, score, tally; audit, inspection of accounts, inspection of books

2 statement, statement of account; bank statement; account rendered, *compte rendu* [Fr], invoice, bill, waybill, manifest; account paid, account settled
▶ *Receipt 492*

3 account book, bankbook, passbook, checkbook, cashbook, petty-cashbook; daybook, journal, ledger, register; books, records
▶ *Record 185*

4 accounts, accountancy, accounting, financial accounting, cost accounting, management accounting; financial records, bookkeeping, commercial arithmetic, creative accounting; item, entry, double entry, single entry, credit, debit; account, profit and loss account *or* income account; balance sheet, debit and credit, receipts and expenditures, payments and receipts; running account, current account, cash account; deposit account, savings account; suspense account, expense account

5 budgeting, budget, capital budget, materials budget, production budget, production cost budget; creditors' budget, debtors' budget, cash budget; zero-based budgeting, budget estimates
▶ *Finance 457*

6 accountant, certified public accountant (CPA), cost accountant, bookkeeper; storekeeper, cashier; paymaster, bursar, purser; treasurer, auditor, inspector of accounts, examiner of accounts, actuary; statistician

ADJECTIVES

7 accounting, bookkeeping, reckoning, computing, calculating; accountable, fiscal, financial, economic, commercial, arithmetical, mathematical, statistical, actuarial; bursarial, budgetary, inventorial, itemized; creative

8 accounted, audited, balanced, tallied; registered, recorded, credited, debited; deposited, saved, received, spent, invoiced, billed, costed; settled, carried forward

VERBS

9 account, keep accounts, keep the books, balance accounts, prepare a balance sheet; make up an account, cast an account, write up, write down, book, enter, journalize, post; carry over, carry forward, debit, credit, record, register; cost, value, estimate, prepare a cash-flow forecast; budget, prepare a budget; practice creative accounting, massage the accounts; falsify the accounts, defraud, garble, fudge, doctor, cook the accounts *or* books [Inf], fiddle [Brit inf]

10 audit, inspect accounts, examine the accounts, go through the books; take stock, check stock, inventory, catalog, list
▶ *List 785*

11 settle accounts, square accounts, pay up, cough up [Inf]; finalize accounts, wind up accounts, write off accounts; prepare a statement, present an account, invoice, bill; charge, surcharge, overcharge, undercharge
▶ *Price 494*

ADVERBS

12 on account, on credit, on the bill, on the tab [Inf]

13 financially, fiscally, economically, commercially; arithmetically, statistically; creatively; in debt, in credit, at a loss, at cost

494 Price

If you have two loaves of bread, sell one and buy a hyacinth. — PERSIAN PROVERB

NOUNS

1 price, cost, charge, price charged, selling price; retail price, wholesale price, factory price, market price, world price; quoted price, quotation, estimate, amount, figure, sum asked for; standard price, list price, current price, offer price; sale price, cut price, discount price, factory discount price, reduced price rate, price cut, price war; price control, fixed price, prix fixe, price range, price list; cheapness, costliness, dearness

▶ *Sale 482; Discount 495; Costliness 496; Cheapness 497*

2 value, monetary value, face value, par value, fair value, market value, scarcity value, exchange value; worth, money's worth, what it will fetch; valuation, assessment

3 fee, rate, going rate, rate for the job, piece rate, flat rate, high rate *or* ceiling, low rate *or* floor, basement price; commission, cut, charge, service fee, demand, surcharge, supplement, extra; dues, subscription, tithe; entrance fee, admission fee, cover charge, service charge, corkage; fare, flat fare, hire, rental, rent, house rent; overcharge, excessive charge, price fixing, extortion, rake-off, ripoff [Inf]

4 bill, invoice, reckoning, statement

5 tax, taxes, taxation, direct tax, indirect tax, progressive tax, proportional tax, capitation tax, regressive tax, punitive tax; income tax, corporate *or* corporation tax, company tax, excess profits tax, windfall profits tax, capital gains tax; inheritance *or* death *or* estate tax; gift tax; property tax, municipal tax, city *or* town tax, local tax, county tax, state tax; sales tax, value-added tax (VAT), octroi, surtax, supertax

6 tax system, tax office *or* bureau, Internal Revenue Service (IRS), withholding tax, Social Security tax (Federal Insurance Contributions Act; FICA); tax return, tax form, 1040 form, tax declaration; tax rate, tax table, tax computation; deduction, exemption; taxable income, tax demand, tax owed, tax payment, tax refund; assessment, appraisal, valorization, estimate

7 levy, duty, impost, toll, excise, customs, US Customs Service, tariff, tonnage and poundage; charge, fine, penalty, imposition, exaction; aid, benevolence, tribute; blackmail, protection money, hush money, ransom; forced saving, involuntary saving

▶ *Payment 489*

8 historical tax, Danegeld, stamp tax, salt tax, gabelle, window tax, scot and lot, feudal tax, scutage, tea tax

9 tax collector, tax assessor, tax consultant; revenuer [Inf]; taxpayer

ADJECTIVES

10 priced, valued, assessed, worth, valued at, taxed

11 chargeable, taxable, dutiable, nontaxable, nondutiable, tax-free, tax-exempt, deductible, tax-deductible

VERBS

12 price, fix the price of, set a price, quote a price; value, valuate, evaluate, appraise, assess; amount to, come to, sell for, fetch, bring in, set one back [Inf]

13 charge, ask, demand, exact; levy, tax, put a tax on; tithe

ADVERBS

14 at a price, for the price of, to the amount of, to the tune of [Inf]

495 Discount

NOUNS

1 discount, reduction, price reduction, cut, decrease, decrement, something off; concession, allowance, margin; rebate, refund, drawback, deduction, deferment; commission, percentage, agio, brokerage, one's cut, rake-off, kickback

▶ *Decrease 747; Subtraction 749*

2 bargain, special offer, loss leader, incentive; knockdown price, bargain price, special price, cut price, cut rate, basement price, bottom price, dumping, sale, bargain sale, grand opening sale, sale of the century, clearance sale, going-out-of-business sale, fire sale; garage sale, yard sale, rummage sale *or* jumble sale [Brit]

▶ *Sale 482; Price 494; Cheapness 497*

ADJECTIVES

3 discounted, marked down, cut-price, cut-rate, bargain, on sale, cheap, rebated, shopworn, irregular

VERBS

4 discount, reduce, lower, reduce the price, mark down, cut, slash, take something off; give a concession, allow a margin, rebate, refund, deduct, subtract, take off, knock off, depreciate, cheapen, dump; offer a bargain, offer a discount, allow a discount, knock down [Inf]

5 take a discount, take one's commission *or* cut, take one's percentage, rake off, kick back [Inf]

6 buy at a discount, pick up cheap, get for a song, make a killing; buy wholesale, buy in bulk; buy on sale, find a bargain

ADVERBS

7 at a discount, at cut price, at half price, at bargain prices, on special offer; below par, less than the going rate, less than the market rate, in the bargain bin

496 Costliness

NOUNS

1 **costliness,** high price, dearness, expensiveness, great price, big price tag, fancy price, luxury price, upmarket price, steep price, stiff price, pretty penny [Inf], ritzy price [Inf]

2 **overpricing,** unfair price, overcharging, excessive charge, overcharge; exorbitance, exorbitant price, extortionate price, highway robbery [Inf]

3 **inflationary price,** rising prices *or* costs, climbing prices, soaring prices *or* costs, spiraling prices, skyrocketing price, mounting costs; inflation, inflationary pressure, inflationary spiral, bullish tendency, bull market, sellers' market, prices going through the ceiling *or* roof

4 **extortion,** usury, profiteering, rack-rent, loansharking, gouging, ripoff [Inf]

◗ *Economics 56; Excess 99; Finance 457; Taking 477; Trade 480; Market 483; Payment 489; Expenditure 491; Price 494*

5 **overcharger,** usurer, extortionist, shark, rack-renter, loan shark, ripoff *or* ripoff artist [Inf], con man [Inf]

◗ *Borrowing 476; Stealing 479; Debt 488*

6 **value,** worth, high value, great worth, valuableness; invaluableness, pricelessness, preciousness, scarcity value

ADJECTIVES

7 **costly,** expensive, high-priced, high-price, big-ticket, dear; extravagant, fancy, luxury, upmarket; exorbitant, excessive, overpriced, overcharging, overcharged, unreasonable, extortionate, prohibitive, beyond one's means, not affordable, more than one can afford, more than one's pocket can stand; inflationary, rising, climbing, soaring, spiraling, mounting, rocketing, high-cost, sky-high, bullish, bull; usurious, profiteering, pricey *or* pricy, gouging, stiff, steep, skyrocketing, going through the roof, out-of-sight, ritzy [Inf]

◗ *Insufficiency 98; Excess 99; Overstepping 712*

8 **valuable,** invaluable, high-value; priceless, beyond price, above price, inestimable, precious, too precious for words; at a premium, worth a pretty penny [Inf], worth a fortune, worth a king's ransom, worth its weight in gold; exclusive, rare, scarce, infrequent, like gold dust, not to be had for love or money

VERBS

9 **cost a lot,** be dear, cost one dear, cost a fortune; hurt one's pocket, make a hole in one's pocket; rise in price, appreciate, escalate, soar, mount, rocket, climb, go through the ceiling *or* roof; run into money, harden, get too dear, price itself out of the market, cost, cost an arm and a leg; [Inf]: cost a pretty penny, cost the earth, cost a packet, cost a bundle

◗ *Economics 56; Finance 457; Payment 489; Price 494; Increase 746*

10 **overcharge,** overprice, sell dear, oversell, ask too much, rack-rent, profiteer; raise the price, put up prices, mark up, set the price tag too high, inflate; hold up, gouge, extort, fleece, swindle; [Inf]: do, commit highway robbery, bleed (white), con, rip off, burn, sting, soak, skin, clip, screw

◗ *Excess 99; Deception 193; Taking 477; Stealing 479; Overstepping 712*

11 **overpay,** overspend, pay too much, pay more than it's worth, pay dearly; ruin oneself, be overdrawn, go into the red; raise the bid, bid up; pay through the nose, be had; get ripped off [Inf], pay a pretty penny [Inf]

◗ *Excess 99; Expenditure 491; Extravagance 500*

ADVERBS

12 **at great cost,** at heavy cost, dearly, dear, at great expense, at huge expense, expensively; grossly, extravagantly, outrageously, exorbitantly; excessively, extortionately; prohibitively, beyond one's means, more than one can afford, usuriously, stiffly, steeply, out of sight [Inf]

13 **valuably,** at great value, invaluably, inestimably, pricelessly, beyond worth; exclusively, rarely, scarcely, infrequently, preciously, at a premium

497 Cheapness

NOUNS

1 **cheapness,** inexpensiveness, reasonableness, reasonable charge, affordability; good value, value for money, money's worth; easy terms, popular price, sensible price, competitive price; low price, sale price, reduced price, discount, budget price, economy price, bargain price, cut rate, price cut, markdown, knockdown price; slashed price, rock-bottom price, giveaway price, nominal price; low *or* small price tag, cheap rate, reduced rate, concessional rate

◗ *Discount 495*

2 **declining prices,** fall, price fall, bear market, bearishness, buyers' market, sluggish market; deflation, slump, plunge, recession, depression; cooling off of the economy, devaluation, depreciation; superfluity, redundance, oversupply, plenty, glut, drug on the market

◗ *Economics 56; Finance 457; Purchase 481; Sale 482; Money 484; Expenditure 491; Price 494; Offer 504*

3 **shoddiness,** cheapness, gaudiness, second-rateness, inferiority; poorness, shabbiness, scruffiness, tackiness, pettiness, paltriness; baseness, lowness, meanness, commonness, vulgarity, kitsch, crumminess [Inf]

◗ *Showiness 404; Meanness 501; Vulgarity 535; Average 742; Inferiority 745*

4 **bargain,** good buy, good deal, steal; special offer, two for the price of one, loss leader; sale goods, sale mer-

chandise, *bon marché* [Fr], seconds, rejects; excursion fare *or* rate, tourist fare *or* rate, second-class fare, coach fare, economy fare, off-season fare, off-peak fare, half fare, standby fare, APEX (Advance Purchase Excursion), cheap ticket, discount ticket, season ticket, twofer [Inf]

▶ *Negotiation 460; Market 483; Transportation 686*

5 **cheap item,** trifle, gewgaw, gimcrack, frippery, bauble, trinket, gaud, curio, knickknack, kickshaw, bagatelle, brummagem, toy, plaything, novelty, bric-a-brac, junk, white elephant

▶ *Decoration 532*

6 **absence of charge,** gift, free gift, giveaway, complimentary gift; throwaway, something for nothing, gratuitousness, gratuity; free lodging *or* quarters, free board, free drink, free lunch; postage paid; free admission *or* entry; free ticket *or* pass, guest ticket *or* pass, complimentary ticket *or* pass, Annie Oakley; free port, free trade; free service, free delivery; volunteer work, voluntary work, charity, labor of love; perquisite; [Inf]: perk, free ride, freebie, paper

▶ *Giving 472; Nonpayment 490; Generosity 498; Offer 504*

7 **discounter,** street trader, wholesaler; cash and carry, warehouse; bargain basement, bargain bin, discount store, secondhand shop, junk shop, thrift shop, charity shop, flea market; rummage sale *or* jumble sale [Brit], yard sale, garage sale; coupons, cents-off coupons; classified ad [Inf]

▶ *Trade 480; Market 483; Discount 495*

8 **bargain hunter,** off-season traveler, pass holder, miser, penny pincher, coupon clipper, skinflint, scrooge, cheap-jack, sponger, freeloader [Inf], gatecrasher [Inf]

▶ *Inactivity 415; Taking 477; Thrift 499; Meanness 501*

ADJECTIVES

9 **cheap,** inexpensive, unexpensive, uncostly; reasonable, sensible, manageable, affordable, within one's means, easy on the pocket; modest, moderate, five-and-ten; low-budget, low-priced, low, brummagem, (well) worth the money; coach-class, economy-class, tourist-class, second-class, third-class, steerage, excursion; concessional, nominal, dirt-cheap, cheapo [Inf]

10 **bargain,** budget, bargain-basement, underpriced, catchpenny; going cheap *or* cheaply, going for a song, cheap at the price, cheap at half the price, on sale, sale-priced; off-season, off-peak; economical, economy, economy-size; discount, knockdown, half-price, cut-rate, markdown, marked down, reduced; reduced to clear, slashed, sacrificial, rock-bottom, giveaway; declining, falling, slumping, bearish, bear; devalued, depreciated, superfluous, redundant, oversupplied, a dime a dozen [Inf]

11 **shoddy,** shabby, scruffy, tacky, base, low, mean, poor, paltry, mangy, gaudy, chintzy, tawdry, tatty, trashy;

second-rate, inferior, low-grade, low-quality; useless, unsalable, unmarketable, valueless, worthless; shopworn, unbought, unwanted, out of fashion, past its sell-by date; [Inf]: crummy, two-bit, lousy, scummy

▶ *Uselessness 802*

12 **free of charge,** free, scot-free, free for the asking, for free, for nothing; without charge, not charged for, uncharged, unchargeable; gratis, given free, given away, given, giveaway; complimentary, on the house, courtesy, gratuitous, honorary; voluntary, unsalaried, unpaid; charity, eleemosynary; untaxed, tax-free, rent-free, postpaid, free on board (f.o.b.)

▶ *Nonpayment 490*

VERBS

13 **be cheap,** cost next to nothing, go for a song, go dirt-cheap; fall in price, depreciate, decline, sag, fall, drift, slump, plunge, plummet

▶ *Lowering 716*

14 **make cheap,** cheapen, devalue; offer value for money, give someone his money's worth; lower the price, reduce the price, lower charges, trim, cut, mark down, slash, discount, offer easy terms; sacrifice, undercharge, undercut, undersell, let go for a song; flood the market, glut the market, dump, unload, depress the market, give away, knock the bottom out of the market, knock down [Inf]

▶ *Sufficiency 97; Lowering 716*

15 **buy cheaply,** economize, shop around, find bargains; buy wholesale, buy in bulk, buy at factory prices, buy at cost, pick up for nothing; travel second-class, travel tourist-class, travel off season, buy for nickels and dimes; haggle, beat down; buy dirt-cheap, sponge (off), freeload [Inf]

▶ *Negotiation 460; Trade 480; Market 483; Thrift 499*

ADVERBS

16 **cheaply,** cheap, inexpensively, unexpensively, reasonably, modestly, moderately, economically; nominally, at cost, wholesale, at a discount, *à bon marché* [Fr], for pennies, for nickels and dimes, for a song, for nothing, on the house, as a gift, on the cheap [Inf]

498 Generosity

NOUNS

1 **generosity,** liberality, charity, openhandedness, beneficence, bounty, bounteousness, hospitality, munificence

2 **magnanimity,** charitableness, benevolence, philanthropy

3 **gift,** contribution, subscription, donation; bonus, tip, lagniappe, alms, baksheesh, handout [Inf]

▶ *Money 484; Payment 489*

4 **abundance,** plenty, plenteousness, profusion, superabundance

5 **generous person,** benefactor, backer, donor, donator,

contributor, subscriber; philanthropist, humanitarian, good Samaritan, willing giver; Lady Bountiful, Father Christmas, Santa Claus, fairy godmother; angel [Inf]

▶ *Giving 472*

ADJECTIVES

6 **generous,** liberal, bountiful, bounteous, openhanded, hospitable, giving; unstinting, ungrudging, beneficent; munificent, lavish, princely, handsome

7 **magnanimous,** charitable, benevolent, humanitarian, philanthropic

8 **abundant,** plentiful, ample, lavish, more than enough, copious, overflowing, profuse, superabundant

▶ *Excess 99*

9 **big,** roomy, large, capacious, spacious, commodious

VERBS

10 **be generous,** give generously, give freely, give away, keep open house, spare no expense, give with both hands; tip well

11 **give,** contribute, subscribe, donate; bequeath, endow; finance, fund, aid, support

▶ *Support 605*

ADVERBS

12 **generously,** liberally, freely, lavishly, copiously, amply, abundantly, plentifully; ungrudgingly, with open hands, with no expense spared

499 Thrift

I knew once a very covetous, sordid fellow, who used frequently to say, "Take care of the pence, for the pounds will take care of themselves." — EARL OF CHESTERFIELD

NOUNS

1 **thrift,** thriftiness, economy; good husbandry, good management, good housekeeping; carefulness, prudence, moderation, frugality, austerity

2 **act of thrift,** economy drive, retrenchment, cutting back, cutback; budget, spending plan

3 **saver,** economizer, scrimper

▶ *Meanness 501*

ADJECTIVES

4 **thrifty,** economical, unlavish, unwasteful; conserving, saving, labor-saving, time-saving, money-saving; good with money, canny, careful, prudent, moderate, economizing; sparing, frugal, Spartan, austere, meager, scrimpy

VERBS

5 **be thrifty,** make do; budget, live on a budget, live *or* keep within one's means, make both ends meet; conserve, husband, husband one's resources; save, save up

6 **economize,** keep costs down; retrench, cut down, cut costs, cut back, cut corners, scrimp, scrape, tighten one's belt, batten down the hatches

ADVERBS

7 **economically,** thriftily, prudently, moderately, frugally, with a sparing hand

500 Extravagance

We're overpaying him but he's worth it.
— SAMUEL GOLDWYN

NOUNS

1 **extravagance,** prodigality, lavishness, conspicuous consumption, unthriftiness, improvidence; wastefulness, profligacy, squandering; spending *or* shopping spree, dissaving

2 **unrestrainedness,** immoderation; exaggeration, hyperbole; profusion, superfluity; dissipation, extremes

3 **spendthrift,** prodigal, prodigal son, profligate, wastrel, squanderer, waster, spender, big spender, big-time spender [Inf], high roller [Inf]

ADJECTIVES

4 **extravagant,** wasteful, lavish, uneconomic; spendthrift, prodigal, profligate, thriftless; unthrifty, improvident, easy come easy go [Inf]

▶ *Generosity 498*

5 **unrestrained,** excessive, inordinate, immoderate; extreme, wild, exaggerated, hyperbolic, magnified; profuse, ostentatious, showy; preposterous, outrageous, fantastical

▶ *Excess 99; Increase 746*

6 **costly,** high-priced, expensive, dear; overpriced, exorbitant, inflationary, sky-high, going through the roof; unaffordable, prohibitive

VERBS

7 **waste,** squander, fritter, fritter away, misspend; dissipate, lavish; go through, use up, exhaust, pour down the drain, blow [Inf]

8 **overspend,** overdraw, live beyond one's means; throw money away, throw good money after bad, go on a spending spree, spend money like water *or* as if it grows on trees, spend money like it's going out of style *or* fashion

ADVERBS

9 **extravagantly,** lavishly, uneconomically; wastefully, excessively, inordinately, immoderately; inexhaustibly, to the full, no end [Inf]

501 Meanness

NOUNS

1 **meanness,** parsimony, parsimoniousness, niggardliness, miserliness; ungenerousness, ungenerosity, tightness, tight-fistedness, close-fistedness; cheeseparing, stinginess, minginess

2 **unpleasantness,** nastiness, hurtfulness, pettiness,

spite; baseness, beastliness, shabbiness, lowliness, squalor

▶ *Unpleasantness 272*

3 **miser,** niggard, skinflint, hoarder, Scrooge, penny pincher, misanthrope; [Inf]: moneygrubber, meany *or* meanie, tightwad

ADJECTIVES

4 **mean,** miserly, parsimonious, ungenerous, grudging, tight, tight-fisted, close, close-fisted, near; niggardly, penurious, penny-pinching, scrimping; cheeseparing, mingy, stingy, moneygrubbing [Inf]

5 **unpleasant,** nasty, unkind, hurtful, spiteful, petty, small, small-minded; despicable, base, shabby, sordid, squalid, lowly, beastly [Inf]

▶ *Unpleasantness 272; Inferiority 745*

VERBS

6 **hoard,** save up, save, stint, scrimp, skimp; starve

7 **grudge,** begrudge, resent

ADVERBS

8 **meanly,** parsimoniously, ungenerously, niggardly, grudgingly; on a shoestring

502 Permission

NOUNS

1 **permission,** authorization, leave, approval, nod of approval, consent, implied consent, approbation, blessing, benevolence; clearance, security clearance, top-secret clearance, authority, legality, law, mandate, sanction; endorsement, confirmation, ratification, verification; corroboration, validation

▶ *Benevolence 305; Approval 437*

2 **tolerance,** toleration, dispensation, exemption; non-liability, connivance; acquiescence, concession, license, free hand, carte blanche, blank check, freedom; easiness, indulgence, leniency, laissez-faire attitude, unconstraint; permissiveness, promiscuity, free love, permissive society, the sixties; green light, go-ahead, the OK *or* O.K. *or* okay, nod, open sesame, magic word; thumbs up

▶ *Authority 52; Leniency 423; Exemption 434; Easiness 823; Freedom 829*

3 **permit,** written permission, grant, warrant, warranty; charter, patent, letters patent; certificate, credentials, diploma; testimonial, recommendation, reference, character reference, seal, signature, endorsement; voucher, ticket, admission ticket, chit; license, fishing license, hunting license, driver's license; release, waiver; imprimatur, nihil obstat; clearance papers; work permit, green card, passport, visa; pass, safe-conduct pass, laissez-passer; leave, sick leave, leave of absence, furlough, sabbatical, parole; stamp, rubber stamp, mark, cross

▶ *Authority 52*

ADJECTIVES

4 **permitted,** allowed, authorized; warranted, sanctioned, licensed; legal, legalized, lawful, licit, decriminalized; chartered, patent; aboveboard, legitimate, acceptable, worthwhile, approved, passed; unconditional, without strings, legit [Inf]

5 **permitting,** permissive, permissible, admissive, admissible; allowing, allowable, printable, sayable, unprohibitive; easygoing, tolerant, lenient, indulgent, laissez-faire; loose, lax, easy come easy go [Inf], overindulgent; irresolute, unassertive; conniving

VERBS

6 **permit,** give permission, allow, let; make possible, authorize, approve, clear, sanction, endorse; confirm, ratify, verify, corroborate, validate; tolerate, exempt, connive, acquiesce, countenance; license, legitimize, legalize, make legal; decriminalize, lift the ban on, not stand in the way of; enable, empower, remove all obstacles, facilitate; say yes, give the OK *or* O.K. *or* okay, give the go-ahead, give the green light, sign on the dotted line, consent, bless, give one's blessing, say the magic word, give the nod to [Inf], give thumbs up; give dispensation, make concessions, grant immunity, compromise

7 **be permissive,** be lax, indulge, spoil, favor, pamper, adopt a laissez-faire attitude; give someone his *or* her head, give someone a free hand, not cramp someone's style [Inf], not stand in the way of, allow to have the run of, make it easy for, give someone a chance; bend the rules, stretch the point, allow someone to take liberties, let someone get away with it; relinquish authority, resign oneself, give carte blanche to, give a blank check to, open the floodgates, let someone get away with murder [Inf]

8 **be permitted,** have permission, receive permission, have authorization, have clearance, have someone's blessing; have a free hand, take liberties, get away with it

9 **ask permission,** beg permission, ask leave, beg leave, ask if one may, ask to be excused; request, petition, seek a favor, seek help, ask for someone's blessing

▶ *Request 505; Help 825*

ADVERBS

10 **with permission,** under authorization, under license, under warrant, under a charter, under a patent; legally, with legal protection, lawfully, legitimately, acceptably; unconditionally, without conditions, without strings; permissively, in a permissive fashion, permissibly; tolerantly, leniently, indulgently, loosely, laxly, with no questions asked; connivingly

503 Prohibition

NOUNS

1 **prohibition,** ban, embargo, injunction, interdiction,

interdict; check, curfew, restriction, circumscription; exclusion, ostracism, excommunication, debarment; crackdown, repression, suppression, prevention, restraint, obstruction, interference, impediment, obstacle; disallowance, abolition, forbidding, taboo; blacklist, impermissibility, illicitness, illegality, illegitimacy

2 **prohibition of alcohol,** temperance, Volstead Act, Eighteenth Amendment

3 **veto,** counterorder, countermand, suspension, cancellation, denial, rejection, refusal, no, pocket veto, rebuff, abrogation, annulment, repeal, red light, thumbs down

> *Rejection 383; Disapproval 438; Refusal 506; Expulsion 709; Exclusion 764; Hindrance 826; Cancellation 834*

4 **censorship,** proscription, deletion; classified document, secret document, top-secret document, restricted information, news blackout; banned book, *Index Librorum Prohibitorum* [L], the Index; movie rating

> *Motion Pictures 137; Literature 139; Concealment 181; Secrecy 182*

ADJECTIVES

5 **prohibited,** prohibitive, prohibiting, prohibitory, interdictive, barred, suppressive, preventive, preventative, obstructive, inhibiting; illicit, illegal, unlawful, illegitimate; excommunicated, banned, blackballed, blacklisted; embargoed, contraband; forbidden, verboten, impermissible, out of bounds, off-limits, taboo; unauthorized, not allowed; repressive, restrictive, circumscriptive, exclusive

6 **vetoed,** injunctive, suspended, canceled, null and void, denied, rejected, refused

7 **censored,** proscriptive, proscribed, banned; deleted, blue-penciled, blacked out, bleeped out; unprintable, unmentionable, unsayable; classified, secretive, secret, top-secret, restrictive, restricted

VERBS

8 **prohibit,** ban, impose a ban, embargo, interdict, forbid, disallow, check, not tolerate; restrict, circumscribe, put out of bounds, make off-limits, prevent, obstruct, impede, inhibit, place an obstacle in someone's path, interfere, withhold *or* refuse permission; exclude, shut *or* close the door on, ostracize, crack down on, excommunicate, blackball, blacklist, debar; abolish, make illegal, outlaw, criminalize, put outside the law

9 **veto,** annul, repeal, revoke, abrogate, counterorder, countermand; suspend, cancel, reject, refuse, rebuff; decide against, turn down, deny, say no, give the red light *or* red-light [Inf], turn *or* give thumbs down, nix [Inf]

10 **censor,** proscribe, delete, blue-pencil; classify secret; taboo, restrict, repress, suppress, restrain, stifle, cancel, kill; ban a book, put on the Index, black out, bleep out; rate a movie

ADVERBS

11 **prohibitively,** interdictively, impermissibly, without

permission, without authorization; illicitly, illegally, unlawfully, illegitimately; repressively, in a repressive way, circumscriptively, exclusively

12 **by veto,** injunctively, under an injunction, preventively, in order to prevent, suppressively, obstructively

13 **under censorship,** proscriptively, with deletions; secretively, in a secret manner; restrictively, with restrictions

504 Offer

I'll make him an offer he can't refuse. — MARIO PUZO

NOUNS

1 **offer,** proffer, proposal, invitation, proposition, bid, approach, lure, come-on [Inf], freebie [Inf]

> *Sociability 408*

2 **tentative offer,** suggestion, presentation, submission; feeler, advance, overture, motion; chance, opening, opportunity, golden opportunity; suit, courting, wooing, offer of one's hand in marriage

> *Persuasion 178; Love 299; Promise 458*

3 **business offer,** merger, bid, takeover bid; final offer, last word, ultimatum, firm price; asking price, fair offer; special offer, sale, special sale

> *Sale 482; Price 494*

4 **illegal offer,** bribe, blood money, kickback, rake-off

5 **offering,** sacrifice, martyrdom; gift, present; dedication, consecration, oblation, offertory, collection, votive offering, peace offering; contribution, donation, subscription, tithe; propitiation, conciliation, appeasement, expiation; self-immolation, burnt offering, sacrificial offering, sacrificial lamb, hecatomb

> *Death 29; Religion 81; Giving 472*

6 **martyr,** willing sacrifice, human sacrifice, sacrificial lamb, suttee; protomartyr

7 **volunteer,** voluntary worker, charity worker, unpaid worker, helper, good Samaritan; philanthropist, humanitarian, benefactor, contributor; altruist, missionary, public servant, do-gooder; wooer

> *Benevolence 305; Philanthropy 307; Giving 472*

ADJECTIVES

8 **offered,** offering, inviting, propositional, bid; persuasive, advertised; bribed, bribable; open to offers, on offer, on special offer, up for sale, for sale; cheap, reduced, up for auction, on auction, open for bid; requested, available, on the market, for rent, to let

9 **voluntary,** unprompted, unforced, of one's own free will, on one's own accord; charitable, unpaid, philanthropic, humanitarian, altruistic

10 **sacrificial,** sacrificed, martyred; consecrated, oblatory, oblational; contributory, donated; propitiatory, conciliatory, expiatory

VERBS

11 **offer,** proffer, propose, bid, approach, submit; suggest,

put out a feeler, advance, make an overture, provide an opportunity, lay before; offer *or* request one's hand in marriage, court, woo, go down on bended knee; make an offer, make a fair offer, keep one's offer open, leave the door open; offer for sale, put up for sale, invite offers, advertise; auction, open the bidding; hand out a sample, hold out an incentive, lure, bait; spur, goad, persuade, induce; bribe, take a kickback, rake off

▶ *Love 299; Negotiation 460; Sale 482*

12 **offer to buy,** attempt to buy; offer a fair price for, make an offer for, make a bid for, bid; negotiate, haggle

13 **volunteer,** do volunteer work, do charity work, do missionary work, work without pay; come forward, take on, lend a helping hand; act on one's own initiative, act without prompting, not wait to be asked; offer help *or* assistance, offer hospitality

14 **sacrifice,** offer *or* sacrifice one's life, sacrifice oneself, become a martyr, die for a cause

15 **offer reparation,** atone, make amends; apologize, offer one's apologies, beg one's pardon; propitiate, conciliate, appease, pacify, expiate; offer satisfaction, give satisfaction

16 **offer worship,** celebrate mass, celebrate communion; administer the sacraments, minister, officiate, lead worship, say prayers

▶ *Religious Ritual 85*

17 **make an offering,** offer a gift, dedicate, consecrate, make a peace offering; contribute, donate, subscribe, tithe; offer a sacrifice, make a burnt offering, make a sacrificial offering, offer a sacrificial lamb

ADVERBS

18 **persuasively,** in a persuasive manner; with no strings attached

19 **voluntarily,** for free, philanthropically, altruistically, like a good Samaritan

20 **sacrificially,** as a sacrifice, conciliatorily

505 Request

NOUNS

1 **request,** asking, entreaty, solemn entreaty, importunity, pressure, persuasion, insistence, urgency, urging, imploring, soliciting, accosting; invitation, application, appeal, bid, cry; desire, expressed desire, special request, favor, wish, want

2 **petition,** round robin; invocation, incantation, prayer, supplication, adjuration, *cri de coeur* [Fr]; begging, beseeching, pestering, solicitation; suggestion, proposition, proposal, motion, approach, offer; requirement, claim, counterclaim

▶ *Persuasion 178; Desire 288; Offer 504*

3 **demand,** requisition, order, summons, call; notice, claim, demand for payment, dunning, dun, final demand, final notice, last time of asking; injunction, command, ultimatum, forcible demand, demand

backed by threats, threat; blackmail, exaction, extortion

▶ *Publication 173; Argument 329; Command 425; Compulsion 428*

4 **solicitation,** fund-raising, appealing, appeal, canvass, canvassing; soliciting money, chain letter, mendicancy, begging; charity appeal, charity event, benefit game, benefit concert *or* gig [Inf], (church) bazaar, telethon; scrounging, sponging, cadging, bumming; [Inf]: panhandling, freeloading, mooching, the touch

▶ *Benevolence 305; Borrowing 476; Taking 477*

5 **requester,** petitioner, appealer, lobbyist; supplicant, suppliant, appellant, solicitor, fund-raiser, charity worker, charity organization, canvasser; claimant, counterclaimant, asker; blackmailer, extortionist, hustler; seeker, inquirer, questioner; borrower, customer, applicant; candidate

6 **beggar,** cadger, mendicant, hanger-on, vagrant, freebooter, tramp, hobo, bum, scrounger, sponger; [Inf]: panhandler, freeloader, moocher

ADJECTIVES

7 **requesting,** requested, asking, insistent, urgent, invitational, inviting, desired; petitioned, round-robin; invocational, incantational, adjuratory, entreating, beseeching; propositional, proposable, proposed, offered, required

8 **demanding,** demanded, claiming, requisitionary, injunctive; forcible, threatening, threatened; blackmailing, blackmailed, extortive, extorting, extorted

9 **begging,** cadging, mendicant; fund-raising; scrounging, sponging, freeloading [Inf], mooching [Inf]

VERBS

10 **request,** make a request, have a need for, lack, want, want to know, demand an answer; ask, ask for, ask if it is possible, ask a favor, ask leave, ask permission, ask to be excused; beg leave, beg permission; make a special request, go cap in hand, entreat, pressure, insist, urge, implore, solicit, accost, hustle; invite, request the pleasure of one's company; apply for, appeal, bid, cry, desire

11 **petition,** sign a petition, sign a round robin; invoke, pray, address one's prayers to, kneel to, go down on one's knees to, supplicate, adjure, beg, beseech; cajole, coax, pester, bug, hawk, suggest, persuade, proposition, propose, move; approach, make an overture, offer, apply, require, claim, counterclaim, issue a suit, tout [Inf]

▶ *Religious Ritual 85*

12 **demand,** requisition, order, summon, call, claim, press a claim, put in a claim; invoice, charge, bill, levy, tax, demand payment, dun, put the squeeze on someone, make a final demand, receive a final notice, receive an injunction; command, issue an ultimatum, threaten; blackmail, exact, extort, bleed, put the bite on [Inf]

13 **solicit money,** beg, cadge, hold out one's hand, go

from door to door; pass around the hat, raise funds, appeal, make a charity appeal, launch an appeal, canvass, hold a charity event; put the squeeze on, scrounge, sponge, bum; [Inf]: panhandle, freeload, mooch, put the touch on

ADVERBS

14 **by request,** insistently, urgently, with urgency; entreatingly, by one's leave, with permission, beseechingly; forcibly, using force, with force

506 Refusal

NOUNS

1 **refusal,** turndown, rejection, denial, repulsion, repulse; lack of consent, negative answer, negation, flat *or* point-blank refusal, red light; noncompliance, resistance, retention, recalcitrance, unwillingness, nonwillingness, noncooperation; nonacceptance, denigration; refusal to work, strike, sit-down strike; lockout; refusal to pay, nonpayment, default, tax evasion, creative accounting; thumbs down

> *Negation 190; Unwillingness 375; Rejection 383; Avoidance 386; Resistance 417; Repulsion 701; Expulsion 709*

2 **dissent,** dissidence; lack of consent, contrary vote, a vote against, veto; disagreement, opposition, objection, discordance; refutation, repudiation, rebuttal, rebuff, kick in the teeth, contradiction, confutation, renunciation, recusancy; confrontation, demonstration, protest, sit-in, civil disobedience, gainsaying, controversy; prohibition, counterorder, interdiction, interdict, ban, embargo

> *Dissent 347; Defiance 416; Prohibition 503; Protest 507; Opposition 828*

3 **abnegation,** relinquishment, self-restraint, self-sacrifice, self-renunciation, self-denial

> *Relinquishment 392; Self-Restraint 455*

4 **refuser,** teetotaler, abstainer; tax evader; draft dodger, conscientious objector, deserter, truant; dissident, recusant, gainsayer, striker; scab

ADJECTIVES

5 **refused,** refusing, uncooperative, noncooperative, unconsenting; uncompliant, noncompliant, noncomplying, resistant, resisting, negative, negating, recalcitrant, unwilling, nonwilling, nonaccepting; turned down, turned away; thrown out, ejected, excluded; withholding, withheld, kept back, not offered, retained; striking, strike-bound, sit-down; given the thumbs down, given the red light, deaf to, not willing to hear of

6 **dissenting,** dissident, disagreeing, repudiating, demurring, opposing, opposite; adversarial, confrontational, controversial, protesting, sit-in, objecting, discordant, refuting, denying, recusant; denied, disallowed, not allowed, not permitted, not granted; con-

tradictory, contrary, contravening, confutative, renunciative, renunciatory; rejecting, rejected, rebuffed, revoking, revocatory; prohibitionary, prohibited, prohibiting, interdictive, banned, embargoed

7 **abnegating,** abnegated, relinquishing, relinquished, self-sacrificing, self-renunciatory, self-denying

VERBS

8 **refuse,** reject, deny, say no, shake one's head; repulse, repel, denigrate, negate, not comply, resist; refuse permission, refuse flatly, refuse point-blank, not cooperate; not be willing to, not accept, decline, turn down, pass up, make one's excuses, send one's apologies, recuse; avoid, turn away, shy away, shrink from, flinch at, balk at, jib at [Brit], keep away, not want anything to do with; refuse to work, strike, go on strike, call a strike, have a sit-down strike; lock out; refuse to pay, default, evade taxes, turn one's back on, turn a deaf ear to, harden one's heart to; give thumbs down, not buy [Inf]; give the red light *or* red-light [Inf]

9 **dissent,** withhold consent, withhold assent; express doubts, disagree, oppose; not allow, disallow, not stand for; reject, repudiate, rebuff, kick someone in the teeth, spurn, snub; object, refute, rebut, contradict, confute, nullify, renunciate; confront, withstand, not comply with, gainsay, demonstrate against; cast a contrary vote, vote against, veto; prohibit, forbid, interdict, embargo, ban; tell someone where to go [Inf], tell someone where to get off [Inf]

10 **refuse oneself,** deny oneself, deprive oneself of; renounce, forbear, demur, abstain, go without, do without; live simply

ADVERBS

11 **uncooperatively,** without a cooperative spirit, on no account, not at all, negatively; resistantly, resistingly, with resistance, unwillingly; dissentingly, dissidently, oppositely, discordantly, contradictorily, in contradiction, contrarily; controversially, in a controversial way, interdictively; no fear, no chance, no way [Inf]

INTERJECTIONS

12 **no!,** no way!, a thousand times no!, never!, not likely!, impossible!, far from it!, over my dead body!, count me out!; [Inf]: nothing doing!, not on your life!, not for all the tea in China!, like hell!, nix!

507 Protest

NOUNS

1 **protest,** opposition, objection, dissent, dissatisfaction, disagreement; disapproval, disapprobation, negation, negativity; contravention, hostility, discontent, recalcitrance, refractoriness, challenge; refusal to obey orders, refutation, noncooperation, noncompliance, disobedience, anger, defiance, recusancy, mutiny; refusal to pay, nonpayment, protestation, expostulation, deprecation, intercession, counteraction, warning, com-

plaint; clamor, outcry, no, nay, denial; contradiction, repudiation, disclaimer, renunciation, disavowal, gainsaying; [Inf]: kick, bitch, beef

> *Negation 190; Unwillingness 375; Disobedience 427; Disapproval 438; Disagreement 463; Refusal 506*

2 **disorder,** agitation, breach of the peace; insurgency, sedition, riot, rioting, rebellion, revolt, mutiny, insurrection, uprising, coup d'état, putsch

> *Defiance 416; Contention 422*

3 **gesture of protest,** peaceful protest, strike, sit-down strike, work to rule [Brit], hunger strike, boycott, picketing, demonstration, protest march, protest meeting, sit-in; raised fist, protest song, boo, hiss, groan, catcall, jeer, howl; [Inf]: raspberry *or* Bronx cheer, the bird, squawk, the finger

> *Labor Relations 57; Sign 183; Demonstration 331*

4 **protester,** objector, conscientious objector; complainer, dissatisfied customer, grumbler, grouser, whiner, moaner, difficult character; mischief-maker, troublemaker, agitator, malcontent, ranter, rabble-rouser; dissident, dissentient, dissenter, critic, detractor, protestant, separatist, sectarian, seditionist, revolter, recusant; dropout, nonconformist, hippie, rebel, demonstrator; striker, picketer, nonstriker, scab; marcher, counterdemonstrator, tub-thumper, suffragette, suffragist; bellyacher [Inf]

ADJECTIVES

5 **protesting,** protestant, opposing, dissenting; dissatisfied, disapproving, negative, negating, hostile, critical, discontent, malcontent, discontented; unconsenting, deprecatory, recalcitrant, refractory, challenging, noncooperative, noncompliant, nonconformist; disobedient, angry, contrary, defiant, recusant, counteractive,

denying, denied, contradictive, repudiated; clamorous, hissing, booing, jeering

6 **disorderly,** insubordinate, insurgent, mutinous, seditious, riotous, rebellious, insurrectionary

VERBS

7 **protest,** oppose, object, raise an objection, dissent, resist, show dissatisfaction, disagree with, disapprove of, show disapproval, gainsay, deprecate, detract, contravene, show discontent, become agitated about; challenge, refuse to obey orders, not cooperate, not comply, disobey; become angry, raise one's fist, defy, mutiny, expostulate; intercede, counteract, warn, complain, clamor, say no, deny, contradict, repudiate, disclaim, renounce, disavow; speak out against, raise one's voice against; [Inf]: raise the roof, kick, bitch, beef

8 **complain,** groan, grumble, grouse, whine, gripe, moan, rant, boo, hiss, tut-tut, give a catcall, fuss *or* kick up a fuss, jeer, howl, yell *or* scream bloody murder; [Inf]: give a raspberry *or* Bronx cheer, give the bird, squawk, bellyache, give someone the finger

9 **cause mischief,** cause trouble; strike, go on strike, walk out, work to rule [Brit], stage a sit-down; boycott, picket, cause disorder, breach the peace, agitate against, demonstrate against, go on a protest march, hold a protest meeting, sit in; riot, rebel, revolt, mutiny, begin an insurrection, lead an uprising, pull off a coup d'état, lead a putsch

ADVERBS

10 **disapprovingly,** without approval, in opposition, negatively, hostilely, with hostility, critically, in a critical way, deprecatorily; disobediently, angrily, with anger, contrarily, defiantly, in defiance of, in the face of, contradictively, in conflict with, insubordinately, mutinously, seditiously, rebelliously, in rebellion against

508 Motivation

NOUNS

1 **motivation,** cause, reason, rationale, grounds, excuse, pretext; motive, driving force, guiding principle, guiding light, guiding star, lodestar, ideal; intention, objective, object, design, purpose, aim, goal; hope, desire, ambition, driving ambition, impetus, what makes one tick, stimulation, impulse, compulsion, inspiration, bright idea; call, calling, vocation, aspiration; selfish motive, ulterior motive

▶ *Hope 281; Intention 374; Duty 433; Selfishness 444; Cause 675*

2 **inducement,** influence, encouragement, invitation, incentive, provocation, enticement, lure, allurement, attraction; attractiveness, charm, fascination, bewitchment, magnetism, magnetic personality, seductiveness, seduction; blandishment, cajolery, coaxing, flattering, teasing, wheedling, pleading, urging; advocacy, advice, persuasion, persuasiveness, propaganda, agitprop, pressure, lobbying; solicitation, advertising, hard sell, soft sell, sales talk, patter, promises, golden handshake

▶ *Advice 176; Flattery 439; Request 505; Influence 512; Attraction 700*

3 **stimulus,** stimulant, arousal, incitation, excitation, provocation, fillip, tonic, sop; gadfly, carrot and stick

4 **negative stimulus,** threat, castigation, irritation, exasperation, big stick; whip, lash, prick, prod, goad, spur, sting, crack of the whip; threat of dismissal

5 **positive stimulus,** flattery, carrot, charm, spell, lure, bait; loss leader, special offer, limited offer, added attraction; incentive, profit, money, cash, pay, payment, salary, wages, benefits, pay increase, raise, bonus, handout, gift, donation, gratuity, tip, lagniappe; bribe, kickback, hush money, political favors, spoils system; inducement, tempting offer, offer one cannot refuse; [Inf]: perk, sweet talk, come-on, turnon, freebie, pork barrel

▶ *Fear 283; Help 825*

6 **motivator,** prime mover, moving spirit; orator, rhetorician, preacher, lawyer, politician; instigator, rabble-rouser, demagogue, agitator, troublemaker, firebrand, ringleader; manipulator, maneuverer, agent provocateur, strategist, tactician, manager, prompter, adviser, counselor, aider and abettor; tempter, temptress, seducer, seductress, femme fatale, vamp, siren, sexpot [Inf]; flatterer, coaxer, spellbinder, hypnotizer, hypnotist, mesmerizer, Svengali, Rasputin; persuader, advertiser, salesman *or* saleswoman, propagandist, public relations (PR) person, publicist, press agent, flack; lobbyist, lobby, pressure group, special-interest group, political action committee (PAC)

ADJECTIVES

7 **motivational,** influential, directional, directive; incentive, attractive, magnetic, persuasive, hortatory, hortative, provocative, incitive, instigative, inflammatory; hypnotic, mesmeric, irresistible, suggestive; motivating, influencing, convincing, compelling, encouraging, challenging, provoking, stimulating, inciting, instigating, electrifying, energizing, kinetic, galvanizing, inflaming, rousing; insinuating, teasing, tantalizing, alluring, tempting, inviting, charming, fascinating, bewitching, spellbinding

8 **motivated,** persuaded, moved, influenced, induced, prompted, impelled, caused, directed, encouraged; exhorted, challenged, urged, egged on, spurred on, pressured, lobbied, prodded, goaded, whipped, provoked, irritated, exasperated; stimulated, electrified, energized, animated, galvanized, inspired, inflamed, incited, roused; charmed, enticed, lured, attracted, seduced, bewitched, coaxed, flattered, spellbound, hypnotized, mesmerized; self-motivated, goal-oriented

VERBS

9 **motivate,** start, initiate, begin, set in motion, instigate; bring about, induce, prompt, actuate, move, cause, bring on, energize, galvanize, electrify, encourage, root for, cheer on; sound the trumpet, rally, inspire, in-

spirit, animate, rouse, arouse, exhort, stimulate, excite; evoke, call forth, challenge, provoke, impel, impress; jolt, jog, irritate, exasperate, prick, spur, spur on, drive on, hurry, hustle, bend, direct; lead, give a lead, set the pace, set a trend, set the fashion, be a trendsetter, turn on [Inf]

10 **be motivated,** be induced, succumb, come *or* fall under the influence of, fall for [Inf]; heed the call, feel the urge, be influenced, be infected; have self-motivation, follow *or* obey one's conscience, follow *or* obey one's instincts

11 **influence,** persuade, convince; suggest, recommend, advocate, advise, counsel; talk into, bring *or* talk someone around, bring over, win over, enlist, recruit, bring to one's side, carry with one, incline, dispose, pull, draw, make one's point, carry one's point, have an impact on; interest, intrigue, prevail upon, act upon, appeal to, attract, captivate, fascinate, charm; coax, cajole, blandish, flatter, tantalize; make things easy for, hold out a carrot, make someone's mouth water, sugar the pill, sweet-talk [Inf]

12 **manipulate,** play on *or* upon, operate on *or* upon, call the tune, put up to, abet, aid and abet; lobby, prejudice, bias, predetermine, predispose, lead astray, misdirect, mislead, insinuate, hint; lead into temptation, tempt, entice, seduce, lure, hypnotize, mesmerize, bewitch, infect; exert pressure, bring pressure to bear, twist someone's arm, force, compel, nag, drive, push, bully, browbeat; override, prevail upon, press, prod, goad, whip, lash; inveigle, incite, egg on, ensnare, entrap, get around someone, needle [Inf]

ADVERBS

13 **influentially,** in order to influence, persuasively, provocatively; hypnotically, irresistibly, suggestively; convincingly, to convince, compellingly, rousingly, hortatorily, hortatively; insinuatingly, teasingly, tantalizingly, alluringly, temptingly, as a temptation, invitingly, charmingly, fascinatingly, bewitchingly, stimulatingly, inspirationally, encouragingly, seductively, in a seductive manner

509 Operation

NOUNS

1 **operation,** implementation, execution, action, performance, exercise, treatment; work, working, doing, course of action, course, procedure, measure, process, movement, motion; power, force, influence, agency; stress, strain, swing, play

 ▶ *Action 412; Activity 414; Vigor 518*

2 **joint operation,** joint venture, cooperation, coordination, interaction; takeover, merger, buyout

3 **business,** office, production, manufacturing, undertaking, venture; matter, cause, affair; task, work, job, position, post

 ▶ *Work 122; Production 522; Completeness 761*

4 **management,** responsibility, effectiveness, effectuality, efficiency, direction; handling, manipulation, maneuvering; maintenance, service, support

 ▶ *Management 126; Influence 512*

5 **operator,** dealer, trader, handler, speculator, agent; worker, coworker, skilled worker, employee; driver, conductor, mechanic, technician; manager, director, administrator, executive

6 **operative,** laborer, hand, unskilled worker, semiskilled worker, machinist

ADJECTIVES

7 **operational,** operating, in operation, functional, functioning, going, working; in working order, usable, running, in running order; in play, in use, active, on the active list, up and going, up and doing [Inf]

8 **workable,** operable, doable, manageable, manipulatable, maneuverable, negotiable; practicable, practical, useful, viable

9 **operative,** in force, carrying force, relevant, significant, important, crucial, critical, key, influential, efficacious, efficient, effective, effectual

VERBS

10 **be operational,** be in action, operate, work, go, run, act, play, be in play, do; serve, perform, function, do one's job; come into operation, come into effect, take effect, be in force, do one's thing [Inf], do one's stuff [Inf]

11 **activate,** actuate, bring into action, bring into operation, make operational, make operate, make work; bring into effect, bring into force, bring into play, make happen, effectuate; influence, stimulate, motivate; wind up, plug in, turn on, switch on, flip the switch, press the button, set going, start up, rev up [Inf]

12 **take action,** use, handle, deal with, manage, manipulate, maneuver, wield, process, treat, employ, implement, execute; move, power, drive, cause, act upon, work upon, bear upon, play upon; maintain, service, sustain, support, crew, man; procure, get done

 ▶ *Use 393*

ADVERBS

13 **operationally,** functionally, actively, in an active manner, usefully; readily, efficaciously, efficiently, with efficiency, effectively, effectually; practically, relevantly, significantly, importantly, crucially, critically, influentially

510 Counteraction

NOUNS

1 **counteraction,** opposing action *or* cause, polarity, polarization, opposition, prevention; remedy, compensation, contravention, reaction, counter, retroaction, return action, repercussion, kickback, boomerang effect, backlash, backfire, recoil, kick

▶ *Compensation 743; Opposition 828*

2 opposing force, countermove, counterintelligence, counteroffensive, counterattack, counterpunch, counterblast; conflict, clash, antagonism, antipathy, hostility, recalcitrance, resistance; deterrent, defense, defensive measure, inhibitor, preventive *or* preventative; headwind, crosscurrent

▶ *Hostility 63; Defense 419; Prohibition 503; Hindrance 826*

3 obstruction, friction, drag, check, block, hindrance, obstacle, barrier, restraint; frustration, interference, counterpressure, repression; intolerance, persecution, suppression

4 neutralization, derestriction, deregulation, decriminalization, demagnetization, deactivation, moderation; invalidation, cancellation, abrogation, negation, nullification, veto; counterweight, counterpoise, counterbalance, offset, countermeasure, countercharm, counterspell

5 counteractant, counteragent, counterirritant; neutralizer, antidote, cure, remedy; defender, protector, nullifier; prophylactic, contraceptive, condom

ADJECTIVES

6 counteracting, counteractive, counter, oppositional, opposing, contravening, opposed to, polarized, contrary; conflicting, clashing, antipathetic, antagonistic, inimical, hostile, resistant, resisting, recalcitrant, intractable; reactionary, retroactive, reactive; frictional, restraining, frustrating, interfering, repressive, suppressive, intolerant, obstructive, counterproductive; corrective, balancing, offsetting, moderating, neutralizing, invalidating, nullifying, compensatory; preventive *or* preventative, antidotal, remedial, contraceptive

VERBS

7 counteract, counter, run counter to, obviate, contravene, oppose, cause opposition, polarize; react against, go against, militate against, agitate against, work against, cross, traverse, thwart, hinder, inhibit, prevent, prohibit, drag, block, check, obstruct; not be conducive to, frustrate, interfere with, repress, persecute, suppress, restrain; resist, fight against, defend against, withstand, conflict with, antagonize, clash; react, recoil, backfire, boomerang, countervail, counterbalance, counterpoise, compensate for, kick back; cancel out, cancel, annul, undo, invalidate, negate, nullify, veto, abrogate; decontrol, derestrict, deregulate, decriminalize, deactivate, demagnetize, neutralize, moderate; cure, find a remedy, recover, get back, retrieve, find a way around

ADVERBS

8 counter, counteractively, contrarily, contrary to, counter to, against; conflictingly, antipathetically, antagonistically, inimically, hostilely, resistantly, resistingly, in opposition to; in contrast, in spite of, despite, although, notwithstanding; intractably; retroactively, reactively, antidotally, remedially, correctively; repressively, intolerantly; preventively

511 Instrumentality

NOUNS

1 instrumentality, agency, operation, responsibility, cause, influence, significance, power, weight, effectiveness, efficacy; performance, achievement, functionality, function, service; promotion, advancement, help, aid, assistance, support, midwifery, intermediacy, intermediateness, intervention, interposition, intercession, mediation; subordination, subservience, employment; use, medium, means, mechanical means, electronic means, use of machinery, instrumentation, mechanization, computerization, automation; application, practicality, serviceability, utility, usefulness, handiness

▶ *Mediation 75; Means 102; Activity 414; Obedience 426; Cause 675; Usefulness 801; Help 825*

2 instrument, means, medium, catalyst; vehicle, agency, influence, mechanism, force, factor, organ; implement, device, tool, machine, apparatus, appliance, equipment, gadget, contrivance; expedient, compromise; contraption [Inf], gismo *or* gizmo [Inf]

▶ *Tool 103; Music 140; Timekeeping 646; Transportation 686; Quantity 738*

3 assistant, helper, help, aide, hand, agent, amanuensis, secretary; servant, lackey, slave, genie; intermediary, mediator, go-between; puppet, creature, cat's-paw, pawn, tool, dupe

▶ *Servant 69; Help 825*

ADJECTIVES

4 instrumental, useful, applicable, employable, utilizable, handy; helping, helpful, assisting, cooperative, advancing, promoting, promotive, promotional, aiding, supportive, subordinate, subservient; effective, efficient, effectual, efficacious, performance-oriented

5 causal, responsible, instrumental, central, powerful, weighty, significant, telling; influential, mediative, intermediate, intervening, interventional, intercessional, interfering, pressuring; maieutic, Socratic

6 practical, applied, servicing, serviceable, general-purpose; working, functioning, functional, operating, operational, operative; hand-operated, manual, mechanical; automatic, automated, electronic, computerized, push-button

VERBS

7 be an instrument, be instrumental, function, operate, work, act, perform, do, serve, be useful; work for, lend oneself to, minister to; help, assist, aid, support, cooperate, promote, advance, have a hand in; cause, control, be responsible for; bridge, channel, interpose, intervene, intercede for, intermediate, mediate, compromise; influence, use one's influence, use one's good offices, pressure, pull strings *or* wires; implement, effect, bring into effect, carry into effect, carry through, carry out, expedite, achieve, pull someone's chestnuts out of the fire, save one's bacon [Inf]

> *Operation 509*

8 **find means,** find a way, obtain assistance, use one's connections, network, get by hook or by crook

ADVERBS

9 **instrumentally,** through the instrumentality of, by means of, by virtue of; usefully, handily, helpfully, with the help of, with the aid of, by way of, by, via, thanks to, with, herewith [Form], through, per; cooperatively, supportively, subserviently; effectively, efficiently, effectually, efficaciously; powerfully, significantly, influentially, by *or* through the good offices of; manually, by the hand of, at the hands of, mechanically, automatically, electronically

512 Influence

NOUNS

1 **influence,** power, powerful influence, potency; potentiality, ability, capability; superior power, strength, might, mightiness, force; predominance, prevalence, greatness, magnitude, importance, significance, advantage, authority; whip hand, upper hand, final say, casting vote, vital role, leading part; leverage, grip, hold, footing, play; weight, impact, pressure, pull, drag, magnetism, gravity; attraction, fascination, repulsion, impulse, motive, motivation, interest, vested interest, emotion; impression, inspiration, persuasion, encouragement, cause; contagion, infection; climate, atmosphere, circumstances, fate, destiny; clout [Inf]

> *Authority 52; Persuasion 178; Compulsion 428; Power 514; Impulsion 695; Attraction 700; Repulsion 701; Superiority 744; Importance 799*

2 **occult influence,** magic, magic spell, witchcraft, sorcery; charm, mesmerism, hypnotism; planetary influence, heaven, stars, astrology, horoscope; malevolence, malign influence, curse, voodoo *or* hoodoo

> *Occultism 86*

3 **personal influence,** personality, magnetic personality, charisma, repute, reputation, credit, prestige; leadership, ascendancy, hegemony, domination, dominance, dominion; tyranny, authority, sway, control, reign

4 **indirect influence,** favor, friend at court, amicus curiae, patronage; wires, wirepulling, strings, lever, hold, hidden influence, secret influence, hidden hand; powerbroker, kingmaker, gray eminence *or* éminence grise, power behind the throne; pull [Inf]

5 **influential person,** president, prime minister, premier, chairman *or* chairwoman, director; parent, best friend, priest, preacher, doctor, lawyer; lobbyist, man-

ager, queen bee, manipulator, influence peddler; [Inf]: big shot, bigwig, big wheel, big cheese, big gun, very important person (VIP), mover and shaker, brass hat, top brass, wheeler-dealer

> *Importance 799; Help 825*

6 **group influence,** self-help group, pressure group, lobby, political action committee (PAC), public opinion; the powers that be, the Establishment, Big Brother; multinational company, superpower

7 **sphere of influence,** area *or* field of influence, territory, orbit, ambit, bailiwick, turf [Inf]

ADJECTIVES

8 **influential,** causal, effectual, effective, persuasive, important, vital; significant, contributing, contributory; decisive, momentous, world-shattering, earthshaking, telling; prestigious, impressive, important, consequential, potent, powerful, strong, mighty, forceful, great, superior, ruling; leading, guiding, directing, instructive, educative; reigning, regnant, in the ascendant, rising, in authority, of authority, commanding, authoritative, tyrannical

9 **appealing,** emotional, moving, affecting, charming, attractive, gripping, fascinating, irresistible, charismatic; magnetic, mesmeric, hypnotic, compelling; inspirational, encouraging, inspiring, motivating; suggestive, tempting, seductive, addictive, habit-forming; infectious, contagious, catching

10 **dominant,** predominant, wide-ranging, international, multinational, monopolistic, prevailing, prevalent; ubiquitous, pervasive, all-pervading, in the driver's seat

VERBS

11 **influence,** have influence, exercise influence, exert influence, command influence, have charisma, impress, motivate, actuate, activate; persuade, carry weight, have importance, be recognized, be listened to, have a voice; make one's voice heard, have a say in, play a role *or* part in, have a part to play, gain a footing *or* foothold, take root, strike root in, gain a hearing, make oneself felt, affect, bear upon, tell upon, work upon; have the right connections, know the right people, have friends in high places, have the ear of; pressurize, put pressure on, lobby, pull strings, pull wires; guide, direct, lead, establish the trend, set the trend, set the fashion, serve as a model, promote; prejudice, bias, brainwash, predispose, dispose, color, lure, tempt, appeal; [Inf]: have pull, have pulling power, have *or* carry clout, wheel and deal

12 **change,** change for the better *or* the worse; counterbalance, turn *or* tip the scale(s), influence positively, make better, improve, leaven; influence negatively, discourage, repulse, disgust, repel, put off, militate against; infect, dilute, contaminate, adulterate, mar, spoil, impair, ruin

13 **be an influence,** be prevalent, prevail, predominate;

fascinate, mesmerize, hypnotize, practice witchcraft; outweigh, override, overbear, gain *or* have the upper hand, have the final say, have the casting vote, have sway; force, compel, pull, drag, tyrannize, dominate, have power over, tower over, have a hold over *or* on, have in one's power, bestride, subdue, subjugate, overawe, overcome; gain full play, master, gain mastery, overmaster, reign supreme, rule; run, control, monopolize, take over, take a firm grip, take (a) hold, rage; be all the rage, be rife, spread, spread like wildfire, run through, pervade, permeate; hold all the cards, hold all the aces, hold the whip hand, be in the driver's seat; lead by the nose, have under one's thumb, wrap *or* twist around one's little finger, wear the pants, throw one's weight around

ADVERBS

14 **influentially,** causally, effectually, to good effect, with great *or* telling effect, persuasively; importantly, vitally, significantly, prestigiously, impressively; potently, powerfully, strongly, forcefully, predominantly, commandingly, authoritatively, with *or* by authority; under someone's influence, within someone's orbit, tyrannically, internationally, encouragingly; decisively, momentously; emotionally, charmingly, irresistibly, charismatically, hypnotically, inspirationally, suggestively, seductively; infectiously, contagiously; ubiquitously, pervasively

513 Tendency

NOUNS

1 **tendency,** tenor, drift, trend, course, direction, current, stream; fashion, taste, the way things are going, sign of the times, spirit of the age, *Zeitgeist* [Ger]; turn, cast, climate, climate of opinion, influence
   ▶ *Direction 697; Attraction 700; Accord 735*

2 **attitude,** cast of mind, turn of mind, mind-set, disposition, predisposition, proclivity, susceptibility, affinity, attraction; liability, probability, proneness, bent, inclination, gravitation, leaning, bias, prejudice, partiality, weakness; readiness, preparedness, propensity, predilection, liking, penchant, humor, mood; vein, grain, strain, tincture, tone, quality, character, idiosyncrasy
   ▶ *Intention 374; Preparation 388; Probability 838*

3 **aptitude,** ability, talent, natural talent, gift, instinct
   ▶ *Skillfulness 127*

ADJECTIVES

4 **tending to,** trending, leading, leading to; inclined toward, inclining toward, inclining, leaning, leaning toward; intending, working toward, aiming at, pointing to, conducive to, calculated to, prejudiced, prejudicial, partial, biased; tendentious, probable, likely, liable to, apt to, prone to, ready, about to, prepared

VERBS

5 **tend,** have a tendency, show a tendency, show a trend, bend; have a bent, develop an attitude, incline, lean, have a leaning, like, show an affinity, have a propensity; have an aptitude, have a genius for, show talent, have natural talent, have a gift, have an instinct; be biased, show prejudice, have a predisposition, be disposed to, gravitate toward, incline toward, lean toward; prepare, approach, affect, contribute, redound, influence; turn to, point to, lead to, conduce to, bid fair, bode well

ADVERBS

6 **probably,** readily, with a strong tendency; prejudicially, tendentiously, from a biased standpoint

514 Power

Power tends to corrupt, and absolute power corrupts absolutely. — LORD ACTON

Power is the ultimate aphrodisiac. — HENRY KISSINGER

NOUNS

1 **power,** powerfulness, potency *or* potence, force, forcefulness, efficacy, energy, might, mightiness, puissance
   ▶ *Strength 516*

2 **vigor,** vitality, push, drive, charge, effort, exertion; strength, brute force *or* strength, muscle power, sinew, might and main; staying power, endurance, stamina, driving force
   ▶ *Vigor 518*

3 **ability,** intelligence, intelligence quotient (IQ), capability, capacity, competence, proficiency, faculty, aptitude, facility, skill; empowerment, enablement
   ▶ *Skillfulness 127; Intellect 315; Influence 512*

4 **powerfulness,** omnipotence, almightiness, all-powerfulness

5 **authority,** sovereignty, dominion, governance, hegemony, jurisdiction, command, control, superiority, predominance, sway, influence, weight, persuasion; the power structure, position of power, political power, the pull [Inf], clout [Inf]
   ▶ *Authority 52; Influence 512*

6 **type of power,** manpower, horsepower, pedal power, engine power, electric power, hydroelectric power, hydraulic power, water power, steam power, geothermal power, solar power, atomic power, nuclear power, thermonuclear power, rocket power, jet power; motive power, pulling power, pushing power, traction, propulsion, thrust, impulse, impulsion, impetus; charisma, mana, special power *or* gift, occult power, magical power, magic, witchcraft, sorcery; power of attorney, work force, fighting force

▶ *Engineering 14; Litigation 54; Occultism 86*

7 energy, internal energy, chemical energy, binding energy, rest energy, potential energy, kinetic energy, radiant energy, solar energy, atomic energy, nuclear energy, electrical energy, mechanical energy, heat

8 force, resistance, friction, force field, force of attraction *or* gravitation, force of inertia, centrifugal force, centripetal force; pressure, head, steam pressure, full head of steam; magnetism, magnetic force, magnetic field, attraction, repulsion, polarity, electromagnetism, electromotive force

9 nuclear power, atomic power, nucleonics, thermonuclear reaction, chain reaction, fission, fusion

10 nuclear power production, stellarator, torus; atomic pile, nuclear reactor *or* nuclear pile, chain-reacting pile, pressurized-water reactor (PWR), light-water reactor (LWR), boiling-water reactor, gas-cooled reactor, heavy-water reactor (HWR), fast-breeder reactor, advanced gas-cooled reactor (AGR); coolant, fuel rod, moderator; radioactivity, fallout, radioactive waste, low-level radioactive waste, waste reprocessing; nuclear-powered submarine, nuclear-powered aircraft carrier, nuclear-powered guided-missile cruiser; nuclear weapon, nuclear warhead, nuclear missile, atomic bomb, hydrogen bomb, fusion bomb, neutron bomb

▶ *Physics 10; Fuel 106*

11 nuclear power agencies, Nuclear Regulatory Commission (NRC), International Atomic Energy Agency (IAEA); nuclear power research, CERN (*Conseil européen pour la recherche nucléaire*, Laboratory for Particle Physics)

12 electrical power, electricity, photoelectricity, thermoelectricity, piezoelectricity, voltaic electricity, galvanic electricity, static electricity, lightning; electrodynamics, electrostatics, induction, inductance, capacitance, resistance, conduction, conductivity, oscillation, frequency, pulse

▶ *Engineering 14*

13 power source, combustion, fossil fuel, coal, gas, natural gas, oil; chemical reaction; nuclear fission, nuclear fusion; renewable energy source, wind power, solar power, solar energy, geothermal power, hydroelectrical power, wave power, tidal power

▶ *Fuel 106*

14 power supplier, windmill, wind farm, solar *or* photoelectric cell, solar battery, solar panel, heat exchanger; hydroelectric plant, waterfall, tidal barrage, water wheel; generator, motor, magneto, dynamo, turbine, turbocharger, turbosupercharger; power line, cable, distributor, lead, cord, pylon, grid, transformer, vacuum tube, cathode-ray tube (CRT), transistor; power pack, battery, cell, wet cell, dry cell; powerhouse, power plant, power station, generating station

▶ *Engineering 14; Fuel 106; Heat 217; Light 246; Air 558; Rotation 682*

ADJECTIVES

15 powerful, potent, forceful, mighty, great, omnipotent, puissant; able, capable, competent, charismatic; empowered, authoritative, sovereign, hegemonic, controlling, compelling, predominating, influential; effectual, effective, efficacious, forcible

16 energetic, dynamic, vigorous, virile

17 nuclear, electric, charged, conductive, magnetic, inductive, propulsive

VERBS

18 be powerful, have power, be able, can, can do, be up to, be capable of, lie in one's power; exercise power, wield power, govern, have *or* exercise authority, take charge, manage, control, maintain control, hold sway, dominate; compel, use force, force; exert energy, endeavor, gain power, prevail, predominate; influence, exert influence; have stamina, have vitality; have charisma, possess special power, possess magical power, practice witchcraft

19 generate power, produce power, combust, radiate, power, fuel, pump, transform energy, amplify, store energy; heat, light

20 empower, give power, enable, authorize, invest with power, vest power in, endow with power, arm, strengthen, energize, animate; electrify, charge, magnetize, plug in, switch on, turn on, power up

ADVERBS

21 powerfully, potently, strongly, mightily, prevailingly, prevalently, predominantly, influentially, omnipotently, irresistibly, authoritatively, virtually, competently, effectually, effectively, efficaciously, efficiently, proficiently, with telling effect, by dint of, by virtue of; forcefully, compellingly, compulsively, cogently; with might and main, with all one's might, forcibly, by force, by force of arms, violently

22 energetically, with energy, dynamically, vigorously, magnetically, electrically

515 Powerlessness

NOUNS

1 powerlessness, lack of power, impotence, absence of power, inability, incapability, incapacity, incompetence, ineptitude, unfitness; power failure, power outage, energy depletion; disarmament, demilitarization

▶ *Weakness 517; Failure 846*

2 lack of authority, unauthorized person, figurehead, titular head, subordinate; ineffectiveness, ineffectuality, invalidity, futility, uselessness, inutility

▶ *Unskillfulness 128; Dissimilarity 734; Uselessness 802; Restraint 830*

3 helplessness, defenselessness, vulnerability, fragility, weakness, frailty; immaturity, minority, infancy; emasculation, defeminization, castration, neutering; feebleness, softness, wimpiness [Inf]

▶ *Youth 26; Innocence 449; Danger 811*

4 **disability,** physical weakness, collapse, handicap, impotence, sterility, infertility; prostration, exhaustion, loss of consciousness, unconsciousness, coma, illness, paralysis; dementia, decrepitude
▶ *Age 27; Insanity 110; Ill Health 114; Deterioration 808; Fatigue 820*

5 **powerless person,** invalid, sick person, weakling, incompetent, straw man, eunuch; [Inf]: pushover, easy mark, patsy, sucker, wimp
▶ *Weakness 517*

ADJECTIVES

6 **powerless,** unable, not able, not enabled, incapable; unemployed, deposed, disqualified, unqualified; unfit, inept, good-for-nothing, unworkable, worthless, useless; ineffective, ineffectual, inefficacious, inefficient, incompetent, out of the running

7 **unauthorized,** not empowered, invalid, invalidated, null and void, not lawful, illegal, disfranchised *or* disenfranchised

8 **inoperative,** not working, switched off, unpowered, suspended, deactivated, out of action, out of order, in abeyance, mothballed, out of circulation, broken, broken down

9 **helpless,** unprotected, undefended, defenseless, indefensible, weaponless, unarmed, disarmed, unfortified, exposed, untenable, dependent, subject; without resource, orphaned, friendless, vulnerable, innocent, meek; out of control, drifting, rudderless, swamped

10 **disabled,** weak, exhausted, used up, decrepit, senile; unconscious, comatose, insensible; incapacitated, on one's back, paralytic, paralyzed; irresolute, spineless, unnerved, demoralized, shell-shocked, *hors de combat* [Fr]; impotent, sterile, infertile

VERBS

11 **be powerless,** be impotent, stand defenseless, be unable, cannot, not work, not operate, not do; be of *or* to no avail, strive in vain, fail; get nowhere, have no resistance, have a hopeless case, have no chance, cut no ice [Inf]; lose consciousness, faint, collapse, pass out

12 **lack authority,** have no power, have no influence, have no say, have no control; look on, stand by

13 **remove power from,** remove authority from, deprive of power *or* authority, veto, invalidate; incapacitate, disable, disqualify, abrogate; disarm, demilitarize, neutralize; weaken, emaciate, make powerless, debilitate, sap, undermine, take the wind out of someone's sails; consume, exhaust, use up; dismiss, fire, recall, impeach; power down, switch off
▶ *Weakness 517*

14 **overpower,** put out of action, prostrate, wind, knock out, tie up; numb, benumb, paralyze, cripple, stifle, suffocate, strangle, deaden, muzzle, silence; spike someone's guns, put out of commission, put the kibosh on [Inf]
▶ *Destruction 523; Subjection 832*

15 **make impotent,** sterilize, make barren, neuter; unnerve, enervate, devitalize

ADVERBS

16 **powerlessly,** illegally, without authority, ineptly, worthlessly, uselessly, ineffectively, ineffectually, inefficiently, incompetently; beyond one, beyond one's power, above one's head, too much for; defenselessly, indefensibly; dependently, harmlessly, innocently, impotently, weakly, feebly, irresolutely, helplessly

516 Strength

My strength is as the strength of ten, / Because my heart is pure. — ALFRED, LORD TENNYSON

NOUNS

1 **strength,** power, potency, might, force, puissance; firmness, authority; fortification, protection; impregnability, impenetrability, inviolability, invincibility, invulnerability, unassailability
▶ *Authority 52; Power 514; Size, Largeness 579*

2 **mechanical strength,** load-bearing capacity, tensile strength, compressive strength, torsional strength
▶ *Physics 10; Engineering 14*

3 **physical strength,** muscularity, athleticism, physical force, brute force, brute strength, musculature, sinews, brawn, burliness, beefiness [Inf]
▶ *Vigor 518*

4 **endurance,** durability, survivability, staying power, tenacity, resilience, resistance, stamina; resolution, stout-heartedness, backbone, assertiveness, courage, pluck, grit, nerve, bravery, toughness, spunk, guts [Inf]
▶ *Vigor 518; Toughness 547*

5 **authority,** greatness, superiority, effectuality, firmness, steadfastness, determination, stability
▶ *Authority 52*

6 **potency,** energy, intensity, capacity; concentration, depth, emphasis, stress, urgency, rashness; potential, resourcefulness, cogency, weight, pressure, severity; persuasiveness, efficacy, effectiveness
▶ *Rashness 286*

7 **strengthening,** toughening, tempering, reinforcing, hardening, stiffening, fortifying, protecting; invigorating, restoring, convalescing, refreshing, reviving, revivifying; revival, reinforcement, invigoration, restoration, tonic, refreshment, revivification, convalescence
▶ *Refreshment 94; Health 113; Repair 809*

8 **person of strength,** strongman, superhero; athlete, weightlifter, boxer, wrestler, sumo wrestler; muscleman, strong-arm man, bouncer, bodybuilder, Mr. Universe; legendary strongman: Atlas, Hercules, Antaeus, Titan, giant, Samson, Goliath, Tarzan; strong woman,

superheroine, amazon, virago [Arch]; bully, bullyboy; [Inf]: bruiser, he-man, tough guy, hunk, beefcake

▸ *Sports 145; Contention 422*

ADJECTIVES

9 **strong,** potent, forceful, powerful, puissant, mighty, redoubtable, formidable, great, high-powered; firm, staunch, authoritative, fortified, impregnable, impenetrable, inviolate, invincible; overpowering, overwhelming, superior; compelling, convincing, persuasive, effective, cogent, telling, trenchant, weighty, distinct, unmistakable, marked; urgent, pressing, severe, intense, vehement; extreme, drastic, draconian; thoroughgoing, deep-rooted, well-founded, well-established; fervent, fervid, fierce

10 **physically strong,** strong, powerful, athletic, muscular, sinewy, burly, husky, brawny, beefy, red-blooded, virile, manly, herculean, amazonian, strapping; healthy, hale, hale and hearty, robust, sound, sound as a bell, fit, in good shape, lusty; hardy, vigorous, sturdy, tough, stalwart, stout; strong as a horse *or* an ox

11 **strong in spirit,** firm, steadfast, determined, resolute, stout-hearted; brave, bold, daring, courageous, plucky, feisty, resilient, resourceful; acute, keen, dedicated, enthusiastic, energetic, zealous, eager; tough, tenacious, unyielding, assertive, self-assertive, aggressive, bellicose, warlike

12 **strong to the senses,** striking, stark, brilliant, bright, dazzling, glaring; loud; strong-smelling; strong-tasting, biting, mordant, sharp, pungent, piquant, spicy, highly flavored, highly seasoned, hot; concentrated, undiluted, pure, neat; intoxicating, heady

13 **strengthened,** toughened, reinforced, fortified, armed, well-armed, well-protected, protective; hard-wearing, heavy-duty; on a firm footing, on a firm foundation, well-built, stout, substantial, durable, tough, resistant; restored, revived; braced, buttressed

VERBS

14 **be strong,** possess strength, have what it takes, come in force; overwhelm, overpower, outmatch, be more than a match for, overmaster; become stronger, rally, recover, revive, convalesce; not weaken, hold out, hold up, bear up, gird up one's loins, never say die, pack a punch [Inf]

15 **strengthen,** make strong, give strength to, lend force to; confirm, underline, underscore, emphasize, stress; reinforce, fortify, protect, entrench; buttress, prop up, sustain, support, brace; toughen, harden, caseharden, temper; energize, animate, quicken, enliven, invigorate, boost; revive, revivify, reinvigorate, refresh; set someone up properly, set someone on his *or* her feet *or* legs, build up, beef up, soup up [Inf]

16 **strengthen oneself,** steel oneself, temper oneself, nerve oneself, screw up one's courage, stiffen, stiffen one's resolve; stiffen the sinews, put life into, put body into, put one's back into, use force, use muscle

ADVERBS

17 **strongly,** powerfully, energetically, forcefully, forcibly, by force, by sheer force, in force, with might and main; soundly, hardily, huskily, sturdily, stoutly, robustly, ruggedly; fiercely, courageously, tenaciously, bravely, assertively, aggressively, boldly; invulnerably, unyieldingly

18 **acutely,** keenly, enthusiastically, energetically, vigorously, zealously, lustily, resolutely, eagerly, heartily, firmly, fervently; urgently, compulsively, by compulsion, intensely, extremely, drastically; brilliantly, brightly, loudly, sharply, pungently, potently; compellingly, convincingly, persuasively, effectively, distinctly, unmistakably

517 Weakness

NOUNS

1 **weakness,** lack of strength, feebleness, impotence, enfeeblement, fatigue, tiredness; strengthlessness, softness, limpness, flaccidity, floppiness, slackness, looseness; weak foundation, dilapidation, impairment, damage, decay, rust, wear; deactivation, neutralization; adulteration, dilution, feet of clay, instability; fragility, brittleness, delicateness, delicacy, helplessness, puniness, smallness, innocence, vulnerability, defenselessness; defect, weak link, Achilles heel; depletion, dissipation, impoverishment

▸ *Powerlessness 515; Lightness 539; Softness 543; Brittleness 548; Imperfection 806; Deterioration 808; Adversity 848*

2 **indecisiveness,** indecision, irresolution, hesitance, doubtfulness; ineffectuality, slowness, sheepishness, spinelessness, nervelessness, nervousness, pusillanimity, timorousness; cowardliness, cowardice, gutlessness [Inf]

▸ *Cowardice 285; Vacillation 378; Changeableness 666; Uncertainty 841*

3 **poor health,** sickliness, debility, frailty, infirmity, invalidism, senility, caducity, decrepitude; weakliness, faintness, dizziness, giddiness, vertigo, shakiness, loss of strength, asthenia, weakened state, enervation, waning, flagging, weariness, exhaustion

▸ *Age 27; Ill Health 114; Thinness 595; Fatigue 820*

4 **weak person,** weakling, ninety-pound weakling, runt; infant, baby, babe in arms; broken reed, small fry, dupe, milksop, doormat, yes-man, namby-pamby; hypochondriac, invalid, sick person; lame duck, burnout, failure; big baby, crybaby, sissy, coward, teacher's pet, mama's boy, straw man; [Inf]: easy mark, softy, pushover, drip, lightweight, weak sister, jellyfish, (poor) fish, wimp, patsy, pansy, chicken

5 **weak thing,** flimsy item, insubstantial thing; lame

dog, kitten; reed, cobweb, gossamer, thread; sand-castle, house built on sand, house of cards; fragile item, paper, tissue paper, matchstick, matchwood, glass, china, eggshell; water, thin gruel, watered-down soup, dishwater, milk and water

❱ *Brittleness 548*

ADJECTIVES

6 **weak,** lacking strength, not strong, pindling, impotent, powerless, feeble, deprived of strength, enfeebled; unhardened, untempered, soft; limp, flaccid, floppy, drooping, hanging, sagging; shoddy, jerry-built, rickety, tottery, tottering, teetering, wobbly, creaky, run-down, seedy; breakable, brittle, fragile, delicate; puny, small, lightweight, ineffectual; helpless, defenseless, unsafe, unprotected, unguarded, unfortified, untenable; weak as a child *or* a baby *or* a kitten *or* water

7 **dilapidated,** broken, broken-down, tumbledown, laid bare, worn, worn out, the worse for wear, on its last legs; rotten, decayed, rusted, withered; diminished, deflated, wasted, depleted, drained, spent, used up

8 **ill,** sickly, faint, pale, pallid, bloodless, white as a sheet, asthenic; groggy, below par, languid, feeble, weakly; wasted, thin, skinny, emaciated, skin-and-bones, skeletal; frail, decrepit, infirm, poorly, crippled, lame, game, limping, hobbling, shaky, unsteady, unsound, weak-minded; gimpy [Inf]

❱ *Ill Health 114*

9 **weakened,** debilitated, etiolated, enervated, unstrung, dissipated, burned-out, sapped, wearied, exhausted, fatigued, tired, laid low, weary, worn out, on one's last legs, on the wane; failed, impoverished

10 **weak-willed,** weakhearted, indecisive, irresolute, wavering, dithering, pusillanimous, vacillating, hesitant, doubtful, half-hearted; nerveless, unnerved, nervous, timid, timorous, cowardly, sheepish, effete, mealy-mouthed, spineless, lily-livered, sissy, namby-pamby, weak-kneed, scared; [Inf]: yellow, gutless, chicken, chicken-hearted, limp-wristed

11 **insufficient,** inadequate, insubstantial, inconclusive; invalid, unconvincing, unsatisfactory, lacking, wanting, deficient; flimsy, slight, small, little, thin, light; shallow, hollow, faulty, substandard, poor, pathetic, understrength, below par; imperceptible, inaudible, invisible, faint, low, distant, muffled, soft, muted, quiet; diluted, runny, tasteless, insipid, watery, milk-and-water, wishy-washy

VERBS

12 **be weak,** be ill, grow weak, weaken, sicken, faint, languish, flag, fail, fall, drop, droop, flop, wilt, fade; decrease, diminish, decline, dwindle; crumble, wear, wear out, wear thin; sag, give way, break, split, come *or* fall apart at the seams; shake, tremble, totter, teeter, stagger, dodder, go lame, limp, halt; yield, collapse, surrender

13 **weaken,** make weak, enfeeble, debilitate, etiolate, enervate, unnerve, rattle, alarm, shake; relax, slacken, loosen; deflate, diminish, reduce, reduce in number, decimate, extenuate, thin, thin out, lessen, deplete, drain, exhaust; impoverish, starve, deprive, rob; sap, undermine, impair, damage, invalidate, spoil, mar, disarm; disable, strain, sprain, lame, maim, cripple, hurt, harm, injure, wound; strip, strip bare, denude, expose; adulterate, dilute, water down; soften up, soften; muffle, mute

ADVERBS

14 **weakly,** impotently, softly, ineffectually, without effect, helplessly, unsafely; faintly, languidly, feebly, weakly, unsteadily, while ill, on one's last legs, unsoundly; indecisively, irresolutely, half-heartedly, nervously, timidly, cowardly, in a cowardly way, sheepishly; insufficiently, inadequately, inconclusively, unsatisfactorily; fragilely, slightly, thinly, lightly, poorly, pathetically; imperceptibly, inaudibly, quietly, tastelessly, insipidly

518 Vigor

NOUNS

1 **vigor,** energy, exertion, effort, activity; excitement, enthusiasm, stimulation, inspiration, dynamism; power, strength, robustness, go, get-up-and-go, force, forcefulness; life, animation, exhilaration, spirit, spunk, pluck, mettle, liveliness, intensity, impetus, dash, élan, éclat, vitality, health, invigoration, refreshment, revitalization, freshness; zest, zing, vim, verve, sparkle, drive, punch, keenness, lustiness, gusto; [Inf]: pep, guts, kick, snap, pizazz, zip, wallop, oomph, balls

❱ *Emphasis 200; Joy, Cheerfulness 269; Courage 284; Resolution 376; Perseverance 377; Activity 414; Power 514; Strength 516; Agitation 684; Haste 818*

ADJECTIVES

2 **vigorous,** energetic, active, dynamic, powerful, strong, forceful, forcible, strenuous; vehement, intense, animated, spirited, spunky, vibrant, brisk, lively; vital, healthy, spry, hale, hale and hearty, hardy, robust, zestful, lusty, feisty, mettlesome, strapping, virile, red-blooded; extrovert, extroverted, outgoing, effective, efficient, enterprising, go-ahead, thrusting, aggressive, keen, punchy, enthusiastic, flourishing, growing; [Inf]: full of beans, full of pep, peppy, snappy, zippy, pushy, go-getting, ballsy, gutsy

3 **invigorating,** healthy, bouncy, bouncing, fresh, exhilarating, rousing, stimulating, inspiring, exciting; bracing, strengthening, reinvigorating, reviving, revivifying, restoring, rejuvenating, refreshing, revitalizing

❱ *Health 113*

VERBS

4 **be full of vigor,** thrive, have zest, enjoy life, enthuse;

burst with energy, burst with health, have a lot of get-up-and-go; never stop, rush around, be up and doing, exert oneself, drive, push, raise the pressure, get up a good head of steam, put on a spurt, pull out all the stops; strike hard, hit hard, tell upon, make an impression; [Inf]: have a lot of pizazz, give it the gun, go like a bat out of hell, come on like gangbusters, have balls, be gutsy

5 **invigorate,** activate, energize, galvanize, exhilarate, electrify, intensify, double, redouble; rouse, kindle, inflame, excite, stimulate, enliven, juice up, turn up the juice, put life into, boost, fire up, step up, wind up; act like a tonic, give heart to, hearten, put heart into, egg on, cheer on, root for, inspire, intoxicate; freshen, refresh, revive, restore, reinvigorate, revitalize; give an edge to, sharpen, make glow; [Inf]: psych up, pep up, step on the gas, soup up, ginger up

ADVERBS

6 **with vigor,** vigorously, energetically, forcefully, forcibly, with telling effect, straight from the shoulder; con brio, lustily, zestfully, hard, full tilt, all out, hammer and tongs, firing on all cylinders, with the throttle wide open, full steam ahead; with a vengeance, with a will; [Inf]: flat out, like mad, like crazy, like hell, like gangbusters, like a bat out of hell

519 Inertness

NOUNS

1 **inertness,** inertia, inactivity, inaction, stillness, motionlessness, lifelessness, deathliness; indolence, idleness, languor, torpor, torpidity, paralysis, insensibility, numbness, vegetation, stagnation, quiescence, dormancy, latency, fallowness; apathy, indifference, dullness, sloth, slowness, sluggishness, laziness, hibernation; laxity, slackness, passivity, passiveness, peacefulness; impassivity, immobility, stolidity, inexcitability; indecisiveness, indecision, irresolution, gutlessness [Inf]

  ▶ *Peace 73; Insensibility 213; Insensitivity 268; Indifference 289; Inaction 413; Inactivity 415; Powerlessness 515; Weakness 517; Lack of Motion 678; Slowness 693; Latency 844*

ADJECTIVES

2 **inert,** inactive, passive, impassive, apathetic, indifferent, unexcitable, peaceful, unreactive; indecisive, irresolute, unresponsive, stolid; idle, lazy, indolent, slack, lax, limp, flaccid, heavy, slothful, lumpish, doltish, sluggish, slow, slumberous, dull, numb, dormant, latent; dead, lifeless, languid, torpid, insensible, hibernating, immobile, unmoving, motionless, still, frozen; static, stagnant, stagnating, vegetating, paralyzed, quiet, quiescent, fallow, gutless [Inf]

3 **suspended,** pending, in abeyance, switched off, on

hold, in reserve, abrogated, off the active list, on ice [Inf]; deactivated, uninfluential, powerless

  ▶ *Powerlessness 515; Weakness 517*

VERBS

4 **be inert,** be immobile, be motionless, lie still, be *or* lie idle; stagnate, vegetate, just sit *or* stand there, just lie there, be dead, be lifeless, not stir, freeze

  ▶ *Inactivity 415; Lack of Motion 678*

ADVERBS

5 **inertly,** inactively, passively, impassively, apathetically, indifferently, peacefully, idly, lazily, indolently; limply, sluggishly, slowly, numbly, latently; lifelessly, languidly, insensibly, motionlessly, quietly, at rest; in suspense, in abeyance, on hold, in reserve, in cold storage, in the deep freeze [Inf], on ice [Inf]

520 Violence

NOUNS

1 **violence,** ferocity, vehemence, excess, severity, virulence, intensity, power, force, strength, vigor; bluster, roughness, rough handling, harshness; fierceness, aggression, furiousness, wildness, fury, frenzy, rage, passion; ferment, agitation, turbulence, storminess, impetuosity; burst, bursting, dissilience; forcefulness, might, energy, boisterousness, destructiveness, murderousness; all hell let loose

  ▶ *Severity 424; Power 514; Strength 516; Vigor 518; Destruction 523; Agitation 684*

2 **violence by person** *or* **animal,** physical cruelty, physical abuse, torture; strong-arm tactics, thuggery, hooliganism, vandalism, terrorism; brute force, brutality, bestiality, savagery, barbarity; bloodlust, bloodthirstiness, bloodletting, slaughter, homicide, murder; rape, battering, assault, pillaging; charge, sortie, attack; commotion, disturbance, tumult, brouhaha, riot, row, flareup, uproar; fight, fisticuffs, fracas, rumpus, clash, crash, donnybrook; twist, sprain, fracture, wrench, dislocation; atrocity, murder, bloodbath, massacre, holocaust; throe, paroxysm, fit, convulsion, spasm, explosion, detonation, blowup, blast

  ▶ *Sex 20; Killing 30; War 76; Physical Pain 215; Malevolence 306; Attack 418; Contention 422; Immorality 432*

3 **natural violence,** tremor, earthquake, quake, tsunami *or* seismic sea wave, cataclysm, volcanic eruption, avalanche; violent weather, storm, tempest, rainstorm, downpour, hailstorm, snowstorm, blizzard; flood, flash flood, gullywasher; thunderstorm, thunder and lightning; squall, tornado, cyclone, hurricane, typhoon; war of the elements, rough weather, dirty weather, foul weather; windstorm, dust storm, sandstorm, sirocco

  ▶ *Meteorology and Climatology 9; Loudness 232; Attack 418*

4 violent animal *or* **person,** beast, wild *or* savage beast, brute, mad dog, raging bull, wolf, tiger, lion; monster, dragon, demon, devil, hellhound, hellcat; ruffian, mugger, thug, savage; terrorist, revolutionary, militant, anarchist; assassin, murderer, rapist, pillager; hangman, executioner, butcher, slaughterer, man of blood, homicidal maniac, madman; arsonist, pyromaniac; firebrand, fire-eater, bravo, desperado, termagant, fury, spitfire, hell-raiser [Inf]

> *Killing 30; Anarchy 51; Insanity 110*

ADJECTIVES

5 violent, ferocious, vehement, excessive, outrageous, severe, virulent, intense, extreme, acute, unmitigated, sharp, rough, harsh, fierce; aggressive, tyrannical, heavy-handed, forceful, forcible; wild, furious, infuriated, angry, on the rampage, on the warpath, fuming, frenzied, frantic, frenetic, hysterical, in hysterics, kicking, struggling, thrashing, roaring, gnashing, howling, desperate; mad, insane, maddened, crazed, enraged, berserk, demented; intemperate, immoderate, unbridled, unrestrained, out of control, uncontrollable, ungovernable, unruly, untamed; raging, rabid, like a mad dog, like a raging *or* mad bull; inextinguishable, irrepressible, heated, inflamed, flaming, scorching, fiery, eruptive, bursting

6 explosive, convulsive, spasmodic; destructive, ruinous, catastrophic, cataclysmic, overwhelming, devastating; volcanic, seismic; tumultuous, tempestuous, stormy; riotous, uproarious, boisterous; rampant, charging

7 murderous, barbarous, savage, brutal, bestial, cruel, vicious; bloody, bloodthirsty, ravening; hotheaded, bellicose, warlike, threatening, tigerish

> *Killing 30; Malevolence 306; Severity 424; Destruction 523; Agitation 684*

VERBS

8 be violent, run riot, run wild, run amuck *or* amok, hurtle, hurl oneself; crash in, burst in, break out, burst out; charge, stampede, break the peace, raise a storm, riot, rampage, go on the rampage, go on the warpath, rage; storm, roar, convulse, erupt, explode, burst, come in like a lion; go berserk, lose control; resort to violence, resort to fisticuffs, take up arms, take to arms, rebel, see red [Inf]

> *Loudness 232; Haste 818*

9 use violence, terrorize, tyrannize, force, use force, strike, hit, mug, beat up, do violence to; assault, attack, savage, murder, slaughter, butcher, massacre, abuse, violate, rape, ravish, pillage, torture; break, smash, destroy; strain, pull, wrench, twist, sprain, dislocate, fracture; force open, blow open, break open, break in, burst in, shock, shake, clobber [Inf]

> *Physical Pain 215; Malevolence 306; Misuse 395; Attack 418; Destruction 523; Agitation 684*

10 make violent, goad, whip, whip up, lash, incite, fire, fire up, inflame, blow on the embers, add fuel to the flames, foment, infuriate, whip into a frenzy, enrage, madden, make mad, wave a red flag; detonate

ADVERBS

11 violently, ferociously, torturously, brutally, viciously, murderously, riotously, vehemently, fiercely, forcefully, forcibly; by storm, by force, hammer and tongs, tooth and nail, like a bull at a gate, like a battering ram; at the point of a gun, at gunpoint, at knifepoint, at swords' points; tyrannously, tyrannically, with a vengeance, beyond all reason; stormily, convulsively, explosively

521 Moderation

By God, Mr. Chairman, at this moment I stand astonished at my own moderation! — ROBERT, LORD CLIVE

Moderation is a fatal thing, Lady Hunstanton. Nothing succeeds like excess. — OSCAR WILDE

NOUNS

1 moderation, moderateness, reasonableness, restraint, check, control, self-control; equanimity, composure, sang-froid, self-possession, sedateness, sobriety, coolness, calmness, quietness, mildness, gentleness, nonviolence, temperance, steadiness; impartiality, neutrality, fairness, justness, judiciousness, justice, due measure; golden mean, average, happy medium, middle way, halfway house; correction, adjustment, modulation, regulation; mutual concession, trade-off, give and take, compromise, mitigation; relaxation, relief, remission, alleviation, easing, assuagement, mollification, calming, quietening, sedation, tranquilization; abatement, lessening, reduction, diminution, decrease, letup [Inf]

> *Remedy 115; Sobriety 120; Silence 231; Compromise 461; Lack of Motion 678; Average 742; Decrease 747; Repair 809; Ease 819*

2 moderator, controller; calming influence, restraining hand, mollifier, peacemaker, pacifier; mediator, arbitrator, arbiter, judge, referee, umpire, chairperson; cushion, buffer, shock absorber, damper; restraint, brake, clamp, killjoy, wet blanket, stopper, downer; sedative, tranquilizer, soporific, sleeping pill, barbiturate, bromide, nightcap [Inf], lullaby, soothing influence, palliative, lenitive, demulcent, alleviative; painkiller, analgesic, anodyne, anesthetic, opiate, opium, laudanum; oil on troubled waters, balm

> *Mediation 75; Remedy 115; Restraint 830*

ADJECTIVES

3 moderate, medium, equable, balanced, steady, not extreme, not excessive, modest; judicious, just, fair; nonviolent, harmless, gentle, gentle as a lamb, mild; weak, poor, middling, mediocre, so-so, indifferent, average, ordinary, passable, unexceptional, unremarkable, limited, restricted, measured; sensible, rational, reasonable, within reason, within limits *or* bounds; restrained, controlled, chastened, subdued; quiet, peaceable, pacific, still, untroubled, peaceful, tranquil, low-key, self-controlled, temperate, tempered, sober, calm, cool, composed; calm, cool, and collected; fair to middling

▸ *Sobriety 120; Silence 231; Lack of Motion 678; Average 742*

4 **politically moderate,** neutral, tolerant, middle-of-the-road, center, nonextreme, nonradical, nonreactionary, mugwumpish, noncommittal, wishy-washy

5 **moderating,** lenitive, soothing, nonirritant, alleviative, assuaging, easing, painkilling, analgesic, anodyne; calming, calmative, sedative, tranquilizing, narcotic, hypnotic, mesmeric, soporific; smooth, soft, bland, emollient, demulcent, lubricating, comforting; disarming, pacificatory

▸ *Pacification 74; Remedy 115*

VERBS

6 **be moderate,** take the middle way, follow the golden mean, stay on an even keel, stay within bounds; sober up, calm down, settle, settle down; keep the peace, give up arms, disarm, go quietly, go out like a lamb; remit, relent, relax, ease off, go easy, compromise

▸ *Sobriety 120; Compromise 461; Ease 819*

7 **moderate,** correct, adjust, modulate, regulate, mediate, judge, arbitrate, chair, take the chair, preside, referee, umpire; curb, tame, check, keep within bounds, restrict, constrict, constrain, limit, keep within limits; repress, restrain, chasten, govern, control, clamp, clamp down on

8 **calm,** pour oil on troubled waters, temper, mollify, soften, cushion, break the fall of; put a damper on, damp, dampen, deaden, cool, subdue; sedate, tranquilize, anesthetize; still, quiet, quieten, hush, lull, rock, rock to sleep; sweeten, dulcify

9 **mitigate,** palliate, extenuate, qualify; weaken, obtund, blunt, dull, take the edge off; assuage, ease, soothe, satisfy, quench, relieve, alleviate, lighten, neutralize, take the sting out of, deactivate, smooth over; disarm, appease, pacify, allay; abate, lessen, reduce, diminish, decrease, play down, moderate one's language, censor, blue-pencil, tone down, euphemize; sober, sober down, throw cold water on, reduce the temperature, bank down the fires, slacken, relax; comfort, soft-pedal [Inf]

▸ *Pacification 74; Mediation 75; Remedy 115; Management 126; Counteraction 510; Decrease 747; Repair 809; Ease 819; Restraint 830*

ADVERBS

10 **moderately,** in *or* with moderation, within limits, within bounds, within reason, reasonably, within range; to a degree, to some extent, fairly, pretty, quite,

rather, somewhat, slightly, at half speed; equably, judiciously, gently, weakly, temperately, calmly; half-heartedly, nervously

522 Production

NOUNS

1 **production,** making, producing; preparation, creation, invention, innovation, origination, original work; originality, creative impulse, creative urge, inspiration, discovery; doing, productivity, productiveness, output, throughput, turnout; effort, endeavor, attempt, try, undertaking, project, enterprise; performance, execution, accomplishment, achievement; art, work of art; assembly of materials, cogitation, conception, formulation, concoction, brewing, fermenting; molding, forming, shaping, casting, technology, workmanship, skill, handiwork, craftsmanship; design, planning, organization, structure

▸ *Fertility 22; Work 122; Skillfulness 127; Attempt 390; Action 412; Newness 652*

2 **manufacture,** manufacturing, making, fabrication; construction, building, engineering, civil engineering, tectonics, architecture; erection, setting up, establishment; business, industry, heavy industry, light industry, sunrise industry; processing, process, treatment; machining, assembly, machine, machinery, plant, conveyor belt, assembly line, production line, workshop, factory; technology, low technology, intermediate technology, industrialization, increased output, mass production, automation, high technology, new technology, computerization, robotics, development, growth; agriculture, growing, market gardening, farming, factory farming; stockbreeding, animal husbandry

▸ *Engineering 14; Agriculture 16; Workplace 124; Architecture 134; Raising 715*

3 **product,** artifact, article, finished article, item, manufactured item, thing, object, creation, creature; result, consequence, effect, outcome, issue, output, turnout; extract, essence, concoction, confection, compound, end product, by-product, spin-off, offshoot; waste product, waste, slag, leavings, fallout

4 **work of art,** brainchild, idea, production, performance, work, *oeuvre* [Fr]; magnum opus, chef-d'oeuvre, masterwork, masterpiece, crowning achievement; painting, drawing, sculpture; ballet, dance, composition, piece, musical composition; literary composition, literary work, work of literature, piece of writing, book, pamphlet, article, poem, work of fiction, story, short story, short novel, novella, novel, full-length novel; theatrical production, play, sketch; film, movie, short, feature film

▸ *Art 133; Dance and Ballet 135; Motion Pictures 137; Literature 139; Music 140; Painting and Drawing 143*

5 **produce,** goods and services, gross national product

(GNP), gross domestic product (GDP), net national product (NNP); interest, return, increase, dividend, gain, profit, revenue, income; offspring, baby, child, young, egg, seed, spawn, young creature

> *Reproduction 21; Gain 467*

6 **merchandise,** goods, wares, commodity; hard goods, durable goods, pottery, earthenware, porcelain, china, stoneware, ironware, kitchenware, hardware; white goods, appliances; brown goods, electronic machines; dry goods, fabric, cloth, textile, drapery, white goods, clothing, hosiery

> *Ceramics 129; Fabrics and Fabric Handling 130*

7 **animal products,** meat, dairy products, eggs, skin, fur, leather, hide

> *Food 90*

8 **plant products,** fruit, flower, blossom, berry, stalk, leaf, heart, head, crop, harvest, vintage, yield, produce

> *Trees 43; Fruits 44; Food 90*

9 **construction,** structure, building, edifice, monument, piece of architecture; stonework, brickwork, bricks and mortar, timbering, half-timbering, wattle and daub

> *Engineering 14; Habitat 60; Architecture 134; Structure 551*

10 **producer,** maker, creator; originator, inventor, discoverer, prime mover, instigator, innovator; founder, founding father, founder member, establisher; begetter, father, mother, parent; artist, author, writer, poet, playwright, dramatist, painter, sculptor, composer, musician; director, stage director, film director, program director; play producer, film producer, radio producer, television producer; designer, planner, architect, engineer, developer, builder, constructor, contractor; fabricator, manufacturer, industrialist, entrepreneur, business executive, businessman, businesswoman, worker, laborer; artificer, artisan, craftsman, craftswoman, craftworker; planter, grower, cultivator, gardener, plantsman, plantswoman, farmer; stockbreeder, sheep farmer, rancher, grazier [Brit]; miner, prospector

> *Agriculture 16; Reproduction 21; Worker 123; Management 126; Motivation 508; Cause 675; Beginning 771*

ADJECTIVES

11 **productive,** creative, innovative, inventive, original, formative; structural, constructive, architectonic; manufacturing, industrial, industrialized, developed, mechanized, automated, high-technology, computerized, robotic, postindustrial; nonindustrial, underdeveloped, developing, low-technology; agricultural, fertile, fruitful, fecund, prolific, rich; profitable, remunerative, lucrative, paying, high-yielding, interest-bearing, worthwhile; high-tech, low-tech

> *Fertility 22; Provision 89; Excess 99; Gain 467; Increase 746*

12 **produced,** created, made, man-made, synthetic, artificial; manufactured, processed, ready-made, machine-made, mass-produced, factory-made; handmade, done by hand, homemade, homespun, tailor-made; architect-designed, craftsman-built, custom-built; invented, thought of, dreamed up, imagined, devised, worked out, discovered; begotten, born, bred, hatched; sown, grown; raised, reared, brought up, educated

VERBS

13 **produce,** make, create, originate, invent, innovate; fabricate, engineer, manufacture, output, mine, quarry, extract, exploit; process, industrialize, develop industrially, mechanize, automate, computerize, mass-produce; synthesize, blend, concoct, combine, put together, cobble together, make up, assemble; build, construct, erect; set up, establish, found, institute, constitute; organize, structure, arrange, stage, direct, bring about, set in motion, cause

14 **bring into existence,** bring into the world, bring into being, generate; engender, beget, bear, give birth to, spawn, breed, hatch; multiply, reproduce, propagate; sow, grow, farm, cultivate; raise, rear, bring up, educate, train

> *Reproduction 21*

15 **dream up,** think of, imagine, think up, conceive, cogitate, cogitate upon; develop, evolve, plan, devise, formulate, design; write, author, compose, paint

> *Literature 139; Music 140; Painting and Drawing 143; Thought 317; Imagination 360*

16 **perform,** give, present, get up; shape, form, mold, fashion, frame; make, spin, weave, knit, sew, run up; carve, chisel, sculpt; forge, cast; coin, mint, mill, machine; prefabricate, turn out, churn out, knock out [Inf]; make by hand, craft, custom-build, customize

> *Sculpture and Engraving 144*

ADVERBS

17 **productively,** creatively, innovatively, inventively; fruitfully, prolifically; profitably, remuneratively

523 Destruction

NOUNS

1 **destruction,** unmaking, undoing, nullification, annihilation, obliteration; deletion, erasure, liquidation, elimination; extermination, extinction, abolition, abolishment, repression, suppression; silencing, stifling, smothering, suffocation, overturning, overthrow, prostration

> *Obliteration 186; Nonexistence 718; Restraint 830*

2 **destroying,** demolition, demolishment, flattening, razing, knocking down, hatchet job; decomposition, dissolution, breaking up, disruption, shattering; crushing, grinding, pulverization, disintegration, shredding; incineration; defoliation; eradication, uprooting, deracination, extirpation; decimation, slaughter, mas-

sacre, genocide, mass murder, mass destruction, killing, murder

> *Killing 30; Crumbliness, Powderiness 553; Disintegration 758*

3 destructiveness, wanton destructiveness, wanton destruction, vandalism, sabotage, arson, iconoclasm

4 ruin, downfall, undoing, crushing blow, knockout blow, knockout punch, fatal blow; ruination, perdition, disaster, calamity, catastrophe, act of God, collapse, debacle, upheaval, cataclysm; breakdown, irretrievable breakdown, crackup, failure, utter failure; meltdown, China syndrome; breakup, crash, smash, smashup, write-off; wreck, shipwreck, sinking, wreckage; ruins, ancient ruins, dilapidation; wrack, rack and ruin, loss, total loss, bankruptcy, insolvency; *coup de grâce* [Fr], end, end of the world, apocalypse, doom, doomsday, crack of doom, knell, death knell

> *Loss 468; Lowering 716; Separation 753; End 773; Failure 846*

5 havoc, damage, turmoil, mayhem, chaos, devastation; laying waste, raid, raiding, despoiling, spoliation, pillage, looting, rape, rapine, depredation; explosion, blitz, nuclear blast, nuclear winter, desolation, scene of desolation, scene of destruction, disaster area, wasteland; desert, desert waste, scorched earth, shambles; carnage, slaughterhouse, holocaust, hecatomb

> *Disorder 766*

6 destroyer, wrecker, spoiler, despoiler, raider, ravager, pillager, looter, arsonist, pyromaniac; demolisher, leveler, iconoclast, destructionist, annihilationist, nihilist, anarchist, revolutionary, revolutionist, saboteur; vandal, defacer, eraser, rubber, eradicator; extinguisher, liquidator, exterminator, killer, murderer, assassin, hatchet man, executioner, hangman, hit man [Inf]; barbarian, hun, Viking, berserker, loose cannon; death, grim reaper, angel of death, time

> *Death 29; Killing 30; Anarchy 51*

7 agent of destruction, plague, pestilence, disease, bubonic plague *or* Black Death, cholera, AIDS; locusts, moth, woodworm, dry rot, wet rot, rust, mildew, blight, potato blight; wear, wear and tear, erosion, decay, corrosion; corrosive, acid; poison, pesticide, defoliant, Agent Orange; radiation, nuclear fallout; natural disaster, landslide, avalanche, earthquake, fire, flood, inundation, storm; the Four Horsemen of the Apocalypse (conquest, war, famine, disease), Fury, avenging angel; weapon, dagger, sword, bow and arrow, crossbow, longbow, slingshot, catapult, gun, cannon, machine gun; explosive, dynamite, blasting powder, nitroglycerine, TNT, bomb; nuclear missile, nuclear warhead, nuclear weapon; blockbuster; bulldozer, battering ram, juggernaut

> *Weapon 78; Ill Health 114; Affliction 117; Deterioration 808*

ADJECTIVES

8 destructive, destroying, devastating, ruinous, internecine, cutthroat, annihilating, consuming, all-consuming, raging, rampaging; suicidal, sacrificial, mortal, life-threatening, deadly, lethal, fatal; disastrous, catastrophic, apocalyptic, cataclysmic, overwhelming; subversive, revolutionary, anarchistic, incendiary, insidious; pernicious, noxious, harmful, injurious, baneful

> *Affliction 117; Disparagement 440*

9 destroyed, wiped out, ruined, devastated, undone, fallen; crushed, ground, pulverized, pulped, shredded, broken up, broken, disintegrated, shattered; wrecked, torpedoed, sunk; in tatters, in ruins, crumbling, dilapidated, falling down, falling apart, tumbledown, coming apart at the seams; failing, not long for this world, sinking fast, doomed; heading for the scrap heap, marked out for destruction, due for demolition; bankrupt, in liquidation, in receivership, in the hands of the receiver, down-and-out; [Inf]: done for, bust, kaput

> *Ill Health 114; Nonexistence 718; Deterioration 808*

VERBS

10 destroy, unmake, undo, bankrupt, destruct; annihilate, liquidate, terminate, end, put an end to, exterminate, put out of his *or* her misery, put away, do away with; make away with, get rid of, dispose of, dispatch; decimate, massacre, slaughter, kill, murder, do for; quell, extinguish, quench, put out, snuff out, blow out, stamp out; extirpate, eradicate, deracinate, uproot, root up, obliterate; [Inf]: zap, do in, chuck out, blow away, total

11 abolish, ax, invalidate, tear up, revoke, abrogate, cancel; efface, expunge, wipe out, wipe off the map, erase, rub out, blot out, strike out, delete, scratch out, nullify, annul; quash, squash, suppress, repress, sit on, keep down, clamp down on; silence, muzzle, muffle, blanket, stifle; smother, suffocate, strangle, drown, submerge; overturn, subvert, overthrow, throw out; scatter, disperse, dispel, dissipate, dissolve, vaporize, evaporate; lose; sacrifice; neutralize, counteract, negate

> *Killing 30; Obliteration 186; Negation 190; Counteraction 510; Nonexistence 718; Dispersion 776*

12 demolish, dismantle, take apart, take to pieces, take to bits; tear apart, rend asunder, tear to pieces, tear to bits, tear to rags, tear to shreds, tear limb from limb, pick *or* pluck to pieces, pull to pieces, cut to pieces; butcher, slaughter; pull apart, unbuild, break, break down, break up; blast, explode, dynamite, blow up, blow to bits, blow to smithereens, blow to kingdom come, bombard, bomb, blitz; shatter, smash, smash up, shiver, smash to matchwood, smash to smithereens, wreck; pulp, crush, crush to pieces, grind, grind *or* turn to dust, grind to powder, pulverize, shred, atomize, make mincemeat of; shake to pieces, batter, ram

13 knock down, fell, cut down, pull down, tear down,

blow down, throw down; bulldoze, steamroller, flatten, level, raze, raze to the ground, lay in the dust, grind into the dust, trample underfoot, grind underfoot, grind under one's heel; beat down, mow down, knock over, topple, kick over; overturn, upset, overthrow, subvert, cause the downfall of, turn upside down, invert, sap *or* undermine the foundations of, mine

◗ *Violence 520; Crumbliness, Powderiness 553; Horizontality 603; Separation 753; Disintegration 758*

14 **lay waste,** devastate, waste, desolate, defoliate, deforest, denude, strip, strip bare, gut; damage, vandalize, run amuck *or* amok, bring destruction, deal destruction; wreak havoc, cause a shambles; lay in ruins, lay in ashes; depopulate, put to the sword; raid, sack, ransack, despoil, pillage, loot, plunder; rape, ravage, violate

15 **ruin,** bring to ruin, spoil; play the devil with; wreck, shipwreck, sink, scupper, torpedo; shoot down in flames; mutilate, deface; knock out, knock flat, floor, flatten; make short work of, make mincemeat of, defeat comprehensively, trounce; hamstring, hobble; nip in the bud, abort, cut off, cut short; [Inf]: KO, put the kibosh on, put the skids under, dish, clobber, play hell with, play merry hell with

◗ *Failure 846*

16 **consume,** eat up, gobble up, devour, swallow up, engulf, envelop, drown, swamp, overwhelm; burn, burn up, incinerate

17 **be destroyed,** self-destruct, go to waste, perish; go down, go under, plunge, sink, sink without a trace, disappear; fail, founder, go on the rocks, disintegrate, split, break up, go to pieces, crumple up; turn to dust, end, come to an end; fall, fall into ruin, go to rack and ruin, tumble, tumble down, crumble, crumble away, crumble to dust; go to the wall, go downhill, go downhill fast, go to pot, go to hell, bite the dust; [Inf]: go to blazes, go to the dogs, come to a sticky end, have bought it, have bought the farm, go west

◗ *Disappearance 265; Disintegration 758; End 773; Deterioration 808; Failure 846*

ADVERBS

18 **destructively,** fatally, lethally; devastatingly, ruinously, catastrophically, disastrously

Material Characteristics

524 Material World

NOUNS

1 **material world,** physical world, real world, empirical world, world of experience, nature, natural world; material existence, materiality, materialness, existence, corporeity, corporeality, corporality; bodiliness, substantiality, physical being, physical existence, physical condition; concreteness, tangibility, palpability, solidity, density, weight, gravity
  ▶ *Heaviness 538; Density 540; Structure 551; Exterior 610; Existence 717; Reality 719*

2 **materialization,** embodiment, incarnation, corporation, epiphany, manifestation; reincarnation, metempsychosis, transmigration; realization; positivism, materialism, dialectical materialism, physical science, empiricism, scientism; unspirituality, worldliness, sensuality, sensualism
  ▶ *Deity 82*

3 **materialist,** dialectical materialist, Marxist, realist, naturalist, humanist, positivist, physical scientist
  ▶ *Philosophy 4; Geology 8; Physics 10; Chemistry 11*

4 **matter,** prime matter, brute matter, material, raw material, basic materials, materials, materiality, stuff; mass, fabric, body, frame, structure, substance, solid substance; corpus, organic matter, flesh, flesh and blood, plasma, protoplasm, cells, organism; element, elementary unit, fundamental particle, building block, principle, first principle, unit of being, origin; four elements: earth, air, fire, and water [Arch]
  ▶ *Materials 104*

5 **physical element,** ingredient, factor, component, constituent, mineral, monad, chemical element, isotope; basic substance, atom, molecule, elementary particle, electron, neutron, proton; minuteness
  ▶ *Physics 10; Chemistry 11; Life Science 13; Essence 723; Part 760*

6 **object,** inanimate object, tangible object; animate being, physical presence, body, human, flesh and blood; thing, something, commodity, article, item, artifact, gadget; [Inf]: thingamabob, thingamajig, thingummy, whatsis
  ▶ *Humankind 18; Life 28; Existence 717; Reality 719*

ADJECTIVES

7 **material,** tangible, substantial, sensible, real, natural; massy, solid, massive, concrete, palpable, ponderable, weighty; physical, empirical, spatiotemporal; objective, impersonal, clinical, neuter; incarnate, embodied; somatic, corporal, corporeal, bodily, fleshly, of flesh and blood, in the flesh, carnal; incarnated, realized, materialized; materialistic, worldly, earthly, unspiritual, nonspiritual, sensual
  ▶ *Reality 719*

VERBS

8 **be material,** exist, materialize, substantialize; substantiate, make concrete, reify, objectify, externalize, realize, make real; corporealize, embody, incarnate, manifest, personify, reincarnate
  ▶ *Existence 717*

ADVERBS

9 **materially,** of material, with material, tangibly, substantially, sensibly; naturally, in a natural way; solidly, concretely, palpably, physically; objectively, with objectivity, impersonally, clinically; corporally, sensually

525 Nonmaterial World

NOUNS

1 **nonmaterial world,** nonphysical world, metaphysical world, ethereal world, other world, another world, imaginary world; eternity, eternal life, afterlife, life after death, perpetuity, hereafter; heaven, hell
  ▶ *Death 29; Religion 81; Deity 82; Imagination 360; Eternity 644; Unreality 720*

2 **immateriality,** immaterialness, immaterialism, unreality, incorporeity *or* incorporeality, incorporealness, insubstantiality *or* unsubstantiality, unsubstantialness, intangibility; disembodiment, disincarnation, demate-

rialization; unworldliness, otherworldliness, unearthliness, spiritualness, spiritualization, spirituality, religion; impalpability, imponderability, shadowiness, ghostliness

> *Death 29; Unreality 720*

3 **spiritual world,** spirit world, world of spirits; occult phenomena, the occult, spiritualism, spiritism, supernaturalism; animism, animatism, astral plane, astral body, spirit; ghost, phantom; extrasensory perception (ESP), sixth sense

> *Occultism 86*

4 **parapsychology,** psychokinesis, precognition, clairvoyance, crystal gazing, fortunetelling, mind reading, telepathy; psychic phenomena, psychic research

> *Occultism 86*

5 **idealism,** philosophical idealism, metaphysical idealism, absolute idealism, transcendental idealism, transcendentalism, Platonism, Neoplatonism, Hegelianism, Kantianism

> *Philosophy 4; Intellect 315; Thought 317; Idea 327*

6 **internal world,** nonexternality, subjectivity, solipsism, selfhood, consciousness, myself, me, yours truly, self; ego, superego, subconscious, unconsciousness, id; psyche, spirit, soul; mind, intellect, psychoanalysis

> *Psychology and Psychiatry 108*

7 **nonmaterialist,** spiritualist, medium, supernaturalist, psychic, occultist, parapsychologist, clairvoyant, crystal gazer, fortuneteller, mind reader, telepathist; animist, solipsist, idealist, religious believer; philosopher, Platonist, Neoplatonist, Hegelian, Kantian; psychoanalyst

> *Religion 81; Occultism 86*

ADJECTIVES

8 **nonmaterial,** nonphysical, unphysical, unworldly; metaphysical, imaginary, illusory, ethereal, heavenly, eternal, perpetual; otherworldly, transcendent, transmundane, extramundane, spiritual, celestial, supernal, psychic, immaterial, immaterialist, immaterialistic, incorporeal, incorporate [Arch], insubstantial *or* unsubstantial, intangible, airy, without mass; disincarnated, disembodied, unembodied, bodiless, without body, unfleshly, dematerializing, dematerialized; impalpable, imponderable, shadowy, ghostly

9 **parapsychological,** extrasensory, supersensible *or* supersensory, precognitive, clairvoyant, telepathic, psychokinetic; psychic, occult, spiritual, spiritualist, spiritualistic, spiritistic, supernatural, animist, animistic, astral, phantom

10 **idealistic,** idealist, Platonic, Neoplatonic, Hegelian, Kantian

11 **internal,** nonexternal, subjective, personal, solipsist *or* solipsistic; conscious, subconscious, unconscious; psychoanalytic(al), mental, abstract

VERBS

12 **dematerialize,** immaterialize, spiritualize, spiritize,

disembody, disincarnate, insubstantialize *or* unsubstantialize; meditate, practice one's religion; dabble in occultism; psychoanalyze

ADVERBS

13 **metaphysically,** ethereally; eternally, for eternity, perpetually, forever; transcendently, spiritually; celestially, religiously; immaterially, incorporeally, insubstantially *or* unsubstantially, intangibly, airily, impalpably, imponderably; occultly, supernaturally, clairvoyantly, telepathically, psychically

14 **subjectively,** personally, internally, within, nonexternally; psychoanalytically, mentally, consciously, unconsciously; abstractly, idealistically, with idealism, Platonically, Neoplatonically

526 Simplicity

NOUNS

1 **simplicity,** simpleness, plainness, ordinariness, commonness, homeyness *or* hominess, homeliness [Brit], humbleness; austerity, severity, spareness, starkness, bareness, no frills; neatness, unclutteredness, cleanness, cleanliness, purity, chastity; ease, easiness, facility, effortlessness, smoothness, painlessness

> *Cleanliness 111; Humility 298; Uncovering 614; Easiness 823*

2 **unpretentiousness,** modesty, unaffectedness; usualness, obviousness, matter-of-factness, mundaneness; intelligibility, clarity, common speech, everyday speech, idiom, vernacular, plain prose, plain words, plain English, household words

> *Clarity 196; Speech, Spoken Language 205; Intelligibility 363; Modesty 403*

3 **unadornment,** unembellishment, lack of decoration, lack of ornamentation, lack of color; unsophistication, unadulteration, unspoiledness

4 **naturalness,** innocence, naiveté, unworldliness; openness, honesty, veracity; artlessness, guilelessness; truth, truthfulness, candidness, candor, frankness, bluntness

> *Truth 721; Naiveté 821*

5 **simpleton,** dullard, dolt, fool, numskull, ninny, dope [Inf], Simple Simon

> *Ignorance 349; Folly 353*

6 **simplification,** refinement, purification; disentanglement, disinvolvement; uncluttering, unscrambling, unsnarling, unknotting; stripping, stripping away *or* down, paring down, getting down to brass tacks, narrowing; streamlining, deconstruction, dismantling

ADJECTIVES

7 **simple,** simplistic, plain, basic, ordinary, commonplace, common *or* garden, everyday, workaday; homey *or* homy, homely [Brit], homespun, humble; austere, severe, Spartan, spare, stark, bare; neat, uncluttered,

stripped down; clear, clean, pure, chaste; uninvolved, uncomplicated; easy, facile, effortless, smooth, painless

> *Cleanliness 111; Clarity 196; Intelligibility 363; Elegance 527; Easiness 823; Undress*

8 **unpretentious,** modest, unaffected; usual, matter-of-fact, mundane, vernacular; unassuming, uninflated; played down, unemphatic, undramatic, unsensational, understated; prosaic, quotidian, unimaginative, uninspired, unpoetical

> *Understatement 195; Modesty 403*

9 **unadorned,** unembellished, undecorated, unornamented, untrimmed, ungarnished; unpainted, uncolored, colorless, unvarnished; unsophisticated, unadulterated, unspoiled

10 **natural,** innocent, simple-hearted, naive, unworldly; open, honest, veracious, unpretentious, unaffected; unassuming, unfeigning, unsophisticated, artless, guileless, ingenuous; forthright, candid, frank, blunt

11 **simpleminded,** dull, slow, dimwitted [Inf]; dense, thick; foolish, silly, witless, half-witted; feeble-minded, empty-headed

> *Ignorance 349; Folly 353*

VERBS

12 **make simple,** simplify, refine, purify; make clear, elucidate, clarify; disentangle, untangle, unsnarl; strip, strip down; naturalize, unfetter, smooth; streamline, dismantle, reduce, reduce to essentials

> *Intelligibility 363*

13 **be simple,** use common speech, use plain English, speak plainly, speak simply, come to the point

> *Clarity 196; Intelligibility 363; Interpretation 365; Truth 721*

ADVERBS

14 **simply,** plainly, basically, ordinarily, commonly; starkly, purely; intelligibly, clearly, prosaically, in the vernacular, in plain words, in common parlance; easily, effortlessly, smoothly, painlessly

15 **unpretentiously,** modestly, undramatically, matter-of-factly; candidly, frankly, bluntly, openly, directly

16 **naturally,** innocently, openly, honestly; artlessly; truthfully, candidly, frankly

527 Elegance

NOUNS

1 **elegance,** elegancy, grace, delicacy; taste, tastefulness, good taste, propriety, politeness, culture; finesse, beauty, exquisiteness; majesty, stateliness, courtliness; sophistication, style, smartness, polish, grooming; purity, clarity, simplicity; restraint, dignity, grandeur, distinctiveness, naturalness; fluidity, flow, smoothness, ease; expressiveness, sensitivity; fluency, aptness; finish, neatness; classicism, Atticism

> *Beauty 529; Refinement 534; Fashion 536; Style 537*

2 **grace,** gracefulness, gentility, refinement, suavity,

suaveness; harmony, euphony, symmetry, balance, proportion, rhythm, ease; well-turned phrase; elaboration, ornament, flourish, fittingness, felicity, right word in the right place, right word at the right time, *mot juste* [Fr]; ease of movement, facility, poetry in motion

> *Skillfulness 127; Clarity 196; Simplicity 526; Symmetry 626; Perfection 805*

ADJECTIVES

3 **elegant,** graceful, delicate, tasteful, proper, polite, cultured, pure; fine, beautiful, exquisite; majestic, stately, courtly, refined, sophisticated, stylish, smart; polished, manicured, soigné, well-groomed, finished; cultivated, clear, plain, simple; restrained, dignified, grand, distinguished, distinctive, natural

> *Beauty 529; Refinement 534; Fashion 536; Style 537*

4 **graceful,** gracile, delicate, gentle, refined, suave; well-proportioned, proportional, symmetrical, balanced, rhythmic, poetic; well-turned, round, readable, neat, neatly put, neatly wrought; facile, agile, nimble, lithe, supple

> *Skillfulness 127; Literature 139*

5 **fluid,** smooth, tripping, easy; expressive, sensitive, classic, proportional, flawless, mellifluous, fluent, apt, fitting, felicitous; unlabored, well-turned, round, neat, neatly put, neatly wrought; artistic, artistically done; classical, Attic, Augustan, Ciceronian

> *Clarity 196; Simplicity 526; Symmetry 626; Perfection 805*

VERBS

6 **be elegant,** be stylish, have taste, be proper; write well, turn a phrase; rewrite, perfect, polish, refine, edit; elaborate, ornament

ADVERBS

7 **elegantly,** stylishly, beautifully, smartly; exquisitely, gracefully, delicately, tastefully, expressively, readably, neatly, artistically, elaborately, decorously; nobly

8 **gracefully,** harmoniously, euphoniously, suavely, clearly, plainly, simply, naturally, symmetrically, rhythmically, easily, smoothly, fluently, aptly

528 Inelegance

NOUNS

1 **inelegance,** inelegancy, stiffness, formality, stiltedness; unnaturalness, artifice; gracelessness, gaucheness, gaucherie, clumsiness, awkwardness, artlessness; lack of refinement, lack of finesse *or* polish *or* style; gawkiness, gawkishness; heaviness, heavy-handedness, klutziness [Inf]

> *Unskillfulness 128; Imperfection 806*

2 **impropriety,** indelicacy, uncouthness, unrefinement; crudeness, rudeness, discourtesy; grossness, coarseness, roughness, boorishness, churlishness

> ▶ *Insolence 400; Discourtesy 411; Vulgarity 535*

3 bad taste, tastelessness, tackiness; garishness, gaudiness, loudness, tawdriness, vulgarity, ugliness; dowdiness, plainness, drabness, shabbiness, commonness

> ▶ *Tastelessness 220; Ugliness 531; Vulgarity 535*

4 inelegance of expression, solecism, incorrectness, bad grammar, clumsy construction, clumsiness, cacology; long-windedness, sesquipedalianism; stiffness, stiltedness, cumbrousness, ponderousness; grandiloquence, turgidity, bombast, pomposity; vulgarism, vulgarity, dysphemism, bad language, cursing

> ▶ *Linguistics, Language 5; Sophistry 330; Equivocation 380*

5 blunder, faux pas, gaffe, gaucherie, misstep, howler; mispronunciation, poor diction, speech defect, speech impediment; [Inf]: boo-boo, screwup, clanger [Brit]

> ▶ *Error 351*

ADJECTIVES

6 inelegant, formal, stiff, stilted, wooden, unfluent, artless; unnatural, artificial, mannered, affected, labored, tortuous; cacological, solecistic, incorrect; grandiose, showy, ostentatious, pretentious, pompous, grandiloquent, bombastic, turgid, rhetorical; ill-sounding, cacophonous, uneuphonious, jarring, grating; dysphemistic, doggerel, vulgar, ludicrous, grotesque

> ▶ *Affectation 367; Formality 406*

7 graceless, ungraceful, gauche; clumsy, awkward, cumbersome, ill-proportioned, ungainly, dumpy; clownish, gawky, gawkish, undignified; unrefined, unpolished; ham-handed, heavy-handed, heavy-footed, all thumbs, having two left feet, klutzy [Inf]

> ▶ *Unskillfulness 128; Imperfection 806*

8 indecorous, unseemly, improper, indelicate; unrefined, unpolished, undignified; crude, vulgar, tasteless, in bad taste, beyond the pale; gaudy, loud, tawdry, meretricious, overdressed; rude, discourteous, impolite; uncouth, gross, coarse, boorish, churlish; barbaric, barbarous, infra dig

> ▶ *Vulgarity 535; Imperfection 806*

9 plain, drab, dreary, dull; shabby, seedy, dingy, squalid, rough, mousy, lank; dowdy, badly dressed, unfashionable; ugly, unattractive, unaesthetic; tacky

> ▶ *Showiness 404; Ugliness 531; Vulgarity 535*

10 unfashionable, out of fashion, out of style, passé, outmoded; outdated, out-of-date, dated; defunct, dead, extinct, obsolete; out, hopeless, out of touch, old hat

ADVERBS

11 inelegantly, gracelessly, clumsily, awkwardly, indecorously, indelicately, grossly, coarsely, shabbily, unfashionably, tastelessly

529 Beauty

She walks in beauty, like the night / Of cloudless climes and starry skies. — LORD BYRON

Beauty is momentary in the mind / The fitful tracing of a portal; / But in the flesh it is immortal.
— WALLACE STEVENS

NOUNS

1 beauty, beauteousness, beautifulness, attractiveness, gorgeousness; gloriousness, ravishingness, exquisiteness; brightness, brilliance, radiance, magnificence; fairness, loveliness, prettiness, delicacy; bonniness, cuteness, sweetness, fineness; grace, gracefulness, nobility, harmony, symmetry; refinement, elegance, glamour, chic, sublimeness, splendidness, splendor

> ▶ *Art 133; Elegance 527; Fashion 536*

2 attractiveness, comeliness, pulchritude, handsomeness, sightliness, good looks; shapeliness, good build, nice body, lovely build, sexy body, sexiness; good bone structure, good features, delicate features

3 beautiful thing, beauty, vision, thing of beauty, cynosure; picture, poem; masterpiece, chef-d'oeuvre, beau ideal; sight for sore eyes, eyeful [Inf], lulu [Inf]

4 appeal, personableness, agreeableness, agreeability, charm; bloom, glow; tastefulness, decorativeness; presentableness, tidiness, trimness

5 attractive female, beauty, belle, belle of the ball, raving beauty; dream, vision, pearl, jewel, treasure; dazzler, pretty woman, beauty queen, pinup girl, glamour girl, cover girl, knockout, smasher; femme fatale, enchantress, lovely, Venus, lady fair, paragon of beauty; [Inf]: looker, babe, doll, dish, cutie

6 attractive male, dream man, dream, beau, charmer, Adonis; [Inf]: looker, dreamboat, hunk

ADJECTIVES

7 beautiful, beauteous, attractive, gorgeous; glorious, ravishing, exquisite, stunning; bright, brilliant, radiant, magnificent; fair, lovely, pretty, delicate; bonny, cute, sweet, fine, winsome; gracile, graceful, noble; refined, elegant, glamorous, chic, heavenly, sublime, resplendent, splendid, dazzling

8 attractive, comely, pulchritudinous, sexy; handsome, sightly, good-looking, easy on the eye, eye-filling, long on looks; well-proportioned, well-made, well-built, shapely, statuesque; goddesslike, godlike, Junoesque, Adonis-like; fit to kill [Inf], dishy [Brit inf]

9 picturesque, scenic, aesthetically pleasing, aesthetic, tasteful; pretty as a picture, pleasing to the eye, lovely to behold

10 appealing, personable, agreeable, charming; peachy, blooming, abloom, rosy; becoming, enchanting, elegant, tasteful, decorative, ornamental; presentable, tidy, trim

> ▶ *Decoration 532*

VERBS

11 be beautiful, shine, beam, bloom, glow, sparkle, dazzle; look good, take the breath away, look fit to kill [Inf]

12 beautify, adorn, grace, decorate

ADVERBS

13 **beautifully,** beauteously, prettily, glamorously, enchantingly, handsomely, attractively, becomingly

14 **gorgeously,** brilliantly, brightly, radiantly, glowingly, dazzlingly, stunningly, exquisitely

15 **elegantly,** exquisitely, gracefully, tastefully, charmingly, nobly; delicately, daintily

16 **magnificently,** splendidly, splendorously, resplendently, ravishingly, sublimely, radiantly

530 Beautification

NOUNS

1 **beautification,** transfiguration, transformation, improvement, refurbishment, restoration, rebuilding, refinement

2 **cosmetic surgery,** plastic surgery, rhinoplasty, rhytidectomy, face-lift, breast reduction, breast enlargement *or* enhancement, breast implant; [Inf]: nose job, boob job, tummy tuck, fanny lift

3 **beauty treatment,** facial, face pack, toilet *or* toilette; manicure, French manicure, nail wrapping, pedicure; wax, body wax

4 **cosmetics,** makeup, beauty products, beauty care products; greasepaint, paint, pancake, rouge, powder; eye shadow, eye makeup, eye liner, kohl, mascara, eyebrow pencil; coverup, foundation, base, blusher, blush; nail polish, nail varnish, nail enamel, basecoat, nail color, top coat, nail tips; lipstick, lip color, lip rouge

5 **cosmetic tool,** makeup brush, brush, powder puff, sponge, wand, pencil, stick; nail clippers, manicure scissors, nail file, emery board, cuticle scissors, cuticle stick, orange stick, cuticle remover; tweezers, eyelash comb, eyelash curler; mirror, vanity, vanity case, makeup case *or* box, paint box, toilet bag, toilet set, manicure set *or* case; nail polish remover, makeup remover, eye makeup remover

6 **toiletries,** perfume, scent, toilet water, eau de toilette, cologne, eau de cologne, perfume oil, essential oil; cold cream, eye cream, moisturizing cream *or* lotion, alpha hydroxy cream, hand cream *or* lotion, vanishing cream; soap, deodorant

7 **hairdressing,** hair cutting, hair styling, hair coloring, hair dyeing, coiffure, shampoo, barbering; hair removal, shave, shaving; depilation, tweezing, electrolysis, waxing; hair replacement, wig, false hair, hairpiece, fall, switch, toupee; hair weaving, minoxidil therapy; [Inf]: rug, divot, weave

8 **coiffure,** haircut, trim, style, hairstyle, hairdo; curls, spit curls, long curls, body wave, wave, marcel waves, marcel, permanent wave, home permanent, perm [Inf]; crop, Eton crop, bob, Dutch bob, short-back-and-sides, shag, straight cut, blunt cut, layered cut, tapered cut, razor cut; wet look, cut and blow-dry;

ponytail, plait, cornrows, braids, pigtails, French braid; bangs, fringe, chignon, French roll *or* twist, bun, beehive, pompadour, pageboy; dreadlocks, sideburns, crewcut, flattop [Inf], ducktail, DA, high-top fade, Mohawk, quiff [Brit], frizz, Afro, 'fro [Inf]; part, cowlick

9 **hairdressing tool,** hairstylist's tool; scissors, razor, comb, brush; curling iron, curler, hair dryer, barrette, bobby pin, hairpin, hair clip, hair band, headband, hair net, snood; hair spray, gel, mousse

10 **hairdressing salon,** beauty parlor, beauty shop, hairdresser's, beauty salon, salon, hair salon; barbershop, barber

11 **beautician,** beauty specialist, makeup artist, cosmetician, hairdresser, shampooer, colorist, barber, trichologist, hairstylist, coiffeur, coiffeuse, manicurist, pedicurist, plastic surgeon; crimper [Brit inf]

▶ *Decoration 532*

ADJECTIVES

12 **beautified,** made beauteous, made beautiful, decorated, adorned, embellished, embroidered, improved; finished, made up, tricked out, decked out; touched up, colored, dyed, highlighted, tinted, shampooed, conditioned, waved, curled, woven, braided, marcelled, styled; dressed up, dressed to the nines, dressed to kill; [Inf]: gussied up, tarted up, done up, dolled up

13 **beautifying,** cosmetic, decorative, restorative, transfiguring

VERBS

14 **beautify,** prettify, glamorize, transform, transfigure, enhance; decorate, ornament, bejewel, adorn, grace; smarten up, spruce up, primp, prink, titivate; make up, put on one's face, paint, manicure, scent, perfume; [Inf]: do up, doll up, gussy up, tart up, apply the war paint

▶ *Beauty 529*

15 **coif,** style, brush, comb, spray; trim, clip, cut; curl, have a body wave, wave, have a permanent *or* a perm, perm [Inf], crimp; braid, plait, weave; dye, color, tint, highlight, rinse

ADVERBS

16 **beautifully,** beauteously, prettily, glamorously; handsomely, attractively, becomingly, cosmetically

531 Ugliness

NOUNS

1 **ugliness,** unsightliness, unattractiveness, homeliness, plainness; hideousness, repulsiveness; hideosity, deformity, contortedness, mutilation, defacement, disfigurement; gracelessness, inelegance, clumsiness, ungainliness; discord, cacophony

▶ *Repulsion 701*

2 **ugly thing,** no beauty, eyesore, blot, blot on the landscape, carbuncle, blemish, slum; scarecrow, gargoyle,

monster, mess, sight, horror, fright, monstrosity; hag, old witch; no Adonis, baboon, ugly duckling; face that would stop a clock, back end of a bus, something the cat dragged in, old bag [Inf and Off], dog [Inf]

ADJECTIVES

3 **ugly,** hideous, horrid, repulsive, unshapely, deformed, contorted, mutilated, defaced, disfigured, ghastly, plain, homely, unsightly, unseemly, not fit to be seen, unlovely; graceless, clumsy, ungainly, inelegant, unaesthetic, unbecoming, unattractive, indelicate, ill-favored; uncouth, distasteful, coarse, awkward; discordant, cacophonous; gross, shoddy, messy, sloppy, unprepossessing; monstrous, misshapen, misbegotten, gruesome, wan, grisly; hard on the eyes, ugly as sin, homely as a mud fence, grotty [Inf]

◗ *Repulsion 701*

VERBS

4 **make ugly,** disfigure, deface, distort, deform, mutilate; blemish, mar, misshape, impair, ruin, spoil, scar

5 **be ugly,** look bad, offend, offend the eye; look a sight *or* a fright, be *or* look a mess, look like hell *or* like the devil

ADVERBS

6 **hideously,** repulsively, repugnantly, revoltingly, ghastly; horridly, horribly, awfully, terribly, dreadfully

7 **inelegantly,** gracelessly, unaesthetically, unbecomingly, unattractively, indelicately, awkwardly, distastefully, grossly, uncouthly, coarsely

532 Decoration

NOUNS

1 **decoration,** decor, style, look; adornment, garnish, ornamentation, embellishment, flourish, patterning, detailing; ornateness, richness, enhancement, enrichment; honor, medal, crown, laurel

◗ *Military Affairs 58*

2 **ornateness,** fanciness, ornamentation; extravagance, luxury, overstatement, exaggeration; ostentation, flamboyance, gaudiness, tackiness, showiness

◗ *Showiness 404; Display 843*

3 **decorative method,** gilding, gilt, gold leaf, filigree, ormolu *or* bronze doré, scrollwork, illumination; lettering, calligraphy, illustration, etching, painting, pyrography, tattooing; molding, fluting, mosaic; fancywork, embroidery, tapestry, cross-stitch, smocking, crewel work, broderie anglaise; crochet, lacework, lace, tatting; patchwork, appliqué, beading, beadwork

◗ *Fabrics and Fabric Handling 130; Architecture 134; Painting and Drawing 143*

4 **interior decoration,** interior design, interior decorating, decor, decorative technique; refurbishment, redoing, refinishing; furnishing, furniture arrangement; home decoration, office decoration, room decoration; painting, stripping, sponging; mural, fresco, wall paint-

ing, wallpaper, wallpapering, wall covering, wall fabric, wall hanging, arras; curtain, shade, blind, window dressing; color, color scheme, color decoration, color design, color coordination, color compatibility, color arrangement, color balance, shading, tones

◗ *Furniture 101; Color 251*

5 **decorative article,** trinket, spangle, sparkler, sequin, frippery, flounce, ruffle, frill, furbelow, fringe, ribbon, braid, feathers; gimcrack, bauble, knickknack, gewgaw, doodad [Inf]

6 **jewelry,** jewel, gem, chain; necklace, pendant, choker, torque; bracelet, bangle, ring, anklet; earring, ear cuff, nose ring; tiara, barrette, hair ornament, hatpin; badge, medallion, pin, brooch; costume jewelry

7 **ornament,** ornamentation, adornment, decoration, garnish, trimming, embellishment, color, flourish, embroidery, frill; decorative arrangement, flower *or* floral arrangement; table setting, place setting, centerpiece, epergne; flower of speech, purple passage, euphemism, metaphor, simile, trope, alliteration

◗ *Architecture 134; Literature 139; Speech, Spoken Language 205; Beautification 530*

8 **decorator,** painter, illustrator, illuminator; jeweler, gilder, scroll worker; embroiderer, crewelist, lacemaker, smocker; interior decorator, interior designer, designer

ADJECTIVES

9 **decorated,** embellished, garnished, enriched, enhanced, bejeweled, gilt, gilded, picked out, embroidered, trimmed, worked, inlaid, enameled, patterned; decorative, rich, fancy, nonfunctional, scenic, picturesque; overdecorated, ornate; honored, crowned, decked out

◗ *Military Affairs 58; Beautification 530*

10 **ornate,** elaborate, fancy, ornamented, ornamental, richly decorated, decorative, adorned, trimmed, beautified; gilded, baroque, rococo, colored, rich, luxuriant, florid, flowery, precious, euphuistic, euphemistic, extravagant, overstated, exaggerated, hyperbolic, affected, pompous, pretentious, ostentatious, flamboyant, meretricious, frothy, fussy, loud, brassy, grandiose, stately; circumlocutory, rhetorical, grandiloquent, magniloquent, orotund; gaudy, tacky, flashy, showy

◗ *Exaggeration 194; Emphasis 200; Speech, Spoken Language 205; Loudness 232; Affectation 367; Showiness 404; Beautification 530; Display 843*

VERBS

11 **decorate,** embellish, adorn, enhance, ornament; bejewel, bedeck, bedizen, array; garland, illuminate, illustrate, emblazon, color, embroider, chase, tool, engrave, festoon, emboss, trace, wreathe, paint, etch, smock; paint and decorate, wallpaper, refurbish, spruce up, give a face-lift, smarten up; honor, knight, crown

◗ *Military Affairs 58; Beautification 530*

12 **ornament,** adorn, decorate, garnish, trim, deck, festoon, embellish, beautify, enhance, grace, embroider,

enrich, gild, overlay, load with ornament, overload, paint *or* gild the lily

▶ *Loudness 232; Affectation 367; Showiness 404; Beautification 530*

13 **decoratively,** ornamentally, prettily, picturesquely; elaborately, flamboyantly, ostentatiously, richly, luxuriously, extravagantly

14 **ornately,** elaborately, floridly, preciously, extravagantly, hyperbolically, pompously, pretentiously, ostentatiously, flamboyantly

533 Blemish

NOUNS

1 **blemish,** defacement, defect, disfigurement, flaw, blight; blot, spot, speck, mark; welt, weal, bruise; taint, imperfection, distortion, damage; scar, stigma, cicatrix, scab, splotch, blotch, crud [Inf]

▶ *Ugliness 531; Imperfection 806*

2 **mark,** birthmark, nevus, strawberry mark, port-wine stain, hemangioma, macula, pockmark, freckle, lentigo, mole, wart, wen, cyst; beauty mark *or* spot, caste mark, tattoo, brand; pimple, spot, blackhead, whitehead, comedo, zit [Inf], hickey [Inf]; pustule, pustulation, rash, sty, boil, swelling, carbuncle, bubo; crazing, crack

3 **stain,** tarnish, smudge, smear, smirch, foxing

4 **blot on the landscape,** eyesore, carbuncle, atrocity; defacement, pollution, blight

ADJECTIVES

5 **blemished,** defaced, defective, disfigured, flawed, marred, blighted, blotted, spotted, speckled; tainted, imperfect, distorted; scarred, stigmatized, cicatrized, splotched, blotched

6 **marked,** pocked, pockmarked, freckled, tattooed, pitted, pimpled, pustular, pustulant; spoiled, soiled, damaged, polluted; crazed, cracked; scabby, scabrous, scablike; smudged, smeared, stained, foxed, tarnished

VERBS

7 **blemish,** deface, disfigure, flaw, blight, mar; blot, spot, speckle, mark, bruise; taint, distort, deform; smudge, smear, soil; damage, mutilate, pustulate, misshape, impair; spoil, ruin

▶ *Ugliness 531; Imperfection 806*

8 **mark,** brand, sully, stain, fox, craze, crack, tarnish, smudge, smear, smirch, maculate, scar, stigmatize

534 Refinement

NOUNS

1 **refinement,** fineness, finesse, elegance, style, grace; taste, good taste, tastefulness; distinction, dignity, quality, polish, finish; culture, propriety, civility, tact, etiquette; good breeding, good manners, correctness;

delicacy, courtesy, decency, seemliness, decorum; urbanity, sophistication, gracious living, connoisseurship

▶ *Education 48; Elegance 527; Beauty 529*

2 **subtlety,** distinction, delicacy, nicety, intricacy; lightness, etherealness, airiness; keenness, shrewdness, sharpness, acumen, discrimination

▶ *Education 48; Elegance 527*

3 **etiquette,** proper etiquette, manners, good manners, politeness; rules, code, code of behavior, custom; fashion, form, good form, convention, conventionality, propriety; ceremony, protocol, formality, decorum; seemliness, what is done, what people do, keeping up appearances

4 **refined person,** connoisseur, aesthete, cognoscente; person of taste, arbiter of taste; gentleman, gentleperson, lady, gentlewoman; epicure, gourmet, gourmand

▶ *Aristocrat 70*

ADJECTIVES

5 **refined,** elegant, graceful, tasteful, cultured; dignified, seemly, polished; delicate, well-finished, well-mannered, well-spoken, courteous, polite, distingué, cosmopolitan, sophisticated, urbane; discriminating, fastidious, critical; sensitive, artistic, aesthetic, appreciative, U [Inf]

6 **cultured,** well-bred, ladylike, gentlemanly, genteel; courtly, noble, classic, aristocratic, gentle; civilized, refined, ennobled, sublimated

VERBS

7 **refine,** cultivate, rarefy, polish, civilize, humanize; uplift, ennoble, sublimate, sensitize; clarify, purify, distill, clear, wash, lave; temper, improve, soften, meliorate, ameliorate

▶ *Simplicity 526*

ADVERBS

8 **elegantly,** stylishly, gracefully, graciously, beautifully, seemly, becomingly

9 **tastefully,** with taste, in good taste, sophisticatedly, fastidiously, aesthetically, artistically

10 **decorously,** courteously, decently, genteelly, correctly, civilly, sensitively, delicately

535 Vulgarity

NOUNS

1 **vulgarity,** tastelessness, no taste, bad taste, coarseness; lack of refinement, indecorum, indecorousness, indelicacy; gaudiness, showiness; inelegance, uncouthness, gaucheness *or* gaucherie, solecism, glitz [Inf]; barbarism, hooliganism

▶ *Showiness 404; Inelegance 528*

2 **tawdriness,** shoddiness, cheapness; tackiness, crudeness; lowness, meanness, baseness, kitsch

3 **grossness,** impropriety, unseemliness; ill-breeding, commonness; incivility, bad form, incorrectness, bad

manners, boorishness, discourtesy; indecency, smuttiness, pornography, obscenity; bad language, curse, swear, cuss [Inf], dirty word, foul language, expletive, four-letter word

4 **vulgar person,** cad, bounder, lout; slob, churl; rascal, rapscallion, scamp, miscreant; barbarian, vulgarian, savage, boor; hooligan, ruffian, hoodlum

5 **vulgar group,** vulgus, hoi polloi; lower class, peasants, rabble, riffraff, scum; huddled masses, great unwashed

ADJECTIVES

6 **vulgar,** tasteless, in bad taste, lacking in taste, crass, coarse, gross; unrefined, ill-bred, indecorous, indelicate; shoddy, cheap, gaudy, showy, loud, glitzy [Inf]; meretricious, ostentatious, garish, tawdry, kitschy; inelegant, uncouth, gauche, uncultivated, solecistic *or* solecistical; barbarous, ungentlemanly, unladylike, unfeminine; infra dig
▶ *Inelegance 528*

7 **discourteous,** boorish, unseemly, gauche; unmannerly, awkward, disorderly; off-color, risqué; unpolished, uncultured, unfashionable; barbaric, parvenu, nouveau riche

8 **ribald,** bawdy, provocative, Rabelaisian; immoral, indecent, offensive, blue; unmentionable, unquotable, unprintable; pornographic, dirty, obscene, filthy, smutty, lewd, scatological; low, mean, base

VERBS

9 **vulgarize,** coarsen, cheapen, lower, lower the tone, commercialize

ADVERBS

10 **vulgarly,** coarsely, grossly, crassly; inelegantly, indecorously; indelicately, crudely; awkwardly, disorderly, roughly, improperly; showily, ostentatiously, garishly, loudly

11 **discourteously,** boorishly, rudely, offensively; uncouthly, unseemly, gauchely, tastelessly, untastefully, in bad taste

12 **ribaldly,** bawdily, provocatively, lewdly, obscenely, pornograhically; indecently, smuttily, scatologically, in the worst possible taste

536 Fashion

As good be out of the world as out of the fashion.
— COLLEY CIBBER

NOUNS

1 **fashion,** design, style, mode, vogue, prevailing taste; look, new look, craze, set, rage, fad; haute couture, high fashion, elegance, designer label; fashionableness, chic, stylishness, trend; manner, way, make, form, kind, sort, practice, custom, general tendency; latest thing, the in thing [Inf]

▶ *Clothing 100; Beautification 530; Style 537*

2 **design,** mode, style, structure, set, mold, aspect, light, appearance, tendency, convention, protocol, form

3 **fashion business,** fashion trade, rag trade [Inf]; fashion designer, designer, clothing designer; fashion model, model, runway model, mannequin; arbiter of fashion, fashion plate, trendsetter, snappy dresser, dandy, fop, Beau Brummel, clotheshorse [Inf]

4 **fashionable elite,** high society, café society, social elite, Four Hundred; upper crust [Inf], cream of the crop, crème de la crème; haut monde, beau monde, clique, coterie; glitterati, beautiful people, jet set, jetsetter; Sloane Ranger [Brit inf]

ADJECTIVES

5 **fashionable,** in fashion, in style, in vogue, all the rage; smart, stylish, modish, à la mode, snazzy; clothes- *or* style-conscious, well-dressed, dressy, dressed up; tasteful, posh, glamorous, well-groomed; chic, dapper, dashing, natty, dressed to the nines, spruce, trim; [Inf]: classy, cool, with it, hip, mod, groovy, in
▶ *Elegance 527; Style 537*

6 **designed,** styled, made, custom-made, bespoke [Brit], formed, fashioned, stylized, overdone, affected
▶ *Style 537*

VERBS

7 **fashion,** shape, produce, figure, design; turn, round, shape; cut, tailor, cut out; create, make, form; chisel, carve, sculpt, hew, mold, cast; hammer out, forge, mint; build, construct, structure, compose

8 **design,** style, model, formulate, invent, originate; shape, pattern, originate, make up, contrive, devise

ADVERBS

9 **fashionably,** stylishly, modishly, à la mode; elegantly, chicly, smartly; glamorously, beautifully, tastefully, exquisitely

10 **dashingly,** jauntily, foppishly; neatly, nattily, sprucely, trimly, sleekly, smartly, swankily

537 Style

NOUNS

1 **style,** cut, line, design, pattern; mode, guise, manner, way, technique, method, approach; tone, tenor, idiom, vein, strain, quality, character; personal style, taste, fashion, mannerism, characteristic, mark; specialty, peculiarity, affectation, idiosyncrasy
▶ *Means 102; Art 133; Architecture 134; Literature 139; Music 140; Emphasis 200; Fashion 536; Specialty 779*

2 **stylishness,** elegance, grace, charm, flair, panache, élan, perfect touch; chic, smartness, nattiness, spruceness, modishness
▶ *Simplicity 526; Elegance 527; Refinement 534; Fashion 536*

3 **mode of expression,** use of language, style, personal style, manner of speaking, form of speech, diction, id-

iolect; literary style, wording, choice of words, word power, vocabulary, sentence structure, phrasing, phraseology, expression of ideas, command of language, command of idiom; oratory, rhetoric; authorial style, editorial style, style sheet, book style, type style

▶ *Linguistics, Language 5; Literature 139; Publication 173; Speech, Spoken Language 205*

4 **stylist,** stylish writer, fine writer, classical author, writer, wordsmith; phrasemonger, rhetorician, orator; craftsman, purist, classicist, artist

▶ *Art 133; Elegance 527; Decoration 532*

ADJECTIVES

5 **designed,** styled, cut, patterned, fashioned, formed; structured, planned, plotted, worked out, drawn up

▶ *Architecture 134; Fashion 536*

6 **styled,** stylized, phrased, worded, expressed, put; stylistic, stylistical, overdone, affected

▶ *Linguistics, Language 5; Literature 139; Speech, Spoken Language 205; Decoration 532; Refinement 534; Fashion 536*

7 **stylish,** elegant, graceful, chic, sophisticated, fashionable, swank, swanky, snazzy, à la mode, ritzy [Inf]

VERBS

8 **style,** show style, demonstrate style, develop a literary style, state, put, phrase, word; express, set out, present; express in words, find words to express, find words for, choose one's words

9 **fashion,** design, make, create; stylize, formulate, frame, block out, couch; shape, arrange, pattern; formalize; ritualize, solemnize

10 **be in style,** be in fashion, be with it [Inf]

ADVERBS

11 **stylistically,** linguistically, rhetorically, idiomatically, idiosyncratically; stylishly, with style, with flair, fluently; ornately, elaborately, gracefully, elegantly

538 Heaviness

NOUNS

1 **heaviness,** weightiness, weight, poundage, tonnage, body weight, solid body, massiveness, mass, lumpiness, lump, bulkiness, bulk; extra weight, fatness, obesity, corpulence, brawn, heftiness, heft; [Inf]: beef, beefiness, chunk

▶ *Density 540; Size, Largeness 579; Thickness 594*

2 **gravity** *or* **g,** specific gravity, gravitation, force of gravity, gravitational pull

3 **displacement,** draft, sinkage; load, loading, freight, cargo, ballast, lading, charge; overload, overloading, overweighting, surcharge

▶ *Contents 577; Transportation 686*

4 **weighing,** hefting, dead weight, dead load, live load, gross weight, net weight; overweight, heavyweight

▶ *Combat Sports 152; Horses, Horseback Riding, Horse Racing 159*

5 **weighing down,** weighting down; saddling, burdensomeness, burdening, burden, overburdening; ponderousness, ponderosity, incubus, onerousness, oppressiveness, oppression; taxing, tax, overtaxing; overbalance, top-heaviness, unwieldiness, pressure; cumbersomeness, cumbrance, encumbrance, handicap, drag, millstone

▶ *Descent 714; Lowering 716; Inequality 741; Difficulty 824; Hindrance 826*

6 **weight measurement,** avoirdupois weight, troy weight, apothecaries' weight; atomic weight, molecular weight; dram, ounce, pound, hundredweight, ton; pennyweight; stone [Brit]; scruple; milligram, gram, kilogram, kilo; carat

▶ *Measurement 589*

7 **weighing instrument,** scales, scale, calibrator, weighing machine, balance, steelyard; counterbalance, counterpoise, makeweight, ballast, ballasting

▶ *Tool 103; Measurement 589*

8 **weight,** sinker, lead, plumb, plummet *or* plumb bob, heavy weight *or* object

ADJECTIVES

9 **heavy,** weighty, having weight, weighted, heavyweight; leaden, solid, dense, massive, massy, considerable, great; stout, large, lumpish, lumpy, bulky, fat, overweight, obese, corpulent, hefty, beefy, chunky; heavy as a horse, heavy as lead

▶ *Density 540; Size, Largeness 579; Thickness 594*

10 **loaded,** laden, charged; overloaded, overladen, overweighed, overweighted

11 **ponderous,** onerous, heavy-handed, cumbersome *or* cumbrous, weighed *or* weighted down, burdensome, burdened, taxed, saddled, overburdened, overloaded, overladen; oppressive, oppressed, taxing, overtaxing, overtaxed; overbalanced, top-heavy, unwieldy; pressing, incumbent on, pressurized, handicapped

▶ *Adversity 848*

VERBS

12 **be heavy,** have weight, gain weight, put on weight, exert weight, carry weight; weigh the same, balance, counterweigh, counterpoise; outweigh, overweigh, outbalance, overbalance, tip the scales, turn the scales, tip the balance; sink, gravitate, settle, founder, descend; weigh a ton [Inf]

13 **weigh on,** weigh *or* lie heavy upon, press upon, weigh one down, oppress, hang like a millstone

14 **make heavy,** load, lade, weigh down, weigh one down, hang weights on, ballast, burden; make overweight, overweigh, overtax, overburden, overload; encumber, cumber, charge, tax; hinder, handicap, hamper, saddle; oppress, lie heavy upon, bear *or* rest hard upon

15 **weigh,** take *or* find the weight of, heft, put *or* stand *or* lay on the scales, measure, weigh oneself, weigh in, weigh out

16 **heavily,** heavy, weightily, with great weight, massively, greatly, stoutly, largely, densely, leadenly; like lead, like a horse, like a ton of bricks [Inf]

17 **burdensomely,** under a burden, oppressively, with oppression, ponderously, onerously, cumbersomely, cumbrously

539 Lightness

NOUNS

1 **lightness,** thinness, portability; airiness, gaseousness, ethereality, rarity; foaminess, frothiness, bubbliness, effervescence, sparkling, yeastiness; downiness, fluffiness, softness; gentleness, tenderness; flimsiness, delicacy, daintiness; imponderableness, imponderability; lack of weight, levity, unheaviness, weightlessness; defiance of gravity, levitation, levitating, floating, floatability, ascent, buoyancy
   ▸ *Sparseness 541; Softness 543; Gas 556; Air 558; Littleness 580; Thinness 595; Unreality 720*

2 **lightening,** easing, easement; aeration; alleviation, relief; unburdening, unloading, unlading, unsaddling, untaxing
   ▸ *Expulsion 709; Easiness 823*

3 **leavening,** leaven, fermentation, ferment; leavening agent: yeast, enzyme, barm, baking powder, self-rising flour
   ▸ *Cooking 91; Raising 715*

ADJECTIVES

4 **light,** weighing little, thin, portable, handy, low-weight, lightweight, featherweight, bantamweight, underweight; light-footed, light on one's feet, light-handed, light-fingered, having a light touch; unheavy, weightless, without weight, unweighable, imponderable, imponderous; light as air, lighter-than-air, light as a feather *or* thistledown, light as a fairy
   ▸ *Thinness 595*

5 **insubstantial,** ethereal, rare, sublime, airy, gaseous; frothy, foamy, foaming, whipped, whisked, bubbly, bubbling, effervescent, *pétillant* [Fr], sparkling; downy, feathery; cobwebby, gossamery; fluffy, uncompressed, soft; gentle, delicate, dainty, tender; flimsy, floaty, floating, floatable, buoyant, buoyed up, unsinkable; levitative, levitational, levitating
   ▸ *Thinness 595*

6 **lightening,** unloading, unloaded, off-loaded; aerating, aerated; easing, relieving, alleviating, alleviative, disburdening, unburdening, disencumbering

7 **leavening,** fermenting, fermentative, rising, self-rising; yeasty, enzymic, zymotic

VERBS

8 **be light,** weigh little, have little weight, lack weight; defy gravity, levitate, ascend, rise, elevate; surface, float to the surface, float; drift, waft, glide, soar, hover

9 **lighten,** make light, make lighter; buoy, buoy up, hold up, uplift, fluff, upraise; leaven, ferment, work, rise; empty, unload, off-load, unlade, lighten ship, unballast; throw overboard, jettison; disencumber, disburden, unburden, unsaddle, untax; relieve, alleviate, ease; reduce weight, lose weight

ADVERBS

10 **lightly,** with a light touch; insubstantially, without substance, ethereally, sublimely; effervescently; softly, gently, with gentleness, delicately, daintily, tenderly, with tenderness; flimsily, fluffily; imponderably; zymotically

540 Density

NOUNS

1 **density,** denseness, solidity, solidness, bulk, mass, thickness, thickening, compactness, concreteness, toughness, hardness, hardening; closeness, cohesion, coalescence, consistency, impenetrability, impermeability, imperviousness; indissolubility, indivisibility, inseparability, coherence; incompressibility
   ▸ *Strength 516; Material World 524; Heaviness 538; Hardness 542; Toughness 547; Thickness 594; Adhesion 755*

2 **concentration,** consolidation, condensation; coagulation, congealment, gelatinization; constriction, hemostasis, thrombosis; concretion, concretization, solidification, constipation; glaciation; ossification, petrifaction, fossilization, crystallization; sedimentation, precipitation

3 **relative density,** specific gravity; densimeter, hydrometer, aerometer
   ▸ *Tool 103*

4 **solid body,** solid mass, solid, mass, block, aggregate, conglomerate; hard core, nucleus; precipitate, deposit, sediment; coagulum, curd, clot, blood clot, thrombosis, thrombus, embolus; concretion, concrete, cement; earth, clay, hardpan, rock, crystal, stone; lump, chunk, clod, clump, cluster, cake, nugget; knot, node, nodule, burl; bone, gristle, cartilage, ossicle; obstacle, wall, forest, thicket
   ▸ *Ill Health 114; Hindrance 826*

5 **condenser,** compressor; thickener, thickening

ADJECTIVES

6 **dense,** thick, compact, cohesive, close-packed; close-knit, close-textured, close-woven; incompressible, close, firm-packed, firm, full; densely arrayed, serried, massed; massive, massy, heavy, weighty, monolithic, solid, concrete; rigid, inelastic; constrictive, styptic, astringent, hemostatic; strong, unbreakable, infrangible, indivisible, inseparable, consistent; impenetrable, thickset, thick-growing, bushy, luxuriant, plenteous; impermeable, impervious, without holes

7 condensed, consolidated, concentrated, solidified, solidifying, binding, constipated, constipating, costive; congealed, congealing, coagulated, coagulating, curdled, clotted, clotting; jelled *or* gelled, jelling *or* gelling, set, setting; freezing, frozen, deep-frozen; unthawed, unmelted, undissolved; insoluble, indissoluble, infusible, crystalline, crystallized; caked, matted; knotted, knotty, ropy, tangled, gnarled, lumpy; compressed, thickened; close, stuffy, foggy, murky, smoky; thick enough to be cut with a knife

VERBS

8 be dense, become thick *or* solid, densify, thicken, cohere; solidify, harden, cement, set; gelatinize, jellify, jell *or* gel; congeal, coagulate, clot, curdle; cake, crust; consolidate, constipate; conglomerate, contract, form a core, form a kernel, nucleate; crystallize, fossilize, petrify, ossify; freeze, glaciate; condense, evaporate, inspissate; precipitate, deposit

9 make dense, bring together, bind; crowd, mass, squeeze *or* pack together, pack, squeeze in, squeeze; load tightly, cram, tamp, ram down, make smaller, compact, compress, concentrate, firm up *or* down

ADVERBS

10 densely, thickly, compactly, cohesively, firmly, with firmness, fully; massively, heavily, solidly, concretely; rigidly, constrictively, strongly; plenteously; imperviously; costively; insolubly

541 Sparseness

NOUNS

1 sparseness, thinness, scarcity, scarceness, rarity, rareness; tenuity, tenuousness, delicacy, fineness, wispiness, lightness; low pressure, windiness, airiness; gaseousness, volatility, volatileness, ethereality, buoyancy; lack of substance, unsubstantiality *or* insubstantiality, immateriality, lack of solidity, slightness, flimsiness, incorporeality; reduced pressure, compressibility, sponginess, softness

  ◗ *Nonmaterial World 525; Lightness 539; Softness 543; Absence 576; Nonexistence 718; Unreality 720*

2 rarefaction, attenuation, etherealization; thinning, dilution, weakness, adulteration

  ◗ *Weakness 517; Contraction 582; Dispersion 776*

ADJECTIVES

3 sparse, thin, scarce, rare; tenuous, delicate, fine, slight, flimsy, wispy, light; low-pressure, windy, airy; gaseous, vaporous, volatile, volatilizable, volatilized, ethereal, buoyant; unsubstantial *or* insubstantial, immaterial, incorporeal; uncompressed, uncompact, compressible, spongy, soft

4 rarefied, rarefactional *or* rarefactive, attenuated, attenuate; etherealized, thinning, thinned; thinned-out, diluted, dilute, weak, adulterated, watered, watered-down, cut

VERBS

5 make sparse, thin, thin out, rarefy; gasify, vaporize, volatilize; reduce pressure, pump out, empty, exhaust; attenuate, etherealize; dilute, water, water down, cut, weaken, adulterate

ADVERBS

6 sparsely, thinly, tenuously, delicately, finely, lightly; airily, ethereally, unsubstantially *or* insubstantially

542 Hardness

NOUNS

1 hardness, strength, firmness; solidity, impenetrability, resistance, density; hard core, hard center, toughness, toughening; steeliness, stoniness, rockiness, cragginess, grittiness; lumpiness, nodularity, nodosity; rigidity, rigidness, rigor, temper, stiffness; stiffening, starchiness, starching; tautness, tightness, inflexibility, inelasticity, inextensibility; tension, tenseness, tensity; backing

  ◗ *Touch 216; Strength 516; Density 540*

2 hardening, solidification, setting; vitrification, crystallization, granulation; petrifaction *or* petrification, fossilization, lapidification [Arch]; glaciation; steeling, tempering, vulcanization; ossification, calcification, sclerosis, atherosclerosis, multiple sclerosis (MS), arteriosclerosis, hardening of the arteries

  ◗ *Geology 8; Ill Health 114*

3 hard substance, diamond, steel, iron, wrought iron, cast iron, metal; hardware, stoneware; rock, stone, adamant, pebble, grit, boulder; silica, flint, granite, quartz, marble; brick, cement, concrete, reinforced concrete *or* ferroconcrete, baked brick; bulletproof glass, armor; hardwood, heartwood *or* duramen; bone, gristle, cartilage, horn, ivory, shell; wart, corn, callus, node, nodule, lump; crust

4 mental hardness, toughness, hardness of heart, hardheartedness, callousness; obduracy, obstinacy, intractability, intransigence, inflexibility, unpliability, unmalleability, unbendingness, unyieldingness, immovability, stubbornness, asperity

  ◗ *Obstinacy 379*

ADJECTIVES

5 hard, diamondlike, steely, steel, iron, wrought-iron, cast-iron; stone, stony, granite, granitic, marble, rock, rocky, rock-hard, rocklike, lithoid *or* lithoidal, lithic, flinty, gritty; lumpy, horny, corneous, callous, leathery, cartilaginous, gristly; bony, osseous, ossific, sclerotic; crusty, encrusted; glassy, crystalline, vitreous; petrifactive, petrifying

6 tough, strong, firm, solid; unbreakable, adamant, indestructible, shatterproof, resistant; starchy, starched, boned, whaleboned; stark, stiff, rigid; inflexible, inelastic, musclebound; unsprung, unrelaxed, tight, taut, tense, pokerlike; stiff as a board *or* a poker *or* a ramrod, stiff as buckram

▸ *Toughness 547*

7 **hardened,** toughened; fortified, strengthened, stiffened, reinforced, backed, braced, buttressed; proofed, tempered, heat-treated, annealed, oil-tempered, indurate, indurated, casehardened; steeled, armored, armor-plated; callous, calloused, ossified, hornified, calcified; crusted, granulated; crystallized, vitrified; petrified, fossilized; sunbaked, solidified, set; frozen, frozen solid, frozen over, icy

8 **mentally hard,** inflexible, stubborn, obdurate, obstinate, firm, tough, intransigent; unadaptable, unpliable, unpliant, unmalleable, intractable, intractile, unbending, unyielding, ungiving, unalterable, immutable, difficult; hardhearted, stony-hearted, heartless; insensitive, callous, thick-skinned, hard-boiled, hard as nails [Inf]

VERBS

9 **harden,** make hard, render hard, toughen, caseharden, strengthen, steel, temper; reinforce, brace, buttress, shore, shore up, back; tense, tighten, tauten, stiffen, starch, wax; crisp, bake, heat, hard-boil; vulcanize, heat-treat, anneal; freeze

10 **solidify,** petrify, fossilize, ossify, calcify; vitrify, crystallize; glaciate; granulate; candy, set, firm, stiffen; condense, thicken, jell *or* gel

11 **be stubborn,** be *or* remain intransigent, not yield, not bend, not give, not alter

ADVERBS

12 **toughly,** strongly, resistantly, by offering resistance; starkly, stiffly, with stiffness, rigidly; tightly, tautly, tensely, in a tense manner; stonily, grittily; crustily; icily

13 **inflexibly,** without flexibility, stubbornly, in a stubborn manner; firmly, with firmness; intransigently, adamantly, intractably, unalterably, immutably; callously, hardheartedly

543 Softness

NOUNS

1 **softness,** pliability, pliableness, pliancy, flexibility, bendability, give; suppleness, willowiness, limberness, litheness; nonrigidity, nonresistiveness, springiness, springing; elasticity, plasticity, ductility, tensileness, tractability; malleability, impressibility, rubberiness, extendibility, extensibility; looseness, slackness, flaccidity, flaccidness, flabbiness, floppiness, limpness

▸ *Elasticity 546*

2 **smoothness,** agreeableness; downiness, featheriness, fluffiness; furriness, woolliness, flocculence, flossiness; silkiness, satininess; velvetiness, plushiness

▸ *Smoothness 545*

3 **compressibility,** sponginess, pulpiness, doughiness;

semiliquidity, sogginess; marshiness, bogginess; squashiness, squelchiness

▸ *Viscosity 561*

4 **soft-heartedness,** gentleness, tenderness, delicacy; mellowness, mildness; kindness, sensitiveness

▸ *Sensitivity 267*

5 **easiness,** easing up, leniency; laxity, laxness, laxation; mollification, mollifying, mitigation, appeasement; compliance, complying, obedience; adaptability

▸ *Anarchy 51; Submission 421; Leniency 423*

ADJECTIVES

6 **soft,** softening, softened; unstarched, unstiffened, nonrigid; flaccid, limp, rubbery, flabby, floppy, flimsy; unstrung, relaxed, slack, lax, loose, sprung; fluid

▸ *Fluid 555*

7 **pliant,** pliable, giving, yielding; melting; flexible, flexile, bendable; stretchable, elastic; lithe, lithesome, willowy, supple, lissome, limber, loose-limbed, double-jointed, springy, acrobatic, athletic; extensile, extensible, extendible; plastic, ductile, tractile, tractable; adaptable, malleable, moldable, shapable; impressible, waxy, doughy, pasty, puttylike

▸ *Elasticity 546*

8 **smooth,** agreeable; satiny, satinlike; silky, silken; velvety, velvet, velvetlike; plushy, plush; downy, feathery, fluffy, flossy; woolly, fleecy, flocculent; furry

▸ *Smoothness 545*

9 **compressible,** squeezable, padded, foam-filled; cushiony, pneumatic, pillowed; spongy, soggy, squashy, squishy, squelchy; juicy, overripe, pulpy, pithy, medullary; muddy, boggy, marshy; mossy, grassy, turfy; loamy, clayey, argillaceous

10 **figurative expressions,** soft as butter *or* as wax *or* as soap, soft as down *or* snow, soft as velvet *or* silk, soft as putty *or* dough, soft *or* smooth as a baby's bottom, soft as a kiss *or* a whisper *or* a sigh

11 **soft-hearted,** tender-hearted, kind-hearted, warm-hearted; sympathetic, compassionate; gentle, tender, kind, delicate, mild, easy; easygoing, relaxed, lenient, lax, complaisant, mellow, laid-back [Inf]

▸ *Sensitivity 267; Pity 308*

12 **impressionable,** susceptible, formable, sensitive; formative, nonresistive

13 **easing,** mollifying, mollified, showing leniency, appeasing, mitigating, complying; adapting, adaptable, moderating

▸ *Ease 819*

VERBS

14 **soften,** soften up, unstiffen; sag, flop; unstring, relax, slacken, loosen, bend; unbend, spring; mold, shape, make an impression in, impress; wax, smooth out; pad, cushion; plump up, plump, fluff up, fluff, shake up; render soft, tenderize; mellow, mature, ripen, over-ripen; oil, grease, lubricate; knead, massage; mash,

whip; pulp, squash, pulverize; chew, masticate, macerate; marinate, steep, drench; melt, thaw, liquefy

15 **ease,** relax, unwind, mellow; temper, lessen, mitigate, assuage, soothe; subdue, soften the tone, tone down, ease up, turn down, simmer down, mollify, moderate; limber up, massage, loosen, loosen up; [Inf]: hang loose, cool it, cool *or* chill out

16 **be kind,** show gentleness, show tenderness; show leniency, have compassion

17 **yield,** give way, give in, give, relent; appease; comply, obey; adapt, submit

ADVERBS

18 **softly,** with softness; limply, flaccidly; flimsily, slackly, loosely, laxly; fluidly, pliantly, flexibly, elastically, lithely, lissomely, limberly, acrobatically, like an acrobat, athletically, like an athlete; waxily, smoothly, silkily; pneumatically; fluffily; soggily

19 **soft-heartedly,** gently, mildly, tenderly, with tenderness; sensitively, delicately; easily, leniently, laxly; compassionately, with compassion, impressionably, susceptibly; complaisantly, compliantly, submissively

544 Roughness

NOUNS

1 **roughness,** unsmoothness; wrinkliness, rugosity, unevenness, corrugation; nonuniformity, irregularity, inequality; joltiness, bumpiness, rough surface, rough ground, ruggedness; raggedness, granulation, coarseness, coarse grain, coarse cloth; cragginess, scraggliness, nodosity, lumpiness; rough air, strong wind, turbulence, rough water, choppiness; hispidity, bristliness, horripilation, villosity, spininess; nubbiness, nubbliness, knobbiness; rough skin, scaliness, scabrousness; hairiness, rough hair, shagginess; scratchiness, rough texture, rough fiber; shattered surface, brokenness, jaggedness, sharp edge; serration, saw edge, rough edge, deckle edge, scalloped edge

▶ *Texture 552; Friction 554; Water 557; Air 558; Covering 613; Edge 618*

2 **rough thing,** sandpaper, emery paper, file; corrugated iron, washboard; grater, steel wool, brush; sackcloth, homespun, tweed, linsey-woolsey, corduroy; knot, kink, bouclé; barbed wire; broken glass, notched wood, splinter; burr, bristle, awn, thistle, prickle, barb, thorn; matted hair, shag; broken water, ripple, big wave, tsunami *or* siesmic sea wave, choppy sea; air pocket, hurricane, tornado, cyclone, twister [Inf]; rough ground, broken ground, canyon, mountain, sierra; rough road, potholed road *or* street, dirt road; dirt track, furrow, rut, crack; undergrowth, overgrowth

3 **rough skin,** chapped hands; scale, scab; bumpy face, acne; creeping flesh, goose flesh, goose pimples, goose bumps; stubble, five o'clock shadow, whiskers

▶ *Blemish 533; Convolution 632; Notch 636; Furrow 638*

4 **rough idea,** rough copy, rough approximation, rough, rough draft, draft, mock-up, preliminary sketch; unfinished piece, crudeness, incompleteness; shapelessness, rudiment, cursoriness, sketchiness, vagueness; approximation

▶ *Diffuseness 199; Lack of Emphasis 201; Idea 327; Plan 387; Imitation 736*

ADJECTIVES

5 **rough,** roughened, rough-hewn, roughcast; unsmooth, textured; corrugated, rippled, rippling, ripply, undulatory; wrinkled, wrinkly, crinkled, crinkly, crumpled, crumply, rugose; uneven, nonuniform, irregular, ruffled; muricate *or* muricated; unequal, rugged, ragged; unsifted

▶ *Texture 552; Friction 554*

6 **coarse,** coarse-grained, rough-grained, cross-grained; grainy, granulated; gravelly, stony, rocky, rock-bound, ironbound, craggy, cragged; scraggly, scraggy; snaggy, snagged, snaggled; hispid, spiny; villous; nodular, lumpy, slubbed; nubby, studded, knobby, knobbly, nodose *or* nodous, knotted, knotty, gnarled, gnarly, knurled; bouclé, tweed, tweedy; shattered, broken, jagged, jaggy, sharp; serrated, ridged, rough-edged, deckle-edged; corrugated, grated; potholed, furrowed, rutty, rutted, pitted; pockmarked, pocked, pocky, pimply; scabby, scabrous, encrusted, scaly; warty; blistered; cracked, chapped

7 **barbed,** prickly, scratchy; notched, hacked; hairy, unshorn, hirsute, shockheaded, bushy; woolly, flocculent, lanate, furry; matted, frizzy, fuzzy, shaggy, shagged; bristly, bristling, bristled, barbellate, setiform, setose, strigose, hispid; unkempt, unshaven, stubbled, stubbly

▶ *Sharpness 549*

8 **bumpy,** jolting; agitated, turbulent, choppy, tempestuous, storm-tossed

9 **unfinished,** incomplete; unpolished, unrefined, shapeless; rudimentary, preliminary, cursory; crude, raw, rough-and-ready; sketchy, vague, approximate

VERBS

10 **be rough,** lack uniformity, lack regularity, lack equality; have a rough surface *or* texture, ripple; crack, chap; have a bumpy face, have acne; creep (of flesh), horripilate, bristle, bristle up, prickle; scale; bump, jolt, jerk

11 **make rough,** rough, rough up, roughen, roughen up; roughcast, rough-hew; ruffle, wrinkle, crease, fold, crinkle, crumple, rumple, corrugate; granulate, coarsen; stud, emboss, boss; break, crack, hack; serrate, crenate, notch, engrail, indent, mill; grate, go against the grain, rub the wrong way, set on edge; knot, kink, tousle, tangle, gnarl; furrow

12 **be unfinished,** leave incomplete; give a rough idea, make a rough copy, approximate; sketch, make a preliminary sketch, draft; rough out, mock up

13 **roughly,** rough, in the rough, unsmoothly; against the grain, against the nap, the wrong way; choppily, unevenly, rugosely, irregularly, without regularity, unequally, without equality; ruggedly, coarsely, stonily, lumpily; turbulently, bumpily, villously; sharply, brokenly, jaggedly

14 **incompletely,** in unfinished form; shapelessly, without shape; preliminarily, crudely, sketchily; vaguely, approximately

545 Smoothness

NOUNS

1 **smoothness,** evenness, flushness; smooth texture, smooth surface; uniformity, regularity; horizontality, levelness, flatness; peacefulness, stillness, calmness, serenity; calm, dead calm, unruffled surface, quiescence; making smooth, levigation; sleekness, silkiness, satininess, velvetiness; softness; shininess, shine, luster, finish, glossiness, glassiness; slickness, slipperiness, slitheriness; unctuousness; lubrication, lubricity, oiliness, greasiness

▶ *Light 246; Oiliness, Lubrication 562; Horizontality 603; Lack of Motion 678; Sameness 730*

2 **smoother,** roller, flattener, trowel; iron, flatiron, tailor's goose, mangle, press, hot press, trouser press; plane, drawknife; rake, harrow; card, comb, brush, hairbrush; sandpaper, emery paper; emery board, file, nail file; buffer, floor polisher, sander; burnisher, chamois, waxer

▶ *Cleanliness 111; Fashion 536; Friction 554*

3 **polish,** varnish, enamel; burnish, gloss, glaze, patina, wax; lubricant, grease, oil

▶ *Oiliness, Lubrication 562*

ADJECTIVES

4 **smooth,** smoothing, smoothed, smooth-surfaced, smooth-textured; streamlined, nonfrictional, frictionless; even, unrough, flush, sleek, slick; bald, clean-shaven, hairless, glabrous *or* glabrate; smooth-haired, combed, brushed, well-brushed, groomed, carded; silken, silky, satiny, velvety; smooth-skinned, peach-like, soft, downy

5 **uniform,** even, regular; horizontal, plane, level, harrowed, rolled, steamrolled, flattened; unsharpened, blunt, edgeless, rounded, curved, waterworn; flat, ironed, pressed, unwrinkled, uncrumpled, unruffled; unbroken

▶ *Bluntness 550; Curve 629; Roundness 633*

6 **soothing,** peaceful, still, quiet, calm; dead, quiescent

7 **polished,** varnished, burnished, waxed, enameled, lacquered, glazed, glacé, gleaming, shiny, glossy, glassy, mirrorlike, reflective; slippery, slick, skiddy, slithery; buttery, lubricated, lubricous, oily, oiled, greasy, greased; soapy

8 **figurative expressions,** smooth as a peach *or* a baby's bottom, smooth as glass *or* marble, smooth as silk *or* velvet *or* satin, satin-smooth; slippery as an eel *or* a greased pig; calm as a millpond

9 **smooth-mannered,** well-mannered, suave, smooth-spoken, sophisticated, urbane, glib, slick, sleek; sycophantic, unctuous, smarmy, ingratiating, creepy [Inf]

VERBS

10 **smooth,** smoothen, smooth out, remove friction, streamline; plane, planish; even, level, harrow, mow, rake; flatten, flatten down, plaster down, comb; rub down, rub, roll; calender, press, hot-press, uncrease, iron, iron out, mangle; shave, cut, shorten; smooth down, file down, sand, sandpaper, emery, levigate; slick down, slick; shine, burnish, make bright, buff, polish, glaze; glacé; butter; gloss, wax; varnish, paint, coat, finish; pave, overlay; lubricate, oil, grease

11 **go smoothly,** glide, skate, roll, ski, float; bowl along, run on rails; slip, slide, skid; coast, freewheel

▶ *Motion 677*

12 **smooth over,** soothe, calm, appease, pacify, allay, ameliorate, assuage; mitigate, alleviate; charm, ingratiate; toady, suck up to [Inf]

ADVERBS

13 **smoothly,** evenly; unroughly, without roughness; flushly; sleekly, slickly; uniformly, on an even keel, regularly, horizontally, levelly; flatly, bluntly

14 **soothingly,** peacefully, without trouble; stilly, quietly, calmly; softly, quiescently

15 **suavely,** sophisticatedly, glibly, urbanely, sleekly; sycophantically, unctuously, smarmily, creepily [Inf]

546 Elasticity

NOUNS

1 **elasticity,** stretchability, stretchiness; stretching, stretch, suppleness, plasticity, rubberiness; extensibility, extension, distension; flexibility, pliancy, pliability, ductility; tensibility, tension, strain; tonicity, tonus, tone; springiness, spring, resilience *or* resiliency; give, snap, snapback, recoil, rebound, bounciness, bounce

▶ *Softness 543; Displacement 574; Change 665*

2 **adaptability,** resilience *or* resiliency, buoyance *or* buoyancy; flexibility, adjustability; responsiveness, liveliness; compliance, accommodation, yielding

▶ *Attention 323; Changeableness 666; Accord 735; Easiness 823; Cooperation 827*

3 **rubber,** gum elastic, elastomer, crude rubber, natural rubber, caoutchouc, plantation rubber, India rubber, foam rubber; hard rubber, vulcanized rubber; vulcanite, ebonite; latex, gutta-percha, sponge rubber; synthetic rubber: cold rubber, nitrile rubber, neoprene, silicone rubber; crepe rubber

4 **spring,** mainspring, hairspring *or* balance spring; coil

spring, spiral spring, volute spring, leaf spring; bed-spring, box spring; suspension system, shock absorber
- *Convolution 632*

ADJECTIVES

5 **elastic,** rubber, rubbery, rubberlike, rubberized; stretchable, stretchy, stretching, stretch, stretched; extending, extended, distensible, distending, distended; supple, plastic, extensible *or* extensile; flexible, flexing, flexed, pliant, pliable, tensile, tensible, ductile, tonic; springy, springing, sprung, well-sprung; coiling, coiled; resilient, giving, yielding; snapping, recoiling, rebounding; bouncy, bouncing

6 **adaptive,** adaptable, adapting, adapted, resilient, buoyant; flexible, adjustable, adjusting, adjusted, responsive, responding; lively; compliant, complying, yielding, accommodating

VERBS

7 **be elastic,** stretch, extend, expand, distend; flex, have flexibility, have tone, show resilience, give; spring, snap, snap back, recoil, rebound, bounce

8 **make elastic,** elasticize, elasticate; rubberize, rubber; vulcanize, plasticize

9 **be adaptable,** adapt, have resilience, have buoyancy; stay flexible, adjust, respond quickly; comply, accommodate, yield; bounce back

ADVERBS

10 **elastically,** with suppleness, plastically; flexibly, pliantly; springily, bouncily

11 **adaptably,** resiliently, flexibly, responsively; compliantly, accommodatingly

547 Toughness

NOUNS

1 **toughness,** strength, ruggedness, solidness, sturdiness, resistance; durability, survivability, lastingness, unbreakableness, unbreakability, infrangibility; hardness, rigidness, stiffness, firmness; cohesiveness, cohesion, coherence
- *Strength 516; Hardness 542; Duration 642; Adhesion 755*

2 **chewiness,** leatheriness, stringiness, rubberiness; inedibility, indigestibility

3 **stalwartness,** stamina; physical strength, physical power, powerful build, athletic build, muscularity, muscles, sinews, brawn; leanness, wiriness, stringiness, vitality, vigorousness, vigor, robustness; tenacity, endurance, resilience, hardiness, staying power
- *Strength 516*

4 **brutality,** physical roughness, brute force, viciousness, bullying
- *Vigor 518; Violence 520*

5 **mental toughness,** mental strength, resolve; single-mindedness, unyieldingness, stubbornness, obstinacy,

obdurateness, inflexibility; hardheartedness, sternness, unfeelingness, callousness, cynicalness
- *Disbelief 88; Will 372; Perseverance 377*

ADJECTIVES

6 **tough,** strong, rugged, solid, sturdy; resistant, resisting; durable, hard-wearing, lasting, long-lasting; unbreakable, nonbreakable, infrangible, untearable, unshatterable; shatterproof, shockproof, chipproof, fractureproof; bulletproof, bombproof, fireproof; indestructible

7 **toughened,** casehardened, tanned, hardened, tempered, annealed, vulcanized; strengthened; stiffened, seasoned

8 **hard,** rock-hard, rigid, stiff, nonelastic, inelastic, unsprung; leathery, leatherlike, coriaceous, firm; tough as old boots *or* leather, hard as nails [Inf]
- *Hardness 542*

9 **chewy,** fibrous, woody, ligneous, gristly, cartilaginous, rubbery; overdone, inedible, indigestible
- *Hardness 542*

10 **stalwart,** hardy; powerful, athletic, muscular, brawny, burly, strapping; sinewy, weather-beaten, lean, wiry, stringy; full of vitality, blessed with stamina, robust; enduring, untiring, unflagging, indefatigable; tenacious, resilient, staying

11 **rough,** brutal, vicious, bullying

12 **mentally tough,** mentally strong, resolved; single-minded, stiff, unyielding, stubborn, obstinate, obdurate, inflexible; hardhearted, stern, unfeeling, callous, cynical; casehardened, thick-skinned; hard-boiled [Inf], hard-nosed [Inf]
- *Disbelief 88; Will 372; Perseverance 377*

VERBS

13 **be tough,** show strength; resist, last, outlast, survive, have survivability, endure, stay the course; resist breaking; have physical strength, have an athletic build, flex one's muscles; show stamina; have tenacity, refuse to yield; have no feelings; hang tough [Inf], tough something out [Inf]
- *Duration 642*

14 **act rough,** brutalize, use brute force, bully
- *Violence 520*

15 **make tough,** strengthen, toughen, harden, stiffen; tan, mercerize, vulcanize, temper, anneal, caseharden; make unbreakable, shatterproof, bulletproof, bombproof, fireproof

ADVERBS

16 **toughly,** strongly, ruggedly; solidly, sturdily; resistantly, resistingly; durably, lastingly, indestructibly, infrangibly; rigidly, stiffly, firmly; indigestibly

17 **stalwartly,** powerfully, athletically, muscularly; leanly, robustly; enduringly, untiringly, lastingly; tenaciously; resiliently, hardily

18 **roughly,** brutally, with brute force

19 **single-mindedly,** stubbornly, obstinately, obdurately;

inflexibly; hardheartedly, sternly, unfeelingly, callously, cynically

548 Brittleness

NOUNS

1 **brittleness,** fragility, fragileness, frangibility, frangibleness; delicacy, flimsiness, frailty, unsturdiness, weakness, vulnerability; breakableness, breakability, breaking, breakup, cracking, crackup, disintegration; splitting, split, splintering, scission; crushability, crumbliness, crumbling, deterioration, friability, friableness, fissility, flakiness; crispness *or* crispiness, crunchiness; inelasticity, rigidness

  ▶ *Weakness 517; Sharpness 549; Crumbliness, Powderiness 553; Separation 753; Deterioration 808*

2 **brittle thing,** eggshell, icicle, ice, old bone, lamina, dead leaf; matchwood, balsa; shale, slate; old paper, parchment, rice paper; glass, crystal, porcelain, pottery; crust, piecrust, pastry, peanut brittle

  ▶ *Weakness 517*

ADJECTIVES

3 **brittle,** fragile, frangible, delicate, papery, wafer-thin, delicate, flimsy, frail; unsturdy, unsteady, weak, insubstantial, vulnerable, breakable; gimcrack, shoddy, jerry-built, dilapidated, tumbledown; ready to break, breaking, broken, crackable, cracking, cracked, crackled, disintegrating, chipping, chipped, shatterable, shattering, shattered; ready to split, splitting, split, splintery, splintering, scissile; tearable, tearing, torn; crushable, crushing, crushed; crumbly, crumbling, crumbled, short, friable, fissile, flaky, flaking, powdery; crispy, crisp, crunchy; inelastic, rigid

VERBS

4 **be brittle,** be fragile, deteriorate, wear thin, crash, give way, fall in, tumble, fall to pieces, break, break down, break apart *or* up *or* off, disintegrate; crack, crack up, disintegrate, fracture, shatter, snap off, snap, split, splinter, chip, chip off, flake, fragment, shiver, crush, crumble

ADVERBS

5 **fragilely,** delicately, flimsily, frailly; unsteadily, insubstantially; shoddily; weakly, vulnerably; crispily, rigidly

549 Sharpness

He'd be sharper than a serpent's tooth, if he wasn't as dull as ditch water. — CHARLES DICKENS

NOUNS

1 **sharpness,** pointedness, acumination, mucronation; spininess, spinosity, thorniness; bristliness, prickliness; denticulation, dentition; serration

  ▶ *Roughness 544*

2 **sharp point,** point, knife point, pencil point, sword point; cusp, vertex; prong, tine; sting; dent, notch

3 **sharp edge,** saw edge, cutting edge, knife edge, razor edge, jagged edge

  ▶ *Weapon 78; Notch 636*

4 **sharp-pointed thing,** pyramid, summit, peak, crag, arête, projection; spire, steeple, flèche; nail, tack, stylus, pin, staple; needle, knitting needle, bodkin, hypodermic needle; pick, pickax, icepick, toothpick; fork, pitchfork; harrow, rake, comb; rowel, cog, sprocket, ratchet; awl, burin, auger, drill, borer, gimlet, broach, perforator; spear, bayonet, sword, dagger, arrowhead, lance, fleam; marlinespike *or* marlinspike; barb, barbed wire; harpoon, fluke, hook, fishhook, gaff; skewer, spit; goad, ankus, prod

5 **sharp-pointed growth,** horn, antler, claw, talon, cockspur *or* spur, quill, spine; prick, sting, spicule *or* spiculum; pine needle, prickle; thorn, brier, burr, bramble, thistle, nettle, awn; cactus, yucca, Adam's-needle, Spanish bayonet

6 **sharp-edged thing,** broken glass, knife, cleaver, razor, razor blade, blade, sword, dagger; wedge; fingernail; edge tool: chisel, plane, scraper, drawknife, spokeshave; cutter: saw, scissors, shears, pinking shears, pruning shears, pruner, clippers, billhook, grasscutter, lawn mower, scythe, sickle; shovel, spade, trowel, adz *or* adze, mattock, plowshare *or* share, colter *or* coulter; hatchet, ax; sticker [Inf]

  ▶ *Edge 618*

7 **tooth,** snaggletooth, fang, tusk, denticle

  ▶ *Human Body 19*

8 **sharpener,** knife sharpener, steel, whetstone, whetter, grindstone, oilstone, hone; file; strap, strop

9 **mental sharpness,** sharp-wittedness, quick-wittedness, acuteness, acuity, astuteness; alertness, brightness, shrewdness, cleverness; intelligence, smartness, perspicacity, perspicaciousness, keenness, discernment, acumen

  ▶ *Intellect 315*

ADJECTIVES

10 **sharp,** sharpened; pointed, pointy, sharp-pointed, needle-pointed, needlelike, acicular, aciculate *or* aciculated, mucronate, acuminate, needle-sharp, sharp as a needle; spearlike, lanceolate, lance-shaped; hastate, arrowlike, sagittal, sagittate *or* sagittiform; fastigiate, conic(al), pyramidal; wedge-shaped, wedgy

11 **spiked,** spiky; star-pointed, starlike *or* star-shaped, stellate, stellular; barbed, spiny, spinose, spinous, acanthoid, acanthous; prickly, pricky, pricking, bristly, bristling, hispid, awned; stinging, stingy, thorny, brambly, briery, thistly

  ▶ *Brittleness 548*

12 **sharp-edged,** sharp-cut, sharp-set; honed, razor-edged, razor-sharp, sharp *or* keen as a razor, keen,

keen-edged; knife-edged, knifelike, cultrate; sword-like, ensiform; double-edged, cutting, saw-edged

13 **toothed,** toothy, fanged, fanglike, tusked, tusklike; horned, hornlike, corniculate, cornute *or* cornuted; toothlike, odontoid, dentiform, denticulate, cusped *or* cuspate, cuspidate; muricate *or* muricated, serrated, notched, emarginate *or* emarginated; comblike, pectinate *or* pectinated; snagged, snaggy, snaggle-toothed, jagged

  ▶ *Notch 636*

14 **mentally sharp,** sharp-witted, quick-witted, keen-minded, acute, astute, alert, bright, shrewd, clever, smart, intelligent; perspicacious, discerning, observant, perceptive, sharp-eyed, keen, acuminous; sharp as a tack, razor-sharp; sharp-tongued, acerbic

  ▶ *Intellect 315*

VERBS

15 **be sharp,** be pointed, have a point, end in a point, taper *or* come to a point; peak, converge, acuminate; spiculate, bristle, bristle with; prickle, prick, stick, pierce, sting; have prongs, have horns, have an edge, have a jagged edge; cut, needle, gore, bite

16 **sharpen,** hone, make sharp, file, grind, stone, strop, strap, whet; taper, edge, put an edge on, point, make pointed, put a point on; notch, serrate, barb, spur

17 **use a sharp tool** *or* **weapon,** scrape, chisel, plane; cut, scissor, saw; shear, clip, prune, scythe, sickle, cut *or* mow the lawn *or* grass; fork, harrow, rake, comb; shovel, spade, trowel, plow; ax, knife, razor, cleave, chop, carve, whittle, slice, skive; drill, bore, perforate; spear, harpoon, hook, gaff, skewer; shoot an arrow; goad, prod; claw, scratch

  ▶ *Attack 418*

18 **be mentally sharp,** show intelligence, have sharp wits, have quick wits; show acuteness, stay alert, discern

  ▶ *Intellect 315*

ADVERBS

19 **sharply,** pointedly; acutely, smartly, astutely, alertly, brightly, shrewdly, cleverly, intelligently, perspicaciously, discerningly, keenly

20 **suddenly,** sharply, cleanly, without warning

  ▶ *Surprise 292*

550 Bluntness

NOUNS

1 **bluntness,** unsharpness, dullness; smoothness, flatness; stubbiness, roundness

  ▶ *Smoothness 545*

2 **outspokenness,** straightforwardness, frankness, directness, candor, candidness; curtness, bluffness, abruptness

  ▶ *Conciseness 198; Insolence 400*

3 **dullness,** obtuseness, obtundity, insensitivity, insensitiveness, hebetude, imperceptibility; numbness

  ▶ *Insensitivity 268; Lack of Intellect 316*

4 **toothlessness,** lack of bite, lack of incisiveness

ADJECTIVES

5 **blunt,** bluntish, blunted, dull, unsharp, unsharpened, unwhetted; worn, smooth, smoothed, faired, stub, stubby; snub, blunt-nosed, rounded, curving, flat, flattened; unedged, edgeless, blunt-edged, dull-edged; unpointed, pointless; blunt-ended, blunt-pointed, dull-pointed

  ▶ *Smoothness 545; Curve 629; Roundness 633*

6 **outspoken,** straightforward, frank, direct, plain-spoken, candid; curt, bluff, abrupt

  ▶ *Conciseness 198; Insolence 400*

7 **dull,** obtuse, insensitive, unperceptive, hebetudinous; dense, slow, numb, unfeeling

  ▶ *Insensibility 213; Insensitivity 268; Lack of Intellect 316*

8 **toothless,** edentate, edental, edentulous, teethless, biteless

VERBS

9 **blunt,** dull, obtund, take the edge off, disedge; flatten, round, smooth, turn, turn the edge; draw the teeth *or* fangs of; take the sting *or* bite out

ADVERBS

10 **smoothly,** dully, stubbily, flatly, roundly; pointlessly, toothlessly

11 **bluntly,** frankly, to the point, candidly, plainly, straightforwardly, directly; curtly, abruptly

12 **obtusely,** insensitively, imperceptively; numbly

551 Structure

NOUNS

1 **structure,** arrangement, organization; organic structure; plan, pattern; tectonics, architecture, architectonics

  ▶ *Plan 387; Arrangement 767*

2 **fabric,** build, texture, contexture, tissue; warp, weft, weave; content, substance, materials, work

  ▶ *Materials 104; Fabrics and Fabric Handling 130; Texture 552*

3 **form,** formation, morphology, architecture; setup, fabrication, creation, fashion, conformation, elevation, configuration, shape, mold, format; composition, makeup, constitution; physique, build, body, anatomy; getup [Inf]

  ▶ *Form 624*

4 **framework,** frame, framing, skeleton; lattice, latticework, scaffold, rack, shell, chassis; cadre; doorframe, window case *or* frame, casement; picture frame

▶ *Support 605*

5 **structuring,** formation, creation; making, shaping, building; production, forging, patterning, molding
▶ *Production 522; Beginning 771*

6 **construction,** building, edifice; construct, erection, complex, establishment; prefab, prefabrication; superstructure, substructure, understructure
▶ *Engineering 14; Architecture 134*

7 **superstructure,** structural framework, skeletal frame, frame, space frame; truss, structural member, supporting member, horizontal member, vertical member; strut, tie, beam, girder, stringer, joist, boom, cantilever, rolled steel joist (RSJ), plate girder, I-beam, H-beam, T-beam, continuous beam, concrete slab; column, pillar, pier, tower, rib, spar, abutment, buttress, arch, vault, dome, shell; bearing, bearing plate, flange, shoe, structural connection, rivet, bolt, weld, web connection, seat connection, pin connection, geodesic dome

8 **substructure,** understructure, underbuilding, foundation, spread foundation, footing, mat, raft, slab, pile, caisson, cofferdam, underpinning, infrastructure; fill, backfill
▶ *Materials 104; Architecture 134*

9 **building,** public building: auditorium, church, theater, stadium; institutional building: hospital, school, courthouse, penitentiary; residential building: house, apartment building *or* complex, condominium, hotel; commercial building: store, shop, department store, mall, office building, storage building, garage, warehouse; industrial building: factory, plant; airport terminal, marine terminal; multistory building: high-rise building, tower block, skyscraper, pyramid, ziggurat
▶ *Habitat 60; Architecture 134; Trade 480*

10 **bridge,** highway bridge, railroad bridge, canal bridge, toll bridge; overpass, flyover [Brit], viaduct, aqueduct; pedestrian bridge, footbridge, catwalk, rope bridge, gangway, gangplank; fixed bridge, beam bridge, girder bridge, box-girder bridge, plate-girder bridge, truss bridge, arched bridge, suspension bridge, cantilever bridge, cable-stayed bridge, concrete bridge, movable bridge, lift bridge, vertical-lift bridge, swing bridge, bascule bridge, drawbridge, ferry bridge, transporter bridge, temporary bridge, Bailey bridge, pontoon bridge, trestle bridge, deck bridge, square bridge, curved bridge, skewed bridge; span, single span, multiple span, deck, flooring, pier, abutment, ramp

11 **tunnel,** vehicular tunnel, railroad *or* rail tunnel, cut-and-cover tunnel, bored tunnel; subway, underpass, channel, culvert, drain, sewer, cloaca

12 **dam,** concrete dam, arch dam, buttress dam, gravity dam, earth dam; reservoir, impoundment, weir, barrage, embankment, levee

13 **water system,** water-supply system, drainage system, sewerage system, irrigation system, flood-control system; barrage, floodgate, sluicegate, sea wall, breakwater, mole, groin *or* groyne, lock, canal, harbor, port; dock wharf, pier, quay, jetty

14 **skeleton,** exoskeleton, carapace, horn; endoskeleton, bone, cartilage; tendon, ligament
▶ *Human Body 19; Density 540; Hardness 542*

15 **science of structure,** anatomy, histology, morphology, osteography, osteology, zootomy; geomorphology, plate tectonics, tectology
▶ *Geology 8; Life Science 13; Medicine 107*

16 **anatomist,** histologist, morphologist; geomorphologist

ADJECTIVES

17 **structural,** constructional, organizational; superstructural, substructural, infrastructural; textural; architectural, tectonic, architectonic

18 **organic,** organismic, organismal, morphological, anatomical, formal

19 **skeletal,** bony

VERBS

20 **structure,** organize, plan; pattern, arrange; prepare; design, draw up; invent

21 **shape,** form, formulate, evolve; make, manufacture, fashion, fabricate; elaborate; mold, frame; compose, create; unify

22 **construct,** build, erect, raise, put up; devise, concoct, set up, get up

23 **assemble,** put together, piece together, patch together

ADVERBS

24 **structurally,** architecturally, tectonically, architectonically; constructionally, superstructurally, substructurally; organically, skeletally, morphologically, anatomically

25 **in production,** under construction, in hand

552 Texture

NOUNS

1 **texture,** surface texture, surface, finish; feel, touch, sensation; intertexture, contexture, structure, constitution; consistency
▶ *Sensation 212; Touch 216; Structure 551*

2 **grain,** fineness *or* coarseness of grain; fineness, refinement, softness, delicacy, daintiness, filminess, gossameriness; smoothness, satin, satininess, silk, silkiness; fluffiness, fluff, downiness, down; fuzziness, peachiness; roughness, coarseness, graininess, granular texture, granulation, grittiness, grit, hardness
▶ *Refinement 534; Hardness 542; Softness 543; Roughness 544; Smoothness 545*

3 **nap,** pile, shag; nub, knub, protuberance; indentation, pit, pock

4 **weave,** weaving; web, network; warp and woof *or* weft

5 **textile,** fabric, cloth, material; tissue; stuff, staple

◗ *Materials 104; Fabrics and Fabric Handling 130*

6 fiber, yarn, thread, string; tow, filament

ADJECTIVES

7 textural, textured, woven, matted

8 rough, coarse, coarse-grained, grained, grainy, granular, granulated, gritty; coarse-woven, ribbed, twilled, tweedy, woolly, hairy, fibrous, homespun, linsey-woolsey

9 smooth, fine, fine-grained, close-woven, fine-woven, refined; satin, satiny, silky, cottony

10 delicate, dainty, filmy, gossamer, gossamery; fine-spun, thin-spun, subtle, fine-drawn, wiredrawn

11 fluffy, downy; fuzzy, velvety, velutinous

VERBS

12 coarsen, roughen, rough up; granulate, grain; gnarl, knob

13 smooth, smooth out, make smooth, flatten, iron, press

14 rumple, wrinkle

ADVERBS

15 texturally, structurally, roughly, coarsely, fibrously; fuzzily; smoothly, finely, silkily, delicately, daintily, subtly; on the surface, to the touch

553 Crumbliness, Powderiness

NOUNS

1 crumbliness, flakiness, friability, friableness, pulverableness, brittleness
◗ *Brittleness 548*

2 graininess, granularity, granulation; mealiness, branniness; grittiness, sandiness, sabulosity; gravelliness
◗ *Texture 552*

3 powderiness, pulverulence, dustiness, chalkiness, flouriness; efflorescence, bloom

4 pulverization, powdering, levigation, trituration, comminution, reducing to dust; dusting, frosting; milling, grinding; crushing, mashing, smashing, beating, pounding, contusion; grating, shredding, crumbling, flaking; granulation, granulization; erosion, abrasion, attrition, detrition; brecciation; fragmentation, sharding; atomization, micronization, disintegration, decomposition
◗ *Disintegration 758; Dispersion 776*

5 crumb, flake, crumble; dandruff, scurf; filings, raspings, fragment; smithereens

6 grain, granule, granulet; speck, mote, particle

7 meal, groats, bran, flour, farina, grist

8 grit, sand, gravel, shingle; detritus, debris
◗ *Geology 8*

9 powder, dust, dirt, chalk; efflorescence, flowers, flowers of sulfur; pounce, talc, talcum powder, face powder; fluff, lint; soot, smut, ash, sawdust, coal dust; airborne particles: fallout, air pollution, smog, cosmic dust, dust cloud, dust storm, dust devil; dust ball, dust kitten, dust bunny, slut's wool [Brit inf]

10 spore, pollen, pollen grain, microspore, sporule
◗ *Reproduction 21; Flowers 42*

11 pulverizer, comminutor, triturator; crusher, rock crusher; food processor, mill, grinder, coffee grinder *or* mill, pepper mill; atomizer; grindstone, millstone, muller, quern, quernstone; masher, pounder, levigator, pestle, mortar and pestle; roller, steamroller

12 grater, cheese grater, nutmeg grater, shredder

13 hammer, sledgehammer *or* sledge, ram, mallet
◗ *Tool 103*

14 abrasive, file, sandpaper, emery paper; emery board, nail file

15 koniology, konimeter

ADJECTIVES

16 crumbly, friable, crumbled, crumbling; crisp, flaky, scaly, scurfy

17 grainy, gritty, granular, sandy, sabulous, arenose, arenaceous, arenarious; gravelly, shingly, shingled, pebbly, pebbled; detrited, detrital

18 mealy, branny, furfuraceous; floury, farinaceous

19 powdery, dusty, dust-covered, pulverulent, pulverous; dirty, sooty; chalky, chalklike, calcareous

20 pulverized, powdered, ground, ground to dust; granulated, disintegrated, crushed, grated, shredded, sifted, pestled; comminuted, triturated, levigated; sharded

21 pulverizable, pulverable, pulverulent, triturable

VERBS

22 crumble, crumb, chip, flake

23 grind, granulate, granulize, grain; mill, flour; mince, kibble

24 grate, shred; abrade, rub down, scrape, rasp, file

25 powder, dust, flour, dredge; sand, sprinkle, scatter

26 pulverize, powder, reduce *or* grind to powder *or* dust, triturate, comminute, levigate; bray, pestle, disintegrate; fragment, shard; atomize, micronize

27 beat, pound, bray; smash, mash, hammer, crush, squash, crunch, scrunch

28 come *or* **fall to dust,** crumble into dust, disintegrate, decompose, fall to bits *or* pieces, break up; granulate, effloresce

29 weather, erode, wear down, rust
◗ *Deterioration 808*

ADVERBS

30 flakily, granularly, grittily, dustily, dirtily

554 Friction

NOUNS

1 friction, rubbing; drag, force, resistance; static friction, rolling friction, internal friction, sliding friction, slip friction; coefficient of friction; skin friction, roughness; rub, frottage; frication
◗ *Physics 10; Resistance 417*

2 wearing away, attrition; abrasion, collision; rubbing against, rubbing together; erosion, wear, corrosion, detrition, ablation; rubbing out *or* off *or* away, erasure, obliteration; sandblasting

▶ *Obliteration 186; Destruction 523; Crumbliness, Powderiness 553*

3 **grinding,** filing, rasping; fretting; chafing, galling, chafe; levigation

▶ *Crumbliness, Powderiness 553*

4 **scraping,** scratching, grazing, scuffing; scrub, scrubbing, scouring; scrape, scratch, scuff

5 **polishing,** rubbing, burnishing; sanding, smoothing; buffing, shining; dressing; elbow grease

6 **massage,** massaging, massotherapy, stroking, rubdown, kneading; facial massage, facial; whirlpool bath; vibrator

▶ *Beautification 530*

7 **eraser,** rubber; scraper; sander, sanding disc, sandpaper, emery paper; emery board, nail file; file, rasp, pumice *or* pumice stone; facial mask *or* masque, facial scrub

▶ *Tool 103*

8 **masseur,** masseuse; massotherapist

▶ *Beautification 530*

9 **irritation,** grating; prickliness, irascibility; tension

▶ *Irascibility 303; Agitation 684*

ADJECTIVES

10 **frictional,** friction, abrasive, irritant, rubbing; attritive, erosive, ablative; gnawing

11 **rough,** rasping, grating, grinding; chafing, fretting, galling

VERBS

12 **rub,** rub up, smooth, polish, burnish, furbish, wax; levigate; buff, scour, scrub; sandpaper, sand, sandblast; dress, brush, curry, currycomb

13 **abrade,** rub against, scuff, graze; scrape, raze, bark, scratch; gnaw, gnaw away; strike (a match)

14 **erode,** corrode, wear, wear away; fray; skin; erase, rub out *or* away, obliterate, frazzle [Inf]

▶ *Obliteration 186*

15 **grind,** rasp, file, plane, grate; chafe, gall; catch, stick; fret, irritate, rub the wrong way

16 **massage,** knead, rub down; pulverize; rub gently; smooth, iron; stroke, caress, pet

ADVERBS

17 **abrasively,** roughly, raspingly; irritatingly

555 Fluid

NOUNS

1 **fluid,** liquid, liquid state; liquor, water, drink, beverage, fluid extract; condensation; compressible fluid, incompressible fluid

▶ *Drinking 93; Water 557; Moisture 559*

2 **juice,** sap, extract, latex; milk, whey, buttermilk, ghee; stock, meat juice, gravy, sauce, soup

▶ *Trees 43; Cooking 91; Viscosity 561*

3 **body fluid,** lymph, plasma, blood, humor; chyle, rheum, serous fluid, serum; pus, matter, purulence, suppuration, ichor, sanies, discharge, gleet; mucus; phlegm; saliva, spittle; urine; excrement; semen, menstrual flow; sweat, perspiration; tear, tears, teardrop; milk, mother's milk, colostrum, lactation; [Inf]: snot, piss, pee, weewee; jism, come

▶ *Excretion 25*

4 **blood,** lifeblood, arterial blood, venous blood; gore, claret [Inf]; blood serum, blood plasma, synthetic plasma, dextran; red blood cell *or* corpuscle, hemoglobin, erythrocyte; white blood cell *or* corpuscle, leukocyte; lymphocyte, plasma cell, B lymphocyte, T lymphocyte, CD4, CD8; granulocyte, neutrophil, basophil, eosinophil; phagocyte, monocyte, macrophage; blood platelet, clot, blood clot, thrombosis; blood group *or* type, O *or* A *or* B *or* AB blood group, Rhesus factor, Rh factor, Rh-positive, Rh-negative; antigen, antibody, isoantibody, globulin, immunoglobulin A (IgA), IgD, IgE, IgG, IgM, opsonin; blood count; blood pressure, circulation, bloodstream; blood bank, bloodmobile, blood transfusion

▶ *Medicine 107; Remedy 115*

5 **fluidity,** fluidness, liquidity, liquidness; wateriness, runniness, rheuminess; nonviscosity, noncoagulation, hemophilia; solubleness; bloodiness, goriness; semiliquidity

6 **flow,** fluency, flux, fluxion; hemorrhage; suppuration, secretion

7 **juiciness,** sappiness, pulpiness, succulence; milkiness, lactescence, lactation; moisture

8 **fluidization,** liquefaction, liquescence; solubility, deliquescence, fluxibility, dissolution, solution, dissolving; decoagulation, unclotting; melting, thaw, thawing, unfreezing, running; fusing, fusion; solubilization, lixiviation, percolation, leaching

9 **solvent,** liquefier, liquefacient, dissolvent, dissolver; dissolving agent, menstruum, anticoagulant, hydragogue; resolvent, resolutive; thinner, diluent; universal solvent, alkahest *or* alcahest

10 **solution,** infusion, decoction; suspension, emulsion, flux; lixivium, lye

▶ *Viscosity 561; Mixture 751*

11 **liquidizer,** blender, food processor, juice extractor

▶ *Cooking 91*

12 **flowmeter,** fluidmeter, sphygmomanometer; hydrometer

13 **fluid mechanics,** hydrodynamics *or* hydromechanics, hydrostatics, hydrokinetics, hydraulics; hydrogeology, hydrology

▶ *Physics 10*

ADJECTIVES

14 **fluid,** liquid, fluidal, fluidic; uncongealed, unclotted

15 **flowing,** fluent, fluxional, fluxionary; watery, runny, juicy, sappy; moist, succulent, squashy

16 **rheumy,** weeping; pussy, purulent, suppurating, suppurative, suppurated, sanious, ichorous, phlegmy; humoral, serous; tearlike, teary, lachrymal, lachrymatory

17 **milky,** lacteal, lacteous [Arch], lactic, lactescent; lactiferous

18 **bloody,** gory, bleeding, sanguineous; hematic *or* hemic, hemal *or* hematal; hemogenic, hemophilic

19 **liquefied,** dissolved, deliquescent; melted, thawed, molten; decoagulated; in solution, in suspension; liquescent, liquefacient, solvent

20 **liquefying,** liquefactive; thawing, melting, fusing; dissolving, dissolutional, anticoagulant

21 **liquefiable,** soluble; meltable, fusible, thawable; dissolvable, dissoluble

VERBS

22 **make fluid,** liquefy, liquidize; fluidize; blend, emulsify; liquate

23 **dissolve,** solve, thin; solubilize; decoagulate, unclot; hold in solution, leach, lixiviate, percolate, decoct, infuse; resolve

24 **melt,** run, thaw; melt down, smelt; defrost, unfreeze; render, clarify; deliquesce, fuse

25 **flow,** flux; run, stream, pour, well up, gush, spout; vomit, spew; bleed; flood; weep; sweat; seep, ooze

ADVERBS

26 **fluidly,** liquidly, fluently; runnily, juicily, moistly, succulently; purulently; weepily, tearfully; lacteally; sanguinely, sanguinarily; sweatily; oozily

556 Gas

NOUNS

1 **gas,** rare *or* inert *or* noble gas; air, atmosphere; vapor, volatile; compressible fluid, ether
   ▶ *Chemistry 11; Air 558*

2 **exhalation,** breath, expiration; effluvium

3 **miasma,** mephitis, malaria [Arch], fetid air, rank air fumes, reek; smoke, wisp *or* puff *or* plume of smoke, smog; poisonous gas, damp, blackdamp, afterdamp, chokedamp *or* firedamp
   ▶ *Odor 224*

4 **water vapor,** steam
   ▶ *Water 557*

5 **belch,** eructation; hiccup; flatulence, flatulency, flatus *or* gas, wind, windiness; burp [Inf], fart [Inf]
   ▶ *Expulsion 709*

6 **gaseousness,** gassiness, gaseity, gaseous state; fizziness, effervescence, fermentation; vaporousness, vaporosity, vaporiness, vapor; pressure

7 **volatility,** vaporability, vaporizability, evaporability
   ▶ *Lightness 539*

8 **aerialness,** aeriality, etherealism, ethereality

▶ *Lightness 539*

9 **vaporization,** evaporation, volatilization, gasification; aeration, etherification, aerification; sublimation; distillation, fractionation; atomization; exhalation; etherealization; steaming, smoking; fumigation

10 **vaporizer,** atomizer, spray, aerosol, aerosol spray; propellant, chlorofluorocarbon (CFC); condenser, retort, still

11 **aerostatics,** aerodynamics; pneumatostatics, pneumatics *or* pneumodynamics
   ▶ *Physics 10*

12 **gasworks,** gas plant, gas tank; gasolier, gaslight, gas lamp

13 **vaporimeter,** manometer, pressure gauge; gasometer, gas meter; aerometer, eudiometer; spirometer, pneumatometer

ADJECTIVES

14 **gaseous,** gaslike, gasiform, gassy, gasified, in the gaseous state; vaporous, vaporlike, vapory, vaporish

15 **airy,** aery, aerial, ethereal, atmospheric

16 **miasmic,** miasmal, miasmatic, mephitic, fetid, reeking; fumy, fuming, effluvial

17 **smoky,** smoking; smoggy; steamy, steaming, vaporing

18 **flatulent,** windy, gassy

19 **gassy,** fizzy, effervescent, bubbly, sparkling, carbonated, aerated

20 **aerostatic,** aerodynamic, pneumatic

21 **volatile,** volatilizable; vaporable, vaporific, vaporizable, vaporescent; evaporable, evaporative

22 **oxygenous,** oxygenic; ozonous, ozoniferous, ozonic

VERBS

23 **gasify,** evaporate, vaporize; volatilize, atomize; sublimate, sublime, distill, fractionate, etherify

24 **aerate,** aerify, etherize; carbonate, oxygenate, hydrogenate; atomize, spray, fumigate; fluidize

25 **give off,** emit, perfume; exhale, reek, fume, smoke, steam; let off *or* blow off steam, turn on the gas

ADVERBS

26 **aerily,** ethereally, atmospherically, vaporously

27 **aerostatically,** aerodynamically; pneumatically, pneumodynamically

28 **smokily,** steamily; effervescently, effervescingly

557 Water

For any ceremonial purposes the otherwise excellent liquid, water, is unsuitable in colour and other respects.
— A. P. HERBERT

NOUNS

1 **water,** H_2O, aqua, *eau* [Fr], Adam's ale *or* wine, fluid, liquid, moisture; heavy water (D_2O), distilled water, soft water, hard water, limewater; rain, rainwater, dew; running water, spring, fountain, spring water, well

water, hydrothermal water; fresh water, seawater, salt water, brine, briny; meltwater, ice, standing water
) *Meteorology and Climatology 9; Fluid 555; Moisture 559; Lakes 568; Rivers 570; Seas 571*

2 **drinking water,** tap water, bottled water; spa water, mineral water; soda water, carbonated water, fizzwater
) *Drinking 93*

3 **wateriness,** wet, wetness, wettishness, damp, dampness, runniness, moistness; raininess, rainfall; dewiness, condensation; vapor, water vapor; haze, mist, fog, cloud
) *Gas 556; Moisture 559*

4 **exudate,** exudation; tears, weeping; sweat, perspiration; saliva, spittle; urine, urination
) *Excretion 25; Fluid 555*

5 **dilution,** solution, adulteration, saturation, watering down

6 **hydrate,** hydration; hydrolysis; wetting agent

7 **hydrotherapy** or **hydrotherapeutics,** hydropathy, water cure, taking the waters
) *Remedy 115*

8 **watering,** irrigation, wetting, hosing, hosing down, sprinkling, spraying, squirting, sparging; splashing, spattering, swashing; affusion, aspersion
) *Dispersion 776*

9 **soaking,** soakage, soak, drenching, drench, sousing, souse; drowning, flooding, inundation; immersion, submersion, ducking, dunking; imbruement, saturation, permeation, impregnation; percolation, leaching, lixiviation
) *Fluid 555*

10 **steeping,** infusion, brewing, maceration, seething, infiltration; pulping

11 **washing,** rinsing, bathing, showering, hot-tubbing
) *Cleanliness 111*

12 **sprinkler,** watering can, nozzle, sparger, sprayer, spray; aspergillum; sprinkling system, sprinkler head; aerosol, atomizer, vaporizer; water pistol or gun, squirt gun
) *Tool 103*

13 **irrigator,** well, oasis; water supply, waterworks, conduit, hydrant, water pipe, tap, garden hose; standpipe, pump, fire engine; shadoof or shaduf, Archimedes' screw
) *Agriculture 16; Horticulture 17*

14 **lavender water,** rose water
) *Fragrance 226*

15 **holy water,** baptism, christening, immersion, religious rite; hydromancy
) *Religious Ritual 85*

16 **water carrier,** water cart, watering cart; water jug, ewer, pitcher, jug, water bouget [Arch]; reservoir, dam; cistern, water tank

) *Container 578*

17 **water cycle,** hydrologic cycle, hydrosphere, hydrometeor; head, hydrostatic head, head of pressure

18 **hydrography,** hydrology; hydrometry, hygrometry; hydrodynamics or hydromechanics, hydraulics, hydrokinetics, hydrostatics; hydroponics, aquiculture
) *Physics 10; Horticulture 17*

19 **measuring instrument,** hygrometer, hygrograph, hygroscope, hygrothermograph; psychrometer, wet-bulb thermometer, dry-bulb thermometer, sling psychrometer; hydrostat; rain gauge or pluviometer; hydrograph; weather station
) *Measurement 589*

20 **hydrologist,** hydrographer; waterfinder, dowser

ADJECTIVES

21 **watery,** waterish, fluid, liquid, aqueous, aquatic; moist, hydrous, hydrated; hydrodynamic, hydraulic, hydrostatic; hydrometric

22 **diluted,** watered-down, thinned, adulterated, weak
) *Thinness 595*

23 **wet,** soaked, soused, drenched; soaking wet, soaked to the skin, like a drowned rat; sodden, soggy, wringing, wringing wet, sopping, sopping wet; saturated, waterlogged, water-soaked; streaming, dripping, dripping wet; bathed, steeped

24 **flooded,** overflowed, awash, swamped, inundated, whelmed, engulfed; deluged, drowned, submerged, submersed; immersed, dipped, ducked, dunked; weltering

25 **seeping,** weeping, oozing, dribbling, dripping

26 **wetting,** watering, moistening, dampening; humectant; irrigational, irriguous [Arch]

27 **cleansing,** hydrotherapeutic

28 **hygric,** hygrometric, hygroscopic; hygrophilous; hygrothermal

VERBS

29 **water,** hydrate, irrigate, sprinkle, rain, pour, shower, moisten, wet; soak, water-soak, drench, douse, souse; drown, immerse, submerse; imbrue, permeate, saturate, impregnate, infiltrate, waterlog; percolate, leach, lixiviate; flood, inundate, deluge, swamp, submerge, duck, dunk; sluice; rain cats and dogs [Inf]
) *Meteorology and Climatology 9; Moisture 559*

30 **dilute,** water down, add water, thin, adulterate, cut; dissolve

31 **steep,** infuse, imbue; macerate, pickle, brine; seethe; injest

32 **sprinkle,** spray, sparge; mist, atomize; splash, slop, splatter; spatter, bespatter

33 **hose,** hose down, squirt; wash, rinse
) *Cleanliness 111*

ADVERBS

34 **wetly,** moistly, damply; fluidly or fluidally, liquidly; weepily, runnily, oozily

35 **hydrodynamically,** hydraulically, hydrostatically; hydrometrically; hydroscopically

558 Air

This most excellent canopy, the air, look you, this brave o'erhanging firmament, this majestic roof fretted with golden fire. — WILLIAM SHAKESPEARE

NOUNS

1 **air,** ether, atmosphere; oxygen, nitrogen, gas; thin air, rarity; air space, gaseous medium *or* environment *or* envelope; sky, blue sky, the heavens, welkin, ozone
   ▶ *Gas 556*

2 **aerosphere,** ecosphere, biosphere, noosphere, anthroposphere

3 **atmospheric layer,** troposphere, substratosphere, tropopause; stratosphere, ozonosphere; chemosphere; mesosphere; thermosphere, ionosphere, D layer *or* region, E *or* Heaviside *or* Kennelly–Heaviside layer *or* region, F_1 layer *or* region, F_2 *or* Appleton layer *or* region; exosphere, magnetosphere, Van Allen radiation belt; lower atmosphere, upper atmosphere, outer atmosphere, stratum, layer, belt
   ▶ *Meteorology and Climatology 9*

4 **airflow,** wind, breeze, gust, blast; air current, current of air, jet stream, updraft, downdraft, crosscurrent; monsoon, roaring forties
   ▶ *Meteorology and Climatology 9; Ascent 713; Descent 714*

5 **open air,** fresh air, ozone, outdoors, exposure, the great outdoors; sea air

6 **ventilation,** airing, fanning, aeration, cross ventilation; air conditioning, air cooling; oxygenation *or* oxygenization
   ▶ *Cold 218*

7 **ventilator,** aerator, fan, blower; air conditioner, air filter; ventilating system, air passage

8 **respiration,** breathing, inhalation, inspiration, exhalation, expiration; airflow, windpipe, trachea, bronchus, bronchiole; exchange of gases; respiratory organ, lung, alveoli, gills

9 **airiness,** lightness, weightlessness, buoyancy, ethereality
   ▶ *Lightness 539*

10 **air bubble,** froth, foam, fluff; sponge; lather, suds; spray, spume, spindrift; cushion of air, air pocket; soufflé, mousse, meringue; balloon, air balloon, air bladder

11 **aeration,** fermentation, leavening
   ▶ *Lightness 539*

ADJECTIVES

12 **airy,** aery, aerial, aeriform; aeriferous; airlike, ethereal; insubstantial, light, lighter-than-air, weightless; exposed, roomy; rare, rarefied, thin

13 **atmospheric,** tropospheric, stratospheric, mesospheric, thermospheric, exospheric

14 **aerial,** buoyant; inflated, blown-up; flatulent; pneumatic

15 **breezy,** windy, blowy, fresh, gusty

16 **open-air,** outdoor, out-of-door, alfresco

17 **ventilated,** well-ventilated, fresh; fanned; air-conditioned, cooled, air-cooled

18 **bubbly,** foamy, frothy, fizzy, effervescent; aerated, yeasty

19 **respiratory,** breathing, respiring, inhaling, exhaling; bronchial, pulmonary, pneumonic

VERBS

20 **aerate,** aerify, oxygenate; air, ventilate, expose, freshen; air-condition, air-cool

21 **respire,** breathe; breathe in, inhale, inspire; breathe out, exhale, expire

22 **blow,** blast, gust; huff, puff; make a draft, fan

23 **whisk,** whip, beat, aerate, leaven

24 **bubble,** froth, foam, fizz, effervesce, sparkle; ferment, gurgle; simmer

ADVERBS

25 **airily,** lightly, frothily, effervescently, effervescingly; atmospherically; pneumatically

26 **out-of-doors,** outside, in the open, in the open air, alfresco; under the open sky, in the sun; abroad, *en plein air* [Fr]

559 Moisture

NOUNS

1 **moisture,** moistness, dampness; wetness, wettishness, wateriness
   ▶ *Fluid 555; Water 557*

2 **mistiness,** fogginess, fog, fog band, cloud; rain, raininess, rainfall, pluviosity, showeriness; Scotch mist, drizzle, mizzle, wet weather
   ▶ *Meteorology and Climatology 9*

3 **humidity,** humidness, dankness, dankishness, mugginess, stickiness, clamminess, closeness; absolute humidity, relative humidity; dew point, saturation, saturation point

4 **seepage,** percolation, permeation, rising damp, wet rot

5 **sprinkle,** sprinkling, spraying, hosing, sparge; aspersion; splash, spatter, splatter, affusion
   ▶ *Water 557; Dispersion 776*

6 **dew,** dewdrops, night dew, dawn dew, evening damp; fog drip; guttation

7 **bogginess,** swampiness, marshiness; muddiness; dewiness

8 **marsh,** swamp, fen, bog, quagmire; wetlands, salt marsh, flood plain; quicksand; mud, slime, ooze, mire, sludge, slush
   ▶ *Viscosity 561; Lowness 597*

ADJECTIVES

9 moist, damp, wet; moistful, dampish, wettish; humid, clammy, sticky, muggy; close, dank, tacky; humectant

10 misty, foggy, cloudy; watery, rainy, showery; drizzling, drizzly, mizzly, dewy, bedewed

11 marshy, swampy, boggy, fenny; oozy, squashy, splashy, sludgy, slushy, muddy

12 seeping, dripping; percolating; splashed, spattered; weeping, tear-stained, tearful; dribbling, drivelling, drooling; sweating, perspiring
> *Water 557*

VERBS

13 moisten, dampen, wet, add water, humidify

14 sprinkle, spatter, splash, dabble, slosh; spray, hose; rain, drizzle, mizzle, mist, fog, dew

15 be moist, be damp, squelch, not have a dry thread *or* stitch

16 seep, drip, percolate, leak, ooze, trickle; shed tears, weep; sweat, perspire, exude; bleed; salivate, dribble, drool, slobber
> *Excretion 25; Water 557*

ADVERBS

17 moistly, wetly, succulently, damply; clammily, humidly, stickily; dankly, oozily

560 Dryness

NOUNS

1 dryness, aridness, aridity, siccity; parchedness, waterlessness, drought

2 thirst, thirstiness, drought [Arch], dryness; dehydration; xerostomia

3 drying, drying up, desiccation, exsiccation, dehydration; airing, air-drying, dehumidification; withering, fading, bleaching, searing, mummification; insolation, sunning; blotting

4 desert, barren land, badlands, dust bowl, salt flat, wasteland
> *Other Geographical Features 572*

5 dryer *or* **drier,** absorbent, blotting paper, blotter; mop, sponge, swab, swabber; towel, toweling; desiccator, desiccative, siccative, exsiccative, exsiccator; dehydrator, dehydrant; dehumidifier; hair dryer; wringer, spin-dryer, clothes dryer, clotheshorse, clothesline

6 dry skin, xeroderma, ichthyosis; xerophthalmia

ADJECTIVES

7 dry, arid, waterless, moistureless; unwatered, unirrigated, unmoistened; needing water, undamped; anhydrous, droughty, high and dry

8 thirsty, thirsting, athirst, dry, dry as a bone, parched

9 dried-up, dried, dehydrated, desiccated, exsiccated; withered, shriveled, sere *or* sear; faded, wizened, parchmentlike, mummified; corky, juiceless, sapless; bone-dry, dry as a bone *or* dust *or* parchment *or* a stick *or* a biscuit *or* a mummy

10 dried-out, drained, evaporated, squeezed dry

11 rainless, fair, hot, sunny, fine, cloudless, pleasant
> *Meteorology and Climatology 9*

12 desert, arid, Saharan; dusty, powdery, sandy; barren, bare, brown, grassless
> *Crumbliness, Powderiness 553; Other Geographical Features 572*

13 adapted to drought, xerophilous, xerophytic, xeromorphic

14 baked, parched, sun-dried, sunbaked; burnt, scorched; bleached, sunned, insolated; aired, wind-dried, air-dried
> *Heat 217*

15 drying, desiccative, desiccant; dehydrating, exsiccative, exsiccant; siccative, siccant; evaporative

16 waterproof, protected from wet, waterproofed; proof, moisture-proof, rainproof, stormproof, flood-proof, showerproof, dampproof; leakproof, watertight, snug; dry-shod

VERBS

17 dry, become dry, dry up, dry off; dry out, dehydrate; drain, evaporate, vaporize; desiccate, exsiccate; freeze-dry; dehumidify; air-dry, wind-dry; smoke, smoke-dry, kipper, cure; drip-dry, spin-dry, tumble-dry; wring; hang out to dry, hang out, air

18 thirst, be thirsty, thirst for; parch

19 bake, sun, expose to sunlight, insolate, sun-dry; toast, roast, scorch, bleach, burn; fire, kiln, torrefy

20 absorb, drink up, soak up, blot, blot up; mop, mop up, swab; wipe, wipe up, wipe dry, sponge, towel

21 dry up, parch, wither, shrivel, wilt, wizen; mummify, preserve

22 keep dry, keep watertight, waterproof; hold off the wet

ADVERBS

23 dryly *or* **drily,** aridly; thirstily; dustily; xerically, xerophytically

561 Viscosity

NOUNS

1 viscosity, viscidity, viscousness; thickening, coagulation, curdling, clotting; inspissation, incrassation; colloidality, emulsification; stickiness, tackiness, glueyness, adhesiveness; glutinousness, glutinosity, gumminess, mucilaginousness; semiliquidity, semifluidity, syrupiness; gelatinousness, jellylikeness, jellification, gelation, gelatinity; clabbering, lobbering *or* loppering

2 doughiness, pastiness, clamminess; ropiness, stringiness, toughness, tenacity, tenaciousness; gooeyness [Inf]
> *Toughness 547; Thickness 594; Adhesion 755*

3 adhesive, glue, gluten; wax, beeswax; gum, chewing gum, bubble gum, chicle *or* chicle gum; guar gum, mastic, resin, birdlime; tar

▶ *Adhesion 755*

4 **paste,** putty; size, gluten, egg white, albumen; glair, slip, glaze; poultice, cataplasm, plaster

5 **emulsion,** emulsoid, colloid; semiliquid, semifluid

6 **mucus,** mucilage, phlegm; clot, grume; gore, pus, matter, snot [Inf]

▶ *Excretion 25; Fluid 555*

7 **semiliquid,** gelatin *or* gelatine, gel, agar, isinglass; aspic, jelly, jam; syrup, honey, molasses; soup, gumbo, gravy, gruel, loblolly, porridge; pulp, purée, pap, mush, mash, squash; dough; clabber, bonnyclabber, curd; batter, paste, mousse, fool, pudding, pith; butter, cream, crème fraîche; junket, yogurt *or* yoghurt *or* yoghourt

▶ *Food 90*

8 **mud,** slush, slosh, muck, sludge, slop, swill; slough, ooze, slime, mire; silt, clay, lava, ash, slip, sediment; grounds, coffee grounds, dregs, lees; [Inf]: goo, gunk, gook, glop, guck

▶ *Moisture 559*

9 **pulpiness,** pulpousness, softness, sponginess; pithiness, squashiness; thickness, heaviness, stodginess; mushiness, mashiness, flabbiness; creaminess, butteriness; fleshiness, overripeness

▶ *Heaviness 538; Softness 543; Fluid 555; Thickness 594*

10 **muddiness,** slushiness, sloshiness, sloppiness; ooziness, miriness, turbidity, turbidness

11 **pulping,** blending, steeping; maceration, mastication; digestion

▶ *Eating 92*

12 **thickener,** starch, flour, cornstarch; rennet, curdler; emulsifier, colloider

13 **pulper,** macerator, blender, food processor, food mill, ricer, masher, beetle

ADJECTIVES

14 **viscous,** viscose, viscid; inspissate, incrassate; glutenous; colloidal, emulsive; gumbo, gumbolike, gummy, gummous, gumlike, waxy; gory, slimy, clammy, ropy, stringy, tough; gooey [Inf], gunky [Inf]

15 **mucilaginous,** adhesive, sticky, pasty, tacky, glutinous, gluey, gluelike

16 **gelatinous,** gelled; jellylike, jellied, jelled, syrupy, jammy

17 **thick,** thickened; coagulated, curdled, clabbered, loppered, clotted; mucous, pussy; snotty [Inf]; stodgy, heavy, lumpy

18 **sludgy,** miry, turbid, dirty, marshy; semiliquid, semifluid; muddy, slushy, sloshy, squelchy, sloppy, oozy; silty, sedimentary

19 **pulpy,** soft, fleshy, sappy, overripe, spongy, doughy, pasty; squashy, stodgy, mushy, flabby; creamy, buttery; soupy, starchy, amylaceous

VERBS

20 **stick,** glue, gum, paste, adhere, gum up [Inf]

▶ *Adhesion 755*

21 **thicken,** gelatinize *or* gelatinate, gel, jell, jellify, jelly; emulsify, curdle, clot, coagulate, congeal, clabber, lopper; churn, whip; incrassate, inspissate

▶ *Thickness 594*

ADVERBS

22 **viscously,** viscidly, gelatinously, thickly; mucilaginously, adhesively, stickily, tackily; tenaciously

23 **slimily,** oozily, slushily, sloppily

562 Oiliness, Lubrication

NOUNS

1 **oiliness,** greasiness, waxiness, unctuousness, unctuosity, lubricity; fatness, fattiness, pinguidity, sebaceousness; adiposis, adiposity; richness, creaminess, butteriness; soapiness, saponaceousness

▶ *Fluid 555; Viscosity 561*

2 **lubrication,** nonfriction, lubricating, oiling, greasing; smoothness, slickness, sleekness, slipperiness, lubricity; lube [Inf]

▶ *Smoothness 545; Nonadhesion 756*

3 **oil,** oleum, mineral oil, fuel oil, vegetable oil, animal oil; fixed oil *or* fatty oil, nonvolatile oil; volatile oil, essential oil; glycerol, wax; drying oil, nondrying oil

▶ *Chemistry 11; Engineering 14*

4 **fat,** adipocere; ester, tallow, animal fat, suet, blubber, lanolin, sebum, wax; saturated fat, unsaturated fat, polyunsaturated fat, hydrogenated fat; soap, carbolic soap, washing soap, scented soap, soap flakes, soap powder; shortening, butter, margarine; cream, light cream, heavy cream, whipping cream, top of the milk, buttermilk; clotted cream, double cream, triple cream

▶ *Food 90; Cleanliness 111*

5 **petroleum,** fossil oil, rock oil, shale oil, coal oil; fuel oil, crude oil *or* crude petroleum; gasoline *or* gas, premium *or* high-test *or* high-octane gas, leaded gas, leadfree gas, regular gas *or* regular, white gas; kerosene, paraffin; diesel fuel *or* oil, motor oil

▶ *Chemistry 11*

6 **resin,** rosin, gum rosin, resinoid, resene, resinate; gum(s), gum resin; oleoresin; tar, bitumen, asphalt; varnish, japan; synthetic resin, hard resin, acaroid resin, coumarone resin; fossil resin, amber; lac, vegetable resin; plastic

7 **lubricant,** lubricator, lubricating oil, lubricating agent, grease, antifriction; graphite *or* black lead *or* plumbago; glycerin *or* glycerine, silicone, wax; mucilage; mucus, spit, spittle, synovia, saliva; soap, lather

▶ *Fluid 555; Viscosity 561*

8 **ointment,** unguent, salve, balm, lotion, cream; spikenard, nard; embrocation, liniment, emollient, lenitive, demulcent; unguent, unguentum, inunction, unction, balsam, chrism *or* chrisom

▶ *Remedy 115*

9 **pomade,** pomatum, brilliantine, hair oil, Macassar oil; hair conditioner, setting lotion, styling mousse, styling gel; cleanser, cold cream; face cream, hand cream *or* lotion, lanolin; eyewash *or* collyrium

▶ *Cleanliness 111; Beautification 530*

10 **lubricator,** oilcan, grease gun

▶ *Tool 103*

ADJECTIVES

11 **oily,** greasy, unctuous, unctional, unguinous, chrismal, oleaginous; oleic, fat, fatty, sebaceous, fleshy, adipose, pinguid; blubbery, tallowy, suety, lardy, lardaceous; rich, creamy, buttery, butyric, butyraceous, milky; paraffinic, waxy, waxen, cereous, cerated; soapy, saponaceous; mucoid, smooth, slick, slippery, slithery, sleek, slimy

12 **lubricational,** lubricating, lubricative, lubricatory, lubricity; lenitive, unguentary, emollient, soothing, moisturizing

13 **resinous,** resiny, resinlike, rosiny, resinoid, resiniferous; bituminous, pitchy, tarry, asphaltic; varnished, japanned; myrrhic, masticic, gummy, gummous, gumlike

14 **lubricated,** well-oiled, well-greased, smooth-running; slippery, oily, greasy, basted; oiled, greased

VERBS

15 **lubricate,** oil, grease, wax, beeswax; soap, lather; spread, baste, butter, cream, lard; glycerinate; moisten, smooth

16 **resinify,** resin, rosin, resinate

17 **anoint,** salve, embrocate, dress; pour oil *or* balm on, smear, daub, slick, slick on, pomade

18 **ease,** smooth over, smooth the way, soap, oil *or* grease the wheels, pour oil on troubled waters

ADVERBS

19 **oilily,** greasily, unctuously, pinguidly; resinously; richly, creamily; soapily; smoothly, slickly, sleekly, moistly

563 Space

Outer space is no place for a person of breeding.
— VIOLET BONHAM CARTER

Space isn't remote at all. It's only an hour's drive away if your car could go straight upwards. — FRED HOYLE

Space – the final frontier. — GENE RODDENBERRY

NOUNS

1 **space,** expanse, expansion, extent, extension, spatial extension, measure, dimensions, proportions, size, length, breadth, width, height, depth, depth of space, surface, area, diameter, circumference, tract, volume, cubic content, capacity
  ▶ *Expansion 581; Distance 585; Measurement 589; Length 590; Depth 598; Quantity 738*

2 **empty space,** emptiness, void, vacuum, nothingness, infinite space, infinity, unlimited space, sky, heavens, aerospace, air space, outer space, interplanetary space, interstellar space, intergalactic space
  ▶ *Astronomy, Astronautics, and Rocketry 7; Nonmaterial World 525; Infinity 798*

3 **geographical space,** region, open space, clear space, clearing, field, glade, open country, wide-open space, wide horizons, expanse, stretch, tract, reach, greenbelt, hinterland, grassland, prairie, steppe, veld, plain, upland, moorland, back country, outback [Aus], wild, wilderness, waste, desert, back o' beyond [Aus inf]
  ▶ *Region 564; Location 565*

4 **spaciousness,** roominess, extensiveness, expansiveness, capaciousness, voluminousness, vastness, immensity
  ▶ *Size, Largeness 579*

5 **reserved space,** room, accommodation, capacity, stowage, storage, storage space, seating capacity, seating, standing room, berthage, place, seat, berth, parking space

6 **available space,** room, latitude, leeway, scope, swing, play, margin, clearance, windage, amplitude, headroom, room overhead, headway, elbowroom, legroom, room to spare, sea room, seaway, air space, breathing space, living space, Lebensraum, turning space, room to maneuver, room to swing a cat
  ▶ *Container 578*

7 **range,** reach, coverage, scope, compass, radius, sweep, stretch, grasp, sphere, field, area, gamut, spectrum, array
  ▶ *Region 564; Limit 620*

8 **intervening space,** distance, interval, gap, remove, break, hiatus, lacuna, blank, pause, interruption, intermission, lapse, time lapse, while, duration, span, spell, stretch, period, turn
  ▶ *Distance 585; Interval 587; Time 639; Period 641; Duration 642; Separation 753*

9 **fourth dimension,** space-time, time-space, space-time continuum, continuum, relativity, Einstein theory, general theory of relativity
  ▶ *Physics 10; Time 639*

10 **space traveler,** spaceman, spacewoman, astronaut, cosmonaut, rocket pilot, astronavigator
  ▶ *Astronomy, Astronautics, and Rocketry 7*

ADJECTIVES

11 **spatial,** spacial, space, dimensional, proportional, two-dimensional, surface, radial, superficial, flat, three-dimensional, cubic, volumetric, stereoscopic, fourth-dimensional, space-time, spatiotemporal

12 **extensive,** regional, widespread, far-reaching, wide-ranging, far-flung, global, worldwide, interstellar, intergalactic, universal, boundless, infinite, unconfined, uncircumscribed, unrestricted

13 **spacious,** roomy, airy, lofty, capacious, voluminous, commodious, cavernous, sizeable, ample, vast, great, immense, enormous, outsized, oversized, expansive, extended, long, broad, wide, deep, high, amplitudinous
  ▶ *Air 558; Size, Largeness 579*

14 extend, expand, lengthen, widen, dilate, distend, deepen, raise, spread out, spread, range, sweep, reach, stretch, cover, encompass, span, straddle, enclose, surround, environ, contain, hold
▶ *Enclosure 619*

15 space, space out, spread out, place at intervals, organize, empty, make room for, order, rank, array, lay out, set out, measure out, proportion, time, mark time, pause, wait, break, lapse, omit, leave out
▶ *Order 765; Arrangement 767*

ADVERBS

16 spatially, spatiotemporally, three-dimensionally

17 spaciously, sizably, amply, voluminously, capaciously, immensely, vastly, deeply, expansively, spatially, spatiotemporally, three-dimensionally

18 extensively, widely, everywhere, globally, universally, intergalactically; here, there, and everywhere; in every place, in all places, in every quarter, in all lands, in all areas, the (whole) world over, throughout the world, on the face of the earth, under the sun, high and low, upstairs and downstairs, near and far, far and wide, inside and out, in every nook and cranny, all around the globe, all around, all over, all over the map, every which way

19 from end to end, from pole to pole, from edge to edge, from coast to coast, from sea to sea; from top to bottom, from north to south, from Land's End to John O'Groat's [Brit], from here to the back o' beyond [Aus inf]

20 from everywhere, from the four corners of the earth *or* world, from every place, from the farthest corners of the earth *or* world, from all points of the compass

21 to all places, to the four winds, to the ends of the earth *or* world, to hell and back

564 Region

NOUNS

1 region, area, territory, territoriality, terrain, zone, belt, section, sector, neighborhood, vicinity, purlieu, place, space, ground, soil, land, heartland, hinterland; plot, patch, field, pale, arena; air space, continental shelf; district, quarter, department, division, salient; nation, nation-state, country, state, republic, kingdom, realm, domain, principality, sultanate, dominion, protectorate, mandate, possession, colony, dependency, empire; sphere, hemisphere, orbit, circle, ambit, round
▶ *Government 49; Politics 50; Country 566*

2 regions, highlands, lowlands, borders, borderland, march, panhandle, corridor, countryside, greenbelt, heartland, provinces, environs, backwater, backwoods, boondocks, outpost, wilderness, wasteland; the sticks [Inf], boonies [Inf]

3 countryside, farm country, farmland, the country, the soil, grass roots, the bush, hinterland, back country, outback [Aus], savannah, plain, prairie, steppe, veld *or* veldt, wide-open spaces
▶ *Other Geographical Features 572*

4 administrative region, country, state, territory, province, metropolitan area, city, town, township, borough, county, shire, division, district, constituency, ward, precinct; canton, duchy, *département, arrondissement* [Fr], eparchy, prefecture, *Kreis, Land* [Ger], oblast, commune, riding, bailiwick; parish, diocese, archdiocese, bishopric, archbishopric
▶ *Government 49; Authority 52; Cities, Towns, and Villages 567; Enclosure 619*

5 administrative headquarters, headquarters (HQ), administrative center, station, seat of government, capital, county seat

---

AMERICAN STATES AND OTHER AREAS, WITH CAPITAL CITIES

States
Alabama (Montgomery)
Alaska (Juneau)
Arizona (Phoenix)
Arkansas (Little Rock)
California (Sacramento)
Colorado (Denver)
Connecticut (Hartford)
Delaware (Dover)
Florida (Tallahassee)
Georgia (Atlanta)
Hawaii (Honolulu)
Idaho (Boise)
Illinois (Springfield)
Indiana (Indianapolis)
Iowa (Des Moines)

Kansas (Topeka)
Kentucky (Frankfort)
Louisiana (Baton Rouge)
Maine (Augusta)
Maryland (Annapolis)
Massachusetts (Boston)
Michigan (Lansing)
Minnesota (St. Paul)
Mississippi (Jackson)
Missouri (Jefferson City)
Montana (Helena)
Nebraska (Lincoln)
Nevada (Carson City)
New Hampshire (Concord)
New Jersey (Trenton)
New Mexico (Santa Fe)

New York (Albany)
North Carolina (Raleigh)
North Dakota (Bismarck)
Ohio (Columbus)
Oklahoma (Oklahoma City)
Oregon (Salem)
Pennsylvania (Harrisburg)
Rhode Island (Providence)
South Carolina (Columbia)
South Dakota (Pierre)
Tennessee (Nashville)
Texas (Austin)
Utah (Salt Lake City)
Vermont (Montpelier)
Virginia (Richmond)
Washington (Olympia)

West Virginia (Charleston)
Wisconsin (Madison)
Wyoming (Cheyenne)

Other Areas
American Samoa (Pago Pago)
Guam (Agaña)
Northern Mariana Islands, Commonwealth of the
Puerto Rico, Commonwealth of (San Juan)
Virgin Islands of the United States (Charlotte Amalie)

CANADIAN PROVINCES AND TERRITORIES, WITH CAPITAL CITIES

Alberta (Edmonton)
British Columbia (Victoria)
Manitoba (Winnipeg)
New Brunswick (Fredericton)
Newfoundland (St. John's)
Northwest Territories (Yellowknife)

Nova Scotia (Halifax)
Ontario (Toronto)
Prince Edward Island (Charlottetown)
Québec (Québec)
Saskatchewan (Regina)
Yukon Territory (Whitehorse)

▶ *Habitat 60; Plan 387; Cities, Towns, and Villages 567*

6 **world region,** zone, clime, tropics, subtropics, doldrums, Torrid Zone, horse latitudes, Temperate Zone, roaring forties, Arctic, Antarctica; Old World, New World, America, North America, Northern Hemisphere, Southern Hemisphere, South America, Latin America, Eastern Hemisphere, Orient, Far East, Western Hemisphere, Occident; Levant, Middle East *or* Mideast, Eurasia, Asia Minor, Africa; Australia, Australasia, antipodes, Oceania, down under [Inf]; Third World, developed world, undeveloped world, underdeveloped world; continent, landmass

▶ *Location 565; Country 566*

7 **regions of the United States,** West, Far West, West Coast, Southern California, Sunbelt, Silicon Valley, Northwest, Pacific Northwest; the Sierras, the Rockies, Rocky Mountain states, Southwest; Middle West *or* Midwest, Middle America, Great Plains, heartland, Plains states, Rust Belt; East, East Coast, Down East, Eastern Seaboard, New England, Northeast, Yankeeland; Appalachia, South, Southeast, Southland, Dixie *or* Dixieland, Deep South, the Old South, the Delta, bayous, Gulf Coast; Bible Belt, borscht belt, Chautauqua Circuit

8 **regions of the British Isles,** Home Counties, Midlands, Lake District *or* Country, the Borders, the Fens, the West Country, the Broads, the Marches, the Mendips, the Pennines, the Black Country, the Potteries, the Peak District, the Weald, the Fylde; Highlands, Lowlands, Hebrides

9 **plot,** plot of ground *or* land, parcel, enclosure, patch, lot acreage, block, square, section, quadrangle, tract, allotment, holding, claim; locality, locale, neighborhood, vicinity, haunt, beat, walk; backyard, stamping ground; neck of the woods [Inf], turf [Inf]

10 **sphere,** field, arena, province, ambit, orbit, theater, jurisdiction, scope, realm, domain, bailiwick, forte, métier

11 **regionalism,** provincialism, parochialism, nationalism

ADJECTIVES

12 **regional,** areal, spatial *or* spacial, geographical, topographic *or* topographical, territorial, zonal, highland, lowland, peninsular, insular, tropical, subtropical, continental, eastern, western, northern, southern, Occidental, Oriental, antipodean

13 **administrative,** divisional, governmental, departmental, constituent, metropolitan, municipal, county, district, provincial, rural, territorial, colonial, national, parochial, diocesan

14 **local,** localized, next-door, neighboring, nearby, insular, confined, limited, back-country, backwoods, small-town, suburban, exurban, rural, countrified, rustic, grass-roots

VERBS

15 **regionalize,** organize, administer, govern, have jurisdiction, survey, countrify

ADVERBS

16 **regionally,** geographically, spatially, territorially, nationally, continentally, tropically, subtropically, provincially, municipally, locally, nearby, colonially, rurally, rustically

565 Location

NOUNS

1 **location,** locality, situation, place, site, position, whereabouts, locale, spot, setting, environs, environment, habitat, parts, haunt, patch, pitch, beat, territory, seat, station, post, base, stamping ground; [Inf]: neck of the woods, hole, turf

▶ *Habitat 60; Region 564; Situation 573; Surroundings 615*

2 **exact location,** spot, point, pinpoint, dot, benchmark, grid reference, map reference, coordinates, bearings, compass direction; latitude, parallel, longitude, meridian, prime meridian, declination, chart, map, plan, address, postal address, postal district, zip code

▶ *Address 209; Plan 387*

3 **locating,** pinpointing, finding the spot *or* place, homing in on, finding, discovering, detecting, unearthing, running to earth, laying one's hands *or* fingers on, turning up, tracking down, pinning down, coming across, chancing upon, hitting on

▶ *Discovery 345; Uncovering 614*

4 **placing,** locating, situating, siting, placement, emplacement, establishment, installation, settling, fixation, fixing, posting, stationing

5 **topography,** geography, cartography, chorography, surveying, triangulation, navigation, orienteering, geodesy

▶ *Geology 8; Region 564; Measurement 589*

ADJECTIVES

6 **located,** situated, placed, positioned, sited, set, stationed, posted, established, installed, settled, fixed, emplaced, planted, ensconced

7 found, located, locatable, discovered, pinpointed, detected, unearthed, tracked down, pinned down

8 locational, situated, positional, topographical, geographical, cartographical, navigational, geodetic, surveyed

VERBS

9 locate, situate, place, site, position, emplace, put, put in place, install *or* instal, establish, set up, plant, ensconce, station, post, billet, quarter, base, fix, spot, stick

10 settle, take up residence, establish residence, move in, ensconce oneself, stay at, inhabit, dwell, reside in, locate, relocate, change address, move

  ▸ *Inhabitant 61; Displacement 574*

11 find, find the spot, pinpoint, zero in on, home in on, discover, detect, unearth, run to earth, lay one's hands *or* fingers on, turn up, track down, pin down, come across, chance upon *or* on, hit upon *or* on, get a fix, get a bearing, calculate *or* fix one's position, navigate, survey, triangulate

  ▸ *Calculation 784*

ADVERBS

12 where, whereabouts, whither, here, hereat, hereabouts, just here, on this spot, at this point, in the vicinity *or* neighborhood, in place, in situ, *in loco* [L], on location, on site, on the spot, there, thereat, in that place, thereabouts, thither, to that place, here and there, in places, in spots, *passim* [L]

13 topographically, geographically, cartographically, geodetically

566 Country

Our country is the world – our countrymen are all mankind. — WILLIAM LLOYD GARRISON

NOUNS

1 country, nation, nationhood, state, statehood, land, body politic, nation-state, sovereign state *or* nation, self-governing state, independent state, free country *or* nation, democracy, dictatorship, oligarchy, monarchy, republic, capitalist country, socialist country, communist country; power, superpower, third-world country, nonaligned *or* unaligned country *or* nation, neutral nation, isolationist nation

2 union of nations, federation, confederation, commonwealth, commonweal, bloc, comity, United Nations

  ▸ *Government 49; Politics 50; Region 564; Union 752*

3 dominion, sovereignty, domain, realm, kingdom, empire; principality, principate, duchy, dukedom, grand duchy, archduchy, archdukedom, earldom, palatinate, sultanate, chieftaincy; city-state, province, territory, occupied country, colony, settlement, protectorate, mandate *or* mandated territory, mandatary, captive nation, buffer state, ally, satellite nation, puppet regime, sphere of influence; imperialism, colonialism

  ▸ *Authority 52; Command 425; Rule 780; Subjection 832*

4 nationalism, nationality, national consciousness, patriotism, chauvinism, jingoism, ultranationalism, isolationism, protectionism, xenophobia, racism

---

COUNTRIES WITH CAPITAL CITIES

Afghanistan (Kabul)
Albania (Tiranë)
Algeria (Algiers)
Andorra (Andorra la Vella)
Angola (Luanda)
Antigua and Barbuda (St. John's)
Argentina (Buenos Aires)
Armenia (Yerevan)
Australia (Canberra)
Austria (Vienna)
Azerbaijan (Baku)
Bahamas, The (Nassau)
Bahrain (Manama)
Bangladesh (Dhaka)
Barbados (Bridgetown)
Belarus (Minsk)
Belgium (Brussels)
Belize (Belmopan)
Benin (Porto-Novo)
Bhutan (Thimphu)
Bolivia (La Paz, Sucre)

Bosnia and Herzegovina (Sarajevo)
Botswana (Gaborone)
Brazil (Brasília)
Brunei Darussalam (Bandar Seri Begawan)
Bulgaria (Sofia)
Burkina Faso (Ouagadougou)
Burma. *See* Myanmar
Burundi (Bujumbura)
Cambodia (Phnom Penh)
Cameroon (Yaoundé)
Canada (Ottawa)
Cape Verde (Praia)
Central African Republic (Bangui)
Chad (N'Djamena)
Chile (Santiago)
China (Beijing)
Colombia (Bogotá)
Comoros (Moroni)
Congo (Brazzaville)
Costa Rica (San José)

Côte d'Ivoire (Yamoussoukro, Abidjan)
Croatia (Zagreb)
Cuba (Havana)
Cyprus (Nicosia)
Czech Republic (Prague)
Denmark (Copenhagen)
Djibouti (Djibouti)
Dominica (Roseau)
Dominican Republic (Santo Domingo)
Ecuador (Quito)
Egypt (Cairo)
El Salvador (San Salvador)
Equatorial Guinea (Malabo)
Eritrea (Asmera)
Estonia (Tallinn)
Ethiopia (Addis Ababa)
Fiji (Suva)
Finland (Helsinki)
France (Paris)
Gabon (Libreville)
Gambia, The (Banjul)

Georgia (Tbilisi)
Germany (Berlin)
Ghana (Accra)
Greece (Athens)
Grenada (St. George's)
Guatemala (Guatemala City)
Guinea (Conakry)
Guinea-Bissau (Bissau)
Guyana (Georgetown)
Haiti (Port-au-Prince)
Honduras (Tegucigalpa)
Hungary (Budapest)
Iceland (Reykjavik)
India (New Delhi)
Indonesia (Jakarta)
Iran (Tehran)
Iraq (Baghdad)
Ireland (Dublin)
Israel (Jerusalem)
Italy (Rome)
Jamaica (Kingston)
Japan (Tokyo)
Jordan (Amman)

Kazakhstan (Almaty)
Kenya (Nairobi)
Kiribati (Tarawa)
Kuwait (Kuwait City)
Kyrgyzstan (Bishkek)
Laos (Vientiane)
Latvia (Riga)
Lebanon (Beirut)
Lesotho (Maseru)
Liberia (Monrovia)
Libya (Tripoli)
Liechtenstein (Vaduz)
Lithuania (Vilnius)
Luxembourg (Luxembourg)
Macedonia (Skopje)
Madagascar (Antananarivo)
Malawi (Lilongwe)
Malaysia (Kuala Lumpur)
Maldives (Male)
Mali (Bamako)
Malta (Valletta)
Marshall Islands (Majuro)
Mauritania (Nouakchott)
Mauritius (Port Louis)
Mexico (Mexico City)
Micronesia (Palikir)
Moldova (Chisinau)
Monaco (Monaco)
Mongolia (Ulaanbaatar)
Morocco (Rabat)

Mozambique (Maputo)
Myanmar (Yangôn)
Namibia (Windhoek)
Nauru (Yaren)
Nepal (Kathmandu)
Netherlands, The (Amsterdam)
New Zealand (Wellington)
Nicaragua (Managua)
Niger (Niamey)
Nigeria (Abuja)
North Korea (Pyongyang)
Norway (Oslo)
Oman (Muscat)
Pakistan (Islamabad)
Panama (Panama City)
Papua New Guinea (Port Moresby)
Paraguay (Asunción)
Peru (Lima)
Philippines (Manila)
Poland (Warsaw)
Portugal (Lisbon)
Qatar (Doha)
Romania (Bucharest)
Russia (Moscow)
Rwanda (Kigali)
St. Kitts and Nevis (Basseterre)
St. Lucia (Castries)

St. Vincent and the Grenadines (Kingstown)
San Marino (San Marino)
São Tomé and Príncipe (São Tomé)
Saudi Arabia (Riyadh)
Senegal (Dakar)
Serbia (Belgrade)
Seychelles (Victoria)
Sierra Leone (Freetown)
Singapore (Singapore)
Slovakia (Bratislava)
Slovenia (Ljubljana)
Solomon Islands (Honiara)
Somalia (Mogadishu)
South Africa (Cape Town, Pretoria, Bloemfontein)
South Korea (Seoul)
South Yemen (Aden)
Spain (Madrid)
Sri Lanka (Colombo)
Sudan (Khartoum, Omdurman)
Suriname (Paramaribo)
Swaziland (Mbabane)
Sweden (Stockholm)
Switzerland (Bern, Lausanne)
Syria (Damascus)
Taiwan (Taipei)
Tajikistan (Dushanbe)

Tanzania (Dar es Salaam)
Thailand (Bangkok)
Togo (Lomé)
Tonga (Nuku'alofa)
Trinidad and Tobago (Port-of-Spain)
Tunisia (Tunis)
Turkey (Ankara)
Turkmenistan (Ashgabat)
Tuvalu (Funafuti)
Uganda (Kampala)
Ukraine (Kiev)
United Arab Emirates (Abu Dhabi)
United Kingdom (London)
United States of America (Washington, D.C.)
Uruguay (Montevideo)
Uzbekistan (Tashkent)
Vanuatu (Vila)
Venezuela (Caracas)
Vietnam (Hanoi)
Western Samoa (Apia)
Yemen or North Yemen (Sanaa)
Zaire (Kinshasa)
Zambia (Lusaka)
Zimbabwe (Harare)

▶ *Pride 297*

5 **internationalism,** internationality, global outlook, universality, universalism, cosmopolitanism

6 **native country,** native land, native soil, country of origin, mother country, motherland, fatherland, *Vaterland* [Ger], *patria* [L], land of our fathers, the old country, one's native ground, birthplace, cradle, home, homeland, home ground, God's country

▶ *Habitat 60*

7 **native,** countryman, countrywoman, citizen, national, local

▶ *Inhabitant 61*

8 **nationalist,** ultranationalist, colonialist, patriot, jingoist, isolationist, protectionist, xenophobe, racist

9 **internationalist,** universalist, cosmopolitan, citizen of the world

ADJECTIVES

10 **national,** federal, state, sovereign, self-governing, independent, self-determining, democratic, republican, welfare, socialist, socialistic, communist, communistic, capitalist, capitalistic, nonaligned *or* unaligned, international, imperialistic, colonial, mandated, buffer, satellite, puppet, nationalistic, ultranational, ultrana-

tionalistic, chauvinistic, jingoistic, isolationistic, protectionistic, xenophobic, gung-ho

VERBS

11 **become a nation,** become independent, declare independence, become self-governing, gain self-determination, have sovereignty; democratize, socialize, communize

12 **exert sovereignty,** rule, occupy, colonize, settle, mandate

ADVERBS

13 **nationally,** federally, independently, democratically, capitalistically, socialistically, communistically, internationally, imperialistically, colonially, nationalistically, patriotically, chauvinistically, jingoistically

567 Cities, Towns, and Villages

The little town that time forgot, that the decades cannot improve. — GARRISON KEILLOR

NOUNS

1 **city,** municipality, metropolis, metropolitan area, greater city, megalopolis, conurbation, urban complex, urban spread *or* sprawl, Standard Metropolitan Statis-

tical Area (SMSA); new city, garden city, cathedral city, industrial city, commercial city, sister city, twinned city [Brit]; seat of government, state capital, capital city, county seat

> *Government 49; Habitat 60; Part 760*

2 town, community, country town, borough, market town [Brit], new town, boom town, ghost town; county town [Brit]; *ville* [Fr]; burg [Inf]

3 village, hamlet, small town, crossroads, whistle stop, tank town, jumping-off place, one-horse town, hick town, Podunk; jerkwater town [Inf], rube town [Inf]

> *Littleness 580*

4 urbanization, gentrification, suburbanization, citifying

5 major US cities, New York, Los Angeles, Chicago, Washington, D.C., San Francisco, Philadelphia, Boston, Detroit, Dallas–Fort Worth, Houston, Miami, Seattle

6 New York, the Big Apple [Inf], Gotham, Greater New York; Manhattan, the Bronx, Queens, Brooklyn, Richmond *or* Staten Island; areas of Manhattan: the Bowery, Central Park, Chinatown, East Side, Greenwich Village, Harlem, Hell's Kitchen, Little Italy, SoHo, Times Square, Tribeca, Wall Street, West Side

7 major British cities, London, Birmingham, Glasgow, Leeds, Sheffield, Liverpool, Manchester, Edinburgh, Bradford, Belfast, Bristol, Cardiff

8 London, the Smoke, the Great Wen, Greater London; areas of London: Belgravia, Bloomsbury, Cheapside, the City *or* the Square Mile, Docklands, Earls Court, East End, Fleet Street, Hampstead, Highgate, Holborn, Hyde Park, the Inns of Court, the Isle of Dogs, Kensington, Knightsbridge, Lambeth, Mayfair, Paddington, Piccadilly Circus, Pimlico, Regents Park, Soho, Southwark, West End, Westminster

9 other famous world cities, Paris, Berlin, Rome, Madrid, Vienna, Budapest, Prague, Athens, Moscow, Calcutta, Hong Kong, Tokyo, Beijing, Rio de Janeiro

> *Country 566*

10 urban area, urban region, built-up area, urban sprawl, metropolitan area; district, quarter, precinct, ward; inner city, central city, city center, main street, high street [Brit]; block, square, market, marketplace, forum, agora; plaza, *piazza* [Ital], *place* [Fr]; uptown, midtown, downtown; shopping area, shopping center, arcade, mall; financial district, business district, business *or* commercial zone; residential area *or* zone, suburb; tenement area *or* district, ghetto, barrio, slum *or* slums, blighted area, shantytown, favela, tenderloin, red-light district, skid row, wrong side of the tracks

> *Government 49; Politics 50; Market 483; Poverty 486; Center 612; Importance 799*

11 suburb, outskirts, suburbia, built-up area, exurb *or* exurbia, greenbelt, commuter belt, bedroom town, streetcar suburb, garden suburb [Brit], faubourg [Fr]

> *Surroundings 615; Edge 618; Circularity 631*

12 municipal resident, citizen, urbanite, urban dweller, city dweller, burgher, downtowner, uptowner, slumdweller; suburbanite, commuter; townsman, townswoman, local, oppidan, villager, parishioner [Brit], city slicker, townie *or* towny [Inf]

13 municipal building, city hall, town hall, firehouse *or* fire station, police station *or* headquarters *or* precinct house, courthouse, community center, school

> *Education 48; Government 49; Region 564*

ADJECTIVES

14 urban, civic, citified, urbane, metropolitan, municipal, interurban, financial, business; downtown, uptown, midtown; inner-city, core-city, ghettoized, blighted, slummy, skid-row; residential, suburban, suburbanized, gentrified, exurban; town, oppidan, local, mainstreet, high-street [Brit]; village, villagelike, communal, county, public, civil, small-town, hick, jerkwater [Inf]

VERBS

15 urbanize, settle, citify, gentrify, suburbanize, charter

ADVERBS

16 municipally, communally, locally, publicly, civically, urbanely

568 Lakes

NOUNS

1 lake, body of water, natural lake, artificial lake, man-

LAKES

Alaotra (Madagascar)	Bear (US)	Constance (Germany)	Foyle (Ireland)
Albano (Italy)	Becharof (US)	Crater (US)	Franklin D. Roosevelt (US)
Albert *or* Mobutu Sese Seko (Uganda, Zaire)	Biwa (Japan)	Dead Sea (Israel, Jordan)	Gairdner (Australia)
Athabasca (Canada)	Broads, the (England)	Derwent Water (England)	Galilee, Sea of (Israel, Jordan)
Atitlán (Guatemala)	Chad (Chad, Niger, Nigeria, Cameroon)	Dubawnt (Canada)	Garda (Italy)
Baikal (Russia)	Champlain (US, Canada)	Edward (Uganda, Zaire)	Geneva, Lake of, *or* Leman (Switzerland, France)
Balaton (Hungary)	Chapala (Mexico)	Ericht (Scotland)	George (US)
Balkhash (Kazakhstan)	Chiem *or* Chiemsee (Germany)	Erie (Canada, US)	Grasmere (England)
Bangweulu (Zambia)		Eyre (Australia)	Great (Australia)
Bay, Laguna de (Philippines)	Como (Italy)	Finger Lakes (US)	
		Flathead (US)	

Great Bear (Canada)
Great Lakes (US, Canada)
Great Salt Lake (US)
Great Slave (Canada)
Hawes Water (England)
Huron (US, Canada)
Ijsselmeer or Ijssel (Netherlands)
Iliamna (US)
Inari (Finland)
Issyk-Kul (Kyrgyzstan)
Kariba (Zambia, Zimbabwe)
Katrine (Scotland)
Khanka or Hanka (China, Russia)
Killarney, Lakes of (Ireland)
Kivu (Zaire, Rwanda)
Klamath Lakes (US)
Koko Nor (China)
Kyoga or Kioga (Uganda)
Ladoga (Russia)
Lake District (England)
Lake of the Woods (Canada)
Leech (US)
Leman or Geneva, Lake of (Switzerland, France)
Leven (Scotland)
Lochy (Scotland)
Lomond, Loch (Scotland)
Lop Nur or Lop Nor (China)
Lucerne or Vierwaldstätter See (Switzerland)

Lugano (Italy, Switzerland)
Maggiore (Italy, Switzerland)
Mai-Ndombe (Zaire)
Mälaren or Malar (Sweden)
Manitoba (Canada)
Manzala (Egypt)
Maracaibo (Venezuela)
Maree (Scotland)
Martin (US)
Mead (US)
Michigan (US)
Mille Lacs (US)
Mjøsa (Norway)
Mobutu Sese Seko or Albert (Uganda, Zaire)
Moosehead (US)
Mweru (Zaire, Zambia)
Naknek (US)
Nasser (Egypt)
Natron (Tanzania)
Neagh (Ireland)
Nemi (Italy)
Ness (Scotland)
Nettilling (Canada)
Neuchâtel (Switzerland)
Neusiedler (Austria, Hungary)
Nicaragua (Nicaragua)
Nipigon (Canada)

Nyasa or Malawi (Malawi, Tanzania, Mozambique)
Okeechobee (US)
Onega (Russia)
Ontario (Canada, US)
Päijänne (Finland)
Patos (Brazil)
Peipus (Russia, Estonia)
Pontchartrain (US)
P'o-yang (China)
Pyramid (US)
Rainy (US)
Rannoch (Scotland)
Reindeer (Canada)
Rudolf or Turkana (Kenya, Ethiopia)
Rydal Water (England)
Saimaa (Finland)
St. Clair (US, Canada)
Salton Sea (US)
Superior (US, Canada)
Tahoe (US)
Tana or Tsana (Ethiopia)
Tanganyika (Zaire, Burundi, Tanzania, Zambia)
Taupo (New Zealand)
Tay (Scotland)
Teshekpuk (US)
Texcoco (Mexico)
Thirlmere (England)

Titicaca (Peru, Bolivia)
Tonle Sap (Cambodia)
Torrens (Australia)
Trasimeno (Italy)
Tung-t'ing (China)
Turkana or Rudolf (Kenya, Ethiopia)
Ullswater (England)
Urmia (Iran)
Utah (US)
Vänern (Sweden)
Van or Van Golu (Turkey)
Vättern (Sweden)
Victoria (Uganda, Tanzania, Kenya)
Vierwaldstätter See or Lucerne (Switzerland)
Volta (Ghana)
Vyrnwy (Wales)
Wakatipu (New Zealand)
Wanaka (New Zealand)
Wast Water (England)
Windermere (England)
Winnebago (US)
Winnibigoshish (US)
Winnipeg (Canada)
Winnipegosis (Canada)
Winnipesaukee (US)
Yellowstone (US)
Zurich (Switzerland)

---

made lake, reservoir, freshwater lake, mountain lake, volcanic lake, glacial lake, oxbow lake, oasis, loch [Scot], lough [Irish], sea loch, salt lake, salina, lagoon, inland sea

2 **small lake,** pool, pond, lakelet, tidal pool, clear pool, muddy pool, millpond, farm pond, village pond, fishpond, dew pond, water hole, swimming hole, swimming pool; landlocked water, standing water, backwater, water pocket, still water, tarn, stagnant water, dead water, bayou, wash, marsh, mere [Brit]

▶ *Geology 8; Meteorology and Climatology 9; Water 557*

3 **lake dwelling,** lake house, lakeside house, lake lodge, lacustrine dwelling, pile house or dwelling, stilt house, crannog [Scot, Irish], lakeside village, stilt village

4 **lake dweller,** lakeside dweller, lacustrine dweller, lacustrian, laker, pile dweller

ADJECTIVES

5 **lakelike,** pondlike, landlocked, tidal, clear, muddy, standing, still, stagnant, marshy; lakeside, lacustrine, lacustrian, lacustral, limnetic, limnologic(al), limnophilous, lake-dwelling

569 Mountains and Hills

Mountains are the beginning and the end of all natural scenery. — JOHN RUSKIN

NOUNS

1 **mountain,** mount, alp, mountain range, mountain chain, range, sierra, cordillera, massif, high country, highlands, heights; mountaintop, precipice, summit, peak, cloud-capped peak, snow-capped peak, pike [Brit], crag, tor, pinnacle, crest; ridge, saddle, spur, slope, scarp, incline; headland, cliff, ness, ben [Scot, Irish]; precipice, scar

▶ *Geology 8; Height 596*

2 **hill,** hillock, mound, hummock, monticule, tumulus, barrow, knob, knoll, butte, foothill, down, hilltop, hillside, brae [Scot], fell [Brit], dune, sand dune, bluff, inselberg, knap, monadnock, moraine, drumlin, climb, ascent

▶ *Animals (General) 34; Habitat 60; Mountaineering 161*

3 **mountain range,** massif, sierra, chain, cordillera; ridge, arête, kame, esker, os, saddle, hogback, watershed, crest, spine; divide, Continental Divide

---

NOTABLE MOUNTAINS, MOUNTAIN RANGES, AND HILLS

Aconcagua (Argentina)
Adirondack Mountains (US)
Ahaggar or Hoggar
  Mountains (Algeria)
Alaska Range (US)
Allegheny Mountains (US)
Alps (France, Switzerland,
  Italy, Austria)
Altay or Altai Mountains
  (Russia, China, Mongolia)
Andes (South America)
Annapurna (Nepal)
Anti-Lebanon Mountains
  (Syria, Lebanon)
Apennines (Italy)
Appalachian Mountains
  (US)
Ararat or Agri Dagi (Turkey)
Aso (Japan)
Athos (Greece)
Atlas Mountains (Morocco,
  Algeria, Tunisia)
Balkan Mountains (Bulgaria)
Bandeira (Brazil)
Bernese Alps or Oberland
  Range (Switzerland)
Bernina (Switzerland)
Bighorn Mountains (US)
Blanc, Mont (France, Italy)
Blue Mountains (Australia;
  Jamaica; US)
Blue Ridge Mountains (US)
Boundary Peak (US)
Brecon Beacons (Wales)
Brocken (Germany)
Cairngorms (Scotland)
Cambrian Mountains (Wales)
Cameroon (Cameroon)
Cantabrian Mountains
  (Spain)
Carmel (Israel)
Carpathian Mountains
  (Czech Republic, Poland,
  Romania, Ukraine)
Carrantuohill (Ireland)
Cascade Range (US, Canada)
Catskill Mountains (US)
Caucasus Mountains (Russia,
  Georgia, Azerbaijan)
Cheviot Hills (England,
  Scotland)
Chimborazo (Ecuador)
Chomo Lhari (Tibet, Bhutan)
Cho Oyu (Nepal, China)
Coast Mountains (Canada)
Communism Peak (Tajikistan)
Cook, Mount or Aorangi
  (New Zealand)
Cotopaxi (Ecuador)
Cotswold Hills (England)

Cumbrian Mountains
  (England)
Damavand or Demavend
  (Iran)
Devils Tower (US)
Dhaulagiri (Nepal)
Dolomites (Italy)
Drakensberg Mountains
  (South Africa)
Egmont, Mount or Taranaki
  (New Zealand)
Eiger (Switzerland)
Elbert, Mount (US)
Elbrus or El'brus (Republic of
  Georgia)
Elburz Mountains (Iran)
Elgon, Mount (Uganda,
  Kenya)
Ellsworth (Antarctica)
Erebus, Mount (Antarctica)
Er Rif or Rif Mountains
  (Morocco)
Erzebirge Range (Germany,
  Czech Republic)
Etna, Mount (Sicily)
Everest, Mount (Nepal,
  Tibet)
Foraker, Mount (US)
Finsteraarhorn (Switzerland)
Fuji or Fujiyama (Japan)
Gasherbrum (Kashmir)
Golan Heights (Israel)
Gongga Shan or Minya Konka
  (China)
Gosainthan (Nepal, Tibet)
Grampian Mountains
  (Scotland)
Grand Teton (US)
Granite Peak (US)
Gran Paradiso (Italy)
Great Dividing Range
  (Australia)
Great Smoky Mountains (US)
Green Mountains (US)
Grossglockner (Austria)
Harz Mountains (Germany)
Helicon (Greece)
Helvellyn (England)
Hermon, Mount (Syria,
  Lebanon)
Highlands (Scotland)
Himalayas (South Asia)
Hindu Kush (Afghanistan,
  Pakistan)
Hood, Mount (US)
Huascaran (Peru)
Humphreys Peak (US)
Hymettus (Greece)
Ida or Kaz Dagi (Turkey)
Illimani (Bolivia)

Jagerhorn (Switzerland)
Jotunheimen (Norway)
Jungfrau (Switzerland)
K2 or Godwin Austen
  (Pakistan, China)
Kamet (India)
Kanchenjunga (Nepal, India)
Karakoram Range (Pakistan,
  India, China)
Katmai, Mount (US)
Kazbek (Republic of
  Georgia)
Kenya (Kenya)
Kilimanjaro (Tanzania)
Kinabalu or Kinabulu
  (Malaysia)
Kings Peak (US)
Kirkpatrick, Mount
  (Antarctica)
Kosciusko, Mount (Australia)
Kunlun Mountains (China)
Lammermuir Hills (Scotland)
Lassen Peak (US)
Laurentian Mountains
  (Canada)
Lebanon Mountains
  (Lebanon)
Lenin Peak (Tajikistan)
Lhotse I (Nepal, China)
Lhotse II (Nepal, China)
Logan, Mount (Canada)
Lomond, Ben (Scotland)
Macdonnell Ranges
  (Australia)
Makalu (China, Nepal)
Manaslu (Nepal)
Matterhorn (Switzerland,
  Italy)
Mauna Kea (US)
Mauna Loa (US)
McKinley, Mount (US), or
  Denali
Mendip Hills (England)
Misti, El (Peru)
Mitchell, Mount (US)
Mourne Mountains (Ireland)
Mulhacén (Spain)
Namcha Barwa (China)
Nanda Devi (India)
Nanga Parbat (India)
Nevis, Ben (Scotland)
Nilgiri Hills (India)
Ojos del Salado (Argentina,
  Chile)
Olives, Mount of (Israel)
Olympic Mountains (US)
Olympus, Mount (Greece)
Orizaba or Citlaltepetl
  (Mexico)
Ossa, Mount (Greece)

Ouachita Mountains (US)
Ozark Mountains (US)
Palomar, Mount (US)
Pamirs Range (Tajikistan,
  China, Afghanistan)
Parnassus, Mount (Greece)
Pennine Chain (England)
Pikes Peak (US)
Pindus Mountains (Greece)
Popocatepetl (Mexico)
Pyrenees (France, Spain)
Rainier, Mount (US)
Ras Dashan (Ethiopia)
Robson, Mount (Canada)
Rocky Mountains or the
  Rockies (US)
Rosa, Monte (Switzerland,
  Italy)
Ruapehu (New Zealand)
Rushmore, Mount (US)
St. Elias Mountains (US,
  Canada)
St. Helens, Mount (US)
Sayan Mountains (Russia)
Shasta, Mount (US)
Sierra de Guadarrama (Spain)
Sierra Madre (US; Mexico)
Sierra Morena Range (Spain)
Sierra Nevada Range (US;
  Spain)
Sikhote Alin Range (Russia)
Snowdon (Wales)
Snowy Mountains (Australia)
Taurus Mountains (Turkey)
Teide, Pico de (Canary
  Islands)
Teton Range (US)
Tian or Tien Shan (Central
  Asia)
Toubkal or Jebel (Morocco)
Tres Cruces (Argentina,
  Chile)
Tupungato (Argentina,
  Chile)
Uinta Mountains (US)
Ural Mountains (Russia,
  Kazakhstan)
Vesuvius, Mount (Italy)
Vinson Massif (Antarctica)
Virunga or Mfumbiro Range
  (Zaire, Uganda, Rwanda)
Viso, Monte (Italy)
Vosges Mountains (France)
Wasatch Range (US)
Weisshorn (Switzerland)
Wheeler Peak (US)
White Mountains (US)
Whitney, Mount (US)
Wilson, Mount (US)
Zagros Mountains (Iran)

4 **study of mountains,** orography, orology; orometer, orologist

▶ Geology 8

ADJECTIVES

5 **mountainous,** high, montane, alpine, alpestrine, altitudinous, elevated, mounting, ascending, towering, soaring, lofty, monumental, snow-capped, cloud-capped, mountain-dwelling; orogenic, orographic, orological, orometric

6 **hilly,** upland, rolling, undulating

VERBS

7 **tower over,** soar, rise, rise above, overtop, surmount

▶ Height 596

570 Rivers

NOUNS

1 **river,** watercourse, waterway, flowing river, running water, meandering river, racing river, navigable river, braided river, underground river, subterranean river; stream, mountain stream, freshet, fresh, small stream, streamlet, rivulet, millstream, rillet, brook, bourn or bourne, burn [Scot], runnel or runlet, run, rill, gill [Brit], kill, brooklet, creek; river system, water system, drainage pattern, confluence, watershed

▶ Geology 8; Motion 677; Water Transportation 690

2 **tributary,** confluent stream, confluent, bayou, branch, feeder, affluent, distributary, fork, effluent, anabranch, headwaters, billabong [Aus]

3 **river parts,** channel, conduit, duct, canal, cut, course, midchannel, midstream; bank, riverbank, sandbank, embankment, levee, riverside, waterside, water's edge; riverbed, bed, bottom, streambed, dry bed, arroyo, wadi; source, riverhead, headstream, head, headwaters, fountainhead; river's end, river mouth, mouth, delta

4 **flow,** river flow, water flow, flowing, flux, fluency; stream, course, current, undercurrent, undertow; drift, driftage, ripple, afflux, inflow, affluence, ingress; flowing together, confluence, convergence, concourse, conflux; outflow, effluence, egress; cross flow, crosscurrent, countercurrent, counterflux; backflow, ebb, reflux, re-

---

RIVERS

Aare or Aar (Switzerland)	Atchafalaya (US)	Chambal (India)	Coppermine (Canada)	Ems (Germany, Netherlands)
Achelous (Greece)	Athabasca (Canada)	Chang Jiang or Yangtze (China)	Courantyne (Guyana, Suriname)	Essequibo (Guyana)
Adda (Italy)	Attawapiskat (Canada)	Chao Phraya (Thailand)	Cumberland (US)	Euphrates (Iraq, Syria, Turkey)
Adige (Italy)	Aube (France)	Charente (France)	Damodar (India)	Fitzroy (Australia)
Ain (France)	Avon (England)	Chari (Central African Republic, Cameroon, Chad)	Danube (Eastern Europe)	Fly (Papua New Guinea)
Aisne (France)	Awash (Ethiopia)		Darling (Australia)	Forth (Scotland)
Alabama (US)	Back (Canada)	Chattahoochee (US)	Delaware (US)	Fraser (Canada)
Albany (Canada)	Balsas (Mexico)	Chenab (Pakistan)	Demerara (Guyana)	Gambia (Gambia, Senegal)
Aldan (Russia)	Barrow (Ireland)	Cheyenne (US)	Derwent (Australia)	
Allegheny (US)	Beas or Bias (India)	Chindwin (Myanmar)	Des Moines (US)	Gan or Kan (China)
Allier (France)	Beni (Bolivia)	Chubut (Argentina)	Diamantina (Australia)	Ganges (India)
Amazon (Peru, Brazil)	Benue (Nigeria)	Chulym (Russia)	Dnieper or Dnepr (Ukraine)	Garonne (France)
Amu Darya (Turkmenistan, Uzbekistan)	Bermejo (Argentina)	Churchill (two, Canada)	Dniester or Dnestr (Ukraine)	Ghaghara (India)
	Big Sioux (US)	Cimarron (US)		Gila (US)
Amur (Mongolia, Russia, China)	Bío-Bío (Chile)	Clark Fork (US)	Don (Russia)	Glomma (Norway)
	Black Warrior (US)	Clutha (New Zealand)	Donets (Ukraine)	Godavari (India)
Androscoggin (US)	Bow (Canada)	Clyde (Scotland)	Dordogne (France)	Grande, Rio, or Río Bravo (US, Mexico)
Angara (Russia)	Brahmaputra (Tibet, India)	Coco (Honduras)	Doubs (France)	
Angerman (Sweden)		Colorado (US; Argentina)	Douro or Duero (Spain, Portugal)	Great Ouse (England)
Apurímac (Peru)	Brandywine Creek (US)	Columbia (US, Canada)	Drava (Italy, Austria, Croatia, Hungary)	Green (US)
Araguaia or Araguaua (Brazil)	Brazos (US)	Conchos (Mexico)	Dvina (Russia)	Guadalquivir (Spain)
	Brenta (Italy)	Congo or Zaire (Congo, Zaire)	Ebro (Spain)	Guadiana (Spain, Portugal)
Aras or Araks (Turkey, Russia)	Bug (Ukraine, Poland, Germany)		Elbe or Labe (Germany, Czech Republic)	Han (China; Korea)
Arkansas (US)	Cagayan (Philippines)	Connecticut (US)		Havel (Germany)
Arno (Italy)	Cam (England)	Cooper Creek (Australia)	Elster (Germany)	Hawkesbury (Australia)
Aruwimi (Zaire)	Canadian (US)			Helmand (Afghanistan)
Assiniboine (Canada)	Cape Fear (US)			
Atbara (Sudan)	Catawba (US)			
	Cauvery (India)			

Herlen or Kerulen (Mongolia)
Hooghly (India)
Housatonic (US)
Huange or Yellow (China)
Hudson (US)
Humbolt (US)
Hunter (Australia)
Ili (China, Russia)
Illinois (US)
Indigirka (Russia)
Indus (India, Pakistan, China)
Irrawaddy (Myanmar)
Irtysh (China, Russia, Kazakhistan)
Isar (Germany)
James (two, US)
Japurá (Brazil)
Jordan (Israel, Jordan)
Juba (Ethiopia, Somalia)
Júcar (Spain)
Jumna (India)
Juruá (Brazil)
Kabul (Afghanistan, Pakistan)
Kama (Russia)
Kansas (US)
Kasai or Cassai (Angola, Zaire)
Kaskaskia (US)
Kemi (Finland)
Klamath (US)
Klondike (Canada)
Koksoak (Canada)
Kolyma (Russia)
Kootenai or Kootenay (US, Canada)
Krishna (India)
Kuban (Russia)
Kura (Turkey, Georgia, Azerbaijan)
Lachlan (Australia)
Lena (Russia)
Liard (Canada)
Liffey (Ireland)
Limpopo (South Africa, Zimbabwe, Mozambique)
Little Bighorn (US)
Little Colorado (US)
Little Missouri (US)
Loire (France)
Lomami (Zaire)
Lualaba (Zaire)

Luapula (Zaire, Zambia)
Luni (India)
Mackenzie (Australia; Canada)
Madeira (Brazil)
Magdalena (Colombia)
Main (Germany)
Mamore (Bolivia)
Manawatu (New Zealand)
Manicouagan (Canada)
Maritsa (Bulgaria, Turkey)
Marne (France)
Medina (US)
Mekong (Laos, China, Vietnam)
Menderes (Turkey)
Merrimack (US)
Mesta (Bulgaria, Greece)
Meuse or Maas (France, Belgium, Netherlands)
Milk (US, Canada)
Minnesota (US)
Miño or Minho (Spain, Portugal)
Mississippi (US)
Missouri (US)
Mohawk (US)
Moselle or Mosel (France, Germany)
Murray (Australia; Canada)
Murrumbidgee (Australia)
Narbada (India)
Neches (US)
Neckar (Germany)
Negro (Argentina, Uruguay; Colombia, Brazil)
Neisse (Poland, Czech Republic, Germany)
Nelson (Canada)
Neman (Russia)
Neuse (US)
Niger (Nigeria, Guinea, Mali)
Nile (Uganda, Sudan, Egypt)
Nueces (US)
Ob (Russia)

Oder (Germany, Czech Republic, Poland)
Ohio (US)
Oise (France)
Oka (Russia)
Onega (Russia)
Orange (South Africa)
Ord (Australia)
Orinoco (Venezuela)
Orontes (Syria, Turkey)
Osage (US)
Ottawa or Outaouais (Canada)
Ouachita (US)
Owyhee (US)
Paraguay (Paraguay)
Paraná (Brazil)
Parnaíba (Brazil)
Peace (Canada)
Pearl (US)
Pechora (Russia)
Pecos (US)
Peel (Canada)
Penobscot (US)
Piave (Italy)
Pilcomayo (Bolivia)
Plata, Río de la (Argentina, Uruguay)
Platte (US)
Po (Italy)
Potomac (US)
Powder (US)
Prut (Romania)
Purus (Colombia, Brazil)
Putumayo (Colombia, Brazil, Peru)
Ravi (India, Pakistan)
Red (US)
Red Deer (Canada)
Red River of the North (US)
Rhine (Switzerland, France, Germany, Netherlands)
Rhône (Switzerland, France)
Ribble (England)
Rímac (Peru)
Roanoke (US)
Rock (US)
Roosevelt, Rio, or Rio da Duvida (Brazil)
Ruhr (Germany)

Saar (Germany, France)
Sabine (US)
Sacramento (US)
Saguenay (Canada)
St. Francis (US)
St. John (Canada, US)
St. Johns (US)
St. Lawrence (Canada)
Salado (Argentina)
Salt (US)
Salween (Tibet, China, Myanmar)
Sangamon (US)
San Joaquin (US)
San Juan (US)
Santee (US)
Santiago (Mexico)
São Francisco (Brazil)
Saône (France)
Sarda (India)
Saskatchewan (Canada)
Sava (Slovenia)
Savannah (US)
Scheldt or Schelde (Belgium, France)
Seine (France)
Selenge (Mongolia)
Senegal (Guinea, Senegal)
Severn (England; Canada)
Shannon (Ireland)
Shenandoah (US)
Siret (Romania, Ukraine)
Skeena (Canada)
Slave (Canada)
Snake (US)
Somme (France)
Songhua or Sungari (China)
Spey (Scotland)
Spree (Germany)
Suriname (Suriname)
Susquehanna (US)
Sutlej (Pakistan)
Suwannee (US)
Syr Darya (Kazakhstan)
Tajo or Tagus (Portugal, Spain)
Tallahatchie (US)
Tanana (US)
Tapajós (Brazil)

Tarim (China)
Tay (Scotland)
Tennessee (US)
Thames and Isis (England)
Tiber (Italy)
Tigris (Iraq, Turkey)
Tisza (Ukraine, Hungary, Yugoslavia)
Tocantins (Brazil)
Trent (England; Canada)
Tungabhadra (India)
Tunguska (Russia)
Tweed (England, Scotland)
Ucayali (Peru)
Uele or Ubangi or Oubangui (Zaire, Central African Republic)
Ural (Russia, Kazakhstan)
Urubamba (Peru)
Uruguay (Uruguay, Brazil, Argentina)
Usumacinta (Guatemala, Mexico)
Vaal (South Africa)
Vistula or Wisla (Poland)
Vltava or Moldau (Czech Republic)
Volga (Russia)
Volta (Ghana)
Volturno (Italy)
Wabash (US)
Waikato (New Zealand)
Warta (Poland)
Weser (Germany)
Wisconsin (US)
Wye (Wales, England)
Xi Jiang or Hsi Chiang (China)
Xingu (Brazil)
Yalu (China, North Korea)
Yellowstone (US)
Yenisey or Yenisei (Russia)
Yukon (Canada, US)
Zambezi (Zambia, Angola, Zimbabwe, Mozambique)

fluence; profluence, surge, gush, rush, onrush, spate, race, run, cascade; torrent, flood, flash flood, inundation, deluge, overflow, overrun, spillage, spillover, flush, washout, engulfment, submersion, alluvion; the Flood, the Deluge

▶ *Geology 8; Meteorology and Climatology 9; Power 514; Forward Motion 679; Backward Motion 680*

5 **river turbulence,** waterfall, falls, cataract, rapids, white water, riffle, chute, shoot, sault, eddy, whirl, twirl, swirl, vortex, maelstrom

▶ *Convolution 632; Rotation 682*

ADJECTIVES

6 **riverlike,** streamlike, brooklike, riverine, fluvial, fluviomarine

7 **flowing,** fluent, fluxive, in flux, effluent, profluent, affluent, confluent, convergent, streaming, running, coursing, winding, meandering; sluggish, snaking, serpentine, rippling, ripply, purling, racing, rushing, gushing, surging, torrential, overflowing, dam-breaking, vortical, inundant, inundatory, falling, ebbing, refluent

8 **flooded,** deluged, inundated, engulfed, swamped, awash, washed, drowned, in *or* at flood, in spate

9 **hydrological,** hydrospheric, hydrostatic

▶ *Water 557; Seas 571*

VERBS

10 **flow,** meander, run, stream, race, braid, course, channel, pour, drift, glide, slide, flow over, babble, bubble, burble, gurgle, purl, trill, murmur, trickle, dribble, slosh, lap, flow together, converge, commingle, flow in, surge, gush, rush, flood, overflow, overrun, spill over, flush, inundate, submerge, swamp, flow out, flow back, ebb; eddy, rotate, whirl, swirl, twirl, fall, cascade

11 **cause to flow,** open the sluice gates, drain, divert, irrigate

12 **stop the flow,** stem, staunch, obstruct, dam, dam up

ADVERBS

13 **fluently,** affluently, flowingly, convergently, sluggishly, torrentially, in *or* at flood, vortically, inundatorily, cataclysmically, hydrologically

571 Seas

For all at last returns to the sea — to Oceanus, the ocean river, like the ever-flowing stream of time, the beginning and the end. — RACHEL CARSON

NOUNS

1 **sea,** ocean, deep sea, deep blue sea, seven seas, the deep, high seas, ocean blue, the blue, main, bounding main, the billow; seawater, salt water, brine, salt sea, salinity; blue water, tide, wave, ocean depths, ocean floor, seabed, sea bottom, benthos; Davy Jones's locker, the briny; [Inf]: the big drink, the pond, the herring pond [Brit]

▶ *Geology 8; Water Transportation 690*

2 **tide,** tidal current, tidal flow, tidal flood, tidal stream, tide race, tidewater, tideway, tide gate, riptide, tiderip, direct tide, opposite tide; high tide, high water, full tide, lunar tide, solar tide, flood tide; spring tide, equinoctial tide, ebb tide *or* ebb, rising tide, flux, flow, flood; low tide, low water, neap tide *or* neap; reflux, refluence, tidal rise and fall, ebb and flow, flux and reflux, tidal range, tidal bore, tidal flat, tidal pool; tide chart, tidal table, tide gauge, thalassometer, tidal power, tideland

▶ *Motion 677; Forward Motion 679; Backward Motion 680; Raising 715; Lowering 716*

3 **wave,** billow, swell, heavy swell, surge, heave, undulation, waviness, rise, trough, wavelet, ripple, riffle, spume, foam, froth, surf, breaker, comber, roller, roll, peak, wave crest, whitecap, white horse, broken water, rough water, rough sea, heavy sea, choppy sea, choppiness, turbulent sea, overfall, angry sea; rogue wave, tidal wave, seiche, tsunami *or* seismic sea wave, undertow, undercurrent

▶ *Oscillation 683*

4 **legendary sea being,** Neptune, Triton, Oceanus, Poseidon, Nereus, Varuna, Oceanid, Nereid, Amphitrite, Thetis, Calypso, Scylla, Charybdis, undine, merman, sea nymph, mermaid, siren, water sprite, water spirit, sea serpent

5 **oceanography,** thalassography, hydrography, bathymetry, marine biology, aquiculture, sea survey, deep-sea drilling, echo sounding, sub-bottom profiling; Admiralty chart [Brit]; research vessel, diving bell, bathysphere, diving vessel, bathyscaphe, bathythermograph, drilling vessel

▶ *Geology 8; Meteorology and Climatology 9*

6 **oceanographer,** thalassographer, hydrographer, marine biologist, deep-sea diver, underwater explorer

OCEANS AND SEAS

Adriatic Sea	Black Sea	Marmara, Sea of
Aegean Sea	Caribbean Sea	Mediterranean
Amundsen Sea	Caspian Sea	Sea
Andaman Sea	China Sea	North Sea
Antarctic Ocean	Coral Sea	Okhotsk, Sea of
Arabian Sea	East China Sea	Pacific Ocean
Arafura Sea	Galilee, Sea of	Philippine Sea
Aral Sea	Greenland Sea	Red Sea
Arctic Ocean	Indian Ocean	Ross Sea
Atlantic Ocean	Inland Sea	Sargasso Sea
Azov, Sea of	Ionian Sea	South China Sea
Baltic Sea	Irish Sea	Tasman Sea
Banda Sea	Japan, Sea of	Timor Sea
Barents Sea	Java Sea	Tyrrhenian Sea
Beaufort Sea	Kara Sea	Weddell Sea
Bellingshausen Sea	Laptev Sea	White Sea
Bering Sea	Ligurian Sea	Yellow Sea

ADJECTIVES

7 **oceanic,** nautical, tidal, sea, salty, briny, equinoctial, lunar, solar, ebb, ebbing, neap, billowing, swelling, surging, breaking, rolling, choppy, heavy, turbulent, angry, dirty, marine, maritime, ocean-going, sea-going, seaworthy, seafaring, undersea, underwater, deep, deep-sea, submarine, subaqueous, subaquatic, sub-aqua, thalassic, pelagic, pelagian, benthic, estuarine, littoral, sublittoral, intertidal, abyssal, terrigenous

8 **oceanographic,** thalassographic, hydrographic, bathymetric

VERBS

9 **billow,** swell, surge, heave, toss, popple, become choppy, become turbulent, undulate, rise, peak, draw to a peak, scend *or* send, ripple, riffle, wave, foam, froth, break, dash, crash, comb, roll, flow in, flow out, surge back, ebb, rise and fall, ebb and flow

ADVERBS

10 **nautically,** at sea, on the sea, on the high seas, afloat, by sea, on water, over the water, across the sea, oversea, overseas, beyond seas, oceanward, seaward, offshore, off soundings, out of soundings, in blue water, tidally

11 **oceanographically,** hydrographically, bathymetrically

572 Other Geographical Features

He loved the desert because there the wind blew out one's footsteps like candle flames. — LAWRENCE DURRELL

NOUNS

1 **landmass,** landform, continent, subcontinent, island; Africa, Antarctica, Asia, Australia, Europe, North America, South America; Eurasia, Oceania, Australasia; Central America, Greenland, India
▸ *Region 564; Country 566; Mountains and Hills 569*

2 **island,** isle, islet, river island, holm [Brit], coral island, atoll, reef, coral reef, cay, key, volcanic island, sandbank *or* bank, sand bar *or* bar, floating island, iceberg, ice floe, island continent, continental island, archipelago, island group, island chain
▸ *Region 564*

3 **marsh,** marshland, wetlands, fen, fenland, flat, mud flat, salt flat, salt marsh, salt pan, salina, playa, bog, peat bog, peatland, moor, swamp, swampland, swamp-forest, bayou, morass, quag, quagmire, quicksand, mudhole, mud, mire, ooze, wallow, slough, slew, slue, sudd
▸ *Water 557; Moisture 559*

4 **coast,** coastline, shoreline, coastland, rocky coast, ironbound coast, sea wall, sea cliff, beach, shore, ocean shore, seashore, seaboard, seaside, strand, sand, pebbles, shingle, submerged coast, continental shelf, coastal plain

▸ *Interface 616; Edge 618; Limit 620*

5 **peninsula,** point of land, point, tongue, neck, spit, sandspit, hook, spur, cape, promontory, foreland, headland, head, projection; land bridge, isthmus
▸ *Union 752*

6 **lowland,** flat country, flats, level, meadow, field, mead [Arch], lea, water meadow, bottom land, plain, the plains, alluvial plain, flood plain, polder, vale, strath [Scot], open country, wide-open spaces, range, heath, grassland, prairie, pampas, llano, veld *or* veldt, savanna *or* savannah, campos, steppe *or* steppes, moor, moorland [Brit]
▸ *Region 564; Lowness 597; Horizontality 603; Sameness 730*

7 **upland,** high country, highland, heights, wold, plateau, mesa, tableland, undulating land, downs, downland
▸ *Mountains and Hills 569*

8 **valley,** vale, dale, dell, dingle, dip, coomb *or* combe *or* comb [Brit], cirque, corrie [Scot], cwm [Welsh], glen, ravine, gorge, canyon, gully, crevasse, chimney, ditch, chine, clough [Brit], couloir
▸ *Opening 583; Concavity 635; Furrow 638*

9 **inlet,** bay, gulf, arm of the sea, natural harbor, port, bight, cove, fiord *or* fjord, firth [Scot], sound, backwater, bayou, outlet, estuary, mouth, delta, channel, gut, strait
▸ *Seas 571; Refuge 812*

10 **desert,** desert sands, sands; waste, barren, wilderness

---

DESERTS

Arabian (Egypt)	Negev (Israel)
Atacama (Chile)	Nubian (Sudan)
Betpak Dala (Kazakhstan)	Painted (US)
Black Rock (US)	Rub' al Khali (Saudi Arabia,
Chihuahuan (US, Mexico)	Oman, Yemen, United Arab
Colorado Plateau (US)	Emirates)
Dasht-e-Kavir (Iran)	Sahara (North Africa)
Dasht-e-Lut (Iran)	Simpson (Australia)
Death Valley (US)	Sinai (Egypt)
Gibson (Australia)	Sonoran (US)
Gobi (Mongolia, China)	Strzelecki (Australia)
Great Basin (US)	Sturt Stony (Australia)
Great Salt Lake (US)	Syrian (Syria, Iraq, Jordan,
Great Sandy (Australia)	Saudi Arabia)
Great Victoria (Australia)	Taklimakan *or* Takla Makan
Kalahari (South Africa,	(China)
Namibia, Botswana)	Thar *or* Indian *or* Great Indian
Kara Kum (Turkmenistan)	(India, Pakistan)
Kyzyl Kum (Uzbekistan)	Turfan Depression (China)
Libyan (Libya, Egypt, Sudan)	Ustyurt *or* Ust Urt
Mojave (US)	(Kazakhstan)
Namib (Namibia)	Yuma (US, Mexico)
Nefud *or* An Nafud (Saudi	
Arabia)	

ISLANDS AND ISLAND CHAINS*

Admiralty Islands (Papua New Guinea; Pacific Ocean)

Aland Island (Finland; Baltic Sea)

Alderney. See Channel Islands

Aleutian Islands (US; Bering Sea): Adak, Amchitka, Attu, Kanaga, Kiska, Tanaga, Umnak, Unalaska, Unimak

Alexander Archipelago (US; Gulf of Alaska)

American Samoa. See Samoa Islands

Andaman Islands (India; Bay of Bengal)

Anticosti (Canada; Atlantic Ocean)

Antigua. See Leeward Islands

Antilles, Greater and Lesser, or West Indies (Caribbean Sea)

Aran Islands (Ireland; Atlantic Ocean)

Aruba (the Netherlands; Caribbean Sea)

Ascension Island (Britain; South Atlantic Ocean)

Auckland Islands (New Zealand; South Pacific Ocean)

Axel Heiberg Island (Canada; Arctic Ocean)

Azores (Portugal; Atlantic Ocean)

Baffin Island (Canada; Arctic Ocean)

Bahamas (Atlantic Ocean)

Bahrain (Persian Gulf)

Balearic Islands or Baleares (Spain; Mediterranean Sea): Ibiza, Majorca or Mallorca, Minorca or Menorca

Bali (Indonesia; Pacific Ocean)

Barbados (Caribbean Sea)

Bathurst Island (Canada; Arctic Ocean)

Bay Islands (Caribbean Sea)

Bermuda Islands (Britain; Atlantic Ocean)

Bikini. See Marshall Islands

Bismarck Archipelago (Papua New Guinea; Pacific Ocean): New Britain, New Ireland

Bora-Bora. See Society Islands

Borneo or Kalimantan (Indonesia; Pacific Ocean)

Bornholm Island (Denmark; Baltic Sea)

Canary Islands (Spain; Atlantic Ocean): Fuerteventura, Gran Canaria, Tenerife

Cape Breton Island (Canada; Atlantic Ocean)

Cape Verde Islands (Atlantic Ocean)

Capri (Italy; Tyrrhenian Sea)

Caroline Islands (Pacific Ocean)

Cayman Islands (Britain; Caribbean Sea)

Channel Islands (Britain; English Channel): Alderney, Guernsey, Jersey, Sark

Christmas Island or Kiritimati (Kiribati; Pacific Ocean)

Clipperton (France; Pacific Ocean)

Cook Islands (South Pacific Ocean)

Corfu (Greece; Mediterranean Sea)

Corsica (France; Mediterranean Sea)

Crete (Greece; Mediterranean Sea)

Cuba (Caribbean Sea)

Curaçao (Netherlands; Caribbean Sea)

Cyclades (Greece; Aegean Sea): Naxos, Thera or Santorin or Santorini

Cyprus (Mediterranean Sea)

Devon (Canada; Arctic Ocean)

Diomede Islands (US and Russia; Pacific Ocean)

Dodecanese (Greece; Aegean Sea): Rhodes

Dominica (Caribbean Sea)

Easter Island (Chile; Pacific Ocean)

Elba (Italy; Mediterranean Sea)

Ellesmere (Canada; Arctic Ocean)

Ellis Island (US)

Eniwetok. See Marshall Islands

Euboea (Greece; Mediterranean Sea)

Faroe Islands (Denmark; Atlantic Ocean)

Fair Isle (Scotland; Atlantic Ocean)

Falkland Islands (Britain; Atlantic Ocean)

Fernando de Noronha Archipelago (Brazil; Atlantic Ocean)

Fiji Islands (Pacific Ocean): Vanua Levu, Viti Levu

Florida Keys (US; Atlantic Ocean): Key Largo, Key West

Franz Josef Land (Russia; Arctic Ocean)

Funafuti (Tuvalu; Pacific Ocean)

Galápagos (Ecuador; Pacific Ocean)

Gotland (Sweden; Baltic Sea)

Great Britain (mainland; Atlantic Ocean)

Greenland (Denmark; Atlantic Ocean)

Grenada (Caribbean Sea)

Grenadines, the (St. Vincent and the Grenadines; Caribbean Sea)

Guadalcanal. See Solomon Islands

Guadeloupe (France; Caribbean Sea)

Guam (US; Pacific Ocean)

Guernsey. See Channel Islands

Hainan (China; Pacific Ocean)

Hawaiian Islands (US; Pacific Ocean): Hawaii, Kahoolawe, Kauai, Lanai, Maui, Molokai, Niihau, Oahu

Hebrides, Outer and Inner (Britain; Atlantic Ocean)

Helgoland (Germany; North Sea)

Hispaniola (Caribbean Sea)

Hokkaido. See Japan

Hong Kong (South China Sea)

Honshu. See Japan

Iceland (Atlantic Ocean)

Indonesia (East Indies)

Ireland (Atlantic Ocean)

Iwo Jima. See Japan

Jamaica (Caribbean Sea)

Japan (Pacific Ocean): Hokkaido, Honshu, Iwo Jima, Kyushu, Okinawa, Shikoku

Java (Indonesia; East Indies)

Jersey. See Channel Islands

Kerguélen Islands (France; Indian Ocean)

Key Largo. See Florida Keys

Key West. See Florida Keys

Kodiak (US; Pacific Ocean)

Kuril Islands (Russia; Pacific Ocean)

Kwajalein. See Marshall Islands

Kyushu. See Japan

Leeward Islands (Caribbean Sea): Antigua, Barbuda, Dominica, Guadeloupe, Nevis, St. Kitts

Lemnos (Greece; Aegean Sea)

Leyte. See Philippines

Liberty Island or Bedloe's Island (US)

Long Island (US)

Luzon. See Philippines

Madagascar (Indian Ocean)

Madeira (Portugal; Atlantic Ocean)

Madura (Indonesia; Pacific Ocean)

Maldives (Indian Ocean)

Malta (Mediterranean Sea)

Man, Isle of (Britain; Atlantic Ocean)

Manhattan (US)

Marajo (Brazil; Atlantic Ocean)

Marianas or Mariana Islands (North Pacific Ocean)

Marquesas Islands (France; South Pacific Ocean)

Marshall Islands (US; Pacific Ocean): Bikini, Eniwetok, Kwajalein

Martha's Vineyard (US; Atlantic Ocean)

Martinique (France; Caribbean Sea)

Matsu (Taiwan; Taiwan Strait)

Maui. See Hawaiian Islands

Mauritius (Indian Ocean)

Melville (Canada; Arctic Ocean)

Midway Islands (Pacific Ocean)

Mindanao. See Philippines

Mindoro. See Philippines

Moluccas or Spice Islands (Pacific Ocean)

Mull, Island of (Scotland; Atlantic Ocean)

Mytilene or Lesbos (Greece; Aegean Sea)

Nantucket (US; Atlantic Ocean)

Nauru (South Pacific Ocean)

Naxos. See Cyclades

New Britain (Papua New Guinea; Pacific Ocean)

New Caledonia (France; South Pacific Ocean)

Newfoundland (Canada; Atlantic Ocean)

New Guinea (Indonesia, Papua New Guinea; Pacific Ocean)

ISLANDS AND ISLAND CHAINS*

New Ireland (Papua New Guinea; Pacific Ocean)

New Zealand (Pacific Ocean): Chatham, North, South, Stewart

Nicobar Islands (India; Bay of Bengal)

Novaya Zemlya (Russia; Arctic Ocean)

Oahu. See Hawaiian Islands

Okinawa. See Japan

Orkney Islands (Scotland; Atlantic Ocean)

Palau (Pacific Ocean)

Palawan. See Philippines

Panay. See Philippines

Parry Islands (Canada; Arctic Ocean)

Pemba (Tanzania; Indian Ocean)

Philippines (Pacific Ocean): Leyte, Luzon, Mindanao, Mindoro, Negros, Palawan, Panay, Samar

Pitcairn Island (Britain; South Pacific Ocean)

Pribilof Islands (US; Bering Sea)

Prince Edward Island (Canada; Atlantic Ocean)

Prince of Wales Island (Canada; Arctic Ocean)

Puerto Rico (US; Caribbean Sea)

Queen Charlotte Islands (Canada; Pacific Ocean)

Queen Elizabeth Islands (Canada; Arctic Ocean)

Quemoy (Taiwan; Taiwan Strait)

Rhodes. See Dodecanese

Roosevelt or Welfare Island (US)

Rügen (Germany; Baltic Sea)

Ryukyu Islands (Japan; Pacific Ocean)

Sable Island (Canada; Atlantic Ocean)

Saipan (Northern Mariana Islands; Pacific Ocean)

St. Helena (Britain; South Atlantic Ocean)

St. Kitts (Caribbean Sea)

St. Lawrence (US; Bering Sea)

St. Lucia (Caribbean Sea)

St. Vincent Island (St. Vincent and the Grenadines; Caribbean Sea)

Sakhalin (Russia; Pacific Ocean)

Samar. See Philippines

Samoa Islands (Pacific Ocean): American Samoa, Western Samoa

Samothrace (Greece; Aegean Sea)

Santa Barbara Islands (US; Pacific Ocean)

Santa Catalina (US; Pacific Ocean)

Sardinia (Italy; Mediterranean Sea)

Sark. See Channel Islands

Scilly Isles (Britain; Atlantic Ocean)

Seychelles (Indian Ocean)

Shetland Islands (Scotland; Atlantic Ocean)

Shikoku. See Japan

Sicily (Italy; Mediterranean Sea)

Singapore (East Indies)

Skye (Scotland; Atlantic Ocean)

Society Islands (France; South Pacific Ocean): Bora-Bora, Tahiti

Solomon Islands (South Pacific Ocean): Guadalcanal, San Cristobal, Malaita, Santa Isabel, New Georgia Group, Bougainville, Choiseul

Somerset (Canada; Arctic Ocean)

Southampton (Canada; Arctic Ocean)

South Georgia (Britain; Atlantic Ocean)

Spitsbergen (Norway; Arctic Ocean)

Sri Lanka or Ceylon (Indian Ocean)

Staten Island (US)

Sulawesi or Celebes (Indonesia; Pacific Ocean)

Sumatra (Indonesia; East Indies)

Tahiti. See Society Islands

Taiwan or Formosa (Pacific Ocean)

Tasmania (Australia; Pacific Ocean)

Tenerife. See Canary Islands

Thera. See Cyclades

Thousand Islands (US and Canada; St. Lawrence River)

Tierra del Fuego (Argentina and Chile; South Atlantic Ocean)

Timor (Indonesia; East Indies)

Tobago (Trinidad and Tobago; Caribbean Sea)

Tonga (South Pacific Ocean)

Trinidad (Trinidad and Tobago; Caribbean Sea)

Tristan da Cunha Islands (Britain; South Atlantic Ocean)

Truk Islands (Federated States of Micronesia; South Pacific Ocean)

Tuamotu Archipelago (South Pacific Ocean)

Tuvalu (South Pacific Ocean)

Unalaska. See Aleutian Islands

Unimak. See Aleutian Islands

Vancouver (Canada; Pacific Ocean)

Vanuatu or New Hebrides (Pacific Ocean)

Victoria (Canada; Arctic Ocean)

Virgin Islands (US and Britain; Caribbean Sea): St. Thomas, St. Croix, St. John, Tortola

Wake Island (US; Pacific Ocean)

Western Samoa. See Samoa Islands

West Indies (Caribbean Sea)

Windward Islands (Caribbean Sea): Barbados, Grenada, Grenadines, Martinique, St. Lucia, St. Vincent

Wrangel (Russia; Arctic Ocean)

Xiamen or Amoy (China; Taiwan Strait)

Zanzibar (Tanzania; Indian Ocean)

*Major islands in island chains are listed at the specific chain as well as in the main listing.

11 **hot spring,** geyser, warm spring, thermal spring, thermae; volcano

▶ *Heat 217; Violence 520; Expulsion 709*

ADJECTIVES

12 **of landmasses,** continental, subcontinental; insular, island, isleted, archipelagic; marshy, fenny, boggy, swampy, paludal, quaggy, undrained, waterlogged, muddy, miry; coastal, littoral, ashore, sandy, pebbled, shingled; peninsular, promontory, isthmian; flat, plain, alluvial, flooded, open, ranging, grassy, campestral, rolling, moory; high, upland, highland, undulating; valleyed, estuarial; desert, wasted, barren; thermal, volcanic

ADVERBS

13 **continentally,** on land, ashore, adrift, subcontinentally, insularly, soggily, muddily, rockily, openly, volcanically, thermally

573 Situation

NOUNS

1 **situation,** position, orientation, direction, bearings; latitude, longitude, aspect, side, frontage; altitude, topography, geography, location, site, setting; place, spot, point, seat, venue, scene, scenery, locale, locality

▶ *Location 565*

2 **circumstances,** setting, background, ground, foot-

ing, basis, stand, standing, standpoint, viewpoint, position, place; context, factor, contingency, condition, juncture, case, state, state of affairs, status, status quo; setup, climate, atmosphere; scene, scenario, lay of the land, way of the world, how things stand, how it is, outfit, layout, kettle of fish, picture, whole picture, size of it, ball game [Inf]

> *Surroundings 615; State 725; Circumstances 726*

3 **employment,** post, position, job, service, station, office, place, livelihood, occupation; berth, billet

> *Work 122*

4 **rank,** sphere, status, class, standing, station, position, position in society, estate

> *Order 765; Class 777*

ADJECTIVES

5 **situated,** positioned, located, set, placed, sited, seated, stationed, orientated, directed toward, pointed, appointed; well-situated, poorly situated

> *Circumstances 726*

6 **situational,** directional, topographical, geographical, local

> *Location 565*

7 **circumstantial,** contextual, contingent, grounded, based, climatic, atmospheric, surrounding

8 **employed,** posted, occupational; classed, ranked, berthed, billeted

VERBS

9 **be situated,** be located, be, lie, stand, rest, sit, take up a position

> *Existence 717*

10 **situate,** position, locate, site, put, put in, install, stand, fix, set, set up, station, post, deploy, direct, orientate

ADVERBS

11 **geographically,** topographically, locally, round about, around, in place, in position, on site, in situ, on location

12 **circumstantially,** contingently, contextually, as it stands, under the circumstances

574 Displacement

NOUNS

1 **displacement,** dislocation, dislodgment, disturbance, disarrangement, derangement, derailment; relocation, translocation, transference, transshipment; shift, shunt, move, switch, swerve, veer, deflection, knocking off course *or* out of place; aberration, perturbation, unseating, unsettling, upsetting, unsaddling

> *Transfer 685; Deviation 698; Disturbance 768*

2 **removal,** forcible removal, extraction, evacuation, extrication, taking away; uprooting, ripping out, tearing out, pulling up, plucking out, pulling out by the roots, eradication, deracination, extirpation

> *Extraction 711; Subtraction 749; Cancellation 834*

3 **replacement,** substitution, supplantation, transfer,

relocation; overthrow, coup, deposition *or* deposal, unseating, takeover; ejection, banishment, expulsion, eviction, deportation, diaspora, repatriation, ethnic cleansing

> *Attack 418; Change 665; Substitution 672; Repulsion 701; Expulsion 709*

4 **relegation,** demotion, downgrading, dismissal, discharge, layoff, marching orders, the elbow, kicking upstairs; [Inf]: sack, boot, heave-ho, bounce

> *Rejection 383; Departure 705; Expulsion 709*

5 **disconnection,** separation, detachment, unhinging, disjointedness, discontinuity, dislocation, luxation, putting out of joint, disarticulation, disengagement, dismemberment

> *Separation 753; Disintegration 758*

6 **misplacement,** mislaying, mislocation, misputting, losing, wrong place

7 **displaced person (DP),** refugee, evacuee, exile, deportee, repatriate, outcast, homeless person, waif, stray; stateless person, man without a country, Wandering Jew

ADJECTIVES

8 **displaced,** dislocated, dislodged, disturbed, disarranged, deranged, derailed; relocated, transferred; shifted, shunted, moved, switched, swerved, veered, deflected, off course, out of place; off-balance, unbalanced; disturbing, perturbing, unsettling, upsetting, shifting, moving, swerving, veering

9 **removed,** extracted, evacuated, extricated, taken away; uprooted, ripped, torn, wrested, pulled, drawn, plucked, pulled out by the roots, eradicated, deracinated, extirpated

10 **replaced,** overthrown, deposed, supplanted, transferred, removed, relocated, banished, thrown out, expelled, deported, repatriated, exiled, ostracized

11 **relegated,** demoted, downgraded, dismissed, discharged, laid off, out of a job; [Inf]: sacked, bounced, booted out, out on one's ear *or* ass

> *Rejection 383*

12 **disconnected,** separated, detached, unhinged, disjointed, discontinuous, out of joint, disarticulated, dislocated, disengaged, dismembered

13 **misplaced,** mislaid, misput, mislocated, lost, missing, gone missing *or* astray

14 **stateless,** outcast, refugee, evicted, evacuated, unhoused, unharbored, houseless, homeless; rootless, of no fixed abode, of no fixed address

VERBS

15 **displace,** dislocate, dislodge, disturb, disorder, disorganize, disrupt, disarrange, derange, derail; relocate, translocate, transship, transfer; move lock, stock, and barrel; shift, shunt, move, switch, swerve, veer, deflect, knock *or* throw off course, throw out of gear; perturb, unseat, unsettle, upset

16 **remove,** extract, evacuate, extricate, take away; draw

out, pull out, pull up, uproot, root out *or* up, pull up by the roots, eradicate, deracinate, extirpate, rip out, tear out, pluck out

17 **replace,** substitute, supplant, overthrow, dethrone, unseat, depose, oust, usurp, stage a coup, take over; eject, banish, expel, evict, turn out, exile, repatriate, ostracize, deport, cast out

18 **relegate,** demote, downgrade, discharge, dismiss, let go, lay off, fire, give the elbow, kick upstairs, show someone the door; [Inf]: sack, boot, bounce, give the heave-ho, kick out, give someone his *or* her walking papers *or* marching orders

19 **disconnect,** separate, detach, unhinge, disjoint, dislocate, luxate, put out of joint, disarticulate, disengage, dismember

20 **misplace,** mislay, misput, mislocate, put in the wrong place, lose, lose track of

ADVERBS

21 **in place of,** instead, in lieu, as an alternative

22 **disconnectedly,** disjointedly, detachedly, separately

575 Presence

NOUNS

1 **presence,** physical *or* actual presence, bodily presence, hereness, being here *or* there; existence, being, manifestation, manifestness, reality, actuality, materialness, materiality, solidity
▶ *Material World 524; Existence 717; Reality 719; Essence 723*

2 **residence,** occupancy, inhabitance, habitation
▶ *Habitat 60; Inhabitant 61*

3 **attendance,** personal attendance, appearance, frequenting, participation, accompaniment, company, companionship
▶ *Appearance 264; Frequency 661*

4 **omnipresence,** ubiquitousness, ubiquity, pervasiveness, pervasion, permeation, diffusion, diffusiveness, imbuement, immanence; ghostly presence, ghost, apparition, manifestation, spiritual presence, specter, phantom, vision, spook [Inf]
▶ *Occultism 86; Vision 242*

5 **availability,** plenty, sufficiency, accessibility, readiness; handiness, convenience, proximity, nearness, immediacy, propinquity, vicinity, neighborhood, immediate area
▶ *Sufficiency 97; Location 565; Situation 573; Surroundings 615*

6 **attender,** spectator, bystander, onlooker, looker-on, witness, eyewitness, watcher, observer, beholder, viewer, passerby; participant, attendee, visitor, patron, audience, churchgoer, theatergoer, moviegoer, *etc.*; frequenter, haunter, habitué, regular customer, regular
▶ *Observance 465; Frequency 661*

ADJECTIVES

7 **present,** existent, existing, extant, being; real, actual, material, solid, manifest

8 **residing,** resident, residential, in residence, on the premises, occupying, in occupation, live-in, in-house, at home

9 **attending,** participating, attendant, in attendance, on hand; accompanying, concomitant, companionable, sociable, associated; regular, habituated
▶ *Sociability 408; Accompaniment 794*

10 **omnipresent,** all-present, all-over, present throughout, ubiquitous, infinite, everywhere; pervasive, pervading, diffusive, imbued, immanent, shot through, filled with; penetrating, permeating, permeative, suffusive, suffusing; ghostly, spectral, haunted
▶ *Time 639; Existence 717; Truth 721*

11 **available,** sufficient, accessible, at hand, on tap [Inf]; ready, handy, convenient, within reach *or* sight *or* call, on the spot, to hand; near, nearby, nearest, close, closest, immediate; in view, at one's fingertips, at one's elbow, under one's nose, before one's eyes

12 **watching,** witnessing, witnessed, beholding, observing

VERBS

13 **be present,** be, exist, occur; be here, be there, be everywhere; pervade, permeate, penetrate, suffuse, diffuse, imbue; impregnate, fill, soak, saturate, leave no space *or* void; run through, filter through, infiltrate, overrun, meet one at every turn; appear, materialize, solidify

14 **attend,** be present at, be there in person, sit in on, be on hand, make one's presence felt; participate, take part, join in

15 **stand by,** spectate, look on, witness, see, watch, observe, view

16 **appear,** visit, turn up, show up, put in an appearance, show one's face, look in on; grace the occasion, honor with one's presence, present oneself; report, report for duty, be all present and correct, be present and accounted for; frequent, haunt, hang around [Inf], hang out [Inf]
▶ *Sociability 408*

17 **reside,** be in residence, occupy, inhabit, live in, dwell

ADVERBS

18 **in person,** personally, live, in existence; really, actually, solidly, materially, bodily, in propria persona, in the flesh

19 **here,** there, where, everywhere, somewhere, anywhere

20 **on the spot,** on the ground, on location, on site, in situ, in place; before one's very eyes, under one's nose, in the face of, in the presence of, before

21 **readily available,** on call, on tap [Inf], to hand, near at hand, within reach, in the vicinity; at home, in residence, on the premises, in

576 Absence

Absence is to love what wind is to fire; it extinguishes the small, it inflames the great.
— ROGER DE BUSSY-RABUTIN

NOUNS

1 **absence,** nonpresence, nonentity, nonbeing, unbeing, nonexistence; disappearance, dematerialization, vanishment, departure, loss; lack, want, deficiency, shortage, scarcity, dearth, insufficiency, paucity, scantiness
  ◗ *Insufficiency 98; Disappearance 265; Loss 468; Nonmaterial World 525; Nonexistence 718*

2 **emptiness,** voidness, vacancy, vacuity; bareness, blankness, hollowness, barrenness, nothingness; void, gap, vacuum, nothing, empty space, empty shell, husk; clean sheet, clean *or* blank slate, tabula rasa
  ◗ *Space 563*

3 **absenteeism,** absentation, nonappearance, nonattendance, desertion, defection, French leave, unauthorized absence, absence without leave (AWOL); truantism, truancy, hooky *or* hookey
  ◗ *Departure 705; Separation 753; Escape 816*

4 **leave of absence,** leave, sick leave, compassionate leave, holiday, vacation; break, time off, day off; furlough, sabbatical
  ◗ *Celebration 405*

5 **absentee,** missing person, defector, deserter, truant, runaway, no-show

6 **nobody,** no one, no man, no woman; nobody present, nobody there, not one, not a soul, not a single person, not a living soul *or* thing
  ◗ *Nonexistence 718; Zero 786*

ADJECTIVES

7 **absent,** not present, nonattendant, unavailable, conspicuous by its absence; nonexistent, inexistent, unreal, nonoccurrent, null, void

8 **away,** out, no longer with us, gone, departed, off; dematerialized, out of sight; absconded, flown, fled; skedaddled [Inf], vamoosed [Inf]

9 **nonresident,** not resident, not in residence, away, away from home, not at home, out of town; on tour, on the road, on location; on leave, on holiday, on vacation, on furlough, on sabbatical, not at work
  ◗ *Death 29*

10 **truant,** absent, absent without leave (AWOL)

11 **missing,** among the missing, lost, nowhere to be found, disappeared, vanished; lacking, wanting, wanted, deficient, minus, short; taken away, deleted, subtracted; omitted, mislaid, excluded, left out, not included

12 **vacant,** vacuous, void, devoid, empty, without content, hollow, barren; bare, blank, clean, clear, featureless, characterless

13 **unoccupied,** empty, vacant, available, unfilled; unlived-in, uninhabited, untenanted, unpeopled, unsettled; unmanned, unstaffed; depopulated, deserted, abandoned, forsaken, godforsaken

VERBS

14 **be absent,** keep away, stay away, take no part in, not come; fail to appear, not turn up, not show up, be conspicuous by one's absence; turn up missing, stay away in droves

15 **absent oneself,** take one's leave, leave, take leave, withdraw, retire, retreat, depart, exit, leave the scene, bow out, vacate; slip away, slip out, sneak out, make oneself scarce; take a leave of absence, go on leave, go on vacation, go on holiday, go on furlough, go on sabbatical, take a day *or* time off
  ◗ *Exit 707*

16 **abscond,** disappear, vanish, dematerialize; decamp, go missing, fly the coop *or* nest, escape, fly, flee, run away, scarper [Brit]; desert, defect, jump ship, be absent without leave (AWOL), take French leave; play truant, play hooky *or* hookey; [Inf]: cut, cut out on, skip, vamoose, skedaddle, bunk off [Brit]

17 **leave empty,** evacuate, vacate, desert, depopulate, abandon, forsake

ADVERBS

18 **absently,** in absentia; vacantly, vacuously, emptily, hollowly, blankly; in one's absence, behind one's back

19 **away,** elsewhere, not here, out of the house, off the premises; on leave, on vacation, on holiday, on furlough, on sabbatical; on tour, on location, out of town; somewhere else, not there, neither here nor there, nowhere, no place

577 Contents

NOUNS

1 **contents,** content, ingredients, components, constituents, constitution; composition, makeup, structure, embodiment, parts, elements, factors, features
  ◗ *Structure 551; Part 760; Arrangement 767*

2 **substance,** sum and substance, stuff, material, matter, spirit, essence, quintessence, gist, meat, nub
  ◗ *Meaning 361; Essence 723*

3 **insides,** inside, inner workings, innards, guts; pith, marrow, heart, core, kernel, entrails, bowels, offal
  ◗ *Interior 611*

4 **stuffing,** filling, filler, facing, wadding, padding, packing, lining, interlining, quilting
  ◗ *Materials 104*

5 **load,** lading, cargo, payload, freight, burden, charge; containerload, carload, truckload, busload, trainload, boatload; shipment, stowage, tonnage
  ◗ *Container 578; Transportation 686*

6 **division,** subdivision, section, chapter, subject matter, theme, topic, item, index, glossary; inventory, table,

list, checklist, tally, chart, catalog, register, schedule, scheme, agenda

▶ *Publication 173; Books 174; Allocation 474; Container 578; Class 777; List 785*

ADJECTIVES

7 **containing,** component, constituent, constituted; composed, made up of, embodying, subsuming, including, inclusive, structured, featuring; elemental, substantial, material, essential, quintessential

8 **loaded,** laden, holding, containing, burdened, burdensome, charged; stuffed, full, lined, padded, packed, stowed, crammed, squeezed, topped up

9 **itemized,** indexed, listed, coded, tabled, tabular, tabulated, charted; cataloged, registered, scheduled, programmed; sectioned, divided, subdivided; thematic, topical, schematic

VERBS

10 **contain,** hold, enclose, conceal, package, parcel, box up, containerize, load, lade, freight, take on board

▶ *Retention 471; Container 578*

11 **embody,** subsume, include, compose, constitute, make up, structure, build, assemble, put together

▶ *Inclusion 763*

12 **stuff,** fill, pad, wad, pack, cram, jam, squeeze; insert, pour in, make full, fill up, top up; line, interline, interlineate; package, quilt

13 **itemize,** index, list, enumerate, tabulate, catalog, classify, divide, subdivide, section, register, file, tally, schedule, schematize, program

ADVERBS

14 **structurally,** elementally, substantially, materially, in essence, essentially, quintessentially

15 **internally,** inside, within, to the core, inclusively, fully, to the brim, to the top

16 **thematically,** indexically, topically, schematically, sectionally, divisionally

578 Container

NOUNS

1 **container,** receptacle, holder, frame, vessel, repository, depository, reservoir, store

▶ *Cooking 91; Store 105; Contents 577; Enclosure 619*

2 **compartment,** cell, cage, cubicle, booth, stall, box; pew, niche, recess, nook, inglenook, cranny, bay, alcove; cubby, cubbyhole, pigeonhole, snuggery [Brit]; rack, shelf, drawer, shelving; luggage rack, overhead rack *or* locker

3 **cabinet,** cupboard, buffet, bookcase, wall unit, entertainment center; file cabinet, desk; kitchen cabinet, refrigerator, freezer, refrigerator-freezer, fridge [Inf]

▶ *Furniture 101; Store 105*

4 **packet,** pack, packaging, cover, wrapper, sheath, jacket; envelope, wallet, file, folder, parcel, bundle; cocoon, sac, nest

▶ *Covering 613*

5 **box,** chest, coffer, casket, caddy, case, locker; canister, tin can, carton, shoebox, mailbox; money box, safe, safe-deposit box, jewelry box, cigarette case, snuffbox; matchbox, tinderbox, ammunition box, powder box; packing box *or* case, crate, freight container, pallet, sea chest, tea chest; coffin, sarcophagus

▶ *Burial 31; Store 105*

6 **basket,** shopping basket, hamper, picnic hamper *or* basket, bread basket, flower basket, fruit basket, punnet [Brit]; pannier, creel, skep, trug; laundry basket, clothes basket, wastepaper basket, wastebasket; bassinet

7 **bag,** sack, bundle; string bag, plastic bag, polyethylene bag, paper bag, shopping bag, freezer bag; carryall, grip, poke, mailbag, pouch, diplomatic pouch; purse, evening bag, clutch purse, handbag, pocketbook, shoulder bag, fanny pack [Inf]; tote bag, duffel bag, saddlebag; makeup bag, toilet kit, sponge bag [Brit], carpetbag, overnight bag; satchel, kit bag, book bag, schoolbag; sports bag, golf bag, game bag; feed bag *or* nose bag

8 **baggage,** luggage, suitcase, travel bag, grip, holdall, carryall, Gladstone bag, portmanteau, valise, trunk, overnight bag, flight bag, carry-on; backpack, knapsack, rucksack, haversack; Boston bag, briefcase, attaché case, dispatch case, portfolio; wallet, money belt

9 **cart,** pushcart, handcart, shopping cart, trolley; barrow, wheelbarrow, wagon

10 **truck,** van, moving van, removal van, semitrailer, full trailer, tractor-trailer, semi [Inf]; lorry [Brit], transit van [Brit]

▶ *Store 105; Transportation 686*

11 **vessel,** urn, jar, caddy, vase, ewer, pitcher, jug, amphora, cookie jar, biscuit jar *or* tin [Brit]; cask, vat, barrel, keg, drum, puncheon, hogshead, firkin [Brit], pipe, tun; tank, cistern, bucket, pail, watering can; garbage can, bin, litter bin [Brit], trash can; scuttle, coal scuttle, hopper

12 **basin,** bowl, trough, sink; washbasin, bathtub, tin bath, tub, washtub, hot tub, Jacuzzi™; hip bath, footbath; sitz bath, bidet, chamber pot

13 **drinking vessel,** cup, mug, beaker, glass, tumbler, tankard, stoup [Scot]

14 **bottle,** flask, flagon, vial, phial, decanter, carafe; wine bottle, demijohn, magnum, jeroboam, rehoboam, methuselah, balthazar; gourd, calabash, wineskin, hip flask; hot-water bottle, thermos, vacuum bottle

15 **pot,** pan, cooking pot, caldron, saucepan, kettle; coffeepot, coffee urn, percolator, coffee maker, teapot, tea urn; jam jar, honeypot, storage jar; flowerpot

▶ *Cooking 91*

16 **crockery,** china, chinaware, dishware, pottery, glassware; tea set, coffee service, dinner service; bowl, finger bowl, mixing bowl, cereal bowl, soup bowl, por-

ringer, sugar bowl, salad bowl, punch bowl, tureen, gravy boat, sauceboat; ramekin, terrine, jelly mold; plate, platter, dish, saucer, charger

▶ *Cooking 91*

17 **ladle,** scoop, dipper, spatula, spoon, wooden spoon; shovel, spade, trowel

▶ *Cooking 91*

ADJECTIVES

18 **containing,** contained, holding, held, enclosing, enclosed; covering, covered, enveloping, enveloped, wrapping, wrapped, sheathed, surrounded, cocooning, cocooned; stabling, stabled, sheltering, sheltered

19 **storing,** storage, stored, reserved; packing, packed, bundled, boxed, caged; canning, canned, tinning, tinned, bottling, bottled; ladled, scooped, spooned, potting, potted, shoveled; binned, shelved, garaged, bagged, in the bag, locked up, entombed

VERBS

20 **contain,** store, put *or* place in a container, reserve, containerize, crate up, bundle, can, tin, pot, box, box up, bottle; cover, wrap, pack, package, sheath, cocoon, envelop, enclose, cage, surround, shelter, stable, garage, entomb

579 Size, Largeness

NOUNS

1 **size,** largeness, magnitude, order of magnitude, amplitude; dimensions, proportions, measurements, measure, gauge, scale; extent, extension, scope, range, reach, limit, expanse, spread, coverage, area; length, breadth, width, height, depth, radius, diameter, caliber, scantling, girth, circumference; mass, bulk, volume, capacity, cubature, cubage, content, tonnage, displacement, burden, tankage; room, space, accommodation, stowage

▶ *Accuracy 350; Heaviness 538; Space 563; Measurement 589; Length 590; Thickness 594; Height 596; Depth 598; Outline 617*

2 **largeness,** bigness, greatness; sizableness, ampleness, generousness, voluminousness, bagginess, capaciousness, spaciousness, roominess; hugeness, enormousness, immenseness, immensity, massiveness; grandness, grandeur, prodigiousness; tallness, bulkiness, unwieldiness, cumbersomeness, broadness, wideness; comprehensiveness, expansiveness, extensiveness, vastness; oversize, outsize, overgrowth

▶ *Whole 759; Completeness 761*

3 **large part,** principal part, main part, main body, the main, chief part; greater part, major part, ninety-nine percent, bulk, mass, majority, lion's share, biggest slice of the cake; almost all, nearly all, everything but the kitchen sink, better *or* best part

4 **gigantism,** giantism, hypertrophy, hyperplasia, acromegaly, elephantiasis

5 **fatness,** obesity, corpulence, portliness, rotundity, roundness; endomorphy, adiposity, grossness, fleshiness, flabbiness, fattishness; bloatedness, puffiness, fullness, plumpness, paunchiness, buxomness, bustiness, plumpishness, pudginess, tubbiness, chubbiness, stoutness, embonpoint; weight problem

6 **squatness,** dumpiness, stockiness, squareness; heavy build, burliness, brawniness, beefiness [Inf], meatiness; heaviness, chunkiness, heftiness, hulkiness, lumpishness, lumpiness

7 **mass,** lump, chunk, hunk, block, clump, cluster; wad, heap, mountain, clod, glob, dollop, gob, gobs [Inf], wodge [Brit inf]

8 **fat,** flab, blubber, lard; double chin, cellulite, paunch, potbelly, beer belly, spare tire [Inf], bay window [Inf]

9 **big thing,** monster, whale, dinosaur, mammoth, mastodon, elephant, hippopotamus, leviathan, behemoth, King Kong; lunker, whopper [Inf], jumbo [Inf]

10 **big person,** hulk, titan, titaness, colossus, amazon, goliath; giant, giantess, ogre, ogress; Brobdingnagian, Gargantua, Pantagruel, Cyclops, Polyphemus, Atlas; tall person [Inf]: highpockets, beanpole, long drink of water; fat person, roly-poly, heavyweight, dumpling, [Inf]: fatty, fatso, tub, blimp, hippo, lardass

▶ *Height 596*

ADJECTIVES

11 **this size,** about this size, so big, this big, about this big, of that order

12 **medium,** medium-size(d), average, average-size(d), standard, regular

▶ *Average 742*

13 **big,** large, great, full-size, full-grown, full-blown, full-scale; life-size, large as life, sizable, good-size, fair-size, large-size, large-scale; heavyweight, considerable, substantial, goodly, tidy, bumper, ample, generous, abundant, plentiful, bountiful, copious; voluminous, baggy, capacious, spacious, roomy; family-size, economy-size, man-size, king-size, queen-size; healthy [Inf]

14 **huge,** giant-size, record-size, great big, larger than life, enormous, immense, massive, massy; gigantic, gigantesque, colossal, titanic, monstrous, mammoth, giant, monster, Gargantuan, Brobdingnagian, Cyclopean; towering, monumental, grand, imposing, Homeric, epic; tremendous, stupendous, prodigious, mountainous, megalithic, macroscopic, astronomical; outsize, extra large, thundering, oversized, too big, overlarge, overgrown; bulky, broad, wide, comprehensive, expansive, extensive, vast, limitless, infinite; [Inf]: jumbo, whopping, walloping, whacking, spanking, mega

15 **fat,** obese, overweight, endomorphic, gross, fleshy, flabby, adipose; bloated, puffy, swollen, distended, full; plump, pudgy, tubby, chubby, stout, corpulent, portly, rotund, round, roly-poly; well-fed, overfed, fat as a pig,

plump as a dumpling *or* partridge, squab, dumpy; round-faced, moon-faced, full-faced, chubby-faced, chubby-cheeked, double-chinned; big-bellied, full-bellied, potbellied, paunchy, abdominous; big-bottomed, steatopygic, steatopygous, hippy; buxom, busty, bosomy, full-bosomed, well-endowed, top-heavy; [Inf]: zaftig, broad in the beam, well-upholstered, fat-assed

16 **stocky,** stout, thickset, heavyset, squat, square; well-built, heavily built, burly, strapping; brawny, beefy, meaty, heavy, chunky, hefty; hulking, hulky, lumbering, elephantine, lumpish, lumpy

VERBS

17 **size,** adjust, grade, gauge, measure; group, rank, sort, match, graduate, proportion; enlarge, fatten, bulk
▶ *Expansion 581*

18 **be big,** bulk, loom, loom large, fill space, tower, soar

ADVERBS

19 **largely,** on a large scale, in the large, greatly, considerably, substantially

20 **amply,** generously, abundantly, plentifully, bountifully, copiously; voluminously, capaciously, spaciously

21 **hugely,** in a big way, enormously, immensely, massively, monstrously, mightily; limitlessly, infinitely, as can be

22 **fatly,** obesely, plumply, stoutly, roundly, buxomly

580 Littleness

NOUNS

1 **littleness,** smallness, smallishness, diminutiveness, shortness, petiteness; small scale, compactness, handiness, portability; tininess, minuteness, fineness, daintiness, thinness, slightness, slenderness, exiguity, tenuousness; imperceptibility, intangibility, impalpability, imponderability, inappreciability, invisibility, evanescence; undersize, stuntedness, puniness, squatness, dumpiness, dwarfishness, runtiness, shrunkenness, scrubbiness, scrawniness, scragginess; meagerness, scantness, scantiness, skimpiness, paltriness, pettiness; snugness, cosiness, pokiness [Inf], dinkiness [Inf]

2 **miniaturization,** microminiaturization, microscopy, micrography, microscope, micrometer

3 **little thing,** particle, grain, grain of sand, seed, mustard seed, granule, point, pinpoint, pinhead, dot; miniature, mini, baby, toy, doll, puppet, model, scaled-down *or* miniaturized version, microcosm; pocket edition, duodecimo, twelvemo; microphotograph, microdot, pixel, microfilm, microfiche; chip, silicon chip, microchip, integrated circuit; molecule, nucleus, monad, atom, subatomic particle, nuclear particle, ion, electron, proton, neutron, neutrino, parton, meson, muon, quark; cell, corpuscle, microbe, bacterium, virus, germ, bacillus, microorganism, animalcule, pro-

tozoan, zoospore, microphyte, amoeba, euglena, plankton

4 **little piece,** bit, fragment, sliver, shaving, filing, jot, tittle, iota, mite; speck, fleck, mote, scrap, crumb, morsel; snippet, minutia, minim, drop, droplet; trace, trace amount, dash, hint, soupçon, suspicion, vestige
▶ *Part 760*

5 **little person** *or* **creature,** dwarf, midget, midge, pygmy, manikin, homunculus, atomy, micromorph, hop-o'-my-thumb; Tom Thumb, Thumbelina, Alberich, Nibelung; hobbit, elf, gnome, fairy, sprite, brownie, leprechaun; runt, minnow, fingerling, slip, wisp; bantam, lightweight, featherweight; [Inf]: shrimp, squirt, snip, half pint, pipsqueak, peewee, shorty

6 **little space,** hole, pigeonhole, cubbyhole, hole-in-the-wall, doll's house; pinch, tight squeeze *or* spot *or* corner; no room to swing a cat in

ADJECTIVES

7 **little,** small, smallish, diminutive, short, petite; small scale, compact, portable; tiny, minute, fine, dainty, elfin, thin, slight, slender, exiguous, tenuous; imperceptible, intangible, impalpable, imponderable, inappreciable, negligible, indiscernible, invisible; petty, trifling, trivial, inconsiderable, insignificant, unimportant, minimal; runty, shrunk, shrunken, shriveled, contracted, scrubby, scrawny, scraggy; meager, scant, scanty, skimpy, paltry, piddling, picayune

8 **undersized,** stunted, puny, squat, dumpy, dwarfish, dwarfed, midget, pygmy; Lilliputian, miniature, sub-miniature, mini, dwarf; bantam, baby, model, small-scale, miniaturized, microcosmic; inadequate, cramped, limited, restricted, snug, cosy, bijou; compact, handy, portable, pocket-size(d), pocket, duodecimo, twelve-mo; [Inf]: two-by-four, poky, dinky, pint-size(d), knee-high to a grasshopper

9 **tiny,** minute, minuscule, infinitesimal, microscopic, ultramicroscopic, rudimentary, rudimental, incipient, embryonic, germinal, granular; corpuscular, molecular, atomic, subatomic, microbic, microbial, bacterial, animalcular, protozoan, amoebic, amoeboid, wee, teeny; [Inf]: weeny, teeny-weeny, bitsy, itty-bitty *or* itsy-bitsy, dinky

VERBS

10 **make little,** diminish, minimize, shrink, shorten, reduce, scale back, contract, miniaturize
▶ *Contraction 582*

11 **be little,** be small, take up no room, fit on the head of a pin

ADVERBS

12 **little,** in a small way, in miniature, on a small scale, in a nutshell; diminutively, daintily, slightly, minimally, minutely, finely, tenuously

13 **infinitesimally,** indiscernibly, imperceptibly, invisibly, intangibly, impalpably, imponderably; inappreciably,

negligibly, inconsiderably, insignificantly, unimportantly

14 **microscopically,** microcosmically, atomically, subatomically

581 Expansion

NOUNS

1 **expansion,** enlargement, increase in size; extension, lengthening, drawing out, stretch, stretching, stretching out, outstretching; spread, spreading, spreading out, outspreading, creeping; sprawl, sprawling, splay, splaying, branching, ramification; fanning, fanning out, dispersion, expansion, widening, broadening, flare, flaring; dilation, diastole, opening

2 **swelling,** swell, swollenness, bloat, bloating, bloatedness, distension *or* distention; tumefaction, tumescence, intumescence, tumidity, tumidness, turgescence, turgidity, turgidness; dropsy, edema, puffiness, inflation, reflation, blowing up, bulging; tympanites, tympany

3 **increase,** building, buildup, augmentation, addition, heightening; rising, raising, elevation, elevating, hiking, upping; magnification, aggrandizement, amplification, waxing, crescendo

4 **growth,** maturation, maturing, development; upgrowth, overdevelopment, hypertrophy, overgrowth; growing up, coming of age, bodily development

5 **germination,** budding, shooting, sprouting, vegetation, burgeoning, blossoming, blooming, flowering; flourishing, thriving, multiplication, reproduction, procreation, breeding, pullulation
  ◗ *Reproduction 21*

6 **enlargeability,** extendability, extendibility, extensibility, extensibleness; stretch, stretchability, elasticity, spreadability, expansibility; dilatability, dilatableness, distensibility

7 **enlargement,** extension, swelling, tumor, bulge, balloon, bubble, inflatable

8 **enlarger,** extensor, lengthener, stretcher, spreader, disperser, expander; widener, broadener, dilator, distender; inflater, pump, increaser, augmenter, developer; stuffing, padding, bulk
  ◗ *Size, Largeness 579*

ADJECTIVES

9 **bigger,** larger, enlarged; extended, lengthened, drawnout, stretched, stretched-out, outstretched; spread, spread-out, outspread, widespread; splayed, fanned, fanned out, dispersed, expanded, widened, broadened, flared; dilated, open, wide-open, unfolded

10 **swelled,** swollen, bloated, distended, tumid, turgid, incrassated, dropsical, edematous; puffedup, puffy, inflated, blown-up, pumped-up; increased, built-up, augmented, heightened; raised, elevated, magnified, am-

plified; full-fledged, fully fledged, full-blown; stuffed, padded, fattened, fatted, fatter, overweight

11 **grown,** full-grown, fully grown, mature, developed; overdeveloped, hypertrophied, overgrown; grown up, of age

12 **growing,** crescent, extending, lengthening, stretching, spreading, creeping, sprawling, splaying, patulous, branching, branching out, fanning; fanlike, fanshaped, flabellate *or* flabelliform; deltoid, expanding, widening, broadening; flaring, dilating, opening, unfolding; swelling, tumescent, turgescent, bulging, bulbous; increasing, waxing, gathering, brewing, mushrooming, snowballing, heightening, rising; developing, maturing, growing up; germinating, budding, shooting, sprouting, burgeoning, blossoming, blooming, flowering; flourishing, thriving, multiplying, pullulating

13 **enlargeable,** extendible, extensible, extensive, extensile, extensional; stretchable, stretchy, elastic; spreadable, dispersive, expandable, expansible, expansive, expansile, expansionary; dilatable, dilational, dilatant, dilative; distensible, distensive, inflatable, inflationary, augmentative; elevatory, multipliable, magnifiable, amplifiable, developable

VERBS

14 **enlarge,** make bigger, make larger, increase in size; extend, lengthen, draw out, stretch, stretch out, outstretch; spread, spread out, outspread, creep; sprawl, splay, ramify; fan, fan out, disperse, expand, widen, broaden, flare; dilate

15 **swell,** bloat, distend; puff up, inflate, blow up, pump, pump up; stuff, pad, fatten, fat, plump, plump up

16 **increase,** build, build up, bulk, augment, add to, heighten; raise, elevate, hike, hike up, up; magnify, aggrandize, amplify; develop, overdevelop, hypertrophy

17 **grow,** become bigger, become larger; branch, branch out, ramify, unfold; tumify, balloon, belly, bulge; fill out, get fat, gain weight, put on weight, become overweight; outgrow, overgrow, grow like a weed, spread like wildfire, mushroom, snowball; wax, greaten, crescendo, gather, brew, rise; mature, grow up, come of age; shoot up, spring up, upspring, sprout up, germinate, bud, shoot, sprout, vegetate, burgeon, blossom, bloom, flower; flourish, thrive, multiply, reproduce, procreate, breed, pullulate

ADVERBS

18 **largely,** broadly, widely, extensively, expansively, increasingly; additionally, reproductively, procreatively; bulbously, puffily, turgidly, tumidly
  ◗ *Size, Largeness 579*

582 Contraction

NOUNS

1 **contraction,** decrease, reduction, lessening; systole,

syneresis, synizesis, shrinking, shrinkage, shrunkenness, preshrinking, preshrinkage; constringency, astringency, astringence, compression, compaction, compactedness; condensation, concentration, miniaturization, scaling-down

2 **shortening,** abbreviation, elision, curtailment, abridgment, editing; pruning, trimming, clipping, shearing, shaving, filing, grinding; narrowing, drawing in, drawing together, closing up, taking in, gathering; puckering, puckering up, pursing, knitting, wrinkling, shriveling, withering, searing; wasting, consumption, tabescence, atrophy, marasmus, emaciation, thinning, slimming, losing weight; decrease, reduction, lessening, diminuendo, wane, waning, leveling off, bottoming out

3 **squeeze,** squeezing, tightening, tightness, pressing, pressure, crush, crushing, pinch, pinching, choking; clenching, clamping, cramping, constriction, coarctation; limitation, restriction, circumscription, strangling, strangulation, stenosis; deflation, flattening, flatness, implosion, collapse, cave-in

4 **contractibility,** contractility, shrinkability, compressibility, compactability; condensibility, crushability, limitability, circumscribability; deflatability, collapsibility

5 **contracted thing,** epitome, compendium, digest, abridgment, condensation, bottleneck, neck, isthmus, cervix, hourglass, hourglass figure, wasp waist

6 **contractor,** astringent, styptic, compressor, compacter, condenser; tourniquet, squeezer, press, crusher, foller, mangle, clamp, vice; corset, straitjacket, constrictor; trimmer, grinder

ADJECTIVES

7 **smaller,** decreased, reduced, lessened; contracted, shrunk, shrunken, preshrunk, Sanforized™; compressed, compact, compacted, condensed, concentrated, boiled-down, miniaturized, scaled-down

8 **shortened,** abbreviated, curtailed, abridged, edited; stunted, pruned, trimmed, clipped, shorn; narrow, narrowed, drawn in, drawn together, closed up, gathered; smocked, tucked, puckered, puckered up, pursed, knitted; wrinkled, shriveled, shriveled up, withered, wizened or wizen, sear, seared; wasted, consumptive, emaciated, thin, slim

9 **squeezed,** tight, tightened, pressed, crushed, pinched; rolled-up, curled-up, huddled, clenched, cramped, constricted, strangled, strangulated; coarctate, limited, restricted, circumscribed; deflated, flat, collapsed, telescoped

10 **contracting,** decreasing, reducing, lessening; contractive, contractional, shrinking, constringent, astringent, styptic; compressive, tightening, crushing, pinching, cramping, constricting, constrictive, limiting, restricting, restrictive, circumscriptive, strangling; deflationary, implosive, collapsing; shortening, stunting, narrowing; gathering, puckering, pursing, shriv-

eling, searing; wasting, tabescent, emaciating, thinning, slimming

11 **contractible,** contractile, shrinkable, compressible, compactable, condensible, crushable; limitable, circumscribable; deflatable, collapsible, foldable, telescopic

VERBS

12 **contract,** make smaller, decrease, reduce, lessen; shrink, preshrink; constringe, compress, compact, condense, concentrate, boil down, miniaturize, scale down; shorten, abbreviate, curtail, abridge, edit; stunt, prune, trim, clip, shear, shave, whittle away, file, grind; narrow, draw, draw in, draw together, close up, take in, gather; smock, tuck, pucker, pucker up, purse, knit, wrinkle, shrivel, sear; waste, emaciate, thin, slim

13 **squeeze,** tighten, press, crush, pinch, cram, jam, roll up, roll up into a ball; clench, clamp, cramp, constrict, limit, restrict, circumscribe, strangle, strangulate; deflate, flatten, implode, collapse, telescope

14 **become smaller,** tighten, roll up, roll up into a ball, curl up, huddle, crowd together; go down, cave in, fall in, fold up; shorten, narrow, draw in, close up, pucker, pucker up, knit; wrinkle, shrivel, shrivel up, wither, wizen; waste, waste away, emaciate; thin *or* trim *or* slim down, diet, lose weight; decrease, reduce, lessen, wane, level off, bottom out

583 Opening

NOUNS

1 **opening,** gap, hole, hollow, cavity, aperture, orifice; gape, duct, passageway, passage, space, open space, interval; door, doorway, window, skylight, entrance, entry; slot, split, crack, hairline crack; crevice, chasm, pass; fault, flaw, breach, break, fracture, rupture, cut, tear, cleft, fissure; perforation, piercing, pricking, puncture, bore

▸ *Space 563; Interval 587; Concavity 635; Notch 636; Passage 692; Entry 706*

2 **opener,** key, master key, skeleton key, passkey, key card, smart card; password, open sesame; can opener, bottle opener, corkscrew; drill, brace and bit, reamer, awl; needle, hypodermic needle, pin; bodkin, punch, leather punch, auger, bit, probe; pick, pickax, ax; saw, trephine, trepan, lance, lancet; bayonet, knife

3 **body orifice,** pore, sweat gland, aural cavity, ear, nasal cavity, nostril, nose, stoma, anus, cloaca, urethra, vagina, oral cavity, mouth, maw; [Inf]: trap, kisser, asshole

4 **hole,** keyhole, peephole, knothole, eyehole; eyelet, eye, buttonhole, pinhole; porthole, borehole, blowhole, air hole; shaft, well, mine, mineshaft, excavation; cavern, cave, volcano

5 **porosity,** porousness; porous thing: sponge, sieve,

colander, teabag, filter, honeycomb; screen, mosquito net, nylon stockings; lattice, grate, grille

6 **open space,** open country, open sea; clearing, meadow; beach, desert; court, yard, glade; stage

7 **openness,** opening up, frankness, bluntness, explicitness, plain words, candor, honesty, sincerity; artlessness, open heart, open face, ingenuousness, naiveté

> *Disclosure 180; Truthfulness 191; Naiveté 821*

8 **opportunity,** opening, open door, toe *or* foot in the door, toehold, foothold, chance, possibility, golden opportunity, occasion; available post, vacancy, position, job, break [Inf], lucky break [Inf]

9 **beginning,** start, commencement, initiation, inception, dawn, birth; inauguration, introduction, launch, debut, premiere

> *Beginning 771*

ADJECTIVES

10 **open,** wide-open, pushed open; pulled open, unclosed, uncovered, unwrapped, unfolded, exposed, visible, ajar; punched open, cut open, split, torn, cracked, creviced, cleft, fissured, breached; gaping, open-mouthed, agape; hacked, hewn, cut, sawed *or* sawn; broken, fractured, ruptured

> *Disclosure 180*

11 **opened up,** unblocked, unlocked, unbolted, unbarred, unlatched, unfastened, unsealed, uncovered, uncorked, unstopped, unobstructed; patent, clear, evident, obvious, apparent, manifest; free, unimpeded, unhindered, unhampered, unrestricted, accessible, open-door, available, vacant, public; unenclosed, unfenced, unprotected, unshielded; extended, extensive, bare, open-plan

12 **holed,** perforated, porous, permeated, riddled with holes, punched full of holes, filled with holes, sievelike, cribriform *or* cribrous, honeycombed, spongy, leaky; injected, penetrated, probed, pierced, pricked, punctured, lanced; bayoneted, knifed, stabbed, stuck, slashed, gashed, shot, peppered with shot; bored, hollowed, drilled, reamed, dug, burrowed, tunneled, sunk, excavated; volcanic

13 **open,** frank, blunt, explicit, plain, candid, unreserved; open-hearted, open-faced, honest, sincere, ingenuous, naive, artless

14 **beginning,** starting, commencing, dawning; initial, inceptive, newborn, inaugural, introductory, first, debut, premiere

VERBS

15 **open,** push open, pull open, open up, open out; unclose, uncover, unwrap, unfold, expose, disclose, reveal, show, leave ajar; punch open, cut open, split, tear, crack, cleave, breach, hack, hew, cut, saw; break, fracture, rupture, burst open; gape; erupt, explode

16 **open up,** unblock, unlock, unbolt, unbar, unlatch, unfasten, unseal, uncover, uncork, unstop; not ob-

struct, clear, free, gain access, access, not enclose; extend, spread

17 **hole,** make porous, perforate, permeate, riddle with holes, punch full of holes, fill with holes, honeycomb; fissure, slot, break the skin, trephine, trepan; inject, penetrate, probe, pierce, prick, puncture, lance; bayonet, knife, stab, run through, stick, slash, gash, shoot, pepper with shot; bore, hollow, drill, ream, dig a hole, burrow, tunnel, sink a mineshaft, excavate

18 **provide passage for,** drain, pipe, funnel, vent; sieve, screen

19 **be open,** open up, speak straight from the shoulder, use plain words, open one's heart

20 **find an opening,** gain a foothold, be in the right place at the right time, get a break [Inf], get a (lucky) break [Inf]

21 **begin,** start, commence, initiate, dawn; introduce, inaugurate, launch, debut, premiere

ADVERBS

22 **openly,** in the open, obviously, apparently, manifestly, visibly, patently, clearly, evidently, plainly; publicly, availably, accessibly; extensively, widely

23 **candidly,** openly, bluntly, plainly, explicitly, frankly, sincerely, honestly, straight from the shoulder, in plain words, ingenuously, naively, artlessly

INTERJECTIONS

24 **open up!,** unlock the door!, open sesame!, make way!, gangway!

584 Closure

NOUNS

1 **closure,** closing, closing up, closing down, shutdown; cloture, finish, cessation, discontinuance, stop, stoppage, conclusion; resolution, fulfillment, completion, termination, end, foreclosure; imperviousness, impermeability, impenetrability, impassability

> *Cessation 668; Completeness 761; End 773*

2 **obstruction,** occlusion, contraction, constriction, congestion, bottleneck, gridlock; strangulation, blockage, constipation, blockade; block, chock, barrier, barricade, roadblock, bar, hindrance, lock, bolt, padlock; impasse, sealing off; standstill, deadlock, stalemate

> *Contraction 582; Limit 620; Hindrance 826*

3 **stopper,** stop, cap, lid, top, cork, covering, cover, seal, plug; bandage, tourniquet; bung, peg, pin, spigot, valve, tap, faucet, stopcock; wad, wadding, stuffing, tampion, tampon, wedge; blood clot, thrombus, embolus, infarct; damper, choke, trip switch, cutout switch, piston

> *Ill Health 114; Covering 613; Connection 754*

4 **closed place,** dead end, cul-de-sac, blind alley, enclosure, enclosed place, prison; reserve, sanctuary, zoo, hutch, cage, kennel, coop, fold; grave, tomb, sepulcher; trap

Prison 55; Enclosure 619

5 closer, doorkeeper, doorman, porter, concierge, gate-keeper; warden, turnkey, jailer; caretaker, zookeeper; sentry, sentinel, night watchman

6 closed-in person, prisoner, inmate, detainee, internee; miner, submariner; shut-in

ADJECTIVES

7 closed, unopened, shut, shut-up; fastened, secured, buttoned, buttoned up, zipped up; sealed, hermetically sealed, airtight, vacuum-packed, watertight, waterproof, lightproof; nonporous, impermeable, impervious

8 obstructed, occluded, blocked up, clogged, clogged up, impenetrable, impassable; locked, bolted, barred, latched, padlocked; constipated, costive, constricted; bottlenecked, gridlocked, congested, choked, choked up; full, stuffed, packed, jammed

9 stopped, stopped up, plugged, capped, corked; dammed, staunched, bandaged; blocked, bunged, bunged up, stuffed up

10 closed down, closed up, shut down; wound up, finished, resolved, completed, ended, clotured

11 enclosed, closed-in, shut up, jailed, imprisoned, confined

VERBS

12 close, close up, shut, shut up, seal; do up, button, button up, zip up; seal off, batten down, batten down the hatches, put the lid on, cover, contain

13 obstruct, occlude, constrict, congest, bottleneck; lock, bolt, padlock; constipate, contract, constrict, congest; strangle, throttle, choke; bar, stay, block, block up, clog, clog up; blockade, barricade, hinder

Restraint 830

14 stop, stopper, plug, cap, top, cork, bung, bung up; dam, staunch, bandage, tampon, stop up

15 close down, close up, shut down, finish, cease, discontinue, cloture, terminate, end, foreclose; conclude, resolve, fulfill, complete, wind up

16 enclose, confine, keep in, lock up *or* in, shut up *or* in, imprison, jail; cage, impound, pen, hutch, kennel, coop, corral, fold; intern, immure, incarcerate; bury, entomb

ADVERBS

17 impermeably, imperviously, impenetrably, impassibly; nonporously, hermetically; costively

18 finally, at last, in the end; completely, over, over and done with

585 Distance

NOUNS

1 distance, farness, far-offness, remoteness, inaccessibility, aloofness; removal, separation, divergence, deviation, dispersion; clearance, margin, leeway, per-spective, long range; astronomical distance, deep space, depth of space, light years, infinity

Space 563; Interval 587; Length 590; Divergence 703; Separation 753

2 great distance, long way, great way, good way, fair way, long run, long haul, long trail, day's march, marathon, far cry, miles away, long shot, long chalk [Brit inf]

3 distant place, background, periphery, circumference, horizon, skyline, offing, vanishing point, apogee, aphelion, where the earth meets the sky, outer space, moon; godforsaken place, outback [Aus], outskirts, outpost, boondocks; antipodes, pole, North Pole, South Pole, Thule, ultima Thule, Pillars of Hercules, Timbuktu, Outer Mongolia, Darkest Africa, Siberia, Pago Pago, the Great Divide, Far East, Far West; four corners of the earth, ends of the earth, world's end, jumping-off place, end of the rainbow; God knows where, middle of nowhere, miles from nowhere; [Inf]: sticks, boonies, back o' beyond [Aus]

Outline 617; Limit 620; Back 622

4 reserve, aloofness, standoffishness, shyness, coldness, coolness

Avoidance 386; Unsociability 409

ADJECTIVES

5 distant, far, far-off, faraway, far-flung, remote; thither, yonder, yon; ulterior, farther, further, outlying, off-shore, inaccessible, out-of-the-way, godforsaken, exotic; antipodean, hyperborean; overseas, transatlantic, transpacific, transoceanic, transmarine, ultramarine, transcontinental, transalpine, transmontane, tramon-tane, ultramontane, transpolar, transpontine, trans-mundane, ultramundane

6 away, apart, asunder, separated, distal, peripheral, long-distance, long-range, out of sight, out of range, out of reach, unreachable, out of this world; farthest, farthermost, furthest, furthermost, ultimate, extreme, terminal

7 reserved, aloof, standoffish, unapproachable, untouchable, shy, cold, cool

VERBS

8 be distant, outlie, outrange, outdistance, stand far away; lie out of the way, stretch to the ends of the earth

9 keep away, keep off, keep one's distance, keep at a distance, remain at a distance; stand off, stand away, stand aloof, stand back; distance oneself, keep away from, keep out of the way of, keep a safe distance from, keep clear of, stand clear, steer clear, give a wide berth to; keep at arm's length, keep apart, separate, space out

10 reach out, stretch out, extend, go, carry out; outreach, outstretch; reach to, stretch to, extend to, go to, lead to, run to, carry to, get to, come to

ADVERBS

11 distantly, remotely, far, afar, far-off, far away, long way off *or* away, over the hills and far away; overseas, abroad, afield, far afield, far and wide, far and near, widely, broadly; to the ends of the earth, out of this world, in the distance, thither, yonder, yon

12 in the offing, in the background; on the horizon, as far as the eye can see, out of sight, out of hearing, out of earshot, out of range; out of reach, beyond reach, out of bounds; too far, further, farther

13 at a distance, at arm's length, apart, asunder, aloof, aside; ahead, in front, behind, way behind, way in front, away, off; astray, clear, wide, wide of the mark, out of the way; in the boondocks; [Inf]: in the sticks, in the boonies, in the back o' beyond [Aus]

14 apart, away, aside, wide apart, way *or* wide away

15 reservedly, aloofly, standoffishly, in a standoffish mood, shyly, coldly, coolly, unapproachably

586 Nearness

NOUNS

1 nearness, closeness, proximity, propinquity, immediacy, intimacy, inseparability; handiness, convenience, accessibility; approximation, approach, convergence, juncture, collision course, conjunction; appulse, perigee, perihelion

 ▶ *Presence 575; Immediacy 645; Convergence 702*

2 short distance, no distance, little way, short way, shortcut; step, stone's throw, spitting distance, striking distance, earshot, close range; brink, verge, hairsbreadth, fingerbreadth, finger's width, inch, centimeter, millimeter; ace, near miss, near thing

 ▶ *Contention 422; Edge 618*

3 near place, vicinity, vicinage, neighborhood, locality, precinct; environs, surroundings, purlieus, confines, approaches; foreground, front, ringside seat; neighbor, next-door neighbor

 ▶ *Surroundings 615*

4 juxtaposition, apposition, adjacency; contiguity, contiguousness, abuttal, abutment, tangency, touching, touch, contact; junction, joining, connection, union; bordering, border, borderland, frontier, buffer state

 ▶ *Touch 216; Edge 618; Limit 620; Union 752; Adhesion 755; Consecutiveness 774*

5 meeting, encounter, interface, intercommunication, impingement, confrontation; nudge, brush, graze

 ▶ *Interface 616*

ADJECTIVES

6 near, nigh, close, proximate, proximal, intimate; side by side, shoulder to shoulder, hand in hand, arm in arm, elbow to elbow; end to end, nose to nose, bumper-to-bumper; cheek by jowl, face to face, hand to hand, neck and neck, close run; nearby, in the vicinity, in the neighborhood, local; wayside, roadside, in-

shore, neighboring, vicinal, next-door; warm, hot, reachable

7 nearer, closer, approximate, approximating; gaining, nearing, approaching, converging, convergent, forthcoming

8 next, immediate, nearest, closest; on the spot, to hand, at hand, handy, convenient, accessible, at one's fingertips

9 juxtaposed, juxtapositional, juxtapositive, adjacent; tangent, tangential, contiguous, adjoining, abutting, touching, in contact, continuous, joined, connecting; bordering, conterminous, coterminous

10 meeting, intercommunicating, linking, interfacing, impinging; rubbing, brushing, grazing, glancing

VERBS

11 be near, stand close to, lie in the vicinity *or* neighborhood of

12 near, come near, get near, get close, move close, bring near, draw near, draw nigh, approach; converge, verge on, close up, move up, get warm, get hot

13 stay near, keep close to, follow, shadow, dog, sit on the tail of, tread on the heels of, breathe down the neck of, hover over, tailgate; stick to, cling to, hug, embrace, skirt; [Inf]: tail, go with, hang around *or* about

14 juxtapose, appose, adjoin, abut, butt, touch; make contact, come into contact, bring into contact, place side by side; join, connect, border, neighbor, be next to, be beside, be side by side

15 meet, encounter, interface, link, intercommunicate, impinge; confront, hit, nudge, jostle, elbow, rub, brush; kiss, graze, scrape, shave, skim, glance, rub shoulders *or* elbows with

ADVERBS

16 near, close, closely, at close quarters, at close range, not far; at hand, near at hand, close at hand, at one's fingertips, at one's elbow, at one's side, at one's feet, under one's nose, nigh

17 nearby, close by, hard by, fast by, in the vicinity, in the neighborhood, locally, next-door; hereabouts, thereabouts, about, around, around and about; within reach, within range, within earshot, within hearing, within call, within sight; a stone's throw away, only a step, just around the corner, on one's doorstep, in one's own backyard, in spitting distance, as near as makes no difference

18 nearly, almost, well-nigh, not quite, just about, all but, as good as, near enough; virtually, practically, for all practical purposes, to all intents and purposes; more *or* less, give *or* take, approximately, roughly, in round numbers, generally speaking, say

19 verging on, on the verge, on the brink, by a hairsbreadth, by the skin of one's teeth [Inf], by a whisker, on the tip of one's tongue

20 beside, alongside, in juxtaposition, adjacently, tangentially, in contact, contiguously, continuously, side by side, cheek by jowl, face to face, nose to nose, eyeball to eyeball, end to end, elbow to elbow, bumper to bumper, nose to tail

587 Interval

NOUNS

1 **interval,** gap, space, distance, room, margin, clearance, interspace, spacing; headroom, leeway, freeboard; distance between, space between, intervening space; interruption, daylight, firebreak, passage, separation; time interval, intermission, discontinuity, hiatus, lacuna, caesura, jump, leap
  ▸ *Space 563; Opening 583; Time 639; Separation 753; Discontinuity 775*

2 **crack,** crevice, cleft, fissure, scissure, interstice, chink, cranny, check, flaw, hairline crack; notch, nick, cut, incision, gash, slit; split, rift, fault, rupture, rent, tear, break, fracture; breach, hole, opening, aperture, orifice, cavity, groove, slot; furrow, trench, ditch, dike, moat, sunk fence, ha-ha
  ▸ *Depth 598; Notch 636; Furrow 638*

3 **gulf,** abyss, chasm, void, gape, gorge, gully, couloir, ravine, gulch, coulee; crevasse, chimney; ghat, pass, defile, col, flumedraw; valley, dell, canyon
  ▸ *Concavity 635; Passage 692*

ADJECTIVES

4 **spaced,** spaced out, interspaced, interspatial, interstitial; separate, separated, parted, set apart, removed, placed at intervals; intervallic, discontinuous

5 **cracked,** cleft, cloven, fissured, fissile, cut, slit; split, riven, ruptured, rent, torn, broken, fractured; open, gaping, grooved, furrowed, rimose, dehiscent

VERBS

6 **space,** space out, interspace, separate, break up, part; set apart, keep apart, place at intervals; make a space, make room, clear

7 **crack,** cleave, check, notch, nick, cut, incise, gash, slit; split, split apart, rive, rupture, rend, tear, break, fracture, breach; open, gape, groove, slot, furrow, trench, ditch

ADVERBS

8 **apart,** separately, discontinuously; at intervals, with a break, with an intermission, with an interval; off and on, now and then, now and again, every so often; interspatially, interstitially

588 Layer

NOUNS

1 **layer,** thickness, bed, stratum, seam, zone, vein, lode, belt, strip, band, course, table; ply, interlining, fold, pleat, lap, flap; superstratum, overlayer, topcoat, topsoil, overlap, substratum, underlayer, underlay, lining, undercoat, bedding

  ▸ *Thickness 594; Horizontality 603; Covering 613*

2 **level,** tier, row, story, floor, landing, deck, terrace, ledge, shelf, step, stage
  ▸ *Base 601; Support 605*

3 **coat,** coating, covering, sheet, blanket; foil, leaf, lamina, lamella, laminate; plate, plating, veneer, facing, fascia, overlay, sheathe, bark, membrane, skin, peel, pellicle, film, patina, bloom, scum, dross; interfacing, undercoat, liner, lining paper
  ▸ *Materials 104; Thinness 595; Covering 613*

4 **slice,** sliver, wafer, disk, chip, rasher, collop, cut, slab; tablet, plaque, plank, slat, lath, panel, pane, tile, slate, shaving, paring, scale, squama; flake, dandruff, scurf, flock, floccus

5 **layering,** stratification, lamination, lamellation, foliation, scaliness, flakiness, squamation; delamination, exfoliation, desquamation

ADJECTIVES

6 **layered,** in layers, stratified, stratiform, straticulate, foliated, laminate, laminated, two-ply, three-ply, *etc.,* two-tiered, three-tiered, *etc.,* two-storied, three-storied, *etc.,* double-decker, triple-decker, *etc.;* terraced, multistage

7 **coated,** undercoated, plated, veneered, faced, overlaid, lined, overlaying, overlapped, overlapping, sheathed, laminated; interlined, interfaced

8 **platelike,** leaflike, foliate, lamellar, lamellate, lamellated, lamelliform, placoid, membranous, pellicular, filmy, scummy, drossy, scaly, furfuraceous, squamous, squamose, squamulose; flaky, scurfy, flocculent, floccose

VERBS

9 **layer,** lay, lay down, arrange in layers, stratify, laminate, tier, deck, shingle, sandwich, coat, spread, cover, plate, veneer, face, line, overlay, overlap; interline, undercoat, interface

10 **scale,** peel off, peel, flake off, flake, strip, shave, delaminate, exfoliate, desquamate

ADVERBS

11 **in layers,** in strips, on several levels, membraneously, furfuraceously, squamously, squamosely, flocculently

589 Measurement

NOUNS

1 **measurement,** measure, measuring, admeasurement, metage; quantification, quantitation, gauging, calibration; calculation, computation, reckoning; assessment, valuation, rating, evaluation, appraisal, appraisement; estimation, estimate, approximation, rough measure, ballpark figure [Inf]; determination, survey, surveying, triangulation, geodesy, geodetics, topography, cartography, oceanography
  ▸ *Space 563; Length 590; Height 596; Quantity 738; Calculation 784*

2 **measurability,** mensurability, quantifiability, determinability; size, magnitude, length, height, altitude, depth, distance, range, scope, breadth, width, volume, capacity, weight, quantity, amount, dosage, degree, extent, value, sound, time, speed

3 **science of measurement,** metrology, mensuration

4 **measuring system,** foot-pound-second (fps) system; metric system, metrication, imperial system [Brit], meter-kilogram-second (mks) system, meter-kilogram-second-ampere (mksa) system; International System of Units *or* SI; linear measure, square measure, surveyor's measure, cubic measure, liquid measure, dry measure, avoirdupois weight, troy weight, apothecaries' measure, apothecaries' weight

5 **unit of measurement,** measure, base *or* fundamental unit, absolute unit, derived unit, supplementary unit, compound unit

6 **coordinates,** ordinate, abscissa, latitude, longitude, azimuth, right ascension, declination; Cartesian coordinates, cylindrical coordinates, rectangular coordinates *or* rectangular coordinate system, spherical coordinates

▶ *Length 590; Depth 598; Timekeeping 646*

7 **standard,** norm, yardstick, touchstone, benchmark, criterion, rule of thumb, canon, test, check, type, model, pattern, prototype

8 **type of measurement,** linear measure, square measure, cubic measure, liquid measure, dry measure, surveyor's measure, board measure, avoirdupois weight, troy weight, apothecaries' weight, apothecaries' measure

9 **scale,** linear scale, logarithmic scale, log scale, temperature scale, Celsius *or* centigrade scale, Fahrenheit scale, Réaumur scale, Rankine scale, absolute scale,

---

FIELDS OF MEASUREMENT (with definitions and related instruments)

acidimetry: degree of acidity; acidimeter

actinometry: radiation; actinometer

aerometry: air; aerometer

alcoholometry: percentage of alcohol; alcoholometer

algometry: pain; algometer

alkalimetry: quantity of carbon dioxide; alkalimeter

altimetry: altitudes; altimeter

anemometry: wind speed; anemometer, wind gauge

anthropometry: human body size and proportions

astrometry: positions of celestial bodies

atmometry: water evaporation; atmometer *or* evaporimeter

audiometry: hearing; audiometer

barometry: atmospheric pressure; barometer

bathymetry: water depth; bathometer, bathymeter

biometry, biometrics: duration of life

calorimetry: heat; calorimeter

cephalometry: human head; cephalometer

chronometry: time; chronometer

clinometry: angles of slope; clinometer

colorimetry: color; colorimeter

coulometry: coulombs; coulometer

craniometry: skull measurement; craniometer

cryometry: low temperature; cryometer

densimetry: density; densimeter, densitometer

dilatometry: expansion; dilatometer

dolorimetry: sensitivity to pain

dosimetry: doses of medicine; dosimeter

dynamometry: mechanical force, power; dynamometer

electrometry: low voltages; electrometer

fluorometry: fluorescence; fluorometer

galvanometry: strength of electric current; galvanometer

goniometry: solid angles; goniometer

hydrometry: specific gravity; hydrometer

hygrometry: humidity; hygrometer

hypsometry: elevation, altitude

interferometry: wavelengths; interferometer

iodometry: analysis of iodine

magnetometry: magnetic field; magnetometer

manometry: fluid pressure; manometer *or* tensimeter

micrometry: minute distances; micrometer, micrometer caliper, micrometer gauge

odometry: distance traveled; odometer

optometry: vision; optometer

phonometry: sound; phonometer

photogrammetry: surveying and mapping through photographs

photometry: light; photometer

piezometry: pressure *or* compressibility; piezometer

planimetry: plane areas; planimeter

plastometry: elasticity; plastometer

pneumatometry: quality of inhaled *or* exhaled air; pneumatometer

polarimetry: amount of light polarization; polarimeter

potentiometry: electromotive force; potentiometer

psychometry: mental traits

pyrometry: high temperatures; pyrometer

radiometry: transformation of radiant energy; radiometer

refractometry: refractive index; refractometer

rheometry: flow of fluids; rheometer

saccharimetry *or* saccharometry: amount of sugar; saccharometer

salinometry: amount of salt; salinometer *or* salimeter

seismometry: earthquakes; seismometer

sensitometry: sensitivity of photographic materials; sensitometer

spectrometry: wavelengths, deviation of refracted rays; spectrometer

spectrophotometry: photometric comparisons between parts of spectra; spectrophotometer

sphygmomanometry: blood pressure; sphygmomanometer

spirometry: lung capacity; spirometer

stereometry: volumes

stoichiometry: amount of elements *or* compounds in chemical reactions

tachometry: speed; tachometer

tachymetry: distances, directions, differences in elevation; tachymeter

telemetry: distances; telemeter

thermometry: temperature; thermometer

tintometry: tints; tintometer

tonometry: tone frequency; intraocular pressure *or* blood pressure; vapor pressure; tonometer

viscometry: viscosity; viscometer

volumetry: volume; volumeter

zoometry: lengths, sizes of animals

Descending Order	Ascending Order
deci (d, 10^{-1})	deca (da, 10)
centi (c, 10^{-2})	hecto (h, 10^2)
milli (m, 10^{-3})	kilo (k, 10^3)
micro (μ, 10^{-6})	mega (M, 10^6)
nano (n, 10^{-9})	giga (G, 10^9)
pico (p, 10^{-12})	tera (T, 10^{12})
femto (f, 10^{-15})	peta (P, 10^{15})
atto (a, 10^{-18})	exa (E, 10^{18})

thermodynamic scale, Kelvin scale, International Practical Temperature Scale (IPTS); Baumé scale

10 **standard,** fundamental standard, standardization; American National Standards Institute (formerly American Standards Association, ASA), *Bureau international des poids et mésures* (BIPM) [Fr], *Deutsche Industrie Normen* (DIN) [Ger], International Standards Organization (ISO), National Bureau of Standards (NBS), National Physical Laboratory (NPL) [Brit]

11 **dimension,** mass, length, time, physical quantity, dimensional analysis

12 **measuring instrument,** length: measuring rod, micrometer, yardstick, foot rule, rule, ruler, tape measure, meter bar, steel rule; clearance: feeler *or* feeler gauge; perpendicularity *or* depth: line, plumb line, lead, chain, Gunter's chain, engineer's chain; weight: scale, graduated scale, calibrated scale, vernier *or* vernier scale, balance, analytic balance, weighing machine, weigh-

bridge; dividers, calipers; set square, try square, T-square, protractor, quadrant, sextant, octant, astrolabe, log; height: altimeter; depth: echo sounder, dipstick; watermark, water line, tidemark, high-water mark, load line *or* Plimsoll line; distance: pedometer, odometer, milestone; time: clock, stopwatch, chronometer; Doppler radar; pressure *or* force: strain gauge, piezoelectric crystal

13 **meter,** gauge, dial gauge, indicator, chart recorder; accelerometer, alidade, ammeter, bolometer, cyclometer, decelerometer, electricity meter, gas meter, Geiger counter, monometer, nitrometer, pressure gauge, pulsimeter, speedometer, tensiometer, theodolite, thermobarometer, thermopile, vaporimeter, variometer, water meter

14 **measurer,** gauger, assessor, valuer, evaluator, appraiser, estimator, surveyor, geodesist, topographer, cartographer, oceanographer, timekeeper, quantifier, actuary

▶ *Mathematics 6*

ADJECTIVES

15 **metrical,** metric, imperial [Brit], avoirdupois, SI, linear, cubic, measuring, mensural, mensurational, mensurative, quantitative, metrological, geodetic, topographic, cartographic, oceanographic

16 **measured,** admeasured, quantified, metered, gauged, calibrated, graduated, reckoned, assessed, valued, rated, estimated, determined, surveyed, triangulated, plotted, mapped

17 **measurable,** mensurable, quantifiable, meterable,

SCIENTIFIC AND TECHNICAL UNITS

ampere	centimeter-gram-	foot-pound	lumen	phon
ampere-hour	second	foot-poundal	lux	phot
ampere-turn	centner	foot-ton	mach *or* mach	poise
angstrom	chronon	fresnel	number	poundal
astronomical unit	circular mil	gal	magneton *or* Bohr	rad
atmosphere	coulomb	gallon	magneton	radian
atomic mass	curie	gamma	maxwell	roentgen
atomic mass unit *or*	cusec (flow rate)	gauge *or* gage	measurement ton *or*	rutherford
amu *or* dalton	cycle	gauss	shipping ton	sabin
barn	darcy	gilbert	meter	siemens *or* mho
baud	decibel	gram	microbar *or* barye	sievert
becquerel	degree	gram atom *or* gram-	micron *or*	slug
bel	degree-day	atomic weight	micrometer	steradian
bit *or* binary digit	diopter	gram molecule *or*	mil	stilb
British thermal unit	dram	gram-molecular	millibar	stoke
(BTU)	dyne	weight	mm Hg	tesla
byte	epoch	gray	mole	therm
calorie *or* calory *or*	erg	henry	neper	torr
gram calorie *or*	farad	hertz	newton	volt
small calorie	faraday	jansky	nit	volt-ampere
Calorie *or* kilocalorie	fathom	joule	oersted	watt
candela	fermi	kelvin	ohm	watt-hour
candle *or*	foot-candle	light-year	parsec	weber
international candle	foot-lambert	line	pascal	x-unit

acre	cup	hank	long ton or gross ton	pipe
acre-foot	degree	hogshead	[Brit]	point (jewelry)
acre-inch	denier	horsepower	man-hour	point (printing)
are	DIN (photography)	horsepower-hour	metric ton or tonne	pole
bar	dram	hundredweight or	mile or statute mile	pound
barleycorn	em	cental or quintal	milline	puncheon
barrel	en	inch	minim	quart
board foot	fathom	international nautical	minute	rod
bushel	fluid dram	mile or air mile	nautical mile or	rood
butt	fluid ounce	kip	geographical mile or	scruple
cable or cable's length	foot	knot	sea mile	second
carat	freight ton	last	net ton	shot
centiare or centare	furlong	lea	ounce	span
chain or surveyor's	gallon	league	peck	stere
chain	gill	liter	pennyweight	stone [Brit]
column inch	grain	long hundredweight	pica	ton
cord	Gunter's chain	[Brit]	pint	yard

gaugeable, calculable, computable, assessable, appraisable, estimable, determinable, perceptible, fathomable

18 **deliberate,** unhurried, leisurely, slow, studied, planned, calculated

19 **metric,** accelerometric, acidimetric, actinometric, aerometric, *etc.*

VERBS

20 **measure,** measure up, take the measurements of, admeasure, quantify, meter, gauge, calibrate, grade, graduate, calculate, compute, count, reckon, assess, value, cost, rate, evaluate, appraise, estimate, determine, survey, triangulate, plumb, sound, fathom, probe, assay, weigh, time, size up, measure off, measure out, mark off, pace off

21 **measure out,** mete out, weigh out, dole out, share, share out, apportion, allot

ADVERBS

22 **measurably,** precisely, perceptibly, noticeably, metrically, quantitatively, metrologically, geodetically, topographically, cartographically, oceanographically

590 Length

NOUNS

1 **length,** extent, span, expanse, stretch, reach, scope, measure, distance, longitude; mileage, yardage, footage, overall length; duration, time
▶ *Distance 585; Measurement 589; Time 639; Duration 642*

2 **piece,** portion, segment, measure, roll, bolt, coil, run, strip, band, stripe, bar, streak, line
▶ *Measurement 589; Part 760*

3 **longness,** tallness, highness, height, full extent, full length; lengthiness, extensiveness, expansiveness; te-

dium, long-windedness, wordiness, prolixity, sesquipedalianism; endlessness, interminability, infinity
▶ *Talkativeness 207; Boredom 296; Expansion 581; Thinness 595; Height 596*

4 **lengthening,** elongation, extension, expansion, prolongation, protraction, longsomeness; stretching out, drawing out, dragging out, stringing out, spinning out
▶ *Boredom 296; Expansion 581*

5 **lengths,** length, extent, efforts

ADJECTIVES

6 **long,** tall, high, long-legged, long-waisted; longish, longer, longest; ankle-length, knee-length, shoulder-length, full-length, unabridged
▶ *Size, Largeness 579; Distance 585; Height 596*

7 **long-lasting,** lasting, long-lived, enduring, long-standing, longtime, long-term, long-range
▶ *Time 639*

8 **lengthwise,** running lengthwise, lengthways, longwise or longways, endways or endwise, longitudinal, linear

9 **lengthy,** extensive, expansive, far-reaching; very long, overlong, too long, tedious, verbose, long-winded, wordy, prolix, sesquipedalian or sesquipedal, polysyllabic; time-consuming, endless, interminable, infinite
▶ *Talkativeness 207; Boredom 296; Expansion 581*

10 **lengthened,** elongated, extended, prolonged, protracted, longsome, stretched out, drawn-out, long-drawn-out, dragged out, strung out, spun out

VERBS

11 **be long,** extend, span, measure, stretch, reach; last, endure
▶ *Distance 585; Time 639; Duration 642*

12 **lengthen,** elongate, extend, expand, stretch, prolong, prolongate, protract, stretch out, draw out, drag out, string out, spin out; keep at arm's length, keep at a distance

Expansion 581

13 **go to any length** or **lengths,** disregard any impediment, put forth every effort

ADVERBS

14 **lengthwise,** lengthways, longwise or longways, endways or endwise, longitudinally, in length, along, in a line, end to end, stem to stern, at full length, *in extenso* [L]; long, for a long time

15 **at length,** to the full extent, completely; after a time, finally; lengthily, extensively, expansively; tediously, verbosely, long-windedly, protractedly, tiresomely, longsomely, endlessly, without end, interminably, ad infinitum, ad nauseam; as long as one's arm, a mile long

16 **at arm's length,** at a distance

591 Shortness

NOUNS

1 **shortness,** diminutiveness, littleness, stubbiness, stumpiness, snubbiness, stockiness, dumpiness, squatness, stuntedness, lowness; transience, briefness, brevity; conciseness, succinctness, compendiousness; skimpiness, scantiness
  ▸ *Conciseness 198; Littleness 580; Nearness 586; Lowness 597; Transience 643*

2 **shortening,** abbreviation, abridgment, compression, telescoping, capsulization, encapsulation, epitomization, foreshortening, cutting, truncation, curtailment, retrenchment, reduction, cut; cutback, docking; elision, apheresis or aphaeresis, contraction, syncope, apocope; clipping, trimming, pruning, mowing
  ▸ *Contraction 582; Decrease 747; Subtraction 749*

3 **shortened version,** synopsis, summary, encapsulation, précis, digest, condensation, abstract, epitome; compendium, abbreviation, abridgment, capsule, outline, ellipsis; résumé, conspectus

4 **abruptness,** shortness, brusqueness, curtness, terseness, rudeness, gruffness, irascibility, short temper
  ▸ *Irascibility 303; Discourtesy 411*

5 **shortcut,** shortest way, beeline, cutoff

ADJECTIVES

6 **short,** diminutive, little, stubby, stumpy, snubby, thickset, stocky, dumpy, squat, stunted, low; short and sweet, transient, brief; concise, succinct, synoptic, summarizing, compendious; skimpy, scant, scanty
  ▸ *Conciseness 198; Littleness 580; Lowness 597; Transience 643*

7 **shortened,** abbreviated, abridged, compressed, telescoped, digested, condensed, abstracted, capsulized, encapsulated, epitomized; elliptical, elided; foreshortened, cut, sawed-off, truncated, cut short, curtailed, curtate; clipped, trimmed, cropped, pruned, mown, mowed

8 **abrupt,** brusque, curt, terse, rude, gruff, irascible, short-tempered
  ▸ *Irascibility 303; Discourtesy 411*

VERBS

9 **shorten,** abbreviate, abridge, compress, condense, telescope, digest, abstract, boil down, capsulize, encapsulate, epitomize, synopsize, summarize, sum up; elide, foreshorten, truncate, cut, cut short, curtail, retrench, reduce, cut back, cut down, cut off, dock; bob, clip, trim, crop, reap, prune, lop, mow; take up, turn up, hem

10 **be short,** be abrupt, be brusque, cut off short, have a short or quick temper

11 **short-cut,** take a shortcut, make a beeline, cut across, cut through, cut a corner, go as the crow flies

ADVERBS

12 **shortly,** diminutively, stubbily, stumpily, stockily; short, briefly, in short, in brief, in a word, in a nutshell, in summary, to summarize; concisely, succinctly, elliptically; for short, as the crow flies

13 **abruptly,** brusquely, curtly, tersely, rudely, gruffly, irascibly

592 Breadth

NOUNS

1 **breadth,** width, size, extent, scope, gauge, range, reach, compass, expanse, span, distance, latitude, wingspan, wingspread, radius, diameter, bore, caliber, handbreadth or hand's breadth, beam; broadness, wideness, extensiveness, expansiveness, vastness, spaciousness, roominess, ampleness, amplitude, boundlessness; comprehensiveness, exhaustiveness; pervasiveness; openness, fullness
  ▸ *Expansion 581; Distance 585; Measurement 589; Thickness 594*

2 **expansion,** extension, enlargement, amplification, opening, dilation; lack of restraint, freedom, excessiveness
  ▸ *Excess 99; Expansion 581; Opening 583*

3 **broad-mindedness,** open-mindedness, liberality, liberalness, catholicity, catholicness, tolerance, latitude, lack of prejudice, impartiality
  ▸ *Lack of Discrimination 338*

4 **plainness,** clarity, explicitness; boldness, directness, forthrightness, candidness, frankness, bluntness
  ▸ *Bluntness 550*

ADJECTIVES

5 **broad,** wide, extensive, expansive, vast, spacious, roomy, ample, boundless, unlimited; broad-based, wide-ranging, comprehensive, exhaustive; splayed, splay, spread-out, wide-spreading, patulous, transverse; widespread, far-reaching, far-flung, pervasive; open, wide-open, full; wide-set, wide-spaced, beamy,

wide-angle, wide-screen, broad-gauge *or* broad-gauged, broadloom

▶ *Expansion 581; Distance 585; Thickness 594*

6 **broad-shaped,** broad-bottomed, wide-bottomed, broad-beamed, broad in the beam [Inf]; broad-winged, broad-tailed, broad-billed, wide-billed, widemouthed, broad-nosed, broadfaced, broad-shouldered, broad-chested, broad-leaved, broadbrimmed; bell-bottomed, wide-cut, flared

7 **broadened,** widened, extended, expanded, enlarged, amplified, opened, dilated

▶ *Expansion 581*

8 **unrestrained,** free, unconfined, unchecked, unrepressed, unbridled, excessive

▶ *Freedom 829*

9 **broad-minded,** open-minded, freethinking, liberal, catholic, tolerant, unprejudiced, unbigoted, unbiased, impartial

▶ *Lack of Discrimination 338*

10 **plain,** clear, explicit; bold, plain-spoken, direct, forthright, candid, frank, blunt

▶ *Bluntness 550*

VERBS

11 **broaden,** widen, extend, expand, enlarge, spread, flare, spread out, splay, open, dilate

▶ *Expansion 581; Opening 583*

12 **span,** extend, reach, stretch, cross, link, straddle, bestride

▶ *Measurement 589*

13 **be broad-minded,** have *or* keep an open mind, be unbiased, lack prejudice

▶ *Lack of Discrimination 338*

14 **speak plainly** *or* **directly,** be candid, be frank *or* blunt

▶ *Bluntness 550*

ADVERBS

15 **broadly,** widely, extensively, expansively, vastly, spaciously; comprehensively, exhaustively; openly, fully; generally, by and large, on the whole; as wide as a barn door, as wide as a truck

16 **breadthways,** breadthwise, widthwise *or* widthways, across, athwart, transversely, crosswise *or* crossways, sideways *or* sidewise, broadside, through, from one side to the other, all the way across, clear across

▶ *Measurement 589; Side 623*

17 **broad-mindedly,** open-mindedly, liberally, catholically, tolerantly, impartially

18 **plainly,** clearly, explicitly; boldly, directly, candidly, frankly, bluntly

593 Narrowness

NOUNS

1 **narrowness,** limitedness, limitation, restrictedness, restriction; incommodiousness, crampedness, tightness, straitness; confinement, circumscription, re-

straint, constraint, repression; compression, contraction, constriction

▶ *Contraction 582; Thinness 595*

2 **narrow place** *or* **thing,** confined space, tight squeeze *or* spot *or* corner, bottleneck, small gap, chink, narrow; narrows, strait, straits, channel, slip, tunnel, passage, defile, ravine, gully, ditch, trench, pass, ridge; isthmus, peninsula, spit; neck, throat, taper, spindle, stick, rod, pipe, tube, narrow gauge, single track

3 **narrowing,** tapering, attenuation, convergence, contraction, stricture, stenosis, strangulation

4 **closeness,** nearness, hairsbreadth, narrow margin, near miss, close call, narrow escape

5 **carefulness,** thoroughness, attentiveness, scrutiny, scrutinization

▶ *Carefulness 325*

6 **meagerness,** smallness, scantiness, exiguity, sparseness, skimpiness, inadequacy; impoverishment, poverty, neediness

▶ *Insufficiency 98; Poverty 486; Sparseness 541; Thinness 595*

7 **narrow-mindedness,** close-mindedness, intolerance, illiberality, bias, bigotry, partiality; shallowness, small-mindedness

▶ *Discrimination 337; Shallowness 599*

ADJECTIVES

8 **narrow,** lacking breadth, limited, restricted; cramped, incommodious, tight, strait, pinched; confined, circumscribed *or* circumscriptive, pent, pent-up, restrained, constrained, repressed; compressed, contracted, constricted, stenosed; clinging, close-fitting, figure-hugging; narrow-leaved, stenophyllous, narrow-petaled, stenopetalous, narrow-beaked, narrow-nosed; narrow-gauge *or* narrow-gauged, single-track, stenopeic, isthmian

▶ *Contraction 582; Thinness 595*

9 **narrowed,** narrowing, tapered, tapering, attenuate *or* attenuating, convergent, fusiform, cone- *or* wedge-shaped; contracted, strictured, stenosed

10 **close,** near, hairsbreadth

11 **careful,** thorough, thoroughgoing, minute, attentive, painstaking, scrutinizing

▶ *Carefulness 325*

12 **meager,** small, scant, scanty, exiguous, sparse, skimpy, inadequate; straitened, impoverished, poor, needy

▶ *Insufficiency 98; Poverty 486; Sparseness 541; Thinness 595*

13 **narrow-minded,** close-minded, intolerant, illiberal, biased, bigoted, partial; shallow, small-minded

▶ *Discrimination 337; Shallowness 599*

VERBS

14 **narrow,** narrow down, limit, restrict; cramp, pinch, tighten, straiten; confine, circumscribe, restrain, constrain, repress; compress, contract, constrict; converge, taper, make narrow *or* narrower, diminish

▶ *Contraction 582; Thinness 595*

15 be careful, be thorough, pay attention to detail, examine, scrutinize
▶ *Carefulness 325*

16 be narrow-minded, have a closed mind, be intolerant, be biased *or* prejudiced, be small-minded
▶ *Discrimination 337*

ADVERBS

17 narrowly, limitedly, restrictedly; incommodiously, tightly, straitly; confinedly, circumscriptively, restrainedly, constrainedly; compressedly, contractedly

18 barely, only just, closely, nearly, hardly, scarcely, by a narrow margin, by a hairsbreadth, by a whisker, by the skin of one's teeth [Inf]

19 meagerly, scantily, exiguously, sparsely, skimpily, inadequately

20 narrow-mindedly, close-mindedly, intolerantly, illiberally; shallowly, small-mindedly

594 Thickness

NOUNS

1 thickness, breadth, broadness, width, wideness, depth, deepness, mass, massiveness, bulk, bulkiness, ampleness; stockiness, solidity, sturdiness; heaviness, stoutness, corpulence, portliness, plumpness, roundness, rotundity, flabbiness, chubbiness, chunkiness, pudginess, tubbiness, fatness, obesity; potbelly, fat, blubber, padding
▶ *Size, Largeness 579; Breadth 592; Depth 598*

2 denseness, density, body, fullness, viscosity, condensation, congealment, coagulation, clotting, thickening, intensification; crowdedness, abundance, teemingness, impenetrability; closeness, tightness
▶ *Friendship 62; Density 540; Viscosity 561*

3 thick-wittedness, thickness, slow-wittedness, slowness, dull-wittedness, dullness, denseness, stupidity, obtuseness, dimness, dumbness, thickheadedness, boneheadedness [Inf]
▶ *Lack of Intellect 316; Folly 353*

4 callousness, insensitivity, hardness, coarseness, thick skin
▶ *Insensitivity 268*

ADJECTIVES

5 thick, broad, wide, deep, massive, substantial, bulky, ample; stocky, solid, sturdy, thickset, thick-bodied, barrel-chested, thick-necked, bull-necked, thick-jawed, thick-legged; thick-leaved, thick-barked, thick-stemmed, thick-stalked; thick-skinned, pachydermatous, thick-coated, thick-walled; heavy, overweight, stout, corpulent, portly, plump, round, rotund, flabby, chubby, chunky, pudgy, tubby, potbellied, well-fed, fat, obese, fat as a pig, big as a house; padded, swollen, incrassate

▶ *Size, Largeness 579; Breadth 592; Depth 598*

6 dense, full-bodied, semiliquid, viscous, condensed, congealed, coagulated, clotted, thickened, intensified, thick with; crowded, abundant, packed, swarming, teeming, jammed, chockablock, impenetrable
▶ *Density 540; Viscosity 561*

7 thick-witted, thick, slow-witted, slow, dull-witted, dull, dense, stupid, obtuse, dim, dumb, thickheaded, boneheaded [Inf]
▶ *Lack of Intellect 316; Folly 353*

8 thick-skinned, callous, insensitive, hard, coarse
▶ *Insensitivity 268*

VERBS

9 thicken, congeal, gel, set, solidify, harden, firm up, condense, coagulate, clot, intensify; crowd, pack, swarm, teem, jam
▶ *Density 540; Viscosity 561*

10 fatten, thicken, fill out, gain *or* put on weight, pad

ADVERBS

11 thick, thickly, broadly, widely, deeply, massively, substantially, heavily, stoutly

12 densely, crowdedly, abundantly, teemingly, impenetrably

13 thick-wittedly, thickly, dully, densely, stupidly, obtusely, dimly, dumbly, thickheadedly

14 callously, insensitively, coarsely

595 Thinness

You can never be too rich or too thin. — SAYING

Yon Cassius hath a lean and hungry look.
 — WILLIAM SHAKESPEARE

NOUNS

1 thinness, slenderness, slimness, gracility, willowiness, twigginess; slightness, slight build, small frame, ectomorphy, puniness; leanness, spareness, lankiness, wiriness, boniness, ranginess, gangliness, weediness; skinniness, scrawniness, scragginess; hourglass figure, narrow *or* wasp waist, girlish figure, boyish figure, thin face, hatchet face, lantern jaw
▶ *Narrowness 593*

2 emaciation, malnutrition, starvation, anorexia nervosa, wasting, atrophy, tabescence, tabes, maramus; gauntness, haggardness, hollow cheeks, hollow eyes, sunken eyes; cadaverousness, boniness, frailty, skin and bones
▶ *Fasting 118*

3 dieting, weight-watching, watching one's weight *or* figure, calorie-counting, reducing, slimming, slenderizing, crash-dieting; diet, crash diet, liquid diet, starvation diet, diet plan
▶ *Fasting 118*

4 thin person, slip, sylph, leptosome, asthenic, ectomorph, weakling, runt; dieter, weight-watcher, calorie counter, slimmer [Brit], anorexic; wraith, shadow, bag of bones, skeleton, walking skeleton, scarecrow; [Inf]: spindlelegs or spindleshanks, beanpole, long drink of water

) *Height 596*

5 **fineness,** delicacy, lightness, filminess, gauziness, laciness, sheerness, diaphaneity, diaphanousness, paperiness; film, gossamer, gauze, muslin, lace; thread, filament, hair, wisp; paper, tissue, wafer, lath, slat, shaving; sensitivity

) *Sensitivity 267; Layer 588*

6 **thinning,** dilution, watering down, wateriness, runniness; weakening, weakness, rarefaction, attenuation; insubstantiality, flimsiness

7 **thinner,** diluter, solvent

8 **sparseness,** scantiness, meagerness, paucity, fewness

) *Sparseness 541*

ADJECTIVES

9 **thin,** slender, slim, svelte, gracile, sylphic, sylphlike, willowy, twiggy; slight, slightly built, small-framed, leptosomic, asthenic, ectomorphic, puny; lean, spare, lank, lanky, wiry, bony, rawboned, rangy, lathy, gawky, spindly or spindling, gangling or gangly, weedy; underweight, skinny, scrawny, scraggy; narrow-waisted, wasp-waisted, thin-legged, spindle-legged or spindle-shanked, thin-fingered, leptodactylous, thin-faced, lean-faced, hatchet-faced, lantern-jawed

) *Narrowness 593*

10 **emaciated,** malnourished, undernourished, underfed, starved, starving, anorectic, wizened, shriveled, withered, wasted, tabescent, wasting away, tabetic, marasmic; gaunt, haggard, hollow-cheeked, hollow-eyed, sunken-eyed, drawn, peaked; cadaverous, corpselike, skeletal, frail, wraithlike, thin as a rail or rake or lath, worn to a shadow

) *Fasting 118*

11 **dieting,** reducing, slenderizing, slimming, weight-watching, calorie-counting

) *Fasting 118*

12 **fine,** delicate, light, filmy, gauzy, gossamer, lacy, sheer, diaphanous, finespun; threadlike, filamentous, filiform, hairlike, wispy; papery, wafer-thin; fine-drawn, wiredrawn; thin-skinned

) *Sensitivity 267; Layer 588*

13 **thinned,** diluted, watered down, watery, runny; weakened, weak, rarefied, rare, attenuated, attenuate; flattened, pressed, rolled out; insubstantial, flimsy

14 **sparse,** scant, scanty, meager, few, few in number

) *Sparseness 541*

VERBS

15 **become thin,** slim down, slim, slenderize, diet, watch one's weight or figure, count calories, crash-diet, lose weight, reduce

) *Fasting 118*

16 **be emaciated,** starve, undereat, waste away, atrophy

) *Fasting 118*

17 **make thin,** thin, thin out, dilute, water down; weaken, rarefy, attenuate; flatten, press, roll out

ADVERBS

18 **thin,** thinly, slenderly, slimly; scrawnily, scraggily, weedily, gauntly, haggardly

19 **finely,** delicately, lightly, filmily, gauzily, lacily, sheerly; diaphanously; sensitively

20 **sparsely,** scantily, meagerly

596 Height

NOUNS

1 **height,** altitude, elevation, rise, lift, uprise, uplift; highness, loftiness, sublimity; tallness, stature, lankiness, ranginess, legginess

) *Size, Largeness 579; Thinness 595; Raising 715*

2 **pinnacle,** peak, pitch, apex, zenith, acme, climax, culmination

) *Summit 600*

3 **exaltation,** eminence, prominence, distinguishment, sublimity, notableness, importance, greatness

) *Importance 799*

4 **heights,** altitudes, highland or highlands, upland or uplands, mesa, tableland, moor, moorland [Brit], downs [Brit], wolds, fell [Scot, Brit]; promontory, headland, escarpment, cliff, bluff, precipice, projection; rising ground, foothill or foothills, mountainside, hillside, slope, incline, acclivity, climb, ascent; summit, top, peak, mountaintop, hilltop, knap, plateau

) *Mountains and Hills 569; Other Geographical Features 572; Summit 600; Verticality 602; Ascent 713*

5 **height measurement,** altimetry, hypsometry, hypsography; topography, relief; altimeter, hypsometer, thermobarometer, orometer

) *Measurement 589*

6 **tall person,** six-footer, seven-footer, amazon, giant, Goliath; [Inf]: beanpole, highpockets, long drink of water

) *Size, Largeness 579; Thinness 595*

ADJECTIVES

7 **high,** altitudinal, altitudinous, elevated, raised, lifted, upraised, upreared, uplifted; high up, lofty, aerial, sky-high, towering, high as a steeple, high-rise, skyscraping, supernal, sublime [Arch]; knee-high, thigh-high, waist-high, chest-high, shoulder-high

) *Measurement 589; Raising 715*

8 **higher,** taller, highest, tallest, superior, upper, upmost, uppermost, topmost, nearest the top

9 **tall,** lanky, gangling or gangly, rangy, towering, leggy, long-legged, long-limbed, giant, amazonian, tall as a maypole

▶ *Size, Largeness 579; Thinness 595*

10 exalted, eminent, prominent, distinguished, sublime, notable, important, grand, great

▶ *Superiority 744; Importance 799*

11 highland, upland; topping, overtopping, overlooking, overhanging, beetling, projecting, clifflike, precipitous

▶ *Mountains and Hills 569*

12 rising, sloping upward, inclining, uprising, climbing, mounting, ascending, soaring, aspiring [Arch]

▶ *Ascent 713*

13 altimetrical, hypsometric *or* hypsometrical, hypsographic *or* hypsographical, topographic *or* topographical

VERBS

14 heighten, make higher, elevate, raise, hoist, lift, rear, hold up, lift up, raise up, uplift, upraise, uprear

▶ *Raising 715*

15 be high, tower, tower above, be at the top, top, overtop, overlook, look down on, overhang, beetle, project, escarp

16 be tall, tower, tower over, stand on tiptoe; grow tall, grow, shoot up, sprout

17 rise, slope upward, incline, climb, mount, scale, ascend, soar, rise up, uprise, aspire [Arch]

▶ *Ascent 713*

18 peak, make it to the top, culminate, climax, reach a climax, complete

▶ *Summit 600; Superiority 744*

19 exalt, promote, elevate, raise, distinguish, ennoble, dignify, glorify, put on a pedestal

ADVERBS

20 high, high up, aloft, sky-high, on high, above, over, overhead, above one's head, in the air, in the clouds, in orbit, at the top, on top, sublimely [Arch]; toweringly, lankily, on stilts, on tiptoe; up to the knees, up to the waist, up to the shoulders; yea high [Inf]

21 higher, up, straight up, upward, skyward, heavenward

22 exaltedly, eminently, prominently, distinguishedly, sublimely, notably, importantly, grandly, greatly

23 altimetrically, hypsometrically, topographically

597 Lowness

NOUNS

1 lowness, flatness, levelness, shallowness; shortness, squatness, stumpiness, stuntedness

▶ *Shortness 591; Shallowness 599*

2 prostration, proneness, recumbency, supineness, reclination; crouch, stoop, bend, bow

▶ *Horizontality 603*

3 lowering, flattening, knockdown, prostration, overthrow, defeat

▶ *Lowering 716*

4 descent, falling, dropping, sinking; decline, grade, declivity, downward inclination, downward slope

▶ *Obliqueness 607; Descent 714*

5 lowest point, lowest level, nadir, bottom, floor, base, foot, depths, low ebb; underside, underneath, subjacency, underlayer, substratum, bottom layer, lowest stratum, bedrock

▶ *Layer 588; Depth 598; Base 601*

6 lowlands, bottom land, piedmont, foothills, hillock, hummock, knoll, molehill; plain, flat *or* flats, level ground; swale, hollow, depression, valley, canyon, gorge, gully, ravine, gulch

▶ *Other Geographical Features 572; Concavity 635*

7 diminishment, decrease, reduction, lessening, ebb; exhaustion, fatigue, weakness, feebleness

▶ *Weakness 517; Decrease 747; Fatigue 820*

8 lowliness, low rank, peasantry, obscurity, humbleness, servility, subservience, subordination, inferiority

▶ *Humility 298; Inferiority 745; Subjection 832*

9 humbling, humiliation, degradation, demotion, subordination, debasement; dishonor, shame, disgrace, disrepute, ignominy

▶ *Humility 298; Lowering 716*

ADJECTIVES

10 low, unelevated, low-lying, flat, level; low-built, low-rise, single-story; shallow, shoal, ankle-high, knee-high, knee-high to a grasshopper [Inf]; short, low-statured, squat, stumpy, stunted; low-necked, low-cut, décolleté

▶ *Clothing 100; Shortness 591; Shallowness 599*

11 prostrate, lying flat, prone, supine, lying down, recumbent, reclining, couchant, crouched, crouching, stooped, stooping, bowed, bowing

▶ *Horizontality 603*

12 lowered, laid low, prostrated, overcome, overthrown, defeated, flattened, knocked down, thrown down, knocked over, knocked flat

▶ *Lowering 716*

13 descending, falling, dropping, sinking; declining, downhill, downward, down

▶ *Obliqueness 607; Descent 714*

14 lower, nether, subjacent, underlying, underlaid, substrative, underneath, underground; lowest, lowermost [Brit], bottom, bottommost, farthest down, bedrock, rock-bottom

▶ *Layer 588; Depth 598; Base 601*

15 lowland, low-lying, flat, level, plain, subalpine, submontane, piedmont; depressed, sunken, submerged

▶ *Other Geographical Features 572; Concavity 635*

16 diminishing, decreasing, ebbing, sinking, dwindling, languishing, flagging, weakening; weak, feeble, weakened, exhausted, fatigued

▶ *Weakness 517; Decrease 747; Deterioration 808; Fatigue 820*

17 **lowly,** low-ranking, obscure, lowborn, plebeian, peasant, humble, servile, subservient, subordinate, inferior
   ‣ *Humility 298; Inferiority 745; Subjection 832*
18 **lowered,** humbled, humiliated, degraded, demoted, subordinated, debased, demeaned, dishonored, shamed, disgraced; disgraceful, shameful, dishonorable, disreputable, base, mean, ignoble, ignomious, lower than low
   ‣ *Humility 298; Lowering 716*
19 **substandard,** low-quality, low-grade, poor, inferior, second-rate
   ‣ *Inferiority 745*

VERBS

20 **be low,** prostrate oneself, lie facedown, lie flat, lie down, recline, lean, couch, crouch, squat, stoop, bend, bow, crawl, creep, grovel
   ‣ *Horizontality 603*
21 **lower,** drop, depress, make lower; lay low, prostrate, make prostrate, overpower, overcome, overthrow, defeat, knock down, throw down, knock over, knock flat, flatten, squash flat, deck [Inf]
   ‣ *Lowering 716*
22 **descend,** climb down, move down, come down, fall, drop, sink; decline, slope downward
   ‣ *Obliqueness 607; Descent 714*
23 **underlie,** lie under *or* beneath, underlay, lay under *or* beneath, go below; bottom out, hit bottom
   ‣ *Layer 588; Depth 598; Base 601*
24 **diminish,** decrease, ebb, sink, dwindle, languish, flag, weaken; reduce, lessen
   ‣ *Weakness 517; Decrease 747; Deterioration 808*
25 **humble,** humiliate, degrade, demote, debase, demean, dishonor, disgrace
   ‣ *Humility 298; Lowering 716*

ADVERBS

26 **low,** near the ground, low down; at the bottom *or* base *or* foot, at the lowest point, at rock bottom; at sea level, near sea level, below sea level; under, below, down below, underneath, beneath, neath *or* 'neath, subjacently, underfoot, underground; down, downward, downhill
27 **humbly,** obscurely, servilely, subserviently, subordinately
28 **disgracefully,** shamefully, dishonorably, ignomiously
29 **of inferior quality,** of low quality, below par, below the mark

598 Depth

NOUNS

1 **depth,** deepness, width, wideness, breadth, broadness, extent, extensiveness, draft, measure; bottomlessness, unfathomableness, fathomlessness, soundlessness

‣ *Measurement 589; Breadth 592*
2 **the depths,** ocean depths, ocean floor *or* bottom, seafloor *or* seabed, bottom of the sea, benthos, Davy Jones's locker; deep water, deep sea, Mariana Trench; vast extent, unfathomable space, infinity, abyss, gulf, cavity, chasm; farthest *or* innermost part, extremity, extremities, bowels, core; the deep, sea, ocean; underground, subterrane
   ‣ *Geology 8; Seas 571; Base 601*
3 **bathymetry,** sounding, depth sounding, probing, echo sounding, sonar, echolocation; bathometer, benthoscope, depth sounder, echo sounder, depth finder, Fathometer™, lead, lead line, plumb, plumb line, sounding line; bathysphere, diving bell; bathyscaphe, submarine, submersible
   ‣ *Seas 571; Measurement 589*
4 **deepening,** lowering, dropping, drop, descent, sinking, sinkage, falling, fall; excavation, digging, mining, tunneling, drilling
   ‣ *Lowness 597; Extraction 711; Descent 714; Lowering 716*
5 **profundity,** profoundness, insightfulness, understanding, astuteness, acuity, perspicacity, shrewdness, wisdom, sagacity, knowledgeableness; insight, penetration, discernment, knowledge; profundities, deep matters, deep thinking, meaningfulness, significance; abstruseness, abstrusity, complexness, complexity, reconditeness, obscurity, esotericism, mysteriousness, esoterica, mystery
   ‣ *Secrecy 182; Wisdom 352; Importance 799*
6 **deepness,** strength, intensity, vividness, darkness; pervasiveness, extensiveness, thoroughness, completeness, exhaustiveness, comprehensiveness
   ‣ *Degree 739; Completeness 761*
7 **depth of feeling,** feeling, emotion, heart, sincerity, genuineness, earnestness, seriousness, gravity; deep-rootedness
   ‣ *Feelings 266; Seriousness 278*
8 **immersion,** engulfment, envelopment, involvement, commitment, absorption, engrossment; submergence, submersion

ADJECTIVES

9 **deep,** wide, broad, great, extensive, deep-reaching, deep-cut; abysmal, abyssal, cavernous, yawning, gaping, deep-set, sunken, plunging, bottomless, soundless, fathomless, infinite, immeasurable, unfathomable, unsoundable; deep as the ocean *or* the sea, deep as a well, deep as hell; ankle-deep, knee-deep, waist-deep
   ‣ *Measurement 589; Breadth 592*
10 **deeper,** lower, under, bottom; deepest, farthest down, lowest, bottommost, rock-bottom; innermost, core
   ‣ *Lowness 597; Base 601*
11 **deep-sea,** deep-water, oceanic, bathyal, bathypelagic, benthic *or* benthal *or* benthonic

◗ *Seas 571*

12 bathymetric, sounding, depth-sounding, depth-finding, probing, echolocating
◗ *Seas 571; Measurement 589*

13 under, underground, subterranean *or* subterraneous, subterrestrial, hypogeal *or* hypogaeal, hypogeous *or* hypogaeous; underwater, subaqueous, subaquatic, undersea, submarine; sunk, submerged, submersed, engulfed, immersed, flooded
◗ *Geology 8; Seas 571; Lowness 597*

14 deepening, lowering, dropping, descending, sinking, falling; intensifying, strengthening, darkening
◗ *Lowness 597; Extraction 711; Descent 714; Lowering 716*

15 profound, deep, penetrating, insightful, astute, acute, discerning, perspicacious, shrewd, wise, sagacious, knowledgeable; meaningful, significant; abstruse, complex, recondite, arcane, esoteric, obscure, mysterious, secret
◗ *Secrecy 182; Wisdom 352; Importance 799*

16 intense, extreme, strong, vivid, dark; pervasive, extensive, thorough, complete, detailed, exhaustive, comprehensive
◗ *Degree 739; Completeness 761*

17 deep-seated, deep-rooted, firmly implanted *or* established; deeply felt, heartfelt, sincere, genuine, earnest, serious, grave
◗ *Feelings 266; Seriousness 278*

18 in deep, engulfed, immersed, enveloped, involved, committed, absorbed, engrossed

19 deep-sounding, low-pitched, hollow, cavernous, sonorous, deep-voiced, resonant
◗ *Lowness 597*

VERBS

20 be deep, extend, measure, stretch wide, yawn, gape
◗ *Breadth 592*

21 deepen, make deeper, lower, drop, become deeper, sink, founder, sink to the bottom, fall, go lower, descend, dive, plunge, reach the bottom, touch bottom; submerge, submerse, immerse, engulf; excavate, dig, mine, tunnel, drill; intensify, strengthen, darken
◗ *Geology 8; Extraction 711; Descent 714; Lowering 716*

22 measure depth, fathom, sound, take soundings, heave the lead, plumb, plumb the depths, probe
◗ *Seas 571; Measurement 589*

23 be profound, be wise, be knowledgeable, have deep understanding, understand, comprehend, fathom, penetrate, discern
◗ *Wisdom 352*

24 immerse, engulf, envelope, involve, commit, absorb, engross

ADVERBS

25 deep, deeply, widely, broadly, extensively; deep down, far down, far back, out of *or* beyond one's depth; abysmally, cavernously, yawningly, gapingly, infinitely, immeasurably, unfathomably

26 under, underground, subterraneanly *or* subterraneously; underwater, underseas *or* undersea

27 profoundly, deeply, penetratingly, insightfully, astutely, acutely, discerningly, perspicaciously, shrewdly, wisely, sagaciously, knowledgeably; meaningfully, significantly; abstrusely, reconditely, esoterically, obscurely, mysteriously, secretly

28 intensely, extremely, strongly, vividly, darkly; pervasively, extensively, thoroughly, completely, in depth, in detail, exhaustively, comprehensively; in deep, up to one's eyes *or* ears

29 with deep feeling, with heart, sincerely, genuinely, earnestly, seriously, gravely

599 Shallowness

NOUNS

1 shallowness, lack of depth, shoaliness; shallows, shallow, shoal, ford, rapids, riffle; wetland *or* wetlands, marshland, marsh, swamp, bog; sandbank, sand bar, shelf, reef, coral reef; flat *or* flats, mud flat, tidal flats
◗ *Moisture 559; Other Geographical Features 572; Lowness 597*

2 superficiality, externality, outwardness, obviousness; surface, outer face, outward appearance, superficies; superficialness, cursoriness, hastiness, lick and a promise, once-over [Inf], once-over-lightly [Inf]; slightness, thinness, weakness, flatness, flimsiness, lightness, insubstantiality, frivolity, unimportance, insignificance, triviality, pettiness, meaninglessness, emptiness
◗ *Exterior 610; Unimportance 800*

ADJECTIVES

3 shallow, not deep, shoal, shoaly, unnavigable, shallow-bottomed, ankle-deep, knee-deep, waist-deep
◗ *Lowness 597*

4 superficial, surface, cosmetic, external, outward, apparent, obvious; skin-deep, epidermal, thin; cursory, hasty, slight, one-dimensional, weak, flat, flimsy, light, lightweight, insubstantial, trifling, frivolous, unimportant, insignificant, trivial, petty, inconsiderable, meaningless, empty
◗ *Exterior 610; Unimportance 800*

VERBS

5 shallow, make shallow, become shallow, shoal, silt up
◗ *Lowness 597*

6 be superficial, be skin-deep, have no depth, have no significance; touch *or* scratch the surface, scrape *or* graze the surface, skim, skim over, slight, trivialize, trifle
◗ *Exterior 610*

7 **shallowly,** near the surface, within one's depth, at *or* on the surface

8 **superficially,** on the surface, externally, outwardly, apparently, obviously; cursorily, lightly, hastily, with a lick and a promise; slightly, one-dimensionally, weakly, flatly, insubstantially, frivolously, unimportantly, insignificantly, trivially

600 Summit

NOUNS

1 **summit,** top, apex, vertex, peak, pinnacle; acme, pitch, zenith, capstone, culmination, climax, highest state, highest degree *or* level, meridian, crest, crest of the wave, maximum, limit; highest point, tiptop, very top, apogee, extremity, upper extremity, utmost height; mountaintop, hilltop, knap, plateau, ridge; point, tip, cusp, spire; top part, head, crown, cap
   ▶ *Height 596; Limit 620; Degree 739*

2 **top of the world,** exosphere, sky, heaven, heavens, seventh heaven, cloud nine [Inf]

3 **summit meeting,** summit conference, summit, summitry, diplomacy, negotiations, talks, dialogue; diplomat, government official, negotiator
   ▶ *Government 49; Politics 50; Negotiation 460*

4 **architectural summit,** capital, head, cap, crown; cornice, cymatium *or* cymation, clerestory; ceiling, roof, rooftop, housetop
   ▶ *Architecture 134*

5 **top layer,** superstratum, topsoil; topside, upper side, upside, surface, top surface, upper surface; topping, icing, frosting, dressing
   ▶ *Layer 588; Covering 613*

ADJECTIVES

6 **top,** upper, uppermost, upmost, topmost, tiptop, highest; summital, apical, vertical; peak, pitch, ultimate, maximum, maximal, consummate, climactic, culminating, crowning, meridian
   ▶ *Height 596; Degree 739*

7 **head,** leading, chief, capital, supreme, paramount, top-level, high-level

8 **topped,** capped, crowned, crested, covered, roofed, overtopped, overarched; tipped, pointed, peaked; topping, capping, crowning, overtopping, overarching
   ▶ *Covering 613*

VERBS

9 **be at the top,** peak, pitch, reach the top, make it to the top; culminate, climax, reach a climax, crest, top off, complete, reach the limit
   ▶ *Height 596; Completeness 761*

10 **top,** cap, cover, overtop, overarch, roof; ice, frost, dress

   ▶ *Covering 613*

11 **summit,** hold a summit meeting, meet, negotiate, hold a dialogue, confer
   ▶ *Negotiation 460*

ADVERBS

12 **at the summit,** at the top, uppermost, upmost, at the highest point, at the peak, on the crest of the wave, consummately, climactically; at the highest level, at the top of the ladder *or* tree

13 **on the top,** on top, topside; atop, on top of

14 **on top of the world,** in heaven, in seventh heaven, on cloud nine [Inf]

601 Base

NOUNS

1 **base,** bottom, foot, floor, bed, nadir, lowest point, depths, the pits [Inf]; lowest level, basement, cellar, ground floor, first floor; ground, earth, ground covering; ocean bottom, ocean floor, seafloor, seabed, riverbed; bottom layer, substratum, lowest stratum, hardpan, rock bottom, bedrock; basecoat, undercoat, underlayer, wainscot, dado; flooring, floor covering, pavement, paving
   ▶ *Layer 588; Lowness 597; Depth 598; Covering 613*

2 **foundation,** base, supporting structure, support, underpinning, substructure, substruction, infrastructure, framework, frame, bedplate *or* baseplate, undercarriage, chassis, keel; platform, stand, plinth, pedestal; sill, baseboard *or* mopboard *or* skirt
   ▶ *Architecture 134; Support 605*

3 **basis,** principle, fundament, foundation, root, footing, groundwork, underpinnings; ground, grounds, reason, cause; principal element, essential, essential quality, main ingredient, constituent
   ▶ *Support 605; Essence 723*

4 **baseline,** standard, gauge, level, rule, guideline, guide, pattern; starting point, point of departure, jumping-off place *or* point; bottom line, net profit *or* loss, deciding factor, outcome

5 **station,** post, home base, home, location, place, situation
   ▶ *Location 565*

ADJECTIVES

6 **bottom,** rock-bottom, bedrock, bottommost, lowest, lowermost [Brit], deepest, farthest down, undermost; underground, ground, ground-level
   ▶ *Lowness 597; Depth 598*

7 **base,** underlying, foundational, basal, basilar *or* basilary, supporting, substructural, substructional
   ▶ *Support 605*

8 **basic,** fundamental, basal, radical, inherent; essential, key, primary, bottom-line; elementary, rudimentary, vestigial

‣ *Essence 723*

9 **based,** stationed, located, placed, situated
‣ *Location 565*

10 **base,** found, establish, anchor, fix, root, ground; support, frame, underpin, undergird, strengthen; layer, underlay, undercoat, coat, cover, pave
‣ *Layer 588; Covering 613*

11 **underlie,** lie under *or* beneath, underlay, lay under *or* beneath, go below; bottom out, hit bottom
‣ *Layer 588; Depth 598*

12 **station,** post, locate, place, situate
‣ *Location 565*

ADVERBS

13 **at the base,** at the bottom *or* base *or* foot, at the lowest point, at rock bottom

14 **basically,** fundamentally, basally, inherently, essentially, in essence, in principle

602   Verticality

NOUNS

1 **verticality,** verticalness, verticalism, uprightness, plumbness, erectness, straightness; steepness, sheerness, precipitousness; fall, drop, plunge, dive
‣ *Depth 598; Straightness 630*

2 **perpendicularity,** orthogonality, squareness, rectangularity *or* rectangularness

3 **vertical,** perpendicular, line, plane, normal, vertical line, vertical axis; upright, pole, post, prop, pier, pile, pylon, column, pillar; precipice, cliff, bluff, escarpment
‣ *Height 596*

4 **plumb line,** plumb, square, try square, T-square, set square
‣ *Measurement 589*

ADJECTIVES

5 **vertical,** upright, bolt upright, plumb, erect, standing, standing up, upstanding, upended; straight, straight up and down, straight up, straight down; steep, sheer, precipitous, plunging
‣ *Height 596; Depth 598; Straightness 630*

6 **perpendicular,** orthogonal, right-angled, square, normal, rectangular

7 **unbowed,** ramping, rampant, rearing, reared, upreared, raising, raised, raised upward, upraised, cocked up, pricked up
‣ *Height 596*

VERBS

8 **be vertical,** stand, stand up, stand upright, stand erect, stand up straight, hold oneself straight, stand to attention, rear, rear up, uprear, rise, rise up, get up, arise, uprise, straighten up, sit up
‣ *Height 596; Straightness 630*

9 **make vertical,** erect, build, elevate, raise, raise up,

upraise, pitch; straighten, plumb, square; upend, stand on end, stick up, cock up, prick up
‣ *Straightness 630; Raising 715*

10 **fall vertically,** drop, drop like a stone, plummet, plunge, dive
‣ *Depth 598*

ADVERBS

11 **vertically,** upright, uprightly, plumb, erectly, at attention; straight, straight up and down, up and down, up, down, on end, endways *or* endwise; steeply, sheerly, precipitously
‣ *Depth 598; Straightness 630*

12 **perpendicularly,** orthogonally, at right angles, square, squarely, rectangularly

603   Horizontality

NOUNS

1 **horizontality,** horizontalness, flatness, levelness, planeness, planarity, flushness, alignment, evenness, smoothness
‣ *Smoothness 545; Lowness 597*

2 **recumbency,** recumbence, decumbence *or* decumbency, accumbency, proneness, prostration, lying flat, lying down, supineness, reclination, reclining, sprawling, sprawl
‣ *Lowness 597; Ease 819*

3 **horizontal surface,** fascia, flat, level, plane, plane surface; sea level, water level, horizon, skyline, rim of the horizon, azimuth; horizontal, horizontal line, horizontal axis, horizontal angle; flat surface, flats, flatland, plain, prairie, pampas, steppe, tableland, level ground, bowling green, floor, platform, table

4 **flattener,** leveler, plane, press, iron, flatiron, steam iron, mangle, rolling pin, sander, sandpaper, roller, steamroller, bulldozer
‣ *Smoothness 545*

5 **planimetry,** planometry, spirit leveling; planimeter, surface plate *or* planometer, spirit level *or* level, straightedge, ruler *or* rule, gauge
‣ *Measurement 589*

ADJECTIVES

6 **horizontal,** flat, level, plane, planar, two-dimensional, flush, aligned, even, smooth, unwrinkled, unruffled, flat as a pancake *or* board, tabular
‣ *Smoothness 545; Lowness 597*

7 **recumbent,** decumbent, accumbent, procumbent, prone, prostrate, lying flat, lying down, supine, reclining, couchant, sprawling, sprawled, spread-eagled
‣ *Lowness 597*

8 **leveled,** flattened, smoothed, smoothened, evened out, graded, pressed, ironed, rolled, spread out, trampled down, trodden, beaten flat, squashed flat, razed, razed to the ground; knocked flat, knocked down, thrown down, prostrated, lowered, laid low

▶ *Lowness 597; Lowering 716*

VERBS

9 **be horizontal,** lie flat, lie down, recline, sprawl, spread-eagle; prostrate oneself, grovel, crawl, kowtow; be flat, be level
   ▶ *Lowness 597; Lowering 716*

10 **make horizontal,** level, flatten, grade, flush, align, even, even out, smooth, smoothen, smooth out, press, iron, roll out, spread out, trample down, beat flat, squash flat, steamroller *or* steamroll, raze, raze to the ground; knock flat, knock down, fell, throw down, prostrate, make prostrate, lower, lay low, deck [Inf]
   ▶ *Smoothness 545; Lowness 597; Lowering 716*

ADVERBS

11 **horizontally,** flat, flatly, even, evenly, smoothly, flush, level, levelly; flatwise *or* flatways, lengthwise *or* lengthways, at full length, in a straight line, from left to right; on the horizon, on a level, on the same level, without a change of plane

12 **recumbently,** decumbently, pronely, supinely, flat on one's back *or* face

604 Suspension

NOUNS

1 **suspension,** hanging, attaching, draping; hovering, dangling, pendulousness, oscillation, swinging, swing, swaying, sway, drooping, droop, sagging, sag; suspensiveness, suspendibility *or* suspensibility
   ▶ *Oscillation 683; Connection 754*

2 **overhanging,** overhang, projection, extension, jut, beetle, protrusion, cantilever
   ▶ *Height 596*

3 **deferment,** deferral, suspension, postponement, adjournment, delay, stay, holdup, tabling, shelving, procrastination; pendency, abeyance, dormancy; indecision, indecisiveness, fluctuation, vacillation, uncertainty, doubt, doubtfulness
   ▶ *Vacillation 378; Inaction 413; Uncertainty 841*

4 **interruption,** intermittence *or* intermittency, intermission, pause, break, cooling-off period, discontinuance, stoppage, stop, arrest, cessation, moratorium, withholding; suspended animation
   ▶ *Cessation 668; Discontinuity 775*

5 **debarment,** exclusion, shutout; hindrance, interference, prevention, prohibition, interdiction
   ▶ *Expulsion 709; Exclusion 764; Hindrance 826*

6 **suspense,** suspensefulness, suspensiveness, excitement, apprehension, apprehensiveness, anxiety
   ▶ *Fear 283*

ADJECTIVES

7 **suspended,** hanging, hung, attached, draped; dangling, dangled, pensile, pendent, pendulous, pendulumlike, oscillating, oscillatory, swinging, swaying, drooping, sagging; suspensive, suspendible *or* suspensible
   ▶ *Oscillation 683*

8 **overhanging,** projecting, jutting, pendent, sticking out, beetling, beetle-browed, cantilevered
   ▶ *Height 596*

9 **deferred,** suspended, postponed, adjourned, delayed, stayed, held up, put off, tabled, shelved; pending, abeyant, dormant, moratory; undecided, indecisive, hovering, fluctuating, wavering, vacillating, uncertain, doubtful, doubting
   ▶ *Vacillation 378; Inaction 413; Uncertainty 841*

10 **interrupted,** intermitted, intermittent, intermissive, broken off, discontinued, stopped, arrested, withheld
   ▶ *Cessation 668; Discontinuity 775*

11 **excluded,** suspended, debarred; exclusive, excluding, debarring; hindering, interfering, preventive, prohibitive, interdictory; hindered, prevented, prohibited, interdicted

12 **in suspense,** anticipatory, excited, apprehensive, anxious; suspenseful, suspensive, exciting, nerve-racking
   ▶ *Fear 283*

VERBS

13 **suspend,** hang, hang up, hook up, fasten, attach, put up, drape; be suspended, hang down, hover, dangle, oscillate, swing, swing from, sway, flap, droop, sag
   ▶ *Oscillation 683; Connection 754*

14 **overhang,** hang over, hover over, project over, extend over, jut over, beetle, stick out over, protrude
   ▶ *Height 596*

15 **defer,** suspend, postpone, adjourn, delay, stay, hold up, table, shelve, put on a shelf, put on hold, put off, proscrastinate; refrain, hold back, keep undetermined; hover, fluctuate, waver, vacillate, be uncertain, doubt
   ▶ *Vacillation 378; Inaction 413; Uncertainty 841*

16 **interrupt,** intermit, discontinue, bring to a stop, stop, arrest, cease, stop payment, withhold; break off, leave off, pause, come to a stop, cease operation
   ▶ *Cessation 668; Discontinuity 775*

17 **debar,** exclude, shut out; hinder, interfere, prevent, prohibit, interdict
   ▶ *Expulsion 709; Exclusion 764; Hindrance 826*

18 **be in suspense,** be excited, be apprehensive, be anxious, be on pins and needles
   ▶ *Fear 283*

ADVERBS

19 **pendulously,** pendently, suspensively, on a string, in midair

20 **interruptedly,** intermittingly, intermittently; on hold, on the shelf [Inf]; undecidedly, indecisively, waveringly, uncertainly, doubtfully, doubtingly

21 **in suspense,** on pins and needles, anticipatorily, excitedly, apprehensively, anxiously; suspensefully, suspensively

605 Support

NOUNS

1 **support,** foundation, base, prop, backing, reinforcement, fortification, strengthening, holding up, propping up, shoring up
▸ *Structure 551; Base 601*

2 **supporting structure,** foundation, base, basement, substratum, substruction, substructure, infrastructure, underpinning, framework, frame, undercarriage, chassis, keel; scaffold, scaffolding, platform; shelf, mantelpiece, pedestal, plinth, stand, music stand, tripod, table, worktable; bulwark, wall, retaining wall, embankment
▸ *Engineering 14; Architecture 134; Structure 551; Base 601*

3 **supporting part,** foundation stone, cornerstone, keystone, linchpin; support, prop, fulcrum, buttress, flying buttress, brace, bracket, stay, strut, abutment; girder, rafter, beam, crossbeam, crossbar, crosspiece, transom, lintel, joist; post, king post, pier, pole, pile, pillar, column, pilaster, caryatid, shaft, baluster, stem
▸ *Engineering 14; Architecture 134; Base 601*

4 **basis,** foundation, root, footing, fundament, principle, premise, reason, grounds, justification, precedent
▸ *Reason 319; Base 601*

5 **ancillary,** auxiliary, helper, subsidiary, supplement, complement, accompaniment, addition

6 **body support,** skeleton, backbone, spine, ribs; sling, cast, splint, bandage, crutch, cane, walking stick, staff, walker; supporting garment, supporter, girdle, garter, corset, brassiere *or* bra, jockstrap *or* athletic supporter
▸ *Human Body 19; Clothing 100; Structure 551*

7 **moral support,** sympathy, empathy, encouragement, heartening, reassurance, supportiveness, strengthening, reinforcement; succor, help, helping hand, assistance, aid, abetment, collaboration, cooperation, support system; approval, favor, endorsement, backing; advocacy, recommendation, praise, promotion, advancement, furtherance; championship, defense, protection; corroboration, validation, authentication, verification, confirmation
▸ *Benevolence 305; Assent 346; Defense 419; Approval 437; Help 825; Cooperation 827*

8 **financial support,** provision, sustainment, sustenance, subsistence, maintenance, preservation, upkeep, child support, alimony; subsidy, pension, contribution; financial aid, pecuniary assistance, grant, stipend, payment; financing, funding, backing, sponsorship, patronage, benefaction, bailout, bankroll [Inf]
▸ *Provision 89; Money 484; Payment 489; Generosity 498*

9 **supporter,** support, bearer, carrier, bulwark, anchor, mainstay, pillar, tower *or* pillar of strength, buttress; helper, helpmate, helping hand, succor, assistant, right arm, aide, auxiliary, sidekick, collaborator, colleague, cooperator, friend, ally, abettor *or* abetter, accomplice, accessory; sympathizer, fellow traveler, empathizer, adherent, follower, disciple, fan, admirer; upholder, corroborator, endorser, backer, seconder; advocate, proponent, promoter; champion, defender, protector, guardian, patron saint, angel, guardian angel, fairy godmother; security blanket
▸ *Relief 275; Help 825; Cooperation 827*

10 **provider,** provisioner, sustainer, maintainer, preserver, keeper; sponsor, patron, benefactor, subsidizer, underwriter, contributor, bankroller [Inf]
▸ *Provision 89; Giving 472; Generosity 498*

ADJECTIVES

11 **supportive,** supporting, foundational, upholding, reinforcing, fortifying, strengthening; sympathetic, empathetic, understanding, kindly, encouraging, heartening, reassuring; helping, helpful, collaborative, cooperative; advocative, advocatory, fostering, promotional, endorsive, approving; protective, guarding, guardian; corroborative, validating, authenticating, verifying, confirming
▸ *Pity 308; Approval 437; Cooperation 827*

12 **foundational,** basal, substrative, substructional, substructural, infrastructural, underpinning, framing
▸ *Structure 551; Base 601*

13 **basic,** root, rooted, fundamental, principled, reasonable, reasoned, justifiable, justified, precedented
▸ *Reason 319; Essence 723*

14 **ancillary,** auxiliary, subsidiary, supplementary *or* supplemental, complementary, accompanying, additional

15 **sustaining,** maintaining, preserving; benevolent, patronly, patronal; subsidized, pensionary, contributory, stipendiary
▸ *Benevolence 305; Giving 472*

VERBS

16 **support,** bear, carry, bear up, sustain, withstand, hold; hold up, prop up, prop, shore up, shore; buttress, reinforce, fortify, strengthen, bolster, underpin, bracket, brace, post, abut, scaffold, frame; bulwark, rampart, wall, embank
▸ *Engineering 14; Architecture 134; Structure 551; Base 601*

17 **bear,** tolerate, countenance, abide, stand, stomach, put up with, brook, endure, submit to, undergo, sustain, suffer
▸ *Submission 421*

18 **give moral support,** sympathize, empathize, stand by, encourage, hearten, reassure, inspirit, buoy up, strengthen, reinforce, shore up, carry; succor, help, lend a helping hand, assist, aid, abet, collaborate, cooperate; uphold, sustain, favor, approve of, give the seal of approval to, endorse, back, second, stand behind; advocate, recommend, praise, promote, advance, foster, further, forward; champion, defend, protect,

guard, fight for, stand up for, stick up for; corroborate, back up, validate, authenticate, verify, confirm

▶ *Benevolence 305; Pity 308; Assent 346; Defense 419; Approval 437; Cooperation 827*

19 **support financially,** provide for, sustain, maintain, preserve, keep; finance, pay for, fund, back, sponsor, patronize, subsidize, underwrite, pension, contribute, grant, bail out, bankroll [Inf]

▶ *Provision 89; Money 484; Payment 489; Help 825*

ADVERBS

20 **supportively,** sympathetically, empathetically, encouragingly, reassuringly; protectively, benevolently, sustainingly; helpfully, collaboratively, cooperatively; endorsingly, corroboratively, corroboratorily

21 **basically,** basally, foundationally, fundamentally, in principle, reasonably, justifiably

606 Parallelism

NOUNS

1 **parallelism,** collaterality, coextension, nonconvergence, nondivergence, equidistance; parallelization, collimation

2 **correspondence,** correlativeness, analogousness, comparability *or* comparableness, similarity, likeness, alikeness, equivalence, equality; comparison, analogy, correlation, parallel, equivalent, equal; balance, alignment, symmetry, harmony

▶ *Symmetry 626; Similarity 733; Equality 740*

3 **correspondent,** counterpart, match, mate, duplicate, twin, double

4 **parallel,** parallel of latitude, parallel line, parallelogram, parallelepiped *or* parallelepipedon, parallel bars, railroad *or* railway tracks

ADJECTIVES

5 **parallel,** parallelistic, collateral, coextensive, nonconvergent, nonconverging, nondivergent, nondiverging, equidistant, collimated

6 **corresponding,** correspondent, correlated, correlative, analogous, comparable, parallel, similar, like, alike, equivalent, equal; balanced, aligned, symmetrical *or* symmetric, harmonious

▶ *Similarity 733; Equality 740*

VERBS

7 **parallel,** be parallel, lie parallel, coextend, run parallel, run side by side, run abreast; make parallel, parallelize, collimate

8 **correspond,** correlate, parallel, be analogous, be similar, be equivalent, equal; draw a parallel, analogize, compare, liken; match, balance, align, symmetrize, harmonize

▶ *Similarity 733; Equality 740*

ADVERBS

9 **in parallel,** abreast, alongside, side by side, collaterally,

coextensively, nonconvergently, nondivergently, equidistantly

10 **correspondingly,** correspondently, analogously, comparably, parallelly, similarly, like, alike, equivalently, equally

607 Obliqueness

NOUNS

1 **obliqueness,** obliquity, slopingness, slope, slant, bias, skew, bevel, inclination, incline, grade, leaning, tilt, tip, pitch, list, camber, cant, askewness, crookedness, cockeyedness

▶ *Height 596; Verticality 602; Angle 628*

2 **divergence,** deviation, digression, tangent, indirectness, indirection, circuitousness, divagation, meandering; zigzag, turn, twist, bend, curve, curvature, swerve, veer, deflection; switchback, hairpin turn, dogleg

▶ *Curve 629; Deviation 698*

3 **indirectness,** circumlocution, periphrasis, convolution, evasion, hedging, ambiguity, equivocation, prevarication, backhandedness, dissemblance, obscureness, distortion, euphemism

▶ *Equivocation 380; Distortion 627*

4 **deviousness,** underhandedness, cunning, slyness, stealth, covertness, furtiveness, shiftiness, shadiness; deviance, aberration, perversity, perverseness; wrongness, immorality, dishonesty, deception, deceptiveness, deceit, deceitfulness, fraudulence, spuriousness

▶ *Deception 193; Wrong 430; Immorality 432*

5 **oblique line,** diagonal, slash, oblique, solidus, virgule, separatrix, cant; beveled edge, oblique angle, oblique triangle, rhomboid, rhombus

ADJECTIVES

6 **oblique,** obliquitous, slanting, skew, sloping, bevel *or* beveled, cant, inclining, inclinational, leaning, tilting, listing; slanted, skewed, sloped, inclined, graded, sidelong, sideways, pitched, tilted, atilt, askew, awry, crooked, cockeyed; diagonal, bias, cater-cornered, catty-corner, kitty-corner; transverse, crosswise *or* crossways, cross

▶ *Height 596; Verticality 602; Angle 628*

7 **divergent,** diverging, deviating, off course, off-target; digressive, tangential, indirect, circuitous, roundabout, meandering, wandering; zigzag, turning, twisting, bending, curving, swerving, deflective; zigzagged, twisted, bent, curved, turned aside, deflected; doglegged

▶ *Curve 629; Deviation 698*

8 **indirect,** roundabout, circumlocutory, periphrastic, convoluted, evasive, hedging, ambiguous, equivocal, sidelong, backhanded *or* backhand, dissembling, veiled, masked, obscured, obscure, distorted, distortive, misleading, euphemistic

◗ *Concealment 181; Equivocation 380; Distortion 627*

9 **devious,** underhand *or* underhanded, cunning, sly, stealthy, covert, furtive, shifty, shady; deviant, aberrational, perverse; wrong, immoral, dishonest, deceptive, deceitful, fraudulent, spurious

◗ *Deception 193; Wrong 430; Immorality 432*

VERBS

10 **be oblique,** slant, slope, bevel, cant, bank, grade, incline, camber, curve, lean, tilt, tip, pitch, list, careen

◗ *Height 596; Verticality 602; Angle 628*

11 **diverge,** deviate, bear off, angle off, digress, meander, wander; zigzag, oblique, wind in and out, turn, twist, bend, curve, skew, swerve, veer, deflect, dogleg, turn aside

◗ *Curve 629; Deviation 698*

12 **circumlocute,** evade, hedge, equivocate, prevaricate, bend the truth, dissemble, veil, mask, obscure, distort, mislead, deceive

◗ *Concealment 181; Deception 193; Equivocation 380; Distortion 627*

ADVERBS

13 **obliquely,** slantingly, bias, slantly, slopingly; toward the side, sidelong, sideways; at an angle, atilt, askew, awry, crookedly, cockeyedly; diagonally, on the bias, cater-cornered, catty-corner, kitty-corner; transversely, crosswise *or* crossways, across

14 **divergently,** off course, off-target; digressively, tangentially, indirectly, circuitously

15 **indirectly,** circumlocutorily, periphrastically, evasively, ambiguously, equivocally, backhandedly, euphemistically

16 **deviously,** underhandedly, stealthily, covertly, furtively; perversely, wrongly, immorally, dishonestly, deceptively, deceitfully, fraudulently, spuriously

608 Inversion

NOUNS

1 **inversion,** reversion, reversal, backwardness, transposition, transposal, inverted order; upside-downness, topsy-turviness, eversion, evagination, invagination, intussusception, introversion, retroversion, retroflexion *or* retroflection

◗ *Reversion 671; Backward Motion 680*

2 **inverse,** reverse, converse, counter, counterpart, antithesis, contrary, opposite

◗ *Oppositeness 731*

3 **act** *or* **instance of inversion,** capsizing, overturn, upset, spill; headstand, handstand, cartwheel, somersault, handspring; atmospheric *or* temperature inversion

◗ *Verticality 602; Horizontality 603*

4 **inverted thing,** inversion, invert, inverse; inverse image, counter image, inverse function, inverse proportion, other side of the coin, inverted arch *or* vault;

anastrophe, palindrome, metathesis, hysteron proteron, chiasmus

◗ *Reversion 671*

ADJECTIVES

5 **inverted,** inversed, reversed, backward, transposed, upside-down, bottom-up, topsy-turvy, head over heels, inside out and back-to-front, back-to-front, inside out, everted, evaginated, invaginated, introverted, retroverted, retroverse, arsy-varsy [Inf]

◗ *Reversion 671; Backward Motion 680*

6 **inverse,** reverse, converse, antithetical, opposite, contrary, counter

◗ *Oppositeness 731*

VERBS

7 **invert,** inverse, reverse, transpose, put in inverted order, put the cart before the horse; turn upside down, turn backward *or* backwards, turn inside out, turn the tables; evert, evaginate, invaginate, intussuscept, turn inward, introvert, retrovert; contrast, counter, oppose

◗ *Reversion 671; Backward Motion 680*

8 **become inverted,** capsize, spill, upset, turn over, overturn; stand on one's head *or* hands, headstand, handstand, cartwheel, somersault, handspring

◗ *Verticality 602; Horizontality 603*

ADVERBS

9 **inversely,** reversedly, in reverse, backward, upside down, bottom up, topsy-turvy, topsy-turvily, head over heels, inside out, inside out and back to front, back to front, in the wrong way; arsy-varsy [Inf], assbackwards [Inf]

◗ *Reversion 671; Backward Motion 680*

10 **reversely,** inversely, conversely, antithetically, oppositely, counter, contrary, contrarily, contrariwise, vice versa

◗ *Oppositeness 731*

609 Interweaving

NOUNS

1 **interweaving,** weaving, crisscross, interlacing, interlacement, intertexture, interwork, lacing intertwining, intertwinement, twining, entanglement, webbing, braiding, plaiting *or* plashing; interlocking, intercommunication, interfusion, interlineation, interdigitation, reticulation, interpenetration

◗ *Decoration 532; Convolution 632; Mixture 751; Disorder 766*

2 **weaving,** loom, hand loom, warp, weft, woof [Brit]; shuttle, distaff, spinning wheel, sewing machine; weaver, knitter, spinner, spider, weaverbird; weave, texture, nap, pile, tissue, fabric, grain, surface, make, feel, touch, fiber

3 **braid,** plait, pigtail, wreath, arabesque, filigree, cat's cradle, web, skein, network, webbing, netting, net, fishnet, mesh; wickerwork, trellis, espalier, lattice, wat-

tle, grid; tracery, fretwork, knitting, crochet, lace, knotting

> *Fabrics and Fabric Handling 130; Beautification 530*

4 **crossroads,** crossing, interchange, intersection, road junction, cloverleaf, traffic circle, rotary, interchange, underpass, overpass, spaghetti junction [Brit]

> *Way 691; Passage 692*

5 **junction,** juncture, unification, accouplement, joining, linking, splicing, uniting, binding, bonding, yoking, connecting, conjoining, coupling

> *Negotiation 460*

ADJECTIVES

6 **interwoven,** woven, handwoven, crosscross, interlaced, laced, lacy, intertwined; twined, webbed, webby, interdigitated, braided, plaited, pleached, wreathed, reticulate *or* reticular, loomed

7 **crossing,** crosswise, crossways, intersecting, interchanging, interconnecting, intersectional, transverse

VERBS

8 **interweave,** inweave, weave, crisscross, interlace, enlace, lace, intertwine, entwine *or* intwine; twine, entangle, web, braid, plait, pleach *or* plash; interlock, interdigitate, reticulate, filigree, net, mesh, mesh together; intercrop, espalier, interfile, interfuse, intermingle; interlay, interline, interpenetrate

9 **cross,** intersect, interchange, meet, come to a junction

10 **join,** interconnect, interlink, bind, unify, couple

ADVERBS

11 **interweavingly,** interlacedly, interlineally, interspatially, interpenetratively, intertwiningly, interchangeably

610 Exterior

NOUNS

1 **exterior,** outer surface, surface, external, outside, outer side, outer face, face, front, facade *or* façade, superficies

> *Front 621*

2 **exteriority,** externality, outward feature; outer layer, overlying layer, superstratum, envelope, outer wall, covering, coating, integument, cortex, involucre, involucrum, shell, rind, pod, hull, husk, crust, skin, epidermis, cuticle, exoskeleton; periphery, circumference, outline, surroundings, border, fringe, edge, rim

> *Layer 588; Covering 613; Surroundings 615*

3 **outside,** out-of-doors, outdoors, the great outdoors, open air, the open; outskirt *or* outskirts, hinterland *or* hinterlands, back country, outland *or* outlands, outback [Aus]

> *Region 564; Distance 585*

4 **appearance,** surface appearance, outward appearance, outwardness, superficies, superficiality *or* superficialness, apparentness, seemingness, aspect, mien,

impression, image, public persona, outer face, facade *or* façade, guise; appearances, externals, superficialities

> *Appearance 264*

5 **externalization,** exteriorization, projection; openness, extroversion *or* extraversion, other-directedness

> *Psychology and Psychiatry 108*

6 **extraneousness,** foreignness, adventitiousness, exteriority, externality; otherworldliness, the other side, the supernatural, the paranormal

> *Occultism 86; Extraneousness 724*

ADJECTIVES

7 **exterior,** external, outer, outermost, surface, superficial, outward, outside, front, facing

> *Front 621*

8 **covering,** coating, integumentary, epidermal, epidermic, cuticular, exoskeletal; peripheral, circumferential, surrounding, bordering

> *Layer 588; Covering 613; Surroundings 615*

9 **outside,** outdoor *or* outdoors, out-of-doors, alfresco, open-air; outlying, extramural, remote, outland, backcountry, outback [Aus]

> *Region 564; Distance 585*

10 **apparent,** surface, external, outward, ostensible, superficial, seeming, appearing, impressional

> *Appearance 264*

11 **externalized,** exteriorized, projected; open, extroverted, extroversive *or* extraversive, extrovertive *or* extravertive, outgoing, other-directed

> *Psychology and Psychiatry 108*

12 **extraneous,** exterior, external, extrinsic, foreign, alien, adventitious; otherworldly, supernatural, paranormal

> *Occultism 86; Extraneousness 724*

VERBS

13 **be exterior,** surface, front, face; layer, overlie, envelop, wrap, cover, coat, encrust; outline, surround, border, fringe, edge, rim; be outside, be out-of-doors *or* outdoors, be in the open air

> *Layer 588; Covering 613; Surroundings 615; Front 621*

14 **appear outwardly,** appear, seem, look, give the impression

> *Appearance 264*

15 **externalize,** make external, exteriorize, make exterior, project; be extroverted, be open, direct outward

> *Psychology and Psychiatry 108*

ADVERBS

16 **exteriorly,** externally, on the surface, outside, on the outside; peripherally, circumferentially

> *Front 621*

17 **outside,** outdoors, out-of-doors, in the open air, alfresco; on the outskirt *or* outskirts, remotely, in the outland *or* outlands, in the back country, outback [Aus], in the outback [Aus]

18 **apparently,** on the surface, externally, outwardly, os-

tensibly, on the face of it, superficially, seemingly, to all appearances

19 **extraneously,** exteriorly, externally, extrinsically, adventitiously

611 Interior

NOUNS

1 **interior,** inside, interior part, inner part, inner side, inner surface, inner layer, inner wall, center, core; endoderm *or* endoblast, endodermis, underlying layer, substratum, subsoil; interiority, internality, internalness, inwardness; the within, the inward
 ▶ *Base 601; Center 612; Enclosure 619*

2 **inland,** inlands, the interior, upcountry, hinterland *or* hinterlands, heartland, Midwest, Midlands
 ▶ *Region 564*

3 **internals,** internal organs, innards, inwards, entrails, bowels, viscera, stomach, intestines, enteron, guts, insides [Inf]
 ▶ *Human Body 19*

4 **inner nature,** inward nature, character, psyche, essence, heart, soul, spirit, anima, inner personality; spirituality, mentality, inner life
 ▶ *Essence 723*

5 **inwardness,** introspection, introspectiveness, soulsearching, self-examination, self-analysis, self-absorption, egocentrism; introversion, shyness
 ▶ *Psychology and Psychiatry 108*

6 **secrecy,** inwardness, intimacy, privacy, confidentiality, confidentialness; secretiveness, covertness, stealth, concealment
 ▶ *Concealment 181; Secrecy 182*

ADJECTIVES

7 **interior,** internal, inner, inside, inward; innermost, inmost, central, center, core, endodermic, endodermal, subcutaneous, subcortical, underlying, substrative *or* substratal
 ▶ *Base 601; Center 612; Enclosure 619*

8 **inland,** interior, central, upcountry, midland, landlocked, continental
 ▶ *Region 564*

9 **internal,** inward, indoor, inside; home, in-house, domestic, local, civil, national

10 **visceral,** internal, bodily, intestinal, enteric, gastric, abdominal
 ▶ *Human Body 19*

11 **intrinsic,** internal, innate, inherent, native, endemic, natural, fundamental, true, real, radical, constitutional
 ▶ *Essence 723*

12 **inward,** introspective, soul-searching, self-examining, self-analyzing, self-absorbed, egocentric; introverted, introversive, introvertive, shy; spiritual, mental, psychological

 ▶ *Psychology and Psychiatry 108*

13 **secret,** inward, private, intimate, inmost, personal, confidential, hidden, concealed, veiled; secretive, covert, stealthy
 ▶ *Concealment 181; Secrecy 182*

VERBS

14 **be interior,** be inside, lie within, lie beneath, underlie, lie below the surface, be at the bottom of

15 **go inside,** go indoors, enter, retreat into, take refuge, seclude oneself

16 **introspect,** look within oneself, search one's soul, self-examine, self-analyze

17 **keep inside,** internalize, turn inward, introvert, bottle up, contain, hold within; hide, conceal

ADVERBS

18 **internally,** inside, into the interior, within, indoors, withindoors; inward *or* inwards, toward the interior, toward the center, centrally, at the core

19 **inland,** in the interior, upcountry, continentally; inhouse, domestically, locally, nationally

20 **intrinsically,** internally, innately, inherently, natively, endemically, naturally, by true nature, basically, fundamentally, constitutionally

21 **inwardly,** internally, introspectively, within the self; spiritually, mentally, psychologically
 ▶ *Psychology and Psychiatry 108*

22 **secretly,** inwardly, privately, intimately, personally, confidentially; secretively, covertly, stealthily

612 Center

NOUNS

1 **center,** middle point, midpoint, center point, navel, dead center, bull's-eye, omphalos; middle, median, mean; center of rotation *or* revolution, pivot, axis, fulcrum, point of rest
 ▶ *Middle 772*

2 **core,** kernal, heart, nucleus, essence, pith, marrow, gist, point, nub, hub, pivot, crux, force, eye of the hurricane
 ▶ *Essence 723*

3 **focus,** focal point *or* principal focus, vital *or* pivotal focus, center of gravity, center of interest, centerpiece, focus of interest, main interest; center of attention *or* attraction, cynosure, star, personality; key figure, principal, primary source, chief, head
 ▶ *Power 514*

4 **center of activity,** hub, epicenter, hotbed, nerve center, headquarters (HQ), general headquarters (GHQ), central office, main office, where the action is [Inf], where it's at [Inf]; principal place, place of pilgrimage, holy place, capital city, capital, market town, town center, public square; forum, marketplace, mart, trading center, trade center, shopping center, mall, shopping mall, shopping plaza, plaza; community center,

civic center, medical center; transportation center, airport, seaport, train station, depot, bus station

> *Market 483; Location 565; Transportation 686*

5 **centrality,** centricity, concentricity, homocentricity; centralization, centralism, concentration, convergence, nucleation, focalization, centering, focalizing, focusing, pinpointing, locating

ADJECTIVES

6 **central,** middle, midmost, equidistant, halfway, midway; medial, median, intermediate, mean; pivotal, axial, key; epicentral, geocentric, heliocentric, centripetal

> *Middle 772*

7 **core,** nuclear, nucleate, essential, pivotal, crucial, pithy, forceful

> *Essence 723*

8 **focal,** principal, primary, vital, pivotal, key, major, main, leading, dominant, chief, head; cynosural, favorite, star

> *Power 514*

9 **centered,** centric or centrical, concentric or concentrical, homocentric or homocentrical; centralized, concentrated, convergent, nucleate, focalized, focused, pinpointed

VERBS

10 **center,** place or put in the middle; center on, center about or around, pivot on, revolve around, rotate around

> *Middle 772*

11 **centralize,** headquarter, nucleate, concentrate, converge, concenter; bring into focus, locate, pinpoint, focalize, focus, focus on, concentrate on, zero in on, home in on

ADVERBS

12 **centrally,** in or at the center of, in the middle of, midmost, in the midmost part, equidistantly, halfway, midway; centrically, concentrically, homocentrically; medially, medianly, intermediately; pivotally, axially

> *Middle 772*

13 **at the core,** at the heart, at the crux; essentially, crucially

14 **focally,** principally, primarily, vitally, pivotally, mainly, dominantly, chiefly

613 Covering

NOUNS

1 **covering,** cover, covering up, covering over, blanketing, cloaking; overlaying, overlay, superimposition, overlapping, imbrication, stratification; overarching, spanning, bridge; coating, topping, paving; enclosure, walling in, walling up; envelopment, enfoldment, wrapping, casing, sheathing; screening, shielding, overshadowing, eclipsing, blotting out, obscuring, hiding

> *Concealment 181; Enclosure 619*

2 **cover,** top, lid, cap, cork, plug, stopper, bung; crust, piecrust, incrustation or encrustation, scab, eschar; flap, shutter; gravestone, pall; topsoil, mulch; cloud, smoke screen

3 **body covering,** clothing, coat, jacket, cloak, robe, sweater, vestment, hood, veil, scarf, comforter; afghan, lap robe, rug [Brit]; hat, cap, bonnet; wig, false hair, periwig, peruke, bagwig, hairpiece, toupee, rug [Inf]; disguise, mask, domino, masquerade, camouflage, protective coloring; shroud

> *Burial 31; Clothing 100; Concealment 181*

4 **medical covering,** dressing, bandage, bandaging, gauze, adhesive tape, adhesive bandage, Band-Aid™, plaster, cast, surgical dressing, surgical mask

> *Medicine 107; Remedy 115*

5 **protective covering,** shield, screen, guard, housing, hood; hard hat, helmet; sun hat, topee or topi or pith helmet, visor, eyeshade, sunglasses, shades [Inf], suntan lotion, sunscreen, sunshade, awning, parasol; umbrella, bumbershoot [Inf], brolly [Brit inf]; tarpaulin, tarp [Inf], mosquito netting; life jacket, life belt; bulletproof vest, armor, mail, bulletproof glass, unbreakable glass; safety or fire curtain; insulation, lagging, fiberglass; blind, Venetian blind, shade; lampshade; tablecloth, place mat, doily, coaster; upholstery, slipcover, antimacassar

> *Safety 810*

6 **shelter,** protection, cover, shield, screen; refuge, retreat, asylum, sanctuary, haven, harbor; concealment, hiding place, hideout, hideaway, safe house; den, lair, covert

> *Habitat 60; Concealment 181*

7 **bed covering,** bedding, bedclothes, bed linens; bedcover, bedspread, spread, blanket, quilt, patchwork quilt, duvet, coverlet, comforter, counterpane [Arch]; bedsheet, sheet, fitted sheet; pillowcase or pillowslip, pillow sham; mattress cover, dust ruffle; canopy, valance

8 **coating,** coat, layer, film, sheet; topping, icing, frosting; plastering; glaze, varnish, shellac, veneer, enamel, lacquer, japan, stain, creosote, paint; wax, furniture polish; plate, electroplate, silver plate, gold plate, copperplate; lamina, overlay

> *Layer 588*

9 **casing,** case, sheath, housing; watchcase; capsule, sac, integument, tegument, cortex, involucre, involucrum, shell, nutshell, artillery shell, pastry shell, eggshell, pod, hull, husk, shuck, chaff, cornhusk, skin, jacket, peel, rind, bark, seed coat, testa, tegmen

> *Layer 588*

10 **wrapping,** wrapping paper, giftwrapping, wrapper, tissue paper, packaging, box, envelope; book cover or jacket, dust cover or jacket, binding; foil, aluminum foil, plastic wrap, wax paper, cellophane, polyethylene

▶ *Enclosure 619*

11 overhead covering, rooftop, housetop, roof, dome, cupola; roofing, slates, tiles, shingles, thatch, sheathing; ceiling; canopy, awning, marquee, ciborium; tent, canvas, big top, tepee, wigwam
▶ *Architecture 134*

12 wall covering, paint, whitewash, wallpaper, wall tile, ceramic tile; plaster, plasterboard, plasterwork, size *or* sizing, stucco, parget *or* pargeting; molding *or* mold, incrustation *or* encrustation; paneling, wainscoting; plywood, wallboard; weatherboard, clapboard, siding, facing, revetment, rendering, cladding; bricks, adobe, mortar, grout, pebble dash; window covering, curtain, drape, drapery; hanging, tapestry, arras

13 floor covering, rug, area rug, throw rug, hooked rug, hearth rug, braided rug; Oriental rug *or* carpet, Persian rug *or* carpet, Turkish rug *or* carpet, Turkoman rug *or* carpet, drugget *or* India drugget; carpet, carpeting, wall-to-wall carpet, broadloom carpet, pile carpet, shag carpet, stair carpet, runner; tile, tiling, linoleum, vinyl; hardwood flooring, planking, boarding, floorboard, parquet; mat, matting, doormat, bathmat; dropcloth, groundsheet *or* ground cloth; duckboard

14 paving, pavement, surfacing, road surface, sidewalk; concrete, cement, Portland cement; tar; blacktop, Tarmac™, asphalt, macadam, gravel, cobblestone, cobble, flagstone, brick

15 animal covering, cortex, epidermis, skin, fell, pelt, hide, hair, fur, fleece; feathers, plumage; exoskeleton, chitin, shell, scale, scute, carapace, lorica, operculum
▶ *Animals (General) 34; Invertebrates 39*

16 coverage, inclusion, incorporation, embodiment, comprehension, comprehensive insurance policy, blanket coverage; handling, fixing; news coverage, publicity
▶ *News 171; Safety 810*

17 substitute, sub [Inf], substitute teacher, replacement, alternate, alternative, surrogate, surrogate mother, proxy, fill-in, stand-in, understudy, double, stunt man *or* woman, ghost writer, backup, relief, reserve, locum tenens [Brit]
▶ *Support 605; Substitution 672*

18 coverer, tailor, furrier, quilter, tanner; giftwrapper, packager, bookbinder; electroplater; roofer, thatcher, plasterer, painter, whitewasher, wallpaperer, tiler, bricklayer; carpetlayer, upholsterer; paver; disguiser, masker, masquerader, camouflager; incorporator, insurer, insurance agent; fixer, handler, publicist, journalist, agent

ADJECTIVES

19 covered, covered up, covered over, blanketed; topped, capped, corked, plugged; glazed, varnished, shellacked, laminated, stained, painted, whitewashed, wallpapered, papered, tiled, paneled, faced, bricked, pebbledashed; roofed, thatched, tented

20 protected, shielded, guarded; insulated, enclosed, wrapped, packaged, boxed, encased, bound, sheathed, swathed, bandaged; screened, masked, veiled, shrouded, enshrouded, cloaked, robed, hooded, obscured, hidden, concealed, disguised, camouflaged

21 covering, overlaying, overlying, superimposed, overlapping; overarching, spanning; epidermal, integumental, tegumental, tegumentary

22 inclusive, incorporated, embodied, comprehensive, encompassing

23 substitute, substitutive, substitutable, alternative, surrogate, stand-in, backup, relief, reserve

VERBS

24 cover, put a lid on, top, cap, crown, cork, plug, bung, stopper, stop

25 overlay, lay over, overlap, imbricate, jut, shingle; span, bridge, overarch, overhang

26 protect, shelter, shield, screen, shade, house, guard, defend, armor, watch over; insulate, lag

27 hide, conceal, keep under cover, cover up, disguise, masquerade, mask, veil, cloak, shroud, hood, camouflage; cloud, overshadow, obscure, eclipse, blot out

28 coat, layer, spread, spread on, spread over, blanket, butter; top, ice, frost; glaze, varnish, shellac, laminate, veneer, enamel, lacquer, japan, stain, creosote, paint; wax, polish; plate, electroplate, gild

29 wrap, enwrap, wrap up, wrap around, surround, envelop, enfold, shroud, enshroud; giftwrap, package, pack, box; enclose, case, encase, sheathe; bandage, bind, jacket, swathe, dress

30 roof, dome, slate, tile, shingle, thatch, sheathe, ceil, canopy

31 face, front, revet, render, clad; brick, lay bricks, mortar, grout; plank, board; panel, paint, whitewash, wallpaper, paper, plaster, size, stucco, parget; mold, incrust *or* encrust; curtain, drape

32 pave, surface, concrete, cement, tar, blacktop, macadamize, gravel, cobble, brick

33 include, incorporate, embody, encompass, contain, comprise; handle, fix, take care of; report, publicize

34 cover for, substitute for, substitute, sub [Inf], replace, surrogate, fill in, stand in for, back up, relieve, alternate, understudy, double for, ghostwrite

ADVERBS

35 inclusively, comprehensively, universally, all around, on all sides, above and below, from all directions

36 alternatively, as a substitute, on behalf of, in behalf of, by proxy, per procurationem *or* per pro

614 Uncovering

NOUNS

1 uncovering, opening, unveiling, exposing, baring, laying bare, defoliation, revealing, disclosing

▸ *Disclosure 180; Opening 583; Display 843*

2 **undressing,** undress, unclothing, disrobing, disrobement, divestment, divestiture; denuding, denudation, stripping, stripping bare, striptease, dance of the seven veils, streaking; strip search *or* skin search, strip poker; [Inf]: skinny-dipping, flashing, mooning
▸ *Vulgarity 535*

3 **bareness,** nakedness, nudity, the nude, birthday suit, state of nature; exposure, indecent exposure, toplessness; [Inf]: the altogether, the buff, the raw
▸ *Vulgarity 535*

4 **nudism,** naturism, gymnosophy; exhibitionism

5 **nude person,** naked person, nude, nudie [Inf]; nude model, nude figure; nudist, naturist, gymnosophist; exposer, exhibitionist, streaker, denuder, disrober, stripper, stripteaser, striptease dancer, striptease artist, ecdysiast, exotic dancer, fan dancer, topless dancer, topless waitress; [Inf]: skinny-dipper, flasher, mooner, peeler
▸ *Light Entertainment 138; Painting and Drawing 143; Sculpture and Engraving 144*

6 **peeling,** shedding, molting, molt, sloughing, exuviation, ecdysis, desquamation, decortication, exfoliation, excoriation; flaying, skinning, abscission, husking, shucking, shelling
▸ *Birds 36; Insects and Arachnids 40; Separation 753*

7 **shedder,** molter; flayer, skinner; scalper

8 **depilation,** hair removal, scalping, shearing, shear, shaving, shave, electrolysis, waxing, wax, plucking, haircut, tonsure; depilatory, depilatory agent, hair remover, wax, denuder; barber, shaver

9 **baldness,** hairlessness, baldheadedness, baldpatedness, calvities, alopecia, hair loss, receding hair, falling hair; beardlessness; bald person, baldhead, baldpate; [Inf]: baldie *or* baldy, skinhead
▸ *Simplicity 526; Smoothness 545*

ADJECTIVES

10 **uncovered,** opened, unveiled, exposed, bared, laid bare, defoliated, revealed, disclosed; hatless, bareheaded; bare-necked, barefaced, barehanded, barelegged, barefoot, unshod, discalced *or* discalceate, barebacked, bare-chested, bare-breasted, topless, barebottomed
▸ *Disclosure 180; Simplicity 526; Opening 583*

11 **undressed,** unclothed, clothesless, unclad, divested, disrobed, unrobed, unattired, undraped, ungarbed

12 **naked,** bare, nude, au naturel, stark naked, naked as the day one was born, naked as a jaybird; denuded, stripped, stripped naked *or* bare; nudist, naturistic, gymnosophical; [Inf]: buck naked, bareass *or* bareassed, starkers [Brit]

13 **peeling,** shedding, sloughy, molting, exuvial, exfoliatory *or* exfoliative, desquamative, ecdysial

14 **shed,** peeled, molted, unfledged, unfeathered, plucked, leafless, exfoliated; flayed, skinned; husked, shucked, shelled

15 **depilatory,** hair-removing, shaved, shaven, beardless, clean-shaven, smooth-shaven, smooth-faced; tonsured, scalped

16 **bald,** hairless, baldheaded, baldpated, balding, thin on top, receding, glabrous *or* glabrate; bald as a billiard ball *or* coot

VERBS

17 **uncover,** open, open up, unveil, expose, bare, lay bare, defoliate, reveal, disclose, exhibit; raise one's hat, doff one's cap, go hatless
▸ *Disclosure 180; Opening 583*

18 **undress,** unclothe, disrobe, unrobe, divest, uncloak, undrape, take off, strip off, slip off, slip out of, step out of, remove, drop; undo, unbutton, unzip, unsnap, unhook, untie, unlace; change one's clothes, change; strip, peel off, bare, strip bare, expose oneself, streak, go topless, practice nudism; [Inf]: strip to the buff, skinny-dip, flash, moon
▸ *Clothing 100*

19 **make nude,** strip, pull *or* rip off someone's clothes, denude, denudate, disrobe, strip-search *or* skin-search, unwrap

20 **depilate,** remove, shave, shear, fleece; pluck, deplume, tear off, scrape off; peel, pare, skin, flay, abrade, rub off, debark, husk, shuck, shell

21 **shed,** peel, slough, molt, lose feathers, throw off, cast off skin, scale off, scale, flake off, decorticate, excoriate, desquamate, exfoliate, exuviate; go bald, recede

ADVERBS

22 **revealingly,** explicitly, nakedly, barely, in the nude, in one's birthday suit, with nothing on, without a stitch on; [Inf]: in the raw *or* buff *or* the altogether

615 Surroundings

NOUNS

1 **surroundings,** environment, environs, area, neighborhood, confines, locale, background, backdrop, setting, arena, stage, scene, scenery, outskirts, outposts, perimeter, periphery, precincts, vicinity
▸ *Region 564; Location 565; Exterior 610; Outline 617; Enclosure 619*

2 **encirclement,** envelopment, enfoldment, encompassment, circumambience *or* circumambiency
▸ *Circularity 631*

3 **ambience,** milieu, aura, atmosphere, feeling, tone, overtone, undertone, situation, vibrations [Inf], vibes [Inf]
▸ *Situation 573*

ADJECTIVES

4 **surrounding,** environmental, neighborhood, neighboring, background, outlying, perimetric *or* perimetrical, peripheral

5 surrounded, encircled, enveloped, wrapped, enfolded, encompassed, girded, circumscribed, circumambient, on all sides, around and about, hemmed-in, enclosed

6 ambient, atmospheric, in the air, aural, situational

VERBS

7 surround, lie around, environ, outlie, encircle, circle, go around, envelop, enfold, encompass, surround, be around, enclose, contain, keep in, edge, border, frame

ADVERBS

8 around, about, on all sides, all around, circumambiently, in the neighborhood, in the vicinity

616 Interface

Something there is that doesn't love a wall.
— ROBERT FROST

NOUNS

1 interface, place of contact, meeting point, adjoining section, contiguity, adjacency, abutment, place of interaction, threshold, shared frontier, common boundary, common border, political border; place of confrontation, battlefront, division line
  ❯ *Touch 216; Defense 419; Nearness 586; Edge 618; Limit 620; Convergence 702; Opposition 828*

2 interaction, common ground, meeting ground, cooperation, compatibility, working together, permeation, interconnection, joint, interpenetration, blend, dovetail, fitting together
  ❯ *Union 752; Adhesion 755; Middle 772*

3 interfacer, confronter, front-line soldier, frontiersman, pioneer, intermediary, middleman, mediator, negotiator, referee, umpire, director, frontbencher [Brit], continuity clerk
  ❯ *Mediation 75*

ADJECTIVES

4 interfacial, contiguous, adjacent, adjoining, meeting, abutting, liminal, interactive, shared, common, same, cooperative, compatible, blended, dovetailed, permeated, interpenetrative, intermediary; confrontational, divisive

VERBS

5 interface, meet, contact, make contact, touch, adjoin, be contiguous, be adjacent, abut, interact, share, hold in common, border, border on; confront, divide

6 cooperate, find common ground, be compatible, work together, blend, dovetail, permeate, interpenetrate, fit together

ADVERBS

7 interfacially, contiguously, adjacently, on the threshold, interactively, commonly, cooperatively, compatibly; confrontationally, divisively

617 Outline

NOUNS

1 outline, plan, summary, synopsis, abstract, epitome, précis, notes; brief impression, single aspect, bare essentials, frame, profile, projection, ground plan, layout, blueprint, representation, limning, emblem, sample; survey, contour line, contour, brief description, illustration, etching, engraving, delineation, depiction; map, chart, graph, diagram; portrayal, picture, simple picture, sketch, thumbnail sketch, tracing, cartoon, stick figure, matchstick figure, skeleton, bare bones, reduction, abridgment, digest, condensation, contraction, abbreviation, long story made short
  ❯ *Painting and Drawing 143; Sculpture and Engraving 144; Representation 187; Description 202; Appearance 264; Plan 387; Form 624*

2 shape, form, relief, shadow, silhouette, profile, contour, figure, frame, framework
  ❯ *Sculpture and Engraving 144; Structure 551; Form 624*

3 edge, horizon, skyline, coastline, outside edge, perimeter, border, fringe, flange, margin, circumference, surround, rim, circumscription
  ❯ *Edge 618; Circularity 631*

ADJECTIVES

4 outlined, summarized, synopsized, brief, impressionistic, representative, emblematic, sample, random, descriptive, delineative, depictive, thumbnail, diagrammatic, skeletal, abridged, abbreviated, circumscriptive, projectional, peripheral, marginal

VERBS

5 outline, plan, sketch out, rough out, block out, summarize, synopsize, abstract, epitomize, précis, present the main points, note, frame, profile, project, lay out, blueprint, draw an outline, picture, portray, sketch, limn, represent, sample, survey, describe briefly, boil down, illustrate, etch, engrave, delineate, depict, map, chart, graph, diagram, make a thumbnail sketch, trace, reduce, abridge, digest, condense, contract, abbreviate, make a long story short

ADVERBS

6 essentially, skeletally, diagrammatically, in outline, in brief, marginally, peripherally

618 Edge

NOUNS

1 edge, border, rim, brim, margin, limit, periphery, frame, lip, skirt, fringe, brink, verge, extremity, bounds, confines, limits, frontier, boundary; water's edge, shoreline, shore, seaside, coast, tideline, waterfront, littoral, strand, beach, riverside, waterside, bank; shoulder, hard shoulder, soft shoulder, roadside, wayside, sideline, curb, ragged edge; gunwale *or* gunnel, coaming

> *Boating Sports 150; Seas 571; Outline 617; Limit 620; End 773*

2 **edging,** hem, hemline, border, selvage *or* selvedge, fringe, flounce, piping, trimming, valance, pinking, furbelow, gimp, crenelation

> *Decoration 532; Fashion 536*

3 **cutting edge,** sharp edge, knife edge, razor edge; blade, sharpness; point of action, forefront

> *Sharpness 549*

4 **advantage,** upper hand, whip hand, little extra something, head start, flying *or* running start; the jump, inside track, ace in the hole

> *Intellect 315; Influence 512; Power 514; Superiority 744*

ADJECTIVES

5 **edging,** edged, bordered, framed, marginal, extreme, seaside, waterfront, coastal, littoral, beach, riverside, waterside, roadside, wayside, sideline, peripheral

> *Outline 617*

6 **edged,** skirted, fringed, valanced, piped, pinked, flounced, hemmed, crenelated

7 **advantaged,** ahead, keen, sharp, acute, biting, pungent, effective, forceful, incisive, powerful

> *Power 514; Superiority 744*

VERBS

8 **edge,** border, frame, hem, fringe, pipe, pink, trim, furbelow, decorate, crenelate, marginalize

> *Outline 617*

9 **border,** rim, limit, skirt, be at the brink, verge on, bind, confine, be on the beach, be on the sideline

10 **have an advantage,** have an edge on, edge out, be ahead, outwit, outthink, outmaneuver, outstrip, outshine, have a head start, have a flying *or* running start; have that little extra something, have the jump on, have the inside track, have an ace in the hole

> *Power 514; Superiority 744*

ADVERBS

11 **marginally,** peripherally, on the edge, at the limit, on the border, at the extreme, extremely, on the threshold

12 **at an advantage,** advantageously

619 Enclosure

NOUNS

1 **enclosure,** confinement, enclosing, closing in, ringing around, walling in, circumvallation, circumscription, quarantine, envelopment, encirclement, wrapping

> *Container 578; Covering 613; Outline 617; Circularity 631*

2 **enclosed area,** enclosed place, yard, park, patio, precinct, enclave, reserve, reserved section, compound, quadrangle, quad [Inf], court, courtyard, walled gar-

den, arena, ghetto, pale; close, sanctuary, holy of holies, sanctum sanctorum, cloister, monastery, convent; stockade, prison, jail, cell, dungeon; harbor, marina; cabin, crib, cage, pen, hutch, kennel, coop, sty, corral, paddock, fold, zoo; grave, tomb, sepulcher

> *Burial 31; Prison 55; Habitat 60; Religion 81; Closure 584*

3 **enclosing thing,** wall, fence, railing, balustrade, barrier, paling, pale, moat, trench, hedge, hedgerow, mole, ditch, dike, fosse, ha-ha; wrapper, wrapping, bandage, cast, wrapping paper, shrinkwrap, foil; package, carton, box, container, envelope, folder; jacket, dust jacket, dust cover [Brit]; frame, framework; scarf, sheath, net, shroud; bookends, parentheses, brackets

> *Clothing 100; Books 174; Container 578; Covering 613*

ADJECTIVES

4 **enclosed,** enclosing, confined, confining, bound, closed-in, fenced-in, walled-in, shut-in, hemmed-in, built-in, penned, framed, pent-up, indoor; cloistered, monastic, conventual; quarantined, jailed, imprisoned

> *Closure 584; Limit 620*

5 **wrapped,** bandaged, sheathed, enveloped, packaged, jacketed

> *Covering 613*

VERBS

6 **enclose,** surround, encompass, circumscribe, frame, close in, fence, fence in, wall, wall in, rail, pale, shut, shut in, hem in, build in, pen, pen up, corral, reserve, confine, quarantine; cloister; jail, imprison; bury, entomb

7 **wrap,** cover, bandage, bind, sheathe, envelop, enfold, package, contain

620 Limit

NOUNS

1 **limit,** end, boundary, confine, border; limiting factor, upper limit, lower limit, speed limit; check, prohibition; restricted area, off-limits area, no-go area [Inf]; ceiling, bottom, stricture, ban, rationing, freeze, curtailment, curb, restrictive practice, closed shop, trading ring, monopoly, cartel, trust, quota, embargo, tariff, allotment; extent, measure, dose, lot, copyright, patent; restraint, hindrance, brake, drag, repression, censorship, veto; self-control, self-restraint

> *Qualification 340; Allocation 474; Refusal 506; Cessation 668; Restraint 830; Subjection 832*

2 **limitation,** limit, restriction, proscription, proviso, condition, inability, circumscription, demarcation, definition, exclusion, restraint, constraint, control; containment, inhibition

3 **farthest point,** furthest point, extremity, edge, outside edge, brink, frontier, outpost; the limit, back o' beyond [Aus inf]

▶ *Distance 585; Edge 618; End 773*

4 limit marker, boundary line, boundary marker, stone, wall, fence, hedge, river, checkpoint; line, line in the sand, high-water mark, low-water mark, failing grade; curfew, time zone, international date line

▶ *Edge 618; Enclosure 619*

ADJECTIVES

5 limited, restricted, restrictive, proscripted, prohibitive, repressive, inhibiting, off-limits, exclusive, no-go [Inf]; controlled, restrained, held back, in check, confined, rationed, frozen, curtailed, finite; copyrighted, patented

6 farthest, furthest, extreme, on the brink, at the limit, bounded, bordered, bordering

VERBS

7 limit, restrict, end, bound, proscribe, prohibit, circumscribe, demarcate, draw the line at; define, exclude, restrain, constrain, control, inhibit, check, hamper, hold in, confine; specify, set parameters, limit one's speed, reach the threshold; hinder, brake, drag, repress, put a stop to, curb, bottle up, censor, veto, ban; place strictures on, ration, freeze, curtail, set curfew, contain, hold back; monopolize, set a quota, embargo, allot, measure out, copyright, patent; have self-control, have self-restraint

ADVERBS

8 within limits, under control, under restrictions, to a certain extent, thus far, off-limits, out of bounds

621 Front

NOUNS

1 front, fore, forepart, foreside, face; frontage, front elevation, foreground, facade or façade; front seat, front yard; head (of coin), obverse; first, beginning

2 front entrance, front door, main entrance, entrance hall, foyer, vestibule, lobby, forecourt, antechamber, anteroom; proscenium

3 waterfront, sea front, shore, promenade, boardwalk, esplanade, strand

▶ *Rivers 570; Seas 571*

4 front matter, preliminaries, prelims [Inf], front page, frontispiece, introduction, foreword, preface, prologue; prefix

▶ *Books 174*

5 vanguard, forefront, spearhead, cutting edge, avant-garde; pioneer, front runner, leader; front line, forward line, battlefront; prow, bow, bowsprit, figurehead, forecastle or fo'c's'le, foredeck, foremast

▶ *Attack 418; Opening 583; Water Transportation 690; Precedence 769*

6 face, visage, physiognomy, countenance, features; forehead, brow; [Inf]: mug, map, pan, puss, mush, kisser, phiz

▶ *Appearance 264*

7 show, surface show, outward appearance, projected image, persona, mask, facade or façade, display, false front, window dressing, disguise

▶ *Exterior 610*

8 assurance, brave front, brave face, self-assurance, confidence, self-confidence, composure, equanimity, authority; boldness, cheek, nerve, audacity, brazenness, brassiness, arrogance, effrontery; [Inf]: sauce, sass, chutzpa or hutzpa

▶ *Authority 52; Insolence 400*

ADJECTIVES

9 front, fore, face, frontal, first, foremost, obverse; anterior, preceding, forward; physiognomic, full-faced, full-frontal; facing, face to face

10 front-running, leading, primary, ahead, in front, pioneering, avant-garde; confrontational, head-on, eyeball to eyeball

11 outward, surface, facial, superficial, displayed, projected, assumed, disguised

12 assured, self-assured, confident, self-confident, composed, authoritative; arrogant, overconfident, bold, brazen, saucy, sassy [Inf]

VERBS

13 be in front, stand in front, front, come to the front, come forward; be ahead of, be first, be in the vanguard; get ahead of, take the lead, lead, head, pioneer, spearhead, challenge, face, confront, face up to, be bold; put on a front, show, display, disguise

▶ *Defiance 416*

ADVERBS

14 before, ahead, in front, up front, forward, to the fore, in the vanguard, in advance, in the forefront, in the lead, frontward

622 Back

NOUNS

1 back, rear, behind, background, hinterland; back end, rear part, back part, wake, train; tail, tailpiece, pigtail, heel, end, end piece, coda; backseat, backyard, back burner; rear guard; tail (of coin), reverse; backstage, backdrop

▶ *Music 140; Side 623; Sequence 770; End 773*

2 back entrance, rear entrance, back door, postern, tradesman's entrance [Brit]

3 back matter, end matter, afterword, epilogue, afterthought, postscript or P.S. or p.s., appendix, supplement, colophon; suffix

▶ *Books 174*

4 rear end, end, behind, stern, after mast; back, backbone, lumbar region, dorsal region, hindquarters, backside; buttocks, rump, gluteus maximus, fundament, posterior, haunches, hunkers, derrière; [Inf]: arse, ass, bottom, bum [Brit], buns, butt, can, cheeks, fanny, hind end, keister, sit-upon [Brit], tail, tushie *or* tush

5 **tail,** cauda, tailpiece, scut, brush

ADJECTIVES

6 **back,** backward, rear, rearward, hind, hindmost, posterior, postern, astern; dorsal, lumbar, gluteal, tail, caudal, latter; back-to-back

VERBS

7 **be in the rear,** be behind, be in the back, tail, bring up the rear, be *or* come last; follow, come after; trail, trail behind, fall behind, fall astern; back, back up, go back, regress
 ❿ *Backward Motion 680*

ADVERBS

8 **behind,** in the rear, to the rear, rearward, hindward, backward, behind the scenes, in the background, after, aftermost, aft, astern

623 Side

NOUNS

1 **side,** flank; laterality, sidedness, edge, border; unilateralism, bilateralism, multilateralism; side entrance, side door; side elevation, hillside, bank, shore, coast, seaside, riverside, sidewalk; surface, siding; side view, profile, side of the face, cheek, jowl, temple, jaw, side whiskers, sideburns; ribs, hips
 ❿ *Other Geographical Features 572; Edge 618*

2 **side direction,** front, back, top, bottom, right-hand, left-hand, south, east, west, north, right, left, other, far, near, offside; windward, weather side, leeward; outside, inside
 ❿ *Front 621; Back 622; Direction 697*

3 **laterality,** right side, right-hand side, dexter side, star-board, Epistle side, right field, right wing, recto page; left side, left-hand side, sinister side, port, Gospel side, left field, left wing, verso page; handedness, right-handedness, left-handedness, ambidexterity
 ❿ *Politics 50; Sports 145; Books 174*

4 **aspect,** feature, facet, element, bright side, funny side, dark side, cruel side
 ❿ *Appearance 264*

5 **group,** team, circle, camp, coterie, home side, away side, visiting side, our side, their side, opposing *or* opposite side, political party
 ❿ *Politics 50; Assembly 59; Sports 145*

ADJECTIVES

6 **side,** lateral, flanking, skirting, facing, oblique; unilateral, bilateral, multilateral; many-sided, multifaceted; front, back, top, bottom, right, left, southern, eastern, western, northern, windward, leeward; collateral, alongside, side-by-side

7 **sided,** handed, right-hand, dextral, left-hand, sinistral; ambidextrous

VERBS

8 **side,** flank, edge, skirt, face, be alongside, be next to, stand side by side

9 **move sideways** *or* **sidewise,** go sideways *or* sidewise, step aside, sidestep, sidle, make a side move, avoid, deviate, dodge, veer
 ❿ *Deviation 698*

10 **side with,** side, support, back, take sides, be partisan

ADVERBS

11 **laterally,** sideways *or* sidewise, sideward, alongside, side by side, hand in hand; to one side, to the side, obliquely; rightward, dextrally, starboard; leftward, sinistrally, larboard, port

624 Form

> It would follow that "significant form" was form behind
> which we catch a sense of ultimate reality.
> — CLIVE BELL

NOUNS

1 **form,** structure, order, system; formation, forming, conformation; format, configuration, construction, composition, composure, gestalt; shape, shaping, figure, profile, contour; frame, lines, outline, silhouette, relief, pattern, patterning, arrangement, design, designing; significant form, inner form, essence, substance, nominalism, Platonism, Platonic form, idea; morphology, isomorphism

   ▶ *Appearance 264; Production 522; Structure 551; Outline 617; Regularity 663; Reality 719; Essence 723; Whole 759; Order 765; Arrangement 767*

2 **prototype,** formula, model, dummy, mold; example, paradigm, pattern, jig, template, stencil, matrix; frame, blank, punch, stamp, cast, die, blueprint

   ▶ *Plan 387; Preparation 388; Originality 737*

3 **kind,** form, type, sort, variety, character, order; genre, art form, verse form, word form, musical form

   ▶ *Literature 139; Music 140; Painting and Drawing 143; Style 537; Order 765; Class 777*

4 **forming,** formulation, creation, morphogenesis, construction, production; expression, fashioning; modeling, molding, tailoring, knitting, weaving, shaping; setup, makeup, composition

   ▶ *Materials 104; Work 122; Production 522*

5 **nature,** health, fitness, condition, shape, fettle, soundness; character, attitude, turn; appearance, features, lineaments, face, expression, look, mien, aspect, demeanor, cast, set; physiognomy, physique, anatomy, body, build, ectomorph, endomorph, mesomorph, figure; trim, posture, stance, cut, cut of one's jib, getup [Inf]

   ▶ *Health 113; Appearance 264; Style 537; Front 621*

ADJECTIVES

6 **formed,** formative, formal, orderly, systematic, conformable, configurational, configurative, creative; created, made, constructed, produced, shaped, sculptured, carved, molded, modeled, tailored, thrown pot, blown glass, turned, rounded, squared; fashioned, set-up, composed, styled, stylized, stylish, expressive; morphological, morphogenic, isomorphic, isomorphous; Platonic; concrete, solid; plastic, fictile

7 **prototypical,** original, exemplary; dummy, paradigmatic *or* paradigmatical, generic, model, custom-built; ready-made, off-the-rack; tailor-made, designer, bespoke [Brit]

8 **in form,** in shape, in good condition, fit; able, capable; healthy, salubrious, hale, in fine fettle, hearty, in the pink

VERBS

9 **form,** structure, order, systematize, formalize, arrange; figure, design, draft, sketch, formulate, draw, format, lay out, rough out, block out, shape, turn, round, square; frame, outline, silhouette; cut out, cut, whittle, hew, rough-hew; carve, chisel, sculpt *or* sculpture, mold, model, knit, weave, knead, throw pots, blow glass; cast, coin, mint, stamp, found, hammer out, punch out, forge, smith; fashion, work up, work, build, construct, create, bring into being, make, produce; express, verbalize, put into words; put into shape, knock into shape, lick into shape [Inf]

ADVERBS

10 **formatively,** formally, systematically; by design, conformably, configurationally; concretely, solidly; plastically, stylishly, creatively; constructively, productively; prototypically, originally, paradigmatically; generically; healthily, heartily; expressively; morphologically; Platonically

625 Shapelessness

NOUNS

1 **shapelessness,** formlessness, featurelessness, amorphousness, amorphism; undevelopment, incompleteness, incompletion, rawness, lack of definition; chaos, confusion, mess, muddle, disorder; obscurity, vagueness, obscureness; unclearness, fuzziness, blurriness, haziness, mistiness, fogginess

  ▶ *Dimness 248; Lack of Preparation 389; Distortion 627; Disorder 766*

ADJECTIVES

2 **shapeless,** formless, featureless, amorphous; unshaped, unformed, undeveloped, underdeveloped, unfinished, incomplete, raw, uncut, unhewn, unlicked [Arch]; undefined, lacking definition, ill-defined, indefinite; chaotic, confused, muddled, disordered; obscure, vague, unclear, fuzzy, blurry, hazy, misty, foggy

VERBS

3 **make shapeless,** deform, distort, misform, misshape; unform, unshape, unmake, knock out of shape, twist, bend; leave undeveloped, keep incomplete; lack definition, be vague, obscure, be unclear, blur, fog

4 **disorder,** put into disorder, cause chaos; muddle, jumble, obfuscate

  ▶ *Destruction 523; Mixture 751; Disturbance 768*

ADVERBS

5 **shapelessly,** formlessly, amorphously; indefinitely, obscurely, vaguely, unclearly; chaotically, confusedly; fuzzily, hazily, mistily, foggily

626 Symmetry

NOUNS

1 **symmetry,** symmetricalness, uniformity, balance, balance of form, bilateral symmetry, proportion, proportionality; rhyme, harmony; chiasmus, counterbalance, equality, equilibrium, equipoise, even sides, congruence; congruity, correspondence, parallelism, correlation, coordinateness; interrelation, interconnectedness, interdependence, interaction; reciprocity, reciprocation, enantiomorphism

  ▶ *Parallelism 606; Sameness 730; Accord 735; Equality 740*

2 **operation of symmetry,** reflection, rotation, inversion, translation; element of symmetry, center of symmetry, reflection plane, rotation axis, rotation-inversion axis, glide plane; rotational symmetry, bilateral symmetry

  ▶ *Chemistry 11*

3 **evenness,** regularity, conformity, regular features, consistency, uniformity; eurhythmy, harmony, beauty, shapeliness

  ▶ *Beauty 529; Conformity 781*

ADJECTIVES

4 **symmetrical,** symmetric, uniform; balanced, well-balanced, proportional, proportionate, well-proportioned, proportioned, harmonious; chiastic, counterbalanced, equal, equilateral, even-sided, isosceles; congruent, correspondent, corresponding; correlational, coordinate, interdependent, interacting; reciprocal, enantiomorphic

5 **even,** even-sided, regular, consistent, uniform; eurhythmic, harmonious; beautiful, shapely; even-steven [Inf]

VERBS

6 **symmetrize,** make uniform; balance, proportion, harmonize; counterbalance, equalize, equilibrate, even, even up, regularize, make consistent; correlate, coordinate

ADVERBS

7 **symmetrically,** uniformly, proportionally; equilaterally; proportionately, correspondingly

8 **equally,** evenly, even-sidedly; reciprocally, on the one hand and on the other

627 Distortion

NOUNS

1 **distortion,** asymmetry, disproportion, lopsidedness, imbalance, difference, irregularity, crookedness, warp; strain, stress; contortion, bias, skewness, twist, torsion, twistedness

  ▶ *Obliqueness 607; Irregularity 664; Inequality 741*

2 **distortion of face,** contortion, grimace, grin, scowl, frown, snarl, sneer, leer, pout, moue, rictus, tic, squint

3 **distortion of body,** deformity, malformation, hunchback, clubfoot, cleft palate, mutation; misshapenness, ugliness, hideousness, disfigurement, grotesquerie, defacement; imperfection, blemish

  ▶ *Ugliness 531; Blemish 533; Nonconformity 782*

4 **distortion of truth,** exaggeration, misrepresentation, perversion, sophistry, misconstruction, false reading, fiction; deception, fabrication, falsity, spuriousness, perfidy, mendacity, deceitfulness, misinformation; disinformation, brainwashing, whitewashing; untruthfulness, lie, falsehood; travesty, burlesque, parody; propaganda, economy with the truth, terminological inexactitude, selective facts, imaginative journalism, poetic license; tall tale, cock-and-bull story, bull [Inf], bullshit [Inf]

  ▶ *Misrepresentation 188; Untruthfulness, Falsehood 192; Deception 193; Exaggeration 194; Sophistry 330; Misinterpretation 366*

5 **distorter,** defacer, spoiler; propagandist, sophister, spin doctor [Inf]; hypocrite, liar; vandal, hooligan, thug, pervert

ADJECTIVES

6 distorted, asymmetric, unsymmetrical, unbalanced; out of balance, out of kilter, out of alignment, out of shape; misshapen, irregular, lopsided, crooked, cock-eyed, askew; disproportionate, unequal; out of context; off-target, off-center

7 deformed, malformed, hunchbacked, clubfooted, disfigured, imperfect; ugly, hideous, grotesque, blemished

8 misrepresented, exaggerated, evasive; fake, perverted, fictitious, deceptive, fabricated, spurious; misinformed, misguided, disinformed, brainwashed; misleading, untruthful, false, perfidious, deceitful, deceiving, mendacious, lying; economical with the truth, burlesqued, parodied, creative

▶ *Misrepresentation 188*

VERBS

9 distort, warp, twist, strain, stress, contort, bias; disproportion, imbalance, misshape; knock out of true alignment, put out of kilter

10 make faces, grimace, grin, leer, scowl, frown, snarl, sneer, pout, contort

11 deform, malform, disfigure, deface, damage; impair, stain, spot, blemish

12 distort the truth, exaggerate, reshape, misrepresent, pervert; misconceive, misconstrue, give a false reading, twist words, read something into it; falsify, fabricate, dissemble, embroider; fake, deceive, dress up, forge, concoct, rig; misinform, mislead, misguide, be false, lie; brainwash, whitewash, propagandize; be economical with the truth, translate the truth, stretch the truth, take out of context, tell a cock-and-bull story, speak with a forked tongue, lead up *or* down the garden path, bullshit [Inf]

ADVERBS

13 asymmetrically, unsymmetrically, differently, irregularly, disproportionately; lopsidedly, crookedly, contortedly, misshapenly; hideously, grotesquely, imperfectly

14 distortedly, evasively, deceptively, hypocritically; falsely, spuriously, deceitfully, untruthfully, mendaciously; perfidiously, perversely

628 Angle

NOUNS

1 angle, bend, corner, sharp corner; fork, intersection, junction; zigzag, obtuse angle, oblique angle, acute angle, right angle, perpendicular; A-frame, V-shape, T-shape, chevron, notch, V-sign, dogleg; angle iron, miter joint; elbow joint, knee joint, gonion

▶ *Mathematics 6; Interweaving 609; Convexity 634*

2 obliquity, skewness, bias, bevel, cant, bezel, edge; wedge, slant, ramp, hill, slope, tilt, declivity; steepness, escarpment, scarp; tangent

3 angled figure, triangle, equilateral triangle, isosceles triangle, scalene triangle, right triangle; quadrangle, quadrilateral, square, rectangle, parallelogram, rhombus, diamond, lozenge, rhomboid; tetragon, pentagon, quincunx, hexagon, hexagram, heptagon, octagon, decagon; tetrahedron, decahedron, dodecahedron, polyhedron; prism, parallepiped, pyramid

4 angular measurement, trigonometry, geometry, goniometry; goniometer, protractor, bevel square, set square, T-square; sundial, sextant, theodolite, quadrant; astrological angle, semisextile, sextile, biquintile, square, quintile, trine; opposition

5 viewpoint, aspect, standpoint, stand; view, impression, slant, bias; premise, theory

▶ *Philosophy 4; Belief 87; Knowledge 348*

6 motive, personal motive, purpose, angle [Inf]

▶ *Selfishness 444; Motivation 508*

ADJECTIVES

7 angular, cornered, sharp-cornered, doglegged; pointed, bent, hooked, jointed, notched, forked, bifurcated; V-shaped, A-framed; mitered

8 oblique, skew, skewed, sloping, beveled, slanting; hilly, sloped, inclined, tilted, steep; tangential, diagonal, transverse, thwart

9 angled, right-angled, perpendicular, oblique-angled, acute-angled, obtuse-angled; scalene, triangular, square, rectangular, quadrilateral, quadrangular, rhomboidal; polygonal, pentagonal, hexagonal, hexagram-moid, heptagonal, octagonal, decagonal; trilateral, cuneate, cuneiform; decahedral, dodecahedral, polyhedral; prismatic, pyramidal; faceted, diamond

10 slanted, biased, angled

VERBS

11 angle, fork, intersect, zigzag, bend, hook over; tip, tilt, slope, lean; cant, bevel, bank, miter; incline, careen; go off on *or* at a tangent

ADVERBS

12 askew, aslant, obliquely, diagonally, at an angle, off on *or* at a tangent, on the bias

629 Curve

NOUNS

1 curve, bend, camber, turn, U-turn, S-curve, detour, curl, arc, arch, crescent; coil, loop, spiral; circuit, circle, oval, rondure, semicircle, meniscus; parabola, hyperbola, roundness, wave, undulation

▶ *Circularity 631*

2 curvature, incurvature, concavity, convexity, bending, arching; circularity, circularness; curliness, curvilinearity, sinuosity

▶ *Convolution 632; Convexity 634; Concavity 635*

3 curved thing, horseshoe, dome, half-moon, archer's

bow, figure eight, bend in the road, smile, rainbow; horizon, earth's orbit; sine wave

ADJECTIVES

4 **curved,** curving, cambered, curviform, curvilinear, bent, flexuous, concave, convex; turning, stooped, bowed; vaulted, arched, arciform; spiraled, curled, coiled, looped; round, oval, semicircular, circular, crescentic, lunar, meniscal; parabolic, hyperbolic, domical; sinusoidal

5 **rounded,** well-rounded; curvy, wavy, undulatory, pear-shaped, sinuous, curvaceous
  ▶ *Roundness 633*

VERBS

6 **curve,** bend, loop, arc, arch, turn, detour; curl, coil, spiral; bow, circle; twine, entwine

ADVERBS

7 **curvedly,** curvilinearly, sinuously, sinusoidally; convexly, concavely, parabolically, hyperbolically; circularly, circuitously, roundly; curvaceously, wavily

630 Straightness

NOUNS

1 **straightness,** directness, linearity, rectilinearity, perpendicularity, horizontality, verticality
  ▶ *Length 590; Verticality 602; Horizontality 603*

2 **straight line,** ray, beeline, horizontal line, vertical line, unbroken line, plumb line, perpendicular; ascending order, descending order; row, column, colonnade
  ▶ *Verticality 602; Horizontality 603*

3 **straightforwardness,** directness, simplicity, plainness, clarity, unambiguousness, unequivocalness
  ▶ *Clarity 196*

4 **honesty,** truthfulness, honorableness, trustworthiness, scrupulousness, fairness
  ▶ *Truthfulness 191*

5 **directness,** candor, frankness, plain speaking, straight talking, openness
  ▶ *Truthfulness 191*

6 **traditionality,** traditionalism, conventionality, conventionalism, moderateness, moderation, conservativeness, conservatism, cautiousness; heterosexuality; squareness [Inf]
  ▶ *Caution 287; Conformity 781; Preservation 815*

7 **straight person,** straight shooter; traditionalist, conventionalist, moderate, conservative; heterosexual, nonuser (of drugs); straight arrow [Inf], square [Inf]
  ▶ *Conformity 781*

ADJECTIVES

8 **straight,** direct, unbending, undeviating, unswerving, straightaway, dead straight, straight as an arrow, rigid; linear, rectilinear, perpendicular, horizontal, vertical; true, right, plumb; straightened, straightened out, uncurled, unbent

  ▶ *Verticality 602; Horizontality 603*

9 **straightforward,** direct, simple, plain, clear, unambiguous, unequivocal, uncomplicated, easy to understand
  ▶ *Clarity 196*

10 **continuous,** unbroken, straight through, uninterrupted, nonstop, one-hop [Inf]

11 **honest,** truthful, honorable, upright, trustworthy, scrupulous, fair, fair and square, as good as one's word
  ▶ *Truthfulness 191*

12 **direct,** candid, frank, plain-speaking, open, up-front
  ▶ *Truthfulness 191*

13 **traditional,** conventional, standard, straight-ahead; moderate, conservative, old-fashioned, cautious; heterosexual, not using (drugs); straight-arrow [Inf], square [Inf]
  ▶ *Caution 287; Conformity 781*

VERBS

14 **straighten,** make straight, iron out, flatten out, straighten out; uncurl, unbend, unroll, unfurl, untangle, unfold; disentangle, comb out, untwist, smooth out, unscramble; tidy up, neaten, make shipshape

15 **talk straight,** talk plainly, speak the truth, stick to the truth; speak one's mind, give it to someone straight, make a clean breast of, mean what one says; keep to the point, not deviate, play it straight [Inf]

ADVERBS

16 **straight,** horizontally, vertically, perpendicularly, directly, unswervingly, straight ahead, as the crow flies, on the beam

17 **straightforwardly,** directly, simply, plainly, clearly, unambiguously, unequivocally

18 **honestly,** truthfully, honorably, scrupulously, fairly, fair and square; directly, candidly, frankly, openly

19 **traditionally,** conventional, moderately, conservatively, cautiously

631 Circularity

All things from eternity are of like forms and come round in a circle. — MARCUS AURELIUS

NOUNS

1 **circularity,** roundness, orbicularity, curvedness, rotundity, annularity
  ▶ *Curve 629; Roundness 633*

2 **circle,** full circle, circumference, ambit; cycle, full cycle, orbit, epicycle; semicircle, half circle, oval; zodiac, mandala; circular path, circular road, circuit, racetrack, traffic circle, rotary; annulus, annulation, ring, loop, figure eight; roundabout way, circuitous route, detour, bypass; round trip, lap
  ▶ *Transportation 686*

3 **circular thing,** hair band, crown, coronet; collar, neckband, dog collar, necklace, choker; belt, waist-

band, cummerbund, sash, girdle; bracelet, wristband, anklet; discus, plate, saucer, disk, ring, hoop, band, tire, wheel; noose, loop, lasso; wreath; equator; halo, corona

4 **parts of a circle,** center, circumference, radius, diameter, quadrant, sextant, sector, segment, chord, crescent, arc

ADJECTIVES

5 **circular,** orbital, cyclic, orbicular, discoid; rounded, round, ring-shaped, annular, annulate; semicircular; elliptic, ovate, oval, ovoid, egg-shaped, rotund; circulatory, circumferential

VERBS

6 **circle,** encircle, surround; go around, travel in a circle, make a round trip, make a circle; circulate, circumambulate, circumnavigate, lap, take a turn; orbit, go into orbit; revolve, rotate; detour, make a detour, bypass, skirt around
  ▶ *Roundness 633*

7 **make circular,** circularize, draw a circle, arrange in a circle, make round; girdle, encompass, round, turn

ADVERBS

8 **circularly,** circuitously, circumferentially; cyclically, orbitally; orbicularly, elliptically, ovately, ovally; annularly, roundly; rotundly

632 Convolution

NOUNS

1 **convolution,** convolutedness, involution, circumvolution; circling upon itself, intricacy, intricateness; twistedness, sinuousness, undulation, anfractuosity
  ▶ *Circularity 631; Deviation 698; Disorder 766*

2 **coil,** turn, twist, twirl, intricacy; spiral, turbination, screw thread *or* worm, corkscrew, spring, whorl, (double) helix; curl, curlicue, ringlet; loop, meandering, squiggle, kink; squirm, shimmy, wriggle
  ▶ *Curve 629; Fold 637*

3 **convoluted thing,** snail shell, ammonite, nautilus, scallop shell, snake; whirlpool, vortex, tornado, twister [Inf]; labyrinth, maze; braid; intestines, cochlea

ADJECTIVES

4 **convolutional,** convoluted, winding, twisted, involutional, circumlocutory; sinuous, undulatory; intricate, braided, wavy, twirled, entwined; tortuous, meandering; labyrinthine, mazelike; serpentine, vermiform, wriggling, squirming, squiggly; coiled, spiral, helical, cochleate, whorled, turbinate

5 **ambiguous,** equivocal, difficult to comprehend; involved, complicated, complex; contorted
  ▶ *Sophistry 330; Equivocation 380*

VERBS

6 **convolute,** convolve, circle upon itself; wind together, twist together, weave together, braid, enlace, twine, entwine; coil, roll, corkscrew, spiral, twirl, curl; wave,

undulate, scallop; distort; meander, loop, snake, twist, turn, twist and turn; wriggle, writhe, squirm, squiggle, shimmy

7 **be ambiguous,** equivocate, complicate, make complex

ADVERBS

8 **circularly,** circuitously, ambiguously, equivocally; complexly, intricately, tortuously; spirally, helically, sinuously, wavily

633 Roundness

Line in nature is not found; / Unit and universe are round.
— RALPH WALDO EMERSON

NOUNS

1 **roundness,** rotundity, orbicularity; sphericity, sphericalness, globosity, globularity; gibbousness, convexity, cylindricality
  ▶ *Circularity 631; Convexity 634*

2 **round body,** well-rounded shape, shapeliness, curvaceousness, pear shape; fatness, corpulence, obesity, fleshiness, stoutness, plumpness, portliness, paunchiness, pudginess, tubbiness, chubbiness, potbelly
  ▶ *Size, Largeness 579*

3 **round thing,** circle, circuit, orbit; sphere, globe, orb, egg, spheroid, hemisphere; ball, bubble, balloon, marble, pellet, shot, bead, pill, pea, bulb, bowl; globule, drop, droplet, dewdrop

4 **cylinder,** roller, rod, rung, tube; cigar, pipe; stalk, trunk, bole; column, rolling pin

5 **cone,** cornet, horn, trumpet, bell shape; top, spinning top

6 **round,** turn, lap, round trip, circuit, daily round; orbit, ambit, circumambulation, circumnavigation; groove, rut

ADJECTIVES

7 **round,** rotund, orbicular; globose, globous, globular; convex, egg-shaped, ovoid; cylindrical, tubular; conical, conic, bell-shaped; bulbous, spherical, spherelike, spheroidal, spheric, hemispherical, round as a ball

8 **well-rounded,** rounded out, round, pear-shaped, shapely, curvaceous, well-proportioned, well-turned; fleshy, fat, overweight, obese, corpulent, stout, plump, portly, paunchy, pudgy, tubby, chubby, potbellied

VERBS

9 **make round,** roll, coil up, roll up, smooth, turn; make spherical, balloon out, ball, round off, round out, fill out

10 **move around,** orbit, circle, circulate, circumambulate, circumnavigate; lap, complete a circuit

ADVERBS

11 **roundly,** orbicularly; spherically, spheroidally, globosely, globularly; convexly; cylindrically, conically; bulbously, rotundly, curvaceously; around

634 Convexity

NOUNS

1 **convexity,** convexness, bulbousness, bulginess, bulge, swelling, gibbousness, billowing; distention, protrusion, protuberance, prominence; excrescence, tumescence, meniscus, camber
▶ *Curve 629; Roundness 633*

2 **bulge,** hump, lens, arc, billow, bump; balloon, bubble; knob, button, boss; bud, nose, wart, knot, edema, swelling, erection, bubo; carbuncle, boil, blister, corn, bunion, tumor, cyst; pregnancy, beer belly; muscle, biceps, pectorals, pecs [Inf]; nipple, papilla, mamilla, bosom, breast, bust, testicles; [Inf]: boobs, knockers, tits, balls
▶ *Reproduction 21; Ill Health 114; Size, Largeness 579*

3 **protuberance,** bump, swelling, protrusion, prominent feature; face, forehead, brow; proboscis, trunk; beak, nose, snout; [Inf]: snoot, bugle, schnoz *or* schnozzle, conk [Brit]
▶ *Front 621*

4 **dome,** cupola, vault, arc, arch, beehive, barrow; mound, hillock, hummock, hill, mountain
▶ *Height 596; Covering 613*

ADJECTIVES

5 **convex,** bulbous, bulgy, bulging, swelling, gibbous, billowing; distended, humped, prominent; excrescent, tumescent, swollen, meniscoid; arcuate, bowed out, arched, vaulted; lenticular, lentiform

6 **protuberant,** protrudent, protruding, sticking out, poking out, jutting out; bumpy, beaked, beaky

VERBS

7 **be convex,** arcuate, arch, cave, camber, bow; protrude, bulge, stick out, swell out, swell, hump; balloon out, round out; distend, billow

8 **protrude,** swell, poke out, project, jut out

ADVERBS

9 **convexly,** bulbously, bulgingly, protuberantly, prominently, excrescently, juttingly

635 Concavity

NOUNS

1 **concavity,** hollowness, curving inward, sinking; incurvation, indentation, indention, depression, impression
▶ *Absence 576; Depth 598; Curve 629; Notch 636*

2 **concave land,** hollow, cove, dip, hole; pothole, borehole, foxhole, crater; valley, vale, dell, glen, dingle, combe [Brit], cwm [Welsh]; col, gap, pass; ravine, gorge, abyss, crevasse, canyon, gully; den, burrow, warren, cave, cavern, tunnel, subway, trough, sap, trench, fosse, moat, grave; quarry, pit, mine; cutting, excavation, canal; inlet, gulf

▶ *Geology 8; Other Geographical Features 572*

3 **cavity,** dent, nook, cranny, niche, recess, alcove, basin, trough, bowl, cup, sump, socket, footprint, dimple, honeycomb, pockmark *or* pock
▶ *Container 578; Opening 583*

4 **digger,** miner, excavator, quarrier, quarryman, tunneler, burrower, gravedigger; driller, borer, dredger, dredge

ADJECTIVES

5 **concave,** hollow, curved inward, incurvate; depressed, sunk, sunken, cavernous; indented, cup-shaped, bowl-shaped; dented, dimpled, pocked, pockmarked, pitted; full of holes, porous, spongy

VERBS

6 **be concave,** curve inward; sink, cave in, collapse, settle

7 **make concave,** hollow, press *or* push inward, press, impress, imprint, indent; punch in, depress, dent, stamp, stave in; excavate, delve into, tunnel, burrow, bore, bore into, dig out, scoop out, gouge out, hollow out, dig, spade, mine, sink a shaft; pockmark, honeycomb

ADVERBS

8 **concavely,** hollowly, cavernously

636 Notch

NOUNS

1 **notch,** indentation, nick, nock, hack, cut, incision, incisure, dent, groove, cleft, slit, split, gash, gouge, score, kerf; serration, serrulation; crenel *or* crenelle; crenation, crenelation, crenature, crenulation
▶ *Defense 419; Sharpness 549; Interval 587; Concavity 635*

2 **notched thing,** leaf, shell, scallop; notched collar *or* lapel, Vandyke collar, arrow, saw blade, pinking shears, rickrack; cog, zigzag, battlement

3 **rung,** peg, step, level, stage, grade, degree, notch [Inf], gradation
▶ *Degree 739*

ADJECTIVES

4 **notched,** notchy, incisural, indented, crenate, crenated, crenulate; cut, slit, split, cogged, dentate, scalloped, pinked, jagged, jaggy, sawlike, saw-toothed, serrate *or* serrated, serriform, zigzag, zigzagged, uneven

VERBS

5 **notch,** indent, nick, nock, cog, hack, cut, incise, dent, slit, split, gash, gouge, score, kerf; serrate, pink, crenelate

6 **notch up,** score, achieve, accomplish, add to, win, gain

ADVERBS

7 **jaggedly,** crenately, dentately, denticulately, unevenly

637 Fold

NOUNS

1 **fold,** bend, turn, overlap, layer, furl, coil, doubling, doubling over, dog-ear; plication *or* plicature, plica; flexure, flection; buckling, geological fold, anticline, syncline
  ▶ *Geology 8; Angle 628*

2 **pleat,** accordion pleat, knife pleat, box pleat, plait; crease, pucker, tuck, gather; ruche, ruffle, shirr, flounce; ruck, rumple, wrinkle, crinkle, crumple, crimp, ripple, furrow, corrugation; paper folding, origami
  ▶ *Convolution 632; Furrow 638; Disturbance 768*

3 **enfoldment,** envelopment, enclosure, wrapping, swathing; entwining, hug, embrace, clasp
  ▶ *Enclosure 619*

4 **closure,** closing, closedown, shutting, shutdown, going out of business; financial failure, business failure, bankruptcy, collapse, going under, striking out, foldup [Inf], bust [Inf]
  ▶ *Nonpayment 490; Destruction 523; Closure 584; Cessation 668*

ADJECTIVES

5 **folded,** folded over, bent, pleated, plicate, plical; flectional, doubled over, turned over *or* down, dog-eared; creased, creasy, rucked up, ruched, flexed, corrugated

6 **closed,** closed down, shut down, failed, bankrupt, collapsed, busted [Inf], folded [Inf]

VERBS

7 **fold,** fold up, fold over, fold around; lap, double, double over *or* under, turn over *or* under, turn up *or* down; dog-ear, bend, buckle, overlap, layer, furl, coil

8 **pleat,** plait, crease, pucker, tuck, tuck up; gather, ruffle, shirr, flounce; ruck, rumple, wrinkle, crinkle, crumple; crimp, ripple, furrow, corrugate

9 **enfold,** envelop, enclose, wrap, swathe; entwine, intertwine, hug, embrace, clasp

10 **close,** close down, shut, shut down, go out of business; collapse, fail, go under, go to the wall, strike out; [Inf]: take it on the chin, go bust, fold up
  ▶ *Closure 584*

638 Furrow

NOUNS

1 **furrow,** trench, trough, scratch, seam, groove, wheel track; slot, fissure, chink, cut, slit; channel, conduit, rut, ditch, gutter, canal; flute, score, corrugation
  ▶ *Record 185; Concavity 635; Notch 636; Fold 637; Separation 753*

2 **wrinkle,** crinkle, crease, rimple, pucker, line, knitted brow, crow's-foot *or* laugh line [Inf]
  ▶ *Age 27; Front 621*

ADJECTIVES

3 **furrowed,** scratched, grooved, wheel-tracked, slotted, chinky, rutty, rutted, rimose; fluted, scored, corrugated, etched, engraved, plowed, rippled

4 **wrinkly,** wrinkled, crinkly, crinkled, creased, rimpled, puckered, lined, seamed, knitted

VERBS

5 **furrow,** trench, trough, scratch, seam, groove, track, slot, fissure, chink; cut, etch, engrave, slit; channel, rut, plow, ditch, gutter, canal; flute, score, corrugate

6 **wrinkle,** crinkle, crease, pucker, line, knit

Time

639 Time

The inaudible and noiseless foot of time.
— WILLIAM SHAKESPEARE

Time is but the stream I go a-fishing in.
— HENRY DAVID THOREAU

NOUNS

1 **time,** passage of time, duration, term, period, interval; tense, tempo; past, present, future; chronology; real time, biological time, psychological time, ontological time, sense of time
  ▶ *Linguistics, Language 5; Music 140; Period 641; Duration 642*

2 **space-time,** space-time continuum, fourth dimension, time warp, time travel, time machine, chronon
  ▶ *Physics 10*

3 **passage of time,** course of time, lapse of time, ravages of time, time and tide; figurative usage: Father Time, time's winged chariot, time the enemy, time the great healer, sands of time

4 **interval,** interlude, intermission, lull, break, coffee break, breather, respite, pause, interim, interregnum, meantime, breathing space, pause for breath, time-out, recess
  ▶ *Interval 587*

5 **time measurement,** chronometry, chronology, chronography, horology, timekeeping
  ▶ *Timekeeping 646*

6 **linguistic time,** tense, past tense, present tense, future tense
  ▶ *Linguistics, Language 5; Present Time 647; Future Time 650; Past Time 651*

7 **musical time,** rhythm, meter, beat, tempo, polyrhythm, pulse, syncopation; time signature
  ▶ *Music 140*

ADJECTIVES

8 **temporal,** time-based, time-related, temporary, pending

9 **lasting,** long-lasting, chronic, constant, durable, enduring; eternal, perpetual, everlasting, immemorial, time-honored

10 **periodic,** periodical, cyclic, repetitive; occasional, sporadic, intermittent, infrequent
  ▶ *Period 641*

11 **interim,** intermediate, intercalary, intercalated, intervalic, interwar, interglacial, interlunar

12 **chronological,** dated, in date order, chronometric, chronographic, chronogrammatic, calendrical, annalistic, of known date
  ▶ *Timekeeping 646*

VERBS

13 **pass,** pass by, elapse, lapse, run its course, roll by, roll on, flow, flow by, flow on, tick away, continue, endure, drag, drag by, drag on, fly, fly by, intervene

14 **spend time,** pass time, put in time, use the time, kill time, take time, while away the time, race against time, buy time, run out of time, make time stand still

15 **time,** keep time, mark time, beat time
  ▶ *Music 140; Timekeeping 646*

ADVERBS

16 **all the time,** in the course of, all along, all through, so long as, till, until, for now, for the time being, for the duration, the whole time, always, ever, forever, day by day, from day to day; day in, day out; week in, week out

17 **at what time,** when, at the time, then, whereupon, at that moment, now, at this moment, at this moment in time, yesterday, today, tonight, tomorrow, this morning, this afternoon, this evening, sometime, someday, any day, anytime, again

18 **meanwhile,** in the meantime, betweentimes, betweenwhiles, in the interim, for the interim, for a time, for a season

19 **sometimes,** often, now and then, now and again, on

and off, occasionally, infrequently, sporadically, intermittently, at times, from time to time, once in a while

20 **one day,** once upon a time, in the days *or* time of; in the year of our Lord, AD (anno Domini), BC (before Christ), AC (ante Christum), AH (anno Hejirae *or* anno Hebraico), AUC (*anno urbis conditae*), CE (Common *or* Christian Era), BCE (before the Common *or* Christian Era)

21 **chronologically,** temporally, annually, biannually, perennially, perpetually, eternally, forever
> *Eternity 644*

640 Timelessness

NOUNS

1 **timelessness,** datelessness, eternity, changelessness, sempiternity; agelessness, datelessness, immortality, deathlessness, everlastingness
> *Eternity 644; Infinity 798*

2 **immutability,** permanence, perpetuity, perpetuation, continuance, continuity
> *Duration 642; Permanence 667*

ADJECTIVES

3 **timeless,** eternal, sempiternal, ageless, dateless, immortal, undying, lasting, everlasting, continuous, perpetual, unceasing, never out of date, never out of fashion

4 **changeless,** permanent, immutable, imperishable, incorruptible, indestructible

VERBS

5 **perpetuate,** hold *or* keep in perpetuity, immortalize, eternalize, keep alive, memorialize, preserve, maintain, make time stand still

ADVERBS

6 **beyond time,** out of time, outside time

7 **ever,** evermore, forever, forevermore, always, eternally, everlastingly, endlessly, incessantly, unceasingly

8 **never,** nevermore, ne'er, not ever, at no time, not *or* never in a million years, not *or* never in a month of Sundays

9 **seldom,** rarely, hardly ever, scarcely, scarcely ever, once in a blue moon

641 Period

NOUNS

1 **period,** interval, span, time, timespan, term, stretch, space, fit, spell, break, pause, breather
> *Time 639*

2 **time period,** moment, instant, second, millisecond, microsecond, nanosecond; minute, hour, day, weekday, weekend, fortnight; term, semester, quarter, cycle, month, calendar month, lunar month, season, year, twelve-month [Brit]; decade, decennium, generation,

quinquennium, century; millennium, chiliad, era, eon, age, epoch
> *Duration 642; Season 654*

3 **geological period,** era, epoch, eon
> *Geology 8*

4 **period of activity,** stint, spell, phase, turn, watch, session, shift, work shift, overtime, halftime, working day, man-hour, tour, tour of duty, term, school term, academic year, semester, tenure, term of office, fiscal *or* financial year; term of imprisonment, sentence; bout, inning, round, go, whack [Inf]
> *Education 48; Sports 145; Punishment 454*

5 **recurrent period,** periodicity, recurrence, return, repetition, repetitiveness, regularity; series, season, cycle, iteration, periodic function, recurrent pattern; menstrual cycle, biorhythm, circadian rhythm, biological clock, photoperiodism
> *Season 654; Repetition 797*

6 **periodical publication,** periodical, magazine, journal, newsletter, bulletin, weekly, monthly, annual, yearbook, almanac
> *Periodicals 175*

ADJECTIVES

7 **periodical,** regular, repetitive, repetitious, iterative, returning, recurrent, quinquennial, millennial, millenary *or* millenarian, cyclic, seasonal, yearly, annual, biannual, biennial, monthly, weekly, daily
> *Regularity 663; Repetition 797*

8 **periodic,** intermittent, sporadic, continual, discontinuous, fitful, irregular
> *Irregularity 664*

VERBS

9 **be periodical,** recur, reappear, repeat, iterate, reiterate, return, come around again

10 **make periodical,** regulate, regularize, modulate

ADVERBS

11 **periodically,** regularly, recurrently, repeatedly, repetitively, repetitiously, cyclically, continually

---

AGES, DECADES, ERAS

Age of Anxiety	Golden Age
Age of Aquarius	Ice Age
Age of Enlightenment	Industrial Revolution
Age of Reason	Iron Age
Ancien Régime [Fr]	Mauve Decade (1890s)
Atomic Age	Middle Ages
Belle Epoque, La [Fr]	Modern Age
Bronze Age	Postmodernism
Classical Age	Prohibition Era (1920s)
Dark Ages	Reconstruction Era
Depression Era (1930s)	Renaissance
Era of Good Feeling	Roaring Twenties
Fin de Siècle [Fr]	Silver Age
Gay Nineties (1890s)	Space Age
Gilded Age	Stone Age

12 for specified periods, hourly, daily, weekly, monthly, quarterly, seasonally, yearly, annually, biannually, biennially, quinquennially

13 for short periods, on occasion, occasionally, at odd times, now and again, now and then, sometimes, fitfully, irregularly, off and on, on and off, by fits and starts

642 Duration

NOUNS

1 duration, length of time, term, course of time, passage of time, lapse of time, march of time, river of time, tide of time, flow of time; continuation, extent, timespan, span, allotted span, life span, lifetime, threescore years and ten; stretch, space, spell, period, limited period, fixed term, stint, reign, office, tenure, tenancy, tour of duty, shift, a bit, while, short while

> *Period 641*

2 continuation, continuousness, continuity, extent, continuum, progress, progression, process; long-lastingness, durability, endurance, staying power, constancy, stability, survival; permanence, permanency, perdurability

> *Timelessness 640*

3 long duration, long time, long while, generation, age, eon, millennium, years on end, month of Sundays, time immemorial, donkey's years [Inf], coon's age [Inf]

ADJECTIVES

4 lasting, durable, enduring, long-lasting, long-lived, abiding, continuing, continuous, continual, long-standing, evergreen, long-term, lifelong

5 permanent, unceasing, incessant, everlasting, eternal, perpetual, perennial, undying, immortal

> *Eternity 644*

VERBS

6 last, endure, stay, stay the course, stand, stand the test of time, abide, remain, last out, hold out, survive, outlive, outlast, persevere, hang on, hang in there [Inf]

7 go on, move on, continue, progress, proceed, run, run the course, elapse, pass

ADVERBS

8 for the duration, to the end, to *or* till the bitter end

> *Eternity 644*

9 for long, for a long time; until *or* till the cows come home, until one is blue in the face, until the Greek calends, until hell freezes over [Inf]

10 everlastingly, permanently, perennially, without end, eternally, without stopping, without pausing for breath, incessantly, continually, continuously

643 Transience

NOUNS

1 transience, transitoriness, impermanence, momentariness, suddenness, quickness, brevity, ephemerality, instability, evanescence, volatility, fugacity

> *Haste 818*

2 transient, passerby, traveler, caller, guest, visitor, drop-in [Inf]; passing fancy, nine days' wonder, flash in the pan, shooting star, meteor, bird of passage, brief encounter, ship that passes in the night

3 short duration, brief span, short time, short space of time, moment, instant, a second or two, a minute or two, just a minute, just a second, half a mo [Inf], just a tick [Brit inf]

> *Duration 642; Immediacy 645*

ADJECTIVES

4 transient, transitory, fleeting, flying, fugitive, fugacious, quick, ephemeral, perishable, unstable, brief, short, short-term, shortlived, evanescent, volatile, disappearing, fading, decaying, passing, meteoric, momentary, sudden, here today gone tomorrow

5 impermanent, temporary, one-off, single-use, throwaway, biodegradable, nondurable, brittle, fragile, mortal

VERBS

6 be transient, visit, drop in, call on, pass, pass by, pass away, flit, fly by *or* away, be fleeting, melt, decay, rot, turn to ashes, come to dust, fade, evanesce, evaporate, vanish, vanish into thin air, disappear, disappear in a puff of smoke, burst like a bubble, burst like a balloon, crumble away, fall to pieces, fall apart, shatter

7 make transient, shorten the life of, cut off, curtail, make disappear, bring to an end, put an end to, shatter the dreams of, burst someone's bubble *or* balloon

ADVERBS

8 transiently, transitorily, ephemerally, quickly, fleetingly, temporarily, impermanently, not long, briefly, shortly, momentarily, for a moment, in a moment, suddenly, in an instant, in a trice, in a twinkling, in the twinkling of an eye; *sic transit gloria mundi* [L]

> *Time 639; Immediacy 645*

644 Eternity

Eternity's a terrible thought. I mean, where's it going to end? — TOM STOPPARD

NOUNS

1 **eternity,** endlessness, infinity, infinitude, everlastingness, time without end, timelessness, perpetuity, sempiternity, permanence, continuity, incorruptibility, imperishability
   ▶ *Timelessness 640*
2 **life without end,** life everlasting, deathlessness, immortality, heaven, paradise, hereafter, afterlife, next world, eternal rest
   ▶ *Death 29; Religion 81; Timelessness 640*
3 **eternalization,** perpetuation, memorialization, remembrance

ADJECTIVES

4 **eternal,** everlasting, never-ending, unending, infinite, perpetual, timeless, sempiternal, permanent, enduring, durable, incorruptible, imperishable, immortal, undying, deathless, unchanging, immutable, evergreen
5 **agelong,** eonian, millennial, immemorial
6 **continuing forever,** ceaseless, unceasing, continuous, constant, unending, nonstop, interminable, incessant, going on and on

VERBS

7 **be eternal,** last forever, outlast, outlive, remain forever, endure *or* go on *or* continue forever, never cease, be permanent, have no end
8 **make eternal,** perpetuate, immortalize, memorialize, remember forever
9 **make permanent,** establish, set up, continue

ADVERBS

10 **eternally,** throughout eternity, forever, for always, for ay *or* aye [Arch], evermore, forevermore, for ever and ever, forever and a day, till *or* until the end of time, crack of doom, doomsday, infinity; without end, on and on, through thick and thin, for better or for worse, from age to age, from generation to generation, world without end, for good, for good and all, for keeps [Inf]
   ▶ *Duration 642*

645 Immediacy

NOUNS

1 **immediacy,** immediateness, lack of delay, instantaneousness, instantaneity, directness, urgency, emergency, exigency, promptness, promptitude
2 **closeness,** nearness, proximity, contiguity
3 **instant,** second, split second, moment, twinkling, twinkling of an eye, flash; [Inf]: jiffy *or* jiff, half a jiffy, mo, half a mo, sec, half a sec, tick [Brit], half a tick [Brit]
4 **point in time,** point, moment, juncture, occasion, instant

ADJECTIVES

5 **immediate,** instantaneous, instant, prompt, quick, fast, rapid, swift, speedy, direct, split-second, urgent, on-the-spot; fast-food, convenience-food, prepared; ready-to-wear, off-the-rack
6 **close,** nearest, proximate, next, contiguous
7 **allowing no delay,** demanding, importunate, burning, imperative, exigent, urgent

ADVERBS

8 **immediately,** instantaneously, instantly, without delay, at once, now, right now, on the spot, swiftly, speedily, rapidly, quick, quickly, as quick as lightning *or* as a flash, promptly, right away, straightaway, forthwith, yesterday, before one knows it, like a shot; [Inf]: before one can say Jack Robinson, like greased lightning, in two shakes of a lamb's tail, on the dot, right off the bat, pronto
9 **in the shortest possible time,** in no time, in an instant, in the same breath, in a twinkling, in the twinkling of an eye, in a trice, in a flash, at the drop of a hat, on the instant, as soon as possible (ASAP), posthaste

646 Timekeeping

The clock, not the steam-engine, is the key-machine of the industrial age. — LEWIS MUMFORD

NOUNS

1 **timekeeping,** timing, dating, scheduling, timetabling, calendar-making
   ▶ *Plan 387; Time 639; Period 641; Duration 642; Order 765; Arrangement 767*
2 **chronology,** chronography, tree-ring dating, dendochronology, radiocarbon dating, radiometric dating, thermoluminescence dating; timetable, almanac, calendar, schedule, diary, journal, order of the day, order

---

FRENCH REVOLUTIONARY CALENDAR*

Vendémiaire (September 22–October 21)
Brumaire (October 22–November 20)
Frimaire (November 21–December 20)
Nivôse (December 21–January 19)
Pluviôse (January 20–February 18)
Ventôse (February 19–March 20)
Germinal (March 21–April 19)
Floréal (April 20–May 19)
Prairial (May 20–June 18)
Messidor (June 19–July 18)
Thermidor (July 19–August 17)
Fructidor (August 18–September 16) (followed by 5 intercalary days; 6 every 4 years)

*The French Revolutionary Convention established this calendar on October 5, 1793. The year begins at the autumnal equinox. The Gregorian calendar was reestablished on January 1, 1806.

of service, program, course, curriculum, list; chronicle, diary, annal, history, record; the time now, the exact time, time of day, time of night, hour

▶ *History 3; Plan 387; Arrangement 767; List 785*

3 **calendar,** Julian calendar, Gregorian calendar, Jewish calendar, Muslim calendar, French Revolutionary calendar, Roman calendar, perpetual calendar, church calendar, ordo calendar

4 **day,** date, calends, nones, ides; birthday, name day, saint's day, red-letter day, anniversary, appointed day, fixed day; era, epoch, age

▶ *Period 641*

5 **time zone,** clock time, local time, astronomical time, solar time, sidereal time; Greenwich Time *or* Greenwich Mean Time (GMT) *or* Universal Time (UT); Alaska-Hawaii Time, Atlantic Time, Bering (Samoa) Time, Central Time, Eastern Time, Mountain Time, Pacific Time, Yukon Time; standard time, daylight-saving time; date line, International Date Line

▶ *Location 565; Time 639*

6 **horology,** clockmaking, watchmaking; horologist, clockmaker, watchmaker

7 **timekeeper,** timepiece, counter, timing device, horologe, clock, 12-hour clock, 24-hour clock; body clock, biological clock

8 **face,** clockface, watchface, dial, analog dial, hands, gnomon, digital display, chronogram

9 **signal,** time signal, hooter, siren, four-minute warning, gong, bell, minute gun, starting gun

▶ *Sign 183*

10 **keeper of time,** timekeeper, chronologist, chronographer, chronicler, diarist, annalist, historian, historiographer, scribe, recorder; referee, time beater, conductor, bandleader

▶ *History 3; Music 140; Record 185*

TIMEPIECES AND TIMERS

alarm clock *or* watch	cuckoo clock	metronome
analog clock *or* watch	digital clock *or* watch	pendulum clock
astronomical clock	egg timer	pocket watch
atomic clock	electric clock	quartz clock *or* watch
box chronometer	electronic clock	repeater
bracket clock	grandfather's *or* grandmother's clock	sandglass
calendar clock		stemwinder watch
cesium clock	half-hunter watch	stopwatch
chronograph	hourglass	sundial
chronometer	hunter *or* hunting watch	tall-case *or* long-case clock
chronoscope	isochronon	traveling clock
clepsydra *or* water clock	journeyman watch	turnip watch
clock radio	marine chronometer	wall clock
clock watch		wristwatch

---

11 **timekeeping,** horological, chronometric, chronographic, chronologic, chronological, annalistic, diaristic, calendric, calendarial, chronogrammatic, temporal

VERBS

12 **keep time,** clock, time, monitor, date, schedule, set a date *or* time for, fix the time, fix the date, fix the day, slate, adjust the clock, put *or* set the clock forward, put *or* set the clock back, set the alarm, synchronize, synchronize watches *or* clocks

13 **chronologize,** calendar, date, be dated, carry a date, bear a date, assign a date; record, chronicle, diarize, keep a journal

14 **measure time,** count the hours, count the minutes, mark time, beat time, keep time, watch the clock, clock in *or* clock on, clock out *or* clock off

ADVERBS

15 **horologically,** by the clock, chronologically, chronographically, annalistically, at this hour, at that hour, at this time, at that time, o'clock, A.M., P.M.

647 Present Time

NOUNS

1 **present time,** today, tonight, the present, here and now, present moment, this moment, this time, this very minute *or* second *or* instant *or* moment *or* hour, this very day, this morning, this afternoon, this evening, this night, nonce; present tense, present participle, historical present

2 **present day,** today, right now; present time, present *or* current situation; contemporary life, the modern day, modernity, modern times, modern world, world of today, today's world, the times, our times; contemporaneousness, newness

▶ *Same Time 649; Newness 652*

3 **modernity,** modernism, currency, up-to-dateness, topicality, actuality, what's happening, state of affairs

ADJECTIVES

4 **present,** current, existent, existing, extant, topical, contemporary, contemporaneous, modern, fashionable, in fashion, up-to-date, instant, happening, taking place, immediate, latest; of this date, of today, of today's date, with it [Inf]

▶ *Immediacy 645; Same Time 649; Newness 652*

5 **occasional,** temporary, provisional, interim, passing, *pro tempore* [L], pro tem

6 **available,** at hand, to hand, ready, here, there, in attendance, nearby, close by, standing by, accounted for, present

VERBS

7 **be present,** exist, be, live, be now

8 **live in the present,** live for today, seize the day, *carpe diem* [L], be modern, be up-to-date, be with it [Inf]

9 **at present,** at this moment, now, at this time, at this moment in time, right now, just now, presently, today, tonight, nowadays, these days; for the present, for the moment; for a while, meanwhile, in the meantime, in the interim; for this occasion, for the occasion, for the time being, for the nonce, not for long; provisionally, temporarily

648 Different Time

NOUNS

1 **different time,** another time, other time, some other time, distant time, better time, more convenient time, any time but this *or* now; past time, former time; future time, later time; time shift, time warp; asynchronism, archaism

▶ *Future Time 650; Past Time 651; Untimeliness 660*

ADJECTIVES

2 **different in time,** asynchronous, unsynchronized, out of sync [Inf], of *or* from another time, of *or* from another age; not contemporary, not modern, unmodern, behind the times, out-of-date, archaic; ahead of the times, avant-garde; mistimed, misdated, anachronistic

▶ *Future Time 650; Past Time 651; Untimeliness 660*

VERBS

3 **be in a different time,** mistime, misdate

ADVERBS

4 **another time,** asynchronously, some other time, not now, not today, not at the moment, not just this minute, sometime, someday, sooner or later, any old time, soon, anon, one of these days

649 Same Time

NOUNS

1 **same time,** same date, same day; simultaneity, contemporaneousness, contemporaneity, contemporariness, coevality, accompaniment, coexistence, existing together, concomitance, concurrence, coincidence

2 **synchronism,** synchronization, isochronism, sync [Inf]

3 **contemporary,** coeval, compeer, peer, friend, classmate, member of one's generation, brother, sister; men *or* women of today, people of today, peer group, one of the boys *or* girls *or* lads *or* lasses, one of the gang; age group, class of

ADJECTIVES

4 **simultaneous,** coeval, contemporary, contemporaneous, coexistent, coexisting, coeternal, concomitant, coincident, coincidental, concurrent, photo-finish, accompanying, of the same generation *or* year *or* age, matched in age, twinned, of the same vintage

5 **synchronized,** synchronous, isochronal, isochronous,

timed, phased, on *or* with the beat, in time, in step, in lock step, in sync [Inf]

VERBS

6 **be simultaneous,** exist simultaneously, be contemporary, happen at the same time, live at the same time, coexist, exist together, accompany, concur, coincide, encounter

7 **synchronize,** keep the same beat, keep in time, keep time with, stay in time, keep in step, keep in step with, keep pace with, march in lock step, go hand in hand, say together, sing together, chorus, harmonize, sync [Inf]

ADVERBS

8 **simultaneously,** at the same time, together, all together, coevally, contemporarily, contemporaneously, coeternally, concomitantly, concomitant with, coincidentally, concurrently, concurrent with

9 **synchronously,** isochronally, isochronously; in time, in step, *pari passu* [L], on *or* with the beat, in unison, in chorus, in concert, harmoniously, at one time, with one voice, as one person, as one, in sync [Inf]

10 **as,** just as, even as, as soon as, at the moment of, just when, in the very moment that, in the same breath as, while

650 Future Time

NOUNS

1 **future time,** future, futurity, time to come, years ahead, time ahead, future years; near future, tomorrow, *mañana* [Sp], tomorrow morning, tomorrow afternoon, tomorrow evening, tomorrow night, morrow [Arch]; the day after tomorrow, next week *or* month *or* year; distant *or* far *or* remote future, long run, long term, after ages, the womb of time, by-and-by, sweet by-and-by; future tense, future perfect

▶ *Distance 585; Nearness 586*

2 **future generation,** descendants, heirs, inheritors, successors, posterity

3 **future condition,** future event, upcoming event, scheduled event; future state, prospectus, outlook, what the future brings *or* holds; uncertainty, uncertain future, fate, destiny, coming events, what fate has in store; latter days, doomsday, crack of doom, end of the world, end of time, eschatology, teleology, last things; millennium, Judgment Day, Day of Judgment, Last Judgment; postexistence, life after death, life to come, hereafter, next world, kingdom come, paradise, nirvana, heaven, underworld, hell, hellfire

▶ *Death 29; Religion 81; Nonmaterial World 525*

4 **looking to the future,** looking ahead, waiting, expectancy, expectation, great expectations, anticipation, preparation, prospect *or* prospects, eventuality, likelihood, outlook; foresight, foreknowledge, prescience,

forecast, prediction, prophecy, premonition, astrology, horoscope, fortunetelling, crystal gazing, second sight
> *Expectation 356; Preparation 388*

5 **predictor,** forecaster, prophet, prophetess, soothsayer, oracle, seer, diviner, augur, geomancer, astrologer, fortuneteller, crystal gazer
> *Occultism 86; Prediction 358*

ADJECTIVES

6 **future,** forthcoming, upcoming, coming, to come, yet to come, to be, yet to be, eventual, later, ahead, futuristic; near, at hand, near at hand, close at hand, just around the corner, approaching, oncoming, due, fated, destined, imminent, threatening, overhanging, impending, pending, waiting, waiting in the wings, nigh

7 **predictable,** foreseeable, probable, possible, potential, likely, certain, sure

8 **foreseen,** foretold, predicted, expected, anticipated, awaited, looked for, hoped for, promised

VERBS

9 **be in the future,** be to come, lie ahead, lie in the future, lie just around the corner, draw near, approach, come soon, overhang, threaten, stare one in the face, cast a shadow before, draw nigh

10 **intend,** have every intention to, be about to, plan to, have in mind to, have an eye to, mean to, shall, will

11 **look ahead,** look forward to, think of the future, hope for, foresee, predict, presage, prophesy, have a premonition, divine, foretell, augur, look into a crystal, read tea leaves, cast bones, haruspicate

12 **expect,** await, wait for, see it coming, prepare for, have prospects, put by for a rainy day, anticipate, forestall, forewarn, take thought for tomorrow, take the long view, take the long-term view

ADVERBS

13 **in the future,** in future, tomorrow, next week, next month, next year, someday, one fine day, futuristically; some other time, not now, soon, imminently, just around the corner, in the offing, in the wind, on the horizon, getting on for, heading for, at the right time, in the fullness of time, eventually, later, later on, ultimately, when the time is right *or* ripe, by and by, in due course, on the morrow [Arch]

14 **after,** afterward, hereafter, hereinafter, henceforth, henceforward, from this time forth, from now on, from this moment on

15 **predictably,** probably, possibly, potentially, likely, in the stars

651 Past Time

Even God cannot change the past. — AGATHON

The past is a foreign country; they do things differently there. — L. P. HARTLEY

NOUNS

1 **past time,** past times, the past, times past, times *or* years gone by, former times; recent past, far past, geological past; history, prehistory, protohistory, ancient history, remote past, ancient times, antiquity; remote age, time immemorial, time out of mind, the long ago and far away, bygone age *or* days, days of old, olden times, olden days, good old days, days of yore, auld lang syne, ancient world
> *History 3; Oldness 653*

2 **past tense,** preterit, perfect tense, past perfect tense, pluperfect, historical present, past participle, aorist
> *Linguistics, Language 5*

3 **retrospection,** memory, retrospective, remembrance, recollection, reminiscence, review, reprise, looking back
> *Memory 354*

4 **recent past,** yesterday, yesterday morning, yesterday afternoon, yesterday evening, last night, the day before yesterday, last week, last month, last year, yesteryear

5 **geological past,** geological era, geological epoch, geological period; age of amphibians, age of reptiles, glacial period, ice age; prehistoric age
> *Geology 8; Period 641*

6 **historical past,** heroic age, golden age, silver age, classical antiquity, Dark Ages, Middle Ages, Renaissance, Age of Reason, Age of Enlightenment, Industrial Revolution
> *History 3; Period 641*

7 **person of the past,** person of antiquity, prehistoric person, cave dweller, caveman, cavewoman, ancient; forerunner, predecessor, progenitor, ancestor, great-great-grandparent; lineage, genealogy, family history, family tree
> *Oldness 653; Sequence 770; Consecutiveness 774*

8 **thing of the past,** survival, remainder, fossil, museum piece, antique, relic, relict, remains, vestige, ancient monument, ancient ruin, artifact *or* artefact, megalith, dolmen, cromlech, menhir, standing stone(s), ancient flint, arrowhead, eolith, microlith, earthwork, barrow, burial chamber, tholos, beehive tomb, pyramid, ziggurat; petrified forest, trilobite, dinosaur, mammoth, amber, coal
> *History 3; Burial 31; Architecture 134; Sign 183; Oldness 653; Remainder 750*

9 **study of the past,** history, antiquarianism, archaeology, paleontology, paleozoology, paleoanthropology, paleogeography, paleontography, paleography, paleoethnology, paleoclimatology, paleometeorology, prehistoric anthropology, fossil record
> *Anthropology 1; History 3; Oldness 653*

10 **historian,** antiquarian, antiquary, archaeologist, paleontologist, paleozoologist, paleoanthropologist, paleogeographer, paleontographer, paleographer, pale-

oethnologist, paleoclimatologist, paleometeorologist, prehistoric anthropologist

▶ *Anthropology 1; History 3*

ADJECTIVES

11 **past,** historical, historic, old, olden, prehistoric, prehistorical, protohistoric, ancient, early, earlier, elder, primitive, primal, primeval

12 **over,** over and done with, gone, gone for good, gone forever, lost forever, lost and gone, completely past, past and gone, bygone, finished, exhausted, ended, done, spent, completed, irrecoverable, dead, dead and gone, dead and buried, extinct, dead as a dodo

▶ *Death 29*

13 **antiquarian,** ancestral, antecedent, preceding, foregoing, out-of-date, outdated, outworn, outmoded, old hat, behind the times, belonging to the past, antiquated, fossilized, old-fashioned, obsolete, passé, past its date, long past, moth-eaten

14 **former,** late, quondam, sometime, obsolescent, retired, emeritus, superannuated, deceased, no longer present, no longer serving

15 **retrospective,** retroactive, diachronic, remembering, reminiscing, looking back, backward-looking

VERBS

16 **be past,** be over, be over and done with, have expired, have had one's day, be in the past, be history, be lost and gone

17 **pass,** pass away, pass into history, finish, end, elapse, expire, become extinct, die out, run out, run its course

18 **look back,** trace back, remember, reminisce, review, reprise, regress, antiquarianize, put the clock back, turn back the clock, turn back time, archaize, return to the past, go back to the past, hark back, relive, live in the past, look over one's shoulder, cast one's eyes backward

19 **excavate,** excavate the past, unearth the past, exhume, unearth, dig up the past

ADVERBS

20 **in the past,** during the past, in past times, in times gone by, formerly, of old, in days of yore, ago, long ago, long since, once upon a time, years ago, ages ago, some time ago, a while ago, a while back, some while back, far back; prehistorically, geologically; in the mists of time, at *or* from the dawn of time, from time immemorial, time out of mind; lately, recently, yesterday, yesterday evening, yestreen [Scot], the day before yesterday, last week, last month, last season, last year, yesteryear, within living memory, only yesterday, the other day, aforetime

21 **before now,** hitherto, heretofore, yet, as yet, until now, till now, up to now, up to this moment, up to this time, ex post facto, already, no longer, not any more

22 **retrospectively,** reminiscently

652 Newness

NOUNS

1 **newness,** recentness, recency, recent occurrence, contemporaneity, topicality, currency, up-to-dateness, new production, mint condition, state of the art; modernism, modernity, innovation, invention, originality; unfamiliarity, unknownness; newfangledness, gimmickry, novelty, neology, neologism, neophilia, new *or* latest wrinkle [Inf]

▶ *Present Time 647; Originality 737*

2 **trendiness,** trend, gimmick, latest craze, latest fashion, fad; high fashion, artistic movement, modernism, postmodernism, new wave, *nouvelle vague* [Fr], New Look, New Thought, Futurism, *nouvelle cuisine* [Fr], the rage, the latest thing; [Inf]: the in thing, what's in, the last word

▶ *Fashion 536; Style 537*

3 **immaturity,** inexperience, youth, virginity, dewiness, callowness, greenness, rawness, naiveté, ingenuousness, innocence, freshness, cleanness, cleanliness

▶ *Youth 26; Cleanliness 111; Lack of Preparation 389*

4 **beginning,** birth, start, inception, commencement, inauguration, initiation, generating, generation, opening, auspication, grand opening, housewarming, unveiling, launching, maiden voyage, first night, premiere

▶ *Beginning 771*

5 **new start,** fresh start, clean slate, tabula rasa, renewal, regeneration, renovation, restoration, refurbishment, rejuvenation, resurrection, revival, revivification, remake, change; reconstruction, rebuilding, repainting, restructure, redesign, reorganization, alteration, modernization, updating, upgrading, revisal, revision; new look, new leaf, new lease on life

▶ *Repair 809*

6 **avant-garde,** vanguard, van, fashionable set, in-group, in-crowd, jet set, trend-setting group, younger generation, new generation, next generation

7 **new arrival,** newborn, baby, newcomer, beginner, fledgling, amateur, novice, tyro, neophyte, greenhorn, recruit, rookie, new member, freshman, new convert, new kid on the block [Inf], new broom, debutante, latecomer, upstart, parvenu, nouveau riche, incomer, immigrant, foreigner, alien, Johnny-come-lately

▶ *Extraneousness 724; Sequence 770*

8 **modern person,** modern man *or* woman, new man *or* woman, trendsetter, avant-gardist, modernist, ultramodernist, postmodernist, futurist, advanced thinker, bright young thing, yuppie, faddist, neophiliac, neologist, neoteric

ADJECTIVES

9 **new,** brand-new, recent, contemporary, topical, cur-

rent, up-to-date, modern, modernistic, futuristic, ultramodern; innovative, revolutionary, inventive, advanced, original; first, latest, most recent, state-of-the-art, newly produced, just out, new-made, oven-fresh, new-minted, hot off the press; neological, neologistic, neologistical, neophytic

10 **unfamiliar,** unknown, not seen before, unheard-of, unprecedented, unused, untried, untested, untrodden, unbeaten, unexplored, out of the ordinary, newfangled, novel, nontraditional, mold-breaking

11 **trendy,** gimmicky, faddish, postmodern; in [Inf]

12 **immature,** inexperienced, budding, aspiring; amateurish, amateur, novice, apprentice, new to the job; embryonic, inchoate, newborn, young, youthful, virginal, virgin, maiden, dewy, callow, green, raw, naive, ingenuous, innocent, fresh, fresh as a daisy, clean, spick-and-span
> *Youth 26; Cleanliness 111*

13 **inaugurated,** initiated, opened, unveiled, launched, premiered, premiere

14 **renewed,** renovated, restored, refurbished, regenerated, rejuvenated, refreshed, freshened up, touched up, repainted, resurrected, revived, revivified, remade, good as new, changed, reconstructed, rebuilt, restructured, redesigned, reorganized, altered, modernized, new-look, updated, upgraded, revised

15 **renewable,** restorable, reconstructible, rebuildable, redesignable, alterable, updatable, upgradable, revisable

16 **avant-garde,** advanced, advance, trendsetting, trendy, fashionable, modish, à la mode, with it [Inf]

VERBS

17 **be new,** begin, commence, generate, inaugurate, initiate, give birth to; open, unveil, launch, make a maiden voyage, premiere

18 **be trendy,** follow the trend, try the latest craze, move with the times, get the new look, go contemporary, go modern; innovate, invent, originate, set a trend, try something new, get with it [Inf]

19 **become new,** begin again, start anew, start from the beginning, renew oneself, get up to date, start afresh, make a fresh or new start, wipe the slate clean, reform, have a new look, turn over a new leaf, start from scratch

20 **make new,** renew, renovate, restore, refresh, freshen up, touch up, refurbish, rejuvenate, regenerate, repaint, resurrect, give a new lease on life, revive, revivify, remake, change, reconstruct, rebuild, restructure, redesign, reorganize, alter, modernize, update, bring up-to-date, upgrade, revise

ADVERBS

21 **newly,** like new, as new, new, lately, latterly, of late, only yesterday, not long ago, a short time ago, just, just now, recently, contemporarily, topically, currently, modernistically, futuristically, innovatively, revolu-

tionarily, inventively, originally, first, firstly, nontraditionally, unusually, neologically, neologistically

22 **again,** anew, afresh, once more, from the top, from the ground up, from the start, from the beginning, all over again, from scratch

23 **immaturely,** aspiringly, amateurishly, youthfully, virginally, maidenly, dewily, rawly, freshly, fresh, cleanly, clean

24 **trendily,** fashionably, in fashion, modishly, in the current mode

653 Oldness

NOUNS

1 **oldness,** antiquity, primitiveness, ancientness, dust or cobwebs of antiquity, olden days, olden times, ancient times, distant past, time out of mind, time immemorial; rust, decay, staleness
> *Past Time 651*

2 **elderliness,** age, hoariness, old age, ripe old age, mellowness, venerableness, maturity, seniority, retirement, dotage, senility, decrepitude, autumn of one's life, burden of years
> *Age 27*

3 **antiquarianism,** classicism, medievalism, archaism, archaeology
> *History 3; Past Time 651*

4 **antiquity,** archaism, antique, heirloom, museum piece, artifact or artefact, relic, thing of the past, monument, ancient manuscript, historic building, fossil, petrified wood

5 **tradition,** custom, common law, lore, folklore, legend, myth, mythology, ancient wisdom, ancient tale
> *History 3*

6 **old people,** the elderly, elders, senior citizens, pensioners, elders and betters, older generation, grandparents, ancestors, forebears
> *Age 27*

7 **prehistoric human,** primitive human, early man, humanoid, protohuman, ape-man, hominid, *Homo erectus*, caveman, cave dweller, *Australopithecus*, *Pithecanthropus*, Neanderthal man, Cro-Magnon man, Heidelberg man, Java man, Peking man, Stone Age man, Bronze Age man, Iron Age man

8 **prehistoric animal,** woolly mammoth, mastodon, saber-toothed tiger or cat, dinosaur, brontosaurus, tyrannosaurus, ichthyosaurus, pterodactyl, giant sloth, ammonite, trilobite

9 **antiquarian,** antiquary, classicist, medievalist, archaeologist, archaist, antique dealer, antique collector

ADJECTIVES

10 **old,** older, elderly, elder, aged, full of years, venerable, veteran, senior, patriarchal, of advanced years, advanced in years, getting on, getting on or along in years, mature, mellow, ripe, gray, old and gray, gray-

haired, white-haired, grizzled, hoary, decrepit, senile, senescent, past one's prime, doddering, over the hill

▶ *Past Time 651*

11 olden, antiquarian, antique, ancient, timeworn, archaic, antiquated, outdated, outmoded, passé, moth-eaten, musty, crumbling, moldering, stale; time-honored, rooted, established, longstanding, traditional, age-old, ancestral, immemorial, antediluvian, from before the Flood, out of the Ark, as old as the hills, as old as time, as old as Adam, adamic, as old as Methuselah; old-world, prewar, antebellum, venerable, inveterate, vintage, classic, classical

12 former, previous, prior, erstwhile, one-time, sometime, quondam, retired, emeritus, emerita

13 historic, historical, of historical interest, heroic, Helladic, Hellenic, classical, Hellenistic, Roman, Etruscan, Ottoman, Persian, Byzantine, medieval, Saxon, Norman, feudal, Romanesque, Gothic, Tudor, Elizabethan, Jacobean, Georgian, Hanoverian, Colonial, Victorian, Edwardian

▶ *History 3; Period 641*

14 primal, primordial, primitive, primeval, early, antediluvian, prelapsarian, Precambrian, Paleozoic, Mesozoic, Cenozoic, preglacial, glacial, prehistoric, Paleolithic, Mesolithic, Neolithic, Chalcolithic, Stone Age, Bronze Age, Iron Age

VERBS

15 be old, belong to the past, survive from the past, go back a long way, go back in time

16 grow old, age, decline, deteriorate, fade, burn out, decay, rot, spoil, wither, molder, decompose, rust, crumble, crumble into dust, become old, become obsolete, be passé, go out of style, lose currency, dodder

▶ *Age 27*

ADVERBS

17 venerably, patriarchally, maturely, mellowly, ripely, decrepitly, senilely, mustily, stalely, rustily

18 anciently, in ancient times, in olden days, in the good old days, of old, of yore, ago, ages ago, way back when, since the big bang, since the world was young, since the world was new, since before the Flood, since the year one, since God knows when, since Adam was a lad

19 formerly, previously, earlier, before, before now

20 archaically, ancestrally, immemorially, old-worldly, inveterately, venerably, classically, historically, primordially, primitively, primevally, primarily, originally, early

654 Season

NOUNS

1 season, season of the year, time of year, spring, summer, fall, autumn, winter; period, annual period, quarterly period; spell, term, interval, seasonality, periodicity

▶ *Time 639; Period 641*

2 seasons, dry season, rainy season, cold season, snow season; social season, the season, dead season; sport season, football season, baseball season, hockey season, hunting season, shooting season, deer season, duck season, cricket season [Brit], open season, closed season; ecclesiastical season, Advent, Christmas, Lent, Easter, Whitsuntide; mating season, estrus, rut, heat; silly season, tourist season

3 spring, springtime, springtide, vernal season, vernal equinox, seedtime, blossom time, bud time, rustle of spring, Maytime *or* Maytide, May Day, month of Maying

4 summer, summertime, summertide, growing season, midsummer, Midsummer Day, summer solstice, high summer, dog days, haymaking, estivation

5 fall, autumn, fall of the leaf, harvest, harvest time, harvest moon, Indian summer, St. Martin's summer, autumnal equinox

6 winter, wintertime, wintertide, midwinter, winter solstice, hibernation

ADJECTIVES

7 seasonal, in season, out of season, off-season, seasonable, equinoctial, solstitial, periodic; spring, vernal, springlike, flowery, blossomy, sappy, juicy, leafy, young; summery, summerlike, estival, midsummer; autumnal, fall-like, golden; wintery, wintry, winterlike, midwinter, hibernal, brumal, boreal, arctic, snowy, icy

8 in season, estrous, rutting, in heat

9 seasoned, ripened, matured, hardened, toughened, accustomed

VERBS

10 spend the season, summer, spend the summer, pass the summer, estivate; winter, overwinter, spend the winter, pass the winter, hibernate

11 season, mature, ripen, condition, dry, harden, toughen, accustom

ADVERBS

12 seasonally, seasonably, vernally, in spring, in summer, autumnally, in autumn, wintrily, in winter, equinoctially, solstitially

655 Daytime

NOUNS

1 daytime, daylight, morning, noon, afternoon

2 morning, morning time, morningtide, forenoon, A.M. (ante meridiem); dawn, daybreak, break of day, false dawn, crack of dawn, sunrise, sunup, morning light, first light, daylight, rosy-fingered dawn, Aurora, Eos, morn, morrow [Arch], dayspring [Arch]; waking time, cockcrow

3 morning things, morning star, morning glory, rooster,

lark, early bird, dawn chorus, reveille, matins, lauds, prime, tierce *or* terce; breakfast, brunch, rush hour, elevenses [Brit]; morning sickness

▶ *Light 246; Earliness 657*

4 **noon,** twelve o'clock, 12 noon, 1200 hours, noonday, noontime, high noon, noontide, midday, middle of the day, noon whistle, lunchtime, sext

5 **afternoon,** P.M. (post meridiem); afternoon things: matinée, afternoon tea, nap, siesta

ADJECTIVES

6 **daily,** daytime, daylight, diurnal; morning, dawning, dawn, auroral, matutinal, antemeridian, forenoon; early, fresh, dewy; midday, high-noon, meridian, twelve-o'clock; afternoon, postmeridian

VERBS

7 **arise,** wake up, get up, wake the dawn, greet the day, rise and shine

ADVERBS

8 **daily,** diurnally; early, in the morning, at sunrise, at sunup, at dawn, at the crack of dawn, at daybreak, at first light, at break of day, at cockcrow, matutinally, aurorally; after noon, in the afternoon

656 Nighttime

NOUNS

1 **nighttime,** evening, night, midnight hours, small *or* wee small hours

2 **evening,** evening time, eve, P.M. (post meridiem), sunset, sundown, setting of the sun, dusk, twilight, gloaming, eventide, vespertide, crepuscule; evening things: rush hour, cocktail hour, suppertime, supper hour, dinner, dinnertime, dinner hour; evening star, Venus, Hesperus; evening news, prime time (TV); vespers, evensong

▶ *Radio and Television 172*

3 **night,** nighttime, nightfall, close of day, day's end, dark, darkness, dark of night, dead of night, blackness; night things: curfew, lights out, taps, nightlight, night person, night owl [Inf], nighthawk [Inf], owl, nightingale, nightjar, night shift, night school, nightlife, nightclub, midnight, pajama party, late-night *or* midnight supper *or* snack; sleep, dream, nightmare; nones, compline

ADJECTIVES

4 **evening,** dusky, twilight, twilit, vespertine, vesperal, crepuscular; nighttime, nocturnal, nightly, dark, benighted, all-night, midnight

VERBS

5 **spend the evening,** spend the night, sleep, rest, dream

ADVERBS

6 **nightly,** every night, at night, after dark, nocturnally, overnight, by night, late, all through the night, in the small *or* wee small hours

657 Earliness

The day shall not be up so soon as I, / To try the fair adventure of tomorrow. — WILLIAM SHAKESPEARE

NOUNS

1 **earliness,** early start, head start; readiness, alacrity, quickness, timeliness, promptness, promptitude, punctuality, punctualness, immediacy, dispatch, expedition

▶ *Immediacy 645; Timeliness 659; Precedence 769; Haste 818*

2 **early hour,** early time, early morning, sunrise, sunup, dawn, crack of dawn, daybreak, unearthly hour

▶ *Daytime 655*

3 **early stage,** beginning, creation, first step, preliminaries; primeval stage, primitive stage, early history, ancient history

▶ *History 3; Past Time 651; Beginning 771*

4 **early comer,** early arrival, first comer, first arrival, premature baby, precursor, predecessor; early riser, early bird, Johnny-on-the-spot [Inf]

▶ *Drama and Theater 136; Untimeliness 660; Precedence 769*

5 **antecedence,** prevenience, foresight, anticipation, expectation, advance notice, preemption

▶ *Foresight 357; Preparation 388*

6 **prematurity,** prematureness, precipitancy *or* precipitance, precipitation, early maturity, precocity, precociousness; haste, hastiness, rush

▶ *Haste 818*

7 **getting ahead,** getting in early, getting in on the ground floor, seizing the chance *or* moment *or* occasion, taking the opportunity, jumping at the chance, moving with the times

▶ *Timeliness 659; Precedence 769*

ADJECTIVES

8 **early,** earliest, first; ready, alacritous, quick, timely, prompt, punctual, immediate, expeditious; good and early, bright and early, at hand

▶ *Timeliness 659*

9 **imminent,** forthcoming, impending, looming, expected, expecting, near, just around the corner

10 **premature,** precipitate, precipitous, precocious, ahead of time, ahead of schedule, advance *or* advanced; antecedent, beforehand, too early, prevenient, preparatory, prophetic, foresighted, anticipatory, anticipative, expectative, precursory, preceding, preliminary, primeval, preemptive; impetuous, hasty, too soon

▶ *Haste 818*

VERBS

11 **be early,** arrive early, arrive first, arrive ahead of time *or* schedule, get there early *or* ahead of time, get there first, jump to it

12 **start early,** get up early, start too soon, jump the gun;

preempt, anticipate, get a head start *or* flying start; rise at the crack of dawn, gain time, be fast (of clocks), have time to spare, be ready and waiting, show readiness, hasten, hurry, dispatch, expedite

13 **precede,** predate, get ahead of, go before

14 **prepare,** precipitate, reserve, order, book in advance, engage, anticipate, expect, foresee; preempt, forestall, nip in the bud, prevent, catch napping, steal a march on, take the words out of one's mouth, step on someone's lines

15 **hasten,** lose no time, go off half-cocked, be half-baked; hop to it [Inf], get a wiggle on [Inf]
 ▶ *Haste 818*

16 **get in early,** get ahead, get in on the ground floor, seize one's chance, seize the moment, seize the occasion, take the opportunity, jump at the chance, move with the times

ADVERBS

17 **early,** first, as soon as possible (ASAP), soon, promptly, punctually, on time; immediately, without delay, forthwith, directly, right away, expeditiously, readily; in advance, ahead of time, ahead of schedule, ahead of oneself, ahead of its time; first thing, at the first opportunity, beforetime, early on, in time, in good time, on time, on schedule, to the minute, to the second, with plenty of time, with time to spare; quickly, hurriedly, hastily, summarily, before the ink is dry, betimes, anon [Arch], good and early, bright and early; on the dot *or* button [Inf]

18 **soon,** presently, shortly, directly, imminently, before long, in a short time, in a while, in a short while, by and by, at short notice, suddenly, without notice, at the drop of a hat

19 **beforehand,** primevally, primitively, anciently, aboriginally, indigenously, colonially, ancestrally

20 **prematurely,** precipitately, precipitously, precociously, forwardly, ahead of its time, beforehand, too early, preveniently, preparatorily, prophetically, foresightedly, anticipatorily, anticipatively, impetuously, hastily, overhastily, too soon

658 Lateness

You used to come at ten o'clock, / And now you come at noon. — NURSERY RHYME

NOUNS

1 **lateness,** tardiness, belatedness, unpunctuality, slowness, retardation, lag, time lag, lagging, delay, unreadiness, unpreparedness, untimeliness, slow development
 ▶ *Lack of Preparation 389; Slowness 693*

2 **late hour,** advanced hour, small hours, wee small hours; day's end, sunset, nighttime; last minute, eleventh hour

 ▶ *Nighttime 656*

3 **delay,** wait, delayed action, delayed reaction, dilatoriness, procrastination, *mañana* [Sp]; delaying, putting off, putting on hold, pigeonholing, tabling, postponement; deferment, deferral, adjournment, prorogation, prolongation, extension, protraction, filibuster, stonewalling, delaying tactics, prevention; hindrance, obstruction, jam, logjam, suspension, holdup, red tape, blockage, block, hang-up [Inf]; restraint, detention, remand, moratorium, halt, pause, cooling-off period, truce, cease-fire, lull, respite, rest and recreation (R and R), grace period, stay of execution, stay, reprieve; last-ditch stand, last word, afterthought; mothballing, putting in cold storage *or* on the back burner, putting on ice [Inf]
 ▶ *Inactivity 415; Duration 642; Cessation 668; Hindrance 826; Cancellation 834*

4 **latecomer,** late arriver, last arriver, Johnny-come-lately, ten o'clock scholar, laggard, late developer, late bloomer, slow starter, slow learner, late riser, slugabed, sluggard, idler, delayer, slowpoke [Inf]

ADJECTIVES

5 **late,** belated, delayed, overdue, unpunctual, dilatory, unready, unprepared, tardy, behind schedule, behind time, behindhand, not on time, never on time; slow, sluggish

6 **held up,** postponed, deferred, adjourned, prorogued, prolonged, extended, protracted, stonewalled, hindered, obstructed, suspended, blocked, tabled, stalled, restrained, detained, remanded; halted, jammed, bogged down, on hold, mothballed, in cold storage *or* on the back burner, on ice [Inf]

7 **late in the day,** last-minute, eleventh-hour

8 **delaying,** slowing, procrastinating, obstructive, obstructing, hindering, retarding, blocking, restraining, detaining, lagging, lagging behind, late-running, following, coming later

9 **later,** future, distant, upcoming

10 **dead,** deceased, late, late lamented, former, previous, past, erstwhile, sometime, old, posthumous

VERBS

11 **be late,** arrive late, arrive last, stay up *or* sit up *or* stay out late, keep late hours, burn the candle at both ends, burn the midnight oil; awake late, oversleep, lag, lag behind, be behindhand, develop late; lose time, be slow (of clocks); drag one's feet, take one's time, take ages, drag on; miss the boat, lose *or* miss one's chance

12 **wait,** pause, stop, stay, tarry, linger, dawdle, waste time, loiter, hang around, hang about, await, be kept waiting, cool one's heels; delay, dally, dilly-dally, hang fire, hang back

13 **delay,** stall, retard, set back, hold back, hold up; obstruct, jam, create a logjam, suspend, halt, block, stonewall; prevent, hinder, restrain, remand, detain, hold over; put off, postpone, reprieve, stay, adjourn,

prorogue, defer; gain time, buy time, play for time, play the waiting game, filibuster; prolong, extend, protract, spin out, procrastinate, temporize; sleep on it, hold one's horses, bide one's time, wait and see, reserve, keep for later, keep *or* save for a rainy day; withhold, file, shelve, pigeonhole, table, lay on the table, hold, hold on, hold the line, make a last-ditch stand, hang on, stand by; put on hold, mothball, put in cold storage *or* on the back burner, put on ice [Inf]

ADVERBS

14 **late,** lately, belatedly, unpunctually, dilatorily, unreadily, unpreparedly, tardily, behind schedule, behind time, behindhand, slowly, leisurely, at one's leisure, sluggishly, extendedly, protractedly, obstructively

15 **at a late hour,** none too soon, at the last minute, at the eleventh hour, at last, at long last, too late

16 **later,** later on, in the future, at a later time, in time, in due course, in a while, after a while

17 **formerly,** lately, posthumously

659 Timeliness

NOUNS

1 **timeliness,** opportuneness, providence, providentiality, suitability, convenience; appropriateness, propitiousness, auspiciousness, favorableness, aptness, fitness; seasonableness, right time, right moment, just the time, perfect moment, readiness, ripeness, maturity, proper time, auspicious moment, good occasion, happy coincidence
▸ *Convenience 803*

2 **opportunity,** good opportunity, fine opportunity, favorable opportunity, golden opportunity, chance, good chance, happy chance, best chance, only chance; luck, good luck, opening, break [Inf], lucky break [Inf], piece of luck, stroke of luck, elbowroom, clear field, clear run, clear view, scope, steppingstone
▸ *Chance 842*

3 **critical time,** critical moment, crucial time, crucial moment, critical juncture, crisis, key point, turning point, pivotal point, nexus, pinch, rub, crux, moment of truth, decisive moment, point of no return, pregnant moment, emergency, eleventh hour, last minute, nick of time
▸ *Lateness 658; Difficulty 824*

ADJECTIVES

4 **timely,** opportune, seasonable, providential, propitious, auspicious, appropriate, apropos, suitable, suited, befitting, fitting, fit, well-timed, convenient, apt, for the occasion, heaven-sent, welcome, favorable, fortunate, lucky, happy, felicitous

5 **critical,** crucial, decisive, momentous, pivotal, key, vital to the occasion, eleventh-hour, last-minute

VERBS

6 **be timely,** suit the occasion, fit the occasion, come at

the right time *or* moment, befit the occasion, befit the time, offer an opportunity, provide a chance

7 **take the opportunity,** profit by, cash in on, capitalize on, turn to good account, exploit, improve the occasion, take time by the forelock, take *or* seize one's chance, seize *or* grab the opportunity, seize the day, *carpe diem* [L], make hay while the sun shines, strike while the iron is hot

ADVERBS

8 **opportunely,** seasonably, providentially, propitiously, auspiciously, appropriate, apropos, suitably, befittingly, fittingly, fitly; conveniently, aptly, for the occasion, favorably, fortunately, luckily, happily, as luck would have it

9 **critically,** crucially, decisively, momentously, pivotally; just in time, in the nick of time, at the last minute, at the eleventh hour

660 Untimeliness

NOUNS

1 **untimeliness,** inopportuneness, inauspiciousness, unpropitiousness, unfavorableness, unseasonableness, ominousness; immaturity, unripeness, poor timing, bad timing, mistiming; bad time, wrong time, unsuitable time; prematurity, earliness, lateness, unpunctuality, bad time of the month, inopportune moment, untimely occurrence, awkward occurrence, untimely action; inexpedience, inappropriateness, unsuitableness, awkwardness; inconvenience, intrusion, interruption, disturbance, disruption
▸ *Earliness 657; Lateness 658; Inconvenience 804*

2 **wrong time,** wrong date, wrong day, chronological error, misdating, parachronism, prochronism, prolepsis, anachronism

3 **lost chance,** lost *or* missed opportunity, misfortune, ill fortune, ill luck, bad luck, hard luck, mischance
▸ *Negligence 326; Failure 846*

4 **mishap,** misadventure, contretemps, accident, disaster, calamity
▸ *Adversity 848*

ADJECTIVES

5 **untimely,** mistimed, ill-timed, inopportune, inauspicious, unpropitious, unfavorable; out of season, unseasonable, immature, unripe; ill-starred, ill-omened, ominous; poorly timed, badly timed, premature, too early, late, tardy, not in time, unpunctual, out of turn, out of order, inexpedient, inappropriate, malapropos, unsuited, inapt, unsuitable, unbefitting, awkward, inconvenient, intrusive, interrupting, disturbing, disrupting
▸ *Earliness 657; Lateness 658*

6 **misdated,** wrongly dated, parachronistic, prochronistic, anachronistic

7 accidental, unlucky, unfortunate, infelicitous, disastrous, calamitous

VERBS

8 be untimely, mistime, time badly, arrive at the wrong time, arrive too early, arrive late, be tardy; lose time, waste time, be late, misjudge, lock the barn door after the horse is stolen; take untimely action, intrude, disturb, disrupt, interrupt, break in, butt in, go off half-cocked

9 misdate, antedate, postdate

10 lose one's chance, be unlucky, have a misfortune, have bad luck, lose *or* miss an opportunity, spoil one's chances, wreck one's chances, throw away an opportunity, throw it all away, let an opportunity slip by, let slip through one's fingers, allow the occasion to go by, miss the boat, blow it [Inf]

11 have a mishap, have a misadventure, have an accident, suffer injury

ADVERBS

12 at the wrong time, too soon, immaturely, too late, inopportunely, inauspiciously, unpropitiously, unfavorably, unseasonably, unripely, ominously, prematurely, late, unpunctually, inexpediently, inappropriately, malapropos, unsuitably, unbefittingly, awkwardly, inconveniently, intrusively, disturbingly, disruptively

13 anachronistically, parachronistically, prochronistically

14 mistakenly, erroneously, accidentally, unluckily, unfortunately, blunderingly, disastrously, calamitously

661 Frequency

NOUNS

1 frequency, frequence, frequentness, oftenness, recurrence, repetition, periodicity; continuity, constancy, persistence, sustainment, steadiness; commonness, numerousness, crowdedness, multitudinousness; incessancy, prevalence, regularity, assiduity, assiduousness, habitualness; frequent occurrence, regular occurrence, common occurrence, everyday occurrence; cycle, pulsation, oscillation

▶ *Regularity 663; Oscillation 683; Repetition 797*

2 frequenting, patronizing, visiting often, coming often, attending regularly, being a regular customer, haunting, hanging out [Inf]

▶ *Sociability 408*

3 radio frequency, radio-frequency band, frequency band, Citizens Band (CB), frequency spectrum, long wave (LW), medium wave (MW), shortwave (SW), very high frequency (VHF), ultrahigh frequency (UHF), frequency modulation (FM), amplitude modulation (AM), wavelength, wave, cycles per second, hertz (Hz), kilohertz (kHz), megahertz (MHz)

▶ *Radio and Television 172*

ADJECTIVES

4 frequent, recurrent, recurring, repetitive, repeated, repetitious, regular, periodic; continual, consecutive, persistent, sustained, steady, constant, nonstop; incessant, common, of common occurrence, run-of-the-mill; many, numerous, crowded, multitudinous; prevalent, often encountered, assiduous, habitual, haunting; cyclic, cyclical

VERBS

5 be frequent, happen often, recur, reoccur, repeat, happen every day, occur regularly, occur periodically, have continuity, continue, go on, prevail, repeat oneself, do habitually, do nothing but

6 frequent, be often seen at, be found at, visit often, come often, attend regularly, be a regular customer of, patronize, haunt, hang out at [Inf]

ADVERBS

7 frequently, often, oftentimes, many a time, repeatedly, repetitively, recurrently, regularly, periodically; commonly, usually, generally, constantly, continually, perpetually; ordinarily, routinely, habitually, incessantly, persistently, sustainingly, steadily; numerously, crowdedly, multitudinously; prevalently, assiduously, hauntingly, without ceasing, without stopping, without stop, thick and fast; all the time, times without number, daily, hourly, every hour, every minute, every second; morning, noon, and night; day and night, night and day; day in, day out; day after day, as often as not, more often than not, in quick succession, in rapid succession, time after time, time and again, again and again, over and over, cyclically; many times, many a time, oft [Arch], many a time and oft [Arch], ever and anon [Arch]

▶ *Regularity 663; Repetition 797; Continuity, Continuation 669*

662 Infrequency

NOUNS

1 infrequency, infrequence, intermittence, seldomness, irregularity, discontinuity, fitfulness, rareness, scarcity, scarceness, uncommonness, unusualness, sparsity, paucity, fewness, uniqueness, infrequent occurrence, rare occurrence, rarity, unrepeatable offer, one-time offer

▶ *Discontinuity 775; Few 796*

ADJECTIVES

2 infrequent, occasional, sometime, sparse, uncommon, unusual, rare, irregular, sporadic, discontinuous, fitful, few and far between, few, intermittent, scarce, seldom seen, seldom met with, almost unheard-of, one of a kind, unique, unprecedented, like gold dust, like snow in August, scarce *or* rare as hen's teeth

VERBS

3 be infrequent, occur infrequently, be occasional, happen now and then

ADVERBS

4 infrequently, irregularly, intermittently, not often, occasionally, now and then, sometimes, from time to time, every so often, seldom, hardly, little, rarely, sparsely, scarcely, scarcely ever, uncommonly, unusually, once or twice; uniquely, once, only once, just this once, once and for all, discontinuously, fitfully, at infrequent intervals, once in a blue moon, once in a month of Sundays, once in a coon's age [Inf]

5 sometimes, occasional, from time to time, every so often, now and then, now and again, every now and again, once in a while, here and there, *passim* [L]

663 Regularity

NOUNS

I regularity, orderliness, usualness, custom, normality; balance, uniformity, evenness, steadiness, levelness, flatness, ordinariness; continuity, continuousness, constance, constancy, consistency; regulation, rule, order, law, custom, tradition, routine
▸ *Habit, Custom 397; Sameness 730; Order 765*

2 frequency, regular recurrence, clockwork regularity, predictability, periodicity; repetition, repetitiveness, return, serialization; timing, phasing, pattern, arrangement, symmetry, alternation, reciprocity, tidal flow, ebb and flow, wave motion, wave frequency, pulsation, oscillation, to-and-fro movement, pendulum movement, piston movement, shuttle movement, undulating motion, undulation, harmonic motion, swing, rhythm, tempo, measure, beat, pulsation, throb, tick
▸ *Repeated Sound 235; Oscillation 683; Consecutiveness 774; Repetition 797*

3 cycle, return, circular return, revolution, rotation, orbital motion, regular return; life cycle, yearly cycle, biorhythm, alpha rhythm, alpha wave, circadian rhythm, menstrual cycle, estrous cycle, menstruation, menses, period, routine, daily round, round, beat, wheel of life, orbit, circuit, lap, shift, relay, turn, go, rota [Brit], Metonic cycle
▸ *Period 641; Orbital Motion 681; Rotation 682*

4 anniversary, commemoration, annual occurrence, centennial *or* centenary, sesquicentennial, bicentennial *or* bicentenary, tricentennial *or* tercentenary *or* tercentennial, millennium; annual holiday, religious holiday
▸ *Religious Ritual 85; Celebration 405*

ADJECTIVES

5 regular, orderly, usual, balanced, uniform, even, steady, level, flat, ordinary, everyday, typical, routine, continual, constant, methodical, metrical, consistent, normal, legal, customary, traditional

6 frequent, recurrent, recurring, repeating, periodic, periodical, repetitive, tidal; reciprocal, alternating, alternate, alternative, every other, to-and-fro, oscillatory, oscillating; revolving, returning, timed, isochronal, isochronous, phasic, phaseal, phased, serial, serialized; rhythmic, rhythmical, measured, swinging, steady, stable, clockwork, beating, ticking, throbbing, pulsating, pulsatory, pulsatile, undulating; constant, even, symmetric, symmetrical, consistent, level, flat, featureless

7 cyclic, cyclical, circular, circling, orbital, revolving, rotational, rotative, rotating; routine, hourly, daily, diurnal, quotidian, nightly, tertian, semiweekly, weekly, hebdomadary, hebdomadal, biweekly, fortnightly, semimonthly, monthly, bimonthly, seasonal, semiannual, biannual, annual, yearly, perennial, bissextile, biennial; biorhythmic, menstrual, estrous, Metonic

8 anniversarial, commemorative, annual, yearly, centennial *or* centenary, sesquicentennial, bicentennial *or* bicentenary, tricentennial *or* tercentenary *or* tercentennial, millennial

VERBS

9 make regular, regularize, make consistent, make uniform, balance, make routine, regulate, time, adjust, set (a clock), order, impose order upon, bring order out of chaos, rule, make ordinary, normalize, rationalize, systematize, steady, serialize, make continual, make constant, level, level out, make even, flatten, flatten out

10 be regular, recur, reoccur, reoccur constantly, repeat, be in order, run on in order, succeed, follow a pattern, intermit, reciprocate, alternate, take one's turn, work a shift, take a turn; beat time, tick, throb, pulse, pulsate, have a regular heartbeat, breathe regularly; undulate, oscillate, swing, sway, swing and sway, go to-and-fro, come and go, ebb and flow, go back and forth, ply, commute, shuttle, vacation, take a holiday

11 be cyclic, cycle, circle, orbit, cycle around, come again, go and return, come around again, return once again, return, walk one's beat, make one's daily round, run a lap, turn, spin, revolve, rotate, occur monthly, menstruate, have one's period, occur annually, happen yearly

12 commemorate, have an anniversary, celebrate an anniversary, have a birthday, celebrate a birthday
▸ *Celebration 405*

ADVERBS

13 orderly, regularly, usually, uniformly, evenly, steadily, flatly, ordinarily, routinely, in an everyday manner, continually, constantly, consistently, normally, legally, according to law, according to order, customarily, by custom, according to rule, traditionally, according to tradition

14 regularly, frequently, periodically, at regular intervals, at fixed intervals, at stated times, at specified times, at fixed periods; repeatedly, repetitiously, reciprocally, alternately, alternatively, by turns, turn and turn about, in a swinging motion, up and down, from side to side, to-and-fro, serially, rhythmically, steadily, like clockwork, pulsatingly, undulatingly, constantly, evenly, symmetrically, consistently, flatly

15 **cyclically,** circularly, orbitally, round and round; routinely, hourly, hour by hour, daily, every day, day by day, diurnally, per diem, nightly, every night, every other day, every other night, semiweekly, twice a week, weekly, every week, biweekly, every other week, fortnightly, semimonthly, twice a month, monthly, every month, bimonthly, every other month, seasonally, semiannually, biannually, twice a year, annually, yearly, per annum, every year, perennially, biennially, every other year, centennially, sesquicentennially, bicentennially, tricentennially, tercentennially, millennially

664 Irregularity

NOUNS

1 **irregularity,** unregularity, nonuniformity, unequalness, inequality, asymmetry, unevenness; roughness, choppiness, spottiness, patchiness, brokenness, disconnection, discontinuation, discontinuity, sporadicalness; infrequency, intermittence, fluctuation, changeableness, change, waver, wavering; variability, variableness, variety, diversity, inconsistency, inconstancy, unpredictability, randomness, fitfulness, fits and starts, capriciousness, caprice, restlessness, desultoriness; unmethodicalness, haphazardness, disorder, instability, unsteadiness, wobbliness, shakiness, jerkiness, flickering, staggering, lurching, careening, veering, bumping

> *Caprice 381; Infrequency 662; Change 665; Agitation 684; Diversity 732; Inequality 741; Disorder 766; Discontinuity 775; Nonconformity 782*

2 **unusualness,** uncommonness, uniqueness, incongruousness; exception, anomaly, aberration, abnormality, eccentricity, nonconformity, unconventionality; oddness, peculiarity, irregularity

> *Diversity 732; Nonconformity 782*

ADJECTIVES

3 **irregular,** unregular, nonuniform, unequal, asymmetric, asymmetrical, unsymmetrical, uneven; rough, choppy, spotty, patchy, broken, disconnected, discontinuous, sporadic; spasmodic, halting; on-again, off-again; stop-and-go, infrequent, intermittent, fluctuating, changeable, changeful, wavering; variable, varying, diverse, inconsistent, erratic, inconstant, unpredictable, random, fitful, capricious, restless, desultory; unmethodical, unsystematic, unsystematical, unrhythmic, unrhythmical, haphazard, disorderly, disordered, unstable, unsteady, wobbly, wobbling, shaky, shaking, jerky, jerking, flickering, staggering,

lurching, careening, veering, bumpy, bumping, herky-jerky

4 **unusual,** uncommon, exceptional, unique, incongruous; anomalous, aberrant, abnormal, eccentric, nonconforming, unconventional; odd, peculiar, irregular

VERBS

5 **be irregular,** lack regularity, intermit, break, disconnect, fluctuate, change, vary, waver, wobble, shake, jerk, go by fits and starts, flicker, stagger, lurch, careen, veer, bump

ADVERBS

6 **irregularly,** unregularly, unequally, asymmetrically, unevenly, roughly, discontinuously, spasmodically, sporadically; in spots, haltingly, off and on, on and off; on-again, off-again; infrequently, once in a while, now and then, every now and again, intermittently, changeably, waveringly; variably, inconsistently, erratically, in a disorderly manner, inconstantly, unpredictably, randomly, at random, fitfully, by fits and starts, unrhythmically, capriciously, restlessly, desultorily, unmethodically, unsystematically, haphazardly; unsteadily, shakily, jerkily, flickeringly, bumpily

7 **unusually,** uncommonly, exceptionally, uniquely, incongruously; anomalously, abnormally, eccentrically; oddly, peculiarly, irregularly

665 Change

Everything flows and nothing stays. — HERACLITUS

NOUNS

1 **change,** transformation, modification, mutation, mutability, alteration, vicissitude; conversion, changeover, switch; exchange, replacement; variation, variety, difference, diversity; adjustment, qualification, variegation, process, activation, fermentation, leavening, modulation, inflection, declension; change ringing

> *Variegation 263; Changeableness 666; Conversion 670*

2 **alteration,** change of course, change of direction, deviation, diversion, detour, turn, U-turn, reversal, shift, eversion, inversion, flip-flop [Inf]; change of position, change of scenery, change of place, relocation, passage; change of mind, change of heart; change of clothes; change of key, transposition, modulation; change of voice; transference, transition, translation, interpretation, adaptation, transcription

> *Interpretation 365; Inversion 608; Deviation 698*

3 **sudden change,** violent *or* radical change, revolution, revolt, coup, overthrow, subversion, reformation, break with the past, break, quantum jump *or* leap, upheaval, sea change

4 **change for the better,** invention, innovation, diversification, modernization, renewal, redecoration, rearrangement, reorganization; restructuring, reordering,

remolding, reshaping, restyling, remodeling, make-over; revision, revisal, emendation, amendment, improvement, betterment, reform; restoration, revival, repairing, repair, amelioration

> *Newness 652; Improvement 807*

5 **change for the worse,** adulteration, dilution, distortion, deterioration, degeneration, worsening, perversion

> *Deterioration 808*

6 **change of mind,** change of opinion, change of belief, change of heart, conversion

> *Belief 87; Changeableness 666; Conversion 670*

7 **transformation,** mutation, transmutation, transfiguration, transubstantiation, metamorphosis, transmogrification, transmigration of souls, metempsychosis, metabolism, conversion

> *Conversion 670*

8 **exchange,** interchange, trade, substitution

> *Trade 480; Exchange 673*

9 **changer,** modifier, activator, influence, converter, transformer, agent, catalyst; enzyme, yeast, ferment, leaven; adapter, editor, reviser, censor, bowdlerizer; innovator, alterer, tailor, dressmaker, decorator; chemist, alchemist, magician, conjurer, sorcerer; restorer, reformer, revolutionary, improver, destroyer

ADJECTIVES

10 **changed,** transformed, modified, mutated, mutable, altered, adjusted, qualified; converted, switched; overthrown, subverted; modernized, renewed, redecorated, rearranged, reorganized, restructured, reordered, restyled, remodeled, remolded, reshaped, revised, emended, amended, improved, repaired, restored, revived; deteriorated, degenerated, worse, perverted, perverse

11 **changeable,** changeful, mutable, variable, alterable; deviatory, turning, reverse, transitional, transitory, transient, revolutionary, subversive, reformative, reformational, inventive, innovative, innovational, ameliorative

12 **transformative,** mutative, transmutative, transubstantial, metamorphic, metamorphous, metabolic, convertive

13 **exchangeable,** interchangeable, tradable, substitutable

> *Exchange 673*

VERBS

14 **change,** transform, alter, modify; convert, change over, switch; adapt, vary; exchange, replace; reorganize, modernize, diversify, adjust; shift, change course, divert, deviate, detour; change position, relocate, change places; change direction, turn, make a U-turn, turn back, reverse; change one's mind, change one's opinion, change one's belief, change one's heart, change one's expression, change one's tune, sing a different tune; change one's clothes; change key, trans-

pose, modulate; ring the changes; transfer, translate, interpret, transcribe; revert, revolt, break with the past, make a break, move with the times, turn over a new leaf; flip-flop [Inf]

15 **be changed,** become different, undergo a change, be varied

16 **cause change,** make a change, effect a change, work a change, make different, convert, influence, cause, affect, alter, divert, diversify, reform, innovate, invent, modify, inflect *or* decline (a word), activate; ferment, leaven, qualify, commute; renew, remodel, restyle, reorganize, restructure, redecorate, rearrange, reorder, remold, reshape, bring in new blood, turn upside down, subvert; revolt, revolutionize, evert, turn inside out, invert, adapt, shift, move, transfer, arrange, change around, translate, interpret, adjust

17 **change for the better,** improve, get better, pass the crisis, get over the worst, turn the corner, better oneself, be converted, convert; better, make better, improve, ameliorate, process, edit, revise, amend, revamp

18 **change for the worse,** adulterate, dilute, weaken, doctor, warp, distort, censor, bowdlerize; deteriorate, degenerate, worsen; impair, wreck, destroy, pervert, spoil; mark, interfere with, tamper *or* meddle *or* tinker with

19 **change back,** repair, reset, restore, revive, turn back

20 **transform,** transmute, transfigure, transubstantiate, transmogrify, mutate, metamorphose, metabolize; perform magic, conjure, dabble in sorcery

21 **exchange,** interchange, trade, substitute

> *Trade 480; Exchange 673*

ADVERBS

22 **changeably,** mutably, variably, alterably, differently, transitionally, subversively; inventively, innovatively

666 Changeableness

NOUNS

1 **changeableness,** changeability, changefulness, mutability, mobility, flexibility, versatility, variety, variegation; iridescence, inconsistency, inconstancy, variability; irregularity, imbalance, disequilibrium; plasticity, pliancy, softness, suppleness; fluidity, flux, fluctuation, waxing and waning; alternation, turning, veering, oscillation; uncertainty, unreliability, unpredictability, vicissitude; unsteadiness, instability, wobbliness, rockiness, shakiness, impermanence, transience, metamorphosis

> *Variegation 263; Change 665*

2 **irresolution,** vacillation, uncertainty, tergiversation, wavering, hesitation, procrastination, fickleness, whim, whimsicality, moodiness, capriciousness, caprice, desultoriness, flightiness, light-mindedness, volatility, erraticism, restlessness, agitation, fitfulness, disquiet, in-

quietude, fidgeting, shilly-shallying, bobbing and weaving, ducking and diving, darting, shiftiness, equivocation, slipperiness, disloyalty, infidelity, treacherousness

▸ *Inattention 324; Vacillation 378; Equivocation 380; Caprice 381; Transience 643; Irregularity 664; Oscillation 683; Agitation 684; Diversity 732; Inequality 741*

ADJECTIVES

3 **changeable,** changeful, mutable, alterable, mobile, versatile, varied, variant, variegated, protean, kaleidoscopic, chameleonic, mercurial, iridescent; inconsistent, inconstant, variable, random, irregular, imbalanced; plastic, pliant, soft, supple; flowing, melting, fluid, fluctuating, in a state of flux, ever-changing, never the same, alternating; tidal, vibrating, oscillating; uncertain, unreliable, unpredictable, unstable, unsteady; floating, loose, unattached, labile; wobbly, rocky, shaky, swaying, tottering, teetering, built on sand, built on weak foundations; unsettled, impermanent, transient, rootless, homeless, of no fixed abode, vagrant, rambling, wandering, roving; precarious, touch and go, fitful, shifting, ephemeral, spasmodic, flickering, wavering

4 **irresolute,** hesitating, vacillating, seesawing, fickle, whimsical, moody, wavering, waffling, wayward, capricious; desultory, malleable, impressionable, yielding, flighty; dizzy, giddy, scatterbrained, light-headed, light-minded; volatile, mercurial, restless, tossing and turning, fidgety, shilly-shallying, shifty, disloyal, unfaithful, traitorous, like putty in one's hands, scatty [Brit inf]

VERBS

5 **be changeable,** change, metamorphose, vary, fluctuate, alternate, oscillate; show variety, show phases, go through phases, ring the changes; flash, flicker, twinkle, gutter; wave, wave in the wind, flutter, whiffle, flap; falter, stagger, teeter, totter, sway, reel, rock; tremble, vibrate, shake, wobble, swing, shuttle; pitch, roll, yaw, tack, turn, veer, back, ebb and flow, wax and wane, have as many phases as the moon

6 **be irresolute,** tergiversate, vacillate, seesaw, blow hot and cold, waver, waffle [Inf]; hesitate, hover, drift, float; dodge about, dart, duck and dive, bob and weave, flit, flitter, fidget, shilly-shally, play fast and loose, change one's mind, change the rules

ADVERBS

7 **changeably,** alterably, back and forth, to and fro, in and out, inconsistently, off and on, on and off, inconstantly, variably, irregularly, iridescently, pliantly, softly, fluidly, alternatively; now this, now that; uncertainly, unreliably, unpredictably, unsteadily, shakily, precariously, fitfully, impermanently; now here, now there; waveringly, ephemerally, spasmodically, irresolutely, round and round, whimsically, moodily, waywardly,

capriciously, desultorily, impressionably; dizzily, shiftily, disloyally, unfaithfully, traitorously

667 Permanence

NOUNS

1 **permanence,** permanency, continuance, continuity; establishment, entrenchment, persistence, perseverance, dependability, steadfastness, reliability, endurance, abidance, durability, survival, subsistence; conservation, conservatism, conservancy, preservation; indestructibility, inalterability, everlastingness, perpetuity, imperishability, immortality, eternity; changelessness, lack of change, constancy, invariability, immutability; finality, fixedness, fixity, firmness, solidity, steadiness, stability; immobility, rigidity, status quo

▸ *Duration 642; Eternity 644; Continuity, Continuation 669; Stability 674; Lack of Motion 678; Preservation 815*

ADJECTIVES

2 **permanent,** lasting, long-lasting, continuing, continuous; established, entrenched, persistent, persevering, durable, surviving, subsisting; conservative, preservative; indestructible, everlasting, perpetual, imperishable, immortal, eternal; changeless, unchanging, unchangeable, cast in stone, constant, invariable, unalterable, immutable; final, fixed, firm, solid, steady, stable; immobile, immovable, rigid, static, stationary

▸ *Preservation 815*

3 **unfailing,** dependable, reliable, steadfast, sustained, perennial, evergreen, abiding, enduring, surviving, subsisting, stable, standing, fixed, established, well-established; entrenched, longstanding, indestructible; conserved, preserved, well-preserved, unbreakable, inviolable, undying, eternal, sempiternal, unfading, firm, solid, steady, rocklike

▸ *Stability 674*

VERBS

4 **be permanent,** last, continue, persist, persevere, stand fast, stand firm, stand pat, stand one's ground, resist change, be *or* remain the same; endure, abide, survive, subsist, outlive, be here for good, last forever, last an eternity, be here for the duration, stay, be here to stay, set in, take root, remain unchanged, remain at rest, refuse to budge, dig in one's toes *or* heels

5 **make permanent,** perpetuate, conserve, preserve, maintain the status quo, oppose change, sustain, keep, keep up, immortalize, fix, finalize, establish, stabilize, immobilize, cast in stone

ADVERBS

6 **permanently,** lastingly, changelessly, *in statu quo* [L], as is, as usual, as ever, still the same, as before, persistently, perseveringly, continuously, constantly, invari-

ably, unalterably, immutably, unfailingly, reliably, steadfastly, perennially, abidingly, enduringly, firmly, solidly, steadily, rigidly, fixedly, at a standstill, indestructibly, imperishably, inviolably, immortally, undyingly, perpetually, eternally, sempiternally, forever, for ever and ever, everlastingly, always, for good, for good and all, once and for all

668 Cessation

NOUNS

1 **cessation,** termination, ceasing, stopping, closing, desistance, discontinuance, discontinuation, discontinuity, completion, relinquishment, withdrawal, abandonment, breakup
▶ *Death 29; End 773*

2 **stop,** end, ending, finish, conclusion, death; dead stop, halt, holdup, standstill, standoff; deadlock, stalemate, draw, checkmate, defeat; failure, breakdown, shutting down, shutdown, closing down, closedown, stoppage, temporary stoppage, blockage, logjam, gridlock; interruption, stay, check, hitch, technical hitch, hindrance; work stoppage, retirement, resignation, dismissal, layoff, strike, general strike, walkout, lockout; permanent stoppage, hanging up, ringing off [Brit], breaking off; closure, closure of debate, cloture
▶ *Death 29; Inactivity 415; Resistance 417; Closure 584; Lack of Motion 678; End 773; Hindrance 826; Resignation 835; Failure 846*

3 **pause,** break, lull, respite, recess, rest, sleep, nap, interruption, breathing space, postponement; stopover, stop-off; interlude, intermission, interval; fermata, caesura; time-out, time off, day off, holiday, vacation, leisure, leisure time, closed season; interim, interim period, cooling-off period, delay, truce, moratorium, suspension, suspension of hostilities, cease-fire, armistice, breather, letup [Inf]
▶ *Pacification 74; Refreshment 94; Leisure 125; Interval 587*

4 **stopping place,** stop, bus stop, flag stop; station, railroad *or* train station, subway station, bus station, service station, gas station; rest stop, highway restaurant, port, port of call, harbor, terminal, air terminal, airport, waiting room
▶ *Arrival 704*

5 **resting place,** bed, hospital, nursing home, retirement home; lodging, hotel, motel, billet; final resting place, cemetery, graveyard, grave
▶ *Death 29; End 773*

ADJECTIVES

6 **ceased,** terminated, stopped, closed, discontinued, complete, relinquished, withdrawn, abandoned, broken up, broken off

7 **stopped,** ended, at an end, finished, concluded;

halted, held up, deadlocked; checkmated, defeated, failed, shut down; closed, closed down, blocked; interrupted, checked, hindered

8 **recessed,** adjourned; pending, on hold, at a pause

VERBS

9 **cease,** terminate, close, desist, discontinue; complete, withdraw, abandon, break up, break off

10 **stop,** end, come to an end, finish, come to a stop, halt, come to a halt, die; stop abruptly, stop dead, stop short, stop in one's tracks, freeze in one's tracks, grind to a halt; brake, put on the brake, pull up, draw up; come to a standstill, stall, stick, jam; discontinue, break down, quit, hold up, refrain from, desist; relinquish, give up, give in, admit defeat; leave off, disappear, fade out, fade away, blow over, run out, run down, peter out, let up, slacken off, tail off, die off, die away, conclude, terminate, break off, stop talking, hang up, ring off [Brit], put the phone down; stop breathing, die

11 **stop work,** retire, resign, dismiss, lay off; strike, go *or* go out on strike, walk out; close down, close, shut up shop, put up the shutters, shut down, lock out; cease trading, go out of business, ring down the curtain, wind up, fail, collapse

12 **cause to cease,** put a stop to, stay, freeze, call a halt, cancel, call off; cut short, interrupt, bring to a standstill, stalemate; catch, hinder, thwart, block, check, stem; arrest, restrain, hold, hold up; checkmate, defeat; close, closure, cloture; exhaust, use up, bring to an end, end, disconnect, break off, see the last of, cut off, cut someone off in his *or* her prime, kill, murder, do in [Inf]

13 **pause,** pause for breath, relax, rest, fall asleep, sleep, nap, interrupt, suspend, stay; adjourn, recess, break, take a break,; call time-out, take a day off, take a holiday, take a vacation, vacation, let up, cool off, hold up, hold back; hang fire, stay one's hand, call a truce, suspend hostilities, cease fire, make peace, take a breather, take five or ten [Inf]

INTERJECTIONS

14 **cease!,** stop!, whoa!, desist!, enough!, that's enough!, stop it!, quit!, that's it!, stop thief!, freeze!, break it up!, leave off!, drop it!, forget it!, let up!, give it up!; lay off!, give over!, knock it off!, cut it out!, pack it in!, cool it!, come off it! [Inf]

669 Continuity, Continuation

NOUNS

1 **continuity,** uninterruption, uninterrupted course, connectedness, connection; series, sequence, succession, flow, progression, run; continuation, continuance
▶ *Consecutiveness 774*

2 **continuation,** prolongation, resumption, repetition,

recurrence, recommencement; supplement, sequel, follow-up

> *Repetition 797*

3 continuance, duration, long duration, continuousness, constancy, stay; perseverance, protraction; preservation, maintenance, sustenance, support

> *Perseverance 377; Duration 642*

4 protraction, prolongation, extension, addition, furtherance, perpetuation, perpetuity, endurance, persistence, perseverance, survival

ADJECTIVES

5 continuous, uninterrupted, connected, unbroken, undivided; flowing, progressive, continuing, in progress, ongoing, constant, steady, incessant

6 progressive, sequent, sequential, additional, supplemental, repetitive, recurrent, flowing, running

7 protracted, prolonged, extended, lengthened, drawn-out, interminable, unvarying, unending, unceasing, undying, unstoppable, unremitting, unrelenting, persistent, unfailing, inexhaustible, endless, enduring, lasting, everlasting, eternal, perpetual

VERBS

8 continue, proceed, advance, make progress, progress, succeed, recur, repeat, connect; add, supplement; flow, run on, go on, follow through, maintain, keep up, sustain, support, uphold, preserve, harp on, keep on, keep alive, keep going, keep things moving, keep the ball rolling, keep the ball in play, keep the pot boiling, not stop, not interfere, let nature take its course, let things take their course, let sleeping dogs lie, let *or* leave alone, let be

9 protract, prolong, further, extend, draw out, spin out, maintain, perpetuate, persist, persist in, persevere, pursue, pursue one's course, resume, follow up, pick up, take up again, continue, recommence, restart, return to, pick up where one left off, last, endure, remain, abide, live on, survive, stay, stay on, haunt, frequent, carry on, keep on, march on, roll on, plod on, keep at it, peg away, stick at it, stick to, go on for a long time, stand the test of time, live out one's time *or* life, see the end of; hang on, stick it out, sit out, hang in there [Inf]

ADVERBS

10 continually, continuously, constantly, repeatedly, endlessly, steadily, incessantly, progressively, sequentially, additionally, supplementally, repetitively, recurrently, without interruption, protractedly, interminably, unendingly, unceasingly, unremittingly, unrelentingly, persistently, inexhaustibly, enduringly, lastingly, everlastingly, eternally, perpetually, without respite, with no letup, nonstop, all the time, always, forever, on and on

INTERJECTIONS

11 go on!, carry on!, drive on!, keep it up!, keep going!, keep up the good work!, keep moving!, stick with it!, never say die!, onward and upward!

670 Conversion

NOUNS

1 conversion, change, converting, convertibility; transition, transposition, changeover; movement, shift, transfer, transference; liquidation; translation, interpretation, alteration, modification, reorganization, rationalization; transformation, metamorphosis, mutation, processing; transmutation, transfiguration

> *Production 522; Change 665; Effect 676*

2 chemical change, reduction, resolution, fermentation, ferment, leaven, dehydration, crystallization, melting; physical change

3 evolution, evolving, growth, life cycle, development, progress; revolution, reformation, reeducation, rebirth, regeneration, rehabilitation, improvement, naturalization, assimilation; degeneration, deterioration, perversion, denaturalization, alienation

> *Improvement 807; Deterioration 808; Repair 809*

4 religious conversion, indoctrination, brainwashing, persuasion, proselytizing, proselytization, evangelism, evangelization, revivalism, revival, spiritual rebirth

> *Religion 81; Persuasion 178; Influence 512*

5 converter, changer, translator, liquidator; reformer, rehabilitator, improver; indoctrinator, teacher, preacher, minister, priest, vicar, proselyter, proselytizer, missionary, apostle, evangelist, television evangelist, televangelist

6 convert, changed person, proselyte, catechumen, neophyte, new man *or* woman, born-again person; apostate, turncoat

ADJECTIVES

7 converted, changed, turned into, transformed, processed, transposed, liquidated; transfigured, born-again, saved; metamorphosed, transmuted, mutated, translated, changed beyond recognition, unrecognizable, brainwashed, proselytized, assimilated, naturalized, improved, modified, regenerated, degenerated

8 converting, changing, becoming, growing, developing, maturing, transferring, altering, transforming, mutating, processing, fermenting, leavening, crystallizing, melting; transmuting, transfiguring, evolving, progressing, regenerating, improving; degenerating, deteriorating

9 convertible, changeable, transformable, impressionable, influenceable, persuadable, transmutable, transposable, transferable, translatable, alterable, improvable, reducible, resolvable

10 influenced, persuaded, brainwashed, revived, proselytized, evangelized

VERBS

11 convert, change, metamorphose, mutate, transpose,

move, shift, transfer, liquidate; translate, alter, transform, process, reduce, resolve, ferment, leaven, dehydrate, crystallize, melt, transmute, transfigure, become, be turned into *or* to; turn into *or* to, get, come to, develop, evolve, pass, shift, slide into; mellow, mature, ripen, melt, merge, dissolve, sink

12 **be converted,** be changed, be transformed; evolve, develop, wax, grow, ripen, mature, mellow, age, progress, improve, naturalize, assimilate, regenerate, be rejuvenated, denaturalize, deteriorate, degenerate, take *or* assume the shape of, assume the character of, assume the nature of, undergo a personality change, not know oneself, suffer a sea change; reform, revolt, enter a new phase, enter a different phase, reach a stage, turn over a new leaf; be saved, be born again, turn to God, change one's ways; turn against, renege, apostatize, desert, turn traitor

13 **transform,** transfigure, change the face of, make into; ferment, leaven, process, reduce, reduce to; turn into, convert, resolve into, conjure into, metamorphose, transmute, alchemize, mold, shape, rehabilitate; paper over, paper over the cracks, paint over, render, translate, interpret, misinterpret, reinterpret, modify; decorate, redecorate, reshape, remodel, reform, reorganize, restructure, reeducate, rationalize, deform, distort, twist, pervert, lick *or* knock into shape [Inf]

14 **persuade,** influence, indoctrinate, brainwash, win over, proselytize, evangelize, preach, convert, save, redeem, revive, convince

ADVERBS

15 **convertibly,** in transition, in transit, en route, on the way to

671 Reversion

NOUNS

1 **reversion,** reversal, turning back *or* backward, going back, return; apostasy, retraction, recantation, repentance, backing down; retreat, retirement, retroversion, retroflexion, looking back, retrospection; reaction, retroaction, retrospective action, counteraction, backfire, ricochet, recoil, boomerang effect, backlash, counterrevolution, counterreformation; about-face, U-turn, volte-face, atavism, recidivism, backsliding, relapse

▶ *Memory 354; Oldness 653; Cause 675; Backward Motion 680; Repetition 797*

2 **restoration,** reconversion, changing back, giving back, reinstatement, transfer, restitution, compensation; revival, new beginning, resumption, recommencement, recovery, retrieval; recycling, taking back, retaliation, reprisal, getting back

▶ *Gain 467; Taking 477; Giving Back 478; Compensation 743; Beginning 771*

3 **return,** regression, recession, retrogression, retrograde state, withdrawal, coming *or* returning home

4 **swing,** swing of the pendulum, give and take, comings and goings, shuttling, shuttle, commuting, round trip; turning point, pivotal point, crucial point *or* moment, crisis, watershed, turn of the tide

▶ *Oscillation 683*

5 **reply,** retort, retortion, answer, response, feedback, confutation, refutation

▶ *Refutation 332; Answer 334*

ADJECTIVES

6 **regressive,** recessive, reversionary, reversional, retroverse, retrograde, restitutive, restitutory, compensatory, retrospective, reflexive, reactive, reactionary, retroactive, atavistic, recidivist, recidivistic, recidivous

7 **reversed,** regressed, retracted, recanted, retreated, reverted, reacted, recoiled, backfired; returned, restored, reinstated, revived, resumed, recovered, retrieved, recycled; replied, retorted, answered, responded, refuted

8 **reversible,** returnable, restorable, recoverable, retrievable, recyclable, refutable

VERBS

9 **reverse,** turn back, turn about, turn, go back, return, revert, regress, recede, retrogress, recidivate, withdraw, retract, back down, retreat, recant, renege, backslide, slide back, slip back, relapse, turn backward *or* backwards, look back, hark back, archaize, turn back the clock, react, counteract, backfire, ricochet, recoil, boomerang, do *or* make an about-face, do *or* make a U-turn

10 **restore,** restore the status quo, reconvert, revive, resume, change back, give back, make restitution, compensate, reinstate, restart, recommence, start again, begin again, go back to the beginning, undo, do again, unmake, remake, start afresh, start anew, recover, retrieve, recycle, take back, retaliate, get back at, take it from the top

11 **return,** return *or* come home, make a round trip

12 **swing,** swing back, swing around, trace back, rebound, recoil, kick back, give and take, come and go, shuttle, commute

13 **reply,** retort, answer, respond, give feedback, confute, refute, recant, repent

ADVERBS

14 **reversibly,** regressively, retrospectively, reflexively, reactively, retroactively, atavistically, retrievably, refutably, invertedly, inside out, wrong side out, back to front, back to the beginning, as you were, from the top

672 Substitution

NOUNS

1 **substitution,** change, exchange, quid pro quo, commutation, alternation, switch, swap, shuffle, representation, replacement; deputing, deputizing, power of attorney, vicariousness, supplanting, supersession, sur-

rogation, surrogacy, alternative choice, equivalence, equivalent, alternative, worse alternative, lesser of two evils, second best, *pis aller* [Fr], expedient, compromise, modus vivendi, temporary measure, stopgap, compensation, expiation

◆ *Deputy 80; Representation 187; Compromise 461; Exchange 673; Equality 740*

2 **substitute,** sub, alternate, proxy, agent, representative, succedaneum; deputy, surrogate, surrogate mother, locum tenens [Brit], fill-in, stand-in, understudy; stunt man *or* woman, double, ringer [Inf]; lookalike, soundalike; impostor, changeling, Doppelgänger; ghost writer, reserve, reservist, pinch hitter, substitute teacher, relief, replacement, rain check; successor, supplanter, foster parent, father figure, father substitute, mother figure, mother substitute, scapegoat, whipping boy, fall guy [Inf], patsy [Inf]; transplant, artificial limb, prosthesis, glass eye, artificial eye, pacemaker; remount, guilt offering, sacrifice, lamb to the slaughter

ADJECTIVES

3 **substitute,** substitutive, substitutional, alternate, alternative, acting, deputy, proxy, reserve, equivalent, lookalike, soundalike, surrogate, second, additional, stopgap, makeshift, temporary, provisional

4 **substituted,** changed, exchanged, switched, swapped, replaced, deputized, supplanted, superseded, compensated

VERBS

5 **substitute,** give in exchange, exchange, switch, swap, shuffle, change for, interchange, put in place of, compensate for, fob off, palm off

6 **be a substitute,** relieve, succeed, supplant, supersede, oust, displace, replace, take the place of, ghostwrite, pinch-hit [Inf], serve as proxy, act as deputy for, represent, act for, do duty for, double for, imitate, fill in, stand in for, understudy, deputize, cover, cover for, hold the fort, take over, foster, take *or* shoulder responsibility for, take the blame, step into the shoes of, take the rap [Inf]

7 **take a substitute,** exchange for, exchange, commute, choose an alternative, compromise, take in exchange, take second best, make do with, put up with, count as, treat as, regard as, take a rain check

ADVERBS

8 **instead,** instead of, in place of, in lieu of, on behalf of, in one's behalf, in one's place, in favor of, at the expense of, as an alternative, alternatively, equivalently, additionally, temporarily, provisionally, for want of anything better, *faute de mieux* [Fr]; in default of, by default, by proxy, *in loco parentis* [L], by *or* through the agency of, in one's shoes

673 Exchange

NOUNS

1 **exchange,** interchange, change, trade, barter, conversion, commutation, commutability; permutation, substitution, transposition, shuffle, shuffling, switch, switching, swap, swapping, pawning, castling (chess); mutuality, reciprocity, reciprocation, banter, give-and-take, tit for tat, quid pro quo, retaliation, blow for blow, eye for an eye, tooth for a tooth, measure for measure; cooperation, logrolling, interplay, two-way traffic, repartee, equivalent, correlation, compensation, recompense, consideration, small consideration, redemption, ransom, trade-off, dealing, financial dealing, transaction, truck

◆ *Answer 334; Retaliation 420; Compromise 461; Trade 480; Cooperation 827*

2 **place of exchange,** place of trade, market, marketplace, stock exchange, bourse, rialto, bank, bureau de change, *cambio* [Ital], *Wechsel* [Ger], pawnshop

◆ *Trade 480; Market 483*

ADJECTIVES

3 **in exchange,** equivalent, complementary, reciprocal, reciprocative, mutual, two-way, tit-for-tat, retaliatory, compensatory, exchangeable, changeable, interchangeable, convertible, commutative, substitutive, substitutable

4 **exchanged,** changed, interchanged, substituted, transposed, traded, bartered, converted, switched, swapped, pawned, reciprocated, requited, compensated, ransomed

VERBS

5 **exchange,** give in exchange, give an equivalent, interchange, shuffle, switch, swap, castle (chess); reciprocate, cooperate, logroll, correlate, requite, give as good as one gets; answer back, retort, bandy, banter, return the compliment; pay in kind, compensate, recompense, exchange for, change places, transpose; substitute, convert, pawn, convert into; change money, barter, trade, trade off, traffic, truck, transact, deal; give in return, give and take, give tit for tat, give blow for blow, take an eye for an eye, rob Peter to pay Paul, take in one another's washing, scratch each other's back

ADVERBS

6 **in exchange,** mutually, reciprocally, equivalently, correlatively, changeably, interchangeably, commutatively, au pair, vice versa, back and forth, backward and forward, to and fro, by turns, turn and turn about, turn about, each in his *or* her turn, in kind, in return, in return for, in exchange for

674 Stability

NOUNS

1 **stability,** stabilization, steadiness, steadfastness, rootedness, fixedness, fixity; solidity, soundness, secureness, strength, durability, permanence; consistency, reliability, constancy, rest, quietude, quiet, dependability, calm; immobilization, immobility, immovability, hardening, stiffening, stiffness; firmness, firming up, inflexibility, steady state, stable equilibrium, homeostasis, balance, equality, stasis; immutability, unchangeableness, unchangeability, changelessness, invariability, incommutability, irreversibility, indestructibility, deathlessness

  ▶ *Density 540; Hardness 542; Duration 642; Eternity 644; Permanence 667; Lack of Motion 678; Sameness 730; Equality 740*

2 **determination,** resolution, resolve, nerve, nerves of steel, iron nerve, iron will, inflexibility, toughness, hardness, steeliness, obstinacy, stubbornness, obduracy, aplomb, imperturbability, coolness

  ▶ *Resolution 376; Obstinacy 379; Certainty 840*

ADJECTIVES

3 **stable,** steady, steadfast, solid, sound, firm, stiff, secure, strong, durable, permanent; consistent, reliable, constant, dependable, predictable, unchangeable, unchanging, unvarying, inalterable, irrevocable, irreversible; restful, quiet, calm; immobile, immovable, held, at rest, at anchor, riding at anchor; aground, stuck fast, high and dry; cast *or* written in stone, wellfounded, frozen; hard, inflexible, unshakable, incontrovertible, indisputable, indefeasible, homeostatic, equal; immutable, changeless, invariable, incommutable, intransmutable; indissoluble, imperishable, inextinguishable, invulnerable, indestructible, ineradicable, indelible, evergreen, perennial, enduring, longlasting, deathless, perpetual, rocklike, steady as a rock

4 **stabilized,** unchanged, unaltered, settled, transfixed, stereotyped, fixed; anchored, moored, tethered, tied, chained, grounded; stranded, pinned down, rooted, rooted to the spot, deep-rooted, well-rooted, established, well-established, ingrained, entrenched, engraved, balanced

5 **determined,** resolute, resolved, certain, sure, nerved, iron-nerved, iron-willed, inflexible, unwavering, tough, hard, steely, obstinate, stubborn, obdurate, imperturbable, cool

VERBS

6 **be stable,** not change, stay in one place, stick fast, hold, remain fixed, adhere; stand, stand up well, hold up, stand firm, stay put; harden, stiffen, stabilize, keep one's balance, set in, settle in, settle down, stay, take root, strike root; quiet down, rest, keep one's cool

7 **make stable,** stabilize, steady, transfix, freeze, balance, equalize; fix, establish, confirm, validate, ratify, make sure, ensure, secure, firm up, set up, set on its feet; found, erect, build on a rock, build on a firm foundation, support, buttress, engrave, stamp, print, stereotype, set, cast *or* write in stone; keep stable, bind, make fast, root, entrench, tie, fasten down, batten down, put at rest, quiet

8 **show determination,** persist, persevere, stand firm, stand pat, stiffen, not budge, be stubborn; hold out, hold out to the bitter end, stay with it, stick with it, stick fast, hold the road, stand *or* hold one's ground, hang on, weather the storm, put one's foot down, stick it out, stick to one's guns

ADVERBS

9 **stably,** unalterably, steadily, steadfastly, solidly, soundly, securely, strongly; permanently, consistently, reliably, constantly; dependably, predictably, irrevocably, irreversibly; restfully, quietly, calmly, stiffly, firmly, on a firm basis, on a firm footing, on a strong foundation; inflexibly, unshakably, indisputably, equally, immutably, indissolubly, imperishably, invulnerably, indestructibly, indelibly; perennially, enduringly, perpetually

10 **determinedly,** with determination, resolutely, in a resolute manner, inflexibly, unwaveringly, toughly, obstinately, stubbornly, obdurately, imperturbably, coolly

675 Cause

NOUNS

1 **cause,** reason, causation, causality, formal cause, underlying cause, motivation; initiation, instigation, determinant, creation, authorship, attribution, origination, occasion, invention, derivation; production, propagation, cultivation, generation, evocation, provocation; compulsion, temptation, impulsion, stimulation, inspiration, fomentation, encouragement, force, spark, etiology, etymology

  ▶ *Compulsion 428; Motivation 508; Originality 737; Beginning 771*

2 **source,** spring, wellspring, mainspring, wellhead, fountainhead, fountain, fount, *fons et origo* [L], headwaters, mine, quarry, home, birthplace; breeding ground, womb, seedbed, hotbed, incubator, hatchery, cradle, nursery; raw material, nucleus, germ, seed

  ▶ *Agriculture 16; Horticulture 17; Beginning 771*

3 **contributory cause,** contributing factor, contribution, agent, leaven, stimulus, factor, hidden cause, influence; butterfly effect, planetary influence, stars, astrological influence; destiny, fate

  ▶ *Effect 676*

4 **reason,** reason why, reason behind, idea behind, the why, the why and wherefore, key, explanation, answer, basis, ground, grounds, rationale, idea, raison

d'être, occasion, motive, object, purpose, aim, opportunity, excuse, pretext; cause and effect
▶ *Answer 334; Effect 676*

5 **undertaking,** cause, enterprise, attempt, action, case, subject, matter, topic, purpose, principle, ideal, worthy cause
▶ *Topic 328*

6 **first cause,** prime mover, God, maker, creator, deity, Supreme Being, *primum mobile* [L]; producer, begetter, only begetter, sire, father, mother, parent, ancestor, progenitor, propagator, instigator, originator, author, founder, inventor, motivator, inspirer
▶ *Reproduction 21; Family 65; Deity 82*

ADJECTIVES

7 **causal,** causative, etiological, creative, inventive; original, aboriginal, primary, primal, primordial, primitive; basic, fundamental, intrinsic, foundational; elemental, elementary, ultimate, radical; effectual, effective, pivotal, determinant, decisive, crucial; central, significant; productive, genetic, generative, germinal, seminal, embryonic, inceptive, rudimentary, formative, initiatory, suggestive, inspiring, inspirational, influential, impelling, compelling, responsible, answerable, blameworthy, at the bottom of, behind the scenes

VERBS

8 **cause,** create, originate, be the author of, be the cause of, author, beget, propagate, father, sire; bring into the world, bring into being; make, produce, invent, derive, cultivate, generate, lie at the bottom of; make or mar, result in, bring about, bring off, bring to pass, make happen, effect, effectuate, have the effect of, lead to, give rise to, occasion, give occasion for

9 **awaken,** stimulate, tempt, excite, kindle, inspire, encourage, motivate, influence, impel; compel, force, make, foment, provoke, incite, set off, touch off, trigger, spark; evoke, bring on, bring out, draw out, induce, precipitate, hasten, elicit, plan, contrive, procure, find means *or* the means, engineer, manage

10 **inaugurate,** initiate, start, begin, launch, instigate, institute, found, lay the foundations; erect, establish, open, broach, set up, set going, set on foot, set afloat, set in motion, sow the seeds, open the door to

11 **determine,** decide, decide the result, decide the outcome, decide the issue; turn *or* tip the scale, have the casting vote, come down on one side or the other, come *or* climb down off the fence, help decide, contribute to, have a hand in, have a large part in, have an effect, promote, advance, foster, aid, abet, help

ADVERBS

12 **causally,** because, by reason of, causatively, creatively, inventively; originally, primarily, primordially, primitively; basically, fundamentally, intrinsically, ultimately, radically, effectually, effectively, pivotally, decisively, crucially, centrally, significantly; productively, genetically, inceptively, suggestively; inspiringly, inspira-

tionally, influentially, compellingly, responsibly, answerably, behind the scenes, in the background

676 Effect

NOUNS

1 **effect,** outcome, logical outcome, counteraction, reaction, action, event, happening, achievement, issue; end, denouement, result, final result, net result, end result, upshot; termination, completion, conclusion, aftermath, aftereffect; culmination, consequence, impact; product, by-product, repercussion, side effect, spin-off, sequel, corollary, inference, derivation; derivative, precipitate, remainder, residue, payoff
▶ *Record 185; Action 412; Remainder 750; Completeness 761; Sequence 770*

2 **visible effect,** handiwork, print, imprint, impress, mark, trace, side effect, footprint, fingerprint, backwash, wake; legacy, inheritance, hereditament; property, belongings, effects, personal effects

3 **growth,** development, expansion, increase, swelling, outgrowth, bud, blossom, florescence, flower, fruit, ear, crop, harvest, produce, gain, profit
▶ *Gain 467; Increase 746*

4 **significance,** import, meaning, purport, sense, tendency, trend, drift

ADJECTIVES

5 **caused,** caused by, effected by, effected, reacting to, reacting; resulting from, resulting, resultant, ensuing, following from, following, coming from, due to, owing to; developing from, developed, deriving from, derived, derivative; evolving from, evolved, arising from, descending from, descended, inheriting from; inherited, hereditary, genetic; depending on, dependent on, dependent, attributed to, attributable to; consequent, consequent upon, consequential, contingent, contingent upon; subject to, subsequent, sequential, secondary, second-generation, next-generation; unoriginal, emergent, eventual, born of, out of, by

6 **growing,** developing, expanding, increasing, swelling, budding, blossoming, flowering, fruit-bearing, producing, gaining, profiting

VERBS

7 **affect,** have an effect, have a side effect, have consequence, have impact, impact upon, counteract; have a visible effect, print, imprint, impress upon, mark, leave a trace, have a side effect, leave a footprint *or* fingerprint

8 **react,** act, happen, achieve, effect, accomplish, issue, end in, result in, eventuate in, terminate, complete, conclude, culminate, produce, precipitate, spin off, pay off

9 **follow from,** follow on from, follow, ensure, supervene, result, result from, spin off from, be the result of, be due to; owe everything to, borrow from, derive

from, be derived from; inherit, descend from, have its roots in, originate in *or* from, come of, come out of, emanate from, emerge, proceed from, issue from; begin from, arise from, spring from, flow from; unfold, evolve, develop, bear the stamp of, depend on, hang upon, turn on, pivot on, center on, be subject to

10 **grow,** grow from, accrue, develop, develop from, expand, increase, swell, sprout, germinate, bud, blossom, flower, bear fruit, harvest, produce, gain, profit

11 **take effect,** come into effect, become law, come about; transpire, arise, happen, occur, take place, end up, turn out, fall out, come to pass, work out, come off [Inf], pan out [Inf]

ADVERBS

12 **with the effect of,** in consequence, as a consequence, consequently, consequentially; derivatively, dependently, attributively, contingently, secondarily, unoriginally; subsequently, eventually, because of, as a result, with the result that, necessarily, naturally, accordingly, of course, and so, and there, ergo, hence, following upon, it follows that

677 Motion

NOUNS

1 **motion,** movement, moving, change of position, migration; movability, movableness, mobility, motility; locomotion, walking, perambulation, pedestrianism; going, running, rushing, marching; riding, equitation; transit, traffic, traffic flow, transport, transportation, travel, land travel, water travel, air travel; kinetic energy, motivity, actuation, motive power; dynamics, laws of motion, kinematics, kinetics, kinesis, kinesiology, kinesiatrics, kinesipathy, kinesitherapy
   ▶ *Physics 10; Transportation 686*

2 **momentum,** propulsion, impulsion, mobilization, motivation, actuation, impetus, stir, stirring, restlessness, unrest; action, activity, agitation, bustle, course, passage, set, trend, career; stream, flow, flux, flight, current, rush, onrush, run, drift, driftage
   ▶ *Action 412; Agitation 684; Transfer 685; Impulsion 695; Propulsion 696*

3 **movement,** motion *or* movement around, rotation, precession, circumnavigation, axial motion, angular motion, radial motion; oscillation, fluctuation, vibration, gyration, agitation, to-and-fro movement, irregular motion; sideward motion, sideways *or* sidewise motion, oblique motion; random motion, Brownian movement
   ▶ *Orbital Motion 681; Rotation 682; Oscillation 683; Agitation 684; Deviation 698*

4 **forward motion,** advance, approach, procession; progress, traversal, traversing, continuation, continuing, continuing on, passing through, traveling through; headway, evolution; motion into, ingress, arrival
   ▶ *Forward Motion 679; Arrival 704; Entry 706*

5 **backward motion,** regression, backing, backflowing, reflowing, refluence, reflux, retreat, withdrawal; departure, exit, motion out of, egress; sternway; recession, following, pursuit
   ▶ *Backward Motion 680; Departure 705; Exit 707*

6 **descending motion,** descent, downward motion, subsiding motion, sinking, plunging
   ▶ *Descent 714*

7 **ascending motion,** upward motion, ascent, ascending, rising, soaring, mounting, climbing, flying
   ▶ *Ascent 713*

8 **rapid motion,** rapidity, speed, velocity
   ▶ *Swiftness 694*

9 **slow motion,** slowness, leisureliness, sluggishness, puttering
   ▶ *Slowness 693*

10 **regular movement,** recurring movement, rhythm, oscillation; uniform movement, continual movement
   ▶ *Regularity 663; Oscillation 683; Repetition 797*

11 **bodily movement,** exercise, athletics, gymnastics, aerobics; gesticulation, wave, gesture; walk, gait, carriage, bearing, tread, pace, clip, step, stride, stroll, saunter, amble, tramp, stamp; run, lope, jog, jog trot, dogtrot, trot, dance step, hop, skip, jump, leap; waddle, shuffle, creep; stalk, strut, swagger, goose step, march, quick march; scamper, scramble, canter, gallop, lick [Inf]
   ▶ *Dance and Ballet 135; Sports 145; Swiftness 694*

ADJECTIVES

12 **moving,** having motion, in motion, motive; mobile, motional, movable, motile; motivational; locomotive, automotive, self-propelled; shifting; impelling, propelling, propellant; driving, traveling, riding, running, rushing, going, passing; fluent, flowing, streaming; transitional, fleeting; mercurial, restless, active, agitated, bustling, scurrying, stirring; wandering, drifting, nomadic; peripatetic, ambulant, erratic, runaway

13 **directional,** advancing, advance, progressive, progressing, processional; backward, regressive, retrogressive, back, backtracking, backflowing, refluent, reflowing, pursuing; downward, sinking, plunging, descending, subsiding; upward, ascending, rising, soaring, mounting, climbing, flying; rapid, speedy, speed-

ing; slow, leisure, sluggish, toddling, puttering; regular, recurring, rhythmic, periodic, uniform, continuous, continual; circuitous, rotary, rotatory, rotational, centripetal, centrifugal, axial, radial; oscillating, fluctuating, vibrating, agitating; irregular, sideward, sideways *or* sidewise; random, to and fro, Brownian; oblique, angular; gyratory, gyrational, gyrating, kinetic, kinematic, dynamic

> *Forward Motion 679; Backward Motion 680; Direction 697*

VERBS

14 **be in motion,** move, have mobility, change position, stir, budge, go; flow, drift, stream; progress, advance, develop, drive forward, evolve, make one's way, proceed, gather way, keep going, go on, pick one's way, fight one's way, wade through; back, back up, regress, retrogress, subside, ebb, wane; change direction, deviate; soar, mount, rise, ascend, climb, fly; descend, sink, plunge; oscillate, go sideways *or* sidewise; gyrate, go around, rotate, spin, whirl; move over, get over, shift, change, change places

> *Forward Motion 679; Backward Motion 680; Rotation 682; Oscillation 683; Divergence 703; Ascent 713; Descent 714*

15 **move,** change places, interchange, move around; travel, roam, wander, drift, stray; shift, dodge, duck, weave; remove, change one's address; motion, gesture, gesticulate, wave

> *Address 209; Slowness 693; Swiftness 694*

16 **set in motion,** move, actuate, push, nudge, shove, drive; hustle, motivate; pull, tug, draw, haul; propel, impel, throw; mobilize, send, dispatch; scatter, disperse; bring together, gather; transfer, transport, convey; transpose, displace

> *Transfer 685; Transportation 686; Impulsion 695; Propulsion 696; Traction 699*

17 **walk,** step, stride, tramp, tread, trip, amble, stroll, saunter, waddle, shuffle, creep; stalk, strut, swagger, march; dance, leap, toddle, patter, putter, stagger, mince; run, jog, lope, rush, gallop, fly, dash, dart

18 **maneuver,** roll, cruise, freewheel, coast, trundle, taxi, chug, stream, tack

ADVERBS

19 **in motion,** kinetically, dynamically, on the move, on the go, up and about, astir, on the march, on the run, on the wing, on the hop; under way, on the road, en route, in transit, under sail; from pillar to post, transitionally, movably; motivationally, progressively, regressively; automotively; mercurially, restlessly, actively, nomadically, peripatetically; rapidly, slowly, circuitously, centripetally, centrifugally

678 Lack of Motion

NOUNS

1 **lack of motion,** motionlessness, immobility, stillness, inactivity, inaction; fixity, fixation, rigidity, stiffness; standstill, stand, stop, halt, pause, dead stop, full stop, lock, dead set; stability, equilibrium, poise, equipoise, balance, stasis, steadiness; inertness, inertia, dormancy, passiveness, passivity, apathy, latency, torpor, indifference, indolence, lotus-eating, languor, stagnancy; vegetation, coma, numbness, catalepsy, catatonia, trance, suspension, stagnation, cessation; deadlock, gridlock, stalemate; truce, lull, suspense, abeyance; stoppage, embargo, freeze, strike

> *Indifference 289; Inaction 413; Inactivity 415; Inertness 519; Cessation 668*

2 **repose,** rest, sleep, slumber, insensibility; eternal rest, death; quiescence, quiescency, silence, quietness, quiet, quietude; placidity, placidness, tranquillity, serenity, peace, composure, quietism, contemplation, nirvana, ataraxia, calmness, calm, restfulness, peacefulness, imperturbability, stillness; still, hush, lull, calm *or* lull before the storm, dead *or* flat calm, windlessness; doldrums, eye of the hurricane, horse latitudes; not a breath of air, nothing stirring, not a mouse stirring

> *Death 29; Peace 73; Silence 231; Latency 844*

3 **sedentary person,** shut-in, stick-in-the-mud, sluggard, couch potato [Inf]

> *Inactivity 415*

ADJECTIVES

4 **motionless,** immobile, still, inactive, unmoving, immotile, static, stationary, stagnant, standing; steady, poised, balanced; immovable, unmovable, fixed, stiff, stuck, paralyzed, unmoved, petrified, transfixed, rooted to the spot, stock-still, spellbound, frozen, still as a statue, quiet as a mouse, still as death; airless, windless, becalmed

> *Inactivity 415*

5 **sedentary,** inert, dormant, passive, latent, languid, languorous, apathetic, indifferent; indolent, phlegmatic, sluggish, vegetating, unaroused; suspended, abeyant, sleeping, slumbering; groggy, dopey [Inf]; heavy, leaden, dull, flat, slack, tame; dead, lifeless, catatonic, cataleptic, numb

> *Inaction 413; Inactivity 415; Inertness 519*

6 **quiescent,** silent, quiet, still, hushed, insensible, soundless; placid, tranquil, calm, serene, easygoing, peaceful, restful, composed; contemplative, smooth, unruffled, untroubled, unperturbed, unagitated, unhurried, unmoved, unstirring; stolid, stoic, impassive, calm as a millpond, quiet as death; inexcitable, imperturbable, cool, pacific, halcyon; undisturbed, sequestered, leisured; at rest, resting, reposing, reposeful, sleepy, stilly, cool as a cucumber

◗ *Peace 73; Silence 231; Indifference 289*

VERBS

7 **be motionless,** stand still, stand, not budge, freeze; remain, abide, stay, stay put; sit, sit down, sit tight, remain seated, remain in situ; perch, land, alight, mark time, wait; stand firm, stand like a post, not stir (a step), not breathe, hold one's breath; keep still, keep quiet, stagnate, vegetate, idle, hang fire; sleep, slumber, repose; die, go to one's eternal rest, go to the happy hunting ground

8 **make motionless,** bring to a standstill, immobilize, suspend, stalemate, call a truce; lock, jam, catch, stick, lodge; put a stop to, embargo, lay an embargo on, prohibit, freeze; soothe, lull, calm down, tranquilize, pacify, assuage, becalm

ADVERBS

9 **motionlessly,** fixedly, stationarily; inertly, inactively, statically, dormantly, passively, latently, stagnantly; calmly, quietly, still, tranquilly, peacefully, placidly, restfully, smoothly, unperturbedly, languidly, languorously; sluggishly, heavily, lifelessly, apathetically, coldly, phlegmatically, stoically, stolidly, impassively; in repose, at a halt, at a stand, far from the madding crowd; after death, posthumously, stilly

679 Forward Motion

NOUNS

1 **forward motion,** motion toward, going forward, step, progress, spurt, sudden progress, leaps and bounds; steady progress, progression, progressiveness, advance, headway, step on the ladder; forward march, forwarding, roll, rolling on, travel
◗ *Motion 677*

2 **course,** march, passage, way, career; march *or* passage *or* course of time, tide, current, flood; onward course, go-ahead, way forward
◗ *Time 639*

3 **advance,** advancement, promotion, preferment; leg up, furtherance, furthering, rise; raise, lift, ascent, elevation, gain, ground gained; enterprise, success, achievement, economic progress, prosperity
◗ *Ascent 713; Raising 715; Prosperity 847*

4 **development,** growth, evolution; furtherance, next step

5 **improvement,** betterment, reform; perfectibility, majestic progress, irresistible progress, irreversibility; getting ahead, overtaking; overstepping, encroachment
◗ *Overstepping 712; Improvement 807*

ADJECTIVES

6 **forward,** onward, progressing; progressive, advanced, advancing, go-ahead, forward-looking, up-to-date, abreast; enterprising, reformist, go-getting [Inf]

7 **ongoing,** continuing; inexorable, irreversible; on-

coming, proceeding, moving, profluent, flowing on, unbroken

VERBS

8 **go forward,** proceed, progress, make progress, make headway, advance, move forward, step forward; pass on, travel, get along, come along, roll, roll on; start, make a good start, make good progress
◗ *Motion 677; Beginning 771*

9 **press on,** push, push on, press forward, drive on, keep on; make strides, gain ground, cover ground, forge *or* shoot ahead, go ahead; climb, gain height, rise, rise higher
◗ *Ascent 713; Raising 715*

10 **make good time,** make up for lost time, make up leeway, recover lost ground, recoup, gain time
◗ *Time 639*

11 **march on,** run on, jog on, roll on, flow, flow on, drift along, go *or* move with the stream

12 **make one's way,** work *or* weave *or* worm *or* thread one's way, inch forward, muddle through, carve *or* force *or* fight one's way; further oneself, get somewhere, climb, reach toward, reach out, raise one's sights

13 **further,** bring on, foster, contribute to, advance, aid, raise, lift, elevate, promote, upgrade, improve, better; forward, hasten, modernize, bring forward, push, force; develop, grow, augment; step up, accelerate, put ahead, put in front; put forward, propose, favor, make for, conduce
◗ *Help 825*

14 **maintain progress,** hold one's lead, overtake, go fast, go ahead, advance by leaps and bounds
◗ *Swiftness 694*

ADVERBS

15 **forward,** onward, forth, on, along, ahead, on the way to, on the road, en route to *or* for, on one's way

16 **in progress,** under way, in transit, going on, progressively; by leaps and bounds, in sight of

680 Backward Motion

NOUNS

1 **backward motion,** going back, regression, regress, recession, reverse direction, backward step *or* motion; retroflexion *or* retroflection, retrocession, retrogression, retrogradation, retroaction
◗ *Reversion 671*

2 **retreat,** motion from; recess, withdrawal, withdrawment, retirement; fallback, pullout, pullback, pulling *or* falling *or* drawing back, advance to the rear, disengagement; resigning, resignation
◗ *Submission 421*

3 **reversal,** reverse, reversing, reversion, inversion; backing, backflow, backing up *or* off *or* out, backup; re-

gurgitation, voidance; reentrance, reentry, turn of the tide, reflux, refluence, ebb

▶ *Reversion 671*

4 **about-face,** rightabout, right about-face, U-turn, turnaround, turnabout; backtracking

5 **decline,** falloff, ebb, falling away; drop, fall, slump, downturn, downward trend; deterioration

▶ *Deterioration 808*

6 **countermotion,** counteraction, countermovement, recoil, rebound, countermarching, reversion, turn, turning point

7 **reflex,** recoil, return to base *or* starting point, resilience, elasticity, kickback, bounceback, rebound

8 **backsliding,** lapse, relapse, recidivism, recidivation; sliding down the slippery slope, going down the tubes *or* chute *or* drain [Inf]

9 **return,** homecoming, homeward journey

ADJECTIVES

10 **backward,** retrograde, retrogressive, retrocessive

11 **receding,** recessive, retreating, retractile; regressive, declining; ebbing, refluent; backsliding, lapsing, relapsing

12 **retroactive,** nostalgic, reactionary, backward-looking, retrospective

13 **reversed,** reverse, reversible, reflex, turned around; wrong way, wrong way around; counter, counterclockwise

▶ *Direction 697*

14 **resilient,** elastic, reflexive, recoiling

15 **returning,** homing, homeward bound

VERBS

16 **go backward,** regress, return, revert, relapse; backslide, slip back, lose ground, slide down the slippery slope; lapse, fall off, decline, recidivate, retrogress; retrograde [Arch], retrocede; go down the tubes *or* chute *or* drain [Inf]

▶ *Reversion 671; Deterioration 808*

17 **retreat,** withdraw, retire, sound *or* beat a retreat, pull back, pull out, advance to the rear, disengage; fall back, fall behind, draw back, run back, move back, stand back; back out, back down, give way, give ground, give place; run away, resign; crawfish [Inf]

▶ *Submission 421*

18 **reverse,** back, turn, back up, go into reverse, back off, back-pedal, back away; backtrack, back-trail, countermarch, reverse one's field, retrace one's steps, go back to the drawing board; take the reciprocal course; turn back, put back, double, double back, return, go *or* come back, go *or* come home; run back, flow back, ebb; regurgitate

19 **slip back,** ebb, fall, drop, decline, descend

▶ *Descent 714*

20 **shrink back,** avoid, shy, shy away, shrink, jib [Brit]

▶ *Avoidance 386*

21 **recoil,** draw back, quail, flinch; bounce back, spring

back, rebound; come back to where one started, box the compass

▶ *Counteraction 510*

22 **turn around** *or* **about,** face about, about-face, right about-face, turn on one's heel; turn one's back, come *or* go *or* fetch about, make a U-turn, turn tail, double, wheel, turn on a dime; veer, veer around, swivel, pivot, swing around

ADVERBS

23 **backward,** hindward, in reverse, rearward, astern, reflexively; back to where one started, against the grain, assbackwards [Inf]

681 Orbital Motion

NOUNS

1 **orbital motion,** orbiting, wheeling, rounding, orbiting, circling; circularity, rotation, turning, spiraling, spiral, gyre; helix, coil, ellipse; circulation, circumnavigation, circumambulation, circummigration

▶ *Curve 629; Rotation 682*

2 **circuitousness,** circulation; roundaboutness, ambages [Arch]; excursion

▶ *Circularity 631; Convolution 632; Deviation 698; Divergence 703*

3 **orbit,** cycle, revolution, circle, full circle; wheel, circuit, round trip, lap, loop, walk, turn, rounds, beat, tour

▶ *Surroundings 615; Circularity 631*

4 **orbiting body,** satellite, moon, planet, sun, star, asteroid, planetoid, comet; spaceship, space capsule, space *or* lunar module

▶ *Astronomy, Astronautics, and Rocketry 7; Space 563; Rotation 682*

ADJECTIVES

5 **orbital,** orbitary, rotary, revolutionary; circuitous, circulatory, turning; ambagious; circumnavigable

6 **circular,** round, O-shaped, wheel-shaped; spiral, helical, elliptical, cyclical, gyratory, coiled, looped

▶ *Circularity 631*

7 **orbiting,** cycling, revolving, wheeling, circling, rotating, spiraling, turning, spinning, gyrating

▶ *Rotation 682*

VERBS

8 **orbit,** go into orbit, circuit, revolve, rotate, turn; make a circuit, describe *or* move in a circle, circulate, go around, wheel around; come full circle, close the circle; make a round trip, return to the starting point; spiral, go around in circles, chase one's tail

9 **ring,** circle, skirt, girdle, loop, curve, flank; go the round, make one's rounds, lap; circumvent, circumambulate, circummigrate; circumnavigate, girdle the earth

▶ *Curve 629; Circularity 631*

ADVERBS

10 **circularly,** wheelwise, in a roundabout way

682 Rotation

NOUNS

1 **rotation,** rotational motion, revolution, rev [Inf], revolutions per minute (rpm); volution, orbit, orbiting, orbital motion, cycle, full circle; circulation, turbination, circumrotation, circumvolution; gyration, spin, spinning motion, axial motion, angular momentum, angular velocity
  ▸ *Circularity 631; Convolution 632; Orbital Motion 681*

2 **dizziness,** giddiness, vertigo

3 **turning,** whirling, swirling, twirling, spinning, pivoting, pirouetting; wheeling, whir, whirring, reeling; centrifugation, rolling, bowling, trolling, trundling, volutation; spiral, spiraling, twisting; torsion, torque

4 **reel,** pirouette, turn, roll, whirl, wheel; swirl, twirl, spin, dance; whirlabout, whirligig, merry-go-round, roundabout [Brit]
  ▸ *Dance and Ballet 135*

5 **rotary,** traffic circle, bypass, ring road [Brit], orbital [Brit], *péripherique* [Fr]
  ▸ *Way 691; Passage 692; Deviation 698*

6 **vortex,** whirl, whirlwind, cyclone, tornado; whirlpool, eddy, swirl, surge, gurge, maelstrom, Charybdis, waterspout; twister [Inf]
  ▸ *Meteorology and Climatology 9; Water 557; Rivers 570; Seas 571*

7 **axle,** shaft, spindle, axletree, universal joint; journal, journal box; axis, swivel, pivot; pin, pintle, hinge, rowlock, oarlock; hub, nave; distaff, mandrel, gimbal; bearing, ball bearing, roller bearing, bushing, jewel, headstock
  ▸ *Engineering 14*

8 **rotator,** wheel, top, spinning top, peg top, humming top, teetotum; bobbin, spindle, spool; drill, rotary drill, Archimedes' screw, rotor, circular saw; gyro, gyroscope, gyrocompass, gyrostabilizer, gyroplane, autogyro; centrifuge, ultracentrifuge; impeller, turbine, propeller, prop, screw, airscrew, winder, capstan, extractor fan; windmill, turntable, treadmill, revolving door; spit, turnspit
  ▸ *Astronomy, Astronautics and Rocketry 7; Engineering 14; Cooking 91; Propulsion 696*

9 **wheel,** cartwheel, wagon wheel; steering wheel, drive wheel; gearwheel, gear, spur wheel *or* gear, cog, cogwheel, pinwheel, flywheel, ratchet wheel, idler wheel, crown wheel, balance wheel, escape wheel, sprocket wheel; mill wheel, paddle wheel, water wheel; spinning wheel, charkha *or* charka, spinning jenny; potter's wheel, buffing wheel; roulette wheel, Catherine wheel, Ferris wheel; prayer wheel; wheel of Ixion

10 **science of rotation** or **rotary motion,** gyrostatics
  ▸ *Physics 10; Engineering 14*

ADJECTIVES

11 **rotating,** rotatory, revolving, gyrating, turning, orbiting, swiveling, pivoting; whirling, spinning, swirling, twirling, reeling, wheeling; rolling, trolling, bowling

12 **rotary,** rotational, rotatory, rotative, orbital, pivotal; circumrotatory, circumgyratory, gyratory, gyrational, gyroscopic, gyrostatic; centrifugal, centripetal, circling, cyclic, cyclical, circulatory, torsional, vortical, vorticose; cyclonic, tornadic

13 **dizzy,** giddy, vertiginous

VERBS

14 **rotate,** revolve, spin, turn, orbit, go around, go into orbit; circle, circulate, circuit, turn around, chase one's tail; spin like a top, twirl, pirouette; gyre, gyrate, circumnutate, circumvolve, circumvolute; swing *or* spin around, whirl, whirl like a dervish, wheel, pivot, swivel
  ▸ *Circularity 631; Orbital Motion 681*

15 **roll,** wind, roll up, fold, scroll, furl, reel; spin yarn, twist, screw, crank, yarn; wamble, roll along; bowl, trundle, troll, trill, set rolling

16 **swirl,** eddy, whirlpool, surge, gurge, seethe; mill around, stir, roil, moil, mix, fold
  ▸ *Mixture 751; Disturbance 768*

ADVERBS

17 **around,** in a circle, around and around, in circles, in a whirl, in a spin, head over heels

18 **clockwise,** counterclockwise, withershins *or* widdershins [Scot], anticlockwise
  ▸ *Circularity 631*

683 Oscillation

NOUNS

1 **oscillation,** alternation, harmonic motion, simple harmonic motion; pendular motion, swing, swing of the pendulum, pendulation; lunar motion, libration, nutation, reciprocation, periodicity; frequency, coming and going, shuttling, to-and-fro, ebb and flow, ups and downs, wax and wane, flux and reflux, systole and diastole, night and day
  ▸ *Parallelism 606; Frequency 661; Regularity 663; Reciprocity 729*

2 **vibration,** resonance, pulsation, rhythm, tempo, pulse, throb, beat, heartbeat, heartthrob, beating, throbbing; staccato, rat-a-tat, rataplan, drumming, flickering, shaking, quivering, shivering, palpitation, flutter, tremor, agitation, pitter-patter, pitapat, fibrillation, arrhythmia
  ▸ *Ill Health 114; Repeated Sound 235; Resonance 236; Fear 283; Agitation 684*

3 **vacillation,** wavering, equivocation, indecision, hesitation, irresolution, dubiety, mental fluctuation
  ▸ *Vacillation 378; Equivocation 380; Uncertainty 841*

4 **wave,** ray, transverse wave, longitudinal wave, electromagnetic wave *or* radiation, light, radio wave, sky

wave, mechanical wave, radiation, heat wave, acoustic wave, sound wave, sawtooth wave, square wave, sine wave; seismic wave, seismicity, earthquake, shock wave, tremor; de Broglie *or* matter wave; diffracted wave, guided wave, one- *or* two- *or* three-dimensional wave, node, antinode, surface wave, tidal wave, amplitude, crest, trough

5 **wavelength,** frequency, frequency band, frequency spectrum, resonance, resonant frequency, period, wave number, diffraction, reinforcement, interference, beat, wave equation, Schrödinger equation, Huygens' principle
  ◗ *Mathematics 6; Physics 10*

6 **measuring instrument,** oscilloscope, oscillograph, oscillometer, harmonograph, vibroscope, vibrograph, kymograph, seismoscope, seismograph, seismometer
  ◗ *Physics 10*

7 **oscillator,** bob, pendulum, vibrator, pendulum wheel, metronome, swing, seesaw, teetertotter, teeterboard, rocker, rocking chair, rocking horse, hobbyhorse, rocking stone, logan *or* loggan *or* logging stone, cradle, shuttlecock *or* shuttle
  ◗ *Furniture 101; Music 140; Timekeeping 646*

ADJECTIVES

8 **oscillating,** oscillatory, swinging, fluctuating, fluctuant, alternating, alternate, reciprocal, reciprocative, back-and-forth, to-and-fro, up-and-down, seesaw, periodical, harmonic, libratory, nutational

9 **vibrating,** vibratory, vibratile, resonant, pulsating, pulsatory, pulsatile, pulsing, pulsative, beating, throbbing, staccato, rhythmic, rhythmical, flickering, quivering, shivering, shaking, palpitating, palpitant

10 **vacillating,** vacillatory, wavering, hesitant, dithering

11 **waving,** undulating, undulatory, undulant, sinusoidal, sinuous, shaking, tremulous; seismic, seismatical, seismological, seismographic, seismometric

VERBS

12 **oscillate,** fluctuate, alternate, vary, swing, sway, move to and fro, pendulate, nutate, reciprocate, come and go, ebb and flow, wax and wane, ride and tie, hitch and hike, back and fill, seesaw, teeter, teetertotter, shuttle, shuttlecock, wigwag, zigzag, pass and repass, leapfrog
  ◗ *Frequency 661; Regularity 663; Reciprocity 729*

13 **vibrate,** resonate, pulsate, pulse, beat, beat time, drum, tick, ticktock, throb, flutter, agitate, shake, quiver, rattle, shiver, flicker, tremble, palpitate, pant, heave, go pitapat
  ◗ *Repeated Sound 235; Fear 283; Timekeeping 646; Motion 677; Agitation 684*

14 **vacillate,** waver, hesitate, fluctuate, dither
  ◗ *Vacillation 378; Uncertainty 841*

15 **wave,** undulate, wave to and fro, wave up and down
  ◗ *Propulsion 696; Display 843*

ADVERBS

16 **to and fro,** back and forth, backward and forward, in

and out, up and down, side to side, left to right, right to left, zigzag, seesaw, shuttlewise, from pillar to post
  ◗ *Orbital Motion 681; Rotation 682; Circularity 631*

684 Agitation

NOUNS

1 **agitation,** perturbation, perturbedness, mental agitation; uneasiness, disquiet, disquietude, inquietude, apprehension, worry, anxiety, nervousness, nerves, nervosity; jitteriness, jitters, edginess, jumpiness, jerkiness, restlessness, pacing, hand-wringing; discomposure, embarrassment; twitter, dither; [Inf]: flap, butterflies, heebie-jeebies, willies, collywobbles
  ◗ *Psychology and Psychiatry 108; Fear 283*

2 **tumult,** turmoil, commotion, racket, din, clamor, uproar, welter; stir, bustle, ado, moil, disturbance; hubbub, hurly-burly, rout, rush, furor, frenzy, fever, excitement, maelstrom, disorder, bobbery, brouhaha; confusion, disconcertment, chagrin, muddle
  ◗ *Anarchy 51; War 76; Argument 329; Disagreement 463; Disorder 766; Disturbance 768*

3 **turbulence,** turbidity, ferment, fermentation, effervescence, seethe, seething; swell, squall, swirl, choppiness, changeableness, pitching, rolling, joltiness, bumpiness; stir, churn, ebullition, boil, boiling, embroilment, roil, fume
  ◗ *Water 557; Seas 571; Disturbance 768*

4 **fuss,** bother, fluster, bluster, flurry, bustle, row, song and dance, to-do [Inf], tizzy [Inf]

5 **restlessness,** unrest, fever, feverishness, dancing, the fidgets, fidgetiness, hopping, twitchiness, itchiness, tossing and turning; jactation, jactitation, formication; pruritus, itching, ants in one's pants [Inf]
  ◗ *Psychology and Psychiatry 108; Ill Health 114; Boredom 296; Changeableness 666*

6 **shaking,** vibrating, quaking, quivering, quavering, shivering, shuddering, juddering [Brit], faltering, throbbing; trembling
  ◗ *Resonance 236*

7 **shake,** tremor, quiver, quake, wriggle, squirm; wag, waggle, wiggle; shudder, judder [Brit], alter, throb; delirium tremens *or* d.t.'s, shivers, cold shivers, rigor; ague, palsy, chorea *or* Huntington's chorea *or* St. Vitus's dance, parkinsonism *or* Parkinson's disease, the shakes [Inf]
  ◗ *Sex 20; Ill Health 114*

8 **spasm,** orgasm, ejaculation, climax; cramp, convulsion, paroxysm, fit, seizure, throes, the jerks; twitch, tic, nervous tic, rictus, vellication; attack, pang, access, grip; epilepsy *or* falling sickness, catalepsy, tarantism, frenzy, staggers, stroke *or* apoplexy, eclampsia
  ◗ *Ill Health 114*

9 **jolt,** jar, knock, tremor, shock; jerk, jump, sudden mo-

tion, start; bump, nudge, dig, jog, joggle, jostle, jounce; bounce, bob, bobbing, jig

10 beat, beating, throb, throbbing; thrill, frisson, palpitation, flutter; pitapat, pitter-patter

▶ *Sudden Sound 234; Repeated Sound 235; Repetition 797*

11 stagger, stumble, totter, falter, flounder, wallow, flounce; rock, roll, lurch, careen, swing, sway, pitch; toss, tumble, plunge

12 flicker, flutter, twinkle, flash, flit, waver, quiver, sputter

▶ *Oscillation 683*

13 atmospheric agitation, tempest, storm, swell, groundswell, squall, heavy sea; vortex, whirlwind, tornado, hurricane, disturbance; magnetic storm, atmospherics

▶ *Meteorology and Climatology 9*

14 agitator, shaker, vibrator, beater, jiggler; paddle, whisk; eggbeater, mixer, blender, food processor; churn

▶ *Rotation 682*

ADJECTIVES

15 agitated, perturbed, troubled, disturbed; nervous, edgy, uneasy, disquieted, apprehensive, worried, anxious, jittery, upset, unsteady; confused, ruffled, flurried, flustered, shaken, shaken up; shocked, stirred up, worked up; discomposed, embarrassed; troublous, hopping, leaping

16 restless, feverish, fevered; fidgety, itchy, unquiet, unpeaceful, twitchy, all aflutter, excited, flustered, fussing, fluttering, fluttery, hot and bothered [Inf], in a flap [Inf]; panting, breathless, giddy, in a spin

17 turbulent, choppy, rough, bumpy, bouncy, pitching, rolling; stormy, tempestuous; boiling, seething, fuming, effervescent

18 shaky, shaking, quaky, quaking, quivery, quivering, quavery, quavering, aspen; unsteady, doddering, shivery, shivering, shuddering, juddering [Brit], joggling; wriggling, wriggly, squirming, squirmy, wiggling, wiggly; faltering, trembling, tremulous, wobbly; successive, successatory; vibratory, vibrating, pulsating, throbbing

19 convulsive, jerky, twitchy, jolting, jarring, jolty, jumping, jumpy; palsied, fitful, spasmodic, paroxysmic, eclamptic, spastic, vellicative; orgasmic; saltatory; choreic, choreal, epileptic, cataleptic

20 flickering, flickery, sputtering, spluttering, guttering, sputtery, wavery

VERBS

21 be agitated, fuss, flap [Inf], flutter, twitter, dither; bustle, rush, mill around; jerk, jump, jump about, hop about, bounce, dance; ripple, effervesce, be in turmoil, bubble, ferment; foam at the mouth, seethe, simmer, boil, boil over; throw a fit, convulse, writhe, squirm, thresh, toss and turn, thrash about; rampage, be angry

▶ *Aggravation 276; Irascibility 303; Activity 414*

22 agitate, shake, wag, waggle, wave, flourish, brandish, fly a flag, flutter; fluster, perturb, disturb, discompose, upset, disquiet, worry, stir, ruffle, rumple, move, trouble; swirl, churn, whip, whisk, beat, paddle, mix; stir up, rile, work up, roil, beat up, churn up, whip up, excite, muddy the waters

23 jolt, shudder, shock, jar, jerk, twitch; bump, jog, joggle, jostle, jounce; bounce, bob, hustle, jump, judder [Brit]

▶ *Impulsion 695; Propulsion 696*

24 shake, vibrate, quake, quiver, quaver, tremble, shiver, falter, shudder; throb, drum, beat, pulse, thrill, pulsate, palpitate, go pitapat; twitter, fidget, twitch, jerk, itch, vellicate; jig, jiggle, shake in one's shoes *or* boots, shake like a leaf, have an ague; wriggle, squirm, wiggle, twist and turn, have ants in one's pants [Inf]

25 pitch, rock, wobble, waggle, totter, teeter, dither, stagger; swing, sway, lurch, swag, roll, reel, careen, plunge; toss and turn, toss and tumble, pitch and plunge, be the sport of wind and waves; flounder, founder, flounce, wallow, welter; stumble, falter, blunder, struggle, labor, thrash about

26 flicker, flutter, twinkle, flash; splutter, sputter, spatter, spit; flick, gutter, bicker, wave, waver, dance

ADVERBS

27 agitatedly, restlessly, uneasily, troublously, unquietly, unpeacefully; nervously, feverishly, in a dither, in a lather [Inf], in a tizzy [Inf]

28 shakily, quiveringly, tremulously, quakily, tremblingly, unsteadily, waveringly, all of a twitter

29 jerkily, convulsively, spasmodically, in fits, in spasms, by fits and starts; with a hop, skip, and a jump; by snatches, saltatorily; like a cat on hot bricks *or* a hot tin roof

685 Transfer

NOUNS

1 transfer, transference, transferral, translocation; transmittal, transmittance, transmigration; transposition, transposal, metathesis; transplantation, removal, relocation, moving, movement; removement, displacement, delocalization, deportation, expulsion, extradition; relegation, shift, shifting, transition; mutual transfer, interchange, trade, exchange, barter, swap; metempsychosis, transmigration of souls

▶ *Trade 480; Motion 677*

2 conveyance, conveying, transport, transshipment; dispatch, sending, mailing, posting [Brit]; export, exportation, import, importation; transit, transition, bridge, passage; vection; vecture; carriage, delivery, handover, haulage, hauling, cartage, portage, porterage; waft, waftage; truckage, drayage, ferriage, lighterage, telpherage *or* telferage, freightage, freight, wagonage [Arch]; expressage, railway express, air express, air freight, airlift; shipment, shipping

> *Transportation 686*

3 **transmission,** conduction, convection, osmosis, transpiration; diapedesis, transduction, transfusion, perfusion; decantation, dispersal; transmission of disease, contagion, infection, contamination; communication, contact, dissemination, spread, spreading, diffusion, dispersion, metastasis

> *Ill Health 114; Dispersion 776*

4 **transferrer,** conveyor *or* conveyer, conveyancer, testator [Form]; carrier, transporter, hauler, carter, drayman, common carrier; trucker, driver, truckdriver, bus driver, taxi driver, cabdriver, cabby [Inf], chauffeur, wagoner; boatman, gondolier, ferryman; importer, exporter; freighter, stevedore, cargo handler; bearer, porter, redcap, skycap, bellboy, page, busboy, litter bearer, stretcher-bearer; shield bearer, gun bearer; cupbearer, Ganymede, water carrier, water boy, Aquarius the Water Carrier; caddy; pallbearer; disease transferrer, infector, vector, transmitter, diffuser, contaminator

> *Ill Health 114; Transportation 686*

5 **messenger,** mail carrier, letter carrier, mailman, postman, expressman, courier, delivery man *or* person, pony express; carrier pigeon, homing pigeon; winged messenger, Mercury, Hermes, Iris

> *Communications 169*

6 **transferred thing,** passenger, fare; freight, freightage, consignment, shipment, goods, load, cargo, cargo load, payload; baggage, luggage, impedimenta, personal belongings; container, pack, backpack, knapsack, rucksack, shopping bag, handbag; message, mail, post [Brit], letter, card, postcard, telegram, telegraph; gift, security, trust, legacy, bequest, pledge; driftwood, flotsam, jetsam; sediment, silt, drift, alluvium, alluvion, loess, moraine, scree, sinter, detritus, debris; infectious disease, contagious disease

> *Geology 8; Contents 577; Container 578*

ADJECTIVES

7 **transferable,** transmittable, transmissible, transmissive, communicable; contagious, infectious, transfusable, importable, metastatic; metathetic, shifting; conveyable, mailable, consignable, conductive, conductional; interchangeable, exchangeable, negotiable; removable, movable, portable, portative, transportable, transportative, transportive, transposable, displaceable; carriageable, roadworthy, airworthy, seaworthy; infectious, contagious

VERBS

8 **transfer,** transmit; translocate, transpose, metathesize; transplant; consign, assign, turn over, hand over, make over, conduct; convect, radiate; transpire, transfuse, diffuse, perfuse, spread, disseminate, disperse, metastasize; infect, contaminate; strain, decant, siphon,

tap, funnel, channel; interchange, exchange, barter, swap, switch; shuffle, castle

9 **convey,** transport, take, freight, dispatch, send, send off *or* away, send forth; remit, consign; transmit, forward, expedite, ship, import, export, carry, deliver, hand over; bear, haul, cart, heave, pack, tote, lug, manhandle, push, propel, lift; waft, whisk, wing, fly, send flying; airlift, truck, bus, ferry, raft, barge, sledge, sled, schlep [Inf]; infect

10 **mail,** post [Brit], airmail, forward, express, airexpress, send; fax, telex, wire

11 **bring,** fetch, get, go and get, go after, go for, pick up, call for; procure, obtain, secure, retain, retrieve; disperse, bequeath, commit, assign, leave, entrust, hand on *or* down, pass on, scatter

12 **take away,** cart away, carry off *or* away, manhandle; set aside, lay *or* put aside, relegate, remove, relocate, move, displace; ladle, scoop, dip, bail, dish, spoon (out), shovel, spade, fork, dig; dislodge, unload, shift, shunt; deport, expel, eject, extradite

ADVERBS

13 **in transit,** en route, on *or* along the way, on the road, on the high seas, on the wing; as one goes, in passing, *en passant* [Fr], in midstream; by hand, by transfer, from door to door; by express, by rail, by special delivery, by remittance, from hand to hand, from pillar to post, conductively; interchangeably, exchangeably, contagiously, infectiously, communicably, metastatically

686 Transportation

NOUNS

1 **transportation,** transport, transfer, conveyance, transportation system; personal transportation, passenger transportation; commercial transportation, carriage, haulage, freightage, portage, shipment, transshipment, cartage, carting; distribution, forwarding, sending, loading, unloading, off-loading; intermodal transportation, containerization, palletization; road transportation, rail transportation, air transportation, water transportation

> *Motion 677; Transfer 685; Road Transportation 687; Rail Transportation 688; Aviation 689; Water Transportation 690; Passage 692*

2 **means of transportation,** vehicle, road vehicle; beast of burden, pack *or* draft animal, pack *or* draft horse, sumpter, cart horse, mule, donkey, camel, ox, sled dog, reindeer, llama, elephant; wagon train, mule train, stagecoach; walking, shanks' mare; people mover, moving sidewalk, driverless car, elevator, lift [Brit], escalator, paternoster, ski lift; automobile, car, truck, lorry [Brit], trailer, bus, taxi, van, bicycle, motorcycle; sleigh, sledge, sled, skis; train, airplane, plane, boat, ship, trolley; stretcher, litter, cart, carriage, perambu-

lator, shopping cart, tea wagon, dolly; skates, roller skates, in-line skates, skateboard, ice skates

> *Road Transportation 687; Rail Transportation 688; Aviation 689; Water Transportation 690*

3 freightage, freight, cargo, goods, lading, load, payload, consignment, shipment; mail, luggage, baggage; container, pallet

4 transporter, hauler, carter, drayman; shipper, conveyor, consignor, distributer; carrier, courier; loader, lader, unloader, consignee, docker, stevedore; trucker, driver, truckdriver, bus driver, taxi driver, cabdriver, cabby [Inf], chauffeur, wagoner; boatman, gondolier, ferryman; importer, exporter; freighter, cargo handler, lader; bearer, porter, redcap, skycap, bellboy, page, busboy, litter bearer, stretcher-bearer; shield bearer, gun bearer; cupbearer, water carrier, water boy, Ganymede, Aquarius; caddy; pallbearer

> *Transfer 685*

5 travel, traveling, journeying, touring; travels, journey, trip, voyage; wanderings, peregrination, tourism, sightseeing, odyssey; tour, excursion, jaunt, junket, outing, expedition, safari; commuting

> *Motion 677; Way 691; Passage 692*

6 traveler, tourer, tourist, journeyer, voyager; wanderer, peregrinator, sightseer; commuter, rider, passenger

ADJECTIVES

7 transportable, transported, movable, portable; roadworthy, airworthy, seaworthy; private, forwarded; freighted, laded, loaded, unloaded; door-to-door, urban, commercial; shipped, bused; biked; main, rural, farm, interstate, truck; railroad, passenger, express, freight, piggyback, elevated, monorail; air-cargo *or* cargo, airplane, short-range, medium-range, long-range, supersonic; waterborne, towed, towing, river, navigational, navigated, navigable, inland, canal, ocean, ocean-going, merchant, dry-cargo, container, oil; piped, pumped; pack, consigned

8 transporting, sending, shipping, carrying, forwarding, loading, lading, unloading, piping, pumping

9 traveling, journeying, touring, moving, wandering, peregrinating, sightseeing; commuting, riding

VERBS

10 transport, send, move, remove; haul, freight, cart, carry, distribute, deliver; ship, convey, consign, forward, dispatch, export; load, lade, unload, off-load; handle cargo; handle a consignment, transfer, transship, reship

> *Transfer 685*

11 travel, journey, adventure, tour, move, wander, peregrinate, sightsee; fly, sail, ride, commute

ADVERBS

12 commercially, door-to-door, hand-to-hand, by road, by rail, by train, by air, by water, by sea

> *Road Transportation 687; Rail Transportation 688; Aviation 689; Water Transportation 690*

687 Road Transportation

The car has become the carapace, the protective and aggressive shell, of urban and suburban man.
— MARSHALL McLUHAN

NOUNS

1 road transportation, road transport; foot transportation, animal transportation, motor transportation, driving, trucking, motor haulage

> *Transportation 686*

2 road, road system, route, highway, thoroughfare, freeway, toll road, turnpike, interstate highway, superhighway, expressway, beltway, ring road [Brit], arterial road; trunk road, feeder road, access road; motorway [Brit], A road [Brit], autobahn [Ger], *autoroute* [Fr], *autopista* [Sp], *autostrada* [Ital]; side road, country road, rural road, farm road, single track, dirt road *or* track

> *Way 691; Passage 692*

3 road attribute, lane, single-lane road, two-lane road; divided *or* dual highway, limited-access highway, dual carriageway [Brit]; slow lane, fast lane, passing lane, breakdown lane, escape lane, exit lane, ramp; corner, bend, curve, S-curve, hairpin bend, chicane, camber; intersection, T-junction, crossroads, cloverleaf *or* cloverleaf junction; rotary, traffic circle, roundabout [Brit]; filter, one-way system; lights, traffic lights, traffic signs; crossing, pedestrian crossing, zebra crossing [Brit]

> *Way 691*

4 road vehicle, wagon, cart, carriage, automobile, car, bus, truck, snow vehicle, bicycle, motorcycle

5 wagon, cart, wain, dray, van, caravan, covered wagon, prairie schooner, stagecoach; handcart, pushcart, dumpcart, barrow, handbarrow, wheelbarrow, baggage cart

6 automobile, auto, motorcar [Brit], (motor) vehicle; car, private car, family car, roadster, runabout, rattletrap, sedan, saloon [Brit], hatchback, coupe, station wagon, estate car [Brit], sports car, convertible, limousine; recreational vehicle (RV), camper, trailer; [Inf]: limo, stretch limo, buggy, wheels, jalopy, tin lizzie, crate, bomb, heap; police car, patrol car, squad car, prowl car, panda car [Brit], unmarked car; police van, patrol wagon, Black Maria, paddy wagon [Inf]; taxicab, taxi, cab, minicab [Brit], hackney *or* hackney cab, hack [Inf]

7 bus, omnibus, single-decker, double-decker, coach, motor coach, luxury coach, char-à-banc [Brit], electric bus *or* trolley bus

8 truck, cart, transporter, articulated vehicle, tractor, semitrailer, semi [Inf], tank truck; van, panel truck, lorry [Brit]

9 snow vehicle, sled, sledge, jumper, sleigh, toboggan, drag, dray, pung [Can]; dogsled, troika; snowmobile, bombardier [Can], skimobile, weasel

▶ *Skiing, Ice Skating, Bobsledding 162*

10 bicycle, two-wheeler, cycle [Brit], bike [Inf], wheel [Inf]; touring bike, racing bike; hybrid bike; mountain *or* off-road bike, all-terrain bike (ATB), velocipede; tandem bicycle; variations: monocycle, unicycle, tricycle, trike [Inf], quadricycle, pedicab *or* trishaw

11 bicycle part, frame, fork, crossbar, wheel, spoke, disk wheel; brake, coaster brake, brake block, rod brake, hand brake, cable brake, caliper brake, cantilever brake; crank, pedal, toeclip; bicycle chain, chainguard, gear, hub gear, derailleur; handlebars, drop handlebars, racing handlebars, straight handlebars; seat, saddle, saddlebag, pannier; kickstand, mudguard, mud flap; bicycle pump, bicycle clips

12 motorcycle, motorbike *or* motorbicycle *or* bike, motorscooter *or* scooter, minibike, moped; motorbike and sidecar; trail *or* dirt bike; chopper [Inf]

13 cyclist, bicyclist, motorcyclist, bike rider, motorcycle courier, bicycle courier, motocross racer, biker

14 miscellaneous automotive terms, air bag, antilock brake system (ABS), autocade, aquaplaning, automotive engineering, body shop, brake fade, carnet, carsickness, car wash, concours d'élégance, cornering, crash barrier, crashworthiness, cruise control, deathtrap, Denver boot, double clutch, double parking, downshift, driver's license, fade, fuel, garage, gasoline, gas, gearshift, grab, gridlock, hardstand, hit-and-run accident, hitchhiker, hot-wiring, jack, Jaws of Life™, jerrycan, jump start, knocking, license plate, lock, mechanic, mileage *or* milage, misfiring, motel, motion sickness, motorcade, nearside, no-claims bonus, overdrive, oversteer, overtaking, parking, parking brake, parking lot, parking meter, parking space, pile up, ping, piston slap, pit, pull in, push start, rack and pinion, registration, roadholding, road test, rustproofing, seat belt, service station, shimmy, sideslip, skid, slip, speed limit, speed trap, spin-out, stall, tailskid, tailspin, test drive, three-point turn, tow, traction, traction control system, traffic, traffic jam, turning circle, understeer, U-turn, vehicle identification number (VIN), weighbridge, wheelbase, wheel wobble

688 Rail Transportation

I like to see it lap up the Miles — / . . . And neigh like Boanerges — / Then punctual as a Star / Stop — docile and omnipotent / At its own stable door. — EMILY DICKINSON

NOUNS

1 railroad system, railroad, main line, railway [Brit]; rolling stock; trolley line, trolley car *or* trolley, streetcar, tram [Brit]; inclined railroad, cog *or* rack railroad, cable railway, cable car, funicular railway; monorail, scenic railroad; elevated railroad, elevated, el [Inf]; subway, underground railway, light-rail rapid-transit system *or* rapid transit, metro, underground [Brit], tube [Brit]

2 track, main line, up line, down line, section, branch line; spur *or* spur track, loop, siding, sidetrack, switch, lay-by [Brit]; cutting, embankment, grade, gradient post; crossing, grade crossing, level crossing [Brit]; signal, lights, semaphore, signal box, fog signal, highball, torpedo; water tower, water trough

3 rail, rails, tracks, metals; gauge, narrow gauge, standard gauge, broad gauge; roadbed, permanent way; ballast, tie, sleeper [Brit], joint bar, fishplate; frog, switch, crossover; turntable, buffer, end of the line

4 train, railroad train, passenger train, express, bullet train, local train, jerkwater train, milk train [Inf]; freight train, goods train [Brit]; locomotive, diesel engine, diesel-electric engine, electric motor, steam engine, steamer, iron horse [Arch]; doubleheader, switch engine *or* switcher, shunting engine *or* shunter [Brit], wildcat; choo-choo [Inf]

5 railroad car, car, day coach, carriage [Brit]; observation car, parlor car, Pullman™, sleeping car *or* sleeper, roomette; dining car, restaurant car [Brit]; baggage car, luggage van [Brit], caboose, mail car; freight car, boxcar, gondola, hopper car, flatcar, container car, piggyback car, rack car, refrigerator car, tank car; rail detector car

6 railroad station, station, depot; terminus, railhead, end of the line; main-line station, whistle stop; platform, bay; ticket office, waiting room, left-luggage office [Brit]; shed, yard, switchyard, snow shed

7 railroad worker, engineer, engine driver [Brit], fireman, motorman; conductor, ticket taker, security officer; switchman, signalman; station manager, stationmaster, ticket agent, porter; trackman, gandy dancer [Inf]

ADJECTIVES

8 rail, funicular, elevated; single-track, main, branch, express, local, coast-to-coast

VERBS

9 travel by train, ride, roll; climb aboard, alight, detrain; shunt

689 Aviation

More beautiful and soft than any moth / With burring furred antennae feeling its huge path / Through dusk, the air-liner with shut-off engines / Glides over suburbs . . .
— STEPHEN SPENDER

1 **aviation,** flying, flight, gliding; piloting, pilotage; aerial reconnaissance, air transportation, air travel; scheduled flight, sortie, air route, air corridor; air freight, air cargo, airmail, payload, airlift, airdrop, paradrop; mercy flight, flying doctor; flying circus, aerobatics, team aerobatics; crop-dusting, skywriting

2 **aeronautics,** aeronautical engineering, aircraft design, avionics, aerothermodynamics, aeroballistics

3 **aircraft,** airplane, plane, airliner, jet plane *or* jet airplane, jumbo jet, aeroplane [Brit]; subsonic transport, supersonic transport (SST); short takeoff and landing (STOL) craft, vertical takeoff and landing (VTOL) craft; helicopter; glider, hang glider; lighter-than-air craft, balloon, hot-air balloon, helium balloon, dirigible, blimp, zeppelin; [Inf]: copter, chopper, eggbeater

4 **airport,** airfield, airbase, air station, airdrome, aerodrome [Brit]; airstrip, landing strip, landing field; terminal, ramp, apron, hardstand, hangar, control tower, taxiway, runway, flight line

5 **flight,** takeoff, liftoff, rollout, climb, flight level, flight formation; airspeed, groundspeed, heading, headwind, tailwind, terminal velocity; ceiling, aeropause, absolute ceiling; descent, approach, flare, glide path, landing, touchdown, run roll; belly-landing, pancake landing, three-point landing; overflight, overshoot, undershoot, crash-landing

6 **flight maneuver,** bank, banking, barrel roll, chandelle, crab, dive, figure eight, flat spin, flutter, heaving, hedgehopping, hunting, Immelmann *or* Immelmann turn, loop, looping the loop, low-level flying, nosedive, pitching, roll, rolling, shock stall, sideslip, skidding, snap roll, soaring, spin, spiral, stall, stalling, turn, vector in flight (VIF), vectoring, victory roll, whipstall, wingover, yawing, zooming

7 **flight control,** ground control, air-traffic control, radar beacon, airborne early warning (AEW), airport surface detection equipment (ASDE), fly-by-wire, fly-by-light, landing beam, standard beam approach (SBA), ground-controlled approach (GCA), talkdown; loran, instrument landing system (ILS), NAVSTAR Global Positioning System (GPS), Teleran™; traffic pattern, stack, stacking, holding

8 **aircraft personnel,** aviator, flyer, pilot, airline pilot, glider pilot, helicopter pilot, test pilot; crew, air crew, captain, copilot, first officer, flight engineer, navigator, observer; flight attendant, purser, steward, stewardess, air hostess; ground crew, ground engineer, air-traffic controller

9 **miscellaneous aviation terms,** air flow, air miss, air pocket, airsickness, angle of bank, angle of incidence, bird strike, boarding pass, dihedral, deicing, dip, downdraft, downwash, drag, drift, driftage, feathering, flameout, flyby, footprint, gremlin, hookup, icing, jet lag, lift, load factor, loading, microburst, moment, rake, reheating, skyjacking, slipstream, spread, sweepback, trim, turbulence, clear-air turbulence, washing, wind shear, wind tunnel, wing loading, wingspan

ADJECTIVES

10 **aviatic,** aviation, aerial, aeronautic, aeronautical, aerospace; aerobatic, aeromechanical, aeromedical; aeroballistic, aerodynamic, aerothermodynamic, avionic; air-traffic, air-transportable, airlift

11 **flying,** rolling, taking off, airborne, climbing, cruising, soaring, gliding, hovering, descending, approaching, landing, touching down, braking, taxiing, parking

12 **flyable,** flightworthy, airworthy; propeller, prop, jet, turbojet, pulsejet; subsonic, supersonic, hypersonic; heavier-than-air, lighter-than-air, hot-air

VERBS

13 **fly,** roll, take off, lift off, climb, gain altitude, cruise, soar, hover, descend, approach, land, touch down, brake, taxi, park; sail, glide, drift, float; go supersonic, break the sound barrier; board, take a flight, travel by air

14 **maneuver,** become *or* be airborne, pull up, nose up, nose down, push down; bank, roll, crab, dive, spin, flutter, heave, hunt, loop, nosedive, pitch, sideslip, skid, spiral, stall, turn, zoom; overfly, overshoot, undershoot, crash-land

15 **pilot,** fly, control, copilot, navigate, crew; trim, feather; fly the corridor, hold, fly the beam, fly on instruments; solo, qualify

16 **service,** hook up, load, deice; assign, clear, stack, divert, talk down

ADVERBS

17 **aeronautically,** aerodynamically, subsonically, supersonically; in flight, on instruments, on the beam, by ground control

690 Water Transportation

NOUNS

1 **water transportation,** shipping, boating, sailing, rowing; sea travel, seafaring, cruising; sea trip, boat trip, voyage, voyaging, passage, crossing; river travel, canal travel; inland navigation, navigation, circumnavigation

2 **waterway,** navigable water, sea *or* shipping lane, seaway, ocean track, steamer route, crossing, ferry crossing; inland waterway, river, lake, canal, cut

3 **vessel,** ship, boat, craft; pleasure boat, yacht; passenger ship, merchant ship, fishing boat, warship
   ◗ *Boating Sports 150*

4 **shipbuilding,** ship design, naval architecture, naval engineering; ship *or* boat materials: wood, steel, medium steel, high-tensile steel, special-treatment steel, aluminum alloy, fiberglass, carbon fiber, reinforced concrete *or* ferroconcrete; ship specifications, structural design, structural model, structural test;

launching, launching ceremony, christening; ship-building contract, shipyard

▶ *Structure 551; Form 624*

5 **navigation,** celestial navigation, astronavigation, inertial navigation, compass reading, piloting, pilotage, pilotship; helmsmanship, seamanship, steering; plane sailing, spherical sailing, great-circle sailing, parallel sailing; dead reckoning, dead-reckoning position, estimated position, plotting

6 **navigational aid,** sailing aid, navigational instrument; marine sextant, sextant, quadrant, angular measure, ephemeris; traverse table, log, ship's log; towed log, submerged log, knotmeter log; lead, line, lead line, depth sounder; compass, ship's compass, magnetic compass, gyrocompass *or* gyroscopic compass, needle, magnetic needle, card, compass card *or* rose, binnacle; chronometer, ship's chronometer, ship's timekeeper; chart, National Ocean and Atmospheric Administration (NOAA) chart, Admiralty chart [Brit], nautical almanac; directional reference, bearing

7 **sea marker,** buoy, nun, can, sonobuoy, bell, gong, whistle, daybeacon; lighthouse, pharos, lightship, light station, fog signal

8 **position finder,** radio direction finder (RDF), radiobeacon station, automatic direction finder (ADF), goniometer; loran, decca [Brit]; radar, navigational radar, sonar; navigational satellite *or* NAVSAT Transit system, NAVSTAR Global Positioning System (GPS), Emergency Position-Indicating Radio Beacon (EPIRB)

9 **ship's steering,** helm, wheel, tiller, rudder, steering oar

10 **navigation laws,** rules of the road, rules of the sea

11 **nautical speed,** ship's speed, speed through the water, speed over the bottom, knot *or* nautical mile per hour, log-line knot

12 **nautical person,** naval officer, sailor, coastguardsman; mariner, seafarer, seafaring man *or* woman, circumnavigator; master mariner, master, ship's master, sailing master, quartermaster; captain, skipper, navigator, pilot, helmsman, steersman, wheelman, man at the wheel; ship's steward, boatswain *or* bosun, bosun's mate, coxswain *or* cox, shipmate *or* mate, deckhand *or* hand, leadsman, lookout, foretopman, reefer, cabin boy, (ship's) crew, (ship's) complement, watch; sea scout, sea cadet [Brit]; fair-weather sailor; salt, old salt, sea dog, sea rover, hearty, jack-tar; boatman, water-

SHIPS AND BOATS

accommodation ship	dinghy	keelboat	pontoon	skin boat
aircraft carrier	diving boat	launch	post-boat [Brit]	slaver *or* slave ship
amphibious landing craft	dragger	Liberty ship	powerboat	smack
ark	dredger	lifeboat	prison ship	steamboat
banana boat	drifter *or* drift boat	lighter	privateer	steamer
barge	dugout	lightship *or* light vessel	PT (patrol torpedo) boat *or* mosquito	steamship
bateau	escort carrier *or* escort ship	longboat	boat *or* motor	submarine
battleship	faltboat *or* foldboat	longliner	torpedo boat	submarine chaser *or* subchaser
bulk carrier	ferry	longship	punt	supertanker
bullboat	fishing boat	mailboat	Q-ship	surf boat
bumboat	flagship	medical ship	racing boat	swamp boat
cabin cruiser	flatboat	merchantman *or*	raft	tanker
caïque	floatel	merchant ship *or*	refrigeration ship	tender
canal boat	freighter	merchant vessel	research vessel	torpedo boat
canoe	galley	motorboat	revenue cutter	towboat
cargo liner	gig	motor yacht	roll-on roll-off	tramp steamer
cockboat *or* cockleboat	gondola	ocean liner	rowboat	transport ship
cockleshell	guard boat	oiler	runabout	trawler
collier	gunboat	oil tanker	sampan	troopship
containership	houseboat	outboard	scallop boat *or* scalloper	tugboat *or* tug
convict ship	hovercraft	outrigger	school ship	umiak
convoy ship	hoy	packet boat *or* packet ship	scow	warship
coracle	hydrofoil	paddleboat	scull	weather ship
crabber	icebreaker *or* iceboat	paddle steamer	sealer	whaleboat
cruiser	inboard	patrol boat	seiner	whaler
currach *or* curagh *or* curragh	inflatable	pilot *or* pilot boat	shell	wherry
cutter	ironclad	pinnace	ship's boat	workboat
destroyer	jet boat *or* jetboat	piragua *or* pirogue	shrimper *or* shrimp boat	votive ship
	jolly boat	pirate ship	skiff	
	kayak *or* kaiak			

man, yachtsman *or* yachtswoman, canoeist, paddler, rower, oarsman *or* oar, sculler, galley slave, punter, gondolier, ferryman, wherryman [Brit], bargeman, [Inf]: tar, gob, swabby

▶ *Boating Sports 150*

13 **marine scientist,** shipbuilder, ship designer, naval architect

ADJECTIVES

14 **nautical,** naval, marine, seafaring, seaworthy, sea-going, ocean-going, at the helm, on board, deep-sea, at sea, on the high seas; seaborne, floating, afloat, launched, aquatic, waterborne, salty; sailing, steaming, plying, ferrying, coasting; rolling, pitching, tossing, wallowing, yawing; like a sailor, sailorly, sailor-like, seamanlike, able-bodied, able; fishing, trawling, dragging, seining; seasick, green; buoyant, fleet, water; shipping, boating, yachting, rowing, cruising; ocean, offshore, bay, coastal, river, canal, inland; ship-building

VERBS

15 **navigate,** circumnavigate; dead-reckon, plot, chart, take a sun *or* moon sight, record one's GPS *or* loran position, take one's bearings; captain a ship, pilot a ship; steer, hold the helm, man a ship, crew, ship out; sail, set sail, launch, push off, cast off, boom off, unmoor, get under way, get up steam, raise steam, put to sea; set a course, hold a course, head for, make way, gather way, carry sail; read the chart, go by the card, take soundings, heave the lead, read the depth sounder; run before the wind, scud, fall to leeward, pay off, put the helm down, head into the wind; change course, reverse course, veer, back, go astern, regress, crab, put about, tack, weather, back and fill, wear, jibe, yaw; race, cross one's bows, outmaneuver, gain the weather gauge, foul, collide

▶ *Boating Sports 150*

16 **sail,** set sail, heave to, lie to, lay to, bring to rest; surface, break water, flood the tanks, dive, plunge; run for port, weather the storm, ride out the storm, ride, ride on an even keel; keep afloat, list, heel over, keel over, overturn, capsize, careen, turn turtle; ground, run aground, wreck, be cast away; sight land, make a landfall; land, make port, drop anchor, cast anchor, wedge, warp, draw, moor, tie up, dock; disembark; get one's sea legs

ADVERBS

17 **nautically,** at sea, on the high seas, afloat, like a sailor; under way, under sail, under steam; before the mast, on board, on deck, on the bridge, on the quarterdeck, at the helm, at the wheel

691 Way

NOUNS

1 **way,** ways and means, mode, manner, wise, means, form; method, methodology, system, technique, procedure, process; proceeding, modus operandi, line, line of action, order, method of operation (MO), manner of working, way of doing things; practice, skill, know-how, conduct, algorithm, approach, tack, line of attack, tactic, tactics; routine, drill, operation, working arrangement, usual way; fashion, style, tone, guise; progress, progression, way of life, modus vivendi, behavior

▶ *Means 102; Order 765*

2 **route,** itinerary, course, track, trail; circuit, round, beat, walk, turn, tour, loop; direction, way to; way in, way out, way through, way over; crossing; line, march, beaten track, beat, road, run, trajectory, orbit; lane, traffic lane, flight lane, sea *or* shipping lane; primrose path, path of least resistance; detour, shortcut; line of advance, line of retreat

▶ *Deviation 698*

3 **access,** means of access, right of way, approach, direct approach; doorway, door, entrance, front door, back door, side door, adit; drive, path, garden path; gangway, gangplank, passage, aisle; staircase, flight of stairs, step, tread, stepladder, ladder, fireman's ladder

---

SAILING SHIPS AND BOATS

advice boat	catboat	galleon	lugger	sailer
bark *or* barque	clipper *or* clipper ship	hermaphrodite brig	merchantman *or*	sailing dinghy
barkentine *or*	convoy ship	or brigantine	merchant ship	schooner
barquentine	corsair	hoy	monohull	shallop
barketta	corvette	iceboat	multihull	ship's boat
bomb ketch *or*	cutter	Indiaman	pink	skiff
bombard *or* mortar	dhow	jackass bark *or* four-	pinnace	slave ship *or* slaver
ketch	dromond *or* dromon	masted brig	piragua	sloop
brig	escort ship	jackass brig	pirate ship	sloop of war
bugeye	felucca	jolly boat	privateer	square-rigger
caïque	fire ship	junk	proa *or* prao	tall ship
caravel *or* carvel	frigate	keelboat	razee	trimaran
carrack	full-rigger	ketch	sailboard	windjammer
catamaran	galiot	lateen	sailboat	xebec *or* zebec

▸ *Transportation 686; Road Transportation 687; Rail Transportation 688; Aviation 689; Water Transportation 690; Entry 706*

4 road, highway; street, drive, avenue, boulevard, thoroughfare, lane; alley, blind alley, alleyway, cul-de-sac, dead end
  ▸ *Road Transportation 687*

5 passage, passageway, path, pathway, footpath, footway, sidewalk, by-path, side path; towpath, bridle path, bicycle *or* cycle path; track, racetrack, racecourse; trail, hiking trail, rut, groove; arcade, colonnade, covered way, gallery, portico, aisle, cloister, triforium, loggia, ambulatory; mall, promenade, esplanade, parade, *prado* [Sp], sea front
  ▸ *Passage 692*

6 tunnel, underpass, subway, railroad tunnel, Channel Tunnel, Chunnel

7 bridge, span, viaduct, aqueduct, overpass, footbridge; suspension bridge, cantilever bridge, humpback bridge, arched bridge; railroad bridge, floating bridge, pontoon bridge, Bailey bridge, drawbridge; steppingstones, catwalk, rope bridge; toll bridge, covered bridge; Bifrost
  ▸ *Engineering 14*

8 railroad, railway [Brit], subway; track, line, railroad line, turnout, switchback, gauge, standard gauge

9 junction, turntable, grade crossing, embankment, trestle, cutting, sidetrack, siding, railroad yard
  ▸ *Rail Transportation 688*

10 channel, canal, conduit, inlet, outlet, culvert, strait, dike *or* dyke, ditch, sewer; waterway, watercourse, stream, river, navigable river, estuary; lock
  ▸ *Rivers 570*

11 cableway, cable railway, funicular (railway); monorail, telpherage *or* telferage, telpherage line; ski lift, chair lift, gondola, aerial tramway
  ▸ *Rail Transportation 688*

12 flight path, flight lane, air lane *or* skyway, air route, airway, air corridor; landing field, runway; launching site, blastoff, trajectory, orbit, earth orbit, parking orbit, docking, reentry, splashdown
  ▸ *Aviation 689*

ADJECTIVES

13 accessible, through, connecting, connected, communicating; linked, bridged, spanned, arched; main, paved, cobbled, well-paved, well-laid, smooth, skidproof; signposted, marked, signaled; well-lit, lit, floodlit, well-used, busy, crowded, overcrowded, jammed; beaten, trodden; bumper to bumper

VERBS

14 find a way, find means, make a way, have a method, do things the usual way; proceed, operate, work
  ▸ *Means 102*

15 find one's way, have a route, draw up an itinerary; approach; take to the road, come to a crossroads; detour, short-cut, take a shortcut, bypass, go around;

cross the street, use a footpath, cross the bridge; enter, use the entrance; take the train, take a plane, fly; blast off, orbit, splash down; come to the end of the line, reach one's destination

ADVERBS

16 how, in this way, after this fashion, along these lines, on the lines of, thus, so, as, like; anyway, anyhow, anywise, by any (manner of) means, in any event, in any case, at any rate; nevertheless, nonetheless, however, regardless, at all; somehow, in some way or other, by some means, somehow or other, in one way or another, after a fashion, no matter how, by hook or by crook, by fair means or foul

17 via, by way of, through, by, over, around, here and there, all through; toward, in the direction of, to, up, on, upon against, over against, on the way, on the road, in transit to, en route to *or* for, on route to, in passage to

692 Passage

NOUNS

1 passage, section, portion, article; selection, excerpt, extract, analects, quotation, citation; paragraph, verse, line, sentence, clause; phrase, measure, strain, bar; verse, stanza, division
  ▸ *Literature 139; Music 140*

2 adoption, authorization, passage, ratification; permission, allowance, grant, warrant, license
  ▸ *Authority 52; Permission 502*

3 passing, passage, movement, transit; transition, transmission, transference, transduction, transfusion, transilience; crossing, traversing, traverse; transportation, journey, voyage, trip
  ▸ *Motion 677; Transfer 685; Transportation 686*

4 passage into, entrance, entry, ingress, penetration, interpenetration, intervention; infiltration, transudation, permeation, percolation, osmosis, endosmosis
  ▸ *Entry 706*

5 passing along, walking, driving, riding, cycling, sailing, flying; perambulation, patrol, round, beat; traffic, circulation, traffic flow, traffic pattern, traffic load, traffic jam
  ▸ *Transportation 686*

6 thoroughfare, road, highway, motorway [Brit], lane, passing lane; track, railroad track, sea *or* shipping lane, channel; route, diversion, detour, alternative route; pass, passageway, access, approach, right of way; path, pathway, footpath, steppingstones, bike path
  ▸ *Transportation 686; Way 691*

7 crossing point, crossing, intersection, junction, crossroads, level crossing [Brit], checkpoint; ford, overpass, bridge, viaduct, underpass, tunnel; pedestrian crossing, school crossing

▸ *Engineering 14; Interweaving 609*

8 passport, visa, pass, safe conduct, laissez-passer, clearance, clearance papers, documentation, permit

ADJECTIVES

9 excerpted, selected, extracted, quoted, cited

10 adopted, authorized, passed, ratified; permitted, allowed, granted, warranted, licensed
▸ *Authority 52; Permission 502*

11 passing, overtaking, moving, proceeding, in transit; transitional, transilient; transmitting, transferring, transducing; crossing, traversing, transporting
▸ *Transfer 685; Transportation 686*

12 penetrating, entering, intervening; infiltrating, transudating, permeating, percolating, osmotic, intervening

VERBS

13 excerpt, select, extract, quote, cite

14 adopt, authorize, pass, ratify; permit, allow, grant, warrant, license
▸ *Authority 52; Permission 502*

15 pass, pass by, flash by, overtake, get past, leave on one side, skirt; pass through, get through, move through, shoot through, come out the other side

16 proceed, go, move along; travel, journey, voyage; circulate, patrol, perambulate, make rounds
▸ *Motion 677*

17 cross, traverse, transit, negotiate, go across, cross over, make a crossing, reach the other side; ford, wade across, step over, bridge; transmit, transfer, translate; carry across, move across, transport, convey, hand over
▸ *Transfer 685; Transportation 686*

18 enter, enter into, penetrate, interpenetrate, intervene; infiltrate, permeate, percolate, osmose, soak through; open a way, force a passage, elbow through, worm one's way in
▸ *Way 691; Entry 706*

ADVERBS

19 passably, acceptably, tolerably, allowingly

20 by the way, in passing, *en passant* [Fr], via, by way of, en route; in transit, transitionally, through, across

693 Slowness

Slow and steady wins the race. — AESOP

NOUNS

1 slowness, leisureliness, unhurriedness, lack of haste, no hurry, drawling; sluggishness, languor, lethargy, inertia, slackness, pokiness [Inf]; sloth, laziness, indolence, inertness, dilatoriness, wasting time; methodicalness, patience, deliberation, deliberateness, circumspection; gradualism, Fabianism, leisurely progress; meticulousness, restraint; time to spare, easy stages

▸ *Carefulness 325; Inactivity 415; Inertness 519*

2 deceleration, brake, curb, restraint, friction, retardation, retardment; slackening, flagging, slowing down *or* up, easing off *or* up, negative *or* minus acceleration

3 slow motion, leisurely gait, walk, amble, stroll, saunter, dawdle; low gear, dragging, lumbering, creeping, snail's pace; creep, crawl, pace, trudge, waddle, slouch, shuffle, plod, limp, hobble, shamble; trot, dogtrot, jog trot, jog, single-foot *or* rack; mincing steps
▸ *Restraint 830*

4 lingering, lagging, dawdling, loitering, dallying, dalliance, dillydallying, shilly-shallying, lallygagging *or* lollygagging [Inf], goofing off [Inf]

5 hesitation, tentativeness, caution, cautiousness, reluctance, foot-dragging, tardiness, procrastination, unwillingness; standing start, slow start; delay, holdup, slowdown, go-slow [Brit], work-to-rule, detention, setback, check, arrest, obstruction; hysteresis
▸ *Caution 287*

6 plodder, slow person, lingerer, loiterer, sloth, tortoise, snail, dawdler; laggard, sloucher, slacker, foot-dragger, idler, procrastinator, slug, sluggard, stick-in-the-mud, drone, slow starter, sleepyhead; [Inf]: slowpoke, goof-off, goldbrick

ADJECTIVES

7 slow, slow-moving, slow-paced, slow-footed, slow-running; ambling, strolling, sauntering, lumbering, easy-paced, tardigrade, snail-paced, snail-like; faltering, flagging, slow-as-slow, slow as death, creeping, crawling, walking, dragging, waddling, shuffling, plodding, limping, halting, hobbling, shambling, tottering, staggering, poking, poky [Inf]
▸ *Lack of Motion 678*

8 unhurried, leisurely, sluggish, languorous, lethargic, inert; slack, slothful, languid, lazy, indolent, sluggardly; listless, idle, apathetic, phlegmatic; methodical, patient, deliberate, circumspect, gradual, Fabian, meticulous, restrained; easy, moderate, gentle, relaxed, taking one's time; imperceptible, stealthy
▸ *Inactivity 415; Inertness 519*

9 hesitant, tentative, cautious, reluctant, lagging, dawdling, drawling, procrastinating, unwilling, slow off the mark, groping, foot-dragging
▸ *Caution 287*

10 delayed, held up, detained, checked, arrested, obstructed, impeded, set back; slowed down, retarded, restrained, slack, backward; behind, late, tardy, hysteretic, dilatory; lingering, dawdling, loitering, dallying, dillydallying, shilly-shallying, lallygagging *or* lollygagging [Inf]
▸ *Hindrance 826*

VERBS

11 move slowly, walk slowly, barely move, go slow *or* slowly, go at a snail's pace, amble, saunter, march in slow time, take it easy, stroll, get nowhere fast [Inf], laze, creep, crawl, inch along, ease along; trickle, ooze, drip; idle, go dead slow; shuffle *or* stagger *or* poke along, wobble, totter *or* toddle along; scuff, take short steps, mince; plod, trudge, shamble, plod *or* stump along; jog, dogtrot; limp, hobble; *festina lente* [L]; [Inf]: traipse, mosey along *or* on, mooch around

▶ *Motion 677*

12 **hesitate,** barely move, grope *or* feel one's way, show caution; speak slowly, drawl; pause, falter, flag; dawdle, linger, loiter, tarry, hover, hang over; delay, dally, waste time, dillydally, shilly-shally, lag, drag, drag one's feet, take one's time, run out of steam, go lame, trail; halt, not get started; lallygag *or* lollygag [Inf], goof off [Inf]

▶ *Caution 287; Vacillation 378; Uncertainty 841*

13 **slow down,** slow up, slow, let up, ease off, slacken *or* slack off, relax, moderate; lose speed, reduce speed, lose momentum, decelerate; retard, delay, detain, impede, arrest, obstruct, hinder, stay, check, curb, hold back, keep back, set back, hold in check, rein in, draw rein; throttle down, take one's foot off the gas, reef, take in sail, shorten sail, back-pedal, clip the wings; brake, put on the drag, lose ground, reverse, regress

▶ *Backward Motion 680; Hindrance 826; Restraint 830*

ADVERBS

14 **slowly,** slow, leisurely, unhurriedly, patiently, easily; moderately, gently; adagio, largo, andante; languidly, sluggishly, languorously, lazily, idly, indolently, lingeringly; dilatorily, loiteringly, haltingly, falteringly; cautiously, deliberately, circumspectly, tentatively, reluctantly; gradually, by degrees, inch by inch, little by little, step by step, bit by bit, by easy stages

▶ *Music 140*

15 **in slow motion,** creepingly, crawlingly, pokingly, pokily [Inf], at a slow pace, at a snail's pace, at a funeral pace, in low gear, at half speed

694 Swiftness

In skating over thin ice, our safety is in our speed.
— RALPH WALDO EMERSON

NOUNS

1 **swiftness,** speed, speediness, velocity, quickness, fastness, fleetness, promptness, promptitude, rapidity, celerity; quick *or* round *or* smart *or* snappy *or* rattling pace, briskness, rapid tempo, fast rate *or* motion, speeding, driving, hard driving, racing, bowling along; dispatch, expedition, expeditiousness, precipitation; hastiness, haste, rashness, hurry, flurry, no loss of time, instantaneity, instantaneousness; agility, nimbleness; career, full career, full pelt, full sail, press of sail, great speed, wide-open speed, blue streak, spanking rate, good *or* fair clip; [Inf]: lick, flat-out speed, nifty pace,

making tracks, barreling along, burning rubber, scorching

2 **speed,** speed of light; speed of sound, sonic speed, sound barrier, subsonic *or* supersonic *or* ultrasonic *or* hypersonic speed; escape velocity; express speed, utmost *or* full *or* top *or* maximum speed, lightning speed; excessive speed, dangerous *or* breakneck *or* reckless speed, illegal speed; speed trap, radar trap; rate of speed: airspeed, groundspeed, miles per hour (mph), kilometers per hour (kph), revolutions per minute (rpm), knot, mach *or* mach number

▶ *Measurement 589*

3 **acceleration,** quickening, speed-up, spurt, burst, burst of speed, burst of energy, thrust, drive, impetus, impulse; jump, spring, bound, pounce, leap; swoop, zoom, dive, power dive; flying start, getaway, rush, headlong rush, headlong plunge, dash, scamper, run, sprint, canter, gallop, tantivy; overtaking, passing, lapping; whiz, zing, zap [Inf], zip [Inf]

4 **quickness of mind,** quick-wittedness, quick study; speed of thought, alacrity, mental quickness, mental agility, brightness, liveliness

▶ *Intellect 315*

5 **speeder,** swift person, runner, sprinter, harrier, speedster, racer, racing driver, Jehu, hustler, courser, courier, messenger, express messenger, speed demon *or* maniac [Inf], scorcher [Inf]

ADJECTIVES

6 **swift,** fast, quick, rapid, fleet, speedy, speeding, swift-moving, high-speed, high-velocity, expeditious; hurried, hasty; double-quick, rapid-fire; alacritous, prompt, sudden, early, immediate, instantaneous, hair-trigger; express, meteoric, jet-propelled, faster than sound, supersonic, hypersonic, ultrasonic; high-geared, streamlined; fleet of foot, light-footed, nimble-footed, nimble, agile, volant, quick-footed, wing-footed; winged, eagle-winged, like an eagle, like a bird; headlong, tempestuous, breakneck, precipitate, precipitous; quick as lightning, quick as a flash, quick as a wink, quick as the wind, faster than a speeding bullet; [Inf]: quick on the draw, quick on the trigger, like greased lightning, zippy, go-go, souped-up, hopped-up

7 **speeding,** darting, dashing, wasting no time, hustling, hurrying, running, charging; racing, galloping, cantering; flying, hurtling, whirling, pelting, rattling, whizzing, flashing, spanking, barreling along [Inf], scorching [Inf]

▶ *Immediacy 645; Motion 677; Impulsion 695; Propulsion 696; Haste 818*

8 **mentally quick,** quick-thinking, quick-witted, nimble-witted, snappy, smart, bright, lively, brisk, vigorous; mercurial, quicksilvery; reckless, rash

▶ *Rashness 286; Intellect 315*

9 **accelerating,** accelerated, quickening, speeding up, getaway; overtaking, passing, lapping

10 be swift, move fast, drive quickly, speed, run, lope, race, chase, hurtle; bowl along, tear along, tear up the road, sweep along, scoot, charge, stampede; ride hard, gallop, canter, trot; expedite, precipitate, cut and run; break the speed limit, fly, wing, burn up the miles, move at the speed of sound, break the sound barrier, move at the speed of light; storm along, thunder along, rattle along, streak, flit, zoom, zing, whiz, hustle; lunge, spring, bound, leap, jump, pounce, swoop, dive, plunge, hie; [Inf]: skedaddle, get a move on, get cracking, step on it, hotfoot it, make tracks, rip along, barrel along, burn rubber, put the hammer down, zip, zap along, scorch, haul *or* shag ass

11 travel at maximum speed, go full tilt *or* full pelt *or* full steam, go all out, go full bat [Brit inf]

12 scamper, scuttle, scurry, rush, dash, hasten, hurry, career, careen, whisk, skirr

13 run, run like a shot *or* like the wind *or* like wildfire; run like a hare *or* like a scared rabbit; run like *or* in a flash; run like lightning *or* a streak of lightning *or* a streak *or* a blue streak; run like the devil, run like a house on fire *or* afire; [Inf]: run like greased lightning, run like sixty, run like mad *or* crazy, run like a bat out of hell, pour it on, highball it, ball the jack
  ◗ *Haste 818*

14 accelerate, quicken, gather speed, speed up, pick up speed; put on speed, spurt, sprint, burst ahead, have a burst of speed, have a burst of energy; gather momentum, impart momentum; step up the pace, raise the tempo, open the throttle; thrust ahead, flash by, whiz by, dash forward, dart off; set off at a run, get off to a flying start; make up time, make up for lost time; bolt, jump ahead, spring forward, spring, bound forward; leave standing, leave at the starting post, run away; gain on, overtake, overhaul, catch up with, make the running; pass, lap, shake off, lose someone, leave behind, romp home, win the race; outdistance, outrun, outpace, outstrip, outmarch, outsail, outdrive, outclass, outdo; [Inf]: get a move on, step on it, let it rip, step on the gas, open up, tear off

15 hurry someone up, hasten, urge on *or* forward, drive, spur, chevy *or* chivy [Brit], put dynamite *or* a bomb under [Inf]
  ◗ *Impulsion 695; Haste 818*

ADVERBS

16 swiftly, quickly, rapidly, expeditiously, fleetly, apace, speedily, snappily; wide open, headlong; with giant strides, with giant leaps, on eagle's wings; roundly, smartly; on *or* at the double, double-quick, in double-time *or* double-quick time, in no time, in nothing flat, as soon as possible (ASAP); by leaps and bounds; meteorically, supersonically, hypersonically, ultrasonically, in high gear; nimbly, agilely, as fast as one's legs can carry one, amain [Arch]; [Inf]: lickety-split, pronto, before one can say Jack Robinson, hell-for-leather, pretty damn quick (PDQ)

17 at full speed, at full throttle, full speed ahead, at one's top speed, at full tilt, at full blast, in full sail, in full career, in high gear, under full steam, for all one is worth; in full gallop, with whip and spur; all out, flat out [Inf]

18 hurryingly, posthaste, hastily, promptly, presto, prestissimo, allegro; suddenly, immediately, instantaneously
  ◗ *Music 140; Haste 818*

695 Impulsion

Give me a firm place to stand, and I will move the earth.
  — ARCHIMEDES

NOUNS

1 impulsion, impulse, impellent, impelling force, impetus, momentum, moment; moment of force; force, irresistible force, driving force, power, motive power, propulsion; compulsion, incentive, incitement; mechanics, dynamics
  ◗ *Power 514; Propulsion 696*

2 collision, head-on collision, meeting, encounter, attack; percussion, concussion, crash, impact, shock, smash; carom, cannon; jolt, nudge, bump

3 ramming, hammering; drumming, rapping, tapping, beating; thrusting, bulling, bulldozing, shouldering, smashing, sledgehammering, butting, bashing; spanking, trouncing, leathering, paddling, pummeling, thrashing, raining blows, dusting off; hiding, whipping, flogging, corporal punishment; licking [Inf]
  ◗ *Punishment 454*

4 assault, assault and battery, grievous bodily harm; attack, exchange of blows, fisticuffs
  ◗ *Attack 418; Contention 422*

5 blow, hit, strike, stroke, rap; punch, thwack, pound, slam, bang, butt, smack, swipe, dash, belt, clout, swat, swing, buffet, drub, jab, knock, poke, thump, pelt; cut, slog, bash, dent; thrust, press, pressure, pressing, push, shove, heave, prod, nudge, dig; jostle, jolt, jog, joggle, hustle, tap, touch, chuck, tip, pat, dab, flick, flip, fillip, peck, brush, whisk; slap, spank, cuff, box, whip, lash, stripe; kick, boot, stomp, punt, stamp, clump, clop, brunt, dint [Arch]; [Inf]: plunk, slug, sock, bonk, biff, whop

6 sporting hit, boxing blow, hook, jab, punch, left, right uppercut, swing, backhand, drive
  ◗ *Sports 145; Combat Sports 152; Golf 156*

7 impeller, ram, rammer, ramrod, battering ram, bulldozer, piledriver, monkey, tamper, tamp, tamping iron; pusher, shover, cue, billiard cue; hammer, sledgehammer *or* sledge, hammerhead, peen, punch, puncher;

knocker, door knocker, carpet beater, tapper; bat, mallet, hockey stick, baseball bat, tennis racket *or* racquet, golf club

▶ *Weapon 78*

ADJECTIVES

8 **impelling,** impellent, impulsive, pulsive, dynamic, motive; moving, thrusting, thrustful; driving, ramming, smashing, thrashing, flogging

VERBS

9 **impel,** give impetus to, impart momentum, accelerate, drive, propel; compel, motivate, incite, urge, spur, start, run; set going, set in motion, move, animate, actuate, galvanize, power; goad, drive on *or* forward, project, thrust, press, stress, push, shove, heave, throw, prod, poke, dig, push around, jostle, jog, joggle, tug, wrench, jerk, jolt; elbow, shoulder, hustle, butt, thwack; press on, bear, bear upon, bring pressure to bear; expel; frogmarch

▶ *Power 514; Motion 677; Propulsion 696*

10 **collide,** impact, crash, crash into, bump into, slam into, smash, impinge upon, clash, carom, cannon; nudge, bump, meet, encounter, bang, percuss; foul, run foul of, hurtle [Arch], cross swords, fence, run one's head against, run up against, knock heads together; ram, ram down, tamp, hammer, bulldoze, sledgehammer, bash; pile up

11 **hit,** strike, stroke, rap, punch, thwack, pound, slam, bang, smack, swipe, dash, belt, clout, swat, swing, buffet; box, box someone's ears, jab, knock, bat, thump, pelt, cut, slog, bash, dent; aim *or* deal a blow, strike at; [Inf]: let have it, sock, slug, clock, clip, whop, bop, bonk, biff, deck, cold-cock, clobber, paste

▶ *Baseball 147; Combat Sports 152; Attack 418; Contention 422*

12 **beat,** trounce, thrash, dust off, hammer, spank, pound, pummel, rain blows on; whip, flog, thrash, flail, lash, cane; baste, lambaste, batter, beat up, wallop; [Inf]: lick, pulverize, give a good hiding, leather

13 **tap,** rap, touch, chuck under the chin, tip, pat, dab, flick, flip, peck, pick, brush, whisk

14 **kick,** boot, knee; stamp *or* stomp, clump, clop; drub, trample, tread on, stamp on, kneel on

15 **club,** cudgel, blackjack, sandbag, cosh, hit over the head, crown, concuss, assail, attack, fight

▶ *Contention 422*

ADVERBS

16 **dynamically,** impulsively, with momentum, with power, percussively; forcefully, violently, shockingly

696 Propulsion

NOUNS

1 **propulsion,** impulsion, propelling, propellant, drive, driving *or* propulsive *or* propelling force; momentum; motive power, impetus, thrust, push, pushing, shove, shoving, butt, bunt, kick, kicking, throwing, shooting

▶ *Impulsion 695*

2 **means of propulsion,** wind, steam, gas, gasoline, diesel, diesel-electric, reaction, jet, turbojet, propfan, turboprop, turbofan, rocket, pulsejet, plasmajet, ramjet, resojet

▶ *Engineering 14*

3 **throwing,** projection, trajection [Arch], jaculation, flinging, slinging, pelting, pitching, casting, hurling, lobbing, heaving, chucking, stone-throwing, precipitation

4 **throw,** toss, pitch, serve, cast, bowl, fling, sling, swipe, shy, cockshy [Brit], hurl, chuck, lob, heave, flip, peg [Inf], put, shot put, pass

▶ *Sports 145*

5 **shooting,** gunnery, ballistics, artillery, firing, musketry; trapshooting, skeet *or* skeet shooting; archery, toxophily

▶ *Hunting and Shooting 160*

6 **shot,** discharge, shooting, gunfire, gunshot, potshot; volley, fusillade, salvo, bombardment, cannonade; ejection, detonation

▶ *Attack 418*

7 **missile,** projectile, weapon; ballistic missile, guided missile, cruise missile; shot, small shot, grapeshot, grape, ball, pellet, bullet, slug; shell, mortar, cannonball; torpedo, heat-seeking missile, rocket; shaft, bolt, stone, brickbat; arrow, dart, discus, quoit, javelin, puck

▶ *Weapon 78; Sports 145*

8 **propeller,** prop, pedal, lever, oar; turbo, turbine, booster, thruster; propellant, propulsor, driver; screw, blade, wheel, paddle wheel, screw propeller, twin screws; fan, impeller, rotor, piston

9 **propellant,** driving force, energy thrust; charge, explosive device, detonator; jet, steam, wind; fuel: coal, peat, gasoline, gas, oil, diesel, electricity, dynamite, cordite, guncotton, gunpowder, solid fuel, rocket fuel, nuclear fuel, hydrogen, helium

▶ *Fuel 106*

10 **thrower,** pitcher, hurler, heaver, tosser, flinger, slinger, bowler, shot putter, javelin thrower, discus thrower, snowballer, knife-thrower, server, striker, curler, stoneslinger, chucker

11 **shooter,** marksman, markswoman, target shooter, trapshooter; shot, crack shot, good shot, dead shot, deadeye; gunner, gunman, sniper, rifleman, musketeer, pistoleer [Arch], carbineer [Arch], cannoneer, artilleryman, gun [Inf]; archer, toxophilite [Form], bowman, hunter, Artemis, Diana, Sagittarius, Nimrod

▶ *Hunting and Shooting 160*

ADJECTIVES

12 **propulsive,** propellant *or* propellent, propulsory, propelling; motive, driving, shoving, pushing

13 **projectile,** jaculatory, ejective, ballistic, missile, expulsive, explosive, trajectile

14 propelled, jet-propelled, steam-propelled, gas-propelled, gasoline-propelled, diesel-propelled, wind-propelled, self-propelled

VERBS

15 propel, push, shove, thrust, impel, launch, traject [Arch], project; drive, kick, pedal, row, pole, treadle, wheel; advance, sweep, sweep before one, hustle, put to flight, butt, bunt, shunt; roll, bowl, trundle, move

16 push, shove, send flying, send headlong, shoulder

17 throw, toss, pitch, cast, hurl, jaculate, fling, sling, chuck, chunk, lob, heave, shy, catapult, pelt, lapidate, stone, shower, snowball, peg [Inf], bung [Brit inf]

18 shoot, discharge, explode, fire, fire at, open fire, fire off, loose off, volley, fire a volley, bombard, cannonade, detonate, let off, let fly; gun, gun down, pistol, shoot at, pull the trigger; strike, hit, shoot down, fell, drop; riddle, pepper, pelt, pump or blast full of lead, blast; snipe, pick off, take a potshot, potshot; plug [Inf], pot [Inf]

▸ *Attack 418; Expulsion 709*

19 blow up, fulminate, dynamite, torpedo

20 start, start off or up, give a start, set or put in motion, launch, set going, start going, jump-start, kick-start, kick off, start the ball rolling, bundle, bundle off, set afloat, float, launch

ADVERBS

21 propulsively, forward, onward, progressively, impulsively, forcefully, powerfully

697 Direction

He flung himself from the room, flung himself upon his horse and rode madly off in all directions.
— STEPHEN LEACOCK

NOUNS

1 direction, bearing or bearings; location, situation, position, lay of the land; quarter, line, line of direction, aim, goal, target, objective; steering, steerage, navigation, piloting, helmsmanship

▸ *Location 565*

2 bearing, heading, trend, tendency, run, set, inclination, bent, tenor, drift, thrust; course, route, line, track, path, way, lay; shortcut, beeline, line of sight; compass direction, compass bearing or heading, relative bearing, true or magnetic bearing or heading or course; tack, vector

▸ *Tendency 513; Way 691*

3 orientation, bearings; collimation, adaptation, adjustment, alignment, accommodation

4 guide, signpost, map, direction finder, compass, tracking device, range finder, gauge; degree, deviation, compass rose, compass card, lubber line; rhumb line, azimuth

▸ *Sign 183*

5 compass direction, degree, cardinal point, half-point, quarter-point; true north, magnetic north, northward; south, southward; east, eastward, Orient, sunrise; west, westward, Occident, sunset; northeast, northwest, southeast, southwest; northing, southing, easting, westing

6 directness, straightness, straightforwardness, uninterruption

▸ *Straightness 630*

7 directions, instructions, direction, pointing out, guidance, instruction, education; guiding, leading, supervising, managing

▸ *Education 48; Management 126; Advice 176*

ADJECTIVES

8 directional, northern, north, northward, northerly, northernmost, northbound, arctic, boreal, hyperborean; southern, south, southward, southerly, southernmost, southbound, meridional, antarctic, austral; eastern, east, eastward, easterly, easternmost, eastbound, Oriental; western, west, westward, westerly, westernmost, westbound, Occidental; northeastern, northeast, northeasterly; southeastern, southeast, southeasterly; northwestern, northwest, northwesterly; southwestern, southwest, southwesterly; aligned, parallel, oblique, axial; cross-country, downwind, upwind, downtown, uptown

9 directed, oriented, pointed for, headed for, bound for, set; signposted, aimed, guided, steered, led, instructed, educated; on the mark, on the nose [Inf], on the money [Inf]

10 directable, steerable, guidable, dirigible, leadable

11 direct, immediate, straight, straightforward, straightaway, undeviating, unswerving, unveering; uninterrupted, unbroken; one-way, unidirectional; irreversible

▸ *Straightness 630*

12 directing, directive, guiding, steering, leading, instructing, educating

▸ *Education 48; Management 126*

VERBS

13 direct, direct to, give directions, point or show the way, indicate, guide, signpost; steer, point, aim, orient, determine, set, fix; present, point at or to, point out, push in the right direction; lead, conduct, steer toward, put on the right track, set straight or right, put right

14 aim, bear, pilot, navigate, collimate; set one's sights on, fix on, train upon, sight on, aim at, point; turn, head, lead, go, hold a heading, direct or align oneself, incline, tend, trend, set, dispose, verge; head for, go for, bear for, steer for, make for; set out or off for, strike out for, take off for; lay for [Inf], bear up to or for, set toward, set one's course for, direct one's course, set one's compass, sail for; dash for, make a break for, run for; go straight, go directly, head straight on, follow one's nose, make a beeline for; get straight to the point, steer a straight course, hold steady, cleave to the line, stay on the beam, hold the line

15 **orient** or **orientate,** orient oneself, take or get one's bearings, get the lay of the land, see which way the wind blows or which way the land lies; adapt, adjust, accommodate; box the compass; take or shoot the sun, check one's course

ADVERBS

16 **directly,** direct, straight, point-blank; straightly, straightforward, unswervingly, undeviatingly, unveeringly; due, due north, right, forthright; in a direct or straight line, in line with, in a beeline, as the crow flies, straight as an arrow, straight across; on course, on the right track, squarely, square, dead ahead, dead, straight ahead, full, flush, plumb, plump; [Inf]: plunk, smack, smack-dab

  ▶ *Straightness 630; Forward Motion 679*

17 **clockwise,** rightward; counterclockwise: leftward, withershins or widdershins [Scot], anticlockwise

  ▶ *Rotation 682*

18 **toward,** homeward, landward, seaward, leeward, windward; earthward, heavenward

19 **in all directions,** in every direction, in all manner of ways, every way, everywhere, every which way, in every quarter, on every side; around, all around, around and about; from every quarter, from or to the four corners of the earth, from or to the four winds

20 **directionally,** upstream, downstream, upwind, downwind; before the wind, close to the wind, near the wind, against the wind, in the wind's eye, close-hauled; downtown, uptown; north, northerly, northward, northwardly; south, southerly, southward, southwardly; east, easterly, eastward, eastwardly; west, westerly, westernly, westward, westwardly; northeast, north-northeast, east-northeast; northeasterly, northeastward, northeastwardly; northwest, north-northwest, west-northwest; northwesterly, northwestward, northwestwardly; southeast, south-southeast, east-southeast; southeasterly, southeastward, southeastwardly; southwest, south-southwest, west-southwest; southwesterly, southwestward, southwestwardly

698 Deviation

NOUNS

1 **deviation,** deviance or deviancy; disorientation, misdirection; aberration, aberrance, aberrancy; nonconformism, eccentricity, exorbitation; wrong course or turning, digression, excursion, departure, declension, tangent, diversion, divergence, deflection, divarication, curvature, branching off; aside, parenthesis, divagation; variation, indirection, obliqueness, obliquity, skew, declination, slant, bias

  ▶ *Obliqueness 607; Curve 629; Divergence 703; Nonconformity 782*

2 **deviating course,** curve, turn, flexure, double; reflection; bend, corner, hairpin bend, dogleg, zigzag; slope, slant, pitch; tack, indirect course; detour, diversion, sheer, bypass, by-path, long way around; winding course, slalom course

  ▶ *Way 691*

3 **deviating motion,** indirect motion, swerve, swerving, veer, veering; skid, side slip; side step, crabwalk; shift, drift, leeway; roll, pitch, yaw, swing; knight's move

4 **wandering,** drifting, circuitousness, deviousness; circumlocution, circumbendibus [Inf], rambling, digression, discursion, discursiveness, excursus; straying, errantry, vagrancy, lapse, error; wandering mind, abstractedness

5 **torsion,** twisting, torque, distortion, warp

  ▶ *Distortion 627*

6 **diffraction,** scatter, refraction, diffusion, dispersion, diaspora, fanning out

  ▶ *Physics 10; Dispersion 776*

7 **deviant,** deviant person, deviate, deviationist; nonconformist, eccentric, tergiversator, dissident, heretic, outcast, outlaw; hermit; extremist, fanatic, pervert, lunatic fringe; [Inf]: queer fish, weirdo, oddball

  ▶ *Disobedience 427; Immorality 432; Irregularity 664; Nonconformity 782*

ADJECTIVES

8 **deviant,** deviative, deviatory, deviating, misdirected, nonconformist; aberrant, aberrational, eccentric; off-center, out of sync [Inf]

  ▶ *Nonconformity 782*

9 **indirect,** turning, curving, roundabout, winding, bending, meandering, snaking, serpentine; labyrinthine, mazy; deflected, reflected, deflective; shifting, swerving, twisting, veering, zigzag, crooked, out-of-the-way; off course, off the beam; off-target, off the mark, wide, wide of the mark, off the fairway, in the rough; lost, stray, astray

10 **undirected,** unguided, random

  ▶ *Chance 842*

11 **oblique,** skewed, biased, slanted, distorted, twisted

  ▶ *Obliqueness 607; Distortion 627*

12 **diverging,** divaricating, branching, divergent, once or twice removed

  ▶ *Divergence 703*

13 **wandering,** drifting, digressive, circuitous, devious; divagatory, rambling, digressing, discursive; straying, errant, erratic, desultory; abstracted, inattentive, off the point, off the subject; vagrant, loose, footloose, footloose and fancy-free

14 **diffractive,** refractive, refractile, refrangible; refracted, diffracted, scattered, diffuse, diffused, dispersed

  ▶ *Physics 10; Dispersion 776*

VERBS

15 deviate, divert, diverge, divaricate, vary, depart from, digress, branch, branch out; detour, go off at a tangent, sheer, curve, heel, trend, bear off; filter, swerve, turn a corner, leave the straight and narrow; turn *or* go out of one's way, alter *or* depart from one's course, change direction, tack, yaw, veer, back

16 divert, change course *or* the course of, pull *or* push *or* draw aside; put rudder on, slice, pull, hook, glance, bowl wide

17 go astray, stray, blunder, get lost, lose *or* miss one's way, lose one's bearings, lose one's sense of direction, take a wrong turn *or* the wrong turning, foul; go adrift, drift; get sidetracked, err, ramble, wander, rove, straggle, divagate

18 lose track of, lose the thread; be inattentive, miss the point, daydream

19 twist, turn, bend, meander, wind; weave, twine; snake, curve, twist and turn; zigzag, crook, dogleg

20 distort, warp, bias, twist, skew, screw
 ▶ *Distortion 627*

21 misdirect, put off the scent, divert, avert, mislead, misaddress, misinform

22 sidestep, sidetrack, turn *or* move *or* draw *or* step aside *or* to one side, sidle; make way for, avoid, turn away, shy, shy off; avert, gee, haw, be oblique, steer clear, get out of the way of, go *or* bear *or* sheer *or* veer *or* ease *or* edge off, fly off

23 shove aside, sidetrack, shunt, switch, shuffle, put on one side

24 slide, slip, sideslip, skid; swing, wobble, oscillate

25 turn around, turn about, about-face, wheel, face about, face the other way, reverse; reverse direction, return, revert, turn back, go back

26 deflect, diffract, bend, diverge, scatter, disperse, diffuse, refract

ADVERBS

27 astray, adrift, off the mark, wide of the mark; discursively

28 indirectly, obliquely, sideways *or* sidewise, diagonally, at a tangent, at one remove

29 erratically, eccentrically, oddly, strangely

699 Traction

NOUNS

1 traction, pulling, draft, drawing, heaving, tugging, pulling *or* tractive power, pull, pulling back, retractiveness, retraction, retractility, retractability, towage, dragging; towing, haulage, hauling, drayage

2 pull, tug, tow, heave, draw, draft, haul, lug, drag, strain, trawl, tug of war

3 jerk, yank, sudden pull, twitch, tweak, pluck, wrench, snatch, hitch, start, jolt, bob, flip, flick, jiggle, jig, jog, joggle

 ▶ *Agitation 684*

4 friction, drag, grip, purchase, adhesion
 ▶ *Friction 554; Adhesion 755*

5 towline, towrope, drawer, puller, hawser, tower, hauler, haulier [Brit], dragnet, windlass; tugboat, tractor, traction engine, locomotive

6 drawing power, attraction, pulling toward, magnetism
 ▶ *Attraction 700*

ADJECTIVES

7 tractional, tractive, pulling, drawing, hauling, tugging, towing, draft, draught [Brit], pulling back, attracting, drawn, horse-drawn

8 retractive, retractable, retractile, ductile

9 attractive, magnetic, pulling toward

VERBS

10 pull, haul, draw, heave, tow, take in tow, hale, lug, tug, warp, kedge; trail, train, trice

11 drag, trawl, dredge, winch, reel in, wind in, wind up, lift, tug, draggle, snake, troll, rake, rake in, rake out, drag up, elevate, drag down

12 pull at, pull out, tug, yank, jerk, tweak, twitch, pluck, snatch, snatch at, wrench, hitch, flip, flick, jiggle, jig, jolt, joggle, jog

13 draw in, pull toward, attract, magnetize

ADVERBS

14 magnetically, attractively, adhesively

700 Attraction

NOUNS

1 attraction, attractiveness, attractivity; mutual attraction, pull, draw, drag, tug, itch, desire, affinity, sympathy
 ▶ *Desire 288; Traction 699*

2 pulling power, magnetism, magnetization; gravity, force of gravity, centripetal force; capillarity, capillary attraction, adhesion, cohesion, adduction; inducement, hypnotism, mesmerism
 ▶ *Traction 699; Adhesion 755*

3 magnet, bar magnet, horseshoe magnet, coil magnet, electromagnet, field magnet, artificial magnet, solenoid, paramagnet, magnetic needle, lodestone *or* loadstone, magnetite; lodestar *or* loadstar, polestar, siderite, magnetized iron
 ▶ *Geology 8; Physics 10*

4 allurement, allure, enticement, charisma, magnetism; seductiveness, temptation; appeal, charm, sex appeal, animal magnetism, come-on [Inf], pull [Inf]

5 lure, bait, decoy, charm, siren song, snare

6 charmer, temptress, tempter, seductress, seducer, enchantress, enchanter, siren, Circe, tantalizer, tease, teaser; flirt, coquette; vamp, femme fatale; Lothario, ladies' *or* lady's man, Don Juan, Casanova, favorite,

Adonis, sex symbol, screen idol, teen idol; [Inf]: man-eater, foxy lady, stud, hunk
 ▶ *Sex 20*

7 **center of attraction,** center of attention, centerpiece, focal point, cynosure, focus, center
 ▶ *Center 612*

ADJECTIVES

8 **attracting,** pulling, drawing, dragging, tugging; adductive, associative, adduouent

9 **magnetic,** magnetized, gravitational, centripetal, convergent, inductive, influential

10 **attractive,** seductive, enticing, tempting, charming, fascinating, captivating, eye-catching, taking, charismatic, enchanting, spellbinding, irresistible; alluring, fetching, appealing, good-looking, sexually attractive, sexy; [Inf]: foxy, hunky, dishy [Brit]
 ▶ *Sex 20; Desire 288; Beauty 529*

VERBS

11 **attract,** pull, draw, adduct, drag, tug, have an attraction, draw toward; influence, persuade; magnetize, be magnetic, exercise a pull, pull toward; appeal, charm, move, pluck at one's heartstrings; induce
 ▶ *Influence 512*

12 **lure,** allure, draw in, coax, bait, ensnare, seduce, decoy, lead on, tempt, entice, tantalize, fascinate, captivate, enthrall, enchant, spellbind, hypnotize, mesmerize

ADVERBS

13 **attractionally,** attractively, centripetally, adhesively, cohesively; inductively, magnetically, mesmerically, hypnotically, irresistibly

14 **attractively,** influentially, sympathetically, appealingly, charismatically, charmingly, enchantingly, seductively, sexily

701 Repulsion

NOUNS

1 **repulsion,** repellence, repellency, repelling; ugliness, repellent quality, repulsiveness; recoil, mutual repulsion, repulsive force, centrifugal force, polarization; disaffinity, magnetic repulsion, diamagnetism, antigravity
 ▶ *Physics 10; Ugliness 531; Oppositeness 731*

2 **repulse,** rebuff, dismissal, snub, cut, cold shoulder, brush-off, spurning; refusal, rejection, ejection, expulsion
 ▶ *Rejection 383; Expulsion 709*

3 **deflection,** defense, foil, counterstroke, parry, counterattack, resistance
 ▶ *Resistance 417; Defense 419*

ADJECTIVES

4 **repulsive,** repellent, repugnant, offensive, noisome, repelling, off-putting, antipathetic, ugly, abhorrent,

obnoxious, disgusting, nauseating, sickening, foul, loathsome, horrible, appalling, hideous, obscene
 ▶ *Unpleasantness 272; Ugliness 531*

5 **abducent,** abductive, centrifugal, repelling, diamagnetic, of opposite polarity
 ▶ *Physics 10*

6 **defensive,** resistant, hostile, dismissive
 ▶ *Rejection 383; Resistance 417; Defense 419*

VERBS

7 **repel,** drive *or* push *or* put away, head off, repulse, turn back, drive *or* push *or* thrust back, chase off *or* away, reject, rebuff, snub, cold-shoulder, slight, cut, spurn, refuse, say no, reject someone's advances, show someone the door, make someone keep his *or* her distance, brush off, shoot someone down [Inf], give someone the bird [Inf]
 ▶ *Rejection 383*

8 **eject,** expel, throw out, dismiss, send packing, pack off, send someone about his *or* her business; [Inf]: give someone his *or* her walking papers *or* marching orders, sack, boot out, give someone the boot, kiss off
 ▶ *Rejection 383; Expulsion 709*

9 **fend off,** deflect, ward off, keep at bay, put off, head off, parry, keep at arm's length, beat *or* fight off, make unwelcome, send away with a flea in one's ear
 ▶ *Counteraction 510*

10 **be repulsive,** disgust, revolt, sicken, nauseate, repel, upset, offend, appall, turn one's stomach, make one's gorge rise
 ▶ *Unpleasantness 272*

ADVERBS

11 **repulsively,** repellently, repugnantly, offensively, antipathetically, abhorrently, noisomely, obnoxiously, horribly, hideously, obscenely

12 **defensively,** resistantly, dismissively, against

702 Convergence

NOUNS

1 **convergence,** converging, confluence, conflux, concurrence, concourse, collision; mutual approach, concentration, meeting, coming together
 ▶ *Accord 735*

2 **approach,** advance, confrontation, collision course

3 **convergent view,** perspective, vanishing point *or* line *or* plane

4 **meeting place,** congress, congregation, assembly, union, junction, crossing, intersection, meeting point
 ▶ *Assembly 59; Union 752*

5 **focus,** center, hub, pivot, centering, coming to the point, concentralization, focalization, asymptote, converging line, radius, tangent, spokes

> *Middle 772*

6 narrowing, narrowing gap, taper, tapering, funnel, bottleneck
> *Narrowness 593*

7 convergent, converging, confluent, uniting, concurrent, meeting, joining, crossing, intersecting; focal, focusing, focused, confocal; centrolineal, centripetal, asymptotic, radial, radiating; tangent, tangential; centering, pointed, tapering, narrowing, conical, pyramidal

8 advancing, oncoming, approaching, mutually approaching, connivent

9 converge, close in, approach, draw near, cross, intersect; be on a collision course, narrow the gap, close, close with *or* in *or* up, funnel, taper, pinch, nip
> *Narrowness 593; Forward Motion 679; Union 752*

10 come together, assemble, congregate, concentrate, gather, cluster, run together, meet, unite, fall in with, get together, roll up, pour in, roll in [Inf]
> *Union 752*

11 focus, bring into focus, home in, zero in, center, centralize, taper, concentralize, concenter, come to a focus, concentrate, corradiate, come to the point

12 convergently, confluently, concurrently, congruently, mutually, together

703 Divergence

1 divergence, divergency, divarication, declination; aberration, deviation, difference; contradiction, contrariety
> *Refutation 332; Deviation 698; Dissimilarity 734*

2 parting, moving *or* going apart, drifting apart, spread, spreading out, splaying, fanning, fanning out, deployment, separation, centrifugence, division, decentralization; parting of the ways
> *Separation 753*

3 radiation, ray, radius, spoke, radiance, scattering, diffusion, dispersion, emanation, ripple effect
> *Dispersion 776*

4 branching, branching out, ramification, arborescence, arborization, treelikeness, forking, furcation, bifurcation, biforking, trifurcation, triforking

5 fork, prong, trident, branch, Y-shape, V-shape, stem, offshoot, fan, delta, crotch, groin, inguen, furcula *or* furculum, wishbone

6 divergent, diverging, divaricate, separated, separate, aberrant, different, contradictory, centrifugal; deviating, divaricating

> *Deviation 698; Dissimilarity 734; Separation 753*

7 radiating, radial, radiate, radiated; radiant, rayed, spoked
> *Dispersion 776*

8 fanlike, fan-shaped, deltoid, deltoidal, delta-like, delta-shaped, palmate, splayed, spread-eagled

9 branched, branching, arborescent, arboreal, arboriform, treelike, tree-shaped, dendriform, dendritic, branchlike, ramose, ramous, Y-shaped, V-shaped, forking, forked, furcate, forklike, biforked, bifurcate, bifurcated, trifurcate, trifurcated, pronged, trident-like

10 diverge, divaricate, aberrate, deviate

11 move apart, part, spread, spread apart, outspread, fan, fan out, deploy; go off *or* away

12 separate, divide, splay, splay apart; go separate ways, split, split off, part company, be disjoined
> *Separation 753*

13 radiate, ray, diffuse, emanate, disperse, scatter
> *Dispersion 776*

14 branch, stem, ramify, branch off *or* out, spread-eagle, straddle, step wide, fork, furcate, bifurcate, trifurcate

15 change direction, switch, fly *or* go off at a tangent, glance, fly off

16 divergently, apart, radiantly, radially, diffusely, ramosely, ramously, aberrantly, differently, separately

704 Arrival

1 arrival, coming, advent, approach, onset, advance, appearance, entrance, emergence, birth, presence, debut, beginning
> *Entry 706; Beginning 771*

2 landing, landfall, touchdown; docking, mooring, tying up, dropping *or* weighing anchor; disembarkation, disembarkment, debarkation, coming *or* going ashore

3 reception, hospitality, welcome, greeting, handshake
> *Sociability 408*

4 return, homecoming, coming back, recursion, reentrance, reentry, prodigal's return

5 meeting, encounter, recounter, rejoining, rendezvous, meeting place

6 destination, goal, objective, bourn; terra firma, harbor, port, haven, home, end, stop, last stop, terminal point, point of arrival, journey's end, end of the line, terminus, terminal, stopping place; winning post, finish, close finish, photo finish, last lap; airport, airdrome, air terminal, heliport, helipad; depot, junction, station
> *End 773*

7 stopover, stage, halt, billet, shelter, dock, port in a storm, dry dock, berth, stable

8 **achievement,** accomplishment, attainment; accession, fulfillment, reaching, making
  ▶ *Success 845*

ADJECTIVES

9 **arriving,** incoming, immigrant, entering, emerging, appearing, born
  ▶ *Appearance 264; Entry 706*

10 **approaching,** impending, imminent, oncoming, advancing, nearing, coming; incoming, inbound, inwardbound, homeward, homeward bound, terminal
  ▶ *Beginning 771*

11 **attainable,** achievable, approachable, accessible

12 **welcoming,** inviting, hospitable
  ▶ *Sociability 408*

VERBS

13 **arrive,** come, appear, make *or* put in an appearance; enter, emerge, be born; be present, be found, turn up, show up, roll up, pull up *or* in, drop in, bob up, hit, blow in [Inf], pop up [Inf]
  ▶ *Appearance 264*

14 **reach,** get there, get to, come to; fetch, fetch up in *or* at, end up in *or* at, make it [Inf], reach one's destination *or* goal, hit the target, come to journey's end; find, discover, arrive at *or* upon, come upon, strike upon, hit upon, fall upon, light upon, pitch upon, stumble upon *or* on, come to rest, finish the race, be in at the death; be received
  ▶ *Discovery 345*

15 **approach,** draw up, sight, near, stand at the door *or* on the threshold, knock at the door, look for a welcome

16 **land,** make port, put into port, dock, beach, berth, moor, tie up, drop anchor; ground, run aground, make a landfall, set foot on dry land, step *or* go ashore, disembark, debark, alight; touch down, disemplane, deplane, get off, detrain, debus; dismount, get down, unharness, unhitch, quit the saddle; emerge, home, return, come *or* get *or* return home, perch; discharge, unload

17 **get in,** come in, set foot in, enter, burst upon, make an entrance, check in, clock in, punch in, ring in, sign in
  ▶ *Entry 706*

18 **stop at,** visit, put in, pull in, stop over, stop off, break one's journey, pause

19 **be brought,** be delivered, come to hand

20 **meet,** join, rejoin, see again, go *or* come to meet, be at the station, keep a date, rendezvous; come upon *or* across, encounter, come into contact, run into *or* across, bump into, meet by chance, butt into, knock into, collide with, gather, assemble, congregate
  ▶ *Assembly 59*

21 **achieve,** accomplish, attain, gain, succeed, be successful, prosper, get to the top, reach the top, get ahead, make good, get somewhere, get there, make the grade, make it [Inf]

▶ *Success 845; Prosperity 847*

ADVERBS

22 **on arrival,** on the doorstep *or* threshold, at the door, here, home, back home, home again, aground, ashore, at journey's end

INTERJECTIONS

23 **hello!,** hail!, hi!, hiya! [Inf], aloha!, *ciao!* [Ital], *salut!* [Fr], how do you do?, how are you?

24 **welcome!,** greetings!, come in!, make yourself at home!, have a seat!, help yourself!, it's a girl!, it's a boy!

705 Departure

He has departed, withdrawn, gone away, broken out.
— CICERO

Depart — be off — excede — evade — erump!
— OLIVER WENDELL HOLMES

NOUNS

1 **departure,** leaving, going, going away; exit, egress; exodus, emigration, migration, hegira *or* hejira; flight, escape, getaway, elopement, flit [Brit]; decampment, abandonment, desertion, defection; withdrawal, retreat, retirement, evacuation, pulling out, voting with one's feet
  ▶ *Exit 707; Escape 816*

2 **start,** starting, startoff, outset; embarkation, embarkment, boarding, going on board, entrainment, enplanement *or* emplanement, takeoff, liftoff
  ▶ *Transportation 686; Beginning 771*

3 **parting,** separation, leave-taking, leave, congé, farewell, goodbye, goodnight, adieu; parting shot, Parthian shot, valediction, valedictory, farewell address, last words, swan song, funeral oration; obituary, epitaph; last handshake, golden handshake, dismissal, viaticum; one for the road, nightcap [Inf], stirrup cup, doch-an-dorrach, send-off

4 **place of departure,** place of embarkation, port, dock, airport, gate, station, railroad station, departure platform, bus station, bus stop; starting point *or* line *or* post *or* gate, outset, base, springboard, jumping-off point
  ▶ *Transportation 686; Exit 707*

ADJECTIVES

5 **departing,** leaving, farewell, valedictory, parting, leave-taking; last, final

6 **departed,** gone, gone away, gone off, left

7 **outgoing,** outward-bound, migratory, emigratory

VERBS

8 **depart,** leave, take *or* make one's leave, take *or* make one's departure, go, go away, get away *or* off, get *or* go along, go *or* get on, clear off *or* out, toddle *or* trot *or* stagger along; walk away, slink off, flounce off *or* out, fling off *or* out, leave in high dudgeon, stamp off, storm

out, get up and go; [Inf]: mosey along, push off, buzz off, make tracks, slope off [Brit]

9 **withdraw,** retreat, beat a retreat, turn back, turn one's back on, pull out, exit, make one's exit, leave the stage; bow out, leave work, clock out, punch out, cease work, retire, receive a golden handshake, resign; sign off, sign out, check out, vacate, evacuate, abandon, relinquish; die, depart this life, pass away, pass over

▸ *Death 29; Relinquishment 392; Cessation 668; Backward Motion 680; Exit 707; Resignation 835*

10 **quit,** quit the scene, leave the country, emigrate, expatriate, defect; move, move house [Brit], remove, relocate; leave home, leave the nest, leave the neighborhood, disappear, vanish, leave no trace, take wing, slip away, elope, escape, give someone the slip, abscond, absent oneself, march out, debouch, decamp, break camp, strike camp, pull up stakes, flit [Brit]

▸ *Disappearance 265; Absence 576; Escape 816*

11 **hurry off,** move fast, make off, run away, run off, flee, bolt, take flight *or* wing, take to one's heels, run for one's life, cut and run, decamp, rush off, hasten off, scamper away, skip, skip off, dash, dash off, nip, nip off, whip off, whiz off, cut, cut away, make oneself scarce; beetle off [Brit], scarper [Brit]; [Inf]: vamoose, absquatulate, skedaddle, beat it, scram, hightail, split, lam, tear off, take it on the lam, take a powder

▸ *Haste 818*

12 **set out,** set forth *or* forward, put *or* go forth, set off, be off, be on one's way, emerge, sally forth, issue, issue forth, start, start out *or* off, strike out, get off, move off, march off, march away; embark, board, entrain, embus, enplane, emplane, go aboard *or* on board, jump on, hop on, mount, set sail, spread sail, spread canvas, hoist the blue peter, weigh anchor, unmoor, cast off, drop the pilot, push off, put to sea, get under way, leave land behind, take off, pull out of the station, hit the road [Inf]

▸ *Transportation 686; Exit 707; Expulsion 709; Beginning 771*

13 **part,** separate, part company, take *or* break oneself off, tear oneself away, take one's leave; say farewell, bid farewell, bid *or* say goodbye *or* goodnight *or* Godspeed, make one's adieus, wave goodbye; speed the parting guest, give someone a good send-off, have one for the road

INTERJECTIONS

14 **goodbye!,** goodnight!, farewell!, by! *or* bye!, Godspeed!, adieu!, *au revoir!* [Fr], *auf Wiedersehen!* [Ger], *ciao!* [Ital], *adios!* [Sp], ta ta! [Brit], cheerio! [Brit], see you!, see you later!, have a nice day!, bon voyage!, cheers!; so long! [Inf], bye-bye! [Inf]

706 Entry

NOUNS

1 **entry,** entrance, ingress, ingression, entrée, access, incoming, ingoing, import; reentry, reentrance, admission, reception, enrollment, enlistment, induction, initiation, introduction, debut, appearance, arrival

▸ *Appearance 264; Transfer 685; Arrival 704; Admittance 708*

2 **influx,** inflow, flood, inflooding, stream, indraught, inhalation, indrawing, indrawal, input, intake, inrush, inrun; afflux, affluxion, affluence

3 **inroad,** encroachment, insertion, penetration, interpenetration, insinuation, infiltration, percolation, seepage, leakage; intrusion, invasion, forced entry, raid, irruption, incursion, attack, illegal entry, trespassing, housebreaking, breaking and entering, burglary

▸ *Attack 418; Insertion 710; Disturbance 768*

4 **right of entry,** nonrestriction, admission, admittance, access, permission, permit, ticket, pass, passport, visa, immigration, in-migration, foreign influx, importation, importing, trade, free trade, free port, open-door policy, free market, expansionism

▸ *Trade 480; Market 483; Permission 502; Admittance 708*

5 **entrance,** way in, entry, access, inlet, ingress, approach, adit, mouth, opening, orifice, conduit, channel, passage

▸ *Opening 583; Way 691; Passage 692*

6 **means of entry** *or* **access,** porch, propylaeum, portico, portal, porte-cochere; doorway, threshold, lintel, doorpost *or* doorjamb, door, front door, side door, French door *or* window, patio door, back door, postern, storm door, cellar door, trapdoor; hatch, hatchway, scuttle; gate, gateway, gatepost, lich *or* lych gate; archway, tollgate, turnstile, turnpike, stile; lobby, vestibule, foyer

7 **entrant,** incomer, comer, arrival, visitor, visitant, caller, guest; immigrant, in-migrant, newcomer, new face, new member, new boy, new girl; intake, beginner, debutante, tyro; settler, colonist; competitor, contender; ticketholder, cardholder, audience, house

▸ *Sociability 408; Contention 422; Beginning 771*

8 **intruder,** invader, raider, attacker, unwelcome guest, trespasser, burglar, housebreaker, picklock, thief, gate-crasher [Inf]

▸ *Stealing 479; Disturbance 768*

ADJECTIVES

9 **entering,** ingressive, inward, incoming, ingoing, inbound, immigrant, imported, allowed in, homing

10 **invasive,** incursive, intrusive, trespassing, attacking, penetrating, irruptive, ingrowing, inflowing, inflooding, inpouring, inrushing

VERBS

11 **enter,** go in *or* into, come in *or* into, get in *or* into, gain admittance, be admitted, open the door, let oneself in, cross the threshold, set foot in, arrive, make an entrance; visit, call, call in, look in, pop in [Inf], drop by *or* in; find one's way into, turn into, put in *or* into; board, embark, go aboard, mount
> *Sociability 408; Arrival 704; Admittance 708*

12 **invade,** irrupt, raid, attack, storm, escalade, encroach, trespass, barge in, rush in, burst in, storm in, butt in, interrupt, muscle in, horn in, outstay one's welcome; break in, break and enter, pick the lock, burgle, gate-crash [Inf]
> *Disturbance 768*

13 **infiltrate,** permeate, percolate, filter in, soak in, leak in, seep, drip, work *or* worm one's way into, have an in, insinuate, creep in, slip in, sneak in, slink in, penetrate, interpenetrate, break through, get *or* pass *or* go through, bore in, pierce, puncture, insert, bite into, eat into, cut into
> *Insertion 710*

14 **flood in,** flow in, inflow, rush in, inrush, pour in, swarm in; pack in, crowd in, throng in, press in, cram in, squeeze in, wedge in, jam in, congregate
> *Assembly 59*

15 **fall into,** drop into, plunge into, dive into, sink into
> *Descent 714; Lowering 716*

16 **enroll,** join, admit, take in, enlist, inscribe, sign on, enter for, contend, induct, initiate, introduce; immigrate, settle, settle in, colonize
> *Contention 422; Beginning 771*

ADVERBS

17 **in,** inward, inwardly, invasively, intrusively, incursively

707 Exit

Exit, pursued by a bear. — WILLIAM SHAKESPEARE

NOUNS

1 **exit,** egress, egression; going out, outgoing, outgo; exodus, departure, walkout, evacuation, exfiltration
> *Departure 705*

2 **way out,** exit, egress, door, back door, gate, port; emergency exit, fire escape, escape hatch, escape route; path, avenue, channel, loophole
> *Way 691; Escape 816*

3 **coming out,** outcoming, outcome, emergence, emerging, emersion; issue, issuance, extrusion, outbreak, breakout, eruption, outburst
> *Departure 705; Expulsion 709; Extraction 711*

4 **outflow,** outflowing, outpouring, outpour, flood, inundation, spill, waste, effluence, effusion, outflux, efflux, effluxion, defluxion, outfall; waterfall, gush, gushing, stream, streaming, jet, fountain, well, spring,

gusher, exhaust, emission, discharge, emanation, exudation, secretion, voidance, excretion, evaporation, perspiration, sweating, sweat, transudation, diaphoresis; running sore, streaming eyes, runny nose, hemorrhage
> *Excretion 25; Waste 96*

5 **leakage,** leak, leaking, seepage, seep, seeping, drip, dripping, dribble, dribbling, trickle, trickling, filtration, filtering, straining; percolation, percolating, leaching, lixiviation, effusion, extravasation; ooze, oozing, weep, weeping

6 **emigration,** out-migration, migration, defection, expatriation, deportation, exile, expulsion, dismissal
> *Expulsion 709*

7 **export,** exporting, exportation, transference, outgoings; outlay, expenditure, spending, loss
> *Loss 468; Trade 480; Expenditure 491; Transfer 685*

8 **outlet,** outfall, chute, spout, tap, drain, drainpipe, gutter, conduit, gargoyle; overflow, flume, sluice, weir, floodgate, opening, orifice, vent, ventage, venthole, pore, blowhole, spiracle, anus
> *Opening 583; Passage 692*

9 **outgoer,** goer, leaver, departer, emigrant, émigré, out-migrant, migrant, colonist, settler, expellee, exile, expatriate, defector, remittance man *or* woman; escapee, walk-off [Inf]

ADJECTIVES

10 **outgoing,** outbound, outward-bound, going, departing, leaving, forthcoming, issuing, egressive, emerging, emergent, coming out, arising, surfacing, erupting, eruptive, volcanic, explosive, expulsive, emanating, emanent, emanative, transeunt, transient
> *Transience 643*

11 **outflowing,** outpouring, effluent, effusive, effused, extravasated, expended, spent

12 **leaky,** oozy, weeping, runny, excretory, porous, permeable, exudative, transudative

VERBS

13 **exit,** make an *or* one's exit, egress, go, leave, depart, withdraw, go away, go out, pass out, get out, walk out, run out, pop out, march out, bow out, walk off; die, expire, pass away, pass over
> *Death 29; Departure 705*

14 **emerge,** come out, issue, issue forth, debouch; sally, sally forth; emanate, effuse; come out in the open, appear, surface, arise, erupt, break out, break forth; project, protrude, jut, break cover, burst out, escape, evacuate, bale out, jump out
> *Appearance 264; Ascent 713; Escape 816*

15 **run out,** drain, drain out, flow out, outflow, flood, flood out, inundate, pour, outpour, pour out, disembogue; surge, well out *or* up *or* over, gush, gush out, jet, spurt, spurt out, spout, spout out, vomit, spew, spew out, blow out, overflow, spill, spill over, slop, slop over

16 **leak,** leak out, drip, dribble, trickle, seep, seep out, weep, ooze, ooze out, extravasate, filter, filtrate, exfiltrate, strain, percolate, leach, lixiviate, effuse, drivel, drool, slaver, slobber, salivate, water at the mouth, emanate, exude, emit, discharge, secrete, excrete, exudate, perspire, sweat, exhale, breathe out
  ◗ *Excretion 25*

17 **emigrate,** out-migrate, migrate, defect, expatriate, deport, exile, expel, dismiss, export, send abroad
  ◗ *Expulsion 709*

18 **be dismissed,** leave, resign, retire, walk out, be laid off, be fired, be pink-slipped; get the boot [Inf], be sacked [Inf]
  ◗ *Expulsion 709*

ADVERBS

19 **forth,** out, outward, apart, away, outwardly, effusively; eruptively, explosively

708 Admittance

NOUNS

1 **admittance,** admission, taking in; receipt, receiving, reception; acceptance, import, importing, importation; immission, intromission; insertion, interjection, invitation, inclusion, interjacence; admissibility, acceptability
  ◗ *Receiving 473; Interface 616; Insertion 710; Inclusion 763*

2 **receptivity,** receptiveness, openness, recipience *or* recipiency, hospitality, welcome, welcoming, welcoming with open arms; access, entrance, entrée, entry
  ◗ *Sociability 408; Entry 706*

3 **refuge,** sanctuary, asylum, shelter, protection, open door
  ◗ *Entry 706; Safety 810*

4 **bringing in,** introduction, initiation, baptism, rite of passage, enrollment, investiture, ordination, induction, registration, enlistment, instatement, installation, inauguration, naturalization
  ◗ *Beginning 771*

5 **intake,** indraft *or* indraught [Brit], ingestion, consumption, eating, drinking, imbibition, ingurgitation, engorgement, swallow, swallowing, gulp, gulping; suck, sucking, suction; aspiration, respiration, breathing in, inspiration, inhalement, inhalation, sniff, sniffing, snuff, snuffle, sniffle, slur, slurping; engulfing, engulfment
  ◗ *Eating 92; Drinking 93; Taste 219; Odor 224*

6 **absorption,** adsorption, sorption, chemisorption, resorption, digestion; engrossment, assimilation, incorporation; absorbency, resorbence, sponging, blotting, seeping, percolation, osmosis, endosmosis

7 **sponge,** blotter, blotting paper, chromatography paper, absorbent, adsorbent

ADJECTIVES

8 **admissive,** admissory, admissible, acceptable, suitable, receivable, receptible, intromissive, intromittent

9 **receptive,** recipient, open, accessible, welcoming, hospitable, inviting, invitatory

10 **introductory,** introductive, initiatory, initiative

11 **absorbent,** absorptive, adsorbent, sorbent, chemisorptive; assimilative, digestive, ingestive, imbibitory, bibulous; soaking, blotting, spongy, spongeous, osmotic, endosmotic

VERBS

12 **admit,** receive, take in, include, let in, allow in, give access to, give a ticket *or* pass to, give admittance *or* entrance to, open the door to, open the hatches; insert, intromit, import, bring in
  ◗ *Receiving 473; Insertion 710; Inclusion 763*

13 **show in,** usher, usher in, introduce, go before, come before, send in

14 **welcome,** embrace, adopt, accept, fling wide the gates, welcome with open arms, put the flags out, invite, call in
  ◗ *Sociability 408*

15 **give refuge to,** give sanctuary to, grant asylum, naturalize, shelter, accommodate, protect, safeguard
  ◗ *Safety 810*

16 **introduce,** bring in, initiate, baptize, register, inscribe, enlist, take on, install, inaugurate, enroll, invest, ordain, show the ropes [Inf]

17 **ingest,** eat, imbibe, drink, drink up *or* in, lap up, engorge, ingurgitate, swallow, gulp, gulp down, wolf down, gobble, slurp; engulf
  ◗ *Eating 92; Drinking 93*

18 **draw in,** suck, suck in *or* up, suckle, aspirate, respire, inhale, inspire, breathe in, sniff, sniffle, snuff, snuffle, smell, scent, scent *or* smell out, detect

19 **absorb,** adsorb, sorb, chemisorb; digest, incorporate, assimilate, internalize; engross, take up, blot, blot up, soak, soak up, sponge, osmose, soak in, seep in, permeate, percolate, infiltrate, reabsorb, resorb

ADVERBS

20 **receptively,** welcomingly, hospitably, invitingly, with open arms

709 Expulsion

NOUNS

1 **expulsion,** ejection, ejectment, throwing out, rejection, propulsion, the push [Brit]; [Inf]: kicking out, booting out, boot, bounce, bum's rush, heave-ho
  ◗ *Propulsion 696; Exclusion 764*

2 **dismissal,** discharge, congé, suspension, laying off, firing, furlough, drumming out, cashiering, pink slip; demotion, degradation, relegation, stripping, depluming *or* displuming; externment, exclusion, excommunication, unfrocking, defrocking, disqualification, dis-

fellowship, striking off; [Inf]: sacking, axing, ax, gate, marching orders, walking papers

▶ *Exclusion 764*

3 **ostracism,** ostracization, exclusion, seclusion, blackballing; snubbing, shunning, sending to Coventry, cold shoulder, brush-off; outlawing, outlawry, banning, proscription, banishment, rustication, exile, expatriation, repatriation, deportation, transportation, extradition

4 **eviction,** ousting, removal, dispossession, expropriation, deprivation, dislodgment, throwing overboard, jettison, precipitation, defenestration, unloading, offloading

5 **removal,** elimination, evacuation, voidance, voiding, clearance, clearing, clearage, cleaning out, scouring out, purging, purgation, catharsis, unfouling, emptying, depletion, exhaustion, draining, drainage, egress

▶ *Excretion 25; Cleanliness 111*

6 **disgorgement,** discharge, disemboguement, ejaculation, extrusion, detrusion, obtrusion; eruption, eruptiveness, blowout, outburst, outpour, effusion; jet, spout, spurt, squirt, excretion, secretion; extravasation, bloodletting, cupping, bleeding, venesection, phlebotomy, paracentesis, tapping, spilling, shedding

▶ *Excretion 25*

7 **vomiting,** vomit, sickness, nausea, regurgitation, egestion, emesis, heaving, retching, gagging, throwing up, puking [Inf], barfing [Inf]

8 **belch,** belching, hiccup, eructation, wind, gas, burp [Inf]

9 **flatulence,** flatulency, flatuosity, flatus, passing gas, breaking wind, fart *or* farting [Inf]

10 **ejector,** expeller, ouster, evictor, dispossessor, depriver, bouncer; propellant, explosive, emitter, radiator, ejecting mechanism, volcano; emetic, purgative, laxative, aperient

▶ *Excretion 25; Propulsion 696*

ADJECTIVES

11 **expulsive,** expellent, ejective, ejaculative, eliminant, explosive, eruptive; radiating, emitting, emissive; secretory, sweaty, sudatory, sudorific, salivary, salivant; sickening, emetic, purgative, laxative, cathartic

12 **vomiting,** sick, nauseated, seasick, airsick, carsick, travel-sick, vomitive, vomitory, pukey [Inf]

13 **eructative,** belching, hiccupping, burping [Inf]; flatulent, flatulous, farting [Inf]

VERBS

14 **expel,** eject, put out, turn out, throw out, cast out, toss out, heave out, hustle out, show someone the door; [Inf]: bounce, chuck *or* kick *or* boot out, give the bum's rush, give the heave-ho, throw out on one's ear

▶ *Exclusion 764*

15 **dismiss,** discharge, disemploy, suspend, lay off, furlough, fire, make redundant [Brit], drop, let go, release, let out, retire, superannuate, pension off; [Inf]: sack, give the sack, give someone his *or* her walking papers *or* marching orders, kick *or* boot out, ax, give the ax to, kick upstairs

16 **disbar,** excommunicate, unfrock, defrock, strip, deplume, displume, disqualify, strike off, strike off the roll, drum out, cashier, depose, dethrone, expel, suspend, send down, rusticate, demote, degrade, downgrade, relegate, bust, kick downstairs [Inf]

▶ *Punishment 454*

17 **ostracize,** exclude, seclude, blackball, spurn, shun, snub, cut, send to Coventry, give the silent treatment, brush off, give the cold shoulder, make unwelcome, outlaw, ban, proscribe, prohibit, banish, rusticate, exile, expatriate, repatriate, deport, transport, extradite, send away

▶ *Rejection 383; Unsociability 409; Exclusion 764*

18 **send away,** send off, see off, order off *or* away, turn away, bundle away, bundle off, pack off, send about one's business, send to the showers, shake off, shoo off *or* away, send packing, send away with a flea in one's ear

19 **drive out,** drum out, chase out, rout out, push out, force out, hunt out, smoke out, freeze out, drive into the open, run out of town, ride on a rail

20 **evict,** oust, remove, dispossess, repossess, expropriate, deprive, dislodge, extirpate, uproot, put out, turn out, turn out of doors, turn out of house and home, turn *or* put out bag and baggage, unhouse, unkennel

▶ *Taking 477*

21 **depopulate,** unpeople, depeople, dispeople, desolate, devastate

▶ *Killing 30*

22 **exterminate,** do away with, purge, liquidate, dispel, eradicate, root out, deracinate, eliminate, get rid of, reject, throw off, cast off, fling off, shake off, shed, destroy, rub out, erase, obliterate, exorcise

▶ *Obliteration 186; Rejection 383*

23 **void,** evacuate, eliminate, remove, deplete, exhaust, empty, empty out, vent, drain, drink up, drain to the dregs, siphon off, pump out, clear out, clean out, curette, purge, gut, disembowel, eviscerate, draw, bone, fillet, unclog, unfoul, blow, blow out, clear off, clear away, sweep out, make a clean sweep, clear the decks

24 **unload,** unburden, disburden, off-load, unlade, unpack, discharge, dump, unship

25 **throw away,** throw out, jettison, throw overboard, discard, scrap, precipitate, defenestrate, get rid of, rid oneself of, junk [Inf]

26 **let out,** give out *or* off, emit, send out, radiate, emit rays, exhaust, give vent to, exhale, expire, respire, breathe out, let one's breath out; blow, puff, fume, smoke, reek, steam, vaporize; stream, turn on the tap, open the floodgates, open the sluice gates; disgorge, debouch, disembogue, discharge, ejaculate, cast forth,

cast out, send forth, extrude, detrude, obtrude; erupt, eruct, blow out, pour out, outpour, spew, spout, jet, spurt, squirt, sputter, splutter; extravasate, bleed; defecate, urinate, excrete, egest, secrete

▶ *Secretion 24; Excretion 25; Propulsion 696; Exit 707*

27 **vomit,** spew, regurgitate, spit, spit up, bring up, be sick, retch, heave, gag, throw up; [Inf]: puke, barf, upchuck, ralph, shoot *or* toss one's cookies, sick up [Brit]

28 **belch,** hiccup, eruct, eructate, burp [Inf]; be flatulent, have *or* pass gas, break wind; fart [Inf]

ADVERBS

29 **expulsively,** explosively, eruptively, emetically, cathartically

INTERJECTIONS

30 **go!,** go away!, begone!, get thee hence!, get you gone!, shoo!, run along!, away!, away with you!, off with you!, off you go!, be off!, on your way!, get out!, get going!, get out of here!, get the hell out of here!, clear out *or* off!, never darken my door again!; [Inf]: buzz off!, push off!, shove off!, bug off!, piss off!, beat it!, scram!, scoot!, scat! vamoose!, skiddoo!, skedaddle!, get lost!, take a walk!, go jump in the lake!, go chase yourself!, cheese it!, take a powder!, blow!, get!, git!

▶ *Departure 705*

710 Insertion

NOUNS

1 **insertion,** introduction, insinuation, addition, interjection, interpolation, intercalation, intromission, embolism; insert, parentheses; import, importation; infixion, impaction, impactment; planting, implantation, transplantation, transplant, graft, grafting, embedment; tessellation

▶ *Addition 748*

2 **injection,** inoculation, vaccination, implantation, impregnation; entry, ingress, penetration, infusion, perfusion, transfusion, shot

▶ *Entry 706*

3 **immersion,** submersion, submergence, plunge, dip, bath, ducking, baptism; interment, burial at sea

▶ *Burial 31*

4 **insert,** insertion, inset, inlay, inclusion, supplement, tip *or* tip-in *or* tip-on; filling, stuffing; plug, stopper, tampon, tampion *or* tompion

▶ *Inclusion 763*

ADJECTIVES

5 **inserted,** introduced, introjected, insinuated, added, interpolated, interpolative, intercalative, intercalated, parenthetical, by-the-by, imported, infixed, impacted, planted, transplanted, grafted, embedded, tessellated

6 **injected,** inoculated, vaccinated, implanted, impregnated, infused, perfused

7 **immersed,** submersed, submerged, baptized, interred, buried at sea

8 **inset,** inlaid, included, tipped *or* tipped-in *or* tipped-on, stuffed, plugged

VERBS

9 **insert,** put in, stick in, introduce, introject, insinuate, add, interject, interpolate, intercalate, put between, intromit, include, drag in, import, bring in, drop in, pot, hole, put in the slot

▶ *Interface 616; Addition 748; Inclusion 763*

10 **inject,** inoculate, vaccinate, implant, impregnate, enter, penetrate, pierce, poke in, squirt in, introduce, pop in, infuse, instill, imbue, perfuse, transfuse, pour in, decant, shoot [Inf]

▶ *Entry 706*

11 **impact,** thrust in, drive in, plunge in, run in, push in, force in, hammer in, knock in, pound in, ram in, jam in, cram in, press in, squeeze in, crowd in, stuff in, pack in

▶ *Contents 577; Container 578*

12 **immerse,** submerge, plunge, dunk, dip, duck, baptize, steep, souse, drench, flood, bury, inter, immerse oneself in, bury oneself in, immerge [Arch]

▶ *Burial 31; Lowering 716*

13 **inset,** set in, inlay, slip in, slide in, ease in, wedge in, infix, dovetail, tip in *or* on; embed, bed in, encapsulate, ensheathe, sheathe, encase, case, box, cover, mount, frame, circumscribe

▶ *Woodworking 131; Covering 613; Surroundings 615*

14 **plant,** implant, transplant, plant out, bed out, graft, engraft, ingraft, bud, imp [Arch]

▶ *Agriculture 16; Horticulture 17*

15 **install,** instate, inaugurate, initiate, invest, ordain, induct, enroll, enlist, sign up, sign on, admit

▶ *Admittance 708*

ADVERBS

16 **in,** inside, parenthetically, in parentheses, in brackets

711 Extraction

NOUNS

1 **extraction,** removal, withdrawal, pull, pulling out, drawing, drawing out; tug, tugging out, wrench, wrenching out, wresting out, evulsion, avulsion, ripping out, tearing out, rooting out, uprooting, deracination, eradication, elimination, dredging, fishing, extrication, disengagement, liberation

▶ *Obliteration 186; Destruction 523; Traction 699; Deliverance 817; Liberation 831*

2 **displacement,** dislodgment, expulsion, expression, squeezing out, pruning, thinning, thinning out, weeding, deforestation

▶ *Displacement 574; Expulsion 709*

3 **digging out,** digging up, unearthing, disinterment, exhumation, disentombment, graverobbing, cutting

out, excision, exsection, excavation, mining, quarrying, drilling
> *Concavity 635; Separation 753*

4 **drawing off,** sucking, sucking out, suction, exsuction, draft, aspiration, vacuuming, pumping, siphoning, tapping, milking, pipetting, broaching, emptying, draining, cupping, bleeding, bloodletting, phlebotomy, venesection, evisceration, gutting, disembowelment, shelling

5 **drawing out,** bringing forth, elicitation, evocation, eduction, calling forth, arousal, stimulation, obtaining, derivation
> *Gain 467*

6 **extortion,** wresting, wrenching, wringing, tearing, ripping, wrest, wrench, wring, exaction, demand, claim
> *Taking 477*

7 **obtaining of an extract,** extraction, separation, refinement, purification, distillation, sublimation, condensation, vaporization, decoction, infusion, squeezing, pressing, expressing, rendering, rendition, steeping, soaking, marinating, concentration

8 **extract,** essence, quintessence, spirit, elixir, decoction, infusion, distillate, sublimate, concentrate, juice
> *Essence 723; Part 760*

9 **extractor,** excavator, miner, quarrier, digger, mechanical digger; shovel, pick, pickax, toothpick, rake, dredge, dredger, shadoof, Persian wheel, scoop, spoon, lever, crowbar, wrench, corkscrew, screwdriver, forceps, pliers, tweezers, pincers
> *Tool 103*

ADJECTIVES

10 **extractive,** eductive, educible, eradicative, eradicable, removable, uprooting, elicitory

11 **dislodged,** displaced, uprooted, deracinated, extricated, disengaged, liberated, eliminated, extracted

12 **exacting,** exactive, extortionate, extortionary, extortive

VERBS

13 **extract,** remove, withdraw, pull out, draw out, take out, get out, tug out, wrench out, wrest out, evulse, avulse, rip out, tear out, root out, uproot, deracinate, eradicate, eliminate, pluck out, pick out, rake out, dredge, fish, fish out, grub out, extricate, disengage, free, liberate, winkle out [Brit inf]
> *Selection 382; Traction 699; Deliverance 817; Liberation 831*

14 **displace,** dislodge, lever out, smoke out, expel, express, squeeze out, wring out, prune, thin, thin out, weed out, deforest
> *Displacement 574; Expulsion 709*

15 **dig out,** dig up, unearth, disinter, exhume, disentomb, gouge out, cut out, excise, excavate, mine, quarry, drill
> *Concavity 635; Separation 753*

16 **draw off,** suck, suck out, draw, aspirate, vacuum,

pump, pump out, siphon, siphon off, tap, milk, pipette, broach, empty, drain, cup, bleed

17 **draw out,** bring forth, elicit, evoke, educe, worm out, bring to light, summon up, call up, rouse, arouse, stimulate, obtain, get, procure, secure, derive, induce, deduce, glean; eviscerate, gut, disembowel, shell

18 **extort,** wrest, wrench, wring, force out, tear out, rip out, exact, demand, claim
> *Taking 477*

19 **obtain an extract,** separate, refine, purify, cream off, distill, condense, vaporize, decoct, infuse, squeeze, press, melt down, render, steep, soak, marinate, concentrate, essentialize

ADVERBS

20 **away,** apart, asunder, removably, exactingly, exigently

712 Overstepping

NOUNS

1 **overstepping,** overrunning, overrun, overpassing, overtaking, overgrowth, overspreading, inundation, overflowing, irruption, flooding, flood

2 **crossing,** crossing-over, transcursion, transcendence, leapfrog, jump, excursion, extravagation

3 **transgression,** trespass, incursion, infringement, infraction, encroachment, intrusion, invasion, infestation, plague, violation, breach, usurpation, taking liberties

4 **excessiveness,** exaggeration, overacting, overplaying, overestimation, overrating, arrogation, hyperbole, excess, overfulfillment, surplus, redundance, overindulgence, intemperance, greed
> *Excess 99; Exaggeration 194; Self-Indulgence 456*

5 **expansionism,** overextension, empire building, imperialism
> *Expansion 581*

ADJECTIVES

6 **overrun,** overspread, overgrown, overtaken, overflowing, brimming, flooding, flooded, inundated, infested, beset, teeming, swarming, plagued, encroaching

7 **transgressing,** trespassing, intrusive, invasive

8 **excessive,** unwarranted, overreaching, undue, uncalled-for, exorbitant, surplus

9 **exaggerated,** overdone, pretentious, affected, hyperbolic, overrated, overindulgent, overambitious, strained, far-fetched, grandiose, grandiloquent, bombastic

10 **surpassing,** overextended, overlong, one up on, in the lead, overtaking; outdone, outclassed, outbid, transcended, surmounted, outmaneuvered

11 **out of reach,** unreachable, far away, cut off, secluded, out of bounds, forbidden

VERBS

12 **overstep,** overrun, overpass, overgrow, overreach,

overstride, overleap, leapfrog, jump, go beyond, go too far, overstep the mark *or* bounds, aim too high, overspread, overflow, irrupt, flood, spill over, brim over
> *Excess 99; Expansion 581; Increase 746*

13 **cross,** cross over, cross the border, cross the Rubicon, pass the point of no return
> *Edge 618; Limit 620*

14 **transgress,** trespass, infringe, encroach, entrench, impinge, violate, breach, usurp, squat, poach, break bounds, make inroads, barge in, intrude, invade, overrun, impair, infest
> *Taking 477; Stealing 479; Violence 520*

15 **exceed,** surpass, outdo, outclass, excel, transcend, surmount, rise above; outrival, overbid, outbid, outmaneuver, outflank, outstrip, steal a march on, make the running, outdistance, outride, outrun, overtake, come in front, shoot ahead, lap, leave standing, leave behind, race, beat all hollow
> *Pursuit 385; Distance 585; Motion 677; Forward Motion 679; Superiority 744; Precedence 769; Improvement 807; Haste 818; Success 845*

16 **exaggerate,** overdo, superabound, overrate, overestimate, strain, stretch, stretch a point, go over the limit, overbid, overcall one's hand, overact, overplay, overindulge
> *Exaggeration 194; Overestimation 343; Showiness 404; Self-Indulgence 456*

ADVERBS

17 **excessively,** overindulgently, hyperbolically, greedily, intrusively, invasively

18 **ahead,** in front, in the lead, across the line, over the border, on the other side, over the hills and far away
> *Distance 585*

713 Ascent

NOUNS

1 **ascent,** ascension, rise, rising, levitation, assumption, uprise, uprising, upward motion; gaining height, defying gravity, surfacing, breaking the surface, floating up
> *Verticality 602; Raising 715*

2 **upturn,** upsurge, surge; spurt, gush, jet, spout, fountain; uptrend, upswing, upsweep, upstroke, upcast, upgrowth, upgrade, uprush, updraft
> *Curve 629; Propulsion 696*

3 **incline,** gradient, slope, upward slope, acclivity; upthrow, upthrust, hill, ramp, rising ground, uphill, highland; increase, spiral, uplift, elevation; rising air, rising current
> *Geology 8; Meteorology and Climatology 9; Summit 600*

4 **sunrise,** sunup, first light, morning, morn; moonrise
> *Daytime 655; Nighttime 656*

5 **ascendancy,** advancement, improvement, step up, rise, betterment, upgrade, uptrade; education, self-improvement, enrichment, enhancement, upward mobility, elevation
> *Improvement 807*

6 **taking off,** leaving ground, takeoff, liftoff; flying up, soaring, gaining altitude, spiraling up; zooming *or* shooting *or* rocketing up
> *Astronomy, Astronautics, and Rocketry 7; Aviation 689; Departure 705*

7 **jump,** vault, leap, bound, leapfrog, quantum jump *or* leap, spring, saltation, bounce, hop, skip; hop, skip, and jump
> *Dance and Ballet 135*

8 **mounting,** mount, climb, climbing, scaling, scaling the heights, clamber; mountaineering, alpinism; going up, skylarking, culmination
> *Mountaineering 161; Height 596*

9 **stairway,** stairs, staircase, escalator; steps, treads and risers, flight of stairs, spiral *or* winding staircase; companionway *or* companion, perron, fire escape; landing, landing stage
> *Way 691; Raising 715*

10 **ladder,** scale; stepladder, folding ladder, rope ladder; loft ladder, fire ladder, extension ladder, roof ladder; companion ladder, accommodation ladder, side ladder, boarding ladder, gangway ladder, quarter ladder, stern ladder, Jacob's ladder *or* jack ladder *or* pilot ladder, ratline

11 **step,** stair, footstep, steppingstone, rest, footrest; rung, rundle, round, spoke, stave, scale; doorstep, tread, riser; bridgeboard, string; stepstool

12 **ascender,** soarer, climber; rocket, skyrocket, eagle, lark, skylark, laverock [Scot]; mountaineer, mountain climber, alpinist, rock climber; steeplejack, roofer, stegophilist, foretopman
> *Mountaineering 161*

ADJECTIVES

13 **ascending,** rising, uprising; in the ascendant, gravity-defying; upturned, surging; spurting, gushing, spouting, fountainlike; upsurging, upswinging, upswept

14 **rising,** mounting, buoyant, rampant, rearing, bullish; escalating, ascending, ascendant, ascensional, ascensive, anabatic
> *Economics 56; Lightness 539*

15 **steep,** sloping, acclivitous, rising, uphill, upgrade, upward; climbing, scansorial, scandent

16 **advanced,** improved, stepped-up, bettered, upcast, uplifted; educated, enriched, enhanced, upwardly mobile, elevated

17 **leaping,** springing, vaulting, jumping, hopping; saltatory, saltant, saltatorial; bounding, bouncing, spiraling, soaring, zooming, skyrocketing, rocketing; lifting, gaining height, airborne

18 **ladderlike,** scalar, scalariform, scalable, climbable, stepped

VERBS

19 **ascend,** rise, rise up, arise, uprise, levitate; spiral, spire, aspire, curl upward, upwind, upspin, go up; upturn, upsurge, surge, upheave, swarm up, sweep up; grow up, reach the top, reach the zenith, culminate
▶ *Summit 600*

20 **upturn,** turn up, take an upturn; advance, improve, step up, rise, get better, upgrade, uptrade; educate, enrich, enhance, elevate; trend upward, slope up, upcast, upsweep
▶ *Improvement 807*

21 **climb,** climb up, mount, walk up, struggle up, climb hand over fist, shin *or* shinny up; scale, escalade, scale the heights, top, breast, clear, hurdle; clamber, clamber up, scramble, scramble up, claw one's way up; work one's way up, climb over, surmount, go over the top

22 **spring up,** shoot up, jump up, leap up, vault up, start up, fly up, pop up, bob up; upspring, upstart; spurt, gush, jet, spout, fountain, upheave; surface, float up, break water; jump, spring, leap, vault, hurdle, bound, bounce; hop, skip, push up

23 **go up,** take off, lift off, rocket, skyrocket; leave the ground, leave the earth behind; gain altitude, gain height, claw skyward, become airborne; soar, zoom, fly, plane, kite, fly aloft, spire

24 **mount,** get on, climb on, back, bestride, climb into the saddle, bestraddle; board, go aboard, go on board; hop in, pile in, hop aboard, jump in

ADVERBS

25 **up,** upward, upstairs, uphill; *excelsior* [L], ever upward *or* higher, onward and upward; skyward, heavenward, hand over fist
▶ *Verticality 602; Direction 697*

714 Descent

Facilis descensus Averni [*Easy is the descent to Hell*].
— VIRGIL

NOUNS

1 **descent,** going down, descension, comedown, descending; lowering, declension, decline, declination, downcome [Arch]; way down, downturn, downdraft, downburst, downgrowth, downthrow, demotion, contraction; abseil, rappel; downer [Inf]
▶ *Mountaineering 161; Curve 629; Way 691; Lowering 716; Decrease 747*

2 **sinkage,** decline, decrease, lowering; downward trend, depression, subsidence; droop, drooping, sag, sagging, catenary, slump; immersion, drowning, submergence, lapse; decurrence, cadence, gravitation, downgrade
▶ *Tendency 513; Heaviness 538; Concavity 635; Deterioration 808*

3 **downflow,** downrush; pour, downpour, deluge, shower, rain; cascade, waterfall, rapids, cataract, chute; defluxion, landslide, avalanche, snowslide
▶ *Water 557; Edge 618*

4 **fall,** falling, dropping, drop, plummeting; plunging, plunge, swooping, swoop, dipping, dip, free fall, bungee jumping; tumble, overturning, stumble, stumbling, titubation, trip; sprawl, crash, flop, spill, header [Inf], pratfall, belly flop *or* belly bust *or* belly whop; dive, nosedive, power dive, skydiving; landing, touchdown, forced landing, crash-landing; slide, sliding, slip, slippage, slither; glide, coast, glissade
▶ *Astronomy, Astronautics, and Rocketry 7; Swimming 164; Destruction 523*

5 **nightfall,** sunset, evening, day's end
▶ *Darkness 247; Nighttime 656*

6 **inclination,** declivity, hill, slope; tilt, dip, precipice, sheer drop

7 **downfall,** collapse, debacle, failure; comedown, demotion, humiliation, ruin, end, death; curtains [Inf]
▶ *Obliteration 186; Humility 298; Error 351; End 773; Failure 846*

8 **descender,** faller, parachutist, paratrooper, aeronaut, sky diver, bungee jumper; diver, frogman, submariner, submarine, diving bell, bathysphere, underwater swimmer; diving bird, merganser, kingfisher
▶ *Birds 36; Swimming 164*

ADJECTIVES

9 **descending,** descendant, on the descendant, down; downward, downhill, declivitous; downflowing, downrushing, pouring; downturning, sinking, declining, bearish, decreasing, lowering, subsiding, slumping; drowning, foundering, tottering, tumbling, crashing, collapsing; submersible, sinkable; katabatic
▶ *Economics 56*

10 **drooping,** droopy, sagging, on the downgrade; depressed, downcast, demoted, down at heart, down in the mouth
▶ *Sorrow 270*

11 **falling,** tumbling, stumbling, titubant, tripping; sprawling, flopping, spilling; diving, plunging, plummeting, dipping, nosediving, dropping, swooping; sliding, slipping, slithering, skidding, gliding, coasting

VERBS

12 **descend,** come *or* go down, dip down; lose height *or* altitude, gravitate, lower, get lower, get lower and lower; decrease, decline, abate, ebb, fall off, drop off, tread downward; go downhill, sink, sink down, seep, seep down, soak in; subside, settle, set; submerge, go under, drown, founder, go underwater, dive, reach a lower level; alight, dismount, get down, get off, climb down, abseil, rappel

13 **drip,** drizzle, patter, shower; cascade, flow down, pour, pour down, rain, precipitate; snow, avalanche; rain cats and dogs [Inf]

14 **droop,** hang down, sag, slouch, swag; slump, slump

down, sit down, flop, flop down, plump, plop, plump down, plop down; prolapse, collapse, cave, cave in, crash, give way

15 **drop,** fall, fall *or* drop down, take a fall *or* spill; fall headlong, measure one's length, fall prostrate, miss one's footing; plummet, pitch, plunge, swoop; titubate, flutter down, spiral, spiral down; dive, belly-flop *or* belly-bust *or* belly-whop, nosedive, power-dive; drop, drop from the sky, fall through the air, bungee jump; parachute, skydive, fly down, pounce; land, light upon, alight upon, come down on, settle on, descend on, touch down, get down, crash-land

16 **trip,** fall over, topple, topple over; overbalance, overturn, capsize, tumble, take a tumble, take a header [Inf]

17 **slide,** slide down, slip, slither, skid, glide, skim; coast, glissade, toboggan, ski; incline, sideslip, slope, tilt, dip, list, be oblique

18 **fail,** fall down, fall in, touch depth, reach the depths; touch bottom, sink to the bottom; reach one's nadir, come down a peg; fall flat on one's face, take a nosedive, bite the dust

ADVERBS

19 **down,** downward, adown [Arch], down below, downhill, downstairs, downgrade
  ▶ *Direction 697*

715 Raising

NOUNS

1 **raising,** elevation, lifting; upping, boosting, hiking up; erection, levitation, escalation, buoyancy; rearing, uprearing, upliftment; rising, elevating; uplift, levitation, hoist, heave, upheaval; upthrow, upcast, upthrust; picking up, ascent, defiance of gravity, antigravity
  ▶ *Ascent 713*

2 **rearing,** raising up, bringing up, nurturing; breeding, stocking, fattening up; farming, growing, planting
  ▶ *Agriculture 16; Horticulture 17*

3 **promotion,** lift, boost, upswinging, upgrading, aid, leg up; exaltation, apotheosis, deification, canonization, beatification, enshrinement, lionization

4 **height,** eminence, sublimity, loftiness, prominence
  ▶ *Height 596; Summit 600*

5 **lifter,** erector, crane, dredger, derrick, hoist, crab, gantry crane, cherry picker, lever, jack, jackscrew; lift, hydraulic lift, forklift, hydraulic tailgate; windlass, winch, tackle, capstan, rope and pulley, block and tackle; elevator, lift [Brit], escalator, moving staircase, dumb waiter; spring, springboard, trampoline; ski lift, funicular, chair lift, conveyor; hot-air balloon, helium balloon, barrage balloon, hydrogen balloon; raising agent, yeast, baking powder, leaven
  ▶ *Engineering 14; Tool 103; Ascent 713*

ADJECTIVES

6 **raised,** elevated, lifted; upraised, boosted, hiked up; erected, erectile, levitated, escalated, buoyant; uplifted, hoisted, heaved, mounted, lobbed, thrown, shot up; upthrown, upcast, upthrust; ascending, antigravitational; supportive, upstanding, vertical
  ▶ *Support 605; Ascent 713*

7 **reared,** raised up, brought up, nurtured, tended; bred, stocked, fattened up; farmed, grown, planted

8 **promoted,** upgraded, elevated; exalted, prominent, eminent, lofty, sublime, high-flown; apotheosized, deified, canonized, beatified, enshrined, lionized

VERBS

9 **raise,** elevate, lift; up, upraise, raise up, set up, lift, levitate, uplift, lift up; hoist, heist, hike, heft, heave, upheave; perk up, buoy up, help up, put on, mount
  ▶ *Height 596; Support 605; Ascent 713*

10 **rear,** raise up, bring up, nurture; incubate, breed, stock, fatten up; farm, grow, plant

11 **erect,** build, build up, put up; jack up, prop up, shoulder, boost; hike up, hold up, uphold, support

12 **send up,** upthrow, upcast; throw in the air, lob, loft, knock up, flight, shoot up, propel; blow up, puff up, swell, increase, escalate
  ▶ *Motion 677; Impulsion 695; Propulsion 696; Ascent 713; Increase 746; Improvement 807*

13 **promote,** heighten, give a lift, give a leg up, boost, enhance, upgrade, elevate; exalt, put on a pedestal, crown; apotheosize, deify, canonize, beatify, enshrine, lionize
  ▶ *Deity 82; Summit 600; Improvement 807; Help 825*

14 **gather up,** pick up, pluck up, take up, draw up; haul up, drag up, dredge up

15 **arise,** rise, rise up, rear, rear up, go on hind legs; lift oneself, stand up; get up, jump up, jump to one's feet, leap up, leap *or* spring to one's feet, pull oneself up; hold oneself up, hold one's head up, draw oneself to one's full height, stand on tiptoe
  ▶ *Verticality 602*

ADVERBS

16 **highly,** on high, aloft; on stilts, on tiptoe, on one's hind legs, on the shoulders of

716 Lowering

NOUNS

1 **lowering,** depression, deflation; reduction, decrease, de-escalation, diminution; deterioration, worsening; descent, drop, downfall; rainfall, shower, precipitation; fall, trip, tumble, spillage
  ▶ *Water 557; Descent 714; Deterioration 808*

2 **downthrow,** downcast; flattening, leveling, grounding; overthrow, overturn, overset, upset, toppling; subversion, revolution, overturning

> *Anarchy 51*

3 **submergence,** sinking; plunging, keeping down, keeping under, suppression, oppression; pushing under, thrusting under, pushing down, detrusion; ducking, swooping, sousing

4 **depression,** indentation, hollow, cavity, concavity; dip, dent, sinkhole
> *Concavity 635*

5 **debasement,** degradation, downgrading, demotion, deterioration, humiliation; bowing and scraping, groveling
> *Humility 298*

6 **bow,** bend, curtsy, nod, bob, duck; crouch, hunch, stoop, squat; genuflection, kneeling, kowtow, salaam, low *or* sweeping bow; reverence, obeisance, prostration, abasement, self-abasement

ADJECTIVES

7 **lowered,** lowering, low, descendent, descending, dropping, falling; depressed, depressing, deflated, flattened; reduced, decreasing, decreased, diminishing, diminished, deteriorating, deteriorated, worse, worsened; grounded, leveled, demolished
> *Decrease 747; Deterioration 808*

8 **fallen,** falling, toppling, tumbling, tripping; downcast, downthrown, sunk, sunken, soused, submerged; showering, sprinkling, scattering, spilling, dropping, precipitous

9 **overthrown,** cast down, overset, upset, toppled; subverted, overturned, revolutionized
> *Anarchy 51; Subjection 832*

10 **degraded,** degrading, debased, debasing, demeaning; downgraded, demoted, humiliated, humiliating; cast down, downcast, depressed, depressive; kowtowing, kneeling, groveling, courteous, deferential
> *Humility 298*

11 **sedentary,** sitting, crouching, stooping, squatting; hunched, hunkered down, bent, bent double; prostrate, supine, prone, spread-eagle
> *Inactivity 415; Lowness 597*

VERBS

12 **lower,** depress, deflate, reduce, decrease, de-escalate, diminish; deteriorate, worsen; let down, take down, lay down, set down, put down
> *Insufficiency 98; Lowness 597; Descent 714; Decrease 747; Deterioration 808*

13 **throw down,** throw, cast down, fling, fling down, shed; pitch, throw overboard, drop over the side, let fall, drop, let drop, let go; let slip, slip through one's fingers; scatter, dust, sow, pour out, pour
> *Dispersion 776*

14 **bring down,** overthrow, overturn, shoot down, shoot down in flames, couch, pull down, take down; overset, upset, topple, subvert; floor, send headlong, lay out, bowl over; torpedo, scuttle, sink, submerge, drown, duck, souse, douse, plunge, send to the bottom; pull *or* fall down about one's ears, trample in the dust; deck [Inf]
> *War 76; Inversion 608*

15 **flatten,** level, lay level, demolish, raze; fell, down, cut down, hew down, chop down, mow down, pull down, tear down; dent, crush, stave in
> *War 76; Obliteration 186; Destruction 523; End 773*

16 **debase,** abase, degrade, demote, put down, humble, reduce to the ranks, cashier; humiliate, snub, deflate, debunk; downgrade, lower standards
> *Humility 298; Inferiority 745*

17 **water down,** dilute, adulterate

18 **bear down on,** push down, thrust down, detrude; weigh on, suppress, keep down, put a lid on, keep under, hold down, squash

19 **lean,** incline, lean over backward, lean forward, bend forward, bend backward, bend over; tip, tilt, trip, topple
> *Backward Motion 680*

20 **sit,** sit down, seat oneself, be seated; perch, alight; squat, hunker down, scrunch down, get down on one's haunches, crouch, hunch down; stoop, bend, duck, get down, scrooch down. park oneself [Inf]
> *Inactivity 415; Lowness 597*

21 **lie down,** prostrate, flatten oneself; couch, recline, drape oneself, spread-eagle
> *Lowness 597*

22 **bow,** make a bow, bend, curtsy, bob, nob, duck, incline one's head; genuflect, kneel, kowtow, salaam, bow low, bow down, kiss hands, kiss rings; revere, pay one's respects, do reverence, make obeisance, prostrate oneself, abase oneself; grovel, cower, cringe, wallow, welter
> *Humility 298; Servility 401; Obedience 426*

23 **lower the flag,** lower the standard, haul down, half-mast, strike, strike the colors
> *Military Affairs 58*

ADVERBS

24 **down,** downward, to the ground, decreasingly, reductively, subversively, oppressively
> *Base 601*

25 **on the ground,** on the floor, in the dirt, on the bottom, at rock bottom, at a low ebb, at half-mast
> *Seas 571; Depth 598*

26 **humbly,** degradingly, on one's knees, on one's back

Abstract Relations

717 Existence

*Row, row, row your boat / Gently down the solution, /
Merrily, merrily, merrily, merrily, / Existence is but a
delusion.* — NURSERY RHYME PARODY

NOUNS

1 **existence,** being, life, subsistence, coexistence, *esse*
[L], occurrence, presence, monadism

2 **philosophy of being,** metaphysics, ontology, existentialism
▶ *Philosophy 4*

3 **thing,** something, ens, entity, being, body, object, substance, item, monad, phenomenon, happening

4 **nature,** fundamental nature, essential nature, essence,
quiddity, innateness, materiality, substantiality
▶ *Essence 723*

5 **demonstrable existence,** reality, actuality, factuality,
truth, authenticity, necessity, historicity, the real thing,
facticity
▶ *Reality 719; Truth 721*

6 **fact,** fact *or* truth of the matter, matter of fact, the
case, basic fact(s); facts, basics, realities, specifics, fundamentals, essentials, whole story, nuts and bolts, bottom line, the picture; [Inf]: what's what, gen [Brit],
nitty-gritty, brass tacks, dope, scoop, score
▶ *Information 170*

7 **continuing existence,** duration, endurance, persistence, continuance, survival, perpetuity

8 **self-existence,** aseity, uncreated being, deity, divinity
▶ *Religion 81*

9 **creation,** coming into being, conception, birth, materialization, actualization, evolution, big bang
▶ *Cause 675; Beginning 771*

10 **mere existence,** vegetable existence, vegetation, stagnation, inertia, torpor, persistent vegetative state *or*
syndrome
▶ *Inertness 519*

ADJECTIVES

11 **existing,** existent, being, living, subsistent, coexistent, occurring, present, prevalent, current, extant,
manifest, necessary, in force, in effect

12 **intrinsic,** innate, inherent, essential, basic, fundamental, natural, material, substantial, substantive, concrete, ontological

13 **lasting,** enduring, persisting, persistent, abiding, continual, continuous, surviving, perpetual

14 **real,** actual, factual, de facto, true, authentic, veritable,
undeniable, indisputable, positive, provable, empirical,
historical, phenomenal

15 **self-existent,** self-existing, uncreated, godlike,
divine

16 **created,** materialized, made, actualized, conceived,
evolved

17 **vegetating,** stagnating, stagnant, inert, torpid

VERBS

18 **exist,** be, live, breathe, coexist, subsist, inhabit, dwell,
occur, be there, be found, be true

19 **come to be,** become, materialize, take shape *or* form,
be born, evolve, arise, come about, grow, develop, unfold; bring into being, create, make, conceive, form,
make up, compose, devise, invent, cause, realize, actualize, factualize, reify

20 **continue to be,** endure, last, persist, abide, continue,
survive, prevail, live on, stand, hold, remain, stay
▶ *Cause 675; Beginning 771*

21 **merely exist,** vegetate, stagnate

ADVERBS

22 **really,** actually, basically, fundamentally, factually,
necessarily, essentially, existentially, inherently,
truly, demonstrably, manifestly, positively, in fact, as a
matter of fact, in point of fact, ipso facto, de facto, to
all intents and purposes, as it happens; no ifs, ands, or
buts

718 Nonexistence

NOUNS

1 **nonexistence,** nonbeing, nonentity, unbeing, non-subsistence, nonoccurrence, nonhappening

2 **nothingness,** nullity, nothing, nil, naught, zero, nothing whatever, nothing at all, nothing on earth, nothing under the sun, no such thing; [Inf]: zilch, zip, sweet Fanny Adams *or* sweet FA [Brit]

3 **negativeness,** negativity, negation, denial, refusal
   ▶ *Negation 190; Refutation 332*

4 **emptiness,** vacuity, vacancy, vacuum, void, limbo, blankness, hole, gap, break, lacuna, interval, space
   ▶ *Space 563; Interval 587*

5 **nonreality,** unreality, imagination, fantasy, make-believe
   ▶ *Imagination 360; Unreality 720*

6 **absence,** no one, nobody, none, not a one, never a one, ne'er a one, nary a one, not a blessed one [Inf]
   ▶ *Absence 576*

7 **not any,** not a bit, not a whit, not a hint, not a speck, not a mite, not a particle, not an iota, not a jot, not a scrap, not a trace, not a suspicion, not a shadow of a suspicion *or* doubt, neither hide nor hair, not a smidgen, not a lick [Inf]

8 **extinction,** obliteration, annihilation, obsolescence, oblivion, death
   ▶ *Obliteration 186; Forgetfulness 355*

ADJECTIVES

9 **nonexistent**, absent, missing, minus, negative, null, void, vacant, empty, blank, devoid, lacking

10 **unreal,** imaginary, illusory, fanciful, fantastical, make-believe
    ▶ *Unreality 720*

11 **no more,** extinct, died out, vanished, dead, passed away, dead and gone, all over, over and done with, defunct, obsolete, dead as a doornail, past, finished, ended, annihilated, obliterated, destroyed, wiped out, kaput [Inf]
    ▶ *History 3; Death 29; Obliteration 186; Destruction 523*

VERBS

12 **not exist,** not be, be null and void

13 **cease to exist,** vanish, disappear, end, leave no trace, disappear without a trace, melt, dissolve, evaporate, melt away, go up in a puff of smoke, die, expire, pass away, die out, die away, peter out, fade away, turn to nothing, pass out of the picture [Inf], kick the bucket [Inf]
    ▶ *Death 29*

14 **cause not to exist,** annihilate, destroy, exterminate, eradicate, wipe out, stamp out, extinguish, snuff out, kill, slay, murder, abort, miscarry, cancel, invalidate, annul, negate, end, veto, vaporize, nuke [Inf]

▶ *Killing 30*

ADVERBS

15 **not at all,** by no means, absolutely not, to no extent, on no account, under no circumstances, not by any stretch of the imagination, in no way, no way [Inf]

16 **not ever,** never, at no time, not at any time, not in a million years

17 **nowhere,** in no place, neither here nor there, not on this earth

719 Reality

Human kind / Cannot bear very much reality.
— T. S. ELIOT

NOUNS

1 **reality,** objective existence, actuality, occurrence, presence, entelechy, material existence, materiality, corporeality, solidity, substantiality, tangibility, substantivity, validity, fact, factuality, matter of fact, the here and now, practicality
   ▶ *Existence 717; Certainty 840*

2 **real world,** substance, matter, thing, physical world, material world, natural world, universe, cosmos
   ▶ *Material World 524*

3 **realism,** real life, naturalism, authenticity, historicity, pragmatism, verisimilitude, documentary, cinema vérité, kitchen-sink drama, slice of life
   ▶ *Accuracy 350; Truth 721*

4 **realist,** pragmatist

5 **realities,** basics, fundamentals, facts of life, home truths, bottom line

ADJECTIVES

6 **real,** actual, occurring, existing, entelechial, true, factual, valid, historical, material, corporeal, tangible, solid, substantial, substantive
   ▶ *Existence 717*

7 **realistic,** natural, naturalistic, lifelike, real-life, true to life, truthful, authentic, genuine, faithful, graphic

8 **practical,** realistic, pragmatic, expedient, sensible, matter-of-fact, no-nonsense, no-frills, down-to-earth, businesslike, levelheaded, sound, functional, utilitarian, usable, serviceable, workable, operative

9 **realizable,** achievable, attainable, practicable, plausible, feasible, possible, probable, likely

VERBS

10 **be real,** exist, occur, happen, loom large

11 **make real,** realize, actualize, materialize, factualize, reify, visualize

12 **establish reality,** validate, authenticate, verify, prove, demonstrate, establish, settle the matter, set at rest, prove one's point, nail down, ascertain, substantiate, corroborate, bear out, confirm, attest, uphold, certify, sustain, reinforce, back up, ratify, endorse, clinch [Inf]

13 **really,** actually, in reality, in fact, de facto, in effect, in actuality, in practice, in all likelihood; when it comes to the crunch, when the chips are down, when push comes to shove, really-truly, honest-to-God

14 **certainly,** indeed, truly, honestly, in truth, undoubtedly, indubitably, no buts about it, nothing else but

720 Unreality

NOUNS

1 **unreality,** nonexistence, unsubstantiality, intangibility, impalpability, incorporeality, ethereality, immateriality, immaterialism

2 **illusion,** fantasy, chimera, phantasmagoria, fancy, flight of fancy, figment, castles in the air *or* in Spain, pipe dream, daydream, dream, nightmare, hallucination, mirage, Fata Morgana, will-o'-the-wisp, ignis fatuus, jack-o'-lantern, vision, appearance, apparition, phantasm, phantom, ghost, specter, spirit, wraith, shade, shadow, fetch, simulacrum, spook [Inf]
   ◗ *Imagination 360*

3 **delusion,** misconception, fallacy, self-deception, false impression, optical illusion, trompe l'oeil, trick of the light, sleight of hand, illusionism, magic, conjuring, trick
   ◗ *Deception 193; Error 351*

4 **theory,** theorization, hypothesis, assumption, speculation, conjecture, guesswork, fiction, empty talk, empty promises, fool's paradise, false dawn, wishful thinking, idealism, utopianism; wind, hot air, gas [Inf], pie in the sky
   ◗ *Supposition 359; Untruth 722*

5 **insubstantial person,** nobody, nothing, nonperson, unperson, nonentity, hollow man, straw man, man of straw [Brit], broken reed, paper tiger, puppet, dummy, jackstraw, nebbish [Inf], windbag [Inf]

6 **unrealistic person,** speculator, theorizer, idealist, romantic, visionary, dreamer

7 **artificiality,** imitation, simulation, shadow, image, fake, sham, artifact
   ◗ *Untruthfulness, Falsehood 192*

ADJECTIVES

8 **unreal,** nonexistent, incorporeal, intangible, impalpable, insubstantial, unsubstantial, ethereal, elusive, fugitive, fleeting, obscure, nebulous, tenuous, vague, flimsy, hollow, airy, hazy, indeterminate, indefinite, undefined, blurred, shadowy, ghostly, spectral, phantasmal

9 **illusory,** fantastic, dreamlike, chimerical, phantasmagorical, fancied, hallucinatory, figmental, visional, delusory

10 **theoretical,** hypothetical, abstract, ideal, speculative, assumed, putative, mythical, fanciful, imaginary, fictional, fictitious, made-up, make-believe

11 **unrealistic,** idealistic, utopian, visionary, romantic

12 **artificial,** synthetic, man-made, simulated, imitation, mock, pretend, pretended, dummy, sham, fake, false, spurious, specious, phony, bogus, counterfeit, so-called, put-on, quasi, pseudo

VERBS

13 **imagine,** fantasize, conjure up, dream, daydream, hallucinate, hear things, see things

14 **theorize,** hypothesize, conceptualize, conjecture, guess

15 **idealize,** romanticize, see through rose-colored glasses, build castles in the air *or* in Spain

16 **delude,** deceive, mislead, give the wrong idea *or* impression, misrepresent, belie, distort, pervert, embroider, embellish, twist, fudge, gild, varnish, whitewash, spin a yarn

17 **fabricate,** manufacture, simulate, imitate, make up, invent, hatch, concoct, cook up [Inf]

ADVERBS

18 **ideally,** in theory, theoretically, hypothetically, perfectly

19 **apparently,** to all appearances, seemingly, ostensibly, allegedly, putatively, purportedly, professedly, avowedly, superficially, in name only

721 Truth

'Tis strange — but true; for truth is always strange; Stranger than fiction. — LORD BYRON

NOUNS

1 **truth,** trueness, veracity, veraciousness, factuality, factualness; fact, indisputable fact, verity, eternal verities, the true, sooth [Arch]
   ◗ *Accuracy 350; Certainty 840*

2 **reality,** realness, actuality, actual existence, existence, substance, substantiality, tangibility; real world, things as they are
   ◗ *Material World 524; Existence 717; Reality 719*

3 **the truth,** facts, facts of the matter, facts of life; plain truth, simple truth, basic truth, home truth; the very truth, the absolute truth, the unalloyed truth, the unvarnished truth, the naked truth, the straight truth, the honest truth *or* honest-to-goodness *or* honest-to-God truth, gospel truth, the whole truth and nothing but the truth, lowdown [Inf]
   ◗ *Truthfulness 191*

4 **trueness,** rightness, correctness, perfection, flawlessness; accuracy, pinpoint accuracy, precision, preciseness, exactness, exactitude, meticulousness, attention to detail
   ◗ *Attention 323; Carefulness 325; Accuracy 350; Perfection 805*

5 **adjustment,** refinement, fine-tuning, truing *or* trueing, squaring, setting

◗ *Improvement 807*

6 truism, basic truth, intrinsic truth, primary premise, principle, axiom; maxim, precept, aphorism, proverb, dictum, adage, platitude, cliché

◗ *Maxim 177*

7 authenticity, genuineness, realness, veritableness, validity, legitimacy, rightfulness; unquestionableness, indisputability, indisputableness, undeniableness, indubitability, indubitableness; purity, unadulteration; genuine article, real thing, not a fake, no imitation, the McCoy *or* the real McCoy

◗ *Affirmation 189; Certainty 840*

8 authentication, validation, certification, verification, confirmation; determination, ascertainment, demonstration, establishment; attestation, substantiation, corroboration, proof, facts, evidence

◗ *Affirmation 189; Demonstration 331; Evidence 339*

9 literalness, literality, literalism, exactness, truthfulness, reliability, reliableness; faithfulness, fidelity, agreement, consistency, conformity, adherence, textualism; literal meaning *or* sense, denotation, literal interpretation, word-for-word translation, transliteration, verbatim account, the very words

◗ *Interpretation 365; Conformity 781*

10 verisimilitude, lifelikeness, look of reality, appearance of truth, ring of truth; realism, absolute realism, representationalism, naturalism; faithful rendering, realistic representation, true portrayal

◗ *Painting and Drawing 143; Representation 187; Reality 719*

ADJECTIVES

11 true, veracious, real, factual, unfallacious, unfictitious, sooth [Arch]

◗ *Truthfulness 191; Certainty 840*

12 real, actual, existing, existent, substantive, substantial, tangible; real-world, real-life

◗ *Material World 524; Existence 717; Reality 719*

13 correct, right, true, flawless, faultless, perfect, letter-perfect; accurate, precise, exact, meticulous; dead-on [Inf]

◗ *Carefulness 325; Accuracy 350*

14 adjusted, finely adjusted, refined, fine-tuned, trued, squared, set, straightened

◗ *Improvement 807*

15 truistic, intrinsic, basic, axiomatic, self-evident; preceptive, aphoristic, proverbial, platitudinous, cliché *or* clichéd

◗ *Maxim 177*

16 authentic, genuine, real, bona fide, veritable, valid, legitimate, rightful, trueborn, pukka; unquestionable, indisputable, undeniable, indubitable, undoubtable; pure, simon-pure, unadulterated, honest-to-goodness *or* honest-to-God, sure enough

◗ *Affirmation 189; Certainty 840*

17 authenticated, validated, certified, verified, confirmed; determined, ascertained, demonstrated, established; attested to, substantiated, corroborated, proved *or* proven

◗ *Affirmation 189; Demonstration 331; Evidence 339*

18 literal, literalistic, exact, truthful, true to fact, true to the facts, reliable; faithful, consistent, conforming, adherent, textual, true to the letter, denotative, word-for-word, verbatim

◗ *Truthfulness 191; Conformity 781*

19 lifelike, verisimilar, realistic, true to life, true-life; realist, representational, representationalistic, naturalist, naturalistic, true to nature, faithfully rendered

◗ *Painting and Drawing 143; Representation 187; Reality 719*

VERBS

20 be true, be the case, conform to facts, square with the facts *or* evidence; hold true, hold water, hold up, stand up, stand the test, stand the test of time, hold up in the wash [Inf], wash [Inf]

◗ *Conformity 781; Certainty 840*

21 be real, exist, be, be tangible, have substance; bring into existence, actualize, make tangible; know the real world, see things as they are; come true, become a reality

◗ *Material World 524; Existence 717; Reality 719*

22 be accurate, be correct, hit the nail on the head, score a bull's-eye [Inf]; be precise, be meticulous, dot one's i's and cross one's t's; make correct, correct, make right, right, perfect, make accurate, pinpoint

◗ *Accuracy 350*

23 adjust, refine, make fine adjustments, true, true up, square, set, straighten, even, even up

◗ *Improvement 807*

24 authenticate, validate, certify, verify, confirm; determine, ascertain, demonstrate, establish, get at the truth; attest to, substantiate, corroborate, prove, show evidence

◗ *Affirmation 189; Demonstration 331; Evidence 339*

25 be literal, follow the letter, follow to the letter, conform, adhere; make literal, literalize, transliterate, interpret literally; give the true story, be true to the facts, give a true report, give a verbatim account, repeat word-for-word, use the very words

◗ *Conformity 781*

26 seem true, seem lifelike, seem real, seem true to life, look real, come alive; give the appearance of truth, have the ring of truth, ring true, sound true; represent realistically, give a true portrayal, render faithfully, copy nature, bring alive

◗ *Painting and Drawing 143; Reality 719*

ADVERBS

27 truly, true, in a true manner, veraciously, verily, factually, unfallaciously, unfictitiously, really, really-truly, certainly, no buts *or* question about it

28 in truth, in fact, in point of fact, as a matter of fact, indeed, actually, in reality, forsooth [Arch]; substantively, substantially, tangibly; in the real world, in real life

29 **correctly,** rightly, truly, flawlessly, faultlessly, perfectly; accurately, precisely, exactly, to the letter, meticulously; squarely, square, plumb, even, evenly, level, levelly, straight; [Inf]: on the nose, on the button

30 **intrinsically,** basically, essentially, axiomatically; preceptively, aphoristically, proverbially

31 **authentically,** genuinely, really, veritably, validly, legitimately, rightfully; unquestionably, indisputably, undeniably, indubitably, undoubtedly, without a doubt, for sure, to be sure; purely, unadulteratedly

32 **literally,** literalistically, strictly speaking, exactly, truthfully, reliably; faithfully, consistently, in conformity, adherently, textually; verbatim, word for word, letter for letter, *verbatim et literatim* [L], in exactly the same words

33 **verisimilarly,** realistically, representationally, naturalistically

INTERJECTIONS

34 **that's for sure!,** for sure!, honest!, ain't it *or* that the truth! [Inf]

722 Untruth

NOUNS

1 **untruth,** falsity, lack of factuality, untrueness, untruthfulness, lack of veracity, fallaciousness
   ◗ *Untruthfulness, Falsehood 192; Uncertainty 841*

2 **unreality,** nonexistence, lack of substance, unsubstantiality, insubstantiality, intangibility, intangibleness, impalpability, vagueness; illusion, illusoriness, delusiveness; fictitiousness, fancifulness, imaginariness, imagination, mythicalness, mythology; invention, myth, illusion, delusion, dream, fancy, fantasy, figment
   ◗ *Imagination 360; Nonexistence 718; Unreality 720*

3 **untrueness,** falseness, incorrectness, erroneousness, faultiness, inaccurateness, imprecision, impreciseness, inexactness, inexactitude; imperfection, fault, distortion, inaccuracy, mistake, error, fallacy; misestimation, overestimation, underestimation; misjudgment, misconstruction, misinterpretation, misapprehension, misimpression, misconception
   ◗ *Misjudgment 342; Overestimation 343; Underestimation 344; Error 351; Misinterpretation 366*

4 **unauthenticity,** inauthenticity, lack of authenticity, ungenuineness, artificiality, counterfeitness, falseness, spuriousness, phoniness *or* phoneyness, hokeyness *or* hokiness, invalidity, illegitimacy; questionableness, disputability, disputableness, deniability, doubtfulness, uncertainty; impurity, adulteration; imitation, copy, fake, phony *or* phoney, counterfeit, forgery

◗ *Imitation 736; Uncertainty 841*

5 **unreliability,** unreliableness, unfaithfulness, infidelity, disagreement, inconsistency, nonconformity
   ◗ *Nonconformity 782*

ADJECTIVES

6 **untrue,** false, unreal, unfactual, untruthful, fallacious, unsound, groundless, unfounded
   ◗ *Untruthfulness, Falsehood 192*

7 **unreal,** nonexistent, inexistent, nonexisting, unsubstantial, insubstantial, intangible, untangible, impalpable, vague; illusive, illusory, delusive, delusory, fictitious, invented, dreamed-up, make-believe, imagined, imaginary, fanciful, fantastic *or* fantastical, mythical *or* mythic, mythological *or* mythologic
   ◗ *Imagination 360; Nonexistence 718; Unreality 720*

8 **incorrect,** untrue, false, erroneous, mistaken, faulty, imperfect, distorted; inaccurate, imprecise, inexact, overestimated, underestimated; misjudged, misconstrued, misinterpreted, misconceived
   ◗ *Misjudgment 342; Overestimation 343; Underestimation 344; Error 351*

9 **unauthentic,** inauthentic, ungenuine, imitation, artificial, synthetic, false, unreal, fake, phony *or* phoney, spurious, sham, bogus, hokey, counterfeit, copied, imitated, forged, invalid, illegitimate; questionable, disputable, deniable, doubtful, uncertain; impure, adulterated
   ◗ *Untruthfulness, Falsehood 192; Imitation 736; Uncertainty 841*

10 **unreliable,** unfaithful, disagreeing, inconsistent, nonconforming
   ◗ *Nonconformity 782*

VERBS

11 **be untrue,** be false, be untruthful, lack factuality, not conform to the facts, not square with the facts; not hold water, not hold up, not hold up in the wash [Inf]
   ◗ *Untruthfulness, Falsehood 192; Uncertainty 841*

12 **be unreal,** not exist, be nonexistent, be intangible, have no substance; delude, invent, dream up, make believe, imagine, fancy, fantasize, pretend, mythologize, mythicize
   ◗ *Imagination 360; Nonexistence 718; Unreality 720*

13 **be incorrect,** be untrue, be erroneous, be mistaken, make a mistake, be inaccurate *or* imprecise; distort, overestimate, underestimate, misjudge, misconstrue, misinterpret, misapprehend
   ◗ *Misjudgment 342; Overestimation 343; Underestimation 344; Error 351*

ADVERBS

14 **without truth,** falsely, unreally, unfactually, untruthfully, fallaciously, unsoundly, without foundation, without grounds
   ◗ *Untruthfulness, Falsehood 192*

15 **unreally,** nonexistently, without substance, unsub-

stantially, insubstantially, intangibly, impalpably, vaguely; illusively, illusorily, fictitiously, fancifully, imaginarily, fantastically, mythically, mythologically

> *Imagination 360; Nonexistence 718; Unreality 720*

16 **incorrectly,** falsely, erroneously, mistakenly, faultily, imperfectly, distortedly, inaccurately, imprecisely, inexactly

> *Misjudgment 342; Overestimation 343; Underestimation 344; Error 351*

17 **unauthentically,** inauthentically, ungenuinely, artificially, synthetically, falsely, unreally, phonily, spuriously, counterfeitly, invalidly, illegitimately; questionably, disputably, doubtfully, uncertainly

> *Untruthfulness, Falsehood 192; Imitation 736; Uncertainty 841*

18 **nonsensically,** pratingly, prattlingly, drivelingly

> *Lack of Meaning 362*

723 Essence

NOUNS

1 **essence,** quiddity, subject, substance, structure, stuff, material, matter, fabric, medium, building blocks

2 **essential content,** basis, core, kernel, gist, meat, heart, backbone, nub, nucleus, marrow, pith, sap, lifeblood, crux, subject matter, principle, issue, gravamen, highlight, high point, center, focus, pivot, keystone, cornerstone, landmark, benchmark, milestone, nuts and bolts, bottom line; nitty-gritty [Inf], name of the game [Inf]

3 **quintessence,** embodiment, incarnation, personification, epitome, archetype, soul, spirit, entelechy, flower, elixir, extract, concentrate, distillate, distillation

> *Existence 717; Reality 719*

4 **nature,** distinguishing feature(s), character, suchness, makeup, constitution, composition, complexion, temperament, disposition, mold, pattern, stamp, type, breed, strain, stripe, humor, mood, trait, hue, quality, attribute, property, nature of the beast

ADJECTIVES

5 **essential,** crucial, vital, necessary, paramount, indispensable, of the essence, prerequisite, requisite, obligatory, mandatory, compulsory, imperative, inalienable, unalienable, uninfringeable, unquestionable

> *Importance 799*

6 **intrinsic,** inherent, basic, primary, fundamental, immanent, innate, inborn, inbred, deep-seated, deep-rooted, ingrained, bred in the bone

7 **integral,** inseparable, ineradicable, built-in, component, constituent, indivisible, integrated

8 **quintessential,** constitutional, structural, organic, peerless, singular, unique, consummate, incarnate, archetypal

9 **characteristic,** distinctive, distinguishing, typical, specific, particular, peculiar, defining, discriminating, idiosyncratic

VERBS

10 **be essential,** be central, be part and parcel of, be crucial

11 **characterize,** identify, depict, portray, represent, delineate, designate, distinguish, differentiate, stamp, inform, mark, demarcate

12 **embody,** incarnate, personify, epitomize, constitute, comprise, incorporate, assimilate, include, embrace, encompass

ADVERBS

13 **in essence,** essentially, intrinsically, per se, primarily, in the main, substantially, materially, by and large, mainly, mostly, chiefly, effectually, for the most part, almost entirely, for all practical purposes, necessarily

14 **at heart,** basically, at the core, fundamentally, at bottom, *au fond* [Fr], radically, in substance

724 Extraneousness

NOUNS

1 **extraneousness,** irrelevance, irrelevancy, immateriality, inessentiality, superfluity, pleonasm, superficiality, redundancy, pointlessness, inapplicability, incidentalness, secondariness, insignificance, triviality, lack of importance

> *Addition 748; Separation 753; Unimportance 800*

2 **foreignness,** alienage, alienism, unrelatedness, unconnectedness, disconnectedness, difference, otherness, exoticness, strangeness, the unknown

3 **separateness,** segregation, dissociation, disaffiliation, nonassimilation, discreteness, isolation, insularity, detachment, noninvolvement, independence, nonconformity

> *Oppositeness 731; Exclusion 764; Nonconformity 782*

4 **externality,** extrinsicality, exteriority, outside, outwardness, surface, periphery, circumference, the external, foreign product, importation, incoming, invasion, infringement, interloping, intrusion, trespass, externalization, projection, the supernatural, the paranormal

> *Attack 418; Entry 706*

5 **foreigner,** outsider, alien, stranger, outlander, ultramontane

> *Distance 585*

6 **new arrival,** newcomer, exile, outcast, refugee, emigrant, émigré, displaced person (DP), settler, new resident, expatriate, guest worker, *Gastarbeiter* [Ger], migrant worker, economic migrant, stateless person, Wandering Jew; immigrant, new face, tenderfoot, greenhorn, new kid on the block [Inf]

7 **intruder,** interloper, trespasser, squatter, uninvited guest, stowaway, cuckoo in the nest, gate-crasher [Inf]

8 **extraneous,** irrelevant, irrelative, immaterial, inessential, nonessential, unessential, unnecessary, superfluous, extra, superficial, redundant, pleonastic, pointless, inapplicable, unrelated, disrelated, unconnected, disconnected, incidental, adventitious, secondary, insignificant, trivial, throwaway

9 **foreign,** alien, unrelated, other, continental, overseas, transatlantic, ultramontane, tramontane *or* transmontane, strange, different, deviating, outlandish, unknown, exotic, barbaric, barbarian, wandering, traveling, rambling, roaming, nomadic, gypsy, migrant, stateless

10 **separate,** separated, apart, dissociated, unaffiliated, disaffiliated, nonassimilated, segregated, removed, isolated, discrete, detached, independent

11 **external,** extrinsic, exterior, extraterrestrial, not of this world, distant, outward, outer, outside, ulterior, peripheral, superficial, foreign-made, imported, importing, incoming, invading, invasive, infringing, interloping, intrusive, trespassing, externalizing, externalized, projecting, projected, supernatural, paranormal

VERBS

12 **be extraneous,** be irrelevant, miss the point, not come to the point, digress, talk off the subject, ramble, go off on a tangent, beat around the bush, have no point, have no relevance, have no relation to, not relate, not apply, not fit

13 **be foreign,** come from another country, live in another land, emigrate, immigrate, flee one's homeland, travel, wander, ramble, roam, live on the road

14 **separate,** keep apart, disassociate, segregate, isolate, remove, detach, divide

15 **be external,** come from without, exist outside, import, invade, infringe, interlope, squat, intrude, trespass, stow away, externalize, project, gate-crash [Inf]

ADVERBS

16 **extraneously,** irrelevantly, immaterially, unessentially, superfluously, superficially, prima facie, pointlessly, beside the point, neither here nor there, inapplicably, incidentally, adventitiously, secondarily, insignificantly, trivially

17 **strangely,** differently, outlandishly, exotically, nomadically, in a foreign country, on foreign soil, overseas

18 **separately,** discretely, independently, apart

19 **externally,** extrinsically, distantly, from a distance, outwardly, on the outside, away from, on the surface, peripherally, intrusively, from outer space, supernaturally

725 State

NOUNS

1 **state,** condition, situation, circumstance *or* circumstances; location, bearings, spot; case, lot, fettle, form, order; estate, position, station, role, status, standing, rank, ranking, place, posture, footing, walk of life, class, echelon; category, structure, aspect, stage, guise, shape, phase, state of the art
  ▸ *Region 564; Situation 573; Essence 723; Circumstances 726*

2 **mode,** manner, way, style, lifestyle, fashion, complexion, appearance, tone, modality, modus vivendi, modus operandi, trend, stamp, fit, mold

3 **predicament,** problem, dilemma, plight, trouble, awkward situation, difficulty *or* difficulties, difficult circumstances, Catch-22; crisis, emergency, exigency, quandary, pretty pass; pinch, corner, hole, spot, time when the chips are down; [Inf]: jam, bind, hot water, fix, pickle
  ▸ *Difficulty 824; Hindrance 826; Opposition 828*

4 **state of affairs,** nature of things, shape of things, status quo, way things shape up, the way things are, how things stand, way of the world, lay of the land; how it is, size of it; [Inf]: where it's at, how things stack up, the way the cookie crumbles

5 **state of mind,** frame of mind, mood, humor, disposition, temper, temperament, attitude, vein, morale, spirits, good spirits, high spirits, good humor, bad spirits, low spirits, bad humor
  ▸ *Joy, Cheerfulness 269; Sorrow 270*

6 **physical state,** state of health, state of repair *or* disrepair, physical condition, shape, physical form, good condition *or* shape, bad *or* poor condition *or* shape, trim, kilter, fettle, fine fettle, fine fig
  ▸ *Health 113; Repair 809*

ADJECTIVES

7 **conditional,** circumstantial, situational, formal; ranked, ranking, placed, situated, classed; stylish, fashionable, trendy; problematic, troubling; high-spirited, good-humored, low-spirited, bad-humored, temperamental, healthy, unhealthy, fit, unfit

VERBS

8 **be in a state of,** be in a certain state, fare, get on *or* along, manage, live, come through, get by, turn out, come out

9 **be in a predicament,** have a predicament *or* a problem *or* a dilemma; run into trouble, have difficulties, labor under, need help, be in a spot, see no way out; [Inf]: get into a jam *or* a fix *or* a bind; be in a pickle, be between a rock and a hard place, be up shit creek

ADVERBS

10 **conditionally,** circumstantially, as it is, as it *or* as the matter stands, in a state of, such being the case, as

things are, in *or* under the circumstances, in the present case, provisionally, contingently; problematically, between a rock and a hard place [Inf]

11 **in good form,** in fine fettle, in good spirits, good-humoredly, in bad form, in bad spirits, bad-humoredly, temperamentally; stylishly, in style, fashionably; healthily, unhealthily, in condition, in order, in repair, in shape; out of order, in disrepair, out of kilter; out of commission, out of whack [Inf]

726 Circumstances

NOUNS

1 **circumstances,** conditions, existing conditions, situation, environment, surroundings, setting, milieu, background; the times, context, status, status quo, state of affairs, position; means, resources, state, posture, attitude, terms, footing, standing, lay of the land; the picture, the whole picture, particulars, full particulars, ins and outs, story thus far, the way it is, blow-by-blow account; contingency, provision, eventuality; setup, the score [Inf]
   ▶ *Situation 573; Surroundings 615; State 725; Relatedness 727; Order 765; Precedence 769*

2 **occurrence,** event, incident, happening, episode, case, occasion, instance, circumstance; juncture, conjuncture, stage, point, milestone, moment, hour

3 **time,** opportunity, steppingstone
   ▶ *Timeliness 659*

4 **aspect,** element, factor, facet, fact, datum, detail, minutia, incidental, item, particular, point, thing

5 **comfortable circumstances,** comfort, security, well-being, ease, prosperity, success, luck, luckiness, good fortune, the good life, life of ease, lap of luxury, halcyon days, golden age
   ▶ *Satisfaction 273; Wealth 485; Prosperity 847*

6 **difficult circumstances,** predicament, awkward *or* tricky situation, plight, trouble
   ▶ *Poverty 486; Situation 573; State 725; Danger 811; Difficulty 824; Hindrance 826*

7 **critical moment,** hour of decision, crossroads, turning point, match point, point of no return, Rubicon
   ▶ *Interface 616; Transience 643; Change 665*

ADJECTIVES

8 **circumstantial,** relative, given, contingent, conditional, dependent on circumstances; indirect, inferential, hearsay, conjectural, presumed, implied, provisional, fitting the circumstances; situational, surrounding, environmental, background, situated, placed, contextual, variable, changeful, transient, incidental, eventual, eventful

9 **detailed,** meticulous, elaborate, minute, precise, exact, specific, incidental, particular, full, special, fussy, finicky, nitpicking, persnickety [Inf]

10 **comfortable,** secure, easy, well, prosperous, lucky, opportune, suitable, auspicious, favorable

11 **difficult,** awkward, critical, pivotal, troublesome, exigent

VERBS

12 **circumstantiate,** itemize, specify, particularize, substantiate, put in context, see the whole picture, get the lay of the land, get the full particulars, detail, go *or* enter into detail, cite, instance, adduce, document, spell out, give *or* quote chapter and verse, atomize, anatomize, know the ins and outs, see how it goes

13 **be in comfortable circumstances,** be comfortable, prosper, enjoy good fortune, get lucky, live a life of ease, live in the lap of luxury, fare well, succeed, flourish, be smiled on by fate

14 **be in difficulties,** get into difficulties, get into trouble, be in a Catch-22 situation, reach a crisis, have an emergency; [Inf]: get into a jam *or* a fix *or* a bind, get into hot water, get in a pickle, be up shit creek

15 **be at a critical moment,** come to a juncture, reach a stage, reach a turning point, come to the point of no return, cross the Rubicon

ADVERBS

16 **under the circumstances,** circumstantially, accordingly, as it is, as it happened, as things stand, as it turns out, as the case may be, that *or* such being the case, in that case, in that event, in this way, given that, and so, thus, so, in the case, if so, provided that, supposing, assuming, granting, allowing, as it may happen, as things may fall, should it be that, by the same token, equally, similarly, consequently, if not, unless, except, without, therefore, like so [Inf]

17 **relatively,** conditionally, under certain conditions *or* circumstances, provisionally, with provisions, indirectly, inferentially, conjecturally, environmentally, contextually, changefully, variably, incidentally, contingently, eventually

18 **meticulously,** with a fine-tooth comb, precisely, exactly, elaborately, minutely, incidentally, particularly, fully, in full, just so, specifically, specially, fussily, sedulously, assiduously

19 **comfortably,** easily, safely, securely, prosperously, luckily, opportunely, suitably, auspiciously, favorably

20 **difficultly,** awkwardly, critically, crucially, at a crucial time *or* point, exigently, when the chips are down

727 Relatedness

NOUNS

1 **relatedness,** relation, relations, relationship, relevance, pertinence, germaneness, bearing, appositeness, connectedness, connection; affinity, friendship, rapport, propinquity; bond, tie, partnership, marriage relationship; link, linkage, involvement, tie-up; casual relationship, liaison, merger, association, affiliation,

alliance, union, mutuality, combination, assemblage; agreement, similarity, something in common, parallel; comparison, reference, analogy, correlation, correspondence, homology, homogeny, implication; addition, adjunct, attachment, appendix, accompaniment

> *Assembly 59; Friendship 62; Marriage 64; Meaning 361; Sameness 730; Similarity 733; Connection 754; Conformity 781; Importance 799*

2 **kinship,** family relationship, blood relationship, consanguinity

> *Family 65*

3 **interrelatedness,** equality, comparability, correlation, reciprocity, interdependence, cross-reference, citation; complementarity, interconnection, relativity, proportionality, interlinkage, interalliance, interassociation, covariation, interaction, interplaying, interworking, intercourse, intercommunication, interweaving, intertwining, interlacing, intermeshing, interpenetration, interchange; alternation, relativeness, ratio, proportion, scale, contrast

> *Interweaving 609; Reciprocity 729; Equality 740; Connection 754*

4 **business relations,** affairs, business, dealings, transactions

> *Labor Relations 57; Finance 457*

5 **relative position,** rank, class, classification, order, degree, echelon, rating, grade, status, level

> *Degree 739; Arrangement 767; Class 777*

ADJECTIVES

6 **related,** relevant, pertinent, germane, apposite, connected; kindred, cognate, agnate, akin to, consanguine, bonded; wedded, married, bound, joined, tied, twinned, paired, involved, implicated; merged, associated, affiliated, allied, linked; parallel, analogous, homologous, homogenous, combined, added, attached, appended, accompanied, spliced [Inf]

7 **interrelated,** similar, equal, comparable, correlated, reciprocal, interdependent, cross-referenced, complementary, corresponding, interconnected, related, relative, proportional, interlinked, interallied, interassociated, interacting, interworking, interweaving, intertwining, intermeshed, interchanged, commensurate

8 **ranked,** classed, classified, ordered, rated

VERBS

9 **relate to,** relate, have a relationship, stand in relation, have relevance, apply to, apply, have a bearing on, bring to bear upon, pertain to, appertain to, affect, interest, have to do with, refer to, make reference to, touch upon, associate, connect, put in context, juxtapose, couple, tie, tie up, link, reconcile, contrast, cross-refer, answer to, have a connection with, liaise, deal with, pair up, belong to, come to the point, address the question; get to the nitty-gritty [Inf], get down to brass tacks [Inf]

10 **correspond to,** correlate, compare, be proportionate to, have a mutual relationship, interconnect, interlock, interpenetrate, interlink, interassociate, interweave, interact, interplay, balance, liken, parallel, draw a parallel to *or* between, equalize, proportion, symmetrize, match, equate, accord, fit, tally

> *Equality 740; Conformity 781*

11 **rank,** class, classify, order, rate

ADVERBS

12 **relevantly,** relatedly, pertinently, germanely, concerning, touching, regarding, as to, as regards, in regard to, in relation to, appositely, mutually, equally, reciprocally, interdependently, respectively, correspondingly, proportionally, proportionately, to scale, similarly, comparably, comparatively, in *or* by comparison, analogously, homologously, homogenously, commensurately, consanguineously, in context, oppositely, in contrast

728 Unrelatedness

NOUNS

1 **unrelatedness,** irrelativeness, irrelevance *or* irrelevancy, impertinence, disrelation; inappositeness, inappropriateness, inaptness, inaptitude, inapplicability; extraneousness, superfluousness; pointlessness, meaninglessness, unimportance, immateriality; illogicality, randomness, arbitrariness, coincidence

> *Unimportance 800; Chance 842*

2 **unconnectedness,** disconnectedness, separateness; disconnection, disjunction, disjuncture, dissociation, disassociation, non sequitur; segregation, separation, divorce

> *Divorce and Widowhood 66; Separation 753; Discontinuity 775*

3 **disparity,** inequality, imbalance, asymmetry, disproportion, distortion; difference, contrast, dissimilarity, unlikeness, foreignness, strangeness; heterogeneity, diversity, variety, nonuniformity; divergence, variance, discrepancy, inconsistency, inconsonance, incongruence, incongruity; gap, credibility gap, generation gap

> *Divergence 703; Oppositeness 731; Diversity 732; Dissimilarity 734*

4 **nonconformity,** nonconformance, individuality, independence, singularity, unilateralism; neutrality, detachment; insularity, isolation, isolationism

> *Nonconformity 782*

5 **no relation,** bad relation, no connection, misconnection, bad connection; misreference, wrong reference; misapplication, misuse, misappropriation; no association, bad association, misalliance, mésalliance, mismatch

> *Divorce and Widowhood 66; Error 351*

ADJECTIVES

6 **unrelated,** irrelative, irrelevant, impertinent, disre-

lated, inapposite, ungermane, inappropriate, inapt, inapplicable, extraneous, extrinsic, nonessential, superfluous, pointless, meaningless, unimportant, immaterial, incidental, unallied, unassociated, unaffiliated
> *Unimportance 800*

7 **illogical,** random, aleatory, arbitrary, coincidental
> *Chance 842*

8 **unconnected,** disconnected, separate, disjunctive, disjoined, disjointed; dissociated, disassociated, segregated, separated, divorced
> *Divorce and Widowhood 66; Separation 753*

9 **disparate,** unequal, imbalanced, asymmetric, asymmetrical, unsymmetrical, disproportionate, disproportional, distorted; different, contrasting, dissimilar, unlike; foreign, alien, strange; heterogeneous, diverse, varied, varying, nonuniform; divergent, variant, discrepant, inconsistent, inconsonant, incongruent
> *Divergence 703; Oppositeness 731; Diversity 732; Dissimilarity 734*

10 **nonconforming,** nonconformist, bohemian, individualistic, independent, singular, unilateral or unilateralist; neutral, detached, uninvolved; insular, isolated, isolationist
> *Deviation 698; Nonconformity 782*

11 **misrelated,** misconnected; misapplied, misused, misappropriated; misallied, mismatched
> *Error 351*

VERBS

12 **be unrelated,** not relate to, be irrelevant, be impertinent, have no bearing on, be inappropriate, be inapplicable, be extraneous, have no point or meaning; stray from the topic, go off on a tangent, digress, get sidetracked, lose the thread
> *Unimportance 800*

13 **not connect,** disconnect, separate, sever, disjoin; dissociate, disassociate, have nothing to do with, segregate, divorce
> *Divorce and Widowhood 66; Separation 753*

14 **be disparate,** be unequal, be imbalanced, be out of proportion; differ, contrast, be dissimilar; diversify, vary, diverge, deviate
> *Divergence 703; Diversity 732; Dissimilarity 734*

15 **misrelate,** relate badly, misconnect, misally; misrefer, misapply, misuse, misappropriate
> *Error 351*

ADVERBS

16 **irrelatively,** irrelevantly, without relevance, impertinently, beside the point, neither here nor there, off the subject, off on a tangent, inappositely, inappropriately, inaptly, inapplicably, extraneously, by the way, extrinsically, nonessentially, superfluously, pointlessly, meaninglessly, unimportantly, immaterially, incidentally
> *Unimportance 800*

17 **illogically,** randomly, arbitrarily, coincidentally

> *Chance 842*

18 **unconnectedly,** disconnectedly, separately, apart, disjunctively, disjointedly
> *Separation 753*

19 **disparately,** unequally, asymmetrically, unsymmetrically, disproportionately, disproportionally, out of proportion, distortedly; differently, contrastingly, without similarity, dissimilarly, strangely; heterogeneously, diversely, nonuniformly; divergently, discrepantly, inconsistently, inconsonantly, incongruently
> *Divergence 703; Oppositeness 731; Diversity 732; Dissimilarity 734*

20 **individualistically,** independently, singularly, unilaterally; neutrally, detachedly; insularly, isolatedly
> *Nonconformity 782; Deviation 698*

729 Reciprocity

NOUNS

1 **reciprocity,** reciprocality, reciprocalness, reciprocation, mutual exchange, exchange, equal exchange, fair exchange, bartering, barter, swap, trade-off; interplay, interworking, interaction, interacting, give and take, compromise; interchange, alternation, seesaw; compensation, repayment, requital, retaliation, payment in kind, tit for tat, an eye for an eye, blow for blow, measure for measure, quid pro quo; return, retort, comeback, response, reaction, counteraction, counterstroke, *tu quoque* [L]
> *Retaliation 420; Compromise 461; Trade 480; Counteraction 510; Exchange 673; Compensation 743*

2 **interrelation,** interrelationship, interconnection, mutual relation or relationship; interdependence, mutual dependence, mutuality, mutualism, mutualization, symbiosis; cooperation, partnership, sharing, bilateralism; complement, counterpart, alter ego
> *Relatedness 727; Accord 735; Connection 754; Cooperation 827*

3 **correlation,** correlativeness or correlativity, correspondence, similarity, parallel, parallelism, comparability; comparison, analogy, analog, allegory; equivalence, symmetry, balance, proportionality, proportion, proportionment
> *Symmetry 626; Sameness 730; Similarity 733; Equality 740*

ADJECTIVES

4 **reciprocal,** reciprocative or reciprocatory, reciprocating, mutual; reciprocated, exchanged, bartered, swapped, traded; interplaying, interworking, interacting, give-and-take, compromising; interchanging, alternating, seesaw, interchanged, alternated, alternate; compensatory, compensational, requited, requitable, retaliatory, tit-for-tat, eye-for-an-eye, blow-for-blow, measure-for-measure; responsive, reactive, reacting, counteracting, counteractive

▷ *Retaliation 420; Compromise 461; Trade 480; Counteraction 510; Exchange 673; Compensation 743*

5 **interrelated,** interconnected, interlinked; interdependent, mutually dependent, mutualistic, symbiotic; cooperative, sharing, two-way, bilateral; complementary, complemental, completing, completive

▷ *Relatedness 727; Connection 754; Cooperation 827*

6 **correlative,** correlational, correlating, correlated, corresponding, correspondent, similar, parallel, comparable, analogous, allegorical; equivalent, symmetric *or* symmetrical, balanced, proportional, proportionate, proportioned; interchanged, converse

▷ *Symmetry 626; Sameness 730; Similarity 733; Equality 740*

VERBS

7 **reciprocate,** exchange, give in exchange, barter, swap, trade, trade off; interplay, interact, give and take, compromise; interchange, counterchange, alternate, take turns; compensate, repay, requite, retaliate, pay in kind, give tit for tat, take an eye for an eye; return, retort, respond, react, counteract, counterstrike

▷ *Retaliation 420; Compromise 461; Trade 480; Counteraction 510; Exchange 673; Compensation 743*

8 **interrelate,** interconnect, interlink; cooperate, partner, share; complement, complete

▷ *Relatedness 727; Connection 754; Cooperation 827*

9 **correlate,** correspond, parallel; parallelize, draw a parallel, draw an analogy, compare; make equivalent, symmetrize, balance, proportion

▷ *Symmetry 626; Similarity 733; Equality 740*

ADVERBS

10 **reciprocally,** mutually; alternatingly, alternately, by turns, turn and turn about; compensatingly; responsively, reactively, counteractingly, counteractively

11 **interrelatedly,** interdependently, symbiotically, cooperatively, bilaterally; complementally, completively

12 **correlatively,** correspondingly, correspondently, similarly, parallelly, comparably, analogously, allegorically; equivalently, symmetrically, in balance, proportionally, proportionately; conversely, vice versa

730 Sameness

NOUNS

1 **sameness,** identity, uniformity; identicalness, selfsameness, one and the same, indistinguishableness, indistinguishability, undifferentiation; the very thing, the exact thing, the very words, *ipsissima verba* [L]; repetition, repetitiveness, redundancy, tautology; lack of variety *or* variation, plainness, homogeneity, uniformness, isotopy, consistency, continuity, evenness, symmetry; merger, mergence, union, consubstantiality, coalescence, absorption, assimilation, synthesis; synchronicity, simultaneousness, coincidence

▷ *Same Time 649; Similarity 733; Union 752; Conformity 781; Repetition 797*

2 **agreement,** harmony, compatibility, accordance, concordance, congruity, congruence *or* congruency; oneness, oneness with, unity, solidarity; accord, consensus, unanimity; birds of a feather

▷ *Agreement 462; Accord 735; One 788*

3 **equivalence,** correspondence, homology, reciprocity; interchangeability, synonymousness, synonymy, synonymity; synonym, homograph, homonym, homophone; equivalent, equal, equipollence, homologue, complement, reciprocation, equal exchange

▷ *Linguistics, Language 5; Meaning 361; Reciprocity 729; Similarity 733; Equality 740*

4 **look-alike,** double, clone, twin, Siamese twin, identical twin, exact likeness, reflection, image, very image, chip off the old block, spit and image *or* spitting image [Inf], dead ringer [Inf]; exact counterpart, alter ego, second self, other self, Doppelgänger; pair, match, two of a kind, two peas in a pod, Tweedledum and Tweedledee

▷ *Appearance 264; Similarity 733; Two 789*

5 **copy,** duplicate, duplication, imitation, replica, facsimile, reduplication, reproduction, photocopy, dupe [Inf], ditto [Inf]; mimic, aper

▷ *Reproduction 21; Photography 132; Imitation 736*

6 **regularity,** routine, daily routine, daily round, habit; steadiness, changelessness, homeostasis, constancy, invariability, invariableness *or* unvariableness, lack of deviation, same old thing, same old story; conformity, standardization, uniformization, regimentation, automation, mass production; orderliness, order, method, pattern, standard; stereotype, cliché

▷ *Habit, Custom 397; Time 639; Timekeeping 646; Regularity 663; Order 765; Conformity 781; Repetition 797*

ADJECTIVES

7 **same,** identical, exactly the same, exactly alike, just alike, like two peas in a pod, indistinguishable, undifferentiated, idem, exact, very, selfsame, one and the same; isotopic; verbatim, repeated, repetitive, repetitious, redundant, tautological; consistent, even, symmetrical, uniform, plain, unvaried, unmixed, homogeneous, of that ilk, of the same kidney, tarred with the same brush; merged, merging, united, uniting, consubstantial, coalesced, coalescent, absorbed, assimilated, assimilating, assimilative *or* assimilatory; synchronous, simultaneous, coinciding, coincident, coincidental

▷ *Same Time 649; Similarity 733; Union 752; Repetition 797*

8 **agreeing,** conforming, harmonious, compatible, accordant, concordant, congruent, congruous; agreed, of the same mind, one, of one resolve, united, solid

▷ *Agreement 462; Accord 735; Conformity 781; One 788*

9 **equivalent,** corresponding, correspondent, homolo-

gous, homological, matching, complementary, reciprocal; interchangeable, synonymous, homographic, homonymic *or* homonymous, homophonic *or* homophonous

▶ *Linguistics, Language 5; Meaning 361; Reciprocity 729; Similarity 733*

10 **look-alike,** twin, identical, matching; matched, paired, cloned

11 **duplicate,** duplicated, reduplicated, reproduced, copied, photocopied; imitated, aped

▶ *Reproduction 21; Photography 132; Imitation 736*

12 **regular,** habitual, routine, established, fixed, constant, steady, unchanging, changeless, homeostatic, constant, invariant *or* invariable, unvariable, unvarying, undeviating; hourly, daily, weekly, monthly, yearly, annual; conforming, standardized, automated, regimented, ordered, orderly, methodical; stereotyped, typecast, patterned; stereotypical, cliché

▶ *Habit, Custom 397; Time 639; Timekeeping 646; Regularity 663; Conformity 781*

VERBS

13 **be the same,** be identical, have no difference; use the same words, iterate, repeat, be redundant; be homogeneous, be uniform, be consistent; conform, run true to type, toe the line *or* mark, follow the crowd, climb *or* jump on the bandwagon; merge, coalesce, be absorbed, be assimilated; be simultaneous, coincide, happen at the same time

▶ *Same Time 649; Similarity 733; Conformity 781; Repetition 797*

14 **agree,** harmonize, be in accord, be congruent; be of the same mind, be united, have a common resolve

▶ *Agreement 462; Accord 735*

15 **be equivalent,** correspond, homologize, match, complement, reciprocate; be interchangeable, be synonymous

▶ *Meaning 361; Reciprocity 729; Similarity 733*

16 **make the same,** equalize, balance, equilibrate, equiponderate, symmetrize, counterbalance, offset; level, even out, smooth; homogenize, uniformize, coalesce, assimilate, absorb; merge, join, unify, unite, consubstantiate; synchronize; equate, match, pair, twin, clone; establish, fix, standardize, regularize, regulate, automate, mass-produce; stereotype, typecast

▶ *Smoothness 545; Equality 740; Union 752; Conformity 781*

17 **copy,** duplicate, reproduce, reduplicate, imitate, photocopy, ditto, mimic, ape

▶ *Reproduction 21; Photography 132; Imitation 736*

ADVERBS

18 **identically,** indistinguishably, exactly, isotopically; verbatim, repeatedly, repetitively, repetitiously, redundantly, tautologically *or* tautologously; consistently, evenly, uniformly, plainly, homogeneously; unitedly, consubstantially; in the same place, ibid, *ibidem* [L]; at

the same time, synchronously, simultaneously, coincidentally

▶ *Same Time 649; Similarity 733; Union 752; Repetition 797*

19 **agreeingly,** harmoniously, compatibly, accordantly, concordantly, congruently, congruously; likewise, ditto, as already stated; unanimously

▶ *Agreement 462; Accord 735; Conformity 781*

20 **equivalently,** correspondingly, correspondently, homologously, homologically, reciprocally; interchangeably, synonymously, homonymously, homophonically

▶ *Linguistics, Language 5; Meaning 361; Reciprocity 729; Similarity 733*

21 **regularly,** habitually, routinely, like clockwork, hourly, daily, weekly, monthly, yearly, annually; steadily, constantly, unchangingly, changelessly, homeostatically, invariantly *or* invariably, without exception, always, unvariably, unvaryingly, undeviatingly

▶ *Habit, Custom 397; Time 639; Regularity 663; Timekeeping 646*

731 Oppositeness

The poet and the dreamer are distinct. / Diverse, sheer opposite, antipodes. / The one pours out a balm upon the world. / The other vexes it. — JOHN KEATS

NOUNS

1 **oppositeness,** polarity, polarization, contrariety, contrariness, antonymy, antithesis, contrast, contraposition, contradiction, opposition, direct opposition, polar opposition; reversal, inversion, obversion

▶ *Inversion 608; Opposition 828*

2 **opposite,** direct opposite, exact opposite, polar opposite, antipode, contrapositive, antonym; opposite pole, antipole, other extreme, other end of the spectrum; opposite side, other side, other side of the fence, other side of the coin, flip side [Inf]; reverse, back, rear, inverse, invert, converse

▶ *Inversion 608; Front 621; Back 622*

ADJECTIVES

3 **opposite,** oppositional, oppositionary, facing, face to face, vis-à-vis, nose to nose, eyeball to eyeball, head to head, toe to toe, back to back; diametrically opposite, diametrical *or* diametric, polar, antipodal; contrary, counter, diametrically opposed, directly opposed, antithetical, contrapositive, contrasted, antonymous; opposing, contrasting, polarized; reverse, reversed, inverse, inverted, obverse, converse

▶ *Inversion 608*

VERBS

4 **be opposite,** face, be *or* stand on the opposite side, lie opposite, subtend; polarize, contrast, contrapose, contradict, run counter to, go contrary to; go to the other

extreme, be on the opposite side, be on the opposite side of the fence; reverse, invert, obvert

ADVERBS

5 **opposite,** oppositely, on opposite sides, on the opposite side, on the other side, on the other side of the fence; in the opposite direction, to the opposite side

6 **diametrically,** contrastively, contrastingly, opposingly, antithetically, contrarily, counter, by contraries; poles apart *or* asunder, at opposite extremes, at the other end of the spectrum; inversely, obversely, conversely, contrariwise, vice versa

732 Diversity

The world is so full of a number of things, / I'm sure we should all be as happy as kings.
— ROBERT LOUIS STEVENSON

NOUNS

1 **diversity,** difference, unlikeness, dissimilarity, contrast; divergence, separateness, deviance, deviation, variation, incongruence, incongruity; exception, exception to the rule, special case; abnormality, freakishness, unusualness, individuality, uniqueness
   ◗ *Deviation 698; Divergence 703; Dissimilarity 734*

2 **variety,** assortment, mixture, mix, medley, hodgepodge, miscellany, miscellanies, sundries, salmagundi, odds and ends, everything but the kitchen sink; miscellaneousness, variousness, sundriness; manifold, multiplicity, multiformity, polymorphism, multifariousness, omnifariousness, nonuniformity, heterogeneity, pluralism, multiculturalism; all shapes and sizes, all sorts and conditions, all colors of the rainbow; diversification, variegation, versatility, versatileness
   ◗ *Variegation 263; Mixture 751*

3 **inconsistency,** nonuniformity, discontinuity, unevenness, bumpiness, unstableness, instability, unpredictability, inconstancy, changeableness, variability *or* variableness, erraticism, irregularity, sporadicalness, fitfulness, haphazardness
   ◗ *Irregularity 664; Changeableness 666; Discontinuity 775*

4 **dissension,** discordance, discord, disagreement, controversy, differing opinions, many voices
   ◗ *Disagreement 463*

ADJECTIVES

5 **diverse,** different, unlike, dissimilar, contrasting; divergent, diverging, separate, deviant, incongruous; abnormal, freakish, unusual, exceptional, individual, unique
   ◗ *Divergence 703; Dissimilarity 734*

6 **varied,** assorted, mixed, various, sundry, divers, miscellaneous; manifold, multiple, multiform, polymorphous, diversiform, multifarious, omnifarious, differ-

ing, nonuniform, heterogeneous, multiethnic, multicultural; motley, mottled, dappled, multicolored
   ◗ *Variegation 263; Mixture 751*

7 **inconsistent,** uneven, bumpy, unstable, unpredictable, inconstant, changeable, variable, erratic, irregular, spasmodic, sporadic, fitful, haphazard

8 **diversified,** variegated, varied, checkered, kaleidoscopic, multifaceted, versatile, all-around; multipurpose
   ◗ *Variegation 263*

9 **dissenting,** disagreeing, discordant, controversial, of different opinions
   ◗ *Disagreement 463*

VERBS

10 **be diverse,** differ, contrast; diverge, deviate; make diverse, vary, ring the changes, separate, differentiate
   ◗ *Divergence 703; Dissimilarity 734*

11 **diversify,** variegate, branch out, spread one's wings, have many irons in the fire, have many strings to one's bow
   ◗ *Variegation 263*

12 **mix,** stir, jumble, shake up, shuffle, scramble, tangle, blend, intermix, intersperse, interleave

13 **dissent,** disagree, have discord, hold opposite opinions, have different opinions, vote against
   ◗ *Disagreement 463*

ADVERBS

14 **diversely,** differently, in different ways, dissimilarly, contrastingly; divergently, separately, deviantly, incongruously; abnormally, freakishly, unusually, exceptionally, individually, uniquely

15 **variously,** sundrily, miscellaneously; nonuniformly, heterogeneously, kaleidoscopically, manifoldly, multifariously, omnifariously

16 **inconsistently,** unevenly, bumpily, unpredictably, inconstantly, changeably, variably, erratically, irregularly, spasmodically, out of step, in fits and starts, sporadically, fitfully, haphazardly, helter-skelter, higgledy-piggledy, harum-scarum, chaotically, without order, willy-nilly

17 **dissentingly,** discordantly, controversially, at sixes and sevens

733 Similarity

NOUNS

1 **similarity,** similitude, resemblance, likeness, semblance; symmetry, proportionality, parity, equality; sameness, alikeness, uniformity, conformity; common feature *or* trait, point of likeness, point in common, parallel, correspondent, equivalent; nearness, closeness, approximation
   ◗ *Parallelism 606; Symmetry 626; Sameness 730; Equality 740; Conformity 781*

2 **comparability,** commensurability, analogousness,

parallelism, correspondence, equivalence; comparison, likening, analogy, analogue *or* analog, simile, metaphor, parable, allegory

▶ *Literature 139; Parallelism 606*

3 **affinity,** connection, compatibility, accordance, agreement; kinship, family relationship, family resemblance, family likeness, genetic likeness; kindred spirit, soul mate, mate, companion, fellow, brother *or* sister under the skin

▶ *Friendship 62; Family 65; Agreement 462; Accord 735*

4 **simulation,** imitation, portrayal, simulacrum; enactment, emulation, aping, mimicking, copying, duplication; duplicate, copy, replica, facsimile

▶ *Reproduction 21; Representation 187; Imitation 736*

5 **counterpart,** similitude, match, semblable, equivalent, equal, the like *or* likes of, suchlike; correspondent, pendant, reciprocal, coordinate, alter ego, second self; twin, double, look-alike, image, reflection, shadow, another edition

▶ *Friendship 62; Sameness 730*

6 **couple,** pair, twins, matched pair, matching set, two of a kind

▶ *Sameness 730*

ADJECTIVES

7 **similar,** resemblant, resembling, quasi, like, alike, not unlike, suchlike, something like [Inf]; symmetrical, proportional, equal; same, much *or* nearly the same, homogeneous, uniform, conforming; common, parallel, equivalent, correspondent, corresponding, matching, reflective; near, close, approximate, approximating

▶ *Sameness 730; Accord 735*

8 **comparable,** akin, commensurable, analogous, like, parallel, correspondent, equivalent; metaphorical *or* metaphoric, allegorical

▶ *Parallelism 606; Equality 740*

9 **connected,** allied, connatural, compatible, accordant, agreeable; akin, related

▶ *Relatedness 727; Accord 735*

10 **matched,** equaled, reciprocated, coordinated; twinned, doubled, reflected, shadowed; coupled, paired

▶ *Sameness 730*

11 **simulated,** imitated, portrayed, enacted, aped, mimicked, copied, replicated, duplicated; imitation, synthetic, ersatz, artificial, false, phony *or* phoney, counterfeit, mock, sham, spurious, pseudo

▶ *Deception 193; Imitation 736*

VERBS

12 **be similar,** be like, resemble; be symmetrical, be proportional, be equal; equal, match, parallel, correspond; bear a resemblance to, take after, favor, look like, reflect, mirror; agree, accord, conform, connect, relate

▶ *Symmetry 626; Relatedness 727; Sameness 730; Accord 735; Equality 740; Conformity 781*

13 **compare,** liken, analogize, draw an analogy, draw a parallel, allegorize; compare with, see no difference

14 **seem like,** smack of, savor of, have all the signs of, have all the appearances *or* features of, have all the earmarks of, have all the hallmarks of; suggest, evoke, put one in mind of, bring to mind, call to mind

15 **make similar,** symmetrize, equalize, assimilate, homogenize, uniformize, approximate

▶ *Symmetry 626; Sameness 730; Equality 740*

16 **simulate,** imitate, portray, enact; emulate, mimic, ape, copy, replicate, duplicate, reproduce, counterfeit

▶ *Reproduction 21; Imitation 736*

ADVERBS

17 **similarly,** resemblingly, alike, in the same manner *or* way, likewise, in like manner, by the same token, just as, to the same degree; symmetrically, proportionally, equally, equivalently, correspondently, correspondingly, reflectively; homogeneously, uniformly; compatibly, accordingly, agreeably

18 **comparably,** commensurably, analogously, metaphorically, allegorically; like, nearly, closely, approximately

19 **seemingly,** apparently, ostensibly, externally, superficially

20 **imitatively,** artificially, falsely, phonily, counterfeitly, spuriously

734 Dissimilarity

NOUNS

1 **dissimilarity,** dissimilitude, unlikeness, difference, dissemblance, unsimilarity, dissimilation; disparity, discrepancy, inconsistency, contradiction, contrast, contrariety, incongruity, incompatibility; asymmetry, imbalance, inequality

▶ *Oppositeness 731; Inequality 741*

2 **nonuniformity,** heterogeneity, variety, multiformity, diversity; divergence, variance, variation; individuality, uniqueness, singularity, distinction, distinguishment, differentiability, discrimination

▶ *Divergence 703; Diversity 732*

3 **incomparability,** incomparableness, uncomparableness, incommensurability, incommensurableness, incommensurateness, unrelatedness, extraneousness; no comparison, no resemblance, nothing in common, no common ground, another matter, another story, quite another thing, something else, different kettle of fish, horse of a different *or* another color

▶ *Unrelatedness 728*

ADJECTIVES

4 **dissimilar,** unlike, different, unsimilar, unresembling, unresemblant, dissimilative, dissimilatory; disparate, discrepant, inconsistent, contradictory, contrasting, contrary, incongruous, incompatible; asymmetric, inequilateral, unequal, imbalanced

> *Oppositeness 731; Inequality 741*

5 nonuniform, unalike, unidentical, heterogeneous, varied, various, multiform, diverse; divergent, variant, variable; individual, unique, singular, cast in a different mold, distinct, distinctive, distinguished, distinguishing, differentiated, differential, differentiable
> *Divergence 703; Diversity 732*

6 incomparable, uncomparable, incommensurable, incommensurate, uncommensurate, unrelated, extraneous
> *Unrelatedness 728*

VERBS

7 be dissimilar, be unlike, differ, not resemble, bear no resemblance, not look like; contrast, contradict, conflict

8 diverge, deviate, depart from; stand out, stand out in a crowd, stick out like a sore thumb [Inf]; not compare with, have little *or* nothing in common

9 make unlike, dissimilate, vary, modify, change, convert; distinguish, differentiate, discriminate, separate the men from the boys, separate the sheep from the goats

ADVERBS

10 dissimilarly, differently, unsimilarly; disparately, discrepantly, inconsistently, contradictorily, contrastingly, contrarily, incongruously, incompatibly; asymmetrically, inequilaterally, unequally

11 nonuniformly, unidentically, heterogeneously, variously, diversely; divergently, in a different direction, deviatingly, variably; individualistically, uniquely, singularly, distinctly, distinctively, distinguishedly, distinguishingly, differentially

12 incomparably, uncomparably, incommensurably, incommensurately, uncommensurately, in a different realm, in a different ballpark [Inf], poles apart *or* asunder, nothing alike, not a bit alike, scarcely *or* hardly alike

735 Accord

NOUNS

1 accord, harmony, proportionality, proportion, correspondence, balance, symmetry, equilibrium
> *Symmetry 626*

2 harmonization, harmony, union, coordination, synchronization, synchrony, sync [Inf], coincidence, concurrence, concomitance; consonance, consonancy, euphony, euphoniousness, assonance, rhyme, alliteration; resonance, echo, resoundingness, soundingness, sonorousness; symphony, symphonization, orchestration, resolution (of a discord), blend, modulation, attunement, chime, chiming, melody, tune, counterpoint, homophony, unison, chorus
> *Linguistics, Language 5; Music 140; Resonance 236*

3 agreement, concurrence, concord, concordance, like-
mindedness, consensus, meeting of minds, concert, consentience, consentaneity, unanimity, unanimousness, unity, one voice, vox populi; adaptation, adjustment, accommodation, compromise, reconciliation; acceptance, compliance, conformance, acquiescence, accedence, concession, capitulation
> *Compromise 461; Agreement 462; Cooperation 827*

4 compatibility, congeniality, kinship, affinity, rapport, closeness, camaraderie, esprit de corps, team spirit, bonding, communion, fellowship, sense of unity, solidarity; mutual understanding, mutuality, similarity, identity, sympathy, empathy
> *Friendship 62; Similarity 733*

5 alliance, entente, federation, league, coalition, cartel, consortium, combination, combo [Inf], union, guild, affiliation, association, society, community, collaborative, cooperative *or* co-op, partnership, fellowship; team, crew, group, band, bunch, gang, posse
> *Government 49; Politics 50; Assembly 59; Union 752*

6 settlement, arrangement, international agreement, entente, entente cordiale, understanding, accord, rapprochement, reconciliation; compact, pact, treaty, covenant, contract, convention, bargain, deal, bond, transaction, pledge, promise
> *Contract 459; Negotiation 460; Compromise 461; Agreement 462; Cooperation 827*

7 conformity, conformance, conformation, uniformity, uniformness, constancy, continuity, consistency, coherence, congruence, congruity, correspondence, correlation, reciprocity, parallelism, likeness, similarity, analogousness
> *Parallelism 606; Reciprocity 729; Sameness 730; Similarity 733; Conformity 781*

8 consent, agreement, assent, hearty assent, affirmation, approval, blessing, sanction, ratification, confirmation, certification, attestation, endorsement, support
> *Affirmation 189; Assent 346; Approval 437; Agreement 462*

9 permission, allowance, vouchsafement, authorization, authority, leave, liberty, clearance, green light, go-ahead, OK *or* O.K. *or* okay; permit, license, charter, warrant, warranty, certificate, patent, exemption, entitlement, dispensation
> *Qualification 340; Exemption 434; Approval 437*

10 grant, bestowal, accordance, vouchsafement, conferment, conferral, presentment; gift, present, donation, endowment, investiture, provision
> *Giving 472*

ADJECTIVES

11 harmonious, proportional, corresponding, balanced, symmetrical, equilibratory
> *Symmetry 626*

12 harmonizing, harmonious, coordinated, synchronized, synchronous, coincident, concurrent, concurring, concomitant, conjoint; consonant, euphonic, eu-

---

phonious, assonant, assonantal, rhyming, alliterative; resonating, resonant, echoing, resounding, sounding, sonorous; symphonic, symphonious, orchestrated, modulated, modulating, attuned; harmonic, enharmonic; melodious, melodic, chiming, contrapuntal, homophonic, unisonous *or* unisonal *or* unisonant, choral

▶ *Linguistics, Language 5; Music 140; Resonance 236*

13 **agreeing,** accordant, concurring, concordant, likeminded, consentient, consentaneous, unanimous, united; adaptable, adaptive, adjustable, accommodating, compromising, conciliatory, reconciling, accepting, acceptant, compliant, conforming, acquiescent, acceding, capitulating

▶ *Compromise 461; Agreement 462; Cooperation 827*

14 **compatible,** congenial, akin, en rapport, close; sympathetic, sympathizing, empathetic, empathizing, understanding; amicable, frictionless, congenial

▶ *Friendship 62; Similarity 733*

15 **allied,** federated, unionized, combined, conjoint, united, merged, affiliated, filiated, associated, partnered, collaborative, cooperative, communal

▶ *Union 752*

16 **settled,** arranged, negotiated, agreed, accorded, reconciled, pledged, promised; contractual, covenantal

▶ *Contract 459; Negotiation 460; Arrangement 767*

17 **conforming,** accordant, uniform, constant, steady, unbroken, consistent, coherent, congruent, correspondent, corresponding, correlative, reciprocal, parallel, like, similar, analogous

▶ *Parallelism 606; Reciprocity 729; Sameness 730; Similarity 733; Conformity 781*

18 **consenting,** agreeing, according, assenting, assentive, affirming, affirmative, confirming, approving, supportive; agreeable, accordable, all-right [Inf]; agreed, affirmed, confirmed, approved, blessed, sanctioned, ratified, confirmed, certified, attested, endorsed, supported

▶ *Affirmation 189; Assent 346; Approval 437; Agreement 462*

19 **permitting,** allowing, authorizing, clearing; permitted, allowed, vouchsafed, authorized, cleared, OK'd; licensed, chartered, warranted, certified, patented, exempt, exempted, entitled

▶ *Qualification 340; Exemption 434; Approval 437*

20 **granted,** bestowed, accorded, vouchsafed, afforded, conferred, presented; gifted, donated, endowed, vested

▶ *Giving 472*

VERBS

21 **be in accord,** be harmonious, be proportional, correspond, balance, symmetrize, equilibrate, counterpoise

▶ *Symmetry 626*

22 **harmonize,** coordinate, synchronize, be in sync [Inf], coincide, concur; euphonize, rhyme, alliterate, res-

onate, resound, echo; symphonize, orchestrate, modulate, attune, chime, melodize

▶ *Linguistics, Language 5; Music 140; Resonance 236*

23 **agree,** concur, be in accord, have no objection, be at one, be in harmony, see eye to eye; adapt, adjust, accommodate, compromise, reconcile, accept, comply, conform, acquiesce, accede, concede, capitulate

▶ *Compromise 461; Agreement 462; Cooperation 827*

24 **have a rapport with,** feel an affinity for, bond, commune with, understand, sympathize with, empathize with, identify with

▶ *Friendship 62; Agreement 462*

25 **form an alliance,** ally, federate, unionize, unite, merge, combine, join, conjoin, collaborate, pull together, associate with, affiliate, side with, team up, partner

▶ *Assembly 59; Union 752*

26 **settle,** arrange, agree, reconcile, make a pact *or* covenant, covenant, pledge, promise, contract, transact, sign a treaty; bargain, deal, negotiate, compromise

▶ *Contract 459; Negotiation 460; Arrangement 767*

27 **conform,** be uniform, match, mirror, tally, square with, be like, correspond, correlate, reciprocate, parallel, complement; be consistent, cohere, hold together, hang together, tie in with; be conventional, toe the line *or* mark, fall in, follow, follow the crowd, go with the flow [Inf], climb *or* jump on the bandwagon

▶ *Parallelism 606; Reciprocity 729; Sameness 730; Similarity 733; Conformity 781*

28 **consent,** agree, assent, affirm, approve, give one's blessing, bless, sanction, ratify, confirm, certify, attest, endorse, support

▶ *Affirmation 189; Assent 346; Approval 437; Agreement 462*

29 **permit,** allow, vouchsafe, authorize, grant leave, clear, say the word, give the OK *or* O.K. *or* okay, give the green light, give the go-ahead, give thumbs up, give the nod to [Inf]; license, charter, warrant, patent, exempt, entitle

▶ *Qualification 340; Exemption 434; Approval 437*

30 **grant,** accord, enable, afford, render, provide, vouchsafe, bestow, confer, present; give, donate, endow, patronize, vest, invest with

▶ *Giving 472*

ADVERBS

31 **harmoniously,** proportionally, in proportion to, according to, accordingly, in accordance, correspondingly, in balance, symmetrically

32 **in harmony,** harmoniously, harmonistically, synchronously, in sync [Inf], coincidently, concurrently, concurringly, concomitantly, conjointly; consonantly, euphonically, euphoniously, in rhyme, alliteratively; resonantly, resoundingly, soundingly, sonorously; symphonically, symphoniously, harmonically, enhar-

monically, melodiously, melodically, homophonically, in tune, in unison, chorally, in concert

33 **in accord,** agreeingly, accordantly, concurringly, concordantly, like-mindedly, by consensus, consentiently, consentaneously, unanimously, *nemine contradicente* or *nem. con.* [L], *nemine dissentiente* or *nem. diss.* [L], with one accord, of one *or* the same mind, with one voice, in concert, concertedly, as one, together, all together, unitedly, solidly; adaptably, adjustably, accommodatingly, compromisingly, conciliatorily, acceptingly, compliantly, acquiescently

34 **compatibly,** congenially, en rapport, closely, sympathetically, sympathizingly, empathetically, empathizingly, understandingly

35 **in alliance,** in association with, in affiliation with, in partnership, conjointly, unitedly, collaboratively, cooperatively, communally; *e pluribus unum* [L]

36 **as agreed upon,** as arranged, as negotiated, as contracted for, as promised *or* pledged; contractually, by covenant

37 **conformingly,** accordantly, uniformly, constantly, steadily, consistently, regularly, coherently, congruently, correspondently, correspondingly, correlatively, reciprocally, like, likewise, similarly, analogously

38 **with consent,** consentingly, of one's own accord, assentingly, affirmingly, affirmatively, in the affirmative, confirmingly, approvingly, supportively; with permission, by *or* with someone's leave, on someone's authority

39 **accordingly,** consequently, as a result, therefore, for this *or* that reason, ergo, so, then, thus, hence, whence, wherefrom, from which, wherefore, for which reason, that *or* such being the case, in that case, at that rate, that being so, on that ground, under the circumstances, as the matter stands
▶ *Consecutiveness 736*

736 Imitation

Imitation is the sincerest flattery.
— CHARLES CALEB COLTON

NOUNS

1 **imitation,** copying, mirroring, following, simulation, repetition; mimesis, parody, emulation, impersonation; conformity, slavishness, literalism, representation; reflection, echo, onomatopoeia; me-tooism [Inf]
▶ *Representation 187; Conformity 781; Repetition 797*

2 **copy,** reproduction, duplicate, image, likeness, replica, model, working model, imitation, dummy, mock-up; picture, portrait, pastiche *or* pasticcio, Doppelgänger, simulation; fair copy, faithful copy, carbon copy, clone; imposture, fake, forgery, sham, bootleg, counterfeit, plagiarism, phony *or* phoney, ripoff [Inf]

▶ *Reproduction 21; Sameness 730*

3 **mimicry,** pantomime, mime, satire, caricature, mockery, travesty, burlesque, impersonation, parody, apery, parrotry, spoof, takeoff, send-up
▶ *Humor 277; Interpretation 365*

4 **duplicate,** duplication, mimeograph, photocopy, photostat, stat [Inf], pantograph, stencil; facsimile, fax, telex, carbon copy, ditto [Inf], replica, model, tracing, rubbing, transfer; transcript, video recording, tape recording, print, offprint *or* separation, photograph, negative
▶ *Sameness 730*

5 **copier,** photocopier, duplicator, facsimile (fax) machine, telex machine, stenciller, computer printer, camera, tape recorder
▶ *Reproduction 21; Photography 132*

6 **imitator,** ventriloquist, impersonator, female impersonator, drag artist, mimic, aper, copycat; plagiarist, counterfeiter, record pirate, forger, faker, imposter, poseur, charlatan, mountebank, phony *or* phoney, illusionist; follower, disciple, slave to fashion, sheep, parrot
▶ *Misrepresentation 188; Untruthfulness, Falsehood 192*

ADJECTIVES

7 **imitative,** copying, imitated, derivative, unoriginal, parodied, transcribed, mimetic, emulating, impersonating, echoing, onomatopoeic; aping, apish, parrotlike, parroting, following, posing

8 **imitation,** mock, sham, fake, forged, plagiarized, copied, counterfeit, ersatz, artificial, synthetic, cultured, man-made, phony *or* phoney, so-called, copycat, pseudo, hokey

VERBS

9 **imitate,** emulate, follow, model oneself upon, ape, parrot, flatter, mirror, repeat, echo, ditto, reflect; copy after, model after, take after, take as a model, pattern after, take a leaf out of one's book; mimic, copycat, mock, caricature, satirize, burlesque, parody, travesty, impersonate, mime, spoof, take off, send up

10 **copy,** reproduce, duplicate, clone, photocopy, photograph, photostat, stat [Inf], mimeograph, stencil, fax, carbon, ditto, replicate; plagiarize, borrow, counterfeit, fake, forge, pirate, crib [Inf]

11 **emulate,** follow, follow on, follow in the footsteps of, walk in the shoes of, follow the example of; follow suit, follow the herd, follow like sheep, climb *or* jump on the bandwagon, play follow the leader

ADVERBS

12 **imitatively,** apishly, like an ape, mockingly, onomatopoetically, unoriginally, artificially, synthetically, derivatively; verbatim, word for word, ditto, like a parrot, to the life, to the letter, letter for letter, literally, literatim

---

The original writer is not one who imitates nobody, but one whom nobody can imitate.

— FRANÇOIS RENÉ DE CHATEAUBRIAND

NOUNS

1 **originality,** creativity, creativeness, creation, dissimilarity, genuineness, authenticity, inventiveness, innovation, initiation, the one and only; imagination, original thought, individuality, independence, idiosyncrasy, eccentricity; novelty, newness, uniqueness, freshness, new departure, precedence, beginning, something new
▶ *Imagination 360; Newness 652; Unrelatedness 728; Dissimilarity 734; Freedom 829*

2 **original,** model, archetype, prototype, pattern, mold, source, paradigm, blueprint; autograph, holograph, signature, one's own hand, manuscript, first edition; test case, precedent, pilot, innovation, invention, patented invention, trademarked product, copyrighted work; real thing, real article, genuine article, absolutely it, the real McCoy
▶ *Essence 723; Precedence 769*

3 **originator,** inventor, creator, innovator, deviser, source, author, creative writer, composer, designer
▶ *Specialty 779*

ADJECTIVES

4 **original,** archetypal, seminal, model, prime, primary, primitive, pristine; creative, inventive, imaginative, innovative; unimitated, uncopied, unduplicated; first, first-hand, first in the field, pioneering

5 **novel,** unique, different, personal, individual, one and only, one of a kind; unparalleled, inimitable, incomparable, new, fresh, avant-garde, revolutionary, transcendent, unprecedented, unheard-of, offbeat, *sui generis* [Lat]

6 **authentic,** genuine, real, *echt* [Ger], bona fide, verified, true, natural, sincere, unadulterated, patented, copyrighted, trademarked

VERBS

7 **originate,** invent, innovate, create, devise, design, imagine, dream up, conceive, generate, pioneer, start, initiate, begin, auspicate, revolutionize, patent, blueprint, copyright, trademark
▶ *Beginning 771*

ADVERBS

8 **originally,** seminally, first, innovatively, conceptually, creatively, inventively, newly, freshly, imaginatively, with imagination; individually, personally, uniquely, differently, with a difference, inimitably, incomparably, without comparison

NOUNS

1 **quantity,** amount, measurement, measure, measured quantity, measuring; extent, dimension, proportions, size, space, area; magnitude, multitude, amplitude, length, width, breadth, thickness, thinness, height, altitude, depth, deepness; capacity, volume, weighing, weight, mass, matter, substance, body, bulk, gravity, heaviness, lightness
▶ *Heaviness 538; Lightness 539; Space 563; Size, Largeness 579; Measurement 589; Length 590; Breadth 592; Height 596; Depth 598; Whole 759; Completeness 761*

2 **container(ful),** armful, handful, mouthful, pocketful, spoon(ful), teaspoon(ful), tablespoon(ful), cup(ful), glass(ful), bottle(ful), jar(ful), pitcher(ful), bowl(ful), pot(ful), plate(ful), bag(ful), sack(ful), basket(ful), box(ful), carton(ful), case(ful), can(ful), bin(ful), crate(ful), barrel(ful), bucket(ful), shovel(ful), roomful, truckload, lorryload [Brit]
▶ *Container 578*

3 **certain amount,** portion, piece, share, lot, load, batch, bunch, pack, packet, parcel, passel, part, mess, limit, stint, quota, quorum, dosage, dose, ration, quantum; upper limit, ceiling, lower limit, floor; great quantity, large amount, mass, chunk, hunk, majority, small quantity, small amount, some, somewhat, few, fewness, pittance, dribble, fraction, minority; [Inf]: heap, gobs, whack
▶ *Contents 577; Limit 620; Increase 746; Decrease 747; Addition 748; Subtraction 749; Number 783; Multitude 795; Few 796*

4 **total,** totality, entirety, aggregate, sum, count, number, net (total), gross (total); whole, all; part and parcel, whole thing, caboodle *or* kit and caboodle [Inf]
▶ *Whole 759; Completeness 761*

5 **numbers,** integers, variable, plurality, zero, infinity, mean, average
▶ *Mathematics 6; Average 742; Number 783; Calculation 784; Zero 786; One 788; Two 789; Three 790; Four 791; Five and Over 792; Plurality 793; Multitude 795; Infinity 798*

ADJECTIVES

6 **quantitative,** quantified, quantized, measured, measuring, weighed, counted, sized; ample, high, deep, long, wide, massive, voluminous; thick, thin, heavy, light, bunched, packed, sparse, mountainous; increased, added, extended, greater; majority, most, many, so many, so much; any, about, approximate, more or less; plural, infinite, all, total, whole, entire, enough, small, some, certain, limited, rationed, finite, few, smaller, least; numbered, fractional, variable, average

Sufficiency 97; Size, Largeness 579; Measurement 589; Number 783; One 788; Plurality 793; Multitude 795; Infinity 798; Certainty 840

VERBS

7 quantify, quantize, measure, weigh, count, number, rate, fix, size; piece, portion, apportion, allot, ration, allocate, dose, divide, share, pack, parcel; limit, set a quota, set an upper limit, set a ceiling, set a lower limit, set a floor; increase, add, extend, decrease, reduce, subtract

Allocation 474; Expansion 581; Contraction 582; Limit 620; Increase 746; Decrease 747; Addition 748; Subtraction 749; Number 783

ADVERBS

8 quantitatively, to such an extent, finitely, about, approximately, some, nearly, as much as, more or less; variably, fractionally, slightly, thinly, sparsely, lightly, mathematically, to the tune of [Inf]

9 wholly, entirely, totally, all of; infinitely, amply, highly, deeply, widely, massively, hugely, enormously, voluminously, thickly, heavily; lock, stock, and barrel

739 Degree

NOUNS

1 degree, extent, measure, amount, frequency, intensity, rate; amplitude, magnitude, value, caliber, quantity, depth, height, altitude, size, breadth, speed; gradualism, gradualness, slowness, scope, range, duration, reach, compass, limitation, stint, scale, pitch, tenor, register, key

Music 140; Size, Largeness 579; Measurement 589; Breadth 592; Height 596; Depth 598; Limit 620; Duration 642; Motion 677; Slowness 693; Quantity 738

2 rank, level, grading, grade, echelon, precedence, order, place, position, the power structure, hierarchy; station, circumstance, footing, standing, status, class, caste; authority

Authority 52; Allocation 474; Circumstances 726; Class 777

3 gradation, graduation, measurement, calibration, valuation, differentiation, differential, degree of difference; classification, rating, ranking, remove, relativeness, relative quantity; comparison, ratio, proportion, ration, standard, grading, shading, notation, bar, line, mark, notch, peg, score

Measurement 589; Relatedness 727; Oppositeness 731; Part 760

4 interval, period, time, stint, shift, portion, part, shade, shadow, nuance; point, place, step, rung, tread, stair, stage; plane, level, plateau, space, steppingstone, milestone, turning point, juncture

Space 563; Interval 587; Ascent 713

ADJECTIVES

5 gradational, graduated, graded, measured, rated,

scaled, in scale, calibrated, classified; valued, sized, sorted, differentiated, differential, relative, comparative, comparable; proportional, proportionable, portioned, standard, within the bounds of, encompassing, limited; majority, minority, level, regular, frequent, extensive; progressive, gradual, slow-ranging, slow-changing, growing, increasing, waxing, reaching, waning, shading off, tapering, fading, fading out, diminishing

6 ranked, hierarchic, hierarchical, leading, preceding, authoritative

VERBS

7 measure, classify, evaluate, rate, rank, order, class, grade, sort, mark, peg, score, scale, shade, graduate; place, position, estimate, quantify, calibrate, calculate, clock, compare, differentiate, precede, lead

8 change by degrees, change gradually, lower, taper off, shade off, cut back, trim, pare, whittle down; abate, die away, melt away, fade out, fade, diminish, decrease, wane, dissolve, evolve, melt into; increase, augment, build up, crescendo, grow, expand, inflate, swell, wax, unfold

Expansion 581; Contraction 582; Increase 746; Decrease 747; Addition 748; Subtraction 749

ADVERBS

9 differentially, relatively, comparatively, by comparison, comparably, proportionally, levelly; regularly, routinely, frequently, often, extensively, hierarchically, authoritatively

10 by degrees, progressively, gradually, slowly, by inches, inchmeal, piecemeal; slowly but surely, a little at a time, in slight measure, inch by inch, just a bit, bit by bit, little by little; by stages, step by step, drop by drop, however little, however much, increasingly, more and more, decreasingly, less and less

11 to a degree, to *or* in some degree, to some extent, in a way, in some measure; somewhat, sort of, kind of, fairly, quite, rather, pretty much, to a great degree, extremely, very; to a small degree, scarcely, slightly, very little, barely, a little, a bit

740 Equality

All animals are equal but some animals are more equal than others. — GEORGE ORWELL

NOUNS

1 equality, equivalence, equivalency, equation, sameness, evenness, levelness, equal footing, same quantity, same degree, correspondence, parallelism, coequality, sharing, going halves, likeness; egalitarianism, fairness, equity, democracy, equal rights, equal opportunity, justice, parity, par; even money, break-even, nothing to choose between, six of one and half a dozen of the other, a distinction without a difference, going Dutch, an eye for an eye; even break, fair shake [Inf]

▶ *Parallelism 606; Exchange 673; Sameness 730; Similarity 733; Accord 735*

2 **equilibrium,** balance, poise, counterpoise, equipoise, equiponderance, even keel, evenness, steadiness, stable state, steady state, balance of power; homeostasis, symmetry, proportion, stability, the same, status quo, stop, stasis

3 **stalemate,** deadlock, standstill, logjam, hung jury; tie, tied score, knotted score, tied game, draw, drawn game *or* match, deuce [Tennis], love all [Tennis], drawn battle; dead heat, photo finish, neck-and-neck race

▶ *Contention 422*

4 **equalization,** equation, equating, equalizing, equilibration; balancing, adjustment, readjustment, weighing up, leveling up *or* down, evening up *or* down, rounding up *or* down; compensation, just compensation, positive discrimination, affirmative action, counteraction, offset; exchange, even exchange, interchange, interchangeability, equipollence, equipollency, isotropy, synonymity, synonym; reciprocation, fair exchange, barter, trade-off, exchange value, fair *or* equal value, fair price, just price

▶ *Trade 480; Price 494; Compensation 743; Repair 809*

5 **equalizer,** counterweight, ballast, makeweight, stopgap, counterpoise, stabilizer, rudder, fin, aileron, spoiler

6 **dividing line,** radius, diameter, coordinate, equator, bisector, longitudinal line, latitudinal line

▶ *Two 789*

7 **equal,** peer, twin, match, mate, fellow; counterpart, opposite number, coequal, shadow, parallel, equivalent, like

▶ *Friendship 62*

ADJECTIVES

8 **equal,** equalized, same, similar, equivalent, like, alike; parallel, convertible, identical, corresponding, correspondent, coequal, egalitarian, democratic, equitable, just, fair, impartial; homologous, congruent, coextensive, equilateral, equidistant, coordinate, coincident, symmetrical, equable, stable; static, homeostatic, self-regulating, steady, balanced, fixed; round, rounded, square, squared, flush, even-sided, regular; well-ordered, commensurate, tantamount, equipollent, proportionate, uniform; unvarying, monotonous, much the same, as broad as long, neither more nor less, on an even keel, even-steven [Inf]

9 **on equal terms,** equally divided, even, par, on a par, at par, level, on the same level, on the same plane, on the same footing, parallel, well-matched, evenly matched; one-to-one, half-and-half, fifty-fifty, neck and neck; abreast, all one, all the same, drawn, tied

10 **equal to,** adequate, capable, fit, able, competent, suitable, apt, appropriate, up to, up to the mark

VERBS

11 **be equal,** be equal to, correspond to, accord with, agree with, coincide with; parallel, tie, draw, break even, run neck and neck, run nip and tuck, run level; make it all square, share, go shares, go halves, go Dutch, go fifty-fifty, share and share alike; measure up to, come up to, match up with, hold one's own, keep up with, keep in step with, keep pace with, keep abreast of, cope with, run abreast

12 **equalize,** synchronize, even, balance, redress the balance; make good, set off, accommodate, adjust, readjust, even up *or* down, level, level up *or* down, square up, equate; strike a balance, poise, counterpoise, counterbalance, countervail, compensate, offset, cancel out, coordinate, integrate, proportion, fit, smooth, stabilize, right oneself; come to the same thing, add up to the same thing, leave no remainder; make no difference, add nothing, detract nothing, hold the road, rob Peter to pay Paul

▶ *Compensation 743*

ADVERBS

13 **equally,** on equal terms, similarly, identically, coequally, correspondingly, equivalently, evenly

14 **as good as,** other things being equal, *ceteris paribus* [L], by the same token, to all intents and purposes, as much as to say, to the same degree; at the same rate, *pari passu* [L], abreast; neck and neck, nip and tuck, in equilibrium, on an even keel

15 **equitably,** justly, with justice, fairly, in a fair way, impartially, without prejudice, democratically; stably, steadily, with a steady pace; congruently, coextensively, equidistantly, symmetrically; roundly, squarely, regularly, uniformly

741 Inequality

We have the religion of inequality. — MATTHEW ARNOLD

NOUNS

1 **inequality,** disparity, difference, degree of difference, contrariety, disproportion, imparity, unlikeness, dissimilarity, superiority, inferiority, inadequacy, insufficiency, insufficience; nonuniformity, heterogeneity, diversity, variability, patchiness; advantage, odds, disadvantage, tilting of the scales, handicap, loaded dice

▶ *Diversity 732; Dissimilarity 734; Compensation 743*

2 **imbalance,** unbalance, overbalance, overcompensation, overload, overkill, top-heaviness; extra, shortage, shortfall, deficiency; tilt, camber, list, unevenness, oddness, odd number, preponderance; asymmetry, lopsidedness, skewness, obliquity, disequilibrium, dizziness, staggers

► *Insufficiency 98; Heaviness 538; Lightness 539; Distortion 627; Superiority 744; Inferiority 745; Addition 748; Subtraction 749*

3 injustice, inequity, unfairness, discrimination, prejudice, bias, partiality, lack of fairness, lack of democracy

► *Misjudgment 342*

ADJECTIVES

4 unequal, disparate, different, disproportionate, disproportioned, incongruent, dissimilar, superior, inferior, inadequate, insufficient; nonuniform, diverse, disagreeing, unlike, uneven, odd, asymmetrical, irregular, scalene, unequaled, inferior, below par, unequable, variable, variegated, deficient, defective, patchy, falling short, mismatched, ill-matched, ill-sorted; at an advantage, at a disadvantage

5 unbalanced, ill-balanced, lopsided, unwieldy, listing, leaning, canting, heeling, off-balance, off-center, overbalanced, overloaded, top-heavy, bottom-heavy; askew, awry, in disequilibrium, swinging, swaying, rocking, unstable, untrimmed, unballasted, uncompensated, losing balance, dizzy, giddy, staggering

6 unjust, unfair, inequitable, discriminatory, prejudiced, biased, partial, undemocratic

VERBS

7 be unequal, not match, not equate, not balance, disagree, preponderate, have the advantage, play above par, be superior, outclass, outstrip, outrank, outvote, outweigh, outdo, surpass; be inferior, be at a disadvantage, play below par, give points to, not suffice, fall short

8 unbalance, throw off *or* out of balance, disbalance, overbalance, unequalize, leave a remainder, make disproportionate, disproportion, skew, destabilize, upset, list, tilt, lean, heel, rock, swing, sway, lilt, fluctuate, vary, change, capsize, miss, overcompensate, overshoot, undershoot; disadvantage, handicap

9 be unjust, lack fairness, discriminate, be prejudiced, show prejudice, be biased, show bias, show partiality, be undemocratic

ADVERBS

10 unequally, disparately, differently, disproportionately, dissimilarly, diversely, nonuniformly, unevenly; at *or* with an advantage, out in front, at *or* with a disadvantage, deficiently, defectively, inadequately, insufficiently; up against it, from behind, from the rear, with a handicap, with the odds stacked against one

11 asymmetrically, irregularly, variously, uniquely, variably, on the light side, on the heavy side

12 unjustly, without justice, unfairly, without fairness, inequitably, discriminatorily, prejudicially, undemocratically

742 Average

I feel like a fugitive from th' law of averages.
— BILL MAULDIN

NOUNS

1 average, norm, standard, par, rule, measure, criterion, yardstick, model; averageness, generality, commonness, commonality, prevalence; ordinariness, familiarity, normality, normalcy, common *or* garden variety; conventionality, conformity, standardness, regularity, the usual, the ordinary, the common lot, the way things are, the way of the world

► *Regularity 663; Generality 778; Conformity 781*

2 medium, happy medium, average, mean, golden mean, *juste-milieu* [Fr], balance; middle, mid [Arch], midpoint, median, center, midsection; middle ground, halfway point, halfway house, midterm, middle term, middle course, middle of the road; via media, moderation, moderateness

► *Moderation 521; Center 612; Middle 772*

3 mediocrity, averageness, passableness, tolerableness, adequacy, mixed blessing, half measure, indifference, unremarkableness; nothing to boast *or* brag about, nothing special, nothing to write home about, no great shakes [Inf]

► *Sufficiency 97; Lack of Emphasis 201; Inferiority 745; Unimportance 800*

4 average person, commoner, boy *or* girl next door, man *or* woman in *or* on the street, John Q. Public, everyman, everywoman, every Tom, Dick, and Harry; commonalty, rank and file, masses, ruck, common folk, small change, small fry, common [Arch]; bourgeoisie, proletariat, working classes; [Inf]: ordinary guy, plain Jane, small potatoes

► *Commoner 71; Worker 123; Class 777; Multitude 795*

ADJECTIVES

5 average, usual, normal, par, typical, general, common, prevailing, current, prevalent, generic, representative; characteristic, ordinary, everyday, run-of-the-mill, familiar, household, common *or* garden, routine; customary, accustomed, traditional, accepted, conventional, standard, stock, set, established, regular, regulation, regulated, classic, orthodox, normative, prescriptive

► *Habit, Custom 397; Regularity 663; Generality 778; Conformity 781*

6 medium, median, medial, mesial, mean, middle, middling, mid, midmost, middlemost, midway; intermediate, intermediary, balanced, halfway, half-and-half, fifty-fifty, central; middle-of-the-road, fence-sitting, middle-ground, moderate, nonextremist

► *Moderation 521; Center 612; Middle 772*

7 mediocre, average, passable, fair, fairish, fair to middling, middling, moderate, tolerable; adequate, not bad, neither good nor bad, all right, indifferent, lukewarm; ordinary, unimpressive, unremarkable, undistinguished, unexceptional, unnoteworthy, unspectacular, commonplace; pedestrian, middle-class, bourgeois, small-town, middle-brow, prosaic; banal, gray, dull, OK or O.K. or okay, small-time, so-so, *comme ci comme ça* [Fr], *così-così* [Ital]

> *Lack of Emphasis 201; Inferiority 745; Conformity 781; Unimportance 800*

VERBS

8 **be average,** be the norm, prevail, predominate, be about right, suffice; be moderate, sit on the fence, not cause a stir, conform, go with the crowd; go unnoticed, blend with the crowd, blur, take a backseat, stay in the background, be a nobody, play second fiddle

> *Sufficiency 97; Lack of Emphasis 201; Inferiority 745; Generality 778*

9 **make average,** even out or up, average out, level, level up or down, normalize, generalize, conventionalize, standardize; balance, balance out, strike a balance, regularize, proportion, smooth out; share, distribute, allocate, divide; split down the middle, split the difference

> *Possession 469; Allocation 474; Center 612; Regularity 663; Middle 772; Calculation 784*

ADVERBS

10 **on average,** chiefly, mainly, commonly, generally, as a rule, in general, generally speaking, broadly, broadly speaking, roughly, roughly speaking; more or less, mostly, for the most part, on the whole, as a whole, by and large, in the long run; altogether, all in all, overall, taking all things together, all things considered, all things being equal, on balance

11 **prevailingly,** predominantly, usually, normally, ordinarily, typically, habitually, routinely, as a matter of course, to be expected, as usual

> *Regularity 663; Sameness 730; Generality 778; Conformity 781*

12 **medianly,** medially, intermediately, centrally, midway, halfway, half-and-half, midmost, middlemost, in the middle; moderately, neither here nor there, in between, betwixt and between

> *Center 612; Middle 772*

743 Compensation

NOUNS

1 **compensation,** recompense, amends, amendment, reparation, indemnity, indemnification, distraint, damages, reimbursement, refund, repayment, meed [Arch]; reward, guerdon, remuneration, remittance, remittal; payoff, golden handshake, golden parachute, settlement, redemption, requital, requitement; replacement, restoration, restitution, recoupment, re-deemability, recovery, replevin, retrieval, rectification, redress, remedy, satisfaction; expiation, atonement, penance, penalty, ransom, blood money, wergild

> *Remedy 115; Atonement 313; Giving Back 478; Money 484; Payment 489*

2 **counterbalance,** setoff, offset, balance, counterweight, ballast, makeweight, counterpoise, equilibration, equilibrant, equalization; correction, self-correction, attunement, tuning, adjustment, readjustment, allowance, countermeasure, trade-off, contraposition, counteraction, return action, retroaction; reprisal, retaliation, revenge, vengeance, eye for an eye, tit for tat, quid pro quo

> *Retaliation 420; Counteraction 510; Equality 740*

ADJECTIVES

3 **compensated,** recompensed, indemnified, reimbursed, refunded, repaid, paid back; rewarded, remunerated, remitted; settled, requited, avenged, revenged; replaced, restored, restituted, recouped, recovered, rectified, redressed, remedied, satisfied, expiated, redeemed, atoned

> *Atonement 313; Giving Back 478; Payment 489*

4 **compensable,** amendable, rectifiable, recoupable, reclaimable, replevisable; redeemable, redemptible, remittable, requitable, restorable, recoverable, satisfiable, atonable

5 **compensatory,** compensative, compensating, compensational; reparatory, reparative, restitutory, restitutive, restorative, restoring; indemnificatory, indemnifying, amendatory, amending; retributive, redemptory, redemptive, redeeming, remedial, expiatory, expiating, propitiatory, propitiating, piacular, penitential, penitentiary; measure for measure, blow for blow, tit-for-tat

> *Atonement 313; Giving Back 478; Payment 489*

6 **counterbalanced,** counterbalancing, set off, offset, balanced, balancing, counterweighted, counterweighing; counterpoised, equiponderant, equilibrated, equilibrating, equalized, equalizing; countervailing, evening up or out, evened up or out; offsetting, corrected, corrective, correcting, self-correcting, attuned, tuned, adjusted, readjusted; counter, counterposed, counterposing, contraposed, contraposing, counteracted, counteracting, counteractive, retroactive; retaliating, retaliatory, avenging

> *Remedy 115; Counteraction 510; Cancellation 834*

VERBS

7 **compensate,** recompense, make amends, indemnify, replevy, reimburse, refund, repay, pay back, pay up; reward, guerdon, remunerate, remit; pay off, settle, settle accounts, settle the score, distrain, redeem, requite; replace, restore, restitute, make restitution, rectify, redress, remedy, mend, satisfy, expiate, atone, do penance, make up for, make good, make it up, put or set straight, put or set right

Atonement 313; Giving Back 478; Payment 489

8 counterbalance, offset, balance, counterweigh, countervail, counterpoise, counterpose, contrapose, equilibrate, equalize, restore to equilibrium; even up *or* out, correct, self-correct, attune, tune, square, square up, adjust, readjust, countermeasure, trade off, counteract; counterblast, return action, retaliate, avenge, revenge

Remedy 115; Counteraction 510; Cancellation 834

9 be compensated, get compensation, recover, retrieve, regain, repossess, recoup, reclaim, retake, redeem, take back, get satisfaction, be avenged

ADVERBS

10 in compensation, remedially, remediably, redemptively, counteractively

11 correctively, redeemably, propitiatorily, penitentially, vengefully

744 Superiority

NOUNS

1 superiority, precedence, eminence, preeminence, primacy, greatness, pride of place, first place, priority, seniority; preponderance, predominance, predomination, prepotence, prepotency, influence, leverage, say, effectiveness; transcendence, prestige, ascendancy, loftiness, altitude, sublimity, excellence, quality, perfection; high caliber, virtuosity, inimitability, incomparability, majority, supremacy, prominence, success, domination, be-all and end-all; clout [Inf], pull [Inf]

Precedence 769; Perfection 805; Success 845

2 leadership, authority, jurisdiction, authorization; rule, sway, control, hegemony, sovereignty, power, imperium, dominion, command, directorship, management, mastership, mastery

Government 49; Politics 50; Authority 52; Management 126

3 advantage, vantage, odds, points, handicap, edge, upper hand, trump hand, something extra, something in reserve, something in hand, ace *or* card up one's sleeve; lead, commanding lead, being ahead, head start, running start, flying start, jump, drop; vantage point, vantage ground, coign of vantage, favor, seeded position, winning position, pole position, inside track, one-upmanship

4 summit, top, top of the pyramid, height, the heights, high ground, lofty ground; acme, zenith, pinnacle, peak, climax, crest; new high, record high, top rung

Height 596; Summit 600

5 superior, master, leader, chief, boss, manager, superintendent, foreman; commander, general, captain; first among equals, *primus inter pares* [L]; [Inf]: Mr. Big, main man, big cheese, big fish *or* frog in a small pond, head honcho

Authority 52; Military Affairs 58; Master 68; Management 126; Importance 799

6 paragon, genius, prodigy, nonpareil, virtuoso, prima donna, diva, first lady, expert, specialist, laureate; high-flier, mastermind, superman, superwoman, star, superstar, the greatest, number one, numero uno, celebrity; champion, victor, winner, prizewinner, world-beater, recordholder, cupholder, record-breaker, chart-topper, ace; whiz kid [Inf], the most [Inf]

Skillfulness 127; Wisdom 352

7 best people, elite, top people, nobility, aristocracy, upper class, cream, cream of the crop, crème de la crème, one's (elders and) betters; chosen few, select few, happy few, brightest and best, pick of the bunch, top drawer; [Inf]: upper crust, the brass, top brass, big boys, nobs [Brit]

Aristocrat 70

ADJECTIVES

8 superior, greater, better, finer, higher, over, super, above, surpassing, eclipsing; overtopping, exceeding, leading, more than a match for, ahead, one step ahead, one up on, capping; outclassing, in a different class, more so, above average, head and shoulders above, ascendant, in ascendancy, preferred, favorite, top-drawer, cut above

9 dominant, dominating, dictatorial, magisterial, authoritative, in authority, ruling, overruling, overriding, governing, ordering, imperial, sovereign

10 best, best ever, greatest, supreme, superlative, crowning, cardinal, capital; matchless, unmatched, unmatchable, peerless, unparalleled, unrivaled, unequaled, without equal, *sans pareil* [Fr], *nulli secundus* [L]; unapproachable, unsurpassed, unsurpassable, unexcelled; inimitable, incomparable, beyond compare, beyond criticism

11 unique, perfect, highest, maximal, maximum, max [Inf], most, uppermost *or* upmost, utmost *or* uttermost

12 elite, top, topmost, topnotch, noble, upper-class; upmost, utmost; prime, primary, paramount, foremost, headmost, main, chief, principal, central, focal; preeminent, supereminent, transcendent, transcending, tiptop [Inf]

13 unbeatable, invincible, dominant, predominant, preponderant, hegemonic, prevailing; first, record, record-breaking, top-ranking, top-ranked, champion, gold-medal, victorious, winning, triumphant, world-beating, recordholding, A one *or* A number one *or* A 1 [Inf], number-one; the last word [Inf], chart-topping, chart-busting, out of this world

14 excellent, major, master, superb, first-rate, first-class, top-flight, upper; prominent, eminent, distinguished, singular, outstanding, banner, star, blue-chip; rare, classic, marked, chosen, of choice, not like the rest, every inch a king *or* queen

15 **be superior,** excel, exceed, predominate, transcend, prevail; win, triumph, defeat, overcome, beat, take command, extinguish, carry the day, batter, thrash, trounce; be laureled, be crowned, bear the palm, win the prize *or* championship *or* blue ribbon *or* cup; beat the record, set a record, improve on, reach new heights, reach a new high; peak, culminate, climax

16 **overtake,** get ahead of, shoot ahead of, come to the front, steal a march on, pass, outdistance, prove too much for; rise above, tower above *or* over, top, trump, overtrump, overplay, overstep, override, overleap, overtop, have it over one, overlook, overshadow, eclipse, throw in the shade, beat someone hollow, run rings *or* circles around; have the last laugh, hold all the cards, hold all the aces, steal someone's thunder, steal the show, out-Herod Herod; [Inf]: lick, whip, clobber
 ▶ *Overstepping 712*

17 **be ahead,** hold *or* have an advantage, have the edge on *or* over, get *or* have the jump on someone, get the drop on, have something extra, have something in reserve, hold the upper hand, hold the trump hand, have something in hand; get a head start *or* flying start, have a running start; have a vantage point, have the pole position, have the inside track, have an ace up one's sleeve

18 **outdo,** outplay, outrank, outvie, outbid, outshine, outstrip, outwit, outgo, outrace, outpace, outmarch, outrun, outride, outjump, outleap, outstep, outrange, outdistance, outreach, outperform, outmaneuver; better, get the better of, go one better, best, surpass, cap

19 **lead,** take the lead, hold *or* have the lead; head, direct, manage, run, front, spearhead, captain; take precedence, come first, rank first, rank, lead the dance, play the lead, star

ADVERBS

20 **superiorly,** with superiority, superlatively, surpassingly, exceedingly, victoriously, triumphantly; dominantly, dominatingly, with a dominating manner, dictatorially, magisterially, authoritatively, with authority, royally

21 **predominantly,** preponderantly, mainly, in the main, chiefly, primarily, principally, paramountly, centrally, eminently, transcendently, transcendentally, excellently, prestigiously

22 **superbly,** masterly, prominently, extremely, importantly, outstandingly, above average, above par, especially, rarely, advantageously, with an advantage, favorably, out of the common run, out of the top drawer

23 **supremely,** superlatively, par excellence, incomparably, without comparison, inimitably, peerlessly, unmatchably, matchlessly, unsurpassedly, unsurpassably, invincibly; at the top of the scale, on the crest, at the peak, at the zenith, above all, to crown all, to the highest degree; far and away, by far, even more, all the

more, still more, more than ever; uniquely, first of all, second to none, *nulli secundus* [L], out of this world, singularly, perfectly, in a perfect way, the most [Inf]

745 Inferiority

No one can make you feel inferior without your consent.
— ELEANOR ROOSEVELT

NOUNS

1 **inferiority,** secondariness, supporting role, second rank, second class, third class, lower class; inferior standing, inferior status, subordinate position, backseat, second best; ordinariness, obscurity, lowliness, baseness, subordination, abasement, dependence; humbleness, humility, subservience, insignificance, unimportance
 ▶ *Humility 298; Unimportance 800*

2 **deficiency,** inadequacy, mediocrity, disadvantage, handicap, impairment; stain, blemish, defect, fault, faultiness, imperfection; failure, failing, decline, worsening, deterioration; insufficiency, shortfall, fewness, poverty, beggarliness; poor quality, badness, cheapness, shoddiness, worthlessness, shabbiness
 ▶ *Insufficiency 98; Lowness 597; Decrease 747; Few 796; Imperfection 806; Deterioration 808; Failure 846*

3 **inferior state,** reduced circumstances, straitened circumstances; low point, low ebb, low, record low, all-time low, nadir, lowest point, minimum, floor, base; bottom, rock bottom, trough, depression, lowness, depths

4 **inferior,** younger, minor, junior, subordinate, subaltern; satellite, vassal, tributary, underling; slave, hireling, subsidiary, deputy; dupe, pawn, flunky, cog, tool, gofer [Inf]; dependent, follower, camp follower, supporter, yes-man; poor relation, the lower classes, hoi polloi, lower orders, lowlife, the masses, canaille, lesser creation; second, poor second, poor third, second-stringer, third-stringer, second-rater, third-rater, benchwarmer, low man on the totem pole [Inf]
 ▶ *Servant 69; Commoner 71; Deputy 80; Submission 421*

ADJECTIVES

5 **inferior,** secondary, supporting; lesser, least, lower, lowest, bottommost; low-standing, backseat; ordinary, obscure, lowly, base, dependent; not up to much, below the salt; unworthy, nothing special, nothing to shout about, nothing out of the ordinary, nothing to write home about
 ▶ *Average 742*

6 **insignificant,** minimal, minimum, small, inconsiderable; humble, humiliated, subservient, unimportant; smaller, smallest, diminished, small-time, lightweight; ordinary, middling, mediocre, common, vulgar, base,

plebeian; small-town, one-horse, hick; [Inf]: jerkwater, penny-ante, dinky, rinky-dink

7 **low quality,** poor quality, substandard, below standard, subnormal; second-rate, second-class, second rank, second-best, third-rate, third class, lower class, low-class, low-grade; defective, deficient, marred, spoiled, shopworn; failed, failing, faulty, imperfect, weak, slight, feeble, unsound; shoddy, tatty, cheap; [Inf]: crummy, crappy, not up to snuff or scratch

8 **subordinate,** minor, junior, dependent, subsidiary, subject, subservient, humble, tributary, ancillary, auxiliary

9 **outclassed,** outshone, bested, worsted, trounced, beaten, defeated, humiliated, humbled, ruined; not fit to hold a candle to, not in the same league

VERBS

10 **be inferior,** fail, lose, fall or come short, fall below, lack, want, not come up to, not come up to scratch, not come up to the mark, not make the grade or cut, not come up to standard, not measure up; lag, trail, fall behind, drag one's feet, not hold a candle to, have nothing on, not make the grade, not pass, not pass the test, not be up to it, not handle it; [Inf]: not make or hack it

11 **become inferior,** get worse, worsen, go from bad to worse, deteriorate, decline, diminish, descend, plunge, sink, sink low, sink without a trace, plumb the depths, touch rock bottom, reach one's nadir, lose face, lose the upper hand, hit the skids [Inf]

12 **follow,** take or play a supporting role, withdraw into the background, sink into obscurity, lapse into oblivion, play second fiddle to, take a backseat; yield to, give in to, cede to, concede the victory to, have to hand it to, hand to on a plate, bow to, knuckle under, submit

ADVERBS

13 **inferiorly,** in an inferior state or place; minimally, at a low ebb, in the lowest position, at one's lowest ebb; below standard, below the mark, under par, short of, less, less than, minus, beneath, under, below

14 **insignificantly,** inconsiderably, unimportantly, commonly, ordinarily

15 **badly,** shoddily, unsoundly, cheaply, defectively, imperfectly, weakly, slightly, feebly, poorly, subnormally

16 **basely,** subordinately, dependently, subserviently, humbly, unworthily

746 Increase

NOUNS

1 **increase,** addition, increment, augmentation, enlargement, growth, development; progress, advancement, advance; accumulation, cumulativeness, cumulative effect, buildup, accretion, snowballing; gain, waxing, bulging, swelling, dilation, expansion, fatten-

ing, thickening, broadening, widening, deepening; improvement, prosperity, profitability, appreciation; excess, overenlargement; magnification, doubling, redoubling, duplication, trebling, triplication, quadruplication, multiplication; reproduction, propagation, proliferation; extension, prolongation, protraction

▶ *Production 522; Expansion 581; Addition 748*

2 **intensification,** escalation, acceleration, speeding, stepping up; concentration, condensation; amplification, enrichment, supplement, heightening, enhancement; exaltation, elevation, aggrandizement, glorification; exaggeration, reinforcement; invigoration, stimulation, stimulus, spur; aggravation, exacerbation; culmination, climax

▶ *Reproduction 21; Exaggeration 194*

3 **spread,** spiral, upswing, upturn, upward curve, upward trend, upsurge, uprush; push, swell, swelling, intumescence, surge, gush; boost, boom; rise, climb, crescendo; leap, jump, takeoff

▶ *Thickness 594; Height 596; Ascent 713; Raising 715*

ADJECTIVES

4 **increasing,** progressive, progressing, expanding, growing, spreading, spreading like wildfire, escalating, bigger and better; crescent, waxing, filling, on the increase; ever-increasing, cumulative, snowballing, augmentative, prolific, additional, supplementary

5 **increased,** enlarged, magnified; accelerated; swollen, bloated, expanded, extended, stretched; intensified, heightened, enhanced, augmented, supplemented; hiked, jazzed up [Inf]

VERBS

6 **increase,** grow, gain, develop, escalate, wax, bulge, dilate, distend, expand, fill, fill out; fatten, thicken, broaden, become larger, grow larger, put on weight; bud, sprout, burgeon, blossom, flower, flourish, thrive; breed, swarm, spawn, proliferate, mushroom, multiply, spread; swell, intumesce; grow up, shoot up, spring up, grow by leaps and bounds; climb, spiral, mount, rise, soar; accumulate, snowball, take off, take off in a big way, rocket, flare up, gain strength, improve, grow rich, prosper, profit, be profitable, earn interest, gain in value, appreciate, rise in price, boom, surge, exceed; rise to a peak, rise to a maximum, crescendo; progress, gain ground, advance, go through the roof or ceiling, skyrocket

7 **make bigger,** make more, augment, supplement, add to, contribute to, bring to, increase, increase numbers, enlist, recruit; enlarge, magnify, double, triple, quadruple, redouble, multiply, duplicate, square, cube, raise to the power of; reproduce, propagate, breed, grow, rear, raise from seed, raise from cuttings; develop, build up, fill up or in or out, pad out, expand, extend; raise, erect, elevate; prolong, stretch, lengthen,

broaden, thicken, deepen; accrue, repay with interest; widen, inflate, blow up

8 **intensify,** heighten, enrich, enhance, amplify; concentrate, condense; aggrandize, exalt, glorify; overrate, exaggerate; raise one's sights, set one's sights higher, raise the stakes; spur on, speed up, accelerate, escalate, step up, energize, stimulate, invigorate, reinforce, boost, give a boost to, maximize, stoke, fuel, add fuel; aggravate, exacerbate; bring to the boil, bring to a head, culminate, climax; heat up, hike up, beef up; [Inf]: jack up, bump up, jazz up

ADVERBS

9 **increasingly,** to an increasing extent, additionally, in addition; progressively, more and more, all the more, more so, even more so; greater and greater, bigger and bigger, bigger and better; cumulatively, prolifically, supplementarily

747 Decrease

NOUNS

1 **decrease,** deduction, subtraction, lessening, decrement, regression, de-escalation, abatement, slackening, moderation, growing soft, diminuendo, decrescendo, dimming, fading, fade-out, evanescence; diminution, waning, shrinking, shrinkage, contraction, detumescence; dwindling, ebb, drain; wasting away, degeneration, atrophy, failure, subsidence; loss of value, depreciation, enfeeblement, weakening, diminishing returns, slowdown, deceleration, retardation, impoverishment; shortage, scarcity, exhaustion

  ▶ *Contraction 582; Subtraction 749*

2 **reduction,** disappearance, evaporation, deliquescence; erosion, attrition, wear, wear and tear, decay, dilapidation, damage; wastage, waste, leakage, loss; extinction, consumption

  ▶ *Poverty 486*

3 **limitation,** restriction, curtailment, squeeze, compression; retrenchment, rationalization; cutback, rollback, economization, economizing; shortening, abbreviation, abridgment, précis; mitigation, extenuation; belittlement, underestimation, undervaluation

  ▶ *Insufficiency 98*

4 **decline,** downturn, downward trend, downward curve, fall, drop, falling off; sinking, plunge, collapse, slump, downward spiral, nosedive, tailspin; deflation, depression; leveling off, leveling out, bottoming out

  ▶ *Finance 457; Discount 495; Lowness 597; Descent 714*

ADJECTIVES

5 **decreasing,** declining, falling, dwindling, waning, wasting away, fading, evanescent, abating; moderating, softening, diminuendo, decrescendo; sinking, going down, subsiding, detumescent, ebbing, decaying; diminished, decreased, on the slide, belittled, on a downer [Inf]

6 **decrescent,** declinate, reductive, depressive, debilitative; deflationary, deflationist, depreciatory, depreciative, loss-making, regressive; corrosive, deliquescent, decompressive; decadent, decayable; declinable, deductible, depreciable

VERBS

7 **decrease,** grow less, lessen, de-escalate, ease, abate, slacken, moderate, die down, fade, fade away, evanesce; grow soft, grow dim; grow smaller, wane, wither, shrink, contract, shrivel, diminish, dwindle; ebb, ebb away, drain, drain away, dry up; waste away, wear away, eat away, corrode, run down, run low, fail; degenerate, atrophy, die away, tail off, taper off; peter out, decline, drop off, fall off, subside, sink, go down, come down, take a turn for the worse; plunge, collapse, slump, spiral downward, take a nosedive, go into a tailspin, go into recession, depreciate; not increase, not grow, level off, level out, bottom out; slow down, decelerate, lose, shed, cast off, cast away; lose one's voice, become invisible, fade from sight *or* view, disappear; evaporate, melt away, become scarce, thin out, thin, detumesce; become endangered, become extinct, die out, pass away, pass into history, pass into oblivion

8 **make smaller,** make less, decrease, whittle, pare down, scrape, shave, trim, prune, dock, clip, slash; reduce, lose weight; cut, cut down, thin out, weed out, rid oneself of; run down, impoverish; cut back, roll back, limit, restrict, curtail, scale down; squeeze, compress, contract, retrench, economize, rationalize, shorten, abbreviate, abridge, condense, précis, edit down; slow down, reduce speed, decelerate, retard, depress, lower; hush, quiet, turn down; weaken, enfeeble, debilitate; dilute, water down; extenuate, mitigate, alleviate; belittle, minimize, undervalue, underestimate, degrade, downgrade, play down

ADVERBS

9 **decreasingly,** diminishingly, in decline, on the wane, at low ebb; less and less, less so, ever less, even less, in descending order, downward; on a declining scale, at a lower rate, at a lower price

748 Addition

NOUNS

1 **addition,** adding, joining, annexation, admixture, superaddition; load, extra load, encumbrance, burden, imposition; superimposition, superposition, interjection, interposition, supervention, insertion, inclusion; attachment, affixture, prefixion, suffixion, supplementation, augmentation, accession, accrual, accretion, increase; increment, supplement, complement; enlargement, extension, addendum, accessory; appurtenance, appendage, appanage; reinforcement, continuation, prolongation

▸ *Excess 99; Expansion 581; Insertion 710; Extraneous-ness 724; Increase 746; Union 752; Hindrance 826*

2 **mathematical addition,** arithmetic, adding up, reckoning up, summation, computation, calculation, totaling, counting up, ringing up; total, toll, tally

▸ *Calculation 784*

3 **additional item,** add-on, adjunct, augmentation, augment; inflection, affix, prefix, suffix, infix, adjective, adverb; additive, attachment, addendum, additament; carry-over, leftover; contribution; reinforcement, patch, padding, stuffing, lining; interpolation, interlineation, interlude, intermezzo, ingredient, component; side effect, side issue, additional part, aftereffect; annex, wing, ell, outhouse, shed, outbuilding, the works [Inf]

4 **appendage,** tail; tailpiece, coda, appendix, postscript *or* P.S. *or* p.s.; ending, epilogue, conclusion, corollary, afterword, envoy *or* envoi; codicil, rider; annotation, footnote, marginal note, marginalia, subscript, superscript

5 **ornamentation,** frill, fringe, edging, border, dingbat; decoration, garnish, garnishing; seasoning, flavoring, sauce, dressing; trimmings, all the trimmings, all that goes with it; accouterments, furnishings, trappings, finish, finishing touch, icing on the cake

▸ *Food 90; Decoration 532; Accompaniment 794*

6 **extra,** little extra, added extra, peripheral, by-product; interest, gain, benefit, bonus, plus, perquisite; tip, gratuity, lagniappe; graft, free gift, giveaway, windfall, find, lucky find, serendipity; supernumerary, surplus, superfluity, extras, sundries; reserves, reserve equipment, spare parts, spares, provisions; items, oddments, odd items, odds and ends; extra help, auxiliaries, auxiliary forces, reinforcements; extra time, injury time, sudden death, extra inning; golden handshake, perk [Inf], freebie [Inf]

7 **extra person,** extra pair of hands; substitute, relief, auxiliary, reinforcement, backup, stand-in, understudy

▸ *Drama and Theater 136; Substitution 672*

ADJECTIVES

8 **additional,** added, included, interpolated, lined, inclusive, annexed, loaded, reinforced, additive, cumulative; adjunctive, adjunct, conjunctive, attached, adjoined, joined, subjoined, inserted, prefixed; adscititious, adventitious, supplemental, supplementary; complementary, accretive, accretionary, subsidiary, incremental; auxiliary, collateral, contributory; another, yet another, further, more

9 **ornamental,** decorative, padded, stuffed, dressed up

10 **extra,** new, fresh, serendipitous; supererogatory, supernumerary, surplus, spare, superfluous

VERBS

11 **add,** add up, count, count up, calculate, total, total up, sum, sum up, do addition, compute; carry, carry over, add to, append, annex, subjoin; attach, pin to, staple to, clip to, stick to, stick onto *or* on, glue onto, tag, tag on, tack on; hitch to, hitch up to, hook up to, yoke to; join, tie to, unite to, conjoin, glue together, accrete; preface, prefix, affix, suffix; tot up, tote up [Inf]

▸ *Union 752; Adhesion 755*

12 **insert,** infix, interpolate, stick in; introduce, interject, interpose, engraft, let in, bring to; contribute to, make one's contribution, add one's share, add *or* put in one's two cents worth

13 **augment,** swell, expand, extend, supplement; crown, complete, put the finishing touches to; make up the shortfall; fill a space, fill the gap; lay on, place on, put upon, impose, burden, load, overload, saddle with, burden *or* load with, heap on, pile on, superadd; superimpose, overlay, paint, paint over, coat, plaster; decorate, ornament, embellish, garnish; season, spice, flavor, mix with, mix in; take to oneself, take in, encompass, absorb, include; add value, accrue, bear interest

14 **support,** add one's support, adhere to; combine with, mix with; join, make an addition to, make one more; reinforce, recruit, make up the numbers, swell the ranks

▸ *Assembly 59; Strength 516*

ADVERBS

15 **additionally,** in addition (to), plus, and, extra, cumulatively, adjunctly, supplementarily, collaterally, superfluously; et cetera, etc., and so on, and so forth; more, over and above, on top of; with interest, with a vengeance; also, as well as, too, to boot, into *or* in the bargain; not to mention, let alone, not forgetting; moreover, furthermore, further; (or) else, besides, on the side, apart from; together with, along with, conjointly, jointly, at the same time, in collaboration, in conjunction with, coupled with, including, inclusive of, even with; despite, in spite of, for all that, beside

749 Subtraction

NOUNS

1 **subtraction,** deduction, taking away, minus; discounting, detraction, devaluation, diminution, decrease, cut, cutting, cutting back, retrenchment, shrinkage, decimation, price cutting, discount, offset; exception, abstraction, exclusion, withdrawal, elimination, expulsion, ejection, extraction, precipitation, sedimentation, removal, alleviation, relief; erosion, corrosion, wear and tear, rubbing out; deletion, erasure, obliteration, extirpation, eradication; editing, bowdlerization, expurgation, striking out, chopping, lopping; docking, curtailment, condensation, abridgment, abbreviation, shortening; mutilation, cutting off, amputation, beheading, decapitation, severance, excision, circumcision, castration, emasculation, altering, fixing [Inf]

▶ *Publication 173; Selection 382; Taking 477; Discount 495; Displacement 574; Shortness 591; Expulsion 709; Extraction 711; Decrease 747; Exclusion 764*

2 subtracted item, thing deducted, decrement, subtrahend, minuend; allowance, remission, discount, price cut, refund, rebate, cut, cutback; limitation, restriction, drawback; shortfall, loss, forfeit, sacrifice, rake-off

▶ *Number 783*

ADJECTIVES

3 subtracted, taken away, removed, deducted, excepted, abstracted, withdrawn, extracted; excluded, expelled, ejected; eliminated, eradicated, extirpated, deleted, rubbed out, erased, obliterated

4 subtractive, reductive, extirpative; deductive, abstract, removable; eradicable

5 reduced, decreased, minus, curtailed; mutilated, headless, beheaded, decapitated, tailless; docked, chopped, lopped, severed, limbless; short, shortened, condensed, abridged, abbreviated; cut-rate, discounted, devalued, diminished, lessened, decimated; eroded, corroded, worn

▶ *Shortness 591*

VERBS

6 subtract, deduct, take away, do subtraction; detract from, devalue, diminish, decrease; condense, abbreviate, abridge, decimate, cut; cut prices, discount, allow, set off, offset; leave out, take out, except, make an exception, abstract, exclude, omit, eliminate, withdraw; throw out, expel, eject, remove, unload, alleviate, relieve, shift, draw off, drain, empty, void; file down, corrode, erode, rub out, cross out, cancel, delete, erase, obliterate, cull, eradicate; thin, thin out, weed, uproot, pull up by the roots, extirpate, pull out, root out, rip out; extract, precipitate; pick, pick out, handpick, put on one side; pick a pocket; censor, blue-pencil, bowdlerize, expurgate

7 take off, sever, cut off, amputate, behead, decapitate; excise, chop off, lop, prune, dock, curtail, shorten; circumcise, castrate, alter, geld, caponize, emasculate, unman, neuter, spay, fix [Inf]; uncover, strip, strip off *or* away, doff, denude, divest; skin, peel, pluck, fleece

ADVERBS

8 by subtraction, at a discount, deductively, in deduction, less; short of, minus, without, bar, barring, save, exclusive of, excluding, except, excepting, with the exception of, save and except [Form]

9 decreasingly, diminishingly, less and less, in a downward curve *or* spiral; deductively, corrosively, removably; eradicably

750 Remainder

NOUNS

1 remainder, remains, rest, relic; relict, remnant, frus-

tum, piece, chunk, shard, sherd; shell, empty shell, husk, stump, rump; stub, plug, dottle *or* dottel, cigarette end, butt, cigarette butt, butt end, roach [Inf]; scrag end, body, torso, trunk, corpse, mortal remains; skeleton, bones, fossil, fragments, bits, debris, wreckage, ruins, all that is left; record, vestige, trace, track, trail, wake, footprint, fingerprint, afterglow, memory, tribal memory, memorabilia, souvenir; reminder, remembrance, survival, effect, aftereffect, result

▶ *History 3; Burial 31; Excess 99; Record 185; Destruction 523; Shortness 591; Part 760; End 773; Calculation 784; Few 796*

2 residue, deposit, sediment, silt, precipitate, alluvium, moraine, loess, detritus, residual, residuum; leavings, leftover, grounds, dregs, lees, dross, heeltap, skimmings; offscourings, scum, slag, ash, cinders, scoria, sludge, bilge; powder, sawdust, shaving, filings, scrapings, crumb, husk, bran, chaff, stubble; scourings, sweepings; peeling, peel, skin; slough, scurf, dandruff, combings; clipping, trimmings, remnant, fag end; castoff, scraps, oddments, odds and ends, bits and pieces, lumber; junk, rubbish, trash, reject, refuse, garbage, litter, dirt, waste, sewage

▶ *Waste 96*

3 difference, discrepancy, surplus, margin; amount *or* sum outstanding, (net) balance, balance carried forward, carry-over, credit; profit, excess; loss, deficit, debit

▶ *Economics 56; Finance 457; Loss 468*

4 surplus, excess, overgrowth, abundance, superabundance, overabundance, oversupply; redundancy, pleonasm; surfeit, superfluity, overload, glut; leftovers, extras, spares, something for a rainy day, bonus, dividend

▶ *Addition 748*

5 estate, effects, hereditament, acquest, bequest, inheritance, patrimony

6 person remaining, survivor, sole survivor, person left, last one out; heir, inheritor, successor; widow, widower, orphan; descendant, offspring, line, lineage

▶ *Sequence 770*

ADJECTIVES

7 remaining, residual, residuary, resultant, left, hereditary, patrimonial, left behind, vestigial; precipitated, deposited, sedimentary; surviving, bereft, widowed, orphan, orphaned; abandoned, discarded, rejected, castoff

8 surplus, net, unused, unspent, unexpired, unconsumed; outcast, on the shelf [Inf], over, left over, passed over, unwanted, odd; still remaining, outstanding, owed, carried over; extra, spare, to spare, excess; excessive, overabundant, superabundant, overloaded, redundant, superfluous, pleonastic, otiose

9 **be left,** be left over, remain, survive, result, continue, subsist, stay, rest

10 **leave,** leave over, owe, leave behind, deposit, bequeath; leave out, exclude, reject, abandon, discard, cast off, cast away, except, not choose

ADVERBS

11 **residually,** vestigially, memorably, discrepantly; excessively, superfluously, abundantly, overabundantly, superabundantly, pleonastically, redundantly

12 **with a remainder,** with the rest, among those remaining, in arrears, in default, outstandingly

751 Mixture

NOUNS

1 **mixture,** admixture, commixture, intermixture; mixing, mingling, intermingling, stirring, shaking, blending; harmonization, association, combination, integration, syncretism, eclecticism; fusion, merger, union, amalgamation, conglomeration, composition; miscibility, solubility, infusion, interfusion, suffusion, transfusion, instillation, infiltration, pervasion, permeation, saturation, penetration, impregnation; contamination, pollution, contagion, infection, adulteration; dilution, watering down; qualification, sophistication, involvement, complexity, complication, entanglement; confusion, disorder, jumble, muddle, scramble, chaos; entropy, randomness, nonuniformity, patchiness; heterogeneity, hybridization, mongrelism, crossbreeding, interbreeding, miscegenation, intermarriage, syngamy, allogamy

2 **mixed thing,** mix, mixture, blend, mélange; composition, harmony, association, synthesis; mixed marriage, interracial marriage, interfaith marriage; combination, compound, alloy, bronze, brass, pewter, billon, electrum, steel, magma, paste, amalgam; fusion, infusion, solution, colloid, suspension; cocktail, punch, brew, witches' brew; medicinal compound, linctus, patent medicine, potion, concoction, confection; potpourri, pastiche or pasticcio, stew, gumbo, soup, broth, goulash, hash, ragout, salmagundi, olla podrida; combo [Inf]

◗ *Food 90; Combination 757*

3 **miscellany,** miscellaneous collection, medley; miscellanea, anthology, collection, thesaurus, chrestomathy; patchwork, mosaic, job lot, hodgepodge, hash, mess, farrago, gallimaufry, mishmash, linsey-woolsey [Arch], ragbag, jumble, grab bag; kaleidoscope, phantasmagoria, babel; menagerie, zoo, circus, variety show; all sorts of things

◗ *Light Entertainment 138; Remainder 750*

4 **variety,** variegation, dappling, speckling, speckled effect, mottled effect, motley; muddle, tangle, entanglement, imbroglio, confusion, complexity, topsy-

turvydom; clatter, clamor, pandemonium; omnium-gatherum, motley crew, assortment

◗ *Variegation 263*

5 **admixture,** ingredient, element; vein, streak, strain; dash, tincture, tinge, infusion, sprinkling, soupçon, touch, smidgen, pinch, smack, modicum, suspicion; flavor, seasoning, condiment, herb, spice, bouquet garni; coloring, color, dye, hue; stain, blot

6 **hybrid,** cross, hybrid flower, crossbreed; mongrel, cur, alley cat, mule

◗ *Mammals 35; Flowers 42*

7 **mixer,** electric mixer, beater, blender, food processor, sifter, shaker, cocktail shaker; stirrer, spoon, whisk, whip, churn, scrambler; mixing bowl, crucible, melting pot

◗ *Cooking 91*

ADJECTIVES

8 **mixed,** intermixed, interracial, interfaith; mingled, intermingled, interspersed, interlaced, interwoven, intertwisted, intertwined, plaited, braided; miscible, soluble, colloidal, dissolved; stirred, shaken, blended, harmonized, combined, integrated, syncretic, eclectic; fused, alloyed, merged, amalgamated, conglomerated; composite, heterogeneous, hybrid, crossbred, crossed, mongrel; of mixed blood, miscegenetic, interbred, intermarried, multiracial, multicultural

◗ *Interweaving 609*

9 **diluted,** dilute, watered-down, tempered, adulterated, weakened, qualified; half-and-half, fifty-fifty

10 **complicated,** involved in, complex, in the melting pot, tangled, entangled; unclassified, unsorted, unordered, disordered, jumbled, confused, out of order, orderless, shuffled, scrambled, chaotic, topsy-turvy; miscellaneous, random, nonuniform, patchy, patched, kaleidoscopic, phantasmagorial; variegated, dappled, speckled, mottled, motley, shot, shot through with; tinged, dyed, colored, pervasive, all-pervading

◗ *Variegation 263*

11 **mixed up,** muddled, jumbled, higgledy-piggledy, scrambled, confused, bewildered, puzzled, confounded, mistaken

VERBS

12 **mix,** admix, commix, immix, mix up, mix and match; stir, sift together, shake, knead, work, brew; infuse, instill, imbue, impregnate; tinge, dye, color; speckle, bespeckle, dapple, variegate; suffuse, combine, integrate, fuse, compound, alloy, amalgamate, merge, blend, harmonize; mingle, commingle, intermingle, intersperse, intermix, interlard, interleave, interlay, intertwine, intertwist, interweave, interlace, plait, braid; sprinkle, besprinkle, dash, dilute, water, water down, qualify, weaken, adulterate, temper; spice, season, fortify, lace, pep up [Inf], spike [Inf]; doctor, meddle with, interfere with, tamper with; spoil, mar, debase, contaminate,

taint; cross, cross-fertilize, crossbreed, interbreed, hybridize, mongrelize

  ▶ *Interweaving 609*

13 **mix up,** muddle, scramble, jumble, shuffle, confuse, bewilder, puzzle, confound, mistake, entangle, do wrong, mess up

14 **mix together,** blend, integrate, run through; penetrate, permeate, pervade, stain, infiltrate; infect, pollute, contaminate; become linked *or* entangled *or* involved with; intermarry, interbreed

15 **be mixed up,** misunderstand, not understand, puzzle over, get wrong, be confused

ADVERBS

16 **mixedly,** intermixedly, complexly, disorderly, complicatedly, chaotically; miscellaneously, randomly, nonuniformly, patchily, heterogeneously, kaleidoscopically, phantasmagorically, pervasively, higgledypiggledy

752 Union

All for one, one for all, that is our motto.
— ALEXANDRE DUMAS THE ELDER

NOUNS

1 **union,** unity, coming together, joining, junction; conjunction, concurrence, confluence, convergence, meeting, rendezvous, liaison; concrescence, coalescence, fusion, synthesis, merger, combination; cohesion, coherence, tenacity, agglutination, concretion, consolidation, solidification, coagulation; condensation, concentration, compaction; closeness, nearness, touching, touch, contact; contiguity, contiguousness, compactness, concentratedness, tightness

  ▶ *Density 540; Mixture 751; Adhesion 755; Combination 757*

2 **association,** collection, congress, concourse, group, gathering, forgathering, assembly, committee; crowd, mob, throng, gang; reunion, alliance, coalition; labor *or* trade union, business union, company, cartel

  ▶ *Trade 480; Cooperation 827*

3 **linkage,** bond, bonding, ligature, link, concatenation, hyphenation, connection, tie-up, hookup, yoke, interconnection, cross connection, anastomosis, inosculation; interlocking, network, communications network, communication; computer network, local area network (LAN), wide area network (WAN), intercommunication, Internet, net [Inf]; exchange, interchange, intercourse, trade, commerce, traffic, cross communication, involvement

  ▶ *Communications 169; Connection 754; Adhesion 755; Cooperation 827*

4 **agreement,** accord, unity, consensus, concurrence; unison, unanimity, solidarity, brotherhood, sisterhood; harmony, peace, concord, concert, entente cordiale

  ▶ *Peace 73; Agreement 462; Accord 735*

5 **unification,** bringing together, joining together, meshing, assemblage, collection, jointing, articulation, structure, organization, composition; knitting, weaving, sewing, stitching, suture; tightening, contraction, ligation, knotting, welding, astriction

  ▶ *Assembly 59; Interweaving 609*

6 **sexual union,** mating, copulation, coition, coitus; procreation, reproduction, syngenesis, syngamy; wedlock, marriage

  ▶ *Sex 20; Marriage 64*

7 **joint,** join, hyphen, conjunction, copula, junction, juncture; tie, knot, hitch, splice, node, link; crease, fold, seam, stitching, suture; bond, weld, welded joint, rivet, screw, staple, pivot, ball-and-socket joint; dovetail joint, dovetail and mortise joint, mortise and tenon joint, miter joint; hasp, latch, catch, hook, fastening, fastener, clasp, clip, paper clip; hinge; bracket; ankle, toe, finger, thumb, knuckle, wrist, knee, hip, elbow, shoulder

  ▶ *Interface 616; Fold 637; Connection 754*

8 **point of union,** junction, junction box, juncture, meeting place, rendezvous; meeting point, focus; intersection, crossroads, decussation

  ▶ *Interface 616*

9 **person who joins,** carpenter, joiner, welder, riveter, weaver, tailor, seamstress, dressmaker; organizer, communicator, continuity person, middleman, intermediary, agent, go-between, pander *or* panderer, pimp, matchmaker; entrepreneur

ADJECTIVES

10 **united,** joined, connected, conjoined; accompanied, partnered; betrothed, promised, engaged, married, wedded, hand in hand, arm in arm; intimate, involved, inextricable, inseparable, intricate, indissoluble, indivisible, thick as thieves [Inf]; associated, symbiotic, (all) rolled into one, incorporated, corporate, cooperative; merged, unified, conjoint, composite, combined, coalescent, collected, cohesive, adhesive, concretive; put-together, made-up, assembled, jointed, articulated, seamed, stitched, sewn, woven, patched, darned

11 **agreeable,** agreed, united, unanimous, solid, harmonious, peaceful, concordant, in concert

12 **conjunctive,** adjunctive, connective, copulative; coagulating, solidifying; condensing, concentrative, astringent; possessive, possessed, copulatory, coital, venereal, sexual

13 **tied,** tied down, tied up, bound, knotted, lashed, hitched, yoked, spliced; gathered, sewn, stitched, woven, interwoven, braided, plaited; roped, secured, fastened, attached; adhering, cohesive, glued, bonded, cemented, rooted; tight, fast, taut, tense, firm, secure; close, close-set, close-packed, tightly packed, tight-fitting; wedged, jammed, stuck, immovable

14 unite, join, conjoin, link, hyphenate, tie in; couple, pair, pair up, have a sister city, pair off, harness together, match, marry, bracket, bracket together; assemble, collect, bring together, draw together, piece together, fit together, put together, lay together, throw together, lump together, gather together, gather, mobilize; combine, mix, mass, amass, mass together, accumulate, add to

15 unify, merge, consolidate, associate, incorporate, roll into one, make one; include, comprise, embrace, unite with, join *or* link with, come together, converge, meet; hold together, hang together, stick together, coalesce, fit well, cohere, adhere, make a good fit, mesh together, interlock, engage; grip, grapple, clinch, hold hands; go with, go steady with, go out with; partner, accompany, associate with, liaise, mix with, be in league with, join (a group)

16 unite closely, pack, compact, impact; compress, condense, concentrate, narrow, constrict; tighten, make firm, make fast, tauten, pull tight, draw tight, truss, lace *or* do up tight(ly)

17 agree, reach an agreement, unite, reach an accord, concur, vote unanimously

18 link, attach, annex, affix, suffix, prefix, infix; fix, stick, tape, staple, pin, pin to, pin on, clip, hang on, hook on; nail, bolt, screw, screw down, rivet, hammer in, knock in, connect; thread, thread *or* string together, rope together, link together, chain together, concatenate; contact, put in contact with, make contact, plug in, ground; network, interconnect, span, bestride, straddle, bridge; connect with, put through to, patch through, put in touch, get in touch, communicate, intercommunicate; tie up with, link up with, yoke, yoke together, harness, leash; tie, splice, knot, lash, hitch, belay, tie together, hook up with [Inf]

➤ *Connection 754*

19 intertwine, braid, baste, plait, twist, crochet, lace, entwine, interlace, interweave; truss, tie up, strap, lace up, lash up; tie to, tie up to, moor to, anchor; tether, pinion, fetter, handcuff, manacle, hobble, shackle; bind, gird, girdle, bandage, swaddle, swathe, wrap, enfold; embrace, clasp, clinch, grip, grapple, articulate; dovetail, mortise, miter, rabbet; fit, wedge, jam, clamp, lock; lock together, interlock, set, gear to, engage, wed, join; weld, solder, fuse, braze, cement, glue; knit, weave, sew, suture, stitch, seam, tack, fasten; fasten up, button, button up, do up, zip up, buckle, close, lock up, seal up; patch, darn, mend, heal over *or* up, form a scab, knit together

➤ *Connection 754*

20 unite sexually, marry, wed, have sexual relations, copulate, mate

➤ *Sex 20; Marriage 64*

21 as one, together, all together, jointly, cooperatively, conjointly, altogether; in conjunction with, in union with, in partnership with, in league with; inseparably, indissolubly, indivisibly, cohesively, with cohesion, adhesively; inextricably, intricately, intimately, conjunctively, connectively; copulatively, sexually; in cahoots [Inf]

22 agreeably, unanimously, solidly, harmoniously, peacefully, concordantly, in concert

23 inextricably, inseparably, intimately; firmly, tightly, tight, fast, tautly, tensely, securely, closely; immovably, without moving

753 Separation

Absence from whom we love is worse than death.
— WILLIAM COWPER

Every parting gives a foretaste of death; every coming together again a foretaste of the resurrection.
— ARTHUR SCHOPENHAUER

1 separation, disconnection, disunion, disunity, discontinuity; disjunction, disjuncture, dislocation, separability; disintegration, breakage, breakup, dispersion, dispersal, scattering; dissolution, decomposition, breakdown; dissection, analysis; resolution, resolving power, high resolution, low resolution; disruption, fragmentation, shattering, splitting, fission, nuclear fission, separating, parting, severance; uncoupling, divorce, divorcement; moving apart, growing apart, divergence, spreading, spread, deviation, split, schism; detachment, unfastening, undoing, untying, unbuttoning, unthreading, unraveling; loosening, loosing, liberating, freeing

➤ *Divorce and Widowhood 66; Disagreement 463; Nonadhesion 756; Disintegration 758; Discontinuity 775; Dispersion 776; Deterioration 808; Liberation 831*

2 setting apart, setting aside, ejection, expulsion; exception, exemption, rejection, boycott, avoidance, exclusion; selection, choice, division, severance, discrimination, apartheid, segregation; zoning, zone, compartment, off-limits area; ghetto, box, cage, prison; isolation, loneliness, seclusion, quarantine, putting aside, keeping to one side, conservation, preservation, reservation; taking away, deprivation, expropriation, removal, withdrawal, resignation; retirement, nonattachment, nonalignment, insularity

➤ *Selection 382; Avoidance 386; Unsociability 409; Expulsion 709; Subtraction 749; Exclusion 764; Resignation 835*

3 separateness, separability, immiscibility, oil and water, severalty, separatism, nationalism, isolationism, difference; dichotomy, division, subdivision, segmentation, partition, cutting, scission, section, break; tear, laceration, dilaceration, tearing apart, rip; rent, fissure, split, gap, breach, rift, crack, cleft, chasm, cleavage, slit, slot, gash, incision; hole, rupture, opening; abscission, decapitation, beheading, amputation, castration, circumcision; docking, curtailment, retrenchment, cutting away, resection

4 **disunity,** disagreement, lack of unity, lack of harmony, dissension; opposition, hostility, no common ground, poles apart

> *Hostility 63; Oppositeness 731*

5 **separator,** dividing line, caesura; comma, semicolon, slash, solidus, dash, hyphen, partition, dieresis, umlaut, period *or* full stop; boundary, fence, hedge, wall, sunk fence *or* ha-ha, screen, curtain; limit, frontier, border, barrier, barricade; former separators: Berlin Wall, Iron Curtain, Mason-Dixon line, Great Wall of China

6 **separates,** coordinates, accessories; peripherals, add-ons

> *Addition 748*

ADJECTIVES

7 **separate,** separated, disunited, disjointed, disjunctive; dislocated, divorced, broken up; disconnected, unplugged; unstuck, untied, undone, unzipped; unloosed, loosened, loose, liberated, released, expelled, ejected; unfettered, unchained, free, open; discontinuous, interrupted, partitioned, bipartite, multipartite, dichotomous, dividing, divided, subdivided, bisected, halved, quartered; dismembered, disemboweled, cut, torn, severed, ruptured

8 **apart,** in pieces *or* bits, asunder, broken, shattered, split, cut up, cut to pieces *or* bits, shot to pieces; rent, riven, cloven, cleft; dispersed, scattered, sundered; fugitive; divergent, radiating

9 **unjoined,** unfastened, adrift, detached; unattached, nonattached, nonaligned, neutral, unfixed, unconnected; discrete, distinct, distinctive, differentiated, separative, excluded, excepted, exempt; abstracted, absent-minded, withdrawn, uninvolved; unmixed, immiscible, unassimilated, unassimilable; not belonging, unrelated, alien, foreign, external, extrinsic; self-sufficient, insular, isolated, secluded, lonely, alone; castoff, cast out, left, abandoned, rejected; selective, picked out, set apart, reclusive

10 **disunited,** disagreeing, unharmonious, dissenting; hostile, adverse, opposite, opposed, antipathetic, inimical

11 **separable,** severable, partible, divisible, fissionable, fissile, scissile, tearable, dissolvable, dissoluble; resolvable, high-resolution, low-resolution, discernible, distinguishable; breakable, biodegradable

VERBS

12 **separate,** part, sever, sunder, break, fracture, chip, crack, rupture, snap, break in two; split up, disunite,

dissociate, disassociate, divorce; unhitch, uncouple, disconnect, unplug; disengage, displace, eject, expel, dispel; wrench, dislocate, throw out of gear; detach, unseat, unhorse, dismount, throw; unstick, untie, unfasten, undo, unbutton, unlace, unhook, unclasp, unzip, unstring, unlock, unlatch, unchain, unbind, unfetter; sever ties, cut the knot, cut the ties that bind, break the link; cut off, remove, take away, detract, subtract, deduct; strip, strip bare, denude, peel, pare, flake, skin, flay, fleece, shear, clip, pluck; behead, decapitate, amputate; curtail, dock, lop, prune

13 **disentangle,** unravel, unstitch, unpick

14 **loosen,** slacken, relax, loose; set free, liberate, release

15 **scatter,** disband, demobilize, disperse, disintegrate, break up; break down, come undone, come unstuck; spring apart, fall apart, come apart, come *or* fall to pieces *or* bits, take to pieces *or* bits

16 **take apart,** cannibalize, slit, split, rive, cleave, rend, tear, tear apart, rip, tear *or* rip to bits *or* pieces; lacerate, dilacerate, hack, hew, cut, chop, stab, slash, gash, cut through, saw, slice; shred, mince, mash, grind, crunch; bite, bite into, bite through, gnaw; carve, carve up, disassemble, dismantle, disjoin, dissolve, unmake; decompose, decay, degrade; blow up, blow to pieces *or* bits, smash, shatter, shiver, splinter; crumble, cave in, pulverize, destroy

17 **set apart,** set aside, put aside, lay up, store, conserve, preserve, reserve; mark out, select, sort, check off, pick out, single out, distinguish, differentiate, discern, resolve; discriminate, exclude, except, boycott, ban, bar, blacklist, blackball, banish, ostracize, send to Coventry, isolate, insulate

18 **divide,** divide up, subdivide, sectionalize, separate the sheep from the goats, separate the wheat from the chaff, segment; fragment, fractionalize, fractionate, fractionize; factorize, analyze, cut up, anatomize, dissect, dismember, disembowel; bisect, halve, quarter; apportion, share out, partition, screen off, compartmentalize, circumscribe; keep apart, segregate, sequester, seclude, quarantine, maroon, keep *or* hold apart; set against, estrange, alienate, make enemies, become enemies

19 **disagree,** lack unity, lack harmony, dissent, oppose, show hostility; find *or* have no common ground, stand poles apart

> *Hostility 63*

20 **diverge,** go away, go separate *or* different ways, follow separate paths, depart; scatter, disperse, deviate, bifurcate, divorce, part, part company; cast adrift, set *or* cut adrift, cut loose; get loose, get free, free oneself, get away, break away, fall away, escape; quit, leave, relinquish, abandon, wash one's hands of

21 **come between,** step between, put asunder, divide, keep *or* hold apart, interpose, flow between; drive apart, drive a wedge between

22 separately, severally, singly, one at a time, one by one, piecemeal, piece by piece, bit by bit; in bits, in pieces, in halves, in two, in twain, dichotomously; discontinuously, disjunctively, loosely, freely

23 apart, asunder, divergently; brokenly, in pieces, in bits; to bits, to smithereens, to shreds, to tatters, to matchwood

24 in isolation, aloof, apart, away, adrift, separatively; distinctly, distinctively, discretely, neutrally, self-sufficiently, abstractly, absent-mindedly; externally, in an alien way, extrinsically, selectively, diagnostically

25 disunitedly, antipathetically, inimically, hostilely, with hostility, unharmoniously; dissentingly, with dissent, adversely, oppositely

754 Connection

Only connect! That was the whole of her sermon. Only connect the prose and the passion, and both will be exalted, and human love will be seen at its height. Live in fragments no longer. Only connect . . .
— E. M. FORSTER

NOUNS

1 connection, union, merger, conjunction, interconnection; attachment, adhesion, graft; link, linking, join, joining, coupling, fastening, cohesion, meeting, involvement, entanglement
▶ *Closure 584; Union 752; Adhesion 755*

2 association, relationship, relation; liaison, nexus, network; intercourse, commerce, communication network, communication, intercommunication, satellite link
▶ *Communications 169*

3 associate, business associate, contact; ally, friend; relation, relative, family member, kin, kinsman, blood kin, kith, clan, tribe
▶ *Friendship 62; Family 65; Sociability 408; Support 605; Relatedness 727*

4 means of connection, bond, chain, fetter, shackle; tie, band, hoop, yoke, link; junction, arch; joint, hinge, ramification, branching, branch, nexus, connective, bonding agent; beam, girder, stretcher, stay, strut; interconnection, stairway, stairs, ladder, stepladder, steps, steppingstone; canal, isthmus, neck, col, ridge; copula, punctuation mark, hyphen, dash, slash, solidus, parenthesis, bracket, square bracket, angle bracket, brace, ampersand, en dash, em dash; road, main road, highway, interstate highway, expressway, arterial road
▶ *Linguistics, Language 5; Transportation 686; Restraint 830*

5 line, cable, hawser, painter, mooring line, cord, whipcord, rope, guy, guy rope, towline, towrope, lifeline; umbilical cord, communication cord, ripcord; string, wire, tape, adhesive tape, twine, binder, binding twine, fiber; ligature, connective tissue, ligament, tendon, muscle; withe, raffia, bast, osier, lashing, binding, thread; band, ribband; bandage, tourniquet, roller bandage; braid, plait, thong, drawstring, lace, shoelace, bootlace, tag, tie, cravat, stock, knot, stitch

6 tackle, chain, anchor chain, rope, cordage; rig, rigging, ratline, shroud, stay, guy, halyard, sheets, bowline, clew line, harness, lanyard

7 fastener, fastening, zipper, button, buttonhole, eyelet, loop, frog, toggle, hook, hook and eye, snaps; stitch, basting, Velcro™; collar stud, cufflink, tiepin, garter, suspenders; brooch, clasp, clip, tie clasp *or* clip; bobby pin, barrette, hairpin, hatpin; thumbtack, pushpin, tack; safety pin, straight pin; toggle pin, cotter pin, linchpin; peg, dowel; nail, treenail, brad, holdfast, staple; brace, batten, clamp, cramp; nut, bolt, rivet, screw;

KNOTS, BENDS, HITCHES, AND SPLICES

barrel knot *or* blood knot	figure eight loop knot	marlinespike hitch	running knot
Blackwall hitch	figure of eight bend	marling hitch	sennit knot
bow *or* bowknot	fisherman's bend *or* anchor	masthead knot	sheepshank
bowline	bend	Matthew Walker	sheet bend *or* becket bend *or*
bowline on the bight	fisherman's knot	monkey's fist	weaver's hitch
bowline with a bight	granny knot	overhand knot *or* single knot	short splice
butcher's knot	half hitch	prolonge knot	shroud knot
carrick bend	half knot	purchase loop knot	slipknot *or* nooseknot
cat's-paw	hangman's knot	reef knot *or* square knot *or*	star knot
clove hitch *or* builder's knot	harness hitch	flat knot	stevedore's knot
constrictor knot	hawser bend	reeving line bend	surgeon's knot
crossing knot	heaving line bend *or* racking	ring hitch *or* lark's head	sword knot
crown knot	bend	ring knot	timber hitch
double sheet bend *or* becket	lanyard knot	rolling hitch	truelove *or* true lover's knot
bend	long splice	round turn and two half	Turk's-head
eye splice	loop knot	hitches	wall knot
figure eight knot	magnus hitch	running bowline	Windsor knot

buckle, hasp, hinge, catch, safety catch, spring catch, latch; lock, lock and key, combination lock, mortise lock, padlock; manacles, handcuffs, bracelets [Inf]; ring, cleat, bollard, post, stake, pile, pale, bar

▶ *Security 464; Union 752; Adhesion 755*

8 **yoke,** coupling, coupler, traces, drawbar; hook, claw, grapple, grappling iron, anchor; sheet anchor, harness, reins *or* ribbons; halter, collar, lead, leash, tether; lasso, lariat, noose, loop

9 **band,** girdle, belt, strap; waistband, cummerbund, bellyband, girth, cinch, sash; shoulder belt, bandoleer, Sam Brown belt; collar, neckband, headband, fillet, ribbon

ADJECTIVES

10 **connective,** conjunctive; cohesive, adhesive, sticky, interconnective; communicative, in contact, liaising, associated, related, joint, coherent

11 **connected,** tied, linked, joined, united, merged, coupled; interfaced, interconnected, interwoven, entangled, laced, braided, plaited; fastened, attached, knotted, lashed, bound, stitched, sewn; tacked, zipped up, buttoned (up); buckled, hooked, wired (up), pinned, nailed, stapled, pegged, riveted, screwed, hinged; stuck, bonded, glued; bracketed, hyphenated, bridged

12 **bound,** tied, chained, fettered, shackled, yoked, harnessed, leashed, tethered, lassoed, manacled, handcuffed; secured, locked, bolted, latched, padlocked, battened; clamped, clasped, gripped

VERBS

13 **connect,** link, join, conjoin, unite, unify, merge, couple, fasten, attach, interconnect; interweave, entwine, entangle, lace, braid, plait, knot, lash, bind, ligate, bandage, tie, stitch, sew, tack; zip up, snap, button (up); buckle, hook, clip, pin, nail, staple, peg, rivet, screw, skewer, bolt, hinge; stick, bond, glue, tape; bracket, bridge, graft

▶ *Union 752; Adhesion 755*

14 **bind,** tie, chain, fetter, shackle, yoke, harness, leash, tether, lasso, manacle, handcuff; secure, lock, bolt, latch, padlock, batten; clamp, clasp, grip; moor, anchor

15 **intercommunicate,** communicate, contact, meet; liaise, network, interface, associate, relate; cohere, adhere, stick together, involve, entangle, form an alliance; pair up, match

ADVERBS

16 **in connection with,** connectively, in relation to *or* with, jointly, conjunctively, cohesively, adhesively, securely

755 Adhesion

NOUNS

1 **adhesion,** adhesiveness, cohesion, cohesiveness; attachment, bonding, connection, connectedness, linkage, magnetism; continuity, coherence, unity; sticki-

ness, cementation, agglutination, conglutination; agglomeration, conglomeration, consolidation; congealment, condensation, concentration, compaction; inseparability, indivisibility, holding together, sticking together; soldering, welding

▶ *Assembly 59; Union 752; Connection 754*

2 **tenacity,** tenaciousness, pertinacity, perseverance, persistence, determination, endurance; stubbornness, obstinacy, headstrongness, bullheadedness; holding on, attachment, adherence, loyalty, fidelity, stick-to-it-iveness [Inf]

▶ *Retention 471; Toughness 547*

3 **adhesive,** glue, mucilage, paste, gum, birdlime, lime, epoxy; fixative *or* fixer, size; luting *or* lute, cement, putty, mortar, plaster, grout, sealing wax, solder, flypaper, sticky tape, masking tape, Scotch™ tape; adhesive tape, sticking plaster, Band-Aid™

4 **adherent,** follower, disciple, apostle, supporter, suitor, fan, satellite, dependent, parasite, hanger-on, sponger, clinger, sycophant; magnet, sticker, sticky label, decal, stamp, barnacle, limpet, remora, leech, burr, brier, bramble, chewing gum, toffee, taffy, molasses; [Inf]: sucker, clinging vine, groupie

ADJECTIVES

5 **adhesive,** adherent, coherent, cohesive, connective; attached, bonded, connected, linked; sticky, gummy, tacky, gluey, viscous, viscid, colloidal, agglutinative; dense, condensed, concentrated, compact, solid, congealed, coagulated, concrete, indivisible, infrangible, inseparable, inextricable; close, thick, side by side, shoulder to shoulder, cheek by jowl, close-fitting, close-packed, continuous, tight, clinging, figure-hugging, molding, skintight

6 **tenacious,** pertinacious, persevering, persistent, determined, enduring, stubborn, obstinate, bullheaded; attached, loyal, faithful, supportive, stick-to-it-ive [Inf], dependent, parasitic, sycophantic, clingy

7 **adhering,** glued, stuck, pasted, epoxied, fixed, cemented; supporting, following, clinging, cleaving

VERBS

8 **adhere,** cohere, hang together, hold together, grow together, hold, hold fast; bunch, bunch up, bunch together, close ranks, stand side by side, stand shoulder to shoulder, sit cheek by jowl, stick, stick close(ly), stick together; grip, clasp, grasp, take hold of, hug, embrace, squeeze, cling to, cling like ivy, twine around, close with, grapple with, clinch, fit, fit tight(ly), fit like a glove, hug *or* mold to the figure; stick to, stick like glue *or* a leech *or* a limpet, cleave to; come *or* rub off on, freeze, condense, coagulate, solidify, consolidate, agglomerate, conglomerate

9 **be tenacious,** persevere, adhere, hold on, hang on, stick to, cling to, attach oneself to, be loyal, hold on like a bulldog

10 **cause to adhere,** stick, stick to, affix to, stick together,

hold together, unite, join; gum, glue, agglutinate, conglutinate, paste, lute, cement, weld, solder, braze

ADVERBS

11 **cohesively,** unitedly, in unison, coherently, indivisibly, solidly, compactly, densely, concretely, inseparably, inextricably, tightly, closely, side by side, shoulder to shoulder, cheek by jowl, stickily, viscously

12 **tenaciously,** pertinaciously, persistently, determinedly, enduringly, stubbornly, obstinately, loyally, faithfully, parasitically, sycophantically

756 Nonadhesion

NOUNS

1 **nonadhesion,** noncohesion, noncoherence, incoherence, nonadherence, noncombination, separation, separability, immiscibility; lack of unity, nonuniformity, disjunction; disorder, confusion, chaos; scattering, dispersion; looseness, bagginess, floppiness, uncondensed state, wateriness, runniness, liquid, liquidity, fluidity, lack of viscosity, slipperiness, frangibility, fragility, crumbliness, friability, atomization
  ◗ *Fluid 555; Separation 753; Disorder 766; Discontinuity 775; Dispersion 776*

2 **aloofness,** privacy, discreteness, separateness, independence, freedom, isolation, seclusion, solitude, unsociability, standoffishness
  ◗ *Unsociability 409; Nonconformity 782; Liberation 831*

3 **individualist,** nonconformist, dissenter, one's own person, free spirit, independent, bohemian, maverick, eccentric, separatist, isolationist, hermit, ascetic, anchorite, monk, nun, loner, lone wolf [Inf]

ADJECTIVES

4 **nonadhesive,** nonadhering, noncohesive, nonadherent, immiscible; broken up, frangible, fragile, noncoherent; uncombined, unconnected, incoherent; not held together, not sticky, nonstick; dry, smooth, slippery, unconsolidated; loose, undone, friable, crumbly, scattered, dispersed; free, wide-ranging, loosely packed; unstuck, lax, slack, relaxed, loose-fitting, baggy, flapping, flopping, floppy, dangling, hanging, peeling off, pulling off, pendulous, waving, flying; uncondensed, streaming, running, runny, watery, liquid, fluid

5 **aloof,** private, discrete, separate, independent, free, isolated, unassimilated, secluded, solitary, unsociable, antisocial, standoffish

VERBS

6 **unstick,** unglue, peel off, unpeel, pull off, pull apart, detach, unfasten, unpin, undo, free, loose, loosen, separate, knock off, shake off, scatter, disperse

7 **come unstuck,** come off, fall off, drop off, peel off, come undone; liquefy, melt, thaw, run, become runny, come adrift, dangle, flap, flop

8 **be aloof,** stay alone, be private, seek privacy, separate from, seek solitude, go into seclusion, hide, resign, become unsociable, keep to oneself, mind one's own business, be reclusive

ADVERBS

9 **noncohesively,** noncoherently, incoherently, fragilely, loosely, in a loose manner, laxly, baggily, pendulously, liquidly, fluidly, immiscibly

10 **aloofly,** privately, in private, discretely, with discretion, separately, alone, independently, without help, freely, in seclusion, in isolation, solitarily, reclusively, unsociably, standoffishly

757 Combination

NOUNS

1 **combination,** combining, joining together, growing together, symphysis, symbiosis, bringing together, composition, synthesis, fusion, coalescence; conflation, blending, blend, mingling, mixing, mixture, mix, syncretism; amalgamation, merger, unification, uniting; assimilation, absorption, digestion, integration, incorporation; centralization, coincidence, concurrence, conjunction, synchronicity, synchronization
  ◗ *Same Time 649; Mixture 751; Union 752*

2 **collaboration,** concurrence, conjunction, coagency, union, alliance, league, marriage; federation, confederation, confederacy, association; plot, conspiracy, cabal; agreement, unity, concord, harmony, chord, counterpoint, orchestration; jigsaw, mosaic, tessellation, collage, patchwork
  ◗ *Music 140; Plan 387; Agreement 462; Accord 735; Union 752; Cooperation 827*

3 **collection,** assembly, assemblage, set, compendium, anthology; aggregation, aggregate, agglomeration, conglomeration, conglomerate, combine, syndicate, consortium; bloc, corporation, company; society, association, club, party; force, army, regiment, brigade, division, squadron, wing, flotilla, fleet; team, group, band, orchestra, chamber orchestra, string quartet; chorus, choir, congregation, audience
  ◗ *Military Affairs 58; Assembly 59; Music 140*

4 **compound,** mixture, suspension, solution, blend, alloy, amalgam, composite, makeup, hybrid, cocktail, portmanteau word
  ◗ *Mixture 751*

ADJECTIVES

5 **combined,** joined, brought together, synthesized, fused, coalesced; conflated, blended, mingled, mixed; amalgamated, merged, unified, united; assimilated, absorbed, digested, integrated, incorporated; synchronous, synchronized

6 **combinatory,** combinative, integrative, composed, syncretic; harmonized, interwoven, intertwined, networked, connected, joint, conjugate, conjoined, conjoint, yoked, linked, united, unified, centralized, in-

corporated, embodied, bred into, bred in the bone, in-bred, ingrained, coalescent, symphystic
    ▶ *Interweaving 609; Mixture 751*

7 **collaborative,** cooperative, symbiotic, in agreement, in harmony, harmonious, on the same wavelength, associated, in association, orchestrated; leagued, in league; conspiratorial, cabalistic; in partnership with, allied, married, wed, federated, confederate, coagent, concurrent, coincident, conjunctive
    ▶ *Agreement 462; Same Time 649; Accord 735; Union 752*

8 **collected,** assembled, heaped up, congregated, aggregated, amalgamated, merged, collective, aggregate, conglomerate, associative, congregational
    ▶ *Assembly 59*

9 **combine,** join together, unite, fit together, put together, assemble, make up, compose, synthesize, integrate; fuse, merge, coalesce, blend, consolidate, grow together, run together, converge; have an affinity, mingle, commingle, mix, mix together, syncretize; interweave, intertwine, network, connect, join, conjoin, link, conjugate, yoke; centralize, unify, incorporate, absorb, digest, assimilate, soak up; amalgamate, pool, collect, heap up, lay up, store, aggregate, congregate, compound, lump together, bracket together, rally, bring together
    ▶ *Interweaving 609; Insertion 710; Addition 748; Mixture 751; Union 752*

10 **come together,** band together, group, group together, brigade, associate, partner, go into partnership with, league with, federate, confederate; join hands, join forces with, team up, cooperate, come to an agreement, agree, concur, make a pact *or* an alliance, ally, collaborate, act together, harmonize, synchronize, make friends with, fraternize, bond, cement a relationship, marry, wed, mate, couple, put heads together; conspire, plot
    ▶ *Assembly 59; Friendship 62; Marriage 64; Plan 387; Sociability 408; Agreement 462; Accord 735; Cooperation 827*

ADVERBS

11 **in combination,** in concert, in league with, in partnership with, jointly, cooperatively, harmoniously, conspiratorially, cabalistically, collectively, associatively, congregationally, concurrently, coincidentally, synchronously, symbiotically, syncretically, together, as one

758 Disintegration

NOUNS

1 **disintegration,** breakup, disorder, chaos, disturbance, deterioration, derangement; incoherence, lack of order; explosion, collapse, wear, wear and tear, erosion;

decay, decomposition, corruption, corrosion, rot, mold, moldering, ruin
    ▶ *Disorder 766; Disturbance 768; Deterioration 808*

2 **deconstruction,** demolition, destruction, breakdown, taking apart, dismantling; disunion, separation, dispersal, scattering, dissolution, dissection, dismemberment, anatomization; dissociation, electrolysis, hydrolysis, catalysis, photolysis, catabolism, atom smashing, fission, nuclear fission, atomization
    ▶ *Physics 10; Chemistry 11; Destruction 523; Separation 753; Dispersion 776*

ADJECTIVES

3 **disintegrated,** smashed, shattered, destroyed, demolished, uncombined, chaotic; disunited, separated, dispersed, scattered, disordered, decayed, decomposed, corrupted, corroded, rotted, rotten, moldering; ruined

4 **deconstructed,** demolished, destroyed, broken up *or* down; dilapidated, decomposable, compostable, biodegradable, recyclable, disposable
    ▶ *Destruction 523; Separation 753; Deterioration 808*

5 **disintegrating,** crumbling, falling apart, tumbledown, dilapidated, decomposing, rotting, decaying, hydrolized, catalyzed, catabolic

VERBS

6 **disintegrate,** come apart, come to pieces, break up *or* down, collapse, fall apart, fall to pieces, go to pieces, explode, blow up, smash to pieces, shatter, splinter, crumble, decompose, corrupt, corrode, decay, molder, rot, waste away, erode, wear away, wear out
    ▶ *Separation 753; Deterioration 808*

7 **deconstruct,** demolish, pull down, wreck, smash, break up, destroy, unsettle, disorder, cause chaos, disturb, derange, pull apart, pull to pieces, take apart, take to pieces, disperse, scatter, dissect, dismember, electrolyze, hydrolyze, catalyze, split, fission, atomize
    ▶ *Physics 10; Chemistry 11; Destruction 523; Separation 753; Disorder 766; Disturbance 768; Dispersion 776*

ADVERBS

8 **to pieces,** to bits, to smithereens, in pieces, in bits, in parts, partitively, analytically, on *or* by analysis, electrolytically, hydrolytically, catalytically, photolytically, catabolically

9 **destructively,** divisively, separately, reductively, explosively, corrosively, chaotically

759 Whole

NOUNS

1 **whole,** wholeness, totality, integrality, integrity, integration, fullness, completeness, indivisibility; oneness, unity, universality, generality, holism, comprehensiveness, inclusiveness, generalization
    ▶ *Completeness 761; Generality 778*

2 **whole thing,** entity, whole number, integer, unit, entirety, Gestalt, totality, sum, total sum, sum total, sum-

mation, total, aggregate, corpus, complete works, complex, ensemble, system, four corners of the earth, world, globe, universe, cosmos, macrocosm, microcosm

▹ *Combination 757; One 788*

3 **whole situation,** grand design, full view, grand view, panorama, bird's-eye view, overview, survey, conspectus, synopsis, world view, world picture, full course, grand unification theory

▹ *Physics 10; Vision 242*

4 **all,** everything, everybody, everyone, one and all, everyone and everything, the world *or* whole world *or* all the world, the whole thing *or* lot, le tout ensemble [Fr], the gross amount, one hundred percent, alpha to omega, be-all and end-all, length and breadth, sum and substance

▹ *Assembly 59; Generality 778; Multitude 795*

5 **unit,** family, ensemble, set, complete set, series, pack, kit, outfit, inventory, full list, complete list, whole list; [Inf]: whole caboodle *or* whole kit and caboodle, whole shooting match, whole shebang, whole nine yards

▹ *Combination 757; List 785*

ADJECTIVES

6 **whole,** integral, total, holistic, general, universal, complete, full, integrated, unified, all, every, any, each, individual, single, one, in one piece, all of a piece, all-inclusive, comprehensive, fully comprehensive, gross, all-embracing, across-the-board, global, worldwide

▹ *Completeness 761; Inclusion 763; Generality 778; One 788*

7 **uncut,** entire, unabridged, unexpurgated, undivided, undiminished, unbroken, intact, unharmed, unscathed, unhurt, uninjured, undamaged, unimpaired, unspoiled, unadulterated, uncontaminated, untouched, inviolate, virgin, pure, faultless, flawless, perfect

▹ *Completeness 761; Perfection 805*

8 **sound,** sound in wind and limb, able-bodied, strong, fit, well, healthy, in good health, hale, hale and hearty, in fine fettle, recovered, fully restored, better

▹ *Health 113; Repair 809*

VERBS

9 **be whole,** form a whole, unite, unify, integrate, total, sum up, add up to, amount to, come to, number, comprise, embrace, encompass

▹ *Union 752*

10 **complete,** fulfill, succeed, accomplish, reach one's goal, achieve one's purpose, leave no loose ends, bring to a head, culminate, climax, take to the limit, carry through, finish off, polish off [Inf], round off, end, finalize, perfect, put the finishing touches to, put the frosting *or* icing on the cake

▹ *Completeness 761*

ADVERBS

11 **wholly,** entirely, integrally, holistically, completely, body and soul, heart and soul, totally, utterly, absolutely, fully, every bit, every inch, pound for pound, in every respect, without exception, without exemption, one hundred percent, universally, *in toto* [L]; lock, stock, and barrel; root and branch; hook, line, and sinker [Inf]

12 **one and all,** as a whole, as a team, as a group, as a unit, comprehensively, collectively, all together, corporately, bodily, and all, in sum, altogether, in the aggregate, in the mass, in bulk, en masse, *en bloc* [Fr]

13 **on the whole,** generally, in general, all in all, by and large, as a rule, predominantly, mostly, for the most part, mainly, in the main, largely, taking everything into consideration, all things considered, when all is said and done, in all truth, essentially, in essence, altogether, quite, substantially, in substance, virtually, practically, almost, nearly, all but, to all intents and purposes, as far as one can tell, in effect, effectively, as good as

▹ *Nearness 586; Essence 723; Generality 778*

14 **completely,** entirely, wholly, totally, absolutely, utterly, quite, thoroughly, clean, plain, plumb, downright, perfectly; in every way, in all, in all respects, on all counts; outright, stark, hollow, unequivocally, unconditionally; root and branch, neck and crop, all around, all the way, heart and soul, body and soul, head over heels, solidly; all in all, *in toto* [L], all told, from wall to wall, from A to Z, from first to last, throughout, from beginning to end, from end to end, from one end to the other, from sea to sea, from coast to coast, from Land's End to John o' Groats [Brit], from the four points of the compass, from the four corners of the world, from far and near; far and wide, high and low, fore-and-aft, from stem to stern, from top to bottom, from top to toe, from head to foot, altogether; warts and all

▹ *Completeness 761*

760 Part

NOUNS

1 **part,** portion, division, piece, section, component; share, quota, percentage, remainder, balance, surplus; part payment, down payment, deposit; advance, earnest, foretaste, preview, appetizer, sample, example, sound bite; element, faction, party, sect, class, category, group, family, phylum, order, genus, species; proportion, fraction, majority, minority; segment, sector, arc, curve, semicircle, hemisphere; stage, phase, leg, lap, round, heat, inning; partition, compartment, department; ward, community, parish, district, county, region, area, quadrant

▹ *Assembly 59; Sports 145; Allocation 474; Region 564; Remainder 750; Separation 753; Arrangement 767; Class 777; Fraction 787*

2 **piece,** portion, part, moiety, share; fragment, fraction; segment, section, sector, division, subdivision, category, class, branch, department; unit, module, building block, building brick; cell, molecule, atom; piece of land, allotment, parcel; patch, insertion, interpolation, addition; length, roll, swatch

3 **component,** constituent, ingredient, aspect, particular, element, detail, item; member, appendage, organ, feeler, antenna, limb, arm, leg, wing, flipper, fin; branch, subbranch, bough, twig, sprig, leaf, shoot, offshoot, switch, scion, sucker, spray, slip, spur, stem, stalk, trunk, bole, stump; part, integral part, integrant, feature, facet, factor, item, link; part and parcel; components, works, workings, mechanism, machinery, engine, innards, guts, insides [Inf]
  ♦ *Human Body 19; Animals (General) 34; Plants (General) 41; Contents 577*

4 **particle,** bit, scrap, rag, fragment, shred, wisp, speck, morsel, bite, crust, crumb; sliver, splinter, snip, snippet; chip, cut, slice, wedge, finger, rasher, cutlet, collop, chop, gobbet, chunk, hunk, lump, slab; bar, block, mass, heap, clod, sod, turf, divot, shard, sherd, potsherd, flake, scale, drop; dose, portion, helping; dollop, smidgen

5 **bits and pieces,** odds and ends, dribs and drabs, miscellanea, oddments, flotsam and jetsam, disjecta membra, bin ends, shavings, filings, clippings, parings, peelings, leavings, rubble, trash, detritus, debris, rags, tatters
  ♦ *Waste 96; Remainder 750*

6 **part of writing,** canto, verse, stanza; act, scene, line; volume, number, issue, edition, fascicle *or* fascicule, installment, article; front matter, text, chapter, episode, section, subsection, passage, paragraph, quotation, quote, extract, sidebar, citation, note, back matter; page, folio, sheet, leaf, signature
  ♦ *Drama and Theater 136; Literature 139; Books 174; Periodicals 175*

7 **part of speech,** noun, pronoun, verb, adverb, adjective, preposition, conjunction, interjection; word, phrase, clause, sentence; grammar, syntax
  ♦ *Linguistics, Language 5*

8 **musical part,** part, section, movement, division; voice part, soprano, second soprano, alto, tenor, baritone, bass
  ♦ *Music 140*

9 **member,** team member, member of the staff, coworker, colleague, associate, fellow, cog in the wheel
  ♦ *Assembly 59; Worker 123*

10 **participation,** role, character, duty, responsibility, function, contribution

ADJECTIVES

11 **partial,** parted, divided, pieced, sectioned, partitioned, apportioned, shared; classed, categorical, grouped; broken, fragmented, fragmentary, crumbly, incomplete; imperfect, inadequate, insufficient, scrappy, bitty [Brit], piecemeal, unfinished, half-finished, fractional, aliquot, proportionate, partitive; sliced, diced, minced, ground, shredded
  ♦ *Insufficiency 98; Incompleteness 762; Fraction 787; Imperfection 806*

12 **component,** constituent, particular, detailed, itemized, fascicular; segmental, segmented, sectional, sectionalized, compartmental, departmental, divided; cellular, molecular, atomic, elemental; departmentalized, compartmentalized, branching, ramifying
  ♦ *Separation 753*

13 **participating,** taking part, involved in, part of, belonging
  ♦ *Sociability 408; Inclusion 763*

VERBS

14 **part,** divide, subdivide, share, apportion, distribute; cut up, dissect, segment, section, sectionalize, compartmentalize, partition, separate, split, bisect, dissect, take apart; sever, fragment, dismantle, break, break up
  ♦ *Allocation 474; Separation 753; Disintegration 758*

15 **particularize,** detail, itemize

16 **participate,** take part in, be involved in, have a role in, be part of, belong to
  ♦ *Sociability 408; Inclusion 763*

ADVERBS

17 **partly,** in part, in some measure, to some extent, to a certain extent, to a *or* some degree, a little, a bit, in bits and pieces, somewhat, slightly, moderately, partially, half, half-and-half, fractionally, not wholly, not fully, incompletely, inadequately, scrappily, piecemeal, part by part, bit by bit, little by little, a little at a time, in *or* by installments, in dribs and drabs, by fits and starts, drop by drop, by degrees, gradually, in parts, in detail, in lots; part for part, proportionally, proportionately, pro rata

761 Completeness

NOUNS

1 **completeness,** entirety, totality, wholeness, unity, sufficiency; integrity, integrality, universality, comprehensiveness, solidarity, solidity; balance, harmony, concord, perfection
  ♦ *Sufficiency 97; Accord 735; Whole 759; End 773; Perfection 805*

2 **completion,** completing, end, ending, finish, finishing, finishing off, finalization, close, conclusion, termination, expiration; culmination, attainment, accomplishment, achievement, arrival, summit, success, fulfillment, consummation, realization, topping-out; finished state, complete cycle, fruition, ripeness, maturity, maturation
  ♦ *Resolution 376; End 773*

3 **conclusion,** finish, termination, end, ending, windup,

mop-up, climax, payoff, close, finality; finis, finale, epilogue, final story, last *or* dying words, final shot, final exam, final chapter, final curtain, last act, swan song, death; resolution, solution, denouement, upshot, result, end result, end product, finished product; finishing touch, final touch, last touch, crowning stroke, finishing stroke, last stroke, *coup de grâce* [Fr], elaboration, capstone, finisher, frosting *or* icing on the cake, clincher; finishing off, rounding off

▶ *Resolution 376; End 773*

4 **limit,** end, extreme, zenith, climax, peak, summit, pinnacle, crown, top, highest point *or* degree, *ne plus ultra* [L], the utmost, culmination, ideal, perfection, the whole hog

▶ *Limit 620; End 773; Perfection 805*

5 **fullness,** plenitude, capacity, full capacity, full size, full length, full extent, full volume, full value, maximum, max [Inf]; saturation, saturation point, satiety, repletion, filling; full complement, full crew, requisite number, quorum, quota, full quota, full house, full load, full measure, bumper, brimmer, bellyful, skinful [Inf]; makeweight, complement, supplement, fill-up, compensation

▶ *Sufficiency 97; Excess 99; Compensation 743; Addition 748*

ADJECTIVES

6 **complete,** entire, total, integral, intact, unbroken, unimpaired, undivided, individual, self-contained, self-sufficient, united, whole, plenary, sufficient, adequate, effective, effectual, lacking nothing, all there; unexpurgated, unabridged, uncut, unabbreviated; all-inclusive, all-embracing, comprehensive, absolute, utter, exhaustive, full-scale, detailed, thorough, thoroughgoing, all-out, wholesale, sweeping, unconfined, unrestricted, unlimited, unqualified; plain, downright, plumb [Inf]; pure, unadulterated, out-and-out, unmitigating, unmitigated, dyed-in-the-wool, consummate, full-blown, full-grown, fully grown, full-fledged, fully fledged, mature, perfect, faultless, perfected

▶ *Whole 759; Perfection 805*

7 **completed,** finished, accomplished, achieved, compleat [Arch], crowning, culminating, supplementary, complementary, finalized, ended, concluded, closed, terminated, over, done

▶ *Sufficiency 97; Whole 759; End 773; One 788*

8 **full,** filled, refilled, replenished, replete, satisfied, topped up, topped off, full, filled up, well-filled, well-stocked, well-lined, bulging, brimming, brimful, full to the brim, level with, flush; overfilled, overfull, overflowing, full to overflowing, running over, full to bursting, bursting at the seams, stuffed, gorged, sated, satiated; chock-full, chockablock, no room to spare, no room to turn around, no room to swing a cat in, crowded, congested, solid, cram-full, crammed, packed, jammed, jam-packed; loaded, laden, fully laden, overloaded, fully charged; all seats taken, standing room only, sold out, overrun, dripping with; coming out of one's ears [Inf], rolling in [Inf]

▶ *Sufficiency 97; Excess 99; Multitude 795*

VERBS

9 **complete,** make complete, make whole, integrate, unite, join, complement, supplement, eke out, fill a gap, fill a need, fill in, fill out, build up, make up, construct, piece together, compose; do, perform, execute, discharge, fulfill, realize, achieve, accomplish, do thoroughly, leave nothing out *or* undone, have nothing to add, leave nothing to chance, carry through, carry out, crown, cap, put the frosting *or* icing on the cake, put the finishing touch *or* touches to, finalize, perfect, finish, end, terminate, close, conclude, round off, wrap up

▶ *Action 412; Production 522; Union 752; Combination 757; End 773; Perfection 805*

10 **be complete,** become complete, be whole, have everything, have it all, say it all, reach *or* touch perfection; climax, culminate, come to an end, come to a close; end, finish, close, terminate, have enough; want *or* lack nothing, fill out, develop fully, reach full growth, grow up, become adult, reach maturity, realize one's potential

11 **fill,** refill, replenish, fill up, top up [Brit], top off, satisfy, sate, satiate, overfill, saturate, soak, drench, overwhelm, swamp, drown, pervade, suffuse, fill to capacity *or* to the brim, cram, jam, stuff, bloat, pack in, pile in, pile on, ram in, ram down, squeeze in, pack, stow, load, charge, lade, freight, stock, supply, fill a space, cover, occupy, spread over, extend *or* reach to, overrun

▶ *Provision 89; Satisfaction 273; Presence 575; Contents 577; Covering 613; Insertion 710*

12 **be full,** be filled, brim with, overflow, run over, slop over, bulge, swell, have *or* eat *or* drink one's fill

▶ *Sufficiency 97; Excess 99; Expansion 581; End 773*

ADVERBS

13 **completely,** entirely, wholly, totally, absolutely, utterly, quite, thoroughly, clean, plain, downright, perfectly, altogether, plumb [Inf]

▶ *Distance 585; Breadth 592; Whole 759*

14 **fully,** in full, every inch, every whit, to capacity, to the maximum, as full as can be, as fully as possible, to the utmost, to the hilt, up to one's neck *or* ears *or* eyes [Inf], to the full, to the brim, to the top, over the top, with a vengeance, with all the trimmings and then some, through and through, to the heart, to the marrow, to the core, full out, at full stretch, through thick and thin, to the last breath, to the last one, for good, for good and all, forever, to the end

▶ *Whole 759; End 773*

761 Completeness

NOUNS

1 **incompleteness,** partialness, partiality, defectiveness; poverty, scantness, scantiness, inadequacy, lack, want, need; ineffectiveness, ineffectuality, imperfection, unfinished state; unpreparedness, unreadiness; underdevelopment, unripeness, immaturity; rawness, roughness, sketchiness, scrappiness, hollowness, superficiality, insubstantiality, perfunctoriness, desultoriness, lick and a promise, half-heartedness, negligence, default, arrears

2 **noncompletion,** incompletion, incompleteness, nonfulfillment, mutilation, impairment, nonsatisfaction, dissatisfaction
▹ *Insufficiency 98; Dissatisfaction 274; Lack of Preparation 389; Part 760; Imperfection 806*

3 **nonachievement,** nonaccomplishment, failure, lack; drawn game, draw, tie, stalemate, deadlock, noncontinuation; procrastination, delay, incomplete work, unfinished task, never-ending story; imperfection, superficiality, rough sketch, perfunctoriness, desultoriness, inattention, neglect, negligence, oversight; loose end, rough edge; underdevelopment, unripeness, immaturity, skimpiness
▹ *Imperfection 806*

4 **omission,** gap, lacuna, hiatus, void, interval, break, breakage, missing part, missing link, loss, deficit, lack, want, need, deficiency, insufficiency, shortfall, slippage, ullage, defalcation, arrears, default
▹ *Insufficiency 98; Loss 468; Interval 587; Exclusion 764; Discontinuity 775; Imperfection 806*

ADJECTIVES

5 **incomplete,** defective, deficient, scant, scanty, skimpy, short, insufficient, inadequate, ineffective, ineffectual; missing, omitting, lacking, wanting, needing, in need of, requiring, short of, shy of, partial; unfinished, not finished, going on, continuing, developing, in progress, in the pipeline; begun, in embryo, in preparation, half-finished, half-done; neglected, uncompleted, underdeveloped, undeveloped, unprepared, unready, unripe, immature, raw, underdone, undercooked; rude, rough, crude, rough-hewn, sketchy, scrappy, thin, poor, meager, hollow, superficial, insubstantial, perfunctory, half-hearted, left hanging, left in the air, interrupted; omitted, lost, missed, manqué, in default, defaulting, in arrears, not up to date, not all there

6 **shortened,** abbreviated, abridged, truncated, curtailed, cropped, docked, lopped, unsatisfactory, blemished, stained, flawed, imperfect
▹ *Necessity 95; Insufficiency 98; Negligence 326; Shortness 591; Part 760; Imperfection 806*

7 **uncompleted,** undone, not finished, unfinished, un-performed, unprocessed, unfulfilled, unconsummated, unrealized, unattained, unachieved, unaccomplished, not accomplished, unexecuted, never-ending, incomplete, imperfect, fragmentary, missing, short, truncated, left unfinished, neglected, not finalized, not cleared up, left hanging, left in the air, up in the air, unelaborated, not worked out, not thought through, unthorough, perfunctory, inattentive, neglectful, desultory, procrastinating, delaying, superficial, half-finished, half-done, half-begun, half-baked, underdone, underdeveloped, immature, unripe, lacking, skimpy, scanty, scrappy, sketchy, in outline

VERBS

8 **be incomplete,** be unfinished, need, want, be wanting, lack, be lacking; miss, be unfulfilled
▹ *Insufficiency 98; Negligence 326; Exclusion 764; Beginning 771; Imperfection 806*

9 **not complete,** not finish, leave undone, leave unfinished, leave out, omit, exclude, not fulfill, not achieve, not accomplish, fall short, leave incomplete, leave hanging, leave in the air, neglect, miss, truncate, not finalize, not clear up, half-finish, half-do, half-begin, draft, rough out, sketch out, outline, do by halves, skimp, scrimp, scrape by, paper over the cracks, give up, not follow up, not follow through, fail to deliver, procrastinate, delay, postpone, put off, give a lick and a promise

ADVERBS

10 **incompletely,** partially, partly, perfunctorily, in part, in *or* by installments, by halves, half, insufficiently, poorly, inadequately, neglectfully, ineffectually, ineffectively, deficiently, insubstantially, scantily, desultorily, roughly, embryonically, sketchily, superficially, skimpily, scrappily, crudely, improperly, imperfectly, negligently, neglectfully, in arrears

763 Inclusion

He chose to include the things that in each other are included, the whole, the complicate, the amassing harmony.
— WALLACE STEVENS

NOUNS

1 **inclusion,** enclosure, encirclement, encapsulation, containment, comprisal, comprehension, involvement, implication, concern, reception, admission, admittance, admissibility, eligibility, participation, membership, presence, accommodation, room, space, capacity, volume; inclusiveness, coverage; global approach, universality, generality, comprehensiveness, no exception, no omission, nothing left out; set, full set, complete set, package, package deal, complement, full complement, full quota, allowance, subsumption, composition, composing, construction, makeup, constitution, incorporation, integration

Production 522; Space 563; Presence 575; Enclosure 619; Admittance 708; Whole 759; Completeness 761; Generality 778

2 **thing** *or* **person included,** ingredient, constituent, factor, additive, appurtenance, feature, component, part, item, element, piece, bit, contents; insider, participant, member, coworker, staff member, crew member, crew, team

Part 760

ADJECTIVES

3 **including,** inclusive, containing, holding, accommodating, having, allowing, considering, counting, consisting of, comprising, composed of, made up of, incorporating, incorporative, all-in, all-inclusive, all-embracing, comprehensive, wholesale, blanket, extensive, widespread, across-the-board, wall-to-wall, sweeping, global, worldwide, universal, expansive, broad-based, covering, umbrella, overall, general, encyclopedic, nonexclusive, nondiscriminatory, without exception, without omission

Whole 759; Completeness 761; Generality 778

4 **included,** built-in, integrated, unsegregated, unseparated, constituent, component, part of, part and parcel of, inherent, intrinsic, belonging, pertinent, pertaining, appurtenant, admissible, admitted, allowed, eligible, in the same class, in the same league, classed with, classified with, subsumed; related, akin, congenerous, congeneric, entered, listed, on the list, noted, recorded, added, linked, joined, combined, merged, inner, interior

Record 185; Possession 469; Interior 611; Admittance 708; Essence 723; Relatedness 727; Addition 748; Union 752; Combination 757; Class 777; List 785

VERBS

5 **include,** contain, hold, have, enclose, encircle, envelop, encapsulate, comprehend, involve, implicate, embrace, cover, encompass, take in, receive, admit, find room for, find space for, accommodate, count, number, boast, take into account, take into consideration, allow for, take account of, take cognizance of, recognize, allow (of), admit of, consist of, comprise, compose, be made up of, incorporate, integrate, embody, constitute, mean

Possession 469; Receiving 473; Container 578; Enclosure 619; Admittance 708; Whole 759; Completeness 761

6 **be included,** be one of, be part of, make up, belong, enter into, become involved with, be mixed up in, be implicated in; participate, take part, share, merge, belong to, appertain to, pertain to, relate to

Possession 469; Relatedness 727

7 **subsume,** place under, count with, reckon among, number with, enumerate with, class with, classify as, categorize as *or* with, enter, list, enter as, put in, put among, arrange in, add to

Insertion 710; Addition 748; Arrangement 767; Class 777

ADVERBS

8 **inclusively,** inherently, intrinsically, pertinently, as well as, comprehensively, universally, globally, generally, from A to Z, alpha to omega, et cetera, etc., and so on, and so forth, inside, within

Interior 611; Contents 577

764 Exclusion

Include me out. — SAMUEL GOLDWYN

NOUNS

1 **exclusion,** noninclusion, omission, suppression, rejection, refusal, denial; forbiddance, prohibition, veto, proscription, interdiction, ban, taboo; embargo, blockade, boycott; bar, exception, exception in favor of, exemption, special case, dispensation, special dispensation, relegation, exclusion order, lockout, picket line, closed door; no entry, nonadmission, inadmissibility; limitation, circumscription; preclusion, preemption, prevention

Misjudgment 342; Rejection 383; Exemption 434; Prohibition 503; Refusal 506; Limit 620

2 **ejection,** eviction, expulsion, dismissal, firing, suspension, disqualification, disbarment, the push [Brit]; removal, riddance, disposal, deletion, cancellation, elimination, obliteration; censorship, bowdlerization, expurgation, eradication; excommunication, deportation, extradition, banishment, exile, expatriation, ostracism; [Inf]: sack, sacking, heave-ho, boot

Obliteration 186; Expulsion 709

3 **exclusion zone,** ghetto, no-man's-land, outer darkness, the outside, pale; economic zone, quarantine, isolation

4 **exclusiveness,** exclusivity, restrictiveness, insularity, ethnicity, ethnic cleansing, xenophobia; shunning, blacklisting, blacklist, blackball, closed shop, private club, clique, inner circle, members only, possessiveness, sole rights, monopoly, dog-in-the-manger policy; segregation, sequestration, seclusion, ghettoization, discrimination, racial discrimination, apartheid, color bar, sexual discrimination

Discrimination 337; Misjudgment 342; Selfishness 444

ADJECTIVES

5 **excluding,** exclusive, exclusionary, exclusory, close, closed, close-knit, clannish, cliquish, cliquey, narrow, restrictive, xenophobic, racist, sexist, restricted, limited, private, elite, select, choice, unique, sole, exemptive, interdictory, prohibitive, preventive, preemptive, preclusive, silent about

Selection 382; Specialty 779

6 **excluded,** not included, absent, missing, not counted, left out, omitted, missed out; excepted, excused, ex-

empt, exempted; barred, banned, embargoed; forbidden, taboo, prohibited; rejected, deleted; dismissed, evicted, expelled, shut out, shunned, blackballed, blacklisted, disbarred, struck off; outcast, exiled; untold, unsaid, unrecounted, unreported, inadmissible; beyond the pale, peripheral, extra, extraneous, foreign, not considered, disregarded, out of account, not in contention, outclassed, not in the same league, out in the cold; precluded, preempted, forestalled, prevented

▸ *Exemption 434; Prohibition 503; Absence 576; Extraneousness 724*

VERBS

7 exclude, leave out, count out, not include, omit, miss, miss out, disregard, ignore, pass over, exempt, excuse, except, make an exception (of), treat as a special case, keep out, warn off, forbid, prohibit, disallow, veto, proscribe, interdict, ban, taboo, embargo, place under an embargo, put an embargo on, bar, suppress, stifle, relegate, put *or* lay aside, leave, give up, abandon, reject, refuse, deny; vote against, vote out, vote down, shut out, shut the door on, deny entry, spurn, blacklist, blackball, rule out, draw the line at; limit, circumscribe, enclose, wall off, fence off, screen off, curtain off, box off, segregate, discriminate against, sequester, quarantine, isolate, seclude, ghettoize, boycott, shun, cold-shoulder, send to Coventry, ostracize, preclude, forestall, preempt, prevent, not entertain (the possibility of), count out

▸ *Rejection 383; Exemption 434; Prohibition 503; Refusal 506; Enclosure 619; Limit 620*

8 eject, evict, expel, throw out, send packing, cast out; dismiss, fire, make redundant [Brit]; suspend, disqualify, disbar, unfrock, defrock, strike off, remove, dispense with; oust, thrust out, get rid of, give the elbow; take out, delete, cross out, strike out, rub out, blot out, cancel, eliminate, obliterate, censor, edit out, blue-pencil; bowdlerize, expurgate, eradicate; uproot, excommunicate, deport, extradite, banish, exile, outlaw, expatriate; [Inf]: sack, kick out, boot out, give the heave-ho

▸ *Obliteration 186; Expulsion 709*

9 be excluded, not belong, stay out, stay outside, be exiled

▸ *Exterior 610*

ADVERBS

10 exclusively, narrowly, with reservations, with restrictions, outside, excluding, exclusive of, except, excepting, except for, with the exception of, bar, barring, save, not counting, ignoring, omitting, outside of, short of, apart from, let alone

765 Order

Order is not pressure which is imposed on society from

without, but an equilibrium which is set up from within.
— JOSÉ ORTEGA Y GASSET

Order is heaven's first law. — ALEXANDER POPE

A place for everything, and everything in its place.
— ISABELLA BEETON

NOUNS

1 order, organization, formalization, formalism, arrangement, array, disposition, layout, pattern, composition, formation, structure, setup, distribution, lineup, putting in order, prioritization, system, scheme, schedule

▸ *Structure 551; Form 624; Arrangement 767*

2 grouping, categorization, classification, codification, specification, pigeonholing, cataloging, indexing, listing, taxonomy

▸ *Class 777*

3 hierarchy, pecking *or* peck order, series, sequence, gradation, progression; alphabetical order, numerical order, serial order, ascending *or* descending order, reverse order, logical order

▸ *Sequence 770; Consecutiveness 774*

4 position, place, class, grade, category, degree, rank, ranking, status, subordination

▸ *Class 777*

5 orderliness, state of order, tidiness, neatness, cleanness, smoothness, straightness, correctness, good condition, good trim, fine fettle, apple-pie order

▸ *Cleanliness 111; Right 429*

6 methodicalness, methodology, meticulousness, punctiliousness, accuracy, straightness, systematization, systematism, systematics, systematology

▸ *Accuracy 350*

7 method, system, discipline, organization, routine, custom, habit, rule, pattern, plan, scheme, structure, coherence, coordination, uniformity, regularity, symmetry, proportion

▸ *Means 102; Plan 387; Habit, Custom 397; Symmetry 626; Sameness 730*

8 harmony, concord, stability, quiet, quietude, peace, peace and quiet, calm, tranquillity, stillness, quietness, detachment

▸ *Accord 735*

9 discipline, law, law and order, rule of law, control, stability

ADJECTIVES

10 ordered, organized, formalized, formal, formalistic, arranged, arrayed, disposed, composed, structured, schematic, systematic, symmetrical, balanced, ordained

▸ *Plan 387; Structure 551; Symmetry 626; Arrangement 767*

11 grouped, categorized, categorical, classified, classifi-

catory, codified, specified, sorted, pigeonholed, indexed, indexical, cataloged, listed
- ▶ *Class 777*

12 **hierarchical,** serial, sequential, gradational, taxonomic, progressive, alphabetical, numerical, in order, graded, ranked
- ▶ *Sequence 770; Consecutiveness 774*

13 **orderly,** tidy, neat, neat and tidy, spick-and-span, clean, smooth, straight, correct, trim, spruce, dapper, smart, sleek, slick, groomed, well-groomed, not a hair out of place, kempt, well-kept, well-cared for, in good order, in perfect order, in good trim, in good condition, in the pink, in fine fettle, shipshape, all shipshape and Bristol fashion, neat as a pin, in apple-pie order
- ▶ *Cleanliness 111; Right 429*

14 **well-ordered,** well-organized, methodical, meticulous, punctilious, systematic, scientific, businesslike, formal, accurate, straight, regular, uniform, coherent, intelligible
- ▶ *Accuracy 350; Intelligibility 363; Sameness 730*

15 **habitual,** routine, usual, regular, customary
- ▶ *Habit, Custom 397*

16 **harmonious,** concordant, stable, steady, quiet, peaceful, calm, tranquil
- ▶ *Accord 735*

17 **disciplined,** controlled, under control, restrained, lawful, law-abiding, peaceable, docile, obedient, well-behaved, well-drilled, well-regulated, according to rule, decorous, mannerly
- ▶ *Conduct 399; Submission 421; Obedience 426*

VERBS

18 **order,** arrange, array, put *or* set in order, dispose, lay out, organize, marshal, manage, run a tight ship, compose, form, structure, set up, line up, align, ordain
- ▶ *Management 126; Structure 551; Arrangement 767*

19 **systematize,** methodize, rationalize, standardize, sort, sort out, sift, group, categorize, class, classify, catalog, codify, index, pigeonhole, rank, grade, place, position, tabulate, prioritize
- ▶ *Class 777*

20 **harmonize,** stabilize, regularize, regulate, synchronize, accord
- ▶ *Accord 735*

21 **tidy,** tidy up, neaten, clean, clean up, smooth, straighten, straighten up, correct, put *or* set to rights, rearrange, untangle, disentangle, unravel, unsnarl, iron out, smarten up, spruce up, groom, whip into shape, lick into shape [Inf], debug [Inf]
- ▶ *Arrangement 767*

22 **restore order,** pacify, calm, cool down, cool off, pour oil on troubled waters, keep order, discipline, take in hand, control, govern, police, clean up, tighten up on, clamp down on

- ▶ *Authority 52; Pacification 74*

23 **be in order,** be in working order, work, function, operate, go, go like clockwork
- ▶ *Operation 509*

24 **line up,** fall in, take one's place, queue up, place oneself, draw up, fall into place, find one's level

ADVERBS

25 **orderly,** in orderly fashion, in order, neatly, tidily, just so

26 **in order,** in turn, hierarchically, formalistically, in series, step by step, by stages, progressively, sequentially, alphabetically, numerically, according to plan

27 **methodically,** systematically, symmetrically, uniformly, regularly, routinely, by the book

766 Disorder

A sweet disorder in the dress / Kindles in clothes a wantonness. — ROBERT HERRICK

NOUNS

1 **disorder,** disorderliness, disorganization, disarrangement, disarray, disjunction, disharmony, discord, disruption, disturbance, upset, discomposure, discomfiture, disconcertedness, discombobulation, disintegration, incoherence, unintelligibility, confusion, derangement
- ▶ *Unintelligibility 364; Disagreement 463; Disintegration 758; Disturbance 768*

2 **irregular order,** irregularity, randomness, haphazardness, nonuniformity, unsymmetry, nonsymmetry, disproportion, misshapenness, shapelessness, no pattern, no rhyme or reason
- ▶ *Shapelessness 625; Diversity 732*

3 **untidiness,** messiness, unkemptness, dishevelment, scruffiness, shabbiness, neglect, negligence, carelessness, slipshodness, shoddiness, sloppiness, sluttishness, dirtiness, uncleanness, grubbiness, slovenliness, slatternliness, sordidness, squalidness
- ▶ *Dirtiness 112; Negligence 326*

4 **confusion,** chaos, muddle, mess, jumble, melee, welter, hodgepodge, hash, mishmash, pickle [Inf]; topsy-turviness, shambles, tohubohu; bedlam, pandemonium, inferno, madhouse, tumult, turmoil, bear garden, turbulence, upheaval, ferment, hullabaloo, hubbub, racket, cacophony, uproar
- ▶ *Waste 96; Loudness 232; Dissonance 241; Uselessness 802*

5 **mix-up,** tangle, snarl, maze, web, jungle; mess, hash; [Inf]: foul-up, ballup, muck-up, fuckup, snafu, cockup [Brit]
- ▶ *Difficulty 824*

6 **lawlessness,** anarchy, chaos, disorder, disobedience, disorderly behavior *or* conduct, unruliness, mob rule, boisterousness, rowdiness, disruptiveness, lack of dis-

cipline, rebelliousness, revolution, uprising, upheaval, vandalism, hooliganism

  ◗ *Anarchy 51; Disobedience 427*

7 **disruption,** disturbance, commotion, pother, stir, fuss, bother, trouble, ado, hurly-burly, all hell let loose, fight, argument, brawl, row, fistfight, fisticuffs, rumpus, ruckus, ruction, rough-and-tumble, free-for-all, donnybrook, affray, breach of the peace, riot, rampage, set-to, roughhouse, dustup; [Inf]: rumble, to-do, aggro [Brit *and* Aus]

  ◗ *Contention 422; Disturbance 768*

8 **derangement,** disorder, disturbance, mental derangement, mental disorder, insanity, madness

  ◗ *Insanity 110; Disturbance 768*

ADJECTIVES

9 **disordered,** orderless, in disorder, in disarray, disarranged, deranged, disrupted, disorganized, muddled, jumbled, shuffled, out of order, displaced, misplaced, out of place, out of joint, disjointed, dislocated; unordered, unorganized, unarranged, ungraded, unsorted, unsifted, unclassified

  ◗ *Displacement 574*

10 **irregular,** random, haphazard, erratic, hit-or-miss, sporadic, spasmodic, desultory, nonuniform, unsymmetrical, nonsymmetrical, misshapen, disproportionate, shapeless, formless

  ◗ *Shapelessness 625*

11 **untidy,** grubby, messy, scruffy, shabby, ragged, in rags, down-at-heel, unsightly, unkempt, disheveled, bedraggled, tousled, uncombed, windblown, like something the cat dragged in, ruffled, crumpled, frumpish, sluttish, slovenly, slatternly, neglectful, negligent, careless, slipshod, shoddy, slack

  ◗ *Negligence 326; Deterioration 808*

12 **confused,** incoherent, convoluted, disorganized, muddleheaded, scatterbrained, featherbrained, unsystematic, unmethodical; discomposed, discomfited, disconcerted, unsettled, disturbed, perturbed, upset, discombobulated

13 **muddled,** jumbled, scrambled, confused, chaotic, tangled, labyrinthine, awry, askew, amiss, topsy-turvy, upside-down, at sixes and sevens, head over heels, higgledy-piggledy, arsy-varsy [Inf], haywire [Inf]

14 **mixed up,** tangled, snarled up, snafu, messed up; [Inf]: balled up, mucked up, fouled up, fucked up

15 **disorderly,** chaotic, lawless, unruly, undisciplined, uncontrolled, out of control, unmanageable, boisterous, disruptive, stroppy [Brit inf], rowdy, hell-raising, harum-scarum, wild, turbulent, rampageous, riotous, rebellious, insubordinate, contumacious, mutinous, obstreperous, disobedient, anarchic, nihilistic, rough-and-tumble

  ◗ *Anarchy 51; Obstinacy 379; Disobedience 427*

16 **deranged,** disordered, disturbed, confused, mentally

deranged, unhinged, unbalanced, disturbed, unstable, insane, mad

  ◗ *Insanity 110; Disturbance 768*

VERBS

17 **disorder,** disorganize, disarrange, derange, throw into disarray, muddle, jumble, shuffle, mix up, scramble, disperse, scatter, break up, disrupt, disturb

  ◗ *Displacement 574; Disturbance 768; Dispersion 776*

18 **discompose,** disconcert, disturb, perturb, upset, hassle, pester, unsettle, disorient, addle, befuddle, confuse, tie in knots

19 **confuse,** muddle, mess up, hash, botch, bungle, mix up, tangle, snarl, snarl up, make a hash *or* mess of; [Inf]: foul up, ball up, fuck up, bollix up, cock up [Brit]

20 **make disorderly,** untidy, mess up, dishevel, bedraggle, tousle, ruffle, rumple, crumple, crease, turn upside down, turn topsy-turvy

21 **be disordered,** lapse into disorder, fall into confusion, fall into disarray, degenerate, disintegrate, come apart, come unstuck, dissolve into chaos

  ◗ *Disintegration 758; Deterioration 808*

22 **be disorderly,** get out of hand, get out of control, disobey, be undisciplined, make trouble, raise a rumpus, run wild, run amuck *or* amok, riot, run riot, rampage, go on the rampage, roister, storm, mob, kick up, raise Cain [Inf], raise hell [Inf]

  ◗ *Anarchy 51; Loudness 232; Disobedience 427*

23 **derange,** disorder, disturb, unhinge, unbalance, drive insane, make mad

  ◗ *Insanity 110*

ADVERBS

24 **in disorder,** in disarray, in confusion, in a muddle, in a mess, in a jumble, by chance, unmethodically, unsystematically, irregularly, haphazardly, erratically, indiscriminately, randomly, at random, sporadically, spasmodically, by fits and starts, without rhyme or reason, chaotically, confusedly

25 **anyhow,** all over, all over the place, upside-down, topsy-turvy, pell-mell, helter-skelter, harum-scarum, off the rails, at sixes and sevens, at cross-purposes, higgledy-piggledy, every which way; all over the lot, arsy-varsy [Inf]

26 **disruptively,** on the rampage, anarchically, rebelliously, boisterously, riotously

767 Arrangement

NOUNS

1 **arrangement,** order, disposition, disposal, placing, placement, location, composition, grouping, alignment, lineup, choreography; ordering, putting in order, arranging, arraying, marshaling, structuring

  ◗ *Structure 551; Location 565; Order 765*

2 **array,** assemblage, arrangement, display, pattern, design, decoration, style, layout, structure, composition

⬧ *Decoration 532; Display 843*

3 organization, method, methodization, system, systematization, routinization, rationalization, standardization, centralization, coordination; planning, charting, structuring
⬧ *Means 102; Management 126; Plan 387*

4 rearrangement, reordering, reorganization, restructuring, realignment; revision, redaction, regrouping; tidying, simplification, streamlining, shake-up
⬧ *Selection 382; Structure 551; Change 665; Order 765*

5 categorization, classification, codification, taxonomy; grouping, placing, placement, pigeonholing, compartmentalization, grading, gradation, ranking, rating, seeding [Sports]; hierarchy, stratification, graduation, sorting, sorting out, sifting, screening, selection, analysis, tabulation, alphabetization, cataloging, listing, indexing, filing
⬧ *Selection 382; Order 765; Class 777; List 785*

6 category, subcategory, class, subclass, group, subgroup, order, suborder, division, subdivision; family, set, bracket, head, heading, department, section, grade, rank, level, position, place, status, slot, niche, pigeonhole, compartment
⬧ *Class 777*

7 catalog, directory, gazetteer, register, digest, compendium, index, list, inventory, record, file, computer file, computer listing
⬧ *Computers 15; Record 185; List 785*

8 chart, diagram, table, graph, flow chart *or* sheet, pie chart, bar chart, scatter diagram, spreadsheet, plan, scheme, schema, schedule, program
⬧ *Plan 387*

9 agreement, understanding, arrangement, settlement, deal, compact, contract, covenant, terms
⬧ *Contract 459; Compromise 461; Agreement 462*

10 arrangements, plans, preparations, groundwork
⬧ *Plan 387; Preparation 388*

ADJECTIVES

11 arranged, ordered, in order, orderly, structured, ranged, arrayed, assembled, marshaled, disposed, placed, grouped, aligned
⬧ *Structure 551; Location 565; Order 765*

12 organized, methodized, systematized, rationalized, planned, prearranged
⬧ *Plan 387*

13 organizational, methodical, systematic, schematic, rational, formational

14 rearranged, reordered, reorganized, restructured, realigned, adjusted, tidied, streamlined, simplified, shaken up
⬧ *Change 665; Order 765*

15 categorized, classified, codified, grouped, pigeonholed, compartmentalized, placed, graded, ranked, rated, seeded [Sports], stratified, sorted, sorted out,

assorted, sifted, screened, selected, analyzed, processed, tabulated, alphabetized, cataloged, indexed, listed, filed
⬧ *Record 185; Selection 382; Class 777; List 785*

16 categorical, classificatory, hierarchical, taxonomic
⬧ *Order 765*

17 diagrammatic, graphic, tabular, schematic, analytic

VERBS

18 arrange, order, put *or* set in order, reduce to order; structure, range, array, marshal; dispose, place, position, locate, set, set out, lay out, display, align, line up, put into shape, compose, group, space, space out; distribute, allocate, settle, choreograph
⬧ *Allocation 474; Structure 551; Location 565; Order 765; Display 843*

19 organize, methodize, systematize, rationalize, standardize, normalize, centralize, coordinate, plan, schematize
⬧ *Management 126; Plan 387*

20 rearrange, reorder, reorganize, restructure, shake up, realign, adjust, tidy, simplify, streamline
⬧ *Change 665; Order 765*

21 categorize, classify, class, codify, digest, program, group, pigeonhole, compartmentalize, place, place in order, put in order, grade, rank, rate, seed, sort, sort out, assort, sift, sift out, sieve, screen, select, analyze, process, process data, tabulate, alphabetize, catalog, index, list, inventory, record, register, file
⬧ *Record 185; Selection 382; Class 777; List 785*

22 come to an arrangement, come to an agreement, come to an understanding, compromise, agree, settle, make a deal, come to terms, fix up [Inf]
⬧ *Compromise 461; Agreement 462*

23 make arrangements, arrange for, prearrange, prepare, plan, schedule, organize, manage, contrive, devise
⬧ *Management 126; Plan 387; Preparation 388*

ADVERBS

24 in place, in order, rationally, tidily, neatly, methodically, systematically, schematically, taxonomically, diagrammatically, indexically, analytically

768 Disturbance

NOUNS

1 disturbance, perturbation, agitation, convulsion, upheaval, upset, disconcertedness, disquiet, discomfiture, discomposure, worry, anxiety, annoyance, bother, nuisance
⬧ *Agitation 684*

2 disarrangement, disorder, disorganization, muddle, confusion
⬧ *Disorder 766*

3 dispersion, displacement, dislodgment, dislocation, disorientation, derailment

> ▸ *Displacement 574; Dispersion 776*

4 **disruption,** disturbance, interruption, intrusion, interference, intervention, molestation, sabotage, hindrance, obstruction, inconvenience, untimeliness, distraction

> ▸ *Inconvenience 804; Hindrance 826*

5 **commotion,** disturbance, breach of the peace, tumult, turmoil, ferment, furor, outcry, outburst; clamor, uproar, fuss, rumpus, ruckus; bedlam, hubbub, hurly-burly, hullabaloo, brouhaha, ado, racket, din, noise; bother, trouble, scuffle, fracas, fray, riot, ruction, to-do [Inf], shemozzle [Brit inf]

> ▸ *Loudness 232; Contention 422; Disorder 766*

ADJECTIVES

6 **disturbed,** perturbed, agitated, convulsed, upset, distressed; unsettled, disconcerted, disquieted, discomfited, discomposed, uncomfortable, uneasy, confused; flustered, ruffled, shaken, rattled, alarmed, concerned, worried, anxious, troubled; bothered, annoyed, irritated, vexed, irked; [Inf]: hassled, spooked, bugged

> ▸ *Sorrow 270; Fear 283; Agitation 684*

7 **disarranged,** deranged, disordered, disorganized, messed up, muddled, confused, roiled; dispersed, displaced, dislodged, dislocated, disoriented, derailed

> ▸ *Displacement 574; Disorder 766; Dispersion 776*

8 **disrupted,** interrupted, interfered with, molested, sabotaged, hindered, obstructed, inconvenienced, distracted

> ▸ *Inconvenience 804; Hindrance 826*

9 **disturbing,** upsetting, distressing, unsettling, disconcerting, alarming, worrying, bothersome, annoying, vexatious, muddling, disruptive, distracting, off-putting

VERBS

10 **disturb,** perturb, agitate, stir, convulse, upset, distress; unsettle, disconcert, disquiet, discomfit, discompose, throw into confusion; fluster, ruffle, shake, rattle; alarm, concern, worry, trouble, bother, pester, harass, annoy, irritate, vex, irk; [Inf]: hassle, spook, bug

> ▸ *Sorrow 270; Fear 283; Agitation 684*

11 **disarrange,** derange, disorder, throw into disorder, disorganize, mess up, muddle, confuse, put out of gear, roil; disperse, displace, dislodge, dislocate, disorient, derail

> ▸ *Displacement 574; Disorder 766; Dispersion 776; Difficulty 824*

12 **disrupt,** interrupt, intrude, butt in on, break in on, interfere, intervene, molest, tamper with, sabotage, hinder, obstruct, inconvenience, put out, distract, put off

> ▸ *Inconvenience 804; Hindrance 826*

ADVERBS

13 **disturbingly,** disconcertingly, confusingly, alarmingly, disquietingly, worryingly; annoyingly, irritatingly, inconveniently, disruptively, intrusively, obstructively, perversely, off the rails, on the wrong track, off course

14 **distractedly,** uneasily, anxiously

769 Precedence

What is today supported by precedents will hereafter become a precedent. — TACITUS

NOUNS

1 **precedence,** antecedence, priority, antecedency, previousness, preceding, going before, coming before, precession, anteriority, anteposition, taking precedence, preemption

> ▸ *Earliness 657; Beginning 771*

2 **priority,** primacy, supremacy, dominion, preeminence, superiority, higher position, higher rank, seniority, prerogative, privilege, advantage; front, front position, forefront, vanguard, head start, head of the line, pole position, first place, lead, pride of place; top priority, urgency, importance, preference, first concern, primary issue

> ▸ *Front 621; Superiority 744; Importance 799*

3 **preparation,** groundwork, foundation, development, exploration; breakthrough, discovery, leap

> ▸ *Discovery 345; Preparation 388*

4 **precedent,** antecedent, lead, example, standard, prototype, model, pattern, paradigm, yardstick, criterion

5 **preface,** foreword, proem, prologue, frontispiece, introduction, opening, opener, preliminaries, prelims [Inf], front matter; prelude, overture, curtain raiser; apéritif, appetizer, hors d'oeuvre; prefix, prefixion, prothesis

> ▸ *Beginning 771*

6 **preview,** foretaste, prediction, premonition, omen, warning, presentiment, presage; prequel, prerelease, sneak preview, trailer

> ▸ *Motion Pictures 137; Prediction 358; Warning 814*

7 **precursor,** forerunner, foregoer, herald, harbinger, messenger, announcer, crier; front runner, lead runner, leader, vanguard, scout, reconnaissance party, guide, pilot, explorer, pathfinder, trailblazer, avant-gardist, groundbreaker, pioneer, frontiersman, founding father, trendsetter, innovator, inventor, discoverer

> ▸ *Discovery 345; Preparation 388; Front 621; Newness 652*

8 **predecessor,** forebear, forefather, ancestor, firstborn, eldest, senior

ADJECTIVES

9 **preceding,** precedent, antecedent, anterior, precessional, first, earliest, preemptive; prior, prior to, former, late, erstwhile, one-time; previous, earlier, foregoing, above, above-mentioned, aforementioned, forenamed, aforesaid

> ▸ *Earliness 657; Beginning 771*

10 **primary,** senior, superior, supreme, preeminent, leading, first, first and foremost, headmost, chief, elder

▶ *Authority 52; Management 126; Superiority 744; Importance 799*

11 **preparatory,** foundational, developmental, leading, guiding, piloting, exploratory, reconnoitering, founding, discovering; innovatory, innovative, avant-garde, pioneering, trailblazing, ground-breaking
▶ *Discovery 345; Preparation 388; Front 621; Newness 652*

12 **precursory,** preliminary, initial, initiatory, introductory, elementary, basic, inaugural, baptismal, prefatory, prefatorial, proemial
▶ *Beginning 771*

VERBS

13 **precede,** antecede, predate, antedate, be before, come before, go before, anticipate, foreshadow; lead, go first, go ahead of, guide, pilot, indicate, show *or* lead the way, point the way, head, spearhead, stand at the head, front, head up
▶ *Management 126; Front 621*

14 **take precedence,** have precedence, outrank, be superior, have priority, take priority, preempt
▶ *Superiority 744; Importance 799*

15 **give priority,** put first, prioritize

16 **forerun,** pioneer, explore, reconnoiter, discover, invent, found, inaugurate, initiate, innovate, set a trend, set the fashion, lead the dance, set the example, influence, pave the way, map out, blaze a trail, scout
▶ *Discovery 345; Influence 512; Newness 652; Beginning 771*

17 **forecast,** foretell, presage, introduce, herald, usher in, ring in, predict, warn
▶ *Prediction 358*

ADVERBS

18 **before,** prior to, formerly, previously, earlier, beforehand, ere; in front of, in the lead

19 **first,** first and foremost, ahead, in front, in advance, in the first place

20 **in anticipation,** in preparation, preparatorily, as a prelude, as a preliminary

21 **primarily,** supremely, preeminently, first, preemptively

770 Sequence

NOUNS

1 **sequence,** succession, successiveness, consecutiveness, consecution, progression, procession, serialization, following, coming after, going after; order, series, arrangement, rank, hierarchy; turn, wake, subsequence, sequel
▶ *Order 765; Consecutiveness 774*

2 **succession,** accession, takeover, changeover, inheritance; assumption, assumption of office, replacement, taking over, taking up the post; descent, lineage, family, family tree

▶ *Beginning 771*

3 **series,** chain, string, train, line, run, course, queue, list; cycle, rota, rotation, alternation
▶ *Rotation 682*

4 **subsequence,** aftermath, aftereffect, afterglow, aftertaste, legacy, by-product, spin-off, fallout; afterthought, second thought

5 **sequel,** continuation, extension, development, series, saga, next installment; follow-through, follow-up, transition, segue; consequence, aftermath, product, outcome, upshot, denouement, effect, result, end result, end, payoff
▶ *Production 522; Continuity, Continuation 669; Effect 676; End 773; Consecutiveness 774*

6 **successor,** follower, descendant, inheritor, heir; progeny, offspring, issue, child, children, fruit, seed, later generation, future generation
▶ *Reproduction 21; Family 65; Future Time 650*

ADJECTIVES

7 **sequential,** sequent, succeeding, successive, successional, following, tailgating; serial, consecutive, sequacious, continuous, in a row, progressive, ranking, hierarchical; next, subsequent
▶ *Continuity, Continuation 669; Order 765; Consecutiveness 774; Succession 845*

8 **next,** near, later, latter, proximate, proximal

9 **consequent,** consequential, resulting, ensuing, caused
▶ *Effect 676*

VERBS

10 **follow,** follow in sequence, follow on, segue, succeed, come after, go after, come next, take one's turn, come in the wake of, follow in the footsteps of, follow in office, tread on the heels of; trail, shadow, dog someone's footsteps, tailgate, tail [Inf]

11 **succeed,** accede, inherit, supersede, supplant, replace, relieve, take over, take the place of, take the role of, step into the shoes of
▶ *Substitution 672*

12 **result,** ensue, arise, spring, emanate, issue, flow, turn out, come to pass
▶ *Effect 676; Beginning 771*

ADVERBS

13 **sequentially,** in sequence, in order, in succession, successively, consecutively, one after the other, running, in waves, in relays, alternately, in turn

14 **after,** afterward, following, as follows, subsequently, in the aftermath, next, then, later, at a later date

15 **consequently,** as a result, in consequence, as a consequence

771 Beginning

Begin at the beginning . . . and go on till you come to the end: then stop. — LEWIS CARROLL

NOUNS

1 **beginning,** start, commencement, opening, launch, onset, outset, outbreak, day one, square one, the word "go"; dawn, daybreak, break of day, morning
▶ *Front 621; Daytime 655*

2 **creation,** genesis, origin, origination, emergence, appearance, arrival
▶ *Appearance 264; Arrival 704*

3 **source,** origin, inchoation, provenance, fountainhead, wellspring; root, seed, seedbed, bud, germ, embryo, egg, nucleus; primordial soup, protoplasm, nest, womb, cradle
▶ *Cause 675*

4 **conception,** pregnancy, birth, nativity, delivery, parturition, nascence, nascency, pullulation, babyhood, cradle, infancy, childhood, youth
▶ *Reproduction 21; Youth 26*

5 **invention,** discovery, formation, creation, origin, origination, conception, innovation, coinage
▶ *Discovery 345; Originality 737*

6 **inauguration,** inception, incipiency, incipience, foundation, institution, establishment, setting up, installation, instigation, setting in motion, launch, embarkation
▶ *Discovery 345; Motion 677*

7 **rudiments,** basics, elements, principles, first principles, preparation, groundwork, spadework, nuts and bolts; ABCs, first steps, outline, first reader, primer
▶ *Preparation 388; Essence 723*

8 **enrollment,** matriculation, investiture, induction, ordination, installation, initiation, initiation ceremony, christening, baptism, wedding
▶ *Marriage 64; Religious Ritual 85; Entry 706*

9 **premiere,** first night, first time, first appearance, debut, coming out, curtain time, curtain raiser, maiden speech, inaugural, presentation, launch, launching, flotation, opening, opening ceremony, unveiling, cutting the ribbon, laying the cornerstone, maiden voyage
▶ *Opening 583*

10 **introduction,** opener, opening line, lead-in, prelude, preamble, preface, proem, exordium, preliminaries, prelims [Inf]
▶ *Precedence 769*

11 **starting point,** point of departure, starting post, starting block, starting pistol, zero hour, blastoff, opening, initiative, kickoff, start, flying start, false start
▶ *Departure 705*

12 **first move,** commencing *or* opening move, gambit, opening gambit, first step, first base, first lap, first round, first stage, first leg, first innings, early stages, early days, first course, starter
▶ *Earliness 657; Precedence 769*

13 **new beginning,** fresh start, new tack, fresh fields, pastures new, new leaf, new page, new chapter

▶ *Newness 652; Change 665*

14 **beginner,** starter, novice, learner, trainee, student, pupil, apprentice, probationer, recruit, raw recruit, tenderfoot, initiate, new boy, new girl, freshman, neophyte, tyro, greenhorn, rookie, debutante, deb [Inf]; baby, newborn, neonate, infant, fledgling, nestling
▶ *Youth 26*

15 **originator,** initiator, maker, creator, inventor, architect, prime mover
▶ *Religion 81; Production 522*

ADJECTIVES

16 **beginning,** starting, commencing, opening, first, primary, initial, initiatory, initiative, maiden, early, formative
▶ *Opening 583; Earliness 657*

17 **front,** frontal, leading, foremost, head

18 **prime,** primal, primordial, primeval, primitive, aboriginal, earliest, original, pristine
▶ *Earliness 657*

19 **embryonic,** budding, in the bud, nascent, germinal, inchoate, developing, fetal, pregnant, gestatory, parturient, dawning, emergent, new, fresh, raw, green; newborn, neonatal, baby, infant, unfledged, young
▶ *Reproduction 21; Youth 26; Newness 652*

20 **inventive,** innovative, creative, original, conceptional, conceptive

21 **inaugural,** inauguratory, incipient, inceptive, inchoative, inchoate, foundational, institutionary, establishing, instigatory, instigative

22 **rudimentary,** rudimental, basic, elementary, fundamental
▶ *Essence 723*

23 **introductory,** preliminary, preparatory, precursory, initiatory, baptismal, prefatory, proemial, preludial, prepositive, prefixed
▶ *Precedence 769*

24 **enrolled,** matriculated, installed, initiated, baptized, christened, wedded, premiered, inaugurated, presented, launched, opened, newly opened, unveiled

VERBS

25 **begin,** start, commence, open, originate, initiate, establish
▶ *Opening 583*

26 **make a beginning,** make a start, get started, debut, set to work, put one's hand to the plow, go at it, get going, embark on, set to *or* about, turn to, fall to, go ahead, tackle, broach, face, get off to a good start, blast off, dive in, take the plunge, plunge into, head into; kick off, get the show on the road, get the ball rolling; [Inf]: go to it, fire away, get one's feet wet, pitch in, get cracking
▶ *Work 122; Action 412; Activity 414*

27 **start off,** start out, set off *or* out, sally forth, make a move, get moving, get under way, set sail, take off, get on the road, hit the road [Inf]

> *Departure 705*

28 **activate,** start up, start going, turn on, switch on, set in motion, prompt, provoke, spark off, trigger off, apply the match, light the fuse, launch, get the ball rolling, kick-start, boot, boot up
> *Cause 675*

29 **pioneer,** explore, guide, pilot, lead, lead the way, set a precedent, head, spearhead, break new ground, open up, blaze a trail, trailblaze, take the first step, take the initiative, make the first move, break the ice
> *Precedence 769*

30 **invent,** discover, innovate, form, create, dream up, call into being, originate, generate, conceive, think of, coin, come up with, sow the seeds
> *Discovery 345; Production 522*

31 **inaugurate,** initiate, auspicate [Arch], establish, found, institute, set up, start up, install, induct, instigate, cause, commission, launch, float, present, be a founding member, be in at the beginning, be in on the ground floor [Inf]
> *Cause 675*

32 **open,** unveil, cut the ribbon, declare open, lay the foundation stone, lay the first stone, cut the first turf

33 **enroll,** matriculate, invest, crown, induct, ordain, install, institute, initiate, blood, baptize, christen, marry

34 **produce,** give birth, bear, mother, father, sire, engender, bring into being, bring into the world, pullulate, breed, teem, bud, germinate
> *Reproduction 21*

35 **emerge,** appear, arrive, originate, arise, issue, issue forth, burst forth, erupt, spring, spring up, crop up, sprout, be born, come into the world, come into being, come into existence, come to be, come forth, see the light of day, dawn, come out, make a debut
> *Appearance 264; Arrival 704; Exit 707*

36 **begin again,** recommence, make a fresh start, start afresh, start anew, turn over a new leaf, go back to square one, go back to the drawing board
> *Newness 652; Change 665*

ADVERBS

37 **first,** firstly, primarily, at first, first thing, in the first place, first of all, first and foremost, before everything, for a start, as a start, for a beginning, primordially, originally, initially, for a kickoff, for starters [Inf]

38 **from the beginning,** from the first, from the foundations, from its inception, from its birth, *ab ovo* [L], *ab initio* [L], *ab origine* [L], from scratch, from the word "go"

39 **in the bud,** in embryo, in infancy

772 Middle

You will be safest in the middle. — OVID

NOUNS

1 **middle,** center, midpoint, core, heart, nucleus, focus, focal point, keystone, linchpin, pivot, fulcrum, bull's-eye, kernel, marrow; inside, interior, midst, heartland, thick, thick of things, nub, heart of the matter
> *Interior 611; Center 612*

2 **midline,** equator, waist, waistline, midriff, diameter; midday, midnight

3 **middle way,** midway, middle course *or* midcourse, middle of the road, center lane, middle ground, midfield, midstream, halfway, halfway point, halfway house, moiety; median, mean, average, golden mean, medium, happy medium

4 **middle ground,** middle distance, equidistance; neutral ground, neutrality, impartiality, compromise; moderation, moderateness, balance, halfway measures; no-man's-land, gray area, mediation, arbitration
> *Mediation 75; Judgment 341; Compromise 461*

5 **middle age,** middle life, middle years, midlife crisis; Middle Ages
> *History 3; Age 27*

6 **middle class,** bourgeoisie, professional class, white-collar class, merchant class, upper middle class, lower middle class, middle management; suburbia, burgherdom, Babbittry
> *Management 126; Average 742*

7 **middleman,** broker, distributor, intermediary, third party, interventionist, intercessor, ombudsperson, negotiator, go-between, mediator, arbitrator, moderator, umpire, referee
> *Mediation 75; Trade 480*

8 **moderate person,** moderate, nonextremist, middle-of-the-roader, centrist, minimalist, neutral person, neutralist; uncommitted person, fence-sitter, agnostic, Laodicean, nonpartisan, mugwump
> *Moderation 521; Average 742; Uncertainty 841*

ADJECTIVES

9 **middle,** mid, central, center, medial, median, mesial, mean, mid- *or* middlemost, core, nuclear, focal, pivotal, inner, inside, interior, internal

10 **midway,** equidistant, midfield, midcourse, midstream; halfway, equatorial, diametral

11 **mediatory,** intermediary, intermediate; neutral, nonpartisan, nonaligned, impartial

12 **moderate,** unextreme, nonextreme, middle-of-the-road, balanced
> *Mediation 75*

13 **irresolute,** half-and-half, even, fifty-fifty, neither one thing nor the other, neither hot nor cold, noncommittal, uncommitted, unattached, fence-sitting, gray, indifferent, detached, lukewarm
> *Indifference 289*

14 **middling,** average, medium, mediocre, ordinary, undistinguished, fair, run-of-the-mill, so-so

▶ *Average 742*

15 **middle-aged,** midlife; middle-class, bourgeois

VERBS

16 **be in the middle,** keep to the middle, steer a middle course, keep to midstream

17 **stand in the middle,** straddle, lie betwixt and between, stand on middle ground, be in between, be *or* go *or* meet halfway, halfway, compromise, equalize, occupy the center (ground), balance, preserve a balance, equivocate, keep to a happy medium, keep the golden mean, show moderation; hedge one's bets, sit on the fence, fall between two stools, be neither one thing nor the other, be neither fish nor fowl, run with the hare and hunt with the hounds

▶ *Equivocation 380; Interface 616*

18 **place in the middle,** center, focus, pivot, center on, balance, interpose, sandwich, interpolate

19 **mediate,** arbitrate, intermediate, umpire, referee, intervene, intercede, come between, negotiate, bargain, compromise

20 **split down the middle,** cut in half, halve, divide fifty-fifty, split in two, split the difference, strike a balance

▶ *Average 742; Separation 753; Fraction 787; Two 789*

ADVERBS

21 **in the middle,** centrally, medially, in the midst of, amid, amidst, among, amongst [Brit], *in medias res* [L], in the thick of, between, in between, meanwhile

22 **midway,** halfway, midstream, amidships, bang in the middle, smack in the middle [Inf]; moderately, in moderation, neutrally, equally, intermediately, impartially

23 **irresolutely,** half-and-half, neither here nor there, betwixt and between, between the devil and the deep blue sea, between Scylla and Charybdis, between a rock and a hard place [Inf]

773 End

This is the way the world ends / Not with a bang but a whimper. — T. S. ELIOT

NOUNS

1 **end,** ending, cessation, conclusion, finish, close, finis, finale, completion, windup

▶ *Completeness 761*

2 **cessation,** ceasing, expiration, termination, stop, stoppage, halt, abrogation, cancellation, annulment, annihilation, expiry; death, demise, decease, passing, departure, exit, release, quietus, last gasp, last breath, last words, swan song, curtains [Inf]

▶ *Death 29; Cessation 668*

3 **conclusion,** end, finish, completion, termination

4 **annihilation,** destruction, extermination, extinction, elimination, dissolution, liquidation, ruin

▶ *Obliteration 186; Destruction 523*

5 **end of time,** fate, destiny, doom, doomsday, crack of doom, end of the world, eschatology, teleology, Last Judgment, Day of Judgment, apocalypse, twilight of the gods, Götterdämmerung

6 **end point,** terminus, terminal, end of the line, last stop, journey's end, destination

7 **limit,** boundary, frontier, border, rim, edge, fringe, verge, extent, extreme, extremity, pole, point, tip, peak, cusp, summit, zenith, top, last frontier, ends of the earth, where the rainbow ends

▶ *Summit 600; Edge 618; Limit 620*

8 **tail,** tail end, butt, butt end, fag end, bin end, bitter end, last penny, last cent, bottom dollar, dregs, lees, heeltap

▶ *Back 622*

9 **close,** closing stage, last stage, final stage, last lap, home stretch, last round, ninth inning, last ball; end of the day, evening, dusk, twilight, decline; end of the road, beginning of the end; deadline, time up, finality, closing time

▶ *Nighttime 656; Deterioration 808*

10 **ending,** finale, finish, climax, culmination, crowning glory, denouement, catastrophe, last act, final curtain; epilogue, envoy *or* envoi, coda, postscript *or* P.S. *or* p.s.; end matter, back matter, appendix, suffix, last word, last laugh, punch line, parting shot, Parthian shot

▶ *Sequence 770*

11 **ender,** stopper, finisher, clincher, settler, crusher, knockout, knockout blow, deathblow, mortal blow, finishing stroke, coup de grâce; period, full stop; last straw, the end [Inf]

12 **aim,** intent, intention, aspiration, goal, target, object, objective, purpose, reason, drift

▶ *Intention 374*

ADJECTIVES

13 **ending,** last, final, ultimate, terminal, concluding, conclusive, completing, completive, closing, finishing, stopping; definitive, culminating, culminative, consummative, consummatory, crowning, capping; apocalyptic, catastrophic, eschatological, teleological

14 **ended,** at an end, finished, complete, completed, finalized, terminated, concluded, decided, settled, done, done with, through, over, all over, done, over and done with; dead, dead and buried, wound up, washed-up [Inf], all over but the shouting, all up

▶ *Cessation 668; Completeness 761*

15 **canceled,** deleted, expunged, annulled; called off, scrapped, off, all off, played out

▶ *Cancellation 834*

16 **annihilated,** destroyed, exterminated, eliminated, dissolved, liquidated, ruined, defunct; doomed, fated, destined

▶ *Destruction 523*

17 limiting, bounding, frontier, bordering, fringing, farthest, extreme, polar

18 hindmost, rear, back, tail, end, endmost, last
▶ *Back 622*

VERBS

19 end, conclude, finish, close, complete, achieve, finalize, resolve, decide, settle, finish off, round off, culminate, consummate, crown, cap, wind up, wrap up, be done with; call it a day, call it quits, call off
▶ *Completeness 761*

20 cease, stop, halt, terminate, discontinue, put an end *or* a stop to, scotch, bring to an end, call a halt, close down, shut down, shut up shop, drop *or* ring down the curtain, make an end to, finish off, kill off, polish off, dispose of; abort, cancel, annul, abrogate, scrap, scratch; [Inf]: put the kibosh on, fold up, pull the plug on, put paid to [Brit]
▶ *Cessation 668; Discontinuity 775; Cancellation 834*

21 die, expire, pass away, pass on, give up the ghost, draw one's last breath; die out, become extinct, end
▶ *Death 29*

22 annihilate, extinguish, destroy, exterminate, eliminate, dissolve, liquidate, wipe out, kill; knock out, shoot down, KO *or* kayo [Inf], zap [Inf]
▶ *Killing 30; Obliteration 186; Destruction 523*

23 come to an end, draw to a close, go out, run out, run out of time, be over, be no more, fade out, fade away, peter out, tail off, die away, come to the end of the road, fizzle out [Inf]
▶ *Disappearance 265*

ADVERBS

24 finally, lastly, terminally, in conclusion, eventually, ultimately, at last, at long last, in the end, at the end of the day, when all is said and done, in the final analysis

25 to the end, to the bitter end, to the last gasp, for always, to the end of the road, till hell freezes over [Inf]

26 conclusively, definitively, once and for all, for good, for good and all, never again

774 Consecutiveness

NOUNS

1 consecutiveness, successiveness, succession, progression, lineup, procession; consecution, sequence, series, nexus, run, course, turn, one thing after another; order, ascending order, descending order, chronological order, catenation, concatenation; chain, train, file, line, queue, string, thread, ladder, stairs, staircase, steps; colonnade, scale, arpeggio, gamut, spectrum
▶ *Order 765; Sequence 770*

2 line, lineage, bloodline, descent, pedigree, dynasty, family tree, genealogy

▶ *Family 65; Relatedness 727; Precedence 769*

3 consequence, result, repercussion, effect, causality, cause and effect, domino theory, snowball effect, chain reaction, aftermath, backlash, reverberation, knock-on effect [Brit]
▶ *Counteraction 510; Cause 675; Effect 676*

4 continuity, continuousness, continualness, continuance, uninterruption, unbrokenness, uniformity, sameness, undifferentiation, monotony, endlessness, ceaselessness, incessancy, constancy, flow, routine, constant flow
▶ *Continuity, Continuation 669; Sameness 730*

5 continuum, continuous motion, cycle, circle, round, endless round, rotation, periodicity, recurrence, assembly line, conveyor belt, treadmill, vicious circle *or* cycle, endless band, Möbius *or* Moebius strip, Klein bottle
▶ *Circularity 631; Rotation 682; Repetition 797*

6 procession, parade, pageant, promenade, cortège, train, line, column, file, stream, steady stream, queue, crocodile [Brit]

ADJECTIVES

7 consecutive, successive, succeeding, following, serial, seriate, sequential, in order, running, ongoing, progressive, chronological, catenary, ordinal, linear, lineal
▶ *Order 765; Sequence 770*

8 repercussive, causal, resultant, consequential, reverberatory
▶ *Cause 675; Effect 676*

9 continuous, continual, constant, incessant, perpetual, nonstop, endless, unending, never-ending, ceaseless, unremitting, interminable, unrelieved, unbroken, solid, smooth, serried, seamless, uninterrupted, uniform, undifferentiated, featureless, monotonous
▶ *Continuity, Continuation 669; Sameness 730*

10 cyclical, periodic, rhythmic, recurrent, repetitive
▶ *Circularity 631; Repetition 797*

VERBS

11 be consecutive, succeed, come after, follow on, run on, progress
▶ *Sequence 770*

12 continue, be continuous, not stop, extend, run, go on and on, carry on, flow
▶ *Continuity, Continuation 669*

13 concatenate, catenate, connect, connect up, join, link, string, string together, thread, chain
▶ *Connection 754*

14 arrange, array, range, rank, line, align, string out; line up, get in line, fall in, form a line, queue, queue up, promenade
▶ *Order 765; Arrangement 767*

ADVERBS

15 consecutively, successively, in succession, serially, in a series, sequentially, in order, chronologically, progressively, one after another, one after the other, one behind the other, in turn, turn and turn about

16 **continuously,** continually, constantly, incessantly, perpetually, nonstop, without stopping, at one go, endlessly, ceaselessly; day in, day out; around the clock, night and day

17 **in a line,** in a row or queue, in file, in single file, in Indian file, bumper to bumper, nose to nose

775 Discontinuity

NOUNS

1 **discontinuity,** discontinuousness, discontinuation, discontinuance, lack of continuity, disconnectedness, disconnection, disjunction, disjointedness, irregularity, intermittence, brokenness, fitfulness, spasmodicalness, sporadicalness, disorder, incoherence, confusion, nonuniformity, unevenness, roughness, jerkiness, bumpiness, joltiness, choppiness
   ▸ *Irregularity 664; Diversity 732; Separation 753; Disorder 766*

2 **interval,** interim, intermission, lull, pause, pause for thought, time-out, break, rest, layover, stopover, letup [Inf]; time lag, time warp, jump in time
   ▸ *Interval 587*

3 **interruption,** break, suspension, gap, breach, fissure, cleft, crevasse, fault, split, crack, fracture, cut, wound
   ▸ *Interval 587; Disturbance 768*

4 **gap,** caesura, hiatus, lacuna, ellipsis, pause, rest, fermata

5 **intervention,** interruption, interjection, interpolation, disturbance, disruption
   ▸ *Disturbance 768*

6 **digression,** non sequitur, parenthesis, nonseriality, nonlinearity, missing link, lost connection

ADJECTIVES

7 **discontinuous,** noncontinuous, unsuccessive, disconnected, disjointed, disunited, discrete, fragmented, broken, unjoined, unconnected; irregular, intermittent, fitful, spasmodic, sporadic, erratic, random, desultory, episodic, stop-and-go; on-again, off-again; incoherent, confused, nonuniform, uneven, rough, choppy, snatchy, jerky, bumpy, jolty, scrappy, patchy, spotty, dotted
   ▸ *Unintelligibility 364; Irregularity 664; Diversity 732; Separation 753*

8 **discontinued,** ended, ceased, stopped, halted, terminated, finished, nonrecurrent, unrepeated
   ▸ *End 773*

9 **interrupted,** disturbed, disrupted, broken off, suspended; digressive, parenthetic, nonserial, nonlinear, nonsequential

VERBS

10 **discontinue,** end, put an end to, cease, stop, halt, terminate, finish, quit, give up, suspend, break off, cut off, cut short, leave off, refrain from, drop
   ▸ *Cessation 668; Completeness 761; End 773*

11 **pause,** pause for thought, take time-out, take a break or vacation or holiday or sabbatical, rest, lay over, stop over, let up, take five or ten [Inf]

12 **disconnect,** break the connection, break off, disjoin, disunite, separate, sever, cut

13 **digress,** lose one's train of thought, stray from the subject, ramble, go off at a tangent, wander, go off the point

14 **interrupt,** disturb, disrupt, intervene, interject, interpolate, interpose, put between, interfere, chip in, chime in, interfere, butt in, cut in, barge in on, put in one's oar
   ▸ *Disturbance 768*

ADVERBS

15 **discontinuously,** periodically, at intervals, intermittently, fitfully, spasmodically, sporadically, irregularly, occasionally, infrequently, once in a while, now and then, off and on, by fits, by fits and starts, by degrees, here and there, *passim* [L], in spots, in dribs and drabs

16 **disconnectedly,** disjointedly, brokenly, desultorily

776 Dispersion

NOUNS

1 **dispersion,** dispersal, diffusion, circumfusion, distribution, dissemination; sowing, strewing, casting, seeding, scattering; circulation, publication, broadcast, broadcasting, spread; deployment, propagation, issuance, giving out, dispensation; decentralization, deconcentration
   ▸ *Publication 173; Allocation 474*

2 **disbandment,** dissolution, demobilization, deactivation, dismissal; migration, emigration, flight, diaspora, dispersed population, population drift; sprawl, urban sprawl

3 **dilution,** watering, watering down, thinning, thinning out, attenuation, liquefaction, deliquescence; evaporation, boiling away, vaporization, volatilization, dissipation, disappearance
   ▸ *Disappearance 265*

4 **sprinkling,** spraying, spattering, splattering, smattering, dusting, powdering, peppering; studding, spotting, dotting, speckling, freckling

5 **divergence,** radiation, branching, branching out, ramification, fanning out, splaying; deflection, diffraction, decomposition, disintegration, fragmentation, pulverizing, shattering, break-up; separation, parting, split-up
   ▸ *Divergence 703; Separation 753; Disintegration 758*

ADJECTIVES

6 **dispersed,** scattered, diffuse, widespread, sparse, infrequent, sporadic, dotted about, few and far between; distributed, disseminated, diffused, broadcast, spread;

deployed, propagated, circulated, published, issued, given out, dispensed; decentralized, deconcentrated

◗ *Publication 173; Allocation 474; Infrequency 662; Few 796*

7 disbanded, dissolved, unassembled, dismissed, demobilized, deactivated; separated, separate, discrete, disintegrated, fragmented, decomposed, broken-up, split-up

◗ *Separation 753; Disintegration 758*

8 diluted, dilute, watered-down, liquefied; evaporated, boiled away, vaporized, dissipated

9 sprinkled, sprayed, spattered, splattered, dusted, powdered, peppered; studded, spotted, dotted, speckled, freckled; sown, seeded, strewn, scattered

10 dispersive, scattering, spreading, diffractive, diffusive, distributive, disseminative, dissipative

11 divergent, forking, radiating, branching, ramiform, dendriform, dendritic, centrifugal; sprawled, sprawling, straggling, straggly, drifting, adrift, astray, wandering, stray, loose, all over the lot

VERBS

12 disperse, scatter, diffract, diffuse, dispel, separate, part, divide, sunder, detach, hive off [Brit]; distribute, disseminate, circulate, put into circulation, publish, broadcast, spread; deploy, propagate, issue, dispense, deal, deal out, dole out; decentralize, deconcentrate

◗ *Publication 173; Allocation 474; Separation 753*

13 disband, dismiss, send away, send off, dissolve, demobilize, demob [Inf], deactivate, discharge, send home, muster out, rout, put to flight; take flight, migrate, spread out, sprawl, stray, straggle; separate, part, break up, split up, part company, go one's separate ways, move apart, drift apart, drift off; bug out [Inf]

◗ *Departure 705; Separation 753*

14 dilute, water down, dissolve, thin, thin out, attenuate, liquefy; evaporate, boil away, vaporize, volatilize, dissipate, disappear, vanish

◗ *Disappearance 265*

15 sprinkle, spray, splash, shower, spatter, splatter, dust, powder, flour, dredge, pepper; stud, spot, dot, speckle, speck, freckle; sow, seed, strew, scatter, scatter around, scatter to the winds, throw around, cast, fling, litter

16 diverge, fork, branch out *or* off, ramify, radiate, fan out, splay; explode, burst, fly apart, fly in all directions, come apart, come unstuck, break up, split up, disintegrate, fragment, decompose

◗ *Disintegration 758*

ADVERBS

17 dispersively, diffractively, diffusively, distributively, disseminatively, dissipatively

18 diffusely, sparsely, infrequently, sporadically, here and there, in places

19 everywhere, all over, in all quarters, wherever you look *or* turn, in all directions, to the four winds, to the four corners of the earth

777 Class

The history of all hitherto existing society is the history of class struggles. — KARL MARX AND FRIEDRICH ENGELS

NOUNS

1 class, subclass, category, subcategory, division, subdivision; bracket, set, subset, slot, pigeonhole, compartment, pocket, section, subsection, group, subgroup, grouping; head, heading, subheading, list, listing, order, branch, department

◗ *Assembly 59; Container 578; Part 760; Order 765; List 785*

2 classification, categorization, grouping, ranking, grading, ordering, hierarchy, taxonomy; classifying, classing, categorizing, compartmentalizing, sectioning, sorting, listing, pigeonholing

◗ *Order 765; Sequence 770*

3 taxonomic classification, kingdom, subkingdom, phylum, subphylum, branch, subbranch, superclass, class, subclass, order, suborder, superfamily, family, subfamily, tribe, subtribe, genus, subgenus, species, subspecies; variety, subvariety, scion

◗ *Life Science 13; Animals (General) 34; Plants (General) 41; Family 65*

4 type, sort, kind, genre, form, variety, version, style, ilk, strain; league, realm, domain, sphere; brand, make, mark, model, marque, label; shape, cast, mold, frame; stripe, feather, line, grain, kidney, stamp, color, complexion, hue, character, nature, manner, persuasion, the like *or* likes of

◗ *Form 624; Similarity 733*

5 social class, social status, standing, station, position; grade, rating, pecking *or* peck order, rank, tier, level, stratum; band, league, order, sphere, caste, group, set, clique, coterie; lower class, middle class, upper class, working class, leisure class

◗ *Sociology 2; Assembly 59*

6 students, class, pupils, grade, year, form [Brit]; track, subject-group, stream, discussion group

7 lecture, class, seminar, lesson, presentation, discussion

◗ *Education 48*

8 distinction, prestige, merit, excellence, presence, bearing, breeding, style, chic

◗ *Refinement 534*

ADJECTIVES

9 classificatory, classificational, categorical, hierarchical, taxonomic, indexical, tabular

10 typical, characteristic, representative, generic, stereotypical, special, specific, particular, peculiar, distinctive, defining, definitive

◗ *Specialty 779*

11 classed, classified, categorized, grouped, ranked,

graded, rated, indexed, sorted, ordered, placed, pigeonholed, filed

VERBS

12 **class,** classify, categorize, group, type, place, pigeonhole, catalog, designate, fix, assign, dispose, distribute, label, brand
  ▶ *Identification 184*

13 **sort,** organize, assort, arrange, range, order, grade, rank, rate, divide, subdivide, analyze, tabulate, index, codify
  ▶ *Separation 753; Order 765; Arrangement 767*

14 **be in a class of one's own,** stand out, shine, be head and shoulders above the rest
  ▶ *Superiority 744*

ADVERBS

15 **taxonomically,** hierarchically, categorically, characteristically, typically, generically, specifically, distinctively, definitively

778 Generality

All generalizations are dangerous, even this one.
— ALEXANDRE DUMAS THE YOUNGER

NOUNS

1 **generality,** universality, cosmicality, general applicability, comprehensiveness, inclusiveness, eclecticism; internationalism, globality, globalism, cosmopolitanism; catholicity, catholicism, ecumenicalism, ecumenicism, ecumenicity
  ▶ *Inclusion 763*

2 **nonspecificness,** broadness, looseness, sweepingness, imprecision, inexactitude; broad canvas, broad spectrum, blanket coverage, dragnet, catchall
  ▶ *Error 351; Breadth 592*

3 **widespreadness,** sweepingness, extensiveness, rifeness, rampantness, pervasiveness, ubiquity, omnipresence
  ▶ *Presence 575*

4 **average,** run-of-the-mill, general run, ordinary run, common run, ruck, lowest common denominator; ordinariness, standardness; general rule, commonality, routine, normality, normalness, habitualness
  ▶ *Habit, Custom 397; Average 742; Conformity 781*

5 **generalization,** general idea, abstract, abstraction, sweeping *or* loose *or* vague generalization *or* statement; cliché, platitude, trite *or* hackneyed expression; generalizing, labeling, stereotyping
  ▶ *Maxim 177*

6 **general public,** populace, common people, grass roots, rank and file; masses, multitude, hoi polloi, vox populi, rabble
  ▶ *Assembly 59; Commoner 71; Multitude 795*

7 **everyone,** everybody, one and all, all hands; all and sundry, each and every one; everywoman, everyman,

common man *or* woman, common type, Mr. *or* Mrs. Average, man *or* woman in the street, John Doe, Jane Doe, John Q. Public; girl *or* boy next door, little man; every mother's son, every man Jack; every Tom, Dick, and Harry; all the world and his wife *or* brother, the whole world, *tout le monde* [Fr], everybody under the sun; whoever, whosoever, whomever, whomsoever, no matter who, anyone, anybody; [Inf]: ordinary Joe, Joe Six-Pack, Joe Blow, Joe Doakes
  ▶ *Humankind 18; Whole 759*

8 **whatever,** whatsoever, what, which, whichever, any, anything; what have you, what you will, no matter what *or* which

ADJECTIVES

9 **general,** universal, whole, comprehensive, inclusive, encyclopedic, extensive; all-inclusive, nonexclusive, all-embracing, all-encompassing, all-covering, all-comprehending, all-pervading; overall, synoptic, heterogenous, diversified, miscellaneous; liberal, catholic, ecumenical, eclectic, cosmopolitan, broad-based; blanket, extensive, wide, broad, sweeping, across-the-board, panoramic, bird's-eye
  ▶ *Breadth 592; Mixture 751; Whole 759; Inclusion 763*

10 **universal,** cosmic, galactic, planetary, worldwide, global, international, cosmopolitan, national, nationwide, countrywide; widespread, extensive, rife, rampant, pervasive, ubiquitous, omnipresent, endemic, epidemic, pandemic; sweeping, far-reaching, wide-reaching, far-ranging, wide-ranging, far-flung
  ▶ *Presence 575; Distance 585*

11 **prevailing,** prevalent, widespread, common, popular, accepted, ruling, predominant, dominant, predominating; public, communal, community, unrestricted

12 **generalized,** nonspecific, unspecific, generic; approximate, inexact, imprecise, indefinite, indeterminate, undetermined, unspecified, ill-defined; broad, loose, vague, sweeping, abstract, nebulous
  ▶ *Error 351; Breadth 592*

13 **common,** regular, standard, normal, usual, ordinary, average, unexceptional, run-of-the-mill; customary, habitual, routine, everyday, quotidian, familiar, accustomed; commonplace, trite, platitudinous, hackneyed, uninspired, unimaginative; jaded, overused, overworked, stereotyped, stereotypical, common or garden
  ▶ *Commoner 71; Maxim 177; Habit, Custom 397; Average 742; Conformity 781*

VERBS

14 **generalize,** universalize, globalize, internationalize

15 **broaden,** widen, spread, expand, extend
  ▶ *Expansion 581; Breadth 592*

16 **broadcast,** diffuse, disperse, disseminate, sow
  ▶ *Dispersion 776*

17 **popularize,** vulgarize, take to the masses

18 **make a generalization,** make a sweeping statement,

generalize, deal in generalities, paint with a broad brush; label, stereotype

19 **prevail,** predominate, dominate, obtain, reign, rule, be the rule, have currency, be the rage
> *Authority 52; Power 514*

ADVERBS

20 **generally,** in general, generally speaking, broadly, broadly speaking, loosely, approximately

21 **usually,** as a rule, almost always, normally, ordinarily, typically, invariably, routinely, habitually, as a matter of course, in the usual course, without exception
> *Habit, Custom 397*

22 **overall,** on balance, on average, all things considered, all in all, on the whole, as a whole, in the long run, for the most part, in the main, mainly, mostly, largely, wholly
> *Whole 759; Part 760*

23 **universally,** cosmically, globally, internationally, nationally, widely, extensively, ecumenically, commonly, predominantly, invariably, everywhere, the world over

779 Specialty

NOUNS

1 **specialty,** specialness, specific quality, specificity, particularity; individuality, originality, uniqueness, distinctiveness; differentness, differentiation; speciality [Brit]
> *Identification 184; Dissimilarity 734; Originality 737; One 788*

2 **special skill,** specialty, expertise, métier, forte, strong point, genius, gift, talent, aptitude, skill
> *Skillfulness 127*

3 **specialization,** particularization, special study, concentration, special interest, pursuit, line, field, area, sphere; school subject, major; vocation, trade, craft
> *Work 122*

4 **special feature,** distinctive feature, singularity, attribute, quality; hallmark, trademark, stamp, seal, badge, brand, cachet; claim to fame

5 **characteristic,** property, nature, trait, quirk, mannerism, peculiarity, idiosyncrasy, eccentricity, trick; mark, earmark, token, mold, cut, shape, figure, configuration; taste, flavor, savor, smell, odor, aroma, touch, feel
> *Taste 219; Odor 224; Form 624; Essence 723*

6 **specifications,** conditions, qualifications, particulars, details, crux, minutiae, essentials, essential facts, fundamentals; basics, fine print, nuts and bolts, ins and outs; specs [Inf], nitty-gritty [Inf]
> *Qualification 340*

7 **special case,** isolated instance, exception, exception to the rule, exemption; anomaly, irregularity, peculiarity, departure

> *Irregularity 664; Nonconformity 782*

8 **the special,** the specific, the particular, the individual, the unique; specialty of the house, *spécialité de la maison* [Fr], chef's special, dish of the day, soup du jour, feature, main feature, leader, leading item

9 **specialist,** authority, consultant, expert, master, connoisseur, maven, professional, scholar, savant
> *Skillfulness 127; Knowledge 348*

ADJECTIVES

10 **special,** especial, specific, particular, express, precise, individual, respective, individualistic, original, unique, quintessential, intrinsic, single, singular, distinct, distinctive, different
> *Clarity 196; Accuracy 350; Essence 723; Dissimilarity 734; Originality 737; One 788*

11 **specialized,** technical, specialist, expert, authoritative, knowledgeable, professional, scholarly
> *Skillfulness 127; Knowledge 348*

12 **characteristic,** distinguishing, personal; peculiar, idiosyncratic, idiomatic, unusual, out of the ordinary, extraordinary; uncommon, curious, marked, quirky, eccentric; typical, in character, true to form
> *Identification 184; Nonconformity 782*

13 **exceptional,** special, one of a kind, unique, *sui generis* [L], inimitable; distinguished, remarkable, notable, noteworthy; esoteric, exotic, way-out [Inf]

14 **customized,** individualized, personalized, custom-built, made to measure, bespoke [Brit]

VERBS

15 **characterize,** distinguish, differentiate, identify, brand, label, mark, earmark, set apart; make special, customize, personalize, individualize, make one's own, put one's mark upon
> *Identification 184; Emphasis 200; Selection 382; Dissimilarity 734*

16 **specialize,** specialize in, pursue, follow, study, major in; excel, stand out, shine, be in a class of one's own
> *Superiority 744*

17 **particularize,** descend to particulars, give details of, treat in detail, go into detail, spell out; come to the point, get down to brass tacks [Inf], get down to the nitty-gritty [Inf]

18 **specify,** stipulate, designate, determine, fix, set, assign; pin down, define, describe, delineate, depict, enumerate, quantify, itemize, list, denominate, name, signify; name names, point to *or* out, mention, cite, quote
> *Description 202; List 785*

ADVERBS

19 **specially,** especially, expressly, exactly, precisely, distinctly, in particular, to be specific

20 **characteristically,** peculiarly, uniquely, singularly, distinctively, markedly, exceptionally, remarkably, like no other, in its own way

21 **particularly,** namely, i.e., that is to say, *videlicet* [L], viz., to wit, for example, e.g., *scilicet* [L]

---

22 specifically, each, apiece, respectively, singly, one by one, in turn, in detail, bit by bit

780 Rule

The exception proves the rule. — SAYING

The golden rule is that there are no golden rules.
  — GEORGE BERNARD SHAW

NOUNS

1 **rule,** regulation, law, bylaw, statute, ordinance; directive, injunction, precept, order, prescription, standing order; edict, ukase, fiat, commandment, act, enactment, covenant
  ▶ *Law 53; Command 425*

2 **ruling,** decision, judgment, decree, opinion, judicial opinion; adjudication, finding, verdict, award, call, penalty, sentence; determination, resolution, outcome, upshot, result

3 **code,** canon, rulebook, statute book, constitution, charter; rubric, doctrine, dogma, belief; moral law, code of conduct, personal code *or* standards
  ▶ *Law 53; Morality 431*

4 **guide,** guideline, direction, instruction; principle, tenet, keynote, axiom, maxim; norm, standard, criterion, precedent, forerunner, example, model, pattern; firm principle *or* condition
  ▶ *Maxim 177; Conformity 781*

5 **custom,** habit, convention, tradition, wont, way, rut, groove; practice, procedure, routine, drill, policy, form; uniformity, constancy, consistency, regularity; usual occurrence, customary practice, matter of course, the thing, way of things, order of things, way things are
  ▶ *Habit, Custom 397; Regularity 663; Way 691; Conformity 781*

6 **authority,** dominion, reign, sovereignty, government, administration, regulation; command, direction, management, influence; control, sway, domination, power, supremacy, mastery
  ▶ *Authority 52; Management 126; Influence 512; Power 514*

7 **formula,** formulary, recipe, method, way, praxis, system; theorem, proposition, corollary; mathematical law, scientific law, law of physics, law of nature; natural *or* universal law; law of the jungle, law of averages; rule of thumb, Murphy's law, Parkinson's law
  ▶ *Mathematics 6; Physics 10*

ADJECTIVES

8 **legal,** statutory, mandatory, compulsory, obligatory, de rigueur, hard-and-fast; regulatory, injunctive, prescriptive, procedural, administrative, official
  ▶ *Law 53*

9 **customary,** habitual, accustomed, wonted; conven-
tional, traditional, regulation, standard, routine, usual, normal, typical, copybook
  ▶ *Habit, Custom 397*

10 **uniform,** constant, consistent, regular, harmonious; regulated, methodical, systematic, orderly
  ▶ *Regularity 663*

11 **ruling,** authoritative, commanding, reigning, sovereign; influential, controlling, powerful, dominant, supreme, masterful

VERBS

12 **rule,** ordain, prescribe, lay down, lay down the law; make a ruling, decide, determine, adjudicate, judge, deem, find, resolve, settle; hand down a judgment, pronounce, declare, decree, establish, rule out, rule against
  ▶ *Judgment 341*

13 **rule over,** govern, reign, hold sway over, dominate, command; be in power, wear the crown, sit on the throne, wield the scepter, rule the roost
  ▶ *Influence 512; Power 514*

14 **direct,** guide, steer, control, regulate, lead, administer, manage, run, preside over, superintend, supervise, oversee
  ▶ *Authority 52; Management 126*

15 **regulate,** standardize, normalize, systematize, organize, order, bring into line
  ▶ *Order 765; Arrangement 767*

16 **be the rule,** hold sway, prevail, predominate

17 **follow the rules,** obey orders, follow the party line, go by the book, stick to the rules; watch one's step, stay *or* keep on the straight and narrow, mind one's p's and q's, toe the line *or* mark, keep one's nose clean
  ▶ *Obedience 426*

ADVERBS

18 **as a rule,** usually, generally, ordinarily, normally, commonly; habitually, customarily, as is one's wont; on the whole, for the most part, mostly, more often than not, mainly, in the main, chiefly, commonly

781 Conformity

When you are in Rome, live in the Roman style; when you are elsewhere, live as they live elsewhere.
  — SAINT AMBROSE

NOUNS

1 **conformity,** conformance, conformation, accord, accordance, agreement, harmony, compatibility; consistency, uniformity, congruity, correspondence, concurrence; similarity, likeness, imitation, emulation, parrotry
  ▶ *Agreement 462; Similarity 733; Accord 735; Imitation 736*

2 **compliance,** obedience, observance, respect, abidance, acquiescence, submission, subordination

⟩ *Submission 421; Obedience 426*

3 **pliancy,** flexibility, malleability, plasticity, softness; adaptability, adaption, adaptation, accommodation, adjustment, assimilation, naturalization, acclimatization; reconciliation, reconcilement
   ⟩ *Softness 543; Conversion 670*

4 **conventionalism,** conservatism, conformism, orthodoxy, traditionalism, Babbittry, bourgeois ethic; etiquette, formality, formalism, strictness, severity, primness, prudery
   ⟩ *Formality 406; Severity 424*

5 **convention,** practice, form, the thing, order of the day, received idea, party line, policy; rule, tradition, custom, fashion, trend, vogue, style
   ⟩ *Habit, Custom 397; Rule 780*

6 **conformist,** conformer, sheep, traditionalist, conventionalist, formalist, pedant, precisian, prude, stick-in-the-mud, old fogey; bourgeois, burgher, Babbitt, Philistine, Mrs. Grundy, Middle American; company man, organization man, follower, loyalist; timeserver, lackey, yes-man; parrot, copycat, imitator, clone; square [Inf]
   ⟩ *Religion 81; Servility 401; Duty 433; Flattery 439; Imitation 736*

ADJECTIVES

7 **conformable,** adaptable, adaptive, adjustable; flexible, pliant, malleable, soft, plastic

8 **conforming,** accordant, concordant, harmonious, compatible; consistent, consonant, congruous, congruent, corresponding; agreeing, in agreement, in accord, in keeping, in line, in step
   ⟩ *Agreement 462; Accord 735*

9 **compliant,** willing, obedient, acquiescent, submissive, yielding, tractable, complaisant, accommodating, agreeable; passive, sheeplike, lemminglike, unmurmuring
   ⟩ *Submission 421; Obedience 426*

10 **conformist,** orthodox, kosher, conservative, law-abiding, conventional, traditional, traditionalist, traditionalistic; bourgeois, provincial, correct, proper, pedantic, formal; old-fashioned, staid, strait-laced, prim, prudish, stuffy, stodgy, square [Inf]
   ⟩ *Habit, Custom 397*

VERBS

11 **conform,** conform to, accord, concur, comply, adapt, adapt to, adjust, accommodate to; fit in, fall in with, go along with, play the game; submit, yield, acquiesce, accede, consent, agree; correspond, match, tally, square with, harmonize, suit, fit, meet, run true to form
   ⟩ *Agreement 462; Accord 735*

12 **abide by,** go by, follow, observe, respect, obey, obey regulations, stick to the rules; toe the line *or* mark, stay in line, keep in step, follow suit; go with the flow, swim *or* go with the stream *or* tide *or* current, run with the pack *or* herd, follow the beaten path; imitate, em-

ulate, copy, do as others do, do as the Romans do, follow the fashion, follow the trend, keep up with the Joneses, jump on the bandwagon, go with the flow [Inf]
   ⟩ *Submission 421; Obedience 426; Imitation 736*

13 **make conform,** accommodate, adjust, straighten, align, fit, fit in, trim; shape, form, mold, press, standardize, stereotype; rectify, correct, discipline; bring into line, cut *or* trim down to size, lick into shape [Inf]

14 **assimilate,** naturalize, acclimatize, rehabilitate, reeducate; imbue, instill, implant, drill, school, teach, train, coach, instruct; indoctrinate, brainwash

ADVERBS

15 **adaptably,** conformably, pliantly, malleably, flexibly; willingly, yieldingly, complaisantly, submissively, compliantly, obediently, passively

16 **conformingly,** harmoniously, compatibly, consistently, congruously, in harmony, in accord, in keeping, in line, in place, in accordance

17 **as usual,** as a matter of course, of course, as always, as before

18 **according to rule,** by the book, conventionally, traditionally, by the numbers

782 Nonconformity

NOUNS

1 **nonconformity,** unconformity, nonconformance, nonconformism, disaccord; incompatibility, disparity, contrast, difference, diversity; inconsistency, incongruity
   ⟩ *Disagreement 463; Diversity 732; Dissimilarity 734*

2 **dissent,** nonconcurrence, disagreement, dissidence, noncompliance, nonobservance; infringement, infraction, disobedience, recalcitrance, contrariety; contumely, protest, recusancy, revolt, rebellion, breaking away
   ⟩ *Dissent 347; Disobedience 427; Disagreement 463; Protest 507*

3 **nonconformism,** unorthodoxy, heterodoxy, heresy, iconoclasm, schism, revisionism, deviationism; unconventionality, unconventional behavior, eccentricity, bohemianism

4 **unusualness,** uncommonness, rareness, rarity, exceptionality, extraordinariness, uniqueness, individuality, singularity, originality; oddity, queerness, curiosity, peculiarity, strangeness, bizarreness, outlandishness, weirdness, freakishness, quirkiness

5 **idiosyncrasy,** quirk, peculiar trait, peculiarity, mannerism, kink

6 **deviation,** deviance, aberration, vagary, abnormality, anomaly, anomalousness, variant, exception, special case
   ⟩ *Diversity 732*

7 **nonconformist,** nonconformer, maverick, uncon-

ventionalist, *enfant terrible* [Fr]; bohemian, free spirit, dropout, hippie, beatnik, flower child, New-Age Traveler, independent, freethinker

◗ *Freedom 829*

8 **dissenter,** dissentient, dissident, protester, recusant; radical, revolutionary, zealot, fanatic, iconoclast, schismatic, apostate, heretic, rebel, anarchist; renegade, young Turk, angry young man, outlaw

◗ *Anarchy 51; Dissent 347; Disagreement 463*

9 **hermit,** loner, lone wolf [Inf]; solitudinarian, solitaire, eremite, anchorite, marabout, ascetic; recluse, isolationist, seclusionist

◗ *Unsociability 409*

10 **eccentric,** character, natural, original, oddity, odd fellow, odd customer, queer specimen, freak, deviant, rum one *or* customer [Brit]; [Inf]: odd stick, wacko, weirdo, crackpot, oddball, screwball, card, case, nut, fruitcake

ADJECTIVES

11 **nonconforming,** unconformable, inconsistent, incongruous, incompatible, contrasting, different

◗ *Extraneousness 724*

12 **dissident,** dissentient, nonconcurring, disagreeing, dissenting, noncompliant, uncompliant, nonobserving; contumacious, recusant, radical, revolutionary, rebellious, anarchic, renegade, unsubmissive, recalcitrant, contrary, defiant

◗ *Disagreement 463*

13 **nonconformist,** unorthodox, heterodox, heretical, iconoclastic, schismatic, schismatical, revisionist; unconventional, eccentric, bohemian

14 **unconventional,** maverick, independent; irregular, nonstandard, not done, out of place; against the rules, out of line, out of step, out of tune, out of one's element, misplaced, displaced, stray; freethinking, bohemian, fringe, beat, hippie, off the wall [Inf]

15 **unusual,** uncommon, rare, rarefied, exceptional, extraordinary, out of the ordinary, unique, individual, individualistic, singular, original; odd, queer, curious, peculiar, strange, bizarre, outlandish, weird, freakish, quirky, idiosyncratic

16 **eccentric,** offbeat, exotic, unique, exceptional, out of this world; odd, queer, curious, peculiar, strange, bizarre, outlandish, weird, freakish, rum [Brit]; [Inf]: far-out, way-out, oddball, kooky, funny

17 **solitary,** standoffish, unsociable, antisocial, lone, reclusive, isolated, aloof

VERBS

18 **not conform,** dissent, protest, rebel, revolt, kick over the traces, get out of line, rock the boat, make waves [Inf]

◗ *Dissent 347; Protest 507*

19 **break the law,** infringe the law, commit a crime, violate, disobey, break the rules, transgress

◗ *Disobedience 427; Immorality 432*

20 **be independent,** break away, break step, break bounds, drop out, opt out, go one's own way, go against the grain, swim against the tide, buck the trend, march to a different drummer; go off the beaten track, deviate, break with custom, break the mold; not fit in with, do one's own thing [Inf], stick out like a sore thumb [Inf]

ADVERBS

21 **unconformably,** inconsistently, incongruously, rebelliously, unconventionally, unusually, uncommonly, singularly, unnaturally, abnormally, oddly, queerly, peculiarly, strangely, outlandishly

22 **out of step,** out of keeping, out of line, out on a limb, independently, off the beaten track, out of the way

783 Number

Round numbers are always false. — SAMUEL JOHNSON

NOUNS

1 **number,** numeral, no. *or* n., figure, digit, cipher, character, decimal, symbol, sign, constant, variable, notation; Arabic numeral, Roman numeral; decimal system, binary system

2 **kind of number,** whole number, integer, odd number, even number, prime number, complex number, imaginary number, real number, rational number, irrational number, transcendental number, algebraic number, cardinal number, ordinal number

3 **large number,** astronomical number, googol, googolplex, infinity; [Inf]: scads, oodles, umpteen, zillion, jillion

◗ *Five and Over 792; Multitude 795; Infinity 798*

4 **mathematical result,** sum, summation, total, running total, score, reckoning, tally, bill, aggregate, whole, amount, quantity; difference, remainder, residual, product, factor

◗ *Remainder 750; Whole 759; Calculation 784*

5 **ratio,** proportion, percentage, percent, fraction; numerator, denominator, decimal fraction, decimal

◗ *Part 760; Fraction 787*

6 **power,** exponent, index, root, square root, cube root, surd, logarithm, common logarithm, log, natural logarithm, mantissa, antilogarithm, antilog

◗ *Mathematics 6*

ADJECTIVES

7 **numerical,** numeric, numerary, numerative, numerate, digital, figurate, figural; odd, *impair* [Fr], even, pair, cardinal, ordinal, imaginary, real, rational, irrational, arithmetical, geometric, algorithmic, round, whole, prime, positive, negative

8 **fractional,** decimal, exponential, logarithmic, logometric, differential, integral, surd, radical, finite, infinite, aliquot

9 number, enumerate, count, tell, tally, reckon, notch up, tot up, add, figure, tick off; [Inf]: tote up, figure out, dope out

10 total, come to, make, equal, amount to, sum
 ▶ *Calculation 784*

ADVERBS

11 numerically, in numerical order, arithmetically, geometrically, digitally

784 Calculation

NOUNS

1 calculation, computation, numeration, enumeration, reckoning, figuring, determining, estimation, assessment; figure work, number work, sums, addition, subtraction, multiplication, division; algebra, geometry, trigonometry, calculus, differentiation, integration, analysis, extraction of roots, reduction, inversion, involution, evolution, convolution, approximation, interpolation, extrapolation, permutation, transformation, equation, algorithm, logarithm, rhabdology
 ▶ *Mathematics 6; Judgment 341; Measurement 589; Addition 748; Subtraction 749; Number 783*

2 statistics, figures, vital statistics, indexes *or* indices, tables, averages

3 count, tally, census, poll, opinion poll, head count, inventory, stocktaking, numbering, counting; accounting, telling, tallying, calculating, ciphering, reckoning, adding, totaling
 ▶ *Accounting 493*

4 computing, computation, data processing (DP), electronic data processing (EDP), computer technology, information technology (IT), information processing, information retrieval, number-crunching [Inf]
 ▶ *Computers 15*

5 calculator, computer, pocket calculator, adding machine, abacus; cash register, till, ready reckoner; table, multiplication table, log table, rule, ruler, slide rule, Napier's bones, tabulator; tape measure, yardstick, gauge, dividers, compass, totalizer, number-cruncher [Inf]
 ▶ *Measurement 589*

6 counter, teller, accountant, bookkeeper, enumerator, census-taker, pollster, reckoner, estimator, abacist; statistician, actuary, computer operator, computer programmer, systems analyst, mathematician
 ▶ *Mathematics 6; Computers 15*

ADJECTIVES

7 calculative, computative, numerative, enumerative, estimative, estimating; calculating, accounting, census-taking, reckoning; computing, computational, numerical, quantifying, statistical, actuarial

8 calculable, computable, reckonable, estimable, countable, numerable, numberable, measurable, mensurable, quantifiable

9 mathematical, arithmetical, algebraic(al), geometric, logarithmic, algorithmic, trigonometrical, differential, integral, analytical

VERBS

10 calculate, compute, work out, solve, cipher, reckon, figure, determine, estimate; [Inf]: guesstimate, figure out, dope out
 ▶ *Number 783*

11 add, add up, sum, sum up, tot up, total; subtract, take away, deduct; multiply, divide, square, cube, extract roots, integrate, differentiate, extrapolate, interpolate

12 total, aggregate, amount to, come to, make, equal

13 number, numerate, enumerate, count, count up, tell, tally, keep a tally, poll, count heads, count hands, count noses, call the roll; score, keep the score, keep count, take stock, inventory, list, quantify, measure, gauge
 ▶ *Measurement 589; List 785*

14 check, verify, audit, balance, balance the books, account, keep accounts
 ▶ *Accounting 493*

ADVERBS

15 mathematically, arithmetically, algebraically, geometrically, trigonometrically, numerically, calculably, computably, estimably, measurably, quantifiably, logarithmically, exponentially

785 List

NOUNS

1 list, listing, enumeration, series, items, itemization, inventory, tally, compendium, stock, repertory, register, registry, table, chart, checklist; reference list, bibliography, book list, reading list, college catalog, course listing, syllabus; filmography, discography, publisher's catalog *or* list, computer listing, menu, window, database, spreadsheet; shopping list, wish list, laundry list [Inf]
 ▶ *Computers 15; Record 185*

2 table, table of contents, contents, index, card index, file, filing system, catalog
 ▶ *Order 765; Arrangement 767*

3 book of lists, dictionary, lexicon, glossary, word list, thesaurus, gazetteer, atlas, encyclopedia, almanac, yearbook, reference book, directory, guidebook, who's who, telephone directory, phone book, white pages, Yellow Pages, address book
 ▶ *Linguistics, Language 5; Books 174*

4 bill, invoice, account, itemized account, statement, ledger, books, account book, daybook, journal, bill of lading, manifest, docket; price list

5 bill of fare, menu, *carte* [Fr], wine list

> *Eating 92; Accounting 493; Price 494*

6 list of dates *or* **events,** diary, engagement diary, engagement book, datebook, day book, calendar; agenda, order of business, docket, program, timetable, schedule, itinerary, prospectus
> *Summary 204*

7 list of names, roll, register, rota, roster, scroll, jury list, panel, census, poll, head count, roll call, muster roll, tax roll, electoral roll, electorate, voting list, property roll, cadastre *or* cadaster, payroll, active list, retired list, civil list [Brit], waiting list, sick list, short list, blacklist, cast list, dramatis personae, credits, lineup

8 listing, enumeration, itemization, registration, enrollment, filing, indexing, cataloging, tabulation, charting, classification, taxonomy
> *Class 777*

ADJECTIVES

9 listed, enumerated, itemized, inventoried, registered, recorded, entered, noted, filed, indexed, cataloged, charted, tabulated, scheduled, programmed

10 of a list, inventorial, glossarial, cadastral, classificatory, taxonomic
> *Class 777*

VERBS

11 list, make a list, enumerate, itemize, inventory, register, record, note, write down, put down, set down, chronicle, put on the agenda, enter, book, post, file, pigeonhole, classify, catalog, index, tabulate, chart, diarize, schedule, bill, invoice, short-list, blacklist
> *Record 185; Class 777*

12 be on a list, be classified, be cataloged; enlist, enroll, matriculate, sign up

ADVERBS

13 inventorially, glossarially, tabularly, encyclopedically; alphabetically, numerically, in order, in series, in sequence; classificatorily, taxonomically

786 Zero

NOUNS

1 zero, naught, 0, cipher, aught; nothing, nil; *nihil* [L], *nada* [Sp], *nichts* [Ger]; nothing at all, not any, none, not a one, nobody, no one, not a soul, not a mite, not an iota, not a jot or tittle, not a whit, no score, love [Tennis]; [Inf]: not a blessed one, not a lick, not a sausage [Brit], zilch, nix, goose egg

2 nothingness, nullity, nonexistence, nonbeing, nihility
> *Nonexistence 718*

3 zero level, nadir, rock bottom, lowest point, last moment, zero hour, crisis point; zero degrees, zero Fahrenheit, zero Celsius, absolute zero
> *Base 601*

4 nonentity, anonymity, nobody, unknown, unperson, nothing

ADJECTIVES

5 zero, nil, no, all gone; null, void, nonexistent, missing, lacking, gone, vanished

VERBS

6 not exist, not be, not occur, be absent, be fictitious, vanish, disappear; annihilate, eradicate, nullify, wipe out, put an end to; hit rock bottom, reach an all-time low
> *Nonexistence 718*

ADVERBS

7 none, no, not, not at all, in no way

787 Fraction

NOUNS

1 fraction, simple fraction, common *or* vulgar fraction, compound fraction, proper fraction, improper fraction, decimal fraction, decimal, ratio
> *Number 783*

2 fractional part, part, percentage, proportion, portion, share, piece, section, segment, division, subdivision, ration
> *Part 760*

3 fragment, particle, chip, shard, sherd, splinter, sliver, scrap, shred, bit, speck, morsel, crumb, atom, iota, whit, jot, tittle

4 less than one, half, third, two thirds, quarter, fourth, three quarters, fifth, sixth, seventh, eighth, ninth, tenth, eleventh, twelfth, thirteenth, fourteenth, fifteenth, sixteenth, seventeenth, eighteenth, nineteenth, twentieth, *etc.*

ADJECTIVES

5 fractional, half, quarter, three-quarter, part, partial, fragmentary, incomplete, proportional, sectional, segmental, divisional, subdivisional
> *Part 760; Incompleteness 762*

6 small, tiny, infinitesimal, insignificant
> *Littleness 580*

VERBS

7 divide, subdivide, split, part, share, fragment
> *Allocation 474; Separation 753*

ADVERBS

8 fractionally, partially, partly, slightly, marginally

788 One

One is one and all alone and ever more shall be so.
— "GREEN GROW THE RUSHES, HO!"

NOUNS

1 one, 1, I; unity, unit, integer, ace, entity, singleton, single, monad, atom, point, item, article, module, individual, person, persona, soul, one and only, no other, nothing else, nobody else

2 **item,** detail, bit, piece, single instance, isolated instance, isolated case, only exception

3 **oneness,** singleness, wholeness, unity, union, undividedness, indivisibility, solidarity, solidity, indissolubility, coherence, integrity
   ◗ *Union 752; Whole 759*

4 **singularity,** individuality, uniqueness, specialness, specialty, particularity, identity, distinctiveness, personhood

5 **aloneness,** loneness, solitude, solitariness, isolation, apartness, separateness, separatism, isolationism, unilateralism; detachment, aloofness, insularity, privacy, seclusion; loneliness, lonesomeness, friendlessness
   ◗ *Unsociability 409*

6 **singleness,** celibacy, divorce, separation, widowhood
   ◗ *Divorce and Widowhood 66; Celibacy 67*

7 **single person,** single, celibate, unmarried man, bachelor, unmarried woman, spinster, maiden aunt, single parent, divorcé, divorcée, widow, widower, only child
   ◗ *Divorce and Widowhood 66*

8 **loner,** solitary, hermit, eremite, anchorite, marabout, stylite, ascetic, recluse, isolationist, seclusionist, lone wolf [Inf]
   ◗ *Nonconformity 782*

9 **soloist,** one-man band, one-man show, one-woman show, solo effort, solo, monologue, soliloquy, monologist, soliloquist
   ◗ *Soliloquy 211*

ADJECTIVES

10 **one,** single, solo, mono, monadic, atomic, individual, solitary, sole, lone, only, one and the same, first, primary

11 **one-sided,** unilateral, uniplanar, one-way, unidirectional, one-size, one-piece, unisex, unisexual, unicellular, unipolar, unicameral, monolingual, monochromatic

12 **whole,** entire, complete, integral, unified, united, joined, rolled into one, undivided, indivisible, inseparable, indissoluble, solid, unanimous
   ◗ *Union 752; Whole 759; Completeness 761*

13 **singular,** individual, special, particular, distinct, unique, one and only, only-begotten, first and last, unrepeated, once-in-a-lifetime

14 **solo,** one-man, one-woman, independent, single-handed, on one's own, alone, unaided, unassisted, unabetted, unsupported, unaccompanied, unescorted, unchaperoned

15 **alone,** lone, solitary, isolated, apart, separate, separated, separatist, isolationist, unilateralist, detached, aloof, insular, withdrawn, reclusive, lonely, lonesome, friendless, companionless, deserted, abandoned, forsaken
   ◗ *Unsociability 409*

16 **single,** unmarried, unwedded, divorced, separated, widowed, chaste, celibate

   ◗ *Divorce and Widowhood 66; Celibacy 67*

VERBS

17 **be one,** stand alone, stand by oneself, stand on one's own two feet, go solo, stand apart, stand aloof, isolate oneself, withdraw, retreat, plow a lonely furrow, go it alone, go one's own way, paddle one's own canoe, hoe one's own row, do one's own thing [Inf]

18 **become one,** make one, unite, unify, integrate, cohere, merge, combine, fuse, join, blend
   ◗ *Union 752; Combination 757; Whole 759*

19 **single out,** pick out, isolate, separate, detach
   ◗ *Selection 382; Separation 753*

ADVERBS

20 **alone,** on its own, uniquely, by itself, per se, on one's own, by oneself, all by oneself, independently, solo, single-handedly, under one's own steam, on one's lonesome [Inf]

21 **one by one,** one at a time, singly, individually, separately, apart, in the singular

22 **wholly,** completely, integrally, indivisibly, unanimously, as one

23 **once,** once only, just once, just this once, never again, once and for all, only, solely, exclusively, simply, purely

789 Two

NOUNS

1 **two,** 2, II; deuce, twain, set of two, pair, couple, brace, span, yoke, team, double harness; duet, duo, dyad, twosome, Darby and Joan; power of two, square

2 **duality,** doubleness, dualism, duplexity, bilingualism, bisexuality, ambidexterity, ambiguity, double meaning, double entendre, irony, ambivalence; dual personality, split personality, double life; double agent, duplicity, two-facedness, double-dealing, double-crossing; double-sidedness *or* double-facedness; Janus, Dr. Jekyll and Mr. Hyde
   ◗ *Equivocation 380*

3 **twosome,** double, doublet, couplet, dimeter, distich, duet, two-hander, diptych, double-decker, tandem, two-seater, two-wheeler, bicycle, biplane, two-dollar bill, tuppence [Brit]; catamaran, bireme, two-piece *or* two-piecer, duplex, bivalve, biped, bipod, binoculars, biathlon, binary system; doubleton, pair, snake eyes

4 **doubling,** pairing, twinning, gemination, cloning; duplication, reproduction, repetition, double exposure
   ◗ *Reproduction 21; Repetition 797*

5 **twin,** double, look-alike, mirror image, Doppelgänger, clone, duplicate, copy, carbon copy, photocopy, counterpart, dead ringer [Inf], spit and image *or* spitting image [Inf]; twins, identical twins, fraternal twins, Siamese twins, Tweedledum and Tweedledee, Castor and Pollux, Gemini, Twin Stars
   ◗ *Sameness 730; Similarity 733; Imitation 736*

6 **halving,** dividing by two, splitting *or* cutting in two,

splitting *or* cutting in half, bifurcation; dichotomy, bisection, bipartition

　　▶ *Separation 753*

7 **half,** fifty percent, moiety, hemisphere, semicircle, diameter, equator, great circle, bisector

　　▶ *Part 760*

ADJECTIVES

8 **two,** dual, dualistic, double, duple, duplex, binary, dyadic, twofold, bifold; paired, coupled, yoked, bracketed, twinned, matched, mated; doubled, squared, two by two, two abreast, in pairs, in twos, à deux, both, the two, second, secondary

9 **two-sided,** double-sided *or* double-faced, two-way, dual-purpose, two-ply; two-stroke, two-story, two-level, two-dimensional; biennial, biannual, biform, bipartite, bifurcate, biped, bipedal, binocular, bifocal, bilateral, bicameral, bilingual, ambidextrous, bisexual; Janus-like

10 **double-edged,** double-barreled, ambiguous, ironic, ambivalent; duplicitous, two-faced, hypocritical, double-dealing, double-crossing, two-timing [Inf]

　　▶ *Equivocation 380*

11 **double,** twin, duplicate, geminate *or* geminated, repeat, second; duplicated, copied, photocopied, repeated, cloned

　　▶ *Reproduction 21; Sameness 730; Similarity 733; Imitation 736; Repetition 797*

12 **half,** halved, bisected, divided by two, split in half, split two ways, dichotomous, dichotomic, bifurcated; halfway, mid, middle, midway

　　▶ *Separation 753; Middle 772*

VERBS

13 **pair,** couple, bracket, yoke, span, double-harness, twin, match, mate, matchmake, pair off, couple, team up

14 **double,** multiply by two, square, duplicate, replicate, clone, twin, geminate, copy, mirror, echo, repeat

　　▶ *Reproduction 21; Repetition 797*

15 **halve,** bisect, transect, divide in half, divide by two, split in half, split in two, cleave, sunder, dichotomize, bifurcate

　　▶ *Separation 753*

16 **go halves,** go fifty-fifty, share, split two ways, split down the middle, go Dutch

　　▶ *Allocation 474*

17 **have it both ways,** have the best of both worlds, have one's cake and eat it too

ADVERBS

18 **twice,** twofold, doubly, dually, twice as much, as much again, twice over, two times, once more, again, over again, yet again, encore, *bis* [Fr]

19 **two by two,** two abreast, in pairs, in twos

20 **second,** secondly, in the second place, secondarily

21 **in half,** in halves, in two, in twain, down the middle, half, fifty percent, half-and-half, fifty-fifty

790　Three

Multiplication is vexation, / Division is as bad; / The rule of three doth puzzle me, / And practice drives me mad.
　— ANONYMOUS

NOUNS

1 **three,** 3, III; trey, trio, threesome, set of three, triad, trinity, triple, power of three, cube

2 **threeness,** triality, trimorphism, triplicity, tripleness, trebleness, threefoldness

3 **triple thing,** trident, tripod, trivet, tricorn, triangle, trihedron, three-wheeler, tricycle, trimaran, trireme, three-decker, three-hander, triumvirate, troika, triennial, triennium, trimester, trinomial, trilogy, triptych, trimeter, terza rima, tristich, triphthong, triplet, trefoil, shamrock, ménage à trois, hat trick

4 **triplication,** tripling, triplicating, trebling, multiplying by three

5 **trisection,** tripartition, trichotomy, trifurcation, dividing by three, splitting in three

　　▶ *Separation 753*

6 **third,** tierce, third part, one third, tertium quid, third class, third party, third person, third power, major third, minor third, Third World, third age, third eye, third degree

ADJECTIVES

7 **three,** triple, triplex, triadic, trinal, trine, triform, trimorphic, ternary, trinary, triune, treble, triplicate, threefold, trifold, three times as much, cubed, third, tertiary

8 **three-sided,** triangular, triangulate, trigonal, trilateral, trihedral, deltoid, fan-shaped, three-pointed, three-pronged, trident, tridentate, three-cornered, tricorn, tricornered, three-leaved, trifoliate, three-legged, three-footed, tripedal, tripodic, three-ply, three-way, three-dimensional, tridimensional, trilingual, trimetric, triennial, trimestrial

9 **trisected,** tripartite, three-part, three-parted, triparted, trichotomous, trifid, trifurcated

VERBS

10 **triple,** triplicate, treble, multiply by three, increase threefold, cube

11 **trisect,** divide by three, split *or* cut in three, trichotomize, trifurcate, split three ways

ADVERBS

12 **thrice,** threefold, three times, trebly, triply, trinely, in triplicate

13 **in threes,** three by three, three abreast

14 **third,** thirdly, in the third place

791　Four

Two and two the mathematician continues to make four, in

spite of the whine of the amateur for three, or the cry of the critic for five. — JAMES MCNEILL WHISTLER

NOUNS

1 **four,** 4, IV *or* IIII; foursome, set of four, quartet, quatre, tetrad, quaternity, quadruple, quadruplet

2 **quadrilateral,** tetragon, quadrangle, square, rectangle, oblong, parallelogram, rhombus, trapezium, trapezoid, tetrahedron; quad [Inf]

3 **foursome,** quadruped, tetrapod, tetradactyl, quadrennium, quadrennial, quadrille, square dance, quatrefoil, four-leaf clover, four-in-hand, four-poster, four winds, four seasons, four corners of the earth, tetrameter, quatrain, tetragram, Tetragrammaton, tetralogy, four-letter word

4 **quadruplication,** quadruplicature, quadrupling, quadruplicating, quadruplicity, fourfoldness

5 **quadrisection,** quadripartition, quartering, dividing by four, splitting in four

6 **quarter,** fourth, fourth part, one fourth, twenty-five percent, quadrant

ADJECTIVES

7 **four,** quaternary, quadratic, quadruple, quadruplex, quadruplicate, fourfold, fourth

8 **quadrilateral,** four-sided, square, rectangular, quadrate, trapezoidal, tetrahedral, foursquare

9 **tetramerous,** quadruped, four-legged, four-footed, quadraphonic, quadrennial, tetravalent, quadrivalent

10 **quartered,** quadrisected, quadripartite, four-part, four-parted, four-handed, four-stroke, quarterly, quadrifid

VERBS

11 **quadruple,** quadruplicate, multiply by four, increase fourfold, quadrate

12 **quadrisect,** quarter, divide by four, divide into four, split four ways

ADVERBS

13 **four times,** fourfold, quadruply, quadrennially, quarterly, squarely, foursquare

14 **in fours,** four by four, on all fours

15 **fourth,** fourthly, in the fourth place

792 Five and Over

Twelve drummers drumming, eleven pipers piping, ten lords a-leaping, nine ladies dancing, eight maids a-milking . . . — "THE TWELVE DAYS OF CHRISTMAS"

NOUNS

1 **five,** 5, V; fivesome, quintet, pentad, cinque, quintuplicate, quintuple, quintuplet, quint [Inf]; fifth, fifth part, one fifth; pentagon, pentahedron, pentagram, pentacle, pentameter, cinquain, pentastich, Pentateuch, pentarchy, pentathlon, pentachord; quinquireme, quincunx, cinquefoil, five-finger; quinquen-

nium, quinquennial, five-dollar bill, five-pound note [Brit]; [Inf]: fiver, five-spot, fin

2 **six,** 6, VI; half-dozen *or* half a dozen, hexad, sextet, sextuplicate, sextuplet, sixth, sixth part, one sixth, sextile; hexagon, hexahedron, hexagram, hexameter, sestet, Hexateuch, hexachord, hexapod, sixth sense, six-footer, six-shooter, Six-Day War, six-pack, sixpence [Brit]

3 **seven,** 7, VII; heptad, septet, septenary, septuplicate, septuple, septuplet, seventh, seventh part, one seventh, hebdomad, heptagon, heptahedron, heptameter, Heptateuch, seven deadly sins, seven seas, Seven Wonders of the World, diminished seventh, seven days, week

4 **eight,** 8, VIII; ogdoad, octad, octet, octonary, octuple, octuplet, octagon, octahedron, octave, octateuch, Eightfold Path, octopus, octarchy, octavo (8vo), figure eight, piece of eight, eighth, eighth part, one eighth; eighter from Decatur [Inf]

5 **nine,** 9, IX; ennead, nonet, nonary, novena, nonuplet, nonagon, enneagon, enneahedron, ninth, ninth part, one ninth, nine days' wonder; niner [Inf], Nina from Carolina [Inf]

6 **ten,** 10, X; decade, decennium, decagon, decahedron, decapod, decagram, decathlon, Decalogue, Ten Commandments, tenth, tenth part, one tenth, tithe, ten-dollar bill, tenner [Inf]

7 **eleven to nineteen,** eleven, undecagon, hendecagon, hendecahedron; twelve, dozen, dodecagon, dodecahedron, duodecimal, duodecimo *or* twelvemo (12mo), Alexandrine, twelfth man, Twelfth Night, Twelfth Day, twelvemonth [Brit]; teens, teenager, thirteen, baker's dozen, long dozen; fourteen, two weeks, fortnight; fifteen, quindecagon, quindecennial; sixteen, sixteenmo (16mo), hexadecimal; nineteen, nineteenth hole [Inf]

8 **twenty and over,** score; twenty-four, four and twenty, two dozen; twenty-five, five and twenty, silver anniversary; forty, twoscore, quadragenarian; fifty, half a hundred, half century, jubilee, quinquagenarian; sixty, threescore, sexagenary, sexagenarian; seventy, threescore and ten, septuagenarian; eighty, fourscore, octogenarian, ninety, fourscore and ten; nonagenarian

9 **hundreds,** hundred, one hundred, C, century, one hundredfold, centuple, centuplicate, hundred percent, centennial, centenary, centennium, centenarian, centurion, centimeter, centigrade, hundredweight, centipede, hecatomb, Hundred Days; one hundred twenty, great *or* long hundred; one hundred forty-four, gross; one hundred fifty, sesquicentennial; two hundred, bicentennial, bicentenary; three hundred, tercentennial, tercentenary; four hundred, quatercentenary; five hundred, five centuries, quincentenary; six centuries, sexcentenary; seven centuries, eight centuries, octocentenary; nine centuries, ten centuries, hundreds and hundreds, hundreds and thousands, C *or* C-note [Inf]

10 **thousand,** M, chiliad, millennium, millenary, millenarian, millipede; milligram, milliliter, millimeter; kilometer, kilogram, kilo, kilobyte; gigabyte, ten thousand, myriad, hundred thousand, lac *or* lakh [India], grand *or* G [Inf]

11 **million,** ten million, crore [India], thousand million, billion, milliard, million million, trillion, quadrillion, quintillion, sextillion, septillion, octillion, nonillion, decillion, undecillion, duodecillion, tredecillion, quattuordecillion, quindecillion, sexdecillion, septendecillion, octodecillion, novemdecillion, vigintillion, googol, googolplex; multimillion, zillion [Inf], jillion [Inf]
▶ *Number 783; Multitude 795*

ADJECTIVES

12 **fifth,** five, fivefold, quintuple, quintuplicate, quinary, quinquennial, quintic, quintile, quinquepartite, pentadic, pentagonal, pentangular, pentahedral, pentatonic

13 **sixth,** six, sixfold, sextuple, sextuplicate, sexennial, sexpartite, hexadic, hexagonal, hexangular, hexahedral, hexatonic

14 **seventh,** seven, sevenfold, septuple, septuplicate, septenary, septennial, heptadic, heptagonal, heptangular, heptahedral, heptatonic, hebdomal

15 **eighth,** eight, eightfold, octuple, octonary, octennial, octadic, octagonal, octangular, octahedral, octatonic

16 **ninth,** nine, ninefold, nonuple, novenary, nonary, enneadic, nonagonal, enneagonal, enneahedral

17 **tenth,** ten, tenfold, decuple, decimal, denary, decennial, decagonal, decahedral

18 **eleventh and above,** undecennial, hendecagonal; twelfth, duodenary, duodecimal; thirteenth, fourteenth, fifteenth, quindecagonal, quindecennial, sixteenth, hexadecimal

19 **twentieth,** vigesimal, vicenary, vicennial, thirtieth, fortieth, fiftieth, sixtieth, seventieth, eightieth, ninetieth

20 **hundredth,** centesimal, centennial, centenary, centenarian, hundredfold, centuple, centuplicate

21 **thousandth,** millenary, millenarian, millennial, thousandfold, four-figure, five-figure, six-figure

22 **millionth,** billionth, trillionth, *etc.;* umpteenth [Inf]

VERBS

23 **quintuple,** quintuplicate, sextuple, sextuplicate, septuple, octuple, centuple, centuplicate, decimalize, decimate

24 **multiply by five,** multiply by six, multiply by seven, *etc.*

25 **divide by five,** divide by six, divide by seven, *etc.*

ADVERBS

26 **fivefold,** fifth, fifthly, quinquennially; sixfold, sixth, sixthly, sexennially; sevenfold, seventh, seventhly, septennially; tenfold, tenth, tenthly, decennially; hundredfold, centennially

793 Plurality

NOUNS

1 **plurality,** pluralness, plural, plural number, many, several, some, a number, a few, a couple, a handful, more than one, (the odd) one or two, two or three, more, a greater number

2 **multiplicity,** multitude, numerousness, multitudinousness, multifariousness, variety, diversity, compositeness, multiformity; many-sidedness, polygon, polyhedron, multilateralism, polygamy, polygyny, polyandry, polytheism, pluralism, multiple personality
▶ *Diversity 732; Multitude 795*

3 **majority,** greater number, more, greatest number, most, more than half, greater *or* best part, greater proportion, bulk, mass, preponderance, lion's share
▶ *Part 760*

4 **multiplication,** proliferation, increase, multiple, product; multiplier, multiplicand, multiplication table
▶ *Increase 746; Calculation 784*

5 **pluralist,** all-rounder, polymath, Renaissance man *or* woman, polyglot, multilateralist, polygamist, polytheist

ADJECTIVES

6 **plural,** in the plural, not singular, more than one, multiple, many, several, some, certain, few, more, most, majority, numerous, multitudinous
▶ *Part 760; Multitude 795*

7 **various,** divers, diverse, sundry, multifarious, multiform, composite, multilateral, polygonal, many-sided, multifaceted, versatile, multipurpose, multirole, polymorphous *or* polymorphic, multinational, multiracial, multilingual, polyglottal
▶ *Diversity 732*

8 **multiplicative,** multiplied, multiple, manifold, multifold, increasing, increased, proliferative, proliferating, proliferated
▶ *Increase 746*

VERBS

9 **pluralize,** make plural, multiply, proliferate, propagate, increase, replicate, clone
▶ *Increase 746*

ADVERBS

10 **plurally,** severally, multiply, multitudinously, variously, diversely, multifariously, multilaterally, upwards of

11 **in the majority,** more, most

12 **et cetera,** etc., and so on, et al., and others, and the rest

794 Accompaniment

NOUNS

1 **accompaniment,** concomitance, coexistence, sym-

biosis; combination, conjunction; association, union, coagency, convoy

▶ *Union 752; Combination 757*

2 **synchronism,** simultaneity, contemporaneity, coincidence, concurrence, co-occurrence, conjunction

▶ *Same Time 649*

3 **companionship,** company, togetherness, fellowship, friendship, partnership, cohabitation, marriage, society, community, mateyness [Brit inf]

▶ *Friendship 62; Marriage 64; Sociability 408*

4 **concomitant,** attribute, feature, fixture, accessory, appendage, adjunct, appurtenance, ornament, attendant, corollary; symptom, syndrome, indication, sign; background, (musical) accompaniment

▶ *Sign 183; Essence 723; Addition 748*

5 **attendance,** cortege, retinue, following, entourage, court, suite, retainers

6 **accompanier,** accompanist, attendant, squire, cavalier, escort, outrider, chaperon, duenna, protector, keeper, guard, bodyguard, muscle [Inf]

▶ *Safety 810*

7 **usher,** shepherd, marshal, conductor, leader, guide, pilot, cicerone

▶ *Management 126*

8 **companion,** colleague, partner, associate, coworker, fellow, classmate, roommate, comrade, friend, chum, traveling companion, fellow traveler, mate, buddy [Inf]

▶ *Friendship 62; Cooperation 827*

9 **partner,** constant companion, escort, date, girlfriend, boyfriend, lover, consort, cohabitant, live-in lover; spouse, husband, wife

▶ *Marriage 64; Love 299*

10 **follower,** shadow, tail, satellite, dependant, hanger-on, parasite, sycophant, camp follower, groupie [Inf]

▶ *Servant 69; Sequence 770*

11 **side dish,** salad, vegetables, condiments, sauce, gravy, dressing, drinks

▶ *Food 90*

ADJECTIVES

12 **accompanying,** concomitant, attending, attendant, belonging, complementary, accessory, collateral, incidental, background, contextual

13 **concurrent,** concurring, coincident, coinciding, simultaneous; contemporary, contemporaneous, parallel, correlative, coexistent, coexisting, symbiotic, cohabiting

14 **associated,** partnered, coupled, paired, wedded, married, combined, joined, inseparable, hand and *or* in glove, thick as thieves [Inf]

▶ *Union 752; Combination 757*

15 **accompanied,** attended, escorted, chaperoned, protected, guarded, ushered, shepherded, marshaled, guided, led, conducted; following, shadowing, dependent

VERBS

16 **accompany,** go together, go with, belong with, complement, go together with; come with, be linked with, go hand in hand, go hand in glove with; concur, coincide, synchronize, keep time with

17 **keep company with,** travel with, run with, work with, partner, escort, go out with, date; consort with, associate with, frequent; befriend, socialize, club together, team up, gang up, pair up; couple, live together, live with, cohabit; hobnob, hang around with [Inf], hang out with [Inf]

▶ *Friendship 62; Sociability 408; Cooperation 827*

18 **escort,** squire, chaperon, protect, guard, safeguard, guide, lead, pilot, usher, shepherd, marshal, conduct, convoy, bring *or* take in tow

▶ *Management 126; Safety 810*

19 **attend,** dance attendance on, wait on, tag along, attach oneself to; follow, dog the footsteps of, shadow, tail, track

▶ *Servant 69; Sequence 770*

ADVERBS

20 **together,** in a body, all together, in unison, collectively, inseparably, unitedly, in convoy, in tow, in someone's wake

21 **hand in hand,** arm in arm, side by side, cheek by jowl, hand in glove

22 **concurrently,** simultaneously, contemporaneously, symbiotically

795 Multitude

Do I contradict myself? / Very well then I contradict myself, / (I am large, I contain multitudes.) — WALT WHITMAN

NOUNS

1 **multitude,** many, great number, large number, quite a few, a lot, lots; large amount, tidy sum; dozens, scores, hundreds, hundreds and thousands, thousands, tens of thousands, hundreds of thousands, millions, billions, trillions, myriads; [Inf]: scads, umpteen, zillions, jillions

▶ *Number 783; Five and Over 792; Plurality 793*

2 **multiplicity,** multitudinousness, numerousness, multifoldness, countlessness, innumerability, infinity

▶ *Infinity 798*

3 **profuseness,** profusion, rifeness, abundance, plenty, barrel; [Inf]: tons, oodles, bags, heap, loads, heck *or* hell of a lot

▶ *Excess 99*

4 **throng,** multitude, mass, mob, crowd, congregation, horde; host, army, troop, legion, fleet; high turnout, large turnout; rout, ruck, jam, clutter, press, crush; swarm, flock, flight; cloud, hail, bevy, covey, shoal; hive, colony, nest, brood, pack, bunch, drove, array,

galaxy; mass *or* masses of, sea of, world *or* worlds of, forest of

> *Assembly 59*

ADJECTIVES

5 **multitudinous,** multitudinal, numerous, legion, multiple, multifold, multifarious, manifold

6 **many,** good many, very many, ever so many, considerable; a good few, not a few, quite a few

7 **myriad,** hundred, a hundred and one, thousand, a thousand and one, million, billion, trillion; [Inf]: umpteen, zillion, jillion

> *Number 783; Five and Over 792; Plurality 793*

8 **numberless,** innumerable, countless, uncountable, incalculable, immeasurable, measureless, beyond measure; unnumbered, uncounted, untold; endless, without end, limitless, without limit, infinite; boundless, inexhaustible, countless, no end [Inf], more than one can shake a stick at [Inf]

> *Eternity 644; Infinity 798*

9 **ample,** abundant, superabundant, profuse, rife, plentiful, plenteous, copious; thick, in abundance, in plenty, in profusion, galore, bumper [Inf]

> *Sufficiency 97; Excess 99*

10 **crowded,** thronged, mobbed, congested, massed, packed, jammed, jam-packed, concentrated, high-density, bursting, pressed, crushed; cluttered, overcrowded, overpopulated, overmanned, overstaffed, overrun

VERBS

11 **crowd,** throng, mob, mass, congregate; pack, jam, press, crush, swarm, teem, crawl, pullulate; hum, buzz, bristle, seethe; mill, troop, flock; pour, stream, flood, brim, overflow; burst

> *Assembly 59*

12 **overcrowd,** overpopulate, overman, overstaff, outnumber, overrun, infest, swamp, overwhelm, snow under

> *Excess 99*

ADVERBS

13 **numerously,** aplenty, multitudinously, multiply, multifariously; innumerably, countlessly, incalculably, immeasurably, beyond measure, beyond count, infinitely; no end [Inf]

14 **in crowds,** in swarms, in masses, en masse, in heaps, in loads, thick and fast

796 Few

Many are called, but few are chosen. — BIBLE: MATTHEW

NOUNS

1 **few,** a few, only *or* just a few, not many, some; small number, one or two, two or three, couple, handful, mere handful; almost none, too few to mention, not enough to count *or* matter; low turnout, poor turnout, low attendance; scattering, sprinkling, trickle,

small quantity, small amount, little, a little, soupçon, dash, hint, suspicion, smidgen

> *Number 783*

2 **least,** minimum, less, minority, the minority

3 **fewness,** sparsity, sparseness, scarcity, scarceness, scantiness; exiguity, paucity, dearth, lack, deficiency, rarity; skimpiness, meagerness, shortage, undersupply, underpopulation, skeleton staff

> *Insufficiency 98*

4 **rarity,** rareness, infrequency, intermittence, sporadicalness

> *Infrequency 662*

ADJECTIVES

5 **few,** a few, some, not many, hardly any, scarcely any, precious few, too few, little, a little, not much, precious little, counted on the fingers of one hand

6 **sparse,** scant, scanty, light, thin, little, minimal, meager, exiguous, measly, niggardly; infrequent, occasional, sporadic, intermittent, rare, seldom seen, seldom met with, uncommon; scarce, few and far between, strung out, spread out, widely spaced, at great intervals; dispersed, scattered, sprinkled, dotted about, underpopulated, low-density, understaffed, undermanned

> *Insufficiency 98; Infrequency 662*

7 **fewer,** less, reduced, diminished, diminishing, least, minimum, minimal, minority, in a minority, too few

VERBS

8 **reduce,** diminish, rarefy, thin, thin out, weed out; decimate, pare *or* cut down, scale down, downsize; cut back, prune, trim, eliminate

9 **scatter,** sprinkle, dot, dot about, string out, space out, spread out, disperse

ADVERBS

10 **in ones and twos,** in twos and threes, here and there, in places, in spots, in a trickle, in dribs and drabs

11 **sparsely,** scantily, lightly, thinly, meagerly, exiguously; little, rarely, infrequently, seldom, occasionally, scarcely, hardly, barely

797 Repetition

NOUNS

1 **repetition,** repeating, doing again; rehearsal, practice, practicing; duplication, reduplication, doubling, redoubling; reproduction, replication, recurrence, imitation, copying, parroting; echo, reecho, ditto; anaphora *or* epanaphora, epistrophe, epiphora, symploce; echolalia

> *Reproduction 21; Imitation 736; Two 789*

2 **iteration,** reiteration, repeating, saying again, recounting, retelling, recapitulation, recap, going over again; review, résumé, summary, summing up, peroration, restatement; tautology, redundancy, padding, filler

▶ *Diffuseness 199; Summary 204*

3 **repetitiveness,** repetitiousness, repetition; monotony, humdrum, tedium, uniformity, regularity, invariability, familiarity; daily grind, same old round, rut, routine, habit, cliché, same old story, old joke, chestnut, twice-told tale

▶ *Habit, Custom 397; Stability 674; Sameness 730*

4 **return,** reappearance, comeback, renewal; starting again, beginning again, starting afresh; reprise, recurrence, rebirth, reincarnation, renaissance; revival, restoration, recycling, cycle, round

5 **repeat,** repetition, repeat performance, encore; rerun, reshowing, replay, replaying; return match, repeat order, second helping, reprint, offprint, reissue, new edition, remake, rehash

6 **reverberation,** echo, reecho, resonance; vibration, oscillation, rhythm, beat, pulse, pulsation, throb, throbbing, drumming, hammering; rhyme, alliteration, assonance

▶ *Repeated Sound 235; Resonance 236*

7 **replica,** double, duplicate, copy, carbon copy, photocopy, print

▶ *Reproduction 21; Sameness 730*

ADJECTIVES

8 **repeated,** duplicated, reduplicated, doubled, redoubled; reproduced, replicated, echoed, reechoed, mirrored, imitative, parrotlike

▶ *Reproduction 21; Imitation 736*

9 **iterated,** reiterated, said again, retold, twice-told, said before, recounted, related, restated

10 **remade,** reissued, reprinted; replayed, reshown; revived, restored, renewed; reborn, reincarnated, reheated, warmed up, recycled, reprocessed, rehashed

11 **repetitious,** repetitive, repetitional, repeating, duplicative, reproductive, doubling, redoubling; echoing, reechoing, iterative, reiterative, reiterant; tautological, redundant, otiose, pleonastic, wordy, prolix; recapitulative; harping

▶ *Diffuseness 199*

12 **monotonous,** tedious, boring, uniform, invariable, changeless; monotone, singsong, familiar, habitual, humdrum; mundane, routine, stale, cliché-ridden, clichéd, hackneyed, trite

▶ *Boredom 296; Habit, Custom 397; Stability 674; Sameness 730*

13 **recurrent,** regular, periodic, cyclical, returning; recurring, reoccurring, reappearing; ubiquitous, haunting, continual, continuous, constant, nonstop, incessant, ceaseless, unremitting

▶ *Permanence 667; Continuity, Continuation 669*

14 **reverberatory,** resonant, vibrational, oscillatory, rhythmical, rhythmic; beating, pulsing, pulsating, throbbing, drumming, hammering, chiming, chanting; rhymed, rhyming, alliterative, alliterating, assonant

▶ *Repeated Sound 235; Resonance 236*

VERBS

15 **repeat,** redo, do again, do a repeat, rehearse, practice, duplicate, reduplicate, double, redouble; reproduce, replicate, copy, echo, mirror, parrot, imitate, mimic

▶ *Reproduction 21; Imitation 736; Two 789*

16 **iterate,** reiterate, repeat, say again, say over again; retell, recapitulate, perorate, go over again, review, summarize, sum up, restate, reemphasize; repeat oneself, go over the same ground, give an encore, recap

▶ *Summary 204*

17 **harp,** harp on, go on about, plug, labor, belabor, go on at, hammer away at; churn out, trot out, sing the same old song, play the same old record, tell the same old story, go over again and again, say over and over, hammer into, nag, go on and on, never hear the last of

▶ *Diffuseness 199*

18 **return to,** go back, retrace one's steps, go over the same ground, relapse, regress, revert, remember, recall

▶ *Memory 354*

19 **renew,** resume, restart, start again, begin again, start afresh, go back to the beginning; come back, stage a comeback, revive, restore, recycle, reprocess; reheat, warm up; reprint, reissue, rerun, replay, play back, remake, rehash

20 **be repeated,** recur, reoccur, happen again, return, reappear, pop up, crop up, show up again, keep coming, come again and again, turn up

21 **resound,** reverberate, echo, reecho; vibrate, oscillate, beat, pulse, pulsate, throb, drum, thrum, hammer, pound, rhyme, alliterate

▶ *Repeated Sound 235; Resonance 236*

ADVERBS

22 **repeatedly,** reiteratively, repetitively, repetitiously, monotonously, recurrently, frequently, often; continually, incessantly, again and again, over and over, time after time, time and again, many times over, day after day; day in, day out; year in, year out, ad nauseam

23 **again,** once more, once again, encore, da capo, from the beginning; afresh, anew, twice over, ditto

798 Infinity

I cannot help it; — in spite of myself, infinity torments me.
— ALFRED DE MUSSET

NOUNS

1 **infinity,** infiniteness, infinitude, boundlessness, limitlessness, illimitability, endlessness, interminability, inexhaustibility, bottomless pit

2 **immeasurability,** measurelessness, incalculability, countlessness, innumerability, numberlessness, indeterminableness, incomprehensibility

> *Multitude 795*

3 **vastness,** immenseness, immensity, space, outer space, infinite space

4 **eternity,** perpetuity, forever, everlastingness, perpetual motion

> *Eternity 644; Permanence 667*

ADJECTIVES

5 **infinite,** boundless, limitless, unlimited, without limit *or* end, illimitable, bottomless, endless, interminable, inexhaustible

6 **immeasurable,** measureless, vast, immense, enormous, astronomical, incalculable, uncountable, countless, innumerable, myriad, numberless, unnumbered, without number, beyond reckoning, untold, indeterminable, inestimable, unfathomable, incomprehensible, beyond comprehension, transcendent, mind-boggling [Inf]

> *Multitude 795*

7 **eternal,** perpetual, everlasting, immortal, undying, forever, ceaseless, endless, unending, never-ending, unremitting, open-ended, no end of *or* to

> *Eternity 644; Permanence 667*

VERBS

8 **have no limit,** have no bounds, know no limit *or* bounds *or* end

9 **be infinite,** last forever, never end, go on and on, never die, never cease, perpetuate, continue, be eternal

ADVERBS

10 **infinitely,** boundlessly, limitlessly, illimitably, endlessly, interminably, indefinitely, without end, without limit, to infinity, ad infinitum

11 **immeasurably,** measurelessly, vastly, immensely, astronomically, incalculably, innumerably, indeterminably, inestimably

12 **eternally,** perpetually, immortally, forever, in perpetuity, until the end of time

799 Importance

Art and religion first, then philosophy; lastly science. That is the order of the great subjects of life, that's their order of importance. — MURIEL SPARK

NOUNS

1 **importance,** primacy, preeminence; priority, urgency, precedence, prominence; distinction, eminence, reputation, repute; paramountcy, supremacy, superiority, essentiality, irreplaceability; import, consequence, significance; weight, weightiness; gravity, seriousness, solemnity; materiality, materialness, substance, pith, moment, substantiality; interest, consideration, concern; business, matter, account; note, notability, noteworthiness, memorability; mark, influence, prestige, size, magnitude, greatness; degree, rank, rating, standing, status; high standing, high approval, value, worth, excellence, merit; use, usefulness, strategic importance, utility; power, stress, emphasis, insistence, affirmation

▶ *Affirmation 189; Influence 512; Power 514; Size, Largeness 579; Reality 719; Degree 739; Superiority 744; Precedence 769; Usefulness 801*

2 **important matter,** vital concern, grave affair; crucial moment, turning point, crisis, crunch; matter of life and death, no joke, no laughing matter; key point, notable point, news, big news, great news; exploit, deed, great doings; important occasion, landmark, milestone, red-letter day, big day, great day, special day; [Inf]: big deal, nothing to sneeze at, not peanuts, not chicken feed, heavy scene

▶ *News 171; Memory 354; Celebration 405; Action 412; Timeliness 659*

3 **chief thing,** what matters, the thing, great thing, main thing; issue, supreme issue, crux of the matter, crux, main topic; fundamentals, basics, grass roots, bedrock, core; hard facts, reality; essential, sine qua non, requirement; priority, first priority; choice, first choice; highlight, main attraction, main feature, high point, best part, cream, crème de la crème, pick, elite

4 **gist,** meaning, substance, essence, essential part, sum and substance, heart, heart of the matter, kernel, nucleus, be-all and end-all; nub, nuts and bolts, center, hub, nexus; fulcrum, pivot, keynote, cornerstone, mainstay, linchpin *or* lynchpin; cardinal point, main point, salient point; half the battle, main part, chief hope; secret weapon, trump card, ace in the hole; big play, main chance, nitty-gritty [Inf]

▶ *Necessity 95; Meaning 361; Selection 382; Support 605; Center 612; Reality 719; Essence 723*

5 **important person,** influential *or* powerful person, personage, notable, personality, somebody; captain of industry, magnate, mogul, tycoon, managing director; head, spearhead; pillar of the community, pillar of society, salt of the earth; expert, key person, top person, top dog, chief, leader; superior, superior person; the greatest, member of the establishment, heavyweight; lord of the manor, local worthy, grandee, noble, aristocrat, great man *or* woman, His *or* Her Highness [Brit], king, queen, monarch, very important person (VIP) [Inf], kingpin [Inf]

▶ *Aristocrat 70; Superiority 744*

6 **celebrity,** big name, newsmaker, leading light, prima donna, star, lion, superman *or* superwoman, catch, great catch, favorite, high-muck-a-muck; [Inf]: top brass, his *or* her nibs, biggie *or* biggy, big guy, big gun, big shot, big noise, big wheel, big cheese, big enchilada, big fish, big chief, big daddy, Mr. Big, big-time operator (BTO), wheeler-dealer, big timer, big man, the man, first fiddle

▶ *Aristocrat 70; Management 126; Skillfulness 127; Wisdom 352; Influence 512; Power 514*

ADJECTIVES

7 **important,** primary, preeminent, urgent, imperative, prominent, distinct, eminent; chief, cardinal, capital, staple, major, main; top, topmost, paramount, supreme, prime, foremost, leading; overriding, over-

ruling, uppermost, most important, superior; worthwhile, taken seriously, not despised, not overlooked; valuable, necessary, vital, indispensable, irreplaceable, key, required; helpful, useful, telling, trenchant, meaningful; taking precedence, high priority, high-level, top-level, summit; top-secret, secret, confidential, hush-hush; high, grand, noble, great; A one *or* A number one *or* A 1 [Inf], not to be sneezed at [Inf]

▸ *Necessity 95; Meaning 361; Size, Largeness 579; Summit 600; Timeliness 659; Relatedness 727; Superiority 744; Precedence 769; Usefulness 801*

8 **serious,** weighty, grave, solemn, pregnant, heavy, big; of consequence, consequential, of importance, of weight; world-shaking, earthshaking, earth-shattering, momentous; critical, crucial, fateful

9 **significant,** of concern, of consideration, considerable, worth considering

10 **essential,** material, to the point, relevant; pivotal, central, basic, fundamental, bedrock; radical, going to the root, grass-roots

▸ *Center 612*

11 **notable,** noteworthy, remarkable, of mark, memorable, unforgettable, signal; first-rate, outstanding, sterling, excellent, superior; top-rank, top ten *or* top-ten, top-flight; ranking, high ranking, prestigious; conspicuous, prominent, eminent; distinguished, exalted, august, dignified; imposing, commanding, leading, impressive, formidable; powerful, influential

▸ *Skillfulness 127; Memory 354; Influence 512; Power 514; Superiority 744*

12 **newsworthy,** front-page, eventful; stirring, breathtaking, shattering, seismic, epoch-making

VERBS

13 **be important,** matter, bulk large, weigh, carry, carry weight; tell, count; cut a dash, cut a figure, make an impression, make someone sit up and take notice, attract attention; cast a long shadow, influence, motivate; signify, represent, import, mean; concern, interest, affect; have priority, take precedence, precede, come before, come first; predominate, take the lead, command respect, take the limelight, deserve notice; make a stir, create a sensation, hit it big; make waves [Inf]

▸ *Persuasion 178; Attention 323; Meaning 361; Respect 435; Influence 512; Relatedness 727; Superiority 744; Precedence 769*

14 **make important,** build up, give weight to, attach *or* ascribe importance to; seize on, fasten on; bring to the fore, place in the foreground; enhance, highlight, stress, emphasize, underline; labor, publicize, promote, advertise; put in bright lights, put in capital letters, headline, splash; bring to notice, bring to attention, put on the map; proclaim, announce, write in letters of gold, celebrate; lionize, honor, glorify, exalt; show respect, respect, value, esteem; regard, consider, take seriously; make a fuss about, make a stir, make much

ado, make much of; put *or* set store by, think everything of; magnify, enlarge, exaggerate, overestimate, overrate

▸ *Publication 173; Affirmation 189; Exaggeration 194; Overestimation 343; Celebration 405; Respect 435; Expansion 581*

ADVERBS

15 **importantly,** primarily, preeminently, urgently, prominently, eminently; seriously, consequentially, significantly, materially, considerably, critically, crucially; largely, mainly, in the main; above all, to crown all, supremely, par excellence; notably, remarkably, memorably; essentially

800 Unimportance

What is Matter? — Never mind. / What is Mind? — No matter. — PUNCH

NOUNS

1 **unimportance,** insignificance, immateriality, unrelatedness, obscurity; irrelevance, irrelevancy; inconsequence, inessentiality, dispensability, expendability; lack of substance, insubstantiality; nothingness, nullity, vacancy, emptiness; secondariness; obscurity

▸ *Understatement 195; Unreality 720; Unrelatedness 728*

2 **triviality,** pettiness, lack of seriousness, frivolousness, frivolity; flippancy, snap of the fingers; superficiality, shallowness; smallness, cheapness, inferiority, worthlessness; uselessness, inutility, mediocrity

▸ *Cheapness 497; Shallowness 599; Uselessness 802*

3 **trifle,** insignificant matter, inessential, nonessential; triviality, technicality, detail, mere detail, petty detail, minutiae, trivia; nothing, mere nothing, bagatelle

4 **little bit,** least bit, whit, jot, iota, tittle, trickle, dab; drop, drop in the bucket, drop in the ocean; damn, tinker's damn *or* dam; straw, rush, chaff; pin, button, feather; dust, cobweb, gossamer; tithe, fraction, small change, cent, penny, dime; fleabite, pinprick, scratch; [Inf]: peanuts, chicken feed, plugged nickel, small potatoes

▸ *Record 185; Littleness 580; Part 760*

5 **trifling fault,** petty sin, venial sin, peccadillo

6 **secondary matter,** accessory, sideshow, diversion, red herring; nothing of note, nothing in particular, matter of indifference, ordinary matter; nothing to boast of, nothing to write home about, nothing to speak of, nothing to worry about; child's play, nothing to it, taking candy from a baby; not the end of the world, no matter, no great matter; mountain out of a molehill, tempest in a teapot *or* teacup, no great shakes [Inf]

▸ *Overestimation 343; Easiness 823*

7 **cheap thing,** bauble, toy, plaything, small toy, rattle; trinket, novelty, gewgaw, geegaw, gimcrack; knick-

knack or nicknack, bibelot, bric-a-brac or bric-à-brac, doodad [Inf]; tinsel, trumpery, frippery, froth

▸ *Cheapness 497*

8 **nonentity,** nobody, unimportant or obscure person, unknown, nonperson; man of straw, figurehead, cipher; zero, nothing, silent partner; fribbler, trifler; beachcomber, smatterer, jack-of-all-trades and master of none; mediocrity, lightweight; small fry, small change, small game; inferior, subordinate, underling, understrapper, second fiddle, stooge, servant; puppet, pawn, instrument; poor relation, weak person, scorned person, object of scorn; scum, scum of the earth, trash; [Inf]: small potatoes, no-account, squirt, wimp, twerp or twirp, pipsqueak

▸ *Servant 69; Disrespect 436; Inferiority 745*

9 **suggestion,** trace, touch, dash, smattering, sprinkling, tinge, taste, jot, iota, suspicion, soupçon, inkling, intimation, smack, taint, thought, shade, tempering, smidgen

ADJECTIVES

10 **unimportant,** without importance; immaterial, circumstantial, not related, not apropos, off the point, irrelevant; ineffectual, uninfluential, forgettable; inessential, nonessential, not vital, unnecessary; dispensable, expendable, inconsiderable, negligible, forgivable, venial, nondescript, inappreciable; not worth considering, not worth worrying about, of little value, out of the running; good-for-nothing, no-account or no-count [Inf]

▸ *Unreality 720; Unrelatedness 728*

11 **not serious,** frivolous, puerile, childish; featherbrained, featherheaded, foolish; windy, airy, frothy

12 **insignificant,** inconsequential, of no consequence, of no great weight, insubstantial

13 **obscure,** disregarded, overlooked, neglected, not considered; beneath notice, beneath contempt

14 **trivial,** petty, trifling, nugatory, picayune, piffling, piddling, peddling, fiddling, niggling, technical, pettifogging, nitpicking; small-time, not worth a second thought; superficial, toy, token, nominal, symbolic; footling [Inf], two-bit [Inf]

15 **secondary,** minor, incidental, subsidiary, peripheral, low-level, of second rank

16 **cheap,** low-priced, five-and-ten or five-and-dime, twopenny; inferior, bad, poor, poor quality, shoddy, jerry-built; tawdry, rubbishy, trashy, trumpery; catchpenny, pinchbeck, gimcrack; potboiling, pulp; worthless, valueless, useless; second-rate, third-rate, mediocre, mickey mouse [Inf], rinky-dink [Inf]

17 **commonplace,** ordinary, usual, limited, parochial, uneventful; one-horse, no great shakes [Inf], jerkwater [Inf]

▸ *Folly 353; Cheapness 497; Shallowness 599; Uselessness 802*

VERBS

18 **be unimportant,** not matter, weigh light upon, have no weight, carry no weight, not weigh, not count, count for nothing, have no clout, have no pull, make no impression, mean little, signify little, cut no ice [Inf]

19 **think unimportant,** disregard, overlook, pass over, underrate, underestimate, shrug off, snap one's fingers at, hold cheap

20 **make unimportant,** trivialize, belittle, degrade, denigrate, demote, downplay, relegate, reduce one's importance, deflate one's ego, trim or cut down to size, knock down a few rungs, kick upstairs, humiliate, disparage, mock, scorn, put down [Inf]

▸ *Humility 298; Insolence 400*

ADVERBS

21 **unimportantly,** insignificantly, circumstantially, irrelevantly, ineffectually, inconsequentially, unnecessarily, negligibly, secondarily, incidentally, trivially, superficially, obscurely

INTERJECTIONS

22 **no matter!,** never mind!, so what!, too bad!, *tant pis!* [Fr], who cares?, who gives a damn!

801 Usefulness

NOUNS

1 **usefulness,** use, purpose, point; utility, handiness, helpfulness; help, aid, service, avail; good stead, good, utilitarianism, practicality; application, functionalism, commodity; convenience, suitability, expediency, applicability; versatility, adaptability; readiness, availability; usage, utilization, employment

▸ *Use 393; Convenience 803; Help 825*

2 **usability,** serviceability, employability, workability; value, worth, merit, good, virtue; function, capacity

▸ *Good 445*

3 **instrumentality,** ability, competence, efficacy; efficiency, power, potency; clout [Inf], influence; adequacy, sufficiency

▸ *Sufficiency 97; Power 514*

4 **benefit,** advantage, gain, profit; profitability, return, earning capacity; productivity, productiveness, fruitfulness; general benefit, public benefit, public good, public utility, commonweal

▸ *Gain 467; Production 522*

ADJECTIVES

5 **useful,** of use, utile, handy, helpful, of help, of service; for everyday use, utilitarian, pragmatic, practical; applied, functional, practicable, commodious, convenient; advisable, sensible, suitable, expedient, applicable; versatile, multipurpose, all-purpose, for all ages, of all work, adaptable; disposable, throwaway; ready, rough-and-ready, at hand, available, on call, ready for use, operative, up; on-line, on-stream, on tap [Inf]

▶ *Use 393; Convenience 803; Help 825*

6 usable, serviceable, fit for, good for, fit for use, approved for use; reusable, recyclable; employable, workable; good, valid, current

7 instrumental, subsidiary, subservient; able, competent; efficacious, effective, effectual; efficient, powerful, conducive, tending; adequate, sufficient

▶ *Sufficiency 97; Power 514*

8 profitable, making a profit, remunerative, lucrative, paying; gainful, productive, fruitful; beneficial, advantageous, salutary, for one's benefit, to one's advantage; good, edifying, worthwhile; worth one's salt, worth one's keep, worth one's weight in gold; worth a mint, worth a million, valuable, invaluable, priceless

▶ *Good 445; Gain 467; Production 522*

VERBS

9 be useful, come in handy, help, aid; advance, promote; prove helpful, bestead [Arch], avail; serve, do service; fill the bill, suit one's purpose, further one's purpose; have some use, perform a function, function, work, operate, perform; do, answer, suffice, make oneself useful; subserve, serve one's turn

▶ *Sufficiency 97; Use 393; Help 825*

10 benefit, advantage, be to one's advantage, serve one well, stand one in good stead, do good; bring results, bear fruit, profit, gain, pay, pay off

▶ *Good 445; Gain 467*

11 find useful, have a use for, find a use for, use, utilize, employ, make use of; take advantage of, turn to good account, capitalize on, make capital out of; profit by, gain from, reap the profit from; reap the benefit of, be the better for

▶ *Use 393; Gain 467; Improvement 807*

ADVERBS

12 usefully, handily, helpfully; practically, conveniently, usably, serviceably, efficiently; advantageously, profitably; *pro bono publico* [L], for the public good

802 Uselessness

NOUNS

1 uselessness, lack of use, inutility, unhelpfulness, disservice; unfitness, unaptness, inaptitude, unsuitability; inapplicability, inconvenience, inexpedience, inexpediency; impracticality, impracticability, unworkability; lack of function, unserviceableness, unemployability; unskillfulness, lack of skill; inability, incompetence, ineptitude, inefficiency, ineffectiveness, inefficacy, ineffectualness; fecklessness, impotence, powerlessness, inadequacy, effeteness; worthlessness, unsalability

2 redundancy, superfluousness, superfluity, expendability, dispensability, disposability

▶ *Excess 99; Unskillfulness 128; Powerlessness 515; Inconvenience 804; Hindrance 826*

3 futility, purposelessness, lack of purpose, pointlessness, hopelessness; vanity, vanity of vanities, idleness; failure, loss, unprofitability, profitlessness, bootlessness, lack of advantage, lack of benefit; unproductiveness, fruitlessness, barrenness, sterility; waste, wastefulness; thanklessness

▶ *Infertility 23; Loss 468; Failure 846*

4 waste of effort, wasted effort, wasted labor, lost labor; waste of time, waste of breath, waste of space; false scent, red herring; wild-goose chase, fool's errand, fool's gold; labor of Sisyphus, blind alley, half measures, tinkering, futilitarianism, dead loss

▶ *Waste 96*

5 refuse, rubbish, trash, junk, litter, scrap; throwaway, disposable, castoff, reject; leftovers, leavings, scraps; stuff, spoilage, wastage, bilge; waste, waste product, wastepaper; scourings, offscourings, sweepings, shavings; chaff, husks, stubble, tares, bran, seeds, cotton seeds; bits, crumbs; offal, carrion; debris, muck, dirt, dust, ash, cinder, clinker; dross, slag, scoria, scum; peel, leaves, weeds, dead wood; effluvia, excrement; odds and ends

▶ *Waste 96; Dirtiness 112; Remainder 750*

6 place for waste, compost, compost heap; dump, refuse dump, garbage dump, garbage pile, trash dump, rubbish heap, midden, landfill; sump, drain, cesspool, septic tank, sewage treatment plant, incinerator; dustheap, slag heap; garbage can, trash can, wastebasket

ADJECTIVES

7 useless, not useful, of no use, inutile, unhelpful, unfit, unapt, inapt, unsuitable, inapplicable, inconvenient, inexpedient, impractical, impracticable, unworkable, unpractical, nonfunctional, functionless, ornamental, unusable, unserviceable, fit for nothing, good-for-nothing; unemployable, unqualified, unskilled, unskillful, unable, incompetent, inept; inefficient, ineffective, ineffectual, feckless, impotent, powerless, inadequate; no good, dud, invalid; void, null, null and void; abrogated, worthless, valueless; rubbishy, trashy, unsalable, not worth the paper it's written on

8 broken down, nonfunctioning, inoperative, not working, out of order, down; worn out, spent, effete, out of action, *hors de combat* [Fr]; [Inf]: no-go, screwed up, fucked up, kaput, past it, mickey mouse

▶ *Excess 99; Unskillfulness 128; Powerlessness 515; Oldness 653; Inconvenience 804; Hindrance 826; Cancellation 834*

9 redundant, superfluous, extra, excessive; unnecessary, not needed, unneeded; unwanted, expendable, dispensable; disposable, throwaway; obsolete, outmoded, old-fashioned, antiquated

10 futile, purposeless, pointless, Sisyphean, hopeless; vain, in vain, idle, unavailing, abortive, unsuccessful; profitless, bootless, not worthwhile, offering no advantage, offering no benefit; unprofitable, not paying, loss-making, uneconomic; unproductive, fruitless, barren, sterile; wasteful, ill-spent, wasted, squandered, time-wasting, effort-wasting; not worth the effort, unrewarding, unrewarded, thankless

▶ *Infertility 23; Waste 96; Loss 468; Failure 846*

VERBS

11 **be useless,** have no use, have no purpose, not help, hinder; achieve nothing, be in vain, have no chance; fail, not work, not function, not go, break down; fall by the wayside, go to waste, go begging

▶ *Excess 99; Hindrance 826; Failure 846*

12 **make useless,** disqualify, disable, render unfit, unfit; unman, disarm, unarm, render harmless; cripple, make lame, lame; dismantle, disassemble, undo, take to pieces, break up, break down; unmount, dismast, unrig, decommission, put out of commission, lay up, deactivate, make inactive; sabotage, obstruct, abrogate; withdraw from currency, devalue, cheapen; impair, deface, pollute, contaminate; destroy, obliterate, lay waste; make barren, sterilize, castrate, emasculate; exhaust, use up, overwork

▶ *Obliteration 186; Inactivity 415; Cheapness 497; Powerlessness 515; Destruction 523; Cancellation 834*

13 **waste effort,** labor the obvious, waste one's breath, waste one's time; go around in circles, beat the air, tilt at windmills, accomplish nothing, get nowhere, labor in vain, sweat for nothing; attempt the impossible, tinker, leave unfinished; talk to a brick wall, beat one's head against a brick wall, carry coals to Newcastle, flog *or* beat a dead horse, search for the end of the rainbow, go on a wild-goose chase, spin one's wheels [Inf]

▶ *Waste 96; Impossibility 837*

ADVERBS

14 **uselessly,** unhelpfully, inconveniently, impractically, incompetently, ineffectively, ineffectually; to no purpose, in vain, to no avail; unsuccessfully, unprofitably; on a wild-goose chase, until one is blue in the face

803 Convenience

NOUNS

1 **convenience,** handiness, helpfulness, practicality, pragmatism, practicability, practicableness; usability, workability, qualification; adaptation, application, suitability, fitness, propriety; expedience, expediency, contrivance, utilitarianism; profit, advantage, benefit; usefulness, utility, prudence; good policy, advisability, desirability; dueness, timeliness, auspiciousness; opportunity, proper time, right time, right time and place, due time

▶ *Qualification 340; Timeliness 659; Usefulness 801; Help 825*

2 **nearness,** proximity, closeness, juxtaposition, adjacency; accessibility, availability

▶ *Nearness 586*

ADJECTIVES

3 **convenient,** handy, helpful, practical, pragmatic, practicable, usable, workable, effective, effectual, qualified, adapted to, cut out for, applicable, to the purpose, suitable, commodious, appropriate; fit, fitting, befitting; seemly, proper, right; expedient, expediential; advantageous, to one's advantage; beneficial, profitable, useful; prudent, politic, judicious, wise; advisable, commendable, desirable, worthwhile, acceptable, approved; owing, due; *in loco* [L]; timely, well-timed; auspicious, opportune, seasonable; right up one's alley [Inf]

▶ *Wisdom 352; Right 429; Approval 437; Timeliness 659; Usefulness 801*

4 **nearby,** next-door, accessible, available, ready; close, adjacent, neighboring, touching, bordering on

VERBS

5 **be convenient,** come in handy, come in useful; fit, befit, suit, suit the occasion; not come amiss, not go amiss; serve the time, expedite one's end, bring about; help, aid, promote, advance, forward; answer; have the desired effect, produce results; do, serve, prove itself, be better than nothing; succeed, achieve one's purpose, fill the bill; qualify for, correspond with, accord; profit, benefit, give an advantage, advantage; do good, hit the spot [Inf], deliver the goods [Inf]

▶ *Sufficiency 97; Good 445; Accord 735; Usefulness 801; Help 825; Success 845*

ADVERBS

6 **conveniently,** handily, practically, fittingly, expediently, opportunely; accessibly, within reach; in the right place at the right time, to fill the bill

7 **nearby,** close by, next to, at hand; in the vicinity *or* neighborhood; within reach, at one's fingertips, on the tip of one's tongue

804 Inconvenience

An adventure is only an inconvenience rightly considered. An inconvenience is only an adventure wrongly considered. — G. K. CHESTERTON

NOUNS

1 **inconvenience,** disadvantage, drawback; detriment, hurt, harm; inexpedience, inexpediency; inadvisability, undesirability, bad policy, imprudence; inappropriateness, unfittingness; impropriety, unseemliness; lack of planning, poor timing; wrongness, wrong, error; unfitness, unsuitability, inaptitude; inopportuneness, untimeliness; disruption, disturbance; impediment, obstacle, hindrance; upset, discomfort, incommodiousness; difficulty, pain [Inf]

2 **annoyance,** irritation, vexation; bother, trouble, nuisance

3 awkwardness, burden, cumbersomeness, unwieldiness, troublesomeness

> *Wrong 430; Untimeliness 660; Disturbance 768; Uselessness 802; Hindrance 826*

4 distance, remoteness, inaccessibility, unapproachability, unavailability

ADJECTIVES

5 inconvenient, discommodious, incommodious, disadvantageous; detrimental, hurtful, harmful; inexpedient, inadvisable, unadvisable, undesirable; uncommendable, not recommended, ill-advised, ill-considered; impolitic, imprudent, injudicious, unwise; inappropriate, unfitting; misapplied, malapropos, out of place; improper, unseemly, undue, not right; objectionable, offensive; wrong, unfit, unsuitable; ineligible, unqualified, inadmissible, unfortunate; unhappy, infelicitous, sad; inept, unapt; inopportune, unseasonable, untimely, ill-timed, poorly timed, wrongly timed; disruptive, disrupting, disturbing, unsettling; useless, unprofitable, unhelpful, hindering, untoward, adverse, unprofessional; ill-contrived, ill-planned

6 awkward, clumsy, cumbersome, lumbering, hulking, unwieldy, burdensome, onerous

> *Unskillfulness 128*

7 annoying, bothersome, troublesome, irritating, irksome, boring, tiresome, vexatious, tedious

> *Folly 353; Wrong 430; Disapproval 438; Untimeliness 660; Disturbance 768; Uselessness 802; Hindrance 826*

8 distant, remote, out-of-the-way, inaccessible, unapproachable, unavailable

> *Distance 585*

VERBS

9 be inconvenient, come amiss, go amiss; not do, not fit, not help, inconvenience; disturb, disrupt, upset; put to inconvenience, put to trouble; discommode, incommode; put out, hinder, obstruct; handicap, disadvantage; penalize, work against, militate against; hurt, harm

10 annoy, bother, trouble; irritate, vex, irk, embarrass; pester, make a nuisance of oneself, hassle [Inf]

ADVERBS

11 inconveniently, discommodiously, incommodiously; inexpediently; inadvisably, injudiciously; improperly, inopportunely, disruptively; uselessly, unhelpfully; awkwardly, clumsily

12 annoyingly, irritatingly, boringly, tediously, tiresomely, vexatiously

805 Perfection

NOUNS

1 perfection, sheer perfection, perfectness; finish, completion, consummation; polish, ripeness, readiness, maturity; exactness, idealness, the ideal; flawlessness, faultlessness, impeccability, infallibility, indefectibility; correctness, correctitude; preciseness, accuracy; irreproachability

2 immaculateness, immaculacy, spotlessness; purity, blamelessness, guiltlessness, innocence

3 perfect condition, wholeness, completeness; excellence, brilliance; mint condition, soundness

4 expertise, mastery, proficiency, skill; superiority, transcendence

5 peak, top, zenith, acme, summit, pinnacle, capstone; height *or* pitch *or* acme *or* peak of perfection

6 ideal, pattern, standard, model, archetype, paragon; *ne plus ultra* [L], ultimate, extreme; last word, crowning achievement, masterpiece, chef-d'oeuvre; flawless performance, ten out of ten, one hundred percent

7 perfectionist, purist, pedant, stickler, perfecter; expert, master

> *Skillfulness 127*

ADJECTIVES

8 perfect, perfected, brought to perfection; finished, completed, fulfilled, polished; ripened, ripe, fully ripe, ready; matured, mature, fully mature; exact, just right, just so; flawless, unflawed, faultless

9 best, very best, optimum; champion, grand-champion, winning, blue-ribbon, gold-medal; nothing like it, first, first-class, first-rate, second to none; a cut above, supreme, incomparable, unequaled; unbeaten, unbeatable, unmatched, matchless, unparalleled, peerless, unsurpassed, unsurpassable; perfect, record, record-breaking, world-class, best-selling, chart-topping, number-one, all-time, crowning; principal, capital, cardinal, important; tops, topnotch, ace, best ever, A one *or* A number one *or* A 1 [Inf], tiptop [Inf]

> *Skillfulness 127; Superiority 744; Importance 799*

10 infallible, impeccable, indefectible, without defect; correct, precise, accurate; irreproachable

11 immaculate, without a stain, unstained, unspotted, spotless; unblemished, without blemish, unmarked; uncontaminated, untainted, pure, unmixed, unalloyed

12 blameless, exemplary, guiltless, innocent, impeccable, sinless; godly, saintly

13 unbroken, sound, uncracked, sound as a bell; right as right can be, right as rain; in perfect condition, undamaged, unmarred, unspoiled *or* unspoilt; safe and sound, unhurt, unscathed, scatheless; unscarred, unscratched, no harm done

14 complete, whole, intact, entire; absolute, utter, total, one hundred percent; undiminished, unreduced, without loss, full; tight, airtight, vacuum-packed, watertight, seaworthy

15 excellent, sublime, superb, dazzling, brilliant

16 expert, proficient, skilled, skillful, masterly; consummate, supreme, transcendent; unrivaled, top, at the peak of perfection

17 ideal, standard, model, archetypal; classic, classical, Augustan; in perfect health, in the pink
- *Health 113; Skillfulness 127; Innocence 449; Superiority 744; Whole 759; Completeness 761*

18 perfectionistic, puristic, puristical, pedantic, precise, punctilious; meticulous, fastidious, scrupulous; particular, exacting, demanding, fussy

VERBS

19 perfect, finish, complete, fulfill; realize, accomplish, achieve, execute, carry out; ripen, mature, bring to perfection, consummate; correct, rectify; improve, ameliorate, elaborate; polish, refine, put on the finishing touch, crown

20 be perfect, leave nothing to be desired, give a flawless performance; score ten out of ten, score one hundred per cent

ADVERBS

21 perfectly, flawlessly, faultlessly, impeccably; exactly, precisely, irreproachably; immaculately, spotlessly; excellently, consummately; to perfection, to just the right degree, to a turn, just as one would wish; verbatim, word for word, to the letter, literally

22 completely, wholly, entirely; absolutely, utterly, totally; quite, thoroughly; unequivocally, unambiguously, purely

806 Imperfection

NOUNS

1 imperfection, imperfectness, faultiness, defectiveness; room for improvement, possibility of perfection, perfectibility; fallibility, peccability; erroneousness, error; peccadillo, irregularity; unevenness, patchiness, adulteration; weakness, vulnerability, frailty, failure; damage, unsoundness, staleness; overripeness, unfitness; infirmity, ill health; inferiority

2 incompleteness, deficiency, want, lack, need; shortfall, inadequacy, insufficiency; perfunctoriness, cursoriness, lack of thoroughness, carelessness; underachievement, immaturity, unripeness; rawness, crudeness; undevelopment, underdevelopment
- *Insufficiency 98; Error 351; Inferiority 745; Incompleteness 762*

3 imperfect item, second, reject; shopworn item, not one's best, second best; poor effort, weak effort; inferior version, incomplete set, broken set; makeshift, stopgap, consolation

4 defect, fault, flaw; blemish, mark, taint, stain; blot, spot, smudge; scratch, chip, tear; mistake, error; rift, leak, loophole; crack, chink, lacuna, gap; deficiency, lack, limitation, shortfall; kink, quirk, idiosyncrasy, eccentricity, foible; failing, shortcoming, weakness; weak point, weak link in the chain; blind spot, soft spot, soft underbelly; tragic flaw, feet of clay, vulnerable point, chink in one's armor, Achilles heel; disadvantage, difficulty, drawback; catch, snag, hindrance, obstacle; fly in the ointment, hang-up [Inf]
- *Error 351; Blemish 533; Interval 587; Hindrance 826*

ADJECTIVES

5 imperfect, not perfect, faulty, defective, not quite right, less than perfect; capable of perfection, perfectible; fallible, peccable, erroneous; irregular, uneven, good and bad, patchy, good in parts; weak, vulnerable, frail, unsteady, wobbly, shaky, rickety; damaged, broken; cracked, leaky, unsound; soiled, shopworn, stained, spotted, marked; scratched, chipped, blemished, tainted; corked, stale, overripe; past its sell date, past its prime; bad, off; off-color, not in the pink; below par, off form, off stride; unfit, unhealthy; not good enough, unsatisfactory, unacceptable, not up to expectations, not up to the mark, unworthy; second-best, second-class, third-class, second-rate, third-rate; inferior, poor
- *Ill Health 114; Unskillfulness 128; Weakness 517; Blemish 533; Inferiority 745; Deterioration 808*

6 incomplete, deficient, wanting, lacking; inadequate, insufficient; perfunctory, cursory, careless; not entire, partial, fragmentary; unfilled, half-filled; unequipped, undermanned, short-staffed, short-handed, below strength; unfinished, half-finished; makeshift, rough-and-ready, provisional; raw, crude; untrained, scratch, immature; undeveloped, unpolished, unrefined
- *Insufficiency 98; Inattention 324; Incompleteness 762*

7 defective, flawed, blemished, marked, tainted, stained, maimed

VERBS

8 be imperfect, have a fault; fall short, fall short of perfection; not live up to expectations, not impress; not bear inspection, not pass muster; fail, fail the test; not make the grade, dissatisfy, not suffice; barely pass, scrape through; have a chink in one's armor, have feet of clay; have a crack, not hold water, leak
- *Insufficiency 98; Dissatisfaction 274; Blemish 533*

9 leave imperfect, finish halfway, leave unfinished; make a weak effort

ADVERBS

10 imperfectly, defectively; below par, irregularly, unevenly; incompletely, insufficiently, to a limited extent; barely, scarcely; almost, not quite, all but; with all its faults

807 Improvement

How doth the little busy bee / Improve each shining hour.
— ISAAC WATTS

NOUNS

1 improvement, betterment, amelioration, melioration; change *or* turn for the better, sea change; transfiguration, transformation, conversion, redemption;

rehabilitation, reform, reformation, radical reform, penitence, new leaf, new resolution; good influence, the making of; polish, perfection; elaboration, enrichment, enhancement; regeneration, refinement; purification, cleansing, sublimation

2 **uplift,** lift, upturn, upswing; upward mobility, success, prosperity, increase; self-improvement, upgrading, elevation, rise, ascent

3 **social improvement,** civilization, socialization, education, enlightenment, cultivation, progress

4 **restoration,** rectification, repair; cure, remedy, recruitment, revival; recovery, recuperation, convalescence; refreshment
  ▶ *Remedy 115; Repair 809*

5 **promotion,** furtherance, advancement, advance, graduation; progress, headway, progression

6 **tidying,** cleaning; renovation, refurbishment, reconditioning, renewal, modernization
  ▶ *Cleanliness 111*

7 **beautification,** embellishment, adornment, ornament, ornamentation, decoration, redecoration; finishing touch, final touch, frosting *or* icing on the cake, last word; face-lift, spruceness, titivation
  ▶ *Beautification 530*

8 **rectification,** putting right, making good, straightening out, adjustment, repair, mending; correction, proofreading; revision, revise, revisal, recension, redaction; blue-penciling, editing, copyediting; amendment, emendation, alteration; reorganization, shake-up
  ▶ *Publication 173; Repair 809*

9 **reconsideration,** reexamination, review, further reflection; better thing, better choice, better idea, new idea, another idea, better thought, second thought; updated model, revised edition, new edition, updated version, improved version, emendation

10 **bodily improvement,** recovery, recuperation; exercise, weight training, aerobics, calisthenics, jogging, walking, swimming, yoga
  ▶ *Health 113*

11 **improver,** reformer, repairer, restorer, progressive; beautifier, rectifier, mender, reviser, redecorator; amender, emender, corrector, rewriter, editor, copyeditor, proofreader
  ▶ *Publication 173; Repair 809*

ADJECTIVES

12 **improved,** better, superior; bettered, enhanced, touched up, beautified, redecorated; reformed, transformed; revised, edited, rewritten; repaired, restored, renovated, modernized; better off, all the better for; better advised, wiser
  ▶ *Superiority 744; Repair 809*

13 **improvable,** perfectible, ameliorable, meliorable; reformable, corrigible, curable

14 **improving,** advancing, ameliorative, meliorative; remedial, restorative; reformative, reformatory, reform-ing, reformist; civilizing, cultural, idealistic; rectifying, emending, correcting, revising; recovering, recuperating, looking up, on the mend; rising, increasing
  ▶ *Repair 809*

VERBS

15 **improve,** make better, better, ameliorate, meliorate; reform, change for the better; make improvements, improve upon; polish, perfect, elaborate, enrich, enhance; work miracles with, transform, transfigure; convert, redeem, rehabilitate; make, be the making of; have a good influence on; leaven, raise, uplift, regenerate; refine, upgrade, elevate, sublimate, purify

16 **civilize,** socialize, educate, teach manners

17 **restore,** mend, repair, straighten, straighten out, rectify, patch up, fix up; make healthy, cure, recruit, revive, infuse new *or* fresh blood into, refresh

18 **promote,** market, hype [Inf]; foster, encourage, forward, further, advance; bring to fruition, mature; profit from, make the most of, get the best out of; take advantage of, use, exploit; develop, open up, reclaim

19 **tidy,** tidy up, make shipshape, make neat, neaten, spruce up, smarten up, freshen up; clean, clean up, shape up, touch up

20 **beautify,** give a face-lift, improve on nature; dress up, make up, titivate; renovate, refurbish, recondition, renew; bring up-to-date, modernize; embellish, adorn, ornament, decorate, gild the lily
  ▶ *Refreshment 94; Influence 512; Beautification 530; Decoration 532; Change 665; Conversion 670; Repair 809*

21 **get better,** grow better, improve, mend, take a turn for the better, turn the corner; pick up, rally, revive, recover, recuperate; get over the worst, pass the crisis, convalesce; make progress, make headway, advance, develop, evolve, progress; mellow, ripen, mature, fructify, bear fruit, increase; rise, ascend, graduate, succeed, rise in the world, better oneself, prosper; mend one's ways, reform, turn over a new leaf, straighten up and fly right [Inf]; improve oneself, learn, study, learn by experience; take advantage of, make capital out of, cash in on, profit by; make the grade, make good
  ▶ *Health 113; Remedy 115; Ascent 713; Increase 746; Repair 809; Success 845; Prosperity 847*

22 **rectify,** put right, set right, remedy, make good, straighten, straighten out; adjust, repair, mend, patch, fix; correct, make corrections, make improvements, make clear, make concise; proofread, remove errors; revise, redact, edit, copyedit, blue-pencil, amend, emend, alter; rewrite, redraft, retell, recast; remold, refashion, remodel, recreate, reform, reorganize; regularize, fine-tune, streamline; review, reexamine

23 **reconsider,** redo, take back to the drawing board, go back to square one; stop and think, think again; think better of, have second thoughts

24 better, for the better, improvably; remedially, restoratively; progressively

808 Deterioration

NOUNS

1 **deterioration,** worsening, turn for the worse, losing ground, retrogradation, retrogression, decay, impairment; regression, reversion to type, throwback, slipping back, backsliding, recidivism, lapse, relapse, setback; descent, downward course, primrose path; deceleration, slowing down; wane, ebb, twilight, fading, dimness; tragedy, misfortune, bad ending, road to hell, going to hell in a handbasket, bad scene; the skids [Inf], bad news [Inf]

▸ *Dimness 248; Poverty 486; Descent 714; Decrease 747*

2 **economic deterioration,** recession, depression, economic downturn, falling off, slump, downturn, downtrend, decline, decrease, depreciation, impoverishment, poverty; law of diminishing returns, bad money driving out good, Gresham's law, exhaustion of supplies, overpopulation, Malthusianism

3 **moral deterioration,** depravity, immorality, degeneration, degeneracy, degenerateness, perversion; prostitution, depravation, addiction, indulgence, substance abuse; promiscuity, impureness, impurity, decadence; ruin, vitiation, corruption, subversion, degradation, debasement, abasement; abuse, brutalization, dehumanization, barbarism; vulgarization, coarsening, devaluation, cheapening; demoralization, loss of morale; draining, depletion, exhaustion

▸ *Misuse 395; Immorality 432; Wickedness 448; Cheapness 497; Distortion 627*

4 **physical deterioration,** wear and tear; infection, contagion, contagious disease, contamination; poisoning, intoxication, autointoxication *or* autotoxemia, ulceration; putrefaction, gangrene, corruption, mold, moldiness, mildew, blight, canker, cancer; decrepitude, old age, senility, ravages of time, one foot in the grave, hardening of the arteries, marasmus, atrophy, disease, illness; lameness, crippling, hobbling; disabling, disablement, weakening, weakness; physical wreck, rambling wreck, shadow of one's former self

▸ *Age 27; Ill Health 114*

5 **dilapidation,** collapse, disintegration, breakdown, ruination, destruction, ruin, rack and ruin; lack of repair, disrepair, lack of maintenance, neglect, negligence, shabbiness; urban blight, slum, inner-city ghetto, rattrap; wreck, mere wreck, perfect wreck

6 **decay,** erosion, corrosion, oxidization, rustiness, rust; rot, rottenness, decomposition; discoloration, weathering, bleaching, patina, verdigris

▸ *Negligence 326; Destruction 523; Disintegration 758*

7 **impairment,** detriment, damage, spoiling, spoilage, waste, loss; ruination, devastation, havoc, demolition, destruction; attack, assault, insult, outrage, sabotage, terrorism; disorganization, derangement; aggravation, exacerbation; adulteration, sophistication, mixture, debasement, watering down; pollution, acid rain, dirtiness, uncleanness, defilement

▸ *Dirtiness 112; Aggravation 276; Attack 418; Destruction 523; Mixture 751; Disturbance 768*

ADJECTIVES

8 **deteriorated,** worsened, worse, getting worse, worse and worse, the worse for, gone from bad to worse; deteriorating, worsening, failing, going downhill, far gone, in a bad way, on the way out; past one's best *or* prime, decreasing, declining, in decline, on the decline, falling off, in recession, going to pot; falling, slipping, sliding, tottering, senile, senescent, aging, degenerate, degenerative; done in [Inf], done for [Inf]

9 **spoiled,** bad, gone bad, gone off, off, rotten, corky; impaired, damaged, ruined, destroyed; effete, worn out, exhausted, tired, overtired, drained; impoverished, poor, run-down, worthless, useless; descending, on the downgrade, on the downward path, downfallen, fallen by the wayside; weakened, undermined, honeycombed, sapped, shaken; faded, discolored; decaying, decayed, decomposed, disintegrated; withered, sere, wasting away, ebbing, at low ebb; retrogressive, regressive, retrograde

▸ *Disintegration 758*

10 **unimproved,** undeveloped, backward; stale, flat, bland, tasteless; old-fashioned, outdated; lapsed, relapsed, recidivist

▸ *Poverty 486; Descent 714; Decrease 747; Uselessness 802; Fatigue 820*

11 **dilapidated,** in disrepair, the worse for wear, falling apart, falling to pieces, in ruins, in shreds, in bits and pieces; beyond repair, cracked, broken, leaking

12 **decrepit,** rickety, tottery, shaky, unsteady; not functioning, not working, out of order, not in proper condition, out of kilter; ruinous, ramshackle, derelict, tumbledown

13 **worn,** battered, weather-beaten, storm-tossed; run-down, on its last legs; dog-eared, worn out, worn to a frazzle, worn to a shadow, worn to the threads; about to go, exhausted, weakened, ruined; slummy, condemned, flea-bitten, rat-infested; worn, well-worn, shopworn, frayed, shabby; unkempt, dingy, holey, in holes, in tatters, in rags, seedy, down-at-heel, down-and-out; rusty, mildewed, moldering; moth-eaten, worm-eaten; [Inf]: kaput, out of whack, on the fritz

VERBS

14 **deteriorate,** worsen, get worse, take a turn for the worse, go from bad to worse; slip, slide, go downhill, lose ground, not maintain one's position, have seen better days, be a shadow of one's former self; fall, fall

off, slump, decline, decrease, decelerate, slow down; wane, ebb, sink, fail, totter, droop, stoop; slip back, retrograde, retrogress, regress, revert, lapse, relapse; degenerate, let oneself go, take it easy, tread the primrose path; become obsolete, lose value, depreciate; go to pieces, self-destruct, ruin oneself, go to the devil, go to rack and ruin, go to the bad, lose control; weaken, lose health, sicken, fall ill; do worse, go farther and fare worse, flop, go to pot, go to the dogs [Inf], hit the skids [Inf]

15 **disintegrate,** crumble, collapse, go to ruin, go or run to seed; break down, come apart, fall apart; contract, shrink; wear out, age, grow old, fade, wither, wilt, shrivel, wrinkle; perish, become dilapidated, fray, become threadbare, become shabby

> *Age 27; Ill Health 114; Weakness 517; Destruction 523; Contraction 582; Descent 714; Decrease 747; Disintegration 758*

16 **decay,** decompose, rot, putrefy; mildew, grow moss; weather, rust, molder, corrode; spoil, go bad, go off, go sour, become rancid, turn; stale, go stale, grow stale, lose taste, lose flavor, go flat; corrupt, rankle, fester, suppurate, go septic, gangrene; smell, stink

> *Stench 227*

17 **make worse,** worsen, make things worse; aggravate, exacerbate, irritate, embitter; adulterate, corrupt, sophisticate, alloy, debase, denature; infect, contaminate, taint; poison, envenom; ulcerate, canker; pollute, foul, dirty, make unclean, defile, desecrate, profane

> *Dirtiness 112; Aggravation 276; Mixture 751*

18 **impair,** damage; make inoperative or inoperable, put out of action; deactivate, make inactive; dismantle, dismast; spoil, mar, maul, ruin, destroy, play havoc with; mess up, untidy, jumble, derange, disorganize, bungle, botch, pull a boner; fool around with, touch, tinker, tamper, trifle with, meddle; wreck, vandalize, ravage, rape, plunder, waste, lay waste, scorch; overthrow, crush, crumble, pulverize; [Inf]: muck up, fuck up, screw up, ball up

> *Unskillfulness 128; Inactivity 415; Destruction 523; Disturbance 768*

19 **eat away,** erode, corrode, shake; honeycomb, fret, bore, gnaw, gnaw at the roots; rust, rot, decay, decompose, mildew, blight, blast, plague; overrun, invade

20 **stain,** spot, blot, blacken, soil; mark, blemish, deface, disfigure, scar, wrinkle; uglify, make ugly

21 **wear out,** reduce to rags; drain, deplete, exhaust, consume, use up; dilapidate, fray, frazzle

22 **pervert,** deform, warp, twist, distort; abuse, misuse, prostitute, deprave, debauch, ruin, vitiate, corrupt; subvert, lower, degrade, debase, abase; treat cruelly, brutalize, dehumanize, barbarize, denature, denaturalize; denationalize, detribalize; propagandize, brain-

wash, misteach; vulgarize, coarsen, make coarse, drag down to one's level, devalue, cheapen

> *Misuse 395; Immorality 432; Wickedness 448; Cheapness 497; Distortion 627; Lowering 716*

ADVERBS

23 **worse,** for the worse, down; downhill, down in the world; badly, poorly; out of the frying pan into the fire

809 Repair

NOUNS

1 **repair,** repairs, reparation, mending, patching up, fixing, putting right, rectification, correction, reactivation, remedy; amendment, editing, emendation; maintenance, service, servicing, correcting faults, overhauling, overhaul, tuning, tune-up, adjustment; renovation, restoration, renewal, reconditioning, reintegration, redintegration, reassembling, do-it-yourself; making like new, putting in mint condition, making as good as new; mend, invisible mending, darn, darning, patch, patching; cobbling, soling, resoling, heeling, resurfacing; splicing, binding; insertion, reinforcement; refit, new look, face-lift, beautification

> *Remedy 115; Beautification 530; Improvement 807*

2 **restoration,** returning, giving back, replacement, putting back, retrocession, repatriation; restitution, redress, amends, reparation, reparations, atonement; finding again, getting back, retrieval, recovery, recall; reinvestment, reinstitution, reinstallation, reinstallment, rehabilitation; replanting, reforestation, reclamation, gentrification; recycling, reprocessing, salvage; redemption, ransom, rescue, salvation; deliverance, reestablishment, reconstitution, reintroduction, relaunching, reformulation; reerection, rebuilding, reformation, reprogramming, reconstruction; reorganization, readjustment, reorientation; remodeling, refashioning; reconversion, reaction, counterreformation, counteraction; resumption, return to normal; recruitment, reinforcement, strengthening, replenishment, provision

> *Provision 89; Atonement 313; Giving Back 478; Counteraction 510; Deliverance 817*

3 **revival,** recovery, renewal, revivification, revitalization, revivescence, reawakening, resurgence; recurrence, comeback, return to fashion; turnabout, turnaround; rally, fresh spurt, new energy, refreshment, new supply, recruitment; financial upturn, economic recovery, economic miracle, boom, prosperity; reactivation, reanimation, resuscitation, artificial respiration; rejuvenation, rejuvenescence, second youth, second honeymoon, second spring, Indian summer; rebirth, renaissance or renascence, new birth, second birth, palingenesis, regeneration, regeneracy; new life, new hope, second chance

▶ *Refreshment 94; Prosperity 847*

4 recuperation, convalescence, recovery, healing, mending, cure, being cured, response to treatment, response to therapy, return to normal; rally, rallying, perking up, upturn, turn for the better; restoration to health, return to health, remedy; moderation, easing, relief; psychological cure, psychotherapy, catharsis, abreaction; curability, curableness

▶ *Health 113; Remedy 115; Relief 275; Improvement 807*

5 repairer, mender, fixer, handyman, mechanic, renovator; amender, emendator, editor, copyeditor, proofreader; rectifier, rebuilder; restorer, refurbisher; reformer, curer, healer

▶ *Remedy 115; Improvement 807*

ADJECTIVES

6 repaired, mended, patched up, fixed, right, correct; restored, reconditioned, renovated, redecorated, remade, rebuilt, reconstructed, reconstituted; refurbished, reequipped, refitted, redone, rectified, put right; reinforced, strengthened, improved; like new, in mint condition, as good as new, renewed; resuscitated, revived, redivivus, renascent, resurgent, phoenixlike, like a phoenix from the ashes; reclaimed, recovered, salvaged, found

▶ *Remedy 115; Improvement 807*

7 repairable, reparable, restorable, mendable, amendable, rectifiable; recoverable, retrievable, redeemable *or* redemptible; curable, operable, treatable, medicable

8 cured, healed, returned to health, healthy; like new, as good as new, none the worse; convalescent, on the mend, better; back on one's feet, back to normal, oneself again; alive and kicking, in one's right mind

▶ *Health 113; Remedy 115*

9 restorative, reparative, analeptic, reviving, recuperative; curative, sanative, healing, medicated, medicinal; remedial, redemptive *or* redemptory

▶ *Refreshment 94; Remedy 115*

VERBS

10 repair, do repairs, mend, patch up, fix, right, put right, set to rights, adjust, tune up, overhaul, service, maintain; rectify, correct, straighten out, put in order; put into working order, get working, put back into operation, reactivate, remedy; amend, edit, emend; cobble, sole, resole, heel, retread; reface, cover, recover, resurface, thatch, line, reline, make good; splice, bind, bind up, tie, tie up; darn, patch, reupholster; stop, fill, fill in, plug, plug up, plug a hole, stop a gap, fill in the cracks, plaster, seal, paper over, caulk; piece together, glue together, reassemble, put back together; cannibalize, join

▶ *Right 429; Closure 584; Covering 613; Union 752; Improvement 807*

11 refurbish, renovate, redecorate, repaint, repaper; recondition, revamp, refit, restore, renew; remodel, refashion, reform; retouch, touch up, freshen up, make over, change, smarten up, give a face-lift; improve,

upgrade, modernize, do wonders with, gentrify; do up [Inf], fix up [Inf]

▶ *Cleanliness 111; Newness 652; Improvement 807*

12 restore, return, replace, retrocede, repatriate; give back, hand back, put back, bring back; yield up, restitute, make amends, pay back, atone; recall, reappoint, reinstall; reintroduce, relaunch, refound; reestablish, reinstitute, rehabilitate, reconstitute, reformulate, reprogram, reform, reorganize, reorient; reinforce, reconstruct, rebuild, reerect, remake, redo; make like new, return to mint condition, make as good as new; service, overhaul, valet, clean; make whole, reintegrate, redintegrate; replant, reclaim, reforest; recycle, reprocess, revalidate; revive, rally, strengthen; replenish, fill up again, restock; reassemble, reconvene, bring together; redeem, ransom, rescue, save, salvage, deliver; release, free, liberate; cough up [Inf]

▶ *Assembly 59; Provision 89; Health 113; Atonement 313; Giving Back 478; Strength 516; Deliverance 817; Liberation 831*

13 be restored, recover, come around, come to, revive; pick up, rally, respond to treatment; pull through, get over, get well, get better, bounce back, make a comeback, sleep off, snap out of it; convalesce, recuperate, regain one's strength, turn the corner, find one's feet again; pick oneself up, get up, weather the storm, survive, live through; undergo repairs

▶ *Refreshment 94; Health 113; Beginning 771; Improvement 807*

14 revive, revivify, revitalize, resuscitate, regenerate; recall to life, awaken, reawaken, resurrect, reanimate; rekindle, enliven, invigorate, reinvigorate; breathe fresh life into, have *or* give a new lease on life, restore vitality, rejuvenate, freshen, refresh, renew, recruit

▶ *Refreshment 94*

15 cure, heal, make well, cure of, break of; nurse, nurse through; treat, physic, medicate, prescribe medication; detoxify, use therapy; doctor; operate, bandage, put a plaster on, bind up one's wounds; work a cure, perform a miracle, snatch from the grave; restore to health, set up, set on one's feet again

▶ *Health 113; Remedy 115; Improvement 807*

ADVERBS

16 repairably; reparably, recoverably, redeemably; remedially

810 Safety

Better safe than sorry. — PROVERB

NOUNS

1 safety, safeness, security, protection; invulnerability, impregnability, immunity, charmed life; lack of danger, lack of risk, harmlessness; safety in numbers, safe place, safe distance, wide berth, avoidance; regained safety, danger past, all clear, coast clear, storm blown over; safe job, secure position, permanent post; guarantee, warranty, warrant; certainty, sense of security, assurance, confidence, faith; means of escape, back door, opt-out clause, escape clause; rescue, negotiated release, deliverance

▸ *Avoidance 386; Refuge 812; Escape 816; Deliverance 817; Certainty 840*

2 **protection,** safeguard, preventive measure; surety, anchor, buffer, cushion; screen, cover, umbrella; defense, defenses, sure defense, guard, tower of strength, armed force; bulwark, bastion, moat, ditch, palisade, stockade; armor, shield, breastplate, armor plate, panoply; deterrent, weapon; precautions, means of safety, precautionary steps

▸ *Weapon 78; Defense 419*

3 **haven,** sanctuary, asylum, refuge, safe house, safe harbor; shelter, halfway house, group home, rest home, assisted-living residence, nursing home, hospice; foster home, orphanage

▸ *Refuge 812*

4 **safe conduct,** passport, pass, permit; escort, convoy

5 **security system,** surveillance, electronic surveillance, alarm system, burglar alarm, security check, vetting; police protection

6 **safekeeping,** grasp, grip, embrace; ward, care, keeping, custody, charge, safe hands, protective custody

▸ *Refuge 812*

7 **patronage,** support, aid, sponsorship, good offices, auspices, aegis; fatherly *or* motherly eye, tutelage, protectorate, guardianship, wardship, wardenship, custodianship, surrogacy

8 **sanitary precaution,** hygiene, immunization, vaccination, inoculation; prophylaxis, contraception, condom, tampon; quarantine, cordon sanitaire, isolation, segregation, seclusion

▸ *Remedy 115; Hygiene 116; Caution 287*

9 **protection from the weather,** oilskin(s), raincoat, rainwear, sou'wester, umbrella; suntan lotion, suntan oil, sunblock, sunshade, parasol; sunglasses, goggles, eyeshade, sun hat, pith helmet, sun helmet, topee *or* topi; snowsuit; tarpaulin, canvas, tent, windbreak; awning, shutter, window shade, blind, Venetian blind, curtain

▸ *Clothing 100*

10 **insurance,** life insurance, life assurance [Brit], fire insurance, car insurance, household insurance; savings, savings account, collateral; nest egg, something for a rainy day, provision, store; Social Security, welfare

▸ *Provision 89; Carefulness 325; Defense 419; Retention 471; Thrift 499; Enclosure 619; Refuge 812; Preservation 815; Help 825*

11 **protector,** guardian, mentor, tutor; guardian angel, patron saint; tutelary saint, liege lord, feudal lord; patron, patroness, benefactor, benefactress, fairy godmother; champion, knight in shining armor, white knight, defender; chaperon, companion, keeper; caregiver, nurse, nursemaid, baby-sitter, sitter, child-minder [Brit]; governess, duenna, au pair, nanny, foster parent; preserver, shepherd, park keeper, gamekeeper; forester, forest ranger, firewatcher, firefighter, fireman, coast guard, lifeguard, lifesaver

12 **surveillant,** curator, conservator, custodian, warden, warder *or* watcher, lookout, watch, watchman, night watchman; vigilante, Guardian Angels, neighborhood watch; guard, security guard, security man *or* woman, sentry, sentinel; doorman, bodyguard, bouncer, strong-arm man

13 **security force,** armed guard, Secret Service, Federal Bureau of Investigation (FBI), National Guard, National Guardsman, militia; customs official; police, policeman, policewoman, police officer, patrolman, constable, sheriff; drug enforcement officer, vice squad member; private investigator (PI), private detective; [Inf]: copper, cop, dick, private eye, weekend warrior

▸ *Defense 419*

14 **watchdog,** guard dog, sniffer dog, police dog, Cerberus

▸ *Defense 419; Preservation 815*

15 **safety device,** alarm, burglar alarm; police barrier, crash barrier, guardrail, railing; pilot *or* cowcatcher; mail, chain mail, armor; bulletproof vest, bulletproof car, bulletproof glass, shatterproof glass, toughened glass; fail-safe device, fail-safe system; respirator, oxygen tent; mask, gas mask, safety goggles, earmuffs, earplugs; safety chain, dead-man's handle *or* pedal; safety catch, safety lock, bolt, dead bolt, deadlock; safety valve, safety pin, safety razor, safety match; lightning rod, ground; fuse, circuit breaker; fire alarm, smoke alarm, fire extinguisher, fire blanket, sprinkler system; fire escape, fire door, fire wall; crash helmet, safety helmet, football helmet, protective clothing; seat belt, safety belt, safety harness, shoulder harness, air bag; ejection seat, escape hatch, means of escape, parachute; safety net; lifeboat, rubber dinghy, life raft; life buoy, lifeline, preserver, life belt, life vest, life jacket, buoyancy jacket, buoyancy aid, Mae West, water wings; breeches buoy, rope, plank; anchor, sheet anchor, kedge, grapnel, grappling iron, killick *or* killock, drogue; lead, reins, brake, fetter; bar, lock, key, stopper; ballast; mole, breakwater, groin, embankment, sea wall; lighthouse, lightship; jury mast, jury rig, emergency part, spare part, spare, extra

▸ *Weapon 78; Clothing 100; Defense 419; Closure 584*

ADJECTIVES

16 **safe,** secure, protected, guarded, defended; not in danger, not at risk, assured, sure, certain, sound, safe and sound, home free, snug; spared, preserved, intact, undamaged, unharmed, uninjured, unhurt, unscathed,

with a whole skin, whole; garrisoned, well-defended; insured, covered; immunized, vaccinated, inoculated; disinfected, salubrious, hygienic; in safety, in security, under guard, on the safe side, on sure ground, on home ground, on the home stretch, on terra firma; in harbor, in port, at anchor, above water; out of danger, out of the woods, out of harm's way, clear; in the clear, unaccused, unthreatened, unmolested; unexposed, under shelter, sheltered, shielded, screened; patronized, under the protection of, under the wing of, in safe hands, in safe keeping

17 **trustworthy,** reliable, dependable; guaranteed, under warrant, warranted; benign, innocent, tame, harmless, innocuous, unthreatening; not dangerous, without risk, risk-free, unhazardous, nonflammable, nontoxic, unpolluted; edible, eatable, drinkable, potable, good

▶ *Hygiene 116; Good 445; Preservation 815; Certainty 840*

18 **invulnerable,** safe, immune, impregnable, sacrosanct, inexpugnable, unassailable, unattackable, ungettable *or* ungetable, unbreakable, unchallengeable, made in heaven; founded on a rock, built like a fortress, defensible, tenable, strong; proof, foolproof, fail-safe; mothproof, childproof, weatherproof, waterproof, leakproof, rustproof, gasproof, fireproof, shatterproof, bulletproof, bombproof; armored, steel-clad, panoplied; snug, tight, seaworthy, airworthy; shrink-wrapped, vacuum-packed, vacuum-sealed, hermetically sealed; freeze-dried, frozen

▶ *Strength 516*

19 **tutelary,** protective, custodial, guardian, surrogate; shepherdlike, watchful, vigilant, keeping, guarding, protecting, preserving; prophylactic, antiseptic, disinfectant, hygienic

▶ *Hygiene 116; Carefulness 325; Preservation 815*

VERBS

20 **be safe,** be out of danger, protect oneself, defend oneself, take precautions, play safe, be on the safe side, hedge one's bets, take no chances, demand assurances, seek safety, find safety, reach safety; go on the lam, cut and run, beat a retreat, shorten sail, run for port; come through, survive, save one's skin, keep a whole skin, live to fight another day; escape, run away, land on one's feet; keep one's head above water, weather the storm, ride it out, see it through; be saved by the bell, live a charmed life, have nine lives; stay at home, be *or* stay under cover, have a roof over one's head, take refuge, hide, lie low, go underground, keep a safe distance, give a wide berth, shy away, avoid; save one's bacon [Inf], skedaddle [Inf]

▶ *Concealment 181; Avoidance 386; Refuge 812; Escape 816*

21 **protect,** safeguard, keep safe, guard, defend; spare, show mercy; support, champion, stand up for, vouch for, stand surety for, go bail for; cover up for, provide an alibi for, shield, harbor, rescue, save; deliver, patronize, grant asylum, afford sanctuary; keep, conserve, preserve, treasure; hoard, store, lock away, lock up, hide away, hide, conceal, put in a safe place, keep under cover; warehouse, garage, take in, house, shelter; ward, watch over, care for, look after, mind, mother, take under one's wing, nurse, tend, foster, cherish; have charge of, take charge of, keep an eye on, ride shotgun, monitor, chaperon; envelop, cocoon, wrap, enclose, insulate; cover, shroud, cloak, shade, screen; make safe, secure, fortify, strengthen, entrench, fence in, fence around, arm, armor; convoy, escort, shepherd, flank, garrison, mount guard, keep order, police, patrol

22 **immunize,** inoculate, vaccinate; pasteurize, chlorinate, fluoridate, fluorinate; disinfect, sanitate, sanitize

23 **assure,** give assurances, promise, give vows; warrant, guarantee, make certain; cushion, buffer, ensconce, enfold, embrace

▶ *Provision 89; Hygiene 116; Concealment 181; Defense 419; Strength 516; Enclosure 619; Preservation 815; Help 825; Certainty 840*

ADVERBS

24 **safely,** securely, in safety, with impunity, without risk; out of danger, out of harm's way, under cover, in the lee of, under the aegis of, under lock and key; invulnerably, impregnably; protectively, watchfully; hygienically

811 Danger

Believe me! The secret of reaping the greatest fruitfulness and the greatest enjoyment from life is to live dangerously! — FRIEDRICH NIETZSCHE

NOUNS

1 **danger,** peril, jeopardy, risk, hazard, dangerousness, perilousness, riskiness, hazardousness, treacherousness, treachery; dangerous situation, unhealthy situation, desperate situation, perilous state, parlous state; shadow of death, jaws of death, lion's mouth, dragon's lair; dire straits, predicament, emergency, urgency, crisis; insecurity, unsoundness, ticklishness, ticklish business, precariousness, slipperiness, shakiness, unsteadiness, uncertainty; slippery slope, road to ruin; acute dilemma, razor edge, impending disaster, sword of Damocles, death trap; snag, pitfall, trap, surprise attack, ambush

▶ *Trap 813*

2 **endangerment,** imperilment, venturesomeness; hazarding, daring, overdaring, rashness, gambling; venture, risky venture, dangerous course; leap in the dark, throw of the dice, spin of the wheel, turn of the card

3 sense of danger, menace, threat, apprehension, anxiety, nervousness, fear
▶ *Fear 283*

4 narrow escape, hairbreadth escape, near tragedy, near miss, near thing, close shave [Inf]
▶ *Fear 283; Rashness 286; Escape 816; Chance 842*

5 danger signal, red light, flashing light, alarm, siren; security alarm, emergency buzzer, panic button, burglar alarm, fire alarm, fire bell, klaxon, alert, red alert; distress signal, SOS, Mayday, distress flare; night sounds, strange noise; gunshot, shout, scream, sudden pain; snarling dog, ticking package; rocks ahead, breakers ahead; storm brewing, gathering storm, gathering clouds, thick fog, rising river, cloud on the horizon
▶ *Fear 283; Danger 811; Warning 814*

6 vulnerability, liability, susceptibility, nonimmunity; openness, exposure, nakedness, pregnability; helplessness, defenselessness, lack of protection, naiveté, innocence; instability, insecurity; easy target, sitting target, sitting duck; exposed part, exposed flank, vulnerable point, undefended part, breach in the wall, chink in one's armor; Achilles heel, weakness, tender spot, soft spot, soft underbelly; unsoundness, failing, flaw, defect, imperfection; defect of character, human failing, feet of clay, tragic flaw, fatal flaw
▶ *Powerlessness 515; Weakness 517; Softness 543; Imperfection 806*

ADJECTIVES

7 dangerous, perilous, treacherous, hazardous, risky, beset with perils, fraught with danger, venturous, venturesome; unknown, uncertain, unlit, difficult, chancy, tricky, snaggy, speculative; crucial, critical, serious; nasty, ugly, menacing, threatening, ominous, foreboding, alarming, frightening; at the boiling point, at the flash point; at stake, in question; inflammable, flammable, explosive, radioactive, toxic, poisonous, deadly, life-threatening; harmful, unhealthy, infectious, unhygienic; [Inf]: sticky, dicey, iffy, hairy
▶ *Fear 283; Uncertainty 841; Chance 842*

8 unsafe, not safe, treacherous, untrustworthy, unreliable, doubtful, shaky, slippery, insecure, unsecure, unsound, precarious, unbalanced, unsteady, unstable, tottering, top-heavy; tumbledown, ramshackle, dilapidated, rickety, frail, falling to pieces, crumbling, condemned; jerry-built, shoddy, gimcrack, crazy, weak, built on sand, on shaky foundations, leaky, waterlogged; critical, delicate, ticklish, risky, heart-stopping, nerve-racking; touch and go, hanging by a thread, trembling in the balance, teetering on the edge, on the edge, on the brink, on the verge; last-second, last-minute
▶ *Weakness 517; Deterioration 808; Uncertainty 841*

9 vulnerable, unprotected, undefended, insecure, in danger; not immune, liable, susceptible, open to; wide open, exposed, naked, bare, uncovered, unarmored, unfortified; expugnable, pregnable, helpless, at the whim of, at the mercy of, defenseless, unarmed; isolated, deserted, abandoned, stranded, left high and dry, out on a limb; unsupported, unshielded, shelterless, guideless, unattended, unguarded, unescorted, unshepherded; unflanked, unwarned, unaware, naive, not on guard, off one's guard, unprepared, unready
▶ *Lack of Preparation 389; Powerlessness 515; Weakness 517; Uncovering 614; Possibility 836*

10 endangered, in danger, in peril, at risk, in jeopardy, in double jeopardy; slipping, drifting, on the rocks, in shallow water, on dangerous ground, on slippery ground, on thin ice; in a bad way, in a tight corner, in a bind, surrounded, trapped, at bay, cornered, with one's back to the wall; under siege, under fire, in the lion's den, thrown to the lions, on the razor's edge; caught both ways, between two fires, between two chairs, between the devil and the deep blue sea, between a rock and a hard place [Inf], between Scylla and Charybdis; on the run, not out of the woods; at the last stand, reduced to the last extremity, facing death, facing the firing squad, under sentence, condemned, with a noose around one's neck, awaiting execution, on death row; [Inf]: in a jam, in the soup, in the hot seat

VERBS

11 be in danger, run the risk of, run into danger, enter the lion's den, put one's head in the lion's mouth, ride a tiger, walk into a trap; tread on dangerous ground, be on slippery ground, skate on thin ice, be out of one's depth, play with fire, feel the ground slip away, feel the ground give way; be up against it, have to run for it; hang by a thread, tremble in the balance, hover on the brink, teeter on the edge, totter, slip, slide, tumble, fall; get lost, wander away, stray, go astray; play with dynamite, sit on a powder keg
▶ *Deviation 698; Descent 714*

12 face danger, face death, take one's life in one's hands, expose oneself, lay oneself open to; stand in the breach, risk, defy, look danger in the face, look down a gun barrel; face heavy odds, have the odds (stacked) against one, have the deck *or* cards stacked against one, have one's back to the wall; engage in a forlorn hope, challenge fate, tempt fate, tempt providence; court disaster, take a tiger by the tail, put one's head in the lion's mouth, play Russian roulette, run the gauntlet, come under fire; venture, dare, hazard, gamble, take a chance, take a flier [Inf], stick one's neck out [Inf]
▶ *Courage 284; Rashness 286; Defiance 416; Chance 842*

13 endanger, expose to danger, put in danger, put at risk, put in jeopardy, put in double jeopardy, jeopardize, imperil, compromise, hazard, risk, stake, gamble; venture, drive headlong, run on the rocks, drive dangerously, drive recklessly, drive without due care and attention; put someone in fear of his *or* her life, threaten one's life, threaten danger; loom, forebode, bode ill, menace, threaten, intimidate, hold over one's head, run one hard

▸ *Fear 283; Chance 842*

ADVERBS

14 **dangerously,** treacherously, perilously, hazardously, riskily, precariously; in the face of death, on the brink; naively, unawares; recklessly, rashly; ominously, threateningly, menacingly; vulnerably, helplessly, defenselessly

812 Refuge

One's home is the safest refuge to everyone. — PANDECTS

NOUNS

1 **refuge,** sanctuary, shelter, asylum, retreat, safe retreat, safe place, safe house, place of safety; resort, recourse, last resort; cache, secret place; rock, Rock of Gibraltar, Rock of Ages, pillar, tower, tower of strength; mainstay, buttress, prop, support, protection

2 **private space,** bed, bedroom, hearth, home, den, nook, lap; inviolable place, privacy; sanctum, chamber, monastery, nunnery, cloister, cell, hermitage; sanctum sanctorum, holy of holies, temple, ark; ivory tower

3 **fortification,** acropolis, citadel, wall, rampart, bulwark, parapet, battlement, barricade, bastion, keep, ward; stronghold, fortress, fastness, fort; foxhole, dugout, pit, bolt-hole, trench; underground shelter, concrete shelter, bunker, blockhouse, bomb shelter, air-raid shelter, fallout shelter

▸ *Concealment 181; Defense 419; Support 605; Safety 810*

4 **shelter,** cover, roof, roof over one's head, home; lee, hedge, wall, fence; camp, stockade, enclosure; shield, screen; burrow; hideout, hiding place, priest hole, hidey-hole [Inf]; animal shelter, kennel, cattery, animal home, bird sanctuary, animal sanctuary; hole, burrow, den, lair, earth, covert, warren, pit, lodge, hive, nest, aerie; fold, pen, sheepfold [Brit], pinfold, pound, sty, pigsty; barn, stall, stable; coop, hutch, cage

5 **safe house,** halfway house, group home, sheltered workshop; almshouse, poorhouse, workhouse; children's home, orphanage, old people's home, retirement home, nursing home, hospice; asylum, mental hospital

▸ *Safety 810*

6 **harbor,** port, harborage, anchorage, haven; quay, jetty; marina, dock

▸ *Enclosure 619; Safety 810; Escape 816*

ADJECTIVES

7 **sheltered,** covered, enclosed, screened; safe, protected, harbored, housed, penned

VERBS

8 **shelter,** seek refuge, take refuge, seek sanctuary, claim sanctuary, seek asylum, ask for political asylum; seek shelter, seek safety, retreat, take to the woods, take to the hills; request aid, turn to, throw oneself in the arms of, clasp the knees of, kiss the hand of, hide behind the skirts of, shelter under the wing of, ask protection from; put up one's umbrella, pull the blankets over one's head; reach home, reach safety, make port, find shelter; lock oneself in, bolt the door, bar the entrance, let down the portcullis, raise the drawbridge; close the blinds, close the shutters, batten down the hatches; go on the lam [Inf]

813 Trap

There was only one catch and that was Catch-22.
— JOSEPH HELLER

NOUNS

1 **trap,** pitfall, pit, snare, gin, springe, trapdoor, trap for the unwary; danger, hazard; catch, snag, Catch-22, obstacle, stumbling block; booby trap, death trap, firetrap, mine, minefield, tank trap; time bomb, terrorist bomb

▸ *Deception 193; Hindrance 826*

2 **trick,** deception, ruse, subterfuge, artifice, stratagem

▸ *Deception 193; Surprise 292*

3 **hidden danger,** unexpected event, surprise, unexpected attack, ambush; sleeping dog, wolf in sheep's clothing; thin ice, bog, quagmire, quicksand, marsh; sandbar, sandbank, shoal, shoal water, breakers, shallows, shallow water, reef, sunken reef, coral reef; rock, ironbound coast, lee shore; steep, chasm, abyss, crevasse, precipice; rapids, white water, current, cross-current, undertow; vortex, maelstrom, whirlpool, eddy; rising water, incoming tide

▸ *Concealment 181*

4 **natural hazard,** tidal wave, flash flood; storm, squall, gale, cyclone, hurricane, whirlwind, tornado, twister [Inf]; volcano, furnace, earthquake

▸ *Affliction 117; Danger 811*

ADJECTIVES

5 **trapped,** caught, attacked, snared, netted, ambushed, tricked, deceived, duped, inveigled; dangerous, hazardous

▸ *Danger 811*

VERBS

6 **trap,** entrap, snare, ensnare, net, catch, catch out [Brit]; catch unawares, surprise, take by surprise, lie in wait, ambush; trick, deceive, dupe, inveigle

▸ *Deception 193; Surprise 292*

814 Warning

Cave canem [*Beware of the dog*].
— INSCRIPTION AT POMPEII

NOUNS

1 **warning,** caution, caveat, alarm; advice, counsel, lesson, object lesson; notice, advance notice, notification; information, intelligence, news; forewarning, word of warning, word in the ear, word to the wise, tip; kick under the table, wink, pinch, nudge, hint; announcement, publication, public warning, storm warning, hurricane watch *or* warning; final warning, final notice, final invoice, final demand, ultimatum, monition; admonition, admonishment, reprimand; deterrent, dissuasion, protest, expostulation; tip-off [Inf]

2 **forewarning,** foreboding, premonition, premonition of disaster; omen, bad omen, evil omen, portent, evil portent; prediction, augury, Mother Carey's chicken *or* storm(y) petrel, bird of ill omen; gathering clouds, gathering storm, rising river, cloud on the horizon, war cloud; conscience, voice of conscience, warning voice, note of warning; murmur of discontent, muttering; sign, symptom, indication, indicator, signal, signs of the times; danger, threat, knell, death knell, menace

▶ *Information 170; News 171; Advice 176; Caution 287; Danger 811*

3 **warning signal,** alarm, warning sign; beacon, light, bell, whistle, horn; honk, toot, ring; storm signal; foghorn, fog signal, bell buoy; car horn, bicycle bell, church bell, curfew bell, tocsin; drumbeat, tattoo, trumpet call; war cry, war whoop; fiery cross; warning light, flashing light, amber light, flare, warning flare, Very lights, red flag, yellow flag; sign of alarm, wide eyes, open mouth, start, tremor, paleness, sweat, hair on end

▶ *Sign 183; Identification 184; Fear 283; Danger 811*

4 **false alarm,** false alert, false warning, alarm test; cry of wolf, scare, hoax; bugbear, bugaboo, bogey *or* bogy; nightmare, bad dream, blank cartridge

▶ *Deception 193; Unpleasantness 272; Unreality 720; Untruth 722*

5 **warner,** cautioner, caveator, adviser, counselor, admonisher; prophet, Ezekiel, Nostradamus, Cassandra; medicine man, witch doctor, shaman, diviner; scaremonger, alarmist; flagman, signaler, lighthouse keeper; watchman, lookout, security guard, security man *or* woman, watch, guard, picket, sentinel, sentry, watchdog, protector; scout, advance guard, vanguard, rear sentry, rear guard; spy, informant, mole; rat [Inf], squealer [Inf]

▶ *Information 170; Advice 176; Caution 287; Prediction 358; Safety 810*

ADJECTIVES

6 **warning,** cautionary, exemplary; advisable, counselable, instructive, informative, notifying, hinting; admonitory *or* monitory, protesting; symptomatic, prognostic; predicting, premonitory, boding, foreboding, ill-omened, ominous, presageful; menacing, minatory, threatening; deterrent, dissuasive, frightening

▶ *Information 170; Advice 176; Fear 283; Caution 287; Prediction 358*

7 **warned,** cautioned, advised, counseled, taught a lesson; cautious, wary, forewarned, forearmed, prepared, once bitten twice shy

▶ *Caution 287; Preparation 388*

VERBS

8 **warn,** caution, issue a caveat, advise, counsel; give a word of warning, give a word in the ear, give a word to the wise, tip, tip off; kick under the table, wink, pinch, nudge, hint, drop a hint; give notice, notify, inform, apprise, issue a public warning; put on one's guard, alert, forewarn, forearm, prepare, spell danger, spell disaster; predict, augur, remind, put one in mind; admonish, reprove, lower, menace, threaten; advise against, dissuade, remonstrate, protest; provoke action, cause panic

▶ *Information 170; Advice 176; Caution 287; Memory 354; Preparation 388; Disapproval 438*

9 **be warned,** receive notice; beware, take heed, watch one's step; learn one's lesson, take someone's words to heart, profit by (the) example, profit by one's mistakes

10 **give warning,** give *or* sound the alarm, sound a warning, sound the fire alarm, sound a siren; sound one's horn, honk, toot, blow the whistle, ring the bell; press the emergency button, fire a warning flare; toll, knell, alert, arouse; give a false alarm, cry wolf, cry too soon

ADVERBS

11 **warningly,** cautionarily, instructively, admonitorily *or* monitorily, predictably, ominously, threateningly

INTERJECTIONS

12 **look out!,** beware!, careful!, watch out!, watch it!, take care!, watch your step!, look where you're going!, fore! [Golf]

815 Preservation

NOUNS

1 **preservation,** conservation, keeping, safekeeping; protection, shelter; maintenance, upkeep, support, service; storage, retention, keeping fresh; saving, provision; self-preservation; environmentalism, ecology, conservancy, salvage; conservatism

2 **conservation,** care, husbandry, protection; renovation, perpetuation, continuation, prolongation, conservancy, permanence; historical preservation, archives, museum, repository, historical monument

3 ecology, environmental movement, green movement, animal rights movement, endangered species act; conservation area, protected area, bird sanctuary, animal sanctuary, wildlife *or* game reserve, nature reserve, forest preserve, arboretum, refuge, sanctuary, preserve, national *or* state park, national seashore, reservation

4 saving, retention, keep, maintenance, support, provision; self-preservation, selfishness; frugality, economy, thrift, saving up

5 upkeep, service, servicing, valeting, cleansing, painting, varnishing, waterproofing

6 preservation of provisions, insulation, heat retention, storage, store; cold storage, freezing, deep-freezing, freeze-drying, refrigeration; boiling, pickling, marination, curing, smoking, dehydration, desiccation, drying, sun-drying, canning, tinning [Brit], processing, packaging, packing, irradiation, sterilization

◗ *Health 113; Hygiene 116*

7 preservation of body, embalming, mummification, taxidermy, stuffing, tanning

8 preservation of status quo, conservatism, conservative politics, right-wing politics, political right, rightism; stubbornness, obstinacy

9 preserver, preservative, formaldehyde, alcohol, camphor, mothball, amber, plastic, salt, brine, spice, pickle, marinade, aspic, pectin, jelly, ice; freezer, refrigerator, vacuum flask, thermos, jar, pot, bottle, can, tin [Brit]; paint, varnish, whitewash, creosote; rescue device, lifeline, life belt, life jacket, safety device, seat belt, safety belt, air bag, gas mask, incubator, respirator, iron lung, life-support system; good-luck charm, charm, amulet, mascot, talisman; silo, cannery, canning factory, bottling plant; fridge [Inf]

◗ *Cooking 91; Cold 218; Safety 810*

10 preserved thing, protected building, registered historic building, listed building [Brit]; protected species, endangered species; mummy, fossil, stuffed animal; frozen food, freeze-dried food, vacuum-packed food, long-life food, dehydrated food, dried food, dried milk, processed food, canned food, tinned food [Brit], preserves, jam, jelly, marmalade, conserve, pickles

◗ *Food 90*

ADJECTIVES

11 preserving, preservative, conserving, conservative, protecting, protective, prophylactic, preventive, preventative, salubrious, hygienic, redemptive, energy-saving, ecological, environment-friendly, environmental, conservational, green

12 preserved, well-preserved, kept, well-kept, alive, fresh, undecayed, intact, whole, perfect; dehydrated, desiccated, dried, sun-dried, freeze-dried, frozen, iced, on ice, in the freezer, in the refrigerator; pickled, marinated, salted, corned, soused, smoked, cured, canned, tinned [Brit], potted, bottled; mummified, embalmed,

stuffed, laid up in lavender; mothballed, stored, conserved, protected; saved, safe, treasured, cherished

◗ *Cooking 91; Store 105; Perfection 805; Safety 810*

13 conservative, traditional, traditionalist, right-wing, rightist, hard-right, reactionary, obstinate, stubborn, old-fashioned, unprogressive, die-hard, dyed-in-the-wool, stick-in-the-mud

VERBS

14 preserve, protect, guard, keep safe, keep alive, perpetuate, continue, prolong, uphold, defend, conserve, keep fresh; freeze, freeze-dry, keep on ice, refrigerate, irradiate, pickle, salt, souse, marinate, cure, smoke, kipper, dehydrate, dry, sun-dry, pot, bottle, can, tin [Brit]; process, season, paint, varnish, whitewash, creosote, waterproof; embalm, mummify, stuff; maintain, service, keep up, keep running, keep in good repair, support, prop up, shore up, bolster; sustain, feed, provision, provide, supply, keep going; safeguard, shelter, keep under cover, warehouse, garage, keep, store, reserve, save, save up, bottle up, withhold; nurse, mother, foster, tend, cherish, treasure, look after; hold, retain, not let go, grasp, hug, hide, spare, rescue, deliver

◗ *Life 28; Provision 89; Store 105; Carefulness 325; Retention 471; Thrift 499; Support 605; Repair 809; Safety 810; Deliverance 817*

15 be conservative, be traditional, remain unchanged

ADVERBS

16 preservatively, conservatively, protectively, prophylactically, preventively, ecologically, environmentally

17 conservatively, traditionally, stubbornly, unprogressively

816 Escape

NOUNS

1 escape, breakout, getaway, freedom, decampment, flight, departure; withdrawal, retreat, hasty retreat, jailbreak; disappearance, disappearing trick, vanishing, vanishing into thin air; French leave, truancy, hooky; elopement, runaway wedding; elusion, evasion, avoidance; reprieve, acquittal, release, setting free, liberation; immunity, impunity, exemption, rescue, deliverance, riddance, relief

◗ *Disappearance 265; Avoidance 386; Departure 705; Deliverance 817*

2 financial escape, nonpayment, tax avoidance, tax evasion, tax dodging, tax shelter, tax haven, creative economy, black economy, moonlighting

◗ *Nonpayment 490*

3 narrow escape, hairbreadth escape, close call, narrow squeak, near miss, near thing; close shave [Inf]

◗ *Exemption 434; Danger 811; Freedom 829; Liberation 831*

4 means of escape, exit, emergency exit, way out,

egress, back door; trapdoor, escape hatch, hidden panel, secret passage, back stairs, ladder, fire escape, drawbridge; vent, safety valve; camouflage, disguise, dodge, device, trick, contrivance; loophole, escape clause, technicality

▶ *Qualification 340; Plan 387; Exit 707; Safety 810*

5 **escaper,** escapee, fugitive, runaway, fleer, retreater, eloper, truant; evader, tax evader, tax dodger; escaped prisoner, jailbreaker; reprieved prisoner, released prisoner; refugee, survivor, escapist; escape artist, escapologist [Brit], Houdini

6 **leak,** leakage, air leakage, gas leakage, water loss, loss; emission, issue, seepage, discharge, outflow

▶ *Exit 707*

ADJECTIVES

7 **escaping,** evasive, elusive, fugitive, runaway, truant; escaped, loose, free, scot-free; relieved, emancipated, liberated, immune, exempt; untied, unbound, unchained

▶ *Freedom 829; Liberation 831*

VERBS

8 **escape,** break out, get out; escape from jail, break out of prison; break loose, break one's chains, break away, get away, make a getaway, decamp, flee, fly, take flight, bolt, run away, abscond, depart, duck and run, get free, win freedom, find freedom; slip one's collar, slip one's lead *or* leash; take to one's heels, retreat, beat a hasty retreat; disappear, vanish, vanish into thin air, make oneself scarce; sneak off *or* out, skip, steal away, go absent without leave (AWOL), take French leave, play truant, play hooky, jump bail, elope; deliver oneself, save oneself, save one's skin; have a narrow escape, have a close call, have a narrow squeak, have a hairbreadth escape; slip through someone's fingers, wiggle *or* wriggle out of, bluff one's way out; scrape through, slip through, break through; [Inf]: vamoose, go over the wall, take it on the lam, have a close shave, escape by the skin of one's teeth, save one's bacon

9 **get a reprieve,** have one's conviction overturned, secure an acquittal; receive immunity, secure exemption; go unpunished, go scot-free, get away with it, get off, get off on a technicality, get off lightly; survive, weather the storm, find relief

▶ *Relief 275; Avoidance 386; Exemption 434; Deliverance 817*

10 **elude,** evade, avoid, dodge, miss; get rid of, rid oneself of; hide, lie low, stay underground; escape detection, give one the slip, shake off, throw off the trail, throw off the scent, give one a run for one's money, escape notice; avoid *or* evade taxes

▶ *Concealment 181; Avoidance 386; Nonpayment 490*

11 **leak,** leak away, leak air, leak gas, lose water; flow out, emerge, issue, seep out, gush, spurt

▶ *Exit 707*

12 **fugitively,** in flight, in hiding; out of range *or* sight, away, over the hills and far away; freely

817 Deliverance

Deliver me from your cold phlegmatic preachers, politicians, friends, lovers and husbands. — ABIGAIL ADAMS

NOUNS

1 **deliverance,** delivery, saving, lifesaving, rescue; extrication, unraveling, untangling, extraction; disencumberment, riddance, good riddance, relief; release, emancipation, freedom, liberation; amnesty, discharge, reprieve, reprieval, acquittal, dispensation, excuse, exemption; escape, way out; salvation, redemption; ransom, bail, buying off, purchase; salvage, retrieval, recovery, restoration; day of grace, respite, delay; truce, standstill, cessation

▶ *Relief 275; Cessation 668; Extraction 711; Escape 816; Freedom 829; Liberation 831*

2 **deliverer,** savior, lifesaver, rescuer, rescue team, lifeboat crew; rescue helicopter, lifeboat; liberator, emancipator; redeemer, salvager

▶ *Safety 810; Liberation 831*

ADJECTIVES

3 **deliverable,** savable, salvable, rescuable, extricable; redeemable, salvageable, fit for release

4 **delivered,** saved, rescued; liberated, free; saving, lifesaving; saved by the bell

VERBS

5 **deliver,** save, rescue, come to the rescue, throw a lifeline to; snatch from the jaws of death, save at the last second *or* minute, rescue at the eleventh hour, save by the bell; extricate, unravel, untangle, extract, get out; unfasten, unloose, untie, unbind, unfetter, unchain; unburden, disburden, disencumber, rid of, save from, relieve; release, emancipate, liberate, free, declare free, set free, set at large; unlock, unbar, let out, let go; let off, get off, reprieve, acquit, exempt, excuse, dispense from, spare; redeem, ransom, bail out, buy off, purchase; salvage, retrieve, recover, bring back, restore

▶ *Relief 275; Exemption 434; Extraction 711; Separation 753; Arrangement 767; Safety 810; Escape 816; Freedom 829; Liberation 831*

ADVERBS

6 **extricably;** redeemably; free; salvably

818 Haste

Hurry! I never hurry. I have no time to hurry. — IGOR STRAVINSKY

NOUNS

1 **haste,** hurry, rush, speed, promptness; briskness,

quickness, swiftness, rapidity, alacrity, celerity, expeditiousness; urge, impulsion, drive, stampede, push, spur, goad, whip; activity, scurry, hurry-scurry, hustle, bustle, hassle, flurry, whirl, scramble, flutter, fidget, fuss, agitation, distress, panic; last-minute rush, rush job, job due yesterday, feverish haste, tearing hurry, deadline, pressure, race against a deadline, race against time, no time to lose, lateness; urgency, immediacy, importance; expedition, dispatch, velocity, hastening, acceleration, dash, spurt, forced march; skedaddle [Inf]

▶ *Lack of Preparation 389; Activity 414; Lateness 658; Agitation 684; Importance 799*

2 **hastiness,** precipitancy *or* precipitance, precipitateness, impetuosity, impetuousness, impulsiveness, recklessness, rashness; inability to wait, impatience; thoughtlessness, carelessness, negligence

▶ *Rashness 286*

ADJECTIVES

3 **hasty,** hurried, rushed; speedy, prompt, brisk, quick, presto, allegro, swift, rapid, fast, fleet, expeditious; impetuous, impulsive, precipitant, precipitate, headlong, overhasty, reckless, heedless, rash, hotheaded, feverish, impatient, all impatience; thoughtless, unthinking, ill-considered; ardent, fervent; rushing, scampering, pushing, shoving, elbowing; uncontrolled, boisterous, furious, violent; breathless, breakneck; without delay, urgent, immediate, in haste, in all haste; hotfoot, running, racing, hastening, speeding; in a hurry, in a rush, unable to wait, pressed for time, hard-pressed, driven; haphazard, slapdash, careless, negligent, cursory, perfunctory, superficial; fleeting, brief; rush, last-minute; rough-and-tumble, rough-and-ready, unprepared, forced, rushed into, stampeded, allowing no time, brooking no delay, pushed through, railroaded [Inf]

▶ *Feelings 266; Rashness 286; Negligence 326; Lack of Preparation 389; Violence 520; Importance 799*

VERBS

4 **hasten,** speed up, accelerate, quicken, hurry, rush; precipitate, expedite, dispatch, urge, impel, propel; drive, stampede, spur, goad, whip, lash, flog, incite; hustle, hustle away, bundle off *or* out, rush along, allow no time, push, press, push forward, brook no delay, breathe down the neck of; railroad [Inf]

▶ *Persuasion 178*

5 **make haste,** hasten, move fast, go fast, speed, rush, spurt, sprint, dash, bolt, race, careen, fly, gallop, run, rush headlong, run helter-skelter, run pell-mell, go like a rocket; scurry, scuttle, scamper, scramble; decamp, hasten away, dash off, rush off *or* away, cut and run; make up for lost time, hurry, catch up, overtake, outrun, outstrip, show one's heels, whirl by, zoom past; make a forced march; accelerate, speed up, burn up the road, go faster, pick up the pace, hustle, bustle; fret, fume, fidget, rush to and fro, dart to and fro; [Inf]: barrel along, tear off, go over the wall, skedaddle, run

like hell *or* blazes, run like mad, fly *or* go like a bat out of hell, go into overdrive, make someone eat dust, make tracks, scat

▶ *Rashness 286; Activity 414; Swiftness 694*

6 **have no time to spare,** have no time to lose; ignore formalities, act without ceremony, cut short, brush aside, rush through, dash through, cut corners, rush one's fences, make short work of; bolt down one's meal; be pressed for time, work against time, work to a deadline, meet a deadline; be behind time, be late; work under pressure, think on one's feet, do at the last moment; lose no time, lose not a moment, make every second count

▶ *Lateness 658; Departure 705*

ADVERBS

7 **hastily,** hurriedly, precipitantly, precipitately, helter-skelter, pell-mell, feverishly, posthaste, hotfoot, apace, quickly, swiftly, rapidly, fast, promptly, speedily, with all haste; like a rocket, in a flash; at short notice, on the spur of the moment, immediately, without delay, straightaway, right away; urgently, with urgency, under pressure, against the clock, by forced march, with not a moment to lose *or* spare, as soon as possible (ASAP); [Inf]: pronto, like greased lightning, like a bat out of hell, lickety-split, pretty damn quick (PDQ), before one can say Jack Robinson

▶ *Immediacy 645*

8 **rashly,** recklessly, impetuously, impulsively, impatiently; heedlessly, thoughtlessly, overhastily

▶ *Rashness 286*

INTERJECTIONS

9 **hurry up!,** faster!, quick!, be quick!, get a move on!, step on it! [Inf], on *or* at the double!, move it!

819 Ease

NOUNS

1 **ease,** relaxation, repose, rest, rest from one's labors, breather, inactivity, idleness, stillness, restfulness; comfort, well-being, content, contentment, eudemonia; peace, quiet, peace and quiet, tranquility, serenity, quiescence; sleep, nap, catnap, snooze, sweet sleep, sweet dreams, happy dreams; breathing space *or* room; refreshment, break, coffee *or* tea break, pause, respite, lull, recess, interval, interim; leave, holiday, vacation, furlough, time off, day off, sabbatical; leisure, free time, spare time, spare hours; day of rest, Sabbath, Lord's day; final rest, eternal peace, peace that passeth all understanding, nirvana, death; [Inf]: letup, forty winks, shuteye

▶ *Refreshment 94; Leisure 125; Physical Pleasure 214; Relief 275; Inactivity 415; Time 639; Cessation 668; Lack of Motion 678; Easiness 823; Prosperity 847*

ADJECTIVES

2 **at ease,** easy, easeful, relaxed, relaxing, reposeful,

easy on, resting, restful; robed, slippered, in one's shirt-sleeves, casual, carefree, unbuttoned [Inf], laid-back [Inf]; content, eudemonic; cushioned, pillowed, snug, comfortable; peaceful, quiet, still, quiescent, tranquil; leisured, leisurely, idle, lazy, sluggish, slow, unhurried; postprandial, after-dinner

▶ *Leisure 125; Physical Pleasure 214; Satisfaction 273; Lack of Motion 678*

VERBS

3 **take it easy,** take one's ease, relax, repose, rest, take a rest, have a rest, rest from one's labors, take a breather, find peace and quiet; come to rest, perch, roost, sit down, sit back, put one's feet up, recline, lie down, lie back, loll, lounge, laze, sprawl; couch, go to bed, bed down, go to sleep, sleep, doze, snooze, drowse, nap, take a nap, have a catnap; unwind, unbend, slow down, let up, slack off, forget one's problems, forget work; put on one's robe and slippers, rest and be thankful, rest on one's laurels, rest on one's oars; take time off *or* out, take a holiday, go on vacation, go on leave, go on a furlough; [Inf]: catch *or* grab some z's, catch forty winks, get some shuteye, take five *or* ten

▶ *Refreshment 94; Inactivity 415; Lack of Motion 678; Easiness 823*

4 **ease,** loosen, slacken, moderate, reduce; relieve, alleviate, comfort

▶ *Relief 275; Moderation 521; Decrease 747*

ADVERBS

5 **easily,** with ease, at rest, restfully, reposefully; quietly, peacefully; casually, in a carefree manner; on leave, on holiday, on vacation, on sabbatical, on furlough

820 Fatigue

Life is one long process of getting tired. — SAMUEL BUTLER

NOUNS

1 **fatigue,** tiredness, weariness, wearifulness, exhaustion, burnout; lassitude, languor, listlessness, lethargy, dullness; staleness, jadedness, boredom; physical fatigue, fatigue syndrome, chronic fatigue syndrome; battle *or* combat fatigue; mental fatigue, tired brain, mental and physical distress, aching muscles; limit of endurance, total exhaustion, collapse, prostration; strain, exertion, work, overtiredness, overexertion, overwork, overdoing it; shortness of breath, hard breathing, labored breathing, panting, gasping, palpitations, heart pain; languishment, weakness, enervation, debilitation; faintness, fainting, faint, swoon, blackout, insensibility, loss of consciousness

▶ *Work 122; Insensibility 213; Boredom 296; Weakness 517; Air 558; Ease 819*

ADJECTIVES

2 **fatigued,** tired, weary, wearied, weariful, jaded; ready

to drop, dropping, exhausted, in need of rest, run-down, all in, tired out, worn out, tired to death, dead, dead tired, dog-tired, fagged, fagged out, stupid from fatigue; faint, spent, weak, drained, dull, stale; strained, overworked, overtired, overfatigued, overstrained, overwrought, burned-out; weakened, enervated, fainting, swooning, flat, prostrate, half-dead, more dead than alive; stiff, aching, sore, footsore, footweary; travel-weary, jet-lagged, wayworn; tired-looking, tired-eyed, heavy-eyed, heavy-lidded, hollow-eyed, haggard, worn, wan, pale; drooping, flagging, languid, languorous; still tired, unrefreshed, unrested; [Inf]: dopey, beat, dead beat, bushed, done for, done in, pooped, washed-out, tuckered out, worn to a frazzle, all in, whacked out

▶ *Inactivity 415; Weakness 517*

3 **panting,** puffing, blowing, puffing and blowing, out of breath *or* wind, short of breath *or* wind, breathless, gasping for breath, wheezing, snorting, winded, broken-winded

▶ *Air 558*

4 **fatiguing,** tiring, exhausting; laborious, toilsome; tiresome, wearisome, wearying; wearing, grueling, punishing; exacting, tough, demanding, physically demanding

▶ *Work 122*

VERBS

5 **be fatigued,** be tired, tire, become weary; flag, droop, languish, fail, sink; stagger, faint, swoon, feel dizzy, feel giddy; succumb, drop, collapse, cry out for rest; have no strength left, have nothing left to give, can do no more, tire oneself out, overdo it, overtax one's strength, overwork, overexert, ache in every muscle *or* limb; gasp, pant, puff, blow, grunt, breathe heavily; get stale, need a rest, need a change, need a break *or* holiday *or* vacation

▶ *Inactivity 415; Weakness 517; Air 558*

6 **fatigue,** exhaust, tire, tire out, tire to death, wear, wear out, fag *or* fag out; wear down, give out, weary; prostrate, double up, wind; work, drive, task, tax, strain, demand too much (of), make extra demands, overwork, jade, overdrive, overtax, overburden, overload, overstrain, burn out, weaken, debilitate, enervate, fall by the wayside, drain, take it out of; keep from sleep, deprive of sleep, allow no rest; do up [Inf], do in [Inf]

ADVERBS

7 **tiredly,** wearily; weakly, listlessly, lethargically, dopily [Inf], good and tired [Inf]

8 **tiringly,** exhaustingly, laboriously, wearisomely

821 Naiveté

NOUNS

1 **naiveté,** artlessness, simplicity, simplemindedness, in-

genuousness, guilelessness, freedom from artifice; youth, innocence, greenness, immaturity, inexperience, ignorance; unworldliness, unsophistication, callowness, credulity, gullibility; plainness, unaffectedness, naturalness; candor, frankness, openness, straightforwardness, bluntness, matter-of-factness, outspokenness; veracity, truth, honesty, probity, sincerity; modesty, unpretentiousness

▶ *Ignorance 349; Modesty 403; Innocence 449; Simplicity 526; Truth 721*

2 **naive person,** naïf, unsophisticated person, ingenuous person, ingenue; child of nature, savage, noble savage; lamb, babe in arms, newborn babe, child, youth, innocent; beginner, novice, greenhorn; simpleton, dolt, clod, fool, ninny, dupe; plain man, simple soul, pure heart, candid speaker; provincial, country cousin, country dweller, rustic, yokel, bumpkin, country bumpkin, hick, hayseed, hillbilly [Off]; rube [Inf], sucker [Inf]

▶ *Commoner 71; Ignorance 349; Folly 353; Innocence 449*

ADJECTIVES

3 **naive,** naïf, artless, without art, simple, simple minded, ingenuous, guileless, free from guile, without artifice, without tricks; childlike, uncontrived, unstudied, uncomplicated; unadorned, unvarnished, plain, homespun, homemade, do-it-yourself, unskilled; unrefined, unpolished; native, natural, unartificial, in a state of nature; untaught, uneducated, untutored, self-taught, self-made; unguided, unlearned, ignorant, Arcadian, young, innocent, unversed, uninitiated, born yesterday, green, immature, inexperienced, unworldly, unsophisticated, callow, wet behind the ears, not dry behind the ears; not on guard, unsuspecting, unsuspicious, trusting, confiding, credulous, gullible; unconstrained, unreserved, uninhibited, unaffected, undissembling, spontaneous, candid, frank, open, straightforward, undesigning, truthful, veracious; single-hearted, single, true, true-blue, loyal, honest, sincere, honorable, aboveboard, out in the open, blunt, outspoken, free-spoken, transparent, undisguised; unpoetical, prosaic, no-nonsense, matter-of-fact, down-to-earth, literal, literal-minded, accurate; modest, shy, inarticulate, unassuming, unpretentious, unpretending; on the up and up [Inf], on the level [Inf]

▶ *Unskillfulness 128; Ignorance 349; Accuracy 350; Folly 353; Improvisation 396; Modesty 403; Innocence 449; Simplicity 526; Vulgarity 535; Truth 721; Display 843*

VERBS

4 **be naive,** live a simple life, live in a state of nature, live in ignorance, know no better, be wet behind the ears; eschew artifice, have no guile, have no tricks, have no affectations; trust, confide, look one in the face, look one straight in the eyes, speak plainly, wear one's heart on one's sleeve; call a spade a spade, say what is in *or* on one's mind, speak one's mind, not mince words *or* matters; have no hang-ups [Inf]

▶ *Innocence 449; Simplicity 526; Truth 721*

ADVERBS

5 **naively,** artlessly, ingenuously, without guile, without artifice, innocently, credulously, gullibly; without pretensions, without affectation, frankly, candidly, sincerely, openly, straightforwardly, bluntly, matter-of-factly, with an open heart

822 Cunning

"I'll be judge, I'll be jury," said cunning old Fury; / "I'll try the whole case, and condemn you to death."
— LEWIS CARROLL

NOUNS

1 **cunning,** cunningness, slyness, wiliness, foxiness, artfulness, craftiness; craft, art, skill, lore, know-how, knowledge, resourcefulness, inventiveness, ingenuity, imagination, knack, guile, cleverness, smartness, sharpness, acuity, shrewdness, caginess, sophistication, intelligence; stealthiness, stealth, subtlety, latency, concealment, caution, wariness; suppleness, slipperiness, shiftiness; chicanery, chicane, trickery, monkey business, imposture; finesse, jugglery, sleight, cheating, circumvention, deception, deceit, duplicity, sophistry, pettifoggery, double-dealing, double-crossing, false promises; smoothness, flattery, beguilement, disguise, insincerity, hypocrisy, evasion, temporizing; policy, diplomacy, Machiavellianism, realpolitik, jobbery, gerrymandering; improbity, sharp practice, underhand *or* underhanded deal, under-the-table deal, under-the-counter purchase; secret influence, backstage dealings, back-room influence, old-boy network, backdoor influence; intrigue, plot, conspiracy, wheeling and dealing [Inf]

▶ *Skillfulness 127; Secrecy 182; Untruthfulness, Falsehood 192; Deception 193; Sophistry 330; Knowledge 348; Imagination 360; Equivocation 380; Plan 387; Conduct 399; Influence 512*

2 **stratagem,** gamesmanship, ruse, wile, art, artifice, device, resource, resort, ploy, shift, dodge, contrivance, expedient, machination; game, (dirty) little game, plot, design, subterfuge; evasion, excuse, pretext, lie, deception, sham; trick, old trick, bag of tricks, box of tricks, tricks of the trade; master stroke, feint, catch, net, web, ambush, Trojan horse, political trick, stalking-horse, trial balloon, trap, ditch, pit, pitfall, Parthian shot; web of cunning, web of deceit, blind, smoke screen, dust thrown in the eyes, red herring, flag of convenience; thin end of the wedge, maneuver, manipulation, move, scheme, stroke, tactic, tactics; [Inf]: wrinkle, con, flimflam

▸ *Deception 193; Plan 387; Conduct 399; Untruth 722; Trap 813*

3 cunning person, wily person, crafty fellow, slyboots, artful dodger, fast talker, sophist, casuist; fox, Reynard; lurker, hider; serpent, snake, snake in the grass, troublemaker, fraud, dissembler, sham *or* shammer, wolf in sheep's clothing; hypocrite, deceiver, liar, cheat, trickster, double-crosser, sharper *or* sharpie, swindler, fly-by-nighter, confidence man, knave, juggler, conjurer; flatterer, glib tongue, smooth talker; diplomat, diplomatist; self-serving politician, timeserver; intriguer, conspirator, plotter, Machiavelli, schemer, strategist, tactician, maneuverer, wirepuller; [Inf]: con man, flimflam man, smoothie *or* smoothy, wheeler-dealer

▸ *Persuasion 178; Concealment 181; Plan 387; Flattery 439; Untruth 722; Trap 813*

ADJECTIVES

4 cunning, sly, wily, foxy, artful, crafty, clever, arch, skillful, knowledgeable; resourceful, inventive, ingenious, guileful, imaginative, disingenuous, subtle; serpentine, vulpine, feline, full of ruses, tricky, tricksy; devious, secret, stealthy, clandestine, underhand *or* underhanded, under-the-table, under-the-counter; scheming, slick, contriving, practicing, plotting, planning, intriguing, conspiring, calculating, Machiavellian; knowing, intelligent, smart, sharp, astute, shrewd, wise, acute, sophisticated, urbane, canny; too clever for, too clever by half, too smart for his *or* her own good; up to everything, not to be caught napping, not born yesterday, experienced; reticent, reserved, not to be drawn, cautious, wary; tactical, strategical, well-laid, well-planned, full of snares; insidious, perfidious, shifty, slippery; timeserving, temporizing, equivocal, sophistical, flattering, beguiling; hypocritical, insincere, deceitful, deceiving; rascally, crooked, dishonest, knavish; no flies on [Inf]

▸ *Skillfulness 127; Secrecy 182; Deception 193; Wisdom 352; Equivocation 380; Plan 387*

VERBS

5 be cunning, finesse, play the fox, shift, dodge, maneuver, jockey, twist, turn, wriggle, hide, lie low, skulk, lurk; scheme, manipulate, intrigue, conspire, plot, plan, design, devise, contrive, wangle, know a trick or two; fix the game, play a dangerous game, spin a web, weave a plot, confuse, muddy the waters, have method in one's madness, have an ulterior motive, have an ax to grind; play tricks with, monkey around *or* about with, tinker, circumvent, gerrymander, overreach; outsmart, outwit, outdo, be too quick for, be too clever for, be one up on; trick, cheat, swindle, defraud, deceive, betray, put one over, steal a march on, snatch from under one's nose; coax, flatter, beguile, cajole, wheedle, fast-talk, smooth-talk, blarney; temporize, play for time, juggle; ambush, waylay, dig a pit for, un-

dermine, bait the trap, get one's foot in the door, create a Catch-22 situation; match in cunning, expose the trick, avoid the trap, see the catch, have a card up one's sleeve, know all the answers, live by one's wits, fly by the seat of one's pants; [Inf]: con, flimflam, double-cross, sweet-talk, pull a fast one, go one better

▸ *Persuasion 178; Concealment 181; Deception 193; Plan 387; Flattery 439; Convolution 632; Overstepping 712; Latency 844*

ADVERBS

6 cunningly, artfully, craftily, slyly, on the sly, secretly, stealthily; shrewdly, astutely; tactically, strategically; deceitfully, dishonestly; with a glib tongue

823 Easiness

It's either easy or impossible. — SALVADOR DALI

NOUNS

1 easiness, ease, facility, effortlessness, lack of difficulty, comfort; proficiency, competence; dexterity, fluency, ability, capability, talent, aptitude, skill, skillfulness; speed, efficiency, readiness

▸ *Skillfulness 127; Ease 819*

2 simplicity, simpleness, plainness, uncomplicatedness, unambiguousness, preciseness, precision; comprehensibility, understandability, clarity, intelligibility, lucidity; facileness, glibness, superficiality

▸ *Clarity 196; Intelligibility 363; Simplicity 526*

3 wieldiness, manageability, handiness, maneuverability, convenience; practicality, feasibility, practicableness, possibility, workability; flexibility, pliability, pliancy, adaptability

4 ease of manner, poise, nonchalance, polish, insouciance, sang-froid, calmness, confidence

▸ *Indifference 289*

5 smoothness, freedom, lack of hindrance, help, assistance

▸ *Help 825*

6 easy thing, simple twist of the wrist, soft option, sinecure; smooth sailing, easy sailing, straight sailing, walkover, easy ride, clear course, clear coast, clear road, smooth road, royal road, the high road; dead certainty, sure thing, soft touch, sitting duck, easy target, no trouble, child's play, duck soup, a pleasure, pie in the sky; [Inf]: cinch, snap, breeze, picnic, setup, velvet, kid stuff, piece of cake, cushy job, no sweat

7 easing, facilitation, smoothing, expediting, hastening, speeding, quickening; streamlining, simplifying, simplification, clarification

▸ *Haste 818*

8 disentanglement, disembarrassment, disinvolvement, extrication, disengagement, freeing, clearing, disencumberment, uncluttering; disburdenment, unburdening, unscrambling, unsnarling

▶ *Order 765; Arrangement 767*

ADJECTIVES

9 **easy,** facile, not difficult, not hard, undemanding, effortless, painless, hands-down, light, moderate, unburdensome, smooth; uncomplicated, simple, uninvolved, straightforward; plain, clear, intelligible, elementary, glib, superficial; dead easy, dead simple, easy as pie, easy as falling off a log, nothing to it, simple as ABC, like shooting fish in a barrel, like taking candy from a baby; with the current *or* tide, with the crowd, downstream, downhill, downhill all the way, no sooner said than done; cushy [Inf], mickey mouse [Inf]

▶ *Clarity 196; Intelligibility 363; Simplicity 526*

10 **feasible,** practicable, workable, practical, possible; facilitating, helpful, useful, laborsaving

▶ *Usefulness 801; Help 825; Possibility 836*

11 **made easy,** made easier, facilitated, simplified, user-friendly, accessible, comprehensive, comprehensible, in plain English *or* language

12 **wieldy,** wieldable, manageable, maneuverable; flexible, pliable, pliant, malleable, ductile, yielding; handy, convenient, foolproof, untroublesome, practical, adaptable; smooth-running, easy-running, easy-flowing, frictionless, lubricated, well-oiled, well-greased

13 **easygoing,** undemanding, lenient, tolerant, permissive, indulgent; tractable, docile, relaxed, calm, serene; acquiescent, compliant, submissive, biddable; comfortable, pain-free, carefree, trouble-free, easy in one's mind; leisurely, unhurried; gentle

▶ *Submission 421; Leniency 423; Slowness 693; Ease 819*

VERBS

14 **be easy,** present no difficulties, give no trouble, make no demands; be had for the asking; have a simple answer, come out easily, be easy as pie

15 **make easy,** make easier, facilitate, ease, assist, aid, help; help on *or* along, smooth, grease, oil, lubricate, iron out, pave the way, smooth the way, prepare the way, grease the way, soap the way, grease the wheels; clear, unclog, unblock, unjam, unbar, free, loose, open up, clear the ground, clear the way; make way for, not stand in the way of, make all clear for, open the door to, bridge the gap; allow, permit, enable, make possible; promote, advance, further, forward, hasten, speed, accelerate, expedite, pioneer, give scope; make clear, explain, clarify, simplify, gloss, popularize, vulgarize, interpret, translate

▶ *Clarity 196; Permission 502; Simplicity 526; Oiliness, Lubrication 562; Haste 818; Help 825*

16 **do easily,** make light *or* little of, make light work of, make short work of, think nothing of, do with both eyes shut, do with one hand tied behind one's back, do standing on one's head; take in one's stride, take to like a duck to water, be in one's element, be quite at home;

have it easy, have it soft, have it all one's own way, have the game in one's hands, carry all before one, have it in the bag, hold all the trumps; coast home, sail home, breeze in, walk over the course, win in a walk, win hands down, win at a canter, have a walkover; swim with the stream, drift with the current, go with the tide *or* flow, save oneself the trouble, take the easy way out, take the line of least resistance, look for a short cut, put one's feet up; [Inf]: go easy, take it easy, easy does it, cool it

▶ *Ease 819; Success 845*

17 **disentangle,** disembarrass, disinvolve, extricate, disengage, free, clear, disencumber, lighten, unload, unclutter, disburden, unburden, alleviate, obviate; cut free, untie, unravel, liberate, unscramble, unsnarl, untangle

▶ *Order 765; Arrangement 767*

18 **go easily,** go smoothly, run smoothly, go *or* run like clockwork, work like a machine, work well, flow, glide, roll, slide, coast, freewheel, sweep, sail, go *or* run on oiled wheels

ADVERBS

19 **easily,** effortlessly, comfortably, facilely, simplistically, superficially, without difficulty, readily, simply; without ado, no problem, like nothing, just like that, by the flick of a switch, with one's eyes closed, with one hand tied behind one's back, freely, smoothly, without let or hindrance [Form], without a hitch, like clockwork; swimmingly, no sweat [Inf]

824 Difficulty

A difficulty for every solution. — HERBERT SAMUEL

NOUNS

1 **difficulty,** hardness, complexity; complication, intricacy, knottiness; technicality, abstruseness, convolution, reconditeness, obscurity, unintelligibility; effort, arduousness, laboriousness, strenuousness, strain; severity, toughness, ruggedness

▶ *Work 122; Obscurity 197; Unintelligibility 364; Severity 424; Disorder 766*

2 **awkwardness,** clumsiness, unwieldiness, lack of ease, lack of grace, lack of skill, ham-handedness

▶ *Unskillfulness 128*

3 **difficult task,** hard task, hard work, labor, toil; struggle, trial, tribulation; tough assignment, tough proposition, no easy task, tall order, large order, big undertaking, hard *or* long row to hoe, tough lineup to buck, hard row of stumps, hard furrow to plow, hard pull, heavy sledding, hard going; rough going, rough ground, difficult terrain, rough terrain, hard road to travel, the hard way; uphill task, uphill struggle, herculean task, superhuman task, brutal task, back-

breaker; [Inf]: handful, no picnic, ball-buster *or* ball-breaker, bitch

▶ *Work 122*

4 **problem,** worry, anxiety, quandary, dilemma, co-nundrum; brainteaser, brain twister, teaser, poser, vexed question, nonplus; nodus, crux, maze, puzzle, perplexity, imbroglio; thorny problem, knotty problem, hard *or* tough nut to crack, Gordian knot, headache, can of worms [Inf]

▶ *Unintelligibility 364; Disorder 766*

5 **predicament,** plight, situation, tangle, snarl, snafu, mess, muddle, hole, spot, tricky situation *or* spot, tick-lish situation, pinch, scrape, squeeze, difficult posi-tion, nice predicament, fine mess, sorry plight, pretty pass, Catch-22, hobble [Arch]; [Inf]: kettle of fish, pickle, pretty pickle, how-do-you-do, unholy mess, hot water, bind, fix, jam, no-win situation

6 **critical situation,** tight corner, tight spot, nowhere to turn, desperate *or* dire *or* parlous straits, clutch, emer-gency, exigency; hard times, hard life, hardship, ad-versity; danger, slippery slope, quagmire, quicksand, swamp, morass, crunch

▶ *Danger 811; Adversity 848*

7 **awkward situation,** awkward position, delicate sit-uation, diplomatic incident, embarrassing situation, embarrassing position, financial embarrassment; bother, bad patch, hard times; dispute, disagreement; sticky wicket [Brit]; tail in a gate [Inf], tit in the wringer [Inf]

▶ *Disagreement 463*

8 **snag,** hitch, catch, drawback, pitfall, teething trou-bles, complication; aggravation, annoyance; inconve-nience, obstacle, hurdle, obstruction, hindrance; im-passe, stalemate, deadlock; standstill, logjam, halt, stop, stoppage; cul-de-sac, blind alley, dead end, blank wall

▶ *Hindrance 826; Impossibility 837*

ADJECTIVES

9 **difficult,** hard, not easy, arduous, strenuous, labori-ous, stiff, toilsome, demanding, exacting, challenging, tough; heavy, hefty, onerous, burdensome; effortful, physically demanding, requiring effort, wearisome, backbreaking, grueling, punishing, exhausting, fa-tiguing; uphill, steep, oppressive, severe; formidable, superhuman, herculean, impossible; impracticable, easier said than done; hairy [Inf]

▶ *Work 122; Fatigue 820; Impossibility 837*

10 **rough,** rugged, craggy, rough-going, heavy-going; im-penetrable, impassable, unnavigable

11 **problematic,** puzzling, baffling, confusing, perplexing, troubling, obfuscating; demanding, exacting, chal-lenging, tough; tricky, sticky, complex, thorny, com-plicated, intricate, delicate, ticklish, convoluted, in-volved, knotty, confused, labyrinthine; skilled, specialized, technical, overspecialized, overtechnical, abstruse, recondite, esoteric; impenetrable, obscure,

unclear, unintelligible, illegible, indecipherable, crabbed, cramped, garbled, jumbled, scrambled; jaw-breaking [Inf]

▶ *Skillfulness 127; Obscurity 197; Unintelligibility 364; Disorder 766*

12 **inconvenient,** awkward, troublesome, bothersome, irksome, vexatious, vexing, annoying, aggravating, exasperating; tedious, tiresome, boring, trying, worry-ing, worrisome, troubling, plaguy *or* plaguey

▶ *Boredom 296; Agitation 684; Disturbance 768*

13 **troublesome,** demanding, contrary, perverse, way-ward, unmanageable, out of hand, beyond control; stubborn, obstinate, obdurate, headstrong, intractable, refractory, difficult to handle; ill-behaved, badly be-haved, naughty, disobedient, disruptive, obstreperous; critical, overcritical, hypercritical, faultfinding, nit-picking, pedantic, censorious, disapproving; grudging, discontented, hard to please, hard to satisfy, fussy, fas-tidious, finicky, particular; difficult to live with, moody, persnickety [Inf]

▶ *Obstinacy 379; Conduct 399; Disobedience 427; Disap-proval 438*

14 **clumsy,** cumbersome, unwieldy, awkward, ungainly, hulking, ponderous, bulky, lumbering

▶ *Size, Largeness 579*

15 **troubled,** beset, worried, anxious, perturbed, both-ered, vexed, annoyed; puzzled, confused, baffled, stumped, perplexed, bewildered, mystified; non-plussed, inconvenienced, put out, harassed, plagued, distressed, embarrassed; in a predicament, in a mess, in a tangle, at a loss, on Queer Street; at a standstill, at an impasse, deadlocked, at one's wits' end, at the end of one's rope *or* tether; in a quandary, in a dilemma *or* on the horns of a dilemma, stuck between the devil and the deep blue sea, between Scylla and Charybdis, between a rock and a hard place [Inf]; in trouble, in a tight spot, in a corner, on the spot; out of one's depth, in deep water, out on a limb, on a tightrope, in diffi-culties, in a scrape, in Dutch; [Inf]: in a jam, in a pickle, in hot water, in the soup, in a fix, behind the eight ball, up a tree

▶ *Unintelligibility 364; Agitation 684*

VERBS

16 **be difficult,** present difficulties, present problems, pose problems; take some doing, require effort; set one a problem, give one trouble, pester, hassle [Inf]

17 **find difficult,** struggle with, get all tangled up, get all snarled up, make heavy weather of, not see the woods for the trees

18 **have difficulty,** have trouble, struggle, flounder, be hard put (to), have one's work cut out, let oneself in for; labor under difficulties, labor under a disadvantage, have one hand tied behind one's back, do it the hard way, swim against the current, swim upstream, walk

or tread on hot coals, come unstuck, invite difficulties, make it hard on oneself

◗ *Work 122*

19 **be in difficulty,** have a problem, face difficulties, get into difficulties, run into trouble, get in a mess, strike a bad patch, hit hard times, have a hard time of it, feel the pinch, paint oneself into a corner, put oneself in a spot; tread carefully, pick one's way, walk on eggs; have one's hands full, bite off more than one can chew, have more than enough, be at a loss, flounder, be at one's wits' end, be at the end of one's rope *or* tether, come to a standstill, have one's back to the wall, not know which way to turn, bear the brunt; go under, go to the wall, be out of one's depth, founder, get one's ass in a bind [Inf], be up a tree

20 **get into trouble,** be asking for trouble, fish in troubled waters, burn one's fingers, bring down on one's head *or* around one's ears; [Inf]: catch it, get it, get *or* catch hell, get into hot water, put one's foot in it

21 **cause trouble,** give trouble, irk, annoy, aggravate, exasperate, bedevil, try one's patience, lead on a merry dance, stir up a hornet's nest, open Pandora's box, raise the devil, raise hob, play hob with, sow the wind and reap the whirlwind; [Inf]: raise the roof, raise Cain, raise hell, have a tiger by the tail, play hell with

◗ *Aggravation 276; Conduct 399*

22 **cause difficulties,** raise *or* create difficulties, make things difficult, trouble; find problems, find fault, criticize, carp, disrupt, put out, disturb, worry, bother, perturb, baffle, perplex, nonplus; stump, puzzle, mystify, confuse, bewilder, inconvenience, discommode, obstruct, hamper, hinder, embarrass, confound, disconcert; corner, box in, trap, put to a lot of trouble, make things awkward, make things *or* matters worse, complicate matters, put to it, give one a hard *or* bad time, make it tough for, force *or* push *or* drive to the wall; tree [Inf]

◗ *Unintelligibility 364; Disapproval 438; Disorder 766; Disturbance 768; Hindrance 826*

ADVERBS

23 **difficultly,** hardly, ill, with difficulty, at a pinch; in spite of, in the teeth of; with much ado; the hard way, against the wind, uphill

24 **arduously,** strenuously, laboriously, punishingly, formidably

25 **problematically,** intricately, delicately; obscurely; unintelligibly

26 **awkwardly,** clumsily, ponderously, unwieldily, unmanageably; inconveniently, annoyingly, tediously

27 **perversely,** waywardly; stubbornly, obstinately; disobediently; disruptively; critically, censoriously, disapprovingly

825 Help

NOUNS

1 **help,** aid, assistance, helping hand, hand, assist, springboard, instrument, means to an end, avail, use, benefit, advantage, improvement, following wind, fair wind, tailwind, leg up

◗ *Means 102; Use 393; Improvement 807*

2 **support,** moral support, succor, relief, comfort, ease, remedy, ministration, ministry, offices, good offices, kind offices; service, benefit, advice, counsel, guidance, constructive criticism, intercession, prayer; lift, boost, good turn, good deed, favor, kindness; rescue, deliverance

◗ *Remedy 115; Advice 176; Relief 275; Good 445; Support 605; Deliverance 817; Ease 819*

3 **sustenance,** support, subsistence, sustainment, sustention, sustentation, maintenance, upkeep, livelihood, living, keep; daily bread, manna, provision, nourishment; nurture, mothering, care, tender loving care (TLC), sympathy

◗ *Provision 89; Support 605*

4 **social assistance,** public assistance, benefit, relief, welfare, unemployment benefit *or* compensation, sickness benefit, disablement benefit, maternity benefit, maternity allowance, maternity grant, child benefit, family allowance, child allowance, family benefit, Aid to Families with Dependent Children (AFDC); pension, retirement pension, state pension, old-age pension, widow's pension, company pension, noncontributory benefit, maintenance, guaranteed annual income, national insurance, state insurance, health insurance, unemployment insurance; Social Security, public provision, state provision, social services, welfare services, protection, dole [Brit]; charity, handout [Inf]

◗ *Sociology 2; Safety 810*

5 **medical assistance,** therapy, treatment, remedy, cure, medicine, first aid

◗ *Medicine 107; Remedy 115; Repair 809*

6 **financial assistance,** subsidy, subvention, grant, allowance, stipend, donation, contribution, endowment, settlement, bestowal, dowry, scholarship, bursary, fellowship, sponsorship, financial backing, funding, loan, advance, credit, monetary aid, economic aid

◗ *Finance 457; Giving 472; Lending 475; Credit 487; Payment 489*

7 **convenience,** facility, amenity, accommodation, appliance, aid, tool, labor-saving device, time-saving device, safeguard

◗ *Tool 103; Convenience 803; Safety 810; Easiness 823*

8 **furtherance,** advancement, facilitation, expediting, forwarding, promotion, preferment, special *or* preferential treatment

9 **patronage,** fosterage, tutelage, auspices, aegis, cham-

pionship, sponsorship, subsidization, seconding, advocacy, encouragement, backing, support, abetment, countenance

▶ *Philanthropy 307; Support 605*

10 **helpfulness,** cooperation, collaboration, willingness, usefulness, utility, benevolence, kindness, goodwill, advantageousness, profitability

▶ *Benevolence 305; Willingness 373; Gain 467; Usefulness 801; Cooperation 827*

11 **self-help,** self-helpfulness, self-sustainment, self-support, self-improvement; independence

12 **helper,** assistant, assister, aider, enabler, aide, mate, abettor; collaborator, colleague, partner, ally, attendant, adjutant, coadjutant, adjuvant, helping hand, facilitator; auxiliary, second, subordinate, deputy, lieutenant, backup, standby, henchman, right-hand man *or* woman, girl *or* man Friday, support, backing, second line, reinforcements, reserves, staff; sidekick, gofer [Inf]

▶ *Servant 69; Deputy 80; Worker 123*

13 **supporter,** mainstay, comfort, prop, succorer, tower of strength, friend in need, good neighbor, good Samaritan, ministering angel, carer, helpmate, helpmeet, friendly critic

▶ *Friendship 62; Good 445*

14 **adviser,** mentor, guide, counselor, minister, pastor, consultant, arbitrator, advocate, troubleshooter

▶ *Mediation 75; Advice 176*

15 **benefactor,** benefactress, philanthropist, patron, sponsor, promoter, backer, guardian angel, patron saint, tutelary, fairy godmother, genie, angel [Inf]

▶ *Philanthropy 307*

ADJECTIVES

16 **helping,** aiding, assisting, adjuvant, serving, supporting, supplementing, of assistance, of service, of help, facilitative, facilitating, instrumental, promoting, favoring

▶ *Support 605; Forward Motion 679; Easiness 823*

17 **supplementary,** auxiliary, subsidiary, ancillary, accessory, subservient, on call, at one's service *or* command, at one's beck and call

18 **supportive,** comforting, reassuring, succoring, morale-boosting, caring, tending, attending, ministering, ministrant, ministrative, encouraging, heartening, sustaining, fostering, nurturing

▶ *Relief 275*

19 **helpful,** useful, utilitarian, serviceable, convenient, handy, informative, practical, constructive, positive, furthering, promoting, contributory, conducive; assistant [Arch]

▶ *Usefulness 801; Convenience 803*

20 **beneficial,** good, salutary, advantageous, favorable, propitious, expedient, profitable, gainful, valuable, remedial, therapeutic

▶ *Remedy 115; Good 445; Gain 467*

21 **benevolent,** kind, kindly, considerate, benign, sympathetic, friendly, neighborly, cooperative, willing, accommodating, obliging, generous, charitable, beneficent, philanthropic, indulgent, well-disposed, favorably disposed, well-affected, well-intentioned, well-meaning, well-meant

▶ *Benevolence 305; Philanthropy 307; Willingness 373; Cooperation 827*

22 **self-helpful,** self-helping, self-supporting, self-sustaining, self-supported, self-sustained, independent

VERBS

23 **help,** aid, assist, abet, aid and abet, help out, make oneself useful; be helpful, be of assistance, be of help, be of use, do something, give a hand, lend *or* bear a hand, give *or* render assistance, give an assist, proffer aid, come to the aid *or* assistance of, rush *or* fly to the assistance of, go *or* come to the relief of, rescue, deliver, save, go for help; serve, avail, profit, gain

▶ *Usefulness 801; Deliverance 817*

24 **support,** succor, comfort, hearten, give relief to, minister to, care for, tend, look after, nurse, alleviate, relieve, ease, remedy, treat, doctor, bolster, strengthen, reinforce, buttress, shore, shore up, prop, prop up, undergird, crutch, boost, lift, rally, revive, restore, give new life to

▶ *Remedy 115; Relief 275; Support 605; Repair 809; Ease 819*

25 **sustain,** support, maintain, keep, provide for, nourish, nurture, mother, hold someone's hand, pamper, coddle, cosset, protect, sympathize

▶ *Provision 89; Safety 810*

26 **improve,** better, ameliorate, enhance, do something for *or* to, do a good turn, do a favor, give a leg up, help a lame dog over a stile, help a lame duck, accommodate, oblige, indulge, favor, collaborate, cooperate

▶ *Duty 433; Improvement 807; Cooperation 827*

27 **advise,** counsel, guide, countenance, encourage, uphold, support, subscribe to [Brit], cultivate, give *or* lend *or* furnish support, lend oneself, endorse, sanction, advocate, champion, argue for, hold a brief for, intercede, take by the hand, hold out a hand to, take under one's wing, patronize, sponsor, take up, propose, second, back, foster, take in hand, take in tow, plump for

▶ *Mediation 75; Advice 176; Support 605*

28 **back,** back up, stand behind, stand back of, get in back of, get in behind, stand by, stick by, take the part of, go to bat for, take up the cudgels for, stick up for, run interference for, side with, align with, associate oneself with, come down *or* range oneself on the side of, ally with

▶ *Union 752*

29 **serve,** attend, wait on, tend, look after, work for, labor in behalf of, cater to *or* for, pander to, do for [Brit]

▶ *Servant 69; Worker 123*

30 **further,** advance, forward, promote, prefer, favor, advantage, facilitate, expedite, subserve, subvene, contribute to, make for, have a hand in, help along, boost, conduce to, ease *or* smooth the way, clear the track, grease the wheels, quicken, hasten, speed, lend wings to

31 **finance,** fund, sponsor, back, support, subsidize, guarantee, endow, settle, bestow, donate, contribute to *or* toward, lend, loan, advance, set up, set *or* put on one's feet, provide the means, be the making of, help out, tide over, see through, bail out, chip in, pitch in [Inf]

▶ *Finance 457; Giving 472; Lending 475; Money 484; Credit 487; Payment 489*

ADVERBS

32 **helpfully,** supportively, usefully, serviceably, conveniently, practically, constructively, positively, beneficially, to the good, advantageously, favorably, profitably, to advantage

33 **in aid of,** for the sake of, on behalf of, by the aid of, thanks to, under the auspices *or* aegis of, in the name of, in the service of

34 **benevolently,** kindly, considerately, sympathetically, cooperatively, willingly, obligingly, charitably

826 Hindrance

NOUNS

1 **hindrance,** hindering, impediment, encumbrance, let or hindrance, obstruction, obstructiveness, restriction, circumscription, restraint, retardation, control, curb, detention, detainment, limitation; friction, interruption, interference, interception, interposition, intervention, meddling, opposition, contrariness, unwillingness, refusal; interdiction, injunction, resistance, counteraction, countermeasure, obviation, determent, dissuasion, discouragement; frustration, foiling, prevention, repression, preclusion, prohibition, stopping, forestalling, hampering

▶ *Dissuasion 179; Unwillingness 375; Resistance 417; Defense 419; Refusal 506; Counteraction 510; Friction 554; Limit 620; Cessation 668; Opposition 828*

2 **obstacle,** block, stumbling block, blockage; blockade, logjam, stoppage, bar; embargo, intervention, impediment, difficulty, deterrent, drawback, joker, inconvenience; not plain sailing, hazard, hurdle, hitch, snag, drag, rub, catch; Catch-22, vicious circle *or* cycle, check, stay, arrest, sabotage, filibuster, delay; trouble, mishap, contretemps, monkey wrench in the works, flaw, impasse, stalemate, deadlock; botch, mix-up, fly in the ointment; [Inf]: foul-up, hang-up, screwup, fuckup

3 **technical problem,** malfunction, accident; breakdown, flat tire, puncture; technical hitch, engine trouble, gremlin, computer malfunction; [Inf]: glitch, bug, hiccup

4 **roadblock,** tollgate, tollbooth, turnstile, bottleneck, jam, traffic jam, gridlock, speed bump

5 **bureaucracy,** red tape, regulations

6 **lockout,** strike, picket line

7 **barrier,** wall, brick wall, stone wall, fence, barbed wire, portcullis; sea wall, jetty, mole, breakwater, levee, dam, dike; bulwark, rampart, bunker, buffer, parapet, breastwork, earthwork, work, embankment; moat, ditch, weir; barrier method contraception *or* prophylactic, condom, female condom, diaphragm, Dutch cap

▶ *Defense 419; Closure 584; Enclosure 619; Refuge 812*

8 **restraint,** curb, check; shackles, chains, ball and chain; tether, fetter, bond, tie, knot; rein, leash, lead; brake, governor (of speed), boot *or* Denver boot; doorstop; anchor

▶ *Prison 55; Subjection 832*

9 **inhibition,** introversion, conservativeness; embarrassment, shyness; negativism; hanging back, foot-dragging

▶ *Unwillingness 375; Avoidance 386; Unsociability 409; Interior 611*

10 **burden,** inconvenience, handicap; encumbrance, debts, mortgage, dependents, family responsibilities; white elephant; overload, last straw, weight on one's shoulders, millstone around one's neck, albatross, dead weight, cross to bear, monkey on one's back [Inf]

▶ *Debt 488; Heaviness 538*

11 **hinderer,** hindrance, interrupter, obstructer, obstructionist, negativist; impeder, marplot, filibuster *or* filibusterer, staller, frustrator; killjoy, spoilsport, heckler, interferer, meddler, intruder, wet blanket, damper; troublemaker, mischief-maker, gremlin, poltergeist; saboteur, snake in the grass, dog in the manger, interfering so-and-so, party pooper [Inf]

ADJECTIVES

12 **hindering,** hindered, impeding, impeded, held back, held up; unhelpful, uncooperative, unwilling, contrary, encumbering, encumbered, obstructive, restrictive, cramping, circumscriptive; limited, interfering, intrusive, interventional, intervening, meddling; deterrent, dissuasive, discouraging, preventive, defensive, prophylactic; counteractive, repressive, preclusive, prohibitive, prohibiting, thwarting

13 **blocked,** barred, in the way, walled in, fenced in, up against a brick wall, with one's back to the wall, in a corner; restraining, restrained, anchored, curbed, shackled, chained, tethered, leashed; deterrent, interventional, inconvenient, bureaucratic, regulatory; hazardous, fraught with difficulties, not easy, accidental; malfunctioning; deadlocked, at a standstill, at an impasse; burdened, overburdened, heavy-laden, handicapped, saddled with, in debt, indebted, overloaded, backbreaking, in a fix [Inf], in a pickle [Inf]

14 **inhibitive,** introversive, conservative, embarrassing, embarrassed; shy, negative, foot-dragging

15 **hinder,** impede, encumber, obstruct, get in the way of, restrict, circumscribe; choke, stifle, restrain, disable, incapacitate, undermine, impair, control, curb; detain, hold back, hold one back, limit, retard, stall; cause friction, interrupt, interfere, intercept, upset, interpose, intervene, come between, meddle, oppose, refuse, resist, counteract, devise countermeasures, obviate, deter, dissuade, discourage; frustrate, thwart, spike, foil, snag, sabotage, foul up, queer, mix up, prevent, repress, preclude, prohibit, forbid, stop, stop one in the act, bring to a standstill, scotch, forestall; hamper, crimp, put a crimp in, dampen, stymie, cripple, hobble, cut the ground from under one's feet, nip in the bud, throw cold water on, clip one's wings, take the wind out of someone's sails, steal someone's thunder, upset one's applecart, spike someone's guns, pull the rug from under one's feet; [Inf]: cramp one's style, snooker, crab one's act or deal, louse up

16 **bother,** heckle, hassle [Inf]

17 **block,** block up, blockade; throw up a roadblock, create an obstacle, create a barrier, wall, wall up, fence; dam, cut off, create a logjam; strike, picket, form a picket line; bar, lock out, embargo, intervene; impede, trip, trip up, stand in the way of, get under one's feet, get in the way, bottleneck, cause a traffic jam, deter, inconvenience; filibuster, delay, stall, drag one's feet, protract, play for time, cause trouble, gum up [Inf], gum up the works [Inf]

18 **have a mishap,** have an accident, have a breakdown, have a flat, develop technical problems, malfunction, develop engine trouble; reach an impasse, reach a stalemate, deadlock; find a joker in the pack, hit a snag, be in a Catch-22 situation, have a fly in the ointment, have a hiccup [Inf]

19 **restrain,** curb, check; shackle, chain, tether, fetter, bind, tie one's hands, tie; rein, leash; brake, act as a brake; anchor

20 **be inhibited,** be introverted, have a conservative outlook, embarrass; shy, hang back, drag, drag one's feet

21 **burden,** inconvenience, handicap; encumber, saddle with, have debts, mortgage one's house, have dependents to support, have family responsibilities; overload, have a weight on one's shoulders, have a millstone around one's neck, have an albatross around one's neck, have a cross to bear, have a monkey on one's back [Inf]

ADVERBS

22 **with delay,** with much ado, without help, unhelpfully, without assistance; uncooperatively, unwillingly, contrarily, obstructively, restrictively, intrusively, in an intrusive manner, dissuasively, discouragingly; preventively, defensively, counteractively, repressively, preclusively, prohibitively

23 **in the way,** interventionally, inconveniently, bu-

reaucratically; hazardously, with difficulty, the hard way; up against a brick wall, with one's back to the wall, in a corner; accidentally

24 **inhibitively,** with inhibitions, in an inhibited way, conservatively; embarrassingly, with embarrassment, shyly; negatively, in a negative manner

827 Cooperation

NOUNS

1 **cooperation,** collaboration, coaction, synergy, synergism; concurrence, cooperativeness; assistance, support, backup, helpfulness, help
  ◗ *Support 605; Help 825*

2 **fellowship,** comradeship, friendship, sodality; solidarity, togetherness, sympathy, fellow feeling, fraternalism, clanship, freemasonry; community spirit, team spirit, morale, esprit de corps, concord, concordance, harmony, accord, consensus, agreement, bipartisanship
  ◗ *Friendship 62; Agreement 462; Accord 735*

3 **mutual relationship,** correlation, interaction, symbiosis, sharing, participation; mutualism, mutualness, mutuality, reciprocity, interplay, mutual assistance, networking, aiding and abetting, logrolling, exchanging favors, back-scratching; compromise, concession, give and take
  ◗ *Sociability 408; Compromise 461; Reciprocity 729*

4 **joint operation,** combined operation, common endeavor, joint effort or venture, combined effort, concerted effort, communal effort; pulling together, joining of forces, pooling of resources, teamwork, working together; joint action, concerted action, collective action, united action, mass action, united front, cooperative enterprise
  ◗ *Economics 56; Work 122; Action 412; Possession 469; Union 752*

5 **joint control,** coagency, coadministration, comanagement, cochairmanship, codirectorship; partnership, copartnership, codetermination, co-ownership; collegialism, federalism, federation, confederation, confederacy; cahoots [Inf]
  ◗ *Management 126*

6 **association,** alliance, alignment, affiliation, sodality; combination, combine, cartel, consortium, union, unification, coalition; cooperative, collective, community, commune; fusion, merging, merger, coalescence, coadunation; amalgamation, consolidation, incorporation, integration; communalism, collectivism, socialism, communism, ecumenicalism or ecumenicism; hookup, tie-up, tie-in
  ◗ *Union 752*

7 **team,** squad, teammates, partners, coworkers, colleagues, associates, fellows, collaborators; community, congregation, brotherhood, fraternity, confraternity, sisterhood, sorority; duet, duumvirate, trio, triumvi-

rate, troika, quartet, quintet, sextet, septet, octet, nonet; league, federation, confederation

▸ *Music 140; Two 789; Three 790; Four 791; Five and Over 792*

8 **cooperator,** helper, assistant, partner, coworker, ally, fellow, coadjutor, collaborator

▸ *Help 825*

ADJECTIVES

9 **cooperative,** cooperating, collaborative, coactive, coacting; concurrent, synergetic, synergistic, synergic, coadjutant, symbiotic *or* symbiotical; helpful, obliging, willing, accommodating, supportive; contributory, participatory

▸ *Support 605; Help 825*

10 **joint,** shared, combined, collective, concerted, united; common, communal, pooled, mutual, reciprocal; correlational, interrelating, interactive; communalistic, collectivistic, communist *or* communistic, socialist *or* socialistic, ecumenical *or* ecumenic

▸ *Possession 469; Reciprocity 729*

11 **associating,** allied, affiliated; comradely, fraternal, friendly, concordant, harmonious, en rapport, concurring; commensal, uncompetitive, noncompetitive; hand and glove *or* hand in glove, shoulder to shoulder, in cahoots [Inf]

▸ *Accord 735; Union 752*

VERBS

12 **cooperate,** collaborate, concur, coact; help, assist, support, play ball

▸ *Support 605; Help 825*

13 **reciprocate,** respond, interrelate, interact, interplay, mesh, lend oneself; requite, repay, give and take, return the compliment, aid and abet, compromise

▸ *Compromise 461; Reciprocity 729*

14 **work together,** act in concert, work as a team, pitch in, rally; pull together, hang together, keep together, hold together, stand together, put *or* get *or* lay heads together; make common cause, unite efforts, sail *or* row in the same boat, stand shoulder to shoulder, stand *or* fall together, sink *or* swim together; contribute, join in, participate, share, pitch in [Inf]

▸ *Work 122; Willingness 373; Sociability 408*

15 **join with,** join up with, join hands with, go in with, do business with, get together with, team up, ally with, align with, range with, line up with, stand in with, cast in one's lot with, join one's fortunes to; get together, band together, club together, gang together, join forces, pool resources, pool interests; merge with, go into partnership with, go partners; throw in with [Inf], string along with [Inf]

▸ *Union 752*

16 **concur,** agree, go along with, harmonize, concert; collude, connive, conspire, be *or* go in cahoots [Inf]

▸ *Agreement 462; Accord 735*

17 **join,** associate, ally, affiliate; combine, amalgamate,

unite, fuse, merge, coalesce, consolidate; federate, confederate; tie up, tie in, hook up [Inf]

▸ *Union 752*

ADVERBS

18 **cooperatively,** cooperatingly, collaboratively, coactively; concurrently, synergistically, synergetically, jointly, together; collectively, combinedly, conjointly, concertedly, communally; harmoniously, concordantly, as one, with one accord, with one voice, unanimously; hand and glove *or* hand in glove, shoulder to shoulder

828 Opposition

NOUNS

1 **opposition,** hostility, antagonism; antipathy, dislike, hate, hatred, aversion, repugnance, repugnancy; disapproval, disapprobation, unfriendliness, stiff opposition, resistance, hindrance

▸ *Hostility 63; Dislike 291; Hate 300; Resistance 417; Disapproval 438; Hindrance 826*

2 **objection,** demurral, demur, remonstration, expostulation, protest, dissent, dissidence; controversy, disputation, disagreement, argument, contradiction, contravention; challenge, impugnment, rebuttal, refutation, denial, refusal, rejection, defiance, animosity

▸ *Dissent 347; Rejection 383; Defiance 416; Disagreement 463; Protest 507*

3 **conflict,** friction, disaccord, dissension, crosscurrent, undercurrent; collision, clashing, confrontation, strife, discord; rivalry, vying, competition, emulation; contention, fighting, fight, battle, war, warfare, attack, defense; bad blood, enmity, adversity

▸ *Hostility 63; War 76; Attack 418; Defense 419; Contention 422*

4 **uncooperativeness,** unhelpfulness, negativeness, negativity, unwillingness; nonacceptance, dissociation; noncooperation, obstructiveness, obstruction, prevention, foot-dragging

▸ *Unwillingness 375; Hindrance 826*

5 **contrariness,** perverseness, perversity, oppugnancy; stubbornness, obstinacy, disobedience, fractiousness, refractoriness, recalcitrance, reaction

▸ *Obstinacy 379; Disobedience 427*

6 **contrariety,** oppositeness, disagreement; difference, discrepancy, inconsistency, disparity, contrast, contradistinction, antithesis, polarity, contraposition

▸ *Oppositeness 731; Dissimilarity 734; Nonconformity 782*

7 **countermeasure,** counterargument, counterproposal, countercheck, countermove, counterattack, counterwork, counteraction

▸ *Counteraction 510*

8 **the opposition,** the other side, opposing party, opposing force, opposite camp, the enemy, the field; faction, minority party *or* group, opposition party

> Government 49; Politics 50

9 opposer, oppositionist, objector, protester, gainsayer, dissenter, dissentient, dissident; agitator, heckler; disputant, litigant, plaintiff, defendant; radical, rebel, revolutionary, counterrevolutionary, resister; intransigent, die-hard, reactionary, conservative, anti, bitterender, last-ditcher; obstructer, obstructionist, filibusterer; negativist, naysayer

> Litigation 54; Negation 190

10 opponent, adversary, antagonist; combatant, enemy, foe; competitor, contestant, contender, player, rival, emulator, corrival

> Hostility 63; Combatant 77; Contention 422

ADJECTIVES

11 oppositional, opposing, opposed, in opposition, hostile, antagonistic, inimical, anti, unfriendly; unfavorable, unpropitious, adverse; counteractive, counteracting, counter, cross; antipathetic, unsympathetic, averse, disapproving; alien, repugnant

> Hostility 63; Dislike 291; Counteraction 510

12 discordant, disagreeing, contentious, dissentient, dissenting, dissident, different; conflicting, clashing, adversarial, confronting, face-to-face, eyeball-to-eyeball, head-on, challenging, defiant; rival, competitive, corrival, emulating, competing, contending, at odds, at cross-purposes, at variance, at issue

> Dissent 347; Defiance 416; Contention 422; Disagreement 463; Dissimilarity 734

13 contrary, contrasting, contrasted, opposite, irreconcilable, polarized, reverse; inconsistent, incompatible; contradictory, repugnant, antithetical, diametric or diametrical, diametrically opposed, adversative

> Oppositeness 731

14 uncooperative, unhelpful, negative, noncooperative, unwilling; obstructive, hindering, contrary, perverse, oppugnant; stubborn, obstinate, disobedient, fractious, refractory, recalcitrant; reactionary, reactionist, conservative, resistant

> Unwillingness 375; Obstinacy 379; Resistance 417; Disobedience 427; Hindrance 826

VERBS

15 oppose, stand against, act against, go or act in opposition, traverse, protest against, fight against, strive against, resist

> Resistance 417; Protest 507

16 be contrary, go against, work against, militate against, counter, run counter to, conflict with

> Oppositeness 731

17 be against, discountenance, disapprove of, disagree with, not support, vote against, object to, not hold with; not abide, not tolerate, not put up with, dissociate oneself from, not have anything to do with, set one's face or oneself against, reject; dislike, hate

> Dislike 291; Hate 300; Rejection 383; Disapproval 438; Disagreement 463

18 object, complain, demur, raise or make objections, make a fuss, gripe, grouse, moan, take exception; protest, remonstrate, expostulate, speak out, deprecate, dissent, express disapproval, assail, criticize; disagree, take issue, beg to differ, call into question, dispute, oppugn, contradict, contravene, belie, rebut, refute, negate, deny, controvert, gainsay, counter, retaliate; defy, challenge, impugn, combat, fight, attack, litigate, kick [Inf]

> Litigation 54; Dissent 347; Defiance 416; Attack 418; Defense 419; Contention 422; Disapproval 438; Disagreement 463; Protest 507

19 confront, front, face, meet head on, take on; conflict, clash, come into conflict, join battle, grapple with; contest with, contend, compete with or against, vie with, rival, emulate; set against, pit against, match against

> Contention 422

20 withstand, stand firm or fast, stand up to, hold one's own, breast the storm, stem the tide, hold out, resist; obstruct, make difficulties, hinder, check, block, bar, dig one's heels in, refuse to budge, stand one's ground; defy, disobey, refuse

> Defiance 416; Resistance 417; Disobedience 427; Hindrance 826; Restraint 830

21 counteract, antagonize, countervail, work against, act against, countercheck, counterattack, countermine; frustrate, cross, thwart, foil, prevent; counterbalance, match, offset, set off against, set in opposition; contrast, compare

> Counteraction 510; Oppositeness 731

ADVERBS

22 opposingly, antagonistically, inimically, adversely, antipathetically, defiantly, competitively, contrastingly, contradictorily, antithetically; uncooperatively, unhelpfully, perversely, stubbornly; in opposition, on the other side

23 at odds, at cross-purposes, at variance, at issue; in confrontation; up in arms, at daggers drawn

24 contrariwise, against the tide, counter, au contraire [Fr]

829 Freedom

I know not what course others may take; but as for me, give me liberty or give me death. — PATRICK HENRY

Live free or die.
— MOTTO OF THE STATE OF NEW HAMPSHIRE

Man is born free and everywhere he is in chains.
— JEAN JACQUES ROUSSEAU

NOUNS

1 freedom, freedom of action, liberty, personal liberty, lack of confinement, freedom of movement, being at large; lack of restraint, unrestraint, noncoercion, nonintimidation; option, choice, freedom of choice, freedom of thought, prerogative, discretion; liberation, release, discharge, deliverance, emancipation; free will, own free will, own account, initiative, own initiative, personal initiative, own responsibility, own volition; license, artistic license, poetic license, privilege; exemption, nonliability, exception, immunity, diplomatic immunity

◗ *Exemption 434; Liberation 831*

2 **freethinking,** broad-mindedness, open-mindedness, toleration, tolerance; liberalism, libertarianism, latitudinarianism, liberated mind; bohemianism, nonconformity

◗ *Will 372; Permission 502; Liberation 831*

3 **noninterference,** nonintervention, laissez faire, free enterprise, free trade, free-trade zone, free port; self-regulating market, open market, free market, capitalism; noninvolvement, seclusion, nonalignment, neutrality, isolationism

◗ *Economics 56; Trade 480; Entry 706*

4 **free rights,** free speech, freedom of religion, freedom of the press, lack of censorship, academic freedom; the Four Freedoms: freedom of speech, freedom of worship, freedom from want, freedom from fear; rights, constitutional rights, legal rights, human rights, inalienable *or* unalienable rights; equal rights, civil rights, civil liberties; Declaration of Independence, Bill of Rights, Magna Carta

5 **independence,** own authority, own way, being in control, self-determination; individualism, self-expression, individuality, self-reliance; self-sufficiency, independent means, private means, wealth; no allegiance; unmarried state, singleness, bachelorhood, spinsterhood; franchise, enfranchisement, citizenship; authority, statehood, nationhood, national status, unilaterality; autonomy, autarky *or* autarchy, self-government, self-rule; independent rule, home rule, states' rights

◗ *Government 49; Authority 52; Will 372; Wealth 485; Originality 737*

6 **informality,** ease, familiarity; relaxation, friendliness, casualness; frankness, candidness, candor, openness, unconstraint

◗ *Informality 407*

7 **scope,** play, free scope *or* play, full scope *or* play *or* opportunity, wide range, free range; maneuverability, room, living room, Lebensraum, living space, elbowroom; wide berth, leverage, leeway, wide margin, latitude, clearance

◗ *Space 563; Possibility 836*

8 **liberality,** carte blanche, blank check, free hand; laxness, laxity, license; excess, excess of freedom, libertinism, immoderation, uninhibitedness, intemperance,

incontinence, free love, illicit love; lack of discipline, unruliness, abandon, abandonment, no holds barred, free fight, free-for-all; licentiousness, wantonness; permissiveness, permissive society; nothing in one's way, one's own way, one's own devices; run of, plenty of rope, enough rope to hang oneself

◗ *Excess 99; Permission 502*

9 **free person,** citizen, free citizen, voter; burgher, burgess, bourgeois; freedman, freedwoman, ex-slave, no slave; ex-convict, released prisoner, parolee; free agent, freelance *or* freelancer, one's own boss, one's own man *or* woman; free spirit, liberal, individualist, rugged individualist; independent, independent voter, undecided voter, undecided, don't-know; nonpartisan, neutral; free trader, capitalist; ex-con [Inf]

◗ *Liberation 831*

10 **freethinker,** rationalist, humanist; atheist, nonbeliever, agnostic, skeptic; latitudinarian, libertarian; bohemian, hippie, libertine, eccentric, nonconformist, maverick, loner, lone wolf [Inf]

ADJECTIVES

11 **free,** unconfined, unrestrained, unregulated, unhindered, unimpeded; unshackled, unfettered, unbridled, uncurbed, unbound, unchained, unmuzzled, unchecked, ungoverned; liberated, released, discharged, delivered, emancipated, freeborn; franchised, enfranchised, authorized; constitutional, inalienable *or* unalienable; acquitted, on the loose, at large, escaped, freed, scot-free; privileged, exempt, nonliable, excepted, immune; noninvolved, secluded, nonaligned, nonpartisan, neutral, isolationist, noninterventional; broad-minded, open-minded, unbiased, unprejudiced, uninfluenced, undecided; moderate, just, tolerant; liberal, libertarian

12 **independent,** individual, self-employed, freelance, wildcat; free-minded, free-spirited, individualistic; self-reliant, self-sufficient, self-contained, self-supporting, self-motivated, inner-directed, one's own master, unsubjected; unwedded *or* unwed, unmarried; footloose and fancy-free, freewheeling, free as air *or* the wind *or* a bird, left to one's own devices, ungoverned; autonomous, self-governing, self-ruling, autarkic *or* autarchic, self-determining; free-trade, self-regulating, self-regulatory, open, capitalistic; uncontrolled, uncompelled, ungovernable, anarchic; uninfluenced, unattached, unaffiliated; detached, indifferent; free to choose, enjoying liberty; unconventional, breakaway, dissenting, freethinking; rationalist, rationalistic; humanist, humanistic; atheistic, nonbelieving; latitudinarian, bohemian, nonconforming, eccentric, nonconformist, maverick

◗ *Will 372; Deviation 698; Originality 737; Nonconformity 782*

13 **free-ranging,** traveling, ranging, free-range, having

full play; unconfined, untethered, unfettered, maneuverable

14 **unconditional,** unconditioned, unrestricted, unlimited; without strings, no strings attached, catch-as-catch-can, no holds barred, free-for-all, anything goes; absolute, discretionary, arbitrary; liberated, lax, excess, excessive, immoderate, loose, uninhibited; unbridled, intemperate, incontinent, unruly, abandoned; licentious, wanton, impure; permissive, wide-open

▶ *Excess 99; Liberation 831*

15 **informal,** relaxed, casual, easy, easygoing, at ease, free and easy; at leisure, at home; out of harness, retired; familiar, frank, candid, open, self-expressive, free-speaking; plain-spoken, plain; uninhibited, unconstrained, spontaneous, willing, dégagé, unbuttoned [Inf]

▶ *Improvisation 396; Informality 407; Bluntness 550*

VERBS

16 **be free,** go free, get free, sample freedom, breathe the air of freedom, escape, enjoy liberty, move freely, lack restraint; have a free mind, speak freely, worship freely, publish freely, have artistic license, be uncensored, teach freely, have freedom of choice, have free will; keep an open mind, have a liberated mind, liberalize, tolerate, think freely

▶ *Will 372; Nonconformity 782; Liberation 831*

17 **set free,** emancipate, manumit, enfranchise, franchise, liberate, release, let go, let off, excuse; grant immunity, give diplomatic immunity, exempt, except; loose, unchain, unfetter, unbind, untie, rescue, deliver, extricate; give scope, allow initiative, give someone his *or* her head, allow full play, give the run of, give someone carte blanche *or* a blank check, facilitate, give a free hand, give the freedom of; give someone leeway, give free rein to, allow enough rope, leave to one's own devices *or* choice; live and let live, keep hands off, not interfere, not tamper, not meddle, not butt in, let sleeping dogs lie; not cramp someone's style [Inf]

▶ *Authority 52; Permission 502*

18 **be independent,** have a will of one's own, go one's own way, have one's way, have *or* do it one's own way; use one's own initiative, fend for oneself, shift for oneself, become a free agent, freelance; stand alone, stand up for one's rights, stand on one's own two feet; stay in control, have authority; have self-reliance, have independent means, stay unmarried, ask no favors, go it alone, call no man master; suit oneself, please oneself, do as one pleases, do as one chooses, do what one likes; vote independent, remain neutral; do one's own thing [Inf], follow one's bent, roam, stray, drift, drop out, paddle one's own canoe, act eccentric, live in a bohemian way

▶ *Authority 52; Will 372; Deviation 698; Originality 737*

19 **be informal,** take it easy, feel at home, make oneself at home; feel free, feel at liberty; let one's hair down [Inf], show candor

▶ *Informality 407*

20 **have scope,** have the run of, have the freedom of, range; have room to breathe, have play, have elbow-room, have one's head; have plenty of rope, have enough rope to hang oneself

▶ *Space 563; Possibility 836*

21 **lack restraint,** live immoderately; have a free hand, have carte blanche, have a blank check; let oneself go, let go; permit oneself, make bold to, take liberties, presume; make free with, cut loose, run wild, sow one's wild oats, have one's fling; go too far, pull out all the stops, lack discipline, go all out, go flat out [Inf], let it all hang out [Inf]

▶ *Excess 99*

ADVERBS

22 **freely,** free, with immunity; autonomously, independently, alone, by oneself, individually, individualistically; on one's own initiative, on one's own say-so, on one's own account, of one's own accord, of one's own volition, of one's own free will, at one's own discretion, on one's own responsibility; self-reliantly, with self-motivation; free-mindedly, broad-mindedly, open-mindedly, tolerantly, moderately, justly; without affiliation, neutrally, indifferently, with an indifferent attitude; rationalistically; atheistically; eccentrically; all by one's lonesome [Inf]

23 **excessively,** unconditionally, with no holds barred, with no strings attached; arbitrarily; immoderately, loosely, without control, without restraint, without stint, unreservedly; with abandon, intemperately, incontinently, licentiously, wantonly, impurely; permissively

24 **informally,** in an informal way; casually, easily, familiarly; frankly, candidly, with candor; freely, openly, plainly; spontaneously, willingly

830 Restraint

NOUNS

1 **restraint,** constraint, suppression, repression, strictness, coercion; hindrance, impediment, obstacle, stumbling block; retardation, deceleration, slowness, slowing down, stopping; prevention, control, strict control, curb, check, rein; veto, ban, bar, blackball, prohibition; restriction, restraint, legal restraint, injunction, interdict; severity, discipline; penalty, fine, punishment; authority, duress, pressure, censorship; putting down, quelling, quashing, suppressant, squelching, smothering, stifling, crackdown

▶ *Authority 52; Severity 424; Obedience 426; Punishment 454; Prohibition 503; Contraction 582; Cessation 668; Hindrance 826; Subjection 832*

2 **limitation,** allotment, stipulation, qualification, requirement, limiting factor, limit, limitations; retrenchment, constriction, squeeze, cuts, curtailment, cir-

cumscription; exclusive rights, exclusivity, copyright; circle, charmed circle, demarcation, restricted area, off-limits area; cramping one's style [Inf]

> *Authority 52; Information 170; Limit 620; Exclusion 764; Hindrance 826*

3 **economic restraint,** economic pressure, rationing, ration; freeze, price freeze, pay freeze, price control, credit squeeze; restrictive practice, restraint of trade, monopoly, cartel, closed shop; intervention, interventionism, protectionism, price fixing, mercantilism; tariff, duty, tariff wall, embargo, antitrust laws

> *Economics 56; Finance 457*

4 **self-restraint,** self-control, self-discipline, discipline, temperance, continence, abstinence, abstemiousness, asceticism, askesis *or* ascesis, Spartanism, moderation; inhibition, introversion, formality, reserved nature, reserve, quietness, modesty; shyness, embarrassment, stiffness

> *Modesty 403; Severity 424; Self-Restraint 455; Moderation 521*

5 **detention,** quarantine; blockade, siege, starving out, guarding; care, custodianship, charge, ward; custody, protective custody, impoundment, restriction of movement, curfew, remand, refusal of bail; arrest, house arrest, sentence, incarceration, imprisonment, internment, confinement, solitary confinement, durance, immurement; captivity, kidnapping; bondage, slavery, servitude; time [Inf], stretch [Inf]

> *Prison 55; Attack 418; Punishment 454*

6 **means of restraint,** diet, fast; ban, veto; damper, governor, drag, cramp, clamp, restraining hand; gag, muzzle; leash, lead; tether, hobble, reins, bridle, bit, halter, harness, collar, yoke; corset, girdle; straitjacket; fetters, bonds, irons, chains, shackles, ball and chain, handcuffs, cuffs, manacles; trammels, bilboes, stocks, pillory; bracelets [Inf]

> *Punishment 454*

7 **one who restrains,** lawmaker, legislator; judge, district attorney (DA); policeman *or* policewoman, enforcer, censor; monopolist, protectionist, restrictionist, disciplinarian; dictator, tyrant; kidnapper; ascetic, Spartan; interventionist, mercantilist, monetarist; warden, jailer, prison guard, screw [Inf]

> *Law 53; Prison 55; Judgment 341*

ADJECTIVES

8 **restraining,** suppressive, suppressing, oppressive, repressive; strict, severe, coercive, preventive; controlling, conditional, constrictive, restrictive, restricting; authoritative, censorial, censorious, censoring; circumscriptive, exclusive, prohibitive; injunctive, interdictive; stifling, limiting

9 **restrained,** under restraint, constrained, kept under constraint, kept under one's thumb, suppressed, repressed; controlled, under control, strictly controlled, prohibited; restricted, tied down, with strings attached; held back, kept in check, slowed, stopped; disciplined, punished, pressurized; censored, banned; limited, required; narrow, cramped, leashed; copyrighted, rationed, frozen, monopolistic; interventional, protective, embargoed

10 **self-restrained,** self-controlled, self-disciplined; dieting, fasting; temperate, continent, abstinent, abstemious; ascetic, Spartan, moderate; inhibiting, inhibited, introversive, quiet, modest, shy, embarrassing, embarrassed; formal, reserved, pent up, stiff; cool, ultracool, uptight [Inf]

> *Fasting 118; Severity 424; Self-Restraint 455*

11 **detained,** quarantined, shut-in, confined, housebound, snowbound, fogbound; besieged; arrested, under arrest, under house arrest; sentenced, incarcerated, imprisoned, in custody, on remand, confined; captive, in captivity, kidnapped, enslaved; gagged, muzzled; in bonds, in irons; serving a sentence; [Inf]: doing time, up the river, in the big house

> *Prison 55; Inactivity 415; Punishment 454*

VERBS

12 **restrain,** constrain, suppress, repress, hold back, hold down; oppress, close down, coerce; hinder, impede, bottle up, clog up, retard, decelerate, slow; stop, put a stop to, vote down, veto, blackball; brake, put the brakes on, act as a brake, prevent, pull back; control, curb, check, hold in check; ban, bar, prohibit; restrict, put a damper on, damper, drag, cramp, clamp down on, clamp; issue an injunction, interdict, regulate, discipline; keep order, police, patrol; impose a fine, punish; pressure; censor, black out; subdue, put down, crack down, quell, quash, squelch, smother, stifle, throttle, crush, smash

> *Severity 424; Compulsion 428*

13 **limit,** allot, stipulate, require qualifications, list requirements, enforce a limit; retrench, constrict, squeeze, cut, curtail; demarcate, draw the line, circumscribe, keep within bounds, stop from spreading, hem in, box in, hold at bay, localize; hold exclusive rights, copyright, join a charmed circle, exclude, keep out, rope out; [Inf]: sit on, put the lid on, cramp one's style

> *Necessity 95; Limit 620*

14 **restrain commerce,** economize, ration, freeze prices, control prices, freeze pay, squeeze credit; restrain trade, monopolize, form a cartel, operate a closed shop; intervene, restrict supplies, restrict consumption; protect, restrict imports, impose a tariff, impose an embargo

> *Economics 56; Finance 457*

15 **restrain oneself,** show self-restraint, control oneself, demonstrate self-control, keep a stiff upper lip; deny oneself, hold oneself back, hold back; diet, slim, fast; stay within one's limits, know when to stop, abstain, take the pledge; keep calm, keep one's cool, stay cool, keep quiet, say nothing; live in a Spartan way, live like

     830 Restraint

a monk, live like a nun, take a cold bath *or* shower; [Inf]: go on the wagon, keep one's shirt on, cool out, chill out

▶ *Fasting 118; Severity 424; Self-Restraint 455*

16 **detain,** quarantine, put into quarantine; blockade, block, siege, besiege, starve out; guard, take custody of, protect; impound, restrict someone's movement, impose a curfew, remand, refuse bail; arrest, make an arrest, put under arrest, take into custody, apprehend, seize, haul in; sentence, incarcerate, imprison, intern, confine, keep under lock and key, keep behind bars; make captive, kidnap, take hostage, hold in captivity, hold incommunicado, hold, put in bondage, send to prison; [Inf]: nab, collar, run in, serve time, serve a stretch, pinch, send up the river, send to the big house

▶ *Prison 55; Punishment 454*

17 **restrain someone,** gag, muzzle, silence, interdict, shout down; leash, lead, tether, hobble; rein in, keep a tight rein on, put a ball and chain on; harness, collar, yoke; girdle, straitjacket; fetter, bind, tie up *or* down, tie hand and foot, tie; throw in irons, chain up *or* down, chain; shackle, handcuff, manacle

ADVERBS

18 **restrainedly,** strictly, coercively, slowly; preventively; controllably; prohibitively; conditionally, restrictively, under restrictions, interdictively; severely, authoritatively; censorially, censoriously; circumscriptively; exclusively, protectively; confinedly

19 **self-restrainedly,** temperately, abstemiously, moderately, in moderation; formally, modestly, with modesty; shyly, embarrassingly, embarrassedly, stiffly

831 Liberation

Men [should have] their rights and nothing more; women their rights and nothing less. — SUSAN B. ANTHONY

Free at last, free at last, / Thank God Almighty, we're free at last. — SPIRITUAL

NOUNS

1 **liberation,** freedom, freeing, setting free; deliverance, delivery; release, disencumberment; emancipation, manumission; unhanding, unbinding, unchaining, unshackling, unfettering, unknotting, unleashing, unbridling, unburdening; mental freedom, independent mind, liberated spirit, liberal thinking; loosing, unloosing; disengagement, decontrol, deregulation; liberalization, relaxation; discharge, dismissal, extrication, parole, bail; demobilization, disbanding; escape, rescue; redemption, pardoning, absolving, salvation; relief, reprieve; exemption, exemptibility; absolution, forgiveness of sins, forgiveness; acquittal, acquittance, quittance, quitclaim; Emancipation Proclamation

▶ *Relief 275; Forgiveness 312; Wisdom 352; Exemption 434; Separation 753; Deliverance 817; Freedom 829; Cancellation 834*

2 **equal opportunity,** equal status, equal rights, antidiscrimination, affirmative action; civil rights, women's liberation, feminism, women's lib [Inf]; minority rights, animal rights activism, gay liberation; Nineteenth Amendment, Equal Rights Amendment (ERA)

▶ *Lack of Discrimination 338; Equality 740*

3 **liberator,** emancipator, manumitter; deliverer, rescuer

▶ *Religion 81; Deliverance 817*

ADJECTIVES

4 **liberated,** free, freed, emancipated, unshackled, unfettered; carefree, independent; deregulated, liberalized; released, paroled, on parole, bailed, out on bail; manumitted, delivered, redeemed, absolved, saved, rescued; exemptible, exempted; acquitted, scot-free

5 **liberating,** redemptive, absolving, acquitting

VERBS

6 **liberate,** free, set free, set at liberty, set at large; deliver, release, emancipate, manumit, disencumber; unhand, untie one's hands, unbind, unchain, unbolt, unlock, uncage, unshackle, unfetter, unknot, unleash, unbridle, unburden; give free rein, have an independent mind; loose, loosen, unloose, unloosen; cast loose, let *or* turn loose, let out, let go of, let go free; disengage; decontrol, deregulate, liberalize, relax restrictions, lift controls; discharge, dismiss, extricate, parole, put on parole; bail, go bail for, let out on bail, grant bail to; demobilize, disband, send home; escape, rescue; redeem, save; relieve, exempt; reprieve, acquit, pardon, absolve, let off the hook

▶ *Freedom 829*

7 **be liberated,** achieve liberty, free oneself, gain one's freedom; go free, go scot-free, go at liberty; extricate oneself, break loose, break out, break away, get away, get free; get off, get off scot-free, get out of; tear loose, get out, break *or* burst one's bonds, throw off the yoke, throw off, shake off, slip the collar; assert oneself, get the bit between one's teeth, stand on one's own two feet; fight for freedom; jump the wall, tunnel out, shake, shake free, go on the lam, pay off a debt, pay off a mortgage; go over the hill [Inf], go over the wall [Inf]

▶ *Freedom 829*

8 **treat equally,** grant equal rights to, grant equality to, enforce civil rights, enfranchise; abolish discrimination, end racial *or* sexual *or* age discrimination; support human rights, support equal rights, support civil rights

▶ *Equality 740*

ADVERBS

9 **free,** freely, fairly, equally

NOUNS

1 **subjection,** subjugation; inferiority, inferior status, lower status, inferior rank; satellite status, subordination, subordinate position, subordinate role, subordinacy, junior rank, juniority; dependence, dependency; wardship, tutelage, apprenticeship; obedience, subservience, servitude, indentureship, servility, service; employment, employ, allegiance; loss of rights, disfranchisement *or* disenfranchisement; loss of battle, defeat; loss of freedom, captivity; compulsory servitude, involuntary servitude, bondage, enslavement, slavery, thralldom, peonage; feudalism, vassalage, serfdom, villeinage

▶ *Prison 55; Servility 401; Obedience 426; Immorality 432; Duty 433; Inferiority 745; Cooperation 827; Failure 846*

2 **domination,** mastery, overpowering, overcoming; discipline, restraint, control; conquest, conquering, suppression, repression; oppression, intimidation; colonialism; tyranny

▶ *Government 49; Politics 50; Authority 52; Severity 424; Influence 512*

3 **subordinate,** inferior; assistant, helper, sidekick; apprentice, student, learner; servant; employee, staff member, right hand, secretary; conscript, substitute; underling, minion, tool, lackey, flunky, stooge, sycophant; [Inf]: low man on the totem pole, gofer, grunt

▶ *Servant 69; Servility 401*

4 **dependent,** child, foster child, orphan, charge, ward; junior, protégé; follower, satellite, hanger-on, parasite

▶ *Youth 26*

5 **subjected person,** loser, surrenderer, captive, hostage, prisoner, prisoner of war (POW), inmate; indentured servant, slave, chattel, bondman, bondmaid, bond servant, bondslave, thrall, galley slave, liege, serf, villein, peon; puppet

▶ *Prison 55; Servant 69*

ADJECTIVES

6 **subject,** subjecting, subjected, in subjection; in one's power, in one's control, in one's pocket, under one's thumb, like putty in one's hands, eating out of one's hands; subjugated, brought to one's knees, brought low, brought to heel; made to grovel, treated like dirt, treated like shit [Inf]; led by the nose, kicked around, browbeaten, henpecked

7 **dominating,** overpowering, overcoming; controlling, controllable, conquering; suppressive, suppressing, repressive, repressing, colonial; oppressive, oppressing, intimidating, tyrannical

8 **subordinate,** inferior, lower, substitute; junior, dependent; tutorial, apprenticed; subservient, obedient, servile; serving, employed, in the pay of, answering to, employable; under one's command, under the sway of; in the hands of, in the clutches of, like a puppet on a string; at one's feet, at one's beck and call, tied to one's apron strings, at one's mercy

▶ *Servility 401; Obedience 426; Inferiority 745*

9 **captive,** in captivity, taken prisoner, in bondage; in bonds, in chains, in harness; unfree, not independent; compulsory, involuntary, indentured; enslaving, enslaved; feudal

▶ *Prison 55; Compulsion 428*

VERBS

10 **subject,** subjugate, subdue, make inferior, lower, humble; subordinate, hold down, keep down, give a subordinate role to; have at one's mercy, do what one likes with; humiliate, walk (all) over, walk on, sit on; regiment, tame, bring into line, bring to one's knees, bring to heel, bring low; keep under one's thumb, twist around one's little finger, keep at one's beck and call, lead by the nose; kick around, browbeat, henpeck; treat like dirt, exploit, treat like shit [Inf], trample on, tread on, use as a doormat; tutor, apprentice, employ; disfranchise *or* disenfranchise, make dependent, reduce to servitude; take away one's freedom, rob of freedom, indenture, colonize; railroad [Inf]

11 **defeat,** vanquish, capture, take prisoner, lead in triumph, lead captive, take hostage; constrain, dominate, overpower, overcome, master, prevail over; discipline, restrain, control; conquer, suppress, oppress, repress; intimidate, tyrannize

▶ *Master 68; Severity 424*

12 **be subject to,** be subjected to, have inferior rank, hold a subordinate position; depend on; pay tribute, pay homage; grovel, serve as a doormat for, eat out of one's hands; obey, bear allegiance, owe loyalty to; serve, wait on; serve involuntarily; lose a battle, lose one's freedom; become a slave, become a hostage, fall into the clutches of, lose one's rights

▶ *Servant 69; Servility 401; Obedience 426; Inferiority 745*

ADVERBS

13 **dependently,** subserviently, servilely; in captivity, in slavery; involuntarily, against one's will

833 Commission

NOUNS

1 **commission,** commissioning, delegation, devolution, devolvement, decentralization; representation, deputation, empowerment, federation; power to act, power, power of attorney, proxy, entrustment, entrusting, responsibility; assignment, assigning, appointment, patronage, accreditation; nomination, election, voting; ordination, ordainment, installation, installment, instatement, induction, inauguration, investiture; enthronement, coronation, crowning

▸ *Government 49; Politics 50; Law 53; Religion 81; Selection 382; Celebration 405; Power 514; Substitution 672*

2 **engagement,** employment, enlistment, enrollment, conscription, recruitment; mission, errand, task, duty, job, office; activity, exercise, undertaking, function, quest

▸ *Undertaking 391; Activity 414*

3 **authority,** written authority, delegated authority, vicarious authority; authorization, permission, warranty, warrant; charge, mandate, trust; permit, charter, writ, license, brevet, diploma, passport

▸ *Authority 52; Command 425; Permission 502*

4 **council,** board, deputation, delegation; committee, subcommittee; crew, establishment, agency; trusteeship, executorship; bureaucracy, public service, civil service; mission, embassy, legation, envoy, governorship; regency

▸ *Delegate 79; Deputy 80*

5 **commissioner,** representative, official representative, elected representative, delegate; nominee, appointee, official, officer; bureaucrat, public servant, civil servant; envoy, ambassador, governor, regent, legate, diplomat, consul, attaché; functionary, emissary, plenipotentiary, deputy, messenger, missionary; agent, proxy, executor, trustee

▸ *Delegate 79*

ADJECTIVES

6 **commissioned,** delegated, devolutionary, decentralized; representational, deputized, empowered, inaugural, responsible; assigned, appointed, accredited, nominated, authorized, vicarious; warranted, mandated; plenipotentiary, ambassadorial, legationary, gubernatorial, official, bureaucratic, agential

▸ *Authority 52; Delegate 79*

7 **engaged,** employed, employable, functional, paid, mercenary

VERBS

8 **commission,** commit, delegate, devolve, decentralize; appoint a representative, appoint, name, assign, accredit, deputize, depute; empower, grant power of attorney, entrust, trust with; patronize; consign, give responsibility, put in one's hands, turn over to, give to, leave it to; nominate, elect, vote; ordain, install, instate, induct, inaugurate; invest, enthrone, crown, anoint

9 **engage,** employ, hire, enlist, enroll; conscript, recruit; post, send on an errand; go on a mission, quest after, undertake

10 **authorize,** give written authority, delegate authority, give permission, permit; warrant, charge, mandate, give a mandate, put in commission; charter, issue a writ, license, brevet, issue a diploma, earn a diploma, appoint a proxy, issue a passport

▸ *Delegate 79*

11 **under commission,** by commission, responsibly, with responsibility; vicariously, by proxy, per procurationem *or* per pro., *in loco parentis* [L]; bureaucratically, like a bureaucracy, officially, with official approval; by delegated authority, under orders

834 Cancellation

The Moving Finger writes; and, having writ, / Moves on; nor all thy Piety nor Wit / Shall lure it back to cancel half a Line, / Nor all thy Tears wash out a Word of it.
— EDWARD FITZGERALD, TRANSLATION OF THE RUBÁIYÁT OF OMAR KHAYYÁM

NOUNS

1 **cancellation,** canceling, nullification, annulment, repealing, repeal, reversion; discontinuation, discontinuance, suspension; waiver, setting aside, invalidation, disallowance; rescinding, rescindment, rescission, abjuration, abrogation, negation, revocation, reversal, recall; rejection, repudiation; amnesty, reprieve; abolition, abolition of sins, salvation; abolishment, elimination, write-off; censorship, deletion, removal; reneging, recantation, retraction; obliteration, defacement

▸ *Religion 81; Obliteration 186; Negation 190; Nonuse 394; Reversion 671*

2 **termination,** cessation, stoppage, discontinuance, nolle prosequi; resignation, honorable discharge, dismissal, discharge, golden handshake, expulsion, firing; suspension, layoff, furlough; services no longer required, cancellation of contract; recall, removal, ejection, dishonorable discharge; [Inf]: ax, sack, boot, bounce, kiss-off, walking papers, marching orders, heave-ho

▸ *Cessation 668; Expulsion 709*

3 **canceling out,** neutralizing, neutralization, making equal, equalizing; balance, equal weight, counterbalance, counterweight, sash weight; counterpoise, counterorder, countermand, counteraction; contradiction, refutation

4 **abrogator,** rescinder, revoker, reverser; rejecter, repudiator; repriever, reformer, new broom, abolitionist; reneger, recanter, retractor; defacer; contradicter, refuter; censor

ADJECTIVES

5 **canceled,** abrogated, stopped, annulled, nullified, null and void, voided, invalid, invalidated, killed, dead; repealed, revoked, rescinded, rescindable, set aside, recalled, negated, reprieved, terminated, abolished; laid off, suspended, discharged, fired; censored, deleted, struck out, struck off, wiped out, defaced; neutralized, equalized, balanced, counteracting, counteractive; contrary; axed [Inf], sacked [Inf]

VERBS

6 **cancel,** nullify, make null and void, void; disallow, reject, negate, abolish, eliminate; suspend, call off, abandon, invalidate, withdraw, set aside, waive, retract; renounce, abjure, quash, overrule; rescind, abrogate, repeal, reverse, recall, revoke; reprieve, offer amnesty to; renege, recant, repudiate, annul; annihilate, obliterate, destroy; delete, cut, erase, efface, write off, do away with, strike out, black out, blot out, cross out, censor; remove all signs of, remove, expunge, scribble out, deface, scrub out, wipe out, kill

▶ *Obliteration 186; Negation 190*

7 **terminate,** stop, dismiss, discontinue, cancel one's contract; resign, remove; bench, suspend, lay off; eject, discharge; give a dishonorable discharge to, cashier, dethrone, depose; divest, unfrock, oust, give someone the golden handshake, demote, bump, fire; [Inf]: ax, give someone the ax, give someone the (old) heave-ho, sack, kiss off, give someone his *or* her walking papers *or* marching orders

8 **cancel out,** cancel, eliminate each other; make neutral, neutralize; make equal, equalize, countervail, offset, weigh equally, counterbalance, counterweigh, balance, counterpoise, work both ways, cut both ways; work against, issue a counterorder, countermand, counteract; turn the tables on, contradict, refute

835 Resignation

NOUNS

1 **resignation,** relinquishment, departure, withdrawal; renouncement, renunciation; surrender; quitting, quitting work, giving notice, handing in one's notice, calling it quits, notice of resignation; forced resignation, voluntary resignation, retirement, abdication; abandonment, throwing in the sponge *or* towel [Inf]

▶ *Relinquishment 392; Reward 453; Departure 705*

2 **resignedness,** acceptance, reconciliation, acquiescence, coming to terms; stoicism, phlegm, indifference, coldness

ADJECTIVES

3 **resigning,** resigned, abdicating, abdicated; retiring, retired, in retirement; past, former, one-time, sometime, late, emeritus; pensioned, pensioned off, forced out; outgoing; renunciatory

4 **resigned,** resigned to one's fate, accepting, reconciled, acquiescent; stoical, phlegmatic, indifferent, cold

VERBS

5 **resign,** offer *or* tender one's resignation, hand in one's resignation, send in one's papers, hand in one's notice, give notice; quit work, quit, call it quits, pack it in; retire, go into retirement, take early retirement, draw one's pension; stand *or* step aside, abdicate, renounce the throne, give up the crown; abandon, desert, leave one's post, leave, depart, withdraw, vacate, tear one-

self away, drop; let go of, give up, resign under pressure; forgo, renounce, surrender, relinquish; [Inf]: throw in the towel, chuck it in, take one's job and shove it

▶ *Politics 50; Relinquishment 392; Reward 453; Departure 705*

6 **resign oneself,** accept, acquiesce, come to terms with

ADVERBS

7 **resignedly,** acquiescently, stoically, phlegmatically, indifferently

836 Possibility

The grand perhaps. — ROBERT BROWNING

Your "if" is the only peacemaker; much virtue in "if." — WILLIAM SHAKESPEARE

NOUNS

1 **possibility,** potential, potentiality, plausibility, likelihood, prospect, chance, odds; promise, opportunity, virtuality, eventuality, contingency

▶ *Probability 838; Chance 842*

2 **possibleness,** realm of possibility, domain of the possible, conceivability, conceivableness, credibility, feasibility; practicability, practicality, workability, operability; accessibility, admissibility, flexibility, approachability, availability; aptitude, ability, capacity, facility

▶ *Thought 317; Action 412; Activity 414; Existence 717; Reality 719; Latency 844*

3 **strong possibility,** probability, good chance, sporting chance, best chance, even chance, opening, luck, good opportunity, sure bet, evens, odds-on, sure thing

▶ *Future Time 650; Probability 838*

4 **remote possibility,** slight *or* faint *or* small hope, small chance, off chance, slim chance, poor prospect, long odds, long shot, outside chance

▶ *Hope 281; Improbability 839; Chance 842*

ADJECTIVES

5 **possible,** potential, conceivable, imaginable, thinkable, credible, believable, feasible, admissible; tenable, reasonable, practical, practicable; doable, workable, performable, operable, achievable, attainable, realizable, likely, accessible, approachable, reachable, available, flexible, able, capable, apt

▶ *Probability 838*

6 **potential,** possible, promising; undeveloped, future, prospective, eventual, virtual, dormant

▶ *Latency 844*

VERBS

7 **make possible,** enable, empower, permit, allow, clear the way, give a chance to, take a chance, gamble, hope

‣ *Power 514; Way 691*

8 be possible, could be, might be, stand a chance, stand a good chance

ADVERBS

9 possibly, perhaps, perchance, peradventure [Arch], haply, maybe, for all one knows, if possible, by chance, on the off chance, by any means

10 practically, workably, tenably, reasonably, within reach, within sight, within one's power
‣ *Probability 838*

11 potentially, virtually, conceivably, imaginably, credibly, believably, feasibly, plausibly, prospectively, eventually, in all likelihood, somehow
‣ *Latency 844*

837 Impossibility

In two words: im–possible. — SAMUEL GOLDWYN

NOUNS

1 impossibility, impossibleness, inconceivability, unthinkability, unimaginability, nonexistence, unreality, self-contradiction, absurdity, paradox, logical impossibility, illogicality, what cannot be
‣ *Disbelief 88; Negation 190; Lack of Thought 318; Refutation 332; Lack of Meaning 362; Unintelligibility 364; Nonexistence 718; Unreality 720; Improbability 839*

2 hopelessness, impossibility, impracticability, impracticality, unfeasibility, unworkability, inoperability, unattainability, insurmountability, insuperability, inaccessibility, unaccessibility, impenetrability, imperviousness, unobtainability, unavailability
‣ *Hopelessness 282; Powerlessness 515*

3 obstacle, prohibition, deadlock, block, impasse, barrier, problem, Sisyphean task, no-no [Inf]
‣ *Difficulty 824; Adversity 848*

ADJECTIVES

4 impossible, not possible, beyond the bounds of possibility, inconceivable, unthinkable, not to be thought of, unimaginable, out of the question, unquestionable, unreasonable, contrary to reason, absurd, ridiculous, preposterous, illogical, irrational, paradoxical, self-contradictory, self-defeating
‣ *Negation 190; Lack of Thought 318; Refutation 332; Unintelligibility 364; Ridiculousness 368; Nonexistence 718*

5 unbelievable, incredible, counterintuitive, beyond belief, fantastic, miraculous, fabulous, bizarre, weird, ineffable, mysterious, mystical
‣ *Disbelief 88; Unreality 720*

6 hopeless, impractical, unfeasible, unworkable, unachievable, untenable, unviable, inoperable, broken, irreparable, irrecoverable, irrevocable, unattainable, insurmountable, insuperable, inaccessible, unaccessible, unapproachable, unreachable, impenetrable, im-

pervious, unobtainable, unavailable, out, away, over, finished, gone
‣ *History 3; Loss 468; Cessation 668; End 773; Uselessness 802; Difficulty 824; Adversity 848*

7 forbidden, prohibited, denied, disallowed, blocked, barred, banned, stopped, canceled, ruled out
‣ *Prohibition 503; Exclusion 764; Cancellation 834*

VERBS

8 make impossible, prohibit, block, bar, ban, forbid, rule out, disqualify, exclude, deny, withhold, negate, disenable, disable, put out of reach, make things difficult, throw a monkey wrench in the works

9 be impossible, fly in the face of reason, be a waste of time, not stand a chance

10 attempt the impossible, waste time, cry for the moon, try for a miracle, look for a needle in a haystack, seek the end of the rainbow, teach an old dog new tricks, make the leopard change its spots, turn back time, turn back the tide, stop the world from turning, make hell freeze over, make rivers run uphill, make a silk purse out of a sow's ear, fetch water in a sieve, walk on water, catch the wind, draw blood from a stone
‣ *Ridiculousness 368*

ADVERBS

11 impossibly, inconceivably, unthinkably, unimaginably, unquestionably, incredibly, illogically, irrationally, absurdly, ridiculously, paradoxically

12 hopelessly, impractically, unworkably, inoperably, irreparably, irrecoverably, irrevocably, unattainably, insurmountably, insuperably, unapproachably

838 Probability

NOUNS

1 probability, likelihood, likeliness, chance, odds, liability, liableness, proneness, predictability; prospect, forecast, outlook, expectation, presumption, anticipation, prognosis, prediction
‣ *Expectation 356; Foresight 357; Prediction 358; Tendency 513; Future Time 650; Chance 842*

2 tendency, propensity, trend, drift, tenor, tone, swing, bearing, tending, general tendency, the way it looks
‣ *Tendency 513; Continuity, Continuation 669; Way 691; Sequence 770*

3 plausibility, probability, possibility, reasonability, credibility, verisimilitude
‣ *Belief 87; Reason 319; Similarity 733; Possibility 836*

4 chance, good chance, sporting chance, main chance, even chance, strong possibility, odds-on chance, best bet, well-grounded hope, fair expectation, favorable prospect
‣ *Expectation 356; Possibility 836; Chance 842*

5 probability theory, mathematical probability, statistical probability, empirical probability, subjective probability, probability distribution, probability function,

probability density function, probability curve, uncertainty principle, law of averages, probabilism
- *Mathematics 6; Calculation 784; Chance 842*

ADJECTIVES

6 **probable,** likely, expected, undoubted, indubitable, unquestionable, apparent, ostensible, evident, presumable, presumed, presumptive, predictive, predictable, prone, liable, apt, anticipated, prospective, tending, drifting, in the cards
- *Expectation 356; Tendency 513*

7 **plausible,** probable, possible, reasonable, credible, believable, persuasive
- *Belief 87; Appearance 264; Reason 319; Possibility 836*

VERBS

8 **be probable,** seem likely, lead one to expect, promise, show a tendency, show signs of, have the makings of, be in the cards, stand a good chance, be in the running, bid fair, stand a fair chance, impend, come as no surprise
- *Promise 458; Tendency 513; Future Time 650*

9 **make probable,** smooth the way, make likely, increase the odds, increase the chances
- *Way 691; Help 825*

10 **think likely,** expect, anticipate, presume, suppose, daresay, predict, prognosticate, foresee, look for, count on, reckon, take for granted, risk, gamble, bet on, take a chance
- *Belief 87; Hope 281; Expectation 356; Foresight 357; Prediction 358; Supposition 359; Chance 842*

ADVERBS

11 **probably,** in all probability, in all likelihood, likely, most likely, as likely as not, doubtless *or* doubtlessly, indubitably, unquestionably, to all intents and purposes, all things considered, ten to one, presumably, apparently, ostensibly, predictably, expectedly, to be expected, as expected, as usual, on average, in anticipation
- *Expectation 356; Habit, Custom 397; Average 742; Sameness 730*

839 Improbability

NOUNS

1 **improbability,** unlikeliness, unlikelihood, uncertainty, doubt, doubtfulness, poor prospect, remote possibility, foolish hope; small chance, hardly a chance, outside chance, ghost of a chance, slim chance, long shot, long odds, chance in a million, hundred-to-one *or* million-to-one chance *or* shot, fat chance [Inf]
- *Hopelessness 282; Impossibility 837; Uncertainty 841; Chance 842*

2 **unexpectedness,** unforeseeableness, unpredictability, miraculousness, rarity, oddity, the unforeseen, the last thing one would expect, more than one bargained for, freak accident, miracle, prodigy, wonder, surprise, lucky shot, fluke, chance
- *Surprise 292; Chance 842*

3 **implausibility,** incredibility, unbelievability, questionableness
- *Disbelief 88; Untruth 722*

ADJECTIVES

4 **improbable,** unlikely, uncertain, doubtful, dubious, dubitable, unpromising, inauspicious, scarcely to be expected, unrealistic, remote, far-fetched, unexpected, not in the cards
- *Uncertainty 841*

5 **questionable,** implausible, unbelievable, fanciful, extraordinary, exceptional, wild, too good to be true, hard to believe, incredible, beyond belief, hard to swallow [Inf]
- *Disbelief 88*

6 **unexpected,** unforeseeable, unpredictable, unanticipated, unguessed, unpredicted, unforeseen, fortuitous, rare, accidental, freakish, chance, fluky
- *Chance 842*

VERBS

7 **be improbable,** go beyond belief, strain one's credulity, go beyond the bounds of reason *or* probability
- *Disbelief 88; Untruthfulness, Falsehood 192; Untruth 722*

ADVERBS

8 **improbably,** incredibly, unbelievably, questionably, doubtfully, dubiously, uncertainly

9 **unexpectedly,** unpredictably, unforeseeably, contrary to expectation, without warning, by accident, out of the blue, never in a month of Sundays; by chance, by accident

10 **rarely,** exceptionally, seldom if ever, once in a blue moon, once in a lifetime, hardly ever, uncommonly, uniquely

840 Certainty

If a man will begin with certainties, he shall end in doubts; but if he will be content to begin with doubts, he shall end in certainties. — FRANCIS BACON

NOUNS

1 **certainty,** surety, knowledge, factuality, reality, actuality, historicity, truth, trueness, verity, veracity, absoluteness, definiteness, authoritativeness, indubitability, indisputability, validity, accuracy, evidence, proof, obviousness, necessity; fact, foregone conclusion, open-and-shut case, winner, safe bet, cinch, sure thing, dead certainty; lead-pipe cinch [Inf], dead cert [Brit inf]
- *Necessity 95; Knowledge 348; Accuracy 350; Reality 719; Truth 721*

2 **conviction,** certainty, certitude, belief, acceptance, credence, trust, faith, assurance, assuredness, sureness, surety, positiveness, confidence, self-assurance, self-confidence; assertiveness, cocksureness, overconfidence, dogmatism, positivism, orthodoxy, narrow-mindedness, obstinacy, stubbornness, bigotry, bias, partisanship
▶ *Belief 87; Discrimination 337; Obstinacy 379*

3 **confirmation,** assurance, verification, affirmation, affirmativeness, demonstration, proof, ascertainment, establishment, evidence, grounds, facts, signs
▶ *Sign 183; Affirmation 189; Demonstration 331; Verification 336; Evidence 339*

4 **guarantee,** assurance, insurance, warrant, warranty, pledge, promise
▶ *Approval 437; Promise 458*

5 **inevitability,** inevitableness, certainty, fate, destiny, fatefulness, predestination, determination, predetermination, ineluctability, necessity, unavoidability, inescapableness, unevasibleness, unpreventability, irrevocability, relentlessness, inexorability
▶ *Necessity 95; Predetermination 384; Power 514; End 773*

6 **infallibility,** reliability, dependability, trustworthiness, predictability, regularity, stability, solidity, security, steadiness, steadfastness, firmness, soundness, staunchness, fidelity, loyalty, stoicism
▶ *Philosophy 4; Prediction 358; Security 464; Regularity 663; Stability 674*

ADJECTIVES

7 **certain,** sure, known, factual, real, actual, historical, true, veracious, absolute, definite, authoritative, indubitable, indisputable, valid, accurate, evident, proven *or* proved, obvious; secure, given, verifiable, demonstrable, well-grounded, well-founded, documented, certified, ascertained, demonstrated, established, tried and true, safe, self-evident, unmistakable, unmistaken, ostensible, necessary, realistic
▶ *Authority 52; Clarity 196; Visibility 244; Verification 336; Knowledge 348; Accuracy 350; Reality 719*

8 **convinced,** certain, positive, believing, accepting, trusting, unquestioning, undoubting, doubtless, unswerving, unhesitating, undeviating, assured, satisfied, persuaded, confident; self-assured, self-confident, opinionated, cocksure, assertive, overconfident, doctrinaire, dogmatic, orthodox, narrow-minded, obstinate, stubborn, bigoted, biased, partisan
▶ *Religion 81; Belief 87; Discrimination 337; Obstinacy 379*

9 **decided,** settled, fixed, established, open-and-shut, undisputed, unrefuted, irrefutable, undeniable, uncontestable, unchallengeable, incontrovertible, indubitable, unimpeachable, unambiguous, unequivocal

▶ *Evidence 339*

10 **guaranteed,** assured, ensured, insured, warranted, pledged, promised
▶ *Promise 458*

11 **inevitable,** destined, predestined, determined, predetermined, fixed, set, fated, fateful, unstoppable, ineluctable, necessary, inescapable, unavoidable, unpreventable, relentless, inflexible, inexorable, unyielding, directed, headed for
▶ *Necessity 95; Predetermination 384*

12 **infallible,** reliable, dependable, trustworthy, predictable, regular, stable, solid, secure, unshakable, unwavering, unchanging, undeviating, steady, steadfast, firm, sound, staunch, faithful, loyal, stoical
▶ *Security 464; Regularity 663; Permanence 667; Stability 674*

VERBS

13 **be certain,** know, know for sure, feel sure, have no doubt, believe, be convinced, accept, credit, rely on, depend on, have faith in, assert oneself, lay down the law, pontificate, stick to one's guns, dogmatize, dig in one's heels, bet one's bottom dollar, bet one's life [Inf]

14 **make certain,** make sure, ensure, insure, confirm, verify, affirm, demonstrate, prove, ascertain, establish, determine, find out, settle, fix, pin down, clear up, check, decide, convince, evince, ground, guarantee, warrant, pledge, promise, authenticate, certify, endorse, substantiate, secure, stabilize, steady, solidify

ADVERBS

15 **certainly,** surely, really, truly, actually, absolutely, positively, firmly, definitely, undoubtedly, indubitably, unquestionably, without question, without a shadow of a doubt

16 **with certainty,** confidently, assuredly, assertively, dogmatically, obstinately, stubbornly

17 **inevitably,** certainly, ineluctably, unavoidably, inescapably, irrevocably, relentlessly, inexorably, surely, fatefully, in the end

INTERJECTIONS

18 **certainly!,** naturally!, definitely!, of course!, by all means!, that's for sure!, no question about it!

841 Uncertainty

NOUNS

1 **uncertainty,** incertitude, unsureness, uncertainness, doubtfulness, dubiousness, disputability, contestability, controvertibility, questionableness, open mind, open verdict, question mark, guesswork, guess, anybody's guess, wild guess, enigma; uncertainty principle
▶ *Physics 10; Disbelief 88; Argument 329; Question 333*

2 **suspicion,** suspiciousness, conjecture, distrust, mistrust, caution, doubt, disbelief, incredulity, denial, rejection, skepticism, agnosticism, atheism

▶ *Philosophy 4; Religion 81; Refutation 332; Rejection 383*

3 irresolution, irresoluteness, indecision, indecisiveness, unsettledness, vacillation, wavering, hesitation, ambivalence, faltering, cleft stick, horns of a dilemma, borderline case
▶ *Vacillation 378*

4 confusion, bewilderment, disconcertion, disconcertedness, confoundment, perplexity, bafflement, puzzlement, predicament, quandary, embarrassment, discomposure, shyness, timidity
▶ *Question 333; Difficulty 824*

5 indemonstrability, unverifiability, unprovability, unconfirmability, unlikelihood, unlikeliness, improbability
▶ *Negation 190; Impossibility 837; Improbability 839*

6 indeterminacy, indefiniteness, vagueness, unclearness, ambiguity, equivocalness, indistinctness, neither one thing nor the other, faintness, haziness, fogginess, mistiness, fuzziness, obscurity, inaccuracy, inexactness, imprecision, looseness, laxity, broadness, generality, amorphousness, incoherence
▶ *Shapelessness 625; Generality 778*

7 unreliability, fallibility, untrustworthiness, treacherousness, insecurity, transience, infirmity, insubstantiality, unsoundness, instability, unstableness, unsteadiness, inconsistency, shiftiness, shakiness, precariousness, eccentricity, irregularity, unpredictability, risk, hazard, adventure, gamble
▶ *Weakness 517; Irregularity 664; Danger 811; Improbability 839; Failure 846*

8 capriciousness, whimsicality, fickleness, volatility, volatileness, fitfulness, changeableness, mutability, fluidity, fluctuation, wavering, inconstancy, flexibility, mobility, variability, randomness, chance
▶ *Caprice 381; Changeableness 666; Motion 677; Oscillation 683; Chance 842*

ADJECTIVES

9 uncertain, unsure, unknown, doubtful, dubious, speculative, conjectural, hypothetical, provisional, disputable, contestable, controversial, controvertible, moot, questionable, suspicious, distrustful, mistrustful, unbelieving, skeptical, agnostic, open-minded
▶ *Religion 81; Disbelief 88; Argument 329; Question 333; Ignorance 349*

10 irresolute, indecisive, vacillating, wavering, hesitant, hesitating, hanging *or* holding back, faltering, undecided, unsettled, ambivalent, unresolved, unanswered
▶ *Vacillation 378; Equivocation 380; Oscillation 683*

11 confused, bewildered, disconcerted, worried, perplexed, nonplussed, confounded, baffled, puzzled, discomposed, in a quandary, at a loss for words, embarrassed; confusing, bewildering, disconcerting, worrying, perplexing, baffling, puzzling, difficult, enigmatic, problematic, cryptic

▶ *Question 333; Unintelligibility 364; Disturbance 768; Difficulty 824; Hindrance 826*

12 indemonstrable, unverifiable, unprovable, unconfirmable, unlikely, improbable, unpredictable
▶ *Wrong 430; Untruth 722; Improbability 839*

13 uncertified, undocumented, unchecked, uncorroborated, unverified, unauthenticated, unsigned, unratified, unascertained, unofficial, unproved, untried, untested, speculative, experimental, apocryphal
▶ *Experiment 335*

14 indeterminate, indefinite, vague, unclear, undefined, unspecified, undetermined, borderline, ambiguous, equivocal, indistinct, faint, hazy, foggy, misty, fuzzy, obscure, inaccurate, inexact, imprecise, loose, lax, broad, general, amorphous, incoherent; unnamed, unmentioned, several, few, many
▶ *Obscurity 197; Diffuseness 199; Faintness of Sound 233; Dimness 248; Sophistry 330; Lack of Discrimination 338; Equivocation 380; Shapelessness 625; Disorder 766; Generality 778*

15 unreliable, fallible, undependable, untrustworthy, treacherous, dishonest, perfidious, insecure, transient, infirm, insubstantial, unsound, unstable, unsteady, inconsistent, shifty, shaky, precarious, slippery, risky, hazardous, dangerous, perilous, eccentric, erratic, irregular, unpredictable
▶ *Deception 193; Weakness 517; Transience 643; Irregularity 664; Danger 811; Failure 846*

16 capricious, whimsical, fickle, irresponsible, skittish, volatile, mercurial, fitful, changeable, mutable, fluid, fluctuating, wavering, flexible, mobile, aleatory, inconstant, variable, random, chancy, haphazard
▶ *Variegation 263; Caprice 381; Change 665; Changeableness 666; Deviation 698; Discontinuity 775; Chance 842*

VERBS

17 be uncertain, have one's doubts, doubt, question, moot, distrust, mistrust, disbelieve, have a suspicion about, suspect, wait and see, wonder about, speculate, conjecture, dispute, contest, controvert
▶ *Argument 329; Question 333*

18 hesitate, vacillate, dither, waver, hang *or* hold back, falter, be irresolute, be in two minds about, equivocate, prevaricate, sit on the fence, keep an open mind
▶ *Sophistry 330; Lack of Discrimination 338; Vacillation 378*

19 make uncertain, obscure, mystify, baffle, faze, confound, confuse, perplex, daze, haze, fog, disturb, disconcert, embarrass, worry, bewilder, flummox [Inf], nonplus, puzzle, stump, keep someone guessing
▶ *Obscurity 197*

20 change, mutate, fluctuate, vary, move, shift, shake, slip, fail, betray
▶ *Change 665; Changeableness 666*

21 risk, chance, gamble, hazard, venture, dare, speculate

◗ *Chance 842*

ADVERBS

22 **uncertainly,** doubtfully, dubiously, suspiciously, skeptically, irresolutely, hesitantly, indecisively, speculatively, conjecturally, disputably, controversially, questionably, in question

◗ *Disbelief 88; Argument 329; Question 333*

23 **confusingly,** bewilderingly, worryingly, puzzlingly, problematically, enigmatically, embarrassingly, in a quandary, on the horns of a dilemma

◗ *Surprise 292; Question 333; Disturbance 768; Difficulty 824*

24 **indeterminately,** indefinitely, vaguely, ambiguously, equivocally, indistinctly, faintly, hazily, foggily, mistily, fuzzily, obscurely, inaccurately, imprecisely, loosely, broadly, generally, amorphously, incoherently

◗ *Obscurity 197; Shapelessness 625*

25 **unreliably,** fallibly, treacherously, dishonestly, insecurely, transiently, insubstantially, unsteadily, inconsistently, shiftily, shakily, precariously, dangerously, perilously, riskily, hazardously, eccentrically, erratically, irregularly, unpredictably, improbably

◗ *Irregularity 664; Danger 811; Improbability 839; Chance 842*

26 **capriciously,** on a whim, whimsically, irresponsibly, fitfully, intermittently, changeably, fluidly, flexibly, inconstantly, variably, randomly

◗ *Caprice 381; Changeableness 666*

842 Chance

NOUNS

1 **chance,** blind chance, randomness, random chance, whatever happens, whatever comes, happenstance; unpredictability, contingency, indeterminacy, indetermination, uncertainty; unaccountability, inexplicability, casualness, flukiness, fluke, freak, coincidence, accident, freak occurrence *or* accident; hazard, risk, gamble, jeopardy; chancing, risktaking, gambling

◗ *Uncertainty 841*

2 **lack of motive,** lack of cause, no attributable cause, lack of intention, nonintention; aimlessness, haphazardness, randomness, purposelessness; no reason, no good reason, arbitrariness, fortuity, fortuitousness, indeterminacy; inexplicability, unaccountability, inconsistency, illogicality, irrationality, quirkiness

◗ *Unintelligibility 364; Possibility 836; Probability 838; Improbability 839; Uncertainty 841*

3 **luck,** lady luck, Fortuna, Moira; fortune, wheel of fortune, providence, destiny, fate, lot, one's lot; good luck, good fortune, luck on one's side, run of good luck, lucky break [Inf]; bad luck, ill fortune, tough luck, rotten luck, worst luck, run of bad luck, bad break [Inf]; bit of luck, lucky shot, lucky strike, chance

hit; chance meeting, chance encounter, chance discovery, serendipity

◗ *Discovery 345; Prosperity 847; Adversity 848*

4 **potluck,** dumb luck, luck of the draw, the way the ball bounces *or* the cookie crumbles [Inf]; random chance, turn of the card, spin of the wheel, throw of the dice; the breaks [Inf]

◗ *Surprise 292*

5 **game of chance,** gambling, risktaking, speculation, gaming; lottery, raffle, drawing, bingo, grab bag, sweepstakes, sweeps [Inf]

6 **good chance,** best chance, main chance, favorable chance, opportunity, occasion, good odds, odds-on, dollars to doughnuts [Inf], probability, likelihood, good possibility; small risk, safe *or* sure bet, sure thing, certainty, dead cert [Brit inf]

◗ *Timeliness 659; Probability 838; Certainty 840*

7 **equal chance,** even chance, fifty-fifty, even odds, tossup, flip *or* spin of the coin; even break [Inf]; fair chance, decent chance, sporting chance, fighting chance, gambling chance, distinct possibility

◗ *Equality 740; Possibility 836*

8 **poor chance,** small chance, rare chance, off chance, half a chance; long shot, long odds, shot in the dark, one chance in a million, improbability; no chance, impossibility, not a prayer, not a snowball's chance in hell [Inf], fat chance [Inf]

◗ *Impossibility 837; Improbability 839*

9 **calculation of chance,** doctrine of chance, law of averages, probability; mathematical probability, theory of probabilities, statistical probability, statistics, stochastics, actuarial calculation

◗ *Mathematics 6; Experiment 335; Probability 838*

ADJECTIVES

10 **chance,** random, unpredictable, aleatory, unforeseeable, indeterminate, incalculable, uncertain; hit-or-miss, catch-as-catch-can, casual; serendipitous, accidental, adventitious; contingent, unexpected, unforeseen; lucky, fortunate, blessed by good fortune; unlucky, unfortunate, cursed; risky, chancy, leaving much to chance; fluky, dicey [Inf], iffy [Inf]

11 **causeless,** groundless, uncaused, unmotivated, undesigned, unplanned, unpremeditated, unmeant, unintended, unintentional, inadvertent, unexplainable, unaccountable, inexplicable; motiveless, undirected, aimless, haphazard, purposeless, arbitrary, fortuitous, indeterminant, undetermined, uncertain, unaccountable; unexpected, unreasonable, coincidental, accidental, casual; stray, incidental; quirky, fifty-fifty

VERBS

12 **chance,** happen, just happen, so happen, hap; turn *or* pop up, crop up; fall to one's lot, befall, betide, bechance [Arch]

◗ *Present Time 647*

13 **chance upon,** encounter by chance, encounter un-

expectedly, meet by accident *or* chance; run into, happen upon, run across, come upon; light upon, hit upon, stumble upon *or* on, blunder upon, fall upon, bump into [Inf]

▶ *Discovery 345*

14 **take a chance,** chance it, chance, take a risk, risk it, risk, hazard; venture, go out on a limb, leave it to chance, leave it to fate; try one's luck, gamble, cast the die, speculate, bet, wager; have luck, be lucky, have a small chance; have *or* stand a chance, not have *or* stand a chance

▶ *Danger 811*

ADVERBS

15 **by chance,** by accident, accidentally, inadvertently, unintentionally, casually, fortuitously, coincidentally, by coincidence

16 **randomly,** at random, haphazardly, unpredictably, unexpectedly, unaccountably, inexplicably, serendipitously

17 **luckily,** as good luck would have it, fortunately; unluckily, as ill luck would have it, unfortunately

18 **perchance,** perhaps, for all one knows, possibly, according to chance, as it may happen, as the case may be, as it may be, as it may chance, whatever happens, in any event

INTERJECTIONS

19 **good luck!,** lots of luck!, hard luck!, better luck next time!; [Inf]: lucky dog!, bingo!, fat chance!

843 Display

That's it, baby, if you've got it, flaunt it. — MEL BROOKS

NOUNS

1 **display,** show, exhibition, exposition, expo; demonstration, manifestation, presentation, spectacle, showing, viewing, collection, retrospective, fair, market; fashion show, motor show, boat show, dog show, cat show, art show, craft show, crafts fair, antique show, antiques fair; parade, array

▶ *Demonstration 331; Showiness 404; Celebration 405*

2 **manifestation,** manifestness, revelation, disclosure, exposure, laying open, unfolding, unrolling; discovery, uncovering, bringing to light, shedding daylight on, visibility; publicity, promotion, advertising; flagrancy, blatancy, conspicuousness, ostentation, showing off; accentuation, emphasis, highlight, spotlight; ceremony, pageant, pageantry, pomp, splash; expression, formulation, affirmation, proof, evidence; confrontation, comparison, projection; representation, symbolization, typification, personification; indication, sign, token, signal, symptom, syndrome, omen; proclamation, publication; apparition, appearance, materialization, epiphany, incarnation, theophany, avatar

▶ *Religion 81; Disclosure 180; Identification 184; Emphasis 200; Vision 242; Attention 323; Prediction 358; Showiness 404*

3 **showpiece,** exhibit, collector's piece, pride, jewel in the crown, collectible, curio, antique, museum piece; model, sample, specimen, example, mock-up, dummy, piece of evidence

4 **showplace,** showroom, exhibition hall, exhibition center, gallery, museum, hall, auditorium, scene; showcase, display case, display cabinet, store window, shop window; notice board, bulletin board, pegboard; billboard, sign, advertisement; poster, placard, sandwich board, label; bill, citation

5 **production,** performance, presentation, enactment, show, spectacle; musical, concert, play, ballet, dance, film, motion picture, cinema; television *or* TV program, radio program; preview

▶ *Drama and Theater 136; Motion Pictures 137; Light Entertainment 138; Radio and Television 172*

6 **openness,** obviousness, open-and-shut case; boldness, daring, brazenness; immodesty, shamelessness, impudence, defiance; barefacedness, bareness, nakedness; flaunt

▶ *Disclosure 180; Truthfulness 191; Showiness 404; Defiance 416*

7 **displayer,** exhibitor, demonstrator, presenter; publicist, publicizer, advertiser, press agent, flack, public relations (PR) person, promotional manager; barker, showman, master of ceremonies *or* emcee *or* M.C.; impresario, stage manager; exhibitionist, flaunter; model, mannequin; vain person, peacock

▶ *Vanity 402; Showiness 404*

ADJECTIVES

8 **displayed,** on display, exhibited, presented, shown, on show, on view, on; made public, brought to public notice, brought to one's notice, brought to attention; manifested, apodictic, featured, visible, apparent, brought forth, produced; mentioned, adduced, cited, quoted; confronted, brought face-to-face; worn, sported; paraded, shown off, flaunted, waved, unfurled, brandished, flourished; advertised, publicized, promoted; published; expressible, producible, showable

▶ *Appearance 264; Showiness 404; Specialty 779*

9 **manifest,** revealed, disclosed, divulged, exposed, uncovered, discovered, declared; overt, palpable, open, in the open, public, on the surface, staring one in the face, unconcealed, uncamouflaged, undisguised; noticeable, conspicuous, notable, apparent, visible, obvious, ostensible, open-and-shut, appearing; patent, evident, self-evident, written all over one for all to see, obtrusive; pronounced, prominent, clear as daylight, marked, striking

10 **identifiable,** recognizable; certain, unmistakable, incontestable, intelligible; signal, token, indicative, typ-

ical; symbolic, personified, representative; definite, defined

11 **accentuated,** in relief, bold, in bold *or* high relief, salient; highlighted, emphasized, in the foreground, in the limelight; flagrant, blatant, arrant, glaring, stark-staring, ostentatious, catching the eye, eye-catching; well-known, notorious, famous, infamous; gaudy, showy, loud
   ◗ *Identification 184; Emphasis 200; Evidence 339; Showiness 404; Certainty 840*

12 **open,** plain, plain as the nose on one's face; clear, crystal-clear; bold, daring, brazen; immodest, shameless, impudent, defiant; barefaced, bare, uncovered, naked, flaunting
   ◗ *Disclosure 180; Truthfulness 191; Showiness 404; Defiance 416*

VERBS

13 **display,** show, exhibit, put on display, put on view, put on show; manifest, present, bring forward, reveal to the public, expose, expose to view, disclose; offer for approval, set out, set before someone's eyes, give a guided tour; bring to notice, draw attention to, feature, spotlight, illuminate, put in bold *or* high relief, headline, emphasize; point out, indicate, teach, instruct, explain; make a show of, flourish, brandish, flash, wave, dangle, flaunt, vaunt, show off; parade, air, sport, model, demonstrate; perform, act, enact, dramatize, put on, stage, screen, televise, broadcast; advertise, release, publish
   ◗ *Drama and Theater 136; Communications 169; Disclosure 180; Identification 184; Representation 187; Emphasis 200; Attention 323; Demonstration 331; Showiness 404*

14 **reveal,** manifest, divulge, disclose, discover, uncover, unearth; bring to light, illuminate, throw light on, shed daylight on, make plain, make obvious; bring up, point up, point out, indicate; accentuate, enhance, make important, throw into relief, emphasize, highlight, spotlight, place in the spotlight, place in the foreground; proclaim, publicize, promote, advertise, publish; cite, mention, make reference to, adduce, quote, extract; invent, develop, formulate, produce, bring out, bring forth; expose, open up, lay bare, lay open, throw open; unmask, unveil, give away, betray; drag out, draw out, draw forth; express, come out with, trot out [Inf]; evidence, show, evince; unfurl, unroll, unfold, spread out, solve, decipher, decode; explain, interpret
   ◗ *Publication 173; Disclosure 180; Affirmation 189; Light 246; Evidence 339; Discovery 345; Interpretation 365; Opening 583; Uncovering 614; Extraction 711; Importance 799*

15 **show oneself,** show one's face, reveal oneself, appear, materialize, rear one's head, show up, be seen; show the flag, come out into the open, come forth; unmask oneself, unveil oneself, tear off the mask, show (oneself in) one's true colors; stand in the open, stand in full view; confront, force a confrontation, come face-to-face, come eyeball-to-eyeball; assert oneself, speak up, speak out, raise one's voice, stand up, stand up and be counted; take a stand, speak plainly, put one's cards on the table; have no secrets, make no mystery, make no secret of, not try to hide, wear one's heart on one's sleeve; have no shame, wash one's dirty linen in public; reveal one's mind *or* thoughts *or* opinions; make no bones about
   ◗ *Appearance 264; Truth 721*

16 **be visible,** attract attention, attract notice, stand out, stand out a mile; have the spotlight on one, be in the limelight, hold center stage, show up, show up well; make an impression, loom large, stare one in the face; openly happen, come to light, transpire, emanate
   ◗ *Visibility 244; Attention 323; Demonstration 331; Intelligibility 363; Simplicity 526; Nearness 586*

ADVERBS

17 **manifestly,** obviously, evidently, plainly, apparently, openly, overtly; publicly, in public, for public notice, for all to see, on show; conspicuously, flagrantly, undisguisedly, palpably, notoriously; externally, on the face of it, on the surface, superficially; open and aboveboard, with one's cards on the table, before one, before all, before God, under the eye of heaven; on exhibition, in full view, in broad daylight, out in the open, in open court, on the stage

18 **frankly,** candidly, honestly; forthrightly, to one's face, face to face; boldly, defiantly

844 Latency

[Russia] is a riddle wrapped in a mystery inside an enigma. — WINSTON CHURCHILL

NOUNS

1 **latency,** latentness, dormancy, dormant condition, sleep, hibernation, estivation; inactivity, passivity, quiescence, abeyance, inertness; delitescence, underdevelopment, potentiality, possibility; virtuality, subconsciousness, subconscious, sublimity; anonymity, no name, unknown person, mystery person, secret society, cabal, clandestineness; depth, hidden depths, deep structure; trope, figure, metaphor, allegory; tip of the iceberg, more than meets the eye, deceptive appearance, hidden fires
   ◗ *Secrecy 182; Inactivity 415; Inertness 519; Depth 598; Lack of Motion 678; Possibility 836*

2 **concealment,** hiding, invisibility, imperceptibility, submergence; skulking, lurking, stealth; privacy, seclusion, sequestration; secrecy, secret document, top-secret document, classified document, restriction; ob-

scurity, code, invisible writing, cryptography; intrigue, undercurrent, plot, ambush

    ◗ *Concealment 181; Secrecy 182; Invisibility 245; Unintelligibility 364; Plan 387; Unsociability 409*

3 **backstage manipulator,** secret influence, power behind the throne, hidden hand, puller of strings, puppeteer, wirepuller, friend at court, amicus curiae, gray eminence *or* éminence grise; old-boy network, boys in the back room

    ◗ *Influence 512*

4 **quietness,** taciturnity, muteness, sealed lips, closed lips; whisper, stage whisper, undertone, faintness, mutter, aside; hint, suggestion, innuendo, nuance, insinuation, connotation, adumbration, implication, inference; inner person, innermost recesses, interiority

    ◗ *Taciturnity 208; Silence 231; Faintness of Sound 233; Meaning 361; Interior 611*

5 **mysteriousness,** mysticism, occultism, occultness; symbolism, symbolization, allegory, anagoge, metaphor, esotericism, cabala; latent meaning, veiled meaning, hidden meaning, occult meaning, unintelligibility, oracle; secret, mystery, dimness, darkness, shadowiness; enigma, riddle

    ◗ *Information 170; Secrecy 182; Darkness 247; Prediction 358; Meaning 361; Unintelligibility 364*

ADJECTIVES

6 **latent,** dormant, sleeping, hibernating, inactive, passive, quiescent, in abeyance, inert; delitescent, undeveloped, potential, possible; virtual, subconscious, subliminal, submerged, underlying, archetypal, unacknowledged; subterranean, below the surface, deep

    ◗ *Inactivity 415; Inertness 519; Depth 598; Lack of Motion 678; Possibility 836*

7 **concealed,** hidden, covert, unseen, unmanifested, unexposed, invisible; screened, behind the scenes, back-room, in the background, underground; skulking, lurking, stealthy, hiding, lying low; private, not public, secluded, sequestered, tucked away, hidden away; unspied, undetected, undisclosed, undercover, under wraps; veiled, muffled, masked, disguised; coded, cryptographic, secret, top-secret, classified, restricted; kept quiet, off-the-record; obscure, murky, dark, arcane, unintelligible, impenetrable, undiscoverable; undiscovered, awaiting discovery, closed, cloaked in secrecy, hush-hush

    ◗ *Concealment 181; Secrecy 182; Invisibility 245; Darkness 247; Ignorance 349; Unintelligibility 364; Unsociability 409*

8 **unsolved,** unknown, undiscovered, unexplained, unrevealed, undivulged; unguessed, unsuspected, unexplored, untracked, untraced, uninvented

    ◗ *Unintelligibility 364*

9 **unsaid,** unspoken, unvoiced, unpronounced, unuttered, unexpressed, unarticulated; unmentioned, un-

told, undivulged, unsung, unpromoted, unproclaimed, undeclared, unprofessed; unwritten, unpublished

10 **tacit,** understood, implied, inferred, inferential; implicit, meant, indicated, suggested, hinted, intimated, insinuated; insinuating, implicative, between the lines, suggestive, allusive, allusory

    ◗ *Taciturnity 208; Silence 231; Meaning 361*

11 **mysterious,** mystic, occult; symbolic, allegorical, tropic *or* tropical, anagogical, metaphorical, figurative; cryptic, esoteric, secret, cabalistic, gnostic; indirect, oblique, clandestine; insidious, treacherous, perfidious, underhand, crooked

    ◗ *Linguistics, Language 5; Obliqueness 607; Specialty 779*

VERBS

12 **be latent,** lie dormant, lie under the surface, lie beneath; sleep, hibernate; smoke, smolder; keep quiet, keep mum

    ◗ *Inactivity 415; Lack of Motion 678*

13 **hide,** conceal; submerge, go below the surface, lie below the surface; skulk, lurk, creep, slink; tiptoe, walk on tiptoe; burrow, go underground; lie low, hunker down, lie hidden, stow away, lie in ambush, keep quiet, make no sign, await discovery; avoid notice, escape observation, evade detection, avoid recognition, stay behind the scenes, dissemble; secretly cause, influence, underlie, stage-manage; go on the lam [Inf]

    ◗ *Concealment 181; Untruthfulness, Falsehood 192; Influence 512; Inertness 519; Cause 675*

14 **imply,** mean, indicate, suggest, carry a suggestion, connote; hint, intimate, insinuate; allude, symbolize

    ◗ *Meaning 361*

ADVERBS

15 **latently,** passively, quiescently, potentially, virtually; subconsciously, subliminally; secretly, covertly; implicitly

16 **tacitly,** implicitly, suggestively

17 **mysteriously,** mystically, symbolically, figuratively, indirectly, obliquely

845 Success

One's religion is whatever he is most interested in, and yours is Success. — J. M. BARRIE

NOUNS

1 **success,** achievement, fame, triumph; accomplishment, attainment, killing, feat, sensation, overnight sensation, breakthrough, mastery, ascendancy; sweet smell of success; momentary *or* brief success, flash in the pan

2 **fame,** recognition, name, fame and fortune, famousness, success story, stardom, celebrity, name in lights, place in history

3 **successfulness,** thriving, plenty, luxury, prosperity, fortune, wealth, riches, affluence; luck, lucky stroke, beginner's luck, run of luck, favorable outcome, happy ending, fairy-tale ending, landing on one's feet, celebration; feather in one's cap; hit, big *or* smash hit; [Inf]: coming up roses, howling success, the big time, smash, lucky break

> *Celebration 405; Wealth 485; Superiority 744; Completeness 761; Prosperity 847*

4 **victory,** triumph, conquest, win, beating, whipping, thrashing, hiding, trouncing; runaway victory, crushing victory, landslide victory; knockout, winning by a mile, walkover, love game, shutout, lurch; overrunning, successful attack, taking by storm, rout; game, set, and match; overtime victory, sudden-death victory, military victory; successful battle, defeat; narrow victory, Pyrrhic victory; [Inf]: licking, pushover, piece of cake, KO, skunk

> *Skillfulness 127; Action 412; Attack 418; Destruction 523; Easiness 823; Certainty 840*

5 **successful thing,** bestseller, chart-topper, blockbuster, box-office success, rave review, number-one ranking *or* rating, good move, checkmate, hole in one, ace, good shot, touchdown, goal, field goal, home run *or* homer, hit, bull's-eye, grand slam, triple crown, hat trick, championship, wow, sellout, box-office hit, number one

6 **successful person,** success, winner, hero, heroine, self-made man *or* woman, achiever, superman, superwoman, man *or* woman of the year, record-breaker, star, celebrity; top of the class, graduate, honors graduate, valedictorian; Most Valuable Player (MVP), crème de la crème, rising star, up-and-coming star, surefire winner, hit, number one, the best; [Inf]: comer, the tops, corker, whiz kid, very important person (VIP)

> *Repute 370; Importance 799*

7 **victor,** winner, conqueror, champion, Olympic champion, world champion, worldbeater, titleholder, medalist, prizewinner, first-place finisher, first; defeater, vanquisher, subjugator, sure winner; champ [Inf], shoo-in [Inf]

ADJECTIVES

8 **successful,** succeeding, winning, crowned with success, wealthy, prosperous, fruitful, thriving, flourishing, favorable; lucky, fortunate, never-failing, surefire, surefooted, certain, rising, crowning, sitting pretty, home free; rewarding, financially rewarding, profitable, lucrative, paying, gainful, remunerative, advantageous, worthwhile

9 **famous,** renowned, efficacious, effective, masterly, best-selling, chart-topping, best ever

10 **victorious,** winning, triumphant, triumphal, flushed with victory, game-winning, prizewinning, on top, top of the league, top of the division, world-beating, always victorious, ever-victorious, undefeated, unbeaten, un-

bowed, unvanquished, unbeatable, unconquerable, invincible, crushing, quelling

VERBS

11 **be successful,** succeed, have success, enjoy success, meet with success, score a success, make a success of; prosper, thrive, flourish, flower, blossom, accomplish, effect, achieve, compass, get results, show results, come off well, become a self-made man *or* woman

12 **do well,** do oneself proud, pass, qualify, graduate, get on, get there, get ahead, get promoted, advance, progress, rise in the world, make good, make one's mark

13 **attain one's goal,** gain one's end, secure one's object, obtain one's objective, arrive, go over; earn a standing ovation, reap the harvest, reap the fruits, make money, get rich, break the bank; bring it off, bring off, pull it off, pull off, hit it off, hit it, carry off, work miracles, make the grade, do wonders, work wonders; not put a foot wrong, get lucky, win one's spurs, top the charts, write a bestseller, come off with flying colors; pull oneself up by one's bootstraps, work one's way up the ladder; have the world at one's feet, set the world on fire, ring the bell, hit the mark, make a hit, bring home the bacon, make a killing, make a go of; [Inf]: hit the jackpot, make the big time, make it, click, go great guns, go over big

14 **overcome obstacles,** overcome difficulties, sweep problems out of the way; manage, prevail, persevere, escape, surmount, get over the *or* a hump, get over a snag, avoid defeat; rise to the occasion, make headway, muddle through, stem the tide, weather the storm, not know the meaning of failure; find a loophole, find a way out, find a way around, cut the Gordian knot, not know when one is beaten, come right in the end, turn out well, land on one's feet, come up smiling, come up roses [Inf]

> *Resolution 376; Escape 816; Hindrance 826*

15 **be effective,** be efficacious, work, go, do, answer the purpose, answer, show results, turn out well, do the job, do wonders, work like magic, work like a charm, pay dividends, pay off, bear fruit, do the trick, ring the bell, fill the bill, come off [Inf]

16 **be victorious,** be triumphant, triumph, conquer, win, win a victory, win by a landslide, win the game, win the match; beat, beat all comers, become champion, take the prize, take the cup, take the championship, win the race, win the battle; achieve victory, claim a victory, win the last battle; force a surrender, defeat, defeat the enemy, vanquish, prevail, quell, subdue, carry the day, carry, take, storm, take by storm, sweep the boards, put down, crush; capture, subject, suppress, subjugate, win on points, win a *or* the point, win on moves; checkmate, check, put in check; wear the crown, wear the laurel wreath *or* laurels, have the

best of it, celebrate a victory; just win, scrape through, scrape home, win by a whisker

17 defeat, defeat easily, rout, put to flight, scatter, win hands down, win going away, romp home, storm home; win in straight sets, sweep the board, sweep, carry all before one, wipe out, break, bankrupt, drive to the wall, destroy, have it all one's way, walk off with; thrash, whip, trounce, overwhelm, crush, drub, give a drubbing, whitewash, trample underfoot, knock out, knock the stuffing out of, beat to a pulp, flatten; [Inf]: knock *or* beat the shit out of, lick, waltz away with, wipe the floor with, cook someone's goose, KO

18 overpower, overmaster, beat, master, overcome, overthrow, overturn, override, outclass, outplay, outpoint, trump, carry a point, score a point, come off best, pass with flying colors, come through with flying colors, outflank, outmaneuver, break through

ADVERBS

19 successfully, prosperously, rewardingly, fruitfully, profitably, lucratively, gainfully, advantageously, favorably, efficaciously, effectively, invincibly, well, marvelously, swimmingly, to some purpose, to good purpose, with good results, with good effect

20 victoriously, triumphantly, in triumph, with flying colors, on top of the heap

846 Failure

She knows there's no success like failure / And that failure's no success at all. — BOB DYLAN

NOUNS

1 failure, lack of success, negative result, hopeless failure; fallibility, inability, inefficiency, ineffectiveness, weakness; unproductiveness, barrenness, nonperformance, noncompletion, discontinuation, dereliction; withdrawal, setback
▶ *Infertility 23; Adversity 848*

2 error, mistake, mess, complete failure, collapse, debacle, fiasco, botch, bungle, bungling, blunder, omission, default, miss, near miss, vain attempt, futile effort; the pits [Inf]
▶ *Unskillfulness 128; Disappointment 293; Error 351*

3 futility, frustration, disappointment, no luck, misfortune, uselessness, lost labor, no result, no answer, no progress
▶ *Powerlessness 515; Incompleteness 762; Uselessness 802*

4 discontinuance, stoppage, shutdown, nonresumption, closure, stalling, stall, breakdown, dead stop, halt, fall, crash
▶ *Hindrance 826*

5 decline, decline in health, failing health, deterioration, failing, ailing, downfall, comedown, letdown; shortage, shortfall, incapacity, insufficiency

▶ *Ill Health 114; Weakness 517; Cessation 668; Descent 714*

6 insolvency, inability to pay, failure to pay, bankruptcy, ruin, nonpayment
▶ *Nonpayment 490*

7 defeat, loss, collapse, reversal, retreat, total defeat, trashing, utter defeat, rout; beating, drubbing, hiding, thrashing, trouncing; subjugation, submission, deathblow, narrow defeat, final defeat, military defeat, lost battle, Waterloo, lost war, lost cause, losing move, fatal move, losing game, nail in one's coffin, licking [Inf]
▶ *Submission 421; Loss 468; Destruction 523*

8 unsuccessful thing, going out of business, bankruptcy, bad idea, lost election, abortion, miscarriage, lost bet, wasted day, wild-goose chase, engine failure, electrical fault, computer fault, mechanical malfunction, crop failure; faux pas, dud, nonstarter, slip-up, flop; [Inf]: washout, wipeout, boo-boo, lemon, turkey, bomb

9 loser, failure, losing person, defeated player, losing general, unsuccessful candidate, unsuccessful competitor, unsuccessful applicant, unsuccessful challenger, deposed champion, nonpaying person, debtor, insolvent, bankrupt, underachiever, slow learner, born loser, misfit, bungler, reject, second-rater, underdog, unfortunate, victim, dupe, dropout, dud, hopeless case, flop, nonstarter, has-been, fly-by-nighter; [Inf]: also-ran, washout, patsy

ADJECTIVES

10 failed, failing, unsuccessful, ineffective, ineffectual, inefficacious; insufficient, unproductive; hopeless, insolvent, bankrupt; unlucky, unfortunate, empty, miscarried, miscarrying; bungled, bungling, blundered, blundering, stillborn, abortive, aborted; shutdown, closed, weak, ailing, fruitless, bootless, profitless, useless, futile; dud, of no effect; [Inf]: on one's beam-ends, washed-up, kaput, on the rocks

11 defeated, beaten, bested, lost, outmaneuvered, outclassed, outmatched, outgunned, outplayed, outshone, outvoted, outwitted, thrashed, on the losing team *or* side, out of the running, in retreat, put to flight, routed, captured, overthrown, wiped-out, down for the count, knocked out; [Inf]: licked, among the also-rans, KO'd

VERBS

12 fail, not succeed, lose out, come to nothing, get no results, not pass, flunk, bite the dust, do badly, fall by the wayside, fall, miss the boat, miss an opportunity, miss, have bad luck, not make the grade, flop, draw a blank, back the wrong horse, return empty-handed; [Inf]: not come off, come a cropper, not come up with the goods

13 blunder, make a bad move, bungle, collapse; slip up, drop the ball, make a hash of; [Inf]: ball up; bollix up, drop a clanger [Brit]

▶ *Error 351*

14 discontinue, shut down, close up, wind up, come to the end of the line, spoil one's reputation, fail in one's duty, let someone down

15 disappoint, disillusion, dash someone's hopes, fall short, not come up to *or* meet expectations, not come up to scratch

16 decline, tire, become fatigued, droop, sink, flag, fail in health, ail, take a turn for the worse, go to the dogs [Inf], fizzle out [Inf]

▶ *Ill Health 114; Fatigue 820*

17 become insolvent, take a loss, go out of business, go bankrupt, go to the wall, go on the rocks; [Inf]: fold, go bust, go belly up

▶ *Loss 468*

18 be defeated, suffer defeat, lose, lose the game, lose the match, lose the race, lose the vote, lose the election, lose the battle, lose the war; retreat, run away, surrender, come out second best, lose out, lose badly, lose hands down, take a beating, take a drubbing; come in last, fail to score, be eliminated, get the worst of it, concede defeat; lose by a whisker, just miss

▶ *Loss 468*

19 miscarry, abort, go wrong, go amiss, go awry, not go well, come to nothing, come to naught, come to grief, go by the board, end in futility, prove a fiasco, fall flat, go *or* end up in smoke, not come off [Inf]

20 malfunction, not start, not work, stop running, stop, come to a dead stop, come to a halt, fail, stall, misfire, jam, seize up, overheat, lose power, go wrong, break, fall to pieces, crash, conk out [Inf], go kaput [Inf]

ADVERBS

21 unsuccessfully, without success, to little purpose, to no purpose, in vain, fruitlessly, bootlessly, ineffectually, ineffectively, inefficaciously, insufficiently, unproductively, hopelessly, insolvently, negligently, neglectfully, unluckily, unfortunately, emptily, blunderingly, abortively, weakly, futilely, uselessly

847 Prosperity

In the day of prosperity be joyful, but in the day of adversity consider. — BIBLE: ECCLESIASTES

NOUNS

1 prosperity, prosperousness, well-being, welfare, wealth, success; fame, fame and fortune, fortune, health and wealth, luxury, lap of luxury, comfort, ease, life of ease, the good life, having it good; thriving, security, plenty, economic prosperity, high standard of living, affluent society, affluence; boom, bull *or* bullish market, booming economy, expanding economy, roaring trade; prestige, glory, honor and glory, happiness, felicity, blessedness, blessings, milk and honey, fat of the land, fleshpots, bed of roses, place in the sun, weal,

land-office business, living in clover, easy street, lap of luxury, life of Riley [Inf]

▶ *Sufficiency 97; Physical Pleasure 214; Joy, Cheerfulness 269; Wealth 485; Success 845*

2 good fortune, happy fortune, fortune, smiles of fortune; luck, good luck, piece of good luck, run of luck, streak of luck, winning streak, bonanza, lucky shot, lucky strike, luck of the draw; auspiciousness, favor, blessings, Midas touch; [Inf]: break, good break, lucky break, the breaks

▶ *Chance 842; Success 845*

3 time of plenty, good times, golden days, golden age, golden time, halcyon days, palmy days, salad days, heyday, honeymoon period, easy times, holiday, summer, prime, youth

4 prosperous person, rich person, successful person, success, self-made man *or* woman, man *or* woman of property, man *or* woman of means, man *or* woman of substance, person of repute, parvenu, nouveau riche, capitalist, plutocrat, tycoon, millionaire, multimillionaire, billionaire; the haves, the upwardly mobile, jet set; lucky fellow, lucky devil, child of fortune, fortune's favorite, favorite of the gods, yuppie, Sloane Ranger [Brit inf], fat cat [Inf]

ADJECTIVES

5 prosperous, prospering, successful, thriving, flourishing, booming, doing well, well-to-do, well-off; rising, up and coming, upwardly mobile, up in the world, famous, affluent, rich, opulent, wealthy; luxurious, in luxury, fat, comfortable, comfortably off, comfortably situated, living *or* eating high on the hog, cozy, at ease, bullish, fortunate, lucky, in luck, felicitous; palmy, balmy, halcyon, golden, rosy, blissful, in bliss, blessed, favorable, promising, auspicious, propitious, cloudless, born with a silver spoon in one's mouth, born under a lucky star; well-heeled [Inf], rolling in it [Inf]

VERBS

6 be prosperous, prosper, enjoy prosperity, do well, succeed, live well, get on well, fare well, make good, make one's mark; rise in the world, get on *or* go up in the world, have everything going one's way, do all right by oneself, get going, progress, advance, arrive; go far, thrive, flourish, blossom, flower, bloom; profit, make a profit, make one's fortune, make money, make a fortune, get rich, grow rich, strike it rich, get *or* grow fat; have a good time of it, rise to fame, become famous, win fame, win glory, win fame and glory; have it easy, live a life of ease, live in the lap of luxury, live off the fat of the land, live *or* eat high on the hog, live in clover, live on easy street; [Inf]: live the life of Riley, make it, have it made, roll in it, hit the big time

▶ *Wealth 485; Credit 487; Payment 489*

7 be fortunate, be lucky, have luck, have all the luck, have a stroke of luck, have a lucky break, have a run of good luck, hit a streak of luck, strike it lucky; strike it rich, come into money, come into an inheritance, be on to a good thing, fall on one's feet, lead a charmed life, be born under a lucky star, be born with a silver spoon in one's mouth, strike oil, get a break [Inf], get on the gravy train [Inf]

8 **be auspicious,** bode well, promise well, augur well, favor, look kindly on, smile on, shine on, bless, shed blessings on

ADVERBS

9 **prosperously,** successfully, famously, affluently, richly, opulently, luxuriously, comfortably, in comfort, cozily, bullishly, fortunately, luckily, with luck, propitiously, happily, felicitously, blissfully, in a blissful manner, blessedly, favorably, promisingly, auspiciously, in clover, on easy street; on velvet [Inf], in the money [Inf]

848 Adversity

Man is born unto trouble, as the sparks fly upward.
— BIBLE: JOB

In adversity remember to keep an even mind. — HORACE

NOUNS

1 **adversity,** difficulty, opposition, struggle, trials, travail; hardship, hard life, adverse circumstances, decline, fall, comedown, trials and tribulations, trouble, troubles; desolation, destitution, homelessness, ruin; predicament, plight, misfortune, affliction, visitation, blight, scourge, curse; misery, wretchedness, bleakness, gloom and doom, pressure, suffering; sorrow, sadness, dejection, despondency, distress, worry, worries, cares; bitter cup, cup of sorrows, bitter pill, bane, load, burden, cross to bear; the worst, hell, living hell; raw deal [Inf], the pits [Inf]
   ▸ *Sorrow 270; Deterioration 808; Difficulty 824; Opposition 828; Failure 846*

2 **misadventure,** mischance, accident, emergency, disaster, calamity, catastrophe; casualty, natural disaster, injury, hard blow; downer [Inf], bad news [Inf]

3 **threat,** trouble ahead, ill wind, gathering clouds, storm clouds, dark clouds

4 **downfall,** defeat, rebuff, humiliation; unrequited love, lost love; lost battle, lost war, retreat
   ▸ *Sorrow 270; Destruction 523; Opposition 828; Failure 846*

5 **adverse health,** decline in health, deterioration, setback; poor health, illness, infection, plague, cancer, pain; terminal illness, death
   ▸ *Ill Health 114; Physical Pain 215; Deterioration 808*

6 **economic adversity,** financial setback, financial reverse, financial disaster, financial ruin; arrears, negative equity, cash-flow problems; need, want, poverty, no money; lost fortune, lost inheritance, bankruptcy;

stock market decline, bear market, slumping market, slump; recession, depression, unemployment
   ▸ *Market 483; Poverty 486*

7 **bad fortune,** misfortune, ill fortune; bad luck, hard luck, rotten luck, no luck, no success; malign influence, evil star, hard fate; mischance, missed chance
   ▸ *Chance 842; Failure 846*

8 **time of adversity,** bad times, hard times, time of sorrow; lean period, rough patch, tough time, bad patch, bad spell; winter of discontent

9 **person in adversity,** poor person, bankrupt, homeless person, destitute; poor wretch, sufferer, unfortunate, unlucky person; loser, born loser, underdog, weakling, lame duck; tramp, down-and-outer, bag lady, poor risk; plaything of the gods, victim of fate, victim; dupe, scapegoat, prey; martyr; sad sack [Inf]

ADJECTIVES

10 **adverse,** contrary, conflicting, opposed, opposing, in opposition; hostile, antagonistic; troublesome, difficult, hard, bleak, cold; detrimental, dreadful, dire; inauspicious, unpropitious, ominous, unfavorable, disadvantageous; bad, harmful, sinister, disastrous, destructive, ruinous, tragic; doomed, unsuccessful; miserable, gloomy, sad, not doing well, in trouble, in difficulties, up against it; in a bad way, in poor shape, in poor health, ill, unwell; on one's last legs, declining, on the wane, on the downgrade, on the slippery slope, washed-up [Inf]

11 **unprosperous,** badly off, in adverse circumstances, poor, penurious, impecunious; poverty-stricken, penniless, broke, stone-broke, bankrupt, in dire straits; homeless, down-and-out, with one's back to the wall, on the road to ruin; [Inf]: on one's beam-ends, hard up, flat broke, stony, belly up

12 **unlucky,** not lucky, out of luck, down on one's luck, luckless, hapless, accident-prone; unfortunate, unblessed, ill-fated, ill-starred, star-crossed, accursed, under a cloud, born under an evil star, born under a bad sign

VERBS

13 **be in trouble,** have trouble, meet adversity, fall foul of, have a bad *or* hard time, have difficulties, bear the brunt, bear more than one's share, not know which way to turn; fail, lose, lose the battle, lose the war, miscarry; endure hardship, fall on hard times, fall on bad days, have seen better days; have no luck, be unlucky, run out of luck; suffer misfortune, have a mishap, have an accident; sink, founder, decline, go down in the world, go downhill, slip, fall from grace, have a comedown; hit rock bottom, run aground, go on the rocks, go to rack and ruin, come to a bad end, come to grief, be humiliated; be ill, have an illness, be in poor health, suffer, feel pain, deteriorate, degenerate, go to pot, die; stew in one's own juice, go to the dogs [Inf], hit the skids [Inf]

14 **need money,** have no money, have a financial setback, have a financial reverse, suffer a financial disaster, come to financial ruin, be ruined; want, fall below the poverty line; lose one's fortune, lose one's inheritance; have a check bounce, be overdrawn; go bankrupt, become insolvent; feel the pinch, have the wolf at one's door, go belly up [Inf]

15 **cause adversity,** cause grief, trouble, cause trouble, create a controversy, create problems; defeat, injure, oppress, sink, humiliate, make ill; burden, overburden, overload, weigh down; cause an accident, cause a death; bring bad luck, jinx, put the jinx on, put the evil eye on, voodoo, hex; [Inf]: put the skids under, put the *or* a whammy on, put the *or* a double whammy on

16 **adversely,** sadly, unhappily, unfortunately, unluckily; in adversity, in adverse circumstances; if worst comes to worst, from bad to worse, out of the frying pan into the fire; as ill luck would have it; conflictingly, contrarily, antagonistically; bleakly, unfavorably, detrimentally, dreadfully, grievously; inauspiciously, unpropitiously, ominously, harmfully, sinisterly, disastrously, tragically; accidentally, by accident, by mischance, by misadventure; unsuccessfully, miserably, poorly

17 **too bad!,** bad luck!, what rotten luck!, tough luck!, terrible!, dreadful!

Index

abnegate *disavow* 190.18, *deny* 332.8, *renounce* 383.13, 392.4
abnegated *relinquished* 392.2, *abnegating* 506.7
abnegating 506.7; *refuting* 332.6
abnegation 506.3; *disavowal* 190.3, *denial* 332.2, *renunciation* 383.4, *relinquishment* 392.1
abnegator *negator* 190.8
abnormal 430.13; *insane* 110.9, *mentally ill* 110.11, *strange* 364.9, *perverted* 432.12, *unusual* 664.4, *diverse* 732.5
abnormality 430.4; *insanity* 110.1, *unusualness* 664.2, *diversity* 732.1, *deviation* 782.6
abnormally *insanely* 110.15, *unusually* 664.7, *diversely* 732.14, *unconformably* 782.21
abnormal psychology Psychological Theories, Schools 108
Abo Nicknames for Inhabitants 61
abode *habitation* 60.2, *place of residence* 209.4
Abode of the Gods *heaven* 82.15
abolish 523.11; *prohibit* 503.8, *cancel* 834.6
abolish discrimination *treat equally* 831.8
abolished *canceled* 834.5
abolishment *destruction* 523.1, *cancellation* 834.1
abolition *prohibition* 503.1, *destruction* 523.1, *cancellation* 834.1
abolitionist *abrogator* 834.4
abolition of sins *cancellation* 834.1
A-bomb *bomb* 78.15
abominable *unclean* 112.8, *detested* 291.11, *hateful* 300.10, *immoral* 430.11
abominableness *hatefulness* 300.4
Abominable Snowman Legendary Creatures 360
abominably *distastefully* 291.19, *hatefully* 300.14, *disgracefully* 371.8
abominate *detest* 291.13, *hate* 300.11
abomination *uncleanness* 112.2, *antipathy* 291.2, *hate* 300.1, *hated thing* 300.5, *wrongdoing* 430.7, *evil thing* 446.2
à bon marché [Fr] *cheaply* 497.16
aboriginal *racial* 1.12, *historical* 3.10, *native* 61.12, *causal* 675.7, *prime* 771.18
aboriginally *historically* 3.17, *beforehand* 657.19
aborigine *race* 1.5, *inhabitant* 61.1
ab origine [L] *from the beginning* 771.38
aborigines *primitive humanity* 18.4
abort *program* 15.29, *be infertile* 23.8, *ruin* 523.15, *cause not to exist* 718.14, *cease* 773.20, *miscarry* 846.19
aborted *failed* 846.10
abortion *infertile state* 23.3, *unsuccessful thing* 846.8
abortive *frustrating* 293.7, *immature* 389.9, *futile* 802.10, *failed* 846.10
abortively *unsuccessfully* 846.21
abound 97.8; *be excessive* 99.9
about *mathematically* 6.93, *offshore* 150.35, *nearby* 586.17, *around* 615.8, *quantitative* 738.6, *quantitatively* 738.8
about-face 680.4; *oppositeness* 190.6, *vacillation* 380.3, *equivocate* 380.8, *reversion* 671.1, *turn around* 680.22, 698.25

about gone *dying* 29.12
about this big *this size* 579.11
about this size *this size* 579.11
about to *tending to* 513.4
about to give birth *pregnant* 21.12
about to go *worn* 808.13
above *stage* 136.18, *high* 596.20, *superior* 744.8, *preceding* 769.9
above all *supremely* 744.23, *importantly* 799.15
above and below *inclusively* 613.35
above average *superior* 744.8, *superbly* 744.22
aboveboard *candid* 191.5, *permitted* 502.4, *naive* 821.3
above expectations *excessively* 99.13
above ground *alive* 28.13
above-mentioned *preceding* 769.9
above one's head *powerlessly* 515.16, *high* 596.20
above par *superbly* 744.22
above price *valuable* 496.8
above reproach *virtuous* 447.5
above suspicion *incorrupt* 449.7
above temptation *virtuous* 447.5
above the horizon *visible* 244.5
above the law *lawless* 53.26
above water *safe* 810.16
ab ovo [L] *from the beginning* 771.38
abracadabra *spell* 86.8, *nonsense* 362.2
abrade 554.13; *erode* 8.67, *grate* 553.24, *depilate* 614.20
abraded *weathered* 8.61
Abraham's bosom *after death* 29.9
abrasion *erosion* 8.41, *painful injury* 215.3, *pulverization* 553.4, *wearing away* 554.2
abrasive 553.14; *cleaning agent* 111.9, *frictional* 554.10
abrasively 554.17
abraxas *spell* 86.8
abreaction *recuperation* 809.4
abreast *in parallel* 203.6, *forward* 679.6, *on equal terms* 740.9, *as good as* 740.14
abridge *be concise* 198.5, *summarize* 204.7, *contract* 582.12, *shorten* 591.9, *outline* 617.5, *make smaller* 747.8, *subtract* 749.6
abridged *concise* 198.4, *summarized* 204.6, *shortened* 582.8, 591.7, 762.6, *outlined* 617.4, *reduced* 749.5
abridged dictionary *word book* 5.27
abridgment *conciseness* 198.1, *outline* 198.2, 204.2, 617.1, *shortening* 582.2, 591.2, *contracted thing* 582.5, *shortened version* 591.3, *limitation* 747.3, *subtraction* 749.1
abroad *out-of-doors* 558.26, *distantly* 585.11
abrogate *acquit* 54.32, *obliterate* 186.6, *disavow* 190.18, *refute* 332.7, *renounce* 383.13, *stop using* 394.10, *veto* 503.9, *counteract* 510.7, *remove power from* 515.13, *abolish* 523.11, *cease* 773.20, *make useless* 802.12, *cancel* 834.6
abrogated *obliterated* 186.4, *renounced* 383.9, *suspended* 519.3, *useless* 802.7, *canceled* 834.5
abrogation *obliteration* 186.1, *disavowal* 190.3, *refutation* 332.1, *renunciation* 383.4, *veto* 503.3, *neutralization* 510.4, *cessation* 773.2, *cancellation* 834.1

abrogative *disavowing* 190.12
abrogator 834.4
abrupt 591.8; *irritable* 304.9, *discourteous* 411.5, *outspoken* 550.6
abruptly 591.13; *explosively* 234.8, *irritably* 304.17, *discourteously* 411.8, *bluntly* 550.11
abruptness 591.4; *irritableness* 304.3, *outspokenness* 550.2
Abruzzi sheepdog Breeds of Dogs 35
abscess *ulcer* 114.18
abscise *be dormant* 41.22
abscisic acid *plant hormone* 12.17
abscissa *coordinates* 6.31, 589.6
abscission *leaf* 41.6, *peeling* 614.6, *separateness* 753.3
abscond 576.16; *run away* 386.21, *not pay* 490.9, *quit* 705.10, *escape* 816.8
absconded *away* 576.8
absconder *nonpayer* 490.6
abseil *climbing techniques* 161.3, *mountaineer* 161.10, *descent* 714.1, *descend* 714.12
absence 576.1, 718.6; *invisibility* 245.1, *disappearance* 265.1, *desertion* 386.7
absence of charge 497.6
absence of color *colorlessness* 252.1
absence of dirt *cleanliness* 111.1
absence of intellect *lack of intellect* 316.1
absence of meaning *lack of meaning* 362.1
absence of power *powerlessness* 515.1
absence without leave (AWOL) *desertion* 386.7, *disobedience* 427.1, *absenteeism* 576.3
absent 576.7; *unprovided* 98.6, *disappeared* 265.4, *unused* 394.5, *truant* 576.10, *nonexistent* 718.9, *excluded* 764.6
absentation *absenteeism* 576.3
absentee 576.5; *avoider* 386.8
absentee ballot *electing* 382.5
absenteeism 576.3; *idleness* 415.3
absentee landlord *nonworker* 415.4
absentee vote *electing* 382.5
absentee voter *electorate* 382.7
absent friends! *cheers!* 93.22
absently 576.18; *unintelligently* 316.9, *resignedly* 392.6
absent-minded 324.6; *forgetful* 186.7, 355.6, *thoughtless* 318.7, *unjoined* 753.9
absent-mindedly *forgetfully* 355.14, *in isolation* 753.24
absent-mindedness 324.2; *forgetfulness* 186.3, 355.1, *lack of thought* 318.1
absent oneself 576.15; *depart* 265.6, *run away* 386.21, *quit* 705.10
absent without leave (AWOL) *truant* 576.10
absinthe *alcoholic drink* 93.9
absolute *authoritative* 52.9, *masterful* 68.15, *divine* 82.16, *definite* 189.8, *correct* 429.8, *complete* 761.6, 805.14, *unconditional* 829.14, *certain* 840.7
absolute age *geological time* 8.47
absolute ceiling *flight* 689.5
absolute contradiction *negation* 190.1
absolute frequency *probability distribution* 6.56

absolute humidity *weather data* 9.6, *humidity* 559.3
absolute idea *idea* 327.1
absolute idealism *idealism* 525.5
absolutely *masterfully* 68.19, *divinely* 82.24, *clean* [Inf] 111.21, *definitely* 189.33, *earnestly* 278.10, *correctly* 429.16, *wholly* 759.11, *completely* 759.14, 761.13, 805.22, *certainly* 840.15
absolutely it *original* 737.2
absolutely not *not at all* 718.15
absolutely not! *no!* 190.28
absolute magnitude *star luminosity* 7.12
absolute monarch *sovereign* 68.2
absolute monarchy *monarchy* 49.6
absolute music *classical music* 140.2
absoluteness *definiteness* 189.6, *right* 429.2, *certainty* 840.1
absolute pitch *tone* 140.24, *hearing* 228.1
absolute rate theory *chemical reaction* 11.8
absolute realism *verisimilitude* 721.10
absolute ruler 68.7
absolutes 6.9
absolute scale *scale* 589.9
absolute truth, the *the truth* 721.3
absolute unit *unit of measurement* 589.5
absolute value *complex number* 6.6, *vector* 6.48
absolute zero *thermodynamics* 10.30, *freezing* 218.2, *zero level* 786.3
absolution 312.2; *favorable verdict* 54.19, *Christian rite* 85.5, *forgiveness* 312.1, *amnesty* 355.5, *acquittal* 434.2, *vindication* 441.1, *legal innocence* 449.3, *liberation* 831.1
absolutism *suppression* 424.2
absolve 312.10; *acquit* 54.32, 434.10, *perform rites* 85.18, *show pity* 308.8, *forgive* 312.8, *vindicate* 441.11, *declare innocent* 449.11, *liberate* 831.6
absolved *acquitted* 54.25, 434.6, *forgiven* 312.5, *declared innocent* 449.8, *liberated* 831.4
absolving *liberation* 831.1, *liberating* 831.5
absorb 11.40, 560.20, 708.19; *observe* 7.34, *interact* 10.73, *eat* 92.21, *use up* 393.12, *immerse* 598.24, *make the same* 730.16, *augment* 748.13, *combine* 757.9
absorbed 11.34; *thoughtful* 4.17, *educated* 48.19, *concentrating* 317.7, *in deep* 598.18, *same* 730.7, *combined* 757.5
absorbed dose *radioactivity* 10.58
absorbency *absorption* 708.6
absorbent 708.11; *dryer* 560.5, *sponge* 708.7
absorption 708.6; *atmospheric process* 9.9, *wave property* 10.12, *emission* 10.56, *process* 11.15, *surface chemistry* 11.20, *physiology* 13.13, *learning* 48.7, *eating* 92.1, *oblivion* 355.4, *immersion* 598.8, *sameness* 730.1, *combination* 757.1
absorption indicator *gravimetric analysis* 11.18
absorption nebula *nebula* 7.6
absorption spectrum *emission* 10.56
absorptive *absorbent* 708.11

absquatulate [Inf] *hurry off* 705.11

abstain 386.16, 455.11; *practice birth control* 23.10, *be continent* 67.10, *fast* 118.8, *be sober* 120.8, *dissociate* 375.14, *renounce* 392.4, *not use* 394.9, *not act* 413.11, *desist* 417.13, *be moral* 431.13, *refuse oneself* 506.10, *restrain oneself* 830.15

abstainer *sober person* 120.4, *reluctant person* 375.7, *avoider* 386.8, *inactive person* 413.8, *resister* 417.5, *self-restrained person* 455.5, *refuser* 506.4

abstain from sex *abstain* 455.11

abstaining 386.11; *inactive* 413.9, *desisting* 417.4, 417.9, *self-restraint* 455.1, *self-restrained* 455.6

abstemious *fasting* 118.5, *sober* 120.5, *desisting* 417.9, *chaste* 431.10, *self-restrained* 455.6, 830.10

abstemiously 118.11, 417.15; *soberly* 120.9, *with self-restraint* 455.14, *self-restrainedly* 830.19

abstemiousness *fasting* 118.1, *sobriety* 120.1, *self-restraint* 455.1, 830.4

abstention *dissociation* 375.4, *abstinence* 386.2, *inaction* 413.1, *self-restraint* 455.1

abstentious *inactive* 413.9

abstergent *cleansing* 111.16

abstinence 386.2, 455.2; *birth control* 23.5, *fasting* 118.1, *sobriety* 120.1, *relinquishment* 392.1, *nonuse* 394.1, *chastity* 431.3, *self-restraint* 455.1, 830.4

abstinence from action *inaction* 413.1

abstinence from food *fasting* 118.1

abstinent 455.7; *celibate* 67.6, *fasting* 118.5, *sober* 120.5, *abstaining* 386.11, *chaste* 431.10, *self-restrained* 455.6, 830.10

abstinently *celibately* 67.12, *away* 386.23, *abstemiously* 417.15

abstract *philosophical* 4.12, *theoretical* 6.66, *portrait* 132.5, *obscure* 197.2, *outline* 198.2, 617.1, 617.5, *be concise* 198.5, *representing* 202.14, *summary* 204.1, *summarize* 204.7, *theoretical* 327.10, 720.10, *supposed* 359.6, *imaginary* 360.12, *choose* 382.14, *internal* 525.11, *shortened version* 591.3, *shorten* 591.9, *subtractive* 749.4, *subtract* 749.6, *generalization* 778.5, *generalized* 778.12

abstract algebra *algebra* 6.21

abstracted *summarized* 204.6, *thoughtless* 318.7, *oblivious* 355.9, *shortened* 591.7, *wandering* 698.13, *subtracted* 749.3, *unjoined* 753.9

abstractedly *theoretically* 327.19, *forgetfully* 355.14

abstractedness *thoughtfulness* 317.2, *oblivion* 355.4, *reverie* 360.6, *wandering* 698.4

abstract expressionism Western Art Styles 133

abstraction *theory* 6.62, *mood disorder* 108.12, *obscurity* 197.1, *idea* 327.1, *reverie* 360.6, *subtraction* 749.1, *generalization* 778.5

Abstraction-Création Western Art Styles 133

---

abstractly *theoretically* 4.24, 327.19, *subjectively* 525.14, *in isolation* 753.24

abstract music *classical music* 140.2

abstract sculptor *sculptor* 144.4

abstract sculpture *sculpture* 144.1

abstract thought *philosophical investigation* 4.4, *thoughtfulness* 317.2

abstruse *mysterious* 182.10, *obscure* 197.2, *difficult* 364.8, *profound* 598.15, *problematic* 824.11

abstrusely *obscurely* 197.4, *profoundly* 598.27

abstruseness *obscurity* 197.1, 250.2, *profundity* 598.5, *difficulty* 824.1

abstrusity *profundity* 598.5

absurd *foolish* 353.5, *fantastic* 360.11, *meaningless* 362.7, *ridiculous* 368.5, *impossible* 837.4

absurd idea *plan* 327.3

absurdism Western Literary Groups 139

absurdity *folly* 353.1, *conception* 360.4, *senseless talk* 362.4, *ridiculousness* 368.1, *impossibility* 837.1

absurdly *foolishly* 353.8, *meaninglessly* 362.13, *ridiculously* 368.8, *impossibly* 837.11

Abu Dhabi Countries 566

Abuja Countries 566

abundance 498.4; *fertility* 22.1, *plenty* 97.2, *excess* 99.1, *quantity* 105.5, *diffuseness* 199.1, *opulence* 485.3, *denseness* 594.2, *surplus* 750.4, *profuseness* 795.3

abundant 498.8; *fertile* 22.8, *plentiful* 97.4, *excessive* 99.5, *available* 105.16, *diffuse* 199.3, *lush* 485.11, *big* 579.13, *dense* 594.6, *ample* 795.9

abundantly *fruitfully* 22.15, *plentifully* 97.11, *excessively* 99.13, *diffusely* 199.7, *generously* 498.12, *amply* 579.20, *densely* 594.12, *residually* 750.11

abuse *expend* 96.16, *vilify* 301.15, 440.14, *malignity* 306.5, *harm* 306.13, *use* 393.1, *exploit* 393.11, *misuse* 395.1, 395.6, *act of discourtesy* 411.3, *be discourteous* 411.7, *personal attack* 418.8, *criticize* 418.26, *suppress* 424.9, *wrongdoing* 430.7, *wrong* 430.19, *seduce* 432.16, *berating* 438.5, *berate* 438.20, *scorn* 440.5, *be evil* 446.10, *be wicked* 448.13, *use violence* 520.9, *moral deterioration* 808.3, *pervert* 808.22

abused *misused* 395.3, *criticized* 438.14

abuse of language *misinformation* 188.3, *language error* 351.10

abuse of power *ill-use* 395.2

abuse of terms *language error* 351.10

abuse one's authority *suppress* 424.9

abuse oneself *stimulate* 20.22

abuse power *ill-use* 395.7

abuser *user* 393.4, *evil person* 446.3

abusive 395.5; *vilifying* 301.9, *malign* 306.11, *discourteous* 411.5, *bad-mannered* 411.6, *critical* 418.16, 438.13, *unlawful* 430.15, *insulting* 436.10, *defamatory* 440.9, *detrimental* 446.8, *villainous* 448.12

abusively 395.8; *vilifyingly* 301.18, *malignly* 306.18, *discourteously* 411.8, *rudely* 411.9

---

abut *adjoin* 216.11, *juxtapose* 586.14, *support* 605.16, *interface* 616.5

abutment Architectural Elements 134, *contiguity* 216.4, *fortification* 419.12, *superstructure* 551.7, *bridge* 551.10, *juxtaposition* 586.4, *supporting part* 605.3, *interface* 616.1

abuttal *juxtaposition* 586.4

abutting *contiguous* 216.8, *juxtaposed* 586.9, *interfacial* 616.4

abysmal *demonic* 446.9, *deep* 598.9

abysmally *deep* 598.25

abyss *evil place* 446.6, *gulf* 587.3, *the depths* 598.2, *concave land* 635.2, *hidden danger* 813.3

abyssal *oceanic* 8.53, 571.7, *deep* 598.9

abyssal hill *ocean floor* 8.18

abyssal plain *ocean floor* 8.18

abyssal waters *ocean* 8.14

Abyssinian Breeds of Sheep 16, Breeds of Cats 35

AC *one day* 639.20

acacia Flowers 42, Trees and Shrubs 43

academia 348.6

academic *sage* 4.11, *educator* 48.4, *educational* 48.17, *educated* 48.19, *intellectual* 315.7, *reasoner* 319.5, *knowledgeable person* 348.5, *literate* 348.8, *theorist* 359.4, *suppositional* 359.5

academically *theoretically* 4.24, *studiously* 48.26, *knowledgeably* 348.14

academicals *formal clothes* 100.5

academic art Western Art Styles 133

academic costume *formal clothes* 100.5

academic dress *formal clothes* 100.5, *formal clothing* 406.5

academic freedom *free rights* 829.4

academic gown *formal clothes* 100.5

academician *visual artist* 133.6, *intellectual* 315.7

academic journal *magazine* 175.3

academic psychology Psychological Theories, Schools 108

academic researcher *theorist* 359.4

academic robe *formal clothes* 100.5

academic year *period of activity* 641.4

academy *type of school* 48.12

Academy Award *motion pictures* 137.1, *prizes* 453.3

Academy of Motion Picture Arts and Sciences *motion pictures* 137.1

acanthoid *spiked* 549.11

acanthous *spiked* 549.11

acanthus Flowers 42, Architectural Elements 134

a cappella Musical Terms and Expression Marks 140

Acapulco gold [Inf] *hemp derivatives* 121.16

acarid or **acarine** *arachnid* 40.4, *arachnidan* 40.12

acaroid *arachnidan* 40.12

acaroid resin Tree Products 43, *resin* 726.6

acarological *arachnological* 40.16

acarologist *entomologist* 40.3

acarology *study of insects* 40.2

acarophobia Phobias 283

---

accede *gain authority* 52.15, *submit* 298.17, *assent to* 346.7, *agree* 735.23, *succeed* 770.11, *conform* 781.11

accedence *agreement* 735.3

acceding *agreeing* 735.13

accelerando Musical Terms and Expression Marks 140

accelerate 694.14; *interact* 10.73, *participate* 166.22, *further* 679.13, *impel* 695.9, *intensify* 746.8, *hasten* 818.4, *make haste* 818.5, *make easy* 823.15

accelerated *accelerating* 694.9, *increased* 746.5

accelerating 694.9

acceleration 694.3; *speed* 10.7, *track event* 166.1, *intensification* 746.2, *haste* 818.1

acceleration due to gravity *speed* 10.7

acceleration path *hammer throwing* 166.14

accelerator *catalysis* 11.16

accelerometer *meter* 589.13

accelerometric *metric* 589.19

accent *language sign* 5.33, *meter* 139.10, *linguistic sign* 183.10, *punctuate* 183.20, *emphasis* 200.1, *emphasize* 200.6, *mode of speech* 205.6, *regional pronunciation* 205.7

accented *punctuated* 183.15, *phonetic* 205.14

accentual *metrical* 139.20

accentual meter *meter* 139.10

accentual-syllabic meter *meter* 139.10

accentuate *emphasize* 200.6, *reveal* 843.14

accentuated 843.11; *emphasized* 200.4

accentuation *syntax* 5.32, *meter* 139.10, *emphasis* 200.1, *manifestation* 843.2

accept *believe* 87.9, *understand* 295.6, *be impartial* 338.11, *assent to* 346.7, *be willing* 373.12, *select* 382.12, *submit* 421.4, *approve* 437.14, *agree with* 462.10, *receive* 473.13, 492.7, *take* 477.14, *welcome* 708.14, *agree* 735.23, *resign oneself* 835.6, *be certain* 840.13

acceptability *sufficiency* 97.1, *desirability* 288.7, *qualification* 340.1, *admittance* 708.1

acceptable *sufficient* 97.3, *satisfactory* 273.6, *expedient* 288.12, *qualified* 340.7, *approvable* 437.13, *permitted* 502.4, *admissive* 708.8, *convenient* 803.3

acceptably *sufficiently* 97.9, *expediently* 288.25, *capably* 340.15, *approvably* 437.22, *with permission* 502.10, *passably* 692.19

accept a charge *be in debt* 488.9

accept a commission or **appointment** *incur a duty* 433.15

accept advice *consult* 176.11

accept a gratification *get paid* 453.17

accept an assignment *incur a duty* 433.15

acceptance *believing* 87.2, *lack of wonder* 295.1, *assent* 346.1, *approval* 437.1, *agreement* 462.1, 735.3, *receiving* 473.1, *admittance* 708.1, *resignedness* 835.2, *conviction* 840.2

---

accept an office *incur a duty* 433.15

acceptant *receiving* 473.9, *agreeing* 735.13

accept a proposal *marry* 64.19, *get engaged to* 458.12

accept battle *battle* 76.33

accepted *believed* 87.8, *undertaken* 391.4, *established* 397.12, *approved* 437.8, *received* 473.11, 492.6, *average* 742.5, *prevailing* 778.11

accepted as one of the family *popular* 408.12

accepted meaning *type of meaning* 361.4

accepted reading *interpretation* 365.1

accepter *recipient* 473.5

accepting *lenient* 423.3, *agreeing* 462.6, 735.13, *receiving* 473.1, 473.9, *resigned* 835.4, *convinced* 840.8

acceptingly *in accord* 735.33

accept invitations *participate* 408.15

accept liability *guarantee* 458.13

accept obligation *guarantee* 458.13

accept on faith *believe* 87.9

acceptor *chemical bond* 11.6, *recipient* 473.5, *purchaser* 481.7

acceptor impurity *semiconductor* 10.34

accept payment *get paid* 453.17

accept responsibility *undertake* 391.7, *guarantee* 458.13

accept stolen property *receive* 473.13

accept the Lord *be religious* 81.25

accept the responsibility *incur a duty* 433.15

access 691.3; *computing terms* 15.22, *program* 15.29, *taking in* 477.7, *open up* 583.16, *spasm* 684.8, *thoroughfare* 692.6, *entry* 706.1, *right of entry* 706.4, *entrance* 706.5, *receptivity* 708.2

accessibility *availability* 575.5, *nearness* 586.1, 803.2, *possibleness* 836.2

accessible 691.13; *communicative* 169.16, *usable* 393.6, *available* 575.11, *opened up* 583.11, *next* 586.8, *attainable* 704.11, *receptive* 708.9, *nearby* 803.4, *made easy* 823.11, *possible* 836.5

accessibly *openly* 583.22, *conveniently* 803.6

accession *acquisition of authority* 52.5, *achievement* 704.8, *addition* 748.1, *succession* 770.2

accessional *authorized* 52.11

accessories *possessions* 470.5, *separates* 753.6

accessory 100.28; *superfluity* 99.4, *supporter* 605.9, *addition* 748.1, *concomitant* 794.4, *accompanying* 794.12, *secondary matter* 800.6, *supplementary* 825.17

access road *road* 687.2

acciaccatura *musical ornament* 140.19

accident *mishap* 660.4, *technical problem* 826.3, *chance* 842.1, *misadventure* 848.2

accidental 660.7; *musical note* 140.15, *blocked* 826.13, *unexpected* 839.6, *chance* 842.10, *causeless* 842.11

accidental death *way of dying* 29.5

accidental discovery *discovery* 345.1

accidental killing 30.9; *killing* 30.1

accidentally *mistakenly* 660.14, *in the way* 826.23, *by chance* 842.15, *adversely* 848.16

accidental shooting *accidental killing* 30.9

accident prevention *bargaining terms* 57.10

accident-prone *unlucky* 848.12

accidents *Phobias* 283

acclaim 437.5, 437.18; *worship* 83.15, *cheer* 239.15, *praise* 435.15, *reward* 453.1, 453.13

acclaimed *rewarded* 453.10

acclamation *cry of praise* 239.3, *acclaim* 437.5, *reward* 453.1

acclamatory 437.10; *approving* 437.9

acclimate *accustom* 397.18

acclimated *habituated* 397.14

acclimatization *habituation* 397.7, *pliancy* 781.3

acclimatize *accustom* 397.18, *assimilate* 781.14

acclimatized *habituated* 397.14

acclivitous *steep* 713.15

acclivity *heights* 596.4, *incline* 713.3

accolade *honor* 72.3, *Architectural Elements* 134, *compliment* 437.4

accommodate *conciliate* 74.10, *provision* 89.9, *be compassionate* 305.11, *compromise* 461.7, *lend* 475.6, *be adaptable* 546.9, *orient* 697.15, *give refuge to* 708.15, *agree* 735.23, *equalize* 740.12, *include* 763.5, *make conform* 781.13, *improve* 825.26

accommodate to *conform* 781.11

accommodate with *give out* 472.12

accommodating *courteous* 410.6, *submitting* 421.3, *lenient* 423.3, *compromising* 461.4, *adaptive* 546.6, *agreeing* 735.13, *including* 763.3, *compliant* 781.9, *benevolent* 825.21, *cooperative* 827.9

accommodatingly *pacifically* 74.12, *courteously* 410.13, *genteelly* 410.14, *leniently* 423.6, *compromisingly* 461.9, *adaptably* 546.11, *in accord* 735.33

accommodation *pacification* 74.1, *compromise* 461.1, *lending* 475.1, *adaptability* 546.2, *reserved space* 563.5, *size* 579.1, *orientation* 697.3, *agreement* 735.3, *inclusion* 763.1, *pliancy* 781.3, *convenience* 825.7

accommodation ladder *ladder* 713.10

accommodations *habitation* 60.2, *provisions* 89.3

accommodation ship *Ships and Boats* 690

accommodative *loaned* 475.5

accompanied 794.1; *related* 727.6, *united* 752.10

accompanier 794.6

accompaniment 794.1; *musical composition* 140.9, *harmonics* 140.13, *attendance* 575.3, *ancillary* 605.5, *same time* 649.1, *relatedness* 727.1

accompanist *accompanier* 794.6

accompanist *or* **accompanyist** *player* 141.2

accompany 794.16; *serve* 69.11, *direct* 126.11, *be simultaneous* 649.6, *unify* 752.15

accompanying 794.12; *attending* 575.9, *ancillary* 605.14, *simultaneous* 649.4

accomplice *guilty person* 450.5, *supporter* 605.9

accomplish *manage* 126.10, *act* 412.11, *secure one's objective* 464.12, *notch up* 636.6, *react* 676.8, *achieve* 704.21, *complete* 759.10, 761.9, *perfect* 805.19, *be successful* 845.11

accomplished *educated* 48.19, *expert* 52.12, 127.12, *skillful* 127.10, *proficient* 445.15, *secured* 464.7, *completed* 761.7

accomplishment *skill* 127.1, *information* 348.2, *action* 412.1, *deed* 412.2, *production* 522.1, *achievement* 704.8, *completion* 761.2, *success* 845.1

accomplishments *learning* 348.3

accomplish nothing *waste effort* 802.13

accord 735.1; *friendly relations* 62.3, *harmonize* 140.28, 765.20, *assent* 346.1, *mean* 361.13, *contract* 459.1, *agreement* 462.1, 730.2, 752.4, *give* 472.10, *correspond to* 727.10, *be similar* 733.12, *settlement* 735.6, *grant* 735.30, *conformity* 781.1, *conform* 781.11, *be convenient* 803.5, *fellowship* 827.2

accordable *consenting* 735.18

accordance *agreement* 462.1, 730.2, *observance* 465.1, *affinity* 733.3, *grant* 735.10, *conformity* 781.1

accordant *agreeing* 462.6, 730.8, 735.13, *connected* 733.9, *conforming* 735.17, 781.8

accordantly *agreeably* 462.14, *agreeingly* 730.19, *similarly* 733.17, *in accord* 735.33, *conformingly* 735.37

accorded *given* 472.8, *settled* 735.16, *granted* 735.20

according *consenting* 735.18

accordingly 735.39; *with the effect of* 676.12, *under the circumstances* 726.16, *harmoniously* 735.31

according to *harmoniously* 735.31

according to chance *perchance* 842.18

according to Hoyle *proper* 429.10

according to law *legal* 53.16, *orderly* 663.13

according to order *orderly* 663.13

according to plan *intentionally* 374.13, *in order* 765.26

according to rule 781.18; *orderly* 663.13, *disciplined* 765.17

according to schedule *as planned* 387.16

according to the agreement *contractually* 459.9

according to the book *meaningfully* 361.16

according to the contract *contractually* 459.9

according to tradition *orderly* 663.13

accordion *Musical Instruments* 142

accordion pleat *pleat* 637.2

accord respect to *show respect* 435.16

accord with *be equal* 740.11

accost *approach* 209.10, *request* 505.10

accosting *request* 505.1

account 493.9; *chronicle* 3.4, *communication* 170.2, *news story* 171.3, *record* 185.1, *description* 202.1, *narration* 202.3, *funds* 484.6, *credit* 487.1, *amount owing* 488.5, *accounts* 493.4, *check* 784.14, *bill* 785.4, *importance* 799.1

accountability *demonstrability* 331.5, *answerability* 334.9, *expectations* 356.2, *sense of duty* 433.2, *debt* 488.1

accountable *answerable* 334.17, *duteous* 433.7, *indebted* 488.7, *accounting* 493.7

accountably *demonstrably* 331.22, *answerably* 334.28, *dutifully* 433.19

accountancy *accounts* 493.4

accountant 493.6; *representative* 75.3, *record keeper* 185.8, *financial adviser* 457.4, *treasurer* 484.18, *counter* 784.6

account book 493.3; *record book* 185.5, *bill* 785.4

accounted 493.8

accounted for *available* 647.6

account for *rationalize* 4.20, *have a sense of duty* 433.13

accounting 493.1, 493.7; *recordkeeping* 185.7, *finance* 457.1, *accounts* 493.4, *count* 784.3, *calculative* 784.7

account paid *statement* 493.2

account rendered *statement* 493.2

accounts 493.4; *recordkeeping* 185.7

account settled *statement* 493.2

accounts payable *credit* 487.1

accounts receivable *amount owing* 488.5, *payment* 489.1

accouplement *junction* 609.5

accouter *clothe* 100.43, *make clothing* 100.44

accoutered *equipped* 388.10, *defended* 419.18

accouterment *provision* 89.1, *clothing* 100.1, *accessory* 100.28

accouterments *equipment* 103.6, *possession of property* 469.3, *possessions* 470.5, *ornamentation* 748.5

Accra *Countries* 566

accredit *authorize* 52.14, *commission* 833.8

accreditation *commission* 833.1

accredited *authorized* 52.11, *believed* 87.8, *established* 397.12, *commissioned* 833.6

accrete *acquire* 467.19, *add* 748.11

accretion *acquisition* 467.4, *increase* 746.1, *addition* 748.1

accretionary *additional* 748.8

accretive *additional* 748.8

accrual *addition* 748.1

accrue *be profitable* 467.21, *receive* 492.7, *grow* 676.10, *make bigger* 746.7, *augment* 748.13

accumbency *recumbency* 603.2

accumbent *recumbent* 603.7

accumulate *assemble* 59.23, *store* 105.17, *acquire* 467.19, *increase* 746.6, *unite* 752.14

accumulated *collected* 59.19, *stored* 105.14

accumulated arrears *amount owing* 488.5

accumulation *assemblage* 59.13, *store* 105.1, *storage* 105.6, *collection* 105.12, *acquisition* 467.4, *increase* 746.1

accumulative *acquisitive* 467.13

accumulatively *gainfully* 467.24

accumulator *collector* 59.17

accumulator [Arch] *computer part* 15.4

accuracy 350.1; *number system* 6.7, *measurement* 10.67, *clarity* 196.1, *right* 429.2, *observance* 465.1, *trueness* 721.4, *methodicalness* 765.6, *perfection* 805.1, *certainty* 840.1

accuracy event *competitive fishing* 154.5

accurate 350.3; *clear* 196.2, *judicious* 341.8, *correct* 429.8, 721.13, *observant* 465.3, *well-ordered* 765.14, *infallible* 805.10, *naive* 821.3, *certain* 840.7

accurately 350.6; *clearly* 196.4, *correctly* 429.16, 721.29

accurateness *right* 429.2

accursed *cursed* 301.8, *unlucky* 848.12

accursedly *execratively* 301.17

accusable *unjust* 53.24, *litigated* 54.22, *villainous* 448.12, *guilty* 450.6

accusation 442.1; *censure* 438.3, *guilt* 450.1

accusative *grammatical term* 5.29

accusatory 442.6

accuse 442.8; *litigate* 54.27, *inform on* 170.13, *tell on* 180.10

accused 442.5; *litigant* 54.4, *condemned* 438.11

accused, the *accused person* 442.4

accused person 442.4; *litigant* 54.4

accuse falsely 442.9

accuse oneself *appear guilty* 450.10, *be penitent* 451.7

accuser 442.3; *informer* 170.8

accusing *litigating* 54.21, *accusation* 442.1, *accusatory* 442.6

accusingly 442.11

accustom 397.18; *season* 654.11

accustomed *habitual* 397.9, *habituated* 397.14, *seasoned* 654.9, *average* 742.5, *common* 778.13, *customary* 780.9

accustom oneself 397.19

AC/DC [Inf] *of sexual nature* 20.17

AC/DC gal [Inf] *bisexual* 33.11

AC/DC guy [Inf] *bisexual* 32.10

ace *expert* 52.8, 68.13, *means* 102.1, *prizewinner* 127.8, *skillful* 127.10, *golfing terms* 156.3, *golf shots* 156.4, *play* 156.8, *tennis terms* 165.5, *cards* 168.2, *superior person* 445.7, *short distance* 586.2, *paragon* 744.6, *one* 788.1, *best* 805.9, *successful thing* 845.5

ace [Inf] *excellent* 68.16, *learn* 68.18

ace in the hole *expedient* 387.5, *advantage* 618.4, *gist* 799.4

Aceldama *battleground* 76.24

acellular *cellular* 13.30

acer *Trees and Shrubs* 43

acerbate *make irritable* 304.15

acerbic *acid* 223.5, *resentful* 302.8, *ill-natured* 303.9, *bitter* 306.9, *discourteous* 411.5, *mentally sharp* 549.14

acerbically *ill-naturedly* 303.18, *bitterly* 306.16

acerbity *sourness* 223.1, *ill nature* 303.2, *bitterness* 306.3, *discourtesy* 411.1

acerophobia *or* **acerbophobia** *Phobias* 283

acetaminophen *analgesic* 115.6

acetate *fiber* 130.2

acetic *Common Fatty Acids* 12

acetic acid *sour thing* 223.3

acetylene lamp *incandescent light* 246.5

ace up one's sleeve *reserves* 102.5, *advantage* 744.3

ache *pain* 117.5, 215.1, *feel pain* 215.8, *be painful* 215.9

ache in every muscle *or* **limb** *be fatigued* 820.5

Achelous *Rivers* 570

achene *botanical fruit* 44.2

Acheron *evil place* 446.6

aches and pains *pain* 215.1

achievable *attainable* 704.11, *realizable* 719.9, *possible* 836.5

achieve 704.21; *manage* 126.10, *act* 412.11, *be an instrument* 511.7, *notch up* 636.6, *react* 676.8, *complete* 761.9, *end* 773.19, *perfect* 805.19, *be successful* 845.11

achieved *completed* 761.7

achieve liberty *be liberated* 831.7

achieve marvels *do wonders* 294.15

achievement 704.8, *Heraldic Terms* 184, *action* 412.1, *deed* 412.2, *instrumentality* 511.1, *production* 522.1, *effect* 676.1, *advance* 679.3, *completion* 761.2, *success* 845.1

achieve nothing *be useless* 802.11

achieve one's purpose *complete* 759.10, *be convenient* 803.5

achieve orgasm *stimulate* 20.22

achiever *doer* 412.3, *successful person* 845.6

achieve victory *be victorious* 845.16

Achilles *Planets and Their Satellites* 7, *Notable Friendships* 62

Achilles heel *weakness* 517.1, *defect* 806.4, *vulnerability* 811.6

aching *painful* 215.4, *feeling pain* 215.6, *fatigued* 820.2

aching all over *feeling pain* 215.6

achingly *painfully* 215.12

aching muscles *fatigue* 820.1

achluophobia *Phobias* 283

achondrite *meteor* 7.21

achromatic *colorless* 252.5, *whitened* 253.8, *dark* 254.6

achromatically *colorlessly* 252.9, *whitely* 253.13

achromaticity *colorlessness* 252.1

achromatism *colorlessness* 252.1, *whiteness* 253.1

achromatize *decolor* 252.8

achy *feeling pain* 215.6

acicular *sharp* 549.10

aciculate *or* **aciculated** *sharp* 549.10

acid 11.10, 11.27, 223.5; *strain* 117.4, *tasty* 219.4, *resentful* 302.8, *ill-natured* 303.9, *bitter* 306.9, *agent of destruction* 523.7

acid [Inf] *hallucinogens* 121.20

acid-base catalysis *catalysis* 11.16

acid dye *dye* 130.8

acid-head [Inf] *drug taker* 121.12

acidic *acid* 11.27, 223.5, *bitter* 306.9

acidify *react* 11.38, *sour* 223.8

acidimeter *Fields of Measurement* 589

acidimetric *metric* 589.19

acidimetry *Fields of Measurement* 589

acidity *gastroenterological disease* 114.11, *sourness* 223.1, *resentment* 302.1, *ill nature* 303.2, *bitterness* 306.3, *Fields of Measurement* 589

acid jazz *jazz* 140.5

acid kiln *ceramic workshop and tools* 129.8

acidly *resentfully* 302.22, *ill-naturedly* 303.18

acidosis *gastroenterological disease* 114.11

acid rain *rain* 9.27, *pollution* 117.8, *impairment* 808.7

acid rock *igneous rock* 8.32, *rock music* 140.6

acid salt *salt* 11.12

acid stop *darkroom equipment* 132.21

acid taste *taste* 219.1

acid test *experiment* 335.1

acid trip [Inf] *drug use* 121.9

acidulated *acid* 223.5

acidulous *acid* 223.5, *resentful* 302.8

acidulousness *sourness* 223.1, *resentment* 302.1

ack-ack [Inf] *ammunition* 78.11, *military defenses* 419.9

acknowledge *correspond* 169.19, *admit* 180.11, *avow* 189.27, *be grateful* 310.6, *apologize* 313.8, *answer* 334.18, *assent* 346.6, *show respect* 435.16, *admire* 437.15, *reward* 453.13, *observe* 465.4, *receive* 473.13, 492.7

acknowledged *disclosed* 180.5, *avowed* 189.19, *answering* 334.11, *rewarded* 453.10, *received* 473.11, 492.6

acknowledged with thanks *received* 492.6

acknowledge guilt *apologize* 313.8

acknowledge one's faults *confess* 451.8

acknowledge one's guilt *be guilty* 450.9

acknowledge one's sins *be guilty* 450.9, *confess* 451.8

acknowledging *thanking* 310.5, *answering* 334.11, *approving* 437.9

acknowledgment 310.3, 334.2; *divulgence* 180.2, *avowal* 189.7, *apology* 313.2, *assent* 346.1, *admiration* 437.2, *reward* 453.1, *observance* 465.1

acknowledgment of guilt *apology* 313.2

acknowledgment of payment 473.3

acknowledgments *book part* 174.5, *acknowledgment* 310.3

aclinic line *geomagnetism* 8.3

acme *superior person* 445.7, *pinnacle* 596.2, *summit* 600.1, 744.4, *peak* 805.5

acmeism *Western Literary Groups* 139

acme of perfection *peak* 805.5

acne *skin disease* 114.16, *rough skin* 544.3

acoelomate *invertebrate* 39.20

acolyte *religious person* 81.9, *ritualist* 85.14

Aconcagua *Mountains and Hills* 569

aconite *alkaloid* 12.19, *Flowers* 42

acorn barnacle *crustacean* 39.10

acorn worm *protochordate* 39.4

acoustic *physical* 10.70, *aural* 228.8, *sounding* 230.7

acoustically *physically* 10.78

acoustic coupler *communications device* 15.26

acoustic guitar *Musical Instruments* 142

acoustic mine *bomb* 78.15

acousticophobia *Phobias* 283

acoustic phenomenon *sound* 230.1

acoustics *classical physics* 10.2, *sound* 10.15, 230.1

acoustic wave *wave* 10.11, 683.4

acquaint *educate* 48.22, *inform* 170.11

acquaintance *friend* 62.2, *information* 170.1, *knowledge* 348.1

acquaintanceship *friendship* 62.1

acquainted with *friendly with* 62.6, *knowledgeable* 348.7

acquaint oneself with *get to know* 348.12

acquest *estate* 750.5

acquiesce 421.5; *submit* 298.17, *assent to* 346.7, *be willing* 373.12, *obey* 426.7, *approve* 437.14, *agree with* 462.10, *permit* 502.6, *agree* 735.23, *conform* 781.11, *resign oneself* 835.6

acquiesced *approved* 437.8

acquiescence 373.3; *submissiveness* 298.3, *assent* 346.1, *submission* 421.1, *obedience* 426.1, *approval* 437.1, *agreement* 462.1, 735.3, *tolerance* 502.2, *compliance* 781.2, *resignedness* 835.2

acquiescent 373.9; *submissive* 298.10, *assenting* 346.4, *submitting* 421.3, *obedient* 426.4, *agreeing* 462.6, 735.13, *compliant* 781.9, *easygoing* 823.13, *resigned* 835.4

acquiescently *submissively* 298.23, *unanimously* 346.8, *obediently* 426.9, *agreeably* 462.14, *in accord* 735.33, *resignedly* 835.7

acquiescing *agreeing* 462.6

acquire 467.19; *learn* 68.18, *find means* 102.6, *detect* 345.12, *gain* 467.15, *receive* 473.13, 492.7, *take over* 477.16, *purchase* 481.10

acquire a reputation *do great deeds* 412.14

acquire credit 487.11

acquired *gainful* 467.10, *received* 473.11

acquired immune deficiency syndrome (AIDS) *sexually transmitted disease (STD)* 114.17

acquired knowledge *learning* 348.3

acquire knowledge *learn* 48.23

acquirement *skill* 127.1, *gain* 467.1

acquirements *learning* 348.3

acquirer *recipient* 473.5

acquire the force of habit *or* **custom** *become a habit* 397.17

acquire the habit *accustom oneself* 397.19

acquiring *gainful* 467.10, *taking* 477.12

acquisition 467.4; *gain* 467.1, *receiving* 473.1, *taking over* 477.3, *purchase* 481.1

acquisitional *acquisitive* 467.13, *taking* 477.12

acquisition of authority *or* **power** 52.5

acquisition of knowledge *learning* 48.7

acquisitive 467.13; *covetous* 288.14, *selfish* 444.4, *gain-seeking* 467.11, *taking* 477.12, *buying* 481.9

acquisitively 481.21; *covetously* 288.28, *selfishly* 444.8, *gainfully* 467.24, *avariciously* 477.22

acquisitiveness *selfishness* 444.1

acquit 54.32, **434.10;** *show pity* 308.8, *absolve* 312.10, *judge* 341.10, *do one's duty* 433.17, *vindicate* 441.11, *declare innocent* 449.11, *perform* 465.5, *deliver* 817.5, *liberate* 831.6

acquit oneself *conduct oneself* 399.17

acquittal 434.2; *favorable verdict* 54.19, *mercy* 308.3, *absolution* 312.2, *verdict* 341.2, *vindication* 441.1, *legal innocence* 449.3, *performance* 465.2, *escape* 816.1, *deliverance* 817.1, *liberation* 831.1

acquittance *promise* 464.2, *payment* 489.1, *liberation* 831.1

acquitted 54.25, **434.6;** *forgiven* 312.5, *vindicated* 441.8, *declared innocent* 449.8, *free* 829.11, *liberated* 831.4

acquitting *liberating* 831.5

Acrania *protochordate* 39.4

acraniate *invertebrate* 39.20

acre General Units 589

acreage *farmland* 16.3, *property* 470.1

acre-foot General Units 589

acre-inch General Units 589

acres *property* 470.1

acrid *acid* 223.5, *bitter* 306.9

acridity *unpalatability* 223.2

Acrilan™ *fiber* 130.2

acrimonious *hostile* 63.6, *hating* 300.7, *resentful* 302.8, *bitter* 306.9, *discourteous* 411.5

acrimoniously *hostilely* 63.13, *with hate* 300.13, *resentfully* 302.22, *bitterly* 306.16, *discourteously* 411.8

acrimony *ill feeling* 63.3, *hate* 300.1, *resentment* 302.1, *bitterness* 306.3

acrobat *circus performer* 138.9

acrobatic *sporting* 145.5, *ski* 162.27, *pliant* 543.7

acrobatically *sportingly* 145.7, *softly* 543.18

acrobatic jump *skiing* 162.1

acrobatic skiing *skiing* 162.1

acromegaly *gigantism* 579.4

acronym *catchword* 5.22

acrophobia Phobias 283

Acropolis *automobile rallies* 146.6

acropolis *fort* 419.13, *fortification* 812.3

acrospire *seed* 41.9

across *breadthways* 592.16, *obliquely* 607.13, *by the way* 692.20

across-the-board *whole* 759.6, *including* 763.3, *general* 778.9

across the counter *in trade* 480.22

across the line *ahead* 712.18

across the sea *nautically* 571.10

acrostic *spelling* 5.26, *puzzle* 182.5

acroterium Architectural Elements 134

acrylic Common Fatty Acids 12, *plastics* 104.6, *painting* 143.3

acrylic fiber *fiber* 130.2

acrylic paint *paint* 251.6

acrylics *material* 143.9

act 136.34, 137.20, 187.13, 412.11; *play part* 136.8, *number* 138.5, *occur* 264.14, *conduct oneself* 399.17, *behave toward* 399.20, *show* 404.12, 404.24, *deed* 412.2, *be active* 414.18, *command* 425.1, *be operational* 509.10, *be an instrument* 511.7, *react* 676.8, *part of writing* 760.6, *rule* 780.1, *display* 843.13

act against *oppose* 828.15, *counteract* 828.21

act aimlessly *mean nothing* 362.10

act as a brake *restrain* 826.19, 830.12

act as agent for *mediate* 75.6

act as a go-between 460.8, *represent* 80.6

act as a magnet *attract attention* 323.12

act as a master of ceremonies *lead* 126.12

act as a middleman *act as a go-between* 460.8

act as a mouthpiece for *represent* 80.6

act as a white knight [Inf] *finance* 457.7, *bargain* 480.20

act as broker for *represent* 80.6

act as deputy for *be a substitute* 672.5

act as guarantor *promise* 464.10

act as guide *interpret* 365.12

act as host *or* **hostess** *be sociable* 408.14, *receive someone* 473.14

act as interpreter *translate* 365.16

act as proxy *represent* 79.7, *substitute for* 80.5

act as security *promise* 464.10

act as spokesperson for *interpret news* 365.17

act curtain *stage set* 136.19

act decisively *be assertive* 189.28

act dishonestly 479.18

act drop *stage set* 136.19

act dumb *be silent* 181.16

act eccentric *be independent* 829.11

act foolishly 128.10

act for *represent* 79.7, *substitute for* 80.5, *stand for* 187.14, *be a substitute* 672.6

act forcefully *be assertive* 189.28

act friendly *agree with* 462.10

act imperiously *have authority* 52.13

act impulsively 318.14, *improvise* 396.6

act in *occur* 264.14

act in concert *work together* 827.14

acting 136.22, 137.12, 187.6, 187.9, 412.9; *governing* 49.25, *deputizing* 80.4, *substitute* 672.3

acting area *stage* 136.18

acting as a law unto oneself *lawless* 53.26

actinide *or* **actinon** *or* **actinoid** *chemical element* 11.3

actinium Chemical Elements and Common Allotropes 11

actinometer Fields of Measurement 589

actinometric *metric* 589.19

actinometry Fields of Measurement 589

actinomycin *fungal antibiotic* 47.7

act in one's own worst interests *act foolishly* 128.10

act in opposition *oppose* 828.15

act insolent *be insubordinate* 416.8

act instead of *substitute for* 80.5

action 412.1; *litigation* 54.1, *battle* 76.23, *dramaturgy* 136.6, *aspect of fiction* 139.5, *painting* 143.3, *conduct* 399.1, *deed* 412.2, *activity* 414.1, *accusation* 442.1, *operation* 509.1, *undertaking* 675.5, *effect* 676.1, *momentum* 677.2

actionable *unjust* 53.24, *litigated* 54.22

action painter *painter* 143.7

action painting Western Art Styles 133

actions *conduct* 399.1, *treatment* 399.11, *deed* 412.2

action sequence *portrait* 132.5

action shot *portrait* 132.5

activate 509.11, 771.28; *react* 11.38, *arouse sensation* 212.11, *influence* 512.11, *invigorate* 518.5, *cause change* 665.16

activated *catalytic* 11.30, *active* 414.13

activated complex *chemical reaction* 11.8

activating *catalytic* 11.30

activation *energy* 414.4, *change* 665.1

activation energy *chemical reaction* 11.8

activator *changer* 665.9

active 414.13; *grammatical term* 5.29, *lively* 28.16, *working* 122.6, *acting* 412.9, *busy* 414.15, *operational* 509.7, *vigorous* 518.2, *moving* 677.12

active army *army* 77.12

active forces *the military* 58.2

active galaxy *galaxy* 7.5

active interest *social activity* 414.2

active list *list of names* 785.7

actively 412.18, 414.24; *operationally* 509.13, *in motion* 677.19

actively involved *active* 414.13

active matrix display *display* 15.9

active member *social person* 408.7

activeness *action* 412.1, *activity* 414.1

active participation *social activity* 414.2

active person *busy person* 414.10

active resistance *defense* 419.1

active site *enzyme* 12.11

active sun *sun* 7.15

active supporter *activist* 412.4

active treatment *treatment* 107.14

active volcano *volcanic activity* 8.26

activewear *informal clothes* 100.7

activism 414.5; *theater movements* 136.9, *action* 412.1

activist 412.4; *motivator* 178.11, *attempter* 390.3, *busy person* 414.10, *defiant person* 416.4

activity 385.4, 414.1; *radioactivity* 10.58, *action* 412.1, *vigor* 518.1, *momentum* 677.2, *haste* 818.1, *engagement* 833.2

act like a bitch [Inf] *be irascible* 303.13

act like a Christian *be charitable* 305.12

act like a gentleman *have good manners* 410.10

act like a lady *have good manners* 410.10

act like a tonic *invigorate* 518.5

act like a vixen *be irascible* 303.13

act negligently *be careless* 289.14

act of charity *benevolent act* 305.5

act of contrition *type of penance* 451.3

act of courage *courageous act* 284.7

act of defiance 416.3

act of discourtesy 411.3

act of dying *dying* 29.3

act of folly 353.2

act of God *necessitarianism* 95.7, *ruin* 523.4

act of grace *benevolent act* 305.5

act of hostility 63.4

act of inversion 608.3

act of kindness *sign of courtesy* 410.5

act of love *sexual intercourse* 20.9

act of malevolence *malignity* 306.5

act of smelling *sense of smell* 224.2

act of thrift 499.2

act of worship 83.2

act on behalf of *substitute for* 80.5, *answer for* 334.24

act one's part *do one's duty* 433.17

act on one's own initiative *volunteer* 504.13

act on the defensive 419.29; *be at war* 76.32

act on the spur of the moment *improvise* 396.6

actor 136.25, 137.13; *artistic worker* 123.12, *speaker* 205.12, *pretender* 367.2, *performer* 412.5

actor-manager *actor* 136.25, *producer* 136.28

actors *cast* 136.26

act recklessly *be careless* 289.14

actress *artistic worker* 123.12, *actor* 136.25, 137.13, *performer* 412.5

act rough 547.14

act rude *exclude* 409.12

act sycophantic *defer to* 410.12

act the fool *play the fool* 353.7

act the grand seigneur *or* **grande dame** *put on airs* 404.27

act the host *be sociable* 408.14

act the hostess *be sociable* 408.14

act the part of *act* 187.13

act the showman *show* 404.24

act together *come together* 757.10

act treasonously *defy* 466.11

actual *factual* 3.14, *correct* 429.8, *present* 575.7, *real* 717.14, 719.6, 721.12, *certain* 840.7

actual existence *reality* 721.2

actuality *historicalness* 3.9, *right* 429.2, *presence* 575.1, *modernity* 647.3, *demonstrable existence* 717.5, *reality* 719.1, 721.2, *certainty* 840.1

actualization *creation* 717.9

actualize *come to be* 717.19, *make real* 719.11, *be real* 721.21

actualized *created* 717.16

actually *biographically* 3.18, *earnestly* 278.10, *in person* 575.18, *really* 717.22, 719.13, *in truth* 721.28, *certainly* 840.15

actual presence *presence* 575.1

actuarial *accounting* 493.7, *calculative* 784.7

actuarial calculation *calculation of chance* 842.9

actuary *accountant* 493.6, *measurer* 589.14, *counter* 784.6

actuate *motivate* 508.9, *activate* 509.11, *influence* 512.11, *set in motion* 677.16, *impel* 695.9

actuation *motion* 677.1, *momentum* 677.2

act upon *motivate* 412.12, *influence* 508.11, *take action* 509.12

act wickedly *be wicked* 448.13

act without ceremony *have no time to spare* 818.6

act without prompting *volunteer* 504.13

act without thinking *lack thought* 318.12

acuity *emphasis* 200.1, *cleverness* 315.3, *accuracy* 350.1, *mental sharpness* 549.9, *profundity* 598.5, *cunning* 542.1

acumen *refinement* 48.10, *way of thinking* 317.4, *judiciousness* 337.2, *wisdom* 352.1, *subtlety* 534.2, *mental sharpness* 549.9

acuminate *sharp* 549.10, *be sharp* 549.15

acumination *sharpness* 549.1

acuminous *mentally sharp* 549.14

acupressure *alternative medicine* 107.4, *therapy* 115.12

acupuncture *alternative medicine* 107.4, *treatment* 107.14, *analgesic* 115.6, *therapy* 115.12, *healing art* 115.13, *anesthetic* 213.3

acupuncturist *healer* 107.22

acutance *composition* 132.17

acute *painful* 215.4, *intelligent* 315.9, *strong in spirit* 516.11, *violent* 520.5, *mentally sharp* 549.14, *profound* 598.15, *advantaged* 618.7, *cunning* 822.4

acute accent Accents and Diacritical Marks 5

acute angle *angle* 6.37, 628.1

acute-angled *angled* 628.9

acute attack *illness* 114.2

acute dilemma *danger* 811.1

acutely 516.18; *intelligently* 315.14, *sharply* 549.19, *profoundly* 598.27

acuteness *cleverness* 315.3, *mental sharpness* 549.9

acute stress disorder *anxiety disorder* 108.11

acute *or* **acute-angled triangle** *triangle* 6.41

acyclic *chemical compound* 11.4

acylate *react* 11.38

acylglycerol *fat* 12.7

AD *one day* 639.20

ad *tennis terms* 165.5

ad [Inf] *advertisement* 173.9

Ada Programming Languages 15

adage *catchword* 5.22, *maxim* 177.1, *moral* 431.5, *truism* 721.6

adagietto Musical Terms and Expression Marks 140

adagio Musical Forms 140, *slowly* 693.14

adagio Musical Terms and Expression Marks 140

adagissimo Musical Terms and Expression Marks 140

Adak Islands 572

Adam *male* 32.1, Furniture Styles 101

adamancy *or* **adamance** *obstinacy* 379.1

adamant *iron-willed* 372.7, *strong-willed* 376.10, *obstinate* 379.5, *hard substance* 542.3, *tough* 542.6

adamantine *obstinate* 379.5

adamantly *inflexibly* 542.13

adamic *olden* 653.11

Adamite *person* 18.8

Adam's ale *or* **wine** *water* 557.1

Adam's apple *figurative usage* 44.4, *speech organ* 205.4

Adam's-needle Flowers 42, *sharp-pointed growth* 549.5

Adam's seed *humankind* 18.1

adapt *produce* 137.21, *compose* 141.18, *modify* 340.13, *translate* 365.16, *accustom* 397.18, *compromise* 461.1, *adopt* 476.11, *yield* 543.17, *be adaptable* 546.9, *change* 665.14, *cause change* 665.16, *orient* 697.15, *agree* 735.23, *conform* 781.11

adaptability 546.2; *skill* 127.1, *compromise* 461.1, *easiness* 543.5, *pliancy* 781.3, *usefulness* 801.1, *wieldiness* 823.3

adaptable *skillful* 127.10, *compromising* 461.4, *pliant* 543.7, *easing* 543.13, *adaptive* 546.6, *agreeing* 735.13, *conformable* 781.7, *useful* 801.5, *wieldy* 823.12

adaptably 546.11, 781.15; *in accord* 735.33

adaptation *musical composition* 140.9, *modification* 340.5, *translation* 365.4, *habituation* 397.7, *compromise* 461.1, *adoption* 476.2, *alteration* 665.2, *orientation* 697.3, *agreement* 735.3, *pliancy* 781.3, *convenience* 803.1

adapted *composed* 141.13, *modified* 340.9, *treated* 388.12, *adaptive* 546.6

adapted to *convenient* 803.3

adapted to drought 560.13

adapter *composer* 141.9, *changer* 665.9

adapt for the stage *dramatize* 136.33

adapting *easing* 543.13, *adaptive* 546.6

adaption *pliancy* 781.3

adaptive 546.6; *agreeing* 735.13, *conformable* 781.7

adapt to *conform* 781.11

ad court *tennis court* 165.3

add 6.86, 748.11, 784.11; *react* 11.38, *continue* 669.8, *insert* 710.9, *quantify* 738.7, *number* 783.9

Adda Rivers 570

add an escape clause *make conditions* 460.7

add commentary *annotate* 365.14

added *inserted* 710.5, *related* 727.6, *quantitative* 738.6, *additional* 748.8, *included* 763.4

added attraction *positive stimulus* 508.5

added extra *extra* 748.6

addend *addition* 6.13

addendum *addition* 748.1, *additional item* 748.3

add explanation *annotate* 365.14

add fuel *fuel* 106.16, *intensify* 746.8

add fuel to the flames *make violent* 520.10

addict *sick person* 114.22, *desirer* 288.9, *creature of habit* 397.8, *compulsive person* 428.5

addicted 121.31; *habituated* 397.14, *overindulgent* 456.8

addicted to alcohol *drunken* 121.28

addiction *affliction* 117.1, *habit* 397.1, *overindulgence* 456.3, *moral deterioration* 808.3

addictive 121.32; *intoxicating* 121.29, *enticing* 178.13, *habit-forming* 397.15, *appealing* 512.9

addictive drug 117.10

adding *addition* 748.1, *count* 784.3

adding machine *calculator* 6.64, 784.5, *computer* 15.1

adding up *mathematical addition* 748.2

add insult to injury *insult* 436.21

Addis Ababa Countries 566

additament *additional item* 748.3

addition 6.13, 748.1; *chemical reaction* 11.8, *increase* 581.3, 746.1, *ancillary* 605.5, *protraction* 669.4, *insertion* 710.1, *relatedness* 727.1, *piece* 760.2, *calculation* 784.1

additional 748.8; *ancillary* 605.14, *progressive* 669.6, *substitute* 672.3, *increasing* 746.4

additional item 748.3

additionally 748.15; *largely* 581.18, *continually* 669.10, *instead* 672.8, *increasingly* 746.9

additional part *additional item* 748.3

addition polymer(ization) *polymer* 11.9

additive *reactive* 11.29, *additional item* 748.3, *additional* 748.8, *thing included* 763.2

additive color *coloring agent* 251.5

addle *be dirty* 112.10, *discompose* 766.18

add nothing *equalize* 740.12

add-on *additional item* 748.3

add one's share *insert* 748.12

add one's support *support* 748.14

add one's two cents worth *insert* 748.12

add-ons *separates* 753.6

address 209.1, 209.8; *data-related concepts* 15.23, *program* 15.29, *manual skill* 127.2, *correspondence* 169.2, *correspond* 169.19, *utterance* 205.10, *public speaking* 205.11, *speak to* 205.19, *appeal to* 209.9, *send* 209.11, *procedure* 387.2, *salute* 435.17, *exact location* 565.2

address book *record book* 185.5, *book of lists* 785.3

addressee *householder* 61.5, *answerer* 334.10, *recipient* 473.5

addresses *courtship* 299.10

addressing 209.6; *nomenclature* 202.7

address of welcome *salutation* 209.2

address oneself to 209.13; *undertake* 391.7

address one's prayers to *petition* 505.11

address the general public *make comprehensible* 363.8

address the question *relate to* 727.9

add strings *make conditions* 460.7

add taste to *make taste* 219.6

add to *increase* 581.16, *notch up* 636.6, *make bigger* 746.7, *add* 748.11, *unite* 752.14, *subsume* 763.7

adduce *circumstantiate* 726.12, *reveal* 843.14

adduced *displayed* 843.8

adducent *attracting* 700.8

adduct *attract* 700.11

adduction *pulling power* 700.2

adductive *attracting* 700.8

add up *add* 6.86, 748.11, 784.11, *be intelligible* 363.10

add up to *mean* 361.13, *be whole* 759.9

add up to the same thing *equalize* 740.12

add value *augment* 748.13

add water *dilute* 557.30, *moisten* 559.13

Aden Countries 566

adenine *nucleotide* 12.10

adenosine diphosphate (ADP) *bioenergetics* 12.23

adenosine monophosphate (AMP) *bioenergetics* 12.23

adenosine triphosphate (ATP) *bioenergetics* 12.23

adept *expert* 68.13, *excellent* 68.16, *occultist* 86.13, *skilled person* 127.7, *skillful* 127.10

adeptly *masterfully* 68.19, *skillfully* 127.16

adeptness *manual skill* 127.2

adequacy *sufficiency* 97.1, *satisfactoriness* 273.3, *qualification* 340.1, *mediocrity* 742.3, *instrumentality* 801.3

adequate *sufficient* 97.3, *satisfactory* 273.6, *qualified* 340.7, *equal to* 740.10, *mediocre* 742.7, *complete* 761.6, *instrumental* 801.7

adequate amount *sufficiency* 97.1

adequate income *sufficiency* 97.1

adequately *sufficiently* 97.9, *satisfactorily* 273.12

à deux *two* 789.8

adhere 755.8; *insist* 376.14, *become a habit* 397.17, *stick* 561.20, *be stable* 674.6, *be literal* 721.25, *unify* 752.15, *intercommunicate* 754.15, *be tenacious* 755.9

adherence *observance* 465.1, *literalness* 721.9, *tenacity* 755.2

adherence to the law *legality* 53.9

adherence to the letter of the law *legality* 53.9

adherent 401.5, 755.4; *supporter* 605.9, *literal* 721.18, *adhesive* 755.5

adherently *literally* 721.32

adherent to *observant* 465.3

adhere to *propound a philosophy* 4.21, *follow* 401.14, *observe* 465.4, *retain* 471.7, *support* 748.14

adhering 755.7; *tied* 752.13

adhering to *observant* 465.3

adhesion 755.1; *retention* 471.1, *friction* 699.4, *pulling power* 700.2, *connection* 754.1

adhesive 561.3, 755.3, 755.5; *retainer* 471.3, *retentive* 471.5, *mucilaginous* 561.15, *united* 752.10, *connective* 754.10

adhesive bandage *medical covering* 613.4

adhesively *tenaciously* 471.11, *viscously* 561.22, *magnetically* 699.14, *attractionally* 700.13, *as one* 752.21, *in connection with* 754.16

adhesiveness *viscosity* 561.1, *adhesion* 755.1

adhesive tape *medical covering* 613.4, *line* 754.5, *adhesive* 755.3

ad hoc *spontaneous* 389.6, *spontaneously* 389.17, *improvised* 396.4, *extempore* 396.7

ad hoc measure *means* 102.1, *method* 387.4, *improvisation* 396.1

adiabatic *atmospheric* 9.40

adiabatic change *heating effect* 10.28

adiabatic cooling *atmospheric process* 9.9

adiabatic lapse rate *atmospheric process* 9.9

adiabatic process *atmospheric process* 9.9

adiaphorism *indifference* 289.1

adieu *parting* 705.3

adieu! *goodbye!* 705.14

Adige Rivers 570

ad infinitum *at length* 590.15, *infinitely* 798.10

adios! [Sp] *goodbye!* 705.14

adipocere *fat* 562.4

adipose *oily* 562.11, *fat* 579.15

adiposis *oiliness* 562.1

adiposity *oiliness* 562.1, *fatness* 579.5

Adirondack Furniture Styles 101

Adirondack Mountains Mountains and Hills 569

adit *access* 691.3, *entrance* 706.5

adjacency *juxtaposition* 586.4, *interface* 616.1, *nearness* 803.2

adjacent *triangle* 6.41, *contiguous* 216.8, *juxtaposed* 586.9, *interfacial* 616.4, *nearby* 803.4
adjacently *beside* 586.20, *interfacially* 616.7
adjectival *of grammar* 5.41
adjectival clause *or* **phrase** *clause* 5.31
adjective *part of speech* 5.30, 760.7, *additional item* 748.3
adjoin 216.11; *juxtapose* 586.14, *interface* 616.5
adjoined *additional* 748.8
adjoining *contiguous* 216.8, *juxtaposed* 586.9, *interfacial* 616.4
adjoining section *interface* 616.1
adjoint *mathematical function* 6.27
adjourn *defer* 604.15, *delay* 658.13, *pause* 668.13
adjourned *deferred* 604.9, *held up* 658.6, *recessed* 668.8
adjournment *deferment* 604.3, *delay* 658.3
adjudge *judge* 341.10
adjudicate *try a case* 54.28, *judge* 341.10, *rule* 780.12
adjudication *legal justice* 53.4, *verdict* 54.18, 341.2, *judgment* 341.1, *ruling* 780.2
adjudicator *judge* 341.5
adjunct *equipment* 103.6, *relatedness* 727.1, *additional item* 748.3, *additional* 748.7, *concomitant* 794.4
adjunctive *additional* 748.8, *conjunctive* 752.12
adjunctly *additionally* 748.15
adjuration *petition* 505.2
adjuratory *requesting* 505.7
adjure *attest* 189.22, *petition* 505.11
adjust 721.23; *conciliate* 74.10, *make clothing* 100.44, *tune* 172.14, *modify* 340.13, *prepare for action* 388.18, *compromise* 461.7, *moderate* 521.7, *be adaptable* 546.9, *size* 579.17, *make regular* 663.9, *change* 665.14, *cause change* 665.16, *orient* 697.15, *agree* 735.23, *equalize* 740.12, *counterbalance* 743.8, *rearrange* 767.20, *conform* 781.11, *make conform* 781.13, *rectify* 807.22, *repair* 809.10
adjustability *adaptability* 546.2
adjustable *type of bed* 101.9, *adaptive* 546.6, *agreeing* 735.13, *conformable* 781.7
adjustable-rate mortgage *mortgage* 476.6
adjustably *in accord* 735.33
adjusted 721.14; *modified* 340.9, *treated* 388.12, *compromising* 461.4, *adaptive* 546.6, *changed* 665.10, *counterbalanced* 743.6, *rearranged* 767.14
adjusting *adaptive* 546.6
adjustment 721.5; *pacification* 74.1, *modification* 340.5, *compromise* 461.1, *moderation* 521.1, *change* 665.1, *orientation* 697.3, *agreement* 735.3, *equalization* 740.4, *counterbalance* 743.2, *pliancy* 781.3, *rectification* 807.8, *repair* 809.1
adjustment disorders *mental disorder* 108.8
adjust the clock *keep time* 646.12
adjutant *helper* 825.12
adjuvant *helper* 825.12, *helping* 825.16
Adler *psychiatrist* 108.34

Adlerian psychology *Psychological Theories, Schools* 108
ad lib *enough* 97.10, *at will* 372.16, *unpremeditation* 389.2, *improvisation* 396.1
ad-lib *act* 136.34, *spontaneous* 389.6, *improvise* 389.15, 396.6, *improvised* 396.4, *extempore* 396.7
ad-libbed *dramatized* 136.32
ad-libber *actor* 136.25, *improviser* 396.3
ad-libbing *improvisation* 396.1
ad libitum *enough* 97.10, *at will* 372.16
ad libitum *Musical Terms and Expression Marks* 140
adman *persuader* 178.9
admeasure *measure* 589.20
admeasured *measured* 589.16
admeasurement *measurement* 589.1
administer *govern* 49.26, *wield authority* 52.16, *practice medicine* 107.32, *manage* 126.10, *direct* 412.16, 780.14, *regionalize* 564.15
administer an oath *attest* 189.22
administer correction *punish* 454.22
administer justice *judge* 53.32, 54.31
administer the sacraments *offer worship* 504.16
administer to *serve* 69.11
administrate *wield authority* 52.16, *direct* 412.16
administration *government* 49.1, *governance* 52.6, *management* 126.1, *management board* 126.2, *treatment* 399.11, *action* 412.1, *authority* 780.6
administrative 564.13; *governmental* 49.24, *authoritative* 52.9, *managerial* 126.9, *effective* 412.10, *legal* 780.8
administrative assistant *office assistant* 69.6, *deputy* 80.1, *clerical worker* 123.5
administrative center *administrative headquarters* 564.5
administrative control *directorship* 126.5
administrative headquarters 564.5
administratively *governmentally* 49.27, *legitimately* 52.19, *managerially* 126.13
administrative management *management system* 126.3
administrative receiver *collector* 473.7
administrative region 564.4
administrative unit *military organization* 58.4
administrator *governor* 49.23, *manager* 126.7, *operator* 412.7, 509.5
admirable *desirable* 288.11, *wondrous* 294.9, *praiseworthy* 437.12, *good* 445.10
admirably *desirably* 288.24, *wondrously* 294.18
Admiral *US Military Ranks* 58, *military title* 72.8
admiral *military leader* 68.10, *person in command* 425.5
admiralty *navy* 77.18
Admiralty chart [Brit] *oceanography* 571.5, *navigational aid* 690.6
admiralty court *type of court* 54.9
Admiralty Islands *Islands* 572

admiration 435.2, 437.2; *liking* 290.1, *wonder* 294.1, *marvel* 294.3, *love* 299.1
admire 437.15; *idolize* 83.16, *like* 290.8, *wonder* 294.12, *love* 299.21, *respect* 435.13, *revere* 435.14
admired *liked* 290.6, *beloved* 299.19, *respected* 435.10, *praiseworthy* 437.12
admirer *idolater* 83.7, *approver* 437.7, *supporter* 605.9
admiring *liking* 290.4, *wondering* 294.7, *loving* 299.15, *reverent* 435.9, *approving* 437.9
admiringly 290.11; *wonderingly* 294.16, *lovingly* 299.29, *approvingly* 437.21
admissibility *admittance* 708.1, *inclusion* 763.1, *possibleness* 836.2
admissible *vindicable* 441.9, *permitting* 502.5, *admissive* 708.8, *included* 763.4, *possible* 836.5
admission *divulgence* 180.2, *avowal* 189.7, *apology* 313.2, *legal evidence* 339.4, *assent* 346.1, *reception* 473.4, *entry* 706.1, *right of entry* 706.4, *admittance* 708.1, *inclusion* 763.1
admission fee *fee* 494.3
admission ticket *permit* 502.3
admissive 708.8; *permitting* 502.5
admissory *admissive* 708.8
admit 180.11, 708.12; *avow* 189.27, *apologize* 313.8, *assent* 346.6, *receive someone* 473.14, *receive* 492.7, *enroll* 706.16, *install* 710.15, *include* 763.5
admit defeat *submit* 421.4, *stop* 668.10
admit no responsibility *exempt oneself* 434.12
admit of *include* 763.5
admittance 708.1; *reception* 473.4, *right of entry* 706.4, *inclusion* 763.1
admitted *disclosed* 180.5, *avowed* 189.19, *rightful* 429.9, *received* 473.11, *included* 763.4
admittedly *avowedly* 189.34
admitting *reception* 473.4
admix *mix* 751.12
admixture 751.5; *addition* 748.1, *mixture* 751.1
admonish *advise* 176.9, *dissuade* 179.7, *caution* 287.15, *condemn* 438.18, *punish* 454.22, *warn* 814.8
admonished *condemned* 438.11
admonisher *adviser* 176.5, *warner* 814.5
admonishing *advisory* 176.7, *condemning* 438.10
admonishingly *advisorily* 176.12, *dissuasively* 179.12
admonishment *condemnation* 438.2, *warning* 814.1
admonition *advice* 176.1, *dissuasion* 179.1, *warning* 287.5, 814.1, *condemnation* 438.2, *punishment* 454.1
admonitorily *advisorily* 176.12, *dissuasively* 179.12, *warningly* 814.11
admonitory *advisory* 176.7, *dissuasive* 179.4, *warning* 287.10, 814.6, *censuring* 438.12, *punitive* 454.18
adnate *of fungi* 47.19
ad nauseam *diffusely* 199.7, *boringly* 296.10, *at length* 590.15, *repeatedly* 797.22

adnexed *of fungi* 47.19
ado *exertion* 122.4, *activity* 414.1, *tumult* 684.2, *disruption* 766.7, *commotion* 768.5
adobe *building materials* 104.2, *material* 129.2, *industrial ceramics* 129.6, *wall covering* 613.12
adolescence *bodily development* 19.17, *youth* 26.1, *age* 27.1
adolescence medicine *Medical Specialties* 107
adolescent *person* 18.8, *young person* 26.7, *young* 26.11
Adonai *God* 82.6
Adonis *Planets and Their Satellites* 7, *boyfriend* 32.4, *attractive male* 529.6, *charmer* 700.6
Adonis-like *attractive* 529.8
adopt 476.11, 692.14; *select* 382.12, *use* 393.9, *approve* 437.14, *welcome* 708.14
adoptability *adoption* 476.2
adoptable *adoption* 476.2
adopt a laissez-faire attitude *be permissive* 502.7
adopted 692.10; *selected* 382.11, *approved* 437.8, *borrowed* 476.8, *adoptive* 476.9
adopting *adoptive* 476.9
adoption 476.2, 692.2; *selection* 382.1, *approval* 437.1
adoptive 476.9
adorability *lovability* 299.5
adorable *likable* 290.7, *lovable* 299.20
adorably *likably* 290.12, *lovably* 299.31
adoration *religiousness* 81.2, *worship* 83.1, *liking* 290.1, *love* 299.1, *admiration* 435.2
adore *revere* 81.26, 435.14, *worship* 83.15, *like* 290.8, *love* 299.21
adored *worshiped* 83.14, *beloved* 299.19
adorer *worshiper* 83.6, *lover* 299.11
adoring *worshipful* 83.12, *liking* 290.4, *loving* 299.15, *reverent* 435.9
adoringly *worshipfully* 83.17, *admiringly* 290.11, *lovingly* 299.29
adorn *beautify* 529.12, 530.14, 807.20, *decorate* 532.11, *ornament* 532.12
adorned *beautified* 530.12, *ornate* 532.10
adornment *decoration* 532.1, *ornament* 532.7, *beautification* 807.7
adown [Arch] *down* 714.19
Adrastea *Planets and Their Satellites* 7
adrenal *of a secretion* 24.5
adrenaline *hormone* 12.16
adrenocorticoid *Human Hormones* 12
adrenocorticotropic hormone *or* **adrenocorticotropin** *Human Hormones* 12
Adriatic Sea *Oceans and Seas* 571
adrift *sailing* 150.25, *offshore* 150.35, *continentally* 572.13, *astray* 698.27, *unjoined* 753.9, *in isolation* 753.24, *divergent* 776.11
adroit *skillful* 127.10, *proficient* 445.15
adroitly *skillfully* 127.16, *proficiently* 445.22
adroitness *manual skill* 127.2, *proficiency* 445.5
adscititious *additional* 748.8
adsorb *absorb* 11.40, 708.19

adsorbed *absorbed* 11.34
adsorbent *sponge* 708.7, *absorbent* 708.11
adsorption *process* 11.15, *surface chemistry* 11.20, *absorption* 708.6
a due *Musical Terms and Expression Marks* 140
adulate *worship* 83.15, *love* 299.21, *praise* 437.16, *flatter* 439.12
adulated *worshiped* 83.14
adulating *worshipful* 83.12
adulation *worship* 83.1, *love* 299.1, *admiration* 435.2, *praise* 437.3, *flattery* 439.1
adulator *worshiper* 83.6, *flatterer* 439.6
adulatory *reverent* 435.9, *approving* 437.9, *flattering* 439.7
adult 27.11; *person* 18.8, *older person* 27.7, *obscene* 112.9
adult education *educational system* 48.2
adult-education center *type of school* 48.12
adulterate *dilute* 220.7, 557.30, *change* 512.12, *weaken* 517.13, *make sparse* 541.5, *change for the worse* 665.3, *water down* 716.17, *mix* 751.12, *make worse* 808.17
adulterated *misrepresentative* 193.14, *tasteless* 220.4, *rarefied* 541.4, *diluted* 557.22, 751.9, *unauthentic* 722.9
adulteration 188.2; *tastelessness* 220.1, *weakness* 517.1, *rarefaction* 541.2, *dilution* 557.5, *change for the worse* 665.5, *unauthenticity* 722.4, *mixture* 751.1, *imperfection* 806.1, *impairment* 808.7
adulterer *hypocrite* 192.9, *sexually immoral person* 432.8
adulteress *sexually immoral person* 432.8
adulterous *dishonorable* 192.14, *unchaste* 432.10
adulterously *dishonorably* 192.28, *promiscuously* 432.19
adultery *sexual intercourse* 20.9, *divorce court* 66.3, *dishonorableness* 192.3, *love affair* 299.9, *fornication* 432.3
adulthood 27.2; *bodily development* 19.17, *age* 27.1
adultness *adulthood* 27.2
adumbrate *describe* 202.15, *make dark* 247.10, *propound* 359.9
adumbration *quietness* 844.4
advance 467.3, 679.3; *educate* 48.22, *military call* 183.9, *propound* 359.9, *attack* 418.17, *better* 445.17, *earnings* 467.5, *improve* 467.18, *lending* 475.1, *lend* 475.6, *borrowing* 476.1, *pay* 489.6, *tentative offer* 504.2, *offer* 504.11, *be an instrument* 511.7, *give moral support* 605.18, *avant-garde* 652.16, *continue* 669.8, *determine* 675.11, *forward motion* 677.4, 679.1, *directional* 677.13, *be in motion* 677.14, *go forward* 679.8, *further* 679.13, 825.30, *propel* 696.15, *approach* 702.2, *arrival* 704.1, *upturn* 713.20, *increase* 746.1, 746.6, *part* 760.1, *be useful* 801.9, *be convenient* 803.5, *promotion* 807.5, *promote* 807.18, *get better* 807.21, *make easy* 823.15, *financial assistance* 825.6, *finance* 825.31, *do well* 845.12, *be prosperous* 847.6
advance *or* **advanced** *premature* 657.10
advance against *attack* 418.17

advance by leaps and bounds *maintain progress* 679.14
advance camp *climbing expedition* 161.2
advanced 713.16; *ski* 162.27, *new* 652.9, *avant-garde* 652.16, *forward* 679.6
advanced gas-cooled reactor (AGR) *nuclear power production* 514.10
advanced hour *late hour* 658.2
advanced in years *aged* 27.15, *old* 653.10
advanced run *ski run* 162.2
advanced thinker *modern person* 652.8
advanced years *old age* 27.5
advance earnings *earnings* 467.5
advance guard *warner* 814.5
advance man *producer* 136.28
advancement *education* 48.1, *surgery* 107.15, *lending* 475.1, *instrumentality* 511.1, *moral support* 605.7, *advance* 679.3, *ascendancy* 713.5, *increase* 746.1, *promotion* 807.5, *furtherance* 825.8
advance notice *notice* 358.3, *antecedence* 657.5, *warning* 814.1
advance on *improve* 467.18
advance one's own interests *be selfish* 444.6
advance party *armed force* 77.10
advance payment *type of payment* 489.3
advance to meet *greet* 410.11, *receive someone* 473.14
advance to the rear *retreat* 680.2, 680.17
advancing 702.8; *lending* 475.1, *instrumental* 511.4, *directional* 677.13, *forward* 679.6, *approaching* 704.10, *improving* 807.14
advancing on royalties *lending* 475.1
advancing on salary *lending* 475.1
advantage 618.4, 744.3; *soccer play* 163.5, *tennis terms* 165.5, *usefulness* 399.2, *tactics* 399.12, *welfare* 445.2, *gain* 467.1, *influence* 512.1, *inequality* 741.1, *priority* 769.2, *benefit* 801.4, 801.10, *convenience* 803.1, *be convenient* 803.5, *help* 825.1, *further* 825.30
advantaged 618.7
advantageous *favorable* 62.8, *desirable* 288.11, *useful* 393.7, *beneficial* 445.11, 825.20, *profitable* 489.13, 801.8, *convenient* 803.3, *successful* 845.8
advantageously *favorably* 62.15, *desirably* 288.24, *usefully* 393.15, 801.12, *all right* 429.19, *well* 445.19, *gainfully* 467.24, *at an advantage* 618.12, *superbly* 744.22, *helpfully* 825.32, *successfully* 845.19
advantageousness *helpfulness* 825.10
advection *atmospheric process* 9.9
advection fog *fog* 9.32
advection frost *frost* 9.25
advective *atmospheric* 9.40
Advent *Christian Holy Days and Seasons* 85, *seasons* 654.2
advent *birth* 264.2, *arrival* 704.1
Adventist churches *Christian Groups* 81
adventitious *extraneous* 610.12, 724.8, *additional* 748.8, *chance* 842.10

adventitious bud *bud* 41.8
adventitiously *extraneously* 610.19, 724.16
adventitiousness *extraneousness* 610.6
adventitious root *root* 41.7
adventure *movie type* 137.3, *venture* 390.2, *undertaking* 391.1, *undertake* 391.7, *travel* 686.11, *unreliability* 841.7
adventurer *militarist* 77.3, *rash move* 286.4, *curious person* 321.3, *rash person* 353.4, *attempter* 390.3, *person who undertakes* 391.3
adventure story *story* 139.4
adventurous 284.12; *reckless* 286.6, *curious* 321.5, *enterprising* 391.5
adventurously 284.20; *recklessly* 286.10, *curiously* 321.9, *ambitiously* 390.10, *enterprisingly* 391.11
adventurousness 284.4; *recklessness* 286.2
adventurous person *attempter* 390.3
adverb *part of speech* 5.30, 760.7, *additional item* 748.3
adverbial *of grammar* 5.41
adverbial clause *or* **phrase** *clause* 5.31
adverbially *grammatically* 5.48
adversarial *combative* 77.32, *dissenting* 506.6, *discordant* 828.12
adversary *hostile person* 63.5, *combatant* 77.1, *contender* 422.13, *opponent* 828.10
adversative *contrary* 828.13
adverse 848.10; *presageful* 358.13, *refusing* 375.9, *critical* 438.13, *disunited* 753.10, *inconvenient* 804.5, *oppositional* 828.11
adverse circumstances *adversity* 848.1
adverse criticism *criticism* 438.4
adverse health 848.5
adversely 848.16; *disunitedly* 753.25, *opposingly* 828.22
adversity 117.2, 848.1; *affliction* 454.9, *critical situation* 824.6, *conflict* 828.3
advertise *publicize* 173.18, 178.19, *predict* 358.14, *show* 404.24, *offer* 504.11, *make important* 799.14, *display* 843.13, *reveal* 843.14
advertised *communicated* 169.15, *broadcast* 172.12, *publicized* 173.14, *offered* 504.8, *displayed* 843.8
advertise for *publicize* 173.18
advertisement 173.9; *public information* 170.5, *publicity* 178.7, *sign* 183.1, *selling* 482.1, *showplace* 843.4
advertise oneself *show off* 404.26
advertiser *publicizer* 173.11, *persuader* 178.9, *motivator* 508.6, *displayer* 843.7
advertising *public relations (PR)* 173.8, *publicity* 178.7, *inducement* 508.2, *manifestation* 843.2
advertising account executive *publicizer* 173.11
advertising agent *publicizer* 173.11
advice 176.1; *education* 48.1, *information* 170.1, *inside information* 170.4, *news source* 171.4, *persuasion* 178.1, *warning* 287.1, 814.1, *inducement* 508.2, *support* 825.2
advice against *communication* 176.3

advice boat *Sailing Ships and Boats* 690
advice column *news story* 171.3
advice for *communication* 176.3
advisability *desirability* 288.7, *convenience* 803.1
advisable 176.8; *warning* 287.10, 814.6, *expedient* 288.12, *preferential* 382.10, *useful* 801.5, *convenient* 803.3
advisably 176.13; *wisely* 4.28, *expediently* 288.25
advise 176.9, 825.27; *educate* 48.22, *practice medicine* 107.32, *treat* 115.17, *direct* 126.11, *inform* 170.11, *persuade* 178.15, *caution* 287.15, *propound* 359.9, *influence* 508.11, *warn* 814.8
advise against *advise* 176.9, *dissuade* 179.7, *warn* 814.8
advised *informed* 170.9, *deliberate* 384.5, *warned* 814.7
advisedly *wisely* 4.28, *educationally* 48.25
advisement *consultation* 176.4
adviser 176.5, 825.14; *sage* 4.11, *educator* 48.4, *lawyer* 54.5, *mediator* 75.2, *representative* 75.3, *expert* 127.9, *informer* 170.8, *news source* 171.4, *motivator* 178.11, 508.6, *judge* 341.5, *meddler* 414.12, *warner* 814.5
advising *advice* 176.1, *advisory* 176.7
advisorily 176.12
advisory 176.7; *educational* 48.17, *mediatory* 75.5, *informative* 170.10, *communication* 176.3, *discussing* 210.9, *warning* 287.10
advisory body 176.6
Advisory Conciliation and Arbitration Service (ACAS) [Brit] *negotiator* 460.4
advocacy *exhortation* 178.2, *approval* 437.1, *inducement* 508.2, *moral support* 605.7, *patronage* 825.9
advocate *politician* 50.7, *lawyer* 54.5, *litigate* 54.27, *adviser* 176.5, 825.14, *advise* 176.9, 825.27, *persuader* 178.9, *persuade* 178.15, *affirmer* 189.9, *speaker* 205.12, *approver* 437.7, *approve* 437.14, *vindicator* 441.5, *influence* 508.11, *supporter* 605.9, *give moral support* 605.18
advocated *approved* 437.8
advocating *recommending* 437.11
advocative *supportive* 605.11
advocatory *supportive* 605.11
adz *woodworking tool* 131.6
adz *or* **adze** *sharp-edged thing* 549.6
aechmea *Flowers* 42
a-effect *dramaturgy* 136.6
Aegean art *Western Art Styles* 133
Aegean Sea *Oceans and Seas* 571
aegis *patronage* 810.7, 825.9
aeolian *windy* 9.42
Aeolian mode *mode* 140.17
Aeolus *wind god* 9.16
Aepyornis *extinct bird* 36.14
aerate 556.24, 558.20; *air* 94.7, *practice hygiene* 116.4, *whisk* 558.23
aerated *lightening* 539.6, *gassy* 556.19, *bubbly* 558.18
aerating *lightening* 539.6
aeration 558.11; *refreshment* 94.1, *lightening* 539.2, *vaporization* 556.9, *ventilation* 558.6
aerator *ventilator* 558.7

aerial 558.14; *floor exercise* 157.4, *ski* 162.27, *airy* 556.15, 558.12, *high* 596.7, *aviatic* 689.10
aerial bombardment *air attack* 418.4
aeriality *aerialness* 556.8
aerialness 556.8
aerial perspective *treatment* 143.6
aerial photography *photographic specialties* 132.2
aerial reconnaissance *aviation* 689.1
aerial root *root* 41.7
aerial tramway *cableway* 691.11
aerial warfare *blockading* 76.22
aerie *dwelling* 36.4, *natural habitat* 60.16, *shelter* 812.4
aeriferous *airy* 558.12
aerification *vaporization* 556.9
aeriform *airy* 558.12
aerify *aerate* 556.24, 558.20
aerily 556.26
aeroacrophobia *Phobias* 283
aeroballistic *aviatic* 689.10
aeroballistics *aeronautics* 689.2
aerobatic *aviatic* 689.10
aerobatics *Sporting Activities* 145, *aviation* 689.1
aerobe *living organism* 13.10
aerobic *physiological* 13.29
aerobic dancing *Dancing Types* 135
aerobic respiration *respiration* 12.24
aerobics *health improvement* 113.3, *Hobbies and Pastimes* 167, *bodily movement* 677.11, *bodily improvement* 807.10
aerodrome [Brit] *airport* 689.4
aerodynamic *physical* 10.70, *aerostatic* 556.20, *aviatic* 689.10
aerodynamically *physically* 10.78, *aerostatically* 556.27, *aeronautically* 689.17
aerodynamics *classical physics* 10.2, *aerostatics* 556.11
aerolite *meteor* 7.21
aerology *meteorology* 9.1
aeromechanical *aviatic* 689.10
aeromedical *aviatic* 689.10
aerometer *relative density* 540.3, *vaporimeter* 556.13, *Fields of Measurement* 589
aerometric *metric* 589.19
aerometry *Fields of Measurement* 589
aeronausiphobia *Phobias* 283
aeronaut *descender* 714.8
aeronautic *aviatic* 689.10
aeronautical *aviatic* 689.10
aeronautical engineer *mechanical engineer* 14.4
aeronautical engineering *mechanical engineering* 14.3, *aeronautics* 689.2
aeronautically 689.17
aeronautics 689.2
aeropause *flight* 689.5
aerophagiaphobia *Phobias* 283
aerophobia *Phobias* 283
aerophone *musical instrument* 142.1
aeroplane [Brit] *aircraft* 689.3
aerosol *phase* 11.13, *vaporizer* 556.10, *sprinkler* 557.12
aerosol spray *vaporizer* 556.10
aerospace *empty space* 563.2, *aviatic* 689.10
aerospace engineer *mechanical engineer* 14.4
aerospace engineering *mechanical engineering* 14.3
aerospace research 7.27
aerosphere 558.2

aerostatic 556.20
aerostatically 556.27
aerostatics 556.11
aerothermodynamic *aviatic* 689.10
aerothermodynamics *aeronautics* 689.2
aery *airy* 556.15, 558.12
Aeschylean tragedy *tragedy* 136.10
Aesculapius *Deities* 82
Aesir *deity* 82.1
aesthesia *sensitivity* 267.1
aesthete *Philosophical Schools of Thought* 4, *refined person* 534.4
aesthetic *Philosophical Schools of Thought* 4, *of a philosophy* 4.13, *artistic* 133.7, *picturesque* 529.9, *refined* 534.5
aesthetically *artistically* 133.10, *tastefully* 534.9
aesthetically pleasing *picturesque* 529.9
aestheticism *Philosophical Schools of Thought* 4, *Western Literary Groups* 139
aesthetic movement *Western Art Styles* 133
afar *distantly* 585.11
Afer *or* Africus *wind god* 9.16
affability *amiability* 271.3, *benevolence* 305.1, *sociability* 407.2, 408.1, *social success* 408.3, *courtesy* 410.1
affable *likable* 271.6, *benevolent* 305.7, *sociable* 407.7, 408.11, *courteous* 410.6
affably *benevolently* 305.13, *sociably* 408.19, *courteously* 410.13
affair *love affair* 299.9, *matter of interest* 328.3, *undertaking* 391.1, *line of duty* 433.3, *business* 509.3
affaire d'amour [Fr] *love affair* 299.9
affaire de coeur [Fr] *love affair* 299.9
affair of honor *duel* 422.12
affair of the heart *love affair* 299.9
affairs *treatment* 399.11, *deed* 412.2, *business relations* 727.4
affannato *Musical Terms and Expression Marks* 140
affannoso *Musical Terms and Expression Marks* 140
affect 676.7; *be untruthful* 192.20, *disdain* 297.14, *move to compassion* 308.9, *be affected* 367.4, *conduct oneself* 399.17, *influence* 512.11, *tend* 513.5, *cause change* 665.16, *relate to* 727.9, *be important* 799.13
affectability *sensitivity* 267.1
affectable *sensitive* 267.3
affectation 367.1; *ungenuineness* 192.2, *arrogance* 297.2, *supposition* 359.1, *mode of behavior* 399.2, *boastfulness* 502.6, *deed* 412.2, *style* 537.1
affected 367.3; *sick* 114.24, *unskilled* 128.5, *ungenuine* 192.13, *arrogant* 297.9, *cocky* 402.11, *inelegant* 528.6, *ornate* 532.10, *designed* 536.6, *styled* 537.6, *exaggerated* 712.9
affectedly 367.5; *arrogantly* 297.18, *cockily* 402.19
affectedness *affectation* 367.1
affecting *emotive* 266.13, *pitiful* 308.5, *appealing* 512.9
affectingly *with feeling* 266.18

affection *friendship* 62.1, *liking* 290.1, *love* 299.1, *demonstrativeness* 331.2, *admiration* 437.2
affectionate *friendly* 62.5, *liking* 290.4, *loving* 299.15, *amorous* 299.18, *benevolent* 305.7, *demonstrative* 331.10, *sociable* 408.11
affectionately *amicably* 62.13, *admiringly* 290.11, *lovingly* 299.29, *amorously* 299.30, *benevolently* 305.13, *demonstratively* 331.21, *sociably* 408.19
affectionateness *lovingness* 299.4
affections *feelings* 266.1
affective disorder *neurosis* 108.9, *mood disorder* 108.12, *psychiatric disease* 114.21
affenpinscher *Breeds of Dogs* 35
affettuoso *Musical Terms and Expression Marks* 140
affiance *marry* 64.19
affianced *marriageable* 64.17, *someone promised* 458.7, *promised* 458.8
affidavit *pretrial proceedings* 54.13, *certificate* 185.2, *attestation* 189.2, *legal evidence* 339.4
affiliate *form an alliance* 735.25, *join* 827.17
affiliated *related* 727.6, *allied* 735.15, *associating* 827.11
affiliation *sociability* 408.1, *relatedness* 727.1, *alliance* 735.5, *association* 827.6
affine geometry *geometry* 6.32
affine transformation *transformation* 6.46
affinity 733.3; *intimacy* 62.4, *liking* 290.1, *agreement* 462.1, *attitude* 513.2, *attraction* 700.1, *relatedness* 727.1, *compatibility* 735.4
affirm 189.21; *legislate* 53.31, *believe* 87.9, *admit* 180.11, *speak* 205.17, *state* 329.13, *prove* 331.17, *testify* 336.10, *give evidence* 339.12, *assent* 346.6, *suppose* 359.8, *mean* 361.13, *conflict* 422.26, *agree with* 462.10, *consent* 735.28, *make certain* 840.14
affirmance *affirmation* 189.1
affirmant *affirmer* 189.9
affirmation 189.1; *mathematical logic* 6.60, *lawmaking* 53.11, *divulgence* 180.2, *emphasis* 200.1, *utterance* 205.10, *line of argument* 329.3, *proof* 331.4, *evidence* 336.3, *assent* 346.1, *promise* 458.1, *agreement* 462.1, *consent* 735.8, *importance* 799.1, *confirmation* 840.3, *manifestation* 843.2
affirmative 189.10; *affirmation* 189.1, *emphatic* 200.3, *yes* 346.2, *assenting* 346.4, *linguistic* 361.9, *agreement* 462.1, *agreeing* 462.6, *consenting* 735.18
affirmative! *yes!* 189.36
affirmative action *equalization* 740.4, *equal opportunity* 831.2
affirmatively 189.29; *unanimously* 346.8, *agreeably* 462.14, *with consent* 735.38
affirmativeness *confirmation* 840.3
affirmatory *affirmative* 189.10
Affirmed *Notable Horses* 159
affirmed 189.11; *logical* 329.9, *proven* 331.13, *verified* 336.7, *consenting* 735.18
affirmer 189.9

affirming *confirming* 189.16, *consenting* 735.18
affirmingly *confirmingly* 189.32, *with consent* 735.38
affirm the contrary *negate* 190.16
affix *part of speech* 5.30, *additional item* 748.3, *add* 748.11, *link* 752.18
affixing *language type* 5.11, *of language* 5.35
affix to *cause to adhere* 755.10
affixture *addition* 748.1
afflatus *inspiration* 360.2
afflict 117.16, 301.16; *be evil* 446.10, *punish* 454.22
afflicted 301.11; *miserable* 117.12, *feeling pain* 215.6
afflicting 117.11
affliction 301.1, 454.9; *illness* 114.2, *infection* 114.7, *pain* 215.1, *misfortune* 301.6, *adversity* 848.1
affluence *wealth* 485.1, *flow* 570.4, *influx* 706.2, *successfulness* 845.3, *prosperity* 847.1
affluent *well-off* 467.12, *wealthy* 485.8, *tributary* 570.2, *flowing* 570.7, *prosperous* 847.5
affluently *gainfully* 467.24, *wealthily* 485.16, *fluently* 570.13, *prosperously* 847.9
affluent society *prosperity* 847.1
afflux *flow* 570.4, *influx* 706.2
affluxion *influx* 706.2
afford *provision* 89.9, *have enough* 97.7, *expend* 491.11, *grant* 735.30
affordability *cheapness* 497.1
affordable *cheap* 497.9
afforded *granted* 735.20
afford sanctuary *protect* 810.10
afforestation *forestry* 43.5
afforested *wooded* 43.12
affray *fight* 422.9, *disruption* 766.7
affrettando *Musical Terms and Expression Marks* 140
affright [Arch] *fear* 283.1, *be afraid* 283.14, *frighten* 283.17
affront *offense* 302.2, *offend* 302.15, *insult* 400.6, 436.5, 436.21, *disdain* 400.16, *be discourteous* 411.7, *defy* 416.7
affronted *offended* 302.9
affronting *maddening* 302.12
affrontive [Arch] *derisive* 400.12
affusion *baptism* 85.6, *watering* 557.8, *sprinkle* 559.5
afghan *body covering* 613.3
Afghan hound *Breeds of Dogs* 35
Afghanistan *Countries* 566
aficionado *idolater* 83.7
afield *distantly* 585.11
aflame *bright* 246.14
afloat *nautically* 571.10, 690.17, *nautical* 690.14
afoot *problematically* 328.12, *in preparation* 388.8, *busy* 414.15
aforementioned *preceding* 769.9
aforesaid *preceding* 769.9
aforethought *intentional* 374.7
aforetime *historically* 3.17, *in the past* 651.20
a fortiori *dialectical* 4.16
afraid *frightened* 283.9, *cowardly* 285.4, *shy* 409.7
afraid of company *shy* 409.7
afraid of one's shadow *fearful* 283.17
A-frame *angle* 628.1
A-framed *angular* 628.7
afreet *evil spirit* 446.4
afresh *again* 652.22, 797.23
Africa *hot place* 217.5, *world region* 564.6, *landmass* 572.1
African American *race* 1.5

Africanism *regional pronunciation* 205.7
African lion hound Breeds of Dogs 35
African Methodist Episcopal churches Christian Groups 81
African Methodist Episcopal Zion churches Christian Groups 81
African violet Flowers 42
Afrikander Breeds of Cattle 16
afrit *evil spirit* 446.4
Afro *coiffure* 530.8
Afro-American *race* 1.5, *racial* 1.12
Afro-Americanism *regional pronunciation* 205.7
Afroasiatic *language family* 5.12
Afro-Caribbean *race* 1.5, *racial* 1.12
aft *sailing* 150.25, *behind* 622.8
after 650.14, 770.14; *aim at* 385.15, *pursuant to* 385.17, *behind* 622.8
after a fashion *how* 691.16
after ages *future time* 650.1
after a time *at length* 590.15
after a while *later* 658.16
aftercare *treatment* 107.14, *therapy* 115.12
afterdamp *miasma* 556.3
after dark *nightly* 656.6
after death 29.9; *fatally* 29.18, *motionlessly* 678.9
after-dinner *culinary* 91.9, *at ease* 819.2
after-dinner speaker *speaker* 205.12
after-dinner speech *public speaking* 205.11
aftereffect *effect* 676.1, *additional item* 748.3, *remainder* 750.1, *subsequence* 770.4
afterglow *remainder* 750.1, *subsequence* 770.4
after him! 385.19
afterimage *image* 187.3, *spectacle* 264.6
afterlife *after death* 29.9, *judgment day* 341.4, *nonmaterial world* 525.1, *life without end* 644.2
after mast *rear end* 622.4
aftermath *effect* 676.1, *subsequence* 770.4, *sequel* 770.5, *consequence* 774.3
aftermost *behind* 622.8
afternoon 655.5; *daytime* 655.1, *daily* 655.6
after noon *daily* 655.8
afternoon tea *meal* 92.8, *drink occasion* 93.14, *social gathering* 408.4, *afternoon* 655.5
afternoon things *afternoon* 655.5
afterpain *physical condition* 215.2
afterpiece *play part* 136.8
aftershaft *plumage* 36.7
aftershave *source of fragrance* 226.2
aftershock *seismic activity* 8.24
aftertaste *taste* 219.1, *subsequence* 770.4
after this fashion *how* 691.16
afterthought *image* 187.3, *vacillation* 380.3, *back matter* 622.3, *delay* 658.3, *subsequence* 770.4
afterward *after* 650.14, 770.14
afterword *back matter* 622.3, *appendage* 748.4
again 652.22, 797.23; *repeatedly* 21.18, *at what time* 639.17, *twice* 789.18
again and again *frequently* 661.7, *repeatedly* 797.22

against *censuring* 438.12, *counter* 510.8, *defensively* 701.12
against one's will *unwillingly* 375.17, *dependently* 832.13
against the clock *hastily* 818.7
against the grain *unwillingly* 375.17, *roughly* 544.13, *backward* 680.23
against the law *illegally* 53.34, *guiltily* 53.38
against the nap *roughly* 544.13
against the rules *violating* 466.8, *unconventional* 782.14
against the tide *contrariwise* 828.24
against the wind *directionally* 697.20, *difficultly* 824.23
Agama *other text* 81.19
agamous *celibate* 67.6
Agaña American States 564
agapanthus Flowers 42
agape *religious festival* 85.13, *wondering* 294.7, *love* 299.1, *open* 583.10
agar *polysaccharide* 12.5, *algal product* 47.15, *semiliquid* 561.7
agarics *fungi* 47.3
agate *variegated thing* 263.5
agateware Ceramics 129
agave Flowers 42
age 27.1, 27.16; *time period* 641.2, *long duration* 642.3, *day* 646.4, *elderliness* 653.2, *grow old* 653.16, *be converted* 670.12, *disintegrate* 808.15
aged 27.15; *old* 653.10
age discrimination *social discrimination* 337.4
agedly *maturely* 27.18
agedness *old age* 27.5
age group *social organization* 2.5, *group* 59.8, *contemporary* 649.3
ageism *social discrimination* 337.4, *unfair treatment* 342.4
ageist *aged* 27.15, *bigot* 337.7, *discriminatory* 337.11, *unjust* 342.7
ageless *timeless* 640.3
agelessness *timelessness* 640.1
agelong 644.5
agency *instrumentality* 102.2, 511.1, *workplace* 124.1, *management* 126.1, *representative* 187.7, *action* 412.1, *operation* 509.1, *instrument* 511.2, *council* 833.4
agenda *issue* 328.2, *predetermination* 384.1, *plan* 387.1, *division* 577.6, *list of dates* 785.6
agent 80.3, 123.15; *lawyer* 54.5, *representative* 75.3, 187.7, *manager* 126.7, *producer* 136.28, *book publishing personnel* 174.12, *motivator* 178.11, *vocal agent* 412.7, 509.5, *salesperson* 482.8, *merchant* 482.10, *assistant* 511.3, *coverer* 613.18, *changer* 665.9, *substitute* 672.2, *contributory cause* 675.3, *person who joins* 752.9, *commissioner* 833.5
agential *commissioned* 833.6
agent of destruction 523.7
Agent Orange *chemical warfare* 76.5, *agent of destruction* 523.7
agent provocateur *motivator* 178.11, 508.6, *troublemaker* 427.5
age of amphibians *geological past* 651.5
Age of Anxiety Ages, Decades, Eras 641
Age of Aquarius Ages, Decades, Eras 641

age of consent *marriageability* 64.4
Age of Enlightenment Ages, Decades, Eras 641, *historical past* 651.6
age of puberty *youth* 26.1
Age of Reason Ages, Decades, Eras 641, *historical past* 651.6
age of reptiles *geological past* 651.5
age-old *olden* 653.11
ageratum Flowers 42
ages ago *in the past* 651.20, *anciently* 653.18
agglomerate *cumulate* 59.20, *assemble* 59.23, *adhere* 755.8
agglomeration *assemblage* 59.13, *adhesion* 755.1, *collection* 757.3
agglutinate *retain* 471.7, *cause to adhere* 755.10
agglutination *union* 752.1, *adhesion* 755.1
agglutinative *language type* 5.11, *of language* 5.35, *adhesive* 755.5
aggrandize *enlarge* 194.12, *increase* 581.16, *intensify* 746.8
aggrandized *enlarged* 194.8
aggrandizement *enlargement* 194.2, *increase* 581.3, *intensification* 746.2
aggravate 276.5; *antagonize* 63.12, *cause hate* 300.12, *irritate* 302.16, *intensify* 746.8, *make worse* 808.17, *cause trouble* 824.21
aggravated 276.3; *resentful* 302.8
aggravated burglary *theft* 479.2
aggravating 276.4; *maddening* 302.12, *inconvenient* 824.12
aggravatingly *maddeningly* 302.25
aggravation 276.1; *dissension* 272.3, *resentment* 302.1, *intensification* 746.2, *impairment* 808.7, *snag* 824.8
aggregate *addition* 6.13, *add* 6.86, *cumulate* 59.20, *assemble* 59.23, *quantity* 105.5, *solid body* 540.4, *total* 738.4, 784.12, *collection* 757.3, *collected* 757.8, *combine* 757.9, *whole thing* 759.2, *mathematical result* 783.4
aggregated *collected* 757.8
aggregate fruit *botanical fruit* 44.2
aggregation *assemblage* 59.13, *collection* 757.3
aggress *have authority* 52.13
aggression *hostility* 63.1, *bellicosity* 76.15, *anger* 302.4, *attack* 418.1, *violence* 520.1
aggressive 63.9, 418.12; *military* 58.10, *warring* 76.26, *warlike* 76.27, *combative* 77.32, *objectionable* 272.7, *heroic* 284.10, *angry* 302.11, *cocky* 402.11, *discourteous* 411.5, *active* 414.13, *defying* 416.6, *contentious* 422.20, *disagreeing* 463.6, *strong in spirit* 516.11, *vigorous* 518.2, *violent* 520.5
aggressively 63.14, 77.38, 418.27; *unpleasantly* 272.10, *heroically* 284.18, *angrily* 302.24, *cockily* 402.19, *discourteously* 411.8, *in defiance* 416.10, *contentiously* 422.27, *in disagreement* 463.12, *strongly* 516.17
aggressiveness *bellicosity* 76.15, *objectionability* 272.2, *heroism* 284.2, *cockiness* 402.3, *energy* 414.4, *attack* 418.1, *divisiveness* 463.2
aggressive war *war* 76.1

aggressor *hostile person* 63.5, *combatant* 77.1, *unpleasant person* 272.5, *attacker* 418.10
aggrieve *offend* 302.15, *wrong* 430.19, *be evil* 446.10
aggro [Brit *and* Aus inf] *quarrel* 272.4, *annoyance* 276.2, *anger* 302.4, *disruption* 766.7
aghast *frightened* 283.9, *wondering* 294.7
agiatamente Musical Terms and Expression Marks 140
agile *skillful* 127.10, *gymnastic* 157.11, *active* 414.13, *graceful* 527.4, *swift* 694.6
agilely *swiftly* 694.16
agility *swiftness* 694.1
agilmente Musical Terms and Expression Marks 140
agin [Inf] *censuring* 438.12
aging 27.13; *deteriorated* 808.8
agio *international finance* 457.2, *currency market* 484.8, *discount* 495.1
agiotage *international finance* 457.2, *trade* 480.1, *currency market* 484.8
agitate 684.22; *arouse sensation* 212.11, *protest* 331.19, *be active* 414.18, *subvert* 427.13, *vibrate* 683.13, *disturb* 768.10
agitate against *cause mischief* 507.9, *counteract* 510.7
agitated 684.15; *susceptible* 212.7, *fearful* 283.10, *fidgety* 414.14, *bumpy* 544.8, *moving* 677.12, *disturbed* 768.6
agitatedly 684.27
agitating *demonstrating* 331.14, *directional* 677.13
agitation 684.1; *sensation* 212.1, *fearfulness* 283.2, *activity* 414.1, *restlessness* 414.7, *subversion* 427.3, *disorder* 507.2, *violence* 520.1, *irresolution* 666.2, *momentum* 677.2, *movement* 677.3, *vibration* 683.2, *disturbance* 768.1, *haste* 818.1
agitator 684.14; *leader* 126.8, *motivator* 178.11, 508.6, *protester* 331.8, 507.4, *troublemaker* 427.5, *opposer* 828.9
agitprop *publicity* 178.7, *subversion* 427.3, *inducement* 508.2
agitpropist *persuader* 178.9
Aglaia Deities 82
aglow *lucent* 246.13
agnate *related* 727.6
agnomen *name* 202.8
agnostic Philosophical Schools of Thought 4, *of a philosophy* 4.13, *disbeliever* 88.5, *disbelieving* 88.6, *negator* 190.8, *unaccepting* 190.13, *questioner* 333.9, *skeptical* 333.14, *nonobservant* 466.5, *moderate person* 772.8, *freethinker* 829.10, *uncertain* 841.9
agnostically *nonacceptantly* 190.25, *questioningly* 333.21
agnosticism Philosophical Schools of Thought 4, *unbelief* 88.4, *unacceptance* 190.4, *uncertainty* 333.6, *suspicion* 841.2
Agnus Dei *prayer* 85.10
ago *historically* 3.17, *in the past* 651.20, *anciently* 653.18
agog *wondering* 294.7, *expecting* 356.4
agon *dramaturgy* 136.6
agonic line *geomagnetism* 8.3
agonist *combatant* 77.1
agonistic *combative* 77.32, *sporting* 145.5, *contending* 422.19

agonistically *aggressively* 77.38, *sportingly* 145.7
agonize *feel pain* 215.8
agonized *miserable* 117.12, *feeling pain* 215.6
agonize over *worry* 283.16
agonizing *painful* 215.4
agony *pain* 117.5, 215.1, *sorrow* 270.1
agony column *newspaper* 175.2
agora *marketplace* 483.7, *urban area* 567.10
agoraphobia *anxiety disorder* 108.11, Phobias 283, *shyness* 409.2
agrarian *agricultural* 16.16
agrarian economics *agriculture* 16.1
agrarianism *agriculture* 16.1
agree 730.14, 735.23, 752.17; *pacify* 74.11, *be persuaded* 178.20, *submit* 298.17, *answer to* 334.22, *assent* 346.6, *be willing* 373.12, *take charge of* 391.8, *approve* 437.14, *contract* 459.8, *agree with* 462.10, *be similar* 733.12, *settle* 735.26, *consent* 735.28, *come together* 757.10, *come to an arrangement* 767.22, *conform* 781.11, *concur* 827.16
agreeability *desirability* 288.7, *lovability* 299.5, *acquiescence* 373.3, *appeal* 529.4
agreeable 752.11; *friendly* 62.5, *harmless* 73.9, *confirming* 189.16, *pleasant* 214.7, 271.5, *lovable* 299.20, *willing* 373.7, *courteous* 410.6, *submitting* 421.3, *contractual* 459.7, *agreeing* 462.6, *appealing* 529.10, *smooth* 543.8, *connected* 733.9, *consenting* 735.18, *compliant* 781.9
agreeableness *pleasantness* 271.1, *courtesy* 410.1, *appeal* 529.4, *smoothness* 543.2
agreeably 462.14, 752.22; *amicably* 62.13, *pacifically* 74.12, *confirmingly* 189.32, *pleasantly* 271.12, *lovably* 299.31, *correspondingly* 334.27, *willingly* 373.15, *courteously* 410.13, *compromisingly* 461.9, *similarly* 733.17
agree beforehand *predetermine* 384.8
agreed 346.5; *confirmed* 189.17, *approved* 437.8, *contractual* 459.7, *compromising* 461.4, *agreeing* 462.6, 730.8, *settled* 735.16, *consenting* 735.18, *agreeable* 752.11
agreed result *predetermination* 384.1
agreeing 462.6, 730.8, 735.13; *confirming* 189.16, *colorful* 251.11, *correspondent* 334.16, *assenting* 346.4, *submission* 421.1, *compromising* 461.4, *consenting* 735.18, *conforming* 781.8
agreeingly 730.19; *confirmingly* 189.32, *in accord* 735.33
agree in meaning *mean* 361.13
agree in principle *assent* 346.6
agreement 462.1, 730.2, 735.3, 752.4, 767.9; *syntax* 5.32, *friendly relations* 62.3, *pacification* 74.1, *confirmation* 189.5, *correspondence* 334.8, *assent* 346.1, *contract* 391.2, 459.1, *approval* 437.1, *compromise* 461.1, *bargaining* 480.10, *literalness* 721.9, *relatedness* 727.1, *affinity* 733.3, *consent* 735.8, *collaboration* 757.2, *conformity* 781.1, *fellowship* 827.2

agreements 459.2
agree to *bargain* 480.20
agree to anything *knuckle under* 401.10
agree to differ *pacify* 74.11, *disagree* 463.8
agree to disagree *pacify* 74.11
agree to half of it *compromise* 461.7
agree to some of it *compromise* 461.7
agree with 462.10; *make pleasant* 271.10, *assent* 346.6, *be equal* 740.11
agrestic *agricultural* 16.16
agribiz [Inf] *agriculture* 16.1
agribusiness *or* **agrobusiness** *agriculture* 16.1
agrichemicals *pest control* 16.13
agricultural 16.16; *productive* 522.11
agricultural chemist *chemist* 11.2
agricultural chemistry Branches of Chemistry 11
agricultural engineer *mechanical engineer* 14.4
agricultural engineering *mechanical engineering* 14.3
agriculturalist *agriculturist* 16.14
agricultural laborer 123.10
agriculturally 16.21
agricultural meteorology *meteorology* 9.1
agricultural sale *agriculture* 16.1
agricultural science *agriculture* 16.1
agricultural tool *tool* 103.1
agriculture 16.1; *manufacture* 522.2
agriculturist 16.14
Agri Dagi Mountains and Hills 569
agrimony Flowers 42
agrizoophobia Phobias 283
agrobiological *agricultural* 16.16
agrobiologist *agriculturist* 16.14, *plant scientist* 41.11
agrobiology *agriculture* 16.1, *plant science* 41.10
agrochemicals *pest control* 16.13
agroecological *agricultural* 16.16
agroecologist *agriculturist* 16.14
agroecology *agriculture* 16.1
agroforestry *agriculture* 16.1, *forestry* 43.5
agrogeologist *agriculturist* 16.14
agrogeology *agriculture* 16.1
agrogeology *agriculture* 16.1
agroindustry *agriculture* 16.1
agrological *agricultural* 16.16
agrologist *agriculturist* 16.14
agrology *agriculture* 16.1
agronomic *agricultural* 16.16
agronomics *agriculture* 16.1
agronomist *agriculturist* 16.14
agronomy *agriculture* 16.1
agroscience *or* **agriscience** *agriculture* 16.1
agrotechnician *agriculturist* 16.14
agrotechnology *agriculture* 16.1
aground *stable* 674.3, *on arrival* 704.22
ague *symptom* 114.3, *tropical disease* 114.10, *shake* 684.7
aguish *of disease* 114.25
agyiophobia Phobias 283
agyrophobia Phobias 283
AH *one day* 639.20
Ahaggar Mountains Mountains and Hills 569
ahead 712.18; *at a distance* 585.13, *advantaged* 618.7, *front-running* 621.10, *before* 621.14, *future* 650.6, *forward* 679.15, *superior* 744.8, *first* 769.19

ahead of its time *early* 657.17, *prematurely* 657.20
ahead of oneself *early* 657.17
ahead of schedule *acquisitive* 467.13, *premature* 657.10, *early* 657.17
ahead of the times *different in time* 648.2
ahead of time *acquisitive* 467.13, *premature* 657.10, *early* 657.17
ahimsa Philosophical Schools of Thought 4, *pacifism* 73.4
A horizon *soil* 8.42
ahull *offshore* 150.35
Ahura Mazda God 82.6
aichurophobia Phobias 283
aid 275.2, 275.10; *represent* 80.6, *remedy* 115.16, 115.16, *mountaineering* 161.9, *charity* 275.3, 307.3, *be compassionate* 305.11, *philanthropize* 307.8, *be eager* 373.13, *motivate* 412.12, *grant* 453.4, 453.14, *gift* 472.2, *levy* 494.7, *give* 498.11, *instrumentality* 511.7, *moral support* 605.7, *give moral support* 605.18, *determine* 675.11, *further* 679.13, *promotion* 715.3, *usefulness* 801.1, *be useful* 801.9, *be convenient* 803.5, *patronage* 810.7, *make easy* 823.15, *help* 825.1, 825.23, *convenience* 825.7
aid and abet *manipulate* 508.12, *help* 825.23, *reciprocate* 827.13
aid climbing *mountaineering* 161.1
aide *deputy* 80.1, *adviser* 176.5, *helper* 275.5, 825.12, *assistant* 511.3, *supporter* 605.9
aide-de-camp *helper* 275.5
aide-mémoire *reminder* 354.4
aider *defender* 419.14, *helper* 825.12
aider and abettor *motivator* 178.11, 508.6
aid for poor sight 243.5
aiding *serving* 69.9, *instrumental* 511.4, *helping* 825.16
aiding and abetting *guilt* 450.1, *mutual relationship* 423.8
aid route *climbing expedition* 161.2
AIDS *agent of destruction* 523.7
AIDS-related complex *sexually transmitted disease (STD)* 114.17
Aid to Families with Dependent Children (AFDC) *social welfare* 307.4, *social assistance* 825.4
aid to the deaf 229.3
aid worker *willing worker* 373.6
aiguillette *insignia* 184.5
aikido 152.16, Sporting Activities 145, *combat sport* 152.1, *wrestling* 152.18
aikido grade *aikido* 152.16
ail *be unhealthy* 114.29, *decline* 846.16
ailanthus Trees and Shrubs 43
aileron *equalizer* 740.5
ailing *sick* 114.24, *decline* 846.5, *failed* 846.10
ailment *illness* 114.2
ailurophobia *or* **aelurophobia** Phobias 283
aim 327.17, 374.10, 697.14, 773.12; *motive* 178.5, *aspiration* 281.3, *aspire* 281.13, *wish* 288.2, *purpose* 327.4, *point* 361.5, *intend* 361.15, *future intention* 374.3, *objective* 374.5, *declaration* 376.2, *venture* 390.2, *fire* 418.18, *motivation* 508.1, *reason* 675.4, *direction* 697.1, *direct* 697.13
aim a blow *hit* 695.11

aim at 385.15; *hunt* 160.12, *aim* 374.10, 697.14
aimed *purposive* 327.11, *directed* 697.9
aim for *aspire to* 288.19
aim for the lowest common denominator *make comprehensible* 363.8
aim high *aim* 327.17
aiming *bowls* 151.7, *purposive* 327.11
aiming at *tending to* 513.4
aiming for the lowest common denominator *simple* 363.6
aiming point *grip* 151.4
aimless 362.8; *circumlocutory* 199.4, *causeless* 842.11
aimless activity *restlessness* 414.7
aimlessly *meaninglessly* 362.13
aimlessness 362.3, 362.6; *circumlocution* 199.2, *restlessness* 414.7, *lack of motive* 842.2
aim to *attempt* 390.6
aim too high *overstep* 712.12
Ain Rivers 570
ain't it *or* **that the truth!** [Inf] *that's for sure!* 721.34
Aintree [Brit] *famous horse races* 159.13
aioli *sauce* 90.17
air 94.7, 558.1; *atmosphere* 9.8, *life* 94.4, *refresher* 94.2, *purify* 111.19, *melody* 140.10, *publish* 173.15, *divulge* 180.9, *odor* 224.1, *transparent thing* 249.4, *external appearance* 264.5, Phobias 283, *demonstrate* 331.15, *mode of behavior* 399.2, *matter* 524.4, *gas* 556.1, *aerate* 558.20, *dry* 560.17, Fields of Measurement 589, *display* 843.13
air ace *attacker* 418.10
air attack 418.4
air bag *miscellaneous automotive terms* 687.14, *safety device* 810.15, *preserver* 815.9
air ball [Inf] *playing terms* 148.4
air balloon *air bubble* 558.10
airbase *airport* 689.4
air bladder *fish characteristic* 38.8, *plant body* 47.13, *air bubble* 558.10
airborne *flying* 689.11, *leaping* 713.17
airborne early warning (AEW) *flight control* 689.7
airborne particles *powder* 553.9
airborne warning and control systems (AWACS) plane *military aircraft* 77.30
air box *racing automobile* 146.2
airbrush *painting* 143.3, *material* 143.9
air bubble 558.10
air campaign *air attack* 418.4
air cargo *aviation* 689.1
air-cargo *transportable* 686.7
air combat *air force commands* 77.28
air-condition *air* 94.7, *make cold* 218.15, *aerate* 558.20
air-conditioned *cooled* 218.11, *ventilated* 558.17
air conditioner *cooler* 218.4, *ventilator* 558.7
air conditioning *refreshment* 94.1, *ventilation* 558.6
air-cool *aerate* 558.20
air-cooled *cooled* 218.11, *ventilated* 558.17
air cooling *ventilation* 558.6
air corridor *aviation* 689.1, *flight path* 691.12

aircraft 689.3; *engine type* 14.11, *military aircraft* 77.30
aircraft carrier *warship* 77.21, Ships and Boats 690
aircraft commander *air force person* 77.31
aircraft design *aeronautics* 689.2
aircraft mechanic *artisan* 123.13
aircraft personnel **689.8**
air crew *air force person* 77.31, *aircraft personnel* 689.8
air current *air movement* 9.11, *airflow* 558.4
air density *weather data* 9.6
air division *air force unit* 77.29
air-dried *baked* 560.14
airdrome *airport* 689.4, *destination* 704.6
airdrop *aviation* 689.1
air-dry *dry* 560.17
air-drying *drying* 560.3
aired *published* 173.12, *baked* 560.14
Airedale terrier Breeds of Dogs 35
air express *conveyance* 685.2
air-express *mail* 685.10
airfield *airport* 689.4
air fight *battle* 76.23
air filter *cleaning tool* 111.10, *deodorant* 225.3, *ventilator* 558.7
airflow **558.4**; *air movement* 9.11, *respiration* 558.8, *miscellaneous aviation terms* 689.9
air force **77.27**; *the military* 58.2, *military* 58.10, *air force unit* 77.29, *security force* 464.3
air force blue *blue* 261.5
air force commands **77.28**
Air Force Cross US Military Medals 58
air force officer *air force person* 77.31
air force person **77.31**
air force staff *military staff* 58.5
air force unit **77.29**
air freight *conveyance* 685.2, *aviation* 689.1
air freshener *cleaning agent* 111.9, *deodorant* 225.3
air frost *frost* 9.25
air gas *gas* 106.6
air gun *banger* 234.3
air-gun shooting Sporting Activities 145
air hole *hole* 583.4
air hostess *aircraft personnel* 689.8
airily **558.25**; *metaphysically* 525.13, *sparsely* 541.6
airiness **558.9**; *subtlety* 534.2, *lightness* 539.1, *sparseness* 541.1
airing *cleaning* 111.2, *ventilation* 558.6, *drying* 560.3
air lane *flight path* 691.12
air layer *propagate* 21.15
air leakage *leak* 816.6
airless *unhygienic* 114.27, *motionless* 678.4
airlift *conveyance* 685.2, *convey* 685.9, *aviation* 689.1, *aviatic* 689.10
airlike *airy* 558.12
airline attendant *attendant* 69.4
airline hostess *attendant* 69.4
airline pilot *aircraft personnel* 689.8
airliner *aircraft* 689.3
airline ticket *means of identification* 184.3
airmail *postal service* 169.5, *correspond* 169.19, *mail* 685.10, *aviation* 689.1
Airman US Military Ranks 58

Airman Basic US Military Ranks 58
Airman First Class US Military Ranks 58
airmanship *art of war* 76.16
Airman's Medal US Military Medals 58
air marshal [Brit] *military leader* 68.10
air mass *atmosphere* 9.8
Air Medal US Military Medals 58
air mile General Units 589
air miss *miscellaneous aviation terms* 689.9
air mobility *air force commands* 77.28
air movement **9.11**; *weather data* 9.6
Air National Guard *air force* 77.27
air operations *offensive warfare* 76.11
air passage *ventilator* 558.7
airplane *military aircraft* 77.30, *means of transportation* 686.2, *transportable* 686.7, *aircraft* 689.3
air plant *plant* 41.2
air pocket *rough thing* 544.2, *air bubble* 558.10, *miscellaneous aviation terms* 689.9
air pollution *unpleasant-smelling thing* 227.2, *powder* 553.9
airport **689.4**; *center of activity* 612.4, *stopping place* 668.4, *destination* 704.6, *place of departure* 705.4
airport police *law enforcement agency* 53.7
airport surface detection equipment (ASDE) *flight control* 689.7
airport terminal *building* 551.9
air pressure *weather data* 9.6
Air Pump Constellations 7
air purifier *deodorant* 225.3
air racing Sporting Activities 145
air raid *air attack* 418.4
air-raid shelter *shelter* 419.11, *fortification* 812.3
air-raid siren *signal* 183.6
air rifle *hunting equipment* 160.4, *banger* 234.3
air-rifle shooting *target shooting* 160.1
air route *aviation* 689.1, *flight path* 691.12
airs **404.2**; *arrogance* 297.2
airs and graces *cockiness* 402.3, *airs* 404.2
airscrew *rotator* 682.8
airsick *vomiting* 709.12
airsickness Phobias 283, *miscellaneous aviation terms* 689.9
air sleeve *indicator* 183.7
air space *air* 558.1, *empty space* 563.2, *available space* 563.6, *region* 564.1
airspeed *flight* 689.5, *speed* 694.2
air station *airport* 689.4
airstream *air movement* 9.11
air strike *air attack* 418.4
airstrip *airport* 689.4
air systems *naval commands* 77.19
air temperature *weather data* 9.6
air terminal *stopping place* 668.4, *destination* 704.6
airtight *closed* 584.7, *complete* 805.14
air-traffic *aviatic* 689.10
air-traffic control *flight control* 689.7
air-traffic controller *aircraft personnel* 689.8
air-transportable *aviatic* 689.10

air transportation *transportation* 686.1, *aviation* 689.1
air travel *motion* 677.1, *aviation* 689.1
air warfare *naval commands* 77.19
airway *flight path* 691.12
airworthy *transferable* 685.7, *transportable* 686.7, *flyable* 689.12, *invulnerable* 810.18
airy **556.15, 558.12**; *spiritual* 86.20, *nonmaterial* 525.8, *insubstantial* 539.5, *sparse* 541.3, *spacious* 563.13, *unreal* 720.8, *not serious* 800.11
airy-fairy [Inf] *fantastic* 360.11
aisle *church interior* 83.9, *church architecture* 134.11, *access* 691.3, *passage* 691.5
Aisne Rivers 570
ajar *open* 583.10
akene *botanical fruit* 44.2
Akhal Teké Horse and Pony Breeds 159
akin *family* 65.6, *comparable* 733.8, *connected* 733.9, *compatible* 735.14, *included* 763.4
akinete *reproductive body* 47.14
akin to *related* 727.6
Akita Breeds of Dogs 35
Aktie Tomaat [Dutch] *theater movements* 136.9
Alabama American States 564, Rivers 570
alabaster *white thing* 253.4, *white* 253.7
à la carte *culinary* 91.9
alacritous *eager* 373.8, *early* 657.8, *swift* 694.6
alacrity **414.3**; *eagerness* 373.2, *earliness* 657.1, *quickness of mind* 694.4, *haste* 818.1
Alambadi Breeds of Cattle 16
à la mode *culinary* 91.9, *dressed up* 100.39, *fashionable* 536.5, *fashionably* 536.9, *stylish* 537.7, *avant-garde* 652.16
Aland Island Islands 572
alanine Amino Acids 12
Alaotra Lakes 568
alarm *signal* 183.6, *burst of sound* 232.4, *fear* 283.1, *frighten* 283.17, *weaken* 517.13, *disturb* 768.10, *safety device* 810.15, *danger signal* 811.5, *warning* 814.1, *warning signal* 814.3
alarm clock *indicator* 183.7
alarm clock *or watch* Timepieces and Timers 646
alarmed *frightened* 283.9, *disturbed* 768.6
alarming *frightening* 283.12, *disturbing* 768.9, *dangerous* 811.7
alarmingly *frighteningly* 283.20, *disturbingly* 768.13
alarmist *frightener* 283.7, *warner* 814.5
alarm system *security* 464.1, *security system* 810.5
alarm test *false alarm* 814.4
alarum [Arch] *signal* 183.6
alarums and excursions *play part* 136.8
Alaska *cold place* 218.7, American States 564
Alaska-Hawaii Time *time zone* 646.5
Alaskan malamute Breeds of Dogs 35
Alaska Range Mountains and Hills 569
Ala-Tau Breeds of Cattle 16
alb *vestment* 84.11
alba Poem or Verse Forms 139

albacore *food fish and shellfish* 90.20
Albania Countries 566
Albanian Breeds of Cattle 16
Albano Lakes 568
Albany American States 564, Rivers 570
albatross *water bird* 36.9, *burden* 117.3, 826.10
albedo Earth 7.17
Alberich *little person* 580.5
Albert Lakes 568
Alberta Canadian Provinces 564
albertype *older photograph* 132.4
albescence *whiteness* 253.1
albescent *white* 253.7
albinic *white* 253.7
albinism *skin disease* 114.16, *paleness* 252.2, *whiteness* 253.1
albinistic *white* 253.7
Albino Horse and Pony Breeds 159
albinotic *drained of color* 252.6
Albion ware Ceramics 129
Al Borak Notable Horses 159
album *record book* 185.5, *compendium* 204.3, *reminder* 354.4
albumen *paste* 561.4
albumin *protein* 12.9
albuminurophobia Phobias 283
alburnum *timber* 43.3
alcahest *solvent* 555.9
alchemical *chemical* 11.24, *witchlike* 86.19
alchemist *occultist* 86.13, *secret person* 182.6, *changer* 665.9
alchemistic *witchlike* 86.19
alchemize *transform* 670.13
alchemy Branches of Chemistry 11, *occultism* 86.1, *witchcraft* 86.6, *mystery* 182.4
alcohol **121.5**; *carbohydrate* 12.3, *alcoholic drink* 93.9, *fuels* 106.2, *addictive drug* 117.10, Phobias 283, Fields of Measurement 589, *preserver* 815.9
alcohol abuse *substance abuse* 121.1
alcoholic *drinkable* 93.18, *sick person* 114.22, *drunkard* 121.8, *drunken* 121.28, *intoxicating* 121.29, *creature of habit* 397.8, *compulsive person* 428.5
alcoholic drink **93.9**; *alcohol* 121.5
alcoholic liquor *alcohol* 121.5
alcoholic psychosis *psychosis* 110.3
Alcoholics Anonymous (AA) *temperance society* 120.3
alcoholic stupor *drunkenness* 121.3
alcoholism *psychiatric disease* 114.21, *substance abuse* 121.1
alcohol lamp *incandescent light* 246.5
alcoholometer Fields of Measurement 589
alcoholometry Fields of Measurement 589
Alcora ware Ceramics 129
alcove *compartment* 578.2, *cavity* 635.3
Aldan Rivers 570
aldaric acid *saccharide* 12.4
al dente *culinary* 91.9
alder Trees and Shrubs 43
aldermanic board *representative body* 79.2
Alderney Islands 572
aldoheptose *saccharide* 12.4
aldohexose *saccharide* 12.4
aldooctose *saccharide* 12.4

aldopentose *saccharide* 12.4
aldose *saccharide* 12.4
aldosterone Human Hormones 12
aldotetrose *saccharide* 12.4
aldotriose *saccharide* 12.4
aldrin *pest control* 16.13
ale *alcoholic drink* 93.9
aleatory *illogical* 728.7, *capricious* 841.16, *chance* 842.10
Alecto Deities 82
alehouse *drink provider* 93.15
Aleksei Vronski Famous Lovers 299
alektorophobia Phobias 283
Alentejo Breeds of Cattle 16, Breeds of Pigs 16
alerce Trees and Shrubs 43
alert *signal* 183.18, *cautious* 287.6, *intelligent* 315.9, 352.5, *curious* 321.5, *watchful* 323.6, *circumspect* 325.8, *prepared* 388.9, *active* 414.13, *mentally sharp* 549.14, *danger signal* 811.5, *warn* 814.8, *give warning* 814.10
alertly *cautiously* 287.16, *intelligently* 315.14, *curiously* 321.9, *attentively* 323.14, *carefully* 325.13, *sharply* 549.19
alertness *caution* 287.1, *cleverness* 315.3, *curiosity* 321.1, *close attention* 323.2, *circumspection* 325.3, *mental sharpness* 549.9
Aleutian Islands Islands 572
alevin *young fish* 38.6
alewife *drink provider* 93.15
Alexander Archipelago Islands 572
Alexandrian school Western Art Styles 133
Alexandrine *meter* 139.10, *eleven to nineteen* 792.7
alfalfa *crop* 16.8, *animal food* 90.2
alfar *sprite* 86.12
Alfardaws *heaven* 82.15
al fine Musical Terms and Expression Marks 140
alfresco *open-air* 558.16, *out-of-doors* 558.26, *outside* 610.9, 610.17
alga 47.10; *lower plant* 41.4, *moss* 46.4
algae 47.11
algal 47.20
algal bloom *alga* 47.10
algal constituent *lichen* 47.16
algal pigment *plant body* 47.13
algal product 47.15
Algarve Churro Breeds of Sheep 16
algebra 6.21; Branches of Mathematics 6, *calculation* 784.1
algebraic(al) *mathematical* 6.65, 784.9
algebraically *mathematically* 784.15
algebraic expression 6.23
algebraic geometry Branches of Mathematics 6, *geometry* 6.32
algebraic number *complex number* 6.6, *kind of number* 783.2
algebraic operation *operation* 6.12
algebraic topology Branches of Mathematics 6, *topology* 6.45
algebraist *mathematician* 6.2
algebra of propositions *algebra* 6.21
Algeria Countries 566
Algerian Arab Breeds of Sheep 16
algicide *killing agent* 30.15
algid *cold* 218.9
algidity *freezing* 218.2

Algiers Countries 566
algin *algal product* 47.15
alginate *algal product* 47.15
algoid *algal* 47.20
Algol Programming Languages 15
algolagnia *sexual perversion* 20.12
algological *algal* 47.20
algologically 47.25; *botanically* 41.25
algologist *plant scientist* 41.11, *study of algae* 47.12
algology *botany* 13.7, *plant science* 41.10, *study of algae* 47.12
Algol variable *variable star* 7.11
algometer Fields of Measurement 589
algometry Fields of Measurement 589
algophobia Phobias 283
algorithm 6.26; *programming concepts* 15.24, *way* 691.1, *calculation* 784.1
algorithmic *numerical* 783.7, *mathematical* 784.9
alias *anonymity* 182.7, *name* 202.8
alibi *evasion* 181.5, *defense* 441.2, *justify* 441.12
Alice B. Toklas Notable Friendships 62
alicyclic *chemical compound* 11.4
alidade *civil engineering tool* 14.18, *meter* 589.13
alien *wild* 41.15, *sprite* 86.12, *spiritual* 86.20, *different* 463.7, *extraneous* 610.12, *new arrival* 652.7, *foreigner* 724.5, *foreign* 724.9, *disparate* 728.9, *unjoined* 753.9, *oppositional* 828.11
alienage *foreignness* 724.2
alienate *antagonize* 63.12, *put off* 179.10, *cause hate* 300.12, *divide* 753.18
alienated *estranged* 63.8, *insane* 110.9, *dissuaded* 179.5, *hated* 300.9
alienation *personal conflict* 63.2, *mood disorder* 108.12, *defense mechanism* 108.23, *disaffection* 179.3, *dislike* 300.2, *evolution* 670.3
alienation effect *dramaturgy* 136.6
alien encounter *occult and psychic phenomena* 86.7
alienism *foreignness* 724.2
alight *on fire* 217.16, *bright* 246.14, *be motionless* 678.7, *travel by train* 688.9, *land* 704.16, *descend* 714.12, *sit* 716.20
alight upon *drop* 714.15
align 6.92; *make horizontal* 603.10, *correspond* 606.8, *order* 765.18, *arrange* 767.18, 774.14, *make conform* 781.13
aligned *horizontal* 603.6, *corresponding* 606.6, *directional* 697.8, *arranged* 767.11
alignment *horizontality* 603.1, *correspondence* 606.2, *orientation* 697.3, *arrangement* 767.1, *association* 827.6
align oneself *aim* 697.14
align with *back* 825.28, *join with* 827.15
alike *vague* 338.9, *corresponding* 606.6, *correspondingly* 606.10, *similar* 733.7, *similarly* 733.17, *equal* 740.8
alikeness *correspondence* 606.2, *similarity* 733.1
aliment *food* 90.1, *feed* 90.41, *income* 492.3
alimental *edible* 92.20

alimentary *physiological* 13.29, *edible* 92.20
alimentation *food* 90.1
alimony *divorce court* 66.3, *earnings* 467.5, *gift* 472.2, *something received* 473.2, *income* 492.3, *financial support* 605.8
A-line skirt *skirt* 100.12
aliphatic *chemical compound* 11.4
aliquot *partial* 760.11, *fractional* 783.8
aliquot part *division* 6.16
alive 28.13; *living* 13.28, *active* 414.13, *preserved* 815.12
alive and kicking *alive* 28.13, *active* 414.13, *cured* 809.8
alive to *sensible* 212.6
alive to opportunity *enterprising* 391.5
alizarin *red pigment* 257.2
alizarin crimson *red pigment* 257.2
alkahest *solvent* 555.9
alkali *base* 11.11
alkali metal *chemical element* 11.3
alkalimeter Fields of Measurement 589
alkalimetry Fields of Measurement 589
alkaline *acid* 11.27
alkaline-earth element *chemical element* 11.3
alkaloid 12.19
alky [Inf] *drinker* 93.16
all 759.4; *total* 738.4, *quantitative* 738.6, *whole* 759.6
alla breve Musical Terms and Expression Marks 140
all aflutter *restless* 684.16
all agog *wondering* 294.7
Allah God 82.6
all along *all the time* 639.16
allamanda Flowers 42
all-American *prizewinner* 127.8, *baseball team* 147.2, *basketball team* 148.2, *football player* 155.15
all and sundry *everyone* 778.7
all and then some *crowd* 59.11
allantoic *developmental* 13.33
allantois *developmental biology* 13.22
allargando Musical Terms and Expression Marks 140
all around *extensively* 563.18, *inclusively* 613.35, *around* 615.8, *in all directions* 697.19, *completely* 759.14
all-around *diversified* 732.8
all-around capacity *skill* 127.1
all around the globe *extensively* 563.18
all at sea *at a loss* 468.11
allay *conciliate* 74.10, *relieve* 275.8, *mitigate* 521.9, *smooth over* 545.12
all but *nearly* 586.18, *on the whole* 759.13, *imperfectly* 806.10
all by oneself *alone* 788.20
all by one's lonesome [Inf] *freely* 829.22
all clear *safety* 810.1
all-clear siren *signal* 183.6
all colors of the rainbow *variety* 732.2
all comers *finalist* 422.16
all-comprehending *general* 778.9
all-consuming *tenacious* 376.9, *destructive* 523.8
all-covering *general* 778.9
all-devouring *gluttonous* 119.3
all ears [Inf] *hearing* 228.9, *diligent* 323.7
allegate *accuse* 442.8

allegation *contention* 189.4, *utterance* 205.10, *accusation* 442.1
allege *contend* 189.24, *speak* 205.17, *give evidence* 339.12
alleged *believed* 87.8, *newsworthy* 171.8, *contended* 189.15, *supposed* 359.6, *reputed* 370.4
allegedly 189.31; *believably* 87.13, *newsworthily* 171.10, *supposedly* 359.10, *reputedly* 370.8, *accusingly* 442.11, *apparently* 720.19
Allegheny Rivers 570
Allegheny Mountains Mountains and Hills 569
allegiance *loyalty* 426.2, *deference* 433.4, *subjection* 832.1
alleging *accusatory* 442.6
allegorical *fictional* 139.16, *symbolic* 361.8, *correlative* 729.6, *comparable* 733.8, *mysterious* 844.11
allegorically *correlatively* 729.12, *comparably* 733.18
allegorical meaning *type of meaning* 361.4
allegorist *author* 139.13
allegorization *interpretation* 365.1
allegorize *compare* 733.13
allegory *correlation* 729.3, *comparability* 733.2, *latency* 844.1, *mysteriousness* 844.5
allegretto Musical Terms and Expression Marks 140
allegro Musical Terms and Expression Marks 140
allegro *hurryingly* 694.18, *hasty* 818.3
allele *genetic material* 13.20
alleluia *cry of praise* 239.3
alleluia! *hallelujah!* 83.18
allemande Dances 135, Musical Forms 140
all-embracing *whole* 759.6, *complete* 761.6, *including* 763.3, *general* 778.9
all-encompassing *general* 778.9
All England Women's Hockey Association (AEWHA) *hockey organizations* 158.7
allergic *of disease* 114.25, *susceptible* 212.7
allergy *ill health* 114.1, *sensitivity* 212.2
allergy [Inf] *dislike* 291.1
Aller Vale pottery Ceramics 129
alleviate *conciliate* 74.10, *remedy* 115.16, *comfort* 121.4, *relieve* 275.8, *mitigate* 521.9, *lighten* 539.9, *smooth over* 545.12, *make smaller* 747.8, *subtract* 749.6, *ease* 819.4, *disentangle* 823.17, *support* 825.24
alleviating *lightening* 539.6
alleviation *ease* 275.1, *moderation* 521.1, *lightening* 539.2, *subtraction* 749.1
alleviative *moderator* 521.2, *moderating* 521.5, *lightening* 539.6
alley *sports ground* 145.2, *tennis court* 165.3, *road* 691.4
alley cat *hybrid* 751.6
all eyes *diligent* 323.7
alleyway *road* 691.4
all fours Card Games 168
all gone *zero* 786.5
all Greek [Inf] *unknown thing* 349.3
Allhallows or **Allhallowmas** Christian Holy Days and Seasons 85
Allhallows Eve Christian Holy Days and Seasons 85
all hands *everyone* 778.7

all hell let loose *tumult* 232.5, *violence* 520.1, *disruption* 766.7
alliance 64.2, 459.5, 735.5; *party* 59.3, *marriage* 64.1, *contract* 459.1, *relatedness* 727.1, *association* 752.2, 827.6, *collaboration* 757.2
alliance of states *nation* 18.14
allied 735.15; *contractual* 459.7, *related* 727.6, *connected* 733.9, *collaborative* 757.7, *associating* 827.11
allied forces *armed forces* 77.9
allied operation *offensive warfare* 76.11
Allier *Rivers* 570
alligator *crocodile* 37.8
all impatience *hasty* 818.3
all in [Inf] *fatigued* 820.2
all-in *including* 763.3
all in a day's work *predictable* 295.4
all in all *on average* 742.10, *on the whole* 759.13, *completely* 759.14, *overall* 778.22
all-inclusive *whole* 759.6, *complete* 761.6, *including* 763.3, *general* 778.9
alliterate *harmonize* 735.22, *resound* 797.21
alliterating *reverberatory* 797.14
alliteration *literary device* 139.12, *ornament* 532.7, *harmonization* 735.2, *reverberation* 797.6
alliterative *metrical* 139.20, *harmonizing* 735.12, *reverberatory* 797.14
alliteratively *in harmony* 735.32
allium *Flowers* 42
alliumphobia *Phobias* 283
all-knowing *divine* 82.16, *knowledgeable* 348.7
all mixed up together *indiscriminately* 338.15
all mouth *effusive* 207.6
all-night *evening* 656.4
allocate 474.5; *have at one's disposal* 393.14, *budget* 457.10, *quantify* 738.7, *make average* 742.9, *arrange* 767.18
allocated 474.4
allocation 474.1; *portion* 474.2
allocation of work *bargaining terms* 57.10
allocution *address* 209.1
allodial *propertied* 470.9
allodium *historical property terms* 470.3
allodoxaphobia *Phobias* 283
all of *wholly* 738.9
all of a piece *whole* 759.6
all of a twitter *shakily* 684.28
all off *canceled* 773.15
allogamy *mixture* 751.1
all one *on equal terms* 740.9
allonym *name* 202.8
allopathic *medical* 107.28
allopathic medicine *medicine* 107.1
allopathy *treatment* 107.14, *healing art* 115.13
allosteric inhibition *enzyme* 12.11
allot *have at one's disposal* 393.14, *own property* 470.11, *give out* 472.12, *allocate* 474.5, *measure out* 589.21, *limit* 620.7, 830.13, *quantify* 738.7
allotment *gift* 472.2, *allocation* 474.1, *portion* 474.2, *plot* 564.9, *limit* 620.1, *piece* 760.2, *limitation* 830.2
allotment [Brit] *garden* 17.2, *property* 470.1

allotted *propertied* 470.9, *receiving* 473.9, *allocated* 474.4
allotted span *old age* 27.5, *life cycle* 28.7, *duration* 642.1
allotted task 474.3
allottee *recipient* 473.5
allotting *allocation* 474.1
all out *tenacious* 376.9, *with vigor* 518.6, *at full speed* 694.17
all-out *complete* 761.6
all-out war *war* 76.1
all over *extensively* 563.18, *no more* 718.11, *anyhow* 766.25, *ended* 773.14, *everywhere* 776.19
all-over *omnipresent* 575.10
all over again *again* 652.22
all over but the shouting *ended* 773.14
all over the lot [Inf] *anyhow* 766.25, *divergent* 776.11
all over the map [Inf] *extensively* 563.18
all over the place *anyhow* 766.25
allow *authorize* 52.14, *make legal* 53.27, *admit* 180.11, *modify* 340.13, *assent* 346.6, *be lenient* 423.5, *budget* 457.10, *permit* 502.6, 735.29, *adopt* 692.14, *subtract* 749.6, *make easy* 823.15, *make possible* 836.7
allow (of) *include* 763.5
allowable *legal* 53.16, *vindicable* 441.9, *permitting* 502.5
allow a discount *discount* 495.4
allow a dismissal *acquit* 54.32
allow a margin *discount* 495.4
allow an appeal *acquit* 54.32
allowance *authorization* 52.3, *modification* 340.5, *leniency* 423.1, *defense* 441.2, *grant* 453.4, *profit* 467.6, *gift* 472.2, *something received* 473.2, *portion* 474.2, *change* 484.3, *income* 492.3, *discount* 495.1, *adoption* 692.2, *permission* 735.9, *counterbalance* 743.2, *subtracted item* 749.2, *inclusion* 763.1, *financial assistance* 825.6
allow credit *lend* 475.6
allowed *authorized* 52.11, 340.8, *given consideration* 423.4, *rightful* 429.9, *permitted* 502.4, *adopted* 692.10, *permitting* 735.19, *included* 763.4
allowed in entering 706.9
allow enough rope *set free* 829.17
allow for *vindicate* 441.11, *include* 763.5
allow full play *set free* 829.17
allow in *be hospitable* 477.21, *admit* 708.12
allowing *permitting* 502.5, 735.19, *under the circumstances* 726.16, *including* 763.3
allowingly *passably* 692.19
allowing no delay 645.7
allowing no time *hasty* 818.3
allow initiative *set free* 829.17
allow no appeal *be severe* 424.8
allow no rest *fatigue* 820.6
allow no time *hasten* 818.4
allow one's mind to wander *be inattentive* 324.10
allow someone to take liberties *be permissive* 502.7
allow the occasion to go by *lose one's chance* 660.10
allow to have the run of *be permissive* 502.7
alloy *chemical compound* 11.4, *metallurgy* 11.32, *extract* 11.41, *mixed thing* 751.2, *mix* 751.12, *compound* 757.4, *make worse* 808.17

alloyed *metallurgical* 11.36, *mixed* 751.8
all-pervading *dominant* 512.10, *complicated* 751.10, *general* 778.9
all points bulletin (APB) *pursuit* 385.1
Allport-Vernon draw-a-person test *Intelligence Tests* 108
Allport-Vernon study of values *Intelligence Tests* 108
all-powerful *divine* 82.16
all-powerfulness *powerfulness* 514.4
all-present *omnipresent* 575.10
all-pro *prizewinner* 127.8, *football player* 155.15
all-purpose *useful* 801.5
all-red *wrestling* 152.18
all right 429.19; *satisfactory* 273.6, *mediocre* 289.11, 742.7, *proper* 429.10
all-right [Inf] *consenting* 735.18
all right! *yes!* 189.36
all-rounder *skilled person* 127.7, *pluralist* 793.5
All Saints' Day *Christian Holy Days and Seasons* 85
all seats taken *full* 761.8
all-seeing *divine* 82.16
all set *prepared* 388.9
all shapes and sizes *variety* 732.2
all shipshape and Bristol fashion *orderly* 765.13
all sorts and conditions *variety* 732.2
all sorts of things *miscellany* 751.3
All Souls' Day *Christian Holy Days and Seasons* 85
allspice *Herbs and Spices* 91
all-square match *golfing terms* 156.3
all-star *baseball team* 147.2, *basketball team* 148.2
all-star game *baseball leagues and championship games* 147.8, *hockey organizations* 158.7
all steamed up [Inf] *healthy* 113.4
all-sufficing *sufficient* 97.3
all-terrain bike (ATB) *bicycle* 687.10
all-terrain ski *ski equipment* 162.10
all-terrain vehicle (ATV) *farm tool* 16.5
all that could be desired *sufficiency* 97.1
all that goes with it *ornamentation* 748.5
all that is left *remainder* 750.1
all that is possible *sufficiency* 97.1
all the better for *improved* 807.12
all the market can bear *excess* 99.1
all the more *supremely* 744.23, *increasingly* 746.9
all the rage *liked* 290.6, *fashionable* 536.5
all there *complete* 761.6
all there [Inf] *sane* 109.3, *intelligent* 352.5
all the same *on equal terms* 740.9
all the time 639.16; *frequently* 661.7, *continually* 669.10
all the time in the world *leisure* 125.1, 413.4
all the trimmings *ornamentation* 748.5
all the way *right away* 429.20, *completely* 759.14
all the way across *breadthways* 592.16
all the world *all* 759.4

all the world and his wife *or brother everyone* 778.7
all things being equal *ideally* 327.22, *considering* 341.13, *on average* 742.10
all things considered *considering* 341.13, *on average* 742.10, *on the whole* 759.13, *overall* 778.22, *probably* 838.11
all those concerned *group* 18.13
all through *all the time* 639.16, *via* 691.17
all through the night *nightly* 656.6
all thumbs *clumsy* 128.6, *graceless* 528.7
all-time *best* 805.9
all-time low *inferior state* 745.3
all together *together* 59.31, 794.20, *simultaneously* 649.8, *in accord* 735.33, *as one* 752.21, *one and all* 759.12
all told *completely* 759.14
allude *propound* 359.9, *imply* 844.14
allude to *speak* 205.17, *mean* 361.13
all up *ended* 773.14
allure *sexual desire* 20.5, *enticement* 178.3, *entice* 178.16, *desirability* 288.7, *cause desire* 288.22, *win the love of* 299.27, *allurement* 700.4, *lure* 700.12
allurement 700.4; *sexual desire* 20.5, *enticement* 178.3, *liking* 290.1, *lovability* 299.5, *inducement* 508.2
alluring *sensual* 20.16, *enticing* 178.13, *desirable* 288.11, *likable* 290.7, *lovable* 299.20, *motivational* 508.7, *attractive* 700.10
alluringly *enticingly* 178.22, *likably* 290.12, *lovably* 299.31, *influentially* 508.13
allusion *obscurity* 197.1
allusive *obscure* 197.2, *suppositional* 359.5, *symbolic* 361.8, *tacit* 844.10
allusively *obscurely* 197.4
allusory *tacit* 844.10
alluvial *coastal* 8.54, *of landmasses* 572.12
alluvial deposit *sediment* 8.29
alluvial plain *lowland* 572.6
alluvion *flow* 570.4, *transferred thing* 685.6
alluvium *soil* 8.42, *transferred thing* 685.6, *residue* 750.2
all-way bet *horse-racing betting terms* 159.11
all wool and a yard wide *truthful* 191.4
all wrapped up in oneself *self-admiring* 402.10
all wrong *mistaken* 351.13, *improper* 430.14, *evilly* 446.12
ally *merge* 64.21, *assenter* 346.3, *contract* 459.8, *dominion* 566.3, *supporter* 605.9, *form an alliance* 735.25, *associate* 754.3, *come together* 757.10, *helper* 825.12, *cooperator* 827.8, *join* 827.17
ally with *back* 825.28, *join with* 827.15
almanac *collection* 105.12, *type of book* 174.3, *plan* 357.2, *periodical publication* 641.6, *chronology* 646.2, *book of lists* 785.3
Almaty *Countries* 566
almightily *divinely* 82.24
almightiness *divine attribute* 82.4, *powerfulness* 514.4
Almighty, the *God* 82.6
almighty *divine* 82.16

---

almighty dollar *finance* 484.7
Almighty God *God* 82.6
almond Trees and Shrubs 43
almoner *benevolent person* 305.6, *philanthropist* 307.5, *giver* 472.7, *treasurer* 484.18
almonry *treasury* 484.19
almost *mathematically* 6.93, *nearly* 586.18, *on the whole* 759.13, *imperfectly* 806.10
almost all *large part* 579.3
almost always *usually* 778.21
almost entirely *in essence* 723.13
almost none *few* 796.1
almost unheard-of *infrequent* 662.2
almost win *lose* 468.12
alms *charity* 275.3, 307.3, *benevolent act* 305.5, *offering* 472.6, *gift* 498.3
almsgiver *benevolent person* 305.6, *philanthropist* 307.5, *giver* 472.7
almsgiving *charity* 275.3, *benevolent act* 305.5, *charitable* 305.9, *philanthropic* 307.6, *giving* 472.1, 472.9
almshouse *safe house* 812.5
aloes *sour thing* 223.3
aloft *sailing* 150.25, *offshore* 150.35, *high* 596.20, *highly* 715.16
aloha! *hello!* 704.23
alone **788.15, 788.20;** *hostilely* 63.13, *lonely* 409.8, *unjoined* 753.9, *aloofly* 756.10, *solo* 788.14, *freely* 829.22
aloneness **788.5**
along *lengthwise* 590.14, *forward* 679.15
alongside *beside* 586.20, *in parallel* 606.9, *side* 623.6, *laterally* 623.11
along these lines *how* 691.16
along the way *in transit* 685.13
along with *additionally* 748.15
aloof **756.5;** *hostile* 63.6, *silent* 181.10, *indifferent* 289.7, *apathetic* 322.4, *away* 386.23, *unsociable* 409.6, *reserved* 585.7, *at a distance* 585.13, *in isolation* 753.24, *solitary* 782.17, *alone* 788.15
aloofly **756.10;** *indifferently* 289.17, *apathetically* 322.7, *unsociably* 409.13, *reservedly* 585.15
aloofness **756.2;** *indifference* 289.1, *incuriosity* 322.1, *avoidance* 386.1, *unsociability* 409.1, *distance* 585.1, *reserve* 585.4, *aloneness* 788.5
alopecia *baldness* 614.9
aloud *aurally* 228.16, *audibly* 230.10
alp *mountain* 569.1
alpaca Fabrics and Fibers 130
alpestrine *mountainous* 569.5
alphabet **5.16;** *language element* 5.13
alphabet game Children's and Party Games 167
alphabetical *written* 5.36, *hierarchical* 765.12
alphabetically *linguistically* 5.44, *in order* 765.26, *inventorially* 785.13
alphabetical order *hierarchy* 765.3
alphabetization *categorization* 767.5
alphabetize *use language* 5.42, *categorize* 767.21
alphabetized *categorized* 767.15
alpha decay *radioactivity* 10.58
alpha emitter *radioactivity* 10.58
alpha helix *protein* 12.9

alpha hydroxy cream *toiletries* 530.6
alpha-naphthol test *sugar test* 12.6
alphanumeric character *character* 15.18
alpha particle *radioactivity* 10.58
alpha rays *radioactivity* 10.58
alpha rhythm *cycle* 663.3
alpha test Intelligence Tests 108
alpha to omega *all* 759.4, *inclusively* 763.8
alpha wave *cycle* 663.3
alphorn *or* **alpenhorn** Musical Instruments 142
Alpine *racial* 1.12, *automobile rallies* 146.6, *ski* 162.27
alpine *ornamental* 17.17, *mountaineering* 161.9, *mountainous* 569.5
alpine chain *mountain building* 8.23
Alpine climbing Sporting Activities 145
Alpine combined event Sporting Activities 145
alpine garden *garden* 17.2
alpine glacier *glacier* 8.44
alpine plant *garden plant* 17.10
Alpine race *ski race* 162.4, *ski* 162.35
Alpine ski *ski equipment* 162.10, *ski* 162.35
Alpine ski championships **162.6**
Alpine skiing Sporting Activities 145, *skiing* 162.1
Alpine ski racing *race* 422.8
Alpine snowboard *snowboarding equipment* 162.12
Alpine-style climbing *mountaineering* 161.1
Alpine type *race* 1.5
alpinism *mountaineering* 161.1, *mounting* 713.8
alpinist *mountaineer* 161.8, *ascender* 713.12
Alps Mountains and Hills 569
already *before now* 651.21
Alsatian Breeds of Dogs 35
al segno Musical Terms and Expression Marks 140
also *additionally* 748.15
also-ran *horse racing* 159.10, *finalist* 422.16
also-ran [Inf] *loser* 846.9
Altai Breeds of Sheep 16
Altamura Breeds of Sheep 16
Altar Constellations 7
altar *church interior* 83.9
altarpiece *painting* 143.3
Altay *or* **Altai Mountains** Mountains and Hills 569
alter *modify* 340.13, *make new* 652.20, *change* 665.14, *cause change* 665.16, *convert* 670.11, *shake* 684.7, *take off* 749.7, *rectify* 807.22
alterable *renewable* 652.15, *changeable* 665.11, 666.3, *convertible* 670.9
alterably *changeably* 665.22, 666.7
alteration **665.2;** *modification* 340.5, *new start* 652.5, *change* 665.1, *conversion* 670.1, *rectification* 807.8
alteration of plan *vacillation* 380.3
altercate *argue* 329.11, *dispute* 463.9
altercation *quarrel* 272.4, 302.7, *argument* 329.1, *dissent* 347.1, *contention* 422.1, *disagreement* 463.1

altered *misrepresentative* 193.14, *modified* 340.9, *renewed* 652.14, *changed* 665.10
alter ego *friend* 62.2, *interrelation* 729.2, *look-alike* 730.4, *counterpart* 733.5
alterer *changer* 665.9
alter *or* **depart from one's course** *deviate* 698.15
altering *converting* 670.8, *subtraction* 749.1
alternate *alternative* 80.2, *substitute* 613.17, 672.2, 672.3, *cover for* 613.34, *frequent* 663.6, *be regular* 663.10, *be changeable* 666.5, *oscillating* 683.8, *oscillate* 683.12, *reciprocal* 729.4, *reciprocate* 729.7
alternate angles *angle* 6.37
alternate breathing *swimming techniques* 164.2
alternated *reciprocal* 729.4
alternate jurors *jury selection* 54.14
alternately *regularly* 663.14, *reciprocally* 729.10, *sequentially* 770.13
alternating *frequent* 663.6, *changeable* 666.3, *oscillating* 683.8, *reciprocal* 729.4
alternating current (a.c.) *electric current* 10.39
alternating current (a.c.) generator *generator* 14.43
alternatingly *reciprocally* 729.10
alternation *mathematical logic* 6.60, *frequency* 663.2, *changeableness* 666.1, *substitution* 672.1, *oscillation* 683.1, *interrelatedness* 727.3, *reciprocity* 729.1, *series* 770.3
alternative 80.2; *means* 102.1, *choice* 382.3, *substitute* 613.17, 613.23, 672.3, *frequent* 663.6, *substitution* 672.1
alternative choice *substitution* 672.1
alternative comedy *comedy* 136.11
alternative hypothesis *hypothesis testing* 6.52
alternatively **613.36;** *by choice* 382.18, *regularly* 663.14, *changeably* 666.7, *instead* 672.8
alternative medicine **107.4;** *healing art* 115.13
alternative practitioner *healer* 107.22
alternative reading *interpretation* 365.1
alternative route *thoroughfare* 692.6
alternator *generator* 14.43
alter *or* **depart from one's course** *deviate* 698.15
alternative theater *drama* 136.1
Alter-Réal Horse and Pony Breeds 159
althaea Flowers 42
althorn *or* **alto horn** Musical Instruments 142
although *counter* 510.8
altimeter Fields of Measurement 589, *measuring instrument* 589.12, *height measurement* 596.5
altimetrical **596.13**
altimetrically **596.23**
altimetry Fields of Measurement 589, *height measurement* 596.5

altitude *line* 6.35, *triangle* 6.41, *celestial sphere* 7.4, *dimension* 10.5, *situation* 573.1, Fields of Measurement 589, *measurability* 589.2, *height* 596.1, *quantity* 738.1, *degree* 739.1, *superiority* 744.1
altitudes Fields of Measurement 589, *heights* 596.4
altitude sickness *climbing dangers* 161.5
altitudinal *high* 596.7
altitudinous *mountainous* 569.5, *high* 596.7
alto *voice* 141.5, *musical part* 760.8
alto clef *written music* 140.21
altocumuliform *cloudy* 9.44
altocumulous *cloudy* 9.44
altocumulus *cloud* 9.17
altogether *clean* [Inf] 111.21, *on average* 742.10, *as one* 752.21, *one and all* 759.12, *on the whole* 759.13, *completely* 759.14, 761.13
altogether [Inf], the *bareness* 614.3
altophobia Phobias 283
alto-relievo *relief carving* 144.2
altostratous *cloudy* 9.44
altostratus *cloud* 9.17
altricial *newly hatched* 36.20
altruism Philosophical Schools of Thought 4, *charity* 305.3, *philanthropy* 307.1, *unselfishness* 443.2, *kindness* 445.3, *virtue* 447.1
altruist Philosophical Schools of Thought 4, *benevolent person* 305.6, *philanthropist* 307.5, *good person* 445.6, *volunteer* 504.7
altruistic *of a philosophy* 4.13, *charitable* 305.9, *philanthropic* 307.6, *unselfish* 443.5, *kind* 445.12, *virtuous* 447.5, *voluntary* 504.9
altruistically *charitably* 305.15, *philanthropically* 307.9, *unselfishly* 443.9, *kindly* 445.20, *virtuously* 447.9, *voluntarily* 504.19
alula *plumage* 36.7
alum *salt* 11.12
aluminum Chemical Elements and Common Allotropes 11, *construction material* 14.21, *electricity* 14.34
aluminum alloy *shipbuilding* 690.4
aluminum foil *cooking equipment* 91.6, *wrapping* 613.10
aluminum hull *sailboat parts and accessories* 150.4
alumna *learner* 48.6
alumnus *learner* 48.6
alveolar arch Human Bones 19
alveolar bone Human Bones 19
alveolar palate *speech organ* 205.4
alveolate *of fungi* 47.19
alveoli *respiration* 558.8
always *for good* 445.23, *all the time* 639.16, *ever* 640.7, *permanently* 667.6, *continually* 669.10, *regularly* 730.21
always ill *unhealthy* 114.23
always victorious *victorious* 845.10
alyssum Flowers 42
Alzheimer's disease *neurological disease* 114.20
A.M. *horologically* 646.15, *morning* 655.2
amah *personal attendant* 69.5
amain [Arch] *swiftly* 694.16
amalgam *chemical compound* 11.4, *mixed thing* 751.2, *compound* 757.4

amalgamate *merge* 64.21, *mix* 751.12, *combine* 757.9, *join* 827.17

amalgamated *mixed* 751.8, *combined* 757.5, *collected* 757.8

amalgamation *alliance* 64.2, *mixture* 751.1, *combination* 757.1, *association* 827.6

Amalthea Planets and Their Satellites 7

amanuensis *record keeper* 185.8, *assistant* 511.3

amaranth *purple pigment* 262.2

amaranthine *purple* 262.6

amaranthus Flowers 42

amaryllis Flowers 42

amass *assemble* 59.23, *heap* 105.19, *acquire* 467.19, *unite* 752.14

amassed *collected* 59.19, *stored* 105.14

amassment *acquisition* 467.4

Amasya Herik Breeds of Sheep 16

amateur *unskilled person* 128.3, *unskilled* 128.5, *bungled* 128.7, *type of wrestling* 152.9, *combat* 152.17, *ignorant person* 349.4, *semiskilled* 349.6, *new arrival* 652.7, *immature* 652.12

Amateur Athletic Association (AAA) swimming *swimming associations* 164.10

Amateur Athletic Union (AAU) *boxing associations* 152.7

Amateur Athletic Union of the United States (AAU) *gymnastics organizations* 157.9

amateur boxer *boxer* 152.8

amateur dramatics *drama* 136.1

amateur hockey *hockey* 158.1

amateurish *unskilled* 128.5, *bungled* 128.7, *semiskilled* 349.6, *immature* 652.12

amateurishly *unskillfully* 128.12, *immaturely* 652.23

amateurishness *lack of knowledge* 349.2

amateurism *unskillfulness* 128.1, *lack of knowledge* 349.2

amateur radio *radio broadcasting* 172.4

amateur rowing *rowing* 150.14

amateur theatricals *drama* 136.1

amateur wrestler *wrestler* 152.12

amathophobia Phobias 283

amative *amorous* 299.18

amatively *amorously* 299.30

amativeness *lovingness* 299.4

amatorily *amorously* 299.30

amatory *amorous* 299.18

amaurosis *blindness* 243.3

amaurotic *blind* 243.11

amaxophobia Phobias 283

amaze *cause disbelief* 88.9, *astonish* 292.10, *be wondrous* 294.14

amazed *astonished* 292.6, *wondering* 294.7

amazement *incredulity* 88.3, *astonishment* 292.2, *wonder* 294.1

amazing *astonishing* 292.8, 294.10

amazing! *wonderful!* 294.20

amazingly *surprisingly* 292.14, *astonishingly* 294.19

Amazon Rivers 570

amazon *mannish female* 33.9, *former servicewoman* 77.6, *person of strength* 516.8, *big person* 579.10, *tall person* 596.6

Amazon Basin *hot place* 217.5

amazonian *female* 33.16, *physically strong* 516.10, *tall* 596.9

Amazon lily Flowers 42

ambages [Arch] *circumlocution* 199.2, *circuitousness* 681.2

ambagious *circumlocutory* 199.4, *orbital* 681.5

ambagiousness *circumlocution* 199.2

ambassador *delegate* 79.1, *representative* 187.7, *negotiator* 460.4, *commissioner* 833.5

ambassadorial *delegated* 79.4, *commissioned* 833.6

ambatch Trees and Shrubs 43

amber *brown* 256.5, *yellow thing* 259.4, *yellow* 259.7, *resin* 562.6, *thing of the past* 651.8, *preserver* 815.9

ambergris *incense* 226.3

amber light *safety light* 246.7, *warning signal* 814.3

ambidexterity *manual skill* 127.2, *laterality* 623.3, *duality* 789.2

ambidextrous *skillful* 127.10, *sided* 623.7, *two-sided* 789.9

ambidextrousness *manual skill* 127.2

ambience 615.3; *treatment* 143.6

ambient 615.6

ambient light *lighting* 132.16

ambiguity *lack of candor* 192.4, *obscurity* 197.1, 250.2, *questionableness* 333.7, *language error* 351.10, *unintelligibility* 364.1, *lack of clarity* 364.2, *equivocation* 380.1, *difference* 463.4, *indirectness* 607.3, *duality* 789.2, *indeterminacy* 841.6

ambiguous 632.5; *uncandid* 192.15, *obscure* 197.2, *inscrutable* 250.5, *questionable* 333.13, *unclear* 364.5, *difficult* 364.8, *equivocal* 380.5, *different* 463.7, *indirect* 607.8, *double-edged* 789.10, *indeterminate* 841.14

ambiguously *uncandidly* 192.29, *obscurely* 197.4, *opaquely* 250.9, *questionably* 333.22, *unintelligibly* 364.16, *equivocally* 380.9, *differently* 463.13, *indirectly* 607.15, *circularly* 632.8, *indeterminately* 841.24

ambiguousness *lack of candor* 192.4, *lack of clarity* 364.2

ambisextrous [Inf] *of sexual nature* 20.17

ambisexual *of sexual nature* 20.17

ambisexuality *sexual nature* 20.4

ambit *sphere of influence* 512.7, *region* 564.1, *sphere* 564.10, *circle* 631.2, *round* 633.6

ambition *motive* 178.5, *aspiration* 281.3, *wish* 288.2, *expectations* 356.2, *social ambition* 408.2, *energy* 414.4, *motivation* 508.1

ambitious *aspiring* 281.8, *desirous* 288.13, *intending* 374.6, *attempting* 390.4, *enterprising* 391.5

ambitiously 390.10; *expectantly* 281.16, *desirously* 288.26, *prospectively* 374.12, *enterprisingly* 391.11

ambivalence *vacillation* 378.1, *equivocation* 380.1, *difference* 463.4, *duality* 789.2, *irresolution* 841.3

ambivalence (of impulse) *anxiety disorder* 108.11

ambivalent *vacillating* 378.5, *equivocal* 380.5, *different* 463.7, *double-edged* 789.10, *irresolute* 841.10

ambivalently 378.14; *equivocally* 380.9, *differently* 463.13

ambiversion *personality type* 108.6

ambivert *personality type* 108.6

amble *bodily movement* 677.11, *walk* 677.17, *slow motion* 693.3, *move slowly* 693.11

ambler *saddle horse* 159.5

ambling *slow* 693.7

amblyopia *faulty vision* 243.1

amblyopic *visually impaired* 243.9

ambrosia *food* 90.1, *sweetener* 222.2

ambrosial *pleasurable* 214.6, *tasty* 219.4, *sweet* 222.5, *fragrant* 226.4

Ambrosian chant *ritual music* 85.9

ambrotype *older photograph* 132.4

ambulance chaser *lawyer* 54.5

ambulance siren *signal* 183.6

ambulant *moving* 677.12

ambulatory *church architecture* 134.11, *passage* 691.5

ambush 292.4, 292.11; *be at war* 76.32, *conceal* 181.12, *attack* 418.17, *danger* 811.1, *hidden danger* 813.3, *trap* 813.6, *stratagem* 822.2, *be cunning* 822.5, *concealment* 844.2

ambushed *surprised* 292.5, *trapped* 813.5

Amchitka Islands 572

ameliorable *improvable* 807.13

ameliorate *refine* 534.7, *smooth over* 545.12, *change for the better* 665.17, *perfect* 805.19, *improve* 807.15, 825.26

amelioration *education* 48.1, *change for the better* 665.4, *improvement* 807.1

ameliorative *changeable* 665.11, *improving* 807.14

Amen *sun* 7.15, Deities 82

amen *yes* 346.2

amen! *hallelujah!* 83.18

amenability *acquiescence* 373.3, *sense of duty* 433.2

amenable *acquiescent* 373.9, *courteous* 410.6, *submitting* 421.3, *obedient* 426.4, *duteous* 433.7

amenably *courteously* 410.13

amend *interpret* 365.12, *put right* 429.14, *change for the better* 665.17, *rectify* 807.22, *repair* 809.10

amendable *compensable* 743.4, *repairable* 809.7

amendatory *compensatory* 743.5

amended *interpreted* 365.9, *changed* 665.10

amender *atoner* 313.4, *improver* 807.11, *repairer* 809.5

amending *compensatory* 743.5

amendment *remedy* 115.1, *interpretation* 365.1, *change for the better* 665.4, *compensation* 743.1, *rectification* 807.8, *repair* 809.1

amends *remedy* 115.1, *reparation* 273.2, *atonement* 313.1, *compensation* 453.7, 478.2, 743.1, *restoration* 809.2

amenities *courtesies* 410.3

amenity *courtesy* 410.1, *convenience* 825.7

amenorrhea *bleeding* 25.10

Amen-Ra *sun* 7.15, Deities 82

ament *flower head* 42.4

Ameraucana Breeds of Fowl 16

amerce *confiscate* 480.21

amerceable *punishable* 604.21

amercement *liability* 604.6

America *world region* 564.6

America First party Political Parties 50

American accent *regional pronunciation* 205.7

American Alpine Club (AAC) *mountaineering associations* 161.7

American Arbitration Association *negotiator* 460.4

American Birkebeiner *cross-country skiing* 162.7

American bobtail Breeds of Cats 35

American bond *masonry* 14.22

American breakfast *meal* 92.8

American Canoe Association (ACA) *canoe associations* 150.13

American Casting Association *fishing associations* 154.11

American Civil War Major Wars 76

American cocker spaniel Breeds of Dogs 35

American crawl *swimming techniques* 164.2

American curl Breeds of Cats 35

American eagle *national emblem* 184.7

American eagle silver *or* **gold bullion coin** *US coinage* 484.10

American Express Industrial Index *or* **AMEX Index** *stock exchange* 457.3

American Federation of Labor–Congress of Industrial Organizations (AFL–CIO) *organized labor* 57.5

American Football Conference (AFC) *football associations* 155.14

American foxhound Breeds of Dogs 35

American Labor party Political Parties 50

American Landrace Breeds of Pigs 16

American League *baseball leagues and championship games* 147.8

American Legion member *former soldier* 77.5

American Merino Breeds of Sheep 16

American National Standards Institute *standard* 589.10

American Quarter Horse Horse and Pony Breeds 159

American Rambouillet Breeds of Sheep 16

American Revolution Major Wars 76

American Rowing Association *rowing associations* 150.17

American Saddle Horse *or* **American Saddlebred** Horse and Pony Breeds 159

American Samoa American States 564, Islands 572

American scene painting Western Art Styles 133

American Shetland pony Horse and Pony Breeds 159

American shorthair Breeds of Cats 35

American Sign Language *artificial language* 5.9, *voiceless speech* 206.4, *aid to the deaf* 229.3

American Staffordshire terrier Breeds of Dogs 35

American Standardbred Horse and Pony Breeds 159

American Standard Code for Information Interchange (ASCII) *character* 15.18

American Stars and Stripes *flag* 184.8

American stroke *rowing techniques* 150.16

American Theatre Wing *drama* 136.1

American Tunis Breeds of Sheep 16

American twist service *tennis strokes* 165.2

American water spaniel Breeds of Dogs 35

American Welsh pony Horse and Pony Breeds 159

American whist Card Games 168

American wirehair Breeds of Cats 35

America's Cup *prizes* 453.3

America's Cup race *competitive sailing* 150.6

America's national sport *baseball* 147.1

America's pastime *baseball* 147.1

americium Chemical Elements and Common Allotropes 11

Amerindian *race* 1.5, *racial* 1.12

Ameslan *artificial language* 5.9, *voiceless speech* 206.4, *aid to the deaf* 229.3

amethyst *purple thing* 262.3

amethystine *purple* 262.6

amiability 271.3; *pleasantness* 271.1, *lovability* 299.5, *benevolence* 305.1, *sociability* 408.1, *courtesy* 410.1

amiable *friendly* 62.5, *harmless* 73.9, *likable* 271.6, *lovable* 299.20, *benevolent* 305.7, *sociable* 408.11, *courteous* 410.6

amiableness *friendship* 62.1

amiably *amicably* 62.13, *lovably* 299.31, *benevolently* 305.13, *sociably* 408.19, *courteously* 410.13

amicability *friendship* 62.1, *good feeling* 266.4, *sociability* 408.1

amicable *friendly* 62.5, *sensitive* 267.3, *likable* 290.7, *loving* 299.15, *sociable* 408.11, *compatible* 735.14

amicableness *friendship* 62.1

amicably 62.13; *likably* 290.12, *lovably* 299.31, *sociably* 408.19

amice *vestment* 84.11

amicus curiae *indirect influence* 512.4, *backstage manipulator* 844.3

amid *in the middle* 772.21

amidships *sailboat parts and accessories* 150.4, *midway* 772.22

amidst *in the middle* 772.21

amigo *friend* 62.2

amino acid 12.8; *food content* 90.3

amino-acid chain *protein* 12.9

amino-acid residue *amino acid* 12.8

amino-acid sequence *molecular biology* 13.18

amiss *wrongly* 351.18, *muddled* 766.13

amity *friendship* 62.1, *coexistence* 73.3, *love* 299.1, *agreement* 462.1

Amman Countries 566

ammeter *electrical instrument* 14.41, *meter* 589.13

ammo dump [Inf] *arsenal* 78.3

ammonia *unpleasant-smelling thing* 227.2

ammoniacal *stinking* 227.3

ammonite *convoluted thing* 632.3, *prehistoric animal* 653.8

ammonium salts *fertilizer* 22.6

ammunition 78.11; *supplies* 102.3, *hunting equipment* 160.4

ammunition box *ammunition* 78.11, *box* 578.5

ammunition chest *arsenal* 78.3

ammunition dump *arsenal* 78.3

ammunition room *arsenal* 78.3

ammunition round *hunting equipment* 160.4

ammunition ship *warship* 77.21, *arsenal* 78.3

ammunition train *arsenal* 78.3

amnesia *trance* 108.18, *forgetfulness* 186.3, 355.1, *mental block* 318.5

amnesiac or **amnesic** *forgetful* 355.6

amnesic disorder *mental disorder* 108.8

amnesty 355.5; *peace treaty* 73.5, *peace offering* 74.5, *obliteration* 186.1, *forgiveness* 312.1, *leniency* 423.1, *deliverance* 817.1, *cancellation* 834.1

Amnesty International *charitable organization* 305.4

amniocentesis *prenatal diagnosis* 107.9

amnion *developmental biology* 13.22

amniotic *developmental* 13.33

amoeba *protozoan* 39.17, *little thing* 580.3

amoebic *protozoan* 39.27, *tiny* 580.9

amoeboid *protozoan* 39.27, *tiny* 580.9

amoeboid protozoan *protozoan* 39.17

among *in the middle* 772.21

amongst [Brit] *in the middle* 772.21

among the also-rans [Inf] *defeated* 846.11

among the missing *missing* 576.11

among those remaining *with a remainder* 750.12

Amor Planets and Their Satellites 7, Deities 82, *goddesses and gods of love* 299.14

amoral *careless* 289.8, *immoral* 430.11, 432.9, *depraved* 448.10

amoralism *immorality* 432.1, *depravity* 448.2

amoralist *badly behaved person* 399.8

amorality *carelessness* 289.2, *immorality* 432.1, *depravity* 448.2

amorally *carelessly* 289.18, *immorally* 432.18, *unvirtuously* 448.16

amorevole Musical Terms and Expression Marks 140

amorist *lover* 299.11

amorous 299.18; *desirous* 20.18

amorously 299.30; *lustfully* 20.24

amorousness *sexual love* 299.3, *lovingness* 299.4

amorphism *shapelessness* 625.1

amorphous *status adjectives* 11.25, *electric* 14.47, *obscure* 197.2, *unemphatic* 201.2, *difficult* 364.8, *shapeless* 625.2, *indeterminate* 841.14

amorphously *chemically* 11.42, *shapelessly* 625.5, *indeterminately* 841.24

amorphousness *obscurity* 197.1, *shapelessness* 625.1, *indeterminacy* 841.6

amount *quantity* 105.5, 738.1, *price* 494.1, *measurability* 589.2, *degree* 739.1, *mathematical result* 783.4

amount of elements or **compounds in chemical reactions** Fields of Measurement 589

amount of light polarization Fields of Measurement 589

amount of salt Fields of Measurement 589

amount of sugar Fields of Measurement 589

amount outstanding *difference* 750.3

amount owing 488.5

amount to *price* 494.12, *be whole* 759.9, *total* 783.10, 784.12

amour *love affair* 299.9, *fornication* 432.3

amour propre [Fr] *proudness* 297.3, *self-admiration* 402.4

Amoy Islands 572

ampere Scientific and Technical Units 589

ampere-hour Scientific and Technical Units 589

Ampère–Laplace law Classical Physical Laws 10

Ampère's law Classical Physical Laws 10

ampere-turn Scientific and Technical Units 589

ampersand Punctuation Marks 5, *means of connection* 754.4

amphetamine *tonic* 115.8, *addictive drug* 117.10, *stimulants* 121.18

Amphibia *amphibian* 37.10

amphibian 37.10, 37.14; *type of animal* 34.5, *warship* 77.21, *military aircraft* 77.30

amphibious force squadron *military organization* 58.4

amphibious landing craft Ships and Boats 690

amphibiousness *skill* 127.1

amphibious operations *offensive warfare* 76.1

amphibious truck or **duck** *warship* 77.21

amphibious warfare *naval warfare* 76.10

amphibolous *equivocal* 380.5

amphibolously *equivocally* 380.9

amphiboly *equivocation* 380.1

amphibrach *meter* 139.10

amphigoric *meaningless* 362.7

amphigory or **amphigouri** *nonsense* 362.2

amphimacer *meter* 139.10

Amphineura *mollusk* 39.13

amphineuran *mollusk* 39.13

amphioxus *protochordate* 39.4

amphipod *crustacean* 39.10

amphisbaena Legendary Creatures 360

amphitheater *theater* 136.16, *rock face* 161.6, *place for viewing* 242.13

Amphitrite *legendary sea being* 571.4

amphora *vessel* 578.11

amphoteric *acid* 11.27

amphoteric compound *acid* 11.10, *base* 11.11

ample 795.9; *plentiful* 97.4, *satisfying* 273.5, *abundant* 498.8, *spacious* 563.13, *big* 579.13, *broad* 592.5, *thick* 594.5, *quantitative* 738.6

ampleness *largeness* 579.2, *breadth* 592.1, *thickness* 594.1

ample time *leisure* 125.1

amplifiable *enlargeable* 581.13

amplification *circuit function* 14.38, *enlargement* 194.2, *diffuseness* 199.1, *clarity* 363.2, *translation* 365.4, *increase* 581.3, *expansion* 592.2, *intensification* 746.2

amplified *broadcast* 172.12, *enlarged* 194.8, *diffuse* 199.3, *swelled* 581.10, *broadened* 592.7

amplifier *circuit* 10.43, *radio reception* 172.2, *sound amplifier* 230.5

amplify *conduct* 14.51, *enlarge* 194.12, *be diffuse* 199.5, *sound* 230.8, *translate* 365.16, *generate power* 514.19, *increase* 581.16, *intensify* 746.8

amplifying *descriptive* 202.11

amplitude *wave form* 10.13, *plenty* 97.2, *diffuseness* 199.1, *sound quality* 230.4, *available space* 563.6, *size* 579.1, *breadth* 592.1, *wave* 683.4, *quantity* 738.1, *degree* 739.1

amplitude modulation (AM) *radio transmission* 172.3, *radio frequency* 661.3

amplitudinous *spacious* 563.13

amply 579.20; *plentifully* 97.11, *generously* 498.12, *spaciously* 563.17, *wholly* 738.9

amputate *practice surgery* 107.33, *take off* 749.7, *separate* 753.12

amputation *surgery* 107.15, *subtraction* 749.1, *separateness* 753.3

Amritmahal Breeds of Cattle 16

AM station *radio broadcasting* 172.4

Amsterdam Countries 566

amtrac *warship* 77.21

amu Scientific and Technical Units 589

Amu Darya Rivers 570

amulet *sacred object* 83.11, *talisman* 86.9, *preserver* 815.9

Amundsen Sea Oceans and Seas 571

Amur Rivers 570

amuse *give pleasure* 214.13, *be humorous* 277.11, *make someone laugh* 368.7

amusement 167.7, 277.2; *game* 167.1, *fun* 269.4, *pleasure* 271.2, *sporting event* 422.6

amusement park *amusement* 167.7

amusement park and playground equipment 167.8

amusing *recreational* 167.10, *cheering* 269.8, *likable* 271.6, *humorous* 277.9, *sociable* 408.11

amusingly *recreationally* 167.15, *humorously* 277.13, *sociably* 408.19

amychophobia Phobias 283

amylaceous *pulpy* 561.19

amylase *enzyme* 12.11

amyloid *of fungi* 47.19

amylopectin *polysaccharide* 12.5

amylose *polysaccharide* 12.5

amyotrophic lateral sclerosis *neurological disease* 114.20

ana *collection* 105.12, *compilation* 174.4

anabatic *rising* 713.14

anabatic wind *wind* 9.12

anabolic *biochemical* 12.25, *physiological* 13.29

anabolically *biochemically* 12.27

anabolic steroid *hormone* 12.16

anabolic steroid test *competition* 166.18

anabolism *metabolism* 12.21, *physiology* 13.13

anabranch *tributary* 570.2

anachronism *wrong time* 660.2

anachronistic *different in time* 648.2, *misdated* 660.6

anachronistically **660.13**

anacoluthia [Form] *language error* 351.10

anaconda *snake* 37.6

anacrusis *meter* 139.10

anaerobe *living organism* 13.10

anaerobic *physiological* 13.29

anaerobic respiration *respiration* 12.24

anagalactic nebula *nebula* 7.6

anaglyph *relief carving* 144.2

anaglyphy *relief carving* 144.2

anaglyptic *sculptural* 144.7

anagnorisis *literary device* 139.12

anagoge *occultism* 86.1, *mysteriousness* 844.5

anagogical *occult* 86.16, *mysterious* 844.11

anagram *spelling* 5.26

anagrammatic *equivocal* 380.5

anagrammatically *linguistically* 5.44

anagrammatism *spelling* 5.26

anagrammatize *word* 5.43

anagrams Children's and Party Games 167

analects *passage* 692.1

analeptic *remedial* 115.14, *restorative* 809.9

anal fin *fish characteristic* 38.8

analgesia *analgesic* 115.6, *insensibility* 213.1

analgesic 115.6; *medicinal* 115.15, *anesthetic* 213.3, 213.6, *reliever* 275.4, *moderator* 521.2, *moderating* 521.5

anal intercourse *sex act* 20.10

analog *chemical compound* 11.4, *correlation* 729.3, *comparability* 733.2

analog clock *or* **watch** Timepieces and Timers 646

analog dial *face* 646.8

analogize *correspond* 606.8, *compare* 733.13

analogous *corresponding* 606.6, *related* 727.6, *correlative* 729.6, *comparable* 733.8, *conforming* 735.17

analogously *correspondingly* 606.10, *relevantly* 727.12, *correlatively* 729.12, *comparably* 733.18, *conformingly* 735.37

analogousness *correspondence* 606.2, *comparability* 733.2, *conformity* 735.7

analogue *comparability* 733.2

analogy *philosophical term* 4.7, *correspondence* 606.2, *relatedness* 727.1, *correlation* 729.3, *comparability* 733.2

anal-retentive *self-restrained* 455.6

anal sex *sex act* 20.10

analysis 11.17; *philosophical investigation* 4.4, Branches of Mathematics 6, *calculus* 6.28, *chemistry* 11.1, *psychotherapy* 108.4, *treatment* 110.7, *identification* 184.1, *reasoning* 319.2, *questioning* 333.2, *experiment* 335.1, *interpretation* 365.1, *separation* 753.1, *categorization* 767.5, *calculation* 784.1

analysis of variance *statistical methods* 6.53

analysis situs [Arch] *topology* 6.45

analyst *mathematician* 6.2, *psychologist* 108.33, *psychiatrist* 108.34, *adviser* 176.5, *questioner* 333.9, *experimenter* 335.5

analytic 11.32; *dialectical* 4.16, *language type* 5.11, *of language* 5.35, *questioning* 333.11, *experimental* 335.8, *diagrammatic* 767.17

analytical *mathematical* 6.65, 784.9, *theoretical* 6.66, *chemical* 11.24, *rational* 319.8

analytical chemist *chemist* 11.2

analytical chemistry Branches of Chemistry 11

analytical journalism *print journalism* 175.4

analytically *philosophically* 4.23, *linguistically* 5.44, *mathematically* 6.93, *chemically* 11.42, *questioningly* 333.21, *experimentally* 335.14, *judiciously* 337.16, *to pieces* 758.8, *in place* 767.24

analytical philosophy Branches of Philosophy 4

analytical psychology Psychological Theories, Schools 108

analytic balance *measuring instrument* 589.12

analytic cubism Western Art Styles 133

analytic geometry *geometry* 6.32

analyze *philosophize* 4.19, *discuss* 4.22, *theorize* 6.84, *psychologize* 108.41, *identify* 184.11, *confer* 210.13, *reason* 319.11, *question* 333.16, *experiment* 335.11, *discriminate* 337.12, *interpret* 365.12, *divide* 753.18, *categorize* 767.21, *sort* 777.13

analyzed *questioned* 333.15, *categorized* 767.15

analyzer *system software* 15.13

anamnesis *prayer* 85.10, *memory* 354.1

anamorphosis *misrepresentation* 188.1

Ananke Planets and Their Satellites 7

anapest *or* **anapaest** *meter* 139.10

anapestic *metrical* 139.20

anaphase *cell division* 13.17

anaphora *literary device* 139.12, *repetition* 797.1

anarch [Arch] *anarchist* 51.4

anarchic 51.5; *of a political philosophy* 4.14, *governmental* 49.24, *lawless* 53.26, *subversive* 427.11, *violating* 466.8, *disorderly* 766.15, *dissident* 782.12, *independent* 829.12

anarchical *anarchic* 51.5, *subversive* 427.11

anarchically 51.10; *lawlessly* 53.35, *defiantly* 466.14, *disruptively* 766.26

anarchism 51.3; *political and economic philosophy* 4.6, *anarchy* 51.1

anarchist 51.4; *political and economic philosopher* 4.10, *malefactor* 306.6, *resister* 417.5, *seditionist* 427.7, *violent animal or person* 520.4, *destroyer* 523.6, *dissenter* 782.8

anarchistic 51.7; *destructive* 523.8

anarcho-syndicalism *anarchism* 51.3

anarcho-syndicalist *political and economic philosopher* 4.10, *of a political philosophy* 4.14, *anarchist* 51.4

anarchy 51.1; *mob rule* 49.12, *subversion* 427.3, *infraction* 466.4, *lawlessness* 766.6

anastomosis *linkage* 752.3

anastrophe *inverted thing* 608.4

anathema *hated thing* 300.5, *curse* 301.1, *condemnation* 438.2

anathematize *curse* 301.1

Anatolian *language family* 5.12

Anatolian Black Breeds of Cattle 16

anatomical *anthropological* 1.10, *biological* 13.27, *organic* 551.18

anatomically *biologically* 13.36, *structurally* 551.24

anatomist 551.16; *life scientist* 13.26

anatomization *deconstruction* 758.2

anatomize *circumstantiate* 726.12, *divide* 753.18

anatomy 13.5, 13.12; *life science* 13.1, *study of life* 28.9, *form* 551.3, *science of structure* 551.15, *nature* 624.5

ancestor *person of the past* 651.7, *first cause* 675.6, *predecessor* 769.8

ancestors *dead person* 29.7, *old people* 653.6

ancestor worship *idolatry* 83.4

ancestor worshiper *idolater* 83.7

ancestor-worshiping *idolatrous* 83.13

ancestral *historical* 3.10, *antiquarian* 651.13, *olden* 653.11

ancestral hall *or* **seat** *mansion* 60.5

ancestrally *historically* 3.17, *archaically* 653.20, *beforehand* 657.19

ancestry *family tree* 65.3, *nobleness* 70.3

anchor *sailing* 150.25, *mountaineer* 161.10, *security* 464.1, *secure* 464.9, *retainer* 471.3, *base* 601.10, *supporter* 605.9, *intertwine* 752.19, *yoke* 754.8, *bind* 754.14, *protection* 810.2, *safety device* 810.15, *restraint* 826.8, *restrain* 826.19

anchorage *harbor* 812.6

anchor bait *fish* 154.14

anchor bend Knots, Bends, Hitches, Splices 754

anchor chain *tackle* 754.6

anchored *stabilized* 674.4, *blocked* 826.13

anchoretic *religious* 81.21

anchorite *religious* 84.9, *unsocial person* 409.5, *individualist* 756.3, *hermit* 782.9, *loner* 788.8

anchor light *safety light* 246.7

anchorman *professional worker* 123.11, *news reporting* 171.5, *broadcasting personnel* 172.11

anchor ring *curved surface* 6.43

anchor rode *sailboat parts and accessories* 150.4

anchorwoman *professional worker* 123.11, *news reporting* 171.5, *broadcasting personnel* 172.11

anchovy *food fish and shellfish* 90.20

anchusa Flowers 42

Ancien Régime [Fr] Ages, Decades, Eras 641,

ancien régime [Fr] *past time* 3.6, *aristocracy* 70.2

ancient *historical* 3.10, *of language* 5.35, *aged* 27.15, *person of the past* 651.7, *past* 651.11, *olden* 653.11

ancient coins 484.12

Ancient Egyptian text *other text* 81.19

ancient flint *thing of the past* 651.8

ancient history *past time* 3.6, 651.1, *early stage* 657.3

ancient language 5.10

anciently 653.18; *beforehand* 657.19

ancient man *primitive humanity* 18.4

ancient manuscript *antiquity* 653.4

ancient monument *monument* 185.10, *thing of the past* 651.8

ancientness *oldness* 653.1

ancient ruin *thing of the past* 651.8

ancient ruins *ruin* 523.4

Ancients Western Art Styles 133

ancient tale *tradition* 653.5

ancient times *past time* 3.6, 651.1, *oldness* 653.1

ancient wisdom *tradition* 1.7, 653.5

ancient woodland *trees* 43.4

ancient world *past time* 651.1

ancillary 605.5, 605.14; *subordinate* 745.8, *supplementary* 825.17

ancon Architectural Elements 134

Ancona Breeds of Fowl 16

ancraophobia *or* **anemophobia** Phobias 283

ancylostomiasis *tropical disease* 114.10

and *additionally* 748.15

and all *one and all* 759.12

Andalusian Breeds of Cattle 16, Breeds of Fowl 16, Horse and Pony Breeds 159

Andalusian Black Breeds of Cattle 16

Andalusian Blond Breeds of Cattle 16, Breeds of Pigs 16

Andalusian-Carthusian Horse and Pony Breeds 159

Andalusian Spotted Breeds of Pigs 16

Andaman Islands Islands 572

Andaman Sea Oceans and Seas 571

andante Musical Terms and Expression Marks 140

andante *slowly* 693.14

Andes Mountains and Hills 569

Andorra Countries 566

Andorra la Vella Countries 566

and others *et cetera* 793.12

androecium *flower part* 42.3

androgen Human Hormones 12, *hormone* 12.16

androgynal *of sexual nature* 20.17

androgyne *sexual nature* 20.4, *mannish female* 33.9

androgynous *of sexual nature* 20.17

androgyny *sexual nature* 20.4

android *humanlike machine* 18.12

Andromeda Constellations 7

androphobia Phobias 283

Androscoggin Rivers 570

androsterone Human Hormones 12

and so *with the effect of* 676.12, *under the circumstances* 726.16

and so forth *additionally* 748.15, *inclusively* 763.8

and so on *additionally* 748.15, *inclusively* 763.8, *et cetera* 793.12

and there *with the effect of* 676.12

and the rest *et cetera* 793.12

anecdotage *old age* 27.5

anecdotal *narrative* 202.12

anecdote *narration* 202.3, *retrospect* 354.2

anecdotist *descriptive writer* 202.10

anemia *blood disease* 114.14, *paleness* 252.2

anemic *unhealthy* 114.23, *of disease* 114.25, *drained of color* 252.6

anemogram *weather data* 9.6

anemograph *weather instrument* 9.7

anemographic *barometric* 9.39

anemological *windy* 9.42

anemology *meteorology* 9.1

anemometer *weather instrument* 9.7, Fields of Measurement 589

anemometric *barometric* 9.39

anemometry *meteorology* 9.1, Fields of Measurement 589

anemone Flowers 42

aneroid barometer *weather instrument* 9.7

anesthesia *surgery* 107.15, *analgesic* 115.6, *insensibility* 213.1, *anesthetic* 213.3

anesthesiologist *medical specialist* 107.20

anesthesiology Medical Specialties 107

anesthetic 213.3, 213.6; *analgesic* 115.6, *medicinal* 115.15, *reliever* 275.4, *soporific* 415.6, *moderator* 521.2

anesthetization *ease* 275.1

anesthetize 213.8; *practice surgery* 107.33, *medicate* 115.18, *relieve* 275.8, *make inactive* 415.16, *calm* 521.8

anesthetized *desensitized* 213.5, *not awake* 415.12

aneurysm *or* aneurism *cardiovascular disease* 114.13

anew *again* 652.22, 797.23

an eye for an eye *reciprocity* 729.1, *equality* 740.1

an eye for an eye and a tooth for a tooth *retaliation* 420.1

anfractuosity *convolution* 632.1

Angara Rivers 570

angel 82.11; *world soul* 82.3, *term of endearment* 299.7, *good person* 445.6, *innocent person* 449.5, *supporter* 605.9

angel [Inf] *producer* 136.28, *defender* 419.14, *giver* 472.7, *generous person* 498.5, *benefactor* 825.15

angel cake *or* angel food cake *cake* 90.36

angel dust [Inf] *tranquilizers* 121.21

angelic 82.21; *virtuous* 447.5, *innocent* 449.6

angelica Herbs and Spices 91

angelica *or* angel lute Musical Instruments 142

angelical *angelic* 82.21

angelically *divinely* 82.24, *virtuously* 447.9, *innocently* 449.13

angelic host *angel* 82.11

angelic order 82.12

angelize *deify* 82.23

Angeln Breeds of Cattle 16

Angeln Saddleback Breeds of Pigs 16

angel of death *personifications and symbols* 29.4, *angel* 82.11, *destroyer* 523.6

angel of mercy *nurse* 107.23, *good person* 445.6

angelology Theologies 81, *angel* 82.11

angels *angelic order* 82.12

Angelus *prayer* 85.10

Angelus bell *signal* 183.6

anger 302.4; *annoyance* 276.2, *annoy* 276.7, *cause dislike* 291.16, *cause hate* 300.12, *make angry* 302.18, *become angry* 302.20, *make irascible* 303.16, *iniquity* 448.3, *protest* 507.1

angered *angry* 302.11

Angerman Rivers 570

angina *cardiovascular disease* 114.13

angina pectoris *cardiovascular disease* 114.13

anginophobia Phobias 283

angiogram *diagnostic radiology* 107.12

angiography *diagnostic radiology* 107.12

angiosperm *seed plant* 41.3, *flowering plant* 42.2

Angiospermae *seed plant* 41.3

angiotensin Human Hormones 12

angle 6.37, 628.1, 628.11; *dimension* 10.5, *kill animals* 30.25, *belief* 87.1, *fish* 154.14, *external appearance* 264.5, *topic* 328.1, *hunt* 385.14

angle [Inf] *motive* 628.6

angle bracket *means of connection* 754.4

angle brackets Punctuation Marks 5, *mathematical symbol* 6.11

angled 628.9; *linear* 6.77, *focused* 328.6, *slanted* 628.10

angled figure 628.3

angle iron *angle* 628.1

angle of bank *miscellaneous aviation terms* 689.9

angle of depression *angle* 6.37

angle of dip *geomagnetism* 10.46

angle of elevation *angle* 6.37

angle off *diverge* 607.11

angle of incidence *miscellaneous aviation terms* 689.9

angle of view *composition* 132.17

angler *fisherman* 154.12, *hunter* 385.6

angler's tale *tall story* 194.5

angle subtended *angle* 6.37

Anglican *Christian* 81.10, *denominational* 81.23

Anglican chant *ritual music* 85.9, *sacred music* 140.3

Anglicanism Christian Groups 81, *Christianity* 81.5

Anglicism *regional pronunciation* 205.7

angling *fishing* 154.1, 154.13

Anglo Nicknames for Inhabitants 61

Anglo-African *race* 1.5, *racial* 1.12

Anglo-Arab Horse and Pony Breeds 159

Anglo-Catholic *Christian* 81.10

Anglo-Catholicism Christian Groups 81, *Christianity* 81.5

Anglo-Indian *race* 1.5, *racial* 1.12

Anglo-Norman Horse and Pony Breeds 159

Anglophobia Phobias 283

Anglo-Saxon *offensive language* 301.5, *profane* 301.10

Anglo-Saxon architecture Architectural Styles 134

Angola Countries 566

Angoni Breeds of Cattle 16

Angora Breeds of Cats 35

angora Fabrics and Fibers 130

angostura bitters *mixed drink* 93.12, *sour thing* 223.3

Angra Mainyu *or* Ahriman *devil* 446.5

angrily 302.24; *crossly* 303.20, *disapprovingly* 507.10

angriness *crossness* 303.4

angry 302.11; *cross* 303.11, *impious* 448.11, *protesting* 507.5, *violent* 520.5, *oceanic* 571.7

angry reply *act of discourtesy* 411.3

angry sea *wave* 571.3

angry young man *dissatisfied person* 274.3, *dissenter* 347.5, 782.8

Angry Young Men Western Literary Groups 139

Angry Young Men *theater* *theater movements* 136.9

angst *strain* 117.4, *worry* 283.4

angstrom Scientific and Technical Units 589

anguilliform *fishlike* 38.10

anguine *snakelike* 37.13

anguish *pain* 215.1, *sorrow* 270.1

anguished *feeling pain* 215.6

angular 628.7; *linear* 6.77, *directional* 677.13

angular acceleration *speed* 10.7

angular deformation *deformation* 14.16

angular direction *angle* 6.37

angular distance *angle* 6.37

angular frequency *frequency* 10.6

angular measure *navigational aid* 690.6

angular measurement 628.4; *angle* 6.37

angular momentum *mass* 10.8, *rotation* 682.1

angular motion *movement* 677.3

angular velocity *speed* 10.7, *rotation* 682.1

anhydride *salt* 11.12

anhydrous *acid* 11.27, *dry* 560.7

anhydrous salt *salt* 11.12

anile *aged* 27.15, *female* 33.16

anilely *maturely* 27.18

aniline *coloring agent* 251.5

anility *old age* 27.5

anima *spirit* 86.10, *psyche* 108.25, *inner nature* 611.4

animadversion *criticism* 438.4, 440.2

animadvert *criticize* 440.12

animadverter *disparager* 440.7

animal 34.1; *living organism* 13.10, *living* 13.28, *animalian* 34.12, *cruel* 306.10

animal breeding *livestock farming* 16.10

animal cell *cell* 13.15

animal charge Heraldic Terms 184

animal conservation *animal welfare* 34.8

animal covering 613.15

animalcular *of animals* 34.13, *tiny* 580.9

animalcule *microorganism* 13.11, *type of animal* 34.5, *little thing* 580.3

animal disease 34.10

animal doctor *veterinarian* 107.27

animal ecology *ecology* 13.25

animal fat *fat* 562.4

animal feed 16.12

animal food 90.2

animal health *livestock farming* 16.10, *animal welfare* 34.8

animal home *shelter* 812.4

animal husbandman *agriculturist* 16.14

animal husbandry *livestock farming* 16.10, *manufacture* 522.2

Animalia *animals* 34.2

animalian 34.12

animalic *animalian* 34.12

animalism *feeling for animals* 34.11

animalistic *animalian* 34.12, *perverted* 432.12

animality *feeling for animals* 34.11, *cruelty* 306.4

animal killer 30.14

animal killing 30.10

animal kingdom *life* 28.1, *animals* 34.2

animal life *living world* 13.9, *life* 28.1, *animals* 34.2

animal-like *animalian* 34.12, *cruel* 306.10

animal lover *animal welfarist* 34.9

animal magnetism *sexuality* 20.3, *allurement* 700.4

animal nutrition *livestock farming* 16.10

animal oil *oil* 562.3

animal painter *painter* 143.7

animal painting *type of painting* 143.5

animal production *livestock farming* 16.10

animal products 522.7

animal protection *animal welfare* 34.8

animal psychology Psychological Theories, Schools 108

animal rearing *or* raising *livestock farming* 16.10

animal rights *rights* 429.4

animal rights activism *equal opportunity* 831.2

animal rights activist *animal welfarist* 34.9

animal rights movement *animal welfare* 34.8, *ecology* 815.3

animals 34.2, Card Games 168, Phobias 283

animal sanctuary *shelter* 812.4, *ecology* 815.3

animal science 34.6

animal scientist 34.7

animal shelter *animal welfare* 34.8, *zoo* 60.14, *shelter* 812.4

animal skin Phobias 283

animal sound 240.1

animal starch *polysaccharide* 12.5

animal suicide *animal killing* 30.10

animal transportation *road transportation* 687.1

animal welfare 34.8; *veterinary medicine* 107.26

animal welfarist 34.9

animal worship *idolatry* 83.4

animal worshiper *idolater* 83.7

anima mundi [L] *world soul* 82.3

animate *living* 13.28, *alive* 28.13, *invigorate* 28.22, *refresh* 94.6, *arouse sensation* 212.11, *bring cheer* 269.12, *inspire* 327.15, *motivate* 508.9, *empower* 514.20, *strengthen* 516.15, *impel* 695.9

animate being *object* 524.6

animated *lively* 28.16, *motion-picture* 137.15, *cheerful* 269.7, *active* 414.13, *motivated* 508.8, *vigorous* 518.2

animated cartoon *drawing* 143.4

animatedly *vitally* 28.23

animated movie *movie type* 137.3

animate existence *life* 28.1

animation *life* 28.1, *liveliness* 28.12, *refreshment* 94.1, *drawing* 143.4, *gaiety* 269.3, *energy* 414.4, *vigor* 518.1

animatism *idolatry* 83.4, *spiritual world* 525.3

animatist *idolater* 83.7

animato Musical Terms and Expression Marks 140

animator *visual artist* 133.6, *drawer* 143.8

animé Tree Products 43

animism Philosophical Schools of Thought 4, *idolatry* 83.4, *occultism* 86.1, *spiritual world* 525.3

animist Philosophical Schools of Thought 4, *idolater* 83.7, *nonmaterialist* 525.7, *parapsychological* 525.9

animistic *of a philosophy* 4.13, *idolatrous* 83.13, *parapsychological* 525.9

animistic spirit *minor deity* 82.2

animosity *hostility* 63.1, *bad feeling* 266.5, *antipathy* 291.2, *hate* 300.1, *resentment* 302.1, *malice* 306.2, *objection* 828.2

animus *hostility* 63.1, *spirit* 86.10, *psyche* 108.25, *antipathy* 291.2, *hate* 300.1

anion *ion* 10.54

anise Herbs and Spices 91

anisogamy *reproductive body* 47.14

Ankara Countries 566

ankh *talisman* 86.9

ankle *appendage* 19.5, *joint* 752.7

anklebone Human Bones 19

ankle-deep *deep* 598.9, *shallow* 599.3

ankle-high *low* 597.10

ankle-length *long* 590.6

ankle socks *legwear* 100.26

anklet *jewelry* 532.6, *circular thing* 631.3

anklets *legwear* 100.26

anklung Musical Instruments 142

Ankole Breeds of Cattle 16

ankus *sharp-pointed thing* 549.4

ankylophobia Phobias 283

Anna Apple Varieties 44

An Nafud Deserts 572

Anna Karenina Famous Lovers 299

annal *chronology* 646.2

annalist *historian* 3.3, *author* 139.13, *record keeper* 185.8, *descriptive writer* 202.10, *keeper of time* 646.10

annalistic *chronological* 639.12, *timekeeping* 646.11

annalistically *horologically* 646.15

annals *history* 3.1, *chronicle* 3.4, *nonfiction* 139.6, *record* 185.1

Annapolis American States 564

Annapurna Mountains and Hills 569

annatto Tree Products 43

anneal *extract* 11.41, *harden* 542.9, *make tough* 547.15

annealed *hardened* 542.7, *toughened* 547.7

annelid *wormlike* 39.24

annelidan *wormlike* 39.24

annex *gain* 467.15, *take over* 477.16, *take back* 477.17, *additional item* 748.3, *add* 748.11, *link* 752.18

annexation *taking over* 477.3, *taking back* 477.4, *addition* 748.1

annexed *taking* 477.12, *additional* 748.8

Annie Oakley *absence of charge* 497.6

annihilate **773.22**; *slaughter* 30.21, *destroy* 186.10, 523.10, *cause to disappear* 265.7, *cause not to exist* 718.14, *not exist* 786.6, *cancel* 834.6

annihilated **773.16**; *destroyed* 186.5, *no more* 718.11

annihilating *destructive* 523.8

annihilation **773.4**; *slaughter* 30.5, *destruction* 186.2, 523.1, *blacking out* 265.2, *extinction* 718.8, *cessation* 773.2

annihilationist *destroyer* 523.6

anniversarial 663.8

anniversary **405.5, 663.4**; *rejoicing* 279.1, *day to remember* 354.5, *commemoration* 405.2, *day* 646.4

anniversary present *gift* 472.2

annotate **365.14**; *identify* 184.11, *dissertate* 203.5

annotated *interpreted* 365.9

annotation **365.2**; *notes* 185.3, *dissertation* 203.1, *appendage* 748.4

annotative **365.10**; *dissertational* 203.4

annotator *dissertator* 203.3, *interpreter* 365.6

announce *communicate* 170.12, *report* 171.9, *broadcast* 172.13, *proclaim* 173.16, *divulge* 180.9, *signal* 183.18, *affirm* 189.21, *predict* 358.14, *make important* 799.14

announced *communicated* 169.15, *broadcast* 172.12, *published* 173.12, *affirmed* 189.11

announcement *communication* 170.2, *publication* 173.1, *advertisement* 173.9, *divulgence* 180.2, *proclamation* 183.8, *affirmation* 189.1, *notice* 358.3, *warning* 814.1

announce one's engagement *propose (marriage)* 299.28

announcer *informer* 170.8, *news reporting* 171.5, *broadcasting personnel* 172.11, *publicizer* 173.11, *discloser* 180.4, *affirmer* 189.9, *speaker* 205.12, *precursor* 769.7

announcing *signaling* 183.14

annoy **276.7, 804.10**; *displease* 272.8, *cause dislike* 291.16, *bore* 296.8, *irritate* 302.16, *make irascible* 303.16, *make irritable* 304.15, *meddle* 414.23, *disturb* 768.10, *cause trouble* 824.21

annoyance **276.2, 804.2**; *unpleasantness* 272.1, *resentment* 302.1, *disturbance* 768.1, *snag* 824.8

annoyed *resentful* 302.8, *cross* 303.11, *disturbed* 768.6, *troubled* 824.15

annoying **804.7**; *unpleasant* 272.6, *aggravating* 276.4, *disliked* 291.10, *maddening* 302.12, *meddling* 414.17, *disturbing* 768.9, *inconvenient* 824.12

annoyingly **276.9, 804.12**; *distastefully* 291.19, *maddeningly* 302.25, *disturbingly* 768.13, *awkwardly* 824.26

annual *garden plant* 17.10, *botanical* 17.15, *plant* 41.2, *of plants* 41.14, *flowering plant* 42.2, *magazine* 175.3, *habitual* 397.9, *periodical publication* 641.6, *periodical* 641.7, *cyclic* 663.7, *anniversarial* 663.8, *regular* 730.12

annual holiday *anniversary* 663.4

annual percentage rate (APR) *interest* 488.4

annually *horticulturally* 17.20, *herbaceously* 41.24, *chronologically* 639.21, *for specified periods* 641.12, *cyclically* 663.15, *regularly* 730.21

annual occurrence *anniversary* 663.4

annual period *season* 654.1

annual report *record* 185.1

annual ring *tree part* 43.2

annuitant *recipient* 473.5

annuity *earnings* 467.5, *something received* 473.2, *pay* 489.6, *income* 492.3

annul *obliterate* 186.8, *disavow* 190.18, *refute* 332.7, *veto* 503.9, *counteract* 510.7, *abolish* 523.11, *cause not to exist* 718.14, *cease* 773.20, *cancel* 834.6

annular *curvilinear* 6.78, *circular* 631.5

annular eclipse *sun* 7.15

annularity *circularity* 631.1

annularly *circularly* 631.8

annulate *circular* 631.5

annulation *circle* 631.2

annulet Architectural Elements 134, Heraldic Terms 184

annulled *disavowing* 190.12, *canceled* 773.15, 834.5

annulment *divorce* 66.1, *obliteration* 186.1, *disavowal* 190.3, *refutation* 332.1, *veto* 503.3, *cessation* 773.2, *cancellation* 834.1

annulus *circle* 6.40, 631.2, *fungal body* 47.4

annunciate *affirm* 189.21

annunciated *affirmed* 189.11

Annunciation Christian Holy Days and Seasons 85

annunciation *type of painting* 143.5, *affirmation* 189.1

annunciative *affirmative* 189.10

annunciator *affirmer* 189.9

annunciatory *affirmative* 189.10

annus mirabilis [L] *marvel* 294.3

anode *electrical conduction* 10.33, *electrochemistry* 11.19, *electron tube* 14.40

anode sludge *electrochemistry* 11.19

anodic *electrochemical* 11.33

anodyne *analgesic* 115.6, *medicinal* 115.15, *reliever* 275.4, *moderator* 521.2, *moderating* 521.5

anoint **562.17**; *gain authority* 52.15, *ordain* 84.16, *perform rites* 85.18, *commission* 833.8

anointed *authorized* 52.11

Anointed One God the Son 82.9

anointing of the sick *Christian rite* 85.5

anointment *acquisition of authority* 52.5

anomalous *unusual* 664.4

anomalously *unusually* 664.7

anomalousness *deviation* 782.6

anomaly *unusualness* 664.2, *special case* 779.7, *deviation* 782.6

anomer *structure* 11.7

anomeric *structural* 11.28

anomerism *structure* 11.7

anon *another time* 648.4

anon [Arch] *right away* 429.20, *early* 657.17

Anon. *anonymity* 182.7

anonymity **182.7**; *cover* 181.4, *unknown thing* 349.3, *nonentity* 786.4, *latency* 844.1

anonymous *disguised* 181.9, *mysterious* 182.10, *unknown* 349.7

anonymously *secretly* 182.14

anopluran *insectile* 40.11

anorak *jacket* 100.18, *ski equipment* 162.10

anorectic *underfed* 98.7, *unhealthy* 114.23, *emaciated* 595.10

anorexia nervosa *delicate eating* 92.3, *eating disorder* 108.15, *dieting* 108.2, *emaciation* 595.2

anorexic *eater* 92.15, *compulsive person* 428.5, *loser* 468.8, *thin person* 595.4

anosmia *lack of sense of smell* 225.2

another *additional* 748.8

another edition *counterpart* 733.5

another idea *reconsideration* 807.9

another matter *incomparability* 734.3

another self *friend* 62.2

another story *incomparability* 734.3

another time **648.4**; *different time* 648.1

another world *nonmaterial world* 525.1

anseriform *avian* 36.19

anserine *foolish* 353.5, *meaningless* 362.7

anserine *or* **anserous** *avian* 36.19

answer **334.1, 334.18**; *rationalize* 4.20, *discuss* 4.22, *pretrial proceedings* 54.13, *suffice* 97.6, *273.10*, *remedy* 115.1, *correspond* 169.19, *utterance* 205.10, *speak* 205.17, *plea* 329.5, *plead* 329.14, *countercharge* 332.3, 332.9, *acknowledgment* 334.2, *response* 334.4, *counterstatement* 334.5, *solution* 334.6, 376.6, *counterevidence* 339.5, *counter* 339.13, *interpretation* 365.1, *expedient* 387.5, *retaliate* 420.4, *atone* 489.24, *reply* 671.5, 671.13, *reason* 675.4, *be useful* 801.9, *be convenient* 803.5, *be effective* 845.15

answerability **334.9**; *sense of duty* 433.2

answerable **334.17**; *solvable* 334.14, *duteous* 433.7, *indebted* 488.7, *causal* 675.7

answerableness *correspondence* 334.8

answerably **334.28**; *correspondingly* 334.27, *causally* 675.12

answer back **334.19**; *countercharge* 332.9, *be insolent* 400.14, *be insubordinate* 416.8, *retaliate* 420.4, *exchange* 673.5

answer book *schoolbook* 48.15

answered *solved* 334.15, *reversed* 671.7

answerer 334.10

answer for **334.24**; *fight* 422.23, *have a sense of duty* 433.13, *guarantee* 458.13

answering **334.11**; *refuting* 332.6, *counterevident* 339.10

answering back *act of defiance* 416.3, *retaliation* 420.1

answering machine *dial* 169.12, *recording instrument* 185.9

answering to *subordinate* 832.8

answer the call *join the army* 76.31, *incur a duty* 433.15

answer the call of nature [Inf] *excrete* 25.20

answer the problem *be desirable* 288.23

answer the purpose *be effective* 845.15

answer to **334.22**; *relate to* 727.9

ant *insect* 40.1, *social insect* 40.6

ant [Inf] *worker* 123.1

anta Architectural Elements 134

antacid *purgative* 115.7

Antaeus *person of strength* 516.8

antagonism *hostility* 63.1, *dissension* 272.3, *antipathy* 291.2, *hate* 300.1, *malice* 306.2, *opposing force* 510.2, *opposition* 828.1

antagonist *hostile person* 63.5, *role* 136.23, *opponent* 828.10

antagonistic *aggressive* 63.9, *418.12*, *combative* 77.32, *antipathetic* 291.7, *hating* 300.7, *malicious* 306.8, *defying* 416.6, *disagreeing* 463.6, *counteracting* 510.6, *oppositional* 828.11, *adverse* 848.10

antagonistically *aggressively* 63.14, 77.38, *discontentedly* 291.17, *with hate* 300.13, *maliciously* 306.15, *argumentatively* 329.15, *in defiance* 416.10, *in disagreement* 463.12, *counter* 510.8, *opposingly* 828.22, *adversely* 848.16
antagonize 63.12; *annoy* 276.7, *cause dislike* 291.16, *cause hate* 300.12, *counteract* 510.7, 828.21
Antananarivo Countries 566
antarctic *directional* 697.8
Antarctica *cold place* 218.7, *world region* 564.6, *landmass* 572.1
Antarctic Circle *cold place* 218.7
Antarctic Ocean Oceans and Seas 571
Antarctic waste *infertile land* 23.2
ant bear *insect-eating mammal* 35.7
ante *gamble* 167.14, *poker* 168.5, *play cards* 168.7
anteater *insect-eating mammal* 35.7
anteating *insectivorous* 35.24
antebellum *harmless* 73.9, *olden* 653.11
antecede *precede* 769.13
antecedence 657.5; *precedence* 769.1
antecedency *precedence* 769.1
antecedent *philosophical term* 4.7, *antiquarian* 651.13, *premature* 657.10, *precedent* 769.4, *preceding* 769.9
antechamber *front entrance* 621.2
antedate *misdate* 660.9, *precede* 769.13
antediluvian *historical* 3.10, *olden* 653.11, *primal* 653.14
antefix Architectural Elements 134
antelope Collective Names 59, *game* 160.6, Heraldic Terms 184
antemeridian *daily* 655.6
antenatal *pregnant* 21.12
antenna *radio telescope* 7.26, *sense organ* 212.4, *receiver* 473.8, *component* 760.3
anteposition *precedence* 769.1
anterior *front* 621.9, *preceding* 769.9
anteriority *precedence* 769.1
anteroom *room* 60.9, *front entrance* 621.2
ante up [Inf] *pay* 489.16
antheap *dwelling* 40.7
anthelmintic *medicine* 115.2
anthem *ritual music* 85.9, Musical Forms 140, *sacred music* 140.3, *song* 140.11
anthemion Architectural Elements 134
anther *organs of reproduction* 21.9, *flower part* 42.3
antheridium *fern plant* 46.2, *moss plant* 46.5, *reproductive body* 47.14
antherozoid *reproductive body* 47.14
anthesis *flowering* 42.5
Anthesteria *religious festival* 85.13
anthill *dwelling* 40.7, *natural habitat* 60.16
anthocyanin *pigment* 12.18
anthologize *compile* 204.8, *select* 382.12
anthology *compilation* 59.14, 174.4, *compendium* 204.3, *selection* 382.1, *miscellany* 751.3, *collection* 757.3
anthophobia Phobias 283
Anthozoa *coelenterate* 39.15
anthozoan *coelenterate* 39.15, 39.25
anthracite *coal* 106.4

anthracosis *respiratory disease* 114.12
anthrax *animal disease* 34.10
anthropocentric *human* 18.15
anthropogenic *anthropological* 1.10
anthropogeny or **anthropogenesis** *anthropology* 1.1
anthropogeographer *anthropologist* 1.3
anthropogeographic *anthropological* 1.10
anthropogeographical *anthropological* 1.10,
anthropogeographically *anthropologically* 1.15
anthropogeography *anthropology* 1.1
anthropographical *anthropological* 1.10
anthropographically *anthropologically* 1.15
anthropography *anthropology* 1.1
anthropoid *human* 18.15, *primate* 35.17, 35.32
anthropoid ape *human ancestor* 18.3, *primate* 35.17
anthropolater *idolater* 83.7
anthropolatry *idolatry* 83.4
anthropological 1.10; *human* 18.15
anthropological linguistics Linguistic Studies 5
anthropologically 1.15; *humanly* 18.18
anthropologist 1.3; *studier of humankind* 18.7
anthropology 1.1; *study of humankind* 18.6, *study of life* 28.9
anthropometric *anthropological* 1.10
anthropometrical *anthropological* 1.10
anthropometrically *anthropologically* 1.15
anthropometrist *anthropologist* 1.3
anthropometry *anthropology* 1.1, *measurement* 1.9, Fields of Measurement 589
anthropomorphic *human* 18.15
anthropomorphize *make human* 18.17
anthropophagite *eater* 92.15
anthropophagy *eating habit* 92.7
anthropophobia Phobias 283
anthroposcopic *anthropological* 1.10
anthroposcopy *measurement* 1.9
anthroposophical *psychic* 86.17
anthroposophist *occultist* 86.13
anthroposophy *supernaturalism* 86.3
anthroposphere *aerosphere* 558.2
anti *oppose* 828.9, *oppositional* 828.11
antiaircraft artillery *guns* 78.9, *military defenses* 419.9
antiaircraft fire *military defenses* 419.9
antiaircraft gun *guns* 78.9
anti-art Western Art Styles 133
antiballistic *strategic* 78.16
antiballistic missile (ABM) *modern missile weapon* 78.4
antibiosis *medicine* 115.2
antibiotic *medicine* 115.2
antibody *medicine* 115.2, *blood* 555.4
antibonding orbital *chemical bond* 11.6
anticathexis *cathexis* 108.32
Antichrist *devil* 446.5

anticipant *expecting* 356.4, *foreseeing* 357.5
anticipate *visualize* 242.24, *expect* 281.12, 356.6, 650.12, *take precautions* 287.14, *foresee* 357.9, *be prepared* 388.17, *push* 414.20, *start early* 657.12, *prepare* 657.14, *precede* 769.13, *think likely* 838.10
anticipated *expected* 356.5, *auspicious* 458.10, *foreseen* 650.8, *probable* 838.6
anticipating *expectant* 281.7, *expecting* 356.4
anticipation *visualization* 242.6, *expectation* 281.2, 356.1, *precaution* 287.4, *preparation* 388.1, *looking to the future* 650.4, *antecedence* 657.5, *probability* 838.1
anticipative *expecting* 356.4, *premature* 657.10
anticipatively *expectantly* 356.10, *prematurely* 657.20
anticipatorily *expectantly* 356.10, *in suspense* 604.21, *prematurely* 657.20
anticipatory *precautionary* 287.9, *expecting* 356.4, *foreseeing* 357.5, *in suspense* 604.12, *premature* 657.10
anticlastic surface *surface* 6.36
anticlimax *lack of emphasis* 201.1
anticline *fold* 8.22, 637.1
anticlockwise *clockwise* 682.18, 697.17
anticoagulant *medicine* 115.2, *solvent* 555.9, *liquefying* 555.20
anticodon *genetic material* 13.20
anticonvulsant *medicine* 115.2
Anticosti Islands 572
antics *bungling* 128.2
anticyclone *weather system* 9.10
anticyclonic *frontal* 9.41
antidiscrimination *impartiality* 338.2, *equal opportunity* 831.2
antidiscriminatory *impartial* 338.6
antidiuretic hormone Human Hormones 12
antidotal *remedial* 115.14, *solved* 334.15, *counteracting* 510.6
antidotally *counter* 510.8
antidote 115.5; *talisman* 86.9, *remedy* 115.1, *solution* 334.6, *expedient* 387.5, *counteractant* 510.5
antielectron *elementary particle* 10.53
antifeminist *misanthrope* 291.5
antiferromagnetism *magnetism* 10.45
antifreeze *heater* 217.3
antifriction *cross-country* 162.31, *lubricant* 562.7
antifriction pad *ski equipment* 162.10
antifungal agent 47.8
antigen *medicine* 115.2, *blood* 555.4
antigravitational *raised* 715.6
antigravity *repulsion* 701.1, *raising* 715.1
anti-G suit *suit* 100.16
Antigua Islands 572
Antigua and Barbuda Countries 566
antihero *role* 136.23
antihistamine *antidote* 115.5
Anti-Lebanon Mountains Mountains and Hills 569
Antilles, Greater and Lesser Islands 572

antilock brake system (ABS) *miscellaneous automotive terms* 687.14
antilog *power* 783.6
antilogarithm *logarithm* 6.17, *power* 783.6
antilogy *sophism* 330.2
antimacassar *protective covering* 613.5
antimasque *dramatic style* 136.3
antimissile *strategic* 78.16
antimissile missile *modern missile weapon* 78.4
antimony Chemical Elements and Common Allotropes 11
antimycotic *antifungal agent* 47.8
antineutron *elementary particle* 10.53
antinode *wave* 10.11, 683.4
antinomian *anarchist* 51.4, *anarchistic* 51.7, *lawless* 53.26
Antinomianism Christian Groups 81
antinomianism *anarchism* 51.3
antinomy *legal injustice* 53.5
antinovel *novel* 139.3
antiparticle *elementary particle* 10.53
antipasto *hors d'oeuvre* 90.13
antipathetic 291.7; *hating* 300.7, *hateful* 300.10, *refusing* 375.9, *counteracting* 510.6, *repulsive* 701.4, *disunited* 753.10
antipathetic or **antipathetical** *oppositional* 828.11
antipathetically *with hate* 300.13, *hatefully* 300.14, *counter* 510.8, *repulsively* 701.11, *disunitedly* 753.25, *opposingly* 828.22
antipathy 291.2; *hostility* 63.1, *dislike* 300.2, *hated thing* 300.5, *dissociation* 375.4, *opposing force* 510.2, *opposition* 828.1
antiperspirant *deodorant* 225.3
antiphon *ritual music* 85.9, *response* 334.4
antiphonal *singing* 85.16, *reactive* 334.12
antiphonal chant *response* 334.4
antipodal *curvilinear* 6.78, *opposite* 731.3
antipode *opposite* 731.2
antipodean *regional* 564.12, *distant* 585.5
antipodes *world region* 564.6, *distant place* 585.3
antipole *opposite* 731.2
antiprivate-language argument *philosophical problem* 4.8
antiproton *elementary particle* 10.53
antipsychotic *psychiatric treatment* 108.3
antipyretic *medicine* 115.2, *remedial* 115.14
antiquarian 651.13, 653.9; *record keeper* 185.8, *historian* 651.10, *olden* 653.11
antiquarianism 653.3; *historicism* 3.7, *study of the past* 651.9
antiquarianize *look back* 651.18
antiquark *elementary particle* 10.53
antiquary *historian* 651.10, *antiquarian* 653.9
antiquated *historical* 3.10, *disused* 394.8, *uncustomary* 398.4, *antiquarian* 651.13, *olden* 653.11, *redundant* 802.9
antique *thing of the past* 651.8, *antiquity* 653.4, *olden* 653.11, *showpiece* 843.3
antique collector *antiquarian* 653.9
antique dealer *antiquarian* 653.9

antiques fair *display* 843.1
antique show *display* 843.1
antiquity 653.4; *past time* 3.6, 651.1, *oldness* 653.1
antirealism Philosophical Schools of Thought 4
antirealist Philosophical Schools of Thought 4
anti-Semite *bigot* 337.7
anti-Semitic *intolerant* 63.7, *discriminatory* 337.11, *unjust* 342.7
anti-Semitism *social discrimination* 337.4, *unfair treatment* 342.4
antisepsis *cleaning* 111.2, *prophylaxis* 115.4, *hygiene* 116.1
antiseptic *cleaning agent* 111.9, *clean* 111.13, *prophylaxis* 115.4, *remedial* 115.14, *hygienic* 116.3, *tutelary* 810.19
antiseptically *hygienically* 116.5
antisepticize *purify* 111.19, *treat* 115.17, *practice hygiene* 116.4
antiserum *medicine* 115.2
antisociability *misanthropy* 291.4
antisocial *hostile* 63.6, *taciturn* 208.4, *misanthropic* 291.8, *unsociable* 409.6, *aloof* 756.5, *solitary* 782.17
antisocial habits *unsociability* 409.1
antisocially *hostilely* 63.13, *misanthropically* 291.18, *unsocially* 409.13
antisocial personality disorder *personality disorder* 108.7
antispasmodic *medicine* 115.2
antistrophe *part of poem* 139.9, *response* 334.4
antisubmarine plane *military aircraft* 77.30
antisymmetric relation *mathematical logic* 6.60
antitank *strategic* 78.16
antitank missile *modern missile weapon* 78.4
antithesis *philosophical argument* 4.5, *philosophical term* 4.7, *oppositeness* 190.6, 731.1, *inverse* 608.2, *contrariety* 828.6
antithetical *reactive* 334.12, *inverse* 608.6, *opposite* 731.3, *contrary* 828.1
antithetically *in answer* 334.25, *reversely* 608.10, *diametrically* 731.6, *opposingly* 828.22
antitoxin *antidote* 115.5
antitrade winds *or* **antitrades** *wind system* 9.15
antitrust laws *economic restraint* 830.4
anti–Vietnam War movement *peace movement* 74.4
antivivisection *animal welfare* 34.8
antivivisectionist *animal welfarist* 34.9
antiwar movement *peace movement* 74.4
antler *sharp-pointed growth* 549.5
Antlia Constellations 7
ant lion *larva* 40.9
antlophobia Phobias 283
antonomasia *literary device* 139.12, *nomenclature* 202.7
Antony Famous Lovers 299
antonym *word* 5.17, *type of meaning* 361.4, *opposite* 731.2
antonym dictionary *word book* 5.27
antonymous *worded* 5.38, *linguistic* 361.9, *opposite* 731.3
antonymy *oppositeness* 731.1

ants Collective Names 59, Phobias 283
ants in one's pants [Inf] *restlessness* 684.5
Antwerp blue *blue pigment* 261.2
Anubis Deities 82
anuptaphobia Phobias 283
Anura *amphibian* 37.10
anuran *amphibian* 37.10, 37.14
anus *internal organ* 19.13, *body orifice* 583.3, *outlet* 707.8
anvil Human Bones 19, *ear* 19.10, 228.2, Musical Instruments 142
anvil cloud *cloud* 9.17
anxiety *anxiety disorder* 108.11, *mental breakdown* 110.4, *strain* 117.4, *fearfulness* 283.2, *worry* 283.4, *suspicion* 314.3, *expectation* 356.1, *suspense* 604.6, *agitation* 684.1, *disturbance* 768.1, *sense of danger* 811.3, *problem* 824.4
anxiety disorder 108.11
anxiety disorders *mental disorder* 108.8
anxiety hysteria *anxiety disorder* 108.11
anxiety reaction *neurosis* 108.9
anxious *strained* 117.13, *fearful* 283.10, *suspicious* 314.6, *expecting* 356.4, *in suspense* 604.21, *agitated* 684.15, *disturbed* 768.6, *troubled* 824.15
anxious for *or* **about** *worried* 283.11
anxiously *fearfully* 283.19, *suspiciously* 314.13, *expectantly* 356.10, *in suspense* 604.21, *distractedly* 768.14
any *quantitative* 738.6, *whole* 759.6, *whatever* 778.8
anybody *everyone* 778.7
anybody's guess *uncertainty* 333.6, *unknown thing* 349.3, *uncertainty* 841.1
any day *at what time* 639.17
anyhow 766.25; *how* 691.16
any old time *another time* 648.4
any old way [Inf] *negligently* 26.8
anyone *everyone* 778.7
anything *whatever* 778.8
anything but! *no!* 190.28
anything goes *unconditional* 829.14
anytime *at what time* 639.17
any time but this *or* **now** *different time* 648.1
anyway *how* 691.16
anywhere *here* 575.19
any which *or* **old way** [Inf] *negligently* 326.8
anywise *how* 691.16
A-OK *or* **A-Okay** [Inf] *great* 445.14
A one *or* **A number one** *or* **A 1** [Inf] *skillful* 127.10, *unbeatable* 744.13, *important* 799.7, *best* 805.9
Aorangi Mountains and Hills 569
aorist *grammatical term* 5.29, *past tense* 651.2
aorta *internal organ* 19.13
Aosta Breeds of Cattle 16
apace *swiftly* 694.16, *hastily* 818.7
Apadana *other text* 81.19
apart 585.14, 587.8, 753.8, 753.23; *without one's spouse* 66.14, *away* 386.23, 585.6, 711.20, *unsociable* 409.6, *at a distance* 585.13, *divergently* 703.16, *forth* 707.19, *separate* 724.10, *separately* 724.18, *unconnectedly* 728.18, *in isolation* 753.24, *alone* 788.15, *one by one* 788.21

apart from *additionally* 748.15, *exclusively* 764.10
apartheid *social discrimination* 337.4, *unfair treatment* 342.4, *separation* 409.3, *setting apart* 753.2, *exclusiveness* 764.4
apartment 60.7; *property* 470.1
apartment building *or* **complex** *apartment house* 60.8, *building* 551.9
apartment house 60.8; *architectural structure* 134.4
apartment-sharing *jointly possessing* 469.12
apartness *unsociability* 409.1, *aloneness* 788.5
apathetic 322.4; *insensible* 213.4, *insensitive* 268.4, *indifferent* 289.7, *wonderless* 295.3, *inattentive* 324.5, *unenthusiastic* 375.10, *avoiding* 386.9, *inactive* 413.9, *not participating* 415.11, *inert* 519.2, *sedentary* 678.5, *unhurried* 693.8
apathetically 322.7; *insensibly* 268.7, *indifferently* 289.17, *without wonder* 295.8, *inattentively* 324.12, *shyly* 386.25, *resignedly* 392.6, *inactively* 413.16, *impassively* 415.18, *inertly* 519.5, *motionlessly* 678.9
apathy 322.2; *mood disorder* 108.12, *insensibility* 213.1, *insensitivity* 268.1, *indifference* 289.1, *lack of wonder* 295.1, *inattention* 324.1, *unenthusiasm* 375.3, *shirking* 386.4, *immobility* 413.2, *idleness* 415.3, *submission* 421.1, *inertness* 519.1, *lack of motion* 678.1
ape *primate* 35.17, *copy* 730.17, *simulate* 733.16, *imitate* 736.9
aped *duplicate* 730.11, *simulated* 733.11
apeirophobia Phobias 283
ape-man *human ancestor* 18.3, *prehistoric human* 653.7
Apennines Mountains and Hills 569
aper *copy* 730.5, *imitator* 736.6
aperçu [Fr] *summary* 204.1
aperient *fecal* 25.14, *cleaning agent* 111.9, *purgative* 115.7, *ejector* 709.10
apéritif *appetizer* 219.2, *preface* 769.5
aperto Musical Terms and Expression Marks 140
aperture *exposure equipment* 132.12, *opening* 583.1, *crack* 587.2
aperture priority *exposure equipment* 132.12
aperture setting *exposure equipment* 132.12
aperture synthesis *radio telescope* 7.26
apery *mimicry* 736.3
apes Collective Names 59
ape-woman *human ancestor* 18.3
APEX (Advance Purchase Excursion) *bargain* 497.4
apex *angle* 6.37, *pinnacle* 596.2, *summit* 600.1
apfelstrudel *notable international dishes* 90.40
aphanitic *types of igneous texture* 8.33
aphasia *trance* 108.18, *speech defect* 206.2
aphasic *inarticulate* 206.6, *silent* 231.2
aphelion *orbit* 7.22, *distant place* 585.3

apheresis *or* **aphaeresis** *shortening* 591.2
aphids *pests and diseases* 17.12
aphonia *speech difficulty* 206.1, *silence* 231.1
aphonic *voiceless* 206.5, *silent* 231.2
aphorism *philosophy* 4.1, *maxim* 177.1, *pithy saying* 198.3, *truism* 721.6
aphoristic *proverbial* 177.2, *concise* 198.4, *truistic* 721.15
aphoristically *proverbially* 177.4, *intrinsically* 721.30
aphorize 177.3; *propound a philosophy* 4.21
aphrodisia *sexual longing* 20.6, *sexual love* 299.1
aphrodisiac *eroticism* 20.7
Aphrodite Deities 82, *goddesses and gods of love* 299.14
Apia Countries 566
a piacere Musical Terms and Expression Marks 140
apiarian *entomological* 40.15
apiarist *entomologist* 40.3
apiary *dwelling* 40.7, *natural habitat* 60.16
apical *top* 600.6
apical bud *bud* 41.8
apiece *specifically* 779.22
aping *simulation* 733.4, *imitative* 736.7
apiphobia Phobias 283
apish *imitative* 736.7
apishly *imitatively* 736.12
APL Programming Languages 15
aplanospore *reproductive body* 47.14
aplastic anemia *blood disease* 114.14
aplenty *numerously* 795.13
aplomb *will* 376.5, *determination* 674.2
apocalypse *disclosure* 180.1, *spectacle* 264.6, *prediction* 358.1, *ruin* 523.4, *end of time* 773.5
apocalyptic *revelatory* 180.7, *appearing* 264.9, *predicting* 358.11, *destructive* 523.8, *ending* 773.13
apocarpous *of a fruit* 44.8
apocope *conciseness* 198.1, *shortening* 591.2
apocrine *secretory* 24.4
apocrine gland *secretory mechanism* 24.3
apocrine secretion *secretion* 24.1
Apocrypha Christian text 81.16
apocryphal *uncertified* 841.13
Apoda *amphibian* 37.10
apodal *or* **apodous** *reptilian* 37.12
apodan *amphibian* 37.10, 37.14
apodeictic *dialectical* 4.16
apodictic *demonstrated* 331.9, *simple* 363.6, *displayed* 843.8
apoenzyme *enzyme* 12.11
apogee *rocketry* 7.32, *distant place* 585.3, *summit* 600.1
Apollo Planets and Their Satellites 7, *sun* 7.15, Deities 82, 82
Apollonius's theorem Mathematical Concepts 6
Apollyon *devil* 446.5
apologetic 313.6, 329.10; *vindicatory* 441.7, *penitent* 451.5
apologetically 313.11, 329.18; *justifyingly* 441.15, *penitently* 451.10
apologetics Theologies 81, *debate* 319.3
apologia *plea* 329.5
apologist *reasoner* 319.5, *vindicator* 441.5

apologize 313.8; recompense 273.11, plead 329.14, succumb 421.7, be penitent 451.7, offer reparation 504.15

apologizer atoner 313.4

apology 313.2; reparation 273.2, plea 329.5, confession 451.2

apophthegm maxim 177.1, moral 431.5

apophyge Architectural Elements 134

apoplectic physical 1.14, angry 302.11

apoplectic build physical type 1.8

apoplexy illness 114.2, spasm 684.8

aporetic dialectical 4.16

aposepalous of flowers 42.11

apostasize not accept 190.19

apostasy unacceptance 190.4, denial 332.2, renunciation 383.4, reversion 671.1

apostate disbeliever 88.5, negator 190.8, equivocator 380.4, equivocating 380.6, relinquished 392.2, convert 670.6, dissenter 782.8

apostatically nonacceptantly 190.25, resignedly 392.6

apostatize disbelieve 88.8, be irresolute 378.9, renounce 383.13, withdraw 392.5, be converted 670.12

apostatized renounced 383.9

a posteriori dialectical 4.16, rational 319.8

a posteriori reasoning reasoning 319.2

apostle converter 670.5, adherent 755.4

apostrophe Punctuation Marks 5, literary device 139.12, address 209.1, soliloquy 211.1

apostrophic soliloquizing 211.3

apostrophize speak to 205.19, address 209.8, soliloquize 211.4

apothecaries' measure measuring system 589.4, type of measurement 589.8

apothecaries' weight weight measurement 538.6, measuring system 589.4, type of measurement 589.8

apothecary druggist 115.10

apothegm maxim 177.1, moral 431.5

apotheosis deification 82.13, praise 437.3, promotion 715.3

apotheosize deify 82.23, revere 435.14, praise 437.16, promote 715.13

apotheosized promoted 715.8

Appalachia regions of the United States 564.7

Appalachian dulcimer Musical Instruments 142

Appalachian Mountain Club (AMC) mountaineering associations 161.7

Appalachian Mountains Mountains and Hills 569

appall displease 272.8, frighten 283.17, be repulsive 701.10

appalling frightening 283.12, repulsive 701.4

Appaloosa Horse and Pony Breeds 159

appanage claim 429.3, property 470.1, addition 748.1

apparat officialdom 49.20

apparatus 103.2; materials 104.1, instrument 511.2

apparatus criticus annotation 365.2

apparel clothing 100.1, clothe 100.43

appareled dressed 100.38

apparent 610.10; visible 242.19, 244.5, appearing 264.9, demonstrable 331.12, evident 339.9, expected 356.5, opened up 583.11, superficial 599.4, probable 838.6, displayed 843.8, manifest 843.9

apparently 264.16, 610.18, 720.19; reportedly 170.16, visibly 242.28, 244.10, evidently 339.16, originally 345.16, openly 583.22, superficially 599.8, seemingly 733.19, probably 838.11, manifestly 843.17

apparent magnitude star luminosity 7.12

apparentness openness 249.6, appearance 610.4

apparent wind sailing terms 150.5

apparition divine manifestation 82.5, ghost 86.11, spectacle 264.6, frightener 283.7, fantasy 360.5, omnipresence 575.4, illusion 720.2, manifestation 843.2

appeal 529.4; enticement 178.3, salutation 209.2, pleasantness 271.1, desirability 288.7, lovability 299.5, win the love of 299.27, question 333.16, offering 472.6, voluntary payment 489.4, grant 489.7, request 505.1, 505.10, solicitation 505.4, solicit money 505.13, influence 512.11, allurement 700.4, attract 700.11

appealer requester 505.5

appealing 512.9, 529.10; sensual 20.16, enticing 178.13, salutatory 209.7, pleasant 271.5, desirable 288.11, likable 290.7, lovable 299.20, solicitation 505.4, attractive 700.10

appealingly enticingly 178.22, desirably 288.24, likably 290.12, lovably 299.31, attractively 700.14

appeal to 209.9; speak to 205.19, influence 508.11

appeal to arms war measures 76.18, go to war 76.29, warfare 422.10

appeal to law litigate 54.27

appear 244.8, 264.12, 331.18, 575.16; act 136.34, 137.20, be published 173.19, be disclosed 180.12, be visible 242.26, become visible 264.13, occur 264.14, be discovered 345.15, be present 575.13, appear outwardly 610.14, arrive 704.13, emerge 707.14, 771.35, show oneself 843.15

appearance 264.1, 610.4; divine manifestation 82.5, indication 339.3, conception 360.4, conduct 399.1, design 536.2, attendance 575.3, nature 624.5, arrival 704.1, entry 706.1, illusion 720.2, mode 725.2, creation 771.2, manifestation 843.2

appearance of truth verisimilitude 721.10

appearances appearance 610.4

appear for substitute for 80.5, answer for 334.24

appear guilty 450.10

appear in occur 264.14

appearing 264.9; appearance 264.1, seeming 264.11, apparent 610.10, arriving 704.9, manifest 843.9

appearing before the judge litigating 54.21

appearing guilty 450.7

appearing in court litigating 54.21

appear like appear 264.12

appear on film or **screen** occur 264.14

appear on stage occur 264.14

appear outwardly 610.14

appear straightforward not cause wonder 295.7

appear to be appear 264.12

appease conciliate 74.10, comfort 214.14, 273.9, relieve 275.8, atone 313.7, submit 421.4, offer reparation 504.15, mitigate 521.9, yield 543.17, smooth over 545.12

appeased relieved 275.6

appeasement pacification 74.1, reparation 273.2, ease 275.1, atonement 313.1, submission 421.1, offering 504.5, easiness 543.5

appeaser mediator 75.2, atoner 313.4, submitter 421.2

appeasing pacificatory 74.8, atoning 313.5, easing 543.13

appeasingly atoningly 313.10

appellant litigant 54.4, accuser 442.3, requester 505.5

appellate court law court 54.8

appellate jurisdiction jurisdiction 54.2

appellation title 72.1, nomenclature 202.7, name 202.8

appellative title 72.1, titled 72.9, name 202.8

appellee litigant 54.4

append add 748.11

appendage 19.5, 748.4; adherent 401.5, addition 748.1, component 760.3, concomitant 794.4

appended related 727.6

appendix book part 174.5, annotation 365.2, back matter 622.3, relatedness 727.1, appendage 748.4, ending 773.10

apperceive think 315.12

apperception intelligence 315.2

appertain to relate to 727.9, be included 763.6

appetence desire 288.1

appetite 92.2, 288.6; taste 219.1, desire 288.1, liking 290.1

appetizer 219.2; hors d'oeuvre 90.13, bite 92.10, part 760.1, preface 769.5

appetizing edible 92.20, pleasurable 214.6, tasty 219.4, piquant 221.6, desirable 288.11

appetizingly desirably 288.24

applaud gesture 183.17, be grateful 310.6, salute 405.13, acclaim 437.18

applauder approver 437.7

applauding rejoicing 279.4, acclamatory 437.10

applause 279.2; play part 136.8, gesture 183.5, cry of praise 239.3, acknowledgment 310.3, tribute 405.6, acclaim 437.5

apple Trees and Shrubs 43, red thing 257.3

apple [Inf] baseball equipment 147.4

apple bob Children's and Party Games 167

apple box Trees and Shrubs 43

apple-cheeked red-faced 257.6

apple cheeks health 113.1

apple of discord figurative usage 44.4

apple of one's eye figurative usage 44.4, loved one 299.13

apple pie notable international dishes 90.40

apple-pie order figurative usage 44.4, orderliness 765.5

apple polisher [Inf] figurative usage 44.4

apple-polishing [Inf] sycophancy 401.2, sycophantic 401.7

applesauce sauce 90.17

applesauce [Inf] figurative usage 44.4, nonsense 192.8

appliance apparatus 103.2, use 393.1, instrument 511.2, convenience 825.7

appliances means 102.1, merchandise 522.6

applicability qualification 340.1, usefulness 393.2, 801.1

applicable usable 393.6, instrumental 511.4, useful 801.5, convenient 803.3

applicant candidate 422.18, requester 505.5

application carefulness 323.3, type of meaning 361.4, interpretation 365.1, commitment 377.2, use 393.1, assiduity 414.8, request 505.1, instrumentality 511.1, usefulness 801.1, convenience 803.1

application software 15.14; software 15.12

applied linguistic 5.34, theoretical 10.71, practical 511.6, useful 801.5

applied arts visual arts 133.1

applied energy exertion 122.4

applied linguistics Linguistic Studies 5

applied load load 14.14

applied mathematics 6.3

applied physics physics 10.1

applied psychology Psychological Theories, Schools 108

applied sociology sociology 2.1

appliqué decorative method 532.3

appliquéing Hobbies and Pastimes 167

apply qualify 340.11, use 393.9, petition 505.11, relate to 727.9

apply a compress medicate 115.18

apply a remedy remedy 115.16

apply a tourniquet treat 115.17

apply for request 505.10

applying committed 377.7

applying pressure touching 216.2

apply oneself to exert oneself 122.11, address oneself to 209.13, undertake 391.7

apply one's mind concentrate 317.10

apply pressure compel 428.8

apply the match activate 771.28

apply the war paint [Inf] beautify 530.14

apply to appeal to 209.9, relate to 727.9

appoggiatura musical ornament 140.19

appoint gain authority 52.15, delegate 79.6, ordain 84.16, select 382.12, predestine 384.9, authorize 425.14, allocate 474.5, commission 833.8

appoint a proxy authorize 833.10

appoint a representative commission 833.8

appointed authorized 52.11, 425.9, delegated 79.4, selected 382.11, predestined 384.6, situated 573.5, commissioned 833.6

appointed day day 646.4

appointed person delegate 79.1

appointee delegate 79.1, commissioner 833.5

appointment *acquisition of authority* 52.5, *delegation* 79.3, *ordination* 84.3, *selection* 382.1, *predestination* 384.2, *social gathering* 408.4, *authorization* 425.4, *allocation* 474.1, *commission* 833.1
appointment of counsel *pretrial proceedings* 54.13
appointments *equipment* 103.6
appointments calendar *plan* 357.2
apportion *have at one's disposal* 393.14, *allocate* 474.5, *measure out* 589.21, *quantify* 738.7, *divide* 753.18, *part* 760.14
apportioned *allocated* 474.4, *partial* 760.11
apportioning *allocation* 474.1
apportionment *allocation* 474.1
appose *juxtapose* 586.14
apposite *qualified* 340.7, *related* 727.6
appositely *relevantly* 727.12
appositeness *qualification* 340.1, *relatedness* 727.1
apposition *syntax* 5.32, *juxtaposition* 586.4
appraisable *measurable* 589.17
appraisal *discrimination* 337.1, *judgment* 341.1, *tax system* 494.6, *measurement* 589.1
appraise *estimate* 341.11, *price* 494.12, *measure* 589.20
appraisement *measurement* 589.1
appraiser *judge* 341.5, *measurer* 589.14
appreciate *taste* 219.5, *take pleasure in* 271.11, *like* 290.8, 299.22, *be grateful* 310.6, *know* 348.10, *respect* 435.13, *admire* 437.15, *augment* 467.16, *cost a lot* 496.9, *increase* 746.6
appreciated *liked* 290.6, *respected* 435.10
appreciation *liking* 290.1, *gratitude* 310.1, *judiciousness* 337.2, *judgment* 341.1, *respect* 435.1, *admiration* 437.2, *augmentation* 467.2, *increase* 746.1
appreciative *liking* 290.4, *grateful* 310.4, *discriminating* 337.9, *judging* 341.7, *respectful* 435.6, *approving* 437.9, *refined* 534.5
appreciatively *admiringly* 290.11, *gratefully* 310.8, *judiciously* 337.16
appreciativeness *gratitude* 310.1
appreciatorily *gratefully* 310.8
appreciatory *grateful* 310.4, *approving* 437.9
apprehend *rationalize* 4.20, *arrest* 55.12, *learn* 68.18, *be fearful* 283.15, *have an idea* 327.13, *know* 348.10, *expect* 356.6, *understand* 363.9, *take away forcefully* 477.19, *detain* 830.16
apprehended *arrested* 55.10
apprehending *conquest* 477.6
apprehensibility *intelligibility* 363.1
apprehensible *intelligible* 363.5
apprehension *pretrial proceedings* 54.13, *arrest* 55.5, *fearfulness* 283.2, *suspicion* 314.3, *idea* 327.1, *knowledge* 348.1, *expectation* 356.1, *understanding* 363.4, *suspense* 604.6, *agitation* 684.1, *sense of danger* 811.3
apprehensive *fearful* 283.10, *suspicious* 314.6, *expecting* 356.4, *in suspense* 604.12, *agitated* 684.15

apprehensively *fearfully* 283.19, *suspiciously* 314.13, *expectantly* 356.10, *in suspense* 604.21
apprehensiveness *fearfulness* 283.2, *suspicion* 314.3, *expectation* 356.1, *suspense* 604.6
apprentice *learner* 48.6, *learn* 48.23, *artisan* 123.13, *unskilled person* 128.3, *untrained* 389.8, *beginner* 398.2, 771.14, *immature* 652.12, *subordinate* 832.3, *subject* 832.10
apprentice chef *cook* 91.3
apprenticed *unskilled* 128.5, *subordinate* 832.8
apprentice oneself *undertake* 391.7
apprenticeship *youth* 26.1, *briefing* 388.4, *subjection* 832.1
apprise *educate* 48.22, *inform* 170.11, *communicate* 176.10, *warn* 814.8
approach 209.3, 209.10, 702.2, 704.15; *means* 102.1, *golf course* 156.2, *jumping* 166.11, *procedure* 387.2, *advance* 467.3, *improve* 467.18, *offer* 504.1, 504.11, *petition* 505.2, 505.11, *tend* 513.5, *style* 537.1, *nearness* 586.1, *near* 586.12, *be in the future* 650.9, *forward motion* 677.4, *flight* 689.5, *fly* 689.13, *way* 691.1, *access* 691.3, *find one's way* 691.15, *thoroughfare* 692.6, *converge* 702.9, *arrival* 704.1, *entrance* 706.5
approachability *possibleness* 836.2
approachable *attainable* 704.11, *possible* 836.5
approach a limit *order* 6.89
approach and hurdle *competitive diving* 164.7
approaches *near place* 586.3
approaching 704.10; *nearer* 586.7, *future* 650.6, *flying* 689.11, *advancing* 702.8
approaching shot *golf shots* 156.4
approach light *safety light* 246.7
approach shot *tennis strokes* 165.2
approbated *approved* 437.8
approbation *assent* 346.1, *repute* 370.1, *respect* 435.1, *approval* 437.1, *agreement* 462.1, *permission* 502.1
approbative *approving* 437.9
approbatory *approving* 437.9
appropriable *adoptive* 476.9
appropriate *expedient* 288.12, *qualified* 340.7, *proper* 429.10, *good* 445.10, *suitable* 462.9, *gain* 467.15, *allocate* 474.5, *adopt* 476.11, *take over* 477.16, *steal* 479.14, *timely* 659.4, *opportunely* 659.8, *equal to* 740.10, *convenient* 803.3
appropriated *borrowed* 476.8, *adoptive* 476.9, *taking* 477.12
appropriately *expediently* 288.25, *capably* 340.15, *properly* 429.18, *well* 445.19, *suitably* 462.17
appropriateness *qualification* 340.1, *properness* 429.5, *good* 445.1, *timeliness* 659.1
appropriating *claiming* 469.2, *adoptive* 476.9
appropriation *claiming* 469.2, *allocation* 474.1, *adoption* 476.2, *taking over* 477.3
appropriator *taker* 477.9
approvable 437.13
approvably 437.22

approval 437.1; *authorization* 52.3, *confirmation* 189.5, *liking* 290.1, *assent* 346.1, *repute* 370.1, *respect* 435.1, *agreement* 462.1, *permission* 502.1, *moral support* 605.7, *consent* 735.8
approve 437.14; *authorize* 52.14, *confirm* 189.25, *like* 290.8, *assent* 346.6, *select* 382.12, *agree with* 462.10, *permit* 502.6, *consent* 735.28
approve a contract *unionize* 57.21
approved 437.8; *authorized* 52.11, *confirmed* 189.17, *liked* 290.6, *reputable* 370.3, *established* 397.12, *agreeing* 462.6, *permitted* 502.4, *consenting* 735.18, *convenient* 803.3
approved for use *usable* 801.6
approved lineage *family tree* 65.3
approved strike *strike* 57.8
approve of *judge* 341.10, *approve* 437.14, *give moral support* 605.18
approver 437.7; *affirmer* 189.9
approving 437.9; *judging* 341.7, *assenting* 346.4, *agreeing* 462.6, *supportive* 605.11, *consenting* 735.18
approvingly 437.21; *confirmingly* 189.32, *admiringly* 290.11, *judicially* 341.12, *agreeably* 462.14, *with consent* 735.38
approximate *equate* 6.88, *unfinished* 544.9, *be unfinished* 544.12, *nearer* 586.7, *similar* 733.7, *make similar* 733.15, *quantitative* 738.6, *generalized* 778.12
approximately *mathematically* 6.93, *wrongly* 351.18, *incompletely* 544.14, *nearly* 586.18, *comparably* 733.18, *quantitatively* 738.8, *generally* 778.20
approximating *nearer* 586.7, *similar* 733.7
approximation *reasoning* 6.61, *inaccuracy* 351.3, *rough idea* 544.4, *nearness* 586.1, *measurement* 589.1, *similarity* 733.1, *calculation* 784.1
appulse *nearness* 586.1
appurtenance *addition* 748.1, *thing included* 763.2, *concomitant* 794.4
appurtenances *possession of property* 469.3
appurtenant *included* 763.4
apricot *orange thing* 258.3, *orange* 258.5
April showers *rain* 9.27
a priori *dialectical* 4.16, *rational* 319.8, *precognitive* 320.7, *supposed* 359.6
a priori knowledge *philosophical problem* 4.8, *precognition* 320.2
a priori reasoning *reasoning* 319.2
apriorism Philosophical Schools of Thought 4
apriorist Philosophical Schools of Thought 4
apron *vestment* 84.11, *accessory* 100.28, Architectural Elements 134, *stage* 136.18, *airport* 689.4
apron stage *stage* 136.18
apropos *timely* 659.4, *opportunely* 659.8
apse *church architecture* 134.11

apt *educatable* 48.18, *skillful* 127.10, *expedient* 288.12, *correspondent* 334.16, *qualified* 340.7, *proper* 429.10, *good* 445.10, *suitable* 462.9, *fluid* 527.5, *timely* 659.4, *equal to* 740.10, *possible* 836.5, *probable* 838.6
apterium *plumage* 36.7
aptitude 127.4, 513.3; *educatability* 48.9, *cleverness* 315.3, *qualification* 340.1, *information* 348.2, *intelligence* 352.2, *ability* 514.3, *special skill* 779.2, *easiness* 823.1, *possibleness* 836.2
aptly *studiously* 48.26, *expediently* 288.25, *correspondingly* 334.27, *capably* 340.15, *properly* 429.18, *well* 445.19, *suitably* 462.17, *gracefully* 527.8, *opportunely* 659.8
aptness *educatability* 48.9, *aptitude* 127.4, *correspondence* 334.8, *qualification* 340.1, *good* 445.1, *suitability* 462.4, *elegance* 527.1, *timeliness* 659.1
apt to *tending to* 513.4
Apulian Breeds of Cattle 16
Apulian Merion Breeds of Sheep 16
Apurímac Rivers 570
Apus Constellations 7
aqua *water* 557.1
aquamarine *green thing* 260.4, *green* 260.7, *blue thing* 261.3, *blue* 261.5
aquaphobia Phobias 283
aquaplaning *miscellaneous automotive terms* 687.14
aquarelle *painting* 143.3
aquarellist *painter* 143.7
aquarist *ichthyologist* 38.9
aquarium *animal welfare* 34.8, *dwelling* 38.4, *cage* 60.15, *repository* 105.13
aquarium fish *fish* 38.5
Aquarius Constellations 7, *transporter* 686.4
Aquarius the Water Carrier *transferrer* 685.4
aquatic *of animals* 34.13, *of plants* 41.14, *watery* 557.21, *nautical* 690.14
aquatic plant *plant* 41.2
aquatint *picture* 133.5, *engraving* 144.3, *engrave* 144.11
aquatinter *engraver* 144.5
aqua vitae *alcohol* 121.5
aqueduct *bridge* 551.10, 691.7
aqueous *watery* 557.21
aqueous humor *eye* 19.9, 242.3
aquicultural *horticultural* 17.14
aquiculture *gardening* 17.5, *hydrography* 557.18
aquifer *groundwater* 8.11
Aquila Constellations 7
aquiline *avian* 36.19
Aquilo *wind god* 9.16
Aquitaine Blond Breeds of Cattle 16
Ara Constellations 7
Arab Horse and Pony Breeds 159
arabesque Architectural Elements 134, Musical Forms 140, *ice-dancing move* 162.19, *braid* 609.3
Arabi Breeds of Sheep 16
Arabian Deserts 572
Arabian Sea Oceans and Seas 571
arabica or **Arabian coffee** *coffee* 93.6
Arabic numeral *numeral* 6.8, *number* 783.1
arabinan *polysaccharide* 12.5
arabinose Common Sugars 12

arable *farmland* 16.3, *farmable* 16.17
arable farm *farm* 16.2
arable farmer *agriculturist* 16.14
arable farming 16.6
arable land *farmland* 16.3
arachidonic acid *fat* 12.7
arachnid 39.8, 40.4; *type of animal* 34.5
Arachnida *arachnid* 39.8, 40.4
arachnidan 40.12; *arthropodal* 39.22
arachnoid *body covering* 19.4, *arthropodal* 39.22, *arachnidan* 40.12
arachnological 40.16; *arthropodal* 39.22
arachnologist *invertebrate zoologist* 39.3, *entomologist* 40.3
arachnology *invertebrate zoology* 39.2, *study of insects* 40.2
arachnophobia *Phobias* 283
Arafura Sea *Oceans and Seas* 571
Aragon *Breeds of Sheep* 16
Araguaia *or* Araguaua *Rivers* 570
Arallu *evil place* 446.6
Aral Sea *Oceans and Seas* 571
Aran Islands *Islands* 572
Aranyaka *other text* 81.19
Ararat *Mountains and Hills* 569
araroba *Tree Products* 43
Aras *or* Araks *Rivers* 570
Araucana *Breeds of Fowl* 16
araucaria *Trees and Shrubs* 43
arbalest *Historical Missile Weapons* 78
arbalester *historical soldier* 77.8
arbiter *judge* 54.10, 341.5, *mediator* 75.2, *adviser* 176.5, *moderator* 521.2
arbiter of fashion *fashion business* 536.3
arbiter of taste *refined person* 534.4
arbitrage *finance* 457.1, 457.7, *trade* 480.1
arbitrager *or* arbitrageur *financial adviser* 457.4
arbitral *mediatory* 75.5
arbitrament of war *war* 76.1
arbitrarily *summarily* 53.36, *erratically* 381.8, *severely* 424.11, *illogically* 728.17, *excessively* 829.23
arbitrariness *capriciousness* 381.2, *unrelatedness* 728.1, *lack of motive* 842.2
arbitrary *refractory* 379.6, *erratic* 381.5, *illogical* 728.7, *unconditional* 829.14, *causeless* 842.11
arbitrary power *severity* 424.1
arbitrate *have an industrial dispute* 57.20, *mediate* 75.6, 772.19, *represent* 80.6, *advise* 176.9, *judge* 341.10, *be right* 429.12, *negotiate* 460.6, *compromise* 461.7, *moderate* 521.7
arbitrated *disputed* 57.15, *negotiated* 460.5
arbitrating *disputed* 57.15
arbitration *strike* 57.8, *pacification* 74.1, *mediation* 75.1, *judgment* 341.1, *negotiation* 460.1, *compromise* 461.1, *middle ground* 772.4
arbitrational *mediatory* 75.5
arbitration award *strike* 57.8
arbitration court *strike* 57.8
arbitration of interests *strike* 57.8
arbitration of rights *strike* 57.8
arbitration tribunal *strike* 57.8

arbitrator *judge* 54.10, 341.5, *employer* 57.3, *mediator* 75.2, *agent* 80.3, *karate* 152.14, *adviser* 176.5, 825.14, *impartial person* 443.3, *negotiator* 460.4, *moderator* 521.2, *middleman* 772.7
arbor *ornamental garden* 17.3, *trees* 43.4
arboraceous *treelike* 43.10
arboreal *horticultural* 17.14, *of animals* 34.13, *treelike* 43.10, *branched* 703.9
arboreous *wooded* 43.12
arborescence *branching* 703.4
arborescent *treelike* 43.10, *branched* 703.9
arboretum *garden* 17.2, *trees* 43.4, *ecology* 815.3
arboricultural 43.13; *horticultural* 17.14
arboriculturally 43.16
arboriculture *horticulture* 17.1, *plant science* 41.10, *forestry* 43.5
arboriculturist *horticulturist* 17.13, *forester* 43.7
arboriform *branched* 703.9
arborio *rice* 90.32
arborist *horticulturist* 17.13, *forester* 43.7
arborization *branching* 703.4
arborous *horticultural* 17.14
arborvitae *Trees and Shrubs* 43
arbutus *Trees and Shrubs* 43
arc *line* 6.35, *circle* 6.40, *rainbow* 9.28, *stage lighting* 136.20, *curve* 629.1, 629.6, *parts of a circle* 631.4, *bulge* 634.2, *dome* 634.4, *part* 760.1
arcade *Architectural Elements* 134, *arch* 134.5, *amusement park and playground equipment* 167.8, *marketplace* 483.7, *urban area* 567.10, *passage* 691.5
Arcadia *dreamland* 360.8
Arcadian *naive* 821.3
arcane *occult* 86.16, *mysterious* 182.10, *obscure* 197.2, *inscrutable* 250.5, *unintelligible* 364.4, *profound* 598.15, *concealed* 844.7
arcanely *occultly* 86.27
arcaneness *unintelligibility* 364.1
arcanum *the occult* 86.2, *mystery* 182.4
arch 134.5, *Architectural Elements* 134, *stimulating* 221.7, *superstructure* 551.7, *curve* 629.1, 629.6, *dome* 634.4, *be convex* 634.7, *means of connection* 754.4, *cunning* 822.4
archaeological *historical* 3.10
archaeological anthropologist *paleoanthropologist* 1.4
archaeological anthropology *prehistoric anthropology* 1.2
archaeologically *historical* 3.17
archaeologist *historian* 3.3, 651.10, *record keeper* 185.8, *discoverer* 345.7, *antiquarian* 653.9
archaeology *history* 3.1, *detection* 345.2, *study of the past* 651.9, *antiquarianism* 653.3
Archaeopteryx *extinct bird* 36.14
Archaeozoic Period *Geologic Time Intervals* 8
archaic *historical* 3.10, *worded* 5.38, *disused* 394.8, *different in time* 648.2, *olden* 653.11
archaically 653.20; *historically* 3.17, *lexically* 5.46
archaicism *Western Art Styles* 133
archaic speech *ancient language* 5.10

archaism *historicism* 3.7, *ancient language* 5.10, *literary device* 139.12, *different time* 648.1, *antiquarianism* 653.3, *antiquity* 653.4
archaist *antiquarian* 653.9
archaize *look back* 651.18, *reverse* 671.9
archangel *angel* 82.11
archangelic *angelic* 82.21
archangels *angelic order* 82.12
archbishop *person in authority* 52.7, *religious leader* 68.9, *priest* 84.8
archbishopric *clerical venue* 84.4, *administrative region* 564.4
arch dam *dam* 551.12
archdeacon *person in authority* 52.7
archdeaconry *clerical dwelling* 84.10
archdiocese *clerical venue* 84.4, *administrative region* 564.4
archduchy *body politic* 50.3, *dominion* 566.3
archdukedom *dominion* 566.3
arched *architectural* 134.12, *curved* 629.4, *convex* 634.5, *accessible* 691.13
arched bridge *bridge* 551.10, 691.7
archegonium *fern plant* 46.2, *moss plant* 46.5
archenemy *hostile person* 63.5
Archer *Constellations* 7
archer *historical soldier* 77.8, *shooter* 696.11
archer's bow *curved thing* 629.3
archery *Sporting Activities* 145, *shooting* 696.5
archetypal *societal* 1.13, *representational* 187.8, *ideal* 327.12, 805.17, *quintessential* 723.8, *original* 737.4, *latent* 844.6
archetypal image *or* symbol *symbol* 108.28
archetypally *societally* 1.17, *ideologically* 327.23
archetypal myth *tradition* 1.7
archetype *tradition* 1.7, *symbol* 108.28, *ideal* 327.6, 805.6, *quintessence* 723.3, *original* 737.2
archetypically *societally* 1.17
Archfiend *devil* 446.5
Archimedean axiom *Mathematical Concepts* 6
Archimedean solid *polyhedron* 6.44
Archimedes' principle *Classical Physical Laws* 10
Archimedes' screw *irrigator* 557.13, *rotator* 682.8
Archimedes' spiral *curve* 6.38
arching *curvature* 629.2
archipelagic *of landmasses* 572.12
archipelago *island* 572.2
architect 134.3; *professional worker* 123.11, *planner* 387.9, *producer* 522.10, *originator* 771.15
architect-designed *produced* 522.12
architectonic *structural* 14.45, 551.17, *architectural* 134.12, *productive* 522.11
architectonically *structurally* 14.52, 551.24, *architecturally* 134.14
architectonics *architecture* 134.1, *structure* 551.1
architectural 134.12; *structural* 14.45, 551.17
architectural artist *visual artist* 133.6

architectural engineer *architect* 134.3
architectural engineering *architecture* 134.1
architecturally 134.14; *structurally* 14.52, 551.24
architectural monstrosity *architectural structure* 134.4
architectural photography *photographic specialties* 132.2
architectural sculptor *sculptor* 144.4
architectural sculpture *sculpture* 144.1
architectural structure 134.4
architectural summit 600.4
architectural tile *industrial ceramics* 129.6
architectural types 134.2
architecture 134.1; *aspect of fiction* 139.5, *manufacture* 522.2, *structure* 551.1, *form* 551.3
architrave *Architectural Elements* 134
archival *chronicled* 3.12
archive *history* 3.1, *chronicle* 3.4, *data-related concepts* 15.23, *program* 15.29, *collection* 105.12, *save* 105.20, *record* 185.13
archived *chronicled* 3.12, *saved* 105.15, *recorded* 185.12
archives *collection* 105.12, *record* 185.1, *conservation* 815.2
archivist *historian* 3.3, *record keeper* 185.8
archivolt *Architectural Elements* 134
archness *stimulation* 221.4
arch types *arch* 134.5
archway *means of entry* 706.6
arciform *curved* 629.4
arc lamp *electric light* 246.6
arc light *stage lighting* 136.20
Arctic *cold place* 218.7, *frozen* 218.10, *world region* 542.6
arctic *cool* 9.49, *seasonal* 654.7, *directional* 697.8
arctic char *food fish and shellfish* 90.20, *game fish* 154.10
Arctic Circle *cold place* 218.7
arctic climate *climate* 9.35
arctic conditions *cold weather* 218.8
Arctic Ocean *Oceans and Seas* 571
Arctic waste *infertile land* 23.2
arcuate *curvilinear* 6.78, *architectural* 134.12, *convex* 634.5, *be convex* 634.7
arcuated *architectural* 134.12
arcuation *arch* 134.5
Ardennais *Horse and Pony Breeds* 159
ardent *friendly* 62.5, *zealous* 81.22, *emphatic* 200.3, *passionate* 266.12, *desirous* 288.13, *amorous* 299.18, *active* 414.13, *hasty* 818.3
ardently *amicably* 62.13, *religiously* 81.29, *emphatically* 200.7, *warmly* 217.20, *with feeling* 266.18, *eagerly* 288.27, 373.16, *amorously* 299.30
ardor *emphasis* 200.1, *emotion* 266.3, *eagerness* 288.3, 373.2, *romantic love* 299.2, *seriousness* 376.3, *energy* 414.4
arduous *laborious* 122.7, *eager* 373.8, *punishing* 454.20, *difficult* 824.9
arduously 824.24; *laboriously* 122.13
arduousness *difficulty* 824.1
are *General Units* 589

area *space* 6.33, 563.1, *surface* 6.36, *dimension* 10.5, *subject* 48.3, *range* 563.7, *region* 564.1, *size* 579.1, *surroundings* 615.1, *quantity* 738.1, *part* 760.1, *specialization* 779.3

area code *dial* 169.12

areal *regional* 564.12

area of disagreement *rivalry* 422.2, *divisiveness* 463.2

area of hostilities *battleground* 76.24

area of influence *sphere of influence* 512.7

area rug *floor covering* 613.13

areca palm Trees and Shrubs 43

arena *slaughterhouse* 30.16, *theater* 136.16, *sports ground* 145.2, *place for viewing* 242.13, *region* 564.1, *sphere* 564.10, *surroundings* 615.1, *enclosed area* 619.2

arenaceous *grainy* 553.17

arenarious *grainy* 553.17

arena theater *theater* 136.16

arenose *grainy* 553.17

Areopagus *place of judgment* 341.3

Ares Deities 82

arête *rock face* 161.6, *sharp-pointed thing* 549.4, *mountain range* 569.3

Argand diagram Mathematical Concepts 6

argent Heraldic Terms 184, *white* 253.7

argental *white* 253.7

Argentina Countries 566

argentine *white* 253.7

Argentine Merino Breeds of Sheep 16

Argentine tango *ice-dancing move* 162.19

Argestes *wind god* 9.16

Argie Nicknames for Inhabitants 61

argil *material* 129.2

argillaceous *compressible* 543.9

arginine Amino Acids 12

argon Chemical Elements and Common Allotropes 11

argosy *naval unit* 77.20

argot *nonstandard language* 5.7, *jargon* 5.21, *regional pronunciation* 205.7, *type of meaning* 361.4

argotic *worded* 5.38, *technical* 361.10

arguable 329.8; *litigated* 54.22, *questionable* 333.13, *vindicable* 441.9

arguably 329.16; *questionably* 333.22

argue 329.11; *discuss* 4.22, *litigate* 54.27, *dissertate* 203.5, *quarrel* 272.9, 302.17, *be irascible* 303.13, *debate* 319.13, *focus on* 328.9, *state* 329.13, *plead* 329.14, *answer back* 334.19, *propound* 359.9, *balance* 378.11, *conflict* 422.26, *justify* 441.12, *dispute* 463.9

argue against *dissuade* 179.7, *deny* 332.8

argued *litigated* 54.22, *disputed* 57.15

argue down *refute* 332.7

argue for *plead for* 419.25, *contend* 422.22, *justify* 441.12, *advise* 825.27

argue into a corner *refute* 332.7

argue one's case *litigate* 54.27

arguer 319.6

argue the toss *discuss* 329.12

argue with *deny* 332.8, *dissent* 347.8

arguing 329.6; *litigating* 54.21, *dissenting* 347.7

argument 329.1; *philosophical argument* 4.5, *complex number* 6.6, *mathematical function* 6.27, *reasoning* 6.61, *claim* 72.2, *aspect of fiction* 139.5, *dissertation* 203.1, *quarrel* 272.4, 302.7, *debate* 319.3, *topic* 328.11, *gist* 329.4, *plea* 329.5, *questioning* 333.2, *counterstatement* 334.5, *supposition* 359.1, *contention* 422.1, *defense* 441.2, *disagreement* 463.1, *dispute* 463.3, *disruption* 766.7, *objection* 828.2

argument ad hominem *philosophical term* 4.7, *sophism* 330.2

argument a fortiori *philosophical term* 4.7

argument a posteriori *philosophical term* 4.7

argument a priori *philosophical term* 4.7

argumentation *debate* 319.3, *logical argument* 329.2

argumentative 319.10, 329.7; *litigating* 54.21, *ill-natured* 303.9, *retaliatory* 334.13, *contentious* 422.20, *vindicatory* 441.7, *disagreeing* 463.6

argumentatively 329.15; *philosophically* 4.23, *ill-naturedly* 303.18, *in answer* 334.25, *contentiously* 422.27, *justifyingly* 441.15, *in disagreement* 463.12

argumentativeness *ill nature* 303.2

argument from design *logical argument* 329.2

argument from first principles *philosophical term* 4.7

argumentum *logical argument* 329.2

Argus *sharp eye* 242.4

Argus-eyed *seeing* 242.17, *suspicious* 314.6

argy-bargy [Brit] *argument* 329.1

argyles *legwear* 100.26

aria *melody* 140.10

arid *infertile* 23.7, *tasteless* 220.4, *boring* 296.6, *dry* 560.7, *desert* 560.12

arid climate *climate* 9.35

aridity *infertility* 23.1, *dilution* 220.2, *boringness* 296.2, *dryness* 560.1

aridly *without taste* 220.8, *dryly* 560.23

aridness *infertility* 23.1, *dryness* 560.1

Ariel Planets and Their Satellites 7

Aries Constellations 7

aright *correctly* 429.16

arise 655.7, 715.15; *become visible* 264.13, *be vertical* 602.8, *take effect* 676.11, *emerge* 707.14, 771.35, *ascend* 713.19, *come to be* 717.19, *result* 770.12

arise from *follow from* 676.9

arising *birth* 264.2, *appearing* 264.9, *outgoing* 707.10

arising from *caused* 676.5

aristocracy 70.2; *oligarchy* 49.10, *best people* 744.7

aristocrat *proud person* 297.7, *important person* 799.5

aristocratic 70.4; *governmental* 49.24, *masterful* 68.15, *majestic* 297.12, *cultured* 534.6

aristocratically 70.6; *masterfully* 68.19, *majestically* 297.12

Aristogiton Notable Friendships 62

Aristophanean comedy *historic comedy* 136.12

Aristotelian Philosophical Schools of Thought 4

Aristotelianism Philosophical Schools of Thought 4

Aristotelian philosophy Philosophical Schools of Thought 4

Arita ware Ceramics 129

arithmancy or **arithmomancy** *divination* 86.5

arithmetic Branches of Mathematics 6, *mathematical addition* 748.2

arithmetical *mathematical* 6.65, 784.9, *accounting* 493.7, *numerical* 783.7

arithmetically *financially* 493.13, *numerically* 783.11, *mathematically* 784.15

arithmetic mean *parameter* 6.57

arithmetic operation *operation* 6.12

arithmetic operator *mathematical symbol* 6.11

arithmetic progression *sequence* 6.18

arithmetic series *sequence* 6.18

arithmophobia Phobias 283

Arizona American States 564

ark Ships and Boats 690, *private space* 812.2

Arkansas American States 564, Rivers 570

Arkansas Black Apple Varieties 44

Arles Merino Breeds of Sheep 16

arm 76.30; *galaxy* 7.5, *appendage* 19.5, *weapon* 78.1, *part of garment* 100.27, *indicator* 183.7, *equip* 388.19, *empower* 514.20, *component* 760.3, *protect* 810.21

armada *naval unit* 77.20

armadillo *toothless mammal* 35.14

Armageddon *world war* 76.2

armament *fitting out* 388.3

armature *generator* 14.43, *material* 144.6

armband *accessory* 100.28, *survival swimming* 164.4

armchair *type of chair* 101.4, *suppositional* 359.5

Armco™ *automobile racing terms* 146.3

armed *warring* 76.26, *martial* 77.33, *equipped* 388.10, *strengthened* 516.13

armed at all points *equipped* 388.10

armed conflict *war* 76.1, *battle* 76.23

armed force 77.10; *force* 59.10, *protection* 810.2

armed forces 77.9; *the military* 58.2, *security force* 464.3

armed guard *guard* 419.15, *security force* 810.13

armed intervention *war* 76.1

armed neutrality *coexistence* 73.3

armed robbery *personal attack* 418.8, *theft* 479.2

armed to the teeth *equipped* 388.10

Armenia Countries 566

armful *container(ful)* 738.2

arm guard *hockey clothing* 158.6

armhole *part of garment* 100.27

arm in arm *intimately* 62.14, *sociably* 408.19, *near* 586.6, *united* 752.10, *hand in hand* 794.21

arming *war measures* 76.18

armistice *truce* 73.2, *pause* 668.3

armlet *accessory* 100.28

arm of the sea *inlet* 572.9

armoire *cabinet* 101.8

armor *reinforce* 419.23, *hard substance* 542.3, *protective covering* 613.5, *protect* 613.26, 810.21, *protection* 810.2, *safety device* 810.15

armored *martial* 77.33, *tenacious* 376.9, *defended* 419.18, *hardened* 542.7, *invulnerable* 810.18

armored attack *land attack* 418.3

armorial *heraldic* 184.10

armorial bearings Heraldic Terms 184

armor-piercing 78.18

armor-piercing ammunition *ammunition* 78.11

armor plate *modern armor* 419.7, *protection* 810.2

armor-plated *defended* 419.18, *hardened* 542.7

armory *arsenal* 78.3, *storehouse* 105.8, *power station* 124.12, Heraldic Terms 184, *insignia* 184.5

arms *war* 76.1, Heraldic Terms 184, *fitting out* 388.3

arms akimbo *gesture* 183.5

arms cache *arsenal* 78.3

arms control *disarmament* 74.3

arms control agreement *alliance* 459.5

arms cuts *disarmament* 74.3

arms depot *arsenal* 78.3

arms race 78.2

arms reduction *disarmament* 74.3

arms sanctions *economic warfare* 76.7

arms trade *arms race* 78.2

arms traffic *arms race* 78.2

arm-twisting *coercive method* 428.3

arm wrestling Sporting Activities 145

army 77.12; *dwelling* 40.7, *the military* 58.2, 58.10, Collective Names 79, *force* 59.10, *army unit* 77.14, *security force* 464.3, *collection* 757.3, *throng* 795.4

army combat specialist 77.16

army commands 77.13

army corps *military organization* 58.4

army formation 77.15

Army General Classification Test Intelligence Tests 108

army group *military organization* 58.4, *army unit* 77.14

army officer *army person* 77.17

army person 77.17

army rule *military government* 49.16

army staff *military staff* 58.5

army unit 77.14

armyworm *larva* 40.9

arnica *analgesic* 115.6

Arno Rivers 570

A road [Brit] *road* 687.2

aroma *piquancy* 221.1, *odor* 224.1, *fragrance* 226.1, *characteristic* 779.5

aromatherapeutic *fragrant* 226.4

aromatherapist *healer* 107.22, *fragrance* 226.1

aromatherapy *alternative medicine* 107.4, *fragrance* 226.1

aromatic *chemical compound* 11.4, *piquant* 221.6, *odorous* 224.5, *fragrant* 226.4

aromatically *piquantly* 221.10, *odorously* 224.10, *fragrantly* 226.7

aromaticity *odor* 224.1

aromatization *chemical reaction* 11.8

aromatize *impart odor to* 224.9, *perfume* 226.6

arondissement [Fr] *administrative region* 564.4

Aron Kodesh [Hebrew] *sacred object* 83.11

Arouca Breeds of Cattle 16

around 615.8, 682.17; *environmentally* 60.26, *geographically* 573.11, *nearby* 586.17, *roundly* 633.11, *via* 691.17, *in all directions* 697.19

around and about *nearby* 586.17, *surrounded* 615.5, *in all directions* 697.19

around and around *around* 682.17

around the clock *continuously* 774.16

around-the-world racing *competitive sailing* 150.6

arousal *physical pleasure* 214.1, *stimulus* 508.3, *drawing out* 711.5

arouse *arouse sensation* 212.11, *give pleasure* 214.13, *cause desire* 288.22, *make angry* 302.18, *motivate* 508.9, *draw out* 711.17, *give warning* 814.10

aroused *desirous* 20.18, *pleasure-seeking* 214.10

arouse jealousy 314.10

arouse no echoes *be nonresonant* 233.10

arouse sensation 212.11

arousing *offensive* 432.11

ARPANET *computer communications* 15.25

arpeggio *musical ornament* 140.19, *consecutiveness* 774.1

arpeggione Musical Instruments 142

arraign *litigate* 54.27, *accuse* 442.8

arraignment *pretrial proceedings* 54.13

arrange 767.18, 774.14; *design* 133.9, *compose* 141.18, *predetermine* 384.8, *plan ahead* 387.13, *produce* 522.13, *fashion* 537.9, *structure* 551.20, *form* 624.9, *cause change* 665.16, *settle* 735.26, *order* 765.18, *sort* 777.13

arrange a fatal accident *murder* 30.20

arrange a marriage *matchmake* 64.22

arrange a mortgage *credit* 487.10

arranged 767.11; *grouped* 59.21, *composed* 141.13, *predetermined* 384.4, *planned* 387.10, *contractual* 459.7, *compromising* 461.4, *settled* 735.16, *ordered* 765.10

arranged marriage *type of marriage* 64.3

arrange for *make arrangements* 767.23

arrange in *subsume* 763.7

arrange in a circle *make circular* 631.7

arrange in layers *layer* 588.9

arrangement 767.1; *assemblage* 59.13, *musical composition* 140.9, *harmonics* 140.13, *treatment* 143.6, *predetermination* 384.1, *preparations* 388.2, *contract* 459.1, *compromise* 461.1, *structure* 551.1, *form* 624.1, *frequency* 663.2, *settlement* 735.6, *order* 765.1, *array* 767.2, *agreement* 767.9, *sequence* 770.1

arrangements 767.10; *preparations* 388.2

arranger *composer* 141.9

arranging *motion-picture editing* 137.8, *arrangement* 767.1

arrant *wicked* 448.9, *accentuated* 843.11

arrantly *wickedly* 448.15

arras *interior decoration* 532.4, *wall covering* 613.12

array 767.2; *radio telescope* 7.26, *army formation* 77.15, *finery* 100.6, *dress up* 100.45, *fitting out* 388.3, *prepare for action* 388.18, *decorate* 532.11, *range* 563.7, *space* 563.15, *order* 765.1, 765.18, *arrange* 767.18, 774.14, *throng* 795.4, *display* 843.1

arrayed *warring* 76.26, *dressed* 100.38, *ordered* 765.10, *arranged* 767.11

arraying *arrangement* 767.1

arrears *amount owing* 488.5, *incompleteness* 762.1, *omission* 762.4, *economic adversity* 848.6

arrest 55.5, 55.12; *pretrial proceedings* 54.13, *mountaineer* 161.10, *accusation* 442.1, *accuse* 442.8, *take away forcefully* 477.19, *interruption* 604.4, *interrupt* 604.16, *cause to cease* 668.12, *hesitation* 693.5, *slow down* 693.13, *obstacle* 826.2, *detention* 830.5, *detain* 830.16

arrested 55.10; *accused* 442.5, *interrupted* 604.10, *delayed* 693.10, *detained* 830.11

arrested development *fixation* 108.21

arresting *conquest* 477.6

arrête *landform* 8.9

Arretine ware Ceramics 129

arrhythmia *vibration* 683.2

arrival 704.1; *appearance* 264.1, *birth* 264.2, *forward motion* 677.4, *entry* 706.1, *entrant* 706.7, *completion* 761.2, *creation* 771.2

arrive 704.13; *become visible* 264.13, *enter* 706.11, *emerge* 771.35, *attain one's goal* 845.13, *be prosperous* 847.6

arrive ahead of time or schedule *be early* 657.11

arrive at a consensus *agree with* 462.10

arrive at or upon *reach* 704.14

arrive at the wrong time *untimely* 660.8

arrive early *be early* 657.11

arrive first *be early* 657.11

arrive last *be late* 658.11

arrive late *be late* 658.11, *be untimely* 660.8

arrive too early *be untimely* 660.8

arriving 704.9; *appearing* 264.9

arrogance 297.2, 400.4; *overestimation* 343.1, *boastfulness* 402.6, *defiance* 416.1, *assurance* 621.8

arrogant 297.9, 400.11; *overestimating* 343.4, *boastful* 402.13, *defiant* 416.5, *contemptuous* 436.12, *assured* 621.12

arrogantly 297.18, 400.21; *authoritatively* 52.18, *overoptimistically* 343.7, *boastfully* 402.21, *defiantly* 416.9

arrogate *be anarchic* 51.8, *gain authority* 52.15

arrogating *anarchic* 51.5

arrogation *anarchy* 51.1, *acquisition of authority* 52.5, *taking over* 477.3, *excessiveness* 712.4

arrow Historical Missile Weapons 78, *sharp weapon* 78.6, *indicator* 183.7, *notched thing* 636.2, *missile* 696.7

arrow case *historical ammunition* 78.12

arrowhead *sharp-pointed thing* 549.4, *thing of the past* 651.8

arrowlike *sharp* 549.10

arrows *guide* 126.6

arroyo *river parts* 570.3

arse [Inf] *rear end* 622.4

arsenal 78.3; *storehouse* 105.8, *power station* 124.12

arsenic Chemical Elements and Common Allotropes 11, *poison* 117.7

arsenic oxide *poison* 117.7

arson *cause of fire* 217.10, *destructiveness* 523.3

arsonist *cause of fire* 217.10, *criminal* 427.6, *violent animal or person* 520.4, *destroyer* 523.6

arsy-varsy [Inf] *inverted* 608.5, *inversely* 608.9, *muddled* 766.13, *anyhow* 766.25

art *masterpiece* 127.5, *artistry* 133.3, *cunning* 330.3, 822.1, *production* 522.1, *stratagem* 822.2

art brut Western Art Styles 133

art collection *collection* 105.12

art college *type of school* 48.12

art-conscious *artistic* 133.7

art deco Furniture Styles 101, Western Art Styles 133, Architectural Styles 134

art director *filmmaker* 137.14

artefact *thing of the past* 651.8, *antiquity* 653.4

arte informel Western Art Styles 133

Artemis *moon* 7.18, Deities 82, *shooter* 696.11

arte povera Western Art Styles 133

arterial blood *blood* 555.4

arterial road *road* 687.2, *means of connection* 774.4

arteries *internal organ* 19.13

arteriography *diagnostic radiology* 107.12

arteriosclerosis *cardiovascular disease* 114.13, *hardening* 542.2

arteritis *cardiovascular disease* 114.13

artesian basin *groundwater* 8.11

artesian spring *groundwater* 8.11

artful 193.13; *cunning* 330.8, 822.4

artful dodger *cunning person* 822.3

artfully *deceptively* 193.21, *hypocritically* 330.15, *cunningly* 822.6

artfulness *guile* 193.3, *cunning* 330.3, 822.1

art gallery *repository* 105.13

art glass *ceramics* 129.1

arthritic *sick person* 114.22, *of disease* 114.25

arthritis *joint disease* 114.19, *painful condition* 115.2

arthrodire *fossil fish* 38.7

arthropod 39.6; *type of animal* 34.5

Arthropoda *arthropod* 39.6

arthropodal 39.22

arthropodan or **arthropodous** *arthropod* 39.22

arthropodlike invertebrate 39.12

article 203.2; *part of speech* 5.30, *news story* 171.3, *basis for negotiations* 460.2, *merchandise* 482.6, *product* 522.3, *work of art* 522.4, *object* 524.6, *passage* 692.1, *part of writing* 760.6, *one* 788.1

article for sale *merchandise* 482.6

article of clothing *clothing* 100.1

article of commerce *merchandise* 482.6

article or **object** or **piece of virtu** *work of art* 133.4

articles of agreement *basis for negotiations* 460.2

articles of faith *belief system* 87.3

articulacy *power of speech* 205.5, *clarity* 363.2

articulate 205.16; *use language* 5.42, *simple* 363.6, *make comprehensible* 363.8, *intertwine* 752.19

articulated *spoken* 205.13, *united* 752.10

articulated vehicle *truck* 687.8

articulately *orally* 205.21, *intelligibly* 363.13

articulateness *power of speech* 205.5, *clarity* 363.2

articulation 205.9; *power of speech* 205.5, *unification* 752.5

artifact *product* 522.3, *object* 524.6, *thing of the past* 651.8, *antiquity* 653.4, *artificiality* 720.7

artifice 193.5; *cunning* 330.3, *affectation* 367.1, *method* 387.4, *inelegance* 528.1, *trick* 813.2, *stratagem* 822.2

artificer *artisan* 123.13, *producer* 522.10

artificial 720.12; *of language* 5.35, *well-made* 127.13, *fishing* 154.13, *mountaineering* 161.9, *ski* 162.27, *ungenuine* 192.13, *affected* 367.3, *produced* 522.12, *inelegant* 528.6, *unauthentic* 722.9, *simulated* 733.11, *imitation* 736.8

artificial coloring *food content* 90.3, *coloring agent* 251.5

artificial dye *coloring agent* 251.5

artificial eye *substitute* 672.2

artificial flavoring *food content* 90.3

artificial fly *bait* 154.6

artificial fly-fishing *fly-fishing* 154.2

artificial grass *stadium* 155.3

artificial insemination *livestock farming* 16.10, *fertilization* 21.6

artificial intelligence 15.21; *philosophical problem* 4.8, *computing* 15.2

artificiality 720.7; *ungenuineness* 192.2, *unauthenticity* 722.4

artificial lake *lake* 568.1

artificial language 5.9

artificial light *electric light* 246.6

artificial lighting *lighting* 132.16

artificial limb *substitute* 672.2

artificial lure *bait* 154.6

artificially *on the water* 154.15, *untruthfully* 192.27, *affectedly* 367.5, *unauthentically* 722.17, *imitatively* 733.20, 736.12

artificial magnet *magnet* 700.3

artificial memory 354.6

artificial minnow *bait* 154.6

artificial respiration *swimming rescue* 164.5, *revival* 809.3

artificial route *climbing expedition* 161.2

artificial satellite 7.30

artificial slope *ski run* 162.2

artificial sweetener *food content* 90.3, *sweetener* 222.2

artillery *guns* 78.9, *burst of sound* 232.4, *shooting* 696.5

artillery bombardment *combined attack* 418.5

artilleryman *army combat specialist* 77.16, *shooter* 696.11

artillery missile *modern missile weapon* 78.4

artillery park *guns* 78.9
artillery shell *casing* 613.9
artillery warfare *blockading* 76.22
artiness [Inf] *artistry* 133.3
artiodactyl *hoofed mammal* 35.16, *ungulate* 35.31
Artiodactyla *hoofed mammal* 35.16
artiodactylous *ungulate* 35.31
artisan 123.13; *expert* 127.9, *visual artist* 133.6, *worker* 412.8, *producer* 522.10
artisanship *artistry* 133.3
artist *artistic worker* 123.12, *expert* 127.9, *visual artist* 133.6, *entertainer* 138.8, *musician* 141.1, *painter* 143.7, *record keeper* 185.8, *visionary* 360.9, *performer* 412.5, *producer* 522.10, *stylist* 537.4
artiste *entertainer* 138.8, *musician* 141.1
artistic 133.7; *well-made* 127.13, *entertaining* 138.12, *gymnastic* 157.11, *representational* 187.8, *representing* 202.14, *acting* 412.9, *fluid* 527.5, *refined* 534.5
artistically 133.10; *skillfully* 127.16, *entertainingly* 138.17, *gymnastically* 157.13, *elegantly* 527.7, *tastefully* 534.9
artistically done *fluid* 527.5
artistic flair *artistry* 133.3
artistic gymnastics *gymnastics* 157.1
artistic invention *artistry* 133.3
artistic license *freedom* 829.1
artistic movement *trendiness* 652.2
artistic person *performer* 412.5
artistic production *or* **creation** *work of art* 133.4
artistic quality *artistry* 133.3
artistic skill *artistry* 133.3
artistic taste *artistry* 133.3
artistic technique *artistry* 133.3
artistic temperament *artistry* 133.3
artistic worker 123.12
artistry 133.3; *masterpiece* 127.5, *imagination* 360.1
artist's colors *paint* 251.6
artless *bungled* 128.7, *ingenuous* 191.6, *raw* 260.9, *unprocessed* 389.10, *naive* 449.9, 821.3, *natural* 526.10, *inelegant* 528.6, *open* 583.13
artlessly *ingenuously* 191.11, *naively* 449.15, 821.5, *naturally* 526.16, *candidly* 583.23
artlessness *ingenuousness* 191.3, *ignorance* 349.1, *naiveté* 449.4, 821.1, *naturalness* 526.4, *inelegance* 528.1, *openness* 583.7
art-minded *artistic* 133.7
art museum *repository* 105.13, *material* 143.9
art nouveau *Furniture Styles* 101, *Western Art Styles* 133, *Architectural Styles* 134
art object *work of art* 133.4
art of dispute *logical argument* 329.2
art of healing *healing art* 115.13
art of illusion *magic* 138.3
art of management *personnel management* 126.4
art of the possible *tactics* 399.12
art of war 76.16; *military affairs* 58.1
artotype *older photograph* 132.4
art paper *paper* 104.5, *material* 143.9
art pottery *ceramics* 129.1
art review *criticism* 365.3

art room *school place* 48.16
arts *learning* 348.3
arts, the *visual arts* 133.1, *literature* 139.1
Arts and Crafts *Furniture Styles* 101
arts and crafts *craft* 133.2
Arts and Crafts movement *Western Art Styles* 133
art show *display* 843.1
arts of design *visual arts* 133.1
artsy-craftiness [Inf] *artistry* 133.3
artsy-craftsy [Inf] *artistic* 133.7
artsy-fartsiness [Inf] *artistry* 133.3
artsy-fartsy [Inf] *artistic* 133.7
artwork *work of art* 133.4, *illustration* 187.2
arty [Inf] *artistic* 133.7
Aruba *Islands* 572
arugula *Herbs and Spices* 91
arum lily *Flowers* 42
Aruwimi *Rivers* 570
Aryan *race* 1.5, *racial* 1.12
as 649.10; *how* 691.16
as a bequest *by transfer* 470.15
as a challenge *in defiance* 416.10
as a compromise *feasibly* 460.9
as a consequence *with the effect of* 676.12, *consequently* 770.15
as a convert *receptively* 473.15
as a cop-out [Inf] *irresolutely* 461.10
as a curse *execratively* 301.17
as a dare *defiantly* 416.9
as a defense *apologetically* 329.18, *in reply* 332.10
as a deterrent *dissuasively* 179.12
asafetida *or* **asafoetida** *unpleasant-smelling thing* 227.2
as a gift 472.17; *cheaply* 497.16
as agreed *responsibly* 391.10, *as promised* 458.16, *contractually* 459.9, *agreeably* 442.14
as agreed upon 735.36; *contractually* 459.9
as a group *one and all* 759.12
as a half-measure *compromisingly* 461.9
as a joke *humorously* 277.13
as already stated *agreeingly* 730.19
as always *regularly* 397.21, *as usual* 781.17
as a matter of course *prevailingly* 742.11, *usually* 778.21, *as usual* 781.17
as a matter of fact *really* 717.22, *in truth* 721.28
as a matter of form *formally* 406.12
as an advance *on loan* 476.14
as an alternative *in place of* 574.21, *instead* 672.8
as an amateur *professionally* 152.22
as an answer *in reply* 332.10
as a new member *receptively* 473.15
as an example *demonstrably* 331.22
as an excuse *justifyingly* 441.15
as an institution *cliquishly* 59.32
as an obligation *contractually* 462.15
ASA number *exposure* 132.15
ASAP *in the shortest possible time* 645.9
as a preliminary *in anticipation* 769.20
as a prelude *in anticipation* 769.20
as a prize *rewardingly* 453.19
as a protest *disobediently* 427.14

as a replacement *answerably* 334.28
as a result *with the effect of* 676.12, *accordingly* 735.39, *consequently* 770.15
as a result of *by virtue of* 447.12
as a reward *rewardingly* 453.19
as arranged *intentionally* 374.13, *as agreed upon* 735.36
as a rule 780.18; *on average* 742.10, *on the whole* 759.13, *usually* 778.21
as a sacrifice *sacrificially* 504.20
as a sign *indicatively* 183.21
as a start *first* 771.37
as a substitute *alternatively* 613.36
as a team *one and all* 759.12
as a temptation *influentially* 508.13
as a thoughtful gesture *genteelly* 410.14
as a token of one's gratitude *gratefully* 310.8
as a trade-off *feasibly* 460.9
as a unit *one and all* 759.12
as a wage earner *receptively* 473.15
as a whole *on average* 742.10, *one and all* 759.12, *overall* 778.22
as before *permanently* 667.6, *as usual* 781.17
asbestosis *respiratory disease* 114.12
as broad as long *equal* 740.8
as can be *hugely* 579.21
ascariasis *tropical disease* 114.10
ascend 713.19; *have authority* 52.13, *mountaineer* 161.10, *be light* 539.8, *rise* 596.17, *be in motion* 677.14, *get better* 807.21
ascendancy 713.5; *authority* 52.1, *personal influence* 512.3, *superiority* 744.1, *success* 845.1
ascendant *authoritative* 52.9, *rising* 713.14, *superior* 744.8
ascender 713.12; *type* 173.5
ascenders *climbing equipment* 161.4
ascending 713.13; *climbing techniques* 161.3, *mountainous* 569.5, *rising* 596.12, 713.14, *ascending motion* 677.7, *directional* 677.13, *raised* 715.6
ascending motion 677.7
ascending order *straight line* 630.2, *hierarchy* 765.3, *consecutiveness* 774.1
ascension *ascent* 713.1
ascensional *rising* 713.14
Ascension Day *Christian Holy Days and Seasons* 85
Ascension Island *Islands* 572
ascensive *rising* 713.14
ascent 713.1; *climbing techniques* 161.3, *lightness* 539.1, *hill* 569.2, *heights* 596.4, *ascending motion* 677.7, *advance* 679.3, *raising* 715.1, *uplift* 807.2
ascertain *learn* 48.23, *prove* 331.17, 336.9, *experiment* 335.11, *find out* 345.13, *establish reality* 719.12, *authenticate* 721.24, *make certain* 840.14
ascertained *proven* 331.13, *authenticated* 721.17, *certain* 840.7
ascertaining *finding out* 345.3
ascertainment *proof* 331.4, 336.2, *experimentation* 335.3, *authentication* 721.8, *confirmation* 840.3
ascesis *unadornment* 424.3, *abstinence* 455.2, *self-restraint* 830.4

ascetic *religious* 81.21, 84.9, *worshipful* 83.12, *fasting* 118.5, *atoner* 313.4, *apologetic* 313.6, *abstaining* 386.11, *unsocial person* 409.5, *unadorned* 424.7, *penitent person* 451.4, *self-restrained person* 455.5, *self-restrained* 455.6, 830.10, *individualist* 756.3, *hermit* 782.9, *loner* 788.8, *one who restrains* 830.7
ascetically *worshipfully* 83.17, *apologetically* 313.11, *plainly* 424.12, *with self-restraint* 455.14
asceticism *act of worship* 83.2, *incompleteness* 98.2, *short rations* 118.3, *unadornment* 424.3, *self-punishment* 454.10, *self-restraint* 455.1, 830.4, *renunciation of wealth* 486.4
ascetism *penitence* 313.3
as changeable as a weathercock *or* **the weather** *or* **the moon** *inconstant* 378.6
ascidian *protochordate* 39.4
as claimed *allegedly* 189.31
as clear as day *clear* 244.6, *simple* 363.6
Asclepius *Deities* 82
ascocarp *fungal body* 47.4
ascogenous *of fungi* 47.19
ascomycetes *fungi* 47.3
Ascomycota *fungi* 47.3
as contracted for *contractually* 459.9, *as agreed upon* 735.36
ascospore *fungal body* 47.4
Ascot [Brit] *famous horse races* 159.13
ascot *neckwear* 100.29
ascribe *recognize* 487.13
ascribe a meaning to *interpret* 365.12
ascribe importance to *be important* 799.13
ascus *fungal body* 47.4
asdic *sound propagation* 230.3
aseity *self-existence* 717.8
asepsis *cleaning* 111.2, *hygiene* 116.1
aseptic *clean* 111.13, *hygienic* 116.3
aseptically *hygienically* 116.5
as ever *permanently* 667.6
as every schoolchild knows *knowledgeably* 348.14
as evidence 339.15; *demonstrably* 331.22
as expected *probably* 838.11
asexual *undersexed* 20.20
asexuality *sexlessness* 20.13
as far as one can *ambitiously* 390.10
as far as one can tell *on the whole* 759.13
as far as one knows *knowledgeably* 348.14
as far as possible *reasonably* 319.15
as far as the eye can see *in the offing* 585.12
as fast as one's legs can carry one *swiftly* 694.16
as follows *after* 770.14
as friends *amicably* 62.13
as full as can be *fully* 761.14
as fully as possible *fully* 761.14
Asgard *heaven* 82.15, *Imaginary Places* 360
as God is my witness! *yes!* 189.36
as good as 740.14; *nearly* 586.18, *on the whole* 759.13
as good as new *repaired* 809.6, *cured* 809.8

as good as one's word *observant* 465.3, *honest* 630.11
as good luck would have it *luckily* 842.17
ash *eruption* 8.27, Trees and Shrubs 43, *dirt* 112.5, *gray thing* 255.3, *powder* 553.9, *mud* 561.8, *residue* 750.2, *refuse* 802.5
ashamed *humiliated* 298.12, *appearing guilty* 450.7, *penitent* 451.5
ashamedly *guiltily* 450.12
Ashcan school Western Art Styles 133
ashen *drained of color* 252.6, *pale* 253.10, *gray* 255.6
ashen-faced *frightened* 283.9
ashen-hued *drained of color* 252.6
ashes *dead person* 29.7
Ashgabat Countries 566
ash-gray *gray* 255.6
ashlar *building materials* 104.2
ashore *of landmasses* 572.12, *continentally* 572.13, *on arrival* 704.22
ashram *clerical dwelling* 84.10
Ash-Shaytan *devil* 446.5
ashtray *tobacco implements* 121.24
Ash Wednesday Christian Holy Days and Seasons 85
ashy *drained of color* 252.6, *pale* 253.10, *gray* 255.6
Asia *landmass* 572.1
Asia Minor *world region* 564.6
Asian *race* 1.5, *racial* 1.12
Asiatic cholera *tropical disease* 114.10
aside *acting* 136.22, *inside information* 170.4, *utterance* 205.10, *soliloquy* 211.1, *undercurrent of sound* 233.3, *faintly* 233.11, *at a distance* 585.13, *apart* 585.14, *deviation* 698.1, *quietness* 844.4
as if one's life depended on it *actively* 414.24
as ill luck would have it *luckily* 842.17, *adversely* 848.16
asinine *ungulate* 35.31, *foolish* 353.5, *meaningless* 362.7, *ridiculous* 368.5
asininity *folly* 353.1
as intended *meaningfully* 361.16
as is *permanently* 667.6
as is befitting *properly* 429.18
as is fitting *properly* 429.18
as is one's wont *regularly* 397.21, *as a rule* 780.18
As I stand here! *yes!* 189.36
as it happened *under the circumstances* 726.16
as it happens *topically* 328.11, *really* 717.22
as it is *conditionally* 725.10, *under the circumstances* 726.16
as it is said *reportedly* 170.16
as it may be *perchance* 842.18
as it may chance *perchance* 842.18
as it may happen *under the circumstances* 726.16, *perchance* 842.18
as it should be *proper* 429.10
as it stands *circumstantially* 573.12, *conditionally* 725.10
as it turns out *conclusively* 334.26, *under the circumstances* 726.16
as it were *supposedly* 359.10
ask *philosophize* 4.19, *question* 333.16, *charge* 494.13, *request* 505.10
ask a favor *request* 505.10

askance or **askant** *reticently* 287.18
Askanian Breeds of Sheep 16
asked *questioned* 333.15
asker *philosopher* 4.9, *questioner* 333.9, *requester* 505.5
askesis *unadornment* 424.3, *abstinence* 455.2, *self-restraint* 830.4
askew **628.12;** *gone wrong* 430.17, *oblique* 607.6, *obliquely* 607.13, *distorted* 627.6, *unbalanced* 741.5, *muddled* 766.13
askewness *obliqueness* 607.1
ask favors of *resort to* 393.13
ask for *desire* 288.17, *demand* 425.11, *bargain* 480.20, *request* 505.10
ask for absolution *ask forgiveness* 312.12
ask for advice *consult* 176.11
ask forgiveness **312.12**
ask for it *be rash* 286.8
ask for mercy **308.10;** *ask forgiveness* 312.2, *capitulate* 421.6
ask for more *eat well* 92.23, *be unsatisfied* 98.10
ask for pity *ask for mercy* 308.10
ask for political asylum *shelter* 812.8
ask for quarter *ask for mercy* 308.10
ask for seconds *eat well* 92.23
ask for someone's blessing *ask permission* 502.9
ask for someone's hand *marry* 64.19, *get engaged to* 458.12
ask for terms *capitulate* 421.6
ask for trouble *be rash* 286.8, *be foolish* 353.6
ask if it is possible *request* 505.10
ask if one may *ask permission* 502.9
ask in *be hospitable* 477.21
asking *philosophical investigation* 4.4, *request* 505.1, *requesting* 505.7
asking for it *reckless* 286.6
asking for trouble *reckless* 286.6
asking price *offer* 504.3
ask leave *ask permission* 502.9, *request* 505.10
ask no favors *be independent* 829.18
ask oneself *speculate* 294.13
ask permission **502.9;** *request* 505.10
ask protection from *shelter* 812.8
ask to be excused *ask permission* 502.9, *request* 505.10
ask too much *overcharge* 496.10
ASL *artificial language* 5.9, *voiceless speech* 206.4, *aid to the deaf* 229.3
aslant *askew* 628.12
asleep *desensitized* 213.5, *not awake* 415.12
asleep in Jesus *dead* 29.11
as likely as not *probably* 838.11
as long as one's arm *at length* 590.15
as luck would have it *opportunely* 659.8
as meant *meaningfully* 361.16
Asmera Countries 566
Asmodeus *evil spirit* 446.4
as much again *twice* 789.18
as much as *quantitatively* 738.8
as much as to say *as good as* 740.14
as near as makes no difference *nearby* 586.17
as negotiated *as agreed upon* 735.36

as never before *inventively* 335.15, *enterprisingly* 391.11
as new *newly* 652.21
Aso Mountains and Hills 569
as often as not *frequently* 661.7
as old as Adam *olden* 653.11
as old as Methuselah *olden* 653.11
as old as the hills *olden* 653.11
as old as time *olden* 653.11
as one **752.21;** *together* 59.31, *cliquishly* 59.32, *matrimonially* 64.23, *unanimously* 346.8, *synchronously* 649.9, *in accord* 735.33, *in combination* 757.11, *wholly* 788.22, *cooperatively* 827.18
as one goes *in transit* 685.13
as one person *synchronously* 649.9
as one pleases or **wishes** *at will* 372.16
as one sees it *ideologically* 327.23
as one thinks fit or **best** *at will* 372.16
as ordered *commandingly* 425.15, *obediently* 426.9, *agreeably* 462.14
asp *snake* 37.6
asparagine Amino Acids 12
asparagus beetle *pests and diseases* 17.12
asparagus fern *fern* 46.1
aspartame *sweetener* 222.2
aspartic acid Amino Acids 12
aspect **623.4, 726.4;** *view* 242.8, *external appearance* 264.5, *conduct* 399.1, *design* 536.2, *situation* 573.1, *appearance* 610.4, *nature* 624.5, *viewpoint* 628.5, *state* 725.1, *component* 760.3
aspect of fiction **139.5**
aspen Trees and Shrubs 43, *shaky* 684.18
as penance *apologetically* 313.11
Asperges Christian rite 85.3, *religious cleansing* 111.3
aspergillosis *fungal disease* 47.6
aspergillum *sacred object* 83.11, *sprinkler* 557.12
asperity *emphasis* 200.1, *resentment* 302.1, *bitterness* 306.3, *discourtesy* 411.1, *severity* 424.1, *mental hardness* 542.4
asperse *perform rites* 85.18, *vilify* 301.15, 440.14, *scorn* 436.19
aspersion **440.4;** *vilification* 301.2, *personal attack* 418.8, *insult* 436.5, *criticism* 438.4, *watering* 557.8, *sprinkle* 559.5
aspersive *defamatory* 440.9
aspersorium *sacred object* 83.11
asphalt *construction material* 14.21, *building materials* 104.2, *resin* 562.6, *paving* 613.14
asphaltic *resinous* 562.13
asphodel Flowers 42
asphyxiant *killing* 30.17, *chemical warfare* 117.9
asphyxiate *murder* 30.20
asphyxiating *stinking* 227.3
asphyxiation *murder* 30.2
aspic *salad* 90.16, *semiliquid* 561.7, *preserver* 815.9
aspirant *hoper* 281.5, *aspiring* 281.8, *desirer* 288.9
aspirate *spoken letter* 5.15, *phonetic* 205.14, *draw in* 708.18, *draw off* 711.16
aspirated *phonetic* 205.14
aspiration **281.3;** *motive* 178.5, *wish* 288.2, *expectations* 130.6, *future intention* 374.3, *motivation* 508.1, *intake* 708.5, *drawing off* 711.4, *aim* 773.12

aspire **281.13;** *aim* 327.17, *ascend* 713.19
aspire [Arch] *rise* 596.17
aspirer *hoper* 281.5
aspire to **288.19;** *aim* 374.10
aspirin *analgesic* 115.6
aspiring **281.8;** *desirous* 288.13, *intending* 374.6, *immature* 652.12
aspiring [Arch] *rising* 596.12
aspiringly *desirously* 288.26, *prospectively* 374.12, *immaturely* 652.23
as plain as the nose on one's face *manifestly* 331.20, *simple* 363.6
as planned **387.16;** *intentionally* 374.13
as promised **458.16;** *contractually* 459.9
as promised or **pledged** *as agreed upon* 735.36
as proof *demonstrably* 331.22
as punishment *vindictively* 441.16
as quick as a flash *immediately* 645.8
as quick as lightning *immediately* 645.8
as regards *relevantly* 727.12
as reported *journalistically* 175.10
as required *commandingly* 425.15
as rumor has it *supposedly* 359.10
ass *unskilled person* 128.3, *foolish person* 353.3
ass [Inf] *rear end* 622.4
assai Musical Terms and Expression Marks 140
assail *combat* 77.34, *attack* 418.17, *fight* 422.23, *berate* 438.20, *club* 695.15, *object* 828.18
assailant *combatant* 77.1, *attacker* 418.10
assailed *criticized* 438.14
assassin *murderer* 30.12, *combatant* 77.1, *attacker* 418.10, *criminal* 427.6, *evil person* 446.3, *villain* 448.5, *punisher* 454.16, *violent animal or person* 520.4, *destroyer* 523.6
assassinate *murder* 30.20, *conquer* 77.36, *be wicked* 448.13, *sin* 450.11
assassinated *killed* 29.13
assassination *way of dying* 29.5, *murder* 30.2, *terrorist attack* 418.7, *wicked act* 448.7
Assateague pony Horse and Pony Breeds 159
Assault Notable Horses 159
assault **695.4;** *combat* 77.34, *vilification* 301.2, *vilify* 301.15, *malignity* 306.5, *malign* 306.11, *harm* 306.6, *ill-use* 395.2, *attack* 418.1, 418.17, *wicked act* 448.7, *violence by person* 520.2, *use violence* 520.9, *impairment* 808.7
assault and battery *personal attack* 418.8, *wicked act* 448.7, *assault* 695.4
assaulted *taking* 477.12
assaulter *combatant* 77.1
assaulting *vilifying* 301.9, *malign* 306.11, *attacking* 418.14
assault sexually *ravish* 477.15
assault troops *armed force* 77.10
assault with a deadly weapon *wicked act* 448.7
assay *experiment* 335.1, 335.11, *attempt* 390.1, 390.6, *measure* 589.20
assayer *experimenter* 335.5
assbackwards [Inf] *inversely* 608.9, *backwards* 680.23
assegai Trees and Shrubs 43, *sharp weapon* 78.6

assemblage 59.13; *assembly* 59.1, *construction* 59.16, *sculpture* 144.1, *acquisition* 467.4, *relatedness* 727.1, *unification* 752.5, *collection* 757.3, *array* 767.2

assemblage of birds 36.18

assemblage of mammals 35.22

assemble 59.23, 551.23; *military call* 183.9, *prepare for action* 388.18, *acquire* 467.19, *produce* 522.13, *embody* 577.11, *come together* 702.10, *meet* 704.20, *unite* 752.14, *combine* 757.9

assembled 59.18; *united* 752.10, *collected* 757.8, *arranged* 767.11

assembler *collector* 59.17

Assemblies of God *Christian Groups* 81

assembling 59.12; *acquisition* 467.4

assembly 59.1; *conference* 59.5, *construction* 59.16, *worshiper* 83.6, *place for conversation* 210.5, *acquisition* 467.4, *manufacture* 522.2, *meeting place* 702.4, *association* 752.2, *collection* 757.3

assembly code *programming language* 15.16

assembly hall *school place* 48.16

assembly language *artificial language* 5.9

assembly line *construction* 59.16, *factory* 124.8, *manufacture* 522.2, *continuum* 774.5

assembly of materials *production* 522.1

assembly plant *construction* 59.16

assent 346.1, 346.6; *admit* 180.11, *confirmation* 189.5, *be willing* 373.12, *submission* 421.1, *submit* 421.4, *obey* 426.7, *approval* 437.1, *approve* 437.14, *ratification* 459.4, *agreement* 462.1, *agree with* 462.10, *consent* 735.8, 735.28

assented *supposed* 359.6

assented to *approved* 437.8

assenter 346.3, 462.5; *affirmer* 189.9, *contractor* 459.6

assenting 346.4; *confirming* 189.16, *willing* 373.7, *submitting* 421.3, *contractual* 459.7, *consenting* 735.18

assentingly *confirmingly* 189.32, *with consent* 735.38

assentive *confirming* 189.16, *consenting* 735.18

assent to 346.7

assert *propound a philosophy* 4.21, *affirm* 189.21, *speak* 205.17, *testify* 336.10, *give evidence* 339.12, *suppose* 359.8, *mean* 361.13

asserted *affirmed* 189.11, *logical* 329.9

assertedly *affirmatively* 189.29

asserter *affirmer* 189.9

assertion *philosophy* 4.1, *mathematical logic* 6.60, *affirmation* 189.1, *utterance* 205.10, *line of argument* 329.3

assertional *affirmative* 189.10

assertion of truth *vindication* 441.1

assertion sign *philosophical term* 4.7

assertive 189.20; *defiant* 416.5, *strong in spirit* 516.11, *convinced* 840.8

assertively 189.35; *defiantly* 416.9, *aggressively* 418.27, *strongly* 516.17, *with certainty* 840.16

assertiveness 189.8; *endurance* 516.4, *conviction* 840.2

assert oneself *appear* 331.18, *impose one's will* 372.14, *push* 414.20, *be liberated* 831.7, *be certain* 840.13, *show oneself* 843.15

assertorily *affirmatively* 189.29

assertory *affirmative* 189.10

assert the truth *vindicate* 441.11

asses *Collective Names* 59

assess *estimate* 341.11, *price* 494.12, *measure* 589.20

assessable *measurable* 589.17

assessed *propertied* 470.9, *priced* 494.10, *measured* 589.16

assessed valuation *personal estate* 470.6

assessment *judgment* 341.1, *value* 494.2, *tax system* 494.6, *measurement* 589.1, *calculation* 784.1

assessor *judge* 54.10, 341.5, *measurer* 589.14

assets *sufficiency* 97.1, *resources* 102.4, *stock in trade* 105.2, *personal estate* 470.6

asseverate *affirm* 189.21

asseverated *affirmed* 189.11

asseveration *affirmation* 189.1

asseverative *affirmative* 189.10

asseveratively *affirmatively* 189.29

asshole [Inf] *body orifice* 583.3

assibilate *hiss* 237.3

assibilation *hiss* 237.1

assiduity 414.8; *exertion* 122.4, *carefulness* 325.1, *commitment* 377.2, *frequency* 661.1

assiduous *working* 122.6, *diligent* 323.7, *careful* 325.6, *committed* 377.7, *industrious* 414.16, *frequent* 661.4

assiduously *attentively* 323.14, *frequently* 661.7, *meticulously* 726.18

assiduousness *carefulness* 323.3, *commitment* 377.2, *frequency* 661.1

assign *delegate* 79.6, *relinquish* 392.3, *have at one's disposal* 393.14, *impose a duty* 433.14, *own property* 470.11, *transfer property* 470.12, *beneficiary* 473.6, *allocate* 474.5, *transfer* 685.8, *bring* 685.11, *service* 689.16, *class* 777.12, *specify* 779.18, *commission* 833.8

assignable *transferring property* 470.10

assign a date *chronologize* 646.13

assignat [Arch] *paper money* 484.14

assignation *social gathering* 408.4

assigned *decentralized* 79.5, *undertaken* 391.4, *duty-bound* 433.8, *contractual* 459.7, *transferring property* 470.10, *allocated* 474.4, *commissioned* 833.6

assigned task *or job allotted task* 474.3

assigned work *work* 122.1

assignee *someone promised* 458.7, *beneficiary* 473.6, *commissioner* 833.5

assigning *commission* 833.1

assignment *delegation* 79.3, *work* 122.1, *task* 122.2, *undertaking* 391.1, *line of duty* 433.3, *transfer of property* 470.4, *allocation* 474.1, *commission* 833.1

assignment of work *delegation* 79.3

assimilate 781.14; *learn* 68.18, *be converted* 670.12, *absorb* 708.19, *embody* 723.12, *make the same* 730.16, *make similar* 733.15, *combine* 757.9

assimilated *converted* 670.7, *same* 730.7, *combined* 757.5

assimilating *same* 730.7

assimilation *syntax* 5.32, *learning* 48.7, *evolution* 670.3, *absorption* 708.6, *sameness* 730.1, *combination* 757.1, *pliancy* 781.3

assimilative *absorbent* 708.11, *same* 730.7

assimilatory *same* 730.7

Assiniboine *Rivers* 570

assist *serve* 69.11, *represent* 80.6, *provision* 89.9, *ice hockey tactics* 158.4, *aid* 275.10, *be eager* 373.13, *grant* 453.14, *be an instrument* 511.7, *give moral support* 605.18, *make easy* 823.15, *help* 825.1, 825.23, *cooperate* 827.12

assistance *aid* 275.2, *charity* 307.3, *social welfare* 307.4, *grant* 453.4, *instrumentality* 511.1, *moral support* 605.7, *smoothness* 823.5, *help* 825.1, *cooperation* 827.1

assistant 511.3; *servant* 69.1, *office assistant* 69.6, *deputy* 80.1, *helper* 275.5, 825.12, *supporter* 605.9, *cooperator* 827.8, *subordinate* 832.3

assistant [Arch] *helpful* 825.19

assistant coach *basketball team* 148.2, *football player* 155.15

assistant editor *filmmaker* 137.14

assistantship *instructorship* 48.5

assisted-living residence *haven* 810.3

assister *helper* 825.12

assisting *instrumental* 511.4, *helping* 825.16

assize *legal process* 54.3

ass-kicking [Inf] *warlike* 76.27

ass-kisser [Inf] *sycophant* 401.3, *flatterer* 439.6, *goody-goody* 445.8

ass-kissing [Inf] *sycophancy* 401.2, *sycophantic* 401.7, 439.11

associate 754.3; *merge* 64.21, *coworker* 123.17, *relate to* 727.9, *unify* 752.15, *intercommunicate* 754.15, *come together* 757.10, *member* 760.9, *companion* 794.8, *join* 827.17

associated 794.14; *attending* 575.9, *related* 727.6, *allied* 735.15, *united* 752.10, *connective* 754.10, *collaborative* 757.7

associate justice *judge* 54.10, 68.4

associates *team* 827.7

associate with *participate* 408.15, *form an alliance* 735.25, *unify* 752.15, *keep company with* 794.17, *back* 825.28

associating 827.11

association 59.4, 480.8, 752.2, **754.2, 827.6;** *correlation* 6.58, *alliance* 64.2, 735.5, *association of ideas* 108.31, *habituation* 397.7, *sociability* 408.1, *relatedness* 727.1, *mixture* 751.1, *mixed thing* 751.2, *collaboration* 757.2, *collection* 757.3, *accompaniment* 794.1

association bargaining *bargaining* 57.9

association by contiguity *association of ideas* 108.31

association by sound *association of ideas* 108.31

association football [Brit] *Sporting Activities* 145, *soccer* 163.1

association of ideas 108.31; *basis of supposition* 359.2

association psychology *Psychological Theories, Schools* 108

association test *Psychological Tests* 108

associative *attracting* 700.8, *collected* 757.8

associatively *in combination* 757.11

associative operation *or law operation* 6.12

assonance *literary device* 139.12, *harmonization* 735.2, *reverberation* 797.6

assonant *metrical* 139.20, *harmonizing* 735.12, *reverberatory* 797.14

assonantal *harmonizing* 735.12

assonate *harmonize* 140.28

as soon as *as* 649.10

as soon as possible (ASAP) *in the shortest possible time* 645.9, *early* 657.17, *swiftly* 694.16, *hastily* 818.7

assort *categorize* 767.21, *sort* 777.13

assorted *indiscriminate* 338.8, *selected* 382.11, *varied* 732.6, *categorized* 767.15

assortment *miscellany* 59.15, *selection* 382.1, *variety* 732.2, 751.4

as stated *reportedly* 170.16

assuage *conciliate* 74.10, *relieve* 275.8, *mitigate* 521.9, *ease* 543.15, *smooth over* 545.12, *make motionless* 678.8

assuaged *relieved* 275.6

assuagement *ease* 275.1, *moderation* 521.1

assuaging *relieving* 275.7, *moderating* 521.5

Assuma *heaven* 82.15

assumable *supposed* 359.6

assume *propound a philosophy* 4.21, *theorize* 6.84, 327.16, *be of the opinion* 87.10, *expect* 281.12, *premise* 319.14, *predict* 356.7, *suppose* 359.8, *be affected* 367.4, *undertake* 391.7, *adopt* 476.11, *take over* 477.16

assume an obligation *take charge of* 391.8

assume authority *gain authority* 52.15

assume command *gain authority* 52.15, *lead* 126.12

assumed *given* 6.74, *theoretical* 327.10, 720.10, *supposed* 359.6, *undertaken* 391.4, *outward* 621.11

assumed name *anonymity* 182.7, *name* 202.8

assume ownership *take over* 477.16

assume responsibility *lead* 126.12, *undertake* 391.7

assume the character of *be converted* 670.12

assume the guise of *be untruthful* 192.20

assume the nature of *be converted* 670.12

assume the offensive *attack* 418.17

assume the role of *act* 187.13

assume the shape of *be converted* 670.12

assuming *under the circumstances* 726.16

assuming ownership *taking* 477.1

Assumption *Christian Holy Days and Seasons* 85

assumption *philosophy* 4.1, *acquisition of authority* 52.5, *expectation* 281.2, 356.1, *explanation* 319.4, *idea* 327.1, *supposition* 359.1, *adoption* 476.2, *taking over* 477.3, *ascent* 713.1, *theory* 720.4, *succession* 770.2

assumption of office *succession* 770.2

assumptive *causal* 319.9, *suppositional* 359.5

assumptively *theoretically* 4.24

assurance 621.8; *believing* 87.2, *vow* 189.3, *encouragement* 284.6, *verification* 336.1, *expectation* 356.1, *contract* 391.2, *audacity* 400.3, *defiance* 416.1, *duty* 433.1, *promise* 458.1, 464.2, *safety* 810.1, *conviction* 840.2, *confirmation* 840.3, *guarantee* 840.4

assure 810.23; *make someone believe* 87.11, *vow* 189.23, *be assertive* 189.28, *comfort* 273.9, *give courage* 284.16, *verify* 336.8, *promise* 458.11, 464.10, *guarantee* 458.13

assured 621.12; *believing* 87.6, *vowed* 189.14, *expectant* 281.7, *verified* 336.7, *audacious* 400.10, *defiant* 416.5, *promised* 458.8, *guaranteeing* 458.9, *guaranteed* 464.6, 840.10, *safe* 810.16, *convinced* 840.8

assuredly 189.30, 336.12; *audaciously* 400.20, *defiantly* 416.9, *correctly* 429.16, *as promised* 458.16, *surely* 464.15, *with certainty* 840.16

assuredness *conviction* 840.2

assuring *encouraging* 284.13, *verificatory* 336.6

assuringly *encouragingly* 284.21

Astarte *goddesses and gods of love* 299.14

astatine *Chemical Elements and Common Allotropes* 11

aster *cell division* 13.17, *Flowers* 42

asterisk *Reference Signs* 183

asterism *constellation* 7.13, *Reference Signs* 183

astern *offshore* 150.35, *back* 622.6, *behind* 622.8, *backward* 680.23

asteroid *planet* 7.16, *echinoderm* 39.5, *orbiting body* 681.4

asteroidal *astronomical* 7.33, *echinodermal* 39.21

asteroid belt *planet* 7.16

asteroidean *echinoderm* 39.5

as the case may be *under the circumstances* 726.16, *perchance* 842.18

as the crow flies *shortly* 591.12, *straight* 630.16, *directly* 697.16

as the fancy takes one *capriciously* 381.7

as the matter stands *accordingly* 735.39

as the mood takes one *capriciously* 381.7

as the saying goes *proverbially* 177.4

as they say *theoretically* 4.24, *proverbially* 177.4

as things are *conditionally* 725.10

as things may fall *under the circumstances* 726.16

as things stand *under the circumstances* 726.16

asthma *respiratory disease* 114.12

asthmatic *sick person* 114.22, *of disease* 114.25, *hissing* 237.2

asthmatically *sibilantly* 237.4

astigmatic *weak-sighted* 243.10

astigmatism *visual acuity* 242.2, *sight defect* 243.2

astilbe *Flowers* 42

astir *busy* 414.15, *in motion* 677.19

as to *relevantly* 727.12

astonish 292.10; *be wondrous* 294.14

astonished 292.6; *wondering* 294.7, *at a loss* 468.11

astonishedly *with surprise* 292.13, *wonderingly* 294.16

astonishing 292.8, 294.10

astonishingly 294.19; *surprisingly* 292.14

astonishment 292.2; *wonder* 294.1, *marvel* 294.3

as to the manner born *skillfully* 127.16

astound *astonish* 292.10, *be wondrous* 294.14

astounded *astonished* 292.6, *wondering* 294.7

astounding *astonishing* 292.8, 294.10

astoundingly *surprisingly* 292.14, *astonishingly* 294.19

astoundment *astonishment* 292.2, *wonder* 294.1

Astraea *Planets and Their Satellites* 7

astragal *Architectural Elements* 134

astragalus *Human Bones* 19

astrakhan *Fabrics and Fibers* 130

astral *astronomical* 7.33, *spiritual* 86.20, *parapsychological* 525.9

astral body *spirit* 86.10, *spiritual world* 525.3

astral plane *the occult* 86.2, *spiritual world* 525.3

astral-project *experience psychic phenomena* 86.23

astral projection *occultism* 86.1

astraphobia *or* **astrapophobia** *Phobias* 283

astray 698.27; *losing* 468.9, *at a loss* 468.11, *at a distance* 585.13, *indirect* 698.9, *divergent* 776.11

astrict *arrest* 55.12

astricted *imprisoned* 55.9

astriction *arrest* 55.5, *unification* 752.5

A string *part of stringed instrument* 142.2

astringence *contraction* 582.1

astringency *sourness* 223.1, *bitterness* 306.3, *contraction* 582.1

astringent *bitter* 306.9, *dense* 540.6, *contractor* 582.6, *contracting* 582.10, *conjunctive* 752.12

astrobiology *astronomy* 7.1, *space biology* 13.8

astrobotany *astronomy* 7.1

astrochemical *chemical* 11.24

astrochemist *chemist* 11.2

astrochemistry *astronomy* 7.1, *Branches of Chemistry* 11

astrodynamics *astronomy* 7.1

astrogeology *astronomy* 7.1, *geology* 8.1

astrolabe *observatory* 7.24, *measuring instrument* 589.12

astrologer *diviner* 86.14, *forecaster* 358.9, *predictor* 650.5

astrological *divinatory* 86.18

astrological angle *angular measurement* 628.4

astrological influence *contributory cause* 675.3

astrologically *occultly* 86.27

astrology *divination* 86.5, 358.2, *occult influence* 512.2, *looking to the future* 650.4

astromancer *diviner* 86.14

astromancy *divination* 86.5

astrometry *astronomy* 7.1, Fields of Measurement 589

astronaut *space travel* 7.29, *space traveler* 563.10

astronautic(al) *astronomical* 7.33

astronautical engineer *mechanical engineer* 14.4

astronautical engineering *mechanical engineering* 14.3

astronautics *aerospace research* 7.27

astronavigation *navigation* 690.5

astronavigator *space traveler* 563.10

astronomer 7.2

astronomical 7.33; *huge* 579.14, *immeasurable* 798.6

astronomical almanac *type of book* 174.3

astronomical clock Timepieces and Timers 646

astronomical distance *distance* 585.1

astronomically 7.36; *immeasurably* 798.11

astronomical number *large number* 783.3

astronomical observatory *observatory* 7.24

astronomical satellite *artificial satellite* 7.30

astronomical telescope *telescope* 7.25

astronomical time *time zone* 646.5

astronomical unit 7.23, Scientific and Technical Units 589

astronomy 7.1

astrophotography *astronomy* 7.1, *photographic specialties* 132.2

astrophysical *astronomical* 7.33

astrophysically *astronomically* 7.36

astrophysicist *astronomer* 7.2

astrophysics *astronomy* 7.1, Fields of Modern Physics 10

Astroturf™ *stadium* 155.3

Asturian Breeds of Cattle 16, Breeds of Pigs 16

astute *refined* 48.20, *intelligent* 315.9, 352.5, *knowledgeable* 348.7, *mentally sharp* 549.14, *profound* 598.15, *cunning* 822.4

astutely *intelligently* 315.14, 352.9, *sharply* 549.19, *profoundly* 598.27, *cunningly* 822.6

astuteness *cleverness* 315.3, *wisdom* 352.1, *mental sharpness* 549.9, *profundity* 598.5

Asunción Countries 566

asunder *away* 585.6, 711.20, *at a distance* 585.13, *apart* 753.8, 753.23

as understood *meaningfully* 361.16

as usual 781.17; *regularly* 397.21, *permanently* 667.6, *prevailingly* 742.11, *probably* 838.11

as well as *additionally* 748.15, *inclusively* 763.8

as well as can be expected *getting well* 113.9

as wide as a barn door *broadly* 592.15

as wide as a truck *broadly* 592.15

as yet *before now* 651.21

asylum *hiding place* 181.2, *security* 464.1, *taking in* 477.7, *shelter* 613.6, *refuge* 708.3, 812.1, *haven* 810.3, *safe house* 812.5

asymmetric *structural* 11.28, *distorted* 627.6, *irregular* 664.3, *disparate* 728.9, *dissimilar* 734.4

asymmetrical *spatial* 6.76, *structural* 11.28, *irregular* 664.3, *disparate* 728.9, *unequal* 741.4

asymmetrically 627.13, 741.11; *irregularly* 664.6, *disparately* 728.19, *dissimilarly* 734.10

asymmetric bars Sporting Activities 145

asymmetric center *structure* 11.7

asymmetric fold *fold* 8.22

asymmetric relation *mathematical logic* 6.60

asymmetry *distortion* 627.1, *irregularity* 664.1, *disparity* 728.3, *dissimilarity* 734.1, *imbalance* 741.2

asymptote *line* 6.35, *focus* 702.5

asymptotic *linear* 6.77, *convergent* 702.7

asynchronism *different time* 648.1

asynchronous *different in time* 648.2

asynchronously *another time* 648.4

asyndeton *syntax* 5.32

as you were *reversibly* 671.14

Atacama Deserts 572

at a crucial time *or* **point** *difficulty* 726.20

atactic *polymeric* 11.35

atactic polymer *polymer* 11.9

at a cut price *at a loss* 468.22

at a cut rate *at a loss* 468.22

at a disadvantage *unequal* 741.4, *unequally* 741.10

at a discount 495.7; *cheaply* 497.16, *by subtraction* 749.8

at a distance 585.13; *at arm's length* 590.16

at a funeral pace *in slow motion* 693.15

at a glance *visibly* 242.28, *originally* 345.16

at a good pace *fast* 166.23

at a guess *supposedly* 359.10

at a gulp *gluttonously* 119.5

at a halt *motionlessly* 678.9

at a late hour 658.15

at a later date *after* 770.14

at a later time 658.16

at all *how* 691.16

at all costs *earnestly* 376.16

at a loose end *not working* 415.10

at a loss 468.11, 468.22; *financially* 493.13, *troubled* 824.15

at a loss for words *confused* 841.11

at a low ebb *on the ground* 716.25, *inferiorly* 745.13

at a lower price *decreasingly* 747.9

at a lower rate *decreasingly* 747.9

at an advantage 618.12; *unequal* 741.4, *unequally* 741.10

at an angle *linear* 6.77, *obliquely* 607.13, *askew* 628.12

at anchor *stable* 674.3, *safe* 810.16

at an end *stopped* 668.7, *ended* 773.14

at an impasse *troubled* 824.15, *blocked* 826.13

at any odd moment *leisurely* 125.6

at any price *earnestly* 376.16

at any rate *how* 691.16

at a pause *recessed* 668.8

at a pinch *difficultly* 824.23
at a premium *profitably* 492.8, *valuable* 496.8, *valuably* 496.13
at a price 494.14
at a profit *gainfully* 467.24
ataractic *indifferent* 289.7
ataraxia *indifference* 289.1, *oblivion* 355.4, *disinterestedness* 443.1, *repose* 678.2
at arms *at war* 76.34
at arm's length 590.16; *at a distance* 585.13
at a slow pace *in slow motion* 693.15
at a snail's pace *in slow motion* 693.15
at a stand *motionlessly* 678.9
at a standstill *inactive* 413.9, *not working* 415.10, *inactively* 415.17, *permanently* 667.6, *troubled* 824.15, *blocked* 826.13
at a start *first* 771.37
at a tangent *circuitously* 199.8, *indirectly* 698.28
at attention *vertically* 602.11
at auction *on sale* 482.24
atavism *reversion* 671.1
atavistic *historical* 3.10, *regressive* 671.6
atavistically *reversibly* 671.14
ataxiophobia Phobias 283
Atbara Rivers 570
at bargain prices *at a discount* 495.7
at bay *defensively* 419.32, *endangered* 811.10
at best *ideally* 327.22
at bottom *at heart* 723.14
at break of day *daily* 655.8
Atchafalaya Rivers 570
at close grips *contentious* 422.20
at close quarters *contentious* 422.20, *near* 586.16
at close range *contentious* 422.20, *near* 586.16
at cockcrow *daily* 655.8
at cost *financially* 493.13, *cheaply* 497.16
at cross-purposes *aggressive* 63.9, *argumentative* 329.7, *disagreeing* 463.6, *anyhow* 766.25, *discordant* 828.12, *at odds* 828.23
at cut price *at a discount* 495.7
at daggers drawn *at odds* 828.23
at dawn *daily* 655.8
at daybreak *daily* 655.8
at each other's throats *aggressive* 63.9
at ease 819.2; *leisurely* 125.4, *pleased* 214.9, *informal* 829.15, *prosperous* 847.5
atelier *studio* 124.6, *material* 143.9
atelophobia Phobias 283
a tempo Musical Terms and Expression Marks 140
Aten Planets and Their Satellites 7, Deities 82
at face value *apparently* 264.16
at fault *mistaken* 351.13, *immoral* 430.11, *wrong* 430.12, *guilty* 450.6
at first *first* 771.37
at first blush *apparently* 264.16
at first hearing *aurally* 228.16
at first light *lightly* 246.23, *daily* 655.8
at first sight *visually* 242.27, *apparently* 264.16, *originally* 345.16
at fixed intervals *regularly* 663.14
at fixed periods *regularly* 663.14
at flood *flooded* 570.8

at full blast *at full speed* 694.17
at full length *lengthwise* 590.14, *horizontally* 603.11
at full pitch *loud* 232.6
at full power *powerfully* 106.19
at full speed 694.17
at full steam *powerfully* 106.19
at full stretch *fully* 761.14
at full stride *fast* 166.23
at full throttle *at full speed* 694.17
at full tilt *at full speed* 694.17
at full volume *loud* 232.6
at great cost 496.12
at great expense *at great cost* 496.12
at great intervals *sparse* 796.6
at great length *diffusely* 199.7
at great value *valuably* 496.13
at grips *warring* 76.26
at gunpoint *compellingly* 428.12, *violently* 520.11
Athabasca Lakes 568, Rivers 570
at half-mast *lamentingly* 280.9, *on the ground* 716.25
at half price *at a discount* 495.7
at half speed *moderately* 521.10, *in slow motion* 693.15
at hand *touchable* 216.5, *available* 575.11, 647.6, *next* 586.8, *near* 586.16, *future* 650.6, *early* 657.8, *useful* 801.5, *nearby* 803.7
Atharvaveda *other text* 81.19
at heart 723.14
at heavy cost *at great cost* 496.12
atheism *unbelief* 88.4, *unacceptance* 190.4, *suspicion* 841.2
atheist *disbeliever* 88.5, *negator* 190.8, *nonobservant* 466.5, *freethinker* 829.10
atheistic *disbelieving* 88.6, *unaccepting* 190.13, *nonobservant* 466.5, *independent* 829.12
atheistically *nonacceptantly* 190.25, *freely* 829.22
Athena *or* **Athene** Deities 82
athenaeum *library* 174.14
Athens Countries 566, *other famous world cities* 567.9
atheroma *cardiovascular disease* 114.13
atherosclerosis *hardening* 542.2
athirst *thirsty* 560.8
athlete 422.15; *sportsman* 145.4, *gymnast* 157.10, *track and field eventer* 166.19, *person of strength* 516.8
athlete's foot *fungal disease* 47.6, *skin disease* 114.16
athlete's heart *cardiovascular disease* 114.13
athletic *keeping fit* 113.10, *sporting* 145.5, *contending* 422.19, *physically strong* 516.10, *pliant* 543.7, *stalwart* 547.10
athletic [Brit] *track and field* 166.20
athletically *sportingly* 145.7, *softly* 543.18, *stalwartly* 547.17
athletic build *stalwartness* 547.3
athletic competition *sports* 422.3
athleticism *physical strength* 516.3
athletics 422.7; *sports* 145.1, 422.3, *bodily movement* 677.11
athletic socks *legwear* 100.26
athletic supporter *underwear* 100.22, *sports equipment* 166.17, *body support* 605.6
at home *inhabiting* 60.18, *habituated* 397.14, *unsocially* 409.13, *residing* 575.8, *readily available* 575.21, *informal* 829.15
at-home *social gathering* 59.7, 408.4, *party* 408.6

at home with *educated* 48.19, *friendly with* 62.6
Athos Mountains and Hills 569
at huge expense *at great cost* 496.12
athwart *offshore* 150.35, *breadthways* 592.16
atilt *oblique* 607.6, *obliquely* 607.13
at infrequent intervals *infrequently* 662.4
at intervals *apart* 587.8, *discontinuously* 775.15
atiptoe *expecting* 356.4
at issue *arguably* 329.16, *questionable* 333.13, *discordant* 828.12, *at odds* 828.23
Atitlán Lakes 568
at journey's end *on arrival* 704.22
at knifepoint *compellingly* 428.12, *violently* 520.11
Atlanta American States 564
atlantes Architectural Elements 134
Atlantic Ocean Oceans and Seas 571
Atlantic Time *time zone* 646.5
Atlantis Imaginary Places 360
at large *free* 829.11
Atlas Planets and Their Satellites 7, *person of strength* 516.8, *big person* 579.10
atlas *schoolbook* 48.15, Architectural Elements 134, *sculpture* 144.1, *type of book* 174.3, *map* 187.5, 387.7, *book of lists* 785.3
Atlas Mountains Mountains and Hills 569
at last *finally* 584.18, 773.24, *at a late hour* 658.15
atlatl Historical Missile Weapons 78
at law *in litigation* 54.34
at leisure *leisurely* 125.4, *informal* 829.15
at length 590.15; *diffusely* 199.7
at liberty *off-duty* 433.11
at loggerheads *aggressive* 63.9, *warring* 76.26, *argumentative* 329.7, *contentious* 422.20, *disagreeing* 463.6
at long last *at a late hour* 658.15, *finally* 773.24
at loose ends *leisurely* 125.4
at low ebb *decreasingly* 747.9, *spoiled* 808.9
Atman God 82.6
atman *spirit* 86.10
at midnight *darkly* 247.11
atmometer Fields of Measurement 589
atmometry Fields of Measurement 589
atmosphere 9.8; *Earth* 8.6, *aspect of fiction* 139.5, *treatment* 143.6, *influence* 512.1, *gas* 556.1, *air* 558.1, *circumstances* 573.2, Scientific and Technical Units 589, *ambience* 615.3
atmospheric 9.40, 558.13; *terrestrial* 8.52, *pictorial* 133.8, *airy* 556.15, *circumstantial* 573.7, *ambient* 615.6
atmospheric agitation 684.13
atmospherically *artistically* 133.10, *aerily* 556.26, *airily* 558.25
atmospheric circulation *air movement* 9.11
atmospheric dust *atmosphere* 9.8
atmospheric electricity *electricity* 10.31
atmospheric inversion *act of inversion* 608.3

atmospheric layer 558.3; *atmosphere* 9.8
atmospheric model *physical law* 10.4
atmospheric physics *meteorology* 9.1
atmospheric pressure *force* 10.9, Fields of Measurement 589
atmospheric process 9.9
atmospherics *atmospheric agitation* 684.13
atmospheric water vapor *atmosphere* 9.8
Atmu Deities 82
at night *nightly* 656.6
at nightfall *darkly* 247.11
at no time *never* 640.8, *not ever* 718.16
at odds 828.23; *aggressive* 63.9, *argumentative* 329.7, *dissenting* 347.7, *contentious* 422.20, *disagreeing* 463.6, *in disagreement* 463.12, *discordant* 828.12
at odd times *for short periods* 641.13
atoll *ocean floor* 8.18, *island* 572.2
atom 10.52; *physical element* 524.5, *little thing* 580.3, *piece* 760.2, *fragment* 787.3, *one* 788.1
atom bomb *bomb* 78.15
atomic *physical* 10.70, *gas* 106.14, *tiny* 580.9, *component* 760.12, *one* 788.10
Atomic Age Ages, Decades, Eras 641
atomically *microscopically* 580.14
atomic bomb *nuclear power production* 514.10
atomic chemistry Branches of Chemistry 11
atomic clock Timepieces and Timers 646
atomic energy *nuclear fusion* 10.61, *nuclear power* 106.8, *energy* 514.7
atomic mass *isotope* 10.57, Scientific and Technical Units 589
atomic mass constant *isotope* 10.57
atomic mass unit Scientific and Technical Units 589
atomic number *isotope* 10.57
atomic orbital *atom* 10.52
atomic physics Fields of Modern Physics 10
atomic pile *nuclear power production* 514.10
atomic power *fuels* 106.2, *nuclear power* 106.8, 514.9, *type of power* 514.6
atomic structure *atom* 10.52
atomic war *warfare* 76.3
atomic warfare 76.4
atomic warhead *explosive* 78.13
atomic waste *waste product* 96.7
atomic weight *isotope* 10.57, *weight measurement* 538.6
atomism Philosophical Schools of Thought 4
atomist Philosophical Schools of Thought 4
atomization *pulverization* 553.4, *vaporization* 556.9, *nonadhesion* 756.1, *deconstruction* 758.2
atomize *demolish* 523.12, *pulverize* 553.26, *gasify* 552.3, *aerate* 556.24, *sprinkle* 557.32, *circumstantiate* 726.12, *deconstruct* 758.7
atomizer *pulverizer* 553.11, *vaporizer* 556.10, *sprinkler* 557.12
atom smashing *nuclear fission* 10.60, *deconstruction* 758.2

atomy *little person* 580.5
Aton *or* **Aten** Deities 82
atonable *compensable* 743.4
atonal *unmelodious* 241.5
atonality *musical dissonance* 241.2
atonally *dissonantly* 241.7
at once *right away* 429.20, *immediately* 645.8
atone **313.7, 489.24;** *worship* 83.15, *recompense* 273.11, *offer reparation* 504.15, *compensate* 743.7, *restore* 809.12
atoned *penitential* 451.6, *compensated* 743.3
atone for *atone* 313.7, *do penance* 451.9
at one go *continuously* 774.16
atonement 313.1; *peace offering* 74.5, *remedy* 115.1, *reparation* 273.2, *type of penance* 451.3, *self-punishment* 454.10, *compensation* 743.1, *restoration* 809.2
atoner 313.4
at one remove *indirectly* 698.28
at one's beck and call *obedient* 426.4, *supplementary* 825.17, *subordinate* 832.8
at one's command *obedient* 426.4, *possessed* 469.13, *possessively* 469.16, *supplementary* 825.17
at one's convenience *leisurely* 125.6
at one's desk *busy* 414.15
at one's disposal *usable* 393.6, *obedient* 426.4, *possessed* 469.13, *possessively* 469.16
at one's elbow *available* 575.11, *near* 586.16
at one's expense *expended* 491.9
at one's feet *near* 586.16, *subordinate* 832.8
at one's fingertips *available* 575.11, *next* 586.8, *near* 586.16, *nearby* 803.7
at one's leisure *leisurely* 125.6, *late* 658.14
at one's lowest ebb *inferiorly* 745.13
at one's mercy *subordinate* 832.8
at one's own discretion *freely* 829.22
at one's own sweet will *capriciously* 381.7
at one's pleasure *at will* 372.16, *obedient* 426.4
at one's service *usable* 393.6, *supplementary* 825.17
at one's side *near* 586.16
at one's top speed *at full speed* 694.17
at one's wits' end *troubled* 824.15
at one time *synchronously* 649.9
atoning 313.5; *penitential* 451.6
atoningly 313.10
atop *on the top* 600.13
at opposite extremes *diametrically* 731.6
at par *on equal terms* 740.9
ATP cycle *bioenergetics* 12.23
at peace *harmless* 73.9, *peacefully* 73.12, *agreeing* 462.6
at present 647.9
atrabilious *depressed* 270.5, *sullen* 304.8
atrabiliousness *sullenness* 304.1
at random *irregularly* 664.6, *in disorder* 766.24, *randomly* 842.14
at regular intervals *regularly* 663.14

at rest *inactively* 413.16, 415.17, *inertly* 519.5, *stable* 674.3, *quiescent* 678.6, *easily* 819.5
atria *internal organ* 19.13
at right angles *perpendicularly* 602.12
at risk *endangered* 811.10
atrocious *cruel* 306.10, *evil* 446.7, *wicked* 448.9
atrociously *cruelly* 306.17, *disgracefully* 371.8, *evilly* 446.12, *wickedly* 448.15
atrociousness *cruelty* 306.4, *evil* 446.1, *wickedness* 448.1
atrocity *cruelty* 306.4, *suppression* 424.2, *evil thing* 446.2, *illegality* 450.4, *violence by person* 520.2, *blot on the landscape* 533.4
at rock bottom *low* 597.26, *at the base* 601.13, *on the ground* 716.25
atrophy *wasting away* 96.4, *neurological disease* 114.20, *fasting* 118.1, *shortening* 582.2, *emaciation* 595.2, *be emaciated* 595.16, *decrease* 747.1, 747.7, *physical deterioration* 808.4
atropine *alkaloid* 12.19
Atropos Deities 82
at sea *nautically* 571.10, 690.17, *nautical* 690.14
at sea level *low* 597.26
at short notice *soon* 657.18, *hastily* 818.7
at sight *visually* 242.27, *apparently* 264.16
at sixes and sevens *aggressive* 63.9, *unprepared* 389.5, *dissentingly* 732.17, *muddled* 766.13, *anyhow* 766.25
at someone's beck and call *obedient* 69.10
at specified times *regularly* 663.14
at stake *dangerous* 811.7
at stated times *regularly* 663.14
at strife *disagreeing* 463.6
at sunrise *daily* 655.8
at sunup *daily* 655.8
at swords' points *at war* 76.34, *compellingly* 428.12, *violently* 520.11
attacca Musical Terms and Expression Marks 140
attach *suspend* 604.13, *add* 748.11, *link* 752.18, *connect* 754.13
attaché *delegate* 79.1, *commissioner* 833.5
attaché case *baggage* 578.8
attached *loving* 299.15, *suspended* 604.7, *related* 727.6, *additional* 748.8, *tied* 752.13, *connected* 754.11, *adhesive* 755.5, *tenacious* 755.6
attach importance to *be important* 799.13
attaching *suspension* 604.1
attachment *liking* 290.1, *love* 299.1, *observance* 465.1, *relatedness* 727.1, *addition* 748.1, *additional item* 748.3, *connection* 754.1, *adhesion* 755.1, *tenacity* 755.2
attach oneself to *love* 299.21, *be tenacious* 755.9, *attend* 794.19

attack 418.1, 418.17; *offensive warfare* 76.11, *battle* 76.23, *be at war* 76.32, *combat* 77.34, *illness* 114.2, *fencing movements* 153.3, *fence* 153.7, *articulation* 205.9, *approach* 209.3, *react against* 291.15, *ambush* 292.4, *vilification* 301.2, *vilify* 301.15, *harm* 306.13, *procedure* 387.2, *ill-use* 395.7, *declare war* 422.25, *berating* 438.5, *berate* 438.20, *violence by person* 520.2, *use violence* 520.9, *spasm* 684.8, *collision* 695.2, *assault* 695.4, *club* 695.15, *inroad* 706.3, *invade* 706.12, *impairment* 808.7, *conflict* 828.3, *object* 828.18
attack bomber *military aircraft* 77.30
attack by the wicked Phobias 283
attacked *surprised* 292.5, *criticized* 438.14, *trapped* 813.5
attacker 418.10; *combatant* 77.1, *disapprover* 438.7, *intruder* 706.8
attacking 418.14; *warring* 76.26, *fencing* 153.6, *vilifying* 301.9, *invasive* 706.10
attacking force *attacker* 418.10
attacking zone *hockey areas* 158.2
attack of nerves *mental breakdown* 110.4
attack submarine *warship* 77.21
attack successfully 418.25
attack tooth and nail *strike* 418.21
attain *manage* 126.10, *gain* 467.15, *achieve* 704.21
attainability *gain* 467.1
attainable 704.11; *touchable* 216.5, *gainful* 467.10, *realizable* 719.9, *possible* 836.5
attainment *skill* 127.1, *learning* 348.3, *gain* 467.1, *achievement* 704.8, *completion* 761.2, *success* 845.1
attain one's goal 845.13
attain one's majority *mature* 27.17
attaint *convict* 54.33
attar *incense* 226.3
Attawapiskat Rivers 570
attempt 390.1, 390.6; *exertion* 122.4, *exert oneself* 122.11, *invent* 335.13, *intentionality* 374.2, *undertaking* 391.1, 675.5, *undertake* 391.7, *action* 412.1, *do something* 412.13, *try* 414.21, *contend* 422.22, *production* 522.1
attempter 390.3
attempting 390.4
attempt the impossible 837.10; *act foolishly* 128.10, *waste effort* 802.13
attempt to buy *offer to buy* 504.12
attend 575.14, 794.19; *practice medicine* 107.32, *treat* 115.17, *hear* 228.13, *appear* 264.12, *be attentive* 323.9, *serve* 825.29
attend a conference *negotiate* 460.6
attend a council meeting *or* **convention** *or* **conference** *represent* 79.7
attendance 575.3, 794.5; *visibility* 264.4, *solicitude* 323.5
attendant 69.4; *wedding party* 64.7, *servant* 69.1, *serving* 69.9, *service worker* 123.7, *attending* 575.9, *concomitant* 794.4, *accompanier* 794.6, *accompanying* 794.12, *helper* 825.12
attend a symphony *enjoy music* 141.19
attend classes *learn* 48.23

attended *accompanied* 794.15
attendee *attender* 575.6
attender 575.6
attending 575.9; *serving* 69.9, *accompanying* 794.12, *supportive* 825.18
attending regularly *frequenting* 661.2
attending to *observance* 465.1
attend regularly *frequent* 661.6
attend to *care for* 325.12, *observe* 465.4
attend upon *serve* 69.11
attention 323.1; *seriousness* 200.2, *hearing* 228.1, *carefully* 325.1, *commitment* 377.2, *assiduity* 414.8, *respect* 435.1
attentions *respectfulness* 435.3
attention to *observance* 465.1
attention to detail *close attention* 323.2, *fastidiousness* 325.4, *accuracy* 350.1, *assiduity* 414.8, *trueness* 721.4
attention to fact *correctness* 350.2
attentive *thoughtful* 4.17, *working* 122.6, *hearing* 228.9, *prudent* 287.7, *compassionate* 305.8, *watchful* 323.6, *solicitous* 323.8, *careful* 325.6, 593.11, *knowledgeable* 348.7, *committed* 377.7, *respectful* 435.6, *observant* 465.3
attentively 323.14; *thoughtfully* 4.27, *aurally* 228.16, *prudently* 287.17, *compassionately* 305.14, *observantly* 465.6
attentiveness *prudence* 287.2, *compassion* 305.2, *attention* 323.1, *carefulness* 325.1, 593.5
attenuate *rarefied* 541.4, *make sparse* 541.5, *thinned* 595.13, *make thin* 595.17, *dilute* 776.14
attenuate *or* **attenuating** *narrowed* 593.9
attenuated *rarefied* 541.4, *thinned* 595.13
attenuation *wave property* 10.12, *rarefaction* 541.2, *narrowing* 593.3, *thinning* 595.6, *dilution* 776.3
attest 189.22; *state* 329.13, *prove* 331.17, *testify* 336.10, *give evidence* 339.12, *guarantee* 458.13, *contract* 459.8, 462.11, *establish reality* 719.12, *consent* 735.28
attestable *demonstrable* 331.12
attestant *affirmer* 189.9, *verifier* 336.4, *witness* 339.7
attestation 189.2; *line of argument* 329.3, *proof* 331.4, *evidence* 336.3, *authentication* 721.8, *consent* 735.8
attestator *affirmer* 189.9, *witness* 339.7
attested 189.13; *logical* 329.9, *proven* 331.13, *verified* 336.7, *evidential* 339.8, *guaranteeing* 458.9, *consenting* 735.18
attested to *authenticated* 721.17
attester *affirmer* 189.9, *witness* 339.7
attestive 189.12
attestor *affirmer* 189.9, *witness* 339.7
attest to *justify* 441.12, *authenticate* 721.24
at that hour *horologically* 646.15
at that moment *at what time* 639.17
at that rate *accordingly* 735.39
at that time *horologically* 646.15
at the base 601.13
at the boiling point *dangerous* 811.7

at the bottom *or* base *or* foot *low* 597.26, *at the base* 601.13
at the bottom of *causal* 675.7
at the breast *young* 26.11
at the center of *centrally* 612.12
at the core 612.13; *internally* 611.18, *at heart* 723.14
at the crack of dawn *daily* 655.8
at the crux *at the core* 612.13
at the dawn of time *in the past* 651.20
at the door *on arrival* 704.22
at the double *swiftly* 694.16
at the double! *hurry up!* 818.9
at the drop of a hat *voluntarily* 373.17, *capriciously* 381.7, *in the shortest possible time* 645.9, *soon* 657.18
at the eleventh hour *at a late hour* 658.15, *critically* 659.9
at the end of one's rope *or* tether *troubled* 824.15
at the end of the day *finally* 773.24
at the expense of *instead* 672.8
at the extreme *marginally* 618.11
at the first opportunity *early* 657.17
at the flash point *dangerous* 811.7
at the front *warring* 76.26, *at war* 76.34
at the hands of *instrumentally* 511.9
at the head *managerially* 126.13
at the heart *at the core* 612.13
at the helm *in authority* 52.20, *managerial* 126.9, *managerially* 126.13, *nautical* 690.14, *nautically* 690.17
at the highest level *at the summit* 600.12
at the highest point *at the summit* 600.12
at the last minute *at a late hour* 658.15, *critically* 659.9
at the last stand *endangered* 811.10
at the limit *marginally* 618.11, *farthest* 620.6
at the lowest point *low* 597.26, *at the base* 601.13
at the mercy of *vulnerable* 811.9
at the mercy of one's creditors *unable to pay* 488.8
at the moment of *as* 649.10
at the other end of the spectrum *diametrically* 731.6
at the peak *at the summit* 600.12, *supremely* 744.23
at the peak of perfection *expert* 805.16
at the Pearly Gates *dead* 29.11
at the planning stage *under discussion* 387.17
at the point of a bayonet *at war* 76.34
at the point of a gun *compellingly* 428.12, *violently* 520.11
at the point of death *dying* 29.12
at the ready *prepared* 388.9
at the reins *in authority* 52.20
at the right time *in the future* 650.13
at the same rate *as good as* 740.14
at the same time *compatibly* 462.16, *simultaneously* 649.8, *identically* 730.18, *additionally* 748.15
at the summit 600.12
at the surface *shallowly* 599.7
at the time *at what time* 639.17

at the top *high* 596.20, *at the summit* 600.12
at the top of one's voice *or* lungs *loudly* 232.11, *vociferously* 239.18
at the top of the ladder *or* tree *at the summit* 600.12
at the top of the scale *supremely* 744.23
at the wheel *in authority* 52.20, *managerial* 126.9, *managerially* 126.13, *nautically* 690.17
at the whim of *vulnerable* 811.9
at the word of command *commandingly* 425.15
at the wrong time 660.12
at the zenith *supremely* 744.23
at this hour *horologically* 646.15
at this moment *at what time* 639.17, *at present* 647.9
at this moment in time *at what time* 639.17, *at present* 647.9
at this point *where* 565.12
at this time *horologically* 646.15, *at present* 647.9
Attic *fluid* 527.5
attic *room* 60.9, *storeroom* 105.7, Architectural Elements 134
Atticism *elegance* 527.1
at times *sometimes* 639.19
attire *clothing* 100.1, *clothe* 100.43
attired *dressed* 100.38
attitude 513.2; *philosophy* 4.1, *religion* 81.1, *belief* 87.1, *feelings* 266.1, *emotion* 266.3, *supposition* 359.1, *conduct* 399.1, *nature* 624.5, *state of mind* 725.5, *circumstances* 726.1
attitudinize *be affected* 367.4
attitudinizer *pretender* 367.2
atto *Decimal Prefixes* 589
attorney *lawyer* 54.5, *court officer* 54.7, *representative* 75.3, *agent* 80.3
attorney-at-law *lawyer* 54.5
Attorney General *law officer* 53.6
attract 700.11; *interact* 10.73, *entice* 178.16, *gesture* 183.17, *cause desire* 288.22, *win the love of* 299.27, *influence* 508.11, *draw in* 699.13
attract attention 323.12; *be important* 799.13, *be visible* 843.16
attracted *liking* 290.4, *enamored* 299.17, *motivated* 508.8
attracting 700.8; *tractional* 699.7
attraction 700.1; *syntax* 5.32, *enticement* 178.3, *manifestation* 244.3, *desirability* 288.7, *liking* 290.1, *inducement* 508.2, *influence* 512.1, *attitude* 513.2, *force* 514.8, *drawing power* 699.6
attractionally 700.13
attractive 477.13, 529.8, 699.9, 700.10; *sensual* 20.16, *enticing* 178.13, *pleasant* 214.7, *likable* 271.6, *290.7, desirable* 288.11, *lovable* 299.20, *motivational* 508.7, *appealing* 512.9, *beautiful* 529.7
attractive female 529.5
attractively 700.14; *enticingly* 178.22, *desirably* 288.24, *likably* 290.12, *lovably* 299.31, *beautifully* 529.13, 530.16, *magnetically* 699.14, *attractionally* 700.13
attractive male 529.6
attractiveness 529.2; *enticement* 178.3, *amiability* 271.3, *lovability* 299.5, *inducement* 508.2, *beauty* 529.1, *attraction* 700.1
attractivity *attraction* 700.1
attract money *get rich* 485.13

attract notice *show off* 404.26, *be visible* 843.16
attributable to *caused* 676.5
attribute *be grateful* 310.6, *ability* 340.2, *property* 470.1, *recognize* 487.13, *nature* 723.4, *special feature* 779.4, *concomitant* 794.4
attributed to *caused* 676.5
attribution *cause* 675.1
attributive *of grammar* 5.41
attributively *grammatically* 5.48, *with the effect of* 676.12
attrition *economic warfare* 76.7, *pulverization* 553.4, *wearing away* 554.2, *reduction* 747.2
attritive *frictional* 554.10
Attu *Islands* 572
Attune *harmonize* 140.28, 735.22, *modify* 340.13, *counterbalance* 743.8
attuned *melodious* 140.26, *modified* 340.9, *agreeing* 462.6, *harmonizing* 735.12, *counterbalanced* 743.6
attunement *melodiousness* 140.12, *modification* 340.5, *agreement* 462.1, *harmonization* 735.2, *counterbalance* 743.2
at variance *estranged* 63.8, *disagreeing* 463.6, *discordant* 828.12, *at odds* 828.23
at war 76.34; *aggressive* 63.9, *warring* 76.26, *martially* 77.39, *contentious* 422.20
at what time 639.17
at will 372.16; *willed* 372.6
at work *acting* 412.9, *busy* 414.15, *on-duty* 433.10
atychiphobia *Phobias* 283
aubade *Poem or Verse Forms* 139, *song* 140.11, *love token* 299.8
Aube *Rivers* 570
aubergine *purple* 262.6
Aubrac *Breeds of Cattle* 16
aubrietia *Flowers* 42
auburn *brown* 256.5, *red-haired* 257.7
AUC *one day* 639.20
Aucassin *Famous Lovers* 299
Auckland Islands *Islands* 572
au contraire [Fr] *to the contrary* 190.27, 339.17, *contrariwise* 828.24
au courant *educated* 48.19, *informed* 170.9, *knowledgeable* 348.7
auction 482.16; *selling* 482.1, *sale* 482.2, *offer* 504.11
auction bridge *Card Games* 168, *bridge* 168.4
auctioneer *seller* 482.7
auction off *auction* 482.16
auction room *market* 483.1
audacious 400.10; *courageous* 284.9, *reckless* 286.6, *defiant* 416.5, *disrespectful* 436.9
audaciously 400.20; *courageously* 284.17, *recklessly* 286.10, *defiantly* 416.9
audaciousness *courage* 284.1, *recklessness* 286.2
audacity 400.3; *courage* 284.1, *recklessness* 286.2, *defiance* 416.1, *assurance* 621.8
audial *aural* 228.8
audibility *sound* 10.15, *hearing* 228.1
audible *huddle* 155.7, *sensate* 212.5, *hearable* 228.12, *sounding* 230.7, *intelligible* 363.5
audibly 230.10; *aurally* 228.16

audience *assembly* 59.1, *theatergoer* 136.30, *interview* 210.4, *audition* 228.6, *hearer* 228.7, *observer* 242.15, *recipient* 473.5, *attender* 575.6, *entrant* 706.7, *collection* 757.3
audience participation *program* 172.10
audio-cassette player *sound reproduction* 230.6
audiofrequency *radio reception* 172.2, *sound propagation* 230.3
audiological *otological* 228.11
audiologist *ear doctor* 228.5
audiology *study of hearing* 228.3
audiometer *study of hearing* 228.3, Fields of Measurement 589
audiometry Fields of Measurement 589
audio signal *television set* 172.6
audiotape *record* 172.15
audit 493.10; *accounting* 493.1, *check* 784.14
audited *accounted* 493.8
audition 228.6; *production* 136.14, *interview* 210.4, *hearing* 228.1, *be heard* 228.15, *questionnaire* 333.3, *question* 333.16, *rehearsal* 335.2, *rehearse* 335.12
auditioner *hearer* 228.7
auditive *aural* 228.8
auditor *hearer* 228.7, *accountant* 493.6
auditorium 136.17; *school place* 48.16, *theater* 136.16, *performance* 141.8, *building* 551.9, *showplace* 843.4
auditory *aural* 228.8
auditory canal *ear* 19.10
auditory nerve *ear* 19.10
auditory organ *ear* 19.10
auditory ossicle *ear* 228.2
auditory phenomenon *sound* 230.1
auditory range *hearing* 228.1
au fait [Fr] *educated* 48.19, *expert* 127.12, *knowledgeable* 348.7, *habituated* 397.14
Aufklärung [Ger] *knowledge* 348.1
au fond [Fr] *at heart* 723.14
auf Wiedersehen! [Ger] *goodbye!* 705.14
auger *construction equipment* 14.23, *sharp-pointed thing* 549.4, *opener* 583.2
aught *zero* 786.1
augment 467.16, 748.13; *store* 105.17, *aggravate* 276.5, *increase* 581.16, *further* 679.13, *change by degrees* 739.8, *make bigger* 746.7, *additional item* 748.3
augmentation 467.2; *aggravation* 276.1, *increase* 581.3, 746.1, *addition* 748.1, *additional item* 748.3
augmentative *part of speech* 5.30, *of grammar* 5.41, *acquisitive* 467.13, *enlargeable* 581.13, *increasing* 746.4
augmented *acquisitive* 467.13, *swelled* 581.10, *increased* 746.5
augmenter *enlarger* 581.8
au gratin *culinary* 91.9
augur *imam* 84.7, *diviner* 86.14, *predict* 358.14, *divine* 358.15, *intend* 361.15, *predictor* 650.5, *look ahead* 650.11, *warn* 814.8
augural *divinatory* 86.18, *presageful* 358.13
augur well *inspire hope* 281.14, *predict* 358.14, *show potential* 458.14, *be auspicious* 847.8

augury *divination* 86.5, 358.2, *expectations* 356.2, *omen* 358.5, *forewarning* 814.2

august *majestic* 297.12, *awe-inspiring* 435.12, *notable* 799.11

Augusta American States 564

Augustan *poetic* 139.19, *fluid* 527.5, *ideal* 805.17

Augustans Western Literary Groups 139

Augustinian Philosophical Schools of Thought 4

Augustinianism Philosophical Schools of Thought 4

Augustinian philosophy Philosophical Schools of Thought 4

augustly *majestically* 297.21

augustness *majesty* 297.5

auk *water bird* 36.9

auld lang syne *past time* 3.6, 651.1

Aulie-Ata Breeds of Cattle 16

aulophobia Phobias 283

aulos Musical Instruments 142

au naturel *culinary* 91.9, *naked* 614.12

aunt *woman in the family* 33.13, *family member* 65.2

auntie [Inf] *woman in the family* 33.13, *family member* 65.2

au pair *personal attendant* 69.5, *domestic worker* 123.4, *in exchange* 673.6, *protector* 810.11

aura *occult and psychic phenomena* 86.7, *reputation* 224.4, *ambience* 615.3

aural 228.8; *sensory* 19.22, *ambient* 615.6

aural cavity *body orifice* 583.3

aurally 228.16

aureate *yellow* 259.7

aureate diction *literary device* 139.12

aureole *highlight* 246.12

au revoir! [Fr] *goodbye!* 705.14

auricle *ear* 19.10, *grass plant* 45.3

auricula Flowers 42

auricular *aural* 228.8, *eared* 228.10

auricularly *aurally* 228.16

auriculate *eared* 228.10

auriform *eared* 228.10

Auriga Constellations 7

auriscope *diagnostic instrument* 107.13, *hearing* 228.3

aurist *ear doctor* 228.5

aurophobia Phobias 283

Aurora Deities 82, *morning* 655.2

aurora Earth 7.17, Phobias 283

aurora australis *natural light* 246.4

aurora borealis Earth 7.17, *natural light* 246.4

auroral *daily* 655.6

aurorally *daily* 655.8

auroraphobia Phobias 283

auscultate *hear* 228.13

auscultation *hearing* 228.1

auscultator *study of hearing* 228.3

auscultatorily *aurally* 228.16

Ausimi Breeds of Sheep 16

auspex *diviner* 86.14

auspicate *launch* 405.14, *originate* 737.7

auspicate [Arch] *inaugurate* 771.31

auspication *beginning* 652.4

auspices *omen* 358.5, *patronage* 810.7, 825.9

auspicial *presageful* 358.13

auspicious 458.10; *favorable* 62.8, *cheering* 281.9, *presageful* 358.13, *celebrative* 405.9, *good* 445.10, *timely* 659.4, *comfortable* 726.10, *convenient* 803.3, *prosperous* 847.5

auspiciously 458.17; *favorably* 62.15, *comfortingly* 281.17, *predictively* 358.16, *well* 445.19, *opportunely* 659.8, *comfortably* 726.19, *prosperously* 847.9

auspicious moment *timeliness* 659.1

auspiciousness *cheer* 281.4, *good* 445.1, *timeliness* 659.1, *convenience* 803.1, *good fortune* 847.2

Aussie Nicknames for Inhabitants 61

Auster *wind god* 9.16

austere *fasting* 118.5, *simple* 195.10, 526.7, *clear* 196.2, *unadorned* 424.7, *thrifty* 499.4

austerely *simply* 195.19, *plainly* 424.12

austereness *simplicity* 195.4

austerities *penitence* 313.3

austerity *incompleteness* 98.2, *fasting* 118.1, *simplicity* 195.4, 526.1, *clarity* 196.1, *unadornment* 424.3, *thrift* 499.1

Austin American States 564

austral *directional* 697.8

Australasia *world region* 564.6, *landmass* 572.1

Australasian *race* 1.5, *racial* 1.12

Australia *world region* 564.6, Countries 566, *landmass* 572.1

Australian cattle dog Breeds of Dogs 35

Australian crawl *swimming techniques* 164.2

Australian English *regional pronunciation* 205.7

Australian GP at Adelaide *Formula 1 World Championship races* 146.5

Australian heeler Breeds of Dogs 35

Australian Illawarra Shorthorn Breeds of Cattle 16

Australian kelpie Breeds of Dogs 35

Australian Masters *golfing associations and tournaments* 156.6

Australian Merino Breeds of Sheep 16

Australian Open *notable tennis competitions* 165.8

Australian pony Horse and Pony Breeds 159

Australian rules football Sporting Activities 145

Australian shepherd Breeds of Dogs 35

Australian Stock Horse Horse and Pony Breeds 159

Australian terrier Breeds of Dogs 35

Australopithecus *prehistoric human* 653.7

Australorp Breeds of Fowl 16

Austria Countries 566

Austrian Brown Breeds of Cattle 16

Austrian Simmental Breeds of Cattle 16

Austrian Tello Breeds of Cattle 16

Austronesian *language family* 5.12

austru Notable Winds 9

autarchic *governmental* 49.24, *independent* 829.12

autarchy *self-government* 49.9, *independence* 829.5

autarkic *independent* 829.12

autarky *economics* 56.1, *independence* 829.5

autecology *ecology* 13.25

auteur *filmmaker* 137.14

authentic 721.16, 737.6; *factual* 3.14, *legitimate* 52.10, 53.21, *attested* 189.13, *verifiable* 336.5, *evidential* 339.8, *correct* 429.8, *contractual* 462.7, *real* 717.14, *realistic* 719.7

authentically 721.31; *biographically* 3.18, *legitimately* 52.19, *verifiably* 336.11, *as evidence* 339.15, *correctly* 429.16, *contractually* 462.15

authenticate 721.24; *identify* 184.11, *attest* 189.12, *verify* 336.8, *prove* 339.14, *assent* 346.6, *contract* 462.11, *certify* 464.11, *give moral support* 605.18, *establish reality* 719.12, *make certain* 840.14

authenticated 721.17; *legitimate* 52.10, *identified* 184.9, *attested* 189.13, *verified* 336.7, *guaranteeing* 458.9, *guaranteed* 464.6

authenticating *attestive* 189.12, *guaranteeing* 458.9, *supportive* 605.11

authentication 721.8; *identification* 184.1, *attestation* 189.2, *verification* 336.1, *contract* 462.2, *promise* 464.2, *moral support* 605.7

authenticator *affirmer* 189.9, *assenter* 462.5

authenticity 721.7; *historicalness* 3.9, *legal power* 52.2, *legality* 53.9, *right* 429.2, *demonstrable existence* 717.5, *realism* 719.3, *originality* 737.1

authentic mode *mode* 140.17

author 139.13; *book publishing personnel* 174.12, *descriptive writer* 202.10, *dissertator* 203.3, *discoverer* 345.7, *producer* 522.10, *dream up* 522.15, *first cause* 675.6, *cause* 675.8, *originator* 737.3

authorial style *mode of expression* 537.3

authoring tool *application software* 15.14

authoritarian *authoritative* 52.9, *masterful* 68.15, *managerial* 126.9, *strict person* 424.4, *severe* 424.5

authoritarianism *suppression* 424.2

authoritative 52.9, 425.8; *educational* 48.17, *believed* 87.8, *managerial* 126.9, *commanding* 425.7, *awe-inspiring* 435.12, *influential* 512.8, *powerful* 514.15, *strong* 516.9, *assured* 621.12, *ranked* 739.6, *dominant* 744.9, *specialized* 779.11, *ruling* 780.11, *restraining* 830.8, *certain* 840.7

authoritatively 52.18; *wisely* 4.28, *educationally* 48.25, *managerially* 126.13, *commandingly* 425.15, *influentially* 512.14, *powerfully* 514.21, *differentially* 739.9, *superiorly* 744.20, *restrainedly* 830.18

authoritativeness *authority* 52.1, *certainty* 840.1

authorities *governing body* 49.19, *governance* 52.6, *power structure* 68.12

authority 52.1, 425.3, 514.5, 516.5, 780.6, 833.3; *sage* 4.11, *educator* 48.4, *jurisdiction* 53.3, *legality* 53.9, *management* 126.1, *expert* 127.9, *information source* 170.6, *documentation* 339.6, *knowledgeable person* 348.5, *severity* 424.1, *claim* 429.3, *respect* 435.1, *promise* 464.2, *permission* 502.1, 735.9, *influence* 512.1, *personal influence* 512.3, *strength* 516.1, *assurance* 621.8, *rank* 739.2, *leadership* 744.2, *specialist* 779.9, *independence* 829.5, *restraint* 830.1

authorization 52.3, 340.4, 425.4; *acquisition of authority* 52.5, *legality* 53.9, *delegation* 79.3, *certificate* 185.2, *permission* 340.3, 502.1, 735.9, *approval* 437.1, *promise* 464.2, *adoption* 692.1, *leadership* 744.2, *authority* 833.3

authorize 52.14, 425.14, 833.10; *make legal* 53.27, *delegate* 79.6, *deputize* 80.7, *permit* 340.12, 502.6, 735.29, *assent* 346.6, *approve* 437.14, *empower* 514.20, *adopt* 692.14

authorized 52.11, 340.8, 425.9; *legal* 53.16, *law-abiding* 53.20, *rightful* 429.9, *approved* 437.8, *permitted* 502.4, *adopted* 692.10, *permitting* 735.19, *free* 829.11, *commissioned* 833.6

Authorized Version *Christian text* 81.16

authorizing *permitting* 735.19

authors Children's and Party Games 167, Card Games 168

authorship *cause* 675.1

autism *defense mechanism* 108.23

autistic *unsociable* 409.6

auto *automobile* 687.6

autobahn [Ger] *road* 687.2

autobiographer *author* 139.13, *record keeper* 185.8

autobiographical *biographical* 3.13, *narrative* 139.18, 202.12

autobiographically *biographically* 3.18

autobiographical novel *novel* 139.3

autobiography *biography* 3.5, *life story* 28.11, *nonfiction* 139.6, *record* 185.1, *factual account* 202.4, *retrospect* 354.2

autocade *miscellaneous automotive terms* 687.14

autocatalysis *catalysis* 11.16

autocatalytic *catalytic* 11.30

autochthon *inhabitant* 61.1

autochthonous or **autochthonic** or **autochthonal** *native* 61.12

autocracy *self-government* 49.9, *suppression* 424.2

autocrat *person in authority* 52.7, *absolute ruler* 68.7, *leader* 126.3, *strict person* 424.4

autocratic *masterful* 68.15, *severe* 424.5, *authoritative* 425.8

autocratically *masterfully* 68.19, *severely* 424.11, *commandingly* 425.15

autocross Sporting Activities 145, *automobile racing* 146.1

auto-da-fé *execution* 30.6, *capital punishment* 454.12

autodidact *learner* 48.6, *knowledgeable person* 348.5

autodidactic *educated* 48.19, *unskilled* 128.5

autodidactics *educational system* 48.2

autoeroticism *sex act* 20.10

autoexposure *exposure equipment* 132.12

autofocus lens *lens* 132.11

autogenesis *genesis* 21.5

autograph *sign* 183.1, 183.19, *personal identification* 184.4, *identify oneself* 184.12, *inscription* 185.4, *name* 202.8, *original* 737.2

autograph collecting Hobbies and Pastimes 167

autogyro *rotator* 682.8

Autoharp™ Musical Instruments 142

autohypnotic *witchlike* 86.19

autohypnotism *occultism* 86.1

autointoxication *physical deterioration* 808.4

Automat™ *eating place* 92.17

automate *employ* 57.18, *produce* 522.13, *make the same* 730.16

automated *hired* 57.17, *mechanical* 103.7, *practical* 511.6, *productive* 522.11, *regular* 730.12

automated teller machine (ATM) *till* 484.21

automatic *computerized* 15.28, *firearm* 78.7, *involuntary* 95.15, *mechanical* 103.7, *hunting* 160.11, *instinctive* 318.8, 320.8, *practical* 511.6

automatically *involuntarily* 95.23, *instrumentally* 103.9, 511.9, *intuitively* 320.11, *systematically* 397.22

automatic buoy *weather station* 9.5

automatic calling unit (ACU) *office automation tools* 15.19

automatic camera *camera* 132.10

automatic direction finder (ADF) *position finder* 690.8

automatic pilot *guide* 126.6

automatic pinsetter *bowling* 151.1

automatic reaction *instinct* 320.4

automatic rifle *hunting equipment* 160.4

automatic shotgun *hunting equipment* 160.4

automatic writing *occult and psychic phenomena* 86.7

automation *economic factor* 56.8, *bargaining terms* 57.10, *instrumentality* 511.1, *manufacture* 522.2, *regularity* 730.6

automatism *occult and psychic phenomena* 86.7, Western Art Styles 133

automatist *occultist* 86.13

automaton *humanlike machine* 18.12, *machinery* 103.5, *figure* 187.4

autometamorphism *metamorphism* 8.35

automobile 687.6; *means of transportation* 686.2, *road vehicle* 687.4

automobile *or* **auto racing** 146.9

automobile mechanic *artisan* 123.13

automobile racer *driver* 146.8

automobile racing 146.1, Sporting Activities 145, *race* 422.8

automobile racing terms 146.3

automobile rallies 146.6

automobile rally *automobile racing* 146.1, *sporting event* 422.6

automotive *engine type* 14.11, *moving* 677.12

automotive engineer *mechanical engineer* 14.4

automotive engineering *mechanical engineering* 14.3, *miscellaneous automotive terms* 687.14

automotively *in motion* 677.19

automysophobia Phobias 283

autonomic *involuntary* 95.15

autonomically *involuntarily* 95.23

autonomous *governmental* 49.24, *free-willed* 372.9, *independent* 829.12

autonomously *freely* 829.22

autonomy *free will* 372.4, *independence* 829.5

autophobia Phobias 283

autopilot *guide* 126.6

autopista [Sp] *road* 687.2

autopsy *after death* 29.9, *postmortem (examination) (PM)* 107.17

auto race *race* 146.10

auto racing *automobile racing* 146.1

autoroute [Fr] *road* 687.2

autosome *chromosome* 13.21

autospore *reproductive body* 47.14

autostrada [Ital] *road* 687.2

autosuggestion *reverie* 360.6

autotoxemia *physical deterioration* 808.4

autumn *season* 654.1, *fall* 654.5

autumnal *seasonal* 654.7

autumnal equinox *fall* 654.5

autumnally *seasonally* 654.12

autumn crocus Flowers 42

autumn of one's life *old age* 27.5, *elderliness* 653.2

autumn sale *sale* 482.2

auxiliaries *reinforcements* 77.11, *extra* 748.6

auxiliary *martial* 77.33, *deputy* 80.1, *helper* 275.5, 825.12, *ancillary* 605.5, 605.14, *supporter* 605.9, *subordinate* 745.8, *extra person* 748.7, *additional* 748.8, *supplementary* 825.17

auxiliary fleet *military organization* 58.4

auxiliary forces *extra* 748.6

auxiliary language *international language* 5.8

auxiliary memory *memory* 15.6

auxin *plant hormone* 12.17

Auxois Horse and Pony Breeds 159

Avadana *other text* 81.19

avail *usefulness* 393.2, 801.1, *better* 445.17, *be profitable* 489.22, *be useful* 801.9, *help* 825.1, 825.23

availability 575.5; *visibility* 244.1, *usefulness* 801.1, *nearness* 803.2, *possibleness* 836.2

available 105.16, 575.11, 647.6; *provisioning* 89.6, *leisurely* 125.4, *visible* 244.5, *usable* 393.6, *not working* 415.10, *gainful* 467.10, *given* 472.8, *salable* 482.13, *offered* 504.8, *unoccupied* 576.13, *opened up* 583.11, *useful* 801.5, *nearby* 803.4, *possible* 836.5

available man *single man* 32.5

available post *opportunity* 583.8

available space 563.6

available to all *simple* 363.6

availably *openly* 583.22

availing *beneficial* 445.11

avail oneself of *frequent* 393.10, *adopt* 476.11

avalanche *mass movement* 8.28, *snow* 9.30, 218.6, *excess* 99.1, *climbing dangers* 161.5, *natural violence* 520.3, *agent of destruction* 523.7, *downflow* 714.3, *drip* 714.13

avalanche! *danger!* 162.39

Avalon *heaven* 82.15, Imaginary Places 360

avant-garde 652.6, 652.16; Western Art Styles 133, *musical* 140.25, *uncustomary* 398.4, *vanguard* 621.5, *front-running* 621.10, *different in time* 648.2, *novel* 737.5, *preparatory* 769.11

avant-garde jazz *jazz* 140.5

avant-gardist *modern person* 652.8, *precursor* 769.7

avarice *covetousness* 288.4, *immorality* 432.1, *selfishness* 444.1, *iniquity* 448.3, *taking* 477.1

avaricious *selfish* 444.4, *impious* 448.11, *gain-seeking* 467.11, *taking* 477.12

avariciously 477.22; *selfishly* 444.8, *gainfully* 467.24

avatar *divine manifestation* 82.5, *manifestation* 843.2

Ave *prayer* 85.10

Avelignese pony Horse and Pony Breeds 159

Ave Maria *prayer* 85.10

avenge 441.14; *retaliate* 420.4, *exact retribution* 454.27, *counterbalance* 743.8

avenged *compensated* 743.3

avenge oneself *retaliate* 489.23

avenger 441.6; *revenger* 420.2, *punisher* 454.16

avenging *vindictive* 441.10, *counterbalanced* 743.6

avenging angel *agent of destruction* 523.7

avens Flowers 42

avenue *road* 691.4, *way out* 707.2

aver *affirm* 189.21, *speak* 205.17, *testify* 336.10, *conflict* 422.26

average 742.1, 742.5, 778.4; *parameter* 6.57, *mediocre* 289.11, 742.7, *vague* 338.9, *moderation* 521.1, *moderate* 521.3, *medium* 579.12, 742.2, *numbers* 738.5, *quantitative* 738.6, *middle way* 772.3, *middling* 772.14, *common* 778.13

averaged out *compromising* 461.4

averagely *unexceptionally* 289.20

averageness *mediocrity* 289.5, 742.3, *average* 742.1

average out *be indiscriminate* 338.10, *compromise* 461.7, *make average* 742.9

average person 18.9, 742.4

averages *statistics* 784.2

average-size(d) *medium* 579.12

average value *parameter* 6.57

averaging out *compromising* 461.4

averment *affirmation* 189.1, *utterance* 205.10, *evidence* 336.3

Avernal *demonic* 446.9

Avernus *evil place* 446.6

averred *affirmed* 189.11, *verified* 336.7

Averroism Philosophical Schools of Thought 4

Averroist Philosophical Schools of Thought 4

averse *disinclined* 291.9, *unwilling* 375.8, *oppositional* 828.11

aversely *with hate* 300.13

averseness *dissociation* 375.4

averse to *hating* 300.7

aversion *fear* 283.1, *dislike* 291.1, 300.2, *hated thing* 300.5, *dissociation* 375.4, *opposition* 828.1

aversive *hateful* 300.10, *fugitive* 386.10

aversively *hatefully* 300.14

avert 386.15; *deter* 179.8, *dissociate* 375.14, *parry* 419.27, *misdirect* 698.21, *sidestep* 698.22

avertable *avoidable* 386.12

avertably *evasively* 386.24

averting *avoidance* 386.1

avert one's gaze *or* **eyes** *be blind to* 243.19

Aves *birds* 36.1

Avesta *other text* 81.19

avian 36.19

avian characteristic 36.6

aviary *farm building* 16.4, *dwelling* 36.4, *cage* 60.15

aviatic 689.10

aviation 689.1; *aviatic* 689.10

aviation beacon *safety light* 246.7

aviation fuel *oil* 106.7

aviation meteorology *meteorology* 9.1

aviation-sensor operations *navy specialties* 77.24

aviatophobia Phobias 283

aviator *professional worker* 123.11, *aircraft personnel* 689.3

avicultural *ornithological* 36.21

aviculture *ornithology* 36.2

aviculturist *ornithologist* 36.3

avid *desirous* 288.13, *eager* 373.8

avidity *or* **avidness** *eagerness* 373.2, *immorality* 432.1

avidly *eagerly* 288.27, 373.16

avifauna *birds* 36.1

avionic *aviatic* 689.10

avionics *aeronautics* 689.2

avitaminosis *vitamin deficiency disease* 12.14

avocado *green thing* 260.4, *green* 260.7

avocation *amusement* 167.7, *activity* 385.4

avocational *recreational* 167.10

avocet *water bird* 36.9

Avogadro's hypothesis Classical Physical Laws 10

avoid 386.13; *conceal oneself* 181.15, *deceive* 193.16, *be neglectful* 326.7, *hesitate* 378.10, *be equivocal* 380.7, *exclude* 383.11, *renounce* 392.4, *not use* 394.9, *escape notice* 403.14, *ignore* 409.11, *not act* 413.11, *parry* 419.27, *be self-restrained* 455.10, *not observe* 466.9, *not perform* 466.10, *lose someone* 468.20, *shrink back* 680.20, *sidestep* 698.22, *be safe* 810.20, *elude* 816.10

avoidable 386.12

avoidably *evasively* 386.24

avoid alcohol *be sober* 120.8

avoidance 386.1; *coexistence* 73.3, *defense mechanism* 108.23, *evasion* 181.5, 380.2, *indifference* 326.2, *rejection* 383.1, *relinquishment* 392.1, *nonuse* 394.1, *unsociability* 409.1, *inaction* 413.1, *self-restraint* 455.1, *nonobservance* 466.1, *setting apart* 753.2, *safety* 810.1, *escape* 816.1

avoidance conditioning *conditioning* 108.24

avoidant personality disorder *personality disorder* 108.7

avoid a parry *fence* 153.7

avoid bloodshed *be at peace* 73.10

avoid defeat *overcome obstacles* 845.14

avoided *rejected* 383.6, *relinquished* 392.2, *lonely* 409.8

avoider 386.8; *visionary* 360.9

avoid excess *be self-restrained* 455.10

avoid financial obligations *not pay* 490.9

avoid food *fast* 118.8

avoid gobbledegook *make comprehensible* 363.8

avoiding 386.9; *indifferent* 326.5, *equivocal* 380.5, *rejecting* 383.2, *nonobservant* 466.5

avoiding financial obligations *nonpayment* 490.1

avoiding the issue *evasiveness* 386.6

avoid notice *hide* 844.13

avoid recognition *hide* 844.13

avoid responsibility for *acquiesce* 421.5

avoid strife *pacify* 74.9

avoid taxes *elude* 816.10

avoid the issue *quibble* 330.13, *be evasive* 386.20

avoid the trap *be cunning* 822.5

avoid war *pacify* 74.9

avoirdupois *metrical* 589.15

avoirdupois weight *weight measurement* 538.6, *measuring system* 589.4, *type of measurement* 589.8

Avon Rivers 570

à votre santé! [Fr] *cheers!* 93.22

avouch *avow* 189.27, *testify* 336.10

avouched *verified* 336.7

avoucher *affirmer* 189.9

avouchment *avowal* 189.7, *evidence* 336.3

avow 189.27; *authorize* 52.14, *admit* 180.11, *testify* 336.10

avowal 189.7; *authorization* 52.3, *divulgence* 180.2, *evidence* 336.3

avowed 189.19; *authorized* 52.11, *disclosed* 180.5, *verified* 336.7, *promised* 458.8

avowedly 189.34; *apparently* 720.19

avower *affirmer* 189.9

Avranchin Breeds of Sheep 16

avulse *extract* 711.13

avulsion *extraction* 711.1

await *expect* 281.12, 650.12, *wait* 356.8, 658.12

await discovery *hide* 844.13

awaited *foreseen* 650.8

awaiting discovery *concealed* 844.7

awaiting execution *punishable* 454.21, *endangered* 811.10

awaiting trial *accused* 442.5

await payment *credit* 487.10

await trial *be accused* 442.10

awake 212.10; *sensible* 212.6, *active* 414.13

awake late *be late* 658.11

awaken 675.9; *revive* 809.14

awaken desire *cause desire* 288.22

awake the echoes *shatter the peace* 232.10

award *legal justice* 53.4, *title* 72.1, *verdict* 341.2, *judge* 341.10, *prize* 453.2, *reward* 453.13, 472.4, *give* 472.10, *ruling* 780.2

award a fellowship *grant* 453.14

awarded *receiving* 473.9

awarder *giver* 472.7

awarding *giving* 472.1

award of damages *favorable verdict* 54.19

aware *sensible* 212.6, *seeing* 242.17, *feeling* 266.9, *sensitive* 267.3, *prudent* 287.7, *ideational* 327.9, *knowledgeable* 348.7, *foreseeing* 357.5

awareness *sensation* 212.1, *visualization* 242.6, *feelings* 266.1, *sensitivity* 267.1, *prudence* 287.2, *idea* 327.1, *knowledge* 348.1, *foresight* 357.1

aware of *sensible* 212.6

Awash Rivers 570

awash *flooded* 557.24, 570.8

Awassi Breeds of Sheep 16

away 386.23, 576.8, 576.19, 585.6, 711.20; *disappeared* 265.4, *fleetingly* 265.8, *nonresident* 576.9, *at a distance* 585.13, *apart* 585.14, *forth* 707.19, *in isolation* 753.24, *fugitively* 816.12, *hopeless* 837.6

away! *go!* 709.30

away from *externally* 724.19

away from home *nonresident* 576.9

away side *group* 623.5

away with you! *go!* 709.30

awe *fear* 283.1, *wonder* 294.1, *be wondrous* 294.14, *admiration* 435.2, *command respect* 435.18

awed *astonished* 292.6, *wondering* 294.7

aweigh *sailing* 150.25

awe-inspiring 435.12; *wondrous* 294.9, *grand* 404.22

aweless *wonderless* 295.3

awelessly *without wonder* 295.8

awesome *fearsome* 283.13, *wondrous* 294.9

awesome! [Inf] *wonderful!* 294.20

awesomely *fearsomely* 283.21, *wondrously* 294.18

awesomeness *wonderfulness* 294.5

awe-stricken or **awestricken** *astonished* 292.6, *shock* 292.3, *wondering* 294.7, *reverent* 435.9

awe-struck or **awestruck** *shock* 292.3, *wondering* 294.7, *reverent* 435.9

awful *silent* 231.2, *without skill* 282.10, *frightening* 283.12, *evil* 446.7

awfully *unskillfully* 282.17, *frighteningly* 283.20, *evilly* 446.12, *hideously* 531.6

awfulness *evil* 446.1

awful silence *silence* 231.1

awkward 804.6; *immature* 26.12, *clumsy* 128.6, 824.14, *raw* 260.9, *ignorant* 349.5, *graceless* 528.7, *ugly* 531.3, *discourteous* 535.7, *untimely* 660.5, *difficult* 726.11, *inconvenient* 824.12

awkward age *youth* 26.1

awkwardly 824.26; *youthfully* 26.14, *unskillfully* 128.12, *inelegantly* 528.11, 531.7, *vulgarly* 535.10, *at the wrong time* 660.12, *difficultly* 726.20, *inconveniently* 804.11

awkwardness 804.3, 824.2; *immaturity* 26.3, *unskillfulness* 128.1, *ignorance* 349.1, *inelegance* 528.1, *untimeliness* 660.1

awkward occurrence *untimeliness* 660.1

awkward position *awkward situation* 824.7

awkward question *difficult question* 333.4

awkward situation 824.7; *predicament* 725.3, *difficult circumstances* 726.6

awl *hand tool* 103.3, *sharp-pointed thing* 549.4, *opener* 583.2

awn *grass plant* 45.3, *rough thing* 544.2, *sharp-pointed growth* 549.5

awned *spiked* 549.11

awning *shade maker* 247.4, *protective covering* 613.5, *overhead covering* 613.11, *protection from the weather* 810.9

awry *wrongly* 351.18, *gone wrong* 430.17, *oblique* 607.6, *obliquely* 607.13, *unbalanced* 741.5, *muddled* 766.13

ax *sharp weapon* 78.6, *hand tool* 103.3, *instrument of execution* 454.15, *abolish* 523.11, *sharp-edged thing* 549.6, *use a sharp tool* 549.17, *opener* 583.2

ax [Inf] *relieve from duty* 275.11, *dismissal* 709.2, *dismiss* 709.15, *termination* 834.2, *terminate* 834.7

axed [Inf] *canceled* 834.5

Axel Heiberg Island Islands 572

axel jump *ice-skating techniques* 162.16

axel lift *ice-skating techniques* 162.16

axial *of stems* 41.17, *central* 612.6, *directional* 677.13, 697.8

axially *centrally* 612.12

axial motion *movement* 677.3, *rotation* 682.1

axial ray *lens system* 10.22

axil *stem* 41.5

axillary *of stems* 41.17

axillary bud *bud* 41.8

axing [Inf] *dismissal* 709.2

axiologically *philosophically* 4.23

axiology Branches of Philosophy 4

axiom *philosophy* 4.1, *philosophical term* 4.7, *theory* 6.62, *physical law* 10.4, *maxim* 177.1, *truism* 721.6, *guide* 780.4

axiomatic *theoretical* 6.66, *proverbial* 177.2, *truistic* 721.15

axiomatically *proverbially* 177.4, *intrinsically* 721.30

axiometric drawing *illustration* 187.2

axis *graph* 6.30, *stem* 41.5, *center* 612.1, *axle* 682.7

axis of symmetry *geometric figure* 6.39

axle 682.7; *machine element* 14.8, *toboggan parts* 162.24

axletree *figurative usage* 43.9, *axle* 682.7

axman *executioner* 30.13

ax murderer *murderer* 30.12

axolotl *young amphibian* 37.11

axon *nervous system* 19.14

ax to grind *intention* 374.1

ayah *personal attendant* 69.5

ayatollah *religious leader* 68.9, *imam* 84.7

aye *yes* 346.2, *electing* 382.5

Ayrshire Breeds of Cattle 16

Ayurvedic medicine *alternative medicine* 107.4

azalea Flowers 42

azan *public worship* 83.3

Azaouak Breeds of Cattle 16

Azazel *evil spirit* 446.4

Azerbaijan Countries 566

Azerbaijan Mountain Merino Breeds of Sheep 16

azimuth *celestial sphere* 7.4, *coordinates* 589.6, *horizontal surface* 603.3, *guide* 697.4

azimuthal equidistant projection *map* 187.5

Azores Islands 572

Azov, Sea of Oceans and Seas 571

Azov Tsigai Breeds of Sheep 16

Azrael *personifications and symbols* 29.4, *angel* 82.11

Aztec two-step [Inf] *defecation* 25.3

azure Heraldic Terms 184, *blueness* 261.1, *blue* 261.5, 261.9

B

B Programming Languages 15

baa *animal sound* 240.1, *make an animal sound* 240.7

baba ghanouj *notable international dishes* 90.40

babassu Trees and Shrubs 43

Baba Yaga *evil spirit* 446.4

Babbage Programming Languages 15

Babbitt *conformist* 781.6

Babbittry *middle class* 772.6, *conventionalism* 781.4

babble *nonstandard language* 5.7, *talk nonsense* 192.26, 362.12, *have difficulty speaking* 206.9, *talk* 207.3, *be talkative* 207.7, *small sound* 233.4, *sound faint* 233.8, *rattle* 235.3, 235.12, *empty talk* 362.5, *be unintelligible* 364.11, *flow* 570.10

babbler *talker* 207.4

babbling *clumsy* 128.6, *nonsensical* 192.19, *speech defect* 206.2, *inarticulate* 206.6, *talkative* 207.5, *unintelligibility* 364.1

Babcock-Levy test Intelligence Tests 108

babe *child* 26.6, *innocent person* 449.5

babe [Inf] *young woman* 26.9, *female* 33.1, *term of endearment* 299.7, *attractive female* 529.5

babe [Inf and Off] *woman considered as a sex object* 33.8

babe in arms *child* 26.6, *weak person* 517.4, *naive person* 821.2

babe in the woods *innocent person* 449.5

babel *dissonance* 241.1, *senseless talk* 362.4, *miscellany* 751.3

baboon *primate* 35.17, *ugly thing* 531.2

babu [Hindu] *male title of address* 32.3

baby *person* 18.8, *progeny* 21.8, *child* 26.6, *young* 26.11, *coward* 285.3, *weak person* 517.4, *produce* 522.5, *little thing* 580.3, *undersized* 580.8, *new arrival* 652.7, *beginner* 771.14, *embryonic* 771.19

baby [Inf] *young woman* 26.9, *term of endearment* 299.7

baby [Inf and Off] *woman considered as a sex object* 33.8

baby blues [Inf] *eye* 19.9, 242.3

baby boom *productiveness* 22.3

baby boomers *the young* 26.10

baby clothes 100.24

baby doll [Inf] *term of endearment* 299.7

baby doll pajamas *nightwear* 100.21

baby food *food* 90.1

babyhood *youth* 26.1, *conception* 771.4

babyish *young* 26.11

babyishly *youthfully* 26.14

baby's-breath Flowers 42

baby-sitter *domestic worker* 123.4, *protector* 810.11

baby talk *nonstandard language* 5.7

baby tooth *teeth* 19.8

baccalaureate *authorization* 340.4

baccarat Card Games 168

bacchanal or **bacchant** *glutton* 119.2, *drunkard* 121.8

bacchanalia *feast* 92.9, *drinking bout* 121.7
bacchius *meter* 139.10
Bacchus Deities 82
bach (it) [Inf] *be celibate* 67.9
Bachaur Breeds of Cattle 16
bachelor *single man* 32.5, *single person* 67.5, 788.7
bachelor girl *single woman* 33.5, *single person* 67.5
bachelorhood *celibacy* 67.1, *independence* 829.5
bachelorlike *celibate* 67.6
bachelorly *celibate* 67.6
bachelor party *general wedding terms* 64.6
bachelor's button Flowers 42
bacillophobia Phobias 283
bacillus *microorganism* 13.11, *disease-causing agent* 114.5, *little thing* 580.3
Back Rivers 570
back 622.1, 622.6, 825.28; *blow* 9.53, *swimming* 164.12, *confirm* 189.25, *side with* 382.15, 623.10, *approve* 437.14, *donate* 491.13, *harden* 542.9, *give moral support* 605.18, *support financially* 605.19, *rear end* 622.4, *be in the rear* 622.7, *side direction* 623.2, *side* 623.6, *be changeable* 666.5, *directional* 677.13, *be in motion* 677.14, *reverse* 680.18, *navigate* 690.15, *deviate* 698.15, *mount* 713.24, *opposite* 731.2, *hindmost* 773.18, *advise* 825.27, *finance* 825.31
backache *painful condition* 215.2
back and fill *oscillate* 683.12, *navigate* 690.15
back and forth *changeably* 666.7, *in exchange* 673.6, *to and fro* 683.16
back-and-forth *oscillating* 683.8
back and front *horizontal bar* 157.5
back another's credit *be in debt* 488.9
back a sail *handle sailboat equipment* 150.30
back away *dissociate* 375.14, *hesitate* 378.10, *shy* 386.17, *reverse* 680.18
backbeat [Inf] *tempo* 140.22
backbencher *elected official* 50.8
backbend *floor exercise* 157.4
backbite *defame* 440.13
backbiter *disparager* 440.7
backbiting *defamation* 440.3, *defamatory* 440.9
backboard *basketball court* 148.3, *green bowling* 151.3
backbone *protein* 12.9, Human Bones 19, *steadfastness* 359.3, *will* 376.5, *stamina* 377.4, *endurance* 516.4, *body support* 605.6, *rear end* 622.4, *essential content* 723.2
backbone of steel *will* 376.5
back boundary line *badminton terms* 165.11
backbreaker *difficult task* 824.3
backbreaking *laborious* 122.7, *punishing* 454.20, *difficult* 824.9, *blocked* 826.13
backbreaking work *work* 122.1
back burner *back* 622.1
backchat [Inf] *chat* 210.2, *answer* 334.1, *answer back* 334.19, *rudeness* 400.2
backchatting *answering* 334.11
backcheck *ice hockey tactics* 158.4
backchecker *hockey player* 158.8
backcloth [Brit] *stage set* 136.19
back country *geographical space*

563.3, *countryside* 564.3, *outside* 610.3
back-country *local* 564.14, *outside* 610.9
backcourt *basketball court* 148.3, *tennis court* 165.3
back crawl *swimming techniques* 164.2
back crawl race *competitive swimming* 164.3
back crawl start *competitive swimming* 164.3
back door *back entrance* 622.2, *access* 691.3, *means of entry* 706.6, *way out* 707.2, *safety* 810.1, *means of escape* 816.4
backdoor influence *cunning* 822.1
back down *relinquish* 392.3, *reverse* 671.9, *retreat* 680.17
backdrop *stage set* 136.19, *surroundings* 615.1, *back* 622.1
backed *confirmed* 189.17, *approved* 437.8, *hardened* 542.7
back emf *electric potential* 10.40
back end *back* 622.1
back end of a bus *ugly thing* 531.2
back entrance 622.2
backer *producer* 136.28, *affirmer* 189.9, *approver* 437.7, *financial adviser* 457.4, *giver* 472.7, *generous person* 498.5, *supporter* 605.9, *benefactor* 825.15
backest *bowls* 151.7
backest bowl *grip* 151.4
backfill *substructure* 551.8
backfire *bang* 234.1, 234.6, *counteraction* 510.1, *counteract* 510.7, *reversion* 671.1, *reverse* 671.9
backfired *reversed* 671.7
backflip *floor exercise* 157.4
back float *swimming techniques* 164.2
backflow *flow* 570.4, *reversal* 680.3
backflowing *backward motion* 677.5, *directional* 677.13
back formation *word* 5.17
back-formed *worded* 5.38
backgammon Board and Table Games 167
background *race* 1.5, *chronicle* 3.4, *refinement* 48.10, *aspect of fiction* 139.5, *description* 202.1, *authorization* 340.4, *circumstances* 573.2, 726.1, *distant place* 585.3, *surroundings* 615.1, *surrounding* 615.4, *back* 622.1, *circumstantial* 726.8, *concomitant* 794.4, *accompanying* 794.12
backhand *bowls* 151.7, *tennis strokes* 165.2, *forehand* 165.12, *sporting hit* 695.6
backhand drive *tennis strokes* 165.2
backhanded *equivocal* 380.5, *insulting* 436.10
backhanded or **backhand** *indirect* 607.8
backhanded compliment *insult* 436.5
backhandedly *indirectly* 607.15
backhandedness *indirectness* 607.3
backhander [Brit inf] *incentive* 178.4
backhand grip *grip* 151.4
backhand shot *grip* 151.4, *ice hockey tactics* 158.4
backhoe *construction equipment* 14.23

back home *on arrival* 704.22
backhouse *place for excretion* 25.11
backing *resources* 102.4, *emulsion* 132.9, *confirmation* 189.5, *approval* 437.1, *recommending* 437.11, *donation* 491.6, *hardness* 542.1, *support* 605.7, *moral support* 605.7, *financial support* 605.8, *backward motion* 677.5, *reversal* 680.3, *patronage* 825.9, *helper* 825.12
backing down *reversion* 671.1
backing or **backup vocalist** *singer* 141.4
backing up or **off** or **out** *reversal* 680.3
backing wind *wind* 9.12
back judge *football player* 155.15
back kick *swimming techniques* 164.2
backlash *response* 334.4, *retaliation* 420.1, *counteraction* 510.1, *reversion* 671.1, *consequence* 774.3
back-layout style *jumping* 166.11
backless dress *dress* 100.11
backlighting *lighting* 132.16
backlog *store* 105.1
back lot *motion-picture studio* 137.7
back matter 622.3; *book part* 174.5, *part of writing* 760.6, *ending* 773.10
back o' beyond [Aus inf] *geographical space* 563.3, *distant place* 585.3, *farthest point* 620.3
back off *shy* 386.17, *reverse* 680.18
back on one's feet *cured* 809.8
back out *be a coward* 285.7, *not observe* 435.4, *retreat* 680.17
backpack *climbing equipment* 161.4, *baggage* 578.8, *transferred thing* 685.6
backpacking Sporting Activities 145, Hobbies and Pastimes 167
back part *back* 622.1
back pass *soccer play* 163.5
back pay *amount owing* 488.5, *pay* 489.6
back-pedal *equivocate* 380.8, *reverse* 680.18, *slow down* 693.13
back-pedaling *vacillation* 380.3, *equivocating* 380.6
backplate *historic armor* 419.8
back rent *amount owing* 488.5
back room *planning* 387.8
back-room *concealed* 844.7
back-room influence *cunning* 822.1
back scratch *be sycophantic* 439.15
back scratcher *assenter* 346.3, *flatterer* 439.6
back scratching *sycophancy* 401.2, 439.5, *sycophantic* 439.11
back-scratching *sycophantic* 401.7, *mutual relationship* 827.3
backseat *back* 622.1, *inferiority* 745.1, *inferior* 745.5
backseat driver *adviser* 176.5, *meddler* 414.12
backside *rear end* 622.4
backsight *visual aid* 242.14
back slang [Brit] *slang* 5.19
backslap *welcome* 408.18
backslapper *social person* 408.7
backslapping *friendly* 62.5, *welcome* 408.10
backslide *be wicked* 448.13, *reverse* 671.9, *go backward* 680.16
backsliding 680.8; *depravity* 448.2, *depraved* 448.10, *reversion* 671.1, *receding* 680.11, *deterioration* 808.1
backspace (BS) *character* 15.18
backspin *golf shots* 156.4
backstabber *malefactor* 306.6

backstage *stage* 136.18, *onstage* 136.39, *private* 245.5, *invisibly* 245.8, *back* 622.1
backstage dealings *cunning* 822.1
backstage manipulator 844.3
back stairs *means of escape* 816.4
backstay *sailboat parts* 150.4
backstretch *racetrack* 159.12
backswing *golf shots* 156.4, *tennis strokes* 165.2
back talk *answer* 334.1, *rudeness* 400.2, *act of defiance* 416.3
back-talk *be insolent* 400.14
back the wrong horse *be in error* 351.15, *fail* 846.12
back to back *manorial* 60.21, *back* 622.6, *opposite* 731.3
back-to-front *inverted* 608.5, *inversely* 608.9, *reversibly* 671.14
back to normal *cured* 809.8
back tooth *teeth* 19.8
back to the beginning *reversibly* 671.14
back to where one started *backward* 680.23
backtrack *take back* 477.17, *reverse* 680.18
backtracking *taking back* 477.4, *directional* 677.13, *about-face* 680.4
back-trail *reverse* 680.18
backup *data-related concepts* 15.23, *alternative* 80.2, *reserves* 102.5, *bowling delivery* 151.2, *bowling* 151.6, *helper* 275.5, 825.12, *substitute* 613.17, 613.23, *reversal* 680.3, *extra person* 748.7, *cooperation* 827.1
backup light *safety light* 246.7
back up *program* 15.29, *substitute for* 80.5, *save* 105.20, *confirm* 189.25, *prove* 339.14, *give moral support* 605.18, *cover for* 613.34, *be in the rear* 622.7, *be in motion* 677.14, *reverse* 680.18, *establish reality* 719.12, *back* 825.28
back wall *squash terms* 165.10
backward 680.10, 680.23; *diving* 164.13, *lacking intellect* 316.5, *intellectually subnormal* 316.7, *ignorant* 349.5, *unenthusiastic* 375.10, *unprepared* 389.5, *reserved* 403.10, *inverted* 608.5, *inversely* 608.9, *back* 622.6, *behind* 622.8, *directional* 677.13, *delayed* 693.10, *unimproved* 808.10
backward and forward *in exchange* 673.6, *to and fro* 683.16
backward dive *competitive diving* 164.7
backward-looking *retrospective* 651.15, *retroactive* 680.12
backward motion 677.5, 680.1
backwardness *unskillfulness* 128.1, *lack of intellect* 316.1, *ignorance* 349.1, *unenthusiasm* 375.3, *reserve* 403.5, *inversion* 608.1
backward somersault *floor exercise* 157.4
backward step or **motion** *backward motion* 680.1
backwash *visible effect* 676.2
backwater *solitary place* 409.4, *regions* 564.2, *small lake* 568.2, *inlet* 572.9
backwood bowl *grip* 151.4
backwoods *regions* 564.2, *local* 564.14
backwoodsman *countryman* 61.8
backyard *plot* 564.9, *back* 622.1
bacon *pork* 90.26
Baconian Philosophical Schools of Thought 4

Baconism Philosophical Schools of Thought 4
bacteria Phobias 283
bacterial *living* 13.28, *tiny* 580.9
bactericide *prophylaxis* 115.4
bacteriological *biological* 13.27
bacteriological warfare *chemical warfare* 76.5
bacteriological weapon *weapon* 78.1
bacteriologist *life scientist* 13.26
bacteriology *biology* 13.2, *medical science* 107.5
bacteriophage *microorganism* 13.11
bacteriophobia Phobias 283
bacterium *microorganism* 13.11, *disease-causing agent* 114.5, *little thing* 580.3
bad *offending* 53.25, *sick* 114.24, *unhygienic* 114.27, *unpalatable* 223.6, *without skill* 282.10, *profane* 301.10, *malevolent* 306.7, *badly behaved* 399.16, *wrongful* 430.10, *immoral* 432.9, *great* 445.14, *evil* 446.1, 446.7, *wicked* 448.9, *cheap* 800.16, *imperfect* 806.5, *spoiled* 808.9, *adverse* 848.10
bad! [Inf] *good!* 445.24
bad air *lack of hygiene* 112.3
Badano Breeds of Sheep 16
bad apple [Inf] *miscreant* 448.6
bad art *misrepresentation* 188.1
bad association *no relation* 728.5
bad atmosphere *bad feeling* 266.5
bad bargain *choice* 382.3
bad behavior *bad conduct* 399.7, *bad manners* 411.2, *wickedness* 448.1
bad blood *hostility* 63.1, *ill feeling* 63.3, *antipathy* 291.2, *hate* 300.1, *malevolence* 306.1, *conflict* 828.3
bad break [Inf] *luck* 842.3
bad breath *unpleasant-smelling thing* 227.2
bad buy *purchase* 481.1
bad character *wickedness* 448.1
bad check *false money* 484.15, *bad payment* 490.3
bad condition or **shape** *physical state* 725.6
bad conduct 399.7
bad connection *no relation* 728.5
bad conscience *sign of guilt* 450.2, *penitence* 451.1
bad day *bungling* 128.2
bad debt *debt* 488.1, *amount owing* 488.5
bad debtor *debtor* 488.6
bad deed *malignity* 306.5, *wrongdoing* 430.7
baddie or **baddy** *evil person* 446.3, *miscreant* 448.6
bad drains *lack of hygiene* 112.3
bad dream *fantasy* 360.5, *false alarm* 814.4
bad ear *hearing* 228.1
bad egg *unpleasant-smelling thing* 227.2, *malefactor* 306.6, *disreputable character* 371.2, *miscreant* 448.6
bad ending *deterioration* 808.1
bad faith *dishonorableness* 192.3, *nonobservance* 466.1
bad-faith *untruthful* 192.12
bad feeling 266.5
bad fit *difference* 463.4
bad form *uncustomary* 398.4, *grossness* 535.3
bad fortune 848.7
badge *military honor* 58.9, Heraldic Terms 184, *means of identification*

184.3, *insignia* 184.5, *jewelry* 532.6, *special feature* 779.4
badge of merit *insignia* 184.5
badge of office *insignia* 184.5
badge of rank *insignia* 184.5
badger *flesh-eating mammal* 35.9
badgers Collective Names 59
bad grammar *grammar* 5.28, *language error* 351.10, *inelegance of expression* 528.4
bad guy [Inf] *role* 136.23
bad habit *habit* 397.1
bad hand *unskilled person* 128.3
bad health *ill health* 114.1
bad heart *cardiovascular disease* 114.13
bad humor *state of mind* 725.5
bad-humored *conditional* 725.7
bad-humoredly *in good form* 725.11
bad idea *unsuccessful thing* 846.8
badinage *wit* 277.3, *derision* 369.1
bad influence *disreputable character* 371.2, *evil thing* 446.2
bad intent or **intention** *malice* 306.2
bad-intentioned *malicious* 306.8
bad job *bungling* 128.2
bad judgment *legal injustice* 53.5
badlands *desert* 560.4
bad language *offensive language* 301.5, *act of discourtesy* 411.3, *inelegance of expression* 528.4, *grossness* 535.3
bad law *legal injustice* 53.5
bad learner *unskilled person* 128.3
bad light *darkness* 247.1, *dimness* 248.1, *disrepute* 371.1
bad likeness *misrepresentation* 188.1
bad lot *disreputable character* 371.2, *miscreant* 448.6
bad luck *lost chance* 660.3, *luck* 842.3, *bad fortune* 848.7
bad luck! *too bad!* 848.17
bad-luck sign 358.7
badly 399.23, 745.15; *unskillfully* 128.12, 282.17, *wrongly* 351.18, 430.24, *abusively* 395.8, *immorally* 432.18, *evilly* 446.12, *wickedly* 448.15, *worse* 808.23
badly behaved 399.16; *bad-mannered* 411.6, *troublesome* 824.13
badly behaved person 399.8
badly done *bungled* 128.7
badly dressed *plain* 528.9
badly lit *dark* 247.5
badly off *poor* 486.8, *unprosperous* 848.11
badly served *disappointed* 293.4
badly timed *untimely* 660.5
bad-mannered 411.6
bad manners 411.2; *objectionability* 272.2, *bad conduct* 399.7, *grossness* 535.3
bad match *difference* 463.4
badminton Sporting Activities 145
badminton court *badminton terms* 165.11
badminton terms 165.11
bad money *false money* 484.15
bad money driving out good *economic deterioration* 808.2
bad mood *sign of irritability* 304.4
bad morals *immorality* 432.1
bad-mouth [Inf] *defame* 440.13
bad move *error* 351.1, *impropriety* 430.5
bad name *disrepute* 371.1
bad nature *malevolence* 306.1
bad-natured *malevolent* 306.7
badness *malevolence* 306.1, *bad*

conduct 399.7, *wrong* 430.1, *immorality* 432.1, *evil* 446.1, *wickedness* 448.1, *deficiency* 745.2
bad news *news* 171.1, *bad outcome* 293.3
bad news [Inf] *badly behaved* 399.16, *miscreant* 448.6, *deterioration* 808.1, *misadventure* 848.2
bad nose *lack of sense of smell* 225.2
bad notice *criticism* 438.4
bad odor *reputation* 224.4, *stench* 227.1, *disrepute* 371.1
bad omen *lack of hope* 282.2, *omen* 358.5, *forewarning* 814.2
bad outcome 293.3
bad patch *awkward situation* 824.7, *time of adversity* 848.8
bad payment 490.3
bad person *malefactor* 306.6
bad policy *inconvenience* 804.1
bad press *criticism* 438.4, 440.2
bad relation *no relation* 728.5
bad reputation *disrepute* 371.1
bad result *bad outcome* 293.3
bad review *criticism* 365.3, 440.2
bad sales *sales* 482.3
bad scene *deterioration* 808.1
bad shot *unskilled person* 128.3
bad spell *evil thing* 446.2, *time of adversity* 848.8
bad spirits *state of mind* 725.5
bad taste 220.3, 528.3; *tastelessness* 338.3, *impropriety* 430.5, *vulgarity* 535.1
bad temper *anger* 302.4, *short temper* 303.5, *sign of irritability* 304.4, *malevolence* 306.1
bad-tempered *ill-natured* 303.9, *irritable* 304.9, *malevolent* 306.7
bad time *untimeliness* 660.1
bad time of the month *untimeliness* 660.1
bad times *insolvency* 486.2, *time of adversity* 848.8
bad timing *untimeliness* 660.1
bad trip [Inf] *drug use* 121.9
bad turn *malignity* 306.5
bad use *misuse* 395.1
bad vibes [Inf] *bad feeling* 266.5
bad visibility *invisibility* 245.1
bad ways *wickedness* 448.1
bad will *malevolence* 306.1
bad-willed *malevolent* 306.7
bad word *vulgarism* 5.20, *curse word* 301.4
bad words *act of discourtesy* 411.3
Baedeker *type of book* 174.3
bael tree Trees and Shrubs 43
Baffin Island Islands 572
baffle *mystify* 182.12, *muffle* 229.11, *sound reducer* 233.5, *obscure* 250.8, *thwart* 293.10, *be wondrous* 294.14, *puzzle* 364.12, *cause difficulties* 824.22, *make uncertain* 841.19
baffled *frustrated* 293.5, *wondering* 294.7, *confused* 364.10, 841.11, *troubled* 824.15
baffle description *be wondrous* 294.14
bafflement *incredulity* 88.3, *frustration* 293.2, *speculation* 294.2, *unintelligibility* 364.1, *confusion* 841.4
baffling *inscrutable* 250.5, *frustrating* 293.7, *astonishing* 294.10, *difficult* 364.8, *problematic* 824.11, *confused* 841.11
baffling attitude *unintelligible thing* 364.3
bafflingly *astonishingly* 294.19
baffy *golf equipment* 156.5

bag 578.7; *receptacle* 105.11, *hunt* 385.14
bag(ful) *container(ful)* 738.2
bag and baggage *possession of property* 469.3, *possessions* 470.5
bagatelle *cheap item* 497.5, *trifle* 800.3
bagel *bread* 90.10
baggage 578.8; *receptacle* 105.11, *possessions* 470.5, *transferred thing* 685.6, *freightage* 686.3
baggage [Inf and Off] *sex object* 20.8, *young woman* 26.9, *woman considered as a sex object* 33.8, *insolent person* 400.7
baggage car *railroad car* 688.5
baggage cart *wagon* 687.3
bagged *storing* 578.19
bagged [Inf] *dead drunk* 121.27
baggily *noncohesively* 756.9
bagginess *largeness* 579.2, *nonadhesion* 756.1
baggy *stylish* 100.42, *big* 579.13, *nonadhesive* 756.4
Baghdad Countries 566
bag job [Inf] *theft* 479.2
bag lady *poor person* 486.6, *person in adversity* 848.9
bag limit *game laws* 160.3
bagman [Brit] *peddler* 482.9
bagnio *brothel* 432.5
bag of bones *thin person* 595.4
bag of tricks *means* 102.1, *collection* 105.12, *artifice* 193.5, *stratagem* 822.2
bagpipe Musical Instruments 142
bags [Inf] *profuseness* 795.3
bag snatcher *taker* 477.9
baguette *bread* 90.10
baguette or **bagnette** Architectural Elements 134
bagwig *body covering* 613.3
bagworm *larva* 40.9
Baha'i *other religious member* 81.13
Baha'ism *other religions* 81.8
Bahamas Countries 566, Islands 572
Bahir *Jewish text* 81.17
Bahrain Countries 566, Islands 572
Baikal Lakes 568
bail *pretrial proceedings* 54.13, *promise* 464.2, *take away* 685.12, *deliverance* 817.1, *liberation* 831.1, *liberate* 831.6
bailed *liberated* 831.4
bailey *fort* 419.13
Bailey bridge *bridge* 551.10, 691.7
bailie [Scot] *judge* 68.4
bailiff *court officer* 54.7, *collector* 473.7
bailiff [Brit] *farm worker* 16.15, *judge* 68.4, *domestic servant* 69.7, *manager* 126.7
bailiwick *subject* 48.3, *habitat* 60.1, *sphere of influence* 512.7, *administrative region* 564.4, *sphere* 564.10
bailout *financial support* 605.8
bail out *support financially* 605.19, *deliver* 817.5, *finance* 825.31
Baily's beads *sun* 7.15
bain-marie *cooking equipment* 91.6
Bairam *religious festival* 85.13
bait 154.6; *enticement* 178.3, *entice* 178.16, *irritate* 302.16, *be severe* 424.8, *reward for service* 453.5, *offer* 504.11, *positive stimulus* 508.5, *lure* 700.5, 700.12
bait casting *fishing* 154.1
baited *fishing* 154.13
baited trap *enticement* 178.3
bait fishing *fishing* 154.1

baiting *fishing* 154.13
bait the hook *fish* 154.14
bait the trap *be cunning* 822.5
baize Fabrics and Fibers 130, *billiards* 149.1
bake 560.19; *cook* 91.10, *heat* 217.17, *harden* 542.9
baked 560.14; *heated* 217.15
baked brick *hard substance* 542.3
baked goods *confectionery* 222.3
baked potatoes *vegetable* 90.33
bake glaze *make ceramics* 129.10
bakehouse *cooking place* 91.4
baker *food provider* 90.6, *cook* 91.3, *retailer* 482.11
baker's dozen *eleven to nineteen* 792.7
bakery *food provider* 90.6, *cooking place* 91.4, *confectionery* 222.3, *source of fragrance* 226.2
bake sale *charitable organization* 305.4
bakeshop *food provider* 90.6
baking *cooking technique* 91.2
baking dish *cooking equipment* 91.6
baking hot *heating* 217.12
baking powder *basic cooking ingredient* 91.8, *leavening* 539.3, *lifter* 715.5
baking soda *basic cooking ingredient* 91.8, *cleaning agent* 111.9
baklava *pastry* 90.37, *notable international dishes* 90.40
baksheesh *bounty* 453.8, *gift* 472.2, 498.3
Baku Countries 566
balaclava *cap* 100.33
balalaika Musical Instruments 142
Balance Constellations 7
balance 378.11; *philosophical attitude* 4.3, *process* 14.50, *superfluity* 99.4, *design* 133.9, *treatment* 143.6, *sailing terms* 150.5, *row* 150.32, *floor exercise* 157.4, *horizontal bar* 157.5, *compromise* 461.1, *deposit* 487.3, *grace* 527.2, *weighing instrument* 538.7, *be heavy* 538.12, *measuring instrument* 589.12, *correspondence* 606.2, *correspond* 606.8, *symmetry* 626.1, *symmetrize* 626.6, *regularity* 663.1, *make regular* 663.9, *stability* 674.1, *make stable* 674.7, *lack of motion* 678.1, *correspond to* 727.10, *correlation* 729.3, *correlate* 729.9, *make the same* 730.16, *accord* 735.1, *be in accord* 735.21, *equilibrium* 740.2, *equalize* 740.12, *medium* 742.6, *make average* 742.9, *counterbalance* 743.2, 743.8, *part* 760.1, *completeness* 761.1, *middle ground* 772.4, *stand in the middle* 772.17, *place in the middle* 772.18, *check* 784.14, *canceling out* 834.3, *cancel out* 834.8
balance accounts *account* 493.9
balance beam 157.3, Sporting Activities 145, *gymnastics equipment* 157.2
balance carried forward *difference* 750.3
balance climbing *climbing techniques* 161.3
balanced *rational* 109.4, *rowing* 150.27, *wise* 352.4, *proper* 429.10, *compromising* 461.4, *accounted* 493.8, *moderate* 521.3, 772.12, *graceful* 527.4, *corresponding* 606.6, *symmetrical* 626.4, *regular* 663.5, *stabilized*
674.4, *motionless* 678.4, *correlative* 729.6, *harmonious* 735.11, *equal* 740.8, *medium* 742.6, *counterbalanced* 743.7, *ordered* 765.10, *canceled* 834.5
balanced diet *diet* 92.5, *health improvement* 113.3
balanced line *offense* 155.6
balanced mind *sanity* 109.1
balance movement *uneven parallel bars* 157.6
balance of form *symmetry* 626.1
balance of mind disturbed *insanity* 110.1
balance of payments *international trade* 56.7, *economic factor* 56.8
balance of power *equilibrium* 740.2
balance of trade *international trade* 56.7
balance out *make average* 742.9
balances *funds* 484.6
balance sheet *accounts* 493.4
balance spring *spring* 546.4
balance the books *check* 784.14
balance to pay *amount owing* 488.5
balance wheel *wheel* 682.9
balancing *rowing* 150.27, *gymnastic* 157.11, *snowboarding* 162.11, 162.30, *compromising* 461.4, *counteracting* 510.6, *equalization* 740.4, *counterbalanced* 743.6
balancing act *equivocation* 380.1, *compromise* 461.1
balancing exercises *gymnastics* 157.1
balata Trees and Shrubs 43
Balaton Lakes 568
Balbas Breeds of Sheep 16
balbriggan Fabrics and Fibers 130
balconet Architectural Elements 134
balcony Architectural Elements 134, *auditorium* 136.17
bald 614.16; *candid* 191.5, *smooth* 545.4
baldachin Architectural Elements 134
bald as a billiard ball *or* **coot** *bald* 614.16
bald cypress Trees and Shrubs 43
Balder Deities 82
balderdash *nonsense* 192.8, *senseless talk* 362.4
baldhead *baldness* 614.9
baldheaded *bald* 614.16
baldheadedness *baldness* 614.9
baldie [Inf] *or* **baldy** [Inf] *baldness* 614.9
balding *bald* 614.16
baldness 614.9; *candor* 191.2, Phobias 283
baldpate *baldness* 614.9
baldpated *bald* 614.16
baldpatedness *baldness* 614.9
bald person *baldness* 614.9
baldric *accessory* 100.28
Baldwin Apple Varieties 44
bale *farm* 16.19, Collective Names 59, *group* 59.24
Baleares Islands 572
Balearic Islands Islands 572
Balearic pony Horse and Pony Breeds 159
bale carrier *farm tool* 16.5
baled *grouped* 59.21
balefire *fire* 246.9
baleful *malicious* 306.8, *detrimental* 446.8
balefully *banefully* 117.19,
maliciously 306.15, *destructively* 446.13
balefulness *malice* 306.2
bale out *emerge* 707.14
baler *farm tool* 16.5
bale sledge *farm tool* 16.5
bale wrapper *farm tool* 16.5
Bali Islands 572
Balinese Breeds of Cattle 16, Breeds of Cats 35
Bali pony Horse and Pony Breeds 159
balk *pitching terms* 147.5, *play baseball* 147.9, *snooker* 149.4, *thwart* 293.10, *oppose* 375.13, *hesitate* 378.10
balkanization *separation* 409.3
Balkan Mountains Mountains and Hills 569
balk at *shy* 386.17, *refuse* 506.8
balked *frustrated* 293.5
Balkhash Lakes 568
Balkhi Breeds of Sheep 16
balking *opposition* 375.2
ball *social gathering* 59.7, Historical Missile Weapons 78, *ammunition* 78.11, *historical ammunition* 78.12, *dance* 135.1, *baseball equipment* 147.4, *pitching terms* 147.5, *football* 155.1, *golf equipment* 156.5, *hockey equipment* 158.3, *toy* 167.9, *formal occasion* 406.4, *party* 408.6, *round thing* 633.3, *make round* 633.9, *missile* 696.7
ball [Inf] *have sex* 20.21
ballad Poem or Verse Forms 139, *popular music* 140.4
ballade Poem or Verse Forms 139
balladeer *author* 139.13, *singer* 141.4, *composer* 141.9
ballad maker *author* 139.13
ballad monger *author* 139.13
ballad opera *musical drama* 136.5
balladry *poetry* 139.8
ballad singer *singer* 141.4
ball and chain *restraint* 826.8, *means of restraint* 830.6
ball-and-socket joint *joint* 752.7
ballast *sailboat parts and accessories* 150.4, *displacement* 538.3, *weighing instrument* 538.7, *make heavy* 538.14, *rail* 688.3, *equalizer* 740.5, *counterbalance* 743.2, *safety device* 810.15
ballasting *weighing instrument* 538.7
ball bearing *machine element* 14.8, *axle* 682.7
ball boy *tennis participant* 165.6
ball-breaker [Inf] *difficult task* 824.3
ball-buster [Inf] *contest* 422.4, *difficult task* 824.3
ball clay *material* 129.2
ball-control offense *playing terms* 148.4
balled up [Inf] *mixed up* 766.14
ballerina *ballet dancer* 135.5
ballet 135.2; *dance* 135.1, *musical drama* 136.5, *classical music* 140.2, *ski* 162.27, *show* 404.12, *work of art* 522.4, *production* 843.5
ballet dancer 135.5
ballet dancing Dancing Types 135, *ballet* 135.2
balletic *dancing* 135.6
balletically *dancingly* 135.8
ballet music *popular music* 140.4
ballet school *type of school* 48.12
ballet shoes *or* **slippers** *shoes* 100.30
ballet skiing *skiing* 162.1
ballet skirt *skirt* 100.12
ball field *baseball field* 147.3
ballflower Architectural Elements 134
ball game *baseball* 147.1, *type of game* 167.2
ball game [Inf] *circumstances* 573.2
ball gown *dress* 100.11, *formal clothing* 406.5
balling [Inf] *sexual intercourse* 20.9
ballista Historical Missile Weapons 78
ballistic *strategic* 78.16, *projectile* 696.13
ballistic missile *modern missile weapon* 78.4, *missile* 696.7
ballistic missile submarine *warship* 77.21, *modern missile weapon* 78.4
ballistics *military training* 76.19, *shooting* 904.3
ballistophobia Phobias 283
ball lightning *thunderstorm* 9.20, *natural light* 246.4
ball milling *ceramic process* 129.5
balloon *air bubble* 558.10, *enlargement* 581.7, *grow* 581.17, *round thing* 633.3, *bulge* 634.2, *aircraft* 689.3
balloon flower Flowers 42
ballooning Sporting Activities 145
balloon mortgage *mortgage* 476.6
balloon out *make round* 633.9, *be convex* 634.7
ballot *electing* 382.5, *election* 382.6
ballot box *election* 382.6
balloter *electorate* 382.7
ballpark *sports ground* 145.2, *baseball field* 147.3
ballpark figure [Inf] *sum* 484.5, *measurement* 589.1
ballpark view *overview* 425.6
ballplayer *baseball team* 147.2
ball return *bowling* 151.1
ballroom *dance hall* 135.3
ballroom dancing Dancing Types 135
ballroom music *popular music* 140.4
balls [Inf] *organs of reproduction* 21.9, *vigor* 518.1, *bulge* 634.2
balls! [Inf] *miscellaneous swearwords* 301.20
ballsy [Inf] *courageous* 284.9, *vigorous* 518.2
ball the jack [Inf] *run* 694.13
ballup [Inf] *bungling* 128.2, *blunder* 351.9, *mix-up* 766.5
ball up [Inf] *err* 351.14, *confuse* 766.19, *impair* 808.18, *blunder* 846.13
ballyhoo *public relations (PR)* 173.8, *publicize* 173.18, *publicity* 178.7, *exaggeration* 194.1, *exaggerate* 194.11, *tumult* 232.5
ballyhooed *exaggerated* 194.7
balm 115.11; *medicine* 115.2, *dose of medicine* 115.3, *analgesic* 115.6, *fragrance* 226.1, *reliever* 275.4, *condolence* 308.2, *moderator* 521.2, *ointment* 562.8
bal masqué [Fr] *cover* 181.4
Balmer series Classical Physical Laws 10
balminess *fragrance* 226.1
balm-of-Gilead Tree Products 43
Balmoral underwear 100.22
balmoral *cap* 100.33
balmy *warm* 9.46, 217.13, *fragrant* 226.1, *prosperous* 845.7
balmy [Inf] *insane* 110.9, *foolish* 353.5
balneal *cleansing* 111.16

baloney [Inf] *nonsense* 192.8, *empty talk* 362.5
baloney! [Inf] *nonsense!* 362.14
balsa Trees and Shrubs 43, *brittle thing* 548.2
balsam Tree Products 43, *medicine* 115.2, *dose of medicine* 115.3, *balm* 115.11, *ointment* 562.8
balsam fir Trees and Shrubs 43
balsamic *medicinal* 115.15, *relieving* 275.7
balsamic vinegar *basic cooking ingredient* 91.8
balsam poplar Trees and Shrubs 43
Balsas Rivers 570
Balt Nicknames for Inhabitants 61
balthazar *bottle* 578.14
Baltic *language family* 5.12
Baltic Black Pied Breeds of Cattle 16
Baltic Sea Oceans and Seas 571
Baluchi Breeds of Sheep 16
baluster Architectural Elements 134, *supporting part* 605.3
balustrade Architectural Elements 134, *enclosing thing* 619.3
Bamako Countries 566
Bambara Breeds of Cattle 16
bambino [Ital] *sacred object* 83.11
Bambocciade Western Art Styles 133
bamboo *grass* 45.1
bamboo pole *fishing tackle* 154.7
bamboozle *deceive* 181.14, *swindle* 193.19, *outtalk* 207.8
bamboozlement *foul play* 193.6
bamboozler *schemer* 193.10
ban *illegality* 53.10, *make illegal* 53.29, *publication* 173.1, *keep secret* 182.11, *curse* 301.1, 301.13, *stop using* 394.10, *exclude* 409.12, 764.7, *command* 425.1, 425.10, *disapproval* 438.1, *withhold approval* 438.17, *exile* 454.24, *be self-restrained* 455.10, *prohibition* 503.1, *prohibit* 503.8, *dissent* 506.2, 506.9, *limit* 620.1, 620.7, *ostracize* 709.17, *set apart* 753.17, *exclusion* 764.1, *restraint* 830.1, *means of restraint* 830.6, *restrain* 830.12, *make impossible* 837.8
ban a book *censor* 503.10
Banach space Mathematical Concepts 4
banal *proverbial* 177.2, *tasteless* 220.4, *boring* 296.6, *meaningless* 362.7, *familiar* 397.10, *mediocre* 742.7
banality *maxim* 177.1, *dilution* 220.2, *boringness* 296.2
banally *boringly* 296.10
banana *yellow thing* 259.4
banana boat Ships and Boats 690
banana bond *chemical bond* 11.6
banana republic [Off] *figurative usage* 44.4, *body politic* 50.3
bananas [Inf] *figurative usage* 44.4, *insane* 110.9
banausic *useful* 393.7
band 754.9; *military organization* 58.4, Collective Names 59, *party* 59.3, *group* 59.8, *team* 59.9, *army unit* 77.14, *neckwear* 100.29, *personnel* 123.16, Architectural Elements 134, *instrumental group* 141.3, *tennis court* 165.3, *stripe* 263.3, *variegate* 263.11, *layer* 588.1, *piece* 590.2, *circular thing* 631.3, *alliance* 735.5, *means of connection* 754.4, *line* 754.5, *collection* 757.3, *social class* 777.5
bandage! *treat* 115.17, *stopper*

584.3, *stop* 584.14, *body support* 605.6, *medical covering* 613.4, *wrap* 613.29, 619.7, *enclosing thing* 619.3, *intertwine* 752.19, *line* 754.5, *connect* 754.13, *cure* 809.15
bandaged *stopped* 584.9, *protected* 613.20, *wrapped* 619.5
bandaging *medical covering* 613.4
Band-Aid™ *medical covering* 613.4, *adhesive* 755.3
bandanna or **bandana** *neckwear* 100.29
Bandar Seri Begawan Countries 566
Banda Sea Oceans and Seas 571
band concert *performance* 141.8
bandeau Heraldic Terms 184
banded *striped* 263.9
Bandeira Mountains and Hills 569
bandelet or **bandlet** Architectural Elements 134
banderole Architectural Elements 134, *flag* 184.8
bandit *criminal* 427.6, *plunderer* 479.9
banditry *plundering* 479.5
bandleader *keeper of time* 646.10
bandmaster *musical director* 141.7
band of cloud *cloud appearance* 9.19
bandoleer *ammunition* 78.11, *accessory* 100.28, *band* 754.9
bandoneon Musical Instruments 142
bandore Musical Instruments 142
band printer *hardcopy device* 15.10
bandsaw *machine tool* 14.9, *woodworking tool* 131.6
band spectrum *emission* 10.56
bandstand *stage* 136.18
band together 59.27; *come together* 757.10, *join with* 827.15
bandurria Musical Instruments 142
bandwidth *computing terms* 15.22
bandy Sporting Activities 145, *exchange* 673.5
bandy about *publish* 173.15
bandy words *quibble* 330.13
bane *lack of hygiene* 112.3, *plague* 114.6, *affliction* 117.1, *hated thing* 300.5, *misfortune* 301.6, *evil thing* 446.2, *evil person* 446.3, *adversity* 848.1
baneful *poisonous* 117.14, *malicious* 306.8, *detrimental* 446.8, *destructive* 523.8
banefully 117.19; *maliciously* 306.15
banefulness *malice* 306.2
bang 234.1, 234.6, *burst of sound* 232.4, *be loud* 232.8, *explosively* 234.8, *blow* 695.5, *collide* 695.10, *hit* 695.11
bang [Inf] Punctuation Marks 5, *drug oneself* 121.37,
banger 234.3; *fire* 246.9
banger [Brit] *sausage* 90.29
banging 234.4; *tumult* 232.5
banging [Inf] *drug use* 121.9
bang in the middle *midway* 772.22
Bangkok Countries 566
Bangladesh Countries 566
bangle *jewelry* 532.6
bang on [Brit inf] *correct* 429.8
bangs *coiffure* 530.8
bangtail [Inf] *racehorse* 159.2
Bangui Countries 566
Bangweulu Lakes 568
banish *exclude* 409.12, *exile* 454.24,

replace 574.17, *ostracize* 709.17, *set apart* 753.17, *eject* 764.8
banished *lonely* 409.8, *replaced* 574.10
banishment *separation* 409.3, *exile* 454.3, *replacement* 574.3, *ostracism* 709.3, *ejection* 764.2
banjo Musical Instruments 142
banjolin Musical Instruments 142
banjo player *player* 141.2
Banjul Countries 566
bank 484.26, 487.4; *assemble* 59.23, *storehouse* 105.8, *deposit* 105.21, *green bowling* 151.3, *lending institution* 475.4, *treasury* 484.19, *river parts* 570.3, *island* 572.2, *be oblique* 607.10, *edge* 618.1, *side* 623.1, *angle* 628.11, *place of exchange* 673.2, *flight maneuver* 689.6, *maneuver* 689.14
bank account *personal finance* 457.5, *funds* 484.6
bank-account number *personal identification* 184.4
bank annuities *funds* 484.6
bankbook *account book* 493.3
bank card *credit card* 487.2, *debt* 488.1
bank deposit *deposit* 487.3
bank down the fires *mitigate* 521.9
banked *saved* 105.15, *racing* 146.9
banked circuit *automobile racing terms* 146.3
banked corner *automobile racing terms* 146.3
banker *financial adviser* 457.4, *lender* 475.3, *merchant* 482.10, *treasurer* 484.18
banker and broker Card Games 168
banker's credit *credit* 487.1
bank failure *insolvency* 490.5
banking *finance* 457.1, *flight maneuver* 689.6
bank loan *loan* 475.2, 476.5, 488.3
bank manager *lender* 475.3
bank note *paper money* 484.14
bank of cloud *cloud appearance* 9.19
Bank of England [Brit] *treasury* 484.19
bank on *believe* 87.9, *hope* 281.10, *predict* 356.7
bank rate *finance* 457.1, *currency market* 484.8, *interest* 488.4
bank robber *lawbreaker* 53.15, *thief* 479.8
bankroll [Inf] *finance* 457.7, *defray* 481.18, *donate* 491.13, *financial support* 605.8, *support financially* 605.19
bankroller [Inf] *provider* 605.10
bankrupt *loser* 468.8, 846.9, *unprofitable* 468.10, *poor person* 486.6, *indebted* 486.9, *impoverish* 486.6, *debtor* 488.6, *nonpayer* 490.6, *nonpaying* 490.7, *destroyed* 523.9, *destroy* 523.10, *closed* 637.6, *defeat* 845.17, *failed* 846.10, *person in adversity* 848.9, *unprosperous* 848.11
bankruptcy *incompleteness* 98.2, *financial loss* 468.4, *insolvency* 486.2, 490.5, 846.6, *ruin* 523.4, *closure* 637.4, *unsuccessful thing* 846.8, *economic adversity* 848.6
bankruptcy court *type of court* 54.9, *insolvency* 490.5
bankruptcy proceedings *insolvency* 490.5
bank shot *playing terms* 148.4, *billiards play* 149.2

banksia Trees and Shrubs 43
bank statement *document* 170.3, *record* 185.1, *receipt* 492.1, *statement* 493.2
bank vault *hiding place* 181.2, *safe* 464.4
banned *cursed* 301.8, *lonely* 409.8, *commanding* 425.7, *disapproved* 438.9, *prohibited* 503.5, *censored* 503.7, *dissenting* 506.6, *excluded* 764.6, *restrained* 830.9, *forbidden* 837.7
banned book *censorship* 503.4
banner *advertisement* 173.9, *sign* 183.1, *flag* 184.8, *excellent* 744.14
banneret or **bannerette** *flag* 184.8
banners *salute* 405.7
banning *exile* 454.3, *ostracism* 709.3
banns *betrothal* 458.2
ban on testing *disarmament* 74.3
banquet *feast* 92.9, *have a meal* 92.25, *rejoicing* 279.1, *rejoice* 279.5, *celebration* 405.1, *party* 408.6
banqueter *eater* 92.15
banquet or **banqueting hall** *eating place* 92.17
banqueting *eating meals* 92.4
banquette *fort* 419.13
banshee Legendary Creatures 360
bantam *livestock* 16.11, *little person* 580.5, *undersized* 580.8
bantamweight *boxing weight divisions* 152.6, *combat* 152.17, *light* 539.4
banter *chat* 210.2, *wit* 277.3, *be humorous* 277.11, *derision* 369.1, *taunt* 436.6, *exchange* 673.1, 673.5
bantering *derisive* 369.5
banteringly *derisively* 369.8
ban-the-bomb movement *peace movement* 74.4
banyan Trees and Shrubs 43
baobab Trees and Shrubs 43
Baoule Breeds of Cattle 16
baptism 85.6; *Christian rite* 85.5, *religious cleansing* 111.3, *nomenclature* 202.7, *ceremony* 405.3, *reception* 473.4, *holy water* 557.15, *bringing in* 708.4, *immersion* 710.3, *enrollment* 771.8
baptismal *ritualistic* 85.15, *precursory* 769.12, *introductory* 771.23
baptismal name *name* 202.8
Baptist churches Christian Groups 81
baptistery or **baptistry** *baptism* 85.6, *church architecture* 134.11
baptize *proselytize* 84.15, *perform rites* 85.18, *introduce* 708.16, *immerse* 710.10, *enroll* 771.33
baptized *immersed* 710.7, *enrolled* 771.24
baptizement *baptism* 85.6
baptizing *nomenclature* 202.7
bar *courtroom* 54.12, *drink provider* 93.15, *written music* 140.21, Heraldic Terms 184, *insignia* 184.5, *stripe* 263.3, *variegate* 263.11, *disapproval* 438.1, *withhold approval* 438.17, *bullion* 484.16, *island* 572.2, *obstruction* 584.2, *obstruct* 584.13, General Units 589, *piece* 590.2, *passage* 692.1, *gradation* 739.3, *by subtraction* 749.8, *set apart* 753.17, *fastener* 754.7, *particle* 760.4, *exclusion* 764.1, *exclude* 764.7, *exclusively* 764.10, *safety device* 810.15, *obstacle* 826.2, *block*

826.17, *withstand* 828.20, *restraint* 830.1, *restrain* 830.12, *make impossible* 837.8

barathea Fabrics and Fibers 130

Barb Horse and Pony Breeds 159

barb Historical Missile Weapons 78, *taunt* 436.6, *rough thing* 544.2, *sharp-pointed thing* 549.4, *sharpen* 549.16

barb [Inf] *sedatives* 121.19

Barbados Breeds of Sheep 16, Countries 566, Islands 572

Barbados Blackbelly Breeds of Sheep 16

barbarian *discourteous person* 411.4, *bad-mannered* 411.6, *destroyer* 523.6, *vulgar person* 535.4, *foreign* 724.9

barbarians *primitive humanity* 18.4

barbaric *worded* 5.38, *cruel* 306.10, *indecorous* 528.8, *discourteous* 535.7, *foreign* 724.9

barbarically *cruelly* 306.17

barbaric art Western Art Styles 133

barbarism *nonstandard language* 5.7, *cruelty* 306.4, *language error* 351.10, *vulgarity* 535.1, *moral deterioration* 808.3

barbarity *cruelty* 306.4, *violence by person* 520.2

barbarize *pervert* 808.22

barbarous *worded* 5.38, *murderous* 520.7, *indecorous* 528.8, *vulgar* 535.6

barbarously *pitilessly* 309.7

barbarousness *pitilessness* 309.1

barbecue *cooking place* 91.4, *cooker* 91.5, *cook* 91.10, *feast* 92.9, *party* 408.6

barbecued *culinary* 91.9

barbecue pit *burner* 217.4

barbecue sauce *sauce* 90.17

barbecuing *cooking technique* 91.2

barbed 544.7; *spiked* 549.11

barbed wire *farm building* 16.4, *rough thing* 544.2, *sharp-pointed thing* 549.4, *barrier* 826.7

barbellate *barbed* 544.7

barber *personal attendant* 69.5, *cleaner* 111.12, *hairdressing salon* 530.10, *beautician* 530.11, *depilation* 614.8

barbering *hairdressing* 530.7

Barber paradox *philosophical problem* 4.8

barberry Herbs and Spices 91

barbershop *hairdressing salon* 530.10

barbershop quartet *singing group* 141.6

barbette *fort* 419.13

barbican *fort* 419.13

barbicel *plumage* 36.7

barbiturate *anesthetic* 213.3, *soporific* 415.6, *moderator* 521.2

barbiturates *sedatives* 121.19

Barbizon school Western Art Styles 133

Barbuda Islands 572

barbule *plumage* 36.7

barcarole *song* 140.11

barchan *dune* 8.43

bar chart *graph* 6.30, *chart* 767.8

bar code *variegated thing* 263.5

bar-code reader *input device* 15.11

bard *author* 139.13, *singer* 141.4

Bardoka Breeds of Sheep 16

bare *infertile* 23.7, *unprovided* 98.6, *disclose* 180.8, *simple* 195.10, *526.7, *desert* 560.12, *vacant* 576.12, *opened up* 583.11, *naked* 614.12, *uncover* 614.17, *undress*

614.18, *vulnerable* 811.9, *open* 843.12

bareass or **bareassed** [Inf] *naked* 614.12

barebacked *uncovered* 614.10

bareback rider *circus performer* 138.9, *horse person* 159.14

bare bones *outline* 617.1

bare-bottomed *uncovered* 614.10

bare-breasted *uncovered* 614.10

bare-chested *uncovered* 614.10

bare cupboard *scarcity* 90.5, *short rations* 118.3, *insolvency* 486.2

bared *uncovered* 614.10

bare essentials *outline* 617.1

barefaced *insolent* 400.8, *uncovered* 614.10, *open* 843.12

barefaced effrontery *defiance* 416.1

barefaced liar *liar* 192.10

barefaced lie *falsehood* 192.6

barefacedly *insolently* 400.18

barefaced lying *lying* 192.5

barefacedness *openness* 843.6

barefoot *beggarly* 486.12

barefoot or **barefooted** *uncovered* 614.10

barehanded *uncovered* 614.10

bareheaded *showing respect* 435.7, *uncovered* 614.10

barelegged *uncovered* 614.10

barely 593.18; *revealingly* 614.22, *to a degree* 739.11, *sparsely* 796.11, *imperfectly* 806.10

barely audible *faint* 233.6

barely heard *faint* 233.6

barely move *move slowly* 693.11, *hesitate* 693.12

barely pass *be imperfect* 806.8

barely sufficient *sufficient* 97.3

bare minimum *sufficiency* 97.1

bare-necked *uncovered* 614.10

bareness 614.3; *simplicity* 195.4, 526.1, *emptiness* 576.2, *openness* 843.6

Barents Sea Oceans and Seas 571

bare one's fangs *hate* 300.11, *be irritable* 304.14

bare one's soul *admit* 180.11

bare one's teeth *be irritable* 304.14, *defy* 416.7

bare subsistence *incompleteness* 98.2, *short rations* 118.3

barf [Inf] *vomit* 709.27

barfing [Inf] *vomiting* 709.7

barfly [Inf] *drunkard* 121.8

Barfoed's test *sugar test* 12.6

bargain 480.20, 481.14, 495.2, 497.4, 497.10; *unionize* 57.21, *confer* 210.13, *deal* 457.9, *contract* 459.8, 462.2, 462.11, *negotiate* 460.6, *compromise* 461.1, *bargaining* 480.10, *purchase* 481.1, *discounted* 495.3, *settlement* 735.6, *settle* 735.26, *mediate* 772.19

bargain basement *store* 483.8, *discounter* 497.7

bargain-basement *bargain* 497.10

bargain bin *discounter* 497.7

bargain collectively *unionize* 57.21

bargained *disputed* 57.15

bargainer *purchaser* 481.7

bargain for *predict* 356.7

bargain hunter 497.8; *purchaser* 481.7

bargaining 57.9, 480.10; *debate* 210.3, *negotiation* 460.1, *buying* 481.9

bargaining session *discussion* 460.3

bargaining terms 57.10

bargain price *bargain* 495.2, *cheapness* 497.1

bargain sale *sale* 482.2, *bargain* 495.2

barge *convey* 685.9, Ships and Boats 690

bargeboard Architectural Elements 134

barge in *invade* 706.12, *transgress* 712.14

barge in on *interrupt* 775.14

bargeman *nautical person* 690.12

bar graph *graph* 6.30, *map* 387.7

Bargur Breeds of Cattle 16

barhop [Inf] *get drunk* 121.35

baring *uncovering* 614.1

baritone *voice* 141.5, Musical Instruments 142, *deepness* 236.3, *musical part* 760.8

barium Chemical Elements and Common Allotropes 11

barium enema *diagnostic radiology* 107.12

barium swallow *diagnostic radiology* 107.12

bark *timber* 43.3, *speak in a particular way* 205.18, *animal sound* 240.1, *animal sound* 240.7, *be angry* 302.19, *abrade* 554.13, *coat* 588.3, *casing* 613.9, Sailing Ships and Boats 690

barkeeper or **barkeep** *attendant* 69.4

barkentine Sailing Ships and Boats 690

barker *circus performer* 138.9, *publicizer* 173.11, *crier* 239.8, *displayer* 843.7

barketta Sailing Ships and Boats 690

Barkhausen effect Classical Physical Laws 10

Barki Breeds of Sheep 16

barking *ululant* 240.4

bark up the wrong tree *be in error* 351.15

barley *crop* 16.8, *animal feed* 16.12, *cereal grass* 45.4, *animal food* 90.2

barleycorn General Units 589

barleycorn lead *fishing tackle* 154.7

barm *leavening* 539.3

bar magnet *magnet* 10.47, 700.3

barmaid *attendant* 69.4, *drink provider* 93.15

barman *drink provider* 93.15

bar mitzvah *non-Christian ritual* 85.8, *ceremony* 405.3

barn *farm building* 16.4, *cage* 60.15, *storehouse* 105.8, Scientific and Technical Units 589, *shelter* 812.4

barnacle *crustacean* 39.10, *sponger* 401.4, *adherent* 755.4

barn dance *dance* 135.1, *party* 408.6

barnlot *farm building* 16.4

barn owl *bird of prey* 36.11

barnstormer *actor* 136.25

barnstorming *engagement* 136.15

barnyard *farm building* 16.4

bar of justice *place of judgment* 341.3

barograph *weather instrument* 9.7

barographic *barometric* 9.39

barometer *weather instrument* 9.7, *indicator* 183.7, Fields of Measurement 589

barometer/altimeter *climbing equipment* 161.4

barometric 9.39

barometry Fields of Measurement 589

baron *nobleman* 70.1, *wealthy person* 485.6

baronet *nobleman* 70.1

baronetcy *aristocracy* 70.2

baronial *aristocratic* 70.4

barony *aristocracy* 70.2

barophobia Phobias 283

baroque Furniture Styles 101, Western Art Styles 133, Architectural Styles 134, *ornate* 532.10

Barotse Breeds of Cattle 16

barque Sailing Ships and Boats 690

barquentine Sailing Ships and Boats 690

barracks *military affairs* 58.1

barracuda *game fish* 154.10

barrage *combined attack* 418.5, *dam* 551.12, *water system* 551.13

barrage balloon *lifter* 715.5

barred *striped* 263.9, *disapproved* 438.9, *prohibited* 503.5, *obstructed* 584.8, *excluded* 764.6, *blocked* 826.13, *forbidden* 837.7

barred spiral galaxy *galaxy* 7.5

barrel Collective Names 59, *type of chair* 101.4, *roof* 134.7, *vault* 134.8, *vessel* 578.11, General Units 589, *profuseness* 795.3

barrel along [Inf] *be swift* 694.10, *make haste* 818.5

barrel-chested *thick* 594.5

barrel(ful) *container(ful)* 738.2

barreling along [Inf] *swiftness* 694.1, *speeding* 694.7

barrel knot Knots, Bends, Hitches, Splices 754

barrel organ Musical Instruments 142

barrel printer *hardcopy device* 15.10

barrel roll *flight maneuver* 689.6

barren *infertile* 23.7, Collective Names 59, *desolate* 96.13, *desert* 560.12, 572.10, *of landmasses* 572.12, *vacant* 576.12, *futile* 802.10

barren cow *livestock* 16.11

barren land *desert* 560.4

barrenness *infertility* 23.1, *emptiness* 576.2, *futility* 802.3, *failure* 846.1

barren waste *infertile land* 23.2

barrette *hairdressing tool* 530.9, *jewelry* 532.6, *fastener* 754.7

barricade *barrier* 419.10, *fence* 419.21, *obstruction* 584.2, *obstruct* 584.13, *separator* 753.5, *fortification* 812.3

barricaded *defended* 419.18

barrier 419.10, 826.7; *hurdles* 166.6, *obstruction* 510.3, 584.2, *enclosing thing* 619.3, *separator* 753.5, *obstacle* 837.3

barrier board *hockey areas* 158.2

barrier contraceptive *contraceptive* 23.6

barrier island *coast* 8.13

barrier method contraception *barrier* 826.7

barrier reef *coast* 8.13

barring *by subtraction* 749.8, *exclusively* 764.10

barrio *urban area* 567.10

barrister [Brit] *lawyer* 54.5, *agent* 80.3

Barroso Breeds of Cattle 16

Barrow Rivers 570

barrow *livestock* 16.11, *burial place* 31.7, *monument* 185.10, *hill* 569.2, *cart* 578.9, *dome* 634.4, *thing of the past* 651.8, *wagon* 687.5

barrow [Brit] *stall* 483.9
bar sinister *Heraldic Terms* 184
barspoon *bait* 154.6
barstool *type of chair* 101.4
bartender *attendant* 69.4, *drink provider* 93.15
barter *trade* 56.12, 480.1, 480.18, *deal* 457.9, *negotiation* 460.1, *negotiate* 460.6, *transfer of property* 470.4, *transfer property* 470.12, *bargain* 481.14, *selling* 482.1, *sell* 482.15, *pay* 489.16, *exchange* 673.1, 673.5, *transfer* 685.1, 685.8, *reciprocity* 729.1, *reciprocate* 729.7, *equalization* 740.4
bartered *exchanged* 673.4, *reciprocal* 729.4
barterer *trader* 480.11
bartering *negotiation* 460.1, *reciprocity* 729.1
bar the entrance *shelter* 812.8
bartizan *fort* 419.13
barye *Scientific and Technical Units* 589
baryon *elementary particle* 10.53
baryton *Musical Instruments* 142
basal *base* 601.7, *basic* 601.8, *foundational* 605.12
basally *basically* 601.14, 605.21
basaltes *Ceramics* 129
basaltic *chalky* 8.59
basaltware *Ceramics* 129
bascule bridge *bridge* 551.10
base 11.11, 601.1, 601.7, 601.10; *number system* 6.7, *logarithm* 6.17, *triangle* 6.41, *tree part* 43.5, *military affairs* 58.1, *habitat* 60.1, *home* 60.3, *armed force* 77.10, *Heraldic Terms* 184, *dastardly* 285.6, *immoral* 432.9, *disregardful* 436.11, *evil* 446.7, *depraved* 448.10, *shoddy* 497.11, *unpleasant* 501.5, *cosmetics* 530.4, *ribald* 535.8, *location* 565.1, *locate* 565.9, *lowest point* 597.5, *lowered* 597.18, *foundation* 601.2, *support* 605.1, *supporting structure* 605.2, *place of departure* 705.4, *inferior state* 745.3, *inferior* 745.5, *insignificant* 745.6
baseball 147.1, *Sporting Activities* 145, *baseball equipment* 147.4, *athletics* 422.7
baseball bat *blunt weapon* 78.5, *impeller* 695.7
baseball cap *cap* 100.33
baseball equipment 147.4
baseball field 147.3
baseball leagues and championship games 147.8
baseball player *baseball team* 147.2
baseball season *seasons* 654.2
baseball shoes *baseball equipment* 147.4
baseball stadium *baseball field* 147.3
baseball team 147.2
baseball uniform *baseball equipment* 147.4
baseboard *foundation* 601.2
base camp *climbing expedition* 161.2
basecoat *cosmetics* 530.4, *base* 601.1
base coin *false money* 484.15
based 601.9; *focused* 328.6, *circumstantial* 573.7
baseless *sophistic* 330.7
baseline 601.4; *basketball court* 148.3, *tennis court* 165.3
basely 745.16; *deviously* 371.9, *unvirtuously* 448.16
basement *room* 60.9, *storeroom*

105.7, *base* 601.1, *supporting structure* 605.2
basement price *fee* 494.3, *bargain* 495.2
baseness *dastardliness* 285.2, *immorality* 432.1, *evil* 446.1, *depravity* 448.2, *shoddiness* 497.3, *unpleasantness* 501.2, *tawdriness* 535.2, *inferiority* 745.1
Basenji *Breeds of Dogs* 35
base on balls *pitching terms* 147.5
baseplate *foundation* 601.2
base runner *baseball team* 147.2
base-spirited *dastardly* 285.6
base troops *armed force* 77.10
base unit *unit of measurement* 589.5
bash *harm* 306.13, *blow* 695.5, *collide* 695.10, *hit* 695.11
bash [Inf] *social gathering* 59.7, *party* 408.6
bashful *unenthusiastic* 375.10, *shy* 403.8, 409.7
bashfully *shyly* 403.16, *unsociably* 409.13
bashfulness *dissociation* 375.4, *shyness* 403.3, 409.2
bashing *ramming* 695.3
Bashkirsky pony *Horse and Pony Breeds* 159
BASIC *Programming Languages* 15
basic 601.8, 605.13; *universal* 6.67, *acid* 11.27, *material* 104.8, *focused* 328.6, *simple* 526.7, *causal* 675.7, *intrinsic* 717.12, 723.6, *truistic* 721.15, *precursory* 769.12, *rudimentary* 771.22, *essential* 799.10
basically 601.14, 605.21; *mathematically* 6.93, *thematically* 328.14, *simply* 526.14, *intrinsically* 611.20, 721.30, *causally* 675.12, *really* 717.22, *at heart* 723.14
basic cooking ingredient 91.8
basic dye *dye* 130.8
basic English *native language* 5.5
basic fact(s) *fact* 717.6
basic materials *materials* 104.1, *matter* 524.4
basic rock *igneous rock* 8.32
basics *supplies* 102.3, *materials* 104.1, *fact* 717.6, *realities* 719.5, *rudiments* 771.7, *specifications* 779.6, *chief thing* 799.7
basic salary *reward for service* 453.5
basic salt *salt* 11.12
basic slag *fertilizer* 16.9
basic substance *physical element* 524.5
basic supplies *supplies* 102.3
basic truth *the truth* 721.3, *truism* 721.6
basidiocarp *fungal body* 47.4
basidiomycetes *fungi* 47.3
Basidiomycota *fungi* 47.3
basidiospore *fungal body* 47.4
basidium *fungal body* 47.4
basidomycetous *of fungi* 47.19
basil *Herbs and Spices* 91
basilar *or* basilary *base* 601.7
basilica *place of worship* 83.8, *church architecture* 134.11
basilisk *lizard* 37.5, *Legendary Creatures* 360
basin 578.12; *moon* 7.18, *landform* 8.9, *bath* 111.6, *cavity* 635.3
basin and ewer *bath* 111.6
basin and pitcher *bath* 111.6
basin and range *fault* 8.21, *mountain building* 8.23
basinet *historic armor* 419.8

Basin Street jazz *jazz* 140.5
basiphobia *Phobias* 283
basis 601.3, 605.4; *motive* 178.5, *explanation* 319.4, *topic* 328.1, *preparations* 388.2, *circumstances* 573.2, *reason* 675.4, *essential content* 723.2
basis for belief *evidence* 339.1
basis for negotiations 460.2
basis of supposition 359.2
bask *Collective Names* 59, *feel pleasure* 214.12, *feel hot* 217.19
basket 578.6; *arch* 134.5, *basketball court* 148.3, *ski equipment* 162.10
basketball 148.1; *Sporting Activities* 145, *athletics* 422.7
basketball associations and tournaments 148.6
basketball court 148.3
basketball game *basketball* 148.1
Basketball Hall of Fame *basketball* 148.1
basketball team 148.2
basket flower *Flowers* 42
basket(ful) *container(ful)* 738.2
basket making *or* basketry *Hobbies and Pastimes* 167
basket-of-gold *Flowers* 42
bask in *feel pleasure* 214.12
basmati *rice* 90.32
basmati rice *notable international dishes* 90.8
bas mitzvah *non-Christian ritual* 85.8
basophil *blood* 555.4
Basque pony *Horse and Pony Breeds* 159
bas-relief *relief carving* 144.2
bas-relief *or* basso-relievo *Architectural Elements* 134
bass *Collective Names* 59, *food fish and shellfish* 90.20, *voice* 141.5, *game fish* 154.10, *sound quality* 230.4, *deepness* 236.3, *musical part* 760.8
bassa *Musical Terms and Expression Marks* 140
bassanello *Musical Instruments* 142
bass-baritone *deepness* 236.3
bass clarinet *Musical Instruments* 142
bass clef *written music* 140.21
bass drum *Musical Instruments* 142
Basseterre *Countries* 566
basset horn *Musical Instruments* 142
basset hound *Breeds of Dogs* 35
bass fiddle *Musical Instruments* 142
bass horn *Musical Instruments* 142
bassinet *type of bed* 101.9, *basket* 578.6
bassist *player* 141.2
bass note *deepness* 236.3
basso *voice* 141.5, *deepness* 236.3
bass oboe *Musical Instruments* 142
basso cantante *voice* 141.5
basso continuo *harmonic element* 140.14
bassoon *Musical Instruments* 142
bassoonist *player* 141.2
basso profundo *voice* 141.5, *deepness* 236.3
basso-relievo *relief carving* 144.2
bass player *player* 141.2
bass viol *Musical Instruments* 142
basswood *Trees and Shrubs* 43
Bast *Deities* 82
bast *line* 754.5

bastard *family member* 65.2
bastard [Inf] *miscreant* 448.6
bastardize *make illegal* 53.29
bastard title *book part* 174.5
bastard wing *plumage* 36.7
baste *cook* 91.10, *sew* 130.18, *lubricate* 562.15, *beat* 695.12, *intertwine* 752.19
basted *lubricated* 562.14
baster *cooking equipment* 91.6
bastille *prison* 55.1
bastinado *corporal punishment* 454.11, *hit* 454.28
basting *sewing* 130.5, *fastener* 754.7
bastion *fort* 419.13, *protection* 810.2, *fortification* 812.3
Basuto pony *Horse and Pony Breeds* 159
bat *baseball equipment* 147.4, *touch* 216.9, *impeller* 695.7, *hit* 695.11
bata *Musical Instruments* 142
Batak pony *Horse and Pony Breeds* 159
batch *assemblage* 59.13, *group* 59.24, *certain amount* 738.3
batch processes *systems and process control* 14.28
batch processing *computing terms* 15.22
bat ear *ear* 228.2
bateau *Ships and Boats* 690
bated *nonresonant* 233.7
bated breath *undercurrent of sound* 233.3
bath 111.6; *privacy* 181.6, *immersion* 710.3
bathe 111.18
bathed *wet* 557.23
bathed in sweat *sweaty* 25.17
bathetic *sensitive* 267.3, *ridiculous* 368.5
bathhouse *swimming equipment* 164.8
bathing *ablutions* 111.4, *Phobias* 283, *washing* 557.11
bathing [Brit] *swimming* 164.12
bathing cap *swimming equipment* 164.8
bathing suit *beachwear* 100.23, *swimming equipment* 164.8
bath mat *floor covering* 613.13
batholith *igneous rock* 8.32
bathometer *Fields of Measurement* 589, *bathymetry* 598.3
bathophobia *Phobias* 283
bathos *emotionalism* 266.6, *ridiculousness* 368.1
bathrobe *robe* 100.20
bathroom *place for excretion* 25.11, *room* 60.9, *bath* 111.6
baths *bath* 111.6
Bathsheba *Famous Lovers* 299
bath sponge *sponge* 39.16
bath towel *cleaning cloth* 111.11
bathtub *bath* 111.6, *basin* 578.12
Bathurst Island *Islands* 572
bathyal *deep-sea* 598.11
bathyal waters *ocean* 8.14
bathymal *oceanic* 8.53
bathymeter *Fields of Measurement* 589
bathymetric 598.12; *geophysical* 8.51, *oceanographical* 571.8
bathymetrically *geologically* 8.68, *oceanographically* 571.11
bathymetrics *ocean* 8.14
bathymetry 598.3; *oceanography* 571.5, *Fields of Measurement* 589
bathypelagic *deep-sea* 598.11
bathyscaphe *oceanography* 571.5, *bathymetry* 598.3

bathysphere *oceanography* 571.5, *bathymetry* 598.3, *descender* 714.8
bathythermograph *oceanography* 571.5
batik *dyeing* 130.9, *craft* 133.2, Hobbies and Pastimes 167
batiste Fabrics and Fibers 130
batman [Brit] *attendant* 69.4
bat *or* **bas mitzvah** *non-Christian ritual* 85.8, *ceremony* 405.3
baton *blunt weapon* 78.5, *instrumental aid* 142.7, *relay racing* 166.5, Heraldic Terms 184, *insignia* 184.5
baton change *or* **changing** *relay racing* 166.5
Baton Rouge American States 564
batophobia Phobias 283
batrachian *amphibian* 37.10, 37.14
batrachophobia Phobias 283
bats [Inf] *insane* 110.9
battalion *military organization* 58.4, *force* 59.10, *army unit* 77.14
batten *stage set* 136.19, *fastener* 754.7, *bind* 754.14
batten down *close* 584.12
batten down the hatches *prepare for action* 388.18, *economize* 499.6, *close* 584.12, *make stable* 674.7, *shelter* 812.8
battened *bound* 754.12
battening down the hatches *preparation* 388.1
batten on *eat well* 92.23, *follow* 401.14
battens *stage lighting* 136.20, *sailboat parts and accessories* 150.4
batter *baseball team* 147.2, *inflict pain* 215.10, *harm* 306.13, *ill-use* 395.7, *demolish* 523.12, *semiliquid* 561.7, *beat* 695.12, *be superior* 744.15
battered *ill-used* 395.4, *worn* 808.13
batterer *criminal* 427.6
battering *violence by person* 520.2
battering ram *blunt weapon* 78.5, *agent of destruction* 523.7, *impeller* 695.7
batter's box *baseball field* 147.3
battery *electrical conduction* 10.33, *electrochemistry* 11.19, *military organization* 58.4, *army unit* 77.14, *guns* 78.9, *electricity* 106.5, *baseball team* 147.2, *malignity* 306.5, *ill-use* 395.2, *power supplier* 514.14
battery hen *or* **chicken** *livestock* 16.11
battery radio *radio* 172.1
battiness [Inf] *insanity* 110.1
batting average *batting terms* 147.6
batting champion *baseball team* 147.2
batting coach *baseball team* 147.2
batting glove *baseball equipment* 147.4
batting helmet *baseball equipment* 147.4
batting terms 147.6
battle 76.23, 76.33; *slaughter* 30.5, *oppose* 63.11, *exertion* 122.4, *exert oneself* 122.11, *action* 412.1, *contention* 422.1, *warfare* 422.10, *contend* 422.22, *conflict* 828.3
battle-ax *sharp weapon* 78.6
battle-ax [Inf] *irascible person* 303.7
battle call *glory of war* 76.17
battle cruiser *warship* 77.21

battle cry *glory of war* 76.17, *military call* 183.9, *cry* 239.1, *act of defiance* 416.3
battledore *badminton terms* 165.11
battle dress *uniform* 100.9, *formal clothing* 406.5
battle fatigue *mental breakdown* 110.4, *fatigue* 820.1
battlefield *slaughterhouse* 30.16, *battleground* 76.24, *field of battle* 422.11
battlefield knowledge *art of war* 76.16
battlefront *field of battle* 422.11, *interface* 616.1, *vanguard* 621.5
battleground 76.24; *slaughterhouse* 30.16, *field of battle* 422.11
battle-hungry *warlike* 76.27
battle jacket *jacket* 100.18
battlemaid *former servicewoman* 77.6
battlement *fort* 419.13, *notched thing* 636.2, *fortification* 812.3
battle orders *word of command* 76.20
battle painting *type of painting* 143.5
battle plan *military affairs* 58.1, *art of war* 76.16
battle plane *military aircraft* 77.30
battler *combatant* 77.1
battle royal *battle* 76.23, *warfare* 422.10
battles *warfare* 76.3
battle-scarred *military* 76.28
battle scene *play part* 136.8
battleship *warship* 77.21, Ships and Boats 690
Battleship™ Board and Table Games 167
battle yell *glory of war* 76.17
battle zone *battleground* 76.24
battling *warring* 76.26, *contending* 422.19
battue *slaughter* 30.5, *hunt* 385.3
batty [Inf] *insane* 110.9
bauble *toy* 167.9, *cheap item* 497.5, *decorative article* 532.5, *cheap thing* 800.7
baud Scientific and Technical Units 589
baud rate *computing terms* 15.22
Bauhaus Furniture Styles 101, Western Art Styles 133, Architectural Styles 134
Baumé scale *scale* 589.9
Baure-Campan Breeds of Sheep 16
Bavarian Warmblood Horse and Pony Breeds 159
bawdily *bluely* 261.11, *profanely* 301.19, *immorally* 432.18, *ribaldly* 535.12
bawdiness *profanity* 301.3, *immorality* 432.1
bawdry [Arch] *immorality* 432.1
bawdy *indecent* 261.8, *profane* 301.10, *offensive* 432.11, *ribald* 535.8
bawdyhouse *brothel* 432.5
bawdy verse *profanity* 301.3
bawl *speak in a particular way* 205.18, *be loud* 232.8, *harsh sound* 238.1, *be strident* 238.7, *cry* 239.1, 239.16, *cry of sorrow* 239.6, *cry out* 239.13, *weep* 280.8
bawled out [Inf] *criticized* 438.14
bawler *crier* 239.8
bawling *tumult* 232.5, *lamentation* 280.1
bawling out [Inf] *berating* 438.5
bawl out [Inf] *hiss* 239.17, *berate* 438.20

Bay, Laguna de Lakes 568
bay *window* 134.10, *horse by color* 159.7, *animal sound* 240.1, *make an animal sound* 240.7, *brown* 256.5, *inlet* 572.9, *compartment* 578.2, *railroad station* 688.6, *nautical* 690.14
bay *or* **bay tree** Trees and Shrubs 43
bayadere *dancer* 135.4
Bayard Notable Horses 159
Bayard-Alpert gauge *surface chemistry* 11.20
bayberry Trees and Shrubs 43
Bayes's theorem Mathematical Concepts 6
Bay Islands Islands 572
bay leaf Herbs and Spices 91
bay leaf garland Architectural Elements 134
bayonet *murder* 30.20, *sharp weapon* 78.6, *stab* 418.22, *sharp-pointed thing* 549.4, *opener* 583.2, *hole* 583.17
bayoneted *holed* 583.12
bayonet-fence *fence* 153.7
bayonet fencing *fencing* 153.1
bayoneting *hit* 418.9
bayou *small lake* 568.2, *tributary* 570.2, *marsh* 572.3, *inlet* 572.9
bayous *regions of the United States* 564.7
bay rum tree Trees and Shrubs 43
bays *insignia* 184.5
bay window [Inf] *fat* 579.8
bazaar 483.10; *sale* 482.2
Bazas Breeds of Cattle 16
bazooka *modern missile weapon* 78.4, *guns* 78.9
B blood group *blood* 555.4
BC *one day* 639.20
BCE *one day* 639.20
BCPL Programming Languages 15
be *live* 28.17, *appear* 264.12, *be situated* 573.9, *be present* 575.13, 647.7, *exist* 717.18, *be real* 721.21
be a bestseller *be sold* 482.22
be abject *be servile* 401.8
be able *find means* 102.6, *qualify* 340.11, *be powerful* 514.18
be able to take it *or* **leave it** *be incurious* 322.5
be a botanist *study plants* 41.23
be about right *be average* 742.8
be about to *intend* 650.10
be a breadwinner *work* 122.8
be abrupt *be short* 591.10
be absent 576.14; *not exist* 786.6
be absent-minded *lack thought* 318.12
be absent without leave (AWOL) *run away* 386.21, *abscond* 576.16
be absorbed *be the same* 730.13
be abstinent *be continent* 67.10
be accountable *have a sense of duty* 433.13
be accurate 350.5, 721.22
be accused 442.10
beach *coast* 8.13, 572.4, *swimming place* 164.9, *open space* 583.6, *edge* 618.1, *edging* 618.5, *land* 704.16
beach-casting *saltwater fishing* 154.3
beachcomber *collector* 59.17, *cleaner* 111.12, *nonentity* 800.8
beachcombing Hobbies and Pastimes 167
beach flea *crustacean* 39.10, *parasite* 39.18
beachhead *battleground* 76.24
beaching *animal killing* 30.10

beach umbrella *shade maker* 247.4
beach volleyball Sporting Activities 145
beachwear 100.23
beacon *signal* 183.6, *safety light* 246.7, *fire* 246.9, *warning signal* 814.3
beacon fire *fire* 217.8
be a coward 285.7
be acquitted *acquit* 54.32
be active 414.18
be active in 412.17
bead Architectural Elements 134, *round thing* 633.3
bead and reel Architectural Elements 134
be adaptable 546.9
beading *decorative method* 532.3
be adjacent *interface* 616.5
beadledom *officialdom* 49.20, *governance* 52.6, *overactivity* 414.9
be admitted *enter* 706.11
beadsman *religious* 84.9
beads of sweat *sweat* 25.8
bead tree Trees and Shrubs 43
beadwork *decorative method* 532.3
be affected 367.4
be afflicted *be miserable* 117.17, *feel pain* 215.8
be a fly on the wall *be informed* 170.15
be a founding member *inaugurate* 771.31
be afraid 283.14
be afraid of *be afraid* 283.14
be after *aim at* 385.15
be against 828.17
be agitated 684.21
beagle Breeds of Dogs 35
be agnostic *not accept* 190.19
be a go-between *mediate* 75.6
be a good citizen *philanthropize* 307.8
be a good mixer *participate* 408.15
be ahead 744.17; *have an advantage* 618.10
be ahead of *be in front* 621.13
be airborne *maneuver* 689.14
beak *avian characteristic* 36.6, *protuberance* 634.3
beak [Inf] *nose* 19.11
beaked *protuberant* 634.6
beaker *drinking vessel* 578.13
beakhead Architectural Elements 134
beaky *protuberant* 634.6
be alert *push* 414.20
be alive *live* 28.17
be alive to *sense* 212.9
be-all and end-all *final intention* 374.4, *superiority* 744.1, *all* 759.4, *gist* 799.4
be all ears [Inf] *hear* 228.13
be all eyes *look* 242.21
be all heart *be sensitive* 267.5
be all present and correct *appear* 575.16
be all the rage *be an influence* 512.13
be alongside *side* 623.8
be aloof 756.8
beam *wood* 131.3, *sailboat parts and accessories* 150.4, *light* 246.1, *quality of light* 246.2, *light up* 246.20, *show joy* 269.10, *be beautiful* 529.11, *superstructure* 551.7, *breadth* 592.1, *supporting part* 605.3, *means of connection* 754.4
be a martyr *feel pain* 215.8
be ambiguous 632.7; *be equivocal* 380.7

be ambivalent *be equivocal* 380.7
beam bridge *bridge* 551.10
beamed *joined* 131.8
be a mess *be ugly* 531.5
beaming *lucent* 246.13, *cheerful* 269.7
beam reach *sail* 150.29
beam reaching *sailing terms* 150.5
beamy *broad* 592.5
bean *vegetable* 17.11
bean [Inf] *head* 19.6
be analogous *correspond* 606.8
be anarchic 51.8
be an architect 134.13
be an authority on 52.17
beanbag toss Children's and Party Games 167
bean curd *meat substitute* 90.23
beanery [Inf] *eating place* 92.17
be an expert on *be an authority on* 52.17
beanfeast [Brit inf] *party* 408.6
be angry 302.19; *be agitated* 684.21
beanie *cap* 100.33
be an influence 512.13
be an instrument 511.7
be annoyed *be irritable* 304.14
be a nobody *be average* 742.8
beanpole *garden tool* 17.7
beanpole [Inf] *big person* 579.10, *thin person* 595.4, *tall person* 596.6
beans *crop* 16.8
be answerable *have a sense of duty* 433.13
bean tree Trees and Shrubs 43
be anxious *be fearful* 283.15, *be in suspense* 604.18
be anxious for *or* **about** *worry* 283.16
be apathetic *be insensible* 213.7
be apprehensive *be in suspense* 604.18
Bear Lakes 568
bear 605.17; *have young* 21.16, *procreate* 22.14, *game* 160.6, *irascible person* 303.7, *sullen person* 304.7, *assent to* 346.7, *discourteous person* 411.4, *succumb* 421.7, *financial* 457.6, *speculate* 480.19, *seller* 482.7, *bargain* 497.10, *bring into existence* 522.14, *support* 605.16, *convey* 685.9, *impel* 695.9, *aim* 697.14, *produce* 771.34
bearable *forgivable* 312.7
bearably *forgivably* 312.7
bear a date *chronologize* 646.13
bear a grudge *be hostile* 63.10, *resent* 302.13, *be malevolent* 306.12
bear a hand *help* 825.23
bear allegiance *obey* 426.7, *be subject to* 832.12
bear a resemblance to *be similar* 733.12
beard *body covering* 19.4, *costume* 100.10, *be courageous* 284.14
bearded *hairy* 19.20
beardless *young* 26.11, *depilatory* 614.15
beardlessness *baldness* 614.9
bear down on 716.18; *attack* 418.17, *compel* 428.8
beards Phobias 283
be a regular customer of *frequent* 393.10, 661.6
bearer *supporter* 605.9, *transferrer* 685.4, *transporter* 686.4
bearer bond *paper money* 484.14
bear false witness *lie* 192.23, *accuse falsely* 442.9
bear for *aim* 697.14

bear fruit *have young* 21.16, *fruit* 44.9, *grow* 676.10, *benefit* 801.10, *get better* 807.21, *be effective* 845.15
bear garden *confusion* 766.4
bear hard upon *make heavy* 538.14
bear hug *communication of love* 299.6, *retention* 471.1
bear-hug *retain* 471.7
bear ill will *be hostile* 63.10, *be malevolent* 306.12
bearing 697.2; *angle* 6.37, *machine element* 14.8, Heraldic Terms 184, *external appearance* 264.5, *meaning* 361.1, *conduct* 399.1, *superstructure* 551.7, *bodily movement* 677.11, *axle* 682.7, *navigational aid* 690.6, *relatedness* 727.1, *distinction* 777.8, *tendency* 838.2
bearing *or* **bearings** *direction* 697.1
bearing arms *military* 76.28
bearing ill will *malevolently* 306.14
bearing in mind *remembering* 354.8
bearing off *sailing terms* 150.5
bearing out *proof* 331.4
bearing plate *superstructure* 551.7
bearings *angle* 6.37, *exact location* 565.2, *situation* 573.1, *orientation* 697.3, *state* 725.1
bearing the cost *payment* 489.1
bear in mind *memorize* 354.11
bear interest *augment* 748.13
bearish *carnivorous* 35.26, *discourteous* 411.5, *bargain* 497.10, *descending* 714.9
bearish [Inf] *cross* 303.11
bearishly [Inf] *crossly* 303.20
bearishness *declining prices* 497.2
bearishness [Inf] *crossness* 303.4
bearlike *carnivorous* 35.26
bear malice *be hostile* 63.10, *resent* 302.13, *be malevolent* 306.12
bear malice toward *hate* 300.11
bear market *scarcity* 98.3, *stock exchange* 457.3, *seller's market* 483.3, *declining prices* 497.2, *economic adversity* 848.6
bear more than one's share *be in trouble* 848.13
Béarnaise *sauce* 90.17
bear no malice *show mercy* 312.11
bear no resemblance *be dissimilar* 734.7
bear off *sail* 150.29, *diverge* 607.11, *navigate* 690.15, *deviate* 698.15, *sidestep* 698.22
bear oneself *conduct oneself* 399.17
be around *surround* 615.7
bear out *prove* 331.17, 336.9, *establish reality* 719.12
bears Collective Names 59
bear the blame *be guilty* 450.9
bear the brunt *survive* 419.31, *be in difficulty* 824.19, *be in trouble* 848.13
bear the cost *defray* 481.18, 489.18, *donate* 491.13
bear the marks of *signify* 183.16
bear the palm *be superior* 744.15
bear the stamp of *signify* 183.16, *follow from* 676.9
bear up *bolster* 377.15, *be strong* 516.14, *support* 605.16
bear upon *take action* 509.12, *influence* 512.11, *impel* 695.9
bear up to *or* **for** *aim* 697.14
bear with *show mercy* 312.11, *be lenient* 423.5
bear witness *accuse* 442.8

bear witness to *signify* 183.16, *attest* 189.22, *give evidence* 339.12
Beas Rivers 570
be a shadow of one's former self *deteriorate* 808.14
be a shining example *or* **light** *be virtuous* 447.8
be asked *be questioned* 333.18
be asking for trouble *get into trouble* 824.20
be assertive 189.28
be assimilated *be the same* 730.13
beast *animal* 34.1, *unpleasant person* 272.5, *violent animal* 520.4
beast fable *story* 139.4
beastings *mammalian characteristic* 35.3, *milk* 93.5
beastlike *animalian* 34.12
beastliness *uncleanness* 112.2, *objectionability* 272.2, *malice* 306.2, *unpleasantness* 501.2
beastliness [Inf] *hatefulness* 300.4
beastly *animalian* 34.12, *unclean* 112.8, *malicious* 306.8, *cruel* 306.10
beastly [Inf] *objectionable* 272.7, *hateful* 300.10, *unpleasant* 501.5
beast of burden *workhorse* 159.3, *means of transportation* 686.2
beast of prey *animal killer* 30.14
beast of venery [Arch] *the hunted* 385.7
beasts *livestock* 16.11
beasts of the field, the *animals* 34.2
be a substitute 672.6
be at *appear* 264.12
beat 553.27, 684.10, 695.12; *master* 68.17, *cook* 91.10, *clean* 111.17, *meter* 139.10, *tempo* 140.22, *sound* 141.15, *sail* 150.29, *fencing movements* 153.3, *hunt* 160.12, 385.3, 385.14, *inflict pain* 215.10, *drumming* 235.1, *drum* 235.10, *harm* 306.13, *ill-use* 395.7, *attack successfully* 418.25, *hit* 454.28, *whisk* 558.23, *plot* 564.9, *location* 565.1, *musical time* 639.7, *frequency* 663.2, *cycle* 663.3, *orbit* 681.3, *vibration* 683.2, *wavelength* 683.5, *vibrate* 683.13, *agitate* 684.22, *shake* 684.24, *route* 691.2, *passing along* 692.5, *be superior* 744.15, *unconventional* 782.14, *reverberation* 797.6, *resound* 797.21, *be victorious* 845.16, *overpower* 845.18
beat [Inf] *fatigued* 820.2
beat about the bush *evade* 181.17, *stall* 419.28
be at a critical moment 726.15
be at a dead horse *waste effort* 802.13
be at a disadvantage *be unequal* 741.7
beat a hasty retreat *retreat* 285.8, *escape* 816.8
beat all comers *be victorious* 845.16
beat all hollow *exceed* 712.15
be at a loss *be in difficulty* 824.19
beat a retreat *signal* 183.18, *retreat* 386.22, 680.17, *withdraw* 705.9, *be safe* 810.20
beat around the bush *be circuitous* 199.6, *quibble* 330.13, *be equivocal* 380.7, *be evasive* 386.20, *be extraneous* 724.12
beat a strategic retreat *survive* 419.31
beat a tattoo *drum* 235.10, *salute* 405.13

beat black and blue *hit* 454.28, *inflict pain* 215.10
beat down *bargain* 480.20, *buy cheaply* 497.15, *knock down* 523.13
be at ease *be satisfied* 273.8
beaten *culinary* 91.9, *ill-used* 395.4, *familiar* 397.10, *punished* 454.19, *accessible* 691.13, *outclassed* 745.9, *defeated* 846.11
beaten flat *leveled* 603.8
beaten track *boring thing* 296.3, *way* 397.3, *route* 691.2
beater *cooking equipment* 91.6, *hunter* 160.9, 385.6, *agitator* 684.14, *mixer* 751.7
be at fault *be guilty* 450.9
beat flat *make horizontal* 603.10
be at home to *receive someone* 473.14
beatification *deification* 82.13, *promotion* 715.3
beatified *deified* 82.20, *promoted* 715.8
beatified soul *deified person* 82.14
beatify *deify* 82.23, *promote* 715.13
beating *hunting* 160.2, *drumming* 235.1, 235.6, Phobias 283, *hunt* 385.3, *ill-use* 395.2, *corporal punishment* 454.11, *pulverization* 553.4, *frequent* 663.6, *vibration* 683.2, *vibrating* 683.9, *beat* 684.10, *ramming* 695.3, *reverberatory* 797.14, *victory* 845.4, *defeat* 846.7
beating around the bush *circumlocution* 199.2, *quibbling* 330.4, *evasion* 368.2
beating heart *life force* 28.2
beating up *tree management* 43.6
beat it [Inf] *retreat* 386.22, *hurry off* 705.11
beat it! [Inf] *hands off!* 386.26, *go!* 709.30
beatnik *nonconformist* 782.7
be at odds with *dissent* 347.8
beat off *fend off* 701.9
be at one *agree* 735.23
beat one's breast *lament* 280.7, *repent* 313.9, *do penance* 451.9
beat one's head against a brick wall *waste effort* 802.13
be at one's wits' end *be in difficulty* 824.19
be at peace 73.10
beat poet *author* 139.13
beat poets Western Literary Groups 139
be a trendsetter *motivate* 508.9
Beatrice Famous Lovers 299
be at sea *find unintelligible* 364.14
beat someone hollow *overtake* 744.16
beat swords into plowshares *make peace* 73.11
be attentive 323.9
beat the air *waste effort* 802.13
beat the big drum *proclaim* 173.16, *flourish* 404.25
be at the bottom of *be interior* 611.14
be at the brink *border* 618.9
beat the drum *battle* 76.33, *signal* 183.18
be at the end of one's rope *or* **tether** *be in difficulty* 824.19
beat the living daylights out of *hit* 454.28
beat the rap [Inf] *acquit* 54.32
beat the record *be superior* 744.15
beat the shit out of [Inf] *defeat* 845.17
be at the station *meet* 704.20

be at the top 600.9; *be high* 596.15

beat time 140.29; *time* 639.15, *measure time* 646.14, *be regular* 663.10, *vibrate* 683.13

beat to a pulp *defeat* 845.17

beat to death *murder* 30.20

beat up *inflict pain* 215.10, *harm* 306.13, *strike* 418.21, *use violence* 520.9, *agitate* 684.22, *beat* 695.12

be at variance *be different* 463.11

be at war 76.32

beau *boyfriend* 32.4, *loved one* 299.13, *attractive male* 529.6

Beau Brummel *fashion business* 536.3

be auditioned *be questioned* 333.18

Beaufort scale *wind strength* 9.13

Beaufort Sea Oceans and Seas 571

beau geste [Fr] *deed* 412.2

beau ideal *beautiful thing* 529.3

beau monde *aristocracy* 70.2, *society* 408.8, *the rich* 485.7, *fashionable elite* 536.4

be auspicious 847.8; *show potential* 458.14

be austere *be unadorned* 424.10

beaut [Inf] *good thing* 445.9

beauteous *beautiful* 529.7

beauteously *beautifully* 529.13, 530.16

beauteousness *beauty* 529.1

be authoritarian *have authority* 52.13

beautician 530.11; *cleaner* 111.12

beautification 530.1, 807.7; *repair* 809.1

beautified 530.12; *ornate* 532.10, *improved* 807.12

beautifier *improver* 807.11

beautiful 529.7; *artistic* 133.7, *lovable* 299.20, *elegant* 527.3, *even* 626.5

beautifully 529.13, 530.16; *lovably* 299.31, *elegantly* 527.7, 534.8, *fashionably* 536.9

beautifulness *beauty* 529.1

beautiful people *the rich* 485.7, *fashionable elite* 536.4

beautiful thing 529.3

beautiful women Phobias 283

beautify 529.12, 530.14, 807.20; *ornament* 532.12

beautifying 530.13

beauty 529.1; *quantum* 10.63, *lovability* 299.5, *elegance* 527.1, *beautiful thing* 529.3, *attractive female* 529.5, *evenness* 626.3

beautybush Flowers 42

beauty care products *cosmetics* 530.4

beauty mark *or* **spot** *mark* 533.2

beauty parlor *hairdressing salon* 530.10

beauty products *cosmetics* 530.4

beauty queen *attractive female* 529.5

beauty salon *hairdressing salon* 530.10

beauty shop *hairdressing salon* 530.10

beauty specialist *beautician* 530.11

beauty treatment 530.3

beaux arts *visual arts* 133.1

Beaux-Arts architecture Architectural Styles 134

be available to one 425.13

be avenged *be compensated* 743.9

beaver *cap* 100.33

beaver [Inf] *worker* 123.1, *hard worker* 414.11

be average 742.8

be aware *sense* 212.9, *be cautious* 287.11

be aware of *sense* 212.9, *see* 242.20, *visualize* 242.24, *feel* 266.14

be a waste of time *be impossible* 837.9

be a wet blanket *discourage* 179.11

be bad *be wicked* 448.13

be beautiful 529.11

bebeeru Trees and Shrubs 43

be before *precede* 769.13

be behind *be in the rear* 622.7

be behindhand *be late* 658.11

be behind time *have no time to spare* 818.6

be benevolent 305.10; *be charitable* 305.12

be bent *or* **hellbent on** *cause* 372.12

Beberbeck Horse and Pony Breeds 159

be bereaved *be widowed* 66.13

be beside *juxtapose* 586.14

be best friends with *befriend* 62.10

be better than nothing *be convenient* 803.5

be between a rock and a hard place [Inf] *be in a predicament* 725.9

be beyond one's reach *be unintelligible* 364.11

be biased *discriminate* 430.21, *tend* 513.5, *be narrow-minded* 593.16, *be unjust* 741.9

be big 579.18

be blind 243.18

be blind to 243.19

be blunt *speak plainly* 592.14

be bold *be in front* 621.13

bebop *jazz* 140.5

be bored 296.7

be boring *bore* 296.8

be born 28.18; *live* 28.17, *arrive* 704.13, *come to be* 717.19, *emerge* 771.35

be born again *recant* 81.27, *be converted* 670.12

be born under a lucky star *be fortunate* 847.7

be born with a silver spoon in one's mouth *be fortunate* 847.7

be brief 204.9

be brittle 548.4

be broad-minded 592.13

be broke *be needy* 95.18, *be poor* 486.14

be brought 704.19

be brought to bed of [Arch] *have young* 21.16

be brushed off *play baseball* 147.9

be brusque *be short* 591.10

be busy 414.19; *work* 122.8

be called *have a title* 72.12

be calm 455.13

becalm *make motionless* 678.8

becalmed *inactive* 413.9, *motionless* 678.4

be candid *speak plainly* 592.14

be capable of *be powerful* 514.18

be capricious 381.6; *equivocate* 380.8

be careful 325.11, 593.15; *be cautious* 287.11

be careful! 287.20

be careless 289.14

be cast away *sail* 690.16

be cataloged *be on a list* 785.12

be caught in a rundown *play baseball* 147.9

be caught in the poverty trap *be poor* 486.14

because *causally* 675.12

because of *by virtue of* 447.12, *with the effect of* 676.12

be cautious 287.11; *be careful* 325.11, *have foresight* 357.8

be celibate 67.9; *be moral* 431.13

be central *be essential* 723.10

be certain 840.13

béchamel *sauce* 90.17

bechance [Arch] *chance* 842.12

be changeable 666.5

be changed 665.15; *be refreshed* 94.8, *be converted* 670.12

be charged *incur a duty* 433.15

be charitable 305.12; *philanthropize* 307.8

becharm *win the love of* 299.27

becharmed *enamored* 299.17

Becharof Lakes 568

be chaste *be continent* 67.10

be chastised *serve one right* 420.5

be cheap 497.13

bêche-de-mer *echinoderm* 39.5

be cheerful *show joy* 269.10

be childless *be infertile* 23.8

be childlike *be naive* 449.12

be circuitous 199.6

be civil *be courteous* 410.9

beck *demand* 425.2

beck and call *demand* 425.2

becket bend Knots, Bends, Hitches, Splices 754

beckon *gesture* 183.17

be clairvoyant *foresee* 357.9

be classified *be on a list* 785.12

be clever *be intelligent* 315.11

becloud *disguise* 181.13, *make dim* 248.8

be clumsy 128.9

be coerced *be compelled* 428.11

be cold 218.13; *be insensitive* 268.6, *be incurious* 322.5

become *be the duty of* 433.16, *convert* 670.11, *come to be* 717.19

become a born-again Christian *confess* 451.8

become acceptable *become a habit* 397.17

become addicted *accustom oneself* 397.19

become adult *be complete* 761.10

become a free agent *be independent* 829.18

become aggravated 276.6

become agitated about *protest* 507.7

become a habit 397.17

become a hostage *be subject to* 832.12

become airborne *maneuver* 689.14, *go up* 713.23

become a karate expert *do martial arts* 152.21

become aloof *be indifferent* 289.12

become a martyr *sacrifice* 504.14

become a nation 566.11

become a new man *or* **woman** *get healthy* 113.12

become angry 302.20; *protest* 507.7

become an heir *or* **heiress** *receive* 473.13

become an in-patient *be unhealthy* 114.29

become annoyed *show impatience* 303.14

become anorectic *lose weight* 468.14

become an out-patient *be unhealthy* 114.29

become a patient *be unhealthy* 114.29

become apparent *be intelligible* 363.10

become a prisoner *forfeit* 468.13

become a reality *be real* 721.21

become a self-made man *or* **woman** *be successful* 845.11

become a slave *be subject to* 832.12

become a teetotaler *give up alcohol* 120.6

become available *occur* 264.14

become aware of *learn* 48.23

become betrothed to *get engaged to* 458.12

become bigger *grow* 581.17

become celebrated *do great deeds* 412.14

become champion *be victorious* 845.16

become choppy *billow* 571.9

become cold 218.14

become complete *be complete* 761.10

become conceited 402.16

become convalescent *get healthy* 113.12

become corrupt *be wicked* 448.13

become dark 247.9

become deeper *deepen* 598.21

become different *be changed* 665.15

become dilapidated *disintegrate* 808.15

become dim *be dim* 248.7

become disenfranchised *or* **disfranchised** *forfeit* 468.13

become dry *dry* 560.17

become enamored with *be in love* 299.23

become endangered *decrease* 747.7

become enemies *divide* 753.18

become engaged *propose (marriage)* 299.28, *incur a duty* 433.15, *get engaged to* 458.12

become extinct *disappear* 265.5, *pass* 651.17, *decrease* 747.7, *die* 773.21

become famous *do great deeds* 412.14, *be prosperous* 847.6

become fatigued *decline* 846.16

become fixed *become a habit* 397.17

become green *green* 260.14

become impoverished *lessen* 468.17

become independent *become a nation* 566.11

become inferior 745.11

become insane 110.12

become inseparable *befriend* 62.10

become insolvent 846.17; *lose money* 468.15, *be unable to pay* 490.11, *need money* 848.14

become inverted 608.8

become invisible 245.6; *disappear* 265.5, *decrease* 747.7

become involved with *be included* 763.6

become irritable *be sensitive* 267.5

become known *be disclosed* 180.12

become known from coast to coast *be published* 173.19

become larger *increase* 467.17, 746.6, *grow* 581.17

become law *take effect* 676.11

become linked *or* **entangled** *or* **involved with** *mix together* 751.14

become long in the tooth *age* 27.16

become new 652.19

become obsolete *disappear* 265.5, *grow old* 653.16, *deteriorate* 808.14

become old *grow old* 653.16

become older *age* 27.16

become one 788.18; *marry* 64.19

become opaque *be opaque* 250.6

become overweight *grow* 581.17

become part of one *become a habit* 397.17

become pregnant *reproduce oneself* 21.14

become proficient *learn* 68.18

become public knowledge *be published* 173.19, *be disclosed* 180.12

become rancid *decay* 808.16

become reconciled *forgive and forget* 312.9

become runny *come unstuck* 756.7

become sane *be sane* 109.5

become scarce *decrease* 747.7

become self-governing *become a nation* 566.11

become shabby *disintegrate* 808.15

become shallow *shallow* 599.5

become silent *be silent* 231.3

become smaller 582.14

become stronger *be strong* 516.14

become the owner of *possess* 469.14

become thick *or* **solid** *be dense* 540.8

become thin 595.15

become threadbare *disintegrate* 808.15

become transparent *be transparent* 249.11

become turbulent *billow* 571.9

become unsociable *be aloof* 756.8

become visible 264.13; *appear* 244.8

become weary *be fatigued* 820.5

be comfortable *be in comfortable circumstances* 726.13

becoming *appealing* 529.10, *converting* 670.8

becoming dim *dimming* 248.3

becoming law *lawmaking* 53.11

becomingly *beautifully* 529.13, 530.16, *elegantly* 534.8

be compassionate 305.11

be compatible 462.12; *cooperate* 616.6

be compelled 428.11

be compensated 743.9

be complete 761.10

be composed *be calm* 455.13

be concave 635.6

be conceited *be vain* 402.14

be concerned *worry* 283.16

be concerned with *focus on* 328.9

be concise 198.5

be confused *be mixed up* 751.15

be confused *or* **challenged** *or* **puzzled** *or* **mystified** *confuse* 333.20

be congruent *agree* 730.14

be consecutive 774.11

be conservative 815.15

be considerate *think* 317.9, *be courteous* 410.9

be consistent *be the same* 730.13, *conform* 735.27

be conspicuous *identify oneself* 184.12

be conspicuous by one's absence *be absent* 576.14

be contagious *cause ill health* 114.30

be contemporary *be simultaneous* 649.6

be contiguous *adjoin* 216.11, *interface* 616.5

be continent 67.10

be continuous *continue* 774.12

be contrary 828.16

be contrite *repent* 313.9

be convenient 803.5

be conventional *conform* 735.27

be converted 670.12; *recant* 81.27, *change for the better* 665.17

be convex 634.7

be convinced *be certain* 840.13

be correct *be right* 429.12, *be accurate* 721.22

be counted *vote* 382.16

be courageous 284.14

be courteous 410.9; *think* 317.9

be covetous of *envy* 314.7

be crazy about *be in love* 299.23

be crestfallen *be disappointed* 293.8

be crowned *be superior* 744.15

be crucial *be essential* 723.10

be cruel *be malevolent* 306.12

be cunning 822.5

be curious 321.7

be cut in *get one's allotment* 474.6

be cut up *grieve* 270.7

be cyclic 663.11

bed *sedimentary rock* 8.34, *practice livestock farming* 16.20, *ornamental garden* 17.3, *cultivate* 17.19, *furniture* 101.1, *river parts* 570.3, *layer* 588.1, *base* 601.1, *resting place* 668.5, *private space* 812.2

be damp *be moist* 559.15

bed and board *hotel* 60.12

bed-and-breakfast (B and B) *hotel* 60.12

bed and lodging *hotel* 60.12

be dark 247.8

be dated *chronologize* 646.13

bedazzle *blind* 243.17, *light* 246.19

bedazzling *blinding* 243.13

bedbug *pest* 40.5

bedchamber *room* 60.9

bedclothes *bed covering* 613.7

bedcover *bed covering* 613.7

bed covering 613.7

bedding *sedimentary rock* 8.34, *layer* 588.1, *bed covering* 613.7

bedding plane *sedimentary rock* 8.34

bedding plant *garden plant* 17.10

bed down *take it easy* 819.3

be dead *die* 29.17, *be inert* 519.4

be deaf 229.8

be dear *cost a lot* 496.9

bedeck *dress up* 100.45, *decorate* 532.11

bedecked *dressed* 100.38

be deep 598.20

be deeply in debt *lose one's money* 486.15

be defeated 846.18; *capitulate* 421.6

be definite 189.26

be delivered *be brought* 704.19

be dense 540.8

be depressed *be disappointed* 293.8

be derived from *follow from* 676.9

be designated *have a title* 72.12

be desirable 288.23

be destroyed 523.17

be determined *be resolute* 376.11

bedevil *bewitch* 86.25, *puzzle* 364.12, *make evil* 446.11, *cause trouble* 824.21

bedeviled *bewitched* 86.21

bedevilment *witchcraft* 86.6

be devoted to *worship* 83.15

bedewed *misty* 559.10

bed-hop *fornicate* 432.14

bed-hopping *fornication* 432.3

be different 463.11

be difficult 824.16

be diffuse 199.5

bedight [Arch] *dress up* 100.45

bedighted [Arch] *dressed* 100.38

be dim 248.7

bedim *make dim* 248.8, *decolor* 252.8

bed in *inset* 710.13

be dirty 112.10

be disappointed 293.8

be disclosed 180.12

be discourteous 411.7; *be inconsiderate* 318.13

be discovered 345.15

be dishonest *be untruthful* 192.20

be dishonorable 192.21

be disinclined 291.14

be disinterested 443.6

be disjoined *separate* 703.12

be disloyal *be dishonorable* 192.21

be dismissed 707.18

be dismissed *or* **discharged** *stop work* 394.12

be disobedient *disobey* 427.12

be disordered 766.21

be disorderly 766.22; *cause confusion* 51.9

be disparate 728.14

be disposed to *propound a philosophy* 4.21, *tend* 513.5

be disquieted *worry* 283.16

be disreputable 371.5

be dissatisfied 274.7

be dissimilar 734.7; *be disparate* 728.14

be dissonant 241.6

be distant 585.8

be disturbed *worry* 283.16

be diverse 732.10

bedizen *dress up* 100.45, *decorate* 532.11

bedizened *dressed up* 100.39

bedizenment *costume* 100.10

bed jacket *informal clothes* 100.7, *nightwear* 100.21

bedlam *mental hospital* 110.6, *tumult* 232.5, *dissonance* 241.1, *confusion* 766.4, *commotion* 768.5

bed linens *bed covering* 613.7

Bedlington terrier *Breeds of Dogs* 35

Bedloe's Island *Islands* 572

bed of roses *figurative usage* 42.8, *idealized pleasure* 214.5, *prosperity* 847.1

be done with *end* 773.19

be dormant 41.22

bed out *cultivate* 17.19, *plant* 710.14

be down in the dumps *be sullen* 304.12

bedpan *place for excretion* 25.11

bedplate *foundation* 601.2

bedraggle *dirty* 112.11, *make disorderly* 766.20

bedraggled *dirty* 112.7, *untidy* 766.11

bedridden *sick* 114.24, *inactive* 415.8

bedrock *rock* 8.30, *lowest point* 597.5, *lower* 597.14, *base* 601.1, *bottom* 601.6, *chief thing* 799.3, *essential* 799.10

bedroom *room* 60.9, *privacy* 181.6, *private space* 812.2

bedroom farce *comedy* 136.11

bedroom town *suburb* 567.11

be drunk 121.34

be dry *give up alcohol* 120.6, *abstain* 455.11

beds *Phobias* 283

bedsheet *bed covering* 613.7

bedside *type of table* 101.5

bedside lamp *electric light* 246.6

bedside manner *therapy* 115.12

bed-sitter [Brit] *apartment* 60.7

bedspread *bed covering* 613.7

bedspring *spring* 546.4

bedstead *type of bed* 101.9

bedstraw *Flowers* 42

be due to *follow from* 676.9

be duteous *have a sense of duty* 433.13

be dutiful 433.12

bed-wetting *urination* 25.4

bee *insect* 40.1, *social insect* 40.6

bee [Inf] *worker* 123.1

be eager 373.13

be early 657.11

be easy 823.14

be easy about *be incurious* 322.5

be easy as pie *be easy* 823.14

bee balm *Flowers* 42

beech *Trees and Shrubs* 43

beech mast *trees* 43.4

be economical with the truth *distort the truth* 627.12

beef 90.24; *meat* 90.22

beef [Inf] *complaint* 304.5, *be irritable* 304.14, *protest* 507.1, 507.7, *heaviness* 538.1

Beefalo *Breeds of Cattle* 16

beefcake [Inf] *sex object* 20.8, *macho man* 32.6, *portrait* 132.5, *person of strength* 516.8

beef farm *farm* 16.2

beef farmer *agriculturist* 16.14

beef farming *livestock farming* 16.10

be effective 845.15

be efficacious *be effective* 845.15

Beef Friesian *Breeds of Cattle* 16

beefiness [Inf] *physical strength* 516.3, *heaviness* 538.1, *squatness* 579.6

Beefmaster *Breeds of Cattle* 16

beef ranch *farm* 16.2

beef sausage *sausage* 90.29

Beef Shorthorn *Breeds of Cattle* 16

beef stroganoff *notable international dishes* 90.40

beef up *reinforce* 419.23, *strengthen* 516.15, *intensify* 746.8

beefwood *Trees and Shrubs* 43

beefy *physically strong* 516.10, *heavy* 538.9

beefy *stocky* 579.16

be egoistic *be egotistic* 444.7

be egotistic 444.7

beehive *dwelling* 40.7, *natural habitat* 60.16, *business* 414.6, *coiffure* 530.8, *dome* 634.4

beehive kiln *ceramic workshop and tools* 129.8

beehive tomb *burial place* 31.7, *thing of the past* 651.8

beekeeper *entomologist* 40.3

beekeeping *study of insects* 40.2, *Hobbies and Pastimes* 167

be elastic 546.7

be elected *run for office* 50.10

be elegant 527.6

be eligible *qualify* 340.11

be eliminated *be defeated* 846.18

beeline *shortcut* 591.5, *straight line* 630.2, *bearing* 697.2

be elsewhere *be inattentive* 324.10

Beelzebub *devil* 446.5

be emaciated 595.16

be employed 57.19

be engraved on one's memory *be remembered* 354.15

be enough *suffice* 97.6

be entitled to **72.13**; *have rights* 429.13
be entrusted *incur a duty* 433.15
be envious of *envy* 314.7
beep *signal* 183.6
beeper *dial* 169.12, *radio* 172.1, *signal* 183.6
beeping *signaling* 183.14
be equal **740.11**; *be similar* 733.12
be equal to *be equal* 740.11
be equivalent **730.15**; *correspond* 606.8
be equivocal **380.7**
beer **93.10**; *alcoholic drink* 93.9, *alcohol* 121.5
beer belly *fat* 579.8, *bulge* 634.2
beer making Hobbies and Pastimes 167
beer party *party* 408.6
be erroneous *be incorrect* 722.13
beery *intoxicating* 121.29
bees Collective Names 59, Phobias 283
be essential **723.10**
be esteemed *have a good reputation* 370.5
beestings *mammalian characteristic* 35.3
beestings *or* beastings *milk* 93.5
be estranged *separate* 66.10
beeswax *dwelling* 40.7, *adhesive* 561.3, *lubricate* 562.15
beet *red thing* 257.3
be eternal **644.7**; *be infinite* 798.9
beetle *pests and diseases* 17.12, *insect* 40.1, *pulper* 561.13, *be high* 596.15, *overhanging* 604.2, *overhang* 604.14
beetle-browed *overhanging* 604.8
beetle off [Brit] *hurry off* 705.11
beetling *highland* 596.11, *overhanging* 604.8
beet-red *red* 257.5
beet sugar Common Sugars 12, *sweetener* 222.2
be evasive **386.20**
be everywhere *be present* 575.13
be evil **446.10**
be examined *be questioned* 333.18
be excessive **99.9**
be excited *be in suspense* 604.18
be excluded **764.9**
be executed **454.32**
be exempt **434.11**
be exiled *be excluded* 764.9
be expert **127.15**
be exterior **610.13**
be external **724.15**
be extinguished *become dark* 247.9
be extraneous **724.12**; *be unrelated* 728.12
be extravagant **194.13**
be extroverted *externalize* 610.15
be fair *be right* 429.12
be faithful *be sincere* 191.8
be faithful to *observe* 465.4
befall *chance* 842.12
be false *be untruthful* 192.20, *distort the truth* 627.12, *be untrue* 722.11
be famished *be hungry* 288.21
be famous *be published* 173.19, *have a good reputation* 370.5
Befana *sprite* 86.12
be farsighted *see badly* 243.16
be fast (of clocks) *start early* 657.12
be fatigued **820.5**
be favorable **62.12**
be fearful **283.16**
be fearful for *worry* 283.16
be fed up *have enough* 97.7
be fertile **22.13**

be festive *make merry* 167.13
be feverish *feel hot* 217.19
be fictitious *not exist* 786.6
be filled *be full* 761.12
be financially worthwhile *be profitable* 467.21
be fined *be punished* 454.31
be finished with *stop using* 394.10
be fired *be dismissed* 707.18
be first *be in front* 621.13
befit *be desirable* 288.23, *be the duty of* 433.16, *be convenient* 803.5
be fit for *be suitable* 462.13
befit the occasion *be timely* 659.6
befit the time *be timely* 659.6
befitting *timely* 659.4, *convenient* 803.3
befittingly *properly* 429.18, *opportunely* 659.8
be flat *be horizontal* 603.9
be flatulent *belch* 709.28
be fleeting *be transient* 643.6
befog *fog* 9.59, *disguise* 181.13, *make dim* 248.8
be fond of *like* 290.8, 299.22
befool *deceive* 193.16, *exploit* 393.11
befooled *deceived* 193.15
be foolish **353.6**
before **621.14**, **769.18**; *on the spot* 575.20, *formerly* 653.19
before all *manifestly* 843.17
before everything *first* 771.37
before God *manifestly* 843.17
beforehand **657.19**; *premature* 657.10, *prematurely* 657.20, *before* 769.18
be foreign **724.13**
before long *soon* 657.18
before now **651.21**; *formerly* 653.19
before one *manifestly* 843.17
before one can say Jack Robinson [Inf] *immediately* 645.8, *swiftly* 694.16, *hastily* 818.7
before one knows it *immediately* 645.8
before one's eyes *visible* 242.19, *available* 575.11
before one's very eyes *on the spot* 575.20
before the bar *judged* 341.9
before the bench *or* bar *or* court *legally* 53.33
before the committee *problematical* 328.12
before the Flood *historical* 3.10
before the house *problematically* 328.12
before the ink is dry *early* 657.17
before the judge *in litigation* 54.34, *accusingly* 442.11
before the mast *nautically* 690.17
before the wind *directionally* 697.20
beforetime *early* 657.17
be forgetful **355.11**
be forgetful of *be ungrateful* 311.5
be forgotten **355.12**
be formal **406.11**
be fortunate **847.7**
befoul *dirty* 112.11, *be evil* 446.10
befouled *dirty* 112.7
be found *arrive* 704.13, *exist* 717.18
be found at *frequent* 661.6
be fragile *be brittle* 548.4
be fragrant **226.5**
be frank *be sincere* 191.8, *speak plainly* 592.14
be free **829.16**
be frequent **661.5**

befriend **62.10**; *better* 445.17, *keep company with* 794.17
be friendly with *befriend* 62.10
be friends **62.9**
be friends of long standing *be friends* 62.9
be frightened *or* terrified *or* horrified *be afraid* 283.14
be fruitful *fruit* 44.9
befuddle *be intoxicating* 121.36, *discompose* 766.18
befuddlement *drunkenness* 121.3
be full **761.12**
be full of oneself *be vain* 402.14
be full of vigor **518.4**
be funny *make someone laugh* 368.7
beg **401.12**; *borrow* 476.10, *petition* 505.11, *solicit money* 505.13
beg, borrow, or steal *find means* 102.6, *gain* 467.15
be gainfully employed *earn* 467.20
be generous **498.10**
beget *propagate* 21.15, *procreate* 22.14, *give birth to* 28.19, *bring into existence* 522.14, *cause* 675.8
begetter *propagator* 21.7, *producer* 522.10, *first cause* 675.6
be getting at *mean* 361.13
beg for crumbs *beg* 401.12
beg for favors *beg* 401.12
beg for forgiveness *ask for mercy* 308.10, *ask forgiveness* 312.12
beg for mercy *ask for mercy* 308.10
beg for more *be unsatisfied* 98.10
beg for one's bread *be poor* 486.14
beg for one's life *ask for mercy* 308.10
beggar **505.6**; *nonworker* 415.4, *recipient* 473.5, *poor person* 486.6, *impoverish* 486.16
beggar description *be wondrous* 294.14
beggardom *beggary* 486.3
beggared *nonpaying* 490.7
beggarliness *beggary* 486.3, *deficiency* 745.2
beggarly **486.12**; *sycophantic* 401.7
beggary **486.3**
begging **505.9**; *borrowing* 476.1, *petition* 505.2, *solicitation* 505.4
begin **583.21**, **771.25**; *be born* 28.18, *work* 122.8, *become visible* 264.13, *undertake* 391.7, *motivate* 508.9, *be new* 652.17, *inaugurate* 675.10, *originate* 737.7
begin again **771.36**; *become new* 652.19, *restore* 671.10, *renew* 797.19
begin an insurrection *cause mischief* 507.9
begin from *follow from* 676.9
beginner **398.2**, **771.14**; *learner* 48.6, *unskilled person* 128.3, *ignorant person* 349.4, *innocent person* 449.5, *new arrival* 652.7, *entrant* 706.7, *naive person* 821.2
beginner's ski 162.27
beginner's luck *successfulness* 845.3
beginner's slope *ski run* 162.2
beginning **583.9**, **583.14**, **652.4**, **771.1**, **771.16**; *appearing* 264.9, *front* 621.1, *early stage* 657.3, *arrival* 704.1, *originality* 737.1
beginning again *return* 797.4
beginning of the end *close* 773.9
beginning of time *philosophical problem* 4.8
begin to understand *understand* 363.9
be given *receive* 473.13

beg leave *ask permission* 502.9, *request* 505.10
be gone *die* 29.17
begone! *go!* 709.30
beg one's pardon *ask forgiveness* 312.12, *offer reparation* 504.15
beg one's pardon *or* forgiveness *apologize* 313.8
begonia Flowers 42
be good **445.16**; *behave well* 399.18, *be moral* 431.13, *be virtuous* 447.8
be good at **445.18**
begotten *produced* 522.12
beg permission *ask permission* 502.9, *request* 505.10
be grammatical *use language* 5.42
be granted a decree of nullity *divorce* 66.9
be granted a final decree *divorce* 66.9
be granted an annulment *divorce* 66.9
be grateful **310.6**
be greedy **119.4**; *be selfish* 444.6
be Greek to [Inf] *not understand* 362.11
begrime *dirty* 112.11
begrimed *dirty* 112.7
be grounded in *know* 48.24
begrudge *hate* 300.11, *be jealous* 314.8, *grudge* 375.15, 501.7
begrudged *hated* 300.9
begrudging *hating* 300.7, *jealous* 314.5
begrudgingly *with hate* 300.13, *jealously* 314.12, *unwillingly* 375.17
begrudgingness *jealousy* 314.2
beg the question *quibble* 330.13
beg to differ *dissent* 347.8, *object* 828.18
beguile *deceive* 193.16, *be cunning* 822.5
beguiled *deceived* 193.15
beguilement *deception* 193.1, *cunning* 822.1
beguiler *deceiver* 193.8
beguiling *deceptive* 193.12, *cunning* 822.4
be guilty **450.9**
beguine Dances 135
begun *incomplete* 762.5
be gunning for *pursue* 385.11
be gutsy [Inf] *be full of vigor* 518.4
be had *overpay* 496.11
be had for the asking *be easy* 823.14
behalf *welfare* 445.2
be half-baked *hasten* 657.15
be halfway *stand in the middle* 772.17
be hanged *be executed* 454.32
be harassed *worry* 283.16
be hard put (to) *have difficulty* 824.18
be harmonious *be in accord* 735.21
be haunted *worry* 283.16
behave *conduct oneself* 399.17, *behave well* 399.18, *occupy oneself* 412.15, *be virtuous* 447.8
behave badly **399.19**; *be discourteous* 411.7
behaved *principled* 447.6
behave in an unsportsmanlike way *exhibit penalty behavior* 155.21
behave oneself *behave well* 399.18
behave properly *have good manners* 410.10
behave toward **399.20**
behave well **399.18**; *have good*

manners 410.10, *obey* 426.7, *better* 445.17

behaving 399.14

behaving badly *wicked* 448.9

behavior *conduct* 399.1, *action* 412.1, *way* 691.1

behavioral *sociological* 2.11, *behaving* 399.14

behaviorally *sociologically* 2.15

behavioral pattern *social environment* 2.4

behavioral psychology or **behaviorism** *Psychological Theories, Schools* 108

behavioral science *anthropology* 1.1, *sociology* 2.1

behavioral scientist *anthropologist* 1.3

behaviorism *study of conduct* 399.3

behavioristic *behaving* 399.14

behavior modification *psychotherapy* 108.4

behavior patterns *custom* 397.4

behavior therapist *psychologist* 108.33

behavior therapy *psychotherapy* 108.4

behead *execute* 30.22, 454.30, *take off* 749.7, *separate* 753.12

be head and shoulders above the rest *be in a class of one's own* 777.14

beheaded *reduced* 749.5

beheading *execution* 30.6, *capital punishment* 454.12, *subtraction* 749.1, *separateness* 753.3

be healthy 113.11

be heard 228.15; *be questioned* 333.18

be heartbroken *be disappointed* 293.8

be heavy 538.12

be helpful *help* 825.23

behemoth *Legendary Creatures* 360, *big thing* 579.9

be here *be present* 575.13

be here for good *be permanent* 667.4

be here for the duration *be permanent* 667.4

be here to stay *be permanent* 667.4

behest *command* 425.1

be high 596.15

be highly thought of *have a good reputation* 370.5

be hilarious *make someone laugh* 368.7

behind 622.8; *unprepared* 389.5, *at a distance* 585.13, *back* 622.1, *rear end* 622.4, *delayed* 693.10

behind bars *in prison* 55.14

behind closed doors *privately* 181.18, *secretly* 182.14, *unsociably* 409.13

behindhand *unprepared* 389.5, *nonpaying* 490.7, *late* 658.5, 658.14

behind one's back *absently* 576.18

behind schedule *late* 658.5, 658.14

behind someone's back *stealthily* 182.15

behind-the-back pass *playing terms* 148.4

behind the eight ball [Inf] *troubled* 824.15

behind the scenes *onstage* 136.39, *private* 245.5, *invisibly* 245.8, *behind* 622.8, *causal* 675.7, *causally* 675.12, *concealed* 844.7

behind the times *different in time* 648.2, *antiquarian* 651.13

behind time *unprepared* 389.5, *late* 658.5, 658.14

be history *be past* 651.16

be hit by a pitch *play baseball* 147.9

be hoist with one's own petard *serve one right* 420.5

behold *see* 242.20

beholden *grateful* 310.4, *answerable* 334.17, *dutiful* 433.6, *indebted* 488.7

beholder *observer* 242.15, *recipient* 473.5, *attender* 575.6

beholding *watching* 575.12

be homogeneous *be the same* 730.13

be honest *be sincere* 191.8

behoove *be the duty of* 433.16

be hopeful 281.11

be hopeless 282.11

be horizontal 603.9

be hospitable 477.21; *be sociable* 408.14

be hospitalized *be unhealthy* 114.29

be hostile 63.10

be hot *feel hot* 217.19

be hot off the press *be published* 173.19

be humble 298.16; *succumb* 421.7

be humiliated *be in trouble* 848.13

be humorous 277.11

be hungry 288.21

be hypocritical *be untruthful* 192.20

be identical *be the same* 730.13

be identified *identify oneself* 184.12

be idle *be inert* 519.4

beige *white* 253.7, *brown* 256.5, *yellow* 259.7

be ignorant 349.8

Beijing *Countries* 566, *other famous world cities* 567.9

be ill *be unhealthy* 114.29, *be weak* 517.12, *be in trouble* 848.13

be illegal 53.30

be imbalanced *be disparate* 728.14

be immobile *be inert* 519.4

be immoral 432.13

be impartial 289.15, 338.11

be impassive *be insensible* 213.7

be impenitent 452.4

be imperfect 806.8

be impertinent *be unrelated* 728.12

be implicated in *be included* 763.6

be important 799.13

be impossible 837.9

be impotent *be powerless* 515.11

be impressed with oneself *be vain* 402.14

be improbable 839.7

be in a bad mood *be irritable* 304.14

be in a Catch-22 situation *be in difficulties* 726.14, *have a mishap* 826.18

be in accord 735.21; *agree* 730.14, 735.23

be inaccurate or **imprecise** *be incorrect* 722.13

be in a certain state *be in a state of* 725.8

be in a class of one's own 777.14; *specialize* 779.16

be in action *be operational* 509.10

be inactive 415.13; *not act* 413.11, *acquiesce* 421.5

be in a different time 648.3

be in a peeve *be irritable* 304.14

be in a pickle [Inf] *be in a predicament* 725.9

be inapplicable *be unrelated* 728.12

be inappropriate *be unrelated* 728.12

be in a predicament 725.9

be in a rut *be bored* 296.7, *have a habit* 397.16

be in a spot *be in a predicament* 725.9

be in a state of 725.8

be inattentive 324.10; *be thoughtless* 324.11, *lose track of* 698.18

be in at the beginning *inaugurate* 771.31

be in at the death *reach* 704.14

be in between *stand in the middle* 772.17

be in bloom *flower* 42.12

be in cahoots [Inf] *concur* 827.16

be incarcerated *be punished* 454.31

be in charge *govern* 49.26, *have authority* 52.13, *direct* 126.11, 412.16

be inclined toward 290.10

be included 763.6

be in comfortable circumstances 726.13

be incomplete 762.8

be inconsiderate 318.13

be inconvenient 804.9

be incorrect 722.13

be incumbent upon *have a sense of duty* 433.13

be incurious 322.5; *be indifferent* 289.12

be in danger 811.11

be in debt 488.9

be in demand *be sold* 482.22

be independent 782.20, 829.18

be indifferent 289.12; *acquiesce* 421.5, *be disinterested* 443.6

be in difficulties 726.14

be in difficulty 824.19

be indirect *lack candor* 192.22

be indiscriminate 338.10

be induced *be motivated* 508.10

be in earnest *take seriously* 278.8

be in error 351.15

be inert 519.4; *not act* 413.11

be in fashion *be in style* 537.10

be infatuated with *like* 290.8, *be in love* 299.23

be infected *be motivated* 508.10

be inferior 745.10; *be unequal* 741.7

be infertile 23.8

be infinite 798.9

be in flower *flower* 42.12

be influenced *be motivated* 508.10

be in force *be operational* 509.10

be informal 407.10, 829.19

be informed 170.15; *know* 48.24, *understand* 363.9

be infrequent 662.3

be in front 621.13

being *living organism* 13.10, *person* 18.8, *life* 28.1, *appearance* 264.1, *visibility* 264.4, *presence* 575.1, *present* 575.7, *thing* 717.3, *existing* 717.11

being ahead *advantage* 744.3

being alive *life* 28.1

being a regular customer *frequenting* 661.2

being at large *freedom* 829.1

being buried alive *Phobias* 283

being by oneself *Phobias* 283

being cured *recuperation* 809.4

being dirty *Phobias* 283

being discussed *in preparation* 388.8

being here or **there** *presence* 575.1

being hit by a pitch *batting terms* 147.6

being in control *independence* 829.5

being in streets *Phobias* 283

being in vehicles *Phobias* 283

being onstage *Phobias* 283

being stared at *Phobias* 283

being there *visibility* 264.4

being under the influence of alcohol *drunkenness* 121.3

be in harmony *agree* 735.23

be inhibited 826.20; *lack candor* 192.22

be in hot pursuit *pursue* 385.11

be in league with *unify* 752.15

be in love 299.23

be in motion 677.14

be innocent 449.10

be in no hurry *have leisure time* 125.5

be in office *run for office* 50.10

be in one's bailiwick *have jurisdiction over* 54.30

be in one's element *do easily* 823.16

be in on the action *act* 412.11

be in on the ground floor [Inf] *inaugurate* 771.31

be in order 765.23; *be regular* 663.10

be in play *be operational* 509.10

be in poor health *be unhealthy* 114.29, *be in trouble* 848.13

be in power *govern* 49.26, *rule over* 780.13

be in prison 55.13

be in residence *reside* 575.17

be insane *become insane* 110.12

be insensible 213.7

be insensitive 268.6

be in service *serve* 69.11

be inside *be interior* 611.14

be insincere *be untruthful* 192.20

be insolent 400.14

be instinctive 320.10

be instructed *learn* 48.23

be instrumental *be an instrument* 511.7

be in style 537.10

be insubordinate 416.8

be insufficient 98.9

be in suspense 604.18

be in sync [Inf] *harmonize* 735.22

be intangible *be unreal* 722.12

be intelligent 315.11, 352.7

be intelligible 363.10

be intentionally walked *play baseball* 147.9

be interchangeable *be equivalent* 730.15

be interior 611.14

be interviewed *be heard* 228.15, *be questioned* 333.18

be in the back *be in the rear* 622.7

be in the cards *be probable* 838.8

be in the chair *direct* 126.11

be in the dark *be ignorant* 349.8

be in the driver's seat *be an influence* 512.13

be in the future 650.9

be in the know *be informed* 170.15, *understand* 295.6

be in the limelight *be published* 173.19, *be visible* 843.16

be in the middle 772.16

be in the news *be published* 173.19

be in the open air *be exterior* 610.13

be in the past *be past* 651.16

be in the pink [Inf] *be healthy* 113.11

be in the rear 622.7

be in the right *be right* 429.12
be in the right place at the right time *find an opening* 583.20
be in the running *be probable* 838.8
be in the shotgun *play offense* 155.18
be in the vanguard *invent* 345.14, *be in front* 621.13
be intimate *have sex* 20.21
be intolerant *be narrow-minded* 593.16
be in touch *communicate* 169.18
be in touch with *hear* 228.13
be intoxicating 121.36
be intransigent *be stubborn* 542.11
be in trouble 848.13
be introverted *be inhibited* 826.20
be intuitive 320.9
be in tune *harmonize* 140.28
be in turmoil *be agitated* 684.21
be in two minds about *hesitate* 841.18
be in vain *be useless* 802.11
be investigated *or* **analyzed** *or* **interrogated** *be questioned* 333.18
be involved in *participate* 760.16
be in working order *be in order* 765.23
be irascible 303.13
be irregular 664.5
be irrelevant *be extraneous* 724.12, *be unrelated* 728.12
be irreparable *be hopeless* 282.11
be irresistible 428.9
be irresolute 378.9, 461.8, 666.6; *hesitate* 841.18
be irritable 304.14; *sense* 212.9
be irritated *sense* 212.9
Beirut *Countries* 566
be itchy *sense* 212.9
be jealous 314.8
be jealous of one's good name *guard one's pride* 297.16
bejewel *beautify* 530.14, *decorate* 532.11
bejeweled *decorated* 532.9
be justified *have rights* 429.13
be just the thing *be the answer* 334.23
be kept waiting *wait* 658.12
be kind 543.16; *be benevolent* 305.10
be knowledgeable *be profound* 598.23
be known to *have a habit* 397.16
bel *sound* 230.1, *Scientific and Technical Units* 589
belabor *hit* 454.28, *harp* 797.17
belabor the obvious *make comprehensible* 363.8
be lacking *be incomplete* 762.8
be laid off *stop work* 394.12, *be dismissed* 707.18
be laid up *be unhealthy* 114.29
Belarus *Countries* 566
be last *be in the rear* 622.7
be late 658.11; *be untimely* 660.8, *have no time to spare* 818.6
belated *late* 658.5
belatedly *late* 658.14
belatedness *lack of preparation* 389.1, *lateness* 658.1
be latent 844.12
bela *or* **belah tree** *Trees and Shrubs* 43
be laureled *be superior* 744.15
be lawless *be illegal* 53.30
be lax *be permissive* 502.7
belay *mountaineering* 161.9,

mountaineer 161.10, *link* 752.18
belay device *climbing equipment* 161.4
belaying *climbing techniques* 161.3, *mountaineering* 161.9
bel canto *classical music* 140.2
belch 556.5, 709.8, 709.28; *hoarseness* 238.2, *sound hoarse* 238.8
belching *belch* 709.8, *eructative* 709.13
beleaguer *be at war* 76.32, *besiege* 418.20
be led to believe *believe* 87.9
be left 750.9
be left over *be left* 750.9
be legal 53.28
be lenient 423.5; *show pity* 308.8, *show mercy* 312.11
be let down *be disappointed* 293.8
be level *be horizontal* 603.9
Belfast *major British cities* 569
Belgian Ardennes *Horse and Pony Breeds* 159
Belgian Black Pied *Breeds of Cattle* 16
Belgian Blue *Breeds of Cattle* 16
Belgian GP at Spa Francorchamps *Formula 1 World Championship races* 146.5
Belgian griffon *Breeds of Dogs* 35
Belgian Heavy Draught *Horse and Pony Breeds* 159
Belgian Landrace *Breeds of Pigs* 16
Belgian shepherd dog *or* **Belgian sheepdog** *Breeds of Dogs* 35
Belgium *Countries* 566
Belgrade *Countries* 566
Belgravia *London* 567.8
be liable (for) *have a sense of duty* 433.13
Belial *devil* 446.5
be liberated 831.7
belie *misrepresent* 188.6, *negate* 190.16, *refute* 332.7, *delude* 720.16, *object* 828.18
belief 87.1; *religion* 81.1, *calling* 178.6, *impression* 266.2, *expectation* 281.2, 356.1, *ideology* 327.5, *judgment* 341.1, *code* 780.3, *conviction* 840.2
beliefs *feelings* 266.1
belief system 87.3; *social organization* 2.5, *philosophical system* 4.2, *religion* 81.1
belie one's expectations *disappoint* 293.9
believability 87.4
believable 87.7; *possible* 836.5, *plausible* 838.7
believably 87.13; *potentially* 836.11
believe 87.9; *be religious* 81.25, *be persuaded* 178.20, *feel* 266.14, *expect* 281.12, *be incurious* 322.5, *theorize* 327.16, *estimate* 341.11, *predict* 356.7, *suppose* 359.8, *be certain* 840.13
believed 87.8
believe in *propound a philosophy* 4.21
believer 87.5; *religious person* 81.9
believing 87.2, 87.6; *religious* 81.21, *convinced* 840.8
believingly 87.12
be lifeless *not act* 413.11, *be inert* 519.4
be light 539.8
be like *be similar* 733.12, *conform* 735.27
be likely *show potential* 458.14

Belinda *Planets and Their Satellites* 7
be linked with *accompany* 794.16
be listened to *influence* 512.11
be literal 721.25
be little 580.11
belittle *disparage* 195.15, 440.11, *be dissatisfied* 274.7, *abase* 298.20, *underestimate* 344.5, *wrong* 430.19, *scorn* 436.19, *criticize* 438.19, *make smaller* 747.8, *make unimportant* 800.20
belittled *abased* 298.13, *undervalued* 436.17, *decreasing* 747.5
belittlement *disparagement* 195.2, 440.1, *abasement* 298.6, *limitation* 747.3
belittler *disparager* 440.7
belittling *debasing* 298.15, *critical* 438.13, *disparaging* 440.8
Belize *Countries* 566
bell *brass instrument* 142.3, *percussion instrument* 142.5, *boxing terms* 152.3, *signal* 183.6, 646.9, *source of resonance* 236.4, *animal sound* 240.1, *animal sound* 240.7, *sea marker* 690.7, *warning signal* 814.3
belladonna *Flowers* 42
Bellary *Breeds of Sheep* 16
bell, book, and candle *talisman* 86.9
bell-bottomed *broad-shaped* 592.6
bell-bottoms *pants* 100.14
bellboy *attendant* 69.4, *transferrer* 685.4, *transporter* 686.4
bell buoy *warning signal* 814.3
belle *attractive female* 529.5
Belleek ware *Ceramics* 129
Belle Epoque, La [Fr] *Ages, Decades, Eras* 641
belle of the ball *attractive female* 529.5
belles-lettres *literature* 139.1
belletrist *literary person* 139.14
belletristic *literary* 139.15
bellflower *Flowers* 42
bellhop *attendant* 69.4
bellicose *military* 58.10, *aggressive* 63.9, *warring* 76.26, *warlike* 76.27, *combative* 77.32, *objectionable* 272.7, *heroic* 284.10, *angry* 302.11, *ill-natured* 303.9, *defying* 416.6, *contentious* 422.20, *disagreeing* 463.6, *strong in spirit* 516.11, *murderous* 520.7
bellicosely *heroically* 284.18, *angrily* 302.24, *ill-naturedly* 303.18, *in defiance* 416.10, *in disagreement* 463.12
bellicosity 76.15; *hostility* 63.1, *heroism* 284.2, *anger* 302.4, *ill nature* 303.2, *attack* 418.1, *divisiveness* 463.2
belligerence *hostility* 63.1, *anger* 302.4, *ill nature* 303.2, *defiance* 416.1, *attack* 418.1, *divisiveness* 463.2
belligerency 76.14; *anger* 302.4, *warfare* 422.10
belligerent *military* 58.10, *aggressive* 63.9, *warring* 76.26, *warlike* 76.27, *combatant* 77.1, *combative* 77.32, *angry* 302.11, *ill-natured* 303.9, *defying* 416.6, *contentious* 422.20, *disagreeing* 463.6
belligerently *at war* 76.34, *aggressively* 77.38, *angrily* 302.24, *ill-naturedly* 303.18, *in defiance* 416.10, *contentiously* 422.27, *in disagreement* 463.12

Bellingshausen Sea *Oceans and Seas* 571
Bellona *Deities* 82
bellow *emphasize* 200.6, *be loud* 232.8, *cry* 239.1, *cry out* 239.13, *animal sound* 240.1, *make an animal sound* 240.7
bellowing *shouting* 232.7, *vociferous* 239.9, *ululant* 240.4
bellows *woodwind* 142.4
bell ringer *player* 141.2
bell ringing *percussion instrument* 142.5, *signaling* 183.14, *ringing* 236.2
bells *Musical Instruments* 142, *percussion instrument* 142.5, *loud tone* 232.3
bell shape *cone* 633.5
bell-shaped *round* 633.7
Bell's inequality *Classical Physical Laws* 10
bell the cat *be courageous* 284.14, *be rash* 286.8, *brace oneself* 376.13
bellwether *leader* 126.8
belly *eating organ* 92.14, *grow* 581.17
bellyache [Inf] *gastroenterological disease* 114.11, *painful injury* 215.3, *be dissatisfied* 274.7, *complaint* 304.5, *to be irritable* 304.14, *complain* 507.8
bellyacher [Inf] *dissatisfied person* 274.3, *sullen person* 304.7, *discourteous person* 411.4, *protester* 507.4
bellyband *band* 754.9
belly-bust *dive* 164.15
belly dancing *Dancing Types* 135
belly flop *or* **belly bust** *or* **belly whop** *diving* 164.6, *fall* 714.4
belly-flop *dive* 164.15, *drop* 714.15
bellyful *immoderation* 99.2, *fullness* 761.5
belly-landing *flight* 689.5
belly laugh [Inf] *joke* 277.6
belly up [Inf] *unprofitable* 468.10, *impoverished* 486.11, *unprosperous* 848.11
belly-whop *dive* 164.15
Belmont Stakes *famous horse races* 159.13
Belmopan *Countries* 566
be located *be situated* 573.9
be long 590.11
belong *be included* 763.6
be long acquainted *be friends* 62.9
be long *or* **short in** *finance* 457.7
belonging *participating* 760.13, *included* 763.4, *accompanying* 794.12
belongings *possession of property* 469.3, *possessions* 470.5, *visible effect* 676.2
belonging to *possessed* 469.13
belonging to the past *antiquarian* 651.13
belong to *be the duty of* 433.16, *relate to* 727.9, *participate* 760.16, *be included* 763.6
belong to a school of thought *propound a philosophy* 4.21
belong to the past *be old* 653.15
belong with *accompany* 794.16
belonophobia *Phobias* 283
be lost *find unintelligible* 364.14
be lost and gone *be past* 651.16
be loud 232.8
beloved 299.19; *loved one* 299.13
beloved disciple *Notable Friendships* 62
be low 597.20

below *stage* 136.18, *low* 597.26, *inferiorly* 745.13
below ground *buried* 31.8
below par *sick* 114.24, *at a discount* 495.7, *ill* 517.8, *insufficient* 517.11, *of inferior quality* 597.29, *unequal* 741.4, *imperfect* 806.5, *imperfectly* 806.10
below sea level *low* 597.26
below standard *low quality* 745.7, *inferiorly* 745.13
below strength *incomplete* 806.6
below the belt *professionally* 152.22, *wrongful* 430.10
below the horizon *invisible* 245.3, *fleetingly* 265.8
below the mark *of inferior quality* 597.29, *inferiorly* 745.13
below the poverty line *poor* 486.8
below the salt *inferior* 745.5
below the surface *fleetingly* 265.8, *latent* 844.6
below zero *cool* 9.49
be loyal *be sincere* 191.8, *be tenacious* 755.9
belt *accessory* 100.28, *instrument of punishment* 454.13, *hit* 454.28, 695.11, *atmospheric layer* 768.5, *region* 564.1, *layer* 588.1, *circular thing* 631.3, *blow* 695.5, *band* 754.9
Beltane *religious festival* 85.13
Belted Galloway Breeds of Cattle 16
belter [Inf] *singer* 141.4
belt holder *prizewinner* 127.8
belt loader *construction equipment* 14.23
belt of cloud *cloud appearance* 9.19
belt out [Inf] *sing* 141.16
belt printer *hardcopy device* 15.10
belt sander *woodworking tool* 131.6
Beltsville Breeds of Fowl 16
Beltsville No. 1 Breeds of Pigs 16
Beltsville No. 2 Breeds of Pigs 16
belt-tightening *incompleteness* 98.2, *insolvency* 486.2
beltway *road* 687.2
be lucky *take a chance* 842.14, *be fortunate* 847.7
belvedere *ornamental garden* 17.3, *place for viewing* 242.13
be made up of *include* 763.5
be magnetic *attract* 700.11
be malevolent 306.12
be manifest *appear* 244.8, *become visible* 264.13
be marvelous *be wondrous* 294.14
be master of one's own ship *conduct oneself* 399.17
be master of one's time *have leisure time* 125.5
be material 524.8
be mediocre 289.16
be melodic *harmonize* 140.28
be mentally sharp 549.18
be merciful *show mercy* 312.11
be meticulous *be accurate* 721.22
be miffed *be offended* 302.14
be mighty *have authority* 52.13
bemire *dirty* 112.11
be miserable 117.17
bemist *fog* 9.59
be mistaken *be incorrect* 722.13
be mixed up 751.15
be mixed up in *be included* 763.6
bemoan *lament* 280.7
be moderate 455.12, 521.6; *be average* 742.8
be modern *live in the present* 647.8
be modest 403.11; *be humble* 298.16

be moist 559.15
be monastic 67.11
be moral 431.13; *be good* 445.16, *be virtuous* 447.8
be more than a match for *be strong* 516.14
be motionless 678.7; *be inert* 519.4
be motivated 508.10
ben [Scot] *mountain* 569.1
be naive 449.12, 821.4
be named *have a title* 72.12
be narrow-minded 593.16
be natural *be informal* 407.10
bench *ornamental garden* 17.3, *judge* 54.10, *courtroom* 541.2, *type of chair* 101.4, *factory* 124.8, *place of judgment* 341.3, *terminate* 834.7
benchmark *computing terms* 15.22
bench mark *indicator* 183.7
benchmark *exact location* 565.2, *standard* 589.7, *essential content* 723.2
bench of judges *place of judgment* 341.3
bench trial *legal process* 54.3
benchwarmer *inferior* 745.4
bench warrant *pretrial proceedings* 54.13, *demand* 425.2
bend *load* 14.49, *automobile racing terms* 146.3, *handle sailboat equipment* 150.30, *fishing tackle* 154.7, Heraldic Terms 184, *be inclined toward* 290.10, *succumb* 421.7, *show obeisance to* 426.8, *mark of respect* 435.4, *show respect* 435.16, *motivate* 508.9, *tend* 513.5, *soften* 543.14, *prostration* 597.2, *be low* 597.20, *divergence* 607.2, *diverge* 607.11, *make shapeless* 625.3, *angle* 628.1, 628.11, *curve* 629.1, 629.6, *fold* 637.1, 637.7, *road attribute* 687.3, *deviating course* 698.2, *twist* 698.19, *deflect* 698.26, *bow* 716.6, 716.22, *sit* 716.20
bendability *softness* 543.1
bendable *pliant* 543.7
bend a rule *be lenient* 423.5
Ben Day process *darkening* 247.2
bend backward *lean* 716.19
bender [Inf] *drinking bout* 121.7, *celebration* 405.1
bend forks *experience psychic phenomena* 86.23
bend forward *lean* 716.19
bending *deformation* 14.16, *inclined toward* 290.5, *submitting* 421.3, *mark of respect* 435.4, *showing respect* 435.7, *divergent* 607.7, *curvature* 629.2, *indirect* 698.9
bending moment *strength of materials* 14.15
bending the knee *mark of respect* 435.4
bend in the road *curved thing* 629.3
bend lines *handle sailboat equipment* 150.30
bend one's elbow [Inf] *get drunk* 121.35
bend over *lean* 716.19
bend over backward *exert oneself* 122.11, *be eager* 373.13, *be unselfish* 443.7
bend sinister Heraldic Terms 184
bend the knee *knuckle under* 401.10, *show respect* 435.16
bend the law *be illegal* 53.30
bend the rules *be permissive* 502.7
bend the truth *circumlocute* 607.12
bend to one's will *have authority* 52.13

be near 586.11
be nearsighted *see badly* 243.16
beneath *low* 597.26, *inferiorly* 745.13
beneath contempt *obscure* 800.13
beneath notice *obscure* 800.13
Benedicite *prayer* 85.10
Benedick Famous Lovers 299
benedict *or* **Benedick** *married man* 64.10
Benedict Arnold *hypocrite* 192.9
benediction *prayer* 85.10, *thanks* 310.2, *welfare* 445.2
Benedict's test *sugar test* 12.6
be needy 95.18
benefaction *charity* 275.3, 307.3, *benevolent act* 305.5, *philanthropy* 307.1, *giving* 472.1, *financial support* 605.8
benefactor 825.15; *philanthropist* 307.5, *doer* 412.3, *giver* 472.7, *generous person* 498.5, *volunteer* 504.7, *provider* 605.10, *protector* 810.11
benefactress *protector* 810.11, *benefactor* 825.15
benefactress *or* **benefactrix** *philanthropist* 307.5
benefice *property* 470.1
beneficence *charity* 305.3, 307.3, *philanthropy* 307.1, *kindness* 445.3, *generosity* 498.1
beneficent *charitable* 305.9, *philanthropic* 307.6, *generous* 498.8, *benevolent* 825.21
beneficently *charitably* 305.15, *philanthropically* 307.9
beneficial 445.11, 825.20; *favorable* 62.8, *health-giving* 113.6, *healthful* 113.7, *remedial* 115.14, *desirable* 288.11, *useful* 393.7, *good* 445.10, *gainful* 467.10, *profitable* 801.8, *convenient* 803.3
beneficially *favorably* 62.15, *desirably* 288.24, *usefully* 393.15, *well* 445.19, *gainfully* 467.24, *helpfully* 825.32
beneficiary 473.6; *gainer* 467.9, *gainful* 467.10, *wealthy person* 485.6
benefit 801.4, 801.10; *theatrical performance* 136.13, *benevolent act* 305.5, *be charitable* 305.12, *philanthropize* 307.8, *usefulness* 393.2, *good* 445.1, *be good* 445.16, *better* 445.17, *gain* 467.1, 467.15, *profit* 467.6, *reward* 472.4, *offering* 472.6, *be profitable* 489.22, *extra* 748.6, *convenience* 803.1, *be convenient* 803.5, *help* 825.1, *support* 825.2, *social assistance* 825.4
benefit concert *or* **gig** [Inf] *solicitation* 505.4
benefit game *solicitation* 505.4
benefit of the doubt *favorable verdict* 54.19
benefit performance *theatrical performance* 136.13, *offering* 472.6
benefits 57.11; *positive stimulus* 508.5
be negative 190.21
be neglectful 326.7
be negligent *be neglectful* 326.7
be neither fish nor fowl *stand in the middle* 772.17
be neither one thing nor the other *stand in the middle* 772.17
Benelux *economic organization* 56.6
be nervous *be fearful* 283.15
be neutral about *be incurious* 322.5

benevolence 305.1; *friendship* 62.1, *philanthropy* 307.1, *pity* 308.1, *forgivingness* 312.3, *goodwill* 373.4, *intention* 374.1, *courtesy* 410.1, *leniency* 423.1, *unselfishness* 443.2, *kindness* 445.3, *virtue* 447.1, *giving* 472.1, *levy* 494.7, *magnanimity* 498.2, *permission* 502.1, *helpfulness* 825.10
benevolent 305.7, 825.21; *friendly* 62.5, *philanthropic* 307.6, *pitying* 308.4, *forgiving* 312.4, *goodwilled* 373.10, *courteous* 410.6, *lenient* 423.3, *unselfish* 443.5, *kind* 445.12, *virtuous* 447.5, *giving* 472.9, *magnanimous* 498.7, *sustaining* 605.15
benevolent act 305.5
benevolent despotism *totalitarianism* 49.13
benevolent disposition *benevolence* 305.1
benevolently 305.13, 825.34; *amicably* 62.13, *philanthropically* 307.9, *pityingly* 308.11, *forgivingly* 312.13, *courteously* 410.13, *genteelly* 410.14, *leniently* 423.6, *unselfishly* 443.9, *kindly* 445.20, *virtuously* 447.9, *as a gift* 472.17, *supportively* 605.20
benevolentness *philanthropy* 307.1
benevolent person 305.6
be new 652.17
be next to *juxtapose* 586.14, *side* 623.8
Bengal Breeds of Cats 35
Beni Rivers 570
Beni Ahsen Breeds of Sheep 16
be nice *be benevolent* 305.10
benighted *blind to* 243.14, *evening* 656.4
benightedness *figurative blindness* 243.8
benign *health-giving* 113.6, *benevolent* 305.7, 825.21, *philanthropic* 307.6, *kind* 445.12, *trustworthy* 810.17
benignity *benevolence* 305.1, *philanthropy* 307.1, *kindness* 445.3
benignly *benevolently* 305.13, *philanthropically* 307.9
benign tumor *cancer* 114.15
Beni Guil Breeds of Sheep 16
Benin Countries 566
benison *prayer* 85.10
be no more *die* 29.17, *come to an end* 773.23
be nonexistent *be unreal* 722.12
be nonpartisan *be impartial* 289.15
be nonresonant 233.10
be nonsense *mean nothing* 362.10
be not all there [Inf] *lack intellect* 316.8
be nothing 190.20
be now *be present* 647.7
bent *aptitude* 127.4, *inclination* 290.2, *ability* 340.2, *intending* 374.6, *tendency* 397.2, *attitude* 513.2, *divergent* 607.7, *angular* 628.7, *curved* 629.4, *folded* 637.5, *bearing* 697.2, *sedentary* 716.11
bent [Brit inf] *offending* 53.25
bent bond *chemical bond* 11.6
bent double *sedentary* 716.11
bent grass *golf course* 156.2
Benthamic *public-spirited* 307.7
Benthamism Philosophical Schools of Thought 4, *political*

and economic philosophy 4.6, *public-spiritedness* 307.2

Benthamite Philosophical Schools of Thought 4, *philanthropist* 307.5

benthic *oceanic* 8.53, 571.7, *deep-sea* 598.11

benthos *sea* 571.1, *the depths* 598.2

benthoscope *bathymetry* 598.3

bent upon *resolute* 376.7

bentwood *type of chair* 101.4

Benue Rivers 570

be null and void *be nothing* 190.20, *not exist* 718.12

benumb *anesthetize* 213.8, *make cold* 218.15, *make indifferent* 289.13, *overpower* 515.14

benumbed *indifferent* 289.7, *inactive* 413.9

benzene hexachloride (BHC) *pest killer* 17.9

benzine *fuels* 106.2

benzoin Tree Products 43

benzoylate *react* 11.38

be objective *be truthful* 191.7, *be impartial* 289.15

be obligated *or* **indebted** *be grateful* 310.6

be obliged to *be grateful* 310.6

be oblique 607.10; *sidestep* 698.22, *slide* 714.17

be oblivious *be insensible* 213.7, *be forgetful* 355.11

be obstinate 379.10, 417.11

be obvious *be visible* 244.7

be occasional *be infrequent* 662.3

be of assistance *help* 825.23

be off *retreat* 386.22, *set out* 705.12

be off! *go!* 709.30

be off-color 251.18

be offended 302.14

be officious *meddle* 414.23

be offside *exhibit penalty behavior* 155.21

be of help *help* 825.23

be of *or* **to no avail** *be powerless* 515.11

be often seen at *frequent* 661.6

be of the opinion 87.10; *propound a philosophy* 4.21

be of the same mind *agree* 730.14

be of *or* **in two minds** *be irresolute* 378.9

be of use *have at one's disposal* 393.14, *help* 825.23

be old 653.15

be old friends *be friends* 62.9

be on a collision course *converge* 702.9

be on a different wavelength *find unintelligible* 364.14

be on a high *awake* 212.10

be on a list 785.12

be on an ego trip [Inf] *pride oneself* 297.13

be on a pension *earn* 467.20

be on call *practice medicine* 107.32, *wait* 356.8, *be prepared* 388.17

be one 788.17

be on edge *be fearful* 283.15

be one of *be included* 763.6

be oneself *be informal* 407.10

be one's own fault *serve one right* 420.5

be one's own man *or* **woman** *follow one's own will* 372.13

be one's own worst enemy *act foolishly* 128.10

be one up on *be cunning* 822.5

be on fire *burn* 217.18

be on guard *fence* 153.7

be on hand *attend* 575.14

be on one's best behavior *have good manners* 410.10

be on one's good *or* **best behavior** *be virtuous* 447.8

be on one's guard *be cautious* 287.11

be on one's high horse *disdain* 297.14

be on one's toes *push* 414.20

be on one's way *set out* 705.12

be on pins and needles *be in suspense* 604.18

be on sale *be sold* 482.22

be on slippery ground *be in danger* 811.11

be on standby *wait* 356.8, *be prepared* 388.17

be on the ball *awake* 212.10

be on the beach *border* 618.9

be on the crest of a wave *be good* 445.16

be on the front page *be published* 173.19

be on the lookout *be cautious* 287.11

be on the opposite side *be opposite* 731.4

be on the opposite side of the fence *be opposite* 731.4

be on the rag [Inf] *bleed* 25.26

be on the run *conceal oneself* 181.15

be on the safe side *be safe* 810.20

be on the same wavelength *agree with* 462.10

be on the sideline *border* 618.9

be on the special team *kick* 155.20

be on the track 146.11

be on the waiting list *wait* 356.8

be on to *understand* 363.9

be on to a good thing *be fortunate* 847.7

be on top of the world *be good* 445.16

be on trial *stand trial* 54.29

be on visiting terms *visit* 408.16

be opaque 250.6

be open 583.19; *be sincere* 191.8, *externalize* 610.15

be open to criticism 438.22

be operational 509.10

be opposite 731.4

be optimistic *hope* 281.10

be ordained *ordain* 84.16

be ostentatious *disdain* 297.14

be out for the count *succumb* 421.7

be out of danger *be safe* 810.20

be out-of-doors *or* **outdoors** *be exterior* 610.13

be out of one's depth *find unintelligible* 364.14, *be in danger* 811.11, *be in difficulty* 824.19

be out of order *go wrong* 430.23

be out of pocket *expend* 491.11

be out of proportion *be disparate* 728.14

be out of sorts *be sullen* 304.12

be outside *be exterior* 610.13

be over *be past* 651.16, *come to an end* 773.23

be over and done with *be past* 651.16

be overcome *be sensitive* 267.5

be overdrawn *overpay* 496.11, *need money* 848.14

be overpossessive *be jealous* 314.8

be overwhelmed *be sensitive* 267.5

be painful 215.9

be parallel *parallel* 606.7

be paralyzed with fear *be afraid* 283.14

be parched *be hungry* 288.21

be parsimonious 490.13

be part and parcel of *be essential* 723.10

be partial to *be inclined toward* 290.10, *like* 299.22

be partisan *side with* 623.10

be part of *participate* 760.16, *be included* 763.6

be passé *grow old* 653.16

be past 651.16

be patient with *show mercy* 312.11

be penalized *exhibit penalty behavior* 155.21

be penitent 451.7; *repent* 313.9

be penny wise and pound foolish *figurative expressions* 128.11

be perfect 805.20

be periodical 641.9

be permanent 667.4; *be eternal* 644.7

be permissive 502.7

be permitted 502.8

be persuaded 178.20

be pessimistic *be negative* 190.21

be pestilential *cause ill health* 114.30

be petrified *be afraid* 283.14

be pink-slipped *be dismissed* 707.18

be piquant 221.9

be pissed *or* **pissed off** [Inf] *be angry* 302.19

be pitiless 309.5

be plagued *worry* 283.16

be pleased with oneself *be vain* 402.14

be plentiful *abound* 97.8

be pointed *be sharp* 549.15

be polite *be courteous* 410.9

be politically correct *be impartial* 338.11

be poor 486.14; *be needy* 95.18

be positive *be definite* 189.26

be possessed by the spirit *revere* 81.26

be possessive *be jealous* 314.8

be possible 836.8

be potent *have authority* 52.13

be powerful 514.18

be powerless 515.11

be precipitous *act impulsively* 318.14

be precise *be accurate* 721.22

be predictable *not cause wonder* 295.7

be prejudiced *be narrow-minded* 593.16, *be unjust* 741.9

be prepared 388.17; *foresee* 357.9

be present 575.13, 647.7; *appear* 264.12, *arrive* 704.13

be present and accounted for *appear* 575.16

be present at *attend* 575.14

be pressed for time *have no time to spare* 818.6

be prevalent *be an influence* 512.13

be prideful *pride oneself* 297.13

be private *escape notice* 403.14, *be aloof* 756.8

be probable 838.8

be productive *be fertile* 22.13

be professional *be expert* 127.15

be proficient in *know* 48.24

be profitable 467.21, 489.22; *increase* 746.6

be profound 598.23

be proper *be elegant* 527.6

be proportional *be similar* 733.12, *be in accord* 735.21

be proportionate to *correspond to* 727.10

be prosperous 847.6

be proud 297.15

be proud of *be proud* 297.15

be public-spirited *philanthropize* 307.8

be published 173.19; *occur* 264.14

be puffed up *be vain* 402.14

be punished 454.31; *serve one right* 420.5

be pure *be moral* 431.13

be qualified *qualify* 340.11

be qualified for *have rights* 429.13

bequeath 372.15; *own property* 470.11, *transfer property* 470.12, *will* 472.11, *make rich* 485.15, *give* 498.11, *bring* 685.11, *leave* 750.10

bequeathable *transferring property* 470.10, *given* 472.8

bequeathal *transfer of property* 470.4, *giving* 472.1, *receiving* 473.1

bequeathed 372.10; *transferring property* 470.10, *given* 472.8, *received* 492.6

bequeather *giver* 472.7

bequeathing *transferring property* 470.10

bequest *final will* 372.5, *profit* 467.6, *transfer of property* 470.4, *gift* 472.2, *receiving* 473.1, *legacy* 492.4, *transferred thing* 685.6, *estate* 750.5

be questioned 333.18

be quick! *hurry up!* 818.9

be quiet *be silent* 231.3

be quite at home *do easily* 823.16

be quits *retaliate* 420.4

berakhah [Hebrew] *prayer* 85.10

be rash 286.8

berate 438.20; *criticize* 418.26

berated *criticized* 438.14

berating 438.5

Berber Breeds of Sheep 16

berceuse Musical Forms 140, *song* 140.11

be ready *be inclined toward* 290.10, *be willing* 373.12, *be prepared* 388.17

be ready and waiting *start early* 657.12

be real 719.10, 721.21

be reasonable 319.12

bereave *widow* 66.12

bereavement *forfeiture* 468.2

be reborn *live* 28.17

be received *reach* 704.14

be reclusive *be aloof* 756.8

be recognizable 363.12

be recognized *influence* 512.11

be redundant *be the same* 730.13

be reflected *resonate* 236.9

be refreshed 94.8

bereft *losing* 468.9, *remaining* 750.7

bereft of life *dead* 29.11

be regular 663.10

be rejuvenated *be converted* 670.12

be relieved *play baseball* 147.9

be religious 81.25

be reluctant *be disinclined* 291.14

be remembered 354.15

Berenice's Hair Constellations 7

be repeated 797.20; *resonate* 236.9

be repulsive 701.10

be resentful *resent* 302.13

be reserved *lack candor* 192.22

be resigned *submit* 421.4

be resolute 376.11
be respected *have a good reputation* 370.5
be responsible *answer for* 334.24, *have a sense of duty* 433.13
be responsible for *be an instrument* 511.7
be rested *be refreshed* 94.8
be restored 809.13; *be refreshed* 94.8
beret *cap* 100.33
be revived *be refreshed* 94.8
be rewarded 453.16
berg *iceberg* 8.45, Notable Winds 9
Bergamo Breeds of Sheep 16
bergenia Flowers 42
Bergmann's rule *measurement* 1.9
bergschrund *rock face* 161.6
Bergsonian Philosophical Schools of Thought 4
Bergsonism Philosophical Schools of Thought 4
beriberi *vitamin deficiency disease* 12.14, *tropical disease* 114.10
be rich 485.12
be ridiculous 368.6
be rife *be an influence* 512.13
be right 429.12
be rightly served *serve one right* 420.5
Bering (Samoa) Time *time zone* 646.5
Bering Sea Oceans and Seas 571
Berkeleyan Philosophical Schools of Thought 4
Berkeleyism Philosophical Schools of Thought 4
berkelium Chemical Elements and Common Allotropes 11
Berkshire Breeds of Pigs 16
Berlin Countries 566, *other famous world cities* 567.9
Berlin Wall *separator* 753.5
Berlin ware Ceramics 129
Bermejo Rivers 570
Bermuda Islands Islands 572
Bermuda shorts *shorts* 100.15
Bern Countries 566
Bernese Alps Mountains and Hills 569
Bernese mountain dog Breeds of Dogs 35
Bernina Mountains and Hills 569
Bernoulli effect Classical Physical Laws 10
Bernoulli trial Mathematical Concepts 6
Bernreuter personality inventory Psychological Tests 108
be rooted to the spot *be afraid* 283.14
be rough 544.10
berry *seed* 41.9, *botanical fruit* 44.2, *fruit* 90.34, *plant products* 522.8
berserk *manic* 110.10, *angry* 302.11, *attacking* 418.14, *violent* 520.5
berserker *destroyer* 523.6
berth *type of bed* 101.9, *reserved space* 563.5, *employment* 573.3, *stopover* 704.7, *land* 704.16
bertha collar *neckwear* 100.29
berthage *reserved space* 563.5
berthed *employed* 573.8
be rude *be inconsiderate* 318.13, *be insolent* 400.14, *disrespect* 436.18
be ruined *need money* 848.14
beryl *green thing* 260.4, *blue thing* 261.3
beryllium Chemical Elements and Common Allotropes 11
be sacked [Inf] *be dismissed* 707.18
be saddened *grieve* 270.7

be safe 810.20
be sane 109.5
be sanguine *hope* 281.10
be satisfied 273.8
be saved *recant* 81.27, *be converted* 670.12
be saved by the bell *be safe* 810.20
be seated *sit* 716.20
beseech *pray* 85.20, *petition* 505.11
beseeching *petition* 505.2, *requesting* 505.7
beseechingly *by request* 505.14
be seen *be visible* 244.7, *show oneself* 843.15
be self-conscious *be shy* 403.13
be selfish 444.6
be self-restrained 455.10
be sensitive 267.5; *sense* 212.9, *be touched by* 216.10
be serious 278.7
be servile 401.8
beset *besiege* 418.20, *overrun* 712.6, *troubled* 824.15
besetting *habit-forming* 397.15
beset with perils *dangerous* 811.7
be severe 424.8
be shamed *be disreputable* 371.5
be sharp 549.15; *be intelligent* 315.11
be short 591.10
be shrill 238.9
be shy 403.13
be sick *be unhealthy* 114.29, *vomit* 709.27
beside 586.20; *additionally* 748.15
be side by side *juxtapose* 586.14
beside oneself *angry* 302.11
besides *additionally* 748.15
beside the point *extraneously* 724.16, *irrelatively* 728.16
besiege 418.20; *be at war* 76.32, *combat* 77.34, *detain* 830.16
besieged *detained* 830.11
besieger *combatant* 77.1, *attacker* 418.10
besieging *blockading* 76.22
be silent 181.16, 231.3; *be voiceless* 206.8
be similar 733.12; *correspond* 606.8
be simple 526.13; *be unadorned* 424.10
be simultaneous 649.6; *be the same* 730.13
be sincere 191.8
be situated 573.9
be skeptical *not accept* 190.19
be skillful 127.14
be skin-deep *be superficial* 599.6
be slave to a habit *accustom oneself* 397.19
beslime *dirty* 112.11
be slow (of clocks) *be late* 658.11
be small *be little* 580.11
be small-minded *be narrow-minded* 593.16
be smart *be intelligent* 315.11, 352.7
besmear *dirty* 112.11, *defame* 440.13
besmeared *dirty* 112.7
be smiled on by fate *be in comfortable circumstances* 726.13
besmirch *dirty* 112.11, *defame* 440.13
besmirched *dirty* 112.7
besmirching *defamatory* 440.9
be snowed in *become cold* 218.14
be snowed under *become cold* 218.14
be sober 120.8
be sociable 408.14, 414.22
be social *be sociable* 408.14

be so cold one's toes *or* fingers drop off *or* one's teeth chatter *become cold* 218.14
be sold 482.22; *be published* 173.19
be solemn *be serious* 278.7
be solicitous 323.13
besom *cleaning tool* 111.10
be (some) years old *age* 27.16
be sorrowful *be miserable* 117.17
be sorry for *feel for* 266.17
besotted with *in love* 299.16
be sour *sour* 223.8
be spared *live* 28.17
bespatter *dirty* 112.11, *defame* 440.13, *sprinkle* 557.32
bespeak *mean* 551.11
bespeak performance [Arch] *theatrical performance* 136.13
bespeckle *mix* 751.12
bespectacled 242.18
bespoke [Brit] *tailored* 100.41, *designed* 536.6, *prototypical* 624.7, *customized* 779.14
bespoke clothes [Brit] *tailor-made clothes* 100.4
besprinkle *mix* 751.12
Bessel functions Mathematical Concepts 6
best 744.10, 805.9; *wondrous* 294.9, *excellence* 445.4, *excellent* 445.13, *outdo* 744.18
best, the *chosen thing or person* 382.8, *successful person* 845.6
be stable 674.6
be starving *be hungry* 288.21
best-ball match *golf* 156.1
best behavior *formality* 406.1
best bet *chance* 838.4
best bib and tucker *formal clothes* 100.5, *formal clothing* 406.5
best boy [Inf] *filmmaker* 137.14
best chance *opportunity* 659.2, *strong possibility* 836.3, *good chance* 842.6
best clothes *formal clothes* 100.5
bestead [Arch] *be useful* 801.9
bested *outclassed* 745.9, *defeated* 846.11
best effort *attempt* 390.1
best ever *excellence* 445.4, *excellent* 445.13, *best* 744.10, 805.9, *famous* 845.9
best forgotten *forgotten* 355.7
best friend *friend* 62.2, *influential person* 512.5
bestial *animalian* 34.12, *cruel* 306.10, *perverted* 432.12, *murderous* 520.7
bestiality *sexual perversion* 20.12, *cruelty* 306.4, *sexual offense* 432.6, *violence by person* 520.2
bestir oneself *exert oneself* 122.11, *be active* 414.18
best man *wedding party* 64.7
best one can do *attempt* 390.1
best option *choice* 382.3
bestow *bequeath* 372.15, *grant* 735.30, *finance* 825.31
bestowable *transferring property* 470.10, *given* 472.8
bestowal *benevolent act* 305.5, *giving* 472.1, *grant* 735.10, *financial assistance* 825.6
bestow alms *give to charity* 472.16
bestowal of love *courtship* 299.10
bestow a medal *reward* 453.13
bestow an honorary degree *reward* 453.13
bestowed *given* 472.8, *granted* 735.20
bestower *giver* 472.7
bestowing *giving* 472.9

bestow in marriage *join in marriage* 64.20
bestow one's hand upon *marry* 64.19
bestow rights *authorize* 52.14
bestow sorrow *be evil* 446.10
bestow upon *give* 472.10
best part *large part* 579.3, *majority* 793.3, *chief thing* 799.3
best people 744.7
bestraddle *mount* 713.24
best regards *courtesies* 410.3
best respects *courtesies* 410.3
bestride *be an influence* 512.13, *span* 592.12, *mount* 713.24, *link* 752.18
be strident 238.7
be strong 516.14; *endure* 377.14
be struck by *have an idea* 327.13
be struck dumb *have difficulty speaking* 206.9, *be silent* 231.1
bestseller *book* 174.1, *good thing* 445.9, *merchandise* 482.6, *successful thing* 845.5
best-selling *best* 805.9, *famous* 845.9
best shot *attempt* 390.1
be stubborn 542.11; *show determination* 674.8
be stuck in a groove *have a habit* 397.16
be stuck on oneself *be vain* 402.14
be stumped *be ignorant* 349.2
be stupid *lack intellect* 316.8
Bestuzhev Breeds of Cattle 16
best wishes *courtesies* 410.3, *greeting* 435.5
be stylish *be elegant* 527.6
be subjected to *be subject to* 832.12
be subject to 832.12; *follow from* 676.9
be submissive *succumb* 421.7
be subservient *be servile* 401.8
be subversive *subvert* 427.13
be successful 845.11; *achieve* 704.21
be suitable 462.13
be sullen 304.12
be superficial 599.6
be superfluous 99.12; *have free time* 413.15
be superior 744.15; *be unequal* 741.7, *take precedence* 769.14
be surprised 292.12
be suspended *suspend* 604.13
be sweet on [Inf] *like* 290.8, *be in love* 299.23
be swept aside *succumb* 421.7
be swift 694.10
be sycophantic 439.15
be symmetrical *be similar* 733.12
be synonymous *be equivalent* 730.15
bet *horse-racing betting terms* 159.11, *gambling* 167.4, *contend* 422.22, *take a chance* 842.14
be taciturn 208.7
be tactful *be sensitive* 267.5, *be courteous* 410.9
beta decay *radioactivity* 10.58
beta emitter *radioactivity* 10.58
beta function *mathematical function* 6.27
be taken aback *be surprised* 292.12
be taken by surprise *be surprised* 292.12
be taken in *be incurious* 322.5
be talkative 207.7
be tall 596.16
be tangible *be real* 721.21
beta particle *radioactivity* 10.58

beta rays *radioactivity* 10.58
be tardy *be untimely* 660.8
be tasteless 220.6
beta test *programming concepts* 15.24, *Intelligence Tests* 108
be taught *learn* 48.23, *be informed* 170.15
be taught a lesson *serve one right* 420.5
be taxed *pay duty on* 433.18
be tedious *bore* 296.8
betel palm *Trees and Shrubs* 43
be temperate *be modest* 403.11, *be moderate* 455.12
be tenacious 755.9
bête noire *adversity* 117.2, *hated thing* 300.5
be termed *have a title* 72.12
be tested *be questioned* 333.18
be thankful *be grateful* 310.6
be thankful for small mercies *be grateful* 310.6
be the answer 334.23
be the author of *cause* 675.8
be the better for *find useful* 801.11
be the boss *manage* 126.10
be the case *be true* 721.20
be the cause of *cause* 675.8
be the center of attention *attract attention* 323.12
be the duty of 433.16
bethel *place of worship* 83.8
be the making of *improve* 807.15, *finance* 825.31
be the norm *be average* 742.8
be the rage *prevail* 778.19
be there *appear* 264.12, *be present* 575.13, *exist* 717.18
be there in person *attend* 575.14
be the result of *follow from* 676.9
be the rule 780.16; *become a habit* 397.17, *prevail* 778.19
be the same 730.13; *be permanent* 667.4
be the sport of wind and waves *pitch* 684.25
be the tool of *knuckle under* 401.10
be thick-skinned *be insensitive* 268.6
be thirsty *be hungry* 288.21, *thirst* 560.18
be thorough *be careful* 593.15
be thoughtful *think* 317.9
be thoughtless 324.11; *be ungrateful* 311.5
be thrifty 499.5
be thrown out *play baseball* 147.9
be ticked *or* **ticked off** [Inf] *be angry* 302.19
betide *chance* 842.12
be timely 659.6
betimes *early* 657.17
be tired *be fatigued* 820.5
be to come *be in the future* 650.9
betoken *signify* 183.16, *state* 329.13, *predict* 358.14, *mean* 361.13
be told *be informed* 170.15, *understand* 363.9
be told by a little bird [Inf] *be informed* 170.15
bet on *think likely* 838.10
bet one's bottom dollar *be certain* 840.13
bet one's life [Inf] *be certain* 840.13
be too clever for *be cunning* 822.5
be too good to be true *overestimate* 343.6
be to one's advantage *benefit* 801.10
be too proud *pride oneself* 297.13

be too quick for *be cunning* 822.5
be tormented *worry* 283.16
be touched by 216.10
be tough 547.13
Betpak Dala *Deserts* 572
be traditional *be conservative* 815.15
be trained (in) *qualify* 340.11
be transferred 470.13
be transformed *be converted* 670.12
be transient 643.6
be transparent 249.11
betray *inform on* 170.13, *tell on* 180.10, *be dishonorable* 192.21, *detect* 345.12, *subvert* 427.13, *be wicked* 448.13, *be cunning* 822.5, *change* 841.20, *reveal* 843.14
betrayal *divulgence* 180.2, *dishonorableness* 192.3
betrayed hopes *frustration* 293.2
betrayer *informer* 170.8, *discloser* 180.4, *hypocrite* 192.9, *malefactor* 306.6, *equivocator* 380.4, *villain* 448.5
betraying *signifying* 183.11, *equivocating* 380.6
betray someone's hopes *thwart* 293.10
be trendy 652.18
be triumphant *be victorious* 845.16
betroth *marry* 64.19, *contract* 459.8
betrothal 458.2; *courtship* 299.10, *contract* 459.1
betrothed *girlfriend* 33.4, *marriageable* 64.17, *loved one* 299.13, *someone promised* 458.7, *promised* 458.8, *united* 752.10
be troubled *be miserable* 117.17, *worry* 283.16
be true 721.20; *be sincere* 191.8, *exist* 717.18
be true to the facts *be literal* 721.25
be truthful 191.7
better 445.17, 807.24; *preferential* 382.10, *excellent* 445.13, *change for the better* 665.17, *further* 679.13, *superior* 744.8, *outdo* 744.18, *sound* 759.8, *improved* 807.12, *improve* 807.15, 825.26, *cured* 809.8
better advised *improved* 807.12
better choice *choice* 382.3, *reconsideration* 807.9
bettered *advanced* 713.16, *improved* 807.12
better half *spouse* 64.8
better idea *reconsideration* 807.9
bettering *educational* 48.17, *beneficial* 445.11
better luck next time! *good luck!* 842.19
betterment *education* 48.1, *welfare* 445.2, *advance* 467.3, *change for the better* 665.4, *improvement* 679.5, 807.1, *ascendancy* 713.5
better off *improved* 807.12
better oneself *change for the better* 665.17, *get better* 807.21
better part *large part* 579.3
better thing *reconsideration* 807.9
better thought *reconsideration* 807.9
better thoughts *vacillation* 380.3
better time *different time* 648.1
betting *horse-racing betting terms* 159.11, *gambling* 167.4, 167.11, *poker* 168.5
betting house *gambling house* 167.5

betting parlor *gambling house* 167.5
bettor *horse person* 159.14, *gambler* 167.6
be turned into *or* **to** *convert* 670.11
be turned on by [Inf] *lust after* 288.20
between *in the middle* 772.21
between a rock and a hard place [Inf] *conditionally* 725.10, *irresolutely* 772.23, *endangered* 811.10, *troubled* 824.15
between jobs *not working* 415.10
between Scylla and Charybdis *irresolutely* 772.23, *endangered* 811.10, *troubled* 824.15
between the devil and the deep blue sea *irresolutely* 772.23, *endangered* 811.10, *troubled* 824.15
between the lines *tacit* 844.10
between the teeth *faintly* 233.11
betweentimes *meanwhile* 639.18
between two chairs *endangered* 811.10
between two fires *endangered* 811.10
betweenwhiles *meanwhile* 639.18
between you, me, and the lamppost *or* **gatepost** *secretly* 182.14
betwixt and between *medianly* 742.12, *irresolutely* 772.23
be two-faced *equivocate* 380.8
be ugly 531.5
be unable *be powerless* 515.11
be unable to pay 490.11
be unable to see something under one's nose *or* **in front of one's eyes** *be blind to* 243.19
be unable to see straight *see badly* 243.16
be unable to see the forest *or* **wood for the trees** *be blind to* 243.19, *misjudge* 342.9
be unaccustomed 398.5
be unadorned 424.10
be unanswered *be unexplained* 364.15
be unappetizing *be tasteless* 220.6
be unappreciative *be ungrateful* 311.5
be unbiased *be impartial* 289.15, *be broad-minded* 592.13
be uncensored *be free* 829.16
be uncertain 841.17; *defer* 604.15
be unclear *make shapeless* 625.3
be uncomfortable with *be unaccustomed* 398.5
be unconscious *be insensible* 213.7
be undeceived *understand* 363.9
be undemocratic *be unjust* 741.9
be under cover *be safe* 810.20
be under the impression *be of the opinion* 87.10
be undisciplined *be disorderly* 766.22
be unemotional *be insensitive* 268.6
be unemployed *have free time* 413.15
be unequal 741.7; *be disparate* 728.14
be unexplained 364.15
be unfaithful *be dishonorable* 192.21, *fornicate* 432.14
be unfeeling *be insensible* 213.7, *be pitiless* 309.5
be unfinished 544.12; *be incomplete* 762.8
be unforgotten *be remembered* 354.15
be unfulfilled *be incomplete* 762.8

be ungrateful 311.5
be unhealthy 114.29
be unheard 229.12
be uniform *be compatible* 462.12, *be the same* 730.13, *conform* 735.27
be unimportant 800.18
be unintelligent *lack intellect* 316.8
be unintelligible 364.11
be united *agree* 730.14
be unjust 342.10, 741.9
be unlike *be dissimilar* 734.7
be unlucky *lose one's chance* 660.10, *be in trouble* 848.13
be unmasked *be discovered* 345.15
be unmoved *have no mercy* 309.6
be unprepared 389.14
be unreal 722.12
be unrelated 728.12
be unresponsive *be insensitive* 268.6
be unruly *cause confusion* 51.9
be unsatisfied 98.10
be unselfish 443.7
be unskillful 128.8
be unsocial 409.10
be unsympathetic *be pitiless* 309.5
be untimely 660.8
be untrue 722.11; *be dishonorable* 192.21, *be incorrect* 722.13
be untruthful 192.20; *be untrue* 722.11
be unused 394.11
be unused to *be unaccustomed* 398.5
be unwilling 375.12
be up against it *be in danger* 811.11
be up and doing *be active* 414.18, *be full of vigor* 518.4
be up a tree *be in difficulty* 824.19
be up in arms *push* 414.20
be up on *know* 48.24, *be an authority on* 52.17
be up shit creek [Inf] *be in a predicament* 725.9, *be in difficulties* 726.14
be up to *be the duty of* 433.16, *be powerful* 514.18
be up-to-date *live in the present* 647.8
be up to something *plot* 387.15
be upwind of *have no smell* 225.7
be useful 801.9; *be an instrument* 511.7
be useless 802.11; *have free time* 413.15
be vague *make shapeless* 625.3
be vain 402.14; *pride oneself* 297.13
be varied *be changed* 665.15
bevel *carpenter's term* 131.5, *obliqueness* 607.1, *be oblique* 607.10, *obliquity* 628.2, *angle* 628.11
bevel *or* **beveled** *oblique* 607.6
beveled *oblique* 628.8
beveled edge *oblique line* 607.5
bevel gear *gear* 14.7
bevel square *angular measurement* 628.4
beverage *drink* 93.2, 121.6, *fluid* 555.1
be vertical 602.8
be victorious 845.16
be vigilant *be careful* 325.11
be violent 520.8
be virtuous 447.8; *be good* 445.16
be visible 242.26, 244.7, 843.16
be voiceless 206.8
be voted in *run for office* 50.10
bevy *assemblage of mammals* 35.22,

Collective Names 59, *group* 59.8, *throng* 795.4
bewail *lament* 280.7
bewail one's sins *be penitent* 451.7
be wanting *be incomplete* 762.8
beware *be cautious* 287.11, *be warned* 814.9
beware! *be careful!* 287.20, *hands off!* 386.26, *look out!* 814.12
be warned 814.9
be wary *suspect* 314.9
be wasted 96.22
be wasteful 468.16
be weak 517.12
bewegt Musical Terms and Expression Marks 140
be well-nourished *eat well* 92.23
be well-preserved *be healthy* 113.11
be well thought of *have a good reputation* 370.5
be wet behind the ears *be naive* 821.4
be whole 759.9; *be complete* 761.10
be wicked 448.13
be widowed 66.13
bewigged *dressed* 100.38
bewilder *mystify* 182.12, *astonish* 292.10, *be wondrous* 294.14, *puzzle* 364.12, *mix up* 751.13, *cause difficulties* 824.22, *make uncertain* 841.19
bewildered *astonished* 292.6, *wondering* 294.7, *confused* 364.10, 841.11, *at a loss* 468.11, *mixed up* 751.11, *troubled* 824.15
bewilderedly *with surprise* 292.13, *speculatively* 294.17
bewildering *mysterious* 182.10, *astonishing* 292.8, 294.10, *confused* 841.11
bewilderingly *surprisingly* 292.14, *astonishingly* 294.19, *confusingly* 841.23
bewilderment *incredulity* 88.3, *astonishment* 292.2, *speculation* 294.2, *confusion* 841.4
be willing 373.12; *be inclined toward* 290.10, *push* 414.20
be wise 352.6; *be skillful* 127.14, *be profound* 598.23
bewitch 86.25; *entice* 178.16, *be wondrous* 294.14, *win the love of* 299.27, *manipulate* 508.12
bewitched 86.21; *wondering* 294.7, *enamored* 299.17, *motivated* 508.8
bewitcher *witch* 86.15
bewitchery *witchcraft* 86.6
bewitching *witchlike* 86.19, *enticing* 178.13, *wondrous* 294.9, *lovable* 299.20, *motivational* 508.7
bewitchingly *wondrously* 294.18, *lovably* 299.31, *execratively* 301.17, *influentially* 508.13
bewitchment *enticement* 178.3, *romantic love* 299.2, *inducement* 508.2
be within one's rights *have rights* 429.13
be within one's sphere *have jurisdiction over* 54.30
be with it [Inf] *understand* 363.9, *be in style* 537.10, *live in the present* 647.8
be wonderful *be wondrous* 294.14
be wondrous 294.14
be worried about or **for** *worry* 283.16
be worthy of *be entitled to* 72.13, *have rights* 429.13

be wrapped up in oneself *be vain* 402.14
be wrong 430.18
beyond, the *death* 29.1
beyond all bounds *self-indulgently* 456.12
beyond all reason *violently* 520.11
beyond belief *disbelieved* 88.7, *astonishing* 294.10, *unbelievable* 837.5, *questionable* 839.5
beyond compare *best* 744.10
beyond comprehension *immeasurable* 798.6
beyond control *troublesome* 824.13
beyond count *numerously* 795.13
beyond criticism *best* 744.10
beyond expectations *plentiful* 97.4
beyond hope *hopeless* 282.6
beyond measure *excessively* 99.13, *numberless* 795.8, *numerously* 795.13
beyond one *difficult* 364.8, *powerlessly* 515.16
beyond one's comprehension *difficult* 364.8
beyond one's means *costly* 496.7, *at great cost* 496.12
beyond one's power *powerlessly* 515.16
beyond price *valuable* 496.8
beyond question *assuredly* 336.12
beyond reach *in the offing* 585.12
beyond recall *hopeless* 282.6, *forgotten* 355.7
beyond reckoning *immeasurable* 798.6
beyond repair *dilapidated* 808.11
beyond seas *nautically* 571.10
beyond the bounds of possibility *impossible* 837.4
beyond the frontiers of knowledge *unknown* 349.7
beyond the pale *indecorous* 528.8, *excluded* 764.6
beyond time 640.6
beyond worth *valuably* 496.13
be young 26.13
bezant *ancient coins* 484.12
bezant or **besant** or **byzant** Architectural Elements 134
bezel *obliquity* 628.2
bezique Card Games 168
bezique pack *cards* 168.2
Bhadarwah Breeds of Sheep 16
Bhagavad-Gita *other text* 81.19
Bhagnari Breeds of Cattle 16
Bhakarwal Breeds of Sheep 16
bhakti *worship* 83.1
bhang [Inf] *drug dose* 121.15
bhikshu *religious person* 81.9
bhikshu or **bhikku** *religious* 84.9
bhikshuni or **bhikkuni** *religious* 84.9
B horizon *soil* 8.42
Bhutan Countries 566
Bhutia pony Horse and Pony Breeds 159
Bianca Planets and Their Satellites 7
biannual *periodical* 641.7, *cyclic* 663.7, *two-sided* 789.9
biannually *chronologically* 639.21, *for specified periods* 641.12, *cyclically* 663.15
Bias Rivers 570
bias 342.11; *population* 6.55, *green bowling* 151.3, *sound quality* 230.4, *inclination* 290.2, *dislike* 291.1, *prejudice* 337.3, *prejudge* 337.13, *unfair treatment* 342.4, *fallibility* 351.6, *opinionatedness*

379.3, *preference* 382.2, *wrong* 430.1, *manipulate* 508.12, *influence* 512.11, *attitude* 513.2, *narrow-mindedness* 593.7, *obliqueness* 607.1, *oblique* 607.6, *obliquely* 607.13, *distortion* 627.1, *distort* 627.9, 698.20, *obliquity* 628.2, *viewpoint* 628.5, *deviation* 698.1, *injustice* 741.3, *conviction* 840.2
biased *misrepresented* 188.4, *inclined toward* 290.5, *discriminatory* 337.11, *unjust* 342.7, 741.6, *mistaken* 351.13, *opinionated* 379.9, *preferential* 382.10, *wrongful* 430.10, *tending to* 513.4, *narrow-minded* 593.13, *slanted* 628.10, *oblique* 698.11, *convinced* 840.8
biased against *displeased* 291.6
biased sample *population* 6.55
Biasro Breeds of Pigs 16
biathlon Sporting Activities 145, *skiing* 162.1, *cross-country* 162.31, *multi-event contest* 166.16, *twosome* 789.3
biathlon race *cross-country skiing* 162.7
biathlon relay race *cross-country skiing* 162.7
bib *baby clothes* 100.24, *part of garment* 100.27
bibber *drinker* 93.16, *drunkard* 121.8
bibbing *drunken* 121.28
bibelot *cheap thing* 800.7
Bible *the Law* 53.2, *Christian text* 81.16, *means of prediction* 358.10
Bible Belt *regions of the United States* 564.7
Bible paper *paper* 104.5
Bible school *religious school* 48.13
Bible-thump [Inf] *proselytize* 84.15
Bible-thumper [Inf] *religionist* 81.14, *moralist* 431.8
Bible-thumping [Inf] *zealous* 81.22
Bible worship *religiousness* 81.2
Bible-worshiping *zealous* 81.22
biblical criticism *criticism* 365.3
biblical interpretation *interpretation* 365.1
Biblicism *religiousness* 81.2
bibliographic *educated* 48.19
bibliography *schoolbook* 48.15, *book part* 174.5, *list* 785.1
bibliolater *religionist* 81.14
bibliolatry *religiousness* 81.2
bibliomancy *divination* 86.5
bibliophage *booklover* 174.16
bibliophagic *bookloving* 174.17
bibliophile *booklover* 174.16
bibliophilic *bookloving* 174.17
bibliophobia Phobias 283
bibliopole *bookshop* 174.15
bibliopolic *bookloving* 174.17
bib pants *ski equipment* 162.10
Bibrik Breeds of Sheep 16
bibulous *drinking* 93.17, *drunken* 121.28, *absorbent* 708.11
bibulousness *drinking* 121.2
bicameral *two-sided* 789.9
bicarpellary *of a fruit* 44.8
bicentenary *day to remember* 354.5, *anniversary* 663.4, *anniversarial* 663.8, *hundreds* 792.9
bicentennial *day to remember* 354.5, *anniversary* 405.5, 663.4, *anniversarial* 663.8, *hundreds* 792.9
bicentennially *cyclically* 663.15
biceps *muscles* 19.3, *bulge* 634.2

Bichon Frise Breeds of Dogs 35
bicker *quarrel* 272.9, *argument* 329.1, *argue* 329.11, *disagree* 463.8, *flicker* 684.26
bickering *dissension* 272.3, *arguing* 329.6, *divisiveness* 463.2, *disagreeing* 463.6
bicolor or **bicolored** *variegated* 263.6
biconditional *philosophical term* 4.7
bicorne or **bicorn** *hat* 100.32
bicuspid *teeth* 19.8
bicycle 687.10; *means of transportation* 686.2, *road vehicle* 687.4, *twosome* 789.3
bicycle bell *warning signal* 814.3
bicycle chain *blunt weapon* 78.5, *instrument of punishment* 454.13, *bicycle part* 687.11
bicycle clips *bicycle part* 687.11
bicycle courier *cyclist* 687.13
bicycle part 687.11
bicycle path *passage* 691.5
bicycle pump *bicycle part* 687.11
bicycle racing *race* 422.8
bicycle riding Hobbies and Pastimes 167
bicycles Phobias 283
bicycling Sporting Activities 145
bicyclist *cyclist* 687.13
bid *bridge* 168.4, *play cards* 168.7, *experiment* 335.1, *intentionality* 374.2, *attempt* 390.1, 390.6, *finance* 457.7, *bargaining* 480.10, *bargain* 480.20, 481.14, *purchasing* 481.9, *offer* 504.1, 504.11, *business offer* 504.3, *offered* 504.8, *offer to buy* 504.12, *request* 505.1, 505.10
biddable *submitting* 421.3, *obedient* 426.4, *easygoing* 823.13
bid defiance to *defy* 416.7
bidder *cardplayer* 168.3, *bridge* 168.4, *attempter* 390.3, *financial adviser* 457.4, *purchaser* 481.7
bidding *card-playing* 168.6, *demand* 425.2, *buying* 481.9
bidding convention *bridge* 168.4
bidding prayer *prayer* 85.10
biddings *Eucharist* 85.7
bide one's time *wait* 356.8, *procrastinate* 413.12, *delay* 658.13
bidet *bath* 111.6, *basin* 578.12
bid fair *inspire hope* 281.14, *predict* 358.14, *show potential* 458.14, *tend* 513.5, *be probable* 838.8
bid farewell *part* 705.13
bid for *aim* 374.10, *bargain* 481.14
bid or **say goodbye** or **goodnight** or **Godspeed** *part* 705.13
bid good day *greet* 410.11
bid price *stock exchange* 457.3
bid up *bargain* 481.14, *overpay* 496.11
bid welcome *be sociable* 408.14
Biedermeier Furniture Styles 101, Western Art Styles 133
Biella Breeds of Sheep 16
biennial *garden plant* 17.10, *botanical* 17.15, *plant* 41.2, *of plants* 41.14, *flowering plant* 42.2, *periodical* 641.7, *cyclic* 663.7, *two-sided* 789.9
biennially *horticulturally* 17.20, *herbaceously* 41.24, *for specified periods* 641.12, *cyclically* 663.15
bier *funeral object* 31.6
biff [Inf] *blow* 695.5, *hit* 695.11
biflagellate *algal* 47.20
bifocal *two-sided* 789.9
bifocals *visual aid* 242.14
bifold *two* 789.8
biforked *branched* 703.9

biforking *branching* 703.4
biform *two-sided* 789.9
Bifrost *bridge* 691.7
bifurcate *branched* 703.9, *branch* 703.14, *diverge* 753.20, *two-sided* 789.9, *halve* 789.15
bifurcated *angular* 628.7, *branched* 703.9, *half* 789.12
bifurcation *branching* 703.4, *halving* 789.6
big 498.9, 579.13; *serious* 799.8
bi-gal [Inf] *bisexual* 33.11
bigamist *married man* 64.10
bigamous *monogamous* 64.18
bigamously *matrimonially* 64.23
bigamy *type of marriage* 64.3
big appetite *gluttony* 119.1
Big Apple Dances 135
Big Apple, the [Inf] *New York* 567.6
big as a house *thick* 594.5
big baby *weak person* 517.4
big band *dance hall* 135.3
big bang *universe* 7.3, *creation* 717.9
big-bellied *fat* 579.15
Big Board [Inf] *stock exchange* 457.3
big-bottomed *fat* 579.15
big boys [Inf] *best people* 744.7
Big Brother *governance* 52.6, *the power structure* 68.12, *strict person* 424.4, *group influence* 512.6
big bucks [Inf] *money* 485.2
big C, the [Inf] *cancer* 114.15
big cat *cat* 35.11
big cheese [Inf] *company leader* 68.8, *manager* 126.7, *influential person* 512.5, *superior* 744.5, *celebrity* 799.6
big chief [Inf] *celebrity* 799.6
big D [Inf] *hallucinogens* 121.20
big daddy [Inf] *celebrity* 799.6
big day *important matter* 799.2
big deal [Inf] *figurative overestimation* 343.3, *important matter* 799.2
big deal! *naturally!* 295.10
Big Dipper Constellations 7
big-eared *eared* 228.10
big earner *wealthy person* 485.6
big eater *eater* 92.15, *glutton* 119.2
big enchilada [Inf] *company leader* 68.8, *celebrity* 799.6
big fish [Inf] *celebrity* 799.6
big fish *or* frog in a small pond [Inf] *superior* 744.5
Bigfoot Legendary Creatures 360
big freeze *cold weather* 9.24
big game *wild animal* 34.4, *the hunted* 385.7
big-game *hunting* 160.11
big-game animals *game* 160.6
big-game fish *fish* 154.14
big-game fisherman *fisherman* 154.12
big-game fishing Sporting Activities 145, *saltwater fishing* 154.3
big-game hunter *hunter* 160.9, 385.6
big-game hunting *hunting* 160.2
bigger 581.9
bigger and better *increasing* 746.4, *increasingly* 746.9
bigger and bigger *increasingly* 746.9
biggest slice of the cake *large part* 579.3
biggie [Inf] *celebrity* 799.6
big government *governance* 52.6
big gun [Inf] *company leader* 68.8, *influential person* 512.5, *celebrity* 799.6

big guy [Inf] *celebrity* 799.6
biggy [Inf] *celebrity* 799.6
big hand *acclaim* 437.5
bigheaded [Inf] *prideful* 297.8, *vain* 402.8
bigheadedness [Inf] *pride* 297.1, *vanity* 402.1
big-hearted *benevolent* 305.7, *unselfish* 443.5
big-heartedly *benevolently* 305.13, *unselfishly* 443.9
big-heartedness *benevolence* 305.1, *unselfishness* 443.2
big hit *successfulness* 845.3
Bighorn Mountains Mountains and Hills 569
big house *the inside* [Inf] 55.2
bight *inlet* 572.9
big lie *falsehood* 192.6
big man [Inf] *celebrity* 799.6
bigmouth *speaker* 205.12, *talkativeness* 207.1, *talker* 207.4
bigmouthed *informative* 170.10, *effusive* 207.6, *shouting* 232.7
big name *celebrity* 799.6
bigness *largeness* 579.2
big news *important matter* 799.2
big noise [Inf] *celebrity* 799.6
bigot 337.7; *hostile person* 63.5, *hater* 300.6, *obstinate person* 379.4
bigoted *intolerant* 63.7, *hating* 300.7, *discriminatory* 337.11, *unjust* 342.7, *opinionated* 379.9, *severe* 424.5, *narrow-minded* 593.13, *convinced* 840.8
bigotry *hostility* 63.1, *hate* 300.1, *prejudice* 337.3, *unfair treatment* 342.4, *opinionatedness* 379.3, *severity* 424.1, *narrow-mindedness* 593.7, *conviction* 840.2
big person 579.10
big picture, the *final intention* 374.1, *overview* 425.6
big play *gist* 799.4
big price tag *costliness* 496.1
big screen, the *motion pictures* 137.1
big shot [Inf] *company leader* 68.8, *manager* 126.7, *person of repute* 370.2, *influential person* 512.5, *celebrity* 799.6
Big Sioux Rivers 570
big spender *waster* 96.8, *spendthrift* 500.3
big stick *incentive* 178.4, *coercive method* 428.3, *instrument of punishment* 454.13, *negative stimulus* 508.4
big thing 579.9
big-ticket *costly* 496.7
big time, the [Inf] *the successfulness* 845.3
big-time operator (BTO) [Inf] *celebrity* 799.6
big timer [Inf] *celebrity* 799.6
big-time spender [Inf] *spendthrift* 500.3
big toe *appendage* 19.5
big top *show* 404.12, *overhead covering* 613.11
big top, the *the circus* 138.2
big tree Trees and Shrubs 43
big undertaking *undertaking* 391.1, *difficult task* 824.3
bi-guy [Inf] *bisexual* 32.10
big wall climbing *mountaineering* 161.1
big wave *rough thing* 544.2
big wheel [Inf] *company leader* 68.8, *influential person* 512.5, *celebrity* 799.6
bigwig [Inf] *company leader* 68.8, *manager* 126.7, *influential person* 512.5

big with *pregnant* 21.12
big with fate *presageful* 358.13
bijective *functional* 6.73
bijou *undersized* 580.8
Bikaneri Breeds of Sheep 16
bike *motorcycle* 687.12
bike [Inf] *bicycle* 687.10
bikeathon *charitable organization* 305.4
biked *transportable* 686.7
bike path *thoroughfare* 692.6
biker *cyclist* 687.13
bike rider *cyclist* 687.13
Bikini Islands 572
bikini *beachwear* 100.23, *swimming equipment* 164.8
bilateral *contractual* 459.7, *side* 623.6, *interrelated* 729.5, *two-sided* 789.9
bilateralism *side* 623.1, *interrelation* 729.2
bilaterally *contractually* 459.9, *interrelatedly* 729.11
bilateral paralysis *neurological disease* 114.20
bilateral symmetry *symmetry* 626.1, *operation of symmetry* 626.2
bilbo [Arch] *sharp weapon* 78.6
bilboes *instrument of punishment* 454.13, *means of restraint* 830.6
Bildungsroman *novel* 139.3
bile *body fluid* 19.16, *secreted substance* 24.2, *unpalatability* 223.2, *sour thing* 223.3, *spleen* 223.4, *irritableness* 304.3, *bitterness* 306.3
bile acid *fat* 12.7
bile pigment *pigment* 12.18
bilge *swill* 112.6, *sailboat parts and accessories* 150.4, *residue* 750.2, *refuse* 802.5
bilge water *swill* 112.6
bilge water *or* bilge [Inf] *senseless talk* 362.4
bilharziasis *tropical disease* 114.10
bilingual *linguist* 5.3, *linguistic* 5.34, *speaking* 205.15, *translational* 365.11, *two-sided* 789.9
bilingualism *duality* 789.2
bilingually *linguistically* 5.44
bilingual text *translation* 365.4
bilious *unhealthy* 114.23, *splenetic* 223.7, *yellow-faced* 259.10, *sick* 260.12, *irritable* 302.10, 304.9, *cross* 303.11
biliously *splenetically* 223.10, *yellowly* 259.13, *irritably* 302.23, 304.17, *crossly* 303.20
biliousness *gastroenterological disease* 114.11, *spleen* 223.4, *yellow skin* 259.3, *irritableness* 302.5, 304.3, *crossness* 303.4
bilirubin *pigment* 12.18
biliverdin *pigment* 12.18
bilk *swindle* 193.19, *thwart* 293.10, *act dishonestly* 479.18, *not pay* 488.10, 490.9
bilked *frustrated* 293.5
bilker *schemer* 193.10, *debtor* 488.6, *nonpayer* 490.6
bill 494.4, 785.4; *avian characteristic* 36.6, *sharp weapon* 78.6, *play part* 136.8, *theatrical performance* 136.13, *dramatize* 136.33, *advertisement* 173.9, *publicize* 173.18, *means of identification* 184.3, *record* 185.1, *paper money* 484.14, *credit* 487.1, *amount owing* 488.5, *statement* 493.2, *settle accounts* 493.11, *demand* 505.12, *mathematical result* 783.4, *list* 785.11, *showplace* 843.4

billabong [Aus] *tributary* 570.2
bill and coo *communicate love* 299.25
billbergia Flowers 42
billboard *advertisement* 173.9, *sign* 183.1, *showplace* 843.4
bill collector *collector* 473.7
billed *accounted* 493.8
billet *military affairs* 58.1, *habitation* 60.2, Architectural Elements 134, *locate* 565.9, *employment* 573.3, *resting place* 668.5, *stopover* 704.7
billet-doux *love token* 299.8
billeted *inhabiting* 60.18, *employed* 573.8
billfold *money storage* 484.20
billhook *garden tool* 103.4, *sharp-edged thing* 549.6
billiard 149.6
billiard ball *billiards* 149.1
billiard cloth *billiards* 149.1
billiard cue *impeller* 695.7
billiards 149.1; Board and Table Games 167
billiards club *billiards* 149.1
billiards play 149.2
billiards player *player* 149.5
billiards saloon [Brit] *billiards* 149.1
billiard table *billiards* 149.1
billing and cooing *communication of love* 299.6
billingsgate *vulgarism* 5.20, *vilification* 301.2
billion *million* 792.11, *myriad* 795.7
billionaire *gainer* 467.9, *wealthy person* 485.6, *prosperous person* 847.4
billions *fortune* 484.4, *multitude* 795.1
billionth *millionth* 792.22
bill of exchange *paper money* 484.14
bill of fare 785.5
bill of lading *means of identification* 184.3, *bill* 785.4
bill of particulars *pretrial proceedings* 54.13
Bill of Rights *the Law* 53.2, *rights* 429.4, *free rights* 829.4
billon *bullion* 484.16, *mixed thing* 751.2
billon coinage *coinage* 484.13
billow 571.9; *wave* 571.3, *bulge* 634.2, *be convex* 634.7
billow, the *the sea* 571.1
billowing *oceanic* 571.7, *convexity* 634.1, *convex* 634.5
billow of cloud *cloud appearance* 9.19
billowy cloud *cloud appearance* 9.19
billposter *or* billsticker *publicizer* 173.11
bills *debt* 488.1
billy *blunt weapon* 78.5
billy goat *livestock* 16.11, *male animal* 32.15, *male mammal* 35.18, *unpleasant-smelling thing* 227.2
bimetallism *economics* 56.1, *international finance* 457.2, *currency market* 484.8
bimodal distribution *probability distribution* 6.56
bimolecular *reactive* 11.29
bimolecular reaction *chemical reaction* 11.8
bimonthly *cyclic* 663.7, *cyclically* 663.15
bin *vessel* 578.11
binary *numerical* 6.68, *chemical*

compound 11.4, *computer information* 15.17, *two* 789.8

binary digit *numeral* 6.8, Scientific and Technical Units 589

binary notation *number system* 6.7

binary number *number system* 6.7

binary star *star* 7.8

binary system *number system* 6.7, *number* 783.1, *twosome* 789.3

binary tree *data-related concepts* 15.23

bind **754.14**; *arrest* 55.12, *group* 59.24, *treat* 115.17, *fencing movements* 153.3, *publish* 174.19, *specify* 340.14, *compel* 428.8, *impose a duty* 433.14, *make dense* 540.9, *join* 609.10, *wrap* 613.29, 619.7, *border* 618.9, *make stable* 674.7, *intertwine* 752.19, *connect* 754.13, *repair* 809.10, *restrain* 826.19, *restrain someone* 830.17

bind [Inf] *predicament* 725.3, 824.5

binder *farm tool* 16.5, *line* 754.5

binding *arrest* 55.5, *necessitate* 95.11, *ski equipment* 162.10, *stage of book production* 174.7, *compelling* 428.6, *duty-bound* 433.8, *agreements* 459.2, *condensed* 540.7, *junction* 609.5, *wrapping* 613.10, *line* 754.5, *repair* 809.1

binding energy *atom* 10.52, *energy* 514.7

binding over *punishment* 454.1

binding twine *line* 754.5

bind oneself *contract* 459.8

bind up *repair* 809.10

bind up one's wounds *cure* 809.15

bindweed Flowers 42

bin end *tail* 773.8

bin ends *bits and pieces* 760.5

Binet-Simon test Intelligence Tests 108

Binet test Intelligence Tests 108

bin(ful) *container(ful)* 738.2

binge [Inf] *appetite* 92.2, *eat well* 92.23, *be greedy* 119.4, *drinking bout* 121.7, *celebration* 405.1, *celebrate* 405.10, *overindulge* 456.11

binge-purge syndrome *gluttony* 119.1

binger [Inf] *glutton* 119.2

Binghi Nicknames for Inhabitants 61

binging [Inf] *appetite* 92.2, *gluttony* 119.1, *gluttonous* 119.3

bingo Board and Table Games 167, *game of chance* 842.5

bingo! [Inf] *good luck!* 842.19

binnacle *navigational aid* 690.6

binned *storing* 578.19

binocular *visual* 242.16, *two-sided* 789.9

binoculars *hunting accessories* 160.5, *visual aid* 242.14, *twosome* 789.3

binomial *algebraic expression* 6.23, *functional* 6.73

binomial coefficient *combinatorics* 6.63

binomial distribution *probability distribution* 6.56

binomial expression *algebraic expression* 6.23

binomial series *sequence* 6.18

binormal *line* 6.35

bint [Brit inf] *sex object* 20.8

bioastronautics *aerospace research* 7.27

Bío-Bío Rivers 570

biochemical **12.25**; *chemical* 11.24, 14.46, *biological* 13.27

biochemical applications **14.30**

biochemical engineer *chemical engineer* 14.25

biochemical engineering *chemical engineering* 14.24

biochemical genetics *genetics* 13.19

biochemical industries *chemical process industries* 14.26

biochemically **12.27**; *biologically* 13.36, *electrochemically* 14.53

biochemical taxonomy *biochemistry* 12.1

biochemist **12.2**; *chemist* 11.2, *life scientist* 13.26

biochemistry **12.1, 13.3**, Branches of Chemistry 11, *life science* 13.1, *cell biology* 13.14, *study of life* 28.9, *medical science* 107.5

biocytin *coenzyme* 12.12

biodegradable *impermanent* 643.5, *separable* 753.11, *deconstructed* 758.4

bioecology *biology* 13.2

bioelectricity *electricity* 10.31

bioenergetic *biochemical* 12.25

bioenergetics **12.23**; *biochemistry* 12.1

biofeedback *occult and psychic phenomena* 86.7, *psychotherapy* 108.4

biogenesis *genesis* 21.5

biogenetic *pertaining to life* 28.14

biogenetics *histology* 13.4

biographer *historian* 3.3, *author* 139.13, *record keeper* 185.8, *descriptive writer* 202.10

biographical **3.13**; *narrative* 139.18, 202.12

biographical dictionary *word book* 5.27

biographically **3.18**

biographical record *biography* 3.5, *record* 185.1

biographical sketch *nonfiction* 139.6

biography **3.5**; *history* 3.1, *life story* 28.11, *nonfiction* 139.6, Children's and Party Games 167, *record* 185.1, *factual account* 202.4

biologic(al) *pertaining to life* 28.14

biological **13.27**

biological anthropology *anthropology* 1.1

biological classification *taxonomy* 13.24

biological clock *life cycle* 28.7, *recurrent period* 641.5, *timekeeper* 646.7

biological death *mortality* 29.2

biological function *life function* 28.6

biologically **13.36**; *vitally* 28.23

biological science *life science* 13.1

biological time *time* 639.1

biological urge *sexual desire* 20.5

biological warfare *chemical warfare* 76.5

biologist *life scientist* 13.26, *animal scientist* 34.7

biology **13.2**; *life science* 13.1, *study of life* 28.9, *animal science* 34.6

bioluminescence *light* 10.17

biomass *renewable energy* 106.9

biomedical *chemical* 14.46

biomedical engineer *chemical engineer* 14.25

biomedical engineering *chemical engineering* 14.24

biomedically *electrochemically* 14.53

biomedicine *medical science* 107.5

biometric *biological* 13.27

biometrics *measurement* 1.9, *biology* 13.2, Fields of Measurement 589

biometrist *life scientist* 13.26

biometry *biology* 13.2, *life cycle* 28.7, Fields of Measurement 589

biomolecular *biochemical* 12.25

bionic *biological* 13.27, *human* 18.15

bionic man *humanlike machine* 18.12

bionics *histology* 13.4

bionic woman *humanlike machine* 18.12

bionomic *biological* 13.27

bionomics *biology* 13.2

biophysical *biological* 13.27

biophysical profile *prenatal diagnosis* 107.9

biophysicist *life scientist* 13.26

biophysics Fields of Modern Physics 10, *biology* 13.2

bioplasm *living matter* 28.4

bioplasma *occult and psychic phenomena* 86.7

bioplast *living matter* 28.4

biopsy *diagnostic procedure* 107.11

biorhythm *life cycle* 28.7, *recurrent period* 641.5, *cycle* 663.3

biorhythmic *cyclic* 663.7

biosphere Earth 8.6, *living world* 13.9, *aerosphere* 558.2

biosynthesis *biochemistry* 12.1

biosynthetic *chemical compound* 11.4, *biochemical* 12.25

biosynthetically *biochemically* 12.27

biosystematic *taxonomic* 13.35

biosystematics *taxonomy* 13.24

biota *living world* 13.9

biotechnological *biological* 13.27

biotechnologist *biochemist* 12.2

biotechnology *industrial chemistry* 11.21, *biochemistry* 12.1, *histology* 13.4, *molecular biology* 13.18

biotic *living* 13.28, *pertaining to life* 28.14

biotically *vitally* 28.23

biotic potential *productiveness* 22.3

biotin *vitamin* 12.13

Biot–Savart law Classical Physical Laws 10

biotype *genetics* 13.19

bipartisan *political* 50.9

bipartisanship *fellowship* 827.2

bipartite *separate* 753.7, *two-sided* 789.9

bipartition *halving* 789.6

biped *type of animal* 34.5, *twosome* 789.3, *two-sided* 789.9

bipedal *of animals* 34.13, *two-sided* 789.9

bipinnate *of leaves* 41.18

biplane *twosome* 789.3

bipod *twosome* 789.3

bipolar disorder *mood disorder* 108.12, *psychosis* 110.3

biquintile *angular measurement* 628.4

birch Trees and Shrubs 43, *instrument of punishment* 454.13, *hit* 454.28

birchbark *canoeing* 150.26

birchbark canoe *canoe* 150.9

birching *corporal punishment* 454.11

bird *animal* 34.1, *type of animal* 34.5, *badminton terms* 165.11

bird [Brit inf] *sex object* 20.8, *young woman* 26.9, *woman considered as a sex object* [Off] 33.8,

bird [Inf] *cry of disapproval* 239.7, *gesture of protest* 507.3

bird banding *ornithology* 36.2

birdbath *ornamental garden* 17.3

birdbrain [Inf] *unintelligent person* 316.4, *foolish person* 353.3

birdbrained [Inf] *foolish* 353.5

birdcage *dwelling* 36.4, *cage* 60.15

birdcage mask *baseball equipment* 147.4

birder *ornithologist* 36.3

birdhouse *dwelling* 36.4, *cage* 60.15

birdie *birds* 36.1, *golfing terms* 156.3, *play* 156.8

bird in the hand *possession* 469.1

birdlife *birds* 36.1

birdlike *avian* 36.19

birdlime *adhesive* 561.3, 755.3

bird of ill omen *forewarning* 814.2

Bird of Paradise Constellations 7

bird-of-paradise Flowers 42

bird of passage *birds* 36.1, *transient* 643.2

bird of peace *birds* 36.1

bird of prey **36.11**; *animal killer* 30.14

bird reserve *dwelling* 36.4

birds **36.1**, Collective Names 59, Phobias 283

bird sanctuary *animal welfare* 34.8, *dwelling* 36.4, *shelter* 812.4, *ecology* 815.3

birdseed *animal food* 90.2

bird's-eye *general* 778.9

bird's-eye view *type of painting* 143.5, *summary* 204.1, *viewpoint* 242.12, *whole situation* 759.3

bird's-mouth joint *carpenter's term* 131.5

birds of a feather *agreement* 730.2

bird song *bird sound* 240.2

bird sound **240.2**

bird strike *miscellaneous aviation terms* 689.9

bird watcher *ornithologist* 36.3, *observer* 242.15

birdwatching *ornithology* 36.2, Hobbies and Pastimes 167

birdy *avian* 36.19

birefringence *polarized light* 10.19

bireme *historical warships* 77.22, *twosome* 789.3

biretta *vestment* 84.11

biretta *or* **berretta** *or* **birretta** *hat* 100.32

Birman Breeds of Cats 35

Birmingham *major British cities* 567.7

birth **264.2**; *bodily development* 19.17, *genesis* 21.5, *life function* 28.6, *beginning* 583.9, 652.4, *arrival* 704.1, *creation* 717.9, *conception* 771.4

birth certificate *personal identification* 184.4, *certificate* 185.2

birth chart *divination* 86.5

birth control **23.5**

birthday *day to remember* 354.5, *anniversary* 405.5, *day* 646.4

birthday party *party* 408.6

birthday present *gift* 472.2

birthday suit *bareness* 614.3

birthmark *skin disease* 114.16, *personal identification* 184.4, *maculation* 263.4, *mark* 533.2

birthplace *home* 60.3, *native country* 566.6, *source* 675.2

birthrate *genesis* 21.5

birthright *claim* 72.2, *rights* 429.4, *receiving* 473.1, *legacy* 492.4

births *news story* 171.3

bis Musical Terms and Expression Marks 140

bis [Fr] *twice* 789.18

bis! [Fr] *bravo!* 437.23

biscuit *bread* 90.10, *brown* 256.5

biscuit [Brit] *cake* 90.36

biscuit barrel [Brit] *kitchen container* 91.7

biscuit *or* **bisque firing** *ceramic process* 129.5

biscuit jar *or* **tin** [Brit] *vessel* 578.11

biscuit ware Ceramics 129

bise Notable Winds 9

bisect *align* 6.92, *allocate* 474.5, *divide* 753.18, *part* 760.14, *halve* 789.15

bisected *separate* 753.7, *half* 789.12

bisection *halving* 789.6

bisectional search *programming concepts* 15.24

bisector *line* 6.35, *dividing line* 740.6, *half* 789.7

bisexual **32.10, 33.11;** *sexual nature* 20.4, *of sexual nature* 20.17, *male* 32.16, *two-sided* 789.9

bisexualism *sexual nature* 20.4

bisexuality *sexual nature* 20.4, *duality* 789.2

Bishkek Countries 566

Bishop *professional title* 72.6

bishop *person in authority* 52.7, *religious leader* 68.9, *priest* 84.8, *board games* 167.3

bishopdom *priesthood* 84.2

bishopric *priesthood* 84.2, *clerical venue* 84.4, *administrative region* 564.4

bishop's palace *clerical dwelling* 84.10

bishop's purple *figurative usage* 262.4

Bismarck American States 564

Bismarck Archipelago Islands 572

Bismarck brown *brown pigment* 256.2

bismuth Chemical Elements and Common Allotropes 11

bison Collective Names 59

bisque *soup* 90.14, *golf shots* 156.4

bisque ware Ceramics 129

Bissau Countries 566

bissextile *cyclic* 663.7

bistable circuit *circuit* 14.37

bistre *or* **bister** *brown pigment* 256.2

bistro *eating place* 92.17, *drink provider* 93.15

bit *numeral* 6.8, *computer information* 15.17, *data-related concepts* 15.23, *riding equipment* 159.9, *little piece* 580.4, *opener* 583.2, Scientific and Technical Units 589, *particle* 760.4, *thing included* 763.2, *fragment* 787.3, *item* 788.2, *means of restraint* 830.6

bit, a *duration* 642.1, *to a degree* 739.11, *partly* 760.17

bit by bit *slowly* 693.14, *by degrees* 739.10, *separately* 753.22, *partly* 760.17, *specifically* 779.22

bitch *female animal* 33.15, *dog* 35.10, *female mammal* 35.19

bitch [Inf] *irascible person* 303.7, *complaint* 304.5, *sullen person* 304.7, *be irritable* 304.14, *miscreant* 448.6, *protest* 507.1, 507.7, *difficult task* 824.3

bitch [Inf *and* Off] *unpleasant woman* 33.7

bitchily [Inf] *ill-naturedly* 303.18, *irritably* 304.17

bitchiness [Inf] *ill nature* 303.2, *irritableness* 304.3, *malice* 306.2

bitchy [Inf] *ill-natured* 303.9, *irritable* 304.9, *malicious* 306.8, *defamatory* 440.9

bite **92.10;** *infest* 40.17, *chew* 92.22, *afflict* 117.16, *engrave* 144.11, *catch* 154.9, *gesture* 183.17, *emphasis* 200.1, *painful injury* 215.3, *be painful* 215.9, *inflict pain* 215.10, *taste* 219.5, *piquancy* 221.1, *be piquant* 221.9, *be angry* 302.19, *fight* 422.23, *be sharp* 549.15, *take apart* 753.16, *particle* 760.4

bite into *infiltrate* 706.13, *take apart* 753.16

biteless *toothless* 550.8

bite off more than one can chew *overdo* 99.11, *figurative expressions* 128.11, *take on too much* 391.9, *be in difficulty* 824.19

bite one's nails *worry* 283.16

bite someone's head off *vent one's anger* 302.21, *show impatience* 303.14

bite the bullet *take courage* 284.15, *brace oneself* 376.13, *succumb* 421.7

bite the dust *die* 29.17, *be destroyed* 523.17, *fail* 714.18, 846.12

bite the hand that feeds one *figurative expressions* 128.11, *be ungrateful* 311.5

bite through *take apart* 753.16

bite to eat *meal* 92.8

bitewing *diagnostic instrument* 107.13

biting *windy* 9.42, *eating* 92.1, *chewing* 92.19, *painful* 215.4, *cold* 218.9, *piquant* 221.6, *acid* 223.5, *bitter* 306.9, *discourteous* 411.5, *strong to the senses* 516.12, *advantaged* 618.7

biting comment *bitterness* 306.3

bitmap *data-related concepts* 15.23

BITNET (Because It's Time NETwork) *computer communications* 15.25

bit of fluff [Brit inf *and* Off] *sex object* 20.8, *woman considered as a sex object* 33.8

bit of luck *luck* 842.3

bit part *or* **bit** *role* 136.23

bit player *actor* 136.25, 137.13

bits *remainder* 750.1, *refuse* 802.5

bits and pieces *miscellany* 59.15, *possessions* 470.5, *residue* 750.2

bitsy [Inf] *tiny* 580.9

bitt *sailboat parts and accessories* 150.4

bitter **306.9;** *windy* 9.42, *hostile* 63.6, *strained* 117.13, *cold* 218.9, *tasty* 219.4, *piquant* 221.6, *acid* 223.5, *splenetic* 223.7, *antipathetic* 291.7, *hating* 300.7, *resentful* 302.8, *jealous* 314.5, *defamatory* 440.9

bitter and twisted *bitter* 306.9

bitter comedy *comedy* 136.11

bitter cup *adversity* 848.1

bitter end *tail* 773.8

bitterender *tenacious person* 377.5, *obstinate person* 379.4, *opposer* 828.9

bitterly **306.16;** *coldly* 218.16, *tastily* 219.7, *piquantly* 221.10, *sourly* 223.9, *splenetically* 223.10, *discontentedly* 291.17, *with hate*

300.13, resentfully 302.22, *jealously* 314.12

bitterly cold *cool* 9.49

bittern *water bird* 36.9

bitterness **306.3;** *ill feeling* 63.3, *strain* 117.4, *flavor* 219.3, *piquancy* 221.1, *sourness* 223.1, *unpalatability* 223.2, *spleen* 223.4, *bad feeling* 266.5, *antipathy* 291.2, *hate* 300.1, *resentment* 302.1, *jealousy* 314.2

Bitter pattern Classical Physical Laws 10

bitter pill *hated thing* 300.5, *affliction* 454.9, *adversity* 848.1

bitter resentment *resentment* 302.1

bitter rot *pests and diseases* 17.12

bitters *sour thing* 223.3

bitter struggle *contest* 422.4

bittersweet Flowers 42, *sweet* 222.5

bitter taste *taste* 219.1

bitter words *berating* 438.5

bitty [Brit] *partial* 760.11

bitumen *construction material* 14.21, *resin* 562.6

bituminous *gas* 106.14, *resinous* 562.13

bituminous coal *coal* 106.4

biuret test *protein* 12.9

bivalence *philosophical term* 4.7

bivalent *chemical compound* 11.4

bivalve *mollusk* 39.13, *twosome* 789.3

bivalved *or* **bivalvular** *molluskan* 39.23

Bivalvia *or* **Lamellibranchia** *mollusk* 39.13

bivouac *take up residence* 60.24, *climbing expedition* 161.2, *mountaineer* 161.10

Biwa Lakes 568

biweekly *magazine* 175.3, *cyclic* 663.7, *cyclically* 663.15

bizarre *astonishing* 294.10, *fantastic* 360.11, *strange* 364.9, *ridiculous* 368.5, *unusual* 782.15, *eccentric* 782.16, *unbelievable* 837.5

bizarrely *eccentrically* 368.9

bizarreness *ridiculousness* 368.1, *unusualness* 782.4

Bizet Breeds of Sheep 16

blab [Inf] *inform on* 170.13, *tell on* 180.10, *talk* 207.3, *be talkative* 207.7

blab *or* **blabber** [Inf] *divulgence* 180.2, *talker* 207.4

blabber [Inf] *informer* 170.8, *discloser* 180.4

blabbermouth [Inf] *speaker* 205.12, *talker* 207.4

blabbing [Inf] *effusive* 207.6

Black *race* 1.5, *racial* 1.12, Breeds of Fowl 16

black **254.5;** *funeral* 31.9, Bean Varieties 90, *drinkable* 93.18, *gravecloth es* 100.25, *dirty* 112.7, *wrestling* 152.18, *horse by color* 159.7, *ski* 162.27, *dark* 247.5, *dark-colored* 247.7, *opaque* 250.3, *blacken* 254.11, *sullen* 304.8

black-and-blue *feeling pain* 215.6, *blackened* 254.7, *bluish* 261.6

Black and Tan [Brit] *black thing* 254.3

black and white *photograph* 132.3, *blackness* 254.1

black-and-white *motion-picture* 137.15, *drawing* 143.4, *checked* 263.8

black-and-white drawing *pen-and-ink sketch* 252.3

black-and-white film *film* 132.8

black-and-white photography *photography* 132.1, *motion-picture photography* 137.9

black-and-white television *television (TV)* 172.5

Black Angus Breeds of Cattle 16, *black thing* 254.3

black armband *clothing* 184.6

black art *witchcraft* 86.6, *figurative usage* 254.4

black as coal *or* **soot** *or* **jet** *or* **pitch** *or* **night** *or* **midnight** *or* **ink** *or* **thunder** *or* **hell** *or* **one's hat** [Brit] *black* 254.5

blackball *figurative usage* 254.4, *blacken* 254.11, *exclude* 383.11, 409.12, 764.7, *separation* 409.3, *disapproval* 438.1, *withhold approval* 438.17, *exile* 454.24, *prohibit* 503.8, *ostracize* 709.17, *set apart* 753.17, *exclusiveness* 764.4, *restraint* 830.1, *restrain* 830.12

blackballed *disapproved* 438.6, *disapproved* 438.9, *prohibited* 503.5, *excluded* 764.6

blackballing *rejecting* 383.2, *disapproval* 438.1, *exile* 454.3, *ostracism* 709.3

blackball vote *rejection* 383.1

black bass *black thing* 254.3

black bean Trees and Shrubs 43

black bear *black thing* 254.3

Black Beauty Notable Horses 159

black beauty [Inf] *sedatives* 121.19

Black Belt *farmland* 16.3

black belt *prizewinner* 127.8, *judo* 152.13, *karate* 152.14, *tae kwon do* 152.15, *black thing* 254.3

blackberry *black thing* 254.3

Black Bess Notable Horses 159

blackbird *black thing* 254.3

blackboard *black thing* 254.3

blackbody *heating effect* 10.28

blackbody radiation *heating effect* 10.28

black book *figurative usage* 254.4

black bottom *figurative usage* 254.4

black-bottom pie *figurative usage* 254.4

black box *recording instrument* 185.9, *figurative usage* 254.4

black card *black thing* 254.3

black cat *talisman* 86.9

black cat crossing one's path *bad-luck sign* 358.7

black checker *black thing* 254.3

blackcock *male bird* 36.15

black coffee *black thing* 254.3

black comedy *comedy* 136.11

Black Country, the *figurative usage* 254.4, *regions of the British Isles* 564.8

black cow *soft drink* 93.8

black currant *black thing* 254.3

blackdamp *miasma* 556.3

Black Death *plague* 114.6, *figurative usage* 254.4, *agent of destruction* 523.7

black diamonds *coal* 106.4, *figurative usage* 254.4

black dress *clothing* 184.6

black economy *figurative usage* 254.4, *trade* 480.1, *seller's market* 483.3, *financial escape* 816.2

blacked out *private* 245.5, *censored* 503.7

blacken **254.11;** *dirty* 112.11, *become dark* 247.9, *condemn* 438.18, *defame* 440.13, *stain* 808.20

blackened 254.7; *culinary* 91.9, *injured* 215.5

blackening *darkening* 247.2, *dimming* 248.3, *blackness* 254.1, *scorn* 440.5, *defamatory* 440.9

black eye *painful injury* 215.3, *black thing* 254.3

black-eyed *black-haired* 254.8

black-eyed Susan Flowers 42, *black thing* 254.3

Blackface Breeds of Sheep 16

blackface *black thing* 254.3

Black-faced Highland Breeds of Sheep 16

blackfish *black thing* 254.3

black flag *automobile racing terms* 146.3, *flag* 184.8, *black thing* 254.3

black fly *black thing* 254.3

Black Forest *figurative usage* 254.4

Black Friar *figurative usage* 254.4

black frost *ice* 218.5

black gold *figurative usage* 254.4

black grouse *black thing* 254.3

blackguard *figurative usage* 254.4, *vilify* 301.15, *malefactor* 306.6, *disreputable character* 371.2, *evil person* 446.3, *villain* 448.5

blackguardly *black-hearted* 254.9

black-haired 254.8

Black Hand *villain* 448.5

black hat *black thing* 254.3

blackhead *skin disease* 114.16, *black thing* 254.3, *mark* 533.2

Blackhead Persian Breeds of Sheep 16

black-hearted 254.9

Black Hills *figurative usage* 254.4

black hole *stellar evolution* 7.10, *prison* 55.1, *dark thing* 247.3, *black thing* 254.3

black humor *figurative usage* 254.4

Black Iberian Breeds of Pigs 16

black ice *frost* 9.25, *ice* 218.5, *figurative usage* 254.4

blacking *cleaning agent* 111.9, *black pigment* 254.2, *black thing* 254.3

blacking out 265.2

blackish *black* 254.5

blackishness *blackness* 254.1

blackjack Trees and Shrubs 43, *blunt weapon* 78.5, Card Games 168, *figurative usage* 254.4, *club* 695.15

black keys *black thing* 254.3

black Labrador Breeds of Dogs 35

blacklead *black pigment* 254.2, *blacken* 254.11

black lead *lubricant* 562.7

blackleg *pests and diseases* 17.12, *animal disease* 34.10

black light *that which makes invisible* 245.2, *black thing* 254.3

blacklist *figurative usage* 254.4, *blacken* 254.11, *separation* 409.3, *exclude* 409.12, 764.1, *withhold approval* 438.17, *prohibition* 503.1, *prohibit* 503.8, *set apart* 753.17, *exclusiveness* 764.4, *list of names* 785.7, *list* 785.11

blacklisted *disapproved* 438.9, *prohibited* 503.5, *excluded* 764.6

blacklisting *exclusiveness* 764.4

black-locked *black-haired* 254.8

black look *look* 242.7, *figurative usage* 254.4, *sign of irascibility* 303.6, *sign of irritability* 304.4, *act of discourtesy* 411.3, *show of disapproval* 438.6

black lung disease *respiratory disease* 114.12

blackly 254.12; *darkly* 247.11, *dismally* 304.19

Black Magellanic Cloud *nebula* 7.6

black magic *witchcraft* 86.6, *figurative usage* 254.4

blackmail *figurative usage* 254.4, *malignity* 306.5, *harm* 306.13, *demand* 425.2, 425.11, 505.3, 505.12, *coercive method* 428.3, *force* 428.10, *taking away* 477.5, *take money away* 477.20, *dishonesty* 479.7, *levy* 494.7

blackmailed *fraudulent* 479.13, *demanding* 505.8

blackmailer *coercer* 428.4, *raider* 477.10, *requester* 505.5

blackmailing *fraudulent* 479.13, *demanding* 505.8

Black Maria *figurative usage* 254.4, *automobile* 687.6

black maria Card Games 168

black mark *expression of dissatisfaction* 274.2, *condemnation* 438.2

black market *figurative usage* 254.4, *trade* 480.1, *seller's market* 483.3

black-market *merchandise* 482.17

black-marketeer *merchandise* 482.17

Black Mass *non-Christian ritual* 85.8, *witchcraft* 86.6, *figurative usage* 254.4

Black Merino Breeds of Sheep 16

black mood *figurative usage* 254.4

Black Muslim Muslim 81.12

Black Muslimism Islam 81.7

blackness 254.1; *dirtiness* 112.1, *invisibility* 245.1, *darkness* 247.1, *opaqueness* 250.1, *night* 656.3

black nightshade *black thing* 254.3

black notes *part of keyboard instrument* 142.6

black olive *black thing* 254.3

blackout *war measures* 76.18, *electricity* 106.5, *drunken behavior* 121.4, *play part* 136.8, Card Games 168, *blindness* 243.3, *darkness* 247.1, *darkening* 247.2, *shade maker* 247.4, *black thing* 254.3, *disappearance* 265.1, *forgetfulness* 355.1, *shelter* 419.11, *fatigue* 820.1

black out *erase* 186.9, *be insensible* 213.7, *be blind* 243.18, *make invisible* 245.7, *make dark* 247.10, *censor* 503.10, *restrain* 830.12, *cancel* 834.6

black out [Inf] *keep secret* 182.11

Black Panthers *figurative usage* 254.4

black pepper Herbs and Spices 91, *seasoning* 221.2, *black thing* 254.3

black pigment 254.2

black pine Trees and Shrubs 43

Black Prince *figurative usage* 254.4

black pudding *sausage* 90.29, *black thing* 254.3

Black Rock Deserts 572

black run *ski run* 162.2

Black Sea *figurative usage* 254.4, Oceans and Seas 571

black sheep *figurative usage* 254.4, *disreputable character* 371.2, *villain* 448.5, *loser* 468.8

Black Shirt *black thing* 254.3

Blacksided Trondheim and Nordland Breeds of Cattle 16

blacksmith *artisan* 123.13, *horse person* 159.14

blacksnake *black thing* 254.3

black spot [Brit] *figurative usage* 254.4

black spruce Trees and Shrubs 43, *black thing* 254.3

black stoneware Ceramics 129

black stuff [Inf] *opiates* 121.17

black swan *black thing* 254.3

blacktail deer *black thing* 254.3

black tea *tea* 93.7

black thing 254.3

blackthorn Trees and Shrubs 43, *black thing* 254.3

blackthorn winter *weather* 9.3

black tie *formal clothes* 100.5, *black thing* 254.3, *formal clothing* 406.5

black-tie *formally dressed* 406.8

blacktop *building materials* 104.2, *black thing* 254.3, *paving* 613.14, *pave* 613.32

Blackwall hitch Knots, Bends, Hitches, Splices 754

black walnut Trees and Shrubs 43

blackware Ceramics 129

Black Warrior Rivers 570

Black Watch [Brit] *black thing* 254.3

blackwater fever *tropical disease* 114.10

Black Welsh Mountain Breeds of Sheep 16

black widow *arachnid* 40.4, *black thing* 254.3

blackwood Trees and Shrubs 43

blad [Inf] *advertisement* 173.9

bladder *clown* 138.10

bladdernut Trees and Shrubs 43

bladderwort Flowers 42

blade *male* 32.1, *grass plant* 45.3, *plant body* 47.13, *combatant* 77.1, *sharp weapon* 78.6, *rowboat parts* 150.15, *fencing equipment* 153.2, *skating equipment* 162.17, *sharp-edged thing* 549.6, *cutting edge* 618.3, *propeller* 696.8

blade of grass *grass plant* 45.3

blade slip *rowing techniques* 150.16

blah [Inf] *be talkative* 207.7, *indifferent* 289.7, *boring* 296.6, *senseless talk* 362.4

blah-blah-blah [Inf] *diffuseness* 199.1, *talk* 207.3, *empty talk* 362.5

blahs, the [Inf] *indifference* 289.1

blain *ulcer* 114.18

blamable *unsatisfactory* 438.15

blame *censure* 438.3, *accusation* 442.1, *accuse* 442.8, *guilt* 450.1

blamed *condemned* 438.11, *accused* 442.5, *guilty* 450.6

blamed [Inf] *miscellaneous euphemisms* 301.12

blameful *guilty* 450.6

blamefully *guiltily* 450.12

blameless 805.12; *incorrupt* 449.7

blamelessly *faultlessly* 449.14

blamelessness *incorruption* 449.2, *immaculateness* 805.2

blame oneself *be penitent* 451.7

blame-shifting *defense mechanism* 108.23

blameworthiness *guilt* 450.1

blameworthy *convicted* 54.26, *immoral* 430.11, *unforgivable* 430.16, *unsatisfactory* 438.15, *villainous* 448.12, *guilty* 450.6, *causal* 675.7

Blanc, Mont Mountains and Hills 569

Blanc du Massif Central Breeds of Sheep 16

blanch *cook* 91.10, *lose color* 252.7, *decolor* 252.8, *whiten* 253.12

blanched *whitened* 253.8, *frightened* 283.9

blancher *color remover* 252.4

blanching *colorlessness* 252.1, *whitening* 253.2

bland *tasteless* 220.4, *good-mannered* 410.7, *moderating* 521.5, *unimproved* 808.10

blandish *persuade* 178.15, *cajole* 439.14, *influence* 508.11

blandishing *cajoling* 439.9

blandishment *persuasion* 178.1, *cajolery* 439.3, *inducement* 508.2

blandishments *cajolery* 439.3

blandly *without taste* 220.8, *genteelly* 410.14

blandness *tastelessness* 220.1, *courtesy* 410.1

blank *clean* 111.13, *opaque* 250.3, *drained of color* 252.6, *wonderless* 295.3, *thoughtless* 318.7, *ignorant* 349.5, *forgetful* 355.6, *unintelligible* 364.4, *new* 394.7, *intervening space* 563.8, *vacant* 576.12, *prototype* 624.2, *nonexistent* 718.9

blank cartridge *false alarm* 814.4

blank check *tolerance* 502.2, *liberality* 829.8

blanket *conceal* 181.12, *abolish* 523.11, *coat* 588.3, 613.28, *bed covering* 613.7, *including* 763.3, *general* 778.9

blanket coverage *print journalism* 175.4, *coverage* 613.16, *nonspecificness* 778.2

blanketed *covered* 613.19

blanket-flower Flowers 42

blanketing *covering* 613.1

blanket mortgage *mortgage* 476.6

blanket of snow *snow* 9.30

blankety-blank [Inf] *miscellaneous euphemisms* 301.12

blankly *colorlessly* 252.9, *without wonder* 295.8, *forgetfully* 355.14, *unintelligibly* 364.16, *newly* 394.14, *absently* 576.18

blank mind *lack of thought* 318.1

blankness *lack of wonder* 295.1, *lack of thought* 318.1, *ignorance* 349.1, *forgetfulness* 355.1, *unintelligibility* 364.1, *newness* 394.2, *emptiness* 576.2, 718.4

blank out *lack thought* 318.12

blank slate *emptiness* 576.2

blank spot *mental block* 318.5

blank verse *poetry* 139.8

blank wall *that which makes invisible* 245.2, *snag* 824.8

blare *speak in a particular way* 205.18, *loud sound* 232.2, *be loud* 232.8, *ringing* 236.2, *harsh sound* 238.1, *be strident* 238.7

blaring *loud* 232.6, *strident* 238.4

blarney 439.2, 439.13; *power of speech* 205.5, *empty talk* 362.5, *talk nonsense* 362.12, *be cunning* 822.5

blarneying *honeyed* 439.8

blasé *indifferent* 289.7, *wonderless* 295.3

blaspheme 301.14; *use language* 5.42, *be wicked* 448.13

blasphemous *of language* 5.35, *profane* 301.10, *disrespectful* 436.9, *impious* 448.11

blasphemously *colloquially* 5.45, *profanely* 301.19, *impiously* 448.17

blasphemy *profanity* 301.3, *disrespect* 436.1, *impiety* 448.4

blast *wind strength* 9.13, *engineer* 14.48, *fight* 77.35, *afflict* 117.16, *proclaim* 173.16, *burst of sound*

232.4, *be loud* 232.8, *bang* 234.1, 234.6, *harsh sound* 238.1, *be strident* 238.7, *vilify* 301.7, *fire* 418.18, *violence by person* 520.2, *demolish* 523.12, *air flow* 558.4, *blow* 558.22, *shoot* 696.18, *eat away* 808.19
blast [Inf] *drug dose* 121.15
blasted *infertile* 23.7, *miscellaneous euphemisms* 301.12
blast full of lead *shoot* 696.18
blast furnace *metallurgy* 11.22, *works* 124.9
blasting *vociferous* 239.9, *vilifying* 301.9
blasting powder *agent of destruction* 523.7
blastoff *flight path* 691.12, *starting point* 771.11
blast off *launch* 7.35, *find one's way* 691.15, *make a beginning* 771.26
blastomycosis *fungal disease* 47.6
blast out *cry out* 239.13
blastulation *developmental biology* 13.12
blatancy 404.6; *clarity* 244.2, *manifestation* 843.2
blatant 404.19; *publicized* 173.14, *clear* 244.6, *accentuated* 843.11
blatantly 404.34; *publicly* 173.20, *visibly* 244.10
blather *empty talk* 362.5, *talk nonsense* 362.12
blather on *be diffuse* 199.5
Blaue Reiter Western Art Styles 133
Blaze Notable Horses 159
blaze *shine* 9.56, *proclaim* 173.16, *sign* 183.19, *identify* 184.11, *fire* 217.8, 246.9, *burn* 217.18, *light up* 246.20
blaze a trail *forerun* 769.16, *pioneer* 771.29
blazer *informal clothes* 100.7, *jacket* 100.18
blazing *bright* 246.14
blazon *proclaim* 173.16, *signify* 183.16, Heraldic Terms 184, *insignia* 184.5, *identify* 184.11
blazoned *heraldic* 184.10
blazonry Heraldic Terms 184
bleach *cleaning agent* 111.9, *clean* 111.17, *treat* 130.21, *color remover* 252.4, *lose color* 252.7, *decolor* 252.8, *whitener* 252.5, *whiten* 253.12, *bake* 560.19
bleached *cleaned* 111.14, *treated* 130.16, *colorless* 252.5, *whitened* 253.8, *baked* 560.14
bleacher *color remover* 252.4
bleachers *baseball field* 147.3, *place for viewing* 242.13
bleaching *fabric treatment* 130.10, *lightening* 246.3, *colorlessness* 252.1, *whitening* 253.2, *drying* 560.3, *decay* 808.6
bleaching powder *color remover* 252.4
bleak *cool* 9.49, *infertile* 23.7, *cold* 218.9, *without hope* 282.7, *adverse* 848.10
bleakly *unhopefully* 282.14, *adversely* 848.16
bleakness *lack of hope* 282.2, *adversity* 848.1
blear *murky* 248.5, *make dim* 248.8
bleared *difficult to see* 245.4, *murky* 248.5
blearily *dimly* 248.10
bleariness *sight defect* 243.2, *murk* 248.2
bleary *weak-sighted* 243.10, *difficult to see* 245.4, *murky* 248.5
bleary-eyed *weak-sighted* 243.10

bleat *animal sound* 240.1, *make an animal sound* 240.7
bleater *dissatisfied person* 274.3
bleed 25.26; *bleed* 25.26, *treat* 115.17, *pity* 308.6, *demand* 505.12, *flow* 555.25, *seep* 559.16, *let out* 709.26, *draw off* 711.16
bleed (white) [Inf] *overcharge* 496.10
bleeder *sick person* 114.22
bleed for *feel for* 266.17, *pity* 308.6
bleeding 25.10, 25.19; *symptom* 114.3, *feeling pain* 215.6, *bloody* 555.18, *disgorgement* 709.6, *drawing off* 711.4
bleeding heart Flowers 42, *benevolent person* 305.6, *philanthropist* 307.5, *goody-goody* 445.8
bleep *shrillness* 238.3
bleeped out *censored* 503.7
bleeper *shrillness* 238.3
bleeping *shrill* 238.6
bleep out *censor* 503.10
blemish 533.1, 533.7; *skin disease* 114.16, *personal identification* 184.4, *view* 242.8, *ugly thing* 531.2, *make ugly* 531.4, *distortion of body* 627.3, *deform* 627.11, *deficiency* 745.2, *defect* 806.4, *stain* 808.20
blemished 533.5; *mottled* 263.10, *deformed* 627.7, *shortened* 762.6, *imperfect* 806.5, *defective* 806.7
blench *whiten* 253.12, *be afraid* 283.14, *oppose* 375.13
blencher *frightened person* 283.8
blend *cook* 91.10, *harmonize* 140.28, *produce* 522.13, *make fluid* 555.22, *interaction* 616.2, *cooperate* 616.6, *mix* 732.12, 751.12, *harmonization* 735.2, *mixed thing* 751.2, *mix together* 751.14, *combination* 757.1, *compound* 757.4, *combine* 757.9, *become one* 788.18
blended *interfacial* 616.4, *mixed* 751.8, *combined* 757.5
blender *cooking equipment* 91.6, *liquidizer* 555.11, *pulper* 561.13, *agitator* 684.14, *mixer* 751.7
blending *pulping* 561.11, *mixture* 751.1, *combination* 757.1
blend into the background *become invisible* 245.6, *disappear* 265.5
blend with the crowd *be average* 742.8
Blenheim spaniel Breeds of Dogs 35
blennophobia Phobias 283
bless *deify* 82.23, *perform rites* 85.18, *pray* 85.20, *give thanks* 310.7, *approve* 437.14, *better* 445.17, *agree with* 462.10, *permit* 502.6, *consent* 735.28, *be auspicious* 847.8
blessed *deified* 82.20, *agreeing* 462.6, *consenting* 735.18, *prosperous* 847.5
blessed [Inf] *miscellaneous euphemisms* 301.12
blessed by good fortune *chance* 842.10
blessed event *genesis* 21.5
blessedly *prosperously* 847.9
blessedness *prosperity* 847.1
Blessed One God 82.6
Blessed Virgin Mary *deified person* 82.9
blessed with stamina *stalwart* 547.10
blessed with talent *gifted* 127.11

blessed with this world's goods *wealthy* 485.8
blessing *act of worship* 83.2, *worshipful* 83.12, *Eucharist* 85.7, *prayer* 85.10, *thanks* 310.2, *thanking* 310.5, *approval* 437.1, *welfare* 445.2, *good thing* 445.9, *agreement* 462.1, *reward* 472.4, *permission* 502.1, *consent* 735.8
blessings *prosperity* 847.1, *good fortune* 847.2
bless my heart! *wonderful!* 294.20
bless my soul! *wonderful!* 294.20
bless one's lucky stars *give thanks* 310.7
bless with *own property* 470.11
bless you! *thank you!* 310.9
blest [Inf] *miscellaneous euphemisms* 301.12
blether *empty talk* 362.5, *talk nonsense* 362.12
Bleue du Nord Breeds of Cattle 16
blight *pests and diseases* 17.12, *tree disease* 43.8, *fungus* 47.1, *infection* 114.7, *affliction* 117.1, *afflict* 117.16, *evil thing* 446.2, *be evil* 446.10, *agent of destruction* 523.7, *blemish* 533.1, 533.7, *blot on the landscape* 533.4, *physical deterioration* 808.4, *eat away* 808.19, *adversity* 848.1
blighted *botanical* 17.15, *fungal* 47.18, *afflicting* 117.11, *blemished* 533.5, *urban* 567.14
blighted area *urban area* 567.10
blighted hopes *frustration* 293.2
blighting *afflicting* 117.11
blimp *military aircraft* 77.30, *aircraft* 689.3
blimp [Inf] *big person* 579.10
blind 243.11, 243.17; *golf course* 156.2, *cover* 181.4, *concealed* 181.8, *artifice* 193.5, *insensible* 213.4, *blinder* 243.7, *that which makes invisible* 245.2, *light* 246.19, *shade maker* 247.4, *oblivious* 355.9, *opinionated* 379.9, *spontaneous* 396.5, *inactive* 413.9, *interior decoration* 532.4, *protective covering* 613.5, *protection from the weather* 810.9, *stratagem* 822.2
blind [Inf] *drinking bout* 121.7
blind alley *closed place* 584.4, *road* 691.4, *waste of effort* 802.4, *snag* 824.8
blind arcade Architectural Elements 134
blind as a bat *or mole blind* 243.11
blind attack *military attack* 418.2
blind chance *chance* 842.1
blind drunk [Inf] *dead drunk* 121.27
blinded 243.12; *opinionated* 379.9
blinded [Inf] *dead drunk* 121.27
blinder 243.7
blinders *blinder* 243.7
blind eye *figurative blindness* 243.8
blind faith *believing* 87.2, *incuriosity* 322.1
blind flying *figurative blindness* 243.8
blindfold *deceive* 181.14, *blinder* 243.7, *blinded* 243.12, *blind* 243.17, *shade maker* 247.4, *make dark* 247.10
blind fury *anger* 302.4, *malevolence* 306.1
blind impulse *spontaneity* 396.2
blinding 243.13; *rainy* 9.50, *bright* 246.14
blindingly 243.21
blindly 243.20

blind man's buff *or bluff* Children's and Party Games 167
blindness 243.3; *darkness* 247.1, *opinionatedness* 379.3
blind oneself *prejudge* 337.13
blind panic *fear* 283.1
blind rage *anger* 302.4
blind side *figurative blindness* 243.8, *opinionatedness* 379.3
blindside [Inf] *ambush* 292.11
blindsided [Inf] *surprised* 292.5
blind spot *eye* 19.9, 242.3, *figurative blindness* 243.8, *mental block* 318.5, *defect* 806.4
blind staggers [Inf] *drunkenness* 121.3
blindstory Architectural Elements 134
blind to 243.14; *indifferent* 289.7, *wonderless* 295.3
blink *see badly* 243.16, *light up* 246.20
blink at *be blind to* 243.19
blinker *indicator* 183.7, *blind* 243.17, *safety light* 246.7
blinkered *blinded* 243.12, *blind to* 243.14, *discriminatory* 337.11
blinkers *riding equipment* 159.9
blinking *faulty vision* 243.1, *weak-sighted* 243.10, *lucent* 246.13
blintz *pancake* 90.11
BLISS Programming Languages 15
bliss *pleasure* 214.2, *joy* 269.1, *pleasantness* 271.1
bliss body *spirit* 86.10
blissful *luscious* 214.8, *joyful* 269.6, *pleasant* 271.5, *prosperous* 847.5
blissfully *pleasingly* 214.15, *joyfully* 269.13, *prosperously* 847.9
blister *symptom* 114.3, *skin disease* 114.16, *effects of hot weather* 217.7, *feel hot* 217.19, *bulge* 634.2
blister beetle *eroticism* 20.7
blistered *feeling pain* 215.6, *coarse* 544.6
blistering *hot* 9.47, 217.11
blister pack *transparent thing* 249.4
blithe *cheerful* 269.7
blithely *cheerfully* 269.14
blithering *meaningless* 362.7
blitz *battle* 76.23, *defensive huddle* 155.10, *play defense* 155.19, *loud sound* 232.2, *combined attack* 418.5, *attack* 418.17, *bomb* 418.19, *havoc* 523.5, *demolish* 523.12
blitz *or blitzkrieg offensive warfare* 76.11
blitzed [Inf] *dead drunk* 121.27
blitzkrieg *land attack* 418.3
blizzard *snow* 9.30, 9.58, 218.6, *natural violence* 520.3
bloat *animal disease* 34.10, Collective Names 59, *swelling* 581.2, *swell* 581.15, *fill* 761.11
bloated *eating* 92.18, *immoderate* 99.6, *prideful* 297.8, *fat* 579.15, *swelled* 581.10, *increased* 746.5
bloatedness *fatness* 579.5, *swelling* 581.2
bloating *swelling* 581.2
Blob, the Legendary Creatures 360
bloc *political party* 50.5, *union of nations* 566.2, *collection* 757.3
Bloch wall Classical Physical Laws 10
block 826.17; *data-related concepts* 15.23, *building materials* 104.2, *defense mechanism* 108.23, *rehearse* 136.37, *material* 144.6, *play basketball* 148.7, *sailboat parts and accessories* 150.4, *bowls* 151.7,

boxing techniques 152.5, box 152.19, play 155.8, play offense 155.18, fence 419.21, stall 419.28, instrument of execution 454.15, stop payment 490.10, obstruction 510.3, 584.2, counteract 510.7, solid body 540.4, plot 564.9, urban area 567.10, mass 579.7, obstruct 584.13, delay 658.3, 658.13, cause to cease 668.12, particle 760.4, obstacle 826.2, 837.3, withstand 828.20, detain 830.16, make impossible 837.8

blockade economic warfare 76.7, be at war 76.32, military attack 418.2, besiege 418.20, barrier 419.10, obstruction 584.2, obstruct 584.13, exclusion 764.1, obstacle 826.2, block 826.17, detention 830.5, detain 830.16

blockader attacker 418.10

blockading 76.22

blockage defense mechanism 108.23, obstruction 584.2, delay 658.3, stop 668.2, obstacle 826.2

block an attack fence 153.7

block and tackle simple machine 14.6, lifter 715.5

blockboard wood 131.3

blockbuster bomb 78.15, agent of destruction 523.7, successful thing 845.5

blockbuster [Inf] drug dose 121.15

block design combinatorics 6.63

blocked 826.13; unconscious 108.40, stopped 584.9, 668.7, held up 658.6, forbidden 837.7

blocked account amount owing 488.5

blocked nose lack of sense of smell 225.2

blocked up obstructed 584.8

blocker basketball team 148.2, offense 155.6

block fault fault 8.21

blockhead unintelligent person 316.4, foolish person 353.3

blockheaded unintelligent 316.6

blockhouse shelter 419.11, fortification 419.12, 812.3

blocking defense mechanism 108.23, production 136.14, playing terms 148.4, combat 152.17, wrestling 152.18, delaying 658.8

block lava eruption 8.27

block out forget 186.11, illustrate 187.11, lay the foundations 388.16, fashion 537.9, outline 617.5, form 624.9

block out light make dark 247.10

block print picture 133.5

blocks toy 167.9

blockship warship 77.21

block shot grip 151.4

block up obstruct 584.13, block 826.17

Bloemfontein Countries 566

blond yellow-haired 259.9

blond or **blonde** white-haired 253.9

Blonde d'Aquitaine Breeds of Cattle 16

blood 555.4; body fluid 19.16, 555.3, life requirement 28.5, family tree 65.3, test 107.10, diagnostic procedure 107.11, red thing 257.3, Phobias 283, enroll 771.33

blood and thunder dramaturgy 136.6

blood bank vault 105.9, blood 555.4

bloodbath slaughter 30.5, military attack 418.2, violence by person 520.2

blood bay horse by color 159.7

blood cell cell 13.15

blood clot cardiovascular disease 114.13, solid body 540.4, blood 555.4, stopper 584.3

blood count blood 555.4

bloodcurdling frightening 283.12

blood disease 114.14

blood donor giver 472.7

blood feud act of hostility 63.4, dispute 463.3

blood fluke parasite 39.18

blood group or **type** blood 555.4

bloodguilt guilt 450.1

bloodguilty guilty 450.6

blood heat heat 217.1

blood horse horse 159.1

bloodhound Breeds of Dogs 35, hunter 385.6

bloodily excrementally 25.27

bloodiness fluidity 555.5

blood kin associate 754.3

blood knot Knots, Bends, Hitches, Splices 754

bloodless peaceful 73.8, of disease 114.25, drained of color 252.6, ill 517.8

bloodless bullfight duel 422.12

bloodlessly peacefully 73.12

bloodlessness paleness 252.2

bloodletting killing 30.1, violence by person 520.2, disgorgement 709.6, drawing off 711.4

bloodline family tree 65.3, line 774.2

bloodlust cruelty 306.4, violence by person 520.2

bloodmobile blood 555.4

blood money atonement 313.1, illegal offer 504.4, compensation 743.1

blood plasma blood 555.4

blood platelet blood 555.4

blood poisoning poisoning 114.8, blood disease 114.14

blood pressure blood 555.4, Fields of Measurement 589

blood pudding sausage 90.29

blood-red red 257.5

blood relationship kinship 727.2

blood running cold symptoms of fear 283.3

blood sausage sausage 90.29

blood serum blood 555.4

bloodshed warfare 76.3, malignity 306.5

bloodshedding killing 30.1

bloodshot weak-sighted 243.10, bloody 257.8

bloodshot eyes faulty vision 243.1

blood-soaked bleeding 25.19

blood sport animal killing 30.10, sporting activity 145.3, hunt 385.3

bloodstained murderous 30.18, bloody 257.8

bloodstock horse 159.1

bloodstream blood 555.4

bloodsucker type of animal 34.5, parasite 39.18

blood test test 107.10

bloodthirst cruelty 306.4

bloodthirstily deadly 30.26, aggressively 77.38

bloodthirstiness cruelty 306.4, violence by person 520.2

bloodthirsty murderous 30.18, 520.7, warlike 77.32, combative 77.32, cruel 306.10, attacking 418.14

blood transfusion blood 555.4

blood vessels internal organ 19.13

bloodworm larva 40.9

bloody 257.8, 555.18; fluid 19.25, bleeding 25.19, bleed 25.26,

murderous 30.18, 520.7, be at war 76.32, inflict pain 215.10, cruel 306.10, attacking 418.14

bloody flux defecation 25.3

bloody hands sign of guilt 450.2

bloody-minded [Brit] objectionable 272.7, willful 372.8, obstinate 379.5

bloody-mindedness [Brit] willfulness 372.3, obstinacy 379.1

bloody nose painful injury 215.3

bloom reproduce oneself 21.14, be fertile 22.13, be young 26.13, vegetate 41.21, flower 42.1, 42.12, grow 43.15, 581.17, health 113.1, be healthy 113.4, redness 257.1, appeal 529.4, be beautiful 529.11, powderiness 553.3, coat 588.3, be prosperous 847.6

bloomer flowering plant 42.2, mistake 342.2, blunder 351.9

bloomers pants 100.14, underwear 100.22

blooming flowering 42.5, 42.10, healthy 113.4, red-faced 257.6, fresh 260.10, first appearance 264.3, appealing 529.10, germination 581.5, growing 581.12

bloom of youth youth 26.1

Bloomsbury London 567.8

Bloomsbury group Western Literary Groups 139

bloomy floral 42.9

blooper [Inf] mistake 342.2, blunder 351.9, act of folly 353.2

blossom be fertile 22.13, vegetate 41.21, flower 42.1, 42.12, plant products 522.8, grow 581.17, 676.10, growth 676.3, increase 746.6, be successful 845.11, be prosperous 847.6

blossoming flowering 42.5, 42.10, germination 581.5, growing 581.12, 676.6

blossom time spring 654.3

blossomy seasonal 654.7

blot dirt 112.5, dirty 112.11, be clumsy 128.9, erase 186.9, blacken 254.11, variegate 263.11, impropriety 430.5, ugly thing 531.2, blemish 533.1, 533.7, absorb 560.20, 708.19, admixture 751.5, defect 806.4, stain 808.20

blotch maculation 263.4, blemish 533.1

blotched blemished 533.5

blot on the landscape 533.4; view 242.8, ugly thing 531.2

blot out erase 186.9, make dark 247.10, cause to disappear 265.7, take away 477.18, abolish 523.11, hide 613.27, eject 764.8, cancel 834.6

blotted blemished 533.5

blotted out concealed 181.8

blotter cleaning tool 111.10, dryer 560.5, sponge 708.7

blotting drying 560.3, absorption 708.6, absorbent 708.11

blotting out taking away 477.5, covering 613.1

blotting paper dryer 560.5, sponge 708.7

blotto [Inf] dead drunk 121.27

blot up absorb 560.20, 708.19

blouse shirt 100.13, make clothing 100.44

blouson shirt 100.13

blow 9.53, 558.22, 695.5; wind strength 9.13, flower 42.1, flowering 42.5, sound 141.15, play an instrument 142.9, type of touch 216.3, sound faint 233.8, bad

outcome 293.3, deed 412.2, be active 414.18, hit 418.9, corporal punishment 454.11, void 709.23, let out 709.26, be fatigued 820.5

blow [Arch] flower 42.12

blow [Inf] waste 96.15, 500.7, drug oneself 121.37, be clumsy 128.9, be wrong 430.18, expend 491.11

blow! [Inf] go! 709.30

blow a fortune [Inf] expend 491.11

blow a fuse or **gasket** [Inf] become angry 302.20

blow a gale storm 9.55

blow a hurricane storm 9.55

blow a kiss communicate love 299.25, greet 410.11

blow a raspberry [Inf] disdain 400.16

blow away [Inf] murder 30.20, be wondrous 294.14, destroy 523.10

blow-by-blow account diffuseness 199.1, factual account 202.4, circumstances 726.1

blow down knock down 523.13

blower ventilator 558.7

blow for blow retaliation 420.1, exchange 673.1, reciprocity 729.1, compensatory 743.5

blow-for-blow reciprocal 729.4

blow glass form 624.9

blowgun Historical Missile Weapons 78

blowhole hole 583.4, outlet 707.8

blow hot and cold vacillate 378.8, be capricious 381.6, stall 419.28, be irresolute 666.6

blow in [Inf] arrive 704.13

blowing flowering 42.5, panting 820.3

blowing [Inf] drug use 121.9

blowing away [Inf] murder 30.2

blowing hot and cold inconstancy 378.2

blowing one's own horn [Inf] overestimation 343.1

blowing up enlargement 194.2, swelling 581.2

blow it [Inf] lose one's chance 660.10

blow job [Inf] sex act 20.10

blown instrumental 142.8

blown [Inf] expended 491.9

blown glass formed 624.6

blown up enlarged 194.8

blown-up aerial 558.14, swelled 581.10

blow off steam give off 556.25

blow or **let off steam** [Inf] vent one's anger 302.21

blow one's cash [Inf] expend 491.11

blow one's cool [Inf] become angry 302.20

blow one's mind [Inf] drug oneself 121.37, be wondrous 294.14

blow one's nose salivate 25.25

blow one's own horn [Inf] show off 402.15

blow one's stack or **top** or **lid** [Inf] become angry 302.20

blow on the embers make violent 520.10

blow open use violence 520.9

blowout bang 234.1, disgorgement 709.6

blowout [Inf] celebration 405.1, party 408.6

blow out destroy 523.10, run out 707.15, void 709.23, let out 709.26

blow out one's brains commit suicide 30.24

blow out the brains of *murder* 30.20

blow out the candle *make dark* 247.10

blow over *stop* 668.10

blowpipe Historical Missile Weapons 78

blows *fight* 422.9

blow smoke [Inf] *drug oneself* 121.37

blow someone's cover *tell on* 180.10

blow the engine *be on the track* 146.11

blow the lid off [Inf] *divulge* 180.9

blow the trumpets *salute* 405.13

blow the whistle *accuse* 442.8, *give warning* 814.10

blow the whistle on *inform on* 170.13, *tell on* 180.10

blow to bits *demolish* 523.12

blow to kingdom come *demolish* 523.12

blow to pieces *or bits take apart* 753.16

blowtorch *cause of fire* 217.10

blow to smithereens *demolish* 523.12

blowup *printing* 132.20, *burst of anger* 302.6, *warfare* 422.10, *violence by person* 520.2

blow up 696.19; *blow* 9.53, *develop* 132.28, *represent* 187.10, *enlarge* 194.12, *bang* 234.6, *become angry* 302.20, *demolish* 523.12, *swell* 581.15, *send up* 715.12, *make bigger* 746.7, *take apart* 753.16, *disintegrate* 758.6

blow up (out of all proportion) *boast* 194.14

blowy *windy* 9.42, *breezy* 558.15

blowzy *red-faced* 257.6

blubber *cry of sorrow* 239.6, *cry* 239.16, *weep* 280.8, *fat* 562.4, 579.8, *thickness* 594.1

blubberer *lamenter* 280.3

blubbering *crying* 239.11

blubbery *oily* 562.11

bludgeon *blunt weapon* 78.5, *coercive method* 428.3, *force* 428.10

bludgeoning *murder* 30.2, *compelling* 428.6

blue 261.5, 261.9; *obscene* 112.9, *musical* 140.25, *ski* 162.27, *spectrum* 251.3, *depressed* 261.7, 270.5, *indecent* 261.8, *without hope* 282.7, *profane* 301.10, *sullen* 304.8, *offensive* 432.11, *ribald* 535.8

blue, the *figurative usage* 261.4, *sea* 571.1

Blue Albian Breeds of Cattle 16

blue alert *figurative usage* 261.4

blue and white ware *ceramics* 129.1

blue baby *blue thing* 261.3

blue ball clay *material* 129.2

blue balls [Inf] *sexual longing* 20.6, *figurative usage* 261.4

Bluebeard *married man* 64.10, *figurative usage* 261.4

bluebell Flowers 42, *blue thing* 261.3

blue belt *tae kwon do* 152.15, *aikido* 152.16

blueberry *blue thing* 261.3

bluebill *blue thing* 261.3

bluebird *blue thing* 261.3

blue-black *black pigment* 254.2, *black* 254.5

blue blazes [Inf] *figurative usage* 261.4

blue blood *nobleman* 70.1, *figurative usage* 261.4

blue-blooded *aristocratic* 70.4

bluebonnet *blue thing* 261.3

blue book *schoolbook* 48.15, *blue thing* 261.3

blue cheer [Inf] *hallucinogens* 121.20, *figurative usage* 261.4

blue cheese *blue thing* 261.3

blue chip *figurative usage* 261.4

blue-chip *excellent* 744.14

blue chips *stock exchange* 457.3

blue-collar *unionized* 57.14

blue-collar union *organized labor* 57.5

blue-collar worker *employee* 57.4, *laborer* 123.9, *figurative usage* 261.4

blue color *blueness* 261.1

blue crab *blue thing* 261.3

Blue Cross *figurative usage* 261.4

blue devils *figurative usage* 261.4, *sign of sullenness* 304.2

blue dye *blue pigment* 261.2

blue-eyed boy [Brit] *figurative usage* 261.4

Bluefaced Leicester Breeds of Sheep 16

Bluefaced Maine Breeds of Sheep 16

bluefish *food fish and shellfish* 90.20, *game fish* 154.10, *blue thing* 261.3

blue flu *figurative usage* 261.4

blue fox *blue thing* 261.3

blue funk [Inf] *figurative usage* 261.4

bluegill *blue thing* 261.3

bluegrass *folk music* 140.7, *blue thing* 261.3, *figurative usage* 261.4

blue-gray *gray* 255.6

blue-green *green* 260.7

blue-green algae *algae* 47.11

blue gum Trees and Shrubs 43

blue heaven *or angel or devil* [Inf] *sedatives* 121.19, *figurative usage* 261.4

blue heron *blue thing* 261.3

blue ice *blue thing* 261.3

blue in the face *bluish* 261.6

bluejacket *naval person* 77.25, *figurative usage* 261.4

blue jay *blue thing* 261.3

blue jeans *informal clothes* 100.7, *pants* 100.14, *blue thing* 261.3

blue joke *joke* 277.6, *profanity* 301.3, *sexual offense* 432.6

blue language *figurative usage* 261.4, *offensive language* 301.5

blue law *figurative usage* 261.4

blue laws *suppression* 424.2

blue line *hockey areas* 158.2

blueline *stage of proof* 174.9

bluely 261.11

blue mold *blue thing* 261.3

blue moon *figurative usage* 261.4

Blue Mountains *figurative usage* 261.4, Mountains and Hills 569

blue movie *figurative usage* 261.4, *pornography* 432.7

blue murder *figurative usage* 261.4

blueness 261.1

Blue Nile *figurative usage* 261.4

blue note *figurative usage* 261.4

blue pencil *obliteration* 186.1, *blue thing* 261.3, *figurative usage* 261.4

blue-pencil 261.10; *purify* 111.19, *obliterate* 186.8, *censor* 503.10, *mitigate* 521.9, *subtract* 749.6, *eject* 764.8, *rectify* 807.22

blue-penciled *expurgated* 111.15, *censored* 503.7

blue-penciling *censorship* 111.5, *rectification* 807.8

Blue Permain Apple Varieties 44

blue peter *flag* 184.8, *blue thing* 261.3

blue pigment 261.2

blue planet Earth 8.6

blue-plate special *figurative usage* 261.4

bluepoint oyster *figurative usage* 261.4

blue-point Siamese cat *blue thing* 261.3

blueprint *stage of proof* 174.9, *illustration* 187.2, *outline* 204.2, 617.1, 617.5, *blue thing* 261.3, *figurative usage* 261.4, *map* 387.7, *preparations* 388.2, *prototype* 624.2, *original* 737.2, *originate* 737.7

blueproof *stage of proof* 174.9

blue racer *blue thing* 261.3

blue ribbon *insignia* 184.5, *blue thing* 261.3, *prize* 453.2

blue-ribbon *best* 805.9

blue-ribbon winner *prizewinner* 127.8

Blue Ridge Mountains *figurative usage* 261.4, Mountains and Hills 569

blue run *ski run* 162.2

blues *uniform* 100.9, *jazz* 140.5, *stage of proof* 174.9

blues, the *ice-dancing move* 162.19, *depression* 270.2, *sign of sullenness* 304.2

blues *or the blues figurative usage* 261.4

blue sea *blue thing* 261.3

Blue Shield *figurative usage* 261.4

blueshift *orbit* 7.22

blue sky *blue thing* 261.3, *air* 558.1

blue-sky *suppositional* 359.5

blue-sky law *figurative usage* 261.4

blue slip *rejection notice* 383.5

bluesman [Inf] *composer* 141.9

blue spruce Trees and Shrubs 43

blues singer *singer* 141.4

bluestocking *figurative usage* 261.4, *intellectual* 315.7, *knowledgeable person* 348.5

bluestone *blue thing* 261.3

blue streak *figurative usage* 261.4, *swiftness* 694.1

bluet Flowers 42

blue thing 261.3

bluetick coonhound Breeds of Dogs 35

blue tit *blue thing* 261.3

blue velvet [Inf] *figurative usage* 261.4

blue water *sea* 571.1

blue whale *blue thing* 261.3

blue with cold *cold* 218.9, *bluish* 261.6

bluff *artifice* 193.5, *deceive* 330.12, *be affected* 367.4, *outspoken* 550.6, *hill* 569.2, *heights* 596.4, *vertical* 602.3

bluffer *schemer* 193.10, *pretender* 367.2

bluffness *discourtesy* 411.1, *outspokenness* 550.2

bluff one's way out *escape* 816.8

bluish 261.6

blunder 351.9, 528.5, 846.13; *be unskillful* 128.8, *be clumsy* 128.9, *act foolishly* 128.10, *negligence* 324.4, *mistake* 342.2, *misjudge* 342.9, *err* 351.14, *act of folly* 353.2, *misinterpret* 366.4, *joke* 368.4, *be wrong* 430.18, *sin* 450.3, *pitch* 684.25, *go astray* 698.17, *error* 846.2

blunderbuss *historical handgun* 78.8, *unskilled person* 128.3

blundered *failed* 846.10

blunderer *unskilled person* 128.3

blundering *failed* 846.10

blunderingly *mistakenly* 660.14, *unsuccessfully* 846.21

blunder upon *chance upon* 842.13

blunge *make ceramics* 129.10

blunged *ceramic* 129.9

blunger *ceramic workshop and tools* 129.8

blunging *ceramic process* 129.5

blunt 550.5, 550.9; *discourage* 179.11, *assertive* 189.20, *candid* 191.5, *anesthetize* 213.8, *insensitive* 268.4, *make indifferent* 289.13, *discourteous* 411.5, *mitigate* 521.9, *natural* 526.10, *uniform* 545.5, *open* 583.13, *plain* 592.10, *naive* 821.3

blunt cut *coiffure* 530.8

blunted *blunt* 550.5

blunt-edged *blunt* 550.5

blunt-ended *blunt* 550.5

blunt instrument *murder weapon* 30.3, *blunt weapon* 78.5

bluntish *blunt* 550.5

bluntly 550.11; *assertively* 189.35, *candidly* 191.10, 583.23, *insensibly* 213.9, *insensitively* 268.7, *discourteously* 411.8, *unpretentiously* 526.15, *smoothly* 545.13, *plainly* 592.18, *naively* 821.5

bluntness 550.1; *assertiveness* 189.8, *candor* 191.2, *insensitivity* 268.1, *discourtesy* 411.1, *naturalness* 526.4, *openness* 583.7, *plainness* 592.4, *naiveté* 821.1

blunt-nosed *blunt* 550.5

blunt-pointed *blunt* 550.5

blunt weapon 78.5

blur *dirty* 112.11, *blind* 243.17, *become invisible* 245.6, *make invisible* 245.7, *murk* 248.2, *make dim* 248.8, *make shapeless* 625.3, *be average* 742.8

blurb *advertisement* 173.9

blurb writer *publicizer* 173.11

blurred *difficult to see* 245.4, *murky* 248.5, *shady* 250.4, *unreal* 720.8

blurred vision *sight defect* 243.2

blurriness *murk* 248.2, *shapelessness* 625.1

blurry *weak-sighted* 243.10, *difficult to see* 245.4, *murky* 248.5, *shapeless* 625.2

blurt *improvise* 396.6

blurt out *tell on* 180.10, *speak* 205.17

blush 403.12; *gesture* 183.5, *heat* 217.1, *feel hot* 217.19, *face color* 251.9, *redness* 257.1, *redden* 257.9, *blushing* 403.2, *sign of guilt* 450.2, *appear guilty* 450.10, *cosmetics* 530.4

blusher *red pigment* 257.2, *cosmetics* 530.4

blushing 403.2, 403.7; *red-faced* 257.6, *Phobias* 283, *chaste* 431.10, *appearing guilty* 450.7

blushing bride *spouse* 64.8

blushingly *ruddily* 257.10, *shyly* 403.16, *guiltily* 450.12

bluster *blow* 9.53, *brag* 400.17, *bravado* 404.8, *be active* 414.18, *defiance* 416.1, *defy* 416.7, *violence* 520.1, *fuss* 684.4

blusterer *exaggerator* 194.6, *proud person* 297.7, *insolent person* 400.7

blustering *swaggering* 400.13

blustery *windy* 9.42

B lymphocyte *blood* 555.4

B-movie *movie type* 137.3
boa *snake* 37.6, *neckwear* 100.29
boar *livestock* 16.11, *male animal* 32.15, *male mammal* 35.18
board *party* 59.3, *take up residence* 60.24, *inhabit* 61.13, *provision* 89.9, *feed* 90.41, *have a meal* 92.25, *type of table* 101.5, *management board* 126.2, *wood* 131.3, *carpenter* 131.10, *stage* 136.18, *sailboard parts* 150.20, *squash terms* 165.10, *advisory body* 176.6, *place of judgment* 341.3, *attack* 418.17, *face* 613.31, *fly* 689.13, *set out* 705.12, *enter* 706.11, *mount* 713.24, *council* 833.4
board, the *governance* 52.6, *the power structure* 68.12
boarded *joined* 131.8
boarder *resident* 61.6, *eater* 92.15, *possessor* 469.10
board foot *General Units* 589
board game *type of game* 167.2
board games 167.3
boarding *wood* 131.3, *ice hockey tactics* 158.4, *combined attack* 418.5, *attacking* 418.14, *floor covering* 613.13, *start* 705.2
boardinghouse *hotel* 60.12
boarding ladder *ladder* 713.10
boarding pass *miscellaneous aviation terms* 689.9
boarding school *type of school* 48.12
board measure *type of measurement* 589.8
board meeting *conference* 59.5
board member *company leader* 68.8
board of advisers *advisory body* 176.6
board of aldermen *governing body* 49.19, *representative body* 79.2
board of directors *management board* 126.2
board of governors *management board* 126.2
boards, the *drama* 136.1, *stage* 136.18
boardsurf *windsurf* 150.33
boardsurfing *windsurfing* 150.19, 150.28
boardwalk *waterfront* 621.3
boars Collective Names 59
boast 194.14; *bombast* 194.4, *object of pride* 297.6, *pride oneself* 297.7, *brag* 400.17, *show off* 402.15, *be egotistic* 444.7, *include* 763.5
boaster *exaggerator* 194.6, *proud person* 297.7, *insolent person* 400.7
boastful 402.13; *prideful* 297.8, *affected* 367.3, *egotistic* 444.5
boastfully 402.21; *pridefully* 297.17, *showily* 367.6
boastfulness 402.6; *pride* 297.1
boasting *bombast* 194.4, *bombastic* 194.10, *swaggering* 400.13, *exhibitionism* 404.9
boat *type of bed* 101.9, *means of transportation* 686.2, *vessel* 690.3
boatbuilder *artisan* 123.13
boater *hat* 100.32, *boating person* 150.24
boating *water transportation* 690.1, *nautical* 690.14
boating person 150.24
boating report *weather forecast* 9.4
boating sports 150.1
boatload *load* 577.5
boatman *transferrer* 685.4, *transporter* 686.4, *nautical person* 690.12

boat materials *shipbuilding* 690.4
boat person *avoider* 386.8
boat racing *race* 422.8
boat show *fair* 483.2, *display* 843.1
boatswain *nautical person* 690.12
boat trip *water transportation* 690.1
bob *boxing techniques* 152.5, *box* 152.19, *bobsledding* 162.23, *swim* 164.14, *mark of respect* 435.4, *show respect* 435.16, *coiffure* 530.8, *shorten* 591.9, *oscillator* 683.7, *jolt* 684.9, 684.23, *jerk* 699.3, *bow* 716.6, 716.22
bob and weave *be irresolute* 666.6
bobber *fishing tackle* 154.7
bobbery *tumult* 684.2
bobbin *fabric-handling tool* 130.12, *fishing tackle* 154.7, *rotator* 682.8
bobbing *combat* 152.17, *swimming techniques* 164.2, *showing respect* 435.7, *jolt* 684.9
bobbing and weaving *irresolution* 666.2
bobble *bungling* 128.2, *be clumsy* 128.9
bobble hat *hat* 100.32
bobby [Brit inf] *law enforcement officer* 53.8
bobby pin *hairdressing tool* 530.9, *fastener* 754.7
bobbysocks *legwear* 100.26
bob down *show respect* 435.16
bobrun *toboggan race* 162.25
bobsled 162.38; *bobsledding* 162.23
bobsled captain *bobsledder* 162.26
bobsledder 162.26
bobsledding 162.23, 162.34; Sporting Activities 145
bob up *arrive* 704.13, *spring up* 713.22
bob up and down *dance* 135.7
bobwhite, masked Endangered US Birds 36
bocage *trees* 43.4
boccie or **bocci** Sporting Activities 145
Boche Nicknames for Inhabitants 61
bod [Inf] *body* 19.1
bode *predict* 358.14
bode ill *endanger* 811.13
bode well *tend* 513.5, *be auspicious* 847.8
Bodhisattva *religious person* 81.9, *God* 82.6
bodhi tree Trees and Shrubs 43, *sacred object* 83.11
bodice *part of garment* 100.27
bodice ripper [Inf] *novel* 139.3
bodiless *nonmaterial* 525.8
bodiliness *material world* 524.1
bodily 19.18; *material* 524.7, *in person* 575.18, *visceral* 611.10, *one and all* 759.12
bodily appetite *sexual desire* 20.5
bodily chastisement *corporal punishment* 454.11
bodily development 19.17; *growth* 581.4
bodily improvement 807.10
bodily movement 677.11
bodily presence *presence* 575.1
boding *warning* 814.6
bodkin *sharp-pointed thing* 549.4, *opener* 583.2
body 19.1; *living organism* 13.10, *person* 18.8, *dead person* 29.7, *party* 59.3, *group* 59.8, *racing automobile* 146.2, *mountaineering* 161.9, *external appearance* 264.5, *matter* 524.4, *object* 524.6, *form* 551.3, *denseness* 594.2, *nature*

624.5, *thing* 717.3, *quantity* 738.1, *remainder* 750.1
body and blood of Christ *Eucharist* 85.7
body and soul *wholly* 759.11, *completely* 759.14
body armor *modern armor* 419.7
body art Western Art Styles 133
body belay *climbing techniques* 161.3
body belt *protective clothing* 419.6
bodybuilder *person of strength* 516.8
bodybuilding *edible* 92.20, *health-giving* 113.6
body-centered *status adjectives* 11.25
body-centered-cubic (b.c.c.) crystal *crystal* 11.14
bodychecking *ice hockey tactics* 158.4
body clock *timekeeper* 646.7
body cord *fencing equipment* 153.2
body count *death count* 29.10
body covering 19.4, 613.3
body dysmorphic disorder *somatoform disorder* 108.19
body English *nonstandard language* 5.7
body fluid 19.16, 555.3
bodyguard *law enforcement officer* 53.8, *personal attendant* 577.5, *defender* 77.2, *guard* 419.15, *security force* 464.3, *accompanier* 794.6, *surveillant* 810.12
body harness *climbing equipment* 161.4
body heat *heat* 217.1
body language *nonstandard language* 5.7, *gesture* 183.5, *articulation* 205.9, *external appearance* 264.5
body odor Phobias 283
body odor or **BO** *unpleasant-smelling thing* 227.2
body of law *law* 53.1
body of water *lake* 568.1
body orifice 583.3
body padding *protective clothing* 419.6
body politic 50.3; *nation* 18.14, *country* 566.1
body process 19.15
body scan *diagnostic radiology* 107.12
body shirt *shirt* 100.13
body shop *miscellaneous automotive terms* 687.14
body slam *wrestling terms* 152.10
body slip *glaze* 129.3
body snatcher *plunderer* 479.9
body snatching *plundering* 479.5, *stolen* 479.12
body stocking *underwear* 100.22
bodysuit *shirt* 100.13, *suit* 100.16
body support 605.6
body type *external appearance* 264.5
body wave *seismic wave* 8.25, *coiffure* 530.8
body wax *beauty treatment* 530.3
body weight *heaviness* 538.1
Boer Wars Major Wars 76
boeuf bourguignon *notable international dishes* 90.40
boffin [Brit inf] *expert* 52.8
bog *dirt* 112.5, *marsh* 559.8, 572.3, *shallowness* 599.1, *hidden danger* 813.3
bog [Brit inf] *place for excretion* 25.11
bogey *golfing terms* 156.3, *play* 156.8, *fantasy* 360.5, *false alarm* 814.4

bogey or **bogy** *adversity* 117.2, *frightener* 283.7
bogeyman or **bogyman** *frightener* 283.7, Legendary Creatures 360
bogged down *held up* 658.6
bogginess 559.7; *compressibility* 543.3
bogging down *inaction* 413.1
boggle *astonish* 292.10, *be wondrous* 294.14, *confuse* 333.20, *sway* 378.12
boggle at *be unwilling* 375.12
boggle the mind *be wondrous* 294.14
boggling *astonishing* 292.8, 294.10, *unsteady* 378.7
boggy *compressible* 543.9, *marshy* 559.11, *of landmasses* 572.12
bog moss *moss* 46.4
Bogotá Countries 566
bogtrotter Nicknames for Inhabitants 61
bogue [Inf] *withdrawal* 121.11, *drugged* 121.30
bogus *hypocritical* 330.10, *artificial* 720.12, *unauthentic* 722.9
bogus check *bad payment* 490.3
bogy *fantasy* 360.5, *false alarm* 814.4
bohemian *dissenter* 347.5, *free* 407.9, *nonobservant* 466.5, *nonconforming* 728.10, *individualist* 756.3, *nonconformist* 782.7, 782.13, *unconventional* 782.14, *freethinker* 829.10, *independent* 829.15
bohemianism *freedom* 407.4, *nonconformism* 782.3, *freethinking* 829.2
Bohr atom Classical Physical Laws 10
Bohr magneton Scientific and Technical Units 589
bohunk Nicknames for Inhabitants 61
boil *heat* 10.74, 217.17, *cook* 91.10, *ulcer* 114.18, *practice hygiene* 116.4, *be angry* 302.19, *mark* 533.2, *bulge* 634.2, *turbulence* 684.3, *be agitated* 684.21
boil away *dilute* 776.14
boil down *summarize* 204.7, *contract* 582.12, *shorten* 591.9, *outline* 617.5
boil down to *mean* 361.13
boiled *culinary* 91.9, *heated* 217.15
boiled away *diluted* 776.8
boiled cabbage *unpleasant-smelling thing* 227.2
boiled-down *smaller* 582.7
boiled fish *fish dish* 90.19
boiled ham *pork* 90.26
boiler *washer* 111.7, *heater* 217.3
boilermaker *power worker* 106.10
boiling *hot* 9.47, *temperature* 10.29, *phase* 11.13, *cooking technique* 91.2, *heating* 217.12, *angry* 302.11, *turbulence* 684.3, *turbulent* 684.17, *preservation of provisions* 815.6
boiling away *dilution* 776.3
boiling mad *angry* 302.11
boiling point *temperature* 10.29, *heat* 217.1
boiling-water reactor *nuclear power production* 514.10
boil over *be agitated* 684.21
Boise American States 564
boisterous *shouting* 232.7, *explosive* 520.6, *disorderly* 766.15, *hasty* 818.3
boisterously *disruptively* 766.26

boisterousness *violence* 520.1, *lawlessness* 766.6

boîte *club* 138.7

boîte de nuit [Fr] *club* 138.7

bola Historical Missile Weapons 78

bold *mountaineering* 161.9, *candid* 191.5, *emphatic* 200.3, *courageous* 284.9, *reckless* 286.6, *imaginative* 360.10, *audacious* 400.10, *defiant* 416.5, *disrespectful* 436.9, *strong in spirit* 516.11, *plain* 592.10, *assured* 621.12, *accentuated* 843.11, *open* 843.12

bold as brass *defiant* 416.5

bold façade *bold front* 284.5

boldface *printed* 173.13

bold-faced *insolent* 400.8

boldface type *type* 173.5

bold front 284.5; *defiance* 416.1

boldly *candidly* 191.10, *courageously* 284.17, *recklessly* 286.10, *audaciously* 400.20, *defiantly* 416.9, *strongly* 516.17, *plainly* 592.18, *frankly* 843.18

bold move *method* 387.4

boldness *candor* 191.2, *emphasis* 200.1, *courage* 284.1, *recklessness* 286.2, *audacity* 400.3, *defiance* 416.1, *plainness* 592.4, *assurance* 621.8, *openness* 843.6

bold relief *that which makes visible* 244.4

bold type *type* 173.5

bole *tree part* 43.2, *cylinder* 633.4, *component* 760.3

bolero *jacket* 100.18, Dances 135

bolide *meteor* 7.21

Bolivia Countries 566

bollard *rock face* 161.6, *fastener* 754.7

bollix up [Inf] *confuse* 766.19, *blunder* 846.13

boll weevil *pests and diseases* 17.12

bologna *sausage* 90.29

bolometer *meter* 589.13

Bolshevist *rebel* 427.8

bolster 377.15; *give courage* 284.16, *support* 605.16, 825.24, *preserve* 815.14

bolt Historical Missile Weapons 78, *eat well* 92.25, *be greedy* 119.4, *climbing equipment* 161.4, *retreat* 386.22, *superstructure* 551.7, *obstruction* 584.2, *obstruct* 584.13, *piece* 590.2, *accelerate* 694.14, *missile* 696.7, *hurry off* 705.11, *link* 752.18, *fastener* 754.7, *connect* 754.11, *bind* 754.14, *safety device* 810.15, *escape* 816.8, *make haste* 818.5

bolt-action 78.17; *hunting* 160.11

bolt-action firearm *firearm* 78.7

bolt-action rifle *hunting equipment* 160.4

bolt-action shotgun *hunting equipment* 160.4

bolt down one's meal *have no time to spare* 818.6

bolted *obstructed* 584.8, *bound* 754.12

bolt from *or* **out of the blue** *shock* 292.3

bolt hammer *climbing equipment* 161.4

bolt-hole *hiding place* 181.2, *fortification* 812.3

bolting *appetite* 92.2, *gluttonous* 119.3

bolt of lightning *thunderstorm* 9.20

bolt route *climbing expedition* 161.2

bolt the door *shelter* 812.8

bolt upright *vertical* 602.5

Boltzmann constant Classical Physical Laws 10

bolus *bite* 92.10, *dose of medicine* 115.3

Bolzano–Weierstrass theorem Mathematical Concepts 6

bomb 78.15, 418.19; *murder weapon* 30.3, *murder* 30.20, *fight* 77.35, *play* 155.8, *banger* 234.3, *shock* 292.3, *agent of destruction* 523.7, *demolish* 523.12

bomb [Inf] *theatrical performance* 136.13, *automobile* 687.6, *unsuccessful thing* 846.8

bombard *historical gun* 78.10, *attack* 418.17, *fire* 418.18, *demolish* 523.12, Sailing Ships and Boats 690, *shoot* 696.18

bombarde Musical Instruments 142

bombardier *air force person* 77.31, *attacker* 418.10

bombardier [Can] *snow vehicle* 687.9

bombardment *bombing* 76.21, *burst of sound* 232.4, *combined attack* 418.5, *shot* 696.16

bombardon Musical Instruments 142

bombast 194.4; *boast* 194.14, *diffuseness* 199.1, *nonsense* 362.2, *flashiness* 404.4, *pomposity* 404.5, *bravado* 404.8, *inelegance of expression* 528.4

bombastic 194.10; *diffuse* 199.3, *articulate* 205.16, *flashy* 404.17, *pompous* 404.18, *inelegant* 528.6, *exaggerated* 712.9

bombastically *exaggeratedly* 194.16, *diffusely* 199.7, *flashily* 404.32, *pompously* 404.33

Bombay Breeds of Cats 35

bomb bay *arsenal* 78.3

bomb dropping *air attack* 418.4

bombe *dessert* 90.35

bombé *type of desk* 101.6

bombed [Inf] *dead drunk* 121.27, *drugged* 121.30

bomber *murderer* 30.12, *military aircraft* 77.30, *attacker* 418.10, *villain* 448.5

bomber jacket *jacket* 100.18

bomber pilot *air force person* 77.31

bombinate *hum* 235.11, *make an insect sound* 240.9

bombination *humming* 235.2, *insect sound* 240.3

bombing 76.21; *air attack* 418.4, *terrorist attack* 418.7, *wicked act* 448.7

bomb ketch Sailing Ships and Boats 690

bombproof *mountaineering* 161.9, *invulnerable* 419.19, 810.18, *tough* 547.6, *make tough* 547.15

bomb rack *arsenal* 78.3

bomb run *air attack* 418.4

bombshell *bomb* 78.15, *shock* 292.3

bomb shelter *hiding place* 181.2, *fortification* 812.3

bomb ship *historical warships* 77.22

bona fide *authentic* 721.16, 737.6

bonanza *source of supply* 105.4, *reward* 472.4, *wealth* 485.1, *good fortune* 847.2

bon appetit! [Fr] *come and get it!* 92.28

bonbon *sweets* 90.39

bond *react* 11.38, *masonry* 14.22, *duty* 433.1, *promise* 458.1, 464.2, *contract* 459.1, 462.2, *paper money* 484.14, *relatedness* 727.1, *settlement* 735.6, *have a rapport with* 735.24, *linkage* 752.3, *joint* 752.7, *means of connection* 754.4, *connect* 754.13, *come together* 757.10, *restraint* 826.8

bondage *detention* 830.5, *subjection* 832.1

bond angle *chemical bond* 11.6

bond broker *financial adviser* 457.4

bonded *related* 727.6, *tied* 752.13, *connected* 754.11, *adhesive* 755.5

bond energy *chemical bond* 11.6

bonding *friendship* 62.1, *junction* 609.5, *compatibility* 735.4, *linkage* 752.3, *adhesion* 755.1

bonding agent *means of connection* 754.4

bonding orbital *chemical bond* 11.6

bondmaid *serf* 69.8, *subjected person* 832.5

bondman *serf* 69.8, *subjected person* 832.5

bond market *stock exchange* 457.3

bond pair *chemical bond* 11.6

bond paper *paper* 104.5

bonds *personal estate* 470.6, *means of restraint* 830.6

bond servant *serf* 69.8, *subjected person* 832.5

bondslave *subjected person* 832.5

bondsman *promise maker* 458.6

bond strength *chemical bond* 11.6

bone *cook* 91.10, *solid body* 540.4, *hard substance* 542.3, *skeleton* 551.14, *void* 709.23

bone ash *material* 129.2

bone cancer *cancer* 114.15

bone carving *sculpture* 144.1

bone cell *cell* 13.15

bone china Ceramics 129

boned *tough* 542.6

bone-dry *dried-up* 560.9

bonefish *game fish* 154.10

boneheaded [Inf] *thick-witted* 594.7

boneheadedness [Inf] *thick-wittedness* 594.3

bone idle *not participating* 415.11

boneless rump *beef* 90.24

bone meal *fertilizer* 16.9, 22.6, *animal feed* 16.12

bone of contention *issue* 328.2, *difficult question* 333.4, *rivalry* 422.2

boner *blunder* 351.9

bones *skeleton* 19.2, Musical Instruments 142, *seat of feelings* 266.7, *remainder* 750.1

bonesetter *healer* 107.22

bonesetting *therapy* 115.12

bone to pick *hostility* 63.1, *divisiveness* 463.2

bone up [Inf] *learn* 48.23

bone urn *funeral object* 31.6

boneyard [Inf] *burial place* 31.7

bonfire *fire* 217.8, 246.9, *salute* 405.7

bong *climbing equipment* 161.4

bongo drums Musical Instruments 142

bonhomie *friendship* 62.1, *benevolence* 305.1, *good company* 408.9

bonhomous *cheerful* 269.7, *benevolent* 305.7

boniness *thinness* 595.1, *emaciation* 595.2

boning up [Inf] *learning* 48.7

bonito *game fish* 154.10

bonk *ski* 162.35

bonk [Inf] *blow* 695.5, *hit* 695.11

bonkers [Inf] *insane* 110.9

bon marché [Fr] *bargain* 497.4

bon mot *wit* 277.3

bonne bouche [Fr] *appetizer* 219.2

bonnet *body covering* 613.3

bonneted *dressed* 100.38

Bonnin and Morris porcelain Ceramics 129

bonniness *beauty* 529.1

bonny *healthy* 113.4, *beautiful* 529.7

bonnyclabber *semiliquid* 561.7

bonsai *garden* 17.2, *tree* 43.1

Bonsmara Breeds of Cattle 16

bonus *superfluity* 99.4, *acknowledgment* 310.3, *reward for service* 453.5, *profit* 467.6, *reward* 472.4, *given* 472.8, *something received* 492.2, *gift* 498.3, *positive stimulus* 508.5, *extra* 748.6, *surplus* 750.4

bonuses *bargaining terms* 57.10

bon vivant *eater* 92.15, *glutton* 119.2, *pleasure-seeker* 214.4, *social person* 408.7, *self-indulgent person* 456.5

bon voyage! *goodbye!* 705.14

bony *bodily* 19.18, *hard* 542.5, *skeletal* 551.19, *thin* 595.9

bony fish *fish* 38.5

bonze *religious* 84.9

boo *gesture* 183.5, 183.17, *cry of disapproval* 239.7, *hiss* 239.17, *expression of dissatisfaction* 274.2, *be dissatisfied* 274.7, *taunt* 436.14, 436.23, *show of disapproval* 438.6, *show disapproval* 438.21, *gesture of protest* 507.3, *complain* 507.8

boob [Inf] *unskilled person* 128.3

boob job [Inf] *cosmetic surgery* 530.2

boo-boo [Inf] *mistake* 342.2, *blunder* 351.9, 528.5, *joke* 368.4, *unsuccessful thing* 846.8

boobs [Inf] *bulge* 634.2

boob tube [Inf] *television set* 172.6

booby *unskilled person* 128.3

booby hatch *the inside* [Inf] 55.2, *mental hospital* 110.6

booby prize *unskillfulness* 128.1, *prize* 453.2

booby trap *bomb* 78.15, *trap* 813.1

booby-trap *fence* 419.21

boodle Card Games 168

boodle [Inf] *profit* 467.6, *takings* 477.8, *stolen goods* 479.4, *cash* 484.2

booed *criticized* 438.14

booer *crier* 239.8

boogie-woogie *jazz* 140.5

boohoo [Inf] *cry of sorrow* 239.6, *cry* 239.16

booing *hissing* 239.12, *taunting* 436.14, *protesting* 507.5

Book, the *Christian text* 81.16

book 174.1; *script* 136.7, 137.5, *part of poem* 139.9, *publication* 173.1, *publication media* 173.6, *register* 185.15, *accuse* 442.8, *reserve* 464.14, *account* 493.9, *work of art* 522.4, *list* 785.11

book bag *bag* 578.7

bookbinder *book publishing personnel* 174.12, *coverer* 613.18

bookbinding 174.11, Hobbies and Pastimes 167

bookcase *cabinet* 101.8, 578.3, *receptacle* 105.11

book club *bookshop* 174.15

book collector *booklover* 174.16

book cover *or* **jacket** *wrapping* 613.10

book dealer *bookshop* 174.15

book depository *library* 174.14
booked *accused* 442.5
bookends *enclosing thing* 619.3
Booker Prize [Brit] *prizes* 453.3
bookie [Inf] *horse person* 159.14
book illustration *illustration* 187.2
book in advance *prepare* 657.14
booking *engagement* 136.15, 138.6, *recordkeeping* 185.7, *accusation* 442.1
booking agent *producer* 136.28
booking clerk *merchant* 482.10
bookish *educated* 48.19
bookishly *studiously* 48.26
bookishness *learnedness* 48.8, *learning* 348.36
book jacket *bookbinding* 174.11
bookkeeper *record keeper* 185.8, *treasurer* 484.18, *accountant* 493.6, *counter* 784.4
bookkeeping *recordkeeping* 185.7, *accounts* 493.4, *accounting* 493.7
book learning *learning* 348.3
book list *list* 785.1
booklover 174.16
bookloving 174.17
bookmaker *horse person* 159.14
bookmaking *book publishing* 174.6
book manufacturing *book publishing* 174.6
bookmobile *library* 174.14
Book of Common Prayer *ritual manual* 85.11
book of hours *ritual manual* 85.11
book of lists 785.3
Book of Mormon *Christian text* 81.16
Book of the Dead *other text* 81.19
book of words *script* 136.7
book part 174.5
bookplate *means of identification* 184.3
book printing 174.10
book production *book publishing* 174.6
book publisher *book publishing personnel* 174.12
book publishing 174.6
book publishing personnel 174.12
book review 174.13; *criticism* 365.3
book reviewer *literary person* 139.14, *book review* 174.13
books *Phobias* 283, *account book* 493.3, *bill* 785.4
book salesman *bookshop* 174.15
bookseller *bookshop* 174.15
bookshelf *receptacle* 105.11
bookshop 174.15
bookstall *bookshop* 174.15
bookstand *bookshop* 174.15
bookstore *bookshop* 174.15
book style *mode of expression* 537.3
book trade *book publishing* 174.6
book wagon *library* 174.14
book-wise *educated* 48.19
bookworm *worm* 39.14, *pest* 40.5, *learner* 48.6, *booklover* 174.16
Boolean algebra *algebra* 6.21
boom *productiveness* 22.3, *be fertile* 22.13, *economic factor* 56.8, *sailboat parts and accessories* 150.4, *sailboard parts* 150.20, *speak in a particular way* 205.18, *burst of sound* 232.4, *burst* 232.9, *bang* 234.1, 234.6, *drum* 235.10, *resonate* 236.9, *barrier* 419.10, *sales* 482.3, *be sold* 482.22, *superstructure* 551.7, *spread* 746.3, *increase* 746.6, *revival* 809.3, *prosperity* 847.1

boom and bust *capitalism* 480.5
boom box [Inf] *radio* 172.1
boom/bust cycle *economic factor* 56.8
boomer [Inf] *warship* 77.21
boomerang *Historical Missile Weapons* 78, *hunting equipment* 160.4, *counteract* 510.7, *reverse* 671.9
boomerang effect *counteraction* 510.1, *reversion* 671.1
booming *productive* 22.9, *loud* 232.6, *banging* 234.4, *deepness* 236.3, *deep* 236.8, *vociferous* 239.9, *prosperous* 847.5
booming economy *prosperity* 847.1
boom off *navigate* 690.15
boom operator *filmmaker* 137.14
boom town *town* 567.2
boom vang *sailboat parts and accessories* 150.4
boon *good* 445.1, *reward* 472.4
boon companion *friend* 62.2
boondocks *regions* 564.2, *distant place* 585.3
boonies [Inf] *regions* 564.2, *distant place* 585.3
boor *unpleasant person* 272.5, *unintelligent person* 316.4, *badly behaved person* 399.8, *discourteous person* 411.4, *vulgar person* 535.4
boorish *clumsy* 128.6, *objectionable* 272.7, *unintelligent* 316.6, *unformed* 389.11, *badly behaved* 399.16, *bad-mannered* 411.6, *indecorous* 528.8, *discourteous* 535.7
boorishly *rudely* 411.9, *discourteously* 535.11
boorishness *objectionability* 272.2, *ignorance* 316.3, *bad conduct* 399.7, *bad manners* 411.2, *impropriety* 528.2, *grossness* 535.3
boost *publicize* 173.18, *compliment* 437.17, *strengthen* 516.15, *invigorate* 518.5, *promotion* 715.3, *erect* 715.11, *promote* 715.13, *spread* 746.3, *intensify* 746.6, *support* 825.2, 825.24, *further* 825.30
boost [Inf] *steal* 479.14
boosted *raised* 715.6
booster *rocketry* 7.32, *radio reception* 172.2, *propeller* 696.8
booster [Inf] *thief* 479.8
booster station *radio broadcasting* 172.4, *television broadcasting* 172.8
boosting *raising* 715.1
boosting [Inf] *stealing* 479.1
boot *program* 15.29, *ski equipment* 162.10, *treatment* 399.11, *blow* 695.5, *kick* 695.14, *activate* 771.28, *restraint* 826.8
boot [Inf] *relegation* 574.4, *relegate* 574.18, *expulsion* 709.1, *ejection* 764.2, *termination* 834.2
bootblack *attendant* 69.4, *cleaner* 111.12
boot camp *military training* 58.3
booted *dressed* 100.38
booted out [Inf] *relegated* 574.11
Boötes *Constellations* 7
booth *shack* 60.10, *stall* 483.9, *compartment* 578.2
boot-ice ax belay *climbing techniques* 161.3
booties *baby clothes* 100.24
booting out [Inf] *expulsion* 709.1
bootlace *line* 754.5
bootleg *alcohol* 121.5, *play* 155.8, *play offense* 155.18, *copy* 736.2
bootlegger *infringer* 479.10

bootlegging *infringement* 479.6
bootless *futile* 802.10, *failed* 846.10
bootlessly *unsuccessfully* 846.21
bootlessness *futility* 802.3
bootlick *fawn* 401.9, *be sycophantic* 439.15
bootlicker *sycophant* 401.3, *flatterer* 439.6
bootlicking *sycophancy* 401.2, *sycophantic* 401.7, 439.11, *submitting* 421.3, *showing respect* 435.7
bootmaker *clothier* 100.37, *horse person* 159.14
bootmaking *the clothing business* 100.36
boot out [Inf] *discard* 383.12, *eject* 701.8, 764.8, *expel* 709.14, *dismiss* 709.15
boot polish *cleaning agent* 111.9
boots 100.31; *climbing equipment* 161.4, *soccer uniform* 163.3
boot-scraper *cleaning tool* 111.10
bootstrap *computing terms* 15.22, *program* 15.29
boot up *program* 15.29, *activate* 771.28
booty *takings* 477.8, *stolen goods* 479.4
booze [Inf] *alcoholic drink* 93.9, *drink* 93.19, *alcohol* 121.5, *get drunk* 121.35
boozed-up [Inf] *drunk* 121.25
boozehound [Inf] *drunkard* 121.8
boozer [Inf] *drinker* 93.16, *drunkard* 121.8
booze-up [Inf] *drinking bout* 121.7
boozing [Inf] *drinking* 93.17, *drunken* 121.28
boozy [Inf] *slightly drunk* 121.26, *drunken* 121.28
bop *jazz* 140.5, *type of touch* 216.3
bop [Inf] *hit* 695.11
bora *Notable Winds* 9
Bora-Bora *Islands* 572
boracic acid *prophylaxis* 115.4
borage *Herbs and Spices* 91
Bordeaux mixture *pest killer* 17.9
Bordelaise *sauce* 90.17
bordello *brothel* 432.5, *wicked place* 448.8
border 618.9; *ornamental garden* 17.3, *stage set* 136.19, *adjoin* 216.11, *juxtaposition* 586.4, *juxtapose* 586.14, *exteriority* 610.2, *be exterior* 610.13, *surround* 615.7, *interface* 616.5, *edge* 617.3, 618.1, 618.8, *edging* 618.2, *limit* 620.1, 773.7, *side* 623.1, *ornamentation* 748.5, *separator* 753.5
Border collie *Breeds of Dogs* 35
bordered *edging* 618.5, *farthest* 620.6
bordering *contiguous* 216.8, *juxtaposition* 586.4, *juxtaposed* 586.9, *covering* 610.8, *farthest* 620.6, *limiting* 773.17
bordering on *nearby* 803.4
borderland *regions* 564.2, *juxtaposition* 586.4
Border Leicester *Breeds of Sheep* 16
borderline *questionable* 333.13, *indeterminate* 841.14
borderline case *irresolution* 841.3
borderline personality disorder *personality disorder* 108.7
border on *interface* 616.5
Borders, the *regions of the British Isles* 564.8
borders *regions* 564.2
Border terrier *Breeds of Dogs* 35
bordure *Heraldic Terms* 184

bore 296.8; *carpenter* 131.10, *be diffuse* 199.5, *be talkative* 207.7, *make indifferent* 289.13, *boring thing* 296.3, *boring person* 296.4, *use a sharp tool* 549.17, *opening* 583.1, *hole* 583.17, *breadth* 592.1, *make concave* 635.7, *eat away* 808.19
boreal *windy* 9.42, *cool* 9.49, *seasonal* 654.7, *directional* 697.8
Boreas *wind god* 9.16
bored 296.5; *incurious* 322.3, *holed* 583.12
boredom 296.1; *lack of emphasis* 201.1, *dilution* 220.2, *incuriosity* 322.1, *fatigue* 820.1
bored out of one's mind *bored* 296.5
bored stiff *bored* 296.5
bored to death *bored* 296.5
bored to distraction *bored* 296.5
bored to tears *bored* 296.5
bored tunnel *tunnel* 551.11
borehole *hole* 583.4, *concave land* 635.2
bore in *infiltrate* 706.13
bore into *make concave* 635.7
borer *pest* 40.5, *woodworking tool* 131.6, *sharp-pointed thing* 549.4, *digger* 635.4
boresome *boring* 296.6
bore stiff *bore* 296.8
bore the pants off *bore* 296.8
bore to death *bore* 296.8
bore to distraction *bore* 296.8
bore to tears *bore* 296.8
boric acid *prophylaxis* 115.4
boring 296.6; *diffuse* 199.3, *unemphatic* 201.2, *tasteless* 220.4, *monotonous* 797.12, *annoying* 804.7, *inconvenient* 824.12
boringly 296.10; *annoyingly* 804.12
boring machine *machine tool* 14.9, *woodworking tool* 131.6
boringness 296.2
boring person 296.4
boring thing 296.3
born *alive* 28.13, *produced* 522.12, *arriving* 704.9
born-again *religious* 81.21, *believing* 87.6, *penitent* 451.5, *converted* 670.7
born-again Christian *Christian* 81.10, *penitent person* 451.4
born-again person *convert* 670.6
born dead *dead* 29.11
Borneo *Islands* 572
borneol *Tree Products* 43
borne out *proven* 331.13
born for *gifted* 127.11
Bornholm Island *Islands* 572
born in *or* **to the purple** *wealthy* 485.8
born loser *hopeless person* 282.5, *loser* 468.8, 846.9, *person in adversity* 848.9
born of *caused* 676.5
born to the purple *figurative usage* 262.4
born to toil *working* 122.6
born under a bad sign *unlucky* 848.12
born under a lucky star *prosperous* 847.5
born under an evil star *unlucky* 848.12
born with a silver spoon in one's mouth *wealthy* 485.8, *prosperous* 847.5
born yesterday *naive* 821.3
boron *Chemical Elements and Common Allotropes* 11

borough *administrative region* 564.4, *town* 567.2
borrow 476.10; *add* 6.86, *take away* 477.18, *steal* 479.14, *acquire credit* 487.11, *copy* 736.10
borrowed 476.8
borrowed word *new word* 5.18
borrower 476.7; *debtor* 488.6, *requester* 505.5
borrow from *follow from* 676.9
borrow illegally 476.12
borrowing 476.1; *borrowed* 476.8, *taking away* 477.5, *loan* 488.3, *indebted* 488.7
borrowing capacity *resources* 102.4, *credit* 487.1
borrow money *be in debt* 488.9
borrow without permission *or* **authorization** *borrow illegally* 476.12
borscht *soup* 90.14, *notable international dishes* 90.40
borscht belt *regions of the United States* 564.7
borscht circuit *or* **belt** *engagement* 138.6
borstal *or* **borstal institution** [Brit] *prison* 55.1
borzoi *Breeds of Dogs* 35
bosal *riding equipment* 159.9
bo-san *religious* 84.9
Bose–Einstein statistics *Classical Physical Laws* 10
bosh *nonsense* 192.8, *senseless talk* 362.4
bosk *trees* 43.4
bosket *trees* 43.4
Boskop man *primitive humanity* 18.4
bosky *wooded* 43.12
Bosnia and Herzegovina *Countries* 566
Bosnian Mountain *Breeds of Sheep* 16
Bosnian pony *Horse and Pony Breeds* 159
bosom *part of garment* 100.27, *seat of feelings* 266.7, *bulge* 634.2
bosom buddy [Inf] *friend* 62.2
bosom friend *friend* 62.2
bosomy *fat* 579.15
boson *elementary particle* 10.53
bosquet *trees* 43.4
boss *person in authority* 52.7, *employer* 57.3, *company leader* 68.8, *master* 68.17, *manager* 126.7, *direct* 126.11, *Architectural Elements* 134, *relief carving* 144.2, *meddle* 414.23, *make rough* 544.11, *bulge* 634.2, *superior* 744.5
bossanova *Dances* 135
boss around *meddle* 414.23, *be severe* 424.8
bosses *management board* 126.2
boss-eyed [Brit inf] *visually impaired* 243.9
bossy *authoritative* 52.9, 425.8, *severe* 424.5
Boston *Card Games* 168, *American States* 564, *major US cities* 567.5
Boston accent *regional pronunciation* 205.7
Boston bag *baggage* 578.8
Boston marriage *sexual nature* 20.4
Boston terrier *Breeds of Dogs* 35
bosun *nautical person* 690.12
bosun's chair *sailboat parts and accessories* 150.4
bosun's mate *nautical person* 690.12

botanical 17.15, 41.20; *biological* 13.27
botanical fruit 44.2
botanical garden *garden* 17.2, *herbarium* 41.12
botanically 41.25; *biologically* 13.36, *horticulturally* 17.20
botanist *life scientist* 13.26, *plant scientist* 41.11
botanize *study plants* 41.23
botanophobia *Phobias* 283
botany 13.7; *biology* 13.2, *study of life* 28.9, *plant science* 41.10
botch *bungling* 128.2, *be clumsy* 128.9, *misrepresentation* 188.1, *misrepresent* 188.6, *mistake* 342.2, *blunder* 351.9, *be wrong* 430.18, *confuse* 766.19, *impair* 808.18, *obstacle* 826.2, *error* 846.2
botched *bungled* 128.7
botcher *unskilled person* 128.3
botching *bungling* 128.2
botch up *err* 351.14, *be wrong* 430.18
botchy *bungled* 128.7
both *two* 789.8
bother 826.16; *annoyance* 276.2, 804.2, *irritate* 302.16, *make irascible* 303.16, *be inconsiderate* 318.13, *alacrity* 414.3, *be active* 414.18, *meddle* 414.23, *fuss* 684.4, *disruption* 766.7, *disturbance* 768.1, *commotion* 768.5, *disturb* 768.10, *annoy* 804.10, *awkward situation* 824.7, *cause difficulties* 824.22
botheration *alacrity* 414.3
bothered *disturbed* 768.6, *troubled* 824.15
bothering *inconsiderate* 318.9
bothersome *disturbing* 768.9, *annoying* 804.7, *inconvenient* 824.12
bo tree *Trees and Shrubs* 43, *sacred object* 83.11
botrytis *pests and diseases* 17.12
Botswana *Countries* 566
bottle 578.14; *blunt weapon* 78.5, *drink container* 93.13, *receptacle* 105.11, *save* 105.20, *contain* 578.20, *preserver* 815.9, *preserve* 815.14
bottled *saved* 105.15, *storing* 578.19, *preserved* 815.12
bottled water *drinking water* 557.2
bottle(ful) *container(ful)* 738.2
bottleful *size of drink* 93.3
bottle garden *garden* 17.2
bottle glass *ceramics* 129.1, *glass* 249.5
bottle-green *green* 260.7
bottle kiln *ceramic workshop and tools* 129.8
bottleneck *contracted thing* 582.5, *obstruction* 584.2, *obstruct* 584.13, *narrow place* 593.2, *narrowing* 702.6, *roadblock* 826.4, *block* 826.17
bottlenecked *obstructed* 584.8
bottle opener *opener* 583.2
bottle tree *Trees and Shrubs* 43
bottle up *conceal* 181.12, *detain* 471.9, *keep inside* 611.17, *limit* 620.7, *preserve* 815.14, *restrain* 830.12
bottling *storage* 105.6, *storing* 578.19
bottling plant *preserver* 815.9
bottling up *detention* 471.2
bottom 601.6; *fishing* 154.13, *river parts* 570.3, *lowest point* 597.5, *lower* 597.14, *deeper* 598.10, *base*

601.1, limit 620.1, *side direction* 623.2, *side* 623.6, *inferior state* 745.3
bottom [Inf] *rear end* 622.4
bottom dollar *tail* 773.8
bottom fishing *fishing* 154.1
bottom-heavy *unbalanced* 741.5
bottoming out *shortening* 582.2, *decline* 747.4
bottom land *lowland* 572.6, *lowlands* 597.6
bottom layer *lowest point* 597.5, *base* 601.1
bottomless *deep* 598.9, *infinite* 798.5
bottomlessness *depth* 598.1
bottomless pit *evil place* 446.6, *infinity* 798.1
bottomless purse *wealth* 485.1
bottom line *return* 453.6, *baseline* 601.4, *fact* 717.6, *realities* 719.5, *essential content* 723.2
bottom-line *basic* 601.8
bottommost *lower* 597.14, *deeper* 598.10, *bottom* 601.6, *inferior* 745.5
bottom of one's heart *seat of feelings* 266.7
bottom of the bill *play part* 136.8
bottom of the sea *the depths* 598.2
bottom out *become smaller* 582.14, *underlie* 597.23, 601.11, *decrease* 747.7
bottom price *bargain* 495.2
bottoms up! *cheers!* 93.22
bottom up *inversely* 608.9
bottom-up *inverted* 608.5
botulism *poisoning* 114.8, *gastroenterological disease* 114.11
bouclé *rough thing* 544.2, *coarse* 544.6
boudoir *room* 60.9, *privacy* 181.6
Bougainville *Islands* 572
bougainvillea *Flowers* 42
bough *tree part* 43.2, *component* 760.3
bought 481.8
bouillabaisse *soup* 90.14, *notable international dishes* 90.40
bouillon *soup* 90.14
boulder *sediment* 8.29, *mountaineer* 161.10, *hard substance* 542.3
boulder clay *glacier* 8.44
bouldering *mountaineering* 161.1
boule *decorative woodwork* 131.2
boule *or* **boulework** *Furniture Styles* 101
boulevard *road* 691.4
boulework *decorative woodwork* 131.2
boulle *decorative woodwork* 131.2
Boulonnais *Breeds of Sheep* 16, *Horse and Pony Breeds* 159
bounce *elasticity* 546.1, *be elastic* 546.7, *jolt* 684.9, 684.23, *be agitated* 684.21, *jump* 713.7, *spring up* 713.22
bounce [Inf] *relegation* 574.4, *relegate* 574.18, *expulsion* 709.1, *expel* 709.14, *termination* 834.2
bounceback *response* 334.4, *reflex* 680.7
bounce back *react* 334.20, *be adaptable* 546.9, *get healthy* 113.12, *recoil* 680.21, *be restored* 809.13
bounced [Inf] *relegated* 574.11
bounced check *false money* 484.15, *amount owing* 488.5, *bad payment* 490.3
bounced light *lighting* 132.16
bounce pass *playing terms* 148.4
bouncer *defender* 77.2, *guard*

419.15, person of strength 516.8, *ejector* 709.10, *surveillant* 810.12
bouncily *elastically* 546.10
bounciness *elasticity* 546.1
bouncing *healthy* 113.4, *cheerful* 269.7, *invigorating* 518.3, *elastic* 546.5, *leaping* 713.17
bouncing baby *child* 26.6
bouncy *cheerful* 269.7, *invigorating* 518.3, *elastic* 546.5, *turbulent* 684.17
bound 754.12; *set* 6.19, *imprisoned* 55.9, *participate* 166.22, *published* 174.18, *conditional* 340.10, *dutiful* 433.6, *promised* 458.8, *guaranteeing* 458.9, *retained* 471.6, *indebted* 488.7, *protected* 613.20, *enclosed* 619.4, *limit* 620.7, *acceleration* 694.3, *be swift* 694.10, *jump* 713.7, *spring up* 713.22, *related* 727.6, *tied* 752.13, *connected* 754.11
boundary *line* 6.35, *green bowling* 151.3, *edge* 618.1, *limit* 620.1, *773.7, separator* 753.5
boundary condition *specification* 340.6
boundary line *limit marker* 620.4
boundary marker *limit marker* 620.4
Boundary Peak *Mountains and Hills* 569
bounded *farthest* 620.6
bounded volume *geometric figure* 6.39
bounden duty *duty* 433.1
bounder *libertine* 32.7, *disreputable character* 371.2, *badly behaved person* 399.8, *vulgar person* 535.4
bound for *directed* 697.9
bound forward *accelerate* 694.14
bounding *jumping* 166.11, *specification* 340.6, *leaping* 713.17, *limiting* 773.17
bounding main *sea* 571.1
boundless *astronomical* 7.33, *extensive* 563.12, *broad* 592.5, *numberless* 795.8, *infinite* 798.5
boundlessly *astronomically* 7.36, *infinitely* 798.8
boundlessness *breadth* 592.1, *infinity* 798.1
bounds *specification* 340.6, *edge* 618.1
bounteous *fertile* 22.8, *generous* 498.6
bounteousness *generosity* 498.1
bountiful *fertile* 22.8, *plentiful* 97.4, *charitable* 305.9, *philanthropic* 307.6, *giving* 472.9, *lush* 485.11, *generous* 498.6, *big* 579.13
bountifully *charitably* 305.15, *philanthropically* 307.9, *as a gift* 472.17, *wealthily* 485.16, *amply* 579.20
bountifulness *fertility* 22.1, *charity* 305.3, *philanthropy* 307.1
bountiful supply *plenty* 97.2
bounty 453.8; *fertility* 22.1, *plenty* 97.2, *philanthropy* 307.1, *giving* 472.1, *offering* 472.6, *opulence* 485.3, *generosity* 498.1
bouquet *flower* 42.1, *assemblage* 59.13, *odor* 224.1, *fragrance* 226.1, *compliment* 437.4, *reward* 453.1
bouquet garni *basic cooking ingredient* 91.8, *admixture* 751.5
Bourbon Red *Breeds of Fowl* 16
bourgeois *commoner* 71.1, *mediocre* 742.7, *middle-aged* 772.15,*

conformist 781.6, 781.10, *free person* 829.9

bourgeois ethic *conventionalism* 781.4

bourgeoisie *common people* 71.2, *average person* 742.4, *middle class* 772.6

bourn *or* **bourne** *river* 570.1, *destination* 704.6

bourse *stock market* 483.6, *place of exchange* 673.2

bout *task* 122.2, *sports* 145.1, *seizure* 418.11, *allotted task* 474.3, *period of activity* 641.4

boutique *store* 483.8

boutique farming *arable farming* 16.6

bout of sickness *illness* 114.2

boutonniere *flower* 42.1

Bouvier des Flandres Breeds of Dogs 35

bouzouki Musical Instruments 142

bovid *hoofed mammal* 35.16, *ungulate* 35.31

Bovidae *hoofed mammal* 35.16

bovine *hoofed mammal* 35.16, *ungulate* 35.31

bovine spongiform encephalopathy (BSE) *animal disease* 34.10

Bow Rivers 570

bow 716.6, 716.22; Historical Missile Weapons 78, *follow rites* 85.19, *sound* 141.15, *part of stringed instrument* 142.2, *play an instrument* 142.9, *sailboat parts and accessories* 150.4, *canoe parts* 150.10, *canoeing* 150.26, *rowing* 150.27, *submissiveness* 298.3, *submit* 298.17, *knuckle under* 401.10, *sign of courtesy* 410.5, *defer to* 410.12, *submission* 421.1, *succumb* 421.7, *obeisance* 426.3, *show obeisance to* 426.8, *mark of respect* 435.4, *show respect* 435.16, *prostration* 597.2, *be low* 597.20, *vanguard* 621.5, *curve* 629.6, *be convex* 634.7

bow *or* **bowknot** Knots, Bends, Hitches, Splices 754

bow and arrow *sharp weapon* 78.6, *hunting equipment* 160.4, *agent of destruction* 523.7

bow and scrape *knuckle under* 401.10, *succumb* 421.7, *show respect* 435.16

bow before the inevitable *succumb* 421.7

bow before the storm *succumb* 421.7

bowdlerization *censorship* 111.5, *self-righteousness* 431.7, *subtraction* 749.1, *ejection* 764.2

bowdlerize *purify* 111.19, *moralize* 431.14, *change for the worse* 665.18, *subtract* 749.6, *eject* 764.8

bowdlerized *expurgated* 111.15, *moralistic* 431.12

bowdlerizer *changer* 665.9

bow down *show respect* 435.16, *bow* 716.22

bowed *instrumental* 142.8, *sycophantic* 401.7, *prostrate* 597.11, *curved* 629.4

bowed out *convex* 634.5

bowed string instrument *musical instrument* 142.1

bowel movement (BM) *defecation* 25.3

bowels *internal organ* 19.13, *eating organ* 92.14, *insides* 577.3, *the depths* 598.2, *internals* 611.3

bower *ornamental garden* 17.3, *trees* 43.4

Bowery, the New York 567.6

bowie knife *sharp weapon* 78.6

bowing *sycophantic* 401.7, *deference* 410.4, *deferential* 410.8, *showing respect* 435.7, *prostrate* 597.11

bowing and scraping *sycophancy* 401.2, *submitting* 421.3, *mark of respect* 435.4, *showing respect* 435.7, *debasement* 716.5

bowl 151.8; *kitchen container* 91.7, *tableware* 92.13, *drink container* 93.13, *green bowling* 151.3, *stadium* 155.3, *historic armor* 419.8, *basin* 578.12, *crockery* 578.16, *round thing* 633.3, *cavity* 635.3, *roll* 682.15, *throw* 696.4, *propel* 696.15

bowl a hook ball *bowl* 151.8

bowl along *go smoothly* 545.11, *be swift* 694.10

bowled over *astonished* 292.6, *wondering* 294.7

bowler 151.5; *hat* 100.32, *thrower* 696.10

bowl(ful) *container(ful)* 738.2

bowl game *football* 155.1

bowline *sailboard parts* 150.20, Knots, Bends, Hitches, Splices 754, *tackle* 754.6

bowline on the bight Knots, Bends, Hitches, Splices 754

bowline with a bight Knots, Bends, Hitches, Splices 754

bowling 151.1, 151.6; Sporting Activities 145, *turning* 682.3, *rotating* 682.11

bowling alley *bowling* 151.1

bowling along *swiftness* 694.1

bowling bag *bowling* 151.1

bowling ball *bowling* 151.1

bowling delivery 151.2

bowling green *green bowling* 151.3, *green place* 260.2, *green thing* 260.4, *horizontal surface* 603.3

bowling lane *bowling* 151.1

bowling pin *bowling* 151.1

bowling rink *green bowling* 151.3

bowling shoes *bowling* 151.1

bowling side *green bowling* 151.3

bowl over *astonish* 292.10, *be wondrous* 294.14, *bring down* 716.14

bow low *bow* 716.22

bowls 151.7; *green bowling* 151.3

bowl-shaped *concave* 635.5

bowls match *green bowling* 151.3

bowls player *bowler* 151.5

bowl wide *divert* 698.16

bowman *historical soldier* 77.8, *shooter* 696.11

bow one's head *show respect* 435.16

bow out *absent oneself* 576.15, *withdraw* 705.9, *exit* 707.13

bow side *rowboat parts* 150.15

bowsprit *vanguard* 621.5

bowstring *instrument of execution* 454.15, *execute* 454.30

bowstringer *punisher* 454.16

bow stroke *canoeing techniques* 150.11

bow tie *formal clothes* 100.5, *neckwear* 100.29

bow to *submit* 421.4, *follow* 745.12

bow wave *wave* 10.11

bowwow [Inf] *dog* 35.10

bowwow theory *linguistic theory* 5.2

box 152.19, 578.5; *farm building* 16.4, Trees and Shrubs 43, *fight* 77.35, *receptacle* 105.11, *tobacco*

implements 121.24, *auditorium* 136.17, *duel* 422.24, *money storage* 484.20, *compartment* 578.2, *contain* 578.20, *wrapping* 613.10, *wrap* 613.29, *enclosing thing* 619.3, *blow* 695.5, *hit* 695.11, *inset* 710.13, *setting apart* 753.2

box, the [Brit] *television set* 172.6

box a round *box* 152.19

boxcar *railroad car* 688.5

box chronometer Timepieces and Timers 646

boxed *storing* 578.19, *protected* 613.20

box elder Trees and Shrubs 43

boxer 152.8; Breeds of Dogs 35, *athlete* 422.15, *person of strength* 516.8

boxer shorts *underwear* 100.22

box(ful) *container(ful)* 738.2

box-girder bridge *bridge* 551.10

box in *cause difficulties* 824.22, *limit* 830.13

boxing 152.2; Sporting Activities 145, *combat sport* 152.1, *self-defense* 419.5, *athletics* 422.7

boxing associations 152.7

boxing blow *sporting hit* 695.6

boxing equipment 152.4

boxing gloves *boxing equipment* 152.4

boxing match *boxing* 152.2

boxing punch *boxing techniques* 152.5

boxing purse *boxing terms* 152.3

boxing ring *boxing terms* 152.3

boxing rules *boxing terms* 152.3

boxing scorecard *boxing terms* 152.3

boxing shorts *boxing equipment* 152.4

boxing techniques 152.5

boxing terms 152.3

boxing weight divisions 152.6

box lunch *meal* 92.8

box off *exclude* 764.7

box office *auditorium* 136.17

box-office hit 137.11; *theatrical performance* 136.13, *successful thing* 845.5

box-office receipts *money received* 492.2

box-office returns *something received* 473.2

box-office staff *stagehand* 136.29

box-office success *successful thing* 845.5

box of tricks *stratagem* 822.2

box one's ears *hit* 454.28

box on the ear *corporal punishment* 454.11

box pleat *pleat* 637.2

box room [Brit] *room* 60.9, *storeroom* 105.7

box seat *auditorium* 136.17

box set *stage set* 136.19

box someone's ears *hit* 695.11

box spring *spring* 546.4

box the compass *recoil* 680.21, *orient* 697.15

box up *contain* 577.10, 578.20

boxwood Trees and Shrubs 43

boy *person* 18.8, *child* 26.6, *young man* 26.8, *male* 32.1, *male title of address* 32.3, *boyfriend* 32.4, *domestic servant* 69.7

boy [Inf] *opiates* 121.17

boycott *strike* 57.8, *have an industrial dispute* 57.20, *blacken* 254.11, *mass demonstration* 331.7, *protest* 331.19, *separation* 409.3, *exclude* 409.12, 764.7, *gesture of protest* 507.3, *cause mischief* 507.9,

setting apart 753.2, *set apart* 753.17, *exclusion* 764.1

boycotted *disputed* 57.15, *lonely* 409.8

boycotting *disputed* 57.15, *demonstrating* 331.14

boyfriend 32.4; *friend* 62.2, *loved one* 299.13, *partner* 794.9

boyhood *youth* 26.1

boyish *young* 26.11

boyish figure *thinness* 595.1

boyishly *youthfully* 26.14

boyishness *youthfulness* 26.2

Boyle's law Classical Physical Laws 10

boylike *young* 26.11

boy next door *average person* 742.4, *everyone* 778.7

boys, the *menfolk* 32.14

Boy Scout uniform *clothing* 184.6

boys in the back room *backstage manipulator* 844.3

boys of summer, the *baseball team* 147.2

boy soprano *voice* 141.5

Bozakh Breeds of Sheep 16

bozo [Inf] *male* 32.1, *unskilled person* 128.3

bra *underwear* 100.22, *body support* 605.6

Brabant Horse and Pony Breeds 159

bra-burner [Inf] *liberated woman* 33.12

brace Collective Names 59, *refresh* 94.6, *written music* 140.21, *bolster* 377.15, *strengthen* 516.15, *harden* 542.9, *supporting part* 605.3, *support* 605.16, *means of connection* 754.4, *fastener* 754.7, *two* 789.1

brace and bit *opener* 583.2

braced *refreshed* 94.5, *strengthened* 516.13, *hardened* 542.7

bracelet *jewelry* 532.6, *circular thing* 631.3

bracelets [Inf] *fastener* 754.7, *means of restraint* 830.6

brace oneself 376.13; *prepare oneself* 388.21

brace root *root* 41.7

braces *mathematical symbol* 6.11

brachiopod *mollusk* 39.13

Brachiopoda *mollusk* 39.13

brachycardia *cardiovascular disease* 114.13

brachycephalic *physical* 1.14

brachycephaly *physical type* 1.8

brachylogous *concise* 198.4

brachylogus *conciseness* 198.1

bracing *fine* 9.43, *refreshing* 94.4, *healthful* 113.7, *cold* 218.9, *invigorating* 518.3

bracken *fern* 46.1

bracket *fungal body* 47.4, *ice-skating techniques* 162.16, *supporting part* 605.3, *support* 605.16, *joint* 752.7, *pair* 752.14, *means of connection* 754.4, *connect* 754.13, *category* 767.6, *class* 777.1, *pair* 789.13

bracket clock Timepieces and Timers 646

bracketed *connected* 754.11, *two* 789.8

bracket fungi *fungi* 47.3

bracketing *framing* 132.18

brackets Punctuation Marks 5, *mathematical symbol* 6.11, *enclosing thing* 619.3

bracket together *unite* 752.14, *combine* 757.9

brackish *unpalatable* 223.6

brackishness *unpalatability* 223.2

bract *leaf* 41.6, *flower part* 42.3
bracteole *leaf* 41.6
bractlet *leaf* 41.6
brad *fastener* 754.7
Bradford *major British cities* 567.7
brae [Scot] *hill* 569.2
Braeburn Apple Varieties 44
Braford Breeds of Cattle 16
Brag Deities 82
brag 400.17; *boast* 194.14, *pride oneself* 297.13, *bravado* 404.8, *be egotistic* 444.7
Braganca Galician Breeds of Sheep 16
braggadocio *exaggerator* 194.6, *insolent person* 400.7, *bravado* 404.8
braggart *exaggerator* 194.6, *proud person* 297.7, *insolent person* 400.7, *vain person* 402.7
bragger *proud person* 297.7, *insolent person* 400.7
bragging *bombast* 194.4, *bombastic* 194.10, *swaggering* 400.13
Bragg's law Classical Physical Laws 10, *crystal* 11.14
Brahlers Breeds of Cattle 16
Brahma Breeds of Fowl 16
Brahman Breeds of Cattle 16, *priest* 84.8
Brahmaputra Rivers 570
Brahma the Creator *God* 82.6
Brahmin *nobleman* 70.1
Brahminic *aristocratic* 70.4
braid 609.3; *spinning* 130.4, *spin* 130.17, *coif* 530.15, *decorative article* 532.5, *flow* 570.10, *interweave* 609.8, *convoluted thing* 632.3, *convolute* 632.6, *mix* 751.12, *intertwine* 752.19, *line* 754.5, *connect* 754.13
braided *spun* 130.13, *woven* 130.15, *beautified* 530.12, *interwoven* 609.6, *convolutional* 632.4, *mixed* 751.8, *tied* 752.13, *connected* 754.11
braided fiber *fiber* 130.2
braided line *fighting chair* 154.8
braided river *river* 570.1
braided rug *floor covering* 613.13
braiding *spinning* 130.4, *interweaving* 609.1
braids *coiffure* 530.8
Braille *aid for poor sight* 243.5
brain 315.6; *head* 19.6, *nervous system* 19.14, *murder* 30.20, *anesthetize* 213.8, *intellect* 348.4
brain [Inf] *expert* 127.9, *intellectual* 315.7
brain or **brains** *intelligence* 315.2, 352.2
brain cancer *cancer* 114.15
brainchild *plan* 327.3, *conception* 360.4, *work of art* 522.4
brain damage *mental deficiency* 316.2
brain-damaged *intellectually subnormal* 316.7
brain death *mortality* 29.2
brain disease *disease* 114.4
brainily *studiously* 48.26
braininess [Inf] *cleverness* 315.3
brainless *lacking intellect* 316.5, *foolish* 353.5
brainlessly *unintelligently* 316.9, *foolishly* 353.8
brainlessness *lack of intellect* 316.1
brain like a sieve *poor memory* 355.2
brain power *intellect* 348.4
brains *variety meat* 90.30, *cleverness* 315.3, *intellect* 348.4
brains [Inf] *planner* 387.9
brainstorm *mental breakdown*

110.4, *creative thought* 317.3, *have an idea* 317.12, *plan* 327.3, *intelligence* 352.2, *caprice* 381.1, *method* 387.4
brainteaser *puzzle* 182.5, *difficult question* 333.4, *problem* 824.4
brain twister *puzzle* 182.5, *problem* 824.4
brainwash *make someone believe* 87.11, *publicize* 178.19, *accustom* 397.18, *influence* 512.11, *distort the truth* 627.12, *persuade* 670.14, *assimilate* 781.14, *pervert* 808.22
brainwashed *misrepresented* 627.8, *converted* 670.7, *influenced* 670.10
brainwasher *persuader* 178.9
brainwashing *publicity* 178.7, *habituation* 397.7, *distortion of truth* 627.4, *religious conversion* 670.4
brain wave [Inf] *creative thought* 317.3, *plan* 327.3, *intelligence* 352.2, *method* 387.4
brainwork *philosophical investigation* 4.4, *learning* 48.7, *thought* 317.1
brainy *educated* 48.19, *intelligent* 315.9, 352.5, *knowledgeable* 348.7
braise *cook* 91.10, *heat* 217.17
braised *culinary* 91.9
braising *cooking technique* 91.2
brake *trees* 43.4, *fern* 46.1, *toboggan parts* 162.24, *pause* 415.15, *be self-restrained* 455.10, *moderator* 521.2, *limit* 620.1, 620.7, *stop* 668.10, *bicycle part* 687.11, *fly* 689.13, *deceleration* 693.2, *slow down* 693.13, *safety device* 810.15, *restraint* 826.8, *restrain* 826.19, 830.12
brake block *bicycle part* 687.11
brake fade *miscellaneous automotive terms* 687.14
brake light *safety light* 246.7
braking *flying* 689.11
braky *wooded* 43.12
bramble *sharp-pointed growth* 549.5, *adherent* 755.4
brambly *spiked* 549.11
Bramley Apple Varieties 44
bran *animal feed* 16.12, *cereal grass* 45.4, *cereal* 90.12, *meal* 753.7, *residue* 750.2, *refuse* 802.5
branch 703.14; *programming concepts* 15.24, *program* 15.29, *stem* 41.5, *tree part* 43.2, *plant body* 47.13, *subject* 48.3, *religious group* 81.4, *educational topic* 328.4, *tributary* 570.2, *grow* 581.17, *rail* 688.8, *deviate* 698.15, *fork* 703.5, *means of connection* 754.4, *piece* 760.2, *component* 760.3, *class* 777.1, *taxonomical classification* 777.3
branched 703.9; *of plants* 41.14
branching 703.4; *treelike* 43.10, *expansion* 581.1, *growing* 581.12, *diverging* 698.12, *branched* 703.9, *means of connection* 754.4, *component* 760.12, *divergence* 776.5, *divergent* 776.11
branching off *deviation* 698.1
branching out *growing* 581.12, *branching* 703.4, *divergence* 776.5
branchiopod *crustacean* 39.10
branchiuran *crustacean* 39.10
branchlet *plant body* 47.13
branchlike *branched* 703.9
branch line *track* 688.2
branch off or **out** *branch* 703.14
branch office *office* 124.2
branch of service *the military* 58.2
branch out *grow* 43.15, 581.17, *deviate* 698.15, *diversify* 732.11

branch out or **off** *diverge* 776.16
brand *practice livestock farming* 16.20, *sign* 183.1, *means of identification* 184.3, *identify* 184.11, *burn* 217.18, *incandescent light* 246.5, *mark* 533.2, 533.8, *type* 777.4, *class* 777.12, *special feature* 779.4, *characterize* 779.15
branded *identified* 184.9
branding iron *heater* 217.3
brandish *demonstrate* 331.15, *use* 393.9, *flourish* 404.25, *agitate* 684.22, *display* 843.13
brandished *displayed* 843.8
brand name *means of identification* 184.3
brand-new *new* 652.9
brandy *alcoholic drink* 93.9
Brandywine Creek Rivers 570
bran flakes *cereal* 90.12
Brangus Breeds of Cattle 16
branniness *graininess* 553.2
branny *mealy* 553.18
brash *reckless* 286.6, *insolent* 400.8, *defiant* 416.5
brashing *tree management* 43.6
brashly *recklessly* 286.10, *insolently* 400.18, *defiantly* 416.9
brashness *recklessness* 286.2, *insolence* 400.1, *defiance* 416.1
Brasília Countries 566
brass *funeral object* 31.6, *musical instrument* 142.1, *ringing* 236.2, *harsh sound* 238.1, *orange thing* 258.3, *mixed thing* 751.2
brass [Inf] *management board* 126.2, *audacity* 400.3, *defiance* 416.1
brass [Brit inf] *cash* 484.2
brass, the [Inf] *best people* 744.7
brassard *historic armor* 419.8
brassard or **brassart** *insignia* 184.5
brass band *instrumental group* 141.3
brass cannon *historical gun* 78.10
brass engraving *engraving* 144.3
brasserie *eating place* 92.17
brass hat [Inf] *military leader* 68.10, *influential person* 512.5
brassica *vegetable* 17.11
brassicaceous *taxonomic* 41.16
brassie *golf equipment* 156.5
brassiere *underwear* 100.22, *body support* 605.6
brassily *audaciously* 400.20
brassiness *loud sound* 232.2, *harsh sound* 238.1, *defiance* 416.1, *assurance* 621.8
brass inlay *decorative woodwork* 131.2
brass instrument 142.3
brass knuckles *blunt weapon* 78.5
brass on shell *decorative woodwork* 131.2
brass plate *means of identification* 184.3
brass ring [Inf] *object of desire* 288.2
brass-rubbing *picture* 133.5, Hobbies and Pastimes 167
brass tacks [Inf] *fact* 717.6
brass wind instrument *brass instrument* 142.3
brassy *loud* 232.6, *strident* 238.4, *orange* 258.5, *audacious* 400.10, *defiant* 416.5, *ornate* 532.10
brat *child* 26.6
Bratislava Countries 566
bratwurst *sausage* 90.29
Braunvieh Breeds of Cattle 16
bravado 404.8; *bold front* 284.5, *defiance* 416.1
brave *combatant* 77.1, *soldier* 77.4,

martial 77.33, *courageous person* 284.8, *courageous* 284.9, *be courageous* 284.14, *acting* 412.9, *defy* 416.7, *strong in spirit* 516.11
brave face *defiance* 416.1, *assurance* 621.8
brave or **bold face** *bold front* 284.5
brave front *resistance* 417.1, *assurance* 621.8
bravely *martially* 77.39, *courageously* 284.17, *strongly* 516.17
braveness *courage* 284.1
brave person *courageous person* 284.8
bravery *courage* 284.1, *endurance* 516.4
brave try *attempt* 390.1
Bravo, Río Rivers 570
bravo *murderer* 30.12, *combatant* 77.1, *cry of praise* 239.3, *violent animal* 520.4
bravo! 437.23
bravura *masterpiece* 127.5, *courageous act* 284.7, *defiance* 416.1
bravura player *skilled person* 127.7
brawl *quarrel* 272.4, 272.9, *activity* 414.1, *fight* 422.9, *dispute* 463.3, 463.9, *disruption* 766.7
brawler *criminal* 427.6
brawling *disagreeing* 463.6
brawn *physical strength* 516.3, *heaviness* 538.1, *stalwartness* 547.3
brawniness *squatness* 579.6
brawny *physically strong* 516.10, *stalwart* 547.10, *stocky* 579.16
bray *loud sound* 232.2, *be loud* 232.8, *harsh sound* 238.1, *strident* 238.7, *cry of amusement* 239.2, *animal sound* 240.1, *make an animal sound* 240.7, *pulverize* 553.26, *beat* 553.27
braying *loud* 232.6, *strident* 238.4, *ululant* 240.4
braze *intertwine* 752.19, *cause to adhere* 755.10
brazen *strident* 238.4, *arrogant* 297.9, *insolent* 400.8, *blatant* 404.19, *defiant* 416.5, *disrespectful* 436.9, *impenitent* 452.2, *assured* 621.12, *open* 843.12
brazen-faced *insolent* 400.8, *disrespectful* 436.9
brazen-facedly *insolently* 400.18
brazen it out *be obstinate* 379.10, *have the audacity* 400.15, *defy* 416.7
brazenly *arrogantly* 297.18, *insolently* 400.18, *blatantly* 404.34, *defiantly* 416.9
brazen-mouthed *shouting* 232.7
brazenness *insolence* 400.1, *blatancy* 404.6, *defiance* 416.1, *assurance* 621.8, *openness* 843.6
brazen out or **through** *be courageous* 284.14
brazier *place for fire* 217.9
Brazil Countries 566
Brazilian Bergamo Breeds of Sheep 16
Brazilian coffee *coffee* 93.6
Brazilian GP at Interlagos *Formula 1 World Championship races* 146.5
Brazilian Polled Breeds of Cattle 16
Brazilian Somali Breeds of Sheep 16
Brazos Rivers 570
Brazzaville Countries 566
breach *lawbreaking* 53.14, *personal conflict* 63.2, *faction* 347.4, *attack*

819

breastwork *military defenses* 419.9, *barrier* 826.7

breath *odor* 224.1, *undercurrent of sound* 233.3, *exhalation* 556.2

breath control *swimming techniques* 164.2

breathe *live* 28.17, *tip* 170.14, *divulge* 180.9, *speak in a particular way* 205.18, *smell* 224.7, *sound faint* 233.8, *respire* 558.21, *exist* 717.18

breathe deeply *be refreshed* 94.8

breathe down the neck of *stay near* 586.13, *hasten* 818.14

breathe fire *be angry* 302.19

breathe fresh life into *revive* 809.14

breathe heavily *be fatigued* 820.5

breathe in *smell* 224.7, *respire* 558.21, *draw in* 708.18

breathe new life into *refresh* 94.6

breathe of *mean* 361.13

breathe one's last *die* 29.17

breathe out *respire* 558.21, *leak* 707.16, *let out* 709.26

breather *refresher* 94.2, *time off* 125.2, *interval* 639.4, *period* 641.1, *pause* 668.3, *ease* 819.1

breathe regularly *be regular* 663.10

breathe the air of freedom *be free* 829.16

breath-freshener *deodorant* 225.3

breathing *metabolic* 19.24, *life function* 28.6, *alive* 28.13, *pertaining to life* 28.14, *respiration* 558.8, *respiratory* 558.19

breathing apparatus *protective clothing* 419.6

breathing difficulty *symptom* 114.3

breathing in *intake* 708.5

breathing-related sleep disorder *sleep disorder* 108.20

breathing space *available space* 563.6, *interval* 639.4, *pause* 668.3

breathing space *or* **room** *leisure* 125.1, *ease* 819.1

breathless *dead* 29.11, *wondering* 294.7, *restless* 684.16, *hasty* 818.3, *panting* 820.3

breathlessly *speculatively* 294.17

breath of air *refresher* 94.2

breath of fresh air *refresher* 94.2, *odorlessness* 225.1

breath of life *life requirement* 28.5

breath of wind *wind strength* 9.13

breath-sweetener *deodorant* 225.3

breathtaking *exciting* 212.8, *wondrous* 294.9, *newsworthy* 799.12

breathtakingly *wondrously* 294.18

brecciation *pulverization* 553.4

Brecon Beacons Mountains and Hills 569

bred *domesticated* 16.18, *produced* 522.12, *reared* 715.7

bred in the bone *intrinsic* 723.6, *combinatory* 757.6

bred into *combinatory* 757.6

bredes *or* **knee breeches** *pants* 100.14

breeches buoy *safety device* 810.15

breeches part *stock part* 136.24

breechloader *firearm* 78.7

breed *practice livestock farming* 16.20, *cultivate* 17.19, *propagate* 21.15, *give birth to* 28.19, *family tree* 65.3, *give into existence* 522.14, *grow* 581.17, *rear* 715.10, *nature* 723.4, *increase* 746.6, *make bigger* 746.7, *produce* 771.34

breeder *agriculturist* 16.14, *horse person* 159.14

Breeders' Cup *famous horse races* 159.13

breeding *propagation* 21.4, *reproductive* 21.11, *refinement* 48.10, *good conduct* 399.5, *social success* 408.3, *good manners* 410.2, *germination* 581.5, *rearing* 715.2, *distinction* 777.8

breeding ground *source* 675.2

breeze *wind strength* 9.13, *refresher* 94.2, *airflow* 558.4

breeze [Inf] *easy question* 333.5, *easy thing* 823.6

breeze in *do easily* 823.16

breezeway *room* 60.9

breezy **558.15;** *windy* 9.42, *cold* 218.9

Breitov Breeds of Pigs 16

Brenta Rivers 570

Breton Horse and Pony Breeds 159

Breton Black Pied Breeds of Cattle 16

Breton Heavy Draught Horse and Pony Breeds 159

breve Accents and Diacritical Marks 5, *notation* 140.20

brevet *authority* 833.3, *authorize* 833.10

breviary *ritual manual* 85.11

brevity *conciseness* 198.1, *summariness* 204.4, *taciturnity* 208.1, *shortness* 591.1, *transience* 643.1

brew *storm* 9.55, *provide drink* 93.21, *grow* 581.17, *mixed thing* 751.2, *mix* 751.12

brew [Inf] *beer* 93.10

brew a plot *plot* 387.15

brewed *drinkable* 93.18

brewery *drink provider* 93.15

brewing *production* 522.1, *steeping* 557.10, *growing* 581.12

brewskie [Inf] *beer* 93.10

Brewster *type of chair* 101.4

Brewster angle Classical Physical Laws 10

Briard Breeds of Dogs 35

bribable *bought* 481.8, *offered* 504.8

bribe **178.18, 472.3;** *incentive* 178.4, *tip* 472.14, *buy off* 481.17, *damages* 489.8, *remunerate* 489.21, *illegal offer* 504.4, *offer* 504.11, *positive stimulus* 508.5

bribed *bought* 481.8, *offered* 504.8

briber *coercer* 428.4, *gainer* 467.9, *giver* 472.7, *purchaser* 481.7

bribery **481.5;** *coercive method* 428.3

bribing *giving* 472.1

bric-a-brac *or* **bric-à-brac** *cheap item* 497.5, *cheap thing* 800.7

brick *construction material* 14.21, *masonry* 14.22, Historical Missile Weapons 78, *building materials* 104.2, *industrial ceramics* 129.6, *make ceramics* 129.10, *red thing* 257.3, *hard substance* 542.3, *paving* 613.14, *face* 613.31, *pave* 613.32

brickbat Historical Missile Weapons 78, *taunt* 436.6, *criticism* 438.4, 440.2, *missile* 696.7

bricked *covered* 613.19

brickfielder Notable Winds 9

bricking *ceramic* 129.9

brick kiln *ceramic workshop and tools* 129.8

bricklayer *artisan* 123.13, *coverer* 613.18

bricklaying *masonry* 14.22

brick-red *red* 257.5

bricks *wall covering* 613.12

bricks and mortar *construction* 522.9

brick wall *that which makes invisible* 245.2, *barrier* 826.7

brickwork *masonry* 14.22, *construction* 522.9

brickworks *works* 124.9

bridal *matrimonial* 64.15

bridal attendant *wedding party* 64.7

bridal bed *marriage* 64.1

bridal bouquet *general wedding terms* 64.6

bridal chamber *general wedding terms* 64.6

bridal outfit *clothing* 100.1

bridal pair *married couple* 64.9

bridal shower *general wedding terms* 64.6

bridal suite *general wedding terms* 64.6

bridal veil *general wedding terms* 64.6

bridal wreath Flowers 42

bride *girlfriend* 33.4, *wedding party* 64.7, *spouse* 64.8

bridebed *marriage* 64.1

bridegroom *boyfriend* 32.4, *wedding party* 64.7, *spouse* 64.8

bride price *marriageability* 64.4

bridesmaid *wedding party* 64.7

bride-to-be *someone promised* 458.7

bridewell [Brit] *prison* 55.1

bridge **168.4, 551.10, 691.7;** *circuit* 14.37, *communications device* 15.26, *teeth* 19.8, *stage* 136.18, *part of stringed instrument* 142.2, Card Games 168, *place for viewing* 242.13, *overview* 425.6, *be an instrument* 511.7, *covering* 613.1, *overlay* 613.25, *conveyance* 685.2, *crossing point* 692.7, *cross* 692.17, *link* 752.18, *connect* 754.13

bridgeboard *step* 713.11

bridged *accessible* 691.13, *connected* 754.11

bridgehead *battleground* 76.24

bridge over *conciliate* 74.10

bridge player *bridge* 168.4

bridges Phobias 283

bridge the gap *make easy* 823.15

Bridgetown Countries 566

bridle *practice livestock farming* 16.20, *riding equipment* 159.9, *ride* 159.16, *become angry* 302.20, *means of restraint* 830.6

bridle path *passage* 691.5

brief **388.20;** *educate* 48.22, *inform* 170.11, *communicate* 176.10, *concise* 198.4, *summary* 204.5, *sparing with words* 208.6, *explain* 331.16, *cause to know* 348.13, *short* 591.6, *outlined* 617.4, *transient* 643.4, *hasty* 818.3

briefcase *baggage* 578.8

brief description **202.2;** *outline* 617.1

briefed *educated* 48.19, *informed* 170.9, *knowledgeable* 348.7, *prepared* 388.9

brief encounter *transient* 643.2

brief impression *outline* 617.1

briefing **388.4;** *information* 170.1, *communication* 176.3, *explanation* 331.3

briefly *concisely* 198.6, *summarily*

204.10, *shortly* 591.12, *transiently* 643.8

briefness *conciseness* 198.1, *summariness* 204.4, *shortness* 591.1

briefs *underwear* 100.22

brief sketch *outline* 198.2

brief span *short duration* 643.3

brief success *success* 845.1

brier *sharp-pointed growth* 549.5, *adherent* 755.4

brier *or* **briar** *tobacco implements* 121.24

briery *spiked* 549.11

brig *prison* 55.1, Sailing Ships and Boats 690

brigade *military organization* 58.4, *force* 59.10, *army unit* 77.14, *collection* 757.3, *come together* 757.10

Brigadier General US Military Ranks 58, *military title* 72.8

brigand *plunderer* 479.9

brigandage *plundering* 479.5

brigandine *historic armor* 419.8

brigandish *stolen* 479.12

brigandism *plundering* 479.5

bright **246.14;** *fine* 9.43, *educatable* 48.18, *clean* 111.13, *clear* 244.6, *colorful* 251.11, *likable* 271.6, *cheering* 281.9, *intelligent* 315.9, 352.5, *auspicious* 458.10, *strong to the senses* 516.12, *beautiful* 529.7, *mentally sharp* 549.14, *mentally quick* 694.8

bright and early *early* 657.8, 657.17

bright as a new pin *clean* 111.13

bright as silver *clean* 111.13

bright-blue *blue* 261.5

bright-colored *colorful* 251.11

brighten *shine* 9.56, *make transparent* 249.10, *color* 251.16, *bring cheer* 269.12

brightened *lit* 246.16

brightening *lightening* 246.3, *lucent* 246.13

brighten one's day *make pleasant* 271.10

brighter *fine* 9.43

brightest and best *best people* 744.7

bright idea *plan* 327.3, *intelligence* 352.2, *method* 387.4, *motivation* 508.1

bright light *quality of light* 246.2

brightly *lightly* 246.23, *colorfully* 251.19, *acutely* 516.18, *gorgeously* 529.14, *sharply* 549.19

bright nebula *nebula* 7.6

brightness *light* 10.17, 246.1, *educatability* 48.9, *clarity* 244.2, *quality of light* 246.2, *cleverness* 315.3, *intelligence* 352.2, *beauty* 529.1, *mental sharpness* 549.9, *quickness of mind* 694.4

bright prospects *potential* 458.4

bright red *red* 257.5

bright side *hope* 281.1, *aspect* 623.4

bright yellow *yellow* 259.7

bright young thing *modern person* 652.8

brilliance *masterpiece* 127.5, *clarity* 244.2, *light* 246.1, *quality of light* 246.2, *hue* 251.4, *cleverness* 315.3, *intelligence* 352.2, *grandeur* 404.10, *beauty* 529.1, *perfect condition* 805.3

brilliant *clear* 244.6, *bright* 246.14, *colorful* 251.11, *intelligent* 315.9, 352.5, *grand* 404.22, *strong to the senses* 516.12, *beautiful* 529.7, *excellent* 805.15

brilliantine *pomade* 562.9

brilliantly *lightly* 246.23, *colorfully* 251.19, *intelligently* 352.9, *grandly* 404.37, *acutely* 516.18, *gorgeously* 529.14

brim *abound* 97.8, *edge* 618.1, *crowd* 795.11

brimful *full* 761.8

brimmer *fullness* 761.5

brimming *overrun* 712.6, *full* 761.8

brimming over *excessive* 99.5

brim over *be excessive* 99.9, *overstep* 712.14

brimstone *yellow thing* 259.4

brim with *be full* 761.12

brim with good health *be healthy* 113.11

brindle *maculation* 263.4, *variegate* 263.11

brindled *mottled* 263.10

brindling *maculation* 263.4

brine *water* 557.1, *steep* 557.31, *sea* 571.1, *preserver* 815.9

brine shrimp *crustacean* 39.10

bring 685.11

bring about *motivate* 178.17, 508.9, *intend* 361.15, *cause* 372.12, 675.8, *produce* 522.13, *be convenient* 803.5

bring a lawsuit *litigate* 54.27

bring alive *seem true* 721.26

bring an indictment *accuse* 442.8

bring around *bring back to life* 28.20, *persuade* 178.15

bring a suit *litigate* 54.27

bring a verdict *judge* 341.10

bring back *remind* 354.13, *give back* 478.5, *restore* 809.12, *deliver* 817.5

bring back to life 28.20

bring bad luck *cause adversity* 848.15

bring before the court *or judge litigate* 54.27

bring charges *accuse* 442.8

bring cheer 269.12

bring coals to Newcastle *be superfluous* 99.12

bring destruction *lay waste* 523.14

bring down 716.14; *cause sorrow* 270.9, *abase* 298.20, *fire* 418.18, *strike* 418.21

bring down on one's head *or around one's ears get into trouble* 824.20

bring down to earth *deflate* 195.16

bring evidence against *accuse* 442.8

bring forth *have young* 21.16, *draw out* 711.17, *reveal* 843.14

bring forward *further* 679.13, *display* 843.13

bring home the bacon *earn* 467.20, *attain one's goal* 845.13

bring in *provision* 89.9, *gain* 467.15, *receive* 473.13, *price* 494.12, *admit* 708.12, *introduce* 708.16, *insert* 710.9

bring in an unfavorable verdict *convict* 54.33

bring in a return *be profitable* 467.21

bring in a verdict *try a case* 54.28

bringing back *giving back* 478.1

bringing forth *drawing out* 711.5

bringing in 708.4; *gain* 467.1

bringing legal action against *litigating* 54.21

bringing of charges *accusation* 442.1

bringing together *collection* 59.2,
acquisition 467.4, *unification* 752.5, *combination* 757.1

bringing to light *manifestation* 843.2

bringing up *rearing* 715.2

bring in new blood *cause change* 665.16

bring into action *activate* 509.11

bring into being *propagate* 21.15, *bring into existence* 522.14, *form* 624.9, *cause* 675.8, *come to be* 717.19, *produce* 771.34

bring into contact *juxtapose* 586.14

bring into disrepute 371.6; *defame* 440.13

bring into effect *activate* 509.11, *be an instrument* 511.7

bring into existence 522.14; *propagate* 21.15, *be real* 721.21

bring into focus *centralize* 612.11, *focus* 702.11

bring into force *activate* 509.11

bring into line *put right* 429.14, *regulate* 780.15, *make conform* 781.13, *subject* 832.10

bring into operation *activate* 509.11

bring into play *activate* 509.11

bring into the open *publish* 173.15, *disclose* 180.8

bring into the world *propagate* 21.15, *bring into existence* 522.14, *cause* 675.8, *produce* 771.34

bring in tow *escort* 794.18

bring it off *secure one's objective* 464.12, *attain one's goal* 845.13

bring legal action *litigate* 54.27

bring legal force to bear *force* 428.10

bring low *subject* 832.10

bring near *near* 586.12

bring off *cause* 675.8, *attain one's goal* 845.13

bring on *motivate* 508.9, *awaken* 675.9, *further* 679.13

bring order out of chaos *make regular* 663.9

bring out *publish* 174.19, *demonstrate* 331.15, *awaken* 675.9, *reveal* 843.14

bring over *influence* 508.11

bring pressure to bear *compel* 428.8, *manipulate* 508.12, *impel* 695.9

bring prosperity *better* 445.17

bring results *benefit* 801.10

bring shame upon *bring into disrepute* 371.6

bring someone around *influence* 508.11

bring suit against *litigate* 54.27

bring the house down *shatter the peace* 232.10, *acclaim* 437.18

bring to *make bigger* 746.7, *insert* 748.12

bring to a head *aggravate* 276.5, *intensify* 746.8, *complete* 759.10

bring to an end *make transient* 643.7, *cause to cease* 668.12, *cease* 773.20

bring to a standstill *cause to cease* 668.12, *make motionless* 678.8, *hinder* 826.15

bring to a stop *interrupt* 604.16

bring to attention *make important* 799.14

bring to bay *attack successfully* 418.25

bring to bear upon *relate to* 727.9

bring to birth *have young* 21.16

bring to book *exact retribution* 454.27

bring to fruition *promote* 807.18

bring together *assemble* 59.23, *conciliate* 74.10, *mediate* 75.6, *acquire* 467.19, *make dense* 540.9, *set in motion* 677.16, *unite* 752.14, *combine* 757.9, *restore* 809.12

bring to heel *subject* 832.10

bring to justice *litigate* 54.27

bring to life *recount* 202.16

bring to light *disclose* 180.8, *make visible* 242.25, 244.9, *detect* 345.12, *draw out* 711.17, *reveal* 843.14

bring to market *sell* 482.15

bring to mind *remind* 354.13, *seem like* 733.14

bring to notice *make important* 799.14, *display* 843.13

bring to one's knees *subject* 832.10

bring to one's side *influence* 508.11

bring to pass *cause* 675.8

bring to perfection *perfect* 805.19

bring to public notice *publish* 173.15

bring to rest *sail* 690.16

bring to ruin *ruin* 523.15

bring to terms *conciliate* 74.10

bring to the bar *litigate* 54.27

bring to the boil *intensify* 746.8

bring to the fore *make important* 799.14

bring to the table *mediate* 75.6

bring to trial *litigate* 54.27

bring under the hammer *auction* 482.16

bring up *educate* 48.22, *publish* 173.15, *bring into existence* 522.14, *vomit* 709.27, *rear* 715.10, *reveal* 843.14

bring up for debate *propound* 359.9

bring up the rear *be in the rear* 622.7

bring up-to-date *brief* 388.20, *make new* 652.20, *beautify* 807.20

bring within the law *make legal* 53.27

brink *short distance* 586.2, *edge* 618.1, *farthest point* 620.3

brinkman *rash move* 286.4

brinkmanship *recklessness* 286.2, *tactics* 399.12

briny *water* 557.1, *sea* 571.1, *oceanic* 571.7

brioche *pastry* 90.37

Briquet's syndrome *somatoform disorder* 108.19

briquette *or* **briquet** *coal* 106.4

briscola *Card Games* 168

brisk *windy* 9.42, *fine* 9.43, *concise* 198.4, *emphatic* 200.3, *active* 414.13, *vigorous* 518.2, *mentally quick* 694.8, *hasty* 818.3

brisket *beef* 90.24

briskly *concisely* 198.6

briskness *conciseness* 198.1, *alacrity* 414.3, *swiftness* 694.1, *haste* 818.1

brisk wind *wind strength* 9.13

bristle *mammalian characteristic* 35.3, *become angry* 302.20, *rough thing* 544.2, *be rough* 544.10, *sharp* 549.15, *crowd* 795.11

bristlecone pine *Trees and Shrubs* 43

bristled *barbed* 544.7

bristles *body covering* 19.4

bristle up *be rough* 544.10

bristle with *abound* 97.8, *be excessive* 99.9, *be sharp* 549.15

bristliness *roughness* 544.1, *sharpness* 549.1

bristling *crowded* 59.22, *excessive* 99.5, *barbed* 544.7, *spiked* 549.11

bristly *barbed* 544.7, *spiked* 549.11

Bristol *major British cities* 567.7

Bristol board *paper* 104.5

britches *pants* 100.14

Brith *or* **Bris** *non-Christian ritual* 85.8

Briticism *regional pronunciation* 205.7

British accent *regional pronunciation* 205.7

British Amateur Gymnastics Association *gymnastics organizations* 157.9

British Boxing Board of Control (BBBC) *boxing associations* 152.7

British Canoe Union *canoe associations* 150.13

British Columbia *Canadian Provinces* 564

British Dane *Breeds of Cattle* 16

British Friesian *Breeds of Cattle* 16

British government 49.22

British GP at Silverstone *Formula 1 World Championship races* 146.5

British Landrace *Breeds of Pigs* 16

British lion and unicorn *national emblem* 184.7

British Market *stock exchange* 457.3

British Open *golfing associations and tournaments* 156.6, *notable tennis competitions* 165.8

British Racing Drivers' Club (BRDC) *racing governing bodies* 146.7

British Saddleback *Breeds of Pigs* 16

British shorthair *Breeds of Cats* 35

British thermal unit (BTU) *heat measurement* 217.2, *Scientific and Technical Units* 589

British Union Jack *flag* 184.8

British White *Breeds of Cattle* 16

Brittany spaniel *Breeds of Dogs* 35

brittle 548.3; *weak* 517.6, *impermanent* 643.5

brittle deformation *fault* 8.21

brittleness 548.1; *weakness* 517.1, *crumbliness* 553.1

brittle star *echinoderm* 39.5

brittle thing 548.2

bro [Inf] *family member* 65.2

broach *sail* 150.29, *sharp-pointed thing* 549.4, *inaugurate* 675.10, *draw off* 711.16, *make a beginning* 771.26

broaching *drawing off* 711.4

broaching machine *machine tool* 14.9

broad 592.5; *Bean Varieties* 90, *spacious* 563.13, *huge* 579.14, *thick* 594.5, *deep* 598.9, *general* 778.9, *generalized* 778.12, *indeterminate* 841.14

broad [Inf *and* Off] *sex object* 20.8, *woman considered as a sex object* 33.8

broad accent *mode of speech* 205.6

broad acres *property* 470.1

broadax *sharp weapon* 78.6

broad-based *broad* 592.5, *including* 763.3, *general* 778.9

broad-beamed *broad-shaped* 592.6

broad-billed *broad-shaped* 592.6

broad-bottomed *broad-shaped* 592.6

Broad-Breasted Bronze Breeds of Fowl 16
Broad-Breasted White Breeds of Fowl 16
broadbrimmed *broad-shaped* 592.6
broad canvas *nonspecificness* 778.2
broadcast 172.12, 172.13, 778.16; *farm* 16.19, *communicate* 169.18, 170.12, *report* 171.9, *broadcast material* 172.9, *publishing* 173.2, *published* 173.12, *publish* 173.15, *divulgence* 180.2, *divulge* 180.9, *public speaking* 205.11, *sound* 230.8, *dispersion* 776.1, *dispersed* 776.6, *disperse* 776.12, *display* 843.13
broadcast dissonance 241.3
broadcast drama 136.4
broadcaster *news reporting* 171.5, *discloser* 180.4, *speaker* 205.12
broadcasting *communications* 169.1, *radio transmission* 172.3, *publishing* 173.2, *publication media* 173.6, *dispersion* 776.1
broadcasting device *sound amplifier* 230.5
broadcasting personnel 172.11
broadcasting station *radio broadcasting* 172.4, *television broadcasting* 172.8
broadcast journalism *news* 171.1
broadcast material 172.9
broadcast news 171.6
broadcast television *television (TV)* 172.5
broad-chested *broad-shaped* 592.6
Broad Church *Christianity* 81.5
broadcloth *fabric* 130.1
broad comedy *comedy* 136.11
broaden 592.11, 778.15; *increase* 467.17, 746.6, *enlarge* 581.14, *make bigger* 746.7
broadened 592.7; *bigger* 581.9
broadener *enlarger* 581.8
broadening *augmentation* 467.2, *expansion* 581.1, *growing* 581.12, *increase* 746.1
broadening the mind *learning* 48.7
broaden the mind *learn* 48.23
broadfaced *broad-shaped* 592.6
broad gauge *rail* 688.3
broad-gauge or **broad-gauged** *broad* 592.5
broad in the beam [Inf] *fat* 579.15, *broad-shaped* 592.6
broad jump *jumping* 166.11
broad-leaved *broad-shaped* 592.6
broad-leaved tree *tree* 43.1
broadloom *fabric* 130.1, *broad* 592.5
broadloom carpet *floor covering* 613.13
broadly 592.15; *largely* 581.18, *distantly* 585.11, *thick* 594.11, *deep* 598.25, *on average* 742.10, *generally* 778.20, *indeterminately* 841.24
broadly speaking *on average* 742.10, *generally* 778.20
broad-minded 592.9; *impartial* 338.6, *wise* 352.4, *free* 829.11
broad-mindedly 592.17; *freely* 829.22
broad-mindedness 592.3; *impartiality* 338.2, *freethinking* 829.2
broadness *largeness* 579.2, *breadth* 592.1, *thickness* 594.1, *depth* 598.1, *nonspecificness* 778.2, *indeterminacy* 841.6
broad-nosed *broad-shaped* 592.6
broad reach *sail* 150.29

broad reaching *sailing terms* 150.5
Broads, the *regions of the British Isles* 564.8
Broads, the Lakes 568
broad-shaped 592.6
broad-shouldered *broad-shaped* 592.6
broadside *guns* 78.9, *offshore* 150.35, *public information* 170.5, *advertisement* 173.9, *newspaper* 175.2, *firing* 418.6, *breadthways* 592.16
broad spectrum *nonspecificness* 778.2
broadsword *sharp weapon* 78.6
broad-tailed *broad-shaped* 592.6
Broadway *drama* 136.1
Broadway melody *melody* 140.10
Broadway musical *musical drama* 136.5
broad-winged *broad-shaped* 592.6
Brobdingnag Imaginary Places 360
Brobdingnagian *big person* 579.10, *huge* 579.14
brocade Fabrics and Fibers 130, *weaving* 130.6
brocatel or **brocatelle** Fabrics and Fibers 130
broccoli *green thing* 260.4
brochure *advertisement* 173.9, *outline* 204.2, *prospectus* 387.3
Brocken Mountains and Hills 569
broderie anglaise *decorative method* 532.3
brogue *mode of speech* 205.6, *regional pronunciation* 205.7
brogues *shoes* 100.30
broil *cook* 91.10, *heat* 217.17, *fight* 422.9
broiled *culinary* 91.9
broiled fish *fish dish* 90.19
broiler *livestock* 16.11, *cooker* 91.5
broiler house *farm building* 16.4
broiling *cooking technique* 91.2
broke *needy* 95.12, *unprofitable* 468.10, *insolvent* 486.10, *unprosperous* 848.11
broken *injured* 215.5, *gone wrong* 430.17, *violating* 466.8, *impoverished* 486.11, *inoperative* 515.8, *dilapidated* 517.7, 808.11, *destroyed* 523.9, *coarse* 544.6, *brittle* 548.3, *open* 583.10, *cracked* 587.5, *irregular* 664.3, *apart* 753.8, *partial* 760.11, *discontinuous* 775.7, *imperfect* 806.5, *hopeless* 837.6
broken bone *painful injury* 215.3
broken chord *musical ornament* 140.19
broken cloud *cloud cover* 9.18
broken down 802.8; *farmable* 16.17, *not working* 415.10, *gone wrong* 430.17, *inoperative* 515.8
broken-down *dilapidated* 517.7
broken English *regional pronunciation* 205.7
broken glass *rough thing* 544.2, *sharp-edged thing* 549.6
broken ground *rough thing* 544.2
brokenhearted *sorrowful* 270.4
broken home *divorce* 66.1
broken in *domesticated* 16.18, *habituated* 397.14
brokenly *roughly* 544.13, *apart* 753.23, *disconnectedly* 775.16
broken man or **woman** *poor person* 486.6
broken marriage *divorce* 66.1
broken mirror *bad-luck sign* 358.7
brokenness *roughness* 544.1, *irregularity* 664.1, *discontinuity* 775.1

broken off *interrupted* 604.10, 775.9, *ceased* 668.6
broken promise *dishonorableness* 192.3, *vacillation* 378.1
broken record *boring thing* 296.3
broken reed *weak person* 517.4, *insubstantial person* 720.5
broken resolve *vacillation* 378.1
broken rhyme *rhyme* 139.11
broken set *imperfect item* 806.3
broken up *destroyed* 523.9, *ceased* 668.6, *separate* 753.7, *nonadhesive* 756.4
broken up or **down** *deconstructed* 758.4
broken-up *disbanded* 776.7
broken vows *dishonorableness* 192.3
broken water *rough thing* 544.2, *wave* 571.3
broken-winded *panting* 820.3
broken word *dishonorableness* 192.3
broker *agent* 80.3, *financial adviser* 457.4, *negotiator* 460.4, *act as a go-between* 460.8, *trader* 480.11, *merchant* 482.10, *middleman* 772.7
brokerage *trade* 480.1, *discount* 495.1
brokering *trade* 480.1
brolly [Brit inf] *protective covering* 613.5
bromeliaceous *taxonomic* 41.16
bromide *maxim* 177.1, *boring thing* 296.3, *boring person* 296.4, *moderator* 521.2
bromide paper *printing* 132.20
bromidrophobia or **bromidrosiphobia** Phobias 283
brominate *react* 11.38
bromine Chemical Elements and Common Allotropes 11
bronchi *internal organ* 19.13
bronchial *of disease* 114.25, *respiratory* 558.19
bronchiole *respiration* 558.8
bronchitic *sick person* 114.22, *of disease* 114.25
bronchitis *respiratory disease* 114.12, *smoking* 121.22
bronchopneumonia *respiratory disease* 114.12
bronchoscope *diagnostic instrument* 107.13
bronchoscopy *diagnostic procedure* 107.11
bronchus *respiration* 558.8
bronco *horse* 159.1
broncobuster *farm worker* 16.15, *horse person* 159.14
brontophobia Phobias 283
brontosaurus *prehistoric animal* 653.8
Bronx, the New York 567.6
bronze *sculpture* 144.1, *material* 144.6, *track and field* 166.20, *brown* 256.5, 256.7, *orange* 258.5, *mixed thing* 751.2
Bronze Age Ages, Decades, Eras 641, *primal* 653.14
Bronze Age man *prehistoric human* 653.7
bronze coinage *coinage* 484.13
bronzed *browned* 256.6
bronze doré *decorative method* 532.3
bronze medal *competition* 166.18, *insignia* 184.5
Bronze Star US Military Medals 58
bronzing *effects of hot weather* 217.7
brooch *jewelry* 532.6, *fastener* 754.7

brood *young animal* 26.4, *young bird* 36.17, *nest* 36.22, Collective Names 59, *family* 65.1, *family circle* 65.4, *despair* 270.8, *be dissatisfied* 274.7, *be sullen* 304.12, *throng* 795.4
brooder *cage* 60.15, *dissatisfied person* 274.3, *sullen person* 304.7
brooding *thoughtful* 4.17, *dissatisfied* 274.4, *sullen* 304.8
broodingly *sullenly* 304.16
broodmare *horse* 159.1
broody *reproductive* 21.11
brook *show mercy* 312.11, *river* 570.1, *bear* 605.17
brookable *forgivable* 312.7
brooking no delay *hasty* 818.3
brooklet *river* 570.1
brooklike *riverlike* 570.6
Brooklyn New York 567.6
Brooklyn accent *regional pronunciation* 205.7
brook no delay *hasten* 818.4
brook no denial *be obstinate* 379.10
brook no rival *be jealous* 314.8
broom Flowers 42, *cleaning tool* 111.10
broth *soup* 90.14, *mixed thing* 751.2
brothel 432.5; *wicked place* 448.8
brothel keeping *prostitution* 432.4
Brother *professional title* 72.6
brother *man in the family* 32.12, *family member* 65.2, *religious* 84.9, *loved one* 299.13, *contemporary* 649.3
Brother Ass *body* 19.1
brotherhood *group* 18.13, *association* 59.4, *friendship* 62.1, *agreement* 752.4, *team* 827.7
brother-in-law *family member* 65.2
brotherly *friendly* 62.5, *family* 65.6, *loving* 299.15, *compassionate* 305.8, *compassionately* 305.14
brotherly interest *friendship* 62.1
brotherly love *love* 299.1, *compassion* 305.2, *philanthropy* 307.1
brother under the skin *affinity* 733.3
brother war *civil war* 76.6
brought before the court or **judge** *litigated* 54.22
brought down *abased* 298.13
brought face-to-face *displayed* 843.8
brought forth *displayed* 843.8
brought low *subject* 832.6
brought to attention *displayed* 843.8
brought together *combined* 757.5
brought to heel *subject* 832.6
brought to one's knees *subject* 832.6
brought to one's notice *displayed* 843.8
brought to perfection *perfect* 805.8
brought to public notice *displayed* 843.8
brought up *produced* 522.12, *reared* 715.7
brouhaha *violence by person* 520.2, *tumult* 684.2, *commotion* 768.5
Brouwer fixed-point theorem Mathematical Concepts 6
brow *face* 621.6, *protuberance* 634.3
browallia Flowers 42
browband *riding equipment* 159.9
browbeat *motivate* 178.17, *intimidate* 283.18, *force* 428.10, *manipulate* 508.12, *subject* 832.10
browbeaten *subject* 832.6

browbeating *incentive* 178.4, *intimidation* 283.6, *coercion* 428.2
brown 256.5, 256.7; *cook* 91.10, *feel hot* 217.19, *desert* 560.12
brown algae *algae* 47.11, *brown thing* 256.3
brown as a berry *or* **a nut** *browned* 256.6
brown-bag *have a meal* 92.25, *brown* 256.7
brown-bagger *figurative usage* 256.4
brown-bagging *eating meals* 92.4
brown-bag lunch *meal* 92.8
brown bat *brown thing* 256.3
brown bear *brown thing* 256.3
brown belt *prizewinner* 127.8, *judo* 152.13, *karate* 152.14, *aikido* 152.16, *brown thing* 256.3
brown betty *brown thing* 256.3
brown-black *black* 254.5
brown bread *bread* 90.10, *brown thing* 256.3
brown coal *coal* 106.4, *brown thing* 256.3
brown color *brownness* 256.1
brown dye *brown pigment* 256.2
browned 256.6; *culinary* 91.9
browned off [Inf] *resentful* 302.8
brown fat *brown thing* 256.3
brown glass *ceramics* 129.1
brown goods *merchandise* 522.6
brown-gray *gray* 255.6
Brownian *directional* 677.13
Brownian movement *movement* 677.3
brownie *sprite* 86.12, *cake* 90.36, *brown thing* 256.3, *figurative usage* 256.4, *little person* 580.5
Brownie Girl Scout *figurative usage* 256.4
Brownie Guide [Brit] *figurative usage* 256.4
Brownie point [Inf] *figurative usage* 256.4
browning *effects of hot weather* 217.7
brownish-red *red* 257.5
brownish-yellow *yellow* 259.7
brown-lung disease *brown thing* 256.3
brownness 256.1
brown-nose *or* **brown-noser** [Inf] *figurative usage* 256.4, *brown* 256.7, *be solicitous* 323.13, *sycophant* 401.3, *fawn* 401.9, *succumb* 521.7, *be sycophantic* 439.15, *goody-goody* 445.8, *submitter* 421.2, *flatterer* 439.6
brown-nosing [Inf] *sycophancy* 401.2, *sycophantic* 401.7, *sycophantic* 439.11
brownout *electricity* 106.5, *figurative usage* 256.4
brown paper bag *brown thing* 256.3
Brown personality inventory Psychological Tests 108
brown pigment 256.2
brown pigmentation *brownness* 256.1
brownprint *stage of proof* 174.9
brown recluse spider *brown thing* 256.3
brown rice *rice* 90.32, *brown thing* 256.3
brown rot *pests and diseases* 17.12, *brown thing* 256.3
brown sauce *sauce* 90.17
brown seaweeds *algae* 47.11
Brown Shirt *figurative usage* 256.4
brownstone *brown thing* 256.3
brown study *figurative usage*

256.4, *thoughtfulness* 317.2, *reverie* 360.6
brown stuff [Inf] *opiates* 121.17
brown sugar *basic cooking ingredient* 91.8, *sweetener* 222.2, *brown thing* 256.3
Brown Swiss Breeds of Cattle 16
Brown Swiss cattle *brown thing* 256.3
brown-tail moth *brown thing* 256.3
brown thing 256.3
brown trout *brown thing* 256.3
brows *body covering* 19.4
browse *graze* 35.35, *eat grass* 45.11, *eat* 92.21
browser *grass eater* 45.6
browsing *grass-eating* 45.9
Brücke Western Art Styles 133
bruise *bleeding* 25.10, *painful injury* 215.3, *inflict pain* 215.10, *black thing* 254.3, *blue thing* 261.3, *lividness* 262.5, *blemish* 533.1, 533.7
bruised *injured* 215.5, *bluish* 261.6
bruiser [Inf] *malefactor* 306.6, *person of strength* 516.8
bruising *bleeding* 25.10, *blueness* 261.1, *lividness* 262.5
bruit about *publish* 173.15
Brumaire French Revolutionary Calendar 646
brumal *seasonal* 654.7
Brumby Horse and Pony Breeds 159
brume *mist* 9.33
brummagem *cheap item* 497.5, *cheap* 497.9
brunch *meal* 92.8, *have a meal* 92.25, *morning things* 655.3
Brunei Countries 566
brunet *or* **brunette** *black-haired* 254.8, *browned* 256.6
brunt *blow* 695.5
brush *trees* 43.4, *battle* 76.23, *cleaning tool* 111.10, *clean* 111.17, *weave* 130.20, *percussion instrument* 142.5, *painting* 143.1, *paint* 143.12, *type of touch* 216.3, *touch* 216.9, *fight* 422.9, *cosmetic tool* 530.5, *hairdressing tool* 530.9, *coif* 530.15, *rough thing* 544.2, *smoother* 545.2, *rub* 554.12, *meeting* 586.5, *meet* 586.15, *tail* 622.5, *blow* 695.5, *tap* 695.13
brush aside *disrespect* 436.18, *have no time to spare* 818.6
brushed *cleaned* 111.14, *woven* 130.15, *painted* 143.10, *smooth* 545.4
brush fire *fire* 246.9
brushing *touching* 216.6, *meeting* 586.10
brushing off the batter *pitching terms* 147.5
brush off *clean* 111.17, *erase* 186.9, *exclude* 383.11, *repel* 701.7, *ostracize* 709.17
brush-off *pitching terms* 147.5, *rejection* 383.1, *repulse* 701.2, *ostracism* 709.3
brush off the batter *play baseball* 147.9
brush the cheek *communicate love* 299.25
brush up *clean* 111.17, *remind* 354.13
brush up on *learn* 48.23
brush with *battle* 76.33
brushwood *timber* 43.3, *fuel starter* 106.3
brushwork *treatment* 143.6
brusque *concise* 198.4, *summary* 204.5, *sparing with words* 208.6,

irritable 304.9, *discourteous* 411.5, *abrupt* 591.8
brusquely *concisely* 198.6, *summarily* 204.10, *irritably* 304.17, *discourteously* 411.8, *abruptly* 591.13
brusqueness *conciseness* 198.1, *summariness* 204.4, *taciturnity* 208.1, *irritableness* 304.3, *discourtesy* 411.1, *abruptness* 591.4
Brussels Countries 566
Brussels griffon Breeds of Dogs 35
brutal *murderous* 30.18, 520.7, *animalian* 34.12, *inflicting pain* 215.7, *cruel* 306.10, *pitiless* 309.3, *discourteous* 411.5, *severe* 424.5, *rough* 547.11
brutalism Architectural Styles 134
brutality 547.4; *cruelty* 306.4, *pitilessness* 309.1, *violence by person* 520.2
brutalization *moral deterioration* 808.3
brutalize *be wicked* 448.13, *act rough* 547.14, *pervert* 808.22
brutally *cruelly* 306.17, *pitilessly* 309.7, *discourteously* 411.8, *severely* 424.11, *violently* 520.11, *roughly* 547.18
brutal murder *murder* 30.2
brutalness *cruelty* 306.4
brutal task *difficult task* 824.3
brute *animal* 34.1, *discourteous person* 411.4, *villain* 448.5, *violent animal* 520.4
brute force *suppression* 424.2, *coercion* 428.2, *physical strength* 516.3, *violence by person* 520.2, *brutality* 547.4
brute force *or* **strength** *vigor* 514.2
brute matter *matter* 524.4
brute strength *physical strength* 516.3
brutish *animalian* 34.12, *cruel* 306.10, *attacking* 418.14
brutishly *cruelly* 306.17
brutishness *cruelty* 306.4
Brutus *hypocrite* 192.9
bryological *mosslike* 46.7
bryologist *plant scientist* 41.11, *moss plant* 46.5
bryology *botany* 13.7, *plant science* 41.10, *moss plant* 46.5
bryony Flowers 42
Bryophyta *lower plant* 41.4
bryophyte *lower plant* 41.4, *moss* 46.4, *mosslike* 46.7
bryophytic *mosslike* 46.7
bryopsid *moss* 46.4
Bryopsida *moss* 46.4
Bryozoa *coelenterate* 39.15
bryozoan *coelenterate* 39.15
B setting *exposure equipment* 132.12
bubble 558.24; *flow* 570.10, *enlargement* 581.7, *round thing* 633.3, *bulge* 634.2, *be agitated* 684.21
bubble bath *bath* 111.6, *cleaning agent* 111.9
bubble gum *adhesive* 561.3
bubble-jet printer *hardcopy device* 15.10
bubble memory *memory* 15.6
bubble pack *transparent thing* 249.4
bubbler *drink provider* 93.15
bubbliness *lightness* 539.1
bubbling *insubstantial* 539.5

bubbly 558.18; *insubstantial* 539.5, *gassy* 556.19
bubbly [Inf] *wine* 93.11
bubo *mark* 533.2, *bulge* 634.2
bubonic plague *plague* 114.6, *agent of destruction* 523.7
buccaneer *militarist* 77.3, *plunderer* 479.9
buccaneering *combative* 77.32, *plundering* 479.5, *stolen* 479.12
buccina Musical Instruments 142
Bucephalus Notable Horses 159
Bucharest Countries 566
buck *male animal* 32.15, *male mammal* 35.18
buck [Inf] *male* 32.1, *libertine* 32.7, *US coinage* 484.10
buckaroo *farm worker* 16.15, *horse person* 159.14
bucket *receptacle* 105.11, *vessel* 578.11
bucket(ful) *container(ful)* 738.2
bucket shop *stock market* 483.6
Buckeye Breeds of Fowl 16
buckeye Trees and Shrubs 43
bucking up *encouragement* 284.6
buckle *fold* 637.7, *intertwine* 752.19, *fastener* 754.7, *connect* 754.13
buckled *connected* 754.11
buckle down *undertake* 391.7, *try* 414.21
buckled shoes *shoes* 100.30
buckle one's seatbelt *prepare for action* 388.18
buckle on one's armor *prepare oneself* 388.21
buckler *historic armor* 419.8
buckle up *prepare for action* 388.18
buckling *fold* 637.1
buck naked [Inf] *naked* 614.12
buckram Fabrics and Fibers 130
bucks [Inf] *cash* 484.2
buckshot *ammunition* 78.11, *historical ammunition* 78.12
buckskin *horse by color* 159.7
buckskins *pants* 100.14
buck the trend *be independent* 782.20
bucktooth *teeth* 19.8
buck up *bring cheer* 269.12, *be hopeful* 281.11, *give courage* 284.16
buckwheat *cereal grass* 45.4
bucolic *agricultural* 16.16, Poem or Verse Forms 139, *poetic* 139.19
bucolically *agriculturally* 16.21
bud 41.8; *cultivate* 17.19, *propagate* 21.15, *age* 27.16, *vegetate* 41.21, *flower* 42.12, *grow* 581.17, 676.10, *bulge* 634.2, *growth* 676.3, *plant* 710.14, *increase* 746.6, *source* 771.3, *produce* 771.34
bud [Inf] *male title of address* 32.3, *family member* 65.2
Budapest Countries 566, *other famous world cities* 567.9
Buddha God 82.6
Buddhic body *spirit* 86.10
Buddhism *other religions* 81.8
Buddhist *other religious member* 81.13, *denominational* 81.23
Buddhist text *other text* 81.19
Buddhology Theologies 81
budding *developmental* 13.33, *gardening* 17.5, *bud* 41.8, *germination* 581.5, *growing* 581.12, 676.6, *immature* 652.12, *embryonic* 771.19
buddleia Flowers 42
buddy [Inf] *male title of address* 32.3, *friend* 62.2, *family member* 65.2, *companion* 794.8

buddy-buddy [Inf] *friendly* 62.5
budge *be in motion* 677.14
budgerigar *or* **budgie** *cage bird* 36.13
budget 457.10; *economize* 56.11, *plan* 387.1, *plan ahead* 387.13, *finance* 457.1, *personal finance* 457.5, *budgeting* 493.5, *account* 493.9, *bargain* 497.10, *act of thrift* 499.2, *be thrifty* 499.5
budget account *credit* 487.1
budgetary *economic* 56.10, *monetary* 484.22, *accounting* 493.7
budget deficit *economic indicator* 56.4
budget estimates *budgeting* 493.5
budgeting 493.5; *home economics* 56.2
budget price *cheapness* 497.1
bud scale *leaf* 41.6
bud stick *plant breeding* 17.6
bud time *spring* 654.3
Budyonny Horse and Pony Breeds 159
Buenos Aires Countries 566
buff *clean* 111.17, *brown* 256.5, *yellow* 259.7, *hard worker* 414.11, *smooth* 545.10, *rub* 554.12
buff, the [Inf] *bareness* 614.3
buffalo chip *feces* 25.5
buffaloes Collective Names 59
buffer 419.22; *safeguard* 419.2, *moderator* 521.2, *smoother* 545.2, *national* 566.10, *rail* 688.3, *protection* 810.2, *assure* 810.23, *barrier* 826.7
buffer state *body politic* 50.3, *dominion* 566.3, *juxtaposition* 586.4
buffet *blow* 9.53, 695.5, *meal* 92.8, *eating place* 92.17, *corporal punishment* 454.11, *cabinet* 578.3, *hit* 695.11
buffing *polishing* 554.5
buffing wheel *wheel* 682.9
buffo *clown* 138.10
buffoon *unskilled person* 128.3, *stock part* 136.24, *clown* 138.10, *humorist* 277.7, *object of ridicule* 368.3
buffoonery *amusement* 277.2, *ridiculousness* 368.1
buffoonish *clownish* 138.14
Bug Rivers 570
bug *programming concepts* 15.24, *pest* 40.5, *cause dislike* 291.16, *petition* 505.11
bug [Inf] *disease-causing agent* 114.5, *recording instrument* 185.9, *disturb* 768.10, *technical problem* 826.3
bugaboo *adversity* 117.2, *false alarm* 814.4
bugbear *adversity* 117.2, *frightener* 283.7, *hated thing* 300.5, *false alarm* 814.4
bug bomb *pest control* 16.13
bugeye Sailing Ships and Boats 690
bugged [Inf] *disturbed* 768.6
bugger [Inf] *stimulate* 20.22
buggered up [Brit inf] *gone wrong* 430.17
bugger it! [Brit inf] *miscellaneous swearwords* 301.20
bugger off! [Brit inf] *miscellaneous swearwords* 301.20
buggery [Inf] *sex act* 20.10, *sexual offense* 432.6
bugging out [Inf] *desertion* 386.7
buggy *verminous* 40.13
buggy [Inf] *automobile* 687.6
bughouse [Inf] *mental hospital* 110.6

bug hunter *entomologist* 40.3
bug-infested *botanical* 17.15
bugle *glory of war* 76.17, Musical Instruments 142, *be loud* 232.8
bugle [Inf] *protuberance* 634.3
bugle call *glory of war* 76.17, *military call* 183.9
bugloss Flowers 42
bug off [Inf] *run away* 386.21
bug off! [Inf] *go!* 709.30
bugout [Inf] *avoider* 386.8
bug out [Inf] *retreat* 386.22, *disband* 776.13
buhl *decorative woodwork* 131.2
build *physical type* 1.8, *engineer* 14.48, *be an architect* 134.13, *produce* 522.13, *fashion* 536.7, *fabric* 551.2, *form* 551.3, 624.9, *construct* 551.22, *embody* 577.11, *increase* 581.16, *make vertical* 602.9, *nature* 624.5, *erect* 715.11
build a bridge *prepare the way* 388.15
build castles in the air *or in* **Spain** *aspire* 281.13, *be inattentive* 324.10, *imagine* 327.14, *fantasize* 360.15, *idealize* 720.15
builder *artisan* 123.13, *producer* 522.10
builder's knot Knots, Bends, Hitches, Splices 754
build in *enclose* 619.6
building 551.9; *structure* 14.20, Collective Names 59, *architectural structure* 134.4, *property* 470.1, *manufacture* 522.2, *construction* 522.9, 551.6, *structuring* 551.5, *increase* 581.3
building and loan association *treasury* 484.19, *bank* 487.4
building block *matter* 524.4, *piece* 760.2
building blocks *toy* 167.9, *essence* 723.1
building brick *piece* 760.2
building contract *purchase contract* 459.3
building design *architecture* 134.1
building designer *architect* 134.3
building material *construction material* 14.21
building materials 104.2; *materials* 104.1
building site *construction workplace* 124.10
building society [Brit] *lending institution* 475.4
building society deposit [Brit] *deposit* 487.3
building stone *masonry* 14.22
building style *architecture* 134.1
build on a firm foundation *make stable* 674.7
build on a rock *make stable* 674.7
buildup *assemble* 59.23, *store* 105.1, *public relations (PR)* 173.8, *increase* 581.3, 746.1
build up *store* 105.17, *publicize* 173.18, *become aggravated* 276.6, *strengthen* 516.15, *increase* 581.16, *erect* 715.11, *change by degrees* 739.8, *make bigger* 746.7, *complete* 761.9, *make important* 799.14
build up hope *show potential* 458.14
build up hopes *predict* 358.14
build up one's stocks *store* 105.17
build utopias *fantasize* 360.15
built *joined* 131.8, *architectural* 134.12
built-in *type of furniture* 101.2,

enclosed 619.4, *integral* 723.7, *included* 763.4
built-in advantage *tactics* 399.12
built like a fortress *invulnerable* 810.18
built on sand *changeable* 666.3, *unsafe* 811.8
built on weak foundations *changeable* 666.3
built-up *environmental* 60.17, *swelled* 581.10
built-up area *urban area* 567.10, *suburb* 567.11
buisine Musical Instruments 142
Bujumbura Countries 566
bulb *garden plant* 17.10, *stem* 41.5, *flowering plant* 42.2, *electric light* 246.6, *round thing* 633.3
bulbous *of plants* 41.14, *of fungi* 47.19, *growing* 581.12, *round* 633.7, *convex* 634.5
bulbously *largely* 581.18, *roundly* 633.11, *convexly* 634.9
bulbousness *convexity* 634.1
Bulgaria Countries 566
Bulgarian Grey Breeds of Cattle 16
Bulgarian Red Breeds of Cattle 16
Bulgarian White Breeds of Pigs 16
bulge 634.2; *battleground* 76.24, *rock face* 161.6, *enlargement* 581.7, *grow* 581.17, *convexity* 634.1, *be convex* 634.7, *increase* 746.6, *be full* 761.12
bulginess *convexity* 634.1
bulging *swelling* 581.2, *growing* 581.12, *convex* 634.5, *increase* 746.1, *full* 761.8
bulgingly *convexly* 634.9
bulgy *convex* 634.5
bulimarexia *gluttony* 119.1
bulimia *appetite* 92.2, *gluttony* 119.1
bulimia nervosa *eating disorder* 108.15, *gluttony* 119.1
bulimic *eater* 92.15, *eating* 92.18, *glutton* 119.2, *gluttonous* 119.3, *compulsive person* 428.5
bulk *food* 90.1, *food content* 90.3, *heaviness* 538.1, *density* 540.1, *size* 579.1, 579.17, *large part* 579.3, *be big* 579.18, *enlarger* 581.8, *increase* 581.16, *thickness* 594.1, *quantity* 738.1, *majority* 793.3
bulk carrier Ships and Boats 690
bulkhead *sailboat parts and accessories* 150.4
bulkiness *heaviness* 538.1, *largeness* 579.2, *thickness* 594.1
bulk large *be important* 799.13
bulk memory *memory* 15.6
bulk strain *load* 14.14
bulk tank *farm tool* 16.5
bulky *heavy* 538.9, *huge* 579.14, *thick* 594.5, *clumsy* 824.14
Bull Constellations 9
bull *livestock* 16.11, *male animal* 32.15, *male mammal* 35.18, *law* 53.1, *command* 425.1, *financial* 457.6, *speculate* 480.19, *purchaser* 481.7, *costly* 496.7
bull [Inf] *law enforcement officer* 53.8, *nonsense* 192.8, *senseless talk* 362.4, *distortion of truth* 627.4
bullboat Ships and Boats 690
bulldog Breeds of Dogs 35
bulldogged *determined* 379.7
bulldoggedness *will* 376.5, *determination* 379.2
bulldoze *intimidate* 283.18, *impose one's will* 372.14, *force* 428.10, *knock down* 523.13, *collide* 695.10

bulldozer *construction equipment* 14.23, *coercer* 428.4, *agent of destruction* 523.7, *flattener* 603.4, *impeller* 695.7
bulldozing *intimidation* 283.6, *compelling* 428.6, *ramming* 695.3
bull-dyke [Inf *and* Off] *homosexual* 33.10
bullet *ammunition* 78.11, *hunting equipment* 160.4, Reference Signs 183, *instrument of execution* 454.15, *missile* 696.7
bullethead *obstinate person* 379.4
bulletin *communication* 170.2, *news event* 171.2, *publication* 173.1, *periodical publication* 641.6
bulletin board *advertisement* 173.9, *showplace* 843.4
bulletin board system (BBS) *communications software* 15.27
bullet pouch *historical ammunition* 78.12
bulletproof *resisting* 417.8, *invulnerable* 419.19, 810.18, *tough* 547.6, *make tough* 547.15
bulletproof car *safety device* 810.15
bulletproof glass *glass* 249.5, *hard substance* 542.3, *protective covering* 613.5, *safety device* 810.15
bulletproof vest *protective clothing* 419.6, *modern armor* 419.7, *protective covering* 613.5, *safety device* 810.15
bullets Phobias 283
bullet train *train* 688.4
bullet tree Trees and Shrubs 43
bullfight *duel* 422.12
bullfighter *animal killer* 30.14, *fighter* 422.14
bullfighting *animal killing* 30.10, Sporting Activities 145
bullheaded *willful* 372.8, *obstinate* 379.5, *tenacious* 755.6
bullheadedness *obstinacy* 379.1, *tenacity* 755.2
bullhorn *sound amplifier* 230.5
bull in a china shop *unskilled person* 128.3
bulling *ramming* 695.3
bullion 484.16; *money* 484.1
bullish *ungulate* 35.31, *hopeful* 281.6, *buying* 481.9, *costly* 496.7, *rising* 713.14, *prosperous* 847.5
bullishly *prosperously* 847.9
bullish market *prosperity* 847.1
bullish tendency *inflationary price* 496.3
bull-like *ungulate* 35.31
bull market *stock exchange* 457.3, *seller's market* 483.3, *inflationary price* 496.3, *prosperity* 847.1
bull mastiff Breeds of Dogs 35
Bull Moose party Political Parties 50
bull-necked *thick* 594.5
bullock *livestock* 16.11, *male animal* 32.15
bullocks Collective Names 59
bull pen [Inf] *prison cell* 55.3, *baseball field* 147.3
bullring *slaughterhouse* 30.16
bull roarer Musical Instruments 142
bull's-eye *objective* 374.5, *center* 612.1, *middle* 772.1, *successful thing* 845.5
bullshit [Inf] *falsehood* 192.6, *nonsense* 192.8, *lie* 192.23, *senseless talk* 362.4, *talk nonsense* 362.12, *distortion of truth* 627.4, *distort the truth* 627.12
bullshitter [Inf] *liar* 192.10

bullshitter *or* **bullshit artist** [Inf] *exaggerator* 194.6

bull terrier Breeds of Dogs 35

bully *combatant* 77.1, *frightener* 283.7, *intimidate* 283.18, *malefactor* 306.6, *harm* 306.13, *impose one's will* 372.14, *meddle* 414.23, *strict person* 424.4, *be severe* 424.8, *coercer* 428.4, *force* 428.10, *villain* 448.5, *manipulate* 508.12, *person of strength* 516.8, *act rough* 547.14

bullyboy *combatant* 77.1, *malefactor* 306.6, *person of strength* 516.8

bullying *incentive* 178.4, *intimidation* 283.6, *malignity* 306.5, *malign* 306.11, *severity* 424.1, *coercion* 428.2, *brutality* 547.4, *rough* 547.11

bully into *motivate* 178.17, *force* 428.10

bullyrag *harm* 306.13

bully tree Trees and Shrubs 43

bulwark *safeguard* 419.2, *fort* 419.13, *retainer* 471.3, *supporting structure* 605.2, *supporter* 605.9, *support* 605.16, *protection* 810.2, *fortification* 812.3, *barrier* 826.7

bum *nonworker* 415.4, *poor person* 486.6, *beggar* 505.6, *solicit money* 505.13

bum [Brit inf] *rear end* 622.4

bum [Inf] *borrow* 476.10, *take* 477.14

bumbershoot [Inf] *protective covering* 613.5

bumble *be clumsy* 128.9

bumbler *unskilled person* 128.3

bumbling *bungling* 128.2, *clumsy* 128.6

bumboat Ships and Boats 690

bum check [Inf] *false money* 484.15, *bad payment* 490.3

bummer [Inf] *bad outcome* 293.3

bumming *solicitation* 505.4

bumming [Inf] *taking* 477.1

bump *skiing snow* 162.3, *painful injury* 215.3, *inflict pain* 215.10, *type of touch* 216.3, *dull sound* 233.2, *be rough* 544.10, *bulge* 634.2, *protuberance* 634.3, *be irregular* 664.5, *jolt* 684.9, 684.23, *collision* 695.2, *collide* 695.10, *terminate* 834.7

bump and run *defensive huddle* 155.10, *play defense* 155.19

bumper *size of drink* 93.3, *sailboard parts* 150.20, *yielding* 467.14, *big* 579.13, *fullness* 761.5

bumper [Inf] *ample* 795.9

bumper crop *yield* 467.8

bumper pool *or* **bumpers** *pool* 149.3

bumper to bumper *near* 586.6, *beside* 586.20, *accessible* 691.13, *in a line* 774.17

bumpily *roughly* 544.13, *irregularly* 664.6, *inconsistently* 732.16

bumpiness *roughness* 544.1, *turbulence* 684.3, *inconsistency* 732.3, *discontinuity* 775.1

bumping *irregularity* 664.1, *irregular* 664.3

bumping off [Inf] *murder* 30.2

bump into *collide* 695.10, *meet* 704.20

bump into [Inf] *chance upon* 842.10

bumpkin *commoner* 71.1, *unskilled person* 128.3, *naive person* 821.2

bump off [Inf] *murder* 30.20

bumptious *arrogant* 297.9,

audacious 400.10, *cocky* 402.11, *defiant* 416.5

bumptiously *arrogantly* 297.18, *audaciously* 400.20, *cockily* 402.19, *defiantly* 416.9

bumptiousness *audacity* 400.3, *cockiness* 402.3, *defiance* 416.1

bump up [Inf] *intensify* 746.8

bumpy **544.8;** *protuberant* 634.6, *irregular* 664.3, *turbulent* 684.17, *inconsistent* 732.7, *discontinuous* 775.7

bumpy face *rough skin* 544.3

bum's rush [Inf] *rejection* 383.1, *expulsion* 709.1

bun *bread* 90.10, *coiffure* 530.8

bunch *party* 59.3, *group* 59.8, 59.24, *assemblage* 59.13, *come together* 59.25, *acquire* 467.19, *alliance* 735.5, *certain amount* 738.3, *adhere* 755.8, *throng* 795.4

bunched *grouped* 59.21, *quantitative* 738.6

bunch light *stage lighting* 136.20

bunch together *adhere* 755.8

bunch up *adhere* 755.8

bunco [Inf] *foul play* 193.6

buncombe *nonsense* 192.8, *empty talk* 362.5, *blarney* 439.2

bundle *assemblage* 59.13, *group* 59.24, *quantity* 105.5, *collection* 105.12, *heap* 105.19, *packet* 578.4, *bag* 578.7, *contain* 578.20, *start* 696.20

bundle [Inf] *acquisition* 467.4, *money* 485.2

bundle away *send away* 709.18

bundled *grouped* 59.21, *stored* 105.14, *storing* 578.19

bundle off *start* 696.20, *send away* 709.18

bundle off *or* **out** *hasten* 818.4

bundle of joy *child* 26.6

bundle of nerves *feeling person* 266.8, *frightened person* 283.8

bundle up *clothe* 100.43

Bundt cake *cake* 90.36

Bundt™ pan *cooking equipment* 91.6

bung *stopper* 584.3, *stop* 584.14, *cover* 1012.7, *stop* 584.14, *cover* 293.2, 613.24

bung [Brit inf] *throw* 696.17

bungalow *house* 60.4, *property* 470.1

bunged *stopped* 584.9

bunged up *stopped* 584.9

bungee jump *drop* 714.15

bungee jumper *descender* 714.8

bungee jumping Sporting Activities 145, *fall* 714.4

bungle *bungling* 128.2, *be clumsy* 128.9, *misjudge* 342.9, *blunder* 351.9, 846.13, *err* 351.14, *misuse* 395.6, *confuse* 766.19, *impair* 808.18, *error* 846.2

bungled **128.7;** *ill-used* 395.4, *failed* 846.10

bungler *unskilled person* 128.3, *ignorant person* 349.4, *loser* 468.8, 846.9

bungling **128.2;** *clumsy* 128.6, *mistake* 342.2, *misuse* 395.1, *error* 846.2, *failed* 846.10

bungling idiot *unskilled person* 128.3

bung up *stop* 584.14

bunion *bulge* 634.2

bunk *type of bed* 101.9

bunk [Inf] *nonsense* 192.8, *senseless talk* 362.4

bunk! [Inf] *nonsense!* 362.14

bunker *room* 60.9, *storeroom* 105.7, *store* 105.17, *golf course* 156.2,

shelter 419.11, *fortification* 812.3, *barrier* 826.7

bunker shot *golf shots* 156.4

bunko [Inf] *foul play* 193.6

bunk off [Brit inf] *abscond* 576.16

bunko steerer [Inf] *schemer* 193.10

bunkum *nonsense* 192.8, *empty talk* 362.5, *blarney* 439.2

buns [Inf] *rear end* 622.4

Bunsen burner *place for fire* 217.9

bunt *batting terms* 147.6, *play baseball* 147.9, *propulsion* 696.1, *propel* 696.15

bunting *songbird* 36.12, Fabrics and Fibers 130, *flag* 184.8, *salute* 405.7

bunya-bunya Trees and Shrubs 43

bunyip Legendary Creatures 360

buoy *indicator* 183.7, *lighten* 539.9, *sea marker* 690.7

buoyance *or* **buoyancy** *adaptability* 546.2

buoyancy *force* 10.9, *hope* 281.1, *lightness* 539.1, *sparseness* 541.1, *airiness* 558.9, *raising* 715.1

buoyancy aid *safety device* 810.15

buoyancy jacket *safety device* 810.15

buoyant *cheerful* 269.7, *hopeful* 281.6, *insubstantial* 539.5, *sparse* 541.3, *adaptive* 546.6, *aerial* 558.14, *nautical* 690.14, *rising* 713.14, *raised* 715.6

buoyantly *cheerfully* 269.14, *hopefully* 281.15

buoyed up *insubstantial* 539.5

buoy up *lighten* 539.9, *give moral support* 605.18, *raise* 715.9

buran Notable Winds 9

burble *small sound* 233.4, *sound faint* 233.8, *flow* 570.10

burden **117.3, 826.10, 826.21;** *overdoing it* 99.3, *afflict* 117.16, *part of poem* 139.9, *weighing down* 538.5, *make heavy* 538.14, *load* 577.5, *size* 579.1, *addition* 748.1, *augment* 748.13, *awkwardness* 804.3, *adversity* 848.1, *cause adversity* 848.15

burdened *ponderous* 538.11, *loaded* 577.8, *blocked* 826.13

burdened with age *aged* 27.15

burdened with debt *indebted* 488.7

burdening *weighing down* 538.5

burden of guilt *sign of guilt* 450.2

burden of years *elderliness* 653.2

burdensome *laborious* 122.7, *ponderous* 538.11, *loaded* 577.8, *awkward* 804.6, *difficult* 824.9

burdensomely **538.17**

burdensomeness *weighing down* 538.5

burden with *augment* 748.13

bureau *cabinet* 101.8, *receptacle* 105.11, *office* 124.2

bureaucracy **826.5;** *officialdom* 49.20, *governance* 52.6, *overdoing it* 99.3, *council* 833.4

bureaucrat *strict person* 424.4, *commissioner* 833.5

bureaucratic *sociological* 2.11, *governmental* 49.24, *authoritative* 52.9, *overdone* 99.7, *blocked* 826.13, *commissioned* 833.6

bureaucratically *sociologically* 2.15, *governmentally* 49.27, *in the way* 826.23, *under commission* 833.11

bureau de change *place of exchange* 673.2

Bureau international des poids et

mésures (BIPM) [Fr] *standard* 589.10

burg [Inf] *town* 567.2

burgage [Arch] *medieval ownership* 469.9, *historical property terms* 470.3

burgee *sailboat parts and accessories* 150.4, *flag* 184.8

burgeon *be fertile* 22.13, *bud* 41.8, *vegetate* 41.21, *flower* 42.12, *mushroom* 47.23, *grow* 581.17, *increase* 746.6

burgeoning *germination* 581.5, *growing* 581.12

burgess *townsperson* 61.7, *free person* 829.9

burgher *townsperson* 61.7, *municipal resident* 567.12, *conformist* 781.6, *free person* 829.9

burgherdom *middle class* 772.6

burglar *lawbreaker* 53.15, *criminal* 427.6, *thief* 479.8, *intruder* 706.8

burglar alarm *signal* 183.6, *self-defense* 419.5, *security system* 810.5, *safety device* 810.15, *danger signal* 811.5

burglarious *stolen* 479.12

burglarize *steal* 479.14

burglarizing *stealing* 479.1

burglary *theft* 479.2, *inroad* 706.3

burgle *steal* 479.14, *invade* 706.12

burgundy *red thing* 257.3

burial **31.1;** *funeral* 31.9, *destruction* 186.2, *blacking out* 265.2

burial at sea *burial* 31.1, *immersion* 710.3

burial chamber *burial place* 31.7, *thing of the past* 651.8

burial clothes *funeral object* 31.6

burial ground *burial place* 31.7

Burial of Jesus Stations of the Cross 85

burial place **31.7**

burial service *funeral* 31.4

buried **31.8;** *imprisoned* 55.9, *destroyed* 186.5, *invisible* 245.3, *disappeared* 265.4

buried at sea *immersed* 710.7

buried treasure *reserve* 105.3, *windfall* 467.7

burin *woodworking tool* 131.6, *material* 144.6, *sharp-pointed thing* 549.4

burka *or* **bourkha** *or* **burkha** *robe* 100.20

burke *murder* 30.20

Burkina Faso Countries 566

burl *tree part* 43.2, *solid body* 540.4

burlap Fabrics and Fibers 130

burlesque *play* 136.2, *comedy* 136.11, 368.2, *dramatic* 136.31, *show business* 138.1, *show* 138.4, 404.12, *variety* 138.13, *misrepresentation* 188.1, *misrepresent* 188.6, *exaggeration* 194.1, *exaggerate* 194.11, *entertainment* 277.4, *ridiculous* 368.5, *form of derision* 369.2, *ridicule* 436.4, 440.6, *ridiculing* 436.13, *distortion of truth* 627.4, *mimicry* 736.3, *imitate* 736.9

burlesqued *misrepresented* 627.8

burlesque queen *entertainer* 138.8

burlesque show *show* 138.4

burletta *comedy* 136.11

burliness *physical strength* 516.3, *squatness* 579.6

burly *physically strong* 516.10, *stalwart* 547.10, *stocky* 579.16

Burma Countries 566

Burma pony Horse and Pony Breeds 159

Burmese Breeds of Cats 35

Burmese cat *brown thing* 256.3
Burmilla Breeds of Cats 35
burn 217.18; *rocketry* 7.32, *shine* 9.56, *murder* 30.20, *be at war* 76.32, *painful injury* 215.3, *be painful* 215.9, *inflict pain* 215.10, *heat* 217.1, *feel hot* 217.19, *light up* 246.20, *blacken* 254.11, *brown* 256.7, *be angry* 302.19, *attack successfully* 418.25, *execute* 454.30, *consume* 523.16, *bake* 560.19
burn [Inf] *overcharge* 496.10
burn [Scot] *river* 570.1
burnable *on fire* 217.16
burn alive *murder* 30.20, *execute* 30.22, 454.30
burn at the stake *burn* 217.18, *execute* 454.30
burn coal *fuel* 106.16
burn down *burn* 217.18
burned *culinary* 91.9, *heated* 217.15
burned down *heated* 217.15
burned-out *heated* 217.15, *weakened* 517.9, *fatigued* 820.2
burned to a cinder *on fire* 217.16
burned to a crisp *on fire* 217.16
burner 217.4
burn gas *fuel* 106.16
burn in *identify* 184.11
burn incense *perfume* 226.6
burning *heat* 10.25, *painful* 215.4, *on fire* 217.16, *lucent* 246.13, *angry* 302.11, *capital punishment* 454.12, *allowing no delay* 645.7
burning alive *execution* 30.6
burning at the stake *capital punishment* 454.12
burning bush Flowers 42
burning glass *fuel starter* 106.3
burning question *difficult question* 333.4
burning resentment *resentment* 302.1
burning rubber [Inf] *swiftness* 694.1
burning the candle at both ends *industrious* 414.16
burning the midnight oil *industrious* 414.16
burning with desire *desirous* 20.18
burnish *glaze* 246.22, *polish* 545.3, *smooth* 545.10, *rub* 554.12
burnished *lustrous* 246.15, *polished* 545.7
burnisher *smoother* 545.2
burnishing *polishing* 554.5
burn one's fingers *be unskillful* 128.8, *get into trouble* 824.20
burn on the pyre *cremate* 31.11
burnout *weak person* 517.4, *fatigue* 820.1
burn out *burn* 217.18, *grow old* 653.16, *fatigue* 820.6
burn rubber [Inf] *be swift* 694.10
burnt *baked* 560.14
burnt almond *brown thing* 256.3
burnt cork *black pigment* 254.2
burnt end *grip* 151.4
burn the candle at both ends *overwork* 122.9, *be busy* 414.19, *overindulge* 496.11, *be late* 658.11
burn the midnight oil *overwork* 122.9, *be busy* 414.19, *be late* 658.11
burn to a cinder *burn* 217.18
burnt offering *penitence* 313.3, *offering* 504.5
burn to the ground *destroy* 186.10, *burn* 217.18
burnt sienna *brown pigment* 256.2
burnt umber *brown pigment* 256.2

burn up *burn* 217.18, *consume* 523.16
burn up the miles *be swift* 694.10
burn up the road *make haste* 818.5
burn with passion *desire* 299.24
burn with zeal *push* 414.20
burp [Inf] *belch* 556.5, 709.8, 709.28
burping [Inf] *eructative* 709.13
burr *tree part* 43.2, *mode of speech* 205.6, *regional pronunciation* 205.7, *rough thing* 544.2, *sharp-pointed growth* 549.5, *adherent* 755.4
burring *voiced* 5.37
burrow *mammal dwelling* 35.21, *natural habitat* 60.16, *take up residence* 60.24, *hole* 583.17, *concave land* 635.2, *make concave* 635.7, *shelter* 812.4, *hide* 844.13
burrowed *holed* 583.12
burrower *digger* 635.4
bursar *provisioner* 89.4, *treasurer* 484.18, *payer* 489.9, *accountant* 493.6
bursarial *accounting* 493.7
bursary *treasury* 484.19, *financial assistance* 825.6
bursary [Brit] *something received* 473.2
bursitis *joint disease* 114.19
burst 232.9; *burst of sound* 232.4, *bang* 234.1, 234.6, *alacrity* 414.3, *be active* 414.18, *firing* 418.6, *violence* 520.1, *be violent* 520.8, *acceleration* 694.3, *diverge* 776.16, *crowd* 795.11
burst ahead *accelerate* 694.14
burst at the seams *be excessive* 99.9
burst forth *emerge* 771.35
burst in *attack* 418.17, *be violent* 520.8, *use violence* 520.9, *invade* 706.12
bursting *immoderate* 99.6, *banging* 234.4, *violence* 520.1, *violent* 520.5, *crowded* 795.10
bursting at the seams *full* 761.8
bursting with health *healthy* 113.4
bursting with pride *prideful* 297.8
burst into flames *burn* 217.18
burst into song *sing* 141.16
burst like a balloon *be transient* 643.6
burst like a bubble *be transient* 643.6
burst of anger 302.6
burst of energy *acceleration* 694.3
burst of sound 232.4
burst of speed *acceleration* 694.3
burst one's bonds *be liberated* 831.7
burst one's bubble *disappoint* 282.12
burst on the ear *bang* 234.6
burst open *open* 583.15
burst out *cry out* 239.13, *be violent* 520.8, *emerge* 707.14
burst someone's bubble *disappoint* 293.9
burst someone's bubble or **balloon** *make transient* 643.7
burst the eardrums *deafen* 229.10
burst upon *get in* 704.17
burst with energy *be full of vigor* 518.4
burst with health *be full of vigor* 518.4
burst with pride *pride oneself* 297.13

Burundi Countries 566
bury 31.10, 105.22, Collective Names 59, *conceal* 181.12, *destroy* 186.10, *make invisible* 245.7, *cause to disappear* 265.7, *enclose* 584.16, 619.6, *immerse* 710.12
bury alive *murder* 30.20
Buryat Breeds of Sheep 16
burying *burial* 31.1
burying the hatchet *peace treaty* 73.5
bury oneself *be unsocial* 409.10
bury oneself in *immerse* 710.12
bury one's head in the sand *be evasive* 386.20
bury one's talents *be infertile* 23.8
bury the hatchet *make peace* 73.11, *pacify* 74.11, *forgive and forget* 312.9, *forgive* 355.13
bus 687.7; *computer part* 15.4, *convey* 685.9, *means of transportation* 686.2, *road vehicle* 687.4
Busa Breeds of Cattle 16
busboy *attendant* 69.4, *service worker* 123.7, *transferrer* 685.4, *transporter* 686.4
bus driver *transferrer* 685.4, *transporter* 686.4
bused *transportable* 686.7
bush *machine element* 14.8, *plant* 41.2, *tree* 43.1, *trees* 43.4, Bean Varieties 90
bush, the *countryside* 564.3
bushed [Inf] *fatigued* 820.2
bushel *make clothing* 100.44, General Units 589
bushel basket *garden tool* 17.7
busheler *clothier* 100.37
bushing *axle* 682.7
bush leagues *baseball leagues and championship games* 147.8
bush lot [Can] *trees* 43.4
bushmen *primitive humanity* 18.4
bushranger [Aus] *thief* 479.8
bush track *racetrack* 159.12
bushwhack *ambush* 292.11
bushy *botanical* 17.15, *treelike* 43.10, *dense* 540.6, *barbed* 544.7
busily *actively* 414.24
business 414.6, 480.6, 509.3; Collective Names 59, *job* 122.3, *dramaturgy* 136.6, *acting* 136.22, *matter of interest* 328.3, *activity* 385.4, *undertaking* 391.1, *action* 412.1, *line of duty* 433.3, *trade* 480.1, *manufacture* 522.2, *urban* 567.14, *business relations* 727.4, *importance* 799.1
business analyst *economist* 56.9
business associate *associate* 754.3
business at hand *issue* 328.2
business borrower *debtor* 488.6
business call *telephone call* 169.11
business card *personal identification* 184.4
business correspondence *correspondence* 169.2
business cycle *economic factor* 56.8
business deal *trade* 480.1
business district *urban area* 567.10
business executive *producer* 522.10
business expenses 491.4
business failure *closure* 637.4
business house *office* 124.2
business income *income* 492.3
business language *international language* 523.11
business law *law* 53.1
businesslike *expert* 127.12, *qualified* 340.7, *behaving* 399.14,

industrious 414.16, *practical* 719.8, *well-ordered* 765.14
business loan *loan* 475.2, 476.5, 488.3
business magazine *magazine* 175.3
businessman *professional worker* 123.11, *trader* 480.11, *producer* 522.10
business management *management* 126.1
business manager *producer* 136.28, *financial adviser* 457.4
business meeting *conference* 59.5
business offer 504.3
business relations 727.4
business school *type of school* 48.12
business suit *suit* 100.16, *dark thing* 247.3
business union *association* 752.2
businesswoman *professional worker* 123.11, *trader* 480.11, *producer* 522.10
business zone *urban area* 567.10
busker [Brit] *musician* 141.1
buskin *costume* 100.10, *tragedy* 136.10
buskined *dramatic* 136.31
buskins *shoes* 100.30, *boots* 100.31
busload *load* 577.5
buss *communicate love* 299.25
bus station *center of activity* 612.4, *stopping place* 668.4, *place of departure* 705.4
bus stop *stopping place* 668.4, *place of departure* 705.4
bust *sculpture* 144.1, *monument* 185.10, *bulge* 634.2, *disbar* 709.16
bust [Inf] *unprofitable* 468.10, *impoverished* 486.11, *destroyed* 523.9, *closure* 637.4
busted [Inf] *needy* 95.12, *impoverished* 486.11, *closed* 637.6
buster [Inf] *male title of address* 32.3
bus ticket *means of identification* 184.3
bustier *shirt* 100.13
bustiness *fatness* 579.5
bustle *underwear* 100.22, *alacrity* 414.3, *be active* 414.18, *momentum* 677.2, *tumult* 684.2, *fuss* 684.4, *be agitated* 684.21, *haste* 818.1, *make haste* 818.5
bustler *busy person* 414.10
bustling *busy* 414.15, *moving* 677.12
bust one's ass [Inf] *overwork* 122.9
busty *fat* 579.15
busy 414.15; *working* 122.6, *acting* 412.9, *on-duty* 433.10, *accessible* 691.13
busy as a beaver *busy* 414.15
busy as a bee *busy* 414.15
busy bee [Inf] *worker* 123.1, *hard worker* 414.11
busybody *adviser* 176.5, *meddler* 321.4, 414.12
busyness *business* 414.6
busy oneself *conduct oneself* 399.17, *occupy oneself* 412.15, *be busy* 414.19
busy person 414.10; *worker* 123.1, *doer* 412.3
busy signal *dial* 169.12
butane *gas* 106.6
butch [Inf and Off] *of sexual nature* 20.17, *homosexual* 33.10, *female* 33.16
butcher *killer* 30.11, *animal killer* 30.14, *slaughter* 30.21, *food*

provider 90.6, *laborer* 123.9, *malefactor* 306.6, *execute* 454.30, *retailer* 482.11, *violent animal* 520.4, *use violence* 520.9, *demolish* 523.12

butchering *animal killing* 30.10

butcher's broom Trees and Shrubs 43

butcher shop *food provider* 90.6

butcher's knot Knots, Bends, Hitches, Splices 754

butchery *slaughter* 30.5

butler *attendant* 69.4, *domestic servant* 69.7, *caterer* 89.5, *domestic worker* 123.4

butt 436.8; *pork* 90.26, *tobacco* 121.23, *unskilled person* 128.3, *boxing techniques* 152.5, *box* 152.19, *object of ridicule* 368.3, *laughingstock* 369.4, *objective* 374.5, *strike* 418.21, *recipient* 473.5, *juxtapose* 586.14, General Units 589, *blow* 695.5, *impel* 695.9, *propulsion* 696.1, *propel* 696.15, *remainder* 750.1, *tail* 773.8

butt [Inf] *tobacco* 121.23, *rear end* 622.4

butt away *retaliate* 419.30

butte *landform* 8.9, *hill* 569.2

butt end *remainder* 750.1, *tail* 773.8

butt-ending *ice hockey tactics* 158.4

butter Bean Varieties 90, *basic cooking ingredient* 91.8, *yellow thing* 259.4, *smooth* 545.10, *semiliquid* 561.7, *fat* 562.4, *lubricate* 562.15, *coat* 613.28

butterbur Flowers 42

Buttercup Breeds of Fowl 16

buttercup Flowers 42, *yellow thing* 259.4

buttercup family *seed plant* 41.3

butterfingered *clumsy* 128.6

butterfingers *unskilled person* 128.3

butterflies [Inf] *gastroenterological disease* 114.11, *acting* 136.22, *agitation* 684.1

butterflies in one's stomach *symptoms of fear* 283.3

butterfly *insect* 40.1, *vacillator* 378.3, *capricious person* 381.3

butterfly collecting Hobbies and Pastimes 167

butterfly effect *causality* 10.66, *contributory cause* 675.3

butterfly flower Flowers 42

butterfly race *competitive swimming* 164.3

butterfly stroke *swimming techniques* 164.2

butteriness *pulpiness* 561.9, *oiliness* 562.1

butter knife *tableware* 92.13

Buttermilk Notable Horses 159

buttermilk *juice* 555.2, *fat* 562.4

buttermilk sky *cloud appearance* 9.19, *variegated thing* 263.5

butternut Trees and Shrubs 43

butterscotch *sweets* 90.39, *brown thing* 256.3

butter up [Inf] *blarney* 439.13

buttery *cooking place* 91.4, *storeroom* 105.7, *honeyed* 439.8, *polished* 545.7, *pulpy* 561.19, *oily* 562.11

butt guide *fishing tackle* 154.7

butt in *answer back* 334.19, *meddle* 414.23, *be untimely* 660.8, *invade* 706.12, *interrupt* 706.11

butting *ramming* 695.3

butt in on *disrupt* 768.12

buttinsky [Inf] *adviser* 176.5

butt into *meet* 704.20

buttocks *rear end* 622.4

button *wear* 100.46, *rowboat parts* 150.15, *dial* 169.12, *close* 584.12, *bulge* 634.2, *intertwine* 752.19, *fastener* 754.7, *little bit* 800.4

buttonball Trees and Shrubs 43

button button Children's and Party Games 167

button-down collar *neckwear* 100.29

button-down shirt *shirt* 100.13

buttoned *closed* 584.7

buttoned-up [Inf] *silent* 181.10, *closed* 584.7, *connected* 754.11

buttonhole *be talkative* 207.7, *approach* 209.10, *touch* 216.9, *bore* 296.8, *retain* 471.7, *hole* 583.4, *fastener* 754.7

buttonhole [Brit] *flower* 42.1

buttonholer *boring person* 296.4

button mushroom *mushroom* 47.2

button one's lip [Inf] *be voiceless* 206.8, *ignore* 413.14

button one's lips *or* **mouth** [Inf] *be silent* 181.16

button up [Inf] *close* 584.12, *intertwine* 752.19, *connect* 754.13

buttonwood Trees and Shrubs 43

buttress Architectural Elements 134, *rock face* 161.6, *bolster* 377.15, *fortification* 419.12, *retainer* 471.3, *strengthen* 516.15, *harden* 542.9, *superstructure* 551.7, *supporting part* 605.3, *supporter* 605.9, *support* 605.16, 825.24, *make stable* 674.7, *refuge* 812.1

buttress dam *dam* 551.12

buttressed *architectural* 134.12, *strengthened* 516.13, *hardened* 542.7

buttress root *root* 41.7

butyraceous *oily* 562.11

butyric Common Fatty Acids 12, *oily* 562.11

buxom *fat* 579.15

buxomly *fatly* 579.22

buxomness *fatness* 579.5

buy *finance* 457.7, *possess* 469.14, *transfer property* 470.12, *purchase* 481.1, 481.10, *expenditure* 491.1, *expend* 491.11

buy [Inf] *believe* 87.9, *be persuaded* 178.20, *submit* 421.4

buy and sell *trade* 480.18

buy a piece of *buy in* 481.13

buy a pig in a poke *be rash* 286.8, *be foolish* 353.6

buy a round *pay one's way* 489.19

buy at a cut price *buy cheaply* 481.11

buy at a discount 495.6

buy at cost *buy cheaply* 497.15

buy at factory prices *buy cheaply* 497.15

buyback *purchasing* 481.2

buy back 481.16

buy cheap and sell dear *trade* 480.18

buy cheaply 481.11, 497.15

buy dirt-cheap *buy cheaply* 497.15

buyer *possessor* 469.10, *person transferring property* 470.8, *recipient* 473.5, *spender* 481.7, *purchaser* 481.7, *spender* 491.7

buyer beware! 481.22

buyers' market *declining prices* 497.2

buyer's market *economic factor* 56.8, *seller's market* 483.3

buy for a song *buy cheaply* 481.11

buy for nickels and dimes *buy cheaply* 497.15

buy from *trade* 480.18

buy in 481.13

buy in bulk *buy at a discount* 495.6, *buy cheaply* 497.15

buying 481.9; *transfer of property* 470.4, *purchasing* 481.2, *expenditure* 491.1

buying and selling *trade* 480.1

buying off *deliverance* 817.1

buying on credit *borrowing* 476.1

buying price *cost(s)* 491.3

buying up *purchasing* 481.2

buy in installments *buy on credit* 476.13

buy off 481.17; *bribe* 178.18, *deliver* 817.5

buy on account *buy on credit* 481.12

buy on approval *buy on credit* 481.12

buy on credit 476.13, 481.12; *be in debt* 488.9

buy oneself in *buy in* 481.13

buy on sale *buy at a discount* 495.6

buy on the installment plan *buy on credit* 476.13, 481.12, *acquire credit* 487.11, *be in debt* 488.9

buy on the spot *purchase* 481.10

buy on time *acquire credit* 487.11

buyout *taking over* 477.3, *joint operation* 509.2

buy out *take over* 477.16, *buy in* 481.13

buy outright *purchase* 481.10

buy over the counter *purchase* 481.10

buy property *own property* 470.11

buy stocks *finance* 457.7, *buy in* 481.13

buy supplies *find means* 102.6

buy the farm [Inf] *die* 29.17

buy time *spend time* 639.14, *delay* 658.13

buyup *taking over* 477.3

buy up *take over* 477.16, *buy in* 481.13

buy up the shop *buy in* 481.13

buy wholesale *buy at a discount* 495.6, *buy cheaply* 497.15

buzuki Musical Instruments 142

buzz *infest* 40.17, Children's and Party Games 167, *publish* 173.15, *stimulus* 212.3, *small sound* 233.4, *sound faint* 233.8, *humming* 235.2, *hum* 235.11, *resonate* 236.9, *insect sound* 240.3, *make an insect sound* 240.9, *crowd* 795.11

buzz [Inf] *drug use* 121.9, *fun* 269.4, *activity* 341.1

buzzard *bird of prey* 36.11

buzzed [Inf] *wasted* 96.14

buzzing *humming* 235.2, 235.7, 240.6, *resonance* 236.1, *resonant* 236.6

buzz off [Inf] *depart* 705.8

buzz off! [Inf] *go!* 709.30

buzzword *catchword* 5.22

bwana [Africa] *master* 68.1

by *by means of* 102.7, *instrumentally* 511.9, *caused* 676.5, *via* 691.17

by! *or* **bye!** *goodbye!* 705.14

by accident *unexpectedly* 839.9, *by chance* 842.15, *adversely* 848.16

by a contract *contractually* 462.15

by a hairsbreadth *verging on* 586.19, *barely* 593.18

by air *commercially* 686.12

by all means! *absolutely!* 840.18

by analysis *to pieces* 758.8

by a narrow margin *barely* 593.18

by and by *in the future* 650.13, *soon* 657.18

by-and-by *future time* 650.1

by and large *broadly* 592.15, *in essence* 723.13, *on average* 742.10, *on the whole* 759.13

by annulment *without one's spouse* 66.14

by any (manner of) means *how* 691.16

by any means *possibly* 836.9

by appointment *preferential* 382.10

by artificial light *lightly* 246.23

by authority *governmentally* 49.27, *authoritatively* 52.18, *influentially* 512.14

by a whisker *verging on* 586.19, *barely* 593.18

by casting *on the water* 154.15

by chance 842.15; *in disorder* 766.24, *possibly* 836.9, *unexpectedly* 839.9

by check *cash down* 489.25

by choice 382.18

by coincidence *by chance* 842.15

by command *commandingly* 425.15

by commission *under commission* 833.11

by comparison *relevantly* 727.12, *differentially* 739.9

by compulsion *acutely* 516.18

by consensus *in accord* 735.33

by contraries *diametrically* 731.6

by conveyance *by transfer* 470.15

by counterattacking *on guard* 153.8

by covenant *as agreed upon* 735.36

by credit *on loan* 476.14

by custom *habitually* 397.20, *actively* 412.18, *orderly* 663.13

by day *lightly* 246.23

by daylight *lightly* 246.23

by decree nisi *or* **absolute** *without one's spouse* 66.14

by decree of nullity *without one's spouse* 66.14

by deed *by transfer* 470.15

by default *instead* 672.8

by deferred payment *on credit* 487.14

by deflection *professionally* 152.22

by degrees 739.10; *slowly* 693.14, *partly* 760.17, *discontinuously* 775.15

by delegated authority *under commission* 833.11

by design *architecturally* 134.14, *intentionally* 374.13, *formatively* 624.10

by dint of *by means of* 102.7, *by virtue of* 447.12, *powerfully* 514.21

by divine right *divinely* 82.24

by ear *aurally* 228.16, *blindly* 243.20

by easy stages *slowly* 693.14

bye-bye! [Inf] *goodbye!* 705.14

bye-byes [Inf] *sleep* 415.5

bye holes *golfing terms* 156.3

by-election [Brit] *election* 382.6

by enactment *actively* 412.18

by express *in transit* 685.13

by eye *visually* 242.27

by fair means or foul *by means of* 102.7, *how* 691.16

by far *supremely* 744.23

by feel *blindly* 243.20

by feinting *professionally* 152.22

by fits *discontinuously* 775.15

by fits and starts *erratically* 381.8, *for short periods* 641.13, *irregularly* 664.6, *jerkily* 684.29, *partly* 760.17, *in disorder* 766.24, *discontinuously* 775.15

by force *compellingly* 428.12,

powerfully 514.21, *strongly* 516.17, *violently* 520.11
by forced march *hastily* 818.7
by force of arms *compellingly* 428.12, *powerfully* 514.21
by force of circumstance *necessarily* 95.22
by force of habit *habitually* 397.20
by God's will *divinely* 82.24
bygone *historical* 3.10, *over* 651.12
bygone age *or days past time* 651.1
bygone days *past time* 3.6
bygones *past time* 3.6
by ground control *aeronautically* 689.17
by guess and by gosh *experimentally* 335.14
by halves *incompletely* 762.10
by hand *laboriously* 122.13, *ornamentally* 129.11, *manually* 216.13, *in transit* 685.13
by heart *memorably* 354.16
by hit and miss *experimentally* 335.14
by hook or by crook *by means of* 102.7, *how* 691.16
by inches *by degrees* 739.10
by installments *on credit* 487.14, *partly* 760.17, *incompletely* 762.10
by instinct *intuitively* 320.11
by itself *alone* 788.20
bylaw *law* 53.1, *rule* 780.1
by law *governmentally* 49.27
by leaps and bounds *in progress* 679.16, *swiftly* 694.16
byline *acknowledgment* 310.3
by main force *compellingly* 428.12
by means of 102.7; *instrumentally* 511.9
by misadventure *adversely* 848.16
by mischance *adversely* 848.16
by mistake *erroneously* 351.17
by necessity *necessarily* 95.22
by negotiating *compromisingly* 461.9
by night *darkly* 247.11, *nightly* 656.6
by no means *not at all* 718.15
by offering resistance *toughly* 542.12
by oneself *celibately* 67.12, *alone* 788.20, *freely* 829.22
by one's leave *by request* 505.14
by open declaration *avowedly* 189.34
by order *legally* 53.33, *commandingly* 425.15
by parrying *on guard* 153.8
bypass *avoid* 386.13, *circle* 631.2, 631.6, *rotary* 682.5, *find one's way* 691.15, *deviating course* 698.2
bypassing *avoidance* 386.1
by-path *passage* 691.5, *deviating course* 698.2
byplay *acting* 136.22
by power *authoritatively* 52.18
by-product *chemical compound* 11.4, *product* 522.3, *effect* 676.1, *extra* 748.6, *subsequence* 770.4
by proxy *indirectly* 80.8, *alternatively* 613.36, *instead* 672.8, *under commission* 833.11
by rail *in transit* 685.13, *commercially* 686.12
byre [Brit] *farm building* 16.4, *cage* 60.15
by reason of *by virtue of* 447.12, *causally* 675.12
by remittance *in transit* 685.13
by request 505.14
by resorting to *by means of* 102.7

by right *legal* 53.16
by rights 429.17
by road *commercially* 686.12
by rote *memorably* 354.16
by rule of thumb *experimentally* 335.14
by sea *nautically* 571.10, *commercially* 686.12
by sheer force *strongly* 516.17
by sight *visually* 242.27
by snatches *jerkily* 684.29
by some means *how* 691.16
by someone's leave *with consent* 735.38
by special delivery *in transit* 685.13
by stages *by degrees* 739.10, *in order* 765.26
bystander *observer* 242.15, *verifier* 336.4, *witness* 339.7, *attender* 575.6
by storm *violently* 520.11
by subtraction 749.8
by surprise *surprisingly* 292.14
byte *numeral* 6.8, *computer information* 15.17, *data-related concepts* 15.23, *Scientific and Technical Units* 589
by the agency of *instead* 672.8
by the aid of *in aid of* 825.33
by the book *religiously* 81.29, *accurately* 350.6, *methodically* 765.27, *according to rule* 781.18
by-the-by *inserted* 710.5
by the clock *horologically* 646.15
by the flick of a switch *easily* 823.19
by the good offices of *instrumentally* 511.9
by the hand of *instrumentally* 511.9
by the numbers *according to rule* 781.18
by the same token *under the circumstances* 726.16, *similarly* 733.17, *as good as* 740.14
by the skin of one's teeth [Inf] *verging on* 586.19, *barely* 593.18
by the sweat of one's brow *laboriously* 122.13
by the way 692.20; *irrelevantly* 728.16
by this token *indicatively* 183.21
by touch *blindly* 243.20
by tradition *habitually* 397.20
by train *commercially* 686.12
by transfer 470.15; *in transit* 685.13
by trial and error *experimentally* 335.14
by trolling *on the water* 154.15
by true nature *intrinsically* 611.20
by turns *regularly* 663.14, *in exchange* 673.6, *reciprocally* 729.10
by use of *by means of* 102.7
by veto 503.12
by virtue of 447.12; *instrumentally* 511.9, *powerfully* 514.21
by virtue of one's authority *authoritatively* 52.18
by warrant of *authoritatively* 52.18
by water *nautically* 571.10, *commercially* 686.12
by way of *instrumentally* 511.9, *via* 691.17, *by the way* 692.20
by way of return *with vengeance* 420.6
byword *maxim* 177.1
by word of mouth *reportedly* 170.16, *orally* 205.21
Byzantine Furniture Styles 101, *historic* 653.13

Byzantine architecture Architectural Styles 134
Byzantine art Western Art Styles 133
Byzantine Revival Architectural Styles 134

C

C Programming Languages 15, *hundreds* 792.9
C [Inf] *stimulants* 121.18
C++ Programming Languages 15
cab *automobile* 687.6
cabal *party* 59.3, *secretiveness* 182.3, *plot* 387.6, 387.15, *subversion* 427.3, *collaboration* 757.2, *latency* 844.1
cabala *the occult* 86.2, *mystery* 182.4, *mysteriousness* 844.5
cabalism *occultism* 86.1, *mystery* 182.4
cabalist *occultist* 86.13, *planner* 387.9
cabalistic *grouped* 59.21, *occult* 86.16, *secretive* 182.9, *obscure* 197.2, *collaborative* 757.7, *mysterious* 844.11
cabalistically *occultly* 86.27, *in combination* 757.11
cabaret *drink provider* 93.15, *musical drama* 136.5, *show* 138.4, *club* 138.7, *variety* 138.13
cabbage *crop* 16.8, *green thing* 260.4
cabbage [Inf] *cash* 484.2
cabbage palm Trees and Shrubs 43
cabbage patch *garden* 17.2
cabbage tree Trees and Shrubs 43
cabbageworms *pests and diseases* 17.12
cabby [Inf] *transferrer* 685.4, *transporter* 686.4
cabdriver *transferrer* 685.4, *transporter* 686.4
cabin *house* 60.4, *sailboat parts and accessories* 150.4, *enclosed area* 619.2
cabin boy *nautical person* 690.12
cabin crew *attendant* 69.4
cabin cruiser Ships and Boats 690
cabinet 101.8, 578.3; *United States government* 49.21, *British government* 49.22, *party* 59.3, *kitchen container* 91.7, *furniture* 101.1, *receptacle* 105.11, *management board* 126.2, *painting* 143.3
cabinetmaker *furniture making* 101.3, *artisan* 123.13, *woodworker* 131.4
cabinetmaking *furniture making* 101.3, *woodworking* 131.1
cabinet meeting *discussion* 460.3
cabinet member *politician* 50.7, *person in authority* 52.7, *delegate* 79.1
cabinet minister *politician* 50.7
cabinetry *woodworking* 131.1
cabinet seat *position of authority* 52.4
cabinet secretary *leader* 68.3
cable *communications device* 15.26, *hand tool* 103.3, *toboggan parts* 162.24, *telecommunication* 169.7, *data transmission* 169.8, *communicate* 169.18, 170.12, *communication* 170.2, *power supplier* 514.14, *line* 754.5
cable *or* **cable's length** General Units 589
cable brake *bicycle part* 687.11

cable car *ski run* 162.2, *railroad system* 688.1
cablegram *data transmission* 169.8, *communication* 170.2
cable movie *movie type* 137.3
cable railway *railroad system* 688.1, *cableway* 691.11
cable release *exposure equipment* 132.12
cable-stayed bridge *bridge* 551.10
cable stitch *knitting* 130.7
cable-stitched sweater *sweater* 100.17
cable television *television (TV)* 172.5
cableway 691.11; *construction equipment* 14.23
caboodle *total* 738.4
caboose *railroad car* 688.5
ca-ca [Inf] *feces* 25.5, *defecate* 25.21
ca'canny [Brit inf] *strike* 57.8
cacao Trees and Shrubs 43
cache *computer part* 15.4, *reserve* 105.3, *bury* 105.22, *hiding place* 181.2, *acquisition* 467.4, *acquire* 467.19, *refuge* 812.1
cache memory *memory* 15.6
cachet *means of identification* 184.3, *repute* 370.1, *special feature* 779.4
cachinnate *be loud* 232.8, *laugh* 239.14
cachinnation *loud sound* 232.2, *cry of amusement* 239.2
cachou *deodorant* 225.3
cackle *speak in a particular way* 205.18, *make a bird sound* 240.8
cacoëthes *habit* 397.1
cacographical *worded* 5.38
cacography *spelling* 5.26
cacological *inelegant* 528.6
cacology *language error* 531.10, *inelegance of expression* 528.4
cacophonous *strident* 238.4, *dissonant* 241.4, *inelegant* 528.6, *ugly* 531.3
cacophonously *dissonantly* 241.7
cacophony *harsh sound* 238.1, *dissonance* 241.1, *ugliness* 531.1, *confusion* 766.4
cactus *plant* 41.2, Flowers 42, *sharp-pointed growth* 549.5
cad *libertine* 32.7, *unpleasant person* 272.5, *disreputable character* 371.2, *badly behaved person* 399.8, *vulgar person* 535.4
cadaster *list of names* 785.7
cadastral *of a list* 785.10
cadastre *list of names* 785.7
cadaver *dead person* 29.7
cadaverous *deathly* 29.15, *emaciated* 595.10
cadaverousness *emaciation* 595.2
caddie *attendant* 69.4, *golfer* 156.7
caddis fly *insect* 40.1
caddish *bad-mannered* 411.6
caddishly *rudely* 411.9
caddishness *bad manners* 411.2
caddisworm *larva* 40.9
caddy *box* 578.5, *vessel* 578.11, *transferrer* 685.4, *transporter* 686.4
cade Trees and Shrubs 43
cadence *harmonic element* 140.14, *mode of speech* 205.6, *sinkage* 714.2
cadenced *harmonic* 140.27
cadenza *musical ornament* 140.19, *improvisation* 396.1
cadge *be inactive* 415.13, *borrow* 476.10, *solicit money* 505.13
cadger *nonworker* 415.4, *borrower* 476.7, *taker* 477.9, *beggar* 505.6

cadging *taking* 477.1, *solicitation* 505.4, *begging* 505.9

cadmium Chemical Elements and Common Allotropes 11

cadmium lemon *yellow pigment* 259.2

cadmium orange *orange pigment* 258.2

cadmium red *red pigment* 257.2

cadmium scarlet *red pigment* 257.2

cadmium yellow *yellow pigment* 259.2

cadre *group* 59.8, *personnel* 123.16, *framework* 551.4

caducity *poor health* 517.3

Caecias *wind god* 9.16

caecilian *amphibian* 37.10

Caelum Constellations 7

caenurus *invertebrate larva* 39.19

Caesar *sovereign* 68.2

Caesar salad *salad* 90.16

caesura *meter* 139.10, *interval* 587.1, *pause* 668.3, *separator* 753.5, *gap* 775.4

café *food provider* 90.6, *eating place* 92.17

café au lait *coffee* 93.6

café-au-lait *brown* 256.5

café society *fashionable elite* 536.4

cafeteria *school place* 48.16, *eating place* 92.17

cafetorium *school place* 48.16

caffeine *alkaloid* 12.19, *tonic* 115.8, *addictive drug* 117.10

caftan *robe* 100.20

Cagayan Rivers 570

cage **60.15**; *mammal dwelling* 35.21, *arrest* 55.12, *hockey areas* 158.2, *compartment* 578.2, *contain* 578.20, *closed place* 584.4, *enclose* 584.16, *enclosed area* 619.2, *setting apart* 753.2, *shelter* 812.4

cage bird **36.13**

caged *imprisoned* 55.9, *storing* 578.19

cageling *cage bird* 36.13

cagey *silent* 181.10, *sparing with words* 208.6, *prudent* 287.7

caginess *caution* 287.1, *prudence* 287.2, *cunning* 822.1

caging *arrest* 55.5

cahoots [Inf] *joint control* 827.5

cainophobia or **cainotophobia** Phobias 283

caïque Sailing Ships and Boats 690, Ships and Boats 690

cairn *burial place* 31.7, *indicator* 183.7, *monument* 185.10

Cairngorms Mountains and Hills 569

cairn terrier Breeds of Dogs 35

Cairo Countries 566

caisson *arsenal* 78.3, *guns* 78.9, *substructure* 551.8

caitiff [Arch] *evil person* 446.3

cajeput Tree Products 43

cajole **439.14**; *persuade* 178.15, *petition* 505.11, *influence* 508.11, *be cunning* 822.5

cajoler *persuader* 178.9, *flatterer* 439.6

cajolery **439.3**; *persuasion* 178.1, *inducement* 508.2

cajoling **439.9**

Cajun dialect *regional pronunciation* 205.7

cake **90.36**; *dessert* 90.35, *dirty* 112.11, *confectionery* 222.3, *solid body* 540.4, *be dense* 540.8

caked *dirty* 112.7, *condensed* 540.7

cake tin *cooking equipment* 91.6, *kitchen container* 91.7

cakewalk Dances 135

calabash Trees and Shrubs 43, *bottle* 578.14

Calabrese Horse and Pony Breeds 159

Calabrian Breeds of Sheep 16

calamari *food fish and shellfish* 90.20

calamite *fern* 46.1

calamitous *detrimental* 446.8, *accidental* 660.7

calamitously *mistakenly* 660.14

calamity *adversity* 117.2, *misfortune* 301.6, *ruin* 523.4, *mishap* 660.4, *misadventure* 848.2

calando Musical Terms and Expression Marks 140

calcaneus Human Bones 19

calcareous *chalky* 8.59, *spongelike* 39.26, *powdery* 553.19

calcareous clay *material* 129.2

calceolaria Flowers 42

calcification *hardening* 542.2

calcified *hardened* 542.7

calcify *react* 11.38, *solidify* 542.10

calcimine *whitener* 253.3, *whiten* 253.12

calcine *react* 11.38, *burn* 217.18

calcitonin Human Hormones 12

calcium Chemical Elements and Common Allotropes 11, *essential element* 12.15, *food content* 90.3

calculable **784.8**; *numerable* 6.70, *measurable* 589.17

calculably *mathematically* 784.15

calculate **784.10**; *rationalize* 4.20, *enumerate* 6.85, *experiment* 10.72, *estimate* 341.11, *predict* 356.7, *intend* 374.8, *measure* 589.20, *739.7*, *add* 784.11

calculated *intentional* 374.7, *deliberate* 384.5, *589.18*

calculated risk *intentionality* 374.2

calculated to *tending to* 513.4

calculate or **fix one's position** *find* 565.11

calculating *artful* 193.13, *planning* 387.11, *accounting* 493.7, *count* 784.3, *calculative* 784.7, *cunning* 822.4

calculating machine *computer* 15.1

calculation **784.1**; *mathematics* 6.1, *numeration* 6.10, *judgment* 341.1, *intentionality* 374.2, *accounting* 493.1, *measurement* 589.1, *mathematical addition* 748.2

calculation of chance **842.9**

calculative **784.7**

calculator **6.64, 784.5**; *computer* 15.1

calculus **6.28**; *mathematics* 6.1, *calculation* 784.1

calculus of variations *calculus* 6.28

Calcutta *other famous world cities* 567.9

caldera *volcanic activity* 8.26

caldron *pot* 578.15

calefacient *heating* 217.12

calendar **646.3**; *record book* 185.5, *chronology* 646.2, *chronologize* 646.13, *list of dates* 785.6

calendar clock Timepieces and Timers 646

calendarial *timekeeping* 646.11

calendar-making *timekeeping* 646.1

calendar month *time period* 641.2

calendar of events *plan* 357.2

calender *smooth* 545.10

calendric *timekeeping* 646.11

calendrical *chronological* 639.12

calends *day* 646.4

calendula Flowers 42

calenture *symptom* 114.3

calescence *heat* 217.1

calf *iceberg* 8.45, *livestock* 16.11, *appendage* 19.5, *young animal* 26.4, *young mammal* 35.20

calf bone Human Bones 19

calf love *romantic love* 299.2

calf's head *variety meat* 90.30

caliber *size* 579.1, *breadth* 592.1, *degree* 739.1

calibrate *experiment* 10.72, *measure* 589.20, 739.7

calibrated *measured* 589.16, *gradational* 739.5

calibrated scale *measuring instrument* 589.12

calibration *measurement* 10.67, 589.1, *gradation* 739.3

calibrator *weighing instrument* 538.7

calico Breeds of Cats 35, Fabrics and Fibers 130

calico cat *variegated thing* 263.5

California American States 564

California spangled Breeds of Cats 35

californium Chemical Elements and Common Allotropes 11

caliper brake *bicycle part* 687.11

calipers *measuring instrument* 589.12

Caliph *priest* 84.8

caliph *sovereign* 68.2

calisaya Tree Products 43

calisthenics *health improvement* 113.3, *floor exercise* 157.4, *bodily improvement* 807.10

call *war measures* 76.18, *ordain* 84.16, *need* 95.4, *gamble* 167.14, *poker* 168.5, *play cards* 168.7, *telephone call* 169.11, *telephone* 169.20, *calling* 178.6, *proclamation* 183.8, *signal* 183.18, *burst of sound* 232.4, *be loud* 232.8, *cry* 239.1, *cry out* 239.13, *animal sound* 240.1, *bird sound* 240.2, *make an animal sound* 240.7, *desire* 288.17, *social gathering* 408.4, *visit* 408.16, *demand* 425.2, 505.3, 505.12, *motivation* 508.1, *enter* 706.11, *ruling* 780.2

call a halt *cause to cease* 668.12, *cease* 773.20

calla lily Flowers 42

call a meeting *call together* 59.28

call an audible *play offense* 155.18

call a spade a spade *be sincere* 191.8, *be naive* 821.4

call a strike *have an industrial dispute* 57.20, *refuse* 506.8

call a truce *make peace* 73.11, *pause* 668.13, *make motionless* 678.8

call attention to *emphasize* 200.6, *speak* 205.31

call box [Brit] *telephone* 169.10

callboy *stagehand* 136.29

called *titled* 72.9, *warring* 76.26, *billiard* 149.6, *named* 202.13

called by God *dead* 29.11

called for *necessary* 95.10, *sold* 482.14

called off *canceled* 773.15

called strike *strike* 57.8

called to eternal rest *dead* 29.11

called-up *assembled* 59.18, *warring* 76.26

caller *telephone personnel* 169.14, *transient* 643.2, *entrant* 706.7

call for *need* 95.4, 95.16, *demand* 356.9, 425.11, *bring* 685.11

call for a fair catch *kick* 155.20

call for a relief pitcher *play baseball* 147.9

call for a showdown *battle* 76.33

call for help *signal* 183.18

call forth *motivate* 508.9

call forwarding *dial* 169.12

call girl *loose woman* 33.6, *sexually immoral person* 432.8

calligraphic *pictorial* 133.8

calligraphy *written letter* 5.14, *craft* 133.2, Hobbies and Pastimes 167, *decorative method* 532.3

Callimachus Notable Friendships 62

call in *herd* 59.29, *have at one's disposal* 393.14, *demonetize* 484.25, *enter* 706.11, *welcome* 708.14

calling **178.6**; *title* 72.1, *job* 122.3, *hunting* 160.2, *signaling* 183.14, *nomenclature* 202.7, *line of duty* 433.3, *business* 480.6, *motivation* 508.1

calling for *demanding* 95.13

calling forth *drawing out* 711.5

calling it quits *resignation* 835.1

call into being *propagate* 21.15, *invent* 771.30

call into play *have at one's disposal* 393.14

call into question *cause disbelief* 88.9, *not accept* 190.19, *doubt* 333.19, *object* 828.18

Calliope Deities 82

calliope Musical Instruments 142

Callisto Planets and Their Satellites 7

call it a day *capitulate* 421.6, *end* 773.19

call it quits *pacify* 74.11, *end* 773.19, *resign* 835.5

call letters *radio broadcasting* 172.4, *means of identification* 184.3

call names *vilify* 301.15, *taunt* 436.23

call no man master *be independent* 829.18

call off *cause to cease* 668.12, *end* 773.19, *cancel* 834.6

call of nature [Inf] *excretion* 25.1, *urination* 25.4

call on *visit* 408.16, *be transient* 643.6

call one's bluff *defy* 416.7

call one's own *possess* 469.14

call on one's time *business* 414.6

call on the carpet *punish* 454.22

callous *pitiless* 309.3, *obstinate* 417.7, *severe* 424.5, *impenitent* 452.2, *hard* 542.5, *hardened* 542.7, *mentally hard* 542.8, *mentally tough* 547.12, *thick-skinned* 594.8

calloused *hardened* 542.7

callously **594.14**; *insensitively* 268.7, *pitilessly* 309.7, *resistingly* 417.14, *severely* 424.11, *inflexibly* 542.13, *single-mindedly* 547.19

callousness **594.4**; *heedlessness* 268.2, *pitilessness* 309.1, *obstinacy* 417.2, *severity* 424.1, *impenitence* 452.1, *mental hardness* 542.4, *mental toughness* 547.5

call out *have an industrial dispute* 57.20, *cry out* 239.13, *fight* 422.23

callow *immature* 26.12, 389.9, 652.12, *unskilled* 128.5, *raw* 260.9, *unaccustomed* 398.3, *naive* 449.9, 821.3

callowness *immaturity* 26.3, 652.3, *unaccustomedness* 398.1, *naiveté* 449.4, 821.1

call sign *radio broadcasting* 172.4, *means of identification* 184.3

call sir *or* **madam** *title* 209.12

call the plays *play offense* 155.18

call the roll *number* 784.13

call the shots [Inf] *wield authority* 52.16, *direct* 126.11, *have authority over* 425.12

call the signals *have authority over* 425.12

call the tune *wield authority* 52.16, *manipulate* 508.12

call time-out *pause* 668.13

call to *approach* 209.10

call to arms *war measures* 76.18, *go to war* 76.29, *military call* 183.9

call together 59.28

call to mind *recollect* 3.16, *remember* 354.12, *imagine* 360.14, *seem like* 733.14

call to prayer *public worship* 83.3, *proclamation* 183.8, *signal* 183.18

call to the colors *enlist* 58.10, *arm* 76.30

call up *call together* 59.28, *arm* 76.30, *telephone* 169.20, *remember* 354.12, *imagine* 360.14, *force* 428.10, *draw out* 711.17

call-up *collection* 59.2, *war measures* 76.18, *coercive method* 428.3

call upon *command* 425.10, *impose a duty* 433.14

call up spirits *conjure* 86.26

callus *hard substance* 542.3

call waiting *dial* 169.12

call witnesses *try a case* 54.28

calm 455.9, 521.8; *detached* 4.18, *wind strength* 9.43, *fine* 9.43, *peaceful* 73.8, *silence* 231.1, *silent* 231.2, *relieve* 275.8, *indifferent* 289.7, *lack of wonder* 295.1, *wonderless* 295.3, *lack of thought* 318.1, *stillness* 413.3, *inactive* 413.9, *moderate* 521.3, *smoothness* 545.1, *soothing* 545.6, *smooth over* 545.12, *stability* 674.1, *stable* 674.3, *repose* 678.2, *quiescent* 678.6, *harmony* 765.8, *harmonious* 765.16, *restore order* 765.22, *easygoing* 823.13

calm as a millpond *figurative expressions* 545.8, *quiescent* 678.6

calmative *moderating* 521.5

calm before the storm *repose* 678.2

calm, cool, and collected *moderate* 521.3

calm down *conciliate* 74.10, *be moderate* 521.6, *make motionless* 678.8

calmed *relieved* 275.6

calming *pacificatory* 74.8, *relieving* 275.7, *moderation* 521.1, *moderating* 521.5

calming influence *moderator* 521.2

calmly 455.16; *stoically* 4.26, *silently* 231.5, *indifferently* 289.17, *without wonder* 295.8, *inactively* 413.16, *moderately* 521.10, *soothingly* 545.14, *stably* 674.9, *motionlessly* 678.9

calmness 455.4; *philosophical attitude* 4.3, *indifference* 289.1, *lack of wonder* 295.1, *stillness* 413.3, *moderation* 521.1, *smoothness* 545.1, *repose* 678.2, *ease of manner* 823.4

calm oneself *not wonder about* 295.5

Calorie Scientific and Technical Units 589

calorie *heat measurement* 217.2

calorie *or* **calory** *or* **gram calorie**

or **small calorie** Scientific and Technical Units 589

calorie-controlled diet *diet* 92.5

calorie counter *dieting* 92.6

calorie-counter *thin person* 595.4

calorie-counting *dieting* 595.3, 595.11

calories *food content* 90.3

calorific *physical* 10.70, *edible* 92.20, *heating* 217.12

calorifically *physically* 10.78, *edibly* 92.26

calorific value *heat measurement* 217.2

calorimeter *heat measurement* 217.2, Fields of Measurement 589

calorimetry Fields of Measurement 589

calorochromic *chromolithographic* 251.14

calotte *vestment* 84.11, Architectural Elements 134

calotype *older photograph* 132.4

caloyer *religious* 84.9

calque *new word* 5.18

caltrop *barrier* 419.10

calumet *peace offering* 74.5, *tobacco implements* 121.24

calumniate *lie* 192.23, *vilify* 301.15, *defame* 440.13, *accuse falsely* 442.9

calumniation *lying* 192.5

calumniator *liar* 192.10

calumniatory *lying* 192.16, *defamatory* 440.9

calumnious *lying* 192.16, *vilifying* 301.9, *defamatory* 440.9, *perjurious* 442.7

calumniously *vilifyingly* 301.18

calumny *lying* 192.5, *vilification* 301.2, *personal attack* 418.8, *defamation* 440.3, *false accusation* 442.2

calve *practice livestock farming* 16.20, *have young* 21.16, *give birth* 35.33

Calvin cycle *photosynthesis* 12.22

Calvinism Christian Groups 81

calvities *baldness* 614.9

Calypso Planets and Their Satellites 7, *legendary sea being* 571.4

calypso *folk music* 140.7, *song* 140.11

calyptra *root* 41.7, *moss plant* 46.5

calyx *leaf* 41.6, *flower part* 42.3

calzone *notable international dishes* 90.40

Cam Rivers 570

camaraderie *friendship* 62.1, *good company* 408.9, *compatibility* 735.4

Camargue pony Horse and Pony Breeds 159

cam belt *machine element* 14.8

camber *obliqueness* 607.1, *be oblique* 607.10, *curve* 629.1, *convexity* 634.1, *be convex* 634.7, *road attribute* 687.3, *imbalance* 741.2

cambered *curved* 629.4

camber inducer *sailboard parts* 150.20

cambio [It] *place of exchange* 673.2

cambist *merchant* 482.10, *financier* 484.17

cambium *stem* 41.5

Cambodia Countries 566

Cambrian Mountains Mountains and Hills 569

Cambrian Period Geologic Time Intervals 8

cambric Fabrics and Fibers 130

camcorder *camera* 132.10, *television recording* 172.7, *recording instrument* 185.9, *imaging device* 242.11

camel *means of transportation* 686.2

camelback couch *couch* 101.7

camel hair *or* **camel's hair** Fabrics and Fibers 130

camelid *hoofed mammal* 35.16, *ungulate* 35.31

Camelidae *hoofed mammal* 35.16

camellia Flowers 42

camel-like *ungulate* 35.31

camelopard [Arch] *hoofed mammal* 35.16

Camelopardalis Constellations 7

Camelot Imaginary Places 360

camel's milk *milk* 93.5

camel spin *ice-skating techniques* 162.16

cameo *role* 136.23, *actor* 137.13, *relief carving* 144.2, *brief description* 202.2

camera 132.10; *recording instrument* 185.9, *imaging device* 242.11, *copier* 736.5

camera angle *motion-picture photography* 137.9

camera case *camera* 132.10

camera crew *filmmaker* 137.14

camera equipment *camera* 132.10

camera lens *lens system* 10.22

camera lucida *material* 143.9

cameraman *photographer* 132.23, *filmmaker* 137.14, *record keeper* 185.8

camera obscura *camera* 132.10, *material* 143.9

camera operator *filmmaker* 137.14

cameraperson *photographer* 132.23, *filmmaker* 137.14

camera position *motion-picture photography* 137.9

camera-ready copy *stage of proof* 174.9

camera-shy *photographic* 132.24

camera strap *camera* 132.10

camerawoman *photographer* 132.23, *filmmaker* 137.14

camera work *motion-picture photography* 137.9

Cameroon Countries 566, Mountains and Hills 569

camiknickers [Brit] *underwear* 100.22

camisole *underwear* 100.22

camming device *climbing equipment* 161.4

camouflage *costume* 100.10, *cover* 181.4, *disguise* 181.13, *blinder* 243.7, *blind* 243.17, *that which makes invisible* 245.2, *cause to disappear* 265.7, *practice sophistry* 330.11, *defensiveness* 419.4, *buffer* 419.22, *body covering* 613.3, *hide* 613.27, *means of escape* 816.4

camouflage clothing *protective clothing* 419.6

camouflaged *disguised* 181.9, *mysterious* 182.10, *hidden* 243.15, *private* 245.5, *protected* 613.20

camouflager *coverer* 613.18

camp *military affairs* 58.1, *party* 59.3, *take up residence* 60.24, *type of chair* 101.4, *type of bed* 101.9, *comedy* 136.11, *climbing expedition* 161.2, *dramatics* 404.3, *blatant* 404.19, *group* 623.5, *shelter* 812.4

campagna *grassland* 45.2

campaign *run for office* 50.10, *military affairs* 58.1, *offensive warfare* 76.11, *be at war* 76.32,

exertion 122.4, *exert oneself* 122.11, *undertaking* 391.1, *tactics* 399.12, *action* 412.1, *motivate* 412.12, *warfare* 422.10, *declare war* 422.25

campaigner *soldier* 77.4, *activist* 412.4

campaigning *warfare* 76.3, *warring* 76.26

campaign plan *art of war* 76.16

Campanian Barbary Breeds of Sheep 16

Campanica Breeds of Sheep 16

campanological *ringing* 236.7

campanologist *player* 141.2

campanology *percussion instrument* 142.5, *ringing* 236.2

campanula Flowers 42

camper *mobile home* 60.11, *automobile* 687.6

camper truck *mobile home* 60.11

campesino [Sp] *farm worker* 16.15

campestral *of landmasses* 572.12

campfire *place for fire* 217.9

camp follower *inferior* 745.4, *follower* 794.10

camphor *terpene* 12.20, Tree Products 43, *incense* 226.3, *preserver* 815.9

camphorated *fragrant* 226.4

camphor tree Trees and Shrubs 43

Campine Breeds of Fowl 16

Campine Red Pied Breeds of Cattle 16

camping Sporting Activities 145

camping it up *acting* 136.22

campion Flowers 42

camp it up *overact* 136.35

campo *grassland* 45.2

Campolino Horse and Pony Breeds 159

campos *lowland* 572.6

camp up *put on a show* 404.28

campus *school place* 48.16

campy *dramatized* 136.32

camwood Trees and Shrubs 43

can *size of drink* 93.3, *drink container* 93.13, *receptacle* 105.11, *save* 105.20, *be powerful* 514.18, *contain* 578.20, *sea marker* 690.7, *preserver* 815.9, *preserve* 815.14

can [Inf] *place for excretion* 25.11, *the inside* 55.2, *relieve from duty* 275.11, *rear end* 622.4

Canaan *promised land* 458.5

Canada Countries 566

Canadian Breeds of Cattle 16, *canoeing* 150.26, Rivers 570

Canadian 5-pin bowling Sporting Activities 145

Canadian Auto Sports Club (CASC) *racing governing bodies* 146.7

Canadian bacon *pork* 90.26

Canadian canoe *canoe* 150.9

Canadian canoe racing Sporting Activities 145

Canadian Corriedale Breeds of Sheep 16

Canadian Coureur des Bois *cross-country skiing* 162.7

Canadian Cutting Horse Horse and Pony Breeds 159

Canadian football Sporting Activities 145

Canadian French *regional pronunciation* 205.7

Canadian GP at Montreal *Formula 1 World Championship races* 146.5

Canadian maple leaf *national emblem* 184.7

Canadian Ski Association (CSA) *skiing associations* 162.13

canaille *inferior* 745.4

canal *water system* 551.13, *river parts* 570.3, *concave land* 635.2, *furrow* 638.1, 638.5, *transportable* 686.7, *waterway* 690.2, *nautical* 690.14, *channel* 691.10, *means of connection* 754.4

canal boat *Ships and Boats* 690

canal bridge *bridge* 551.10

canalize *direct* 126.11

canal travel *water transportation* 690.1

canapé *hors d'oeuvre* 90.13, *appetizer* 219.2

canard *partial truth* 192.7

canary *cage bird* 36.13

canary [Inf] *accuser* 442.3

Canary Islands *Islands* 572

canary-yellow *yellow* 259.7

can a shot [Inf] *play basketball* 148.7

canasta *Card Games* 168

canasta pack *cards* 168.2

Canastra *Breeds of Pigs* 16

Canastrao *Breeds of Pigs* 16

Canberra *Countries* 566

can-can *Dances* 135

can-can dancer *dancer* 135.4

cancel 834.6; *manipulate* 6.87, *obliterate* 186.8, *disavow* 190.18, *cause to disappear* 265.7, *renounce* 383.13, *stop using* 394.10, *veto* 503.9, *censor* 503.10, *counteract* 510.7, *abolish* 523.11, *cause to cease* 668.12, *subtract* 749.6, *eject* 764.8, *cease* 773.20, *cancel out* 834.8

cancel a debt *forgive a debt* 490.12

canceled 773.15, **834.5**; *obliterated* 186.4, *disavowing* 190.12, *renounced* 383.9, *relinquished* 392.2, *vetoed* 503.6, *forbidden* 837.7

canceled check *receipt* 492.1

canceling *cancellation* 834.1

canceling out 834.3

cancellation 834.1; *evaluation* 6.22, *postal communication* 169.4, *obliteration* 186.1, *disavowal* 190.3, *blacking out* 265.2, *renunciation* 383.4, *relinquishment* 392.1, *veto* 503.3, *neutralization* 510.4, *ejection* 764.2, *cessation* 773.2

cancellation of contract *termination* 834.2

cancellation of debts *nonpayment* 490.1

cancel one's contract *terminate* 834.7

cancel out 834.8; *counteract* 510.7, *equalize* 740.12

Cancer *Constellations* 7

cancer 114.15; *Phobias* 283, *physical deterioration* 808.4, *adverse health* 848.5

cancerous *of disease* 114.25

cancerous growth *cancer* 114.15

cancerous tumor *cancer* 114.15

cancerphobia *or* **cancerophobia** *Phobias* 283

cancer stick [Inf] *tobacco* 121.23

candela *Scientific and Technical Units* 589

candent *hot* 217.11

candescence *light* 246.1

candescent *lucent* 246.13

candid 191.5; *photograph* 132.3, *communicative* 169.16, *informative* 170.10, *disclosing* 180.6, *effusive* 207.6, *easily seen through* 249.10,

---

demonstrative 331.10, *natural* 526.10, *outspoken* 550.6, *open* 583.13, *plain* 592.10, *direct* 630.12, *naive* 821.3, *informal* 829.15

candidate 422.18; *person questioned* 333.10, *chosen thing* 382.8, *requester* 505.5

candidiasis *fungal disease* 47.6

candidly 191.10, 583.23; *openly* 180.13, *effusively* 207.10, *demonstratively* 331.21, *unpretentiously* 526.15, *naturally* 526.16, *bluntly* 550.11, *plainly* 592.18, *honestly* 630.18, *naively* 821.5, *informally* 829.24, *frankly* 843.18

candidness *candor* 191.2, *naturalness* 526.4, *outspokenness* 550.2, *plainness* 592.4, *informality* 829.6

candid speaker *naive person* 821.2

candied *sweet* 222.5

candied fruit *sweets* 90.39, *sweetener* 222.2

candle *sacred object* 83.11, *incandescent light* 246.5, *Scientific and Technical Units* 589

candleberry *Trees and Shrubs* 43

candle flame *flickering light* 246.10

candlelight *incandescent light* 246.5

candlelit *lit* 246.16

candle making *Hobbies and Pastimes* 167

Candlemas *Christian Holy Days and Seasons* 85

candlenut tree *Trees and Shrubs* 43

candlepin *bowling* 151.1, 151.6

candlepin bowler *bowler* 151.5

candlepins *Sporting Activities* 145, *bowling* 151.1

candlewood *Trees and Shrubs* 43

can do *be powerful* 514.18

can do no more *be fatigued* 820.5

candor 191.2; *openness* 180.3, 583.7, *effusiveness* 207.2, *demonstrativeness* 331.2, *naturalness* 526.4, *outspokenness* 550.2, *directness* 630.5, *naiveté* 821.1, *informality* 829.6

candy *sweets* 90.39, *confectionery* 222.3, *sweeten* 222.7, *love token* 299.8, *solidify* 542.10

candy [Inf] *stimulants* 121.18

candy man [Inf] *drug pusher* 121.13

candy store *food provider* 90.6, *confectionery* 222.3

candy thermometer *cooking equipment* 91.6

candytuft *Flowers* 42

cane *grass* 45.1, *grass plant* 45.3, *type of chair* 101.4, *fencing* 153.1, *instrument of punishment* 454.13, *hit* 454.28, *body support* 605.6, *beat* 695.12

canella *Tree Products* 43

canephora *or* **canephoros** *Architectural Elements* 134

caner *punisher* 454.16

canescence *whiteness* 253.1, *grayness* 255.1

canescent *gray* 255.6

cane sugar *Common Sugars* 12, *sweetener* 222.2

Canes Venatici *Constellations* 7

can(ful) *container(ful)* 738.2

canid *flesh-eating mammal* 35.9

Canidae *flesh-eating mammal* 35.9

canine *teeth* 19.8, *type of animal*

34.5, *flesh-eating mammal* 35.9, *dog* 35.10, *carnivorous* 35.26

canine distemper *animal disease* 34.10

caning *Hobbies and Pastimes* 167, *corporal punishment* 454.11

Canis Major *Constellations* 7

Canis Minor *Constellations* 7

canister *kitchen container* 91.7, *box* 578.5

canister (shot) *historical ammunition* 78.12

can it [Inf] *silence* 231.4

can it! [Inf] *hush!* 231.6

canker *pests and diseases* 17.12, *tree disease* 43.8, *fungus* 47.1, *physical deterioration* 808.4, *make worse* 808.17

cankered *fungal* 47.18

canna *Flowers* 42

cannabis *addictive drug* 117.10, *hemp derivatives* 121.16

canned *saved* 105.15, *storing* 578.19, *preserved* 815.12

canned [Inf] *drunk* 121.25

canned food *food* 90.1, *preserved thing* 815.10

canned goods *merchandise* 482.6

cannel coal *coal* 106.4

cannery *preserver* 815.9

cannibal *killer* 30.11, *eater* 92.15

cannibalism *eating habit* 92.7, *cruelty* 306.4

cannibalistic *murderous* 30.18, *eating* 92.18, *cruel* 306.10

cannibalistically *carnivorously* 92.27

cannibalize *harm* 306.13, *take apart* 753.16, *repair* 809.10

cannily *precautiously* 287.19

canniness *precaution* 287.4, *cleverness* 315.3

canning *cooking technique* 91.2, *storage* 105.6, *storing* 578.19, *preservation of provisions* 815.6

canning factory *preserver* 815.9

cannon *Historical Missile Weapons* 78, *weapon* 78.1, *historical gun* 78.10, *agent of destruction* 523.7

cannon [Brit] *collision* 695.2, *collide* 695.10

cannonade *combined attack* 418.5, *fire* 418.18, *shot* 696.6, *shoot* 696.18

cannonball *historical ammunition* 78.12, *diving* 164.13, *dive* 164.15, *missile* 696.7

cannonball jump *diving* 164.6

cannoneer *historical soldier* 77.8, *shooter* 696.11

cannon fodder *army person* 77.17

cannonry *guns* 78.9

cannot *be powerless* 515.11

cannot be helped *be compelled* 428.11

cannot do otherwise *be compelled* 428.11

cannot help but *be compelled* 428.11

canny *precautionary* 287.9, *intelligent* 352.5, *thrifty* 499.4, *cunning* 822.4

canoe 150.9, 150.31; *canoeing* 150.26, *Ships and Boats* 690

canoe associations *canoeing* 150.13

canoeing 150.8, 150.26; *boating sports* 150.1

canoeing techniques 150.11

canoeist *boating person* 150.24, *nautical person* 690.12

canoe parts 150.10

canoe polo *Sporting Activities* 145

---

canoe race *canoe racing* 150.12

canoe racing 150.12

canoe sailing *Sporting Activities* 145

canoe slalom racing *Sporting Activities* 145

canoe sprint racing *Sporting Activities* 145

can of worms [Inf] *problem* 824.4

canola oil *basic cooking ingredient* 91.8

canon *philosophy* 4.1, *law* 53.1, *religious text* 81.15, *member of the clergy* 84.5, *belief system* 87.3, *Musical Forms* 140, *command* 425.1, *standard* 589.7, *code* 780.3

canoness *religious* 84.9

canonical *universal* 6.67, *curricular* 48.21, *theological* 81.24, *priestly* 84.12

canonically *educationally* 48.25, *religiously* 81.29

canonicals *vestment* 84.11, *uniform* 100.9

canonical writings *religious text* 81.15

canonization *deification* 82.13, *promotion* 715.3

canonize *deify* 82.23, *promote* 715.13

canonized *deified* 82.20, *promoted* 715.8

canonized person *deified person* 82.14

canon law *law* 53.1

can opener *cooking equipment* 91.6, *opener* 583.2

canopic urn *or* **jar** *or* **vase** *funeral object* 31.6

canopied *type of bed* 101.9

canopy *bed covering* 613.7, *overhead covering* 613.11, *roof* 613.30

cant *jargon* 5.21, *worded* 5.38, *use language* 5.42, *grip* 151.4, *ungenuineness* 192.2, *be untruthful* 192.20, *vernacular* 205.8, *obliqueness* 607.1, *oblique line* 607.5, *oblique* 607.6, *be oblique* 607.10, *obliquity* 628.2, *angle* 628.11

cantabile *Musical Terms and Expression Marks* 140

Cantabrian Mountains *Mountains and Hills* 569

cantaloupe *orange thing* 258.3

cantankerous *objectionable* 272.7, *irascible* 303.8, *irritable* 304.9, *argumentative* 329.7, *disagreeing* 463.6

cantankerously *irascibly* 303.17, *irritably* 304.17, *in disagreement* 463.12

cantankerousness *objectionability* 272.2, *irascibility* 303.1, *irritableness* 304.3, *divisiveness* 463.2

cantata *ritual music* 85.9, *Musical Forms* 140, *sacred music* 140.3

can't bear *detest* 291.13

canteen *room* 60.9, *eating place* 92.17, *drink container* 93.13

canter *ride* 159.16, *hypocrite* 192.7, *bodily movement* 677.11, *acceleration* 694.3, *be swift* 694.10

Canterbury *cabinet* 101.8

Canterbury bell *Flowers* 42

cantering *speeding* 694.7

cantharides *eroticism* 20.7

cantharis *eroticism* 20.7

canticle *ritual music* 85.9, *Musical Forms* 140, *sacred music* 140.3, *song* 140.11

cantilever *Architectural Elements*

134, superstructure 551.7, *overhanging* 604.2

cantilever brake *bicycle part* 687.11

cantilever bridge *bridge* 551.10, 691.7

cantilevered *overhanging* 604.8

canting *worded* 5.38, *zealous* 81.22, *unbalanced* 741.5

canto *part of poem* 139.9, *melody* 140.10, *part of writing* 760.6

canton Heraldic Terms 184, *administrative region* 564.4

Canton crepe Fabrics and Fibers 130

cantor *rabbi* 84.6, *singer* 141.4

Cantor set Mathematical Concepts 6

cantus *or* **cantus firmus** *melody* 140.10

Canuck Nicknames for Inhabitants 61

canvas Fabrics and Fibers 130, *painting* 143.3, *material* 143.9, *overhead covering* 613.11, *protection from the weather* 810.9

canvass *confer* 210.13, *plead* 329.14, *question* 333.16, *motivate* 412.12, *sell* 482.15, *solicitation* 505.4, *solicit money* 505.13

canvassed *questioned* 333.15

canvasser *questioner* 333.9, *activist* 412.4, *merchant* 482.10, *requester* 505.5

canvas shoes *shoes* 100.30

canvassing *selling* 482.1, *solicitation* 505.4

canyon *landform* 8.9, *rough thing* 544.2, *valley* 572.8, *gulf* 587.3, *lowlands* 597.6, *concave land* 635.2

can you beat that! *wonderful!* 294.20

canzone Musical Forms 140

caoutchouc *rubber* 546.3

cap 100.33; *moss plant* 46.5, *fungal body* 47.4, *explosive* 78.13, *clothe* 100.43, *fuel starter* 106.3, *baseball equipment* 147.4, *golf equipment* 156.5, *type* 173.5, *retaliate* 420.4, *stopper* 584.3, *stop* 584.14, *summit* 600.1, *architectural summit* 600.4, *top* 600.10, *cover* 613.2, 613.24, *body covering* 613.3, *outdo* 744.18, *complete* 761.9, *end* 773.10

capability *means* 102.1, *skill* 127.1, *qualification* 340.1, *ability* 340.2, 514.3, *potential* 458.4, *influence* 512.1, *easiness* 823.1

capable *qualified* 340.7, *intelligent* 352.5, *powerful* 514.15, *in form* 624.8, *equal to* 740.10, *possible* 836.5

capableness *qualification* 340.1

capable of being used *adoptive* 476.9

capable of life *alive* 28.13

capable of perfection *imperfect* 806.5

capable of solution *solvable* 334.14

capably 340.15; *skillfully* 127.16

capacious *big* 498.9, 579.13, *spacious* 563.13

capaciously *spaciously* 563.17, *amply* 579.20

capaciousness *spaciousness* 563.4, *largeness* 579.2

capacitance *resistance* 10.41, *electrical power* 514.12

capacitive *electric* 14.47

capacitor *circuit* 10.43, *circuit element* 14.39

capacity *running water* 8.10, *means*

102.1, skill 127.1, *ability* 340.2, 514.3, *potential* 458.4, *potency* 516.6, *space* 563.1, *reserved space* 563.5, *size* 579.1, *measurability* 589.2, *quantity* 738.1, *fullness* 761.5, *inclusion* 763.1, *usability* 801.2, *possibleness* 836.2

capacity for life *life cycle* 28.7

cap and bells *costume* 100.10, *clown* 138.10

cap and gown *formal clothes* 100.5, *clothing* 184.6, *formal clothing* 406.5

caparison *finery* 100.6

cape *coat* 100.19, *peninsula* 572.5

Cape Breton Island Islands 572

Cape doctor Notable Winds 9

Cape Fear Rivers 570

caper *dance* 135.7, *joke* 277.6

caper [Inf] *theft* 479.2

capers Herbs and Spices 91

Cape Town Countries 566

Cape Verde Countries 566

Cape Verde Islands Islands 572

capillaries *internal organ* 19.13

capillarity *pulling power* 700.2

capillary attraction *pulling power* 700.2

cap in hand *showing respect* 435.7

capital *killing* 30.17, *resources* 102.4, *stock in trade* 105.2, Architectural Elements 134, *type* 173.5, *printed* 173.13, *punitive* 454.18, *personal estate* 470.6, *funds* 484.6, *administrative headquarters* 564.5, *architectural summit* 600.4, *head* 600.7, *center of activity* 612.4, *best* 744.10, 805.9, *important* 799.7

capital accumulation *economic development* 56.5

capital budget *budgeting* 493.5

capital city *city* 567.1, *center of activity* 612.4

capital crime *wicked act* 448.7

capital gains *profit* 467.6, *money received* 472.6

capital gains tax *tax* 494.5

capital goods *merchandise* 482.6

capital investment *economic development* 56.5

capitalism 480.5; *political and economic philosophy* 4.6, *economics* 56.1, *plutocracy* 485.5, *noninterference* 829.3

capitalist *political and economic philosopher* 4.10, *of a political philosophy* 4.14, *gainer* 467.9, *financier* 484.17, *wealthy person* 485.6, *national* 566.10, *free person* 829.9, *prosperous person* 847.4

capitalist country *country* 566.1

capitalistic *masterful* 68.15, *gainful* 467.10, *national* 566.10, *independent* 829.12

capitalistically *nationally* 566.13

capitalist system *economics* 56.1

capitalize on *exploit* 393.11, *profit* 467.22, *take the opportunity* 659.7, *find useful* 801.11

capital letter *type* 173.5

capital market *economic factor* 56.8

capital murder *murder* 30.2

capital punishment 454.12; *way of dying* 29.5, *execution* 30.6

capital reserves *funds* 484.6

capital ship *warship* 77.21

capital sin *iniquity* 448.3

capitation tax *tax* 494.5

Capitol, the *the power structure* 68.12

Capitol Hill *the power structure* 68.12

---

capitulate 421.6; *submit* 298.17, *agree* 735.23

capitulating *agreeing* 735.13

capitulation *submission* 421.1, *agreement* 735.3

capitulum *flower head* 42.4

capnomancer *diviner* 86.14

cap of darkness *talisman* 86.9

capon *livestock* 16.11

caponize *take off* 749.7

capote *coat* 100.19

capped *dressed* 100.38, *stopped* 584.9, *topped* 600.8, *covered* 613.19

capping *dentistry* 107.6, *topped* 600.8, *superior* 744.8, *ending* 773.13

cappuccino *coffee* 93.6

Capri Islands 572

capric Common Fatty Acids 12

caprice 381.1; *imprudence* 286.3, *conception* 360.4, *vacillation* 380.3, *irregularity* 664.1, *irresolution* 666.2

capricious 381.4, 841.16; *imprudent* 286.7, *inconstant* 378.6, *irregular* 664.3, *irresolute* 666.4

capriciously 381.7, 841.26; *imprudently* 286.11, *irregularly* 664.6, *changeably* 666.7

capriciousness 381.2, 841.8; *imprudence* 286.3, *inconstancy* 378.2, *irregularity* 664.1, *irresolution* 666.2

capricious person 381.3

Capricorn Constellations 7

caprine *ungulate* 35.31

Capri pants *or* **Capris** *pants* 100.14

caproic Common Fatty Acids 12

caprylic Common Fatty Acids 12

capsicum Herbs and Spices 91

capsize *become inverted* 608.8, *sail* 690.16, *trip* 714.16, *unbalance* 741.8

capsizing *act of inversion* 608.3

capstan *rotator* 682.8, *lifter* 715.5

capstan lathe *machine tool* 14.9

capstone Architectural Elements 134, *summit* 600.1, *conclusion* 761.3, *peak* 805.5

capsule *botanical fruit* 44.2, *dose of medicine* 115.3, *shortened version* 591.3, *casing* 613.9

capsulization *shortening* 591.2

capsulize *shorten* 591.9

capsulized *shortened* 591.7

Captain US Military Ranks 58, *military title* 72.8

captain *leader* 126.8, *lead* 126.12, 744.19, *basketball team* 148.2, *boating person* 150.24, *sail* 150.29, *bowler* 151.5, *football player* 155.15, *soccer participant* 163.4, *aircraft personnel* 689.8, *nautical person* 690.12, *superior* 744.5

captain a ship *navigate* 690.15

captaincy *directorship* 126.5

captain of industry *company leader* 68.8, *important person* 799.5

captain's *type of chair* 101.4

captainship *directorship* 126.5

caption *brief description* 202.2

captious *quibbling* 330.9, *critical* 438.13

captiously *sophistically* 330.14

captiousness *quibbling* 330.4, *criticism* 438.4

captivate *cause joy* 269.11, *win the love of* 299.27, *influence* 508.11, *lure* 700.12

captivated *joyful* 269.6, *liking* 290.4, *enamored* 299.17

---

captivating *delightful* 271.7, *likable* 290.7, *wondrous* 294.9, *lovable* 299.20, *attractive* 477.13, 700.10

captivatingly *likably* 290.12, *wondrously* 294.18, *lovably* 299.31, *takingly* 477.23

captivation *liking* 290.1

captive 832.9; *prisoner* 55.7, *imprisoned* 55.9, *serf* 69.8, *detained* 830.11, *subjected person* 832.5

captive nation *dominion* 566.3

captivity *arrest* 55.5, *detention* 830.5, *subjection* 832.1

captor *absolute ruler* 68.7, *raider* 477.10

capture *arrest* 55.5, 55.12, *board games* 167.3, *play* 167.12, *represent* 187.10, *ambush* 292.4, 292.11, *imagine* 360.14, *attack successfully* 418.25, *taking* 477.1, *takings* 477.8, *take* 477.14, *take away forcefully* 477.19, *defeat* 832.11, *be victorious* 845.16

capture an expression *describe* 202.15

captured *arrested* 55.10, *surprised* 292.5, *defeated* 846.11

capture on film *record* 185.13

capture the flag Children's and Party Games 167

capturing *conquest* 477.6

capuche *vestment* 84.11

car *means of transportation* 686.2, *road vehicle* 687.4, *automobile* 687.6, *railroad car* 688.5

carabineer *historical soldier* 77.8

carabiner *climbing equipment* 161.4

carabiner-ice ax belay *climbing techniques* 161.3

caracara, Audubon's crested Endangered US Birds 36

Caracas Countries 566

Caracu Breeds of Cattle 16

carafe *bottle* 578.14

car alarm *signal* 183.6, *self-defense* 419.5

caramel *sweets* 90.39, *brown thing* 256.3

carapa Trees and Shrubs 43

carapace *skeleton* 551.14, *animal covering* 613.15

carat *weight measurement* 538.6, General Units 589

caravan *wagon* 687.5

caravan [Brit] *mobile home* 60.11

caravel *or* **carvel** Sailing Ships and Boats 690

caraway seed Herbs and Spices 91

carbine *firearm* 78.7

carbineer [Arch] *shooter* 696.11

carbocyclic *chemical compound* 11.4

carbohydrate 12.3

carbohydrate diet *diet* 92.5

carbohydrates *food content* 90.3

carbolic *prophylaxis* 115.4

carbolic acid *cleaning agent* 111.9

carbolic soap *fat* 562.4

carbolize *clean* 111.17

car bomb *bomb* 78.15

car bombing *terrorist attack* 418.7

carbon Chemical Elements and Common Allotropes 11, *essential element* 12.15, *copy* 736.10

carbon-14 dating *dating* 8.48

carbonaceous *gas* 106.14

carbonaceous chondrite *meteor* 7.21

carbonate *mineral types* 8.38, *react* 11.38, *aerate* 556.24

carbonated *gassy* 556.19

---

carbonated water *water* 93.4, *drinking water* 557.2

carbon copy *reprint* 21.3, *recording* 185.6, *illustration* 187.2, *copy* 736.2, *duplicate* 736.4, *twin* 789.5, *replica* 797.7

carbon dioxide *pollution* 117.8, Fields of Measurement 589

carbon dioxide laser *laser* 10.18

carbon fiber *shipbuilding* 690.4

carboniferous *gas* 106.14

Carboniferous Period Geologic Time Intervals 8

carbonize *burn* 217.18

carbon monoxide *pollution* 117.8

carbon paper *paper* 104.5

carboxylic acid *acid* 11.10, *fat* 12.7

carbuncle *ulcer* 114.18, *ugly thing* 531.2, *mark* 533.2, *blot on the landscape* 533.4, *bulge* 634.2

carburetor *racing automobile* 146.2

carburize *react* 11.38

carcass *body* 19.1, *dead person* 29.7

carcinogen *poison* 117.7

carcinogenic *of disease* 114.25

carcinoma *cancer* 114.15

carcinomatoid *of disease* 114.25

carcinomatous *of disease* 114.25

carcinophobia Phobias 283

car coat *coat* 100.19

card 15.7; *computer part* 15.4, *type of table* 101.5, *correspondence* 169.2, *means of identification* 184.3, *record book* 185.5, *smoother* 545.2, *transferred thing* 685.6, *navigational aid* 690.6

card [Inf] *male* 32.1, *eccentric* 782.10

cardamon Herbs and Spices 91

Cardano's formula Mathematical Concepts 6

cardboard *paper* 104.5, *misrepresented* 188.4

carded *smooth* 545.4

card game *type of game* 167.2, *card playing* 168.1

cardholder *debtor* 488.6, *entrant* 706.7

cardiac arrest *cardiovascular disease* 114.13

cardiac disease *cardiovascular disease* 114.13

cardiac hypertrophy *cardiovascular disease* 114.13

cardiac surgery Medical Specialties 107

cardialgia *gastroenterological disease* 114.11

Cardiff *major British cities* 567.7

cardigan *sweater* 100.17

cardigan or **cardigan jacket** *jacket* 100.18

cardinal *number* 6.4, *ranked* 6.72, *person in authority* 52.7, *religious leader* 68.9, *masterful* 68.15, *priest* 84.8, *red thing* 257.3, *best* 744.10, 805.9, *numerical* 783.7, *important* 799.7

cardinal flower Flowers 42

cardinal number *number* 6.4, *kind of number* 783.2

cardinal point *compass direction* 697.5, *gist* 799.4

cardinal red *red* 257.5

cardinal's hat *vestment* 84.11

cardinalship *priesthood* 84.2

cardinal virtues *virtues* 447.2

card index *table* 785.2

cardioid *curve* 6.38

cardiology Medical Specialties 107

cardiophobia Phobias 283

cardiopulmonary disease *disease* 114.4

cardiovascular disease 114.13; *disease* 114.4

carditis *cardiovascular disease* 114.13

cardplayer 168.3

card playing 168.1

card-playing 168.6

card punch *peripheral* 15.8

card reader *peripheral* 15.8

cards 168.2; *means of prediction* 358.10

card shark *gambler* 167.6

cardsharp *gambler* 167.6

card toss Children's and Party Games 167

card up one's sleeve *reserves* 102.5, *expedient* 387.5, *advantage* 744.3

care *provision* 89.1, *management* 126.1, *rock face* 161.6, *caution* 287.1, *solicitude* 323.5, *carefulness* 325.1, *consideration* 325.2, *foresight* 357.1, *be courteous* 410.9, *line of duty* 433.3, *observance* 465.1, *observe* 465.4, *safekeeping* 810.6, *conservation* 815.2, *sustenance* 825.3, *detention* 830.5

careen *be oblique* 607.10, *angle* 628.11, *be irregular* 664.5, *stagger* 684.11, *pitch* 684.25, *sail* 690.16, *scamper* 694.12, *make haste* 818.5

careening *irregularity* 664.1, *irregular* 664.3

career *job* 122.3, *activity* 385.4, *line of action* 399.4, *momentum* 677.2, *course* 679.2, *swiftness* 694.1, *scamper* 694.12

careerist *hard worker* 414.11

career of crime *wicked act* 448.7

career woman *liberated woman* 33.12, *professional worker* 123.11

care for 325.12; *serve* 69.11, *practice medicine* 107.32, *like* 290.8, *be attentive* 323.9, *protect* 810.21, *support* 825.24

carefree *unskillful* 128.4, *cheerful* 269.7, *thoughtless* 318.7, *unpremeditated* 389.7, *at ease* 819.2, *easygoing* 823.13, *liberated* 831.4

careful 325.6, 593.11; *cautious* 287.6, *watchful* 323.6, *foreseeing* 357.5, *active* 414.13, *thrifty* 499.4

careful! *look out!* 814.12

careful consideration *prudence* 287.2

carefully 325.13; *thoughtfully* 4.27, *cautiously* 287.16, *attentively* 323.14

carefulness 323.3, 325.1, 593.5; *caution* 287.1, *use* 393.1, *thrift* 499.1

careful of *observant* 465.3

caregiver *nurse* 107.23, *protector* 810.11

caregiving *consideration* 325.2, *considerate* 325.7

careless 289.8, 324.8; *clumsy* 128.6, *unemphatic* 201.2, *imprudent* 286.7, *negligent* 326.4, *unrefined* 338.7, *unthinking* 355.8, *unpremeditated* 389.7, *nonobservant* 466.5, *untidy* 766.11, *incomplete* 806.6, *hasty* 818.3

careless dress *dressing* 100.2

carelessly 289.18; *dressily* 100.47, *unskillfully* 128.12, *unemphatically* 201.4, *imprudently* 286.11, *inattentively* 324.12, 466.13, *negligently* 326.8, *wrongly* 351.18, *forgetfully* 355.14

carelessly dressed *in dishabille* 100.40

carelessness 289.2; *lack of emphasis* 201.1, *imprudence* 286.3, *inattention* 324.1, *negligence* 326.1, *tastelessness* 338.3, *inaccuracy* 351.3, *unthinkingness* 355.3, *nonobservance* 466.1, *untidiness* 766.3, *incompleteness* 806.2, *hastiness* 818.2

care nothing for *be indifferent* 289.12

carer *feeling person* 266.8, *supporter* 825.13

cares *adversity* 848.1

caress *gesture* 183.17, *type of touch* 216.3, *touch* 73.9, *communication of love* 299.6, *communicate love* 299.25, *massage* 554.16

caressable *lovable* 299.20

caressing *touching* 216.2, *communication of love* 299.6

caret Reference Signs 393

caretaker *animal welfarist* 34.9, *prison officer* 55.8, *attendant* 69.4, *leader* 126.8, *observer* 242.15, *closer* 584.5

caretaker government 49.14

cargo *merchandise* 482.6, *displacement* 283.3, *load* 577.5, *transferred thing* 685.6, *freightage* 686.3, *transportable* 686.7

cargo handler *transferrer* 685.4, *transporter* 686.4

cargo liner Ships and Boats 690

cargo load *transferred thing* 685.6

carhop *attendant* 69.4

car horn *signal* 183.6, *warning signal* 814.3

Caribbean Community and Common Market (CARICOM) *economic organization* 56.6

Caribbean Sea Oceans and Seas 571

caribou *game* 160.6

caricatural *ridiculing* 436.13

caricature *drawing* 143.4, *draw* 143.13, *illustration* 187.2, *illustrate* 187.11, *misrepresentation* 188.1, *misrepresent* 188.6, *exaggeration* 194.1, *exaggerate* 194.11, *entertainment* 277.4, *be humorous* 277.11, *form of derision* 369.2, *deride* 369.7, *ridicule* 436.4, 436.22, 440.6, 440.15, *mimicry* 736.3, *imitate* 736.9

caricatured *drawn* 143.11, *misrepresented* 188.4

caricaturist *visual artist* 133.6, *humorist* 277.7, *derider* 369.3, *disparager* 440.7

carillon Musical Instruments 142, *percussion instrument* 142.5, *source of resonance* 236.4

Carina Constellations 7

carina *avian characteristic* 36.6

caring *sensitive* 266.11, 267.3, *worried* 283.11, *pitying* 308.4, *solicitous* 323.8, *considerate* 325.7, *observance* 465.1, *supportive* 825.18

caring father *liberated man* 32.13

caringly 325.14; *sensitively* 267.6

car insurance *insurance* 810.10

carioca Dances 135

carious *unclean* 112.5

carload *load* 577.5

Carme Planets and Their Satellites 7

car mechanic *artisan* 123.13

Carmel Mountains and Hills 569

carminative *purgative* 115.7

carmine *red pigment* 257.2, *red* 257.5

carnage *slaughter* 30.5, *havoc* 523.5

carnal *sensual* 20.16, *pleasurable* 214.6, *unchaste* 432.10, *depraved* 448.10, *self-indulgent* 456.6, *material* 524.7

carnal desire *sexual desire* 20.5, 288.5

carnality *sexuality* 20.3, *physical pleasure* 214.1, *sexual immorality* 432.2, *depravity* 448.2, *self-indulgence* 456.1

carnally *promiscuously* 432.19, *unvirtuously* 448.16

carnal sin *iniquity* 448.3

carnassial *teeth* 19.8

carnation Flowers 42, *red thing* 257.3, *red* 257.5

carnauba Tree Products 43

carnelian *red thing* 257.3

carnet *miscellaneous automotive terms* 687.14

carnival *religious festival* 85.13, *circus* 138.2, *amusement* 167.7, *show* 404.12, *celebration* 405.1

carnival-like *festive* 408.13

Carnivora *flesh-eating mammal* 35.9

carnivore *type of animal* 34.5, *flesh-eating mammal* 35.9, *eater* 92.15

carnivorous 35.26; *of animals* 34.13, *of plants* 41.14, *eating* 92.18

carnivorously 92.27

carnivorousness *eating habit* 92.7

carnophobia Phobias 283

Carnot cycle Classical Physical Laws 10, *engine cycle* 14.13

carol *ritual music* 85.9, *song* 140.11, *sing* 141.16, *make a bird sound* 240.8

Caroline Islands Islands 572

Carolingian architecture Architectural Styles 134

Carolingian art Western Art Styles 133

carom *billiards play* 149.2, *play* 149.7, *collision* 695.2, *collide* 695.10

carom billiards Sporting Activities 145

caroms Board and Table Games 167

caron Accents and Diacritical Marks 5

carotene *pigment* 12.18, *plant body* 47.13, *orange pigment* 258.2

carotenoid *pigment* 12.18, *terpene* 12.20

carousal *celebration* 405.1, *dissipation* 456.2

carouse *rejoice* 279.5, *celebrate* 405.10, *overindulge* 456.11

carousel *amusement park and playground equipment* 167.8

carouser *drunkard* 121.8

carousing *drunken* 121.28

carp *food fish and shellfish* 90.20, *be dissatisfied* 274.7, *complaint* 304.5, *be irritable* 304.14, *criticize* 438.19, *cause difficulties* 824.22

carpal bones or **carpus** Human Bones 19

car papers *certificate* 185.2

carp at *criticize* 438.19

Carpathian Mountains Mountains and Hills 569

carpe diem [L] *live in the present* 647.8, *take the opportunity* 659.7

carpel *flower part* 42.3

carpenter 131.10; *artisan* 123.13, *woodworker* 131.4, *person who joins* 752.9

carpenter's term 131.5
carpentry *woodworking* 131.1
carper *dissatisfied person* 274.3
carpet *fabric* 130.1, *floor covering* 613.13
carpet [Inf] *stadium* 155.3
carpet [Brit inf] *condemn* 438.18
carpetbag *bag* 578.7
carpet beater *impeller* 695.7
carpet-bomb *bomb* 418.19
carpet bombing *bombing* 76.21, *air attack* 418.4
carpeting *fabric* 130.1, *floor covering* 613.13
carpeting [Brit inf] *condemnation* 438.2
carpetlayer *coverer* 613.18
carpet sweeper *cleaning tool* 111.10
car phone *telephone* 169.10
carping *criticism* 438.4, *critical* 438.13
carplike *fishlike* 38.10
carpogonium *reproductive body* 47.14
carpophore *fungal body* 47.4
carpospore *reproductive body* 47.14
car racing *automobile racing* 146.1
carrack Sailing Ships and Boats 690
car radio *radio* 172.1
carrageen *moss* 46.4
Carrantuohill Mountains and Hills 569
carriage *external appearance* 264.5, *conduct* 399.1, *bodily movement* 677.11, *conveyance* 685.2, *transportation* 686.1, *means of transportation* 686.2, *road vehicle* 687.4
carriage [Brit] *railroad car* 688.5
carriageable *transferable* 685.7
carriage dog Breeds of Dogs 35
carriage horse *workhorse* 159.3
carriage return (CR) *character* 15.18
carrick bend Knots, Bends, Hitches, Splices 754
carried *agreed* 346.5, *agreeing* 462.6
carried away *imaginative* 360.10
carried forward *accounted* 493.8
carried over *surplus* 750.8
carrier *analysis* 11.17, *disease-causing agent* 114.5, *infectious person* 114.9, *conductor* 399.13, *supporter* 605.9, *transferrer* 685.4, *transporter* 686.4
carrier pigeon *messenger* 685.5
carrion *dead person* 29.7, *dirt* 112.5, *refuse* 802.5
carrot *incentive* 178.4, *orange thing* 258.3, *positive stimulus* 508.5
carrot and stick *incentive* 178.4, *coercive method* 428.3, *stimulus* 508.3
carrot family *seed plant* 41.3
carrot-top [Inf] *red thing* 257.3
carroty *red-haired* 257.7, *orange* 258.5
carry *add* 6.86, 748.11, *cause ill health* 114.30, *golf shots* 156.4, *be heard* 228.15, *conduct* 399.21, *attack successfully* 418.25, *merchandise* 482.17, *support* 605.16, *give moral support* 605.18, *convey* 685.9, *transport* 686.10, *be important* 799.13, *be victorious* 845.16
carry across *cross* 692.17
carry a date *chronologize* 646.13
carryall *receptacle* 105.11, *bag* 578.7, *baggage* 578.8

carry all before one *do easily* 823.16, *defeat* 845.17
carry a point *overpower* 845.18
carry a suggestion *imply* 844.14
carry clout [Inf] *influence* 512.11
carry coals to Newcastle *waste effort* 802.13
carry forward *account* 493.9
carrying *hearable* 228.12, *loud* 232.6, *resonant* 236.6, *transporting* 686.8
carrying force *operative* 509.9
carrying out *performance* 465.2
carrying the puck *ice hockey tactics* 158.4
carrying too far *extravagance* 194.3
carry into effect *be an instrument* 511.7
Carry Nation *moralist* 431.8
carry no weight *be unimportant* 800.13
carry off *take away* 477.18, *attain one's goal* 845.13
carry off *or* **away** *kidnap* 479.15, *take away* 685.12
carry on *live* 28.17, *manage* 126.10, *maintain* 377.12, *follow up* 385.16, *behave badly* 399.19, *behave toward* 399.20, *occupy oneself* 412.15, *protract* 669.9, *continue* 774.12
carry-on *baggage* 578.8
carry on! *go on!* 669.11
carry on a conversation *converse* 210.11
carry on a vendetta *dispute* 463.9
carry oneself *conduct oneself* 399.17
carry one's liquor *be sober* 120.8
carry one's point *influence* 508.11
carry on regardless *be rash* 286.8
carry on the line *propagate* 21.15
carry out *suffice* 97.6, *take charge of* 391.8, *behave toward* 399.20, *act* 412.11, *perform* 465.5, *be an instrument* 511.7, *reach out* 585.10, *complete* 761.9, *perfect* 805.19
carry out goals *manage* 126.10
carry out *or* **perform** *or* **fulfill one's duty** *do one's duty* 433.17
carry out orders *obey* 426.7
carry out to the letter *perform* 465.5
carry over *account* 493.9, *add* 748.11
carry-over *additional item* 748.3, *difference* 750.3
carry sail *navigate* 690.15
carry shoulder high *salute* 405.13
carry the can [Brit inf] *be open to criticism* 438.22
carry the day *be superior* 744.15, *be victorious* 845.16
carry through *be resolute* 376.11, *endure* 377.14, *behave toward* 399.20, *act* 412.11, *be an instrument* 511.7, *complete* 759.10, 761.9
carry to *reach out* 585.10
carry too far *be extravagant* 194.13
carry weight *influence* 512.11, *be heavy* 538.12, *be important* 799.13
carry with one *influence* 508.11
carsick *vomiting* 709.12
carsickness *miscellaneous automotive terms* 687.14
Carson City American States 564
cart 578.9; *convey* 685.9, *means of transportation* 686.2, *transport* 686.10, *road vehicle* 687.4, *wagon* 687.5, *truck* 687.8

cartage *conveyance* 685.2, *transportation* 686.1
cart away *take away* 685.12
carte [Fr] *bill of fare* 785.5
carte blanche *tolerance* 502.2, *liberality* 829.8
cartel *economic factor* 56.8, *alliance* 459.5, 735.5, *association* 480.8, 752.2, 827.6, *limit* 620.1, *economic restraint* 830.3
carter *transferrer* 685.4, *transporter* 686.4
Cartesian Philosophical Schools of Thought 4
Cartesian coordinates *coordinates* 6.31, 589.6
Cartesianism Philosophical Schools of Thought 4
Cartesian space *space* 6.33
car thief *lawbreaker* 53.15
cart horse *workhorse* 159.3, *means of transportation* 686.2
Carthusian Horse and Pony Breeds 159
cartilage *muscles* 19.3, *solid body* 540.4, *hard substance* 542.3, *skeleton* 551.14
cartilageous *bodily* 19.18
cartilaginous *hard* 542.5, *chewy* 547.9
cartilaginous fish *fish* 38.5
carting *transportation* 686.1
cartogram *map* 187.5
cartographer *measurer* 589.14
cartographic *metrical* 589.15
cartographical *locational* 565.8
cartographically *topographically* 565.13, *measurably* 589.22
cartography *map* 187.5, *topography* 565.5, *measurement* 589.1
carton *receptacle* 105.11, *tobacco implements* 121.24, *box* 578.5, *enclosing thing* 619.3
carton(ful) *container(ful)* 738.2
cartoon *movie type* 137.3, *drawing* 143.4, *draw* 143.13, *illustration* 187.2, *entertainment* 277.4, *form of derision* 369.2, *outline* 617.1
cartooned *drawn* 143.11
cartooning *(act of) drawing* 143.2
cartoonist *visual artist* 133.6, *drawer* 143.8, *humorist* 277.7, *derider* 369.3
cartouche *historical ammunition* 78.12, Architectural Elements 134
cartridge *ammunition* 78.11, *film* 132.8
cartridge belt *ammunition* 78.11
cartridge case *ammunition* 78.11
cartulary *record book* 185.5
cartwheel *floor exercise* 157.4, *act of inversion* 608.3, *become inverted* 608.8, *wheel* 682.9
carve *work wood* 131.9, *sculpt* 144.10, *ski* 162.35, *inscribe* 185.14, *illustrate* 187.11, *perform* 522.16, *fashion* 536.7, *use a sharp tool* 549.17, *form* 624.9, *take apart* 753.16
carved *woodcrafted* 131.7, *sculpted* 144.8, *engraved* 144.9, *snowplow* 162.29, *formed* 624.6
carved turn *skiing techniques* 162.5
carve letters *word* 5.43
carve *or* **force** *or* **fight one's way** *make one's way* 679.12
carver *type of chair* 101.4, *artisan* 123.13, *woodworker* 131.4, *sculptor* 144.4
carvery *eating place* 92.17
carve up *allocate* 474.5, *take apart* 753.16

carving *woodworking* 131.1, *sculpture* 144.1, *snowboarding* 162.11, 162.30
carving knife *tableware* 92.13
carvone *terpene* 12.20
car wash *washer* 111.7, *miscellaneous automotive terms* 687.14
caryatid Architectural Elements 134, *sculpture* 144.1, *supporting part* 605.3
caryopsis *botanical fruit* 44.2
Casanova *libertine* 32.7, *tempter* 178.10, *lover* 299.11, *sexually immoral person* 432.8, *charmer* 700.6
cascade *flow* 570.4, 570.10, *downflow* 714.3, *drip* 714.13
cascade loops *systems and process control* 14.28
Cascade Range Mountains and Hills 569
cascara Tree Products 43, *purgative* 115.7
case *grammatical term* 5.29, *litigation* 54.1, *patient* 107.25, *infectious person* 114.9, *sick person* 114.22, *instrumental aid* 142.7, *issue* 328.2, *line of argument* 329.3, *accusation* 442.1, *circumstances* 573.2, *box* 578.5, *casing* 613.9, *wrap* 613.29, *undertaking* 675.5, *inset* 710.13, *state* 725.1, *occurrence* 726.2
case, the *fact* 717.6
case [Inf] *eccentric* 782.10
case binding *bookbinding* 174.11
case book *schoolbook* 48.15
case dismissed *or* **thrown out of court** *favorable verdict* 54.19
case for decision *litigation* 54.1
case for the prosecution *accusation* 442.1
case(ful) *container(ful)* 738.2
case grammar *grammar* 5.28
case harden *extract* 11.41
caseharden *accustom* 397.18, *strengthen* 516.15, *harden* 542.9, *make tough* 547.15
casehardened *determined* 379.7, *habituated* 397.14, *hardened* 542.7, *toughened* 547.7, *mentally tough* 547.12
casein *protein* 12.9
casemate *fort* 419.13
casement *window* 134.10, *framework* 551.4
Caserta Breeds of Pigs 16
case shot *historical ammunition* 78.12
caseworker *philanthropist* 307.5
cash 484.2; *resources* 102.4, *bank* 484.26, *money* 485.2, *positive stimulus* 508.5
cash account *accounts* 493.4
cash a check *bank* 484.26
cash and carry *store* 483.8, *discounter* 497.7
cash-and-carry *buying* 481.9
cashbook *record book* 185.5, *account book* 493.3
cash box *money storage* 484.20
cash budget *budgeting* 495.5
cash cow [Inf] *wealth* 485.1
cash crop *crop* 16.8, *yield* 467.8
cash desk *till* 484.21
cash dispenser *till* 484.21
cash down 489.25
cash flow *funds* 484.6
cash-flow crisis *insolvency* 490.5

cash-flow problems *economic adversity* 848.6

cashier *exile* 454.24, *treasurer* 484.18, *payer* 489.9, *accountant* 493.6, *disbar* 709.16, *debase* 716.16, *terminate* 834.7

cashiering *dismissal* 709.2

cashier's check *paper money* 484.14

cash in on *exploit* 393.11, *profit* 467.22, *take the opportunity* 659.7, *get better* 807.21

cash in one's chips [Inf] *die* 29.17

cashmere Fabrics and Fibers 130

cashmere coat *coat* 100.19

cashmere sweater *sweater* 100.17

cash *or* **collect on delivery (C.O.D.)** *postal service* 169.5, *buying* 481.9

cash payment *type of payment* 489.3

cash-poor *unprofitable* 468.10

cash prize *prize* 453.2

cash purchase *purchasing* 481.2

cash register *calculator* 6.64, 784.5, *recording instrument* 185.9, *till* 484.21

cash supplies *funds* 484.6

cash transaction *finance* 457.1, 484.7

casing 613.9; *covering* 613.1

casino *dance hall* 135.3, *gambling house* 167.5, *Card Games* 168

cask *vessel* 578.11

casket *funeral object* 31.6, *box* 578.5

Caspian pony Horse and Pony Breeds 159

Caspian Sea Oceans and Seas 571

casque *historic armor* 419.8

Cassai Rivers 570

Cassandra *hopeless person* 282.5, *warner* 814.5

Cassegrain telescope *telescope* 7.25

casserole *meat dish* 90.21, *cooking equipment* 91.6

casseroling *cooking technique* 91.2

cassette *film* 132.8, *recording* 185.6, *sound reproduction* 230.6

cassette recorder *recording instrument* 185.9, *sound reproduction* 230.6

cassette tape *recording* 185.6

cassia Trees and Shrubs 43, Herbs and Spices 91

cassia bark Tree Products 43

cassimere *or* **casimere** *or* **casimire** Fabrics and Fibers 130

Cassiopeia Constellations 7

cassock *vestment* 84.11, *robe* 100.20

cassone *cabinet* 101.8

cassowary *flightless bird* 36.8

cast 136.26; *group* 18.13, Collective Names 59, *team* 59.9, *personnel* 123.16, *make ceramics* 129.10, *dramatized* 136.32, *dramatize* 136.33, *produced* 137.17, *produce* 137.21, *sculpture* 144.1, *sculpted* 144.8, *sculpt* 144.10, *fishing* 154.13, *fish* 154.14, *illustrate* 187.11, *faulty vision* 243.1, *hue* 251.4, *tendency* 513.1, *perform* 522.16, *fashion* 536.7, *body support* 605.6, *medical covering* 613.4, *enclosing thing* 619.3, *prototype* 624.2, *nature* 624.5, *form* 624.9, *throw* 696.4, 696.17, *sprinkle* 776.15, *type* 777.4

cast about *pursue* 385.11

cast a contrary vote *dissent* 506.9

cast adrift *diverge* 753.20

cast a horoscope *divine* 358.15

cast a long shadow *be important* 799.13

cast a lure *fish* 154.14

cast an account *account* 493.9

cast anchor *sail* 690.16

cast a negative vote *discard* 383.12

castanets Musical Instruments 142

cast a shadow *make dark* 247.10, *make dim* 248.8

cast a shadow before *be in the future* 650.9

cast a slur *bring into disrepute* 371.6, *vilify* 440.14

cast aspersions on *vilify* 301.15, 440.14, *criticize* 418.26

cast a vote *vote* 382.16

castaway *relinquished* 392.2, *unsocial person* 409.5

cast away *decrease* 747.7, *leave* 750.10

cast bait *fish* 154.14

cast bones *look ahead* 650.11

cast doubt *cause disbelief* 88.9, *doubt* 333.19

cast down *overthrown* 716.9, *degraded* 716.10, *throw down* 716.13

caste *rank* 739.2, *social class* 777.5

caste mark *personal identification* 184.4, *mark* 533.2

cast envious eyes *envy* 314.7

caster *sculptor* 144.4

caster sugar *basic cooking ingredient* 91.8, *sweetener* 222.2

cast forth *let out* 709.26

castigate *dissuade* 179.7, *condemn* 438.18, *punish* 454.22

castigated *condemned* 438.11, *punished* 454.19

castigating *condemning* 438.10

castigation *condemnation* 438.2, *punishment* 454.1, *negative stimulus* 508.4

castigator *disapprover* 438.7, *punisher* 454.16

castigatory *censuring* 438.12, *punitive* 454.18

Castilian Breeds of Sheep 16

cast in a different mold *nonuniform* 734.5

casting *production* 136.14, 137.6, 522.1, *sculpture* 144.1, *fishing* 154.1, 154.13, *hunt* 385.3, *throwing* 696.3, *dispersion* 776.1

casting a shadow *darkening* 247.6

casting director *filmmaker* 137.14

casting nativities *divination* 358.2

casting rod *fishing tackle* 154.7

casting vote *influence* 512.1

cast in one's lot with *side with* 382.15, *join with* 827.15

cast in stone *permanent* 667.2, *make permanent* 667.5, *stable* 674.3, *make stable* 674.7

cast iron *construction material* 14.21, *hard substance* 542.3

cast-iron *strong-willed* 376.10, *hard* 542.5

castle *mansion* 60.5, *architectural structure* 134.4, *board games* 167.3, *play* 167.12, *fort* 419.13, *property* 470.1, *transfer* 685.8

castle (chess) *exchange* 673.5

Castleford ware Ceramics 129

castles in the air *or* **in Spain** *aspiration* 281.3, *figurative overestimation* 343.3, *idealism* 360.7, *illusion* 720.2

Castle walk Dances 135

castling *board games* 167.3

castling (chess) *exchange* 673.1

cast list *list of names* 785.7

cast loose *liberate* 831.6

cast lots *divine* 358.15

cast nativities *divine* 86.24

castoff *dirt* 112.5, *design and makeup* 174.8, *relinquished* 392.2, *unused thing* 394.4, *disused* 394.8, *residue* 750.2, *remaining* 750.7, *refuse* 802.5

cast off *sail* 150.29, *disavow* 190.18, *renounce* 392.4, *stop using* 394.10, *navigate* 690.15, *set out* 705.12, *exterminate* 709.22, *decrease* 747.7, *leave* 750.10, *unjoined* 753.9

castoffs *old clothes* 100.8

castoff skin *dirt* 112.5

cast off skin *shed* 614.21

cast of mind *inclination* 290.2, *attitude* 513.2

cast of thousands *cast* 136.26

cast one's ballot *vote* 382.16

cast one's eye(s) over *inspect* 242.22

cast one's eyes backward *look back* 651.18

cast one's net *hunt* 385.14

Castor Notable Friendships 62, Deities 82

castor Fabrics and Fibers 130

Castor and Pollux *twin* 789.5

castor oil *purgative* 115.7

Castor ware Ceramics 129

cast out *discarded* 383.8, *discard* 383.12, *exclude* 409.12, *replace* 574.17, *expel* 709.14, *let out* 709.26, *unjoined* 753.9, *eject* 764.8

cast pearls before swine *misspend* 96.17

castrate *practice livestock farming* 16.20, *make infertile* 23.9, *eunuch* 32.11, *take off* 749.7, *make useless* 802.12

castrated *undersexed* 20.20, *male* 32.16

castration *that which makes infertile* 23.4, *type of complex* 108.22, *helplessness* 515.3, *subtraction* 749.1, *separateness* 753.3

castrato *sexlessness* 20.13, *eunuch* 32.11, *voice* 141.5

Castries Countries 566

cast spells *bewitch* 86.25

cast steel *construction material* 14.21

cast the die *take a chance* 842.14

cast the I Ching *divine* 86.24

casual *stylish* 100.42, *perfunctory* 324.9, *indifferent* 326.5, *unrefined* 338.7, *informal* 407.6, 829.15, *nonobservant* 466.5, *at ease* 819.2, *chance* 842.10, *causeless* 842.11

casual clothes *informal clothes* 100.7, *informal clothing* 407.5

casual clothing *informal clothing* 407.5

casual labor *personnel* 123.16

casual laborer *laborer* 123.9

casually *dressily* 100.47, *informally* 407.11, 829.24, *inattentively* 466.13, *easily* 819.5, *by chance* 842.15

casually dressed *in dishabille* 100.40

casualness *dressing* 100.2, *indifference* 326.2, *informality* 407.1, 829.6, *nonobservance* 466.1, *chance* 842.1

casual relationship *relatedness* 727.1

casual sex *sexual intercourse* 20.9

casualty *dead person* 29.7, *misadventure* 848.2

casualty list *death count* 29.10

casual wear *informal clothes* 100.7

casuarina Trees and Shrubs 43

casuist *arguer* 319.6, *sophist* 330.6, *cunning person* 822.3

casuistical *sophistic* 330.7

casuistically *sophistically* 330.14

casuistry Branches of Philosophy 4, *lack of candor* 192.4, *sophistry* 330.1

casus belli *act of hostility* 63.4, *rivalry* 422.2, *divisiveness* 463.2

cat 35.11; *instrument of punishment* 454.13

cat [Inf] *composer* 141.9

catabolic *biochemical* 12.25, *physiological* 13.29, *disintegrating* 758.5

catabolically *biochemically* 12.27, *to pieces* 758.8

catabolism *metabolism* 12.21, *physiology* 13.13, *deconstruction* 758.2

catachresis *language error* 351.10

cataclasis *metamorphism* 8.35

cataclysm *natural violence* 520.3, *ruin* 523.4

cataclysmic *explosive* 520.6, *destructive* 523.8

cataclysmically *fluently* 570.13

cataclysmic variable *variable star* 7.11

catacomb *burial place* 31.7

catadioptric system *lens system* 10.22

catafalque *burial place* 31.7

catagelophobia Phobias 283

Catalanas Breeds of Fowl 16

catalectic *metrical* 139.20

catalepsy *trance* 108.18, *sleep* 415.5, *lack of motion* 678.1, *spasm* 684.8

cataleptic *sedentary* 678.5, *convulsive* 684.19

catalexis *meter* 139.10

catalog 767.7; *type of book* 174.3, *identify* 184.11, *record book* 185.5, *record* 185.13, *audit* 493.10, *division* 577.6, *itemize* 577.13, *systematize* 765.19, *categorize* 767.21, *class* 777.12, *table* 785.2, *list* 785.11

cataloged *itemized* 577.9, *grouped* 765.11, *categorized* 767.15, *listed* 785.9

cataloging *identification* 184.1, *identified* 184.9, *recordkeeping* 185.7, *grouping* 765.2, *categorization* 767.5, *listing* 785.8

Cataloging in Publication (CIP) data *book part* 174.5

catalog selling *selling* 482.1

catalog shopping *shopping* 481.3

catalpa Trees and Shrubs 43

catalysis 11.16; Branches of Chemistry 11, *systems and process control* 14.28, *deconstruction* 758.2

catalyst *catalysis* 11.16, *instrument* 511.2, *changer* 665.9

catalytic 11.30; *chemical* 11.24, 14.46

catalytically *chemically* 11.42, *electrochemically* 14.53, *to pieces* 758.8

catalytic reactions *chemical reaction thermodynamics* 14.29

catalyze *react* 11.38, *metabolize* 12.26, *deconstruct* 758.7

catalyzed *disintegrating* 758.5

catamaran *sailboat* 150.3, *canoe* 150.9, Sailing Ships and Boats 690, *twosome* 789.3

catamenia *bleeding* 25.10

catamenial *bleeding* 25.19

catamenial discharge *bleeding* 25.10

catamite *sexually immoral person* 432.8

cataphract *historical soldier* 77.8

cataplasm *paste* 561.4

cataplexy *trance* 108.18

catapult Historical Missile Weapons 78, *weapon* 78.1, *agent of destruction* 523.7, *throw* 696.17

cataract *blindness* 243.3, *murk* 248.2, *river turbulence* 570.5, *downflow* 714.3

catarrh *saliva* 25.9, *respiratory disease* 114.12

catastrophe *play part* 136.8, *disclosure* 180.1, *ruin* 523.4, *ending* 773.10, *misadventure* 848.2

catastrophic *detrimental* 446.8, *explosive* 520.6, *destructive* 523.8, *ending* 773.13

catastrophically *destructively* 523.18

catastrophism *geological time* 8.47, *evolution* 13.23

catatonia *psychosis* 110.3, *oblivion* 355.4, *lack of motion* 678.1

catatonic *mentally ill* 110.11, *desensitized* 213.5, *oblivious* 355.9, *sedentary* 678.5

catatonic stupor *mood disorder* 108.12

catatonic trance *trance* 108.18

catatonic-type schizophrenia *psychosis* 108.10

Catawba Rivers 570

catboat *sailboat* 150.3, Sailing Ships and Boats 690

cat burglar *thief* 479.8

catcall *gesture* 183.5, 183.17, *be loud* 232.8, *shrillness* 238.3, *be shrill* 238.9, *cry of disapproval* 239.7, *hiss* 239.17, *taunt* 436.6, 436.23, *show of disapproval* 438.6, *show disapproval* 438.21, *gesture of protest* 507.3

catcalling *hissing* 237.2, *taunting* 436.14

catch 154.9; Collective Names 59, *rowing techniques* 150.16, *row* 150.32, *kick* 155.12, Children's and Party Games 167, *represent* 187.10, *touch* 216.9, *hear* 228.13, *object of desire* 288.8, *lover* 299.11, *difficult question* 333.4, *detection* 345.2, *detect* 345.12, *acquisition* 467.4, *detain* 471.9, *takings* 477.8, *grind* 554.15, *cause to cease* 668.12, *make motionless* 678.8, *joint* 752.7, *fastener* 754.7, *celebrity* 799.6, *defect* 806.4, *trap* 813.1, 813.6, *stratagem* 822.2, *snag* 824.8, *obstacle* 826.2

Catch-22 *futility* 282.3, *difficult question* 333.4, *predicament* 725.3, 824.5, *trap* 813.1, *obstacle* 826.2

catchable *contagious* 114.26

catch a crab [Inf] *row* 150.32

catch a fly *play baseball* 147.9

catch a glimpse of *see* 242.20, *discover* 345.11

catch a likeness *represent* 187.10, *describe* 202.15

catchall *nonspecificness* 778.2

catch an infection *be unhealthy* 114.29

catch-as-catch-can *type of wrestling* 152.9, *wrestling* 152.18, *improvised* 396.4, *unconditional* 829.14, *chance* 842.10

catch at *be eager* 373.13

catch a Tartar *be unskillful* 128.8

catch a whiff of *smell* 224.7

catch cold *be cold* 218.13

catch crop *crop* 16.8

catcher *baseball team* 147.2

catcher's box *baseball field* 147.3

catcher's mask *baseball equipment* 147.4

catcher's mitt *baseball equipment* 147.4

catcher's sign *pitching terms* 147.5

catch exactly *represent* 187.10

catch fire *burn* 217.18

catch fish *fish* 154.14

catchfly Flowers 42

catch forty winks [Inf] *take it easy* 819.3

catch hell [Inf] *get into trouble* 824.20

catching *contagious* 114.26, *detection* 345.2, *appealing* 512.9

catching a crab [Inf] *rowing techniques* 150.16

catching glove *hockey clothing* 158.6

catching the eye *accentuated* 843.11

catch in the act *detect* 345.12

catch it [Inf] *be punished* 454.31, *get into trouble* 824.20

catchment area *running water* 8.10

catch napping *surprise* 292.9, *prepare* 657.14

catch off guard *surprise* 292.9

catch on *know* 48.24, 348.10, *understand* 295.6, 363.9, *find out* 345.13, *become a habit* 397.17

catch oneself doing *accustom oneself* 397.19

catch out [Brit] *surprise* 292.9, *trap* 813.6

catchpenny *bargain* 497.10, *cheap* 800.16

catchphrase *catchword* 5.22, *maxim* 177.1

catch red-handed *surprise* 292.9, *detect* 345.12

catch sight of *see* 242.20

catch something *be unhealthy* 114.29

catch some z's [Inf] *take it easy* 819.3

catch the drift of *understand* 363.9

catch the eye *be visible* 242.26, *attract attention* 323.12

catch the wind *attempt the impossible* 837.10

catch unawares *surprise* 292.9, *be unprepared* 389.14, *trap* 813.6

catch up *make haste* 818.5

catch up with *accelerate* 694.14

catch-waist *ice-skating* 162.9

catch-waist camel spin *ice-skating techniques* 162.16

catchword 5.22; *maxim* 177.1, *proclamation* 183.8

catchy *melodious* 140.26

cat cracking *industrial chemistry* 11.21

catechism *subject* 48.3, *belief system* 87.3, *questionnaire* 333.3

catechismic *problematic* 333.12

catechization *education* 48.1

catechize *question* 333.16

catecholamine *hormone* 12.16

catechu Tree Products 43

catechumen *religious person* 81.9, *convert* 670.6

categorical 767.16; *family* 65.6, *definite* 189.18, *emphatic* 200.3, *duty-bound* 641.38, *partial* 760.11, *grouped* 765.11, *classificatory* 777.9

categorical imperative *philosophical problem* 4.8

categorically *philosophically* 4.23, *definitely* 189.33, *taxonomically* 777.15

categoricalness *definiteness* 189.6

categorical proposition *philosophical term* 4.7

categorization 767.5; *identification* 184.1, *grouping* 765.2, *classification* 777.2

categorize 767.21; *identify* 184.11, *systematize* 765.19, *class* 777.12

categorize as or with *subsume* 763.7

categorized 767.15; *identified* 184.9, *grouped* 765.11, *classed* 777.11

categorizing *classification* 777.2

category 767.6; *family* 65.1, *topic* 328.1, *state* 725.1, *part* 760.1, *piece* 760.2, *position* 765.4, *class* 777.1

category mistake *philosophical problem* 4.8

category theory Branches of Mathematics 6

catenary *curve* 6.38, *arch* 134.5, *sinkage* 714.2, *consecutive* 774.7

catenate *concatenate* 774.13

catenation *consecutiveness* 774.1

cater *provision* 89.9, *feed* 90.41

cater-cornered *oblique* 607.6, *obliquely* 607.13

catered *supplied* 89.7

caterer 89.5; *provisioner* 89.4, *food provider* 90.6, *cook* 91.3

catering *provisioning* 89.2, 89.6, *cooking* 91.1

caterpillar *young animal* 26.4, *worm* 39.14, *larva* 40.9

caterpillars *pests and diseases* 17.12, Collective Names 59

cater to *pander to* 401.11

cater to or for *sell* 482.15, *serve* 825.29

caterwaul *be loud* 232.8, *cry* 239.1, *cry out* 239.13, *make an animal sound* 240.7

caterwauling *dissonance* 241.1

catfish *food fish and shellfish* 90.20

cat food *animal food* 90.2

catharsis *defecation* 25.3, *tragedy* 136.10, *aspect of fiction* 139.5, *removal* 709.5, *recuperation* 809.4

cathartic *fecal* 25.14, *purgative* 115.7, *medicinal* 115.15, *dramatic* 136.31, *expulsive* 709.11

cathartically *dramatically* 136.38, *expulsively* 709.29

cathectic energy *cathexis* 108.32

cathection *cathexis* 108.32

cathedral *place of worship* 83.8, *architectural structure* 134.4

cathedral city *city* 567.1

Catherine wheel *fire* 246.9, *wheel* 682.7

catheterization *therapy* 115.12

catheterize *purify* 111.19

cathexis 108.32

cathisophobia Phobias 283

cathode *electrical conduction* 10.33, *electrochemistry* 11.19, *electron tube* 14.40

cathode-ray tube (CRT) *electron tube* 14.40, *display* 15.9, *television set* 172.6, *power supplier* 514.14

cathodic *electrochemical* 11.33

Catholic *Christian* 81.10, *denominational* 81.23

catholic *undiscriminating* 338.5, *broad-minded* 592.9, *general* 778.9

catholically *broad-mindedly* 592.17

Catholic Charities *charitable organization* 305.4

Catholic Church Christianity 81.5

Catholicism Christianity 81.5

catholicism *generality* 778.1

catholicity *lack of discrimination* 338.1, *broad-mindedness* 592.3, *generality* 778.1

catholicness *broad-mindedness* 592.3

catholicon *remedy* 115.1

catholic school *religious school* 48.13

catholic tastes *lack of discrimination* 338.1

cathouse [Inf] *brothel* 432.5, *wicked place* 448.8

Cathy Famous Lovers 299

cation *ion* 10.54

catkin *flower head* 42.4

catlike *carnivorous* 35.26

cat lover *animal welfarist* 34.9

catnap *desensitization* 213.2, *sleep* 415.5, 415.14, *ease* 819.1

cat-o'-nine-tails *instrument of punishment* 454.13

catoptrophobia Phobias 283

cats Collective Names 59, Phobias 283

CAT scanner *imaging device* 242.11

cat's concert *dissonance* 241.1

cat's cradle Children's and Party Games 167, *braid* 609.3

cat's-eye *reflector* 242.10

cat show *display* 843.1

cat sitter *animal welfarist* 34.9

Catskill Mountains Mountains and Hills 569

cat's pajamas or **meow** [Inf], the *superior person* 445.7

cat's-paw *sycophant* 401.3, *assistant* 511.3, Knots, Bends, Hitches, Splices 754

catsup *sauce* 90.17, *red thing* 257.3

Cattalo Breeds of Cattle 16

Cattell's Infant Intelligence Scale Intelligence Tests 108

cattery *cage* 60.15, *shelter* 812.4

cattily *maliciously* 306.15

cattiness *malice* 306.2

cattish *carnivorous* 35.26

cattle *livestock* 16.11, *domestic animal* 34.3, Collective Names 59

cattle breeder *agriculturist* 16.14

cattle cake *animal food* 90.2

cattleman *agriculturist* 16.14

cattle ranch *farm* 16.2

cattle rustler *thief* 479.8

cattle rustling *stealing* 479.1

cattleya orchid Flowers 42

catty *carnivorous* 35.26, *malicious* 306.8, *defamatory* 440.9

catty-corner *obliquely* 607.13, *oblique* 607.6

catwalk *bridge* 551.10, 691.7

Caucasian *race* 1.5, *racial* 1.12, Breeds of Sheep 16

Caucasian Brown Breeds of Cattle 16

Caucasoid *racial* 1.12

Caucasoid race *race* 1.5

Caucasus Mountains Mountains and Hills 569

Cauchy–Schwarz inequality Mathematical Concepts 6

Cauchy sequence Mathematical Concepts 6

caucus *political organization* 50.4, *conference* 59.5, *election* 382.6

cauda *tail* 622.5

caudal *back* 622.6

caudal fin *fish characteristic* 38.8

Caudata *amphibian* 37.10

caudate *amphibian* 37.10, 37.14

caudex *stem* 41.5

caught *guilty* 450.6, *trapped* 813.5
caught both ways *endangered* 811.10
caught in the act *or* **red-handed** *or* **with one's pants down** [Inf] *guilty* 450.6
caught napping *surprised* 292.5, *unprepared* 389.5
caught unawares *surprised* 292.5, *unprepared* 389.5
cauliflower ear *ear* 228.2
cauliflower-eared *eared* 228.10
cauline *of stems* 41.17
caulk *repair* 809.10
Caurus *wind god* 9.16
causal 319.9, 511.5, 675.7; *apologetic* 329.10, *influential* 512.8, *repercussive* 774.8
causal body *spirit* 86.10
causality 10.66; *cause* 675.1, *consequence* 774.3
causal law *causality* 10.66
causally 675.12; *apologetically* 329.18, *influentially* 512.14
causal relationship *basis of supposition* 359.2
causal theory of perception *philosophical problem* 4.8
causation *motive* 178.5, *cause* 675.1
causative *causal* 675.7
causatively *causally* 675.12
cause 372.12, 675.1, 675.8; *interact* 10.73, *motive* 178.5, *motivate* 178.17, 508.9, *explanation* 319.4, *plea* 329.5, *intend* 361.15, *energy* 414.4, *defense* 441.2, *business* 509.3, *take action* 509.12, *instrumentality* 511.1, *be an instrument* 511.7, *influence* 512.1, *produce* 522.13, *basis* 601.3, *cause change* 665.16, *undertaking* 675.5, *come to be* 717.19, *inaugurate* 771.31
cause a death *cause adversity* 848.15
cause adversity 848.15
cause an accident *cause adversity* 848.15
cause anarchy *be anarchic* 51.8, *violate the law* 466.12
cause and effect *philosophical problem* 4.8, *causality* 10.66, *reason* 675.4, *consequence* 774.3
cause a sensation *arouse sensation* 212.11
cause a shambles *lay waste* 523.14
cause a traffic jam *block* 826.17
cause célèbre *marvel* 294.3
cause change 665.16
cause chaos *disorder* 625.4, *deconstruct* 758.7
cause confusion 51.9
caused 676.5; *apologetic* 329.10, *motivated* 508.8, *consequent* 770.9
caused by *caused* 676.5
cause desire 288.22
cause difficulties 824.22
cause disarray *cause confusion* 51.9
cause disbelief 88.9
cause dislike 291.16
cause disorder *cause confusion* 51.9, *cause mischief* 507.9
cause doubt *puzzle* 364.12
cause friction *hinder* 826.15
cause grief *cause adversity* 848.15
cause hate 300.12
cause ill health 114.30
cause joy 269.11
causeless 842.11
cause mischief 507.9
cause not to exist 718.14

cause of action *litigation* 54.1, *motive* 178.5
cause offense *antagonize* 63.12, *be discourteous* 411.7
cause of fire 217.10
cause of wonder 294.4; *marvel* 294.3
cause opposition *counteract* 510.7
cause panic *warn* 814.8
causerie *chat* 210.2
cause sorrow 209.9
cause the downfall of *knock down* 523.13
cause to adhere 755.10
cause to cease 668.12
cause to disappear 265.7
cause to flow 570.11
cause to know 348.13
cause trouble 824.21; *cause mischief* 507.9, *block* 826.17, *cause adversity* 848.15
cause turmoil *cause confusion* 51.9
causing death *killing* 30.1
caustic *lens system* 10.22, *on fire* 217.16, *resentful* 302.8, *bitter* 306.9, *satirical* 369.6, *defamatory* 440.9
caustically *resentfully* 302.22, *bitterly* 306.16, *satirically* 369.9
causticity *bitterness* 306.3
causticness *bitterness* 306.3
caustic reply *bitterness* 306.3
cauterize *burn* 217.18
cauterizing *heating* 217.12
caution 287.1, 287.15; *inside information* 170.4, *advice* 176.1, *advise* 176.9, *dissuasion* 179.1, *dissuade* 179.7, *carefulness* 325.1, *foresight* 357.1, *omen* 358.5, *hesitation* 693.5, *warning* 814.1, *warn* 814.8, *cunning* 822.1, *suspicion* 841.2
cautionarily *warningly* 814.11
cautionary *informative* 170.10, *advisory* 176.7, *dissuasive* 179.4, *predicting* 358.11, *warning* 814.6
cautioned *warned* 814.7
cautioner *warner* 814.5
cautious 287.6; *sparing with words* 208.6, *careful* 325.6, *foreseeing* 357.5, *unenthusiastic* 375.10, *traditional* 630.13, *hesitant* 693.9, *warned* 814.7, *cunning* 822.4
cautiously 287.16; *carefully* 325.13, *foresightedly* 357.10, *traditionally* 630.19, *slowly* 693.14
cautiousness *traditionality* 630.6, *hesitation* 693.5
Cauvery *Rivers* 570
cavalier *horse person* 159.14, *lover* 299.11, *discourteous* 411.5, *accompanier* 794.6
Cavalieri's principle Mathematical Concepts 6
Cavalier poets Western Literary Groups 139
cavalier servente [Ital] *lover* 299.11
cavalry *horse person* 159.14
cavalry horse *war-horse* 159.4
cavalryman *army combat specialist* 77.16, *horse person* 159.14
cavalry sword *sharp weapon* 78.6
cavatate *windsurf* 150.33
cavatation *windsurfing terms* 150.21
cavatina *song* 140.11
cave *groundwater* 8.11, *natural habitat* 60.16, *painting* 143.3, *hiding place* 181.2, *solitary place* 409.4, *hole* 583.4, *be convex* 634.7, *concave land* 635.2, *droop* 714.14
caveat *advice* 176.1, *warning* 814.1

caveat emptor! *buyer beware!* 481.22
caveator *warner* 814.5
cave dweller *primitive humanity* 18.4, *unsocial person* 409.5, *person of the past* 651.7, *prehistoric human* 653.7
cave exploring Hobbies and Pastimes 167
cave in *become smaller* 582.14, *be concave* 635.6, *droop* 714.14, *take apart* 753.16
cave in [Inf] *succumb* 421.7
cave-in *submission* 421.1, *squeeze* 582.3
caveman *macho man* 32.6, *person of the past* 651.7, *prehistoric human* 653.7
caveman *or* **cavewoman** *primitive humanity* 18.4
cavern *hole* 583.4, *concave land* 635.2
cavernous *spacious* 563.13, *deep* 598.9, *deep-sounding* 598.19, *concave* 635.5
cavernously *deep* 598.25, *concavely* 635.8
cavesson *riding equipment* 159.9
cavetto Architectural Elements 134
cavewoman *person of the past* 651.7
caviar *fish product* 38.9, *fish dish* 90.19
cavicorn *ungulate* 35.31
cavil *be dissatisfied* 274.7, *discuss* 329.12, *sophism* 330.2, *quibble* 330.13, *censure* 438.3, *criticize* 438.19
caviler *sophist* 330.6, *dissenter* 347.5
caviling *quibbling* 330.4, 330.9, *criticism* 438.4, *critical* 438.13
caving in [Inf] *submission* 421.1
cavity 635.3; *opening* 583.1, *crack* 587.2, *the depths* 598.2, *depression* 716.4
cavort *dance* 135.7
caw *hoarseness* 238.2, *sound hoarse* 238.8, *bird sound* 240.2, *make a bird sound* 240.8
cawing *hoarse* 238.5
cay *island* 572.2
cayenne pepper Herbs and Spices 91
Cayley–Hamilton theorem Mathematical Concepts 6
cayman *crocodile* 37.8
Cayman Islands Islands 572
cayuse *horse* 159.1
C clef *written music* 140.21
CD4 *blood* 555.4
CD8 *blood* 555.4
CD-ROM (compact disk read-only memory) *recording* 185.6
CdS meter *exposure equipment* 132.12
CE *one day* 639.20
ceanothus Flowers 42
cease 668.9, 773.20; *disappear* 265.5, *stop using* 394.10, *not act* 413.11, *pause* 415.15, *close down* 584.15, *interrupt* 604.16, *discontinue* 775.10
cease! 668.14
ceased 668.6; *discontinued* 775.8
cease fire *pause* 668.13
cease-fire *truce* 73.2, *treaty* 74.2, *delay* 658.3, *pause* 668.3
ceaseless *constant* 377.8, *continuing forever* 644.6, *continuous* 774.9, *recurrent* 797.13, *eternal* 798.7
ceaseless energy *energy* 414.4

ceaselessly *continually* 377.17, *continuously* 774.16
ceaselessness *constancy* 377.3, *continuity* 774.4
cease operation *interrupt* 604.16
cease publication *disappear* 265.5
cease resistance *capitulate* 421.6
cease to be *disappear* 265.5
cease to be *or* **live** *die* 29.17
cease to exist 718.13; *disappear* 265.5
cease trading *stop work* 668.11
cease work *withdraw* 705.9
ceasing *cessation* 668.1, 773.2
cedar Trees and Shrubs 43
cedar of Lebanon Trees and Shrubs 43
cede *relinquish* 392.3, *transfer property* 470.12, *give out* 472.12
cede to *follow* 765.12
cedilla Accents and Diacritical Marks 5
ceil *roof* 613.30
ceiling Architectural Elements 134, *fee* 494.3, *architectural summit* 600.4, *overhead covering* 613.11, *limit* 620.1, *flight* 689.5, *certain amount* 738.3
ceiling light *electric light* 246.6
celadon *green* 260.7
celadonite *green pigment* 260.3
celandine Flowers 42
Celebes Islands 572
celebrant *worshiper* 83.6, *ritualist* 85.14, *rejoicer* 279.3
celebrate 405.10, 406.10; *worship* 83.15, *perform rites* 85.18, *enjoy* 269.9, *rejoice* 279.5, *commemorate* 354.14, *greet* 410.11, *make important* 799.14
celebrate a birthday *commemorate* 663.12
celebrate a marriage *join in marriage* 64.20
celebrate an anniversary *commemorate* 663.12
celebrate a victory *be victorious* 845.16
celebrate communion *offer worship* 504.16
celebrated *publicized* 173.14, *known* 348.9
celebratedly *eminently* 370.7
celebrate mass *offer worship* 504.16
celebrating *worshipful* 83.12, *rejoicing* 279.1, *celebration* 405.1
celebration 405.1; *social gathering* 59.7, *act of worship* 83.2, *religious festival* 85.13, *rejoicing* 279.1, *day to remember* 354.5, *formal occasion* 406.4, *successfulness* 845.3
celebrative 405.9
celebrator *rejoicer* 279.3
celebratory *ritualistic* 85.15, *joyful* 269.6, *rejoicing* 279.4, *memorial* 354.10, *ceremonious* 404.23, *celebrative* 405.9
celebrity 799.6; *important person* 18.11, *idol* 83.5, *person of repute* 370.2, *paragon* 744.6, *fame* 845.2, *successful person* 845.6
celerity *swiftness* 694.1, *haste* 818.1
celery pine Trees and Shrubs 43
celery salt Herbs and Spices 91
celery seed Herbs and Spices 91
celesta Musical Instruments 142
celestial *astronomical* 7.33, *world soul* 82.3, *angel* 82.11, *heavenly* 82.22, *nonmaterial* 525.8
celestial being *world soul* 82.3
celestial bodies Fields of Measurement 589
Celestial City *heaven* 82.15

celestial equator *celestial sphere* 7.4

celestial kingdom *heaven* 82.15

celestial latitude *celestial sphere* 7.4

celestial longitude *celestial sphere* 7.4

celestially *astronomically* 7.36, *metaphysically* 525.13

celestial mechanics *astronomy* 7.1

celestial navigation *navigation* 690.5

celestial poles *celestial sphere* 7.4

celestial sphere 7.4

celibacy 67.1; *birth control* 23.5, *unsociability* 409.1, *abstinence* 455.2, *singleness* 788.6

celibate 67.4, 67.6; *chaste person* 431.6, *chaste* 431.10, *abstinent* 455.7, *single person* 788.7, *single* 788.16

celibately 67.12

celibate order *monasticism* 67.3

celibate person *celibate* 67.4

celibatic *celibate* 67.6

cell 13.15; *electrochemistry* 11.19, *living organism* 13.10, *cellular* 13.30, *living matter* 28.4, *place of worship* 83.8, *solitary place* 409.4, *instrument of punishment* 454.13, *power supplier* 514.14, *compartment* 578.2, *little thing* 580.3, *enclosed area* 619.2, *piece* 760.2, *private space* 812.2

cella *shrine* 83.10, Architectural Elements 134

cellar *room* 60.9, *cooking place* 91.4, *storeroom* 105.7, *hiding place* 181.2, *dark thing* 247.3, *base* 601.1

cellar door *means of entry* 706.6

cell biologist *life scientist* 13.26

cell biology 13.14; *histology* 13.4

cellblock *prison cell* 55.3

cell cycle *cell division* 13.17

cellhouse *prison cell* 55.3

cellist *player* 141.2

cell membrane *cell structure* 13.16

cell nucleus *cell structure* 13.16

cello Musical Instruments 142

cellophane *transparent thing* 249.4, *wrapping* 613.10

cell physiology *cell biology* 13.14

cell plate *cell structure* 13.16

cell respiration *respiration* 12.24

cells *matter* 524.4

cell structure 13.16; *cell biology* 13.14

cellular 13.30; *component* 760.12

cellular phone *telephone* 169.10

cellular physiology *biochemical applications* 14.30

cellular slime molds *fungi* 47.3

cellule *cell* 13.15

cellulite *fat* 579.8

celluloid *plastics* 104.6

cellulose *carbohydrate* 12.3, *polysaccharide* 12.5, *cell structure* 13.16, *timber* 43.3

cell wall *cell structure* 13.16

celosia Flowers 42

Celsius *scale* 589.9

Celsius scale *heat measurement* 217.2

Celtic *language family* 5.12

Celtic art Western Art Styles 133

Celtic twilight Western Literary Groups 139

cement *lithify* 8.66, *construction material* 14.21, *masonry* 14.22, *building materials* 104.2, *industrial ceramics* 129.6, *make ceramics*

129.10, *solid body* 540.4, *be dense* 540.8, *hard substance* 542.3, *paving* 613.14, *pave* 613.32, *intertwine* 752.19, *adhesive* 755.3, *cause to adhere* 755.10

cement a relationship *come together* 757.10

cementation *petrogenesis* 8.31, *adhesion* 755.1

cemented *tied* 752.13, *adhering* 755.7

cement kiln *ceramic workshop and tools* 129.8

cemeteries Phobias 283

cemetery *burial place* 31.7, *resting place* 668.5

cenobite *celibate* 67.4, *religious* 84.9, *unsocial person* 409.5

cenobitic *monastic* 67.8

cenophobia Phobias 283

cenotaph *funeral object* 31.6, *burial place* 31.7

Cenozoic *primal* 653.14

cense *perfume* 226.6

censer *sacred object* 83.11, *incense* 226.3

censor 503.10; *defense mechanism* 108.23, *purify* 111.19, *conceal* 181.12, *keep secret* 182.11, *obliterate* 186.8, *judge* 341.5, 341.10, *suppress* 424.9, *moralist* 431.8, *moralize* 431.14, *disapprover* 438.7, *mitigate* 521.9, *limit* 620.7, *changer* 665.9, *change for the worse* 665.18, *subtract* 749.6, *eject* 764.8, *one who restrains* 830.7, *restrain* 830.12, *abrogator* 834.4, *cancel* 834.6

censored 503.7; *concealed* 181.8, *secret* 182.8, *obliterated* 186.4, *suppressed* 424.6, *moralistic* 431.12, *restrained* 830.9, *canceled* 834.5

censorial *severe* 424.5, *restraining* 830.8

censorially *restrainedly* 830.18

censoring *restraining* 830.8

censorious *judging* 341.7, *critical* 418.16, 438.13, *severe* 424.5, *moralistic* 431.12, *troublesome* 824.13, *restraining* 830.8

censoriously *moralistically* 431.16, *disapprovingly* 438.23, *perversely* 824.27, *restrainedly* 830.18

censoriousness *criticism* 438.4

censorship 111.5, 503.4; *war measures* 76.18, *verbal concealment* 181.3, *secrecy* 182.1, *obliteration* 186.1, *suppression* 424.2, *self-righteousness* 431.7, *limit* 620.1, *ejection* 764.2, *restraint* 830.1, *cancellation* 834.1

censurable *unforgivable* 430.16, *guilty* 450.6

censure 438.3; *dissatisfaction* 274.1, *dislike* 300.2, *hate* 300.11, *vilification* 301.2, *vilify* 301.15, *judgment* 341.1, *judge* 341.10, *personal attack* 418.8, *criticize* 418.26, *condemn* 438.18, *guilt* 450.1

censured *hated* 300.9, *censuring* 438.12, *guilty* 450.6

censurer *disapprover* 438.7

censuring 438.12

census *numeration* 6.10, *questionnaire* 333.3, *count* 784.3, *list of names* 785.7

census-taker *counter* 784.6

census-taking *calculative* 784.7

cent *US coinage* 484.10, *little bit* 800.4

cental General Units 589

centare General Units 589

Centaur *or* **Centaurus** Constellations 7

centaur Legendary Creatures 360

centavo *national coins* 484.11

centenarian *older person* 27.7, *hundreds* 792.9, *hundredth* 792.20

centenary *day to remember* 354.5, *anniversary* 663.4, *anniversarial* 663.8, *hundreds* 792.9, *hundredth* 792.20

centennial *day to remember* 354.5, *anniversary* 405.5, 663.4, *anniversarial* 663.8, *hundreds* 792.9, *hundredth* 792.20

centennially *cyclically* 663.15, *fivefold* 792.26

centennium *hundreds* 792.9

center 612.1, 612.10; *political party* 50.5, *armed force* 77.10, *basketball team* 148.2, *offense* 155.6, *play offense* 155.18, *hockey player* 158.8, *politically moderate* 521.4, *interior* 611.1, 611.7, *parts of a circle* 631.4, *center of attraction* 700.7, *focus* 702.5, 702.11, *essential content* 723.2, *medium* 742.2, *middle* 772.1, 772.9, *place in the middle* 772.18, *gist* 799.4

center about *or* **around** *center* 612.10

center back *soccer participant* 163.4

centerboard *sailboat* 150.3

center circle *stadium* 163.2

center court *basketball court* 148.3

centered 612.9; *arch* 134.5

centered dot Reference Signs 183

center field *baseball field* 147.3

center fielder *baseball team* 147.2

center forward *hockey player* 158.8, *soccer participant* 163.4

center half *hockey player* 158.8, *soccer participant* 163.4

centering *centrality* 612.5, *focus* 702.5, *convergent* 702.7

center lane *middle way* 772.3

center line *hockey areas* 158.2, *badminton terms* 165.11

center mark *tennis court* 165.3

center of activity 612.4

center of attention *center of attraction* 700.7

center of attention *or* **attraction** *focus* 612.3

center of attraction 700.7

center of effort (CE) *windsurfing terms* 150.21

center of gravity *mass* 10.8, *load* 14.14, *focus* 612.3

center of interest *focus* 612.3

center of lateral resistance (CLR) *windsurfing terms* 150.21

center of mass *mass* 10.8

center of rotation *or* **revolution** *center* 612.1

center of symmetry *geometric figure* 6.39, *operation of symmetry* 626.2

center on *focus on* 328.9, *center* 612.10, *follow from* 676.9, *place in the middle* 772.18

centerpiece *ornament* 532.7, *focus* 612.3, *center of attraction* 700.7

center-pin *fishing* 154.13

center-pin reel *fishing tackle* 154.7

center point *center* 612.1

center spot *billiards* 149.1, *hockey areas* 158.2

center stage *stage* 136.18, *onstage* 136.39

center zone *hockey areas* 158.2

centesimal *hundredth* 792.20

centesimo *national coins* 484.11

centi Decimal Prefixes 589

centiare General Units 589

centigrade *hundreds* 792.9

centigrade scale *heat measurement* 217.2, *scale* 589.9

centime *national coins* 484.11

centimeter *short distance* 586.2, *hundreds* 792.9

centimeter-gram-second Scientific and Technical Units 589

centipede *hundreds* 792.9

centner Scientific and Technical Units 589

cento Poem or Verse Forms 139

centophobia Phobias 283

central 612.6; *curvilinear* 6.78, *focused* 328.6, *causal* 511.5, 675.7, *interior* 611.7, *internal* 611.8, *medium* 742.6, *elite* 744.12, *middle* 772.9, *essential* 799.10

Central African Republic Countries 566

Central America *landmass* 572.1

Central and Upper Belgian Breeds of Cattle 16

central casting *filmmaker* 137.14

central city *urban area* 567.10

central heating *heater* 217.3

Central Intelligence Agency (CIA) *law enforcement agency* 53.7, *secretiveness* 182.3

centralism *centrality* 612.5

centrality 612.5

centralization *management system* 126.3, *planning* 387.8, *centrality* 612.5, *combination* 757.1, *organization* 767.3

centralize 612.11; *plan* 387.12, *focus* 702.11, *combine* 757.9, *organize* 767.19

centralized *governmental* 49.24, *centered* 612.9, *combinatory* 757.6

centrally 612.12; *thematically* 328.13, *internally* 611.18, *causally* 675.12, *medianly* 742.12, *predominantly* 744.21, *in the middle* 772.21

centrally heated *heated* 217.15

centrally planned economy *economics* 56.1

central nervous system *nervous system* 19.14

central office *center of activity* 612.4

Central Park *New York* 567.6

central position *compromise* 461.1

central processing unit (CPU) *computer part* 15.4

Central Pyrenean Breeds of Sheep 16

Central Time *time zone* 646.5

centric *or* **centrical** *centered* 612.9

centrically *centrally* 612.12

centricity *centrality* 612.5

centrifugal *avoiding* 386.9, *directional* 677.13, *rotary* 682.12, *abducent* 701.5, *divergent* 703.6, 776.11

centrifugal force *force* 10.9, 514.8, *repulsion* 701.1

centrifugally *in motion* 677.19

centrifugation *biochemical applications* 14.30, *turning* 682.3

centrifuge *rotator* 682.8

centrifuge *or* **centrifugalize** *process* 14.50

centrifugence *parting* 703.2

centripetal *central* 612.6, *directional* 677.13, *rotary* 682.12, *magnetic* 700.9, *convergent* 702.7

centripetal force *force* 10.9, 514.8, *pulling power* 700.2

centripetally *in motion* 677.19, *attractionally* 700.13

centrist *moderate person* 772.8

centroid *triangle* 6.41
centrolineal *convergent* 702.7
centromere *cell division* 13.17
centrosome *cell structure* 13.16, *cell division* 13.17
cents-off coupons *discounter* 497.7
centuple *hundreds* 792.9, *hundredth* 792.20, *quintuple* 792.23
centuplicate *hundreds* 792.9, *hundredth* 792.20, *quintuple* 792.23
centurion *hundreds* 792.9
century *historical soldier* 77.8, *time period* 641.2, *hundreds* 792.9
century [Inf] *US coinage* 484.10
century plant Flowers 42
cephalin *fat* 12.7
Cephalochordata *protochordate* 39.4
cephalochordate *protochordate* 39.4, *invertebrate* 39.20
cephalometer Fields of Measurement 589
cephalometry Fields of Measurement 589
cephalopod *mollusk* 39.13
Cephalopoda *mollusk* 39.13
cephalopodan *molluscan* 39.23
cephalopodic *molluscan* 39.23
cephalopodous *molluscan* 39.23
Cepheid variable *variable star* 7.11
Cepheus Constellations 7
ceramic 129.9; *chemical compound* 11.4, *chemical* 14.46, *sculptural* 144.7
ceramic armor *modern armor* 419.7
ceramic composites *chemical process industries* 14.26
ceramicist *ceramist* 129.7
ceramic process 129.5
ceramics 129.1; *chemical process industries* 14.26, *craft* 133.2
ceramics manufacturing *chemical process industries* 14.26
ceramic tile *wall covering* 613.12
ceramic ware *ceramics* 129.1
ceramic workshop and tools 129.8
ceramist 129.7; *visual artist* 133.6
cerate *balm* 115.11
cerated *oily* 562.11
Cerberus Legendary Creatures 360, *watchdog* 810.14
cercaria *invertebrate larva* 39.19
cereal 90.12; *horticultural* 17.14, *plant* 41.2, *cereal grass* 45.4
cereal bowl *crockery* 578.16
cereal grass 45.4; *grass* 45.1
cereals *seed plant* 41.3
cerebellum *head* 19.6, *nervous system* 19.14
cerebral *internal* 19.23, *intellectual* 315.8, *thoughtful* 317.5, *ideational* 327.9
cerebral death *mortality* 29.2
cerebral edema *climbing dangers* 161.5
cerebrally *mentally* 315.13
cerebral palsy *neurological disease* 114.20
cerebral spinal fluid (CSF) *test* 107.10
cerebrate *think* 317.9
cerebration *thought* 317.1
cerebroside *fat* 12.7
cerebrum *head* 19.6, *nervous system* 19.14, *brain* 315.6
cerecloth *funeral object* 31.6
cerements *funeral object* 31.6, *graveclothes* 100.25

ceremonial 404.11; *ritual* 85.1, *ritualistic* 85.15, *ceremonious* 404.23, 406.7, *commemoration* 405.2, *celebrative* 405.9, *formal occasion* 406.4, *formal* 406.6, *performance* 465.2
ceremonial attire *vestment* 84.11
ceremonial function *ceremony* 405.3
ceremonialism *ritualism* 85.2, *formalism* 406.2
ceremonialist *ritualist* 85.14
ceremonially *ritually* 85.21, *ceremoniously* 404.38, *formally* 406.12
ceremonious 404.23, 406.7; *majestic* 404.21, *formal* 406.6, *good-mannered* 410.7, *respectful* 435.6
ceremoniously 404.38; *majestically* 404.36, *formally* 406.12, *genteelly* 410.14
ceremoniousness *ceremonial* 404.11, *formality* 406.1
ceremony 405.3; *ritual* 85.1, *custom* 397.4, *ceremonial* 404.11, *formal occasion* 406.4, *performance* 465.2, *etiquette* 534.3, *manifestation* 843.2
cereous *oily* 562.11
Ceres Planets and Their Satellites 7, Deities 82
cerise *red* 257.5
cerium Chemical Elements and Common Allotropes 11
CERN *nuclear power agencies* 514.11
cerography *engraving* 144.3
ceroplastic *sculptural* 144.7
ceroplastics *sculpture* 144.1
certain 840.7; *legitimate* 52.10, *believing* 87.6, *inevitable* 95.14, *definite* 189.18, *emphatic* 200.3, *demonstrable* 331.12, *verified* 336.7, *evidential* 339.8, *known* 348.9, *expecting* 356.4, *expected* 356.5, *intelligible* 363.5, *correct* 429.8, *guaranteeing* 458.9, *auspicious* 458.10, *guaranteed* 464.6, *predictable* 650.7, *determined* 674.5, *quantitative* 738.6, *plural* 793.6, *safe* 810.16, *convinced* 840.8, *identifiable* 843.10, *successful* 845.8
certain amount 738.3
certain cure *remedy* 115.1
certainly 719.14, 840.15; *legitimately* 52.19, *necessarily* 95.22, *definitely* 189.33, *earnestly* 278.10, *demonstrably* 331.22, *assuredly* 336.12, *as evidence* 339.15, *correctly* 429.16, *as promised* 458.16, *auspiciously* 458.17, *truly* 721.27, *inevitably* 840.17
certainly! 840.18; *yes!* 189.36
certainly not! *no!* 190.28
certain places Phobias 283
certainty 840.1; *probability* 6.59, *legal power* 52.2, *belief* 87.1, *inevitability* 95.6, 840.5, *horse racing* 159.10, *definiteness* 189.6, *demonstrability* 331.5, *proof* 339.2, *expectation* 356.1, *prediction* 358.1, *intelligibility* 363.1, *right* 429.2, *safety* 810.1, *conviction* 840.2, *good chance* 842.6
certifiable *verifiable* 336.5
certifiable [Inf] *insane* 110.9
certifiably *verifiably* 336.11
certificate 185.2; *document* 170.3, *means of identification* 184.3, *authorization* 340.4, *prize* 453.2, *promise* 464.2, *paper money*

484.14, *permit* 502.3, *permission* 735.9
certificate of deposit account *funds* 484.6, *deposit* 487.3
certificate of exemption *license* 434.4
certification *attestation* 189.2, *verification* 336.1, *authorization* 340.4, *yes* 346.2, *approval* 437.1, *authentication* 721.8, *consent* 735.8
certificatory *attestive* 189.12
certified *mentally ill* 110.11, *attested* 189.13, *verified* 336.7, *authorized* 340.8, *approved* 437.8, *guaranteeing* 458.9, *guaranteed* 464.6, *authenticated* 721.17, *consenting* 735.18, *permitting* 735.19, *certain* 840.7
certified check *paper money* 484.14
certified mail *postal service* 169.5
certified public accountant (CPA) *accountant* 493.6
certifier *affirmer* 189.9
certify 110.14, 464.11; *inform* 170.11, *attest* 189.22, *verify* 336.8, *prove* 339.14, *permit* 340.12, *approve* 437.14, *guarantee* 458.13, *establish reality* 719.12, *authenticate* 721.24, *consent* 735.28, *make certain* 840.14
certifying *attestive* 189.12
certiorari *legal process* 54.3
certitude *conviction* 840.2
certosina work *decorative woodwork* 131.2
cerulean *blue* 261.5
cerulean blue *blue pigment* 261.2
cervical *reproductive* 21.11
cervical cancer *cancer* 114.15
cervical smear *diagnostic procedure* 107.11
cervid *hoofed mammal* 35.16, *ungulate* 35.31
Cervidae *hoofed mammal* 35.16
cervine *ungulate* 35.31
cervix *organs of reproduction* 21.9, *contracted thing* 582.5
cesious *bluish* 261.6
cesium Chemical Elements and Common Allotropes 11
cesium clock Timepieces and Timers 646
cespitose *of fungi* 47.19
cessation 668.1, 773.2; *truce* 73.2, *obliteration* 186.1, *disappearance* 265.1, *inactivity* 415.1, *closure* 584.1, *interruption* 604.4, *lack of motion* 678.1, *end* 773.1, *deliverance* 817.1, *termination* 834.2
cession *relinquishment* 392.1, *submission* 421.1
cesspit *unpleasant-smelling thing* 227.2
cesspool *unpleasant-smelling thing* 227.2, *place for waste* 802.6
cestoid *wormlike* 39.24
Cetacea *marine mammal* 35.12
cetacean 35.27; *marine mammal* 35.12
cetaceous *cetacean* 35.27
cete Collective Names 59
ceteris paribus [L] *as good as* 740.14
Cetus Constellations 7
Ceylon Islands 572
Ceylon tea *tea* 93.7
cha-cha Dances 139
chaconne Musical Forms 140
Chad Countries 566, Lakes 568
chaetophobia Phobias 283
chafe *feel pain* 215.8, *heat* 217.17,

irritate 302.16, *grinding* 554.3, *grind* 554.15
chafer *pest* 40.5
chaff *cereal grass* 45.4, *taunt* 436.6, *casing* 613.9, *residue* 750.2, *little bit* 800.4, *refuse* 802.5
chaffer [Arch] *bargain* 480.20
chaffing *taunting* 436.14
chafing *grinding* 554.3, *rough* 554.11
Chagas' disease *tropical disease* 114.10
chagrin *disappointment* 293.1, *humiliation* 298.5, *indignity* 436.7, *tumult* 684.2
chagrined *disappointed* 293.4, *humiliated* 298.12
chain *polymer* 11.9, *instrument of punishment* 454.13, *jewelry* 532.6, *mountain range* 569.3, General Units 589, *measuring instrument* 589.12, *means of connection* 754.4, *tackle* 754.6, *bind* 754.14, *series* 770.3, *consecutively* 774.1, *concatenate* 774.13, *restrain* 826.19, *restrain someone* 830.17
chain armor *historic armor* 419.8
chained *stabilized* 674.4, *bound* 754.12, *blocked* 826.13
Chained Lady Constellations 7
chain gang *imprisonment* 454.2
chain gang [Inf] *football player* 155.15
chain-gang member *prisoner* 55.7
chainguard *bicycle part* 687.11
chain letter *solicitation* 505.4
chain mail *historic armor* 419.8, *safety device* 810.15
chain of office *insignia* 184.5
chain plates *sailboat parts and accessories* 150.4
chain printer *hardcopy device* 15.10
chain-reacting pile *nuclear power production* 514.10
chain reaction *nuclear fission* 10.60, *chemical reaction* 11.8, *nuclear power* 514.9, *consequence* 774.3
chains *stadium* 155.3, *restraint* 826.8, *means of restraint* 830.6
chain saw *hand tool* 103.3
chainsaw mortiser *woodworking tool* 131.6
chain shot *historical ammunition* 78.12
chain-smoke *smoke* 121.38
chain-smoking *smoking* 121.22
chain stitch *knitting* 130.7
chain store *store* 483.8
chain together *link* 752.18
chain up or **down** *restrain someone* 830.17
chair *instructorship* 48.5, *position of authority* 52.4, *company leader* 68.8, *furniture* 101.1, *manager* 126.7, *direct* 126.11, *moderate* 521.7
chair, the *instrument of execution* 454.15
chairing *managerial* 126.9
chairlift *ski run* 162.2, *cableway* 691.11, *lifter* 715.5
chairman *company leader* 68.8, *manager* 126.7, *influential person* 512.5
chairman of the board *company leader* 68.8
chairman of the Federal Reserve System *treasurer* 484.18
chairmanship *position of authority* 52.4, *directorship* 126.5

chairperson *company leader* 68.8, *manager* 126.7, *moderator* 521.2

chair socket *fighting chair* 154.8

chairwoman *company leader* 68.8, *manager* 126.7, *influential person* 512.5

chaise longue *couch* 101.7

chakram *Historical Missile Weapons* 78

chalaza *eggs* 36.5

chalcogen *chemical element* 11.3

chalcography *engraving* 144.3

Chalcolithic *primal* 653.14

chalet *property* 470.1

chalice *sacred object* 83.11

chalk *material* 143.9, *draw* 143.13, *billiards* 149.1, *climbing equipment* 161.4, *identify* 184.11, *white thing* 253.4, *powder* 553.9

chalk a stick *play* 149.7

chalk bag *climbing equipment* 161.4

chalkily *whitely* 253.13

chalkiness *whiteness* 253.1, *powderiness* 553.3

chalklike *powdery* 553.19

chalk mark *grip* 151.4

chalk out *sign* 183.19, *plan out* 387.14

chalky 8.59; *white* 253.7, *powdery* 553.19

challenge *philosophical investigation* 4.4, *philosophize* 4.19, *disbelieve* 88.8, *participate* 145.6, *negation* 190.1, *negate* 190.16, *logical argument* 329.2, *discuss* 329.12, *question* 333.1, *questioning* 333.3, *confuse* 333.20, *undertake* 391.7, *disobedience* 416.2, *act of defiance* 416.3, *defy* 416.7, *be insubordinate* 416.8, *resistance* 417.1, *resist* 417.10, *counterattack* 418.24, *contend* 422.22, *pick a fight* 463.10, *protest* 507.1, 507.7, *motivate* 508.9, *be in front* 621.13, *objection* 828.2, *object* 828.18

challenged *negated* 190.10, *problematic* 328.7, *questioned* 333.15, *resistant* 417.6, *defending* 419.17, *motivated* 508.8

challenge fate *face danger* 811.12

challenge for cause *jury selection* 54.14

challenger *sportsman* 145.4, *boxer* 152.8, *negator* 190.8, *attempter* 390.3, *defiant person* 416.4, *contender* 422.13

challenging *problematic* 328.7, 333.12, 824.11, *arguable* 329.8, *defying* 416.6, *resistant* 417.6, *counterattacking* 418.15, *contending* 422.19, *protesting* 507.5, *motivational* 508.7, *difficult* 824.9, *discordant* 828.12

challengingly *problematically* 328.12, *questionably* 333.22, *in defiance* 416.10, *resistingly* 417.14

challis *Fabrics and Fibers* 130

chalone *secreted substance* 24.2

chalumeau *Musical Instruments* 142

Chamaeleon *Constellations* 7

Chambal *Rivers* 570

chamber *room* 60.9, *storehouse* 105.8, *private space* 812.2

chamber concert *performance* 141.8

chamber group *instrumental group* 141.3

chamberlain *domestic servant* 69.7

chambermaid *domestic servant* 69.7

chamber music *classical music* 140.2

chamber of commerce *economic zone* 480.4

chamber orchestra *instrumental group* 141.3, *collection* 757.3

chamber pot *place for excretion* 25.11, *basin* 578.12

chambray *Fabrics and Fibers* 130

Chameleon *Constellations* 7

chameleon *lizard* 37.5, *variegated thing* 263.5, *vacillator* 378.3

chameleonic *variegated* 263.6, *changeable* 666.3

chamfer *Architectural Elements* 134

chamois *leather* 104.7, *smoother* 545.2

chamois or **chammy** or **shammy** *cleaning cloth* 111.11

chamomile or **camomile** *Flowers* 42, *Herbs and Spices* 91

chamomile tea *tea* 93.7

champ *chew* 92.22, *boxer* 152.8, **champ** [Inf] *expert* 68.13, *victor* 845.7

champac *Trees and Shrubs* 43

champaca *Trees and Shrubs* 43

champagne *wine* 93.11, *yellow* 259.7

champaign *grassland* 45.2

champignon *mushroom* 47.2

champing *eating* 92.1

champing at the bit *eager* 373.8

Champion *Notable Horses* 159

champion *expert* 68.13, *excellent* 68.16, *titleholder* 72.4, *prizewinner* 127.8, *boxer* 152.8, *combat* 152.17, *defender* 419.14, *plead for* 419.25, *approver* 437.7, *approve* 437.14, *vindicator* 441.5, *justify* 441.12, *superior person* 445.7, *supporter* 605.9, *give moral support* 605.18, *paragon* 744.6, *unbeatable* 744.13, *best* 805.9, *protector* 810.11, *protect* 810.21, *advise* 825.27, *victor* 845.7

championed *approved* 437.8

championing *recommending* 437.1

championship *honor* 72.3, *contest* 422.4, *approval* 437.1, *moral support* 605.7, *patronage* 825.9, *successful thing* 845.5

championship fight *boxing* 152.2

Champlain *Lakes* 568

champlevé *Ceramics* 129

chance 838.4, 842.1, 842.10, 842.12; *probability* 6.59, 838.1, *doubt* 333.19, *invent* 335.13, *tentative offer* 504.2, *opportunity* 583.8, 659.2, *possibility* 836.1, *unexpectedness* 839.2, *unexpected* 839.6, *capriciousness* 841.8, *risk* 841.21, *take a chance* 842.14

chanced *tested* 335.10

chance discovery *luck* 842.3

chance encounter *luck* 842.3

chance hit *luck* 842.3

chance in a million *improbability* 839.1

chance it *take a chance* 842.14

chancel *church architecture* 134.11

chancellor *educator* 48.4, *person in authority* 52.7, *leader* 68.3, *educational leader* 68.11, *person in command* 425.5

chance meal *meal* 92.8

chance meeting *luck* 842.3

chance upon 842.13

chance upon or on *find* 565.11

chancing *chance* 842.1

chancing upon *locating* 565.3

chancre *sexually transmitted disease (STD)* 114.17

chancy *questionable* 333.13,

original 335.9, *dangerous* 811.7, *capricious* 841.16, *chance* 842.10

chandelle *flight maneuver* 689.6

change 484.3, 512.12, 665.1, 665.14, 841.20; *interact* 10.73, *wear* 100.46, *percussion instrument* 142.5, *ice-skating* 162.32, *Phobias* 283, *modification* 340.5, *modify* 340.13, *vacillate* 378.8, *caprice* 381.1, *be capricious* 381.6, *bank* 484.26, *undress* 614.18, *new start* 652.5, *make new* 652.20, *irregularity* 664.1, *be irregular* 664.5, *be changeable* 666.5, *conversion* 670.1, *convert* 670.11, *substitution* 672.1, *exchange* 673.1, *be in motion* 677.14, *make unlike* 734.9, *unbalance* 741.8, *refurbish* 809.11

changeability *capriciousness* 381.2, *changeableness* 666.1

changeable 665.11, 666.3; *variegated* 263.6, *inconstant* 378.6, *capricious* 381.4, 841.16, *irregular* 664.3, *convertible* 670.9, *in exchange* 673.3, *inconsistent* 732.7

changeableness 666.1; *inconstancy* 378.2, *capriciousness* 381.2, 841.8, *irregularity* 664.1, *turbulence* 684.3, *inconsistency* 732.3

changeably 665.22, 666.7; *irregularly* 664.6, *in exchange* 673.6, *inconsistently* 732.16, *capriciously* 841.26

change address *settle* 565.10

change around *cause change* 665.16

change back 665.19; *restore* 671.10

change by degrees 739.8

change color *grow* 43.15

change countenance *lose color* 252.7

change course *change* 665.14, *navigate* 690.15

change course or **the course of** *divert* 698.16

changed 665.10; *modified* 340.9, *renewed* 652.14, *converted* 670.7, *substituted* 672.4, *exchanged* 673.4

changed beyond recognition *converted* 670.7

change direction 703.15; *change* 665.14, *be in motion* 677.14, *deviate* 698.15

changed meaning *type of meaning* 361.4

change down *be on the track* 146.11

changed person *convert* 670.6

change for *substitute* 672.5

change for the better 665.4, 665.17; *improvement* 807.1, *improve* 807.15

change for the better or **the worse** *change* 512.12

change for the worse 665.5, 665.18

changeful *irregular* 664.3, *changeable* 665.11, 666.3, *circumstantial* 726.8

changefully *relatively* 726.17

changefulness *changeableness* 666.1

change gradually *change by degrees* 739.8

change hands *transfer property* 470.12, *be transferred* 470.13, *be sold* 482.22

change key *change* 665.14

changeless 640.4; *permanent* 667.2, *stable* 674.3, *regular* 730.12, *monotonous* 797.12

changelessly *permanently* 667.6, *regularly* 730.21

changelessness *timelessness* 640.1, *permanence* 667.1, *stability* 674.1, *regularity* 730.6

changeling *substitute* 672.2

change loop *ice-skating techniques* 162.16

change money *exchange* 673.5

change moods *equivocate* 380.8

change of belief *change of mind* 665.6

change of clothes *alteration* 665.2

change of course *alteration* 665.2

change of direction *vacillation* 380.3, *alteration* 665.2

change of hands *transfer of property* 470.4

change of heart *confession* 451.2, *alteration* 665.2, *change of mind* 665.6

change of key *alteration* 665.2

change of life *infertile state* 23.3, *middle age* 27.4

change of mind 665.6; *vacillation* 380.3, *caprice* 381.1, *alteration* 665.2

change of mood *vacillation* 380.3

change of opinion *change of mind* 665.6

change of ownership *transfer of property* 470.4

change-of-pace *pitching terms* 147.5

change of place *alteration* 665.2

change of position *alteration* 665.2, *motion* 677.1

change of purpose *vacillation* 380.3

change of scene *refresher* 94.2

change of scenery *alteration* 665.2

change of voice *alteration* 665.2

change one's address *move* 677.15

change one's belief *change* 665.14

change one's clothes *wear* 100.46, *undress* 614.18, *change* 665.14

change one's expression *change* 665.14

change one's heart *change* 665.14

change one's mind *hesitate* 378.10, *equivocate* 380.8, *renounce* 392.4, *change* 665.14, *be irresolute* 666.6

change one's opinion *change* 665.14

change one's tune *equivocate* 380.8, *change* 665.14

change one's ways *be converted* 670.12

changeover *relay racing* 166.5, *change* 665.1, *conversion* 670.1, *succession* 770.2

change over *change* 665.14

change ownership *be transferred* 470.13

change places *change* 665.14, *exchange* 673.5, *be in motion* 677.14, *move* 677.15

change position *change* 665.14, *be in motion* 677.14

change purse *money storage* 484.20

changer 665.9; *converter* 670.5

change ringing *percussion instrument* 142.5, *change* 665.1

change sides *be irresolute* 378.9

change the face of *transform* 670.13

change the rules *be irresolute* 666.6

change the station *or* **channel** tune 172.14

change the tires *be on the track* 146.11

change-up *pitching terms* 147.5

changing *converting* 670.8

changing back *restoration* 671.2

changing down *automobile racing terms* 146.3

changing voice *speech difficulty* 206.1

Chang Jiang *Rivers* 570

channel 691.10; *computing terms* 15.22, *direct* 126.11, *information source* 170.6, *be an instrument* 511.7, *tunnel* 551.11, *river parts* 570.3, *flow* 570.10, *inlet* 572.9, *narrow place* 593.2, *furrow* 638.1, 638.5, *transfer* 685.8, *thoroughfare* 692.6, *entrance* 706.5, *way out* 707.2

Channel Islands *Islands* 572

channel-surf [Inf] *tune* 172.14

Channel Tunnel *tunnel* 691.6

Chanothar *Breeds of Sheep* 16

chanson *Poem or Verse Forms* 139, *song* 140.11

chant *ritual music* 85.9, *follow rites* 85.19, *spell* 86.8, *sacred music* 140.3, *song* 140.11, *sing* 141.16, *speak in a particular way* 205.18

Chantecler *Breeds of Fowl* 16

chanter *singer* 141.4, *woodwind* 142.4

chanteuse *singer* 141.4

chantey *or* **chanty** *or* **shantey** *song* 140.11

chanticleer *male bird* 36.15

Chantilly ware *Ceramics* 129

chanting *singing* 85.16, *tumult* 232.5, *reverberatory* 797.14

chantry *place of worship* 83.8

Chao Phraya *Rivers* 570

chaos *causality* 10.66, *confusion* 51.2, 766.4, *havoc* 523.5, *shapelessness* 625.1, *mixture* 751.1, *nonadhesion* 756.1, *disintegration* 758.1, *lawlessness* 766.6

chaos magic *witchcraft* 86.6

chaos theory *causality* 10.66

chaotic *disorderly* 51.6, 766.15, *lawless* 53.26, *indiscriminate* 338.8, *shapeless* 625.2, *complicated* 751.10, *disintegrated* 758.3, *muddled* 766.13

chaotically *confusedly* 51.11, *shapelessly* 625.5, *inconsistently* 732.16, *mixedly* 751.16, *destructively* 758.9, *in disorder* 766.24

chap *be rough* 544.10

chap [Inf] *average person* 18.9, *male* 32.1

Chapala *Lakes* 568

chaparral *plants* 41.1, *trees* 43.4

chapati *bread* 90.10

chapeau *hat* 100.32

chapel *place of worship* 83.8, *church architecture* 134.11

chapel de fer *helmet* 100.34

chapelgoer *worshiper* 83.6

chapel of remembrance *burial place* 31.7

chapel of rest *place of worship* 83.8

chaperon *personal attendant* 69.5, *accompanier* 794.6, *escort* 794.18, *protector* 810.11, *protect* 810.21

chaperoned *accompanied* 794.15

chaplain *member of the clergy* 84.5

chaplaincy *priesthood* 84.2

chaplainship *priesthood* 84.2

chaplet *flower* 42.1, *sacred object* 83.11, Architectural Elements

134, Heraldic Terms 184, *insignia* 184.5

chapman [Arch] *peddler* 482.9

chapped *coarse* 544.6

chapped hands *rough skin* 544.3

chaps *legwear* 100.26

chapter *religious group* 81.4, *book part* 174.5, *division* 577.6, *part of writing* 760.6

Chapter 11 *insolvency* 490.5

chapterhouse *clerical dwelling* 84.10

char *burn* 217.18, *blacken* 254.11, *brown* 256.7

char [Brit] *domestic servant* 69.7, *serve* 69.11

char-à-banc [Brit] *bus* 687.7

character 15.18; *written letter* 5.14, *computer information* 15.17, *someone* 18.10, *role* 136.23, *sort* 202.6, *reputation* 224.4, *morals* 431.2, *virtues* 447.2, *attitude* 513.2, *style* 537.1, *inner nature* 611.4, *kind* 624.3, *nature* 624.5, 723.4, *participation* 760.10, *type* 777.4, *eccentric* 782.10, *number* 783.1

character acting *acting* 136.22

character actor *actor* 136.25

character actor *or* **actress** *actor* 137.13

character actress *actor* 136.25

character assassination *defamation* 440.3

character dress *costume* 100.10

characteristic 723.9, 779.5, 779.12; *logarithm* 6.17, *parameter* 6.57, *given* 6.74, *symbolic* 183.12, *identification* 184.1, *representational* 187.8, *external appearance* 264.5, *property* 470.1, *style* 537.1, *average* 742.5, *typical* 777.10

characteristically 779.20; *indicatively* 183.21, *representationally* 187.15, *taxonomically* 777.15

characteristic curve *exposure* 132.15

characterization *dramaturgy* 136.6, *acting* 136.22, 187.6, *script* 137.5, *aspect of fiction* 199.5, *identification* 184.1, *description* 202.1

characterize 723.11, 779.15; *write* 139.21, *signify* 183.16, *identify* 184.11, *act* 187.13, *describe* 202.15, *recount* 202.16

characterized *dramatized* 136.32, *identified* 184.9

characterizing *acting* 187.6

characterless *tasteless* 220.4, *vacant* 576.12

character recognition 15.20

character reference *documentation* 339.6, *recommendation* 437.6, *permit* 502.3

characters *cast* 136.26

character set *character* 15.18

character sketch *description* 202.1

charade *number* 138.5, *puzzle* 182.5, *acting* 187.6

charades *Children's and Party Games* 167

charbroil *cook* 91.10

charbroiling *cooking technique* 91.2

charcoal *fuels* 106.2, *coal* 106.4, *material* 143.9, *black thing* 254.3

charcoal burner *power worker* 106.10

charcoal drawing *drawing* 143.4

charcoal-gray *gray* 255.6

Charente *Rivers* 570

charge 494.13; *electric charge* 10.38, 14.36, *quantum* 10.63, *conduct* 14.51, *litigate* 54.27, *battle* 76.33, *fight* 77.35, *explosive* 78.13, *deputize* 80.7, *power* 106.17, *cathexis* 108.32, *burden* 117.3, *management* 126.1, *play field hockey* 158.10, *communication* 176.3, *military call* 183.9, Heraldic Terms 184, *identify* 184.11, *attest* 189.22, *military attack* 418.2, *attack* 418.17, *command* 425.1, 425.10, *authorization* 425.14, *authorize* 425.14, 833.10, *line of duty* 433.3, *payment* 433.5, *impose a duty* 433.14, *censure* 438.3, *accusation* 442.1, *accuse* 442.8, *bargain* 480.20, *acquire credit* 487.11, *debt* 488.1, *be in debt* 488.9, *expense* 491.2, *settle accounts* 493.11, *price* 494.1, *fee* 494.3, *levy* 494.7, *demand* 505.12, *vigor* 514.2, *empower* 514.20, *violence by person* 520.2, *be violent* 520.8, *displacement* 538.13, *make heavy* 538.14, *load* 577.5, *be swift* 694.10, *propellant* 696.9, *fill* 761.11, *safekeeping* 810.6, *detention* 830.5, *dependent* 832.4, *authority* 833.3

chargeable 494.11; *guilty* 450.6

charge account *credit* 487.1, *debt* 488.1

charge account payment *type of payment* 493.3

charge against *attack* 418.17

charge a jury *communicate* 176.10

charge at *chase* 385.13

charge attraction *electric charge* 10.38

charge card *credit* 476.4, *credit card* 487.2, *debt* 488.1

charge-card purchase *purchasing* 481.2

charge carrier *semiconductor* 10.34, *electric charge* 14.36

charged 487.9; *fired* 106.13, *duty-bound* 433.8, *condemned* 438.11, *accused* 442.5, *bought* 481.8, *nuclear* 514.17, *loaded* 538.10, 577.8

chargé d'affaires *delegate* 79.1, *negotiator* 460.4

charged body *electric charge* 10.38

charge density *electric charge* 10.38, 14.36

charged particle *electric charge* 10.38

charged substance *electric charge* 10.38

charge hand *manager* 126.7

charge number *ion* 10.54

charge nurse *nurse* 107.23

charger *war-horse* 159.4, *accuser* 442.3, *crockery* 578.16

charge repulsion *electric charge* 10.38

charge the jury *try a case* 54.28, *judge* 341.10

charge to one's account *acquire credit* 487.11, *be in debt* 488.9

charge to the jury *closing arguments* 54.17, *communication* 176.3

charge withdrawn *favorable verdict* 54.19

charging *ice hockey tactics* 158.4, *field hockey tactics* 158.5, *soccer play* 163.5, *attacking* 418.14, *explosive* 520.6, *speeding* 694.7

Chari *Rivers* 570

charily *cautiously* 287.16, *carefully* 325.13

chariness *caution* 287.1

Charioteer *Constellations* 7

charisma *enticement* 178.3, *personal influence* 512.3, *type of power* 514.6, *allurement* 700.4

charismatic *religious person* 81.9, *enticing* 178.13, *sociable* 408.11, *appealing* 512.9, *powerful* 514.15, *attractive* 700.10

charismatically *influentially* 512.14, *attractively* 700.14

charismatic leader *leader* 126.8

charismatize *entice* 178.16

charitable 305.9; *loving* 299.15, *philanthropic* 307.6, *pitying* 308.4, *courteous* 410.6, *lenient* 423.3, *unselfish* 443.5, *kind* 445.12, *principled* 447.6, *giving* 472.9, *magnanimous* 498.7, *voluntary* 504.9, *benevolent* 825.21

charitable act *or* **deed** *benevolent act* 305.5

charitable foundation *charity* 307.3

charitableness *charity* 305.3, *philanthropy* 307.1, *leniency* 423.1, *magnanimity* 498.2

charitable organization 305.4

charitable work *voluntary work* 373.5

charitably 305.15; *lovingly* 299.29, *philanthropically* 307.9, *pityingly* 308.11, *courteously* 410.13, *genteelly* 410.14, *leniently* 423.6, *unselfishly* 443.9, *kindly* 445.20, *ethically* 447.10, *as a gift* 472.17, *benevolently* 825.34

charity 275.3, 305.3, 307.3; *love* 299.1, *philanthropy* 307.1, *pity* 308.1, *courtesy* 410.1, *leniency* 423.1, *unselfishness* 443.2, *kindness* 445.3, *virtues* 447.2, *giving* 472.1, *absence of charge* 497.6, *free of charge* 497.12, *generosity* 498.1, *social assistance* 825.4

charity appeal *solicitation* 505.4

charity bazaar *sale* 482.2

charity case *recipient* 473.5

charity event *charity* 307.3, *solicitation* 505.4

charity gala *theatrical performance* 136.13

charity game *offering* 472.6

charity organization *requester* 505.5

charity performance *theatrical performance* 136.13

charity raffle *charitable organization* 305.4

charity sale *sale* 482.2

charity shop *discounter* 497.7

charity that begins at home *selfishness* 444.1

charity work *giving* 472.1

charity worker *independent worker* 123.3, *philanthropist* 307.5, *willing worker* 373.6, *volunteer* 504.7, *requester* 505.5

charka *wheel* 682.9

charkha *wheel* 682.9

charlatan *unskilled person* 128.3, *unskilled* 128.5, *deceiver* 193.8, *pretender* 367.2, *imitator* 736.6

charlatanism *unskillfulness* 128.1, *hypocrisy* 330.5

charlatanism *or* **charlatanry** *deception* 193.1

Charles Parnell *Famous Lovers* 299

Charles's law *Classical Physical Laws* 10

Charleston *Dances* 135, *American States* 564

charley horse *painful condition* 215.2

Charlotte Amalie American States 564

Charlottetown Canadian Provinces 564

charm *quantum* 10.63, Collective Names 59, *sacred object* 83.11, *spell* 86.8, *talisman* 86.9, *bewitch* 86.25, *enticement* 178.3, *entice* 178.16, *give pleasure* 214.13, *cause joy* 269.11, *pleasantness* 271.1, *make pleasant* 271.10, *lovability* 299.5, *win the love of* 299.27, *curse* 301.1, 301.13, *blarney* 439.13, *inducement* 508.2, *positive stimulus* 508.5, *influence* 508.11, *occult influence* 512.2, *appeal* 529.4, *stylishness* 537.2, *smooth over* 545.12, *allurement* 700.4, *lure* 700.5, *attract* 700.11, *preserver* 815.9

charmed *bewitched* 86.21, *enamored* 299.17, *motivated* 508.8
charmed circle *limitation* 830.2
charmed life *safety* 810.1
charmer 700.6; *witch* 86.15, *tempter* 178.10, *pleasant thing* 271.4, *flatterer* 439.6, *attractive male* 529.6
charming *witchlike* 86.19, *enticing* 178.13, *pleasant* 214.7, 271.5, *delightful* 271.7, *lovable* 299.20, *sociable* 408.11, *motivational* 508.7, *appealing* 512.9, 529.10, *attractive* 700.10
charming fellow *social person* 408.7
charmingly *enticingly* 178.22, *lovably* 299.31, *sociably* 408.19, *influentially* 508.13, 512.14, *elegantly* 529.15, *attractively* 700.14
charmlessly *discourteously* 411.8
Charmoise Breeds of Sheep 16
charms *lovability* 299.5
charnel house *after death* 29.9, *mortuary* 31.3
Charolais Breeds of Cattle 16
Charollais Half-bred Horse and Pony Breeds 159
Charon Planets and Their Satellites 7
charred *blackened* 254.7, *browned* 256.6
chart 767.8; *graph* 6.30, *illustration* 187.2, *map* 187.5, 187.12, 387.7, *plan out* 387.14, *exact location* 565.2, *division* 577.6, *outline* 617.1, 617.5, *navigational aid* 690.6, *navigate* 690.15, *list* 785.1, 785.11
chart [Inf] *written music* 140.21
chart-busting *unbeatable* 744.13
charted *planned* 387.10, *itemized* 577.9, *listed* 785.9
charter *authorization* 52.3, *authorize* 52.14, 833.10, *law* 53.1, *certificate* 185.2, *license* 434.4, *permit* 502.3, 735.29, *urbanize* 567.15, *permission* 735.9, *code* 780.3, *authority* 833.3
chartered *authorized* 52.11, *permitted* 502.4, *permitting* 735.19
charting *organization* 767.3, *listing* 785.8
chart recorder *meter* 589.13
chartreuse *yellow* 259.7, *green* 260.7
chart-topper *paragon* 744.6, *successful thing* 845.5
chart-topping *unbeatable* 744.13, *best* 805.9, *famous* 845.9
chartulary *record book* 185.5

charwoman *domestic servant* 69.7, *cleaner* 111.12, *domestic worker* 123.4
chary *cautious* 287.6, *circumspect* 325.8, *unenthusiastic* 375.10
Charybdis *legendary sea being* 571.4, *vortex* 682.6
chase 385.2, 385.13; *animal killing* 30.10, *avenge* 144.11, *lust after* 288.20, *court* 299.26, *decorate* 532.11, *be swift* 694.10
chased *engraved* 144.9, *pursued* 385.10
chase down *pursue* 377.11
chase fame and fortune *seek riches* 485.14
chase off or **away** *repel* 701.7
chase one's tail *be busy* 414.19, *orbit* 681.8, *rotate* 682.14
chase out *drive out* 709.19
chaser *drink* 93.2, 121.6, *engraver* 144.5, *racehorse* 159.2
chaser [Inf] *play part* 136.8
chasing *relief carving* 144.2, *engraving* 144.3, *chase* 385.2, *pursuing* 385.8
chasing one's own tail *overactivity* 414.9
chasm *opening* 583.1, *gulf* 587.3, *the depths* 598.2, *separateness* 753.3, *hidden danger* 813.3
chassepot *historical handgun* 78.8
chassis *racing automobile* 146.2, *framework* 551.4, *foundation* 601.2, *supporting structure* 605.2
chaste 431.10; *virginal* 67.7, *pure* 253.11, *principled* 447.6, *innocent* 449.6, *abstinent* 455.7, *simple* 526.7, *single* 788.16
chastely *celibately* 67.12, *morally* 431.15, *ethically* 447.10, *innocently* 449.13, *with self-restraint* 455.14
chasten *rebuke* 298.21, *punish* 454.22, *moderate* 521.7
chastened *abased* 298.13, *moderate* 521.3
chastener *punisher* 454.16
chasteness *virginity* 67.2
chastening *punishment* 454.1
chaste person 431.6
chaste tree Trees and Shrubs 43
chastise *be severe* 424.8, *condemn* 438.18, *punish* 454.22
chastised *condemned* 438.11
chastisement *condemnation* 438.2, *punishment* 454.1
chastisement of the flesh *corporal punishment* 454.11
chastiser *punisher* 454.16
chastising *condemning* 438.10, *censuring* 438.12
chastity 431.3; *virginity* 67.2, *purity* 253.6, *virtues* 447.2, *innocence* 449.1, *abstinence* 455.2, *simplicity* 526.1
chasuble *vestment* 84.11
chat 210.2, 210.12; *vernacular* 205.8, *talk* 207.3, *be talkative* 207.7, *conversation* 210.1
château *mansion* 60.5
chatelaine *master* 68.1
Chatham Islands 572
chatoyancy *variegation* 263.1
chatoyant *iridescent* 263.7
chat show [Brit] *program* 172.10
Chattahoochee Rivers 570
chattel *possession of property* 469.3, *possessions* 470.5, *subjected person* 832.5
chattel mortgage *mortgage* 476.6
chatter *vernacular* 205.8, *talk* 207.3, *be talkative* 207.7, *chat* 210.12, *rattle* 235.3, 235.12, *bird*

sound 240.2, *make a bird sound* 240.8
chatterbox *talker* 207.4
chatterer 210.7; *speaker* 205.12, *talker* 207.4, *answerer* 334.10
chattering Collective Names 59, *talk* 207.3, *talkative* 207.5, *rattling* 235.8, *singing* 240.5
chattering teeth *symptoms of fear* 283.3
chattily *effusively* 207.10
chattiness *talkativeness* 207.1
chatting *conversing* 210.8
chatty *informative* 170.10, *effusive* 207.6, *conversational* 210.10
chauffeur *personal attendant* 69.5, *domestic worker* 123.4, *transferrer* 685.4, *transporter* 686.4
chauffeur's uniform *clothing* 184.6
chaulmoogra Trees and Shrubs 43
Chautauqua Circuit *regions of the United States* 564.7
chauvinism *bellicosity* 76.15, *social discrimination* 337.4, *unfair treatment* 342.4, *nationalism* 566.4
chauvinist *militarist* 77.3, *bigot* 337.7
chauvinistic *discriminatory* 337.11, *unjust* 342.7, *national* 566.10
chauvinistically *prejudicially* 337.17, *unjustly* 342.13, *nationally* 566.13
cheap 497.9, 800.16; *underestimated* 344.4, *discounted* 495.3, *cheaply* 497.16, *offered* 504.8, *vulgar* 535.6, *low quality* 745.7
cheap at half the price *bargain* 497.10
cheap at the price *bargain* 497.10
cheapen *desecrate* 436.24, *discount* 495.4, *make cheap* 497.14, *vulgarize* 535.9, *make useless* 802.12, *pervert* 808.22
cheapening *moral deterioration* 808.3
cheap item 497.5
cheap-jack *peddler* 482.9, *bargain hunter* 497.8
cheaply 481.19, 497.16; *badly* 745.15
cheapness 497.1; *price* 494.1, *shoddiness* 497.3, *tawdriness* 535.2, *deficiency* 745.2, *triviality* 800.2
cheapo [Inf] *cheap* 497.9
cheap rate *cheapness* 497.1
Cheapside London 567.8
cheap thing 800.7
cheap ticket *bargain* 497.4
cheat *be dishonorable* 192.21, *deceiver* 193.9, *deceive* 193.16, *wrong* 430.19, *do wrong* 430.20, *villain* 448.5, *be wicked* 448.13, *infringer* 479.10, *dishonest person* 479.11, *act dishonestly* 479.18, *cunning person* 822.3, *be cunning* 822.5
cheat [Inf] *fornicate* 432.14
cheat death *live* 28.17
cheated *deceived* 193.15, *fraudulent* 479.13
cheater *hypocrite* 192.9, *deceiver* 193.8
cheating *dishonorableness* 192.3, *dishonorable* 192.14, *deception* 193.1, *deceptive* 193.12, *villainous* 448.12, *infringement* 479.6, *dishonesty* 479.7, *fraudulent* 479.13, *cunning* 822.1
cheating [Inf] *fornication* 432.3
cheatingly *deceptively* 193.21

cheat on [Inf] *be dishonorable* 192.21
cheat one's creditors *not pay* 488.10
Chebyshev's inequality Mathematical Concepts 6
check 263.2, 784.14; *ice hockey tactics* 158.4, *play ice hockey* 158.9, *board games* 167.3, *deter* 179.8, *identify* 184.11, *record* 185.1, *variegate* 263.11, *care for* 325.12, *question* 333.16, *experiment* 335.1, 335.11, *verification* 336.1, *verify* 336.8, *specification* 340.6, *specify* 340.14, *estimate* 341.11, *pause* 415.15, *loss* 468.1, *paper money* 484.14, *prohibition* 503.1, *prohibit* 503.8, *obstruction* 510.3, *counteract* 510.7, *moderation* 521.1, *moderate* 521.7, *crack* 587.2, 587.7, *standard* 589.7, *limit* 620.1, 620.7, *stop* 668.2, *cause to cease* 668.12, *hesitation* 693.5, *slow down* 693.13, *obstacle* 826.2, *restraint* 826.8, 830.1, *restrain* 826.19, 830.12, *withstand* 828.20, *make certain* 840.14, *be victorious* 845.16
checkbook *record book* 185.5, *account book* 493.3
checked 263.8; *tested* 335.10, *verified* 336.7, *conditional* 340.10, *stopped* 668.7, *delayed* 693.10
checker *board games* 167.3, *check* 263.2, *variegate* 263.11
checkerboard *board games* 167.3, *variegated thing* 263.5
checkered *checked* 263.8, *diversified* 732.8
checkered flag *automobile racing terms* 146.3
checkers Board and Table Games 167, *board games* 167.3
check in *get in* 704.17
checking *poker* 168.5, *verificatory* 336.6
checking account *personal finance* 457.5, *funds* 484.6
checking account deposit *deposit* 487.3
checklist *questionnaire* 333.3, *division* 577.6, *list* 785.1
checkmate *board games* 167.3, *play* 167.12, *stop* 668.2, *cause to cease* 668.12, *successful thing* 845.5, *be victorious* 845.16
checkmated *stopped* 668.7
check off *identify* 184.11, *set apart* 753.17
check off names *register* 185.15
check one's course *orient* 697.15
check out *experiment* 335.11, *estimate* 341.11, *withdraw* 705.9
checkpoint *limit marker* 620.4, *crossing point* 692.7
check register *record* 185.1
checkrein *riding equipment* 159.9
checkroom *room* 60.9
check stock *audit* 493.10
check stub *record* 185.1, *promise* 464.2, *acknowledgment of payment* 473.3, *receipt* 492.1
checkup *health care* 107.7
cheek *wall* 134.9, *audacity* 400.3, *bad manners* 411.2, *defiance* 416.1, *assurance* 621.8, *side* 623.1
cheekbone Human Bones 19
cheek by jowl *near* 586.6, *beside* 586.20, *adhesive* 755.5, *cohesively* 755.11, *hand in hand* 794.21
cheekily *audaciously* 400.20, *rudely* 411.9, *defiantly* 416.9
cheekiness *audacity* 400.3, *defiance* 416.1

cheeks *head* 19.6
cheeks [Inf] *rear end* 622.4
cheeky *audacious* 400.10, *bad-mannered* 411.6, *defiant* 416.5, *disrespectful* 436.9
cheep *bird sound* 240.2, *make a bird sound* 240.8
cheeping *singing* 240.5
cheer 239.15, 281.4; *food* 90.1, *refresh* 94.6, *gesture* 183.5, *give pleasure* 214.13, *cry of praise* 239.3, *cheerfulness* 269.2, *bring cheer* 269.12, *applause* 279.2, *inspire hope* 281.14, *salute* 405.13, *sociability* 408.1, *acclaim* 437.5, 437.18
cheerer *crier* 239.8, *rejoicer* 279.3
cheer for *cheer* 239.15
cheerful 269.7; *rejoicing* 279.4, *hopeful* 281.6, *sociable* 408.11
cheerful giver *giver* 472.7
cheerfully 269.14; *hopefully* 281.15, *willingly* 373.15, *sociably* 408.19
cheerfulness 269.2; *hope* 281.1
cheerful person *joyful person* 269.5
cheerily *cheerfully* 269.14
cheeriness *cheerfulness* 269.2
cheering 239.10, 269.8, 281.9; *rejoicing* 279.4, *tribute* 405.6, *acclaim* 437.5, *acclamatory* 437.10
cheerio! [Brit] *goodbye!* 705.14
cheerleader *miscellaneous terms* 155.16, *crier* 239.8
cheerless *without hope* 282.7, *sullen* 304.8
cheerlessly *unhopefully* 282.14, *sullenly* 304.16
cheerlessness *depression* 270.2, *lack of hope* 282.2, *sullenness* 304.1
cheer on *motivate* 508.9, *invigorate* 518.5
cheers! 93.22; *hurrah!* 279.8, *goodbye!* 705.14
cheer up *bring cheer* 269.12, *be hopeful* 281.11, *inspire hope* 281.14
cheery *cheerful* 269.7, *rejoicing* 279.4
cheese *dish* 90.7, *snack* 90.8, *dessert* 90.35
cheeseburger *sandwich* 90.9
cheesecake *cake* 90.36
cheesecake [Inf and Off] *sex object* 20.8, *woman considered as a sex object* 33.8, *portrait* 132.5
cheesecloth Fabrics and Fibers 130
cheese grater *grater* 553.12
cheese it! [Inf] *go!* 709.30
cheeseparing *meanness* 501.1, *mean* 501.4
chef *caterer* 89.5, *food provider* 90.6, *cook* 91.3
chef-d'oeuvre *masterpiece* 68.14, 127.5, *work of art* 133.4, *marvel* 294.3, *good thing* 445.9, *work of art* 522.4, *beautiful thing* 529.3, *ideal* 805.6
chef's salad *salad* 90.16
chef's special *the special* 779.8
cheimaphobia or cheimatophobia Phobias 283
chela *religious* 84.9
chelate *chemical compound* 11.4
chelicerate *arthropodal* 39.22
chelonian *turtle* 37.7, *reptilian* 37.12
chelonid *turtle* 37.7
Chelsea porcelain Ceramics 129
chemical 11.24, 14.46
chemical bond 11.6

chemical change 670.2
chemical compound 11.4
chemical contraceptive *contraceptive* 23.6
chemical dye *dye* 130.8
chemical element 11.3; *physical element* 524.5
chemical energy *energy* 10.10, 514.7
chemical engineer 14.25; *engineer* 14.2
chemical engineering 14.24, Branches of Chemistry 11, *industrial chemistry* 11.21, *engineering* 14.1
chemical formula *structure* 11.7
chemically 11.42
chemical manufacturing *chemical process industries* 14.26
chemical manufacturing processes *industrial processes* 14.27
chemical messenger *hormone* 12.16
chemical physics Fields of Modern Physics 10, Branches of Chemistry 11
chemical porcelain *industrial ceramics* 129.6
chemical process industries 14.26
chemical pulping recovery *chemical reaction thermodynamics* 14.29
chemical reaction 11.8; *power source* 514.13
chemical reaction engineer *chemical engineer* 14.25
chemical reaction engineering *chemical engineering* 14.24
chemical reaction thermodynamics 14.29
chemical reactor *systems and process control* 14.28
chemical science *chemistry* 11.1
chemical scientist *chemist* 11.2
chemical toilet *place for excretion* 25.11
chemical warfare 76.5, 117.9
chemical weapon *weapon* 78.1, *chemical warfare* 117.9
chemical weathering *weathering* 8.40
chemiluminescence *light* 10.17
chemin de fer Card Games 168
chemise *underwear* 100.22
chemisette *neckwear* 100.29
chemisorb *absorb* 11.40, 708.19
chemisorbed *absorbed* 11.34
chemisorption *surface chemistry* 11.20, *absorption* 708.6
chemisorptive *absorbent* 708.11
chemist 11.2; *changer* 665.9
chemist [Brit] *druggist* 115.10
chemistry 11.1; *sexual desire* 20.5
chemosphere *atmospheric layer* 558.3
chemotherapy *treatment* 107.14, *therapy* 11.12
chemurgy [Arch] Branches of Chemistry 11
Chenab Rivers 570
chenille Fabrics and Fibers 130
chenopodiaceous *taxonomic* 41.16
cheongsam *dress* 100.11
Cher Berrichon Breeds of Sheep 16
cherish *like* 290.8, *love* 299.21, *revere* 435.14, *detain* 471.9, *protect* 810.21, *preserve* 815.14
cherish a grudge *be malevolent* 306.12

cherished *liked* 290.6, *beloved* 299.19, *preserved* 815.12
cherishing *detention* 471.2
Cherkasy Breeds of Sheep 16
cheroot *tobacco* 121.23
cherophobia Phobias 283
cherry *red thing* 257.3, *red* 257.5
cherry [Inf] *figurative usage* 44.4
cherry-lipped *red-faced* 257.6
cherry picker *figurative usage* 44.4, *lifter* 715.5
cherry-red *red* 257.5
cherub *angel* 82.11
cherubic *angelic* 82.21
cherubically *divinely* 82.24
cherubim *angelic order* 82.12
chervil Herbs and Spices 91
Chesapeake Bay retriever Breeds of Dogs 35
chess Board and Table Games 167, *board games* 167.3
chessboard *board games* 167.3, *variegated thing* 263.5
chessman *board games* 167.3
chess piece *board games* 167.3
chest *cabinet* 101.8, *receptacle* 105.11, *money storage* 484.20, *box* 578.5
chesterfield *coat* 100.19
chesterfield couch *couch* 101.7
Chester White Breeds of Pigs 16
chest-high *high* 596.7
chestnut Trees and Shrubs 43, *horse by color* 159.7, *maxim* 177.1, *brown* 256.5, *red-haired* 257.7, *boring thing* 296.3, *repetitiveness* 797.3
chest of drawers *cabinet* 101.8, *receptacle* 105.11
chest pain *cardiovascular disease* 114.13
chest protector *baseball equipment* 147.4, *fencing equipment* 153.2, *hockey clothing* 158.6
chest spasm *cardiovascular disease* 114.13
chest X ray *diagnostic radiology* 107.12
cheval glass *reflector* 242.10
chevaux-de-frise *barrier* 419.10
chevet *church architecture* 134.11
Cheviot Breeds of Sheep 16
cheviot Fabrics and Fibers 130
Cheviot Hills Mountains and Hills 569
chevron Architectural Elements 134, Heraldic Terms 184, *insignia* 184.5, *angle* 628.1
chevy [Brit] *pursue* 385.11, *hurry someone up* 694.15
chew 92.22; *bite* 92.10, *smoke* 121.38, *soften* 543.14
chewiness 547.2
chewing 92.19; *eating* 92.1
chewing gum *adhesive* 561.3, *adherent* 755.4
chewing out [Inf] *punishment* 454.1
chewing the cud *eating habit* 92.7
chewing tobacco *tobacco* 121.23
chew one's nails *worry* 283.16
chew the cud *graze* 35.35, *eat grass* 45.11, *chew* 92.22
chew the fat [Inf] *converse* 210.11
chew the scenery *overact* 136.35, *exaggerate* 194.11
chew the string Children's and Party Games 167
chew up *chew* 92.22
chewy 547.9
Cheyenne American States 564, Rivers 570
Chiana Breeds of Cattle 16
Chianina Breeds of Cattle 16

chiaramente Musical Terms and Expression Marks 140
chiaroscuro *treatment* 143.6, *highlight* 246.12, *blackness* 254.1
chiasmus *literary device* 139.12, *inverted thing* 608.4, *symmetry* 626.1
chiastic *symmetrical* 626.4
chic *dressed up* 100.39, *beauty* 529.1, *beautiful* 529.7, *fashion* 536.1, *fashionable* 536.5, *stylishness* 537.2, *stylish* 537.7, *distinction* 777.8
Chicago Card Games 168, *major US cities* 567.5
Chicago jazz *jazz* 140.5
Chicago School Architectural Styles 134
chicane *automobile racing terms* 146.3, *deception* 193.1, *deceive* 193.16, *road attribute* 687.3, *cunning* 822.1
chicanery *deception* 193.1, *hypocrisy* 330.5, *cunning* 822.1
chichi *affected* 367.3
chick *livestock* 16.11, *progeny* 21.8, *young animal* 26.4, *young bird* 36.17
chick [Inf] *young woman* 26.9
chick [Inf and Off] *sex object* 20.8, *woman considered as a sex object* 33.8
chicken *livestock* 16.11, *table bird* 36.10, *meat* 90.22
chicken [Inf] *chicken-hearted* 259.11, *frightened person* 283.8, *coward* 285.3, *cowardly* 285.4, *inactive person* 413.8, *weak person* 517.4, *weak-willed* 517.10
chicken coop *farm building* 16.4, *cage* 60.15
chicken farm *farm* 16.2
chicken farming *livestock farming* 16.10
chicken feed *animal feed* 16.12, *animal food* 90.2
chicken feed [Inf] *change* 484.3, *little bit* 800.4
chicken-hearted 259.11; *weak-willed* 517.10
chicken-hearted [Inf] *cowardly* 285.4
chicken-heartedly [Inf] *cowardly* 285.9
chicken-heartedness [Inf] *cowardice* 285.1
chicken-livered [Inf] *cowardly* 285.4
chicken out [Inf] *be a coward* 285.7
chickenpox *infection* 114.7, *skin disease* 114.16
chicken run *farm building* 16.4
chickens Collective Names 59, Phobias 283
chicken wire *farm building* 16.4
chicle Tree Products 43, *adhesive* 561.3
chicle gum *adhesive* 561.3
chicly *dressily* 100.47, *fashionably* 536.9
chicory Herbs and Spices 91
chide *condemn* 438.18, *punish* 454.22
chiding *condemnation* 438.2, *condemning* 438.10, *censuring* 438.12, *punishment* 454.1
chief *person in authority* 52.7, *leader* 68.3, *company leader* 68.8, *masterful* 68.15, Heraldic Terms 184, *head* 600.7, *focus* 612.3, *focal* 612.8, *superior* 744.5, *elite* 744.12, *primary* 769.10, *important person* 799.5, *important* 799.7

chief constable [Brit] *law enforcement officer* 53.8
chief cook and bottlewasher *domestic worker* 123.4
chief executive *leader* 68.3, *operator* 412.7, *person in command* 425.5
chief executive officer (CEO) *company leader* 68.8, *manager* 126.7, *person in command* 425.5
chief financial officer (CFO) *company leader* 68.8
chief hope *gist* 799.4
chief justice *judge* 54.10, 68.4, 341.5
chiefly *focally* 612.14, *in essence* 723.13, *on average* 742.10, *predominantly* 744.21, *as a rule* 780.18
chief magistrate *judge* 68.4
Chief Master Sergeant US Military Ranks 58
Chief Master Sergeant of the Air Force US Military Ranks 58
chief meaning *type of meaning* 361.4
chief of police *law enforcement officer* 53.8
chief of staff *military staff* 58.5
chief of state *leader* 68.3
chief operating officer (COO) *manager* 126.7
chief part *role* 136.23, *large part* 579.3
Chief Petty Officer US Military Ranks 58
chief rabbi *priest* 84.8
chieftain *leader* 68.3
chieftaincy *dominion* 566.3
chieftainship *position of authority* 52.4
chief thing 799.3
Chief Warrant Officer W-2 US Military Ranks 58
Chief Warrant Officer W-3 US Military Ranks 58
Chief Warrant Officer W-4 US Military Ranks 58
chief whip *elected official* 50.8
chief whip [Brit] *party official* 68.5
Chiem Lakes 568
Chiemsee Lakes 568
chiffon Fabrics and Fibers 130, *transparent thing* 249.4
chigger *pest* 40.5
chignon *coiffure* 530.8
Chihuahua Breeds of Dogs 35
Chihuahuan Deserts 572
chilblain *ulcer* 114.18, *chills* 218.3
child 26.6; *person* 18.8, *progeny* 21.8, *family member* 65.2, *loved one* 299.13, *innocent person* 449.5, *produce* 522.5, *successor* 770.6, *naive person* 821.2, *dependent* 832.4
child abuse *malignity* 306.5
child abuser *villain* 448.5
child abuser or **molester** *sexually immoral person* 432.8
child allowance *social assistance* 825.4
child-bearing *female* 33.16
child benefit *social assistance* 825.4
childcare worker *domestic worker* 123.4
childhood *bodily development* 19.17, *youth* 26.1, *age* 27.1, *naiveté* 449.4, *conception* 771.4
child image *symbol* 108.28
childish *of language* 5.35, *young* 26.11, *unintelligent* 316.6, *foolish*

353.5, *immature* 389.9, *not serious* 800.11
childishly *youthfully* 26.14, *immaturely* 389.18
childishness *youthfulness* 26.2, *ignorance* 316.3, *folly* 353.1, *immaturity* 389.3
childless *infertile* 23.7
childlessness *infertility* 23.1
childlike *young* 26.11, *unintelligent* 316.6, *immature* 389.9, *naive* 449.9, 821.3
child-minder [Brit] *protector* 810.11
child of fortune *prosperous person* 847.4
child of God *religious person* 81.9
child of nature *naive person* 821.2
child porn [Inf] *pornography* 432.7
child pornography *pornography* 432.7
child prodigy *wonderful person* 294.6
childproof *invulnerable* 810.18
child psychologist *psychologist* 108.33
child psychology Psychological Theories, Schools 108, *therapy* 115.12
children *progeny* 21.8, *the young* 26.10, Phobias 283, *successor* 770.6
children's book *type of book* 174.3
children's dentist *dentist* 107.21
children's dictionary *word book* 5.27
children's game *type of game* 167.2
children's home *safe house* 812.5
children's hospital *hospital* 107.16
children's nurse *nurse* 107.23
children's rights *rights* 429.4
children's swimming pool *swimming place* 164.9
children's wear *dry goods* 130.3
child's play *easy question* 333.5, *secondary matter* 800.6, *easy thing* 823.6
child support *divorce court* 66.3, *income* 492.3, *financial support* 605.8
child welfare *social welfare* 307.4
Chile Countries 566
Chilean pine Trees and Shrubs 43
chiliad *time period* 641.2, *thousand* 792.10
chili powder Herbs and Spices 91
CHILL Programming Languages 15
chill *cold weather* 9.24, *cool* 9.49, *air* 94.7, *symptom* 114.3, *discourage* 179.11, *cold* 218.1, 218.9, *make cold* 218.15, *unsociability* 409.1
chilled *refreshed* 94.5, *discouraged* 179.6, *cold* 218.9, *cooled* 218.11
chilled to the bone or **marrow** *cold* 218.9
chill factor *weather data* 9.6, *cold weather* 218.8
chilliness *cold weather* 9.24, *hostility* 63.1, *cold* 218.1, *unsociability* 409.1
chilling *dissuasive* 179.4, *cold* 218.1
chilling effect *deterrence* 179.2
chill in the air *cold weather* 9.24
chill out [Inf] *ease* 543.15, *restrain oneself* 830.15
chills 218.3
chilly *cool* 9.49, *hostile* 63.6, *cold* 218.9, *unsociable* 409.6
chilopod *myriapod* 39.11
Chilopoda *myriapod* 39.11

Chimborazo Mountains and Hills 569
chime *melodiousness* 140.12, *harmonize* 140.28, 735.22, *ring* 235.14, 236.10, *ringing* 236.2, *harmonization* 735.2
chime in *assent* 346.6, *interrupt* 775.14
chimera *self-deception* 193.2, *spectacle* 264.6, Legendary Creatures 360, *fantasy* 360.5, *illusion* 720.2
chimerical *deceptive* 193.12, *seeming* 264.11, *imaginary* 360.12, *illusory* 720.9
chimes Musical Instruments 142, *percussion instrument* 142.5, *loud tone* 232.3, *source of resonance* 236.4
chiming *ringing* 235.5, 236.7, *pealing* 235.9, *harmonization* 735.2, *harmonizing* 735.12, *reverberatory* 797.14
chimney *rock face* 161.6, *mountaineer* 161.10, *place for fire* 217.9, *valley* 572.8, *gulf* 587.3
chimney corner *place for fire* 217.9
chimneying *climbing techniques* 161.3
chimney sweep *cleaner* 111.12
chin *head* 19.6
China Countries 566
china *tableware* 92.13, *ceramics* 129.1, *weak thing* 517.5, *merchandise* 522.6, *crockery* 578.16
china or **chinaware** Ceramics 129
chinaberry or **China tree** Trees and Shrubs 43
china cabinet *cabinet* 101.8
china clay or **stone** *material* 129.2
china decorator *ceramist* 129.7
china doll *figure* 187.4
China ink *black pigment* 254.2
china painter *ceramist* 129.7
china plumbing ware *industrial ceramics* 129.6
China rose Flowers 42
China Sea Oceans and Seas 571
china stone *material* 129.2
China syndrome *ruin* 523.4
China tea *tea* 93.7
Chinatown New York 567.6
chinaware *ceramics* 129.1, *crockery* 578.16
chinbone Human Bones 19
chinchilla Fabrics and Fibers 130
Chincoteague pony Horse and Pony Breeds 159
Chindwin Rivers 570
chine *valley* 572.8
Chinese Phobias 283
Chinese architecture Architectural Styles 134
Chinese character *written letter* 5.14
Chinese checkers Board and Table Games 167, *board games* 167.3
Chinese chess Board and Table Games 167
Chinese Chippendale Furniture Styles 101
Chinese crested Breeds of Dogs 35
Chinese fan-tan Card Games 168
Chinese lantern Flowers 42
Chinese or **Japanese lantern** *lantern* 246.8
Chinese lanterns *salute* 405.7
Chinese New Year *religious festival* 85.13
Chinese puzzle *puzzle* 182.5

Chinese remainder theorem Mathematical Concepts 6
Chinese white *whitener* 253.3
Ch'ing porcelain Ceramics 129
Chink Nicknames for Inhabitants 61
chink *small sound* 233.4, *sound faint* 233.8, *ringing* 236.2, *crack* 587.2, *narrow place* 593.2, *furrow* 638.1, 638.5, *defect* 806.4
chink in one's armor *defect* 806.4, *vulnerability* 811.6
chinky *furrowed* 638.3
chino Fabrics and Fibers 130
chinoiserie Furniture Styles 101
chinook Notable Winds 9
chins Phobias 283
chintz Fabrics and Fibers 130
chintzy *shoddy* 497.11
chinwag [Inf] *speech* 205.1, *talk* 207.3
chionophobia Phobias 283
Chios Breeds of Sheep 16
chip *circuit* 14.37, *computer part* 15.4, *computing terms* 15.22, *sculpt* 144.10, *golf shots* 156.4, *play* 156.8, *play soccer* 163.8, *poker* 168.5, *be brittle* 548.4, *crumble* 553.22, *little thing* 580.3, *slice* 588.4, *separate* 753.12, *particle* 760.4, *fragment* 787.3, *defect* 806.4
chipboard *wood* 131.3
chip in *give out* 472.12, *interrupt* 775.14, *finance* 825.31
chip off *be brittle* 548.4
chip off the old block *look-alike* 730.4
chipped *brittle* 548.3, *imperfect* 806.5
chipped beef *beef* 90.24
Chippendale Furniture Styles 101
chipping *brittle* 548.3
chipproof *tough* 547.6
chippy [Inf] *drug taker* 121.12, *drug oneself* 121.37, *sexually immoral person* 432.8
chiral *structural* 11.28
chiral center *structure* 11.7
chirality *structure* 11.7
chiromancer *diviner* 86.14
chiromancy *divination* 86.5
Chiron Planets and Their Satellites 7
chiropractic *alternative medicine* 107.4, *treatment* 107.14, *therapy* 115.12, *touching* 216.2
chiropractor *healer* 107.22
Chiroptera *flying mammal* 35.8
chiropteran 35.25
chiropteran or **chiropter** *flying mammal* 35.8
chirp *bird sound* 240.2, *make a bird sound* 240.8
chirping *singing* 240.5
chirpy *cheerful* 269.7
chirr *insect sound* 240.3, *make an insect sound* 240.9
chirring *humming* 240.6
chirrup *bird sound* 240.2, *make a bird sound* 240.8
Chisel Constellations 7
chisel *farm tool* 16.5, *hand tool* 103.3, *woodworking tool* 131.6, *carpenter* 131.10, *material* 144.6, *sculpt* 144.10, *swindle* 193.19, *act dishonestly* 479.18, *perform* 522.16, *fashion* 536.7, *sharp-edged thing* 549.6, *use a sharp tool* 549.17, *form* 624.9
chiseler *schemer* 193.10
chisel plow *farm tool* 16.5
Chisinau Countries 566

chi-square distribution
probability distribution 6.56
chi-square test hypothesis testing
6.52
chit young woman 26.9, means of
identification 184.3, documentation
339.6, guarantee 458.3, permit
502.3
chitarra Musical Instruments 142
chitarra battente Musical
Instruments 142
chitchat chat 210.2
chitin polysaccharide 12.5, animal
covering 613.15
chitinoid arthropodal 39.22
chitinous arthropodal 39.22
chiton robe 100.20
chittamwood Trees and Shrubs
43
chittarone Musical Instruments
142
chitterlings variety meat 90.30
chivalrous male 32.16, military
76.28, heroic 284.10, courteous
410.6, virtuous 447.5
chivalrously heroically 284.18,
courteously 410.13, virtuously
447.9
chivalrousness courtesy 410.1
chivalry glory of war 76.17, heroism
284.2, courtesy 410.1, virtue 447.1
chivalry [Arch] courageous act
284.7
chives Herbs and Spices 91
chivvy along hurry someone up
694.15
chivy hurry someone up 694.15
chlamydia sexually transmitted
disease (STD) 114.17
Chloë Famous Lovers 299
chloramphenicol fungal antibiotic
47.7
chloride of lime color remover
252.4
chlorinate react 11.38, purify
111.19, practice hygiene 116.4,
immunize 810.22
chlorinated hygienic 116.3
chlorinated lime color remover
252.4
chlorination cleaning 111.2,
hygiene 116.1
chlorine Chemical Elements and
Common Allotropes 11, essential
element 12.15
chlorofluorocarbon (CFC)
atmosphere 9.8, pollution 117.8,
vaporizer 556.10
chlorophyll pigment 12.18, plant
body 47.13, green pigment 260.3
chlorophyll a photosynthesis 12.22
chlorophyll b photosynthesis 12.22
Chlorophyta algae 47.11
chlorophyte algae 47.11
chloroplast cell structure 13.16
chloroprene rubber polymer 11.9
chlorosis pests and diseases 17.12
Chnoumis Deities 82
chock sailboat parts and accessories
150.4, climbing equipment 161.4,
obstruction 584.2
chockablock crowded 59.22, filled
97.5, dense 594.6, full 761.8
chock-full filled 97.5, full 761.8
chockstone rock face 161.6
chocolate sweets 90.39, brown
thing 256.3, brown 256.5
chocolate milk milk 93.5
chocolate-point Siamese cat
brown thing 256.3
chocolates love token 299.8
choice 382.3; means 102.1, likes
290.3, judgment 341.1, will 372.1,
selection 382.1, selected 382.11,

excellence 445.4, excellent 445.13,
setting apart 753.2, excluding
764.5, chief thing 799.3, freedom
829.1
choice, the finalist 422.16
choice of expression phrasing
5.25
choice of words phrasing 5.25,
mode of expression 537.3
choir church interior 83.9, church
architecture 134.11, singing group
141.6, collection 757.3
choir invisible angel 82.11
choirmaster musical director 141.7
choir robe robe 100.20
choir school type of school 48.12
Choiseul Islands 572
choke murder 30.20, be excessive
99.9, wrestling terms 152.10,
wrestle 152.20, sound hoarse
238.8, stopper 584.3, obstruct
584.13, hinder 826.15
choked speechless 206.7, obstructed
584.8
chokedamp miasma 556.3
choked up obstructed 584.8
choker neckwear 100.29, jewelry
532.6, circular thing 631.3
chokey or choky [Brit] the inside
[Inf] 55.2
choking Phobias 283, squeeze
582.3
cholagogic inducing secretion 24.6
cholecystokinin or cholecysto-
kinin-pancreozymin or
pancreozymin Human
Hormones 12
choler anger 302.4, irritableness
302.5, irascibility 303.1
cholera tropical disease 114.10,
gastroenterological disease 114.11,
Phobias 283, agent of destruction
523.7
choleric personality type 108.6,
irritable 302.10, irascible 303.8,
bitter 306.9, argumentative 329.7
cholerically irascibly 303.17
cholerophobia Phobias 283
cholesterol fat 12.7
choline vitamin 12.13
Chomo Lhari Mountains and
Hills 569
chomp chew 92.22
chomping eating 92.1
Chondrichthyes fish 38.5
chondrite meteor 7.21
choo-choo [Inf] train 688.4
choose 382.14; discriminate
337.12, will 372.11, select 382.12
choose an alternative take a
substitute 672.7
choose by ballot vote 382.16
choose one's ground battle 76.33
choose one's words style 537.8
choose the military solution go
to war 76.29
choose to enjoy 290.9
choosing selecting 384.2, 382.9
choosy discriminating 337.9,
selecting 382.9
Cho Oyu Mountains and Hills 569
chop meat dish 90.21, pork 90.26,
lamb 90.27, cook 91.10, tennis
strokes 165.2, play tennis 165.13,
use a sharp tool 549.17, take apart
753.16, particle 760.4
chop and change be capricious
381.6
chop down flatten 716.15
chophouse eating place 92.17
choplogic sophistry 330.1, faulty
reasoning 351.4
chop logic practice sophistry 330.11
chop off take off 749.7

chopped culinary 91.9, reduced
749.5
chopper [Inf] motorcycle 687.12,
aircraft 689.3
choppily roughly 544.13
choppiness roughness 544.1, wave
571.3, irregularity 664.1,
turbulence 684.3, discontinuity
775.1
chopping subtraction 749.1
chopping board cooking equipment
91.6
chopping bowl cooking equipment
91.6
choppy bumpy 544.8, oceanic
571.7, irregular 664.3, turbulent
684.17, discontinuous 775.7
choppy sea rough thing 544.2,
wave 571.3
chops veal 90.25
chopsticks tableware 92.13
chop the air gesture 183.17
choragus producer 136.28
choral dramatic 136.31, musical
141.11, harmonizing 735.12
chorale Musical Forms 140, sacred
music 140.3, song 140.11, singing
group 141.6
choral group singing group 141.6
chorally dramatically 136.38, in
harmony 735.32
choral music making Hobbies
and Pastimes 167
chord 140.18; line 6.35, circle 6.40,
parts of a circle 631.4, collaboration
757.2
Chordata protochordate 39.4
chordate type of animal 34.5, of
animals 34.13, protochordate 39.4
chordophone musical instrument
142.1
chore task 122.2, line of duty 433.3,
allotted task 474.3
chorea neurological disease 114.20,
shake 684.7
choreal convulsive 684.19
choregus producer 136.28
choreic convulsive 684.19
choreograph dance 135.7, arrange
767.18
choreographed dramatized 136.32
choreographer dancer 135.4,
producer 136.28
choreographic dancing 135.6,
dramatic 136.31
choreographically dancingly
135.8, dramatically 136.38
choreography ballet 135.2,
dramaturgy 136.6, representation
187.1, arrangement 767.1
chores work 122.1
choriamb meter 139.10
choric Poem or Verse Forms 139
chorine dancer 135.4
chorion developmental biology 13.22
chorionic developmental 13.33
chorionic villus sampling (CVS)
prenatal diagnosis 107.9
C horizon soil 8.42
chorography map 187.5,
topography 565.5
chorophobia Phobias 283
chortle cry of amusement 239.2,
laugh 239.14, 277.12, laughter
277.8
chorus play part 136.8, role 136.23,
cast 136.26, part of poem 139.9,
song 140.11, singing group 141.6,
sing 141.16, speaker 205.12,
synchronize 649.7, harmonization
735.2, collection 757.3
chorus boy dancer 135.4,
entertainer 138.8

chorus girl dancer 135.4,
entertainer 138.8
chorus line dancer 135.4
chorus master musical director
141.7
chose legal property terms 470.2
chose in action legal property terms
470.2
chose in possession legal
ownership 469.8, legal property
terms 470.2
chosen authorized 52.11, expected
356.5, willed 372.6, selected
382.11, excellent 744.14
chosen, the chosen thing 382.8
chosen few best people 744.7
chosen people chosen thing or
person 382.8
chosen person 382.8
chosen thing 382.8
choughs Collective Names 59
chow [Inf] food 90.1
chow chow or chow Breeds of
Dogs 35
chowder soup 90.14
chow down! come and get it! 92.28
chrematophobia Phobias 283
chrestomathy compilation 59.14,
compendium 204.3, miscellany
751.3
chrism sacred object 83.11
chrism or chrisom ointment 562.8
chrismal oily 562.11
Christ God the Son 82.9
Christ! miscellaneous swearwords
301.20
Christ Almighty! miscellaneous
swearwords 301.20
christen perform rites 85.18, enroll
771.33
Christendom Christianity 81.5
christened enrolled 771.24
christening baptism 85.6,
nomenclature 202.7, ceremony
405.3, reception 473.4, holy water
557.15, shipbuilding 690.4,
enrollment 771.8
Christian 81.10; denominational
81.23, loving 299.15, benevolent
person 305.6, charitable 305.9,
virtuous 447.5
Christian charity love 299.1,
charity 305.3
Christian conduct virtues 447.2
Christian door Architectural
Elements 134
Christianity 81.5
Christianize proselytize 84.15
Christian love love 299.1
Christian name name 202.8
Christian prayers prayer 85.10
Christian rite 85.5
Christian Science Christian
Groups 81, Christianity 81.5
Christian Science practitioner
healer 107.22
Christian Science text Christian
text 81.16
Christian text 81.16
christie skiing techniques 162.5,
snowplow 162.29
Christ Jesus God the Son 82.9
Christlike 82.18
Christly Christlike 82.18
Christmas Christian Holy Days
and Seasons 85, seasons 654.2
Christmas account personal
finance 457.5
Christmas box [Brit] gift 472.2
Christmas cactus Flowers 42
Christmas carol song 140.11
Christmas dinner feast 92.9
Christmas Island Islands 572
Christmas present gift 472.2

Christmastide Christian Holy Days and Seasons 85
Christmas tree *tree* 43.1
Christmas tree lights *electric light* 246.6
Christological *theological* 81.24
Christology Theologies 81
chroma *hue* 251.4
chromascope *chromatics* 251.8
chromatic *colored* 251.10
chromatic aberration *chromaticism* 251.2
chromaticism 251.2
chromaticity *hue* 251.4
chromaticity chart *chromatics* 251.8
chromaticity diagram *chromatics* 251.8
chromatic painting *color image* 251.7
chromatics 251.8
chromatic scale *scale* 140.16
chromatid *chromosome* 13.21
chromatin *cell structure* 13.16
chromatism *chromaticism* 251.2
chromatograph *analysis* 11.17
chromatographic *analytic* 11.32
chromatography *process* 11.15, *analysis* 11.17, *biochemical applications* 14.30
chromatography paper *sponge* 708.7
chromatological *chromolithographic* 251.14
chromatology *chromatics* 251.8
chrome yellow *yellow pigment* 259.2
chromium Chemical Elements and Common Allotropes 11, *essential element* 12.15
chromogenic film *film* 132.8
chromolithographic **251.14**
chromolithography *printing* 173.3, *color image* 251.7
chromonema *cell structure* 13.16
chromophobia or **chromatophobia** Phobias 283
chromosomal *genetic* 13.32
chromosome **13.21;** *genetic material* 13.20
chromosome mutation *chromosome* 13.21
chromosphere *sun* 7.15
chromotypography *printing* 173.3
chronic *sick* 114.24, *painful* 215.4, *unyielding* 379.8, *habituated* 397.14, *lasting* 639.9
chronically *unhealthily* 114.31
chronically ill *unhealthy* 114.23
chronically sick *unhealthy* 114.23
chronic complaint *ill health* 114.1
chronic fatigue syndrome *fatigue* 820.1
chronic ill health *ill health* 114.1
chronic illness *ill health* 114.1
chronic invalid *sick person* 114.22
chronicle **3.4, 3.15;** *history* 3.1, *nonfiction* 139.6, *record* 185.1, 185.13, *recount* 202.16, *chronology* 646.2, *chronologize* 646.13, *list* 785.11
chronicled **3.12;** *recorded* 185.12
chronicler *historian* 3.3, *author* 139.13, *record keeper* 185.8, *descriptive writer* 202.10, *keeper of time* 646.10
chronogram *face* 646.8
chronogrammatic *chronological* 639.12, *timekeeping* 646.11
chronograph Timepieces and Timers 646

chronographer *keeper of time* 646.10
chronographic *chronological* 639.12, *timekeeping* 646.11
chronographically *horologically* 646.15
chronography *time measurement* 639.5, *chronology* 646.2
chronologic *timekeeping* 646.11
chronological **639.12;** *timekeeping* 646.11, *consecutive* 774.7
chronological error *wrong time* 660.2
chronologically **639.21;** *horologically* 646.15, *consecutively* 774.11
chronological order *consecutiveness* 774.1
chronologist *keeper of time* 646.10
chronologize 646.13
chronology 646.2; *time* 639.1, *time measurement* 639.5
chronometer Fields of Measurement 589, *measuring instrument* 589.12, Timepieces and Timers 646, *navigational aid* 690.6
chronometric *chronological* 639.12, *timekeeping* 646.11
chronometry Fields of Measurement 589, *time measurement* 639.5
chronon Scientific and Technical Units 589, *space-time* 639.2
chronophobia Phobias 283
chronoscope Timepieces and Timers 646
chronostratigraphic unit *geological time* 8.47
chrysalid *immature* 40.14
chrysalis *developmental biology* 13.22, *young animal* 26.4, *insect metamorphal stage* 40.8
chrysanthemum Flowers 42
Chrysophyta *algae* 47.11
chrysophyte *algae* 47.11
chrysoprase *green thing* 260.4
chthonian or **chthonic** *demonic* 446.9
chubbiness *fatness* 579.5, *thickness* 594.1, *round body* 633.2
chubby *fat* 579.15, *thick* 594.5, *well-rounded* 633.8
chubby-cheeked *fat* 579.15
chubby-faced *fat* 579.15
Chubut Rivers 570
chuck *beef* 90.24, *stone* 418.23, *blow* 695.5, *throw* 696.4, 696.17
chuck [Inf] *food* 90.1
chucker *thrower* 696.10
chucking *throwing* 696.3
chuck it in [Inf] *resign* 835.5
chuckle *cry of amusement* 239.2, *laugh* 239.14, 277.12, *make a bird sound* 240.8, *show joy* 269.10, *laughter* 277.8
chuckling *cheering* 239.10
chuck out [Inf] *discard* 383.12, *destroy* 523.10, *expel* 709.14
chuck under the chin *communicate love* 299.25, *tap* 695.13
chuck-wagon cook *cook* 91.3
chuff *rattle* 235.12
chug *rattle* 235.12, *maneuver* 677.18
chug-a-lug [Inf] *drink* 93.19, *get drunk* 121.35
chukka boots *boots* 100.31
Chulym Rivers 570
chum *friend* 62.2, *bait* 154.6, *social person* 408.7, *companion* 794.8
chumminess [Inf] *friendship* 62.1
chummy [Inf] *friendly* 62.5

Ch'un Chiu *other text* 81.19
chunk *solid body* 540.4, *mass* 579.7, *throw* 696.17, *certain amount* 738.3, *remainder* 750.1, *particle* 760.4
chunk [Inf] *heaviness* 538.1
chunkiness *squatness* 579.6, *thickness* 594.1
chunky *heavy* 538.9, *stocky* 579.16, *thick* 594.5
Chunnel *tunnel* 691.6
Church, the *priesthood* 84.2
church *social institution* 2.8, *party* 59.3, *religious group* 81.4, *place of worship* 83.8, *architectural structure* 134.4, Phobias 283, *building* 551.9
church architecture **134.11**
church bazaar *sale* 482.2
church bell *signal* 183.6, *source of resonance* 236.4, *warning signal* 814.3
church book *ritual manual* 85.11
church calendar *calendar* 646.3
Churches of Christ Christian Groups 81
Churches of God Christian Groups 81
Churches of the Brethren Christian Groups 81
Churches of the Nazarene Christian Groups 81
church furniture *furniture* 101.1
churchgoer *worshiper* 83.6, *attender* 575.6
churchgoing *religious* 81.21
church government *theocracy* 49.4
Churchill Rivers 570
churchiness *religiousness* 81.2
church interior **83.9**
churchly *priestly* 84.12
churchman *priest* 84.8
church mode *mode* 140.17
church music *sacred music* 140.3
Church of Christ, Scientist Christian Groups 81
Church of England *Christianity* 81.5, *denominational* 81.23
church property *property* 470.1
church service *public worship* 83.3
churchwarden *tobacco implements* 121.24
church wedding *wedding* 64.5
churchy *zealous* 81.22
churchyard *burial place* 31.7
churl *commoner* 71.1, *sullen person* 304.7, *vulgar person* 535.4
churlish *common* 71.3, *clumsy* 128.6, *ill-natured* 303.9, *irritable* 304.9, *bad-mannered* 411.6, *indecorous* 528.8
churlishly *vulgarly* 71.5, *ill-naturedly* 303.18, *irritably* 304.17, *rudely* 411.9
churlishness *ill nature* 303.2, *irritableness* 304.3, *bad manners* 411.2, *impropriety* 528.2
churn *farm tool* 16.5, *thicken* 561.21, *turbulence* 684.3, *agitator* 684.14, *agitate* 684.22, *mixer* 751.7
churn out *perform* 522.16, *harp* 797.17
churn up *agitate* 684.22
churrigueresque architecture Architectural Styles 134
Churro do Campo Breeds of Sheep 16
Chushka Breeds of Sheep 16
chute *river turbulence* 570.5, *outlet* 707.8, *downflow* 714.3
chute-the-chute *amusement park and playground equipment* 167.8

chutney *side dish* 90.15
chutzpa [Inf] *audacity* 400.3, *defiance* 416.1, *assurance* 621.8
chutzpadik [Yiddish] *insolent person* 400.7
chyle *body fluid* 19.16, 555.3
chypre *incense* 226.3
ciao! [Ital] *hello!* 704.23, *goodbye!* 705.14
cibophobia Phobias 283
ciborium *sacred object* 83.11, *overhead covering* 613.11
cicatrix *blemish* 533.1
cicatrized *blemished* 533.5
cicerone *usher* 794.7
Ciceronian *fluid* 527.5
cicisbeo *lover* 299.11
cigar *tobacco* 121.23, *cylinder* 633.4
cigarette *tobacco* 121.23
cigarette butt *remainder* 750.1
cigarette case *tobacco implements* 121.24, *box* 578.5
cigarette end *tobacco* 121.23, *remainder* 750.1
cigarette holder *tobacco implements* 121.24
cigarette lighter *tobacco implements* 121.24
cigarette machine *tobacco implements* 121.24
cigarette paper *tobacco* 121.23
cigarette smoke *unpleasant-smelling thing* 227.2
cigarillo *tobacco* 121.23
cilantro Herbs and Spices 91
cilia *body covering* 19.4, *eye* 242.3
ciliary *hairy* 19.20
Ciliata *protozoan* 39.17
ciliate *protozoan* 39.17, 39.27
ciliate protozoan *protozoan* 39.17
Cimarron Rivers 570
cimbalom or **cymbalom** Musical Instruments 142
Cimmerian *dark* 247.5
cinch *riding equipment* 159.9, Card Games 168, *band* 754.9, *certainty* 840.1
cinch [Inf] *easy question* 333.5, *easy thing* 823.6
cinchona Tree Products 43
cincin! [Ital] *cheers!* 93.22
cincture *accessory* 100.28
cinder *dirt* 112.5, *refuse* 802.5
cinder block *masonry* 14.22, *building materials* 104.2
cinder cone *volcanic activity* 8.26
Cinderella *poor person* 486.6
cinders *residue* 750.2
cinema *motion pictures* 137.1, *motion-picture theater* 137.10, *place for viewing* 242.13, *production* 843.5
cinemactor or **cinemactress** *actor* 137.13
CinemaScope™ *motion-picture photography* 137.9
cinematic *motion-picture* 137.15
cinematics *motion-picture photography* 137.9
cinematize *produce* 137.21
cinematographer *photographer* 132.23, *filmmaker* 137.14
cinematography *photographic specialties* 132.2, *motion-picture photography* 137.9
cinéma vérité *movie type* 137.3, *realism* 719.3
cineraria Flowers 42
cinerarium *burial place* 31.7
cinerary *funeral* 31.9
cinerary urn *funeral object* 31.6
cinereous *gray* 255.6
cingulum *vestment* 84.11
cinnabar *red pigment* 257.2

cinnamon Herbs and Spices 91, *brown thing* 256.3
cinquain Poem or Verse Forms 139, *five* 792.1
cinque *five* 792.1
cinquecento architecture Architectural Styles 134
cinquefoil Flowers 42, Heraldic Terms 184, *five* 792.1
cipher *absolutes* 6.9, *the occult* 86.2, *puzzle* 182.5, *make mysterious* 182.13, *symbol* 183.3, *negator* 190.8, *unintelligible thing* 364.3, *number* 783.1, *calculate* 784.10, *zero* 786.1, *nonentity* 800.8
ciphering *count* 784.3
circadian rhythm *recurrent period* 641.5, *cycle* 663.3
circadian rhythm sleep disorder *sleep disorder* 108.20
Circe *witch* 86.15, *tempter* 178.10, *charmer* 700.6
Circean *witchlike* 86.19
Circinus Constellations 7
circle 6.40, 631.2, 631.6; *align* 6.92, *group* 59.8, 623.5, *auditorium* 136.17, *pommel horse* 157.7, *stationary rings* 157.8, *hammer throwing* 166.14, *place for viewing* 242.13, *region* 564.1, *surround* 615.7, *curve* 629.1, 629.6, *round thing* 633.3, *move around* 633.10, *be cyclic* 663.11, *orbit* 681.3, *ring* 681.9, *rotate* 682.14, *continuum* 774.5, *limitation* 830.2
circle chat Children's and Party Games 167
circle of friends *friend* 62.2
circle of least confusion *lens system* 10.22
circle of wagons *barrier* 419.10
circle theater *theater* 136.16
circle upon itself *convolute* 632.6
circling *cyclic* 663.7, *orbital motion* 681.1, *orbiting* 681.7, *rotary* 682.12
circling upon itself *convolution* 632.1
circuit 10.43, 14.37; *combinatorics* 6.63, *engagement* 136.15, 138.6, *automobile racing terms* 146.3, *curve* 629.1, *circle* 631.2, *round thing* 633.3, *round* 633.6, *cycle* 663.3, *orbit* 681.3, 681.8, *rotate* 682.14, *route* 691.2
circuit breaker *safety device* 810.15
circuit court of appeals *type of court* 54.9
circuit design *circuit* 14.37
circuit diagram *circuit* 14.37
circuit element 14.39; *circuit* 10.43
circuit function 14.38
circuitous *superfluous* 99.8, *circumlocutory* 199.4, *divergent* 607.7, *directional* 677.13, *orbital* 681.5, *wandering* 698.13
circuitously 199.8; *superfluously* 99.15, *divergently* 607.14, *curvedly* 629.7, *circularly* 631.8, 632.8, *in motion* 677.19
circuitousness 681.2; *divergence* 607.2, *wandering* 698.4
circuitous route *circle* 631.2
circuitous writing *circumlocution* 199.2
circuitry *circuit* 14.37
circular 631.5, 681.6; *curvilinear* 6.78, *advertisement* 173.9, *sophistic* 330.7, *curved* 629.4, *cyclic* 663.7
circular argument *sophism* 330.2, *faulty reasoning* 351.4

circular decimal *division* 6.16
circular function *trigonometric function* 6.50
circularity 631.1; *sophistry* 330.1, *curvature* 629.2, *orbital motion* 681.1
circularize *make circular* 631.7
circularized *published* 173.12
circularly 631.8, 632.8, 681.10; *sophistically* 330.14, *curvedly* 629.7, *cyclically* 663.15
circularly polarized light *polarized light* 10.19
circular mil Scientific and Technical Units 589
circular motion *frequency* 10.6
circularness *curvature* 629.2
circular parry *fencing movements* 153.3
circular path *circle* 631.2
circular polarization *wave property* 10.12
circular return *cycle* 663.3
circular road *circle* 631.2
circular saw *machine tool* 14.9, *woodworking tool* 131.6, *rotator* 682.8
circular triangle *triangle* 6.41
circulate *publish* 173.15, *be published* 173.19, *report* 175.9, *be sociable* 414.22, *monetize* 484.24, *circle* 631.6, *move around* 633.10, *orbit* 681.8, *rotate* 682.14, *proceed* 692.16, *disperse* 776.12
circulated *published* 173.12, *dispersed* 776.6
circulating *metabolic* 19.24, *published* 173.12, 174.18, 175.8
circulating library *library* 174.14
circulating medium *money* 484.1
circulation *body process* 19.15, *publishing* 173.2, *publicity* 173.7, *blood* 555.4, *orbital motion* 681.1, *circuitousness* 681.2, *rotation* 682.1, *passing along* 692.5, *dispersion* 776.1
circulation pattern *ocean current* 8.15
circulatory *metabolic* 19.24, *circular* 631.5, *orbital* 681.5, *rotary* 682.12
circulatory disease *disease* 114.4
circumambience or circumambiency *encirclement* 615.2
circumambient *surrounded* 615.5
circumambiently *around* 615.8
circumambulate *circle* 631.6, *move around* 633.10, *ring* 681.9
circumambulation *non-Christian ritual* 85.8, *round* 633.6, *orbital motion* 681.1
circumbendibus [Inf] *wandering* 698.4
circumcenter *triangle* 6.41
circumcircle *circle* 6.40
circumcise *take off* 749.7
Circumcision Christian Holy Days and Seasons 85
circumcision *non-Christian ritual* 85.8, *subtraction* 749.1, *separateness* 753.3
circumference *line* 6.35, *circle* 6.40, 631.2, *space* 563.1, *size* 579.1, *distant place* 585.3, *exteriority* 610.2, *edge* 617.3, *parts of a circle* 631.4, *externality* 724.4
circumferential *covering* 610.8, *circular* 631.5
circumferentially *exteriorly* 610.16, *circularly* 631.8
circumflex Accents and Diacritical Marks 5
circumfusion *dispersion* 776.1

circumgyratory *rotary* 682.12
circumlocute 607.12
circumlocution 199.2; *phrasing* 5.25, *misinformation* 188.3, *equivocation* 380.1, *indirectness* 607.3, *wandering* 698.4
circumlocutorily *indirectly* 607.15
circumlocutory 199.4; *phrased* 5.39, *equivocal* 380.5, *ornate* 532.10, *indirect* 607.8, *convolutional* 632.4
circummigrate *ring* 681.9
circummigration *orbital motion* 681.1
circumnavigable *orbital* 681.5
circumnavigate *circle* 631.6, *move around* 633.10, *ring* 681.9, *navigate* 690.15
circumnavigation *round* 633.6, *movement* 677.3, *orbital motion* 681.1, *water transportation* 690.1
circumnavigator *nautical person* 690.12
circumnutate *rotate* 682.14
circumpolar star *star* 7.8
circumrotation *rotation* 682.1
circumrotatory *rotary* 682.12
circumscribability *contractibility* 582.4
circumscribable *contractible* 582.11
circumscribe *align* 6.92, *specify* 340.14, *fence* 419.21, *be moderate* 455.12, *prohibit* 503.8, *squeeze* 582.13, *narrow* 593.14, *enclose* 619.6, *limit* 620.7, 830.13, *inset* 710.13, *divide* 753.18, *exclude* 764.7, *hinder* 826.15
circumscribed *conditional* 340.10, *temperate* 455.8, *retained* 471.6, *squeezed* 582.9, *narrow* 593.8, *surrounded* 615.5
circumscribed figure *geometric figure* 6.39
circumscription *specification* 340.6, *prohibition* 503.1, *squeeze* 582.3, *narrowness* 593.1, *edge* 617.3, *enclosure* 619.1, *limitation* 620.2, 830.2, *exclusion* 764.1, *hindrance* 826.1
circumscriptive *prohibited* 503.5, *contracting* 582.10, *narrow* 593.8, *outlined* 617.4, *hindering* 826.12, *restraining* 830.8
circumscriptively *prohibitively* 503.11, *narrowly* 593.17, *restrainedly* 830.18
circumspect 325.8; *prudent* 287.7, *thoughtful* 315.10, *watchful* 323.6, *wise* 352.4, *foreseeing* 357.5, *unhurried* 693.8
circumspection 325.3; *prudence* 287.2, *thought* 315.5, *carefulness* 323.3, *foresight* 357.1, *slowness* 693.1
circumspectly *prudently* 287.17, *attentively* 323.14, *slowly* 693.14
circumstance *pomp* 404.7, *formality* 406.1, *occurrence* 726.2, *rank* 739.2
circumstance or circumstances *state* 725.1
circumstances 573.2, 726.1; *personal estate* 470.6, *influence* 512.1
circumstances beyond one's control *necessitarianism* 95.7
circumstantial 573.7, 726.8; *verificatory* 336.6, *evidential* 339.8, *conditional* 725.7, *unimportant* 800.10
circumstantial evidence *evidence* 54.15, *legal evidence* 339.4

circumstantiality *diffuseness* 199.1
circumstantially 573.12; *verifiably* 336.11, *as evidence* 339.15, *conditionally* 725.10, *under the circumstances* 726.16, *unimportantly* 800.21
circumstantiate 726.12; *prove* 331.17, 336.9, 339.14
circumstantiation *proof* 336.2
circumvallation *fortification* 419.12, *enclosure* 619.1
circumvent *deceive* 193.16, *avoid* 386.13, *ring* 681.9, *be cunning* 822.5
circumvention *guile* 193.3, *avoidance* 386.1, *cunning* 822.1
circumvent the law *be illegal* 53.30
circumvolute *rotate* 682.14
circumvolution *convolution* 632.1, *rotation* 682.1
circumvolve *rotate* 682.14
circus 138.2; *theater* 136.16, *show* 404.12, *miscellany* 751.3
circus animal *domestic animal* 34.3
circus clown *circus performer* 138.9
circus horse *horse* 159.1
circus performer 138.9
circus troupe *circus* 138.2
cire perdue *sculpture* 144.1
cirque *landform* 8.9, *rock face* 161.6, *valley* 572.8
cirque glacier *glacier* 8.44
cirriform *cloudy* 9.44
cirripede *crustacean* 39.10
cirrocumuliform *cloudy* 9.44
cirrocumulous *cloudy* 9.44
cirrocumulus *cloud* 9.17
cirrose or cirrous *cloudy* 9.44
cirrostratous *cloudy* 9.44
cirrostratus *cloud* 9.17
cirrus *cloud* 9.17
cissoid *curve* 6.38
cist *funeral object* 31.6
cistern *storehouse* 105.8, *water carrier* 557.16, *vessel* 578.11
cis-trans isomer(ism) *structure* 11.7
citadel *fort* 419.13, *fortification* 812.3
Citation Notable Horses 159
citation *pretrial proceedings* 54.13, *demand* 425.2, *compliment* 437.4, *accusation* 442.1, *passage* 692.1, *interrelatedness* 727.3, *part of writing* 760.6, *showplace* 843.4
cite *litigate* 54.27, *speak* 205.17, *explain* 331.16, *accuse* 442.8, *excerpt* 692.13, *circumstantiate* 726.12, *specify* 779.18, *reveal* 843.14
cited *accused* 442.5, *excerpted* 692.9, *displayed* 843.8
cithara *Musical Instruments* 142
citified *urban* 567.14
citify *urbanize* 567.15
citifying *urbanization* 567.4
citizen *national* 61.3, *native* 566.7, *municipal resident* 567.12, *free person* 829.9
citizen by adoption *national* 61.3
citizen of the world *national* 61.3, *internationalist* 566.9
citizenry *group* 18.13, *inhabitants* 61.2
citizen's army *the military* 58.2
Citizens Band (CB) *radio broadcasting* 172.4, *radio frequency* 661.3
citizenship *national* 61.3, *public-spiritedness* 307.2, *independence* 829.5
Citizens party Political Parties 50

Citlaltepetl Mountains and Hills 569

citric *fruitlike* 44.6

citric acid cycle *bioenergetics* 12.23, *respiration* 12.24

citriculture *horticulture* 17.1

citrine *fruitlike* 44.6, *yellow* 259.7

citron *yellow thing* 259.4, *yellow* 259.7

citrous *fruitlike* 44.6

citrulline Amino Acids 12

citrus *fruitlike* 44.6

Citrus Belt *farmland* 16.3

citrus fruit *fruits* 44.1, *botanical fruit* 44.2, *fruit* 90.34

citrus grove *garden* 17.2

cittern Musical Instruments 142

City, the [Brit] *stock market* 483.6, *London* 567.8

city 567.1; *body politic* 50.3, *administrative region* 564.4

city center *urban area* 567.10

city council *governing body* 49.19, *representative body* 79.2

city dweller *townsperson* 61.7, *municipal resident* 567.12

city editor *print journalist* 175.5

city farm *farm* 16.2

city hall *municipal building* 567.13

city hospital *hospital* 107.16

city jail *prison* 55.1

city magistrate *judge* 54.10

city map *map* 187.5

City of God *heaven* 82.15

city of the dead *burial place* 31.7

city person *townsperson* 61.7

cityscape *view* 242.8

city slicker *townsperson* 61.7, *municipal resident* 567.12

city-state *nation* 18.14, *body politic* 50.3, *dominion* 566.3

city tax *tax* 494.5

civet *incense* 226.3

civic *national* 18.16, *governmental* 49.24, *political* 50.9, *architectural types* 134.2, *sociable* 408.11, *urban* 567.14

civic affairs *politics* 50.1

civically *politically* 50.11, *municipally* 567.16

civic center *center of activity* 612.4

civic garden *garden* 17.2

civic-minded *public-spirited* 307.7

civic-mindedly *for the public good* 307.10

civics *subject* 48.3, *political science* 50.2

civil *national* 18.16, *governmental* 49.24, *sociable* 408.11, *courteous* 410.6, *urban* 567.14, *internal* 611.9

civil architect *architect* 134.3

civil ceremony *wedding* 64.5

civil code *law* 53.1

civil court *law court* 54.8

civil disobedience *resistance movement* 417.3, *disobedience* 427.1, *dissent* 506.2

civil disturbance *violation of the law* 427.2

civil engineer 14.19; *engineer* 14.2, *professional worker* 123.11

civil engineering 14.17; *engineering* 14.1, *manufacture* 522.2

civil engineering tool 14.18

civil government *government* 49.1

civilian *pacific* 74.7

civilian clothes *informal clothes* 100.7

civilian evacuation *war measures* 76.18

civilities *etiquette* 406.3, *courtesies* 410.3

civility *courtesy* 410.1, *refinement* 534.1

civilization *civilized humanity* 18.5, *education* 48.1, *learning* 348.3, *social improvement* 807.3

civilize 807.16; *socialize* 2.14, *make human* 18.17, *educate* 48.22, *refine* 534.7

civilized *human* 18.15, *refined* 48.20, *cultured* 534.6

civilized humanity 18.5

civilized world *civilized humanity* 18.5

civilizing *improving* 807.14

civil law *law* 53.1

civil liberties *free rights* 829.4

civil list [Brit] *list of names* 785.7

civilly *sociably* 408.19, *courteously* 410.13, *decorously* 534.10

civil rights *rights* 429.4, *free rights* 829.4, *equal opportunity* 831.2

civil servant *public servant* 69.3, *commissioner* 833.5

civil service *officialdom* 49.20, *council* 833.4

civil society *nation* 18.14

civil trial *legal process* 54.3

civil war 76.6; *revolution* 427.4

civil wedding *wedding* 64.5

civism *public-spiritedness* 307.2

civit Bean Varieties 90

civitas Dei [L] *heaven* 82.15

civvies *informal clothes* 100.7, *informal clothing* 407.5

clabber *semiliquid* 561.7, *thicken* 561.21

clabbered *thick* 561.17

clabbering *viscosity* 561.1

clack *rattle* 235.3, 235.12, *make a bird sound* 240.8

clad *dressed* 100.38, *face* 613.31

cladding *wall covering* 613.12

clade *taxonomy* 13.24

cladism *taxonomy* 13.24

cladist *life scientist* 13.26

cladistic *taxonomic* 13.35

cladistics *taxonomy* 13.24, *classification of life* 28.10

cladode *leaf* 41.6

cladophyll *leaf* 41.6

claim 72.2, 429.3; *litigation* 54.1, *litigate* 54.27, *industrial dispute* 57.7, *be entitled to* 72.13, *contention* 189.4, *contend* 189.24, *line of argument* 329.3, *plea* 329.5, *state* 329.13, *plead* 329.14, *demand* 425.2, 425.11, 505.3, 505.12, *have rights* 429.13, *possess* 469.14, *property* 470.1, *petition* 505.2, 505.11, *plot* 564.9, *extortion* 711.6, *extort* 711.18

claimant *litigant* 54.4, *accuser* 442.3, *requester* 505.5

claim a victory *be victorious* 845.16

claimed *litigated* 54.22, *contended* 189.15, *logical* 329.9

claiming 469.2; *litigating* 54.21, *demanding* 505.8

claim sanctuary *shelter* 812.8

claims of conscience *sense of duty* 433.2

claim squatter's rights *possess* 469.14

claim to fame *repute* 370.1, *special feature* 779.4

clairaudience *psychic power* 86.4

clairaudient *diviner* 86.14, *divinatory* 86.18

clairsentience *psychic power* 86.4

clairsentient *diviner* 86.14, *divinatory* 86.18

clairvoyance *divine manifestation* 82.5, *psychic power* 86.4,

divination 86.5, 358.2, *sensation* 212.1, *impression* 266.2, *precognition* 320.2, *parapsychology* 525.4

clairvoyant *diviner* 86.14, *divinatory* 86.18, *observer* 242.15, *intuitive* 266.10, *intuitive person* 320.5, *precognitive* 320.7, *predictor* 357.4, *foreseeing* 357.5, *oracle* 358.8, *predicting* 358.11, *nonmaterialist* 525.7, *parapsychological* 525.9

clairvoyantly *occultly* 86.27, *foresightedly* 357.10, *metaphysically* 525.13

clam *food fish and shellfish* 90.20

clamant *shouting* 232.7

clambake *feast* 92.9

clamber *mounting* 713.8, *climb* 713.21

clamber up *climb* 713.21

clamlike *molluskan* 39.23, *noncommittal* 181.11

clammed up [Inf] *silent* 231.2

clammily *moistly* 559.17

clamminess *humidity* 559.3, *doughiness* 561.2

clammy *sweaty* 25.17, *moist* 559.9, *viscous* 561.14

clamor *loudness* 232.1, *harsh sound* 238.1, *cry* 239.1, *dissonance* 241.1, *show of disapproval* 438.6, *protest* 507.1, 507.7, *tumult* 684.2, *variety* 751.4, *commotion* 768.5

clamorous *shouting* 232.7, *strident* 238.4, *vociferous* 239.9, *protesting* 507.5

clamorously *vociferously* 239.18

clamp *hand tool* 103.3, *retention* 471.1, *retainer* 471.3, *retain* 471.7, *moderator* 521.2, *moderate* 521.7, *contractor* 582.6, *squeeze* 582.13, *intertwine* 752.19, *fastener* 754.7, *bind* 754.14, *means of restraint* 830.6, *restrain* 830.12

clampdown *severity* 424.1

clamp down on *be severe* 424.8, *moderate* 521.7, *abolish* 523.11, *restore order* 765.22, *restrain* 830.12

clamped *bound* 754.12

clamping *squeeze* 582.3

clamshell *construction equipment* 14.23

clam up [Inf] *keep secret* 182.11, *lack candor* 192.22, *be silent* 231.3

clan *society* 1.6, *social organization* 2.5, *group* 18.13, 59.8, *inhabitants* 61.2, *family* 65.1, *associate* 754.3

clandestine *secretive* 182.9, *private* 245.5, *cunning* 822.4, *mysterious* 844.11

clandestinely *stealthily* 182.15

clandestineness *secretiveness* 182.3, *latency* 844.1

clang *loud tone* 232.3, *be loud* 232.8, *ring* 235.14, *ringing* 236.2

clang association *association of ideas* 108.31

clanger [Brit inf] *blunder* 528.5

clangor *loud tone* 232.3, *ringing* 236.2

clangorous *loud* 232.6

clank *sound hoarse* 238.8

clanking *hoarse* 238.5

clannish *family* 65.6, *dissenting* 347.7, *excluding* 764.5

clannishly *cliquishly* 59.32

clanship *fellowship* 827.2

clan system *tribalism* 49.2

clap *gesture* 183.17, *burst of sound* 232.4, *crack* 234.2, 234.7, *acclaim* 437.5, 437.18

clap [Inf] *sexually transmitted disease (STD)* 114.17

clapboard *wood* 131.3, *wall covering* 613.12

clap eyes on [Inf] *see* 242.20

clap of thunder *thunderstorm* 9.20, *bang* 234.1

clap one's hands *acclaim* 437.18

clapper *source of resonance* 236.4, *approver* 437.7

clappers Musical Instruments 142

clapping *gesture* 183.5, *gestural* 183.13, *acclaim* 437.5, *acclamatory* 437.10

claptrap *nonsense* 192.8, *empty talk* 362.5

claque *theatergoer* 136.30, *approver* 437.7

claqueur *theatergoer* 136.30, *approver* 437.7

claret *red thing* 257.3

claret [Inf] *blood* 555.4

clarification *cleaning* 111.2, *explanation* 331.3, *proof* 336.2, *interpretation* 365.1, *easing* 823.7

clarified *transparent* 249.7, *explanatory* 331.11, *interpreted* 365.9

clarifier *demonstrator* 331.6, *interpreter* 365.6

clarify 196.3; *rationalize* 4.20, *purify* 111.19, *make visible* 244.9, *make transparent* 249.12, *explain* 331.16, *prove* 336.9, *make comprehensible* 363.8, *interpret* 365.12, *make simple* 526.12, *refine* 534.7, *melt* 555.24, *make easy* 823.15

clarifying *interpretive* 365.8

clarinet Musical Instruments 142

clarinettist *player* 141.2

clarion Musical Instruments 142

clarion call *war measures* 76.18, *exhortation* 178.2, *burst of sound* 232.4

clarity 196.1, 244.2, 363.2; *light* 10.17, *transparency* 249.1, *comprehensibility* 361.3, *unpretentiousness* 526.2, *elegance* 527.1, *plainness* 592.4, *straightforwardness* 630.3, *simplicity* 823.2

Clark Fork Rivers 570

clarkia Flowers 42

clash *hostility* 63.1, *oppose* 63.11, *battle* 76.23, *sound* 141.15, *tumult* 232.5, *be loud* 232.8, *bang* 234.1, 234.6, *be strident* 238.7, *dissonance* 241.1, *be dissonant* 241.6, *be off-color* 251.18, *quarrel* 272.4, 272.9, *argue* 329.11, *dissent* 347.8, *contention* 422.1, *warfare* 422.10, *dispute* 463.3, 463.9, *disagree* 463.8, *opposing force* 510.2, *counteract* 510.7, *violence by person* 520.2, *collide* 695.10, *confront* 828.19

clashing *hostility* 63.1, *aggressive* 63.9, *dissonant* 241.4, *gaudy* 251.12, *off-color* 251.15, *divisiveness* 463.2, *counteracting* 510.6, *conflict* 828.3, *discordant* 828.12

clasp *gesture* 183.5, 183.17, *retention* 471.1, *retainer* 471.3, *retain* 471.7, *enfoldment* 637.3, *enfold* 637.9, *joint* 752.7, *intertwine* 752.19, *fastener* 754.7, *bind* 754.14, *adhere* 755.8

clasped *retained* 471.6, *bound* 754.12

clasp hands *greet* 410.11

clasping *retentive* 471.5
clasp the knees of *shelter* 812.8
class **777.1, 777.12;** *set* 6.19, *group* 18.13, 59.8, *family* 65.1, *rank* 573.4, 727.11, 739.2, *state* 725.1, *relative position* 727.5, *measure* 739.7, *part* 760.1, *piece* 760.2, *position* 765.4, *systematize* 765.19, *category* 767.6, *categorize* 767.21, *taxonomical classification* 777.3, *students* 777.6, *lecture* 777.7
class boundary *social stratification* 2.7
class conflict *social stratification* 2.7
class discrimination *social discrimination* 337.4
classed **777.11;** *employed* 573.8, *conditional* 725.7, *ranked* 727.8, *partial* 760.11
classed with *included* 763.4
classic *historic* 3.11, *masterpiece* 68.14, *stylish* 100.42, *workmanlike job* 127.6, *mountaineering* 161.9, *book* 174.1, *fluid* 527.5, *cultured* 534.6, *olden* 653.11, *average* 742.5, *excellent* 744.14, *ideal* 805.17
classical *of language* 5.35, *physical* 10.70, *curricular* 48.21, *literary* 139.15, *musical* 140.25, *fluid* 527.5, *olden* 653.11, *historic* 653.13, *ideal* 805.17
Classical Age Ages, Decades, Eras 641
classical antiquity *historical past* 651.6
classical architecture Architectural Styles 134
classical author *stylist* 537.4
classical ballet *ballet* 135.2
classical conditioning *conditioning* 108.24
classical dancer *dancer* 135.4
classical economics *economics* 56.1
classical genetics *genetics* 13.19
classical guitar Musical Instruments 142
classical language *ancient language* 5.10
classically *physically* 10.78, *archaically* 653.20
classical mathematics *mathematics* 6.1
classical music **140.2**
classical physics **10.2**
Classical Revival Architectural Styles 134
classical riding *equestrianism* 159.8
classical taxonomy *taxonomy* 13.24
classical tragedy *tragedy* 136.10
classicism Western Art Styles 133, Western Literary Groups 139, *elegance* 527.1, *antiquarianism* 653.3
classicist *stylist* 537.4, *antiquarian* 653.17
classic murder *murder* 30.2
classic route *climbing expedition* 161.2
classics, the *literature* 139.1
classification **777.2;** *identification* 184.1, *nomenclature* 202.7, *relative position* 727.5, *gradation* 739.3, *grouping* 765.2, *categorization* 767.5, *listing* 785.8
classificational *classificatory* 777.9
classification of life **28.10**
classificatorially *inventorially* 785.13
classificatory **777.9;** *grouped*

765.11, *categorical* 767.16, *of a list* 785.10
classified *secret* 182.8, *identified* 184.9, *censored* 503.7, *ranked* 727.8, *gradational* 739.5, *grouped* 765.11, *categorized* 767.15, *classed* 777.11, *concealed* 844.7
classified ad [Inf] *advertisement* 173.9, *discounter* 497.7
classified advertisement *advertisement* 173.9
classified document *censorship* 503.4, *concealment* 844.2
classified information *inside information* 170.4, *verbal concealment* 181.3, *secret* 182.2
classified with *included* 763.4
classify *keep secret* 182.11, *identify* 184.11, *itemize* 577.13, *rank* 727.11, *measure* 739.7, *systematize* 765.19, *categorize* 767.21, *class* 777.12, *list* 785.11
classify as *subsume* 763.7
classifying *identification* 184.1, *classification* 777.2
classify secret *censor* 503.10
classing *classification* 777.2
classism *social discrimination* 337.4
classist *discriminatory* 337.11
classless *governmental* 49.24
classmate *learner* 48.6, *friend* 62.2, *contemporary* 649.3, *companion* 794.8
class of *contemporary* 649.3
class photo *portrait* 132.5
class prejudice *social discrimination* 337.4
class project *educational topic* 328.4
class reunion *social gathering* 408.4
class ring *clothing* 184.6
classroom *school place* 48.16
class structure *social stratification* 2.7
class war *social discrimination* 337.4
class with *subsume* 763.7
classy [Inf] *aristocratic* 70.4, *fashionable* 536.5
clastic *petrographic* 8.58
clastic rock *sedimentary rock* 8.34
clathrate *chemical compound* 11.4
clatter *tumult* 232.5, *be loud* 232.8, *crack* 234.7, *rattle* 235.3, 235.12, *variety* 751.4
clattering *rattling* 235.8
Claude tint *yellow pigment* 259.2
clausal *phrased* 5.39
clause **5.31;** *basis for negotiations* 460.2, *passage* 692.1, *part of speech* 760.7
claustrophobia Phobias 283
claves Musical Instruments 142
clavicembalo Musical Instruments 142
clavichord Musical Instruments 142
clavichordist *player* 141.2
clavicle Human Bones 19
clavicytherium Musical Instruments 142
clavier *part of keyboard instrument* 142.6
claw *inflict pain* 215.10, *retainer* 471.3, *sharp-pointed growth* 549.5, *use a sharp tool* 549.17, *yoke* 754.8
claw, the *grip* 154.4
claw chisel *material* 144.6
clawed *carnivorous* 35.26
claw hammer [Inf] *jacket* 100.18
claw one's way up *climb* 713.21
claw skyward *go up* 713.23

clay *sediment* 8.29, *soil* 8.42, *masonry* 14.22, *building materials* 104.2, *dirt* 112.5, *material* 129.2, *solid body* 540.4, *mud* 561.8
clay court *tennis court* 165.3
clayey *earthy* 8.60, *compressible* 543.9
claymation *movie type* 137.3
claymore *sharp weapon* 78.6
clay pigeon shooting Sporting Activities 145
clay pipe *tobacco implements* 121.24
clay sculpture *sculpture* 144.1
clayware Ceramics 129
clean **111.13, 111.17;** *hygienic* 116.3, *practice hygiene* 116.4, *work* 122.8, *mountaineering* 161.9, *mountaineer* 161.10, *odorless* 225.4, *deodorize* 225.6, *make transparent* 249.12, *pure* 253.11, 431.11, *whiten* 253.12, *new* 394.7, *right* 429.7, *innocent* 449.6, *simple* 526.7, *vacant* 576.12, *immature* 652.12, *immaturely* 652.23, *completely* 759.14, *761.13, orderly* 765.19, *tidy* 765.21, 807.19, *restore* 809.12
clean [Inf] **111.21**
clean as a whistle *clean* 111.13
clean bill of health *health* 113.1
clean climbing *mountaineering* 161.1
clean dry air *atmosphere* 9.8
cleaned **111.14**
cleaned out *cleaned* 111.14, *impoverished* 486.11
cleaned up *cleaned* 111.14, *expurgated* 111.15
cleaner **111.12;** *cleaning agent* 111.9, *domestic worker* 123.4
clean for *serve* 69.11
clean forget [Inf] *forget* 355.10
clean-handed *incorrupt* 449.7
clean hands *incorruption* 449.2
cleaning **111.2;** *cleansing* 111.16, *fabric treatment* 130.10, *climbing techniques* 161.3, *tidying* 807.6
cleaning agent **111.9**
cleaning cloth **111.11**
cleaning out *removal* 709.5
cleaning tool **111.10;** *climbing equipment* 161.4
cleaning up *cleaning* 111.2
cleaning woman *domestic servant* 69.7
cleanliness **111.1;** *hygiene* 116.1, *rightfulness* 429.1, *purity* 431.4, *innocence* 449.1, *simplicity* 526.1, *immaturity* 652.3
cleanly **111.20;** *clean* 111.13, *odorlessly* 225.8, *newly* 394.14, *suddenly* 549.20, *immaturely* 652.23
cleanness *cleanliness* 111.1, *hygiene* 116.1, *odorlessness* 225.1, *transparency* 249.1, *purity* 253.6, *newness* 394.2, *innocence* 449.1, *simplicity* 526.1, *immaturity* 652.3, *orderliness* 765.5
clean one's plate *eat well* 92.23
clean out *clean* 111.17, *purify* 111.19, *void* 709.23
cleanse *purify* 111.19, *practice hygiene* 116.4, *deodorize* 225.6, *make transparent* 249.12
cleanse oneself of sin *or* **guilt** *repent* 313.9
cleansed *cleaned* 111.14
cleanser *cleaning agent* 111.9, *cleaner* 111.12, *pomade* 562.9
clean-shaven *smooth* 545.4, *depilatory* 614.15
clean sheet *emptiness* 576.2

cleansing **111.16, 557.27;** *Christian rite* 85.5, *cleaning* 111.2, *medicinal* 115.15, *deodorizing* 225.5, *penitence* 313.3, *apologetic* 313.6, *improvement* 807.1, *upkeep* 815.5
cleansing agent *cleaning agent* 111.9
cleansing cream *cleaning agent* 111.9
clean slate *obliteration* 186.1, *emptiness* 576.2, *new start* 652.5
clean teeth *practice dentistry* 107.34
cleanup *cleaning* 111.2
cleanup [Inf] *profit* 467.6
clean up *clean* 111.17, *purify* 111.19, *tidy* 765.21, 807.19, *restore order* 765.22
clean up [Inf] *profit* 467.22, *get rich* 485.13
cleanup man *baseball team* 147.2
Clear Programming Languages 15
clear **196.2, 244.6;** *fine* 9.43, *shine* 9.56, *manage trees* 43.14, *acquitted* 54.25, 434.6, *acquit* 54.32, *clean* 111.17, *sailing* 150.25, *informative* 170.10, *disclosed* 180.5, *visible* 242.19, 244.5, *sunny* 246.17, *transparent* 249.7, *demonstrated* 331.9, *evident* 339.9, *meaningful* 361.6, *simple* 363.6, 526.7, *away* 386.23, *vindicate* 441.11, *declare innocent* 449.11, *profit* 467.22, *receive* 473.13, *pay off* 489.17, *permit* 502.6, 735.29, *elegant* 527.3, *refine* 534.7, *lakelike* 568.5, *vacant* 576.12, *opened up* 583.11, *open up* 583.16, *at a distance* 585.13, *space* 587.6, *plain* 592.10, *straightforward* 630.9, *service* 689.16, *climb* 713.21, *safe* 810.16, *easy* 823.9, *make easy* 823.15, *disentangle* 823.17, *open* 843.12
clear accounts with *pay off* 489.17
clear across *breadthways* 592.16
clearage *removal* 709.5
clear-air turbulence *miscellaneous aviation terms* 689.9
clearance *defecation* 25.3, *favorable verdict* 54.19, *jumping* 166.11, *vindication* 441.1, *sale* 482.2, *payment* 489.1, *permission* 502.1, 735.9, *available space* 563.6, *distance* 585.1, *interval* 587.1, *measuring instrument* 589.12, *passport* 692.8, *removal* 709.5, *scope* 829.7
clearance papers *permit* 502.3, *passport* 692.8
clearance sale *sale* 482.2, *bargain* 495.2
clear as air *transparent* 249.7
clear as crystal *transparent* 249.7
clear as daylight *manifest* 843.9
clear as mud *obscure* 197.2, *inscrutable* 250.5, *difficult* 364.8
clear away *void* 709.23
clear bulb *electric light* 246.6
clear coast *easy thing* 823.6
clear conscience *virtue* 447.1, *incorruption* 449.2
clear course *easy thing* 823.6
clear-cut *clear* 196.2, 244.6, *visible* 242.19, *demonstrable* 331.12, *intelligible* 363.5
cleared *authorized* 52.11, *acquitted* 54.25, *vindicated* 441.8, *incorrupt* 449.7, *declared innocent* 449.8, *paid* 489.11, *permitting* 735.19
cleared up *explanatory* 331.11, *solved* 334.15

clear-eyed *seeing* 242.17
clear field *opportunity* 659.2
clear glass *glass* 249.5
clear handwriting *clarity* 363.2
clear head *sobriety* 120.1
clearheaded *rational* 4.15, 109.4, *sober* 120.5, *intelligent* 352.5
clear image *image* 187.3
clearing *farmland* 16.3, *trees* 43.4, *field hockey tactics* 158.5, *geographical space* 563.3, *open space* 583.6, *removal* 709.5, *permitting* 735.19, *disentanglement* 823.8
clearing agent *darkroom equipment* 132.21
clearing from guilt *vindication* 441.1
clearinghouse *treasury* 484.19
clearing of one's name *vindication* 441.1
clearing up *cleaning* 111.2, *solution* 334.6
clearly 196.4; *visibly* 242.28, 244.10, *transparently* 249.13, *apparently* 264.16, *manifestly* 331.20, *evidently* 339.16, *meaningfully* 361.16, *intelligibly* 363.13, *simply* 526.14, *gracefully* 527.8, *openly* 583.22, *plainly* 592.18, *straightforwardly* 630.17
clearly handwritten *simple* 363.6
clearly printed *simple* 363.6
clear message *comprehensibility* 361.3
clearness *clarity* 196.1, 244.2, 363.2, *transparency* 249.1
clear off *depart* 705.8, *void* 709.23
clear one's head *be refreshed* 94.8, *sober up* 120.7
clear one's name *absolve* 312.10, *vindicate* 441.11
clear one's throat *salivate* 25.25, *sound hoarse* 238.8
clear out *clean* 111.17, *depart* 705.8, *void* 709.23
clear out *or* **off!** *go!* 709.30
clear pool *small lake* 568.2
clear printing *clarity* 363.2
clear profit *profit* 467.6
clear road *easy thing* 823.6
clear run *opportunity* 659.2
clear shot *badminton terms* 165.11
clear-sighted *seeing* 242.17
clear sky *sun* 9.21
clear soup *soup* 90.14
clear space *geographical space* 563.3
clear stock *sell off* 482.20
clearstory *church architecture* 134.11
clear the air *deodorize* 225.6, *atone* 313.7
clear the cobwebs out *be refreshed* 94.8
clear the decks *void* 709.23
clear the ground *make easy* 823.15
clear the track *further* 825.30
clear the water *row* 150.32
clear the way *make easy* 823.15, *make possible* 836.7
clear thinking *common sense* 315.4
clear to anyone *simple* 363.6
clear up *rationalize* 4.20, *clean* 111.17, *solve* 334.21, *prove* 336.9, *make comprehensible* 363.8, *make certain* 840.14
clear varnish *transparent thing* 249.4
clear view *opportunity* 659.2
cleat *sailboat parts and accessories* 150.4, *sailboard parts* 150.20, *fastener* 754.7

cleats *shoes* 100.30, *baseball equipment* 147.4, *football uniform* 155.2
cleavage *rock* 8.30, *mineral* 8.37, *developmental biology* 13.22, *separateness* 753.3
cleave *use a sharp tool* 549.17, *open* 583.15, *crack* 587.7, *take apart* 753.16, *halve* 789.15
cleaver *sharp-edged thing* 549.6
cleavers *or* **clivers** Flowers 42
cleave to *retain* 471.7, *adhere* 755.8
cleave to the line *aim* 697.14
cleaving *adhering* 755.7
cleek *golf equipment* 156.5
clef *written music* 140.21
cleft *dispute* 463.3, *opening* 583.1, *open* 583.10, *crack* 587.2, *cracked* 587.5, *notch* 636.1, *separateness* 753.3, *apart* 753.8, *interruption* 775.3
cleft palate *distortion of body* 627.3
cleft stick *irresolution* 841.3
clematis Flowers 42, *purple thing* 262.3
clemency *peace offering* 74.5, *compassion* 305.2, *mercy* 308.3, *forgiveness* 312.3, *leniency* 423.1
clement *warm* 217.13, *pitying* 308.4, *forgiving* 312.4, *lenient* 423.3
clementine *orange thing* 258.3
clemently *pacifically* 74.12, *pityingly* 308.11, *forgivingly* 312.13
clench *retention* 471.1, *retain* 471.7, *squeeze* 582.13
clenched *squeezed* 582.9
clenched fist *gesture* 183.5, *retainer* 471.3
clenched jaw *gesture* 183.5, *will* 376.5
clenched teeth *gesture* 183.5, *will* 376.5
clenching *squeeze* 582.3
clench one's fist *gesture* 183.17
clench one's jaw *gesture* 183.17
clench one's teeth *gesture* 183.17, *be silent* 231.3, *brace oneself* 376.13
Cleopatra Famous Lovers 299
clepsydra Timepieces and Timers 646
clerestory *church architecture* 134.11, *architectural summit* 600.4
clergy 84.1
clergyman *member of the clergy* 84.5
clergyperson *ritualist* 85.14
clergywoman *member of the clergy* 84.5
cleric *member of the clergy* 84.5
clerical *priestly* 84.12
clerical collar *vestment* 84.11, *neckwear* 100.29
clerical dress *uniform* 100.9, *formal clothing* 406.5
clerical dwelling 84.10
clerical garb *uniform* 100.9
clerical hat *hat* 100.32
clericalism *theocracy* 49.4, *priesthood* 84.2
clerically 84.17
clerical robe *robe* 100.20
clericals [Inf] *vestment* 84.11
clerical venue 84.4
clerical worker 123.5
clerihew Poem or Verse Forms 139
clerisy, the *literary person* 139.14
clerk *attendant* 69.4, *office assistant* 69.6, *record keeper* 185.8, *salesperson* 482.8

clerk of the court *court officer* 54.7
clerk-typist *clerical worker* 123.5
Cleveland Bay Horse and Pony Breeds 159
clever *educatable* 48.18, *educated* 48.19, *skillful* 127.10, *well-made* 127.13, *witty* 277.10, *intelligent* 315.9, 352.5, *imaginative* 360.10, *mentally sharp* 549.14, *cunning* 822.4
clever hands *manual skill* 127.2
cleverly *studiously* 48.26, *skillfully* 127.16, *intelligently* 315.14, 352.9, *sharply* 549.19
cleverness 315.3; *educatability* 48.9, *manual skill* 127.2, *intelligence* 352.2, *mental sharpness* 549.9, *cunning* 822.1
clew Collective Names 59, *sailboard parts* 150.20
clew line *tackle* 754.6
clianthus Flowers 42
cliché *catchword* 5.22, *worded* 5.38, *maxim* 177.1, *lack of emphasis* 201.1, *nonsense* 362.2, *truism* 721.6, *regularity* 730.6, *regular* 730.12, *generalization* 778.5, *repetitiveness* 797.3
cliché *or* **clichéd** *truistic* 721.15
clichéd *worded* 5.38, *proverbial* 177.2, *unemphatic* 201.2, *meaningless* 362.7, *familiar* 397.10, *monotonous* 797.12
cliché-ridden *unemphatic* 201.2, *monotonous* 797.12
click *small sound* 233.4, *sound faint* 233.8, *crack* 234.2, 234.7
click [Inf] *attain one's goal* 845.13
clicking *crackling* 234.5, *rattling* 235.8
client *computer communications* 15.25, *patient* 107.25, *user* 393.4, *purchaser* 481.7
client-centered therapy *psychotherapy* 108.4
clientele *custom* 480.12, *purchaser* 481.7
clients *custom* 480.12
cliff *coast* 8.13, *mountain* 569.1, *heights* 596.4, *vertical* 602.3
cliff-hanger *novel* 139.3
cliff-hanging *competitive* 422.21
clifflike *highland* 596.11
Cliffs Notes™ *schoolbook* 48.15
climacophobia Phobias 283
climacteric *middle age* 27.4, *middle-aged* 27.14
climacterically *maturely* 27.18
climactic *top* 600.6
climactically *at the summit* 600.12
climate 9.35; *weather* 9.3, *influence* 512.1, *tendency* 513.1, *circumstances* 573.2
climate modification *climatic change* 9.37
climate of opinion *belief* 87.1, *tendency* 513.1
climate zone 9.36
climatic *meteorologic* 9.38, *circumstantial* 573.7
climatically *meteorologically* 9.60
climatic change 9.37
climatic trend *climatic change* 9.37
climatic variation *climatic change* 9.37
climatological *geophysical* 8.51, *meteorologic* 9.38
climatologically *meteorologically* 9.60
climatologist *geophysicist* 8.5, *meteorologist* 9.2
climatology *geophysics* 8.2, *meteorology* 9.1

climax *sex act* 20.10, *stimulate* 20.22, *play part* 136.8, *physical pleasure* 214.1, *feel pleasure* 214.12, *pinnacle* 596.2, *peak* 596.18, *summit* 600.1, 744.4, *be at the top* 600.9, *spasm* 684.8, *be superior* 744.15, *intensification* 746.2, *intensify* 746.8, *complete* 759.10, *conclusion* 761.3, *limit* 761.4, *be complete* 761.10, *ending* 773.10
climb 713.21; *mountaineer* 161.10, *skiing techniques* 162.5, *ski* 162.35, *cost a lot* 496.9, *hill* 569.2, *heights* 596.4, *rise* 596.17, *be in motion* 677.14, *press on* 679.9, *make one's way* 679.12, *flight* 689.5, *fly* 689.13, *mounting* 713.8, *spread* 746.3, *increase* 746.6
climbable *ladderlike* 713.18
climb aboard *travel by train* 688.9
climb a mountain *mountaineer* 161.10
climb a rock *mountaineer* 161.10
climb down *humble oneself* 298.18, *descend* 597.22, 714.12
climb-down *humiliation* 298.5
climb down off the fence *determine* 675.11
climber *garden plant* 17.10, *plant* 41.2, *mountaineer* 161.8, *ascender* 713.12
climb hand over fist *climb* 713.21
climbing *of plants* 41.14, *mountaineering* 161.1, 161.9, *snowplow* 162.29, *costly* 496.7, *rising* 596.12, *ascending motion* 677.7, *directional* 677.13, *flying* 689.11, *mounting* 713.8, *steep* 713.15
climbing boots *climbing equipment* 161.4
climbing dangers 161.5
climbing equipment 161.4
climbing expedition 161.2
climbing gear *climbing equipment* 161.4
climbing plant *garden plant* 17.10
climbing prices *inflationary price* 496.3
climbing shoes *climbing equipment* 161.4
climbing techniques 161.3
climb into the saddle *mount* 713.24
climb on *mount* 713.24
climb on the bandwagon *be the same* 730.13, *conform* 735.27, *emulate* 736.11
climb over *climb* 713.21
climb up *climb* 713.21
clime *world region* 564.6
clinch *fencing movements* 153.3, *fence* 153.7, *prove* 331.17, *retention* 471.1, *retain* 471.7, *unify* 752.15, *intertwine* 752.19, *adhere* 755.8
clinch [Inf] *establish reality* 719.12
clincher *workmanlike job* 127.6, *refutation* 332.1, *conclusion* 761.3, *ender* 773.11
cling *hold out* 397.13, *become a habit* 397.17
clinger *adherent* 755.4
clinging *habit-forming* 397.15, *retentive* 471.5, *narrow* 593.8, *adhesive* 755.5, *adhering* 755.7
clinging on *or* **to** *retention* 471.1
clinging vine [Inf] *adherent* 755.4
cling like ivy *adhere* 755.8
cling on *or* **to** *retain* 471.7
cling to *observe* 465.4, *stay near*

586.13, *adhere* 755.8, *be tenacious* 755.9

cling to custom *be obstinate* 379.10, *have a habit* 397.16

cling to hope *hope* 281.10

clingy *tenacious* 755.6

clinic *hospital* 107.16

clinical *medical* 107.28, *material* 524.7

clinical death *mortality* 29.2

clinical depression *mood disorder* 108.12, *mental breakdown* 110.4

clinical disorder *mental disorder* 108.8

clinical educator *nurse* 107.23

clinically *medically* 107.35, 115.20, *materially* 524.9

clinical psychologist *psychologist* 108.33

clinical psychology Psychological Theories, Schools 108, *therapy* 115.12

clinical thermometer *heat measurement* 217.2

clinical treatment *treatment* 107.14, *therapy* 115.12

clinician *medical specialist* 107.20, *psychologist* 108.33

clink *small sound* 233.4, *sound faint* 233.8, *ringing* 236.2

clink [Inf] *the inside* 55.2

clinker *dirt* 112.5, *refuse* 802.5

clinker [Inf] *musical dissonance* 241.2

clinking *hoarse* 238.5

clinking gold *money* 484.1

clinometer *civil engineering tool* 14.18, Fields of Measurement 589

clinometry Fields of Measurement 589

clinophobia Phobias 283

Clio Deities 82

cliometric *historical* 3.10

cliometrician *historian* 3.3

cliometrics *history* 3.1

clip *ammunition* 78.11, *be on the track* 146.11, *exhibit penalty behavior* 155.21, *flag* 184.8, *be concise* 198.5, *retainer* 471.3, *demonetize* 484.25, *coif* 530.15, *use a sharp tool* 549.17, *contract* 582.12, *shorten* 591.9, *bodily movement* 677.11, *make smaller* 747.8, *joint* 752.7, *link* 752.18, *separate* 753.12, *fastener* 754.7, *connect* 754.13

clip [Inf] *overcharge* 496.10, *hit* 695.11

clip-fed *bolt-action* 78.17

clip-fed rifle *firearm* 78.7

clip one's wings *hinder* 826.15

clipped *worded* 5.38, *concise* 198.4, *summarized* 204.6, *monetary* 484.22, *shortened* 582.8, 591.7

clipped accent *regional pronunciation* 205.7

clipped coinage *false money* 484.15

clipped form *or* **word** *word* 5.17, *conciseness* 198.1

clipper Sailing Ships and Boats 690

clippers *sharp-edged thing* 549.6

clipper ship Sailing Ships and Boats 690

Clipperton Islands 572

clipping *penalty* 155.13, *record* 185.1, *shortening* 582.2, 591.2, *residue* 750.2

clippings *bits and pieces* 760.5

clip the apex *be on the track* 146.11

clip the wings *slow down* 693.13

clip to *add* 748.11

clique *group* 18.13, 59.8, *fashionable elite* 536.4, *exclusiveness* 764.4, *social class* 777.5

cliquey *excluding* 764.5

cliquish *excluding* 764.5

cliquishly 59.32

clitoral *reproductive* 21.11

clitoridectomy *non-Christian ritual* 85.8

clitoris *organs of reproduction* 21.9

clivia Flowers 42

cloaca *tunnel* 551.11, *body orifice* 583.3

cloak *vestment* 84.11, *occult* 86.22, *coat* 100.19, *clothe* 100.43, *conceal* 181.12, *blinder* 243.7, *make invisible* 245.7, *buffer* 419.22, *body covering* 613.3, *hide* 613.27, *protect* 810.21

cloak-and-dagger [Inf] *secretive* 182.9

cloaked *dressed* 100.38, *protected* 613.20

cloaked in secrecy *concealed* 844.7

cloaking *covering* 613.1

cloakroom *room* 60.9

cloakroom attendant *attendant* 69.4

clobber [Inf] *use violence* 520.9, *ruin* 523.15, *hit* 695.11, *overtake* 744.16

cloche *nursery* 17.4, *hat* 100.32

Clock Constellations 7

clock *computing terms* 15.22, *furniture* 101.1, *stadium* 155.3, *indicator* 183.7, *measuring instrument* 589.12, *timekeeper* 646.7, *keep time* 646.12, *measure* 739.7

clock [Inf] *hit* 695.11

clock cycle *computing terms* 15.22

clockface *face* 646.8

clock in *work* 122.8, *measure time* 646.14, *get in* 704.17

clockmaker *artisan* 123.13, *horology* 646.6

clockmaking *horology* 646.6

clock off *measure time* 646.14

clock on *measure time* 646.14

clock out *work* 122.8, *measure time* 646.14, *withdraw* 705.9

clock radio *radio* 1050.11, Timepieces and Timers 646

clock rate *computing terms* 15.22

clock time *time zone* 646.5

clock watch Timepieces and Timers 646

clock watcher *nonworker* 415.4

clockwise **682.18, 697.17**

clockwork *machinery* 1040.5, *frequent* 847.6

clockwork precision *accuracy* 973.1

clockwork regularity *frequency* 847.2

clod *unskilled person* 128.3, *unintelligent person* 316.4, *solid body* 1045.6, *mass* 1047.7, *particle* 1051.4, *naive person* 954.2

clodhoppers *shoes* 100.30

clog *be dirty* 112.10, *dirty* 112.11, *detain* 471.9, *obstruct* 584.13

clog dancer *dancer* 705.4

clog dancing Dancing Types 705

clogged *dirty* 112.7, *retentive* 471.5, *obstructed* 584.8

clogged up *obstructed* 584.8

clogs *shoes* 100.30

clog up *obstruct* 584.13, *restrain* 1012.12

cloisonné Ceramics 742

cloister *clerical dwelling* 703.10, *solitary place* 584.4, *enclosed area* 1009.2, *enclose* 1009.6, *passage* 1075.5, *private space* 1052.2

cloistered *secluded* 584.9, *enclosed* 1009.4

clone *reprint* 548.3, *reproduce* 548.13, *image* 349.3, *impression* 517.7, *look-alike* 784.4, *make the same* 790.16, *copy* 942.2, 990.10, *conformist* 867.6, *twin* 873.5, *double* 873.14, *pluralize* 883.9

cloned *look-alike* 784.10, *double* 873.10

cloning *biochemistry* 684.1, *doubling* 873.4

cloning vector *molecular biology* 705.18

clop *blow* 901.5, *kick* 901.14

close **584.12, 765.10, 847.10, 849.6, 1011.9;** *humid* 1065.48, *crowded* 770.22, *intimate* 587.7, *silent* 51.10, *noncommittal* 344.11, *secretive* 345.9, *warm* 1018.13, *disappear* 34.5, *unsociable* 583.6, *contentious* 457.20, *mean* 651.4, *dense* 1043.6, *condensed* 1043.7, *moist* 1063.9, *available* 472.11, *near* 223.6, 223.16, *enclosed area* 1009.2, *cease* 856.9, *stop work* 856.11, *cause to cease* 856.12, *converge* 907.9, *similar* 783.7, *compatible* 788.14, *tied* 1006.13, *intertwine* 1006.19, *adhesive* 802.5, *completion* 816.2, *conclusion* 816.3, *complete* 816.9, *be complete* 816.10, *excluding* 765.5, *end* 819.1, 819.19, *nearby* 223.4

close a deal *contract* 591.8

close at hand *near* 223.16, *future* 838.6

close attention 983.2

close binary *star* 8.8

close by *nearby* 223.17, 1008.7, *available* 472.6

close call *closeness* 850.4, *narrow escape* 369.3

closed **584.7, 708.6;** *unionized* 57.14, *hunting* 382.11, *snowplow* 181.29, *secret* 345.8, *ceased* 856.6, *stopped* 856.7, *completed* 816.7, *excluding* 765.5, *concealed* 346.7, *failed* 1010.10

closed book *unknown thing* 930.3, *predetermination* 964.1

closed circuit *circuit* 1032.37

closed-circuit television *television (TV)* 1035.5

closed couplet *part of poem* 720.9

closed door *deterrence* 379.2, *exclusion* 773.1

closed down **584.10;** *closed* 857.6, *stopped* 1012.8

closed-face *fishing* 382.13

closed-face reel *fishing tackle* 382.7

closed figure *geometric figure* 278.9

closed gate *ski race* 753.4

closed-in *enclosed* 584.11, 1009.4

closed-in person 584.6

closed lips *quietness* 51.4

closed mind *unfair treatment* 650.2, *opinionatedness* 970.3, *predetermination* 964.1

closed-minded *opinionated* 970.9

closed mortgage *mortgage* 438.6

closed order *privacy* 583.6

closedown *closure* 857.4, *stop* 1012.2

close down **584.15;** *disappear* 34.5, *close* 857.10, *stop work* 856.11, *cease* 857.20, *restrain* 1012.12

closed place 584.4

closed primary *election* 609.6

closed season *game laws* 673.3, *seasons* 313.2, *pause* 402.3

closed session *secret* 345.2

closed shop *organized labor* 727.5, *limit* 210.1, *exclusiveness* 764.4, *economic restraint* 1011.3

closed surface *surface* 206.36, *curved surface* 279.13

closed universe *universe* 1070.3

closed up *shortened* 582.8, *closed down* 857.10

close examination *close attention* 983.2

close fight *contest* 457.4

close fighting *fight* 457.9

close finish *contest* 457.4, *destination* 186.6

close-fisted *mean* 651.4

close-fistedness *meanness* 651.1

close-fitting *narrow* 270.8, *adhesive* 802.5

close friend *friend* 588.2

close friendship *intimacy* 587.4

close grips *fight* 457.9, *duel* 457.12

close-hauled *sailing* 182.25, *directionally* 161.20

close hauling *sailing terms* 182.5

close in *enclose* 1009.6, *converge* 907.9

close-knit *dense* 1043.6, *excluding* 765.5

closely *intimately* 587.14, *near* 223.16, *barely* 248.18, *comparably* 943.18, *compatibly* 788.34, *inextricably* 1006.23, *cohesively* 802.11

close-minded *discriminatory* 980.11, *narrow-minded* 980.13

close-mindedly *prejudicially* 980.17, *narrow-mindedly* 980.20

close-mindedness *prejudice* 980.3, *narrow-mindedness* 980.7

closemouthed *uncandid* 354.15

close-mouthed *secretive* 345.9

closeness **587.4, 850.2;** *intimacy* 587.4, *verbal concealment* 345.3, *density* 1043.1, *humidity* 1063.9, *nearness* 223.1, 1008.2, *denseness* 1043.2, *similarity* 783.1, *compatibility* 788.4, *union* 799.1

close observance *close attention* 983.2

close of day *night* 315.3

close one's ears *fail to hear* 49.9

close one's eyes to *be indifferent* 102.4

close one's mind *prejudge* 980.13

close-packed *status adjectives* 159.25, *dense* 1043.6, *tied* 1006.13, *adhesive* 802.5

close quarters *fight* 457.9, *duel* 457.12

closer **584.5;** *baseball team* 745.2, *nearer* 223.7

close range *short distance* 223.2

close ranks *adhere* 802.8

close reach *sail* 182.29

close reaching *sailing terms* 182.5

close run *near* 223.6

close-run *competitive* 457.21

close-set *tied* 1006.13

close shave [Inf] *narrow escape* 369.4, 1013.3

closest *available* 472.11, *next* 223.8

closestool *place for excretion* 12.11

closet *room* 60.9, *receptacle* 195.11, *hiding place* 346.2, *privacy* 583.6

closet drama *dramatic style* 704.6

close-textured *dense* 1043.6

close the blinds *shelter* 1008.8

close the circle *orbit* 1070.8

close the door on *exclude* 772.4

close the eyes *bury* 31.10
close the proceedings *try a case* 54.28
close the ranks *battle* 76.33
close the shutters *make dark* 247.10, *shelter* 812.8
close to the wind *directionally* 697.20
closeup *portrait* 132.5, *news story* 171.3
close up *contract* 582.12, *become smaller* 582.14, *close* 584.12, *close down* 584.15, *near* 586.12, *discontinue* 846.14
closeup shot *composition* 132.17
close with *strike* 418.21, *contend* 422.22, *adhere* 755.8
close with *or* in *or* up *converge* 702.9
close-woven *dense* 540.6, *smooth* 552.9
closing *closure* 584.1, 637.4, *cessation* 668.1, *ending* 773.13
closing arguments 54.17
closing down *closure* 584.1, *stop* 668.2
closing-down sale *sale* 482.2
closing in *fencing movements* 153.3, *enclosure* 619.1
closing stage *close* 773.9
closing the grave *funeral* 31.4
closing time *close* 773.9
closing up *shortening* 582.2, *closure* 584.1
closure 584.1, 637.4; *set* 6.19, *stop* 668.2, *cause to cease* 668.12, *discontinuance* 846.4
closure of debate *stop* 668.2
clot *dirty* 112.11, *cardiovascular disease* 114.13, *solid body* 540.4, *be dense* 540.8, *blood* 555.4, *mucus* 561.6, *thicken* 561.21, 594.9
cloth *vestment* 84.11, *fabric* 104.4, 130.1, *woven* 130.15, *stage set* 136.19, *merchandise* 522.6, *textile* 552.5
cloth, the *clergy* 84.1
clothe 100.43; *provision* 89.9
clothed *dressed* 100.38
clothes *clothing* 100.1, *external appearance* 264.5
clothes basket *basket* 578.6
clothes brush *cleaning tool* 111.10
clothes-conscious *fashionable* 536.5
clothes dryer *dryer* 560.5
clotheshorse *dryer* 560.5
clotheshorse [Inf] *fashion business* 536.3
clothes label *personal identification* 184.4
clothesless *undressed* 614.11
clothesline *dryer* 560.5
clothes marking *personal identification* 184.4
clothier 100.37; *artisan* 123.13
clothing 100.1, 184.6; *provisions* 89.3, *dry goods* 130.3, *external appearance* 264.5, Phobias 283, *merchandise* 522.6, *body covering* 613.3
clothing business, the 100.36
clothing designer *fashion business* 536.3
clothing maker *fabric handler* 130.11
Clotho Deities 82
clotted *dirty* 112.7, *condensed* 540.7, *thick* 561.17, *dense* 594.6
clotted cream *fat* 564.4
clotting *condensed* 540.7, *viscosity* 561.1, *denseness* 594.2
cloture *closure* 584.1, *close down*

584.15, *stop* 668.2, *cause to cease* 668.12
clotured *closed down* 584.10
cloud 9.17, 9.54, Collective Names 59, *disguise* 181.13, *dark thing* 247.3, *make dim* 248.8, *opaque* 250.7, *variegate* 263.11, *wateriness* 557.3, *mistiness* 559.2, *cover* 613.2, *hide* 613.27, *throng* 795.4
cloud appearance 9.19
cloud base *cloud* 9.17
cloudburst *rain* 9.27
cloud-capped *cloudy* 9.44, *mountainous* 569.5
cloud-capped peak *mountain* 569.1
cloud ceiling *cloud cover* 9.18
cloud cover 9.18
cloud-covered *cloudy* 9.44
cloud-crossed *cloudy* 9.44
cloud-cuckoo-land *aspiration* 281.3, *marvel* 294.3, Imaginary Places 360
clouded *dimmed* 248.6, *shady* 250.4, *overcast* 304.11
cloud-flecked *cloudy* 9.44
cloudily *meteorologically* 9.60, *dimly* 248.10, *opaquely* 250.9, *grayly* 255.10
cloudiness *cloud cover* 9.18, *dirtiness* 112.1, *obscurity* 197.1, *murk* 248.2, *opaqueness* 250.1, *dullness* 255.5, *overcast* 304.6
clouding over *dimming* 248.3
cloud-laden *cloudy* 9.44
cloudless *fine* 9.43, *sunny* 246.17, *transparent* 249.7, *rainless* 560.11, *prosperous* 847.5
cloudlessness *transparency* 249.1
cloudless sky *cloud cover* 9.18
cloud nine [Inf] *top of the world* 600.2
cloud of words *diffuseness* 199.1
cloud on the horizon *danger signal* 811.5, *forewarning* 814.2
cloud over *cloud* 9.54, *become dark* 247.9, *be dim* 248.7, *be opaque* 250.6
clouds Phobias 283
cloudscape *portrait* 132.5, *type of painting* 143.5
cloud seeding *rain* 9.27
cloud street *cloud appearance* 9.19
cloud-topped *cloudy* 9.44
cloud tower *cloud appearance* 9.19
cloudy 9.44; *dirty* 112.7, *obscure* 197.2, *dark* 247.5, *dim* 248.4, *murky* 248.5, *shady* 250.4, *dull* 255.8, *mottled* 263.10, *overcast* 304.11, *imaginary* 360.12, *misty* 559.10
clough [Brit] *valley* 572.8
clout *corporal punishment* 454.11, *hit* 454.28, 695.11, *blow* 695.5, *instrumentality* 801.3
clout [Inf] *authority* 52.1, 514.5, *influence* 512.1, *superiority* 744.1
clove Herbs and Spices 91
clove hitch Knots, Bends, Hitches, Splices 754
cloven *cracked* 587.5, *apart* 753.8
cloven-hoofed *ungulate* 35.31
clover *crop* 16.8, *animal feed* 16.12, Flowers 42, *animal food* 90.2
cloverleaf *crossroads* 609.4, *road attribute* 687.3
cloverleaf junction *road attribute* 687.3
clowder Collective Names 59
clown 138.10; *unskilled person* 128.3, *entertain* 138.16, *humorist* 277.7, *be humorous* 277.11, *play*

the fool 353.7, *object of ridicule* 368.3, *be ridiculous* 368.6
clown around *play the fool* 353.7
clowning *amusement* 277.2, *ridiculousness* 368.1
clownish 138.14; *clumsy* 128.6, *ridiculous* 368.5, *graceless* 528.7
clownishly *entertainingly* 138.17
cloy *overindulge* 99.10, *bore* 296.8
cloyed *immoderate* 99.6
cloying *immoderate* 99.6, *sweet* 222.5
club 138.7, 695.15; *association* 59.4, *blunt weapon* 78.5, *type of chair* 101.4, *baseball team* 147.2, *golf equipment* 156.5, Card Games 168, *instrument of punishment* 454.13, *collection* 757.3
clubbishness *sociability* 408.1
clubby *sociable* 408.11
club circuit *engagement* 136.15, 138.6
club cover *golf equipment* 156.5
clubfoot *distortion of body* 627.3
clubfooted *deformed* 627.7
club fungi *fungi* 47.3
clubman *social person* 408.7
club moss *fern* 46.1
clubroot *pests and diseases* 17.12
clubs *cards* 168.2
club sandwich *sandwich* 90.9
club tie *clothing* 184.6
club together *fraternize* 408.17, *keep company with* 794.17, *join with* 827.15
clubwoman *social person* 408.7
cluck *bird sound* 240.2, *make a bird sound* 240.8
clue *inside information* 170.4, *signs* 183.2, *theory* 327.2, *indication* 339.3, *basis of supposition* 359.2, *interpretation* 365.1
clued in *educated* 48.19, *informed* 170.9, *sensible* 212.6
clue in *inform* 170.11
clueless [Inf] *ignorant* 349.5
clumber spaniel Breeds of Dogs 35
clump *grassland* 45.2, *assemblage* 59.13, *group* 59.24, *solid body* 540.4, *mass* 579.7, *blow* 695.5, *kick* 695.14
clumped *grouped* 59.21
clumsily *unskillfully* 128.12, *inelegantly* 528.11, *inconveniently* 804.11, *awkwardly* 824.26
clumsily built *clumsy* 128.6
clumsiness *unskillfulness* 128.1, *insensibility* 213.1, *inelegance* 528.1, *inelegance of expression* 528.4, *ugliness* 531.1, *awkwardness* 824.2
clumsy 128.6, 824.14; *insensible* 213.4, *handling* 216.7, *graceless* 528.7, *ugly* 531.3, *awkward* 804.6
clumsy construction *inelegance of expression* 528.4
clumsy lout *unskilled person* 128.3
clumsy oaf *unskilled person* 128.3
Clun Forest Colbred Breeds of Sheep 16
clunk *dull sound* 233.2, *be nonresonant* 233.10, *crack* 234.7
clupeoid *fishlike* 38.10
cluricaune *sprite* 86.12
cluster *galaxy* 7.5, Collective Names 59, *assemblage* 59.13, *group* 59.24, *come together* 59.25, 702.10, *solid body* 540.4, *mass* 579.7
cluster analysis *statistical methods* 6.53
cluster bomb *bomb* 78.15
clustered *grouped* 59.21

clutch *young animal* 26.4, *eggs* 36.5, *young bird* 36.17, *racing automobile* 146.2, *touch* 216.9, *retention* 471.1, *retain* 471.7, *critical situation* 824.6
clutch at *take* 477.14
clutched *retained* 471.6
clutches *governance* 52.6
clutching *touching* 216.2, *taking* 477.1
clutch purse *bag* 578.7
clutch-slip *automobile racing terms* 146.3, *be on the track* 146.11
Clutha Rivers 570
clutter Collective Names 59, *throng* 795.4
cluttered *crowded* 795.10
Clyde Rivers 570
Clydesdale Horse and Pony Breeds 159
Cnidaria *coelenterate* 39.15
cnidarian *coelenterate* 39.15, 39.25
cnidophobia Phobias 283
C-note [Inf] *US coinage* 484.10, *hundreds* 882.9
coach *educator* 48.4, *educate* 48.22, *basketball team* 148.2, *football player* 155.15, *soccer participant* 163.4, *track and field eventer* 166.19, *compete in track and field* 166.21, *adviser* 176.5, *advise* 176.9, *motivator* 178.11, *cause to know* 348.13, *preparer* 388.6, *brief* 388.20, *bus* 687.7, *assimilate* 781.14
coach builder *artisan* 123.13
coach-class *cheap* 497.9
coach dog Breeds of Dogs 35
coach fare *bargain* 497.4
coach horse *workhorse* 159.3
coaching *education* 48.1
coact *cooperate* 827.12
coacting *cooperative* 827.9
coaction *cooperation* 827.1
coactive *cooperative* 827.9
coactively *cooperatively* 827.18
coadjutant *helper* 825.12, *cooperative* 827.9
coadjutor *cooperator* 827.8
coadministration *joint control* 827.5
coadunation *association* 827.6
coagency *collaboration* 757.2, *accompaniment* 794.1, *joint control* 827.5
coagent *collaborative* 757.7
coagulate *be dense* 540.8, *thicken* 561.21, 594.9, *adhere* 755.8
coagulated *condensed* 540.7, *thick* 561.17, *dense* 594.6, *adhesive* 755.5
coagulating *condensed* 540.7, *conjunctive* 752.12
coagulation *concentration* 540.2, *viscosity* 561.1, *denseness* 594.2, *union* 752.1
coagulum *solid body* 540.4
coal 106.4; *fuels* 106.2, *dark thing* 247.3, *black thing* 254.3, *power source* 514.13, *thing of the past* 651.8, *propellant* 696.9
coal bed *coal* 106.4
coalbin *coal* 106.4
coal-black *black* 254.5
coal bunker *coal* 106.4
coal-burning *heated* 217.15
coal dust *coal* 106.4, *powder* 553.9
coalesce *be the same* 730.13, *make the same* 730.16, *unify* 752.15, *combine* 757.9, *join* 827.17
coalesced *same* 730.7, *combined* 757.5
coalescence *density* 540.1,

sameness 730.1, union 752.1, combination 757.1, association 827.6

coalescent same 730.7, united 752.10, combinatory 757.6

coal field coal 106.4

coal fire place for fire 217.9

coal-fired fired 106.13, heated 217.15

coalfish food fish and shellfish 90.20

coal gas gas 106.6

coal heaver power worker 106.10

coal hod coal 106.4

coaling station coal 106.4

coalition political party 50.5, alliance 735.5, association 752.2, 827.6

coalition government caretaker government 49.14

coal measures coal 106.4

coal merchant power worker 106.10

coal mine coal 106.4, works 124.9

coal miner power worker 106.10, laborer 123.9

coal oil oil 106.7, petroleum 562.5

coal pit coal 106.4

Coalport Ceramics 129

coal-powered fired 106.13

Coalsack nebula nebula 7.6

coal scuttle coal 106.4, vessel 578.11

coal seam coal 106.4

coaly gas 106.14

coaming sailboat parts and accessories 150.4, edge 618.1

coarctate squeezed 582.9

coarctation squeeze 582.3

coarse 544.6; unclean 112.8, woven 130.15, fishing 154.13, indecent 261.8, unrefined 338.7, unformed 389.11, bad-mannered 411.6, offensive 432.11, indecorous 528.8, ugly 531.3, vulgar 535.6, rough 552.8, thick-skinned 594.8

coarse cloth roughness 544.1

coarse fishing Sporting Activities 145, fishing 154.1

coarse grain exposure 132.15, roughness 544.1

coarse-grained coarse 544.6, rough 552.8

coarsely vulgarly 71.5, 535.10, dirtily 112.12, tastelessly 338.14, immaturely 389.18, rudely 411.9, inelegantly 528.11, 531.7, roughly 544.13, texturally 552.15, callously 594.14

coarsen 552.12; vulgarize 535.9, make rough 544.11, pervert 808.22

coarseness uncleanness 112.2, immaturity 389.3, bad manners 411.2, impropriety 528.2, vulgarity 535.1, roughness 544.1, grain 552.2, plainness 592.4, callousness 594.4

coarseness of grain grain 552.2

coarsening moral deterioration 808.3

coarse pottery ceramics 129.1

coarse-woven rough 552.8

coast 8.13, 572.4; not act 413.11, pause 415.15, go smoothly 545.11, edge 618.1, side 623.1, maneuver 677.18, fall 714.4, slide 714.17, go easily 823.18

coastal 8.54; of landmasses 572.12, edging 618.5, nautical 690.14

coastal cruiser sailboat 150.3

coastal dune dune 8.43

coastal fog fog 9.32

coastal plain landform 8.9, coast 572.4

coastal racer sailboat 150.3

coastal station weather station 9.5

coastal waters ocean 8.14

coast artillery guns 78.9

coast clear safety 810.1

coaster protective covering 613.5

coaster brake bicycle part 687.11

coast guard protector 810.11

coastguardsman naval person 77.25, nautical person 690.12

coast home do easily 823.16

coasting nautical 690.14, falling 714.11

coastland coast 572.4

coastline coast 8.13, 572.4, edge 617.3

Coast Mountains Mountains and Hills 569

coast-to-coast rail 688.8

coat 100.19, 588.3, 613.28; paint 143.12, opaque 250.7, color 251.16, smooth 545.10, layer 588.9, base 601.10, be exterior 610.13, body covering 613.3, coating 613.8, augment 748.13

coated 588.7; treated 130.16, painted 143.10, opaque 250.3

coating 613.8; coat 588.3, exteriority 610.2, covering 610.8, 613.1

coat of arms Heraldic Terms 184, insignia 184.5

coat of mail historic armor 419.8

coattail part of garment 100.27

coax persuade 375.18, cajole 439.14, petition 505.11, influence 508.11, lure 700.12, be cunning 822.5

coaxed motivated 508.8

coaxer persuader 178.9, motivator 508.6

coaxial cable or **coax** telecommunication 169.7

coaxing persuasion 178.1, cajoling 439.9, inducement 508.2

Cob Horse and Pony Breeds 159

cob male bird 36.15, cereal grass 45.4, pony 159.6

cobalt Chemical Elements and Common Allotropes 11, essential element 12.15

cobalt blue blue pigment 261.2

cobalt-blue blue 261.5

cobalt violet purple pigment 262.2

cobble make clothing 100.44, building materials 104.2, paving 613.14, pave 613.32, repair 809.10

cobbled accessible 691.13

cobbled together bungled 128.7

cobbler dessert 90.35, clothier 100.37, repair worker 123.8

cobblestone paving 613.14

cobble together produce 522.13

cobbling the clothing business 100.36, repair 809.1

COBOL Programming Languages 15

cobra snake 37.6

Cobra group Western Art Styles 133

cobweb spinner 40.10, dirt 112.5, weak thing 517.5, little bit 800.4

cobwebby dirty 112.7, insubstantial 539.5

cobwebs of antiquity oldness 653.1

Coca-Cola™ soft drink 93.8

cocaine alkaloid 12.19, stimulants 121.18, anesthetic 213.3

coccidioidomycosis fungal disease 47.6

coccus microorganism 13.11

coccyx Human Bones 19

cochairmanship joint control 827.5

Cochin Breeds of Fowl 16

cochineal red pigment 257.2

cochlea ear 19.10, 228.2, convoluted thing 632.3

cochlear nerve ear 228.2

cochleate convolutional 632.4

cock livestock 16.11, male animal 32.15, male bird 36.15, prepare for action 388.18

cock [Inf] organs of reproduction 21.9

cockade insignia 184.5

cock-a-doodle-doo bird sound 240.2

Cockaigne Imaginary Places 360

cock-a-leekie notable international dishes 90.40

cockalorum insolent person 400.7

cock-and-bull story falsehood 192.6, distortion of truth 627.4

cockatoo cage bird 36.13

cockatrice Heraldic Terms 184, Legendary Creatures 360

cockboat or **cockleboat** Ships and Boats 690

cockcrow morning 655.2

cocked hat hat 100.32

cocked up unbowed 602.7

cockerel male animal 32.15, male bird 36.15, young bird 36.17

cocker spaniel Breeds of Dogs 35

cockeye faulty vision 243.1

cockeyed visually impaired 243.9, oblique 607.6, distorted 627.6

cockeyedly obliquely 607.13

cockeyedness obliqueness 607.1

cockfight duel 422.12

cockfighting animal killing 30.10, Sporting Activities 145

cockily 402.19; arrogantly 297.18, 400.21, defiantly 416.9

cockiness 402.3; arrogance 400.4, defiance 416.1

cocking preparation 388.1

cockleshell Ships and Boats 690

cockles of one's heart seat of feelings 266.7

cockney accent regional pronunciation 205.7

cock of the walk company leader 68.8, proud person 297.7, insolent person 400.7

cockpit sailboat parts and accessories 150.4, canoe parts 150.10, overview 425.6

cockroach insect 40.1, pest 40.5

cock-robin male bird 36.15

cockscomb Flowers 42, cap 100.33

cockshy [Brit] throw 696.4

cock-sparrow male bird 36.15

cockspur Trees and Shrubs 43, sharp-pointed growth 549.5

cocksure convinced 840.8

cocksureness conviction 840.2

cocktail drink 93.2, 121.6, mixed drink 93.12, mixed thing 751.2, compound 757.4

cocktail dress dress 100.11, formal clothing 406.5

cocktail hour drink occasion 93.14, evening 656.2

cocktailing [Inf] drug use 121.9

cocktail lounge drink provider 93.15

cocktail party drink occasion 93.14, party 408.6

cocktail sausage sausage 90.29

cocktail shaker mixer 751.7

cock the float fish 154.14

cock up make vertical 602.9

cockup [Brit inf] mix-up 766.5

cock up [Brit inf] confuse 766.19

cocky 402.11; arrogant 297.9, 400.11, defiant 416.5

Coco Rivers 570

cocoa milk 93.5, sweet drink 222.4

coco de mer Trees and Shrubs 43

coconut crab crustacean 39.10

coconut milk soft drink 93.8

coconut palm Trees and Shrubs 43

cocoon young animal 26.4, insect metamorphal stage 40.8, spinner 40.10, packet 578.4, contain 578.20, protect 810.21

cocooned containing 578.18

cocooning containing 578.18

cocotte cooking equipment 91.6

Cocytus evil place 446.6

cod food fish and shellfish 90.20

coda back 622.1, appendage 748.4, ending 773.10

coddle cook 91.10, comfort 214.14, love 299.21, sustain 825.25

coddled culinary 91.9, pleased 214.9, beloved 299.19

coddled egg egg dish 90.18

coddling cooking technique 91.2

code 780.3; philosophical system 4.2, nonstandard language 5.7, artificial language 5.9, combinatorics 6.63, the occult 86.2, puzzle 182.5, make mysterious 182.13, symbol 183.3, sign 183.1, vernacular 205.8, unintelligible thing 364.3, etiquette 534.3, concealment 844.2

code cracking interpretation 365.1

coded disguised 181.9, mysterious 182.10, itemized 577.9, concealed 844.7

codefendant litigant 54.4

codeine analgesic 115.6

code name anonymity 182.7

code of behavior etiquette 534.3

code of conduct philosophical system 4.2, code 780.3

code of duty or **honor** sense of duty 433.2

Code of Hammurabi the Law 53.2

code of practice philosophical system 4.2

codetermination joint control 827.5

codex rare book 174.2

Codex Juris Canonici the Law 53.2

codger [Inf] male 32.1

codicil appendage 748.4

codification law 53.1, lawmaking 53.11, grouping 765.2, categorization 767.5

codified disguised 181.9, grouped 765.11, categorized 767.15

codified law law 53.1

codify legislate 53.31, systematize 765.19, categorize 767.21, sort 777.13

coding stage of book production 174.7

codirectorship joint control 827.5

codlike fishlike 38.10

codling moth pests and diseases 17.12

cod-liver oil fish product 38.9

codomain mathematical function 6.27

codon genetic material 13.20

codpiece part of garment 100.27

coefficient algebraic expression 6.23

coefficient of friction friction 554.1

coelacanth fossil fish 38.7

coelenterate 39.15, 39.25

coelomate invertebrate 39.20

coenobial algal 47.20

coenobium reproductive body 47.14

---

coenocytic *cellular* 13.30
coenzyme 12.12; *enzyme* 12.11, *vitamin* 12.13
coenzyme A (CoA) *coenzyme* 12.12
coenzyme Q (CoQ) *coenzyme* 12.12
coequal *equal* 740.7, 740.8
coequality *equality* 740.1
coequally *equally* 740.13
coerce *necessitate* 95.17, *motivate* 178.17, *suppress* 424.9, *compel* 428.8, *restrain* 830.12
coerced *suppressed* 424.6
coercer 428.4
coercion 428.2; *necessitation* 95.5, *incentive* 178.4, *suppression* 424.2, *restraint* 830.1
coercive *masterful* 68.15, *severe* 424.5, *compelling* 428.6, *restraining* 830.8
coercively *compellingly* 428.12, *restrainedly* 830.18
coercive method 428.3
coeternal *simultaneous* 649.4
coeternally *simultaneously* 649.8
coeval *contemporary* 649.3, *simultaneous* 649.4
coevality *same time* 649.1
coevally *simultaneously* 649.8
coexist *be simultaneous* 649.6, *exist* 717.18
coexistence 73.3; *agreement* 462.1, *same time* 649.1, *existence* 717.1, *accompaniment* 794.1
coexistent *agreeing* 462.6, *simultaneous* 649.4, *existing* 717.11, *concurrent* 794.13
coexisting *agreeing* 462.6, *simultaneous* 649.4, *concurrent* 794.13
coextend *parallel* 606.7
coextension *parallelism* 606.1
coextensive *parallel* 606.5, *equal* 740.8
coextensively *in parallel* 606.9, *equitably* 740.15
cofactor *enzyme* 12.11, *vitamin* 12.13
co-favorite *horse racing* 159.10
C of E *denominational* 81.23
coffee 93.6; *type of table* 101.5, *brown thing* 256.3, *brown* 256.5, *social gathering* 408.4
coffee bar [Brit] *eating place* 92.17
coffee break *drink occasion* 93.14, *interval* 639.4, *ease* 819.1
coffeecake *bread* 90.10
coffee-colored *brown* 256.5
coffee cup *drink container* 93.13
coffee estate *farm* 16.2
coffee grinder *cooking equipment* 91.6, *sailboat parts and accessories* 150.4, *source of fragrance* 226.2
coffee grinder or **mill** *pulverizer* 553.11
coffee grounds *mud* 561.8
coffee hour *drink occasion* 93.14
coffeehouse *eating place* 92.17, *drink provider* 93.15
coffee maker *pot* 578.15
coffee plantation *farm* 16.2
coffee planter *agriculturist* 16.14
coffeepot *cooking equipment* 91.6, *pot* 578.15
coffee service *crockery* 578.16
coffee shop *eating place* 92.17, *drink provider* 93.15
coffee spoon *tableware* 92.13
coffee-table book *type of book* 174.3
coffee tree Trees and Shrubs 43
coffee urn *pot* 578.15
coffee with cream *coffee* 93.6

coffee with milk *coffee* 93.6
coffer *vault* 105.9, *safe* 464.4, *money storage* 484.20, *box* 578.5
cofferdam *substructure* 551.8
coffering Architectural Elements 134
coffers *storehouse* 105.8
coffin *funeral object* 31.6, *bury* 31.10, *box* 578.5
coffined *buried* 31.8
coffin lead *fishing tackle* 154.7
coffin nail [Inf] *tobacco* 121.23
cog *carpenter* 131.10, *sharp-pointed thing* 549.4, *notched thing* 636.2, *notch* 636.5, *wheel* 682.9, *inferior* 745.4
cogency *persuasion* 178.1, *power* 447.4, *potency* 516.6
cogent *dialectical* 4.16, *persuasive* 178.12, *emphatic* 200.3, *compelling* 428.6, *strong* 516.9
cogently *persuasively* 178.21, *compellingly* 428.12, *powerfully* 514.21
cogged *joined* 131.8, *notched* 636.4
cogging *carpenter's term* 131.5
cog in the wheel *member* 760.9
cogitate *philosophize* 4.19, *think* 317.9, *dream up* 522.15
cogitate upon *dream up* 522.15
cogitation *philosophical investigation* 4.4, *thought* 317.1, *production* 522.1
cogitative *thoughtful* 4.17
cogitatively *thoughtfully* 4.27
cognac *alcoholic drink* 93.9
cognate *word* 5.17, *worded* 5.38, *related* 727.6
cognition *intellect* 315.1, *knowledge* 348.1
cognitive *thoughtful* 317.5
cognitive disorders *mental disorder* 108.8
cognitively *knowledgeably* 348.14
cognitive psychology Psychological Theories, Schools 108
cognizability *recognizability* 363.3
cognizable *unjust* 53.24
cognizance *jurisdiction* 54.2, *knowledge* 348.1
cognizant *educated* 48.19, *knowledgeable* 348.7
cognomen *name* 202.8
cognoscente *expert* 127.9, *refined person* 534.4
cog railroad *railroad system* 688.1
cogwheel *wheel* 682.9
cohabit *keep company with* 794.17
cohabitant *common-law wife* 64.12, *partner* 794.9
cohabitation *marriage* 64.1, *companionship* 794.3
cohabiting *concurrent* 794.13
coheir *beneficiary* 473.6
Cohen *rabbi* 84.6
cohere *be dense* 540.8, *conform* 735.27, *unify* 752.15, *intercommunicate* 754.15, *adhere* 755.8, *become one* 788.18
coherence *rationality* 109.2, *clarity* 196.1, *intelligibility* 363.1, *density* 540.1, *toughness* 547.1, *conformity* 735.7, *union* 752.1, *adhesion* 755.1, *method* 765.7, *oneness* 788.3
coherent *rational* 109.4, *clear* 196.2, *intelligible* 363.5, *conforming* 735.17, *connective* 754.10, *adhesive* 755.5, *well-ordered* 765.14
coherent light *light* 246.1
coherently *sanely* 109.6, *clearly* 196.4, *intelligibly* 363.13,

conformingly 735.37, *cohesively* 755.11
coherent radiation *laser (light amplification by stimulated emission of radiation)* 10.18
cohesion *density* 540.1, *toughness* 547.1, *pulling power* 700.2, *union* 752.1, *connection* 754.1, *adhesion* 755.1
cohesive *retentive* 471.5, *dense* 540.6, *united* 752.10, *tied* 752.13, *connective* 754.10, *adhesive* 755.5
cohesively 755.11; *tenaciously* 471.11, *densely* 540.10, *attractionally* 700.13, *as one* 752.21, *in connection with* 754.16
cohesiveness *toughness* 547.1, *adhesion* 755.1
cohesive strength *strength of materials* 14.15
cohort *group* 59.8, *historical soldier* 77.8
coif 530.15; *cap* 100.33, *clothe* 100.43, *historic armor* 419.8
coifed *dressed* 100.38
coiffeur *beautician* 530.11
coiffeuse *beautician* 530.11
coiffure 530.8; *hairdressing* 530.7
coign Architectural Elements 134
coign of vantage *advantage* 744.3
coil 632.2; *magnet* 10.47, *contraceptive* 23.6, *piece* 590.2, *curve* 629.1, 629.6, *convolute* 632.6, *fold* 637.1, 637.7, *orbital motion* 681.1
coiled *elastic* 546.5, *curved* 629.4, *convolutional* 632.4, *circular* 681.6
coiling *elastic* 546.5
coil magnet *magnet* 700.3
coil spring *spring* 546.4
coil up *make round* 633.9
coimetrophobia Phobias 283
coin *imagine* 360.14, *money* 484.1, *coinage* 484.13, *monetize* 484.24, *perform* 522.16, *form* 624.9, *invent* 771.30
coin [Inf] *cash* 484.2
coinage 484.13; *new word* 5.18, *money* 484.1, *cash* 484.2, *invention* 771.5
coin a phrase *aphorize* 177.3
coin a word *word* 5.43
coincide *mean* 361.13, *be compatible* 462.12, *be simultaneous* 649.6, *be the same* 730.13, *harmonize* 735.22, *accompany* 794.16
coincidence *aspect of fiction* 139.5, *same time* 649.1, *unrelatedness* 728.1, *sameness* 730.1, *harmonization* 735.2, *combination* 757.1, *synchronism* 794.2, *chance* 842.1
coincident *simultaneous* 649.4, *same* 730.7, *harmonizing* 735.12, *equal* 740.8, *collaborative* 757.7, *concurrent* 794.13
coincidental *simultaneous* 649.4, *illogical* 728.7, *same* 730.7, *causeless* 842.11
coincidentally *simultaneously* 649.8, *illogically* 728.17, *identically* 730.18, *in combination* 757.11, *by chance* 842.15
coincidently *in harmony* 735.32
coincide with *be equal* 740.11
coinciding *compatibility* 462.3, *compatible* 462.8, *same* 730.7, *concurrent* 794.13
coin collecting Hobbies and Pastimes 167, *coinage* 484.13
coin collection *collection* 105.12
coin collector *financier* 484.17

coined *worded* 5.38, *monetary* 484.22
coiner *financier* 484.17
coin money *get rich* 485.13
coin of the realm *coinage* 484.13
coins *change* 484.3, *coinage* 484.13
coin-toss *miscellaneous terms* 155.16
coital *desirous* 20.18, *conjunctive* 752.12
coition *sexual intercourse* 20.9, *propagation* 21.4, *sexual union* 752.6
coitophobia Phobias 283
coitus *sexual intercourse* 20.9, Phobias 283, *sexual union* 752.6
coitus interruptus *sex act* 20.10, *birth control* 23.5
coke *fuels* 106.2, *coal* 106.4
coke [Inf] *stimulants* 121.18
Coke™ *soft drink* 93.8
cokehead [Inf] *drug taker* 121.12
cokernel *mathematical function* 6.27
col *rock face* 161.6, *gulf* 587.3, *concave land* 635.2, *means of connection* 754.4
cola *soft drink* 93.8
colander *cooking equipment* 91.6, *porosity* 583.5
col arco Musical Terms and Expression Marks 140
colascione Musical Instruments 142
colchicine *alkaloid* 12.19
cold 10.26, 218.1, 218.9; *cold weather* 9.24, *windy* 9.42, *cool* 9.49, *undersexed* 20.20, *dead* 29.11, *hostile* 63.6, *refreshing* 94.4, *respiratory disease* 114.12, *insensitive* 268.4, Phobias 283, *indifferent* 289.7, *pitiless* 309.3, *unsociable* 409.6, *inactive* 413.9, *reserved* 585.7, *resigned* 835.4, *adverse* 848.10
cold air *atmosphere* 9.8
cold as the grave or **marble** or **charity** *frozen* 218.10
cold bath *bath* 111.6
cold-blooded 218.12; *murderous* 30.18, *reptilian* 37.12, *fishlike* 38.10, *insensible* 213.4, *heedless* 268.5, *indifferent* 289.7, *pitiless* 309.3
cold-blooded animal *reptile* 37.1
cold-bloodedly *indifferently* 289.17, *pitilessly* 309.7
cold-blooded murderer *murderer* 30.12
cold-bloodedness *indifference* 289.1, *cruelty* 306.4, *pitilessness* 309.1
cold body *cold* 10.26
cold climate *climate* 9.35
cold-cock [Inf] *hit* 695.11
cold cream *cleaning agent* 111.9, *toiletries* 530.6, *pomade* 562.9
colder *cool* 9.49
cold feet [Inf] *symptoms of fear* 283.3, *cowardice* 285.1
cold fingers of death *personifications and symbols* 29.4
cold fish [Inf] *insensitive person* 268.3, *indifferent person* 289.6
cold frame *nursery* 17.4
cold front *air movement* 9.11, *cold weather* 218.8
cold heart *insensitive person* 268.3
cold-hearted *heedless* 268.5, *indifferent* 289.7, *cruel* 306.10, *pitiless* 309.3, *selfish* 444.4, *impenitent* 452.2
cold-heartedly *indifferently* 289.17, *cruelly* 306.17, *pitilessly*

309.7, selfishly 444.8, impenitently 452.5

cold-heartedness heedlessness 268.2, indifference 289.1, cruelty 306.4, pitilessness 309.1, impenitence 452.1

cold in the head chills 218.3

cold in the nose or **head** lack of sense of smell 225.2

coldish cool 9.49

coldly 218.16; meteorologically 9.60, hostilely 63.13, insensitively 268.7, indifferently 289.17, pitilessly 309.7, unsocially 409.13, reservedly 585.15, motionlessly 678.9

coldness sexlessness 20.13, hostility 63.1, cold 218.1, insensitivity 268.1, indifference 289.1, pitilessness 309.1, unsociability 409.1, reserve 585.4, resignedness 835.2

cold occlusion air movement 9.11

cold place 218.7

cold reception rejection 383.1

cold rubber rubber 546.3

cold season cold weather 218.8, seasons 654.2

cold shivers shake 684.7

cold shoulder indifference 289.1, rejection 383.1, avoidance 386.1, act of discourtesy 411.3, insult 436.5, disapproval 438.1, repulse 701.2, ostracism 709.3

cold-shoulder exclude 383.11, 764.7, shun 386.14, ignore 409.11, be discourteous 411.7, insult 436.21, withhold approval 438.17, repel 701.7

cold-shouldered lonely 409.8

cold shower refresher 94.2, bath 111.6

cold snap cold weather 9.24, 218.8

cold spell cold weather 9.24, 218.8

cold storage storage 105.6, preservation of provisions 815.6

cold store storage 105.6

cold substance cold 10.26

cold sweat sweat 25.8, symptoms of fear 283.3

cold things Phobias 283

cold turkey [Inf] withdrawal 121.11

cold-type typesetting typesetting 173.4

cold war psychological warfare 76.13, contention 422.1

cold-water cure therapy 115.12

cold wave cold weather 9.24

cold weather 9.24, 218.8

coleopteran or **coleopterous** insectile 40.11

coleoptile seed 41.9

coleorhiza seed 41.9

coleslaw salad 90.16

coleus Flowers 42

colic gastroenterological disease 114.11

colitis gastroenterological disease 114.11

collaborate be eager 373.13, federate 480.21, give moral support 605.18, form an alliance 735.25, come together 757.10, improve 825.26, cooperate 827.12

collaborate with submit 421.4

collaborating assenting 346.4

collaboration 757.2; goodwill 373.4, submission 421.1, moral support 605.7, helpfulness 825.10, cooperation 827.1

collaborative 757.7; goodwilled 373.10, supportive 605.11, alliance

735.5, allied 735.15, cooperative 827.9

collaboratively supportively 605.20, in alliance 735.35, cooperatively 827.18

collaborator assenter 346.3, adherent 401.5, seditionist 427.7, supporter 605.9, helper 825.12, cooperator 827.8

collaborators team 827.7

collage construction 59.16, picture 133.5, sculpture 144.1, Hobbies and Pastimes 167, variegated thing 263.5, collaboration 757.2

collagen protein 12.9

collapse symptom 114.3, be unhealthy 114.29, succumb 421.7, failure 430.9, forfeit 488.13, insolvency 490.5, be unable to pay 490.11, disability 515.4, be powerless 515.11, be weak 517.12, ruin 523.4, squeeze 582.3, 582.13, be concave 635.6, closure 637.4, close 637.10, stop work 668.11, downfall 714.7, droop 714.14, decline 747.4, decrease 747.7, disintegration 758.1, disintegrate 758.6, 808.15, dilapidation 808.5, fatigue 820.1, be fatigued 820.5, error 846.2, defeat 846.7, blunder 846.13

collapsed sick 114.24, squeezed 582.9, closed 637.6

collapsibility contractibility 582.4

collapsible contractible 582.11

collapsing contracting 582.10, descending 714.9

collar part of garment 100.27, neckwear 100.29, rowboat parts 150.15, circular thing 631.3, yoke 754.8, band 754.9, means of restraint 830.6, restrain someone 830.17

collar [Inf] arrest 55.5, 55.12, prisoner 55.7, detain 830.16

collarbone Human Bones 19

collaring ceramic process 129.5

collar stud fastener 754.7

collate verify 336.8

collated verified 336.7

collateral promise 464.2, personal estate 470.6, propertied 470.9, parallel 606.5, side 623.6, additional 748.8, accompanying 794.12, insurance 810.10

collaterality parallelism 606.1

collateral loan loan 475.2

collaterally proprietarily 470.14, in parallel 606.9, additionally 748.15

collateral security loan 488.3

collation meal 92.8, verification 336.1

collative verificatory 336.6

colleague friend 62.2, coworker 123.17, supporter 605.9, member 760.9, companion 794.8, helper 825.12

colleagues team 827.7

colleagueship friendship 62.1

collect assemble 59.23, come together 59.25, prayer 85.10, store 105.17, select 382.12, acquire 467.19, receive 473.13, unite 752.14, combine 757.9

collect(s) Eucharist 85.7

collectable receivable 473.12

collectanea miscellany 59.15

collect call telephone call 169.11

collect dust be dirty 112.10

collected 59.19, 757.8; detached 4.18, stored 105.14, summarized 204.6, wonderless 295.3, received 473.11, united 752.10

collectedly without wonder 295.8

collectedness lack of wonder 295.1

collected works compilation 174.4

collect funds gain 467.15

collectible showpiece 843.3

collecting collection 59.2, Hobbies and Pastimes 167, receiving 473.1

collecting unemployment unemployed 413.10

collection 59.2, 105.12, 757.3; assemblage 59.13, compilation 59.14, 174.4, store 105.1, compendium 204.3, selection 382.1, acquisition 467.4, offering 472.6, 504.5, receiving 473.1, voluntary payment 489.4, grant 489.7, miscellany 751.3, association 752.2, unification 752.5, display 843.1

collective communal 2.12, grammatical term 5.29, industrial 57.13, cumulate 59.20, sociable 408.11, negotiated 460.5, acquisitive 467.13, collected 757.8, association 827.6, joint 827.10

collective action joint operation 827.4

collective adaptation society 2.6

collective agreement bargaining 57.9

collective bargain negotiate 460.6

collective bargaining bargaining 57.9, negotiation 460.1

collective creation dramatic style 136.3

collective farm farm 16.2

collectively sociologically 2.15, industrially 57.22, together 59.31, 794.20, feasibly 460.9, gainfully 467.24, in combination 757.11, one and all 759.12, cooperatively 827.18

collective memory memory 354.1

collective noun part of speech 5.30

collective unconscious tradition 1.7, psyche 108.25

collectivism political and economic philosophy 4.6, association 827.6

collectivist political and economic philosopher 4.10

collectivistic of a political philosophy 4.14, joint 827.10

collectivity society 2.6

collect on delivery (COD) type of payment 489.3, cash down 489.25

collect oneself not wonder about 295.5

collector 59.17, 473.7; gainer 467.9

collectorship receiving 473.1

collector's item good thing 445.9

collector's piece showpiece 843.3

collector's piece or **item** workmanlike job 127.6

collect plants study plants 41.23

collect together compile 204.8

college school 48.11, university 48.14

college baseball baseball 147.1

college basketball basketball 148.1

college catalog list 785.1

college days youth 26.1

college dictionary word book 5.27

college football football 155.1

college president educational leader 68.11

college radio radio broadcasting 172.4

collegialism joint control 827.5

collegiate curricular 48.21, varsity 155.17, soccer 163.7

col legno Musical Terms and Expression Marks 140

collembolan insectile 40.11

collide 695.10; interact 10.73, oppose 63.11, navigate 690.15

collide with attack 418.17, meet 704.20

colliding contiguous 216.8

collie Breeds of Dogs 35

collier laborer 123.9, Ships and Boats 690

colliery works 124.9

colligate put together 59.30

colligation collection 59.2

colligative status adjectives 11.25

colligative property phase 11.13

collimate parallel 606.7, aim 697.14

collimated parallel 606.5

collimation parallelism 606.1, orientation 697.3

collinear linear 6.77

collineation transformation 6.46

collision 695.2; nuclear reaction 10.59, hostility 63.1, battle 76.23, wearing away 554.2, convergence 702.1, conflict 828.3

collision course nearness 586.1, approach 702.2

collisions and diffusion chemical reaction thermodynamics 14.29

collision theory chemical reaction 11.8

collocated phrased 5.39

collocating phrased 5.39

collocation collection 59.2

colloid phase 11.13, emulsion 561.5, mixed thing 751.2

colloidal status adjectives 11.25, viscous 561.14, mixed 751.8, adhesive 755.5

colloidality viscosity 561.1

colloidally chemically 11.42

colloidal solution phase 11.13

colloider thickener 561.12

collop slice 588.4, particle 760.4

colloquial of language 5.35, conversational 210.10

colloquialism spoken language 205.2

colloquialize use language 5.42

colloquial language nonstandard language 5.7

colloquially 5.45; conversationally 210.14

colloquial speech vernacular 205.8

colloquist conversationalist 210.6

colloquium conference 59.5, debate 210.3

colloquize discuss 4.22

colloquy philosophical argument 4.5, speech 205.1, conversation 210.1

collotype older photograph 132.4, illustration 187.2

collude scheme 193.18, plot 387.15, concur 827.16

collusion collection 59.2

collyrium balm 115.11, pomade 562.9

collywobbles [Inf] symptoms of fear 283.3, agitation 684.1

cologne source of fragrance 226.2, toiletries 530.6

Colombia Countries 566

Colombian coffee coffee 93.6

Colombo Countries 566

colon Accents and Diacritical Marks 5, internal organ 19.13

Colonel US Military Ranks 58

colonette Architectural Elements 134

Colonial historic 653.13

colonial of animals 34.13, algal 47.20, governing 49.25, settler 61.4, Furniture Styles 101, administrative 564.13, national 566.10, dominating 832.7

colonial architecture Architectural Styles 134

colonial government 49.15

colonialism colonial government 49.15, dominion 566.3, domination 832.2

colonialist nationalist 566.8

colonially algologically 47.25, regionally 564.16, nationally 566.13, beforehand 657.19

Colonial Revival Architectural Styles 134

colonist settler 61.4, entrant 706.7, outgoer 707.9

colonization taking over 477.3

colonize settle 61.14, take over 477.16, exert sovereignty 566.12, enroll 706.16, subject 832.10

colonized inhabited 61.10

colonizer settler 61.4

colonnade column 134.6, straight line 630.2, passage 691.5, consecutiveness 774.1

colony body politic 50.3, Collective Names 59, inhabitants 61.2, possession of property 469.3, region 564.1, dominion 566.3, throng 795.4

colophon book part 174.5, means of identification 184.3, back matter 622.3

color 251.1, 251.16; race 1.5, motion-picture 137.15, treatment 143.6, paint 143.12, television set 172.6, identification 184.1, misrepresent 188.6, redden 257.9, Phobias 283, modify 340.13, influence 512.11, coif 530.15, interior decoration 532.4, ornament 532.7, decorate 532.11, Fields of Measurement 589, admixture 751.5, mix 751.12, type 777.4

colorable colored 251.10

Colorado American States 564, Rivers 570

Colorado Plateau Deserts 572

Colorado potato beetle pests and diseases 17.12

colorant dye 130.8, coloring agent 251.5

color arrangement interior decoration 532.4

coloration color 251.1

coloratura soprano voice 141.5

color balance composition 132.17, interior decoration 532.4

color-balancing filter filter 132.14

color bar hostility 63.1, exclusiveness 764.4

colorbearer soldier 77.4

color-blind visually impaired 243.9, undiscriminating 338.5

color blindness faulty vision 243.1, chromaticism 251.2, lack of discrimination 338.1

colorcast 251.17; spectrum 251.3

color cast composition 132.17

color chart spectrum 251.3

color circle spectrum 251.3

color code spectrum 251.3

color-code color 251.16

color compatibility interior decoration 532.4

color-coordinated stylish 100.42

color coordination spectrum 251.3, interior decoration 532.4

color-correcting or **compensating filter** filter 132.14

color decoration interior decoration 532.4

color design interior decoration 532.4

color disk spectrum 251.3

colored 251.10; treated 130.16, painted 143.10, beautified 530.12, ornate 532.10, complicated 751.10

colored chalk paint 251.6

colored crayon paint 251.6

colored glaze glaze 129.3

colored paper paint 251.6

colored pencil paint 251.6

colorfast colored 251.10

colorfastness coloring agent 251.5

color-field painting Western Art Styles 133, color image 251.7

color film film 132.8, color image 251.7

color filter stage lighting 136.20, color image 251.7

colorful 251.11; variegated 263.6, profane 301.10, flashy 404.17

colorful language offensive language 301.5

colorfully 251.19; profanely 301.19, flashily 404.32

colorfulness spectrum 251.3, flashiness 404.4

color harmony spectrum 251.3

color highly exaggerate 194.11

color hologram stereoscopic image 132.7

colorific colored 251.10

color image 251.7

colorimeter chromatics 251.8, Fields of Measurement 589

colorimetric chromolithographic 251.14

colorimetry chromatics 251.8, Fields of Measurement 589

color in color 251.16

coloring dyeing 130.9, (act of) painting 143.1, identification 184.1, misrepresentation 188.1, color 251.1, coloring agent 251.5, meaning 361.1, blushing 403.2, admixture 751.5

coloring agent 251.5

coloring book type of book 174.3

coloring matter coloring agent 251.5

coloring the truth misrepresentation 366.2

colorist visual artist 133.6, beautician 530.11

coloristically colorfully 251.19

colorization motion-picture photography 137.9, color image 251.7

colorize paint 143.12, color 251.16

colorized motion-picture 137.15, painted 143.10, colored 251.10

colorizing (act of) painting 143.1

colorless 252.5; unhealthy 114.23, unemphatic 201.2, transparent 249.7, whitened 253.8, unadorned 526.9

colorlessly 252.9; unemphatically 201.4

colorlessness 252.1; transparency 249.1, whiteness 253.1

color negative film 132.8, color image 251.7

color painting color image 251.7

color perception chromaticism 251.2

color photograph photograph 132.3

color photography photography 132.1, motion-picture photography 137.9, color image 251.7

colorpoint shorthair Breeds of Cats 35

color print printing 132.20, picture 133.5, color image 251.7

color-print color 251.16

color printer hardcopy device 15.10

color printing printing 173.3, color image 251.7

color processing development 132.19

color proof stage of proof 174.9

color purple Phobias 283

color quality hue 251.4

color red Phobias 283

color remover 252.4; color remover 252.4

color reproduction color image 251.7

colors costume 100.10, flag 184.8

color scheme spectrum 251.3, interior decoration 532.4

color slides color image 251.7

color supplement newspaper 175.2

color television television (TV) 172.5, color image 251.7

color temperature lighting 132.16, hue 251.4

color theory chromatics 251.8

color transparency color image 251.7

color up redden 257.9, blush 403.12

color vision chromaticism 251.2

colorwash coloring agent 251.5, color 251.16

color wheel stage lighting 136.20, spectrum 251.3

color white Phobias 283

colossal huge 579.14

colossus big person 579.10

Colossus of Rhodes Seven Wonders of the Ancient World 294

colostrum body fluid 19.16, 555.3, secreted substance 24.2, mammalian characteristic 35.3

colporteur peddler 482.9

colposcope diagnostic instrument 107.13

colposcopy diagnostic procedure 107.11

colt young animal 26.4, male animal 32.15, male mammal 35.18, young mammal 35.20, unskilled person 128.3, horse 159.1

colter sharp-edged thing 549.6

coltish active 414.13

colts Collective Names 59

colubriform snakelike 37.13

colubrine snakelike 37.13

Columba Constellations 7

columbarium burial place 31.7, dwelling 36.4

columbary cage 60.15

Columbia Breeds of Sheep 16, American States 564, Rivers 570

columbiform avian 36.19

Columbine stock part 136.24, clown 138.10, Famous Lovers 299

columbine avian 36.19, Flowers 42

Columbus American States 564

column 134.6; matrix 6.20, army formation 77.15, Architectural Elements 134, news story 171.3, monument 185.10, superstructure 551.7, vertical 602.3, supporting part 605.3, straight line 630.2, cylinder 633.4, procession 774.6

columnar architectural 134.12

columnated architectural 134.12

column chromatography analysis 11.17

columned architectural 134.12

columniation column 134.6

column inch General Units 589

columnist print journalist 175.5, record keeper 185.8, descriptive writer 202.10, news interpreter 365.7

coma comet 7.20, illness 114.2, desensitization 213.2, oblivion 355.4, sleep 415.5, forfeiture 468.2, disability 515.4, lack of motion 678.1

Coma Berenices Constellations 7

COMAL Programming Languages 15

comanagement joint control 827.5

comatose sick 114.24, desensitized 213.5, indifferent 289.7, not awake 415.12, disabled 515.10

comb practice livestock farming 16.20, cleaning tool 111.10, clean 111.17, hairdressing tool 530.9, coif 530.15, smoother 545.2, smooth 545.10, sharp-pointed thing 549.4, use a sharp tool 549.17, billow 571.9

combat 77.34, 152.17; battle 76.33, contention 422.1, warfare 422.10, contend 422.22, declare war 422.25, object 828.18

combatant 77.1; killer 30.11, enlisted 58.11, hostile person 63.5, contender 422.13, opponent 828.10

combat boots boots 100.31

combat fatigue fatigue 820.1

combative 77.32; military 58.10, warlike 76.27, combat 152.17, militant 418.13, contentious 422.20, disagreeing 463.6

combatively aggressively 77.38, in disagreement 463.12

combativeness bellicosity 76.15, attack 418.1, divisiveness 463.2

combative sport combat sport 152.1

combat-ready forces armed forces 77.9

combat sport 152.1

combat team military organization 58.4

combat troops armed forces 77.9

combat unit military organization 58.4

combat zone battleground 76.24

combe [Brit] concave land 635.2

combed smooth 545.4

comber wave 571.3

combination 757.1; set 6.19, collection 59.2, relatedness 727.1, alliance 735.5, mixture 751.1, mixed thing 751.2, union 752.1, accompaniment 794.1, association 827.6

combination lock fastener 754.7

combinative combinatory 757.6

combinatorial mathematical 6.65

combinatorics 6.63, Branches of Mathematics 6

combinatory 757.6

combine 757.9; farm tool 16.5, put together 59.30, produce 522.13, form an alliance 735.25, mix 751.12, unite 752.14, collection 757.3, become one 788.18, association 827.6, join 827.17

combined 757.5; cumulate 59.20, related 727.6, allied 735.15, mixed 751.8, united 752.10, included 763.4, associated 794.14, joint 827.10

combined attack 418.5

combined effort joint operation 827.4

combinedly cooperatively 827.18

combined operation offensive

warfare 76.11, *joint operation* 827.4

combined training *equestrianism* 159.8

combine with *support* 748.14

combings *residue* 750.2

combining *combination* 757.1

comb jelly *coelenterate* 39.15

comblike *toothed* 549.13

combo [Inf] *team* 59.9, *dance hall* 135.3, *alliance* 735.5, *mixed thing* 751.2

comb out *straighten* 630.14

combust *generate power* 514.19

combustibility *fire* 217.8

combustible 106.12; *on fire* 217.16

combustibly *powerfully* 106.19

combustion *heat* 10.25, *fire* 217.8, *power source* 514.13

combustion light *incandescent light* 246.5

come *become visible* 264.13, *arrive* 704.13

come [Inf] *stimulate* 20.22, *body fluid* 555.3

come about *sail* 150.29, *take effect* 676.11, *turn around* 680.22, *come to be* 717.19

come a cropper [Inf] *be unskillful* 128.8, *fail* 846.12

come across *discover* 345.11, *win an award* 467.23, *find* 565.11

come across [Inf] *pay* 489.16

come adrift *come unstuck* 756.7

come after *be in the rear* 622.7, *follow* 770.10, *be consecutive* 774.11

come again *be unsatisfied* 98.10, *be cyclic* 663.11

come again and again *be repeated* 797.20

come alive *be intelligible* 363.10, *seem true* 721.26

come along *go forward* 679.8

come amiss *be inconvenient* 804.9

come and get it! 92.28

come and go *be active* 414.18, *be regular* 663.10, *swing* 671.12, *oscillate* 683.12

come apart *scatter* 753.15, *disintegrate* 758.6, 808.15, *be disordered* 766.21, *diverge* 776.16

come apart at the seams *be weak* 517.12

come around *live* 28.17, *be refreshed* 94.8, *be persuaded* 178.20, *be restored* 809.13

come around again *occur* 264.14, *be periodical* 641.9, *be cyclic* 663.11

come as a surprise *astonish* 292.10

come as no surprise *be probable* 838.8

come as you are *be informal* 407.10

come at someone's call *obey* 426.7

come at the right time *or moment be timely* 659.6

comeback *countercharge* 332.3, *answer* 334.1, *counterevidence* 339.5, *retaliation* 420.1, *reciprocity* 729.1, *return* 797.4, *revival* 809.3

come back *be unsatisfied* 98.10, *answer* 334.18, *be remembered* 354.15, *retaliate* 419.30, *reverse* 680.18, *renew* 797.19

come back to where one started *recoil* 680.21

come before *lead* 126.12, *predict* 358.14, *show in* 708.13, *precede* 769.13, *be important* 799.13

come before the court *stand trial* 54.29

come between 753.21; *be active in* 412.17, *mediate* 772.19, *hinder* 826.15

come by *gain* 467.15, *receive* 473.13, *purchase* 481.10

come cap in hand *apologize* 313.8

come clean *admit* 180.11

comedian *actor* 136.25, *dramatist* 136.27, *entertainer* 138.8, *humorist* 277.7

comédie larmoyante [Fr] *comedy* 136.11

comedienne *actor* 136.25, *entertainer* 138.8

comédie rosse [Fr] *comedy* 136.11

comedo *mark* 533.2

comedown *humiliation* 298.5, *descent* 714.1, *downfall* 714.7, *decline* 846.5, *adversity* 848.1

come down *descend* 597.22, 714.12, *decrease* 747.7,

come down a peg *fail* 714.18

come down hard on *penalize* 454.26

come down in buckets *or torrents or sheets rain* 9.57

come down in the world *lose one's money* 486.15

come down off the fence *determine* 675.11

come down on *be severe* 424.8, *penalize* 454.26, *drop* 714.15

come down on one side or the other *determine* 675.11

come down on the side of *back* 825.28

come down with *be unhealthy* 114.29

comedy 136.11, 368.2; *movie type* 137.3, *entertainment* 277.4

comedy actor *actor* 136.25

comedy actress *actor* 136.25

comedy of character *comedy* 136.11

comedy of humors *comedy* 136.11

comedy of ideas *comedy* 136.11

comedy of intrigue *comedy* 136.11

comedy of manners *comedy* 136.11

comedy of morals *comedy* 136.11

comedy show *show* 138.4

come eyeball-to-eyeball *show oneself* 843.15

come face-to-face *show oneself* 843.15

come first *lead* 744.19, *be important* 799.13

come forth *become visible* 264.13, *appear* 331.18, *emerge* 771.35, *show oneself* 843.15

come forward *become visible* 264.13, *volunteer* 504.13, *be in front* 621.13

come from another country *be foreign* 724.13

come from without *be external* 724.15

come full circle *orbit* 681.8

come hat in hand *humble oneself* 298.18

come hell or high water [Inf] *earnestly* 376.16

come-hither look *look* 242.7, *communication of love* 299.6

come home *return* 671.11, *reverse* 680.18, *land* 704.16

come in *get in* 704.17

come in *or into enter* 706.11

come in! welcome! 704.24

come in first *compete in track and field* 166.21

come in for *receive* 473.13

come in force *be strong* 516.14

come in front *exceed* 712.15

come in handy *be useful* 801.9, *be convenient* 803.5

come in last *be defeated* 846.18

come in like a lion *be violent* 520.8

come in sight *become visible* 264.13

come in the wake of *follow* 770.10

come into *receive* 473.13, 492.7

come into an inheritance *be fortunate* 847.7

come into being *emerge* 771.35

come into conflict *confront* 828.19

come into contact *adjoin* 216.11, *juxtapose* 223.11, *meet* 704.20

come into effect *be operational* 509.10, *take effect* 676.11

come into existence *be born* 28.18, *emerge* 771.35

come into focus *appear* 244.8

come into money *profit* 472.12, *get rich* 485.13, *be fortunate* 847.7

come into operation *act* 412.11, *be operational* 509.10

come into the hands of *be transferred* 470.13

come into the picture *become visible* 264.13

come into the world *be born* 28.18, *emerge* 771.35

come into use *or fashion become a habit* 397.17

come into view *be visible* 242.26

come in useful *be convenient* 803.5

come last *be in the rear* 622.7

comeliness *attractiveness* 529.2

comely *attractive* 529.8

come near *near* 586.12

come next *follow* 770.10

come of *follow from* 676.9

come of age *mature* 27.17, *grow* 581.17

come off *come unstuck* 756.7

come off [Inf] *take effect* 676.11, *be effective* 387.2

come off best *overpower* 845.18

come off it! [Inf] *cease!* 668.14

come off on *adhere* 755.8

come off well *be successful* 845.11

come off with flying colors *attain one's goal* 845.13

come often *frequent* 661.6

come-on [Inf] *enticement* 178.3, *offer* 504.1, *positive stimulus* 508.5, *allurement* 700.4

come on bended knee *humble oneself* 298.18

come on like gangbusters [Inf] *be full of vigor* 518.4

come on the scene *become visible* 264.13

come on the stage *occur* 264.14

come out *be published* 173.19, *be disclosed* 180.12, *become visible* 264.13, *occur* 264.14, *launch* 405.14, *emerge* 707.14, 771.35, *be in a state of* 725.8

come out easily *be easy* 823.14

come out for *side with* 382.15

come out from the woodwork *appear* 244.8

come out in the open *emerge* 707.14

come out in the wash *lose color* 252.7

come out into the open *show oneself* 843.15

come out of *follow from* 676.9

come out of nowhere *astonish* 292.10

come out of the blue *astonish* 292.10

come out of the closet *divulge* 180.9

come out on one side *side with* 382.15

come out second best *be defeated* 846.18

come out the other side *pass* 692.15

come out with *divulge* 180.9, *improvise* 396.6, *reveal* 843.14

come over the horizon *appear* 244.8, *become visible* 264.13

comer *entrant* 706.7

comer [Inf] *successful person* 845.6

come rain or shine *earnestly* 376.16

come right in the end *overcome obstacles* 845.14

come short *be insufficient* 98.9, *be inferior* 745.10

come soon *be in the future* 650.9

comestible *edible* 92.20, *tasty* 219.4

comestibles *food* 90.1

comet 7.20; *natural light* 246.4, *orbiting body* 681.4

cometary *astronomical* 7.33

comet cloud *comet* 7.20

come through *live* 28.17, *be in a state of* 725.8, *be safe* 810.20

come through loud and clear *be intelligible* 363.10

come through with flying colors *overpower* 845.18

comet nucleus *comet* 7.20

come to *live* 28.17, *be refreshed* 94.8, *price* 494.12, *reach out* 585.10, *convert* 670.11, *reach* 704.14, *be whole* 759.9, *total* 783.10, 784.12, *be restored* 809.13

come to a bad end *be in trouble* 848.13

come to a close *be complete* 761.10

come to a conclusion *or decision or determination resolve* 376.12

come to a crossroads *find one's way* 691.15

come to a dead stop *malfunction* 846.20

come to a focus *focus* 702.11

come to a halt *pause* 415.15, *stop* 668.10, *malfunction* 846.20

come to a head *fester* 25.23

come to a junction *cross* 609.9

come to a juncture *be at a critical moment* 726.15

come to an agreement *contract* 459.8, *come together* 757.10, *come to an arrangement* 767.22

come to an arrangement 767.22

come to an end 773.23; *be destroyed* 523.17, *stop* 668.10, *be complete* 761.10

come to an understanding *pacify* 74.11, *come to an arrangement* 767.22

come to a parting of the ways *divorce* 66.9, *disagree* 463.8

come to a point *be sharp* 549.15

come to a standstill *pause* 415.15, *stop* 668.10, *be in difficulty* 824.19

come to a sticky end [Inf] *be destroyed* 523.17

come to a stop *interrupt* 604.16, *stop* 668.10

come to bat *play baseball* 147.9

come to be 717.19; *emerge* 771.35

come to blows *oppose* 63.11, *fight* 422.23

come to close quarters *fight* 422.23

come to dust 553.28; *die* 29.17, *be transient* 643.6

come to financial ruin *need money* 848.14

come together 59.25, 702.10, 757.10; *unify* 752.15

come to grief *miscarry* 846.19, *be in trouble* 848.13

come to grips *fight* 422.23

come to grips with *undertake* 391.7

come to hand *receive* 473.13, *be brought* 704.19

come to heel *obey* 426.7

come to journey's end *pause* 415.15, *reach* 704.14

come to know *be informed* 170.15

come to life *live* 28.17, *be born* 28.18

come to light *be disclosed* 180.12, *be visible* 242.26, 843.16, *appear* 244.8, *become visible* 264.13, *be discovered* 345.15

come to meet *meet* 704.20

come to mind *have an idea* 327.13

come to naught *be infertile* 23.8, *go to waste* 468.19, *miscarry* 846.19

come to nothing *be infertile* 23.8, *go to waste* 468.19, *fail* 846.12, *miscarry* 846.19

come to one *have an idea* 327.13, *receive* 473.13

come to one's senses *be sane* 109.5, *awake* 212.10

come to pass *take effect* 676.11, *result* 770.12

cometophobia Phobias 283

come to pieces *disintegrate* 758.6

come or fall to pieces or bits *scatter* 753.15

come to rest *pause* 415.15, *reach* 704.14, *take it easy* 819.3

come to terms *contract* 459.8, *negotiate* 460.6, *come to an arrangement* 767.22

come to terms with *resign oneself* 835.6

come to the aid or assistance of *help* 825.23

come to the end of the line *find one's way* 691.15, *discontinue* 846.14

come to the end of the road *come to an end* 773.23

come to the front *be in front* 621.13, *overtake* 744.16

come to the point *be concise* 198.5, *be brief* 204.9, *be simple* 526.13, *focus* 702.11, *relate to* 727.9, *particularize* 779.17

come to the point of no return *be at a critical moment* 726.15

come to the relief of *help* 825.23

come to the rescue *rescue* 419.26, *deliver* 817.5

come to the rescue of *save* 275.9

come to the same thing *equalize* 740.12

come to the surface *appear* 244.8, *become visible* 264.13

come to understand *understand* 363.9

come true *be real* 721.21

comets Phobias 283

come under fire *face danger* 811.12

come under the hammer *be sold* 482.22

come under the influence of *be persuaded* 178.20, *be motivated* 508.10

come undone *scatter* 753.15, *come unstuck* 756.7

come unstuck 756.7; *be unskillful* 128.8, *scatter* 753.15, *be disordered* 766.21, *diverge* 776.16, *have difficulty* 824.18

come up *become visible* 264.13

come up or back for more *endure* 377.14

come up for trial *stand trial* 54.29

come upon *discover* 345.11, *reach* 704.14, *chance upon* 842.13

come upon or across *meet* 704.20

comeuppance [Inf] *retaliation* 420.1, *compensation* 453.7, *reckoning* 454.8

come up roses [Inf] *overcome obstacles* 845.14

come up smiling *overcome obstacles* 845.14

come up to *be equal* 740.11

come up to scratch *meet with approval* 437.20

come up with *improvise* 396.6, *invent* 771.30

come what may *necessarily* 95.22, *earnestly* 376.16

come with *accompany* 794.16

come within earshot *be heard* 228.15

come within the law *be legal* 53.28

comfort 214.14, 273.9; *pleasure* 214.2, 271.2, *make pleasant* 271.10, *satisfaction* 273.1, *ease* 275.1, 819.1, 819.4, *relieve* 275.8, *cheer* 281.4, *inspire hope* 281.14, *be compassionate* 305.11, *condolence* 308.2, *grieve* 308.7, *opulence* 485.3, *mitigate* 521.9, *comfortable circumstances* 726.5, *easiness* 823.1, *support* 825.2, 825.24, *supporter* 825.13, *prosperity* 847.1

comfortable 271.8, 726.10; *fit for habitation* 60.19, *getting well* 113.9, *pleasant* 214.7, 271.5, *pleased* 214.9, *satisfied* 273.4, *wealthy* 485.8, *at ease* 819.2, *easygoing* 823.13, *prosperous* 847.5

comfortable circumstances 726.5; *opulence* 485.3

comfortably 726.19; *pleasingly* 214.15, *wealthily* 485.16, *easily* 823.19, *prosperously* 847.9

comfortably drunk *drunk* 121.25

comfortably off *well-off* 467.12, *wealthy* 485.8, *prosperous* 847.5

comfortably situated *prosperous* 847.5

comforted *relieved* 275.6

Comforter *God the Holy Ghost* 82.10

comforter *neckwear* 100.29, *reliever* 275.4, *body covering* 613.3, *bed covering* 613.7

comforting *refreshing* 94.4, *pleasant* 214.7, *satisfying* 273.5, *relieving* 275.7, *cheering* 281.9, *pitying* 308.4, *moderating* 521.5, *supportive* 825.18

comfortingly 275.14, 281.17; *pityingly* 308.11

comfortless *without hope* 282.7

comfort station *place for excretion* 25.11, *room* 60.9

comfrey Herbs and Spices 91

comfy [Inf] *comfortable* 271.8

comic *dramatic* 136.31, 137.16, *entertainer* 138.8, *poetic* 139.19, *drawing* 143.4, *humorist* 277.7, *humorous* 277.9, *ridiculous* 368.5

comic or comical *variety* 138.13

comical *humorous* 277.9, *ridiculous* 368.5

comicality *ridiculousness* 368.1

comically *dramatically* 136.38, *entertainingly* 138.17, *humorously* 277.13, *funnily* 368.10

comic book *magazine* 175.3

comic business *comedy* 136.11

comic magazine *magazine* 175.3

comic opera *musical drama* 136.5, *opera* 140.8

comic performer *clown* 138.10

comic poet *author* 139.13

comic poetry *poetry* 139.8

comic relief *comedy* 136.11, *aspect of fiction* 139.5

comics *newspaper* 175.2

comic strip *drawing* 143.4, *entertainment* 277.4

comic-strip artist *visual artist* 133.6

coming *appearance* 264.1, *birth* 264.2, *appearing* 264.9, *future* 650.6, *arrival* 704.1, *approaching* 704.10

coming about *sailing terms* 150.5

coming across *locating* 565.3

coming after *sequence* 770.1

coming and going *busy* 414.15, *oscillation* 683.1

coming apart at the seams *destroyed* 523.9

coming ashore *landing* 704.2

coming back *return* 704.4

coming before *precedence* 769.1

coming by *gain* 467.1

coming down in buckets or torrents or sheets *rainy* 9.50

coming down with *sick* 114.24

coming events *future condition* 650.3

coming from *caused* 676.5

coming home *return* 671.3

coming into being *birth* 264.2, *appearing* 264.9, *creation* 717.9

coming into sight *appearing* 264.9

coming into view *appearance* 264.1, *appearing* 264.9

coming later *delaying* 658.8

coming of age *growth* 581.4

coming often *frequenting* 661.2

coming on the scene *appearing* 264.9

coming out 707.3; *outgoing* 707.10, *premiere* 771.9

coming-out *party* 408.6

coming out of one's ears [Inf] *full* 761.8

coming-out party *party* 408.6

comings and goings *swing* 671.4

coming through loud and clear *intelligible* 363.5

coming together *collection* 59.2, *convergence* 702.1, *union* 752.1

coming to terms *resignedness* 835.2

coming to the point *focus* 702.5

coming up roses [Inf] *successfulness* 845.3

Comiso Breeds of Sheep 16

comity *etiquette* 406.3, *courtesy* 410.1, *loyalty* 426.2, *deference* 433.4, *respectfulness* 435.3,

agreement 462.1, *union of nations* 566.2

comma Accents and Diacritical Marks 5, *separator* 753.5

command 425.1, 425.10; *computing terms* 15.22, *know* 48.24, *governance* 49.18, *govern* 49.26, *authority* 52.1, 514.5, 780.6, *have authority* 52.13, *military organization* 58.4, *master* 68.17, *word of command* 76.20, *directorship* 126.5, *direct* 126.11, *skill* 127.1, *military call* 183.9, *signal* 183.18, *wish* 288.2, *desire* 288.17, *impose one's will* 372.14, *have at one's disposal* 393.14, *treatment* 399.11, *coercion* 428.2, *compel* 428.8, *impose a duty* 433.14, *possess* 469.14, *demand* 505.3, 505.12, *leadership* 744.2, *rule over* 780.13

commandant *military leader* 68.10, *person in command* 425.5

command capital *be rich* 485.12

commanded *authorized* 425.9

commandeer *take away* 275.13, *force* 428.10

commandeering *taking* 477.12

Commander US Military Ranks 58, *military title* 72.8

commander *person in authority* 52.7, *military staff* 58.5, *military leader* 68.10, *person in command* 425.5, *superior* 744.5

commander in chief *person in authority* 52.7, *military leader* 68.10, *person in command* 425.5

command influence *influence* 512.11

commanding 425.7; *governing* 49.25, *authoritative* 52.9, *masterful* 68.15, *believable* 87.7, *signaling* 183.14, *compelling* 428.6, *influential* 512.8, *ruling* 780.11, *notable* 799.11

commanding lead *advantage* 744.3

commandingly 425.15; *authoritatively* 52.18, *advisorily* 176.12, *compellingly* 428.12, *influentially* 512.14

commanding officer *person in authority* 52.7, *military position* 58.6, *military leader* 68.10

commanding officer (CO) *person in command* 425.5

commandment *command* 425.1, *rule* 780.1

command of idiom *mode of expression* 537.3

command of language *power of speech* 205.5, *mode of expression* 537.3

command of the air *military affairs* 58.1

command of the sea *military affairs* 58.1

commandos *armed force* 77.10

commando unit *military organization* 58.4

command performance *theatrical performance* 136.13

command respect 435.18; *be important* 799.13

Command Sergeant Major US Military Ranks 58

command ship *warship* 77.21

comme ci comme ça [Fr] *mediocre* 742.7

commedia dell'arte *dramatic style* 136.3, *historic comedy* 136.12

comme il faut [Fr] *proper* 429.10

commemorate 354.14, 405.11, 663.12

commemoration **405.2;** *memento* 354.3, *anniversary* 663.4
commemorative *memorial* 354.10, *celebrative* 405.9, *anniversarial* 663.8
commemoratively *memorably* 354.16
commence *begin* 583.21, 771.25, *be new* 652.17
commencement *beginning* 583.9, 652.4, 771.1
commencing *beginning* 583.14, 771.16
commencing move *first move* 771.12
commend *advise* 176.9, *compliment* 437.17
commendable *praiseworthy* 437.12, *worthy* 447.7, *convenient* 803.3
commendably *worthily* 447.11
commendation *compliment* 437.4
Commendation Medal US Military Medals 58
commendatory *approving* 437.9
commender *approver* 437.7
commending *approving* 437.9
commensal *ecology* 13.25, *associating* 827.11
commensalism *ecology* 13.25
commensurability *comparability* 733.2
commensurable *divisible* 6.71, *comparable* 733.8
commensurably *comparably* 733.18
commensurate *sufficient* 97.3, *interrelated* 727.7, *equal* 740.8
commensurately *relevantly* 727.12
comment *dissertation* 203.1, *utterance* 205.10, *judgment* 341.1, *annotation* 365.2
commentarial *annotative* 365.10
commentary *nonfiction* 139.6, *dissertation* 203.1, *annotation* 365.2
commentate *dissertate* 203.5
commentator *broadcasting personnel* 172.11, *dissertator* 203.3, *judge* 341.5, *interpreter* 365.6, *news interpreter* 365.7
commented on *interpreted* 365.9
comment on *discuss* 4.22, *dissertate* 203.5, *estimate* 341.11, *interpret* 365.12, *annotate* 365.14, *interpret news* 365.17
commerce *international trade* 56.7, *trade* 480.1, *linkage* 752.3, *association* 754.2
commercial *economic* 56.10, *broadcast material* 172.9, *advertisement* 173.9, *mercantile* 480.13, *accounting* 493.7, *transportable* 686.7
commercial arithmetic *accounts* 493.4
commercial art *visual arts* 133.1
commercial artist *visual artist* 133.6
commercial bank *treasury* 484.19, *bank* 487.4
commercial break *broadcast material* 172.9
commercial building *building* 551.9
commercial city *city* 567.1
commercial intercourse *commercial trade* 480.2
commercialistic *economic* 56.10, *mercantile* 480.13
commercialize *trade in* 457.8, *trade* 480.18, *vulgarize* 535.9
commercial law *law* 53.1

commercial listing *advertisement* 173.9
commercially 686.12; *economically* 56.13, *marketably* 482.23, *financially* 493.13
commercial paper *paper money* 484.14
commercial radio *radio broadcasting* 172.4
commercial time-out *game time* 155.4
commercial trade 480.2
commercial transaction *trade* 480.1
commercial transportation *transportation* 686.1
commercial traveler *salesperson* 482.8
commercial zone *urban area* 567.10
commie [Inf] *political party member* 50.6
comminate *curse* 301.13
commination *curse* 301.1
comminative *cursing* 301.7
comminatory *ritualistic* 85.15, *cursing* 301.7
commingle *flow* 570.10, *mix* 751.12, *combine* 757.9
comminute *pulverize* 553.26
comminuted *pulverized* 553.20
comminution *pulverization* 553.4
comminutor *pulverizer* 553.11
commiserable *pitiful* 308.5
commiserate *feel for* 266.17, *be sensitive* 267.5, *pity* 308.6, *grieve* 308.7
commiserating *pitying* 308.4
commiseration *sensitivity* 267.1, *pity* 308.1, *condolence* 308.2
commiserative *pitying* 308.4
commiseratively *pityingly* 308.11
commissarial *provisioning* 89.6
commissariat *food provider* 90.6
commissary *provisioner* 89.4, *food provider* 90.6
commission 833.1, 833.8; *party* 59.3, *join the army* 76.31, *delegate* 79.6, *task* 122.2, *management* 126.1, *selection* 382.1, *select* 382.12, *fitting out* 388.3, *prepare for action* 388.18, *action* 412.1, *act* 412.11, *authorization* 425.4, *authorize* 425.14, *line of duty* 433.3, *impose a duty* 433.14, *reward for service* 453.5, *profit* 467.6, *give out* 472.12, *something received* 473.2, *pay* 489.6, *fee* 494.3, *discount* 495.1, *inaugurate* 771.31
commissioned 833.6; *enlisted* 58.11, *masterful* 68.15, *authorized* 425.9, *duty-bound* 433.8
commissioned officer *military leader* 68.10
commissioner 833.5; *person in authority* 52.7, *leader* 68.3, *delegate* 79.1
commissioner of police *law enforcement officer* 53.8
commissioning *commission* 833.1
commit *certify* 110.14, *do something* 412.13, *impose a duty* 433.14, *immerse* 598.24, *bring* 685.11, *commission* 833.8
commit a crime *be illegal* 53.30, *disobey* 427.12, *do wrong* 430.20, *sin* 450.11, *break the law* 782.19
commit adultery *have sex* 20.21, *be dishonorable* 192.21, *fornicate* 432.14
commit a felony *sin* 450.11
commit a foul *do wrong* 430.20

commit a misdemeanor *sin* 450.11
commit an atrocity *suppress* 424.9
commit an offense *do wrong* 430.20
commit a sacrilege *blaspheme* 301.14
commit a white-collar crime *sin* 450.11
commit bigamy *marry* 64.19
commit burglary *steal* 479.14
commit for trial *try a case* 54.28, *judge* 341.10
commit genocide *slaughter* 30.21, *execute* 454.30
commit hara-kiri or **seppuku** *commit suicide* 30.24
commit highway robbery [Inf] *overcharge* 496.10
commitment 377.2; *intimacy* 62.4, *vow* 189.3, *earnestness* 278.2, *seriousness* 376.3, *contract* 391.2, 459.1, *duty* 433.1, *promise* 458.1, *giving* 472.1, *debt* 488.1, *immersion* 598.8
commit money *give to charity* 472.16
commit murder *murder* 30.20
commit oneself *vow* 189.23, *side with* 382.15, *take charge of* 391.8, *incur a duty* 433.15, *promise* 458.11, *guarantee* 458.13, *contract* 459.8, *fund* 472.15
commit perjury *accuse falsely* 442.9
commit robbery *steal* 479.14
commit sacrilege *desecrate* 436.24
commit sin *be wicked* 448.13
commit suicide 30.24
commit suttee *commit suicide* 30.24
committal *pretrial proceedings* 54.13
committed 377.7; *intimate* 62.7, *vowed* 189.14, *earnest* 278.5, *steady* 376.8, *dutiful* 433.6, *promised* 458.8, *guaranteeing* 458.9, *contractual* 459.7, *indebted* 488.7, *in deep* 598.18
committedly *intimately* 62.14
committed to memory *memorized* 354.9
committee *party* 59.3, *representative body* 79.2, *management board* 126.2, *association* 752.2, *council* 833.4
committeeman *political party member* 50.6
committeewoman *political party member* 50.6
committer *doer* 412.3
commit time *give to charity* 472.16
commit to memory *memorize* 354.11
commit to writing *inscribe* 185.14
commix *mix* 751.12
commixture *mixture* 751.1
commode *place for excretion* 25.11, *cabinet* 101.8
commodious *big* 498.9, *spacious* 563.13, *useful* 801.5, *convenient* 803.3
commodities broker *financial adviser* 457.4
commodities exchange *stock exchange* 457.3
commodity *merchandise* 482.6, 522.6, *object* 524.6, *usefulness* 801.1
commodity exchange *stock market* 483.6

commodity market *stock market* 483.6
Commodore US Military Ranks 58, *military title* 72.8
common 71.3, 778.13; *of language* 5.35, *grassland* 45.2, *green place* 260.2, *predictable* 295.4, *lowly* 298.9, *known* 348.9, *familiar* 397.10, 407.8, *sociable* 408.11, *joint possession* 469.6, *property* 470.1, *interfacial* 616.4, *frequent* 661.4, *similar* 733.7, *average* 742.5, *insignificant* 745.6, *prevailing* 778.11, *joint* 827.10
common [Arch] *average person* 742.4
Common Albanian Breeds of Sheep 16
commonality *group* 18.13, *average* 742.1, 778.4
commonalty *common people* 71.2, *average person* 742.4
common border *interface* 616.1
common boundary *interface* 616.1
common carrier *transferrer* 685.4
common chord *chord* 140.18
common cold *respiratory disease* 114.12
common courtesy *courtesy* 410.1
common denominator *division* 6.16
common endeavor *joint operation* 827.4
Common Enemy *devil* 446.5
commoner 71.1; *average person* 742.4
common feature or **trait** *similarity* 733.1
common folk *average person* 742.4
common fraction *division* 6.16, *fraction* 787.1
common friend *mediator* 75.2
common good *welfare* 445.2
common grave *burial place* 31.7
common ground *interaction* 616.2
common jury *jury* 54.11
common knowledge *public information* 170.5, *publicity* 173.7, *information* 348.2
common land *joint possession* 469.6, *property* 470.1
common law *tradition* 1.7, 653.5, *law* 53.1
common-law husband *common-law wife* 64.12
common-law jurisdiction *jurisdiction* 54.2
common-law marriage *type of marriage* 64.3
common-law wife 64.12; *married woman* 64.11
common logarithm *logarithm* 6.17, *power* 783.6
common lot, the *average* 742.1
commonly 71.4; *predictably* 295.9, *indiscriminately* 338.15, *in common* 469.17, *simply* 526.14, *interfacially* 616.7, *frequently* 661.7, *on average* 742.10, *insignificantly* 745.14, *universally* 778.23, *as a rule* 780.18
common man *average person* 18.9, *commoner* 71.1
common man or **woman** *everyone* 778.7
commonness *predictability* 295.2, *lowliness* 298.2, *shoddiness* 497.3, *simplicity* 499.1, *bad taste* 528.3, *grossness* 535.3, *frequency* 661.1, *average* 742.1
common noun *part of speech* 5.30
common occurrence *frequency* 661.1

common or garden *simple* 526.7, *average* 742.5, *common* 778.13
common or garden variety *average* 742.1
common ownership *joint possession* 469.6
common people 71.2; *group* 18.13, *general public* 778.6
common persons *group* 18.13
commonplace 800.17; *catchword* 5.22, *worded* 5.38, *maxim* 177.1, *proverbial* 177.2, *lack of emphasis* 201.1, *unemphatic* 201.2, *mediocre* 289.11, *742.7, predictable* 295.4, *boring* 296.6, *nonsense* 362.2, *meaningless* 362.7, *familiar* 397.10, *simple* 526.7, *common* 778.13
commonplace book *record book* 185.5
commonplacely *boringly* 296.10
commonplaceness *boringness* 296.2
common practice *standard procedure* 397.6
common property *joint possession* 469.6, *property* 470.1
common room *school place* 48.16
common rule *bargaining* 57.9
common run *average* 778.4
common sense 315.4; *philosophical attitude* 4.3, *rationality* 109.2, *social skill* 127.3, *intelligence* 352.2
commonsense Branches of Philosophy 4
commonsensical *rational* 4.15, 109.4
common soldier *soldier* 77.4, *army person* 77.17
common speech *spoken language* 205.2, *unpretentiousness* 526.2
common stock *stock exchange* 457.3, *joint possession* 469.6
common supplies *joint possession* 469.6
common touch *mode of behavior* 399.2, *familiarity* 407.3, *courtesy* 410.1
common type *everyone* 778.7
commonweal *union of nations* 566.2, *benefit* 801.4
Commonwealth, the *nation* 18.14
commonwealth *nation* 18.14, *constitutional government* 49.8, *body politic* 50.3, *union of nations* 566.2
Commonwealth Games *competition* 166.18
Commonwealth of Nations *nation* 18.14
commotion 768.5; *exaggeration* 194.1, *burst of anger* 302.6, *activity* 414.1, *violence by person* 520.2, *tumult* 684.2, *disruption* 766.7
communal 2.12; *societal* 1.13, *sociological* 2.11, *national* 18.16, *inhabited* 61.10, *sociable* 408.11, *urban* 567.14, *allied* 735.15, *prevailing* 778.11, *joint* 827.10
communal eating *eating meals* 92.4
communal effort *joint operation* 827.4
communalism *association* 827.6
communalistic *joint* 827.10
communalize *deposit* 105.21, *take over* 477.16
communally *societally* 1.17, *sociologically* 2.15, *cliquishly* 59.32, *ritually* 85.21, *municipally* 567.16, *in alliance* 735.35, *cooperatively* 827.18

commune *inhabitants* 61.2, *worship* 83.15, *follow rites* 85.19, *converse* 210.11, *administrative region* 564.4, *association* 827.6
commune with *have a rapport with* 735.24
communicable *contagious* 114.26, *communicational* 169.17, *transferable* 685.7
communicable disease *disease* 114.4
communicably *in transit* 685.13
communicant *Christian* 81.10, *worshiper* 83.6
communicate 169.18, 170.12, 176.10; *socialize* 2.14, *use language* 5.42, *educate* 48.22, *publish* 173.15, *divulge* 180.9, *signal* 183.18, *recount* 202.16, *speak* 205.17, *converse* 210.11, *mean* 361.13, *negotiate* 460.6, *link* 752.18, *intercommunicate* 754.15
communicated 169.15; *published* 173.12
communicated insanity *delusion* 110.2
communicate love 299.25
communicate with *communicate* 169.18
communicate with aliens *experience psychic phenomena* 86.23
communicating *communicational* 169.17, *accessible* 691.13
communication 170.2, 176.3; *news event* 171.2, *publication media* 173.6, *advice* 176.1, *divulgence* 180.2, *conversation* 210.1, *sociability* 408.1, *negotiation* 460.1, *transmission* 685.3, *linkage* 752.3, *association* 754.2
communicational 169.17
communication channel *telecommunication* 169.7
communication cord *line* 754.5
communication network *association* 754.2
communication of love 299.6
communications 169.1; *navy specialties* 77.24
communications adapter *card* 15.7
communications device 15.26
communications engineering *telecommunication* 169.7
communications line *telecommunication* 169.7
communications link *telecommunication* 169.7
communications medium *communications* 169.1
communications network *linkage* 752.3
communications protocol *computer communications* 15.25
communications satellite *artificial satellite* 7.30
communications software 15.27; *application software* 15.14
communications system *telecommunication* 169.7
communicative 169.16; *socioeconomic* 2.13, *educational* 48.17, *informative* 170.10, *disclosing* 180.6, *effusive* 207.6, *conversing* 210.8, *sociable* 408.11, *negotiated* 460.5, *connective* 754.10
communicatively *sociologically* 2.15, *effusively* 207.10, *conversationally* 210.14, *sociably* 408.19, *feasibly* 460.9
communicativeness *effusiveness* 207.2, *sociability* 408.1
communicator *informer* 170.8,

discloser 180.4, *speaker* 205.12, *person who joins* 752.9
Communion *Eucharist* 85.7
communion *act of worship* 83.2, *conversation* 210.1, *sociability* 408.1, *compatibility* 735.4
communion with God *religiousness* 81.2
communiqué *communication* 170.2, 176.3, *news event* 171.2, *publication* 173.1
communism *political and economic philosophy* 4.6, *totalitarianism* 49.13, *economics* 56.1, *association* 827.6
Communism Peak Mountains and Hills 569
communist *political and economic philosopher* 4.10, *of a political philosophy* 4.14, *governmental* 49.24, *national* 566.10
communist *or* **communistic** *joint* 827.10
communist country *country* 566.1
communistic *national* 18.16, 566.10, *governmental* 49.24
communistically *governmentally* 49.27, *nationally* 566.10
Communist party Political Parties 50
community *society* 1.6, 2.6, *social organization* 2.5, *ecology* 13.25, *group* 18.13, 59.8, *inhabitants* 61.2, *family* 65.1, *town* 567.2, *alliance* 735.5, *part* 760.1, *prevailing* 778.11, *companionship* 794.3, *association* 827.6, *team* 827.7
community at large *group* 18.13
community center *municipal building* 567.13, *center of activity* 612.4
community chest *stock in trade* 105.2, *charity* 307.3
community college *type of school* 48.12
community drama *dramatic style* 136.3
community hospital *hospital* 107.16
community medicine *medicine* 107.1, *health care* 107.7
community of interest *friendly relations* 62.3
community of nations *group* 18.13
community physician *doctor* 107.19
community relations *society* 2.6
community service *social services* 2.10
community service worker *philanthropist* 307.5
community spirit *fellowship* 827.2
community study *sociological research* 2.2
community theater *theater movements* 136.9
communitywide *sociological* 2.11
community work *voluntary work* 373.5
communize *become a nation* 566.11
commutability *exchange* 673.1
commutation *substitution* 672.1, *exchange* 673.1
commutative *in exchange* 673.3
commutative algebra Branches of Mathematics 6
commutatively *in exchange* 673.6
commutative operation *or law operation* 6.12

commute *be regular* 663.10, *cause change* 665.16, *swing* 671.12, *take a substitute* 672.7, *travel* 686.11
commuter *municipal resident* 567.12, *traveler* 686.6
commuter belt *suburb* 567.11
commuting *swing* 671.4, *travel* 686.5, *traveling* 686.9
Como Lakes 568
Comoros Countries 566
comp [Inf] *book publishing personnel* 174.12
compact *concise* 198.4, *be concise* 198.5, *summary* 204.5, *promise* 458.1, *contract* 459.1, 462.2, *582.12, dense* 540.6, *make dense* 540.9, *little* 580.7, *undersized* 580.8, *smaller* 582.7, *settlement* 735.6, *unite closely* 752.16, *adhesive* 755.5, *agreement* 767.9
compactability *contractibility* 582.4
compactable *contractible* 582.11
compact camera *camera* 132.10
compact dictionary *word book* 5.27
compact disk *or CD recording* 185.6, *sound reproduction* 230.6
compact disk *or CD player sound reproduction* 230.6
compact-disk read-only memory (CD-ROM) *disk* 15.5
compacted *summarized* 204.6, *smaller* 582.7
compactedness *contraction* 582.1
compacter *contractor* 582.6
compaction *petrogenesis* 8.31, *contraction* 582.1, *union* 752.1, *adhesion* 755.1
compactly *concisely* 198.6, *densely* 540.10, *cohesively* 755.11
compactness *conciseness* 198.1, *summariness* 204.4, *density* 540.1, *littleness* 580.1, *union* 752.1
compactor *construction equipment* 14.23
companion 794.8; *friend* 62.2, *personal attendant* 69.5, *stairway* 713.9, *affinity* 733.3, *protector* 810.11
companionability *sociability* 408.1
companionable *friendly* 62.5, *sociable* 408.11, *attending* 575.9
companionably *sociably* 408.19
companionate marriage *type of marriage* 64.3
companion ladder *ladder* 713.10
companionless *alone* 788.15
companionship 794.3; *attendance* 575.3
companionway *sailboat parts and accessories* 150.4, *stairway* 713.9
company 480.7; *military organization* 58.4, Collective Names 59, *party* 59.3, *group* 59.8, *team* 59.9, *army unit* 77.14, *personnel* 123.16, *workplace* 124.1, *cast* 136.26, *good company* 408.9, *attendance* 575.3, *association* 752.2, *collection* 757.3, *companionship* 794.3
company director *manager* 126.7
company grade officer *military position* 58.6
company headquarters *office* 124.2
company leader 68.8
company man *conformist* 781.6
company official *company leader* 68.8
company pension *social assistance* 825.4
company policy *procedure* 387.2

company promoter *merchant* 482.10

company report *record* 185.1

company tax *tax* 494.5

company-wide bargaining *bargaining* 57.9

comparability 733.2; *correspondence* 606.2, *interrelatedness* 727.3, *correlation* 729.3

comparable 733.8; *corresponding* 606.6, *interrelated* 727.7, *correlative* 729.6, *gradational* 739.5

comparableness *correspondence* 606.2

comparably 733.18; *correspondingly* 606.10, *relevantly* 727.12, *correlatively* 729.12, *differentially* 739.9

comparative *linguistic* 5.34, *of grammar* 5.41, *gradational* 739.5

comparative anatomy *anatomy* 13.12

comparative grammar *syntax* 5.32

comparative linguistics Linguistic Studies 5

comparatively *sociologically* 2.15, *linguistically* 5.44, *grammatically* 5.48, *relevantly* 727.12, *differentially* 739.9

comparative macrosociology *sociology* 2.1

comparative psychology Psychological Theories, Schools 108

comparative sociology *sociology* 2.1

compare 733.13; *correspond* 606.8, *correspond to* 727.10, *correlate* 729.9, *measure* 739.7, *counteract* 828.21

compare and contrast *discriminate* 337.12

compare with *compare* 733.13

comparison *correspondence* 606.2, *relatedness* 727.1, *correlation* 729.3, *comparability* 733.2, *gradation* 739.3, *manifestation* 843.2

comparison-shop *shop* 481.15

comparison shopping *shopping* 481.3

compartment 578.2; *setting apart* 753.2, *part* 760.1, *category* 767.6, *class* 777.1

compartmental *component* 760.12

compartmentalization *categorization* 767.5

compartmentalize *divide* 753.18, *part* 760.14, *categorize* 767.21

compartmentalized *component* 760.12, *categorized* 767.15

compartmentalizing *classification* 777.2

compass *geometric construction* 6.47, *guide* 126.6, 697.4, *climbing equipment* 161.4, *indicator* 183.7, *range* 563.7, *breadth* 592.1, *navigational aid* 690.6, *degree* 739.1, *calculator* 784.5, *be successful* 845.11

compass bearing *or* **heading** *bearing* 697.2

compass card *navigational aid* 690.6, *guide* 697.4

compass direction 697.5; *exact location* 565.2, *bearing* 697.2

Compasses Constellations 7

compasses *geometric construction* 6.47

compassion 305.2; *sensitivity* 267.1, *philanthropy* 307.1, *pity*

308.1, *mercy* 308.3, *forgivingness* 312.3, *consideration* 325.2, *leniency* 423.1, *unselfishness* 443.2, *kindness* 445.3

compassionate 305.8; *sensitive* 267.3, *philanthropic* 307.6, *pitying* 308.4, *forgiving* 312.4, *lenient* 423.3, *unselfish* 443.5, *kind* 445.12, *soft-hearted* 543.11

compassionate leave *license* 434.4, *leave of absence* 576.4

compassionately 305.14; *sensitively* 267.6, *philanthropically* 307.9, *pityingly* 308.11, *forgivingly* 312.13, *caringly* 325.14, *leniently* 423.6, *unselfishly* 443.9, *kindly* 445.20, *soft-heartedly* 543.19

compassionateness *philanthropy* 307.1, *pity* 308.1, *forgivingness* 312.3

compass needle *indicator* 183.7

compass reading *navigation* 690.5

compass rose *guide* 697.4

compatibility 462.3, 735.4; *reasoning* 6.61, *computing terms* 15.22, *friendly relations* 62.3, *amiability* 271.3, *love* 299.1, *sociability* 408.1, *interaction* 616.2, *agreement* 730.2, *affinity* 733.3, *conformity* 781.1

compatible 462.8, 735.14; *logical* 6.83, *friendly* 62.5, *likable* 271.6, *loving* 299.15, *lovable* 299.20, *interfacial* 616.4, *agreeing* 730.8, *connected* 733.9, *conforming* 781.8

compatibly 462.16, 735.34; *amicably* 62.13, *lovably* 299.31, *interfacially* 616.7, *agreeingly* 730.19, *similarly* 733.17, *conformingly* 781.16

compatriot *national* 61.3

compeer *contemporary* 649.3

compeers *group* 59.8

compel 428.8; *necessitate* 95.17, *persuade* 178.15, *direct* 384.10, *have authority over* 425.12, *be irresistible* 428.9, *manipulate* 508.12, *be an influence* 512.13, *be powerful* 514.18, *awaken* 675.9, *impel* 695.9

compelled *directed* 384.7

compelling 428.6; *persuasive* 178.12, *emphatic* 200.3, *commanding* 425.7, *motivational* 508.7, *appealing* 512.9, *powerful* 514.15, *strong* 516.9, *causal* 675.7

compelling force *direction* 384.3

compellingly 428.12; *commandingly* 425.15, *influentially* 508.13, *powerfully* 514.21, *acutely* 516.18, *causally* 675.12

compel respect *command respect* 435.18

compendious *concise* 198.4, *summary* 204.5, *short* 591.6

compendiously *concisely* 198.6

compendiousness *conciseness* 198.1, *summariness* 204.4, *shortness* 591.1

compendium 204.3; *compilation* 59.14, *outline* 198.2, *contracted thing* 582.5, *shortened version* 591.3, *collection* 757.3, *catalog* 767.7, *list* 785.1

compensable 743.4

compensate 478.6, 743.7; *recompense* 273.11, *atone* 313.7, *put right* 429.14, *pay* 453.15, *profit* 467.22, *pay back* 489.20, *restore* 671.10, *exchange* 673.5, *reciprocate* 729.7, *equalize* 740.12

compensated 743.3; *receiving* 473.9, *substituted* 672.4, *exchanged* 673.4

compensate for *counteract* 510.7, *substitute* 672.5

compensating *compensatory* 743.5

compensatingly *reciprocally* 729.10

compensation 453.7, 478.2, 743.1; *bargaining terms* 57.10, *peace offering* 74.5, *defense mechanism* 108.23, *snowplow* 162.29, *reparation* 273.2, *atonement* 313.1, *reward for service* 453.5, *liability* 454.6, *profit* 467.6, *something received* 473.2, *repayment* 489.5, *counteraction* 510.1, *restoration* 671.2, *substitution* 672.1, *exchange* 673.1, *reciprocity* 729.1, *equalization* 740.4, *fullness* 761.5

compensational *atoning* 313.5, *reciprocal* 729.4, *compensatory* 743.5

compensation technique *skiing techniques* 162.5

compensative *atoning* 313.5, *receivable* 473.12, *compensatory* 743.5

compensator *atoner* 313.4, *returner* 478.3

compensatory 453.11, 743.5; *atoning* 313.5, *gainful* 467.10, *receivable* 473.12, *restoring* 478.4, *paying in return* 489.15, *counteracting* 510.6, *regressive* 671.6, *in exchange* 673.3, *reciprocal* 729.4

compensatory payment *liability* 454.6

compère [Brit] *direct* 126.11

compete *participate* 145.6, *compete in track and field* 166.21, *be jealous* 314.8, *contend* 422.22

compete in gymnastics *exercise* 157.12

compete in track and field 166.21

competence *running water* 8.10, *sufficiency* 97.1, *skill* 127.1, *qualification* 340.1, *proficiency* 445.5, *ability* 514.3, *instrumentality* 801.3, *easiness* 823.1

competence *or* **competency** *governance* 52.6

competency *satisfactoriness* 273.3

competent *law-abiding* 53.20, *excellent* 68.16, *sufficient* 97.3, *skillful* 127.10, *expert* 127.12, *satisfactory* 273.6, *qualified* 340.7, *knowledgeable* 348.7, *proficient* 445.15, *powerful* 514.15, *equal to* 740.10, *instrumental* 801.7

competently *masterfully* 68.19, *skillfully* 127.16, *satisfactorily* 273.12, *capably* 340.15, *proficiently* 445.22, *powerfully* 514.21

compete with *or* **against** *confront* 828.19

competing *jealous* 314.5, *contending* 422.19, *discordant* 828.12

competition 166.18; *ecology* 13.25, *economic factor* 56.8, *sports* 145.1, *jealousy* 314.2, *rivalry* 422.2, *contest* 422.4, *conflict* 828.3

competition aikido *aikido* 152.16

competition judo *judo* 152.13

competitive 422.21; *skillful* 127.10, *sporting* 145.5, *wrestling* 152.18, *gymnastic* 157.11, *swimming* 164.12, *track and field* 166.20, *jealous* 314.5,

argumentative 329.7, *discordant* 828.12

competitive casting *competitive fishing* 154.5

competitive diver *swimmer* 164.11

competitive diving 164.7; *diving* 164.6

competitive diving marks *competitive diving* 164.7

competitive fishing 154.5

competitive gymnastics *gymnastics* 157.1

competitive ice dancing *ice dancing* 162.18

competitive ice skating *ice skating* 162.15

competitive inhibition *enzyme* 12.11

competitive lugeing *toboggan race* 162.25

competitively *sportingly* 145.7, *professionally* 152.22, *on the water* 154.15, *gymnastically* 157.13, *jealously* 314.12, *opposingly* 828.22

competitiveness *jealousy* 314.2, *rivalry* 422.2

competitive price *cheapness* 497.1

competitive rowing *rowing* 150.14

competitive sailing 150.6; *sailing* 150.2

competitive scoring *ice-dancing move* 162.19

competitive skiing *skiing* 162.1

competitive spirit *jealousy* 314.2

competitive swimmer *swimmer* 164.11

competitive swimming 164.3; *swimming* 164.1

competitive tae kwon do *tae kwon do* 152.15

competitive trail riding *equestrianism* 159.8

competitor *hostile person* 63.5, *tae kwon do* 152.15, *track and field eventer* 166.19, *contender* 422.13, *entrant* 706.7, *opponent* 828.10

compilation 59.14, 174.4; *compendium* 204.3

compile 204.8; *program* 15.29, *put together* 59.30

compiled language *programming language* 15.16

compiler *system software* 15.13

complacency *satisfaction* 273.1, *incuriosity* 322.1, *self-satisfaction* 402.2

complacent *satisfied* 273.4, *incurious* 322.3, *self-satisfied* 402.9

complacently *apathetically* 322.7, *smugly* 402.18

complain 507.8; *have an industrial dispute* 57.20, *be dissatisfied* 274.7, *lament* 280.7, *be irritable* 304.14, *refuse* 347.9, *accuse* 442.8, *protest* 507.7, *object* 828.18

complain about *protest* 331.19

complainant *accuser* 442.3

complainer *sad person* 270.3, *dissatisfied person* 274.3, *lamenter* 280.3, *sullen person* 304.7, *protester* 507.4

complaining *dissatisfied* 274.4

complain of *be unhealthy* 114.29

complaint 304.5; *pretrial proceedings* 54.13, *industrial dispute* 57.7, *illness* 114.2, *Poem or Verse Forms* 139, *expression of dissatisfaction* 274.2, *lament* 280.2, *disapproval* 347.2, *fault* 430.2,

censure 438.3, accusation 442.1, protest 507.1
complaisance *deference* 410.4, *obedience* 426.1
complaisant *deferential* 410.8, *obedient* 426.4, *soft-hearted* 543.11, *compliant* 781.9
complaisantly *deferentially* 410.15, *obediently* 426.9, *soft-heartedly* 543.19, *adaptably* 781.15
compleat [Arch] *completed* 761.7
complement *part of speech* 5.30, *set* 6.19, *team* 59.9, *personnel* 123.16, *ancillary* 605.5, *interrelation* 729.2, *interrelate* 729.8, *equivalence* 730.3, *be equivalent* 730.15, *conform* 735.27, *addition* 748.1, *fullness* 761.5, *complete* 761.9, *inclusion* 763.1, *accompany* 794.16
complemental *interrelated* 729.5
complementally *interrelatedly* 729.11
complementarity *interrelatedness* 727.3
complementary *of grammar* 5.41, *ancillary* 605.14, *in exchange* 673.3, *interrelated* 727.7, 729.5, *equivalent* 730.9, *additional* 748.8, *completed* 761.7, *accompanying* 794.12
complementary angle *angle* 6.37
complementary color *color* 251.1
complementary medicine *alternative medicine* 107.4
complete 759.10, 761.6, 761.9, 805.14; *logical* 6.83, *sufficient* 97.3, *endure* 377.14, *act* 412.11, *secure one's objective* 464.12, *close down* 584.15, *peak* 596.18, *intense* 598.16, *be at the top* 600.9, *ceased* 668.6, *cease* 668.9, *react* 676.8, *interrelate* 729.8, *augment* 748.13, *whole* 759.6, 788.12, *ended* 773.14, *end* 773.19, *perfect* 805.19
complete a circuit *move around* 633.10
complete a purchase *purchase* 481.10
complete blank *unknown thing* 349.3
complete cycle *completion* 761.2
completed 761.7; *secured* 464.7, *closed down* 584.10, *over* 651.12, *ended* 773.14, *perfect* 805.8
complete failure *error* 846.2
complete list *unit* 759.5
completely 759.14, 761.13, 805.22; *clean* [Inf] 111.21, *right away* 429.20, *finally* 584.18, *at length* 590.15, *intensely* 598.28, *wholly* 759.11, 788.22
completely past *over* 651.12
completeness 761.1; *reasoning* 6.61, *deepness* 598.6, *whole* 759.1, *perfect condition* 805.3
complete pass *play* 155.8
complete set *unit* 759.5, *inclusion* 763.1
complete works *compilation* 174.4, *whole thing* 759.2
completing *interrelated* 729.5, *completion* 761.2, *ending* 773.13
completion 761.2; *sufficiency* 97.1, *action* 412.1, *ratification* 459.4, *closure* 584.1, *cessation* 668.1, *effect* 676.1, *end* 773.1, *conclusion* 773.3, *perfection* 805.1
completive *interrelated* 729.5, *ending* 773.13
completively *interrelatedly* 729.11
complex 6.69; *chemical compound*

11.4, *delusion* 110.2, *mysterious* 182.10, *obscure* 197.2, *difficult* 364.8, *habit* 397.1, *construction* 551.6, *profound* 598.15, *ambiguous* 632.5, *complicated* 751.10, *whole thing* 759.2, *problematic* 824.11
complex analysis *calculus* 6.28
complex conjugate *complex number* 6.6
complex fraction *division* 6.16
complexion *face color* 251.9, *external appearance* 264.5, *nature* 723.4, *mode* 725.2, *type* 777.4
complexion [Arch] *personality type* 108.6
complexity *obscurity* 197.1, *profundity* 598.5, *mixture* 751.1, *variety* 751.4, *difficulty* 824.1
complex lipid *fat* 12.7
complexly *circularly* 632.8, *mixedly* 751.16
complexness *profundity* 598.5
complex number 6.6; *kind of number* 783.2
complex sugar *saccharide* 12.4
compliance 781.2; *submissiveness* 298.3, *willingness* 324.1, *acquiescence* 373.3, *servility* 401.1, *deference* 410.4, 433.4, *submission* 421.1, *obedience* 426.1, *agreement* 462.1, 735.3, *observance* 465.1, *easiness* 543.5, *adaptability* 546.2
compliant 781.9; *submissive* 298.10, *assenting* 346.4, *willing* 373.7, *servile* 401.6, *deferential* 410.8, 433.9, *obedient* 426.4, *showing respect* 435.7, *agreeing* 462.6, 735.13, *observant* 465.3, *adaptive* 546.6, *easygoing* 823.13
compliantly *submissively* 298.23, *unanimously* 346.8, *deferentially* 410.15, *obediently* 426.9, *agreeably* 462.14, *observantly* 465.6, *soft-heartedly* 543.19, *adaptably* 546.11, 781.15, *in accord* 735.33
complicate *make obscure* 197.3, *make unintelligible* 364.13, *be ambiguous* 632.7
complicated 751.10; *difficult* 364.8, *ambiguous* 632.5, *problematic* 824.11
complicatedly *mixedly* 751.16
complicate matters *cause difficulties* 824.22
complication *illness* 114.2, *aspect of fiction* 139.5, *mixture* 751.1, *difficulty* 824.1, *snag* 824.8
complicity *guilt* 450.1
compliment 437.4, 437.17; *pleasant thing* 271.4, *flatter* 439.12
complimentary *phrased* 5.39, *celebrative* 405.9, *approving* 437.9, *flattering* 439.7, *given* 472.8, *free of charge* 497.12
complimentary gift *absence of charge* 497.6
complimentary phrase *phrasing* 5.25
complimentary or flattering remark *compliment* 437.4
complimentary ticket *or* **pass** *absence of charge* 497.6
complimenting *greeting* 435.8
compliments *courtesies* 410.3, *greeting* 435.5, *flattery* 439.1
compliments of the season *courtesies* 410.3
compline *public worship* 83.3, *night* 656.3
comply *submit* 298.17, 421.4, *assent to* 346.7, *be willing* 373.12, *be servile* 401.8, *defer to* 410.12,

obey 426.7, *yield* 543.17, *be adaptable* 546.9, *agree* 735.23, *conform* 781.11
complying *obedient* 426.4, *easiness* 543.5, *easing* 543.13, *adaptive* 546.6
comply with *obey* 426.7, *agree with* 462.10, *observe* 465.4
component 760.3, 760.12; *vector* 6.48, *circuit element* 14.39, *machinery* 103.5, *physical element* 524.5, *containing* 577.7, *integral* 723.7, *additional item* 748.3, *part* 760.1, *thing included* 763.2, *included* 763.4
components *materials* 104.1, *contents* 577.1, *component* 760.3
comportment *conduct* 399.1
comport oneself *conduct oneself* 399.17
comport oneself well *behave well* 399.18
compose 141.18; *put together* 59.30, *conciliate* 74.10, *design* 133.9, *produce* 137.21, *write* 139.21, *print* 173.17, *imagine* 360.14, *dream up* 522.15, *fashion* 536.7, *shape* 577.11, *come to be* 717.19, *combine* 757.9, *complete* 761.9, *include* 763.5, *order* 765.18, *arrange* 767.18
compose a photograph 132.27
composed 141.13; *detached* 4.18, *printed* 173.13, *wonderless* 295.3, *calm* 455.9, *moderate* 521.3, *containing* 577.7, *assured* 621.12, *formed* 624.6, *quiescent* 678.6, *combinatory* 757.6, *ordered* 765.10
composedly *stoically* 4.26
composed of *including* 763.3
compose oneself *not wonder about* 295.5, *prepare oneself* 388.21
composer 141.9; *filmmaker* 137.14, *visionary* 360.9, *producer* 522.10, *originator* 737.3
composing *typesetting* 173.4, *inclusion* 763.1
Composite *column* 134.6
composite *divisible* 6.71, *taxonomic* 41.16, *fencing* 153.6, *mixed* 751.8, *united* 752.10, *compound* 757.4, *various* 793.7
composite attack *fencing movements* 153.3
composite fruit *botanical fruit* 44.2
composite function *mathematical function* 6.27
compositeness *multiplicity* 793.2
composite number *number* 6.4
composite parry *fencing movements* 153.3
composite volcano *volcanic activity* 8.26
composition 132.17; *mathematical function* 6.27, *rock* 8.30, *compilation* 59.14, *work of art* 133.4, 522.4, (act of) painting 143.1, *treatment* 143.6, *printing* 173.3, *dissertation* 203.1, *repayment* 489.5, *form* 551.3, 624.1, *contents* 577.1, *forming* 624.4, *nature* 723.4, *mixture* 751.1, *mixed thing* 751.2, *unification* 752.5, *combination* 757.1, *inclusion* 763.1, *order* 765.1, *arrangement* 767.1, *array* 767.2
compositor *printer* 173.10, *book publishing personnel* 174.12
compos mentis [L] *sane* 109.3
compost *fertilizer* 16.9, 17.8, 22.6, *cultivate* 17.19, *fertilize* 22.12, *place for waste* 802.6

compostable *deconstructed* 758.4
compost heap *place for waste* 802.6
composting *gardening* 17.5
compost pile *or* **heap** *nursery* 17.4
composure *philosophical attitude* 4.3, *lack of wonder* 295.1, *calmness* 455.4, *moderation* 521.1, *assurance* 621.8, *form* 624.1, *repose* 678.2
compotation *drinking* 121.2
compound 757.4; *divisible* 6.71, *of leaves* 41.18, *prison* 55.1, *product* 522.3, *enclosed area* 619.2, *mixed thing* 751.2, *mix* 751.12, *combine* 757.9
compound epithet *literary device* 139.12
compound fraction *division* 6.16, *fraction* 787.1
compound interest *profit* 467.6, *interest* 488.4
compound lens *lens system* 10.22
compound unit *unit of measurement* 589.5
comprehend *rationalize* 4.20, *know* 48.24, 348.10, *learn* 68.18, *understand* 363.9, *be profound* 598.23, *include* 763.5
comprehensibility 361.3; *clarity* 196.1, *intelligibility* 363.1, *simplicity* 823.2
comprehensible *clear* 196.2, *meaningful* 361.6, *intelligible* 363.5, *made easy* 823.11
comprehensibly *clearly* 196.4, *intelligibly* 363.13
comprehension *intelligence* 315.2, *knowledge* 348.1, *wisdom* 352.1, *understanding* 363.4, *coverage* 613.16, *inclusion* 763.1
comprehensive *huge* 579.14, *broad* 592.5, *intense* 598.16, *inclusive* 613.22, *whole* 759.6, *complete* 761.6, *including* 763.3, *general* 778.9, *made easy* 823.11
comprehensive insurance policy *coverage* 613.16
comprehensively *broadly* 592.15, *intensely* 598.28, *inclusively* 613.35, 763.8, *one and all* 759.12
comprehensiveness *largeness* 579.2, *breadth* 592.1, *deepness* 598.6, *whole* 759.1, *completeness* 761.1, *inclusion* 763.1, *generality* 778.1
comprehensive school *type of school* 48.12
comprehensive test ban *disarmament* 74.3
compress *be concise* 198.5, *retain* 471.7, *make dense* 540.9, *contract* 582.12, *shorten* 591.9, *narrow* 593.14, *make smaller* 747.8, *unite closely* 752.16
compressed *concise* 198.4, *condensed* 540.7, *smaller* 582.7, *shortened* 591.7, *narrow* 593.8
compressedly *narrowly* 593.17
compressibility 543.3; *heating effect* 10.28, *sparseness* 541.1, *contractility* 582.4, Fields of Measurement 589
compressible 543.9; *sparse* 541.3, *contractible* 582.11
compressible fluid *fluid* 555.1, *gas* 556.1
compression *heating effect* 10.28, *load* 14.14, *deformation* 14.16, *computer communications* 15.25, *cross-country* 162.31, *conciseness* 198.1, *outline* 204.2, *retention* 471.1, *contraction* 582.1,

shortening 591.2, narrowness 593.1, limitation 747.3
compression wood timber 43.3
compressive contracting 582.10
compressive strength mechanical strength 516.2
compressor engine type 14.11, condenser 540.5, contractor 582.6
comprisal inclusion 763.1
comprise include 613.33, 763.5, embody 723.12, unify 752.15, be whole 759.9
comprising including 763.3
compromise 461.1, 461.7; pacification 74.1, pacify 74.11, defame 440.13, negotiation 460.1, negotiate 460.6, permit 502.6, instrument 511.2, be an instrument 511.7, moderation 521.1, be moderate 521.6, substitution 672.1, take a substitute 672.7, reciprocity 729.1, reciprocate 729.7, 827.13, agreement 735.3, agree 735.23, settle 735.26, come to an arrangement 767.22, middle ground 772.4, stand in the middle 772.17, mediate 772.19, endanger 811.13, mutual relationship 827.3
compromising 461.4; negotiation 460.1, negotiated 460.5, reciprocal 729.4, agreeing 735.13
compromisingly 461.9; feasibly 460.9, in accord 735.33
compte rendu [Fr] document 170.3, statement 493.2
Compton effect Classical Physical Laws 10
comptroller treasurer 484.18
compulsion 108.13, 428.1; necessitation 95.5, involuntariness 95.9, type of complex 108.22, delusion 110.2, work 122.1, habit 397.1, motivation 508.1, cause 675.1, impulsion 695.1
compulsive compelling 428.6
compulsive cease-fire treaty 74.2
compulsive eater or **gambler** or **talker** or **liar** or **shopper** compulsive person 428.5
compulsive eating appetite 92.2
compulsively compellingly 428.12, powerfully 514.21, acutely 516.18
compulsiveness compulsion 428.1
compulsive person 428.5
compulsory 428.7; necessitative 95.11, involuntary 95.15, ice-skating 162.32, commanding 425.7, duty-bound 433.8, essential 723.5, legal 780.8, captive 832.9
compulsory arbitration strike 57.8
compulsory dancing ice dancing 162.18
compulsory exercise gymnastics 157.1
compulsory figure ice-skating techniques 162.16
compulsory marriage type of marriage 64.3
compulsory payment liability 454.6
compulsory service military affairs 58.1
compulsory servitude subjection 832.1
compunction penitence 313.3, 451.1
compunctious penitent 451.5
compunctiously penitently 451.10
compurgation favorable verdict 54.19, vindication 441.1
computable numerable 6.70, measurable 589.17, calculable 784.8

computably mathematically 784.15
computation mathematics 6.1, numeration 6.10, accounting 493.1, measurement 589.1, mathematical addition 748.2, calculation 784.1, computing 784.4
computational linguistic 5.34, calculative 784.7
computational linguistics Linguistic Studies 5
computative calculative 784.7
compute rationalize 4.20, enumerate 6.85, experiment 10.72, measure 589.20, add 748.11, calculate 784.10
computed value measurement 10.67
computer 15.1; calculator 6.64, 784.5, recording instrument 185.9
computer-aided design (CAD) computing 15.2
computer-aided manufacturing (CAM) computing 15.2
computer-aided molecular design (CAMD) computing 15.2
computer-aided testing (CAT) computing 15.2
computer-assisted learning (CAL) computing 15.2
computer-based learning (CBL) computing 15.2
computer chip semiconductor 10.34
computer communications 15.25
computer composition typesetting 173.4
computer crime dishonesty 479.7
computer criminal dishonest person 479.11
computer dating matchmaker 64.13
computer electronics electronics 14.33
computer engineer computer user 15.3
computerese vernacular 205.8
computer fault unsuccessful thing 846.8
computer file record book 185.5, catalog 767.7
computer game application software 15.14, type of game 167.2
computer games Hobbies and Pastimes 167
computer hobbyist computer user 15.3
computer information 15.17
computer-integrated manufacture (CIM) computing 15.2
computerization bargaining terms 57.10, instrumentality 511.1, manufacture 522.2
computerize employ 57.18, produce 522.13
computerized 15.28; hired 57.17, practical 511.6, productive 522.11
computerized axial tomography (CAT or CT) scan diagnostic radiology 107.12
computerized information information technology (IT) 170.7
computerized typesetting typesetting 173.4
computer language artificial language 5.9
computer listing catalog 767.7, list 785.1
computer malfunction technical problem 826.3

computer-managed instruction (CMI) computing 15.2
computer memory artificial memory 354.6
computer network linkage 752.3
computer networking telecommunication 169.7
computer network surfing Hobbies and Pastimes 167
computer operator computer user 15.3, record keeper 185.8, counter 784.6
computer paper paper 104.5
computer part 15.4
computer printer copier 736.5
computer programmer professional worker 123.11, counter 784.6
computer repairman artisan 123.13
computers Phobias 283
computer scanner imaging device 242.11
computer science computing 15.2
computer scientist computer user 15.3
computer technician technical worker 123.14
computer technology computing 784.4
computer user 15.3
computer war warfare 76.3
computing 15.2, 784.4; accounting 493.7, calculative 784.7
computing terms 15.22
comrade friend 62.2, companion 794.8
comradely friendly 62.5, associating 827.11
comradeship friendship 62.1, good company 408.9, fellowship 827.2
Comtism Philosophical Schools of Thought 4
Comtois Horse and Pony Breeds 159
con learn 48.23, rehearse 136.37, act 137.20, get to know 348.12
con [Inf] lawbreaker 53.15, prisoner 55.7, foul play 193.6, swindle 193.19, disreputable action 371.3, overcharge 496.10, stratagem 822.2, be cunning 822.5
con abbandono Musical Terms and Expression Marks 140
Conakry Countries 566
con amore Musical Terms and Expression Marks 140
con artist [Inf] schemer 193.10
conation will 372.1
conative willed 372.6
con brio Musical Terms and Expression Marks 140
con brio with vigor 518.6
concatenate 774.13; link 752.18
concatenation linkage 752.3, consecutiveness 774.1
concave 635.5; curvilinear 6.78, curved 629.4
concave land 635.2
concavely 635.8; curvedly 629.7
concave surface surface 6.36
concavity 635.1; surface 6.36, curvature 629.2, depression 716.4
conceal 181.12; bury 105.22, keep secret 182.11, obliterate 186.8, be untruthful 192.20, misrepresent 193.17, make invisible 245.7, cause to disappear 265.7, exclude 409.12, buffer 419.22, contain 577.10, keep inside 611.17, hide 613.27, 844.13, protect 810.21
concealed 181.8, 844.7; mysterious 182.10, obliterated 186.4, ungenuine 192.13, private 245.5,

disappeared 265.4, secret 611.13, protected 613.20
concealer one who conceals 181.7
concealing equivocal 380.5
concealment 181.1, 844.2; secrecy 182.1, 611.6, obliteration 186.1, misrepresentation 193.4, invisibility 245.1, blacking out 265.2, evasion 380.2, separation 409.3, shelter 613.6, cunning 822.1
conceal oneself 181.15
concede be persuaded 178.20, admit 180.11, assent 346.6, acquiesce 421.5, be lenient 423.5, compromise 461.7, agree with 462.10, agree 735.23
concede a hole play 156.8
concede defeat be defeated 846.18
conceded hole golfing terms 156.3
concede the victory to follow 745.12
conceding compromising 461.4
conceit literary device 139.12, pride 297.1, overestimation 343.1, folly 353.1, supposition 359.1, conception 360.4, vanity 402.1, boastfulness 402.6, egotism 444.2
conceited prideful 297.8, affected 367.3, vain 402.8, boastful 402.13, egotistic 444.5
conceitedly pridefully 297.17, vainly 402.17, boastfully 402.21, egoistically 444.9
conceitedness vanity 402.1
conceivability possibleness 836.2
conceivable imaginable 360.13, possible 836.5
conceivableness possibleness 836.2
conceivably potentially 836.11
conceive reproduce oneself 21.14, procreate 22.14, give birth to 28.19, imagine 327.14, 360.14, know 348.10, suppose 359.8, recognize 363.11, dream up 522.15, come to be 717.19, originate 737.7, invent 771.30
conceive a plan plan 387.12
conceived ideational 327.9, created 717.16
conceive of have an idea 317.12
concenter centralize 612.11, focus 702.11
concentralization focus 702.5
concentralize focus 702.11
concentrate 317.10; solidify 11.37, extract 11.41, 711.8, learn 48.23, hear 228.13, try 414.21, make dense 540.9, contract 582.12, centralize 612.11, come together 702.10, focus 702.11, obtain an extract 711.19, quintessence 723.3, intensify 746.8, unite closely 752.16
concentrated thoughtful 4.17, status adjectives 11.25, committed 377.7, strong to the senses 516.12, condensed 540.7, smaller 582.7, centered 612.9, adhesive 755.5, crowded 795.10
concentrated attack combined attack 418.5
concentratedness union 752.1
concentrated solution phase 11.13
concentrate on focus on 328.9, centralize 612.11
concentrating 317.7; thoughtful 4.17
concentration 540.2; philosophical investigation 4.4, subject 48.3, Children's and Party Games 167, Card Games 168, thoughtfulness 317.2, carefulness 323.3, commitment 377.2, assiduity 414.8,

potency 516.6, contraction 582.1, centrality 612.5, convergence 702.1, obtaining of an extract 711.7, intensification 746.2, union 752.1, adhesion 755.1, specialization 779.3

concentration camp prison 55.1
concentration cell electrochemistry 11.19
concentrative conjunctive 752.12
concentric curvilinear 6.78
concentric or **concentrical** centered 612.9
concentrically centrally 612.12
concentric circles circle 6.40
concentricity centrality 612.5
concept philosophy 4.1, idea 327.1, conception 360.4
conceptacle reproductive body 47.14
conception 360.4, 771.4; genesis 21.5, intellect 315.1, idea 327.1, production 522.1, creation 717.9, invention 771.5
conceptional inventive 771.20
conceptive philosophical 4.12, intellectual 315.8, inventive 771.20
conceptual philosophical 4.12, intellectual 315.8, speculative 317.8, theoretical 327.10, imaginary 360.12
conceptual art Western Art Styles 133
conceptualism Philosophical Schools of Thought 4
conceptualist Philosophical Schools of Thought 4
conceptualization imagination 327.8, 360.1
conceptualize philosophize 4.19, think 315.12, imagine 327.14, 360.14, theorize 720.14
conceptualized ideational 327.9
conceptually theoretically 4.24, 327.19, artistically 133.10, mentally 315.13, originally 737.8
conceptual realism Philosophical Schools of Thought 4
conceptual realist Philosophical Schools of Thought 4
conceptual thought philosophical investigation 4.4
concern workplace 124.1, worry 283.4, attention 323.1, consideration 325.2, topic 328.1, issue 328.2, claim 429.3, line of duty 433.3, company 480.7, store 483.8, inclusion 763.1, disturb 768.10, importance 799.1, be important 799.13
concerned worried 283.11, solicitous 323.8, disturbed 768.6
concerned with focused 328.6
concerning relevantly 727.12
concert performance 141.8, lay the foundations 388.16, show 404.12, agreement 735.3, 752.4, concur 827.16, production 843.5
concerted joint 827.10
concerted action joint operation 827.4
concerted effort joint operation 827.4
concertedly in accord 735.33, cooperatively 827.18
concertgoer music lover 141.10
concert hall performance 141.8
concertina Musical Instruments 142
concertina wire barrier 419.10
concertmaster artistic worker 123.12, musical director 141.7
concert music classical music 140.2
concerto Musical Forms 140

concerto grosso Musical Forms 140
concert pitch tone 140.24
concession submission 421.1, leniency 423.1, basis for negotiations 460.2, compromise 461.1, giving 472.1, discount 495.1, tolerance 502.2, agreement 735.3, mutual relationship 827.3
concessional cheap 497.9
concessional rate cheapness 497.1
concessionary submitting 421.3, negotiated 460.5
conch church architecture 134.11
conch or **concha** Architectural Elements 134
concha ear 19.10
conchological molluskan 39.23
conchologist invertebrate zoologist 39.3
conchology invertebrate zoology 39.2
Conchos Rivers 570
concierge attendant 69.4, closer 584.5
conciliate 74.10; mediate 75.6, atone 313.7, negotiate 460.6, offer reparation 504.15
conciliatingly atoningly 313.10
conciliation strike 57.8, pacification 74.1, mediation 75.1, atonement 313.1, negotiation 460.1, offering 504.5
conciliative atoning 313.5
conciliator employer 57.3, mediator 75.2, atoner 313.4
conciliatorily industrially 57.22, mediatorially 75.7, atoningly 313.10, feasibly 460.9, sacrificially 504.20, in accord 735.33
conciliatory disputed 57.15, pacificatory 74.8, mediatory 75.5, atoning 313.5, negotiated 460.5, sacrificial 504.10, agreeing 735.13
concise 198.4; summary 204.5, sparing with words 208.6, short 591.6
concise dictionary word book 5.27
concisely 198.6; summarily 204.10, intelligibly 363.13, shortly 591.12
concisely styled concise 198.4
conciseness 198.1; summariness 204.4, guarded speech 208.3, shortness 591.1
concise style conciseness 198.1
concise version outline 204.2
concision conciseness 198.1
conclave conference 59.5, representative body 79.2, place for conversation 210.5
conclude propound a philosophy 4.21, theorize 6.84, have an idea 317.12, solve 334.21, judge 341.10, suppose 359.8, resolve 376.12, close down 584.15, stop 668.10, react 676.8, complete 761.9, end 773.10
concluded solved 334.15, predetermined 384.4, stopped 668.7, completed 761.7, ended 773.14
concluding ending 773.13
conclusion 761.3, 773.3; philosophy 4.1, reasoning 6.61, solution 334.6, verdict 341.2, closure 584.1, stop 668.2, effect 676.1, appendage 748.4, completion 761.2, end 773.1
conclusive legitimate 52.10, demonstrable 331.12, ending 773.13
conclusive argument refutation 332.1

conclusively 334.26, 773.26; legitimately 52.19, in reply 332.10
conclusiveness legal power 52.2
concoct fabricate 192.24, 720.17, imagine 360.14, plan 387.12, plot 387.15, produce 522.13, construct 551.22, distort the truth 627.12
concocted fabricated 192.17
concoction drink 93.2, falsehood 192.6, production 522.1, product 522.3, mixed thing 751.2
concomitance same time 649.1, harmonization 735.2, accompaniment 794.1
concomitant 794.4; attending 575.9, simultaneous 649.4, harmonizing 735.12, accompanying 794.12
concomitantly simultaneously 649.8, in harmony 735.32
concomitant with simultaneously 649.8
Concord American States 564
concord friendship 62.1, peace 73.1, melodiousness 140.12, agreement 462.1, 735.3, 752.4, collaboration 757.2, completeness 761.1, harmony 765.8, fellowship 827.2
concordance word book 5.27, type of book 174.3, assent 346.1, agreement 462.1, 730.2, 735.3, fellowship 827.2
concordant assenting 346.4, agreeing 462.6, 730.8, 735.13, agreeable 765.16, harmonious 765.16, conforming 781.8, associating 827.11
concordantly agreeably 462.14, 752.22, agreeingly 730.19, in accord 735.33, cooperatively 827.18
concordat alliance 459.5, contract 462.2
concours d'élégance miscellaneous automotive terms 687.14
concourse conference 59.5, worshiper 83.6, flow 570.4, convergence 702.1, association 752.2
concrescence union 752.1
concrete construction material 14.21, building materials 104.2, industrial ceramics 129.6, make ceramics 129.10, touchable 216.5, visible 244.5, material 524.7, solid body 540.4, dense 540.6, hard substance 542.3, paving 613.14, pave 613.32, formed 624.6, intrinsic 717.12, adhesive 755.5
concrete art Western Art Styles 133
concrete bridge bridge 551.10
concrete dam dam 551.12
concretely materially 524.9, densely 540.10, formatively 624.10, cohesively 755.11
concreteness touch 216.1, material world 524.1, density 540.1
concrete poetry poetry 139.8
concrete shelter shelter 419.11, fortification 812.3
concrete slab superstructure 551.7
concretion concentration 540.2, solid body 540.4, union 752.1
concretive united 752.10
concretization concentration 540.2
concubinage type of marriage 64.3, fornication 432.3
concubinal matrimonial 64.15
concubinary matrimonial 64.15
concubine girlfriend 33.4, married woman 64.11, sexually immoral person 432.8
concupiscence sexual longing 20.6,

sexual desire 288.5, sexual immorality 432.2, overindulgence 456.3
concupiscent desirous 20.18, lustful 288.15, unchaste 432.10, overindulgent 456.8
concupiscible desirable 288.11
concur 827.16; assent 346.6, approve 437.14, agree with 462.10, be simultaneous 649.6, harmonize 735.22, agree 735.23, 752.17, come together 757.10, conform 781.11, accompany 794.16, cooperate 827.12
concurred approved 437.8
concurrence assent 346.1, approval 437.1, agreement 462.1, 735.3, 752.4, same time 649.1, convergence 702.1, harmonization 735.2, union 752.1, combination 757.1, collaboration 757.2, conformity 781.1, synchronism 794.2, cooperation 827.1
concurrent 794.13; agreeing 462.6, simultaneous 649.4, convergent 702.7, harmonizing 735.12, collaborative 757.7, cooperative 827.9
concurrent jurisdiction jurisdiction 54.2
concurrently 794.22; agreeably 462.14, simultaneously 649.8, convergently 702.12, in harmony 735.32, in combination 757.11, cooperatively 827.18
concurrent resolution declaration 376.2
concurrent with simultaneously 649.8
concurring assenting 346.4, agreeing 462.6, 735.13, harmonizing 735.12, concurrent 794.13, associating 827.11
concurringly agreeably 462.14, in harmony 735.32, in accord 735.33
concuss anesthetize 213.8, club 695.15
concussed desensitized 213.5
concussion collision 695.2
condemn 438.18; execute 30.22, convict 54.33, be dissatisfied 274.7, dislike 291.12, hate 300.11, vilify 301.15, judge 341.10, criticize 418.26, be evil 446.10, make evil 446.11, penalize 454.26
condemnable unforgivable 430.16
condemnation 438.2; unfavorable verdict 54.20, dislike 291.1, 300.2, vilification 301.2, verdict 341.2, penalty 454.5
Condemnation of Jesus by Pilate Stations of the Cross 85
condemnatory judging 341.7
condemned 438.11; convicted 54.26, disliked 291.10, hated 300.9, cursed 301.8, guilty 450.6, punishable 454.21, worn 808.13, unsafe 811.8, endangered 811.10
condemned, the dying person 29.6
condemned housing lack of hygiene 112.3
condemned man or **woman** dying person 29.6
condemned prisoner prisoner 55.7
condemned to die dying 29.12
condemning 438.10; vilifying 301.9
condemningly vilifyingly 301.18
condemn oneself be penitent 451.7
condemn to death execute 454.30
condemn to the galleys imprison 454.23

condensation atmospheric process 9.9, dew 9.34, chemical reaction 11.8, phase 11.13, outline 198.2, 617.1, murk 248.2, concentration 540.2, fluid 555.1, wateriness 557.3, contraction 582.1, contracted thing 582.5, shortened version 591.3, denseness 594.2, obtaining of an extract 711.7, intensification 746.2, subtraction 749.1, union 752.1, adhesion 755.1

condensation nuclei atmosphere 9.8

condensation polymer(ization) polymer 11.9

condensation trail sign 183.1

condense solidify 11.37, 542.10, react 11.38, be concise 198.5, summarize 204.7, be dense 540.8, contract 582.12, shorten 591.9, thicken 594.9, outline 617.5, obtain an extract 711.19, intensify 746.8, make smaller 747.8, subtract 749.6, unite closely 752.16, adhere 755.8

condensed 540.7; atmospheric 9.40, status adjectives 11.25, concise 198.4, smaller 582.7, shortened 591.7, dense 594.6, reduced 749.5, adhesive 755.5

condensed milk milk 93.5

condenser 540.5; lens system 10.22, vaporizer 556.10, contractor 582.6

condensibility contractibility 582.4

condensible contractible 582.11

condensing conjunctive 752.12

condescend disdain 297.14, defer to 410.12

condescending arrogant 297.9, deferential 410.8

condescendingly arrogantly 297.18

condescension arrogance 297.2, deference 410.4

condign rightful 429.9

condiment seasoning 221.2, admixture 751.5

condiments side dish 90.15, 794.11

condition reasoning 6.61, provision 89.1, psychologize 108.41, health 113.1, illness 114.2, supposition 359.1, accustom 397.18, circumstances 573.2, limitation 620.2, nature 624.5, season 654.11, state 725.1

conditional 340.10, 725.7; philosophical term 4.7, grammatical term 5.29, mathematical logic 6.60, logical 6.83, provisional 89.8, negotiated 460.5, circumstantial 726.8, restraining 830.8

conditionally 340.16, 725.10; provisionally 89.12, feasibly 460.9, relatively 726.17, restrainedly 830.18

conditional phrase or clause clause 5.31

conditional probability probability 6.59

conditioned modified 340.9, habituated 397.14, beautified 530.12

conditioned reflex conditioning 108.24, instinct 318.3, habit 397.1

conditioning 108.24; habituation 397.7

conditions specification 340.6, basis for negotiations 460.2, circumstances 726.1, specifications 779.6

conditions of employment bargaining terms 57.10

condo [Inf] apartment house 60.8

condole be compassionate 305.11

condolence 308.2; compassion 305.2

condolences condolence 308.2

condolent compassionate 305.8, pitying 308.4

condole with grieve 308.7

condom contraceptive 23.6, counteractant 510.5, sanitary precaution 810.8, barrier 826.7

condominium apartment house 60.8, architectural structure 134.4, joint possession 469.6, property 470.1, building 551.9

condominium owner possessor 469.10

condonable forgivable 312.7, vindicable 441.9

condonation or condonance forgivingness 312.3

condone show mercy 312.11, submit 421.4, approve 437.14

condoned overlooked 312.6

condoning forgiving 312.4

condor bird of prey 36.11

condor, California Endangered US Birds 36

condottiere militarist 77.3

conduce further 679.13

conduce to tend 513.5, further 825.30

conducive instrumental 801.7, helpful 825.19

conducive to tending to 513.4

conduct 14.51, 141.17, 399.1, 399.21; interact 10.73, manage 126.10, direct 126.11, 697.13, tradition 397.5, behave toward 399.20, action 412.1, transfer 685.8, way 691.1, escort 794.18

conductance resistance 10.41

conduct an experiment experiment 335.11

conduct an inquiry question 333.16

conducted directed 141.12, accompanied 794.15

conduct employee relations employ 57.18

conducting medium electrical conduction 10.33, electricity 14.34

conductiometric titration gravimetric analysis 11.18

conduction atmospheric process 9.9, heat flow 10.27, electricity 14.34, electrical power 514.12, transmission 685.3

conductional transferable 685.7

conduction band semiconductor 10.34

conduction current electric current 10.39

conductive nuclear 514.17, transferable 685.7

conductively in transit 685.13

conductivity electrical conduction 10.33, resistance 10.41, electricity 14.34, electrical power 514.12

conduct of affairs management 126.1

conduct one's affairs conduct oneself 399.17

conduct oneself 399.17; occupy oneself 412.15

conduct oneself properly behave well 399.18

conductor 399.13; electrical conduction 10.33, electricity 14.34, leader 126.8, musical director 141.7, operator 509.5, keeper of time 646.10, railroad worker 688.7, usher 794.7

conduct the ceremony join in marriage 64.20

conduct the wedding join in marriage 64.20

conduct unbecoming bad manners 411.2

conduct unbecoming an officer military honor 58.9

conduit irrigator 557.13, river parts 570.3, furrow 638.1, channel 691.10, entrance 706.5, outlet 707.8

cone 633.5; curved surface 6.43, eye 19.9, 242.3, tree part 43.2

cone-bearing taxonomic 41.16

coneflower Flowers 42

cone-shaped spherical 6.80, narrowed 593.9

confab [Inf] chat 210.2

confabulate deceive 193.16, converse 210.11

confabulation self-deception 193.2, chat 210.2

confabulator conversationalist 210.6

confabulatory deceptive 193.12, conversing 210.8

confection product 522.3, mixed thing 751.2

confectioner's food provider 90.6, confectionery 222.3

confectioner's sugar basic cooking ingredient 91.8

confectionery 222.3; sweets 90.39

confederacy collaboration 757.2, joint control 827.5

confederate collaborative 757.7, come together 757.10, join 827.17

Confederate flag flag 184.8

confederation body politic 50.3, union of nations 566.2, collaboration 757.2, joint control 827.5, team 827.7

confer 210.13; consult 176.11, bequeath 372.15, negotiate 460.6, transfer property 470.12, summit 600.11, grant 735.30

conference 59.5, 75.4; representative body 79.2, publicity 173.7, consultation 176.4, place for conversation 210.5, discussion 460.3

conference call telephone call 169.11

conference delegate delegate 79.1

conferential discussing 210.9

confer holy orders on ordain 84.16

conferment ordination 84.3, transfer of property 470.4, giving 472.1, grant 735.10

confer ownership upon transfer property 470.12

conferral transfer of property 470.4, giving 472.1, grant 735.10

conferred bequeathed 372.10, granted 735.20

conferrer giver 472.7

conferring discussing 210.9

confer upon give 472.10

conferval algal 47.20

confervoid algal 47.20

confess 451.8; convict 54.33, follow rites 85.19, pray 85.20, believe 87.9, admit 180.11, avow 189.27, apologize 313.8, assent 346.6, be guilty 450.9

confessed disclosed 180.5, avowed 189.19, penitent 451.5

confessed criminal guilty person 450.5

confessing convicted 54.26, penitent 451.5

confession 451.2; Christian rite 85.5, prayer 85.10, divulgence 180.2, secret 182.2, avowal 189.7, apology 313.2, legal evidence 339.4, assent 346.1

confessional prayerful 85.17, church architecture 134.11, privacy 181.6, place of judgment 341.3

confessional poetry poetry 139.8

confessions nonfiction 139.6

confess one's sins confess 451.8

confessor member of the clergy 84.5, discloser 180.4, affirmer 189.9, penitent person 451.4

confess the truth be sincere 191.8

confetti variegated thing 263.5

confidant or confidante friend 62.2, personal attendant 69.5, stock part 136.24, adviser 176.5, secret person 182.6

confide inform 170.11, divulge 180.9, be naive 821.4

confide in believe 87.9, consult 176.11

confidence maturity 27.3, believing 87.2, secret 182.2, expectation 281.2, 356.1, steadfastness 284.3, security 464.1, repute 487.7, assurance 621.8, safety 810.1, ease of manner 823.4, conviction 840.2

confidence game foul play 193.6, dishonesty 479.7

confidence level parameter 6.57

confidence limits parameter 6.57

confidence man schemer 193.10, dishonest person 479.11, cunning person 822.3

confident adult 27.11, believing 87.6, expectant 281.7, steadfast 284.11, expecting 356.4, assured 621.12, convinced 840.8

confidential intimate 62.7, secret 182.8, 611.13, important 799.7

confidential information secret 182.2

confidentiality verbal concealment 181.3, secrecy 182.1, 611.6

confidentially secretly 182.14, 611.22

confidentialness secrecy 611.6

confidently believingly 87.12, assertively 189.35, expectantly 281.16, 356.10, steadfastly 284.19, with certainty 840.16

confiding naive 821.3

configuration geometric figure 6.39, geometric construction 6.47, constellation 7.13, perceptual concept 108.30, form 551.3, 624.1, characteristic 779.5

configurational formed 624.6

configurationally formatively 624.10

configurationism Psychological Theories, Schools 108

configurative formed 624.6

configure represent 6.91

confine imprison 55.11, conceal 181.12, specify 340.14, exclude 409.12, be moderate 455.12, enclose 584.11, 619.6, narrow 593.14, border 618.9, limit 620.1, 620.7, detain 830.16

confined imprisoned 55.9, sick 114.24, conditional 340.10, temperate 455.8, local 564.14, enclosed 584.11, 619.4, narrow 593.8, limited 620.5, detained 830.11

confinedly narrowly 593.17, restrainedly 830.18

confined space narrow place 593.2

confinement prison cell 55.3, imprisonment 55.4, 454.2, specification 340.6, narrowness

593.1, *enclosure* 619.1, *detention* 830.5

confines *near place* 586.3, *surroundings* 615.1, *edge* 618.1

confining *enclosed* 619.4

confirm 189.25; *legislate* 53.31, *perform rites* 85.18, *prove* 331.17, 339.14, *answer* 334.18, *experiment* 335.11, *verify* 336.8, *assent* 346.6, *promise* 458.11, *contract* 459.8, *agree with* 462.10, *permit* 502.6, *strengthen* 516.15, *give moral support* 605.18, *make stable* 674.7, *establish reality* 719.12, *authenticate* 721.24, *consent* 735.28, *make certain* 840.14

confirmability *demonstrability* 331.5

confirmable *demonstrable* 331.12

confirmation 189.5, 840.3; *lawmaking* 53.11, *Christian rite* 85.5, *proof* 331.4, 339.2, *acknowledgment* 334.2, *verification* 336.1, *evidence* 336.3, *assent* 346.1, *ceremony* 405.3, *ratification* 459.4, *agreement* 462.1, *reception* 473.4, *permission* 502.1, *moral support* 605.7, *authentication* 721.8, *consent* 735.8

confirmational *ritualistic* 85.15

confirmative *assenting* 346.4, *agreeing* 462.6

confirmatory proof *stage of proof* 174.9

confirmation name *name* 202.8

confirmed 189.17; *proven* 331.13, *answering* 334.11, *verified* 336.7, *evidential* 339.8, *habituated* 397.14, *authenticated* 721.17, *consenting* 735.18

confirmed bachelor *single person* 67.5

confirmed habit *habit* 397.1

confirmed liar *liar* 192.10

confirmer *affirmer* 189.9

confirming 189.16; *answering* 334.11, *verificatory* 336.6, *supportive* 605.11, *consenting* 735.18

confirmingly 189.32; *with consent* 735.38

confiscate 454.25; *take away* 275.13, *take over* 477.16, *take back* 477.17

confiscation 454.4; *taking over* 477.3, *taking back* 477.4

confiscator *collector* 473.7, *taker* 477.9

confiscatory *taking* 477.12

conflagration *fire* 217.8, 246.9

conflate *interpret* 365.12

conflated *interpreted* 365.9, *combined* 757.5

conflation *interpretation* 365.1, *combination* 757.1

conflict 422.26, 828.3; *hostility* 63.1, *act of hostility* 63.4, *oppose* 63.11, *war* 76.1, *anxiety disorder* 108.11, *be off-color* 251.18, *quarrel* 272.4, 272.9, *argue* 329.11, *dissent* 347.1, 347.8, *contention* 422.1, *dispute* 463.3, 463.9, *opposing force* 510.2, *be dissimilar* 734.7, *confront* 828.19

conflicting *aggressive* 63.9, *off-color* 251.15, *dissenting* 347.7, *counteracting* 510.6, *discordant* 828.12, *adverse* 848.10

conflictingly *counter* 510.8, *adversely* 848.16

conflict in meaning *mean* 361.13

conflict with *counteract* 510.7, *be contrary* 828.16

confluence *contiguity* 216.4, *river*

570.1, *flow* 570.4, *convergence* 702.1, *union* 752.1

confluent *cumulate* 59.20, *tributary* 570.2, *flowing* 570.7, *convergent* 702.7

confluently *convergently* 702.12

confluent stream *tributary* 570.2

conflux *flow* 570.4, *convergence* 702.1

confocal *curvilinear* 6.78, *convergent* 702.7

conform 735.27, 781.11; *answer to* 334.22, *assent to* 346.7, *be formal* 406.11, *obey* 426.7, *be compatible* 462.12, *be literal* 721.25, *be the same* 730.13, *be similar* 733.12, *agree* 735.23, *be average* 742.8

conformable 781.7; *observant* 465.3, *formed* 624.6

conformably *observantly* 465.6, *formatively* 624.10, *adaptably* 781.15

conformance *observance* 465.1, *agreement* 735.3, *conformity* 735.7, 781.1

conformation *compatibility* 462.3, *form* 551.3, 624.1, *conformity* 735.7, 781.1

conformational *structural* 11.28

conformer *believer* 87.5, *conformist* 781.6

conforming 735.17, 781.8; *correspondent* 334.16, *obedient* 426.4, *compatible* 462.8, *observant* 465.3, *literal* 721.18, *agreeing* 730.8, 735.13, *regular* 730.12, *similar* 733.7

conformingly 735.37, 781.16; *correspondingly* 334.27, *obediently* 426.9, *compatibly* 462.16, *observantly* 465.6

conformism *conventionalism* 781.4

conformist 781.6, 781.10; *Christian* 81.10, *believer* 87.5, *believing* 87.6, *assenter* 346.3, 462.5

conformity 735.7, 781.1; *correspondence* 334.8, *obedience* 426.1, *compatibility* 462.3, *observance* 465.1, *evenness* 626.3, *literalness* 721.9, *regularity* 730.6, *similarity* 733.1, *imitation* 736.1, *average* 742.1

conform to *observe* 465.4, *conform* 781.11

conform to facts *be true* 721.20

confound *make obscure* 197.3, *be wondrous* 294.14, *refute* 332.7, *be indiscriminate* 338.10, *puzzle* 364.12, *be wrong* 430.18, *mix up* 751.13, *cause difficulties* 824.22, *make uncertain* 841.19

confounded *wondering* 294.7, *miscellaneous euphemisms* 301.12, *confused* 364.10, 841.11, *mixed up* 751.11

confoundedly *speculatively* 294.17, *wrongfully* 430.25

confounding *refutation* 332.1, *refuting* 332.6

confoundment *confusion* 841.4

confraternal *friendly* 62.5

confraternally *cliquishly* 59.32

confraternity *association* 59.4, *friendship* 62.1, *team* 827.7

confront 828.19; *battle* 76.33, *be courageous* 284.14, *undertake* 391.7, *be insubordinate* 416.8, *resist* 417.10, *counterattack* 418.24, *disagree* 463.8, *dissent* 506.9, *meet* 586.15, *interface* 616.5, *be in front* 621.13, *show oneself* 843.15

confrontation *disobedience* 416.2,

disagreement 463.1, *dissent* 506.2, *meeting* 586.5, *approach* 702.2, *conflict* 828.3, *manifestation* 843.2

confrontational *disagreeing* 463.6, *dissenting* 506.6, *interfacial* 616.4, *front-running* 621.10

confrontationally *interfacially* 616.7

confronted *displayed* 843.8

confronter *interfacer* 616.3

confronting *discordant* 828.12

Confucian *other religious member* 81.13

Confucianism Philosophical Schools of Thought 4, *other religions* 81.8

Confucian text *other text* 81.19

con fuoco Musical Terms and Expression Marks 140

confuse 333.20, 766.19; *be anarchic* 51.8, *make insane* 110.13, *deceive* 181.14, *mystify* 182.12, *make obscure* 197.3, *not understand* 362.11, *puzzle* 364.12, *make unintelligible* 364.13, *be wrong* 430.18, *mix up* 751.13, *discompose* 766.18, *disarrange* 768.11, *be cunning* 822.5, *cause difficulties* 824.22, *make uncertain* 841.19

confused 364.10, 766.12, 841.11; *anarchic* 51.5, *obscure* 197.2, *problematic* 333.12, 824.11, *indiscriminate* 338.8, *unclear* 364.5, *shy* 403.8, *at a loss* 468.11, *shapeless* 625.2, *agitated* 684.15, *complicated* 751.10, *mixed up* 751.11, *muddled* 766.13, *deranged* 766.16, *disturbed* 768.6, *disarranged* 768.7, *discontinuous* 775.7, *troubled* 824.15

confusedly 51.11; *anarchically* 51.10, *wrongfully* 430.25, *shapelessly* 625.5, *in disorder* 766.24

confused message *lack of clarity* 364.2

confusing *mysterious* 182.10, *problematic* 333.12, 824.11, *difficult* 364.8, *confused* 841.11

confusingly 841.23; *disturbingly* 768.13

confusion 51.2, 766.4, 841.4; *anarchy* 51.1, *obscurity* 197.1, *question* 333.1, *indiscrimination* 338.4, *unintelligibility* 364.1, *shapelessness* 625.1, *tumult* 684.2, *mixture* 751.1, *variety* 751.4, *nonadhesion* 756.1, *disorder* 766.1, *disarrangement* 768.2, *discontinuity* 775.1

confutability *refutability* 332.4

confutable *refutable* 332.5

confutably *refutably* 332.11

confutation *negation* 190.1, *denial* 332.2, *counterevidence* 339.5, *dissent* 506.2, *reply* 671.5

confutative *refuting* 332.6, *dissenting* 506.6

confute *dissuade* 179.7, *negate* 190.16, *refute* 332.7, *doubt* 333.19, *answer back* 334.19, *dissent* 347.8, 506.9, *reply* 671.13

confuted *negated* 190.10

confuting *refuting* 332.6

conga Dances 135

conga drums Musical Instruments 142

con game [Inf] *dishonesty* 479.7

congé *parting* 705.3, *dismissal* 709.2

congé or **congee** Architectural Elements 134

congeal *become cold* 218.14, *be dense* 540.8, *thicken* 561.21, 594.9

congealed *condensed* 540.7, *dense* 594.6, *adhesive* 755.5

congealing *condensed* 540.7

congealment *concentration* 540.2, *denseness* 594.2, *adhesion* 755.1

congeneric *included* 763.4

congenerous *included* 763.4

congenial *friendly* 62.5, *pleasant* 214.7, *likable* 271.6, 290.7, *lovable* 299.20, *benevolent* 305.7, *agreeing* 462.6, *compatible* 735.14

congeniality *friendship* 62.1, *amiability* 271.3, *sociability* 408.1, *agreement* 462.1, *compatibility* 735.4

congenially *likably* 290.12, *lovably* 299.31, *benevolently* 305.13, *agreeably* 462.14, *compatibly* 735.34

congenital disease *disease* 114.4

congeries *assemblage* 59.13

congest *be excessive* 99.9, *obstruct* 584.13

congested *excessive* 99.5, *obstructed* 584.8, *full* 761.8, *crowded* 795.10

congestion *excess* 99.1, *symptom* 114.3, *obstruction* 584.2

conglomerate *cumulate* 59.20, *company* 480.7, *association* 480.8, *solid body* 540.4, *be dense* 540.8, *adhere* 755.8, *collection* 757.3, *collected* 757.8

conglomerated *mixed* 751.8

conglomeration *assemblage* 59.13, *mixture* 751.1, *adhesion* 755.1, *collection* 757.3

conglutinate *cause to adhere* 755.10

conglutination *adhesion* 755.1

Congo Countries 566, Rivers 570

congratulate 405.12; *fete* 279.6, *compliment* 437.17

congratulate oneself *pride oneself* 297.13

congratulation *compliment* 437.4

congratulations *applause* 279.2, *tribute* 405.6

congratulatory *celebrative* 405.9, *approving* 437.9

congregate *assembled* 59.18, *come together* 59.25, 702.10, *meet* 704.20, *flood in* 706.14, *combine* 757.9, *crowd* 795.11

congregated *assembled* 59.18, *collected* 757.8

congregation Collective Names 59, *assembly* 59.1, *religious group* 81.4, *worshiper* 83.6, *hearer* 228.7, *meeting place* 702.4, *collection* 757.3, *throng* 795.4, *team* 827.7

congregational *grouped* 59.21, *collected* 757.8

Congregationalism Christian Groups 81

congregationally *in combination* 757.11

Congress United States government 49.21, *representative body* 79.2

congress *conference* 59.5, *place for conversation* 210.5, *meeting place* 702.4, *association* 752.2

congressional *governmental* 49.24, *grouped* 59.21, *delegated* 79.4

congressional committee *advisory body* 176.6

congressionally *representatively* 79.8

Congressional Medal of Honor US Military Medals 58

congressional offices *government office* 124.13

Congressional Record *record* 185.1

congressional seat *position of authority* 52.4

congressman *elected official* 50.8, *person in authority* 52.7, *delegate* 79.1, *representative* 187.7

congresswoman *elected official* 50.8, *person in authority* 52.7, *delegate* 79.1, *representative* 187.7

congruence *equality* 6.24, *transformation* 6.46, *correspondence* 334.8, *symmetry* 626.1, *agreement* 730.2, *conformity* 735.7

congruency *agreement* 730.2

congruent *correspondent* 334.16, *compatible* 462.8, *symmetrical* 626.4, *agreeing* 730.8, *conforming* 735.17, 781.8, *equal* 740.8

congruently *correspondingly* 334.27, *compatibly* 462.16, *convergently* 702.12, *agreeingly* 730.19, *conformingly* 735.37, *equitably* 740.15

congruent triangles *triangle* 6.41

congruity *compatibility* 462.3, *symmetry* 626.1, *agreement* 730.2, *conformity* 735.7, 781.1

congruous *compatible* 462.8, *agreeing* 730.8, *conforming* 781.8

congruously *agreeingly* 730.19, *conformingly* 781.16

conic *round* 633.7

conic(al) *sharp* 549.10

conical *spherical* 6.80, *vault* 134.8, *round* 633.7, *convergent* 702.7

conically *roundly* 633.11

conic projection *map* 187.5

conic section or conic *curve* 6.38

conidium *fungal body* 47.4

conifer *tree* 43.1

coniferous *taxonomic* 41.16, *treelike* 43.10

coniferous forest *trees* 43.4

coniferous tree *tree* 43.1

coniine *alkaloid* 12.19

conjectural *philosophical* 4.12, *speculative* 317.8, *theoretical* 327.10, *skeptical* 333.14, *experimental* 335.8, *suppositional* 359.5, *circumstantial* 726.8, *uncertain* 841.9

conjecturally *speculatively* 294.17, *theoretically* 327.19, *questionably* 333.22, *experimentally* 335.14, *supposedly* 359.10, *relatively* 726.17, *uncertainly* 841.22

conjecture 359.3; *philosophy* 4.1, *philosophize* 4.19, *theory* 6.62, 327.2, 720.4, *belief* 87.1, *speculation* 294.2, *speculate* 294.13, *have an idea* 317.12, *theorize* 327.16, 720.14, *uncertainty* 333.6, *doubt* 333.19, *experimentation* 335.3, *experiment* 335.11, *judgment* 341.1, *estimate* 341.11, *suppose* 359.8, *suspicion* 841.2, *be uncertain* 841.17

conjectured *supposed* 359.6

conjecturing *speculative* 294.8

conjoin *form an alliance* 735.25, *add* 748.11, *unite* 752.14, *connect* 754.13, *combine* 757.9

conjoined *united* 752.10, *combinatory* 757.6

conjoining *contiguous* 216.8, *junction* 609.5

conjoint *harmonizing* 735.12, *allied* 735.15, *united* 752.10, *combinatory* 757.6

conjointly *cliquishly* 59.32, *in harmony* 735.32, *in alliance* 735.35, *additionally* 748.15, *as one* 752.21, *cooperatively* 827.18

conjoint therapy *psychotherapy* 108.4

conjugal *matrimonial* 64.15, *contractual* 459.7

conjugal bliss *marriage* 64.1

conjugal bond *marriage* 64.1

conjugality *marriage* 64.1

conjugally *matrimonially* 64.23, *contractually* 459.9

conjugate *combinatory* 757.6, *combine* 757.9

conjugate angles *angle* 6.37

conjugated protein *protein* 12.9

conjugation *grammatical term* 5.29

conjunction *philosophical term* 4.7, *part of speech* 5.30, 760.7, *mathematical logic* 6.60, *contiguity* 216.4, *nearness* 586.1, *union* 752.1, *joint* 752.7, *connection* 754.1, *combination* 757.1, *collaboration* 757.2, *accompaniment* 794.1, *synchronism* 794.2

conjunctiva *eye* 19.9, 242.3

conjunctive 752.12; *of grammar* 5.41, *additional* 748.8, *connective* 754.10, *collaborative* 757.7

conjunctively *grammatically* 5.48, *as one* 752.21, *in connection with* 754.16

conjunctivitis *eye disease* 243.4

conjuncture *occurrence* 726.2

conjural *witchlike* 86.19

conjuration *spell* 86.8

conjurator *witch* 86.15

conjure 86.26; *entertain* 138.16, *transform* 665.20

conjure into *transform* 670.13

conjure man *witch* 86.15

conjurer *changer* 665.9, *cunning person* 822.3

conjure up *conjure* 86.26, *imagine* 327.14, 360.14, 720.13, *remember* 354.12

conjure up a vision *imagine* 360.14

conjuring *magic* 138.3, *magical* 138.15, *delusion* 720.3

conjuror *magician* 138.11

conk *fungal body* 47.4

conk [Brit inf] *nose* 19.11, *protuberance* 634.3

conked out [Inf] *gone wrong* 430.17

conk out [Inf] *go wrong* 430.23, *malfunction* 846.20

con man [Inf] *schemer* 193.10, *villain* 448.5, *dishonest person* 479.11, *overcharger* 496.5, *cunning person* 822.3

connatural *connected* 733.9

connect 754.13; *conduct* 14.51, *put together* 59.30, *merge* 64.21, *adjoin* 216.11, *juxtapose* 586.14, *continue* 669.8, *relate to* 727.9, *be similar* 733.12, *link* 752.18, *combine* 757.9, *concatenate* 774.13

connected 733.9, 754.11; *cumulate* 59.20, *continuous* 669.5, *accessible* 691.13, *related* 727.6, *united* 752.10, *adhesive* 755.5, *combinatory* 757.6

connectedness *continuity* 669.1, *relatedness* 727.1, *adhesion* 755.1

Connecticut *American States* 564, *Rivers* 570

connecting *contiguous* 216.8, *juxtaposed* 586.9, *junction* 609.5, *accessible* 691.13

connection 754.1; *construction* 59.16, *alliance* 64.2, *juxtaposition* 586.4, *continuity* 669.1, *relatedness* 727.1, *affinity* 733.3, *linkage* 752.3, *adhesion* 755.1

connection [Inf] *drug pusher* 121.13

connective 754.10; *conjunctive*

752.12, *means of connection* 754.4, *adhesive* 755.5

connectively *as one* 752.21, *in connection with* 754.16

connective tissue *line* 754.5

connect up *concatenate* 774.13

connect with *link* 752.18

Connemara pony *Horse and Pony Breeds* 159

Conner Prairie *Breeds of Pigs* 16

conning tower *place for viewing* 242.13

conniption or conniption fit [Inf] *burst of anger* 302.6

connivance *tolerance* 502.2

connive *scheme* 193.18, *show mercy* 312.11, *plot* 387.15, *permit* 502.6, *concur* 827.16

connivent *advancing* 702.8

connivery *forgivingness* 312.3

conniving *deceptive* 193.12, *forgiving* 312.4, *permitting* 502.5

connivingly *with permission* 502.10

connoisseur *expert* 52.8, 127.9, *collector* 59.17, *eater* 92.15, *pleasure-seeker* 214.4, *discriminator* 337.6, *judge* 341.5, *refined person* 534.4, *specialist* 779.9

connoisseurship *refinement* 48.10, 534.1, *artistry* 133.3, *judiciousness* 337.2

connotation *word* 5.17, *sign* 183.1, *meaning* 361.1, *type of meaning* 361.4, *interpretation* 365.1, *quietness* 844.4

connotative *signifying* 183.11, *similar* 361.7

connote *signify* 183.16, *mean* 361.13, *imply* 844.14

connubial *matrimonial* 64.15

connubially *matrimonially* 64.23

conquer 77.36; *master* 68.17, *make peace* 73.11, *take over* 477.16, *take away forcefully* 477.19, *defeat* 832.11, *be victorious* 845.16

conquering *taking over* 477.3, *domination* 832.2, *dominating* 832.7

conqueror *victor* 845.7

conquest 477.6; *truce* 73.2, *lover* 299.11, *domination* 832.2, *victory* 845.4

conquistador *militarist* 77.3

consanguine *related* 727.6

consanguineous *family* 65.6

consanguineously *relevantly* 727.12

consanguinity *kinship* 727.2

conscience *calling* 178.6, *morals* 431.2, *sense of duty* 433.2, *forewarning* 814.2

conscienceless *impenitent* 452.2

conscience money *bribe* 472.3, *compensation* 478.2

conscience-stricken *appearing guilty* 450.7, *penitent* 451.5

conscientious *duteous* 433.7, *observant* 465.3

conscientiously *dutifully* 433.19, *virtuously* 447.9, *observantly* 465.6

conscientiousness *carefulness* 325.1, *observance* 465.1

conscientious objection *disobedience* 427.1

conscientious objector (CO) *pacifist* 74.6, *dissenter* 347.5, *defiant person* 416.4, *resister* 417.5, *refuser* 506.4, *protester* 507.4

conscionable *moral* 431.9, *virtuous* 447.5

conscious *alive* 28.13, *sensible* 212.6, *feeling* 266.9,

knowledgeable 348.7, *internal* 525.11

consciously *occultly* 86.27, *knowledgeably* 348.14, *subjectively* 525.14

conscious mind *psyche* 108.25

consciousness *life force* 28.2, *sensation* 212.1, *feelings* 266.1, *knowledge* 348.1, *internal world* 525.6

conscious of one's place *showing respect* 435.7

conscious self *psyche* 108.25

conscript *enlist* 58.13, *join the army* 76.31, *soldier* 77.4, *force* 428.10, *subordinate* 832.3, *engage* 833.9

conscript army *army* 77.12

conscripted *enlisted* 58.11, *warring* 76.26, *martial* 77.33

conscript forces *armed forces* 77.9

conscripting *military affairs* 58.1

conscription *military affairs* 58.1, *war measures* 76.18, *coercive method* 428.3, *engagement* 833.2

conscripts *reinforcements* 77.11

consecrate *gain authority* 52.15, *deify* 82.23, *ordain* 84.16, *give praise to* 472.13, *make an offering* 504.17

consecrated *authorized* 52.11, *deified* 82.20, *ritualistic* 85.15, *sacrificial* 504.10

consecrated elements *Eucharist* 85.7

consecration *acquisition of authority* 52.5, *deification* 82.13, *Eucharist* 85.7, *offering* 472.6, 504.5

consecution *sequence* 770.1, *consecutiveness* 774.1

consecutive 774.7; *frequent* 661.4, *sequential* 770.7

consecutively 774.15; *sequentially* 770.13

consecutiveness 774.1; *sequence* 770.1

consensual *contractual* 459.7

consensually *contractually* 459.9

consensus *assent* 346.1, *agreement* 462.1, 730.2, 735.3, 752.4, *fellowship* 827.2

consent 735.8, 735.28; *be persuaded* 178.20, *assent* 346.1, *willingness* 373.1, *be willing* 373.12, *submission* 421.1, *submit* 421.4, *obey* 426.7, *approval* 373.1, *approve* 437.14, *ratification* 459.4, *agreement* 462.1, *agree with* 462.10, *permission* 502.1, *permit* 502.6, *conform* 781.11

consent [Arch] *melodiousness* 140.12

consentaneity *agreement* 735.3

consentaneous *agreeing* 735.13

consentaneously *in accord* 735.33

consented to *approved* 437.8

consenter *assenter* 346.3

consentience *agreement* 735.3

consentient *agreeing* 735.13

consentiently *in accord* 735.33

consenting 735.18; *confirming* 189.16, *assenting* 346.4, *willing* 373.7, *agreeing* 462.6

consentingly *confirmingly* 189.32, *with consent* 735.38

consenting party *contractor* 459.6

consent to *assent* 346.6

consequence 774.3; *importance* 278.3, 799.1, *product* 522.3, *effect* 676.1, *sequel* 770.5

consequences *Children's and Party Games* 167

consequent 770.9; *caused* 676.5

consequentalist Philosophical Schools of Thought 4

consequential *significant* 361.11, *influential* 512.8, *caused* 676.5, *consequent* 770.9, *repercussive* 774.8, *serious* 799.8

consequentialism Philosophical Schools of Thought 4

consequently *with the effect of* 676.12, *importantly* 799.15

consequently 770.15; *with the effect of* 676.12, *under the circumstances* 726.16, *accordingly* 735.39

consequent upon *caused* 676.5

conservancy *permanence* 667.1, *preservation* 815.1, *conservation* 815.2

conservation 815.2; *forestry* 43.5, *home economics* 56.2, *storage* 105.6, *permanence* 667.1, *setting apart* 753.2, *preservation* 815.1

conservational *preserving* 815.11

conservation area *ecology* 815.3

conservationism *green politics* 260.6

conservationist *animal welfarist* 34.9, *environmental* 260.13

conservation land *trees* 43.4

conservation of charge *electric charge* 10.38

conservation of energy *energy* 10.10

conservation of mass *mass* 10.8

conservation of mass and energy *energy* 10.10

conservatism *traditionality* 630.6, *permanence* 667.1, *conventionalism* 781.4, *preservation* 815.1, *preservation of status quo* 815.8

Conservative *denominational* 81.23

conservative 815.13; *understated* 195.8, *underestimating* 344.3, *obstinate person* 379.4, *creature of habit* 397.8, *resister* 417.5, *obstinate* 417.7, *reactionary* 427.9, *straight person* 630.7, *traditional* 630.13, *permanent* 667.2, *conformist* 781.10, *preserving* 815.11, *inhibitive* 826.14, *opposer* 828.9, *uncooperative* 828.14

conservative estimate *understatement* 195.1, *underestimation* 344.1

Conservative Jew *Jew* 81.11

Conservative Judaism *Judaism* 81.6

conservatively 815.17; *pessimistically* 344.6, *resistingly* 417.14, *traditionally* 630.19, *preservatively* 815.16, *inhibitively* 826.24

conservativeness *traditionality* 630.6, *inhibition* 826.9

Conservative party Political Parties 50

conservative politics *preservation of status quo* 815.8

conservative treatment *treatment* 107.14

Conservative Union party Political Parties 50

conservator *surveillant* 810.12

conservatory *nursery* 17.4, *type of school* 48.12, *room* 60.9, *transparent thing* 249.4

conserve *economize* 56.11, *sweets* 90.39, *save* 105.20, *practice hygiene* 116.4, *sweetener* 222.2, *be thrifty* 499.5, *make permanent* 667.5, *set apart* 753.17, *protect* 810.21, *preserved thing* 815.10, *preserve* 815.14

conserved *saved* 105.15, *unfailing* 667.3, *preserved* 815.12

conserving *home economics* 56.2, *thrifty* 499.4, *preserving* 815.11

consider *philosophize* 4.19, *propound a philosophy* 4.21, *be of the opinion* 87.10, *visualize* 242.24, *think* 317.9, *be attentive* 323.9, *discuss* 329.12, *estimate* 341.11, *have foresight* 357.8, *imagine* 360.14, *show respect* 435.16, *make important* 799.14

considerable *heavy* 538.9, *big* 579.13, *many* 795.6, *significant* 799.9

considerably *largely* 579.19, *importantly* 799.15

consider as important *take seriously* 278.8

considerate 325.7; *compassionate* 305.8, *thoughtful* 317.5, *solicitous* 323.8, *courteous* 410.6, *lenient* 423.3, *respectful* 435.6, *unselfish* 443.5, *benevolent* 825.21

considerately *compassionately* 305.14, *thoughtfully* 317.13, *courteously* 410.13, *genteelly* 410.14, *leniently* 423.6, *unselfishly* 443.9, *benevolently* 825.34

considerateness *unselfishness* 443.2

consideration 325.2; *philosophical investigation* 4.4, *visualization* 242.6, *compassion* 305.2, *thought* 315.5, *thoughtfulness* 317.2, *attention* 323.1, *solicitude* 323.5, *logical argument* 329.2, *plea* 329.5, *judgment* 341.1, *foresight* 357.1, *courtesy* 410.1, *leniency* 423.1, *respect* 435.1, *unselfishness* 443.2, *compensation* 453.7, *exchange* 673.1, *importance* 799.1

considered *deliberate* 384.5

considering 341.13; *including* 763.3

consider the pros and cons *confer* 210.13

consign *delegate* 79.6, *send* 209.11, *transfer property* 470.12, *give* 472.10, *transfer* 685.8, *convey* 685.9, *transport* 686.10, *commission* 833.8

consignable *transferring property* 470.10, *transferable* 685.7

consignation *delegation* 79.3

consigned *decentralized* 79.5, *transportable* 686.7

consignee *manager* 126.7, *recipient* 473.5, *purchaser* 481.7, *treasurer* 484.18, *transporter* 686.4

consignment *transfer of property* 470.4, *giving* 472.1, *transferred thing* 685.6, *freightage* 686.3

consignment goods *merchandise* 482.6

consignor *seller* 482.7, *transporter* 686.4

consign to earth *bury* 31.10

consign to oblivion *forget* 355.10

consistency *reasoning* 6.61, *touch* 216.1, *compatibility* 462.3, *density* 540.1, *texture* 552.1, *evenness* 626.3, *regularity* 663.1, *stability* 674.1, *literalness* 721.9, *sameness* 730.1, *conformity* 735.7, 781.1, *custom* 780.5

consistent *logical* 6.83, *compatible* 462.8, *dense* 540.6, *even* 626.5, *regular* 663.5, *frequent* 663.6, *stable* 674.3, *literal* 721.18, *same* 730.7, *conforming* 735.17, 781.8, *uniform* 780.10

consistently *compatibly* 462.16, *orderly* 663.13, *regularly* 663.14,

stably 674.9, *literally* 721.32, *identically* 730.18, *conformingly* 735.37, 781.16

consisting of *including* 763.3

consist of *include* 763.5

consociation *sociability* 408.1

consolation *ease* 275.1, *condolence* 308.2, *imperfect item* 806.3

consolation prize *prize* 453.2

console *type of table* 101.5, *cabinet* 101.8, *part of keyboard instrument* 142.6, *radio* 172.1, *relieve* 275.8, *inspire hope* 281.14, *grieve* 308.7

consoled *relieved* 275.6

consoler *reliever* 275.4

consolidate *lithify* 8.66, *merge* 64.21, *compile* 204.8, *be dense* 540.8, *unify* 752.15, *adhere* 755.8, *combine* 757.9, *join* 827.17

consolidated *petrographic* 8.58, *condensed* 540.7

consolidated snow *snow* 9.30

consolidation *petrogenesis* 8.31, *alliance* 64.2, *concentration* 540.2, *union* 752.1, *adhesion* 755.1, *association* 827.6

consoling *relieving* 275.7, *pitying* 308.4

consolingly *pityingly* 308.11

consommé *soup* 90.14

consonance *literary device* 139.12, *melodiousness* 140.12, *harmonization* 735.2

consonancy *harmonization* 735.2

consonant *spoken letter* 5.15, *harmonizing* 735.12, *conforming* 781.8

consonantal *voiced* 5.37

consonantly *in harmony* 735.32

consort *spouse* 64.8, *partner* 794.9

consorting *sociability* 408.1

consortium *alliance* 459.5, 735.5, *association* 480.8, 827.6, *collection* 757.3

consort with *participate* 408.15, *keep company with* 794.17

conspectus *summary* 204.1, *shortened version* 591.3, *whole situation* 759.3

conspicuous *visible* 242.19, 244.5, *appearing* 264.9, *notable* 799.11, *manifest* 843.9

conspicuous by its absence *absent* 576.7

conspicuous consumption *use* 393.1, *extravagance* 500.1

conspicuously *visibly* 242.28, 244.10, *eminently* 370.7, *manifestly* 843.17

conspicuousness *visibility* 244.1, *manifestation* 843.2

conspiracy *secretiveness* 182.3, *artifice* 193.5, *plot* 387.6, *overactivity* 414.9, *subversion* 427.3, *collaboration* 757.2, *cunning* 822.1

conspirator *one who conceals* 181.7, *schemer* 193.10, *planner* 387.9, *seditionist* 427.7, *cunning person* 822.3

conspiratorial *artful* 193.13, *planning* 387.11, *subversive* 427.11, *collaborative* 757.7

conspiratorially 387.18; *stealthily* 182.15, *subversively* 427.15, *contractually* 459.9, *in combination* 757.11

conspiratory *secretive* 182.9

conspire *scheme* 193.18, *plot* 387.15, *subvert* 427.13, *come together* 757.10, *be cunning* 822.5, *concur* 827.16

conspirer *schemer* 193.10

conspiring *cunning* 822.4

constable *person in authority* 52.7, *judge* 68.4, *security force* 810.13

constable [Brit] *law enforcement officer* 53.8

constabulary *law enforcement agency* 53.7

Constance Lakes 568

constance *regularity* 663.1

constancy 377.3; *intimacy* 62.4, *truthfulness* 191.1, *seriousness* 376.3, *loyalty* 426.2, *morals* 431.2, *continuation* 642.2, *frequency* 661.1, *regularity* 663.1, 730.6, *permanence* 667.1, *continuance* 669.3, *stability* 674.1, *conformity* 735.7, *continuity* 774.4, *custom* 780.5

constant 377.8; *algebraic expression* 6.23, *given* 6.74, *intimate* 62.7, *truthful* 191.4, *colored* 251.10, *steady* 376.8, *habitual* 397.9, *loyal* 426.5, *moral* 431.9, *observant* 465.3, *lasting* 639.9, *continuing forever* 644.6, *frequent* 661.4, 663.6, *regular* 663.5, 730.12, *permanent* 667.2, *continuous* 669.5, 774.9, *stable* 674.3, *conforming* 735.17, *uniform* 780.10, *number* 783.1, *recurrent* 797.13

constant companion *partner* 794.9

constant flow *continuity* 774.4

constantly *intimately* 62.14, *obediently* 426.9, *observantly* 465.6, *frequently* 661.7, *orderly* 663.13, *regularly* 663.14, 730.21, *permanently* 667.6, *continually* 669.10, *stably* 674.9, *conformingly* 735.37, *continuously* 774.16

constellation 7.13

consternate *be wondrous* 294.14

consternation *dissatisfaction* 274.1, *fear* 283.1, *speculation* 294.2

constipate *detain* 471.9, *be dense* 540.8, *obstruct* 584.13

constipated *retentive* 471.5, *condensed* 540.7, *obstructed* 584.8

constipating *condensed* 540.7

constipation *defecation* 25.3, *gastroenterological disease* 114.11, Phobias 283, *retentiveness* 471.4, *concentration* 540.2, *obstruction* 584.2

constituency *administrative region* 564.4

constituent *material* 104.8, *electorate* 382.7, *physical element* 524.5, *administrative* 564.13, *containing* 577.7, *basis* 601.3, *integral* 723.7, *component* 760.3, *thing included* 763.2, *included* 763.4

constituents *materials* 104.1, *contents* 577.1

constitute *produce* 522.13, *embody* 577.11, 723.12, *include* 763.5

constituted *legitimate* 52.10, *containing* 577.7

constituted authority *legal power* 52.2

constitutent *component* 760.12

Constitution *rights* 429.4

constitution *law* 53.1, *health* 113.1, *form* 551.3, *texture* 552.1, *contents* 577.1, *nature* 723.4, *inclusion* 763.1, *code* 780.3

constitutional *types of history* 3.2, *governmental* 49.24, *health improvement* 113.3, *way* 397.3, *intrinsic* 611.11, *quintessential* 723.8, *free* 829.11

constitutional anthropology *measurement* 1.9

constitutional government 49.8
constitutionalism *jurisprudence* 53.13
constitutionality *lawmaking* 53.11
constitutional law *law* 53.1
constitutionally *governmentally* 49.27, *intrinsically* 611.20
constitutional monarchy *monarchy* 49.6
constitutional psychology Psychological Theories, Schools 108
constitutional rights *rights* 429.4, *free rights* 829.4
Constitution of the United States of America *the Law* 53.2
constrain *arrest* 55.12, *play down* 195.17, *compel* 428.8, *force* 428.10, *moderate* 521.7, *narrow* 593.14, *limit* 620.7, *restrain* 830.12, *defeat* 832.11
constrained *imprisoned* 55.9, *reserved* 195.11, 403.10, *downplayed* 195.13, *narrow* 593.8, *restrained* 830.9
constrainedly *narrowly* 593.17
constraining *compelling* 428.6
constrain oneself *be self-restrained* 455.10
constraint *arrest* 55.5, *necessitation* 95.5, *reserve* 195.5, 403.5, *downplaying* 195.6, *coercion* 428.2, *self-restraint* 455.1, *narrowness* 593.1, *limitation* 620.2, *restraint* 830.1
constrict *moderate* 521.7, *squeeze* 582.13, *obstruct* 584.13, *narrow* 593.14, *unite closely* 752.16, *limit* 830.13
constricted *squeezed* 582.9, *obstructed* 584.8, *narrow* 593.8
constricting *contracting* 582.10
constriction *concentration* 540.2, *squeeze* 582.3, *obstruction* 584.2, *narrowness* 593.1, *limitation* 830.2
constrictive *dense* 540.6, *contracting* 582.10, *restraining* 830.8
constrictively *densely* 540.10
constrictor *snake* 37.6, *contractor* 582.6
constrictor knot Knots, Bends, Hitches, Splices 754
constringe *contract* 582.12
constringency *contraction* 582.1
constringent *contracting* 582.10
construct 551.22; *represent* 6.91, *engineer* 14.48, *put together* 59.30, *be an architect* 134.13, *idea* 327.1, *produce* 522.13, *fashion* 536.7, *construction* 551.6, *form* 624.9, *complete* 761.9
construct a model *plan out* 387.14
constructed *formed* 624.4
construction 59.16, 522.9, 551.6; *geometric construction* 6.47, *civil engineering* 14.17, *structure* 14.20, *construction* 59.16, *navy specialties* 77.24, *conjecture* 359.3, *type of meaning* 361.4, *interpretation* 365.1, *manufacture* 522.2, *form* 624.1, *forming* 624.4, *inclusion* 763.1
constructional *structural* 14.45, 551.17
constructionally *structurally* 14.52, 551.24, *architecturally* 134.14
construction coordinator *filmmaker* 137.14
construction engineer *civil engineer* 14.19

construction engineering *civil engineering* 14.17
construction equipment 14.23
construction material 14.21
construction site *construction workplace* 124.10
construction worker *laborer* 123.9
construction workplace 124.10
constructive *evidential* 339.8, *interpretive* 365.8, *productive* 522.11, *helpful* 825.19
constructive criticism *recommendation* 176.2, *judgment* 341.1, *support* 825.2
constructively *formatively* 624.10, *helpfully* 825.32
constructivism Western Art Styles 133, *theater movements* 136.9
constructor *producer* 522.10
construe *rationalize* 4.20, *interpret* 365.12
construing *syntax* 5.32
consubstantial *ritualistic* 85.15, *same* 730.7
consubstantiality *sameness* 730.1
consubstantially *identically* 730.18
consubstantiate *make the same* 730.18
consubstantiation *Eucharist* 85.7
consuetude *tradition* 397.5
consul *person in authority* 52.7, *leader* 68.3, *delegate* 79.1, *commissioner* 833.5
consular *delegated* 79.4
consular agent *agent* 80.3
consulate *position of authority* 52.4, *official residence* 60.6, *representative body* 79.2
consul general *person in authority* 52.7, *leader* 68.3
consult 176.11; *health care* 107.7, *practice medicine* 107.32, *confer* 210.13
consultant *sage* 4.11, *expert* 52.8, 68.13, 127.9, *representative* 75.3, *doctor* 107.19, *medical specialist* 107.20, *independent worker* 123.3, *adviser* 176.5, 825.14, *forecaster* 358.9, *specialist* 779.9
consultation 176.4; *health care* 107.7, *advice* 176.1, *debate* 210.3, *preparation* 388.1
consultative *advisory* 176.7
consultative or consultatory *discussing* 210.9
consultative body *advisory body* 176.6
consultatively *advisorily* 176.12
consultatory *advisory* 176.7
consulting room *hospital* 107.16
consult the Tarot *divine* 86.24
consumable *edible* 92.20, *useful* 393.7
consumably *edibly* 92.26
consume 491.12, 523.16; *eat* 92.21, *use up* 393.12, *lose* 468.12, *take* 477.14, *remove power from* 515.13, *wear out* 808.21
consumed 96.11; *used* 393.5
consumer *ecology* 13.25, *eater* 92.15, *user* 393.4, *purchaser* 481.7
consumer demand *need* 95.4, *custom* 481.6
consumer durables *merchandise* 482.6
consumer goods *merchandise* 482.6
consumer price index (CPI) *economic indicator* 56.4
consumer questionnaire *market* 482.5

consumer research *questioning* 333.2
consumer researcher *questioner* 333.9
consumer savings *economic factor* 56.8
consumer spending *economic factor* 56.8
consuming *eating* 92.1, *destructive* 523.8
consummate *have sex* 20.21, *excellent* 68.16, *top* 600.6, *quintessential* 723.8, *complete* 761.6, *end* 773.19, *expert* 805.16, *perfect* 805.19
consummate liar *liar* 192.10
consummately *masterfully* 68.19, *at the summit* 600.12, *perfectly* 805.21
consummate one's marriage *marry* 64.19
consummation *sexual intercourse* 20.9, *completion* 761.2, *perfection* 805.1
consummative *ending* 773.13
consummatory *ending* 773.13
consumption *eating* 92.1, *respiratory disease* 114.12, *use* 393.1, *taking* 477.1, *shortening* 582.2, *intake* 708.5, *reduction* 747.2
consumptive *sick person* 114.22, *of disease* 114.25, *shortened* 582.8
contact *socialize* 2.14, *agent* 80.3, *informer* 170.8, *news source* 171.4, *touch* 216.9, *adjoin* 216.11, *juxtaposition* 586.4, *interface* 616.5, *transmission* 685.3, *union* 752.1, *link* 752.18, *associate* 754.3, *intercommunicate* 754.15
contact again *follow up* 385.16
contact herbicide *pest control* 16.13
contact insecticide *pest control* 16.13
contact lenses *visual aid* 242.14, *aid for poor sight* 243.5
contact metamorphism *metamorphism* 8.35
contact print *printing* 132.20
contacts *visual aid* 242.14, *aid for poor sight* 243.5
contact sheet *printing* 132.20
contact sport *sporting activity* 145.3
contagion *disease* 114.4, *plague* 114.6, *infection* 114.7, *influence* 512.1, *transmission* 685.3, *mixture* 751.1, *physical deterioration* 808.4
contagious 114.26; *appealing* 512.9, *transferable* 685.7
contagious disease *disease* 114.4, *transferred thing* 685.6, *physical deterioration* 808.4
contagiously *unhygienically* 114.32, *influentially* 512.14, *in transit* 685.13
contagiousness *lack of hygiene* 112.3, *infection* 114.7
contagium *disease-causing agent* 114.5
contain 577.10, 578.20; *focus on* 328.9, *detain* 471.9, *extend* 563.14, *close* 584.12, *keep inside* 611.17, *include* 613.33, 763.5, *surround* 615.7, *wrap* 619.7, *limit* 620.7
contained *retained* 471.6, *containing* 578.18
container 578.1; *receptacle* 105.11, *enclosing thing* 619.3, *transferred thing* 685.6, *freightage* 686.3, *transportable* 686.7

container(ful) 738.2
container car *railroad car* 688.5
containerization *transportation* 686.1
containerize *contain* 577.10, 578.20
containerload *load* 577.5
containership Ships and Boats 690
containing 577.7, 578.18; *loaded* 577.8, *including* 763.3
containment *detention* 471.2, *limitation* 620.2, *inclusion* 763.1
contaminant *pollution* 117.8
contaminate *infest* 40.17, *dirty* 112.11, *poison* 117.18, *change* 512.12, *transfer* 685.8, *mix* 751.12, *mix together* 751.14, *make useless* 802.12, *make worse* 808.17
contaminated *unclean* 112.8, *sick* 114.24, *contagious* 114.26, *polluting* 117.15, *unpalatable* 223.6
contamination *uncleanness* 112.2, *pollution* 117.8, *transmission* 685.3, *mixture* 751.1, *physical deterioration* 808.4
contaminator *transferrer* 685.4
conte [Fr] *story* 139.4
contemn *hate* 300.11, *disdain* 400.16
contemplate *philosophize* 4.19, *learn* 48.23, *worship* 83.15, *visualize* 242.24, *concentrate* 317.10, *expect* 356.6, *have foresight* 357.8, *imagine* 360.14, *mean* 361.13, *intend* 374.8
contemplated *expected* 356.5
contemplation *philosophical investigation* 4.4, *learning* 48.7, *act of worship* 83.2, *visualization* 242.6, *thoughtfulness* 317.2, *expectation* 356.1, *foresight* 357.1, *repose* 678.2
contemplative *thoughtful* 4.17, *educated* 48.19, *worshipful* 83.12, *concentrating* 317.7, *quiescent* 678.6
contemplatively *thoughtfully* 4.27, 317.13, *studiously* 48.26, *worshipfully* 83.17
contemporaneity *same time* 649.1, *newness* 652.1, *synchronism* 794.2
contemporaneous *present* 647.4, *simultaneous* 649.4, *concurrent* 794.13
contemporaneously *simultaneously* 649.8, *concurrently* 794.22
contemporaneousness *present day* 647.2, *same time* 649.1
contemporarily *simultaneously* 649.8, *newly* 652.21
contemporariness *same time* 649.1
contemporary 649.3, Furniture Styles 101, *topical* 328.5, *present* 647.4, *simultaneous* 649.4, *new* 652.9, *concurrent* 794.13
contemporary life *present day* 647.2
contempt 436.3; *dissatisfaction* 274.1, *hate* 300.1, *arrogance* 400.4, *disobedience* 416.2, *scorn* 440.5, *nonobservance* 466.1
contemptibility *hatefulness* 300.4
contemptible *hateful* 300.10, *unforgivable* 430.16, *disregardful* 436.11, *evil* 446.7
contemptibly *hatefully* 300.14, *disgracefully* 371.8

contemptuous 436.12; *dissatisfied* 274.4, *hating* 300.7, *arrogant* 400.11, *defiant* 416.5, *scornful* 440.10, *nonobservant* 466.5

contemptuously 436.27; *discontentedly* 274.8, *with hate* 300.13, *arrogantly* 400.21, *defiantly* 416.9, *disparagingly* 440.16

contemptuousness *dissatisfaction* 274.1, *disobedience* 416.2, *contempt* 436.3

contemputously *derisively* 369.8

contend 189.24, 422.22; *discuss* 4.22, *battle* 76.33, *participate* 145.6, *compete in track and field* 166.21, *raise the point* 328.10, *disagree* 463.8, *enroll* 706.16, *confront* 828.19

contended 189.15

contender 422.13; *hostile person* 63.5, *combatant* 77.1, *sportsman* 145.4, *attempter* 390.3, *entrant* 706.7, *opponent* 828.10

contending 422.19; *warring* 76.26, *discordant* 828.12

contend with *resist* 417.10

content *pacificatory* 74.8, *conciliate* 74.10, *sufficiency* 97.1, *filled* 97.5, *suffice* 97.6, *pleased* 214.9, *comfort* 214.14, *satisfaction* 273.1, *satisfied* 273.4, *satisfy* 273.7, *willing* 373.7, *approved* 437.8, *fabric* 551.2, *contents* 577.1, *size* 579.1, *ease* 819.1, *at ease* 819.2

contented *filled* 97.5, *pleased* 214.9, *joyful* 269.6, *satisfied* 273.4, *proud* 297.10, *self-satisfied* 402.9

contentedly *joyfully* 269.13, *with satisfaction* 273.13

contentedness *satisfaction* 273.1, *willingness* 373.1

contenting *sufficient* 97.3

contention 189.4, 422.1; *hostility* 63.1, *argument* 329.1, *denial* 332.2, *disagreement* 463.1, *divisiveness* 463.2, *conflict* 828.3

contentious 422.20; *aggressive* 63.9, 418.12, *ill-natured* 303.9, *arguable* 329.8, *dissenting* 347.7, *disagreeing* 463.6, *discordant* 828.12

contentiously 422.27; *aggressively* 63.14, *ill-naturedly* 303.18, *dissentiently* 347.10, *in disagreement* 463.12

contentiousness *ill nature* 303.2, *disagreement* 463.1

contentment *sufficiency* 97.1, *pleasure* 214.2, *joy* 269.1, *satisfaction* 273.1, *proudness* 297.3, *ease* 819.1

contents 577.1; *topic* 328.1, *meaning* 361.1, *personal estate* 470.6, *thing included* 763.2, *table* 785.2

conterminous *juxtaposed* 586.9

contest 422.4; *discuss* 4.22, *litigation* 54.1, *battle* 76.33, *sports* 145.1, *participate* 145.6, *compete in track and field* 166.21, *negate* 190.16, *argue* 329.11, *doubt* 333.19, *contend* 422.22, *be uncertain* 841.17

contestability *uncertainty* 841.1

contestable *uncertain* 841.9

contestant *attempter* 390.3, *contender* 422.13, *opponent* 828.10

contested *litigated* 54.22, *negated* 190.10

contesting *litigating* 54.21, *contending* 422.19

contest with *confront* 828.19

context *meaning* 361.1, *type of meaning* 361.4, *circumstances* 573.2, 726.1

contextual *circumstantial* 573.7, 726.8, *accompanying* 794.12

contextualism Philosophical Schools of Thought 4

contextualist Philosophical Schools of Thought 4

contextually *circumstantially* 573.12, *relatively* 726.17

contexture *fabric* 551.2, *texture* 552.1

contiguity 216.4; *juxtaposition* 586.4, *interface* 616.1, *closeness* 645.2, *union* 752.1

contiguous 216.8; *juxtaposed* 586.9, *interfacial* 616.4, *close* 645.6

contiguously *beside* 586.20, *interfacially* 616.7

contiguousness *juxtaposition* 586.4, *union* 752.1

continence *celibacy* 67.1, *chastity* 431.3, *abstinence* 455.2, *self-restraint* 830.4

continent 8.8; *excremental* 25.13, *celibate* 67.6, *chaste* 431.10, *abstinent* 455.7, *world region* 564.6, *landmass* 572.1, *self-restrained* 830.10

continental *terrestrial* 8.52, *regional* 564.12, *of landmasses* 572.12, *inland* 611.8, *foreign* 724.9

continental breakfast *meal* 92.8

continental climate *climate* 9.35

continental crust *earth zone* 8.7

Continental Divide *mountain range* 569.3

continental divide *running water* 8.10

continental drift *continent* 8.8, *plate tectonics* 8.19

continental glacier *glacier* 8.44

continental ice sheet *glacier* 8.44

continental island *island* 572.2

continentally 572.13; *geologically* 8.68, *regionally* 564.16, *inland* 611.19

continental margin *continent* 8.8, *ocean floor* 8.18

continental rise *ocean floor* 8.18

continental shelf *continent* 8.8, *ocean floor* 8.18, *region* 564.1, *coast* 572.4

continental slope *continent* 8.8, *ocean floor* 8.18

continental zone *climate zone* 9.36

continently *celibately* 67.12

contingency *reasoning* 6.61, *expectations* 356.2, *circumstances* 573.2, 726.1, *possibility* 836.1, *chance* 842.1

contingency plan *plan* 357.2, *procedure* 387.2

contingent *logical* 6.83, *conditional* 340.10, *circumstantial* 573.7, 726.8, *caused* 676.5, *chance* 842.10

contingently *conditionally* 340.16, 725.10, *circumstantially* 573.12, *with the effect of* 676.12, *relatively* 726.17

contingent truth *philosophical term* 4.7

contingent upon *caused* 676.5

continual *periodic* 641.8, *lasting* 642.4, 717.13, *frequent* 661.4, *regular* 663.5, *directional* 677.13, *continuous* 774.9, *recurrent* 797.13

continually 377.17, 669.10; *periodically* 641.11, *everlastingly*

642.10, *frequently* 661.7, *orderly* 663.13, *continuously* 774.16, *repeatedly* 797.22

continual movement *regular movement* 677.10

continualness *continuity* 774.4

continuance 669.3; *constancy* 377.3, *immutability* 640.2, *permanence* 667.1, *continuity* 669.1, 774.4, *continuing existence* 717.7

continuation 642.2, 669.2; *duration* 642.1, *continuity* 669.1, *forward motion* 677.4, *addition* 748.1, *sequel* 770.5, *conservation* 815.2

continue 669.8, 774.12; *live* 28.17, *persevere* 377.10, *maintain* 377.12, *follow up* 385.16, *pass* 639.13, *go on* 642.7, *make permanent* 644.9, *be frequent* 661.5, *be permanent* 667.4, *protract* 669.9, *continue to be* 717.20, *be left* 750.9, *be infinite* 798.9, *preserve* 815.14

continued fraction *division* 6.16

continue to be 717.20

continue working *work* 122.8

continuing *constant* 377.8, *lasting* 642.4, *permanent* 667.2, *continuous* 669.5, *forward motion* 677.4, *ongoing* 679.7, *incomplete* 762.5

continuing existence 717.7

continuing forever 644.6

continuing on *forward motion* 677.4

continuity 669.1, 774.4; *aspect of fiction* 139.5, *immutability* 640.2, *continuation* 642.2, *eternity* 644.1, *frequency* 661.1, *regularity* 663.1, *permanence* 667.1, *sameness* 730.1, *conformity* 735.7, *adhesion* 755.1

continuity clerk *interfacer* 616.3

continuity of germ plasm *evolution* 13.23

continuity person *person who joins* 752.9

continuo *harmonic element* 140.14

continuous 630.10, 669.5, 774.9; *universal* 6.67, *status adjectives* 11.25, *juxtaposed* 586.9, *timeless* 640.3, *lasting* 642.4, 717.13, *continuing forever* 644.6, *permanent* 667.2, *directional* 677.13, *adhesive* 755.5, *sequential* 770.7, *recurrent* 797.13

continuous beam *superstructure* 551.7

continuous digester *systems and process control* 14.28

continuous distortion *topology* 6.45

continuous distribution *probability distribution* 6.56

continuous function *mathematical function* 6.27

continuously 774.16; *mathematically* 6.93, *beside* 586.20, *everlastingly* 642.10, *permanently* 667.6, *continually* 669.10

continuous motion *continuum* 774.5

continuousness *continuation* 642.2, *regularity* 663.1, *continuance* 669.3, *continuity* 774.4

continuous phase *phase* 11.13

continuous spectrum *emission* 10.56

continuum 774.5; *fourth dimension* 563.9, *continuation* 642.2

contort *distort* 627.9, *make faces* 627.10

contorted *ugly* 531.3, *ambiguous* 632.5

contortedly *asymmetrically* 627.13

contortedness *ugliness* 531.1

contortion *distortion* 627.1, *distortion of face* 627.2

contortionist *circus performer* 138.9

contour *line* 6.35, *external appearance* 264.5, *outline* 617.1, *shape* 617.2, *form* 624.1

contour farming *arable farming* 16.6

contour feather *plumage* 36.7

contour line *outline* 617.1

contra *rebel* 427.8

contraband *prohibited* 503.5

contrabass Musical Instruments 142

contrabassoon Musical Instruments 142

contraception *birth control* 23.5, *prophylaxis* 115.4, *sanitary precaution* 810.8

contraceptive 23.6; *counteractant* 510.5, *counteracting* 510.6

contraceptive foam *contraceptive* 23.6

contraceptive injection *contraceptive* 23.6

contraceptive sponge *contraceptive* 23.6

contract 391.2, 459.1, 459.8, 462.2, 462.11, 582.12; *be concise* 198.5, *summarize* 204.7, *take charge of* 391.8, *duty* 433.1, *impose a duty* 433.14, *promise* 458.1, 458.11, *guarantee* 458.3, *basis for negotiations* 460.2, *bargaining* 480.15, *bargain* 480.20, *be dense* 540.8, *make little* 580.10, *obstruct* 584.13, *narrow* 593.14, *outline* 617.5, *settlement* 735.6, *settle* 735.26, *decrease* 747.7, *make smaller* 747.8, *agreement* 767.9, *disintegrate* 808.15

contract a disease *be unhealthy* 114.29

contract a marriage *contract* 459.8

contract bridge Card Games 168, *bridge* 168.4

contracted *industrial* 57.13, *concise* 198.4, *summarized* 204.6, *dutiful* 433.6, *guaranteeing* 458.9, *contractual* 459.7, 462.7, *little* 580.7, *smaller* 582.7, *narrow* 593.8, *narrowed* 593.9

contractedly *narrowly* 593.17

contracted thing 582.5

contract for employment *be employed* 57.19

contractibility 582.4

contractible 582.11

contractile *contractible* 582.11

contractility *contractibility* 582.4

contracting 582.10; *industrial* 57.13, *contractual* 462.7

contracting party *contractor* 459.6, *assenter* 462.5

contraction 582.1; *conciseness* 198.1, *outline* 204.2, 617.1, *obstruction* 584.2, *shortening* 591.2, *narrowness* 593.1, *narrowing* 593.3, *descent* 714.1, *decrease* 747.1, *unification* 752.5

contractional *contracting* 582.10

contractive *contracting* 582.10

contract killer *murderer* 30.12

contract matrimony *marry* 64.19

contract murder *murder* 30.2

contractor 459.6, 582.6; *civil*

engineer 14.19, *attempter* 390.3, *operator* 412.7, *assenter* 462.5, *producer* 522.10

contracts law *law* 53.1

contract theory of morality *philosophical problem* 4.8

contractual 459.7, 462.7, 480.16; *industrial* 57.13, *undertaken* 391.4, *settled* 735.16

contractually 459.9, 462.15; *industrially* 57.22, *responsibly* 391.10, *as agreed upon* 735.36

contractual obligations *bargaining terms* 57.10

contradict *discuss* 4.22, *negate* 190.16, *argue* 329.11, *deny* 332.8, *answer back* 334.19, *counter* 339.13, *refuse* 347.9, *mean* 361.13, *renounce* 383.13, *dissent* 506.9, *protest* 507.7, *be opposite* 731.4, *be dissimilar* 734.7, *object* 828.18, *cancel out* 834.8

contradicted *negated* 190.10, *renounced* 383.9

contradicter *abrogator* 834.4

contradicting *renunciation* 383.4, *censuring* 438.12

contradiction *reasoning* 6.61, *negation* 190.1, *denial* 332.2, *counterstatement* 334.5, *counterevidence* 339.5, *renunciation* 383.4, *censure* 438.3, *dissent* 506.2, *protest* 507.1, *divergence* 703.1, *oppositeness* 731.1, *dissimilarity* 734.1, *objection* 828.2, *canceling out* 834.3

contradiction in terms *sophism* 330.2

contradictive *protesting* 507.5

contradictive *or* **contradictory** *negational* 190.9

contradictively *disapprovingly* 507.10

contradictively *or* **contradictorily** *negatively* 190.22

contradict oneself *practice sophistry* 330.11

contradictor *negator* 190.8

contradictorily *uncooperatively* 506.11, *dissimilarly* 734.10, *opposingly* 828.22

contradictory *logical* 6.83, *dissuasive* 179.4, *sophistic* 330.7, *refuting* 332.6, *counterevident* 339.10, *censuring* 438.12, *dissenting* 506.6, *divergent* 703.6, *dissimilar* 734.4, *contrary* 828.13

contradictory law *legal injustice* 53.5

contradictory meaning *type of meaning* 361.4

contradistinction *contrariety* 828.6

contrail *sign* 183.1

contraindicate *dissuade* 179.7

contraindication *dissuasion* 179.1, *counterevidence* 339.5

contralto *voice* 141.5, *deepness* 236.3

contrapose *be opposite* 731.4, *counterbalance* 743.8

contraposed *counterbalanced* 743.6

contraposing *counterbalanced* 743.6

contraposition *oppositeness* 731.1, *counterbalance* 743.2, *contrariety* 828.6

contrapositive *opposite* 731.2, 731.3

contraption *tool* 103.1

contraption [Inf] *instrument* 511.2

contrapuntal *harmonic* 140.27, *harmonizing* 735.12

contrariety 828.6; *divergence* 703.1, *oppositeness* 731.1, *dissimilarity* 734.1, *inequality* 741.1, *dissent* 782.2

contrarily *negatively* 190.22, *arguably* 329.16, *to the contrary* 339.17, *uncooperatively* 506.11, *disapprovingly* 507.10, *counter* 510.8, *reversely* 608.10, *diametrically* 731.6, *dissimilarly* 734.10, *with delay* 826.22, *adversely* 848.16

contrariness 828.5; *oppositeness* 190.6, 731.1, *obstinacy* 379.1, *defiance* 416.1, *hindrance* 826.1

contrariwise 828.24; *reversely* 608.10, *diametrically* 731.6

contrary 828.13; *dissuasive* 179.4, *oppositeness* 190.6, *negational* 190.9, *argumentative* 329.7, *refuting* 332.6, *obstinate* 379.5, *refractory* 379.6, *dissenting* 506.6, *protesting* 507.5, *counteracting* 510.6, *inverse* 608.2, 608.6, *reversely* 608.10, *opposite* 731.3, *dissimilar* 734.4, *dissident* 782.12, *troublesome* 824.13, *hindering* 826.12, *uncooperative* 828.14, *canceled* 834.5, *adverse* 848.10

contrary advice *dissuasion* 179.1

contrary assertion *negation* 190.1

contrary to *counter* 510.8

contrary to expectation *unexpectedly* 839.9

contrary to law *illegally* 53.34

contrary to orders *disobediently* 427.14

contrary to reason *impossible* 837.4

contrary vote *dissent* 506.2

contrast *light* 10.17, *composition* 132.17, *television set* 172.6, *invert* 608.7, *interrelatedness* 727.3, *relate to* 727.9, *disparity* 728.3, *be disparate* 728.14, *oppositeness* 731.1, *be opposite* 731.4, *diversity* 732.1, *be diverse* 732.10, *dissimilarity* 734.1, *be dissimilar* 734.7, *nonconformity* 782.1, *contrariety* 828.6, *counteract* 828.21

contrasted *opposite* 731.3, *contrary* 828.13

contrasting *disparate* 728.9, *opposite* 731.3, *diverse* 732.5, *dissimilar* 734.4, *nonconforming* 782.11, *contrary* 828.13

contrastingly *disparately* 728.19, *diametrically* 731.6, *diversely* 732.14, *dissimilarly* 734.10, *opposingly* 828.22

contrastive *linguistic* 5.34

contrastive linguistics Linguistic Studies 5

contrastively *diametrically* 731.6

contrasty *exposed* 132.25

contravene *negate* 190.16, *deny* 332.8, *violate the law* 466.12, *protest* 507.7, *counteract* 510.7, *object* 828.18

contravening *refuting* 332.6, *violating* 466.8, *dissenting* 506.6, *counteracting* 510.6

contravention *lawbreaking* 53.14, *negation* 190.1, *denial* 332.2, *infraction* 466.4, *protest* 507.1, *counteraction* 510.1, *objection* 828.2

contrectophobia Phobias 283

contredanse *or* **contradance** Dances 135

contre-partie *decorative woodwork* 131.2

contretemps *mishap* 660.4, *obstacle* 826.2

contribute *provision* 89.9, *defray* 489.18, *donate* 491.13, *give* 498.11, *make an offering* 504.17, *tend* 513.5, *support financially* 605.19, *work together* 827.14

contributed *expended* 491.9

contribute to *give to charity* 472.16, *determine* 675.11, *further* 679.13, 825.30, *make bigger* 746.7, *insert* 748.12

contribute to *or* **toward** *finance* 825.31

contributing *giving* 472.1, *influential* 512.8

contributing factor *contributory cause* 675.3

contribution *utterance* 205.10, *benevolent act* 305.5, *giving* 472.1, *offering* 472.6, 504.5, *voluntary payment* 489.4, *grant* 489.7, *donation* 491.6, *gift* 498.3, *financial support* 605.8, *contributory cause* 675.3, *additional item* 748.3, *participation* 760.10, *financial assistance* 825.6

contributor *dissertator* 203.3, *benevolent person* 305.6, *giver* 472.7, *generous person* 498.5, *volunteer* 504.7, *provider* 605.10

contributory *given* 472.8, *sacrificial* 504.10, *influential* 512.8, *sustaining* 605.15, *additional* 748.8, *helpful* 825.19, *cooperative* 827.9

contributory cause 675.3

con trick [Inf] *disreputable action* 371.3

contrite *apologetic* 313.6, *appearing guilty* 450.7, *penitent* 451.5

contritely *apologetically* 313.11, *guiltily* 450.12, *penitently* 451.10

contriteness *penitence* 313.3

contrite sinner *penitent person* 451.4

contrition *penitence* 313.3, 451.1, *sign of guilt* 450.2

contrivance *means* 102.1, *tool* 103.1, *social skill* 127.3, *aspect of fiction* 139.5, *artifice* 193.5, *sophism* 330.2, *solution* 334.6, *invention* 345.4, *expedient* 387.5, *planning* 387.8, *tactics* 399.12, *instrument* 511.2, *convenience* 803.1, *means of escape* 816.4, *stratagem* 822.2

contrive *find means* 102.6, *scheme* 193.18, *practice sophistry* 330.11, *solve* 334.21, *invent* 345.14, *predetermine* 384.8, *plan* 387.12, *lay the foundations* 388.16, *improvise* 396.6, *design* 536.8, *awaken* 675.9, *make arrangements* 767.23, *be cunning* 822.5

contrived *ungenuine* 192.13, *sophistic* 330.7, *solved* 334.15, *imaginary* 360.12, *deliberate* 384.5, *planned* 387.10

contriver *planner* 387.9

contriving *planning* 387.11, *cunning* 822.4

control *philosophical attitude* 4.3, *process* 14.50, *governance* 49.18, *govern* 49.26, *authority* 52.1, 425.3, 514.5, 780.6, *have authority* 52.13, *master* 68.17, *management* 126.1, *directorship* 126.5, *manage* 126.10, *skill* 127.1, *rehearsal* 338.7, *specification* 340.6, *specify* 340.14, *use* 393.1, *have at one's disposal* 393.14, *treatment* 399.11, *behave toward* 399.20, *action* 412.1, *direct*

412.16, 780.14, *have authority over* 425.12, *claiming* 469.2, *be an instrument* 511.7, *personal influence* 512.3, *be an influence* 512.13, *be powerful* 514.18, *moderation* 521.1, *moderate* 521.7, *limitation* 620.2, *limit* 620.7, *pilot* 689.15, *leadership* 744.2, *discipline* 765.9, *restore order* 765.22, *hindrance* 826.1, *hinder* 826.15, *restraint* 830.1, *restrain* 830.12, *domination* 832.2, *defeat* 832.11

control character *character* 15.18

controllable *dominating* 832.7

controllably *restrainedly* 830.18

controlled *detached* 4.18, *unconscious* 108.40, *bowls* 151.7, *conditional* 340.10, *deliberate* 384.5, *moderate* 521.3, *limited* 620.5, *disciplined* 765.17, *restrained* 830.9

controlled association *association of ideas* 108.31

controlled-association test Psychological Tests 108

controlled blur *framing* 132.18

controlled nuclear fusion *nuclear fusion* 10.61

controlled shot *grip* 151.4

controlled substance *drug* 115.9, 121.14

controller *computing terms* 15.22, *governor* 49.23, *company leader* 68.8, *operator* 412.7, *treasurer* 484.18, *moderator* 521.2

controller card *card* 15.7

controllers *management board* 126.2

controller tuning *systems and process control* 14.28

controlling *governing* 49.25, *authoritative* 52.9, 425.8, *masterful* 68.15, *managerial* 126.9, *powerful* 514.15, *ruling* 780.11, *restraining* 830.8, *dominating* 832.7

controlling body *management board* 126.2

control one's appetite *eat less* 118.9, *abstain* 455.11

control oneself *be virtuous* 447.8, *be self-restrained* 455.10, *restrain oneself* 830.15

control one's lusts *abstain* 455.11

control one's passions *be virtuous* 447.8

control prices *restrain commerce* 830.14

control results *manage* 126.10

controls *guide* 126.6, *television set* 172.6

control sequence *character* 15.18

control the finances *manage* 126.10

control theory Branches of Mathematics 6

control the purse strings *wield authority* 52.16

control tower *airport* 689.4

controversial *arguable* 329.8, *questionable* 333.13, *disagreeing* 463.6, *dissenting* 506.6, 732.9, *uncertain* 841.9

controversially *arguably* 329.16, *questionably* 333.22, *in disagreement* 463.12, *uncooperatively* 506.11, *dissentingly* 732.17, *uncertainly* 841.22

controversy *argument* 329.1, *difficult question* 333.4, *dissent* 347.1, 506.2, *contention* 422.1, *disagreement* 463.1, *dissension* 732.4, *objection* 828.2

controvert *negate* 190.16, *deny*

332.8, object 828.18, be uncertain 841.17

controvertibility uncertainty 841.1

controvertible uncertain 841.9

contumacious obstinate 379.5, refractory 379.6, insulting 436.10, disorderly 766.15, dissident 782.12

contumacy obstinacy 379.1, disobedience 416.2

contumelious arrogant 400.11, contemptuous 436.12, scornful 440.10

contumeliously arrogantly 400.21

contumely arrogance 400.4, insult 400.6, act of defiance 416.3, contempt 436.3, dissent 782.2

contuse inflict pain 215.10

contusion painful injury 215.3, pulverization 553.4

conundrum mystery 182.4, difficult question 333.4, unintelligible thing 364.3, equivocation 380.1, problem 824.4

conurbation city 567.1

convalesce get healthy 113.12, be strong 516.14, get better 807.21, be restored 809.13

convalescence health 113.1, strengthening 516.7, restoration 807.4, recuperation 809.4

convalescent getting well 113.9, infectious person 114.9, cured 809.8

convalescent home nursing home 107.18

convalescing strengthening 516.7

convect transfer 685.8

convection atmospheric process 9.9, heat flow 10.27, transmission 685.3

convection cell air movement 9.11

convection heater heater 217.3

convective atmospheric 9.40

convene call together 59.28

convened assembled 59.18

convenience 803.1, 825.7; place for excretion 25.11, leisure 125.1, desirability 288.7, ready-made 388.13, availability 575.5, nearness 586.1, timeliness 659.1, usefulness 801.1, wieldiness 823.3

convenience food food 90.1

convenience-food immediate 645.5

conveniences means 102.1

convenience store store 483.8

convenient 803.3; expedient 288.12, ready-made 388.13, usable 393.6, available 575.11, next 586.8, timely 659.4, useful 801.5, wieldy 823.8, helpful 825.19

conveniently 803.6; leisurely 125.6, expediently 288.25, usefully 393.15, 801.12, opportunely 659.8, helpfully 825.32

convenor union member 57.6

convent monasticism 667.3, place of worship 83.8, clerical dwelling 84.10, privacy 181.6, enclosed area 619.2

conventicle place of worship 83.8

convention 781.5; conference 59.5, pacification 74.1, representative body 79.2, lack of emphasis 201.1, place for conversation 210.5, tradition 397.5, standard procedure 397.6, ceremonial 404.11, etiquette 406.3, 534.3, good manners 410.2, alliance 459.5, performance 465.2, design 536.2, settlement 735.6, custom 780.5

conventional unemphatic 201.2, customary 397.11, 780.9, formal 406.6, good-mannered 410.7, observant 465.3, traditional 630.13, traditionally 630.19, average 742.5, conformist 781.10

conventionalism 781.4; formalism 406.2, traditionality 630.6

conventionalist creature of habit 397.8, straight person 630.7, conformist 781.6

conventionality formality 406.1, formalism 406.2, etiquette 534.3, traditionality 630.6, average 742.1

conventionalize formalize 406.9, make average 742.9

conventionally unemphatically 201.4, habitually 397.20, formally 406.12, genteelly 410.14, observantly 465.6, according to rule 781.18

conventional medicine medicine 107.1

conventional representation representation 187.1

conventional symbol sign 183.1

conventional weapon weapon 78.1

convention delegate delegate 79.1, agent 123.15

conventions way of life 399.9

convent school religious school 48.13

conventual religious 84.9, monastic 84.13, enclosed 619.4

converge 702.9; align 6.92, be sharp 6.92, flow 570.10, near 586.12, narrow 593.14, centralize 612.11, unify 752.15, combine 757.9

convergence 702.1; contiguity 216.4, flow 570.4, nearness 586.1, narrowing 593.3, centrality 612.5, union 752.1

convergence zone plate tectonics 8.19

convergent 702.7; linear 6.77, cumulate 59.20, flowing 570.7, nearer 586.7, narrowed 593.9, centered 612.9, magnetic 700.9

convergent evolution evolution 13.23

convergently 702.12; fluently 570.13

convergent series sequence 6.18

convergent strabismus faulty vision 243.1

convergent view 702.3

converging contiguous 216.8, nearer 586.7, convergence 702.1, convergent 702.7

converging line focus 702.5

converging lines line 6.35

conversableness social success 408.3

conversant habituated 397.14

conversant with educated 48.19, knowledgeable 348.7

conversation 210.1; philosophical argument 4.5, speech 205.1, sociability 408.1

conversational 210.10; of language 5.35, communicative 169.16, effusive 207.6

conversationalist 210.6; speaker 205.12, answerer 334.10, social person 408.7

conversationally 210.14; colloquially 5.45, in answer 334.25

conversation piece type of painting 143.5

conversation poem Poem or Verse Forms 139

converse 210.11; reasoning 6.61, logical 6.83, react 334.20, inverse 608.2, 608.6, correlative 729.6, opposite 731.2, 731.3

conversely reversely 608.10, correlatively 729.12, diametrically 731.6

converser conversationalist 210.6

converse with approach 209.10

conversing 210.8

conversion 670.1; scoring 155.5, reuse 393.3, confession 451.2, transfer of property 470.4, change 665.1, change of mind 665.6, transformation 665.7, exchange 673.1, improvement 807.1

conversion disorder somatoform disorder 108.19, mental breakdown 110.4

convert 670.6, 670.11; religious person 81.9, recant 81.27, proselytize 84.15, make someone believe 87.11, play offense 155.18, publicize 178.19, exploit 393.11, transfer property 470.12, change 665.14, cause change 665.16, change for the better 665.17, transform 670.13, persuade 670.14, exchange 673.5, make unlike 734.9, improve 807.15

converted 670.7; believing 87.6, bowling 151.6, penitent 451.5, changed 665.10, exchanged 673.4

converted split bowling delivery 151.2

converter 670.5; electricity 106.5, ceramic workshop and tools 129.8, changer 665.9

convertibility usefulness 393.2, conversion 670.1

convertible 670.9; in exchange 673.3, automobile 687.6, equal 740.8

convertible bond paper money 484.14

convertible couch couch 101.7

convertible sofa type of bed 101.9

convertibly 670.15; usefully 393.15

converting 670.8; conversion 670.1

convert into exchange 673.5

convertive transformative 665.12

convex 634.5; curvilinear 6.78, curved 629.4, round 633.7

convexity 634.1; surface 6.36, curvature 629.2, roundness 633.1

convexly 634.9; curvedly 629.7, roundly 633.11

convexness convexity 634.1

convex surface surface 6.36

convey 685.9; communicate 170.12, speak 205.17, mean 361.13, conduct 399.21, contract 459.8, transfer property 470.12, give 472.10, sell 482.15, set in motion 677.16, transport 686.10, cross 692.17

conveyable negotiated 460.5, transferring property 470.10, transferable 685.7

convey a meaning or a message or an idea mean 361.13

conveyance 685.2; transfer of property 470.4, giving 472.1, selling 482.1, transportation 686.1

conveyancer person transferring property 470.8, transferrer 685.4

conveyancing transfer of property 470.4

conveyed transferring property 470.10

conveying conveyance 685.2

conveyor construction equipment 14.23, transporter 686.4, lifter 715.5

conveyor or **conveyer** transferrer 685.4

conveyor belt manufacture 522.2, continuum 774.5

convict 54.33; lawbreaker 53.15, prisoner 55.7, guilty person 450.5

convicted 54.26; guilty 450.6

convicted criminal guilty person 450.5

conviction 840.2; unfavorable verdict 54.20, religion 81.1, belief 87.1, calling 178.6, expectation 281.2, guilt 450.1

conviction of guilt guilt 450.1

convict oneself convict 54.33

convict ship Ships and Boats 690

convince proselytize 84.15, make someone believe 87.11, persuade 178.15, 670.14, emphasize 200.6, comfort 273.9, be irresistible 428.9, influence 508.11, make certain 840.14

convinced 840.8; believing 87.6, persuadable 178.14

convince oneself suppose 359.8

convince otherwise dissuade 179.7

convincer persuader 178.9

convince to the contrary dissuade 179.7

convincibility persuadability 178.8

convincible persuadable 178.14

convincing believable 87.7, persuasive 178.12, emphatic 200.3, descriptive 202.11, compelling 428.6, motivational 508.7, strong 516.9

convincingly believably 87.13, persuasively 178.21, compellingly 428.12, influentially 508.13, acutely 516.18

convincingness persuasion 178.1

convivial pleasant 214.7, cheerful 269.7, celebrative 405.9, sociable 408.11

conviviality pleasure 214.2, cheerfulness 269.2, celebration 405.1, sociability 408.1

convivially sociably 408.19

convivial person social person 408.7

convocation Collective Names 59, conference 59.5, ceremony 405.3

convoke call together 59.28

convolute 632.6

convoluted obscure 197.2, indirect 607.8, convolutional 632.4, confused 766.12, problematic 824.11

convolutedness convolution 632.1

convoluted thing 632.3

convolution 632.1; differentiation 6.29, obscurity 197.1, indirectness 607.3, calculation 784.1, difficulty 824.1

convolutional 632.4

convolve convolute 632.6

convolvulus Flowers 42

convoy naval unit 77.20, accompaniment 794.1, escort 794.18, safe conduct 810.4, protect 810.21

convoy ship Sailing Ships and Boats 690, Ships and Boats 690

convulse inflict pain 215.10, be violent 520.8, be agitated 684.21, disturb 768.10

convulsed feeling pain 215.6, disturbed 768.6

convulsion burst of anger 302.6, violence by person 520.2, spasm 684.8, disturbance 768.1

convulsive 684.19; angry 302.11, explosive 520.6

convulsively *violently* 520.11, *jerkily* 684.29

convulsive therapy *psychiatric treatment* 108.3

coo *speak in a particular way* 205.18, *bird sound* 240.2, *make a bird sound* 240.8

co-occurrence *synchronism* 794.2

cooch *Dances* 135

Cook, Mount *Mountains and Hills* 569

cook **91.3, 91.10;** *domestic servant* 69.7, *air force person* 77.31, *caterer* 89.5, *food provider* 90.6, *domestic worker* 123.4, *heat* 217.17

cookbook *cooking* 91.1, *type of book* 174.3

cooked *culinary* 91.9

cooked-up [Inf] *perjurious* 442.7

cooked-up charge [Inf] *false accusation* 442.2

cooker **91.5;** *cook* 91.3, *burner* 217.4

cookery *cooking* 91.1, *cooking place* 91.4

cookery book [Brit] *cooking* 91.1

cook for *provision* 89.9, *feed* 90.41

cookhouse *cooking place* 91.4

cookie *cake* 90.36

cookie [Inf] *term of endearment* 299.7

cookie cutter *cooking equipment* 91.6

cookie jar *kitchen container* 91.7, *vessel* 578.11

cookie press *cooking equipment* 91.6

cookies *confectionery* 222.3

cookie sheet *cooking equipment* 91.6

cooking **91.1,** *Hobbies and Pastimes* 167

cooking equipment 91.6

cooking place 91.4

cooking pot *pot* 578.15

cooking technique 91.2

Cook Islands *Islands* 572

cookout *feast* 92.9, *party* 408.6

cookroom *cooking place* 91.4

cook someone's goose [Inf] *defeat* 845.17

cook the accounts *or* **books** [Inf] *account* 493.9

cook the books [Inf] *act dishonestly* 479.18

cook the evidence [Inf] *accuse falsely* 442.9

cook up [Inf] *plot* 387.15, *fabricate* 720.17

cook up a charge [Inf] *accuse falsely* 442.9

cool **9.49;** *detached* 4.18, *hostile* 63.6, *refreshing* 94.4, *refreshed* 94.5, *air* 94.7, *musical* 140.25, *discourage* 179.11, *cold* 218.9, *indifferent* 289.7, *lack of wonder* 295.1, *wonderless* 295.3, *unsociable* 409.6, *disinterested* 443.4, *moderate* 521.3, *calm* 521.8, *reserved* 585.7, *determined* 674.5, *quiescent* 678.6, *self-restrained* 830.10

cool [Inf] *great* 445.14, *fashionable* 536.5

cool! [Inf] *wonderful!* 294.20

coolabah *Trees and Shrubs* 43

coolant *machine tool* 14.9, *cooler* 218.4, *nuclear power production* 514.10

cool as a cucumber *wonderless* 295.3, *quiescent* 678.6

cool breeze *refresher* 94.2

cool climate *climate* 9.35

cool down *air* 94.7, *become cold* 218.14, *restore order* 765.22

cooled **218.11;** *discouraged* 179.6, *ventilated* 558.17

cooled off *refreshed* 94.5

cooler **218.4;** *cool* 9.49

cooler [Inf] *the inside* 55.2

cool-headed *detached* 4.18, *rational* 109.4

cool-headedness *philosophical attitude* 4.3

cool hue *hue* 251.4

coolie *or* **cooly** [Off] *laborer* 123.9

coolie *or* **cooly** *Nicknames for Inhabitants* 61

coolie hat *hat* 100.32

cooling *windy* 9.42, *refreshing* 94.4, *cold* 218.1

cooling down *refreshment* 94.1

cooling fluid *machine tool* 14.9

coolingly *meteorologically* 9.60

cooling off *refreshment* 94.1

cooling off of the economy *declining prices* 497.2

cooling-off period *interruption* 604.4, *delay* 658.3, *pause* 668.3

cooling system *cold* 10.26

cooling tower *cooler* 218.4

coolish *cold* 218.9

cool it! *cease!* 668.14

cool it [Inf] *submit* 421.4, *ease* 543.15, *do easily* 823.16

cool jazz *jazz* 140.5

coolly *stoically* 4.26, *hostilely* 63.13, *refreshingly* 94.9, *coldly* 218.16, *indifferently* 289.17, *without wonder* 295.8, *unsocially* 409.13, *disinterestedly* 443.8, *reservedly* 585.15, *determinedly* 674.10

cool million [Inf] *money* 485.2

coolness *philosophical attitude* 4.3, *cold weather* 9.24, *hostility* 63.1, *refreshment* 94.1, *cold* 218.1, *indifference* 289.1, *lack of wonder* 295.1, *unsociability* 409.1, *moderation* 521.1, *reserve* 585.4, *determination* 674.2

cool off *air* 94.7, *be refreshed* 94.8, *become cold* 218.14, *pause* 668.13, *restore order* 765.22

cool one's heels *wait* 658.12

cool one's temper *conciliate* 74.10

cool out [Inf] *ease* 543.15, *restrain oneself* 830.15

cool welcome *rejection* 383.1

coomb *or* **combe** *or* **comb** [Brit] *valley* 572.8

cooncan *or* **conquian** *Card Games* 167

coonhound *Breeds of Dogs* 35

coon's age [Inf] *long duration* 642.3

coonskin cap *or* **hat** *cap* 100.33

coop *cage* 60.15, *closed place* 584.4, *enclose* 584.16, *enclosed area* 619.2, *shelter* 812.4

coop [Inf] *the inside* 55.2

co-op *apartment house* 60.8, *alliance* 735.5

cooped up *imprisoned* 55.9

cooper *artisan* 123.13, *woodworker* 131.4

cooperate **616.6, 827.12;** *be willing* 373.12, *negotiate* 460.6, *compromise* 461.7, *agree with* 462.10, *federate* 480.21, *be an instrument* 511.7, *give moral support* 605.18, *exchange* 673.5, *interrelate* 729.8, *come together* 757.10, *improve* 825.26

cooperating *agreeing* 462.6, *cooperative* 827.9

cooperatingly *cooperatively* 827.18

cooperation **827.1;** *friendship*

62.1, *willingness* 373.1, *sociability* 408.1, *contract* 459.1, *compromise* 461.1, *agreement* 462.1, *joint operation* 509.2, *moral support* 605.7, *interaction* 616.2, *exchange* 673.1, *interrelation* 729.2, *helpfulness* 825.10

cooperative **827.9;** *association* 59.4, 827.6, *friendly* 62.5, *assenting* 346.4, *willing* 373.7, *goodwilled* 373.10, *agreeing* 462.6, *instrumental* 511.4, *supportive* 605.11, *interfacial* 616.4, *interrelated* 729.5, *alliance* 735.5, *allied* 735.15, *united* 752.10, *collaborative* 757.7, *benevolent* 825.21

cooperative apartment house *apartment house* 60.8

cooperative enterprise *joint operation* 827.4

cooperative hospital *hospital* 107.16

cooperatively **827.18;** *cliquishly* 59.32, *amicably* 62.13, *agreeably* 462.14, *instrumentally* 511.9, *supportively* 605.20, *interfacially* 616.7, *interrelatedly* 729.11, *in alliance* 735.35, *as one* 752.21, *in combination* 757.11, *benevolently* 825.34

cooperativeness *willingness* 373.1, *cooperation* 827.1

cooperator **827.8;** *assenter* 462.5, *supporter* 605.9

Cooper Creek *Rivers* 570

cooping *arrest* 55.5

coopt *select* 382.12

cooptation *selection* 382.1

cooption *selection* 382.1

coop up *arrest* 55.12

Coopworth *Breeds of Sheep* 16

coordinate *of grammar* 5.41, *react* 11.38, *modify* 340.13, *symmetrical* 626.4, *symmetrize* 626.6, *counterpart* 733.5, *harmonize* 735.22, *dividing line* 740.6, *equal* 740.8, *equalize* 740.12, *organize* 767.19

coordinate bond *chemical bond* 11.6

coordinate clause *clause* 5.31

coordinated *modified* 340.9, *matched* 733.10, *harmonizing* 735.12

coordinate geometry *geometry* 6.32

coordinateness *symmetry* 626.1

coordinates **6.31, 589.6;** *dimension* 10.5, *suit* 100.16, *exact location* 565.2, *separates* 753.6

coordinates (of a point) *point* 6.34

coordinate system *coordinates* 6.31

coordinating conjunction *part of speech* 5.30

coordination *chemical compound* 11.4, *modification* 340.5, *joint operation* 509.2, *harmonization* 735.2, *method* 765.7, *organization* 767.3

coot *water bird* 36.9

cootie [Inf] *pest* 40.5

coots *Collective Names* 59

co-ownership *joint control* 827.5

cop [Inf] *law enforcement officer* 53.8, *security force* 810.13

copacetic [Inf] *great* 445.14

copaiba *Tree Products* 43

copal *Tree Products* 43

copartner *possessor* 469.10

copartnership *joint possession* 469.6, *joint control* 827.5

cope *vestment* 84.11

Copenhagen *Notable Horses* 159, *Countries* 566

Copenhagen interpretation *quantum theory* 10.64

copepod *crustacean* 39.10

Copernican universe *universe* 7.3

copestone *Architectural Elements* 134

cope with *behave toward* 399.20, *be equal* 740.11

copied *reproduced* 21.10, *drawn* 143.11, *recorded* 185.12, *borrowed* 476.8, *unauthentic* 722.9, *duplicate* 730.11, *simulated* 733.11, *imitation* 736.8, *double* 789.11

copier **736.5;** *infringer* 479.10

copilot *air force person* 77.31, *aircraft personnel* 689.8, *pilot* 689.15

coping stone *Architectural Elements* 134

copious *fertile* 22.8, *plentiful* 97.4, *diffuse* 199.3, *abundant* 498.8, *big* 579.13, *ample* 795.9

copiously *plentifully* 97.11, *diffusely* 199.7, *generously* 498.12, *amply* 579.20

copiousness *plenty* 97.2, *diffuseness* 199.1

coplanar *spatial* 6.76

copolymer(ization) *polymer* 11.9

copolymeric *polymeric* 11.35

cop out *cover up* 441.13

cop out [Inf] *shirk* 386.18, *be irresolute* 461.8

cop-out [Inf] *shirking* 386.4, *cover-up* 441.3, *irresolution* 461.3

copper *Chemical Elements and Common Allotropes* 11, *essential element* 12.15, *electricity* 14.34, *brown* 256.5, *orange* 258.3

copper [Inf] *law enforcement officer* 53.8, *security force* 810.13

copper coinage *coinage* 484.13

copper-colored *brown* 256.5

copper engraving *engraving* 144.3

Coppermine *Rivers* 570

copper plate *material* 144.6

copperplate *coating* 613.8

coppers *change* 484.3

coppery *brown* 256.5, *orange* 258.5

coppice *trees* 43.4, *manage trees* 43.14

coppicing *tree management* 43.6

coprocessor *computer part* 15.4

coprolalia *vulgarism* 5.20

coprolite *feces* 25.5

coprology *vulgarism* 5.20, *profanity* 301.3

coprophilia *sexual perversion* 20.12

coprophilous *of fungi* 47.19

coprophobia *Phobias* 283

coprostasophobia *Phobias* 283

copse *trees* 43.4

copsy *wooded* 43.12

copter [Inf] *aircraft* 689.3

Coptic art *Western Art Styles* 133

Coptic Church *Christian Groups* 81

copula *part of speech* 5.30, *joint* 752.7, *means of connection* 754.4

copular *of grammar* 5.41

copulate *have sex* 20.21, *unite sexually* 752.20

copulating *coupling* 20.19

copulation *sexual intercourse* 20.9, *propagation* 21.4, *sexual union* 752.6

copulative *conjunctive* 752.12

copulatively *as one* 752.21

copulatory *conjunctive* 752.12

copy 730.5, 730.17, 736.2, 736.10; *program* 15.29, *reproduction* 21.1, *reprint* 21.3, *reproduce* 21.13, *picture* 133.5, *draw* 143.13, *means of identification* 184.3, *recording* 185.6, *record* 185.13, *image* 187.3, *represent* 187.10, *impression* 264.7, *appear* 264.12, *borrow illegally* 476.12, *infringe* 479.17, *unauthenticity* 722.4, *simulation* 733.4, *simulate* 733.16, *abide by* 781.12, *twin* 789.5, *double* 789.14, *replica* 797.7, *repeat* 797.15
copy after *imitate* 736.9
copy aide *office assistant* 69.6
copybook *schoolbook* 48.15, *customary* 780.9
copycat *imitator* 736.6, *imitation* 736.8, *imitate* 736.9, *conformist* 781.6
copy DNA (cDNA) *nucleotide* 12.10
copyedit *publish* 174.19, *report* 175.9, *interpret* 365.12, *rectify* 807.22
copyediting *stage of book production* 174.7, *rectification* 807.8
copyeditor *book publishing personnel* 174.12, *print journalist* 175.5, *interpreter* 365.6, *improver* 807.11, *repairer* 809.5
copyhold [Brit] *historical property terms* 470.3, *propertied* 470.9
copying *(act of) drawing* 143.2, *illegal borrowing* 476.3, *infringement* 479.6, *simulation* 733.4, *imitation* 736.1, *imitative* 736.7, *repetition* 797.1
copyist *visual artist* 133.6
copy nature *seem true* 721.26
copyreader *print journalist* 175.5
copyright *means of identification* 184.3, *property* 470.1, *limit* 620.1, 620.7, 830.13, *originate* 737.7, *limitation* 830.2
copyrighted *propertied* 470.9, *limited* 620.5, *authentic* 737.6, *restrained* 830.9
copyrighted work *original* 737.2
copyright page *or* **copyright notice** *book part* 174.5
copywriter *publicizer* 173.11
coq au vin *notable international dishes* 90.40
coquet *court* 299.26, *be capricious* 381.6
coquetry *courtship* 299.10, *caprice* 381.1
coquette *lover* 299.11, *capricious person* 381.3, *charmer* 700.6
coquettish *amorous* 299.18, *capricious* 381.4
coquettish glance *communication of love* 299.6
coquettishly *amorously* 299.30
coquettishness *capriciousness* 381.2
coquito *Trees and Shrubs* 43
coracle *Ships and Boats* 690
CORAL *Programming Languages* 15
coral *red* 257.5
coral island *island* 572.2
coralline *coelenterate* 39.25
coralloid *coelenterate* 39.25
coral-pink *red* 257.5
coral reef *island* 572.2, *shallowness* 599.1, *hidden danger* 813.3
Coral Sea *Oceans and Seas* 571
coral tree *Trees and Shrubs* 43

coram judice [L] *litigated* 54.22, *in litigation* 54.34
cor anglais *Musical Instruments* 142
corbel *Architectural Elements* 134, *arch* 134.5
cord *timber* 43.3, *electricity* 106.5, *Fabrics and Fibers* 130, *power supplier* 514.14, *General Units* 589, *line* 754.5
cordage *timber* 43.3, *tackle* 754.6
cordate *of leaves* 41.18
Cordelia *Planets and Their Satellites* 7
cordial *friendly* 62.5, *alcoholic drink* 93.9, *tonic* 115.8, *stimulant* 221.5, *sweet drink* 222.4, *sensitive* 267.3, *likable* 271.6, *benevolent* 305.7, *goodwilled* 373.10, *sociable* 407.7, 408.11, *agreeing* 462.6
cordiality *friendship* 62.1, *good feeling* 266.4, *amiability* 271.3, *benevolence* 305.1, *goodwill* 373.4, *sociability* 407.2, 408.1, *good company* 408.9, *agreement* 462.1
cordially *amicably* 62.13, *pleasantly* 271.12, *benevolently* 305.13, *sociably* 408.19, *agreeably* 462.14
cordial relations *coexistence* 73.3
cordial welcome *welcome* 408.10
cordillera *mountain* 569.1, *mountain range* 569.3
cordite *explosive* 78.13, *propellant* 696.9
cordless phone *telephone* 169.10
cordon *Architectural Elements* 134
cordon bleu *prizewinner* 127.8
cordon bleu chef *cook* 91.3
cordon sanitaire *prophylaxis* 115.4, *hygiene* 116.1, *sanitary precaution* 810.8
cords *pants* 100.14
corduroy *Fabrics and Fibers* 130, *rough thing* 544.2
corduroys *pants* 100.14
cordwainer [Arch] *clothier* 100.37
cordwood *timber* 43.3, *wood* 131.3
core 612.2, 612.7; *cook* 91.10, *nuclear power* 106.8, *meaning* 361.1, *insides* 577.3, *the depths* 598.2, *deeper* 598.10, *interior* 611.1, 611.7, *essential content* 723.2, *middle* 772.1, 772.9, *chief thing* 799.3
core-city *urban* 567.14
core curriculum *subject* 48.3
core enzyme *enzyme* 12.11
core of one's being *seat of feelings* 266.7
coreopsis *Flowers* 42
corespondent *litigant* 54.4, *divorce court* 66.3, *accused person* 442.4
Corfu *Islands* 572
corgi *Breeds of Dogs* 35
coriaceous *hard* 547.8
coriander *Herbs and Spices* 91
Corinthian *column* 134.6
Coriolis force *atmospheric process* 9.9
cork *timber* 43.3, *fishing tackle* 154.7, *sound reducer* 233.5, *detention* 471.2, *detain* 471.9, *stopper* 584.3, *stop* 584.14, *cover* 613.2, 613.24
corkage *fee* 494.3
corked *unpalatable* 223.6, *stopped* 584.9, *covered* 613.19, *imperfect* 806.5
corker [Inf] *good thing* 445.9, *successful thing* 409.8
corking [Inf] *great* 445.14
cork oak *Trees and Shrubs* 43
corkscrew *opener* 583.2, *coil*

632.2, *convolute* 632.6, *extractor* 711.9
cork tip *tobacco* 121.23
cork-tip *tobacco* 121.33
corkwood *Trees and Shrubs* 43
corky *dried-up* 560.9, *spoiled* 808.9
Corlay *Horse and Pony Breeds* 159
corm *garden plant* 17.10, *stem* 41.5, *flowering plant* 42.2
cormorant *water bird* 36.9
cormous *of plants* 41.14
corn *crop* 16.8, *animal feed* 16.12, *cereal grass* 45.4, *animal food* 90.2, *ulcer* 114.18, *snow* 162.28, *hard substance* 542.3, *bulge* 634.2
Corn Belt *farmland* 16.3
corn bread *bread* 90.10
corncob *cereal grass* 45.4
corncrib *farm building* 16.4
cornea *eye* 19.9, 242.3
corned *preserved* 815.12
corned beef *beef* 90.24
cornel *Trees and Shrubs* 43
cornemuse *Musical Instruments* 142
corneous *hard* 542.5
corner *angle* 6.37, 628.1, *automobile racing terms* 146.3, *boxing terms* 152.3, *wrestling terms* 152.10, *rock face* 161.6, *ski* 162.35, *soccer* 163.7, *attack successfully* 418.25, *instrument of punishment* 454.13, *monopoly* 469.4, *possess* 469.14, *buy in* 481.13, *road attribute* 687.3, *deviating course* 698.2, *predicament* 725.3, *cause difficulties* 824.22
corner area *stadium* 163.2
cornerback *defense* 155.9
cornered *angular* 628.7, *endangered* 811.10
corner flag *stadium* 163.2
cornering *purchasing* 481.2, *miscellaneous automotive terms* 687.14
cornering of the market *monopoly* 469.4
corner judge *judo* 152.13
corner kick *or* **corner** *soccer play* 163.5
cornerstone *Architectural Elements* 134, *supporting part* 605.3, *essential content* 723.2, *gist* 799.4
corner store *store* 483.8
corner the market *trade in* 457.8, *possess* 469.14, *buy in* 481.13
cornet *Musical Instruments* 142, *Card Games* 168, *cone* 633.5
cornett *Musical Instruments* 142
corn exchange *market* 483.1
cornfield *farmland* 16.3
cornflakes *cereal* 90.12
cornflower *Flowers* 42, *blue thing* 261.3
corn god *minor deity* 82.2
cornhusk *casing* 613.9
cornice *Architectural Elements* 134, *rock face* 161.6, *architectural summit* 600.4
corniculate *toothed* 549.13
Cornish *Breeds of Fowl* 16
Cornish accent *regional pronunciation* 205.7
Cornish rex *Breeds of Cats* 35
Cornish stone *material* 129.2
corn market *market* 483.1
cornmeal *basic cooking ingredient* 91.8
corn oil *basic cooking ingredient* 91.8
corn pone *bread* 90.10
cornrows *coiffure* 530.8

corn snow *snow* 9.30
cornstarch *basic cooking ingredient* 91.8, *thickener* 561.12
corn sugar *Common Sugars* 12
cornu *Musical Instruments* 142
cornucopia *fertility* 22.1, *plenty* 90.4, 97.2, *quantity* 105.5, *opulence* 485.3
cornute *or* **cornuted** *toothed* 549.13
corny [Inf] *humorous* 277.9
corolla *flower part* 42.3
corollary *theory* 6.62, *judgment* 341.1, *effect* 676.1, *appendage* 748.4, *formula* 780.7, *concomitant* 794.4
corona *sun* 7.15, *tobacco* 121.23, *Architectural Elements* 134, *highlight* 246.12, *circular thing* 631.3
Corona Australis *Constellations* 7
Corona Borealis *Constellations* 7
coronach [Scot, Irish] *lament* 280.2
corona discharge *flickering light* 246.10
coronary *cardiovascular disease* 114.13
coronary heart disease *cardiovascular disease* 114.13
coronary thrombosis *cardiovascular disease* 114.13
coronate *gain authority* 52.15
coronated *authorized* 52.11
coronation *acquisition of authority* 52.5, *ceremony* 405.3, *formal occasion* 406.4, *commission* 833.1
coroner *person dealing with the dead* 29.8, *law enforcement officer* 53.8, *questioner* 333.9
coroner's court *type of court* 54.9
coroner's jury *jury* 54.11, 341.6
coronet *headdress* 100.35, *Heraldic Terms* 184, *circular thing* 631.3
Corporal *military title* 72.8
corporal *punitive* 454.18, *material* 524.7
corporality *material world* 524.1
corporally *materially* 524.9
corporal punishment 454.11; *ramming* 695.3
Corporal/Specialist 4 *US Military Ranks* 58
corporate 480.17; *jointly possessing* 469.12, *united* 752.10
corporate bond *paper money* 484.14
corporate income *earnings* 467.5
corporately *cliquishly* 59.32, *one and all* 759.12
corporate plan *plan* 387.1
corporate sector *economy* 56.3
corporate tax *tax* 494.5
corporation *company* 480.7, *association* 480.8, *materialization* 524.2, *collection* 757.3
corporation tax *tax* 494.5
corporative state *body politic* 50.3
corporeal *bodily* 19.18, *material* 524.7, *real* 719.6
corporeal entity *body* 19.1
corporeality *material world* 524.1, *reality* 719.1
corporealize *be material* 524.8
corporeity *material world* 524.1
corps *team* 59.9, *force* 59.10, *army unit* 77.14
corps à corps [Fr] *fencing movements* 153.3
corps de ballet *ballet dancer* 135.5
corpse *dead person* 29.7, *remainder* 750.1

corpselike *deathly* 29.15, *emaciated* 595.10

corpses Phobias 283

corps of engineers *army commands* 77.13

corpulence *heaviness* 538.1, *fatness* 579.5, *thickness* 594.1, *round body* 633.2

corpulent *heavy* 538.9, *fat* 579.15, *thick* 594.5, *well-rounded* 633.8

corpus *compilation* 59.14, *compendium* 204.3, *matter* 524.4, *whole thing* 759.2

Corpus Christi Christian Holy Days and Seasons 85

corpuscle *cell* 13.15, *little thing* 580.3

corpuscular *tiny* 580.9

corpus juris *law* 53.1

Corpus Juris Civilis *the Law* 53.2

corradiate *focus* 702.11

corral *farm building* 16.4, *practice livestock farming* 16.20, *mammal dwelling* 35.21, *herd* 59.29, *enclose* 584.16, 619.6, *enclosed area* 619.2

corraling *assembling* 59.12

correct 350.4, 429.8, 721.13; *of language* 5.35, *remedy* 115.16, *inform* 170.11, *accurate* 350.3, *be accurate* 350.5, 721.22, *ceremonious* 404.23, *formal* 406.6, *good-mannered* 410.7, *proper* 429.10, *put right* 429.14, *moral* 431.9, *punish* 454.22, *moderate* 521.7, *counterbalance* 743.8, *orderly* 765.13, *tidy* 765.21, *conformist* 781.10, *make conform* 781.13, *infallible* 805.10, *perfect* 805.19, *rectify* 807.22, *repaired* 809.6, *repair* 809.10

correct behavior *formality* 406.1

corrected *counterbalanced* 743.6

correct English *grammar* 5.28

correct for *equate* 6.88

correcting *counterbalanced* 743.6, *improving* 807.14

correcting faults *repair* 809.1

correction *remedy* 115.1, *righting wrong* 429.6, *punishment* 454.1, *moderation* 521.1, *counterbalance* 743.2, *rectification* 807.8, *repair* 809.1

correctional *communal* 2.12, *punitive* 454.18

correctional institution *social institution* 2.8, *prison* 55.1

correction fluid *that which makes invisible* 245.2

corrections officer *prison officer* 55.8

correctitude *formality* 406.1, *properness* 429.5, *perfection* 805.1

corrective *remedy* 115.1, *remedial* 115.14, *punitive* 454.18, *counteracting* 510.6, *counterbalanced* 743.6

correctively 743.11; *remedially* 115.19, *counter* 510.8

corrective training *imprisonment* 55.4

correctly 429.16, 721.29; *grammatically* 5.48, *gymnastically* 157.13, *accurately* 350.6, *ceremoniously* 404.38, *formally* 406.12, *genteelly* 410.14, *morally* 431.15, *decorously* 534.10

correctness 350.2; *reasoning* 6.61, *gymnastics* 157.1, *formality* 406.1, *good manners* 410.2, *right* 429.2, *properness* 429.5, *morals* 431.2, *refinement* 534.1, *trueness* 721.4, *orderliness* 765.5, *perfection* 805.1

corrector *punisher* 454.16, *improver* 807.11

correct speech *standard language* 5.6

correlate 729.9; *equate* 6.88, *answer to* 334.22, *correspond* 606.8, *symmetrize* 626.6, *exchange* 673.5, *correspond to* 727.10, *conform* 735.27

correlated *corresponding* 606.6, *interrelated* 727.7, *correlative* 729.6

correlating *correlative* 729.6

correlation 6.58, 729.3; *correspondence* 334.8, 606.2, *symmetry* 626.1, *exchange* 673.1, *relatedness* 727.1, *interrelatedness* 727.3, *conformity* 735.7, *mutual relationship* 827.3

correlational *symmetrical* 626.4, *correlative* 729.6, *joint* 827.10

correlation coefficient *correlation* 6.58

correlative 729.6; *correspondent* 334.16, *corresponding* 606.6, *conforming* 735.17, *concurrent* 794.13

correlatively 729.12; *correspondingly* 334.27, *in exchange* 673.6, *conformingly* 735.37

correlativeness *correspondence* 606.2, *correlation* 729.3

correlativity *correlation* 729.3

correspond 169.19, 606.8; *communicate* 170.12, *recount* 202.16, *answer to* 334.22, *compatible* 462.12, *correlate* 729.9, *be equivalent* 730.15, *be similar* 733.12, *be in accord* 735.21, *conform* 735.27, 781.11

correspondence 169.2, 334.8, 606.2; *communications* 169.1, *record* 185.1, *compatibility* 462.3, *symmetry* 626.1, *relatedness* 727.1, *correlation* 729.3, *equivalence* 730.3, *comparability* 733.2, *accord* 735.1, *conformity* 735.7, 781.1, *equality* 740.1

correspondence course *educational system* 48.2

correspondent 169.3, 334.16, 606.3; *informer* 170.8, *news reporting* 171.5, *print journalist* 175.5, *descriptive writer* 202.10, *answerer* 334.10, *corresponding* 606.6, *symmetrical* 626.4, *correlative* 729.6, *equivalent* 730.9, *similarity* 733.1, *counterpart* 733.5, *similar* 733.7, *comparable* 733.8, *conforming* 735.17, *equal* 740.8

correspondently *correspondingly* 606.10, *correlatively* 729.12, *equivalently* 730.20, *similarly* 733.17, *conformingly* 735.37

corresponding 606.6; *correspondent* 334.16, *compatible* 462.8, *symmetrical* 626.4, *interrelated* 727.7, *correlative* 729.6, *equivalent* 730.9, *similar* 733.7, *harmonious* 735.11, *conforming* 735.17, 781.8, *equal* 740.8

correspondingly 334.27, 606.10; *compatibly* 462.16, *symmetrically* 626.7, *relevantly* 727.11, *correlatively* 729.12, *equivalently* 730.20, *similarly* 733.17, *harmoniously* 735.31, *conformingly* 735.37, *equally* 740.13

correspond to 727.10; *be equal* 740.11

correspond with *correspond* 169.19, *be convenient* 803.5

corridor *room* 60.9, *regions* 564.2

corridors of power *the power structure* 68.12

corrie [Scot] *valley* 572.8

Corriedale Breeds of Sheep 16

Corriente Breeds of Cattle 16

corrigible *improvable* 807.13

corrival *opponent* 828.10, *discordant* 828.12

corroborate *identify* 184.11, *attest* 189.22, *prove* 331.17, 336.9, 339.14, *assent* 346.6, *justify* 441.12, *permit* 502.6, *give moral support* 605.18, *establish reality* 719.12, *authenticate* 721.24

corroborated *identified* 184.9, *attested* 189.13, *proven* 331.13, *authenticated* 721.17

corroboration *identification* 184.1, *attestation* 189.2, *proof* 331.4, 336.2, 339.2, *assent* 346.1, *defense* 441.2, *permission* 502.1, *moral support* 605.7, *authentication* 721.8

corroborative *proven* 331.13, *verificatory* 336.6, *evidential* 339.8, *vindicatory* 441.7, *supportive* 605.11

corroborative or **corroboratory** or **corroborating** *attestive* 189.12

corroboratively *verifiably* 336.11, *supportively* 605.20

corroborator *affirmer* 189.9, *supporter* 605.9

corroboratorily *supportively* 605.20

corrode *erode* 554.14, *decrease* 747.7, *subtract* 749.6, *disintegrate* 758.6, *decay* 808.16, *eat away* 808.19

corroded *reduced* 749.5, *disintegrated* 758.3

corrosion *deformation* 14.16, *agent of destruction* 523.7, *wearing away* 554.2, *subtraction* 749.1, *disintegration* 758.1, *decay* 808.6

corrosive *detrimental* 446.8, *agent of destruction* 523.7, *decrescent* 747.6

corrosively *decreasingly* 749.9, *destructively* 758.9

corrugate *make rough* 544.11, *pleat* 637.8, *furrow* 638.5

corrugated *rough* 544.5, *coarse* 544.6, *folded* 637.5, *furrowed* 638.3

corrugated iron *rough thing* 544.2

corrugation *roughness* 544.1, *pleat* 637.2, *furrow* 638.1

corrupt *offending* 53.25, *unclean* 112.8, *dirty* 112.11, *bribe* 178.18, *immoral* 430.11, 432.9, *demoralize* 432.15, *evil* 446.7, *be evil* 446.10, *depraved* 448.10, *be wicked* 448.13, *deprave* 448.14, *buy off* 481.17, *disintegrate* 758.6, *decay* 808.16, *make worse* 808.17, *pervert* 808.22

corrupted *worded* 5.38, *disintegrated* 758.3

corrupting *unhygienic* 114.27

corruption *uncleanness* 112.2, *unpleasant-smelling thing* 227.2, *immorality* 432.1, *evil* 446.1, *depravity* 448.2, *bribery* 481.5, *disintegration* 758.1, *moral deterioration* 808.3, *physical deterioration* 808.4

corruptive *detrimental* 446.8

corruptly *immorally* 432.18, *evilly* 446.12, *unvirtuously* 448.16

corsage *flower* 42.1, *part of garment* 100.27

corsair *plunderer* 479.9, Sailing Ships and Boats 690

corselet *historic armor* 419.8

corset *underwear* 100.22, *contractor* 582.6, *body support* 605.6, *means of restraint* 830.6

Corsica Islands 572

Corsican Breeds of Sheep 16

corslet *historic armor* 419.8

cortege *funeral* 31.4, *attendance* 794.5

cortège *procession* 774.6

cortex *stem* 41.5, *exteriority* 610.2, *casing* 613.9, *animal covering* 613.15

corticoid Human Hormones 12

corticolous *lichenoid* 47.21

corticosteroid *hormone* 12.16

corticosterone Human Hormones 12

cortisol Human Hormones 12

cortisone Human Hormones 12

Cortland Apple Varieties 44

coruscate *light up* 246.20

coruscating *bright* 246.14

coruscation *quality of light* 246.2

corvée *work* 122.1

corvette *warship* 77.21, Sailing Ships and Boats 690

corvine *avian* 36.19

Corvus Constellations 7

corydalis Flowers 42

corymb *flower head* 42.4

corymbose *of flowers* 42.11

coryza *respiratory disease* 114.12

Cosa Nostra *villain* 448.5

cosecant (cosec or **csc)** *trigonometric function* 6.50

cosh *blunt weapon* 78.5, *instrument of punishment* 454.13, *club* 695.15

così-così [Ital] *mediocre* 742.7

cosign *contract* 459.8

cosign a loan *be in debt* 488.9

cosign a note *guarantee* 458.13

cosignatory *promise maker* 458.6

cosignature *ratification* 459.4

cosigned *guaranteeing* 458.9, *contractual* 459.7

cosigner *promise maker* 458.6, *contractor* 459.6, *debtor* 488.6

cosine (cos) *trigonometric function* 6.50

cosiness *littleness* 580.1

cosmetic *beautifying* 530.13, *superficial* 599.4

cosmetically *beautifully* 530.16

cosmetician *beautician* 530.11

cosmetics 530.4; *face color* 251.9

cosmetic surgery 530.2

cosmetic tool 530.5

cosmic *astronomical* 7.33, *psychic* 86.17, *universal* 778.10

cosmicality *generality* 778.1

cosmically *astronomically* 7.36, *universally* 778.23

cosmic background *universe* 7.3

cosmic consciousness *psychic power* 86.4

cosmic dust *interstellar matter* 7.7, *powder* 553.9

cosmic rays *interstellar matter* 7.7, *radioactivity* 10.58

cosmic vibration *occult and psychic phenomena* 86.7

cosmochemist *astronomer* 7.2

cosmochemistry *astronomy* 7.1

cosmogenist *astronomer* 7.2

cosmogeny *astronomy* 7.1

cosmoid scale *fish characteristic* 38.8

cosmological *astronomical* 7.33

cosmologically *astronomically* 7.36

cosmological model *universe* 7.3, *physical law* 10.4

cosmologist *philosopher* 4.9, *astronomer* 7.2

cosmology Branches of Philosophy 4, *astronomy* 7.1
cosmonaut *space travel* 7.29, *space traveler* 563.10
cosmonautics *aerospace research* 7.27
cosmopolitan *refined* 534.5, *internationalist* 566.9, *general* 778.9, *universal* 778.10
cosmopolitanism *internationalism* 566.5, *generality* 778.1
cosmos *universe* 7.3, Flowers 42, *real world* 719.2, *whole thing* 759.2
Cossack *horse person* 159.14
cosset *comfort* 214.14, *love* 299.21, *sustain* 825.25
cosseted *pleased* 214.9
cost *account* 493.9, *price* 494.1, *cost a lot* 496.9, *measure* 589.20
cost(s) 491.3
costa Human Bones 19
cost a bundle [Inf] *cost a lot* 496.9
cost accountant *accountant* 493.6
cost accounting *accounts* 493.4
cost a fortune *cost a lot* 496.9
cost a lot 496.9
cost an arm and a leg *cost a lot* 496.9
cost a packet [Inf] *cost a lot* 496.9
cost a pretty penny [Inf] *cost a lot* 496.9
costar *act* 136.34, 137.20
Costa Rica Countries 566
costarring *starring* 137.18
costed *accounted* 493.8
costermonger or **coster** [Brit] *peddler* 482.9
costing nothing *given* 472.8
costive *self-restrained* 455.6, *retentive* 471.5, *condensed* 540.7, *obstructed* 584.8
costively *densely* 540.10, *impermeably* 584.17
costliness 496.1; *price* 494.1
costly 496.7, 500.6; *grand* 404.22, *opulent* 485.10
costmary Herbs and Spices 91
cost next to nothing *be cheap* 497.13
cost of living *cost(s)* 491.3
cost-of-living *negotiated* 57.16
cost-of-living adjustment *bargaining terms* 57.10
cost-of-living index *economic indicator* 56.4, *cost(s)* 491.3
cost one dear *cost a lot* 496.9
costs *liability* 454.6
cost the earth [Inf] *cost a lot* 496.9
costume 100.10; *suit* 100.16, *make clothing* 100.44, *cover* 181.4
costume ball *dance* 135.1
costumed *dressed* 100.38, *disguised* 181.9
costume designer *clothier* 100.37, *producer* 136.28, *filmmaker* 137.14
costume drama *program* 172.10
costume jewelry *jewelry* 532.6
costume party *cover* 181.4, *party* 408.6
costumer *clothier* 100.37, *producer* 136.28, *filmmaker* 137.14
costumery *costume* 100.10
costumes *motion-picture studio* 137.7
costumier *clothier* 100.37
costumier or **costumière** *producer* 136.28
cosy *undersized* 580.8
cot *type of bed* 101.9
cotangent (cot or **ctn)** *trigonometric function* 6.50
cote *cage* 60.15

Côte d'Ivoire Countries 566
co-tenant *possessor* 469.10
Cotentin Breeds of Sheep 16
coterie *group* 59.8, 623.5, *fashionable elite* 536.4, *social class* 777.5
coterminous *juxtaposed* 586.9
cothurnus *costume* 100.10, *tragedy* 136.10
cothurnuses *shoes* 100.30
cotillion or **cotillon** *dance* 135.1
Cotopaxi Mountains and Hills 569
Cotswold Breeds of Sheep 16
Cotswold Hills Mountains and Hills 569
cottage *house* 60.4, *architectural structure* 134.4, *property* 470.1
cottager [Brit] *countryman* 61.8
cotter pin *fastener* 754.7
cotton *crop* 16.8, Fabrics and Fibers 130
Cotton Belt *farmland* 16.3
Cotton Bowl *football* 155.1
cotton or **cottonseed cake** *animal feed* 16.12
cotton mill *factory* 124.8
cotton paper *paper* 104.5
cotton seeds *refuse* 802.5
cotton to [Inf] *like* 299.22
cotton to or **on to** [Inf] *seek friendship* 62.11
cottonwood Trees and Shrubs 43
cottony *smooth* 552.9
cottony cloud *cloud appearance* 9.19
cotyledon *leaf* 41.6, *seed* 41.9
couch 101.7; *mammal dwelling* 35.21, *natural habitat* 60.16, *furniture* 101.1, *fashion* 537.9, *be low* 597.20, *bring down* 716.14, *lie down* 716.21, *take it easy* 819.3
couch, the [Inf] *psychotherapy* 108.4
couchant Heraldic Terms 184, *prostrate* 597.11, *recumbent* 603.7
couch potato [Inf] *nonworker* 415.4, *sedentary person* 678.3
cough *saliva* 25.9, *salivate* 25.25, *symptom* 114.3, *respiratory disease* 114.12, *hoarseness* 238.2, *sound hoarse* 238.8
coughing *saliva* 25.9, *salivating* 25.18
cough up *salivate* 25.25
cough up [Inf] *relinquish* 392.3, *pay* 489.16, *settle accounts* 493.11, *restore* 809.12
could be *be possible* 836.8
could not care less *be incurious* 322.5
couldn't care less *be insensitive* 268.6, *be indifferent* 289.12
couldn't-care-less *imprudent* 286.7
coulee *gulf* 587.3
couloir *rock face* 161.6, *valley* 572.8, *gulf* 587.3
coulomb Scientific and Technical Units 589
coulombs Fields of Measurement 589
Coulomb's law Classical Physical Laws 10
coulometer Fields of Measurement 589
coulometry Fields of Measurement 589
coulter *sharp-edged thing* 549.6
coumarone resin *resin* 562.6
council 833.4; *party* 59.3, *conference* 59.5, *representative body* 79.2, *management board* 126.2, *advisory body* 176.6, *place for*

conversation 210.5, *place of judgment* 341.3
Council for Mutual Economic Assistance (COMECON) *economic organization* 56.6
councilor *union member* 57.6
councilor or **councillor** *delegate* 79.1
counsel *lawyer* 54.5, *psychologize* 108.41, *direct* 126.11, *advice* 176.1, *consultation* 176.4, *advise* 176.9, 825.27, *persuade* 178.15, *warning* 287.5, 814.1, *caution* 287.15, *influence* 508.11, *warn* 814.8, *support* 825.2
counselable *warning* 814.6
counseled *warned* 814.7
counseling *psychotherapy* 108.4, *treatment* 110.7, *advice* 176.1, *advisory* 176.7, *persuasion* 178.1
Counselor God the Holy Ghost 82.10
counselor *sage* 4.11, *lawyer* 54.5, *employer* 57.3, *mediator* 75.2, *representative* 75.3, *psychologist* 108.33, *adviser* 176.5, 825.14, *motivator* 178.11, 508.6, *judge* 341.5, *warner* 814.5
counselor-at-law *lawyer* 54.5
count 784.3; *numeration* 6.10, *enumerate* 6.85, *nobleman* 70.1, *boxing techniques* 152.5, *accusation* 442.1, *measure* 589.20, *total* 738.4, *quantify* 738.7, *add* 748.11, *include* 763.5, *number* 783.9, 784.13, *be important* 799.13
countable *numerable* 6.70, *calculable* 784.8
count as *take a substitute* 672.7
count calories *taste* 92.24, *eat less* 118.9, *become thin* 595.15
count down *prepare for action* 388.18
counted *quantitative* 738.6
counted on the fingers of one hand *few* 796.5
countenance *external appearance* 264.5, *approval* 437.1, *approve* 437.14, *permit* 502.6, *bear* 605.17, *face* 621.6, *patronage* 825.9, *advise* 825.27
counter 339.13, 419.3, 510.8, 784.6; *discuss* 4.22, *computing terms* 15.22, *be at war* 76.32, *ice-skating techniques* 162.16, *negational* 190.9, *negate* 190.16, *negatively* 190.22, *countercharge* 332.9, *parry* 419.27, *retaliation* 420.1, *retaliate* 420.4, *stall* 483.9, *counteraction* 510.1, *counteracting* 510.6, *counteract* 510.7, *inverse* 608.2, 608.6, *invert* 608.7, *reversely* 608.10, *timekeeper* 646.7, *reversed* 680.13, *opposite* 731.3, *diametrically* 731.6, *counterbalanced* 743.6, *oppositional* 828.11, *be contrary* 828.16, *object* 828.18, *contrariwise* 828.24
counteraccusation *countercharge* 332.3
counteract 510.7, 828.21; *protest* 507.1, *abolish* 523.11, *reverse* 671.9, *affect* 676.7, *reciprocate* 729.7, *counterbalance* 743.8, *hinder* 826.15, *cancel out* 834.8
counteractant 510.5; *remedial* 115.14
counteracted *counterbalanced* 743.6
counteracting 510.6; *reciprocal* 729.4, *counterbalanced* 743.6, *oppositional* 828.11, *canceled* 834.5

counteractingly *reciprocally* 729.10
counteraction 510.1; *countercharge* 332.3, *counter* 419.3, *retaliation* 420.1, *protest* 507.1, *reversion* 671.1, *effect* 676.1, *countermotion* 680.6, *reciprocity* 729.1, *equalization* 740.4, *counterbalance* 743.2, *restoration* 809.2, *hindrance* 826.1, *countermeasure* 828.7, *canceling out* 834.3
counteractive *refuting* 332.6, *protesting* 507.5, *counteracting* 510.6, *reciprocal* 729.4, *counterbalanced* 743.6, *hindering* 826.12, *oppositional* 828.11, *canceled* 834.5
counteractively *counter* 510.8, *reciprocally* 729.10, *in compensation* 743.10, *with delay* 826.22
counteragent *counteractant* 510.5
counterargument *evidence* 54.15, *countercharge* 332.3, *defense* 441.2, *countermeasure* 828.7
counterattack 418.24; *be at war* 76.32, *fencing movements* 153.3, *fence* 153.7, *military attack* 418.2, *opposing force* 510.2, *deflection* 701.3, *countermeasure* 828.7, *counteract* 828.21
counterattacking 418.15; *fencing* 153.6
counterbalance 743.2, 743.8; *neutralization* 90.4, *counteract* 510.7, 828.21, *change* 512.12, *weighing instrument* 538.7, *symmetry* 626.1, *symmetrize* 626.6, *make the same* 730.16, *equalize* 740.12, *canceling out* 834.3, *cancel out* 834.8
counterbalanced 743.6; *symmetrical* 626.4
counterbalancing *counterbalanced* 743.6
counterblast *countercharge* 332.3, 332.9, *counterstatement* 334.5, *answer back* 334.19, *counterevidence* 339.5, *counter* 339.13, *retaliation* 420.1, *opposing force* 510.2, *counterbalance* 743.8
counterblasted *retaliatory* 334.13
countercathexis *cathexis* 108.32
counterchange *reciprocate* 729.7
countercharge 332.3, 332.9; *counterstatement* 334.5, *answer back* 334.19, *counterevidence* 339.5, *counter* 339.13, *retaliate* 420.4, *accusation* 442.1, *accuse* 442.8
countercharged *retaliatory* 334.13, *accused* 442.5
countercharm *neutralization* 510.4
countercheck *countermeasure* 828.7, *counteract* 828.21
counterclaim *litigation* 54.1, *countercharge* 332.3, 332.9, *counterevidence* 339.5, *counter* 339.13, *petition* 505.2, 505.11
counterclaimant *requester* 505.5
counterclockwise *reversed* 680.13, *clockwise* 682.18, 697.17
counterconditioning *conditioning* 108.24
counterculture *dissentience* 347.3
countercurrent *flow* 570.4
counterdemonstrator *protester* 507.4
countered *fencing* 153.6
counter emf *electric potential* 10.40
counterevidence 339.5; *evidence* 54.15, 336.3

counterevident 339.10
counterexample *philosophical term* 4.7
counterfactual *philosophical term* 4.7
counterfeit *misrepresent* 193.17, *hypocritical* 330.10, *act dishonestly* 479.18, *monetize* 484.24, *artificial* 720.12, *unauthenticity* 722.4, *unauthentic* 722.9, *simulated* 733.11, *simulate* 733.16, *copy* 736.2, 736.10, *imitation* 736.8
counterfeited *misrepresentative* 193.14
counterfeiter *one who misrepresents* 193.9, *dishonest person* 479.11, *imitator* 736.6
counterfeiting *adulteration* 188.2, *misrepresentation* 193.4, *dishonesty* 479.7
counterfeitly *unauthentically* 722.17, *imitatively* 733.20
counterfeit money *false money* 484.15, *depreciation* 490.4
counterfeitness *unauthenticity* 722.4
counterflux *flow* 570.4
counterfoil [Brit] *promise* 464.2, *acknowledgment of payment* 473.3, *receipt* 492.1
counterforce *counter* 419.3
counterglow *solar system* 7.14, *natural light* 246.4
counter image *inverted thing* 608.4
countering *fencing* 153.6, *counterevident* 339.10
counterintelligence *secretiveness* 182.3, *opposing force* 510.2
counterintuitive *unbelievable* 837.5
counterinvestment *cathexis* 108.32
counterirritant *antidote* 115.5, *counteractant* 510.5
counterman *attendant* 69.4
countermand *disavowal* 190.3, *disavow* 190.18, *command* 425.1, 425.10, *veto* 503.3, 503.9, *canceling out* 834.3, *cancel out* 834.8
countermanded *disavowing* 190.12, *commanding* 425.7
countermarch *be at war* 76.32, *reverse* 680.18
countermarching *countermotion* 680.6
countermeasure 828.7; *antidote* 115.5, *neutralization* 510.4, *counterbalance* 743.2, 743.8, *hindrance* 826.1
countermeasures *procedure* 387.2
countermine *plot* 387.6, 387.15, *retaliation* 420.1, *counteract* 828.21
countermotion 680.6
countermove *opposing force* 510.2, *countermeasure* 828.7
countermovement *countermotion* 680.6
counteroffensive *military attack* 418.2, *opposing force* 510.2
counterorder *veto* 503.3, 503.9, *dissent* 506.2, *canceling out* 834.3
counterpane [Arch] *bed covering* 613.7
counter parry *fencing movements* 153.3
counterpart 733.5; *correspondent* 606.3, *inverse* 608.2, *interrelation* 729.2, *equal* 740.7, *twin* 789.5
counterplot *plot* 387.6, 387.15, *retaliation* 420.1
counterpoint *meter* 139.10,

harmonic element 140.14, harmonization 735.2, collaboration 757.2
counterpoint rhythm *tempo* 140.22
counterpoise *neutralization* 510.4, *counteract* 510.7, *weighing instrument* 538.7, *be heavy* 538.12, *be in accord* 735.21, *equilibrium* 740.2, *equalizer* 740.5, *equalize* 740.12, *counterbalance* 743.2, 743.8, *canceling out* 834.3, *cancel out* 834.8
counterpoised *counterbalanced* 743.6
counterpose *counterbalance* 743.8
counterposed *counterbalanced* 743.6
counterposing *counterbalanced* 743.6
counterpressure *obstruction* 510.3
counterproductive *counteracting* 510.6
counterproposal *countermeasure* 828.7
counterpunch *retaliation* 420.1, *opposing force* 510.2
counterreformation *reversion* 671.1, *restoration* 809.2
counterreply *counterevidence* 339.5, *counter* 339.13
counterrevisionist *types of history* 3.2
counterrevolution *reversion* 671.1
counterrevolutionary *reactionary* 427.9, *opposer* 828.9
counter-riposte *or* counter-ripost *fencing movements* 153.3
counterscarp *fort* 419.13
countersign *symbol* 183.3, *sign* 183.19, *means of identification* 184.3, *identify oneself* 184.12, *verify* 336.8, *prove* 339.14, *assent* 346.6, *contract* 459.8, *promise* 464.10
countersignature *ratification* 459.4
countersigned *agreed* 346.5, *contractual* 459.7
countersigner *contractor* 459.6
counterspell *neutralization* 510.4
counterstaining *cell biology* 13.14
counterstate *answer back* 334.19, *counter* 339.13
counterstated *retaliatory* 334.13
counterstatement 334.5; *countercharge* 332.3, *counterevidence* 339.5
counterstrike *reciprocate* 729.7
counterstroke *counter* 419.3, *retaliation* 420.1, *deflection* 701.3, *reciprocity* 729.1
countersue *retaliate* 420.4
countersuit *litigation* 54.1, *retaliation* 420.1
countertenor *voice* 141.5
counterterrorist *reactionary* 427.9
counter to *counter* 510.8
countervail *counteract* 510.7, 828.21, *equalize* 740.12, *counterbalance* 743.8, *cancel out* 834.8
countervailing *counterbalanced* 743.6
counterweigh *be heavy* 538.12, *counterbalance* 743.8, *cancel out* 834.8
counterweighing *counterbalanced* 743.6
counterweight *neutralization* 510.4, *equalizer* 740.5, *counterbalance* 743.2, *canceling out* 834.3

counterweighted *counterbalanced* 743.6
counterword *catchword* 5.22
counterwork *countermeasure* 828.7
countess *nobleman* 70.1
Count Fleet *Notable Horses* 159
count for nothing *be unimportant* 800.18
count hands *number* 784.13
count heads *number* 784.13
counting *numeration* 6.10, *including* 763.3, *count* 784.3
counting calories *dieting* 118.2
counting hands *electing* 382.5
counting heads *electing* 382.5
counting house *treasury* 484.19
counting noses *electing* 382.5
counting system *number system* 6.7
counting up *mathematical addition* 748.2
countless *numberless* 795.8, *immeasurable* 798.6
countlessly *numerously* 795.13
countlessness *multiplicity* 795.2, *immeasurability* 798.2
count me out! *no!* 506.12
count noses *number* 784.13
count on *believe* 87.9, *hope* 281.10, *predict* 356.7, *think likely* 838.10
count one's beads *pray* 85.20
count one's blessings *give thanks* 310.7
count one's chickens before they are hatched *be rash* 286.8, *predict* 356.7
count out *exclude* 383.11, 764.7
countrified *local* 564.14
countrify *regionalize* 564.15
country 566.1; *nation* 18.14, *body politic* 50.3, *musical* 140.25, *region* 564.1, *administrative region* 564.4
country, the *countryside* 564.3
country-and-western *folk music* 140.7
country-and-western singer *singer* 141.4
country bumpkin *countryman* 61.8, *commoner* 71.1, *unskilled person* 128.3, *naive person* 821.2
country-club set, the *the rich* 485.7
country cousin *countryman* 61.8, *commoner* 71.1, *naive person* 821.2
country dance *dance* 135.1
country dancing *Dancing Types* 135
country dweller *countryman* 61.8, *naive person* 821.2
country gentleman *countryman* 61.8
country house *house* 60.4
countryman 61.8; *native* 566.7
country music *folk music* 140.7
country of origin *native country* 566.6
country road *road* 687.2
country rock *rock music* 140.6
countryside 564.3; *regions* 564.2
country town *town* 567.2
countrywide *universal* 778.10
countrywide circulation *publicity* 173.7
countrywoman *countryman* 61.8, *native* 566.7
count the hours *measure time* 646.14
count the minutes *measure time* 646.14
count up *add* 748.11, *number* 784.13
count with *subsume* 763.7
county *body politic* 50.3,

administrative region 564.4, administrative 564.13, urban 567.14, part 760.1
county board *representative body* 79.2
county court *type of court* 54.9
county hospital *hospital* 107.16
county jail *prison* 55.1
county library *library* 174.14
county map *map* 187.5
county seat *administrative headquarters* 564.5, *city* 567.1
county set, the [Brit] *the rich* 485.7
county tax *tax* 494.5
county town [Brit] *town* 567.2
coup *anarchy* 51.1, *acquisition of authority* 52.5, *workmanlike job* 127.6, *deed* 412.2, *revolution* 427.4, *taking over* 477.3, *replacement* 574.3, *sudden change* 665.3
coup de grâce *ender* 773.11
coup de grâce [Fr] *execution* 30.6, *deed* 412.2, *ruin* 523.4, *conclusion* 761.3
coup de main [Fr] *deed* 412.2, *military attack* 418.2
coup de maître [Fr] *masterpiece* 127.5
coup d'état *anarchy* 51.1, *acquisition of authority* 52.5, *deed* 412.2, *revolution* 427.4, *taking over* 477.3, *disorder* 507.2
coup de théâtre [Fr] *dramaturgy* 136.6
coup d'oeil [Fr] *look* 242.7
coupe *automobile* 687.6
coupé *fencing movements* 153.3
couped *Heraldic Terms* 184
couple 733.6; *have sex* 20.21, *Collective Names* 59, *marry* 64.19, *join* 609.10, *relate to* 727.9, *unite* 752.14, *connect* 754.13, *come together* 757.10, *two* 789.1, *pair* 789.13, *keep company with* 794.17, *few* 796.1
couple, a *plurality* 793.1
coupled *married* 64.16, *matched* 733.10, *connected* 754.11, *two* 789.8, *associated* 794.14
coupled with *additionally* 748.15
coupler *yoke* 754.8
couplet *part of poem* 139.9, *twosome* 789.3
coupling 20.19; *machine element* 14.8, *sexual intercourse* 20.9, *junction* 609.5, *connection* 754.1, *yoke* 754.8
coupling circuit *circuit* 14.37
coupon *promise* 464.2, *paper money* 484.14
coupon clipper *bargain hunter* 497.8
coupons *discounter* 497.7
courage 284.1; *proudness* 297.3, *tenacity* 376.4, *will* 376.5, *stamina* 377.4, *defiance* 416.1, *security* 464.1, *endurance* 516.4
courageous 284.9; *proud* 297.10, *tenacious* 376.9, *enduring* 377.9, *enterprising* 391.5, *defiant* 416.5, *strong in spirit* 516.11
courageous act 284.7
courageously 284.17; *proudly* 297.19, *defiantly* 416.9, *strongly* 516.17
courageousness *courage* 284.1, *tenacity* 376.4
courageous person 284.8
courante *Dances* 135, *Musical Forms* 140
Courantyne *Rivers* 570
courier *office assistant* 69.6, *horse*

person 159.14, *postal worker* 169.6, *messenger* 685.5, *transporter* 686.4, *speeder* 694.5
course 92.12, 679.2; *subject* 48.3, *dish* 90.7, *dieting* 92.6, *means* 102.1, *therapy* 115.12, *sports ground* 145.2, *sailing terms* 150.5, *racetrack* 159.12, *hunt* 160.12, 385.14, *educational topic* 328.4, *line of action* 399.4, *operation* 509.1, *tendency* 513.1, *river parts* 570.3, *flow* 570.4, 570.10, *layer* 588.1, *chronology* 646.2, *momentum* 677.2, *route* 691.2, *bearing* 697.2, *series* 770.3, *consecutiveness* 774.1
course listing *list* 785.1
course of action *procedure* 387.2, *operation* 509.1
course of law *legal process* 54.3
course of time *passage of time* 639.3, *duration* 642.1
courser *war-horse* 159.4, *hunting dog* 160.7, *hunter* 160.9, *speeder* 694.5
courses *bleeding* 25.10
coursing *hunting* 160.2, *flowing* 570.7
court 299.26; *law court* 54.8, *judge* 54.10, *courtroom* 54.12, *seek friendship* 62.11, *sports ground* 145.2, *basketball court* 148.3, *tennis court* 165.3, *lust after* 288.20, *be solicitous* 323.13, *aim at* 385.15, *cajole* 439.14, *offer* 504.11, *open space* 583.6, *enclosed area* 619.2, *attendance* 794.5
court award *liability* 454.6
court card *cards* 168.2
court case *accusation* 442.1
court costs *unfavorable verdict* 54.20
court disaster *be courageous* 284.14, *be rash* 286.8, *face danger* 811.12
court dress *formal clothing* 406.5
courteous 410.6; *friendly* 62.5, *likable* 271.6, *submissive* 298.10, *benevolent* 305.7, *thoughtful* 317.5, *solicitous* 323.8, *well-behaved* 399.15, *sociable* 408.11, *obeisant* 426.6, *showing respect* 435.7, *refined* 534.5, *degraded* 716.10
courteously 410.13; *amicably* 62.13, *submissively* 298.23, *benevolently* 305.13, *thoughtfully* 317.13, *well* 399.22, *sociably* 408.19, *obediently* 426.9, *respectfully* 435.19, *decorously* 534.10
courteousness *benevolence* 305.1, *thoughtfulness* 317.2, *courtesy* 410.1
courtesan *sexually immoral person* 432.8
courtesies 410.3
courtesy 410.1; *friendship* 62.1, *amiability* 271.3, *submissiveness* 298.3, *benevolent act* 305.5, *thoughtfulness* 317.2, *solicitude* 323.5, *good conduct* 399.5, *social success* 408.3, *obeisance* 426.3, *respectfulness* 435.3, *given* 472.8, *free of charge* 497.12, *refinement* 534.1
courtesy call *social gathering* 408.4
courtesy light *safety light* 246.7
court fine *liability* 454.6
courthouse *courtroom* 54.12, *building* 551.9, *municipal building* 567.13
courthouse wedding *wedding* 64.5

courting *courtship* 299.10, *tentative offer* 504.2
courting disaster *recklessness* 286.2
courtliness *courtesy* 410.1, *elegance* 527.1
courtly *courteous* 410.6, *courteously* 410.13, *elegant* 527.3, *cultured* 534.6
court-martial *type of court* 54.9, *military law* 58.7
court of appeals *type of court* 54.9
court of conscience *place of judgment* 341.3
court officer 54.7
court of general jurisdiction *law court* 54.8
court of justice *law court* 54.8
court of law *law court* 54.8
court of limited jurisdiction *law court* 54.8
court of original jurisdiction *law court* 54.8
court of record *law court* 54.8
court of sessions *law court* 54.8
court payment *liability* 454.6
court reporter *court officer* 54.7
courtroom 54.12
court sessions *legal process* 54.3
courtship 299.10
court sitting *legal process* 54.3
court tennis *Sporting Activities* 145, *tennis* 165.1
courtyard *enclosed area* 619.2
couscous *notable international dishes* 90.40
cousin *family member* 65.2
cousin-german *family member* 65.2
cousin once removed *family member* 65.2
cousin twice removed *family member* 65.2
couturier or **couturière** *clothier* 100.37
couvade *non-Christian ritual* 85.8
covalent *chemical compound* 11.4
covalent bond *chemical bond* 11.6
covalently *chemically* 11.42
covariance *parameter* 6.57
covariation *interrelatedness* 727.3
cove *Architectural Elements* 134, *inlet* 572.9, *concave land* 635.2
coven *witchcraft* 86.6
covenant *duty* 433.1, *promise* 458.1, 458.11, 464.2, *contract* 459.1, 459.8, 462.2, 462.11, *settlement* 735.6, *settle* 735.26, *agreement* 767.9, *rule* 780.1
covenantal *contractual* 459.7, *settled* 735.16
covenantally *contractually* 459.9
covenanted *contractual* 459.7, *guaranteed* 464.6
covenanter *contractor* 459.6, *assenter* 462.5
cover 181.4, 613.2, 613.24; *have sex* 20.21, *Collective Names* 59, *clothe* 100.43, *play defense* 155.19, *broadcast* 172.13, *report* 175.9, *concealment* 181.1, *conceal* 181.12, *obliteration* 186.1, *obliterate* 186.8, *recount* 202.16, *blinder* 243.7, *shade maker* 247.4, *opaque* 250.7, *interpret news* 365.17, *buffer* 419.22, *security* 464.1, *certify* 464.11, *extend* 563.14, *packet* 578.4, *contain* 578.20, *stopper* 584.3, *close* 584.12, *layer* 588.9, *top* 600.10, *base* 601.10, *be exterior* 610.13, *covering* 613.1, *shelter* 613.6, 812.4, *wrap* 619.7, *be a substitute* 672.6, *inset* 710.13, *fill* 761.11, *include* 763.5, *repair*

809.10, *protection* 810.2, *protect* 810.21
cover (over) *make dark* 247.10
cover (up) *make invisible* 245.7
cover a blade *row* 150.32
coverage 613.16; *news reporting* 171.5, *publicity* 173.7, *print journalism* 175.4, *range* 563.7, *size* 579.1, *inclusion* 763.1
coveralls *suit* 100.16
cover charge *fee* 494.3
cover crop *crop* 16.8
covered 613.19; *architectural* 134.12, *concealed* 181.8, *obliterated* 186.4, *private* 245.5, *opaque* 250.3, *guaranteed* 464.6, *containing* 578.18, *topped* 600.8, *safe* 810.16, *sheltered* 812.7
covered bridge *bridge* 691.7
covered market *marketplace* 483.7
covered over *covered* 613.19
covered up *covered* 613.19
covered wagon *wagon* 687.5
covered way *passage* 691.5
coverer 613.18
cover for 613.34; *be a substitute* 672.6
cover girl *attractive female* 529.5
cover ground *press on* 679.9
covering 610.8, 613.1, 613.21; *dressing* 100.2, *roof* 134.7, *blinder* 243.7, *external appearance* 264.5, *containing* 578.18, *stopper* 584.3, *coat* 588.3, *exteriority* 610.2, *including* 763.3
covering over *covering* 613.1
covering up *obliteration* 186.1, *covering* 613.1
coverlet *bed covering* 613.7
cover oneself *proceed with caution* 287.12
cover one's tracks *conceal oneself* 181.15
coversine (covers) *trigonometric function* 6.50
covert *mammal dwelling* 35.21, *dwelling* 36.4, *plumage* 36.7, *assemblage of birds* 36.18, *trees* 43.4, *natural habitat* 60.16, *occult* 86.16, *disguised* 181.9, *secretive* 182.9, *private* 245.5, *devious* 607.9, *secret* 611.13, *shelter* 613.6, 812.4, *concealed* 844.7
cover the ground *improve* 467.18
covertly *stealthily* 182.15, *deviously* 607.16, *secretly* 611.22, *latently* 844.15
covertness *secretiveness* 182.3, *deviousness* 607.4, *secrecy* 611.6
coverture [Form] *marriage* 64.1
coverup *beachwear* 100.23, *cosmetics* 530.4
cover-up 441.13; *cover* 181.4, *evasion* 181.5, *misrepresentation* 193.4
cover up *conceal* 181.12, *keep secret* 182.11, *obliterate* 186.8, *misrepresent* 193.17, *hide* 613.27
cover up for *protect* 810.21
cover with dust *dirty* 112.11
covet 288.18; *envy* 314.7, *be selfish* 444.6
coveted *desired* 288.10
coveter *desirer* 288.9
coveting *covetous* 288.14
covetingly *covetously* 288.28
covetous 288.14; *green-eyed* 260.11, *envious* 314.4, *selfish* 444.4, *impious* 448.11
covetously 288.28; *enviously* 314.11, *selfishly* 444.8
covetousness 288.4; *envy* 314.1, *selfishness* 444.1, *iniquity* 448.3

covey *assemblage of birds* 36.18, *Collective Names* 59, *throng* 795.4
cow *livestock* 16.11, *female animal* 33.15, *female mammal* 35.19, *daunt* 179.9, *intimidate* 283.18
cow [Inf and Off] *unpleasant woman* 33.7
coward 285.3; *cowardly* 285.4, *avoider* 386.8, *inactive person* 413.8, *submitter* 421.2, *weak person* 517.4
cowardice 285.1; *yellow streak* [Inf] 259.6, *defeatism* 413.7, *indecisiveness* 517.2
cowardliness *cowardice* 285.1, *indecisiveness* 517.2
cowardly 285.4, 285.9; *inactive* 413.9, *weak-willed* 517.10, *weakly* 517.14
cowbell *Flowers* 42, *Musical Instruments* 142, *source of resonance* 236.4
cowboy *farm worker* 16.15, *horse person* 159.14
cowboy [Inf] *unskilled person* 128.3
cowboy boots *boots* 100.31
cowboy hat *hat* 100.32
cowboys and Indians *Children's and Party Games* 167
cowcatcher *safety device* 810.15
cow chip *feces* 25.5
cowed *cowardly* 285.4
cower *be a coward* 285.7, *evade* 386.19, *knuckle under* 401.10, *bow* 716.22
cowering *cowardly* 285.4, *evasion* 386.5, *fugitive* 386.10, *sycophantic* 401.7
cow flop *feces* 25.5
cowgirl *farm worker* 16.15, *horse person* 159.14
cowhand *farm worker* 16.15
cowherd *farm worker* 16.15
cowhide *leather* 104.7, *instrument of punishment* 454.13
cowing *intimidation* 283.6
cowish *ungulate* 35.31
cowl *headdress* 100.35
cowlick *coiffure* 530.8
cowlike *ungulate* 35.31
cowling *toboggan parts* 162.24
coworker 123.17; *operator* 509.5, *member* 760.9, *thing included* 763.2, *companion* 794.8, *cooperator* 827.8
coworkers *team* 827.7
cow pat *feces* 25.5
cowpoke *farm worker* 16.15
cow pony *workhorse* 159.3
cowpuncher *farm worker* 16.15, *horse person* 159.14
cowrie *money* 484.1
cowshed *farm building* 16.4, *cage* 60.15
cowslip *Flowers* 42, *yellow thing* 259.4
cow's milk *milk* 93.5
cox *lead* 126.12, *row* 150.32, *nautical person* 690.12
coxed *rowing* 150.27
Cox's Orange Pippin *Apple Varieties* 44
coxswain *boating person* 150.24, *nautical person* 690.12
coxswainless *rowing* 150.27
coy *amorous* 299.18, *shy* 403.8
coyly *amorously* 299.30, *shyly* 403.16
coyness *shyness* 403.3
coz [Inf] *family member* 65.2
cozen *deceive* 181.14, 193.16
cozenage *deception* 193.1

cozener *deceiver* 193.8
cozily *pleasingly* 214.15, *prosperously* 847.9
coziness *pleasure* 214.2
cozy *fit for habitation* 60.19, *luscious* 214.8, *comfortable* 271.8, *prosperous* 847.5
cozy chat *chat* 210.2
CPL Programming Languages 15
Crab Constellations 7
crab *crustacean* 39.10, *food fish and shellfish* 90.20, *flight maneuver* 689.6, *maneuver* 689.14, *navigate* 690.15, *lifter* 715.5
crab [Inf] *irascible person* 303.7, *sullen person* 304.7, *be irritable* 304.14
crab apple *sour thing* 223.3
crabbed *splenetic* 223.7, *objectionable* 272.7, *cross* 303.11, *unintelligible* 364.4, *problematic* 824.11
crabbedness *spleen* 223.4, *crossness* 303.4
crabber Ships and Boats 690
crabbily *splenetically* 223.10
crabbily [Inf] *crossly* 303.20, *irritably* 304.17
crabbiness [Inf] *crossness* 303.4, *irritableness* 304.3
crabbing [Inf] *critical* 438.13, *criticism* 438.4
crabby *splenetic* 223.7
crabby [Inf] *objectionable* 272.7, *cross* 303.11, *irritable* 304.9
crablike *arthropodal* 39.22
Crab nebula *nebula* 7.6
crab one's act *or* **deal** [Inf] *hinder* 826.15
crabs *sexually transmitted disease (STD)* 114.17
Crabstock ware Ceramics 129
crabwalk *deviating motion* 698.3
crabwood Trees and Shrubs 43
crack 234.2, 234.7, 587.2, 587.7; *skillful* 127.10, *rock face* 161.6, *stripe* 263.3, *variegate* 263.11, *decipher* 365.13, *great* 445.14, *mark* 533.2, 533.8, *rough thing* 544.2, *be rough* 544.11, *make rough* 544.11, *be brittle* 548.4, *opening* 583.1, *open* 583.15, *separateness* 753.3, *separate* 753.12, *interruption* 775.3, *defect* 806.4
crack [Inf] *stimulants* 121.18, *utterance* 205.10, *experiment* 335.1, *attempt* 390.1
crackable *brittle* 548.3
crack a bottle *get drunk* 121.35
crack a bottle with *participate* 408.15
crack a code *or* **cipher** *decipher* 365.13
crackajack [Inf] *superior person* 445.7, *great* 445.14
crack a joke *be humorous* 277.11
crack a safe *steal* 479.14
crackback block *penalty* 155.13
crack-brained [Inf] *insane* 110.9
crack climbing *climbing techniques* 161.3
crack cocaine [Inf] *stimulants* 121.18
crackdown *prohibition* 503.1, *restraint* 830.1
crack down *restrain* 830.12
crack down on *prohibit* 503.8
cracked 587.5; *voiceless* 206.5, *hoarse* 238.5, *unmelodious* 241.5, *interpreted* 365.9, *marked* 533.6, *coarse* 544.6, *brittle* 548.3, *open* 583.10, *imperfect* 806.5, *dilapidated* 808.11

cracked glass *variegated thing* 263.5
cracked ice *ice* 218.5
cracked voice *hoarseness* 238.2
cracker *computer user* 15.3, *bread* 90.10, *banger* 234.3
cracker [Inf *and* Off] *countryman* 61.8
crackerjack [Inf] *superior person* 445.7, *great* 445.14
cracker race Children's and Party Games 167
crackers *snack* 90.8
crackers and cheese *hors d'oeuvre* 90.13
cracking *industrial chemistry* 11.21, *oil* 106.7, *brittleness* 548.1, *brittle* 548.3
crackle *glaze* 129.3, *burn* 217.18, *crack* 234.2, 234.7, *stripe* 263.3
crackled *brittle* 548.3
crackleware Ceramics 129
crackling 234.5; *crack* 234.2
crack of dawn *morning* 655.2, *early hour* 657.2
crack of doom *death* 29.1, *ruin* 523.4, *eternally* 644.10, *future condition* 650.3, *end of time* 773.5
crack of the whip *incentive* 178.4, *negative stimulus* 908.1
crack one's voice *be loud* 232.8, *sound hoarse* 238.8
crackpot [Inf] *insane person* 110.5, *eccentric* 782.10
crack shot *prizewinner* 127.8, *shooter* 696.11
cracksman [Inf] *thief* 479.8
crack the whip *have authority* 52.13, *direct* 126.11
crackup *mental breakdown* 110.4, *ruin* 523.4, *brittleness* 548.1
crack up *be brittle* 548.4
cradle *home* 60.3, *type of bed* 101.9, *native country* 566.6, *source* 675.2, 771.3, *oscillator* 683.7, *conception* 771.4
cradle song *song* 140.11
craft 133.2; *job* 122.3, *manual skill* 127.2, *business* 480.6, *perform* 522.16, *vessel* 690.3, *specialization* 779.3, *cunning* 822.1
craftily *deceptively* 193.21, *hypocritically* 330.15, *cunningly* 822.6
craftily contrived *well-made* 127.13
craftiness *manual skill* 127.2, *guile* 193.3, *cunning* 330.3, 822.1
crafting *furniture making* 101.3
crafts fair *display* 843.1
craft show *display* 843.1
craftsman *artisan* 123.13, *expert* 127.9, *visual artist* 133.6, *worker* 412.8, *producer* 522.10, *stylist* 537.4
craftsman-built *produced* 522.12
craftsmanship *manual skill* 127.2, *artistry* 133.3, *learning* 348.3, *production* 522.1
craftswoman *artisan* 123.13, *expert* 127.9, *visual artist* 133.6, *worker* 412.8, *producer* 522.10
craft union *organized labor* 57.5
craftworker *producer* 522.10
crafty *skillful* 127.10, *artful* 193.13, *cunning* 330.8, 822.4
crafty fellow *cunning person* 822.3
crag *rock face* 161.6, *sharp-pointed thing* 549.4, *mountain* 569.1
cragged *coarse* 544.6
cragginess *hardness* 542.1, *roughness* 544.1
craggy *coarse* 544.6, *rough* 824.10
crake *water bird* 36.9

cram *crowd* 59.26, *be excessive* 99.9, *be greedy* 119.4, *make dense* 540.9, *stuff* 577.12, *squeeze* 582.13, *fill* 761.11
cram [Inf] *learn* 48.23
crambo Children's and Party Games 167
Cramer's rule Mathematical Concepts 6
cram-full *full* 761.8
cram in *flood in* 706.14, *impact* 710.11
crammed *crowded* 59.22, *immoderate* 99.6, *loaded* 577.8, *full* 761.8
cramming *gluttonous* 119.3
cramming [Inf] *learning* 48.7
cramoisy [Arch] *red* 257.5
cramp *pain* 215.1, *be painful* 215.9, *squeeze* 582.13, *narrow* 593.14, *spasm* 684.8, *fastener* 754.7, *means of restraint* 830.6, *restrain* 830.12
cramped *not enough* 98.5, *unintelligible* 364.4, *undersized* 580.8, *squeezed* 582.9, *narrow* 593.8, *problematic* 824.11, *restrained* 830.9
crampedness *narrowness* 593.1
cramping *painful* 215.4, *squeeze* 582.3, *contracting* 582.10, *hindering* 826.12
cramping one's style [Inf] *limitation* 830.2
cramp one's style [Inf] *be insufficient* 98.9, *hinder* 826.15, *limit* 830.13
crampon *mountaineer* 161.10
crampons *climbing equipment* 161.4
cramps *gastroenterological disease* 114.11, *painful condition* 215.2
cranberry sauce *sauce* 90.17
Crane Constellations 7
crane *construction equipment* 14.23, *water bird* 36.9, *lifter* 715.5
crane, Mississippi sandhill Endangered US Birds 36
crane, whooping Endangered US Birds 36
cranefly *insect* 40.1
cranes Collective Names 59
cranesbill Flowers 42
Craniata *protochordate* 39.4
craniate *protochordate* 39.4
craniologer *anthropologist* 1.3
craniological *anthropological* 1.10
craniologically *anthropologically* 1.15
craniology *anthropology* 1.1
craniometer Fields of Measurement 589
craniometric *anthropological* 1.10
craniometrical *anthropological* 1.10
craniometrically *anthropologically* 1.15
craniometrist *anthropologist* 1.3
craniometry *anthropology* 1.1, *measurement* 1.9, Fields of Measurement 589
cranium Human Bones 19
crank *machine element* 14.8, *engine type* 14.11, *visionary* 360.9, *caprice* 381.1, *capricious person* 381.3, *prepare for action* 388.18, *roll* 682.15, *bicycle part* 687.11
crank [Inf] *irascible person* 303.7, *sullen person* 304.7
crank call *telephone call* 169.11
crankily *irritably* 304.17
crankiness *crossness* 303.4, *irritableness* 304.3, *capriciousness* 381.2

crank over *be on the track* 146.11
crankshaft *engine type* 14.11
crank up *prepare for action* 388.18
cranky *cross* 303.11, *irritable* 304.9
crannog [Scot, Irish] *lake dwelling* 568.3
cranny *hiding place* 181.2, *compartment* 578.2, *crack* 587.2, *cavity* 635.3
crap [Inf] *feces* 25.5, *defecate* 25.21, *dirt* 112.5, *senseless talk* 362.4
crap *or* **crapola** [Inf] *nonsense* 192.8
crapper [Inf] *place for excretion* 25.11
crappily [Inf] *excrementally* 25.27
crappy [Inf] *fecal* 25.14, *low quality* 745.7
craps Board and Table Games 167, *gambling* 167.4
craps bet *gambling* 167.4
crapshooter *gambler* 167.6
crapulence *drunkenness* 121.3, *overindulgence* 456.3
crapulent *drunk* 121.25, *overindulgent* 456.8
crapulently *drunkenly* 121.39
crapulous *drunk* 121.25
crapulously *drunkenly* 121.39
crapulousness *drunkenness* 121.3
crash *programming concepts* 15.24, *program* 15.29, Collective Names 59, Fabrics and Fibers 130, *tumult* 232.5, *be loud* 232.8, *bang* 234.1, 234.6, *be dissonant* 241.6, *insolvency* 490.5, *be unable to pay* 490.11, *violence by person* 520.2, *ruin* 523.4, *be brittle* 548.4, *billow* 571.9, *collision* 695.2, *collide* 695.10, *fall* 714.4, *droop* 714.14, *discontinuance* 846.4, *malfunction* 846.20
crash [Inf] *take up residence* 60.24, *settle* 61.14
crash barrier *miscellaneous automotive terms* 687.14, *safety device* 810.15
crash diet *diet* 92.5, *dieting* 118.2, 595.3
crash-diet *become thin* 595.15
crash-dieting *dieting* 595.3
crasher [Inf] *illegal occupant* 61.9
crash helmet *helmet* 100.34, *protective clothing* 419.6, *safety device* 810.15
crash in *be violent* 520.8
crashing *contiguous* 216.8, *loud* 232.6, *banging* 234.4, *descending* 714.9
crashing bore *boring person* 296.4
crash into *collide* 695.10
crash-land *maneuver* 689.14, *drop* 714.15
crash-landing *flight* 689.5, *fall* 714.4
crash pad [Inf] *habitation* 60.2
crashworthiness *miscellaneous automotive terms* 687.14
crass *vulgar* 535.6
crassly *vulgarly* 535.10
crate *receptacle* 105.11, *box* 578.5
crate [Inf] *automobile* 687.6
crate(ful) *container(ful)* 738.2
Crater Constellations 7, Lakes 568
crater *moon* 7.18, *volcanic activity* 8.26, *concave land* 635.2
crate up *contain* 578.20
cravat *neckwear* 100.29, *line* 754.5
crave *aspire* 281.13, *desire* 288.17, *envy* 314.7
craved *desired* 288.10
craven *coward* 285.3, *dastardly* 285.6
cravenly *cowardly* 285.9

cravenness *yellow streak* [Inf] 259.6, *dastardliness* 285.2
craver *desirer* 288.9
craving *appetite* 92.2, 288.6, *compulsion* 108.13, *delusion* 110.2, *aspiration* 281.3, *aspiring* 281.8, *desire* 288.1, *desirous* 288.13, *likes* 290.3
crawfish *crustacean* 39.10
crawfish [Inf] *retreat* 680.17
crawfish *or* **crawdad** *food fish and shellfish* 90.20
crawl *crowd* 59.26, 795.11, *swimming techniques* 164.2, *swim* 164.14, *humble oneself* 298.18, *be solicitous* 323.13, *fawn* 441.9, *succumb* 421.7, *be sycophantic* 439.15, *be low* 597.20, *be horizontal* 603.9, *slow motion* 693.3, *move slowly* 693.11
crawler *sycophant* 401.3
crawling *crowded* 59.22, *excessive* 99.5, *unclean* 112.8, *radio reception* 172.2, *sycophancy* 401.2, *sycophantic* 401.7, 439.11, *submitting* 421.3, *slow* 693.7
crawlingly *in slow motion* 693.15
crawl into one's shell *escape notice* 403.14
crawl out of the woodwork *become visible* 264.13
crawl with *infest* 40.17, *abound* 97.8, *be excessive* 99.9
crayfish *crustacean* 39.10, *food fish and shellfish* 90.20
crayon *material* 143.9, *color* 251.16
crayon drawing *drawing* 143.4
craze *compulsion* 108.13, *delusion* 110.2, *stripe* 263.3, *variegate* 263.11, *likes* 290.3, *caprice* 381.1, *mark* 533.8, *fashion* 536.1
crazed *violent* 520.5, *marked* 533.6
crazily *insanely* 110.15
craziness *insanity* 110.1, *folly* 353.1
crazing *glaze* 129.3, *mark* 533.2
crazy *insane* 110.9, *foolish* 353.5, *meaningless* 362.7, *unsafe* 811.8
crazy about [Inf] *in love* 299.16
crazy eights *Card Games* 168
crazy idea *creative thought* 317.3, *plan* 327.3
crazy paving [Brit] *variegated thing* 263.5
creak *small sound* 233.4, *sound faint* 233.8, *shrillness* 238.3, *be shrill* 238.9
creakiness *shrillness* 238.3
creaking *shrill* 238.6
creaky *shrill* 238.6, *weak* 517.6
cream *basic cooking ingredient* 91.8, *milk* 93.5, *dose of medicine* 115.3, *balm* 115.11, *choose* 382.14, *excellence* 445.4, *semiliquid* 561.7, *fat* 562.4, *ointment* 562.8, *lubricate* 562.15, *best people* 744.7, *chief thing* 799.3
cream, the *chosen thing or person* 382.8
cream-colored *yellow* 259.7
creamcups *Flowers* 42
creamery *farm* 124.11
creamily *whitely* 253.13, *yellowly* 259.13, *oilily* 562.19
creaminess *whiteness* 253.1, *pulpiness* 561.9, *oiliness* 562.1
cream off *obtain an extract* 711.19
cream of society, the *the rich* 485.7
cream of the crop *excellence* 445.4, *fashionable elite* 536.4, *best people* 744.7
cream puff *pastry* 90.37
cream soda *sweet drink* 222.4
cream soup *soup* 90.14

cream tea [Brit] *meal* 92.8
creamware *ceramics* 129.1
creamy *soft-hued* 251.13, *white* 253.7, *yellow* 259.7, *pulpy* 561.19, *oily* 562.11
crease *make rough* 544.11, *pleat* 637.2, 637.8, *wrinkle* 638.2, 638.6, *joint* 752.7, *make disorderly* 766.20
creased *folded* 637.5, *wrinkly* 638.4
crease-resistant *treated* 130.16
creasy *folded* 637.5
create *design* 133.9, *imagine* 327.14, 360.14, *invent* 335.13, 345.14, 771.30, *produce* 522.13, *fashion* 536.7, *shape* 551.21, *form* 624.9, *cause* 675.8, *come to be* 717.19, *originate* 737.7
create a barrier *block* 826.17
create a Catch-22 situation *be cunning* 822.5
create a controversy *cause adversity* 848.15
create a logjam *delay* 658.13, *block* 826.17
create anarchy *subvert* 427.13
create an obstacle *block* 826.17
create a role *or* **part** *act* 136.34
create a scene *become angry* 302.20
create a sensation *be important* 799.13
create a tempest in a teapot *or* **teacup** *exaggerate* 194.11
create bad blood *cause hate* 300.12
created 717.16; *imaginary* 360.12, *produced* 522.12, *formed* 624.6
create difficulties *cause difficulties* 824.22
create life *give birth to* 28.19
create problems *cause adversity* 848.15
create resentment *arouse jealousy* 314.10
creatine phosphate *bioenergetics* 12.23
creating a role *or* **part** *acting* 136.22
creation 717.9, 771.2; *universe* 7.3, *life* 28.1, *masterpiece* 127.5, *invention* 345.4, 771.5, *production* 522.1, *product* 522.3, *form* 551.3, *structuring* 551.5, *forming* 624.4, *early stage* 657.3, *cause* 675.1, *originality* 737.1
creation of genius *masterpiece* 127.5
creative *enriching* 22.11, *artistic* 133.7, *ideational* 327.9, *imaginative* 360.10, *acting* 412.9, *accounting* 493.7, *productive* 522.11, *formed* 624.6, *misrepresented* 627.8, *causal* 675.7, *original* 737.4, *inventive* 771.20
creative accountant *dishonest person* 479.11
creative accounting *nonpayment* 490.1, *accounts* 493.4, *refusal* 506.1
creative composition *fictional account* 202.5
creative economy *financial escape* 816.2
creative exercise *conception* 360.4
creative force *imagination* 360.1
creative impulse *production* 522.1
creatively *fruitfully* 22.15, *artistically* 133.10, *thoughtfully* 317.13, *imaginatively* 327.21, 360.17, *inventively* 335.15, *financially* 493.13, *productively* 522.17, *formatively* 624.10, *causally* 675.12, *originally* 737.8

creativeness *imagination* 360.1, *originality* 737.1
creative person *performer* 412.5
creative thought 317.3; *imagination* 360.1
creative urge *production* 522.1
creative work *imagination* 360.1
creative worker *visionary* 360.9, *performer* 412.5
creative writer *descriptive writer* 202.10, *originator* 737.3
creative writing *fictional account* 202.5, *conception* 360.4
creativity *enrichment* 22.5, *imagination* 327.8, 360.1, *originality* 335.4, 737.1
Creator *God* 82.6
creator *experimenter* 335.5, *producer* 522.10, *first cause* 675.6, *originator* 737.3, 771.15
creature *living organism* 13.10, *person* 18.8, *animal* 34.1, *sycophant* 401.3, *assistant* 511.3, *product* 522.3
creature comforts *food* 90.1
creaturely *human* 18.15
creature of habit 397.8
creature of impulse *improviser* 396.3
crèche [Brit] *school* 48.11
credence *believing* 87.2, *conviction* 840.2
credential *authorization* 52.3, *certificate* 185.2, *evidence* 336.3, *documentation* 339.6, *recommendation* 437.6
credentials *personal identification* 184.4, *authorization* 340.4, *permit* 503.3
credibility *believability* 87.4, *truthfulness* 191.1, *repute* 370.1, *possibleness* 836.2, *plausibility* 838.3
credibility gap *difference* 463.4, *disparity* 728.3
credible *believable* 87.7, *possible* 836.5, *plausible* 838.7
credibly *believably* 87.13, *potentially* 836.11
credit 476.4, 487.1, 487.10; *believing* 87.2, *believe* 87.9, *resources* 102.4, *acknowledgment* 310.3, *be grateful* 310.6, *repute* 370.1, *admiration* 437.2, *admire* 437.15, *worth* 447.3, *reward* 453.1, 453.13, *promise* 464.2, *receive* 473.13, 492.7, *solvency* 485.4, *deposit* 487.3, *accounts* 493.4, *account* 493.9, *personal influence* 512.3, *difference* 750.3, *financial assistance* 825.6, *be certain* 840.13
creditability *desirability* 288.7
creditable *believable* 87.7, *desirable* 288.11, *reputable* 370.3, *praiseworthy* 437.12, *worthy* 447.7
creditably *desirably* 288.24, *reputably* 370.6, *worthily* 447.11
credit account *credit* 476.4, 487.1, *deposit* 487.3, *debt* 488.1
credit balance *deposit* 487.3
credit bureau *bank* 487.4
credit buyer *debtor* 488.6
credit card 487.2; *credit* 476.4, *debt* 488.1
credit-card *borrowed* 476.8
credit-card company *lending institution* 475.4
credit-card holder *borrower* 476.7
credit-card number *personal identification* 184.4
credit company *lending institution* 475.4

credit control *credit* 487.1
credited *rewarded* 453.10, *received* 492.6, *accounted* 493.8
credit facility *credit* 476.4
crediting *thanking* 310.5
credit limit *resources* 102.4, *credit* 487.1
credit line *acknowledgment* 310.3
credit note *credit card* 487.2
credit one's account *deposit* 487.12
creditor *provisioner* 89.4, *lender* 475.3
creditors' budget *budgeting* 493.5
credit purchase *purchasing* 481.2
credit rating *resources* 102.4, *credit* 487.1
credits *acknowledgment* 310.3, *something received* 473.2, *money received* 492.2, *list of names* 785.7
credit squeeze *economic restraint* 830.3
credit to one's account *earn* 467.20
credit union *lending institution* 475.4, *treasury* 484.19, *bank* 487.4
credit user *borrower* 476.7
creditworthiness *resources* 102.4, *solvency* 485.4, *credit* 487.1
creditworthy *reputable* 370.3, *solvent* 485.9, *in credit* 487.8
credo *philosophical system* 4.2, *religion* 81.1, *Eucharist* 85.7, *belief system* 87.3, *ideology* 327.5
credulity *believing* 87.2, *persuadability* 178.8, *incuriosity* 322.1, *naiveté* 821.1
credulous *believing* 87.6, *persuadable* 178.14, *raw* 260.9, *incurious* 322.3, *naive* 449.9, 821.3
credulously *believingly* 87.12, *incuriously* 322.6, *naively* 449.15, 821.5
credulousness *believing* 87.2, *persuadability* 178.8, *naiveté* 449.4
creed *philosophical system* 4.2, *religion* 81.1, *Eucharist* 85.7, *belief system* 87.3, *ideology* 327.5
creedal *believed* 87.8
creek *river* 570.1
creel *basket* 578.6
creep *mass movement* 8.28, *deformation* 14.16, *conceal oneself* 181.15, *be sycophantic* 439.15, *enlarge* 581.14, *be low* 597.20, *bodily movement* 677.11, *walk* 677.17, *slow motion* 693.3, *move slowly* 693.11, *hide* 844.13
creep (of flesh) *be rough* 544.10
creeper *garden plant* 17.10, *baby clothes* 100.24
creepily [Inf] *suavely* 545.15
creep in *infiltrate* 706.13
creeping *reptilian* 37.12, *of plants* 41.14, *radio reception* 172.2, *sycophantic* 439.11, *expansion* 581.1, *growing* 581.12, *slow motion* 693.3, *slow* 693.7
creeping flesh *rough skin* 544.3
creeping Jenny *Flowers* 42
creepingly *in slow motion* 693.15
creeping thing *animal* 34.1
creep into a corner *be unsocial* 409.10
creep into one's shell *escape notice* 403.14
creep off *retreat* 386.22
creeps, the [Inf] *stimulus* 212.3, *symptoms of fear* 283.3
creep up on *ambush* 292.11
creepy *spiritual* 86.20, *frightening* 283.12

C
G

creepy [Inf] smooth-mannered 545.9

creepy-crawly [Inf] insect 40.1

creese sharp weapon 78.6

cremate 31.11; burn 217.18

cremated buried 31.8

cremation 31.2

crematorial funeral 31.9

crematorium cremation 31.2, place for fire 217.9

crematory funeral 31.9

crème de la crème masterpiece 68.14, chosen thing 382.8, fashionable elite 536.4, best people 744.7, chief thing 799.3, successful person 845.6

crème fraîche semiliquid 561.7

cremnophobia Phobias 283

cremocarp botanical fruit 44.2

crenate of leaves 41.18, make rough 544.11, notched 636.4

crenated notched 636.4

crenately jaggedly 636.7

crenation notch 636.1

crenature notch 636.1

crenel fort 419.13

crenel or **crenelle** notch 636.1

crenelate edge 618.8, notch 636.5

crenelated edged 618.6

crenelation Architectural Elements 134, edging 618.2, notch 636.1

crenulate notched 636.4

crenulation notch 636.1

Creole international language 5.8

creophagous eating 92.18

creophagously carnivorously 92.27

creophagy eating habit 92.7

creosote coating 613.8, coat 613.28, preserver 815.9, preserve 815.14

crepe fabric 130.1, clothing 184.6, black thing 254.3

crêpe pancake 90.11

crepe de Chine Fabrics and Fibers 130

crêpe pan cooking equipment 91.6

crepe paper paper 104.5

crêperie eating place 92.17

crepe rubber rubber 546.3

crepe-soled or **crepe rubber-soled shoes** shoes 100.30

crepitant crackling 234.5

crepitate crack 234.7

crepitation crack 234.2

crepon fabric 130.1

Crepuscolari Western Literary Groups 139

crepuscular dim 248.4, evening 656.4

crepuscule evening 656.2

crescendo Musical Terms and Expression Marks 140

crescendo loud tone 232.3, loud 232.6, loudly 232.11, increase 581.3, 746.6, grow 581.17, change by degrees 739.8, spread 746.3

crescent circle 6.40, wrestling 152.18, Heraldic Terms 184, growing 581.12, curve 629.1, parts of a circle 631.4, increasing 746.4

crescent dune dune 8.43

crescentic curved 629.4

crescent moon moon 7.18

crescent-shaped curvilinear 6.78

Cressida Planets and Their Satellites 7, Famous Lovers 299

crest plumage 36.7, Architectural Elements 134, Heraldic Terms 184, insignia 184.5, mountain 569.1, mountain range 569.3, summit 600.1, 744.4, be at the top 600.9, wave 683.4

crested heraldic 184.10, topped 600.8

crestfallen sorrowful 270.4, disappointed 293.4, humiliated 298.12

cresting Architectural Elements 134

crest of the wave summit 600.1

Cretaceous Period Geologic Time Intervals 8

Crete Islands 572

cretic meter 139.10

cretin unintelligent person 316.4

cretinous intellectually subnormal 316.7

cretonne Fabrics and Fibers 130

crevasse glacier 8.44, rock face 161.6, valley 572.8, gulf 587.3, concave land 635.2, interruption 775.3, hidden danger 811.8

Crevecoeur Breeds of Fowl 16

crevice opening 583.1, crack 587.2

creviced open 583.10

crew farm worker 16.15, team 59.9, force 59.10, personnel 123.16, sail 150.29, equip 388.19, take action 509.12, aircraft personnel 689.8, pilot 689.15, navigate 690.15, alliance 735.5, thing included 763.2, council 833.4

crew chief air force person 77.31

crewcut coiffure 530.8

crewel fiber 130.2

crewelist decorator 532.8

crewelwork sewing 130.5

crewel work decorative method 532.3

crew member thing included 763.2

crew-neck sweater sweater 100.17

crew socks legwear 100.26

crib schoolbook 48.15, type of bed 101.9, brothel 432.5, enclosed area 619.2

crib [Inf] habitation 60.2, gambling house 167.5, translation 365.4, borrow illegally 476.12, infringe 479.17, copy 736.10

cribbage Card Games 168

cribber [Inf] infringer 479.10

cribbing [Inf] illegal borrowing 476.3, infringement 479.6

cribbing strap riding equipment 159.9

cribriform or **cribrous** holed 583.12

cricket [Brit] Sporting Activities 145

cricket season [Brit] seasons 654.2

cri de coeur [Fr] petition 505.2

crier 239.8; publicizer 173.11, precursor 769.7

crikey! miscellaneous euphemisms 301.21

crime lawbreaking 53.14, malignity 306.5, errancy 351.7, bad conduct 399.7, deed 412.2, violation of the law 427.2, wrongdoing 430.7, immorality 432.1, evil thing 446.2, wicked act 448.7, illegality 450.4

crime against humanity cruelty 306.4

Crimean War Major Wars 76

crime of passion murder 30.2

crime story story 139.4

crime writer author 139.13, descriptive writer 202.10

criminal 427.6; lawbreaker 53.15, offending 53.25, malefactor 306.6, malign 306.11, skeptical 333.14, the hunted 385.7, badly behaved person 399.8, evildoer 412.6, disobedient 427.10, wrongdoer 430.8, unlawful 430.15, immoral

432.9, unsatisfactory 438.15, evil person 446.3, villain 448.5, wicked 448.9, guilty person 450.5, sinful 450.8, dishonest person 479.11

criminal act deed 412.2, wicked act 448.7

criminal conversation fornication 432.3

criminal court law court 54.8

criminal insanity insanity 110.1

criminal intent intention 374.1

criminal investigation army commands 77.13, questioning 333.2

criminality lawbreaking 53.14, violation of the law 427.2, unlawfulness 430.6, immorality 432.1, wickedness 448.1, guilt 450.1

criminalize make illegal 53.29, prohibit 503.8

criminal law law 53.1

criminally illegally 53.34, cruelly 306.17, malignly 306.18, disobediently 427.14, immorally 432.18, wickedly 448.15, villainously 448.18, guiltily 450.12

criminal offense wicked act 448.7, illegality 450.4

criminal psychology Psychological Theories, Schools 108

criminal record record 185.1

criminal trial legal process 54.3

criminal world villain 448.5

crimp thief 479.8, kidnap 479.15, coif 530.15, pleat 637.2, 637.8, hinder 826.15

crimper [Brit inf] beautician 530.11

crimping kidnapping 479.3

crimson red 257.5, redden 257.9, blush 403.12

crimsoning blushing 403.2, 403.7

crimson lake red pigment 257.2

cringe be afraid 283.14, be a coward 285.7, knuckle under 401.10, succumb 421.7, bow 716.22

cringing cowardly 285.4, sycophancy 401.2, sycophantic 401.7, submitting 421.3

crinkle make rough 544.11, pleat 637.2, 637.8, wrinkle 638.2, 638.6

crinkled rough 544.5, wrinkly 638.4

crinkle leaf pests and diseases 17.12

crinkly rough 544.5, wrinkly 638.4

crinoid echinoderm 39.5

crinoidal echinodermal 39.21

crinoline skirt 100.12, underwear 100.22, Fabrics and Fibers 130

Criollo Horse and Pony Breeds 159

cripes! miscellaneous euphemisms 301.21

cripple sick person 114.22, overpower 515.14, weaken 517.13, make useless 802.12, hinder 826.15

crippled ill 517.8

crippling physical deterioration 808.4

crisis difficult question 333.4, critical time 659.3, swing 671.4, predicament 725.3, important matter 799.2, danger 811.1

crisis point zero level 786.3

crisis theology Theologies 81

crisp fine 9.43, concise 198.6, harden 542.9, brittle 548.3, crumbly 553.16

crispily fragilely 548.5

crisply concisely 198.6, summarily 204.10

crispness conciseness 198.1

crispiness or **crispiness** brittleness 548.1

crisps [Brit] snack 90.8

crispy brittle 548.3

crisscross weaving 130.6, interweaving 609.1, interweave 609.8

criteria specification 340.6

Criterion Apple Varieties 44

criterion theory 6.62, physical law 10.4, standard 589.7, average 742.1, precedent 769.4, guide 780.4

critic theatergoer 136.30, book review 174.13, print journalist 175.5, dissertator 203.3, discriminator 337.6, judge 341.5, dissenter 347.5, 463.5, theorist 359.4, interpreter 365.6, disapprover 438.7, disparager 440.7, protester 507.4

critical 418.16, 438.13, 659.5; refined 48.20, 534.5, sick 114.24, literary 139.15, advisory 176.7, dissertational 203.4, important 278.6, discriminating 337.9, judging 341.7, annotative 365.10, disparaging 440.8, protesting 507.5, operative 509.9, difficult 726.11, serious 799.8, dangerous 811.7, unsafe 811.8, troublesome 824.13

critical care medicine Medical Specialties 107

critical care unit (CCU) hospital 107.16

critical edition interpretation 365.1

critical juncture critical time 659.3

critically 659.9; advisorily 176.12, discursively 203.6, judiciously 337.16, judicially 341.12, disapprovingly 438.23, 507.10, disparagingly 440.16, operationally 509.13, difficultly 726.20, importantly 799.15, perversely 824.27

critical mass nuclear fission 10.60

critical moment 726.7; critical time 659.3

critical of dissatisfied 274.4

critical remarks criticism 438.4

critical review criticism 438.4

critical situation 824.6

critical state thermodynamics 10.30

critical success theatrical performance 136.13, box-office hit 137.11

critical temperature thermodynamics 10.30

critical time 659.3

criticism 365.3, 438.4, 440.2; nonfiction 139.6, book review 174.13, recommendation 176.2, article 203.2, expression of dissatisfaction 274.2, judiciousness 337.2, judgment 341.1, personal attack 418.8, disagreement 463.1

criticize 365.15, 418.26, 438.19, 440.12; discuss 4.22, advise 176.9, dissertate 203.5, be dissatisfied 274.7, discriminate against 337.14, judge 341.10, estimate 341.11, disagree 463.8, cause difficulties 824.22, object 828.18

criticized 438.14

criticizer disapprover 438.7

criticizing judging 341.7, disagreeing 463.6

critique nonfiction 139.6, book

review 174.13, *article* 203.2, *judgment* 341.1, *criticism* 365.3, *criticize* 365.15
critter [Inf] *animal* 34.1
croak *hoarseness* 238.2, *sound hoarse* 238.8, *bird sound* 240.2, *make an animal sound* 240.7
croakiness *speech difficulty* 206.1
croaking *voiceless* 206.5, *hoarse* 238.5
croaky *hoarse* 238.5
Croatia *Countries* 566
croc [Inf] *crocodile* 37.8
crochet *knitting* 130.7, *sew* 130.18, *knit* 130.19, *decorative method* 532.3, *braid* 609.3, *intertwine* 752.19
crochet hook *fabric-handling tool* 130.12
crocheting *Hobbies and Pastimes* 167
crockery 578.16; *ceramics* 129.1
crocket *Architectural Elements* 134, *arch* 134.5
Crockpot™ *cooking equipment* 91.6
crocodile 37.8
crocodile [Brit] *procession* 774.6
crocodiles *Collective Names* 59
crocodile tears *ungenuineness* 192.2
Crocodilia *reptile* 37.1
crocodilian *crocodile* 37.8, *reptilian* 37.12
crocus *Flowers* 42, *yellow thing* 259.4
Croesus *wealthy person* 485.6
croft [Brit] *farm* 16.2
crofter [Brit] *agriculturist* 16.14, *countryman* 61.8
Crohn's disease *gastroenterological disease* 114.11
croissant *pastry* 90.37
Cro-Magnon man *primitive humanity* 18.4, *prehistoric human* 653.7
cromlech *burial place* 31.7, *monument* 185.10, *thing of the past* 651.8
Cronus or **Cronos** *Deities* 82
crony *friend* 62.2
crook *lawbreaker* 53.15, *vestment* 84.11, *brass instrument* 142.3, *schemer* 193.10, *wrongdoer* 430.8, *evil person* 446.3, *villain* 448.5, *raider* 477.10, *dishonest person* 479.11, *twist* 698.19
crooked *offending* 53.25, *dishonorable* 192.14, *unlawful* 430.15, *villainous* 448.12, *fraudulent* 479.13, *oblique* 607.6, *distorted* 627.6, *indirect* 698.9, *cunning* 822.4, *mysterious* 844.11
crookedly *dishonorably* 192.28, *obliquely* 607.13, *asymmetrically* 627.13
crookedness *lawbreaking* 53.14, *dishonorableness* 192.3, *dishonesty* 479.7, *obliqueness* 607.1, *distortion* 627.1
croon *sing* 141.16, *sound faint* 233.8
crooner *singer* 141.4
crop 16.8; *farm* 16.19, *cultivate* 17.19, *avian characteristic* 36.6, *fruits* 44.1, *eat grass* 45.11, *eating organ* 92.14, *eat* 92.21, *store* 105.1, *riding equipment* 159.9, *yield* 467.8, *plant products* 522.8, *coiffure* 530.8, *shorten* 591.9, *growth* 676.3
crop circle *occult and psychic phenomena* 86.7

crop-dusting *cultivation* 16.7, *aviation* 689.1
crop-eared *eared* 228.10
crop failure *unsuccessful thing* 846.8
crop farming *agriculture* 16.1, *arable farming* 16.6
crop husbandry *arable farming* 16.6, *plant science* 41.10
cropland *farm* 16.2
cropped *farmable* 16.17, *shortened* 591.7, 762.6
cropping *eating habit* 92.7, *framing* 132.18
crop rotation *arable farming* 16.6
crop-spraying *cultivation* 16.7
crop top *shirt* 100.13
crop up *appear* 244.8, *become visible* 264.13, *emerge* 771.35, *be repeated* 797.20, *chance* 842.12
croquet *Sporting Activities* 145
crore [India] *million* 792.11
crosier *vestment* 84.11
cross 303.11, 609.9, 692.17, 712.13; *funeral object* 31.6, *sacred object* 83.11, *adversity* 117.2, *stationary rings* 157.8, *punctuate* 183.20, *Heraldic Terms* 184, *insignia* 184.5, *irritable* 302.10, 304.9, *argumentative* 329.7, *instrument of execution* 454.15, *permit* 502.3, *counteract* 510.7, 828.21, *span* 592.12, *oblique* 607.6, *converge* 702.9, *hybrid* 751.6, *mix* 751.12, *oppositional* 828.11
crossbar *stadium* 155.3, 163.2, *supporting part* 605.3, *bicycle part* 687.11
crossbeam *supporting part* 605.3
cross block *play* 155.8, *play offense* 155.18
crossbow *Historical Missile Weapons* 78, *agent of destruction* 523.7
crossbow archery *Sporting Activities* 145
crossbowman *historical soldier* 77.8
crossbred *domesticated* 16.18, *mixed* 751.8
crossbreed *dog* 35.10, *hybrid* 751.6, *mix* 751.12
crossbreeding *mixture* 751.1
cross-Channel *swimming* 164.12
crosscheck *verification* 336.1, *verify* 336.8
cross-checked *verified* 336.7
crosschecking *ice hockey tactics* 158.4
cross-checking *verificatory* 336.6
cross communication *linkage* 752.3
cross connection *linkage* 752.3
cross-country 162.31; *equine* 159.15, *directional* 697.8
cross-country racing 166.8
cross-country running *Sporting Activities* 145
cross-country skier *skier* 162.14
cross-country skiing 162.7, *Sporting Activities* 145, *skiing* 162.1
cross-country skiing championships 162.9
cross-country ski racing *race* 422.8
cross-country techniques 162.8
crosscross *interwoven* 609.6
crosscurrent *opposing force* 510.2, *air flow* 558.4, *flow* 570.4, *hidden danger* 813.3, *conflict* 828.3
crosscut *carpenter* 131.10

crosscut saw *woodworking tool* 131.6
cross-dissolve *motion-picture editing* 137.8
cross-dresser *sexual nature* 20.4, *bisexual* 32.10
cross-dressing *sexual nature* 20.4
crossed *mixed* 751.8
crossed eyes *faulty vision* 243.1
crossed legs *gesture* 183.5
crossed out *obliterated* 186.4
crossed over *dead* 29.11
cross-examination *witness* 54.16, *questioning* 333.2
cross-examine *try a case* 54.28, *interrogate* 333.17
cross-examined *questioned* 333.15
cross-examiner *conversationalist* 210.6, *questioner* 333.9
cross-eye *faulty vision* 243.1
cross-eyed *visually impaired* 243.9
cross-fertilize *mix* 751.12
cross fire *firing* 418.6
cross flow *flow* 570.4
cross-foot spin *ice-skating techniques* 162.16
cross-grained *refractory* 379.6, *coarse* 544.6
cross hairs *visual aid* 242.14
cross handstand *uneven parallel bars* 157.6
cross-hatch *draw* 143.13, *make dark* 247.10
cross-hatching *darkening* 247.2
crossing 609.7, 712.2; *church architecture* 134.11, *crossroads* 609.4, *road attribute* 687.3, *track* 688.2, *water transportation* 690.1, *waterway* 690.2, *route* 691.2, *passing* 692.3, 692.11, *crossing point* 692.7, *meeting place* 702.4, *convergent* 702.7
crossing knot *Knots, Bends, Hitches, Splices* 754
crossing out *obliteration* 186.1
crossing over *cell division* 13.17, *dying* 29.3
crossing-over *crossing* 712.2
crossing point 692.7
crossing streets *Phobias* 283
crossing the bar *dying* 29.3
crossing the picket lines *strike* 57.8
crossing the Styx or **Lethe** or **Jordan** *dying* 29.3
cross linking *polymer* 11.9
crossly 303.20; *irritably* 302.23, 304.17, *argumentatively* 329.15, *discourteously* 411.8
cross-multiplication *evaluation* 6.22
cross multiply *add* 6.86
cross my heart and hope to die! *yes!* 189.36
crossness 303.4; *irritableness* 302.5, 304.3
cross one's bows *navigate* 690.15
cross oneself *follow rites* 85.19
cross one's fingers *be hopeful* 281.11
cross one's heart (and hope to die) *vow* 189.23, *promise* 458.11
cross one's legs *gesture* 183.17
cross one's mind *have an idea* 327.13
cross one's palm with silver *remunerate* 489.21
crossopterygian *fish* 38.5, *fossil fish* 38.7
cross out *punctuate* 183.20, *erase* 186.9, *subtract* 749.6, *eject* 764.8, *cancel* 834.6
cross-out fortunes *Children's and Party Games* 167

crossover *rail* 688.3
cross over *die* 29.17, *cross* 692.17, 712.13
crosspatch [Inf] *irascible person* 303.7, *sullen person* 304.7, *discourteous person* 411.4
cross picket lines *have an industrial dispute* 57.20
crosspiece *supporting part* 605.3
cross-pollination *pollination* 42.6
cross product *vector* 6.48
cross purposes *misjudgment* 342.1
cross-question *interrogate* 333.17
cross-questioned *questioned* 333.15
cross-questioning *questioning* 333.2
cross-refer *relate to* 727.9
cross-reference *interrelatedness* 727.3
cross-referenced *punctuated* 183.15, *interrelated* 727.7
crossroads 609.4; *village* 567.3, *road attribute* 687.3, *crossing point* 692.7, *critical moment* 726.7, *point of union* 752.8
crossroad sign *indicator* 183.7
crossruff *bridge* 168.4, *play cards* 168.7
cross section *geometric figure* 6.39, *nuclear reaction* 10.59, *representative* 187.7
cross someone's palm (with silver) *tip* 472.14
cross-stitch *decorative method* 532.3
cross-stitching *sewing* 130.5
cross swords *collide* 695.10
cross swords with *battle* 76.33, *quarrel* 272.9, *contend* 422.22
cross the bar *die* 29.17
cross the border *cross* 712.13
cross the bridge *find one's way* 691.15
cross the floor *be irresolute* 378.9
cross the Rubicon *brace oneself* 376.13, *cross* 712.13, *be at a critical moment* 726.15
cross the street *find one's way* 691.15
cross the Styx or **Lethe** or **Jordan** *die* 29.17
cross the threshold *enter* 706.11
cross through *erase* 186.9
cross to bear *adversity* 117.2, 848.1, *burden* 826.10
crosstree *figurative usage* 43.9
cross ventilation *ventilation* 558.6
crossways *oblique* 607.6, *obliquely* 607.13, *crossing* 609.7
crosswind *wind* 9.12
crosswise or **crossways** *oblique* 607.6, *obliquely* 607.13, *crossing* 609.7
crosswise *oblique* 607.6, *obliquely* 607.13, *crossing* 609.7
crosswise or **crossways** *breadthways* 592.16
crossword puzzle *spelling* 5.26, *puzzle* 182.5
crossword puzzles *Hobbies and Pastimes* 167
crotch *part of garment* 100.27, *fork* 703.5
crotched *billiard* 149.6
crotchet *notation* 140.20, *caprice* 381.1
crotchetiness *crossness* 303.4
crotchety *cross* 303.11, *refractory* 379.6, *erratic* 381.5
croton *Trees and Shrubs* 43
crotonic *Common Fatty Acids* 12
crouch *knuckle under* 401.10, *succumb* 421.7, *prostration* 597.2, *be low* 597.20, *bow* 716.6, *sit* 716.20
crouched *prostrate* 597.11

crouching *submitting* 421.3, *prostrate* 597.11, *sedentary* 716.11
crouchware Ceramics 129
croup *respiratory disease* 114.12, *pommel horse* 157.7
croupy *of disease* 114.25
crouton *bread* 90.10
Crow Constellations 7
crow *songbird* 36.12, *speak in a particular way* 205.18, *bird sound* 240.2, *make a bird sound* 240.8, *black thing* 254.3
crowbar *hand tool* 103.3, *extractor* 711.9
crowd 59.11, 59.26, 795.11; *group* 59.8, *excess* 99.1, *disrespect* 436.18, *make dense* 540.9, *thicken* 594.9, *association* 752.2, *throng* 795.4
crowd, the *society* 408.8
crowded 59.22, 795.10; *dense* 594.6, *frequent* 661.4, *accessible* 691.13, *full* 761.8
crowdedly *densely* 594.12, *frequently* 661.7
crowdedness *denseness* 594.2, *frequency* 661.1
crowd in *flood in* 706.14, *impact* 710.11
crowds Phobias 283
crowd together *become smaller* 582.14
crowfoot Flowers 42
crowlike *avian* 36.19
crown *teeth* 19.8, *tree part* 43.2, *gain authority* 52.11, *honor* 58.14, 72.3, *headdress* 100.35, *practice dentistry* 107.34, *treat* 115.17, Architectural Elements 134, *play* 167.12, Heraldic Terms 184, *insignia* 184.5, *objective* 374.5, *launch* 405.14, *greet* 410.11, *prize* 453.2, *decoration* 532.1, *decorate* 532.11, *summit* 600.1, *architectural summit* 600.4, *cover* 613.24, *circular thing* 631.3, *club* 695.15, *promote* 715.13, *augment* 748.13, *limit* 761.4, *complete* 761.9, *enroll* 771.33, *end* 773.19, *perfect* 805.19, *commission* 833.8
Crown attorney [Can] *law officer* 53.6
Crown Derby porcelain Ceramics 129
crowned *authorized* 52.11, *masterful* 68.15, *decorated* 532.9, *topped* 600.8
crowned head *sovereign* 68.2
crowned with success *successful* 845.8
crown gall *tree disease* 43.8
crown glass *glass* 249.5
crown-green *bowls* 151.7
crown-green bowls *green bowling* 151.3
crowning *dentistry* 107.6, *board games* 167.3, *celebrative* 405.9, *top* 600.6, *topped* 600.8, *best* 744.10, 805.19, *completed* 761.7, *ending* 773.13, *commission* 833.1, *successful* 845.8
crowning achievement *work of art* 522.4, *ideal* 805.6
crowning glory *ending* 773.10
crowning stroke *conclusion* 761.3
crown knot Knots, Bends, Hitches, Splices 754
crown of thorns Flowers 42
crown-of-thorns *echinoderm* 39.5
crown rot *pests and diseases* 17.12
crown rust *pests and diseases* 17.12
crown wheel *wheel* 682.9
crow over *defy* 416.7
crows Collective Names 59

crow's-foot *wrinkle* 638.2
crow's nest *place for viewing* 242.13, *overview* 425.6
crucial *important* 278.6, *problematic* 333.12, *operative* 509.9, *core* 612.7, *critical* 659.5, *causal* 675.7, *essential* 723.5, *serious* 799.8, *dangerous* 811.7
crucially *operationally* 509.13, *at the core of* 612.13, *critically* 659.9, *causally* 675.12, *difficultly* 726.20, *importantly* 799.15
crucial moment *critical time* 659.3, *important matter* 799.2
crucial point or **moment** *swing* 671.4
crucial time *critical time* 659.3
crucible *heater* 217.3, *mixer* 751.7
crucifer *ritualist* 85.14
cruciferous *taxonomic* 41.16
crucifix *sacred object* 83.11
crucifixes Phobias 283
crucifixion *ritual killing* 30.7, *type of painting* 143.5, *capital punishment* 454.12
Crucifixion, the Stations of the Cross 85
cruciform church *church architecture* 134.11
crucify *kill ritually* 30.23, *inflict pain* 215.10, *execute* 454.30
crud [Inf] *dirt* 112.5, *blemish* 533.1
crud, the [Inf] *disease* 114.4
crude *gas* 106.14, *bungled* 128.7, *gaudy* 251.12, *unformed* 389.11, *blatant* 404.19, *bad-mannered* 411.6, *indecorous* 528.8, *unfinished* 544.9, *incomplete* 762.5, 806.6
crude data *population* 6.55
crude estimate *conjecture* 359.3
crudely *immaturely* 389.18, *blatantly* 404.34, *rudely* 411.9, *vulgarly* 535.10, *incompletely* 544.14, 762.10
crudeness *immaturity* 389.3, *blatancy* 404.6, *bad manners* 411.2, *impropriety* 528.2, *tawdriness* 535.2, *rough idea* 544.4, *incompleteness* 806.2
crude oil or **crude** or **crude petroleum** *oil* 106.7, *petroleum* 562.5
crude rubber *rubber* 546.3
crudités *hors d'oeuvre* 90.13
crudity *immaturity* 389.3
cruel 306.10; *murderous* 30.18, 520.7, *warlike* 76.27, *inflicting pain* 215.7, *pitiless* 309.3, *attacking* 418.14, *severe* 424.5, *wicked* 448.9
cruelhearted *cruel* 306.10, *pitiless* 309.3
cruelly 306.17; *pitilessly* 309.7, *severely* 424.11, *wickedly* 448.15
cruelness *cruelty* 306.4, *pitilessness* 309.1, *wickedness* 448.1
cruel side *aspect* 623.4
cruelty 306.4; *divorce court* 66.3, *pitilessness* 309.1, *severity* 424.1
cruise *maneuver* 677.18, *fly* 689.13
cruise control *miscellaneous automotive terms* 687.14
cruise missile *modern missile weapon* 78.4, *missile* 696.7
cruiser *warship* 77.21, Ships and Boats 690
cruiserweight *boxing weight divisions* 152.6, *combat* 152.17
cruising *sailing* 150.2, 150.25, *canoeing* 150.26, *flying* 689.11, *water transportation* 690.1, *nautical* 690.14
cruising canoe *canoe* 150.9

cruising hook *canoeing techniques* 150.11
cruising stroke *canoeing techniques* 150.11
crumb 553.5; *bread* 90.10, *crumble* 553.22, *little piece* 580.4, *residue* 750.2, *particle* 760.4, *fragment* 787.3
crumble 553.22; *be weak* 517.12, *be destroyed* 523.17, *be brittle* 548.4, *crumb* 553.5, *grow old* 653.16, *take apart* 753.16, *disintegrate* 758.6, 808.15, *impair* 808.18
crumble away *be destroyed* 523.17, *be transient* 643.6
crumbled *brittle* 548.3, *crumbly* 553.16
crumble into dust *come to dust* 553.28, *grow old* 653.16
crumble to dust *be destroyed* 523.17
crumbliness 553.1; *brittleness* 548.1, *nonadhesion* 756.1
crumbling *destroyed* 523.9, *brittleness* 548.1, *brittle* 548.3, *pulverization* 553.4, *crumbly* 553.16, *olden* 653.11, *disintegrating* 758.5, *unsafe* 811.8
crumbly 553.16; *brittle* 548.3, *nonadhesive* 756.4, *partial* 760.11
crumbs *refuse* 802.5
crumhorn Musical Instruments 142
crumminess [Inf] *shoddiness* 497.3
crummy [Inf] *sick* 114.24, *shoddy* 497.11, *low quality* 745.7
crumpet *bread* 90.10
crumple *make rough* 544.11, *pleat* 637.2, 637.8, *make disorderly* 766.20
crumpled *rough* 544.5, *untidy* 766.11
crumple up *be destroyed* 523.17
crumply *rough* 544.5
crunch *chew* 92.22, *sound hoarse* 238.8, *beat* 553.27, *take apart* 753.16, *important matter* 799.2, *critical situation* 824.6
crunchiness *brittleness* 548.1
crunchy *brittle* 548.3
crupper strap *riding equipment* 159.9
crusade *holy war* 76.8, *combat* 77.34, *proselytize* 84.15, *action* 412.1
crusader *militarist* 77.3, *activist* 412.4, *attacker* 418.10
Crusades Major Wars 76
crusading *combative* 77.32, *zealous* 81.22, *acting* 412.9
crush *crowd* 59.11, 795.11, *master* 68.17, *deter* 179.8, *disappoint* 282.12, 293.9, *abase* 298.20, *refute* 332.7, *business* 414.6, *be severe* 424.8, *demolish* 523.12, *be brittle* 548.4, *beat* 553.27, *squeeze* 582.3, 582.13, *flatten* 716.15, *throng* 795.4, *impair* 808.18, *restrain* 830.12, *be victorious* 845.16, *defeat* 845.17
crush [Inf] *likes* 290.3, *romantic love* 299.2
crushability *brittleness* 548.1, *contractibility* 582.4
crushable *brittle* 548.3, *contractible* 582.11
crushed *disappointed* 293.4, *abased* 298.13, *destroyed* 523.9, *brittle* 548.3, *pulverized* 553.20, *squeezed* 582.9, *crowded* 795.10
crusher *pulverizer* 553.11, *contractor* 582.6, *ender* 773.11
crushing *laborious* 122.7, *destroying*

523.2, *brittle* 548.3, *pulverization* 553.4, *squeeze* 582.3, *contracting* 582.10, *victorious* 845.10
crushing blow *ruin* 523.4
crushing device *instrument of torture* 454.14
crushing victory *victory* 845.4
crush note *musical ornament* 140.19
crush someone's hopes *thwart* 293.10
crush to pieces *demolish* 523.12
crust *earth zone* 8.7, *bread* 90.10, *be dense* 540.8, *hard substance* 542.3, *brittle thing* 548.2, *exteriority* 610.2, *cover* 613.2, *particle* 760.4
crust [Inf] *audacity* 400.3
Crustacea *crustacean* 39.10
crustacean 39.10; *arthropodal* 39.22
crustaceous *arthropodal* 39.22
crustal *solid-earth* 8.55
crustal movement *earth movement* 8.20
crustal plate *earth zone* 8.7
crusted *hardened* 542.7
crustily *ill-naturedly* 303.18, *toughly* 542.12
crustiness *ill nature* 303.2, *discourtesy* 411.1
crustose *lichenoid* 47.21
crustose lichen *lichen* 47.16
crusty *ill-natured* 303.9, *discourteous* 411.5, *hard* 542.5
crutch *tree part* 43.2, *body support* 605.6, *support* 825.24
Crux Constellations 7
crux *difficult question* 333.4, *core* 612.2, *critical time* 659.3, *essential content* 723.2, *specifications* 779.6, *chief thing* 799.3, *problem* 824.4
crux of the matter *chief thing* 799.3
cruzado *national coins* 484.11
crwth Musical Instruments 142
cry 239.1, 239.16; *secrete* 24.7, *proclaim* 173.16, *signal* 183.18, *speak in a particular way* 205.18, *express pain* 215.11, *tumult* 232.5, *be loud* 232.8, *cry of sorrow* 239.6, *make an animal sound* 240.7, *grieve* 290.7, *applause* 279.2, *lament* 280.2, *weep* 280.8, *plea* 329.5, *request* 505.1, 505.10
crybaby *lamenter* 280.3, *weak person* 517.4
cry craven *be a coward* 285.7
cry down *berate* 438.20, *disparage* 440.11
cry for help *proclamation* 183.8
cry for the moon *attempt the impossible* 837.10
crying 239.11; *secretion* 24.1, *secretory* 24.4, *demanding* 95.13, *shouting* 232.17, *cry of sorrow* 239.6, *lamentation* 280.1, *lamenting* 280.4
crying down *disparagement* 440.1
crying out for *demanding* 95.13
crying shame *impropriety* 430.5
cryobiological *biological* 13.27
cryobiologist *life scientist* 13.26
cryobiology *biology* 13.2
cry of amusement 239.2
cry of disapproval 239.7
cry of greeting 239.4
cry of pain 239.5
cry of praise 239.3
cry of sorrow 239.6
cry of wolf *false alarm* 814.4
cryogen *cooler* 218.4
cryogenic *physical* 10.70, *cooled* 218.11
cryogenically *physically* 10.78

cryogenic memory *memory 15.6*
cryogenic pump *surface chemistry 11.20*
cryogenics Fields of Modern Physics 10, *cold 218.1*
cryohydrate *chemical compound 11.4*
cryometer Fields of Measurement 589
cryometry Fields of Measurement 589
cry one's eyes out *weep 280.8*
cryonic *cooled 218.11*
cryonics *freezing 218.2*
cryophobia Phobias 283
cryostat *cooler 218.4*
cry out *239.13*
cry out for *desire 288.17*
cry out for rest *be fatigued 820.5*
crypt *burial place 31.7, church architecture 134.11*
cryptanalysis *artificial language 5.9, science of interpretation 365.5*
cryptanalyst *interpreter 365.6*
cryptic *occult 86.16, disguised 181.9, mysterious 182.10, 844.11, obscure 197.2, inscrutable 250.5, unintelligible 364.4, confused 841.11*
cryptically *obscurely 197.4, opaquely 250.9, unintelligibly 364.16*
cryptogam *lower plant 41.4*
cryptogamic *taxonomic 41.16*
cryptogram *puzzle 182.5*
cryptographer *secret person 182.6, interpreter 365.6*
cryptographic *disguised 181.9, concealed 844.7*
cryptography *artificial language 5.9, puzzle 182.5, science of interpretation 365.5, concealment 844.2*
cryptologist *interpreter 365.6*
cryptology *navy specialties 77.24, science of interpretation 365.5*
cryptomeria Trees and Shrubs 43
cry quits *pacify 74.11, capitulate 421.6*
crystal *8.39, 11.14; transparent thing 249.4, glass 249.5, transparent 249.7, solid body 540.4, brittle thing 548.2*
crystal axis *crystal 8.39*
crystal ball *divination 86.5, means of prediction 358.10*
crystal boundary *crystal 11.14*
crystal-clear *clear 244.6, transparent 249.7, simple 363.6, open 843.12*
crystal-field theory *valence 11.5*
crystal-gaze *divine 86.24*
crystal gazer *diviner 86.14, observer 242.1, nonmaterialist 525.7, predictor 650.5*
crystal gazing *parapsychology 525.4, looking to the future 650.4*
crystal-gazing *divination 86.5*
crystal glass *glass 249.5*
crystal growth *crystal 8.39, industrial processes 14.27*
crystal lattice *crystal 8.39*
crystalline *status adjectives 11.25, transparent 249.7, condensed 540.7, hard 542.5*
crystalline element *or compound mineral 8.37*
crystallinity *transparency 249.1*
crystallite *crystal 11.14*
crystallization *petrogenesis 8.31, crystal 8.39, 11.14, process 11.15, concentration 540.2, hardening 542.2, chemical change 670.2*
crystallize *lithify 8.66, interact*

10.73, solidify 11.37, 542.10, make ceramics 129.10, be transparent 249.11, make transparent 249.12, be dense 540.8, convert 670.11
crystallized *status adjectives 11.25, ceramic 129.9, sweet 222.5, condensed 540.7, hardened 542.7*
crystallized glass *industrial ceramics 129.6*
crystallize out *solidify 11.37*
crystallizing *converting 670.8*
crystallographer *geologist 8.4*
crystallographic *physical 10.70, chemical 11.24*
crystallographically *physically 10.78*
crystallography *geology 8.1, Fields of Modern Physics 10, Branches of Chemistry 11, crystal 11.14*
crystalloid *status adjectives 11.25*
crystallophobia Phobias 283
crystal-oriented *electric 14.47*
crystals Phobias 283
crystal set *radio 172.1*
crystal symmetry *crystal 8.39*
crystal system *crystal 8.39, 11.14*
crystal vision *psychic power 86.4*
cry too soon *give warning 814.10*
cry uncle [Inf] *capitulate 421.6*
cry up *compliment 437.17*
cry wolf *give warning 814.10*
CSF *diagnostic procedure 107.11*
Ctenophora *coelenterate 39.15*
ctenophoran *coelenterate 39.25*
ctenophore *or ctenophoran coelenterate 39.15*
cub *have young 21.16, young animal 26.4, young man 26.8, young mammal 35.20, give birth 35.33, beginner 398.2*
Cuba Countries 566, Islands 572
cubage *size 579.1*
Cubalaya Breeds of Fowl 16
Cuban heels *shoes 100.30*
cubature *size 579.1*
cubby *compartment 578.2*
cubbyhole *hiding place 181.2, compartment 578.2, little space 580.6*
cube *multiplication 6.15, polyhedron 6.44, add 6.86, 784.11, make bigger 746.7, three 790.1, triple 790.10*
cubed *three 790.7*
cube root *multiplication 6.15, power 783.6*
cubic *6.81; functional 6.73, status adjectives 11.25, spatial 563.11, metrical 589.15*
cubic close-packed *status adjectives 11.25*
cubic close packing *crystal 11.14*
cubic content *space 563.1*
cubic crystal *crystal 11.14*
cubic equation *equation 6.25*
cubicle *compartment 578.2*
cubic measure *measuring system 589.4, type of measurement 589.8*
cubiform *cubic 6.81*
cubism Western Art Styles 133
cubitiere *historic armor 419.8*
cuboid *polyhedron 6.44, cubic 6.81*
cuboid bone Human Bones 19
cub reporter *print journalist 175.5*
cucking stool *instrument of punishment 454.13*
cuckold *married man 64.10, fornicate 432.14*
cuckolding *fornication 432.3*
cuckoldry *love affair 299.9, fornication 432.3*
cuckoo *bird sound 240.2*
cuckoo [Inf] *insane 110.9*

cuckoo clock Timepieces and Timers 646
cuckoo flower Flowers 42
cuckoo in the nest *intruder 724.7*
cuckoolike *avian 36.19*
cuckoopint Flowers 42
cuculiform *avian 36.19*
cucumber tree Trees and Shrubs 43
cud-chewer *hoofed mammal 35.16*
cud-chewing *ungulate 35.31*
cuddle *give pleasure 214.13, comfort 214.14, communicate love 299.25, retention 471.1, retain 471.7*
cuddlesome *luscious 214.8, lovable 299.20*
cuddling *communication of love 299.6*
cuddly *luscious 214.8, lovable 299.20*
cudgel *blunt weapon 78.5, instrument of punishment 454.13, hit 454.28, club 695.15*
cue *acting 136.22, dramatize 136.33, billiard 149.6, signs 183.2, reminder 354.4, impeller 695.7*
cue *or cue stick billiards 149.1*
cue ball *snooker 149.4*
cued *billiard 149.6*
cue rest *or bridge billiards 149.1*
cuff *part of garment 100.27, corporal punishment 454.11, hit 454.28, blow 695.5*
cufflink *fastener 754.7*
cuffs *means of restraint 830.6*
cuirass *historic armor 419.8*
cuisine *cooking 91.1*
cuisinier [Fr] *cook 91.3*
cuisinière [Fr] *cook 91.3*
cuisse *historic armor 419.8*
cul-de-sac *closed place 584.4, road 691.4, snag 824.8*
culinarily *91.11*
culinary *91.9*
culinary art *cooking 91.1*
culinary artist *cook 91.3*
culinary herb *vegetable 17.11, plant 41.2*
culinary masterpiece *dish 90.7*
cull *animal killing 30.10, kill animals 30.25, hunt 160.12, choose 382.14, subtract 749.6*
culled *hunting 160.11*
culling *hunting 160.2*
culm *grass plant 45.3*
culminate *peak 596.18, be at the top 600.9, react 676.8, ascend 713.19, be superior 744.15, intensify 746.8, complete 759.10, be complete 761.10, end 773.19*
culminating *top 600.6, completed 761.7, ending 773.13*
culmination *pinnacle 596.2, summit 600.1, effect 676.1, mounting 713.8, intensification 746.2, completion 761.2, limit 761.4, ending 773.10*
culminative *ending 773.13*
culottes *skirt 100.12*
culpability *lawbreaking 53.14, errancy 351.7, guilt 450.1*
culpable *offending 53.25, errant 351.12, immoral 430.11, unsatisfactory 438.15, villainous 448.12, guilty 450.6*
culpable omission *sin 450.3*
culpably *guiltily 53.38, villainously 448.18*
culprit *lawbreaker 53.15, wrongdoer 430.8, accused person 442.4, evil person 446.3, villain 448.5, guilty person 450.5*
cult *religious group 81.4, idolatry*

83.4, symbolics 85.4, belief system 87.3
cultish *idolatrous 83.13*
cultism *idolatry 83.4, symbolics 85.4*
cultist *religionist 81.14, idolater 83.7*
cultivable *farmable 16.17*
cultivar *plant breeding 17.6*
cultivate *17.19; farm 16.19, garden 17.18, educate 48.22, bring into existence 522.14, refine 534.7, cause 675.8, advise 825.27*
cultivate a friendship *befriend 62.10*
cultivate a habit *accustom oneself 397.19*
cultivated *ornamental 17.17, wild 41.15, refined 48.20, good-mannered 410.7, elegant 527.3*
cultivated land *farmland 16.3*
cultivated mushroom *mushroom 47.2*
cultivated plant *plant 41.2*
cultivating *cultivation 16.7*
cultivation *16.7; education 48.1, refinement 48.10, learning 348.3, cause 675.1, social improvement 807.3*
cultivator *farm tool 16.5, agriculturist 16.14, garden tool 17.7, 103.4, propagator 21.7, preparer 388.6, producer 522.10*
cult movie *movie type 137.3*
cultrate *sharp-edged 549.12*
cultural *societal 1.13, improving 807.14*
cultural anthropology *anthropology 1.1*
cultural commentator *literary person 139.14*
cultural ecology *sociology 2.1*
culturally *societally 1.17, sociologically 2.15*
culture *society 1.6, cultivation 16.7, civilized humanity 18.5, literature 139.1, learning 348.3, good manners 410.2, elegance 527.1, refinement 534.1*
cultured *534.6; ornamental 17.17, refined 48.20, 534.5, good-mannered 410.7, elegant 527.3, imitation 736.8*
cultures of *diagnostic procedure 107.11*
culverin *historical gun 78.10*
culvert *tunnel 551.11, channel 691.10*
cumber *make heavy 538.14*
Cumberland Rivers 570
cumbersome *clumsy 128.6, 824.14, graceless 528.7, ponderous 538.11, awkward 804.6*
cumbersomely *burdensomely 538.17*
cumbersomeness *weighing down 538.5, largeness 579.2, awkwardness 804.3*
cumbrance *weighing down 538.5*
Cumbrian Mountains Mountains and Hills 569
cumbrous *ponderous 538.11*
cumbrously *burdensomely 538.17*
cumbrousness *inelegance of expression 528.4*
cumin Herbs and Spices 91
cummerbund *formal clothes 100.5, circular thing 631.3, band 754.9*
cumshaw *gift 472.2*
cumulate *59.20; acquire 467.19*
cumulation *acquisition 467.4*
cumulative *acquisitive 467.13, increasing 746.4, additional 748.8*

cumulative distribution function *probability distribution* 6.56

cumulative effect *increase* 746.1

cumulatively *gainfully* 467.24, *increasingly* 746.9, *additionally* 748.15

cumulativeness *increase* 746.1

cumuliform *cloudy* 9.44

cumulonimbiform *cloudy* 9.44

cumulonimbus *cloud* 9.17

cumulostratus *cloud* 9.17

cumulous *cloudy* 9.44

cumulus *cloud* 9.17

cunctative *inactive* 413.9

cuneal *written* 5.36

cuneate *angled* 628.9

cuneiform *written letter* 5.14, *written* 5.36, *angled* 628.9

cuneiform church *church architecture* 134.11

cunnilingus *sex act* 20.10

cunning 330.3, **330.8, 822.1, 822.4;** *manual skill* 127.2, *skillful* 127.10, *well-made* 127.13, *guile* 193.3, *artful* 193.13, *planning* 387.11, *tactics* 399.12, *deviousness* 607.4, *devious* 607.9

Cunningham *sailing* 150.25

Cunningham tackle *sailboat parts and accessories* 150.4

cunningly **822.6;** *hypocritically* 330.15, *conspiratorially* 387.18

cunningness *cunning* 822.1

cunning person **822.3**

cunt [Inf] *organs of reproduction* 21.9

cunt [Inf *and* Off] *woman considered as a sex object* 33.8

Cup *Constellations* 7

cup *tableware* 92.13, *size of drink* 93.3, *drink container* 93.13, *golf course* 156.2, *monument* 185.10, *objective* 374.5, *prize* 453.2, *drinking vessel* 578.13, *General Units* 589, *cavity* 635.3, *draw off* 711.16

cup and ball *Children's and Party Games* 167

cupbearer *transferrer* 685.4, *transporter* 686.4

cupboard *receptacle* 105.11, *cabinet* 578.3

cupboard love *ungenuineness* 192.2

cupboard lover *hypocrite* 192.9

cupcake *cake* 90.36

cupcake [Inf *and* Off] *sex object* 20.8, *woman considered as a sex object* 33.8

cup(ful) *container(ful)* 738.2

cupful *size of drink* 93.3

cup fungi *fungi* 47.3

cupholder *prizewinner* 127.8, *paragon* 744.6

Cupid *Deities* 82, *goddesses and gods of love* 299.14

cupidinous *jealous* 314.5

cupidity *covetousness* 288.4, *jealousy* 314.2, *immorality* 432.1

cup of sorrows *adversity* 848.1

cupola *Architectural Elements* 134, *overhead covering* 613.11, *dome* 634.4

cupping *disgorgement* 709.6, *drawing off* 711.4

cupreous *brown* 256.5

cup-shaped *concave* 635.5

cup that cheers *drink* 121.6

cur *dog* 35.10, *hybrid* 751.6

Curaçao *Islands* 572

curability *recuperation* 809.4

curable *improvable* 807.13, *repairable* 809.7

curableness *recuperation* 809.4

curacy *priesthood* 84.2

curagh *Ships and Boats* 690

curate *member of the clergy* 84.5

curative *therapeutic* 107.30, *remedial* 115.14, *hygienic* 116.3, *relieving* 275.7, *restorative* 809.9

curatively *remedially* 115.19

curator *leader* 126.8, *surveillant* 810.12

curb *be self-restrained* 455.10, *moderate* 521.7, *edge* 618.1, *limit* 620.1, 620.7, *deceleration* 693.2, *slow down* 693.13, *hindrance* 826.1, *restraint* 826.8, 830.1, *hinder* 826.15, *restrain* 826.19, 830.12

curbed *conditional* 340.10, *blocked* 826.13

curb market *seller's market* 483.3

curd *solid body* 540.4, *semiliquid* 561.7

curdle *sour* 223.8, *be dense* 540.8, *thicken* 561.21

curdled *unpalatable* 223.6, *condensed* 540.7, *thick* 561.17

curdler *thickener* 561.12

curdling *viscosity* 561.1

cure **809.15;** *conciliate* 74.10, *means* 102.1, *practice medicine* 107.32, *make healthy* 113.13, *remedy* 115.1, 115.16, *therapy* 115.12, *season* 221.8, *therapy* 275.4, *disaccustom* 398.6, *put right* 429.14, *counteractant* 510.5, *counteract* 510.7, *dry* 560.17, *restoration* 807.4, *restore* 807.17, *recuperation* 809.4, *preserve* 815.14, *medical assistance* 825.5

cure-all *remedy* 115.1

cured **809.8;** *getting well* 113.9, *piquant* 221.6, *relieved* 275.6, *treated* 388.12, *preserved* 815.12

cured fish *fish dish* 90.19

cured ham *pork* 90.26

cure of *cure* 809.15

curer *repairer* 809.5

curette *void* 709.23

curfew *prohibition* 503.1, *limit marker* 620.4, *night* 656.3, *detention* 830.5

curfew bell *warning signal* 814.3

curia *place of judgment* 341.3

curie *Scientific and Technical Units* 589

Curie's law *Classical Physical Laws* 10

Curie–Weiss law *Classical Physical Laws* 10

curing **221.3;** *cooking technique* 91.2, *remedial* 115.14, *preservation of provisions* 815.6

curio *cheap item* 497.5, *showpiece* 843.3

curio cabinet *cabinet* 101.8

curiosa *mystery* 182.4

curiosity **321.1, 333.8;** *educatability* 48.9, *eagerness* 288.3, *wonderful person* 294.6, *unusualness* 782.4

curious **321.5;** *educatable* 48.18, *astonishing* 294.10, *watchful* 323.6, *problematic* 328.7, *questioning* 333.11, *characteristic* 779.12, *unusual* 782.15, *eccentric* 782.16

curiously **321.9;** *astonishingly* 294.19, *problematically* 328.12, *questioningly* 333.21

curiousness *curiosity* 321.1

curious person **321.3**

curium *Chemical Elements and Common Allotropes* 11

curl *vector* 6.48, *coif* 530.15, *curve*

629.1, 629.6, *coil* 632.2, *convolute* 632.6

curled *beautified* 530.12, *curved* 629.4

curled-up *squeezed* 582.9

curler *hairdressing tool* 530.9, *thrower* 696.10

curlew *water bird* 36.9

curlews *Collective Names* 59

curlicue *coil* 632.2

curliness *curvature* 629.2

curling *Sporting Activities* 145

curling iron *hairdressing tool* 530.9

curl one's lip *gesture* 183.17

curl pass *play* 155.8

curls *coiffure* 530.8

curl up *become smaller* 582.14

curl upward *ascend* 713.19

curly braces *Punctuation Marks* 5

curly-coated retriever *Breeds of Dogs* 35

curmudgeon *sullen person* 304.7, *discourteous person* 411.4

curmudgeonly *irritable* 304.9

currach *Ships and Boats* 690

curragh *Ships and Boats* 690

currency *publicity* 173.7, *money* 484.1, *modernity* 647.3, *newness* 652.1

currency market **484.8;** *stock exchange* 457.3

current *electric current* 10.39, *published* 173.12, *topical* 328.5, *familiar* 397.10, *tendency* 513.1, *flow* 570.4, *present* 647.4, *new* 652.9, *momentum* 677.2, *course* 679.2, *existing* 717.11, *average* 742.5, *usable* 801.6, *hidden danger* 813.3

current account *accounts* 493.4

current affairs *news* 171.1

current assets stock *personal estate* 470.6

current density *electric current* 10.39

current electricity *electricity* 10.31, 14.34

currently *topically* 328.11, *newly* 652.21

current of air *air flow* 558.4

current price *price* 494.1

currents *erosion* 8.41

current situation *present day* 647.2

curricular **48.21**

curriculum *subject* 48.3, *chronology* 646.2

curriculum vitae (CV) *biography* 3.5, *record* 185.1, *summary* 204.1, *documentation* 339.6

curried *culinary* 91.9

curry *cook* 91.10, *ride* 159.16, *season* 221.8, *rub* 554.12

currycomb *riding equipment* 159.9, *rub* 554.12

curry favor *fawn* 401.9, *cajole* 439.14

curry powder *Herbs and Spices* 91

curse **301.1, 301.13;** *use language* 5.42, *perform rites* 85.18, *bewitch* 86.25, *affliction* 117.1, *afflict* 117.16, *cry of disapproval* 239.7, *hiss* 239.17, *hate* 300.11, *blaspheme* 301.14, *evil thing* 446.2, *make evil* 446.11, *occult influence* 512.2, *grossness* 535.3, *adversity* 848.1

curse, the [Inf] *bleeding* 25.10

cursed **301.8;** *ritualistic* 85.15, *bewitched* 86.21, *afflicting* 117.11, *chance* 842.10

curse of Eve, the [Inf] *bleeding* 25.10

curse word **301.4**

cursing **301.7;** *hissing* 239.12, *profanity* 301.3, *profane* 301.10, *bad-mannered* 411.6, *inelegance of expression* 528.4

cursive *printed* 173.13

cursive type *type* 173.5

cursive writing *written letter* 5.14

cursor *computing terms* 15.22, *indicator* 183.7

cursorily *negligently* 326.8, *superficially* 599.8

cursoriness *rough idea* 544.4, *superficiality* 599.2, *incompleteness* 806.2

cursory *unrefined* 338.7, *unfinished* 544.9, *superficial* 599.4, *incomplete* 806.6, *hasty* 818.3

curt *concise* 198.4, *summary* 204.5, *sparing with words* 208.6, *discourteous* 411.5, *outspoken* 550.6, *abrupt* 591.8

curtail *play down* 195.17, *contract* 582.12, *shorten* 591.9, *limit* 620.7, 830.13, *make transient* 643.7, *make smaller* 747.8, *take off* 749.7, *separate* 753.12

curtailed *downplayed* 195.13, *shortened* 582.8, 591.7, 762.6, *limited* 620.5, *reduced* 749.5

curtailment *downplaying* 195.6, *shortening* 582.2, 591.2, *limit* 620.1, *limitation* 747.3, 830.2, *subtraction* 749.1, *separateness* 753.3

curtain *wall* 134.9, *play part* 136.8, *stage set* 136.19, *conceal* 181.12, *blinder* 243.7, *that which makes invisible* 245.2, *fort* 419.13, *buffer* 419.22, *interior decoration* 532.4, *wall covering* 613.12, *face* 613.31, *separator* 753.5, *protection from the weather* 810.9

curtain call *play part* 136.8, *acclaim* 437.5

curtain-lifter *play part* 136.8

curtain music *play part* 136.8

curtain off *exclude* 764.7

curtain raiser *preface* 769.5, *premiere* 771.9

curtain-raiser *play part* 136.8

curtains [Inf] *death* 29.1, *downfall* 714.7, *cessation* 773.2

curtain time *premiere* 771.9

curtal *Musical Instruments* 142

curtate *shortened* 591.7

Curtis Cup *golfing associations and tournaments* 156.6

curtly *concisely* 198.6, *discourteously* 411.8, *bluntly* 550.11, *abruptly* 591.13

curtness *conciseness* 198.1, *taciturnity* 208.1, *outspokenness* 550.2, *abruptness* 591.4

curtsy *submissiveness* 298.3, *submit* 298.17, *sign of courtesy* 410.5, *defer to* 410.12, *submission* 421.1, *succumb* 421.7, *obeisance* 426.3, *show deference to* 426.8, *mark of respect* 435.4, *show respect* 435.16, *bow* 716.6, 716.22

curtsying *showing respect* 435.7

curvaceous *rounded* 629.5, *well-rounded* 633.8

curvaceously *curvedly* 629.7, *roundly* 633.11

curvaceousness *round body* 633.2

curvature **629.2;** *surface* 6.36, *curve* 6.38, *divergence* 607.2, *deviation* 698.1

curve **6.38, 629.1, 629.6;** *graph* 6.30, *line* 6.35, *align* 6.92,

automobile racing terms 146.3, bowling delivery 151.2, divergence 607.2, be oblique 607.10, diverge 607.11, ring 681.9, road attribute 687.3, deviating course 698.2, deviate 698.15, twist 698.19, part 760.1
curve ball *pitching terms* 147.5
curved 629.4; *curvilinear* 6.78, *bowling* 151.6, *uniform* 545.5, *divergent* 607.7
curved bridge *bridge* 551.10
curved inward *concave* 635.5
curved line *line* 6.35
curvedly 629.7
curvedness *circularity* 631.1
curved surface 6.43; *surface* 6.36
curved thing 629.3
curve inward *be concave* 635.6
curve running *track event* 166.1
curviform *curved* 629.4
curvilinear 6.78; *curved* 629.4
curvilinearity *curvature* 629.2
curvilinearly *curvedly* 629.7
curving *blunt* 550.5, *divergent* 607.7, *curved* 629.4, *indirect* 698.9
curving inward *concavity* 635.1
curvy *rounded* 629.5
cusec *Scientific and Technical Units* 589
cushion *billiards* 149.1, *snooker* 149.4, *buffer* 419.22, *moderator* 521.2, *calm* 521.8, *soften* 543.14, *protection* 810.2, *assure* 810.23
cushioned *at ease* 819.2
cushion of air *air bubble* 558.10
cushiony *compressible* 543.9
cushy [Inf] *luscious* 214.8, *easy* 823.9
cushy job [Inf] *easy thing* 823.6
cusk *food fish and shellfish* 90.20
cusp *angle* 6.37, *Architectural Elements* 134, *sharp point* 549.2, *summit* 600.1, *limit* 773.7
cusped *or* **cuspate** *toothed* 549.13
cuspid *teeth* 19.8
cuspidate *toothed* 549.13
cuss [Inf] *blaspheme* 301.14, *grossness* 535.3
cuss *or* **cussword** [Inf] *curse word* 301.4
cussed [Inf] *obstinate* 379.5
cussedness [Inf] *obstinacy* 379.1, *defiance* 416.1
custard *egg dish* 90.18, *dessert* 90.35
custard pie *pie* 90.38
Custer's Last Stand *slaughter* 30.5
custodial *tutelary* 810.19
custodian *attendant* 69.4, *leader* 126.8, *protector* 419.16, *surveillant* 810.12
custodianship *patronage* 810.7, *detention* 830.5
custody *storage* 105.6, *possession of property* 469.3, *safekeeping* 810.6, *detention* 830.5
custody of children *divorce court* 66.3
custom 397.4, 480.12, 481.6, 780.5; *tradition* 1.7, 653.5, *expected thing* 356.3, *habit* 397.1, *etiquette* 406.3, 534.3, *good manners* 410.2, *action* 412.1, *performance* 465.2, *fashion* 536.1, *regularity* 663.1, *method* 765.7, *convention* 781.5
custom and practice *work practices* 57.2
customarily *societally* 1.17, *predictably* 295.9, *habitually* 397.20, *orderly* 663.13, *as a rule* 780.18

customariness *predictability* 295.2
customary 397.11, 780.9; *societal* 1.13, *predictable* 295.4, *habitual* 397.9, 765.15, *regular* 663.5, *average* 742.5, *common* 778.13
customary practice *custom* 780.5
custom board *sailboard parts* 150.20
custom-build *perform* 522.16
custom-built *produced* 522.12, *prototypical* 624.7, *customized* 779.14
customer *someone* 18.10, *user* 393.4, *recipient* 473.5, *purchaser* 481.7, *requester* 505.5
customer account *credit* 487.1
customer credit *credit* 487.1
customers *custom* 480.12
custom house *market* 483.1
custom *or* **customs house** *treasury* 484.19
customize *perform* 522.16, *characterize* 779.15
customized 779.14
custom-made *tailored* 100.41, *designed* 536.6
custom-made clothes *tailor-made clothes* 100.4
custom-make *make clothing* 100.44
customs *sailboard parts* 150.20, *way of life* 399.9, *morals* 431.2, *payment* 433.5, *money received* 492.2, *levy* 494.7
customs barrier *international trade* 56.7, *protectionism* 480.3
customs officer *collector* 473.7
customs official *security force* 810.13
cut *ornamental* 17.17, *cultivate* 17.19, *manage grassland* 45.10, *cook* 91.10, *woven* 130.15, *woodworking* 131.10, *carpenter* 131.10, *sculpt* 144.10, *play basketball* 148.7, *fencing movements* 153.3, *card playing* 168.1, *play cards* 168.7, *inscribe* 185.14, *illustrate* 187.11, *concise* 198.4, *be concise* 198.5, *summarized* 204.6, *painful injury* 215.3, *injured* 215.5, *inflict pain* 215.10, *external appearance* 264.5, *shun* 386.14, *ignore* 409.11, *be discourteous* 411.7, *hit* 418.9, 695.11, *stab* 418.22, *insult* 436.5, *allocate* 474.5, *taking away* 477.5, *take away* 477.18, *fee* 494.3, *discount* 495.1, 495.4, *make cheap* 497.14, *coif* 530.15, *fashion* 536.7, *style* 537.1, *designed* 537.5, *rarefied* 541.4, *make sparse* 541.5, *smooth* 545.10, *be sharp* 549.15, *use a sharp tool* 549.17, *dilute* 557.30, *river parts* 570.3, *opening* 583.1, *open* 583.10, 583.15, *crack* 587.2, 587.7, *cracked* 587.5, *slice* 588.4, *shortening* 591.2, *shortened* 591.7, *shorten* 591.9, *nature* 624.5, *form* 624.9, *notch* 636.1, 636.5, *notched* 636.4, *furrow* 638.1, 638.5, *waterway* 690.2, *blow* 695.5, *repulse* 701.2, *repel* 701.7, *hurry off* 705.11, *ostracize* 709.17, *make smaller* 747.8, *subtraction* 749.1, *subtracted item* 749.2, *subtract* 749.6, *separate* 753.7, *take apart* 753.16, *particle* 760.4, *interruption* 775.3, *disconnect* 775.12, *characteristic* 779.5, *limit* 830.13, *cancel* 834.6
cut [Inf] *winnings* 492.5, *abscond* 576.16
cut above *superior* 744.8
cut above, a *best* 805.9

cut a corner *short-cut* 591.11
cut across *short-cut* 591.11
cut a dash *show off* 404.26, *be important* 799.13
cut a dash *or* **swath** *or* **figure** *put on a show* 404.28
cut a deal [Inf] *contract* 459.8
cut adrift *diverge* 753.20
cut a figure *be important* 799.13
cut a long story short *be concise* 198.5, *be brief* 204.9
cut and blow-dry *coiffure* 530.8
cut-and-cover tunnel *tunnel* 551.11
cut-and-dried *predetermined* 384.4, *ready-made* 388.13
cut and run *retreat* 285.8, 386.22, *be swift* 694.10, *hurry off* 705.11, *be safe* 810.20, *make haste* 818.5
cut-and-try *experimental* 335.8
cutaneous *skin* 19.19
cutaneous disease *skin disease* 114.16
cutaway *jacket* 100.18, *formal clothing* 406.5
cut away *hurry off* 705.11
cutaway dive *competitive diving* 164.7
cutback *play* 155.8, *play offense* 155.18, *act of thrift* 499.2, *shortening* 591.2, *limitation* 747.3, *subtracted item* 749.2
cut back *deflated* 195.12, *deflate* 195.16, *economize* 499.6, *shorten* 591.9, *change by degrees* 739.8, *make smaller* 747.8, *reduce* 796.8
cut both ways *be equivocal* 380.7, *cancel out* 834.8
cut corners *economize* 499.6, *have no time to spare* 818.6
cut costs *economize* 499.6
cut dead *be discourteous* 411.7, *insult* 436.21
cut down *slaughter* 30.21, *be at war* 76.32, *deflated* 195.12, *deflate* 195.16, *stab* 418.22, *economize* 499.6, *knock down* 523.13, *shorten* 591.9, *flatten* 716.15, *make smaller* 747.8, *reduce* 796.8
cut down to size *deflate* 195.16, *abased* 298.13, *abase* 298.20, *make conform* 781.13
cute *beautiful* 529.7
cuteness *beauty* 529.1
cut flowers *flower* 42.1
cut free *disentangle* 823.17
cuticle *body covering* 19.4, *exteriority* 610.2
cuticle remover *cosmetic tool* 530.5
cuticle scissors *cosmetic tool* 530.5
cuticle stick *cosmetic tool* 530.5
cuticular *covering* 610.8
cutie [Inf] *attractive female* 529.5
cut in *interrupt* 775.14
cut in half *split down the middle* 772.20, *halve* 789.15
cut in three *trisect* 790.11
cut into *infiltrate* 706.13
cut in two *halve* 789.15
cut it out! *cease!* 668.14
cutlass *sharp weapon* 78.6
cutlery *tableware* 92.13
cutlet *meat dish* 90.21, *veal* 90.25, *particle* 760.4
cut loose *diverge* 753.20, *lack restraint* 829.21
cut no ice [Inf] *be powerless* 515.11, *be unimportant* 800.18
cutoff *shortcut* 591.5
cut off *kill* 30.19, *be at war* 76.32, *be concise* 198.5, *exclude* 409.12, *ruin* 523.15, *shorten* 591.9, *make transient* 643.7, *cause to cease*

668.12, *out of reach* 712.11, *take off* 749.7, *separate* 753.12, *discontinue* 775.10, *block* 826.17
cut off one's head *execute* 454.30
cut off one's nose to spite one's face *figurative expressions* 128.11
cut off short *be short* 591.10
cut off without a penny *impoverish* 486.16
cut of one's jib *nature* 624.5
cut one's own throat *figurative expressions* 128.11
cut one's throat *commit suicide* 30.24
cut open *open* 583.10, 583.15
cutout *darkening* 247.2
cut out *lay the foundations* 388.16, *fashion* 536.7, *form* 624.9, *dig out* 711.15
cut out [Inf] *run away* 386.21
cut out for *gifted* 127.11, *qualified* 340.7, *convenient* 803.3
cut out on [Inf] *abscond* 576.16
cutout switch *stopper* 584.3
cutover *fencing movements* 153.3, *fencing* 153.6
cut price *financial loss* 468.4, *buying* 481.9, *price* 494.1, *bargain* 495.2
cut-price *unprofitable* 468.10, *discounted* 495.3
cut prices *lose money* 468.15, *subtract* 749.6
cutpurse [Arch] *thief* 479.8
cut rate *financial loss* 468.4, *bargain* 495.2, *cheapness* 497.1
cut-rate *unprofitable* 468.10, *discounted* 495.3, *bargain* 497.10, *reduced* 749.5
cuts *limitation* 830.2
cut short *be concise* 198.5, *summarized* 204.6, *summarize* 204.7, *ruin* 523.15, *shortened* 591.7, *shorten* 591.9, *cause to cease* 668.12, *discontinue* 775.10, *have no time to spare* 818.6
cut someone off in his *or* **her prime** *cause to cease* 668.12
cut someone out of one's will *take back* 477.17
cut steps *mountaineer* 161.10
cutter *livestock* 16.11, *warship* 77.21, *clothier* 100.37, *artisan* 123.13, *sailboat* 150.3, *cardplayer* 168.3, *sharp-edged thing* 549.6, *Sailing Ships and Boats* 690, *Ships and Boats* 690
cut the cackle [Inf] *be concise* 198.5
cut the first turf *open* 771.32
cut the Gordian knot *overcome obstacles* 845.14
cut the ground from under one's feet *hinder* 826.15
cut the knot *separate* 753.12
cut *or* **mow the lawn** *or* **grass** *use a sharp tool* 549.17
cut the ribbon *open* 771.32
cut the throat of *slaughter* 30.21
cut the ties that bind *separate* 753.12
cutthroat *murderer* 30.12, *malefactor* 306.6, *competitive* 422.21, *evil person* 446.3, *destructive* 523.8
cutthroat competition *rivalry* 422.2
cut through *short-cut* 591.11, *take apart* 753.16
cut timber *manage trees* 43.14
cutting *plant breeding* 17.6, *garden plant* 17.10, *motion-picture editing* 137.8, *card playing* 168.1, *card-playing* 168.6, *emphatic* 200.3,

---

bitter 306.9, unsociability 409.1, attacking 418.14, insulting 436.10, sharp-edged 549.12, shortening 591.2, concave land 635.2, track 688.2, junction 691.9, subtraction 749.1, separateness 753.3
cutting away separateness 753.3
cutting back gardening 17.5, deflation 195.7, act of thrift 499.2, subtraction 749.1
cutting board cooking equipment 91.6
cutting corners home economics 56.2
cutting down deflation 195.7
cutting down to size downplaying 195.6
cutting edge 618.3; sharp edge 549.3, vanguard 621.5
cutting fluid machine tool 14.9
cutting in half halving 789.6
cutting in two halving 789.6
cutting off subtraction 749.1
cutting out digging out 711.3
cutting remark insult 436.5
cuttings compendium 204.3
cutting the ribbon premiere 771.9
cutting torch material 144.6
cutting words berating 438.5
cut to pieces slaughter 30.21, demolish 523.12
cut to pieces or **bits** apart 753.8
cut to ribbons slaughter 30.21
cut to the quick inflict pain 215.10
cut up sorrowful 270.4, harm 306.13, apart 753.8, divide 753.18, part 760.14
cutworm larva 40.9
cutworms pests and diseases 17.12
CV biography 3.5
cwm landform 8.9
cwm [Welsh] valley 572.8, concave land 635.2
cyan blueness 261.1, blue 261.5
cyanic blue 261.5
cyanide poison 117.7
cyanobacteria algae 47.11
Cyanophyta algae 47.11
cyanosed bluish 261.6
cyanosis blueness 261.1
cyanotic bluish 261.6
cyanotically bluely 261.11
Cybele Deities 82
cybernetically instrumentally 103.9
cybernetics histology 13.4, computing 15.2, artificial intelligence (AI) 15.21, data transmission 169.8
cyberphobia Phobias 283
cyberspace computer communications 15.25
cyborg humanlike machine 18.12
cycad fern 46.1
cycad fern fern 46.1
Cyclades Islands 572
cyclamate sweetener 222.2
cyclamen Flowers 42, red 257.5
cycle 663.3; be healthy 113.11, Scientific and Technical Units 589, circle 631.2, time period 641.2, recurrent period 641.5, frequency 661.1, be cyclic 663.11, orbit 681.3, rotation 682.1, series 770.3, continuum 774.5, return 797.4
cycle [Brit] bicycle 687.10
cycle around be cyclic 663.11
cycle path passage 691.5
cycle racing Sporting Activities 145
cycles per second radio frequency 661.3

cyclic 6.82, 663.7; chemical compound 11.4, reactive 11.29, habitual 397.9, circular 631.5, periodic 639.10, periodical 641.7, frequent 661.4, rotary 682.12
cyclic adenosine monophosphate (cAMP) bioenergetics 12.23
cyclical 774.10; frequent 661.4, cyclic 663.7, circular 681.6, rotary 682.12, recurrent 797.13
cyclically 663.15; circularly 631.8, periodically 641.11, frequently 661.7
cycling health improvement 113.3, orbiting 681.7, passing along 692.5
cycling shorts shorts 100.15
cyclist 687.13
cyclization chemical reaction 11.8
cyclize react 11.38
cycloid curve 6.38, personality type 108.6
cyclometer meter 589.13
cyclone weather system 9.10, wind vortex 9.14, natural violence 520.3, rough thing 544.2, vortex 682.6, natural hazard 813.4
cyclonic frontal 9.41, rotary 682.12
Cyclopean huge 579.14
Cyclopean construction Architectural Styles 134
cyclophobia Phobias 283
Cyclops Legendary Creatures 360, big person 579.8
cyclops crustacean 39.10
cyclorama stage set 136.19
cyclostome fish 38.5
cyclothyme personality type 108.6
cyclothymia psychosis 110.3
cyclothymic disorder mood disorder 108.12
cygnet young animal 26.4, young bird 36.17
Cygnus Constellations 7
cylinder 633.4; curved surface 6.43, engine type 14.11
cylindrical spherical 6.80, round 633.7
cylindrical coordinates coordinates 6.31, 589.6
cylindricality roundness 633.1
cylindrically roundly 633.11
cyma Architectural Elements 134
cyma recta Architectural Elements 134
cyma reversa Architectural Elements 134
cymatium Architectural Elements 134
cymatium or **cymation** architectural summit 600.4
cymbal percussion instrument 142.5
cymbalist player 141.2
cymbals Musical Instruments 142
cymbidium Flowers 42
cyme flower head 42.4
cymophobia Phobias 283
cymose of flowers 42.11
cymose inflorescence flower head 42.4
cymric Breeds of Cats 35
cynic Philosophical Schools of Thought 4, hopeless person 282.5, misanthrope 291.5, underestimator 344.2
cynical without hope 282.7, misanthropic 291.8, mentally tough 547.12
cynically unhopefully 282.14, misanthropically 291.18, pessimistically 344.6, satirically 369.9, single-mindedly 547.19
cynicalness mental toughness 547.5

Cynicism Philosophical Schools of Thought 4
cynicism lack of hope 282.2, misanthropy 291.4, underestimation 344.1
cynophobia Phobias 283
cynosural focal 612.8
cynosure indicator 183.7, manifestation 244.3, beautiful thing 529.3, focus 612.3, center of attraction 700.7
Cynthia moon 7.18
cyperaceous taxonomic 41.16
cypress Trees and Shrubs 43
cypress pine Trees and Shrubs 43
Cyprian sexually immoral person 432.8
cyprianophobia Phobias 283
cypridophobia Phobias 283
cyprinoid fishlike 38.10
Cyprus Countries 566, Islands 572
Cyprus Fat-tailed Breeds of Sheep 16
cypsela botanical fruit 44.2
Cyrenaic Philosophical Schools of Thought 4
Cyrenaic philosophy Philosophical Schools of Thought 4
cyst reproductive body 47.14, skin disease 114.16, ulcer 114.18, mark 533.2, bulge 634.2
cysteine Amino Acids 12
cysticercus invertebrate larva 39.19
cystic fibrosis respiratory disease 114.12
cystoscope diagnostic instrument 107.13
cystoscopy diagnostic procedure 107.11
cytochemistry cell biology 13.14
cytogenetics genetics 13.19
cytokinesis cell division 13.17
cytokinin plant hormone 12.17
cytological biological 13.27
cytologically biologically 13.36
cytologist life scientist 13.26
cytology histology 13.4, cell biology 13.14
cytoplasmic cellular 13.30
cytosine nucleotide 12.10
cytoskeleton cell structure 13.16
cytosol cell structure 13.16
cytosome cell structure 13.16
cytotaxonomy taxonomy 13.24
czar sovereign 68.2
czardas Dances 135
czarina sovereign 68.2
Czechoslovakian Improved White Breeds of Pigs 16
Czech Pied Breeds of Cattle 16
Czech Republic Countries 566

D

DA coiffure 530.8
dab type of touch 216.3, touch 216.9, blow 695.5, tap 695.13, little bit 800.4
dabble sprinkle 559.14
dabble in know little 349.9
dabble in occultism dematerialize 525.12
dabble in sorcery transform 665.20
dabble in stocks speculate 480.19
dabbler unskilled person 128.3, ignorant person 349.4, meddler 414.12
dabbling lack of knowledge 349.2, meddling 414.17
dabbling duck water bird 36.9

dab hand or **dab** [Inf] expert 52.8, 68.13
da capo Musical Terms and Expression Marks 140
da capo again 797.23
dachshund Breeds of Dogs 35
Dacron™ fiber 130.2
dactyl meter 139.10
dactylic metrical 139.20
dactylic hexameter meter 139.10
dactylographic gestural 183.13
dactylology gesture 183.5, aid to the deaf 229.3
dad [Inf] man in the family 32.12, family member 65.2
Dada Western Art Styles 133
Dadaism Western Literary Groups 139
dad-blamed miscellaneous euphemisms 301.12
dad-blasted miscellaneous euphemisms 301.12
dad-burned miscellaneous euphemisms 301.12
daddy [Inf] man in the family 32.12, family member 65.2
daddy-longlegs arachnid 40.4
dad-gummed miscellaneous euphemisms 301.12
dado Architectural Elements 134, base 601.1
daedal well-made 127.13
daemon system software 15.13, minor deity 82.2
daffodil Flowers 42, yellow thing 259.4
daft insane 110.9, unintelligent 316.6, foolish 353.5, ridiculous 368.5
daftly ridiculously 368.8
daftness folly 353.1, ridiculousness 368.1
Dagestan Mountain Breeds of Sheep 16
dagger sharp weapon 78.6, Reference Signs 183, agent of destruction 523.7, sharp-pointed thing 549.4, sharp-edged thing 549.6
daggerboard sailboat 150.3, sailboard parts 150.20
Daglic Breeds of Sheep 16
dago Nicknames for Inhabitants 61
dagoba shrine 83.10
daguerreotype older photograph 132.4
daguerreotypist photographer 132.23
Dagwood sandwich sandwich 90.9
dahlia Flowers 42
daily 655.6, 655.8; newspaper 175.2, magazine 175.3, habitual 397.9, periodical 641.7, for specified periods 641.12, frequently 661.7, cyclic 663.7, cyclically 663.15, regular 730.12, regularly 730.21
daily [Brit] domestic servant 69.7
daily bread life requirement 28.5, food 90.1, sustenance 825.3
daily double horse-racing betting terms 159.11
daily grind work 122.1, repetitiveness 797.3
daily habit way 397.3
daily help domestic servant 69.7
daily market market 483.1
daily paper newspaper 175.2
daily round way 397.3, round 633.6, cycle 663.3, regularity 730.6
daily routine regularity 730.6

dainties *hors d'oeuvre* 90.13
daintily *elegantly* 529.15, *lightly* 539.10, *texturally* 552.15, *little* 580.12
daintiness *cleanliness* 111.1, *lightness* 539.1, *grain* 552.2, *littleness* 580.1
dainty *edible* 92.20, *clean* 111.13, *appetizer* 219.2, *tasty* 219.4, *insubstantial* 539.5, *delicate* 552.10, *little* 580.7
dainty eater *eater* 92.15
dainty palate *delicate eating* 92.3
dairy *farm building* 16.4, *farm* 124.11
dairy farm *farm* 16.2
dairy farmer *agriculturist* 16.14
dairy farming *livestock farming* 16.10
dairyhand *farm worker* 16.15
dairying *livestock farming* 16.10
dairyland *farmland* 16.3
dairymaid *farm worker* 16.15
dairyman *farm worker* 16.15
dairy products *animal products* 522.7
Dairy Shorthorn Breeds of Cattle 16
dairywoman *farm worker* 16.15
dais *stage* 136.18
daisy Flowers 42
daisy and sunflower families *seed plant* 41.3
daisy chain *flower* 42.1
daisy-cutter *figurative usage* 42.8
daisy wheel *figurative usage* 42.8
daisy-wheel printer *hardcopy device* 15.10
Dakar Countries 566
dakhma *burial place* 31.7
Dala Breeds of Sheep 16
Dalai Lama *sovereign* 68.2, *priest* 84.8
dale *valley* 572.8
Dalesbred Breeds of Sheep 16
Dales pony Horse and Pony Breeds 159
Dallas–Fort Worth *major US cities* 567.5
dalliance *courtship* 299.10, *lingering* 693.4
dally *court* 299.26, *be irresolute* 378.9, *wait* 658.12, *hesitate* 693.12
dallying *courtship* 299.10, *lingering* 693.4, *delayed* 693.10
Dalmatian Breeds of Dogs 35, *variegated thing* 263.5
Dalmatian Karst Breeds of Sheep 16
dal segno Musical Terms and Expression Marks 140
dalton Scientific and Technical Units 589
daltonism *faulty vision* 243.1
Dalton's law Classical Physical Laws 10
dam 551.12; *propagator* 21.7, *horse* 159.1, *water carrier* 557.16, *stop the flow* 570.12, *stop* 584.14, *barrier* 826.7, *block* 826.17
damage *erosion* 96.3, *ill-use* 395.2, 395.7, *criticize* 438.19, *defame* 440.13, *be evil* 446.10, *affliction* 454.9, *loss* 468.1, *destroy* 468.18, *weakness* 517.1, *weaken* 517.13, *havoc* 523.5, *lay waste* 523.14, *blemish* 533.1, 533.7, *deform* 627.11, *reduction* 747.2, *imperfection* 806.1, *impairment* 808.7, *impair* 808.18
damaged *marked* 533.6, *imperfect* 806.5, *spoiled* 808.9
damages 489.8; *compensation*

453.7, 478.2, 743.1, *liability* 454.6, *business expenses* 491.4
damages [Inf] *cost(s)* 491.3
damaging *abusive* 395.5, *critical* 438.13, *defamatory* 440.9, *detrimental* 446.8, *irresolute* 461.6
damagingly *devastatingly* 96.24
Damani Breeds of Sheep 16
damascene *check* 263.2, *variegate* 263.11
Damascus Breeds of Cattle 16, Countries 566
damask Fabrics and Fibers 130, *red* 257.5
Damavand *or* **Demavend** Mountains and Hills 569
dam-breaking *flowing* 570.7
Dame *female title of address* 33.3, *honorific* 72.5
dame *noblewoman* 70.1
dame [Inf *and* Off] *sex object* 20.8, *woman considered as a sex object* 33.8
Damietta Breeds of Cattle 16
dammed *stopped* 584.9
damn *curse* 301.13, *vilify* 301.15, *condemn* 438.18, *make evil* 446.11, *little bit* 800.4
damn! *miscellaneous swearwords* 301.20
damnation *curse* 301.1, *condemnation* 438.2
damnation! *miscellaneous swearwords* 301.20
damned *cursed* 301.8, *condemned* 438.11, *demonic* 446.9
damned soul *loser* 468.8
damning *cursing* 301.7, *condemning* 438.10
damningly *execratively* 301.17
damn it! *miscellaneous swearwords* 301.20
damn the torpedoes — full speed ahead! *here goes!* 376.18
damn with faint praise *disparage* 195.15
Damodar Rivers 570
Damon Notable Friendships 62
damp *weather data* 9.6, *humid* 9.48, *calm* 521.8, *miasma* 556.3, *wateriness* 557.3, *moist* 559.9
damp down *mute* 233.9
damped *nonresonant* 233.7
dampen *discourage* 179.11, *mute* 233.9, *cause sorrow* 270.9, *calm* 521.8, *moisten* 559.13, *hinder* 826.15
dampened *discouraged* 179.6, *nonresonant* 233.7
dampener *sound reducer* 233.5
dampening *wetting* 557.26
dampen the spirits *cause sorrow* 270.9
damper *disaffection* 179.3, *sound reducer* 233.5, *moderator* 521.2, *stopper* 584.3, *hinderer* 826.11, *means of restraint* 830.6, *restrain* 830.12
damping-off *pests and diseases* 17.12, *fungal disease* 47.6
dampish *moist* 559.9
damply *wetly* 557.34, *moistly* 559.17
dampness *weather data* 9.6, Phobias 283, *wateriness* 557.3, *moisture* 559.1
dampproof *waterproof* 560.16
damsel [Arch] *female* 33.1
damson-colored *purple* 262.6
damson plum *purple thing* 262.3
dam up *stop the flow* 570.12
dan *prizewinner* 127.8
dance 135.1, 135.7; *social gathering* 59.7, *dancing* 135.6, *entertain*

138.16, *boxing techniques* 152.5, *rejoice* 279.5, *party* 408.6, *work of art* 522.4, *walk* 677.17, *reel* 682.4, *be agitated* 684.21, *flicker* 684.26, *production* 843.5
dance about *box* 152.19
dance around the issue *lack candor* 192.22
dance attendance on *serve* 69.11, *be attentive* 323.9, *pander to* 401.11, *attend* 794.19
dance band *dance hall* 135.3
dance drama *dance* 135.1
dance floor *dance hall* 135.3
dance hall 135.3
dance lift *ice-dancing move* 162.19
dance music *popular music* 140.4
dance notation *representation* 187.1
dance of death *personifications and symbols* 29.4
dance of the seven veils *undressing* 614.2
dance on ice *ice-skate* 162.36
dancer 135.4; *artistic worker* 123.12
dance step *ice-dancing move* 162.19, *bodily movement* 677.11
dancing 135.6; *dance* 135.1, *combat* 152.17, Phobias 283, *fidgety* 414.14, *restlessness* 684.5
dancing light *variegated thing* 263.5
dancingly 135.8
dancing on ice *ice dancing* 162.18
dandelion Flowers 42, *yellow thing* 259.4
dander [Inf] *anger* 302.4
Dandie Dinmont Breeds of Dogs 35
dandle *love* 299.21
dandruff *dirt* 112.5, *crumb* 553.5, *slice* 588.4, *residue* 750.2
dandy *fashion business* 536.3
dandy [Inf] *good thing* 445.9, *great* 445.14
Danegeld *historical tax* 494.8
dang *or* **danged** *miscellaneous euphemisms* 301.12
danger 811.1; *trap* 813.1, *forewarning* 814.2, *critical situation* 824.6
danger-loving *adventurous* 284.12, *reckless* 286.6
dangerous 811.7; *unhygienic* 114.27, *trapped* 813.5, *unreliable* 841.15
dangerous age *middle age* 27.4
dangerous course *endangerment* 811.2
dangerous game *rash move* 286.4
dangerously 811.14; *unreliably* 841.25
dangerousness *danger* 811.1
dangerous situation *danger* 811.1
dangerous speed *speed* 694.2
dangerous subject *provocation* 302.3
danger past *safety* 810.1
danger sign *signs* 183.2
danger signal 811.5; *signal* 183.6, *red thing* 257.3, *notice* 358.3
Dangi Breeds of Cattle 16
dangle *suspend* 604.13, *come unstuck* 756.7, *display* 843.13
dangle before one's eyes *entice* 178.16, *flourish* 604.25
dangled *suspended* 604.7
dangler *adherent* 401.5
dangling *suspension* 604.1,

suspended 604.7, *nonadhesive* 756.4
dangling participle *language error* 351.10
dan grade *judo* 152.13, *karate* 152.14
Daniel *judge* 54.10
Danish Black Pied Breeds of Cattle 16
Danish Landrace Breeds of Pigs 16
Danish pastry *pastry* 90.37
Danish Red Breeds of Cattle 16
Danish Red Pied Breeds of Cattle 16
dank *unpalatable* 223.6, *moist* 559.9
dankishness *humidity* 559.3
dankly *moistly* 559.17
dankness *unpalatability* 223.2, *humidity* 559.3
danseur *ballet dancer* 135.5
danseuse *ballet dancer* 135.5
Dante Famous Lovers 299
Dantesque *poetic* 139.19
Danube Rivers 570
Danube Merino Breeds of Sheep 16
Danubian Horse and Pony Breeds 159
Daphne *figurative usage* 43.9
daphne Trees and Shrubs 43
daphnia *crustacean* 39.10
Daphnis Famous Lovers 299
dapper *dressed up* 100.39, *clean* 111.13, *fashionable* 536.5, *orderly* 765.13
dapping *fly-fishing* 154.2
dapple *variegate* 263.11, *mix* 751.12
dappled *mottled* 263.10, *varied* 732.6, *complicated* 751.10
dapple-gray *horse by color* 159.7, *gray* 255.6
dapple horse *variegated thing* 263.5
dappling *maculation* 263.4, *variety* 751.4
Darashomi Horse and Pony Breeds 159
Darashouri Horse and Pony Breeds 159
Darby and Joan *two* 789.1
darcy Scientific and Technical Units 589
dare *be courageous* 284.14, *take courage* 284.15, *invent* 335.13, *brace oneself* 376.13, *undertake* 391.7, *have the audacity* 400.15, *act of defiance* 416.3, *defy* 416.7, *be insubordinate* 416.8, *face danger* 811.12, *risk* 841.21
D area *snooker* 149.4
daredevil *courageous person* 284.8, *rash move* 286.4, *reckless* 286.6, *rash person* 353.4, *foolish* 353.5
daredeviltry *or* **daredevilry** *recklessness* 286.2
daresay *suppose* 359.8, *think likely* 838.10
Dar es Salaam Countries 566
daring *courage* 284.1, *courageous* 284.9, *recklessness* 286.2, *reckless* 286.6, *originality* 335.4, *original* 335.9, *attempting* 390.4, *enterprising* 391.5, *dramatic* 404.16, *defiance* 416.1, *defiant* 416.5, *strong in spirit* 516.1, *endangerment* 811.2, *openness* 843.6, *open* 843.12
daringly *recklessly* 286.10, *inventively* 335.15, *enterprisingly* 391.11, *dramatically* 404.31, *defiantly* 416.9

daringness *defiance* 416.1
dark 247.5, 254.6; *cloudy* 9.44, *funeral* 31.9, *exposed* 132.25, *hidden* 243.15, *difficult to see* 245.4, *private* 245.5, *darkness* 247.1, *dark-colored* 247.7, *dim* 248.4, *opaque* 250.3, *shady* 250.4, *blackness* 254.1, *dull* 255.8, *browned* 256.6, *Phobias* 283, *overcast* 304.11, *intense* 598.16, *night* 656.3, *evening* 656.4, *concealed* 844.7
Dark Ages Ages, Decades, Eras 641, *historical past* 651.6
dark-blue *blue* 261.5
dark brown *brown* 256.5
dark clothes *darkness* 247.3
dark cloud *cloud* 9.17
dark clouds *threat* 848.3
dark color *blackness* 254.1
dark-colored 247.7
dark coloring *blackness* 254.1
dark comedy *comedy* 136.11
dark complexion *brownness* 256.1
dark-complexioned *dark* 254.6
darken *cloud* 9.54, *disguise* 181.13, *blind* 243.13, *become invisible* 245.6, *make invisible* 245.7, *become dark* 247.9, *make dark* 247.10, *be dim* 248.7, *make dim* 248.8, *opaque* 250.7, *color* 251.16, *blacken* 254.11, *deepen* 598.21
darkened *difficult to see* 245.4
darkening 247.2, 247.6; *blinding* 243.13, *blackness* 254.1, *deepening* 598.14
Darkest Africa *distant place* 585.3
darkest hour *darkness* 247.1
dark glasses *visual aid* 242.14, *dark thing* 247.3, *shade maker* 247.4
dark-gray *gray* 255.6
dark-green *green* 260.7
dark-haired *dark-colored* 247.7, *black-haired* 254.8
dark-headed *black-haired* 254.8
dark horse *horse racing* 159.10
darkish *dark* 247.5, *dim* 248.4
dark lantern *lantern* 246.8, *dark thing* 247.3
darkle *become dark* 247.9
darkling *dark* 247.5
darkly 247.11; *dimly* 248.10, *blackly* 254.12, *dismally* 304.19, *intensely* 598.28
dark matter *universe* 7.3, *dark thing* 247.3
dark meat *poultry* 90.28
dark nebula *nebula* 7.6
darkness 247.1; *blindness* 243.3, *invisibility* 245.1, *that which makes invisible* 245.2, *opaqueness* 250.1, *hue* 251.4, *blackness* 254.1, *dullness* 255.5, *Phobias* 283, *deepness* 598.6, *night* 656.3, *mysteriousness* 844.5
dark of night *night* 656.3
dark purple *purple* 262.6
dark reaction *photosynthesis* 12.22
darkroom *dark thing* 247.3
darkroom equipment 132.21
dark side *aspect* 623.4
dark skin *brownness* 256.1
dark-skinned *dark-colored* 247.7
dark star *dark thing* 247.3
dark thing 247.3
Darling *Rivers* 570
darling *child* 26.6, *idol* 83.5, *term of endearment* 299.7, *beloved* 299.19
darn *sew* 130.18, *intertwine* 752.19, *repair* 809.1, 809.10
darn *or* **darned** [Inf] *miscellaneous euphemisms* 301.12

darn! [Inf] *miscellaneous euphemisms* 301.21
darned *united* 752.10
darning *sewing* 130.5, *repair* 809.1
darshan *imam* 84.7
dart Historical Missile Weapons 78, *be irresolute* 666.6, *walk* 677.17, *missile* 696.7
darting *irresolution* 666.2, *speeding* 694.7
Dartmoor Breeds of Sheep 16
Dartmoor pony Horse and Pony Breeds 159
dart off *accelerate* 694.14
darts Sporting Activities 145
darts game *type of game* 167.2
dart to and fro *make haste* 818.5
Darussalam Countries 566
Darvaz Breeds of Sheep 16
Darwinian *evolutionary* 13.34
Darwinism *evolution* 13.23
Darwinist *life scientist* 13.26
Darwin's finch *songbird* 36.12
Dasehra *religious festival* 85.13
dash *punctuate* 183.20, *emphasis* 200.1, *emphasize* 200.6, *will* 376.5, *flashiness* 404.4, *alacrity* 414.3, *be active* 414.18, *vigor* 518.1, *billow* 571.9, *little piece* 580.4, *walk* 677.17, *acceleration* 694.3, *scamper* 694.12, *blow* 695.5, *hit* 695.11, *hurry off* 705.11, *admixture* 751.5, *mix* 751.12, *separator* 753.5, *means of connection* 754.4, *few* 796.1, *suggestion* 800.9, *haste* 818.1, *make haste* 818.5
dash! [Brit] *miscellaneous euphemisms* 301.21
dash at *attack* 418.17
dashed hopes *lack of hope* 282.2, *frustration* 293.2
dash for *aim* 697.14
dash forward *accelerate* 694.14
dashiki *shirt* 100.13
dashing *emphatic* 200.3, *swaggering* 404.20, *active* 414.13, *fashionable* 536.5, *speeding* 694.7
dashingly 536.10; *swaggeringly* 404.35
dash off *accelerate* 694.14, *hurry off* 705.11, *make haste* 818.5
dash someone's hopes *thwart* 293.10, *disappoint* 846.15
dash the cup from one's lips *disappoint* 282.12, *thwart* 293.10
dash through *have no time to spare* 818.6
dastard *coward* 285.3, *dastardly* 285.6
dastardliness 285.2
dastardly 285.6
Dastur *priest* 84.8
data *computer information* 15.17, *data-related concepts* 15.23, *information* 170.1, 348.2, *evidence* 339.1, *basis of supposition* 359.2
data bank *vault* 105.9
database 15.15; *schoolbook* 48.15, *information technology (IT)* 170.7, *record book* 185.5, *list* 785.1
database management system (DBMS) *database* 15.15
database program *application software* 15.14
data collection *population* 6.55
data communications *information technology (IT)* 170.7
data entry *computing* 15.2
data-entry clerk *office assistant* 69.6
data processing (DP) *computing*

15.2, 784.4, *information technology (IT)* 170.7, *recordkeeping* 185.7
data-processing language *artificial language* 5.9
data-related concepts 15.23
data structure *programming concepts* 15.24
data summarization *population* 6.55
data systems *navy specialties* 77.24
data tablet *input device* 15.11
data transmission 169.8; *artificial satellite* 7.30
date *seek friendship* 62.11, *engagement* 136.15, 138.6, *lover* 299.11, *court* 299.26, *social gathering* 408.4, *fraternize* 408.17, *day* 646.4, *keep time* 646.12, *chronologize* 646.13, *partner* 794.9, *keep company with* 794.17
datebook *record book* 185.5, *list of dates* 785.6
dated *historical* 3.10, *unfashionable* 528.10, *chronological* 839.12
date in history *day to remember* 354.5
dateless *timeless* 640.3
datelessness *timelessness* 640.1
date line *time zone* 646.5
date palm Trees and Shrubs 43
date rape *personal attack* 418.8, *sexual offense* 432.6
dating 8.48; *courtship* 299.10, *timekeeping* 646.1
dating agency *matchmaker* 64.13
dating service *matchmaker* 64.13
dative *grammatical term* 5.29
dative bond *chemical bond* 11.6
datum *basis of supposition* 359.2, *aspect* 726.4
daub *dirty* 112.11, *painting* 143.3, *paint* 143.12, *misrepresent* 188.6, *nonsense* 362.2, *mean nothing* 362.10, *anoint* 562.17
daubed *painted* 143.10
dauber *unskilled person* 128.3, *visual artist* 133.6
daubing (*act of*) *painting* 143.1, *misrepresentation* 188.1
daughter *woman in the family* 33.13, *family member* 65.2, *loved one* 299.13
daughter-in-law *family member* 65.2
daughter nuclide *radioactivity* 10.58
daughter product *radioactivity* 10.58
daunt 179.9; *intimidate* 283.18
daunted *dissuaded* 179.5, *cowardly* 285.4
daunting *dissuasive* 179.4, *fearsome* 283.13
dauntingly *dissuasively* 179.12, *fearsomely* 283.21
dauntless *courageous* 284.9, *tenacious* 376.9
dauntlessly *courageously* 284.17
dauntlessness *courage* 284.1, *tenacity* 376.4
davenport *couch* 101.7
davenport [Brit] *type of desk* 101.6
David Notable Friendships 62, Famous Lovers 299
Davis Cup *notable tennis competitions* 165.8
Davy Jones's locker *sea* 571.l, *the depths* 598.2
Davy lamp *lantern* 246.8
dawdle *be inactive* 415.13, *wait* 658.12, *slow motion* 693.3, *hesitate* 693.12

dawdler *nonworker* 415.4, *plodder* 693.6
dawdling *restlessness* 414.7, *idleness* 415.3, *not participating* 415.11, *lingering* 693.4, *hesitant* 693.9, *delayed* 693.10
dawn *grow light* 246.21, *red thing* 257.3, *become visible* 264.13, *Phobias* 283, *beginning* 583.9, 771.1, *begin* 583.21, *morning* 655.2, *daily* 655.6, *early hour* 657.2, *emerge* 771.35
dawn chorus *morning things* 655.3
dawn dew *dew* 559.6
dawning *beginning* 583.14, *daily* 655.6, *embryonic* 771.19
dawn on *be intelligible* 363.10
dawn redwood Trees and Shrubs 43
dawn upon *have an idea* 327.13
day 646.4; *time period* 641.2
day after day *frequently* 661.7, *repeatedly* 797.22
day after tomorrow, the *future time* 650.1
day and night *frequently* 661.7
day-and-night attack *combined attack* 418.5
daybeacon *sea marker* 690.7
daybed *type of bed* 101.9
day before yesterday, the *recent past* 651.4, *in the past* 651.20
day-blind *visually impaired* 243.9
day blindness *faulty vision* 243.1
daybook *periodical* 175.1, *certificate* 185.2, *record book* 185.5, *account book* 493.3, *bill* 785.4
day book *list of dates* 785.6
daybreak *morning* 655.2, *early hour* 657.2, *beginning* 771.1
day by day *all the time* 639.16, *cyclically* 663.15
day-care center *school* 48.11
day coach *railroad car* 688.5
daydream *lack thought* 318.12, *be inattentive* 324.10, *imagine* 327.14, 720.13, *conception* 360.4, *reverie* 360.6, *fantasize* 360.15, *lose track of* 698.18, *illusion* 720.2
daydreamer *visionary* 360.9, *inactive person* 413.8
daydreaming *trance* 108.18, *inattention* 329.2, *thoughtfulness* 317.2, *absent-mindedness* 324.2, *absent-minded* 324.6, *idealism* 327.7, *imaginative* 360.10
Day-Glo™ clothing *protective clothing* 419.6
Day-Glo™ vest *hunting accessories* 160.5
day hospital *hospital* 107.16
day in, day out *all the time* 639.16, *frequently* 661.7, *continuously* 774.16, *repeatedly* 797.22
day laborer *laborer* 123.9
daylight *lighting* 132.16, *natural light* 246.4, *sunny* 246.17, *Phobias* 283, *interval* 587.1, *daytime* 655.1, *morning* 655.2, *daily* 655.6
daylight-saving time *time zone* 646.5
daylily Flowers 42
day nurse *nurse* 107.23
day of abstinence *fast* 118.4
Day of Atonement Jewish Holy Days and Seasons 85, *penitence* 313.3
day off *time off* 125.2, *leave of absence* 576.4, *pause* 668.3, *ease* 819.1
day of grace *deliverance* 817.1

Day of Judgment *future condition* 650.3, *end of time* 773.5
day of judgment *judgment day* 341.4, *reckoning* 454.8
day of reckoning *reckoning* 454.8
day of rest *ease* 819.1
day one *beginning* 771.1
daypack *climbing equipment* 161.4
day sailing *sailing* 150.2
day sailor *sailboat* 150.3
day school *type of school* 48.12
day's end *night* 656.3, *late hour* 658.2, *nightfall* 714.5
days gone by *past time* 3.6
day's march *great distance* 585.2
days of innocence *naiveté* 449.4
days of old *past time* 3.6, 651.1
days of yore *past time* 3.6, 651.1
dayspring [Arch] *morning* 655.2
daystar *sun* 7.15
daytime 655.1; *daily* 655.6
daytime drama *program* 172.10
Daytona 500 race *races* 146.4
day to remember 354.5; *anniversary* 405.5
daze *trance* 108.18, *be wondrous* 294.14, *make uncertain* 841.19
dazed *wondering* 294.7
dazzle *blind* 243.17, *quality of light* 246.2, *light* 246.19, *be wondrous* 294.14, *flashiness* 404.4, *put on a show* 404.28, *be beautiful* 529.11
dazzled *blinded* 243.12, *wondering* 294.7
dazzler *attractive female* 529.5
dazzling *blinding* 243.13, *bright* 246.14, *wondrous* 294.9, *flashy* 404.17, *strong to the senses* 516.12, *beautiful* 529.7, *excellent* 805.15
dazzlingly *blindingly* 243.21, *lightly* 246.23, *flashily* 404.32, *gorgeously* 529.14
d-block *chemical element* 11.3
D.C. Musical Terms and Expression Marks 140
DDT *pest control* 16.13
deacon *member of the clergy* 84.5
deaconess *member of the clergy* 84.5
deaconry *priesthood* 84.2
deaconship *priesthood* 84.2
deactivate *make inactive* 415.16, *counteract* 510.7, *mitigate* 521.9, *disband* 776.13, *make useless* 802.12, *impair* 808.18
deactivated *reactive* 11.29, *catalytic* 11.30, *inoperative* 515.8, *suspended* 519.3, *disbanded* 776.7
deactivation *catalysis* 11.16, *neutralization* 510.4, *weakness* 517.1, *disbandment* 776.2
dead 29.11, 658.10; *infertile* 23.7, *bowls* 151.7, *nonresonant* 233.7, *disappeared* 265.4, *accurately* 350.6, *inactive* 413.9, *correct* 429.8, *inert* 519.2, *unfashionable* 528.10, *soothing* 545.6, *over* 651.12, *sedentary* 678.5, *directly* 697.16, *no more* 718.11, *ended* 773.14, *fatigued* 820.2, *canceled* 834.5
dead, the *dead person* 29.7
dead ahead *directly* 697.16
dead and buried *forgotten* 355.7, *losing* 468.9, *over* 651.12, *ended* 773.14
dead and gone *over* 651.12, *no more* 718.11
dead as a dodo *over* 651.12
dead as a doornail *dead* 29.11, *no more* 718.11
dead ball *playing terms* 148.4, *billiards* 749.2
dead-ball foul *penalty* 155.13
deadbeat *sponger* 401.4

dead beat [Inf] *fatigued* 820.2
dead body *dead person* 29.7
dead bolt *safety device* 810.15
dead bowl *grip* 151.4
dead broke *needy* 95.12, *insolvent* 486.10
dead calm *smoothness* 545.1, *repose* 678.2
dead center *center* 612.1
dead cert [Brit inf] *certainty* 840.1, *good chance* 842.6
dead certainty *easy thing* 823.6, *certainty* 840.1
dead drunk 121.27
dead duck [Inf] *dying person* 29.6, *hopeless person* 282.5
dead easy *easy* 823.9
deaden *discourage* 179.11, *strike dumb* 206.10, *anesthetize* 213.8, *muffle* 229.11, *mute* 233.9, *tarnish* 248.9, *decolor* 252.8, *make indifferent* 289.13, *make inactive* 415.16, *overpower* 515.14, *calm* 521.8
dead end *closed place* 584.4, *road* 691.4, *snag* 824.8
deadened *discouraged* 179.6, *desensitized* 213.5, *nonresonant* 233.7
deadening *anesthetic* 213.6
deadeye *shooter* 696.11
dead hand *legal property terms* 470.2
deadhead *cultivate* 17.19
deadhead [Inf] *theatergoer* 136.30
deadheading *gardening* 17.5
dead heat *horse racing* 159.10, *stalemate* 740.3
dead jack *grip* 151.4
dead language *ancient language* 5.10
dead leaf *brown thing* 256.3, *brittle thing* 548.2
dead letter *postal communication* 169.4, *nonsense* 362.2
dead-letter office *postal service* 169.5
deadline *close* 773.9, *haste* 818.1
deadliness *lack of hygiene* 112.3, *evil* 446.1
dead load *load* 14.14, *weighing* 538.4
deadlock *inaction* 413.1, *obstruction* 584.2, *stop* 668.2, *lack of motion* 678.1, *stalemate* 740.3, *nonachievement* 762.3, *safety device* 810.15, *snag* 824.8, *obstacle* 826.2, 837.3, *have a mishap* 826.18
deadlocked *inactive* 413.9, *stopped* 668.7, *troubled* 824.15, *blocked* 826.13
dead loss *loss* 468.1, *waste of effort* 802.4
deadly 29.14, 30.26; *killing* 30.17, *unhygienic* 114.27, *toxic* 114.28, *boring* 396.6, *detrimental* 446.8, *sinful* 450.8, *destructive* 523.8, *dangerous* 811.7
deadly crime *wicked act* 448.7
deadly sin *iniquity* 448.3, *sin* 450.3
deadman *climbing equipment* 161.4
dead-man's float *swimming techniques* 164.2
dead-man's handle or **pedal** *safety device* 810.15
dead march *funeral* 31.4
deadness *hue* 251.4
dead of night *night* 656.3
dead or **depths of winter** *cold weather* 218.8
dead-on [Inf] *correct* 429.8, 721.13

dead on arrival (DOA) *dead* 29.11
deadpan *serious* 278.4, *apathetic* 322.4, *unintelligible* 364.4
dead person 29.7
dead pigeon [Inf] *dying person* 29.6
dead puck *ice hockey tactics* 158.4
dead-reckon *navigate* 690.15
dead reckoning *navigation* 690.5
dead-reckoning position *navigation* 690.5
dead-right *accurate* 350.3, *correct* 429.8
dead ringer [Inf] *image* 187.3, *look-alike* 730.4, *twin* 789.5
Dead Sea Lakes 568
dead season *seasons* 654.2
dead set *military attack* 418.2, *lack of motion* 678.1
dead set upon *resolute* 376.7
dead shot *prizewinner* 127.8, *shooter* 696.11
dead silence *silence* 231.1
dead simple *easy* 823.9
dead stop *stop* 668.2, *lack of motion* 678.1, *discontinuance* 846.4
dead straight *straight* 630.8
dead tired *fatigued* 820.2
dead to *wonderless* 295.3
dead to the world *desensitized* 213.5, *unhearing* 229.5, *not awake* 415.12
dead water *small lake* 568.2
dead weight *weighing* 538.4, *burden* 826.10
dead wood *timber* 43.3, *refuse* 802.5
dead-wrong *wrong* 430.12
deaf 229.4; *insensible* 213.4, *oblivious* 355.9, *opinionated* 379.9, *inactive* 413.9
deaf aid *aid to the deaf* 229.3
deaf-and-dumb [Off] *deaf* 229.4
deaf as a post *deaf* 229.4
deaf ears *inattention* 229.2
deafen 229.10; *shatter the peace* 232.10
deafened *deaf* 229.4
deafening 229.6; *loud* 232.6, *vociferous* 239.9
deafeningly *deafly* 229.13, *vociferously* 239.18
deafening row *tumult* 232.5
deafly 229.13
deaf-mute *deaf* 229.4
deaf-mutism *mutism* 206.3, *deafness* 229.1
deafness 229.1; *opinionatedness* 379.3
deaf to *unhearing* 229.5, *indifferent* 289.7, *wonderless* 295.3, *refused* 506.5
de-air *make ceramics* 129.10
de-airing *ceramic process* 129.5
deal 457.9; *wood* 131.3, *card playing* 168.1, *play cards* 168.7, *deed* 412.2, *occupy oneself* 412.15, *contract* 459.1, 459.8, 462.2, 462.11, *negotiation* 460.1, *negotiate* 460.6, *compromise* 461.1, *allocate* 474.5, *trade* 480.1, 480.18, *bargaining* 480.10, *bargain* 480.20, *selling* 482.1, *sell* 482.15, *exchange* 673.5, *settlement* 735.6, *settle* 735.26, *agreement* 767.9, *disperse* 776.12
deal a blow *hit* 695.11
deal a deathblow *execute* 30.22
deal destruction *lay waste* 523.14
dealer *cardplayer* 168.3, *contractor* 459.6, *trader* 480.11, *merchant* 482.10, *retailer* 482.11, *operator* 509.5

dealer in real estate *person transferring property* 470.8
deal gently *be lenient* 423.5
deal harshly with *be severe* 424.8
deal in *be active in* 412.17, *trade* 480.18, *merchandise* 482.17
deal in futures *finance* 457.7, *speculate* 480.19
dealing *card playing* 168.1, *card-playing* 168.6, *trade* 480.1, *selling* 482.1, *exchange* 673.1
dealing death *killing* 30.1
deal in generalities *make a generalization* 778.18
dealing out *allocation* 474.1
dealings *treatment* 399.11, *deed* 412.2, *business relations* 727.4
dealing with *focused* 328.6
deal in the black market *trade* 480.18
deal out *give out* 472.12, *allocate* 474.5, *disperse* 776.12
deal with *raise the point* 328.10, *behave toward* 399.20, *be active in* 412.17, *trade* 480.18, *take action* 509.12, *relate to* 727.9
deal with in depth *dissertate* 203.5
dean *educator* 48.4, *person in authority* 52.7, *religious leader* 68.9, *educational leader* 68.11, *member of the clergy* 84.5
deanery *official residence* 60.6, *priesthood* 84.2, *clerical dwelling* 84.10
deanship *priesthood* 84.2
dear *term of endearment* 299.7, *beloved* 299.19, *overestimated* 343.5, *opulent* 485.10, *costly* 496.7, 500.6, *at great cost* 496.12
dear departed, the *dead person* 29.7
dear heart *term of endearment* 299.7
Dear John or **Jane letter** *rejection notice* 383.5
dearly *lovingly* 299.29, *expensively* 481.20, *at great cost* 496.12
dearly beloved *loved one* 299.13
dearly love *love* 299.21
dearly loved *beloved* 299.19
dearly love to *enjoy* 290.9
dearness *price* 494.1, *costliness* 496.1
dearth *infertile state* 23.3, *scarcity* 98.3, *inadequacy* 486.5, *absence* 576.1, *fewness* 796.3
dear to one's heart *beloved* 299.19
deary or **dearie** [Inf] *term of endearment* 299.7
death 29.1; *bodily development* 19.17, *life function* 28.6, *illness* 114.2, *disappearance* 265.1, Phobias 283, *forfeiture* 473.4, *destroyer* 523.6, *stop* 668.2, *repose* 678.2, *downfall* 714.7, *extinction* 718.8, *conclusion* 761.3, *cessation* 773.2, *ease* 819.1, *adverse health* 848.5
deathbed *dying* 29.3
deathbed confession *dying* 29.3, *confession* 451.2
deathbed repentance *dying* 29.3, *confession* 451.2
deathblow *execution* 30.6, *ender* 773.11, *defeat* 846.7
death-bringing *killing* 30.17
death by a thousand cuts *corporal punishment* 454.11
death by misadventure *way of dying* 29.5, *accidental killing* 30.9
death camp *slaughterhouse* 30.16
death cell *prison cell* 55.3

death certificate *after death* 29.9, *personal identification* 184.4, *certificate* 185.2

death column *death count* 29.10

death count **29.10**

death-dealing *murderous* 30.18

death-defying *reckless* 286.6

death from old age *way of dying* 29.5

death grapple *warfare* 422.10

death grip *retention* 471.1

death in action *way of dying* 29.5

death instinct *compulsion* 108.13

death knell *death* 29.1, *ruin* 523.4, *forewarning* 814.2

deathless *eternal* 644.4, *stable* 674.3

deathlessness *timelessness* 640.1, *life without end* 644.2, *stability* 674.1

deathlike *dying* 29.12, *deathly* 29.15, *silent* 231.2, *drained of color* 252.6

deathlike silence *silence* 231.1

deathliness *inertness* 519.1

deathly **29.15;** *killing* 30.17, *drained of color* 252.6

deathly hush *silence* 231.1

death notice *death count* 29.10

death penalty *execution* 30.6, *capital punishment* 454.12

death rate *death count* 29.10

death rattle *dying* 29.3

death ray *weapon* 78.1

death record *death count* 29.10

death register *death count* 29.10

death roll *death count* 29.10

death row *prison cell* 55.3

death's bright angel *personifications and symbols* 29.4, *angel* 82.11

death sentence *prison sentence* 55.6, *capital punishment* 454.12

death's-head *personifications and symbols* 29.4

death spiral *ice-skating techniques* 162.16

death struggle *dying* 29.3, *warfare* 422.10

death tax *tax* 494.5

death throes *dying* 29.3

death toll *death count* 29.10

deathtrap *miscellaneous automotive terms* 687.14

death trap *danger* 811.1, *trap* 813.1

Death Valley *hot place* 217.5, *Deserts* 572

death warrant *capital punishment* 454.12

deathwatch *dying* 29.3

death wish *compulsion* 108.13, *depression* 270.2

deb [Inf] *beginner* 771.14

debacle *failure* 430.9, *ruin* 523.4, *downfall* 714.7, *error* 846.2

debar **604.17;** *prohibit* 503.8

debark *depilate* 614.20, *land* 704.16

debarkation *landing* 704.2

debarment **604.5;** *prohibition* 503.1

debarred *excluded* 604.11

debarring *excluded* 604.11

debase **716.16;** *abase* 298.20, *bring into disrepute* 371.6, *demoralize* 432.15, *vilify* 440.14, *demonetize* 484.25, *humble* 597.25, *mix* 751.12, *make worse* 808.17, *pervert* 808.22

debased *abased* 298.13, *disreputable* 371.4, *depraved* 448.10, *lowered* 597.18, *degraded* 716.10

debasement **716.5;** *abasement* 298.6, *scorn* 440.5, *humbling* 597.9, *moral deterioration* 808.3, *impairment* 808.7

debasing *298.15; degraded* 716.10

debatable *problematic* 328.7, *arguable* 329.8, *questionable* 333.13

debatably *problematically* 328.12, *questionably* 333.22

debate 210.3, 319.3, 319.13; *philosophical argument* 4.5, *discuss* 4.22, *confer* 210.13, *raise the point* 328.10, *logical argument* 329.2, *doubt* 333.19, *balance* 378.11, *contention* 422.1, *conflict* 422.26, *discussion* 460.3, *dispute* 463.3, 463.9

debater **422.17;** *arguer* 319.6

debating *debate* 210.3

debauch *celebration* 405.1, *celebrate* 405.10, *demoralize* 432.15, *deprave* 448.14, *overindulge* 456.11, *pervert* 808.22

debauched *unchaste* 432.10, *depraved* 448.10, *dissipated* 456.7

debauchedly *promiscuously* 432.19

debauchee *sexually immoral person* 432.8, *self-indulgent person* 456.5

debauchery *sexual immorality* 432.2, *depravity* 448.2, *dissipation* 456.2

debauching *dissipated* 456.7

debenture *purchase contract* 459.3, *promise* 464.2, *paper money* 484.14

debenture bond *purchase contract* 459.3

debilitate *remove power from* 515.13, *weaken* 517.13, *make smaller* 747.8, *fatigue* 820.6

debilitated *consumed* 96.11, *weakened* 517.9

debilitation *fatigue* 820.1

debilitative *decrescent* 747.6

debility *ill health* 114.1, *poor health* 517.3

debit *financial loss* 468.4, *debt* 488.1, *accounts* 493.4, *account* 493.9, *difference* 750.3

debit and credit *accounts* 493.4

debited *accounted* 493.8

deblossom *cultivate* 17.19

debouch *quit* 705.10, *emerge* 707.14, *let out* 709.26

Debouillet *Breeds of Sheep* 16

debris *grit* 553.8, *transferred thing* 685.6, *remainder* 750.1, *bits and pieces* 760.5, *refuse* 802.5

debris flow *mass movement* 8.28

de Broglie principle *Classical Physical Laws* 10

de Broglie wave *wave* 683.4

debt **488.1;** *loan* 476.5, *insolvency* 486.2, 490.5, *credit* 487.1

debt capital *loan* 488.3

debt collector *collector* 473.7, *lender* 487.5

debt-free *paid* 489.11

debt of honor *promise* 458.1, *debt* 488.1

debtor **488.6;** *borrower* 476.7, *nonpayer* 490.6, *loser* 846.9

debtors' budget *budgeting* 493.5

debtor's colony or **prison** *prison* 55.1

debts *burden* 826.10

debt to society *imprisonment* 454.2

debud *cultivate* 17.19

debug [Inf] *program* 15.29, *tidy* 765.21

debugger [Inf] *system software* 15.13

debugging [Inf] *programming concepts* 15.24

debunk *abase* 298.20, *deride* 369.7, *debase* 716.16

debunked *abased* 298.13

debus *land* 704.16

debut *theatrical performance* 136.13, *birth* 264.2, *attempt* 390.1, *ceremony* 405.3, *launch* 405.14, *party* 408.6, *reception* 473.4, *beginning* 583.9, 583.14, *begin* 583.21, *arrival* 704.1, *entry* 706.1, *premiere* 771.9, *make a beginning* 771.26

debutante *social person* 408.7, *new arrival* 652.7, *entrant* 706.7, *beginner* 771.14

deca *Decimal Prefixes* 589

decade *time period* 641.2, *ten* 792.6

Decadence *Western Literary Groups* 139

decadence *immorality* 432.1, *moral deterioration* 808.3

decadent *literary* 139.15, *immoral* 432.9, *decrescent* 747.6

decaf [Inf] *coffee* 93.6

decaffeinated coffee *coffee* 93.6

decagon *polygon* 6.42, *angled figure* 628.3, *ten* 792.6

decagonal *angled* 628.9, *tenth* 792.17

decagram *ten* 792.6

decahedral *angled* 628.9, *tenth* 792.17

decahedron *angled figure* 628.3, *ten* 792.6

decal *adherent* 755.4

decalcomania *decoration* 129.4

Decalogue *ten* 792.6

decamp *depart* 265.6, *run away* 386.21, *not pay* 490.9, *abscond* 576.16, *quit* 705.10, *hurry off* 705.11, *escape* 816.8, *make haste* 818.5

decampment *departure* 705.1, *escape* 816.1

decant *purify* 111.19, *transfer* 685.8, *inject* 710.10

decantation *transmission* 685.3

decanter *drink container* 93.13, *bottle* 578.14

decapitate *execute* 454.30, *take off* 749.7, *separate* 753.12

decapitated *reduced* 749.5

decapitation *capital punishment* 454.12, *subtraction* 749.1, *separateness* 753.3

decapod *ten* 792.6

decarbonize *purify* 111.19

decathlon *Sporting Activities* 145, *multi-event contest* 166.16, *ten* 792.6

decay **808.6, 808.16;** *radioactivity* 10.58, *wasting away* 96.4, *waste away* 96.20, *lack of hygiene* 112.3, *dirt* 112.5, *be dirty* 112.10, *ulcer* 114.18, *afflict* 117.16, *unpleasant-smelling thing* 227.2, *weakness* 517.1, *agent of destruction* 523.7, *be transient* 643.6, *oldness* 653.1, *grow old* 653.16, *reduction* 747.2, *take apart* 753.16, *disintegration* 758.1, *disintegrate* 758.6, *deterioration* 808.1, *eat away* 808.19

decayable *decrescent* 747.6

decay constant *radioactivity* 10.58

decayed *unhygienic* 114.27, *dilapidated* 517.7, *disintegrated* 758.3, *spoiled* 808.9

decaying *of disease* 114.25, *putrid* 227.4, *transient* 643.4, *decreasing* 747.5, *disintegrating* 758.5, *spoiled* 808.9

decaying matter *Phobias* 283

decca [Brit] *position finder* 690.8

Deccani *Breeds of Sheep* 16

decease *death* 29.1, *die* 29.17, *cessation* 773.2

deceased *dead* 29.11, 658.10, *former* 651.14

deceased, the *dead person* 29.7

deceit *Collective Names* 59, *deception* 193.1, *hypocrisy* 330.5, *deviousness* 607.4, *cunning* 822.1

deceitful *deceptive* 193.12, *hypocritical* 330.10, *questionable* 333.13, *devious* 607.9, *misrepresented* 627.8, *cunning* 822.4

deceitfully *deceptively* 193.21, *hypocritically* 330.15, *questionably* 333.22, *deviously* 607.16, *distortedly* 627.14, *cunningly* 822.6

deceitfulness *evasion* 181.5, *deception* 193.1, *questionableness* 333.7, *deviousness* 607.4, *distortion of truth* 627.4

deceive 181.14, 193.16, 330.12; *make someone believe* 87.11, *mystify* 182.12, *hoax* 193.20, *blind* 243.17, *confuse* 333.20, *be equivocal* 380.7, *act dishonestly* 479.18, *circumlocute* 607.12, *distort the truth* 627.12, *delude* 720.16, *trap* 813.6, *be cunning* 822.5

deceived 193.15; *misjudging* 342.6, *trapped* 813.5

deceive oneself *deceive* 193.16

deceiver **193.8;** *one who conceals* 181.7, *pretender* 367.2, *cunning person* 822.3

deceiving *deceptive* 193.12, *misrepresented* 627.8, *cunning* 822.4

decelerate *interact* 10.73, *pause* 415.15, *slow down* 693.13, *decrease* 747.7, *make smaller* 747.8, *deteriorate* 808.14, *restrain* 830.12

deceleration **693.2;** *decrease* 747.1, *deterioration* 808.1, *restraint* 830.1

decelerometer *meter* 589.13

decencies *etiquette* 406.3

decency *courtesy* 410.1, *properness* 429.5, *morals* 431.2, *virtue* 447.1, *refinement* 534.1

decennial *tenth* 792.17

decennially *fivefold* 792.26

decennium *time period* 641.2, *ten* 792.6

decent *courteous* 410.6, *proper* 429.10, *in the right* 429.11, *moral* 431.9, *virtuous* 447.5

decent chance *equal chance* 842.7

decently *courteously* 410.13, *genteelly* 410.14, *morally* 431.15, *virtuously* 447.9, *decorously* 534.18

Décentralisation Dramatique [Fr] *theater movements* 136.9

decentralization *delegation* 79.3, *management system* 126.3, *parting* 703.2, *dispersion* 776.1, *commission* 833.1

decentralize *delegate* 79.6, *disperse* 776.12, *commission* 833.8

decentralized **79.5;** *dispersed* 776.6, *commissioned* 833.6

deception **193.1;** *evasion* 181.5, *misrepresentation* 188.1, *hoax* 193.7, *hypocrisy* 330.5, *misjudgment* 342.1, *dishonesty* 479.7, *deviousness* 607.4, *distortion of truth* 627.4, *trick* 813.2, *cunning* 822.1, *stratagem* 822.2

deceptive 193.12; *blinding*

243.13, *seeming* 264.11, *hypocritical* 330.10, *questionable* 333.13, *affected* 367.3, *fraudulent* 479.13, *devious* 607.9, *misrepresented* 627.8

deceptive appearance *latency* 844.1

deceptively 193.21; *hypocritically* 330.15, *questionably* 333.22, *thievishly* 479.19, *deviously* 607.16, *distortedly* 627.14

deceptiveness *deception* 193.1, *questionableness* 333.7, *affectation* 367.1, *deviousness* 607.4

deci Decimal Prefixes 589

decibel *sound* 230.1, Scientific and Technical Units 589

decidable *numerable* 6.70

decide *judge* 53.32, 54.31, 341.10, *try a case* 54.28, *will* 372.11, *resolve* 376.12, *select* 382.12, *determine* 675.11, *end* 773.19, *rule* 780.12, *make certain* 840.14

decide against *veto* 503.9

decide beforehand *predetermine* 384.8

decided 840.9; *willed* 372.6, *resolute* 376.7, *ended* 773.14

decided beforehand *predetermined* 384.4

decidedly *selectively* 382.17, *correctly* 429.16

decidedness *resolution* 376.1

decided upon *selected* 382.11

decide on *select* 382.12

decide the issue *determine* 675.11

decide the outcome *determine* 675.11

decide the result *determine* 675.11

deciding *selecting* 382.9

deciding factor *baseline* 601.4

deciding on *selecting* 382.4

deciding vote *electing* 382.5

decidophobia Phobias 283

deciduous *of plants* 41.14, *treelike* 43.10

deciduous tooth *teeth* 19.8

deciduous tree *tree* 43.1

decillion *million* 792.11

decimal *division* 6.16, *numerical* 6.68, *computer information* 15.17, *monetary* 484.22, *number* 783.1, *ratio* 783.5, *fractional* 783.8, *fraction* 787.1, *tenth* 792.17

decimal currency *money* 484.1

decimal fraction *division* 6.16, *ratio* 783.5, *fraction* 787.1

decimalize *add* 6.86, *quintuple* 792.23

decimal notation *number system* 6.7

decimal number *number system* 6.7

decimal point Punctuation Marks 5, *number system* 6.7, *symbol* 183.3

decimal system *number system* 6.7, *number* 783.1

decimate *slaughter* 30.21, *execute* 454.30, *weaken* 517.13, *destroy* 523.10, *subtract* 749.6, *quintuple* 792.23, *reduce* 796.8

decimated *reduced* 749.5

decimation *slaughter* 30.5, *destroying* 523.2, *subtraction* 749.1

decipher 365.13; *clarify* 196.3, *translate* 365.16, *reveal* 843.14

decipherability *clarity* 363.2

decipherable *solvable* 334.14, *simple* 363.6

deciphered *interpreted* 365.9

decipherer *interpreter* 365.6

decipherment *interpretation* 365.1, *translation* 365.4

decision *boxing terms* 152.3, *verdict* 341.2, *will* 372.1, *intentionality* 374.2, *declaration* 376.2, *selection* 382.1, *choice* 382.3, *ruling* 780.2

decision making *management* 126.1

decisions Phobias 283

decisive *assertive* 189.20, *resolute* 376.7, *selecting* 382.9, *influential* 512.8, *critical* 659.5, *causal* 675.7

decisively *assertively* 189.35, *resolutely* 376.15, *influentially* 512.14, *critically* 659.9, *causally* 675.12

decisive moment *critical time* 659.3

decisiveness *assertiveness* 189.8, *resolution* 376.1

deck *type of chair* 101.4, *sailboat parts and accessories* 150.4, *diving* 164.13, *cards* 168.2, *ornament* 532.12, *bridge* 551.10, *level* 588.2, *layer* 588.9

deck [Inf] *lower* 597.21, *make horizontal* 603.10, *hit* 695.11, *bring down* 716.14

deck bridge *bridge* 551.10

deck dives *diving* 164.6

decked *canoeing* 150.26

decked-canoe race *canoe racing* 150.12

decked kayak *canoe* 150.9

decked out *dressed* 100.38, *beautified* 530.12, *decorated* 532.9

deckhand *nautical person* 690.12

deckle edge *roughness* 544.1

deckle-edged *coarse* 544.6

deck out *dress up* 100.45

deck-stepped *sailing* 150.25

deck-stepped mast *sailboat parts and accessories* 150.4

deck well *canoe parts* 150.10

deck with flowers *salute* 405.13

declaim *proclaim* 173.16, *address* 209.8

declaimer *public speaker* 209.5

declamation *public speaking* 205.11, *address* 209.7

declamatory *articulate* 205.16, *addressing* 209.6

declarant *affirmer* 189.9

declaration 376.2; *authorization* 52.3, *publication* 173.1, *divulgence* 180.2, *affirmation* 189.1, *utterance* 205.10, *public speaking* 205.11, *legal evidence* 339.4, *command* 425.1, *promise* 458.1

declaration of faith *belief system* 87.3

Declaration of Independence *free rights* 829.4

declaration of intent *betrothal* 458.2

declaration of war *act of hostility* 63.4, *belligerence* 76.14, *act of defiance* 416.3

declarative *affirmative* 189.10

declaratively *affirmatively* 189.29

declaratory *affirmative* 189.10, *meaningful* 361.6

declare *propound a philosophy* 4.21, *authorize* 52.14, *believe* 87.9, *proclaim* 173.16, *divulge* 180.9, *signal* 183.18, *affirm* 189.21, *speak* 205.17, *give evidence* 339.12, *mean* 361.13, *command* 425.10, *pay duty on* 433.18, *rule* 780.12

declare as true *attest* 189.22

declare Chapter 11 *lose one's money* 486.15

declared *authorized* 52.11,

published 173.12, *affirmed* 189.11, *manifest* 843.9

declared innocent 449.8

declaredly *avowedly* 189.34

declare free *deliver* 817.5

declare independence *become a nation* 566.11

declare innocent 449.11

declare one's love *communicate love* 299.25

declare open *open* 771.32

declarer *bridge* 168.4, *affirmer* 189.9

declare war 422.25; *go to war* 76.29, *combat* 77.34, *be insubordinate* 416.8

declaring war *warfare* 76.3

declension *grammatical term* 5.29, *change* 665.1, *deviation* 698.1, *descent* 714.1

declinable *decrescent* 747.6

declinate *decrescent* 747.6

declination *celestial sphere* 7.4, *geomagnetism* 8.3, *rejection* 383.1, *exact location* 565.2, *coordinates* 589.6, *deviation* 698.1, *divergence* 703.1, *descent* 714.1

decline 680.5, 747.4, 846.5, 846.16; *old age* 27.5, *age* 27.16, *wasting away* 96.4, *waste away* 96.20, *become aggravated* 276.6, *reject* 383.10, *withdraw* 392.5, *not use* 394.9, *be cheap* 497.13, *refuse* 506.8, *be weak* 517.12, *descent* 597.4, 714.1, *descend* 597.22, 714.12, *grow old* 653.16, *go backward* 680.16, *slip back* 680.19, *sinkage* 714.2, *deficiency* 745.2, *become inferior* 745.11, *decrease* 747.7, *close* 773.9, *economic deterioration* 808.2, *deteriorate* 808.14, *adversity* 848.1, *be in trouble* 848.13

decline (a word) *cause change* 665.16

declined *rejected* 383.6

decline in fortune *lose one's money* 486.15

decline in health *decline* 846.5, *adverse health* 848.5

declining *aging* 27.13, *rejecting* 383.2, *bargain* 497.10, *descending* 597.13, 714.9, *receding* 680.11, *decreasing* 747.5, *deteriorated* 808.8, *adverse* 848.10

declining prices 497.2

declining years *old age* 27.5

declivitous *descending* 714.9

declivity *descent* 597.4, *obliquity* 628.2, *inclination* 714.6

decoagulate *dissolve* 555.23

decoagulated *liquefied* 555.19

decoagulation *fluidization* 555.8

decoct *dissolve* 555.23, *obtain an extract* 711.19

decoction *drink* 93.2, *dose of medicine* 115.3, *solution* 555.10, *obtaining of an extract* 711.7, *extract* 711.8

decode *program* 15.29, *solve* 334.21, *decipher* 365.13, *reveal* 843.14

decoded *solved* 334.15, *simple* 363.6, *interpreted* 365.9

decoder *secret person* 182.6, *answerer* 334.10, *interpreter* 365.6

decoding *solution* 334.6, *clarity* 363.2, *interpretation* 365.1, *translation* 365.4

decollate *execute* 454.30

decollation *capital punishment* 454.12

décolletage *part of garment* 100.27

décolleté *stylish* 100.42, *low* 597.10

decolor 252.8

decolorant *color remover* 252.4

decoloration *colorlessness* 252.1

decolored *colorless* 252.5

decolorization *colorlessness* 252.1

decolorize *decolor* 252.8, *whiten* 253.12

decolorized *whitened* 253.8

decommission *stop using* 394.10, *make useless* 802.12

decommissioned *disused* 394.8

decompensation *anxiety disorder* 108.11, *defense mechanism* 108.23

decompile *program* 15.29

decomposable *deconstructed* 758.4

decompose *erode* 8.67, *mold* 47.22, *come to dust* 553.28, *grow old* 653.16, *take apart* 753.16, *disintegrate* 758.6, *diverge* 776.16, *decay* 808.16, *eat away* 808.19

decomposed *of disease* 114.25, *putrid* 227.4, *disintegrated* 758.5, *disbanded* 776.7, *spoiled* 808.9

decomposing *disintegrating* 758.5

decomposition *weathering* 8.40, *uncleanness* 112.2, *unpleasant-smelling thing* 227.2, *destroying* 523.2, *pulverization* 553.4, *separation* 753.1, *disintegration* 758.1, *divergence* 776.5, *decay* 808.6

decompressive *decrescent* 747.6

deconcentrate *disperse* 776.12

deconcentrated *dispersed* 776.6

deconcentration *dispersion* 776.1

deconstruct 758.7

deconstructed 758.4

deconstruction 758.2; Western Literary Groups 139, *criticism* 365.3, *simplification* 526.6

deconstructionism Philosophical Schools of Thought 4

deconstructionist Philosophical Schools of Thought 4

decontaminate *purify* 111.19, *practice hygiene* 116.4

decontaminated *cleaned* 111.14

decontamination *nuclear problem* 10.62, *cleaning* 111.2, *hygiene* 116.1

decontrol *counteract* 510.7, *liberation* 831.1, *liberate* 831.6

decor *stage set* 136.19, *decoration* 532.1, *interior decoration* 532.4

decorate 532.11; *honor* 58.14, *make ceramics* 129.10, *be an architect* 134.13, *reward* 453.13, *beautify* 529.12, 530.14, 807.20, *ornament* 532.12, *edge* 618.8, *transform* 670.13, *augment* 748.13

decorated 532.9; *honored* 58.12, 72.11, *architectural* 134.12, *beautified* 530.12

Decorated style Architectural Styles 134

decoration 129.4, 532.1; *military honor* 58.9, *honor* 72.3, *visual arts* 133.1, *insignia* 184.5, *monument* 185.10, *reward* 453.1, *ornament* 532.7, *ornamentation* 748.5, *array* 767.2, *beautification* 807.7

decorations *salute* 405.7

decorative *artistic* 133.7, *appealing* 529.10, *beautifying* 530.13, *decorated* 532.9, *ornate* 532.10, *ornamental* 748.9

decorative arrangement *ornament* 532.7

decorative article 532.5

decorative arts *visual arts* 133.1

decorative glass *ceramics* 129.1

decoratively **532.13**; *artistically* 133.10, *architecturally* 134.14
decorative method **532.3**
decorativeness *appeal* 529.4
decorative technique *interior decoration* 532.4
decorative woodwork **131.2**
decorator **532.8**; *artisan* 123.13, *changer* 665.9
decorous *formal* 406.6, *proper* 429.10, *disciplined* 765.17
decorously **534.10**; *elegantly* 527.7
decorousness *formality* 406.1
decorticate *shed* 614.21
decortication *peeling* 614.6
decorum *literary device* 139.12, *formality* 406.1, *etiquette* 406.3, 534.3, *properness* 429.5, *refinement* 534.1
découpage Hobbies and Pastimes 167
decoupling of multiple control loops *systems and process control* 14.28
decoy *hunting accessories* 160.5, *enticement* 178.3, *entice* 178.16, *lure* 700.5, 700.12
decoy duck *enticement* 178.3
decrease **747.1, 747.7**; *wasting away* 96.4, *waste away* 96.20, *loss* 468.1, *lose* 468.12, *discount* 495.1, *be weak* 517.12, *moderation* 521.1, *mitigate* 521.9, *contraction* 582.1, *shortening* 582.2, *contract* 582.12, *become smaller* 582.14, *diminishment* 597.7, *diminish* 597.24, *sinkage* 714.2, *descend* 714.12, *lowering* 716.1, *lower* 716.12, *quantify* 738.7, *change by degrees* 739.8, *make smaller* 747.8, *subtraction* 749.1, *subtract* 749.6, *economic deterioration* 808.2, *deteriorate* 808.14
decreased *smaller* 582.7, *lowered* 716.7, *decreasing* 747.5, *reduced* 749.5
decreasing **747.5**; *contracting* 582.10, *diminishing* 597.16, *descending* 714.9, *lowered* 716.7, *deteriorated* 808.8
decreasingly **747.9, 749.9**; *down* 716.24, *by degrees* 739.10
decree *law* 53.1, *legislate* 53.31, *judge* 53.32, 54.31, 341.10, *publication* 173.1, *verdict* 341.2, *impose one's will* 372.14, *declaration* 376.2, *predestination* 384.2, *predestine* 384.9, *command* 425.1, 425.10, *impose a duty* 433.14, *ruling* 780.2, *rule* 780.12
decree absolute *divorce* 66.1, *verdict* 341.2
decreed *predestined* 384.6
decree nisi *divorce* 66.1, *verdict* 341.2
decree of nullity *divorce* 66.1
decrement *differentiation* 6.29, *loss* 468.1, *discount* 495.1, *decrease* 747.1, *subtracted item* 749.2
decrepit **808.12**; *aged* 27.15, *unhealthy* 114.23, *disabled* 515.10, *ill* 517.8, *old* 653.10
decrepitly *venerably* 653.17
decrepitude *disability* 515.4, *poor health* 517.3, *elderliness* 653.2, *physical deterioration* 808.4
decrescendo *decrease* 747.1, *decreasing* 747.5
decrescendo or *decr.* or *decresc.* Musical Terms and Expression Marks 140
decrescent **747.6**
decretal *legislative* 53.17

decrial *personal attack* 418.8, *disparagement* 440.1
decried *censuring* 438.12
decrier *disparager* 440.7
decriminalization *legality* 53.9, *neutralization* 510.4
decriminalize *make legal* 53.27, *permit* 502.6, *counteract* 510.7
decriminalized *legal* 53.16, *permitted* 502.4
decry *criticize* 418.26, *berate* 438.20, *disparage* 440.11
decrying *critical* 418.16, *berating* 438.5, *disparaging* 440.8
decumbence or decumbency *recumbency* 603.2
decumbent *recumbent* 603.7
decumbently *recumbently* 603.12
decuple *tenth* 792.17
decurrence *sinkage* 714.2
decurrent *of fungi* 47.19
decury *historical soldier* 77.8
decussation *point of union* 752.8
Dedham pottery Ceramics 129
dedicate *give praise to* 472.13, *make an offering* 504.17
dedicated *intimate* 62.7, *religious* 81.21, *worshipful* 83.12, *earnest* 278.5, *steady* 376.8, *deferential* 433.9, *strong in spirit* 516.11
dedicated to *loyal* 426.5
dedicate oneself to *worship* 83.15
dedication *intimacy* 62.4, *religiousness* 81.2, *worship* 83.1, *book part* 174.5, *earnestness* 278.2, *seriousness* 376.3, *deference* 433.4, *offering* 472.6, 504.5
dedication to duty *sense of duty* 433.2
deduce *rationalize* 4.20, *theorize* 6.84, *think* 315.12, *have an idea* 317.12, 327.13, *reason* 319.11, *discuss* 329.12, *estimate* 341.11, *suppose* 359.8, *infer* 361.14, *interpret* 365.12, *draw out* 711.17
deduced *supposed* 359.6
deduct *take away* 477.18, *discount* 495.4, *subtract* 749.6, *separate* 753.12, *add* 784.11
deducted *subtracted* 749.3
deductible *chargeable* 494.11, *decrescent* 747.6
deduction *philosophical investigation* 4.4, *philosophical term* 4.7, *reasoning* 6.61, 319.2, *thought* 317.1, *way of thinking* 317.4, *logical argument* 329.2, *judgment* 341.1, *basis of supposition* 359.2, *taking away* 477.5, *stoppage* 490.2, *tax system* 494.6, *discount* 495.1, *decrease* 747.1, *subtraction* 749.1
deductive *logical* 4.28, *intellectual* 315.8, *rational* 319.8, *taking* 477.12, *subtractive* 749.4
deductively *philosophically* 4.23, *logically* 329.17, *avariciously* 477.22, *by subtraction* 749.8, *decreasingly* 749.9
deductive reasoning *reasoning* 319.2
deed **412.2**; *task* 122.2, *certificate* 185.2, *courageous act* 284.7, *cause of wonder* 294.4, *tactics* 399.12, *contract* 459.1, 459.8, *promise* 464.2, *transfer property* 470.12, *important matter* 799.2
deeded *contractual* 459.7
deeded over *transferring property* 470.10
deeding *transfer of property* 470.4
deed of arms *warfare* 422.10
deed of trust *purchase contract* 459.3
deed over *transfer property* 470.12

deeds *treatment* 399.11
deeds of blood *warfare* 76.3
deejay *broadcasting personnel* 172.11
deejay or D.J. *broadcasting personnel* 172.11
deem *propound a philosophy* 4.21, *be of the opinion* 87.10, *estimate* 341.11, *rule* 780.12
de-emphasis *downplaying* 195.6
de-emphasize **201.3**; *play down* 195.17
de-emphasized *downplayed* 195.13
deep **236.8, 598.9, 598.25**; *phrased* 5.39, *obscure* 197.2, *colorful* 251.11, *dark* 254.6, *thoughtful* 315.10, *wise* 352.4, *unintelligible* 364.4, *spacious* 563.13, *oceanic* 571.7, *thick* 594.5, *profound* 598.15, *quantitative* 738.6, *latent* 844.6
deep, the *sea* 571.1, *the depths* 598.2
deep as a well *deep* 598.9
deep as hell *deep* 598.9
deep as the ocean or the sea *deep* 598.9
deep-blue *blue* 261.5
deep blue sea *sea* 571.1
deep-colored *dark-colored* 247.7, *colorful* 251.11
deep-cut *deep* 598.9
deep-dish pie *pie* 90.38
deep diver *bait* 154.6
deep down *deep* 598.25
deepen **598.21**; *become dark* 247.9, *blacken* 254.11, *aggravate* 276.5, *extend* 563.14, *make bigger* 746.7
deepened *aggravated* 276.3
deepening **598.4, 598.14**; *aggravation* 276.1, *increase* 746.1
deeper **598.10**
deepest *deeper* 598.10, *bottom* 601.6
deepest feelings *seat of feelings* 266.7
deep-fat frier *cooking equipment* 91.6
deep-fat frying *cooking technique* 91.2
deep freezer *kitchen container* 91.7, *refrigerator* 105.10, *cooler* 218.4
deep-freezing *preservation of provisions* 815.6
deep-fried *culinary* 91.9
deep-frozen *condensed* 540.7
deep-fry *cook* 91.10
deep in debt *indebted* 488.7
deep-laid *well-made* 127.13
deeply *wisely* 4.28, *resonantly* 236.11, *blackly* 254.12, *spaciously* 563.17, *thick* 594.11, *deep* 598.25, *profoundly* 598.27, *wholly* 738.9
deeply felt *emotive* 266.13, *deep-seated* 598.17
deeply involved *active* 414.13
deep matters *profundity* 598.5
deepness **236.3, 598.6**; *unintelligibility* 364.1, *thickness* 594.1, *depth* 598.1, *quantity* 738.1
deep note *deepness* 236.3
deep-pitched *deep* 236.8
deep purple *purple* 262.6
deep-reaching *deep* 598.9
deep red *red* 257.5
deep-rooted *fixed* 397.13, *strong* 516.9, *deep-seated* 598.17, *stabilized* 674.4, *intrinsic* 723.6
deep-rootedness *depth of feeling* 598.7
deeps, the *the depths* 598.2

deep sea *sea* 571.1, *the depths* 598.2
deep-sea **598.11**; *oceanic* 8.53, 571.7, *fishing* 154.13, *nautical* 690.14
deep-sea diver *oceanographer* 571.6
deep-sea drilling *oceanography* 571.5
deep-sea fish *fish* 154.14
deep-sea fisherman *fisherman* 154.12
deep-sea fishing Sporting Activities 145, *saltwater fishing* 154.3
deep-seated **598.17**; *fixed* 397.13, *intrinsic* 723.6
deep-sea trolling *saltwater fishing* 154.3
deep-set *deep* 598.9
deep-six [Inf] *murder* 30.20
deep-sixed [Inf] *dead* 29.11
deep-sounding **598.19**; *deep* 236.8
Deep South *regions of the United States* 564.7
deep space *universe* 7.3, *distance* 585.1
deep structure *grammar* 5.28, *meaning* 361.1, *latency* 844.1
deep thinking *thought* 317.1, *profundity* 598.5
deep tone *blackness* 254.1
deep-toned *deep* 236.8
deep-voiced *deep* 236.8, *deep-sounding* 598.19
deep water *the depths* 598.2
deep-water *deep-sea* 598.11
deer Collective Names 59, *game* 160.6
deer farm *farm* 16.2
deerhound Breeds of Dogs 35
deerlike *ungulate* 35.31
deer season *seasons* 654.2
deerstalker *cap* 100.33
de-escalate *lower* 716.12, *decrease* 747.7
deescalation *disarmament* 74.3
de-escalation *lowering* 716.1, *decrease* 747.1
deface *obliterate* 186.8, *ruin* 523.15, *make ugly* 531.4, *blemish* 533.7, *deform* 627.11, *make useless* 802.12, *stain* 808.20, *cancel* 834.6
defaced *ugly* 531.3, *blemished* 533.5, *canceled* 834.5
defacement *obliteration* 186.1, *ugliness* 531.1, *blemish* 533.1, *blot on the landscape* 533.4, *distortion of body* 627.3, *cancellation* 834.1
defacer *destroyer* 523.6, *distorter* 627.5, *abrogator* 834.4
de facto *real* 717.14, *really* 717.22, 719.13
de facto possession *legal ownership* 469.8
defalcate [Form] *not pay* 490.9
defalcation *omission* 762.4
defalcation [Form] *nonpayment* 490.1
defalcator *nonpayer* 490.6
defamation **440.3**; *misinformation* 188.3, *lying* 192.5, *vilification* 301.2, *personal attack* 418.8, *disrespect* 436.1, *false accusation* 442.2
defamation of character *defamation* 440.3
defamatorily *accusingly* 442.11
defamatory **440.9**; *lying* 192.16, *vilifying* 301.9, *critical* 418.16, 438.13, *insulting* 436.10, *perjurious* 442.7

defamatory remark *aspersion* 440.4

defame 440.13; *lie* 192.23, *be dissatisfied* 274.7, *vilify* 301.15, *criticize* 418.26, 438.19, *wrong* 430.19, *scorn* 436.19, *accuse falsely* 442.9

defamed *perjurious* 442.7

defamer *liar* 192.10, *disparager* 440.7

defamingly *vilifyingly* 301.18

default *be insufficient* 98.9, *nonperformance* 466.2, *not perform* 466.10, *not pay* 488.10, 490.9, *nonpayment* 490.1, *refusal* 506.1, *refuse* 506.8, *incompleteness* 762.1, *omission* 762.4, *error* 846.2

defaulted *nonperforming* 466.6

defaulted match *golfing terms* 156.3

defaulter *loser* 468.8, *debtor* 488.6, *nonpayer* 490.6

defaulting *nonperforming* 466.6, *amount owing* 488.5, *unable to pay* 488.8, *nonpaying* 490.7, *incomplete* 762.5

defeasibility *refutability* 332.4

defeasible *refutable* 332.5

defeasibly *refutably* 332.11

defeat 832.11, 845.17, 846.7; *master* 68.17, *bad outcome* 293.3, *disappoint* 293.9, *abase* 298.20, *refute* 332.7, *discarding* 383.3, *discard* 383.12, *loss* 468.1, *lowering* 597.3, *lower* 597.21, *stop* 668.2, *cause to cease* 668.12, *be superior* 744.15, *subjection* 832.1, *victory* 845.4, *be victorious* 845.16, *downfall* 848.4, *cause adversity* 848.15

defeat comprehensively *ruin* 523.15

defeat easily *defeat* 845.17

defeated 846.11; *without hope* 282.7, *disappointed* 293.4, *abased* 298.13, *discarded* 383.8, *lowered* 597.12, *stopped* 668.7, *outclassed* 745.9

defeatedly *disappointedly* 293.11

defeated player *loser* 846.9

defeater *victor* 845.7

defeatism 413.7; *negativism* 190.7, *lack of hope* 282.2, *cowardice* 285.1, *underestimation* 344.1

defeatist *negator* 190.8, *negative* 190.15, *hopeless person* 282.5, *without hope* 282.7, *cowardly* 285.4, *underestimator* 344.2, *underestimating* 344.3, *inactive person* 413.8, *inactive* 413.9, *submitter* 421.2

defeat of the prosecution *favorable verdict* 54.19

defeat the enemy *be victorious* 845.16

defecate 25.21; *relieve oneself* 275.12, *let out* 709.26

defecation 25.3

defect 806.4; *insufficiency* 98.1, *disobey* 427.12, *failure* 430.9, *iniquity* 448.3, *nonperformance* 466.2, *defy* 466.11, *weakness* 517.1, *blemish* 533.1, *abscond* 576.16, *quit* 705.10, *emigrate* 707.17, *deficiency* 745.2, *vulnerability* 811.6

defected *relinquished* 392.2, *impious* 448.11

defecting *defiant* 466.7

defection *relinquishment* 392.1, *disobedience* 427.1, *defiance* 466.3, *absenteeism* 576.3, *departure* 705.1, *emigration* 707.6

defective 806.7; *gone wrong*

430.17, *nonperforming* 466.6, *blemished* 533.5, *unequal* 741.4, *low quality* 745.7, *incomplete* 762.5, *imperfect* 806.5

defective hearing *deafness* 229.1

defectively *inattentively* 466.13, *unequally* 741.10, *badly* 745.15, *imperfectly* 806.10

defectiveness *incompleteness* 762.1, *imperfection* 806.1

defect of character *vulnerability* 811.6

defector *absentee* 576.5, *outgoer* 707.9

defeminization *helplessness* 515.3

Defence Council [Brit] *military staff* 58.5

defend 77.37, 419.20; *be at war* 76.32, *confirm* 189.25, *premise* 319.14, *plead* 329.14, *answer back* 334.19, *justify* 441.12, *secure* 464.9, *give moral support* 605.18, *protect* 613.26, 810.21, *preserve* 815.14

defend against *counteract* 510.7

defend an action *stand trial* 54.29

defendant *litigant* 54.4, *arguer* 319.6, *person questioned* 333.10, *answerer* 334.10, *witness* 339.7, *accused person* 442.4, *opposer* 828.9

defended 419.18; *confirmed* 189.17, *causal* 319.9, *safe* 810.16

defender 77.2, 419.14; *sportsman* 145.4, *hockey player* 158.8, *soccer participant* 163.4, *affirmer* 189.9, *resister* 417.5, *vindicator* 441.5, *counteractant* 510.5, *supporter* 605.9, *protector* 810.11

defending 419.17; *warring* 76.26, *counterevident* 339.10, *vindicatory* 441.7

defend one's attitude *have an idea* 317.12

defend oneself *revolt* 417.12, *be accused* 442.10, *be safe* 810.16

defenestrate *throw away* 709.25

defenestration *eviction* 709.4

defense 155.9, 419.1, 441.2; *preventive warfare* 76.12, *battle* 76.23, *arms race* 78.2, *confirmation* 189.5, *explanation* 319.4, *plea* 329.5, *countercharge* 332.3, *counterstatement* 334.5, *counterevidence* 339.5, *security* 464.1, *opposing force* 510.2, *moral support* 605.7, *deflection* 701.3, *protection* 810.2, *conflict* 828.3

defense cuts *disarmament* 74.3

defenseless *helpless* 515.9, *weak* 517.6, *vulnerable* 811.9

defenselessly *powerlessly* 515.16, *dangerously* 811.14

defenselessness *helplessness* 515.3, *weakness* 517.1, *vulnerability* 811.6

defense mechanism 108.23; *evasion* 386.5, *defensiveness* 419.4

defense reaction *defense mechanism* 108.23

defenses *protection* 810.2

defense zone *hockey areas* 158.2

defensible *in the right* 429.11, *vindicable* 441.9, *invulnerable* 810.18

defensive 701.6; *military* 58.10, *strategic* 78.16, *varsity* 155.17, *suspicious* 314.6, *causal* 319.9, *apologetic* 329.10, *retaliatory* 334.13, *defending* 419.17, *vindicatory* 441.7, *hindering* 826.12

defensive, the *defense* 419.1

defensive backfield *defense* 155.9

defensive backs *defense* 155.9

defensive battle *battle* 76.23

defensive circle *barrier* 419.10

defensive coordinator *football player* 155.9

defensive end *defense* 155.9

defensive formation *defense* 155.9

defensive foul *penalty* 155.13

defensive halfback *soccer participant* 163.4

defensive huddle 155.10

defensive line *defense* 155.9, *military defenses* 419.9

defensive lineman *defense* 155.9

defensively 419.32, 701.12; *militarily* 58.15, *suspiciously* 314.13, *in reply* 332.10, *in answer* 334.25, *justifyingly* 441.15, *with delay* 826.22

defensive measure *opposing force* 510.2

defensive missile *modern missile weapon* 78.4

defensive move *defense* 419.1

defensiveness 419.4; *suspicion* 314.3

defensive reaction *evasion* 386.5

defensive tackle *defense* 155.9

defensive tactic *defense* 419.1

defensive team *defense* 155.9

defer 604.15; *submit* 298.17, *assent* to 346.7, *be servile* 401.48, *procrastinate* 413.12, *obey* 426.7, *delay* 658.13

deference 410.4, 433.4; *submissiveness* 298.3, *servility* 401.1, *submission* 421.1, *obedience* 426.1, *respectfulness* 435.3

deferent *submissive* 298.10

deferential 410.8, 433.9; *servile* 401.6, *obedient* 426.4, *showing respect* 435.7, *degraded* 716.10

deferentially 410.15; *submissively* 298.23, *obediently* 426.9, *respectfully* 435.19

deferment 604.3; *discount* 495.1, *delay* 658.3

defer payment *acquire credit* 487.11

deferral *deferment* 604.3, *delay* 658.3

deferred 604.9; *idle* 394.6, *charged* 487.9, *held up* 658.6

deferred payment *purchasing* 481.2, *credit* 487.1, *type of payment* 489.3

defer to 410.12; *knuckle under* 401.10, *submit* 421.4, *obey* 426.7, *show respect* 435.16

defiance 416.1, 466.3; *negation* 190.1, *audacity* 400.5, *resistance* 417.1, *disobedience* 427.1, *protest* 507.1, *objection* 828.2, *openness* 843.6

defiance of authority *anarchy* 51.1

defiance of gravity *lightness* 539.1, *raising* 715.1

defiance of orders *disobedience* 427.1

defiant 416.5, 466.7; *anarchic* 51.5, *negational* 190.9, *audacious* 400.10, *resistant* 417.6, *counterattacking* 418.15, *disobedient* 427.10, *protesting* 507.5, *dissident* 782.12, *discordant* 828.12, *open* 843.12

defiantly 416.9, 466.14; *negatively* 190.22, *courageously* 284.17, *audaciously* 400.20, *resistingly* 417.14, *disobediently* 427.14, *disapprovingly* 507.10, *opposingly* 828.22, *frankly* 843.18

defiant person 416.4

deficiency 745.2; *insufficiency* 98.1, *financial loss* 468.4, *inadequacy* 486.5, *absence* 576.1, *imbalance* 741.2, *omission* 762.4, *fewness* 796.3, *incompleteness* 806.2, *defect* 806.4

deficiency disease *disease* 114.4

deficient *insufficient* 98.4, 517.11, *unequipped* 389.13, *unprofitable* 468.10, *inadequate* 486.13, *missing* 576.11, *unequal* 741.4, *low quality* 745.7, *incomplete* 762.5, 806.6

deficiently *at a loss* 468.22, *unequally* 741.10, *incompletely* 762.10

deficit *insufficiency* 98.1, *financial loss* 468.4, *amount owing* 488.5, *difference* 750.3, *omission* 762.4

deficit finance *finance* 457.1

deficit financing *economic factor* 56.8

deficit spending *economic factor* 56.8

defied *negated* 190.10

defile *dirty* 112.11, *bring into disrepute* 371.6, *misuse* 395.6, *wrong* 430.19, *demoralize* 432.15, *desecrate* 436.24, *vilify* 440.14, *be evil* 446.10, *gulf* 587.3, *narrow place* 593.2, *make worse* 808.17

defiled *dirty* 112.7, *misused* 395.3, *immoral* 432.9

defilement *dirtiness* 112.1, *misuse* 395.1, *immorality* 432.1, *scorn* 440.5, *evil* 446.1, *impairment* 808.7

defiling *immoral* 432.9

define *rationalize* 4.20, *word* 5.43, *clarify* 196.3, *name* 202.17, *dissertate* 203.5, *specify* 340.14, *779.18, *interpret* 365.12, *limit* 620.7

defined *clear* 244.6, *conditional* 340.10, *recognizable* 363.7, *interpreted* 365.9, *identifiable* 843.10

definer *interpreter* 365.6

defining *interpretive* 365.8, *characteristic* 723.9, *typical* 777.10

definite 189.18; *of grammar* 5.41, *informative* 170.10, *clear* 196.2, *emphatic* 200.3, *intelligible* 363.5, *recognizable* 363.7, *correct* 429.8, *certain* 840.7, *identifiable* 843.10

definite article *part of speech* 5.30

definite integral *differentiation* 6.29

definitely 189.33; *earnestly* 278.10, *correctly* 429.16, *certainly* 840.15

definitely! *certainly!* 840.18

definiteness 189.6; *clarity* 196.1, *intelligibility* 363.3, *right* 429.2, *certainty* 840.1

definition *word* 5.17, *clarity* 196.1, 244.2, *specification* 340.6, *type of meaning* 361.4, *recognizability* 363.3, *interpretation* 365.1, *limitation* 620.2

definitional *conditional* 340.10, *interpretive* 365.8

definitive *legitimate* 52.10, *interpretive* 365.8, *ending* 773.13, *typical* 777.10

definitively *conclusively* 773.26, *taxonomically* 777.15

deflatability *contractibility* 582.4

deflatable *contractible* 582.11

deflate 195.16; *humiliate* 298.19, *refute* 332.7, *deride* 369.7, *weaken* 517.13, *squeeze* 582.13, *lower* 716.12, *debase* 716.16

deflated 195.12; *humiliated* 298.12, *dilapidated* 517.7, *squeezed* 582.9, *lowered* 716.7

deflate one's ego *make unimportant* 800.20

deflation 195.7; *economic factor* 56.8, *humiliation* 298.5, *inflation* 484.9, *squeeze* 582.3, *lowering* 716.1, *decline* 747.4

deflationary *economic* 56.10, *financial* 457.6, *monetary* 484.22, *contracting* 582.10, *decrescent* 747.6

deflationist *decrescent* 747.6

deflect 698.26; *deter* 179.8, *evade* 386.19, *parry* 419.27, *displace* 574.15, *diverge* 607.11, *fend off* 701.9

deflected *dissuaded* 179.5, *displaced* 574.8, *divergent* 607.7, *indirect* 698.9

deflection 701.3; *wave property* 10.12, *deterrence* 179.2, *evasion* 386.5, *displacement* 574.1, *divergence* 607.2, 776.5, *deviation* 698.1

deflective *dissuasive* 179.4, *divergent* 607.7, *indirect* 698.9

defloration *sexual immorality* 432.2

deflower *seduce* 432.16, *ravish* 477.15

deflowered *unchaste* 432.10

deflowerment *sexual possession* 477.2

defluxion *outflow* 707.4, *downflow* 714.3

defoliant *chemical warfare* 76.5, *agent of destruction* 523.7

defoliate *waste* 23.11, *lay waste* 523.14, *uncover* 614.17

defoliated *uncovered* 614.10

defoliation *infertile land* 23.2, *tree disease* 43.8, *destroying* 523.2, *uncovering* 614.1

deforest *waste* 23.11, *lay waste* 523.14, *displace* 711.14

deforestation *infertile land* 23.2, *forestry* 43.5, *displacement* 711.2

deform 627.11; *load* 14.49, *misrepresent* 188.6, *make ugly* 531.4, *blemish* 533.7, *make shapeless* 625.3, *transform* 670.13, *pervert* 808.22

deformation 14.16; *earth movement* 8.20, *misrepresentation* 188.1

deformational *tectonic* 8.56

deformed 627.7; *mechanical* 14.44, *misrepresented* 188.4, *ugly* 531.3

deformity *ugliness* 531.1, *distortion of body* 627.3

defraud *deceive* 181.14, *swindle* 193.19, *misuse* 395.6, *wrong* 430.19, *act dishonestly* 479.18, *not pay* 490.9, *account* 493.9, *be cunning* 822.5

defrauder *schemer* 193.10, *dishonest person* 479.11, *nonpayer* 490.6

defrauding *nonpayment* 490.1

defray 481.18, 489.18; *donate* 491.13

defrayal *payment* 489.1

defraying *payment* 489.1

defrayment *payment* 489.1

defray the cost *defray* 489.18

defrock *disbar* 709.16, *eject* 764.8

defrocking *dismissal* 709.2

defrost *heat* 217.17, *melt* 555.24

defrosted *heated* 217.15

deft *skillful* 127.10, *proficient* 445.15

deft fingers *manual skill* 127.2

deftly *skillfully* 127.16, *proficiently* 445.22

deftness *manual skill* 127.2, *proficiency* 445.5

defunct *dead* 29.11, *uncustomary* 398.4, *unfashionable* 528.10, *no more* 718.11, *annihilated* 773.16

defunct, the *dead person* 29.7

defuse *make inactive* 415.16

defy 416.7, 466.11; *negate* 190.16, *be courageous* 284.14, *brace oneself* 376.13, *push* 414.20, *resist* 417.10, *counterattack* 418.24, *disobey* 427.12, *protest* 507.7, *face danger* 811.12, *object* 828.18, *withstand* 828.20

defy authority *be anarchic* 51.8

defy comprehension *be unintelligible* 364.11

defy danger *be rash* 286.8

defy gravity *be light* 539.8

defying 416.6; *defiance* 416.1

defying comprehension *difficult* 364.8

defying gravity *ascent* 713.1

defy the law *be illegal* 53.30

dégagé *informal* 829.15

degas *absorb* 11.40

degassed *absorbed* 11.34

degassing *surface chemistry* 11.20

degeneracy *sexual immorality* 432.2, *depravity* 448.2, *moral deterioration* 808.3

degenerate *become aggravated* 276.6, *sexually immoral person* 432.8, *unchaste* 432.10, *be immoral* 432.13, *miscreant* 448.6, *depraved* 448.10, *deprave* 448.14, *change for the worse* 665.18, *be converted* 670.12, *decrease* 747.7, *be disordered* 766.21, *deteriorated* 808.8, *deteriorate* 808.14, *be in trouble* 848.13

degenerated *changed* 665.10, *converted* 670.7

degenerateness *moral deterioration* 808.3

degenerating *depraved* 448.10, *converting* 670.8

degeneration *depravity* 448.2, *change for the worse* 665.5, *evolution* 670.3, *decrease* 747.1, *moral deterioration* 808.3

degenerative *of disease* 114.25, *depraved* 448.10, *deteriorated* 808.8

degenerative disease *disease* 114.4

degenerative joint disease *joint disease* 114.19

degeneratively *promiscuously* 432.19, *unvirtuously* 448.16

Degeres *Breeds of Sheep* 16

deglaciation *glaciation* 8.46

deglutition *eating* 92.1

degradation *abasement* 298.6, *disrepute* 371.1, *indignity* 436.7, *scorn* 440.5, *depravity* 448.2, *humbling* 597.9, *dismissal* 709.2, *debasement* 716.5, *moral deterioration* 808.3

degrade *react* 11.38, *abase* 298.20, *desecrate* 436.24, *vilify* 440.14, *deprave* 448.14, *punish* 454.22, *humble* 597.25, *disbar* 709.16, *debase* 716.16, *make smaller* 747.8, *take apart* 753.16, *make unimportant* 800.20, *pervert* 808.22

degraded 716.10; *abased* 298.13, *depraved* 448.10, *lowered* 597.18

degrade oneself *be disreputable* 371.5

degrading *debasing* 298.15, *disreputable* 371.4, *humiliating* 436.15, *depraved* 448.10, *punishment* 454.1, *degraded* 716.10

degradingly *humiliatingly* 298.25, *unvirtuously* 448.16, *humbly* 716.26

degree 739.1; *equation* 6.25, *authorization* 340.4, *General Units* 589, *Scientific and Technical Units* 589, *measurability* 589.2, *rung* 636.3, *guide* 697.4, *compass direction* 697.5, *relative position* 727.5, *position* 765.4, *importance* 799.1

degree-day *Scientific and Technical Units* 589

degree-granting institution *university* 48.14

degree of difference *gradation* 739.3, *inequality* 741.1

degust *taste* 219.5

degustation *appetizer* 219.2

dehisce *vegetate* 41.21, *fruit* 44.9

dehiscent *of a fruit* 44.8, *cracked* 587.5

dehiscent fruit *botanical fruit* 44.2

dehorn *practice livestock farming* 16.20

dehors *Musical Terms and Expression Marks* 140

dehumanization *moral deterioration* 808.3

dehumanize *deprave* 448.14, *pervert* 808.22

dehumanized *cruel* 306.10

dehumidification *drying* 560.3

dehumidifier *dryer* 560.5

dehumidify *dry* 560.17

dehydrant *dryer* 560.5

dehydrate *dry* 560.17, *convert* 670.11, *preserve* 815.14

dehydrated *hungry* 288.16, *dried-up* 560.9, *preserved* 815.17

dehydrated food *food* 90.1, *preserved thing* 815.10

dehydrating *drying* 560.15

dehydration *thirst* 560.2, *drying* 560.3, *chemical change* 670.2, *preservation of provisions* 815.6

dehydrator *dryer* 560.5

dehydrogenase *enzyme* 12.11

deice *service* 689.16

de-ice *heat* 217.17

deicer *heater* 217.3

deicing *miscellaneous aviation terms* 689.9

deictic *dialectical* 4.16

deification 82.13; *praise* 437.3, *promotion* 715.3

deified 82.20; *promoted* 715.8

deified person 82.14

deify 82.23; *idolize* 83.16, *revere* 435.14, *praise* 437.16, *promote* 715.13

deifying *reverent* 435.9

deil [Scot] *devil* 446.5

Deimos *Planets and Their Satellites* 7

deipnophobia *Phobias* 283

deism *Philosophical Schools of Thought* 4, *religiousness* 81.2

deist *Philosophical Schools of Thought* 4

deity 82.1; *idol* 83.5, *first cause* 675.6, *self-existence* 717.8

déjà vu *recollection* 3.8, *occult and psychic phenomena* 86.7, *reappearance* 264.8, *retrospect* 354.2

deject *discourage* 179.11, *disappoint* 293.9, *make sullen* 304.13

dejecta *excrement* 25.2

dejected *discouraged* 179.6, *depressed* 261.7, 270.5, *without hope* 282.7, *disappointed* 293.4, *sullen* 304.8

dejectedly *dishearteningly* 179.13, *bluely* 261.11, *unhopefully* 282.14, *disappointedly* 293.11, *sullenly* 304.16

dejectedness *depression* 270.2

dejection *excrement* 25.2, *defecation* 25.3, *mood disorder* 108.12, *disaffection* 179.3, *depression* 270.2, *lack of hope* 282.2, *disappointment* 293.1, *sullenness* 304.1, *adversity* 848.1

dejecture *excrement* 25.2

de jure *legal* 53.16

de jure possession *legal ownership* 469.8

deke *ice hockey tactics* 158.4, *play ice hockey* 158.9

del *vector* 6.48

Delaine Merino *Breeds of Sheep* 16

delaminate *scale* 588.10

delamination *layering* 588.5

Delaware *Breeds of Fowl* 16, *American States* 564, *Rivers* 570

delay 375.6, 375.16, 658.3, 658.13; *indifference* 326.2, *be neglectful* 326.7, *be irresolute* 378.9, *be evasive* 386.20, *tactics* 399.12, *do-nothingism* 413.6, *procrastinate* 413.12, *idleness* 415.3, *be inactive* 415.13, *stall* 419.28, *deferment* 604.3, *defer* 604.15, *lateness* 658.1, *wait* 658.12, *pause* 668.3, *hesitation* 693.5, *hesitate* 693.12, *slow down* 693.13, *nonachievement* 762.3, *not complete* 762.9, *deliverance* 817.1, *obstacle* 826.2, *block* 826.17

delayed 693.10; *deferred* 604.9, *late* 658.5

delayed action *delay* 658.3

delayed reaction *delay* 658.3

delayer *latecomer* 658.4

delaying 658.8; *indifferent* 326.5, *procrastinating* 375.11, *inactive* 413.9, *delay* 658.3, *uncompleted* 762.7

delaying action *evasiveness* 386.6

delaying tactics *delay* 658.3

delay of game *penalty* 155.13

dele *obliteration* 186.1, *obliterate* 186.8

delectable *pleasant* 214.7, *tasty* 219.4

d-electron *atom* 10.52

delegable *delegated* 79.4

delegate 79.1, 79.6; *gain authority* 52.15, *representative* 75.3, 187.7, *agent* 80.3, 123.15, *speaker* 205.12, *select* 382.12, *transfer property* 470.12, *give out* 472.12, *commissioner* 833.5, *commission* 833.8

delegate authority *authorize* 52.14, 833.10

delegated 79.4; *legitimate* 52.10, *authorized* 52.11, *commissioned* 833.6

delegated authority *legal power* 52.2, *authority* 833.3

delegation 79.3; *acquisition of authority* 52.5, *representative body* 79.2, *transfer of property* 470.4, *commission* 833.1, *council* 833.4

delegation of power *delegation* 79.3

delegation of work *delegation* 79.3

delete *program* 15.29, *obliterate* 186.8, *take away* 477.18, *censor*

503.10, *abolish* 523.11, *subtract* 749.6, *eject* 764.8, *cancel* 834.6

deleted *obliterated* 186.4, *censored* 503.7, *missing* 576.11, *subtracted* 749.4, *excluded* 764.6, *canceled* 773.15, 834.5

deleterious *detrimental* 446.8

deleteriously *destructively* 446.13

deletion *obliteration* 186.1, *taking away* 477.5, *censorship* 503.4, *destruction* 523.1, *subtraction* 749.1, *ejection* 764.2, *cancellation* 834.1

delft *or* **delftware** Ceramics 129

Delhi belly [Inf] *defecation* 25.3

deli [Inf] *food provider* 90.6

deliberate 384.5, 589.18; *philosophize* 4.19, *leisurely* 125.4, *soccer* 163.7, *consult* 176.11, *confer* 210.13, *think* 317.9, *imagine* 327.14, *discuss* 329.12, *meant* 361.12, *willed* 372.6, *intentional* 374.7, *resolute* 376.7, *negotiate* 460.6, *unhurried* 693.8

deliberately *purposively* 327.20, *logically* 329.17, *intentionally* 374.13, *resolutely* 376.15, *slowly* 693.14

deliberateness *intentionality* 374.2, *resolution* 376.1, *slowness* 693.1

deliberation *philosophical investigation* 4.4, *consultation* 176.4, *prudence* 287.2, *thoughtfulness* 317.2, *logical argument* 329.2, *slowness* 693.1

deliberative *thoughtful* 4.17, *advisory* 176.7, *speculative* 317.8

deliberatively *thoughtfully* 4.27, *advisorily* 176.12

delicacies *hors d'oeuvre* 90.13

delicacy *ill health* 114.1, *manual skill* 127.2, *subtlety* 195.3, 534.2, *sensitivity* 212.2, 267.1, *appetizer* 219.2, *sweetener* 222.2, *judiciousness* 337.2, *weakness* 517.1, *elegance* 527.1, *beauty* 529.1, *refinement* 534.1, *lightness* 539.1, *sparseness* 541.1, *soft-heartedness* 543.4, *brittleness* 548.1, *grain* 552.2, *fineness* 595.5

delicate 552.10; *unhealthy* 114.23, *subtle* 195.9, *susceptible* 212.7, *handling* 216.7, *soft-hued* 251.13, *sensitive* 267.3, *discriminating* 337.9, *weak* 517.6, *elegant* 527.3, *graceful* 527.4, *beautiful* 529.7, *refined* 534.5, *insubstantial* 539.5, *sparse* 541.3, *soft-hearted* 543.11, *brittle* 548.3, *fine* 595.12, *unsafe* 811.8, *problematic* 824.11

delicate eating 92.3

delicate features *attractiveness* 529.2

delicate flavor *flavor* 219.3

delicate health *ill health* 114.1

delicately *sensitively* 267.6, *judiciously* 337.16, *elegantly* 527.7, 529.15, *decorously* 534.10, *lightly* 539.10, *sparsely* 541.6, *soft-heartedly* 543.19, *fragilely* 548.5, *texturally* 552.15, *finely* 595.19, *problematically* 824.25

delicateness *weakness* 517.1

delicate situation *awkward situation* 824.7

delicatessen *food provider* 90.6, *eating place* 92.17

Delicious Apple Varieties 44

delicious *edible* 92.20, *pleasurable* 214.6, *tasty* 219.4

deliciously *edibly* 92.26, *tastily* 219.7

deliciousness *taste* 219.1

delight *pleasure* 214.2, *give pleasure* 214.13, *gaiety* 269.3, *cause joy* 269.11, *pleasantness* 271.1, *pleasant thing* 271.4, *make pleasant* 271.10, *rejoicing* 279.1, *likes* 290.3

delighted *pleased* 214.9, *joyful* 269.6

delightful 271.7; *pleasant* 214.7, 271.5

delightfulness *pleasantness* 271.1

delight in *enjoy* 269.9, 290.9, *take pleasure in* 271.11, *be satisfied* 273.8, *like* 299.22

delimit *identify* 184.11, *specify* 340.14, *allocate* 474.5

delimitation *specification* 340.6, *allocation* 474.1

delimited *conditional* 340.10

delineate *write* 139.21, *draw* 143.13, *sign* 183.19, *represent* 187.10, *describe* 202.15, *explain* 331.16, *outline* 617.5, *characterize* 723.11, *specify* 779.18

delineated *drawn* 143.11, *explanatory* 331.11

delineating *(act of) drawing* 143.2

delineation *(act of) drawing* 143.2, *drawing* 143.4, *representation* 187.1, *description* 202.1, *explanation* 331.3, *outline* 617.1

delineative *outlined* 617.4

delineator *visual artist* 133.6, *drawer* 143.8

delineatory *representational* 187.8

delinquency *lawbreaking* 53.14, *disobedience* 427.1, *unlawfulness* 430.6, *immorality* 432.1, *wickedness* 448.1, *wicked act* 448.7, *guilt* 450.1, *infraction* 466.4

delinquent *lawbreaker* 53.15, *disobedient* 427.10, *wrongdoer* 430.8, *unlawful* 430.15, *immoral* 432.9, *wicked* 448.9, *guilty person* 450.5, *violating* 466.8

delinquently *resignedly* 392.6, *disobediently* 427.14, *immorally* 432.18, *wickedly* 448.15

Deli pony Horse and Pony Breeds 159

deliquesce *mold* 47.22, *melt* 555.24

deliquescence *fluidization* 555.8, *reduction* 747.2, *dilution* 776.3

deliquescent *of fungi* 47.19, *liquefied* 555.19, *decrescent* 747.6

delirious *psychologically disturbed* 108.39, *manic* 110.10, *of disease* 114.25, *meaningless* 362.7

delirium *mental disorder* 108.8, *delusion* 110.2, *symptom* 114.3, *reverie* 360.6, *nonsense* 362.2

delirium tremens *or* **d.t.'s** *delusion* 110.2, *drunken behavior* 121.4, *shake* 684.7

delitescence *latency* 844.1

delitescent *latent* 844.6

deliver 817.5; *provision* 89.9, *correspond* 169.19, *report* 175.9, *save* 275.9, *absolve* 312.10, *rescue* 419.26, *transfer property* 470.12, *give* 472.10, *give back* 478.5, *convey* 685.9, *transport* 686.10, *restore* 809.12, *protect* 810.21, *preserve* 815.14, *help* 825.23, *set free* 829.17, *liberate* 831.6

deliverable 817.3

deliver an address *address* 209.8

deliverance 817.1; *favorable verdict* 54.19, *aid* 275.2, *absolution* 312.2, *restoration* 809.2, *safety* 810.1, *escape* 816.1, *support* 825.2, *freedom* 829.1, *liberation* 831.1

deliver a speech *speak to* 205.19

delivered 817.4; *forgiven* 312.5, *free* 829.11, *liberated* 831.4

deliverer 817.2; *liberator* 831.3

deliver oneself *escape* 816.8

deliver the goods [Inf] *be convenient* 803.5

delivery *grip* 151.4, *articulation* 205.9, *conduct* 399.1, *transfer of property* 470.4, *giving* 472.1, *conveyance* 685.2, *conception* 771.4, *deliverance* 817.1, *liberation* 831.1

delivery date *promise* 458.1

delivery man *or* **person** *messenger* 685.5

dell *valley* 572.8, *gulf* 587.3, *concave land* 635.2

dell pony *pony* 159.6

delocalization *transfer* 685.1

delocalized *chemical compound* 11.4

delousing *cleaning* 111.2

Delphic oracle *diviner* 86.14

delphinium Flowers 42

Delphinus Constellations 7

Delta, the *regions of the United States* 564.7

delta *sediment* 8.29, *river parts* 570.3, *inlet* 572.9, *fork* 703.5

delta-like *fanlike* 703.8

delta-shaped *fanlike* 703.8

deltoid *growing* 581.12, *fanlike* 703.8, *three-sided* 790.8

deltoidal *fanlike* 703.8

delubrum *shrine* 83.10

delude 720.16; *deceive* 193.16, *be unreal* 722.12

deluded *psychologically disturbed* 108.39, *manic* 110.10, *deceived* 193.15, *misjudging* 342.6, *mistaken* 351.13

deluder *deceiver* 193.8

Deluge, the *flow* 570.4

deluge *rain* 9.27, *crowd* 59.11, *excess* 99.1, *be excessive* 99.9, *water* 557.29, *flow* 570.4, *downflow* 714.3

deluged *flooded* 557.24, 570.8

delusion 110.2, 720.3; *deception* 193.1, *self-deception* 193.2, *fallibility* 351.6, *fantasy* 360.5, *unreality* 722.2

delusional *or* **delusionary** *deceptive* 193.12

delusional disorder *psychosis* 108.10

delusions of grandeur *delusion* 110.2, *airs* 404.2

delusive *unreal* 722.7

delusive *or* **delusory** *deceptive* 193.12

delusively *deceptively* 193.21

delusiveness *deception* 193.1, *self-deception* 193.2, *unreality* 722.2

delusory *illusory* 720.9, *unreal* 722.7

de luxe *luscious* 214.8, *grand* 404.22

deluxe *opulent* 485.10

delve [Arch] *farm* 16.19, *cultivate* 17.19

delve into *make concave* 635.7

demagnetization *neutralization* 510.4

demagnetize *counteract* 510.7

demagogic *addressing* 209.6, *cunning* 330.8

demagogical *addressing* 209.6

demagogically *oratorically* 209.14, *hypocritically* 330.15

demagogue *leader* 126.8, *motivator* 178.11, 508.6, *speaker* 205.12, *public speaker* 209.5

demagoguery *cunning* 330.3

demagogy *totalitarianism* 49.13

demand 356.9, 425.2, 425.11, 505.3, 505.12; *need* 95.4, 95.16, *wish* 288.2, *desire* 288.17, *harm* 306.13, *impose one's will* 372.14, *compel* 428.8, *custom* 481.6, *fee* 494.3, *charge* 494.13, *extortion* 711.6, *extort* 711.18

demand an answer *request* 505.10

demand assurances *be safe* 810.20

demand backed by threats *demand* 505.3

demand bid *bridge* 168.4

demanded *necessary* 95.10, *desired* 288.10, *demanding* 505.8

demand for payment *demand* 505.3

demanding 95.13, 505.8; *desirous* 288.13, *punishing* 454.20, *allowing no delay* 645.7, *perfectionistic* 805.18, *fatiguing* 820.4, *difficult* 824.9, *problematic* 824.11, *troublesome* 824.13

demandingly 356.12

demand one's rights *have rights* 429.13

demand payment *demand* 425.11, 505.12

demands *expectations* 356.2

demand too much (of) *fatigue* 820.6

demarcate *sign* 183.19, *discriminate* 337.13, *specify* 340.14, *allocate* 474.5, *limit* 620.7, 830.13, *characterize* 723.11

demarcated *judged* 337.10, *conditional* 340.10

demarcation *discrimination* 337.1, *specification* 340.6, *allocation* 474.1, *limitation* 620.2, 830.2

dematerialization *disappearance* 265.1, *immateriality* 525.2, *absence* 576.1

dematerialize 525.12; *occult* 86.22, *disappear* 265.5, *abscond* 576.16

dematerialized *nonmaterial* 525.8, *away* 576.8

dematerializing *nonmaterial* 525.8

demean *abase* 298.20, *disdain* 400.16, *humble* 597.25

demeaned *lowered* 597.18

demeaning *debasing* 298.15, *degraded* 716.10

demean oneself *humble oneself* 298.18, *be disreputable* 371.5, *behave badly* 399.19, *knuckle under* 401.10

demeanor *gesture* 183.5, *external appearance* 264.5, *conduct* 399.1, *nature* 624.5

dement *make insane* 110.13

demented *psychologically disturbed* 108.39, *insane* 110.9, *manic* 110.10, *violent* 520.5

dementedly *insanely* 110.15

dementia *mental disorder* 108.8, *disability* 515.4

dementia praecox *psychosis* 110.3

dementophobia Phobias 283

Demerara Rivers 570

demerara *brown thing* 256.3

demerara sugar *basic cooking ingredient* 91.8, *sweetener* 222.2

demerit *iniquity* 448.3

demesne *farm* 16.2, *property* 470.1

Demeter Deities 82

demibastion *fort* 419.13

demigod *minor deity* 82.2

demijohn *bottle* 578.14

demilitarization *powerlessness* 515.1

demilitarize *make peace* 73.11, *remove power from* 515.13

demilune *fort* 419.13

Demiourgos *God* 82.6

Demi-Sang Horse and Pony Breeds 159

demise *death* 29.1, *cessation* 773.2

demised *dead* 29.11

demisemiquaver *notation* 140.20

demist *make transparent* 249.12

demiurge *God* 82.6

demo [Inf] *rally* 59.6, *mass demonstration* 331.7

demob [Inf] *enlist* 58.13

demobilization *truce* 73.2, *peace movement* 74.4, *disbandment* 776.2, *liberation* 831.1

demobilize *enlist* 58.13, *make peace* 73.11, *make inactive* 415.16, *scatter* 753.15, *disband* 776.13, *liberate* 831.6

demobilized *disbanded* 776.7

democracy *constitutional government* 49.8, *country* 566.1, *equality* 740.1

democratic *national* 18.16, 566.10, *governmental* 49.24, *equal* 740.8

democratically *governmentally* 49.27, *nationally* 566.13, *equitably* 740.15

democratic behavior *mode of behavior* 399.2

Democratic party Political Parties 50

Democratic whip *party official* 68.5

democratize *become a nation* 566.11

demographer *anthropologist* 1.3, *sociologist* 2.3

demographic *anthropological* 1.10

demographic(al) *socioeconomic* 2.13

demographically *anthropologically* 1.15, *sociologically* 2.15

demographic research *sociological research* 2.2

demographic survey *sociological research* 2.2

demographic transition *economic development* 56.5

demography *anthropology* 1.1, *sociology* 2.1, *sociological research* 2.2

de Moivre–Laplace theorem Mathematical Concepts 6

de Moivre's formula Mathematical Concepts 6

demolish 523.12; *be at war* 76.32, *destroy* 186.10, *refute* 332.7, *flatten* 716.15, *deconstruct* 758.7

demolished *destroyed* 186.5, *lowered* 716.7, *disintegrated* 758.3, *deconstructed* 758.4

demolisher *destroyer* 523.6

demolishment *destroying* 523.2

demolition *destruction* 186.2, *destroying* 523.2, *deconstruction* 758.2, *impairment* 808.7

demon *ghost* 86.11, *evil spirit* 446.4, *violent animal* 520.4

demonetize 484.25; *devalue the currency* 490.14

demonetized *monetary* 484.22

demonetized coinage *false money* 484.15

demon for work *hard worker* 414.11

demoniac *demonic* 446.9

demoniacal *demonic* 446.9

demonic 446.9; *idolatrous* 83.13, *witchlike* 86.19, *fidgety* 414.14

demonical *witchlike* 86.19, *demonic* 446.9

demonically *magically* 86.28, *devilishly* 446.14

demonism *idolatry* 83.4

demonize *bewitch* 86.25, *make evil* 446.11

demonology *witchcraft* 86.6

demonophobia Phobias 283

demons Phobias 283

demonstrability 331.5

demonstrable 331.12; *certain* 840.7

demonstrable existence 717.5

demonstrableness *demonstrability* 331.5

demonstrably 331.22; *really* 717.22

demonstrate 331.15; *rationalize* 4.20, *propound a philosophy* 4.21, *theorize* 6.84, *be expert* 127.15, *clarify* 196.3, *make visible* 242.25, 244.9, *state* 329.13, *protest* 331.19, *prove* 336.9, *interpret* 365.12, *show* 404.24, *push* 414.20, *be insubordinate* 416.8, *justify* 441.12, *establish reality* 719.12, *authenticate* 721.24, *make certain* 840.14, *display* 843.13

demonstrate against *dissent* 506.9, *cause mischief* 507.9

demonstrated 331.9; *explanatory* 331.11, *proven* 331.13, *authenticated* 721.17, *certain* 840.7

demonstrate self-control *be disinterested* 443.6, *restrain oneself* 830.15

demonstrate style *style* 537.8

demonstrating 331.14

demonstration 331.1; *reasoning* 6.61, *evidence* 54.15, *rally* 59.6, *manifestation* 244.3, *explanation* 331.3, *proof* 331.4, 336.2, 339.2, *interpretation* 365.1, *show* 404.12, *act of defiance* 416.3, *dissent* 506.2, *gesture of protest* 507.3, *authentication* 721.8, *confirmation* 840.3, *display* 843.1

demonstrative 331.10; *friendly* 62.5, *symbolic* 183.12, *amorous* 299.18, *verificatory* 336.6, *evidential* 339.8, *interpretive* 365.8

demonstratively 331.21; *indicatively* 183.21, *amorously* 299.30, *verifiably* 336.11, *as evidence* 339.15

demonstrativeness 331.2; *lovingness* 299.4

demonstrator 331.6; *protester* 331.8, 507.4, *defiant person* 416.4, *troublemaker* 427.5, *displayer* 843.7

demophobia Phobias 283

demoralization *intimidation* 283.6, *moral deterioration* 808.3

demoralize 432.15; *intimidate* 283.18, *deprave* 448.14

demoralized *disabled* 515.10

demoralizing *fearsome* 283.13

de Morgan's rules Mathematical Concepts 6

demote *employ* 57.18, *punish* 454.22, *relegate* 574.18, *humble* 597.25, *disbar* 709.16, *debase* 716.16, *make unimportant* 800.20, *terminate* 834.7

demoted *relegated* 574.11, *lowered* 597.18, *drooping* 714.10, *degraded* 716.10

demotion *punishment* 454.1, *relegation* 574.4, *humbling* 597.9,

---

dismissal 709.2, *descent* 714.1, *downfall* 714.7, *debasement* 716.5

demulcent *analgesic* 115.6, *medicinal* 115.15, *moderator* 521.2, *moderating* 521.5, *ointment* 562.8

demur *disbelief* 88.1, *negation* 190.1, *negate* 190.16, *countercharge* 332.9, *counter* 339.13, *disapproval* 347.2, *refuse* 347.9, *opposition* 375.2, *oppose* 375.13, *shy* 386.17, *refuse oneself* 506.10, *objection* 828.2, *object* 828.18

demure *shy* 403.8

demurely *modestly* 403.15

demureness *shyness* 403.3

demurral *disbelief* 88.1, *negation* 190.1, *countercharge* 332.3, *counterevidence* 339.5, *disapproval* 347.2, *objection* 828.2

demurrer *pretrial proceedings* 54.13, *countercharge* 332.3

demurring *disbelieving* 88.6, *unwilling* 375.8, *dissenting* 506.6

demystify *decipher* 365.13

demythologization *interpretation* 365.1

demythologizer *interpreter* 365.6

demythologizing *interpretive* 365.8

den *mammal dwelling* 35.21, *room* 60.9, *natural habitat* 60.16, *home workplace* 124.3, *privacy* 181.6, *solitary place* 409.4, *wicked place* 448.8, *shelter* 613.6, 812.4, *concave land* 635.2, *private space* 812.2

denarius *ancient coins* 484.12

denary *numerical* 6.68, *tenth* 792.17

denationalization *economics* 56.1

denationalize *pervert* 808.22

denaturalization *evolution* 670.3

denaturalize *be converted* 670.12, *pervert* 808.22

denature *make worse* 808.17, *pervert* 808.22

denaturization *protein* 12.9

dendochronology *chronology* 646.2

dendriform *treelike* 43.10, *branched* 703.9, *divergent* 776.11

dendrite *nervous system* 19.14

dendritic *treelike* 43.10, *branched* 703.9, *divergent* 776.11

dendrochronological *arboricultural* 43.13

dendrochronologically *arboriculturally* 43.16

dendrochronology *dating* 8.48, *forestry* 43.5

dendroid *horticultural* 17.14, *algal* 47.20

dendroid or **dendroidal** *treelike* 43.10

dendrolater *idolater* 83.7

dendrolatrous *idolatrous* 83.13

dendrolatry *idolatry* 83.4

dendrologic(al) *arboricultural* 43.13

dendrologically *botanically* 41.25, *arboriculturally* 43.16

dendrologist *plant scientist* 41.11, *forester* 43.7

dendrologous *arboricultural* 43.13

dendrology *botany* 13.7, *plant science* 41.10, *forestry* 43.5

dendrophobia Phobias 283

dengue *tropical disease* 114.10

deniability *unauthenticity* 722.4

deniable *unauthentic* 722.9

denial 332.2; *mathematical logic* 6.60, *incredulity* 88.3, *defense*

---

mechanism 108.23, *negation* 190.1, *refusal* 190.2, 506.1, *frustration* 293.2, *counterevidence* 339.5, *disapproval* 347.2, *rejection* 383.1, *renunciation* 383.4, *evasiveness* 386.6, *desisting* 417.4, *forfeiture* 468.2, *veto* 503.3, *protest* 507.1, *negativeness* 718.3, *exclusion* 764.1, *objection* 828.2, *suspicion* 841.2

denied *negated* 190.10, *disagreeing* 190.11, *frustrated* 293.5, *rejected* 383.6, *renounced* 383.9, *vetoed* 503.6, *dissenting* 506.6, *protesting* 507.5, *forbidden* 837.7

denier *fiber* 130.2, General Units 589

denigrate *criticize* 418.26, *wrong* 430.19, *scorn* 436.19, *berate* 438.20, *disparage* 440.11, *refuse* 506.8, *make unimportant* 800.20

denigrated *undervalued* 436.17

denigrating *critical* 418.16

denigration *personal attack* 418.8, *disparagement* 440.1, *refusal* 506.1

denigratory *disparaging* 440.8

denim Fabrics and Fibers 130

denim jacket *jacket* 100.18

denims *informal clothes* 100.7, *pants* 100.14

denizen *inhabitant* 61.1

Denmark Countries 566

den of iniquity or *vice* *wicked place* 448.8

denominate *specify* 779.18

denominated *titled* 72.9

denomination *party* 59.3, *title* 72.1, *religious group* 81.4, *identification* 184.1, *nomenclature* 202.7

denominational 81.23

denominationally *cliquishly* 59.32, *religiously* 81.29

denominational school *type of school* 48.12

denominator *division* 6.16, *ratio* 783.5

denotation *word* 5.17, *meaning* 361.1, *type of meaning* 361.4, *literalness* 721.9

denotative *signifying* 183.11, *linguistic* 361.9, *literal* 721.18

denote *signify* 183.16, *stand for* 187.14, *state* 329.13, *mean* 361.13

denoted *identified* 184.9

denouement *play part* 136.8, *aspect of fiction* 139.5, *disclosure* 180.1, *solution* 334.6, *effect* 676.1, *conclusion* 761.3, *sequel* 770.5, *ending* 773.10

denounce *perform rites* 85.18, *inform on* 170.13, *hate* 300.11, *vilify* 301.15, *deride* 369.7, *criticize* 418.26, *condemn* 438.18, *accuse* 442.8

denounced *condemned* 438.11, *censuring* 438.12, *accused* 442.5

denouncement *vilification* 301.2, *condemnation* 438.2, *censure* 438.3, *accusation* 442.1

denouncer *accuser* 442.3

denouncing *vilifying* 301.9, *condemning* 438.10

dense 540.6, 594.6; *plantlike* 41.13, *crowded* 59.22, *opaque* 250.3, *unintelligent* 316.6, *simpleminded* 526.11, *heavy* 538.9, *dull* 550.7, *thick-witted* 594.7, *adhesive* 755.5

dense cloud *cloud cover* 9.18

dense fog *fog* 9.32, *murk* 248.2

densely 540.10, 594.12; *opaquely*

250.9, *heavily* 538.16, *thick-wittedly* 594.13, *cohesively* 755.11
densely arrayed *dense* 540.6
denseness 594.2; *density* 540.1, *thick-wittedness* 594.3
densify *be dense* 540.8
densimeter *relative density* 540.3, Fields of Measurement 589
densimetry Fields of Measurement 589
densitometer Fields of Measurement 589
density 540.1; *mass* 10.8, *opaqueness* 250.1, *material world* 524.1, *hardness* 542.1, Fields of Measurement 589, *denseness* 594.2
density current *ocean current* 8.15
dent *sharp point* 549.2, *cavity* 635.3, *make concave* 635.7, *notch* 636.1, 636.5, *blow* 695.5, *hit* 695.11, *depression* 716.4, *flatten* 716.15
dental 107.31; *toothed* 19.21
dental auxiliary *paramedic* 107.24
dental floss *cleaning tool* 111.10, *prophylaxis* 115.4
dental hygienist *paramedic* 107.24
dentally *medically* 107.35
dental powder *cleaning agent* 111.9
dental record *means of identification* 184.3
dental surgeon *dentist* 107.21
dental surgery *dentistry* 107.6, *therapy* 115.12
dental surgery assistant *paramedic* 107.24
dental technician *paramedic* 107.24
dentate *of leaves* 41.18, *notched* 636.4
dentately *jaggedly* 636.7
dented *concave* 635.5
denticle *tooth* 549.7
denticulate *toothed* 549.13
denticulately *jaggedly* 636.7
denticulation *sharpness* 549.1
dentiform *toothed* 549.13
dentifrice *cleaning agent* 111.9, *prophylaxis* 115.4
dentil Architectural Elements 134
dentist 107.21
dentistry 107.6
dentists Phobias 283
dentition *teeth* 19.8, *sharpness* 549.1
dentoid *toothed* 19.21
dentophobia Phobias 283
denture *teeth* 19.8
denudate *make nude* 614.19
denudation *erosion* 8.41, *destruction* 468.7, *undressing* 614.2
denude *erode* 8.67, *disclose* 180.8, *destroy* 468.18, *weaken* 517.13, *lay waste* 523.14, *make nude* 614.19, *take off* 749.7, *separate* 753.12
denuded *naked* 614.12
denuder *nude person* 614.5, *depilation* 614.8
denuding *undressing* 614.2
denumerable *numerable* 6.70
denunciate *vilify* 301.15, *accuse* 442.8
denunciated *accused* 442.5
denunciation *Christian rite* 85.5, *vilification* 301.2, *form of derision* 369.2, *personal attack* 418.8, *censure* 438.3, *accusation* 442.1
denunciative *vilifying* 301.9
denunciatively *vilifyingly* 301.18

denunciatory *vilifying* 301.9, *critical* 418.16, *accusatory* 442.6
Denver American States 564
Denver boot *miscellaneous automotive terms* 687.14, *restraint* 826.81
deny 332.8; *discuss* 4.22, *disbelieve* 88.8, *negate* 190.16, *refuse* 190.17, 347.9, 506.8, *not accept* 190.19, *thwart* 293.10, *counter* 339.13, *reject* 383.10, *renounce* 383.13, *be evasive* 386.20, *veto* 503.9, *protest* 507.7, *exclude* 764.7, *object* 828.18, *make impossible* 837.8
deny entry *exclude* 764.7
denying *negational* 190.9, *disagreeing* 190.11, *counterevident* 339.10, *renunciation* 383.4, *desisting* 417.9, *dissenting* 506.6, *protesting* 507.5
denyingly 190.23
denying oneself *desisting* 417.4
deny oneself *abstain* 386.16, *renounce* 392.4, *desist* 417.13, *be self-restrained* 455.10, *refuse oneself* 506.10, *restrain oneself* 830.15
deny oneself nothing *indulge oneself* 456.10
deodar Trees and Shrubs 43
deodorant 225.3; *cleaning agent* 111.9, *deodorizing* 225.5, *toiletries* 530.6
deodorization *cleaning* 111.2, *odorlessness* 225.1
deodorize 225.6; *purify* 111.19
deodorized *odorless* 225.4
deodorizer *deodorant* 225.3
deodorizing 225.5
Deoni Breeds of Cattle 16
deontology Branches of Philosophy 4
Deo volente [L] *divinely* 82.24
deoxycorticosterone Human Hormones 12
deoxynucleotide *nucleotide* 12.10
deoxyribonucleic acid (DNA) *nucleotide* 12.10, *cell structure* 13.16
depaganize *proselytize* 84.15
depart 265.6, 705.8; *die* 29.17, *run away* 386.21, *absent oneself* 576.15, *exit* 707.13, *diverge* 753.20, *escape* 816.8, *resign* 835.5
departed 705.6; *dead* 29.11, *away* 576.8
département *administrative region* 564.4
departer *outgoer* 707.9
depart from *deviate* 698.15, *diverge* 734.8
departing 705.5; *dying* 29.3, *disappearing* 265.3, *outgoing* 707.10
department *subject* 48.3, *educator* 48.4, *region* 564.1, *part* 760.1, *piece* 760.2, *category* 767.6, *class* 777.1
departmental *administrative* 564.13, *component* 760.12
departmentalized *component* 760.12
department chairman or **chairwoman** or **chair** *educational leader* 68.11
department head *employer* 57.3, *educational leader* 68.11
Department of Defense *military organization* 58.4
department store *store* 124.4, 483.8, *building* 551.9
department store account *credit* 487.1
depart this life *withdraw* 705.9

departure 705.1; *death* 29.1, *circumlocution* 199.2, *disappearance* 265.1, *desertion* 386.7, *absence* 576.1, *backward motion* 677.5, *deviation* 698.1, *exit* 707.1, *cessation* 773.2, *special case* 779.7, *escape* 816.1, *resignation* 835.1
departure platform *place of departure* 705.4
dependability *observance* 465.1, *permanence* 667.1, *stability* 674.1, *infallibility* 840.6
dependable *steady* 376.8, *observant* 465.3, *unfailing* 667.3, *stable* 674.3, *trustworthy* 810.17, *infallible* 840.12
dependably *observantly* 465.6, *stably* 674.9
dependant *follower* 794.10
dependence *believing* 87.2, *habit* 397.1, *insolvency* 486.2, *inferiority* 745.1, *subjection* 832.1
dependency *body politic* 50.3, *possession of property* 469.3, *property* 470.1, *region* 564.1, *subjection* 832.1
dependent 832.4; *given* 6.74, *adherent* 401.5, 755.4, *servile* 401.6, *recipient* 473.5, *helpless* 515.9, *caused* 676.5, *inferior* 745.4, 745.5, *subordinate* 745.8, 832.8, *tenacious* 755.6, *accompanied* 794.15
dependently 832.13; *in a trance* 121.40, *powerlessly* 515.16, *with the effect of* 676.12, *basely* 745.16
dependent on *caused* 676.5
dependent on circumstances *circumstantial* 726.8
dependent personality disorder *personality disorder* 108.7
dependents *burden* 826.10
dependent variable *mathematical function* 6.27
depending on *caused* 676.5
depend on *believe* 87.9, *follow from* 676.9, *be subject to* 832.12, *be certain* 840.13
depeople *depopulate* 709.21
depersonalization *oblivion* 355.4
depersonalization disorder *dissociative disorder* 108.17
depersonalized *oblivious* 355.9
depict *draw* 143.13, *represent* 187.10, *describe* 202.15, *explain* 331.16, *outline* 617.5, *characterize* 723.11, *specify* 779.18
depicted *explanatory* 331.11
depict in glowing terms *boast* 194.14
depiction *representation* 187.1, *description* 202.1, *explanation* 331.3, *outline* 617.1
depictive *descriptive* 139.17, *representational* 187.8, *outlined* 617.4
depilate 614.20
depilation 614.8; *hairdressing* 530.7
depilatory 614.15; *depilation* 614.8
depilatory agent *depilation* 614.8
deplane *land* 704.16
deplete *expend* 626.5, *lessen* 468.17, *consume* 491.12, *weaken* 517.13, *void* 709.23, *wear out* 808.21
depleted *consumed* 96.11, *losing* 468.9, *used* 491.10, *dilapidated* 517.7
depletion *lessening* 468.6, *weakness*

517.1, *removal* 709.5, *moral deterioration* 808.3
deplorable *lamentable* 280.6, *unforgivable* 430.16, *evil* 446.7
deplorably *lamentably* 280.10, *disgracefully* 371.8, *evilly* 446.12
deplore *be dissatisfied* 274.7, *lament* 280.7, *hate* 300.11
deploy *have at one's disposal* 393.14, *situate* 573.10, *move apart* 703.11, *disperse* 776.12
deployed *dispersed* 776.6
deployment *use* 393.1, *parting* 703.2, *dispersion* 776.1
deplume *depilate* 614.20, *disbar* 709.16
depluming *dismissal* 709.2
deponent *witness* 339.7
depopulate 709.21; *lay waste* 523.14, *leave empty* 576.17
depopulated *unoccupied* 576.13
deport *exclude* 409.12, *exile* 454.24, *replace* 574.17, *take away* 685.12, *emigrate* 707.17, *ostracize* 709.17, *eject* 764.8
deportation *separation* 409.3, *exile* 454.3, *replacement* 574.3, *transfer* 685.1, *emigration* 707.6, *ostracism* 709.3, *ejection* 764.2
deported *lonely* 409.8, *replaced* 574.10
deportee *displaced person* 574.7
deportment *external appearance* 264.5, *conduct* 399.1
deport oneself *conduct oneself* 399.17
deposal *replacement* 574.3
depose *be anarchic* 51.8, *attest* 189.22, *give evidence* 339.12, *discard* 383.12, *replace* 574.17, *disbar* 709.16, *terminate* 834.7
deposed *avowed* 189.19, *powerless* 515.16, *replaced* 574.10
deposed champion *loser* 846.9
deposit 105.21, 487.3, 487.12; *sediment* 8.29, *ore* 11.23, *reserve* 105.3, *source of supply* 105.4, *dirt* 112.5, *personal finance* 457.5, *budget* 457.10, *bank* 484.26, *type of payment* 489.3, *solid body* 540.4, *be dense* 540.8, *residue* 750.2, *leave* 750.10, *part* 760.1
deposit account *funds* 484.6, *accounts* 493.4
depositary *treasurer* 484.18
deposited *accounted* 493.8, *remaining* 750.7
deposition *petrogenesis* 8.31, *certificate* 185.2, *attestation* 189.2, *avowal* 189.7, *legal evidence* 339.4, *replacement* 574.3
deposition on oral or **written questions** *pretrial proceedings* 54.13
depositor 487.6
depository *storehouse* 105.8, *money storage* 484.20, *container* 578.1
depot *storehouse* 105.8, *marketplace* 483.7, *center of activity* 612.4, *railroad station* 688.6, *destination* 704.6
depot ship *warship* 77.21
depravation *moral deterioration* 808.3
deprave 448.14; *demoralize* 432.15, *pervert* 808.22
depraved 448.10; *unchaste* 432.10, *evil* 446.7
depravity 448.2; *sexual immorality* 432.2, *evil* 446.1, *moral deterioration* 808.3
deprecate *negate* 190.16, *play down* 195.17, *be dissatisfied* 274.7, *abase* 298.20, *resist* 417.10,

criticize 438.19, disparage 440.11, protest 507.7, object 828.18

deprecating *underestimating* 344.3, *resistant* 417.6

deprecatingly *humiliatingly* 298.25, *resistingly* 417.14

deprecation *dissatisfaction* 274.1, *abasement* 298.6, *underestimation* 344.1, *resistance* 417.1, *disparagement* 440.1, *protest* 507.1

deprecative *resistant* 417.6

deprecatorily *disapprovingly* 507.10

deprecatory *critical* 438.13, *disparaging* 440.8, *protesting* 507.5

depreciable *decrescent* 747.6

depreciate *deflate* 195.16, *scorn* 436.19, *criticize* 438.19, *disparage* 440.11, *lessen* 468.17, *demonetize* 484.25, *discount* 495.4, *be cheap* 497.13, *decrease* 747.7, *deteriorate* 808.14

depreciated *deflated* 195.12, *financial* 457.6, *monetary* 484.22, *bargain* 497.10

depreciated currency *false money* 484.15

depreciate the currency *devalue the currency* 490.14

depreciation 490.4; *deflation* 195.7, *underestimation* 344.1, *use* 393.1, *disparagement* 440.1, *international finance* 457.2, *lessening* 468.6, *currency market* 484.8, *decrease* 747.1, *economic deterioration* 808.2

depreciative *decrescent* 747.6

depreciator *disparager* 440.7

depreciatory *underestimating* 344.3, *disparaging* 440.8, *decrescent* 747.6

depredate *plunder* 479.16

depredation *plundering* 479.5, *havoc* 523.5

depredator *plunderer* 479.9

depress *discourage* 179.11, *cause sorrow* 270.9, *disappoint* 293.9, *make sullen* 304.13, *predict* 358.14, *be evil* 446.10, *lower* 597.21, 716.12, *make concave* 635.7, *make smaller* 747.8

depressed 261.7, 270.5; *infertile* 23.7, *psychologically disturbed* 108.39, *mentally ill* 110.11, *arch* 134.5, *discouraged* 179.6, *sad* 254.10, *lamenting* 280.4, *without hope* 282.7, *disappointed* 293.4, *sullen* 304.8, *lowland* 597.15, *concave* 635.5, *drooping* 714.10, *lowered* 716.7, *degraded* 716.10

depressed person *sad person* 270.3

depressed population *the poor* 486.7

depressing *dissuasive* 179.4, *sad* 254.10, *distressing* 270.6, *lamentable* 280.6, *disappointing* 293.6, *overcast* 304.11, *lowered* 716.7

depressingly *dishearteningly* 179.13, *disappointingly* 293.12, *dismally* 304.19, *destructively* 446.13

depression 270.2, 716.4; *weather system* 9.10, *infertile state* 23.3, *economic factor* 56.8, *neurosis* 108.9, *mood disorder* 108.12, *mental breakdown* 110.4, *symptom* 114.3, *psychiatric disease* 114.21, *lack of hope* 282.2, *disappointment* 293.1, *sullenness* 304.1, *unemployment* 415.2, *sales* 482.3, *insolvency* 486.2, *lowlands* 597.6, *concavity* 635.1, *sinkage* 714.2,

lowering 716.1, *inferior state* 745.3, *decline* 747.4, *economic deterioration* 808.2, *economic adversity* 848.6

Depression Era *Ages, Decades, Eras* 641

depressive *insane person* 110.5, *mentally ill* 110.11, *sad person* 270.3, *degraded* 716.10, *decrescent* 747.6

depressively *psychologically* 108.42

depress the market *make cheap* 497.14

deprivation *confiscation* 454.4, *loss* 468.1, *taking back* 477.4, *poverty* 486.1, *eviction* 709.4, *setting apart* 753.2

deprive *confiscate* 454.25, *lose* 468.12, *take back* 477.17, *impoverish* 486.16, *weaken* 517.13, *evict* 709.20

deprived *needy* 95.12, *losing* 468.9, *poor* 486.8

deprived, the *the poor* 486.7

deprived of strength *weak* 517.6

deprived of vision *blind* 243.11

deprive of life *kill* 308.19

deprive of power *or* **authority** *remove power from* 515.13

deprive of sight *blind* 243.17

deprive of sleep *fatigue* 820.6

deprive oneself of *refuse oneself* 506.10

depriver *ejector* 709.10

depriving *losing* 468.9

depth 598.1; *line* 6.35, *obscurity* 197.1, *Phobias* 283, *thought* 315.5, *potency* 516.6, *space* 563.1, *size* 579.1, *Fields of Measurement* 589, *measurability* 589.2, *measuring instrument* 589.12, *thickness* 594.1, *quantity* 738.1, *degree* 739.1, *latency* 844.1

depth charge *naval mine* 77.23, *bomb* 78.15

depth finder *bathymetry* 598.3

depth-finding *bathymetric* 598.12

depth indicator *indicator* 183.7

depth of feeling 598.7

depth of field *lens system* 10.22, *composition* 132.17

depth of focus *exposure equipment* 132.12

depth of space *space* 563.1, *distance* 585.1

depth psychology *Psychological Theories, Schools* 108

depths *lowest point* 597.5, *base* 601.1, *inferior state* 745.3

depths, the 598.2

depth sounder *bathymetry* 598.3, *navigational aid* 690.6

depth sounding *sounding* 10.16, *bathymetry* 598.3

depth-sounding *bathymetric* 598.12

depurate *purify* 111.19

deputation *acquisition of authority* 52.5, *delegation* 79.3, *commission* 833.1, *council* 833.4

deputative *deputizing* 80.4

depute *delegate* 79.6, *deputize* 80.7, *commission* 833.8

deputed *decentralized* 79.5

deputing *delegation* 79.3, *substitution* 672.1

deputize 80.7; *gain authority* 52.15, *delegate* 79.6, *answer for* 334.24, *be a substitute* 672.6, *commission* 833.8

deputized *authorized* 52.11, *substituted* 672.4, *commissioned* 833.6

deputize for *aid* 275.10

deputizing 80.4; *delegation* 79.3, *substitution* 672.1

deputy 80.1; *delegated* 79.4, *agent* 123.15, *representative* 187.7, *helper* 275.5, 825.12, *substitute* 672.2, 672.3, *inferior* 745.4, *commissioner* 833.5

deputy chief of staff *military staff* 58.5

deputy sheriff *deputy* 80.1

deracinate *destroy* 523.10, *remove* 574.16, *exterminate* 709.22, *extract* 711.13

deracinated *removed* 574.9, *dislodged* 711.11

deracination *destroying* 523.2, *removal* 574.2, *extraction* 711.1

derail *displace* 574.15, *disarrange* 768.11

derailed *displaced* 574.8, *disarranged* 768.7

derailleur *bicycle part* 687.11

derailment *displacement* 574.1, *dispersion* 768.3

derange 766.23; *make insane* 110.13, *displace* 574.15, *deconstruct* 758.7, *disorder* 766.17, *disarrange* 768.11, *impair* 808.18

deranged 766.16; *insane* 110.9, *displaced* 574.8, *disordered* 766.9, *disarranged* 768.7

derangement 766.8; *displacement* 574.1, *disintegration* 758.1, *disorder* 766.1, *impairment* 808.7

derby *hat* 100.32

Derby porcelain *Ceramics* 129

Derbyshire Gritstone *Breeds of Sheep* 16

deregulate *counteract* 510.7, *liberate* 831.6

deregulated *liberated* 831.4

deregulation *neutralization* 510.4, *liberation* 831.1

dereism *defense mechanism* 108.23

derelict *relinquished* 392.2, *disused* 394.8, *decrepit* 808.12

dereliction *negligence* 326.1, *disobedience* 375.5, *relinquishment* 392.1, *disuse* 394.3, *failure* 846.1

dereliction of duty *self-exemption* 434.3, *sin* 450.3, *nonperformance* 466.2

derestrict *counteract* 510.7

derestriction *neutralization* 510.4

deride 369.7; *be dissatisfied* 274.7, *exclude* 383.11, *disdain* 400.16, *ridicule* 436.22, 440.15, *show disapproval* 438.21

derided *criticized* 438.14

derider 369.3

de rigueur *necessitative* 95.11, *established* 397.12, *good-mannered* 410.7, *duty-bound* 433.8, *legal* 780.8

derision 369.1, 400.5; *dissatisfaction* 274.1, *joke* 368.4, *discourtesy* 411.1, *disobedience* 416.2, *ridicule* 436.4, *show of disapproval* 438.6, *scorn* 440.5

derisive 369.5, 400.12; *dissatisfied* 274.4, *defiant* 416.5, *ridiculing* 436.13, *scornful* 440.10

derisively 369.8, 400.22; *rudely* 411.9, *defiantly* 416.9, *mockingly* 436.26, *disparagingly* 440.16

derisiveness *derision* 369.1

derisory *dissatisfied* 274.4, *ridiculous* 368.5, *ridiculing* 436.13

derivation *reasoning* 6.61, *type of meaning* 361.4, *cause* 675.1, *effect* 676.1, *drawing out* 711.5

derivative *differentiation* 6.29, *effect* 676.1, *caused* 676.5, *imitative* 736.7

derivatively *with the effect of* 676.12, *imitatively* 736.12

derive *theorize* 6.84, *cause* 675.8, *draw out* 711.17

derived *caused* 676.5

derived authority *legal power* 52.2

derived unit *unit of measurement* 589.5

derive from *follow from* 676.9

deriving from *caused* 676.5

dermal *skin* 19.19

Dermantsi Pied *Breeds of Pigs* 16

dermapteran *insectile* 40.11

dermatitis *skin disease* 114.16

dermatological disease *disease* 114.4

dermatology *Medical Specialties* 107

dermatopathophobia *Phobias* 283

dermatophyte *fungal association* 47.5

dermatophytosis *fungal disease* 47.6

dermatosiophobia *Phobias* 283

dermis *body covering* 19.4

Dermoptera *flying mammal* 35.8

dermopteran *flying mammal* 35.8, *chiropteran* 35.25

derogate *criticize* 438.19, *disparage* 440.11

derogation *disparagement* 440.1

derogator *disparager* 440.7

derogatorily *derisively* 400.22, *disparagingly* 440.16

derogatory *derisive* 400.12, *critical* 438.13, *disparaging* 440.8

derrick *construction equipment* 14.23, *lifter* 715.5

derrière *rear end* 622.4

derring-do *courage* 284.1, *courageous act* 284.7

derringer *firearm* 78.7

derris *pest killer* 17.9

dervish *religious* 84.9

Derwent *Rivers* 570

Derwent Water *Lakes* 568

desalinate *purify* 111.19

desalination *cleaning* 111.2

desalinize *purify* 111.19

desalt *purify* 111.19

Desargues's theorem *Mathematical Concepts* 6

descale *practice dentistry* 107.34

descant *melody* 140.10, *dissertation* 203.1, *dissertate* 203.5

descend 597.22, 714.12; *mountaineer* 161.10, *be transferred* 470.13, *be heavy* 538.12, *deepen* 598.21, *be in motion* 677.14, *slip back* 680.19, *fly* 689.13, *become inferior* 745.11

descendant *descending* 714.9, *person remaining* 750.6, *successor* 770.6

descendants *future generation* 650.2

descended *caused* 676.5

descendent *lowered* 716.7

descender 714.8; *type* 173.5

descend from *follow from* 676.9

descending 597.13, 714.9; *climbing techniques* 161.3, *deepening* 598.14, *directional* 677.13, *flying* 689.11, *descent* 714.1, *lowered* 716.7, *spoiled* 808.9

descending from *caused* 676.5

descending motion 677.6

descending order *straight line* 630.2, *hierarchy* 765.3, *consecutiveness* 774.1

descend into the arena *contend* 422.22

descend on *drop* 714.15

descend to particulars *particularize* 779.17

descension *descent* 714.1

descent 597.4, 714.1, Collective Names 59, *family tree* 65.3, *climbing techniques* 161.3, *humiliation* 298.5, *deepening* 598.4, *descending motion* 677.6, *flight* 689.5, *lowering* 716.1, *succession* 770.2, *line* 774.2, *deterioration* 808.1

describe 202.15; *chronicle* 3.15, *write* 139.21, *communicate* 170.12, *illustrate* 187.11, *explain* 331.16, *interpret* 365.12, *specify* 779.18

describe or **move in a circle** *orbit* 681.8

describe briefly *outline* 617.5

described *chronicled* 3.12, *named* 202.13, *explanatory* 331.11

description 202.1; *chronicle* 3.4, *aspect of fiction* 139.5, *representation* 187.1, *nomenclature* 202.7, *explanation* 331.3, *interpretation* 365.1

descriptive 139.17, 202.11; *chronicled* 3.12, *philosophical* 4.12, *linguistic* 5.34, *of grammar* 5.41, *representational* 187.8, *explanatory* 331.11, *intelligible* 363.5, *interpretive* 365.8, *outlined* 617.4

descriptive grammar *grammar* 5.28

descriptive linguistics Linguistic Studies 5

descriptively 139.24, 202.18; *linguistically* 5.44, *grammatically* 5.48, *representationally* 187.15, *demonstrably* 331.22

descriptiveness *intelligibility* 363.1

descriptive statistics *statistics* 6.51

descriptive writer 202.10

descriptive writing *nonfiction* 139.6, *fictional account* 202.5

descriptivism Philosophical Schools of Thought 4

descriptivist Philosophical Schools of Thought 4

descry see 242.20, *discover* 345.11, *recognize* 363.11

Desdemona Planets and Their Satellites 7

desecrate 436.24; *dirty* 112.11, *bring into disrepute* 371.6, *misuse* 395.6, *wrong* 430.19, *make worse* 808.17

desecrated *misused* 395.3

desecrating *impious* 448.11

desecration *misuse* 395.1, *impiety* 448.4

desensitization 213.2

desensitize *anesthetize* 213.8, *make indifferent* 289.13

desensitized 213.5

desert 66.11, 96.6, 560.4, 560.12, 572.10; *infertile land* 23.2, *infertile* 23.7, Collective Names 59, *desolate* 96.13, *hot place* 217.5, *retreat* 285.8, *run away* 386.21, *retaliation* 420.1, *disobey* 427.12, *claim* 429.3, *worth* 447.3, *not perform* 466.10, *defy* 466.11, *havoc* 523.5, *geographical space* 563.3, *of landmasses* 572.12, *abscond* 576.16, *leave empty* 576.17, *open space* 583.6, *be converted* 670.12, *resign* 835.5

desert climate *climate* 9.35

desert dune *dune* 8.43

deserted *divorced* 66.7, *relinquished* 392.2, *lonely* 409.8, *secluded* 409.9, *unoccupied* 576.13, *alone* 788.15, *vulnerable* 811.9

deserter *coward* 285.3, *the hunted* 385.7, *avoider* 386.8, *refuser* 506.4, *absentee* 576.5

desertification *climatic change* 9.37, *infertile land* 23.2

deserting *disobedient* 427.10, *nonperforming* 466.6, *defiant* 466.7

desertion 386.7; *separation* 66.2, *divorce court* 66.3, *disappearance* 265.1, *dastardliness* 285.2, *relinquishment* 392.1, *disobedience* 427.1, *defiance* 466.3, *absenteeism* 576.3, *departure* 705.1

desertion of principles *irresolution* 461.3

desert island *infertile land* 23.2, *privacy* 181.6, *solitary place* 409.4

desert one's principles *be irresolute* 461.8

deserts *mode of behavior* 399.2, *retaliation* 420.1, *reward* 453.1, *retribution* 454.7

desert sands *desert* 572.10

desert warfare *warfare* 76.3

desert waste *havoc* 523.5

deserve *be entitled to* 72.13, *qualify* 340.11, *have rights* 429.13

deserved *qualified* 340.7, *rightful* 429.9

deservedly *capably* 340.15, *right* 429.15

deservedness *qualification* 340.1, *claim* 429.3

deserved reward *reward* 453.1

deserved tribute *reward* 453.1

deserve ill of *behave badly* 399.19

deserve notice *be important* 799.13

deserve well of *behave well* 399.18

deserving *honored* 72.11, *desirable* 288.11, *praiseworthy* 437.12

deservingly *worthily* 72.14, *desirably* 288.24

deserving punishment *punishable* 454.21

desiccant *drying* 560.15

desiccate *dry* 560.17

desiccated *dried-up* 560.9, *preserved* 815.12

desiccation *drying* 560.3, *preservation of provisions* 815.6

desiccation cracks *sedimentary rock* 8.34

desiccative *dryer* 560.5, *drying* 560.15

desiccator *dryer* 560.5

desiderate *need* 95.16, *be unsatisfied* 98.10

desideratum *necessity* 95.1, *object of desire* 288.8

design 133.9, 536.2, 536.8; *combinatorics* 6.63, *engineer* 14.48, *make clothing* 100.44, *visual arts* 133.1, *work of art* 133.4, *be an architect* 134.13, *drawing* 143.4, *treatment* 143.6, *stage of book production* 174.7, *publish* 174.19, *illustrate* 187.11, *describe* 202.15, *purpose* 327.4, *aim* 327.17, *invention* 345.4, *invent* 345.14, *point* 361.5, *intend* 361.15, 374.8, *future intention* 374.3, *plan* 387.1, 387.12, *plan out* 387.14, *undertaking* 391.1, *motivation* 508.1, *production* 522.1, *dream up* 522.15, *fashion* 536.1, 536.7, 537.9, *style* 537.1, *structure* 551.20, *form* 624.1, 624.9,

originate 737.7, *array* 767.2, *stratagem* 822.2, *be cunning* 822.5

design and makeup 174.8

design a prototype *plan out* 387.14

designate *deputize* 80.7, *identify* 184.11, *mean* 361.13, *selected* 382.11, *select* 382.12, *characterize* 723.11, *class* 777.12, *specify* 779.18

designated *titled* 72.9, *identified* 184.9, *expected* 356.5

designated hitter *baseball team* 147.2

designated runner *baseball team* 147.2

designation *title* 72.1, *identification* 184.1, *nomenclature* 202.7, *selection* 382.1

design body *spirit* 86.10

designed 536.6, 537.5; *architectural* 134.12, *drawn* 143.11, *published* 174.18, *purposive* 327.11, *meant* 359.7, 361.12, *intentional* 374.7, *deliberate* 384.5, *planned* 387.10

designer *tailored* 100.41, *visual artist* 133.6, *producer* 136.28, 522.10, *drawer* 143.8, *book publishing personnel* 174.12, *discoverer* 345.7, *planner* 387.9, *decorator* 532.8, *fashion business* 536.3, *prototypical* 624.7, *originator* 737.3

designer drug *drug* 115.9, 121.14

designer gene *molecular biology* 13.18

designer label *fashion* 536.1

designing *invention* 345.4, *planning* 387.11, *form* 624.1

design school *type of school* 48.12

desirability 288.7; *lovability* 299.5, *preference* 382.2, *convenience* 803.1

desirable 288.11; *sensual* 20.16, *object of desire* 288.8, *lovable* 299.20, *preferential* 382.10, *convenient* 803.3

desirableness *desirability* 288.7

desirably 288.24; *lovably* 299.31

desire 288.1, 288.17, 299.24; *sexual longing* 20.6, *be unsatisfied* 98.10, *aspiration* 281.3, *aspire* 281.13, *lust after* 288.20, *liking* 290.1, *like* 290.8, *sexual love* 299.3, *envy* 314.1, 314.7, *curiosity* 321.1, *reverie* 360.6, *will* 372.1, 372.11, *prefer* 382.13, *request* 505.1, 505.10, *motivation* 508.1, *attraction* 700.1

desire concentration *cathexis* 108.32

desired 288.10; *liked* 290.6, *expected* 356.5, *willed* 372.6, *requesting* 505.7

desire for knowledge *curiosity* 333.8

desire for oneself *envy* 314.7

desire knowledge *be curious* 321.7

desirer 288.9

desires *expectations* 356.2

desires of the flesh *sexual desire* 20.5, *sexual love* 299.3

desiring *envious* 314.4, *expecting* 356.4

desirous 20.18, 288.13; *aspiring* 281.8, *liking* 290.4, *envious* 314.4

desirously 288.26; *lustfully* 20.24, *admiringly* 290.11, *enviously* 314.11

desist 417.13; *not act* 413.11, *cease* 668.9, *stop* 668.10, *cease* 668.14

desist! *cease!* 668.14

desistance *desisting* 417.4, *cessation* 668.1

desisting 417.4, 417.9; *chaste* 431.10

desk *furniture* 101.1, *cabinet* 578.3

desk dictionary *word book* 5.27

desk lamp *electric light* 246.6

desk sergeant *law enforcement officer* 53.8

desktop publishing (DTP) *computing* 15.2

desktop publishing (DTP) program *application software* 15.14

desk worker *clerical worker* 123.5

Des Moines American States 564, Rivers 570

desolate 96.13; *infertile* 23.7, *waste* 23.11, *sorrowful* 270.4, *without hope* 282.7, *lonely* 409.8, *secluded* 409.9, *lay waste* 523.14, *depopulate* 709.21

desolation *infertile land* 23.2, *sorrow* 270.1, *lack of hope* 282.2, *havoc* 523.5, *adversity* 848.1

desorb *absorb* 11.40

desorbed *absorbed* 11.34

desorption *surface chemistry* 11.20

despair 270.8; *be negative* 190.21, *depression* 270.2, *lack of hope* 282.2, *be hopeless* 282.11, *disappointment* 293.1, *be disappointed* 293.8

despairing *negative* 190.15, *without hope* 282.7

despairingly *pessimistically* 190.26, *unhopefully* 282.14

desperado *murderer* 30.12, *rash move* 286.4, *villain* 448.5, *violent animal* 520.4

desperate *without hope* 282.7, *reckless* 286.6, *active* 414.13, *villainous* 448.12, *violent* 520.5

desperately *unhopefully* 282.14, *recklessly* 286.10

desperateness *recklessness* 286.2

desperate remedy *means* 102.1

desperate situation *danger* 811.1

desperate straits *critical situation* 824.6

desperation *lack of hope* 282.2, *recklessness* 286.2

despicability *hatefulness* 300.4

despicable *dastardly* 285.6, *detested* 291.11, *hateful* 300.10, *unforgivable* 430.16, *disregardful* 436.11, *evil* 446.7, *unpleasant* 501.5

despicably *cowardly* 285.9, *hatefully* 300.14, *disgracefully* 371.8

Despina Planets and Their Satellites 7

despise *detest* 291.13, *disdain* 297.14, 400.16, *hate* 300.11, *scorn* 436.19

despised *detested* 291.11, *hated* 300.9

despite *contempt* 436.3, *in disagreement* 463.12, *counter* 510.8, *additionally* 748.15

despiteful *bitter* 306.9

despitefully *bitterly* 306.16

despitefulness *hostility* 63.1, *bitterness* 306.3

despiteous [Arch] *bitter* 306.9

despoil *desecrate* 436.24, *be evil* 446.10, *destroy* 468.18, *take away forcefully* 477.19, *plunder* 479.16, *lay waste* 523.14

despoiler *raider* 477.10, *plunderer* 479.9, *destroyer* 523.6

despoiling *conquest* 477.6, *plundering* 479.5, *havoc* 523.5

despoilment *destruction* 468.7, *plundering* 479.5

despoliation *plundering* 479.5

despond *despair* 270.8, *lack of hope* 282.2

despondence *or* **despondency** *negativism* 190.7

despondency *depression* 270.2, *lack of hope* 282.2, *sullenness* 304.1, *adversity* 848.1

despondent *negative* 190.15, *depressed* 261.7, 270.5, *without hope* 282.7, *sullen* 304.8

despondently *pessimistically* 190.26, *bluely* 261.11, *unhopefully* 282.14, *sullenly* 304.16

despot *person in authority* 52.7, *absolute ruler* 68.7, *strict person* 424.4

despotic *lawless* 53.26, *masterful* 68.15, *managerial* 126.9, *severe* 424.5

despotically *summarily* 53.36

despotism *totalitarianism* 49.13, *suppression* 424.2

desquamate *scale* 588.10, *shed* 614.21

desquamation *layering* 588.5, *peeling* 614.6

desquamative *peeling* 614.13

dessert 90.35; *dish* 90.7, *course* 92.12, *confectionery* 222.3

dessert spoon *tableware* 92.13

dessert wine *sweet drink* 222.4

destabilize *solidify* 11.37, *unbalance* 741.8

destabilized *status adjectives* 11.25

destabilizer *phase* 11.13

de Stijl *Furniture Styles* 101, *Western Art Styles* 133, *Architectural Styles* 134

destination 704.6; *objective* 374.5, *predestination* 384.2, *end point* 773.6

destine *intend* 361.15, *predestine* 384.9

destined *inevitable* 95.14, 840.11, *meant* 361.12, *predestined* 384.6, *auspicious* 458.10, *future* 650.6, *annihilated* 773.16

destine for *intend for* 374.11

destiny *inevitability* 95.6, 840.5, *predestination* 384.2, *influence* 512.1, *future condition* 650.3, *contributory cause* 675.3, *end of time* 773.5, *luck* 842.3

destitute *needy* 95.12, *poor* 486.8, *person in adversity* 848.9

destitution *neediness* 95.3, *poverty* 486.1, *adversity* 848.1

destrier [Arch] *war-horse* 159.4

destroy 186.10, 468.18, 523.10; *kill* 30.19, *slaughter* 30.21, *be at war* 76.32, *cause to disappear* 265.7, *refute* 332.7, *be evil* 446.10, *use violence* 520.9, *change for the worse* 665.18, *exterminate* 709.22, *cause not to exist* 718.14, *take apart* 753.16, *deconstruct* 758.7, *annihilate* 773.22, *make useless* 802.12, *impair* 808.18, *cancel* 834.6, *defeat* 845.17

destroyed 186.5, 523.9; *losing* 468.9, *no more* 718.11, *disintegrated* 758.3, *deconstructed* 758.4, *annihilated* 773.16, *spoiled* 808.9

destroyer 523.6; *warship* 77.21, *changer* 665.9, *Ships and Boats* 690

destroyer escort *warship* 77.21

destroyer flotilla *military organization* 58.4

destroy goodwill *cause hate* 300.12

destroying 523.2; *destructive* 523.8

destruct *destroy* 523.10

destruction 186.2, 468.7, 523.1; *killing* 30.1, *slaughter* 30.5, Collective Names 59, *blacking out* 265.2, *deconstruction* 758.2, *annihilation* 773.4, *dilapidation* 808.5, *impairment* 808.7

destructionist *destroyer* 523.6

destruction of life *killing* 30.1

destruction of weapons *disarmament* 74.3

destructive 523.8; *murderous* 30.18, *attacking* 418.14, *defamatory* 440.9, *detrimental* 446.8, *explosive* 520.6, *adverse* 848.10

destructively 446.13, 523.18, 758.9; *in reply* 332.10

destructiveness 523.3; *violence* 520.1

desuetude *relinquishment* 392.1, *disuse* 394.3

desultorily *irregularly* 664.6, *changeably* 666.7, *incompletely* 762.10, *disconnectedly* 775.16

desultoriness *inattention* 324.1, *restlessness* 414.7, *irregularity* 664.1, *irresolution* 666.2, *incompleteness* 762.1, *nonachievement* 762.3

desultory *perfunctory* 324.9, *vague* 338.9, *irregular* 664.3, 766.10, *irresolute* 666.4, *wandering* 698.13, *uncompleted* 762.7, *discontinuous* 775.7

detach *disconnect* 574.19, *separate* 724.14, 753.12, *unstick* 756.6, *disperse* 776.12, *single out* 788.19

detached 4.18; *manorial* 60.21, *indifferent* 289.7, *incurious* 322.3, *inattentive* 324.5, *oblivious* 355.9, *unsociable* 409.6, *disinterested* 443.4, *disconnected* 574.12, *separate* 724.10, *nonconforming* 728.10, *unjoined* 753.9, *irresolute* 772.13, *alone* 788.15, *independent* 829.12

detached house *house* 60.4

detachedly *disconnectedly* 574.22, *individualistically* 728.20

detached retina *sight defect* 243.2

detachment *philosophical attitude* 4.3, *military organization* 58.4, *army unit* 77.14, *mood disorder* 108.12, *indifference* 289.1, *incuriosity* 322.1, *inattention* 324.1, *oblivion* 355.4, *unsociability* 409.1, *disinterestedness* 443.1, *disconnection* 574.5, *separateness* 724.3, *nonconformity* 728.4, *separation* 753.1, *harmony* 765.8, *aloneness* 788.5

detach oneself *be indifferent* 289.12, *be incurious* 322.5

detail *military organization* 58.4, *army unit* 77.14, *diffuseness* 199.1, *be diffuse* 199.5, *recount* 202.16, *name* 202.17, *choose* 382.14, *allocate* 474.5, *aspect* 726.4, *circumstantiate* 726.12, *component* 760.3, *particularize* 760.15, *item* 788.2, *trifle* 800.3

detailed 726.9; *laborious* 122.7, *diffuse* 199.3, *descriptive* 202.11, *accurate* 350.3, *intense* 598.16, *component* 760.12, *complete* 761.6

detailed account *diffuseness* 199.1

detailed description *or* **account** *description* 202.1

detailing *decoration* 532.1

details *description* 202.1, *specifications* 779.6

detain 471.9, 830.16; *imprison* 55.11, *delay* 658.13, *slow down* 693.13, *hinder* 826.15

detained 830.11; *imprisoned* 55.9, *retained* 471.6, *held up* 658.6, *delayed* 693.10

detainee *prisoner* 55.7, *closed-in person* 584.6

detaining *delaying* 658.8

detainment *imprisonment* 55.4, *hindrance* 826.1

detect 345.12; *identify* 184.11, *sense* 212.9, *recognize* 363.11, *find* 565.11, *draw in* 708.18

detectability *visibility* 31.1

detectable *visible* 242.19, 244.5, *discoverable* 345.10

detected *found* 565.7

detecting *locating* 565.3

detection 345.2; *identification* 184.1

detective *law enforcement officer* 53.8, *curious person* 321.3, *questioner* 333.9, *discoverer* 345.7

detective story *story* 139.4

detector 345.6

detente *agreement* 462.1

détente *pacification* 74.1

detention 471.2, 830.5; *pretrial proceedings* 54.13, *imprisonment* 55.4, 454.2, *delay* 658.3, *hesitation* 693.5, *hindrance* 826.1

detention cell *prison cell* 55.3

detention center *or* **camp** *prison* 55.1

detention home *prison* 55.1

deter 179.8; *hinder* 826.15, *block* 826.17

detergent *cleaning agent* 111.9, *cleansing* 111.16

deteriorate 808.14; *age* 27.16, *waste away* 96.20, *be unhealthy* 114.29, *become aggravated* 276.6, *be unused* 394.11, *be unaccustomed* 398.5, *lessen* 468.17, *be brittle* 548.4, *grow old* 653.16, *change for the worse* 665.18, *be converted* 670.12, *lower* 716.12, *become inferior* 745.11, *be in trouble* 848.13

deteriorated 808.8; *depraved* 448.10, *changed* 665.10, *lowered* 716.7

deteriorating *depraved* 448.10, *converting* 670.8, *lowered* 716.7, *deteriorated* 808.8

deterioration 808.1; *wasting away* 96.4, *aggravation* 276.1, *unaccustomedness* 398.1, *depravity* 448.2, *international finance* 457.2, *lessening* 468.6, *brittleness* 548.1, *change for the worse* 665.5, *evolution* 670.3, *decline* 680.5, 846.5, *lowering* 716.1, *debasement* 716.5, *deficiency* 745.2, *disintegration* 758.1, *adverse health* 848.5

determent *hindrance* 826.1

determinability *measurability* 589.2

determinable *experimental* 335.8, *measurable* 589.17

determinant *matrix* 6.20, *cause* 675.1, *causal* 675.7

determination 379.2, 674.2; *earnestness* 278.2, *steadfastness* 284.3, *proof* 331.4, 336.2, *experimentation* 335.3, *specification* 340.6, *will* 372.1, *willpower* 372.2, *intentionality* 374.2, *resolution* 376.1, *perseverance* 377.1, *selection* 382.1, *assiduity*

414.8, *authority* 516.5, *measurement* 589.1, *authentication* 721.8, *tenacity* 755.2, *ruling* 780.2, *inevitability* 840.5

determine 675.11; *enumerate* 6.85, *experiment* 10.72, 335.11, *prove* 331.17, 336.9, *specify* 340.14, 779.18, *judge* 341.10, *find out* 345.13, *will* 372.11, *resolve* 374.9, 376.12, *select* 382.12, *measure* 589.20, *direct* 697.13, *authenticate* 721.24, *rule* 780.12, *calculate* 784.10, *make certain* 840.14

determined 379.7, 674.5; *earnest* 278.5, *steadfast* 284.11, *proven* 331.13, *tested* 335.10, *conditional* 340.10, *willed* 372.6, *iron-willed* 372.7, *intending* 374.6, *resolute* 376.7, *persevering* 377.6, *active* 414.13, *strong in spirit* 516.11, *measured* 589.16, *authenticated* 721.17, *tenacious* 755.6, *inevitable* 840.11

determined effort *attempt* 390.1

determinedly 674.10; *prospectively* 374.12, *tenaciously* 755.12

determinedness *resolution* 376.1

determine once and for all *resolve* 376.12

determine to *resolve* 374.9

determining *experimental* 335.8, *verificatory* 336.6, *willed* 372.6, *selecting* 382.9, *calculation* 784.1

determinism Philosophical Schools of Thought 4, *causality* 10.66, *necessitarianism* 95.7

determinist Philosophical Schools of Thought 4, *necessitarian* 95.8

deterministic *inevitable* 95.14

deterministic law *causality* 10.66

deterred *dissuaded* 179.5

deterrence 179.2

deterrent *deterrence* 179.2, *dissuasive* 179.4, *security* 461.1, *secure* 464.5, *opposing force* 510.2, *protection* 810.2, *warning* 814.1, 814.6, *obstacle* 826.2, *hindering* 826.12, *blocked* 826.13

detest 291.13; *hate* 300.11

detestability *hatefulness* 300.4

detestable *detested* 291.11, *hateful* 300.10, *evil* 446.7

detestably *hatefully* 300.14

detestation *antipathy* 291.2, *hate* 300.1, *hated thing* 300.5

detested 291.11; *hated* 300.9

detester *hater* 300.6

dethrone *replace* 574.17, *disbar* 709.16, *terminate* 834.7

detonate *fuel* 106.16, *burst* 232.9, *bang* 234.6, *make violent* 520.10, *shoot* 696.18

detonation *bang* 234.1, *violence by person* 520.2, *shot* 696.6

detonator *explosive* 78.13, *fuel starter* 106.3, *propellant* 696.9

detour *curve* 629.1, 629.6, *circle* 631.2, 631.6, *alteration* 665.2, *change* 665.14, *route* 691.2, *find one's way* 691.15, *thoroughfare* 692.6, *deviating course* 698.2, *deviate* 698.15

detoxify *sober up* 120.7, *cure* 809.15

detract *disparage* 440.11, *protest* 507.7, *separate* 753.12

detract from *disparage* 195.15, *subtract* 749.6

detracting *underestimating* 344.3

detraction *disparagement* 195.2,

440.1, *underestimation* 344.1, *subtraction* 749.1
detract nothing *equalize* 740.12
detractor *disbeliever* 88.5, *questioner* 333.9, *underestimator* 344.2, *dissenter* 347.5, *disparager* 440.7, *protester* 507.4
detractory *disparaging* 440.8
detrain *travel by train* 688.9, *land* 704.16
detribalize *pervert* 808.22
detriment *loss* 468.1, *inconvenience* 804.1, *impairment* 808.7
detrimental 446.8; *inconvenient* 804.5, *adverse* 848.10
detrimentally *adversely* 848.16
detrimental to health *unhygienic* 114.27
detrital *petrographic* 8.58, *grainy* 553.17
detrited *grainy* 553.17
detrition *pulverization* 553.4, *wearing away* 554.2
detritus *grit* 553.8, *transferred thing* 685.6, *residue* 750.2, *bits and pieces* 760.5
Detroit *major US cities* 567.5
detrude *let out* 709.26, *bear down on* 716.18
detrusion *disgorgement* 709.6, *submergence* 716.3
detumesce *decrease* 747.7
detumescence *decrease* 747.1
detumescent *decreasing* 747.5
deuce *tennis terms* 165.5, *cards* 168.2, *evil spirit* 446.4, *two* 789.1
deuce [Tennis] *stalemate* 740.3
deuce court *tennis court* 165.3
deuced [Brit] *miscellaneous euphemisms* 301.12
deus ex machina *play part* 136.8, *literary device* 139.12
deuteragonist *role* 136.23
deuteranopia *faulty vision* 243.1
deuteranopic *visually impaired* 243.9
deuterate *react* 11.38
deuterogamous *monogamous* 64.18
deuterogamy *type of marriage* 64.3
deuteromycetes *fungi* 47.3
Deuteromycota *fungi* 47.3
Deutsche Industrie Normen (DIN) [Ger] *standard* 589.10
Deutschmark *national coins* 484.11
deva *minor deity* 82.2
devaloka *heaven* 82.15
devaluated *financial* 457.6
devaluation *international finance* 457.2, *currency market* 484.8, *depreciation* 490.4, *subtraction* 749.1, *moral deterioration* 808.3
devalue *demonetize* 484.25, *make cheap* 497.14, *subtract* 749.6, *make useless* 802.12, *pervert* 808.22
devalued *financial* 457.6, *monetary* 484.22, *bargain* 497.10, *reduced* 749.5
devalued currency *false money* 484.15, *depreciation* 490.4
devalue the currency 490.14
devastate *lay waste* 96.21, 523.14, *disappoint* 293.9, *depopulate* 709.21
devastated 96.12; *disappointed* 293.4, *destroyed* 523.9
devastating *explosive* 520.6, *destructive* 523.8
devastatingly 96.24; *destructively* 523.18
devastation 96.5; *bad outcome*

293.3, *military attack* 418.2, *havoc* 523.5, *impairment* 808.7
develop 40.18, 132.28; *mature* 27.17, *educate* 48.22, *show potential* 458.14, *increase* 467.17, 581.16, 746.6, *dream up* 522.15, *convert* 670.11, *be converted* 670.12, *follow from* 676.9, *grow* 676.10, *be in motion* 677.14, *further* 679.13, *come to be* 717.19, *make bigger* 746.7, *promote* 807.18, *get better* 807.21, *reveal* 843.14
developable *enlargeable* 581.13
develop a habit *accustom oneself* 397.19
develop a literary style *style* 537.8
develop a method *find means* 102.6
develop an attitude *tend* 513.5
develop a thesis *dissertate* 203.5
developed *adult* 27.11, *productive* 522.11, *grown* 581.11, *caused* 676.5
developed country *economic development* 56.5
developed world *world region* 564.6
develop engine trouble *have a mishap* 826.18
developer *darkroom equipment* 132.21, *person transferring property* 470.8, *producer* 522.10, *enlarger* 581.8
develop from *grow* 676.10
develop fully *be complete* 761.10
develop industrially *produce* 522.13
developing *developmental* 13.33, *maturing* 27.12, *development* 132.19, *appearing* 264.9, *productive* 522.11, *growing* 581.12, 676.6, *converting* 670.8, *incomplete* 762.5, *embryonic* 771.19
developing from *caused* 676.5
develop late *be late* 658.11
development 132.19, 679.4; *education* 48.1, *aspect of fiction* 139.5, *augmentation* 467.2, *manufacture* 522.2, *growth* 581.4, 676.3, *evolution* 670.3, *increase* 746.1, *preparation* 769.3, *sequel* 770.5
developmental 13.33; *preparatory* 769.11
developmental biologist *life scientist* 13.26
developmental biology 13.6, 13.22
developmental psychology *Psychological Theories, Schools* 108
develop technical problems *have a mishap* 826.18
deviance *deviousness* 607.4, *diversity* 732.1, *deviation* 782.6
deviance or **deviancy** *deviation* 698.1
deviancy *errancy* 351.7
deviant 698.7, 698.8; *sexual perversion* 20.12, *errant* 351.12, *abnormal* 430.13, *perverted* 432.12, *devious* 607.9, *diverse* 732.5, *eccentric* 782.10
deviantly *promiscuously* 432.19, *diversely* 732.14
deviant person *deviant* 698.7
deviate 698.15; *sexual perversion* 20.12, *be circuitous* 199.6, *transgress* 351.16, *equivocate* 380.8, *be different* 463.11, *diverge* 607.11, 703.10, 734.8, 753.20,

move sideways 623.9, *change* 665.14, *be in motion* 677.14, *deviant* 698.7, *be disparate* 728.14, *be diverse* 732.10, *be independent* 782.20
deviate from the path of virtue *be wicked* 448.13
deviating *circumlocutory* 199.4, *equivocating* 380.6, *different* 463.7, *divergent* 607.7, 703.6, *deviant* 698.8, *foreign* 724.9
deviating course 698.2
deviatingly *nonuniformly* 734.11
deviating motion 698.3
deviation 698.1, 782.6; *circumlocution* 199.2, *vacillation* 380.3, *abnormality* 430.4, *difference* 463.4, *distance* 585.1, *divergence* 607.2, 703.1, *alteration* 665.2, *guide* 697.4, *diversity* 732.1, *separation* 753.1
deviationism *nonconformism* 782.3
deviationist *troublemaker* 427.5, *deviant* 698.7
deviation of refracted rays *Fields of Measurement* 589
deviative *deviant* 698.8
deviatory *changeable* 665.11, *deviant* 698.8
device *means* 102.1, *apparatus* 103.2, *aspect of fiction* 139.5, *Heraldic Terms* 184, *invention* 345.4, *method* 387.4, *instrument* 511.2, *means of escape* 816.4, *stratagem* 822.2
device driver *system software* 15.13
devil 446.5; *cook* 91.10, *evil spirit* 446.4, *violent animal* 520.4
devil, the *tempter* 178.10
deviled *culinary* 91.9
deviled egg *egg dish* 90.18
Devil Incarnate *devil* 446.5
devilish *witchlike* 86.19, *evil* 446.7, *demonic* 446.9, *impious* 448.11
devilishly 446.14; *impiously* 448.17
devilize *make evil* 446.11
devil-like *demonic* 446.9
devil-may-care *imprudent* 286.7, *careless* 289.8, *thoughtless* 318.7, *foolish* 353.5
devilry *evil* 446.1
devil's advocate *defiant person* 416.4
devil's food cake *cake* 90.36
Devils Tower *Mountains and Hills* 569
devil tree *Trees and Shrubs* 43
deviltry *evil* 446.1, *impiety* 448.4
devil worship *idolatry* 83.4, *impiety* 448.4
devil worshiper *idolater* 83.7
devious 607.9; *artful* 193.13, *disreputable* 371.4, *wandering* 698.13, *cunning* 822.8
deviously 371.9, 607.16; *deceptively* 193.21
deviousness 607.4; *guile* 193.3, *wandering* 698.4
devisable [Form] *transferring property* 470.10
devise *invent* 345.14, *imagine* 360.14, *plan* 387.12, *improvise* 396.6, *own property* 470.11, *dream up* 522.15, *design* 536.8, *construct* 551.22, *come to be* 717.19, *originate* 737.7, *make arrangements* 767.23, *be cunning* 822.5
devise countermeasures *hinder* 826.15

devised *imaginary* 360.12, *deliberate* 384.5, *produced* 522.12
devisee *beneficiary* 473.6
deviser *planner* 387.9, *originator* 737.3
devisor [Form] *giver* 472.7
devitalize *make impotent* 515.15
devitrified *ceramic* 129.9
devitrified glass *industrial ceramics* 129.6
devitrify *make ceramics* 129.10, *opaque* 250.7
devoid *vacant* 576.12, *nonexistent* 718.9
devoir *duty* 433.1
devoirs *greeting* 435.5
devolution *delegation* 79.3, *transfer of property* 470.4, *commission* 833.1
devolutionary *commissioned* 833.6
devolve *delegate* 79.6, *transfer property* 470.12, *be transferred* 470.13, *commission* 833.8
devolved *decentralized* 79.5
devolvement *delegation* 79.3, *commission* 833.1
devolve upon *be the duty of* 433.16
Devon *Breeds of Cattle* 16, *Islands* 572
Devon Closewool *Breeds of Sheep* 16
Devonian Period *Geologic Time Intervals* 8
Devon Longwool *Breeds of Sheep* 16
devote *give praise to* 472.13
devoted *intimate* 62.7, *religious* 81.21, *worshipful* 83.12, *liking* 290.4, *loving* 299.15, *steady* 376.8, *loyal* 426.5
devotedly *intimately* 62.14, *worshipfully* 83.17, *admiringly* 290.11, *lovingly* 299.29, *obediently* 426.9, *dutifully* 433.19
devotedness *intimacy* 62.4, *worship* 83.1, *seriousness* 376.3, *assiduity* 414.8
devoted to *loyal* 426.5
devotee *religious person* 81.9, *idolater* 83.7, *desirer* 288.9, *busy person* 414.10
devotee of Bacchus *drunkard* 121.8
devote oneself *revere* 81.26
devote oneself to *address oneself to* 209.13, *undertake* 391.7
devotion *intimacy* 62.4, *religiousness* 81.2, *worship* 83.1, *prayer* 85.10, *good feeling* 266.4, *liking* 290.1, *love* 299.1, *seriousness* 376.3, *loyalty* 426.2, *deference* 433.4, *respectfulness* 435.3
devotional *religious* 81.21, *worshipful* 83.12, *prayerful* 85.17
devotionally *worshipfully* 83.17
devotion to duty *sense of duty* 433.2
devour *eat* 92.21, *eat well* 92.23, *be greedy* 119.4, *consume* 523.16
devoured or **consumed** or **obsessed** or **eaten up with jealousy** *jealous* 314.5
devourer *eater* 92.15
devouring *appetite* 92.2, *eating* 92.18, *gluttonous* 119.3
devour with one's eyes *look* 242.21
devout *religious* 81.21, *worshipful* 83.12, *observant* 465.3
devoutly *religiously* 81.29, *ritually* 85.21, *observantly* 465.6

dew 9.34, 559.6; *moisture 9.31, water 557.1, sprinkle 559.14*
dewdrop *dew 9.34, round thing 633.3*
dewdrops *dew 559.6*
dewily *immaturely 652.23*
dewiness *cleanliness 111.1, wateriness 557.3, bogginess 559.7, immaturity 652.3*
dewpoint *weather data 9.6*
dew point *dew 9.34, humidity 559.3*
dew pond *small lake 568.2*
dewy *foggy 9.51, clean 111.13, misty 559.10, immature 652.12, daily 655.6*
dex [Inf] *stimulants 121.18*
dexie [Inf] *stimulants 121.18*
dexo [Inf] *stimulants 121.18*
Dexter *Breeds of Cattle 16*
dexter *Heraldic Terms 184*
dexterity *manual skill 127.2, easiness 823.1*
dexterous *skillful 127.10, proficient 445.15*
dexterously *skillfully 127.16, proficiently 445.22*
dexterousness *manual skill 127.2, proficiency 445.5*
dexter side *laterality 623.3*
dextral *sided 623.7*
dextrally *laterally 623.11*
dextran *polysaccharide 12.5, blood 555.4*
dextro form *structure 11.7*
dextrophobia *Phobias 283*
dextrose *Common Sugars 12*
D-form *structure 11.7*
Dhaka *Countries 566*
Dhamma *other text 81.19*
dhammaduta *imam 84.7*
Dhammapada *other text 81.19*
Dhaulagiri *Mountains and Hills 569*
dhobie itch *fungal disease 47.6, tropical disease 114.10, skin disease 114.16*
dhow *Sailing Ships and Boats 690*
diabetes *Phobias 283*
diabetic *sick person 114.22, of disease 114.25*
diabetic diet *diet 92.5*
diabetic retinopathy *eye disease 243.4*
diabetophobia *Phobias 283*
diable [Fr] *devil 446.5*
diablerie *witchcraft 86.6*
diablo [Sp] *devil 446.5*
diabolic *idolatrous 83.13, witchlike 86.19, demonic 446.9, impious 448.11*
diabolical *witchlike 86.19, demonic 446.9*
diabolically *magically 86.28, devilishly 446.14, impiously 448.17*
diabolism *idolatry 83.4, impiety 448.4*
diabolist *idolater 83.7*
diabolize *bewitch 86.25, make evil 446.11, deprave 448.14*
Diabolus *devil 446.5*
diachronic *historical 3.10, retrospective 651.15*
diachronic linguistics *Linguistic Studies 5*
diacidic *acid 11.27*
diacidic base *base 11.11*
diacritical *of grammar 5.41*
diacritical mark *language sign 5.33, linguistic sign 183.10*
diagnose *practice medicine 107.32,*

disclose 180.8, identify 184.11, discriminate 337.12
diagnosed *judged 337.10*
diagnosis 107.8; *disclosure 180.1, identification 184.1, experiment 335.1, discrimination 337.1*
diagnostic 107.29; *computing terms 15.22, symbolic 183.12, discriminating 337.9*
diagnostically *medically 107.35, indicatively 183.21, discriminatingly 337.15, in isolation 753.24*
diagnostician *medical specialist 107.20*
diagnostic instrument 107.13
diagnostic procedure 107.11
diagnostic radiology 107.12
diagnostics *diagnosis 107.8, science of interpretation 365.5*
diagnostic test *diagnosis 107.8*
diagonal *Accents and Diacritical Marks 5, line 6.35, cross-country 162.31, oblique line 607.5, oblique 607.6, 628.8*
diagonal gate *ski race 162.4*
diagonally *obliquely 607.13, askew 628.12, indirectly 698.28*
diagonal matrix *matrix 6.20*
diagonal side step *cross-country techniques 162.8*
diagram *drawing 143.4, illustration 187.2, map 187.5, 187.12, 387.7, illustrate 187.11, outline 617.1, 617.5, chart 767.8*
diagrammatic 767.17; *pictorial 6.75, symbolic 183.12, representational 187.8, representing 202.14, outlined 617.4*
diagrammatically *essentially 617.6, in place 767.24*
dial 169.12; *face 646.8*
dialect 5.24; *native language 5.5, nonstandard language 5.7, vernacular 205.8*
dialectal *of language 5.35*
dialect geography *Linguistic Studies 5*
dialectic *philosophical argument 4.5, philosophical term 4.7, debate 210.3, logical argument 329.2*
dialectical 4.16; *argumentative 319.10, logical 329.9*
dialectically *philosophically 4.23, logically 329.17, in answer 334.25*
dialectical materialism *Philosophical Schools of Thought 4, materialization 524.2*
dialectical materialist *Philosophical Schools of Thought 4, materialist 524.3*
dialectician *philosopher 4.9, reasoner 319.5, answerer 334.10*
dialecticism *debate 319.3*
dialectics *debate 319.3*
dialectology *Linguistic Studies 5, regional pronunciation 205.7*
dial gauge *meter 589.13*
dialing *dial 169.12*
dialing code *dial 169.12*
dialogical theology *Theologies 81*
dialogue *philosophical argument 4.5, play 136.2, dramaturgy 136.6, script 137.5, speech 205.1, conversation 210.1, logical argument 329.2, question and answer 334.3, summit meeting 600.3*
dial telephone *telephone 169.10*
dial tone *dial 169.12*
dialyse *practice surgery 107.33*
dialysis *analysis 11.17, treatment 107.14, cleaning 111.2*

dialyze *purify 111.19*
diamagnetic *abducent 701.5*
diamagnetism *magnetism 10.45, repulsion 701.1*
Diamantina *Rivers 570*
diameter *line 6.35, circle 6.40, dimension 10.5, space 563.1, size 579.1, breadth 592.1, parts of a circle 631.4, dividing line 740.6, midline 772.2, half 789.7*
diametral *curvilinear 6.78, midway 772.10*
diametral pitch *gear 14.7*
diametric *curvilinear 6.78*
diametric *or* **diametrical** *contrary 828.13*
diametrical *or* **diametric** *opposite 731.3*
diametrically 731.6
diametrically opposed *opposite 731.3, contrary 828.13*
diametrically opposite *opposite 731.3*
diamond *polygon 6.42, Chemical Elements and Common Allotropes 11, baseball field 147.3, hard substance 542.3, angled figure 628.3, angled 628.9*
diamond fret *Architectural Elements 134*
diamond in the rough *natural state 389.4*
diamond jubilee *anniversary 405.5*
diamondlike *hard 542.5*
diamonds *cards 168.2*
diamond-shaped *polygonal 6.79*
diamond-studded *grand 404.22, opulent 485.10*
diamond wedding anniversary *anniversary 405.5*
Diana *moon 7.18, Deities 82, type of complex 100.22, hunter 160.9, 385.6, shooter 696.11*
dianthus *Flowers 42*
diapason *loud tone 232.3*
diapedesis *transmission 685.3*
diaper *baby clothes 100.24, Architectural Elements 134*
diaphaneity *fineness 595.5*
diaphanous *translucent 249.8, fine 595.12*
diaphanously *transparently 249.13, finely 595.19*
diaphanousness *translucency 249.2, fineness 595.5*
diaphoresis *sweat 25.8, outflow 707.4*
diaphoretic *sweaty 25.17*
diaphragm *internal organ 19.13, contraceptive 23.6, exposure equipment 132.12, stage lighting 136.20, barrier 826.7*
diapositive *printing 132.20*
diaresis *Accents and Diacritical Marks 5*
diarist *author 139.13, record keeper 185.8, descriptive writer 202.10, keeper of time 646.10*
diaristic *timekeeping 646.11*
diarize *chronologize 646.13, list 785.11*
diarrhea *defecation 25.3, symptom 114.3, gastroenterological disease 114.11*
diary *chronicle 3.4, collection 105.12, nonfiction 139.6, periodical 175.1, record book 185.5, reminder 354.4, chronology 646.2, list of dates 785.6*
diaspora *replacement 574.3, diffraction 698.6, disbandment 776.2*
diastase *enzyme 12.11*

diaster *cell division 13.17*
diastole *expansion 581.1*
diastrophic *tectonic 8.56*
diastrophism *earth movement 8.20*
diathesis *ill health 114.1*
diatomaceous *algal 47.20*
diatomaceous earth *algal product 47.15*
diatomic *chemical compound 11.4*
diatonic scale *scale 140.16*
diatribe *public speaking 205.11, address 209.1, attack 418.1, berating 438.5*
diavolo [Ital] *devil 446.5*
diazotize *react 11.38*
dibasic *acid 11.27*
dibasic base *acid 11.10*
dibber *garden tool 103.4*
dibble *garden tool 17.7, 103.4, cultivate 17.19*
dibbuk *evil spirit 446.4*
dibrach *meter 139.10*
dibs [Inf] *cash 484.2*
dice *cook 91.10, Board and Table Games 167, gambling 167.4, means of prediction 358.10*
dice bet *gambling 167.4*
diced *partial 760.11*
dice game *type of game 167.2*
dicey [Inf] *dangerous 811.7, chance 842.10*
dichasial cyme *flower head 42.4*
dichasium *flower head 42.4*
dichotomic *half 789.12*
dichotomize *halve 789.15*
dichotomous *separate 753.7, half 789.12*
dichotomously *separately 753.22*
dichotomy *philosophical term 4.7, separateness 753.3, halving 789.6*
dichroic *variegated 263.6*
dichroism *variegation 263.1*
dichromatic *variegated 263.6*
dichromatism *variegation 263.1*
dick [Inf] *organs of reproduction 21.9, law enforcement officer 53.8, security force 810.13*
dickens *evil spirit 446.4*
dicker *bargain 480.20*
dickey *shirt 100.13, neckwear 100.29*
dicotyledon *or* **dicot** *or* **dicotyl** *seed plant 41.3*
Dicotyledonae *seed plant 41.3*
dicotyledonous *taxonomic 41.16*
Dictaphone™ *recording instrument 185.9*
dictate *govern 49.26, master 68.17, direct 126.11, command 425.1, 425.10, compel 428.8*
dictate of conscience *calling 178.6*
dictate to *have authority over 425.12*
dictating *governing 49.25*
dictator *person in authority 52.7, absolute ruler 68.7, leader 126.8, strict person 424.4, one who restrains 830.7*
dictatorial *national 18.16, governmental 49.24, lawless 53.26, masterful 68.15, managerial 126.9, severe 424.5, commanding 425.7, compelling 428.6, dominant 744.9*
dictatorially *governmentally 49.27, summarily 53.36, masterfully 68.19, severely 424.11, commandingly 425.15, superiorly 744.20*
dictatorship *totalitarianism 49.13, directorship 126.5, suppression 424.2, country 566.1*
dictatorship of the proletariat *totalitarianism 49.13*

diction *articulation* 205.9, *meaning* 361.1, *mode of expression* 537.3

dictionary *word book* 5.27, *schoolbook* 48.15, *collection* 105.12, *type of book* 174.3, *book of lists* 785.3

dictionary of dialects *word book* 5.27

dictionary of names *word book* 5.27

dictionary of quotations *word book* 5.27

dictionary program *application software* 15.14

dictum *maxim* 177.1, *affirmation* 189.1, *utterance* 205.10, *command* 425.1, *truism* 721.6

dictyopteran *insectile* 40.11

didactic *educational* 48.17, *advisory* 176.7, *persuasive* 178.12

didactically *advisorily* 176.12

didacticism *advice* 176.1

didactic poetry *poetry* 139.8

didaskaleinophobia *Phobias* 283

diddle [Inf] *have sex* 20.21, *swindle* 193.19

diddling [Inf] *sexual intercourse* 20.9

did you ever! *wonderful!* 294.20

die 29.17, 773.21; *Architectural Elements* 134, *gambling* 167.4, *disappear* 265.5, *not act* 413.11, *forfeit* 468.13, *prototype* 624.2, *stop* 668.10, *be motionless* 678.7, *withdraw* 705.9, *exit* 707.13, *cease to exist* 718.13, *be in trouble* 848.13

die at one's post *hold out* 377.13

die away *sound faint* 233.8, *stop* 668.10, *cease to exist* 718.13, *change by degrees* 739.8, *decrease* 747.7, *come to an end* 773.23

die before one's spouse *widow* 66.12

die by one's own hand *commit suicide* 30.24

died out *no more* 718.11

die down *pause* 415.15, *decrease* 747.7

die for *desire* 288.17

die for a cause *sacrifice* 504.14

die for food *starve* 118.10

die-hard *tenacious person* 377.5, *obstinate person* 379.4, *resister* 417.5, *obstinate* 417.7, *conservative* 815.13, *opposer* 828.9

die in the attempt *tackle* 390.8

die in the ear *sound faint* 233.8

dieldrin *pest control* 16.13

dielectric *insulation* 10.36, *nonconductor* 14.35

dielectric coefficient *insulation* 10.36

dielectric constant *insulation* 10.36, *nonconductor* 14.35

dielectric polarization *insulation* 10.36

die of embarrassment *be shy* 403.13

die off *stop* 668.10

die of shame *be shy* 403.13

die out *disappear* 265.5, *pass* 651.17, *cease to exist* 718.13, *decrease* 747.7, *die* 773.21

dieresis *separator* 753.5

die Roman fashion *commit suicide* 30.24

diesel *engine type* 14.11, *gas* 106.14, *means of propulsion* 696.2, *propellant* 696.9

diesel cycle *Classical Physical Laws* 10, *engine cycle* 14.13

diesel-electric *means of propulsion* 696.2

diesel-electric engine *train* 688.4

diesel engine *train* 688.4

diesel fuel *or oil fuels* 106.2, *oil* 106.7, *petroleum* 562.5

diesel-propelled *propelled* 696.14

Dies Irae [L] *funeral* 31.4

diet 92.5; *conference* 59.5, *food* 90.1, *taste* 92.24, *therapy* 115.12, *dieting* 118.2, 595.3, *eat less* 118.9, *abstain* 455.11, *lose weight* 468.14, *become smaller* 582.14, *become thin* 595.15, *means of restraint* 830.6, *restrain oneself* 830.15

dietary *dieting* 92.6, *edible* 92.20

dietary expert *dietitian* 92.16

dietary plan *dieting* 92.6

dieter *eater* 92.15, *self-restrained person* 455.5, *loser* 468.8, *thin person* 595.4

dietetic *edible* 92.20

dietetics *diet* 92.5, *health care* 107.7

dietician *dietitian* 92.16, *paramedic* 107.24

dieting 92.6, 118.2, 595.3, 595.11; *delicate eating* 92.3, *abstinence* 455.2, *abstinent* 455.7, *loss of weight* 468.3, *self-restrained* 830.10

dietitian 92.16

dietitian *or dietician hygienist* 116.2

diet of bread and water *short rations* 118.3

diet plan *dieting* 595.3

diet regimen *or regime dieting* 92.6

diet sheet *dieting* 92.6

die without issue *or offspring be infertile* 23.8

differ *oppose* 63.11, *argue* 329.11, *dissent* 347.8, *conflict* 422.26, *disagree* 463.8, *be disparate* 728.14, *be diverse* 732.10, *be dissimilar* 734.7

difference 463.4, 750.3; *subtraction* 6.14, *Heraldic Terms* 184, *identify* 184.11, *variegation* 263.1, *argument* 329.1, *numerical answer* 334.7, *dissent* 347.1, *disagreement* 463.1, *distortion* 627.1, *change* 665.1, *divergence* 703.1, *foreignness* 724.2, *disparity* 728.3, *diversity* 732.1, *dissimilarity* 734.1, *inequality* 741.1, *separateness* 753.3, *nonconformity* 782.1, *mathematical result* 783.4, *contrariety* 828.6

difference of opinion *quarrel* 272.4, *dissent* 347.1, *disagreement* 463.1

differences *dissent* 347.1

difference set *combinatorics* 6.63

differences in elevation *Fields of Measurement* 589

differencing *or dimidiation Heraldic Terms* 184

different 463.7; *arguing* 329.6, *divergent* 703.6, *foreign* 724.9, *disparate* 728.9, *diverse* 732.5, *dissimilar* 734.4, *novel* 737.5, *unequal* 741.4, *special* 779.10, *nonconforming* 782.11, *discordant* 828.12

differentiability *nonuniformity* 734.2

differentiable *nonuniform* 734.5

differential *differentiation* 6.29, *functional* 6.73, *machine element* 14.8, *discriminating* 337.9, *nonuniform* 734.5, *gradation* 739.3, *gradational* 739.5, *fractional* 783.8, *mathematical* 784.9

differential calculus *calculus* 6.28

differential diagnosis *diagnosis* 107.8

differential equation *equation* 6.25, *differentiation* 6.29

differential erosion *erosion* 8.41

differential focusing *framing* 132.18

differential geometry *Branches of Mathematics* 6, *geometry* 6.32

differentially 739.9; *discriminatingly* 337.15, *nonuniformly* 734.11

differential operator *vector* 6.48

differential psychology *Psychological Theories, Schools* 108

differential weathering *weathering* 8.40

differentiate *evaluate* 6.90, *identify* 184.11, *discriminate* 337.12, *characterize* 723.11, 779.15, *be diverse* 732.10, *make unlike* 734.9, *measure* 739.7, *set apart* 753.17, *add* 784.11

differentiated *judged* 337.10, *nonuniform* 734.5, *gradational* 739.5, *unjoined* 753.9

differentiation 6.29; *identification* 184.1, *discrimination* 337.1, *judgment* 341.1, *gradation* 739.3, *specialty* 779.1, *calculation* 784.1

differentness *specialty* 779.1

different in time 648.2

different kettle of fish *incomparability* 734.3

differently 463.13; *argumentatively* 329.15, *asymmetrically* 627.13, *changeably* 665.22, *divergently* 703.16, *strangely* 724.17, *disparately* 728.19, *diversely* 732.14, *dissimilarly* 734.10, *originally* 737.8, *unequally* 741.10

differing *dissenting* 347.7, *disagreeing* 463.6, *different* 463.7, *varied* 732.6

differing opinions *dissension* 732.4

differ with *disagree* 463.8

difficult 364.8, 726.11, 824.9; *laborious* 122.7, *ice-skating* 162.32, *mysterious* 182.10, *obscure* 197.2, *problematic* 333.12, *bad-mannered* 411.6, *mentally hard* 542.8, *dangerous* 811.7, *confused* 841.11, *adverse* 848.10

difficult character *protester* 507.4

difficult choice *choice* 382.3

difficult circumstances 726.6; *predicament* 725.3

difficulties *poverty* 486.1

difficult language *obscurity* 197.1

difficultly 726.20, 824.23

difficult position *predicament* 824.5

difficult problem *puzzle* 182.5

difficult question 333.4

difficult task 824.3

difficult terrain *difficult task* 824.3

difficult to comprehend *ambiguous* 632.5

difficult to handle *troublesome* 824.13

difficult to hear *unheard* 229.7

difficult to live with *troublesome* 824.13

difficult to see 245.4

difficult word *word* 5.17

difficulty 824.1; *gymnastics* 157.1, *ice-dancing move* 162.19, *competitive diving* 164.7, *question* 333.1, *unintelligibility* 364.1, *disagreement* 463.1, *inconvenience* 804.1, *defect* 806.4, *obstacle* 826.2, *adversity* 848.1

difficulty *or* **difficulties** *predicament* 725.3

difficulty in speaking *speech difficulty* 206.1

diffidence *reserve* 195.5, *taciturnity* 208.1, *shyness* 403.3, 409.2

diffident *reserved* 195.11, *taciturn* 208.4, *shy* 403.8

diffidently *reservedly* 195.20, *shyly* 403.16

diffract *reflect* 10.76, *deflect* 698.26, *disperse* 776.12

diffracted *diffractive* 698.14

diffracted wave *wave* 683.4

diffraction 698.6; *wave property* 10.12, *optical element* 10.20, *optical characteristic* 10.21, *wavelength* 683.5, *divergence* 776.5

diffraction grating *optical element* 10.20

diffractive 698.14; *dispersive* 776.10

diffractively *dispersively* 776.17

diffractive optical element *optical element* 10.20

diffuse 199.3; *phrased* 5.39, *superfluous* 99.8, *obscure* 197.2, *be present* 575.13, *transfer* 685.8, *diffractive* 698.14, *deflect* 698.26, *radiate* 703.13, *dispersed* 776.6, *disperse* 776.12, *broadcast* 778.16

diffused *murky* 248.5, *diffractive* 698.14, *dispersed* 776.6

diffusely 199.7, 776.18; *superfluously* 99.15, *divergently* 703.16

diffuse nebula *nebula* 7.6

diffuseness 199.1; *phrasing* 5.25, *superfluity* 99.4, *obscurity* 197.1, *empty talk* 362.5

diffuser *lighting* 132.16, *racing automobile* 146.2, *transferrer* 685.4

diffusing filter *filter* 132.14

diffusion *wave property* 10.12, *diffuseness* 199.1, *omnipresence* 575.4, *transmission* 685.3, *diffraction* 698.6, *radiation* 703.3, *dispersion* 776.1

diffusionist *anthropological* 1.10

diffusion pump *surface chemistry* 11.20

diffusive *diffuse* 199.3, *omnipresent* 575.10, *dispersive* 776.10

diffusively *diffusely* 199.7, *dispersively* 776.17

diffusiveness *diffuseness* 199.1, *omnipresence* 575.4

dig *engineer* 14.48, *farm* 16.19, *cultivate* 17.19, *work* 122.8, *Card Games* 168, *taunt* 436.6, *deepen* 598.21, *make concave* 635.7, *jolt* 684.9, *take away* 685.12, *blow* 695.5, *impel* 695.9

dig [Inf] *understand* 363.9

dig a hole *hole* 583.17

digamous *monogamous* 64.18

digamy *type of marriage* 64.3

dig a pit for *be cunning* 822.5

dig at *taunt* 436.23

dig coal *mine coal* 106.18

digest *eat* 92.21, *summary* 204.1, *summarize* 204.7, *succumb* 421.7, *contracted thing* 582.5, *shortened version* 591.3, *shorten* 591.9, *outline* 617.1, 617.5, *absorb*

708.19, combine 757.9, catalog 767.7, categorize 767.21

digested *shortened* 591.7, *combined* 757.5

digestible *edible* 92.20

digestibly *edibly* 92.26

digestion *body process* 19.15, *eating* 92.1, *pulping* 561.11, *absorption* 708.6, *combination* 757.1

digestive *metabolic* 19.24, *purgative* 115.7, *medicinal* 115.15, *absorbent* 708.11

digestive juice *secreted substance* 24.2

Digest of Justinian *the Law* 53.2

dig for *pursue* 385.11

digger 635.4; *construction equipment* 14.23, *extractor* 711.9

digging *deepening* 598.4

digging in one's toes *or* **heels** *refusing* 375.9

digging out 711.3

digging up *detection* 345.2, *digging out* 711.3

digging up the past *historicism* 3.7

dig in *battle* 76.33, *insist* 376.14, *entrench* 419.24

dig in one's toes *or* **heels** *insist* 376.14, *hold out* 377.13, *be obstinate* 379.10, 471.11, *retain* 471.7, *be permanent* 667.4, *withstand* 828.20, *be certain* 840.13

digit *numeral* 6.8, *number* 783.1

digital *numerical* 6.68, 783.7

digital circuit *circuit* 14.37

digital clock *or* **watch** Timepieces and Timers 646

digital display *face* 646.8

digitally *mathematically* 6.93, *numerically* 783.11

digitizer *input device* 15.11

diglyceride *fat* 12.7

dignification *worship* 83.1

dignified 297.11; *well-behaved* 399.15, *majestic* 404.21, *formal* 406.6, *elegant* 527.3, *refined* 534.5, *notable* 799.11

dignify *worship* 83.15, *celebrate* 406.10, *exalt* 596.19

dignifying *worshipful* 83.12

dignitary *official* 68.6

dignities *courtesies* 410.3

dignity 297.4; *proudness* 297.3, *good conduct* 399.5, *formality* 406.1, *elegance* 527.1, *refinement* 534.1

dig out 711.15; *make concave* 635.7

digraph *written letter* 5.14, *spoken letter* 5.15

digraphic *voiced* 5.37

digress 775.13; *be circuitous* 199.6, *diverge* 607.11, *deviate* 698.15, *be extraneous* 724.12, *be unrelated* 728.12

digressing *wandering* 698.13

digression 775.6; *aspect of fiction* 139.5, *circumlocution* 199.2, *divergence* 607.2, *deviation* 698.1, *wandering* 698.4

digressive *circumlocutory* 199.4, *divergent* 607.7, *wandering* 698.13, *interrupted* 813.3

digressively *circuitously* 199.8, *divergently* 607.14

digs [Inf] *habitation* 60.2

dig up *disclose* 180.8, *detect* 345.12, *acquire* 467.19, *dig out* 711.15

dig up the dirt [Inf] *report* 171.9

dig up the past *recollect* 3.16, *excavate* 651.19

dihedral *rock face* 161.6, *miscellaneous aviation terms* 689.9

dihedral angle *angle* 6.37

dihydrogen Chemical Elements and Common Allotropes 11

Dike Deities 82

dike *igneous rock* 8.32, *crack* 587.2, *enclosing thing* 619.3, *channel* 691.10, *barrier* 826.7

dikephobia Phobias 283

dilacerate *take apart* 753.16

dilaceration *separateness* 753.3

dilapidate *wear out* 808.21

dilapidated 517.7, 808.11; *used* 393.5, *beggarly* 486.12, *destroyed* 523.9, *brittle* 548.3, *deconstructed* 758.4, *disintegrating* 758.5, *unsafe* 811.8

dilapidation 808.5; *use* 393.1, *beggary* 486.3, *weakness* 517.1, *ruin* 523.4, *reduction* 747.2

dilatability *enlargeability* 581.6

dilatable *enlargeable* 581.13

dilatableness *enlargeability* 581.6

dilatant *enlargeable* 581.13

dilatation *transformation* 6.46

dilate *enlarge* 194.12, 581.14, *be diffuse* 199.5, *increase* 467.17, 746.6, *extend* 563.14, *broaden* 592.11

dilated *enlarged* 194.8, *bigger* 581.9, *broadened* 592.7

dilating *growing* 581.12

dilation *transformation* 6.46, *augmentation* 467.2, *expansion* 581.1, 592.2, *increase* 746.1

dilation *or* **dilatation** *enlargement* 194.2

dilational *enlargeable* 581.13

dilative *enlargeable* 581.13

dilatometer Fields of Measurement 589

dilatometry Fields of Measurement 589

dilator *enlarger* 581.8

dilatorily *late* 658.14, *slowly* 693.14

dilatoriness *delay* 658.3, *slowness* 693.1

dilatory *not participating* 415.11, *late* 658.5, *delayed* 693.10

dilemma *futility* 282.3, *difficult question* 333.4, *choice* 382.3, *predicament* 725.3, *problem* 824.4

dilettante *ignorant person* 349.4, *semiskilled* 349.6

dilettantism *lack of knowledge* 349.2

diligence 323.4; *carefulness* 325.1, *constancy* 377.3, *assiduity* 414.8, *observance* 465.1

diligent 323.7; *working* 122.6, *careful* 325.6, *constant* 377.8, *industrious* 414.16, *observant* 465.3

diligently *attentively* 323.14, *carefully* 325.13, *observantly* 465.6

dill Herbs and Spices 91

dill seed Herbs and Spices 91

dilly [Inf] *good thing* 445.9

dillydally *hesitate* 693.12

dilly-dally *be irresolute* 378.9, *wait* 658.12

dillydallying *lingering* 693.4, *delayed* 693.10

diluent *solvent* 555.9

dilute 220.7, 557.30, 776.14; *status adjectives* 11.25, *solidify* 11.37, *play down* 195.17, *tasteless* 220.4, *change* 512.12, *weaken* 517.13, *rarefied* 541.4, *make sparse* 541.5, *make thin* 595.17, *change for the worse* 665.18, *water down* 716.17, *make smaller* 747.8, *diluted* 751.9, 776.8, *mix* 751.12

diluted 557.22, 751.9, 776.8;

drinkable 93.18, *downplayed* 195.13, *tasteless* 220.4, *insufficient* 517.11, *rarefied* 541.4, *thinned* 595.13

diluter *thinner* 595.7

dilute solution *phase* 11.13

dilution 220.2, 557.5, 776.3; *downplaying* 195.6, *tastelessness* 220.1, *weakness* 517.1, *rarefaction* 541.2, *thinning* 595.6, *change for the worse* 665.5, *mixture* 751.1

dim 248.4; *disguise* 181.13, *difficult to see* 245.4, *become invisible* 245.6, *make invisible* 245.7, *dark* 247.5, 254.6, *become dark* 247.9, *make dark* 247.10, *shady* 250.4, *opaque* 250.7, *colorless* 252.5, *decolor* 252.8, *difficult* 364.8, *lessen* 468.17, *thick-witted* 594.7

dim [Inf] *unintelligent* 316.6

dim and distant past *past time* 3.6

dim-bulb [Inf] *unintelligent person* 316.4

dime *US coinage* 484.10, *little bit* 800.4

dime a dozen [Inf], *a bargain* 497.10

dime bag *drug dose* 121.15

dime defense *defense* 155.9

dimension 10.5, 589.11; *space* 6.33, *quantity* 738.1, *size* 579.1

dimensional *spatial* 563.11

dimensional analysis *dimension* 589.11

dimensions *space* 6.33, *external appearance* 264.5, *space* 563.1

dimeter *meter* 139.10, *twosome* 789.3

dimethoate *pest killer* 17.9

dimidiate *identify* 184.11

diminish 597.24; *waste away* 96.20, *play down* 195.17, *relieve* 275.8, *humiliate* 298.19, *lessen* 468.17, *be weak* 517.12, *weaken* 517.13, *mitigate* 521.9, *make little* 580.10, *narrow* 593.14, *lower* 716.12, *change by degrees* 739.8, *become inferior* 745.11, *decrease* 747.7, *subtract* 749.6, *reduce* 796.8

diminished *downplayed* 195.13, *humiliated* 298.12, *dilapidated* 517.7, *lowered* 716.7, *insignificant* 745.6, *decreasing* 747.5, *reduced* 749.5, *fewer* 796.7

diminished responsibility *insanity* 110.1

diminished seventh *chord* 140.18, *seven* 792.3

diminishing 597.16; *lowered* 716.7, *gradational* 739.5, *fewer* 796.7

diminishingly *decreasingly* 747.9, 749.9

diminishing returns *financial loss* 468.4, *decrease* 747.1

diminishment 597.7; *downplaying* 195.6, *abasement* 298.6

diminuendo *shortening* 582.2, *decrease* 747.1, *decreasing* 747.5

diminuendo *or* **dim.** Musical Terms and Expression Marks 140

diminution *wasting away* 96.4, *outline* 204.2, *lessening* 468.6, *moderation* 521.1, *lowering* 716.1, *decrease* 747.1, *subtraction* 749.1

diminutive *part of speech* 5.30, *of grammar* 5.41, *name* 202.8, *little* 580.7, *short* 591.6

diminutively *little* 580.12, *shortly* 591.12

diminutiveness *littleness* 580.1, *shortness* 591.1

dimity Fabrics and Fibers 130

dim lighting *dimness* 248.1

dimly 248.10; *invisibly* 245.8, *darkly* 247.11, *colorlessly* 252.9, *thick-wittedly* 594.13

dimly lit *dim* 248.4

dimmed 248.6

dimmed headlights *safety light* 246.7

dimmed lights *dimness* 248.1

dim memory *poor memory* 355.2

dimmer switch *darkening* 247.2

dimming 248.3; *darkening* 247.2, 247.6, *lessening* 468.6, *decrease* 747.1

dimness 248.1; *darkness* 247.1, *opaqueness* 250.1, *ignorance* 316.3, *fantasy* 360.5, *thick-wittedness* 594.3, *deterioration* 808.1, *mysteriousness* 844.5

dim-out *darkening* 247.2

dimple *cavity* 635.3

dimpled *concave* 635.5

dim sight *faulty vision* 243.1

dim-sighted *visually impaired* 243.9

dim sum *hors d'oeuvre* 90.13

dim view *disapproval* 438.1

dimwit [Inf] *unintelligent person* 316.4

dimwitted [Inf] *unskillful* 128.4, *unintelligent* 316.6, *foolish* 353.5, *simpleminded* 526.11

dimwittedness *ignorance* 316.3

DIN General Units 589

din *loudness* 232.1, *burst* 232.9, *dissonance* 241.1, *tumult* 684.2, *commotion* 768.5

dinar *national coins* 484.11

dine *have a meal* 92.25

dined *popular* 408.12

dine out *have a meal* 92.25, *participate* 408.15

diner *eater* 92.15, *eating place* 92.17

dinette *room* 60.9, *eating place* 92.17

ding *sailboard parts* 150.20, *ringing* 235.5

dingbat *ornamentation* 748.5

dingbat [Inf] *foolish person* 353.3

ding-dong *ringing* 235.5, *competitive* 422.21

ding-dong battle *contention* 422.1

ding-dong theory *linguistic theory* 5.2

dinghy Ships and Boats 690

dingily *dimly* 248.10, *colorlessly* 252.9

dinginess *dirtiness* 112.1, *murk* 248.2

dingle *valley* 572.8, *concave land* 635.2

dingleberry [Inf] *feces* 25.5

dingo *dog* 35.10

dingy *dirty* 112.7, *dark* 247.5, 254.6, *dimmed* 248.6, *colorless* 252.5, *plain* 528.9, *worn* 808.13

din in *emphasize* 200.6

dining *eating meals* 92.4, *eating* 92.18, *type of chair* 101.4, *type of table* 101.5, Phobias 283

dining car *eating place* 92.17, *railroad car* 688.5

dining hall *room* 60.9, *eating place* 92.17

dining out *eating meals* 92.4

dining room *school place* 48.16, *room* 60.9, *eating place* 92.17

dinkiness [Inf] *littleness* 580.1

dinky [Inf] *undersized* 580.8, *tiny* 580.9, *insignificant* 745.6

dinner *social gathering* 59.7, *meal* 92.8, *feast* 92.9, *party* 408.6, *evening* 656.2

dinner bell *signal* 183.6
dinner dance *feast* 92.9, *dance* 135.1
dinner dress *or* **gown** *formal clothes* 100.5, *dress* 100.11
dinner gong *signal* 183.6
dinner hour *evening* 656.2
dinner jacket *formal clothes* 100.5, *jacket* 100.18, *formal clothing* 406.5
dinner party *feast* 92.9, *party* 408.6
dinner service *crockery* 578.16
dinner theater *drama* 136.1
dinnertime *evening* 656.2
dinning *loud* 232.6
DIN number *exposure* 132.15
dinophobia Phobias 283
dinosaur *extinct reptile* 37.9, *big thing* 579.9, *thing of the past* 651.8, *prehistoric animal* 653.8
dint *power* 447.4
dint [Arch] *blow* 695.5
diocesan *priest* 84.8, *priestly* 84.12, *administrative* 564.13
diocese *clerical venue* 84.4, *administrative region* 564.4
diode *semiconductor* 10.34, *circuit* 10.43, *circuit element* 14.39
dioecious *of flowers* 42.11
Diomede Islands Islands 572
Diomedes Notable Friendships 62
Dione Planets and Their Satellites 7
Dionysia *religious festival* 85.13
Dionysus Deities 85
Diophantine equation Mathematical Concepts 6
diopter Scientific and Technical Units 589
dioptric *transparent* 249.7
dioxin *pollution* 117.8
dioxygen Chemical Elements and Common Allotropes 11
dip [Inf] *geomagnetism* 8.3, *hors d'oeuvre* 90.13, *ablutions* 111.4, *bathe* 111.18, *valley* 572.8, *concave land* 635.2, *take away* 685.12, *miscellaneous aviation terms* 689.9, *immersion* 710.3, *immerse* 710.12, *fall* 714.4, *inclination* 714.6, *slide* 714.17, *depression* 716.4
dip [Inf] *thief* 479.8
dip a toe in the water *test* 390.9
Dipavamsa *other text* 81.19
dip down *descend* 714.12
dipeptide *amino acid* 12.8
diphtheria *respiratory disease* 114.12
diphthong *spoken letter* 5.15
dip into capital *expend* 491.11
diplegia *neurological disease* 114.20
diploid *plant breeding* 17.6
diploma *certificate* 185.2, *authorization* 340.4, *permit* 502.3, *authority* 833.3
diplomacy *politics* 50.1, *mediation* 75.1, *treatment* 399.11, *tactics* 399.12, *good manners* 410.2, *negotiation* 460.1, *summit meeting* 600.3, *cunning* 822.1
diplomat *politician* 50.7, *mediator* 75.2, *delegate* 79.1, *agent* 123.15, *expert* 127.9, *summit meeting* 600.3, *cunning person* 822.3, *commissioner* 833.5
diplomat *or* **diplomatist** *negotiator* 460.4
diplomatic *political* 50.9, *mediatory* 75.5, *delegated* 79.4, *skillful* 127.10, *wise* 352.4, *good-mannered* 410.7, *negotiated* 460.5
diplomatic agent *agent* 80.3
diplomatically *politically* 50.11,
mediatorially 75.7, *representatively* 79.8, *indirectly* 80.8, *wisely* 352.8, *genteelly* 410.14, *feasibly* 460.9
diplomatic code *etiquette* 406.3
diplomatic corps *representative body* 79.2
diplomatic immunity *exemption* 434.1, *freedom* 829.1
diplomatic incident *awkward situation* 824.7
diplomatic language *international language* 5.8
diplomatic officer *delegate* 79.1
diplomatic pouch *postal communication* 169.4, *bag* 578.7
diplomatist *mediator* 75.2, *cunning person* 822.3
diplopia *sight defect* 243.2
diplopod *myriapod* 39.11
Diplopoda *myriapod* 39.11
dipluran *insectile* 40.11
dipnoan *fish* 38.5
dipody *meter* 139.10
dipolar ions *amino acid* 12.8
dipole *electric charge* 10.38
dipole-dipole interaction *chemical bond* 11.6
dipole moment *electric charge* 10.38
dipped *flooded* 557.24
dipper *ladle* 578.17
dipping *ablutions* 111.4, *fall* 714.4, *falling* 714.11
dipping the colors *mark of respect* 435.4
dippy [Inf] *insane* 110.9
dipsomania *compulsion* 108.13, *substance abuse* 121.1
dipsomaniac *drunkard* 121.8
dipsomaniac(al) *drunken* 121.28
dipsomaniacal *drinking* 93.17
dipsophobia Phobias 283
dipstick *measuring instrument* 589.12
dipstick [Inf] *unskilled person* 128.3
dipteran *or* **dipterous** *insectile* 40.11
diptych *painting* 143.3, *twosome* 789.3
Dirac notation *quantum theory* 10.64
Dirac's equation Classical Physical Laws 10
dire *frightening* 283.12, *detrimental* 446.8, *adverse* 848.10
direct **126.11, 384.10, 412.16, 630.12, 697.11, 697.13, 780.14;** *of grammar* 5.41, *educate* 48.22, *govern* 49.26, *have authority* 52.13, *wield authority* 52.16, *master* 68.17, *manage* 126.10, *dramatize* 136.33, *produce* 137.21, 522.13, *conduct* 141.17, 399.21, *cross-country* 162.31, *soccer* 163.7, *disclosing* 180.6, *sign* 183.19, *candid* 191.5, *clear* 196.2, *send* 209.11, *easily seen through* 249.10, *evidential* 339.8, *simple* 363.6, *take charge of* 391.8, *behave toward* 399.20, *effective* 412.10, *command* 425.10, *motivate* 508.9, *influence* 512.11, *outspoken* 550.6, *situate* 573.10, *plain* 592.10, *straight* 630.8, *straightforward* 630.9, *immediate* 645.5, *directly* 697.16, *lead* 744.19
directable **697.10**
direct access *data-related concepts* 15.23
direct approach *access* 691.3
direct carving *sculpture* 144.1
direct current (d.c.) *electric current* 10.39
direct current (d.c.) generator *generator* 14.43
direct descent *cross-country techniques* 162.8
direct distance dialing *dial* 169.12
direct dye *dye* 130.8
directed **141.12, 384.7, 697.9;** *dramatized* 136.32, *produced* 137.17, *motivated* 508.8, *inevitable* 840.11
directed energy *exertion* 122.4
directed number *number* 6.4
directed toward *situated* 573.5
directed verdict *verdict* 54.18
direct examination *witness* 54.16
direct-examine *try a case* 54.28
direct free kick *soccer play* 163.5
direct hit *grip* 151.4
directing **697.12;** *governing* 49.25, *authoritative* 52.9, *directorship* 126.5, *managerial* 126.9, *influential* 512.8
direction **384.3, 697.1;** *line* 6.35, *vector* 6.48, *education* 48.1, *government* 49.1, *governance* 49.18, 52.6, *authority* 52.1, 780.6, *management* 126.1, 509.4, *directorship* 126.5, *guide* 126.6, 780.4, *production* 136.14, 137.6, *motive* 178.5, *treatment* 399.11, *action* 412.1, *command* 425.1, *tendency* 513.1, *situation* 573.1, *route* 691.2, *directions* 697.7
directional **677.13, 697.8;** *managerial* 126.9, *signifying* 183.11, *motivational* 508.7, *situational* 573.6
directionally **697.20**
directional reference *navigational aid* 690.6
directional sign *sign* 183.1
directional signal light *safety light* 246.7
direction finder *guide* 697.4
direction indicator *indicator* 183.7
directions **697.7,** Fields of Measurement 589
directive *command* 425.1, *commanding* 425.7, *motivational* 508.7, *directing* 697.12, *rule* 780.1
directly **697.16;** *grammatically* 5.48, *openly* 180.13, *candidly* 191.10, *clearly* 196.4, *transparently* 249.13, *meaningfully* 361.16, *effectively* 412.19, *right away* 429.20, *unpretentiously* 526.15, *bluntly* 550.11, *plainly* 592.18, *straight* 630.16, *straightforwardly* 630.17, *honestly* 630.18, *early* 657.17, *soon* 657.18
directly opposed *opposite* 731.3
direct mail *postal communication* 169.4, *publicity* 178.7
direct-mailer *persuader* 178.9
direct marketing *publicity* 178.7
directness **630.5, 697.6;** *openness* 180.3, *candor* 191.2, *clarity* 196.1, 363.2, *outspokenness* 550.2, *plainness* 592.4, *straightness* 630.1, *straightforwardness* 630.3, *immediacy* 645.1
direct object *part of speech* 5.30
Directoire Furniture Styles 101
direct one's course *aim* 697.14
direct oneself *aim* 697.14
direct opposite *opposite* 731.2
direct opposition *oppositeness* 731.1
director *governor* 49.23, *person in authority* 52.7, *employer* 57.3, *company leader* 68.8, *artistic worker* 123.12, *manager* 126.7, *producer*
136.28, 522.10, *filmmaker* 137.14, *conductor* 399.13, *operator* 412.7, 509.5, *influential person* 512.5, *interfacer* 616.3
directorate *management board* 126.2
direct order *command* 425.1
directorial *managerial* 126.9
director of photography *filmmaker* 137.14
directors *management board* 126.2
director's *type of chair* 101.4
directorship **126.5;** *position of authority* 52.4, *leadership* 744.2
directorship, the *governance* 52.6, *the power structure* 68.12
directory *computing terms* 15.22, *data-related concepts* 15.23, *dial* 169.12, *information source* 170.6, *type of book* 174.3, *record book* 185.5, *catalog* 767.7, *book of lists* 785.3
direct outward *externalize* 610.15
direct primary *election* 382.6
direct proof *reasoning* 6.61
direct radiation *sun* 9.21
directrix *curve* 6.38
direct tax *money received* 492.2, *tax* 494.5
direct tide *tide* 571.2
direct to *direct* 697.13
direct vote *electing* 382.5
dire necessity *poverty* 486.1
dire straits *poverty* 486.1, *danger* 811.1, *critical situation* 824.6
dirge *funeral* 31.4, Poem or Verse Forms 139, *lament* 280.2
dirgeful *funeral* 31.9
dirgelike *funeral* 31.9, *lamenting* 280.4
dirham *national coins* 484.11
Dirichlet series Mathematical Concepts 6
dirigible *aircraft* 689.3, *directable* 697.10
dirk *sharp weapon* 78.6
dirndl *skirt* 100.12
dirt **112.5;** *feces* 25.5, *building materials* 104.2, Phobias 283, *immorality* 432.1, *powder* 553.9, *residue* 750.2, *refuse* 802.5
dirt [Inf] *inside information* 170.4
dirt bike *motorcycle* 687.12
dirt-cheap *cheap* 497.9
dirt-encrusted *dirty* 112.7
dirt farmer *agriculturist* 16.14
dirt-free *clean* 111.13
dirtily **112.12;** *unhygienically* 114.32, *flakily* 553.30
dirtiness **112.1;** *lack of hygiene* 112.3, *untidiness* 766.3, *impairment* 808.7
dirt road *rough thing* 544.2, *road* 687.2
dirt track *racetrack* 159.12, *rough thing* 544.2
dirt-track *racing* 146.9
dirty **112.7, 112.11;** *stormy* 9.45, *obscene* 112.9, *contagious* 114.26, *unhygienic* 114.27, *dimmed* 248.6, *tarnish* 248.9, *shady* 250.4, *blacken* 254.11, *profane* 301.10, *indifferent* 326.5, *immoral* 432.9, *beggarly* 486.12, *ribald* 535.8, *powdery* 553.19, *sludgy* 561.18, *oceanic* 571.7, *make worse* 808.17
dirty book *obscenity* 112.4
dirty clothes *laundry* 111.8
dirty dancing Dancing Types 135
dirty dishes *laundry* 111.8
dirty film *obscenity* 112.4
dirty habits *uncleanness* 112.2

dirty hands *sign of guilt* 450.2
dirty joke *obscenity* 112.4,
  profanity 301.3, *act of discourtesy*
  411.3
dirty joke *or* **story** *sexual offense*
  432.6
dirty liar *liar* 192.10
dirty lie *falsehood* 192.6
dirty linen *laundry* 111.8
dirty look *look* 242.7, *show of*
  disapproval 438.6
dirty magazine *obscenity* 112.4,
  pornography 432.7
dirty mouth [Inf] *profanity* 301.3
dirty old man [Inf] *sexually*
  immoral person 432.8
dirty pictures *pornography* 432.7
dirty story *joke* 277.6
dirty talk [Inf] *profanity* 301.3
dirty trick *artifice* 193.5,
  disreputable action 371.3
dirty water *swill* 112.6
dirty weather *natural violence*
  520.3
dirty word *curse word* 301.4,
  grossness 535.3
Dis *evil place* 446.6
disability 515.4; *bargaining terms*
  57.10, *illness* 114.2
disability insurance *benefits*
  57.11
disable *make inactive* 415.16,
  remove power from 515.13, *weaken*
  517.13, *make useless* 802.12,
  hinder 826.15, *make impossible*
  837.8
disabled 515.10; *inactive* 415.8
disabled person *sick person*
  114.22
disablement *physical deterioration*
  808.4
disablement benefit *social*
  assistance 825.4
disabling *physical deterioration*
  808.4
disabuse *inform* 170.11
disaccharide *saccharide* 12.4
disaccord *disagreement* 463.1,
  nonconformity 782.1, *conflict* 828.3
disaccustom 398.6; *be unskillful*
  128.8, *renounce* 392.4
disaccustomed *unaccustomed*
  398.3
disadvantage *loss* 468.1, *inequality*
  741.1, *unbalance* 741.8, *deficiency*
  745.2, *inconvenience* 804.1, *be*
  inconvenient 804.9, *defect* 806.4
disadvantaged, the *the poor*
  486.7
disadvantageous *inconvenient*
  804.5, *adverse* 848.10
disaffect *put off* 179.10
disaffected *estranged* 63.8,
  dissuaded 179.5, *dissatisfied* 274.4,
  displeased 291.6, *hated* 300.9
disaffectedly *hostilely* 63.13,
  dissuasively 179.12
disaffection 179.3; *hostility* 63.1,
  antipathy 291.2, *dislike* 300.2,
  dissentience 347.3
disaffiliated *separate* 724.10
disaffiliation *separateness* 724.3
disaffinity *hostility* 63.1, *repulsion*
  701.1
disaffirm *negate* 190.16, *deny*
  332.8
disaffirmation *refutation* 332.1,
  denial 332.2, *renunciation* 383.4
disaffirmation *or* **disaffirmance**
  negation 190.1
disagree 463.8, 753.19; *disbelieve*
  88.8, *negate* 190.16, *quarrel*
  272.9, *react against* 291.15, *be*
  irascible 303.13, *argue* 329.11,

doubt 333.19, *dissent* 347.8,
  506.9, 732.13, *mean* 361.13,
  oppose 375.13, *be insubordinate*
  416.8, *conflict* 422.26, *be unequal*
  741.7, *object* 828.18
disagreeable *unpalatable* 223.6,
  unpleasant 272.6, *antipathetic*
  291.7, *ill-natured* 303.9, *irritable*
  304.9, *argumentative* 329.7,
  discourteous 411.5
disagreeableness *unpleasantness*
  272.1, *antipathy* 291.2,
  irritableness 304.3, *discourtesy*
  411.1
disagreeably *unpleasantly* 272.10,
  discontentedly 291.17, *ill-naturedly*
  303.18, *irritably* 304.17,
  argumentatively 329.15,
  discourteously 411.8
disagreebleness *ill nature* 303.2
disagreeing 190.11, 463.6;
  negational 190.9, *gaudy* 251.12,
  arguing 329.6, *refusing* 375.9,
  defying 416.6, *censuring* 438.12,
  dissenting 506.6, 732.9, *unreliable*
  722.10, *unequal* 741.4, *disunited*
  753.10, *dissident* 782.12,
  discordant 828.12
disagreement 463.1; *disbelief*
  88.1, *negation* 190.1, *dissension*
  272.3, 732.4, *argument* 329.1,
  dissent 347.1, 506.2, 782.2,
  opposition 375.2, *disobedience*
  416.2, *censure* 438.3, *protest*
  507.1, *unreliability* 722.5, *disunity*
  753.4, *awkward situation* 824.7,
  objection 828.2, *contrariety* 828.6
disagree with *protest* 507.7, *be*
  against 828.17
disallow *refuse* 190.17, *refute*
  332.7, *reject* 383.10, *withhold*
  approval 438.17, *prohibit* 503.8,
  dissent 506.9, *exclude* 764.7, *cancel*
  834.6
disallowal *refutation* 332.1
disallowance *refusal* 190.2,
  rejection 383.1, *prohibition* 503.1,
  cancellation 834.1
disallowed *disagreeing* 190.11,
  rejected 383.6, *dissenting* 506.6,
  forbidden 837.7
disallow payment *stop payment*
  490.10
disambiguate *clarify* 196.3,
  interpret 365.12
disappear 265.5; *conceal oneself*
  181.15, *become invisible* 245.6, *be*
  destroyed 523.17, *abscond* 576.16,
  be transient 643.6, *stop* 668.10,
  quit 705.10, *cease to exist* 718.13,
  decrease 747.7, *dilute* 776.14, *not*
  exist 786.6, *escape* 816.8
disappearance 265.1; *concealment*
  181.1, *invisibility* 245.1, *absence*
  576.1, *reduction* 747.2, *dilution*
  776.3, *escape* 816.1
disappeared 265.4; *missing*
  576.11
disappear in a puff of smoke *be*
  transient 643.6
disappearing 265.3; *disappearance*
  265.1, *transient* 643.4
disappearing act *disappearance*
  265.1
disappearing trick *escape* 816.1
disappear into thin air *disappear*
  265.5
disappear without a trace *cease*
  to exist 718.13
disappoint 282.12, 293.9, 846.15;
  be insufficient 98.9, *dissatisfy* 274.6
disappointed 293.4; *dissatisfied*
  274.4, *disapproving* 438.8
disappointedly 293.11

disappointing 293.6; *insufficient*
  98.4, *unsatisfactory* 274.5
disappointingly 293.12;
  insufficiently 98.11
disappointment 293.1;
  insufficiency 98.1, *dissatisfaction*
  274.1, *lack of hope* 282.2, *futility*
  846.3
disapprobation *dissatisfaction*
  274.1, *dislike* 291.1, 300.2,
  resentment 302.1, *disapproval*
  347.2, 438.1, *disesteem* 436.2,
  protest 507.1, *opposition* 828.1
disapprobatory *disapproving*
  438.8
disapproval 347.2, 438.1;
  dissatisfaction 274.1, *dislike* 291.1,
  300.2, *resentment* 302.1, *rejection*
  383.1, *disesteem* 436.2, *protest*
  507.1, *opposition* 828.1
disapprove 438.16; *be dissatisfied*
  274.7, *dislike* 291.12, *rebuke*
  298.21, *hate* 300.11, *refuse* 347.9,
  reject 383.10
disapproved 438.9; *disliked*
  291.10, *hated* 300.9
disapprove of *judge* 341.10,
  disapprove 438.16, *protest* 507.7,
  be against 828.17
disapprover 438.7
disapproving 438.8; *dissatisfied*
  274.4, *displeased* 291.6, *resentful*
  302.8, *judging* 341.7, *rejecting*
  383.2, *protesting* 507.5, *oppositional*
  828.11
disapprovingly 438.23, 507.10;
  discontentedly 274.8, *judicially*
  341.12, *perversely* 824.27
disarm *make peace* 73.11, *conciliate*
  74.10, *move to compassion* 308.9,
  remove power from 515.13, *weaken*
  517.13, *be moderate* 521.6,
  mitigate 521.9, *make useless*
  802.12
disarmament 74.3; *powerlessness*
  515.1
disarmament treaty *peace treaty*
  73.5
disarmed *helpless* 515.9
disarming *pacificatory* 74.8,
  moderating 521.5
disarrange 768.11; *displace*
  574.15, *disorder* 766.17
disarranged 768.7; *displaced*
  574.8, *disordered* 766.9
disarrangement 768.2;
  displacement 574.1, *disorder* 766.1
disarray *disorder* 766.1
disarticulate *disconnect* 574.19
disarticulated *disconnected* 574.12
disarticulation *disconnection* 574.5
disassemble *program* 15.29, *take*
  apart 753.16, *make useless* 802.12
disassociate *separate* 724.14,
  753.12, *not connect* 728.13
disassociated *disavowing* 190.12,
  unconnected 728.8
disassociate oneself *disavow*
  190.18
disassociation *disavowal* 190.3,
  unconnectedness 728.2
disaster *adversity* 117.2, *bad*
  outcome 293.3, *ruin* 523.4, *mishap*
  660.4, *misadventure* 848.2
disaster area *devastation* 96.5,
  havoc 523.5
disaster relief *charity* 275.3, 307.3
disastrous *detrimental* 446.8,
  destructive 523.8, *accidental* 660.7,
  adverse 848.10
disastrously *destructively* 446.13,
  523.18, *mistakenly* 660.14,
  adversely 848.16

disavow 190.18; *deny* 332.8,
  renounce 383.13, *protest* 507.7
disavowal 190.3; *denial* 332.2,
  renunciation 383.4, *protest* 507.1
disavowed *disavowing* 190.12,
  renounced 383.9
disavowedly *retractively* 190.24
disavowing 190.12
disbalance *unbalance* 741.8
disband 776.13; *scatter* 753.15,
  liberate 831.6
disbanded 776.7
disbanding *peace movement* 74.4,
  liberation 831.1
disbandment 776.2
disbar 709.16; *exclude* 409.12, *eject*
  764.8
disbarment *ejection* 764.2
disbarred *lonely* 409.8, *excluded*
  764.6
disbelief 88.1; *unacceptance* 190.4,
  suspicion 841.2
disbelieve 88.8; *not accept* 190.19,
  doubt 333.19, *not observe* 466.9, *be*
  uncertain 841.17
disbelieved 88.7; *unaccepting*
  190.13
disbeliever 88.5; *negator* 190.8
disbelieving 88.6; *unaccepting*
  190.13, *nonobservant* 466.5
disbelievingly 88.10;
  nonacceptantly 190.25
disburden *lighten* 539.9, *unload*
  709.24, *deliver* 817.5, *disentangle*
  823.17
disburdening *lightening* 539.6
disburdenment *disentanglement*
  823.8
disburse *pay* 489.16, *expend*
  491.11
disbursed *expended* 491.9
disbursement *payment* 489.1,
  expenditure 491.1
disburser *payer* 489.9
disbursing *paying* 490.10
discalced *or* **discalceate** *uncovered*
  614.10
discard 383.12; *renounce* 392.4,
  unused thing 394.4, *stop using*
  394.10, *throw away* 709.25, *leave*
  750.10
discarded 383.8; *disused* 394.8,
  uncustomary 398.4, *remaining*
  750.7
discarding 383.3; *disuse* 394.3
discern *know* 48.24, 348.10, *see*
  242.20, *visualize* 242.24,
  discriminate 337.12, *be wise* 352.6,
  recognize 363.11, *be mentally sharp*
  549.18, *be profound* 598.23, *set*
  apart 753.17
discernibility *visibility* 244.1
discernible *visible* 242.19, 244.5,
  separable 753.11
discernibly *visibly* 244.10
discerning *refined* 48.20,
  discriminating 337.9, *judging*
  341.7, *judicious* 341.8, *foreseeing*
  357.5, *selecting* 382.9, *mentally*
  sharp 549.14, *profound* 598.15
discerningly 48.27; *judiciously*
  337.16, *judicially* 341.12,
  foresightedly 357.10, *sharply*
  549.19, *profoundly* 598.27
discernment *refinement* 48.10,
  visualization 242.6, *common sense*
  315.4, *judiciousness* 337.2,
  judgment 341.1, *knowledge* 348.1,
  wisdom 352.1, *foresight* 357.1,
  mental sharpness 549.9, *profundity*
  598.5
discharge *conduct* 14.51, *secretion*
  24.1, *secrete* 24.7, *excretion* 25.1,
  pus 25.7, *excrete* 25.20, *favorable*

verdict 54.19, acquit 54.32, 434.10, symptom 114.3, ulcer 114.18, bang 234.1, 234.6, absolution 312.2, absolve 312.10, disuse 394.3, occupy oneself 412.15, obey 426.7, acquittal 434.2, vindication 441.1, vindicate 441.11, ratification 459.4, performance 465.2, perform 465.5, payment 489.1, pay off 489.17, body fluid 555.3, relegation 574.4, relegate 574.18, shot 696.6, shoot 696.18, land 704.16, outflow 707.4, leak 707.16, 816.6, dismissal 709.2, disgorgement 709.6, dismiss 709.15, unload 709.24, let out 709.26, complete 761.9, disband 776.13, deliverance 817.1, freedom 829.1, liberation 831.1, liberate 831.6, termination 834.2, terminate 834.7

discharge a bankrupt forgive a debt 490.12

discharged acquitted 54.25, 434.6, forgiven 312.5, vindicated 441.8, paid 489.11, relegated 574.11, free 829.11, canceled 834.5

discharged bankrupt nonpayer 490.6

discharge one's duty do one's duty 433.17

discharge one's obligations be virtuous 447.8

discharge one's responsibility or **function** perform 465.5

disciple religious person 81.9, supporter 605.9, imitator 736.6, adherent 755.4

disciplinarian manager 126.7, strict person 424.4, one who restrains 830.7

disciplinary hired 57.17, punitive 454.18

disciplinary action punishment 454.1

disciplinary procedure bargaining terms 57.10

discipline 765.9; subject 48.3, educate 48.22, government 49.1, bargaining terms 57.10, employ 57.18, educational topic 328.4, treatment 399.11, severity 424.1, be severe 424.8, compel 428.8, punishment 454.1, punish 454.22, method 765.7, restore order 765.22, make conform 781.13, restraint 830.1, self-restraint 830.4, restrain 830.12, domination 832.2, defeat 832.11

disciplined 765.17; hired 57.17, severe 424.5, obedient 426.4, punished 454.19, restrained 830.9

discipline oneself be self-restrained 455.10

discipliner punisher 454.16

disciplining hired 57.17

disc jockey broadcasting personnel 172.11

disclaim disavow 190.18, deny 332.8, renounce 383.13, protest 507.7

disclaimed disavowing 190.12, renounced 383.9

disclaimer disavowal 190.3, denial 332.2, renunciation 383.4, protest 507.1

disclaiming refuting 332.6, renunciation 383.4

disclamation disavowal 190.3, renunciation 383.4

disclamatory disavowing 190.12

disclose 180.8; educate 48.22, report 171.9, publish 173.15, signify 183.16, avow 189.27, speak 205.17, make visible 244.9, present 264.15, demonstrate 331.15, detect 345.12, open 583.15, uncover 614.17, display 843.13, reveal 843.14

disclosed 180.5; published 173.12, avowed 189.19, demonstrated 331.9, uncovered 614.10, manifest 843.9

discloser 180.4; affirmer 189.9

disclosing 180.6; signifying 183.11, uncovering 614.1

disclosure 180.1; publishing 173.2, avowal 189.7, first appearance 264.3, demonstration 331.1, detection 345.2, manifestation 843.2

disco dance hall 135.3, popular music 140.4

disco dance dance 135.1

disco dancer dancer 135.4

disco dancing Dancing Types 135

discography list 785.1

discoid circular 631.5

discolor color 251.16, decolor 252.8, variegate 263.11

discoloration hue 251.4, decay 808.6

discolored soft-hued 251.13, off-color 251.15, colorless 252.5, spoiled 808.9

discombobulated confused 766.12

discombobulation disorder 766.1

discomfit humiliate 298.19, disturb 768.10

discomfited confused 766.12, disturbed 768.6

discomfiting humiliating 298.14

discomfiture disorder 766.1, disturbance 768.1

discomfort pain 215.1, unpleasantness 272.1, displease 272.8, unaccustomedness 398.1, inconvenience 804.1

discomforting objectionable 272.7

discommode be inconvenient 804.9, cause difficulties 824.22

discommodious inconvenient 804.5

discommodiously inconveniently 804.11

discompose 766.18; agitate 684.22, disturb 768.10

discomposed agitated 684.15, confused 766.12, 841.11, disturbed 768.6

discomposure agitation 684.1, disorder 766.1, disturbance 768.1, confusion 841.4

disconcert astonish 292.10, humiliate 298.19, discompose 766.18, disturb 768.10, cause difficulties 824.22, make uncertain 841.19

disconcerted astonished 292.6, humiliated 298.12, confused 766.12, 841.11, disturbed 768.6

disconcertedly with surprise 292.13

disconcertedness disorder 766.1, disturbance 768.1, confusion 841.4

disconcerting astonishing 292.8, humiliating 298.14, disturbing 768.9, confused 841.11

disconcertingly surprisingly 292.14, humiliatingly 298.25, disturbingly 768.13

disconcertion astonishment 292.2, confusion 841.4

disconcertment astonishment 292.2, tumult 684.2

disconfirm refute 332.7

disconfirmation refutation 332.1

disconformity nonobservance 466.1

disconnect 574.19, 775.12; conduct 14.51, be irregular 664.5, cause to cease 668.12, not connect 728.13, separate 753.12

disconnected 574.12; psychologically disturbed 108.39, unemphatic 201.2, irregular 664.3, extraneous 724.8, unconnected 728.8, separate 753.7, discontinuous 775.7

disconnectedly 574.22, 775.16; unconnectedly 728.18

disconnectedness foreignness 724.2, unconnectedness 728.2, discontinuity 775.1

disconnection 574.5; dissociative disorder 108.17, lack of emphasis 201.1, irregularity 664.1, unconnectedness 728.2, separation 753.1, discontinuity 775.1

disconsolate sorrowful 270.4, lamenting 280.4, without hope 282.7

disconsolately unhopefully 282.14

disconsolation lack of hope 282.2

discontent insufficiency 98.1, dissatisfaction 274.1, dissatisfied 274.4, dislike 291.1, displeased 291.6, disappointment 293.1, disappoint 293.9, resentment 302.1, irritableness 304.3, make irritable 304.15, envy 314.1, disapproval 438.1, protest 507.1, protesting 507.5

discontented unprovided 98.6, dissatisfied 274.4, disappointed 293.4, resentful 302.8, irritable 304.9, envious 314.4, discourteous 411.5, disapproving 438.8, protesting 507.5, troublesome 824.13

discontentedly 274.8, 291.17; disappointedly 293.11, enviously 314.11, discourteously 411.8

discontentedness irritableness 304.3, disapproval 438.1

discontenting disappointing 293.6

discontently irritably 304.17

discontentment dissatisfaction 274.1, envy 314.1, disapproval 438.1

discontinuance 846.4; relinquishment 392.1, unaccustomedness 398.1, closure 584.1, interruption 604.4, cessation 668.1, discontinuity 775.1, cancellation 834.1, termination 834.2

discontinuation irregularity 664.1, cessation 668.1, discontinuity 775.1, cancellation 834.1, failure 846.1

discontinue 775.10, 846.14; close down 584.15, interrupt 604.16, cease 668.9, 773.20, stop 668.10, terminate 834.7

discontinued 775.8; relinquished 392.2, disused 394.8, interrupted 604.10, ceased 668.6

discontinuity 775.1; earth zone 8.7, disconnection 574.5, interval 587.1, infrequency 662.1, irregularity 664.1, cessation 668.1, inconsistency 732.3, separation 753.1

discontinuous 775.7; disconnected 574.12, spaced 587.4, periodic 641.8, infrequent 662.2, irregular 664.3, separate 753.7

discontinuously 775.15; apart 587.8, infrequently 662.4,

irregularly 664.6, separately 753.22

discontinuousness discontinuity 775.1

discord harsh sound 238.1, be strident 238.7, dissonance 241.1, musical dissonance 241.2, dissension 272.3, 732.4, argument 329.1, dissentience 347.3, dispute 463.3, difference 463.4, ugliness 531.1, disorder 766.1, conflict 828.3

discordance harsh sound 238.1, dissonance 241.1, dissension 272.3, 732.4, dissentience 347.3, disagreement 463.1, dissent 506.2

discordant 828.12; hostile 63.6, strident 238.4, dissonant 241.1, gaudy 251.12, off-color 251.15, unpleasant 272.6, arguing 329.6, disagreeing 463.6, different 463.7, dissenting 506.6, 732.9, ugly 531.3

discordantly hostilely 63.13, stridently 238.10, dissonantly 241.7, argumentatively 329.15, in disagreement 463.12, differently 463.13, uncooperatively 506.11, dissentingly 732.17

discotheque dance hall 135.3

discount 495.1, 495.4; financial loss 468.4, bargain 497.10, make cheap 497.14, subtraction 749.1, subtracted item 749.2, subtract 749.6

discounted 495.3; reduced 749.5

discountenance disapprove 438.16, be against 828.17

discounter 497.7

discounting subtraction 749.1

discount price price 494.1

discount store store 483.8, discounter 497.7

discount ticket bargain 497.4

discourage 179.11; dissuade 179.7, deter 179.8, disappoint 293.9, change 512.12, hinder 826.15

discouraged 179.6; dissuaded 179.5, without hope 282.7, disappointed 293.4

discouragement dissuasion 179.1, lack of hope 282.2, disappointment 293.1, hindrance 826.1

discouraging dissuasive 179.4, disappointing 293.6, hindering 826.12

discouragingly dissuasively 179.12, disappointingly 293.12, with delay 826.22

discourse nonfiction 139.6, dissertation 203.1, dissertate 203.5, speech 205.1, speak to 205.19, address 209.1, 209.8, conversation 210.1, converse 210.11, logical argument 329.2, explanation 331.3

discourse at length be diffuse 199.5

discourser public speaker 209.5, conversationalist 210.6

discourteous 411.5, 535.7; clumsy 128.6, objectionable 272.7, ungrateful 311.2, inconsiderate 318.9, badly behaved 399.16, rude 400.9, unsociable 409.6, disrespectful 436.9, nonobservant 466.5, indecorous 528.8

discourteously 411.8, 535.11; unpleasantly 272.10, ungratefully 311.6, thoughtlessly 318.15, badly 399.23, rudely 400.19, unsocially 409.13, disrespectfully 436.25, defiantly 466.14

discourteousness ingratitude 311.1, discourtesy 411.1

discourteous person 411.4

discourtesy 411.1; *objectionability* 272.2, *inconsideration* 318.4, *bad conduct* 399.7, *rudeness* 400.2, *unsociability* 409.1, *disrespect* 436.1, *nonobservance* 466.1, *impropriety* 528.2, *grossness* 535.3

discover 345.11; *learn* 48.23, *be informed* 170.15, *disclose* 180.8, *see* 242.20, *surprise* 292.9, *solve* 334.21, *get to know* 348.12, *find* 565.11, *reach* 704.14, *forerun* 769.16, *invent* 771.30, *reveal* 843.14

discoverable 345.10; *visible* 244.5

discover a treasure trove *win an award* 467.23

discovered 345.9; *solved* 334.15, *known* 348.9, *produced* 522.12, *found* 565.11, *manifest* 843.9

discoverer 345.7; *discloser* 180.4, *producer* 522.10, *precursor* 769.7

discovering 345.8; *locating* 565.3, *preparatory* 769.11

discovery 345.1; *pretrial proceedings* 54.13, *source of supply* 105.4, *disclosure* 180.1, *solution* 334.6, *find* 345.5, *divination* 358.2, *windfall* 467.7, *production* 522.1, *preparation* 769.3, *invention* 771.5, *manifestation* 843.2

discredit *incredulity* 88.3, *disbelieve* 88.8, *cause disbelief* 88.9, *refute* 332.7, *disrepute* 371.1, *bring into disrepute* 371.6, *defame* 440.13

discreditably *disreputably* 371.7

discredited *disbelieved* 88.7, *disused* 394.8, *irresolute* 461.6

discrediting *refutation* 332.1, *refuting* 332.6

discreet *silent* 181.10, *noncommittal* 181.11, *soft-hued* 251.13, *prudent* 287.7, *wise* 352.4, *courteous* 410.6

discreetly *prudently* 287.17, *wisely* 352.8, *courteously* 410.13, *genteelly* 410.14

discreteness *prudence* 287.2

discrepancy *difference* 463.4, 750.3, *disparity* 728.3, *dissimilarity* 734.1, *contrariety* 828.6

discrepant *different* 463.7, *disparate* 728.9, *dissimilar* 734.4

discrepantly *differently* 463.13, *disparately* 728.19, *dissimilarly* 734.10, *residually* 750.11

discrete *universal* 6.67, *judged* 337.10, *separate* 724.10, *unjoined* 753.9, *aloof* 756.5, *discontinuous* 775.7, *disbanded* 776.7

discrete component *circuit element* 14.39

discrete distribution *probability distribution* 6.56

discretely *mathematically* 6.93, *separately* 724.18, *in isolation* 753.24, *aloofly* 756.10

discrete mathematics *combinatorics* 6.63

discreteness *separateness* 724.3, *aloofness* 756.2

discrete representations of continuous systems *systems and process control* 14.28

discretion *social skill* 127.3, *verbal concealment* 181.3, *prudence* 287.2, *judiciousness* 337.2, *judgment* 341.1, *wisdom* 352.1, *will* 372.1, *free will* 372.4, *selection* 382.1, *courtesy* 410.1, *freedom* 829.1

discretionary *willed* 372.6, *unconditional* 829.14

discretionary *or* **discretional** *selecting* 382.9

discriminate 337.12, 430.21; *know* 48.24, *be skillful* 127.14, *be wise* 352.6, *select* 382.12, *make unlike* 734.9, *be unjust* 741.9, *set apart* 753.17

discriminate against 337.14; *be unjust* 342.10, *discriminate* 430.21, *exclude* 764.7

discriminated against *judged* 337.10

discriminating 337.9; *rational* 4.15, *refined* 48.20, 534.5, *subtle* 195.9, *judging* 341.7, *judicious* 341.8, *selecting* 382.9, *characteristic* 723.9

discriminatingly 337.15; *wisely* 4.28, *discerningly* 48.27, *judicially* 341.12, *selectively* 382.17

discrimination 337.1; *refinement* 48.10, *social skill* 127.3, *subtlety* 195.3, 534.2, *judiciousness* 337.2, *prejudice* 337.3, *judgment* 341.1, *injustice* 342.3, 741.3, *wisdom* 352.1, *selection* 382.1, *selectivity* 430.1, *nonuniformity* 734.2, *setting apart* 753.2, *exclusiveness* 764.4

discriminator 337.6

discriminatorily *unjustly* 342.13, 741.12

discriminatory 337.11; *unjust* 342.7, 741.6, *wrongful* 430.10

discursion *circumlocution* 199.2, *wandering* 698.4

discursive *circumlocutory* 199.4, *dissertational* 203.4, *wandering* 698.13

discursively 203.6; *circuitously* 199.8, *astray* 698.27

discursiveness *wandering* 698.4

discursive reasoning *reasoning* 319.2

discus *discus throwing* 166.13, *circular thing* 631.3, *missile* 696.7

discuss 4.22, 329.12; *consult* 176.11, *dissertate* 203.5, *confer* 210.13, *raise the point* 328.10, *doubt* 333.19, *balance* 378.11, *negotiate* 460.6

discussable *logical* 329.9

discussing 210.9

discussion 460.3; *philosophical argument* 4.5, *consultation* 176.4, *dissertation* 203.1, *debate* 210.3, *logical argument* 329.2, *negotiation* 460.1, *lecture* 777.7

discussion group *conference* 59.5, *students* 777.6

discus throw *discus throwing* 166.13

discus thrower *thrower* 696.10

discus throwing 166.13, Sporting Activities 145, *field event* 166.10

disdain 297.14, 400.16; *arrogance* 297.2, 400.4, *hate* 300.1, 300.11, *exclude* 383.11, *disobedience* 416.2, *contempt* 436.3, *scorn* 436.19, 440.5, *nonobservance* 466.1

disdainful *arrogant* 297.9, 400.11, *hating* 300.7, *defiant* 416.5, *contemptuous* 436.12, *nonobservant* 466.5

disdainfully *arrogantly* 297.18, 400.21, *with hate* 300.13, *unsocially* 409.13, *defiantly* 416.9, *contemptuously* 436.27

disdainfulness *contempt* 436.3

disease 114.4; *illness* 114.2, *affliction* 117.1, *Phobias* 283, *agent of destruction* 523.7, *physical deterioration* 808.4

disease-causing agent 114.5

diseased *sick* 114.24

disease prevention *hygiene* 116.1

disease transferrer *transferrer* 685.4

disect *align* 6.92

disedge *blunt* 550.9

disembark *sail* 690.16, *land* 704.16

disembarkation *landing* 704.2

disembarkment *landing* 704.2

disembarrass *disentangle* 823.17

disembarrassment *disentanglement* 823.8

disembodied *spiritual* 86.20, *nonmaterial* 525.8

disembodiment *disappearance* 265.1, *immateriality* 525.2

disembody *cause to disappear* 265.7, *dematerialize* 525.12

disembogue *run out* 707.15, *let out* 709.26

disemboguement *disgorgement* 709.6

disembowel *void* 709.23, *draw out* 711.17, *divide* 753.18

disemboweled *separate* 753.7

disembowelment *drawing off* 711.4

disemplane *land* 704.16

disemploy *dismiss* 709.15

disemployed *discarded* 383.8

disemployment *discarding* 383.3

disenable *make impossible* 837.8

disenchant *discourage* 179.11, *disappoint* 293.9

disenchanted *discouraged* 179.6, *displeased* 291.6, *disappointed* 293.4

disenchantedly *disappointedly* 293.11

disenchanting *dissuasive* 179.4, *disappointing* 293.6

disenchantingly *dishearteningly* 179.13

disenchantment *disaffection* 179.3, *disappointment* 293.1

disencumber *take away* 275.13, *lighten* 539.9, *deliver* 817.5, *disentangle* 823.17, *liberate* 831.6

disencumbering *lightening* 539.6

disencumberment *deliverance* 817.1, *disentanglement* 823.8, *liberation* 831.1

disendow *impoverish* 486.16

disenfranchise *subject* 832.10

disenfranchised *unauthorized* 515.7

disenfranchisement *forfeiture* 468.2, *subjection* 832.1

disengage *fencing movements* 153.3, *fence* 153.7, *be incurious* 322.7, *disconnect* 574.19, *retreat* 680.17, *extract* 711.13, *separate* 753.12, *disentangle* 823.17, *liberate* 831.6

disengaged *leisurely* 125.4, *fencing* 153.6, *apathetic* 322.4, *not working* 415.10, *disconnected* 574.12, *dislodged* 711.11

disengagement *disconnection* 574.5, *retreat* 680.2, *extraction* 711.1, *disentanglement* 823.8, *liberation* 831.1

disentangle 753.13, 823.17; *decipher* 365.13, *make simple* 526.12, *straighten* 630.14, *tidy* 765.21

disentanglement 823.8; *solution* 376.6, *simplification* 526.3

disentitlement *forfeiture* 468.2

disentomb *dig out* 711.15

disentombment *digging out* 711.3

disequilibrium *changeableness* 666.1, *imbalance* 741.2

disesteem 436.2; *dislike* 291.1, 291.12, *disapproval* 438.1

disesteemed *disliked* 291.10

disfavor *be dissatisfied* 274.7, *dislike* 291.1, 291.12, 300.2, *abasement* 298.6, *disrepute* 371.1, *disesteem* 436.2, *disapproval* 438.1, *disapprove* 438.16

disfavorable *disapproving* 438.8

disfavored *disliked* 291.10, *disapproved* 438.9

disfellowship *dismissal* 709.2

disfigure *identify* 184.11, *make ugly* 531.4, *blemish* 533.7, *deform* 627.11, *stain* 808.20

disfigured *ugly* 531.3, *blemished* 533.5, *deformed* 627.7

disfigurement *ugliness* 531.1, *blemish* 533.1, *distortion of body* 627.3

disfranchise *subject* 832.10

disfranchised *unauthorized* 515.7

disfranchisement *forfeiture* 468.2, *subjection* 832.1

disgorge *let out* 709.26

disgorgement 709.6

disgorger *fishing tackle* 154.7

disgrace *honor* 58.14, *humiliation* 298.5, *humiliate* 298.19, *vilify* 301.15, *disrepute* 371.1, *impropriety* 400.5, *demoralize* 432.15, *dishonor* 436.20, *humbling* 597.9, *humble* 597.25

disgraced *honored* 58.12, *humiliated* 298.12, *disreputable* 371.4, *lowered* 597.18

disgracedly *with honor* 58.16

disgraceful *honored* 58.12, *immoral* 430.11, *wicked* 448.9, *lowered* 597.18

disgracefully 371.8, 597.28; *with honor* 58.16, *improperly* 430.26, *wickedly* 448.15

disgrace oneself *be disreputable* 371.5, *be wicked* 448.13

disgrace to one's uniform *military honor* 58.9

disgruntle *dissatisfy* 274.6

disgruntled *dissatisfied* 274.4, *disapproving* 438.8

disgruntlement *dissatisfaction* 274.1, *disapproval* 438.1

disguise 181.13; *costume* 100.10, *concealment* 181.1, *cover* 181.4, *conceal* 181.12, *be untruthful* 192.20, *that which makes invisible* 245.2, *make invisible* 245.7, *spectacle* 264.6, *cause to disappear* 265.7, *practice sophistry* 330.11, *body covering* 613.3, *hide* 613.27, *show* 621.7, *be in front* 621.13, *means of escape* 816.4, *cunning* 822.1

disguised 181.9; *mysterious* 182.10, *ungenuine* 192.13, *private* 245.5, *protected* 613.20, *outward* 621.11, *concealed* 844.7

disguise oneself as *appear* 264.12

disguiser *one who conceals* 181.7, *coverer* 613.18

disgust *put off* 179.10, *displease* 272.8, *dissatisfaction* 274.1, *dissatisfy* 274.6, *antipathy* 291.2, *cause dislike* 291.16, *dislike* 300.2, *cause hate* 300.12, *change* 512.12, *be repulsive* 701.10

disgusted *dissuaded* 179.5, *dissatisfied* 274.4, *antipathetic* 291.7, *hating* 300.7

disgustedly *dissuasively* 179.12, *discontentedly* 274.8

disgusting *unclean* 112.8, *dissuasive* 179.4, *unpalatable* 223.6, *unpleasant* 272.6, *detested* 291.11, *hateful* 300.10, *repulsive* 701.4

disgustingly *distastefully* 291.19, *hatefully* 300.14

dish 90.7; *course* 92.12, *tableware* 92.13, *crockery* 578.16, *take away* 685.12

dish [Inf] *ruin* 523.15, *attractive female* 529.5

dishabille *dressing* 100.2

disharmonious *disagreeing* 463.6

disharmoniously *dissonantly* 241.7, *in disagreement* 463.12

disharmony *dissonance* 241.1, *dissension* 272.3, *dissentience* 347.3, *disagreement* 463.1, *disorder* 766.1

dishcloth *cleaning tool* 111.10, *cleaning cloth* 111.11

dishearten *discourage* 179.11, *cause sorrow* 270.9, *disappoint* 293.9, *make sullen* 304.13

disheartened *discouraged* 179.6, *sorrowful* 270.4, *without hope* 282.7, *disappointed* 293.4, *sullen* 304.8

disheartening *dissuasive* 179.4, *disappointing* 293.6

dishearteningly 179.13

disheartenment *disaffection* 179.3, *disappointment* 293.1, *sullenness* 304.1

dishevel *make disorderly* 766.20

disheveled *untidy* 766.11

dishevelment *untidiness* 766.3

dish fit for a king or **queen** *dish* 90.7

dish of the day *dish* 90.7, *the special* 779.8

dishonest *offending* 53.25, *untruthful* 192.12, *hypocritical* 330.10, *immoral* 430.11, 432.9, *fraudulent* 479.13, *devious* 607.9, *cunning* 822.4, *unreliable* 841.15

dishonestly *untruthfully* 192.27, *hypocritically* 330.15, *immorally* 430.27, 432.18, *unvirtuously* 448.16, *thievishly* 479.19, *deviously* 607.16, *cunningly* 822.6, *unreliably* 841.25

dishonest person 479.11

dishonesty 479.7; *lawbreaking* 53.14, *evasion* 181.5, *untruthfulness* 192.1, *immorality* 432.1, *iniquity* 448.3, *deviousness* 607.4

dishonor 436.20; *honor* 58.14, *abasement* 298.6, *disrepute* 371.1, *bring into disrepute* 371.6, *impropriety* 430.5, *wrong* 430.19, *demoralize* 432.15, *disesteem* 436.2, *defame* 440.13, *irresolution* 461.3, *humbling* 597.9, *humble* 597.25

dishonorable 192.14; *honored* 58.12, *disreputable* 371.4, *immoral* 430.11, *disregardful* 436.11, *irresolute* 461.6, *lowered* 597.18

dishonorable discharge *military honor* 58.9, *termination* 834.2

dishonorableness 192.3

dishonorably 192.28; *with honor* 58.16, *disreputably* 371.7, *immorally* 430.27, *irresolutely* 461.10, *disgracefully* 597.28

dishonor a check *stop payment* 490.10

dishonored *honored* 58.12, *irresolute* 461.6, *lowered* 597.18

dishonored check *bad payment* 490.3

dish out [Inf] *give out* 472.12, *allocate* 474.5, *remunerate* 489.21

dishrag *cleaning cloth* 111.11

dish towel *cleaning cloth* 111.11

dishware *tableware* 92.13, *crockery* 578.16

dishwasher *domestic servant* 69.7, *washer* 111.7, *cleaner* 111.12, *service worker* 123.7

dishwashing *cleaning* 111.2

dishwashing liquid *cleaning agent* 111.9

dishwater *swill* 112.6, *weak thing* 517.5

dishy [Brit inf] *attractive* 529.8, *attractive* 700.10

disillusion *inform* 170.11, *discourage* 179.11, *dissatisfy* 274.6, *disappoint* 293.9, 846.15

disillusioned *discouraged* 179.6, *dissatisfied* 274.4, *displeased* 291.6, *disappointed* 293.4

disillusioning *disappointing* 293.6

disillusionment *disaffection* 179.3, *dissatisfaction* 274.1, *disappointment* 293.1

disincarnate *dematerialize* 525.12

disincarnated *nonmaterial* 525.8

disincarnation *immateriality* 525.2

disincentive *deterrence* 179.2

disinclination 291.3; *disaffection* 179.3, *unwillingness* 375.1

disincline *put off* 179.10, *cause dislike* 291.16

disinclined 291.9; *estranged* 63.8, *dissuaded* 179.5, *unwilling* 375.8

disinfect *clean* 111.17, *purify* 111.19, *treat* 115.17, *practice hygiene* 116.4, *deodorize* 225.6, *immunize* 810.22

disinfectant *cleaning agent* 111.9, *cleansing* 111.16, *prophylaxis* 115.4, *remedial* 115.14, *deodorant* 225.3, *deodorizing* 225.5, *tutelary* 810.19

disinfected *cleaned* 111.14, *hygienic* 116.3, *odorless* 225.4, *safe* 810.16

disinfection *cleaning* 111.2, *prophylaxis* 115.4, *hygiene* 116.1

disinfestation *cleaning* 111.2

disinflation *economic factor* 56.8, *inflation* 484.9

disinflationary *financial* 457.6

disinform *misinform* 188.7, *misrepresent* 193.17

disinformation *misinformation* 188.3, *misrepresentation* 193.4, *sophism* 330.2, *distortion of truth* 627.4

disinformed *misrepresentative* 193.14, *misrepresented* 627.8

disinformer *one who misrepresents* 193.9

disingenuous *ungenuine* 192.13, *hypocritical* 330.10, *cunning* 822.4

disingenuously *untruthfully* 192.27, *hypocritically* 330.15

disingenuousness *ungenuineness* 192.2, *hypocrisy* 330.5

disinherit *renounce* 383.13, *take back* 477.17, *impoverish* 486.16

disinheritance *renunciation* 383.4, *taking back* 477.4, *insolvency* 486.2

disinherited *renounced* 383.9, *impoverished* 486.11

disinheriting *renunciation* 383.4

disintegrate 758.6, 808.15; *erode* 8.67, *interact* 10.73, *be destroyed* 523.17, *be brittle* 548.4, *pulverize* 553.26, *come to dust* 553.28, *scatter* 753.15, *be disordered* 766.21, *diverge* 776.16

disintegrated 758.3; *destroyed* 523.9, *pulverized* 553.20, *disbanded* 776.7, *spoiled* 808.9

disintegrating 758.5; *brittle* 548.3

disintegration 758.1; *weathering* 8.40, *nuclear reaction* 10.59, *destroying* 523.2, *brittleness* 548.1, *pulverization* 553.4, *separation* 753.1, *disorder* 766.1, *divergence* 776.5, *dilapidation* 808.5

disintegration of personality *dissociative disorder* 108.17

disinter *disclose* 180.8, *detect* 345.12, *dig out* 711.15

disinterest *philosophical attitude* 4.3, *indifference* 289.1, *lack of wonder* 295.1, *incuriosity* 322.1, *disinterestedness* 443.1

disinterested 443.4; *detached* 4.18, *indifferent* 289.7, *impartial* 289.9, 338.6, *wonderless* 295.3, *self-abasing* 298.11, *incurious* 322.3

disinterestedly 443.8; *indifferently* 289.17, *impartially* 289.19, 338.12, *without wonder* 295.8, *incuriously* 322.6

disinterestedness 443.1; *impartiality* 289.3, 338.2, *self-abasement* 298.4

disinterment *digging out* 711.3

disinvest *expend* 491.11

disinvolve *disentangle* 823.17

disinvolvement *simplification* 526.6, *disentanglement* 823.8

disjecta membra *bits and pieces* 760.5

disjoin *not connect* 728.13, *take apart* 753.16, *disconnect* 775.12

disjoined *unconnected* 728.8

disjoint *disconnect* 574.19

disjointed *unemphatic* 201.2, *disconnected* 574.12, *unconnected* 728.8, *separate* 753.7, *disordered* 766.9, *discontinuous* 775.7

disjointedly *disconnectedly* 574.22, 775.16, *unconnectedly* 728.18

disjointedness *disconnection* 574.5, *discontinuity* 775.1

disjoint sets *set* 6.19

disjunction *philosophical term* 4.7, *mathematical logic* 6.60, *unconnectedness* 728.2, *separation* 753.1, *nonadhesion* 756.1, *disorder* 766.1, *discontinuity* 775.1

disjunctive *unconnected* 728.8, *separate* 753.7

disjunctively *unconnectedly* 728.18, *separately* 753.22

disjuncture *unconnectedness* 728.2, *separation* 753.1

disk 15.5; *circle* 6.40, *galaxy* 7.5, *computer part* 15.4, *peripheral* 15.8, *record book* 185.5, *sound reproduction* 230.6, *slice* 588.4, *circular thing* 631.3

disk flower or **floret** *flower head* 42.4

disk harrow *farm tool* 16.5

disk jockey (DJ) *broadcasting personnel* 172.11

disklike *spherical* 6.80

disk sander *woodworking tool* 131.6

disk-shaped *spherical* 6.80

disk wheel *bicycle part* 687.11

dislikable *disliked* 291.10

dislike 291.1, 291.12, 300.2; *hostility* 63.1, *bad feeling* 266.5, *dissatisfaction* 274.1, *be dissatisfied* 274.7, *boredom* 296.1, *hate* 300.11, *unwillingness* 375.1, *be unwilling* 375.12, *disapproval* 438.1, *disapprove* 438.16, *opposition* 828.1, *be against* 828.17

disliked 291.10; *unpleasant* 272.6, *hated* 300.9

dislike or **distrust of humankind** *misanthropy* 291.4

disliking *disapproving* 438.8

dislocate *use violence* 520.9, *displace* 574.15, *disconnect* 574.19, *separate* 753.12, *disarrange* 768.11

dislocated *displaced* 574.8, *disconnected* 574.12, *separate* 753.7, *disordered* 766.9, *disarranged* 768.7

dislocation *violence by person* 520.2, *displacement* 574.1, *disconnection* 574.5, *separation* 753.1, *dispersion* 768.3

dislocation metamorphism *metamorphism* 8.35

dislodge *displace* 574.15, 711.14, *take away* 685.12, *evict* 709.20, *disarrange* 768.11

dislodged 711.11; *displaced* 574.8, *disarranged* 768.7

dislodgment *displacement* 574.1, 711.2, *eviction* 709.4, *dispersion* 768.3

disloyal *estranged* 63.8, *dishonorable* 192.14, *equivocating* 380.6, *disobedient* 427.10, *defiant* 466.7, *irresolute* 666.4

disloyal friend *equivocator* 380.4

disloyally *hostilely* 63.13, *dishonorably* 192.28, *disobediently* 427.14, *defiantly* 466.14, *changeably* 666.7

disloyalty *personal conflict* 63.2, *dishonorableness* 192.3, *disobedience* 427.1, *defiance* 466.3, *irresolution* 666.2

dismal *depressed* 270.5, *overcast* 304.11

dismally 304.19; *sorrowfully* 270.10

dismalness *overcast* 304.6

dismantle *make inactive* 415.16, *demolish* 523.12, *make simple* 526.12, *take apart* 753.16, *part* 760.14, *make useless* 802.12, *impair* 808.18

dismantled *unequipped* 389.13

dismantling *simplification* 526.6, *deconstruction* 758.2

dismast *make useless* 802.12, *impair* 808.18

dismasted *unequipped* 389.13

dismay *fear* 283.1, *frighten* 283.17

dismaying *frightening* 283.12

dismember *execute* 454.30, *disconnect* 574.19, *divide* 753.18, *deconstruct* 758.7

dismembered *disconnected* 574.12, *separate* 753.7

dismemberment *disconnection* 574.5, *deconstruction* 758.2

dismiss 709.15; *employ* 57.18, *cause to disappear* 265.7, *relieve from duty* 275.11, *be indifferent* 289.12, *absolve* 312.10, *refute* 332.7, *discard* 383.12, *make inactive* 415.16, *acquit* 434.10, *vindicate* 441.11, *remove power from* 515.13, *relegate* 574.4, *stop work* 668.11, *eject* 701.8, 764.8, *emigrate* 707.17, *disband* 776.13, *liberate* 831.6, *terminate* 834.7

dismissal 709.2; *Eucharist* 85.7, *absolution* 312.2, *refutation* 332.1, *discarding* 383.3, *disuse* 394.3, *vindication* 441.1, *relegation* 574.4, *stop* 668.2, *repulse* 701.2, *parting* 705.3, *emigration* 707.6, *ejection* 764.2, *disbandment* 776.2, *liberation* 831.1, *termination* 834.2

dismissal for lack of evidence *favorable verdict* 54.19

dismiss charges *acquit* 54.32

dismissed *hired* 57.17, *forgiven* 312.5, *discarded* 383.8, *vindicated*

441.8, *relegated* 574.11, *excluded* 764.6, *disbanded* 776.7
dismissive *defensive* 701.6
dismissively *in reply* 332.10, *defensively* 701.12
dismiss out of hand *reject* 383.10
dismount *exercise* 157.12, *land* 704.16, *descend* 714.12, *separate* 753.12
disobedience 375.5, 416.2, 427.1; *anarchy* 51.1, *unacceptance* 190.4, *dissentience* 347.3, *obstinacy* 379.1, *defiance* 466.3, *protest* 507.1, *lawlessness* 766.6, *dissent* 782.2, *contrariety* 828.5
disobedient 427.10; *anarchic* 51.5, *unaccepting* 190.13, *obstinate* 379.5, *refractory* 379.6, *defying* 416.6, *defiant* 466.7, *protesting* 507.5, *disorderly* 766.15, *troublesome* 824.13, *uncooperative* 828.14
disobediently 427.14; *anarchically* 51.10, *nonacceptantly* 190.25, *in defiance* 416.10, *defiantly* 466.14, *disapprovingly* 507.10, *perversely* 824.27
disobey 427.12; *be anarchic* 51.8, *not accept* 190.19, *dissociate* 375.14, *be insubordinate* 416.8, *defy* 466.11, *protest* 507.7, *be disorderly* 766.22, *break the law* 782.19, *withstand* 828.20
disobeyed *unaccepting* 190.13
disobeying *disobedient* 427.10
D-isomer *amino acid* 12.8
disorder 507.2, 625.4, 766.1, 766.17; *confusion* 51.2, *illness* 114.2, Phobias 283, *violation of the law* 427.2, *infraction* 466.4, *displace* 574.15, *shapelessness* 625.1, *irregularity* 664.1, *tumult* 684.2, *mixture* 751.1, *nonadhesion* 756.1, *disintegration* 758.1, *deconstruct* 758.7, *lawlessness* 766.6, *derangement* 766.8, *derange* 766.23, *disarrangement* 768.2, *disarrange* 768.11, *discontinuity* 775.1
disordered 766.9; *disorderly* 51.6, *indiscriminate* 338.8, *shapeless* 625.2, *irregular* 664.3, *complicated* 751.10, *disintegrated* 758.3, *deranged* 766.16, *disarranged* 768.7
disorderliness *confusion* 51.2, *disorder* 766.1
disorderly 51.6, 507.6, 766.15; *shouting* 232.7, *disobedient* 427.10, *violating* 466.8, *discourteous* 535.7, *vulgarly* 535.10, *irregular* 664.3, *mixedly* 751.16
disorderly behavior *or* **conduct** *lawlessness* 766.6
disorganization *confusion* 51.2, *lack of preparation* 389.1, *disorder* 766.1, *disarrangement* 768.2, *impairment* 808.7
disorganize *displace* 574.15, *disorder* 766.17, *disarrange* 768.11, *impair* 808.18
disorganized *disorderly* 51.6, *indiscriminate* 338.8, *unprepared* 389.5, *disordered* 766.9, *confused* 766.12, *disarranged* 768.7
disorganized-type schizophrenia *psychosis* 108.10
disorient *discompose* 766.18, *disarrange* 768.11
disorientation *deviation* 698.1, *dispersion* 768.3
disoriented *at a loss* 468.11, *disarranged* 768.7

disown *disavow* 190.18, *deny* 332.8, *renounce* 383.13, *be evasive* 386.20
disowned *disavowing* 190.12, *renounced* 383.9
disowning *disavowal* 190.3, *refuting* 332.6, *renunciation* 383.4
disownment *disavowal* 190.3, *denial* 332.2
disparage 195.15, 440.11; *abase* 298.20, *vilify* 301.15, *underestimate* 344.5, *disdain* 400.16, *criticize* 418.26, 438.19, *wrong* 430.19, *scorn* 436.19, *make unimportant* 800.20
disparaged *abased* 298.13, *undervalued* 436.17
disparagement 195.2, 440.1; *abasement* 298.6, *vilification* 301.2, *derision* 400.5, *personal attack* 418.8
disparager 440.7
disparaging 440.8; *debasing* 298.15, *vilifying* 301.9, *underestimating* 344.3, *derisive* 400.12, *critical* 418.16, 438.13
disparagingly 440.16; *humiliatingly* 298.25, *vilifyingly* 301.18, *pessimistically* 344.6, *derisively* 400.22
disparaging remark *aspersion* 440.4
disparate 728.9; *dissimilar* 734.4, *unequal* 741.4
disparately 728.19; *dissimilarly* 734.10, *unequally* 741.10
disparity 728.3; *difference* 463.4, *dissimilarity* 734.1, *inequality* 741.1, *nonconformity* 782.1, *contrariety* 828.6
dispassion *philosophical attitude* 4.3, *indifference* 289.1, *disinterestedness* 443.1
dispassionate *detached* 4.18, *indifferent* 289.7, *judicious* 341.8, *disinterested* 443.4
dispassionately *stoically* 4.26, *indifferently* 289.17, *judicially* 341.12, *disinterestedly* 443.8
dispatch *execution* 30.6, *kill* 30.19, *eat well* 92.23, *correspond* 169.19, *communication* 170.2, *news event* 171.2, *report* 171.9, *send* 209.11, *behave toward* 399.20, *action* 412.1, *act* 412.11, *alacrity* 414.3, *try* 414.21, *give out* 472.12, *destroy* 523.10, *earliness* 657.1, *start early* 657.12, *set in motion* 677.16, *conveyance* 685.2, *convey* 685.9, *transport* 686.10, *swiftness* 694.1, *haste* 818.1, *hasten* 818.4
dispatch box *postal communication* 169.4
dispatch case *baggage* 578.8
dispatcher *news reporting* 171.5
dispel *refresh* 94.6, *cause to disappear* 265.7, *abolish* 523.11, *exterminate* 709.22, *separate* 753.12, *disperse* 776.12
dispensability *unimportance* 800.1, *redundancy* 802.2
dispensable *vindicable* 441.9, *unimportant* 800.10, *redundant* 802.9
dispensary *hospital* 107.16
dispensation *forgiveness* 312.1, *exemption* 434.1, *allocation* 474.1, *tolerance* 502.2, *permission* 735.9, *exclusion* 764.1, *dispersion* 776.1, *deliverance* 817.1
dispense *exempt* 434.9, *give out* 472.12, *allocate* 474.5, *disperse* 776.12

dispensed *exempt* 434.5, *dispersed* 776.6
dispense from *deliver* 817.5
dispenser *druggist* 115.10
dispense with *eject* 764.8
dispensing *allocation* 474.1
dispeople *depopulate* 709.21
dispersal *disappearance* 265.1, *transmission* 685.3, *separation* 753.1, *deconstruction* 758.2, *dispersion* 776.1
disperse 776.12; *status adjectives* 11.25, *solidify* 11.37, *waste* 96.15, *cause to disappear* 265.7, *abolish* 523.11, *enlarge* 581.14, *set in motion* 677.16, *transfer* 685.8, *bring* 685.11, *deflect* 698.26, *radiate* 703.13, *scatter* 753.15, *796.9, *diverge* 753.20, *unstick* 756.6, *deconstruct* 758.7, *disorder* 766.17, *disarrange* 768.11, *broadcast* 778.16
dispersed 776.6; *disappeared* 265.4, *bigger* 581.9, *diffractive* 698.14, *apart* 753.8, *nonadhesive* 756.4, *disintegrated* 758.3, *disarranged* 768.7, *sparse* 796.6
dispersed population *disbandment* 776.2
disperse phase *phase* 11.13
disperser *enlarger* 581.8
dispersion 768.3, 776.1; *parameter* 6.57, *wave property* 10.12, *waste* 96.1, *disappearance* 265.1, *expansion* 581.1, *distance* 585.1, *transmission* 685.3, *diffraction* 698.6, *radiation* 703.3, *separation* 753.1, *nonadhesion* 756.1
dispersion force *chemical bond* 11.6
dispersive 776.10; *enlargeable* 581.13
dispersively 776.17
dispirit *discourage* 179.11, *cause sorrow* 270.9, *disappoint* 293.9, *humiliate* 298.19, *make sullen* 304.13
dispirited *discouraged* 179.6, *depressed* 270.5, *disappointed* 293.4, *humiliated* 298.12, *sullen* 304.8
dispiritedly *dishearteningly* 179.13, *disappointedly* 293.11
dispiritedness *depression* 270.2, *sullenness* 304.1
dispiriting *distressing* 270.6
displace 574.15, 711.14; *exclude* 409.12, *be a substitute* 672.6, *set in motion* 677.16, *take away* 685.12, *separate* 753.12, *disarrange* 768.11
displaceable *transferable* 685.7
displaced 574.8; *lonely* 409.8, *dislodged* 711.11, *disordered* 766.9, *disarranged* 768.7, *unconventional* 782.14
displaced person (DP) 574.7; *avoider* 386.8, *new arrival* 724.6
displacement 538.3, 574.1, 711.2; *electric field* 10.42, *chemical reaction* 11.8, *defense mechanism* 108.23, *windsurfing* 150.28, *size* 579.1, *transfer* 685.1, *dispersion* 768.3
displacement activity *overactivity* 414.9
displacement board *sailboard parts* 150.20
displacement current *electric current* 10.39
displacement sailing *windsurfing* 150.19
display 15.9, 843.1, 843.13; *computer part* 15.4, *peripheral* 15.8, *computing terms* 15.22,

compilation 59.14, *public relations (PR)* 173.8, *view* 242.8, *make visible* 242.25, 244.9, *manifestation* 244.3, *visibility* 264.4, *present* 264.15, *demonstration* 331.1, *demonstrate* 331.15, *show* 404.12, 404.24, 621.7, *be in front* 621.13, *array* 767.2, *arrange* 767.18
display bad manners *be discourteous* 411.7
display board *advertisement* 173.9
display cabinet *showplace* 843.4
display case *showplace* 843.4
displayed 843.8, Heraldic Terms 184, *appearing* 264.9, *demonstrated* 331.9, *outward* 621.11
displayer 843.7; *demonstrator* 331.6
display of disapproval *show of disapproval* 438.6
display one's skill *be expert* 127.15
displease 272.8; *dissatisfy* 274.6, *cause dislike* 291.16, *cause hate* 300.12, *make irritable* 304.15
displeased 291.6; *dissatisfied* 274.4, *resentful* 302.8, *disapproving* 438.8
displeasing *unpleasant* 272.6, *disliked* 291.10, *maddening* 302.12
displeasingly *distastefully* 291.19, *maddeningly* 302.25
displeasure *dissatisfaction* 274.1, *dislike* 291.1, 300.2, *resentment* 302.1, *disapproval* 438.1
displume *disbar* 709.16
displuming *dismissal* 709.2
disposability *redundancy* 802.2
disposable *usable* 393.6, *deconstructed* 758.4, *useful* 801.5, *refuse* 802.5, *redundant* 802.9
disposable camera *camera* 132.10
disposable income *economic factor* 56.8
disposable lenses *visual aid* 242.14
disposal *relinquishment* 392.1, *use* 393.1, *disuse* 394.3, *transfer of property* 470.4, *selling* 482.1, *ejection* 764.2, *arrangement* 767.1
disposal of the dead *burial* 31.1
dispose *transfer property* 470.12, *influence* 508.11, 512.11, *aim* 697.14, *order* 765.18, *arrange* 767.18, *class* 777.12
disposed *inclined toward* 290.5, *willed* 372.6, *willing* 373.7, *intending* 374.6, *ordered* 765.10, *arranged* 766.11
disposed of *relinquished* 392.2
dispose of *refute* 332.7, *relinquish* 392.3, *sell* 482.15, *destroy* 523.10, *cease* 733.20
disposition *inclination* 290.2, *will* 372.1, *transfer of property* 470.4, *attitude* 723.4, *nature* 723.4, *state of mind* 725.5, *order* 765.1, *arrangement* 767.1
dispossess *take away* 275.13, *lose* 468.12, *take back* 477.17, *impoverish* 486.16, *evict* 709.20
dispossessed *impoverished* 486.11
dispossession *loss* 468.1, *taking back* 477.4, *insolvency* 486.2, *eviction* 709.4
dispossessor *ejector* 709.10
dispraise *criticism* 438.4, *criticize* 438.19, 440.12
dispraised *criticized* 438.14
dispraising *critical* 438.13
disproof *evidence* 54.15, *negation* 190.1, *refutation* 332.1

disproportion *distortion* 627.1, *distort* 627.9, *disparity* 728.3, *inequality* 741.1, *unbalance* 741.8, *irregular order* 766.2
disproportional *disparate* 728.9
disproportionally *disparately* 728.19
disproportionate *excessive* 99.5, *distorted* 627.6, *disparate* 728.9, *unequal* 741.4, *irregular* 766.10
disproportionately *excessively* 99.13, *asymmetrically* 627.13, *disparately* 728.19, *unequally* 741.10
disproportionation *chemical reaction* 11.8
disproportioned *unequal* 741.4
disprovability *refutability* 332.4
disprovable *refutable* 332.5
disprovably *refutably* 332.11
disproval *refutation* 332.1
disprove *theorize* 6.84, *negate* 190.16, *refute* 332.7, *renounce* 383.13
disproved *negated* 190.10
disproven *renounced* 383.9
disproving *refuting* 332.6, *renunciation* 383.4
disputability *unauthenticity* 722.4, *uncertainty* 841.1
disputable *litigated* 54.22, *disbelieved* 88.7, *arguable* 329.8, *questionable* 333.13, *unauthentic* 722.9, *uncertain* 841.9
disputableness *unauthenticity* 722.4
disputably *unbelievably* 88.11, *questionably* 333.22, *unauthentically* 722.17, *uncertainly* 841.22
disputant *arguer* 319.6, *opposer* 828.9
disputation *philosophical argument* 4.5, *debate* 319.3, *logical argument* 329.2, *objection* 828.2
disputatious *legalistic* 53.22, *ill-natured* 303.9, *argumentative* 329.7, *dissenting* 347.7, *aggressive* 418.12, *disagreeing* 463.6
disputatiously *ill-naturedly* 303.18, *in disagreement* 463.12
disputatiousness *ill nature* 303.2
dispute 463.3, 463.9; *discuss* 4.22, *litigation* 54.1, *battle* 76.33, *disbelieve* 88.8, *dissuade* 179.7, *negate* 190.16, *quarrel* 302.7, 302.17, *be irascible* 303.13, *debate* 319.3, 319.13, *argument* 329.1, *argue* 329.11, *deny* 332.8, *doubt* 333.19, *dissent* 347.1, 347.8, *contention* 422.1, *conflict* 422.26, *awkward situation* 824.7, *object* 828.18, *be uncertain* 841.17
disputed 57.15; *litigated* 54.22, *negated* 190.10
disputed area *divisiveness* 463.2
disputedly *arguably* 329.16, *refutably* 332.11
disputer *dissenter* 347.5, 463.5
disputes procedure *strike* 57.8
disputing *litigating* 54.21, *argumentative* 319.10, *arguing* 329.6, *disagreeing* 463.6
disqualification *unskillfulness* 128.1, *track event* 166.1, *forfeiture* 468.2, *dismissal* 709.2, *ejection* 764.2
disqualified *unskillful* 128.4, *powerless* 515.6
disqualified athlete *loser* 468.8
disqualify *remove power from* 515.13, *disbar* 709.16, *eject* 764.8, *make useless* 802.12, *make impossible* 837.8

disquiet *fearfulness* 283.2, *irresolution* 666.2, *agitation* 684.1, *agitate* 684.22, *disturbance* 768.1, *disturb* 768.10
disquieted *fearful* 283.10, *agitated* 684.15, *disturbed* 768.6
disquietingly *disturbingly* 768.13
disquietude *fearfulness* 283.2, *agitation* 684.1
disquisition *dissertation* 203.1, *address* 209.1
disquisitional *dissertational* 203.4
disregard *downplaying* 195.6, *play down* 195.17, *figurative blindness* 243.8, *be blind to* 243.19, *carelessness* 289.2, *be careless* 289.14, *forgivingness* 312.3, *show mercy* 312.11, *be incurious* 322.5, *inattention* 324.1, *thoughtlessness* 324.3, *be inattentive* 324.10, *be thoughtless* 324.11, *negligence* 326.1, *be neglectful* 326.7, *be indiscriminate* 338.10, *unthinkingness* 355.3, *rejection* 383.1, *exclude* 383.11, 764.7, *not use* 394.9, *ignore* 413.14, *disobedience* 416.2, *be insubordinate* 416.8, *disesteem* 436.2, *dishonor* 436.20, *nonobservance* 466.1, *not observe* 466.9, *think unimportant* 800.19
disregardable *forgivable* 312.7
disregard any impediment *go to any length* 590.13
disregarded *downplayed* 195.13, *overlooked* 312.6, *neglected* 326.6, *rejected* 383.6, *undervalued* 436.17, *excluded* 764.6, *obscure* 800.13
disregardful 436.11; *negligent* 326.4, *nonobservant* 466.5
disregarding *careless* 289.8, *inattentive* 324.5, *unthinking* 355.8, *nonobservant* 466.5
disregard of orders *defiance* 466.3
disregard orders *defy* 466.11
disrelated *extraneous* 724.8, *unrelated* 728.6
disrelation *unrelatedness* 728.1
disrelish *dislike* 291.1, 291.12, 300.2, *hate* 300.11
disrelished *disliked* 291.10, *hated* 300.9
disrepair *dilapidation* 808.5
disreputability *disrepute* 371.1
disreputable 371.4; *disregardful* 436.11, *wicked* 448.9, *lowered* 597.18
disreputable action 371.3
disreputable character 371.2
disreputably 371.7; *unvirtuously* 448.16
disrepute 371.1; *abasement* 298.6, *disesteem* 436.2, *depravity* 448.2, *humbling* 597.9
disreputed *depraved* 448.10
disrespect 436.1, 436.18; *dislike* 291.1, 291.12, *disrepute* 371.1, *rudeness* 400.2, *be insolent* 400.14, *disapproval* 438.1, *defiance* 466.3
disrespected 436.16; *disliked* 291.10
disrespectful 436.9; *rude* 400.9, *discourteous* 411.5, *disapproving* 438.8, *defiant* 466.7
disrespectfully 436.25; *rudely* 400.19, 411.9, *unsocially* 409.13, *defiantly* 466.14
disrespectfulness *rudeness* 400.2, *disrespect* 436.1
disrobe *undress* 614.18, *make nude* 614.19
disrobed *undressed* 614.11
disrobement *undressing* 614.2

disrober *nude person* 614.5
disrobing *undressing* 614.2
disrupt 768.12; *cause confusion* 51.9, *displace* 574.15, *be untimely* 660.8, *disorder* 766.17, *interrupt* 775.14, *be inconvenient* 804.9, *cause difficulties* 824.22
disrupted 768.8; *disordered* 766.9, *interrupted* 775.9
disrupting *untimely* 660.5, *inconvenient* 804.5
disruption 766.7, 768.4; *confusion* 51.2, *destroying* 523.2, *untimeliness* 660.1, *separation* 753.1, *disorder* 766.1, *intervention* 775.5, *inconvenience* 804.1
disruptive *disorderly* 51.6, 766.15, *disturbing* 768.9, *inconvenient* 804.5, *troublesome* 824.13
disruptively 766.26; *confusedly* 51.11, *at the wrong time* 660.12, *disturbingly* 768.13, *inconveniently* 804.11, *perversely* 824.27
disruptiveness *lawlessness* 766.6
dissatisfaction 274.1; *dilution* 220.2, *dislike* 291.1, *disappointment* 293.1, *boredom* 296.1, *resentment* 302.1, *irritableness* 304.3, *envy* 314.1, *disapproval* 347.2, 438.1, *protest* 507.1, *noncompletion* 762.2
dissatisfactory *unsatisfactory* 274.5
dissatisfied 274.4; *displeased* 291.6, *disappointed* 293.4, *bored* 296.5, *resentful* 302.8, *irritable* 304.9, *envious* 314.4, *dissenting* 347.7, *disapproving* 438.8, *protesting* 507.5
dissatisfied customer *dissatisfied person* 274.3, *protester* 507.4
dissatisfiedly *disappointedly* 293.11
dissatisfied person 274.3
dissatisfy 274.6; *cause dislike* 291.16, *disappoint* 293.9, *bore* 296.8, *make irritable* 304.15, *be imperfect* 806.8
dissatisfying *disliked* 291.10, *disappointing* 293.6, *maddening* 302.12
dissatisfyingly *maddeningly* 302.25
dissave *expend* 491.11
dissaving *extravagance* 500.1
dissect *divide* 753.18, *deconstruct* 758.7, *part* 760.14
dissection *anatomy* 13.12, *separation* 753.1, *deconstruction* 758.2
dissemblance *ungenuineness* 192.2, *indirectness* 607.3, *dissimilarity* 734.1
dissemble *deceive* 181.14, 330.12, *be untruthful* 192.20, *be equivocal* 380.7, *do great deeds* 412.14, *circumlocute* 607.12, *distort the truth* 627.12, *hide* 844.13
dissembler *one who conceals* 181.7, *hypocrite* 192.9, *cunning person* 822.3
dissembling *ungenuine* 192.13, *hypocritical* 330.10, *indirect* 607.8
dissemblingly *untruthfully* 192.27
disseminate *communicate* 170.12, *publish* 173.15, *transfer* 685.8, *disperse* 776.12, *broadcast* 778.16
disseminated *published* 173.12, 175.8, *dispersed* 776.6
disseminated sclerosis *neurological disease* 114.20
dissemination *communication* 170.2, *public information* 170.5,

publishing 173.2, *transmission* 685.3, *dispersion* 776.1
disseminative *dispersive* 776.10
disseminatively *dispersively* 776.17
dissension 272.3, 732.4; *hostility* 63.1, *dissentience* 347.3, *contention* 422.1, *disobedience* 427.1, *censure* 438.3, *disagreement* 463.1, *disunity* 753.4, *conflict* 828.3
dissent 347.1, 347.8, 506.2, 506.9, 732.13, 782.2; *discuss* 4.22, *oppose* 63.11, 375.13, *disbelief* 88.1, *disbelieve* 88.8, *negation* 190.1, *negate* 190.16, *quarrel* 272.9, *react against* 291.15, *debate* 319.3, 319.13, *argue* 329.11, *protest* 331.19, 507.1, 507.7, *doubt* 333.19, *opposition* 375.2, *disobedience* 416.2, *be insubordinate* 416.8, *resistance* 417.1, *resist* 417.10, *contention* 422.1, *conflict* 422.26, *disobey* 427.12, *disagreement* 463.1, *disagree* 463.8, 753.19, *not observe* 466.9, *not conform* 782.18, *objection* 828.2, *object* 828.18
dissenter 347.5, 463.5, 782.8; *disbeliever* 88.5, *negator* 190.8, *protester* 331.8, 507.4, *questioner* 333.9, *individualist* 756.3, *opposer* 828.9
dissenters 347.6
dissentience 347.3
dissentient *arguing* 329.6, *dissenter* 347.5, 463.5, 782.8, *dissenting* 347.7, *disagreeing* 463.6, *protester* 507.4, *dissident* 782.12, *opposer* 828.9, *discordant* 828.12
dissentiently 347.10
dissenting 347.7, 506.6, 732.9; *aggressive* 63.9, *disbelieving* 88.6, *negational* 190.9, *argumentative* 319.10, *arguing* 329.6, *demonstrating* 331.14, *dissentience* 347.3, *refusing* 375.9, *resistant* 417.6, *disobedient* 427.10, *censuring* 438.12, *disagreeing* 463.6, *protesting* 507.5, *disunited* 753.10, *dissident* 782.12, *discordant* 828.12, *independent* 829.12
dissentingly 732.17; *negatively* 190.22, *dissentiently* 347.10, *resistingly* 417.14, *disobediently* 427.14, *in disagreement* 463.12, *uncooperatively* 506.11, *disunitedly* 753.25
dissentious *objectionable* 272.7, *argumentative* 329.7
dissertate 203.5
dissertation 203.1; *nonfiction* 139.6, *public speaking* 205.11, *judgment* 341.1
dissertational 203.4
dissertator 203.3
disservice *malignity* 306.5, *uselessness* 802.1
dissidence *dissentience* 347.3, *disagreement* 463.1, *defiance* 466.3, *dissent* 506.2, 782.2, *objection* 828.2
dissident 782.12; *disbeliever* 88.5, *protester* 331.8, 507.4, *dissenter* 347.5, 463.5, 782.8, *dissenting* 347.7, 506.6, *refusing* 375.9, *troublemaker* 427.5, *disagreeing* 463.6, *nonobservant* 466.5, *defiant* 466.7, *refuser* 506.4, *deviant* 698.7, *opposer* 828.9, *discordant* 828.12
dissidently *uncooperatively* 506.11
dissidents *dissenters* 347.6

dissilience *violence* 520.1

dissimilar 734.4; *misrepresented* 188.4, *different* 463.7, *disparate* 728.9, *diverse* 732.5, *unequal* 741.4

dissimilarity 734.1; *difference* 463.4, *disparity* 728.3, *diversity* 732.1, *originality* 737.1, *inequality* 741.1

dissimilarly 734.10; *differently* 463.13, *disparately* 728.19, *diversely* 732.14, *unequally* 741.10

dissimilate *make unlike* 734.9

dissimilation *syntax* 5.32, *dissimilarity* 734.1

dissimilative *dissimilar* 734.4

dissimilatory *dissimilar* 734.4

dissimilitude *dissimilarity* 734.1

dissimulate *be untruthful* 192.20, *deceive* 330.12

dissimulating *ungenuine* 192.13, *hypocritical* 330.10

dissimulation Collective Names 59, *evasion* 181.5, *ungenuineness* 192.2, *deed* 412.2

dissimulator *hypocrite* 192.9

dissipate *waste* 96.15, 500.7, *cause to disappear* 265.7, *overindulge* 456.11, *be wasteful* 468.16, *go to waste* 468.19, *expend* 491.11, *abolish* 523.11, *dilute* 776.14

dissipated 456.7; *disappeared* 265.4, *immoral* 432.9, *weakened* 517.9, *diluted* 776.8

dissipatedly *immorally* 432.18

dissipated person *loser* 468.8

dissipating *dissipated* 456.7

dissipation 456.2; *wave property* 10.12, *waste* 96.1, 468.5, *physical pleasure* 214.1, *disappearance* 265.1, *immorality* 432.1, *unrestrainedness* 500.2, *weakness* 517.1, *dilution* 776.3

dissipative *dispersive* 776.10

dissipatively *dispersively* 776.17

dissociability *unsociability* 409.1

dissociable *unsociable* 409.6

dissocial *unsociable* 409.6

dissociate 375.14; *react* 11.38, *not connect* 728.13, *separate* 753.12

dissociated *psychologically disturbed* 108.39, *disavowing* 190.12, *separate* 724.10, *unconnected* 728.8

dissociate oneself *disavow* 190.18

dissociate oneself from *be against* 828.17

dissociation 375.4; *dissociative disorder* 108.17, *disavowal* 190.3, *separateness* 724.3, *unconnectedness* 728.2, *deconstruction* 758.2, *uncooperativeness* 828.4

dissociation energy *chemical bond* 11.6

dissociation reaction *neurosis* 108.9

dissociative *disavowing* 190.12

dissociative amnesia *dissociative disorder* 108.17

dissociative disorder 108.17

dissociative disorders *mental disorder* 108.8

dissociative fugue *dissociative disorder* 108.17

dissociative identity disorder *dissociative disorder* 108.17

dissoluble *liquefiable* 555.21, *separable* 753.11

dissolute *immoral* 432.9, *dissipated* 456.7

dissolutely *immorally* 432.18

dissoluteness *immorality* 432.1, *dissipation* 456.2

dissolution *mortality* 29.2,

---

disappearance 265.1, *destroying* 523.2, *fluidization* 555.8, *separation* 753.1, *deconstruction* 758.2, *annihilation* 773.4, *disbandment* 776.2

dissolutional *liquefying* 555.20

dissolution of marriage *divorce* 66.1

dissolvable *liquefiable* 555.21, *separable* 753.11

dissolve 555.23; *solidify* 11.37, *motion-picture editing* 137.8, *disappear* 265.5, *abolish* 523.11, *dilute* 557.30, 776.14, *convert* 670.11, *cease to exist* 718.13, *change by degrees* 739.8, *take apart* 753.16, *annihilate* 773.22, *disband* 776.13

dissolved *divorced* 66.7, *liquefied* 555.19, *mixed* 751.8, *annihilated* 773.16, *disbanded* 776.7

dissolve into chaos *be disordered* 766.21

dissolvent *solvent* 555.9

dissolve one's marriage *divorce* 66.9

dissolver *solvent* 555.9

dissolving *disappearing* 265.3, *fluidization* 555.8, *liquefying* 555.20

dissolving agent *solvent* 555.9

dissonance 241.1; *harsh sound* 238.1, *disagreement* 463.1

dissonant 241.4; *strident* 238.4, *disagreeing* 463.6

dissonant chord *musical dissonance* 241.2

dissonantly 241.7; *in disagreement* 463.12

dissuade 179.7; *advise* 176.9, *warn* 814.8, *hinder* 826.15

dissuaded 179.5

dissuading *dissuasive* 179.4

dissuasion 179.1; *communication* 176.3, *warning* 814.1, *hindrance* 826.1

dissuasive 179.4; *advisory* 176.7, *warning* 814.6, *hindering* 826.12

dissuasively 179.12; *advisorily* 176.12, *with delay* 826.22

distaff *weaving* 609.2, *axle* 682.7

distaff side *womenfolk* 33.14

distal *away* 585.6

distance 585.1, 804.4; *swimming* 164.12, *that which makes invisible* 245.2, *murk* 248.2, *avoidance* 386.1, *unsociability* 409.1, *intervening space* 563.8, *interval* 587.1, Fields of Measurement 589, *measurability* 589.2, *measuring instrument* 589.12, *length* 590.1, *breadth* 592.1

distance between *interval* 587.1

distance event *competitive fishing* 154.5

distance freestyle race *competitive swimming* 164.3

distance oneself *keep away* 585.9

distances Fields of Measurement 589

distance swimmer *swimmer* 164.11

distant 585.5, 804.8; *estranged* 63.8, *faint* 233.6, *difficult to see* 245.4, *murky* 248.5, *apathetic* 322.4, *unsociable* 409.6, *insufficient* 517.11, *later* 658.9, *external* 724.11

distantly 585.11; *faintly* 233.11, *away* 386.23, *resignedly* 392.6, *unsocially* 409.13, *externally* 724.19

distant past *oldness* 653.1

---

distant place 585.3

distant sound *faintness of sound* 233.1

distant time *different time* 648.1

distaste *dislike* 291.1, 300.2, *disapproval* 438.1

distasteful *unpleasant* 272.6, *disliked* 291.10, *ugly* 531.3

distastefully 291.19; *unpleasantly* 272.10, *inelegantly* 517.1

distastefulness *unpleasantness* 272.1

distemper *animal disease* 34.10, *illness* 114.2, *material* 143.9, *coloring agent* 251.5, *color* 251.16

distend *enlarge* 194.12, *be elastic* 546.7, *extend* 563.14, *swell* 581.15, *be convex* 634.7, *increase* 746.6

distended *elastic* 546.5, *fat* 579.15, *swelled* 581.10, *convex* 634.5

distender *enlarger* 581.8

distending *elastic* 546.5

distensibility *enlargeability* 581.6

distensible *elastic* 546.5, *enlargeable* 581.13

distension *elasticity* 546.1

distension *or* **distention** *swelling* 581.2

distensive *enlargeable* 581.13

distention *convexity* 634.1

distich *part of poem* 139.9, *twosome* 789.3

distill *extract* 11.41, *provide drink* 93.21, *purify* 111.19, *refine* 534.7, *gasify* 556.23, *obtain an extract* 711.19

distillate *extract* 711.8, *quintessence* 723.3

distillation *process* 11.15, *oil* 106.7, *cleaning* 111.2, *vaporization* 556.9, *obtaining of an extract* 711.7, *quintessence* 723.3

distilled *status adjectives* 11.25, *drinkable* 93.18, *cleaned* 111.14

distilled liquor *alcoholic drink* 93.9

distilled water *water* 557.1

distillery *drink provider* 93.15

distinct *universal* 6.67, *clear* 196.2, 244.6, *visible* 242.19, 244.5, *demonstrable* 547.1, *simple* 363.6, *recognizable* 337.10, *simple* 363.6, *recognizable* 363.7, *excellent* 445.13, *strong* 516.9, *nonuniform* 734.5, *unjoined* 753.9, *special* 779.10, *singular* 788.13, *important* 799.7

distinction 777.8; *nobleness* 70.3, *dignity* 297.4, *discrimination* 337.1, *judgment* 341.1, *recognizability* 363.3, *repute* 370.1, *excellence* 445.4, *refinement* 534.1, *subtlety* 534.2, *nonuniformity* 734.2, *importance* 799.1

distinction without a difference, a *equality* 740.1

distinctive *elegant* 527.3, *characteristic* 723.9, *nonuniform* 734.5, *unjoined* 753.9, *typical* 777.10, *special* 779.10

distinctive feature *special feature* 779.4

distinctively *eminently* 370.7, *nonuniformly* 734.11, *in isolation* 753.24, *taxonomically* 777.15, *characteristically* 779.20

distinctiveness *identity* 184.2, *recognizability* 363.3, *elegance* 527.1, *specialty* 779.1, *singularity* 788.4

distinctly *clearly* 196.4, *visibly* 242.28, 244.10, *discriminatingly* 337.15, *intelligibly* 363.13, *excellently* 445.21, *acutely* 516.18,

---

nonuniformly 734.11, *in isolation* 753.24, *specially* 779.19

distinctness *clarity* 196.1, 363.2, *visibility* 244.1

distinct possibility *equal chance* 842.7

distingué *refined* 534.5

distinguish *identify* 184.11, *see* 242.20, *discriminate* 337.12, *know* 348.10, *be wise* 352.6, *recognize* 363.11, *choose* 382.14, *exalt* 596.19, *characterize* 723.11, *779.15, *make unlike* 734.9, *set apart* 753.17

distinguishability *recognizability* 363.3

distinguishable *visible* 244.5, *recognizable* 363.7, *separable* 753.11

distinguished *dignified* 297.11, *reputable* 370.3, *elegant* 527.3, *exalted* 596.10, *nonuniform* 734.5, *excellent* 744.14, *exceptional* 779.13, *notable* 799.11

Distinguished Flying Cross US Military Medals 58

distinguishedly *exaltedly* 596.22, *nonuniformly* 734.11

Distinguished Service Cross US Military Medals 58

Distinguished Service Medal US Military Medals 58

distinguishing *identification* 184.1, *characteristic* 723.9, 779.12, *nonuniform* 734.5

distinguishing feature(s) *nature* 723.4

distinguishingly *nonuniformly* 734.11

distinguishment *exaltation* 596.3, *nonuniformity* 734.2

distort 627.9, 698.20; *misrepresent* 188.6, 193.17, 366.5, *practice sophistry* 330.11, *misjudge* 342.9, *err* 351.14, *misuse* 395.6, *deprave* 448.14, *make ugly* 531.4, *blemish* 533.7, *circumlocute* 607.12, *make shapeless* 625.3, *convolute* 632.6, *change for the worse* 665.18, *transform* 670.13, *delude* 720.16, *be incorrect* 722.13, *pervert* 808.22

distorted 627.6; *spatial* 6.76, *misrepresented* 188.4, *partially true* 192.18, *misrepresentative* 193.14, *sophistic* 330.7, *erroneous* 351.11, *misinterpreted* 366.3, *misused* 395.3, *blemished* 533.5, *indirect* 607.8, *oblique* 698.11, *incorrect* 722.8, *disparate* 728.9

distorted image *misrepresentation* 188.1

distortedly 627.14; *misrepresentedly* 366.7, *abusively* 395.8, *incorrectly* 722.16, *disparately* 728.19

distorted truth *partial truth* 192.7

distorter 627.5; *one who misrepresents* 193.9

distorting mirror *reflector* 242.10, *visual distortion* 243.6

distortion 627.1; *deformation* 14.16, *radio reception* 172.2, *misrepresentation* 188.1, 193.4, 351.5, 366.2, *partial truth* 192.7, *sophistry* 330.1, *misjudgment* 342.1, *misuse* 395.1, *blemish* 533.1, *indirectness* 607.3, *change for the worse* 665.5, *torsion* 698.5, *untrueness* 722.3, *disparity* 728.3

distortion of body 627.3

distortion of face 627.2

distortion of truth 627.4

distortive *misrepresentative* 193.14, *indirect* 607.8

---

distort the truth 192.25, 627.12
distract *disrupt* 768.12
distracted *inattentive* 324.5, *oblivious* 355.9, *disrupted* 768.8
distractedly 768.14; *forgetfully* 355.14
distracting *disturbing* 768.9
distraction *inattention* 324.1, *disruption* 768.4
distrain *take back* 477.17, *compensate* 743.7
distraint *taking back* 477.4, *compensation* 743.1
distress *affliction* 117.1, *pain* 215.1, *sorrow* 270.1, *lamentation* 280.1, *be evil* 486.1, *poverty* 486.1, *disturb* 768.10, *haste* 818.1, *adversity* 848.1
distress call *proclamation* 183.8
distressed *afflicting* 117.11, *feeling pain* 215.6, *sorrowful* 270.4, *fearful* 283.11, *disturbed* 768.6, *troubled* 824.15
distress flare *danger signal* 811.5
distressing 270.6; *painful* 215.4, *lamentable* 280.6, *pitiful* 308.5, *disturbing* 768.9
distressingly *destructively* 446.13
distress signal *signal* 183.6, *danger signal* 811.5
distributary *tributary* 570.2
distribute *provision* 89.9, *publish* 174.19, *report* 175.9, *allocate* 474.5, *remunerate* 489.21, *transport* 686.10, *make average* 742.9, *part* 760.14, *arrange* 767.18, *disperse* 776.12, *class* 777.12
distributed *published* 173.12, 174.18, *allocated* 474.4, *dispersed* 776.6
distributer *transporter* 686.4
distribution *economic factor* 56.8, *allocation* 474.1, *selling* 482.1, *transportation* 686.1, *order* 765.1, *dispersion* 776.1
distributive *dispersive* 776.10
distributively *dispersively* 776.17
distributive operation *or* **law** *operation* 6.12
distributor *garden tool* 17.7, *agent* 123.15, *trader* 480.11, *power supplier* 514.14, *middleman* 772.7
distributor of largesse *giver* 472.7
district *body politic* 50.3, *place of residence* 209.4, *region* 564.1, *administrative region* 564.4, *administrative* 564.13, *urban area* 567.10, *part* 760.1
district attorney (DA) *law officer* 53.6, *accuser* 442.3, *one who restrains* 830.7
district court *type of court* 54.9
district magistrate *judge* 54.10
district nurse *nurse* 107.23
district official *union member* 57.6
distrust *disbelief* 88.1, *disbelieve* 88.8, *suspicion* 314.3, 841.2, *suspect* 314.9, *uncertainty* 333.6, *doubt* 333.19, *be uncertain* 841.17
distrustful *disbelieving* 88.6, *suspicious* 314.6, *skeptical* 333.14, *uncertain* 841.9
distrustfully *disbelievingly* 88.10, *suspiciously* 314.12
distrustfulness *suspicion* 314.3
disturb 768.10; *arouse sensation* 212.11, *displease* 272.8, *displace* 574.15, *be untimely* 660.8, *agitate* 684.22, *deconstruct* 758.7, *disorder* 766.17, *discompose* 766.18, *derange* 766.23, *interrupt* 775.14, *be inconvenient* 804.9, *cause*

difficulties 824.22, *make uncertain* 841.19
disturbance 768.1; *activity* 414.1, *violence by person* 520.2, *displacement* 574.1, *untimeliness* 660.1, *tumult* 684.2, *atmospheric agitation* 684.13, *disintegration* 758.1, *disorder* 766.1, *disruption* 766.7, 768.4, *derangement* 766.8, *commotion* 768.5, *intervention* 775.5, *inconvenience* 804.1
disturbed 768.6; *insane* 110.9, *mentally ill* 110.11, *worried* 283.11, *displaced* 574.8, *agitated* 684.15, *confused* 766.12, *deranged* 766.16, *interrupted* 775.9
disturbing 768.9; *displaced* 574.8, *untimely* 660.5, *inconvenient* 804.5
disturbingly 768.13; *at the wrong time* 660.12
disulfide bonds *protein* 12.9
disunion *dissentience* 347.3, *separation* 753.1, *deconstruction* 758.2
disunite *antagonize* 63.12, *separate* 753.12, *disconnect* 775.12
disunited 753.10; *estranged* 63.8, *separate* 753.7, *disintegrated* 758.3, *discontinuous* 775.7
disunitedly 753.25
disunity 753.4; *dissension* 272.3, *disagreement* 463.1, *separation* 753.1
disusage *unaccustomedness* 398.1
disuse 394.3; *discarding* 383.3, *discard* 383.12, *relinquishment* 392.1, *stop using* 394.10, *unaccustomedness* 398.1
disused 394.8; *discarded* 383.8
dital harp Musical Instruments 142
ditch *green bowling* 151.3, *discard* 383.12, *stop using* 394.10, *military defenses* 419.9, *valley* 572.8, *crack* 587.2, 587.7, *narrow place* 593.2, *enclosing thing* 619.3, *furrow* 638.1, 638.5, *channel* 691.10, *protection* 810.2, *stratagem* 822.2, *barrier* 826.7
ditch [Inf] *renounce* 392.4
ditchwater *swill* 112.6
diterpene *terpene* 12.20
dither *sway* 378.12, *vacillate* 683.14, *agitation* 684.1, *be agitated* 684.21, *pitch* 684.25, *hesitate* 841.18
ditherer *vacillator* 378.3, *inactive person* 413.8
dithering *unsteady* 378.7, *weak-willed* 517.10, *vacillating* 683.10
dithyramb Poem or Verse Forms 139
dithyrambic *articulate* 205.16
dithyrambist *author* 139.13
ditto *agree with* 462.10, *copy* 730.17, 736.10, *agreeingly* 730.19, *imitate* 736.9, *imitatively* 736.12, *repetition* 797.1, *again* 797.23
ditto [Inf] *copy* 730.5, *duplicate* 736.4
ditto mark Reference Signs 183
ditty Poem or Verse Forms 139
diuretic *urinary* 25.15, *purgative* 115.7
diurnal *of animals* 34.13, *daily* 655.6, *cyclic* 663.7
diurnally *daily* 655.8, *cyclically* 663.15
diva *skilled person* 127.7, *actor* 136.25, *singer* 141.4, *paragon* 744.6
divagate *go astray* 698.17

divagation *divergence* 607.2, *deviation* 698.1
divagatory *wandering* 698.13
divalent *chemical compound* 11.4
divan *couch* 101.7, *type of bed* 101.9
divaricate *deviate* 698.15, *divergent* 703.6, *diverge* 703.10
divaricating *diverging* 698.12, *divergent* 703.6
divarication *deviation* 698.1, *divergence* 703.1
dive 164.15; *row* 150.32, *play soccer* 163.8, *deepen* 598.21, *verticality* 602.1, *fall vertically* 602.10, *flight maneuver* 689.6, *maneuver* 689.14, *sail* 690.16, *acceleration* 694.3, *be swift* 694.10, *fall* 714.4, *descend* 714.12, *drop* 714.15
dive [Inf] *hotel* 60.12, *gambling house* 167.5
dive bomber *attacker* 418.10
dive bombing *air attack* 418.4
dive categories *competitive diving* 164.7
dive difficulty *competitive diving* 164.7
dive in *make a beginning* 771.26
dive into *fall into* 706.15
dive positions *competitive diving* 164.7
diver *water bird* 36.9, *swimmer* 164.11, *descender* 714.8
diverge 607.11, 703.10, 734.8, 753.20, 776.16; *align* 6.92, *be circuitous* 199.6, *be different* 463.11, *deviate* 698.15, *deflect* 698.26, *be disparate* 728.14, *be diverse* 732.10
divergence 607.2, 703.1, 776.5; *vector* 6.48, *difference* 463.4, *distance* 585.1, *deviation* 698.1, *disparity* 728.3, *diversity* 732.1, *nonuniformity* 734.2, *separation* 753.1
divergence zone *plate tectonics* 8.19
divergency *divergence* 703.1
divergent 607.7, 703.6, 776.11; *linear* 6.77, *different* 463.7, *diverging* 698.12, *disparate* 728.9, *diverse* 732.5, *nonuniform* 734.5, *apart* 753.8
divergently 607.14, 703.16; *differently* 463.13, *disparately* 728.19, *diversely* 732.14, *nonuniformly* 734.11, *apart* 753.23
divergent series *sequence* 6.18
divergent strabismus *faulty vision* 243.1
diverging 698.12; *divergent* 607.7, 703.6, *diverse* 732.5
diverging lines *line* 6.35
divers *varied* 732.6, *various* 793.7
diverse 732.5; *arguing* 329.6, *irregular* 664.3, *disparate* 728.9, *nonuniform* 734.5, *unequal* 741.4, *various* 793.7
diversely 732.14; *variedly* 263.12, *argumentatively* 329.15, *disparately* 728.19, *nonuniformly* 734.11, *unequally* 741.10, *plurally* 793.10
diversification *variegation* 263.1, *change for the better* 665.4, *variety* 732.2
diversified 732.8; *general* 778.9
diversiform *varied* 732.6
diversify 732.11; *variegate* 263.11, *change* 665.14, *cause change* 665.16, *be disparate* 728.14
diversion *game* 167.1, *amusement* 167.7, 277.2, *artifice* 193.5, *pleasure* 271.2, *misuse* 395.1, *alteration* 665.2, *thoroughfare*

692.6, *deviation* 698.1, *deviating course* 698.2, *secondary matter* 800.6
diversity 732.1; *variegation* 263.1, *irregularity* 664.1, *change* 665.1, *disparity* 728.3, *nonuniformity* 734.2, *inequality* 741.1, *nonconformity* 782.1, *multiplicity* 793.2
diversity of colors *variegation* 263.1
divert 698.16; *be humorous* 277.11, *misuse* 395.6, *not pay* 490.9, *cause to flow* 570.11, *change* 665.14, *cause change* 665.16, *service* 689.16, *deviate* 698.15, *misdirect* 698.21
diverted *misused* 395.3
divertimento *play* 136.2, Musical Forms 140
diverting *recreational* 167.10, *cheering* 269.8, *humorous* 277.9
divertissement *play* 136.2
Dives *wealthy person* 485.6
dives *diving* 164.6
divest *lose* 468.12, *take back* 477.17, *undress* 614.18, *take off* 749.7, *terminate* 834.7
divested *undressed* 614.11
divestiture *undressing* 614.2
divestment *loss* 468.1, *taking back* 477.4, *undressing* 614.2
dividable *allocated* 474.4
divide 753.18, 787.7; *add* 6.86, 784.11, *antagonize* 63.12, *practice surgery* 107.33, *discriminate* 337.12, *dissent* 347.8, *withdraw* 392.5, *disagree* 463.8, *pick a fight* 463.10, *allocate* 474.5, *mountain range* 569.3, *itemize* 577.13, *interface* 616.5, *separate* 703.12, 724.14, *quantify* 738.7, *make average* 742.9, *come between* 753.21, *part* 760.14, *disperse* 776.12, *sort* 777.13
divide by five 792.25
divide by four *quadrisect* 791.12
divide by seven *divide by five* 792.25
divide by six *divide by five* 792.25
divide by three *trisect* 790.11
divide by two *halve* 789.15
divided *estranged* 63.8, *judged* 337.10, *allocated* 474.4, *itemized* 577.9, *separate* 753.7, *partial* 760.11, *component* 760.12
divided by two *half* 789.12
divided highway *road attribute* 687.3
divide fifty-fifty *split down the middle* 772.20
divide in half *halve* 789.15
divide into four *quadrisect* 791.12
dividend *division* 6.16, *something received* 473.2, *portion* 474.2, *produce* 522.5, *surplus* 750.4
dividends *stock exchange* 457.3, *profit* 467.6
divide proportionately *allocate* 474.5
divider *wall* 134.9
dividers *geometric construction* 6.47, *measuring instrument* 589.12, *calculator* 784.5
divide up *allocate* 474.5, *divide* 753.18
dividing *separate* 753.7
dividing by four *quadrisection* 791.5
dividing by three *trisection* 790.5
dividing by two *halving* 789.6
dividing line 740.6; *separator* 753.5
divi-divi Trees and Shrubs 43

divination 86.5, 358.2; *divine manifestation* 82.5, *impression* 266.2, *precognition* 320.2, *prediction* 357.3
divinatory 86.18; *precognitive* 320.7
divine 82.16, 86.24, 358.15; *masterful* 68.15, *theologian* 81.20, *theological* 81.24, *priest* 84.8, *idyllic* 214.11, *pleasant* 271.5, *be intuitive* 320.9, *suppose* 359.8, *look ahead* 650.11, *self-existent* 717.15
divine afflatus *inspiration* 360.2
divine attribute 82.4
divine essence *deity* 82.1
divine justice *retribution* 454.7
divinely 82.24
divine manifestation 82.5
Divine Mind *God* 82.6
divine nature *divine attribute* 82.4
divineness *deity* 82.1
divine office *public worship* 83.3
divine principle *deity* 82.1
diviner 86.14; *intuitive person* 320.5, *predictor* 357.4, 650.5, *forecaster* 358.9, *visionary* 360.9, *interpreter* 365.6, *warner* 814.5
divine right *legal power* 52.2, *claim* 429.3
divine service *public worship* 83.3
diving 164.6, 164.13, Sporting Activities 145, *rowing techniques* 150.16, *rowing* 150.27, *swimming* 164.1, *falling* 714.11
diving bell *oceanography* 571.5, *bathymetry* 598.3, *descender* 714.8
diving bird *water bird* 36.9, *descender* 714.8
diving board *swimming equipment* 164.8
diving boat Ships and Boats 690
diving duck *water bird* 36.9
diving vessel *oceanography* 571.5
divining *divination* 86.5, *interpretive* 365.8
divining rod *detector* 345.6
divining rods *divination* 86.5
divinity *deity* 82.1, *self-existence* 717.8
divinity student *theologian* 81.20
divinization *deification* 82.13
divinize *deify* 82.23
divisi Musical Terms and Expression Marks 140
divisibility *division* 6.16
divisible 6.71; *allocated* 474.4, *separable* 753.11
division 6.16, 577.6; *military organization* 58.4, *force* 59.10, *army unit* 77.14, *naval unit* 77.20, *surgery* 107.15, *sportsman* 145.4, *discrimination* 337.1, *faction* 347.4, *divisiveness* 463.2, *allocation* 474.1, *region* 564.1, *administrative region* 564.4, *passage* 692.1, *parting* 703.2, *setting apart* 753.2, *separateness* 753.3, *collection* 757.3, *part* 760.1, *piece* 760.2, *musical part* 760.8, *category* 767.6, *class* 777.1, *calculation* 784.1, *fractional part* 787.2
Division I *windsurfing classes* 150.22
Division II *windsurfing classes* 150.22
Division III *windsurfing classes* 150.22
divisional *discriminating* 337.9, *administrative* 564.13, *fractional* 787.5
divisionally *thematically* 577.16
divisionism Western Art Styles 133

division line *interface* 616.1
division sign *mathematical symbol* 6.11, *symbol* 183.3
divisive *dissenting* 347.7, *disagreeing* 463.6, *interfacial* 616.4
divisively *discriminatingly* 337.15, *dissentiently* 347.10, *in disagreement* 463.12, *interfacially* 616.7, *destructively* 758.9
divisiveness 463.2
divisor *division* 6.16
divorce 66.1, 66.9; *personal conflict* 63.2, *unconnectedness* 728.2, *not connect* 728.13, *separation* 753.1, *separate* 753.12, *diverge* 753.20, *singleness* 788.6
divorcé *single man* 32.5, *divorced person* 66.4, *single person* 788.7
divorce case *divorce court* 66.3
divorce court 66.3
divorced 66.7; *unconnected* 728.8, *separate* 753.7, *single* 788.16
divorce decree *divorce* 66.1
divorced man *divorced person* 66.4
divorced person 66.4
divorced woman *divorced person* 66.4
divorcée *single woman* 33.5, *divorced person* 66.4, *single person* 788.7
divorcement *divorce* 66.1, *separation* 753.1
divorcer *divorced person* 66.4
divorce settlement *divorce court* 66.3, *transfer of property* 470.4
divot *grassland* 45.2, *golfing terms* 156.3, *particle* 760.4
divot [Inf] *hairdressing* 530.7
divulge 180.9; *educate* 48.22, *publish* 173.15, *detect* 345.12, *reveal* 843.14
divulged *manifest* 843.9
divulgement *divulgence* 180.2
divulgence 180.2
divulging *disclosing* 180.6
divvied [Inf] *allocated* 474.4
divvy [Inf] *allocate* 474.5
divvying [Inf] *allocation* 474.1
Diwali *religious festival* 85.13
Dixie or **Dixieland** *regions of the United States* 564.7
Dixiecrats Political Parties 50
Dixieland *musical* 140.25
Dixieland jazz *jazz* 140.5
dizzily *changeably* 666.7
dizziness 682.2; *symptom* 114.3, *drunken behavior* 121.4, Phobias 283, *absent-mindedness* 324.2, *poor health* 517.3, *imbalance* 741.2
dizzy 682.13; *slightly drunk* 121.26, *careless* 324.8, *irresolute* 666.4, *unbalanced* 741.5
djellabah *robe* 100.20
Djibouti Countries 566
djin *ghost* 86.11
D layer or **region** *atmospheric layer* 558.3
DNA *genetic material* 13.20, *means of identification* 184.3
DNA double helix *molecular biology* 13.18
DNA probe *molecular biology* 13.18
Dnieper or **Dnepr** Rivers 570
Dniester or **Dnestr** Rivers 570
do *suffice* 97.6, 273.10, *undertake* 391.7, *conduct oneself* 399.17, *behave toward* 399.20, *act* 412.11, *be active* 414.18, *perform* 465.5, *be operational* 509.10, *be an instrument* 511.7, *complete* 761.9, *be useful* 801.9, *be convenient* 803.5, *be effective* 845.15
do [Brit] *social gathering* 59.7

do [Inf] *overcharge* 496.10
do a bad job *be clumsy* 128.9
doable *workable* 509.8, *possible* 836.5
do a christie *ski* 162.35
do addition *add* 748.11
do a deal *negotiate* 460.6, *contract* 462.11, *bargain* 480.20
do a favor *be charitable* 305.12, *improve* 825.26
do again *restore* 671.10, *repeat* 797.15
do a good deed *philanthropize* 307.8
do a good turn *philanthropize* 307.8, *better* 445.17, *improve* 825.26
do a handspring *exercise* 157.12
do a handstand *exercise* 157.12
do a job [Inf] *steal* 479.14
do a job on [Inf] *contend* 422.22
do a kindness *be benevolent* 305.10
do all one can *exert oneself* 122.11
do all right by oneself *be prosperous* 847.6
do all that is possible *suffice* 97.6
do all the talking *monopolize the conversation* 211.5
do an about-face *reverse* 671.9
do and no more *suffice* 97.6
do a nine-to-five [Inf] *work* 122.8
do a paper *dissertate* 203.5
do a portrait *describe* 202.15
do a prescribed *or an optional* **exercise** *exercise* 157.12
do a project on *raise the point* 328.10
do a repeat *repeat* 797.15
do a slow burn [Inf] *become angry* 302.20
do as one chooses *be independent* 829.18
do as one is told *obey* 426.7
do as one likes *or chooses or pleases* *follow one's own will* 372.13
do as one pleases *be independent* 829.18
do as one would be done by *be benevolent* 305.10
do as others do *abide by* 781.12
do as the Romans do *abide by* 781.12
do a swap *trade* 480.18
do at the last moment *have no time to spare* 818.6
do a U-turn *equivocate* 380.8, *reverse* 671.9
do away with *kill* 30.19, *destroy* 523.10, *exterminate* 709.22, *cancel* 834.6
do away with oneself *commit suicide* 30.24
do a world of good *better* 445.17
do badly *be clumsy* 128.9, *fail* 846.12
do battle *battle* 76.33
dobbin *horse* 159.1
Doberman pinscher Breeds of Dogs 35
Dobrojea Breeds of Cattle 16
do business *occupy oneself* 412.15, *negotiate* 460.6, *trade* 480.18
do business with *trade* 480.18, *join with* 827.15
do by halves *not complete* 762.9
doc [Inf] *doctor* 107.19
docent *educator* 48.4
doch-an-dorrach *drink* 93.2, *parting* 705.3
do charity work *volunteer* 504.13
do chores *serve* 69.11

docile *educatable* 48.18, *acquiescent* 373.9, *submitting* 421.3, *obedient* 426.4, *deferential* 433.9, *disciplined* 765.17, *easygoing* 823.13
docilely *studiously* 48.26, *obediently* 426.9
docility *educatability* 48.9, *acquiescence* 373.3, *submission* 421.1, *obedience* 426.1, *deference* 433.4
dock *courtroom* 54.12, *storehouse* 105.8, *construction workplace* 124.10, *shorten* 591.9, *sail* 690.16, *stopover* 704.7, *land* 704.16, *place of departure* 705.4, *make smaller* 747.8, *take off* 749.7, *separate* 753.12, *harbor* 812.6
docked *summarized* 204.6, *reduced* 749.5, *shortened* 762.6
docker *laborer* 123.9, *transporter* 686.4
docket *means of identification* 184.3, *identify* 184.11, *record* 185.1, *register* 185.15, *bill* 785.4, *list of dates* 785.6
docking *rocketry* 7.32, *shortening* 591.2, *flight path* 691.12, *landing* 704.2, *subtraction* 749.1, *separateness* 753.3
Docklands *London* 567.8
dock wharf *water system* 551.13
dockyard *construction workplace* 124.10
do compulsory figures *ice-skate* 162.36
do credit to *meet with approval* 437.20
Doctor *professional title* 72.6
doctor 107.19; *person dealing with the dead* 29.8, *educator* 48.4, *practice medicine* 107.32, *professional worker* 123.11, *helper* 275.5, *account* 493.9, *influential person* 512.5, *change for the worse* 665.18, *mix* 751.12, *cure* 809.15, *support* 825.24
doctoral *curricular* 48.21
doctoral candidate *dissertator* 203.3
doctored *misrepresentative* 193.14
doctors Phobias 283
doctrinaire *theorist* 359.4, *convinced* 840.8
doctrinal *curricular* 48.21, *theological* 81.24, *believed* 87.8
doctrinally *religiously* 81.29
doctrinal theology Theologies 81
doctrine *philosophy* 4.1, *religion* 81.1, *belief system* 87.3, *code* 780.3
doctrine of chance *calculation of chance* 842.9
docudrama *movie type* 137.3, *program* 172.10
document 170.3; *chronicle* 3.15, *communication* 170.2, *communicate* 170.12, *report* 171.9, *broadcast* 172.13, *record* 185.1, 185.13, *verify* 336.8, *documentation* 339.6, *prove* 339.14, *circumstantiate* 726.12
documentary *chronicle* 3.4, *dramatic* 137.16, *broadcast news* 171.6, *recorded* 185.12, *factual account* 202.4, *narrative* 202.12, *evidential* 339.8, *realism* 719.3
documentary account *factual account* 202.4
documentary evidence *legal evidence* 339.4
documentary film *movie type* 137.3
documentary photography *photographic specialties* 132.2

documentary theater *theater movements* 136.9

documentation 339.6; *chronicle* 3.4, *record* 185.1, *verification* 336.1, *authorization* 340.4, *passport* 692.8

documented *chronicled* 3.12, *recorded* 185.12, *verifiable* 336.5, *verified* 336.7, *evidential* 339.8, *authorized* 340.8, *certain* 840.7

documents *record* 185.1, *verification* 336.1

dodder *age* 27.16, *be weak* 517.12, *grow old* 653.16

dodderer *older person* 27.7

doddering *aged* 27.15, *old* 653.10, *shaky* 684.18

dodecagon *eleven to nineteen* 792.7

dodecahedral *angled* 628.9

dodecahedron *polyhedron* 6.44, *angled figure* 628.3, *eleven to nineteen* 792.7

Dodecanese Islands 572

dodecaphonism *musical dissonance* 241.2

dodecaphony *musical dissonance* 241.2

dodge *social skill* 127.3, *conceal oneself* 181.15, *artifice* 193.5, *deceive* 193.16, 330.12, *scheme* 193.18, *sophism* 330.2, *evasion* 380.2, 386.5, *be equivocal* 380.7, *evade* 386.11, *method* 387.4, *not perform* 466.10, *lose someone* 468.20, *move sideways* 623.9, *move* 677.15, *means of escape* 816.4, *elude* 816.10, *stratagem* 822.2, *be cunning* 822.5

dodge about *be irresolute* 666.6

dodge ball Children's and Party Games 167

dodger *deceiver* 193.8, *avoider* 386.8

dodgery *deception* 193.1

dodge the issue *lack candor* 192.22

dodgily *hypocritically* 330.15

dodging *evasion* 181.5, *nonperforming* 466.6

dodging the issue *lack of candor* 192.4

dodgy *cunning* 330.8, *disreputable* 371.4

do dirt-track racing *race* 146.10

dodo *extinct bird* 36.14, *creature of habit* 397.8

do duty for *substitute for* 80.5, *aid* 275.10, *be a substitute* 672.6

doe *female animal* 33.15, *female mammal* 35.19

do easily 823.16

do easy work *work* 122.8

doer 412.3; *agent* 123.15, *manager* 126.7, *busy person* 414.10

doeskin *leather* 104.7, Fabrics and Fibers 130

do evil *be evil* 446.10

doff *stop using* 394.10, *take off* 749.7

doffing one's cap *deference* 410.4

doff one's cap *show respect* 435.16, *uncover* 614.17

doff one's hat *defer to* 410.12

doff one's hat to *compliment* 437.17

do for *destroy* 523.10

do for [Brit] *serve* 69.11, 825.29

do for effect *show off* 404.26, *put on a show* 404.28

do Formula 1 racing *race* 146.10

dog 35.10; *male animal* 32.15, *male mammal* 35.18, *defensive huddle* 155.10, *play defense* 155.19, *hunt*

160.12, follow 385.12, *stay near* 586.13

dog [Inf] *ugly thing* 531.2

dogbane Flowers 42

dog brush *cleaning tool* 111.10

dog collar *circular thing* 631.3

dog collar [Inf] *vestment* 84.11, *neckwear* 100.29

dog days *weather* 9.3, *hot weather* 9.22, *summer* 654.4

dog-ear *fold* 637.1, 637.7

dog-eared *used* 393.5, *folded* 637.5, *worn* 808.13

dog eat dog *anarchism* 51.3

dog-eat-dog *competitive* 422.21

dog-eat-dog competition *rivalry* 422.2

dogfight *battle* 76.23, *fight* 422.9, *duel* 422.12

dogfish *food fish and shellfish* 90.20

dog food *animal food* 90.2

dog fox *male animal* 32.15

dogged *steadfast* 284.11, *willful* 372.8, *tenacious* 376.9, *persevering* 377.6, *determined* 379.7

doggedly *steadfastly* 284.19, *persistently* 376.17, *perseveringly* 377.16, *obstinately* 379.11

doggedness *willfulness* 372.3, *resolution* 376.1, *tenacity* 376.4, *perseverance* 377.1, *determination* 379.2

dogger *pursuer* 385.5

doggerel *poetry* 139.8, *poetic* 139.19, *inelegant* 528.6

dogging *hunting* 160.2, *pursuit* 385.1

doggish *carnivorous* 35.26

doggone [Inf] *or* **doggoned** [Inf] *miscellaneous euphemisms* 301.12

doggy *carnivorous* 35.26

doghouse *cage* 60.15

dogie *young mammal* 35.20

dog in the manger *obstinate person* 379.4, *selfish person* 444.3, *hinderer* 826.11

dog-in-the-manger policy *exclusiveness* 764.4

dog Latin *slang* 5.19

dogleg *divergence* 607.2, *diverge* 607.11, *angle* 628.1, *deviating course* 698.2, *twist* 698.19

doglegged *divergent* 607.7, *angular* 628.7

dogleg hole *golf course* 156.2

doglike *carnivorous* 35.26

dog lover *animal welfarist* 34.9

dogma *philosophy* 4.1, *religion* 81.1, *belief system* 87.3, *code* 780.3

dogmatic *believing* 87.6, *emphatic* 200.3, *discriminatory* 337.11, *opinionated* 379.9, *convinced* 840.8

dogmatically *believingly* 87.12, *emphatically* 200.7, *prejudicially* 337.17, *with certainty* 840.16

dogmatic theology Theologies 81

dogmatism *opinionatedness* 379.3, *conviction* 840.2

dogmatist *bigot* 337.7, *obstinate person* 379.4

dogmatize *be obstinate* 379.10, *be certain* 840.13

dognap *steal* 479.14

dognapper *thief* 479.8

dognapping *kidnapping* 479.3

dog one's footsteps *follow* 385.12

do good *philanthropize* 307.8, *better* 445.17, *be virtuous* 447.8, *benefit* 801.10, *be convenient* 803.5

do-gooder *benevolent person* 305.6, *philanthropist* 307.5, *volunteer* 504.7

do-gooderism *philanthropy* 307.1

do-goodism *philanthropy* 307.1

do good works *be charitable* 305.12

dog-paddle *swim* 164.14

dog-paddling *survival swimming* 164.4, *swimming* 164.12

dog pound *cage* 60.15

dog racing *race* 422.8

do grasstrack racing *race* 146.10

do great deeds 412.14

dog rose Flowers 42

dogs Collective Names 59, Phobias 283

dogsbody [Brit inf] *office assistant* 69.6

dog's breath *unpleasant-smelling thing* 227.2

dog show *display* 843.1

dog sitter *animal welfarist* 34.9

dogsled *snow vehicle* 687.9

dog someone's footsteps *follow* 770.10

dog tag [Inf] *means of identification* 184.3

dog the footsteps of *attend* 794.19

dog-tired *fatigued* 820.2

dogtooth ornament Architectural Elements 134

dogtooth violet Flowers 42

dogtrot *bodily movement* 677.11, *slow motion* 693.3, *move slowly* 693.11

dog violet Flowers 42

dogwood Trees and Shrubs 43

Doha Countries 566

do habitually *be frequent* 661.5

do hard work *work* 122.8

do homage *succumb* 421.7, *show respect* 435.16

do housework *serve* 69.11

do ill *be evil* 446.10

doily *protective covering* 613.5

do impressions *entertain* 138.16

do in [Inf] *murder* 30.20, *destroy* 523.10, *cause to cease* 668.12, *fatigue* 820.6

doing *action* 412.1, *acting* 412.9, *operation* 590.1, *production* 522.1

doing again *repetition* 797.1

doing away with oneself *suicide* 30.8

doing business *trade* 480.1

doing chores *busy* 414.15

doing fine *well-off* 467.12

doing it [Inf] *sexual intercourse* 20.9

doing nicely thank you *wealthy* 485.8

doing nothing *inactive* 413.9

doing one's best *attempting* 390.4

doing one's duty for God and country *war measures* 76.18

doing penance *penitential* 451.6

doings *deed* 412.2

doing the right thing *formality* 406.1

doing time [Inf] *imprisoned* 55.9, *detained* 830.11

doing very nicely *or* **great** *well-off* 467.12

doing well *prosperous* 847.5

doing without *abstaining* 386.11, *desisting* 417.4

do insider dealing *act dishonestly* 479.18

do insider trading *act dishonestly* 479.18

do it [Inf] *have sex* 20.21

do it one's own way *be independent* 829.18

do it the hard way *have difficulty* 824.18

do-it-yourself *bungled* 128.7, *repair* 809.1, *naive* 821.3

dojo (practice hall) *judo* 152.13, *karate* 152.14

do justice to *eat well* 92.23, *vindicate* 441.11

dolce Musical Terms and Expression Marks 140

dolce far niente [Ital] *leisure* 125.1, 413.4

doldrums *wind system* 9.15, *depression* 270.2, *immobility* 413.2, *world region* 564.6, *repose* 678.2

dole *security* 464.1, *offering* 472.6, *portion* 474.2

dole [Brit] *incompleteness* 98.2, *social assistance* 825.4

dole, the *social welfare* 307.4

doleful *sorrowful* 270.4, *lamenting* 280.4

dolefully *sorrowfully* 270.10, *lamentingly* 280.9

dolefulness *lamentation* 280.1

dolente *or* **doloroso** Musical Terms and Expression Marks 140

dole out *give out* 472.12, *allocate* 474.5, *remunerate* 489.21, *measure out* 589.21, *disperse* 776.12

dolicocephalic *physical* 1.14

dolicocephaly *physical type* 1.8

doling out *allocation* 474.1

doll *little thing* 580.3

doll [Inf] *term of endearment* 299.7, *attractive female* 529.5

doll [Inf and Off] *sex object* 20.8, *woman considered as a sex object* 33.8

dollar *money* 484.1, *US coinage* 484.10

dollar reserves *funds* 484.6

dollars to doughnuts [Inf] *good chance* 842.6

doll carriage *toy* 167.9

dolled up [Inf] *dressed up* 100.39, *flashy* 404.17, *formally dressed* 406.8, *beautified* 530.12

dollhouse *toy* 167.9

dollop *portion* 474.2, *mass* 579.7, *particle* 760.4

dolls Phobias 283

doll's house *little space* 580.6

doll up [Inf] *beautify* 530.14

dolly *means of transportation* 686.2

dolly *or* **dolly peg** *ceramic workshop and tools* 129.8

dolly grip *filmmaker* 137.14

dolly up [Inf] *dress up* 100.45

dolman jacket *jacket* 100.18

dolman sleeve *part of garment* 100.27

dolmen *burial place* 31.7, *monument* 185.10, *thing of the past* 651.8

Dolomites Mountains and Hills 569

dolor *sorrow* 270.1

dolor [Form] *pain* 215.1

dolorimetry Fields of Measurement 589

dolorous *sorrowful* 270.4

Dolphin Constellations 7

dolphin *swimming* 164.12

dolphin kick *swimming techniques* 164.2

dolt *unskilled person* 128.3, *unintelligent person* 316.4, *foolish person* 353.3, *simpleton* 526.5, *naive person* 821.2

doltish *unintelligent* 316.6, *foolish* 353.5, *inert* 519.2

Dom *male title of address* 32.3, *professional title* 72.6

domain *mathematical function* 6.27, *subject* 48.3, *habitat* 60.1, *property*

470.1, *legal property terms* 470.2, *region* 564.1, *sphere* 564.10, *dominion* 566.3, *type* 777.4
domain of the possible *possibleness* 836.2
do martial arts 152.21
dome 634.4; *observatory* 7.24, Architectural Elements 134, *church architecture* 134.11, *superstructure* 551.7, *overhead covering* 613.11, *roof* 613.30, *curved thing* 629.3
dome [Inf] *head* 19.6
domestic 60.20; *domesticated* 16.18, *servant* 69.1, *domestic servant* 69.7, *domestic worker* 123.4, *architectural types* 134.2, *local* 328.8, *unsociable* 409.6, *internal* 611.9
domestically *topically* 328.11, *unsociably* 409.13, *inland* 611.19
domestic animal 34.3
domestic architect *architect* 134.3
domesticate *accustom* 397.18
domesticated 16.18; *of animals* 34.13, *housebound* 415.9
domestic cat *cat* 35.11
domestic fowl *table bird* 36.10
domestic mail *postal service* 169.5
domestic science *cooking* 91.1
domestic servant 69.7; *domestic worker* 123.4
domestic trade *commercial trade* 480.2
domestic tragedy *tragedy* 136.10
domestic worker 123.4
domical *vault* 134.8, *curved* 629.4
domicile *habitation* 60.2, *home* 60.3, *settle* 61.14, *place of residence* 209.4
domiciled *inhabiting* 60.18, *inhabited* 61.10
domiciliary *domestic* 60.20
dominance *genetics* 13.19, *authority* 52.1, *personal influence* 512.3
dominant 512.10, 744.9; *genetic* 13.32, *authoritative* 52.9, *musical note* 140.15, *focal* 612.8, *unbeatable* 744.13, *prevailing* 778.11, *ruling* 780.11
dominantly *authoritatively* 52.18, *focally* 612.14, *superiorly* 744.20
dominate *have authority* 52.13, *master* 68.17, *impose one's will* 372.14, *have authority over* 425.12, *be an influence* 512.13, *be powerful* 514.18, *prevail* 778.19, *rule over* 780.13, *defeat* 832.11
dominating 832.7; *masterful* 68.15, *severe* 424.5, *dominant* 744.9
dominatingly *masterfully* 68.19, *superiorly* 744.20
domination 832.2; *authority* 52.1, 425.3, 780.6, *personal influence* 512.3, *superiority* 744.1
dominations *angelic order (highest to lowest)* 82.12
domineer *have authority* 52.13
domineering *authoritative* 52.9, 425.8, *masterful* 68.15, *severe* 424.5
domineeringly *masterfully* 68.19, *commandingly* 425.15
Dominica Countries 566, Islands 572
Dominican Republic Countries 566
dominion 566.3; *governance* 49.18, 52.6, *body politic* 50.3, *jurisdiction* 54.2, *authority* 425.3, 514.5, 780.6, *possession* 469.1, *possession of property* 469.3,

property 470.1, *personal influence* 512.3, *region* 564.1, *leadership* 744.2, *priority* 769.2
Dominique Breeds of Fowl 16
dominium *legal ownership* 469.8
domino *that which makes invisible* 245.2, *body covering* 613.3
dominoes Board and Table Games 167
domino theory *consequence* 774.3
do mischief *be evil* 446.10
do missionary work *volunteer* 504.13
do more than enough *overdo* 99.11
Don *male title of address* 32.3, Horse and Pony Breeds 159, Rivers 570
don *educator* 48.4, *expert* 52.8, *wear* 100.46, *knowledgeable person* 348.5
don [Brit] *educational leader* 68.11
donate 491.13; *provision* 89.9, *philanthropize* 307.8, *give to charity* 472.16, *defray* 489.18, *give* 498.11, *make an offering* 504.17, *grant* 735.30, *finance* 825.31
donated *supplied* 89.7, *sacrificial* 504.10, *granted* 735.20
donation 491.6; *charity* 275.3, 307.3, *benevolent act* 305.7, *giving* 472.1, *offering* 472.6, 504.5, *voluntary payment* 489.4, *grant* 489.7, 735.10, *gift* 498.3, *positive stimulus* 508.5, *financial assistance* 825.6
donative *offering* 472.6, *given* 472.8
donator *giver* 472.7, *generous person* 498.5
done *culinary* 91.9, *undertaken* 391.4, *established* 397.12, *secured* 464.7, *over* 651.12, *completed* 761.7, *ended* 773.14
done by hand *produced* 522.12
donee [Form] *recipient* 473.5
done for *destroyed* 523.9
done for [Inf] *dead* 29.11, *deteriorated* 808.8, *fatigued* 820.2
Donegal tweed Fabrics and Fibers 130
done in [Inf] *deteriorated* 808.8, *fatigued* 820.2
done thing, the *expected thing* 356.3
Donets Rivers 570
done up [Inf] *beautified* 530.12
done with *disused* 394.8, *ended* 773.14
Don Juan *sexual perversion* 20.12, *libertine* 32.7, *desirer* 288.9, *lover* 299.11, *sexually immoral person* 432.8, *charmer* 700.6
Don Juanism *sexual perversion* 20.12, *sexual desire* 288.5, *sexual immorality* 432.2
donkey Card Games 167, *obstinate person* 379.4, *means of transportation* 686.2
donkey-gray *gray* 255.6
donkey's years [Inf] *long duration* 642.3
donkey work [Inf] *work* 122.1
Donna *female title of address* 33.3
donnish *literate* 348.5
donnybrook *dispute* 463.3, *violence by person* 520.2, *disruption* 766.7
do no evil *be virtuous* 447.8
donor *chemical bond* 11.6, *provisioner* 89.4, *giver* 472.7, *generous person* 498.5
donor impurity *semiconductor* 10.34
do nothing *not act* 413.11, *be inactive* 415.13

do-nothing *inactive* 413.9
do nothing but *be frequent* 661.5
do nothing in excess *be moderate* 455.12
do-nothingism 413.6
do no wrong *be moral* 431.13
Don Quixote Notable Friendships 62, *visionary* 360.9
don't-know *vacillator* 378.3, *free person* 829.9
do number one [Inf] *urinate* 25.22
do number two [Inf] *defecate* 25.21
doodad [Inf] *tool* 103.1, *decorative article* 532.5, *cheap thing* 800.7
doodle *drawing* 143.4, *draw* 143.13, *describe* 202.15, *nonsense* 362.2, *make unintelligible* 364.13
doodlebug *larva* 40.9
doodler *visual artist* 133.6, *drawer* 143.8
doodlesack Musical Instruments 142
doodling *(act of) drawing* 143.2
doohickey [Inf] *tool* 103.1
Døøle Gudbrandshal Horse and Pony Breeds 159
Døøle Trotter Horse and Pony Breeds 159
doom *death* 29.1, *inevitability* 95.6, *lack of hope* 282.2, *afflict* 301.16, *predestination* 384.2, *be evil* 446.10, *reckoning* 454.8, *ruin* 523.4, *end of time* 773.5
doomed *inevitable* 95.14, *inauspicious* 282.8, *afflicted* 301.11, *predestined* 384.6, *destroyed* 523.9, *annihilated* 773.16, *adverse* 848.10
doomed to die *dying* 29.12
doomsayer *frightener* 283.7, *oracle* 358.8
Doomsday *judgment day* 341.4
doomsday *reckoning* 454.8, *ruin* 523.4, *eternally* 644.10, *future condition* 650.3, *end of time* 773.5
doomster *oracle* 358.8
doom watcher *oracle* 358.8
do one a bad turn *be malevolent* 306.12
do one proud *guard one's pride* 297.16, *salute* 405.13
do one's best *try hard* 390.7, *try* 414.21
do one's bit *do one's duty* 433.17
do one's damnedest [Inf] *try hard* 390.7, *try* 414.21
do one's duty 433.17; *obey* 426.7, *be dutiful* 433.12, *be virtuous* 447.8, *perform* 465.5
do oneself in [Inf] *commit suicide* 30.24
do oneself proud *do well* 845.12
do one's homework *prepare oneself* 388.21
do one's job *be operational* 509.10
do one's own thing [Inf] *not observe* 466.9, *be independent* 782.20, 829.18, *be one* 788.17
do one's stuff [Inf] *be operational* 509.10
do one's thing [Inf] *be operational* 509.10
do one's utmost *exert oneself* 122.11
door Architectural Elements 134, *opening* 583.1, *access* 691.3, *means of entry* 706.6, *way out* 707.2
door, the *discarding* 383.3
doorbell *signal* 183.6, *source of resonance* 236.4
door buzzer *signal* 183.6
do-or-die *reckless* 286.6

doorframe *framework* 551.4
doorjamb *means of entry* 706.6
doorkeeper *stagehand* 136.29, *closer* 584.5
door knocker *signal* 183.6, *impeller* 695.7
doorman *guard* 419.15, *closer* 584.5, *surveillant* 810.12
doormat *cleaning tool* 111.10, *hiding place* 181.2, *sycophant* 401.3, *submitter* 421.2, *weak person* 517.4, *floor covering* 613.13
doorpost *means of entry* 706.6
doorstep *step* 713.11
doorstop *restraint* 826.8
door-to-door *transportable* 686.7, *commercially* 686.12
door-to-door salesman *salesperson* 482.8
doorway *opening* 583.1, *access* 691.3, *means of entry* 706.6
do out of [Inf] *swindle* 193.19
doo-wop *popular music* 140.4
doozie [Inf] *or* **doozy** [Inf] *good thing* 445.9
dopamine *hormone* 12.16
dope *medicate* 115.18, *anesthetic* 213.3, *make inactive* 415.16, *addictive drug* 117.10, *drug* 115.9, 121.14, *inside information* 170.4, *unintelligent person* 316.4, *foolish person* 353.3, *simpleton* 526.5
dope, the [Inf] *fact* 717.6
doped [Inf] *drugged* 121.30, *not awake* 415.12
dope fiend [Inf] *drug taker* 121.12
do penance 451.9; *repent* 313.9, *be penitent* 451.7, *compensate* 743.7
dope out [Inf] *number* 783.9, *calculate* 784.10
dopey [Inf] *anesthetic* 213.6, *unintelligent* 316.6, *not awake* 415.12, *sedentary* 678.5, *fatigued* 820.2
dopily [Inf] *in a trance* 121.40, *sleepily* 415.19, *tiredly* 820.7
doping *semiconductor* 10.34
Doppelgänger *substitute* 672.2, *look-alike* 730.4, *copy* 736.2, *twin* 789.5
dopping Collective Names 59
doppio Musical Terms and Expression Marks 140
Doppler effect Classical Physical Laws 10
Doppler radar *measuring instrument* 589.12
do public relations *interpret news* 365.17
Dorado Constellations 7
doraphobia Phobias 283
d-orbital *chemical bond* 11.6
Dordogne Rivers 570
do regularly *have a habit* 397.16
do-re-mi [Inf] *cash* 484.2
do repairs *repair* 809.10
do reverence *bow* 716.22
Dorian mode *mode* 140.17
Doric column 134.4
Doric mode *mode* 140.17
Dorking Breeds of Fowl 16
dorm [Inf] *school place* 48.16, *hotel* 60.12
dormancy *bud* 41.8, *inaction* 413.1, *sleep* 415.5, *inertness* 519.1, *deferment* 604.3, *lack of motion* 678.1, *latency* 844.1
dormant *inactive* 413.9, *not awake* 415.12, *inert* 519.2, *deferred* 604.9, *sedentary* 678.5, *potential* 836.6, *latent* 844.6
dormant condition *latency* 844.1
dormantly *motionlessly* 678.9

dormant volcano *volcanic activity* 8.26

dormer *window* 134.10

dormie side *golfing terms* 156.3

dormitory *school place* 48.16, *room* 60.9, *hotel* 60.12

dorm room [Inf] *room* 60.9

Dorper Breeds of Sheep 16

dorsal *back* 622.6

dorsal fin *fish characteristic* 38.8

dorsal region *rear end* 622.4

Dorset Breeds of Pigs 16, Breeds of Sheep 16

Dorset Down Breeds of Sheep 16

Dorset Golden Apple Varieties 44

Dorset Horn Breeds of Sheep 16

dosage *dose of medicine* 115.3, *portion* 474.2, *measurability* 589.2, *certain amount* 738.3

dose *dose of medicine* 115.3, *medicate* 115.18, *affliction* 454.9, *portion* 474.2, *allocate* 474.5, *limit* 620.1, *certain amount* 738.3, *quantify* 738.7, *particle* 760.4

dose [Inf] *sexually transmitted disease (STD)* 114.17

dose equivalent *radioactivity* 10.58

dose of medicine 115.3

do service *serve* 69.11, *pander to* 401.11, *obey* 426.7, *be useful* 801.9

doses of medicine Fields of Measurement 589

do set pattern dancing *ice-skate* 162.36

dosimeter Fields of Measurement 589

dosimetry Fields of Measurement 589

do someone's bidding *obey* 426.7

do something 412.13; *help* 825.23

do something about *attempt* 390.6

do something for or *to improvc* 825.26

dossier *chronicle* 3.4, *document* 170.3, *record* 185.1

do standing on one's head *do easily* 823.16

do stunt-skiing *ski* 162.35

do subtraction *subtract* 749.6

dot *punctuate* 183.20, *maculation* 263.4, *variegate* 263.11, *exact location* 565.2, *little thing* 580.3, *sprinkle* 776.15, *scatter* 796.9

dot about *scatter* 796.9

dotage *old age* 27.5, *folly* 353.1, *elderliness* 653.2

dotard *older person* 27.7, *foolish person* 353.3

dote on *love* 299.21

do the bidding of *pander to* 401.11

do the cleaning *clean* 111.17

do the deed *do something* 412.13

do the dirty work of *pander to* 401.11

do the fair thing *be disinterested* 443.6

do the groundwork *prepare the way* 388.15

do the honors *be sociable* 408.14, *show respect* 435.16

do the job *be effective* 845.15

do the laundry *clean* 111.17

do the needful *do something* 412.13, *do one's duty* 433.17

do the needful [Inf] *pay* 489.16

do the prep work *prepare* 388.14

do the right or **proper thing** *be dutiful* 433.12

do the right thing *be right* 429.12, *be good* 445.16

do the right thing by *be unselfish* 443.7

do the same old thing *be bored* 296.7

do the splits *exercise* 157.12

do the trick *be the answer* 334.23, *be effective* 845.15

do the washing *clean* 111.17

do the will of *obey* 426.7

do the work *work* 122.8

do things backward *be unskillful* 128.8

do things by halves *be unskillful* 128.8

do things by the book *be formal* 406.11

do things halfway *be unskillful* 128.8

do things the usual way *find a way* 691.14

do thoroughly *complete* 761.9

do time [Inf] *be in prison* 55.13

doting *loving* 299.15

dot-matrix printer *hardcopy device* 15.10

dot one's i's and cross one's t's *punctuate* 183.20, *be accurate* 350.5, 721.22

dot product *vector* 6.48

dotted *mottled* 263.10, *discontinuous* 775.7, *sprinkled* 776.9

dotted about *dispersed* 776.6, *sparse* 796.6

dotted swiss *fabric* 130.1

dottel *remainder* 750.1

dotting *sprinkling* 776.4

dottle *remainder* 750.1

dotty [Inf] *insane* 110.9

do twice over *be superfluous* 99.12

do two jobs *work* 122.8

Douay Bible *Christian text* 81.16

double 789.11, **789.14**; *alternative* 80.2, *type of bed* 101.9, *actor* 137.13, *batting terms* 147.6, *play baseball* 147.9, *rowing* 150.27, *gambling* 167.4, *bridge* 168.4, *play cards* 168.7, *image* 187.3, *representation* 202.9, *impression* 264.7, *invigorate* 518.5, *correspondent* 606.3, *substitute* 613.17, 672.2, *fold* 637.7, *reverse* 680.18, *turn around* 680.22, *deviating course* 698.2, *look-alike* 730.4, *counterpart* 733.5, *make bigger* 746.7, *twosome* 789.3, *twin* 789.5, *two* 789.8, *replica* 797.7, *repeat* 797.15

double agent *secret person* 182.6, *hypocrite* 192.9, *duality* 789.2

Double-A league *baseball leagues and championship games* 147.8

double axel *ice-skating techniques* 162.16

double back *reverse* 680.18

double-barreled *hunting* 160.11, *double-edged* 789.10

double bass Musical Instruments 142

double bassoon Musical Instruments 142

double bill *play* 136.2

double-black *ski* 162.27

double-black run *ski run* 162.2

double-bladed *canoeing* 150.26

double-bladed paddle *canoe parts* 150.10

double-blade race *canoe racing* 150.12

double-blind experiment or **trial** *rehearsal* 335.2

double bogey *golfing terms* 156.3

double boiler *cooking equipment* 91.6

double bond *chemical bond* 11.6

double-breasted *tailored* 100.41

double-breasted suit *suit* 100.16

double check *verification* 336.1

double-check *verify* 336.8

double-checked *verified* 336.7

double-checking *verificatory* 336.6

double chin *fat* 579.8

double-chinned *fat* 579.15

double clutch *miscellaneous automotive terms* 687.14

double-clutch *be on the track* 146.11

double-clutching *automobile racing terms* 146.3

double coverage *defense* 155.9

double cream *fat* 562.4

double cross *dishonorableness* 192.3

double-cross *be dishonorable* 192.21, *be cunning* 822.5

double-crosser *hypocrite* 192.9, *malefactor* 306.6, *cunning person* 822.3

double-crossing *duality* 789.2, *double-edged* 789.10, *cunning* 822.1

double-crust pie *pie* 90.38

doubled *matched* 733.10, *two* 789.8, *repeated* 797.8

double dactyl Poem or Verse Forms 139

double date *social gathering* 408.4

double-deal *deceive* 193.16

double-dealer *deceiver* 193.8, *equivocator* 380.4

double-dealing *deception* 193.1, *deceptive* 193.12, *hypocrisy* 330.5, *hypocritical* 330.10, *equivocating* 380.6, *duality* 789.2, *double-edged* 789.10, *cunning* 822.1

double-decker *sandwich* 90.9, *layered* 588.6, *bus* 687.7, *twosome* 789.3

double-dig *cultivate* 17.19

doubled over *folded* 637.5

double dresser *cabinet* 101.8

double-dribble *play basketball* 148.7

double-dribbling *violations* 148.5

double eagle *golfing terms* 156.3

double-edged **789.10**; *sharp-edged* 549.12

double-ended *canoeing* 150.26

double-ended paddle *canoe parts* 150.10

double-ender *sailboat* 150.3

double entendre *joke* 277.6, *equivocation* 380.1, *sexual offense* 432.6, *duality* 789.2

double entry *accounts* 493.4

double-entry bookkeeping *recordkeeping* 185.7

double exposure *doubling* 789.4

double-faced *two-sided* 789.9

double-facedness *duality* 789.2

double flat *musical note* 140.15

double for *substitute for* 80.5, *cover for* 613.34, *be a substitute* 672.6

double foul *playing terms* 148.4

double-glazed *heated* 217.15

double glazing *heater* 217.3, *sound reducer* 233.5

double-handed *fishing* 154.13

double-handed rod *fishing tackle* 154.7

double harness *two* 789.1

double-harness *pair* 789.13

doubleheader *other game terms* 147.7, *train* 688.4

double helix *nucleotide* 12.10

double hook *fishing tackle* 154.7

double integral *differentiation* 6.29

double-jointed *pliant* 543.7

double kayak (K-2) race *canoe racing* 150.12

double life *duality* 789.2

double meaning *lack of clarity* 364.2, *equivocation* 380.1, *duality* 789.2

double-minded *vacillating* 378.5

double-mindedness *vacillation* 378.1

double negative *language error* 351.10

doubleness *deception* 193.1, *duality* 789.2

double-oar *rowing* 150.27

double-oar rowing *rowing* 150.14

double one's efforts *persevere* 377.10, *try hard* 390.7

double over or **under** *fold* 637.7

double-paddle *canoeing* 150.26

double-paddle canoeing *canoeing* 150.8

double parking *miscellaneous automotive terms* 687.14

double play *other game terms* 147.7

double-pole *cross-country techniques* 162.8, *cross-country* 162.31, *ski* 162.35

double-pole with leg kick *cross-country techniques* 162.8

double-quick *swift* 694.6, *swiftly* 694.16

double rainbow *rainbow* 9.28

double recessiveness *genetics* 13.19

double reed *woodwind* 142.4

double rhyme *rhyme* 139.11

doubles *tennis terms* 165.5, *forehand* 165.12

double salt *salt* 11.12

doubles court *squash terms* 165.10

double sculling *rowing* 150.14

double sharp *musical note* 140.15

double sheet bend Knots, Bends, Hitches, Splices 754

double-sided *snowplow* 162.29, *two-sidcd* 789.9

double-sidedness *duality* 789.2

double-sided skating *ski race* 162.4

double somersault *competitive diving* 164.7

doublespeak *senseless talk* 362.4

doubles player *tennis participant* 165.6

doubles sideline *tennis court* 165.3

double star *star* 7.8

double-strength *intoxicating* 121.29

doublet *word* 5.17, *twosome* 789.3

doublet [Arch] *shirt* 100.13

double-talk *wordiness* 5.23, *senseless talk* 362.4, *talk nonsense* 362.12, *equivocation* 380.1, *be equivocal* 380.7

double-talk or **doubletalk** *lack of candor* 192.4, *lack candor* 192.22

double-talker *liar* 192.10, *equivocator* 380.4

double-talking *equivocating* 380.6

double tenoner *woodworking tool* 131.6

double throw axel *ice-skating techniques* 162.16

doubleton *twosome* 789.3

double-tongue *sound* 141.15

double-tongued *ungenuine* 192.13, *equivocal* 380.5

double up *fatigue* 820.6

double vision *sight defect* 243.2
double whammy [Inf] *curse* 301.1
double-wing formation *offense* 155.6
doubling 789.4; *fold* 637.1, *increase* 746.1, *repetition* 797.1, *repetitious* 797.11
doubling over *fold* 637.1
doubly *twice* 789.18
Doubs Rivers 570
doubt 287.13, 333.19; *disbelief* 88.1, *disbelieve* 88.8, *not accept* 190.19, *lack of hope* 282.2, *be hopeless* 282.11, *reticence* 287.3, *speculation* 294.2, *speculate* 294.13, *suspicion* 314.3, 841.2, *suspect* 314.9, *logical argument* 329.2, *discuss* 329.12, *question* 333.1, *uncertainty* 333.6, *dissociation* 375.4, *vacillation* 378.1, *vacillate* 378.8, *deferment* 604.3, *defer* 604.15, *improbability* 839.1, *be uncertain* 841.17
doubted *unaccepting* 190.13
doubter *disbeliever* 88.5, *negator* 190.8, *questioner* 333.9
doubtful *disbelieving* 88.6, *unaccepting* 190.13, *reticent* 287.8, *suspicious* 314.9, *arguable* 329.8, *questionable* 333.13, *vacillating* 378.5, *weak-willed* 517.10, *deferred* 604.9, *unauthentic* 722.9, *unsafe* 811.8, *improbable* 839.4, *uncertain* 841.9
doubtfully *disbelievingly* 88.10, *nonacceptantly* 190.25, *reticently* 287.18, *speculatively* 294.17, *suspiciously* 314.13, *arguably* 329.16, *questionably* 333.22, *ambivalently* 378.14, *interruptedly* 604.20, *unauthentically* 722.17, *improbably* 839.8, *uncertainly* 841.22
doubtfulness *disbelief* 88.1, *unacceptance* 190.4, *uncertainty* 333.6, 841.1, *questionableness* 333.7, *indecisiveness* 517.2, *deferment* 604.3, *unauthenticity* 722.4, *improbability* 839.1
doubting *disbelieving* 88.6, *unaccepting* 190.13, *speculative* 294.8, *questioning* 333.11, *skeptical* 333.14, *deferred* 604.9
doubtingly *nonacceptantly* 190.25, *interruptedly* 604.20
doubting Thomas *disbeliever* 88.5, *negator* 190.8, *questioner* 333.9
doubtless *convinced* 840.8
doubtless *or* **doubtlessly** *probably* 838.11
douceur *bribe* 472.3
douche *bath* 111.6, *bathe* 111.18, *dose of medicine* 115.3, *purgative* 115.7
dough *bread* 90.10, *semiliquid* 561.7
dough [Inf] *cash* 484.2
doughboy [Inf] *soldier* 77.4
doughiness 561.2; *compressibility* 543.3
doughnut *cake* 90.36
doughtily *steadfastly* 284.19
doughtiness *steadfastness* 284.3
doughty *steadfast* 284.11
doughy *drained of color* 252.6, *pliant* 543.7, *pulpy* 561.19
Douglas fir Trees and Shrubs 43
Doulton ware Ceramics 129
doum palm Trees and Shrubs 43
do up *close* 584.12, *intertwine* 752.19
do up [Inf] *beautify* 530.14, *refurbish* 809.11, *fatigue* 820.6

do up tightly *unite closely* 752.16
dour *serious* 278.4, *sullen* 304.8, *obstinate* 379.5
dourly *sullenly* 304.16
dourness *seriousness* 278.1, *sullenness* 304.1, *obstinacy* 379.1
Douro Rivers 570
douse *make dark* 247.10, *water* 557.29, *bring down* 716.14
douse the flames *conciliate* 74.10
dout Collective Names 59
Dove Constellations 7, *God the Holy Ghost* 82.10
dove *birds* 36.1, *symbol of peace* 73.6, *pacifist* 74.6, *mediator* 75.2, *innocent person* 449.5
dovecote *dwelling* 36.4, *cage* 60.15
dove-gray *gray* 255.6
dovelike *avian* 36.19, *peaceful* 73.8, *pacificatory* 74.8, *innocent* 449.6
Dover American States 564
doves Collective Names 59
dovetail *carpenter* 131.10, *interaction* 616.2, *cooperate* 616.6, *inset* 710.13, *intertwine* 752.19
dovetail and mortise joint *joint* 752.7
dovetailed *joined* 131.8, *interfacial* 616.4
dovetailing *carpenter's term* 131.5
dovetail joint *joint* 752.7
do violence to *ill-use* 395.7, *use violence* 520.9
do volunteer work *volunteer* 504.13
dowager *female* 33.1, *surviving spouse* 66.6, *master* 68.1
dowager queen *surviving spouse* 66.6
dowdiness *bad taste* 528.3
dowdy *plain* 528.9
dowel *fastener* 754.7
do well 845.12; *be skillful* 127.14, *be good* 445.16, *be prosperous* 847.6
do well at *be good at* 445.18
dower *own property* 470.11, *will* 472.11, *legacy* 492.4
dowered *propertied* 470.9, *given* 472.8
dowerless *impoverished* 486.11
do what comes naturally *improvise* 396.6
do what is expected *do one's duty* 433.17
do what is necessary *do one's duty* 433.17
do what is required *suffice* 97.6
do what is required *or* **needed** *do something* 412.13
do what one can with *have at one's disposal* 393.14
do what one has to do *do one's duty* 433.17
do what one likes *be independent* 829.18
do what one likes with *have at one's disposal* 393.14, *subject* 832.10
do with a heavy heart *grudge* 375.15
do with both eyes shut *do easily* 823.16
do with one hand tied behind one's back *do easily* 823.16
do without *not use* 394.9, *desist* 417.13, *be self-restrained* 455.10, *refuse oneself* 506.10
Dow Jones Industrial Index *or* **Dow Industrials** *or* **the Dow** *stock exchange* 457.3
down 714.19, 716.24; *plumage* 36.7, Collective Names 59, *drink*

93.19, *depressed* 270.5, *lamenting* 280.4, *without hope* 282.7, *grain* 552.2, *hill* 569.2, *descending* 597.13, 714.9, *low* 597.26, *vertically* 602.11, *flatten* 716.15, *broken down* 802.8, *worse* 808.23
down-and-out *beggarly* 486.12, *destroyed* 523.9, *worn* 808.13, *unprosperous* 848.11
down-and-outer *loser* 468.8, *poor person* 486.6, *person in adversity* 848.9
down at heart *drooping* 714.10
down-at-heel *used* 393.5, *beggarly* 486.12, *untidy* 766.11, *worn* 808.13
downbeat *tempo* 140.22
down below *low* 597.26, *down* 714.19
downburst *descent* 714.1
downcast *depressed* 261.7, 270.5, *without hope* 282.7, *sullen* 304.8, *drooping* 714.10, *downthrow* 716.2, *fallen* 716.8, *degraded* 716.10
downclimb *mountaineer* 161.10
downclimbing *climbing techniques* 161.3
down coat *coat* 100.19
downcome [Arch] *descent* 714.1
downdraft *air movement* 9.11, *air flow* 558.4, *miscellaneous aviation terms* 689.9, *descent* 714.1
down-drawn *ceramic* 129.9
down-drawn kiln *ceramic workshop and tools* 129.8
Down East *regions of the United States* 564.7
downer *moderator* 521.2
downer [Inf] *drug* 115.9, *sedatives* 121.19, *futility* 282.3, *descent* 714.1, *misadventure* 848.2
downfall 714.7, 848.4; *rain* 9.27, *failure* 430.9, *ruin* 523.4, *lowering* 716.1, *decline* 846.5
downfallen *spoiled* 808.9
down feathers *plumage* 36.7
downflow 714.3
downflowing *descending* 714.9
down for the count *defeated* 846.11
downgrade *program* 15.29, *punish* 454.22, *relegate* 574.18, *disbar* 709.16, *sinkage* 714.2, *down* 714.19, *debase* 716.16, *make smaller* 747.8
downgraded *relegated* 574.11, *degraded* 716.10
downgrading *punishment* 454.1, *relegation* 574.4, *debasement* 716.5
downgrowth *descent* 714.1
downhaul *sailboat parts and accessories* 150.4, *windsurfing* 150.28
downhaul line *sailboard parts* 150.20
downhearted *sorrowful* 270.4, *without hope* 282.7, *sullen* 304.8
downheartedly *sullenly* 304.16
downheartedness *sorrow* 270.1, *sullenness* 304.1
downhill *ski* 162.27, *descending* 597.13, 714.9, *low* 597.26, *down* 714.19, *worse* 808.23, *easy* 823.9
downhill all the way *easy* 823.9
downhill race *ski race* 162.4
downhill racer *skier* 162.14
downhill racing Sporting Activities 145
downhill ski *ski equipment* 162.10, *ski* 162.35
downhill skier *skier* 162.14
downhill skiing *skiing* 162.1
downhill ski run *ski run* 162.2

downiness *lightness* 539.1, *smoothness* 543.2, *grain* 552.2
downing *eating* 92.1
Downing Street [Brit] *the power structure* 68.12
down in the dumps *depressed* 270.5, *without hope* 282.7
down in the mouth *without hope* 282.7, *drooping* 714.10
down in the world *worse* 808.23
downland *grassland* 45.2, *upland* 572.7
downlight *highlight* 246.12
down line *track* 688.2
download *computing terms* 15.22, *program* 15.29
down on one's luck *unlucky* 848.12
down on the farm *agriculturally* 16.21
down payment *type of payment* 489.3, *part* 760.1
downplay *play down* 195.17, *make unimportant* 800.20
downplayed 195.13
downplaying 195.6
downpour *rain* 9.27, *natural violence* 520.3, *downflow* 714.3
downright *disclosing* 180.6, *candid* 191.5, *simple* 363.6, *completely* 759.14, 761.13, *complete* 761.6
downright lie *falsehood* 192.6
downrightness *openness* 180.3, *candor* 191.2, *clarity* 363.2
downrush *downflow* 714.3
downrushing *descending* 714.9
downs *grassland* 45.2, *upland* 572.7
downs [Brit] *heights* 596.4
downshift *miscellaneous automotive terms* 687.14
down side *golfing terms* 156.3
downsize *reduce* 796.8
downstage *stage* 136.18, *onstage* 136.39
downstairs *down* 714.19
downstream *directionally* 697.20, *easy* 823.9
downsweep method *relay racing* 166.5
downswing *golf shots* 156.4
down the hatch! *cheers!* 93.22
down-the-line shooting Sporting Activities 145
down the middle *in half* 789.21
downthrow 716.2; *descent* 714.1
downthrown *fallen* 716.8
downtime *computing terms* 15.22, *leisure* 125.1
down-to-earth *rational* 4.15, *practical* 719.8, *naive* 821.3
down to one's last penny *insolvent* 486.10
downtown *urban area* 567.10, *urban* 567.14, *directional* 697.8, *directionally* 697.20
downtowner *municipal resident* 567.12
downtrend *economic deterioration* 808.2
downturn *decline* 680.5, 747.4, *descent* 714.1, *economic deterioration* 808.2
downturning *descending* 714.9
down under [Inf] *world region* 564.6
downward *socioeconomic* 2.13, *descending* 597.13, 714.9, *low* 597.26, *directional* 677.13, *down* 714.19, 716.24, *decreasingly* 747.9
downward course *deterioration* 808.1
downward curve *decline* 747.4

downward inclination *descent* 597.4

downward mobility *social stratification* 2.7

downward motion *descending motion* 677.6

downward slope *descent* 597.4

downward spiral *decline* 747.4

downward trend *decline* 680.5, 747.4, *sinkage* 714.2

downwash *miscellaneous aviation terms* 689.9

downwelling *ocean current* 8.15

downwind *directional* 697.8, *directionally* 697.20

downwind of *odorous* 224.5

downy *insubstantial* 539.5, *smooth* 543.8, 545.4, *fluffy* 552.11

downy mildew *pests and diseases* 17.12

do wonders 294.15; *attain one's goal* 845.13, *be effective* 845.15

do wonders with *refurbish* 809.11

do worse *deteriorate* 808.14

do wrong 430.20; *be illegal* 53.30, *be immoral* 432.13, *be evil* 446.10, *be wicked* 448.13, *mix up* 751.13

dowry *marriageability* 64.4, *profit* 467.6, *transfer of property* 470.4, *giving* 472.1, *financial assistance* 825.6

dowse *divine* 86.24

dowser *diviner* 86.14, *discoverer* 345.7, *forecaster* 358.9, *hydrologist* 557.20

dowsing *divination* 86.5, 358.2

dowsing rod *detector* 345.6

dowsing rods *divination* 86.5

Doxology *prayer* 85.10

doxology *ritual music* 85.9, *sacred music* 140.3

doyen *company leader* 68.8, *expert* 127.9

doyen *or* **doyenne** *older person* 27.7

doyenne *company leader* 68.8

doylt *Collective Names* 59

doze *desensitization* 213.2, *be insensible* 213.7, *sleep* 415.5, 415.14, *take it easy* 819.3

dozen *eleven to nineteen* 792.7

dozens *multitude* 795.1

dozer *construction equipment* 14.23, *sleeper* 415.7

dozily *sleepily* 415.19

doziness *sleep* 415.5

dozing *not awake* 415.12

dozy *not awake* 415.12

DP manager *computer user* 15.3

drab *dark-colored* 247.7, *dimmed* 248.6, *dull* 255.8, *boring* 296.6, *plain* 528.9

drabble *dirty* 112.11

drably *dimly* 248.10, *grayly* 255.10, *boringly* 296.10

drabness *darkness* 247.1, *murk* 248.2, *dullness* 255.5, *bad taste* 528.3

drachma *national coins* 484.11

Draco *Constellations* 7

Draconian *severe* 424.5

draconian *strong* 516.9

Draconian measures *severity* 424.1

Dracula *Legendary Creatures* 360

Dracula's Castle *Imaginary Places* 360

draff *dirt* 112.5

draft *enlist* 58.13, *join the army* 76.31, *size of drink* 93.3, *dose of medicine* 115.3, *drawing* 143.4, *draw* 143.13, *basketball team* 148.2, *sailboat parts and accessories*

150.4, *illustration* 187.2, *illustrate* 187.11, *describe* 202.15, *suppose* 359.8, *plan out* 387.14, *preparations* 388.2, *lay the foundations* 388.16, *coercive method* 428.3, *force* 428.10, *paper money* 484.14, *displacement* 538.3, *rough idea* 544.4, *be unfinished* 544.12, *depth* 598.1, *form* 624.9, *traction* 699.1, *pull* 699.2, *tractional* 699.7, *drawing off* 711.4, *not complete* 762.9

draft, the *military affairs* 58.1, *war measures* 76.18

draft animal *means of transportation* 686.2

draft beer *beer* 93.10

draft dodger *avoider* 386.8, *refuser* 506.4

drafted *enlisted* 58.11, *warring* 76.26, *martial* 77.33, *drawn* 143.11

draftee *soldier* 77.4

draftees *reinforcements* 77.11

drafter *drawer* 143.8

draft horse *workhorse* 159.3, *means of transportation* 686.2

drafting *(act of) drawing* 143.2

draft pick *basketball team* 148.2, *football player* 155.15

drafts *Phobias* 283

draftsman *visual artist* 133.6

draftsmanship *(act of) drawing* 143.2, *treatment* 143.6

draftswoman *visual artist* 133.6

drag 699.11; *smoking* 121.22, *smoke* 121.38, *bobsled* 162.38, *obstruction* 510.3, *counteract* 510.7, *influence* 512.1, *be an influence* 512.13, *weighing down* 538.5, *friction* 554.1, 699.4, *limit* 620.1, 620.7, *pass* 639.13, *snow vehicle* 687.9, *miscellaneous aviation terms* 689.9, *hesitate* 693.12, *pull* 699.2, *attraction* 700.1, *attract* 700.11, *obstacle* 826.2, *be inhibited* 826.20, *means of restraint* 830.6, *restrain* 830.12

drag [Inf] *hopeless person* 282.5, *boring thing* 296.3, *boring person* 296.4

drag artist *entertainer* 138.8, *imitator* 736.6

drag by *pass* 639.13

drag down *drag* 699.11

drag down to one's level *pervert* 808.22

dragée *dose of medicine* 115.3

drag from *force* 428.10

dragged out *lengthened* 590.10

dragger *Ships and Boats* 690

dragging *toboggan race* 162.25, *bobsledding* 162.34, *nautical* 690.14, *slow motion* 693.3, *slow* 693.7, *traction* 699.1, *attracting* 700.8

dragging of the feet *unenthusiasm* 375.3

dragging out *lengthening* 590.4

dragging over the coals *condemnation* 438.2

draggle *dirty* 112.11, *drag* 699.11

drag in *insert* 710.9

drag in the mud [Inf] *dishonor* 436.20

dragline *construction equipment* 14.23

dragnet *pursuit* 385.1, *towline* 699.5, *nonspecificness* 778.2

Dragon *Constellations* 7

dragon *Legendary Creatures* 360, *violent animal* 520.4

drag on *pass* 639.13, *be late* 658.11

drag one's feet *delay* 375.16, *shy*

386.17, *be late* 658.11, *hesitate* 693.12, *be inferior* 745.10, *block* 826.17, *be inhibited* 826.20

dragonfly *insect* 40.1, *variegated thing* 263.5

dragonnade *military attack* 418.2

dragon's blood *Tree Products* 43, *red pigment* 257.2

dragon's lair *danger* 811.1

dragon tree *Trees and Shrubs* 43

dragoon *horse person* 159.14, *force* 428.10

drag out *lengthen* 590.12, *reveal* 843.14

drag over the coals *condemn* 438.18

drag-race *race* 146.10

drag racer *driver* 146.8

drag racing *Sporting Activities* 145, *automobile racing* 146.1

drag through the gutter *defame* 440.13

drag through the mud [Inf] *defame* 440.13

drag up *drag* 699.11, *gather up* 715.14

drain 8.64; *drink* 93.19, *expend* 96.16, *purify* 111.19, *practice hygiene* 116.4, *unpleasant-smelling thing* 227.2, *exploit* 393.11, *lessening* 468.6, *lessen* 468.17, *weaken* 517.13, *tunnel* 551.11, *dry* 560.17, *cause to flow* 570.11, *provide passage for* 583.18, *outlet* 707.8, *run out* 707.15, *void* 709.23, *draw off* 711.16, *decrease* 747.1, 747.7, *subtract* 749.6, *place for waste* 802.6, *wear out* 808.21, *fatigue* 820.6

drain a bumper *congratulate* 405.12

drainage *cleaning* 111.2, *swill* 112.6, *removal* 709.5

drainage basin *running water* 8.10

drainage pattern *running water* 8.10, *river* 570.1

drainage system *running water* 8.10, *water system* 551.13

drain away *decrease* 747.7

drain cleaner *deodorant* 225.3

drained *consumed* 96.11, *dilapidated* 517.7, *dried-out* 560.10, *spoiled* 808.9, *fatigued* 820.2

drained of color 252.6

draining *lessening* 468.6, *removal* 709.5, *drawing off* 711.4, *moral deterioration* 808.3

drain of color *decolor* 252.8

drain out *run out* 707.15

drainpipe *cleaning tool* 111.10, *outlet* 707.8

drain the lifeblood of *slaughter* 30.21

drain tile *industrial ceramics* 129.6

drain to the dregs *void* 709.23

drake *livestock* 16.11, *male animal* 32.15, *male bird* 36.15

drake [Arch] *Legendary Creatures* 360

Drakensberger *Breeds of Cattle* 16

Drakensberg Mountains *Mountains and Hills* 569

dram *size of drink* 93.3, *drink* 121.6, *weight measurement* 538.6, *General Units* 589, *Scientific and Technical Units* 589

drama 136.1; *play* 136.2, *movie type* 137.3, *fiction* 139.2, *marvel* 294.3, *activity* 414.1

drama, the *drama* 136.1

drama college *type of school* 48.12

drama of fate *tragedy* 136.10

drama of suspense *dramatic style* 136.3

drama series *program* 172.10

dramatherapist *psychologist* 108.33

dramatic 136.31, 137.16, 404.16; *poetic* 139.19, *wondrous* 294.9, *demonstrative* 331.10, *acting* 412.9

dramatically 136.38, 404.31; *descriptively* 139.24, *demonstratively* 331.21

dramatic art *drama* 136.1, *dramaturgy* 136.6

dramatic conflict *dramaturgy* 136.6

dramatic convention *dramaturgy* 136.6

dramatic coup *dramaturgy* 136.6

dramatic cycle *play* 136.2

dramatic entertainment *drama* 136.1

dramatic form *dramaturgy* 136.6

dramatic irony *dramaturgy* 136.6, *aspect of fiction* 139.5

dramatic monologue *play* 136.2, *Poem or Verse Forms* 139

dramatic poet *author* 139.13

dramatic poetry *poetry* 139.8

dramatic recital *play* 136.2

dramatic representation *play* 136.2

dramatics 404.3; *drama* 136.1, *dramaturgy* 136.6, *Hobbies and Pastimes* 167, *demonstrativeness* 331.2

dramatic soprano *voice* 141.5

dramatic stroke *dramaturgy* 136.6

dramatic structure *dramaturgy* 136.6

dramatic style 136.3

dramatic tension *dramaturgy* 136.6

dramatic unities *dramaturgy* 136.6

dramatis personae *group* 18.13, *cast* 136.26, *list of names* 785.7

dramatist 136.27; *author* 139.13, *descriptive writer* 202.10, *producer* 522.10

dramatize 136.33; *write* 139.21, *act* 187.13, *recount* 202.16, *appear* 331.18, *display* 843.13

dramatized 136.32

dramatize oneself *show off* 404.26

dramaturge *dramatist* 136.27, *author* 139.13

dramaturgic *dramatic* 136.31

dramaturgically *dramatically* 136.38

dramaturgy 136.6

drape *clothe* 100.43, *stage set* 136.19, *shade maker* 247.4, *suspend* 604.13, *wall covering* 613.12, *face* 613.31

draped *dressed* 100.38, *suspended* 604.7

drape oneself *lie down* 716.21

drapery *fabric* 130.1, *merchandise* 522.6, *wall covering* 613.12

draping *suspension* 604.1

drastic *strong* 516.9

drastically *acutely* 516.18

draught [Brit] *tractional* 699.7

draughts *Board and Table Games* 167

Drava *Rivers* 570

draw 143.13; *represent* 6.91, *cook* 91.10, *treat* 115.17, *smoking* 121.22, *smoke* 121.38, *design* 133.9, *bowls* 151.7, *play* 155.8, *golf shots* 156.4, *ice hockey tactics* 158.4, *illustrate* 187.11, *describe*

202.15, *desirability* 288.7, *cause desire* 288.22, *bank* 484.26, *income* 492.3, *influence* 508.11, *contract* 582.12, *form* 624.9, *stop* 668.2, *set in motion* 677.16, *sail* 690.16, *pull* 699.2, 699.10, *attraction* 700.1, *attract* 700.11, *void* 709.23, *draw off* 711.16, *stalemate* 740.3, *be equal* 740.11, *nonachievement* 762.3

draw a bead on *hunt* 160.12, *fire* 418.18

draw a blank *be wasteful* 468.16, *fail* 846.12

draw a blueprint *illustrate* 187.11

draw a circle *make circular* 631.7

draw a kiln *make ceramics* 129.10

draw a large income *be rich* 485.12

draw a meaning *infer* 361.14

draw a mental picture *suppose* 359.8

draw an allowance *profit* 467.22

draw an analogy *correlate* 729.9, *compare* 733.13

draw an outline *outline* 617.5

draw a parallel *correspond* 606.8, *correlate* 729.9, *compare* 733.13

draw a parallel to *or* **between** *correspond to* 727.10

draw a pay check *earn* 467.20

draw a pension *receive* 473.13

draw a personal foul *play basketball* 148.7, *exhibit penalty behavior* 155.21

draw a salary *get paid* 453.17, *earn* 467.20

draw a shot *bowl* 151.8

draw aside *divert* 698.16

draw a technical foul *play basketball* 148.7

draw attention *attract attention* 323.12

draw attention to *emphasize* 200.6, *display* 843.13

draw attention to oneself *appear* 331.18

draw a veil over *conceal* 181.12

drawback *discount* 495.1, *subtracted item* 749.2, *inconvenience* 804.1, *defect* 806.4, *snag* 824.8, *obstacle* 826.2

draw back *be afraid* 283.14, *shy* 386.17, *retreat* 680.17, *recoil* 680.21

drawbar *yoke* 754.8

draw blood *inflict pain* 215.10

draw blood from a stone *attempt the impossible* 837.10

draw blueprints *be an architect* 134.13

draw breath *live* 28.17, *be born* 28.18, *be refreshed* 94.8

drawbridge *for* 419.13, *bridge* 551.10, 691.7, *means of escape* 816.4

draw close to jack *bowl* 151.8

drawee *debtor* 488.6

drawer 143.8; *receptacle* 105.11, *visual artist* 133.6, *compartment* 578.2, *towline* 699.5

drawers *underwear* 100.22

draw forth *reveal* 843.14

draw in 699.13, 708.18; *contract* 582.12, *become smaller* 582.14, *lure* 700.12

drawing 143.4; *geometric construction* 6.47, *craft* 133.2, *picture* 133.5, *architecture* 134.1, *illustration* 187.2, *representation* 202.9, *view* 242.8, *map* 387.7, *work of art* 522.4, *traction* 699.1, *tractional* 699.7, *attracting* 700.8,

extraction 711.1, *game of chance* 842.5

drawing back *retreat* 680.2

drawing board *planning* 387.8

drawing frame *material* 143.9

drawing in *shortening* 582.2

drawing off 711.4

drawing out 711.5; *expansion* 581.1, *lengthening* 590.4, *extraction* 711.1

drawing paper *material* 143.9

drawing pencil *material* 143.9

drawing power 699.6

drawing room *room* 60.9, *meeting place* 408.5

drawing-room comedy *historic comedy* 136.12

drawing together *shortening* 582.2

draw *or* **pull in one's horns** *doubt* 287.13, *humble oneself* 298.18

draw interest *profit* 467.22

drawknife *smoother* 545.2, *sharp-edged thing* 549.6

drawknife *or* **drawshave** *woodworking tool* 131.6

drawl *mode of speech* 205.6, *speak in a particular way* 205.18, *hesitate* 693.12

drawling *slowness* 693.1, *hesitant* 693.9

drawn 143.11; *removed* 574.9, *emaciated* 595.10, *tractional* 699.7, *on equal terms* 740.9

drawn battle *stalemate* 740.3

draw near *near* 586.12, *be in the future* 650.9, *converge* 702.9

drawn game *nonachievement* 762.3

drawn game *or* **match** *stalemate* 740.3

draw nigh *near* 586.12, *be in the future* 650.9

drawn in *shortened* 582.8

drawn-out *diffuse* 199.3, *bigger* 581.9, *lengthened* 590.10, *protracted* 669.7

drawn together *shortened* 582.8

drawn up *planned* 387.10, *designed* 537.5

draw off 711.16; *subtract* 749.6

draw on *resort to* 393.13

draw oneself to one's full height *arise* 715.15

draw one's last breath *die* 773.21

draw one's pension *resign* 835.5

draw on one's savings *expend* 491.11

draw out 711.17; *be diffuse* 199.5, *bore* 296.8, *remove* 574.16, *enlarge* 581.14, *lengthen* 590.12, *protract* 669.9, *awaken* 675.9, *extract* 711.13, *reveal* 843.14

draw poker *Card Games* 168, *poker* 168.5

draw rein *slow down* 693.13

draw retirement pay *earn* 467.20

draw shot *or* **draw** *grip* 151.4

drawstring *line* 754.5

draw stroke *canoeing techniques* 150.11

draw the curtains *make dark* 247.10

draw the line *detain* 471.9, *limit* 830.13

draw the line at *reject* 383.10, *limit* 620.7, *exclude* 764.7

draw the teeth *or* **fangs of** *blunt* 550.9

draw tight *unite closely* 752.16

draw to a close *come to an end* 773.23

draw to a peak *billow* 571.9

draw together *assemble* 59.23, *contract* 582.12, *unite* 752.14

draw to scale *map* 187.12

draw toward *attract* 700.11

draw up *plan out* 387.14, *structure* 551.20, *stop* 668.10, *approach* 704.15, *gather up* 715.14, *line up* 765.24

draw up a design *or* **plan** *plan out* 387.14

draw up an itinerary *find one's way* 691.15

draw up a schedule *plan out* 387.14

draw up a will *will* 472.11

draw up birth *or* **natal charts** *divine* 86.24

draw-weight *bowls* 151.7

dray *Collective Names* 59, *wagon* 687.5, *snow vehicle* 687.9

drayage *conveyance* 685.2, *traction* 699.1

dray horse *workhorse* 159.3

drayman *transferrer* 685.4, *transporter* 686.4

dread *fear* 283.1, *be afraid* 283.14, *expectation* 356.1, *expect* 356.6

dreaded *expected* 356.5, *evil* 446.7

dreadful *frightening* 283.12, *evil* 446.7, *adverse* 848.10

dreadful! *too bad!* 848.17

dreadfully *frighteningly* 283.20, *evilly* 446.12, *hideously* 531.6, *adversely* 848.16

dreadfulness *evil* 446.1

dreading *expecting* 356.4

dreadlocks *coiffure* 530.8

dreadnought *historical warships* 77.22

dream *spectacle* 264.6, *aspiration* 281.3, *aspire* 281.13, *wish* 288.2, *ideal* 327.6, *imagine* 327.14, 360.14, 720.13, *expectations* 356.2, *suppose* 359.8, *fantasy* 360.5, *objective* 374.5, *attractive female* 529.5, *attractive male* 529.6, *night* 656.3, *spend the evening* 656.5, *illusion* 720.2, *unreality* 722.2

dream anxiety disorder *sleep disorder* 108.20

dreamboat [Inf] *attractive male* 529.6

dream dreams *fantasize* 360.15

dreamed up *produced* 522.12

dreamed-up *imaginary* 360.12, *unreal* 722.7

dreamer *philosopher* 4.9, *hoper* 281.5, *desirer* 288.9, *visionary* 360.9, *avoider* 386.8, *inactive person* 413.8, *nonworker* 415.4, *unrealistic person* 720.6

dream factory [Inf] *motion-picture studio* 137.7

dreamily *imaginatively* 327.21

dreaming *thoughtful* 4.17, *aspiring* 281.8, *imaginative* 360.10, *not awake* 415.12

dream interpretation *divination* 86.5

dream interpreter *diviner* 86.14

dreamland 360.8; *sleep* 415.5

dreamlike *seeming* 264.11, *imaginary* 360.12, *illusory* 720.9

dreamlike thinking *defense mechanism* 108.23

dream man *attractive male* 529.6

dream of *aspire to* 288.19, *aim* 374.10

dream of other worlds *fantasize* 360.15

dreams *Phobias* 283

dream state *trance* 108.18

dream-symbol interpretation *symbol* 108.28

dream up 522.15; *imagine* 327.14, 360.14, *improvise* 396.6, *be unreal* 722.12, *originate* 737.7, *invent* 771.30

dream world *aspiration* 281.3, *dreamland* 360.8

dreamy *speculative* 317.8, *ideal* 327.12, *imaginative* 360.10, *imaginary* 360.12

drearily *grayly* 255.10, *sorrowfully* 270.10, *boringly* 296.10

dreariness *dullness* 255.5, *depression* 270.2, *boringness* 296.3

dreary *dull* 255.8, *depressed* 270.5, *boring* 296.6, *plain* 528.9

dreary routine *work* 122.1

dreck [Inf] *dirt* 112.5

dredge *construction equipment* 14.23, *engineer* 14.48, *powder* 553.25, *digger* 635.4, *drag* 699.11, *extractor* 711.9, *extract* 711.13, *sprinkle* 776.15

dredger *construction equipment* 14.23, *digger* 635.4, *Ships and Boats* 690, *extractor* 711.9, *lifter* 715.5

dredge up *gather up* 715.14

dredging *extraction* 711.1

dregs *dirt* 112.5, *mud* 561.8, *residue* 750.2, *tail* 773.8

dregs of society *villain* 448.5

dreidel game *Children's and Party Games* 167

drench *practice livestock farming* 16.20, *be excessive* 99.9, *bathe* 111.18, *soften* 543.14, *soaking* 557.9, *water* 557.29, *immerse* 710.12, *fill* 761.11

drenched *excessive* 99.5, *wet* 557.23

drenched with sweat *sweaty* 25.17

drenching *soaking* 557.9

drenching rain *rain* 9.27

Dresden china *Ceramics* 129

dress 100.11; *fertilize* 22.12, *cook* 91.10, *clothing* 100.1, *clothe* 100.43, *equipment* 103.6, *treat* 115.17, *medicate* 115.18, *make taste* 219.6, *external appearance* 264.5, *equip* 388.19, *rub* 554.12, *anoint* 562.17, *top* 600.10, *wrap* 613.29

dress a fly *fish* 154.14

dressage *Sporting Activities* 145, *equestrianism* 159.8

dress blue *uniform* 100.9

dress circle *auditorium* 136.17, *place for viewing* 242.13

dress coat *jacket* 100.18

dress down *condemn* 438.18, *punish* 454.22

dressed 100.38; *culinary* 91.9, *fishing* 154.13, *equipped* 388.10

dressed down *condemned* 438.11

dressed fly *bait* 154.6

dressed for battle *equipped* 388.10

dressed to kill *dressed up* 100.39, *flashy* 404.17, *formally dressed* 406.8, *beautified* 530.12

dressed to the nines *dressed up* 100.39, *flashy* 404.17, *formally dressed* 406.8, *beautified* 530.12, *fashionable* 536.5

dressed up 100.39; *formally dressed* 406.8, *beautified* 530.12, *fashionable* 536.5, *ornamental* 748.9

dresser *cabinet* 101.8, *receptacle* 105.11, *stagehand* 136.29

dress formally *be formal* 406.11

dressily 100.47
dress in *wear* 100.46
dressing 100.2; *fertilizer* 22.6, *side dish* 90.15, 794.11, *type of table* 101.5, *polishing* 554.5, *top layer* 600.5, *medical covering* 613.4, *ornamentation* 748.5
dressing-down *condemnation* 438.2, *punishment* 454.1
dressing gown *robe* 100.20
dressing room *room* 60.9, *stage* 136.18
dressing ship *salute* 405.7
dressing-table mirror *reflector* 242.10
dressing up *dressing* 100.2
dress in one's best bib and tucker *dress up* 100.45
dressmaker *clothier* 100.37, *fabric handler* 130.11, *changer* 665.9, *person who joins* 752.9
dressmaking *the clothing business* 100.36, Hobbies and Pastimes 167
dress rehearsal *production* 136.14, *preparations* 388.2
dress ship *salute* 405.13
dress shirt *shirt* 100.13
dress suit *formal clothes* 100.5, *suit* 100.16, *formal clothing* 406.5
dress to kill *dress up* 100.45
dress to the nines *dress up* 100.45
dress uniform *uniform* 100.9, *formal clothing* 406.5
dress up 100.45; *practice sophistry* 330.11, *be formal* 406.11, *distort the truth* 627.12, *beautify* 807.20
dress up as *appear* 264.12
dress warmly *feel hot* 217.19
dress whites *uniform* 100.9
dressy *dressed up* 100.39, *stylish* 100.42, *fashionable* 536.5
drey *mammal dwelling* 35.21
Dreyer's New General Catalog (NGC) *star catalog* 7.9
dribble *saliva* 25.9, *salivate* 25.25, *play basketball* 148.7, *ice hockey tactics* 158.4, *field hockey tactics* 158.5, *play field hockey* 158.10, *seep* 559.16, *flow* 570.10, *leakage* 707.5, *leak* 707.16, *certain amount* 738.3
dribble away *lessen* 468.17
dribbled *soccer* 163.7
dribbler *batting terms* 147.6
dribbling *salivating* 25.18, *playing terms* 148.4, *soccer play* 163.5, *soccer* 163.7, *seeping* 557.25, 559.12, *leakage* 707.5
dribbling away *lessening* 468.6
dribs and drabs *bits and pieces* 760.5
dried *dried-up* 560.9, *preserved* 815.12
dried beef *beef* 90.24
dried flower *flower* 42.1
dried food *food* 90.1, *preserved thing* 815.10
dried fruit *fruits* 44.1, *sweets* 90.39
dried grass *animal feed* 16.12
dried milk *milk* 93.5, *preserved thing* 815.10
dried-out 560.10
dried-up 560.9
dried vegetable *vegetable* 17.11
drier *fine* 9.43, *dryer* 560.5
drift *glacier* 8.44, Collective Names 59, *automobile racing terms* 146.3, *radio reception* 172.2, *summary* 204.1, *topic* 328.1, *meaning* 361.1, *not act* 413.11, *be inactive* 415.13, *be cheap* 497.13, *tendency* 513.1, 838.2, *be light* 539.8, *flow* 570.4, 570.10, *be irresolute* 666.9,

significance 676.4, *momentum* 677.2, *be in motion* 677.14, *move* 677.15, *transferred thing* 685.6, *miscellaneous aviation terms* 689.9, *fly* 689.13, *bearing* 697.2, *deviating motion* 698.3, *go astray* 698.17, *aim* 773.12, *be independent* 829.18
driftage *flow* 570.4, *momentum* 677.2, *miscellaneous aviation terms* 689.9
drift along *march on* 679.11
drift apart *disband* 776.13
drift boat Ships and Boats 690
drifter *nonworker* 415.4, Ships and Boats 690
drifting *helpless* 515.9, *moving* 677.12, *wandering* 698.4, 698.13, *divergent* 776.11, *endangered* 811.10, *probable* 838.6
drifting apart *parting* 703.2
drifting snow *snow* 9.30
drift off *disband* 776.13
drift with the current *do easily* 823.16
driftwood *timber* 43.3, *transferred thing* 685.6
drill *machine tool* 14.9, *engineer* 14.48, *farmland* 16.3, *farm tool* 16.5, *farm* 16.19, *garden tool* 17.7, *cultivate* 17.19, *educate* 48.22, *military training* 76.19, *hand tool* 103.3, *practice dentistry* 107.34, *training* 122.5, *train* 122.12, Fabrics and Fibers 130, *woodworking tool* 131.6, *carpenter* 131.10, *material* 144.6, *climbing equipment* 161.4, *burst* 232.9, *briefing* 388.4, *brief* 388.20, *standard procedure* 397.6, *formal occasion* 406.4, *sharp-pointed thing* 549.4, *use a sharp tool* 549.17, *opener* 583.2, *hole* 583.17, *deepen* 598.21, *rotator* 682.8, *way* 691.1, *dig out* 711.15, *custom* 780.5, *assimilate* 781.14
drilled *holed* 583.12
driller *digger* 635.4
drilling *education* 48.1, *habituation* 397.7, *deepening* 598.4, *digging out* 711.3
drilling machine *machine tool* 14.9
drilling vessel *oceanography* 571.5
drillmaster *preparer* 388.6
drill rig *oil* 106.7
drill sergeant *preparer* 388.6
drily *sourly* 223.9, *dryly* 560.23
drink 93.2, 93.19, 121.6; *refreshments* 94.3, *alcohol* 121.5, *get drunk* 121.35, *taste* 219.5, Phobias 283, *celebrate* 405.10, *fluid* 555.1, *ingest* 708.17
drinkable 93.18; *tasty* 219.4, *trustworthy* 810.17
drink container 93.13
drink deep *get drunk* 121.35
drinker 93.16; *farm tool* 16.5, *drunkard* 121.8
drink hard *get drunk* 121.35
drinking 93.1, 93.17, 121.2; *substance abuse* 121.1, Phobias 283, *intake* 708.5
drinking bout 121.7; *celebration* 405.1
drinking place *drink provider* 93.15
drinking vessel 578.13
drinking water 557.2; *water* 93.4
drink like a fish *drink* 93.19, *get drunk* 121.35
drink moderately *be sober* 120.8
drink occasion 93.14
drink of the gods *drink* 93.2

drink one's fill *drink* 93.19, *have enough* 97.7, *be full* 761.12
drink provider 93.15
drinks *side dish* 794.11
drinks cabinet *cabinet* 101.8
drink seller *drink provider* 93.15
drink sociably *be sober* 120.8
drink the cup of humiliation *humble oneself* 298.18
drink the health of *drink to* 93.20, *congratulate* 405.12
drink to 93.20; *congratulate* 405.12, *participate* 408.15
drink up *drink* 93.19, *absorb* 560.20, *void* 709.23
drink up or in *ingest* 708.17
drink water *be sober* 120.8
drip 714.13; *dose of medicine* 115.3, *therapy* 115.12, Architectural Elements 134, *knock* 235.4, 235.13, *seep* 559.16, *move slowly* 693.11, *infiltrate* 706.13, *leakage* 707.5, *leak* 707.16
drip [Inf] *boring person* 296.4, *weak person* 517.4
drip-dry *clean* 111.17, *treated* 130.16, *dry* 560.17
drip-feed *feed* 90.41, *therapy* 115.12
dripping *knock* 235.4, *wet* 557.23, *seeping* 557.25, 559.12, *leakage* 707.5
drippings *basic cooking ingredient* 91.8
dripping wet *wet* 557.23
dripping with *full* 761.8
dripping with wealth *wealthy* 485.8
dripstone Architectural Elements 134
drip with wealth *be rich* 485.12
drive *practice livestock farming* 16.20, *herd* 59.29, *exertion* 122.4, *play basketball* 148.7, *grip* 151.4, *golf shots* 156.4, *play* 156.8, *ride* 159.16, *hunt* 160.12, 385.3, *badminton terms* 165.11, *play tennis* 165.13, *emphasis* 200.1, *seriousness* 376.3, *direction* 384.3, *direct* 384.10, *use* 399.9, *energy* 414.4, *push* 414.20, *military attack* 418.2, *attack* 418.17, *compulsion* 428.1, *compel* 428.8, *manipulate* 508.12, *take action* 509.12, *vigor* 514.2, 518.1, *be full of vigor* 518.4, *set in motion* 716.16, *access* 691.3, *road* 691.4, *acceleration* 694.3, *hurry someone up* 694.15, *sporting hit* 695.6, *impel* 695.9, *propulsion* 696.9, *propel* 696.15, *haste* 818.1, *hasten* 818.4, *fatigue* 820.6
drive against *attack* 418.17
drive a hard bargain *deal* 457.9, *bargain* 480.20
drive apart *come between* 753.21
drive a trade *trade* 480.18
drive away *repel* 701.7
drive a wedge between *come between* 753.21
drive back *repel* 701.7
drive-by shooting *accidental killing* 30.9
drive crazy *make insane* 110.13
drive dangerously *endanger* 811.13
drive-foot landing *discus throwing* 166.13
drive forward *be in motion* 677.14
drive headlong *endanger* 811.13
drive home *emphasize* 200.6
drive in *impact* 710.11
drive-in *eating place* 92.17

drive-in *or* **drive-in theater** *motion-picture theater* 137.10
drive in a run *play baseball* 147.9
drive insane *derange* 766.23
drive into *motivate* 178.17
drive into a frenzy *make angry* 302.18
drive into the open *drive out* 709.19
drivel *saliva* 25.9, *salivate* 25.25, *nonsense* 192.8, *talk nonsense* 192.26, 362.12, *senseless talk* 362.4, *leak* 707.16
driveler *talker* 207.4
driveling *clumsy* 128.6, *nonsensical* 192.19
drivelingly *nonsensically* 192.30, 722.18
drivelling *seeping* 559.12
drive mad *make insane* 110.13
driven *desirous* 20.18, *fired* 106.13, *steady* 376.8, *directed* 384.7, *hasty* 818.3
driven snow *snow* 9.30, 218.6
drive on *motivate* 508.9, *press on* 679.9
drive on *or* **forward** *impel* 695.9
drive on! *go on!* 669.11
drive out 709.19
drive out of balk *play* 149.7
drive quickly *be swift* 694.10
driver 146.8; *personal attendant* 69.5, *golf equipment* 156.5, *user* 393.4, *conductor* 399.13, *operator* 509.5, *transferrer* 685.4, *transporter* 686.4, *propeller* 696.8
drive recklessly *endanger* 811.13
driverless car *means of transportation* 686.2
drive round the bend [Inf] *make insane* 110.13
driver's license *permit* 502.3, *miscellaneous automotive terms* 687.14
driver's license number *personal identification* 184.4
drive through *exert oneself* 122.11
drive to death *kill* 30.19
drive to despair *disappoint* 282.12
drive together *herd* 59.29
drive to the wall *cause difficulties* 824.22, *defeat* 845.17
drive up the wall [Inf] *make insane* 110.13, *irritate* 302.16
drive wheel *wheel* 682.9
drive without due care and attention *endanger* 811.13
drive with the bowl *bowl* 151.8
driving *rainy* 9.50, *assembling* 59.12, *hunting* 160.2, *tenacious* 376.9, *compelling* 428.6, *moving* 677.12, *road transportation* 687.1, *passing along* 692.5, *swiftness* 694.1, *impelling* 695.8, *propulsive* 696.12
driving ambition *motivation* 508.1
driving force *motive* 178.5, *motivation* 508.1, *vigor* 514.2, *impulsion* 695.1, *propulsion* 696.1, *propellant* 696.9
driving rain *rain* 9.27
drizzle *rain* 9.27, 9.57, *mistiness* 559.2, *sprinkle* 559.14, *drip* 714.13
drizzling *rainy* 9.50, *misty* 559.10
drizzly *rainy* 9.50, *misty* 559.10
Dr. Jekyll and Mr. Hyde *duality* 789.2
drogue *weather instrument* 9.7, *safety device* 810.15
droll *humorous* 277.9, *ridiculous* 368.5

drollery *humor* 277.1, *ridiculousness* 368.1
drolly *humorously* 277.13
dromond *or* **dromon** Sailing Ships and Boats 690
dromophobia Phobias 283
drone *male animal* 32.15, *social insect* 40.6, *infest* 40.17, *tone* 140.24, *woodwind* 142.4, *undercurrent of sound* 233.3, *sound faint* 233.8, *humming* 235.2, *hum* 235.11, *insect sound* 240.3, *make an insect sound* 240.9, *be dissonant* 241.6, *nonworker* 415.4, *plodder* 693.6
drone on *be talkative* 207.7, *bore* 296.8
droning *humming* 235.7, 240.6, *unmelodious* 241.5
drool *saliva* 25.9, *salivate* 25.25, *eat well* 92.23, *seep* 559.16, *leak* 707.16
drooling *salivating* 25.18, *seeping* 559.12
drool over *communicate love* 299.25
droop 714.14; *be unhealthy* 114.29, *despair* 270.8, *be weak* 517.12, *suspension* 604.1, *suspend* 604.13, *sinkage* 714.2, *deteriorate* 808.14, *be fatigued* 820.5, *decline* 846.16
droopiness *depression* 270.2
drooping 714.10; *sick* 114.24, *weak* 517.6, *suspension* 604.1, *suspended* 604.7, *sinkage* 714.2, *fatigued* 820.2
droopy *depressed* 270.5, *drooping* 714.10
drop 714.15; *have young* 21.16, *give birth* 35.33, *be unhealthy* 114.29, *drink* 121.6, *be clumsy* 128.9, Architectural Elements 134, *stage set* 136.19, *appetizer* 219.2, *relinquish* 392.3, *stop using* 394.10, *succumb* 421.7, *be weak* 517.12, *little piece* 580.4, *lower* 597.21, *descend* 597.22, *deepening* 598.4, *deepen* 598.21, *verticality* 602.1, *fall vertically* 602.10, *undress* 614.18, *round thing* 633.3, *decline* 680.5, 747.4, *slip back* 680.19, *shoot* 696.18, *dismiss* 709.15, *fall* 714.4, *drop* 714.15, *lowering* 716.1, *throw down* 716.13, *advantage* 744.3, *particle* 760.4, *discontinue* 775.10, *little bit* 800.4, *be fatigued* 820.5, *resign* 835.5
drop [Inf] *drug oneself* 121.37
drop a bomb *or* **bombshell** *surprise* 292.9
drop a catch *be clumsy* 128.9
drop acid [Inf] *drug oneself* 121.37
drop a clanger [Brit inf] *blunder* 846.13
drop a habit *disaccustom* 398.6
drop a hint *warn* 814.8
drop a line *or* **card** *or* **note** *correspond* 169.19
drop anchor *handle sailboat* 150.30, *sail* 690.16, *land* 704.16
drop and oar *row* 150.32
drop a pop-up *be clumsy* 128.9
drop ball *soccer play* 163.5
drop bombs 418.19
drop by *visit* 408.16
drop by *or* **in** *enter* 706.11
drop by drop *by degrees* 739.10, *partly* 760.17
dropcloth *floor covering* 613.13
drop-crotching *tree management* 43.6

drop curtain *stage set* 136.19
drop down *drop* 714.15
drop from the sky *drop* 714.15
drop from view *be forgotten* 355.12
drop handlebars *bicycle part* 687.11
drop in *visit* 408.16, *be transient* 643.6, *arrive* 704.13, *insert* 710.9
drop-in [Inf] *social gathering* 408.4, *transient* 643.2
drop in the bucket *incompleteness* 98.2, *little bit* 800.4
drop in the ocean *incompleteness* 98.2, *little bit* 800.4
drop into *fall into* 706.15
drop it *renounce* 392.4
drop it! *cease!* 668.14
drop kick *kick* 155.12
drop-kick *kick* 155.20
drop-kicker *special team* 155.11
drop-leaf *type of table* 101.5
drop leaves *grow* 43.15
droplet *little piece* 580.4, *round thing* 633.3
drop like a stone *fall vertically* 602.10
drop off *be insensible* 213.7, *descend* 714.12, *decrease* 747.7, *come unstuck* 756.7
drop of the curtain *play part* 136.8
drop one's eyes *be blind to* 243.19
drop one's guard *be unprepared* 389.14
drop one's jaw *wonder* 294.12
drop one's voice *sound faint* 233.8
drop ornament Architectural Elements 134
dropout *dissenter* 347.5, *reluctant person* 375.7, *nonperforming* 466.6, *protester* 507.4, *nonconformist* 782.7, *loser* 846.9
drop out *dissociate* 375.14, *withdraw* 392.5, *not perform* 466.10, *be independent* 782.20, 829.18
drop over the side *throw down* 716.13
drop pass *ice hockey tactics* 158.4
dropped *ice-skating* 162.32, *relinquished* 392.2
dropped catch *bungling* 128.2
dropped egg *egg dish* 90.18
dropped mohawk *ice-dancing move* 162.19
dropped three *ice-dancing move* 162.19
dropping *descent* 597.4, *descending* 597.13, *deepening* 598.4, 598.14, *fall* 714.4, *falling* 714.11, *lowered* 716.7, *fallen* 716.8, *fatigued* 820.2
dropping anchor *landing* 704.2
droppings *feces* 25.5, *dirt* 112.5
drops *dose of medicine* 115.3
drop scene *stage set* 136.19
drop shot *tennis strokes* 165.2, *badminton terms* 165.11
dropsical *of disease* 114.25, *swelled* 581.10
dropsy *symptom* 114.3, *swelling* 581.2
drop the ball *blunder* 846.13
drop the bomb *be at war* 76.32
drop *or* **ring down the curtain** *cease* 773.20
drop *or* **give up the idea** *renounce* 392.4
drop the payload *bomb* 418.19
drop the pilot *set out* 705.12
dross *dirt* 112.5, *coat* 588.3, *residue* 750.2, *refuse* 802.5
drossy *platelike* 588.8

drought *dryness* 9.23, 560.1, *scarcity* 98.3
drought [Arch] *thirst* 560.2
Droughtmaster Breeds of Cattle 16
drought-stricken *infertile* 23.7
drought-stricken land *infertile land* 23.2
droughty *dry* 560.7
drove *practice livestock farming* 16.20, *assemblage of mammals* 35.22, Collective Names 59, *throng* 795.4
drover *farm worker* 16.15
drown *murder* 30.20, *destroy* 186.10, *abolish* 523.11, *consume* 523.16, *water* 557.29, *descend* 714.12, *bring down* 716.14, *fill* 761.11
drowned *flooded* 557.24, 570.8
drowning *way of dying* 29.5, *murder* 30.2, *capital punishment* 454.12, *soaking* 557.9, *sinkage* 714.2, *descending* 714.9
drown oneself *commit suicide* 30.24
drown one's sorrows *get drunk* 121.35
drown out *muffle* 229.11
drown-proofed *swimming* 164.12
drown-proofing *survival swimming* 164.4, *swimming* 164.12
drowse *be insensible* 213.7, *sleep* 415.14, *take it easy* 819.3
drowser *sleeper* 415.7
drowsily *insensibly* 213.9, *sleepily* 415.19
drowsiness *sleep* 415.5
drowsy *anesthetic* 213.6, *not awake* 415.12
drub *hit* 454.28, *blow* 695.5, *kick* 695.14, *defeat* 845.17
drubbing *corporal punishment* 454.11, *defeat* 846.7
drudge *servant* 69.1, *work* 122.8, *worker* 123.1, *persevere* 377.10, *hard worker* 414.11
drudgery *work* 122.1, *assiduity* 414.8
drudging *working* 122.6
drug 115.9, 121.14; *medicine* 115.2, *medicate* 115.18, *poison* 117.18, *anesthetic* 213.3, *make inactive* 415.16
drug abuse *substance abuse* 121.1, *drug use* 121.9
drug addict *sick person* 114.22, *drug taker* 121.12, *creature of habit* 397.8
drug addiction *drug use* 121.9
drug dealer *drug pusher* 121.13
drug dependence *drug use* 121.9
drug-dependent *addicted* 121.31
drug dose 121.15
drug enforcement officer *security force* 810.13
drugged 121.30; *desensitized* 213.5, *not awake* 415.12
drugget Fabrics and Fibers 130, *floor covering* 613.13
druggie [Inf] *drug taker* 121.12
druggist 115.10
drug house *wicked place* 448.8
drug oneself 121.37
drug peddler *drug pusher* 121.13
drug peddler *or* **dealer** *villain* 448.5
drug peddling *drug pushing* 121.10
drug peddling *or* **dealing** *wicked act* 448.7
drug pusher 121.13
drug pushing 121.10

drugs *drug* 121.14, Phobias 283
drug scorer [Inf] *drug taker* 121.12
drugstore *druggist* 115.10
drugstore counter *eating place* 92.17
drug taker 121.12
drug taking *substance abuse* 121.1
drug test *competition* 166.18
drug traffic *trade* 480.1
drug trafficking *drug pushing* 121.10
drug treatment *treatment* 107.14, *psychiatric treatment* 108.3
drug use 121.9
drug user *drug taker* 121.12
druid *occultist* 86.13
druidess *occultist* 86.13
druidic *witchlike* 86.19
drum 235.10; *rain* 9.57, Architectural Elements 134, *percussion instrument* 142.5, *mean nothing* 362.10, *vessel* 578.11, *vibrate* 683.13, *shake* 684.24, *resound* 797.21
drumbeat *military call* 183.9, *drumming* 235.1, *warning signal* 814.3
drumhead *percussion instrument* 142.5
drumlin *glacier* 8.44, *hill* 569.2
drummer *player* 141.2
drumming 235.1, 235.6; *rainy* 9.50, *ceremonial* 404.11, *vibration* 683.2, *ramming* 695.3, *reverberation* 797.6, *reverberatory* 797.14
drumming fingers *gesture* 183.5
drumming out *dismissal* 709.2
drum one's fingers *gesture* 183.17, *be active* 414.18
drum out *exile* 454.24, *disbar* 709.16, *drive out* 709.19
drum printer *hardcopy device* 15.10
drumroll *drumming* 235.1, *salute* 405.7
drums *glory of war* 76.17
drumstick *poultry* 90.28, *percussion instrument* 142.5
drunk 121.25; *wasted* 96.14, *drunkard* 121.8, *overindulgent* 456.8
drunk and disorderly *drunk* 121.25
drunkard 121.8; *drinker* 93.16
drunk as a fiddler *drunk* 121.25
drunk as a lord *drunk* 121.25
drunk as an owl *drunk* 121.25
drunk as a skunk *drunk* 121.25
drunken 121.28; *drinking* 93.17, *drunk* 121.25
drunken behavior 121.4
drunkenly 121.39
drunkenness 121.3; *immoderation* 99.2, *overindulgence* 456.3
drunken stupor *drunkenness* 121.3
drunk tank *prison cell* 55.3
drupe *botanical fruit* 44.2, *fruit* 90.34
Druze *Muslim* 81.12
Druzism *Islam* 81.7
dry 560.7, 560.17; *fine* 9.43, *domesticated* 16.18, *infertile* 23.7, *political party member* 50.6, *drinkable* 93.18, *clean* 111.17, *practice hygiene* 116.4, *sober* 120.5, *make ceramics* 129.10, *unemphatic* 201.2, *tasteless* 220.4, *season* 221.8, 654.11, *acid* 223.5, *hoarse* 238.5, *hungry* 288.16, *boring* 296.6, *abstaining* 386.11, *strict person* 424.4, *self-restrained person*

455.5, *abstinent* 455.7, *thirsty* 560.8, *nonadhesive* 756.4, *preserve* 815.14

dryad *figurative usage* 43.9, *minor deity* 82.2

dry air *atmosphere* 9.8

dry as a bone *thirsty* 560.8

dry as a bone *or* **dust** *or* **parchment** *or* **a stick** *or* a biscuit *or* **a mummy** *dried-up* 560.9

dry-as-dust *tasteless* 220.4, *boring* 296.6

dry bed *river parts* 570.3

dry-bulb thermometer *measuring instrument* 557.19

dry-cargo *transportable* 686.7

dry cell *electrochemistry* 11.19, *power supplier* 514.14

dry-clean *clean* 111.17, *treat* 130.21

dry-cleaned *treated* 130.16

dry cleaner *cleaner* 111.12, *fabric handler* 130.11

dry cleaning *cleaning* 111.2, *fabric treatment* 130.10

dry climate *climate* 9.35

dry county *prohibition of alcohol* 120.2

dry cow *livestock* 16.11

dry dock *stopover* 704.7

dryer 560.5; *fabric-handling tool* 130.12, *darkroom equipment* 132.21

dry farming *arable farming* 16.6

dry feed *animal food* 90.2

dry-fly *fishing* 154.13

dry fly-fishing *fly-fishing* 154.2

dry fruit *botanical fruit* 44.2

dry goods 130.3; *store-bought clothes* 100.3, *merchandise* 482.6, 522.6

dry-goods dealer *clothier* 100.37

dry humor *humor* 277.1

dry ice *ice* 218.5

drying 560.3, 560.15; *ceramic process* 129.5, *preservation of provisions* 815.6

drying oil *oil* 562.3

drying out *sober* 120.5

drying up *drying* 560.3

dryly 560.23; *without taste* 220.8, *humorously* 277.13, *boringly* 296.10

dry measure *measuring system* 589.4, *type of measurement* 589.8

dryness 9.23, 560.1; *infertility* 23.1, *dilution* 220.2, *sourness* 223.1, *Phobias* 283, *appetite* 288.6, *boringness* 296.2, *thirst* 560.2

dry off *practice livestock farming* 16.20, *dry* 560.17

dry out *sober up* 120.7, *drug oneself* 121.37, *dry* 560.17

drypoint *engraving* 144.3

dry rot *fungus* 47.1, *dirt* 112.5, *agent of destruction* 523.7

dry run *rehearsal* 335.2

dry season *seasons* 654.2

dry-shod *waterproof* 560.16

dry skin 560.6

dry snow *snow* 218.6

dry spell *dryness* 9.23

dry state *prohibition of alcohol* 120.2

dry up 560.21; *waste away* 96.20, *be insufficient* 98.9, *underact* 136.36, *lapse into silence* 208.8, *be forgetful* 355.11, *dry* 560.17, *decrease* 747.7

dry up! [Inf] *hush!* 231.6

dry wine *wine* 93.11, *sour thing* 223.3

dry wit *wit* 277.3

dry-witted *witty* 277.10

D string *part of stringed instrument* 142.2

dual *two* 789.8

dual carriageway [Brit] *road attribute* 687.3

dual citizenship *or* **nationality** *national* 61.3

dual highway *road attribute* 687.3

dualism Philosophical Schools of Thought 4, *duality* 789.2

dualist Philosophical Schools of Thought 4

dualistic *two* 789.8

duality 789.2

dually *twice* 789.18

dual personality *duality* 789.2

dual-purpose *two-sided* 789.9

dub [Inf] *golfer* 156.7

Dubawnt Lakes 568

dubbed shot *golf shots* 156.4

dubiety *disbelief* 88.1, *vacillation* 683.3

dubious *disbelieving* 88.6, *arguable* 329.8, *sophistic* 330.7, *questionable* 333.13, *improbable* 839.4, *uncertain* 841.9

dubiously *disbelievingly* 88.10, *sophistically* 330.14, *questionably* 333.22, *improbably* 839.8, *uncertainly* 841.22

dubiousness *disbelief* 88.1, *questionableness* 333.7, *uncertainty* 841.1

dubitable *improbable* 839.4

Dublin Countries 566

Dubrovnik Breeds of Sheep 16

ducal *aristocratic* 70.4

ducat *ancient coins* 484.12

duce *absolute ruler* 68.7

duchess *nobleman* 70.1

duchy *body politic* 50.3, *administrative region* 564.4, *dominion* 566.3

duck *livestock* 16.11, *water bird* 36.9, *female bird* 36.16, *meat* 90.22, Fabrics and Fibers 130, *game* 160.6, *dissociate* 375.14, *evasion* 386.5, *evade* 386.19, *punish* 454.22, *water* 557.29, *move* 677.15, *immerse* 710.12, *bow* 716.6, 716.22, *bring down* 716.14, *sit* 716.20

duck and dive *be irresolute* 666.6

duck and run *escape* 816.8

duck-billed platypus *or* **duckbill** *egg-laying mammal* 35.4

duckboard *floor covering* 613.13

duck duck goose Children's and Party Games 167

ducked *flooded* 557.24

duck farming *livestock farming* 16.10

ducking *punishment* 454.1, *soaking* 557.9, *immersion* 710.3, *submergence* 716.3

ducking and diving *irresolution* 666.2

ducking stool *instrument of punishment* 454.13

duckling *livestock* 16.11, *young animal* 26.4, *young bird* 36.17

duckpin *bowling* 151.1, 151.6

duckpin bowler *bowler* 151.5

duckpins Sporting Activities 145, *bowling* 151.1

duck responsibility *be irresolute* 461.8

ducks Collective Names 59, *pants* 100.14

duck season *seasons* 654.2

duck soup *easy thing* 823.6

ducktail *coiffure* 530.8

duck the issue *be evasive* 386.20

ducky *or* **ducks** [Brit inf] *term of endearment* 299.7

duct *river parts* 570.3, *opening* 583.1

ductile *pliant* 543.7, *elastic* 546.5, *retractive* 699.8, *wieldy* 823.12

ductility *softness* 543.1, *elasticity* 546.1

ductless gland *secretory mechanism* 24.3

dud *useless* 802.7, *unsuccessful thing* 846.8, *loser* 846.9, *failed* 846.10

dude [Inf] *male* 32.1

dudelsack Musical Instruments 142

dudgeon *resentment* 302.1

dudgeon [Arch] *sharp weapon* 78.6

duds [Inf] *clothing* 100.1

due *title* 72.1, *qualified* 340.7, *expected* 356.5, *claim* 429.3, *rightful* 429.9, *indebted* 488.7, *payable* 489.12, *future* 650.6, *directly* 697.16, *convenient* 803.3

due credit *reward* 453.1

due for demolition *destroyed* 523.9

duel 422.12, 422.24; *slaughter* 30.5, *fence* 153.7

dueler *combatant* 77.1

dueler *or* **duelist** *fencer* 153.5

dueling *fencing* 153.1, *duel* 422.12

dueling pistol *historical handgun* 78.8

dueling sword *fencing equipment* 153.2

duelist *combatant* 77.1

duel to the death *duel* 422.12

due measure *moderation* 521.1

dueness *qualification* 340.1, *mode of behavior* 399.2, *retaliation* 420.1, *convenience* 803.1

duenna *accompanier* 794.6, *protector* 810.11

due north *directly* 697.16

due payment *type of payment* 489.3

due process *legal process* 54.3

due recognition *reward* 453.1

due respect *respectfulness* 435.3

Duero Rivers 570

dues *payment* 433.5, *money received* 492.2, *fee* 494.3

duet *instrumental group* 141.3, *two* 789.1, *twosome* 789.3, *team* 827.7

due time *convenience* 803.1

due to *by virtue of* 447.12, *caused* 676.5

duffel Fabrics and Fibers 130, *possessions* 470.5

duffel *or* **duffle coat** *coat* 100.19

duffel bag *bag* 578.7

duffer [Inf] *male* 32.1, *unskilled person* 128.3, *golfer* 156.7, *ignorant person* 349.4

dug *mammalian characteristic* 35.3, *holed* 583.12

dug in *defended* 419.18

dugout *baseball field* 147.3, *canoeing* 150.26, *hiding place* 181.2, *military defenses* 419.9, Ships and Boats 690, *fortification* 812.3

dugout canoe *canoe* 150.9

duke *nobleman* 70.1

dukedom *body politic* 50.3, *aristocracy* 70.2, *dominion* 566.3

Duke of Perth Dances 135

dukes [Inf] *retainer* 471.3

dulcet *melodious* 140.26, *pleasurable* 214.6, *comfortable* 271.8

dulcet [Arch] *sweet* 222.5

dulcify *sweeten* 222.7, *calm* 521.8

dulcinea *loved one* 299.13

dule Collective Names 59

dull 255.8, 550.7; *cloudy* 9.44, *discourage* 179.11, *unemphatic* 201.2, *tasteless* 220.4, *nonresonant* 233.7, *mute* 233.9, *dim* 248.4, *dimmed* 248.6, *tarnish* 248.9, *shady* 250.4, *colorless* 252.5, *decolor* 252.8, *insensitive* 268.4, *indifferent* 289.7, *make indifferent* 289.13, *wonderless* 295.3, *boring* 296.6, *overcast* 304.11, *lacking intellect* 316.5, *apathetic* 322.4, *foolish* 353.5, *inactive* 413.9, *not participating* 415.11, *inert* 519.2, *mitigate* 521.9, *simpleminded* 526.11, *plain* 528.9, *blunt* 550.5, 550.9, *thick-witted* 594.7, *sedentary* 678.5, *mediocre* 742.7, *fatigued* 820.2

dullard *unintelligent person* 316.4, *simpleton* 526.5

dull as ditchwater *or* **dishwater** *tasteless* 220.4

dulled *dimmed* 248.6

dull-edged *blunt* 550.5

dull-green *green* 260.7

dullness 255.5, 550.3; *lack of emphasis* 201.1, *insensibility* 213.1, *tastelessness* 220.1, *murk* 248.2, *opaqueness* 250.1, *hue* 251.4, *insensitivity* 268.1, *indifference* 289.1, *lack of wonder* 295.1, *boringness* 296.2, *overcast* 304.6, *idleness* 415.3, *inertness* 519.1, *bluntness* 550.1, *thick-wittedness* 594.3, *fatigue* 820.1

dull-pointed *blunt* 550.5

dull sound 233.2

dull speech *boring thing* 296.3

dull-witted *thick-witted* 594.7

dull-wittedness *thick-wittedness* 594.3

dully *without taste* 220.8, *colorlessly* 252.9, *grayly* 255.10, *without wonder* 295.8, *boringly* 296.10, *apathetically* 322.7, *impassively* 415.18, *smoothly* 550.10, *thick-wittedly* 594.13

Dülmen pony Horse and Pony Breeds 159

Dulong and Petit's law Classical Physical Laws 10

duly *properly* 429.18

dumb *animalian* 34.12, *unskillful* 128.4, *speechless* 206.7, *silent* 208.5, 231.2, *wondering* 294.7, *unintelligent* 316.6, *thick-witted* 594.7

dumb animal *animal* 34.1

dumbbell *unintelligent person* 316.4

dumb crambo Children's and Party Games 167

dumbfound *strike dumb* 206.10, *silence* 231.4, *astonish* 292.10, *be wondrous* 294.14

dumbfounded *speechless* 206.7, *silent* 231.2, *astonished* 292.6, *wondering* 294.7

dumbfoundment *wonder* 294.1

dumb luck *potluck* 842.4

dumbly *silently* 231.5, *speculatively* 294.17, *thick-wittedly* 594.13

dumbness *mutism* 206.3, *silence* 208.2, 231.1, *thick-wittedness* 594.3

dumb show *dramatic style* 136.3, *acting* 187.6

dumbstruck *wondering* 294.7, *at a loss* 468.11

dumb waiter *lifter* 715.5

dumdum *armor-piercing* 78.18
dum-dum [Inf] *unintelligent person* 316.4
dumdum bullet *ammunition* 78.11
dummy *bridge* 168.4, *stage of book production* 174.7, *figure* 187.4, *experimental* 335.8, *nonworker* 415.4, *prototype* 624.2, *prototypical* 624.7, *insubstantial person* 720.5, *artificial* 720.12, *copy* 736.2, *showpiece* 843.3
dummy [Inf] *unintelligent person* 316.4
dummy run *rehearsal* 335.2
dump *programming concepts* 15.24, *program* 15.29, *stop using* 394.10, *sell* 482.15, *discount* 495.4, *make cheap* 497.14, *unload* 709.24, *place for waste* 802.6
dump [Inf] *shack* 60.10
dumpcart *wagon* 687.5
dumpiness *squatness* 579.6, *littleness* 580.1, *shortness* 591.1
dumping *disuse* 394.3, *bargain* 495.2
dumpling *pasta* 90.31, *big person* 579.10
dump on [Inf] *insult* 436.21
dump on the market *overdo* 99.11
dumps, the *sign of sullenness* 304.2
dump truck *construction equipment* 14.23
dumpy *graceless* 528.7, *fat* 579.15, *undersized* 580.8, *short* 591.6
dun *horse by color* 159.7, *gray* 255.6, *brown* 256.5, *meddle* 414.23, *lender* 487.5, *credit* 487.10, *demand* 505.3, 505.12
Duncan Phyfe *Furniture Styles* 101
dunce *unintelligent person* 316.4, *ignorant person* 349.4, *foolish person* 353.3
dunce cap *clothing* 184.6
dunce cap *or* **dunce's cap** *or* **fool's cap** *cap* 100.33
dunce's cap *instrument of punishment* 454.13
dunderhead *unintelligent person* 316.4
dune 8.43; *hill* 569.2
dune face *dune* 8.43
dune field *dune* 8.43
dung *fertilizer* 16.9, 22.6, *farm* 16.19, *cultivate* 17.19, *feces* 25.5, *dirt* 112.5, *unpleasant-smelling thing* 227.2
dungaree *Fabrics and Fibers* 130
dungarees *pants* 100.14
dungeon *prison* 55.1, *dark thing* 247.3, *fort* 419.13, *enclosed area* 619.2
dunghill *fertilizer* 16.9
dunging *cultivation* 16.7
dungy *fecal* 25.14, *unclean* 112.8
dunk *bathe* 111.18, *playing terms* 148.4, *play basketball* 148.7, *play* 156.8, *water* 557.29, *immerse* 710.12
dunked *flooded* 557.24
dunking *playing terms* 148.4, *soaking* 557.9
dunning *demand* 505.3
duo *two* 789.1
duodecillion *million* 792.11
duodecimal *eleven to nineteen* 792.7, *eleventh and above* 792.18
duodecimal notation *number system* 6.7
duodecimo *little thing* 580.3, *undersized* 580.8, *eleven to nineteen* 792.7

duodenal ulcer *gastroenterological disease* 114.11
duodenary *eleventh and above* 792.18
duodenitis *gastroenterological disease* 114.11
duodenum *internal organ* 19.13
duodrama *play* 136.2
duologue *play* 136.2, *conversation* 210.1
duomo [Ital] *place of worship* 83.8
dupe *make someone believe* 87.11, *deceive* 181.14, 193.16, *laughingstock* 369.4, *sycophant* 401.3, *butt* 436.8, *loser* 468.8, 846.9, *act dishonestly* 479.18, *assistant* 511.3, *weak person* 517.4, *inferior* 745.4, *trap* 813.6, *naive person* 821.2, *person in adversity* 848.9
dupe [Inf] *copy* 730.5
duped *deceived* 193.15, *trapped* 813.5
duper *deceiver* 193.8
duple *two* 789.8
duple meter *meter* 139.10
duplex *house* 60.4, *apartment* 60.7, *manorial* 60.21, *twosome* 789.3, *two* 789.8
duplexity *duality* 789.2
duplicate 730.11, 736.4; *reprint* 21.3, *reproduce* 21.13, *be superfluous* 99.12, *means of identification* 184.3, *recording* 185.6, *image* 187.3, *represent* 187.10, *representation* 202.9, *correspondent* 606.3, *copy* 730.5, 730.17, 736.2, 736.10, *simulation* 733.4, *simulate* 733.16, *make bigger* 746.7, *twin* 789.5, *double* 789.11, 789.14, *replica* 797.7, *repeat* 797.15
duplicate bridge *bridge* 168.4
duplicated *reproduced* 21.10, *duplicate* 730.11, *simulated* 733.11, *double* 789.11, *repeated* 797.8
duplication *reproduction* 21.1, *superfluity* 99.4, *copy* 730.5, *simulation* 733.4, *duplicate* 736.4, *increase* 746.1, *doubling* 789.4, *repetition* 797.1
duplicative *superfluous* 99.8, *repetitious* 797.11
duplicator *copier* 736.5
duplicitous *deceptive* 193.12, *double-edged* 789.10
duplicitously *deceptively* 193.21
duplicity *evasion* 181.5, *deception* 193.1, *hypocrisy* 330.5, *duality* 789.2, *cunning* 822.1
durability *endurance* 516.4, *toughness* 547.1, *continuation* 642.2, *permanence* 667.1, *stability* 674.1
durable *strengthened* 516.13, *tough* 547.6, *lasting* 639.9, 642.4, *eternal* 644.4, *permanent* 667.2, *stable* 674.3
durable goods *merchandise* 522.6
durables *merchandise* 482.6
durably *toughly* 547.16
dura mater *body covering* 19.4
duramen *timber* 43.3, *hard substance* 542.3
durance *imprisonment* 55.4, *detention* 830.5
durance vile *imprisonment* 55.4
duration 642.1; *intervening space* 563.8, *length* 590.1, *time* 639.1, *continuance* 669.3, *continuing existence* 717.7, *degree* 739.1
duration of time *Phobias* 283

duress *coercion* 428.2, *restraint* 830.1
Durga-puja *religious festival* 85.13
Durham Rule *insanity* 110.1
during the past *in the past* 651.20
durmast *or* **durmast oak** *Trees and Shrubs* 43
durn *or* **durned** [Inf] *miscellaneous euphemisms* 301.12
Duroc *Breeds of Pigs* 16
Duroc Jersey *Breeds of Pigs* 16
Dushanbe *Countries* 566
dusk *darkness* 247.1, *dimness* 248.1, *evening* 656.2, *close* 773.9
duskily *blackly* 254.12
duskiness *dimness* 248.1, *blackness* 254.1
dusky *dark* 247.5, 254.6, *dim* 248.4, *evening* 656.4
dust *fertilizer* 16.9, *cultivate* 17.19, *clean* 111.17, *dirt* 112.5, *variegate* 263.11, *Phobias* 283, *powder* 553.9, 553.25, *throw down* 716.13, *sprinkle* 776.15, *little bit* 800.4, *refuse* 802.5
dust ball *powder* 553.9
dust bowl *infertile land* 23.2, *desert* 560.4
dust bunny *powder* 553.9
dust cloth *cleaning tool* 111.10, *cleaning cloth* 111.11
dust cloud *powder* 553.9
dust cover *bookbinding* 174.11
dust cover [Brit] *enclosing thing* 619.3
dust cover *or* **jacket** *wrapping* 613.10
dust-covered *powdery* 553.19
dust devil *wind vortex* 9.14, *powder* 553.9
dusted *mottled* 263.10, *sprinkled* 776.9
duster *coat* 100.19
dustheap *place for waste* 802.6
dustily *flakily* 553.30, *dryly* 560.23
dustiness *powderiness* 553.3
dusting *cleaning* 111.2, *corporal punishment* 454.11, *pulverization* 553.4, *sprinkling* 776.4
dusting off *ramming* 695.3
dusting off the batter *pitching terms* 147.5
dust jacket *bookbinding* 174.11, *enclosing thing* 619.3
dust kitten *powder* 553.9
dustman [Brit] *cleaner* 111.12
dust of antiquity *oldness* 653.1
dust off *hit* 454.28, *beat* 695.12
dust-off *pitching terms* 147.5
dustpan and brush *cleaning tool* 111.10
dust ruffle *bed covering* 613.7
dust storm *wind* 9.12, *natural violence* 520.3, *powder* 553.9
dust thrown in the eyes *stratagem* 822.2
dustup *dispute* 463.3, *disruption* 766.7
dusty *dirty* 112.7, *murky* 248.5, *dimmed* 248.6, *shady* 250.4, *whitened* 253.8, *mottled* 263.10, *powdery* 553.19, *desert* 560.12
dusty air *murk* 248.2
Dutch *arch* 134.5
Dutch auction *sale* 482.2
Dutch Belted *Breeds of Cattle* 16
Dutch Black Pied *Breeds of Cattle* 16
Dutch bob *coiffure* 530.8
Dutch cap *contraceptive* 23.6, *barrier* 826.7
Dutch courage [Inf] *drinking* 121.2, *bold front* 284.5

Dutch door *Architectural Elements* 134
Dutch Draught *Horse and Pony Breeds* 159
Dutch elm *Trees and Shrubs* 43
Dutch elm disease *tree disease* 43.8, *fungal disease* 47.6
Dutch Landrace *Breeds of Pigs* 16
Dutchman's breeches *Flowers* 42
Dutch oven *cooking equipment* 91.6, *burner* 217.4
Dutch rush *fern* 46.1
Dutch uncle *adviser* 176.5, *strict person* 424.4
Dutch Yorkshire *Breeds of Pigs* 16
duteous 433.7; *obedient* 426.4, *observant* 465.3
duteously *dutifully* 433.19, *observantly* 465.6
duteousness *sense of duty* 433.2
dutiable *chargeable* 494.11
dutiful 433.6; *prayerful* 85.17, *answerable* 334.17, *obedient* 426.4, *showing respect* 435.7, *kind* 445.12, *principled* 447.6, *observant* 465.3
dutifully 433.19; *ritually* 85.21, *answerably* 334.28, *obediently* 426.9, *kindly* 445.20, *ethically* 447.10, *observantly* 465.6
dutifulness *obedience* 426.1, *kindness* 445.3
duty 433.1; *international trade* 56.7, *title* 72.1, *ritual* 85.1, *necessitation* 95.5, *burden* 117.3, *work* 122.1, *calling* 178.6, *answerability* 334.9, *obedience* 426.1, *virtues* 447.2, *observance* 465.1, *money received* 492.2, *levy* 494.7, *participation* 760.10, *economic restraint* 830.3, *engagement* 833.2
duty-bound 433.8; *answerable* 334.17
duty-free *tax-free* 434.8, *with impunity* 434.13
duumvirate *oligarchy* 49.10, *team* 827.7
duvet *bed covering* 613.7
duvetyn *or* **duvetyne** *or* **duvetine** *Fabrics and Fibers* 130
Duvida, Rio da *Rivers* 570
Dvina *Rivers* 570
dwarf *sprite* 86.12, *little person* 580.5, *undersized* 580.8
dwarfed *undersized* 580.8
dwarf elliptical *galaxy* 7.5
dwarfish *undersized* 580.8
dwarfishness *littleness* 580.1
dwarf tree *tree* 43.1
dwell *inhabit* 60.22, 61.13, *settle* 565.10, *reside* 575.17, *exist* 717.18
dweller *inhabitant* 61.1
dwellers *inhabitants* 61.2
dwell in *possess* 469.14
dwelling 36.4, 38.4, 40.7; *habitation* 60.2, *inhabiting* 60.18, *resident* 61.11
dwelling place *habitation* 60.2
dwell on *emphasize* 200.6
dwindle *waste away* 96.20, *disappear* 265.5, *lessen* 468.17, *be weak* 517.12, *diminish* 597.24, *decrease* 747.7
dwindle away *disappear* 265.5
dwindling *disappearance* 265.1, *lessening* 468.6, *diminishing* 597.16, *decrease* 747.1, *decreasing* 747.5
DX code *exposure* 132.15

dyad *two* 789.1
dyadic *dialectical* 4.16, *two* 789.8
dyarchy *oligarchy* 49.10
dybbuk *evil spirit* 446.4
dye 130.8; *treat* 130.21, *coloring agent* 251.5, *color* 251.16, *coif* 530.15, *admixture* 751.5, *mix* 751.12
dye blue *blue* 261.9
dyed *treated* 130.16, *colored* 251.10, *fixed* 397.13, *beautified* 530.12, *complicated* 751.10
dyed-in-the-wool *treated* 130.16, *fixed* 397.13, *complete* 761.6, *conservative* 815.13
dyed-in-the-yarn *treated* 130.16
dyeing 130.9
dye laser *laser (light amplification by stimulated emission of radiation)* 10.18
dyer's-broom Flowers 42
dyestuff *dye* 130.8, *fabric-handling tool* 130.12, *coloring agent* 251.5
dyestuffs *industrial chemistry* 11.21
dyewood *fabric-handling tool* 130.12
dying 29.3, 29.12; *sick* 114.24, *disappearance* 265.1, *disappearing* 265.3
dying away *faint* 233.6
dying breath *dying* 29.3
dying by one's own hand *suicide* 30.8
dying day *dying* 29.3
dying for *desirous* 288.13
dying for food *underfed* 118.7
dying out *disappearance* 265.1
dying patient *dying person* 29.6
dying person 29.6
dying race *infertile state* 23.3
dying star *stellar evolution* 7.10
dying words *conclusion* 761.3
dyke *channel* 691.10
dyke [Inf and Off] *homosexual* 33.10
dykey [Inf and Off] *of sexual nature* 20.17, *female* 33.16
dynamic *physical* 10.70, *mechanical* 14.44, *lively* 28.16, *active* 414.13, *energetic* 514.16, *vigorous* 518.2, *directional* 677.13, *impelling* 695.8
dynamically 695.16; *physically* 10.78, *energetically* 514.22, *in motion* 677.19
dynamic belay *climbing techniques* 161.3
dynamic energy *energy* 414.4
dynamic friction *force* 10.9
dynamic load *load* 14.14
dynamic memory *memory* 15.6
dynamic metamorphism *metamorphism* 8.35
dynamic psychology Psychological Theories, Schools 108
dynamic random-access memory (DRAM) *memory* 15.6
dynamic range *exposure* 132.15
dynamics *classical physics* 10.2, *motion* 677.1, *impulsion* 695.1
dynamic structure 14.5
dynamic system *dynamic structure* 14.5
dynamism Philosophical Schools of Thought 4, *energy* 414.4, *vigor* 518.1
dynamist Philosophical Schools of Thought 4
dynamite *explosive* 78.13, *agent of destruction* 523.7, *demolish* 523.12, *propellant* 696.9, *blow up* 696.19
dynamo *generator* 14.43, *electricity*

106.5, *busy person* 414.10, *power supplier* 514.14
dynamometer Fields of Measurement 589
dynamometry Fields of Measurement 589
dynastic *governing* 49.25, *family* 65.6
dynasty *governance* 49.18, *family tree* 65.3, *nobleness* 70.3, *line* 774.2
dyne Scientific and Technical Units 589
dysentery *defecation* 25.3, *gastroenterological disease* 114.11
dysfunction *failure* 430.9
dysmenorrhea *bleeding* 25.10, *painful condition* 215.2
dyspepsia *gastroenterological disease* 114.11
dyspeptic *sick person* 114.22, *cross* 303.11, *irritable* 304.9
dyspeptically *crossly* 303.20, *irritably* 304.17
dysphasia *speech defect* 206.2
dysphasic *inarticulate* 206.6
dysphemia *speech defect* 206.2
dysphemic *inarticulate* 206.6
dysphemism *curse word* 301.4, *inelegance of expression* 528.4
dysphemistic *profane* 301.10, *inelegant* 528.6
dysphonia *speech difficulty* 206.1
dysphonic *voiceless* 206.5
dyspnea *cardiovascular disease* 114.13
dysprosium Chemical Elements and Common Allotropes 11
dyssomnia *sleep disorder* 108.20
dysthymic disorder *mood disorder* 108.12
dystopian novel *novel* 139.3
dystychiphobia Phobias 283

E

E1 *chemical reaction* 11.8
E2 *chemical reaction* 11.8
each *whole* 759.6, *specifically* 779.22
each and every one *everyone* 778.7
each in his or **her turn** *in exchange* 673.6
eager 373.8; *earnest* 278.5, *desirous* 288.13, *inclined toward* 290.5, *expecting* 356.4, *steady* 376.8, *active* 414.13, *strong in spirit* 516.11
eager beaver *willing worker* 373.6, *hard worker* 414.11
eagerly 288.27, 373.16; *admiringly* 290.11, *expectantly* 356.10, *actively* 414.24, *acutely* 516.18
eagerness 288.3, 373.2; *earnestness* 278.2, *inclination* 290.2, *expectation* 356.1, *seriousness* 376.3, *energy* 414.4
Eagle Constellations 7
eagle *bird of prey* 36.11, *golfing terms* 156.3, *play* 156.8, *Heraldic Terms* 184, *US coinage* 484.10, *ascender* 713.12
eagle, bald Endangered US Birds 36
eagle eye *sharp eye* 242.4
eagle-eyed *seeing* 242.17
eagles Collective Names 59
eaglet *young bird* 36.17
eagle-winged *swift* 694.6
ear 19.10, 228.2; *cereal grass* 45.4, *sense organ* 212.4, *hearing*

228.1, *body orifice* 583.3, *growth* 676.3
earache *painful condition* 215.2, *ear problem* 228.4
ear canal *ear* 19.10
ear cuff *jewelry* 532.6
ear doctor 228.5
ear drops *ear problem* 228.4
eardrum *body covering* 19.4, *ear* 19.10, 228.2
eared 228.10
ear for *aptitude* 127.4
earful *public speaking* 205.11, *address* 209.1, *condemnation* 438.2
earhole *ear* 228.2
earl *nobleman* 70.1
earldom *aristocracy* 70.2, *dominion* 566.3
earless *deaf* 229.4
Earliblaze Apple Varieties 44
earlier *past* 651.11, *formerly* 653.19, *preceding* 769.9, *before* 769.18
earlies *crop* 16.8
earliest *early* 657.8, *preceding* 769.9, *prime* 771.18
earliest inhabitant *inhabitant* 61.1
earlike *eared* 228.10
earliness 657.1; *untimeliness* 660.1
earlobe *ear* 19.10, 228.2
Earl of Coventry Card Games 168
Earls Court London 567.8
early 657.8, 657.17; *past* 651.11, *primal* 653.14, *archaically* 653.20, *daily* 655.6, 655.8, *swift* 694.6, *beginning* 771.16
early agreement *predetermination* 384.1
early American Furniture Styles 101, Architectural Styles 134
early arrival *early comer* 657.4
early bird *morning things* 655.3, *early comer* 657.4
early Christian architecture Architectural Styles 134
early Christian art Western Art Styles 133
early comer 657.4
early days *first move* 771.12
early edition *newspaper* 175.2
early English style Architectural Styles 134
early history *early stage* 657.3
early Homo Sapiens *primitive humanity* 18.4
early hour 657.2
early humanity *primitive humanity* 18.4
early life *youth* 26.1
early man *primitive humanity* 18.4, *prehistoric human* 653.7
early maturity *prematurity* 657.6
early morning *dimness* 248.1, *early hour* 657.2
early on *early* 657.17
early-onset personality dysfunction *personality disorder* 108.7
early retirement *bargaining terms* 57.10
early riser *early comer* 657.4
early settlement or **decision** or **resolution** *predetermination* 384.1
early stage 657.3
early stages *first move* 771.12
early start *earliness* 657.1
early time *early hour* 657.2
early wood *timber* 43.3
earmark *means of identification* 184.3, *identify* 184.11, *intend for*

374.11, *choose* 382.14, *allocate* 474.5, *take over* 477.16, *characteristic* 779.5, *characterize* 779.15
earmarked *identified* 184.9
earmarking *allocation* 474.1
earmuffs *accessory* 100.28, *safety device* 810.15
earn 467.20; *be entitled to* 72.13, *gain* 467.15, *receive* 473.13, 492.7
earn a black belt *do martial arts* 152.21
earn a diploma *authorize* 833.10
earn a dividend *profit* 467.22
earn a living *earn* 467.20
earn an income *get paid* 453.17
earn a standing ovation *attain one's goal* 845.13
earn a wage *work* 122.8
earned income *earnings* 467.5
earned-run average (ERA) *pitching terms* 147.5
earned-run-average (ERA) leader *baseball team* 147.2
earner *breadwinner* 123.2, *gainer* 467.9, *recipient* 473.5
earnest 278.5; *emphatic* 200.3, *serious* 278.4, *steady* 376.8, *type of payment* 489.3, *deep-seated* 598.17, *part* 760.1
earnestly 278.10, 376.16; *emphatically* 200.7, *with deep feeling* 598.29
earnest money *type of payment* 489.3
earnestness 278.2; *seriousness* 278.1, 376.3, *assiduity* 414.8, *depth of feeling* 598.7
earning *receiving pay* 489.14
earning capacity *benefit* 801.4
earnings 467.5; *reward for service* 453.5, *gain* 467.1, *something received* 473.2, *takings* 477.8, *pay* 489.6, *income* 492.3
earnings per share *stock exchange* 457.3
earning status *social stratification* 2.7
earn interest *increase* 746.6
earn little or **nothing** *be poor* 486.14
ear, nose, and throat (ENT) *study of hearing* 228.3, *otological* 228.11
earphone *sound amplifier* 230.5
earphones *receiver* 473.8
earpiece *telephone* 169.10
ear-piercing *shrill* 238.6
earplug *sound reducer* 233.5, *safety device* 810.15
ear problem 228.4
ear-rending *loud* 232.6
earring *jewelry* 532.6
ears *head* 19.6
ear shape *ear* 228.2
ear-shaped *eared* 228.10
ear-shattering *deafening* 229.6
earshot *hearing* 228.1, *short distance* 586.2
ear-splitting *hearable* 228.12, *deafening* 229.6, *loud* 232.6, *strident* 238.4
ear-splitting noise *loudness* 232.1
Earth 7.17, 8.6; Planets and Their Satellites 7, *planet* 7.16
earth *soil* 8.42, *electric potential* 10.40, *mammal dwelling* 35.21, Collective Names 59, *natural habitat* 60.16, *dirt* 112.5, *solid body* 540.4, *base* 601.1, *shelter* 812.4
earth art Western Art Styles 133, *sculpture* 144.1
earthborn *human* 18.15

earth closet *place for excretion* 25.11

earth dam *dam* 551.12

earthenware Ceramics 129, *ceramics* 129.1, *merchandise* 522.6

earthenware mark *decoration* 129.4

earthflow *mass movement* 8.28

earth goddess *minor deity* 82.2

earth light *Earth* 7.17

earthling *person* 18.8

earthlings *humankind* 18.1

earthly *material* 524.7

earthly paradise *idealized pleasure* 214.5

earth movement 8.20

earthmover *construction equipment* 14.23

earth orbit *rocketry* 7.32, *flight path* 691.12

earthquake *seismic activity* 8.24, *natural violence* 520.3, *agent of destruction* 523.7, *wave* 683.4, *natural hazard* 813.4

earthquake magnitude *seismic activity* 8.24

earthquakes Fields of Measurement 589

earthquake zone *seismic activity* 8.24

earth satellite *artificial satellite* 7.30

earth science *geology* 8.1

earth scientist *geologist* 8.4

earthshaking *influential* 512.8, *serious* 799.8

earth-shattering *serious* 799.8

earthshine *Earth* 7.17, *natural light* 246.4

earth's magnetism *geomagnetism* 10.46

earth's orbit *curved thing* 629.3

earth tremor *seismic activity* 8.24

earthward *toward* 697.18

earthwork *monument* 185.10, *military defenses* 419.9, *fort* 419.13, *thing of the past* 651.8, *barrier* 826.7

earthy 8.60

earth zone 8.7

ear trumpet *aid to the deaf* 229.3

ear wax *body fluid* 19.16, *ear problem* 228.4

earwig *pests and diseases* 17.12, *insect* 40.1

earwitness *hearer* 228.7

ease 275.1, 543.15, 562.18, 819.1, 819.4; *conciliate* 74.10, *refreshment* 94.1, *refresh* 94.6, *practice medicine* 107.32, *remedy* 115.16, *leisure* 125.1, *manual skill* 127.2, *handle sailboat equipment* 150.30, *pleasure* 214.2, 271.2, *comfort* 214.14, *satisfaction* 273.1, *relieve* 275.8, *freedom* 407.4, *justify* 441.12, *opulence* 485.3, *mitigate* 521.9, *simplicity* 526.1, *elegance* 527.1, *grace* 527.2, *lighten* 539.9, *comfortable circumstances* 726.5, *decrease* 747.7, *easiness* 823.1, *make easy* 823.15, *support* 825.2, 825.24, *informality* 829.6, *prosperity* 847.1

ease along *move slowly* 693.11

eased *relieved* 275.6

easeful *pleasant* 214.7, *at ease* 819.2

ease in *inset* 710.13

easel *painting* 143.3, *material* 143.9

easel painter *painter* 143.7

easement *lightening* 539.2

ease off *be moderate* 521.6, *slow down* 693.13

ease or **edge off** *sidestep* 698.22

ease of manner 823.4

ease of movement *grace* 527.2

ease of viewing *clarity* 244.2

ease oneself *excrete* 25.20

ease the way *further* 825.30

ease up *ease* 543.15

easier said than done *difficult* 824.9

easily 819.5, 823.19; *sociably* 408.19, *leniently* 423.6, *simply* 526.14, *gracefully* 527.8, *soft-heartedly* 543.19, *slowly* 693.14, *comfortably* 726.19, *informally* 829.24

easily detected *easily seen through* 249.10

easily distinguished *visible* 244.5

easily excused *forgivable* 312.7

easily mistaken *unrecognizable* 364.7

easily seen through 249.10

easily understood *simple* 363.6

easiness 543.5, 823.1; *clarity* 363.2, *leniency* 423.1, *tolerance* 502.2, *simplicity* 526.1

easing 543.13, 823.7; *relieving* 275.7, *moderation* 521.1, *moderating* 521.5, *lightening* 539.2, 539.6, *recuperation* 809.4

easing off or **up** *deceleration* 693.2

easing up *easiness* 543.5

East *bridge* 168.4, *regions of the United States* 564.7

east side *direction* 623.2, *compass direction* 697.5, *directional* 697.8, *directionally* 697.20

East African Safari *automobile rallies* 146.6

East Balkan Breeds of Pigs 16

eastbound *directional* 697.8

East Bulgarian Horse and Pony Breeds 159

East China Sea Oceans and Seas 571

East Coast *regions of the United States* 564.7

East End *London* 567.8

Easter Christian Holy Days and Seasons 85, *seasons* 654.2

Easter bonnet *hat* 100.32

Easter Even Christian Holy Days and Seasons 85

Easter Island Islands 572

Easter lily Flowers 42

easterly *windy* 9.42, *directional* 697.8, *directionally* 697.20

eastern *regional* 564.12, *side* 623.6, *directional* 697.8

Eastern Christianity *Christianity* 81.5

Eastern cutoff style *jumping* 166.11

Eastern Hemisphere *world region* 564.6

easternmost *directional* 697.8

Eastern Orthodoxy Christian Groups 81

Eastern Red Pied Breeds of Cattle 16

Eastern Seaboard *regions of the United States* 564.7

Eastern Time *time zone* 646.5

Easter offering *offering* 472.6

Eastertide Christian Holy Days and Seasons 85

East Friesian Breeds of Sheep 16, Horse and Pony Breeds 159

easting *compass direction* 697.5

east-northeast *directionally* 697.20

East Side *New York* 567.6

east-southeast *directionally* 697.20

eastward *compass direction* 697.5,

directional 697.8, *directionally* 697.20

eastwardly *directionally* 697.20

easy 823.9; *type of chair* 101.4, *leisurely* 125.4, *comfortable* 271.8, 726.10, *simple* 363.6, 526.7, *sociable* 408.11, *lenient* 423.3, *unchaste* 432.10, *fluid* 527.5, *soft-hearted* 543.11, *unhurried* 693.8, *at ease* 819.2, *informal* 829.15

easy as falling off a log *easy* 823.9

easy as pie *simple* 363.6, *easy* 823.9

easy circumstances *opulence* 485.3

easy come easy go [Inf] *extravagant* 500.4, *permitting* 502.5

easy death *way of dying* 29.5

easy does it [Inf] *do easily* 823.16

easy does it! [Inf] *be careful!* 287.20

easy-flowing *wieldy* 823.12

easygoing 823.13; *harmless* 73.9, *unskillful* 128.4, *likable* 271.6, *thoughtless* 318.7, *unpremeditated* 389.7, *free* 407.9, *sociable* 408.11, *lenient* 423.3, *permitting* 502.5, *soft-hearted* 543.11, *quiescent* 678.6, *informal* 829.15

easygoingness *freedom* 407.4

easy in one's mind *easygoing* 823.13

easy-listening *hearable* 228.12

easy manner *social success* 408.3

easy mark [Inf] *butt* 436.8, *powerless person* 515.5, *weak person* 517.4

easy money *windfall* 467.7

easy on *at ease* 819.2

easy on the ear *hearable* 228.12

easy on the eye *visible* 242.19, *attractive* 529.8

easy on the pocket *cheap* 497.9

easy-paced *slow* 693.7

easy question 333.5

easy ride *easy thing* 823.6

easy-running *wieldy* 823.12

easy sailing *easy thing* 823.6

easy stages *slowness* 693.1

easy street *idealized pleasure* 214.5, *opulence* 485.3, *prosperity* 847.1

easy target *vulnerability* 811.6, *easy thing* 823.6

easy temper *courtesy* 410.1

easy terms *peace offering* 74.5

easy thing 823.6

easy times *time of plenty* 847.3

easy to comprehend *simple* 363.6

easy to follow *simple* 363.6

easy to grasp *simple* 363.6

easy to read *simple* 363.6

easy to see *clear* 244.6

easy to understand *straightforward* 630.9

easy virtue *sexual immorality* 432.2

easy word *word* 5.17

easy work *work* 122.1, *unemployment* 413.5

eat 92.21; *taste* 219.5, *ingest* 708.17

eatable *edible* 92.20, *trustworthy* 810.17

eatables *food* 90.1

eatably *edibly* 92.26

eat away 808.19; *decrease* 747.7

eat between meals *have a meal* 92.25

eat crow [Inf] *humble oneself* 298.18, *succumb* 421.7

eat dirt [Inf] *humble oneself* 298.18, *succumb* 421.7

eat, drink, and be merry *enjoy* 269.9

eater 92.15

eatery [Inf] *eating place* 92.17

eat everything in sight *eat well* 92.23

eat grass 45.11

eat high on the hog *be prosperous* 847.6

eat humble pie *humble oneself* 298.18, *succumb* 421.7, *take back* 477.17

eating 92.1, 92.18; *pertaining to life* 28.14, Phobias 283, *intake* 708.5

eating alone *eating meals* 92.4

eating disorder 108.15; *neurosis* 108.9, *psychiatric disease* 114.21

eating disorders *mental disorder* 108.8

eating for two *pregnant* 21.12

eating habit 92.7

eating habits *tradition* 397.5

eating high on the hog *prosperous* 847.5

eating in bed *eating meals* 92.4

eating meals 92.4

eating on the run *eating meals* 92.4

eating organ 92.14

eating out *eating meals* 92.4

eating out of one's hands *subject* 832.6

eating place 92.17

eating together *eating meals* 92.4

eat in moderation *abstain* 455.11

eat into *infiltrate* 706.13

eat less 118.9; *taste* 92.24

eat like a bird *fast* 118.8

eat like a horse *be greedy* 119.4

eat like a pig *eat well* 92.23

eat no meat *fast* 118.8

eat nothing *fast* 118.8

eat off the same platter *participate* 408.15

eat one's fill *have enough* 97.7, *be full* 761.12

eat one's head off *be greedy* 119.4

eat one's heart out *grieve* 270.7, *be jealous* 314.8

eat one's words *disavow* 190.18, *humble oneself* 298.18, *take back* 477.17

eat out *have a meal* 92.25

eat out of house and home *be greedy* 119.4

eat out of one's hands *be subject to* 832.12

eats [Inf] *food* 90.1

eat sparingly *fast* 118.8, *abstain* 455.11

eat to live *abstain* 455.11

eat up *eat well* 92.23, *be greedy* 119.4, *consume* 523.16

eat up! *come and get it!* 92.28

eat well 92.23

eau [Fr] *water* 557.1

eau de cologne *toiletries* 530.6

eau de toilette *toiletries* 530.6

eavesdrop *hear* 228.13, *meddle* 321.8

eavesdropper *hearer* 228.7, *meddler* 321.4

eavesdropping *hearing* 228.1

ebb *drain* 8.64, *wasting away* 96.4, *disappearance* 265.1, *disappear* 265.5, *flow* 570.4, 570.10, *oceanic* 571.1, *billow* 571.9, *diminishment* 597.7, *diminish* 597.24, *be in motion* 677.14, *reversal* 680.3, *decline* 680.5, *reverse* 680.18, *slip back* 680.19, *descend* 714.12, *decrease* 747.1, 747.7, *deterioration* 808.1, *deteriorate* 808.14

ebb and flow *swaying* 378.4, *tide* 571.2, *billow* 571.9, *frequency* 663.2, *be regular* 663.10, *be* changeable 666.5, oscillation 683.1, oscillate 683.12

ebb away waste away 96.20, decrease 747.7

ebbing flowing 570.7, oceanic 571.7, diminishing 597.16, receding 680.11, decreasing 747.5, spoiled 808.9

ebb tide or **ebb** tide 571.2

Eblis devil 446.5

ebon black 254.5

ebonite rubber 546.3

ebony Trees and Shrubs 43, dark thing 247.3, black thing 254.3, black 254.5

Ebro Rivers 570

ebullience joy 269.1

ebullient joyful 269.6

ebullition temperature 10.29, turbulence 684.3

écarté Card Games 168

eccentric 782.10, 782.16; curvilinear 6.78, rash person 353.4, foolish 353.5, visionary 360.9, strange 364.9, object of ridicule 368.3, ridiculous 368.5, capricious person 381.3, capricious 381.4, unsocial person 409.5, unusual 664.4, deviant 698.7, 698.8, individualist 756.3, characteristic 779.12, nonconformist 782.13, freethinker 829.10, independent 829.12, unreliable 841.15

eccentrically 368.9; unusually 398.9, 664.7, erratically 698.29, freely 829.22, unreliably 841.25

eccentric circles circle 6.40

eccentricity curve 6.38, orbit 7.22, insanity 110.1, folly 353.1, ridiculousness 368.1, caprice 381.1, capriciousness 381.2, unusualness 664.2, deviation 698.1, originality 737.1, characteristic 779.5, nonconformism 782.3, defect 806.4, unreliability 841.7

ecchymose bleed 25.26

ecchymosed bleeding 25.19

ecchymosis excretion 25.1, bleeding 25.10

ecclesiarch religious leader 68.9, priest 84.8

ecclesiastic priest 84.8

ecclesiastic(al) priestly 84.12

ecclesiastical law law 53.1

ecclesiastically religiously 81.29, clerically 84.17

ecclesiastical season seasons 654.2

ecclesiastical vestments clothing 184.6

ecclesiasticism theocracy 49.4, priesthood 84.2

ecclesiological theological 81.24

ecclesiology Theologies 81

ecclesiophobia Phobias 283

eccrine secretory 24.4, of a secretion 24.5

eccrine gland secretory mechanism 24.3

eccrine secretion secretion 24.1

ecdysial peeling 614.13

ecdysiast entertainer 138.8, pornography 432.7, nude person 614.5

ecdysis peeling 614.6

echelon state 725.1, relative position 727.5, rank 739.2

echidna egg-laying mammal 35.4, insect-eating mammal 35.7

echinoderm 39.5

echinodermal 39.21

Echinodermata echinoderm 39.5

echinodermatous echinodermal 39.21

echinoid echinoderm 39.5, echinodermal 39.21

echinus Architectural Elements 134

echo reproduce 21.13, be heard 228.15, sound quality 230.4, sound 230.8, bang 234.6, drumming 235.1, drum 235.10, resonance 236.1, resonate 236.9, response 334.4, react 334.20, assent 346.6, agree with 462.10, harmonization 735.2, harmonize 735.22, imitation 736.1, imitate 736.9, double 789.14, repetition 797.1, reverberation 797.6, repeat 797.15, resound 797.21

echo chamber resonator 236.5

echoed repeated 797.8

echoic worded 5.38, hearable 228.12, resonant 236.6

echoic word word 5.17

echoing hearable 228.12, resonant 236.6, reactive 334.12, harmonizing 735.12, imitative 736.7, repetitious 797.11

echoingly in answer 334.25

echolalia repetition 797.1

echolocating bathymetric 598.12

echolocation sound propagation 230.3, bathymetry 598.3

echo sounder measuring instrument 589.12, bathymetry 598.3

echo sounding sounding 10.16, oceanography 571.5, bathymetry 598.3

echt [Ger] authentic 737.6

éclair pastry 90.37

eclampsia spasm 684.8

eclamptic convulsive 684.19

éclat acclaim 437.5, vigor 518.1

eclectic selecting 382.9, mixed 751.8, general 778.9

eclectically selectively 382.17

eclecticism Western Art Styles 133, selection 382.1, mixture 751.1, generality 778.1

eclipse orbit 7.22, observe 7.34, concealment 181.1, disguise 181.13, blinder 243.7, blind 243.17, that which makes invisible 245.2, make invisible 245.7, darkness 247.1, darkening 247.2, make dark 247.10, blacking out 265.2, hide 613.27, overtake 744.16

eclipsed concealed 181.8, invisible 245.3, disappeared 265.4

eclipse of the moon darkness 247.1

eclipse of the sun darkness 247.1

eclipsing covering 613.1, superior 744.8

eclipsing binary star 7.8

ecliptic celestial sphere 7.4

eclogue Poem or Verse Forms 139

École Spéciale Militaire [Fr] military training 58.3

ecological anthropological 1.10, biological 13.27, preserving 815.11

ecologically biologically 13.36, agriculturally 16.21, botanically 41.25, preservatively 815.16

ecological psychology Psychological Theories, Schools 108

ecologist life scientist 13.26, animal scientist 34.7

ecology 13.25, 815.3; biology 13.2, study of life 28.9, animal science 34.6, preservation 815.1

econometrics economic indicator 56.4

economic 56.10, 480.14; socioeconomic 2.13, types of history 3.2, financial 457.6, accounting 493.7

economic adversity 848.6

economic aid financial assistance 825.6

economical precautionary 287.9, self-restrained 455.6, bargain 497.10, thrifty 499.4

economically 56.13, 499.7; sociologically 2.15, managerially 126.13, precautiously 287.19, with self-restraint 455.14, financially 457.17, 493.13, cheaply 497.16

economically worded concise 198.4

economical with the truth misrepresented 627.8

economic analysis economic indicator 56.4

economic analyst economist 56.9

economic anthropology anthropology 1.1

economic biologist plant scientist 41.11

economic boom productiveness 22.3

economic botany plant science 41.10

economic decline infertile state 23.3

economic deterioration 808.2

economic determinist sociologist 2.3

economic development 56.5

economic downturn economic factor 56.8, economic deterioration 808.2

economic expert economist 56.9

economic factor 56.8

economic force economic factor 56.8

economic geology geology 8.1

economic growth economics 56.1, economic development 56.5

economic indicator 56.4

economic integration economic zone 480.4, free market 483.4

economic materialism social stratification 2.7

economic migrant new arrival 724.6

economic miracle revival 809.3

economic organization 56.6

economic policy economics 56.1

economic power social stratification 2.7

economic pressure economic restraint 830.3

economic productivity economic indicator 56.4

economic progress advance 679.3

economic prosperity prosperity 847.1

economic recovery revival 809.3

economic restraint 830.3

economics 56.1

economic sanctions economic warfare 76.7

economic sector economy 56.3

economic stagnation infertile state 23.3

economic statistics economic indicator 56.4

economic status social stratification 2.7

economic system economics 56.1

economic theory economics 56.1

economic union international trade 56.7

economic upturn productiveness 22.3, economic factor 56.8

economic warfare 76.7

economic zone 480.4; international trade 56.7, free market 483.4, exclusion zone 764.3

economist 56.9

economization limitation 747.3

economize 56.11, 499.6; deposit 105.21, take precautions 287.14, be self-restrained 455.10, budget 457.10, be parsimonious 490.13, buy cheaply 497.15, make smaller 747.8, restrain commerce 830.14

economizer saver 499.3

economizing home economics 56.2, thrifty 499.4, limitation 747.3

economy 56.3; self-restraint 455.1, bargain 497.10, thrift 499.1, saving 815.4

economy-class cheap 497.9

economy drive act of thrift 499.2

economy fare bargain 497.4

economy of words conciseness 198.1

economy-size bargain 497.10, big 579.13

economy with the truth partial truth 192.7, distortion of truth 627.4

ecophobia Phobias 283

ecophysiology ecology 13.25

ecosphere Earth 8.6, living world 13.9, aerosphere 558.2

écossaise Dances 135

ecosystem ecology 13.25, habitat 60.1

ecru white 253.7, gray 255.6, brown 256.5

ecstasy delusion 110.2, emotion 266.3, oblivion 355.4, inspiration 360.2

ecstasy [Inf] stimulants 121.18

ecstatic occultist 86.13, passionate 266.12, rejoicing 279.4, oblivious 355.9

ecstatically with feeling 266.18, rejoicingly 279.7, forgetfully 355.14

ectohormone hormone 12.16, secreted substance 24.2

ectomorph physical type 1.8, personality type 108.6, thin person 595.4, nature 624.5

ectomorphic physical 1.14, thin 595.9

ectomorphism personality type 108.6

ectomorphy physical type 1.8, personality type 108.6, thinness 595.1

ectoplasm cell structure 13.16, occult and psychic phenomena 86.7, spectacle 264.6

ectoplasmic cellular 13.30

ectoplasy occult and psychic phenomena 86.7

ectoproct coelenterate 39.15

Ectoprocta coelenterate 39.15

ectotrophic mycorrhiza fungal association 47.5

Ecuador Countries 566

ecumenical general 778.9

ecumenical or **ecumenic** joint 827.10

ecumenicalism generality 778.1, association 827.6

ecumenically universally 778.23

ecumenicism generality 778.1, association 827.6

ecumenicity generality 778.1

eczema skin disease 114.16

edacious gluttonous 119.3

edaciously gluttonously 119.5

edacity *gluttony* 119.1
eddy *wind vortex* 9.14, *river turbulence* 570.5, *flow* 570.10, *vortex* 682.6, *swirl* 682.16, *hidden danger* 813.3
eddy current *electric current* 10.39
edelweiss *Flowers* 42
edema *swelling* 581.2, *bulge* 634.2
edematous *swelled* 581.10
edematous or edematose *of disease* 114.25
edental *toothless* 550.8
Edentata *toothless mammal* 35.14
edentate *toothless mammal* 35.14, *insectivorous* 35.24, *toothless* 550.8
edentulous *toothless* 550.8
edge 617.3, 618.1, 618.8; *line* 6.35, *mountaineer* 161.10, *skiing techniques* 162.5, *sharpen* 549.16, *exteriority* 610.2, *be exterior* 610.13, *surround* 615.7, *farthest point* 620.3, *side* 623.1, 623.8, *obliquity* 628.2, *advantage* 744.3, *limit* 773.7
edge away *dissociate* 375.14
edged 618.6; *edging* 618.5
edged tool *hand tool* 103.3
edgeless *uniform* 545.5, *blunt* 550.5
edge of sight *that which makes invisible* 245.2
edge out *have an advantage* 618.10
edger *garden tool* 17.7
edge tool *sharp-edged thing* 549.6
edginess *agitation* 684.1
edging 618.2, 618.5; *part of garment* 100.27, *climbing techniques* 161.3, *ornamentation* 748.5
edging iron or knife *garden tool* 103.4
edging tool *garden tool* 17.7
edgy *fearful* 283.10, *agitated* 684.15
edible 92.20; *trustworthy* 810.17
edible or eatable *tasty* 219.4
edibles *food* 90.1
edibly 92.26
edict *law* 53.1, *publication* 173.1, *verdict* 341.2, *command* 425.1, *rule* 780.1
edification *education* 48.1, *welfare* 445.2
edifice *architectural structure* 134.4, *construction* 522.9, 551.6
edificial *structural* 14.45, *architectural* 134.12
edify *better* 445.17
edifying *educational* 48.17, *beneficial* 445.11, *profitable* 801.8
edifyingly *educationally* 48.25
Edilbaev *Breeds of Sheep* 16
Edinburgh *major British cities* 567.7
edit *program* 15.29, *film* 137.19, *produce* 137.21, *publish* 174.19, *report* 175.9, *blue-pencil* 261.10, *be accurate* 350.5, *interpret* 365.12, *be elegant* 527.6, *contract* 582.12, *change for the better* 665.17, *rectify* 807.22, *repair* 809.10
edit down *make smaller* 747.8
edited *expurgated* 111.15, *produced* 137.17, *published* 174.18, *obliterated* 186.4, *interpreted* 365.9, *shortened* 582.8, *improved* 807.12
edited text *interpretation* 365.1
editing *censorship* 111.5, *obliteration* 186.1, *interpretation* 365.1, *shortening* 582.2, *subtraction* 749.1, *rectification* 807.8, *repair* 809.1
edition *reprint* 21.3, *book* 174.1, *newspaper* 175.2, *magazine* 175.3,

interpretation 365.1, *translation* 365.4, *part of writing* 760.6
editor *professional worker* 123.11, *book publishing personnel* 174.12, *print journalist* 175.5, *judge* 341.5, *interpreter* 365.6, *changer* 665.9, *improver* 807.11, *repairer* 809.5
editorial *news story* 171.3, *newsworthy* 175.7, *article* 203.2, *dissertational* 203.4, *annotative* 365.10
editorial change *obliteration* 186.1
editorial comment *article* 203.2, *annotation* 365.2
editorialist *dissertator* 203.3
editorialize *report* 171.9
editorially *newsworthily* 171.10, *journalistically* 175.10, *discursively* 203.6
editorial style *mode of expression* 537.3
editorial writer *news interpreter* 365.7
editor in chief *book publishing personnel* 174.12
edit out *purify* 111.19, *obliterate* 186.8, *eject* 764.8
Edmonton *Canadian Provinces* 564
educability *educatability* 48.9
educable *educatable* 48.18
educatability 48.9
educatable 48.18
educate 48.22; *inform* 170.11, *divulge* 180.9, *cause to know* 348.13, *brief* 388.20, *bring into existence* 522.14, *upturn* 713.20, *civilize* 807.16
educated 48.19; *of language* 5.35, *refined* 48.20, *informed* 170.9, *literate* 348.8, *produced* 522.12, *directed* 697.9, *advanced* 713.16
educated palate *delicate eating* 92.3
educating *directing* 697.12
education 48.1; *refinement* 48.10, *learning* 348.3, *briefing* 388.4, *directions* 697.7, *ascendancy* 713.5, *social improvement* 807.3
educational 48.17; *sociological* 2.11, *dramatic* 137.16, *informative* 170.10
educational broadcasting *broadcast material* 172.9
educational film *movie type* 137.3
educational institution *social institution* 2.8, *school* 48.11
educationalist *educator* 48.4
educational leader 68.11
educationally 48.25; *sociologically* 2.15
educational psychologist *educator* 48.4
educational psychology *Psychological Theories, Schools* 108
educational status *social stratification* 2.7
educational system 48.2
educational topic 328.4
education and training *naval commands* 77.19, *air force commands* 77.28
educationist *educator* 48.4
educative *educational* 48.17, *influential* 512.8
educator 48.4; *person in authority* 52.7, *literary person* 139.14
educatory *educational* 48.17
educe *draw out* 711.17
educible *extractive* 711.10
eduction *drawing out* 711.5
eductive *extractive* 711.10
edulcorate *purify* 111.19

edulcoration *cleaning* 111.2
Edward *Lakes* 568
Edwardian *historic* 653.13
Edwardian style *Architectural Styles* 134
Edward Rochester *Famous Lovers* 299
Edward VIII *Famous Lovers* 299
eel *food fish and shellfish* 90.20
eel-like *fishlike* 38.10
eels *Collective Names* 59
eerie *spiritual* 86.20
eerily *magically* 86.28
eeriness *the occult* 86.2
Eeyore *sad person* 270.3, *hopeless person* 282.5
Eeyorish *depressed* 270.5
efface *obliterate* 186.8, *abolish* 523.11, *cancel* 834.6
effaced *obliterated* 186.4
efface from one's memory *forget* 355.10
effacement *obliteration* 186.1
effect 676.1; *physical law* 10.4, *interact* 10.73, *manage* 126.10, *impression* 264.7, *meaning* 361.1, *cause* 372.12, 675.8, *action* 412.1, *power* 447.4, *be an instrument* 511.7, *product* 522.3, *react* 676.8, *remainder* 750.1, *sequel* 770.5, *consequence* 774.3, *be successful* 845.11
effect a change *cause change* 665.16
effect a result *predetermine* 384.8
effected *caused* 676.5
effected by *caused* 676.5
effective 412.10; *soldier* 77.4, *persuasive* 178.12, *emphatic* 200.3, *appearing* 264.9, *operative* 509.9, *instrumental* 511.4, 801.7, *influential* 512.8, *powerful* 514.15, *strong* 516.9, *vigorous* 518.2, *advantaged* 618.7, *causal* 675.7, *complete* 761.6, *convenient* 803.3, *famous* 845.9
effectively 412.19; *medicinally* 115.21, *persuasively* 178.21, *operationally* 509.13, *instrumentally* 511.9, *powerfully* 514.21, *acutely* 516.18, *causally* 675.12, *on the whole* 759.13, *successfully* 845.19
effectiveness *power* 447.4, *management* 509.4, *instrumentality* 511.1, *potency* 516.6, *superiority* 744.1
effective procedure *algorithm* 6.26
effective rate *finance* 457.1
effect of use *use* 393.1
effects *possession of property* 469.3, *possessions* 470.5, *visible effect* 676.2, *estate* 750.5
effects of hot weather 217.7
effectual *operative* 509.9, *instrumental* 511.4, 801.7, *influential* 512.8, *powerful* 514.15, *causal* 675.7, *complete* 761.6, *convenient* 803.3
effectuality *power* 447.4, *management* 509.4, *authority* 516.5
effectually *operationally* 509.13, *instrumentally* 511.9, *influentially* 512.14, *powerfully* 514.21, *causally* 675.12, *in essence* 723.13
effectuate *activate* 509.11, *cause* 675.8
effectuation *action* 412.1
effeminacy *femaleness* 33.2
effeminate *of sexual nature* 20.17, *male* 32.16, *female* 33.16
effeminate male 32.8

effervesce *crack* 234.7, *hiss* 237.3, *bubble* 558.24, *be agitated* 684.21
effervescence *hiss* 237.1, *lightness* 539.1, *gaseousness* 556.6, *turbulence* 684.3
effervescent *hissing* 237.2, *insubstantial* 539.5, *gassy* 556.19, *bubbly* 558.18, *turbulent* 684.17
effervescently *sibilantly* 237.4, *lightly* 539.10, *smokily* 556.28, *airily* 558.25
effervescingly *smokily* 556.28, *airily* 558.25
effete *weak-willed* 517.10, *broken down* 802.8, *spoiled* 808.9
effeteness *uselessness* 802.1
efficacious *qualified* 340.7, *operative* 509.9, *instrumental* 511.4, 801.7, *powerful* 514.15, *famous* 845.9
efficaciously *operationally* 509.13, *instrumentally* 511.9, *powerfully* 514.21, *successfully* 845.19
efficaciousness *power* 447.4
efficacy *qualification* 340.1, *power* 447.4, 514.1, *instrumentality* 511.1, 801.3, *potency* 516.6
efficiency *work* 14.10, *skill* 127.1, *qualification* 340.1, *proficiency* 445.5, *management* 509.4, *instrumentality* 801.3, *easiness* 823.1
efficient *skillful* 127.10, *expert* 127.12, *qualified* 340.7, *knowledgeable* 348.7, *industrious* 414.16, *proficient* 445.15, *operative* 509.9, *instrumental* 511.4, 801.7, *vigorous* 518.2
efficiently *skillfully* 127.16, *capably* 340.15, *proficiently* 445.22, *operationally* 509.13, *instrumentally* 511.9, *powerfully* 514.21, *usefully* 801.12
effigy *idol* 83.5, *image* 187.3
effloresce *flower* 42.12, *come to dust* 553.28
efflorescence *fertilization* 21.6, *flowering* 42.5, *powderiness* 553.3, *powder* 553.9
efflorescent *horticultural* 17.14, *flowering* 42.10
effluence *flow* 570.4, *outflow* 707.7
effluent *fertilizer* 16.9, *excrement* 25.2, *tributary* 570.2, *flowing* 570.7, *outflowing* 707.11
effluvia *waste product* 96.7, *refuse* 802.5
effluvial *miasmic* 556.16
effluvium *occult and psychic phenomena* 86.7, *pollution* 117.8, *stench* 227.1, *exhalation* 556.2
efflux *outflow* 707.4
effluxion *outflow* 707.4
effort *work* 14.10, *exertion* 122.4, *experiment* 335.1, *commitment* 377.2, *attempt* 390.1, *undertaking* 391.1, *action* 412.1, *contest* 422.4, *vigor* 514.2, 518.1, *production* 522.1, *difficulty* 824.1
effortful *difficult* 824.9
effortless *simple* 526.7, *easy* 823.9
effortlessly *simply* 526.14, *easily* 823.19
effortlessness *simplicity* 526.1, *easiness* 823.1
efforts *lengths* 590.5
effort-wasting *futile* 802.10
effrontery *insolence* 400.1, *defiance* 416.1, *assurance* 621.8
effulgence *quality of light* 246.2
effulgent *bright* 246.14
effuse *diffuse* 199.3, *emerge* 707.14, *leak* 707.16
effused *outflowing* 707.11

effusion *excretion* 25.1, *diffuseness* 199.1, *effusiveness* 207.2, *outflow* 707.4, *leakage* 707.5, *disgorgement* 709.6

effusive 207.6; *friendly* 62.5, *overdone* 99.7, *diffuse* 199.3, *passionate* 266.12, *demonstrative* 331.10, *outflowing* 707.11

effusively 207.10; *amicably* 62.13, *diffusely* 199.7, *demonstratively* 331.21, *forth* 707.19

effusiveness 207.2; *overdoing it* 99.3, *diffuseness* 199.1, *demonstrativeness* 331.2

e.g. *particularly* 779.21

egalitarian *equal* 740.8

egalitarianism *isocracy* 49.11, *equality* 740.1

egest *excrete* 25.20, *let out* 709.26

egesta *excrement* 25.2

egestion *excretion* 25.1, *vomiting* 709.7

egestive *excretory* 25.12

egg *organs of reproduction* 21.9, *eggs* 36.5, *insect metamorphal stage* 40.8, *produce* 522.5, *round thing* 633.3, *source* 771.3

egg and dart *or* **egg and tongue** *or* **egg and anchor** *Architectural Elements* 134

egg and spoon race *Children's and Party Games* 167, *sporting event* 422.6

eggbeater *cooking equipment* 91.6, *agitator* 684.14

eggbeater [Inf] *aircraft* 689.3

egg carry race *Children's and Party Games* 167

egg dish 90.18

egged on *persuadable* 178.14, *motivated* 508.8

egghead [Inf] *expert* 127.9, *intellectual* 315.7, *knowledgeable person* 348.5

egg-laying mammal 35.4

egg on *manipulate* 508.12, *invigorate* 518.5

egg on one's face [Inf] *humiliation* 298.5, *indignity* 436.7

eggplant *purple thing* 262.3

eggs 36.5; *basic cooking ingredient* 91.8, *animal products* 522.7

egg salad *egg dish* 90.18

eggs Benedict *egg dish* 90.18

egg-shaped *circular* 631.5, *round* 633.7

eggshell *eggs* 36.5, *weak thing* 517.5, *brittle thing* 548.2, *casing* 613.9

eggshell glaze *glaze* 129.3

eggshell porcelain *Ceramics* 129

egg timer *Timepieces and Timers* 646

egg white *paste* 561.4

eglantine *Flowers* 42

Egmont, Mount *Mountains and Hills* 569

ego *psyche* 108.25, *egotism* 444.2, *internal world* 525.6

ego analysis *psychotherapy* 108.4

egocentric *selfish* 402.12, *egotistic* 444.5, *inward* 611.12

egocentrically *smugly* 402.18, *selfishly* 402.20, *egoistically* 444.9

egocentricity *egotism* 444.2

egocentrism *egotism* 444.2, *inwardness* 611.5

ego-id conflict *psyche* 108.25

ego ideal *psyche* 108.25

egoism *Philosophical Schools of Thought* 4, *misanthropy* 291.4, *pride* 297.1, *selfishness* 402.5, *egotism* 444.2, *self-absorption* 456.4

egoist *Philosophical Schools of Thought* 4, *misanthrope* 291.5, *boring person* 296.4, *proud person* 297.7, *vain person* 402.7, *selfish person* 444.3, *self-indulgent person* 456.5

egoistic *misanthropic* 291.8, *egotistic* 444.5, *self-absorbed* 456.9

egoistical *egotistic* 444.5

egoistically 444.9; *misanthropically* 291.18

egomania *compulsion* 108.13, *overestimation* 343.1, *vanity* 402.1

egomaniac *badly behaved person* 399.8, *vain person* 402.8, *selfish person* 444.3

egotism 444.2; *misanthropy* 291.4, *pride* 297.1, *love* 299.1, *selfishness* 402.5, *self-absorption* 456.4

egotist *misanthrope* 291.5, *boring person* 296.4, *proud person* 297.7, *vain person* 402.7, *selfish person* 444.3, *self-indulgent person* 456.5

egotistic 444.5; *self-absorbed* 456.9

egotistical *misanthropic* 291.8, *prideful* 297.8, *loving* 299.15, *selfish* 402.12, *egotistic* 444.5

egotistically *misanthropically* 291.18, *pridefully* 297.17, *selfishly* 402.20, *egoistically* 444.9

ego trip [Inf] *selfishness* 402.5, *egotism* 444.2

ego-trip [Inf] *be egotistic* 444.7

egress *flow* 570.4, *backward motion* 677.5, *departure* 705.1, *exit* 707.1, *707.13*, *way out* 707.2, *removal* 709.5, *means of escape* 816.4

egression *exit* 707.1

egressive *outgoing* 707.10

Egypt *Countries* 566

Egyptian *Breeds of Cattle* 16, *Furniture Styles* 101

Egyptian architecture *Architectural Styles* 134

Egyptian mau *Breeds of Cats* 35

eiderdown *plumage* 36.7

eidetic *representational* 187.8, *descriptive* 202.11, *imaginative* 360.10

eidetic image *image* 187.3

Eiger *Mountains and Hills* 569

eight 792.4; *numeral* 6.8, *eighth* 792.15

Eight, the *Western Art Styles* 133

eight all *squash terms* 165.10

eightball *pool* 149.3

eight-card stud *poker* 168.5

eight centuries *hundreds* 792.9

eighteenth *less than one* 787.4

Eighteenth Amendment *prohibition of alcohol* 120.2, 503.2

eighter from Decatur [Inf] *eight* 792.4

eightfold *eighth* 792.15

Eightfold Path *eight* 792.4

eighth 792.15; *ranked* 6.72, *less than one* 787.4, *eight* 792.4

eighth note *notation* 140.20

eighth part *eight* 792.4

eightieth *twentieth* 792.19

eights *Card Games* 168

eight-sided *polygonal* 6.79

eighty *twenty and over* 792.8

eighty-day injunction *strike* 57.8

eighty-eights [Inf] *part of keyboard instrument* 142.6

Ein Shemer *Apple Varieties* 44

Einsteinian universe *universe* 7.3

einsteinium *Chemical Elements and Common Allotropes* 11

Einstein theory *fourth dimension* 563.9

Eir *Deities* 82

Eirene *Deities* 82

eisegesis *interpretation* 365.1

Eisenhower jacket *jacket* 100.18

eisoptrophobia *Phobias* 283

ejaculate *stimulate* 20.22, *excrete* 25.20, *speak* 205.17, *cry out* 239.13, *let out* 709.26

ejaculation *sex act* 20.10, *excretion* 25.1, *utterance* 205.10, *cry* 239.1, *spasm* 684.8, *disgorgement* 709.6

ejaculative *expulsive* 709.11

ejaculatory *coupling* 20.19, *vociferous* 239.9

eject 701.8, 764.8; *secrete* 24.7, *excrete* 25.20, *discard* 383.12, *stop using* 394.10, *replace* 574.17, *take away* 685.12, *expel* 709.14, *subtract* 749.6, *separate* 753.12, *terminate* 834.7

ejecta *eruption* 8.27, *excrement* 25.2

ejectamenta *excrement* 25.2

ejected *discarded* 383.8, *refused* 506.5, *subtracted* 749.3, *separate* 753.7

ejecting mechanism *ejector* 709.10

ejection 764.2; *secretion* 24.1, *excretion* 25.1, *soccer play* 163.5, *discarding* 383.3, *replacement* 574.3, *shot* 696.6, *repulse* 701.2, *expulsion* 709.1, *subtraction* 749.1, *setting apart* 753.2, *termination* 834.2

ejection seat *safety device* 810.15

ejective *excretory* 25.12, *projectile* 696.13, *expulsive* 709.11

ejectment *expulsion* 709.1

ejector 709.10

eke out *complete* 761.9

eke out a livelihood *be poor* 486.14

el [Inf] *railroad system* 688.1

elaborate *laborious* 122.7, *distort the truth* 192.25, *be diffuse* 199.5, *grand* 404.22, *be elegant* 527.6, *ornate* 532.10, *shape* 551.21, *detailed* 726.9, *perfect* 805.19, *improve* 807.15

elaborated *partially true* 192.18

elaborately *grandly* 404.37, *elegantly* 527.7, *decoratively* 532.13, *ornately* 532.14, *stylistically* 537.11, *meticulously* 726.18

elaborateness *grandeur* 404.10

elaboration *exertion* 122.4, *partial truth* 192.7, *diffuseness* 199.1, *grace* 527.2, *conclusion* 761.3, *improvement* 807.1

elaborative *untruthful* 192.12

elaboratively *untruthfully* 192.27

elaborator *gossip* 192.11

élan *vigor* 518.1, *stylishness* 537.2

élan vital *life force* 28.2

elapse *pass* 639.13, 651.17, *go on* 642.7

Elara *Planets and Their Satellites* 7

elasmobranch *fish* 38.5

elastic 546.5; *pliant* 543.7, *enlargeable* 581.13, *resilient* 680.14

elastically 546.10; *softly* 543.18

elasticate *make elastic* 546.8

elastic board *pommel horse* 157.7

elasticity 546.1; *force* 10.9, *strength of materials* 14.15, *softness* 543.1, *enlargeability* 581.6, *Fields of Measurement* 589, *reflex* 680.7

elasticize *make elastic* 546.8

elastic scattering *nuclear reaction* 10.59

elastic strain *load* 14.14

elastomer *rubber* 546.3

elated *joyful* 269.6

elater *moss plant* 46.5

elation *transformation* 6.46, *delusion* 110.2, *joy* 269.1

E *or* **Heaviside** *or* **Kennelly–Heaviside layer** *or* **region** *atmospheric layer* 558.3

Elba *Islands* 572

Elbe *Rivers* 570

Elbert, Mount *Mountains and Hills* 569

elbow *Human Bones* 19, *appendage* 19.5, *gesture* 183.17, *type of touch* 216.3, *touch* 216.9, *meet* 586.15, *impel* 695.9, *joint* 752.7

elbow, the *relegation* 574.4

elbow aside *disrespect* 436.18

elbow-cop *historic armor* 419.8

elbow grease *exertion* 122.4, *polishing* 554.5

elbow guard *fencing equipment* 153.2

elbowing *ice hockey tactics* 158.4, *hasty* 818.3

elbow joint *angle* 628.1

elbow one's way *exert oneself* 122.11, *follow up* 385.16, *push* 414.20

elbow pad *hockey clothing* 158.6

elbowroom *available space* 563.6, *opportunity* 659.2, *scope* 829.7

elbow through *enter* 692.18

elbow to elbow *near* 586.6, *beside* 586.20

Elbrus *or* **El'brus** *Mountains and Hills* 569

Elburz Mountains *Mountains and Hills* 569

eld [Arch] *past time* 3.6

elder *older person* 27.7, *Trees and Shrubs* 43, *masterful* 68.15, *member of the clergy* 84.5, *past* 651.11, *old* 653.10, *primary* 769.10

elderliness 653.2; *old age* 27.5

elderly *aged* 27.15, *old* 653.10

elderly, the *old people* 27.10, 653.6

elders *old people* 653.6

elder statesman *intellectual* 315.7

eldest *predecessor* 769.8

El Dorado *Imaginary Places* 360, *objective* 374.5, *wealth* 485.1

eldritch *spiritual* 86.20

Eleaticism *Philosophical Schools of Thought* 4

Eleaticist *Philosophical Schools of Thought* 4

elecampane *Herbs and Spices* 91

elect *gain authority* 52.15, *delegate* 79.6, *ordain* 84.16, *selected* 382.11, *vote* 382.16, *commission* 833.8

elected *authorized* 52.11, *delegated* 79.4, *selected* 382.11

elected official 50.8; *chosen thing* 382.8

elected person *delegate* 79.1

elected representative *union member* 57.6, *delegate* 79.1, *commissioner* 833.5

electing 382.5

election 382.6; *acquisition of authority* 52.5, *delegation* 79.3, *ordination* 84.3, *selection* 382.1, *commission* 833.1

election day *election* 382.6

electioneer *run for office* 50.10

election returns *election* 382.6

elector *electorate* 382.7

electoral college *electorate* 382.7

electoral defeat *discarding* 383.3

electoral mandate *acquisition of authority* 52.5, *authorization* 425.4
electoral roll *list of names* 785.7
electorate 382.7; *place of judgment* 341.3, *list of names* 785.7
Electra *type of complex* 108.22
electric 14.47; *physical* 10.70, *gas* 106.14, *fencing* 153.6, *exciting* 212.8, *nuclear* 514.17
electrical *physical* 10.70, *electric* 14.47, *gas* 106.14
electrical conduction 10.33
electrical energy 10.44; *energy* 10.10, 514.7
electrical engineer 14.32; *engineer* 14.2, *professional worker* 123.11
electrical engineering 14.31; *engineering* 14.1
electrical fault *unsuccessful thing* 846.8
electrical instrument 14.41
electrically *physically* 10.78, *electronically* 14.54, *powerfully* 106.19, *energetically* 514.22
electrical oscillation *wave* 10.11
electrical porcelain *industrial ceramics* 129.6
electrical power 514.12
electrical wheel *ceramic workshop and tools* 129.8
electric battery *electricity* 106.5
electric blanket *heater* 217.3
electric-blue *blue* 261.5
electric bus or **trolley bus** *bus* 687.7
electric chair *electricity* 106.5, *instrument of execution* 454.15
electric charge 10.38, 14.36; *electricity* 106.5
electric circuit *circuit* 10.43, 14.37
electric clock *Timepieces and Timers* 646
electric constant *electric charge* 10.38, *fundamental constant* 10.69
electric current 10.39; *electricity* 106.5, *Fields of Measurement* 589
electric drill *hand tool* 103.3
electric épée *fencing equipment* 153.2
electric fence *farm building* 16.4, *farm tool* 16.5, *barrier* 419.10
electric field 10.42
electric field strength *electric field* 10.42
electric fire *place for fire* 217.9
electric flux *electric field* 10.42
electric foil *fencing equipment* 153.2
electric guitar *Musical Instruments* 142
electrician *electrical engineer* 14.32, *power worker* 106.10, *artisan* 123.13, *stagehand* 136.29
electricity 10.31, 14.34, 106.5; *classical physics* 10.2, *fuels* 106.2, *Phobias* 283, *electrical power* 514.12, *propellant* 696.9
electricity meter *electricity* 106.5, *meter* 589.13
electricity supply *electricity* 106.5
electric lead *electricity* 106.5
electric light 246.6
electric mixer *cooking equipment* 91.6, *mixer* 751.7
electric motor *electrical energy* 10.44, *electricity* 106.5, *train* 688.4
electric organ *Musical Instruments* 142
electric potential 10.40
electric power *electrical energy* 10.44, *type of power* 514.6

electric storm *thunderstorm* 9.20
electric switch *electricity* 106.5
electrification *electricity* 106.5
electrified *fired* 106.13, *motivated* 508.8
electrify *interact* 10.73, *power* 106.17, *be wondrous* 294.14, *motivate* 508.9, *empower* 514.20, *invigorate* 518.5
electrifying *gas* 106.14, *exciting* 212.8, *wondrous* 294.9, *motivational* 508.7
electro *rock music* 140.6
electroacoustics *Fields of Modern Physics* 10
electrobiology *biology* 13.3
electrocardiogram (EKG) *diagnostic procedure* 107.11
electrocardiography *diagnostic procedure* 107.11
electrochemical 11.33; *chemical* 14.46
electrochemically 14.53
electrochemical separation *biochemical applications* 14.30
electrochemical series *electrochemistry* 11.19
electrochemistry 11.19, *Branches of Chemistry* 11
electroconvulsive shock therapy (EST) *psychiatric treatment* 108.3
electroconvulsive therapy (ECT) *psychiatric treatment* 108.3, *treatment* 110.7, *therapy* 115.12
electrocute *conduct* 14.51, *murder* 30.20, *execute* 30.22, 454.30
electrocution *execution* 30.6, *electricity* 106.5, *capital punishment* 454.12
electrocutioner *executioner* 30.13
electrode *electrical conduction* 10.33
electrodeposit *electrolyze* 11.39
electrodeposited *electrochemical* 11.33
electrodeposition *electrochemistry* 11.19
electrode potential (ΔE) *electrochemistry* 11.19
electrodynamic *physical* 10.70, *electric* 14.47
electrodynamically *physically* 10.78, *electronically* 14.54
electrodynamics *classical physics* 10.2, *electrical power* 514.12
electroencephalogram (EEG) *diagnostic procedure* 107.11
electroencephalogy *diagnostic procedure* 107.11
electroform *electrolyze* 11.39
electroformed *electrochemical* 11.33
electrolysis *electrical conduction* 10.33, *electrochemistry* 11.19, *hairdressing* 530.7, *depilation* 614.8, *deconstruction* 758.2
electrolyte *electrical conduction* 10.33, *electrochemistry* 11.19, *electricity* 14.34
electrolytic *electrochemical* 11.33, *electric* 14.47
electrolytically *electronically* 14.54, *to pieces* 758.8
electrolytic cell *electrical conduction* 10.33, *electrochemistry* 11.19
electrolytic conductor *electrical conduction* 10.33
electrolytic corrosion *electrochemistry* 11.19
electrolytic extraction *metallurgy* 11.22
electrolytic forming *electrochemistry* 11.19

electrolytic refining *electrochemistry* 11.19
electrolyze 11.39; *deconstruct* 758.7
electromagnet *magnet* 10.47, 700.3
electromagnetic(al) *electric* 14.47
electromagnetically *electronically* 14.54
electromagnetic induction 10.37; *magnetic phenomenon* 10.50
electromagnetic interaction *fundamental interaction* 10.65
electromagnetic radiation 10.14, 10.49; *light* 246.1
electromagnetic spectrum *electromagnetic radiation* 10.14, 10.49
electromagnetic theory *theory* 10.3
electromagnetic wave *electromagnetic radiation* 10.49
electromagnetic wave or **radiation** *wave* 683.4
electromagnetism *classical physics* 10.2, *magnetism* 10.45, *force* 514.8
electromechanically *electronically* 14.54
electrometallurgy *metallurgy* 11.22
electrometer *electrical instrument* 14.41, *Fields of Measurement* 589
electrometry *Fields of Measurement* 589
electromotive *electrochemical* 11.33, *electric* 14.47
electromotive force *force* 514.8, *Fields of Measurement* 589
electromotive force (emf) *electric potential* 10.40, *electrochemistry* 11.19
electromotive series *electrochemistry* 11.19
electromyogram (EMG) *diagnostic procedure* 107.11
electromyography *diagnostic procedure* 107.11
electron *semiconductor* 10.34, *electric charge* 10.38, *atom* 10.52, *elementary particle* 10.53, *physical element* 524.5, *little thing* 580.3
electron conduction *semiconductor* 10.34
electron configuration *atom* 10.52
electron-deficient *chemical compound* 11.4
electron-deficient bond *chemical bond* 11.6
electron emission 14.42
electron gun *electron emission* 14.42
electronic *electric* 14.47, *mechanical* 103.7, *ceramic* 129.9, *practical* 511.6
electronically 14.54; *instrumentally* 103.9, 511.9
electronic brain *computer* 15.1
electronic circuit *circuit* 10.43, 14.37
electronic clock *Timepieces and Timers* 646
electronic communication *communications* 169.1
electronic component *circuit* 10.43
electronic data interchange (EDI) *computer communications* 15.25
electronic data processing (EDP) *computing* 15.2, 784.4

electronic device *circuit* 10.43, *circuit element* 14.39
electronic engineer *electrical engineer* 14.32
electronic engineering *electrical engineering* 14.31
electronic flash *flash* 132.13
electronic listening device *recording instrument* 185.9
electronic machines *merchandise* 522.6
electronic mail *office automation tools* 15.19, *communications software* 15.27, *data transmission* 169.8
electronic means *instrumentality* 511.1
electronics 14.33, *Fields of Modern Physics* 10, *circuit* 14.37
electronics industries *chemical process industries* 14.26
electronic surveillance *security system* 810.5
electronic systems *naval commands* 77.19
electronic timer *swimming equipment* 164.8
electronic tube *industrial ceramics* 129.6
electron lens *electron emission* 14.42
electron mass *fundamental constant* 10.69
electron microscopy *cell biology* 13.14
electron multiplier *electron emission* 14.42
electron nuclear double resonance (ENDOR) *analysis* 11.17
electron shell *atom* 10.52
electron spectroscopy *analysis* 11.17
electron spin resonance (ESR) *analysis* 11.17
electron-transport chain *respiration* 12.24
electron tube 14.40; *electron emission* 14.42
electro-optical effect *photosensitivity* 10.23
electro-optics *Fields of Modern Physics* 10
electro-osmosis *analysis* 11.17
electrophile *chemical reaction* 11.8
electrophilic *reactive* 11.29
electrophilic reaction *chemical reaction* 11.8
electrophobia *Phobias* 283
electrophone *musical instrument* 142.1
electrophoresis *analysis* 11.17
electrophoretic *analytic* 11.32
electrophotographic printer *hardcopy device* 15.10
electroplate *electrolyze* 11.39, *coating* 613.8, *coat* 613.28
electroplated *electrochemical* 11.33
electroplater *coverer* 613.18
electroplating *electrochemistry* 11.19, *metallurgy* 11.22
electrorefining *metallurgy* 11.22
electroshock *treatment* 110.7
electrostatic *electric* 14.47
electrostatically *electronically* 14.54
electrostatic force *force* 10.9
electrostatic generator *generator* 14.43
electrostatic induction *electromagnetic induction* 10.37
electrostatic printer *hardcopy device* 15.10

---

electrostatics *electrical power* 514.12

electrostriction *electromagnetic induction* 10.37

electrotechnician *electrical engineer* 14.32

electrotechnics *electrical engineering* 14.31

electrotechnology *electrical engineering* 14.31

electrotherapy *therapy* 115.12

electrothermodynamics Fields of Modern Physics 10

electrovalent *chemical compound* 11.4

electrovalent bond *chemical bond* 11.6

electrovalently *chemically* 11.42

electrovoltaic *electrochemical* 11.33

electroweak interaction *fundamental interaction* 10.65

electrowinning *metallurgy* 11.22

electrum *bullion* 484.16, *mixed thing* 751.2

electrum coinage *coinage* 484.13

eleemosynary *philanthropic* 307.6, *free of charge* 497.12

elegance 527.1; *phrasing* 5.25, *refinement* 48.10, 534.1, *social skill* 127.3, *subtlety* 195.3, *grandeur* 404.10, *good manners* 410.2, *beauty* 529.1, *fashion* 536.1, *stylishness* 537.2

elegancies *etiquette* 406.3, *courtesies* 410.3

elegancy *elegance* 527.1

elegant 527.3; *phrased* 5.39, *well-made* 127.13, *subtle* 195.9, *grand* 404.22, *formal* 406.6, *good-mannered* 410.7, *beautiful* 529.7, *appealing* 529.10, *refined* 534.5, *stylish* 537.7

elegantly 527.7, 529.15, 534.8; *phraseologically* 5.47, *discerningly* 48.27, *dressily* 100.47, *tastily* 219.7, *grandly* 404.37, *genteelly* 410.14, *fashionably* 536.9, *stylistically* 537.11

elegantly upholstered *opulent* 485.10

elegant phrase *phrasing* 5.25

elegiac *funeral* 31.9, *poetic* 139.19, *lamenting* 280.4

elegiacal *funeral* 31.9

elegiacally *funereally* 31.13

elegiac couplet *meter* 139.10

elegiac distich *meter* 139.10

elegiac pentameter *meter* 139.10

elegiac poem Poem or Verse Forms 139

elegiac poetry *poetry* 139.8

elegist *funeral person* 31.5, *author* 139.13, *lamenter* 280.3

elegize *write* 139.21, *lament* 280.7

elegized *lamented* 280.5

elegy *funeral* 31.4, Poem or Verse Forms 139, Musical Forms 140, *lament* 280.2

element *set* 6.19, *chemical element* 11.3, *group* 18.13, *habitat* 60.1, *air force unit* 77.29, *matter* 524.4, *aspect* 623.4, 726.4, *admixture* 751.5, *part* 760.1, *component* 760.3, *thing included* 763.2

elemental 11.26; *meteorologic* 9.38, *spiritual* 86.20, *material* 104.8, *containing* 577.7, *causal* 675.7, *component* 760.12

elementally *structurally* 577.14

elemental spirit *sprite* 86.12

elementary *immature* 389.9, *basic* 601.8, *causal* 675.7, *precursory*

769.12, *rudimentary* 771.22, *easy* 823.9

elementary backstroke *swimming techniques* 164.2

elementary charge *fundamental constant* 10.69

elementary particle 10.53; *atom* 10.52, *physical element* 524.5

elementary unit *matter* 524.4

element of symmetry *operation of symmetry* 626.2

elements *weather data* 9.6, *materials* 104.1, *contents* 577.1, *rudiments* 771.7

elements, the *weather* 9.3

elenchic *dialectical* 4.16

elenchus *philosophical term* 4.7, *logical argument* 329.2, *refutation* 332.1

elephant *game* 160.6, *big thing* 579.9, *means of transportation* 686.2

elephant bird *extinct bird* 36.14

elephantiasis *gigantism* 579.4

elephantine *elephantlike* 35.30, *stocky* 579.16

elephantlike 35.30

elephantoid *elephantlike* 35.30

elephants Collective Names 59

eleutherophobia Phobias 283

elevate *deify* 82.23, *be intoxicating* 121.36, *be light* 539.8, *increase* 581.16, *heighten* 596.14, *exalt* 596.19, *make vertical* 602.9, *further* 679.13, *drag* 699.11, *upturn* 713.20, *raise* 715.9, *promote* 715.13, *make bigger* 746.7, *improve* 807.15

elevated *deified* 82.20, *serious* 200.5, *dignified* 297.11, *mountainous* 569.5, *swelled* 581.10, *high* 596.7, *transportable* 686.7, *railroad system* 688.1, *rail* 688.8, *advanced* 713.16, *raised* 715.6, *promoted* 715.8

elevated railroad *railroad system* 688.1

elevating *increase* 581.3, *raising* 715.1

elevation *continent* 8.8, *deification* 82.13, *drunken behavior* 121.4, *map* 187.5, *seriousness* 200.2, *external appearance* 264.5, *form* 551.3, *increase* 581.3, Fields of Measurement 589, *height* 596.1, *advance* 679.3, *incline* 713.3, *ascendancy* 713.5, *raising* 715.1, *intensification* 746.2, *uplift* 807.2

elevation of the Host *Eucharist* 85.7

elevator *construction equipment* 14.23, *means of transportation* 686.2, *lifter* 715.5

elevatory *enlargeable* 581.13

eleven *eleven to nineteen* 792.7

elevenses [Brit] *meal* 92.8, *morning things* 655.3

eleventh *less than one* 787.4

eleventh and above 792.18

eleventh hour *late hour* 658.2, *critical time* 659.3

eleventh-hour *late in the day* 658.7, *critical* 659.5

eleventh-hour rescue *expedient* 387.5

eleven to nineteen 792.7

elf *sprite* 86.12, *little person* 580.5

elfin *little* 580.7

Elgon, Mount Mountains and Hills 569

elicit *awaken* 675.9, *draw out* 711.17

elicitation *drawing out* 711.5

elicitory *extractive* 711.10

elide *shorten* 591.9

elided *shortened* 591.7

eligibility *qualification* 340.1, *inclusion* 763.1

eligible *marriageable* 64.17, *qualified* 340.7, *included* 763.4

eligible bachelor *marriageability* 64.4

eligible party *marriageability* 64.4

eliminant *excretory* 25.12, *expulsive* 709.11

eliminate *manipulate* 6.87, *react* 11.38, *excrete* 25.20, *murder* 30.20, *purify* 111.19, *obliterate* 186.8, *cause to disappear* 265.7, *discard* 383.12, *exterminate* 709.22, *void* 709.23, *extract* 711.13, *subtract* 749.6, *eject* 764.8, *annihilate* 773.22, *reduce* 796.8, *cancel* 834.6

eliminated *obliterated* 186.4, *discarded* 383.8, *dislodged* 711.11, *subtracted* 749.3, *annihilated* 773.16

eliminate each other *cancel out* 834.8

eliminate the alternatives *choose* 382.14

elimination *evaluation* 6.22, *chemical reaction* 11.8, *excretion* 25.1, *obliteration* 186.1, *blacking out* 265.2, *discarding* 383.3, *destruction* 523.1, *removal* 709.5, *extraction* 711.1, *subtraction* 749.1, *ejection* 764.2, *annihilation* 773.4, *cancellation* 834.1

eliminative *excretory* 25.12

elision *literary device* 139.12, *conciseness* 198.1, *shortening* 582.2, 591.2

elite 744.12; *aristocracy* 70.2, *chosen thing* 382.8, *selected* 382.11, *excellence* 445.4, *excellent* 445.13, *best people* 744.7, *excluding* 764.5, *chief thing* 799.3

elite troops *armed force* 77.10

elitism *oligarchy* 49.10, *social discrimination* 337.4

elitist *bigot* 337.7, *discriminatory* 337.11

elixir *remedy* 115.1, *dose of medicine* 115.3, *extract* 711.8, *quintessence* 723.3

Elizabethan Furniture Styles 101, *historic* 653.13

Elizabethan architecture Architectural Styles 134

Elizabethan poets Western Literary Groups 139

Elizabethan theater *theater* 136.16

Elizabethan tragedy *tragedy* 136.10

Elizabeth Bennet Famous Lovers 299

elk *game* 160.6

elkhound Breeds of Dogs 35

elks Collective Names 59

ell *additional item* 748.3

Ellesmere Islands 572

ellipse *curve* 6.38, *orbital motion* 681.1

ellipsis Punctuation Marks 5, *syntax* 5.32, *obscurity* 197.1, *conciseness* 198.1, *shortened version* 591.3, *gap* 775.4

ellipsoid *curved surface* 6.43

ellipsoidal *spherical* 6.80

elliptic *concise* 198.4, *circular* 631.5

elliptic(al) *curvilinear* 6.78

elliptical *arch* 134.5, *obscure* 197.2, *shortened* 591.7, *circular* 681.6

elliptical galaxy *galaxy* 7.5

elliptically *obscurely* 197.4, *concisely* 198.6, *shortly* 591.12, *circularly* 631.8

elliptically polarized light *polarized light* 10.19

elliptical orbit *orbit* 7.22

elliptical polarization *wave property* 10.12

elliptic curve *curve* 6.38

elliptic geometry *geometry* 6.32

Ellis Island Islands 572

Ellsworth Mountains and Hills 569

elm Trees and Shrubs 43

elocution *articulation* 205.9

Elohim *God* 82.6

Elohistic *Jehovan* 82.17

elongate *lengthen* 590.12

elongated *lengthened* 590.10

elongation *deformation* 14.16, *lengthening* 590.4

elope *marry* 64.19, *run away* 386.21, *quit* 705.10, *escape* 816.8

elopement *wedding* 64.5, *desertion* 386.7, *departure* 705.1, *escape* 816.1

eloper *escaper* 816.5

elope with *take away* 477.18

eloquence *seriousness* 200.2, *power of speech* 205.5, *talkativeness* 207.1

eloquent *emphatic* 200.3, *articulate* 205.16, *talkative* 207.5, *meaningful* 361.6

eloquently *orally* 205.21, *talkatively* 207.9

El Salvador Countries 566

elsewhere *away* 576.19

Elster Rivers 570

eluant *analysis* 11.17

elucidate *rationalize* 4.20, *clarify* 196.3, *dissertate* 203.5, *make visible* 244.9, *explain* 331.16, *make comprehensible* 363.8, *interpret* 365.12, *make simple* 526.12

elucidated *explanatory* 331.11, *interpreted* 365.9

elucidation *explanation* 331.3, *interpretation* 365.1

elucidative *interpretive* 365.8

elucidatory *descriptive* 202.11

eludable *avoidable* 386.12

elude 816.10; *conceal oneself* 181.15, *deceive* 193.16, 330.12, *dissociate* 375.14, *evade* 386.19, *not perform* 466.10, *lose someone* 468.20

elude one *be unintelligible* 364.11

eluding *equivocal* 380.5

elusion *guile* 193.3, *evasion* 380.2, 386.5, *escape* 816.1

elusive *cunning* 330.8, *difficult* 364.8, *avoiding* 386.9, *unreal* 720.8, *escaping* 816.7

elusive or elusory *artful* 193.13

elusively *deceptively* 193.21, *hypocritically* 330.15, *equivocally* 380.9, *evasively* 386.24

elusiveness *guile* 193.3, *evasiveness* 386.6, *defensiveness* 419.4

elution *analysis* 11.17

elutriate *purify* 111.19

elver *young fish* 38.6

Elysian *idyllic* 214.11, *pleasant* 271.5

Elysian fields *after death* 29.9, *heaven* 82.15, *idealized pleasure* 214.5

Elysium *heaven* 82.15, *idealized pleasure* 214.5

em General Units 589

emaciate *waste away* 96.20, *remove power from* 515.13, *contract* 582.12, *become smaller* 582.14

emaciated 595.10; *underfed* 98.7, *unhealthy* 114.23, *ill* 517.8, *shortened* 582.8
emaciating *contracting* 582.10
emaciation 595.2; *wasting away* 96.4, *shortening* 582.2
e-mail *office automation tools* 15.19, *data transmission* 169.8, *communication* 170.2
e-mail reader *communications software* 15.27
emanate *secrete* 24.7, *have odor* 224.8, *radiate* 703.13, *emerge* 707.14, *leak* 707.16, *result* 770.12, *be visible* 843.16
emanate from *follow from* 676.9
emanating *outgoing* 707.10
emanation *secretion* 24.1, *excretion* 25.1, *occult and psychic phenomena* 86.7, *odor* 224.1, *reputation* 224.4, *spectacle* 264.6, *radiation* 703.3, *outflow* 707.4
emanational *secretory* 24.4
emanative *secretory* 24.4, *odorous* 224.5, *outgoing* 707.10
emanatory *secretory* 24.4
emancipate *save* 275.9, *deliver* 817.5, *set free* 829.17, *liberate* 831.6
emancipated *escaping* 816.7, *free* 829.11, *liberated* 831.4
emancipation *aid* 275.2, *deliverance* 817.1, *freedom* 829.1, *liberation* 831.1
Emancipation Proclamation *liberation* 831.1
emancipator *deliverer* 817.2, *liberator* 831.3
emanent *outgoing* 707.10
emarginate *or* **emarginated** *toothed* 549.13
emasculate *make infertile* 23.9, *take off* 749.7, *make useless* 802.12
emasculated *undersexed* 20.20
emasculation *helplessness* 515.3, *subtraction* 749.1
embalm *bury* 31.10, *perfume* 226.6, *preserve* 815.14
embalmed *posthumous* 29.16, *buried* 31.8, *preserved* 815.12
embalmed body *dead person* 29.7
embalmer *person dealing with the dead* 29.8, *funeral person* 31.5
embalming *after death* 29.9, *burial* 31.1, *preservation of body* 815.7
embalmment *burial* 31.1
embank *support* 605.16
embankment *military defenses* 419.9, *retainer* 471.3, *dam* 551.12, *river parts* 570.3, *supporting structure* 605.2, *track* 688.2, *junction* 691.9, *safety device* 810.15, *barrier* 826.7
embargo *command* 425.1, 425.10, *stoppage* 490.2, *prohibition* 503.1, *prohibit* 503.8, *dissent* 506.2, 506.9, *limit* 620.1, 620.7, *lack of motion* 678.1, *make motionless* 678.8, *exclusion* 764.1, *exclude* 764.7, *obstacle* 826.2, *block* 826.17, *economic restraint* 830.3
embargoed *commanding* 425.7, *prohibited* 503.5, *dissenting* 506.6, *excluded* 764.6, *restrained* 830.9
embark *set out* 705.12, *enter* 706.11
embarkation *start* 705.2, *inauguration* 771.6
embarkment *start* 705.2
embark on *undertake* 391.7, *make a beginning* 771.26
embarras de choix [Fr] *selection* 382.1
embarras de richesses [Fr] *fertility* 22.1, *excess* 99.1, *selection* 382.1

embarrass *humiliate* 298.19, *annoy* 804.10, *cause difficulties* 824.22, *be inhibited* 826.20, *make uncertain* 841.19
embarrassed *humiliated* 298.12, *shy* 403.8, *agitated* 684.15, *troubled* 824.15, *inhibitive* 826.14, *self-restrained* 830.10, *confused* 841.11
embarrassedly 298.24; *self-restrainedly* 830.19
embarrassing *humiliating* 298.14, 436.15, *inhibitive* 826.14, *self-restrained* 830.10
embarrassingly *humiliatingly* 298.25, *inhibitively* 826.24, *self-restrainedly* 830.19, *confusingly* 841.23
embarrassing position *awkward situation* 824.7
embarrassing situation *awkward situation* 824.7
embarrassment *humiliation* 298.5, *shyness* 403.3, *indignity* 436.7, *sign of guilt* 450.2, *agitation* 684.1, *inhibition* 826.3, *self-restraint* 830.4, *confusion* 841.4
embarrassment of riches *fertility* 22.1
embassy *official residence* 60.6, *representative body* 79.2, *government office* 124.13, *council* 833.4
embattled *warring* 76.26
Embden–Meyerhof pathway *respiration* 12.24
embed *inset* 710.13
embedded *inserted* 710.5
embedment *insertion* 710.1
embellish *distort the truth* 192.25, *exaggerate* 194.11, *decorate* 532.11, *ornament* 532.12, *delude* 720.16, *augment* 748.13, *beautify* 807.20
embellished *partially true* 192.18, *exaggerated* 194.7, *beautified* 530.12, *decorated* 532.9
embellisher *gossip* 192.11
embellishment *partial truth* 192.7, *exaggeration* 194.1, *decoration* 532.1, *ornament* 532.7, *beautification* 807.7
embers *fire* 246.9
embezzle *misuse* 395.6, *take money away* 477.20, *act dishonestly* 479.18, *not pay* 490.9
embezzled *misused* 395.3
embezzlement *misuse* 395.1, *taking away* 477.5, *dishonesty* 479.7, *nonpayment* 490.1
embezzler *raider* 477.10, *dishonest person* 479.11, *nonpayer* 490.6
embiopteran *insectile* 40.11
embitter *antagonize* 93.12, *cause hate* 300.12, *make angry* 302.18, *make irritable* 304.15, *make worse* 808.17
embittered *resentful* 302.8
emblazon *identify* 184.11, *color* 251.16, *flourish* 404.25, *decorate* 532.11
emblazoned *heraldic* 184.10
emblem *talisman* 86.9, *sign* 183.1, *means of identification* 184.3, *insignia* 184.5, *outline* 617.1
emblematic *heraldic* 184.10, *representational* 187.8, *representing* 202.14, *outlined* 617.4
emblematically *identifiably* 184.13, *representationally* 187.15
embodied *appearing* 264.9, *material* 524.7, *inclusive* 613.22, *combinatory* 757.6
embodiment *body* 19.1, *divine*

manifestation 82.5, *representation* 187.1, *appearance* 264.1, *materialization* 524.2, *contents* 577.1, *coverage* 613.16, *quintessence* 723.3
embody 577.11, 723.12; *represent* 187.1, *be material* 524.8, *include* 613.33, 763.5
embodying *containing* 577.7
embolden *give courage* 284.16
embolism *cardiovascular disease* 114.13, *insertion* 710.1
embolus *solid body* 540.4, *stopper* 584.3
embonpoint *fatness* 579.5
emboss *sculpt* 144.10, *identify* 184.11, *decorate* 532.11, *make rough* 544.11
embossed *sculpted* 144.8
embossing *relief carving* 144.2
embossment *relief carving* 144.2
embouchure *brass instrument* 142.3
embrace *communication of love* 299.6, *communicate love* 299.25, *side with* 382.15, *welcome* 408.10, 408.18, 708.14, *be sociable* 408.14, *sign of courtesy* 410.5, *greet* 410.11, *retention* 471.1, *retain* 471.7, *stay near* 586.13, *enfoldment* 637.3, *enfold* 637.9, *embody* 723.12, *unify* 752.15, *intertwine* 752.19, *adhere* 755.8, *be whole* 759.9, *include* 763.5, *safekeeping* 810.6, *assure* 810.23
embracing *communication of love* 299.6
embrasure *fort* 419.13
embrocate *anoint* 562.17
embrocation *balm* 115.11, *ointment* 562.8
embroider *sew* 130.18, *distort the truth* 192.25, 627.12, *exaggerate* 194.11, *practice sophistry* 330.11, *decorate* 532.11, *ornament* 532.12, *delude* 720.16
embroidered *sewn* 130.14, *partially true* 192.18, *exaggerated* 194.7, *variegated* 263.6, *beautified* 530.12, *decorated* 532.9
embroiderer *fabric handler* 130.11, *gossip* 192.11, *decorator* 532.8
embroidering Hobbies and Pastimes 167
embroidery *sewing* 130.5, *craft* 133.2, *partial truth* 192.7, *exaggeration* 194.1, *decorative method* 532.3, *ornament* 532.7
embroidery hoop *fabric-handling tool* 130.12
embroilment *turbulence* 684.3
embrown *brown* 256.7
embryo *developmental biology* 13.22, *seed* 41.9, *source* 771.3
embryogenesis *developmental biology* 13.22
embryogeny *developmental biology* 13.22
embryological *biological* 13.27, *of animals* 34.13
embryologically *biologically* 13.36
embryologist *life scientist* 13.26, *animal scientist* 34.7
embryology *life science* 13.1, *developmental biology* 13.6, 13.22, *study of life* 28.9, *animal science* 34.6
embryonic 771.19; *developmental* 13.33, *immature* 389.9, 652.12, *tiny* 580.9, *causal* 675.7
embryonically *immaturely* 389.18, *incompletely* 762.10
embus *set out* 705.12
emcee *leader* 126.8, *lead* 126.12,

entertainer 138.8, *entertain* 138.16, *broadcasting personnel* 172.11
em dash Punctuation Marks 5, *means of connection* 754.4
emend *be accurate* 350.5, *interpret* 365.12, *put right* 429.14, *rectify* 807.22, *repair* 809.10
emendation *interpretation* 365.1, *change for the better* 665.4, *rectification* 807.8, *reconsideration* 807.9, *repair* 809.1
emendator *interpreter* 365.6, *repairer* 809.5
emended *interpreted* 365.9, *changed* 665.10
emender *interpreter* 365.6, *improver* 807.11
emending *improving* 807.14
emerald *green thing* 260.4, *green* 260.7
Emerald City Imaginary Places 360
emerge 707.14, 771.35; *be disclosed* 180.12, *be visible* 242.26, *become visible* 264.13, *follow from* 676.9, *arrive* 704.13, *land* 704.16, *set out* 705.12, *leak* 816.11
emergence *birth* 264.2, *arrival* 704.1, *coming out* 707.3, *creation* 771.2
emergency *immediacy* 645.1, *critical time* 659.3, *predicament* 725.3, *danger* 811.1, *critical situation* 824.6, *misadventure* 848.2
emergency aid *charity* 275.3
emergency buzzer *danger signal* 811.5
emergency exit *way out* 707.2, *means of escape* 816.4
emergency funds *reserves* 102.5
emergency medical technician (EMT) *paramedic* 107.24
emergency medicine Medical Specialties 107
emergency part *safety device* 810.15
emergency plan *plan* 357.2, *procedure* 387.2
Emergency Position-Indicating Radio Beacon (EPIRB) *position finder* 690.8
emergency practitioner *medical specialist* 107.20
emergency procedure *procedure* 387.2
emergency reserves *reserve* 105.3
emergent *appearing* 264.9, *caused* 676.5, *outgoing* 707.10, *embryonic* 771.19
emerging *arriving* 704.9, *coming out* 707.3, *outgoing* 707.10
emerita *former* 653.12
emeritus *former* 651.14, 653.12, *resigning* 835.3
emersion *coming out* 707.3
emery *smooth* 545.10
emery board *cosmetic tool* 530.5, *smoother* 545.2, *abrasive* 553.14, *eraser* 554.7
emery paper *rough thing* 544.2, *smoother* 545.2, *abrasive* 553.14, *eraser* 554.7
emesis *vomiting* 709.7
emetic *purgative* 115.7, *medicinal* 115.15, *ejector* 709.10, *expulsive* 709.11
emetically *expulsively* 709.29
emetophobia Phobias 283
emigrant *outgoer* 707.9, *new arrival* 724.6
emigrate 707.17; *quit* 705.10, *be foreign* 724.13

emigration 707.6; *departure* 705.1, *disbandment* 776.2
emigratory *outgoing* 705.7
émigré *outgoer* 707.9, *new arrival* 724.6
eminence *repute* 370.1, *person of repute* 370.2, *excellence* 445.4, *exaltation* 596.3, *height* 715.4, *superiority* 744.1, *importance* 799.1
éminence grise *deputy* 80.1, *one who conceals* 181.7, *figurative usage* 255.4, *indirect influence* 512.4, *backstage manipulator* 844.3
eminent *legitimate* 52.10, *reputable* 370.3, *excellent* 445.13, 744.14, *exalted* 596.10, *promoted* 715.8, *important* 799.7, *notable* 799.11
eminent domain *legal power* 52.2
eminently 370.7; *aristocratically* 70.6, *excellently* 445.21, *exaltedly* 596.22, *predominantly* 744.21, *importantly* 799.15
emissary *delegate* 79.1, *agent* 80.3, *commissioner* 833.5
emission 10.56; *secretion* 24.1, *excretion* 25.1, *outflow* 707.4, *leak* 816.6
emission nebula *nebula* 7.6
emission spectrum *emission* 10.56
emissive *secretory* 24.4, *expulsive* 709.11
emit *observe* 7.34, *secrete* 24.7, *excrete* 25.20, *give off* 556.25, *leak* 707.16, *let out* 709.26
emit rays *let out* 709.26
emitter *ejector* 709.10
emitting *expulsive* 709.11
Emmanuel *God the Son* 82.9
Emmy *prizes* 453.3
emollient *pacificatory* 74.8, *dose of medicine* 115.3, *balm* 115.11, *medicinal* 115.15, *reliever* 275.4, *moderating* 521.5, *ointment* 562.8, *lubricational* 562.12
emolument *reward for service* 453.5, *profit* 467.6, *pay* 489.6, *income* 492.3
emotion 266.3; *sensation* 212.1, *influence* 512.1, *depth of feeling* 598.7
emotional *sensitive* 266.11, 267.3, *amorous* 299.18, *demonstrative* 331.10, *spontaneous* 396.5, *appealing* 512.9
emotional instability *emotionalism* 266.6
emotionalism 266.6; *demonstrativeness* 331.2
emotionalistic *demonstrative* 331.10
emotionality *emotionalism* 266.6, *demonstrativeness* 331.2
emotionalize *appear* 331.18
emotionally *sensationally* 212.12, *with feeling* 266.18, *sensitively* 267.6, *amorously* 299.30, *demonstratively* 331.21, *influentially* 512.14
emotionally disturbed person *personality disorder* 108.7
emotional person *feeling person* 266.8
emotional shock *anxiety disorder* 108.11
emotional strain *or* **tension** *anxiety disorder* 108.11
emotive 266.13; *exciting* 212.8
emotiveness *emotionalism* 266.6
emotivism Philosophical Schools of Thought 4
emotivist Philosophical Schools of Thought 4

empanel *record* 185.13, *register* 185.15
empanelment *recordkeeping* 185.7
empathetic *sensitive* 266.11, 267.3, *liking* 290.4, *compassionate* 305.8, *pitying* 308.4, *agreeing* 462.6, *supportive* 605.11, *compatible* 735.14
empathetically *admiringly* 290.11, *compassionately* 305.14, *pityingly* 308.11, *agreeably* 462.14, *supportively* 605.20, *compatibly* 735.34
empathize *feel for* 266.17, *be sensitive* 267.5, *be compassionate* 305.11, *pity* 308.6, *have insight* 360.16, *agree with* 462.10, *give moral support* 605.18
empathizer *supporter* 605.9
empathize with *like* 290.8, *pity* 308.6, *have a rapport with* 735.24
empathizing *compatible* 735.14
empathizingly *compatibly* 735.34
empathy *good feeling* 266.4, *sensitivity* 267.1, *liking* 290.1, *compassion* 305.2, *pity* 308.1, *insight* 360.3, *agreement* 462.1, *moral support* 605.7, *compatibility* 735.4
emperor *person in authority* 52.7, *sovereign* 68.2
empery *governance* 49.18
emphasis 200.1; *meter* 139.10, *affirmation* 189.1, *mode of speech* 205.6, *potency* 516.6, *importance* 799.1, *manifestation* 843.2
emphasize 200.6; *signify* 183.16, *punctuate* 183.20, *affirm* 189.21, *make comprehensible* 363.8, *contend* 422.22, *compel* 428.8, *strengthen* 516.15, *make important* 799.14, *display* 843.13, *reveal* 843.14
emphasized 200.4; *affirmed* 189.11, *accentuated* 843.11
emphatic 200.3; *affirmed* 189.11, *colorful* 251.11, *defiant* 416.5
emphatically 200.7; *affirmatively* 189.29, *defiantly* 416.9
emphatically deny *negate* 190.16
emphatic denial *negation* 190.1
emphysema *respiratory disease* 114.12, *smoking* 121.22
Empire Apple Varieties 44, Furniture Styles 101
empire *governance* 49.18, *body politic* 50.3, *region* 564.1, *dominion* 566.3
empire building *expansionism* 712.5
Empire style Architectural Styles 134
empire waist *part of garment* 100.27
empirical *theoretical* 6.66, *experimental* 335.8, *evidential* 339.8, *material* 524.7, *real* 717.14
empirical formula *structure* 411.7
empirically *experimentally* 335.14
empirical probability *probability* 6.59, *probability theory* 838.5
empirical psychology Psychological Theories, Schools 108
empirical sociologist *sociologist* 2.3
empirical world *material world* 524.1
empiricism Philosophical Schools of Thought 4, *experimentation* 335.3, *materialization* 524.2
empiricist Philosophical Schools of Thought 4, *experimenter* 335.5
emplace *locate* 565.9

emplaced *located* 565.6
emplacement *fortification* 419.12, *placing* 565.4
emplane *set out* 705.12
emplanement *start* 705.2
employ 57.18; *socialize* 2.14, *work for* 122.10, *use* 393.1, 393.9, *take* 477.14, *take action* 509.12, *find useful* 801.11, *subjection* 832.1, *subject* 832.10, *engage* 833.9
employability *usability* 801.2
employable *industrial* 57.13, *usable* 393.6, 801.6, *instrumental* 511.4, *subordinate* 832.8, *engaged* 833.7
employed 573.8; *industrial* 57.13, *working* 122.6, *used* 393.5, *busy* 414.15, *subordinate* 832.8, *engaged* 833.7
employee 57.4; *industrial* 57.13, *servant* 69.1, *office assistant* 69.6, *worker* 123.1, *operator* 509.5, *subordinate* 832.3
employee at will *worker* 123.1
employee claim *industrial dispute* 57.7
employee compensation *bargaining terms* 57.10
employee demands *bargaining* 57.9
employee incentive programs *bargaining terms* 57.10
employee jurisdiction *labor relations* 57.1
employee management *personnel management* 126.4
employee negotiations *bargaining* 57.9
employee planning *personnel management* 126.4
employee practices *bargaining* 57.9
employee relations *labor relations* 57.1, *personnel management* 126.4
employee rights *labor relations* 57.1
employees *personnel* 123.16
employer 57.3; *industrial* 57.13, *company leader* 68.8, *manager* 126.7
employer contributions *benefits* 57.11
employer–employee relations *labor relations* 57.1
employer jurisdiction *labor relations* 57.1
employer rights *labor relations* 57.1
employers *management board* 126.2
employer's liability *bargaining terms* 57.10
employers' organization *or* **association** *labor relations* 57.1
employing *industrial* 57.13
employment 573.3; *industrial* 57.13, *job* 122.3, *use* 393.1, *action* 412.1, *taking* 477.1, *instrumentality* 511.1, *usefulness* 801.1, *subjection* 832.1, *engagement* 833.2
employment contract *work practices* 57.2, *purchase contract* 459.3
employment laws *work practices* 57.2
employment manager *employer* 57.3
employment rate *economic factor* 56.8
employment relations *labor relations* 57.1
employment rules *work practices* 57.2

employment standards *bargaining terms* 57.10
employment status *social stratification* 2.7
employment training *educational system* 48.2
employ oneself *occupy oneself* 412.15
employ tactics *conduct oneself* 399.17
emporium *marketplace* 483.7
empower 514.20; *gain authority* 52.15, *delegate* 79.6, *deputize* 80.7, *permit* 340.12, 502.6, *commission* 833.8, *make possible* 836.7
empowered *authoritative* 52.9, *authorized* 52.11, 340.8, *rightful* 429.9, *powerful* 514.15, *commissioned* 833.6
empowerment *acquisition of authority* 52.5, *permission* 340.3, *ability* 514.3, *commission* 833.1
empress *person in authority* 52.7, *sovereign* 68.2
emprise *undertaking* 391.1
emptily *absently* 576.18, *unsuccessfully* 410.18
emptiness 576.2, 718.4; *nonentity* 190.5, *ungenuineness* 192.2, *lack of emphasis* 201.1, *nonsense* 362.2, *empty space* 563.2, *superficiality* 599.2, *unimportance* 800.1
emptiness of mind *forgetfulness* 355.1
emptor *purchaser* 481.7
empty *infertile* 23.7, *expend* 96.15, *unprovided* 98.6, *fasting* 118.5, *nonexistent* 190.14, *ungenuine* 192.13, *diffuse* 199.3, *unemphatic* 201.2, *hungry* 288.16, *meaningless* 362.7, *not working* 415.10, *lighten* 539.9, *make sparse* 541.5, *space* 563.15, *vacant* 576.12, *unoccupied* 576.13, *superficial* 599.4, *void* 709.23, *draw off* 711.16, *nonexistent* 718.9, *subtract* 749.6, *failed* 846.10
empty chatter *empty talk* 362.5
empty gesture *ungenuineness* 192.2
empty gossip *or* **talk** *partial truth* 192.7
empty-handed *unprovided* 98.6
empty head *lack of thought* 318.1, *vain person* 402.7
empty-headed *unintelligent* 316.6, *thoughtless* 318.7, *ignorant* 349.5, *foolish* 353.5, *forgetful* 355.6, *simpleminded* 922.9
empty-headedly *unintelligently* 316.9
empty-headedness *ignorance* 316.3, 349.1, *lack of thought* 318.1, *forgetfulness* 355.1
emptying *removal* 709.5, *drawing off* 711.4
empty one's pocket *pay* 489.16, *expend* 491.11
empty out *void* 709.23
empty pantry *insolvency* 486.2
empty phrase *nonstandard language* 5.7
empty pride *vanity* 402.1
empty promises *theory* 720.4
empty purse *insolvency* 486.2
empty rooms Phobias 283
empty set *set* 6.19
empty shell *emptiness* 576.2, *remainder* 750.1
empty sound *nonsense* 362.2
empty space 563.2; *emptiness* 576.2
empty talk 362.5; *nonstandard language* 5.7, *diffuseness* 199.1,

---

talk 207.3, senseless talk 362.4, theory 720.4
empty words *sophistry* 330.1, *nonsense* 362.2
empurple 262.7
empyreal *heavenly* 82.22
empyrean *universe* 7.3, *heaven* 82.15, *heavenly* 82.22
Ems *Rivers* 570
emu *flightless bird* 36.8
emulate 736.11; *program* 15.29, *contend* 422.22, *simulate* 733.16, *imitate* 736.9, *abide by* 781.12, *confront* 828.19
emulating *imitative* 736.7, *discordant* 828.12
emulation *rivalry* 422.2, *simulation* 733.4, *imitation* 736.1, *conformity* 781.1, *conflict* 828.3
emulative *envious* 314.4
emulator *computing terms* 15.22, *contender* 422.13, *opponent* 828.10
emulous *envious* 314.4
emulously *enviously* 314.11
emulousness [Arch] *envy* 314.1
emulsification *viscosity* 561.1
emulsifier *food content* 90.3, *thickener* 561.12
emulsify *solidify* 11.37, *make fluid* 555.22, *thicken* 561.21
emulsion 132.9, 561.5; *phase* 11.13, *solution* 555.10
emulsion paint *paint* 251.6
emulsive *viscous* 561.14
emulsoid *status adjectives* 11.25, *emulsion* 561.5
en *General Units* 589
enable *find means* 102.6, *permit* 340.12, 502.6, *empower* 514.20, *grant* 735.30, *make easy* 823.15, *make possible* 836.7
enabled *authorized* 340.8
enablement *permission* 340.3, *ability* 514.3
enabler *helper* 825.12
enact *legislate* 53.31, *act* 136.34, 187.13, 412.11, *behave toward* 399.20, *command* 425.10, *simulate* 733.16, *display* 843.13
enacted *dramatized* 136.32, *commanding* 425.7, *simulated* 733.11
enacting *lawmaking* 53.11, *acting* 412.9
enactment *lawmaking* 53.11, *acting* 136.22, 187.6, *action* 412.1, *command* 425.1, *simulation* 733.4, *rule* 780.1, *production* 843.5
enamel *make ceramics* 129.10, *coloring agent* 251.5, *color* 251.16, *variegate* 263.11, *polish* 545.3, *coating* 613.8, *coat* 613.28
enamel *or* **enamelware** *Ceramics* 129
enameled *ceramic* 129.9, *decorated* 532.9, *polished* 545.7
enameler *visual artist* 133.6
enameler *or* **enamelist** *ceramist* 129.7
enameling *ceramic* 129.9, *craft* 133.2, *Hobbies and Pastimes* 167
enamelist *visual artist* 133.6
enamel kiln *ceramic workshop and tools* 129.8
enamelwork *variegated thing* 263.5
enamor *win the love of* 299.27
enamored 299.17
enamored of *or* **with** *in love* 299.17
enantiomorph *transformation* 6.46
enantiomorphic *symmetrical* 626.4

enantiomorphism *symmetry* 626.1
en bloc [Fr] *one and all* 759.12
encaenia *religious festival* 85.13
encamp *take up residence* 60.24
encapsulate *summarize* 204.7, *shorten* 591.9, *inset* 710.13, *include* 763.5
encapsulated *shortened* 591.7
encapsulation *shortening* 591.2, *shortened version* 591.3, *inclusion* 763.1
encase *wrap* 613.29, *inset* 710.13
encased *protected* 613.20
encaustic *ceramic* 129.9, *painting* 143.3
encaustically *ornamentally* 129.11
enceinte *pregnant* 21.12
Enceladus *Planets and Their Satellites* 7
encephalitis lethargica *tropical disease* 114.10
enchant *bewitch* 86.25, *cause joy* 269.11, *be wondrous* 294.14, *win the love of* 299.27, *lure* 700.12
enchanted *bewitched* 86.21, *joyful* 269.6, *wondering* 294.7, *enamored* 299.17
enchantedly *wonderingly* 294.16
enchanter *witch* 86.15, *charmer* 700.6
enchanting *witchlike* 86.19, *delightful* 271.7, *wondrous* 294.9, *lovable* 299.20, *appealing* 529.10, *attractive* 700.10
enchantingly *wondrously* 294.18, *lovably* 299.31, *beautifully* 529.13, *attractively* 700.14
enchantment *witchcraft* 86.6, *joy* 269.1, *wonder* 294.1, *romantic love* 299.2
enchantress *witch* 86.15, *attractive female* 529.5, *charmer* 700.6
enchilada *notable international dishes* 90.40
encipher *make mysterious* 182.13, *make unintelligible* 364.13
encircle *align* 6.92, *besiege* 418.20, *surround* 615.7, *circle* 631.6, *include* 763.5
encircled *surrounded* 615.5
encirclement 615.2; *military attack* 418.2, *enclosure* 619.1, *inclusion* 763.1
enclave *enclosed area* 619.2
enclitic *word* 5.17, *worded* 5.38
enclose 584.16, 619.6; *besiege* 418.20, *fence* 419.21, *detain* 471.9, *extend* 563.14, *contain* 577.10, 578.20, *wrap* 613.29, *surround* 615.7, *enfold* 637.9, *include* 763.5, *exclude* 764.7, *protect* 810.21
enclosed 584.11, 619.4; *containing* 578.18, *protected* 613.20, *surrounded* 615.5, *sheltered* 812.7
enclosed area 619.2
enclosed land *farmland* 16.3
enclosed place *closed place* 584.4, *enclosed area* 619.2
enclosed places *Phobias* 283
enclosed space *space* 6.33
enclosing *detention* 471.2, *containing* 578.18, *enclosure* 619.1, *enclosed* 619.4
enclosing thing 619.3
enclosure 619.1; *farm building* 16.4, *blockading* 76.22, *plot* 564.9, *closed place* 584.4, *covering* 613.1, *enfoldment* 637.3, *inclusion* 763.1, *shelter* 812.1

encoded *occult* 86.16, *unintelligible* 364.4
encoffin *bury* 31.10
encomiastic *approving* 437.9
encomium *public speaking* 205.11, *praise* 437.3
encompass *extend* 563.14, *include* 613.33, 763.5, *surround* 615.7, *enclose* 619.6, *make circular* 631.7, *embody* 723.12, *augment* 748.13, *be whole* 759.9
encompassed *surrounded* 615.5
encompassing *inclusive* 613.22, *gradational* 739.5
encompassment *encirclement* 615.2
encore *play part* 136.8, *acclaim* 437.5, 437.18, *twice* 789.18, *repeat* 797.5, *again* 797.23
encore! *bravo!* 437.23
encounter *discovery* 345.1, *discover* 345.11, *contention* 422.1, *warfare* 422.10, *fight* 422.23, *meeting* 586.5, 704.5, *meet* 586.15, 704.20, *be simultaneous* 649.6, *collision* 695.2, *collide* 695.10
encounter aliens *experience psychic phenomena* 86.23
encounter by chance *chance upon* 842.13
encounter unexpectedly *chance upon* 842.13
encourage *educate* 48.22, *advise* 176.9, 825.27, *persuade* 178.15, *inspire hope* 281.14, *give courage* 284.16, *be benevolent* 305.10, *motivate* 508.9, *give moral support* 605.18, *awaken* 675.9, *promote* 807.18
encouraged *persuadable* 178.14, *motivated* 508.8
encouragement 284.6; *exhortation* 178.2, *cheer* 281.4, *inducement* 508.2, *influence* 512.1, *moral support* 605.7, *cause* 675.1, *patronage* 825.9
encouraging 284.13; *advisory* 176.7, *persuasive* 178.12, *cheering* 269.8, 281.9, *motivational* 508.7, *appealing* 512.9, *supportive* 605.11, 825.18
encouragingly 284.21; *educationally* 48.25, *advisorily* 176.12, *comfortingly* 281.17, *influentially* 508.13, 512.14, *supportively* 605.20
Encratite *chaste person* 431.6
encroach *exhibit penalty behavior* 155.21, *besiege* 418.20, *invade* 706.12, *transgress* 712.14
encroaching *offending* 53.25, *overrun* 712.6
encroachment *lawbreaking* 53.14, *penalty* 155.13, *military attack* 418.2, *improvement* 679.5, *inroad* 706.3, *transgression* 712.3
encrust *be exterior* 610.13, *face* 613.31
encrustation *dirtiness* 112.1, *cover* 613.2, *wall covering* 613.12
encrusted *dirty* 112.7, *hard* 542.5, *coarse* 544.6
encryption *computer communications* 15.25
encumber *make heavy* 538.14, *hinder* 826.15, *burden* 826.21
encumbered *indebted* 488.7, *hindering* 826.12
encumbering *hindering* 826.12
encumbrance *debt* 488.1, *weighing down* 538.5, *addition* 748.1, *hindrance* 826.1, *burden* 826.10
encyclical *law* 53.1, *publication*

173.1, *command* 425.1, *commanding* 425.7
encyclopedia *schoolbook* 48.15, *collection* 105.12, *type of book* 174.3, *book of lists* 785.3
encyclopedic *knowledgeable* 348.7, *including* 763.3, *general* 778.9
encyclopedically *inventorially* 785.13
Encyclopédistes *Western Literary Groups* 139
end 773.1, 773.19; *death* 29.1, *die* 29.17, 773.21, *type of table* 101.5, *green bowling* 151.3, *motive* 178.5, *disappearance* 265.1, *disappear* 265.5, *purpose* 327.4, *point* 361.5, *objective* 374.5, *solution* 376.6, *ruin* 523.4, *destroy* 523.10, *be destroyed* 523.17, *closure* 584.1, *close down* 584.10, *limit* 620.1, 620.7, 761.4, *back* 622.1, *rear end* 622.4, *pass* 651.17, *stop* 668.2, 668.10, *cause to cease* 668.12, *effect* 676.1, *destination* 704.6, *downfall* 714.7, *cease to exist* 718.13, *cause not to exist* 718.14, *complete* 759.10, 761.9, *completion* 761.2, *conclusion* 761.3, 773.3, *be complete* 761.10, *sequel* 770.5, *hindmost* 773.18, *discontinue* 775.10
end, the [Inf] *ender* 773.11
end an affair *withdraw* 392.5
endanger 811.11
endangered 811.10
endangered species *preserved thing* 815.10
endangered species act *ecology* 815.3
endangerment 811.2
end around *play* 155.8
en dash *Punctuation Marks* 5, *means of connection* 754.4
endboards *hockey areas* 158.2
endearing *likable* 290.7, *loving* 299.15, *lovable* 299.20
endearingly *likably* 290.12, *lovingly* 299.29, *lovably* 299.31
endearing qualities *lovability* 299.5
endearment *love* 299.1
endearments *communication of love* 299.6, *empty talk* 362.5
endeavor *exertion* 122.4, *exert oneself* 122.11, *experiment* 335.1, *invent* 335.13, *attempt* 390.1, *try hard* 390.7, *undertaking* 391.1, *undertake* 391.7, *action* 412.1, *be powerful* 514.18, *production* 522.1
ended 773.14; *closed down* 584.10, *over* 651.12, *stopped* 668.7, *no more* 718.11, *completed* 761.7, *discontinued* 775.8
endemic *contagious* 114.26, *intrinsic* 611.11, *universal* 778.10
endemically *intrinsically* 611.20
endemic disease *disease* 114.4
ender 773.11
end game *board games* 167.3
end-grain wood *wood* 131.3
end hostilities *make peace* 73.11
end in *react* 676.8
end in a point *be sharp* 549.15
end in futility *miscarry* 846.19
ending 773.10, 773.13; *death* 29.1, *stop* 668.2, *appendage* 748.4, *completion* 761.2, *conclusion* 761.3, *end* 773.1
end in view *objective* 374.5
end leaf *bookbinding* 174.11
endless *lengthy* 590.9, *protracted* 669.7, *continuous* 774.9, *numberless* 795.8, *infinite* 798.5, *eternal* 798.7

endless band *continuum* 774.5
endlessly *at length* 590.15, *ever* 640.7, *continually* 669.10, *continuously* 774.16, *infinitely* 798.10
endlessness *longness* 590.3, *eternity* 644.1, *continuity* 774.4, *infinity* 798.1
endless round *continuum* 774.5
end line *stadium* 155.3
end matter *book part* 174.5, *back matter* 622.3, *ending* 773.10
endmost *hindmost* 773.18
endoblast *interior* 611.1
endocarp *fruit structure* 44.3
endocrine *biological* 13.27, *of a secretion* 24.5
endocrine disease *disease* 114.4
endocrine gland *secretory mechanism* 24.3
endocrinological *biological* 13.27
endocrinologist *life scientist* 13.26, *medical specialist* 107.20
endocrinology *biochemistry* 13.3, Medical Specialties 107, *medical science* 107.5
endoderm *interior* 611.1
endodermal *interior* 611.7
endodermic *interior* 611.7
endodermis *interior* 611.1
endodontic *dental* 107.31
endodontics *dentistry* 107.6
endodontist *dentist* 107.21
end of hostilities *truce* 73.2
end of life *death* 29.1
end of the day *close* 773.9
end of the line *rail* 688.3, *railroad station* 688.6, *destination* 704.6, *end point* 773.6
end of the rainbow *idealism* 360.7, *dreamland* 360.8, *distant place* 585.3
end of the road *close* 773.9
end of the world *ruin* 523.4, *future condition* 650.3, *end of time* 773.5
end of time 773.5; *philosophical problem* 4.8, *future condition* 650.3
end of war *truce* 73.2
endogamy *type of marriage* 64.3
endogenous depression *mental breakdown* 110.4
endogenous depression or melancholia *mood disorder* 108.12
endomorph *physical type* 1.8, *personality type* 108.6, *nature* 624.5
endomorphic *physical* 1.14, *fat* 579.15
endomorphism *personality type* 108.6
endomorphy *physical type* 1.8, *personality type* 108.6, *fatness* 579.5
endoplasm *cell structure* 13.16
endoplasmic *cellular* 13.30
endoplasmic reticulum (ER) *cell structure* 13.16
endorse *legislate* 53.31, *identify oneself* 184.12, *confirm* 189.25, *verify* 336.8, *prove* 339.14, *assent* 346.6, *side with* 382.15, *approve* 437.14, *contract* 459.8, 462.11, *promise* 464.10, *permit* 502.6, *give moral support* 605.18, *establish reality* 719.12, *consent* 735.28, *advise* 825.27, *make certain* 840.14
endorse a check *bank* 484.26
endorsed *confirmed* 189.17, *approved* 437.8, *contractual* 462.7, *consenting* 735.18
endorsee *recipient* 473.5
endorsement *personal*

identification 184.4, *confirmation* 189.5, *yes* 346.2, *approval* 437.1, *contract* 462.2, *promise* 464.2, *permission* 502.1, *permit* 502.3, *moral support* 605.7, *consent* 735.8
endorser *affirmer* 189.9, *assenter* 346.3, 462.5, *contractor* 459.6, *supporter* 605.9
endorsingly *confirmingly* 189.32, *supportively* 605.20
endorsive *confirming* 189.16, *supportive* 605.11
endoscope *diagnostic instrument* 107.13
endoscopy *diagnostic procedure* 107.11
endoskeleton *skeleton* 551.14
endosmosis *passage into* 692.4, *absorption* 708.6
endosmotic *absorbent* 708.11
endosperm *seed* 41.9
endothelium *body covering* 19.4
endotrophic mycorrhiza *fungal association* 47.5
endow *provision* 89.9, *permit* 340.12, *own property* 470.11, *will* 472.11, *make rich* 485.15, *give* 498.11, *grant* 735.30, *finance* 825.31
endowed *gifted* 127.11, *qualified* 340.7, *propertied* 470.9, *given* 472.8, *granted* 735.20
endowing *giving* 472.1
endowment *provision* 89.1, *aptitude* 127.4, *ability* 340.2, *permission* 340.3, *profit* 467.6, *giving* 472.1, *grant* 735.10, *financial assistance* 825.6
endow with power *empower* 514.20
end paper *bookbinding* 174.11
end piece *back* 622.1
end point 773.6; *gravimetric analysis* 11.18
end product *product* 522.3, *conclusion* 761.3
end racial or sexual or age discrimination *treat equally* 831.8
end result *solution* 376.6, *effect* 676.1, *conclusion* 761.3, *sequel* 770.5
end rhyme *rhyme* 139.11
end sheet *bookbinding* 174.11
ends of the earth *distant place* 585.3, *limit* 773.7
end someone's life *kill* 30.19
end to end *near* 586.6, *beside* 586.20, *lengthwise* 590.14
end up *take effect* 676.11
end up in *or* *at reach* 704.14
end up in smoke *go to waste* 468.19, *miscarry* 846.19
endurable *forgivable* 312.7
endurably *forgivably* 312.14
endurance 516.4; *racing* 146.9, *steadfastness* 284.3, *forgivingness* 312.3, *tenacity* 376.4, 755.2, *stamina* 377.4, *vigor* 514.2, *stalwartness* 547.3, *continuation* 642.2, *permanence* 667.1, *protraction* 669.4, *continuing existence* 717.7
endurance event *automobile racing* 146.1
endurance racing *automobile racing* 146.1
endure 377.14; *live* 28.17, *feel pain* 215.8, *take courage* 284.15, *show mercy* 312.11, *resist* 417.10, *succumb* 421.7, *be tough* 547.13, *be long* 590.11, *bear* 605.17, *pass* 639.13, *last* 642.6, *be permanent*

667.4, *protract* 669.9, *continue to be* 717.20
endure *or* *go on* *or* *continue forever* *be eternal* 644.7
endured *overlooked* 312.6
endure hardship *be in trouble* 848.13
endure longer *improve* 467.18
enduring 377.9; *detached* 4.18, *steadfast* 284.11, *tenacious* 376.9, 755.6, *stalwart* 547.10, *long-lasting* 590.7, *lasting* 639.9, 642.4, 717.13, *eternal* 644.4, *unfailing* 667.3, *protracted* 669.7, *stable* 674.3
enduringly *stoically* 4.26, *stalwartly* 547.17, *permanently* 667.6, *continually* 669.10, *stably* 674.9, *tenaciously* 755.12
end use *usefulness* 393.2
endways *vertically* 602.11
endways *or* *endwise* *lengthwise* 590.8, 590.14
endwise *vertically* 602.11
end zone *stadium* 155.3
enema *cleaning agent* 111.9, *purgative* 115.7
Enemy *devil* 446.5
enemy *hostile person* 63.5, *opponent* 828.10
enemy, the *the opposition* 828.8
enemy forces *armed forces* 77.9
enemy *or* *hater of marriage single person* 67.5
energetic 514.16; *lively* 28.16, *healthy* 113.4, *working* 122.6, *emphatic* 200.3, *active* 414.13, *industrious* 414.16, *strong in spirit* 516.11, *vigorous* 518.2
energetically 514.22; *laboriously* 122.13, *emphatically* 200.7, *strongly* 516.17, *acutely* 516.18, *with vigor* 518.6
energetic person *busy person* 414.10
energize *invigorate* 28.22, 518.5, *motivate* 508.9, *empower* 514.20, *strengthen* 516.15, *intensify* 746.8
energized *motivated* 508.8
energizing *motivational* 508.7
energy 10.10, 414.4, 514.7; *liveliness* 28.12, *health* 113.1, *exertion* 122.4, *emphasis* 200.1, *power* 447.4, 514.1, *potency* 516.6, *vigor* 518.1, *violence* 520.1
energy balance *atmospheric process* 9.9
energy balances *chemical reaction thermodynamics* 14.29
energy band *semiconductor* 10.34
energy charge *cathexis* 108.32
energy crisis *scarcity* 98.3
energy depletion *powerlessness* 515.1
energy gap *semiconductor* 10.34
energy imparted *radioactivity* 10.58
energy level *atom* 10.52
energy-rich bond *bioenergetics* 12.23
energy-saving *preserving* 815.11
energy source *fuel* 106.1
energy states *chemical reaction thermodynamics* 14.29
energy thrust *propellant* 696.9
enervate *de-emphasize* 201.3, *make impotent* 515.15, *weaken* 517.13, *fatigue* 820.6
enervated *weakened* 517.9, *fatigued* 820.2
enervated style *lack of emphasis* 201.1
enervation *lack of emphasis* 201.1, *poor health* 517.3, *fatigue* 820.1

enetophobia Phobias 283
en famille [Fr] *informally* 407.11, *sociably* 408.19
enfant terrible [Fr] *nonconformist* 782.7
enfeeble *weaken* 517.13, *make smaller* 747.8
enfeebled *weak* 517.6
enfeeblement *weakness* 517.1, *decrease* 747.1
enfeoffment *giving* 472.1
enfilade *land attack* 418.3, *fire* 418.18
enflé Card Games 168
enfold 637.9; *clothe* 100.43, *wrap* 613.29, 619.7, *surround* 615.7, *intertwine* 752.19, *assure* 810.23
enfolded *surrounded* 615.5
enfoldment 637.3; *covering* 613.1, *encirclement* 615.2
enforce *compel* 428.8
enforce a limit *limit* 830.13
enforce civil rights *treat equally* 831.8
enforcement *coercion* 428.2
enforcer *one who restrains* 830.7
enforcing *compelling* 428.6
enfranchise *set free* 829.17, *treat equally* 831.8
enfranchised *free* 829.11
enfranchisement *independence* 829.5
engage 833.9; *marry* 64.19, *battle* 76.33, *resolve* 374.9, *take charge of* 391.8, *attack* 418.17, *fight* 422.23, *impose a duty* 433.14, *take* 477.14, *prepare* 657.14, *unify* 752.15, *intertwine* 752.19
engagé *active* 414.13
engaged 833.7; *marriageable* 64.17, *warring* 76.26, *busy* 414.15, *dutiful* 433.6, *duty-bound* 433.8, *on-duty* 433.10, *promised* 458.8, *united* 752.10
engaged in war *warring* 76.26
engaged man *boyfriend* 32.4
engaged person *someone promised* 458.7
engaged woman *girlfriend* 33.4
engage in *address oneself to* 209.13, *undertake* 391.7
engage in a forlorn hope *face danger* 811.12
engage in conversation *converse* 210.11
engage in dialectic *discuss* 4.22
engage in fisticuffs *box* 152.19, *duel* 422.24, *dispute* 463.9
engage in war *or* *hostilities* *be at war* 76.32
engagement 136.15, 138.6, 833.2; *battle* 76.23, *courtship* 299.10, *intentionality* 359.4, *undertaking* 391.1, *contract* 391.2, *social gathering* 408.4, *contention* 422.1, *warfare* 422.10, *line of duty* 433.3, *betrothal* 458.2, *taking* 477.1
engagement book *list of dates* 785.6
engagement calendar *reminder* 354.4
engagement diary *list of dates* 785.6
engagement ring *love token* 299.8
engage oneself *incur a duty* 433.15
engage with *contend* 422.22
engaging *likable* 271.6, 290.7, *lovable* 299.20
engagingly *lovably* 299.31
en garde *fencing movements* 153.3
engender *propagate* 21.15,

procreate 22.14, *bring into existence* 522.14, *produce* 771.34

engendering *propagation* 21.4

engine *rocketry* 7.32, *dynamic structure* 14.5, *component* 760.3

engine cycle 14.13

engine driver [Brit] *railroad worker* 688.7

engineer 14.2, 14.48; *air force person* 77.31, *professional worker* 123.11, *plan* 387.12, *producer* 522.10, *produce* 522.13, *awaken* 675.9, *railroad worker* 688.7

engineering 14.1; *naval commands* 77.19, *manufacture* 522.2

engineer's chain *measuring instrument* 589.12

engine failure *unsuccessful thing* 846.8

engine lathe *machine tool* 14.9

engine part *engine type* 14.11

engine power *type of power* 514.6

engine trouble *technical problem* 826.3

engine type 14.11

England Phobias 283

English *billiards play* 149.2

English, the Phobias 283

English architecture Architectural Styles 134

English as it is spoken *spoken language* 205.2

English billiards *billiards* 149.1

English bond *masonry* 14.22

English breakfast *meal* 92.8

English Civil War Major Wars 76

English Classics [Brit] *famous horse races* 159.13

English cocker spaniel Breeds of Dogs 35

English daisy Flowers 42

English foxhound Breeds of Dogs 35

English horn Musical Instruments 142

English Longwool Breeds of Sheep 16

English muffin *bread* 90.10

English rose *national emblem* 184.7

English saddle *riding equipment* 159.9

English setter Breeds of Dogs 35

English springer spaniel Breeds of Dogs 35

English stroke *rowing techniques* 150.16

English toy spaniel Breeds of Dogs 35

engobe *material* 129.2

engorge *eat well* 92.23, *be greedy* 119.4, *ingest* 708.17

engorged *gluttonous* 119.3

engorgement *appetite* 92.2, *immoderation* 99.2, *intake* 708.5

engraft *plant* 710.14, *insert* 748.12

engrail *make rough* 544.11

engram *memory* 108.27

engrave 144.11; *design* 133.9, *identify* 184.11, *inscribe* 185.14, *illustrate* 187.11, *decorate* 532.11, *outline* 617.5, *furrow* 638.5, *make stable* 674.7

engraved 144.9; *furrowed* 638.3, *stabilized* 674.4

engraver 144.5; *record keeper* 185.8

engrave wood *work wood* 131.9

engraving 144.3; *craft* 133.2, *picture* 133.5, *relief carving* 144.2, Hobbies and Pastimes 167, *recordkeeping* 185.7, *illustration* 187.2, *outline* 617.1

engross *possess* 469.14, *buy in*

481.13, *immerse* 598.24, *absorb* 708.19

engrossed *diligent* 323.7, *in deep* 598.18

engrossment *monopoly* 469.4, *immersion* 598.8, *absorption* 708.6

engulf *eat* 92.21, *be excessive* 99.9, *consume* 523.16, *deepen* 598.21, *immerse* 598.24, *ingest* 708.17

engulfed *flooded* 557.24, 570.8, *under* 598.13, *in deep* 598.18

engulfing *intake* 708.5

engulfment *flow* 570.4, *immersion* 598.8, *intake* 708.5

enhance *exaggerate* 194.11, *emphasize* 200.6, *make taste* 219.6, *aggravate* 276.5, *make rich* 485.15, *beautify* 530.14, *decorate* 532.11, *ornament* 532.12, *upturn* 713.20, *promote* 715.13, *intensify* 746.8, *make important* 799.14, *improve* 807.15, 825.26, *reveal* 843.14

enhanced *exaggerated* 194.7, *emphasized* 200.4, *aggravated* 276.3, *decorated* 532.9, *advanced* 713.16, *increased* 746.5, *improved* 807.12

enhanced radiation bomb *bomb* 78.15

enhancement *exaggeration* 194.4, *aggravation* 276.1, *decoration* 532.1, *ascendancy* 713.5, *intensification* 746.2, *improvement* 807.1

enharmonic *harmonizing* 735.12

enharmonically *in harmony* 735.32

enharmonic scale *scale* 140.16

enigma *the occult* 86.2, *mystery* 182.4, *obscurity* 197.1, *wonderful person* 294.6, *difficult question* 333.4, *unknown thing* 349.3, *unintelligible thing* 364.3, *equivocation* 380.1, *uncertainty* 841.1, *mysteriousness* 844.5

enigmatic *occult* 86.16, *proverbial* 177.2, *mysterious* 182.10, *obscure* 197.2, *inscrutable* 250.5, *astonishing* 294.10, *problematic* 333.12, *unintelligible* 364.4, *difficult* 364.8, *confused* 841.11

enigmatically *occultly* 86.27, *obscurely* 197.4, *astonishingly* 294.19, *questionably* 333.22, *unintelligibly* 364.16, *confusingly* 841.23

Eniwetok Islands 572

enjoin *impose a duty* 433.14

enjoy 269.9, 290.9; *feel pleasure* 214.12, *taste* 219.5, *take pleasure in* 271.11, *like* 299.22, *have at one's disposal* 393.14, *possess* 469.14

enjoyable *pleasant* 214.7, 271.5

enjoyably *pleasingly* 214.15

enjoy company *be sociable* 408.14

enjoyer *user* 393.4

enjoy friendship with *befriend* 62.10

enjoy good fortune *be in comfortable circumstances* 726.13

enjoy good health *be healthy* 113.11

enjoying *possessing* 469.11

enjoying liberty *independent* 829.12

enjoy liberty *be free* 829.16

enjoy life *be full of vigor* 518.4

enjoyment *pleasure* 214.2, 271.2, *gaiety* 269.3, *fun* 269.4, *satisfaction* 273.1, *amusement* 277.2, *likes* 290.3, *proudness* 297.3, *use* 393.1, *sociability* 408.1, *possession* 469.1

enjoy music 141.19

enjoy oneself *feel pleasure* 214.12

enjoy peace *be at peace* 73.10, *pacify* 74.9

enjoy prosperity *be prosperous* 847.6

enjoy sex *feel pleasure* 214.12

enjoy success *be successful* 845.11

enlace *interweave* 609.8, *convolute* 632.6

enlarge 194.12, 581.14; *develop* 132.28, *represent* 187.10, *size* 579.17, *broaden* 592.11, *make bigger* 746.7, *make important* 799.14

enlargeability 581.6

enlargeable 581.13

enlarged 194.8; *aggravated* 276.3, *bigger* 581.9, *broadened* 592.7, *increased* 746.5

enlarged heart *cardiovascular disease* 114.13

enlargement 194.2, 581.7; *printing* 132.20, *diffuseness* 199.1, *expansion* 581.1, 592.2, *increase* 746.1, *addition* 748.1

enlarger 581.8; *darkroom equipment* 132.21

enlarge upon *be diffuse* 199.5

enlarging *printing* 132.20

enlighten *educate* 48.22, *inform* 170.11, *clarify* 196.3, *moralize* 431.14

enlightened *educated* 48.19, *holy* 82.19, *informed* 170.9, *knowledgeable* 348.7

enlightening *educational* 48.17, *informative* 170.10

enlightenment *education* 48.1, *divine attribute* 82.4, *finding out* 345.3, *knowledge* 348.1, *wisdom* 352.1, *interpretation* 365.1, *social improvement* 807.3

enlist 58.13; *join the army* 76.31, *publicize* 178.19, *register* 185.15, *influence* 508.11, *enroll* 706.16, *introduce* 708.16, *install* 710.15, *make bigger* 746.7, *be on a list* 785.12, *engage* 833.9

enlisted 58.11; *martial* 77.33

enlisted man *soldier* 77.4, *air force person* 77.31

enlisted person *army person* 77.17, *naval person* 77.25

Enlisted Personnel US Military Ranks 58

enlisting *war measures* 76.18

enlist in one's service *resort to* 393.13

enlistment *recordkeeping* 185.7, *entry* 706.1, *bringing in* 708.4, *engagement* 833.2

enliven *invigorate* 28.22, 518.5, *refresh* 94.6, *arouse sensation* 212.11, *bring cheer* 269.12, *inspire* 327.15, *strengthen* 516.15, *revive* 809.14

enlivened *alive* 28.13, *refreshed* 94.5

en masse *together* 59.31, *one and all* 759.12, *in crowds* 795.14

enmist *fog* 9.59

enmity *hostility* 63.1, *antipathy* 291.2, *hate* 300.1, *malice* 306.2, *divisiveness* 463.2, *conflict* 828.3

ennead *nine* 792.5

enneadic *ninth* 792.16

enneagon *nine* 792.5

enneagonal *ninth* 792.16

enneahedral *ninth* 792.16

enneahedron *nine* 792.5

ennoble *make noble* 70.5, *refine* 534.7, *exalt* 596.19

ennobled *aristocratic* 70.4, *cultured* 534.6

ennui *boredom* 296.1

enormity *wickedness* 448.1, *illegality* 450.4

enormous *spacious* 563.13, *huge* 579.14, *immeasurable* 798.6

enormously *hugely* 579.21, *wholly* 738.9

enormousness *largeness* 579.2

enough 97.10; *sufficiency* 97.1, *sufficient* 97.3, *satisfactory* 273.6, *satisfactorily* 273.12, *quantitative* 738.6

enough! *I/we surrender!* 421.9, *cease!* 668.14

enough and to spare *plentiful* 97.4, *excessively* 99.13

enough noise to wake the dead *tumult* 232.5

enough rope to hang oneself *liberality* 829.8

enough to get by *sufficiency* 97.1

enough to go around *sufficient* 97.3

enough to keep body and soul together *sufficiency* 97.1

enough to live on *sufficiency* 97.1

enough to wake the dead *loudly* 232.11

en passant [Fr] *in transit* 685.13, *by the way* 692.20

enplane *set out* 705.12

enplanement *start* 705.2

en plein air [Fr] *out-of-doors* 558.26

enprint *printing* 132.20

enquire *philosophize* 4.19, *be curious* 321.7, *question* 333.16, *experiment* 335.11

enquire after *be curious* 321.7

enquirer *curious person* 321.3, *experimenter* 335.5

enquiring mind *curiosity* 333.8

enquiry *philosophical investigation* 4.4, *curiosity* 321.1, *questioning* 333.2, *experiment* 335.1

enrage *displease* 272.8, *cause dislike* 291.16, *cause hate* 300.12, *make angry* 302.18, *make violent* 520.10

enraged *angry* 302.11, *violent* 520.5

enraging *maddening* 302.12

en rapport *agreeing* 462.6, *compatible* 735.14, *compatibly* 735.34, *associating* 827.11

enrapture *cause joy* 269.11, *win the love of* 299.27

enraptured *enamored* 299.17

enrich *fertilize* 22.12, *give* 472.10, *make rich* 485.15, *ornament* 532.12, *upturn* 713.20, *intensify* 746.8, *improve* 807.15

enriched *decorated* 532.9, *advanced* 713.16

enriched uranium *nuclear power* 106.8

enricher *fertilizer* 22.6

enriching 22.11

enrichment 22.5; *decoration* 532.1, *ascendancy* 713.5, *intensification* 746.2, *improvement* 807.1

enrich oneself *get rich* 485.13

enrobe *clothe* 100.43

enroll 706.16, 771.33; *join the army* 76.31, *record* 185.13, *register* 185.15, *introduce* 708.16, *install* 710.15, *be on a list* 785.12, *engage* 833.9

enrolled 771.24; *recorded* 185.12

enrollment 771.8; *recordkeeping* 185.7, *entry* 706.1, *bringing in* 708.4, *listing* 785.8, *engagement* 833.2

en route *convertibly* 670.15, *in*

motion 677.19, in transit 685.13, by the way 692.20
en route to or **for** forward 679.15, via 691.17
ens thing 717.3
ensanguined murderous 30.18, bloody 257.8
ensconce conceal 181.12, locate 565.9, assure 810.23
ensconced located 565.6
ensconce oneself settle 565.10
ensemble family 65.1, suit 100.16, cast 136.26, instrumental group 141.3, whole thing 759.2, unit 759.5
ensepulcher bury 31.10
ensheathe inset 710.13
enshrine deify 82.23, promote 715.13
enshrined deified 82.20, promoted 715.8
enshrinement deification 82.13, promotion 715.3
enshroud fog 9.59, wrap 613.29
enshrouded foggy 9.51, protected 613.20
ensiform sharp-edged 549.12
Ensign US Military Ranks 58, military title 72.8
ensign sailboat parts and accessories 150.4, flag 184.8
ensilage animal feed 16.12, storage 105.6
enslave suppress 424.9, take away forcefully 477.19
enslaved detained 830.11, captive 832.9
enslavement subjection 832.1
enslaving captive 832.9
ensnare ambush 292.11, detect 345.12, hunt 385.14, take away forcefully 477.19, manipulate 508.12, lure 700.12, trap 813.6
ensnared surprised 292.5
ensue result 770.12
ensuing caused 676.5, consequent 770.9
ensure verify 336.8, be prepared 388.17, promise 464.10, make stable 674.7, follow from 676.9, make certain 840.14
ensure a result predetermine 384.8
ensured guaranteed 840.10
entablature Architectural Elements 134
entail intend 361.15, legal property terms 470.2
entameba parasite 39.18
entangle puzzle 364.12, interweave 609.8, mix up 751.13, connect 754.13, intercommunicate 754.15
entangled complicated 751.10, connected 754.11
entanglement love affair 299.9, interweaving 609.1, mixture 751.1, variety 751.4, connection 754.1
entanglements barrier 419.10
entangle one's line fish 154.14
entelechial real 719.6
entelechy reality 719.1, quintessence 723.3
entente friendly relations 62.3, pacification 74.1, alliance 459.5, 735.5, contract 462.2, settlement 735.6
entente cordiale friendly relations 62.3, alliance 459.5, contract 462.2, settlement 735.6, agreement 752.4
enter 692.18, 706.11; act 136.34, participate 145.6, register 185.15, become visible 264.13, contend 422.22, account 493.9, go inside 611.15, find one's way 691.15,

arrive 704.13, get in 704.17, inject 710.10, subsume 763.7, list 785.11
enter a different phase be converted 670.12
enter a new phase be converted 670.12
enter as subsume 763.7
entered recorded 185.12, included 763.4, listed 785.9
enter for contend 422.22, enroll 706.16
enteric visceral 611.10
enter in a book inscribe 185.14
entering 706.9; appearing 264.9, penetrating 692.12, arriving 704.9
enter into enter 692.18, be included 763.6
enter into a contract contract 459.8
enter into an agreement promise 458.11
enter into an alliance contract 459.8
enter into argument debate 319.13
enter into detail circumstantiate 726.12
enter into the spirit of feel for 266.17
enteritis gastroenterological disease 114.11
enter names register 185.15
enterogastrone Human Hormones 12
enteron internals 611.3
enter one's head have an idea 327.13
enter orbit launch 7.35
enterprise imagination 360.1, future intention 374.3, undertaking 391.1, 675.5, social activity 414.2, energy 414.4, business 480.6, association 480.8, production 522.1, advance 679.3
enterpriser planner 387.9
enterprising 391.5; original 335.9, imaginative 360.10, attempting 390.4, active 414.13, vigorous 518.2, forward 679.6
enterprising businessman or **businesswoman** person who undertakes 391.3
enterprisingly 391.11
entertain 138.16; provision 89.9, give pleasure 214.13, be humorous 277.11, be sociable 408.14, give 472.10, receive someone 473.14
entertained popular 408.12, received 473.14
entertainer 138.8
entertaining recreational 167.10, cheering 269.8, humorous 277.9, festive 408.13, reception 473.4
entertainingly 138.17; recreationally 167.15, sociably 408.19
entertainment 277.4; eating meals 92.4, show business 138.1, game 167.1, amusement 167.7, 277.2, fun 269.4, pleasure 271.2, social gathering 408.4, party 408.6
entertainment center cabinet 101.8, 578.3
entertainment industry show business 138.1
enter the church be religious 81.25
enter the lion's den be in danger 811.11
enter the lists contend 422.22
enter the ring box 152.19
enthalpy thermodynamics 10.30

enthrall cause joy 269.11, win the love of 299.27, lure 700.12
enthralled enamored 299.17
enthralling delightful 271.7
enthrone launch 405.14, commission 833.8
enthronement ceremony 405.3, commission 833.1
enthuse be full of vigor 518.4
enthusiasm religiousness 81.2, emphasis 200.1, eagerness 373.2, energy 414.4, vigor 518.1
enthusiast collector 59.17, visionary 360.9, busy person 414.10
enthusiastic emphatic 200.3, desirous 288.13, imaginative 360.10, eager 373.8, active 414.13, strong in spirit 516.11, vigorous 518.2
enthusiastically emphatically 200.7, eagerly 373.16, actively 414.24, acutely 516.18
entice 178.16; manipulate 508.12, lure 700.12
enticed motivated 508.8
enticement 178.3; reward for service 453.5, inducement 508.2, allurement 700.1
enticing 178.13; attractive 700.10
enticingly 178.22
entire of leaves 41.18, quantitative 738.6, uncut 759.7, complete 761.6, 805.14, whole 788.12
entire horse male animal 32.15
entirely clean [Inf] 111.21, wholly 738.9, 759.11, completely 759.14, 761.13, 805.22
entirety total 738.4, whole thing 759.2, completeness 761.1
entitle title 209.12, permit 735.29
entitled honored 72.11, qualified 340.7, authorized 340.8, rightful 429.9, permitting 735.19
entitledness claim 429.3
entitlement title 72.1, qualification 340.1, claim 429.3, guarantee 458.3, permission 735.9
entity living organism 13.10, living being 28.3, thing 717.3, whole thing 759.2, one 788.1
entomb bury 31.10, contain 578.20, enclose 584.16, 619.6
entombed buried 31.8, storing 578.19
entombment burial 31.1
entomological 40.15; arthropodal 39.22
entomologist 40.3; animal scientist 34.7, invertebrate zoologist 39.3
entomology animal science 34.6, invertebrate zoology 39.2, study of insects 40.2
entomophobia Phobias 283
entoproct coelenterate 39.15
Entoprocta coelenterate 39.15
entourage attendance 794.5
entr'acte play part 136.8
entrails internal organ 19.13, means of prediction 358.10, insides 577.3, internals 611.3
entrain set out 705.12
entrainment start 705.2
entrance 706.5; acting 136.22, birth 264.2, be wondrous 294.14, opening 583.1, access 691.3, passage into 692.4, arrival 704.1, entry 706.1, receptivity 708.2
entranced bewitched 86.21, wondering 294.7
entrance fee fee 494.3
entrance hall room 60.9, front entrance 621.2
entrancing witchlike 86.19, delightful 271.7

entrant 706.7; candidate 422.18
entrap arrest 55.12, ambush 292.11, manipulate 508.12, trap 813.6
entrapment arrest 55.5, ambush 292.4
entrapped imprisoned 55.9
entreat persuade 178.15, appeal to 209.9, plead 329.14, question 333.16, request 505.10
entreating requesting 505.7
entreatingly by request 505.14
entreaty exhortation 178.2, plea 329.5, question 333.1, request 505.1
entrée dish 90.7, course 92.12, entry 706.1, receptivity 708.2
entremets dish 90.7, course 92.12
Entre Minho e Douro Breeds of Sheep 16
entrench 419.24; strengthen 516.15, make stable 674.7, transgress 712.14, protect 810.21
entrenched defended 419.18, permanent 667.2, unfailing 667.3, stabilized 674.4
entrenchment military defenses 419.9, permanence 667.1
entre nous secretly 182.14
entrepôt storehouse 105.8, marketplace 483.7
entrepreneur attempter 390.3, person who undertakes 391.3, operator 412.7, contractor 459.6, producer 522.10, person who joins 752.9
entropy frequency 10.6, thermodynamics 10.30, mixture 751.1
entrust delegate 79.6, impose a duty 433.14, give out 472.12, bring 685.11, commission 833.8
entrusted duty-bound 433.8
entrusting commission 833.1
entrustment commission 833.1
entry 706.1; horse racing 159.10, competitive diving 164.7, record 185.1, recordkeeping 185.7, accounts 493.4, opening 583.1, passage into 692.4, entrance 706.5, receptivity 708.2, injection 710.2
entryway room 60.9
ENT specialist ear doctor 228.5
entwine interweave 609.8, curve 629.6, convolute 632.6, enfold 637.9, intertwine 752.19, connect 754.13
entwined convolutional 632.4
entwining enfoldment 637.3
enucleate [Arch] decipher 365.13
enumerable numerable 6.70
enumerate 6.85; itemize 777.13, specify 779.18, number 783.9, 784.13, list 785.11
enumerated listed 785.9
enumerate with subsume 763.7
enumeration numeration 6.10, accounting 493.1, calculation 784.1, list 785.1, listing 785.8
enumerative calculative 784.7
enumerator counter 784.6
enunciate affirm 189.21, speak 205.17
enunciated affirmed 189.11, spoken 205.13
enunciation affirmation 189.1, articulation 205.9
enunciative or **enunciatory** affirmative 189.10
enunciatively affirmatively 189.29
enunciator affirmer 189.9
enuresis urination 25.4
enuretic urinary 25.15
envelop clothe 100.43, detain

471.9, consume 523.16, contain 578.20, be exterior 610.13, wrap 613.29, 619.7, surround 615.7, enfold 637.9, include 763.5, protect 810.21

envelope correspondence 169.2, packet 578.4, immerse 598.24, exteriority 610.2, wrapping 613.10, enclosing thing 619.3

enveloped containing 578.18, in deep 598.18, surrounded 615.5, wrapped 619.5

enveloping containing 578.18

envelopment fencing movements 153.3, detention 471.2, immersion 598.8, covering 613.1, encirclement 615.2, enclosure 619.1, enfoldment 637.3

envenom cause hate 300.12, make angry 302.18, make irritable 304.15, make worse 808.17

envenomed toxic 114.28, poisonous 117.14, bitter 306.9

envied desired 288.10, hated 300.9

envier desirer 288.9

envious 314.4; hostile 63.6, green-eyed 260.11, passionate 266.12, covetous 288.14, hating 300.7, resentful 302.8, selfish 444.4, impious 448.11

enviously 314.11; hostilely 63.13, covetously 288.28, with hate 300.13, resentfully 302.22, selfishly 444.8

enviousness envy 314.1

environ extend 563.14, surround 615.7

environment habitat 60.1, location 565.1, surroundings 615.1, circumstances 726.1

environmental 60.17, 260.13; sociological 2.11, chemical 14.46, surrounding 615.4, circumstantial 726.8, preserving 815.6

environmental abuse misuse 395.1

environmental engineer chemical engineer 14.25

environmental engineering chemical engineering 14.24

environmentalism green politics 260.6, preservation 815.1

environmentally 60.26; sociologically 2.15, electrochemically 14.53, relatively 726.17, preservatively 815.16

environmental movement ecology 815.3

environment art Western Art Styles 133

environment-friendly preserving 815.11

environments matrix management system 126.3

environs habitat 60.1, regions 564.2, location 565.1, near place 586.3, surroundings 615.1

envisage imagine 327.14, 360.14, expect 356.6, foresee 357.9, plan ahead 387.13

envision imagine 327.14, 360.14, foresee 357.9, aim 374.10

envoi appendage 748.4, ending 773.10

envoy delegate 79.1, agent 80.3, representative 187.7, appendage 748.4, ending 773.10, council 833.4, commissioner 833.5

envoy or **envoi** part of poem 139.9

envy 314.1, 314.7; personal conflict 63.2, bad feeling 266.5, covet 288.18, hate 300.1, 300.11, resentment 302.1, selfishness 444.1, be selfish 444.6, iniquity 448.3

envying envious 314.4

enwrap wrap 613.29

enzootic contagious 114.26

enzymatically biochemically 12.27

enzyme 12.11; catalysis 11.16, leavening 539.3, changer 665.9

enzyme class enzyme 12.11

enzymic biochemical 12.25, leavening 539.7

enzymologist biochemist 12.2

enzymology biochemistry 12.1, 13.3

Eocene Epoch Geologic Time Intervals 8

eolian deposit sediment 8.29

eolith thing of the past 651.8

eon geological time 8.47, time period 641.2, geological period 641.3, long duration 642.3

eonian agelong 644.5

eonism sexual nature 20.4

eonothem geological time 8.47

Eos Deities 82, morning 655.2

eosinophil blood 555.4

eosophobia Phobias 283

Eostre Deities 82

EP (extended-play record) recording 185.6

Epaminondas Notable Friendships 62

epanaphora repetition 797.1

eparchy administrative region 564.4

epaulet or **epaulette** insignia 184.5

épée sharp weapon 78.6, fencing equipment 153.2, fencing 153.6

épée-fence fence 153.7

épée fencing fencing 153.1

épéeist fencer 153.5

épée prongs fencing equipment 153.2

epeirogenic tectonic 8.56

epeirogeny earth movement 8.20

epergne ornament 532.7

epexegesis interpretation 365.1

ephemera compendium 204.3

ephemeral plant 41.2, of plants 41.14, flowering plant 42.2, transient 643.4, changeable 666.3

ephemerality transience 643.1

ephemerally herbaceously 41.24, transiently 643.8, changeably 666.7

ephemeris star catalog 7.9, type of book 174.3, navigational aid 690.6

ephemeropteran insectile 40.11

ephod vestment 84.11

epic masterpiece 68.14, dramatic 137.16, poetic 139.19, narrative 202.12, huge 579.14

epicalyx flower part 42.3

epicarp fruit structure 44.3

epicene of sexual nature 20.17

epicenter seismic activity 8.24, center of activity 612.4

epicentral central 612.6

epic film movie type 137.3

epic length diffuseness 199.1

epic novel novel 139.3

epic poem Poem or Verse Forms 139

epic poet author 139.13

epic poetry poetry 139.8

epic simile literary device 139.12

epic theater theater movements 136.9

epicure eater 92.15, pleasure-seeker 214.4, discriminator 337.6, self-indulgent person 456.5, refined person 534.4

Epicurean Philosophical Schools of Thought 4

epicurean culinary 91.9, pleasure-seeker 214.4, tasty 219.4,

discriminating 337.9, self-indulgent 456.6

Epicureanism Philosophical Schools of Thought 4

epicureanism delicate eating 92.3, pleasure 214.2, self-indulgence 456.1

epic work masterpiece 127.5

epicycle circle 631.2

epicycloid curve 6.38

epidemic plague 114.6, contagious 114.26, universal 778.10

epidemic disease disease 114.4

epidemiological medical 107.28

epidemiologist medical specialist 107.20

epidemiology medical science 107.5

epidermal skin 19.19, superficial 599.4, covering 610.8, 613.21

epidermic covering 610.8

epidermis body covering 19.4, stem 41.5, exteriority 610.2, animal covering 613.15

epigeal of fungi 47.19

epiglottis throat 19.12, speech organ 205.4

epigram Poem or Verse Forms 139, maxim 177.1, pithy saying 198.3, moral 431.5

epigrammatic proverbial 177.2, concise 198.4, summary 204.5

epigrammatical summary 204.5

epigrammatically proverbially 177.4, summarily 204.10

epigrammatize aphorize 177.3, be concise 198.5, summarize 204.7

epigraph book part 174.5, maxim 177.1

epigrapher paleoanthropologist 1.4, historian 3.3

epigraphic paleoanthropological 1.11

epigraphical paleoanthropological 1.11

epigraphically paleoanthropologically 1.16, historically 3.17, linguistically 5.44

epigraphist paleoanthropologist 1.4, interpreter 365.6

epigraphy history 3.1, inscription 185.4, science of interpretation 365.5

epigynous of flowers 42.11

epilepsy neurological disease 114.20, spasm 684.8

epileptic of disease 114.25, convulsive 684.19

epilithic algal 47.20

epilogue play part 136.8, back matter 622.3, appendage 748.4, conclusion 771.3, ending 773.10

epimenorrhea bleeding 25.10

epimer structure 11.7

epimeric structural 11.28

epimerism structure 11.7

Epimetheus Planets and Their Satellites 7

epinephrine hormone 12.16

epiphanic Christlike 82.18, revelatory 180.7, appearing 264.9

Epiphany Christian Holy Days and Seasons 85

epiphany divine manifestation 82.5, disclosure 180.1, spectacle 264.6, materialization 524.2, manifestation 843.2

epiphenomenalism Philosophical Schools of Thought 4

epiphenomenalist Philosophical Schools of Thought 4

epiphora repetition 797.1

epiphyllum Flowers 42

epiphyte plant 41.2

epiphytic of plants 41.14, algal 47.20

epiphytically herbaceously 41.24, algologically 47.25

episcopal priestly 84.12

Episcopalian Christian 81.10, denominational 81.23

Episcopalianism Christian Groups 81

episcopal ring vestment 84.11

episcopal vestment vestment 84.11

episcopate priesthood 84.2

episode play part 136.8, aspect of fiction 139.5, occurrence 726.2, part of writing 760.6

episodic discontinuous 775.7

epistaxiophobia Phobias 283

epistemologically philosophically 4.23

epistemology Branches of Philosophy 4

Epistle Eucharist 85.7

epistle correspondence 169.2

Epistles Christian text 81.16

Epistle side laterality 623.3

epistolary communicational 169.17

epistolary novel novel 139.3

epistrophe literary device 139.12, repetition 797.1

epistyle Architectural Elements 134

epitaph funeral object 31.6, inscription 185.4, parting 705.3

epitaphic phrased 5.39, funeral 31.9

epitaphist funeral person 31.5

epithalamion general wedding terms 64.6, Poem or Verse Forms 139

epitheca plant body 47.13

epithelioma cancer 114.15

epithelium body covering 19.4

epithet maxim 177.1, name 202.8

epitome representation 187.1, pithy saying 198.3, summary 204.1, ideal 327.6, translation 365.4, contracted thing 582.5, shortened version 591.3, outline 617.1, quintessence 723.3

epitomical concise 198.4, ideal 327.12

epitomization shortening 591.2

epitomize 327.18; represent 187.10, be concise 198.5, summarize 204.7, shorten 591.9, outline 617.5, embody 723.12

epitomized shortened 591.7

epizootic contagious 114.26

e pluribus unum [L] in alliance 735.35

epoch geological time 8.47, Scientific and Technical Units 589, time period 641.2, geological period 641.3, day 646.4

epoch-making newsworthy 799.12

epode Poem or Verse Forms 139, part of poem 139.9

epos poetry 139.8

eponym name 202.8

eponymy nomenclature 202.7

epoxide resin polymer 11.9

epoxied adhering 755.7

epoxy plastics 104.6, adhesive 755.3

epoxy resin adhesive 755.3

Epsom Derby [Brit] famous horse races 159.13

Epsom salt or **salts** purgative 115.7

equable detached 4.18, moderate 521.3, equal 740.8

equably stoically 4.26, moderately 521.10

equal 740.7, 740.8; *ranked* 6.72, *equate* 6.88, *sufficient* 97.3, *right* 429.7, *compatible* 462.8, *be compatible* 462.12, *correspondence* 606.2, *corresponding* 606.6, *correspond* 606.8, *symmetrical* 626.4, *stable* 674.3, *interrelated* 727.7, *equivalence* 730.3, *counterpart* 733.5, *similar* 733.7, *be similar* 733.12, *total* 783.10, 784.12

equal chance 842.7

equal contest *contest* 422.4

equaled *matched* 733.10

equal exchange *reciprocity* 729.1, *equivalence* 730.3

equal footing *equality* 740.1

equality 6.24, 740.1; *rightfulness* 429.1, *compatibility* 462.3, *correspondence* 606.2, *symmetry* 626.1, *stability* 674.1, *interrelatedness* 727.3, *similarity* 733.1

equalization 740.4; *sound quality* 230.4, *counterbalance* 743.2

equalization fund *finance* 457.1

equalize 740.12; *equate* 6.88, *symmetrize* 626.6, *make stable* 674.7, *correspond to* 727.10, *make the same* 730.16, *make similar* 733.15, *counterbalance* 743.8, *stand in the middle* 772.17, *cancel out* 834.8

equalized *equal* 740.8, *counterbalanced* 743.6, *canceled* 834.5

equalizer 740.5

equalizer [Inf] *firearm* 78.7

equalizing *equalization* 740.4, *counterbalanced* 743.6, *canceling out* 834.3

equally 626.8, 740.13; *mathematically* 6.93, *right* 429.15, *compatibly* 462.16, *correspondingly* 606.10, *stably* 674.9, *under the circumstances* 726.16, *relevantly* 727.12, *similarly* 733.17, *midway* 772.22, *free* 831.9

equally divided *on equal terms* 740.9

equal opportunity 831.2; *equality* 740.1

equal rights *rights* 429.4, *equality* 740.1, *free rights* 829.4, *equal opportunity* 831.2

Equal Rights Amendment (ERA) *equal opportunity* 831.2

equal or equals sign *mathematical symbol* 6.11, *symbol* 183.3

equal status *equal opportunity* 831.2

equal swap *compromise* 461.1

equal to 740.10; *sufficient* 97.3

equal value *equalization* 740.4

equal weight *canceling out* 834.3

equanimity *philosophical attitude* 4.3, *satisfaction* 273.1, *impartiality* 338.2, *moderation* 521.1, *assurance* 621.8

equanimous *detached* 4.18, *impartial* 338.6

equanimously *impartially* 338.13

equate 6.88; *solve* 334.21, *correspond to* 727.10, *make the same* 730.16, *equalize* 740.12

equating *equalization* 740.4

equation 6.25; *theory* 6.62, *physical law* 10.4, *equality* 740.1, *equalization* 740.4, *calculation* 784.1

equational division *cell division* 13.17

equation of state *physical law* 10.4, *thermodynamics* 10.30

equator *cell division* 13.17, *hot place* 217.5, *circular thing* 631.3, *dividing line* 740.6, *midline* 772.2, *half* 789.7

equatorial *warm* 217.13, *midway* 772.10

Equatorial Guinea Countries 566

equatorial low *wind system* 9.15

equatorial rainy zone *climate zone* 9.36

equestrian *horse person* 159.14, *equine* 159.15

equestrian director *circus performer* 138.9

equestrianism 159.8

equestrian painter *painter* 143.7

equestrian painting *type of painting* 143.5

equestrienne *horse person* 159.14

equidistance *parallelism* 606.1, *middle ground* 772.4

equidistant *linear* 6.77, *parallel* 606.5, *central* 612.6, *equal* 740.8, *midway* 772.10

equidistantly *in parallel* 606.9, *centrally* 612.12, *equitably* 740.15

equilateral *linear* 6.77, *symmetrical* 626.4, *equal* 740.8

equilaterally *symmetrically* 626.7

equilateral triangle *triangle* 6.41, *angled figure* 628.3

equilibrant *counterbalance* 743.2

equilibrate *symmetrize* 626.6, *make the same* 730.16, *be in accord* 735.21, *counterbalance* 743.8

equilibrated *reactive* 11.29, *counterbalanced* 743.6

equilibrating *counterbalanced* 743.6

equilibration *equalization* 740.4, *counterbalance* 743.2

equilibratory *harmonious* 735.11

equilibrist *circus performer* 138.9

equilibrium 740.2; *force* 10.9, *chemical reaction* 11.8, *symmetry* 626.1, *lack of motion* 678.1, *accord* 735.1

equilibrium constant *chemical reaction* 11.8

equine 159.15; *ungulate* 35.31, *horse* 159.1

equine distemper *animal disease* 34.10

equinoctial *oceanic* 571.7, *seasonal* 654.7

equinoctially *seasonally* 654.12

equinoctial tide *tide* 571.2

equip 388.19; *educate* 48.22, *provision* 89.9, *find means* 102.6, *procure* 104.9, *permit* 340.12

equipment 103.6; *provision* 89.1, *supplies* 102.3, *apparatus* 103.2, *materials* 104.1, *qualification* 340.1, *permission* 340.3, *fitting out* 388.3, *instrument* 511.2

equipment rack *climbing equipment* 161.4

equipoise *symmetry* 626.1, *lack of motion* 678.1, *equilibrium* 740.2

equipollence *equivalence* 730.3, *equalization* 740.4

equipollency *equalization* 740.4

equipollent *equal* 740.8

equiponderance *equilibrium* 740.2

equiponderant *counterbalanced* 743.6

equiponderate *make the same* 730.16

equipped 388.10; *supplied* 89.7, *qualified* 340.7

equipper *preparer* 388.6

equipping *provisioning* 89.2, 89.6

equisetum *fern* 46.1

equitable *right* 429.7, *in the right* 429.11, *moral* 431.9, *disinterested* 443.4, *equal* 740.8

equitable jurisdiction *jurisdiction* 54.2

equitableness *rightfulness* 429.1, *disinterestedness* 443.1

equitably 740.15; *right* 429.15, *morally* 431.15, *disinterestedly* 443.8

equitation *equestrianism* 159.8, *motion* 677.1

equity *legal justice* 53.4, *rightfulness* 429.1, *claim* 429.3, *morals* 431.2, *equality* 740.1

equity court *law court* 54.8

equivalence 730.3; *philosophical term* 4.7, *equality* 6.24, 740.1, *mathematical logic* 6.60, *correspondence* 334.8, 606.2, *type of meaning* 361.4, *substitution* 672.1, *correlation* 729.3, *comparability* 733.2

equivalence point *gravimetric analysis* 11.18

equivalence relation *mathematical logic* 6.60

equivalency *equality* 740.1

equivalent 730.9; *logical* 6.83, *analytic* 11.32, *correspondent* 334.16, *similar* 361.7, 733.7, *translational* 365.11, *correspondence* 606.2, *corresponding* 606.6, *substitution* 672.1, *substitute* 672.3, *exchange* 673.1, *in exchange* 673.3, *correlative* 729.6, *equivalence* 730.3, *similarity* 733.1, *counterpart* 733.5, *comparable* 733.8, *equal* 740.7, 740.8

equivalent circuit *circuit* 14.37

equivalently 730.20; *correspondingly* 334.27, 606.10, *instead* 672.8, *in exchange* 673.6, *correlatively* 729.12, *similarly* 733.17, *equally* 740.13

equivalent meaning *type of meaning* 361.4

equivalent triangles *triangle* 6.41

equivocal 380.5; *worded* 5.38, *uncandid* 192.15, *obscure* 197.2, *sophistic* 330.7, *quibbling* 330.9, *questionable* 333.13, *unclear* 364.5, *difficult* 364.8, *vacillating* 378.5, *avoiding* 386.9, *indirect* 607.8, *ambiguous* 632.5, *cunning* 822.4, *indeterminate* 841.14

equivocally 380.9; *lexically* 5.46, *uncandidly* 192.29, *obscurely* 197.4, *sophistically* 330.14, *questionably* 333.22, *irresolutely* 378.13, *evasively* 386.24, *indirectly* 607.15, *circularly* 632.8, *indeterminately* 841.24

equivocalness *wordiness* 5.23, *obscurity* 197.1, *circumlocution* 199.2, *equivocation* 380.1, *indeterminacy* 841.6

equivocate 380.8; *evade* 181.17, *lack candor* 192.22, *quibble* 330.13, *vacillate* 378.8, *be equivocal* 380.7, *be evasive* 386.20, *circumlocute* 607.12, *be ambiguous* 632.7, *stand in the middle* 772.17, *hesitate* 841.18

equivocating 380.6; *quibbling* 330.9, *equivocal* 380.5

equivocation 380.1; *wordiness* 5.23, *evasion* 181.5, *lack of candor* 192.4, *obscurity* 197.1, *circumlocution* 199.2, *sophistry* 330.1, *quibbling* 330.4, *unintelligibility* 364.1, *lack of clarity* 364.2, *vacillation* 378.1,

683.3, *evasiveness* 386.6, *indirectness* 607.3, *irresolution* 666.2

equivocator 380.4; *liar* 192.10, *sophist* 330.6

equivoque *or* **equivoke** *lack of candor* 192.4, *equivocation* 380.1

Equuleus Constellations 7

era *geological time* 8.47, *time period* 641.2, *geological period* 641.3, *day* 646.4

eradicable *extractive* 711.10, *subtractive* 749.4

eradicably *decreasingly* 749.9

eradicate *destroy* 186.10, 523.10, *take away* 477.18, *remove* 574.16, *exterminate* 709.22, *extract* 711.13, *cause not to exist* 718.14, *subtract* 749.6, *eject* 764.8, *not exist* 786.6

eradicated *destroyed* 186.5, *removed* 574.9, *subtracted* 749.3

eradication *destruction* 186.2, *taking away* 477.5, *destroying* 523.2, *removal* 574.2, *extraction* 711.1, *subtraction* 749.1, *ejection* 764.2

eradicative *extractive* 711.10

eradicator *destroyer* 523.6

Era of Good Feeling Ages, Decades, Eras 641

erasable *computerized* 15.28

erasable programmable read-only memory (EPROM) *memory* 15.6

erase 186.9; *program* 15.29, *clean* 111.17, *cause to disappear* 265.7, *take away* 477.18, *abolish* 523.11, *erode* 554.14, *exterminate* 709.22, *subtract* 749.6, *cancel* 834.6

erased Heraldic Terms 184, *obliterated* 186.4, *subtracted* 749.3

erased from the record *forgiven* 312.5

erase from one's memory *forget* 355.10

erase from the record *absolve* 312.10

eraser 554.7; *cleaning tool* 111.10, *destroyer* 523.6

erasing *obliteration* 186.1

erasure *obliteration* 186.1, *blacking out* 265.2, *taking away* 477.5, *destruction* 523.1, *wearing away* 554.2, *subtraction* 749.1

erathem *geological time* 8.47

Erato Deities 82

Eratosthenes, sieve of Mathematical Concepts 6

erbium Chemical Elements and Common Allotropes 11

ere *before* 769.11

Erebus *evil place* 446.6

Erebus, Mount Mountains and Hills 569

erect 715.11; *engineer* 14.48, *of plants* 41.14, *put together* 59.30, *be an architect* 134.13, *arrogant* 297.9, *produce* 522.13, *construct* 551.22, *vertical* 602.5, *make vertical* 602.9, *make stable* 674.7, *inaugurate* 675.10, *make bigger* 746.7

erected *architectural* 134.12, *raised* 715.6

erectile *raised* 715.6

erection *construction* 159.16, 551.6, *architectural structure* 134.4, *manufacture* 522.2, *bulge* 634.2, *raising* 715.1

erectly *vertically* 602.11

erectness *verticality* 602.1

erector *lifter* 715.5

eremite *celibate* 67.4, *unsocial*

person 409.5, *hermit* 782.9, *loner* 788.8
eremitophobia Phobias 283
eremophobia *or* **eremiophobia** Phobias 283
Erewhon *aspiration* 281.3, Imaginary Places 360
erg Scientific and Technical Units 589
ergo *with the effect of* 676.12, *accordingly* 735.39
ergonomics *exertion* 122.4
ergophobia Phobias 283
ergotism *fungal disease* 47.6
Ericht Lakes 568
Eridanus Constellations 7
Erie Lakes 568
Erinyes Deities 82
Eris Deities 82
eristic Philosophical Schools of Thought 4, *philosophical argument* 4.5, *logical argument* 329.2
eristic school Philosophical Schools of Thought 4
Eritrea Countries 566
ermine Heraldic Terms 184
erminois Heraldic Terms 184
erode 8.67, 96.19, 554.14; *lessen* 468.17, *weather* 553.29, *subtract* 749.6, *disintegrate* 758.6, *eat away* 808.19
eroded *weathered* 8.61, *infertile* 23.7, *disappeared* 265.4, *reduced* 749.5
erogenously *sexily* 20.23
eromania *eroticism* 20.7
Eros Planets and Their Satellites 7, Deities 82, *libido* 108.26, Famous Lovers 299, *goddesses and gods of love* 299.14
erosion 8.41, 96.3; *disappearance* 265.1, *lessening* 468.16, *agent of destruction* 523.7, *pulverization* 553.4, *wearing away* 554.2, *reduction* 747.2, *subtraction* 749.1, *disintegration* 758.1, *decay* 808.6
erosive *frictional* 554.10
erotic *pleasurable* 214.6, *offensive* 432.11
erotica *pornography* 432.7
erotically *sexily* 20.23
erotic desire *libido* 108.26
eroticism 20.7; *libido* 108.26, *physical pleasure* 214.1, *sexual love* 299.3, *pornography* 432.7
erotic novel *novel* 139.3
erotic poetry *poetry* 139.8
erotism *eroticism* 20.7, *pornography* 432.7
erotomania *eroticism* 20.7, *sexual love* 299.3
erotomanic-type delusional disorder *psychosis* 108.10
erotophobia Phobias 283
err 351.14; *be unskillful* 128.8, *transgress* 351.16, *misinterpret* 366.4, *be wrong* 430.18, *sin* 430.22, *be immoral* 432.13, *go astray* 698.17
errancy 351.7
errand *engagement* 833.2
errant 351.12; *wandering* 698.13
errantry *wandering* 698.4
erratic 381.5, 381.9; *glacier* 8.44, *inconstant* 378.6, *irregular* 664.3, 766.10, *moving* 677.12, *wandering* 698.13, *inconsistent* 732.7, *discontinuous* 775.7, *unreliable* 841.15
erratically 381.8, 698.29; *irregularly* 664.6, *inconsistently* 732.16, *in disorder* 766.24, *unreliably* 841.25
erraticism *inconstancy* 378.2,

caprice 381.1, *irresolution* 666.2, *inconsistency* 732.3
Er Rif Mountains and Hills 569
erring *errant* 351.4
erroneous 351.11; *sophistic* 330.7, *wrong* 430.12, *incorrect* 722.8, *imperfect* 806.5
erroneously 351.17; *sophistically* 330.14, *mistakenly* 366.6, 660.14, *wrongfully* 430.25, *incorrectly* 722.16
erroneousness 351.2; *incorrectness* 430.3, *untrueness* 722.3, *imperfection* 806.1
error 351.1, 846.2; *reasoning* 6.61, *measurement* 10.67, *bungling* 128.2, *bowling delivery* 151.2, Phobias 283, *negligence* 324.4, *mistake* 342.2, *act of folly* 353.2, *fantasy* 360.5, *misinterpretation* 366.1, *incorrectness* 430.3, *wandering* 698.4, *untrueness* 722.3, *inconvenience* 804.1, *imperfection* 806.1, *defect* 806.4
error of law *legal injustice* 53.5
ersatz *deputizing* 80.4, *borrowed* 476.8, *simulated* 733.11, *imitation* 736.8
erstwhile *former* 653.12, *dead* 658.10, *preceding* 769.9
eruct *let out* 709.26, *belch* 709.28
eructate *belch* 709.28
eructation *belch* 556.5, 709.8
eructative 709.13
erudite *educated* 48.19, *literary* 139.15, *intelligent* 315.9, *knowledgeable* 348.7, *wise* 352.4
erudition *learning* 48.7, 348.3, *learnedness* 48.8, *literature* 139.1, *cleverness* 315.3, *wisdom* 352.1
erupt *quake* 8.65, *be violent* 520.8, *open* 583.15, *emerge* 707.14, 771.35, *let out* 709.26
erupting *outgoing* 707.10
eruption 8.27; *skin disease* 114.16, *burst of anger* 302.6, *coming out* 707.3, *disgorgement* 709.6
eruptive *volcanic* 8.57, *violent* 520.5, *outgoing* 707.10, *expulsive* 709.11
eruptively *forth* 707.19, *expulsively* 709.29
eruptiveness *disgorgement* 709.6
erysipelas *skin disease* 114.16
erysipelatous *of disease* 114.25
erythema *skin disease* 114.16, *redness* 257.1
erythrocyte *blood* 555.4
erythrophobia Phobias 283
erythropoietin Human Hormones 12
Erzebirge Range Mountains and Hills 569
escalade *military attack* 418.2, *attack* 418.17, *invade* 706.12, *climb* 713.21
escalader *combatant* 77.1, *attacker* 418.10
escalate *augment* 467.16, *cost a lot* 496.9, *send up* 715.12, *increase* 746.6, *intensify* 746.8
escalated *raised* 715.6
escalating *rising* 713.14, *increasing* 746.4
escalation *augmentation* 467.2, *raising* 715.1, *intensification* 746.2
escalator *means of transportation* 686.2, *stairway* 713.9, *lifter* 715.5
escallop *veal* 90.25
escapable *avoidable* 386.12
escapade *caprice* 381.1
escape 816.1, 816.8; *plant* 41.2, *evasion* 181.5, 386.5, *guile* 193.3, *deceive* 193.16, *disappearance*

265.1, *depart* 265.6, *evade* 386.19, *run away* 386.21, *survive* 419.31, *exempt oneself* 434.12, *lose someone* 468.20, *abscond* 576.16, *departure* 705.1, *quit* 705.10, *emerge* 707.14, *diverge* 753.20, *be safe* 810.20, *deliverance* 817.1, *be free* 829.16, *liberation* 831.1, *liberate* 831.6, *overcome obstacles* 845.14
escape artist *magician* 138.11, *escaper* 816.5
escape by the skin of one's teeth [Inf] *escape* 816.8
escape character *character* 15.18
escape clause *specification* 340.6, *basis for negotiations* 460.2, *safety* 810.1, *means of escape* 816.4
escaped *wild* 41.15, *fugitive* 386.10, *escaping* 816.7, *free* 829.11
escape detection *elude* 816.10
escaped prisoner *escaper* 816.5
escapee *the hunted* 385.7, *avoider* 386.8, *outgoer* 707.9, *escaper* 816.5
escape from jail *escape* 816.8
escape hatch *way out* 707.2, *safety device* 810.15, *means of escape* 816.4
escape lane *road attribute* 687.3
escape notice 403.14; *become invisible* 245.6, *elude* 816.10
escape observation *hide* 844.13
escape one *be unintelligible* 364.11
escaper 816.5; *avoider* 386.8
escape route *way out* 707.2
escape sequence *character* 15.18
escape velocity *rocketry* 7.32, *speed* 694.2
escape wheel *wheel* 682.9
escaping 816.7; *disappearing* 265.3
escapism *defense mechanism* 108.23, *reverie* 360.6, *evasiveness* 386.6, *self-exemption* 434.3
escapist *visionary* 360.9, *avoider* 386.8, *fugitive* 386.10, *escaper* 816.5
escapologist [Brit] *magician* 138.11, *escaper* 816.5
escapology [Brit] *magic* 138.3
escargot [Fr] *food fish and shellfish* 90.20
escarp *fort* 419.13, *be high* 596.15
escarpment *landform* 8.9, *heights* 596.4, *vertical* 602.3, *obliquity* 628.2
eschar *cover* 613.2
eschatological *theological* 81.24, *ending* 773.13
eschatology Theologies 81, *future condition* 650.3, *end of time* 773.5
escheat *confiscation* 454.4, *confiscate* 454.25
eschew *exclude* 383.11, *shun* 386.14, *be self-restrained* 455.10
eschewal *self-restraint* 455.1
eschew artifice *be naive* 821.4
eschewed *rejected* 383.6
eschewing *rejecting* 383.2
escort 794.18; *boyfriend* 32.4, *lead* 126.12, *lover* 299.11, *court* 299.26, *conductor* 399.3, *conduct* 399.21, *guard* 419.15, *accompanier* 794.6, *partner* 794.9, *keep company with* 794.17, *safe conduct* 810.4, *protect* 810.21
escort carrier *warship* 77.21, Ships and Boats 690
escorted *accompanied* 794.15
escort ship Sailing Ships and Boats 690, Ships and Boats 690
escribed figure *geometric figure* 6.39
escrime [Fr] *fencing* 153.1

escritoire *type of desk* 101.6
escrow *storage* 105.6, *contract* 459.1, *promise* 464.2
escudo *national coins* 484.11
esculent *edible* 92.20, *tasty* 219.4
escutcheon Heraldic Terms 184
esker *glacier* 8.44, *mountain range* 569.3
Eskimo dog Breeds of Dogs 35
Eskimo roll *canoeing techniques* 150.11
esodophobia Phobias 283
esophagus *internal organ* 19.13, *eating organ* 92.14
esoteric *philosophical* 4.12, *occultist* 86.13, *occult* 86.16, *mysterious* 182.10, 844.11, *obscure* 197.2, *unintelligible* 364.4, *profound* 598.15, *exceptional* 779.13, *problematic* 824.11
esoterica *occultism* 86.1, *the occult* 86.2, *mystery* 182.4, *profundity* 598.5
esoterically *theoretically* 4.24, *occultly* 86.27, *unintelligibly* 364.16, *profoundly* 598.27
esotericism *occultism* 86.1, *mystery* 182.4, *unintelligibility* 364.1, *profundity* 598.5, *mysteriousness* 844.5
esoteric sense *type of meaning* 361.4
esoterism *occultism* 86.1
esotery *occultism* 86.1
esotropia *faulty vision* 243.1
espadrilles *shoes* 100.30
espalier *braid* 609.3, *interweave* 609.8
especial *special* 779.10
especially *superbly* 744.22, *specially* 779.19
Esperanto *international language* 5.8
espionage *secretiveness* 182.3, *observation* 242.5, *subversion* 427.3
esplanade *waterfront* 621.3, *passage* 691.5
espousal *courtship* 299.10
espouse *marry* 64.19, *side with* 382.15, *get engaged to* 458.12
espouse a theory *propound a philosophy* 4.21
espoused *spouse* 64.8, *married* 64.16
espouser *spouse* 64.8
espresso *coffee* 93.6
espresso café *eating place* 92.17
esprit de corps *friendly relations* 62.3, *compatibility* 735.4, *fellowship* 827.2
espy *see* 242.20, *discover* 345.11
Esq. *male title of address* 32.3
Esquire *professional title* 72.6
essay *nonfiction* 139.6, *narration* 202.3, *dissertation* 203.1, *experiment* 335.1, 335.11, *attempt* 390.1, 390.6, *contest* 422.4, *contend* 422.22
essayed *tested* 335.10
essayer *attempter* 390.3
essaying *attempting* 390.4
essayist *author* 139.13, *descriptive writer* 202.10, *dissertator* 203.3
esse [L] *existence* 717.1
essence 723.1; *idea* 327.1, *topic* 328.1, *gist* 329.4, 799.4, *meaning* 361.1, *excellence* 445.4, *product* 522.3, *substance* 577.2, *inner nature* 611.4, *core* 612.2, *form* 624.1, *extract* 711.8, *nature* 717.4
Essene *Jew* 81.11
essential 723.5, 799.10; *necessity* 95.1, *necessary* 95.10, *material*

104.8, *compulsion* 428.1, *excellent* 445.13, *containing* 577.7, *basis* 601.3, *basic* 601.8, *core* 612.7, *intrinsic* 717.12, *chief thing* 799.3
essential amino acid *amino acid* 12.8
essential clause *basis for negotiations* 460.2
essential content 723.2
essential element 12.15
essential facts *specifications* 779.6
essential fatty acid *fat* 12.7
essentialism Philosophical Schools of Thought 4
essentialist Philosophical Schools of Thought 4
essentiality *importance* 799.1
essentialize *obtain an extract* 711.19
essentially 617.6; *with need* 95.20, *thematically* 328.13, *structurally* 577.14, *basically* 601.14, *at the core of* 612.13, *really* 717.22, *intrinsically* 721.30, *in essence* 723.13, *on the whole* 759.13, *importantly* 799.15
essential nature *nature* 717.4
essentialness *indispensability* 95.2
essential oil *toiletries* 530.6, *oil* 562.3
essential part *gist* 799.4
essential quality *basis* 601.3
essentials *materials* 104.1, *fact* 717.6, *specifications* 779.6
Essequibo Rivers 570
establish *legislate* 53.31, *identify* 184.11, *attest* 189.22, *state* 329.13, *prove* 331.17, 336.9, *lay the foundations* 388.16, *produce* 522.13, *locate* 565.9, *base* 601.10, *make permanent* 644.9, 667.5, *make stable* 674.7, *inaugurate* 675.10, 771.31, *establish reality* 719.12, *authenticate* 721.24, *make the same* 730.16, *begin* 771.25, *rule* 780.12, *make certain* 840.14
established 397.12; *societal* 1.13, *masterful* 68.15, *identified* 184.9, *attested* 189.13, *propertied* 470.9, *located* 565.6, *olden* 653.11, *permanent* 667.2, *unfailing* 667.3, *stabilized* 674.4, *authenticated* 721.17, *regular* 730.12, *average* 742.5, *certain* 840.7, *decided* 840.9
established custom *custom* 397.4
established ways *way* 397.3
establisher *producer* 522.10
establishing *identification* 184.1, *verificatory* 336.6, *inaugural* 771.21
Establishment, the *governance* 52.6, *the power structure* 68.12, *group influence* 512.6
establishment *plant* 124.7, *identification* 184.1, *attestation* 189.2, *proof* 336.2, *association* 480.8, *store* 483.8, *manufacture* 522.2, *construction* 551.6, *placing* 565.4, *permanence* 667.1, *authentication* 721.8, *inauguration* 771.6, *council* 833.4, *confirmation* 840.3
establish reality 719.12
establish residence *settle* 565.10
establish the trend *influence* 512.11
estate 750.5; *farm* 16.2, *mansion* 60.5, *possession of property* 469.3, *property* 470.1, *wealth* 485.1, *rank* 573.4, *state* 725.1
estate agent [Brit] *person transferring property* 470.8
estate car [Brit] *automobile* 687.6
estate tax *tax* 494.5

esteem *worship* 83.1, 83.15, *be of the opinion* 87.10, *liking* 290.1, *like* 290.8, *dignity* 297.4, *love* 299.1, 299.21, *estimate* 341.11, *repute* 370.1, *respect* 435.1, 435.13, *admiration* 437.2, *admire* 437.15, *make important* 799.14
esteemed *worshiped* 83.14, *liked* 290.6, *dignified* 297.11, *beloved* 299.19, *reputable* 370.3, *respected* 435.10
esteeming *worshipful* 83.12
ester *fat* 562.4
esterify *react* 11.38
esthesia *sensation* 212.1
esthesis *sensation* 212.1
estimable *respectable* 435.11, *praiseworthy* 437.12, *measurable* 589.17, *calculable* 784.8
estimably *reputably* 370.6, *mathematically* 784.15
estimate 341.11; *equate* 6.88, *experiment* 10.72, 335.11, *document* 170.3, *recommendation* 176.2, *theorize* 327.16, *judgment* 341.1, *predict* 356.7, *interpretation* 365.1, *interpret* 365.12, *account* 493.9, *price* 494.1, *tax system* 494.6, *measurement* 589.1, *measure* 589.20, 739.7, *calculate* 784.10
estimated *theoretical* 327.10, *tested* 335.10, *measured* 589.16
estimated position *navigation* 690.5
estimated value *measurement* 10.67
estimating *calculative* 784.7
estimation *reasoning* 6.61, *idea* 327.1, *experimentation* 335.3, *judgment* 341.1, *repute* 370.1, *measurement* 589.1, *calculation* 784.1
estimative *calculative* 784.7
estimator *judge* 54.10, *measurer* 589.14, *counter* 784.6
estinto Musical Terms and Expression Marks 140
estival *seasonal* 654.7
estivate *sleep* 415.14, *spend the season* 654.10
estivating *not awake* 415.12
estivation *sleep* 415.5, *summer* 654.4, *latency* 844.1
Estonia Countries 566
Estonian Bacon Breeds of Pigs 16
Estonian Darkheaded Breeds of Sheep 16
Estonian Red Breeds of Cattle 16
estradiol Human Hormones 12
estral *desirous* 20.18
estrange *antagonize* 63.12, *cause hate* 300.12, *divide* 753.18
estranged 63.8; *divorced* 66.7, *hated* 300.9
estrangement *personal conflict* 63.2, *separation* 66.2, *dislike* 300.2, *disagreement* 463.1
Estre Deities 82
E string *part of stringed instrument* 142.2
estriol Human Hormones 12
estrogen Human Hormones 12, *hormone* 12.16
estrone Human Hormones 12
estrous *desirous* 20.18, *in season* 654.8, *cyclic* 663.7
estrous cycle *sexual desire* 20.5, *cycle* 663.3
estrus *sexual desire* 20.5, *seasons* 654.2
estuarial *of landmasses* 572.12
estuarine *oceanic* 571.7
estuary *inlet* 572.9, *channel* 691.10

esurient *gluttonous* 119.3
et al. *et cetera* 793.12
etc. *additionally* 748.15, *inclusively* 763.8, *et cetera* 793.12
et cetera 793.12; *additionally* 748.15, *inclusively* 763.8
etch *engrave* 144.11, *identify* 184.11, *inscribe* 185.14, *illustrate* 187.11, *decorate* 532.11, *outline* 617.5, *furrow* 638.5
etchant *material* 144.6
etched *engraved* 144.9, *furrowed* 638.3
etcher *engraver* 144.5
etching *craft* 133.2, *engraving* 144.3, *illustration* 187.2, *decorative method* 532.3, *outline* 617.1
etching point *material* 144.6
eternal 644.4, 798.7; *divine* 82.16, *nonmaterial* 525.8, *lasting* 639.9, *timeless* 640.3, *permanent* 642.5, 667.2, *unfailing* 667.3, *protracted* 669.7
Eternal, the *God* 82.6
eternal damnation *evil place* 446.6
eternalization 644.3
eternalize *perpetuate* 640.5
eternal life *new life* 28.8, *nonmaterial world* 525.1
eternally 644.10, 798.12; *divinely* 82.24, *for good* 445.23, *metaphysically* 525.13, *chronologically* 639.21, *ever* 640.7, *everlastingly* 642.10, *permanently* 667.6, *continually* 669.10
eternal peace *ease* 819.1
eternal rest *death* 29.1, *life without end* 644.2, *repose* 678.2
eternal triangle *jealousy* 314.2
eternal verities *truth* 721.1
eternity 644.1, 798.4; *divine attribute* 82.4, *nonmaterial world* 525.1, *timelessness* 640.1, *permanence* 667.1
etesian Notable Winds 9
ethane *fuels* 106.2
ethanol *fuels* 106.2
ethene *plant hormone* 12.17
ether *anesthetic* 213.3, *gas* 556.1, *air* 558.1
ethereal *heavenly* 82.22, *spiritual* 86.20, *imaginary* 360.12, *nonmaterial* 525.8, *insubstantial* 539.5, *sparse* 541.3, *airy* 556.15, 558.12, *unreal* 720.8
etherealism *aerialness* 556.8
ethereality *lightness* 539.1, *sparseness* 541.1, *aerialness* 556.8, *airiness* 558.9, *unreality* 720.1
etherealization *rarefaction* 541.2, *vaporization* 556.9
etherealize *occult* 86.22, *make sparse* 541.5
etherealized *rarefied* 541.4
ethereally *metaphysically* 525.13, *lightly* 539.10, *sparsely* 541.6, *aerily* 556.26
etherealness *subtlety* 534.2
ethereal world *nonmaterial world* 525.1
etheric body *spirit* 86.10
etherification *vaporization* 556.9
etherify *gasify* 556.23
etherize *anesthetize* 213.8, *aerate* 556.24
etherized *desensitized* 213.5
Ethernet *computer communications* 15.25
ethical *philosophical* 4.12, *well-behaved* 399.15, *right* 429.7, *proper* 429.10, *moral* 431.9, *virtuous* 447.5, *principled* 447.6
ethical drug *medicine* 115.2

ethicality *morality* 431.1
ethically 447.10; *theoretically* 4.24, *well* 399.22, *morally* 431.15, *dutifully* 433.19, *virtuously* 447.9
ethicalness *morality* 431.1, *virtue* 447.1
ethical self *psyche* 108.25
ethical system *philosophical system* 4.2
ethics Branches of Philosophy 4, *religion* 81.1, *morality* 431.1, *morals* 431.2, *virtues* 447.2
Ethiopia Countries 566
ethmoid bone Human Bones 19
ethnic *racial* 1.12, *societal* 1.13, *human* 18.15, *native* 61.12
ethnically *societally* 1.13, *sociologically* 2.15, *humanly* 18.18
ethnic cleansing *slaughter* 30.5, *social discrimination* 337.4, *replacement* 574.3, *exclusiveness* 764.4
ethnic group *society* 1.6, *social organization* 2.5, *group* 18.13
ethnicity *exclusiveness* 764.4
ethnic minority *group* 18.13
ethnic music *folk music* 140.7
ethnic origin *race* 1.5
ethnic psychology Psychological Theories, Schools 108
ethnobiological *biological* 13.27
ethnobiologist *life scientist* 13.26
ethnobotanical *botanical* 41.20
ethnobotanist *plant scientist* 41.11
ethnobotany *anthropology* 1.1, *plant science* 41.10
ethnocentric *discriminatory* 337.11
ethnocentrically *prejudicially* 337.17
ethnocentricity *social discrimination* 337.4
ethnogenic *anthropological* 1.10
ethnogenist *anthropologist* 1.3
ethnogeny *anthropology* 1.1
ethnographer *anthropologist* 1.3
ethnographic *anthropological* 1.10
ethnographical *human* 18.15
ethnographically *anthropologically* 1.15, *humanly* 18.18
ethnography *anthropology* 1.1
ethnological *anthropological* 1.10
ethnologically *anthropologically* 1.15
ethnologist *anthropologist* 1.3
ethnology *anthropology* 1.1
ethnomusicologist *anthropologist* 1.3
ethnomusicology *anthropology* 1.1
ethnoscientific *anthropological* 1.10
ethnoscientific studies *anthropology* 1.1
ethological *of animals* 34.13, *behaving* 399.14
ethologist *animal scientist* 34.7
ethology *animal science* 34.6
ethos *philosophical system* 4.2, *way of life* 399.9, *morality* 431.1
ethylene *plant hormone* 12.17
ethylene glycol *heater* 217.3
etiolate *decolor* 252.8, *whiten* 253.12, *weaken* 517.13
etiolated *colorless* 252.5, *whitened* 253.8, *weakened* 517.9
etiolation *colorlessness* 252.1, *whitening* 253.2
etiological *causal* 675.7
etiology *medical science* 107.5, *cause* 675.1
etiquette 406.3, 534.3; *tradition* 397.5, *good conduct* 399.5, *formality* 406.1, *good manners*

essential amino acid — etiquette

410.2, *properness* 429.5, *refinement* 534.1, *conventionalism* 781.4

Etna, Mount Mountains and Hills 569

Eton collar *neckwear* 100.29

Eton crop *coiffure* 530.8

Eton jacket *jacket* 100.18

Etruscan *historic* 653.13

Etruscan architecture Architectural Styles 134

Etruscan art Western Art Styles 133

étude Musical Forms 140

etymological *linguistic* 361.9

etymologically *linguistically* 5.44

etymologist *linguist* 5.3

etymology Linguistic Studies 5, *language* 5.4, *type of meaning* 361.4, *cause* 675.1

etymon *word* 5.17, *part of speech* 5.30

Euboea Islands 572

eucalyptus Trees and Shrubs 43, *incense* 226.3

eucaryotic *cellular* 13.30

eucaryotic cell *cell* 13.15

eucharis Flowers 42

Eucharist 85.7; *Christian rite* 85.5

eucharist *thanks* 310.2

eucharistic *ritualistic* 85.15

euchre Card Games 168

euchromosome *chromosome* 13.21

Euclidean geometry *geometry* 6.32

Euclidean space *space* 6.33

Euclid's axioms Mathematical Concepts 6

eucryphia Trees and Shrubs 43

eudemonia *ease* 819.1

eudemonic *at ease* 819.2

eudemonism Philosophical Schools of Thought 4

eudemonist Philosophical Schools of Thought 4

eudiometer *vaporimeter* 556.13

eugenics *genetics* 13.19, *medical science* 107.5

euglena *little thing* 580.3

euhemerism Philosophical Schools of Thought 4, *interpretation* 365.1

euhemerist Philosophical Schools of Thought 4, *interpreter* 365.6

euhemeristic *interpretive* 365.8

eukaryotic *cellular* 13.30

eukaryotic cell *cell* 13.15

Euler angles *angle* 6.37

Eulerian circuit *combinatorics* 6.63

Euler's constant Mathematical Concepts 6

Euler's formula Mathematical Concepts 6

eulogia *prayer* 85.10

eulogist *funeral person* 31.5, *approver* 437.7

eulogistic *funeral* 31.9, *approving* 437.9

eulogistical *funeral* 31.9

eulogistically *funereally* 31.13

eulogize *praise* 437.16

eulogized *lamented* 280.5

eulogizer *funeral person* 31.5, *approver* 437.7

eulogy *funeral* 31.4, *public speaking* 205.11, *lament* 280.2, *praise* 437.3

Eumenides Deities 82

Eumycota *fungi* 47.3

Eunomia Planets and Their Satellites 7, Deities 82

eunuch 32.11; *sexlessness* 20.13, *powerless person* 515.5

eunuchized *undersexed* 20.20

euonymus Trees and Shrubs 43

eupepsia *health* 113.1

eupeptic *healthy* 113.4

euphemism *ornament* 532.7, *indirectness* 607.3

euphemistic *ornate* 532.10, *indirect* 607.8

euphemistically *indirectly* 607.15

euphemize *mitigate* 521.9

euphobia Phobias 283

euphonic *harmonizing* 735.12

euphonically *in harmony* 735.32

euphonious *pleasurable* 214.6, *harmonizing* 735.12

euphoniously *tunefully* 140.30, *gracefully* 527.8, *in harmony* 735.32

euphoniousness *melodiousness* 140.12, *harmonization* 735.2

euphonium Musical Instruments 142

euphonize *harmonize* 735.22

euphony *literary device* 139.12, *melodiousness* 140.12, *grace* 527.2, *harmonization* 735.2

euphorbia Flowers 42

euphoria *pleasure* 214.2, *joy* 269.1

euphoric *pleased* 214.9, *joyful* 269.6, *rejoicing* 279.4

euphorically *rejoicingly* 279.7

Euphrates Rivers 570

Euphrosyne Planets and Their Satellites 7, Deities 82

euphuism Western Literary Groups 139, *obscurity* 197.1, *affectation* 367.1

euphuistic *obscure* 197.2, *affected* 367.3, *ornate* 532.10

Eurasia *world region* 564.6, *landmass* 572.1

eurhythmic *even* 626.5

eurhythmics *dance* 135.1

eurhythmy *evenness* 626.3

Euripidean tragedy *tragedy* 136.10

Euroclydon Notable Winds 9

Euronet *computer communications* 15.25

Europa Planets and Their Satellites 7

Europe *landmass* 572.1

Europe (SHAPE) *military staff* 58.5

European Bank *lending institution* 475.4, *finance* 484.7

European Boxing Union *boxing associations* 152.7

European Cup *soccer associations and awards* 163.6

European Cup Winners' Cup *soccer associations and awards* 163.6

European Free Trade Association (EFTA) *economic organization* 56.6

European Games *competition* 166.18

European Union (EU) *economic organization* 56.6

europium Chemical Elements and Common Allotropes 11

Eurus *wind god* 9.16

Euryalus Notable Friendships 62

eurypterid *extinct arthropod* 39.7

Eustachian tube *ear* 19.10, 228.2

eutectic *chemical compound* 11.4, *phase* 11.13, *metallurgy* 11.22, *status adjectives* 11.25

Euterpe Deities 82

euthanasia *way of dying* 29.5, *killing* 30.1

euthanasiast *killer* 30.11

Eutheria *placental mammal* 35.6

eutherian *placental mammal* 35.6, *mammalian* 35.23

eutherian characteristic *placental mammal* 35.6

eutrophication *alga* 47.10

evacuate *defecate* 25.21, *withdraw* 392.5, 705.9, *remove* 574.16, *leave empty* 576.17, *emerge* 707.14, *void* 709.23

evacuated *removed* 574.9, *stateless* 574.14

evacuation *defecation* 25.3, *relinquishment* 392.1, *removal* 574.2, 709.5, *departure* 705.1, *exit* 707.1

evacuee *displaced person* 574.7

evadable *avoidable* 368.12

evade 181.17, 386.19; *conceal oneself* 181.15, *lack candor* 192.22, *deceive* 330.12, *hesitate* 378.10, *be equivocal* 380.7, *not perform* 466.10, *lose someone* 468.20, *circumlocute* 607.12, *elude* 816.10

evade detection *hide* 844.13

evade liability *exempt oneself* 434.12

evade one's creditors *not pay* 490.9

evade one's responsibilities *exempt oneself* 434.12, *be irresolute* 461.8

evader *one who conceals* 181.7, *liar* 192.10, *avoider* 386.8, *escaper* 816.5

evade taxes *not pay* 490.9, *refuse* 506.8, *elude* 816.10

evading *nonperforming* 466.6

evaginate *invert* 608.7

evaginated *inverted* 608.5

evagination *inversion* 608.1

evaluate 6.90; *rationalize* 4.20, *enumerate* 6.85, *estimate* 341.11, *criticize* 365.15, *price* 494.12, *measure* 589.20, 739.7

evaluation 6.22; *reasoning* 6.61, *judgment* 341.1, *measurement* 589.1

evaluation of returns *election* 382.6

evaluator *measurer* 589.14

evanesce *disappear* 265.5, *be transient* 643.6, *decrease* 747.7

evanescence *disappearance* 265.1, *littleness* 580.1, *transience* 643.1, *decrease* 747.1

evanescent *disappearing* 265.3, *transient* 643.4, *decreasing* 747.5

evanescently *fleetingly* 265.8

evangel *news* 171.1

Evangelical *Christian* 81.10

evangelical *zealous* 81.22

Evangelicalism Christian Groups 81, *Christianity* 81.5

evangelism *religious conversion* 670.4

evangelist *religious person* 81.9, *religionist* 81.14, *converter* 670.5

evangelization *religious conversion* 670.4

evangelize *proselytize* 84.15, *make someone believe* 87.11, *moralize* 431.14, *persuade* 670.14

evangelized *influenced* 670.10

evaporability *volatility* 556.7

evaporable *volatile* 556.21

evaporate *drain* 8.64, *heat* 10.74, *solidify* 11.37, *disappear* 265.5, *lessen* 468.17, *abolish* 523.11, *be dense* 540.8, *gasify* 556.23, *dry* 560.17, *be transient* 643.6, *cease to exist* 718.13, *decrease* 747.7, *dilute* 776.14

evaporated *atmospheric* 9.40,

status adjectives 11.25, *dried-out* 560.10, *diluted* 776.8

evaporated milk *milk* 93.5

evaporating *disappearing* 265.3

evaporation *water cycle* 8.12, *atmospheric process* 9.9, *temperature* 10.29, *phase* 11.13, *disappearance* 265.1, *lessening* 468.6, *vaporization* 556.9, Fields of Measurement 589, *outflow* 707.14, *reduction* 747.2, *dilution* 776.3

evaporative *volatile* 556.21, *drying* 560.15

evaporimeter Fields of Measurement 589

evasion 181.5, 380.2, 386.5; *concealment* 181.1, *lack of candor* 192.4, *quibbling* 330.4, *hypocrisy* 330.5, *method* 387.4, *indirectness* 607.3, *escape* 816.1, *cunning* 822.1, *stratagem* 822.2

evasion of responsibility *self-exemption* 434.3, *irresolution* 461.3

evasive *silent* 181.10, *noncommittal* 181.11, *uncandid* 192.15, *sparing with words* 208.6, *cunning* 330.8, *equivocal* 380.5, *avoiding* 386.9, *irresolute* 461.6, *indirect* 607.8, *misrepresented* 627.8, *escaping* 816.7

evasively 386.24; *professionally* 152.22, *privately* 181.18, *uncandidly* 192.29, *hypocritically* 330.15, *equivocally* 380.9, *irresolutely* 461.10, *indirectly* 607.15, *distortedly* 627.14

evasiveness 386.6; *evasion* 181.5, *secrecy* 182.1, *lack of candor* 192.4

Eve *female* 33.1, *tempter* 178.10

eve *evening* 656.2

even 626.5; *numerical* 6.68, 783.7, *smooth* 545.4, 545.10, *uniform* 545.5, *horizontal* 603.6, *make horizontal* 603.10, *horizontally* 603.11, *symmetrize* 626.6, *regular* 663.5, *frequent* 663.6, *adjust* 721.23, *correctly* 721.29, *same* 730.7, *on equal terms* 740.9, *equalize* 740.12, *irresolute* 772.13

even as *as* 649.10

even break *equality* 740.1, *equal chance* 842.7

even chance *strong possibility* 836.3, *chance* 838.4, *equal chance* 842.7

evened out *leveled* 603.8

evened up *or out* *counterbalanced* 743.6

even exchange *equalization* 740.4

evening 656.2, 656.4; *nighttime* 656.1, *nightfall* 714.5, *close* 773.9

evening bag *bag* 578.7

evening damp *dew* 559.6

evening dress *formal clothes* 100.5, *formal clothing* 406.5

evening gown *formal clothes* 100.5, *dress* 100.11, *formal clothing* 406.5

evening light *dimness* 248.1

evening meal *meal* 92.8

evening news *evening* 656.2

evening of one's life *old age* 27.5

evening paper *newspaper* 175.2

evening prayer *public worship* 83.3

evening service *public worship* 83.3

evening shirt *shirt* 100.13

evening star *star* 7.8, *evening* 656.2

evening things *evening* 656.2

evening time *evening* 656.2

evening up or **down** *equalization* 740.4
evening up or **out** *counterbalanced* 743.6
even keel *equilibrium* 740.2
even less *decreasingly* 747.9
evenly *smoothly* 545.13, *horizontally* 603.11, *equally* 626.8, 740.13, *orderly* 663.13, *regularly* 663.14, *correctly* 721.29, *identically* 730.18
evenly matched *on equal terms* 740.9
even match *contest* 422.4
even money *horse-racing betting terms* 159.11, *equality* 740.1
even more *supremely* 744.23
even more so *increasingly* 746.9
evenness 626.3; *smoothness* 545.1, *horizontality* 603.1, *regularity* 663.1, *sameness* 730.1, *equality* 740.1, *equilibrium* 740.2
even number *number* 6.4, *kind of number* 783.2
even odds *equal chance* 842.7
even out *make horizontal* 603.10, *make the same* 730.16
even out or **up** *make average* 742.9
evens *strong possibility* 836.3
even-sided *symmetrical* 626.4, *even* 626.5, *equal* 740.8
even-sidedly *equally* 626.8
even sides *symmetry* 626.1
evensong *public worship* 83.3, *evening* 656.2
even-steven [Inf] *even* 626.5, *equal* 740.8
event *probability* 6.59, *sports* 145.1, *prize competition* 422.5, *effect* 676.1, *occurrence* 726.2
even temper *courtesy* 410.1
even temperament *key* 140.23
even-tempered *detached* 4.18, *harmonic* 140.27, *courteous* 410.6
eventer *horse person* 159.14
eventful *busy* 414.15, *circumstantial* 726.8, *newsworthy* 799.12
event horizon *stellar evolution* 7.10
eventide *evening* 656.2
eventing *equestrianism* 159.8, *equine* 159.15
even-toed *ungulate* 35.31
even-toed ungulate *hoofed mammal* 35.16
events *matter of interest* 328.3
eventual *auspicious* 458.10, *future* 650.6, *caused* 676.5, *circumstantial* 726.8, *potential* 836.6
eventuality *looking to the future* 650.4, *circumstances* 726.1, *possibility* 836.1
eventually *auspiciously* 458.17, *in the future* 650.13, *with the effect of* 676.12, *relatively* 726.17, *finally* 773.24, *potentially* 836.11
eventuate in *react* 676.8
even up *symmetrize* 626.6, *adjust* 721.23
even up or **down** *equalize* 740.12
even up or **out** *counterbalance* 743.8
even with *additionally* 748.15
ever 640.7; *all the time* 639.16
ever and anon [Arch] *frequently* 661.7
ever-changing *changeable* 666.3
Everest, Mount *Mountains and Hills* 569
evergreen *plant* 41.2, *of plants* 41.14, *tree* 43.1, *treelike* 43.10, *green thing* 260.4, *fresh* 260.10,

lasting 642.4, *eternal* 644.4, *unfailing* 667.3, *stable* 674.3
ever-increasing *increasing* 746.4
everlasting *lasting* 639.9, *timeless* 640.3, *permanent* 642.5, 667.2, *eternal* 644.4, 798.7, *protracted* 669.7
Everlasting Father *God the Father* 82.8
everlasting flower *flower* 42.1
everlastingly 642.10; *ever* 640.7, *permanently* 667.6, *continually* 669.10
everlastingness *timelessness* 640.1, *eternity* 644.1, 798.4, *permanence* 667.1
ever less *decreasingly* 747.9
evermore *ever* 640.7, *eternally* 644.10
ever so many *many* 795.6
evert *invert* 608.7, *cause change* 665.16
everted *inverted* 608.5
ever upward or **higher** *up* 713.25
ever-victorious *victorious* 845.10
every *whole* 759.6
every bit *wholly* 759.11
everybody *humankind* 18.1, *all* 759.4, *everyone* 778.7
everybody under the sun *everyone* 778.7
everyday *of language* 5.35, *predictable* 295.4, *habitual* 397.9, *simple* 526.7, *regular* 663.5, *average* 742.5, *common* 778.13
every day *cyclically* 663.15
everyday knowledge *manual skill* 127.2
everyday occurrence *frequency* 661.1
everyday practice *way* 399.10
everyday speech *unpretentiousness* 526.2
everyday work *work* 122.1
every hour *frequently* 661.7
every inch *wholly* 759.11, *fully* 761.14
every inch a king or **queen** *excellent* 744.14
every living soul *humankind* 18.1
everyman *average person* 18.9, 742.4, *commoner* 71.1, *everyone* 778.7
every man for himself *anarchism* 51.3, *lawless* 53.26
every man Jack *everyone* 778.7
every minute *frequently* 661.7
every month *cyclically* 663.15
every mother's son *everyone* 778.7
every night *nightly* 656.6, *cyclically* 663.15
every now and again *sometimes* 662.5, *irregularly* 664.6
everyone 778.7; *humankind* 18.1, *all* 759.4
everyone and everything *all* 759.4
every other *frequent* 663.6
every other day *cyclically* 663.15
every other month *cyclically* 663.15
every other night *cyclically* 663.15
every other week *cyclically* 663.15
every other year *cyclically* 663.15
every second *frequently* 661.7
every so often *apart* 587.8, *infrequently* 662.4, *sometimes* 662.5

everything *Phobias* 283, *all* 759.4
everything being equal *considering* 341.13
everything but the kitchen sink *large part* 579.3, *variety* 732.2
every Tom, Dick, and Harry *average person* 742.4, *everyone* 778.7
every way *in all directions* 697.19
every week *cyclically* 663.15
everywhere 776.19; *extensively* 563.18, *omnipresent* 575.10, *here* 575.19, *in all directions* 697.19, *universally* 778.23
every which way [Inf] *extensively* 563.18, *in all directions* 697.19, *anyhow* 766.25
every whit *fully* 761.14
everywoman *average person* 18.9, 742.4, *everyone* 778.7
every year *cyclically* 663.15
evict 709.20; *lose* 468.12, *take back* 477.17, *replace* 574.17, *eject* 764.8
evicted *stateless* 574.14, *excluded* 764.6
eviction 709.4; *loss* 468.1, *taking back* 477.4, *replacement* 574.3, *ejection* 764.2
evictor *ejector* 709.10
evidence 54.15, 336.3, 339.1; *authorization* 52.3, *sign* 183.1, *attestation* 189.2, *visibility* 244.1, *line of argument* 329.3, *proof* 331.4, *prove* 331.17, *indication* 339.3, *basis of supposition* 359.2, *mean* 361.13, *accusation* 442.1, *authentication* 721.8, *certainty* 840.1, *confirmation* 840.3, *manifestation* 843.2, *reveal* 843.14
evident 339.9; *visible* 242.19, 244.5, *easily seen through* 249.10, *appearing* 264.9, *outer* 264.10, *demonstrable* 331.12, *opened up* 583.11, *probable* 838.6, *certain* 840.7, *manifest* 843.9
evidential 339.8; *symbolic* 183.12, *proven* 331.13, *verificatory* 336.6
evidentially *indicatively* 183.21
evidentiary *authorized* 52.11, *evidential* 339.8
evidently 339.16; *mathematically* 6.93, *visibly* 242.28, 244.10, *apparently* 264.16, *openly* 583.22, *manifestly* 843.17
evil 446.1, 446.7; *affliction* 117.1, *afflicting* 117.11, *black-hearted* 254.9, *malevolent* 306.7, *wrong* 430.1, *wrongful* 430.10, *immoral* 432.9, *demonic* 446.9, *wicked* 448.9
evil act *malignity* 306.5
evil deed *wrongdoing* 430.7
evil disposition *malevolence* 306.1
evildoer 412.6; *malefactor* 306.6, *evil person* 446.3, *villain* 448.5
evildoing *wickedness* 448.1, *wicked* 448.9
evil eye *spell* 86.8, *look* 242.7, *curse* 301.1, *evil thing* 446.2
evil genius *evil person* 446.3
evil intent *malice* 306.2
evilly 446.12; *malevolently* 306.14, *abusively* 395.8, *immorally* 432.18, *wickedly* 448.15
evil-minded *malevolent* 306.7
evilness *malevolence* 306.1, *wrong* 430.1, *immorality* 432.1, *evil* 446.1, *wickedness* 448.1
evil omen *forewarning* 814.2
Evil One *devil* 446.5
evil person 446.3
evil place 446.6
evil plight *evil thing* 446.2

evil portent *forewarning* 814.2
evil power *evil thing* 446.2
evil-smelling *stinking* 227.3
evil spell *curse* 301.1, *evil thing* 446.2
evil spirit 446.4
evil star *evil thing* 446.2, *bad fortune* 848.7
evil thing 446.2
evil ways *wickedness* 448.1
evil will *malevolence* 306.1
evil-willed *malevolent* 306.7
evil wish *evil thing* 446.2
evince *state* 329.13, *prove* 331.17, 336.9, *make evident* 339.11, *make certain* 840.14, *reveal* 843.14
eviscerate *void* 709.23, *draw out* 711.17
evisceration *drawing off* 711.4
evocation *developmental biology* 13.22, *spell* 86.8, *representation* 187.1, *memory* 354.1, *cause* 675.1, *drawing out* 711.5
evocative *representational* 187.8, *descriptive* 202.11, *memorable* 354.7, *symbolic* 361.8
evoke *conjure* 86.26, *represent* 187.10, *recount* 202.16, *motivate* 508.9, *awaken* 675.9, *draw out* 711.17, *seem like* 733.14
evolute *curve* 6.38
evolution 13.23, 670.3; *developmental biology* 13.6, *life* 28.1, *action* 412.1, *deed* 412.2, *forward motion* 677.4, *development* 679.4, *creation* 717.9, *calculation* 784.1
evolutionary 13.34; *biological* 13.27
evolutionist *life scientist* 13.26
evolve *show potential* 458.14, *dream up* 522.15, *shape* 551.21, *convert* 670.11, *be converted* 670.12, *follow from* 676.9, *be in motion* 677.14, *come to be* 717.19, *change by degrees* 739.8, *get better* 807.21
evolved *caused* 676.5, *created* 717.16
evolving *evolution* 670.3, *converting* 670.8
evolving from *caused* 676.5
evulse *extract* 711.13
evulsion *extraction* 711.1
ewe *livestock* 16.11, *female animal* 33.15, *female mammal* 35.19
ewe lamb *female animal* 33.15
ewer *water carrier* 557.16, *vessel* 578.11
exa *Decimal Prefixes* 589
exacerbate *aggravate* 276.5, *make irritable* 304.15, *intensify* 746.8, *make worse* 808.17
exacerbated *aggravated* 276.3
exacerbation *aggravation* 276.1, *intensification* 746.2, *impairment* 808.7
exact *clear* 196.2, *concise* 198.4, *fastidious* 325.9, *accurate* 350.3, *formal* 406.6, *severe* 424.5, *demand* 425.11, 505.12, *force* 428.10, *correct* 429.8, 721.13, *observant* 465.3, *charge* 494.13, *extort* 711.18, *literal* 721.18, *detailed* 726.9, *same* 730.7, *perfect* 805.8
exacta *horse-racing betting terms* 159.11
exact amount *sufficiency* 97.1
exact a penalty *penalize* 454.26
exact compensation *retaliate* 420.4
exact counterpart *look-alike* 730.4

exact image *image* 187.3
exacting 711.12; *demanding* 95.13, *severe* 424.5, *perfectionistic* 805.18, *fatiguing* 820.4, *difficult* 824.9, *problematic* 824.11
exactingly *severely* 424.11, *away* 711.20
exaction *levy* 494.7, *demand* 505.3, *extortion* 711.6
exaction of penalty *penalty* 454.5
exactitude *fastidiousness* 325.4, *accuracy* 350.1, *right* 429.2, *trueness* 721.4
exactive *exacting* 711.12
exact likeness *image* 187.3, *look-alike* 730.4
exact location 565.2
exactly *clearly* 196.4, *concisely* 198.6, *accurately* 350.6, *correctly* 429.16, 721.29, *observantly* 465.6, *literally* 721.32, *meticulously* 726.18, *identically* 730.18, *specially* 779.19, *perfectly* 805.21
exactly alike *same* 730.7
exactly enough *enough* 97.10
exactly the same *same* 730.7
exactness *clarity* 196.1, *conciseness* 198.1, *carefulness* 325.1, *accuracy* 350.1, *right* 429.2, *trueness* 721.4, *literalness* 721.9, *perfection* 805.1
exact opposite *opposite* 731.2
exact picture *image* 187.3
exact retribution 454.27
exact revenge *be malevolent* 306.12
exact science *physics* 10.1
exact thing, the *sameness* 730.1
exact time, the *chronology* 646.2
exacum *Flowers* 42
exaggerate 194.11, 712.16; *overdo* 99.11, *misrepresent* 188.6, 366.5, *distort the truth* 192.25, 627.12, *aggravate* 276.5, *overestimate* 343.6, *imagine* 360.14, *fantasize* 360.15, *put on airs* 404.27, *intensify* 746.8, *make important* 799.14
exaggerated 194.7, 712.9; *overdone* 99.7, *misrepresented* 188.4, 627.8, *partially true* 192.18, *overestimated* 343.5, *imaginative* 360.10, *meaningless* 362.7, *misinterpreted* 366.3, *unrestrained* 500.5, *ornate* 532.10
exaggerated lengths *exaggeration* 194.1
exaggeratedly 194.16; *misrepresentedly* 366.7
exaggerating *exaggeration* 194.1
exaggeratingly *untruthfully* 192.27
exaggeration 194.1; *excess* 99.1, *public relations (PR)* 173.8, *misrepresentation* 188.1, 366.2, *misinformation* 188.3, *partial truth* 192.7, *aggravation* 276.1, *overestimation* 343.1, *conception* 360.4, *empty talk* 362.5, *unrestrainedness* 500.2, *ornateness* 532.2, *distortion of truth* 627.4, *excessiveness* 712.4, *intensification* 746.2
exaggerative *or* **exaggeratory** *untruthful* 192.12
exaggeratively *untruthfully* 192.27
exaggerator 194.6; *gossip* 192.11, *overestimator* 343.2
exalt 596.19; *deify* 82.23, *worship* 83.11, *praise* 435.15, 437.16, *promote* 715.13, *intensify* 746.8, *make important* 799.14
exaltation 596.3, Collective

Names 59, *deification* 82.13, *worship* 83.1, *joy* 269.1, *praise* 437.3, *promotion* 715.3, *intensification* 746.2
exalted 596.10; *deified* 82.20, *worshiped* 83.14, *dignified* 297.11, *promoted* 715.8, *notable* 799.11
exaltedly 596.22; *with dignity* 297.20
exam book *schoolbook* 48.15
examination *philosophical investigation* 4.4, *witness* 54.16, *dissertation* 203.1, *interview* 210.4, *observation* 242.5, *questionnaire* 333.3, *experimentation* 335.3
examinational *problematic* 333.12
examination results *authorization* 340.4
examine *philosophize* 4.19, *try a case* 54.28, *practice medicine* 107.32, *inspect* 242.22, *take note of* 323.10, *question* 333.16, *interrogate* 333.17, *experiment* 335.11, *estimate* 341.11, *be careful* 593.15
examined *questioned* 333.15
examinee *person questioned* 333.10, *candidate* 422.18
examiner *conversationalist* 210.6, *curious person* 321.3, *questioner* 333.9, *judge* 341.5
examiner of accounts *accountant* 493.6
examine the accounts *audit* 493.10
examining *questioning* 333.11
example *representative* 187.7, *ideal* 327.6, *explanation* 331.3, *interpretation* 365.1, *mode of behavior* 399.2, *punishment* 454.1, *prototype* 624.2, *part* 760.1, *precedent* 769.4, *guide* 780.4, *showpiece* 843.3
exanimate *dead* 29.11
exasperate *annoy* 276.7, *cause hate* 300.12, *irritate* 302.16, *make irritable* 304.15, *motivate* 508.9, *cause trouble* 824.21
exasperated *resentful* 302.8, *motivated* 508.8
exasperating *aggravating* 276.4, *maddening* 302.12, *inconvenient* 824.12
exasperatingly *maddeningly* 302.25
exasperation *annoyance* 276.2, *resentment* 302.1, *negative stimulus* 508.4
ex cathedra *authoritatively* 52.18
excavate 651.19; *recollect* 3.16, *engineer* 14.48, *hole* 583.17, *deepen* 598.21, *make concave* 635.7, *dig out* 711.15
excavated *holed* 583.12
excavate the past *excavate* 651.19
excavation *historicism* 3.7, *detection* 345.2, *hole* 583.4, *deepening* 598.4, *concave land* 635.2, *digging out* 711.3
excavation site *construction workplace* 124.10
excavator *construction equipment* 14.23, *laborer* 123.9, *digger* 635.4, *extractor* 711.9
exceed 712.15; *be superior* 744.15, *increase* 746.6
exceeding *superior* 744.8
exceedingly *superiorly* 744.20
exceed one's authority *be illegal* 53.30
exceed requirements *be superfluous* 99.12

445.18, *exceed* 712.15, *be superior* 744.15, *specialize* 779.16
excellence 445.4; *skill* 127.1, *worth* 447.3, *superiority* 744.1, *distinction* 777.8, *importance* 799.1, *perfect condition* 805.3
excellent 68.16, 445.13, 744.14, 805.15; *skillful* 127.10, *wondrous* 294.9, *good* 445.10, *worthy* 447.7, *notable* 799.11
excellently 445.21; *masterfully* 68.19, *worthily* 447.11, *predominantly* 744.21, *perfectly* 805.21
excelsior [L] *up* 713.25
except *exclude* 383.11, 764.7, *exempt* 434.9, *under the circumstances* 726.16, *subtract* 749.6, *by subtraction* 749.8, *leave* 750.10, *set apart* 753.17, *exclusively* 764.10, *set free* 829.17
excepted *rejected* 383.6, *exempt* 434.5, *subtracted* 749.3, *unjoined* 753.9, *excluded* 764.6, *free* 829.11
except for *exclusively* 764.10
excepting *by subtraction* 749.8, *exclusively* 764.10
exception *marvel* 294.3, *rejection* 383.1, *exemption* 434.1, *censure* 438.3, *unusualness* 664.2, *diversity* 732.1, *subtraction* 749.1, *setting apart* 753.2, *exclusion* 764.1, *special case* 779.7, *deviation* 782.6, *freedom* 829.1
exceptional 779.13; *wondrous* 294.9, *unusual* 664.4, 782.15, *diverse* 732.5, *eccentric* 782.16, *questionable* 839.5
exceptionality *unusualness* 782.4
exceptionally *wondrously* 294.18, *unusually* 664.7, *diversely* 732.14, *characteristically* 779.20, *rarely* 839.10
exception in favor of *exclusion* 764.1
exception to the rule *diversity* 732.1, *special case* 779.7
excerpt 692.13; *compile* 204.8, *chosen thing* 382.8, *choose* 382.14, *passage* 692.1
excerpted 692.9
excerpts *compendium* 204.3
excess 99.1; *employ* 57.18, *waste* 96.10, *superfluous* 99.8, *exaggeration* 194.1, *diffuseness* 199.1, *overactivity* 414.9, *overindulgence* 456.3, *violence* 520.1, *excessiveness* 712.4, *increase* 746.1, *difference* 750.3, *surplus* 750.4, 750.8, *liberality* 829.8, *unconditional* 829.14
excessed *hired* 57.17
excessing *bargaining terms* 57.10
excessive 99.5, 712.8; *exaggerated* 194.7, *extravagant* 194.9, *diffuse* 199.3, *overindulgent* 456.8, *costly* 496.7, *unrestrained* 500.5, 592.8, *violent* 520.5, *surplus* 750.8, *redundant* 802.9, *unconditional* 829.14
excessive charge *fee* 494.3, *overpricing* 496.2
excessive consumption *appetite* 92.2
excessive drinking *drinking* 121.2
excessive frankness *discourtesy* 411.1
excessive interest *interest* 488.4
excessively 99.13, 194.17, 712.17, 829.23; *self-indulgently* 456.12, *at great cost* 496.12, *extravagantly* 500.9, *residually* 750.11

excessiveness 712.4; *excess* 99.1, *exaggeration* 194.1, *extravagance* 194.3, *overindulgence* 456.3, *expansion* 592.2
excessive praise *flattery* 439.1
excessive speed *speed* 694.2
excess of freedom *liberality* 829.8
excess profits tax *tax* 494.5
exchange 665.8, 665.21, 673.1, 673.5; *question and answer* 334.3, *react* 334.20, *stock exchange* 457.3, *negotiation* 460.1, *negotiate* 460.6, *transfer of property* 470.4, *transfer property* 470.12, *trade* 480.1, 480.18, *selling* 482.1, *sell* 482.15, *market* 483.1, *bank* 484.26, *change* 665.1, 665.14, *substitution* 672.1, *substitute* 672.5, *take a substitute* 672.7, *transfer* 685.1, 685.8, *reciprocity* 729.1, *reciprocate* 729.7, *equalization* 740.4, *linkage* 752.3
exchangeable 665.13; *negotiated* 460.5, *transferring property* 470.10, *mercantile* 480.13, *in exchange* 673.3, *transferable* 685.7
exchangeably *in answer* 334.25, *in transit* 685.13
exchange blows *fight* 422.23
exchange broker *financial adviser* 457.4
exchange control *currency market* 484.8
exchanged 673.4; *substituted* 672.4, *reciprocal* 729.4
exchange for *take a substitute* 672.7, *exchange* 673.5
exchange force *fundamental interaction* 10.65
exchange ideas *discuss* 4.22
exchange letters *correspond* 169.19
exchange of blows *assault* 695.4
exchange of gases *respiration* 558.8
exchange of goods *trade* 480.1
exchange of views *consultation* 176.4, *debate* 210.3, *discussion* 460.3
exchange of vows *betrothal* 458.2
exchange opinions *debate* 319.13, *discuss* 329.12
exchange pleasantries *converse* 210.11
exchange premium *international finance* 457.2
exchange rate *economic indicator* 56.4, *economic factor* 56.8, *international finance* 457.2, *currency market* 484.8
exchange rate mechanism (ERM) *economic indicator* 56.4
exchange rate parity *currency market* 484.8
exchange shots *declare war* 422.25
exchange value *value* 494.2, *equalization* 740.4
exchange views *consult* 176.11, *confer* 210.13, *negotiate* 460.6
exchange vows *get engaged to* 458.12
exchange words *converse* 210.11
exchanging *mercantile* 480.13
exchanging favors *mutual relationship* 827.3
exchequer *storehouse* 105.8
exchequer [Brit] *treasury* 484.19
excise *practice surgery* 107.33, *payment* 433.5, *levy* 494.7, *dig out* 711.15, *take off* 749.7
exciseman *collector* 473.7
excise officer *collector* 473.7

excision *surgery* 107.15, *digging out* 711.3, *subtraction* 749.1

excitability *emotionalism* 266.6, *touchiness* 303.3, *restlessness* 414.7

excitable *passionate* 266.12, *touchy* 303.10, *fidgety* 414.14

excitably *touchily* 303.19

excitation *excited atom* 10.55, *drunken behavior* 121.4, *activity* 414.1, *stimulus* 508.3

excitation energy *excited atom* 10.55

excitation state *excited atom* 10.55

excite *be intoxicating* 121.36, *arouse sensation* 212.11, *give pleasure* 214.13, *be piquant* 221.9, *cause desire* 288.22, *motivate* 508.9, *invigorate* 518.5, *awaken* 675.9, *agitate* 684.22

excited *desirous* 20.18, *susceptible* 212.7, *pleasure-seeking* 214.10, *expecting* 356.4, *in suspense* 604.12, *restless* 684.16

excited atom 10.55

excitedly *exaggeratedly* 194.16, *in suspense* 604.21

excited state *excited atom* 10.55

excite expectations *predict* 358.14

excite hate *cause hate* 300.12

excitement *exaggeration* 194.1, *sensation* 212.1, *vigor* 518.1, *suspense* 604.6, *tumult* 684.2

excite the attention of *attract attention* 323.12

exciting 212.8; *intoxicating* 121.29, *descriptive* 202.11, *stimulating* 221.7, *invigorating* 518.3, *in suspense* 604.12

excitingly *sensationally* 212.12

exclaim *speak* 205.17, *speak in a particular way* 205.18, *cry out* 239.13

exclamation *utterance* 205.10, *cry* 239.1

exclamation point or **exclamation mark** Punctuation Marks 5

exclamatory *vociferous* 239.9

exclude 383.11, 409.12, 764.7; *discriminate* 337.12, *exempt* 434.9, *withhold approval* 438.17, *prohibit* 503.8, *debar* 604.17, *limit* 620.7, *830.13*, *ostracize* 709.17, *subtract* 749.6, *leave* 750.10, *set apart* 753.17, *not complete* 762.9, *make impossible* 837.8

excluded *604.11, 764.6; judged* 337.10, *rejected* 383.6, *exempt* 434.5, *disapproved* 438.9, *refused* 506.5, *missing* 576.11, *subtracted* 749.3, *unjoined* 753.9

excluding 764.5; *disapproving* 438.8, *excluded* 604.11, *by subtraction* 749.8, *exclusively* 764.10

exclusion 764.1; *discrimination* 337.1, *rejection* 383.1, *separation* 409.3, *exemption* 434.1, *disapproval* 438.1, *prohibition* 503.1, *debarment* 604.5, *limitation* 620.2, *dismissal* 709.2, *ostracism* 709.3, *subtraction* 749.1, *setting apart* 753.2

exclusionary *excluding* 764.5

exclusion order *exclusion* 764.1

exclusion zone 764.3

exclusive *news story* 171.3, *newsworthy* 171.8, *unsociable* 409.6, *possessing* 469.11, *possessed* 469.13, *valuable* 496.8, *prohibited* 503.5, *excluded* 604.11, *limited* 620.5, *excluding* 764.5, *restraining* 830.8

exclusive jurisdiction *jurisdiction* 54.2

exclusively 764.10; *cliquishly* 59.32, *unsocially* 409.13, *possessively* 469.16, *prohibitively* 503.11, *once* 788.23, *restrainedly* 830.18

exclusiveness 764.4

exclusive of *by subtraction* 749.8, *exclusively* 764.10

exclusive possession *monopoly* 469.4

exclusive rights *limitation* 830.2

exclusive sale *selling* 482.1

exclusivity *unsociability* 409.1, *exclusiveness* 764.4, *limitation* 830.2

exclusory *excluding* 764.5

excogitate *philosophize* 4.19, *imagine* 360.14

excogitation *philosophical investigation* 4.4

excommunicate *perform rites* 85.18, *curse* 301.13, *prohibit* 503.8, *disbar* 709.16, *eject* 764.8

excommunicated *ritualistic* 85.15, *cursed* 301.8, *prohibited* 503.5

excommunication *Christian rite* 85.5, *curse* 301.1, *prohibition* 503.1, *dismissal* 709.2, *ejection* 764.2

ex-con [Inf] *free person* 829.9

ex-convict *free person* 829.9

excoriate *condemn* 438.18, *shed* 614.21

excoriating *condemning* 438.10

excoriation *condemnation* 438.2, *peeling* 614.6

excrement 25.2; *waste product* 96.7, *dirt* 112.5, *unpleasant-smelling thing* 227.2, *body fluid* 555.3, *refuse* 802.5

excremental 25.13

excrementally 25.27

excrementary *excremental* 25.13

excrementitious or **excremental** *unclean* 112.8

excrescence *superfluity* 99.4, *convexity* 634.1

excrescent *convex* 634.5

excrescently *convexly* 634.9

excreta *excrement* 25.2

excrete 25.20; *secrete* 24.7, *leak* 707.16, *let out* 709.26

excretion 25.1; *physiology* 13.13, *body process* 19.15, *secretion* 24.1, *life function* 28.6, *uncleanness* 112.2, *outflow* 707.4, *disgorgement* 709.6

excretionary *excretory* 25.12

excretive *metabolic* 19.24, *excretory* 25.12

excretory 25.12; *physiological* 13.29, *secretory* 24.4, *leaky* 707.12

excruciate *inflict pain* 215.10

excruciatingly *painfully* 215.12

exculpable *forgivable* 312.7

exculpate *acquit* 54.32, 434.10, *absolve* 312.10, *vindicate* 441.11, *declare innocent* 449.11

exculpated *acquitted* 54.25, *forgiven* 312.5, *declared innocent* 449.8

exculpating *vindicatory* 441.7

exculpation *favorable verdict* 54.19, *absolution* 312.2, *vindication* 441.1, *legal innocence* 449.3

exculpatory *vindicatory* 441.7

excursion *circumlocution* 199.2, *cheap* 497.9, *circuitousness* 681.2, *travel* 686.5, *deviation* 698.1, *crossing* 712.2

excursion fare or **rate** *bargain* 497.4

excursive *circumlocutory* 199.4

excursus *circumlocution* 199.2, *wandering* 698.4

excusable *forgivable* 312.7, *in the right* 429.11, *vindicable* 441.9

excusably *forgivingly* 312.14

excusatory *vindicatory* 441.7

excuse *forgiveness* 312.1, *forgive* 312.8, *apology* 313.2, *explanation* 319.4, *premise* 319.14, *plea* 329.5, *acquittal* 434.2, *acquit* 434.10, *defense* 441.2, *vindicate* 441.11, *motivation* 508.1, *reason* 675.4, *exclude* 764.7, *deliverance* 817.1, *deliver* 817.5, *stratagem* 822.2, *set free* 829.17

excused *forgiven* 312.5, *causal* 319.9, *acquitted* 434.6, *excluded* 764.6

excuse oneself *exempt oneself* 434.12

excuser *vindicator* 441.5

excusing *defending* 419.17, *vindicatory* 441.7

exec [Inf] *military leader* 68.10

execrable *hateful* 300.10

execrably *hatefully* 300.14, *disgracefully* 371.8

execrate *detest* 291.13, *hate* 300.11, *curse* 301.13, *berate* 438.20

execrated *hated* 300.9, *cursed* 301.8

execration *hate* 300.1, *hated thing* 300.5, *curse* 301.1, *berating* 438.5

execrative *hating* 300.7, *cursing* 301.7

execratively 301.17; *with hate* 300.13

execratory *cursing* 301.7, *critical* 438.13

executant *artistic worker* 123.12, *doer* 412.3

execute 30.22, 454.30; *follow up* 385.16, *take charge of* 391.8, *behave toward* 399.20, *act* 412.11, *suppress* 424.9, *perform* 465.5, *take action* 509.12, *complete* 761.9, *perfect* 805.19

execute a contract *contract* 459.8

execute or **carry out a sentence** *penalize* 454.26

execute a will *will* 472.11

executed *undertaken* 391.4, *suppressed* 424.6, *punished* 454.19

execute justice *penalize* 454.26

execution 30.6; *way of dying* 29.5, *killing* 30.1, *manual skill* 127.2, *gymnastics* 157.1, *action* 412.1, *suppression* 424.2, *capital punishment* 454.12, *ratification* 459.4, *performance* 465.2, *operation* 509.1, *production* 522.1

executioner 30.13; *killer* 30.11, *punisher* 454.16, *violent animal* 520.4, *destroyer* 523.6

execution of judgment *verdict* 341.2

execution of justice *penalty* 454.5

execution of sentence *penalty* 454.5

executive *governor* 49.23, *governmental* 49.24, *person in authority* 52.7, *company leader* 68.8, *masterful* 68.15, *professional worker* 123.11, *manager* 126.7, *managerial* 126.9, *operator* 412.7, 509.5, *effective* 412.10

executive branch *United States government* 49.21

executive director *filmmaker* 137.14

executively *masterfully* 68.19

executive office *office* 124.2

executive officer *person in authority* 52.7, *military leader* 68.10

executive producer *filmmaker* 137.14

executives *management board* 126.2

executive session *secret* 182.2

executor *agent* 123.15, *manager* 126.7, *operator* 412.7, *commissioner* 833.5

executorship *council* 833.4

executrix *agent* 123.15

exegesis *dissertation* 203.1, *explanation* 331.3, *interpretation* 365.1

exegete *dissertator* 203.3, *interpreter* 365.6

exegete or **exegetist** *demonstrator* 331.6

exegetic *explanatory* 331.11

exegetic or **exegetical** *interpretive* 365.8

exegetical *dissertational* 203.4

exegetically *linguistically* 5.44, *discursively* 203.6, *demonstrably* 331.22, *in other words* 365.18

exegetics *science of interpretation* 365.5

exegetist *interpreter* 365.6

exemplar *representative* 187.7, *ideal* 327.6

exemplary *representational* 187.8, *ideal* 327.12, *interpretive* 365.8, *worthy* 447.7, *prototypical* 624.7, *blameless* 805.12, *warning* 814.6

exemplification *explanation* 331.3, *interpretation* 365.1

exemplificatory *explanatory* 331.11

exemplified *explanatory* 331.11

exemplify *rationalize* 4.20, *stand for* 187.14, *epitomize* 327.18, *explain* 331.16, *interpret* 365.12

exemplifying *explanatory* 331.11

exempt 434.5, 434.9; *acquitted* 54.25, *acquit* 54.32, *forgive* 312.8, *exclude* 383.11, 764.7, *permit* 502.6, 735.29, *permitting* 735.19, *unjoined* 753.9, *excluded* 764.6, *escaping* 816.7, *deliver* 817.5, *free* 829.11, *set free* 829.17, *liberate* 831.6

exempted *acquitted* 54.25, *forgiven* 312.5, *rejected* 383.6, *exempt* 434.5, *permitting* 735.19, *excluded* 764.6, *liberated* 831.4

exemptibility *liberation* 831.1

exemptible *vindicable* 441.9, *liberated* 831.4

exemption 434.1; *favorable verdict* 54.19, *forgiveness* 312.1, *rejection* 383.1, *tax system* 494.6, *tolerance* 502.2, *permission* 735.9, *setting apart* 753.2, *exclusion* 764.1, *special case* 779.7, *escape* 816.1, *deliverance* 817.1, *freedom* 829.1, *liberation* 831.1

exemptive *excluding* 764.5

exempt oneself 434.12

exequies *funeral* 31.4

exercise 157.12; *health improvement* 113.3, *be healthy* 113.11, *task* 122.2, *training* 122.5, *train* 122.12, *briefing* 388.4, *brief* 388.20, *prepare oneself* 388.21, *venture* 390.2, *undertaking* 391.1, *use* 393.1, *393.9, deed* 412.2, *occupy oneself* 412.15, *operation* 509.1, *bodily* movement 677.11, bodily improvement 807.10, engagement 833.2

exercise a pull *attract* 700.11

exercise authority *be powerful* 514.18

exercise book *schoolbook* 48.15

exercised *used* 393.5

exercised in arms *military* 76.28

exercise discretion *be skillful* 127.14

exercise influence *influence* 512.11

exercise judgment *judge* 53.32

exercise one's discretion *select* 382.12

exercise one's intellect *think* 317.9

exercise one's rights or **prerogative** *have rights* 429.13

exercise power *have authority* 52.13, *be powerful* 514.18

exerciser *gymnast* 157.10

exercise self-control *be self-restrained* 455.10

exercising *keeping fit* 113.10, Hobbies and Pastimes 167

exert authority *be severe* 424.8

exert energy *be powerful* 514.18

exert influence *influence* 512.11, *be powerful* 514.18

exertion 122.4; *commitment* 377.2, *action* 412.1, *contest* 422.4, *vigor* 514.2, 518.1, *fatigue* 820.1

exert oneself 122.11; *try hard* 390.7, *try* 414.21, *be full of vigor* 518.4

exert pressure *manipulate* 508.12

exert sovereignty 566.12

exert weight *be heavy* 538.12

exfiltrate *leak* 707.16

exfiltration *exit* 707.1

exfoliate *scale* 588.10, *shed* 614.21

exfoliated *shed* 614.14

exfoliation *weathering* 8.40, *layering* 588.5, *peeling* 614.6

exfoliatory or **exfoliative** *peeling* 614.13

ex gratia payment *giveaway* 472.5, *pay* 489.6

exhalation 556.2; *life function* 28.6, *odor* 224.1, *stench* 227.1, *murk* 248.2, *vaporization* 556.9, *respiration* 558.8

exhale *have odor* 224.8, *give off* 556.25, *respire* 558.21, *leak* 707.16, *let out* 709.26

exhaling *respiratory* 558.19

exhaust *expend* 96.16, *use up* 393.12, *consume* 491.12, *waste* 500.7, *remove power from* 515.13, *weaken* 517.13, *make sparse* 541.5, *cause to cease* 668.12, *outflow* 707.4, *void* 709.23, *let out* 709.26, *make useless* 802.12, *wear out* 808.21, *fatigue* 820.6

exhausted *consumed* 96.11, *unhealthy* 114.23, *unemphatic* 201.2, *used* 393.5, 491.10, *disabled* 515.10, *weakened* 517.9, *diminishing* 597.16, *over* 651.12, *spoiled* 808.9, *worn* 808.13, *fatigued* 820.2

exhaust fumes *pollution* 117.8, *unpleasant-smelling thing* 227.2

exhausting *laborious* 122.7, *punishing* 454.20, *fatiguing* 820.4, *difficult* 824.9

exhaustingly *tiringly* 820.8

exhausting work *work* 122.1

exhaustion *lack of emphasis* 201.1, *use* 393.1, *lessening* 468.6, *disability* 515.4, *poor health* 517.3, *diminishment* 597.7, *removal*

709.5, *decrease* 747.1, *moral deterioration* 808.3, *fatigue* 820.1

exhaustion of supplies *economic deterioration* 808.2

exhaustive *broad* 592.5, *intense* 598.16, *complete* 761.6

exhaustively *broadly* 592.15, *intensely* 598.28

exhaustiveness *breadth* 592.1, *deepness* 598.6

exhaust the possibilities of *exploit* 393.11

exhibit *propound a philosophy* 4.21, *repository* 105.13, *identify* 184.11, *make visible* 242.25, 244.9, *present* 264.15, *demonstrate* 331.15, *legal evidence* 339.4, *show* 404.24, *uncover* 614.17, *showpiece* 843.3, *display* 843.13

exhibited *demonstrated* 331.9, *displayed* 843.8

exhibition *compilation* 59.14, *repository* 105.13, *theatrical performance* 136.13, *public relations (PR)* 173.8, *view* 242.8, *manifestation* 244.3, *visibility* 264.4, *demonstration* 331.1, *affectation* 367.1, *show* 404.12, *fair* 483.2, *display* 843.1

exhibitional *demonstrated* 331.9

exhibition center *showplace* 843.4

exhibition game *football* 155.1, *prize competition* 422.5

exhibition hall *showplace* 843.4

exhibitionism 404.9; *sexual disorder* 108.14, *demonstrativeness* 331.2, *boastfulness* 402.6, *nudism* 614.4

exhibitionist *demonstrator* 331.6, *demonstrative* 331.10, *pretender* 367.2, *vain person* 402.7, *show-off* 404.13, *nude person* 614.5, *displayer* 843.7

exhibitionistic *demonstrative* 331.10, *boastful* 402.13, *flashy* 404.17

exhibitor *displayer* 843.7

exhibit penalty behavior 155.21

exhilarate *refresh* 94.6, *be intoxicating* 121.36, *inspire* 327.15, *invigorate* 518.5

exhilarated *refreshed* 94.5, *joyful* 269.6

exhilarating *refreshing* 94.4, *intoxicating* 121.29, *invigorating* 518.3

exhilaratingly *refreshingly* 94.9

exhilaration *refreshment* 94.1, *drunken behavior* 121.4, *joy* 269.1, *vigor* 518.1

exhort *advise* 176.9, *persuade* 178.15, *give courage* 284.16, *motivate* 508.9

exhortation 178.2; *recommendation* 176.2, *public speaking* 205.11, *salutation* 209.2, *encouragement* 284.6

exhortative *advisory* 176.7

exhortatively *oratorically* 209.14

exhorted *motivated* 508.8

exhorting *advisory* 176.7, *persuasive* 178.12, *salutatory* 209.7

exhortingly *oratorically* 209.14

exhumation *historicism* 3.7, *digging out* 711.3

exhume *recollect* 3.16, *excavate* 651.19, *dig out* 711.15

ex-husband *single man* 32.5

ex hypothesi *theoretically* 4.24

exigency *necessity* 95.1, *immediacy* 645.1, *predicament* 725.3, *critical situation* 824.6

exigent *necessary* 95.10, *allowing no delay* 645.7, *difficult* 726.11

exigently *away* 711.20, *difficultly* 726.20

exiguity *littleness* 580.1, *meagerness* 593.6, *fewness* 796.3

exiguous *little* 580.7, *meager* 593.12, *sparse* 796.6

exiguously *meagerly* 593.19, *sparsely* 796.11

exile 454.3, 454.24; *separation* 409.3, *exclude* 409.12, *displaced person* 574.7, *replace* 574.17, *emigration* 707.6, *outgoer* 707.9, *emigrate* 707.17, *ostracism* 709.3, *ostracize* 709.17, *new arrival* 724.6, *ejection* 764.2, *eject* 764.8

exiled *lonely* 409.8, *replaced* 574.10, *excluded* 764.6

exist 717.18; *live* 28.17, *be dormant* 41.22, *be material* 524.8, *be present* 575.13, 647.7, *be real* 719.10, 721.21

existence 717.1; *life* 28.1, *visibility* 264.4, *material world* 524.1, *presence* 575.1, *reality* 721.2

existence of God *philosophical problem* 4.8

existence/relatedness/growth (ERG) theory *management system* 126.3

existent *present* 575.7, 647.4, *existing* 717.11, *real* 721.12

existentialism Philosophical Schools of Thought 4, Western Literary Groups 139, *philosophy of being* 717.2

existentialist Philosophical Schools of Thought 4

existentially *really* 717.22

existential psychology Psychological Theories, Schools 108

existential quantifier *mathematical logic* 6.60

existential theology Theologies 81

existing 717.11; *life* 28.1, *alive* 28.13, *present* 575.7, 647.4, *real* 719.6, 721.12

existing conditions *circumstances* 726.1

existing together *same time* 649.1

exist outside *be external* 724.15

exist simultaneously *be simultaneous* 649.6

exist together *be simultaneous* 649.6

exit 707.1, 707.13; *death* 29.1, *acting* 136.22, *act* 136.34, *conceal oneself* 181.15, *disappearance* 265.1, *absent oneself* 576.15, *backward motion* 677.5, *departure* 705.1, *withdraw* 705.9, *way out* 707.2, *cessation* 773.2, *means of escape* 816.4

exit lane *road attribute* 687.3

ex libris *means of identification* 184.3

Exmoor Horn Breeds of Sheep 16

Exmoor pony Horse and Pony Breeds 159

exobiology *astronomy* 7.1, *space biology* 13.8

exocarp *fruit structure* 44.3

exocrine *of a secretion* 24.5

exocrine gland *secretory mechanism* 24.3

exodontic *dental* 107.31

exodontics *dentistry* 107.6

exodontist *dentist* 107.21

exodus *play part* 136.8, *departure* 705.1, *exit* 707.1

ex officio *managerially* 126.13

exogamy *type of marriage* 64.3

exon *genetic material* 13.20

exonerate *acquit* 54.32, 434.10, *absolve* 312.10, *vindicate* 441.11, *declare innocent* 449.11

exonerated *acquitted* 54.25, 434.6, *forgiven* 312.5, *declared innocent* 449.8

exonerating *vindicatory* 441.7

exoneration *favorable verdict* 54.19, *absolution* 312.2, *acquittal* 434.2, *vindication* 441.1, *legal innocence* 449.3

exonerative *vindicatory* 441.7

exorbitance *excess* 99.1, *exaggeration* 194.1, *overpricing* 496.2

exorbitant *excessive* 99.5, 712.8, *exaggerated* 194.7, *extravagant* 194.9, *costly* 496.7, 500.6

exorbitantly *excessively* 99.13, 194.17, *at great cost* 496.12

exorbitant price *overpricing* 496.2

exorbitation *deviation* 698.1

exorcise *perform rites* 85.18, *exterminate* 709.22

exorcised *ritualistic* 85.15

exorciser *occultist* 86.13

exorcism *Christian rite* 85.5

exorcist *occultist* 86.13

exordium *introduction* 771.10

exoskeletal *covering* 610.8

exoskeleton *skeleton* 551.14, *exteriority* 610.2, *animal covering* 613.15

exosphere *atmosphere* 9.8, *atmospheric layer* 558.3, *top of the world* 600.2

exospheric *atmospheric* 558.13

exoteric *simple* 363.6

exotic *ornamental* 17.17, *plant* 41.2, *wild* 41.15, *astonishing* 294.10, *distant* 585.5, *foreign* 724.9, *exceptional* 779.13, *eccentric* 782.16

exotically *horticulturally* 17.20, *herbaceously* 41.24, *astonishingly* 294.19, *strangely* 724.17

exotic dancer *entertainer* 138.8, *pornography* 432.7, *nude person* 614.5

exoticness *foreignness* 724.2

exotic shorthair Breeds of Cats 35

exoticness *foreignness* 724.2

exotropia *faulty vision* 243.1

expand *manipulate* 6.87, *have authority* 52.13, *enlarge* 194.12, 581.14, *be diffuse* 199.5, *increase* 467.17, 746.6, *be elastic* 546.7, *extend* 563.14, *lengthen* 590.12, *broaden* 592.11, 778.15, *grow* 676.10, *change by degrees* 739.8, *make bigger* 746.7, *augment* 748.13

expandable *enlargeable* 581.13

expanded *enlarged* 194.8, *diffuse* 199.3, *bigger* 581.9, *broadened* 592.7, *increased* 746.5

expanded polystyrene *polymer* 11.9

expander *enlarger* 581.8

expanding *armor-piercing* 78.18, *growing* 581.12, 676.6, *increasing* 746.4

expanding bullet *ammunition* 78.11

expanding economy *prosperity* 847.1

expanding the mind *learning* 48.7

expanding universe *universe* 7.3

expanse *geographical space* 563.3, *size* 579.1, *length* 590.1, *breadth* 592.1

expansibility *enlargeability* 581.6

expansible *enlargeable* 581.13

expansile *enlargeable* 581.13
expansion 581.1, 592.2;
evaluation 6.22, *heating effect*
10.28, *enlargement* 194.2,
diffuseness 199.1, *augmentation*
467.2, *space* 563.1, *expansion*
581.1, *Fields of Measurement*
589, *lengthening* 590.4, *growth*
676.3, *increase* 746.1
expansionary *enlargeable* 581.13
expansion coefficient *heating*
effect 10.28
expansionism 712.5; *bellicosity*
76.15, *right of entry* 706.4
expansionist *militarist* 77.3
expansive *effusive* 207.6,
demonstrative 331.10, *acquisitive*
467.13, *spacious* 563.13, *huge*
579.14, *enlargeable* 581.13,
lengthy 590.9, *broad* 592.5,
including 763.3
expansively *effusively* 207.10,
demonstratively 331.21, *gainfully*
467.24, *spaciously* 563.17, *largely*
581.18, *at length* 590.15, *broadly*
592.15
expansiveness *demonstrativeness*
331.2, *spaciousness* 563.4,
largeness 579.2, *longness* 590.3,
breadth 592.1
expatiate *be diffuse* 199.5, *be*
talkative 207.7
expatiation *diffuseness* 199.1
expatriate *quit* 705.10, *outgoer*
707.9, *emigrate* 707.17, *ostracize*
709.17, *new arrival* 724.6, *eject*
764.8
expatriation *emigration* 707.6,
ostracism 709.3, *ejection* 764.2
expect 281.12, 356.6, 650.12; *be*
entitled to 72.13, *not wonder about*
295.5, *foresee* 357.9, *intend* 374.8,
plan ahead 387.13, *be prepared*
388.17, *impose a duty* 433.14,
prepare 657.14, *think likely*
838.10
expectancy *expectation* 281.2,
looking to the future 650.4
expectancy *or* **expectance**
expectation 356.1
expectant 281.7; *pregnant* 21.12,
expecting 356.4, *foreseeing* 357.5
expectantly 281.16, 356.10;
foresightedly 357.10
expectant theory *management*
system 126.3
expectation 281.2, 356.1; *title*
72.1, *believing* 87.2, *prediction*
357.3, 358.1, *looking to the future*
650.4, *antecedence* 657.5,
probability 838.1
expectations 356.2; *expectation*
281.2
expectative *premature* 657.10
expected 356.5; *predictable* 295.4,
meant 359.7, *foreseen* 650.8,
imminent 657.9, *probable* 838.6
expectedly 356.11; *predictably*
295.9, *probably* 838.11
expectedness *lack of wonder* 295.1
expected thing 356.3
expected value *parameter* 6.57
expecting 356.4; *pregnant* 21.12,
expectant 281.7, *imminent* 657.9
expecting a baby *pregnant* 21.12
expecting a blessed event
pregnant 21.12
expect it of *impose a duty* 433.14
expect more *or* **better** *be*
disappointed 293.8
expectorant *salivating* 25.18,
purgative 115.7
expectorate *excrete* 25.20, *salivate*
25.25

expectoration *excretion* 25.1,
saliva 25.9
expect the worst *expect* 356.6
expedience *convenience* 803.3
expediency *desirability* 288.7,
usefulness 801.1, *convenience* 803.1
expedient 288.12, 387.5; *means*
102.1, *advisable* 176.8, *artifice*
193.5, *instrument* 511.2,
substitution 672.1, *practical* 719.8,
useful 801.5, *convenient* 803.3,
stratagem 822.2, *beneficial* 825.20
expediential *convenient* 803.3
expediently 288.25; *advisably*
176.13, *conveniently* 803.6
expedient plan *expedient* 387.5
expedite *be an instrument* 511.7,
start early 657.12, *convey* 685.9, *be*
swift 694.10, *hasten* 818.4, *make*
easy 823.15, *further* 825.30
expedite one's end *be convenient*
803.5
expediting *easing* 823.7,
furtherance 825.8
expedition *offensive warfare* 76.11,
alacrity 414.3, *earliness* 657.1,
travel 686.5, *swiftness* 694.1, *haste*
818.1
expeditionary force *armed force*
77.10
expeditious *active* 414.13, *early*
657.8, *swift* 694.6, *hasty* 818.3
expeditiously *early* 657.17, *swiftly*
694.16
expeditiousness *swiftness* 694.1,
haste 818.1
expel 709.14; *excrete* 25.20, *cause to*
disappear 265.7, *discard* 383.12,
exclude 409.12, *exile* 454.24,
replace 574.17, *take away* 685.12,
impel 695.9, *eject* 701.8, 764.8,
emigrate 707.17, *disbar* 709.16,
displace 711.14, *subtract* 749.6,
separate 753.12
expelled *discarded* 383.8, *lonely*
409.8, *replaced* 574.10, *subtracted*
749.3, *separate* 753.7, *excluded*
764.6
expellee *outgoer* 707.9
expellent *expulsive* 709.11
expeller *ejector* 709.10
expend 96.16, 491.11; *use up*
393.12, *shop* 481.15, *pay* 489.16
expendability *unimportance*
800.1, *redundancy* 802.2
expendable *unimportant* 800.10,
redundant 802.9
expended 491.9; *outflowing*
707.11
expender *payer* 489.9
expending 491.8; *paying* 489.10
expenditure 491.1; *shopping*
481.3, *payment* 489.1, *cost(s)*
491.3, *export* 707.7
expense 491.2
expense account *reward for service*
453.5, *profit* 467.6, *reward* 472.4,
expense 491.2, *accounts* 493.4
expenses *expense* 491.2, *cost(s)*
491.3
expensive *overestimated* 343.5,
grand 404.22, *opulent* 485.10,
costly 496.7, 500.6
expensively 481.20; *grandly*
404.37, *at great cost* 496.12
expensiveness *costliness* 496.1
experience *maturity* 27.3, *skill*
127.1, *sensation* 212.1, *sense*
212.9, *taste* 219.5, *feelings* 266.1,
feel 266.14, *authorization* 340.4,
learning 348.3, *get to know*
348.12, *wisdom* 352.1
experienced *adult* 27.11, *educated*
48.19, *excellent* 68.16, *expert*

127.12, *qualified* 340.7,
knowledgeable 348.7, *cunning*
822.4
experienced hand *expert* 127.9
experience psychic phenomena
86.23
experiences *biography* 3.5
experiential *theoretic(al)* 6.66
experiment 10.72, 335.1, 335.11;
invention 345.4, *venture* 390.2, *test*
390.9
experimental 335.8; *theoretical*
10.71, *clumsy* 128.6, *skeptical*
333.14, *original* 335.9, *discovering*
345.8, *tentative* 390.5, *uncustomary* 398.4, *uncertified*
841.13
experimentalism *experimentation*
335.3
experimentalist *experimenter*
335.5
experimentalize *experiment*
335.11
experimentally 335.14;
questioningly 333.21, *inventively*
335.15, *originally* 345.16,
ambitiously 390.10, *unusually*
398.9
experimental method *way*
399.10
experimental psychology
Psychological Theories, Schools
108
experimental scientist *theorist*
359.4
experimental subject 335.7
experimental taxonomy
taxonomy 13.24
experimental theater *drama*
136.1
experimentation 335.3;
originality 335.4
experimented upon *tested* 335.10
experimentee *experimental subject*
335.7
experimenter 335.5; *demonstrator*
331.6, *questioner* 333.9, *theorist*
359.4, *attempter* 390.3
experimenting *experimental* 335.8
experiment on *kill animals* 30.25
expert 52.8, 52.12, 68.13, 127.9,
127.12, 805.16; *sage* 4.11,
educator 48.4, *educational* 48.17,
excellent 68.16, *skilled person*
127.7, *skillful* 127.10, *shooter*
160.10, *ski* 162.27, *adviser* 176.5,
qualified 340.7, *judge* 341.5,
knowledgeable person 348.5,
knowledgeable 348.7, *proficient*
445.15, *paragon* 744.6, *specialist*
779.9, *specialized* 779.11, *important person* 799.5,
perfectionist 805.7
expertise 805.4; *learnedness* 48.8,
skill 127.1, *authorization* 340.4,
information 348.2, *proficiency*
445.5, *special skill* 779.2
expertly 52.21; *wisely* 4.28,
educationally 48.25, *masterfully*
68.19, *skillfully* 127.16,
proficiently 445.22
expertly made *well-made* 127.13
expertness *skill* 127.1
expert run *ski run* 162.2
expert system *artificial intelligence*
(AI) 15.21
expert witness *witness* 54.16
expiate *recompense* 273.11, *atone*
313.7, *offer reparation* 504.15,
compensate 743.7
expiated *compensated* 743.3
expiating *compensatory* 743.5
expiation *remedy* 115.1, *reparation*
273.2, *atonement* 313.1, *offering*

504.5, *substitution* 672.1,
compensation 743.1
expiational *atoning* 313.5
expiator *atoner* 313.4
expiatory *atoning* 313.5, *sacrificial*
504.10, *compensatory* 743.5
expiatory offering *penitence*
313.3
expiration *exhalation* 556.2,
respiration 558.8, *completion*
761.2, *cessation* 773.2
expiration [Arch] *death* 29.1
expire *die* 29.17, 773.21, *disappear*
265.5, *respire* 558.21, *pass*
651.17, *exit* 707.13, *let out*
709.26, *cease to exist* 718.13
expiring *dying* 29.12
expiry *death* 29.1, *cessation* 773.2
explain 331.16; *rationalize* 4.20,
name 202.17, *dissertate* 203.5,
premise 319.14, *plead* 329.14,
solve 334.21, *make comprehensible*
363.8, *interpret* 365.12, *moralize*
431.14, *justify* 441.12, *make easy*
823.15, *display* 843.13, *reveal*
843.14
explainable *vindicable* 441.9
explained *apologetic* 329.10,
explanatory 331.11, *solved* 334.15,
simple 363.6, *interpreted* 365.9
explainer *demonstrator* 331.6,
interpreter 365.6
explaining *interpretive* 365.8
explain wrongly *misrepresent*
366.5
explanation 319.4, 331.3;
philosophy 4.1, *disclosure* 180.1,
description 202.1, *dissertation*
203.1, *apology* 313.2, *plea* 329.5,
solution 334.6, 376.6, *supposition*
359.1, *type of meaning* 361.4,
clarity 363.2, *interpretation* 365.1,
defense 441.2, *reason* 675.4
explanatorily *discursively* 203.6
explanatory 331.11; *revelatory*
180.7, *signifying* 183.11,
descriptive 202.11, *causal* 319.9,
solved 334.15, *intelligible* 363.5,
interpretive 365.8, *annotative*
365.10, *vindicatory* 441.7
explanatory remark *annotation*
365.2
expletive *vulgarism* 5.20,
superfluity 99.4, *diffuseness* 199.1,
curse word 301.4, *grossness* 535.3
explicability *intelligibility* 363.1
explicable *apologetic* 329.10,
intelligible 363.5
explicably *apologetically* 329.18
explicate *rationalize* 4.20, *clarify*
196.3, *make comprehensible* 363.8,
interpret 365.12
explication *interpretation* 365.1,
solution 376.6
explicative *interpretive* 365.8
explicator *demonstrator* 331.6
explicatory *revelatory* 180.7,
descriptive 202.11, *explanatory*
331.11, *intelligible* 363.5,
interpretive 365.8
explicit *given* 6.74, *informative*
170.10, *assertive* 189.20, *clear*
196.2, *demonstrated* 331.9,
meaningful 361.6, *simple* 363.6,
open 583.13, *plain* 592.10
explicitly *assertively* 189.35, *clearly*
196.4, *meaningfully* 361.16,
intelligibly 363.13, *candidly*
583.23, *plainly* 592.18, *revealingly*
614.22
explicitness *assertiveness* 189.8,
clarity 196.1, 363.2,
comprehensibility 361.3, *openness*
583.7, *plainness* 592.4

explode *fuel* 106.16, *burst* 232.9, *bang* 234.6, *cry out* 239.13, *feel deeply* 266.16, *become angry* 302.20, *refute* 332.7, *renounce* 383.13, *be active* 414.18, *be violent* 520.8, *demolish* 523.12, *open* 583.15, *shoot* 696.18, *disintegrate* 758.6, *diverge* 776.16

exploded *disbelieved* 88.7, *renounced* 383.9

exploding *banging* 234.4, *refuting* 332.6, *renunciation* 383.4

exploit 393.11; *workmanlike job* 127.6, *be skillful* 127.14, *courageous act* 284.7, *cause of wonder* 294.4, *discriminate against* 337.14, *ill-use* 395.7, *deed* 412.2, *direct* 412.16, *suppress* 424.9, *wrong* 430.19, *be good at* 445.18, *produce* 522.13, *take the opportunity* 659.7, *important matter* 799.2, *promote* 807.18, *subject* 832.10

exploitable *usable* 393.6

exploitation *social skill* 127.3, *ill-use* 395.2, *suppression* 424.2

exploitative *abusive* 395.5, *severe* 424.5

exploitatively *offensively* 395.9

exploited *judged* 337.10, *used* 393.5, *ill-used* 395.4, *suppressed* 424.6

exploited, the *victim of discrimination* 337.8

exploiter *user* 393.4

exploration *experimentation* 335.3, *invention* 345.4, *preparation* 769.3

exploratory *questioning* 333.11, *experimental* 335.8, *discovering* 345.8, *preparatory* 769.11

explore *philosophize* 4.19, *experiment* 335.11, *invent* 345.14, *forerun* 769.16, *pioneer* 771.29

explored *known* 348.9

explorer *curious person* 321.3, *discoverer* 345.7, *precursor* 769.7

explosion *burst of sound* 232.4, *bang* 234.1, *burst of anger* 302.6, *violence by person* 520.2, *havoc* 523.5, *disintegration* 758.1

explosive 78.13, 520.6; *armor-piercing* 78.18, *combustible* 106.12, *banger* 234.3, *banging* 234.4, *angry* 302.11, *agent of destruction* 523.7, *projectile* 696.13, *outgoing* 707.10, *ejector* 709.10, *expulsive* 709.11, *dangerous* 811.7

explosive ammunition *ammunition* 78.11

explosive device *bomb* 78.15, *propellant* 696.9

explosively 234.8; *powerfully* 106.19, *angrily* 302.24, *violently* 520.11, *forth* 707.19, *expulsively* 709.29, *destructively* 758.9

explosives *industrial chemistry* 11.21

explosive shot *historical ammunition* 78.12

expo *demonstration* 331.1, *display* 843.1

exponent *multiplication* 6.15, *representative* 187.7, *dissertator* 203.3, *demonstrator* 331.6, *interpreter* 365.6, *power* 783.6

exponential *functional* 6.73, *fractional* 783.8

exponential distribution *probability distribution* 6.56

exponential function *mathematical function* 6.27

exponentially *mathematically* 6.93, 784.15

exponential series *sequence* 6.18

exponentiation *multiplication* 6.15

export 707.7; *international trade* 56.7, *economic* 56.10, *trade* 56.12, *trade in* 457.8, *conveyance* 685.2, *convey* 685.9, *transport* 686.10, *emigrate* 707.17

export and import *commercial trade* 480.2, *trade* 480.18

exportation *conveyance* 685.2, *export* 707.7

exporter *trader* 480.11, *merchant* 482.10, *transferrer* 685.4, *transporter* 686.4

exporting *export* 707.7

exporting and importing *commercial trade* 480.2

expose *compose a photograph* 132.27, *publish* 173.15, *disclose* 180.8, *make visible* 242.25, 244.9, *present* 264.15, *demonstrate* 331.15, *refute* 332.7, *detect* 345.12, *weaken* 517.13, *aerate* 558.20, *open* 583.15, *uncover* 614.17, *display* 843.13, *reveal* 843.14

exposé *divulgence* 180.2, *brief description* 202.2

exposed 132.25; *mountaineering* 161.9, *published* 173.12, *disclosed* 180.5, *visible* 244.5, *clear* 244.6, *appearing* 264.9, *demonstrated* 331.9, *discovered* 345.9, *unprepared* 389.5, *helpless* 515.9, *airy* 558.12, *open* 583.10, *uncovered* 614.10, *vulnerable* 811.9, *manifest* 843.9

exposed flank *vulnerability* 811.6

exposed part *vulnerability* 811.6

exposed to view *clear* 244.6

expose oneself *present* 264.15, *undress* 614.18, *face danger* 811.12

exposer *discloser* 180.4, *nude person* 614.5

expose the trick *be cunning* 822.5

expose to danger *endanger* 811.13

expose to sunlight *bake* 560.19

expose to view *display* 843.13

exposing *uncovering* 614.1

exposing oneself *sexual offense* 432.6

exposition *dissertation* 203.1, *manifestation* 244.3, *demonstration* 331.1, *explanation* 331.3, *interpretation* 365.1, *fair* 483.2, *display* 843.1

expositional *demonstrated* 331.9

expositive *descriptive* 202.11, *interpretive* 365.8

expositively *discursively* 203.6

expositor *dissertator* 203.3, *public speaker* 209.5, *demonstrator* 331.6

expositorily *discursively* 203.6

expository *revelatory* 180.7, *descriptive* 202.11, *dissertational* 203.4, *demonstrated* 331.9, *interpretive* 365.8

expository prose *prose* 139.7

expository scene *play part* 136.8

expository writer *author* 139.13

ex post facto *before now* 651.21

expostulate *dissuade* 179.7, *protest* 507.7, *object* 828.18

expostulatingly *dissuasively* 179.12

expostulation *dissuasion* 179.1, *protest* 507.1, *warning* 814.1, *objection* 828.2

expostulatory *dissuasive* 179.4

exposure 132.15; *publicity* 173.7, *disclosure* 180.1, *clarity* 244.2, *manifestation* 244.3, 843.2, *first appearance* 264.3, *detection* 345.2,

open air 558.5, *bareness* 614.3, *vulnerability* 811.6

exposure equipment 132.12

exposure meter *photoelectricity* 10.32

exposure scene *play part* 136.8

expound *rationalize* 4.20, *propound a philosophy* 4.21, *dissertate* 203.5, *explain* 331.16, *interpret* 365.12

expounded *explanatory* 331.11

expounder *dissertator* 203.3, *public speaker* 209.5, *demonstrator* 331.6, *interpreter* 365.6

expounding *explanation* 331.3

express *use language* 5.42, *write* 139.21, *speak* 205.17, *demonstrated* 331.9, *explain* 331.16, *meaningful* 361.6, *mean* 361.13, *style* 537.8, *form* 624.9, *mail* 685.10, *transportable* 686.7, *train* 688.4, *rail* 688.8, *swift* 694.6, *displace* 711.14, *special* 779.10, *reveal* 843.14

expressage *conveyance* 685.2

express disapprobation *disapprove* 438.16

express disapproval *disapprove* 438.16, *object* 828.18

express doubts *not accept* 190.19, *dissent* 506.9

expressed *styled* 537.6

expressed desire *request* 505.1

express gratitude *be grateful* 310.6

expressible *displayed* 843.8

expressing *obtaining of an extract* 711.7

express in words *style* 537.8

expression *algebraic expression* 6.23, *utterance* 205.10, *external appearance* 264.5, *meaning* 361.1, *forming* 624.4, *nature* 624.5, *displacement* 711.2, *manifestation* 843.2

expressionism *Western Art Styles* 133, *theater movements* 136.9, *Western Literary Groups* 139

expressionless *unintelligible* 364.4

expressionlessly *unintelligibly* 364.16

expression of dissatisfaction 274.2

expression of ideas *mode of expression* 537.3

expression of regret *apology* 313.2

expressive *descriptive* 139.17, 202.11, *symbolic* 183.12, 361.8, *fluid* 527.5, *formed* 624.6

expressively *descriptively* 139.24, *indicatively* 183.21, *demonstratively* 331.21, *intelligibly* 363.13, *elegantly* 527.7, *formatively* 624.10

expressiveness *elegance* 527.1

expressly *specially* 779.19

express mail *postal service* 169.5

expressman *messenger* 685.5

express messenger *speeder* 694.5

express pain 215.11

express pithily *be concise* 198.5

express regret *apologize* 313.8

express regrets *be penitent* 451.7

express speed *speed* 694.2

express sympathy for *grieve* 308.7

expressway *road* 687.2, *means of connection* 754.4

expropriate *misuse* 395.6, *lose* 468.12, *take back* 477.17, *evict* 709.20

expropriation *confiscation* 454.4, *loss* 468.1, *taking back* 477.4, *eviction* 709.4, *setting apart* 753.2

expropriator *taker* 477.9

expropriatory *taking* 477.12

expugnable *vulnerable* 811.9

expulsion 709.1; *excretion* 25.1, *discarding* 383.3, *separation* 409.3, *exile* 454.3, *replacement* 574.3, *transfer* 685.1, *repulse* 701.2, *emigration* 707.6, *displacement* 711.2, *subtraction* 749.1, *setting apart* 753.2, *ejection* 764.2, *termination* 834.2

expulsive 709.11; *projectile* 696.13, *outgoing* 707.10

expulsively 709.29

expunction *obliteration* 186.1, *self-righteousness* 431.7

expunge *erase* 186.9, *moralize* 431.14, *abolish* 523.11, *cancel* 834.6

expunged *obliterated* 186.4, *moralistic* 431.12, *canceled* 773.15

expunged from the record *forgiven* 312.5

expunge from the record *absolve* 312.10

expurgate *purify* 111.19, *suppress* 424.9, *moralize* 431.14, *subtract* 749.6, *eject* 764.8

expurgated 111.15; *suppressed* 424.6, *moralistic* 431.12

expurgation *censorship* 111.5, *suppression* 424.2, *self-righteousness* 431.7, *subtraction* 749.1, *ejection* 764.2

exquisite *luscious* 214.8, *painful* 215.4, *wondrous* 294.9, *excellent* 445.13, *elegant* 527.3, *beautiful* 529.7

exquisitely *excellently* 445.21, *elegantly* 527.7, 529.15, *gorgeously* 529.14, *fashionably* 536.9

exquisiteness *excellence* 445.4, *elegance* 527.1, *beauty* 529.1

exsecant (exsec) *trigonometric function* 6.50

exsection *digging out* 711.3

ex-serviceman *former soldier* 77.5

ex-servicewoman *former soldier* 77.5

exsiccant *drying* 560.15

exsiccate *dry* 560.17

exsiccated *dried-up* 560.9

exsiccation *drying* 560.3

exsiccative *dryer* 560.5, *drying* 560.15

exsiccator *dryer* 560.5

ex-slave *free person* 829.9

exsuction *drawing off* 711.4

extant *alive* 28.13, *present* 575.7, 647.4, *existing* 717.11

extemporaneous *improvised* 396.4

extemporaneously *extempore* 396.7

extemporary *improvised* 396.4

extempore 396.7; *spontaneously* 389.17, *improvised* 396.4

extemporization *unpremeditation* 389.2, *improvisation* 396.1

extemporize *improvise* 389.15, 396.6

extemporized *spontaneous* 389.6, *improvised* 396.4

extemporizer *improviser* 396.3

extemporizing *improvisation* 396.1

extend 563.14; *align* 6.92, *be excessive* 99.9, *be diffuse* 199.5, *be elastic* 546.7, *enlarge* 581.14, *open up* 583.16, *reach out* 585.10, *be long* 590.11, *lengthen* 590.12, *broaden* 592.11, 778.15, *span* 592.12, *be deep* 598.20, *delay* 658.13, *protract* 669.9, *quantify*

738.7, *make bigger* 746.7, *augment* 748.13, *continue* 774.12

extendability *enlargeability* 581.6

extend credit *credit* 487.10

extended *diffuse* 199.3, *linguistic* 361.9, *elastic* 546.5, *spacious* 563.13, *bigger* 581.9, *opened up* 583.11, *lengthened* 590.10, *broadened* 592.7, *held up* 658.6, *protracted* 669.7, *quantitative* 738.6, *increased* 746.5

Extended Binary Coded Decimal Interchange Code (EBCDIC) *character* 15.18

extended family *family circle* 65.4

extendedly *late* 658.14

extended meaning *lack of clarity* 364.2

extend gratitude *or* **thanks** *be grateful* 310.6

extendibility *softness* 543.1, *enlargeability* 581.6

extendible *pliant* 543.7, *enlargeable* 581.13

extending *elastic* 546.5, *growing* 581.12

extend over *overhang* 604.14

extend the hand of friendship *seek friendship* 62.11

extend to *reach out* 585.10, *fill* 761.11

extensibility *softness* 543.1, *elasticity* 546.1, *enlargeability* 581.6

extensible *pliant* 543.7, *enlargeable* 581.13

extensible *or* **extensile** *elastic* 546.5

extensibleness *enlargeability* 581.6

extensile *pliant* 543.7, *enlargeable* 581.13

extensin *polysaccharide* 12.5

extension *dial* 169.12, *diffuseness* 199.1, *elasticity* 546.1, *space* 563.1, *size* 579.1, *expansion* 581.1, 592.2, *enlargement* 581.7, *lengthening* 590.4, *overhanging* 604.2, *delay* 658.3, *protraction* 669.4, *increase* 746.1, *addition* 748.1, *sequel* 770.5

extensional *enlargeable* 581.13

extension ladder *ladder* 713.10

extensive 563.12; *huge* 579.14, *enlargeable* 581.13, *opened up* 583.11, *lengthy* 590.9, *broad* 592.5, *deep* 598.16, *intense* 598.16, *gradational* 739.5, *including* 763.3, *general* 778.9, *universal* 778.10

extensively 563.18; *largely* 581.18, *openly* 583.22, *at length* 590.15, *broadly* 592.15, *deep* 598.25, *intensely* 598.28, *differentially* 739.9, *universally* 778.23

extensiveness *spaciousness* 563.4, *largeness* 579.2, *longness* 590.3, *breadth* 592.1, *depth* 598.1, *deepness* 598.6, *widespreadness* 778.3

extensive study *learning* 48.7

extensor *enlarger* 581.8

extent *space* 6.33, 563.1, *surface* 6.36, *size* 579.1, *measurability* 589.2, *length* 590.1, *lengths* 590.5, *breadth* 592.1, *depth* 598.1, *limit* 620.1, 773.7, *duration* 642.1, *continuation* 642.2, *quantity* 738.1, *degree* 739.1

extenuate *modify* 340.13, *justify* 441.12, *weaken* 517.13, *mitigate* 521.9, *make smaller* 747.8

extenuating *defending* 419.17, *vindicatory* 441.7

extenuating circumstances *modification* 340.5, *defense* 441.2

extenuatingly *justifyingly* 441.15

extenuation *defense* 441.2, *limitation* 747.3

extenuatory *vindicatory* 441.7

exterior 610.1, 610.7; *space* 6.33, *type of painting* 143.5, *external appearance* 264.5, *outer* 264.10, *extraneous* 610.12, *external* 724.11

exterior angle *angle* 6.37

exteriority 610.2; *extraneousness* 610.6, *externality* 724.4

exteriorization *externalization* 610.5

exteriorize *externalize* 610.15

exteriorized *externalized* 610.11

exteriorized protoplasm *occult and psychic phenomena* 86.7

exteriorly 610.16; *extraneously* 610.19

exterior product *vector* 6.48

exterminate 709.22; *kill* 30.19, *slaughter* 30.21, *kill animals* 30.25, *destroy* 186.10, 523.10, *cause not to exist* 718.14, *annihilate* 773.22

exterminated *destroyed* 186.5, *annihilated* 773.16

extermination *pest control* 16.13, *slaughter* 30.5, *animal killing* 30.10, *destruction* 186.2, 523.1, *annihilation* 773.4

exterminator *destroyer* 523.6

external 724.11; *visible* 244.5, *outer* 264.10, *superficial* 599.4, *exterior* 610.1, 610.7, *apparent* 610.10, *extraneous* 610.12, *unjoined* 753.9

external, the *externality* 724.4

external appearance 264.5

external-combustion *engine type* 14.11

external gear *gear* 14.7

external geometric form *crystal* 8.39

externality 724.4; *superficiality* 599.2, *exteriority* 610.2, *extraneousness* 610.6

externalization 610.5; *externality* 724.4

externalize 610.15; *be material* 524.8, *be external* 724.15

externalized 610.11; *external* 724.11

externalizing *external* 724.11

externally 724.19; *visibly* 244.10, *apparently* 264.16, 610.18, *superficially* 599.8, *exteriorly* 610.16, *extraneously* 610.19, *seemingly* 733.19, *in isolation* 753.24, *manifestly* 843.17

externally acting hormone *hormone* 12.16

external organ *appendage* 19.5

external respiration *respiration* 12.24

externals *external appearance* 264.5, *appearance* 610.4

external work *thermodynamics* 10.30

externment *dismissal* 709.2

extinct *dead* 29.11, *disappeared* 265.4, *inactive* 413.9, 415.8, *unfashionable* 528.10, *over* 651.12, *no more* 718.11

extinct arthropod 39.7

extinct bird 36.14

extinction 718.8; *mortality* 29.2, *disappearance* 265.1, *inactivity* 415.1, *destruction* 523.1, *reduction* 747.2, *annihilation* 773.4

extinct reptile 37.9

extinguish *discourage* 179.11, *make dark* 247.10, *make inactive* 415.16, *destroy* 523.10, *cause not to exist* 718.14, *be superior* 744.15, *annihilate* 773.22

extinguisher *destroyer* 523.6

extinguishing *darkening* 247.6

extinguishment *darkening* 247.2

extirpate *destroy* 186.10, 523.10, *remove* 574.16, *evict* 709.20, *subtract* 749.6

extirpated *destroyed* 186.5, *removed* 574.9, *subtracted* 749.3

extirpation *destruction* 186.2, *destroying* 523.2, *removal* 574.2, *subtraction* 749.1

extirpative *subtractive* 749.4

extol *worship* 83.15, *publicize* 173.18, *praise* 435.15, 437.16

extolled *worshiped* 83.14, *ritualistic* 85.15

extoller *approver* 437.7

extolling *worshipful* 83.12

extolment *worship* 83.1, *praise* 437.3

extort 711.18; *suppress* 424.9, *demand* 425.11, 505.12, *force* 428.10, *lend* 475.6, *take money away* 477.20, *act dishonestly* 479.18, *overcharge* 496.10

extorted *demanding* 505.8

extorting *taking away* 477.5, *demanding* 505.8

extortion 496.4, 711.6; *suppression* 424.2, *demand* 425.2, 505.3, *violation of the law* 427.2, *coercive method* 428.3, *lending* 475.1, *taking away* 477.5, *dishonesty* 479.7, *fee* 494.3

extortionary *exacting* 711.12

extortionate *loaned* 475.5, *taking* 477.12, *costly* 496.7, *exacting* 711.12

extortionately *avariciously* 477.22

extortionate price *overpricing* 496.2

extortioner *raider* 477.10

extortionist *criminal* 427.6, *coercer* 428.4, *raider* 477.10, *lender* 487.5, *overcharger* 496.5, *requester* 505.5

extortive *demanding* 505.8, *exacting* 711.12

extort protection money *take money away* 477.20

extra 748.6, 748.10; *waste* 96.10, *superfluity* 99.4, *superfluous* 99.8, *actor* 136.25, 137.13, *news story* 171.3, *diffuseness* 199.1, *unused thing* 394.4, *unused* 394.5, *profit* 467.6, *fee* 494.3, *extraneous* 724.8, *imbalance* 741.2, *additionally* 748.15, *surplus* 750.8, *excluded* 764.6, *redundant* 802.9, *safety device* 810.15

extrachromosomal genetic element *genetic material* 13.20

extract 11.41, 711.8, 711.13; *practice dentistry* 107.34, *treat* 115.17, *exploit* 393.11, *take away* 477.18, *product* 522.3, *produce* 522.13, *juice* 555.2, *remove* 574.16, *passage* 692.1, *excerpt* 692.13, *quintessence* 723.3, *subtract* 749.6, *part of writing* 760.6, *deliver* 817.5, *reveal* 843.14

extract a root *add* 6.86

extracted *removed* 574.9, *excerpted* 692.9, *dislodged* 711.11, *subtracted* 749.3

extraction 711.1; *metallurgy* 11.22, *dentistry* 107.6, *taking away* 477.5, *removal* 574.2, *obtaining of an extract* 711.7, *subtraction* 749.1, *deliverance* 817.1

extraction of roots *multiplication* 6.15, *calculation* 784.1

extractive 711.10; *metallurgical* 11.36

extractive metallurgy *metallurgy* 11.22

extractor 711.9

extractor fan *rotator* 682.8

extract roots *add* 784.11

extracts *compendium* 204.3

extracurricular *curricular* 48.21

extradite *give back* 478.5, *take away* 685.12, *ostracize* 709.17, *eject* 764.8

extradition *giving back* 478.1, *transfer* 685.1, *ostracism* 709.3, *ejection* 764.2

extrados Architectural Elements 134

extra edition *or* **extra** *newspaper* 175.2

extraembryonic membrane *developmental biology* 13.22

extragalactic *astronomical* 7.33

extragalactically *astronomically* 7.36

extra help *extra* 748.6

extra inning *other game terms* 147.7, *extra* 748.6

extrajudicial *unlawful* 53.23

extrajudicial execution *execution* 30.6

extrajudicial oath *vow* 189.3

extra large *huge* 579.14

extra load *addition* 748.1

extramarital relations *fornication* 432.3

extra money *profit* 467.6

extramundane *astronomical* 7.33, *spiritual* 86.20, *nonmaterial* 525.8

extramural *curricular* 48.21, *outside* 610.9

extraneous 610.12, 724.8; *unrelated* 728.6, *incomparable* 734.6, *excluded* 764.6

extraneously 610.19, 724.16; *irrelatively* 728.16

extraneousness 610.6, 724.1; *unrelatedness* 728.1, *incomparability* 734.3

extraordinarily *wondrously* 294.18

extraordinariness *wonderfulness* 294.5, *unusualness* 782.4

extraordinary *wondrous* 294.9, *characteristic* 779.12, *unusual* 782.15, *questionable* 839.5

extra pair of hands *extra person* 748.7

extra person 748.7

extra point *scoring* 155.5

extrapolate *equate* 6.88, *add* 784.11

extrapolation *reasoning* 6.61, *calculation* 784.1

extras *expense* 491.2, *extra* 748.6, *surplus* 750.4

extrasensory *psychic* 86.17, *precognitive* 320.7, *parapsychological* 525.9

extrasensory perception (ESP) *psychic power* 86.4, *sensation* 212.1, *impression* 266.2, *precognition* 320.2, *divination* 358.2, *spiritual world* 525.3

extraterrestrial *astronomical* 7.33, *spiritual* 86.20, *external* 724.11

extraterrestrial (ET) *sprite* 86.12

extraterrestrially *astronomically* 7.36

extra time *extra* 748.6

extravagance 194.3, 491.5, 500.1; *waste* 96.1, *superfluity* 99.4, *folly* 353.1, *misuse* 395.1, *flashiness* 404.4, *blatancy* 404.6, *overindulgence* 456.3, *ornateness* 532.2

extravagant 194.9, 500.4; *wasteful* 96.9, *superfluous* 99.8, *entertaining* 138.12, *fantastic* 360.11, *abusive* 395.5, *flashy* 404.17, *blatant* 404.19, *overindulgent* 456.8, *expending* 491.8, *costly* 496.7, *ornate* 532.10

extravagantly 500.9; *wastefully* 96.23, *entertainingly* 138.17, *excessively* 194.17, *abusively* 395.8, *flashily* 404.32, *blatantly* 404.34, *generously* 491.14, *at great cost* 496.12, *decoratively* 532.13, *ornately* 532.14

extravaganza *show* 138.4, *conception* 360.4

extravagation *crossing* 712.2

extravasate *excrement* 25.2, *excrete* 25.20, *bleed* 25.26, *leak* 707.16, *let out* 709.26

extravasation *outflowing* 707.11

extravasation *excretion* 25.1, *leakage* 707.5, *disgorgement* 709.6

extravasation of blood *bleeding* 25.10

extravehicular activity (EVA) *space travel* 7.29

extraversion *externalization* 610.5

extraversive *externalized* 610.11

extravertive *externalized* 610.11

extra weight *heaviness* 538.1

extra work *task* 122.2

extreme *excessive* 99.5, *mountaineering* 161.9, *exaggerated* 194.7, *painful* 215.4, *unrestrained* 500.5, *strong* 516.9, *violent* 520.5, *away* 585.6, *intense* 598.16, *edging* 618.5, *farthest* 620.6, *limit* 761.4, *773.7, limiting* 773.17, *ideal* 805.6

extremely *excessively* 99.13, *194.17, acutely* 516.18, *intensely* 598.28, *marginally* 618.11, *to a degree* 739.11, *superbly* 744.22

extreme penalty *capital punishment* 454.12

extremes *excess* 99.1, *exaggeration* 194.1, *unrestrainedness* 500.2

extreme unction *dying* 29.3, *Christian rite* 85.5

extremism *exaggeration* 194.1

extremist *seditionist* 427.7, *deviant* 698.7

extremities *the depths* 598.2

extremity *the depths* 598.2, *summit* 600.1, *edge* 618.1, *farthest point* 620.3, *limit* 773.7

extricable *deliverable* 817.3

extricably 817.6

extricate *remove* 574.16, *extract* 711.13, *deliver* 817.5, *disentangle* 823.17, *set free* 829.17, *liberate* 831.6

extricated *removed* 574.9, *dislodged* 711.11

extricate oneself *be liberated* 831.7

extrication *removal* 574.2, *extraction* 711.1, *deliverance* 817.1, *disentanglement* 823.8, *liberation* 831.1

extrinsic *extraneous* 610.12, *external* 724.11, *unrelated* 728.6, *unjoined* 753.9

extrinsicality *externality* 724.4

extrinsically *extraneously* 610.19, *externally* 724.19, *irrelatively* 728.16, *in isolation* 753.24

extroversion *personality type* 108.6, *externalization* 610.5

extroversive *extroverted* 108.38, *externalized* 610.11

extrovert *personality type* 108.6, *extroverted* 108.38, *vigorous* 518.2

extroverted 108.38; *sociable* 408.11, *vigorous* 518.2, *externalized* 610.11

extrovertedness *personality type* 108.6

extrovertive *externalized* 610.11

extrudable *spun* 130.13

extrude *excrete* 25.20, *spin* 130.17, *let out* 709.26

extruded *spun* 130.13

extruder *fabric-handling tool* 130.12

extrusion) *petrogenesis* 8.31

extrusion *excretion* 25.1, *spinning* 130.4, *coming out* 707.3, *disgorgement* 709.6

extrusive *petrographic* 8.58

extrusive rock *igneous rock* 8.32

exuberance *fertility* 22.1, *excess* 99.1, *diffuseness* 199.1, *joy* 269.1

exuberant *fertile* 22.8, *excessive* 99.5, *diffuse* 199.3, *joyful* 269.6

exuberantly *excessively* 99.13

exudate 557.4; *excrement* 25.2, *sweat* 25.8, *leak* 707.16

exudation *secretion* 24.1, *excretion* 25.1, *excrement* 25.2, *sweat* 25.8, *exudate* 557.4, *outflow* 707.4

exudative *secretory* 24.4, *excretory* 25.12, *leaky* 707.12

exude *secrete* 24.7, *excrete* 25.20, *sweat* 25.24, *seep* 559.16, *leak* 707.16

exult *rejoice* 279.5

exultant *worshipful* 83.12, *rejoicing* 279.4

exultation *rejoicing* 279.1, *405.8

exultet *ritual music* 85.9

exult in *be proud* 297.15

exurb or **exurbia** *suburb* 567.11

exurban *local* 564.14, *urban* 567.14

exuviae *dirt* 112.5

exuvial *peeling* 614.13

exuviate *shed* 614.21

exuviation *peeling* 614.6

ex-wife *single woman* 33.5

eyas *young bird* 36.17

eye 19.9, 242.3; *fishing tackle* 154.7, *sense organ* 212.4, *look* 242.21, *hole* 583.4

eyeball *eye* 19.9, 242.3

eyeball [Inf] *inspect* 242.22

eyeball-to-eyeball *beside* 586.20, *front-running* 621.10, *opposite* 731.3, *discordant* 828.12

eyebrow *eye* 242.3

eyebrow pencil *cosmetics* 530.4

eyebrows *body covering* 19.4, *head* 19.6

eye-catching *visible* 242.19, *clear* 244.6, *attractive* 700.10, *accentuated* 843.11

eye clinic *aid for poor sight* 243.5

eye cream *toiletries* 530.6

eyed *seeing* 242.17

eye disease 243.4

eye drops *aid for poor sight* 243.5

eye-filling *attractive* 529.8

eye for *aptitude* 127.4

eye for an eye *atonement* 313.1, *exchange* 673.1, *counterbalance* 743.2

eye-for-an-eye *reciprocal* 729.4

eyeful *view* 242.8

eyeful [Inf] *beautiful thing* 529.3

eyeglass *visual aid* 242.14, *transparent thing* 249.4

eyehole *hole* 583.4

eye hospital *aid for poor sight* 243.5

eyelash *eye* 19.9, 242.3

eyelash comb *cosmetic tool* 530.5

eyelash curler *cosmetic tool* 530.5

eyelashes *body covering* 19.4

eyeless *blind* 243.11

eyelessness *blindness* 243.3

eyelet *hole* 583.4, *fastener* 754.7

eyelid *eye* 19.9, 242.3

eyelike *visual* 242.16

eye liner *cosmetics* 530.4

eye makeup *cosmetics* 530.4

eye makeup remover *cosmetic tool* 530.5

eye muscle *eye* 242.3

eye of the hurricane *core* 612.2, *repose* 678.2

eye of the storm *wind vortex* 9.14

eyeopener *view* 242.8, *detection* 345.2

eye-opening *educational* 48.17, *visible* 242.19

eye pain *Phobias* 283

eyepatch *blinder* 243.7

eyepiece *lens system* 10.22

eye-popper [Inf] *marvel* 294.3

eye rhyme *rhyme* 139.11

eyes *head* 19.6, *Phobias* 283

eyeshade *visual aid* 242.14, *shade maker* 247.4, *protective covering* 613.5, *protection from the weather* 810.9

eye shadow *cosmetics* 530.4

eyeshot *viewpoint* 242.12, *visibility* 244.1

eyesight *vision* 242.1, *visibility* 244.1

eyesocket *eye* 242.3

eyesore *architectural structure* 134.4, *view* 242.8, *ugly thing* 531.2, *blot on the landscape* 533.4

eye splice Knots, Bends, Hitches, Splices 754

eyespot *plant body* 47.13

eyestrain *sight defect* 243.2

Eyetie Nicknames for Inhabitants 61

eye to eye *agreeably* 462.14

eyetooth *teeth* 19.8

eyewash *balm* 115.11, *aid for poor sight* 243.5, *pomade* 562.9

eyewash [Inf] *nonsense* 192.8, *senseless talk* 362.4, *flattery* 439.1

eyewitness *newsworthy* 171.8, *affirmer* 189.9, *observer* 242.15, *verifier* 336.4, *witness* 339.7, *attender* 575.6

eyewitness account *news story* 171.3

Eyre Lakes 568

eyrie *dwelling* 36.4, *natural habitat* 60.16

Ezekiel *warner* 814.5

F

fab! [Inf] *wonderful!* 294.20, *good!* 445.24

Fabian *unhurried* 693.8

Fabianism *slowness* 693.1

fable *story* 139.4, *falsehood* 192.6, *fabricate* 192.24, *idealism* 360.7, *empty talk* 362.5

fabled *fabricated* 192.17, *supposed* 359.6, *imaginary* 360.12, *reputable* 370.3

fabler *author* 139.13

fabliau *story* 139.4

fabric 104.4, 130.1, 551.2; *rock* 8.30, *materials* 104.1, *dry goods* 130.3, *woven* 130.15, *Phobias* 283, *merchandise* 522.6, *matter* 524.4, *textile* 552.5, *weaving* 609.2, *essence* 723.1

fabricate 192.24, 720.17; *put together* 59.30, *be an architect* 134.13, *imagine* 360.14, *produce* 522.13, *shape* 551.21, *distort the truth* 627.12

fabricated 192.17; *structural* 14.45, *imaginary* 360.12, *misrepresented* 627.8

fabrication *construction* 59.16, *falsehood* 192.6, *fantasy* 360.5, *manufacture* 522.2, *form* 551.3, *distortion of truth* 627.4

fabricator *liar* 192.10, *producer* 522.10

fabric dealer *clothier* 100.37

fabric handler 130.11

fabric-handling tool 130.12

fabric treatment 130.10

fabula [L] *dramatic style* 136.3

fabulist *author* 139.13, *descriptive writer* 202.10

fabulous *fictional* 139.16, *imaginary* 360.12, *unbelievable* 837.5

fabulous! *wonderful!* 294.20

fabulous [Inf] *great* 445.14

fabulously [Inf] *excellently* 445.21

faburden *harmonic element* 140.14

facade or **façade** *ungenuineness* 192.2, *blinder* 243.7, *external appearance* 264.5, *exterior* 610.1, *appearance* 610.4, *front* 621.1, *show* 621.7

face 613.31, 621.6, 646.8; *surface* 6.36, *head* 19.6, *golf equipment* 156.5, *type* 173.5, *external appearance* 264.5, *be courageous* 284.14, *expect* 356.6, *brace oneself* 376.13, *audacity* 400.3, *layer* 588.9, *exterior* 610.1, *be exterior* 610.13, *front* 621.1, 621.9, *be in front* 621.13, *side* 623.8, *nature* 624.5, *protuberance* 634.3, *be opposite* 778.4, *make a beginning* 771.26, *confront* 828.19

face about *turn around* 680.22, *698.25

face a total loss *forfeit* 468.13

face bankruptcy *lose money* 468.15

face both ways *equivocate* 380.8

face card *cards* 168.2

face-centered *status adjectives* 11.25

face-centered-cubic (f.c.c.) crystal *crystal* 11.14

face climbing *climbing techniques* 161.3

face color 251.9

face cream *cleaning agent* 111.9, *balm* 115.11, *pomade* 562.9

faced *coated* 588.7, *covered* 613.19

face danger 811.12; *defy* 416.7

face death *face danger* 811.12

face defeat *lose* 468.12

face difficulties *be in difficulty* 824.19

face disaster *be unskillful* 128.8

face disqualification *forfeit* 468.13

face down *be courageous* 284.14

face float *swimming techniques* 164.2

faceguard *exhibit penalty behavior* 155.21

faceguarding *penalty* 155.13

face heavy odds *face danger* 811.12

face in the crowd *one who conceals* 181.7

face-lift *cosmetic surgery* 530.2, *beautification* 807.7, *repair* 809.1
facemask *football uniform* 155.2, *penalty* 155.13, *exhibit penalty behavior* 155.21, *hockey clothing* 158.6, *modern armor* 419.7
face off *play ice hockey* 158.9
face-off *ice hockey tactics* 158.4
face-off circle *hockey areas* 158.2
face pack *beauty treatment* 530.3
face powder *powder* 553.9
face reality *submit* 421.4
facet *external appearance* 264.5, *aspect* 623.4, 726.4, *component* 760.3
faceted *angled* 628.9
face that would stop a clock *ugly thing* 531.2
face the cameras *act* 137.20
face the facts *submit* 421.4
face the firing squad *be executed* 454.32
face the issue *brace oneself* 376.13
face the music *be courageous* 284.14, *be punished* 454.31
face the odds *brace oneself* 376.13
face the other way *turn around* 698.25
facetious *humorous* 277.9
facetiously *humorously* 277.13
facetiousness *humor* 277.1
face to face *near* 586.6, *beside* 586.20, *front* 621.9, *opposite* 731.3, *discordant* 828.12, *frankly* 843.18
face up to *be in front* 621.13
face value *impression* 264.7, *value* 494.2
facial *beauty treatment* 530.3, *massage* 554.6, *outward* 621.11
facial expression *external appearance* 264.5
facially *apparently* 264.16
facial mask *or* **masque** *eraser* 554.7
facial massage *massage* 554.6
facial scrub *eraser* 554.7
facies *rock* 8.30, *external appearance* 264.5
facile *simple* 526.7, *graceful* 527.4, *easy* 823.9
facilely *easily* 823.19
facileness *simplicity* 823.2
facilitate *find means* 102.6, *make comprehensible* 363.8, *interpret* 365.12, *permit* 502.6, *make easy* 823.15, *further* 825.30, *set free* 829.17
facilitated *made easy* 823.11
facilitating *feasible* 823.10, *helping* 825.16
facilitation *easing* 823.7, *furtherance* 825.8
facilitative *helping* 825.16
facilitator *helper* 825.12
facilities *naval commands* 77.19, *provisions* 89.3, *means* 102.1
facility *manual skill* 127.2, *ability* 340.2, 514.3, *clarity* 363.2, *simplicity* 526.1, *grace* 527.2, *easiness* 823.1, *convenience* 825.7, *possibleness* 836.2
facing *external appearance* 264.5, *stuffing* 577.4, *coat* 588.3, *exterior* 610.7, *wall covering* 613.12, *front* 621.9, *side* 623.6, *opposite* 731.3
facing both ways *equivocal* 380.5
facing death *endangered* 811.10
facing machine *machine tool* 14.9
facing the firing squad *endangered* 811.10
facsimile *reprint* 21.3, *image* 187.3, *representation* 202.9, *copy* 730.5,

simulation 733.4, *duplicate* 736.4
facsimile (fax) machine *office automation tools* 15.19, *copier* 736.5
facsimile transmission *data transmission* 169.8
fact 717.6; *historicalness* 3.9, *right* 429.2, *reality* 719.1, *truth* 721.1, *aspect* 726.4, *certainty* 840.1
fact checker *book publishing personnel* 174.1
fact-find *question* 333.16
fact-finding *questioning* 333.11
facticity *demonstrable existence* 717.5
faction 347.4; *party* 59.3, *religious group* 81.4, *program* 172.10, *calling* 178.6, *dissenters* 347.6, *subversion* 427.3, *part* 760.1, *the opposition* 828.8
faction [Inf] *fictional account* 202.5
factional *grouped* 59.21, *subversive* 427.11
factionalism *dissentience* 347.3
factionalist *dissenter* 347.5
factious *argumentative* 329.7, *disagreeing* 463.6
factitious disorders *mental disorder* 108.8
fact of the matter *fact* 717.6
factor *multiplication* 6.15, *genetics* 13.19, *genetic material* 13.20, *manager* 126.7, *instrument* 511.2, *physical element* 524.5, *circumstances* 573.2, *contributory cause* 675.3, *aspect* 726.4, *component* 760.3, *thing included* 763.2, *mathematical result* 783.4
factorage *trade* 480.1
factor analysis *statistical methods* 6.53
factorial *multiplication* 6.15, *genetic* 13.32
factorization *multiplication* 6.15
factorize *add* 6.86, *divide* 753.18
factors *contents* 577.1
factorship *trade* 480.1
factory 124.8; *social institution* 2.8, *place of experimentation* 335.6, *manufacture* 522.2, *building* 551.9
factory discount price *price* 494.1
factory farm *farm* 16.2
factory farming *agriculture* 16.1, *manufacture* 522.2
factory floor *force* 59.10
factory hand *laborer* 123.9
factory-made *produced* 522.12
factory mark *decoration* 129.4
factory price *price* 494.1
factory worker *laborer* 123.9
factotum *servant* 69.1, *worker* 123.1, *hard worker* 414.11
facts *information* 170.1, 348.2, *news* 171.1, *evidence* 339.1, *fact* 717.6, *the truth* 721.3, *authentication* 721.8, *confirmation* 840.3
facts and figures *information* 170.1
facts of life *realities* 719.5, *the truth* 721.3
facts of the matter *the truth* 721.3
factual 3.14; *narrative* 202.12, *evidential* 339.8, *correct* 350.4, 429.8, *real* 717.14, 719.6, *true* 721.11, *certain* 840.7
factual account 202.4
factualism *correctness* 350.2
factuality *right* 429.2, *demonstrable existence* 717.5, *reality* 719.1, *truth* 721.1, *certainty* 840.1

factualize *come to be* 717.19, *make real* 719.11
factually *biographically* 3.18, *as evidence* 339.15, *correctly* 429.16, *really* 717.22, *truly* 721.27
factualness *historicalness* 3.9, *correctness* 350.2, *truth* 721.1
facula *sun* 7.15
faculty *educator* 48.4, *governance* 52.6, *skill* 127.1, *aptitude* 127.4, *ability* 340.2, 514.3, *intellect* 348.4
faculty of judgment *judgment* 341.1
faculty of sight *vision* 242.1
faculty psychology *Psychological Theories, Schools* 108
fad *likes* 290.3, *caprice* 381.1, *fashion* 536.1, *trendiness* 652.2
faddish *capricious* 381.4, *trendy* 652.11
faddishness *capriciousness* 381.2
faddism *capriciousness* 381.2
faddist *modern person* 652.8
fade *waste away* 96.20, *motion-picture editing* 137.8, *golf shots* 156.4, *play* 156.8, *play cards* 168.7, *become invisible* 245.6, *be dim* 248.7, *make dim* 248.8, *color* 251.16, *lose color* 252.7, *decolor* 252.8, *whiten* 253.12, *disappear* 265.5, *be weak* 517.12, *be transient* 643.6, *grow old* 653.16, *miscellaneous automotive terms* 687.14, *change by degrees* 739.8, *decrease* 747.7, *disintegrate* 808.15
fade *or* **fading** *radio reception* 172.2
fadeaway *pitching terms* 147.5
fade away *be unhealthy* 114.29, *sound faint* 233.8, *become invisible* 245.6, *disappear* 265.5, *stop* 668.10, *cease to exist* 718.13, *decrease* 747.7, *come to an end* 773.23
faded *dimmed* 248.6, *colorless* 252.5, *whitened* 253.8, *dried-up* 560.9, *spoiled* 808.9
faded hue *hue* 251.4
fade from one's memory *be forgotten* 355.12
fade from sight *or* **view** *decrease* 747.7
fade in *become visible* 264.13
fade-in *motion-picture editing* 137.8
fade into the background *conceal oneself* 181.15, *acquiesce* 421.5
fadeout *darkening* 247.2
fade out *be dim* 248.7, *disappear* 265.5, *lessen* 468.17, *stop* 668.10, *change by degrees* 739.8, *come to an end* 773.23
fade-out *motion-picture editing* 137.8, *disappearance* 265.1, *decrease* 747.1
fading *dying* 29.12, *colorlessness* 252.1, *colorless* 252.5, *disappearance* 265.1, *disappearing* 265.3, *drying* 560.3, *transient* 643.4, *gradational* 739.5, *decrease* 747.1, *decreasing* 747.5, *deterioration* 808.1
fading away *disappearance* 265.1
fading out *disappearance* 265.1, *lessening* 468.6, *gradational* 739.5
fag *work* 122.8, *hard worker* 414.11
fag *or* **fag out** *fatigue* 820.6
fag [Inf] *tobacco* 121.23
fag [Inf *and* Off] *homosexual* 32.9
fag end *residue* 750.2, *tail* 773.8
fagged *fatigued* 820.2
fagged out *fatigued* 820.2
faggot *timber* 43.3

faggot [Inf *and* Off] *homosexual* 32.9
faggoty [Inf *and* Off] *of sexual nature* 20.17
fagot *fuel starter* 106.3
Fahrenheit scale *heat measurement* 217.2, *scale* 589.9
faience *Ceramics* 129
fail 714.18, 846.12; *load* 14.49, *be infertile* 23.8, *be insufficient* 98.9, *be unhealthy* 114.29, *be unskillful* 128.8, *be clumsy* 128.9, *disappoint* 293.9, *be wrong* 430.18, *go wrong* 430.23, *not perform* 466.10, *lose* 468.12, *be unable to pay* 490.11, *be powerless* 515.11, *be weak* 517.12, *be destroyed* 523.17, *close* 637.10, *stop work* 668.11, *be inferior* 745.10, *decrease* 747.7, *be useless* 802.11, *be imperfect* 806.8, *deteriorate* 808.14, *be fatigued* 820.5, *change* 841.20, *malfunction* 846.20, *be in trouble* 848.13
failed 846.10; *unskillful* 128.4, *gone wrong* 430.17, *nonperforming* 466.6, *losing* 468.9, *weakened* 517.9, *closed* 637.6, *stopped* 668.7, *low quality* 745.7
fail in duty *defy* 466.11
failing *aged* 27.15, *iniquity* 448.3, *impious* 448.11, *nonperforming* 466.6, *losing* 468.9, *destroyed* 523.9, *deficiency* 745.2, *low quality* 745.7, *defect* 806.4, *deteriorated* 808.8, *vulnerability* 811.6, *decline* 846.5, *failed* 846.10
failing grade *limit marker* 620.4
failing health *ill health* 114.1, *decline* 846.5
failing sight *faulty vision* 243.1
fail in health *decline* 846.16
fail in one's duty *exempt oneself* 434.12, *discontinue* 846.14
faille *Fabrics and Fibers* 130
fail-safe *invulnerable* 810.18
fail-safe device *safety device* 810.15
fail-safe system *safety device* 810.15
fail the test *be imperfect* 806.8
fail to act *be indifferent* 289.12, *not act* 413.11
fail to amaze *not cause wonder* 295.7
fail to appear *depart* 265.6, *be absent* 576.14
fail to appreciate *be ungrateful* 311.5
fail to comprehend *lack intellect* 316.8
fail to deliver *disappoint* 293.9, *not complete* 762.9
fail to hear 229.9
fail to heed *be careless* 289.14
fail to inspire *make indifferent* 289.13
fail to interest *bore* 296.8
fail to move *make indifferent* 289.13
fail to score *be defeated* 846.18
fail to see *lack intellect* 316.8
fail to take advantage of *not use* 394.9
failure 430.9, 846.1; *probability* 6.59, *deformation* 14.16, *insufficiency* 98.1, *bungling* 128.2, *unskilled person* 128.3, *theatrical performance* 136.13, *hopeless person* 282.5, *Phobias* 283, *bad outcome* 293.3, *sin* 450.3, *nonperformance* 466.2, *loss* 468.1, *loser* 468.8, 846.9, *insolvency* 490.5, *weak person* 517.4, *ruin* 523.4, *stop* 668.2, *downfall* 714.7,

deficiency 745.2, decrease 747.1, nonachievement 762.3, futility 802.3, imperfection 806.1
failure of credit insolvency 490.5
failure to act inaction 413.1
failure to arouse lack of wonder 295.1
failure to hear deafness 229.1
failure to meet one's obligations insolvency 490.5
failure to pay insolvency 846.6
fainéant nonworker 415.4
faint 233.6; be unhealthy 114.29, desensitization 213.2, be insensible 213.7, unheard 229.7, silent 231.2, nonresonant 233.7, difficult to see 245.4, murky 248.5, colorless 252.5, succumb 421.7, forfeit 468.13, be powerless 515.11, ill 517.8, insufficient 517.11, be weak 517.12, fatigue 820.1, fatigued 820.2, be fatigued 820.5, indeterminate 841.14
faint-colored drained of color 252.6
faintheart coward 285.3
fainthearted cowardly 285.4
faintheartedly cowardly 285.9
faintheartedness cowardice 285.1, unenthusiasm 375.3
faint hope hope 281.1, questionableness 333.7, remote possibility 836.4
fainting symptom 114.3, Phobias 283, fatigue 820.1, fatigued 820.2
faintly 233.11; silently 231.5, dimly 248.10, colorlessly 252.9, weakly 517.14, indeterminately 841.24
faintness silence 231.1, faintness of sound 233.1, invisibility 245.1, dimness 248.1, paleness 252.2, unintelligibility 364.1, poor health 517.3, fatigue 820.1, indeterminacy 841.6, quietness 844.4
faintness of sound 233.1
faint praise disparagement 195.2, 440.1
faint smell odor 224.1
faint sound faintness of sound 233.1
fair 483.2; fine 9.43, circus 138.2, amusement 167.7, warm 217.13, white-haired 253.9, satisfactory 273.6, impartial 289.9, 338.6, mediocre 289.11, 742.7, judicious 341.8, celebration 405.1, courteous 410.6, right 429.7, in the right 429.11, moral 431.9, disinterested 443.4, principled 447.6, moderate 521.3, beautiful 529.7, rainless 560.11, honest 630.11, equal 740.8, middling 772.14, display 843.1
fair and square honest 630.11, honestly 630.18
fair ball batting terms 147.6
fair catch kick 155.12
fair chance equal chance 842.7
fair clip swiftness 694.1
fair copy copy 736.2
faired blunt 550.5
fair exchange trade 480.1, reciprocity 729.1, equalization 740.4
fair expectation chance 838.4
fair game butt 436.8
fair-haired white-haired 253.9
fairish mediocre 742.7
Fair Isle Islands 572
fairlead sailboat parts and accessories 150.4
fairly rationally 4.25, stoically 4.26, impartially 289.19, 338.13, unexceptionally 289.20, judicially

341.12, right 429.15, morally 431.15, disinterestedly 443.8, ethically 447.10, moderately 521.10, honestly 630.18, to a degree 739.11, equitably 740.15, free 831.9
fair-minded impartial 338.6, wise 352.4, disinterested 443.4
fair-mindedness impartiality 338.2, rightfulness 429.1, disinterestedness 443.1
fairness legal justice 53.4, whiteness 253.1, impartiality 289.3, 338.2, rightfulness 429.1, morals 431.2, disinterestedness 443.1, virtues 447.2, moderation 521.1, beauty 529.1, honesty 630.4, equality 740.1
fair offer peace offering 74.5, business offer 504.3
fair play legal justice 53.4, morals 431.2
fair price equalization 740.4
fair shake [Inf] equality 740.1
fair-size big 579.13
fair-skinned white 253.7
fair territory baseball field 147.3
fair to middling getting well 113.9, moderate 521.3, mediocre 742.7
fair trial legal process 54.3
fair value value 494.2, equalization 740.4
fairway golf course 156.2
fair way great distance 585.2
fair-weather ungenuine 192.13
fair-weather friend hypocrite 192.9, assenter 346.3, equivocator 380.4, capricious person 381.3
fair-weather sailor unskilled person 128.3, nautical person 690.12
fair wind help 825.1
fairy sprite 86.12, spiritual 86.20, little person 580.5
fairy [Inf and Off] homosexual 32.9
fairy godmother wonderful person 294.6, giver 472.7, generous person 498.5, supporter 605.9, protector 810.11, benefactor 825.15
fairyland marvel 294.3, dreamland 360.8
fairy lights electric light 246.6
fairy ring mushroom 47.2, talisman 86.9
fairy shrimp crustacean 39.10
fairy tale story 139.4, conception 360.4
fairy-tale ending successfulness 845.3
faith believing 87.2, belief system 87.3, expectation 281.2, virtues 447.2, security 464.1, observance 465.1, safety 810.1, conviction 840.2
faith cure therapy 115.12
faithful intimate 62.7, religious 81.21, prayerful 85.17, believer 87.5, believing 87.6, truthful 191.4, correct 350.4, translational 365.11, constant 377.8, loyal 426.5, moral 431.9, deferential 433.9, principled 447.6, observant 465.3, realistic 719.7, literal 721.18, tenacious 755.6, infallible 840.12
faithful copy copy 736.2
faithfully intimately 62.14, religiously 81.29, believingly 87.12, truthfully 191.9, accurately 350.6, obediently 426.9, morally 431.15, ethically 447.10, observantly 465.6, literally 721.32, tenaciously 755.12

faithfully rendered lifelike 721.19
faithfulness religiousness 81.2, truthfulness 191.1, correctness 350.2, loyalty 426.2, morals 431.2, deference 433.4, observance 465.1, literalness 721.9
faithful rendering verisimilitude 721.10
faithful spouse spouse 64.8
faith healer occultist 86.13, healer 107.22
faith healing occultism 86.1, alternative medicine 107.4, healing art 115.13
faithless disbelieving 88.6
faithlessness disobedience 427.1
fake play offense 155.18, ice hockey tactics 158.4, hoax 193.7, 193.20, deceiver 193.8, hoaxer 193.11, deceptive 193.14, misrepresentative 193.14, hypocritical 330.10, deceive 330.12, illegal borrowing 476.3, borrowed 476.8, borrow illegally 476.12, infringement 479.6, misrepresented 627.8, distort the truth 627.12, artificiality 720.7, artificial 720.12, unauthenticity 722.4, unauthentic 722.9, copy 736.2, 736.10, imitation 736.8
fake a confession accuse falsely 442.9
fake confession false accusation 442.2
faked misrepresentative 193.14
fake kick kick 155.12
faker liar 192.10, hoaxer 193.11, imitator 736.6
fakery ungenuineness 192.2, deception 193.1, hypocrisy 330.5
fake someone out [Inf] swindle 193.19
fake the evidence accuse falsely 442.9
faking hypocritical 330.10
fakir religious person 81.9, religious 84.9, occultist 86.13
Falabella pony Horse and Pony Breeds 159
falafel notable international dishes 90.40
Falak al Aflak heaven 82.15
falchion sharp weapon 78.6
falcon bird of prey 36.11, hunt 160.12, Heraldic Terms 184
falcon, American peregrine Endangered US Birds 36
falcon, Arctic peregrine Endangered US Birds 36
falcon, northern aplomado Endangered US Birds 36
falconer hunter 160.9
falconry Sporting Activities 145, hunting 160.2
Falkland Islands Islands 572
Falklands War Major Wars 76
fall 654.5, 714.4; meteor 7.21, rain 9.57, Collective Names 59, wrestling terms 152.10, transgress 351.16, be immoral 432.13, declining prices 497.2, be cheap 497.13, be weak 517.12, be destroyed 523.17, hairdressing 530.7, flow 570.10, descend 597.22, deepening 598.4, deepen 598.21, verticality 602.1, season 654.1, decline 680.5, 747.4, slip back 680.19, drop 714.15, lowering 716.1, deteriorate 808.14, be in danger 811.11, discontinuance 846.4, fail 846.12, adversity 848.1
fallacious sophistic 330.7, erroneous

351.11, equivocal 380.5, wrong 430.12, untrue 722.6
fallaciously sophistically 330.14, without truth 722.14
fallaciousness sophistry 330.1, erroneousness 351.2, incorrectness 430.3, untruth 722.1
fallacy sophistry 330.1, sophism 330.2, misjudgment 342.1, faulty reasoning 351.4, equivocation 380.1, delusion 720.3, untrueness 722.3
fall apart be transient 643.6, scatter 753.15, disintegrate 758.6, 808.15
fall apart at the seams be weak 517.12
fall asleep be insensible 213.7, pause 668.13
fall astern be in the rear 622.7
fall at a person's feet pander to 401.11
fall at the feet of show respect 435.16
fall away diverge 753.20
fallback retreat 680.2
fall back retreat 680.17
fall back on resort to 393.13, survive 419.31
fall behind be in the rear 622.7, retreat 680.17, be inferior 745.10
fall below be insufficient 98.9, be inferior 745.10
fall below the poverty line be poor 486.14, need money 848.14
fall between two stools stand in the middle 772.17
fall by the wayside be useless 802.11, fatigue 820.6, fail 846.12
fall dead on the ear be nonresonant 233.10
fall down drop 714.15, fail 714.18
fall down before show respect 435.16
fallen 716.8; unchaste 432.10, demonic 446.9, depraved 448.10, destroyed 523.9
fallen angel angel 82.11, evil spirit 446.4, loser 468.8
fallen by the wayside losing 468.9, spoiled 808.9
fallen nature depravity 448.2
fallen woman sexually immoral person 432.8
faller descender 714.8
fall flat miscarry 846.19
fall flat on one's face fail 714.18
fall for [Inf] believe 87.9, be in love 299.23, be motivated 508.10
fall foul of fight 422.23, be in trouble 848.13
fall from grace sin 430.22, be immoral 432.13, be wicked 448.13, be in trouble 848.13
fall from grace or favor be disreputable 371.5
fall guy [Inf] laughingstock 369.4, butt 436.8, loser 468.8, substitute 672.2
fall headlong drop 714.15
fall head over heels in love be in love 299.23
fall heir to profit 467.22
fallibility 351.6; misjudgment 342.1, imperfection 806.1, unreliability 841.7, failure 846.1
fallible misjudging 342.6, errant 351.12, imperfect 806.5, unreliable 841.15
fallibly misguidedly 342.12, unreliably 841.25
fall ill be unhealthy 114.29, deteriorate 808.14
fall in band together 59.27, be brittle 548.4, become smaller 582.14, fail

714.18, *conform* 735.27, *line up* 765.24, *arrange* 774.14

falling 714.11; *mountaineering* 161.9, *financial* 457.6, *bargain* 497.10, *flowing* 570.7, *descent* 597.4, *descending* 597.13, *deepening* 598.4, 598.14, *fall* 714.4, *lowered* 716.7, *fallen* 716.8, *decreasing* 747.5, *deteriorated* 808.8

falling apart *destroyed* 523.9, *disintegrating* 758.5, *dilapidated* 808.11

falling away *decline* 680.5

falling back *retreat* 680.2

falling birth rate *infertile state* 23.3

falling down *destroyed* 523.9

falling exchange rate *international finance* 457.2, *currency market* 484.8

falling hair *baldness* 614.9

falling in love *romantic love* 299.2

falling off *lessening* 468.6, *decline* 747.4, *economic deterioration* 808.2, *deteriorated* 808.8

falling-out *quarrel* 302.7, *argument* 329.1, *dispute* 463.3

falling pressure *weather data* 9.6

falling rocks *climbing dangers* 161.5

falling short *disappointing* 293.6, *unequal* 741.4

falling sickness *neurological disease* 114.20, *spasm* 684.8

falling star *meteor* 7.21

falling to pieces *dilapidated* 808.11, *unsafe* 811.8

fall in love *be in love* 299.23

fall in one's own trap *act foolishly* 128.10

fall in price *be cheap* 497.13

fall into 706.15

fall into a habit *accustom oneself* 397.19

fall into arrears *be unable to pay* 490.11

fall into confusion *be disordered* 766.21

fall into disarray *be disordered* 766.21

fall into disuse *be unaccustomed* 398.5

fall into evil ways *be wicked* 448.13

fall into one's hands *receive* 473.13

fall into place *line up* 765.24

fall into ruin *be destroyed* 523.17

fall into the clutches of *be subject to* 832.12

fall in with *agree with* 462.10, *come together* 702.10, *conform* 781.11

fall-like *seasonal* 654.7

fall line *ski run* 162.2

falloff *decline* 680.5

fall off *sail* 150.29, *go backward* 680.16, *descend* 714.12, *decrease* 747.7, *come unstuck* 756.7, *deteriorate* 808.14

fall off the roof [Inf] *bleed* 25.26

fall of the leaf *fall* 654.5

fall on bad days *be in trouble* 848.13

fall on deaf ears *be unheard* 229.12

fall on hard times *lose one's money* 486.15, *be in trouble* 848.13

fall on one's feet *be fortunate* 847.7

fall on one's knees *ask for mercy*

308.10, *knuckle under* 401.10, *show respect* 435.16

fall on one's sword *commit suicide* 30.24

fall on the ear *be heard* 228.15

Fallopian tubes *organs of reproduction* 21.9

fallout *nuclear problem* 10.62, *lack of hygiene* 112.3, *nuclear power production* 514.10, *product* 522.3, *powder* 553.9, *subsequence* 770.4

fall out *oppose* 63.11, *disagree* 463.8, *take effect* 676.11

fall out of love *be indifferent* 289.12

fallout shelter *shelter* 419.11, *fortification* 812.3

fall out with *dissent* 347.8

fall over *trip* 714.16

fall over backward [Inf] *be unselfish* 443.7

fallow *farmable* 16.17, *infertile* 23.7, *yellow* 259.7, *thoughtless* 318.7, *unprocessed* 389.10, *idle* 394.6, *inactive* 413.9, *not working* 415.10, *inert* 519.2

fallow mind *lack of thought* 318.1

fallowness *infertility* 23.1, *inertness* 519.1

fall prostrate *drop* 714.15

falls *river turbulence* 570.5

fall short *be insufficient* 98.9, *disappoint* 293.9, 846.15, *lose money* 468.15, *be unequal* 741.7, *be inferior* 745.10, *not complete* 762.9, *be imperfect* 806.8

fall short of perfection *be imperfect* 806.8

fall sick *be unhealthy* 114.29

fall silent *be silent* 231.3

fall through the air *drop* 714.15

fall to *eat well* 92.23, *be the duty of* 433.16, *make a beginning* 771.26

fall to bits *or pieces* *come to dust* 553.28

fall to dust *come to dust* 553.28

fall together *work together* 827.14

fall to leeward *navigate* 690.15

fall to one *receive* 492.7

fall to one's lot *receive* 473.13, *chance* 842.12

fall to one's share *receive* 473.13

fall to pieces *be brittle* 548.4, *be transient* 643.6, *disintegrate* 758.6, *malfunction* 846.20

fall to the lot of *be the duty of* 433.16

fall under the influence of *be persuaded* 178.20, *be motivated* 508.10

fall upon *strike* 418.21, *reach* 704.14, *chance upon* 842.13

fall vertically **602.10**

false *logical* 6.83, *arch* 134.5, *fencing* 153.6, *misrepresented* 188.4, 627.8, *ungenuine* 192.13, *hypocritical* 330.10, *erroneous* 351.11, *affected* 367.3, *equivocal* 380.5, *wrong* 430.5, *artificial* 720.12, *untrue* 722.6, *incorrect* 722.8, *unauthentic* 722.9, *simulated* 733.11

false acacia *Trees and Shrubs* 43

false accusation 442.2

false alarm 814.4

false alert *false alarm* 814.4

false arrest *legal injustice* 53.5

false attack *fencing movements* 153.3

false charge *false accusation* 442.2

false colors *ungenuineness* 192.2

false conclusion *error* 351.1

false construction *misinterpretation* 366.1

false dawn *morning* 655.2, *theory* 720.4

false depiction *misrepresentation* 188.1

false depiction *or* **impression** *misrepresentation* 366.2

false display *affectation* 367.1

false evidence *evasion* 181.5, *false accusation* 442.2

false face *ungenuineness* 192.2

false friend *hypocrite* 192.9

false front *affectation* 367.1, *show* 621.7

false fruit *botanical fruit* 44.2

false gold *bullion* 484.16

false hair *hairdressing* 530.7, *body covering* 613.3

false-hearted *ungenuine* 192.13

false-heartedly *untruthfully* 192.27

false-heartedness *ungenuineness* 192.2

falsehood 192.6; *misrepresentation* 188.1, *conception* 360.4, *empty talk* 362.5, *evasion* 380.2, *distortion of truth* 627.4

false hope *hope* 281.1

false hopes *frustration* 293.2

false idea *misinformation* 188.3

false image *misrepresentation* 188.1

false impression *misrepresentation* 188.1, *fallibility* 351.6, *delusion* 720.3

false information *misinformation* 188.3

false light *misrepresentation* 188.1

falsely *unrepresentatively* 188.8, *untruthfully* 192.27, *sophistically* 330.14, *mistakenly* 366.6, *equivocally* 380.9, *wrongfully* 430.25, *distortedly* 627.14, *without truth* 722.14, *incorrectly* 722.16, *unauthentically* 722.17, *imitatively* 733.20

falsely color *distort the truth* 192.25

falsely colored *partially true* 192.18

falsely modest *moralistic* 431.12

false mildew *pests and diseases* 17.12

false modesty *self-righteousness* 431.7

false money 484.15

false move *error* 351.1

false name *name* 202.8

falseness *ungenuineness* 192.2, *erroneousness* 351.2, *incorrectness* 430.3, *untrueness* 722.3, *unauthenticity* 722.4

false note *musical dissonance* 241.2

false oath *lying* 192.5

false piety *ungenuineness* 192.2

false plea *lying* 192.5

false pretenses *misrepresentation* 193.4

false pride *arrogance* 297.2

false promises *cunning* 822.1

false reading *misjudgment* 342.1, *misinterpretation* 366.1, *distortion of truth* 627.4

false reasoning *sophistry* 330.1

false rumor *partial truth* 192.7

false scent *waste of effort* 802.4

false scorpion *arachnid* 40.4

false sense *misinformation* 188.3

false shame *self-righteousness* 431.7

false start *penalty* 155.13, *track event* 166.1, *starting point* 771.11

false-start *exhibit penalty behavior* 155.21

false statement *falsehood* 192.6

false statements *Phobias* 283

false step *error* 351.1

false tooth *teeth* 19.8

falsetto *voice* 141.5, *shrillness* 238.3

false warning *false alarm* 814.4

false witness *liar* 192.10, *accuser* 442.3

falsies [Inf] *underwear* 100.22

falsification *misrepresentation* 188.1, 193.4, 351.5, *lying* 192.5

falsified *misrepresentative* 193.14, *erroneous* 351.11, *misinterpreted* 366.3

falsifier *liar* 192.10, *one who misrepresents* 193.9

falsify *misrepresent* 188.6, 193.17, *lie* 192.23, *practice sophistry* 330.11, *err* 351.14, *distort the truth* 627.12

falsify the accounts *account* 493.9

falsifying *lying* 192.16

falsity *mathematical logic* 6.60, *reasoning* 6.61, *erroneousness* 351.2, *affectation* 367.1, *distortion of truth* 627.4, *untruth* 722.1

faltboat *canoe* 150.9, *Ships and Boats* 690

falter *vacillate* 378.8, *be changeable* 666.5, *stagger* 684.11, *shake* 684.24, *pitch* 684.25, *hesitate* 693.12, 841.18

faltering *vacillation* 378.1, *vacillating* 378.5, *shaking* 684.6, *shaky* 684.18, *slow* 693.7, *irresolution* 841.3, *irresolute* 841.10

falteringly *ambivalently* 378.14, *slowly* 693.14

fame 845.2; *publicity* 173.7, *success* 845.1, *prosperity* 847.1

fame and fortune *fame* 845.2, *prosperity* 847.1

famed *historic* 3.11, *publicized* 173.14

familial *family* 65.6

familiar 397.10, 407.8; *educated* 48.19, *friend* 62.2, *friendly with* 62.6, *talisman* 86.9, *sprite* 86.12, *local* 328.8, *habituated* 397.14, *discourteous* 411.5, *disrespectful* 436.9, *average* 742.5, *common* 778.13, *monotonous* 797.12, *informal* 829.15

familiarity 407.3; *friendly relations* 62.3, *knowledge* 348.1, *habit* 397.1, *sociability* 408.1, *average* 742.1, *repetitiveness* 797.3, *informality* 829.6

familiarize *accustom* 397.18

familiarized *habituated* 397.14

familiarize oneself with *get to know* 348.12

familiarly *intimately* 62.14, *informally* 407.11, 829.24

familiar name *name* 202.8

familiar spirit *talisman* 86.9

familiar with *knowledgeable* 348.7

family 65.1, 65.6; *social organization* 2.5, *social institution* 2.8, *chemical element* 11.3, *group* 18.13, 59.8, *inhabitants* 61.2, *society* 408.8, *unit* 759.5, *part* 760.1, *category* 767.6, *succession* 770.2, *taxonomical classification* 777.3

family allowance *social assistance* 825.4

family benefit *social assistance* 825.4

family car *automobile* 687.6

family circle 65.4; *society* 408.8
family court *type of court* 54.9
family doctor *doctor* 107.19
family farm *farm* 16.2
family feeling *agreement* 462.1
family group *social organization* 2.5
family history *person of the past* 651.7
family likeness *affinity* 733.3
family man *man in the family* 32.12
family meal *meal* 92.8
family member 65.2; *associate* 754.3
family name *name* 202.8
family of curves *curve* 6.38
family of humankind *human family* 65.5
family of man *humankind* 18.1
family of nations *human family* 65.5
family-oriented *sociably* 408.19
family planning *birth control* 23.5
family plot *burial place* 31.7
family practice Medical Specialties 107
family practitioner *doctor* 107.19, *medical specialist* 107.20
family relationship *kinship* 727.2, *affinity* 733.3
family resemblance *affinity* 733.3
family responsibilities *burden* 826.10
family reunion *social gathering* 408.4
family room *room* 60.9
family secret *secret* 182.2
family-size *big* 579.13
family therapy *psychotherapy* 108.4
family tree 65.3; *figurative usage* 43.9, *person of the past* 651.7, *succession* 770.2, *line* 774.2
famine *infertile state* 23.3, *scarcity* 90.5, 98.3, *beggary* 486.3, *agent of destruction* 523.7
famine relief *charity* 275.3
famine-stricken *underfed* 98.7
famish *starve* 118.10
famished *underfed* 98.7, 118.7, *hungry* 288.16
famishing *underfed* 118.7
famous 845.9; *historic* 3.11, *publicized* 173.14, *known* 348.9, *reputable* 370.3, *accentuated* 843.11, *prosperous* 847.5
famous horse races 159.13
famously *eminently* 370.7, *prosperously* 847.9
famousness *publicity* 173.7, *fame* 845.2
fan *idolater* 83.7, *refreshment* 94.1, *air* 94.7, *purify* 111.19, *vault* 134.8, *theatergoer* 136.30, *soccer participant* 163.4, *cooler* 218.4, *make cold* 218.15, *approver* 437.7, *ventilator* 558.7, *blow* 558.22, *enlarge* 581.14, *supporter* 605.9, *propeller* 696.8, *fork* 703.5, *move apart* 703.11, *adherent* 755.4
fanatic *religionist* 81.14, *exaggerator* 194.6, *bigot* 337.7, *obstinate person* 379.4, *busy person* 414.10, *deviant* 698.7, *dissenter* 782.8
fanatical *zealous* 81.22, *passionate* 266.12, *discriminatory* 337.11, *unjust* 342.7, *opinionated* 379.9, *active* 414.13
fanatically *religiously* 81.29, *prejudicially* 337.17, *unjustly* 342.13
fanatical worker *hard worker* 414.11

fanaticism *emotion* 266.3, *social discrimination* 337.4, *unfair treatment* 342.4, *opinionatedness* 379.3
fancied *supposed* 359.6, *imaginary* 360.12, *illusory* 720.9
fancier *ornithologist* 36.3, *collector* 59.17, *expert* 127.9, *desirer* 288.9
fanciful *speculative* 317.8, *ideational* 327.9, *supposed* 359.6, *fantastic* 360.11, *imaginary* 360.12, *capricious* 381.4, *unreal* 718.10, 722.7, *theoretical* 720.10, *questionable* 839.5
fancifully *imaginatively* 360.17, *capriciously* 381.7, *unreally* 722.15
fancifulness *imagination* 360.1, *unreality* 722.2
fanciness *ornateness* 532.2
fan club *approver* 437.7
fancy *be of the opinion* 87.10, *impression* 266.2, *desire* 288.17, *likes* 290.3, *enjoy* 290.9, *romantic love* 299.2, *like* 299.22, *theory* 327.2, *imagine* 327.14, 360.14, *supposition* 359.1, *suppose* 359.8, *imagination* 360.1, *conception* 360.4, *fantasy* 360.5, *will* 372.1, 372.11, *caprice* 381.1, *preference* 382.2, *preferential* 382.10, *prefer* 382.13, *costly* 496.7, *decorated* 532.9, *ornate* 532.10, *illusion* 720.2, *unreality* 722.2, *be unreal* 722.12
fancy dress *costume* 100.10
fancy-dress ball *dance* 135.1
fancy-dress party *party* 408.6
fancy-free *celibate* 67.6
fancy price *costliness* 496.1
fancy that! *wonderful!* 294.20
fancywork *sewing* 130.5, *decorative method* 532.3
fan dancer *dancer* 135.4, *nude person* 614.5
fan dancing Dancing Types 135
fandango Dances 135
fane [Arch] *place of worship* 83.8
fanfare Musical Forms 140, *military call* 183.9, *burst of sound* 232.4, *ringing* 236.2, *applause* 279.2, *salute* 405.7
fanfaron *exaggerator* 194.6
fanfaronade *bravado* 404.8
fang *teeth* 19.8, *tooth* 549.7
fanged *toothed* 549.13
fanglike *toothed* 549.13
fangs *retainer* 471.3
fan heater *heater* 217.3
fanlight Architectural Elements 134
fanlike 703.8; *growing* 581.12
fan mail *postal communication* 169.4
fanned *ventilated* 558.17, *bigger* 581.9
fanned out *bigger* 581.9
fanning *ventilation* 558.6, *expansion* 581.1, *growing* 581.12, *parting* 703.2
fanning out *expansion* 581.1, *diffraction* 696.8, *parting* 703.2, *divergence* 776.5
fanny [Inf] *rear end* 622.4
fanny lift [Inf] *cosmetic surgery* 530.2
fanny pack [Inf] *bag* 578.7
fanon *vestment* 84.11
fan out *enlarge* 581.14, *move apart* 703.11, *diverge* 776.16
fan-shaped *growing* 581.12, *fanlike* 703.8, *three-sided* 790.8
fantabulous [Inf] *wondrous* 294.9
fantail Architectural Elements 134

fan-tan Card Games 168
fantasia *reverie* 360.6
fantasist *visionary* 360.9
fantasize 360.15; *aspire* 281.13, *imagine* 327.14, 720.13, *be unreal* 722.12
fantast *visionary* 360.9
fantastic 360.11; *wondrous* 294.9, *ideal* 327.12, *capricious* 381.4, *illusory* 720.9, *unreal* 722.7, *unbelievable* 837.5
fantastic! *wonderful!* 294.20
fantastical *fantastic* 360.11, *unrestrained* 500.5, *unreal* 718.10, 722.7
fantasticality *or* **fantasticalness** *imagination* 360.1
fantastically *wondrously* 294.18, *imaginatively* 327.21, *unreally* 722.15
fantasy 360.5; *defense mechanism* 108.23, Musical Forms 140, *aspiration* 281.3, *marvel* 294.3, *imagination* 360.1, *conception* 360.4, *nonreality* 718.5, *illusion* 720.2, *unreality* 722.2
fantasyland *marvel* 294.3, *dreamland* 360.8
fantasy novel *novel* 139.3
fanwork Architectural Elements 134
far *domesticated* 16.18, *fast* 166.23, *distant* 585.5, *distantly* 585.11, *side direction* 623.2
farad Scientific and Technical Units 589
faraday Scientific and Technical Units 589
Faraday effect Classical Physical Laws 10
Faraday's laws Classical Physical Laws 10
far afield *distantly* 585.11
far and away *supremely* 744.23
far and near *distantly* 585.11
farandole Dances 135
far and wide *extensively* 563.18, *distantly* 585.11, *completely* 759.14
faraway *distant* 585.5
far away *distantly* 585.11, *out of reach* 712.11
far back *deep* 598.25, *in the past* 651.20
farce *dramatic style* 136.3, *comedy* 136.11, 368.2, *entertainment* 277.4
farceur *actor* 136.25, *dramatist* 136.27
farceuse *dramatist* 136.27
farcical *dramatic* 136.31, *variety* 138.13, *humorous* 277.9, *ridiculous* 368.5
farcically *entertainingly* 138.17, *humorously* 277.13
far cry *great distance* 585.2
farcy *animal disease* 34.10
far down *deep* 598.25
fare *food* 90.1, *eat* 92.21, *fee* 494.3, *transferred thing* 685.6, *be in a state of* 725.8
Far East *world region* 564.6, *distant place* 585.3
farewell *parting* 705.3, *departing* 705.5
farewell! *goodbye!* 705.14
fare well *be in comfortable circumstances* 726.13, *be prosperous* 847.6
farewell address *public speaking* 205.11, *parting* 705.3
farewell oration *public speaking* 205.11
farewell performance *theatrical performance* 136.13

farewell-to-spring Flowers 42
far-fetched *disbelieved* 88.7, *exaggerated* 194.7, 712.9, *improbable* 839.4
far-flung *extensive* 563.12, *distant* 585.5, *broad* 592.5, *universal* 778.10
far from it *to the contrary* 190.27
far from it! *no!* 506.12
far from the madding crowd *motionlessly* 678.9
far future *future time* 650.1
far gone *dying* 29.12, *deteriorated* 808.8
farina *meal* 553.7
farinaceous *horticultural* 17.14, *grasslike* 45.7, *mealy* 553.18
far infrared *electromagnetic radiation* 10.14
farm 16.2, 16.19, 124.11; *agricultural* 16.16, *property* 470.1, *bring into existence* 522.14, *transportable* 686.7, *rear* 715.10
farmable 16.17
farm agent *farm worker* 16.15
farm animal *domestic animal* 34.3
Farm Belt *farmland* 16.3
farmboy *farm worker* 16.15
farm building 16.4
farm business *agriculture* 16.1
farm club *baseball leagues and championship games* 147.8
farm country *countryside* 564.3
farmed *farmable* 16.17, *reared* 715.7
farmer *agriculturist* 16.14, *countryman* 61.8, *food provider* 90.6, *agricultural laborer* 123.10, *producer* 522.10
farmer's lung *fungal disease* 47.6
farmers' market *agriculture* 16.1, *food provider* 90.6, *market* 483.1
farmery [Brit] *farm building* 16.4
farmhand *farm worker* 16.15, *servant* 69.1
farm hand *agricultural laborer* 123.10
farmhouse *farm building* 16.4, *agricultural* 16.16, *house* 60.4
farm implement *farm tool* 16.5
farming *agriculture* 16.1, *agricultural* 16.16, *manufacture* 522.2, *rearing* 715.2
farmland 16.3; *farm* 16.2, *green place* 260.2, *countryside* 564.3
farm machinery *farm tool* 16.5
farm manager *farm worker* 16.15
farm office *farm building* 16.4
farm pond *small lake* 568.2
farm road *road* 687.2
farmstead *farm* 16.2
farm tool 16.5
farmwork *work* 122.1
farm worker 16.15; *agricultural laborer* 123.10
farmyard *farm building* 16.4, *unpleasant-smelling thing* 227.2
farnesol *terpene* 12.20
farness *distance* 585.1
faro Card Games 168
Faroe Islands Islands 572
far-off *distant* 585.5, *distantly* 585.11
far-offness *distance* 585.1
far-out [Inf] *uncustomary* 398.4, *eccentric* 782.16
far past *past time* 651.1
farrago *miscellany* 751.3
far-ranging *universal* 778.10
far-reaching *extensive* 563.12, *lengthy* 590.9, *broad* 592.5, *universal* 778.10
farrier *horse person* 159.14
farriery *riding equipment* 159.9

farrow *have young* 21.16, *young animal* 26.4, *young mammal* 35.20, *give birth* 35.33
farrowing crate *farm building* 16.4
farrowing house *farm building* 16.4
farseeing *seeing* 242.17, *foreseeing* 357.5
far sight *sight defect* 243.2
farsighted *weak-sighted* 243.10, *intelligent* 352.5, *foreseeing* 357.5
farsightedly *foresightedly* 357.10
farsightedness *visual acuity* 242.2, *visualization* 242.6, *sight defect* 243.2, *wisdom* 352.1, *foresight* 357.1
fart [Inf] *unpleasant-smelling thing* 227.2, *belch* 556.5, 709.28, *flatulence* 709.9
farther *distant* 585.5, *in the offing* 585.12
farthermost *away* 585.6
farther throw *advance* 467.3
farthest 620.6; *away* 585.6, *limiting* 773.12
farthest down *lower* 597.14, *deeper* 598.10, *bottom* 601.6
farthest part *the depths* 598.2
farthest point 620.3
farthingale *skirt* 100.12, *underwear* 100.22
farting [Inf] *flatulence* 709.9, *eructative* 709.13
far ultraviolet *electromagnetic radiation* 10.14
Far West *regions of the United States* 564.7, *distant place* 585.3
fascia *Architectural Elements* 134, *coat* 588.3, *horizontal surface* 603.3
fasciate *checked* 263.8
fasciately *variedly* 263.12
fascicle or **fascicule** *part of writing* 760.6
fascicular *component* 760.12
fasciculate *grouped* 59.21
fascinate *entice* 178.16, *be wondrous* 294.14, *win the love of* 299.27, *influence* 508.11, *be an influence* 512.13, *lure* 700.12
fascinated *bewitched* 86.21, *liking* 290.4, *wondering* 294.7, *enamored* 299.17
fascinating *witchlike* 86.19, *enticing* 178.15, *likable* 290.7, *wondrous* 294.9, *lovable* 299.20, *motivational* 508.7, *appealing* 512.9, *attractive* 700.10
fascinatingly *likably* 290.12, *wondrously* 294.18, *lovably* 299.31, *influentially* 508.13
fascination *sexual desire* 20.5, *enticement* 178.3, *eagerness* 288.3, *liking* 290.1, *wonder* 294.1, *romantic love* 299.2, *inducement* 508.2, *influence* 512.1
fascism *totalitarianism* 49.13, *social discrimination* 337.4, *suppression* 424.2
fascist *governmental* 49.24, *bigot* 337.7, *discriminatory* 337.11, *severe* 424.5
Fascist aesthetic movement *Western Art Styles* 133
fascistic *governmental* 49.24
fashion 536.1, 536.7, 537.9; *dressing* 100.2, *describe* 202.15, *external appearance* 264.5, *custom* 397.4, *mode of behavior* 399.2, *tendency* 513.1, *perform* 522.16, *etiquette* 534.3, *style* 537.1, *form* 551.3, 624.9, *shape* 551.21, *way* 691.1, *mode* 725.2, *convention* 781.5

fashionable 536.5; *dressed up* 100.39, *established* 397.12, *stylish* 537.7, *present* 647.4, *avant-garde* 652.16, *conditional* 725.7
fashionable elite 536.4
fashionableness *fashion* 536.1
fashionable set *avant-garde* 652.6
fashionably 536.9; *dressily* 100.47, *trendily* 652.24, *in good form* 725.11
fashion artist *visual artist* 133.6
fashion boots *boots* 100.31
fashion business 536.3
fashion designer *clothier* 100.37, *fashion business* 536.3
fashion designing *dressing* 100.2
fashioned *designed* 536.6, 537.5, *formed* 624.6
fashioning *forming* 624.4
fashion magazine *magazine* 175.3
fashion model *fashion business* 536.3
fashion photography *photographic specialties* 132.2
fashion plate *fashion business* 536.3
fashion reporter *print journalist* 175.5
fashion show *display* 843.1
fashion trade *fashion business* 536.3
fashion world, the *dressing* 100.2
fast 118.4, 118.8, 166.23, 464.8; *reactive* 11.29, *intimate* 62.7, *worship* 83.15, *incompleteness* 98.2, *fasting* 118.1, *colored* 251.10, *repent* 313.9, *active* 414.13, *actively* 414.24, *abstinence* 455.2, *abstain* 455.11, *lose weight* 468.14, *retained* 471.6, *immediate* 645.5, *swift* 694.6, *tied* 752.13, *inextricably* 752.23, *hasty* 818.3, *hastily* 818.7, *means of restraint* 830.6, *restrain oneself* 830.15
fast asleep *not awake* 415.12
fast ball *pitching terms* 147.5
fast break offense *playing terms* 148.4
fast-breeder reactor *nuclear power production* 514.10
fast by *nearby* 586.17
fast day *holy day* 85.12, *fast* 118.4, *anniversary* 405.5
fast dye *coloring agent* 251.5
fasten *suspend* 604.13, *intertwine* 752.19, *connect* 754.13
fasten down *make stable* 674.7
fastened *closed* 584.7, *tied* 752.13, *connected* 754.11
fastener 754.7; *retainer* 471.3, *joint* 752.7
fastening *joint* 752.7, *connection* 754.1, *fastener* 754.7
fasten on *retain* 471.7, *make important* 799.14
fasten one's seatbelt *prepare for action* 388.18
fasten up *intertwine* 752.19
faster *self-restrained person* 455.5, *loser* 468.8
faster! *hurry up!* 818.9
faster race *advance* 467.3
faster than a speeding bullet *swift* 694.6
faster than sound *swift* 694.6
fast film *exposure* 132.15
fast food *food* 90.1
fast-food *immediate* 645.5
fast-food cook *cook* 91.3
fast-food counter *eating place* 92.17
fast-food place *food provider* 90.6
fast-food restaurant *eating place* 92.17

fast friendship *intimacy* 62.4
fast green *green bowling* 151.3
fastidious 325.9; *clean* 111.13, *subtle* 195.9, *diligent* 323.7, *discriminating* 337.9, *selecting* 382.9, *formal* 406.6, *severe* 424.5, *critical* 438.13, *observant* 465.3, *refined* 534.5, *perfectionistic* 805.18, *troublesome* 824.13
fastidiously *attentively* 323.14, *judiciously* 337.16, *severely* 424.11, *observantly* 465.6, *tastefully* 534.9
fastidiousness 325.4; *cleanliness* 111.1, *subtlety* 195.3, *carefulness* 323.3, *judiciousness* 337.2, *accuracy* 350.1, *selection* 382.1, *formality* 406.1, *severity* 424.1, *criticism* 438.4
fastigiate *sharp* 549.10
fasting 118.1, 118.5; *act of worship* 83.2, *worshipful* 83.12, *delicate eating* 92.3, *underfed* 98.7, *penitence* 313.3, *abstinence* 455.2, *abstinent* 455.7, *loss of weight* 468.3, *beggary* 486.3, *self-restrained* 830.10
fast lane *road attribute* 687.3
fast lane [Inf] *dissipation* 456.2
fast-living *dissipated* 456.7
fastly 464.16; *intimately* 62.14
fastness *fortification* 419.12, 812.3, *swiftness* 694.1
Fast of Av *Jewish Holy Days and Seasons* 85
fastoso *Musical Terms and Expression Marks* 140
fast rate or **motion** *swiftness* 694.1
fast reaction *chemical reaction* 11.8
fast-talk *be cunning* 822.5
fast talker *cunning person* 822.3
fat 12.7, 562.4, 579.8, 579.15; *food content* 90.3, *basic cooking ingredient* 91.8, *plentiful* 97.4, *immoderation* 99.2, *lush* 485.11, *heavy* 538.9, *oily* 562.11, *swell* 581.15, *thickness* 594.1, *thick* 594.5, *well-rounded* 633.8, *prosperous* 847.5
fatal 29.14, *killing* 30.17, *detrimental* 446.8, *destructive* 523.8
fatal accident *way of dying* 29.5, *accidental killing* 30.9
fatal blow *ruin* 523.4
fatal car or **train** or **plane crash** *accidental killing* 30.9
fatal flaw *iniquity* 448.3, *vulnerability* 811.6
fatal illness *illness* 114.2
fatal or **mortal** or **terminal illness** or **disease** *way of dying* 29.5
fatalism *Philosophical Schools of Thought* 4, *necessitarianism* 95.7, *submission* 421.1
fatalist *Philosophical Schools of Thought* 4, *necessitarian* 95.8, *inactive person* 413.8
fatalistic *submitting* 421.3
fatality *way of dying* 29.5, *dead person* 29.7
fatality list *death count* 29.10
fatally 29.18; *deadly* 30.26, *destructively* 446.13, 523.18
fatally ill *dying* 29.12
fatal move *defeat* 846.7
Fata Morgana *illusion* 720.2
fat as a pig *fat* 579.15, *thick* 594.5
fat-assed [Inf] *fat* 579.15
fat cat [Inf] *person of repute* 370.2, *gainer* 467.9 *wealthy person* 485.6, *prosperous person* 847.4

fat chance [Inf] *improbability* 839.1, *poor chance* 842.8
fat chance! [Inf] *good luck!* 842.19
fat clay *material* 129.2
Fate *minor deity* 82.2
fate *inevitability* 95.6, 840.5, *predestination* 384.2, *influence* 512.1, *future condition* 650.3, *contributory cause* 675.3, *end of time* 773.5, *luck* 842.3
fated *inevitable* 95.14, 840.11, *predestined* 384.6, *auspicious* 458.10, *future* 650.6, *annihilated* 773.16
fatedly *necessarily* 95.22
fated to die *dying* 29.12
fateful *presageful* 358.13, *serious* 799.8, *inevitable* 840.11
fatefully *predictively* 358.16, *inevitably* 840.17
fatefulness *inevitability* 840.5
Fates, the *Deities* 82
fat-free diet *diet* 92.5
fathead *sailboard parts* 150.20
Father *male title of address* 32.3, *professional title* 72.6
father *propagator* 21.7, *propagate* 21.15, *man* 27.8, *man in the family* 32.12, *family member* 65.2, *member of the clergy* 84.5, *type of complex* 108.22, *loved one* 299.13, *producer* 522.10, *first cause* 675.6, *cause* 675.8, *produce* 771.34
Father Almighty *God the Father* 82.8
Father Christmas *giver* 472.7, *generous person* 498.5
father figure *substitute* 672.2
father figure or **image** or **surrogate** *surrogate* 108.29
father fixation *fixation* 108.21
fatherhood *maleness* 32.2
father image *symbol* 108.28
fathering *propagation* 21.4
father-in-law *family member* 65.2
fatherland *home* 60.3, *native country* 566.6
fatherly *middle-aged* 27.14, *family* 65.6, *loving* 299.15
fatherly eye *patronage* 810.7
Father/Mother God *God* 82.6
father of the bride *wedding party* 64.7
father of the groom *wedding party* 64.7
father substitute *substitute* 672.2
father symbol *symbol* 108.28
Father Time *passage of time* 639.3
fathom *rationalize* 4.20, *know* 48.24, *be wise* 352.6, *understand* 363.9, *General Units* 589, *Scientific and Technical Units* 589, *measure* 589.20, *measure depth* 598.22, *be profound* 598.23
fathomable *intelligible* 363.5, *measurable* 589.17
fathomableness *intelligibility* 363.1
Fathometer™ *bathymetry* 598.3
fathomless *deep* 598.9
fathomlessness *depth* 598.1
fatidic or **fatidical** *predicting* 358.11
fatigue 820.1, 820.6; *symptom* 114.3, *work for* 122.10, *Phobias* 283, *bore* 296.8, *use up* 393.12, *ill-use* 395.2, 395.7, *weakness* 517.1, *diminishment* 597.7
fatigue or **fatigue duty** *work* 122.1
fatigued 820.2; *unhealthy* 114.23, *bored* 296.5, *weakened* 517.9, *diminishing* 597.16
fatigues *uniform* 100.9

fatigue syndrome *fatigue* 820.1
fatiguing 820.4; *boring* 296.6, *difficult* 824.9
fatling *livestock* 16.11
fatly 579.22
fatness 579.5; *heaviness* 538.1, *oiliness* 562.1, *thickness* 594.1, *round body* 633.2
fat of the land *opulence* 485.3, *prosperity* 847.1
fat part [Inf] *role* 136.23
fatso [Inf] *big person* 579.10
fatstock [Brit] *livestock* 16.11
fatted *swelled* 581.10
fatten 594.10; *practice livestock farming* 16.20, *feed* 90.41, *size* 579.17, *swell* 581.15, *increase* 746.6
fattened *swelled* 581.10
fattened up *reared* 715.7
fattening *edible* 92.20, *increase* 746.1
fattening house *farm building* 16.4
fatten on *eat well* 92.23, *sponge* 401.13
fatten up *feed* 90.41, *rear* 715.10
fatter *swelled* 581.10
fattiness *immoderation* 99.2, *oiliness* 562.1
fattishness *fatness* 579.5
fatty *oily* 562.11
fatty [Inf] *big person* 579.10
fatty acid *fat* 12.7
fatty-acid ester *fat* 12.7
fatty degeneration of the heart *cardiovascular disease* 114.13
fatty oil *oil* 562.3
fatuity *ignorance* 316.3, *lack of thought* 318.1, *ridiculousness* 368.1
fatuous *unintelligent* 316.6, *thoughtless* 318.7, *foolish* 353.5, *meaningless* 362.7, *ridiculous* 368.5
fatuously *unintelligently* 316.9, *ridiculously* 368.8
fatuousness *folly* 353.1, *ridiculousness* 368.1
faubourg [Fr] *suburb* 567.11
faucet *stopper* 584.3
fault 8.21, 430.2; *tennis terms* 165.5, *badminton terms* 165.11, *play tennis* 165.13, *error* 351.1, *sin* 430.22, 450.3, *immorality* 432.1, *criticize* 438.19, *iniquity* 448.3, *opening* 583.1, *crack* 587.2, *untrueness* 722.3, *deficiency* 745.2, *interruption* 775.3, *defect* 806.4
fault-block mountain *mountain building* 8.23
faulted *immoral* 432.9, *impious* 448.11
faultfinder *discourteous person* 411.4, *disapprover* 438.7, *disparager* 440.7
faultfinding *criticism* 438.4, *critical* 438.13, *disparagement* 440.1, *troublesome* 824.13
faultily *wrongly* 351.18, *incorrectly* 722.16
faultiness *untrueness* 722.3, *deficiency* 745.2, *imperfection* 806.1
faultless *correct* 429.8, 721.13, *pure* 431.11, *incorrupt* 449.7, *uncut* 759.7, *complete* 761.6, *perfect* 805.8
faultlessly 449.14; *correctly* 721.29, *perfectly* 805.21
faultlessness *right* 429.2, *purity* 431.4, *incorruption* 449.2, *perfection* 805.1
fault scarp *fault* 8.21
fault system *fault* 8.21

faulty *bungled* 128.7, *sophistic* 330.7, *erroneous* 351.11, *insufficient* 517.11, *incorrect* 722.8, *low quality* 745.7, *imperfect* 806.5
faulty logic *sophistry* 330.1
faulty reasoning 351.4
faulty syntax *syntax* 5.32, *language error* 351.10
faulty vision 243.1
fault zone *fault* 8.21
faun *minor deity* 82.2
fauna *living world* 13.9, *animals* 34.2
Faunus *Deities* 82
faute de mieux [Fr] *instead* 672.8
fauvism *Western Art Styles* 133
fauxbourdon *harmonic element* 140.14
faux pas *bungling* 128.2, *mistake* 342.2, *blunder* 351.5, 528.5, *sin* 450.3, *unsuccessful thing* 846.8
fava *Bean Varieties* 90
favela *urban area* 567.10
Faverolle *Breeds of Fowl* 16
favonian *windy* 9.42
Favonius *wind god* 9.16
favor *desire* 288.17, *inclination* 290.2, *be inclined toward* 290.10, *benevolent act* 305.5, *mercy* 308.3, *show pity* 308.8, *discriminate* 337.12, 430.21, *repute* 370.1, *will* 372.11, *preference* 382.2, *prefer* 382.13, *leniency* 423.1, *be lenient* 423.5, *respect* 435.1, 435.13, *approval* 437.1, *approve* 437.14, *welfare* 445.2, *good* 445.10, *welfare* 445.9, *better* 445.17, *reward* 453.1, 472.4, *be permissive* 502.7, *request* 505.1, *indirect influence* 512.4, *moral support* 605.7, *give moral support* 605.18, *further* 679.13, 825.30, *be similar* 733.12, *advantage* 744.3, *support* 825.2, *improve* 825.26, *good fortune* 847.2, *be auspicious* 847.8
favorable 62.8; *friendly* 62.5, *cheering* 281.9, *desirable* 288.11, *presageful* 358.13, *approving* 437.9, *good* 445.10, *auspicious* 458.10, *timely* 659.4, *comfortable* 726.10, *beneficial* 825.20, *successful* 845.8, *prosperous* 847.5
favorable attitude *liking* 290.1
favorable auspices *potential* 458.4
favorable chance *good chance* 842.6
favorable critic *approver* 437.7
favorableness *willingness* 373.1, *good* 445.1, *timeliness* 659.1
favorable opportunity *opportunity* 659.2
favorable outcome *probability* 6.59, *successfulness* 845.3
favorable prospect *chance* 838.4
favorable review *criticism* 365.3, *compliment* 437.4
favorable toward *inclined toward* 290.5
favorable verdict 54.19
favorable wind *wind* 9.12
favorably 62.15; *desirably* 288.24, *admiringly* 290.11, *all right* 429.19, *well* 445.19, *auspiciously* 458.17, *opportunely* 659.8, *comfortably* 726.19, *superbly* 744.22, *helpfully* 825.32, *successfully* 845.19, *prosperously* 847.9
favorably disposed *benevolent* 825.21
favored *liked* 290.6, *reputable* 370.3, *approved* 437.8
favoring *inclined toward* 290.5, *preferential* 382.10, *wrongful*

430.10, *beneficial* 445.11, *helping* 825.16
favorite *intimate* 62.7, *idol* 83.5, *horse racing* 159.10, *object of pride* 297.6, *person of repute* 370.2, *preferential* 382.10, *finalist* 422.16, *focal* 612.8, *charmer* 700.6, *superior* 744.8, *celebrity* 799.6
favorite of the gods *prosperous person* 847.4
favoritism 337.5; *friendship* 62.1, *injustice* 342.3, *preference* 382.2
favor with *give* 472.10
favus *fungal disease* 47.6
fawn 401.9; *young animal* 26.4, *young mammal* 35.20, *brown* 256.5, *be sycophantic* 439.15
fawner *assenter* 346.3, *flatterer* 439.6
fawning *sycophancy* 401.2, 439.5, *sycophantic* 401.7, 439.11, *showing respect* 435.7
fawningly *sycophantically* 401.16
fawn on *defer to* 410.12, *be sycophantic* 439.15
fawn over *be solicitous* 323.13
fax *data transmission* 169.8, *communicate* 169.18, 170.12, *communication* 170.2, *mail* 685.10, *duplicate* 736.4, *copy* 736.10
Faxflói pony *Horse and Pony Breeds* 159
fax machine *copier* 736.5
fax-modem *communications device* 15.26
fay *sprite* 86.12
faze *make uncertain* 841.19
f-block *chemical element* 11.3
F clef *written music* 140.21
fealty *loyalty* 426.2, *deference* 433.4, *admiration* 435.2
fear 283.1; *strain* 117.4, *Phobias* 283, *be afraid* 283.4, *antipathy* 291.2, *detest* 291.13, *speculation* 294.2, *wonder* 294.12, *hated thing* 300.5, *expectation* 356.1, *expect* 356.6, *sense of danger* 811.3
fear and trembling *fear* 283.1
feared *detested* 291.11, *expected* 356.5
fear for *worry* 283.16
fearful 283.10; *frightening* 283.12, *cowardly* 285.4, *antipathetic* 291.7, *wondering* 294.7
fearfully 283.19; *cowardly* 285.9
fearfulness 283.2; *cowardice* 285.1
fear God *revere* 81.26
fearing *antipathetic* 291.7
fearless *courageous* 284.9, *tenacious* 376.9
fearlessly *courageously* 284.17
fearlessness *courage* 284.1, *tenacity* 376.4
fearnought or **fearnaught** *coat* 100.19
fear of animals *feeling for animals* 34.11
fear of God *religiousness* 81.2
fearsome 283.13; *detested* 291.11, *astonishing* 294.10
fearsomely 283.21
fear-stricken *frightened* 283.9
feasibility *wieldiness* 823.3, *possibleness* 836.2
feasible 823.10; *negotiated* 460.5, *realizable* 719.9, *possible* 836.5
feasibly 460.9; *potentially* 836.11
feast 92.9; *holy day* 85.12, *feed* 90.41, *have a meal* 92.25, *rejoicing* 279.1, *rejoice* 279.5, *celebration* 405.1, *celebrate* 405.10, *party* 408.6

feast day *holy day* 85.12, *rejoicing* 279.1, *anniversary* 405.5
feaster *eater* 92.15
feasting *appetite* 92.2, *eating meals* 92.4
Feast of Lights *Jewish Holy Days and Seasons* 85
Feast of Tabernacles *Jewish Holy Days and Seasons* 85
Feast of the Dedication *Jewish Holy Days and Seasons* 85
Feast of Weeks *Jewish Holy Days and Seasons* 85
feast one's eyes *look* 242.21
feat *task* 122.2, *workmanlike job* 127.6, *courageous act* 284.7, *cause of wonder* 294.4, *method* 387.4, *undertaking* 391.1, *deed* 412.2, *success* 845.1
feather *plumage* 36.7, *type of bed* 101.9, *row* 150.32, *pilot* 689.15, *type* 777.4, *little bit* 800.4
feather ball or **feathery** *golf equipment* 156.5
featherbedded *negotiated* 57.16
featherbedding *work practices* 57.2, *negotiated* 57.16
featherbrain *capricious person* 381.3
featherbrained *inconstant* 378.6, *capricious* 381.4, *confused* 766.12, *not serious* 800.11
feather duster *cleaning tool* 111.10
feathered friend *birds* 36.1
featherheaded *not serious* 800.11
featheriness *smoothness* 543.2
feathering *rowing techniques* 150.16, *rowing* 150.27, *miscellaneous aviation terms* 689.9
feather in one's cap *successfulness* 845.3
feather one's nest *be selfish* 444.6, *get rich* 485.13
feathers *avian characteristic* 36.6, *plumage* 36.7, *badminton terms* 165.11, *Phobias* 283, *decorative article* 532.5, *animal covering* 613.15
feather star *echinoderm* 39.5
featherweight *boxing weight divisions* 152.6, *combat* 152.17, *light* 539.4, *little person* 580.5
feathery *insubstantial* 539.5, *smooth* 543.8
feathery cloud *cloud appearance* 9.19
feat of arms *warfare* 422.10
feat of skill *workmanlike job* 127.6
feature *dramatize* 136.33, *produce* 137.21, *publicize* 173.18, *emphasize* 200.6, *external appearance* 264.5, *aspect* 623.4, *component* 760.3, *thing included* 763.2, *the special* 779.8, *concomitant* 794.4, *display* 843.13
feature article *news story* 171.3
featured *displayed* 843.8
featured player *actor* 137.13
feature film *movie type* 137.3, *work of art* 522.4
featureless *vacant* 576.12, *shapeless* 625.2, *frequent* 663.6, *continuous* 774.9
featurelessness *shapelessness* 625.1
features *external appearance* 264.5, *contents* 577.1, *face* 621.6, *nature* 624.5
features editor *print journalist* 175.5
feature story *news story* 171.3
feature writer *print journalist* 175.5

featuring *starring* 137.18,
containing 577.7
febrifugal *remedial* 115.14
febrifuge *medicine* 115.2
febrile *of disease* 114.25
febrile disease *disease* 114.4
febriphobia *Phobias* 283
fecal 25.14; *unclean* 112.8
fecally *excrementally* 25.27
feces 25.5; *waste product* 96.7, *dirt*
112.5, *Phobias* 283
feckless *unskillful* 128.4, *capricious*
381.4, *useless* 802.7
fecklessness *capriciousness* 381.2,
uselessness 802.1
feculence *feces* 25.5, *dirt* 112.5
feculent *fecal* 25.14
fecund *fertile* 22.8, *procreative*
22.10, *imaginative* 360.10, *lush*
485.11, *productive* 522.11
fecundate *propagate* 21.15, *fertilize*
22.12
fecundation *fertilization* 21.6,
procreation 22.4
fecundative *reproductive* 21.11
fecundity *fertility* 22.1
fedayeen *guerrilla* 77.7
Federal *Furniture Styles* 101
federal *governmental* 49.24,
national 566.10
**Federal Bureau of
Investigation (FBI)** *law
enforcement agency* 53.7, *security
force* 810.13
federal court *type of court* 54.9
federal debt *national debt* 488.2
federal depository *money storage*
484.20
federal district court *type of court*
54.9
federal election *election* 382.6
federal government 49.7; *United
States government* 49.21
federalism *federal government* 49.7,
joint control 827.5
Federalist party *Political Parties*
50
federally *nationally* 566.13
federal marshal *law officer* 53.6
federal post *position of authority*
52.4
federal prison *prison* 55.1
Federal Reserve System *treasury*
484.19
federate 480.21; *form an alliance*
735.25, *come together* 757.10, *join*
827.17
federated *allied* 735.15,
collaborative 757.7
federation *federal government* 49.7,
body politic 50.3, *party* 59.3, *union
of nations* 566.2, *alliance* 735.5,
collaboration 757.2, *joint control*
827.5, *team* 827.7, *commission*
833.1
**Fédération Internationale de
Football Association (FIFA)**
soccer associations and awards
163.6
**Fédération Internationale de
Gymnastique** *gymnastics
organizations* 157.9
**Fédération Internationale de
Hockey (FIH)** *hockey
organizations* 158.7
**Fédération Internationale de
l'Automobile (FIA)** *racing
governing bodies* 146.7
**Fédération Internationale
d'Escrime (FIE)** [Fr] *fencing
association* 153.4
**Fédération Internationale
Sociétés d'Aviron (FISA)**
rowing associations 150.17

fedora *hat* 100.32
feds [Inf] *law enforcement agency*
53.7
fed up *displeased* 291.6, *bored*
296.5
fee 494.3; *payment* 433.5, *reward
for service* 453.5, *earnings* 467.5,
gift 472.2, *pay* 489.6, *expense*
491.2
fee *or* **feud** *medieval ownership*
469.9, *historical property terms*
470.3
feeble *unemphatic* 201.2, *tasteless*
220.4, *faint* 233.6, *murky* 248.5,
weak 517.6, *ill* 517.8, *diminishing*
597.16, *low quality* 745.7
feeble-minded *intellectually
subnormal* 316.7, *simpleminded*
526.11
feeble-mindedly *unintelligently*
316.9
feeble-mindedness *mental
deficiency* 316.2
feebleness *lack of emphasis* 201.1,
tastelessness 220.1, *helplessness*
515.3, *weakness* 517.1,
diminishment 597.7
feebly *unemphatically* 201.4,
powerlessly 515.16, *weakly*
517.14, *badly* 745.15
feed 90.41; *machine tool* 14.9,
practice livestock farming 15.6,
fertilize 22.12, *support life* 28.21,
manage grassland 45.10, *provision*
89.9, *animal food* 90.2, *eat* 92.21,
refresh 94.6, *preserve* 815.14
feed [Inf] *feast* 92.9, *role* 136.23
feed *or* **feeder** [Inf] *role* 136.23,
entertainer 138.8
feedback *circuit function* 14.38,
reply 671.5
feedback inhibition *enzyme*
12.11
feed bag *bag* 578.7
feedbin *farm tool* 16.5
feeder *farm tool* 16.5, *eater* 92.15,
tributary 570.2
feeder [Inf] *role* 136.23
feeder road *road* 687.2
feed-forward control *systems and
process control* 14.28
feeding *gardening* 17.5, *eating*
92.1, 92.18, *edible* 92.20
feeding frenzy *feast* 92.9
feedlot *farm building* 16.4
feed on *sponge* 401.13
feed one's face [Inf] *eat well*
92.23
feedstuff *animal feed* 16.12
feedyard *farm building* 16.4
feel 266.14; *propound a philosophy*
4.21, *sense* 212.9, *touch* 216.1,
216.9, *be touched by* 216.10, *be
intuitive* 320.9, *imagine* 327.14,
judiciousness 337.2, *texture* 552.1,
weaving 609.2, *characteristic*
779.5
feel an affinity for *have a rapport
with* 735.24
feel an obligation *be grateful*
310.6
feel at home *be informal* 407.10,
829.19
feel at liberty *be informal* 829.19
feel bad *be unhealthy* 114.29
feel cheated *be unsatisfied* 98.10
feel concern for *be curious* 321.7
feel confident *expect* 281.12
feel contrite *be penitent* 451.7
feel deeply 266.16; *be sensitive*
267.5
feel dissatisfied *be unsatisfied*
98.10
feel dizzy *be fatigued* 820.5

feeler *sense organ* 212.4, *experiment*
335.1, *retainer* 471.3, *tentative
offer* 504.2, *component* 760.3
feeler *or* **feeler gauge** *measuring
instrument* 589.12
feel fear *detest* 291.13
feel fine *be healthy* 113.11
feel for 266.17; *be sensitive* 267.5,
love 299.21, *pity* 308.6
feel free *be informal* 829.19
feel giddy *be fatigued* 820.5
feel good *be healthy* 113.11, *feel
pleasure* 214.12
feel great *be healthy* 113.11
feel guilty *appear guilty* 450.10, *be
penitent* 451.7
feel hot 217.19
feel hurt *be offended* 302.14
feel ill *be unhealthy* 114.29
feeling 266.9; *philosophy* 4.1,
sensory 19.22, *belief* 87.1, *emphasis*
200.1, *sensible* 212.6, *touch* 216.1,
emotion 266.3, *sensitive* 266.11,
267.3, *amorous* 299.18, *pity*
308.1, *intuition* 320.1, *insight*
320.3, *idea* 327.1, *theory* 327.2,
prediction 358.1, *conduct* 399.1,
depth of feeling 598.7, *ambience*
615.3
feeling fine *feeling well* 113.8
feeling for *aptitude* 127.4
feeling for animals 34.11
feeling good *feeling well* 113.8
feeling great *feeling well* 113.8
feeling guilty *appearing guilty*
450.7
feeling like a million dollars
feeling well 113.8
feelingly *sensationally* 212.12, *with
feeling* 266.18, *sensitively* 267.6
feeling of identity *agreement*
462.1
feeling pain 215.6
feeling person 266.8
feelings 266.1; *sensitivity* 212.2
feeling well 113.8
feel in one's bones *or* **guts** *feel
instinctively* 266.15
feel instinctively 266.15
feel insulted *be offended* 302.14
feel it coming *foresee* 357.9
feel it in one's bones *be intuitive*
320.9, *foresee* 357.9
feel kinship for *agree with* 462.10
feel like a kid again *be refreshed*
94.8
feel like a million dollars *be
healthy* 113.11
feel like a new person *be
refreshed* 94.8
feel like hell [Inf] *be unhealthy*
114.29
feel like oneself again *get healthy*
113.12
feel no concern for *be incurious*
322.5
feel no obligation *be ungrateful*
311.5
feel no pity *be pitiless* 309.5
feel no remorse *be impenitent*
452.4
feel nothing *be impenitent* 452.4
feel offended *be offended* 302.14
feel oneself again *be refreshed*
94.8
feel one's way *have foresight*
357.8, *hesitate* 693.12
feel pain 215.8; *be in trouble*
848.13
feel piqued *be offended* 302.14
feel pity *pity* 308.6
feel pleasure 214.12
feel pride *show off* 402.15
feel refreshed *be refreshed* 94.8

feel remorse *be penitent* 451.7
feel resentment *resent* 302.13
feel rotten *be unhealthy* 114.29
feel shame *be shy* 403.13, *be
penitent* 451.7
feel sick *be unhealthy* 114.29, *react
against* 291.15
feel something is missing *be
unsatisfied* 98.10
feel sorrow for *pity* 308.6
feel sorry *be penitent* 451.7
feel sorry for *pity* 308.6
feel sure *be certain* 840.13
feel the ground give way *be in
danger* 811.11
feel the ground slip away *be in
danger* 811.11
feel the lack *be unsatisfied* 98.10
feel the pinch *be poor* 486.14, *be
in difficulty* 824.19, *need money*
848.14
feel the pulse *experiment* 335.11
feel the spirit *revere* 81.26
feel the urge *be persuaded* 178.20,
be motivated 508.10
feel unfulfilled *be unsatisfied*
98.10
feel up [Inf] *touch* 216.9
feel well *be healthy* 113.11
fees *income* 492.3
fee simple *legal ownership* 469.8,
legal property terms 470.2
fee tail *legal property terms* 470.2
feet of clay *weakness* 517.1, *defect*
806.4, *vulnerability* 811.6
Fehling's test *sugar test* 12.6
feign *be untruthful* 192.20, *deceive*
330.12, *do great deeds* 412.14
feigned *ungenuine* 192.13
feigning *hypocritical* 330.10
feint *boxing techniques* 152.5, *box*
152.19, *fencing movements* 153.3,
fence 153.7, *artifice* 193.5,
stratagem 822.2
feinting *combat* 152.17, *fencing*
153.6
feistiness *obstinacy* 379.1
feisty *obstinate* 379.5, *strong in
spirit* 516.11, *vigorous* 518.2
feldspar *material* 129.2
f-electron *atom* 10.52
felicitate *congratulate* 405.12
felicitation *compliment* 437.4
felicitous *approving* 437.9, *fluid*
527.5, *timely* 659.4, *prosperous*
847.5
felicitously *prosperously* 847.9
felicitousness *pleasantness* 271.1
felicity *pleasure* 214.2, *joy* 269.1,
grace 527.2, *prosperity* 847.1
felid *flesh-eating mammal* 35.9
Felidae *flesh-eating mammal* 35.9
feline *type of animal* 34.5, *flesh-
eating mammal* 35.9, *cat* 35.11,
carnivorous 35.26, *cunning*
822.4
fell *killing* 30.17, *manage trees*
43.14, *knock down* 523.13, *make
horizontal* 603.10, *animal covering*
613.15, *shoot* 696.18, *flatten*
716.15
fell [Brit] *hill* 569.2
fell [Scot] *heights* 596.4
fella [Inf] *loved one* 299.13
fellate *stimulate* 20.22
fellatio *or* **fellation** *sex act* 20.10
felling *tree management* 43.6
fellow *male* 32.1, *educator* 48.4,
friend 62.2, *educational leader*
68.11, *recipient* 473.5, *affinity*
733.3, *equal* 740.7, *member*
760.9, *companion* 794.8,
cooperator 827.8

---

fellow [Inf] *male title of address* 32.3, *loved one* 299.13
fellow citizen *national* 61.3
fellow countryman *or* **countrywoman** *national* 61.3
fellow creature *person* 18.8
fellow feeling *friendly relations* 62.3, *good feeling* 266.4, *love* 299.1, *pity* 308.1, *agreement* 462.1, *fellowship* 827.2
fellows *team* 827.7
fellow servant *coworker* 123.17
fellowship **827.2;** *instructorship* 48.5, *party* 59.3, *association* 59.4, *friendship* 62.1, *compassion* 305.2, *good company* 408.9, *grant* 453.4, *agreement* 462.1, *profit* 467.6, *gift* 472.2, *something received* 473.2, *income* 492.3, *compatibility* 735.4, *alliance* 735.5, *companionship* 794.3, *financial assistance* 825.6
fellowship winner *recipient* 473.5
fellow student *learner* 48.6
fellow tenant *possessor* 469.10
fellow traveler *assenter* 346.3, *supporter* 605.9, *companion* 794.8
fellow worker *coworker* 123.17
Fell pony Horse and Pony Breeds 159, *pony* 159.6
felo-de-se *suicide* 30.8, *self-punishment* 454.10
felon *lawbreaker* 53.15, *wrongdoer* 430.8, *evil person* 446.3, *villain* 448.5, *guilty person* 450.5
felonious *offending* 53.25, *unlawful* 430.15, *villainous* 448.12
feloniously *villainously* 448.18
felony *violation of the law* 427.2, *wicked act* 448.7, *illegality* 450.4
felsic rock *igneous rock* 8.32
felt Fabrics and Fibers 130, *weave* 130.20
felted *woven* 130.15
felt hat *hat* 100.32
felucca Sailing Ships and Boats 690
female 33.1, 33.16; *sex* 20.1, *sexual* 20.15, *of flowers* 42.11
female animal 33.15
female bird 36.16
female circumcision *non-Christian ritual* 85.8
female condom *contraceptive* 23.6, *barrier* 826.7
female impersonator *entertainer* 138.8, *imitator* 736.6
female mammal 35.19
femaleness 33.2; *sex* 20.1
female person *female* 33.1
female sex organs *organs of reproduction* 21.9
female title of address 33.3
female transvestite *bisexual* 33.11
female warrior *former servicewoman* 77.6
feme covert [Form] *married woman* 64.11
femidom *contraceptive* 23.6
feminacy *femaleness* 33.2
femineity *femaleness* 33.2
feminine *grammatical term* 5.29, *of grammar* 5.41, *sexual* 20.15, *female* 33.16
feminine gender *femaleness* 33.2
feminine intuition *intuition* 320.1
feminineness *femaleness* 33.2
feminine rhyme *rhyme* 139.11
femininity *sex* 20.1, *femaleness* 33.2
feminism *femaleness* 33.2, *equal opportunity* 831.2

feminist *liberated woman* 33.12, *female* 33.16
feministic *female* 33.16
feminist theater *theater movements* 136.9
feminist theology Theologies 81
feminophobia Phobias 283
femme fatale *loose woman* 33.6, *tempter* 178.10, *lover* 299.11, *motivator* 508.6, *attractive female* 529.5, *charmer* 700.6
femto Decimal Prefixes 589
femur Human Bones 19
fen *marsh* 559.8, 572.3
fence 153.7, 419.21; *farm building* 16.4, *ornamental garden* 17.3, *fight* 77.35, *evade* 181.17, *lack candor* 192.22, *be equivocal* 380.7, *be evasive* 386.20, *barrier* 419.10, 826.7, *parry* 419.27, *duel* 422.24, *retainer* 471.3, *enclosing thing* 619.3, *enclose* 619.6, *limit marker* 620.4, *collide* 695.10, *separator* 753.5, *shelter* 812.4, *barrier* 826.7, *block* 826.17
fence [Inf] *recipient* 473.5, *receive* 473.13, *dishonest person* 479.11, *trader* 480.11, *trade* 480.18, *merchant* 482.10
fence around *protect* 810.21
fenced in *retained* 471.6, *blocked* 826.13
fenced-in *enclosed* 619.4
fence in *detain* 471.9, *enclose* 619.6, *protect* 810.21
fence off *exclude* 764.7
fencer 153.5; *athlete* 422.15
fence-sitter *indifferent person* 289.6, *moderate person* 772.8
fence-sitting *inconstancy* 378.2, *irresolution* 461.3, *medium* 742.6, *irresolute* 772.13
fence-straddling *inconstancy* 378.2
fencing 153.1, 153.6, Sporting Activities 145, *lack of candor* 192.4, *duel* 422.12
fencing area *fencing* 153.1
fencing assault *fencing* 153.6
fencing associations 153.4
fencing bout *fencing* 153.1
fencing clothes *fencing equipment* 153.2
fencing equipment 153.2
fencing movements 153.3
fencing sword *sharp weapon* 78.6
fencing weapon *fencing equipment* 153.2
fender board *sailboat parts and accessories* 150.4
fenders *sailboat parts and accessories* 150.4
fend for oneself *be independent* 829.18
fend off 701.9; *parry* 419.27
fenestra Architectural Elements 134
fenestration *window* 134.10
fen farming *arable farming* 16.6
fenland *marsh* 572.3
fennel Herbs and Spices 91
fenny *marshy* 559.11, *of landmasses* 572.12
Fens, the *regions of the British Isles* 564.8
Fensalir *heaven* 82.15
fenugreek Herbs and Spices 91
feral *of animals* 34.13
fermata *written music* 140.21, *pause* 668.3, *gap* 775.4
Fermat prime Mathematical Concepts 6
Fermat's last theorem Mathematical Concepts 6

Fermat's principle Classical Physical Laws 10
ferment *react* 11.38, *mold* 47.22, *sour* 223.8, *burst of anger* 302.6, *violence* 520.1, *leavening* 539.3, *lighten* 539.9, *bubble* 558.24, *changer* 665.9, *cause change* 665.16, *chemical change* 670.2, *convert* 670.11, *transform* 670.13, *turbulence* 684.3, *be agitated* 684.21, *confusion* 766.4, *commotion* 768.5
fermentation *leavening* 539.3, *gaseousness* 556.6, *aeration* 558.11, *change* 665.1, *chemical change* 670.2, *turbulence* 684.3
fermentative *leavening* 539.7
fermented *fungal* 47.18, *drinkable* 93.18, *unpalatable* 223.6
fermented drink *alcoholic drink* 93.9
fermenting *production* 522.1, *leavening* 539.7, *converting* 670.8
fermi Scientific and Technical Units 589
fermion *elementary particle* 10.53
fermium Chemical Elements and Common Allotropes 11
fern 46.1
fern ally *fern* 46.1
Fernando de Noronha Archipelago Islands 572
fernlike 46.6
fernlike plant *fern* 46.1
fern plant 46.2
fern seed *fern plant* 46.2
ferny *fernlike* 46.6
ferocious *cruel* 306.10, *violent* 520.5
ferociously *cruelly* 306.17, *violently* 520.11
ferociousness *cruelty* 306.4
ferocity *cruelty* 306.4, *violence* 520.1
Ferrers diagram *combinatorics* 6.63
ferreting out *detection* 345.2
ferret out *detect* 345.12
ferrets Collective Names 59
ferriage *conveyance* 685.2
ferrimagnetism *magnetism* 10.45
Ferris wheel *amusement park and playground equipment* 167.8, *wheel* 682.9
ferrite *magnet* 10.47
ferroconcrete *hard substance* 542.3
ferroconcrete hull *sailboat parts and accessories* 150.4
ferromagnetic core *magnet* 10.47
ferromagnetism *magnetism* 10.45
ferrotype *older photograph* 132.4
ferruginous *brown* 256.5
ferrule *fishing tackle* 154.7
ferry *convey* 685.9, Ships and Boats 690
ferry bridge *bridge* 551.10
ferry crossing *waterway* 690.2
ferrying *nautical* 690.14
ferryman *transferrer* 685.4, *transporter* 686.4, *nautical person* 690.12
fertile 22.8; *farmable* 16.17, *fruiting* 44.5, *plentiful* 97.4, *imaginative* 360.10, *yielding* 467.14, *lush* 485.11, *productive* 522.11
fertile land 22.2
fertilely *gainfully* 467.24
fertile nuclide *nuclear fission* 10.60
fertility 22.1
fertility cult 22.7
fertility drug *fertilizer* 22.6

fertility god *minor deity* 82.2
fertility rite *fertility cult* 22.7, *non-Christian ritual* 85.8
fertility symbol *fertility cult* 22.7, *symbol* 108.28
fertilization 21.6; *procreation* 22.4
fertilize 22.12; *farm* 16.19, *cultivate* 17.19, *propagate* 21.15, *manage grassland* 45.10
fertilizer 16.9, 17.8, 22.6; *propagator* 21.7
fertilizers *industrial chemistry* 11.21
fertilizer spreader *farm tool* 16.5
fertilizing *cultivation* 16.7
ferule *instrument of punishment* 454.13
fervent *zealous* 81.22, *emphatic* 200.3, *passionate* 266.12, *desirous* 288.13, *eager* 373.8, *active* 414.13, *strong* 516.9, *hasty* 818.3
fervently *emphatically* 200.7, *with feeling* 266.18, *eagerly* 288.27, *acutely* 516.18
fervent patriotism *bellicosity* 76.15
fervid *strong* 516.9
fervidity *eagerness* 373.2
fervor *religiousness* 81.2, *emphasis* 200.1, *emotion* 266.3, *eagerness* 288.3, 373.2, *liking* 290.1, *energy* 414.4
fescue *crop* 16.8
fesse point Heraldic Terms 184
festa *celebration* 405.1
festal *ritualistic* 85.15, *celebrative* 405.9
festal cheer *plenty* 90.4
festally *ritually* 85.21
fester 25.23; *be dirty* 112.10, *ulcer* 114.18, *decay* 808.16
festering *pus* 25.7, *purulent* 25.16, *unclean* 112.8, *infection* 114.7, *of disease* 114.25, *toxic* 114.28
festina lente [L] *move slowly* 693.11
festival *social gathering* 59.7, *religious festival* 85.13, *rejoicing* 279.1, *celebration* 405.1
Festival of Lights *religious festival* 85.13
festive 408.13; *ritualistic* 85.15, *celebrative* 405.9
festive board *plenty* 90.4
festive gathering *feast* 92.9
festively *sociably* 408.19
festive occasion *celebration* 405.1
festivities *celebration* 405.1
festivity *social gathering* 59.7, *amusement* 167.7, *rejoicing* 279.1, *celebration* 405.1, *sociability* 408.1, *party* 408.6
festoon *flower* 42.1, Architectural Elements 134, *decorate* 532.11, *ornament* 532.12
festoon blind *shade maker* 247.4
festschrift *compilation* 174.4
fetal *developmental* 13.33, *embryonic* 771.19
fetal heart rate monitor *prenatal diagnosis* 107.9
fetch *ghost* 86.11, *sail* 150.29, *artifice* 193.5, *scheme* 193.18, *price* 494.12, *bring* 685.11, *reach* 704.14, *illusion* 720.2
fetch a blow *strike* 418.21
fetch about *turn around* 680.22
fetch a good price *be sold* 482.22
fetch and carry *knuckle under* 401.10, *pander to* 401.11
fetching *attractive* 700.10
fetch up in *or* **at** *reach* 704.14
fetch water in a sieve *attempt the impossible* 837.10
fete 279.6; *social gathering* 59.7,

feed 90.41, *show* 404.12,
celebration 405.1, *celebrate* 405.10,
salute 405.13, *formal occasion*
406.4, *greet* 410.11
fête champêtre [Fr] *feast* 92.9, *party*
408.6
feted *popular* 408.12
fête galante [Fr] *type of painting*
143.5
fetichism *idolatry* 83.4, *witchcraft*
86.6
fetichistic *witchlike* 86.19
fetid *unclean* 112.8, *miasmic*
556.16
fetid *or* **foetid** *stinking* 227.3
fetid air *miasma* 556.3
fetidness *or* **foetidness** *stench*
227.1
fetish *minor deity* 82.2, *idol* 83.5,
sacred object 83.11, *talisman* 86.9
fetishism *idolatry* 83.4, *witchcraft*
86.6, *sexual disorder* 108.14,
delusion 110.2
fetishist *idolater* 83.7
fetishistic *idolatrous* 83.13,
ritualistic 85.15, *witchlike* 86.19
fetishize *idolize* 83.16
fetor *uncleanness* 112.2
fetor *or* **foetor** *stench* 227.1
fetoscope *diagnostic instrument*
107.13
fetoscopy *prenatal diagnosis* 107.9
fetter *intertwine* 752.19, *means of*
connection 754.4, *bind* 754.14,
safety device 810.15, *restraint*
826.8, *restrain* 826.19, *restrain*
someone 830.17
fettered *bound* 754.12
fetters *instrument of punishment*
454.13, *means of restraint* 830.6
fettle *health* 113.1, *make ceramics*
129.10, *nature* 624.5, *state* 725.1,
physical state 725.6
fettling *ceramic process* 129.5
fettuccine *pasta* 90.31
fetus *developmental biology* 13.22
feud *act of hostility* 63.4, *oppose*
63.11, *quarrel* 272.4, 272.9,
dissent 347.1, *dispute* 463.3, 463.9
feudal *governmental* 49.24,
propertied 470.9, *historic* 653.13,
captive 832.9
feudalism **49.5;** *subjection* 832.1
feudality *feudalism* 49.5, *medieval*
ownership 469.9, *historical property*
terms 470.3
feudal lord *protector* 810.11
feudal tax *historical tax* 494.8
feudatory *propertied* 470.9
feuilleton *newspaper* 175.2
fever *symptom* 114.3, *tropical disease*
114.10, *heat* 217.1, *Phobias* 283,
restlessness 414.7, 684.5, *tumult*
684.2
fevered *of disease* 114.25, *red-faced*
257.6, *restless* 684.16
feverish *sick* 114.24, *of disease*
114.25, *red-faced* 257.6, *fidgety*
414.14, *restless* 684.16, *hasty*
818.3
feverish haste *haste* 818.1
feverishly *warmly* 217.20,
agitatedly 684.27, *hastily* 818.7
feverishness *symptom* 114.3, *heat*
217.1, *restlessness* 684.5
fever tree Trees and Shrubs 43
few 796.1, **796.5;** *incompleteness*
98.2, *scarce* 98.8, *sparse* 595.14,
infrequent 662.2, *certain amount*
738.3, *quantitative* 738.6, *plural*
793.6, *indeterminate* 841.14
few, a *plurality* 793.1, *few* 796.1,
796.5
few and far between *scarce* 98.8,

infrequent 662.2, *dispersed* 776.6,
sparse 796.6
few bricks short of a full load, a
insane 110.9
fewer 796.7
few in number *sparse* 595.14
fewness **796.3;** *sparseness* 595.8,
infrequency 662.1, *certain amount*
738.3, *deficiency* 745.2
few words *conciseness* 198.1
fey *spiritual* 86.20, *intuitive* 266.10
feyness *psychic power* 86.4
fez *cap* 100.33
fiancé *boyfriend* 32.4, *someone*
promised 458.7
fiancée *girlfriend* 33.4, *someone*
promised 458.7
fiancée *or* **fiancé** *loved one* 299.13
Fianna Fáil Political Parties 50
fiasco *bad outcome* 293.3, *error*
846.2
fiat *command* 425.1, *rule* 780.1
fiat money *paper money* 484.14
fib *misrepresentation* 188.1,
falsehood 192.6, *lie* 192.23
fibber *liar* 192.10
fibbing *lying* 192.5, 192.16
fiber 104.3, 130.2, **552.6;** *food*
content 90.3, *materials* 104.1,
weaving 609.2, *line* 754.5
fiberboard *paper* 104.5
fiber cable *telecommunication* 169.7
fiberglass *construction material*
14.21, *fiber* 104.3, *sailing* 150.25,
snowplow 162.29, *protective*
covering 613.5, *shipbuilding* 690.4
fiberglass hull *sailboat parts and*
accessories 150.4
fiberglass ski *ski equipment* 162.10
fiberoptic cable *telecommunication*
169.7
fiber optics *photometry* 10.24
fiber-optics transmission
photometry 10.24
fiber paper *paper* 104.5
fibers *industrial chemistry* 11.21
fiberscope *diagnostic instrument*
107.13
Fibonacci numbers
Mathematical Concepts 6
fibrillation *vibration* 683.2
fibrin *protein* 12.9
fibrositis *joint disease* 114.19
fibrous *spongelike* 39.26, *chewy*
547.9, *rough* 552.8
fibrously *texturally* 552.15
fibrous protein *protein* 12.9
fibrous root *root* 41.7
fibrous-rooted *of roots* 41.19
fibster *liar* 192.10
fibula Human Bones 19
FICA *tax system* 494.6
Fichtean Philosophical Schools of
Thought 4
Fichteanism Philosophical
Schools of Thought 4
fichu *neckwear* 100.29
fickle *inconstant* 378.6, *capricious*
381.4, 841.16, *irresolute* 666.4
fickleness *inconstancy* 378.2,
capriciousness 381.2, 841.8,
irresolution 666.2
fictile *formed* 624.6
fiction **139.2;** *falsehood* 192.6,
conception 360.4, *distortion of truth*
627.4, *theory* 720.4
fictional **139.16;** *fabricated* 192.17,
narrative 202.12, *imaginative*
360.10, *imaginary* 360.12,
theoretical 720.10
fictional account **202.5**
fictional biography *novel* 139.3
fictionalization *partial truth* 192.7

fictionalize *fabricate* 192.24,
recount 202.16, *fantasize* 360.15
fictionalized *fictional* 139.16,
fabricated 192.17
fiction editor *book publishing*
personnel 174.12
fictionist *descriptive writer* 202.10
fiction writer *author* 139.13,
descriptive writer 202.10
fictitious *sophistic* 330.7, *imaginary*
360.12, *misrepresented* 627.8,
theoretical 720.10, *unreal* 722.7
fictitiously *unreally* 722.15
fictitiousness *unreality* 722.2
fictive *imaginary* 360.12
fiddle *sound* 141.15, *play an*
instrument 142.9, *touch* 216.9,
mean nothing 362.10, *method*
387.4, *meddle* 414.23
fiddle [Brit inf] *account* 493.9
fiddler *player* 141.2
fiddler crab *crustacean* 39.10
fiddlestick *part of stringed*
instrument 142.2
fiddle with *touch* 216.9
fiddling *laborious* 122.7, *restlessness*
414.7, *meddling* 414.17, *trivial*
800.14
fidelity *truthfulness* 191.1,
correctness 350.2, *constancy* 377.3,
loyalty 426.2, *morals* 431.2, *virtues*
447.2, *observance* 465.1, *literalness*
721.9, *tenacity* 755.2, *infallibility*
840.6
fidget *busy person* 414.10, *be*
irresolute 666.6, *shake* 684.24,
haste 818.1, *make haste* 818.5
fidgetiness *restlessness* 414.7,
684.5
fidgeting *irresolution* 666.2
fidgets, the *restlessness* 414.7,
684.5
fidgety **414.14;** *irresolute* 666.4,
restless 684.16
FidoNet *computer communications*
15.25
fiducial point *point* 6.34, *orbit*
7.22
fiduciary *agent* 123.15, *monetary*
484.22
fiduciary currency *paper money*
484.14
fiduciary heir *beneficiary* 473.6
fief *medieval ownership* 469.9,
historical property terms 470.3
fiefdom *historical property terms*
470.3
field *set* 6.19, *algebra* 6.21, *data-*
related concepts 15.23, *farmland*
16.3, *grassland* 45.2, *subject* 48.3,
Collective Names 59, *sports*
ground 145.2, *stadium* 155.3,
163.2, *hockey areas* 158.2, *track*
and field 166.20, *television set*
172.6, Heraldic Terms 184,
educational topic 328.4,
geographical space 563.3, *range*
563.7, *region* 563.1, *sphere*
564.10, *lowland* 572.6,
specialization 779.3
field, the *horse racing* 159.10,
finalist 422.16, *the opposition*
828.8
field archery Sporting Activities
145
field army *military organization*
58.4, *armed force* 77.10
field army commander *military*
position 58.6
field day *celebration* 405.1, *sporting*
event 422.6
field desorb *absorb* 11.40
field desorption *surface chemistry*
11.20

field emission *electron emission*
14.42
fielder *baseball team* 147.2
field event 166.10
field general [Inf] *offense* 155.6
field glasses *visual aid* 242.14
field goal *playing terms* 148.4,
scoring 155.5, *successful thing*
845.5
field-goal kicker *special team*
155.11
field grade officer *military*
position 58.6
field guide *type of book* 174.3
field gun *guns* 78.9
field hockey Sporting Activities
145, *hockey* 158.1
field hockey tactics **158.5**
field ionize *absorb* 11.40
field judge *football player* 155.15
field magnet *magnet* 700.3
field marshal [Brit] *military leader*
68.10
field mushroom *mushroom* 47.2
field of battle **422.11;**
slaughterhouse 30.16, *battleground*
76.24
field of blood *battleground* 76.24
field of conflict *battleground*
76.24
field of influence *sphere of*
influence 512.7
field of vision *viewpoint* 242.12,
visibility 244.1
field peas *crop* 16.8
field piece *guns* 78.9
field spaniel Breeds of Dogs 35
field sports *hunting* 160.2, *sports*
422.3
field station *weather station* 9.5,
place of experimentation 335.6
field trial *hunting* 160.2
fieldwork *work* 122.1, *military*
defenses 419.9
fiend *malefactor* 306.6, *evil person*
446.3, *evil spirit* 446.4
fiendish *witchlike* 86.19, *cruel*
306.10, *demonic* 446.9, *wicked*
463.9
fiendishly *cruelly* 306.17, *devilishly*
446.14, *wickedly* 448.15
fiendishness *cruelty* 306.4,
wickedness 448.1
fiendlike *cruel* 306.10, *demonic*
446.9
fierce *warlike* 76.27, *heating*
217.12, *angry* 302.11, *active*
414.13, *strong* 516.9, *violent*
520.5
fiercely *angrily* 302.24, *strongly*
516.17, *violently* 520.11
fierceness *violence* 520.1
fierily *warmly* 217.20
fiery *emphatic* 200.3, *heating*
217.12, *bright* 246.14, *red-faced*
257.6, *passionate* 266.12, *violent*
520.5
fiery cross *warning signal* 814.3
fiesta *social gathering* 59.7, *religious*
festival 85.13, *celebration*
405.1
Fiesta Bowl *football* 155.1
fife Musical Instruments 142
fifteen *eleven to nineteen* 792.7
fifteenth *less than one* 787.4,
eleventh and above 792.18
fifth **792.12;** *ranked* 6.72, *chord*
140.18, *less than one* 787.4, *five*
792.1, *fivefold* 792.26
fifth column *subversion* 427.3
fifth columnism *subversion*
427.3
fifth columnist *informer* 170.8,
hypocrite 192.9, *seditionist* 427.7

fifthly *fivefold* 792.26
fifth part *five* 792.1
fifth wheel *superfluity* 99.4
fiftieth *twentieth* 792.19
fifty *twenty and over* 792.8
fifty cents *US coinage* 484.10
fifty-dollar bill *US coinage* 484.10
fifty-fifty *on equal terms* 740.9, *medium* 742.6, *diluted* 751.9, *irresolute* 772.13, *in half* 789.21, *equal chance* 842.7, *causeless* 842.11
fifty percent *half* 789.7, *in half* 789.21
fig *finery* 100.6
fight 77.35, 422.9, 422.23; *oppose* 63.11, 375.13, *battle* 76.23, 76.33, *go to war* 76.29, *boxing* 152.2, *box* 152.19, *be off-color* 251.18, *quarrel* 272.9, 302.7, 302.17, *react against* 291.15, *contention* 422.1, *contend* 422.22, *subvert* 427.13, *dispute* 463.3, 463.9, *disagree* 463.8, *violence by person* 520.2, *club* 695.15, *disruption* 766.7, *conflict* 828.3, *object* 828.18
fight a defensive battle *act on the defensive* 419.29
fight against *counteract* 510.7, *oppose* 828.15
fight a pitched battle *declare war* 422.25
fight as a heavyweight *box* 152.19
fight back *counterattack* 418.24, *retaliate* 419.30
fighter 422.14; *warrior* 76.25, *combatant* 77.1, *military aircraft* 77.30, *boxer* 152.8, *unpleasant person* 272.5, *attempter* 390.3
fighter-bomber *military aircraft* 77.30
fighter pilot *air force person* 77.31, *attacker* 418.10
fight fire with fire *retaliate* 420.4
fight for *plead for* 419.25, *give moral support* 605.18
fight for freedom *be liberated* 831.7
fight hand-to-hand *fight* 422.23
fight hard *declare war* 422.25
fight-hungry *contentious* 422.20
fighting *military* 58.10, *warfare* 76.3, *warring* 76.26, *combat sport* 152.1, *boxing* 152.2, *combat* 152.17, *ice hockey tactics* 158.4, *dissension* 272.3, *attacking* 418.14, *contention* 422.1, *contending* 422.19, *divisiveness* 463.2, *disagreeing* 463.6, *conflict* 828.3
Fighting Bull *Breeds of Cattle* 16
fighting chair 154.8
fighting chance *equal chance* 842.7
fighting cock *fighter* 422.14
fighting drunk *drunk* 121.25
fighting fit *healthy* 113.4
fighting force *type of power* 514.6
fighting forces *armed forces* 77.9
fighting mad *angry* 302.11
fighting man *combatant* 77.1, *soldier* 77.4
fighting skill *combat sport* 152.1
fighting spirit *bellicosity* 76.15, *courage* 284.1
fighting sport *combat sport* 152.1
fight it out *battle* 76.33, *declare war* 422.25
fight like cats and dogs *disagree* 463.8
fight like devils *or* **fiends** *declare war* 422.25

fight off *revolt* 417.12, *parry* 419.27, *fend off* 701.9
fight on! 417.16
fight one's way *follow up* 385.16, *be in motion* 677.14
fight shy *shy* 386.17
fight the good fight *battle* 76.33, *preach* 84.14, *declare war* 422.25, *be moral* 431.13, *be virtuous* 447.8
fight to the death *contention* 422.1
fight to the finish *battle* 76.33, *declare war* 422.25
fight to the last man *battle* 76.33, *contention* 422.1, *declare war* 422.25
figment *conception* 360.4, *illusion* 720.2, *unreality* 722.2
figmental *illusory* 720.9
figment of the imagination *conception* 360.4
figural *numerical* 783.7
figurate *numerical* 783.7
figuration *representation* 187.1
figurative *representational* 187.8, *representing* 202.14, *symbolic* 361.8, *mysterious* 844.11
figurative art *Western Art Styles* 133
figurative blindness 243.8
figurative expressions 128.11, 543.10, 545.8
figurative language *literary device* 139.12
figuratively *pictorially* 133.11, *representationally* 187.15, *meaningfully* 361.16, *mysteriously* 844.17
figurative meaning *type of meaning* 361.4
figurative overestimation 343.3
figurative usage 42.8, 43.9, 44.4, 253.5, 254.4, 255.4, 256.4, 257.4, 258.4, 259.5, 260.5, 261.4, 262.4; *passage of time* 639.3
figure 187.4; *numeral* 6.8, *geometric figure* 6.39, *perceptual concept* 108.30, *harmonic element* 140.14, *sculpture* 144.1, *external appearance* 264.5, *sum* 484.5, *price* 494.1, *fashion* 536.7, *shape* 617.2, *form* 624.1, 624.9, *nature* 624.5, *characteristic* 779.5, *number* 783.1, 783.9, *calculate* 784.10, *latency* 844.11
figured bass *harmonic element* 140.14
figure eight *curved thing* 629.3, *circle* 631.2, *flight maneuver* 689.6, *eight* 792.4
figure eight knot *Knots, Bends, Hitches, Splices* 754
figure eight loop knot *Knots, Bends, Hitches, Splices* 754
figure-ground *perceptual concept* 108.30
figurehead *lack of authority* 515.2, *vanguard* 621.5, *nonentity* 800.8
figure-hugging *narrow* 593.8, *adhesive* 755.5
figure of eight bend *Knots, Bends, Hitches, Splices* 754
figure of fun *object of ridicule* 368.3, *laughingstock* 369.4, *butt* 436.8
figure out *rationalize* 4.20
figure out [Inf] *number* 783.9, *calculate* 784.10
figures *mathematics* 6.1, *statistics* 784.2
figure-skate *ice-skate* 162.36
figure skater *ice skater* 162.22

figure skating *Sporting Activities* 145, *ice skating* 162.15
figure-skating *ice-skating* 162.32
figure-watching *loss of weight* 468.3
figure work *calculation* 784.1
figurine *sculpture* 144.1, *figure* 187.4
figuring *numeration* 6.10, *sculpture* 144.1, *calculation* 784.1
figurist *sculptor* 144.4
Fiji *Countries* 566
Fiji Islands *Islands* 572
filament *galaxy* 7.5, *sun* 7.15, *flower part* 42.3, *fiber* 104.3, 130.2, 552.6, *fineness* 595.5
filamentary cloud *cloud appearance* 9.19
filament lamp *incandescent light* 246.5
filamentous *algal* 47.20, *fine* 595.12
filch *steal* 479.14
filcher *thief* 479.8
filching *stealing* 479.1
file *chronicle* 3.4, 3.15, *data-related concepts* 15.23, *army formation* 77.15, *collection* 105.12, *save* 105.20, *document* 170.3, *record* 185.1, 185.13, *rough thing* 544.2, *smoother* 545.2, *sharpener* 549.8, *sharpen* 549.16, *abrasive* 553.14, *grate* 553.24, *eraser* 554.7, *grind* 554.15, *itemize* 577.13, *packet* 578.4, *contract* 582.12, *delay* 658.13, *catalog* 767.7, *categorize* 767.21, *consecutiveness* 774.1, *procession* 774.6, *table* 785.2, *list* 785.11
file a brief *litigate* 54.27
file a claim *litigate* 54.27
file cabinet *cabinet* 101.8, 578.3
file clerk *record keeper* 185.8
filed *chronicled* 3.12, *saved* 105.15, *recorded* 185.12, *categorized* 767.15, *classed* 777.11, *listed* 785.9
file down *smooth* 545.10, *subtract* 749.6
file (suit) for divorce *divorce* 66.9
file server *computer communications* 15.25
file transfer protocol (ftp) program *communications software* 15.27
filial love *love* 299.1
filiated *allied* 735.15
filibeg *skirt* 100.12
filibuster *outtalk* 207.8, *quibble* 330.13, *opposition* 375.2, *oppose* 375.13, *delay* 658.3, 658.13, *obstacle* 826.2, *block* 826.17
filibuster *or* **filibusterer** *hinderer* 826.11
filibusterer *opposer* 828.9
Filicinae *fern* 46.1
filiform *fine* 595.12
filigree *decorative method* 532.3, *braid* 609.3, *interweave* 609.8
filing *recordkeeping* 185.7, *grinding* 554.3, *little piece* 580.4, *shortening* 582.2, *categorization* 767.5, *listing* 785.8
filing an appeal *unfavorable verdict* 54.20
filings *crumb* 553.5, *residue* 750.2, *bits and pieces* 760.5
filing system *table* 785.2
fill 761.11; *replenish* 89.10, *suffice* 97.6, *be excessive* 99.9, *store fuel* 105.18, *practice dentistry* 107.34, *treat* 115.17, *satisfy* 273.7, *substructure* 551.8, *be present*

575.13, *stuff* 577.12, *increase* 746.6, *repair* 809.10
fill a gap *complete* 761.9
fill a need *complete* 761.9
fill a space *augment* 748.13, *fill* 761.11
filled 97.5; *full* 761.8
filled to overflowing *excessive* 99.5
filled to the brim *filled* 97.5
filled up *full* 761.8
filled with *omnipresent* 575.10
filled with holes *holed* 583.12
filler *diffuseness* 199.1, *stuffing* 577.4, *iteration* 797.2
fillet *cook* 91.10, *headdress* 100.35, *Architectural Elements* 134, *void* 709.23, *band* 754.9
fill in *clarify* 196.3, *cover for* 613.34, *be a substitute* 672.6, *complete* 761.9, *repair* 809.10
fill in [Inf] *inform* 170.11
fill-in *substitute* 613.17, 672.2
filling *superfluity* 99.4, *satisfying* 273.5, *stuffing* 577.4, *insert* 710.4, *increasing* 746.4, *fullness* 761.5
fillings *dentistry* 107.6
filling station *storehouse* 105.8, *gas* 106.6
fill-in light *lighting* 132.16
fill in the cracks *repair* 809.10
fillip *incentive* 178.4, *stimulus* 508.3, *blow* 695.5
fill oneself *be greedy* 119.4
fill one's glass *congratulate* 405.12
fill one's lungs *be refreshed* 9.4
fill one's stomach *eat well* 92.23
fill out *grow* 581.17, *fatten* 594.10, *make round* 633.9, *increase* 746.6, *complete* 761.9, *be complete* 761.10
fill space *be big* 579.18
fill the air *shatter the peace* 232.10
fill the bill *suffice* 97.6, *be desirable* 288.23, *be useful* 801.9, *be convenient* 803.5, *be effective* 845.15
fill the gap *augment* 748.13
fill to capacity *or* **to the brim** *fill* 761.11
fill up *suffice* 97.6, *store fuel* 105.18, *fuel* 106.16, *stuff* 577.12, *fill* 761.11
fill up *or* **in** *or* **out** *make bigger* 746.7
fill-up *fullness* 761.5
fill up again *restore* 809.12
fill with desire *cause desire* 288.22
fill with holes *hole* 583.17
fill with longing *cause desire* 288.22
filly *young animal* 26.4, *female animal* 33.15, *female mammal* 35.19, *young mammal* 35.20, *horse* 159.1
film 132.8, 137.19; *photograph* 132.26, *motion picture* 137.2, *motion-picture* 137.15, *recording* 185.6, *record* 185.13, *represent* 187.10, *that which makes invisible* 245.2, *murk* 248.2, *make dim* 248.8, *transparent thing* 249.4, *work of art* 522.4, *coat* 588.3, *fineness* 595.5, *coating* 613.8, *production* 843.5
film actor *or* **actress** *actor* 137.13
film advance *film* 132.8
film case *camera* 132.10
film company *motion-picture studio* 137.7
film crew *filmmaker* 137.14
film director *producer* 522.10
filmdom *motion pictures* 137.1
filmed *produced* 137.17, *recorded* 185.12

film editing *motion-picture editing* 137.8

film editor *filmmaker* 137.14

filmic *motion-picture* 137.15

filmily *finely* 595.19

filminess *murk* 248.2, *translucency* 249.2, *grain* 552.2, *fineness* 595.5

filmmaker 137.14

film noir *movie type* 137.3

filmography *list* 785.1

film over *be dim* 248.7

film plane *film* 132.8

film processing *development* 132.19

film producer *producer* 522.10

film proof *stage of proof* 174.9

film-rating system 137.4

film *or* **television review** *criticism* 365.3

film rewind *film* 132.8

films, the *motion pictures* 137.1

film school *type of school* 48.12

film speed *exposure* 132.15

film star *actor* 137.13

film studio *motion-picture studio* 137.7

filmy *difficult to see* 245.4, *murky* 248.5, *translucent* 249.8, *shady* 250.4, *delicate* 552.10, *platelike* 588.8, *fine* 595.12

filo *pastry* 90.37

filoplume *plumage* 36.7

filter 132.14; *circuit* 10.43, *extract* 11.41, *process* 14.50, *system software* 15.13, *cleaning tool* 111.10, *purify* 111.19, *sound reducer* 233.5, *porosity* 583.5, *road attribute* 687.3, *deviate* 698.15, *leak* 707.16

filterable virus *microorganism* 13.11

filter cloth *ceramic workshop and tools* 129.8

filtered *status adjectives* 11.25, *cleaned* 111.14

filtered water *water* 93.4

filter in *infiltrate* 706.13

filtering *circuit function* 14.38, *leakage* 707.5

filter press *ceramic workshop and tools* 129.8

filter pressing *ceramic process* 129.5

filter pump *surface chemistry* 11.20

filter through *be present* 575.13

filter tip *tobacco* 121.23

filter-tip *tobacco* 121.33

filth *lack of hygiene* 112.3, *dirt* 112.5, *profanity* 301.3, *immorality* 432.1

filthily *unhygienically* 114.32, *profanely* 301.19

filthiness *dirtiness* 112.1, *immorality* 432.1

filthy *dirty* 112.7, *obscene* 112.9, *unhygienic* 114.27, *profane* 301.10, *immoral* 432.9, *ribald* 535.8

filthy language *offensive language* 301.5

filthy lucre *profit* 467.6, *cash* 484.2

filthy mouth *or* **language** *or* **talk** *sexual offense* 432.6

filthy rich *well-off* 467.12, *wealthy* 485.8

filtrate *leak* 707.16

filtration *process* 11.15, *cleaning* 111.2, *leakage* 707.5

fin *fish characteristic* 38.8, *sailboard parts* 150.20, *swimming equipment* 164.8, *equalizer* 740.5, *component* 760.3

fin [Inf] *US coinage* 484.10, *five* 792.1

final *track event* 166.1, *prize competition* 422.5, *permanent* 667.2, *departing* 705.5, *ending* 773.13

final attempt *attempt* 390.1

final battle *warfare* 422.10

final cause *final intention* 374.4

final chapter *conclusion* 761.3

final curtain *play part* 136.8, *conclusion* 761.3, *ending* 773.10

final decision *intentionality* 374.2

final defeat *defeat* 846.7

final demand *demand* 425.2, *505.3, warning* 814.1

finale *play part* 136.8, *conclusion* 761.3, *end* 773.1, *ending* 773.10

final exam *conclusion* 761.3

final intention 374.4

final invoice *warning* 814.1

finalist 422.16

finality *permanence* 667.1, *conclusion* 761.3, *close* 773.9

finalization *completion* 761.2

finalize *make permanent* 667.5, *complete* 759.10, *761.9, end* 773.19

finalize accounts *settle accounts* 493.11

finalized *completed* 761.7, *ended* 773.14

finally 584.18, 773.24; *at length* 590.15

final notice *demand* 505.3, *warning* 814.1

final objective *objective* 374.5

final offer *business offer* 504.3

final rest *ease* 819.1

final resting place *burial place* 31.7, *resting place* 668.5

final result *effect* 676.1

final say *influence* 512.1

final shot *conclusion* 761.3

Final Solution *slaughter* 30.5

final stage *close* 773.9

final story *conclusion* 761.3

final stroke *execution* 30.6

final touch *conclusion* 761.3, *beautification* 807.7

final warning *demand* 425.2, *warning* 814.1

final will 372.5

final wishes *final will* 372.5

final word *intentionality* 374.2

final words *dying* 29.3

finance 457.1, 457.7, 484.7, 825.31; *find means* 102.6, *finance* 457.7, *fund* 472.15, *defray* 481.18, *489.18, donation* 491.6, *donate* 491.13, *give* 498.11, *support financially* 605.19

finance a purchase *borrow* 476.10

finance company *bank* 487.4

finance company *or* **corporation** *lending institution* 475.4

finances *resources* 102.4, *funds* 484.6

financial 457.6; *economic* 56.10, *480.14, monetary* 484.22, *accounting* 493.7, *urban* 567.14

financial accounting *finance* 457.1, *accounts* 493.4

financial adviser 457.4

financial affairs *finance* 457.1

financial aid *financial support* 605.8

financial analysis *economic indicator* 56.4

financial analyst *economist* 56.9

financial assistance 825.6; *gift* 472.2

financial backing *financial assistance* 825.6

financial collapse *insolvency* 486.2

financial company *treasury* 484.19

financial consultant *or* **adviser** *adviser* 176.5

financial control *authority* 52.1, *finance* 457.1, 484.7

financial crisis *insolvency* 490.5

financial dealing *exchange* 673.1

financial disaster *economic adversity* 848.6

financial district *urban area* 567.10

financial embarrassment *insolvency* 486.2, *awkward situation* 824.7

financial escape 816.2

financial failure *closure* 637.4

financial forecaster *forecaster* 358.9

financial institution *lending institution* 475.4

financial loss 468.4

financially 457.11, 493.13; *economically* 56.13, *monetarily* 484.27, *profitably* 492.8

financially embarrassed *indebted* 486.9

financially rewarding *rewarding* 453.9, *successful* 845.8

financially ruined *indebted* 486.9

financially sound *solvent* 485.9

financially stable *solvent* 485.9

financially worthwhile *gainful* 467.10

financial management *management system* 126.3, *finance* 457.1

financial plan *plan* 387.1

financial power *wealth* 485.1

financial provision *funds* 484.6

financial records *accounts* 493.4

financial resources *resources* 102.4

financial reverse *economic adversity* 848.6

financial reward *reward* 453.1

financial right *or* **rights** *claim* 429.3

financial ruin *insolvency* 486.2, *490.5, economic adversity* 848.6

financial sector *economy* 56.3

financial setback *economic adversity* 848.6

financial soundness *solvency* 485.4

financial stability *solvency* 485.4

financial statement *document* 170.3

financial support 605.8; *income* 492.3

financial unsoundness *insolvency* 486.2

financial upturn *revival* 809.3

financial year *finance* 457.1, *period of activity* 641.4

financier 484.17; *financial adviser* 457.4, *giver* 472.7, *lender* 475.3, *merchant* 482.10, *treasurer* 484.18

financing *borrowing* 476.1, *financial support* 605.8

finch *songbird* 36.12

finches Collective Names 59

finchlike *avian* 36.19

find 345.5, 565.11; *meteor* 7.21, *try a case* 54.28, *find means* 102.6, *judge* 341.10, *discover* 345.11, *good thing* 445.9, *windfall* 467.7, *purchase* 481.1, *reach* 704.14, *extra* 748.6, *rule* 780.12

find a bargain *buy at a discount* 495.6

findable *discoverable* 345.10

find a clue *detect* 345.12

find against *convict* 54.33, *judge* 341.10

find agreement *mediate* 75.6

find a husband *or* **wife for** *matchmake* 64.22

find a joker in the pack *have a mishap* 826.18

find a lack of evidence *acquit* 54.32

find a loophole *overcome obstacles* 845.14

find a mate for *matchmake* 64.22

find an opening 583.20

find an out *justify* 441.12

find a remedy *counteract* 510.7

find a solution *or* **resolution** *decipher* 365.13

find a use for *find useful* 801.11

find a way 691.14; *find means* 102.6, 511.8

find a way around *counteract* 510.7, *overcome obstacles* 845.14

find a way out *overcome obstacles* 845.14

find a way to *appeal to* 209.9

find bargains *buy cheaply* 497.15

find common ground *cooperate* 616.6

find difficult 824.17

finder *discoverer* 345.7

Fin de Siècle [Fr] Ages, Decades, Eras 641

fin-de-siècle art Western Art Styles 133

find fault *criticize* 438.19, 440.12, *cause difficulties* 824.22

find fault with *be dissatisfied* 274.7

find favor with *meet with approval* 437.20

find for *acquit* 54.32, *judge* 341.10

find freedom *escape* 816.8

find guilty *convict* 54.33, *judge* 341.10

find hard to understand *find unintelligible* 364.14

finding *legal justice* 53.4, *verdict* 54.18, 341.2, *discovery* 345.1, *discovering* 345.8, *solution* 376.6, *windfall* 467.7, *locating* 565.3, *ruling* 780.2

finding again *restoration* 809.2

finding a penny *good-luck sign* 358.6

finding of fact *verdict* 54.18

finding of innocence *legal innocence* 449.3

finding out 345.3

finding the spot *or* **place** *locating* 565.3

find innocent *declare innocent* 449.11

find in the cross hairs *fire* 418.18

find liable *convict* 54.33

find means 102.6, 511.8; *find a way* 691.14

find means *or* **the means** *awaken* 675.9

find no case to answer *acquit* 54.32

find no common ground *disagree* 753.19

find no fault *admire* 437.15

find not guilty *acquit* 54.32, *declare innocent* 449.11

find not to one's taste *dislike* 291.12

find one's El Dorado *get rich* 485.13

find one's feet again *be restored* 809.13

find one's level *line up* 765.24

find one's match *serve one right* 420.5

find one's way 691.15

find one's way into *enter* 706.11

find out 345.13; *learn* 48.23, *get to know* 348.12, *make certain* 840.14

find out about *find out* 345.13

find peace and quiet *take it easy* 819.3

find problems *cause difficulties* 824.22

find relief *get a reprieve* 816.9

find room for *include* 763.5

find safety *be safe* 810.20

find shelter *shelter* 812.8

find space for *include* 763.5

find the case not proven *acquit* 54.32

find the key to *decipher* 365.13

find the meaning *decipher* 365.13

find the philosophers' stone *get rich* 485.13

find the pot of gold *win an award* 467.23

find the pot of gold at the end of the rainbow *get rich* 485.13

find the sense of *decipher* 365.13

find the spot *find* 565.11

find the very thing *be suitable* 462.13

find the weight of *weigh* 538.15

find time for *have leisure time* 125.5

find time hangs heavy on one's hands *have leisure time* 125.5

find too difficult *find unintelligible* 364.14

find unintelligible 364.14

find useful 801.11; *exploit* 393.11

find words for *word* 5.43, *speak* 205.17, *style* 537.8

find words to express *speak* 205.17, *style* 537.8

fine 9.43, 595.12; *unfavorable verdict* 54.20, *healthy* 113.4, *ceramic* 129.9, *woven* 130.15, *translucent* 249.8, *majestic* 404.21, *coercive method* 428.3, *proper* 429.10, *excellent* 445.13, *principled* 447.6, *liability* 454.6, *confiscate* 454.25, *levy* 494.7, *elegant* 527.3, *beautiful* 529.7, *sparse* 541.3, *smooth* 552.9, *rainless* 560.11, *little* 580.7, *restraint* 830.1

fine and dandy [Inf] *great* 445.14

fine art *illustration* 187.2

fine arts *visual arts* 133.1

fine chemicals *industrial chemistry* 11.21

fined *punished* 454.19

fine-drawn *delicate* 552.10, *fine* 595.12

fine fettle *physical state* 725.6, *orderliness* 765.5

fine fig *physical state* 725.6

Fine Gael *Political Parties* 50

fine grain *exposure* 132.15

fine-grained *smooth* 552.9

finely 595.19; *ethically* 447.10, *sparsely* 541.6, *texturally* 552.15, *little* 580.12

finely adjusted *adjusted* 721.14

fine mess *predicament* 824.5

fineness 595.5; *translucency* 249.2, *beauty* 529.1, *refinement* 534.1, *sparseness* 541.1, *grain* 552.2, *littleness* 580.1

fineness of grain *grain* 552.2

fine opportunity *opportunity* 659.2

fine print *specifications* 779.6

fine qualities *virtues* 447.2

finer *superior* 744.8

fine rain *rain* 9.27

finer feelings *feelings* 266.1, *sensitivity* 267.1

finery 100.6; *formal clothing* 406.5

finespun *delicate* 552.10, *fine* 595.12

finesse *refinement* 48.10, 534.1, *social skill* 127.3, *bridge* 168.4, *play cards* 168.7, *subtlety* 195.3, *judiciousness* 337.2, *plot* 387.15, *elegance* 527.1, *cunning* 822.1, *be cunning* 822.5

finest class *excellence* 445.4

fine-structure constant *Classical Physical Laws* 10

fine-tune *be accurate* 350.5, *rectify* 807.22

fine-tuned *adjusted* 721.14

fine-tuning *radio reception* 172.2, *accuracy* 350.1, *adjustment* 721.5

fine-weave *woven* 130.15

fine workmanship *manual skill* 127.2

fine-woven *smooth* 552.9

fine writer *stylist* 537.4

finger *appendage* 19.5, *drink* 121.6, *play an instrument* 142.9, *painting* 143.3, *indicator* 183.7, *sense organ* 212.4, *touch* 216.9, *use up* 393.12, *retainer* 471.3, *joint* 752.7, *particle* 760.4

finger [Inf] *sign* 183.19

finger, the [Inf] *gesture of protest* 507.3

finger alphabet *aid to the deaf* 229.3

fingerboard *part of stringed instrument* 142.2

finger bowl *crockery* 578.16

fingerbreadth *short distance* 586.2

finger crack *rock face* 161.6

finger in every pie, a *overactivity* 414.9

fingering *touching* 216.2

Finger Lakes *Lakes* 568

finger-licking *edible* 92.20

fingerling *young fish* 38.6, *little person* 580.5

fingernail *body covering* 19.4, *sharp-edged thing* 549.6

fingernails *retainer* 471.3

finger painter *painter* 143.7

finger post *indicator* 183.7

fingerprint *sign* 183.1, 183.19, *means of identification* 184.3, *identify* 184.11, *vestige* 185.11, *visible effect* 676.2, *remainder* 750.1

fingerprinted *identified* 184.9

fingerprinting *means of identification* 184.3

finger puppet *figure* 187.4

fingers *retainer* 471.3

finger sandwich *sandwich* 90.9

finger's width *short distance* 586.2

fingertip *sense organ* 212.4

finial *Architectural Elements* 134

finickiness *carefulness* 323.3, *fastidiousness* 325.4, *selection* 382.1

finicky *fastidious* 325.9, *discriminating* 337.9, *selecting* 382.9, *detailed* 726.9, *troublesome* 824.13

fining *liability* 454.6

finis *conclusion* 761.3, *end* 773.1

finish *make clothing* 100.44, *manual skill* 127.2, *rowing techniques* 150.16, *row* 150.32, *horizontal bar* 157.5, *horse racing* 159.10, *racetrack* 159.12, *participate* 166.22, *elegance* 527.1,

refinement 534.1, *smoothness* 545.1, *smooth* 545.10, *texture* 552.1, *closure* 584.1, *close down* 584.15, *pass* 651.17, *stop* 668.2, *668.10, destination* 704.6, *ornamentation* 748.5, *completion* 761.2, *conclusion* 761.3, 773.3, *complete* 761.9, *be complete* 761.10, *end* 773.1, 773.19, *ending* 773.10, *discontinue* 775.10, *perfection* 805.1, *perfect* 805.19

finished *historical* 3.10, *dead* 29.11, *excellent* 68.16, *skillful* 127.10, *expert* 127.12, *well-made* 127.13, *rowing* 150.27, *elegant* 527.3, *beautified* 530.12, *closed down* 584.10, *over* 651.12, *stopped* 668.7, *no more* 718.11, *completed* 761.7, *ended* 773.14, *discontinued* 775.8, *perfect* 805.8, *hopeless* 837.6

finished article *product* 522.3

finished product *conclusion* 761.3

finished state *completion* 761.2

finisher *clothier* 100.37, *furniture making* 101.3, *doer* 412.3, *conclusion* 761.3, *ender* 773.11

finish halfway *leave imperfect* 806.9

finishing *furniture making* 101.3, *track event* 166.1, *completion* 761.2, *ending* 773.13

finishing off *completion* 761.2, *conclusion* 761.3

finishing school *type of school* 48.12

finishing stroke *conclusion* 761.3, *ender* 773.11

finishing touch *ornamentation* 748.5, *conclusion* 761.3, *beautification* 807.7

finish line *objective* 374.5

finish off *complete* 759.10, *end* 773.19, *cease* 773.20

finish one's preparations *prepare for action* 388.18

finish tape *track event* 166.1, *objective* 374.5

finish the job *work* 122.8

finish the race *reach* 704.14

finite *complex* 6.69, *human* 18.15, *limited* 620.5, *quantitative* 738.6, *fractional* 783.8

finitely *mathematically* 6.93, *quantitatively* 738.8

finite number *number* 6.4

finite sequence *sequence* 6.18

finite set *set* 6.19

fink [Inf] *informer* 170.8, *accuser* 442.3, *accuse* 442.8

fin keel *sailboat* 150.3

Finland *Countries* 566

Finnish *Breeds of Cattle* 16, *Horse and Pony Breeds* 159

Finnish Ayrshire *Breeds of Cattle* 16

Finnish Landrace *Breeds of Pigs* 16, *Breeds of Sheep* 16

Finnsheep *Breeds of Sheep* 16

Finno-Ugric *language family* 5.12

Finsteraarhorn *Mountains and Hills* 569

fiord *inlet* 572.9

fioritura *Musical Terms and Expression Marks* 140

fipple flute *Musical Instruments* 142

fir *Trees and Shrubs* 43

fir cone *tree part* 43.2

fire 217.8, 246.9, 418.18; *employ* 57.18, *fight* 77.35, *fuel* 106.16, *make ceramics* 129.10, *signal* 183.6, *emphasis* 200.1, *burn* 217.18, *burst of sound* 232.4,

incandescent light 246.5, *light* 246.19, *red thing* 257.3, *emotion* 266.3, *relieve from duty* 275.11, *Phobias* 283, *discard* 383.12, *make inactive* 415.16, *firing* 418.6, *remove power from* 515.13, *make violent* 520.10, *agent of destruction* 523.7, *bake* 560.19, *relegate* 574.18, *shoot* 696.18, *dismiss* 709.15, *eject* 764.8, *terminate* 834.7

fire! *after him!* 385.19

fire alarm *signal* 183.6, *safety device* 810.15, *danger signal* 811.5

firearm 78.7, *Historical Missile Weapons* 78, *banger* 234.3

firearms *hunting equipment* 160.4

fire a salute *greet* 410.11, *salute* 435.17

fire a salvo *salute* 405.13

fire a shot *bowl* 151.8

fire at *battle* 76.33, *hunt* 160.12, *fire* 418.18, *shoot* 696.18

fire a volley *shoot* 696.18

fire a warning flare *give warning* 814.10

fire a warning shot *signal* 183.18

fire away [Inf] *make a beginning* 771.26

fireball *meteor* 7.21, *fire* 217.8

fire bell *source of resonance* 236.4, *danger signal* 811.5

fire blanket *safety device* 810.15

fire blight *pests and diseases* 17.12

firebomb *bomb* 78.15, *cause of fire* 217.10

firebomber *cause of fire* 217.10

firebox *place for fire* 217.9

firebrand *fuel starter* 106.3, *motivator* 178.11, 508.6, *cause of fire* 217.10, *violent animal* 520.4

firebreak *interval* 587.1

firebrick *industrial ceramics* 129.6

firebug [Inf] *cause of fire* 217.10

firecracker *banger* 234.3

fire curtain *stage set* 136.19, *protective covering* 613.5

fired 106.13; *hired* 57.17, *ceramic* 129.9, *heated* 217.15, *discarded* 383.8, *canceled* 834.5

firedamp *miasma* 556.3

fire door *safety device* 810.15

firedrake *Legendary Creatures* 360

fire-eater *combatant* 77.1, *circus performer* 138.9, *violent animal* 520.4

fire engine *red thing* 257.3, *irrigator* 557.13

fire-engine red *red* 257.5

fire-engine siren *signal* 183.6

fire escape *way out* 707.2, *stairway* 713.9, *safety device* 810.15, *means of escape* 816.4

fire extinguisher *safety device* 810.15

firefight *contention* 422.1, *warfare* 422.10

firefighter *protector* 810.11

firefighter's uniform *uniform* 100.9

firefly *flickering light* 246.10

firehouse *municipal building* 567.13

fire insurance *insurance* 810.10

fire ladder *ladder* 713.10

firelight *fire* 246.9

fire lighter *fuel starter* 106.3, *fire* 246.9

firelit *lit* 246.16

fireman *railroad worker* 688.7, *protector* 810.11

fireman's ladder *access* 691.3

fire off *shoot* 696.18

fire on *fire* 418.18
fire one's imagination *inspire* 327.15
fireplace *place for fire* 217.9
fireproof *tough* 547.6, *make tough* 547.15, *invulnerable* 810.18
fireproof clothing *protective clothing* 419.6
firer *ceramist* 129.7
fire-resistant suit *modern armor* 419.7
fire sale *sale* 482.2, *bargain* 495.2
fire ship *historical warships* 77.22, *Sailing Ships and Boats* 690
fireside *home* 60.3
fireside chat *chat* 210.2
fire station *municipal building* 567.13
firestorm *cause of fire* 217.10
fire the first shot *attack* 418.17
fire the parting shot *answer back* 334.19
firethorn *Flowers* 42
firetrap *trap* 813.1
fire up *fuel* 106.16, *invigorate* 518.5, *make violent* 520.10
fire wall *safety device* 810.15
firewatcher *protector* 810.11
firewater [Inf] *alcoholic drink* 93.9
firewood *timber* 43.3, *fuel starter* 106.3
fireworks *propellant* 78.14, *masterpiece* 127.5, *fire* 246.9, *show* 404.12, *salute* 405.7
fire worship *idolatry* 83.4
fire worshiper *idolater* 83.7
firing 418.6; *bargaining terms* 57.10, *ceramic process* 129.5, *bowls* 151.7, *discarding* 383.3, *shooting* 696.5, *dismissal* 709.2, *ejection* 764.2, *termination* 834.2
firing line *battleground* 76.24
firing on all cylinders *with vigor* 518.6
firing shot *grip* 151.4
firing squad *execution* 30.6, *instrument of execution* 454.15
firing squad member *executioner* 30.13
firkin [Brit] *vessel* 578.11
firm *intimate* 62.7, *workplace* 124.1, *truthful* 191.4, *emphatic* 200.3, *iron-willed* 372.7, *resolute* 376.7, *unyielding* 379.8, *obstinate* 417.7, *severe* 424.5, *retentive* 471.5, *company* 480.7, *store* 483.8, *strong* 516.9, *strong in spirit* 516.11, *dense* 540.6, *tough* 542.6, *mentally hard* 542.8, *solidify* 542.10, *hard* 547.8, *permanent* 667.2, *unfailing* 667.3, *stable* 674.3, *tied* 752.13, *infallible* 840.12
firmament *universe* 7.3, *heaven* 82.15
firm control *severity* 424.1
firm date *promise* 458.1
firm hand *severity* 424.1
firm hold *retention* 471.1
firming up *stability* 674.1
firmly *intimately* 62.14, *truthfully* 191.9, *resistingly* 417.14, *severely* 424.11, *tenaciously* 471.11, *acutely* 516.18, *densely* 540.10, *inflexibly* 542.13, *toughly* 547.16, *permanently* 667.6, *stably* 674.9, *inextricably* 752.23, *certainly* 840.15
firmly implanted *or* **established** *deep-seated* 598.17
firm-minded *resolute* 376.7
firmness *truthfulness* 191.1, *resolution* 376.1, *obstinacy* 417.2, *severity* 424.1, *strength* 516.1, *authority* 516.5, *hardness* 542.1,

toughness 547.1, *permanence* 667.1, *stability* 674.1, *infallibility* 840.6
firmness of mind *or* **spirit** *resolution* 376.1
firmness of purpose *willpower* 372.2, *resolution* 376.1
firm-packed *dense* 540.6
firm price *business offer* 504.3
firm principle *or* **condition** *guide* 780.4
firm resolve *resolution* 376.1
firm up *thicken* 594.9, *make stable* 674.7
firm up *or* **down** *make dense* 540.9
firn *snow* 9.30, *rock face* 161.6
first 769.19, 771.37; *ranked* 6.72, *beginning* 583.14, 771.16, *front* 621.1, 621.9, *new* 652.9, *newly* 652.21, *early* 657.8, 657.17, *original* 737.4, *originally* 737.8, *unbeatable* 744.13, *preceding* 769.9, *primary* 769.10, *primarily* 769.21, *one* 788.10, *best* 805.9, *victor* 845.7
first aid *therapy* 115.12, *medical assistance* 825.5
first-aid *remedial* 115.14
first among equals *superior* 744.5
first and foremost *primary* 769.10, *first* 769.19, 771.37
first and last *singular* 788.13
first appearance 264.3; *premiere* 771.9
first arrival *early comer* 657.4
first assistant director *filmmaker* 137.14
first attempt *attempt* 390.1
first base *baseball field* 147.3, *first move* 771.12
first baseman *baseball team* 147.2
first-base umpire *baseball team* 147.2
firstborn *predecessor* 769.8
First Cause *God* 82.6
first cause 675.6; *philosophical problem* 4.8
first chair *skilled person* 127.7
first choice *chosen thing* 382.8, *chief thing* 799.3
first class *excellence* 445.4
first-class *aristocratic* 70.4, *excellent* 445.13, 744.14, *opulent* 485.10, *best* 805.9
first-class mail *postal service* 169.5
first comer *inhabitant* 61.1, *early comer* 657.4
first concern *priority* 769.2
first course *dish* 90.7, *course* 92.12, *first move* 771.12
first cousin *family member* 65.2
first-degree burn *heat* 217.1
first-degree murder *murder* 30.2
first derivative *differentiation* 6.29
first early *crop* 16.8
first echelon *armed force* 77.10
first edition *rare book* 174.2, *original* 737.2
first fiddle [Inf] *celebrity* 799.6
first finger *appendage* 19.5
first floor *base* 601.1
first go *attempt* 390.1
first-hand *original* 737.4
first house *theatrical performance* 136.13
first impression *impression* 264.7
first innings *first move* 771.12
first in the field *original* 737.4
first lady *paragon* 744.6
first lap *first move* 771.12
first law *thermodynamics* 10.30
first leg *first move* 771.12
First Lieutenant *US Military Ranks* 58
fished *fishing* 154.13

first light *dimness* 248.1, *morning* 655.2, *sunrise* 713.4
first love *romantic love* 299.2
firstly *newly* 652.21, *first* 771.37
first mortgage *mortgage* 476.6
first move 771.12
first name *name* 202.8
first night *theatrical performance* 136.13, *beginning* 652.4, *premiere* 771.9
firstnighter *theatergoer* 136.30
first-night nerves *or* **jitters** *acting* 136.22
first of all *supremely* 744.23, *first* 771.37
first officer *aircraft personnel* 689.8
first-order *reactive* 11.29
first payment *type of payment* 489.3
first performance *theatrical performance* 136.13
first-person narrative *aspect of fiction* 139.5
first place *superiority* 744.1, *priority* 769.2
first-place finisher *victor* 845.7
first principle *matter* 524.4
first principles *theory* 6.62, *rudiments* 771.7
first priority *chief thing* 799.3
first quarter *moon* 7.18
first-rate *excellent* 68.16, 445.13, 744.14, *skillful* 127.10, *notable* 799.11, *best* 805.9
first-rater *superior person* 445.7
first reader *rudiments* 771.7
first refusal *purchasing* 481.2
first round *first move* 771.12
First Sergeant *US Military Ranks* 58
first stage *first move* 771.12
first step *early stage* 657.3, *first move* 771.12
first steps *rudiments* 771.7
first-stringer *prizewinner* 127.8
first-string player *prizewinner* 127.8
first-team player *basketball team* 148.2
first thing *early* 657.17, *first* 771.37
first time *premiere* 771.9
first tooth *teeth* 19.8
firth [Scot] *inlet* 572.9
fiscal *economic* 56.10, 480.14, *financial* 457.6, *monetary* 484.22, *accounting* 493.7, *period of activity* 641.4
fiscal competence *solvency* 485.4
fiscal incompetence *insolvency* 486.2
fiscally *economically* 56.13, *financially* 457.11, 493.13, *monetarily* 484.27
fiscal policy *economics* 56.1, *economic factor* 56.8
fiscal year *finance* 457.1
fish 38.5, 154.14; *kill animals* 30.25, *animal* 34.1, *type of animal* 34.5, *fishes* 38.1, *Collective Names* 59, *Card Games* 168, *Phobias* 283, *hunt* 385.14, *extract* 711.13
fish and chips [Brit] *fish dish* 90.19
fishbowl *dwelling* 38.4
fish breeding *study of fish* 38.2
fish cake *or* **fish ball** *fish dish* 90.19
fish characteristic 38.8
fish course *dish* 90.7, *course* 92.12
fish day *fast* 118.4
fish dish 90.19

fisher *fisherman* 154.12, *hunter* 385.6
fisherman 154.12; *food provider* 90.6, *hunter* 385.6
fisherman's bend *Knots, Bends, Hitches, Splices* 754
fisherman's knot *Knots, Bends, Hitches, Splices* 754
fisherman's tale *tall story* 194.5
fisherman sweater *sweater* 100.17
Fishes *Constellations* 7
fishes 38.1
fisheye lens *lens* 132.11, *visual aid* 242.14
fish farm *farm* 16.2, *dwelling* 38.4
fish farming *livestock farming* 16.10
fish finger *fish dish* 90.19
fish food *animal food* 90.2
fish for *pursue* 385.11
fish for compliments *be vain* 402.14, *show off* 404.26
fish for invitations *participate* 408.15
fish fork *tableware* 92.13
fish glue *food product* 38.9
fishhook *fishing tackle* 154.7, *sharp-pointed thing* 549.4
fishing 154.1, 154.11; *hunt* 385.3, *hunting* 385.9, *nautical* 690.14, *extraction* 711.1
fishing associations 154.11
fishing bird *water bird* 36.9
fishing boat *Ships and Boats* 690, *vessel* 690.3
fishing license *permit* 502.3
fishing pole *fishing tackle* 154.7
fishing rod *fishing tackle* 154.7
fishing tackle 154.7
fishing the water *fly-fishing* 154.2
fishing to the rise *fly-fishing* 154.2
fishing trip *or* **expedition** [Inf] *pretrial proceedings* 54.13
fish in troubled waters *get into trouble* 824.20
fish joint *carpenter's term* 131.5
fish knife *tableware* 92.13
fishlike 38.10
fish-liver oil *fish product* 38.9
fish louse *crustacean* 39.10, *parasite* 39.18
fish lover *ichthyologist* 38.3
fish market *market* 483.1
fish meal *fertilizer* 16.9, 17.8, 22.6, *animal feed* 16.12
fishmeal *fish product* 38.9
fishmonger [Brit] *food provider* 90.6, *retailer* 482.11
fishnet *braid* 609.3
fishnet tights *legwear* 100.26
fish of the sea, the *animals* 34.2
fish out *extract* 711.13
fish pie *fish dish* 90.19
fishplate *rail* 688.3
fishpond *dwelling* 38.4, *small lake* 568.2
fish product 38.9
fish roe *fish product* 38.9
fish soup *soup* 90.14
fish stick *fish dish* 90.19
fish store *food provider* 90.6
fish story [Inf] *tall story* 194.5
fishtank *dwelling* 38.4, *cage* 60.15
fish the water *fish* 154.14
fish to the rise *fish* 154.14
fishwife *irascible person* 303.7
fish with bait *fish* 154.14
fishy *fishlike* 38.10
fissile *brittle* 548.3, *cracked* 587.5, *separable* 753.11
fissile nuclide *nuclear fission* 10.60
fissility *brittleness* 548.1

fission *nuclear fission* 10.60, *nuclear power* 514.9, *separation* 753.1, *deconstruction* 758.2, *deconstruct* 758.7

fissionable *separable* 753.11

fissionable material *explosive* 78.13

fissionable nuclide *nuclear fission* 10.60

fission product *nuclear fission* 10.60

fission reaction *nuclear fission* 10.60, *chemical reaction* 11.8

fissure *volcanic activity* 8.26, *opening* 583.1, *hole* 583.17, *crack* 587.2, *furrow* 638.1, 638.5, *separateness* 753.3, *interruption* 775.3

fissured *open* 583.10, *cracked* 587.5

fissure sealing *dentistry* 107.6

fist *weapon* 78.1, *Reference Signs* 183, *gesture* 183.5, *retainer* 471.3

fistfight *disruption* 766.7

fisticuffs *boxing* 152.2, *quarrel* 272.4, *dispute* 463.3, *violence by person* 520.2, *assault* 695.4, *disruption* 766.7

fistula *ulcer* 114.18

fit *make clothing* 100.44, *healthy* 113.4, *illness* 114.2, *part of poem* 139.9, *burst of anger* 302.6, *be the answer* 334.23, *qualified* 340.7, *qualify* 340.11, *caprice* 381.1, *equip* 388.19, *alacrity* 414.3, *seizure* 418.11, *rightful* 429.9, *suitable* 462.9, *physically strong* 516.10, *violence by person* 520.2, *in form* 624.8, *period* 641.1, *timely* 659.4, *spasm* 684.8, *mode* 725.2, *conditional* 725.7, *correspond to* 727.10, *equal to* 740.10, *equalize* 740.12, *intertwine* 752.19, *adhere* 755.8, *sound* 759.8, *conform* 781.11, *make conform* 781.13, *convenient* 803.3, *be convenient* 803.5

fit a beam *carpenter* 131.10

fit and ready *healthy* 113.4

fit as a fiddle *feeling well* 113.8

fit badly *be different* 463.11

fit for *usable* 801.6

fit for habitation 60.19

fit for marriage *marriageable* 64.17

fit for nothing *useless* 802.7

fit for release *deliverable* 817.3

fit for use *in hand* 388.11, *usable* 801.6

fitful *capricious* 381.4, 841.16, *erratic* 381.5, *periodic* 641.8, *infrequent* 662.2, *irregular* 664.3, *changeable* 666.3, *convulsive* 684.19, *inconsistent* 732.7, *discontinuous* 775.7

fitfully *erratically* 381.8, *for short periods* 641.13, *infrequently* 662.4, *irregularly* 664.6, *changeably* 666.7, *inconsistently* 732.16, *discontinuously* 775.15, *capriciously* 841.26

fitfulness *capriciousness* 381.2, 841.8, *infrequency* 662.1, *irregularity* 664.1, *irresolution* 666.2, *inconsistency* 732.3, *discontinuity* 775.1

fit in *conform* 781.11, *make conform* 781.13

fit like a glove *adhere* 755.8

fitly *opportunely* 659.8

fitness *health* 113.1, *aptitude* 127.4, *correspondence* 334.8, *qualification* 340.1, *preparedness* 388.5, *properness* 429.5, *suitability*

462.4, *nature* 624.5, *timeliness* 659.1, *convenience* 803.1

fitness for marriage *marriageability* 64.4

fitness walking Sporting Activities 145

fit of anger *burst of anger* 302.6

fit of temper *burst of anger* 302.6

fit of terror *fear* 283.1

fit of the sulks *sign of sullenness* 304.2

fit on the head of a pin *be little* 580.11

fit out *find means* 102.6, *equip* 388.19

fit perfectly *be suitable* 462.13

fits and starts *irregularity* 664.1

fitted *qualified* 340.7, *treated* 388.12

fittedness *qualification* 340.1

fitted sheet *bed covering* 613.7

fitter *clothier* 100.37, *artisan* 123.13, *preparer* 388.6

fit the occasion *be timely* 659.6

fit tight(ly) *adhere* 755.8

fitting *sufficient* 97.3, *expedient* 288.12, *correspondent* 334.16, *qualified* 340.7, *proper* 429.10, *suitable* 462.9, *fluid* 527.5, *timely* 659.4, *convenient* 803.3

fittingly *expediently* 288.25, *correspondingly* 334.27, *capably* 340.15, *properly* 429.18, *opportunely* 659.8, *conveniently* 803.6

fittingness *properness* 429.5, *grace* 527.2

fitting out 388.3

fitting retribution *revenge* 441.4, *retribution* 454.7

fittings *equipment* 103.6, *possessions* 470.5

fitting the circumstances *circumstantial* 726.8

fitting together *construction* 59.16, *interaction* 616.2

fit to be tied [Inf] *resentful* 302.8

fit together *put together* 59.30, *cooperate* 616.6, *unite* 752.14, *combine* 757.9

fit to kill [Inf] *attractive* 529.8

fit well *be suitable* 462.13, *unify* 752.15

Fitzroy Rivers 570

Fitzwilliam Darcy Famous Lovers 299

five 792.1; *numeral* 6.8, *basketball team* 148.2, *cards* 168.2, *fifth* 792.12

five-act play *play* 136.2

five-and-dime *cheap* 800.16

five-and-ten *cheap* 497.9, 800.16

five and twenty *twenty and over* 792.8

five-card stud *poker* 168.5

five cents *US coinage* 484.10

five centuries *hundreds* 792.9

five-dollar bill *US coinage* 484.10, *five* 792.1

five-figure *thousandth* 792.21

five-finger *five* 792.1

fivefold 792.26; *fifth* 792.12

five hundred Card Games 168, *hundreds* 792.9

five o'clock shadow *body covering* 19.4, *rough skin* 544.3

five of a kind *poker* 168.5

five-pound note [Brit] *five* 792.1

fiver [Inf] *US coinage* 484.10, *five* 792.1

five-sided *polygonal* 6.79

fivesome *five* 792.1

five-spot *cards* 168.2

five-spot [Inf] *five* 792.1

five-year plan *plan* 387.1

fix *remedy* 115.16, *prove* 331.17, *resolve* 376.12, *prepare for action* 388.18, *put right* 429.14, *exact retribution* 454.27, *locate* 565.9, *situate* 573.10, *base* 601.10, *include* 613.33, *make permanent* 667.5, *make stable* 674.7, *direct* 697.13, *make the same* 730.16, *quantify* 738.7, *link* 752.18, *class* 777.12, *specify* 779.18, *rectify* 807.22, *repair* 809.10, *make certain* 840.14

fix [Inf] *drug dose* 121.15, *foul play* 193.6, *predetermine* 384.8, *predicament* 725.3, 824.5, *take off* 749.7

fixated *mentally ill* 110.11, *diligent* 323.7

fixation 108.21; *cell biology* 13.14, *delusion* 110.2, *diligence* 323.4, *prejudgment* 342.5, *habit* 397.1, *placing* 565.4, *lack of motion* 678.1

fixation of affect *fixation* 108.21

fixative *material* 143.9, *adhesive* 755.3

fixed 397.13; *phrased* 5.39, *mountaineering* 161.9, *unjust* 342.7, *unyielding* 379.8, *deliberate* 384.5, *correct* 429.8, *fast* 464.8, *propertied* 470.9, *located* 565.6, *permanent* 667.2, *unfailing* 667.3, *stabilized* 674.4, *motionless* 678.4, *regular* 730.12, *equal* 740.8, *adhering* 755.7, *repaired* 809.6, *decided* 840.9, *inevitable* 840.11

fixed assets *personal estate* 470.6

fixed bridge *bridge* 551.10

fixed day *day* 646.4

fixed disk *disk* 15.5

fixed expression *phrasing* 5.25

fixed fight *boxing* 152.2

fixed-focus lens *lens* 132.11

fixed idea *prejudgment* 342.5

fixedly *fastly* 464.16, *permanently* 667.6, *motionlessly* 678.9

fixedness *right* 429.2, *permanence* 667.1, *stability* 674.1

fixed oil *oil* 562.3

fixed point *point* 6.34

fixed-point notation *number system* 6.7

fixed position *military defenses* 419.9

fixed price *price* 494.1

fixed-rate mortgage *mortgage* 476.6

fixed resolve *resolution* 376.1

fixed seat *rowboat parts* 150.15

fixed-seat *rowing* 150.27

fixed-seat rowing *rowing* 150.14

fixed-spool *fishing* 154.13

fixed-spool reel *fishing tackle* 154.7

fixed star *star* 7.8

fixed term *duration* 642.1

fixed up [Inf] *predetermined* 384.4

fixed ways *way* 397.3

fixer *darkroom equipment* 132.21, *coverer* 613.18, *adhesive* 755.3, *repairer* 809.5

fixer [Inf] *lawyer* 54.5

fixing *placing* 565.4, *coverage* 613.16, *repair* 809.1

fixing [Inf] *subtraction* 749.1

fixing solution *darkroom equipment* 132.21

fix in one's mind *memorize* 354.11

fixity *determination* 379.2, *permanence* 667.1, *stability* 674.1, *lack of motion* 678.1

fixity of purpose *resolution* 376.1

fix on *aim* 697.14

fix one's teeth into *retain* 471.7

fix the date *keep time* 646.12

fix the day *keep time* 646.12

fix the game *be cunning* 822.5

fix the price of *price* 494.12

fix the time *keep time* 646.12

fix to *make fast* 464.13

fixture *concomitant* 794.4

fixtures *equipment* 103.6, *possessions* 470.5

fix up *restore* 807.17

fix up [Inf] *predetermine* 384.8, *come to an arrangement* 767.22, *refurbish* 809.11

fix upon *scrutinize* 323.11

fizz *soft drink* 93.8, *hiss* 237.1, 237.3, *bubble* 558.24

fizziness *gaseousness* 556.6

fizzle *hiss* 237.3

fizzle out [Inf] *come to an end* 773.23, *decline* 846.16

fizzling *hissing* 237.2

fizzwater *water* 93.4, *drinking water* 557.2

fizzy *drinkable* 93.18, *hissing* 237.2, *gassy* 556.19, *bubbly* 558.18

fjord *landform* 8.9, *glacier* 8.44, *inlet* 572.9

Fjord pony Horse and Pony Breeds 159

flab *fat* 579.8

flabbergast *astonish* 292.10, *be wondrous* 294.14

flabbergasted *astonished* 292.6, *wondering* 294.7

flabbiness *softness* 543.1, *pulpiness* 561.9, *fatness* 579.5, *thickness* 594.1

flabby *soft* 543.6, *pulpy* 561.19, *fat* 579.15, *thick* 594.5

flabellate *or* **flabelliform** *growing* 581.12

flaccid *unemphatic* 201.2, *weak* 517.6, *inert* 519.2, *soft* 543.6

flaccidity *lack of emphasis* 201.1, *weakness* 517.1, *softness* 543.1

flaccidly *softly* 543.18

flaccidness *softness* 543.1

flack *publicizer* 173.11, *news interpreter* 365.7, *criticism* 440.2, *motivator* 508.6, *displayer* 843.7

flackery *public relations (PR)* 173.8, *publicity* 178.7

flack suit *modern armor* 419.7

flack vest *modern armor* 419.7

flag 184.8, *Flowers* 42, *be unhealthy* 114.29, *sailboat parts and accessories* 150.4, *golf course* 156.2, *signal* 183.18, *despair* 270.8, *be weak* 517.12, *diminish* 597.24, *hesitate* 693.12, *be fatigued* 820.5, *decline* 846.16

flag down *gesture* 183.17

flagellant *atoner* 313.4, *penitent person* 451.4

flagellate *protozoan* 39.17, 39.27, *algal* 47.20, *hit* 454.28

flagellate oneself *repent* 313.9, *do penance* 451.9

flagellate protozoan *protozoan* 39.17

flagellation *penitence* 313.3, *type of penance* 451.3, *corporal punishment* 454.11

flagellator *punisher* 454.16

flageolet Bean Varieties 90, Musical Instruments 142

flagging *sick* 114.24, *poor health* 517.3, *diminishing* 597.16, *deceleration* 693.2, *slow* 693.7, *fatigued* 820.2

flagitious *evil* 446.7, *wicked* 448.9

flagitiously *evilly* 446.12, *wickedly* 448.15

flagitiousness *evil* 446.1, *wickedness* 448.1

flagman *warner* 814.5

flag of convenience *flag* 184.8, *expedient* 387.5, *stratagem* 822.2

flag officer *military position* 58.6

flag of surrender *flag* 184.8

flag of truce *symbol of peace* 73.6, *peace offering* 74.5, *flag* 184.8

flagon *bottle* 578.14

flagpole *flag* 184.8

flagrancy *blatancy* 404.6, *wickedness* 448.1, *manifestation* 843.2

flagrant *publicized* 173.14, *blatant* 404.19, *wicked* 448.9, *accentuated* 843.11

flagrante delicto *actively* 412.18, *guiltily* 450.12

flagrantly *blatantly* 404.34, *wickedly* 448.15, *manifestly* 843.17

flags *salute* 405.7

flagship *warship* 77.21, Ships and Boats 690

flag signals *signaling* 169.9

flagstaff *flag* 184.8

flagstick *golf course* 156.2

flagstone *building materials* 104.2, *paving* 613.14

flag stop *stopping place* 668.4

flag waving *tribute* 405.6

flail *farm tool* 16.5, *blunt weapon* 78.5, *strike* 418.21, *hit* 454.28, *beat* 695.12

flailing *attacking* 418.14

flair *aptitude* 127.4, *cleverness* 315.3, *judiciousness* 337.2, *ability* 340.2, *stylishness* 537.2

flak *ammunition* 78.11, *criticism* 438.4, 440.2

flake *rock face* 161.6, *be brittle* 548.4, *crumb* 553.5, *crumble* 553.22, *slice* 588.4, *scale* 588.10, *separate* 753.12, *particle* 760.4

flake [Inf] *stimulants* 121.18, *capricious person* 381.3

flaked out [Inf] *not awake* 415.12

flake off *scale* 588.10, *shed* 614.21

flake pastry *pastry* 90.37

flake white *whitener* 253.3

flakily 553.30

flakiness *brittleness* 548.1, *crumbliness* 553.1, *layering* 588.5

flakiness [Inf] *capriciousness* 381.2

flaking *brittle* 548.3, *pulverization* 553.4

flak jacket *football uniform* 155.2

flaky *brittle* 548.3, *crumbly* 553.16, *platelike* 588.8

flaky [Inf] *capricious* 381.4

flam [Inf] *foul play* 193.6, *swindle* 193.19

flambeau *incandescent light* 246.5

flamboyance *extravagance* 194.3, *demonstrativeness* 331.2, *flashiness* 404.4, *ornateness* 532.2

flamboyant *extravagant* 194.9, *demonstrative* 331.10, *flashy* 404.17, *ornate* 532.10

flamboyantly *excessively* 194.17, *demonstratively* 331.21, *flashily* 404.32, *decoratively* 532.13, *ornately* 532.14

flamboyant style Architectural Styles 134

flame *fire* 217.8, 246.9, *burn* 217.18, *light up* 246.20

flame [Inf] *loved one* 299.13

flame-colored *red* 257.5, *orange* 258.5

flamen *priest* 84.8

flamenco Dancing Types 135

flame-of-the-forest Trees and Shrubs 43

flameout *miscellaneous aviation terms* 689.9

flameproof *treated* 130.16, *treat* 130.21

flameproofing *fabric treatment* 130.10

flames *fire* 217.8, *incandescent light* 246.5

flames of love *sexual love* 299.3

flamethrower *firearm* 78.7, *cause of fire* 217.10

flame tree Trees and Shrubs 43

flaming *on fire* 217.16, *bright* 246.14, *violent* 520.5

flamingo *water bird* 36.9

flammability *fire* 217.8

flammable *combustible* 106.12, *on fire* 217.16, *dangerous* 811.7

flammer [Inf] *schemer* 193.10

flamming [Inf] *artful* 193.13

flan *dessert* 90.35

flanch Heraldic Terms 184

flâneur [Fr] *nonworker* 415.4

flange *superstructure* 551.7, *edge* 617.3

flank *side* 623.1, 623.8, *ring* 681.9, *protect* 810.21

flanker *offense* 155.6

flanking *side* 623.6

flanking attack *land attack* 418.3

flannel Fabrics and Fibers 130

flannelet *or* **flannelette** Fabrics and Fibers 130

flannels *pants* 100.14

flan ring *cooking equipment* 91.6

flap *part of garment* 100.27, *layer* 588.1, *suspend* 604.13, *cover* 613.2, *be changeable* 666.5, *come unstuck* 756.7

flap [Inf] *dispute* 463.3, *agitation* 684.1, *be agitated* 684.21

flapdoodle [Inf] *empty talk* 362.5

flapjack *pancake* 90.11

flapping *nonadhesive* 756.4

flare *composition* 132.17, *signal* 183.6, *burn* 217.18, *quality of light* 246.2, *fire* 246.9, *light up* 246.20, *expansion* 581.1, *enlarge* 581.14, *broaden* 592.11, *flight* 689.5, *warning signal* 814.3

flared *mountaineering* 161.9, *bigger* 581.9, *broad-shaped* 592.6

flared skirt *skirt* 100.12

flare pass *play* 155.8

flare path *safety light* 246.7

flare star *variable star* 7.11

flareup *burst of anger* 302.6, *violence by person* 520.2

flare up *light up* 246.20, *become angry* 302.20, *increase* 746.6

flaring *on fire* 217.16, *bright* 246.14, *gaudy* 251.12, *expansion* 581.1, *growing* 581.12

flash 132.13; *news event* 171.2, *quality of light* 246.2, *natural light* 246.4, *light up* 246.20, *become visible* 264.13, *insight* 320.3, *spontaneity* 396.2, *flourish* 404.25, *instant* 645.3, *be changeable* 666.5, *flicker* 684.12, 684.26, *display* 843.13

flash [Inf] *undress* 614.18

flash attachment *camera* 132.10

flashback *recollection* 3.8, *retrospect* 354.2

flashbulb *flash* 132.13, *electric light* 246.6

flash by *pass* 692.15, *accelerate* 694.14

flashcube *flash* 132.13

flash desorption *surface chemistry* 11.20

flasher [Inf] *sexually immoral person* 432.8, *nude person* 614.5

flash flood *natural violence* 520.3, *flow* 570.4, *natural hazard* 813.4

flashgun *flash* 132.13, *electric light* 246.6

flashily 404.32; *showily* 367.6

flashiness 404.4; *demonstrativeness* 331.2

flashing *signaling* 183.14, *quality of light* 246.2, *lucent* 246.13, *bright* 246.14, *speeding* 694.7

flashing [Inf] *sexual offense* 432.6, *undressing* 614.2

flashing light *signal* 183.6, *safety light* 246.7, *danger signal* 811.5, *warning signal* 814.3

flashing lights Phobias 283

flash in the pan *transient* 643.2, *success* 845.1

flash lamp *electric light* 246.6

flashlight *lantern* 246.8

flashlit *lit* 246.16

flash of inspiration *creative thought* 317.3

flash photography *photographic specialties* 132.2

flash point *heat* 217.1

flashtube *flash* 132.13

flashy 404.17; *gaudy* 251.12, *demonstrative* 331.10, *ornate* 532.10

flask *drink container* 93.13, *bottle* 578.14

flask fungi *fungi* 47.3

flat *spatial* 6.76, 563.11, *linear* 6.77, *exposed* 132.25, *roof* 134.7, *stage set* 136.19, *musical note* 140.15, *unemphatic* 201.2, *tasteless* 220.4, *nonresonant* 233.7, *strident* 238.4, *unmelodious* 241.5, *soft-hued* 251.13, *boring* 296.6, *uniform* 545.5, *blunt* 550.5, *marsh* 572.3, *of landmasses* 572.12, *squeezed* 582.9, *low* 597.10, *lowland* 597.15, *superficial* 599.4, *horizontal surface* 603.3, *horizontal* 603.6, *horizontally* 603.11, *regular* 663.5, *frequent* 663.6, *sedentary* 678.5, *unimproved* 808.10, *fatigued* 820.2

flat *or* **flats** *lowlands* 597.6, *shallowness* 599.1

flat [Brit] *apartment* 60.7, *property* 470.1

flat [Inf] *insolvent* 486.10

flat as a pancake *or* **board** *horizontal* 603.6

flat-bed plotter *hardcopy device* 15.10

flatboard *sailboard parts* 150.20

flatboat Ships and Boats 690

flat broke *needy* 95.12, *insolvent* 486.10, *unprosperous* 848.11

flat calm *repose* 678.2

flatcar *railroad car* 688.5

flat contradiction *negation* 190.1

flat country *lowland* 572.6

flat denial *negation* 190.1

flat fare *fee* 494.3

flatfish *fish* 38.5, *food fish and shellfish* 90.20

flatfoot *mountaineer* 161.10

flatfoot [Inf] *law enforcement officer* 53.8

flat-footing *climbing techniques* 161.3

Flathead Lakes 568

flatiron *fabric-handling tool* 130.12, *smoother* 545.2, *flattener* 603.4

flat knot Knots, Bends, Hitches, Splices 754

Flatland Imaginary Places 360

flatland *horizontal surface* 603.3

flatly *without taste* 220.8, *boringly* 296.10, *smoothly* 545.13, 550.10, *superficially* 599.8, *horizontally* 603.11, *orderly* 663.13, *regularly* 663.14

flatmate [Brit] *resident* 61.6

flatness *surface* 6.36, *lack of emphasis* 201.1, *dilution* 220.2, *musical dissonance* 241.2, *boringness* 296.2, *smoothness* 545.1, *bluntness* 550.1, *squeeze* 582.3, *lowness* 597.1, *superficiality* 599.2, *horizontality* 603.1, *regularity* 663.1

flat on one's back *or* **face** *recumbently* 603.12

flat out [Inf] *with vigor* 518.6, *at full speed* 694.17

flat-out speed [Inf] *swiftness* 694.1

flat race *horse racing* 159.10

flat rate *fee* 494.3

flat refusal *refusal* 506.1

flats *lowland* 572.6, *horizontal surface* 603.3

flat service *tennis strokes* 165.2

flat shoes *or* **flats** 100.30

flat spin *flight maneuver* 689.6

flat surface *surface* 6.36, *horizontal surface* 603.3

flatten 716.15; *knock down* 523.13, *ruin* 523.15, *smooth* 545.10, 552.13, *blunt* 550.9, *squeeze* 582.13, *make thin* 595.17, *lower* 597.21, *make horizontal* 603.10, *make regular* 663.9, *defeat* 845.17

flatten down *smooth* 545.10

flattened *uniform* 545.5, *blunt* 550.5, *thinned* 595.13, *lowered* 597.12, 716.7, *leveled* 603.8

flattener 603.4; *smoother* 545.2

flattening *destroying* 523.2, *squeeze* 582.3, *lowering* 597.3, *downthrow* 716.2

flatten oneself *lie down* 716.21

flatten out *straighten* 630.14, *make regular* 663.9

flatter 439.12; *persuade* 178.15, *boast* 194.14, *talk nonsense* 362.12, *fawn* 401.9, *compliment* 437.17, *influence* 508.11, *imitate* 736.9, *be cunning* 822.5

flattered *exaggerated* 194.7, *motivated* 508.8

flatterer 439.6; *persuader* 178.9, *humble person* 298.7, *assenter* 346.3, *sycophant* 401.8, *motivator* 508.6, *cunning person* 822.3

flattering 439.7; *misrepresentation* 188.1, *unmeant* 362.9, *sycophantic* 401.7, *good-mannered* 410.7, *approving* 437.9, *inducement* 508.2, *cunning* 822.4

flatteringly 439.16

flatter oneself *pride oneself* 297.13, *be vain* 402.14

flatter to deceive *blarney* 439.13

flattery 439.1; *persuasion* 178.1, *misrepresentation* 188.1, *bombast* 194.4, *pleasant thing* 271.4, *empty talk* 362.5, *sycophancy* 401.2, *courtesy* 410.1, *compliment* 437.4, *positive stimulus* 508.5, *cunning* 822.1

flat tire *technical problem* 826.3

flattop [Inf] *warship* 77.21, *coiffure* 530.8

flatulence 709.9; *gastroenterological disease* 114.11, *lack of emphasis* 201.1, *belch* 556.5

flatulency *belch* 556.5, *flatulence* 709.9

flatulent 556.18; *diffuse* 199.3,

unemphatic 201.2, aerial 558.14, eructative 709.13
flatulous eructative 709.13
flat universe universe 7.3
flatuosity flatulence 709.9
flatus gastroenterological disease 114.11, unpleasant-smelling thing 227.2, belch 556.5, flatulence 709.9
flatware tableware 92.13
flatways horizontally 603.11
flatwise horizontally 603.11
flatworm worm 39.14
flaunt disdain 297.14, demonstrate 331.15, openness 843.6, display 843.13
flaunted displayed 843.8
flaunter proud person 297.7, displayer 843.7
flaunting gaudy 251.12, exhibitionism 404.9, open 843.12
flauntingly arrogantly 297.18
flaunt oneself show off 404.26
flaunty arrogant 297.9
flautist player 141.2
flavescent yellowish 259.8
flavin adenine dinucleotide (FAD) coenzyme 12.12
flavone pigment 12.18
flavonoid pigment 12.18
flavonol pigment 12.18
flavoprotein protein 12.9, coenzyme 12.12
flavor 219.3; cook 91.10, make taste 219.4, season 221.8, augment 748.13, admixture 751.5, characteristic 779.5
flavored coffee coffee 93.6
flavor enhancer food content 90.3, flavor 219.3
flavorful pleasurable 214.6, piquant 221.6
flavorful or **flavorsome** tasty 219.4
flavorfully culinarily 91.11
flavoring flavor 219.3, seasoning 221.2, ornamentation 748.5
flavorless tasteless 220.4
flaw iniquity 448.3, blemish 533.1, 533.7, opening 583.1, crack 587.2, defect 806.4, vulnerability 811.6, obstacle 826.2
flawed blamable 330.7, erroneous 351.11, impious 448.11, blemished 533.5, shortened 762.6, defective 806.7
flawed argument sophism 330.2
flawed logic faulty reasoning 351.4
flawless correct 429.8, 721.13, excellent 445.13, fluid 527.5, uncut 759.7, perfect 805.8
flawlessly correctly 429.16, 721.29, perfectly 805.21
flawlessness right 429.2, trueness 721.4, perfection 805.1
flawless performance ideal 805.6
flax crop 16.8
flaxen-haired white-haired 253.9
flay condemn 438.18, hit 454.28, execute 454.30, depilate 614.20, separate 753.12
flay alive execute 454.30
flayed shed 614.14
F₁ layer or **region** atmospheric layer 558.3
F₂ or **Appleton layer** or **region** atmospheric layer 558.3
flayer shedder 614.7
flaying condemnation 438.2, peeling 614.6
flaying alive capital punishment 454.12
flay one's back hit 454.28
flea pest 40.5, dirt 112.5

fleabag [Inf] hotel 60.12, club 138.7
fleabane Flowers 42
flea beetle pests and diseases 17.12
fleabite little bit 800.4
flea-bitten verminous 40.13, unclean 112.8, worn 808.13
flea-flicker 155.8
flea in one's ear public speaking 205.11, condemnation 438.2
flea in the ear communication 176.3
fleam sharp-pointed thing 549.4
flea market bazaar 483.10, discounter 497.7
fleapit [Brit inf] theater 136.16, motion-picture theater 137.10
flèche church architecture 134.11, fencing movements 153.3, sharp-pointed thing 549.4
fléchette Historical Missile Weapons 78
fléchette ammunition ammunition 78.11
fleck maculation 263.4, little piece 580.4
flection fold 637.1
flectional folded 637.5
fled away 576.8
fledgling young animal 26.4, young 26.11, young bird 36.17, new arrival 652.7, beginner 771.14
flee depart 265.6, retreat 285.8, 386.22, abscond 576.16, hurry off 705.11, escape 816.8
fleece Fabrics and Fibers 130, swindle 193.19, take money away 477.20, act dishonestly 479.18, impoverish 486.16, overcharge 496.10, animal covering 613.15, depilate 614.20, take off 749.7, separate 753.12
fleeced impoverished 486.11
fleecer schemer 193.10
fleecy smooth 543.8
fleecy cloud cloud appearance 9.19
flee one's homeland be foreign 724.13
fleer escaper 816.5
fleet military organization 58.4, force 59.10, naval unit 77.20, nautical 690.14, swift 694.6, collection 757.3, throng 795.4, hasty 818.3
Fleet Admiral US Military Ranks 58
fleet admiral military leader 68.10
fleet auxiliary vessels warship 77.21
fleet blockade naval warfare 76.10
fleeting disappearing 265.3, transient 643.4, moving 677.12, unreal 720.8, hasty 818.3
fleetingly 265.8; transiently 643.8
fleetly swiftly 694.16
fleetness swiftness 694.1
fleet of foot swift 694.6
Fleet Street print journalism 175.4, London 567.8
Flemish Breeds of Cattle 16
Flemish bond masonry 14.22
flesh human fallibility 18.2, body 19.1, sexuality 20.3, fruit structure 44.3, meat 90.22, matter 524.4
flesh and blood person 18.8, body 19.1, matter 524.4, object 524.6
flesh-colored red 257.5
flesh-eater type of animal 34.5, eater 92.15
flesh eating eating habit 92.7
flesh-eating carnivorous 35.26, eating 92.18
flesh-eating mammal 35.9

fleshiness pulpiness 561.9, fatness 579.5, round body 633.2
fleshliness sexuality 20.3, sexual immorality 432.2
fleshly human 18.15, bodily 19.18, sensual 20.16, unchaste 432.10, material 524.7
fleshly lust sexual longing 20.6
flesh one's sword be at war 76.32
flesh-pink red 257.5
fleshpot wicked place 448.8, opulence 485.3
fleshpots prosperity 847.1
fleshy of a fruit 44.8, pulpy 561.19, oily 562.11, fat 579.15, well-rounded 633.8
fleur-de-lis Flowers 42, Architectural Elements 134, Heraldic Terms 184
fleury Heraldic Terms 184
flex be elastic 546.7
flex defense defense 155.9
flexed elastic 546.5, folded 637.5
flexibility manual skill 127.2, softness 543.1, elasticity 546.1, adaptability 546.2, changeableness 666.1, pliancy 781.3, wieldiness 823.3, possibleness 836.2, capriciousness 841.8
flexible skillful 127.10, unsteady 378.7, pliant 543.7, elastic 546.5, adaptive 546.6, conformable 781.7, wieldy 823.12, possible 836.5, capricious 841.16
flexibly softly 543.18, elastically 546.10, adaptably 546.11, 781.15, capriciously 841.26
flexile pliant 543.7
flexing elastic 546.5
flex one's muscles prepare oneself 388.21, be tough 547.13
flextime or **flexitime** benefits 57.11
flexuous curved 629.4
flexure fold 8.22, 637.1, deviating course 698.2
flick play field hockey 158.10, play soccer 163.8, type of touch 216.3, touch 216.9, flicker 684.26, blow 695.5, tap 695.13, jerk 699.3, pull at 699.12
flick [Inf] motion picture 137.2
Flicka Notable Horses 159
flicker 684.12, 684.26; quality of light 246.2, light up 246.20, be irregular 664.5, be changeable 666.5, vibrate 683.13
flickering 684.20; quality of light 246.2, lucent 246.13, irregularity 664.1, irregular 664.3, changeable 666.3, vibration 683.2, vibrating 683.9
flickering light 246.10
flickeringly irregularly 664.6
flickery lucent 246.13, flickering 684.20
flicking touching 216.6
flicks, the [Inf] motion pictures 137.1
flick stroke field hockey tactics 158.5
flier advertisement 173.9, newspaper 175.2
flies Collective Names 59, stage 136.18
flight 689.5; assemblage of birds 36.18, military organization 58.4, Collective Names 59, air force unit 77.29, defense mechanism 108.23, disappearance 265.1, desertion 386.7, momentum 677.2, aviation 689.1, departure 705.1, send up 715.12, disbandment 776.2, throng 795.4, escape 816.1

flight attendant attendant 69.4, aircraft personnel 689.8
flight bag baggage 578.8
flight control 689.7
flight engineer aircraft personnel 689.8
flight feather plumage 36.7
flight formation flight 689.5
flightiness absent-mindedness 324.2, capriciousness 381.2, irresolution 666.2
flight lane route 691.2, flight path 691.12
flightless avian 36.19
flightless bird 36.8
flight level flight 689.5
flight line airport 689.4
flight maneuver 689.6
flight of fancy tall story 194.5, conception 360.4, illusion 720.2
flight of stairs access 691.3, stairway 713.9
flight path 691.12
flight reaction neurosis 108.9
flight recorder recording instrument 185.9
flight suit 100.16
flight test rehearsal 335.2
flight-test rehearse 335.12
flightworthy flyable 689.12
flighty careless 324.8, capricious 381.4, irresolute 666.4
flimflam [Inf] foul play 193.6, swindle 193.19, empty talk 362.5, dishonesty 479.7, stratagem 822.2, be cunning 822.5
flimflam man [Inf] schemer 193.10, dishonest person 479.11, cunning person 822.3
flimflammer [Inf] schemer 193.10
flimflamming [Inf] artful 193.13
flimsily transparently 249.13, lightly 539.10, softly 543.18, fragilely 548.5
flimsiness translucency 249.2, lightness 539.1, sparseness 541.1, brittleness 548.1, thinning 595.6, superficiality 599.2
flimsy translucent 249.8, insufficient 517.11, insubstantial 539.5, sparse 541.3, soft 543.6, brittle 548.3, thinned 595.13, superficial 599.4, unreal 720.8
flimsy item weak thing 517.5
flinch feel pain 215.8, be afraid 283.14, oppose 375.13, recoil 680.21
flinch at refuse 506.8
fling experiment 335.1, attempt 390.1, throw 696.4, 696.17, throw down 716.13, sprinkle 776.15
fling down throw down 716.13
flinger thrower 696.10
flinging throwing 696.3
fling money around expend 491.11
fling off exterminate 709.22
fling off or **out** depart 705.8
fling wide the gates salute 405.13, welcome 708.14
flint fuel starter 106.3, material 129.2, hard substance 542.3
flint glass glass 249.5
flintiness relentlessness 309.2, tenacity 803.1
flintlock historical handgun 78.8
flint pebbles material 129.2
flinty chalky 35.9, relentless 309.4, tenacious 376.9, hard 542.5
flip cook 91.10, swimming 164.12, blow 695.5, tap 695.13, throw 696.4, jerk 699.3, pull at 699.12
flip [Inf] effusive 207.6, rude 400.9
flip-flop floor exercise 157.4

flip-flop [Inf] *caprice* 381.1, *be capricious* 381.6, *alteration* 665.2, *change* 665.14
flip-flop circuit *circuit* 14.37
flip-flops *shoes* 100.30
flip of the coin *equal chance* 842.7
flip one's lid [Inf] *become angry* 302.20
flippancy *humor* 277.1, *imprudence* 286.3, *folly* 353.1, *rudeness* 400.2, *triviality* 800.2
flippant *humorous* 277.9, *imprudent* 286.7, *foolish* 353.5, *rude* 400.9
flippantly *imprudently* 286.11, *rudely* 400.19
flipper *stage set* 136.19, *swimming equipment* 164.8, *sense organ* 212.4, *component* 760.3
flip side [Inf] *opposite* 731.2
flip the switch *activate* 509.11
flip turn *competitive swimming* 164.3
flirt *lover* 299.11, *court* 299.26, *be solicitous* 323.13, *capricious person* 381.3, *be capricious* 381.6, *charmer* 700.6
flirtation *love affair* 299.9, *courtship* 299.10, *caprice* 381.1
flirtatious *amorous* 299.18, *capricious* 381.4
flirtatiously *amorously* 299.30
flirtatiousness *capriciousness* 381.2
flirtingly *amorously* 299.30
flirting with death *recklessness* 286.2
flirt with death *be rash* 286.8
flirty *amorous* 299.18
flit *be transient* 643.6, *be irresolute* 666.6, *flicker* 684.12, *be swift* 694.10
flit [Brit] *desertion* 386.7, *run away* 386.21, *departure* 705.1, *quit* 705.10
flitch *timber* 43.3
flitched *joined* 131.8
flitched joint *carpenter's term* 131.5
flitter *be irresolute* 666.6
float *plant body* 47.13, *soft drink* 93.8, *find means* 102.6, *fishing tackle* 154.7, *swimming techniques* 164.2, *survival swimming* 164.4, *swim* 164.14, *finance* 457.7, *trade* 480.18, *be light* 539.8, *go smoothly* 545.11, *be irresolute* 666.6, *fly* 689.13, *start* 696.20, *inaugurate* 771.31
floatability *lightness* 539.1
floatable *insubstantial* 539.5
float a loan *lend* 475.6
floated *swimming* 164.12
floatel *Ships and Boats* 690
floater *sailboard parts* 150.20, *windsurfing* 150.28
float fishing *fishing* 154.1
floating *fishing* 154.13, *swimming* 164.12, *monetary* 484.22, *lightness* 539.1, *insubstantial* 539.5, *changeable* 666.3, *nautical* 690.14
floating bridge *bridge* 691.7
floating currency *international finance* 457.2
floating debt *debt* 488.1
floating device *survival swimming* 164.4
floating diver *bait* 154.6
floating exchange rate *currency market* 484.8
floating island *island* 572.2
floating plug *bait* 154.6
floating-point notation *number system* 6.7

floating-point operation (FLOP) *computing terms* 15.22
floating rib *Human Bones* 19
floating up *ascent* 713.1
floating voter [Brit] *vacillator* 378.3
float on the air *sound faint* 233.8
float rod *fishing tackle* 154.7
float tackle *fishing tackle* 154.7
float to the surface *be light* 539.8
float up *spring up* 713.22
floaty *insubstantial* 539.5
floccose *platelike* 588.8
flocculate *solidify* 11.37
flocculence *smoothness* 543.2
flocculent *status adjectives* 11.25, *smooth* 543.8, *barbed* 544.7, *platelike* 588.8
flocculently *in layers* 588.11
flocculent precipitate *phase* 11.13
floccus *slice* 588.4
flock *assemblage of mammals* 35.22, *assemblage of birds* 36.18, *Collective Names* 59, *come together* 59.25, *worshiper* 83.6, *slice* 588.4, *throng* 795.4, *crowd* 795.11
floe *iceberg* 8.45
flog *inflict pain* 215.10, *hit* 454.28, *beat* 695.12, *hasten* 818.4
flog a dead horse *be superfluous* 99.12, *waste effort* 802.13
flogger *punisher* 454.16
flogging *corporal punishment* 454.11, *ramming* 695.3, *impelling* 695.8
Flood, the *flow* 570.4
flood *rain* 9.27, *crowd* 59.11, 59.26, 795.11, *excess* 99.1, *be excessive* 99.9, *stage lighting* 136.20, *natural violence* 520.3, *agent of destruction* 523.7, *flow* 555.25, 570.4, 570.10, *water* 557.29, *tide* 571.2, *course* 679.2, *influx* 706.2, *outflow* 707.4, *run out* 707.15, *immerse* 710.12, *overstepping* 712.1, *overstep* 712.12
flood-control system *water system* 551.13
flooded 557.24, **570.8**; *of landmasses* 572.12, *under* 598.13, *overrun* 712.6
floodgate *water system* 551.13, *outlet* 707.8
flood in **706.14**
flooding *excessive* 99.5, *soaking* 557.9, *overstepping* 712.1, *overrun* 712.6
floodlight *lighting* 132.16, *stage lighting* 136.20, *electric light* 246.6, *light* 246.19
floodlit *lit* 246.16, *accessible* 691.13
flood of words *obscurity* 197.1
flood out *run out* 707.15
flood plain *landform* 8.9, *marsh* 559.8, *lowland* 572.6
flood-proof *waterproof* 560.16
floods *Phobias* 283
flood the market *overdo* 99.11, *make cheap* 497.14
flood the tanks *sail* 690.16
flood tide *tide* 571.2
floor *Architectural Elements* 134, *astonish* 292.10, *refute* 332.7, *fee* 494.3, *ruin* 523.15, *level* 588.2, *lowest point* 597.5, *base* 601.1, *horizontal surface* 603.3, *bring down* 716.14, *certain amount* 738.3, *inferior state* 745.3
floorboard *floor covering* 613.13
floor covering **613.13**; *base* 601.1
floorer [Inf] *refutation* 332.1

floor exercise **157.4**; *gymnastics* 157.1
floor exercises *Sporting Activities* 145
flooring *bridge* 551.10, *base* 601.1
floor plan *map* 387.7
floor polish *cleaning agent* 111.9
floor polisher *smoother* 545.2
floor show *show* 138.4
floor tile *industrial ceramics* 129.6
floorwalker *salesperson* 482.8
floozy [Inf] *sexually immoral person* 432.8
flop *bungling* 128.2, *theatrical performance* 136.13, *jumping* 166.11, *loser* 468.8, 846.9, *be sold* 482.22, *be weak* 517.12, *soften* 543.14, *fall* 714.4, *droop* 714.14, *come unstuck* 756.7, *deteriorate* 808.14, *unsuccessful thing* 846.8, *loser* 846.9, *fail* 846.12
flop down *droop* 714.14
flophouse *hotel* 60.12
floppiness *weakness* 517.1, *softness* 543.1, *nonadhesion* 756.1
flopping *falling* 714.11, *nonadhesive* 756.4
floppy *weak* 517.6, *soft* 543.6, *nonadhesive* 756.4
floppy disk *magnetic recording* 10.51, *disk* 15.5
floptical disk *disk* 15.5
flora *living world* 13.9, *plants* 41.1, *herbarium* 41.12
floral **42.9**; *horticultural* 17.14, *fragrant* 226.4
floral arrangement *ornament* 532.7
floral charge *Heraldic Terms* 184
floral envelope *flower part* 42.3
floral leaf *leaf* 41.6
florally **42.13**; *horticulturally* 17.20, *fragrantly* 226.7
floral marquetry *decorative woodwork* 131.2
Floréal *French Revolutionary Calendar* 646
floreate *floral* 42.9
Florence Nightingale *nurse* 107.23
Florentine school *Western Art Styles* 133
florescence *fertilization* 21.6, *flowering* 42.5, *growth* 676.3
florescent *horticultural* 17.14, *flowering* 42.10
floret *flower* 42.1
floriate *or* **floriated** *floral* 42.9
floricultural *horticultural* 17.14
floriculture *horticulture* 17.1, *plant science* 41.10, *flower culture* 42.7
floriculturist *horticulturist* 17.13, *flower culture* 42.7
florid *floral* 42.9, *healthy* 113.4, *colorful* 251.11, *red-faced* 257.6, *variegated* 263.6, *ornate* 532.10
Florida *American States* 564
Florida Keys *Islands* 572
floridity *redness* 257.1
floridly *florally* 42.13, *ruddily* 257.10, *variedly* 263.12, *ornately* 532.14
floridness *redness* 257.1
florist *flower culture* 42.7, *retailer* 482.11
floristic *floral* 42.9
floristically *florally* 42.13
floristics *flower culture* 42.7
flossiness *smoothness* 543.2
flossy *smooth* 543.8
flotation *premiere* 771.9
flotilla *military organization* 58.4, *naval unit* 77.20, *collection* 757.3
flotilla leader *warship* 77.21

flotsam *transferred thing* 685.6
flotsam and jetsam *bits and pieces* 760.5
flounce *decorative article* 532.5, *edging* 618.2, *pleat* 637.2, 637.8, *stagger* 684.11, *pitch* 684.25
flounced *edged* 618.6
flounce off *or* **out** *depart* 705.8
flounder *food fish and shellfish* 90.20, *be clumsy* 128.9, *game fish* 154.10, *be wrong* 430.18, *stagger* 684.11, *pitch* 684.25, *have difficulty* 824.18, *be in difficulty* 824.19
floundering *at a loss* 468.11
flour *basic cooking ingredient* 91.8, *meal* 553.7, *grind* 553.23, *powder* 553.25, *thickener* 561.12, *sprinkle* 776.15
flouriness *powderiness* 553.3
flourish **404.25**; *be fertile* 22.13, *vegetate* 41.21, *flower* 42.12, *mushroom* 47.23, *be healthy* 113.11, *military call* 183.9, *burst of sound* 232.4, *ringing* 236.2, *demonstrate* 331.15, *ceremonial* 404.11, *be good* 445.16, *grace* 527.2, *decoration* 532.1, *ornament* 532.7, *grow* 581.17, *agitate* 684.22, *be in comfortable circumstances* 726.13, *increase* 746.6, *display* 843.13, *be successful* 845.11, *be prosperous* 847.6
flourished *displayed* 843.8
flourishing *fertile* 22.8, *plantlike* 41.13, *flowering* 42.10, *healthy* 113.4, *fresh* 260.10, *vigorous* 518.2, *germination* 581.5, *growing* 581.12, *successful* 845.8, *prosperous* 847.5
flour sifter *cooking equipment* 91.6
floury *mealy* 553.18
flout *defy* 416.7, 466.11
flout authority *disobey* 427.12
flout etiquette *be discourteous* 411.7
flouting *taunting* 436.14
flow **555.6, 555.25, 570.4, 570.10**; *drain* 8.64, *excretion* 25.1, *crowd* 59.26, *abound* 97.8, *be excessive* 99.9, *diffuseness* 199.1, *be diffuse* 199.5, *sound faint* 233.8, *be active* 414.18, *elegance* 527.1, *tide* 571.2, *pass* 639.13, *continuity* 669.1, *774.4, *continue* 669.8, 774.12, *momentum* 677.2, *be in motion* 677.14, *march on* 679.11, *result* 770.12, *go easily* 823.18
flow back *flow* 570.10, *reverse* 680.18
flow between *come between* 753.21
flow by *pass* 639.13
flow chart *map* 387.7
flow chart *or* **sheet** *chart* 767.8
flow diagram *map* 387.7
flow down *drip* 714.13
flower **42.1, 42.12**; *garden plant* 17.10, *reproduce oneself* 21.14, *age* 27.16, *plant* 41.2, *vegetate* 41.21, *grow* 43.15, 581.17, 676.10, *source of fragrance* 226.2, *excellence* 445.4, *increase* 467.17, 746.6, *plant products* 522.8, *growth* 676.3, *quintessence* 723.3, *be successful* 845.11, *be prosperous* 847.6
flowerage *plants* 41.1, *flowering* 42.5
flower arrangement *flower* 42.1, *ornament* 532.7
flower arranging *Hobbies and Pastimes* 167
flower basket *basket* 578.6

flower bed *ornamental garden* 17.3
flower bud *bud* 41.8
flower child *figurative usage* 42.8, *nonconformist* 782.7
flower cluster *flower head* 42.4
flower culture 42.7
flowered *floral* 42.9
flowerer *flowering plant* 42.2
floweret *flower* 42.1
flower garden *garden* 17.2, *ornamental garden* 17.3, *source of fragrance* 226.2
flower gardening *horticulture* 17.1
flower girl *wedding party* 64.7
flower grower *horticulturist* 17.13, *flower culture* 42.7
flower growing *horticulture* 17.1, *flower culture* 42.7
flower head 42.4
flowering 42.5, 42.10; *fertilization* 21.6, *taxonomic* 41.16, *germination* 581.5, *growing* 581.12, 676.6
flowering ash Trees and Shrubs 43
flowering plant 42.2; *seed plant* 41.3
flowering quince Flowers 42
flowerlet *flower* 42.1
flowerlike *floral* 42.9
flower market *market* 483.1
flower of speech *ornament* 532.7
flower painter *painter* 143.7
flower painting *type of painting* 143.5
flower part 42.3
flowerpot *nursery* 17.4, *pot* 578.15
flower power *figurative usage* 42.8
flower pressing Hobbies and Pastimes 167
flowers *funeral object* 31.6, Phobias 283, *love token* 299.8, *powder* 553.9
flowers [Arch] *bleeding* 25.10
flower seller *flower culture* 42.7
flower selling *flower culture* 42.7
flowers of sulfur *powder* 553.9
flower stalk *stem* 41.5
flower vegetable *vegetable* 90.33
flowery *horticultural* 17.14, *floral* 42.9, *fragrant* 226.4, *ornate* 532.10, *seasonal* 654.7
flowery speech *power of speech* 205.5
flow from *follow from* 676.9
flow in *flow* 570.10, *billow* 571.9, *flood in* 706.14
flowing 555.15, 570.7; *excessive* 99.5, *diffuse* 199.3, *flow* 570.4, *changeable* 666.3, *continuous* 669.5, *progressive* 669.6, *moving* 677.12
flowing bowl *drink* 121.6
flowingly *fluently* 570.13
flowing on *ongoing* 679.7
flowing river *river* 570.1
flowing together *flow* 570.4
flowing with milk and honey *lush* 485.11
flowmeter 555.12
flown *away* 576.8
flow of electricity *electric current* 10.39
flow of fluids Fields of Measurement 589
flow of ideas *creative thought* 317.3
flow of time *duration* 642.1
flow of words *talkativeness* 207.1
flow on *pass* 639.13, *march on* 679.11
flow out *waste away* 96.20, *be excessive* 99.5, *flow* 570.10, *billow*

571.9, *run out* 707.15, *leak* 816.11
flow over *flow* 570.10
flow stress *load* 14.14
flow together *flow* 570.10
flow with milk and honey *abound* 97.8
flu *respiratory disease* 114.12
flub *bungling* 128.2, *be wrong* 430.18
fluctuant *oscillating* 683.8
fluctuate *vacillate* 378.8, 683.14, *be capricious* 381.6, *defer* 604.15, *be irregular* 664.5, *be changeable* 666.5, *oscillate* 683.12, *unbalance* 741.8, *change* 841.20
fluctuating *inconstant* 378.6, *deferred* 604.9, *irregular* 664.3, *changeable* 666.3, *directional* 677.13, *oscillating* 683.8, *capricious* 841.16
fluctuating currency *money* 484.1
fluctuation *inconstancy* 378.2, *capitalism* 480.5, *deferment* 604.3, *irregularity* 664.1, *changeableness* 666.1, *movement* 677.3, *capriciousness* 841.8
flue *place for fire* 217.9
fluency *gymnastics* 157.1, *power of speech* 205.5, *talkativeness* 207.1, *elegance* 527.1, *flow* 555.6, 570.4, *easiness* 823.1
fluent *diffuse* 199.3, *articulate* 205.16, *talkative* 207.5, *fluid* 527.5, *flowing* 555.15, 570.7, *moving* 677.12
fluently 570.13; *talkatively* 207.9, *gracefully* 527.8, *stylistically* 537.11, *fluidly* 555.26
fluent tongue *talkativeness* 207.1
Fluer Breeds of Fowl 16
fluff *bungling* 128.2, *be clumsy* 128.9, *underact* 136.36, *blunder* 351.9, *lighten* 539.9, *soften* 543.14, *grain* 552.2, *powder* 553.9, *air bubble* 558.10
fluffily *lightly* 539.10, *softly* 543.18
fluffiness *lightness* 539.1, *smoothness* 543.2, *grain* 552.2
fluff one's lines *be unskillful* 128.8, *be forgetful* 355.11
fluff up *soften* 543.14
fluffy 552.11; *insubstantial* 539.5, *smooth* 543.8
flügelhorn Musical Instruments 142
fluid 19.25, 527.5, 555.1, 555.14; *soft* 543.6, *water* 557.1, *watery* 557.21, *changeable* 666.3, *nonadhesive* 756.4, *capricious* 841.16
fluidal *fluid* 555.14
fluid dram General Units 589
fluid dynamics *classical physics* 10.2
fluid extract *fluid* 555.1
fluidic *fluid* 555.14
fluid intake *drinking* 93.1
fluidity 555.5; *elegance* 527.1, *changeableness* 666.1, *nonadhesion* 756.1, *capriciousness* 841.8
fluidization 555.8
fluidize *make fluid* 555.22, *aerate* 556.24
fluidly 555.26; *softly* 543.18, *changeably* 666.7, *noncohesively* 756.9, *capriciously* 841.26
fluidly *or* **fluidally** *wetly* 557.34
fluid mechanics 555.13; *classical physics* 10.2, *industrial processes* 14.27
fluidmeter *flowmeter* 555.12
fluidness *fluidity* 555.5

fluid ounce General Units 589
fluid pressure Fields of Measurement 589
fluke *parasite* 39.18, *sharp-pointed thing* 549.4, *unexpectedness* 839.2, *chance* 842.1
flukiness *chance* 842.1
fluky *wormlike* 39.24, *unexpected* 839.6, *chance* 842.10
flume *outlet* 707.8
flumedraw *gulf* 587.3
flummery *empty talk* 362.5
flummox [Inf] *puzzle* 364.12, *make uncertain* 841.19
flummoxed [Inf] *confused* 364.10
flunk *fail* 846.12
flunky *servant* 90.1, *domestic worker* 123.4, *inferior* 745.4
fluoresce *reflect* 10.76, *light up* 246.20
fluorescence *light* 10.17, 246.1, Fields of Measurement 589
fluorescent *lucent* 246.13
fluorescent lamp *electron tube* 14.40
fluorescent light *electric light* 246.6
fluorescent paint *or* **clothing** *that which makes visible* 244.4
fluorescent tube *industrial ceramics* 129.6
fluoridate *react* 11.38, *immunize* 810.22
fluoridation *health care* 107.7
fluoride *prophylaxis* 115.4
fluoride treatment *dentistry* 107.6
fluorinate *react* 11.38, *immunize* 810.22
fluorine Chemical Elements and Common Allotropes 11
fluorometer Fields of Measurement 589
fluorometry Fields of Measurement 589
flurried *agitated* 684.15
flurry *snow* 9.30, *alacrity* 414.3, *fuss* 684.4, *swiftness* 694.1, *haste* 818.1
flush *filled* 97.5, *clean* 111.17, *hunt* 160.12, *snowplow* 162.29, *poker* 168.5, *heat* 217.1, *feel hot* 217.19, *face color* 251.9, *redness* 257.1, *redden* 257.9, *blushing* 403.2, *blush* 403.17, *well-off* 467.12, *wealthy* 485.8, *smooth* 545.4, *flow* 570.4, 570.10, *horizontal* 603.6, *make horizontal* 603.10, *horizontally* 603.11, *directly* 697.16, *equal* 740.8, *full* 761.8
flush bead Architectural Elements 134
flushed *red-faced* 257.6, *blushing* 403.7
flushed with pride *prideful* 297.8
flushed with rage *angry* 302.11
flushed with victory *victorious* 845.10
flush gate *ski race* 162.4
flushing *red-faced* 257.6, *blushing* 403.2
flushing out *cleaning* 111.2
flushly *smoothly* 545.13
flushness *smoothness* 545.1, *horizontality* 603.1
flush out *clean* 111.17, *purify* 111.19
fluster *fuss* 684.4, *agitate* 684.22, *disturb* 768.10
flustered *slightly drunk* 121.26, *agitated* 684.15, *restless* 684.16, *disturbed* 768.6
flute *drink container* 93.13, Architectural Elements 134,

Musical Instruments 142, *speak in a particular way* 205.18, *furrow* 638.1, 638.5
fluted *furrowed* 638.3
fluted armor *historic armor* 419.8
flutes Phobias 283
fluther Collective Names 59
fluting Architectural Elements 134, *decorative method* 532.3
flutist *player* 141.2
flutter *swimming* 164.12, *broadcast dissonance* 241.3, *be fearful* 283.15, *be changeable* 666.5, *vibration* 683.2, *vibrate* 683.13, *beat* 684.10, *flicker* 684.12, 684.26, *be agitated* 684.21, *agitate* 684.22, *flight maneuver* 689.6, *maneuver* 689.14, *haste* 818.1
flutter board *swimming equipment* 164.8
flutter down *drop* 714.15
fluttering *stimulus* 212.3, *restless* 684.16
flutter kick *swimming techniques* 164.2
flutter one's eyelashes at *look* 242.21
fluttery *restless* 684.16
fluvial *riverlike* 570.6
fluviomarine *riverlike* 570.6
flux *force* 10.9, *excretion* 25.1, *defecation* 25.3, *flow* 555.6, 555.25, 570.4, *solution* 555.10, *tide* 571.2, *changeableness* 666.1, *momentum* 677.2
flux and reflux *swaying* 378.4, *tide* 571.2, *oscillation* 683.1
flux collector *telescope* 7.25
flux density *force* 10.9
fluxibility *fluidization* 555.8
fluxion *differentiation* 6.29, *flow* 555.6
fluxional *flowing* 555.15
fluxionary *flowing* 555.15
fluxive *flowing* 570.7
fluxus Western Art Styles 133
Fly Constellations 7, Rivers 570
fly 36.23, 689.13; *insect* 40.1, *part of garment* 100.27, *batting terms* 147.6, *bait* 154.6, *flag* 184.8, *depart* 265.6, *retreat* 386.22, *be active* 414.18, *abscond* 786.16, *pass* 639.13, *be in motion* 677.14, *walk* 677.17, *convey* 685.9, *travel* 686.11, *pilot* 689.15, *find one's way* 691.15, *be swift* 694.10, *go up* 713.23, *escape* 816.8, *make haste* 818.5
flyable 689.12
fly a flag *agitate* 684.22
fly against *attack* 418.17
fly a kite *test* 390.9
fly aloft *go up* 713.23
fly apart *diverge* 776.16
fly ball *batting terms* 147.6
flyblow *infest* 40.17
flyblown *verminous* 40.13, *unclean* 112.8
flyby *rocketry* 7.32, *miscellaneous aviation terms* 689.9
fly by *pass* 639.13
fly by *or* **away** *be transient* 643.6
fly-by-light *flight control* 689.7
fly-by-nighter *cunning person* 822.3, *loser* 846.9
fly by the seat of one's pants *be cunning* 822.5
fly-by-wire *flight control* 689.7
fly casting *fishing* 154.1
flycatcher *songbird* 36.12
fly dick [Inf] *law enforcement officer* 53.8
fly down *drop* 714.15
flyer *aircraft personnel* 689.8

fly-fish *fish* 154.14
fly-fisher *fisherman* 154.12
fly-fishing 154.2, Sporting Activities 145
fly floor *or* **gallery** *stage* 136.18
fly in all directions *diverge* 776.16
flying 689.11; *chiropteran* 35.25, *wrestling* 152.18, *ice-skating* 162.32, *Phobias* 283, *transient* 643.4, *ascending motion* 677.7, *directional* 677.13, *aviation* 689.1, *passing along* 692.5, *speeding* 694.7, *nonadhesive* 756.4
flying axel *ice-skating techniques* 162.16
flying boat *military aircraft* 77.30
flying bomb *bomb* 78.15
flying buttress Architectural Elements 134, *supporting part* 605.3
flying circus *circus* 138.2, *aviation* 689.1
flying column *armed force* 77.10
flying doctor *aviation* 689.1
Flying Fish Constellations 7
flying fish *fish* 38.5
flying mammal 35.8
flying mare *wrestling terms* 152.10
flying picket *strike* 57.8
flying reptile *extinct reptile* 37.9
flying start *automobile racing terms* 146.3, *advantage* 618.4, 744.3, *acceleration* 694.3, *starting point* 771.11
flying up *taking off* 713.6
fly in the face of *defy* 416.7
fly in the face of reason *be impossible* 837.9
fly in the ointment *defect* 806.4, *obstacle* 826.2
fly into a rage *become angry* 302.20
flyleaf *bookbinding* 174.11
fly like a bat out of hell [Inf] *make haste* 818.5
flyman *stagehand* 136.29
fly off *sidestep* 698.22, *change direction* 703.15
fly off at a tangent *change direction* 703.15
fly off the handle [Inf] *become angry* 302.20
fly on instruments *pilot* 689.15
fly out *play baseball* 147.9
fly-out *other game terms* 147.7
flyover [Brit] *bridge* 551.10
flypaper *adhesive* 755.3
fly pattern *play* 155.8
fly right *be virtuous* 447.8
fly rod *fishing tackle* 154.7
fly spoon *bait* 154.6
fly-spotted *mottled* 263.10
fly the beam *pilot* 689.15
fly the coop *or* **nest** *abscond* 576.16
fly the corridor *pilot* 689.15
fly to arms *go to war* 76.29
fly to the assistance of *help* 825.23
fly up *spring up* 713.22
flyweight *boxing weight divisions* 152.6, *combat* 152.17
flywheel *wheel* 682.9
FM station *radio broadcasting* 172.4
f-number *or* **f number** *lens system* 10.22, *exposure equipment* 132.12
foal *have young* 21.16, *young animal* 26.4, *young mammal* 35.20, *give birth* 35.33, *horse* 159.1
foam *saliva* 25.9, *air bubble* 558.10, *bubble* 558.24, *wave* 571.3, *billow* 571.9

foam at the mouth *salivate* 25.25, *be angry* 302.19, *be agitated* 684.21
foam-filled *compressible* 543.9
foam-flecked *whitened* 253.8
foam glass *industrial ceramics* 129.6
foaminess *lightness* 539.1
foaming *salivating* 25.18, *whitened* 253.8, *insubstantial* 539.5
foaming at the mouth *manic* 110.10, *angry* 302.11
foam rubber *rubber* 546.3
foamy *insubstantial* 539.5, *bubbly* 558.18
fob off *substitute* 672.5
fob off on *force* 428.10
focaccia *bread* 90.10
focal 612.8; *curvilinear* 6.78, *convergent* 702.7, *elite* 744.12, *middle* 772.9
focalization *centrality* 612.5, *focus* 702.5
focalize *centralize* 612.11
focalized *centered* 612.9
focalizing *centrality* 612.5
focal length *lens system* 10.22, *composition* 132.17
focally 612.14
focal plane *lens system* 10.22
focal point *lens system* 10.22, *composition* 132.17, *focus* 612.3, *center of attraction* 700.7, *middle* 772.1
fo'c's'le *vanguard* 621.5
focus 612.3, 702.5, 702.11; *curve* 6.38, *lens system* 10.22, *learn* 48.23, *composition* 132.17, *compose a photograph* 132.27, *clarity* 244.2, *make visible* 244.9, *issue* 328.2, *prepare for action* 388.18, *centralize* 612.11, *center of attraction* 700.7, *essential content* 723.2, *point of union* 752.8, *middle* 772.1, *place in the middle* 772.18
focused 328.6; *intelligible* 363.5, *centered* 612.9, *convergent* 702.7
focusing *centrality* 612.5, *convergent* 702.7
focusing screen *exposure equipment* 132.12
focus of interest *focus* 612.3
focus on 328.9; *look* 242.21, *make visible* 244.9, *aim* 374.10, *centralize* 612.11
fodder *animal feed* 16.12, *practice livestock farming* 16.20, *eat grass* 45.11, *animal food* 90.2
fodderbeets *crop* 16.8, *animal feed* 16.12
fodder crop *crop* 16.8
fodder grass *grass* 45.1
foe *hostile person* 63.5, *opponent* 828.10
foehn Notable Winds 9
fog 9.32, 9.59; *moisture* 9.31, *phase* 11.13, *composition* 132.17, *disguise* 181.13, *invisibility* 245.1, *that which makes invisible* 245.4, *murk* 248.2, *make dim* 248.8, *be opaque* 250.6, *Phobias* 283, *wateriness* 557.3, *mistiness* 559.2, *sprinkle* 559.14, *make shapeless* 625.3, *make uncertain* 841.19
fog band *mistiness* 559.2
fog bank *fog* 9.32
fogbound *foggy* 9.51, *detained* 830.11
fogbow *rainbow* 9.28
fogdog *rainbow* 9.28
fog drip *fog* 9.32, *dew* 559.6
foggily *meteorologically* 9.60, *dimly* 248.10, *opaquely* 250.9, *grayly*

255.10, *shapelessly* 625.5, *indeterminately* 841.24
fogginess *obscurity* 197.1, *invisibility* 245.1, *murk* 248.2, *opaqueness* 250.1, *mistiness* 559.2, *shapelessness* 625.1, *indeterminacy* 841.6
foggy 9.51; *obscure* 197.2, *difficult to see* 245.4, *murky* 248.5, *shady* 250.4, *dull* 255.8, *difficult* 364.8, *condensed* 540.7, *misty* 559.19, *shapeless* 625.2, *indeterminate* 841.14
foghorn *signal* 183.6, *warning signal* 814.3
fog level *exposure* 132.15
fog light *safety light* 246.7
fogou *burial place* 31.7
fog signal *track* 688.2, *sea marker* 690.7, *warning signal* 814.3
foible *defect* 806.4
foil *sharp weapon* 78.6, Architectural Elements 134, *entertainer* 138.8, *fencing equipment* 153.2, *fencing* 153.6, *thwart* 293.10, *avert* 386.15, *coat* 588.3, *wrapping* 613.10, *enclosing thing* 619.3, *deflection* 701.3, *hinder* 826.15, *counteract* 828.21
foil button *fencing equipment* 153.2
foiled *frustrated* 293.5
foil-fence *fence* 153.7
foil fencing *fencing* 153.1
foil grip *fencing equipment* 153.2
foil guard *fencing equipment* 153.2
foiling *hindrance* 826.1
foilsman *fencer* 153.5
foist on *force* 428.10
fold 8.22, 637.1, 637.7; *farm building* 16.4, *cage* 60.15, *worshiper* 83.6, *part of garment* 100.27, *make clothing* 100.44, *gamble* 167.14, *play cards* 168.7, *make rough* 544.11, *closed place* 584.4, *enclose* 584.16, *layer* 588.1, *enclosed area* 619.2, *roll* 682.15, *swirl* 682.16, *joint* 752.7, *shelter* 812.4
fold [Inf] *become insolvent* 846.17
foldable *contractible* 582.11
fold around *fold* 637.7
foldaway *type of bed* 101.9
fold belt *fold* 8.22
fold-belt mountain *mountain building* 8.23
foldboat *canoe* 150.9, Ships and Boats 690
folded 637.5
folded [Inf] *closed* 637.6
folded and gathered sheets (F and Gs) *stage of proof* 174.9
folded arms *gesture* 183.5
folded hands *gesture* 183.5
folded over *folded* 637.5
folder *collection* 105.12, *packet* 578.4, *enclosing thing* 619.3
fold in *cook* 91.10
folding *livestock farming* 16.10, *type of chair* 101.4, *canoeing* 150.26
folding canoe *canoe* 150.9
folding green [Inf] *cash* 484.2
folding ladder *ladder* 713.10
folding money [Inf] *cash* 484.2
fold mountain *mountain building* 8.23
fold nappe *fold* 8.22
fold one's arms *gesture* 183.17
fold over *fold* 637.7
foldup [Inf] *closure* 637.4, *close* 637.10, *cease* 773.20
fold up *save* 105.20, *become smaller* 582.14, *fold* 637.7

foliage *leaf* 41.6, *green thing* 260.4
foliage bud *bud* 41.8
foliar *horticultural* 17.14
foliate *of plants* 41.14, *platelike* 588.8
foliated *petrographic* 8.58, *layered* 588.6
foliated rock *metamorphic rock* 8.36
foliation *petrogenesis* 8.31, Architectural Elements 134, *layering* 588.5
folic acid *vitamin* 12.13
folie à deux *delusion* 110.2
folio *book part* 174.5, *part of writing* 760.6
foliose *lichenoid* 47.21
foliose lichen *lichen* 47.16
folium *curve* 6.38
folk *society* 1.6, *societal* 1.13, *group* 18.13, *musical* 140.25
folk art *tradition* 1.7, Western Art Styles 133
folk ballad *folk music* 140.7
folk dancing Dancing Types 135, Hobbies and Pastimes 167
folk etymology *language error* 351.10
folk group *instrumental group* 141.3
folk history *tradition* 1.7, *chronicle* 3.4
folk literature *literature* 139.1
folklore *tradition* 1.7, 653.5, *study of humankind* 18.6, *custom* 397.4
folklorist *studier of humankind* 18.7
folk medicine *alternative medicine* 107.4, *healing art* 115.13
folk motif *tradition* 1.7
folk music 140.7
folk play *dramatic style* 136.3
folk poetry *poetry* 139.8
folk psychology Psychological Theories, Schools 108
folk rock *rock music* 140.6, *folk music* 140.7
folk-rock singer *singer* 141.4
folks, the [Inf] *family circle* 65.4
folksiness *familiarity* 407.3
folk singer *singer* 141.4
folk society *society* 2.6
folk song *tradition* 1.7, *folk music* 140.7, *song* 140.11
folk story *story* 139.4
folksy *musical* 140.25, *familiar* 407.8
folk tale *tradition* 1.7, *chronicle* 3.4, *story* 139.4
folk Victorian style Architectural Styles 134
folkways *custom* 397.4
foller *contractor* 582.6
follicle *botanical fruit* 44.2
follicle-stimulating hormone Human Hormones 12
follies *show* 138.4
follow 385.12, 401.14, 745.12, 770.10; *rationalize* 4.20, *propound a philosophy* 4.21, *serve* 69.11, *understand* 363.9, *observe* 465.4, *stay near* 586.13, *be in the rear* 622.7, *follow from* 676.9, *conform* 735.27, *imitate* 736.9, *emulate* 736.11, *specialize* 779.16, *abide by* 781.12, *attend* 794.19
follow a course *conduct oneself* 399.17
follow advice *consult* 176.11
follow a pattern *be regular* 663.10
follow a plan *plan ahead* 387.13
follow a procedure *perform* 465.5

follow a Spartan regimen *fast* 118.8

follow custom *have good manners* 410.10

followed *pursued* 385.10

follower 794.10; *servant* 69.1, *worshiper* 83.6, *pursuer* 385.5, *adherent* 401.5, 755.4, *approver* 437.7, *assenter* 462.5, *supporter* 605.9, *imitator* 736.6, *inferior* 745.4, *successor* 770.6, *conformist* 781.6, *dependent* 832.4

follow from 676.9

following *pursuit* 385.1, *pursuing* 385.8, *observance* 465.1, *delaying* 658.8, *caused* 676.5, *backward motion* 677.5, *imitation* 736.1, *imitative* 736.7, *adhering* 755.7, *sequence* 770.1, *sequential* 770.7, *after* 770.14, *consecutive* 774.7, *attendance* 794.5, *accompanied* 794.15

following from *caused* 676.5

following spot [Inf] *stage lighting* 136.20

following up *pursuit* 385.1

following upon *with the effect of* 676.12

following wind *wind* 9.12, *help* 825.1

follow in office *follow* 770.10

follow in sequence *follow* 770.10

follow in the footsteps of *emulate* 736.11, *follow* 770.10

follow like sheep *obey* 426.7, *emulate* 736.11

follow on *emulate* 736.11, *follow* 770.10, *be consecutive* 774.11

follow one's bent *be independent* 829.18

follow one's career *conduct oneself* 399.17

follow one's conscience *be persuaded* 178.20, *be virtuous* 447.8, *be motivated* 508.10

follow one's hunch *be intuitive* 320.9

follow one's instincts *be motivated* 508.10

follow one's nose *smell* 224.7, *aim* 697.14

follow one's own will 372.13

follow on from *follow from* 676.9

follow orders *obey* 426.7

follow protocol *be formal* 406.11

follow rites 85.19

follow separate paths *diverge* 753.20

follow suit *emulate* 736.11, *abide by* 781.12

follow that car! *after him!* 385.19

follow the beaten path *abide by* 781.12

follow the book *obey* 426.7

follow the crowd *assent to* 346.7, *follow* 401.14, *be the same* 730.13, *conform* 735.27

follow the example of *emulate* 736.11

follow the fashion *abide by* 781.12

follow the golden mean *be moderate* 521.6

follow the herd *emulate* 736.11

follow the hounds *hunt* 385.14

follow the law *be legal* 53.28

follow the leader Children's and Party Games 167

follow the letter *be literal* 721.25

follow the letter of the law *be legal* 53.28

follow the party line *obey* 426.7, *follow the rules* 780.17

follow the rules 780.17

follow the scent *hunt* 160.12, *smell* 224.7, *follow* 385.12

follow or **keep to the straight and narrow** *be moral* 431.13

follow the trail *follow* 385.12

follow the trend *be trendy* 652.18, *abide by* 781.12

follow through *maintain* 377.12, *continue* 669.8

follow-through *bowling delivery* 151.2, *grip* 151.4, *bowling* 151.6, *bowls* 151.7, *golf shots* 156.4, *tennis strokes* 165.2, *sequel* 770.5

follow to the ends of the earth *obey* 426.7

follow to the letter *be literal* 721.25

follow up 385.16; *practice medicine* 107.32, *pursue* 377.11, *protract* 669.9

follow-up *health care* 107.7, *continuation* 669.2, *sequel* 770.5

folly 353.1; *recklessness* 286.2, *ignorance* 316.3, 349.1, *lack of thought* 318.1, *ridiculousness* 368.1

foment *make violent* 520.10, *awaken* 675.9

fomentation *heater* 217.3, *cause* 675.1

Fomorian Legendary Creatures 360

fond *sensitive* 267.3, *loving* 299.15

fond feeling *liking* 290.1

fond illusion *self-deception* 193.2

fondle *give pleasure* 214.13, *type of touch* 216.3, *touch* 216.9, *communicate love* 299.25

fondling *touching* 216.2, *communication of love* 299.6

fondly *lovingly* 299.29

fondness *good feeling* 266.4, *liking* 290.1, *love* 299.1

fondness for company *sociability* 408.1

fondness for the bottle *drinking* 121.2

fond of *desirous* 288.13, *liking* 290.4

fond of a drink *drunken* 121.28

fond of company *sociable* 408.11

fondue fork *tableware* 92.13

fons et origo [L] *source* 675.2

font *church interior* 83.9, *type* 173.5

food 90.1; *life requirement* 28.5, *provisions* 89.3, *refreshments* 94.3, *fuels* 106.2, Phobias 283

foodaholic *glutton* 119.2

food aid *offering* 472.6

food bank *charitable organization* 305.4

food chain *ecology* 13.25, *food content* 90.3

food-combining diet *diet* 92.5

food content 90.3

food drive *charitable organization* 305.4

food fish *fish* 38.5

food fish and shellfish 90.20

food for powder *army person* 77.17

foodie [Inf] *eater* 92.15

food mill *pulper* 561.13

food mountain *plenty* 90.4

food of the gods *food* 90.1

food parcel *offering* 472.6

food plant *plant* 41.2

food poisoning *poisoning* 114.8, *gastroenterological disease* 114.11

food preparation *cooking* 91.1

food processing *chemical process industries* 14.26, *cooking* 91.1

food processor *cooking equipment* 91.6, *pulverizer* 553.11, *liquidizer*

555.11, *pulper* 561.13, *agitator* 684.14, *mixer* 751.7

food provider 90.6

food pyramid *ecology* 13.25, *food content* 90.3, *diet* 92.5

food stamps *social welfare* 307.4, *offering* 472.6

food store *plant body* 47.13

foodstuffs *food* 90.1

food web *ecology* 13.25

fool *unskilled person* 128.3, *stock part* 136.24, *clown* 138.10, *deceive* 181.14, 193.16, *unintelligent person* 316.4, *ignorant person* 349.4, *foolish person* 353.3, *object of ridicule* 368.3, *laughingstock* 369.4, *butt* 436.8, *simpleton* 526.5, *semiliquid* 561.7, *naive person* 821.2

fool around *occupy oneself* 412.15, *fornicate* 432.14

fool around with *impair* 808.18

fooled *deceived* 193.15

foolery *act of folly* 353.2

foolhardily *adventurously* 284.20, *recklessly* 286.10

foolhardiness *adventurousness* 284.4, *recklessness* 286.2, *impulsiveness* 318.6

foolhardy *adventurous* 284.12, *reckless* 286.6, *impulsive* 318.11, *foolish* 353.5

fooling around *communication of love* 299.6, *fornication* 432.3

foolish 353.5; *unskillful* 128.4, *clownish* 138.14, *imprudent* 286.7, *unintelligent* 316.6, *thoughtless* 318.7, *misjudged* 342.8, *meaningless* 362.7, *ridiculous* 368.5, *simpleminded* 526.11, *not serious* 800.11

foolish hope *improbability* 839.1

foolishly 353.8; *unskillfully* 128.12, *imprudently* 286.11, *unintelligently* 316.9, *misguidedly* 342.12, *meaninglessly* 362.13, *ridiculously* 368.8

foolishness *imprudence* 286.3, *ignorance* 316.3, *folly* 353.1, *ridiculousness* 368.1

foolish person 353.3

foolish talk *senseless talk* 362.4

foolproof *invulnerable* 810.18, *wieldy* 823.12

foolscap *paper* 104.5

fool's cap *clown* 138.10

fool's errand *futility* 282.3, *waste* 468.5, *waste of effort* 802.4

fool's gold *bullion* 484.16, *waste of effort* 802.4

fool's paradise *aspiration* 281.3, *misjudgment* 342.1, *figurative overestimation* 343.3, *theory* 720.4

fool with *be clumsy* 128.9

foot *appendage* 19.5, *moss plant* 46.5, *army person* 77.17, *part of poem* 139.9, *meter* 139.10, General Units 589, *lowest point* 597.5, *base* 601.1

footage *motion-picture photography* 137.9, *length* 590.1

foot-and-mouth disease *animal disease* 34.10

football 155.1, Sporting Activities 145, *soccer* 163.1, 163.7, *athletics* 422.7

football associations 155.14

footballer [Brit] *soccer participant* 163.4

football game *football* 155.1

football helmet *safety device* 810.15

football player 155.15

football season *seasons* 654.2

football uniform 155.2

footbath *bath* 111.6, *basin* 578.12

footboard *type of bed* 101.9

footbridge *bridge* 551.10, 691.7

foot-candle Scientific and Technical Units 589

foot-dragger *plodder* 693.6

foot-dragging *unenthusiasm* 375.3, *unenthusiastic* 375.10, *hesitation* 693.5, *hesitant* 693.9, *inhibition* 826.9, *inhibitive* 826.14, *uncooperativeness* 828.4

footfault *play tennis* 165.13

foot fault *grip* 151.4, *tennis terms* 165.5

foot-first surface dive *diving* 164.6

footgear *shoes* 100.30

foothill *hill* 569.2

foothill or **foothills** *heights* 596.4

foothills *lowlands* 597.6

foothold *rock face* 161.6, *retention* 471.1, *opportunity* 583.8

footing *retention* 471.1, *influence* 512.1, *substructure* 551.8, *circumstances* 573.2, 726.1, *basis* 601.3, 605.4, *state* 725.1, *rank* 739.2

foot in the door *opportunity* 583.8

foot-lambert Scientific and Technical Units 589

footlights *stage lighting* 136.20, *electric light* 246.6

footlights, the *the drama* 136.1

footling [Inf] *trivial* 800.14

foot locker *receptacle* 105.11

footloose *wandering* 698.13

footloose and fancy-free *wandering* 698.13, *independent* 829.12

footman *domestic servant* 69.7

footnote *annotation* 365.2, *annotate* 365.14, *appendage* 748.4

footpath *passage* 691.5, *thoroughfare* 692.6

foot-pound Scientific and Technical Units 589

foot-poundal Scientific and Technical Units 589

foot-pound-second (fps) system *measuring system* 589.4

footprint *means of identification* 184.3, *vestige* 185.11, *indication* 339.3, *cavity* 635.3, *visible effect* 676.2, *miscellaneous aviation terms* 689.9, *remainder* 750.1

foot race *race* 422.8

footrest *step* 713.11

foot rule *measuring instrument* 589.12

foots *stage lighting* 136.20

footslogger *army person* 77.17

foot soldier *army person* 77.17

footsore *fatigued* 820.2

foot steering *windsurfing terms* 150.21

footstep *vestige* 185.11, *step* 713.11

footstone *funeral object* 31.6

footstool *sycophant* 401.3

footstrap *sailboard parts* 150.20

foot the bill *defray* 489.18

foot-ton Scientific and Technical Units 589

foot transportation *road transportation* 687.1

foot warmer *heater* 217.3

footway *passage* 691.5

footwear *shoes* 100.30

footweary *fatigued* 820.2

footwork *boxing techniques* 152.5

foozle *bungling* 128.2, *be clumsy* 128.9

foozled *bungled* 128.7

fop *vain person* 402.7, *fashion business* 536.3

foppish *cocky* 402.11, *flashy* 404.17

foppishly *cockily* 402.19, *flashily* 404.32, *dashingly* 536.10
foppishness *dressing* 100.2
for *indirectly* 80.8, *recommending* 437.11
for a beginning *first* 771.37
forage *animal feed* 16.12, *eat grass* 45.11, *animal food* 90.2
Foraker, Mount *Mountains and Hills* 569
for a kickoff *first* 771.37
for all ages *useful* 801.5
for all one is worth *laboriously* 122.13, *actively* 414.24, *at full speed* 694.17
for all one knows *possibly* 836.9, *perchance* 842.18
for all practical purposes *nearly* 586.18, *in essence* 723.13
for all that *additionally* 748.15
for all to see *publicly* 173.20, *clear* 244.6, *manifestly* 331.20, 843.17, *evidently* 339.16
for a long time *lengthwise* 590.14, *for long* 642.9
for always *tenaciously* 471.11, *eternally* 644.10, *to the end* 773.25
for a moment *transiently* 643.8
for a purpose *intentional* 374.7, *with the intention of* 374.14
for a rainy day *foresightedly* 357.10
for a reason *intentional* 374.7
for a season *meanwhile* 639.18
for a song *buying* 481.9, *cheaply* 497.16
for a start *first* 771.37
for a time *meanwhile* 639.18
for a while *at present* 647.9
foray *military attack* 418.2, *attack* 418.17, *plundering* 479.5, *plunder* 479.16
for ay *or* **aye** [Arch] *eternally* 644.10
forbear *show pity* 308.8, *abstain* 386.16, *not use* 394.9, *desist* 417.13, *be lenient* 423.5, *be self-restrained* 455.10, *refuse oneself* 506.10
forbear! *hands off!* 386.26
forbearance *mercy* 308.3, *forgivingness* 312.3, *abstinence* 386.2, *nonuse* 394.1, *freedom* 407.4, *desisting* 417.4, *leniency* 423.1, *self-restraint* 455.1
forbearer *resister* 417.5
forbearing *pitying* 308.4, *forgiving* 312.4, *desisting* 417.4, 417.9, *lenient* 423.3, *chaste* 431.10, *self-restrained* 455.6
forbearingly *pityingly* 308.11, *forgivingly* 312.13, *abstemiously* 417.15, *with self-restraint* 455.14
for better or for worse *perseveringly* 377.16, *eternally* 644.10
forbid *make illegal* 53.29, *refute* 332.7, *reject* 383.10, *prohibit* 503.8, *dissent* 506.9, *exclude* 764.7, *hinder* 826.15, *make impossible* 837.8
forbiddance *rejection* 383.1, *exclusion* 764.1
forbidden 837.7; *rejected* 383.6, *prohibited* 503.5, *out of reach* 712.11, *excluded* 764.6
forbidden fruit *figurative usage* 44.4, *object of desire* 288.8
forbidden love *love affair* 299.9
forbidden love *or* **fruit** *fornication* 432.3
forbidding *unsociable* 409.6, *prohibition* 503.1
forbiddingly *unsocially* 409.13

f-orbital *chemical bond* 11.6
force 10.9, 59.10, 428.10, 514.8; *party* 59.3, *necessitate* 95.17, *exertion* 122.4, *motivate* 178.17, *emphasis* 200.1, *meaning* 361.1, *impose one's will* 372.14, *tenacity* 376.4, *ill-use* 395.2, 395.7, *action* 412.1, *coercion* 428.2, *seduce* 432.16, *manipulate* 508.12, *operation* 509.1, *instrument* 511.2, *influence* 512.1, *be an influence* 512.13, *power* 514.1, *be powerful* 514.18, *strength* 516.1, *vigor* 518.1, *violence* 520.1, *use violence* 520.9, *friction* 554.1, *measuring instrument* 589.12, *core* 612.2, *cause* 675.1, *awaken* 675.9, *further* 679.13, *impulsion* 695.1, *collection* 757.3
force, the *law enforcement agency* 53.7
force a confrontation *show oneself* 843.15
force a passage *enter* 692.18
force a surrender *be victorious* 845.16
forced *ornamental* 17.17, *immature* 389.9, *hasty* 818.3
forced entry *inroad* 706.3
forced labor *imprisonment* 55.4, *work* 122.1, *coercive method* 428.3
forced landing *fall* 714.4
forced march *haste* 818.1
forced out *other game terms* 147.7, *resigning* 835.3
forced reconciliation *treaty* 74.2
forced resignation *resignation* 835.1
forced saving *levy* 494.7
forced vibration *wave* 10.11
forced wedding *wedding* 64.5
force-feed *feed* 90.41, *force* 428.10
force-feeding *coercive method* 428.3
force field *force* 10.9, 514.8
forceful *persuasive* 178.12, *assertive* 189.20, *emphatic* 200.3, *descriptive* 202.11, *tenacious* 376.9, *abusive* 395.5, *effective* 412.10, *active* 414.13, *compelling* 428.6, *influential* 512.8, *powerful* 514.15, *strong* 516.9, *vigorous* 518.2, *violent* 520.5, *core* 612.7, *advantaged* 618.7
forcefully *persuasively* 178.21, *assertively* 189.35, *emphatically* 200.7, *offensively* 395.9, *effectively* 412.19, *actively* 414.24, *aggressively* 418.27, *compellingly* 428.12, *influentially* 512.14, *powerfully* 514.21, *strongly* 516.17, *with vigor* 518.6, *violently* 520.11, *dynamically* 695.16, *propulsively* 696.21
forcefulness *persuasion* 178.1, *assertiveness* 189.8, *emphasis* 200.1, *power* 514.1, *vigor* 518.1, *violence* 520.1
forceful person *coercer* 428.4
force in *impact* 710.11
force into oblivion *destroy* 186.10
force of attraction *or* **gravitation** *force* 514.8
force of circumstance *necessitarianism* 95.7
force of gravity *gravity* 538.2, *pulling power* 700.2
force of habit *habit* 397.1
force of inertia *force* 514.8
force oneself *grudge* 375.15
force one's way *exert oneself* 122.11, *follow up* 385.16
force open *use violence* 520.9

force out *play baseball* 147.9, *drive out* 709.19, *extort* 711.18
forcep *fishing tackle* 154.7
force play *other game terms* 147.7
forceps *retainer* 471.3, *extractor* 711.9
forcer *coercer* 428.4
for certain *assuredly* 336.12
forces *load* 14.14, *army commands* 77.13
forces of law and order *law enforcement agency* 53.7
force someone's hand *compel* 428.8
force to accept *force* 428.10
force to step down *refute* 332.7
force to the wall *cause difficulties* 824.22
force upon *force* 428.10
forcible *compelling* 428.6, *demanding* 505.8, *powerful* 514.15, *vigorous* 518.2, *violent* 520.5
forcible demand *demand* 505.3
forcible removal *removal* 574.2
forcibly *compellingly* 428.12, *by request* 505.14, *powerfully* 514.21, *strongly* 516.17, *with vigor* 518.6, *violently* 520.11
forcing *coercion* 428.2
forcing a run *pitching terms* 147.5
forcing bed *nursery* 17.4
forcing house *nursery* 17.4
ford *shallowness* 599.1, *crossing point* 692.7, *cross* 692.17
for dear life *actively* 414.24
fore *front* 621.1, 621.9
fore! 156.9; *look out!* 814.12
fore-and-aft *sailing* 150.25, *completely* 759.14
fore-and-after *cap* 100.33
forearm *appendage* 19.5, *be prepared* 388.17, *warn* 814.8
forearmed *expecting* 356.4, *prepared* 388.9, *warned* 814.7
forebear *predecessor* 769.8
forebears *old people* 653.6
forebode *foresee* 357.9, *predict* 358.14, *endanger* 811.13
foreboding *fearfulness* 283.2, *insight* 320.3, *expectation* 356.1, *prediction* 358.1, *predicting* 358.10, *dangerous* 811.7, *forewarning* 814.2, *warning* 814.6
forecaddie *golfer* 156.7
forecast 9.52, 769.17; *weather forecast* 9.4, *divine* 86.24, *expectations* 356.2, *predict* 356.7, 358.14, *foreseeable* 357.7, *prediction* 358.1, *predicted* 358.12, *plan ahead* 387.13, *looking to the future* 650.4, *probability* 838.1
forecaster 358.9; *diviner* 86.14, *predictor* 358.5, 650.5
forecasting *divination* 86.5, *prediction* 358.1
forecastle *vanguard* 621.5
forechecker *hockey player* 158.8
foreclose *take back* 477.17, *close down* 584.15
foreclosed *unable to pay* 488.8
foreclosing *taking back* 477.4
foreclosure *taking back* 477.4, *amount owing* 488.5, *closure* 584.1
foreconscious *psyche* 108.25
forecourt *tennis court* 165.3, *front entrance* 621.2
foredeck *vanguard* 621.5
forefather *predecessor* 769.8
forefathers *dead person* 29.7
for effect *showily* 367.6
forefinger *appendage* 19.5, *indicator* 183.7

forefront *cutting edge* 618.3, *vanguard* 621.5, *priority* 769.2
Forego *Notable Horses* 159
foregoer *precursor* 769.7
foregoing *antiquarian* 651.13, *preceding* 769.9
foregone conclusion *prejudgment* 342.5, *predetermination* 384.1, *certainty* 840.1
foreground *near place* 586.3, *front* 621.1
forehand 165.12; *bowls* 151.7, *tennis strokes* 165.2
forehand drive *tennis strokes* 165.2
forehand grip *grip* 151.4
forehead *face* 621.6, *protuberance* 634.3
foreign 724.9; *extraneous* 610.12, *disparate* 728.9, *unjoined* 753.9, *excluded* 764.6
foreign accent *mode of speech* 205.6
foreign affairs *politics* 50.1
foreign correspondent *print journalist* 175.5
foreign currency reserves *international finance* 457.2
foreigner 724.5; *new arrival* 652.7
foreigners *Phobias* 283
foreign exchange dealer *merchant* 482.10
foreign *or* **foreign-language film** *movie type* 137.3
foreign influx *right of entry* 706.4
foreign language dictionary *word book* 5.27
foreign loan *loan* 475.2
foreign-made *external* 724.11
foreign market *international trade* 56.7, *international finance* 457.2
foreignness 724.2; *extraneousness* 610.6, *disparity* 728.2
foreign policy *politics* 50.1
foreign product *externality* 724.4
foreign sector *economy* 56.3
foreign service *representative body* 79.2
foreign trade *commercial trade* 480.2
forejudge *foresee* 357.9
foreknow *foresee* 357.9
foreknowledge *knowledge* 348.1, *prediction* 357.3, *looking to the future* 650.4
foreland *peninsula* 572.5
foreman *manager* 126.7, *superior* 744.5
foreman *or* **foreperson of the jury** *jury* 341.6, 54.11
foremast *sailboat parts and accessories* 150.4, *vanguard* 621.5
foremost *front* 621.9, 771.17, *elite* 744.12, *important* 799.7
forename *name* 202.8
forenamed *preceding* 769.9
forenoon *morning* 655.2, *daily* 655.6
forensic *judicatory* 54.24, *medical* 107.28
forensic medicine *medical science* 107.5
foreordain *predestine* 384.9
foreordained *predestined* 384.6
foreordination *predestination* 384.2
forepart *front* 621.1
foreperson of the jury *jury* 54.11
foreplay *sex act* 20.10
forerun 769.16; *predict* 358.14
forerunner *discoverer* 345.7, *omen* 358.5, *person of the past* 651.7, *precursor* 769.7, *guide* 780.4
foresee 357.9; *divine* 86.24,

visualize 242.24, predict 356.7, 358.14, intend 374.8, plan ahead 387.13, look ahead 650.11, prepare 657.14, think likely 838.10

foreseeable 357.7; *expected* 356.5, *predicted* 358.12, *auspicious* 458.10, *predictable* 650.7

foreseeably *expectedly* 356.11, *predictively* 358.16

foreseeing 357.5; *predicting* 358.11

foreseen 650.8; *expected* 356.5

foreshadow *foresee* 357.9, *predict* 358.14, *precede* 769.13

foreshock *seismic activity* 8.24

foreshorten *design* 133.9, *shorten* 591.9

foreshortened *pictorial* 133.8, *shortened* 591.7

foreshortening *treatment* 143.6, *shortening* 591.2

foreshow *predict* 358.14

foreside *front* 621.1

foresight 357.1; *psychic power* 86.4, *visualization* 242.6, *visual aid* 242.14, *precaution* 287.4, *knowledge* 348.1, *wisdom* 352.1, *prediction* 358.1, *procedure* 387.2, *preparation* 388.1, *looking to the future* 650.4, *antecedence* 657.5

foresighted 357.6; *precautionary* 287.9, *foreseeing* 357.5, *premature* 657.17

foresightedly 357.10; *prematurely* 657.20

foreskin *organs of reproduction* 21.9

forest *plants* 41.1, *trees* 43.4, *solid body* 540.4

forestage *stage* 136.18

forestal *wooded* 43.12

forestall *foresee* 357.9, *possess* 469.14, *expect* 650.12, *prepare* 657.14, *exclude* 764.7, *hinder* 826.15

forestalled *excluded* 764.6

forestalling *purchasing* 481.2, *hindrance* 826.1

forestallment *monopoly* 469.4

forestay *sailboat parts and accessories* 150.4

forested *plantlike* 41.13, *wooded* 43.12

forester 43.7; *protector* 810.11

forest fire *fire* 217.8

forest-green *green* 260.7

forest manager *forester* 43.7

forest of *throng* 795.4

forest preserve *ecology* 815.3

forest ranger *forester* 43.7, *protector* 810.11

forestry 43.5; *arable farming* 16.6, *plant science* 41.10

forests *Phobias* 283

foretaste *prediction* 358.1, *part* 760.1, *preview* 769.6

foretell *divine* 86.24, *foresee* 357.9, *predict* 358.14, *look ahead* 650.11, *forecast* 769.17

foreteller *diviner* 86.14

foretelling *prediction* 358.1, *predicting* 358.11

for eternity *metaphysically* 525.13

forethought *precaution* 287.4, *wisdom* 352.1, *foresight* 357.1, *procedure* 387.2, *preparation* 388.1

forethoughtful *precautionary* 287.9

foretime *past time* 3.6

foretoken *omen* 358.5, *predict* 358.14

foretold *predicted* 358.12, *foreseen* 650.8

foretopman *nautical person* 690.12, *ascender* 713.12

forever *for good* 445.23, *tenaciously* 471.11, *metaphysically* 525.13, *all the time* 639.16, *chronologically* 639.21, *ever* 640.7, *eternally* 644.10, 798.12, *permanently* 667.6, *continually* 669.10, *fully* 761.14, *eternity* 798.4, *eternal* 798.7

forever and a day *eternally* 644.10

forever and ever *eternally* 644.10, *permanently* 667.6

forever in one's memory *memorable* 354.7

forevermore *ever* 640.7, *eternally* 644.10

for everyday use *useful* 801.5

for everyone *simple* 363.6

forewarn *caution* 287.15, *foresee* 357.9, *predict* 358.14, *expect* 650.12, *warn* 814.8

forewarned *expecting* 356.4, *prepared* 388.9, *warned* 814.7

forewarning 814.2; *warning* 287.5, 814.1, *prediction* 358.1, *omen* 358.5, *predicting* 358.11

forewoman *manager* 126.7

foreword *public speaking* 205.11, *front matter* 621.4, *preface* 769.5

for example *particularly* 779.21

forfeit 468.13; *relinquishment* 392.1, *relinquish* 392.3, *confiscation* 454.4, *confiscate* 454.25, *forfeiture* 468.2, *subtracted item* 749.2

forfeited *relinquished* 392.2

forfeit one's reputation *be disreputable* 371.5

forfeiture 468.2; *confiscation* 454.4

for free *as a gift* 472.17, *free of charge* 497.12, *voluntarily* 504.19

for fun *humorously* 277.13

forgather *come together* 59.25

forgathering *collection* 59.2, *association* 752.2

forge *works* 124.9, *misrepresent* 193.17, *place for fire* 217.9, *act dishonestly* 479.18, *monetize* 484.24, *perform* 522.16, *fashion* 536.7, *form* 624.9, *distort the truth* 627.12, *copy* 736.10

forge ahead *press on* 679.9

forged *misrepresentative* 193.14, *unauthentic* 722.9, *imitation* 736.8

forged note *false money* 484.15

forger *artisan* 123.13, *one who misrepresents* 193.9, *dishonest person* 479.11, *financier* 484.17, *imitator* 736.6

forgery *adulteration* 188.2, *misrepresentation* 193.4, *dishonesty* 479.7, *false money* 484.15, *unauthenticity* 722.4, *copy* 736.2

forget 186.11, 355.10; *be ungrateful* 311.5, *forgive and forget* 312.9, *lack thought* 318.12, *be neglectful* 326.7, *be lenient* 423.5, *lose* 468.12

forgetful 186.7, 355.6; *insensible* 213.4, *ungrateful* 311.2, *inattentive* 324.5, *negligent* 326.4, *nonobservant* 466.5

forgetfully 186.12, 355.14; *ungratefully* 311.6, *inattentively* 324.12, *466.13*

forgetfulness 186.3, 355.1; *ingratitude* 311.1, *inattention* 324.1, *negligence* 326.1, *nonobservance* 466.1

forget grievances *pacify* 74.11

forget it *renounce* 392.4

forget it! *no!* 190.28, *who cares?* 289.21, *cease!* 668.14

forget-me-not *Flowers* 42, *blue thing* 261.3

forget one's differences *make peace* 73.11

forget one's lines *underact* 136.36, *be forgetful* 355.11

forget one's problems *take it easy* 819.3

forget one's words *be unskillful* 128.8

forgettable *forgotten* 355.7, *unimportant* 800.10

forgetting *memory* 108.27, *forgetfulness* 186.3, *forgetful* 355.6

forget work *take it easy* 819.3

forgivable 312.7; *in the right* 429.11, *vindicable* 441.9, *unimportant* 800.10

forgivably 312.14; *justifyingly* 441.15

forgive 312.8, 355.13; *acquit* 54.32, 434.10, *be compassionate* 305.11, *show pity* 308.8, *be lenient* 423.5

forgive a debt 490.12

forgive and forget 312.9; *pacify* 74.11, *forgive* 355.13

forgiven 312.5; *acquitted* 54.25, *given consideration* 423.4

forgiveness 312.1; *favorable verdict* 54.19, *peace treaty* 73.5, *peace offering* 74.5, *compassion* 305.2, *mercy* 308.3, *amnesty* 355.5, *leniency* 423.1, *liberation* 831.1

forgiveness of debts *nonpayment* 490.1

forgiveness of sin *forgiveness* 312.1

forgiveness of sins *liberation* 831.1

forgive one's sins *forgive* 312.8

forgiving 312.4; *compassionate* 305.8, *pitying* 308.4, *lenient* 423.3

forgivingly 53.37, 312.13; *pacifically* 74.12, *compassionately* 305.14, *pityingly* 308.11

forgiving nature *forgivingness* 312.3

forgivingness 312.3; *mercy* 308.3

forgo *relinquish* 392.3, *be self-restrained* 455.10, *resign* 835.5

forgoing *relinquishment* 392.1

forgone *relinquished* 392.2

for good 445.23; *tenaciously* 471.11, *eternally* 644.10, *permanently* 667.6, *fully* 761.14, *conclusively* 773.26

for good and all *for good* 445.23, *tenaciously* 471.11, *eternally* 644.10, *permanently* 667.6, *fully* 761.14, *conclusively* 773.26

forgo repayment *acquire credit* 487.11

forgo sex *be continent* 67.10, *be moral* 431.13

forgotten 186.6, 355.7; *unthanked* 311.3, *losing* 468.9

for humane reasons *pityingly* 308.11

forjudge *prejudge* 337.13

fork 703.5; *garden tool* 17.7, 103.4, *cultivate* 17.19, *tree part* 43.2, *tableware* 92.13, *board games* 167.3, *sharp-pointed thing* 549.4, *use a sharp tool* 549.17, *tributary* 570.2, *angle* 628.1, 628.11, *take away* 685.12, *bicycle part* 687.11, *branch* 703.14, *diverge* 776.16

fork *or* **forked lightning** *thunderstorm* 9.20

fork bender *occultist* 86.13

fork bending *occult and psychic phenomena* 86.7

forked *angular* 628.7, *branched* 703.9

forked lightning *natural light* 246.4

for keeps *tenaciously* 471.11

for keeps [Inf] *eternally* 644.10

for kicks *pleasingly* 214.15

fork in *eat well* 92.23

forking *branching* 703.4, *branched* 703.9, *divergent* 776.11

forklift *lifter* 715.5

forklike *branched* 703.9

fork out [Inf] *expend* 491.11

fork out *or* **over** *or* **up** [Inf] *give out* 472.12, *pay* 489.16

for long 642.9

forlorn *sorrowful* 270.4, *without hope* 282.7, *lonely* 409.8

forlornly *unhopefully* 282.14

forlornness *lack of hope* 282.2

form 551.3, 624.1, 624.9; *crystal* 11.14, *anatomy* 13.12, *mammal dwelling* 35.21, *educate* 48.22, *jurisprudence* 53.13, *ritual* 85.1, *perceptual concept* 108.30, *health* 113.1, *treatment* 143.6, *sculpt* 144.10, *competitive diving* 164.7, *identification* 184.1, *record* 185.1, *illustrate* 187.11, *describe* 202.15, *external appearance* 264.5, *plan out* 387.14, *tradition* 397.5, *formality* 406.1, *perform* 522.16, *etiquette* 534.3, *fashion* 536.1, 536.7, *design* 536.2, *shape* 551.21, 617.2, *kind* 624.3, *way* 691.1, *come to be* 717.19, *state* 725.1, *order* 765.18, *invent* 771.30, *type* 777.4, *custom* 780.5, *convention* 781.5, *make conform* 781.13

form [Brit] *students* 777.6

formable *impressionable* 543.12

form a cartel *contract* 459.8, *restrain commerce* 830.14

form a community *socialize* 2.14

form a core *be dense* 540.8

form a hypothesis *suppose* 359.8

form a kernel *be dense* 540.8

formal 406.6; *of language* 5.35, *theoretic(al)* 6.66, *formal clothes* 100.5, *dance* 135.1, *literary* 139.15, *majestic* 404.21, *ceremonious* 404.23, *formal* 406.5, *good-mannered* 410.7, *severe* 424.5, *agreements* 459.2, *inelegant* 528.6, *organic* 551.18, *formed* 624.6, *conditional* 725.7, *ordered* 765.10, *well-ordered* 765.14, *conformist* 781.10, *self-restrained* 830.10

formal agreement *approval* 437.1

formal argument *debate* 319.3

formal attire *formal clothing* 406.5

formal cause *cause* 675.1

formal clothes 100.5

formal clothing 406.5

formal contract *contract* 459.1

formal dance *dance* 135.1

formaldehyde *preserver* 815.9

formal dining *eating meals* 92.4

formal dinner *feast* 92.9

formal expression *theory* 6.62

formal garden *garden* 17.2

form a line *arrange* 774.14

formal intention *or* **opinion** *declaration* 376.2

formalism 406.2; *sacramentalism* 85.3, *theater movements* 136.9, *order* 765.1, *conventionalism* 781.4

formalist *religionist* 81.14, *conformist* 781.6

formalistic *zealous* 81.22, *formal* 406.6, *ordered* 765.10

formalistically *in order* 765.26
formalities *ceremonial* 404.11, *etiquette* 406.3, *courtesies* 410.3
formality 406.1; *jurisprudence* 53.13, *easy question* 333.5, *tradition* 397.5, *pomp* 404.7, *good manners* 410.2, *severity* 424.1, *inelegance* 528.1, *etiquette* 534.3, *conventionalism* 781.4, *self-restraint* 830.4
formalization *order* 765.1
formalize 406.9; *legislate* 53.31, *fashion* 537.9, *form* 624.9
formalized *ordered* 765.10
formal language *standard language* 5.6, *grammar* 5.28
formal logic *mathematical logic* 6.60
formally 406.12; *grammatically* 5.48, *majestically* 404.36, *ceremoniously* 404.38, *genteelly* 410.14, *severely* 424.11, *formatively* 624.10, *self-restrainedly* 830.19
formally dressed 406.8
formal meal *meal* 92.8
formalness *formality* 406.1
formal occasion 406.4; *feast* 92.9
formal reasoning *way of thinking* 317.4
formal sanction *approval* 437.1
formal speech *address* 209.1
formal usage *grammar* 5.28
formal visit *social gathering* 408.4
form an alliance 735.25; *intercommunicate* 754.15
form an image of *imagine* 360.14
form a partnership *merge* 64.21, *contract* 459.8, *federate* 480.21
form a picket line *block* 826.17
form a plan *plan* 387.12
form a scab *intertwine* 752.19
format *data-related concepts* 15.23, *program* 15.29, *external appearance* 264.5, *form* 551.3, 624.1, 624.9
formation *rock* 8.30, *form* 551.3, 624.1, *structuring* 551.5, *order* 765.1, *invention* 771.5
formational *organizational* 767.13
formative *part of speech* 5.30, *of grammar* 5.41, *productive* 522.11, *impressionable* 543.12, *formed* 624.6, *causal* 675.7, *beginning* 771.16
formatively 624.10
form a whole *be whole* 759.9
form criticism *criticism* 365.3
formed 624.6; *architectural* 134.12, *designed* 536.6, 537.5
form engraver *woodworker* 131.4
former 651.14, 653.12; *historical* 3.10, *dead* 658.10, *preceding* 769.9, *resigning* 835.3
for mercy's sake! *have pity!* 308.13
formerly 653.19, 658.17; *historically* 3.17, *in the past* 651.20, *before* 769.18
former separators *separator* 753.5
former servicewoman 77.6
former soldier 77.5
former time *different time* 648.1
former times *past time* 3.6, 651.1
formic *Common Fatty Acids* 12
formication *skin disease* 114.16, *stimulus* 212.3, *restlessness* 684.5
formidable *fearsome* 283.13, *strong* 516.9, *notable* 799.11, *difficult* 824.9
formidably *fearsomely* 283.21, *arduously* 824.24
forming 624.4; *production* 522.1, *form* 624.1

formless *shapeless* 625.2, *irregular* 766.10
formlessly *shapelessly* 625.5
formlessness *shapelessness* 625.1
form letters *word* 5.43
form of derision 369.2
form of government *government* 49.1
form of law *jurisprudence* 53.13
form of speech *mode of expression* 537.3
form of worship *public worship* 83.3
for money or **profit** or **gain** *gainfully* 467.24
Formosa *Islands* 572
form teacher [Brit] *educator* 48.4
formula 780.7; *clause* 5.31, *operation* 6.12, *theory* 6.62, *structure* 11.7, *jurisprudence* 53.13, *ritual* 85.1, *remedy* 115.1, *maxim* 177.1, *procedure* 387.2, *prototype* 624.2
Formula 1 *racing* 146.9
Formula 1 (F1) races *races* 146.4
Formula 1 racer *driver* 146.8
Formula 1 World Championship races 146.5; *races* 146.4
Formula 2 *racing* 146.9
Formula 2 (F2) races *races* 146.4
Formula 2000 races *races* 146.4
Formula 3 (F3) races *races* 146.4
Formula 3000 races *races* 146.4
formula car *racing automobile* 146.2
Formula car racer *driver* 146.8
Formula car racing *automobile racing* 146.1
formulaic *ritualistic* 85.15
formulary *ritual* 85.1, *formula* 780.7
Formula Super Vee races *races* 146.4
formulate *use language* 5.42, *aphorize* 177.3, *speak* 205.17, *imagine* 327.14, *plan* 387.12, *dream up* 522.15, *design* 536.8, *fashion* 537.9, *shape* 551.21, *form* 624.9, *reveal* 843.14
formulation *production* 522.1, *forming* 624.4, *manifestation* 843.2
Fornax *Constellations* 7
fornicate 432.14; *have sex* 20.21
fornication 432.3; *sexual intercourse* 20.3
for nickels and dimes *cheaply* 497.16
for noble reasons *virtuously* 447.9
for nothing *given* 472.8, *free of charge* 497.12, *cheaply* 497.16
for now *all the time* 639.16
for one's benefit *profitable* 801.8
for one's own sake *selfishly* 444.8
for one's service *rewardingly* 453.19
for pennies *cheaply* 497.16
for pity's sake! *have pity!* 308.13
for private ends *selfishly* 444.8
for public notice *manifestly* 843.17
for rent *offered* 504.8
for revenge *evilly* 446.12
forsake *leave empty* 576.17
forsaken *relinquished* 392.2, *unoccupied* 576.13, *alone* 788.15
forsake one's duties *withdraw* 392.5
for sale *given* 472.8, *on sale* 482.24, *offered* 504.8
Forseti *Deities* 82
for short *shortly* 591.12
for short periods 641.13
forsooth [Arch] *in truth* 721.28

for specified periods 641.12
for starters [Inf] *first* 771.37
for sure *assuredly* 336.12, *authentically* 721.31
for sure! *that's for sure!* 721.34
forswear *disavow* 190.18, *abstain* 386.16, *renounce* 392.4
forswearer *equivocator* 380.4
forswearing *disavowal* 190.3, *disavowing* 190.12, *abstinence* 386.2
forsythia *Flowers* 42
fort 419.13; *fortification* 812.3
fortalice *fort* 419.13
forte *skill* 127.1, *loud tone* 232.3, *loud* 232.6, *loudly* 232.11, *information* 348.2, *sphere* 564.10, *special skill* 779.2
forte or **f** *Musical Terms and Expression Marks* 140
fortepiano *Musical Instruments* 142
forte-piano *Musical Terms and Expression Marks* 140
Forth *Programming Languages* 15, *Rivers* 570
forth 707.19; *forward* 679.15
forthcoming *disclosing* 180.6, *in preparation* 388.8, *nearer* 586.7, *future* 650.6, *imminent* 657.9, *outgoing* 707.10
forthcomingly *openly* 180.13
forthcomingness *openness* 180.3
for the asking *given* 472.8
for the benefit of others *virtuously* 447.9
for the better *better* 807.24
for the count *professionally* 152.22
for the duration 642.8; *all the time* 639.16
for the first time *inventively* 335.15
for the general public *simple* 363.6, *intelligibly* 363.13
for the interim *meanwhile* 639.18
for the layman *simple* 363.6
for the layperson *intelligibly* 363.13
for the love of God! *have pity!* 308.13
for the moment *at present* 647.9
for the most part *in essence* 723.13, *on average* 742.10, *on the whole* 759.13, *overall* 778.22, *as a rule* 780.18
for the nonce *at present* 647.9
for the occasion *at present* 647.9, *timely* 659.4, *opportunely* 659.8
for the present *at present* 647.9
for the price of *at a price* 494.14
for the public good 307.10; *usefully* 801.12
for the sake of *in aid of* 825.33
for the sake of appearances *apparently* 264.16
for the sake of others *unselfishly* 443.9
for the time being *all the time* 639.16, *at present* 647.9
for the worse *worse* 808.23
for this occasion *at present* 647.9
for this or **that reason** *accordingly* 735.39
forthright *disclosing* 180.6, *candid* 191.5, *easily seen through* 249.10, *simple* 363.6, *natural* 526.10, *plain* 592.10, *directly* 697.16
forthrightly *openly* 180.13, *candidly* 191.10, *frankly* 843.18
forthrightness *openness* 180.3, *candor* 191.6, *clarity* 363.2, *plainness* 592.4
forthwith *right away* 429.20, *immediately* 645.8, *early* 657.17

fortieth *twentieth* 792.19
fortification 419.12, 812.3; *art of war* 76.16, *strength* 516.1, *support* 605.1
fortified *refreshed* 94.5, *tenacious* 376.9, *defended* 419.18, *strong* 516.9, *strengthened* 516.13, *hardened* 542.7
fortified line *military defenses* 419.9
fortified wine *wine* 93.11
fortify *refresh* 94.6, *reinforce* 419.23, *make fast* 464.13, *strengthen* 516.15, *support* 605.16, *mix* 751.12, *protect* 810.21
fortifying *refreshing* 94.4, *strengthening* 516.7, *supportive* 605.11
fortissimo *loud tone* 232.3, *loud* 232.6, *loudly* 232.11
fortissimo or **ff** *Musical Terms and Expression Marks* 140
fortitude *steadfastness* 284.3, *willpower* 372.2, *tenacity* 376.4, *will* 376.5, *stamina* 377.4, *virtues* 447.2
Fort Knox *money storage* 484.20
fortnight *time period* 641.2, *eleven to nineteen* 792.7
fortnightly *magazine* 175.3, *cyclic* 663.7, *cyclically* 663.15
Fortran *Programming Languages* 15
fortress *fort* 419.13, *fortification* 812.3
fortuitous *unexpected* 839.6, *causeless* 842.11
fortuitously *by chance* 842.15
fortuitousness *lack of motive* 842.2
fortuity *lack of motive* 842.2
Fortuna *Deities* 82, *luck* 842.3
fortunate *presageful* 358.13, *auspicious* 458.10, *timely* 659.4, *chance* 842.10, *successful* 845.8, *prosperous* 847.5
Fortunate Isles *Imaginary Places* 360
fortunately *auspiciously* 458.17, *opportunely* 659.8, *luckily* 842.17, *prosperously* 847.9
fortune 484.4; *prediction* 358.1, *good thing* 445.9, *wealth* 485.1, *luck* 842.3, *successfulness* 845.3, *prosperity* 847.1, *good fortune* 847.2
fortune's favorite *prosperous person* 847.4
fortunes of war *war* 76.1
fortuneteller *diviner* 86.14, *forecaster* 358.9, *nonmaterialist* 525.7, *predictor* 650.5
fortunetelling *divination* 86.5, 358.2, *predicting* 358.11, *parapsychology* 525.4, *looking to the future* 650.4
forty *twenty and over* 792.8
forty-something *middle-aged* 27.14
forty winks [Inf] *sleep* 415.5, *ease* 819.1
forum *representative body* 79.2, *place for conversation* 210.5, *place of judgment* 341.3, *marketplace* 483.7, *urban area* 567.10, *center of activity* 612.4
for want of anything better *instead* 672.8
forward 679.6, 679.15; *basketball team* 148.2, *sailing* 150.25, *hockey player* 158.8, *diving* 164.13, *correspond* 169.19, *send* 209.11, *audacious* 400.10, *bad-mannered* 411.6, *disrespectful* 436.9, *give moral support* 605.18, *front* 621.9,

before 621.14, *further* 679.13, 825.30, *convey* 685.9, *mail* 685.10, *transport* 686.10, *propulsively* 696.21, *be convenient* 803.5, *promote* 807.18, *make easy* 823.15

forward bow *canoeing* 150.26

forward dive *competitive diving* 164.7

forwarded *transportable* 686.7

forwarded mail *postal service* 169.5

forwarding *forward motion* 679.1, *transportation* 686.1, *transporting* 686.8, *furtherance* 825.8

forward line *vanguard* 621.5

forward-looking *forward* 679.6

forwardly *audaciously* 400.20, *prematurely* 657.20

forward march *forward motion* 679.1

forward motion 677.4, 679.1

forwardness *audacity* 400.3

forward planning *plan* 357.2

forward progress *offense* 155.6

forward somersault *floor exercise* 157.4

for which reason *accordingly* 735.39

for your ears only *secretly* 182.14

fosse *military defenses* 419.9, *enclosing thing* 619.3, *concave land* 635.2

fossil 8.49; *thing of the past* 651.8, *antiquity* 653.4, *remainder* 750.1, *preserved thing* 815.10

fossil algae *algal product* 47.15

fossil bird *extinct bird* 36.14

fossil fish 38.7

fossil fuel *fuel* 106.1, *power source* 514.13

fossil hunting Hobbies and Pastimes 167

fossiliferous *fossilized* 8.63

fossilization *fossil* 8.49, *concentration* 540.2, *hardening* 542.2

fossilize *lithify* 8.66, *be dense* 540.8, *solidify* 542.10

fossilized 8.63; *posthumous* 29.16, *hardened* 542.7, *antiquarian* 651.13

fossil oil *petroleum* 562.5

fossil record *fossil* 8.49, *evolution* 13.23, *study of the past* 651.9

fossil reptile *extinct reptile* 37.9

fossil resin *resin* 562.6

fossils *sedimentary rock* 8.34

foster *educate* 48.22, *give moral support* 605.18, *be a substitute* 672.6, *determine* 675.11, *further* 679.13, *promote* 807.18, *protect* 810.21, *preserve* 815.14, *advise* 825.27

fosterage *patronage* 825.9

foster brother *family member* 65.2

foster child *family member* 65.2, *dependent* 832.4

foster home *haven* 810.3

fostering *supportive* 605.11, 825.18

foster parent *substitute* 672.2, *protector* 810.11

foster sister *family member* 65.2

fought to the death *competitive* 422.21

fought to the finish *competitive* 422.21

foul *stormy* 9.45, *defecate* 25.21, *dirty* 112.7, 112.11, *unclean* 112.8, *unhygienic* 114.27, *play baseball* 147.9, *playing terms* 148.4, *play basketball* 148.7, *billiard* 149.6, *sailing* 150.25,

bowling 151.6, *boxing techniques* 152.5, *box* 152.19, *soccer play* 163.5, *play soccer* 163.8, *detested* 291.11, *profane* 301.10, *evil* 446.7, *be evil* 446.10, *wicked* 448.9, *navigate* 690.15, *collide* 695.10, *go astray* 698.17, *repulsive* 701.4, *make worse* 808.17

foulard Fabrics and Fibers 130

foul ball *batting terms* 147.6

fouled *dirty* 112.7, *soccer* 163.7

fouled up [Inf] *bungled* 128.7, *mixed up* 766.14

Foul Fiend *devil* 446.5

fouling *soccer play* 163.5, *soccer* 163.7

foul language *offensive language* 301.5, *grossness* 535.3

foul line *baseball field* 147.3, *basketball court* 148.3, *bowling* 151.1

foully *wickedly* 448.15

foul mouth *profanity* 301.3

foul-mouthed *profane* 301.10, *bad-mannered* 411.6

foulness *dirtiness* 112.1, *uncleanness* 112.2, *evil* 446.1, *wickedness* 448.1

foul off *play baseball* 147.9

foul out *play baseball* 148.7

foul play 193.6; *malignity* 306.5, *unfair treatment* 342.4, *disreputable action* 371.3, *deed* 412.2, *personal attack* 418.8, *fault* 430.2, *unlawfulness* 430.6, *evil thing* 446.2, *wicked act* 448.9

foul shooter *basketball team* 148.2

foul shot *playing terms* 148.4

foul-smelling *stinking* 227.3

foul taste *unpalatability* 223.2

foul-tasting *unpalatable* 223.6

foul territory *baseball field* 147.3

foul tip *batting terms* 147.6

foul up *be dirty* 112.10, *hinder* 826.15

foul up [Inf] *be clumsy* 128.9, *err* 351.14, *confuse* 766.19

foul-up [Inf] *bungling* 128.2, *blunder* 351.9, *mix-up* 766.5, *obstacle* 826.2

foul weather *natural violence* 520.3

found 565.7; *discovered* 345.9, *lay the foundations* 388.16, *produce* 522.13, *base* 601.10, *form* 624.9, *make stable* 674.7, *inaugurate* 675.10, 771.31, *forerun* 769.16, *repaired* 809.6

foundation 601.2; *topic* 328.1, *preparations* 388.2, *association* 480.8, *cosmetics* 530.4, *substructure* 551.8, *basis* 601.3, 605.4, *support* 605.1, *supporting structure* 605.2, *preparation* 769.3, *inauguration* 771.6

foundational 605.12; *structural* 14.45, *base* 601.7, *supportive* 605.11, *causal* 675.7, *preparatory* 769.11, *inaugural* 771.21

foundationally *basically* 605.21

foundation garment *underwear* 100.22

foundation stone *supporting part* 605.3

founded *focused* 328.6

founded on a rock *invulnerable* 810.18

founder *discoverer* 345.7, *planner* 387.9, *producer* 522.10, *be destroyed* 523.17, *be heavy* 538.12, *deepen* 598.21, *first cause* 675.6, *pitch* 684.25, *descend* 714.12, *be in difficulty* 824.19, *be in trouble* 848.13

foundering *descending* 714.9

founder member *producer* 522.10

found guilty *guilty* 450.6

founding *preparatory* 769.11

founding father *producer* 522.10, *precursor* 769.7

found innocent *declared innocent* 449.8

found not guilty *declared innocent* 449.8

found object *sculpture* 144.1

foundry *works* 124.9

foundry proof *stage of proof* 174.9

foundry worker *laborer* 123.9

found wanting *insufficient* 98.4, *unsatisfactory* 438.15

fount *source of supply* 105.4, *source* 675.2

fount [Brit] *type* 173.5

fountain *ornamental garden* 17.3, *source of supply* 105.4, *water* 557.1, *source* 675.2, *outflow* 707.4, *upturn* 713.2, *spring up* 713.22

fountainhead *river parts* 570.3, *source* 675.2, 771.3

fountainlike *ascending* 713.13

Fountain of Youth Imaginary Places 360, *objective* 374.5

four 791.1, 791.7; *numeral* 6.8, *cards* 168.2

four and twenty *twenty and over* 792.8

four bits [Inf] *US coinage* 484.10

four by four *in fours* 791.14

four-coloring *combinatorics* 6.63

four-color printing *printing* 173.3

four-color process printing *book printing* 174.10

four-color theorem *combinatorics* 6.63

four corners of the earth *distant place* 585.3, *whole thing* 759.2, *foursome* 791.3

four corners of the law *jurisprudence* 53.13

four-dimensional continuum *dimension* 10.5

four-dimensional space *space* 6.33, *dimension* 10.5

four elements *matter* 524.4

four-eyed [Inf] *bespectacled* 242.18

four-figure *thousandth* 792.21

fourfold *four* 791.7, *four times* 791.13

fourfoldness *quadruplication* 791.4

four-footed *tetramerous* 791.9

Four Freedoms, the *free rights* 829.4

four-handed *quartered* 791.10

Four Horsemen of the Apocalypse the *agent of destruction* 523.7

Four Hundred *fashionable elite* 536.4

four hundred *hundreds* 792.9

Fourier analysis Branches of Mathematics 6, Mathematical Concepts 6

Fourier series *sequence* 6.18

four-in-hand *neckwear* 100.29, *foursome* 791.3

four-leaf clover *talisman* 86.9, *good-luck sign* 358.6, *foursome* 791.3

four-legged *tetramerous* 791.9

four-legged friend *animal* 34.1

four-letter *of language* 5.35

four-letter word *vulgarism* 5.20, *curse word* 301.4, *grossness* 535.3, *foursome* 791.3

four-man bobsled *bobsledding* 162.23

four-man kayak (K-4) race *canoe racing* 150.12

four-masted brig Sailing Ships and Boats 690

four-minute warning *signal* 646.9

four-o'clock Flowers 42

four of a kind *poker* 168.5

four-part *quartered* 791.10

four-parted *quartered* 791.10

four-poster *type of bed* 101.9, *foursome* 791.3

fours *bowls* 151.7

fourscore *twenty and over* 792.8

fourscore and ten *twenty and over* 792.8

four seasons *foursome* 791.3

four-sided *polygonal* 6.79, *quadrilateral* 791.8

fours match *or* **fours** *green bowling* 151.3

foursome 791.3; *golf* 156.1, *four* 791.1

four-spot *cards* 168.2

foursquare *quadrilateral* 791.8, *four times* 791.13

four-stroke *quartered* 791.10

four-stroke cycle *engine cycle* 14.13

fourteen *eleven to nineteen* 792.7

fourteenth *less than one* 787.4, *eleventh and above* 792.18

fourth 791.15; *ranked* 6.72, *chord* 140.18, *less than one* 787.4, *quarter* 791.6, *four* 791.7

fourth-class mail *postal service* 169.5

fourth dimension 563.9; *space-time* 639.2

fourth-dimensional *spatial* 563.11

fourth estate, the *news* 171.1, *print journalism* 175.4

fourth finger *appendage* 19.5

fourth-generation language *programming language* 15.16

fourthly *fourth* 791.15

fourth part *quarter* 791.6

fourth power *multiplication* 6.15

four times 791.13

four winds *foursome* 791.3

fowl *livestock* 16.11, *birds* 36.1

fowling piece *firearm* 78.7

fowl-like *avian* 36.19

fowl of the air *birds* 36.1

fowl of the air, the *animals* 34.2

fox *game* 160.6, *variegate* 263.11, *mark* 533.8, *cunning person* 822.3

fox and geese Board and Table Games 167

foxed *mottled* 263.10, *marked* 533.6

foxes Collective Names 59

foxglove Flowers 42

foxhole *hiding place* 181.2, *military defenses* 419.9, *concave land* 635.2, *fortification* 812.3

foxhound Breeds of Dogs 35

foxiness *cunning* 330.3, 822.1

foxing *maculation* 263.4, *stain* 533.3

foxlike *carnivorous* 35.26

fox terrier Breeds of Dogs 35

fox trot Dances 135

fox-trot *dance* 135.7

foxtrotter *dancer* 135.4

foxy *carnivorous* 35.26, *brown* 256.5, *cunning* 330.8, 822.4

foxy [Inf] *attractive* 700.10

foxy lady [Inf] *charmer* 700.6

foyer *room* 60.9, *auditorium* 136.17, *front entrance* 621.2, *means of entry* 706.6

Foyle Lakes 568

fp Musical Terms and Expression Marks 140
Frabosa Breeds of Sheep 16
fracas *fight* 422.9, *dispute* 463.3, *violence by person* 520.2, *commotion* 768.5
fractal *curve* 6.38, *geometric figure* 6.39, *curvilinear* 6.78
fraction 787.1; *real number* 6.5, *division* 6.16, *industrial chemistry* 11.21, *certain amount* 738.3, *part* 760.1, *piece* 760.2, *ratio* 783.5, *little bit* 800.4
fractional 783.8, 787.5; *numerical* 6.68, *quantitative* 738.6, *partial* 760.11
fractional crystallization *process* 11.15
fractional currency *coinage* 484.13
fractional distillation *process* 11.15, *industrial chemistry* 11.21
fractionalize *divide* 753.18
fractionally 787.8; *quantitatively* 738.8, *partly* 760.17
fractional part 787.2
fractionate *extract* 11.41, *gasify* 556.23, *divide* 753.18
fractionation *industrial chemistry* 11.21, *oil* 106.7, *vaporization* 556.9
fractionize *divide* 753.18
fractious *ill-natured* 303.9, *argumentative* 329.7, *uncooperative* 828.14
fractiously *ill-naturedly* 303.18
fractiousness *ill nature* 303.2, *disobedience* 375.5, *contrariness* 828.5
fracture *fault* 8.21, *mineral* 8.37, *deformation* 14.16, *load* 14.49, *painful injury* 215.3, *inflict pain* 215.10, *violence by person* 520.2, *use violence* 520.9, *be brittle* 548.4, *opening* 583.1, *open* 583.15, *crack* 587.2, 587.7, *separate* 753.12, *interruption* 775.3
fractured *injured* 215.5, *open* 583.10, *cracked* 587.5
fractureproof *tough* 547.6
fragile *weak* 517.6, *brittle* 548.3, *impermanent* 643.5, *nonadhesive* 756.4
fragile item *weak thing* 517.5
fragilely 548.5; *weakly* 517.14, *noncohesively* 756.9
fragileness *brittleness* 548.1
fragility *helplessness* 515.3, *weakness* 517.1, *brittleness* 548.1, *nonadhesion* 756.1
fragment 787.3; *be brittle* 548.4, *crumb* 553.5, *pulverize* 553.26, *little piece* 580.4, *divide* 753.18, 787.7, *piece* 760.2, *particle* 760.4, *part* 760.14, *diverge* 776.16
fragmentary *partial* 760.11, *uncompleted* 762.7, *fractional* 787.5, *incomplete* 806.6
fragmentation *armor-piercing* 78.18, *pulverization* 553.4, *separation* 753.1, *divergence* 776.5
fragmentation ammunition *ammunition* 78.11
fragmentation bomb *bomb* 78.15
fragmented *partial* 760.11, *discontinuous* 775.7, *disbanded* 776.7
fragments *remainder* 750.1
fragrance 226.1; *physical pleasure* 214.1, *sweetness* 222.1, *odor* 224.1
fragrance-free *odorless* 225.4
fragrancy *fragrance* 226.1
fragrant 226.4; *floral* 42.9,

pleasurable 214.6, *pleasant* 222.6, *odorous* 224.5
fragrantly 226.7; *florally* 42.13, *sweetly* 222.8
fraidy-cat [Inf] *frightened person* 283.8, *coward* 285.3
frail *human* 18.15, *immoral* 432.9, *impious* 448.11, *ill* 517.8, *brittle* 548.3, *emaciated* 595.10, *imperfect* 806.5, *unsafe* 811.8
frailly *fragilely* 548.5
frailty *old age* 27.5, *immorality* 432.1, *iniquity* 448.3, *helplessness* 515.3, *poor health* 517.3, *brittleness* 548.1, *emaciation* 595.2, *imperfection* 806.1
frambesia *tropical disease* 114.10, *skin disease* 114.16
frame *skeleton* 19.2, *fabric-handling tool* 130.12, *carpenter* 131.10, *racing automobile* 146.2, *snooker* 149.4, *bowling* 151.1, *television set* 172.6, *specify* 340.14, *plan out* 387.14, *preparations* 388.2, *perform* 522.16, *matter* 524.4, *fashion* 537.9, *framework* 551.4, *superstructure* 551.7, *shape* 551.21, 617.2, *container* 578.1, *foundation* 601.2, *base* 601.10, *supporting structure* 605.2, *support* 605.16, *surround* 615.7, *outline* 617.1, 617.5, *edge* 618.1, 618.8, *enclosing thing* 619.3, *enclose* 619.6, *form* 624.1, 624.9, *prototype* 624.2, *bicycle part* 687.11, *inset* 710.13, *type* 777.4
frame [Inf] *predetermine* 384.8, *false accusation* 442.2, *accuse falsely* 442.9
framed *joined* 131.8, *edging* 618.5, *enclosed* 619.4
framed [Inf] *predetermined* 384.4, *perjurious* 442.7
frame of mind *emotion* 266.3, *state of mind* 725.5
frame of reference *coordinates* 6.31, *specification* 340.6, *basis for negotiations* 460.2
framer *planner* 387.9
frames *visual aid* 242.14
frame-up [Inf] *predetermination* 384.1, *false accusation* 442.2
framework 551.4; *skeleton* 19.2, *preparations* 388.2, *foundation* 601.2, *supporting structure* 605.2, *shape* 617.2, *enclosing thing* 619.3
framing 132.18; *carpenter's term* 131.5, *composition* 132.17, *framework* 551.4, *foundational* 605.12
François Premier style Architectural Styles 134
franc *national coins* 484.11
France Phobias 283, Countries 566
Francesca Famous Lovers 299
franchise *license* 434.4, *independence* 829.5, *set free* 829.17
franchised *free* 829.11
francium Chemical Elements and Common Allotropes 11
Francophobia Phobias 283
Franco-Prussian War Major Wars 76
frangibility *brittleness* 548.1, *nonadhesion* 756.1
frangible *brittle* 548.3, *nonadhesive* 756.4
frangibleness *brittleness* 548.1
frangipani Flowers 42, *incense* 226.3
Franglais *regional pronunciation* 205.7
frank *postal communication* 169.4,

correspond 169.19, *disclosing* 180.6, *candid* 191.5, *effusive* 207.6, *send* 209.11, *easily seen through* 249.10, *demonstrative* 331.10, *exempt* 434.9, *natural* 526.10, *outspoken* 550.6, *open* 583.13, *plain* 592.10, *direct* 630.12, *naive* 821.3, *informal* 829.15
frankalmoign [Arch] *medieval ownership* 469.9, *historical property terms* 470.3
franked *tax-free* 434.8
Frankenstein's monster Legendary Creatures 360
Frankfort American States 564
frankfurter *sausage* 90.29
frankincense Tree Products 43, *incense* 226.3
Frankish style Architectural Styles 134
Franklin D. Roosevelt Lakes 568
frankly 843.18; *openly* 180.13, *candidly* 191.10, 583.23, *effusively* 207.10, *demonstratively* 331.21, *unpretentiously* 526.15, *naturally* 526.16, *bluntly* 550.11, *plainly* 592.18, *honestly* 630.18, *naively* 821.5, *informally* 829.24
frankness *openness* 180.3, 249.6, *583.7, candor* 191.2, *effusiveness* 207.2, *demonstrativeness* 331.2, *naturalness* 526.4, *outspokenness* 550.2, *plainness* 592.4, *directness* 630.5, *naiveté* 821.1, *informality* 829.6
frantic *manic* 110.10, *reckless* 286.6, *fidgety* 414.14, *violent* 520.5
frantically *recklessly* 286.10
frantic haste *alacrity* 414.3
Franz Josef Land Islands 572
frappe *milk* 93.5
frappe or **frappé** *milk* 93.5
frappé *frozen* 218.10
Fraser Rivers 570
fraternal *friendly* 62.5, *family* 65.6, *loving* 299.15, *associating* 827.11
fraternalism *friendship* 62.1, *fellowship* 827.2
fraternally *cliquishly* 59.32, *amicably* 62.13
fraternal order *association* 59.4
fraternal society *association* 59.4
fraternal twins *twin* 789.5
fraternity *group* 18.13, *association* 59.4, *friendship* 62.1, *good company* 408.9, *team* 827.7
fraternity house *school place* 48.16
fraternization *friendship* 62.1, *sociability* 408.1
fraternize 408.17; *be friends* 62.9, *come together* 757.10
frat house [Inf] *school place* 48.16
fratricide *homicide* 30.4
Frau [Ger] *female title of address* 33.3
fraud *lawbreaking* 53.14, *deception* 193.1, *artifice* 193.5, *hoax* 193.7, *deceiver* 193.8, *hoaxer* 193.11, *pretender* 367.2, *disreputable action* 371.3, *misuse* 395.1, *dishonesty* 479.7, *cunning person* 822.3
fraudulence *deviousness* 607.4
fraudulence or **fraudulency** *deception* 193.1
fraudulent 479.13; *offending* 53.25, *deceptive* 193.12, *hypocritical* 330.10, *disreputable* 371.4, *abusive* 395.5, *devious* 607.9
fraudulent alteration *adulteration* 188.2

fraudulently *deceptively* 193.21, *offensively* 395.9, *thievishly* 479.19, *deviously* 607.16
fraught with danger *dangerous* 811.7
fraught with difficulties *blocked* 826.13
Fraulein *female title of address* 33.3
Fraunhofer diffraction Classical Physical Laws 10
Fraunhofer lines *sun* 7.15
fray *exertion* 122.4, *activity* 414.1, *warfare* 422.10, *erode* 554.14, *commotion* 768.5, *disintegrate* 808.15, *wear out* 808.21
frayed *worn* 808.13
frazzle *wear out* 808.21
frazzle [Inf] *erode* 554.14
freak *wonderful person* 294.6, *caprice* 381.1, *capricious person* 381.3, *eccentric* 782.10, *chance* 842.1
freak [Inf] *drug taker* 121.12, *desirer* 288.9
freak accident *unexpectedness* 839.2
freaked out [Inf] *drugged* 121.30
freaking out [Inf] *desirous* 288.13
freakish *astonishing* 294.10, *capricious* 381.4, *diverse* 732.5, *unusual* 782.15, *eccentric* 782.16, *unexpected* 839.6
freakishly *astonishingly* 294.19, *diversely* 732.14
freakishness *insanity* 110.1, *capriciousness* 381.2, *diversity* 732.1, *unusualness* 782.4
freak occurrence or **accident** *chance* 842.1
freak out [Inf] *drug oneself* 121.37, *feel deeply* 266.16
freaky [Inf] *astonishing* 294.10
freckle *skin disease* 114.16, *brownness* 256.1, *maculation* 263.4, *variegate* 263.11, *mark* 533.2, *sprinkle* 776.15
freckled *mottled* 263.10, *marked* 533.6, *sprinkled* 776.9
freckling *maculation* 263.4, *sprinkling* 776.4
Fredericton Canadian Provinces 564
Frederiksborg Horse and Pony Breeds 159
free 407.9, 829.11, 831.9; *acquit* 54.32, 434.10, *celibate* 67.6, *leisure* 125.3, *leisurely* 125.4, *billiard* 149.6, *gymnastic* 157.11, *mountaineering* 161.9, *ice-skating* 162.32, *soccer* 163.7, *candid* 191.5, *save* 275.9, *absolve* 312.10, *translational* 365.11, *not working* 415.10, *acquitted* 434.6, *independent* 434.7, *vindicate* 441.11, *free of charge* 497.12, *opened up* 583.11, *open up* 583.16, *unrestrained* 592.8, *extract* 711.13, *separate* 753.7, *nonadhesive* 756.4, *aloof* 756.5, *unstick* 756.6, *restore* 809.12, *escaping* 816.7, *delivered* 817.4, *deliver* 817.5, *extricably* 817.6, *make easy* 823.15, *disentangle* 823.17, *freely* 829.22, *liberated* 831.4, *liberate* 831.6
free admission or **entry** *absence of charge* 497.6
free agent *football player* 155.15, *free person* 829.9
free and easy *imprudent* 286.7, *free* 407.9, *sociable* 408.11, *informal* 829.15
free as air or **the wind** or **a bird** *independent* 829.12

977

free association *association of ideas* 108.31

free-association test Psychological Tests 108

free ball *snooker* 149.4

freebase [Inf] *drug oneself* 121.37

freebasing [Inf] *drug use* 121.9

freebie [Inf] *windfall* 467.7, *giveaway* 472.5, *absence of charge* 497.6, *offer* 504.1, *positive stimulus* 508.5, *extra* 748.6

freeboard *sailboat parts and accessories* 150.4, *interval* 587.1

free board *absence of charge* 497.6

freeboot *plunder* 479.16

freebooter *militarist* 77.3, *plunderer* 479.9, *beggar* 505.6

freebooting *plundering* 479.5

freeborn *free* 829.11

free citizen *free person* 829.9

free city *body politic* 50.3

free climbing *mountaineering* 161.1

free country or **nation** *country* 566.1

freed *acquitted* 54.25, *forgiven* 312.5, *free* 829.11, *liberated* 831.4

free dancing *ice dancing* 162.18

free delivery *absence of charge* 497.6

freed from blame *acquitted* 434.6

free diving [Brit] *Sporting Activities* 145, *swimming* 164.1

freedman *free person* 829.9

Freedom Apple Varieties 44

freedom 407.4, 829.1; *favorable verdict* 54.19, *leisure* 125.1, *candor* 191.2, *Phobias* 283, *acquittal* 434.2, *tolerance* 502.2, *expansion* 592.2, *aloofness* 756.2, *escape* 816.1, *deliverance* 817.1, *smoothness* 823.5, *liberation* 831.1

freedom fighter *guerrilla* 77.7, *resister* 417.5

freedom from artifice *naïveté* 821.1

freedom from blame *incorruption* 449.2

freedom from dirt *cleanliness* 111.1

freedom from fear *free rights* 829.4

freedom from sin *incorruption* 449.2

freedom from want *free rights* 829.4

freedom from war *peace* 73.1, *peace movement* 74.4

freedom of action *freedom* 407.4, 829.1

freedom of choice *means* 102.1, *free will* 372.4, *freedom* 829.1

freedom of movement *freedom* 829.1

freedom of religion *free rights* 829.4

freedom of speech *free rights* 829.4

freedom of the press *free rights* 829.4

freedom of thought *freedom* 829.1

freedom of worship *free rights* 829.4

free drink *absence of charge* 497.6

freedwoman *free person* 829.9

free economy *capitalism* 480.5

free enterprise *capitalism* 480.5, *noninterference* 829.3

free exchange rate *currency market* 484.8

free exercises *gymnastics* 157.1

free fall *space travel* 7.29, *speed* 10.7, *fall* 714.4

freefalling Sporting Activities 145

free fight *fight* 422.9, *liberality* 829.8

free-for-all *fight* 422.9, *disruption* 766.7, *liberality* 829.8, *unconditional* 829.14

free for the asking *free of charge* 497.12

free from blame *vindicate* 441.11

free from guile *naive* 821.3

free from impurities *purify* 111.19

free from sin *incorrupt* 449.7

free gift *windfall* 467.7, *giveaway* 472.5, *absence of charge* 497.6, *extra* 748.6

free goods *international trade* 56.7

free hand *free will* 372.4, *freedom* 407.4, *tolerance* 502.2, *liberality* 829.8

freehand drawing *representation* 202.9

free hit *field hockey tactics* 158.5

freehold *resident* 61.11, *possession of property* 469.3, *property* 470.1, *propertied* 470.9

freeholder *householder* 61.5, *property owner* 470.7

freeing *absolution* 312.2, *separation* 753.1, *disentanglement* 823.8, *liberation* 831.1

free kick *kick* 155.12, *soccer play* 163.5

freelance *work* 122.8, *independent worker* 123.3, *write* 139.21, *independent* 829.12, *be independent* 829.18

freelance or **freelancer** *free person* 829.9

freelance pay *income* 492.3

freelancer *independent worker* 123.3

freelance reporter *print journalist* 175.5

freelance worker *employee* 57.4

freelance writer *print journalist* 175.5

free liver *self-indulgent person* 456.5

free-living *dissipated* 456.7

freeload [Inf] *participate* 408.15, *buy cheaply* 497.15, *solicit money* 505.13

freeloader [Inf] *sponger* 401.4, *nonworker* 415.4, *poor person* 486.6, *bargain hunter* 497.8, *beggar* 505.6

freeloading [Inf] *sycophantic* 401.7, *solicitation* 505.4, *begging* 505.9

free lodging or **quarters** *absence of charge* 497.6

free love *sexology* 20.14, *fornication* 432.3, *tolerance* 502.2, *liberality* 829.8

free lunch *absence of charge* 497.6

freely 407.12, 829.22; *forgivingly* 53.37, *celibately* 67.12, *openly* 180.13, *candidly* 191.10, *with impunity* 434.13, *generously* 498.12, *separately* 753.22, *aloofly* 756.10, *fugitively* 816.12, *easily* 823.19, *informally* 829.24, *free* 831.9

free market 483.4; *right of entry* 706.4, *noninterference* 829.3

free-market economy *economy* 56.3, *capitalism* 480.5

freemasonry *fellowship* 827.2

free meal *offering* 472.6

free-minded *independent* 829.12

free-mindedly *freely* 829.22

free moments *leisure* 125.1

free of charge 497.12

free (of charge) *given* 472.8, *as a gift* 472.17

free on board (f.o.b.) *free of charge* 497.12

free oneself *diverge* 753.20, *be liberated* 831.7

free person 829.9

free port *international trade* 56.7, *marketplace* 483.7, *absence of charge* 497.6, *right of entry* 706.4, *noninterference* 829.3

free range *scope* 829.7

free-range *free-ranging* 829.13

free-range hen or **chicken** *livestock* 16.11

free-ranging 829.13

free ride [Inf] *absence of charge* 497.6

free rider [Inf] *nonworker* 415.4

free-riding snowboard *snowboarding equipment* 162.12

free rights 829.4

free scope or **play** *scope* 829.7

free service *absence of charge* 497.6

freesia Flowers 42

free-skate *ice-skate* 162.36

free skating *ice skating* 162.15

free-skating *ice-skating* 162.32

free-skating movement *ice-skating techniques* 162.16

free socage *medieval ownership* 469.9, *historical property terms* 470.3

free space *dimension* 10.5

free-speaking *speaking* 205.15, *informal* 829.15

free speech *freedom* 407.4, *free rights* 829.4

free spirit *free will* 372.4, *individualist* 756.3, *nonconformist* 782.7, *free person* 829.9

free-spirited *independent* 829.12

free-spoken *naive* 821.3

freestyle *windsurfing* 150.28, *type of wrestling* 152.9, *wrestling* 152.18, *professionally* 152.22, *ski* 162.27, *swimming* 164.12

freestyle relay race *competitive swimming* 164.3

freestyle sailing *windsurfing* 150.19

freestyle skier *skier* 162.14

freestyle skiing Sporting Activities 145, *skiing* 162.1

freestyle snowboard *snowboarding equipment* 162.12

freestyle wrestler *wrestler* 152.12

freethinker 829.10; *disbeliever* 88.5, *nonconformist* 782.7

freethinking 829.2; *free* 407.9, *broad-minded* 592.9, *unconventional* 782.14, *independent* 829.12

free thought *freedom* 407.4

free throw *playing terms* 148.4

free throw lane *basketball court* 148.3

free throw line *basketball court* 148.3

free ticket or **pass** *absence of charge* 497.6

free time *leisure* 125.1, *ease* 819.1

free to choose *independent* 829.12

Freetown Countries 566

free trade *international trade* 56.7, *capitalism* 480.5, *absence of charge* 497.6, *right of entry* 706.4, *noninterference* 829.3

free-trade *independent* 829.12

free trader *free person* 829.9

free-trade zone *international trade* 56.7, *economic zone* 480.4, *free market* 483.4, *noninterference* 829.3

free translation *translation* 365.4

free verse Poem or Verse Forms 139, *poetry* 139.8

freeway *road* 687.2

freewheel *not act* 413.11, *go smoothly* 545.11, *maneuver* 677.18, *go easily* 823.18

freewheeling *independent* 829.12

free will 372.4; *philosophical problem* 4.8, *freedom* 407.4, 829.1

free-willed 372.9

freezable *cooled* 218.11

freeze 10.75; *snow* 9.58, *solidify* 11.37, *save* 105.20, *anesthetize* 213.8, *be cold* 218.13, *become cold* 218.14, *make cold* 218.15, *stop using* 394.10, *stoppage* 490.2, *stop payment* 490.10, *be inert* 519.4, *be dense* 540.8, *harden* 542.9, *limit* 620.1, 620.7, *cause to cease* 668.12, *make stable* 674.7, *lack of motion* 678.1, *be motionless* 678.7, *make motionless* 678.8, *adhere* 755.8, *preserve* 815.14, *economic restraint* 830.3

freeze! *cease!* 668.14

freeze-dried *frozen* 218.10, *invulnerable* 810.18, *preserved* 815.12

freeze-dried food *food* 90.1, *preserved thing* 815.10

freeze-dry *make cold* 218.15, *dry* 560.17, *preserve* 815.14

freeze-drying *preservation of provisions* 815.6

freeze in one's tracks *stop* 668.10

freeze out *exclude* 383.11, 409.12, *drive out* 709.19

freeze over *become cold* 218.14

freeze pay *restrain commerce* 830.14

freeze prices *restrain commerce* 830.14

freezer *kitchen container* 91.7, *refrigerator* 105.10, *cooler* 218.4, *cold place* 218.7, *cabinet* 578.3, *preserver* 815.9

freezer bag *bag* 578.7

freezer stock *food* 90.1

freeze tag Children's and Party Games 167

freeze to death *become cold* 218.14

freeze-up *cold weather* 9.24, *ice* 218.5

freeze with horror *be afraid* 283.14

freezing 218.2; *windy* 9.42, *cool* 9.49, *cold* 10.26, 218.9, *temperature* 10.29, *phase* 11.13, *storage* 105.6, *unhygienic* 114.27, *cooled* 218.11, *bluish* 261.6, *condensed* 540.7, *preservation of provisions* 815.6

freezing cold *freezing* 218.2

freezing fog *fog* 9.32

freezing point *temperature* 10.29

freezing rain *precipitation* 9.26

freezing weather *cold weather* 9.24

Fregean Philosophical Schools of Thought 4

Fregeanism Philosophical Schools of Thought 4

Freiberger Saddle Horse Horse and Pony Breeds 159

freight *merchandise* 482.6, *displacement* 538.3, *load* 577.5, *contain* 577.10, *conveyance* 685.2, *transferred thing* 685.6, *convey* 685.9, *freightage* 686.3, *transportable* 686.7, *transport* 686.10, *fill* 761.11

freightage 686.3; *business expenses* 491.4, *conveyance* 685.2,

transferred thing 685.6, *transportation* 686.1
freight car *railroad car* 688.5
freight charges *business expenses* 491.4
freight container *box* 578.5
freighted *transportable* 686.7
freighter *transferrer* 685.4, *transporter* 686.4, Ships and Boats 690
freight ton General Units 589
freight train *train* 688.4
French Bean Varieties 90, *window* 134.10
French, the Phobias 283
French and Indian War Major Wars 76
French architecture Architectural Styles 134
French billiards *billiards* 149.1
French braid *coiffure* 530.8
French bread *bread* 90.10
French bulldog Breeds of Dogs 35
French coffee *coffee* 93.6
French colonial style Architectural Styles 134
French cricket Sporting Activities 145
French curve Mathematical Concepts 6
French dip sandwich *sandwich* 90.9
French disease [Inf] *sexually transmitted disease (STD)* 114.17
French door Architectural Elements 134
French door *or* **window** *means of entry* 706.6
French farce *comedy* 136.11
French fleur-de-lis *national emblem* 184.7
French fries *vegetable* 90.33
French Friesian Breeds of Cattle 16
French GP at Bandol Formula 1 World Championship races 146.5
French heels *shoes* 100.30
French horn Musical Instruments 142
French kiss *communication of love* 299.6
French-kiss *communicate love* 299.25
French leave *desertion* 386.7, *disobedience* 427.1, *absenteeism* 576.3, *escape* 816.1
French letter [Inf] *contraceptive* 23.6
French manicure *beauty treatment* 530.3
French Open *notable tennis competitions* 165.8
French Provincial Furniture Styles 101
French Renaissance Furniture Styles 101
French Revolution Major Wars 76
French Revolutionary calendar *calendar* 646.3
French roll *or* **twist** *coiffure* 530.8
French Saddle Horse Horse and Pony Breeds 159
French tricolor *flag* 184.8
French Trotter Horse and Pony Breeds 159
frenetic *manic* 110.10, *fidgety* 414.14, *violent* 520.5
frenzied *manic* 110.10, *angry* 302.11, *meaningless* 362.7, *fidgety* 414.14, *attacking* 418.14, *violent* 520.5
frenzy *delusion* 110.2, *burst of anger* 302.6, *inspiration* 360.2, *reverie*

360.6, *nonsense* 362.2, *activity* 414.1, *energy* 414.4, *violence* 520.1, *tumult* 684.2, *spasm* 684.8
frequence *frequency* 661.1
frequency **10.6, 661.1, 663.2;** *probability distribution* 6.56, *wave form* 10.13, *electric current* 10.39, *tone* 230.2, *electrical power* 514.12, *oscillation* 683.1, *wavelength* 683.5, *degree* 739.1
frequency band *wave form* 10.13, *radio transmission* 172.3, *radio frequency* 661.3, *wavelength* 683.5
frequency distribution *probability distribution* 6.56
frequency function *probability distribution* 6.56
frequency modulation (FM) *radio transmission* 172.3, *radio frequency* 661.3
frequency response *measurement* 10.67
frequency spectrum *wave form* 10.13, *radio frequency* 661.3, *wavelength* 683.5
frequent **60.25, 393.10, 661.4, 661.6, 663.6;** *habitual* 397.9, *have a habit* 397.16, *appear* 575.16, *protract* 669.9, *gradational* 739.5, *keep company with* 794.17
frequenter *user* 393.4, *creature of habit* 397.8, *attender* 575.6
frequenting **661.2;** *attendance* 575.3
frequently **661.7;** *regularly* 663.14, *differentially* 739.9, *repeatedly* 797.22
frequentness *frequency* 661.1
frequent occurrence *frequency* 661.1
frequent patron *creature of habit* 397.8
fresco *painting* 143.3, *interior decoration* 532.4
fresh **260.10;** *windy* 9.42, *fine* 9.43, *refreshing* 94.4, *clean* 111.13, *healthy* 113.4, *cold* 218.9, *pleasant* 222.6, *odorless* 225.4, *verdant* 260.8, *new* 394.7, *unaccustomed* 398.3, *pure* 431.11, *invigorating* 518.3, *breezy* 558.15, *ventilated* 558.17, *river* 570.1, *immature* 652.12, *immaturely* 652.23, *daily* 655.6, *novel* 737.5, *extra* 748.10, *embryonic* 771.19, *preserved* 815.12
fresh [Inf] *audacious* 400.10, *disrespectful* 436.9
fresh air *odorlessness* 225.1, *open air* 558.5
fresh-air fiend [Inf] *hygienist* 116.2
fresh as a daisy *clean* 111.13, *immature* 652.12, *feeling well* 113.8
fresh breeze *wind strength* 9.13
freshen *blow* 9.53, *provide drink* 93.21, *refresh* 94.6, *clean* 111.17, *purify* 111.19, *practice hygiene* 116.4, *make cold* 218.15, *deodorize* 225.6, *invigorate* 518.5, *aerate* 558.20, *revive* 809.14
freshened *cleaned* 111.14
freshened up *refreshed* 94.5, *renewed* 852.7
freshener *cleaning agent* 111.9
freshening *cleaning* 111.2, *deodorizing* 225.5
freshening up *refreshment* 94.1
freshen up *refresh* 94.6, *clean* 111.17, *make new* 652.20, *tidy* 807.19, *refurbish* 809.11
freshet *river* 570.1
fresh fields *new beginning* 771.13

fresh ham *pork* 90.26
freshly *refreshingly* 94.9, *sweetly* 222.8, *odorlessly* 225.8, *greenly* 260.15, *newly* 394.14, *immaturely* 652.23, *originally* 737.8
freshly [Inf] *audaciously* 400.20
freshman *learner* 48.6, *new arrival* 652.7, *beginner* 771.14
fresh milk *milk* 93.5
freshness *youthfulness* 26.2, *refreshment* 94.1, *cleanliness* 111.1, *cold* 218.1, *sweetness* 222.1, *odorlessness* 225.1, *newness* 394.2, *unaccustomedness* 398.1, *purity* 431.4, *vigor* 518.1, *immaturity* 652.3, *originality* 737.1
freshness [Inf] *audacity* 400.3
fresh smell *odor* 224.1
fresh spurt *revival* 809.3
fresh start *new start* 652.5, *new beginning* 771.13
freshwater *fishing* 154.13
fresh water *water* 557.1
freshwater bait fishing *fishing* 154.1
freshwater fish *fish* 154.14
freshwater fisherman *fisherman* 154.12
freshwater fishes *fishes* 38.1
freshwater fishing Sporting Activities 145
freshwater lake *lake* 568.1
freshwater sailor *unskilled person* 128.3
fresh wind *wind strength* 9.13
fresnel Scientific and Technical Units 589
Fresnel diffraction Classical Physical Laws 10
fret Architectural Elements 134, *part of stringed instrument* 142.2, Heraldic Terms 184, *cry* 239.16, *worry* 283.16, *irritate* 302.16, *be irascible* 303.13, *be sullen* 304.12, *restlessness* 414.7, *be active* 414.18, *grind* 554.15, *eat away* 808.19, *make haste* 818.5
fretful *irascible* 303.8, *fidgety* 414.14
fretfully *irascibly* 303.17
fretfulness *irascibility* 303.1, *capriciousness* 381.2
fret saw *hand tool* 103.3
fretsome *irascible* 303.8
fretting *worry* 283.4, *worried* 283.11, *grinding* 554.3, *rough* 554.11
fretwork *braid* 609.3
Freud *psychiatrist* 108.34
Freudian fixation *fixation* 108.21
Freudian psychology Psychological Theories, Schools 108
Freudian slip *trivial error* 351.8
Frey *or* **Freyr** Deities 82
Freya *goddesses and gods of love* 299.14
Freya *or* **Freyja** Deities 82
friability *brittleness* 548.1, *crumbliness* 553.1, *nonadhesion* 756.1
friable *brittle* 548.3, *crumbly* 553.16, *nonadhesive* 756.4
friableness *brittleness* 548.1, *crumbliness* 553.1
friar *religious* 84.9
friar's lantern *flickering light* 246.10
friary *clerical dwelling* 84.10
fribbler *nonentity* 800.8
Fribourg Breeds of Cattle 16
fricassee *meat dish* 90.21
frication *friction* 554.1

fricative *spoken letter* 5.15, *voiced* 5.37
friction **554.1, 699.4;** *force* 10.9, 514.8, *hostility* 63.1, *hoarseness* 238.2, *dissension* 272.3, *dissent* 347.1, *disagreement* 463.1, *obstruction* 510.3, *frictional* 554.10, *deceleration* 693.2, *hindrance* 826.1, *conflict* 828.3
frictional **554.10;** *counteracting* 510.6
frictional electricity *electricity* 10.31
frictionless *voiced* 5.37, *smooth* 545.4, *compatible* 735.14, *wieldy* 823.12
frictionless continuant *spoken letter* 5.15
friction match *fuel starter* 106.3, *fire* 246.9
Friday Notable Friendships 62, *fast* 118.4
fridge [Inf] *kitchen container* 91.7, *refrigerator* 105.10, *cooler* 218.4, *cabinet* 578.3, *preserver* 815.9
fried *culinary* 91.9
fried [Inf] *drunk* 121.25
fried egg *egg dish* 90.18
fried fish *fish dish* 90.19
fried potatoes *vegetable* 90.33
fried rice *notable international dishes* 90.40
friend **62.2;** *adviser* 176.5, *feeling person* 266.8, *social person* 408.7, *good person* 445.6, *supporter* 605.9, *contemporary* 649.3, *associate* 754.3, *companion* 794.8
friend at court *indirect influence* 512.4, *backstage manipulator* 844.3
friend in need *supporter* 825.13
friendless *lonely* 409.8, *helpless* 515.9, *alone* 788.15
friendlessness *aloneness* 788.5
friendlike *friendly* 62.5
friendlily *amicably* 62.13, *benevolently* 305.13
friendliness *friendship* 62.1, *peace offering* 74.5, *good feeling* 266.4, *amiability* 271.3, *liking* 290.1, *sociability* 408.1, *courtesy* 410.1, *kindness* 445.3, *informality* 829.6
friendly **62.5;** *amicably* 62.13, *harmless* 73.9, *pacificatory* 74.8, *sensitive* 267.3, *likable* 271.6, *290.7, *loving* 299.15, *benevolent* 305.7, 825.21, *benevolently* 305.13, *sociable* 408.11, *courteous* 410.6, *kind* 445.12, *agreeing* 462.6, *associating* 827.11
friendly approach *peace offering* 74.5
friendly critic *supporter* 825.13
friendly relations **62.3**
friendly takeover *deal* 457.9
friendly talk *chat* 210.2
friendly with **62.6**
Friends Christian Groups 81
friends and acquaintances *society* 408.8
friends and relations *society* 408.8
friendship **62.1;** *social environment* 2.4, *coexistence* 73.3, *liking* 290.1, *love* 299.1, *benevolence* 305.1, *good company* 408.9, *agreement* 462.1, *relatedness* 727.1, *companionship* 794.3, *fellowship* 827.2
Friends of the Earth [Brit] *green politics* 260.6
friends with *friendly with* 62.6
frier *cooking equipment* 91.6
Friesian Breeds of Cattle 16, Horse and Pony Breeds 159

frieze Fabrics and Fibers 130, Architectural Elements 134
frigate *historical warships* 77.22, Sailing Ships and Boats 690
frigate bird *water bird* 36.9
Frigg *gods and goddesses of marriage* 64.14, Deities 82
fright *view* 242.8, *fear* 283.1, *frighten* 283.17, *shock* 292.3, *ugly thing* 531.2
frighten 283.17; *cause dislike* 291.16, *surprise* 292.9, *harm* 306.13, *be severe* 424.8
frighten away *daunt* 179.9
frightened 283.9; *surprised* 292.5, *wondering* 294.7, *shy* 403.8
frightened out of one's wits *frightened* 283.9
frightened person 283.8
frightened to death *frightened* 283.9
frightener 283.7
frightening 283.12; *detested* 291.11, *surprising* 292.7, *astonishing* 294.10, *dangerous* 811.7, *warning* 814.6
frighteningly 283.20
frighten off *daunt* 179.9
frighten someone to death *frighten* 283.17
frightful *frightening* 283.12
frightful bore *boring person* 296.4
frightfully *frighteningly* 283.20
frigid *cool* 9.49, *undersexed* 20.20, *cold* 218.9, *insensitive* 268.4, *indifferent* 289.7, *unsociable* 409.6
frigidity *sexlessness* 20.13, *freezing* 218.2, *unsociability* 409.1
frigidly *coldly* 218.16, *unsocially* 409.13
frigophobia Phobias 283
frigorific *cooled* 218.11
frill *plumage* 36.7, *superfluity* 99.4, *decorative article* 532.5, *ornament* 532.7, *ornamentation* 748.5
frilly *flashy* 404.17
Frimaire French Revolutionary Calendar 646
fringe *negotiated* 57.16, *coiffure* 530.8, *decorative article* 532.5, *exteriority* 610.2, *be exterior* 610.13, *edge* 617.3, 618.1, 618.8, *edging* 618.2, *ornamentation* 748.5, *limit* 773.7, *unconventional* 782.14
Fringe, the *drama* 136.1
fringe benefit *profit* 467.6, *something received* 473.2
fringe benefits *benefits* 57.11, *reward for service* 453.5
fringed *edged* 618.6
fringe medicine *alternative medicine* 107.4
fringe theater *drama* 136.1
fringe tree Trees and Shrubs 43
fringilline *or* **fringillid** *avian* 36.19
fringing *limiting* 773.17
fringing forest *trees* 43.4
frippery *finery* 100.6, *cheap item* 497.5, *decorative article* 532.5, *cheap thing* 800.7
Frisbee™ Sporting Activities 145
frisky *active* 414.13
frisson *stimulus* 212.3, *beat* 684.10
fritillary Flowers 42
frittata *egg dish* 90.18
fritted glaze *glaze* 129.3
fritter *misuse* 395.6, *waste* 500.7
fritter away *waste* 96.15, 500.7, *be wasteful* 468.16, *expend* 491.11
frittering away *waste* 96.1
frivolity *imprudence* 286.3, *absent-mindedness* 324.2, *folly* 353.1,

capriciousness 381.2, *superficiality* 599.2, *triviality* 800.2
frivolous *imprudent* 286.7, *foolish* 353.5, *capricious* 381.4, *superficial* 599.4, *not serious* 800.11
frivolously *imprudently* 286.11, *capriciously* 381.7, *superficially* 599.8
frivolousness *capriciousness* 381.2, *triviality* 800.2
frizz *coiffure* 530.8
Frizzle Breeds of Fowl 16
frizzy *barbed* 544.7
frock *vestment* 84.11, *ordain* 84.16, *dress* 100.11
frock coat *or* **frock** *coat* 100.19
frocked *dressed* 100.38
Froebel system *educational system* 48.2
Frog Nicknames for Inhabitants 61
frog *swimming* 164.12, Card Games 168, *rail* 688.3, *fastener* 754.7
froggy *amphibian* 37.14
frog in the middle Children's and Party Games 167
frog in the pond Card Games 168
frog in the throat *hoarseness* 238.2
frog kick *swimming techniques* 164.2
froglet *young amphibian* 37.11
froglike *amphibian* 37.14
frogman *descender* 714.8
frogmarch *impel* 695.9
frogs Collective Names 59, Phobias 283
frogspawn *young amphibian* 37.11
frog spit *alga* 47.10
frolic *dance* 135.7
frolic about *occupy oneself* 412.15
from a biased standpoint *probably* 513.6
from a distance *externally* 724.19
from age to age *eternally* 644.10
from a historical perspective *historically* 3.17
from all directions *inclusively* 613.35
from all points of the compass *from everywhere* 563.20
from another age *different in time* 648.2
from another time *different in time* 648.2
from A to Z *completely* 759.14, *inclusively* 763.8
from bad to worse 276.8; *adversely* 848.16
from before the Flood *olden* 653.11
from beginning to end *completely* 759.14
from behind *unequally* 741.10
from coast to coast *from end to end* 563.19, *completely* 759.14
from day to day *all the time* 639.16
from door to door *in transit* 685.13
from edge to edge *from end to end* 563.19
from end to end 563.19; *completely* 759.14
from every place *from everywhere* 563.20
from every quarter *in all directions* 697.19
from everywhere 563.20
from far and near *completely* 759.14
from first to last *completely* 759.14

from generation to generation *eternally* 644.10
from hand to hand *in transit* 685.13
from head to foot *completely* 759.14
from here to the back o' beyond [Aus inf] *from end to end* 563.19
from its birth *from the beginning* 771.38
from its inception *from the beginning* 771.38
from Land's End to John O'Groat's [Brit] *from end to end* 563.19
from Land's End to John o' Groats [Brit] *completely* 759.14
from left to right *horizontally* 603.11
from north to south *from end to end* 563.19
from now on *after* 650.14
from one end to the other *completely* 759.14
from one extreme to the other *capriciously* 381.7
from one side to the other *breadthways* 592.16
from outer space *externally* 724.19
from personal motives *selfishly* 444.8
from pillar to post *irresolutely* 378.13, *in motion* 677.19, *to and fro* 683.16, *in transit* 685.13
from pole to pole *from end to end* 563.19
from scratch *again* 652.22, *from the beginning* 771.38
from sea to sea *from end to end* 563.19, *completely* 759.14
from side to side *regularly* 663.14
from stem to stern *completely* 759.14
from the beginning 771.38; *again* 652.22, 797.23
from the bottom of one's heart *with feeling* 266.18
from the context *meaningfully* 361.16
from the dawn of time *in the past* 651.20
from the farthest corners of the earth *or* **world** *from everywhere* 563.20
from the first *from the beginning* 771.38
from the foundations *from the beginning* 771.38
from the four corners of the earth *in all directions* 697.19
from the four corners of the earth *or* **world** *from everywhere* 563.20
from the four corners of the world *completely* 759.14
from the four points of the compass *completely* 759.14
from the four winds *in all directions* 697.19
from the grapevine *reportedly* 170.16
from the ground up *again* 652.22
from the rear *unequally* 741.10
from the start *again* 652.22
from the top *again* 652.22, *reversibly* 671.14
from the word go *from the beginning* 771.38
from this moment on *after* 650.14
from this time forth *after* 650.14

from time immemorial *in the past* 651.20
from time to time *sometimes* 639.19, 662.5, *infrequently* 662.4
from top to bottom *from end to end* 563.19, *completely* 759.14
from top to toe *completely* 759.14
from wall to wall *completely* 759.14
from what one can gather *reportedly* 170.16
from which *accordingly* 735.39
frond *leaf* 41.6, *fern plant* 46.2, *plant body* 47.13
frondeur *troublemaker* 427.5
front 621.1, 621.9, 771.17; *air movement* 9.11, *battleground* 76.24, *bowls* 151.7, *ungenuineness* 192.2, *that which makes invisible* 245.2, *external appearance* 264.5, *near place* 586.3, *exterior* 610.1, 610.7, *be exterior* 610.13, *face* 613.31, *be in front* 621.13, *side direction* 623.2, *side* 623.6, *lead* 744.19, *priority* 769.2, *precede* 769.13, *confront* 828.19
frontage *situation* 573.1, *front* 621.1
frontal 9.41; *front* 621.9, 771.17
frontal bone Human Bones 19
frontal system *weather system* 9.10
frontbencher [Brit] *interfacer* 616.3
front bowls *grip* 151.4
front court *basketball court* 148.3
front door *front entrance* 621.2, *access* 691.3, *means of entry* 706.6
front elevation *front* 621.1
front-end loader *construction equipment* 14.23, *farm tool* 16.5
front entrance 621.2
front for *substitute for* 80.5
front four, the *defense* 155.9
frontier *juxtaposition* 586.4, *edge* 618.1, *farthest point* 620.3, *separator* 753.5, *limit* 773.7, *limiting* 773.17
frontiersman *countryman* 61.8, *interfacer* 616.3, *precursor* 769.7
frontispiece Architectural Elements 134, *book part* 174.5, *front matter* 621.4, *preface* 769.5
frontlighting *lighting* 132.16
front line *battleground* 76.24, *armed force* 77.10, *vanguard* 621.5
front-line soldier *interfacer* 616.3
front-loader *farm tool* 16.5
front matter 621.4; *book part* 174.5, *part of writing* 760.6, *preface* 769.5
front of house *auditorium* 136.17
front page *front matter* 621.4
front-page *newsworthy* 171.8, 175.7, 799.12
front-page news *news* 171.1
front-point *mountaineer* 161.6
front-pointing *climbing techniques* 161.3
front position *priority* 769.2
front room *room* 60.9
front rows *auditorium* 136.17
front runner *finalist* 422.16, *precursor* 769.7, *vanguard* 621.5
front-running 621.10
front scale *balance beam* 157.3
front seat *front* 621.1
front stage *stage* 136.18, *onstage* 136.39
front tooth *teeth* 19.8
frontward *before* 621.14
front yard *front* 621.1
frost 9.25; *snow* 9.58, *freezing* 218.2, *ice* 218.5, *sweeten* 222.7, *opaque* 250.7, *white thing* 253.4,

whiten 253.12, gray 255.9, Phobias 283, top 600.10, coat 613.28
frost and root wedging weathering 8.40
frostbite climbing dangers 161.5, chills 218.3
frostbitten frozen 218.10
frost-covered cool 9.49
frost damage frost 9.25
frosted cool 9.49, frozen 218.10, sweet 222.5, murky 248.5, semitransparent 249.9, shady 250.4, whitened 253.8
frosted bulb electric light 246.6
frosted glass murk 248.2, glass 249.5
frost heave frost 9.25
frostily meteorologically 9.60, hostilely 63.13, coldly 218.16
frostiness hostility 63.1, ice 218.5, unsociability 409.1
frosting ice 218.5, confectionery 222.3, pulverization 553.4, top layer 600.5, coating 613.8
frosting or **icing on the cake** conclusion 761.3, beautification 807.7
frosty cool 9.49, hostile 63.6, cold 218.9, whitened 253.8, indifferent 289.7, unsociable 409.6
froth saliva 25.9, dirt 112.5, air bubble 558.10, bubble 558.24, wave 571.3, billow 571.9, cheap thing 800.7
froth at the mouth salivate 25.25
froth flotation metallurgy 11.22
frothily airily 558.25
frothiness lightness 539.1
frothing salivating 25.18
frothy flashy 404.17, ornate 532.10, insubstantial 539.5, bubbly 558.18, not serious 800.11
frottage picture 133.5, friction 554.1
frotteurism sexual disorder 108.14
froufrou small sound 233.4, hiss 237.1
froward obstinate 379.5
frown 303.15; gesture 183.5, 183.17, be serious 278.7, react against 291.15, be angry 302.19, sign of irascibility 303.6, sign of irritability 304.4, act of discourtesy 411.3, show of disapproval 438.6, show disapproval 438.21, distortion of face 627.2, make faces 627.10
frowning 303.12, 304.10; serious 278.4
frowningly 304.18
frown on exclude 409.12, disapprove 438.16
frowstiness stench 227.1
frowsty stinking 227.3
frowziness stench 227.1
frowzy dirty 112.7, stinking 227.3
frozen 218.10; status adjectives 11.25, saved 105.15, desensitized 213.5, disused 394.8, inactive 413.9, propertied 470.9, inert 519.2, condensed 540.7, hardened 542.7, limited 620.5, stable 674.3, motionless 678.4, invulnerable 810.18, preserved 815.12, restrained 830.9
frozen assets personal estate 470.6, amount owing 488.5
frozen balance amount owing 488.5
frozen ball billiards play 149.2
frozen corn snow skiing snow 162.3

frozen food food 90.1, preserved thing 815.10
frozen over hardened 542.7
frozen rain ice 218.5
frozen shoulder joint disease 114.19
frozen solid hardened 542.7
frozen solid or **stiff** frozen 218.10
frozen yogurt dessert 90.35
fructan polysaccharide 12.5
Fructidor French Revolutionary Calendar 646
fructiferous fertile 22.8, fruiting 44.5
fructiferously 44.10
fructification fertilization 21.6, procreation 22.4
fructify have young 21.16, fertilize 22.12, be fertile 22.13, give birth to 28.19, fruit 44.9, get better 807.21
fructose Common Sugars 12, food content 90.3
fructuous fruiting 44.5
fructuously fructiferously 44.10
frugal precautionary 287.9, self-restrained 455.6, thrifty 499.4
frugality precaution 287.4, self-restraint 455.1, thrift 499.1, saving 815.4
frugally precautiously 287.19, with self-restraint 455.14, economically 499.7
frugivore eater 92.15
frugivorous fruit-eating 44.7, eating 92.18
frugivorousness eating habit 92.7
fruit 44.9, 90.34; progeny 21.8, organs of reproduction 21.9, have young 21.16, Tree Products 43, grow 43.15, dish 90.7, snack 90.8, sweetener 222.2, yield 467.8, plant products 522.8, growth 676.3, successor 770.6
fruitage horticulture 17.1
fruit basket basket 578.6
fruit-bearing fertile 22.8, fruiting 44.5, growing 676.6
fruitcake cake 90.36
fruitcake [Inf] insane person 110.5, eccentric 782.10
fruit cocktail fruit 90.34
fruit compote fruit 90.34
fruit crush sweet drink 222.4
fruit cup fruit 90.34, sweet drink 222.4
fruit diet diet 92.5
fruit dish fruit 90.34
fruit dot fern plant 46.2
fruit-eating 44.7
fruiter horticulturist 17.13
fruit farm farm 16.2, garden 17.2
fruit farmer agriculturist 16.14, horticulturist 17.13
fruit farming arable farming 16.6
fruit fork tableware 92.13
fruitful farmable 16.17, fertile 22.8, fruiting 44.5, yielding 467.14, productive 522.11, profitable 801.8, successful 845.8
fruitfully 22.15; agriculturally 16.21, fructiferously 44.10, gainfully 467.24, productively 522.17, successfully 845.19
fruitfulness fertility 22.1, benefit 801.4
fruit growing horticulture 17.1
fruitily fructiferously 44.10
fruitiness odor 224.1
fruiting 44.5
fruiting body botanical fruit 44.2, fungal body 47.4
fruition fertilization 21.6, completion 761.2

fruit juice soft drink 93.8, sweet drink 222.4
fruit knife tableware 92.13
fruitless infertile 23.7, futile 282.9, 802.10, thankless 311.4, failed 846.10
fruitlessly unproductively 23.12, futilely 282.16, thanklessly 311.7, unsuccessfully 846.21
fruitlessness infertility 23.1, futility 282.3, 802.3, waste 468.5
fruitlike 44.6
fruit painter painter 143.7
fruit painting type of painting 143.5
fruit pie pie 90.38
fruits 44.1
fruit salad salad 90.16, fruit 90.34
fruits of the earth fruits 44.1
fruit squash [Brit] sweet drink 222.4
fruit structure 44.3
fruit sugar Common Sugars 12
fruit tree tree 43.1
fruit wall fruit structure 44.3
fruity botanical 17.15, fruitlike 44.6, fragrant 226.4
frumpish untidy 766.11
frustrate thwart 293.10, counteract 510.7, 828.21, hinder 826.15
frustrated 293.5; desirous 20.18
frustrating 293.7; counteracting 510.6
frustratingly disappointingly 293.12
frustration 293.2; anxiety disorder 108.11, failure 430.9, obstruction 510.3, hindrance 826.1, futility 846.3
frustration test Psychological Tests 108
frustrator hinderer 826.11
frustule plant body 47.13
frustum curved surface 6.43, polyhedron 6.44, remainder 750.1
fruticose lichenoid 47.21
fruticose lichen lichen 47.16
fry young animal 26.4, young fish 38.6, cook 91.10, heat 217.17
frying cooking technique 91.2
frying pan cooking equipment 91.6
frypan cooking equipment 91.6
f-stop or **f stop** exposure equipment 132.12
f-test hypothesis testing 6.52
fuchsia Flowers 42, red 257.5, purple 262.6
fuck [Inf] have sex 20.21
fuck! [Inf] miscellaneous swearwords 301.20
fuck around [Inf] fornicate 432.14
fucked up [Inf] bungled 128.7, mixed up 766.14, broken down 802.8
fucking [Inf] sexual intercourse 20.9
fucking around [Inf] fornication 432.3
fuck it! [Inf] miscellaneous swearwords 301.20
fuck me! [Inf] miscellaneous swearwords 301.20
fuck off! [Inf] miscellaneous swearwords 301.20
fuckup [Inf] blunder 351.9, mix-up 766.5, obstacle 826.2
fuck up [Inf] err 351.14, confuse 766.19, impair 808.18
fuck you! [Inf] miscellaneous swearwords 301.20
fucoid algal 47.20
fucose Common Sugars 12
fucoxanthin pigment 12.18
fuddle get drunk 121.35, be intoxicating 121.36

fuddled slightly drunk 121.26
fudge sweets 90.39, practice sophistry 330.11, be equivocal 380.7, be evasive 386.20, account 493.9, delude 720.16
fudge the issue lack candor 192.22
fudging the issue lack of candor 192.4
fuel 106.1, 106.16; heat 10.25, food 90.1, materials 104.1, store fuel 105.18, be on the track 146.11, generate power 514.19, miscellaneous automotive terms 687.14, propellant 696.9, intensify 746.8
fuel cell electrical conduction 10.33, electrochemistry 11.19, electricity 106.5
fueled 106.11
fueled up fueled 106.11
fuel-efficient fueled 106.11
fuel filter cleaning tool 111.10
fuel injection oil 106.7
fuel oil oil 562.3, petroleum 562.5
fuel rod nuclear power 106.8, nuclear power production 514.10
fuels 106.2
fuel ship warship 77.21
fuel starter 106.3
fuel up store fuel 105.18, fuel 106.16
Fuerteventura Islands 572
fug lack of hygiene 112.3, heat 217.1, stench 227.1
fugacious transient 643.4
fugacity transience 643.1
fuggy hot 217.11, stinking 227.3
fugitive 386.10; disappearing 265.3, the hunted 385.7, avoider 386.8, transient 643.4, unreal 720.8, apart 753.8, escaper 816.5, escaping 816.7
fugitively 816.12; fleetingly 265.8
fugue trance 108.18, Musical Forms 140
fugue state trance 108.18
Führer [Ger] absolute ruler 68.7
Fuji or **Fujiyama** Mountains and Hills 569
Fulani Breeds of Sheep 16
fulcrum supporting part 605.3, center 612.1, middle 772.1, gist 799.4
fulfill suffice 97.6, satisfy 273.7, do something 412.13, perform 465.5, close down 584.15, complete 759.10, 761.9, perfect 805.19
fulfill a code of duty or **honor** have a sense of duty 433.13
fulfill a commitment or **promise** be dutiful 433.12
fulfill a contract be dutiful 433.12
fulfill an obligation be dutiful 433.12
fulfilled sufficient 97.3, satisfied 273.4, proud 297.10, perfect 805.8
fulfill expectations be the answer 334.23
fulfilling satisfying 273.5
fulfillment sufficiency 97.1, satisfaction 273.1, proudness 297.3, ratification 459.4, performance 465.2, closure 584.1, achievement 704.8, completion 761.2
fulguration thunderstorm 9.20
fuliginous black 254.5, gray 255.6
full 761.8; eating 92.18, filled 97.5, excessive 99.5, descriptive 202.11, loud 232.6, deep 236.8, satisfied 273.4, dense 540.6, loaded 577.8, fat 579.15, obstructed 584.8, broad 592.5, directly 697.16, detailed 766.9, whole 759.6, full 761.8, complete 805.14

full armor *historic armor* 419.8
fullback *offense* 155.6, *hockey player* 158.8, *soccer participant* 163.4
full-ball *billiard* 149.6
full-ball aim *billiards play* 149.2
full-bellied *fat* 579.15
full blast *loud tone* 232.3, *loudly* 232.11
full bloom *flowering* 42.5
full blow *flowering* 42.5
full-blown *big* 579.13, *swelled* 581.10, *complete* 761.6
full-bodied *drinkable* 93.18, *dense* 594.6
full-bosomed *fat* 579.15
full capacity *fullness* 761.5
full career *swiftness* 694.1
full chorus *loud tone* 232.3, *loudly* 232.11
full circle *circle* 631.2, *orbit* 681.3, *rotation* 682.1
full-colored *colorful* 251.11
full complement *fullness* 761.5, *inclusion* 763.1
full course *whole situation* 759.3
full crew *fullness* 761.5
full cycle *circle* 631.2
full dress *formal clothes* 100.5, *formal clothing* 406.5
full-dress uniform *uniform* 100.9
full extent *longness* 590.3, *fullness* 761.5
full-faced *fat* 579.15, *front* 621.9
full-face portrait *type of painting* 143.5
full fig *finery* 100.6
full-fledged *swelled* 581.10, *complete* 761.6
full-frontal *front* 621.9
full gale *wind strength* 9.13
full-grown *adult* 27.11, *big* 579.13, *grown* 581.11, *complete* 761.6
full growth *bodily development* 19.17, *adulthood* 27.2
full head of steam *force* 514.8
full house *theatrical performance* 136.13, *theatergoer* 136.30, *poker* 168.5, *fullness* 761.5
full length *longness* 590.3, *fullness* 761.5
full-length *long* 590.6
full-length mirror *reflector* 242.10
full-length novel *work of art* 522.4
full-length portrait *type of painting* 143.5
full list *unit* 759.5
full load *fullness* 761.5
full meal *meal* 92.8
full measure *sufficiency* 97.1, *fullness* 761.5
full military rites *burial* 31.1
full moon *moon* 7.18, *natural light* 246.4
full name *name* 202.8
full nelson *wrestling terms* 152.10, *retention* 471.1
fullness 761.5; *plenty* 97.2, *deepness* 236.3, *fatness* 579.5, *breadth* 592.1, *denseness* 594.2, *whole* 759.1
full of beans [Inf] *healthy* 113.4, *active* 414.13, *vigorous* 518.2
full of difficult words *obscure* 197.2
full of flavor *tastily* 219.7
full of grace *angelic* 82.21
full of guilt *penitent* 451.5
full of hate *hostile* 63.6, *hating* 300.7
full of holes *concave* 635.5

full of hope *hopeful* 281.6, *expecting* 356.4
full of labor *laborious* 122.7
full of loathing *malevolent* 306.7
full of meaning *meaningful* 361.6
full of noise *loud* 232.6
full of oneself *cocky* 402.11
full of pep [Inf] *vigorous* 518.2
full of potential *auspicious* 458.10
full of promise *auspicious* 458.10
full of regrets *penitent* 451.5
full of remorse *penitent* 451.5
full of ruses *cunning* 822.4
full of snares *cunning* 822.4
full of stamina *industrious* 414.16
full of steam [Inf] *healthy* 113.4
full of the milk of human kindness *benevolent* 305.7
full of vitality *healthy* 113.4, *active* 414.13, *stalwart* 547.10
full of years *old* 653.10
full out *fully* 761.14
full pardon *peace offering* 74.5
full particulars *circumstances* 726.1
full pelt *swiftness* 694.1
full pressure *exertion* 122.4
full quota *fullness* 761.5, *inclusion* 763.1
full report *divulgence* 180.2
full-rigger *Sailing Ships and Boats* 690
full sail *swiftness* 694.1
full satisfaction *payment* 489.1
full-scale *big* 579.13, *complete* 761.6
full scope *or* **play** *or* **opportunity** *scope* 829.7
full set *inclusion* 763.1
full settlement *payment* 489.1
full size *big* 579.13, *fullness* 761.5
full skirt *skirt* 100.12
full slip *underwear* 100.22
full speed *speed* 694.2
full speed ahead *at full speed* 694.17
full steam ahead *with vigor* 518.6
full stop *lack of motion* 678.1, *separator* 753.5, *ender* 773.11
full stop [Brit] *Punctuation Marks* 5
full stride *track event* 166.1
full-throated *shouting* 232.7
full tide *tide* 571.2
full tilt *actively* 414.24, *with vigor* 518.6
full to bursting *full* 761.8
full to overflowing *full* 761.8
full to the brim *full* 761.8
full trailer *truck* 578.10
full-up *eating* 92.18, *filled* 97.5, *satisfied* 273.4
full value *fullness* 761.5
full view *whole situation* 759.3
full volume *fullness* 761.5
fully **761.14;** *densely* 540.10, *internally* 577.15, *broadly* 592.15, *meticulously* 726.18, *wholly* 759.11
fully armed *equipped* 388.10
fully charged *full* 761.8
fully comprehensive *whole* 759.6
fully dressed *equipped* 388.10
fully engaged *busy* 414.15
fully fledged *swelled* 581.10, *complete* 761.6
fully furnished *equipped* 388.10
fully grown *grown* 581.11, *complete* 761.6
fully laden *full* 761.8
fully mature *perfect* 805.8
fully occupied *busy* 414.15
fully occupied person *busy person* 414.10

fully restored *sound* 759.8
fully ripe *perfect* 805.8
fully trained *prepared* 388.9
fulmar *water bird* 36.9
fulminate *burst* 232.9, *vilify* 301.15, *condemn* 438.18, *blow up* 696.19
fulmination *vilification* 301.2, *condemnation* 438.2
fulminatory *vilifying* 301.9, *condemning* 438.10
fulsome *excessive* 99.5, *exaggerated* 194.7, *detested* 291.11
fulsomely *excessively* 99.13, *distastefully* 291.19
fulsomeness *excess* 99.1, *exaggeration* 194.1
fulvous *brown* 256.5, *yellowish* 259.8
fumaric *Common Fatty Acids* 12
fumarole *eruption* 8.27
fumble *bungling* 128.2, *be clumsy* 128.9, *play* 155.8, *touch* 216.9
fumbler *unskilled person* 128.3
fumbling *clumsy* 128.6
fume *burn* 217.18, *be angry* 302.19, *be active* 414.18, *give off* 556.25, *turbulence* 684.3, *let out* 709.26, *make haste* 818.5
fumigant *pest control* 16.13, *prophylaxis* 115.4
fumigate *purify* 111.19, *practice hygiene* 116.4, *deodorize* 225.6, *aerate* 556.24
fumigated *odorless* 225.4
fumigation *cleaning* 111.2, *hygiene* 116.1, *odorlessness* 225.1, *vaporization* 556.9
fumigator *deodorant* 225.3
fuming *angry* 302.11, *violent* 520.5, *miasmic* 556.16, *turbulent* 684.17
fumy *miasmic* 556.16
fun **269.4;** *pleasure* 214.2, *luscious* 214.8, *gaiety* 269.3, *amusement* 277.2, *festive* 408.13
Funafuti *Countries* 566, *Islands* 572
funboard *sailboard parts* 150.20
funboard storm sail *sailboard parts* 150.20
function *philosophical term* 4.7, *mathematical function* 6.27, *social gathering* 59.7, *purpose* 327.4, *usefulness* 393.2, *ceremonial* 404.11, *celebration* 405.1, *ceremony* 405.3, *act* 412.11, *line of duty* 433.3, *be operational* 509.10, *instrumentality* 511.1, *be an instrument* 511.7, *participation* 760.10, *be in order* 765.23, *usability* 801.2, *be useful* 801.9, *engagement* 833.2
functional *mathematical function* 6.27, *purposive* 327.11, *useful* 393.7, *801.5, *effective* 412.10, *operational* 509.7, *practical* 511.6, *719.8, *engaged* 833.7
functional analysis *Branches of Mathematics* 6, *calculus* 6.28
functional calculus *mathematical logic* 6.60
functional disease *disease* 114.4
functional equation *equation* 6.25
functionalism *Philosophical Schools of Thought* 4, *Architectural Styles* 134, *usefulness* 801.1
functionalist *anthropological* 1.10, *Philosophical Schools of Thought* 4

functionality *instrumentality* 511.1
functionally *mathematically* 6.93, *purposively* 327.20, *effectively* 412.19, *operationally* 509.13
functional psychology *Psychological Theories, Schools* 108
functionary *official* 68.6, *agent* 123.15, *commissioner* 833.5
functioning *purposive* 327.11, *usefulness* 393.2, *usable* 393.6, *action* 412.1, *operational* 509.7, *practical* 511.6
function key *data-related concepts* 15.23
functionless *useless* 802.7
fund **472.15;** *find means* 102.6, *stock in trade* 105.2, *source of supply* 105.4, *deposit* 105.21, *charity* 307.3, *philanthropize* 307.8, *treasury* 484.19, *defray* 489.18, *give* 498.11, *support financially* 605.19, *finance* 825.31
fundament *basis* 601.3, *605.4, *rear end* 622.4
fundamental *universal* 6.67, *necessity* 95.1, *necessary* 95.10, *severe* 424.5, *basic* 601.8, *605.13, *intrinsic* 611.11, *717.12, *723.6, *causal* 675.7, *rudimentary* 771.22, *essential* 799.10
fundamental constant 10.69
fundamental interaction 10.65
fundamentalism *religiousness* 81.2, *Christianity* 81.5, *severity* 424.1
fundamentalist *religionist* 81.14, *zealous* 81.22, *denominational* 81.23, *moralist* 431.8
fundamentally *mathematically* 6.93, *with need* 95.20, *severely* 424.11, *basically* 601.14, *605.21, *intrinsically* 611.20, *causally* 675.12, *really* 717.22, *at heart* 723.14
fundamental nature *nature* 717.4
fundamental particle *elementary particle* 10.53, *matter* 524.4
fundamentals *fact* 717.6, *realities* 719.5, *specifications* 779.6, *chief thing* 799.3
fundamental standard *standard* 589.10
fundamental unit *unit of measurement* 589.5
fund drive *charitable organization* 305.4
funded *saved* 105.15
funded debt *national debt* 488.2
funder *giver* 472.7
fund finance *finance* 457.7
funding *financial support* 605.8, *financial assistance* 825.6
fund-raiser *charitable organization* 305.4, *charity* 307.3, *gainer* 467.9, *requester* 505.5
fund-raising *charitable organization* 305.4, *charity* 307.3, *gain* 467.1, *gainful* 467.10, *solicitation* 505.4, *begging* 505.9
funds **484.6;** *resources* 102.4, *personal estate* 470.6
funds for investment *funds* 484.6
funds in hand *funds* 484.6
funeral **31.4, 31.9;** *after death* 29.9, *lamentation* 280.1, *formal occasion* 406.4
funeral ceremony *funeral* 31.4
funeral color *purpleness* 262.1
funeral director *person dealing*

with the dead 29.8, *funeral person* 31.5
funeral home *after death* 29.9
funeral home *or house mortuary* 31.3
funeral hymn *funeral* 31.4
funeral object 31.6
funeral oration *funeral* 31.4, *parting* 705.3
funeral palm Trees and Shrubs 43
funeral person 31.5
funeral procession *funeral* 31.4
funeral pyre *place for fire* 217.9
funeral rites *after death* 29.9, *funeral* 31.4
funeral sermon *funeral* 31.4
funeral service *funeral* 31.4
funeral urn *funeral object* 31.6
funerary *funeral* 31.9
funerary sculpture *sculpture* 144.1
funereal *posthumous* 29.16, *funeral* 31.9, *ritualistic* 85.15, *dark-colored* 247.7, *sad* 254.10
funereally 31.13
fungal 47.18
fungal antibiotic 47.7
fungal association 47.5
fungal body 47.4
fungal constituent *lichen* 47.16
fungal disease 47.6
fungi 47.3
fungicidal *herbicidal* 17.16
fungicide *pest control* 16.13, *pest killer* 17.9, *killing agent* 30.15, *antifungal agent* 47.8
fungiform *fungal* 47.18
Fungi Imperfecta *fungi* 47.3
fungistat *antifungal agent* 47.8
fungoid *fungal* 47.18
fungologist *plant scientist* 41.11
fungology *plant science* 41.10
fungosity *fungus* 47.1
fungous *fungal* 47.18
fungus 47.1; *lower plant* 41.4, *dirt* 112.5
fungus root *fungal association* 47.5
funhouse *amusement park and playground equipment* 167.8
funicle *or* **funiculus** *stem* 41.5, *seed* 41.9
funicular *ski run* 162.2, *rail* 688.8, *lifter* 715.5
funicular (railway) *cableway* 691.11
funicular railway *railroad system* 688.1
funk *depression* 270.2, *fear* 283.1, *be afraid* 283.14
funk art Western Art Styles 133
fun-loving *pleasure-seeking* 214.10
funnel *cooking equipment* 91.6, *direct* 126.11, *be on the track* 146.11, *provide passage for* 583.18, *transfer* 685.8, *narrowing* 702.6, *converge* 702.9
funnies, the *entertainment* 277.4
funnily 368.10; *humorously* 277.13
funniness *humor* 277.1, *humorous* 277.9, *ridiculous* 368.5
funny [Inf] *joke* 277.6, *eccentric* 782.16
funny bone Human Bones 19, *sense of humor* 277.5
funny farm [Inf] *mental hospital* 110.6
funnyman *humorist* 277.7
funny money [Inf] *false money* 484.15
funny paper *entertainment* 277.4
funny side *aspect* 623.4
funny story *joke* 277.6

fun time *good time* 214.3
fur *mammalian characteristic* 35.3, Heraldic Terms 184, *Phobias* 283, *animal products* 522.7, *animal covering* 613.15
furanose *saccharide* 12.4
furbelow *decorative article* 532.5, *edging* 618.2, *edge* 618.8
furbish *rub* 554.12
furcate *branched* 703.9, *branch* 703.14
furcation *branching* 703.4
fur coat *coat* 100.19
furcula *fork* 703.5
furculum *fork* 703.5
furfuraceous *mealy* 553.18, *platelike* 588.8
furfuraceously *in layers* 588.11
fur hat *hat* 100.32
Furies Deities 82
Furioso Horse and Pony Breeds 159
furious *angry* 302.11, *malevolent* 306.7, *bitter* 306.9, *violent* 520.5, *hasty* 818.3
furiously *angrily* 302.24, *malevolently* 306.14
furiousness *violence* 520.1
furl *handle sailboat equipment* 150.30, *fold* 637.1, 637.7, *roll* 682.15
furlong General Units 589
furlough *time off* 125.2, *permit* 502.3, *leave of absence* 576.4, *dismissal* 709.2, *dismiss* 709.15, *ease* 819.1, *termination* 834.2
Furnace Constellations 7
furnace *works* 124.9, *ceramic workshop and tools* 129.8, *heater* 217.3, *hot place* 217.5, *place for fire* 217.9, *natural hazard* 813.4
furnish *provision* 89.9, *find means* 102.6, *equip* 388.19
furnish a good excuse *justify* 441.12
furnish credit *credit* 487.10
furnished *supplied* 89.7, *equipped* 388.10
furnishing *provisioning* 89.2, 89.6, *furniture* 101.1, *equipment* 103.6, *fitting out* 388.3, *interior decoration* 532.4
furnishings *ornamentation* 748.5
furnish support *advise* 825.27
furniture 101.1; *provisions* 89.3, *typesetting* 173.4, *possessions* 470.5
furniture arrangement *interior decoration* 532.4
furniture designing *furniture making* 101.3
furniture factory *furniture making* 101.3
furniture maker *furniture making* 101.3
furniture making 101.3
furniture polish *cleaning agent* 111.9, *coating* 613.8
furniture shop *or store furniture making* 101.3
furor *tumult* 684.2, *commotion* 768.5
furrier *clothier* 100.37, *coverer* 613.18
furriness *smoothness* 543.2
furrow 638.1, 638.5; *farmland* 16.3, *rough thing* 544.2, *make rough* 544.11, *crack* 587.2, 587.7, *pleat* 637.2, 637.8
furrowed 638.3; *coarse* 544.6, *cracked* 587.5
furrowing *cultivation* 16.7
furry *smooth* 543.8, *barbed* 544.7
furry friend *animal* 34.1
further 679.13, 825.30; *educate*

48.22, *distant* 585.5, *in the offing* 585.12, *give moral support* 605.18, *protract* 669.9, *additional* 748.8, *additionally* 748.15, *promote* 807.18, *make easy* 823.15
furtherance 825.8; *moral support* 605.7, *protraction* 669.4, *advance* 679.3, *development* 679.4, *promotion* 807.5
furthering *advance* 679.3, *helpful* 825.19
furthermore *additionally* 748.15
furthermost *away* 585.6
further oneself *make one's way* 679.12
further one's purpose *be useful* 801.9
further reflection *reconsideration* 807.9
furthest *away* 585.6, *farthest* 620.6
furthest point *farthest point* 620.3
furtive *secretive* 182.9, *artful* 193.13, *devious* 607.9
furtively *stealthily* 182.15, *deceptively* 193.21, *deviously* 607.16
furtiveness *secretiveness* 182.3, *guile* 193.3, *deviousness* 607.4
furuncle *ulcer* 114.18
Fury *agent of destruction* 523.7
fury *bad feeling* 266.5, *anger* 302.4, *malevolence* 306.1, *violence* 520.1, *violent animal* 520.4
fuscous *brown* 256.5
fuse *interact* 10.73, *conduct* 14.51, *explosive* 78.13, *fuel starter* 106.3, *heat* 217.17, *melt* 555.24, *mix* 751.12, *intertwine* 752.19, *combine* 757.9, *become one* 788.18, *safety device* 810.15, *join* 827.17
fused *mixed* 751.8, *combined* 757.5
fusible *liquefiable* 555.21
fusiform *of fungi* 47.19, *narrowed* 593.9
fusil *historical handgun* 78.8, Heraldic Terms 184
fusilier *historical soldier* 77.8
fusillade *firing* 418.6, *fire* 418.18, *shot* 696.6
fusing *fluidization* 555.8, *liquefying* 555.20
fusion *temperature* 10.29, *nuclear fusion* 10.61, *rock music* 140.6, *nuclear power* 514.9, *fluidization* 555.8, *mixture* 751.1, *mixed thing* 751.2, *union* 752.1, *combination* 757.1, *association* 827.6
fusional *language type* 5.11
fusion bomb *nuclear power production* 514.10
fusion reaction *nuclear fusion* 10.61
fuss 684.4; *exaggeration* 194.1, *figurative overestimation* 343.3, *blatancy* 404.6, *alacrity* 414.3, *be active* 414.18, *criticize* 438.19, *dispute* 463.3, 463.9, *complain* 507.8, *be agitated* 684.21, *disruption* 766.7, *commotion* 768.5, *haste* 818.1
fuss and bother *alacrity* 414.3
fuss and feathers *exhibitionism* 404.9
fussbudget *meddler* 414.12
fussily *blatantly* 404.34, *meticulously* 726.18
fussing *criticism* 438.4, *restless* 684.16
fussing like a hen with chickens *busy* 414.15
fussing over *solicitude* 323.5
fuss over *be solicitous* 323.13
fussy *laborious* 122.7, *solicitous*

323.8, *selecting* 382.9, *blatant* 404.19, *fidgety* 414.14, *critical* 438.13, *ornate* 532.10, *detailed* 726.9, *perfectionistic* 805.18, *troublesome* 824.13
fussy eater *eater* 92.15
fust *stench* 227.1
fustian Fabrics and Fibers 130, *bombastic* 194.10, *diffuse* 199.3
fustic Tree Products 43
fustigate *condemn* 438.18, *hit* 454.28
fustigation *condemnation* 438.2
fustily *stinkingly* 227.6
fustiness *stench* 227.1
fusty *dirty* 112.7, *unhygienic* 114.27, *stinking* 227.3
futhark *or* **futharc** *alphabet* 5.16
futile 282.9, 802.10; *unskillful* 128.4, *aimless* 362.8, *failed* 846.10
futile activity *overactivity* 414.9
futile effort *error* 846.2
futilely 282.16; *unsuccessfully* 846.21
futilitarianism *waste of effort* 802.4
futility 282.3, 802.3, 846.3; *aimlessness* 362.3, 362.6, *lack of authority* 515.2
futon *type of bed* 101.9
future 650.6; *grammatical term* 5.29, *expected* 356.5, *time* 639.1, *future time* 650.1, *later* 658.9, *potential* 836.6
future condition 650.3
future event *future condition* 650.3
future generation 650.2; *successor* 770.6
future intention 374.3
future perfect *grammatical term* 5.29, *future time* 650.1
future state *future condition* 650.3
futures trader *financial adviser* 457.4
future tense *linguistic time* 639.6, *future time* 650.1
future time 650.1; *different time* 648.1
future years *future time* 650.1
Futurism *trendiness* 652.2
futurism Western Art Styles 133, Western Literary Groups 139
futurist *modern person* 652.8
futuristic *dramatic* 137.16, *literary* 139.15, *future* 650.6, *new* 652.9
futuristically *in the future* 650.13, *newly* 652.21
futuristic film *movie type* 137.3
futurity *future time* 650.1
futurologist *predictor* 357.4, *forecaster* 358.9
futurology *foresight* 357.1
fuzz, the [Inf] *law enforcement agency* 53.7
fuzzily *obscurely* 197.4, *texturally* 552.15, *shapelessly* 625.5, *indeterminately* 841.24
fuzziness *obscurity* 197.1, *invisibility* 245.1, *murk* 248.2, *opaqueness* 250.1, *grain* 552.2, *shapelessness* 625.1, *indeterminacy* 841.6
fuzzy *obscure* 197.2, *anesthetic* 213.6, *difficult to see* 245.4, *murky* 248.5, *shady* 250.4, *difficult* 364.8, *barbed* 544.7, *fluffy* 552.11, *shapeless* 625.2, *indeterminate* 841.14
fuzzy tongue *drunken behavior* 121.4
Fylde, the *regions of the British Isles* 564.8
fylfot *talisman* 86.9

G

G *film-rating system* 137.4
G [Inf] *thousand* 792.10
g *gravity* 538.2
gab [Inf] *talk* 207.3, *be talkative* 207.7
gabardine *or* gaberdine Fabrics and Fibers 130
gabardine *or* gaberdine coat *coat* 100.19
gabber [Inf] *talker* 207.4
gabbiness *talkativeness* 207.1
gabble *talk* 207.3, *be talkative* 207.7, *empty talk* 362.5, *talk nonsense* 362.12
gabbling *talkative* 207.5
gabby [Inf] *talkative* 207.5
gabelle *historical tax* 494.8
gabion *fortification* 419.12
gable Architectural Elements 134, *roof* 134.7
gableboard Architectural Elements 134
Gabon Countries 566
gaboon Trees and Shrubs 43
Gaborone Countries 566
Gabriel *angel* 82.11
gadfly *stimulus* 508.3
gadget *tool* 103.1, *instrument* 511.2, *object* 524.6
gadget play *play* 155.8
gadid *or* gadoid *fishlike* 38.10
gadolinium Chemical Elements and Common Allotropes 11
gadroon Architectural Elements 134
Gaea Deities 82
Gaelic football Sporting Activities 145
gaff *sharp weapon* 78.6, *sailboat parts and accessories* 150.4, *sailing* 150.25, *fishing tackle* 154.7, *sharp-pointed thing* 549.4, *use a sharp tool* 549.17
gaffe *bungling* 128.2, *blunder* 351.9, 528.5, *act of folly* 353.2
gaffer *filmmaker* 137.14
gaffer [Inf] *male* 32.1
gaffer [Brit] *manager* 126.7
gaff-rigged *sailing* 150.25
gaff-rigged sailboat *sailboat* 150.3
gaffsail *sailboat parts and accessories* 150.4
gag *strike dumb* 206.10, *silence* 231.4, *sound reducer* 233.5, *joke* 277.6, 368.4, *vomit* 709.27, *means of restraint* 830.6, *restrain someone* 830.17
gaga [Inf] *aged* 27.15, *foolish* 353.5
gage Scientific and Technical Units 589
gagged *speechless* 206.7, *detained* 830.11
gagging *vomiting* 709.7
gaggle *assemblage of birds* 36.18, Collective Names 59
gagman *dramatist* 136.27
gagster *humorist* 277.7
gag writer *dramatist* 136.27, *humorist* 277.7
Gaia *Earth* 8.6
gaiety 269.3, Phobias 283, *celebration* 405.1, *sociability* 408.1
gaillardia Flowers 42
gaily *cheerfully* 269.14
gain 453.18, 467.1, 467.15; *circuit function* 14.38, *good* 445.1, *be good* 445.16, *return* 453.6, *profit* 467.6, *receive* 473.13, 492.7, *sell at a profit* 482.18, *get rich* 485.13, *money received* 492.2, *produce* 522.5, *notch up* 636.6, *growth*

676.3, *grow* 676.10, *advance* 679.3, *achieve* 704.21, *increase* 746.1, 746.6, *extra* 748.6, *benefit* 801.4, 801.10, *help* 825.23
gain access *open up* 583.16
gain admittance *enter* 706.11
gain a foothold *find an opening* 583.20
gain a footing *or* foothold *influence* 512.11
gain a hearing *influence* 512.11
gain altitude *fly* 689.13, *go up* 713.23
gain a reward *be rewarded* 453.16
gain authority 52.15
gain credit *meet with approval* 437.20
gained *received* 473.11, 492.6
gain employment *be employed* 57.19
gainer 467.9
gain from *find useful* 801.11
gainful 467.10; *good* 445.10, *rewarding* 453.9, *received* 492.6, *profitable* 801.8, *beneficial* 825.20, *successful* 845.8
gain full play *be an influence* 512.13
gainfully 467.24; *profitably* 453.20, 492.8, *successfully* 845.19
gainfulness *gain* 467.1
gain ground *improve* 467.18, *press on* 679.9, *increase* 746.6
gain height *increase* 467.17, *press on* 679.9, *go up* 713.23
gaining *gain* 467.1, *acquisitive* 467.13, *nearer* 586.7, *growing* 676.6
gaining altitude *taking off* 713.6
gaining ground *advance* 467.3
gaining height *ascent* 713.1, *leaping* 713.7
gaining on *advance* 467.3
gaining time *advance* 467.3
gaining weight Phobias 283
gaining wisdom *aging* 27.13
gain in value *augmentation* 467.2, *augment* 467.16, *increase* 746.6
gain mastery *be an influence* 512.13
gain on *improve* 467.18, *accelerate* 694.14
gain one's end *attain one's goal* 845.17
gain one's freedom *be liberated* 831.7
gain one's spurs *meet with approval* 437.20
gain power *be powerful* 514.18
gains *profit* 467.6
gainsay *negate* 190.16, *argue* 329.11, *deny* 332.8, *dissent* 506.9, *protest* 507.7, *object* 828.18
gainsayer *negator* 190.8, *refuser* 506.4, *opposer* 828.9
gainsaying *dissent* 506.2, *protest* 507.1
gain-seeking 467.11
gain self-determination *become a nation* 566.11
gain strength *increase* 746.6
gain the friendship of *befriend* 62.10
gain the upper hand *gain authority* 52.15, *be an influence* 512.13
gain the weather gauge *navigate* 690.15
gain time *improve* 467.18, *start early* 657.12, *delay* 658.13, *make good time* 679.10
gain weight *increase* 467.17, *be heavy* 538.12, *grow* 581.17

gain *or* put on weight *fatten* 594.10
Gairdner Lakes 568
gait *bodily movement* 677.11
gaiters *legwear* 100.26, *climbing equipment* 161.4, *ski equipment* 162.10
gal Scientific and Technical Units 589
gal [Inf] *female* 33.1
Gala Apple Varieties 44
gala *show* 404.12, *celebration* 405.1, *celebrative* 405.9, *formal occasion* 406.4, *party* 408.6
galactic *astronomical* 7.33, *universal* 778.10
galactically *astronomically* 7.36
galactic center *galaxy* 7.5
galactic latitude *celestial sphere* 7.4
galactic longitude *celestial sphere* 7.4
galactic nebula *nebula* 7.6
galactose Common Sugars 12
gala night *theatrical performance* 136.13
Galápagos Islands 572
Galapagos finch *songbird* 36.12
gala performance *formal occasion* 406.4
Galatea Planets and Their Satellites 7, Famous Lovers 299
galaxy 7.5; *throng* 795.4
gale *wind strength* 9.13, *natural hazard* 813.4
gale-force *windy* 9.42
galenical *medicine* 115.2
gale warning *warning signal* 814.3
gale watch *or* warning *weather forecast* 9.4
Galiceño Horse and Pony Breeds 159
Galician Blond Breeds of Cattle 16
Galilean satellite *satellite* 7.19
Galilean telescope *telescope* 7.25
Galilee, Sea of Lakes 568, Oceans and Seas 571
galilee porch *church architecture* 134.11
galimatias *empty talk* 362.5
galiot Sailing Ships and Boats 690
gall *secreted substance* 13.2, *sour thing* 117.4, *unpalatability* 223.2, *sour thing* 223.3, *hate* 300.1, *resentment* 302.1, *bitterness* 306.3, *audacity* 400.3, *grind* 554.15
gall and wormwood *sour thing* 223.3, *antipathy* 291.2, *resentment* 302.1, *bitterness* 306.3
gallant *heroic* 284.10, *lover* 299.11, *amorous* 299.18, *solicitous* 323.8, *swaggering* 404.20, *courteous* 410.6
gallant company *army person* 77.17
Gallant Fox Notable Horses 159
gallantly *heroically* 284.18, *amorously* 299.30, *swaggeringly* 404.35, *courteously* 410.13
gallantry *heroism* 284.2, *courageous act* 284.7, *solicitude* 323.5, *courtesy* 410.1
gallbladder *internal organ* 19.13
galleass *historical warships* 77.22
galleon *historical warships* 77.22, Sailing Ships and Boats 690
gallery *repository* 105.13, *auditorium* 136.17, *place for viewing* 242.13, *passage* 691.5, *showplace* 843.4
gallery forest *trees* 43.4
galley *room* 60.9, *cooking place* 91.4, Ships and Boats 690

galley proof *stage of proof* 174.9
galley slave *serf* 69.8, *hard worker* 414.11, *nautical person* 690.12, *subjected person* 832.5
galliard Dances 135, Musical Forms 140
Gallicism *regional pronunciation* 205.7
galliform *avian* 36.19
galligaskins *pants* 100.14, *legwear* 100.26
gallimaufry *miscellany* 751.3
gallinaceous *avian* 36.19
galling *grinding* 554.3, *rough* 554.11
gallium Chemical Elements and Common Allotropes 11
gallon General Units 589, Scientific and Technical Units 589
gallop *ride* 159.16, *bodily movement* 677.11, *walk* 677.17, *acceleration* 694.3, *be swift* 694.10, *make haste* 818.5
gallop at *attack* 418.17
galloping *speeding* 694.7
galloping *or* gallop rhythm *cardiovascular disease* 114.13
Galloway Breeds of Cattle 16, Horse and Pony Breeds 159, *pony* 159.6
Galois group Mathematical Concepts 6
galoot [Inf] *unskilled person* 128.3
galop Dances 135
galore *plenty* 97.2, *ample* 795.9
galoshes *boots* 100.31
gals, the [Inf] *womenfolk* 33.14
galumph *be clumsy* 128.9
galvanic electricity *electrical power* 514.12
galvanize *arouse sensation* 212.11, *motivate* 508.9, *invigorate* 518.5, *impel* 695.9
galvanized *motivated* 508.8
galvanizing *motivational* 508.7
galvanometer *electrical instrument* 14.41, Fields of Measurement 589
galvanometry Fields of Measurement 589
Galway Breeds of Sheep 16
gam Collective Names 59
Gambia Rivers 570
Gambia, The Countries 566
gambit *board games* 167.3, *artifice* 193.5, *experiment* 335.1, *attempt* 390.1, *tactics* 399.12, *first move* 771.12
gamble 167.14; *play cards* 168.7, *rash move* 286.6, *be rash* 286.8, *invent* 335.13, *divine* 358.15, *conjecture* 359.3, *suppose* 359.8, *tackle* 390.8, *undertaking* 391.1, *speculate* 480.19, *face danger* 811.12, *endanger* 811.13, *make possible* 836.7, *think likely* 838.10, *unreliability* 841.7, *risk* 841.21, *chance* 842.1, *take a chance* 842.14
gambler 167.6; *rash move* 286.4, *forecaster* 358.9, *theorist* 359.4
gambling 167.4, 167.11; *card playing* 168.1, *conjecture* 359.3, *speculation* 480.9, *endangerment* 811.2, *chance* 842.1, *game of chance* 842.5
gambling chance *equal chance* 842.7
gambling den *gambling house* 167.5, *wicked place* 448.8
gambling game *type of game* 167.2, *card playing* 168.1
gambling house 167.5

gamboge Tree Products 43, *yellow pigment* 259.2

gambol *dance* 135.7

gambrel *roof* 134.7

game 160.6, 167.1; *wild animal* 34.4, *meat* 90.22, *sports* 145.1, *tennis terms* 165.5, *bridge* 168.4, *adventurous* 284.12, *willing* 373.7, *objective* 374.5, *enduring* 377.9, *the hunted* 385.7, *plot* 387.6, *attempting* 390.4, *tactics* 399.12, *prize competition* 422.5, *butt* 436.8, *ill* 517.8, *stratagem* 822.2

game [Inf] *job* 122.3

game at which two can play *retaliation* 420.1

game bag *bag* 578.7

gamebird *table bird* 36.10

gamecock *fighter* 422.14

game fish 154.10; *fish* 38.5

game fishing Sporting Activities 145, *fishing* 154.1

game fowl *table bird* 36.10

gamekeeper *protector* 419.16, 810.11

game laws 160.3

game license *game laws* 160.3

gamely *adventurously* 284.20

gameness *adventurousness* 284.4, *willingness* 373.1, *stamina* 377.4

game of chance 842.5

game of golf *golf* 156.1

game participant *athlete* 422.15

game plan *miscellaneous terms* 155.16, *plan* 387.1, *tactics* 399.12

game point *tennis terms* 165.5

game reserve *animal welfare* 34.8, *ecology* 815.3

game room *room* 60.9

game rules *tactics* 399.12

games *competition* 166.18, *sports* 422.3

game, set, and match *victory* 845.4

game shooting *hunting* 160.2

game show *program* 172.10

game-show guest *person questioned* 333.10

game show host *broadcasting personnel* 172.11

game-show host *questioner* 333.9

gamesmanship *tactics* 399.12, *rivalry* 422.2, *stratagem* 822.2

gamester *gambler* 156.7

gamete *cell* 13.15, *fertilizer* 22.6, *reproductive body* 47.14

game theory *artificial intelligence* 15.21

game time 155.4

gametogenesis *cell division* 13.17

gametophobia *or* **gamophobia** Phobias 283

gametophyte *moss plant* 46.5

game warden *animal welfarist* 34.9

game-winning *victorious* 845.10

gamic *sexual* 20.15

gaminess *piquancy* 221.1, *unpleasant-smelling thing* 227.2

gaming *type of table* 101.5, *game of chance* 842.5

gaming house *gambling house* 167.5

gamma *exposure* 132.15, Scientific and Technical Units 589

gammadion *talisman* 86.9

gamma distribution *probability distribution* 6.56

gamma function *mathematical function* 6.27

gamma-ray astronomy *astronomy* 7.1

gamma rays *electromagnetic radiation* 10.14, *radioactivity* 10.58

gamma ray spectrum *emission* 10.56

gammon *pork* 90.26

gamut *scale* 140.16, *range* 563.7, *consecutiveness* 774.1

gamy *piquant* 221.6, *putrid* 227.4

Gan Rivers 570

gander *livestock* 16.11, *male animal* 32.15, *male bird* 36.15

gander [Inf] *look* 242.7

gandy dancer [Inf] *railroad worker* 688.7

ganef [Inf] *dishonest person* 479.11

gang Collective Names 59, *party* 59.3, *group* 59.8, *personnel* 123.16, *alliance* 735.5, *association* 752.2

gangbang [Inf] *sex act* 20.10, *sexual offense* 432.6

ganger [Brit] *manager* 126.7

Ganges Rivers 570

gangland *villain* 448.5

gangliness *thinness* 595.1

gangling *clumsy* 128.6

gangling *or* **gangly** *thin* 595.9, *tall* 596.9

ganglion *nervous system* 19.14

gang member *murderer* 30.12, *criminal* 427.6, *evil person* 446.3, *dishonest person* 479.11

gang murder *murder* 30.2

gangplank *bridge* 551.10, *access* 691.3

gang rape *sexual offense* 432.6

gangrene *be dirty* 112.10, *infection* 114.7, *ulcer* 114.18, *physical deterioration* 808.4, *decay* 808.16

gangrenous *of disease* 114.25

gangster *murderer* 30.12, *combatant* 77.1, *evildoer* 412.6, *criminal* 427.6, *evil person* 446.3, *villain* 448.5, *dishonest person* 479.11

gang together *join with* 827.15

gangue *ore* 11.23

gang up *band together* 59.27, *keep company with* 794.17

gang warfare *fight* 422.9, *violation of the law* 427.2

gangway *bridge* 551.10, *access* 691.3

gangway! *open up!* 583.24

gangway ladder *ladder* 713.10

ganja *hemp derivatives* 121.16

gannet *water bird* 36.9

ganoid scale *fish characteristic* 38.8

gantry crane *lifter* 715.5

Ganymede Planets and Their Satellites 7, *transferrer* 685.4, *transporter* 686.4

gaol [Brit] *prison* 55.1

Gaolao Breeds of Cattle 16

gaolbird [Brit inf] *prisoner* 55.7

gaoler [Brit] *prison officer* 55.8

gap 775.4; *need* 95.4, *intervening space* 563.8, *emptiness* 576.2, 718.4, *opening* 583.1, *interval* 587.1, *concave land* 635.2, *disparity* 728.3, *separateness* 753.3, *omission* 762.4, *interruption* 775.3, *defect* 806.4

gape *look* 242.7, 242.21, *wonder* 294.12, *opening* 583.1, *open* 583.15, *gulf* 587.3, *crack* 587.7, *be deep* 598.20

gaper *observer* 242.15

gaping *wondering* 294.7, *open* 583.10, *cracked* 587.5, *deep* 598.9

gapingly *deep* 598.25

gap in the market *need* 95.4

garage *storehouse* 105.8, *building* 551.9, *contain* 578.20,

---

miscellaneous automotive terms 687.14, *protect* 810.21, *preserve* 815.14

garaged *storing* 578.19

garage sale *sale* 482.2, *bazaar* 483.10, *bargain* 495.2, *discounter* 497.7

garb *clothing* 100.1, *clothe* 100.43, *external appearance* 264.5

garbage *waste product* 96.7, *dirt* 112.5, *residue* 750.2

garbage can *vessel* 578.11, *place for waste* 802.6

garbage collector *cleaner* 111.12

garbage disposal unit *cleaning tool* 111.10

garbage dump *place for waste* 802.6

garbage goal *ice hockey tactics* 158.4

garbageman *laborer* 123.9

garbage pile *place for waste* 802.6

garbed *dressed* 100.38

garble *misinform* 188.7, *distort the truth* 192.25, *make obscure* 197.3, *lack of emphasis* 201.1, *talk nonsense* 362.12, *make unintelligible* 364.13, *misinterpret* 366.4, *account* 493.9

garbled *misinformed* 188.5, *partially true* 192.18, *unemphatic* 201.2, *unintelligible* 364.4, *misinterpreted* 366.3, *problematic* 824.11

garbling *misinformation* 188.3

Garda Lakes 568

gardant Heraldic Terms 184

garden 17.2, 17.18; *farm* 124.11

garden apartment *garden* 17.2

garden center *garden* 17.2

garden chair *ornamental garden* 17.3

garden city *garden* 17.2, *city* 567.1

gardener *horticulturist* 17.13, *domestic servant* 69.7, *domestic worker* 123.4, *agricultural laborer* 123.10, *producer* 522.10

garden flower *flower* 42.1

garden gnome *ornamental garden* 17.3

garden hose *irrigator* 557.13

gardenia Flowers 42

gardening 17.5; *horticulture* 17.1, Hobbies and Pastimes 167

Garden of Eden *garden* 17.2, Imaginary Places 360

garden of remembrance *garden* 17.2, *burial place* 31.7

garden of rest *garden* 17.2, *burial place* 31.7

Garden of the Hesperides *garden* 17.2

garden party *party* 408.6

garden path *ornamental garden* 17.3, *access* 691.3

garden plant 17.10; *plant* 41.2

garden sculpture *sculpture* 144.1

garden seat *ornamental garden* 17.3

garden shed *nursery* 17.4

garden shop *garden* 17.2

garden suburb [Brit] *suburb* 567.11

garden tool 17.7, 103.4; *tool* 103.1

garden-variety *familiar* 397.10, *simple* 526.7

garden work *work* 122.1

Garfagnana Breeds of Cattle 16, Breeds of Sheep 16

gargantua *big person* 579.10

Gargantuan *huge* 579.14

gargle *cleaning agent* 111.9, *prophylaxis* 115.4

---

gargoyle Architectural Elements 134, *image* 187.3, *ugly thing* 531.2, *outlet* 707.8

garish *clear* 244.6, *gaudy* 251.12, *flashy* 404.17, *vulgar* 535.6

garishly *colorfully* 251.19, *flashily* 404.32, *vulgarly* 535.10

garishness *flashiness* 404.4, *bad taste* 528.3

garland *flower* 42.1, Architectural Elements 134, Heraldic Terms 184, *insignia* 184.5, *salute* 405.13, *greet* 410.11, *decorate* 532.11

garlic *talisman* 86.9, Herbs and Spices 91, Phobias 283

garlic press *cooking equipment* 91.6

garlic salt Herbs and Spices 91

garlic sausage *sausage* 90.29

garment *clothing* 100.1, *clothe* 100.43

Garment Center *the clothing business* 100.36

Garment District *the clothing business* 100.36

garmentmaker *fabric handler* 130.11

garment-making *the clothing business* 100.36

garner *storehouse* 105.8, *store* 105.17

garnering *storage* 105.6

garnet *red thing* 257.3

garnish *cook* 91.10, *make taste* 219.6, *decoration* 532.1, *ornament* 532.7, 532.12, *ornamentation* 748.5, *augment* 748.13

garnished *decorated* 532.9

garnishing *ornamentation* 748.5

garniture *part of garment* 100.27

Garonne Rivers 570

Garrano pony Horse and Pony Breeds 159

garret *room* 60.9

garrison *armed force* 77.10, *entrench* 419.24, *protect* 810.21

garrisoned *safe* 810.16

garrote *murder weapon* 30.3, *murder* 30.20, *execute* 30.22, 454.30, *capital punishment* 454.12, *instrument of execution* 454.15

garroter *murderer* 30.12

garroting *murder* 30.2

garrotter *punisher* 454.16

garrulity *talkativeness* 207.1

garrulous *talkative* 207.5

garrulously *talkatively* 207.9

garrulousness *talkativeness* 207.1

garter *military honor* 58.9, *underwear* 100.22, *body support* 605.6, *fastener* 754.7

garter belt *underwear* 100.22

garter stitch *knitting* 130.7

garuda Legendary Creatures 360

gas 106.6, 106.14, 556.1; *phase* 11.13, *turbine type* 14.12, *murder* 30.20, *execute* 30.22, 454.30, *fuels* 106.2, *gastroenterological disease* 114.11, *stench* 227.1, *capital punishment* 454.12, *instrument of execution* 454.15, *power source* 514.13, *belch* 556.5, 709.8, *air* 558.1, *petroleum* 562.5, *miscellaneous automotive terms* 687.14, *means of propulsion* 696.2, *propellant* 696.9

gas [Inf] *talk* 207.3, *be talkative* 207.7, *empty talk* 362.5, *theory* 720.4

gas analysis *gravimetric analysis* 11.18

gasbag [Inf] *talker* 207.4, *chatterer* 210.7

gas burner *gas* 106.6

---

gas can *gas* 106.6
gas chamber *execution* 30.6, *slaughterhouse* 30.16
Gascony Breeds of Cattle 16
gas-cooled reactor *nuclear power production* 514.10
gas-discharge tube *electron tube* 14.40
gaseity *gaseousness* 556.6
gaseous 556.14; *status adjectives* 11.25, *gas* 106.14, *insubstantial* 539.5, *sparse* 541.3
gaseous medium *or* **environment** *or* **envelope** *air* 558.1
gaseous nebula *nebula* 7.6
gaseousness 556.6; *lightness* 539.1, *sparseness* 541.1
gaseous state *gaseousness* 556.6
gases Phobias 283
gas field *source of supply* 105.4, *gas* 106.6
gas fire *place for fire* 217.9
gas-fired *fired* 106.13, *heated* 217.15
gas fitter *power worker* 106.10
gas-guzzling [Inf] *gas* 106.14
gash *painful injury* 215.3, *inflict pain* 215.10, *hole* 583.17, *crack* 587.2, 587.7, *notch* 636.1, 636.5, *separateness* 753.3, *take apart* 753.16
gas heater *heater* 217.3
gashed *holed* 583.12
Gasherbrum Mountains and Hills 569
gasification *vaporization* 556.9
gasified *gaseous* 556.14
gasiform *gaseous* 556.14
gasify 556.23; *make sparse* 541.5
gas jet *place for fire* 217.9, *incandescent light* 246.5
gas lamp *incandescent light* 246.5, *gasworks* 556.12
gas laser *laser (light amplification by stimulated emission of radiation)* 10.18
gas leakage *leak* 816.6
gaslight *incandescent light* 246.5, *gasworks* 556.12
gaslike *gaseous* 556.14
gas main *gas* 106.6
gasman *power worker* 106.10, *artisan* 123.13
gas mantle *incandescent light* 246.5
gas mask *protective clothing* 419.6, *modern armor* 419.7, *safety device* 810.15, *preserver* 815.9
gas meter *gas* 106.6, *vaporimeter* 556.13, *meter* 589.13
gasolier *gasworks* 556.12
gasoline *engine type* 14.11, *fuels* 106.2, *petroleum* 562.5, *miscellaneous automotive terms* 687.14, *means of propulsion* 696.2, *propellant* 696.9
gasoline *or* **gas** *oil* 106.7
gasoline-propelled *propelled* 696.14
gasolinic *gas* 106.14
gasometer *gas* 106.6, *vaporimeter* 556.13
gasometer [Brit] *storehouse* 105.8
gas oneself *commit suicide* 30.24
gas-operated *bolt-action* 78.17
gas-operated firearm *firearm* 78.7
gas oven *place for fire* 217.9
gasp *utterance* 205.10, *speak in a particular way* 205.18, *express pain* 215.11, *sound hoarse* 238.8, *cry of pain* 239.5, *cry* 239.16, *wonder* 294.12, *be fatigued* 820.5

gasping *wondering* 294.7, *fatigue* 820.1
gasping for breath *panting* 820.3
gas pipe *gas* 106.6
gas plant *gasworks* 556.12
gas-powered *fired* 106.13
gasproof *invulnerable* 810.18
gas-propelled *propelled* 696.14
gas pump *storehouse* 105.8, *gas* 106.6
gasser [Inf] *talker* 207.4, *chatterer* 210.7
gassiness *gaseousness* 556.6
gassiness [Inf] *talkativeness* 207.1
gassing oneself *suicide* 30.8
gas/solid chromatography (GSC) *analysis* 11.17
gas station *storehouse* 105.8, *gas* 106.6, *service workplace* 124.5, *stopping place* 668.4
gassy 556.19; *stinking* 227.3, *gaseous* 556.14, *flatulent* 556.18
gassy [Inf] *talkative* 207.5
gas tank *storehouse* 105.8, *gas* 106.6, *gasworks* 556.12
gathered skirt *skirt* 100.12
Gastarbeiter [Ger] *new arrival* 724.6
gasteropod *mollusk* 39.13
gastralgia *gastroenterological disease* 114.11
gastric *metabolic* 19.24, *of a secretion* 24.5, *visceral* 611.10
gastric juice *secreted substance* 24.2
gastric ulcer *gastroenterological disease* 114.11
gastrin Human Hormones 12
gastritis *gastroenterological disease* 114.11
gastroenteritis *gastroenterological disease* 114.11
gastroenterological disease 114.11
gastroenterology Medical Specialties 107
gastrointestinal disease *disease* 114.4
gastronome *eater* 92.15
gastronomic *culinary* 91.9
gastronomically *culinarily* 91.11
gastronomy *cooking* 91.1, *eating* 92.1
gastropod *type of animal* 34.5, *mollusk* 39.13
Gastropoda *mollusk* 39.13
gastropodous *molluskan* 39.23
gastroscope *diagnostic instrument* 107.13
gastroscopy *diagnostic procedure* 107.11
gastrulation *developmental biology* 13.22
gas turbine *gas* 106.6
gas vent *eruption* 8.27
gas warfare *chemical warfare* 76.5
gasworks 556.12; *gas* 106.6, *power station* 124.12
gat [Inf] *firearm* 78.7
gate *circuit* 14.37, *farm building* 16.4, *canoe racing* 150.12, *ski race* 162.4, *fort* 419.13, *money received* 492.2, *place of departure* 705.4, *means of entry* 706.6, *way out* 707.2
gate [Inf] *discarding* 383.3, *dismissal* 709.2
gate, the *something received* 473.2
gâteau [Brit, Fr] *cake* 90.36
gate-crash [Inf] *invade* 706.12, *be external* 724.15
gate-crasher [Inf] *illegal occupant* 61.9, *dissenter* 463.5, *bargain hunter* 497.8, *intruder* 706.8, 724.7
gatehouse *fort* 419.13

gatekeeper *closer* 584.5
gate-leg *type of table* 101.5
gate money *something received* 473.2, *money received* 492.2
gate money *or* **winnings** *earnings* 467.5
gatepost *means of entry* 706.6
gateway *communications device* 15.26, *means of entry* 706.6
gather *storm* 9.55, *farm* 16.19, *assemble* 59.23, *come together* 59.25, 702.10, *make clothing* 100.44, *store* 105.17, *hear* 228.13, *suppose* 359.8, *select* 382.12, *grow* 581.17, *contract* 582.12, *pleat* 637.2, 637.8, *set in motion* 677.16, *meet* 704.20, *unite* 752.14
gather around *come together* 59.25
gather around the table *confer* 210.13
gather dust *have free time* 413.15, *be sold* 482.22
gathered *assembled* 59.18, *shortened* 582.8, *tied* 752.13
gathered skirt *skirt* 100.12
gathered to one's fathers *dead* 29.11
gatherer *collector* 59.17, *gainer* 467.9
gather in *gain* 467.15, *acquire* 467.19
gathering *collection* 59.2, *conference* 59.5, *worshiper* 83.6, *storage* 105.6, *ulcer* 114.18, *toxic* 114.28, *sewing* 130.5, *place for conversation* 210.5, *selection* 382.1, *social gathering* 408.4, *acquisition* 467.4, *growing* 581.12, *shortening* 582.2, *contracting* 582.10, *association* 752.2
gathering clouds *danger signal* 811.5, *forewarning* 814.2, *threat* 848.3
gathering in *gain* 467.1
gathering of the clans *social gathering* 59.7
gathering storm *danger signal* 811.5, *forewarning* 814.2
gather momentum *accelerate* 694.14
gather notes *lay the foundations* 388.16
gather speed *accelerate* 694.14
gather the news *report* 171.9
gather together *acquire* 467.19, *unite* 752.14
gather up 715.14
gather way *be in motion* 677.14, *navigate* 690.15
gator [Inf] *crocodile* 37.8
Gator Bowl *football* 155.1
gauche *clumsy* 128.6, *raw* 260.9, *ignorant* 349.5, *uncustomary* 398.4, *graceless* 528.7, *vulgar* 535.6, *discourteous* 535.7
gauchely *discourteously* 535.11
gaucheness *inelegance* 528.1, *vulgarity* 535.1
gaucherie *unskillfulness* 128.1, *ignorance* 349.1, *inelegance* 528.1, *blunder* 528.5, *vulgarity* 535.1
gaucho *farm worker* 16.15, *horse person* 159.14
gaud *cheap item* 497.5
gaudily *colorfully* 251.19, *flashily* 404.32
gaudiness *flashiness* 404.4, *bad taste* 528.3, *ornateness* 532.2, *vulgarity* 535.1
gaudy 251.12; *clear* 244.6, *flashy* 404.17, *shoddy* 497.11, *indecorous* 528.8, *ornate* 532.10, *vulgar* 535.6, *accentuated* 843.11
gauge *fabric-handling tool* 130.12,

indicator 183.7, *recording instrument* 185.9, *estimate* 341.11, *size* 579.1, 579.17, Scientific and Technical Units 589, *meter* 589.13, *measure* 589.20, *breadth* 592.1, *baseline* 601.4, *planimetry* 603.5, *rail* 688.3, *railroad* 691.8, *guide* 697.4, *calculator* 784.5, *number* 784.13
gaugeable *measurable* 589.17
gauged *measured* 589.16
gauger *measurer* 589.14
gauging *measurement* 589.1
gauleiter *absolute ruler* 68.7
gaunt *infertile* 23.7, *underfed* 98.7, *emaciated* 595.10
gauntlet *accessory* 100.28, *historic armor* 419.8
gauntlets *protective clothing* 419.6
gauntly *thin* 595.18
gauntness *emaciation* 595.2
gauss Scientific and Technical Units 589
Gaussian distribution *probability distribution* 6.56
Gauss's lemma Mathematical Concepts 6
Gauss's theorem Mathematical Concepts 6
gauze Fabrics and Fibers 130, *stage set* 136.19, *transparent thing* 249.4, *fineness* 595.5, *medical covering* 613.4
gauzily *finely* 595.19
gauziness *translucency* 249.2, *fineness* 595.5
gauzy *translucent* 249.8, *fine* 595.12
gavel *insignia* 184.5
gavotte Dances 135, Musical Forms 140
gawk *look* 242.21, *wonder* 294.12
gawkiness *inelegance* 528.1
gawkish *clumsy* 128.6, *graceless* 528.7
gawkishness *inelegance* 528.1
gawky *clumsy* 128.6, *graceless* 528.7, *thin* 595.9
gawp *wonder* 294.12
gawp [Dial] *look* 242.21
gawper *observer* 242.15
gay *sexual nature* 20.4, *of sexual nature* 20.17, *homosexual* 32.9, 33.10, *male* 32.16, *colorful* 251.11, *cheerful* 269.7, *flashy* 404.17, *celebrative* 405.9
gay dog [Inf] *male* 32.1
gay liberation *equal opportunity* 831.2
Gay-Lussac's law Classical Physical Laws 10
Gay Nineties Ages, Decades, Eras 641
Gayoe pony Horse and Pony Breeds 159
gay rights *rights* 429.4
gazania Flowers 42
gaze *gesture* 183.17, *look* 242.7, 242.21, *wonder* 294.12, *be discourteous* 411.7
gazebo *ornamental garden* 17.3, Architectural Elements 134, *place for viewing* 242.13
gazehound Breeds of Dogs 35
gaze into a crystal ball *divine* 358.15
gazelle *game* 160.6
gazelle hound Breeds of Dogs 35
gazer *observer* 242.15
gazette *periodical* 175.1
gazetteer *type of book* 174.3, *catalog* 767.7, *book of lists* 785.3
gazing *wondering* 294.7
GCF [Brit] *multiplication* 6.15

G clef *written music* 140.21
Ge Deities 82
gean Trees and Shrubs 43
gear 14.7; *simple machine* 14.6, *machine element* 14.8, *costume* 100.10, *equipment* 103.6, *be on the track* 146.11, *fitting out* 388.3, *possession of property* 469.3, *possessions* 470.5, *wheel* 682.9, *bicycle part* 687.11
gear box *racing automobile* 146.2
gearing *automobile racing terms* 146.3
gear oneself up *prepare oneself* 388.21
gearshift *miscellaneous automotive terms* 687.14
gear sling *climbing equipment* 161.4
gear to *intertwine* 752.19
gear tooth *gear* 14.7
gear train *gear* 14.7
gear up *prepare for action* 388.18
gearwheel *machine element* 14.8, *wheel* 682.9
Geb Deities 82
gecko *lizard* 37.5
gee *sidestep* 698.22
gee! [Inf] *wonderful!* 294.20, *miscellaneous euphemisms* 301.21
geegaw *cheap thing* 800.7
geese Collective Names 59
gee whillikers! [Inf] *miscellaneous euphemisms* 301.21
gee whiz! [Inf] *miscellaneous euphemisms* 301.21
geezer [Inf] *male* 32.1
gefilte fish *fish dish* 90.19
gegenschein *solar system* 7.14, *natural light* 246.4
Gehenna *evil place* 446.6
geigenwerk Musical Instruments 142
Geiger counter *meter* 589.13
geisha *girlfriend* 33.4
geist *spirit* 86.10
gekkin Musical Instruments 142
gel *phase* 11.13, *solidify* 11.37, 542.10, *dose of medicine* 115.3, *hairdressing tool* 530.9, *be dense* 540.8, *semiliquid* 561.7, *thicken* 561.21, 594.9
gelatin *protein* 12.9, *dessert* 90.35, *emulsion* 132.9
gelatin or gel *stage lighting* 136.20
gelatin or gelatine *semiliquid* 561.7
gelatinity *viscosity* 561.1
gelatinization *concentration* 540.2
gelatinize *be dense* 540.8
gelatinize or gelatinate *thicken* 561.21
gelatinous 561.16
gelatinously *viscously* 561.22
gelatinousness *viscosity* 561.1
gelation *viscosity* 561.1
gelato *dessert* 90.35
Gelbvieh Breeds of Cattle 16
geld *make infertile* 23.9, *take off* 749.7
Gelderland Horse and Pony Breeds 159
gelding *sexlessness* 20.13, *that which makes infertile* 23.4, *eunuch* 32.11, *horse* 159.1
gel electrophoresis *analysis* 11.17
gel filtration *analysis* 11.17
gelid *frozen* 218.10
gelidity *freezing* 218.2
gelignite *explosive* 78.13
geliophobia Phobias 283
gelled *status adjectives* 11.25, *condensed* 540.7, *gelatinous* 561.16
gelling *condensed* 540.7

gelt [Inf] *cash* 484.2
gem *ore* 11.23, *good thing* 445.9, *jewelry* 532.6
Gemara *Jewish text* 81.17
gemeinschaft *social organization* 2.5
gem engraver *engraver* 144.5
gem engraving *engraving* 144.3
geminate *double* 789.14
geminate or geminated *double* 789.11
gemination *doubling* 789.4
Gemini Constellations 7, *twin* 789.5
gemma *bud* 41.8, *moss plant* 46.5
gemma cup *moss plant* 46.5
gemmate *vegetate* 41.21
gemmation *bud* 41.8
gemmulation *bud* 41.8
gemmule *bud* 41.8
gem of the first water *excellence* 445.4
gen [Brit inf] *information* 170.1, *fact* 717.6
gendarme *law enforcement officer* 53.8
gendarmerie *law enforcement agency* 53.7
gender *grammatical term* 5.29, *sex* 20.1
gender identity disorder *sexual disorder* 108.14
gene *genetic material* 13.20, *genetic* 13.32, *living matter* 28.4
genealogical *family* 65.6
genealogical tree *figurative usage* 43.9
genealogy *family tree* 65.3, Hobbies and Pastimes 167, *person of the past* 651.7, *line* 774.2
gene cloning *molecular biology* 13.18
genecology *genetics* 13.19
gene complement *genetic material* 13.20
gene complex *genetics* 13.19
gene flow *genetics* 13.19
gene frequency *genetics* 13.19
gene manipulation *genetics* 13.19
gene mapping *molecular biology* 13.18
gene mutation *genetic material* 13.20
gene pool *genetics* 13.19
gene probe *molecular biology* 13.18
General US Military Ranks 58, *military title* 72.8
general 778.9; *universal* 6.67, *computer communications* 15.25, *national* 18.16, *military leader* 68.10, *person in command* 425.5, *average* 742.5, *superior* 744.5, *whole* 759.6, *including* 763.3, *indeterminate* 841.14
General Agreement on Tariffs and Trade (GATT) *international trade* 56.7
general anesthesia *analgesic* 115.6
general anesthetic *analgesic* 115.6
general applicability *generality* 778.1
General Aptitude Test Battery Intelligence Tests 108
general benefit *benefit* 801.4
general confession *Eucharist* 85.7
general consent *agreement* 462.1
general court-martial *military law* 58.7
general delivery *postal service* 169.5
general dictionary *word book* 5.27

general election *election* 382.6
general headquarters (GHQ) *center of activity* 612.4
general hospital *hospital* 107.16
general idea *generalization* 778.5
generalissimo *military leader* 68.10
generality 778.1; *group* 18.13, *indiscrimination* 338.4, *average* 742.1, *whole* 759.1, *inclusion* 763.1, *indeterminacy* 841.6
generalization 778.5; *theory* 6.62, *reasoning* 319.2, *inaccuracy* 351.3, *whole* 759.1
generalize 778.14; *theorize* 6.84, *reason* 319.11, *make average* 742.9, *make a generalization* 778.18
generalized 778.12
generalized anxiety disorder *anxiety disorder* 108.11
generalizing *generalization* 778.5
general knowledge *information* 348.2
general linguistics Linguistic Studies 5
generally 778.20; *mathematically* 6.93, *indiscriminately* 338.15, *broadly* 592.15, *frequently* 661.7, *on average* 742.10, *on the whole* 759.13, *inclusively* 763.8, *as a rule* 780.18, *indeterminately* 841.24
generally speaking *nearly* 586.18, *on average* 742.10, *generally* 778.20
general manager *operator* 412.7
general market *marketplace* 483.7
general medicine *medicine* 107.1
general officer *military position* 58.6
General of the Air Force US Military Ranks 58
General of the Army US Military Ranks 58
general outlook *weather forecast* 9.4
general paralysis *neurological disease* 114.20
general paresis *neurological disease* 114.20
general policy *military affairs* 58.1
general population *group* 18.13
general practice *medical practice* 107.3
general practitioner (G.P.) *doctor* 107.19
general principle *theory* 6.62
general procedure *standard procedure* 397.6
general proposition *theory* 6.62
general public 778.6; *group* 18.13, *inhabitants* 61.2
general-purpose *practical* 511.6
general relativity *universe* 7.3
general rule *average* 778.4
general run *average* 778.4
general semantics Linguistic Studies 5, *meaning* 361.1
generalship *art of war* 76.16, *tactics* 399.12
general staff *military staff* 58.5
general strike *strike* 57.8, *stop* 668.2
general studies *subject* 48.3
general synopsis *weather forecast* 9.4
general tendency *fashion* 536.1, *tendency* 838.2
general theory of relativity *theory* 10.3, *fourth dimension* 563.9
general union *organized labor* 57.5
general verdict *verdict* 54.18
general war *war* 76.1

general wedding terms 64.6
general welfare *welfare* 445.2
generate *represent* 6.91, *process* 14.50, *conduct* 14.51, *propagate* 21.15, *procreate* 22.14, *bring into existence* 522.14, *be new* 652.17, *cause* 675.8, *originate* 737.7, *invent* 771.30
generate power 514.19
generating *beginning* 652.4
generating function *combinatorics* 6.63
generating station *electricity* 106.5, *power supplier* 514.14
generation *propagation* 21.4, *time period* 641.2, *long duration* 642.3, *beginning* 652.4, *cause* 675.1
generation gap *disparity* 728.3
generation of Adam *humankind* 18.1
generations of man *humankind* 18.1
generative *metabolic* 19.24, *reproductive* 21.11, *causal* 675.7
generative grammar *linguistic theory* 5.2
generator 14.43; *electrical energy* 10.44, *electricity* 106.5, *power supplier* 514.14
gene replacement therapy *treatment* 107.14
generic *taxonomic* 13.35, *prototypical* 624.7, *average* 742.5, *typical* 777.10, *generalized* 778.12
generically *biologically* 13.36, *formatively* 624.10, *taxonomically* 777.15
generic drug *medicine* 115.2
generosity 498.1; *charity* 305.3, *philanthropy* 307.1, *courtesy* 410.1, *unselfishness* 443.2, *kindness* 445.3, *virtue* 447.1, *giving* 472.1, *donation* 491.6
generous 498.6; *friendly* 62.5, *plentiful* 97.4, *charitable* 305.9, *philanthropic* 307.6, *courteous* 410.6, *lenient* 423.3, *unselfish* 443.5, *kind* 445.12, *virtuous* 447.5, *giving* 453.12, 472.9, *expending* 491.8, *big* 579.13, *benevolent* 825.21
generous endowment *wealth* 485.1
generous giver *giver* 472.7
generous giving *giving* 472.1
generous-hearted *receptive* 473.10
generously 491.14, 498.12; *amicably* 62.13, *charitably* 305.15, *philanthropically* 307.9, *courteously* 410.13, *genteelly* 410.14, *leniently* 423.6, *unselfishly* 443.9, *kindly* 445.20, *virtuously* 447.9, *as a gift* 472.17, *amply* 579.20
generous nature *giving* 472.1
generousness *charity* 305.3, *leniency* 423.1, *largeness* 579.2
generous person 498.5
gene sequence *genetic material* 13.20
gene sequencing *molecular biology* 13.18
genesis 21.5; *creation* 771.2
gene splicing *molecular biology* 13.18, *genetic material* 13.20
gene structure *molecular biology* 13.18
gene therapy *biochemistry* 12.1, *treatment* 107.14
genetic 13.32; *biological* 13.27, *reproductive* 21.11, *causal* 675.7, *caused* 676.5
genetically *biologically* 13.36,

reproductively 21.17, causally 675.12

genetic code *genetic material* 13.20

genetic constitution *genetics* 13.19

genetic counseling *health care* 107.7

genetic drift *genetics* 13.19

genetic element *genetic material* 13.20

genetic engineering *histology* 13.4, *molecular biology* 13.18

genetic fingerprinting *means of identification* 184.3

genetic *or* **DNA fingerprinting** *molecular biology* 13.18

geneticist *life scientist* 13.26

genetic likeness *affinity* 733.3

genetic map *genetic material* 13.20, *map* 187.5

genetic material 13.20

genetic psychology Psychological Theories, Schools 108

genetics 13.19; *histology* 13.4, *study of life* 28.9, *medical science* 107.5

Geneva, Lake of Lakes 568

Geneva Bible *Christian text* 81.16

genial *friendly* 62.5, *cheerful* 269.7, *likable* 271.6, 290.7, *benevolent* 305.7, *sociable* 408.11, *courteous* 410.6

geniality *friendship* 62.1, *cheerfulness* 269.2, *amiability* 271.3, *benevolence* 305.1, *sociability* 408.1

genially *amicably* 62.13, *cheerfully* 269.14, *pleasantly* 271.12, *likably* 290.12, *benevolently* 305.13, *sociably* 408.19

genic *genetic* 13.32

genie *ghost* 86.11, *assistant* 511.3, *benefactor* 825.15

geniophobia Phobias 283

genital *metabolic* 19.24, *sexual* 20.15, *reproductive* 21.11

genitalia *internal organ* 19.13, *sexual organs* 20.2, *organs of reproduction* 21.9

genitals *internal organ* 19.13, *sexual organs* 20.2, *organs of reproduction* 21.9

genitive *grammatical term* 5.29

genius *sage* 4.11, *expert* 52.8, 68.13, *minor deity* 82.2, *sprite* 86.12, *aptitude* 127.4, *skilled person* 127.7, *artistry* 133.3, *wonderful person* 294.6, *cleverness* 315.3, *intellectual* 315.7, *ability* 340.2, *knowledgeable person* 348.5, *intelligence* 352.2, *inspiration* 360.2, *superior person* 445.7, *paragon* 744.6, *special skill* 779.2

genned up [Brit inf] *informed* 170.9

Genoa *sailboat parts and accessories* 150.4

genocidal *murderous* 30.18

genocide *slaughter* 30.5, *capital punishment* 454.12, *destroying* 523.2

genome *genetic material* 13.20

genomic *genetic* 13.32

genophobia Phobias 283

genotype *molecular biology* 13.18, *genetics* 13.19

genotypic(al) *genetic* 13.32

genre *sort* 202.6, *kind* 624.3, *type* 777.4

genre painter *painter* 143.7

genre painting Western Art Styles 133, *type of painting* 143.5

gent [Inf] *male* 32.1, *nobleman* 70.1

genteel *good-mannered* 410.7, *cultured* 534.6

genteelly 410.14; *decorously* 534.10

genteelness *good manners* 410.2

gentian Flowers 42

gentian blue *blue pigment* 261.2

gentian violet *purple pigment* 262.2

gentilities *courtesies* 410.3

gentility *nobleness* 70.3, *good manners* 410.2, *grace* 527.2

gentle *faint* 233.6, *pitying* 308.4, *courteous* 410.6, *lenient* 423.3, *innocent* 449.6, *moderate* 521.3, *graceful* 527.4, *cultured* 534.6, *insubstantial* 539.5, *soft-hearted* 543.11, *unhurried* 693.8, *easygoing* 823.13

gentle as a lamb *moderate* 521.3

gentle breeze *wind strength* 9.13

gentlefolk *aristocracy* 70.2

gentle handling *treatment* 399.11

gentleman *male* 32.1, *male title of address* 32.3, *domestic servant* 69.7, *nobleman* 70.1, *well-behaved person* 399.6, *refined person* 534.4

gentleman farmer *agriculturist* 16.14

gentlemanliness *good manners* 410.2

gentlemanly *male* 32.16, *aristocratic* 70.4, *well-behaved* 399.15, *good-mannered* 410.7, *cultured* 534.6

gentlemanly behavior *good conduct* 399.5

gentleman's *agreements* 459.2

gentleman's agreement *contract* 391.2, 462.2, *duty* 433.1, *promise* 458.1

gentleman's gentleman *domestic servant* 69.7

gentleness *pity* 308.1, *courtesy* 410.1, *leniency* 423.1, *moderation* 521.1, *lightness* 539.1, *soft-heartedness* 543.4

gentleperson *refined person* 534.4

gentlewoman *nobleman* 70.1, *refined person* 534.4

gently *pityingly* 308.11, *courteously* 410.13, *leniently* 423.6, *moderately* 521.10, *lightly* 539.10, *soft-heartedly* 543.19, *slowly* 693.14

gentrification *urbanization* 567.4, *restoration* 809.2

gentrified *urban* 567.14

gentrify *urbanize* 567.15, *refurbish* 809.11

gentry *aristocracy* 70.2

gents', the [Inf] *place for excretion* 25.11

genuflect *worship* 83.15, *follow rites* 85.19, *submit* 298.17, *show obeisance to* 426.8, *show respect* 435.16, *bow* 716.22

genuflection *act of worship* 83.2, *submissiveness* 298.3, *submission* 421.1, *obeisance* 426.3, *mark of respect* 435.4, *bow* 716.6

genuine *factual* 3.14, *legitimate* 52.10, 53.21, *truthful* 191.4, *earnest* 278.5, *correct* 429.8, *deep-seated* 598.17, *realistic* 719.7, *authentic* 721.16, 737.6

genuine article *authenticity* 721.7, *original* 737.2

genuinely *biographically* 3.18, *legitimately* 52.19, *truthfully* 191.9, *earnestly* 278.10, *verifiably* 336.11, *correctly* 429.16, *with deep*

feeling 598.29, *authentically* 721.31

genuineness *historicalness* 3.9, *legal power* 52.2, *legality* 53.9, *truthfulness* 191.1, *right* 429.2, *depth of feeling* 598.7, *authenticity* 721.7, *originality* 737.1

genuphobia Phobias 283

genus *part* 760.1, *taxonomical classification* 777.3

geocentric *astronomical* 7.33, *central* 612.6

geochemical *geologic* 8.50

geochemist *geologist* 8.4

geochemistry *geology* 8.1, Branches of Chemistry 11

geochronological *geologic* 8.50

geochronological unit *geological time* 8.47

geochronologist *geologist* 8.4

geochronology *geology* 8.1

geodesic *line* 6.35, *roof* 134.7

geodesic dome *roof* 134.7, *superstructure* 551.7

geodesist *geophysicist* 8.5, *measurer* 589.14

geodesy *geophysics* 8.2, *topography* 565.5, *measurement* 589.1

geodetic *geologic* 8.50, *locational* 565.8, *metrical* 589.15

geodetically *geologically* 8.68, *topographically* 565.13, *measurably* 589.22

geodetics *measurement* 589.1

geographical *regional* 564.12, *locational* 565.8, *situational* 573.6

geographically 573.11; *anthropologically* 1.15, *geologically* 8.68, *regionally* 564.16, *topographically* 565.13

geographical mile General Units 589

geographical space 563.3

geography *geology* 8.1, Children's and Party Games 167, *topography* 565.5, *situation* 573.1

geoid Earth 8.6

geolinguistics Linguistic Studies 5

geologic 8.50; *chemical* 11.24

geological *geologic* 8.50

geological epoch *geological past* 651.5

geological era *geological past* 651.5

geological fold *fold* 637.1

geologically 8.68; *in the past* 651.20

geological past 651.5; *past time* 651.1

geological period 641.3; *geological past* 651.5

geological time 8.47

geological time scale *geological time* 8.47

geological time unit *geological time* 8.47

geologist 8.4

geology 8.1

geomagnetic *geophysical* 8.51

geomagnetic field *geomagnetism* 8.3

geomagnetic pole *geomagnetism* 8.3

geomagnetism 8.3, 10.46; *geophysics* 8.2

geomagnetist *geophysicist* 8.5

geomancer *diviner* 86.14, *predictor* 650.5

geomancy *divination* 86.5

geometer *mathematician* 6.2

geometric *mathematical* 6.65, 784.9, *pictorial* 133.8, *numerical* 783.7

geometrically *pictorially* 133.11,

numerically 783.11, *mathematically* 784.15

geometric art Western Art Styles 133

geometric construction 6.47

geometric figure 6.39

geometrician *mathematician* 6.2

geometric instrument *geometric construction* 6.47

geometric mean *parameter* 6.57

geometric optics *classical physics* 10.2

geometric perspective *treatment* 143.6

geometric progression *sequence* 6.18

geometric series *sequence* 6.18

geometric shape *geometric figure* 6.39

geometry 6.32, Branches of Mathematics 6, *angular measurement* 628.4, *calculation* 784.1

geomorphic feature *landform* 8.9

geomorphological *geologic* 8.50

geomorphologically *geologically* 8.68

geomorphologist *geologist* 8.4, *anatomist* 551.16

geomorphology *geology* 8.1, *science of structure* 551.15

geophysical 8.51

geophysical satellite *artificial satellite* 7.30

geophysicist 8.5

geophysics 8.2; Fields of Modern Physics 10

geopolitical *political* 50.9

geopolitically *politically* 50.11

geopolitics *geology* 8.1, *political science* 50.2

geoponic *agricultural* 16.16

geoponics *agriculture* 16.1

George Lakes 568

Georgetown Countries 566

Georgette crepe Fabrics and Fibers 130

Georgia American States 564, Countries 566

Georgian Furniture Styles 101, *historic* 653.13

Georgian architecture Architectural Styles 134

Georgian poetry Western Literary Groups 139

georgic *agricultural* 16.16, Poem or Verse Forms 139

geospheric *terrestrial* 8.52

geostationary orbit *artificial satellite* 7.30

geostrophic *atmospheric* 9.40

geostrophic force *atmospheric process* 9.9

geostrophic wind *wind* 9.12

geosynchronous orbit *artificial satellite* 7.30

geosyncline *fold* 8.22

geotechnical engineer *civil engineer* 14.19

geotechnical engineering *civil engineering* 14.17

geothermal *or* **geothermic** *renewable* 106.15

geothermal energy *renewable energy* 106.9

geothermal power *type of power* 514.6, *power source* 514.13

gephyrophobia Phobias 283

geraniol *terpene* 12.20

geranium Flowers 42, *red thing* 257.3

gerascophobia Phobias 283

gerbera daisy Flowers 42

Gerda Deities 82

geriatric *older person* 27.7, *aged* 27.15

geriatric center *nursing home* 107.18

geriatrician *gerontology* 27.6

geriatric medicine *gerontology* 27.6

geriatric patient *sick person* 114.22

geriatrics Medical Specialties 107

germ *microorganism* 13.11, *developmental biology* 13.22, *developmental* 13.33, *disease-causing agent* 114.5, *little thing* 580.3, *source* 675.2, 771.3

German architecture Architectural Styles 134

German Blackheaded Mutton Breeds of Sheep 16

German Black Pied Breeds of Cattle 16

German Brown Breeds of Cattle 16

germander Flowers 42

germane *related* 727.6

germanely *relevantly* 727.12

germaneness *relatedness* 727.1

German GP at Hockenheim *Formula 1 World Championship races* 146.5

German gymnastics *gymnastics* 157.1

German Heath Breeds of Sheep 16

Germanic *language family* 5.12

Germanic art Western Art Styles 133

germanium Chemical Elements and Common Allotropes 11

German Landrace Breeds of Pigs 16

German measles *infection* 114.7

German Mutton Merino Breeds of Sheep 16

Germanophobia Phobias 283

German Red Pied Breeds of Cattle 16

Germans Phobias 283

German shepherd Breeds of Dogs 35

German shorthaired pointer Breeds of Dogs 35

German Simmental Breeds of Cattle 16

German solo Card Games 168

German Trotter Horse and Pony Breeds 159

German wirehaired pointer Breeds of Dogs 35

Germany Countries 566

German Yellow Breeds of Cattle 16

German Yorkshire Breeds of Pigs 16

germ-carrier *infectious person* 114.9

germ-carrying *contagious* 114.26

germ cell *cell* 13.15

germen *cell* 13.15

germ-free *hygienic* 116.3

germicide *killing agent* 30.15, *prophylaxis* 114.4

Germinal French Revolutionary Calendar 646

germinal *developmental* 13.33, *reproductive* 21.11, *tiny* 580.9, *causal* 675.7, *embryonic* 771.19

germinant *developmental* 13.33

germinate *reproduce oneself* 21.14, *fertilize* 22.12, *vegetate* 41.21, *mushroom* 47.23, *grow* 581.17, 676.10, *produce* 771.34

germinating *developmental* 13.33, *growing* 581.12

germinating seed *seed* 41.9

germination **581.5**; *developmental biology* 13.22, *fertilization* 21.6, *seed* 41.9

germinative *developmental* 13.33

germ-laden *toxic* 114.28

germ plasm *cell structure* 13.16

germ warfare *chemical warfare* 76.5

gerontocracy *oligarchy* 49.10

gerontologic(al) *aged* 27.15

gerontologist *gerontology* 27.6

gerontology **27.6**

gerontophobia Phobias 283

gerrymander *run for office* 50.10, *be cunning* 822.5

gerrymandering *politics* 50.1, *cunning* 822.1

Gertrude Stein Notable Friendships 62

gerund *part of speech* 5.30

Gesamtkunstwerke Western Art Styles 133

gesellschaft *social organization* 2.5

Gesell's development schedule Psychological Tests 108

gesso *material* 143.9

gest *or* **geste** *story* 139.4

Gestalt *whole thing* 759.2

gestalt *philosophical term* 4.7, *perceptual concept* 108.30, *form* 624.1

Gestalt psychology Psychological Theories, Schools 108

gestation *genesis* 21.5

gestatory *embryonic* 771.19

gesticulate *gesture* 183.17, *have difficulty speaking* 206.9, *conduct oneself* 399.17, *move* 677.15

gesticulation *gesture* 183.5, *articulation* 205.9, *voiceless speech* 206.4, *conduct* 399.1, *deed* 412.2, *bodily movement* 677.11

gesticulative *gestural* 183.13

gestural **183.13**

gesture **183.5, 183.17**; *nonstandard language* 5.7, *dramaturgy* 136.6, *inside information* 170.4, *sign* 183.19, *articulation* 205.9, *voiceless speech* 206.4, *have difficulty speaking* 206.9, *conduct* 399.1, *conduct oneself* 399.17, *deed* 412.2, *bodily movement* 677.11, *move* 677.15

gesture of equality *mode of behavior* 399.2

gesture of protest 507.3

get *understand* 363.9, *gain* 467.15, *receive* 473.13, 492.7, *take* 477.14, *purchase* 481.10, *convert* 670.11, *bring* 685.11, *draw out* 711.17

get [Inf] *have an idea* 327.13

get! [Inf] *go!* 709.30

get a bad name *be open to criticism* 438.22

get a bad press *be open to criticism* 438.22

get a bargain *buy cheaply* 481.11

get a bearing *find* 565.11

get about *undertake* 391.7

get about *or* **around** *participate* 408.15

get above oneself *be vain* 402.14

get a break [Inf] *find an opening* 583.20, *be fortunate* 847.7

get a (lucky) break [Inf] *find an opening* 583.20

get a corner on *possess* 469.14

get acquainted *befriend* 62.10

get across *mean* 361.13, *make*

---

comprehensible 363.8, *be intelligible* 363.10

get a dose of one's own medicine *serve one right* 420.5

get a firm hold *retain* 471.7

get a firm hold on *detain* 471.9

get a fix *find* 565.11

get a fix on *know* 48.24

get a foothold *retain* 471.7

get agitated about *feel deeply* 266.16

get a half nelson on *retain* 471.7

get ahead *get in early* 657.16, *achieve* 704.21, *do well* 845.12

get a headlock on *retain* 471.7

get ahead of *be in front* 621.13, *precede* 657.13, *overtake* 744.16

get a head start *or* **flying start** *start early* 657.12, *be ahead* 744.17

get a kick out of [Inf] *feel pleasure* 214.12

get all snarled up *find difficult* 824.17

get all tangled up *find difficult* 824.17

get along *go forward* 679.8, *depart* 705.8

get along with *fraternize* 408.17

get a medal *be rewarded* 453.16, *win an award* 467.23

get a mental picture of *imagine* 360.14

get a middle-aged spread *age* 27.16

get a move on! *hurry up!* 818.9

get a move on [Inf] *be swift* 694.10, *accelerate* 694.14

get an advance *earn* 467.20

get an earful *hear* 228.13

get angry *become angry* 302.20, *show impatience* 303.14

get a piece of the action [Inf] *be sociable* 414.22, *get one's allotment* 474.6

get a reprieve 816.9

get a reward *be rewarded* 453.16

get around *be skillful* 127.14

get around *or* **about** *be published* 173.19

get around someone *manipulate* 508.12

get a share *get one's allotment* 474.6

get a stranglehold on *retain* 471.7

get a tan *feel hot* 217.19

get a tight grip *retain* 471.7

get a toehold *retain* 471.7

get at the truth *authenticate* 721.24

getaway *acceleration* 694.3, *accelerating* 694.9, *departure* 705.1, *escape* 816.1

get away *diverge* 753.20, *escape* 816.8, *be liberated* 831.7

get away *or* **off** *depart* 705.8

get away with *exempt oneself* 434.12

get away with it *be permitted* 502.8, *get a reprieve* 816.9

get away with murder [Inf] *exempt oneself* 434.12

get a wiggle on [Inf] *hasten* 657.15

get back *counteract* 510.7

get back at *restore* 671.10

get back on one's feet *get healthy* 113.12

get behindhand *be unable to pay* 490.11

get better **807.21**; *be good* 445.16, *show potential* 458.14, *change for*

---

the better 665.17, *upturn* 713.20, *be restored* 809.13

get by *be mediocre* 289.16, *be in a state of* 725.8

get by any means *find means* 102.6

get by fair means or foul *find means* 102.6

get by hook or by crook *find means* 102.6, 511.8

get by on *have at one's disposal* 393.14

get caught *be guilty* 450.9

get caught in the act *or* **red-handed** *or* **with one's pants down** [Inf] *be guilty* 450.9

get changed *wear* 100.46

get close *near* 586.12

get cold feet [Inf] *be fearful* 283.15, *be a coward* 285.7

get compensation *be compensated* 743.9

get cracking [Inf] *do something* 412.13, *be swift* 694.10, *make a beginning* 771.26

get credit *be in debt* 488.9

get crow's feet *age* 27.16

get dirty *be dirty* 112.10

get divorced *divorce* 66.9

get done *take action* 509.12

get down *eat* 92.21, *land* 704.16, *descend* 714.12, *drop* 714.15, *sit* 716.20

get down from one's high horse *humble oneself* 298.18

get down on one's haunches *sit* 716.20

get down on one's knees *apologize* 313.8, *show respect* 435.16

get down to *tackle* 390.8, *undertake* 391.7

get down to brass tacks [Inf] *be concise* 198.5, *relate to* 727.9, *particularize* 779.17

get down to it *work* 122.8

get down to the nitty-gritty [Inf] *be concise* 198.5, *particularize* 779.17

get down to the nuts and bolts *be concise* 198.5

get dressed *wear* 100.46

get drunk **121.35**; *celebrate* 405.10

get egg on one's face [Inf] *be clumsy* 128.9

get engaged to **458.12**

get even *retaliate* 509.15

get even with *retaliate* 420.4, *exact retribution* 454.27

get fat *grow* 581.17, *be prosperous* 847.6

get fatter *increase* 467.17

get for a song *buy at a discount* 495.6

get free *diverge* 753.20, *escape* 816.8, *be free* 829.16, *be liberated* 831.7

get fresh [Inf] *have the audacity* 400.15

get frostbite *become cold* 218.14

get going *undertake* 391.7, *do something* 412.13, *make a beginning* 771.26, *be prosperous* 847.6

get going! *go!* 709.30

get heads together *work together* 827.14

get healthy **113.12**

get hell [Inf] *get into trouble* 824.20

get hitched [Inf] *marry* 64.19

get hold of *understand* 363.9, *gain* 467.15, *take* 477.14

get hold of the wrong end of the stick *misjudge* 342.9

get home *land* 704.16
get hot *near* 586.12
get hot under the collar [Inf] *become angry* 302.20
get huffy *be offended* 302.14
get ideas *aim* 327.17
get in 704.17
get in *or* into *enter* 706.11
get in a mess *be in difficulty* 824.19
get in a pickle [Inf] *be in difficulties* 726.14
get in back of *back* 825.28
get in behind *back* 825.28
get in early 657.16
get in line *arrange* 774.14
get in on the act *act* 412.11
get in on the ground floor *get in early* 657.16
get in the cross hairs *fire* 418.18
get in the way *be clumsy* 128.9, *block* 826.17
get in the way of *hinder* 826.15
get into *wear* 100.46
get into a habit *accustom oneself* 397.19
get into a jam *or* a fix *or* a bind [Inf] *be in a predicament* 725.9, *be in difficulties* 726.14
get into character *rehearse* 136.37
get into debt *be in debt* 488.9, *be unable to pay* 490.11
get into difficulties *be in difficulties* 726.14, *be in difficulty* 824.19
get into gear *prepare for action* 388.18
get into hot water [Inf] *be in difficulties* 726.14, *get into trouble* 824.20
get into mischief *disobey* 427.12
get into one's head *suppose* 359.8
get into one's stride *accustom oneself* 397.19
get into the final *qualify* 340.11
get into the good graces of *fawn* 401.9
get into the papers *be published* 173.19
get into trouble 824.20; *be in difficulties* 726.14
get in touch *communicate* 169.18, *link* 752.11
get involved *take charge of* 391.8
get it [Inf] *find out* 345.13, *get into trouble* 824.20
get it into one's head *be of the opinion* 87.10
get it off one's chest *admit* 180.11
get it wrong *be in error* 351.15
get job satisfaction *be rewarded* 453.16
get laid [Inf] *have sex* 20.21
get laryngitis *be silent* 231.3
get light *grow light* 246.21
get loose *diverge* 753.20
get lost *go astray* 698.17, *be in danger* 811.11
get lost! [Inf] *go!* 709.30
get lower *descend* 714.12
get lower and lower *descend* 714.12
get lucky *be in comfortable circumstances* 726.13, *attain one's goal* 845.13
get mad *become angry* 302.20
get married *marry* 64.19, *propose (marriage)* 299.28
get miffed *be offended* 302.14
get mileage out of *use up* 393.12
get mixed up in *be active in* 412.17
get moving *start off* 771.27

get near *near* 586.12
get nearer *improve* 467.18
get no results *fail* 846.12
get nowhere *be powerless* 515.11, *waste effort* 802.13
get nowhere fast [Inf] *move slowly* 693.11
get off *acquit* 54.32, *land* 704.16, *set out* 705.12, *descend* 714.12, *get a reprieve* 816.9, *deliver* 817.5, *be liberated* 831.7
get off [Inf] *stimulate* 20.22
get off lightly *get a reprieve* 816.9
get off on a technicality *get a reprieve* 816.9
get off scot-free *exempt oneself* 434.12, *be liberated* 831.7
get off the subject *be circuitous* 199.6
get off to a flying start *accelerate* 694.14
get off to a good start *make a beginning* 771.26
get old *age* 27.16
get older *age* 27.16
get on *age* 27.16, *depart* 705.8, *mount* 713.24, *do well* 845.12
get on *or* along *be in a state of* 725.8
get on credit *buy on credit* 476.13
get one by *suffice* 97.6
get one's allotment 474.6
get one's ass in a bind [Inf] *be in difficulty* 824.19
get one's ass in gear [Inf] *be active* 414.18
get one's back up [Inf] *be offended* 302.14
get one's bearings *orient* 697.15
get one's breath back *be refreshed* 94.8
get one's call-up papers *join the army* 76.31
get one's comeuppance [Inf] *be rewarded* 453.16, *be punished* 454.31
get one's dander up [Inf] *become angry* 302.20
get one's deserts *serve one right* 420.5, *be rewarded* 453.16, *be punished* 454.31
get oneself into a sulk *be sullen* 304.12
get oneself killed *commit suicide* 30.24
get one's feet wet [Inf] *make a beginning* 771.26
get one's fingers on *gain* 467.15
get one's footing *retain* 471.7
get one's foot in the door *be cunning* 822.5
get one's goat [Inf] *cause dislike* 291.16
get one's hands dirty *work* 122.8
get one's head down *undertake* 391.7
get *or* keep one's hopes *or* spirits up *be hopeful* 281.11
get one's Irish up *become angry* 302.20
get one's mind into *undertake* 391.7
get one's money's worth *use up* 393.12, *buy cheaply* 481.11
get one's own back *retaliate* 420.4, 489.23
get one's sea legs *sail* 690.16
get one's second wind *be refreshed* 94.8
get one's share *get one's allotment* 474.6
get one's teeth into *eat well* 92.23, *undertake* 391.7
get one wrong *misinterpret* 366.4

get on in the world *be prosperous* 847.6
get on in years *age* 27.16
get on one's high horse *defy* 416.7
get on one's nerves *cause dislike* 291.16, *irritate* 302.16
get on the gravy train [Inf] *work* 122.8, *be fortunate* 847.7
get on the right side of *fawn* 401.9
get on the road *start off* 771.27
get on well *be prosperous* 847.6
get on well with *fraternize* 408.17
get on with *do something* 412.13
get out *be disclosed* 180.12, *exit* 707.13, *extract* 711.13, *escape* 816.8, *deliver* 817.5, *be liberated* 831.7
get out! *go!* 709.30
get out of *shirk* 386.18, *be liberated* 831.7
get out of control *be disorderly* 766.22
get out of hand *be disorderly* 766.22
get out of here! *go!* 709.30
get out of line *not conform* 782.18
get out of practice *be unskillful* 128.8
get out of the way *avoid* 386.13
get out of the way of *sidestep* 698.22
get out while the going is good *survive* 419.31
get over *be in motion* 677.14, *be restored* 809.13
get over a snag *overcome obstacles* 845.14
get overheated *feel hot* 217.19
get over the *or* a hump *overcome obstacles* 845.14
get over the worst *change for the better* 665.17, *get better* 807.21
get paid 453.17; *earn* 467.20
get past *pass* 692.15
get pinned *court* 299.26
get pissed [Inf] *drink* 93.19
get pregnant *reproduce oneself* 21.14
get promoted *do well* 845.12
get ready *prepare* 388.14, *prepare oneself* 388.21
get ready for action *prepare oneself* 388.21
get religion *be religious* 81.25
get results *be successful* 845.11
get rich 485.13; *be good* 445.16, *attain one's goal* 845.13, *be prosperous* 847.6
get rid of *kill* 30.19, *cause to disappear* 265.7, *discard* 383.12, *renounce* 392.4, *sell* 482.15, *destroy* 523.10, *exterminate* 709.22, *throw away* 709.25, *eject* 764.8, *elude* 816.10
get rid of a hangover *sober up* 120.7
get ripped off [Inf] *overpay* 496.11
get royalties *earn* 467.20
get sacked *play offense* 155.18
get satisfaction *retaliate* 420.4, *be compensated* 743.9
get set *prepare oneself* 388.21
get sidetracked *be circuitous* 199.6, *go astray* 698.17, *be unrelated* 728.12
get smart *be insolent* 400.14
get Social Security payments *earn* 467.20
get some shuteye [Inf] *take it easy* 819.3

get something for nothing *win an award* 467.23
get something through *negotiate* 460.6
get somewhere *make one's way* 679.12, *achieve* 704.21
get sore [Inf] *become angry* 302.20, *show impatience* 303.14
get spliced [Inf] *marry* 64.19
get stale *be fatigued* 820.5
get started *make a beginning* 771.26
get straight to the point *aim* 697.14
gettable *receivable* 473.12
getter *absorb* 11.40, *recipient* 473.5
gettering *surface chemistry* 11.20
getter-ion pump *surface chemistry* 11.20
get the ball rolling *make a beginning* 771.26, *activate* 771.28
get the best out of *use up* 393.12, *promote* 807.18
get the better of *outdo* 744.18
get the bit between one's teeth *be liberated* 831.7
get the boot [Inf] *be dismissed* 707.18
get the checkered flag *be on the track* 146.11
get the color back in one's cheeks *get healthy* 113.12
get the drop on *be ahead* 744.17
get thee hence! *go!* 709.30
get the feel of *accustom oneself* 397.19
get the full particulars *circumstantiate* 726.12
get the fumes out of one's brain *sober up* 120.7
get the giggles *laugh* 277.12
get the gist of *understand* 363.9
get the green light *be on the track* 146.11
get the hang of [Inf] *know* 48.24, *understand* 363.9, *accustom oneself* 397.19
get the hell out of here! *go!* 709.30
get the hungries [Inf] *eat well* 92.23
get the idea *understand* 363.9
get the job done *suffice* 97.6
get the jump on someone *be ahead* 744.17
get the knack of *accustom oneself* 397.19
get the lay of the land *proceed with caution* 287.12, *orient* 697.15, *circumstantiate* 726.12
get the lead out [Inf] *be active* 414.18
get the new look *be trendy* 652.18
get the picture *understand* 363.9
get there *reach* 704.14, *achieve* 704.21, *do well* 845.12
get there early *or* ahead of time *be early* 657.11
get there first *be early* 657.11
get the show on the road *make a beginning* 771.26
get the whip hand *gain authority* 52.15
get the worst of it *be defeated* 846.18
get the wrong idea *find unintelligible* 364.14
get through *qualify* 340.11, *consume* 491.12, *pass* 692.15, *infiltrate* 189.7
getting *gain* 467.1, *receiving* 473.1, *taking* 477.1
getting ahead 657.7; *gain* 467.1, *improvement* 679.5

getting a middle-aged spread *aging* 27.13

getting back *restoration* 671.2, 809.2

getting crow's feet *aging* 27.13

getting down *eating* 92.1

getting down to brass tacks *simplification* 526.6

getting drunk *drinking* 121.2

getting even *reckoning* 454.8

getting hitched [Inf] *marriage* 64.1

getting in early *getting ahead* 657.7

getting in on the ground floor *getting ahead* 657.7

getting old *aging* 27.13

getting on *old* 653.10

getting one's hands dirty *work* 122.1

getting on for *in the future* 650.13

getting on *or along in years* *aging* 27.13, *old* 653.10

getting pinned *courtship* 299.10

getting ready *preparation* 388.1

getting spliced [Inf] *marriage* 64.1

getting well 113.9

getting worse *deteriorated* 808.8

get to *improve* 467.18, *reach out* 585.10, *reach* 704.14

get together *band together* 59.27, *pacify* 74.11, *participate* 408.15, *acquire* 467.19, *come together* 702.10, *join with* 827.15

get-together *social gathering* 59.7, 408.4

get together with *join with* 827.15

get to know 348.12; *befriend* 62.10, *understand* 363.9

get too dear *cost a lot* 496.9

get to one's feet *be vertical* 602.8

get to the bottom of *understand* 363.9

get to the heart of the matter *raise the point* 328.10

get to the nitty-gritty [Inf] *relate to* 727.9

get to the top *achieve* 704.21

get tough *be severe* 424.8

get tough with *suppress* 424.9

get under one's feet *block* 826.17

get under way *navigate* 690.15, *set out* 705.12, *start off* 771.27

get up *blow* 9.53, *be active* 414.18, *perform* 522.16, *construct* 551.22, *be vertical* 602.8, *arise* 655.7, 715.15, *be restored* 809.13

getup [Inf] *costume* 100.10, *form* 551.3, *nature* 624.5

get up a good head of steam *be full of vigor* 518.4

get up and go *depart* 705.8

get-up-and-go *energy* 414.4, *vigor* 518.1

get up early *start early* 657.12

get up on the wrong side of the bed *be irascible* 303.13, *be irritable* 304.14

get up steam *navigate* 690.15

get up to date *become new* 652.19

get used to *accustom oneself* 397.19

get warm *detect* 345.12, *near* 586.12

get well *get healthy* 113.12, *be restored* 809.13

get what is coming to one *be rewarded* 453.14

get what one deserves *serve one right* 420.5

get what one is asking for *be punished* 454.31

get what was coming *serve one right* 420.5

get what was due *serve one right* 420.5

get wind of *be informed* 170.15, *smell* 224.7, *detect* 345.12

get wise to [Inf] *understand* 295.6, 363.9, *get to know* 348.12

get with it [Inf] *be trendy* 652.18

get working *repair* 809.10

get worse *be unhealthy* 114.29, *become aggravated* 276.6, *become inferior* 745.11, *deteriorate* 808.14

get wrong *misjudge* 342.9, *find unintelligible* 364.14, *misinterpret* 366.4, *be mixed up* 751.15

get you gone! *go!* 709.30

geumaphobia Phobias 283

geumatophobia Phobias 283

geumophobia Phobias 283

gewgaw *cheap item* 497.5, *decorative article* 532.5, *cheap thing* 800.7

geyser *eruption* 8.27, *hot spring* 572.11

geyser [Brit] *heater* 217.3

Ghaghara Rivers 570

Ghana Countries 566

ghastly *deathly* 29.15, *drained of color* 252.6, *pale* 253.10, *frightening* 283.12, *ugly* 531.3, *hideously* 531.6

ghat *gulf* 587.3

ghee *juice* 555.2

ghetto *group* 18.13, *urban area* 567.10, *enclosed area* 619.2, *setting apart* 753.2, *exclusion zone* 764.3

ghetto blaster [Inf] *radio* 172.1

ghettoization *social discrimination* 337.4, *exclusiveness* 764.4

ghettoize *exclude* 764.7

ghettoized *urban* 567.14

ghetto resident *poor person* 486.6

ghibli Notable Winds 9

ghost 86.11; *substitute for* 80.5, Children's and Party Games 167, *spectacle* 264.6, *frightener* 283.7, *fantasy* 360.5, *evil spirit* 446.4, *spiritual world* 525.3, *omnipresence* 575.4, *illusion* 720.2

ghost dance *non-Christian ritual* 85.8

ghost-fire *make ceramics* 129.10

ghost firing *ceramic process* 129.5

ghostliness *the occult* 86.2, *immateriality* 525.2

ghostly *spiritual* 86.20, *devastated* 96.12, *nonmaterial* 525.8, *omnipresent* 575.10, *unreal* 720.8

ghostly presence *omnipresence* 575.4

ghost of a chance *improbability* 839.1

ghostridden *bewitched* 86.21

ghosts Phobias 283

ghost story *story* 139.4

ghost town *town* 567.2

ghostweed Flowers 42

ghost word *new word* 5.18

ghostwrite *substitute for* 80.5, *write* 139.21, *cover for* 613.34, *be a substitute* 672.6

ghost writer *alternative* 80.2, *book publishing personnel* 174.12, *descriptive writer* 202.10, *substitute* 613.17, 672.2

ghoul *ghost* 86.11, *frightener* 283.7, Legendary Creatures 360, *evil spirit* 446.4

ghoulish *frightening* 283.12

ghoulishly *magically* 86.28

GI *soldier* 77.4

giant *star luminosity* 7.12, Legendary Creatures 360, *person*

---

of strength 516.8, *big person* 579.10, *huge* 579.14, *tall person* 596.6, *tall* 596.9

giant circles *horizontal bar* 157.5

giant elliptical *galaxy* 7.5

giantess *big person* 579.10

giantism *gigantism* 579.4

giant reptile *extinct reptile* 37.9

giant schnauzer Breeds of Dogs 35

giant-size *huge* 579.14

giant slalom Sporting Activities 145

giant slalom race *ski race* 162.4

giant slalom racer *skier* 162.14

giant slalom ski *ski equipment* 162.10

giant sloth *prehistoric animal* 653.8

giant spiral *galaxy* 7.5

Giant's Ridge International Classic Marathon *cross-country skiing championships* 162.9

giant star *star luminosity* 7.12

giardia *parasite* 39.18

gib *cat* 35.11

gibber *be talkative* 207.7, *talk nonsense* 362.12, *be unintelligible* 364.11

gibbering *obscure* 197.2, *talkative* 207.5, *meaningless* 362.7, *unintelligible* 364.4

gibberish *nonstandard language* 5.7, *obscurity* 197.1, *senseless talk* 362.4, *unintelligible thing* 364.3

gibbet *execute* 454.30

gibbous *convex* 634.5

gibbous moon *moon* 7.18

gibbousness *roundness* 633.1, *convexity* 634.1

Gibbs function Classical Physical Laws 10

gibe *joke* 368.4, *derision* 400.5, *disdain* 400.16, *taunt* 436.6, 436.23

giberellin *plant hormone* 12.17

gibing *derisive* 400.12, *taunting* 436.14

gibingly *derisively* 400.22

gibli Notable Winds 9

GI bride *spouse* 64.8

Gibson Deserts 572

giddiness *folly* 353.1, *capriciousness* 381.2, *poor health* 517.3, *dizziness* 682.2

giddy *slightly drunk* 121.26, *unskillful* 128.4, *capricious* 381.4, *irresolute* 666.4, *dizzy* 682.13, *restless* 684.16, *unbalanced* 741.5

Gidran Horse and Pony Breeds 159

gift 472.2, 498.3; *aptitude* 127.4, 513.3, *pleasant thing* 271.4, *charity* 275.3, 307.3, *benevolent act* 305.5, *ability* 340.2, *good* 445.1, *proficiency* 445.5, *bounty* 453.8, *windfall* 467.7, *transfer of property* 470.4, *give* 472.10, *something received* 473.2, *absence of charge* 497.6, *offering* 504.5, *positive stimulus* 508.5, *transferred thing* 685.6, *grant* 735.10, *special skill* 779.2

gifted 127.11; *skillful* 127.10, *intelligent* 315.9, 352.5, *qualified* 340.7, *proficient* 445.15, *granted* 735.20

gifted child *skilled person* 127.7

gifting *giving* 472.1

gift of healing *healing art* 115.13

gift of the gab [Inf] *power of speech* 205.5, *talkativeness* 207.1

gift tax *tax* 494.5

gift token *gift* 472.2

gift voucher *gift* 472.2

---

giftwrap *wrap* 613.29

giftwrapper *coverer* 613.18

giftwrapping *wrapping* 613.10

gig [Inf] *engagement* 138.6, 136.15, Ships and Boats 690, *performance* 141.8

giga Decimal Prefixes 589

gigabyte (gig) *data-related concepts* 15.23, *thousand* 792.10

gigantesque *huge* 579.14

gigantic *huge* 579.14

gigantism 579.4

giggle *cry of amusement* 239.2, *laugh* 239.14, 277.12, *show joy* 269.10, *laughter* 277.8

giggling *cheering* 109.11

gigolo *libertine* 32.7, *lover* 299.11, *sponger* 401.4, *sexually immoral person* 432.8

gigue Dances 135, Musical Forms 140

Gila Rivers 570

gilbert Scientific and Technical Units 589

gild *make ceramics* 129.10, *color* 251.16, *make yellow* 259.12, *practice sophistry* 330.11, *ornament* 532.12, *coat* 613.28, *delude* 720.16

gilded *ceramic* 129.9, *yellow* 259.7, *opulent* 485.10, *decorated* 532.9, *ornate* 532.10

Gilded Age Ages, Decades, Eras 641

gilded decoration *decoration* 129.4

gilder *decorator* 532.8

gilding *decorative method* 532.3

gilding the lily *exaggeration* 194.1

gild the lily *be superfluous* 99.12, *exaggerate* 194.11, *ornament* 532.12, *beautify* 807.20

gill *fish characteristic* 38.8, *fungal body* 47.4, *loved one* 299.13, General Units 589

gill [Brit] *size of drink* 93.3, *river* 570.1

gill cover *fish characteristic* 38.8

gills *respiration* 558.8

gill slit *fish characteristic* 38.8

gillyflower Flowers 42

gilt *livestock* 16.11, *female animal* 33.15, *female mammal* 35.19, *yellow* 259.7, *decorative method* 532.3, *decorated* 532.9

gilt-edged *guaranteed* 464.6

gilt-edged security *promise* 464.2

gimbal *axle* 682.7

gimcrack *cheap item* 497.5, *decorative article* 532.5, *brittle* 548.3, *cheap thing* 800.7, *cheap* 800.16, *unsafe* 811.8

gimlet *sharp-pointed thing* 549.4

gimlet eye *sharp eye* 242.4

gimlet-eyed *seeing* 242.17

gimmick *social skill* 127.3, *artifice* 193.5, *method* 387.4, *trendiness* 652.2

gimmickry *newness* 652.1

gimmicky *trendy* 652.11

gimp *edging* 618.2

gimpy [Inf] *ill* 517.8

gin *alcoholic drink* 93.9, *trap* 813.1

ginger Herbs and Spices 91, *orange* 258.5

ginger [Inf] *liveliness* 28.12

ginger ale *soft drink* 93.8

gingerbread *cake* 90.36

gingerbread man *figure* 187.4

gingerbread style Architectural Styles 134

gingerbread woman *figure* 187.4

ginger-haired *red-haired* 257.7

gingerly *reticent* 287.8, *reticently* 287.18, *carefully* 325.13
ginger up [Inf] *invigorate* 518.5
gingery [Inf] *lively* 28.16
gingham Fabrics and Fibers 130
gingko Trees and Shrubs 43
ginned up [Inf] *drunk* 121.25
gin rummy Card Games 168
ginseng Herbs and Spices 91, *tonic* 115.8
gin-sodden *drunken* 121.28
giocoso Musical Terms and Expression Marks 140
gip *foul play* 193.6, *swindle* 193.19
Giraffe Constellations 7
giraffe *hoofed mammal* 35.16, *game* 160.6
giraffes Collective Names 59
gird *intertwine* 752.19
girded *surrounded* 615.5
girder *superstructure* 551.7, *supporting part* 605.3, *means of connection* 754.4
girder bridge *bridge* 551.10
girdle *underwear* 100.22, *body support* 605.6, *circular thing* 631.3, *make circular* 631.7, *ring* 681.9, *intertwine* 752.19, *band* 754.9, *means of restraint* 830.6, *restrain someone* 830.17
girdle the earth *ring* 681.9
gird up one's loins *prepare oneself* 388.21, *be strong* 516.14
girl *person* 18.8, *child* 26.6, *young woman* 26.9, *female* 33.1, *girlfriend* 33.4, *loved one* 299.13
girl [Inf] *stimulants* 121.18
girl Friday *office assistant* 69.6, *deputy* 80.1, *clerical worker* 123.5
girl or **man Friday** *office assistant* 69.6, *deputy* 80.1, *clerical worker* 123.5, *helper* 275.5, 825.12
girlfriend 33.4; *friend* 62.2, *loved one* 299.13, *partner* 794.9
girlhood *youth* 26.1
girlie show [Inf] *show* 138.4
girlish *young* 26.11, *female* 33.16
girlish figure *thinness* 595.1
girlishly *youthfully* 26.14
girlishness *youthfulness* 26.2, *femaleness* 33.2
girl-like *young* 26.11
girl next door *average person* 742.4, *everyone* 778.7
girls, the *womenfolk* 33.14
girth *riding equipment* 159.9, *size* 579.1, *band* 754.9
GI's [Inf] *defecation* 25.3
gismo [Inf] *tool* 103.1, *instrument* 511.2
gist 329.4, 799.4; *summary* 204.1, *topic* 328.1, *meaning* 361.1, *intention* 374.1, *substance* 577.2, *core* 612.2, *essential content* 723.2
git! [Inf] *go!* 709.30
gittern Musical Instruments 142
givable *given* 478.25
give 472.10, 498.11; *provision* 89.9, *philanthropize* 307.8, *pay* 453.15, *own property* 470.11, *defray* 489.18, *donate* 491.13, *perform* 522.16, *softness* 543.1, *yield* 543.17, *elasticity* 546.1, *be elastic* 546.7, *grant* 735.30
give a big hand *acclaim* 437.18
give a blank check to *be permissive* 502.7
giveable *transferring property* 470.10
give a bonus *be grateful* 310.6
give a boost to *intensify* 746.8
give a bouquet or **posy** *compliment* 437.17
give a break *refresh* 94.6

give (someone) a break [Inf] *show pity* 308.8
give a breather [Inf] *refresh* 94.6
give a Bronx cheer *disdain* 400.16, *complain* 507.8
give a catcall *complain* 507.8
give access to *be hospitable* 477.21, *admit* 708.12
give a chance to *make possible* 836.7
give a cold reception to *exclude* 383.11
give a commission *join the army* 76.31
give a concession *discount* 495.4
give a cool welcome to *exclude* 383.11
give a deserved reward *reward* 453.13
give a direction *command* 425.10
give a dishonorable discharge to *terminate* 834.7
give admittance or **entrance to** *admit* 708.12
give a dressing-down *punish* 454.22
give a drubbing *defeat* 845.17
give advice *advise* 176.9
give a face-lift *decorate* 532.11, *beautify* 807.20, *refurbish* 809.11
give a false alarm *give warning* 814.10
give a false depiction or **impression** *misrepresent* 366.5
give a false idea *misrepresent* 366.5
give a false impression *be untruthful* 192.20
give a false reading *distort the truth* 627.12
give a firm date *promise* 458.11
give a flawless performance *be perfect* 805.20
give a free hand *set free* 829.17
give a gift *give* 472.10
give a good hiding [Inf] *beat* 695.12
give a good reason *justify* 441.12
give a good word to *compliment* 437.17
give a gratuity *tip* 472.14
give a guided tour *display* 843.13
give a hand *help* 825.23
give a hand or **big hand** *be grateful* 310.6
give a hand signal *signal* 183.18
give a hearing *hear* 228.13
give a helping hand *philanthropize* 307.8
give a hero's welcome *greet* 410.11
give a hiding [Inf] *hit* 454.28
give a job to *employ* 57.18
give a lead *motivate* 508.9
give a leg up *promote* 715.13, *improve* 825.26
give a lesson *punish* 454.22
give a lethal injection *execute* 30.22, 454.30
give a lick and a promise *be neglectful* 326.7, *not complete* 762.9
give a lift *promote* 715.13
give allegiance to *obey* 426.7
give alms *philanthropize* 307.8, *give to charity* 472.16
give a long-term loan *lend* 475.6
give a look *gesture* 183.17
give a low rating *disapprove* 438.16
give a mandate *command* 425.10, *authorize* 833.10
give a miss *shy* 386.17

give an account of *report* 171.9
give an advantage *be convenient* 803.5
give a name to *identify* 184.11
give an assist *help* 825.23
give and go *ice hockey tactics* 158.4
give-and-go *play ice hockey* 158.9
give and take *mediation* 75.1, *retaliate* 420.4, *fight* 422.9, 422.23, *compromise* 461.7, *moderation* 521.1, *swing* 671.4, 671.12, *exchange* 673.5, *reciprocity* 729.1, *reciprocate* 729.7, 827.13, *mutual relationship* 827.3
give an edge to *invigorate* 518.5
give an encore *iterate* 797.16
give an equivalent *exchange* 673.5
give a new lease on life *make new* 652.20, *revive* 809.14
give an example *interpret* 365.12
give an order *command* 425.10
give an outline of *summarize* 204.7
give a party *be sociable* 408.14
give a password *sign* 183.19
give a piece of one's mind [Inf] *condemn* 438.18
give a pill *medicate* 115.18
give approval to *confirm* 189.25
give a present *give* 472.10
give a prize *reward* 453.13, *give* 472.10
give a promise *promise* 458.11
give a quid pro quo *retaliate* 420.4
give a raspberry [Inf] *complain* 507.8
give a rebel yell *be insubordinate* 416.8
give a receipt *receive* 473.13
give a reference for *recommend* 437.19
give a referral *authorize* 52.14
give a report *report* 171.9
give a reward *reward* 453.13
give a rough idea *be unfinished* 544.12
give a ruling *have authority over* 425.12
give a scholarship *grant* 453.14
give a second or **last chance to show pity** 308.8
give a sense of security *secure* 464.9
give a sense to *interpret* 365.12
give as good as one gets *fight* 422.23, *exchange* 673.5
give as good as one got *retaliate* 420.4
give a short-term loan *lend* 475.6
give a shot *medicate* 115.18
give a shot in the arm *invigorate* 28.22
give a sop to Cerberus *bribe* 178.18
give a spin to [Inf] *interpret news* 365.17
give assent to *confirm* 189.25
give assistance *help* 825.23
give assurances *assure* 810.23
give a standing ovation *acclaim* 437.18
give a start *start* 696.20
give a subordinate role to *subject* 832.10
give a sworn statement *attest* 189.22

give asylum to *be hospitable* 477.21
give a talk *address* 209.8
give a talking-to *condemn* 438.18
give a ticket or **pass to** *admit* 708.12
give a tongue lashing *berate* 438.20
give a true portrayal *seem true* 721.26
give a true report *be literal* 721.25
give attention to *observe* 465.4
give a verbatim account *be literal* 721.25
give a warm reception to *retaliate* 419.30
giveaway 472.5; *newspaper* 175.2, *divulgence* 180.2, *gainful* 467.10, *windfall* 467.7, *given* 472.8, *bargain* 497.10, *free of charge* 497.12, *absence of charge* 497.6, *extra* 748.6
give away *join in marriage* 64.20, *tell on* 180.10, *give* 472.10, *make cheap* 497.14, *be generous* 498.10, *reveal* 843.14
give a wide berth *be safe* 810.20
give a wide berth to *avoid* 386.13, *keep away* 585.9
give a word in the ear *warn* 814.8
give a word of warning *warn* 814.8
give a word to the wise *communicate* 176.10, *warn* 814.8
give a written guarantee *guarantee* 438.13
give back 478.5; *restore* 671.10, 809.12
give back one's position *give back* 478.5
give battle *battle* 76.33, *declare war* 422.25
give birth 35.33; *have young* 21.16, *procreate* 22.14, *produce* 771.34
give birth to 28.19; *bring into existence* 522.14, *be new* 652.17
give blow for blow *exchange* 673.5
give by will *will* 472.11
give carte blanche to *be permissive* 502.7
give chapter and verse *circumstantiate* 726.12
give chase *chase* 385.13
give constructive criticism *criticize* 365.15
give counsel *advise* 176.9
give courage 284.16
give credit *lend* 475.6, *credit* 487.10
give credit to *be grateful* 310.6
give credit where credit is due *recognize* 487.13
give criticism *criticize* 365.15
give delivery *transfer property* 470.12
give details of *particularize* 779.17
give diplomatic immunity *set free* 829.17
give directions *direct* 697.13
give dispensation *permit* 502.6
give ear *hear* 228.13
give enlightenment *interpret* 365.12
give evidence 339.12; *testify* 336.10
give evidence of *signify* 183.16
give false evidence *accuse falsely* 442.9
give false information *misinform* 188.7

give feedback *reply* 671.13
give final notice *demand* 425.11
give financial reward *reward* 453.13
give financial support *be charitable* 305.12
give first aid *treat* 115.17
give fitting retribution *avenge* 441.14
give food and drink *refresh* 94.6
give forgiveness *forgive* 312.8
give formal sanction *approve* 437.14
give free *give* 472.10
give freely *be charitable* 305.12, *give to charity* 472.16, *be generous* 498.10
give free rein *liberate* 831.6
give free rein to *set free* 829.17
give generously *be unselfish* 443.7, *give to charity* 472.16, *be generous* 498.10
give ground *retreat* 680.17
give hard knocks *fight* 422.23
give head [Inf] *stimulate* 20.22
give heart to *invigorate* 518.5
give his *or* her comeuppance [Inf] *exact retribution* 454.27
give hope *predict* 358.14
give impetus to *impel* 695.9
give in *assent* 346.6, *withdraw* 392.5, *submit* 421.4, *yield* 543.17, *stop* 668.10
give in exchange *substitute* 672.5, *exchange* 673.5, *reciprocate* 729.7
give in marriage *join in marriage* 64.20
give in return *exchange* 673.5
give insight *interpret* 365.12
give instances *explain* 331.16
give in to *follow* 745.12
give it a go *experiment* 335.11
give it a try *contend* 422.22
give it a try *or* go *or* whirl *attempt* 390.4
give it one's all *try hard* 390.7
give it one's best shot *try hard* 390.7
give it the gun [Inf] *be full of vigor* 518.4
give it to someone straight *talk straight* 630.15
give it up! *cease!* 668.14
give it your best shot! *here goes!* 390.11
give job satisfaction *reward* 453.13
give laws *legislate* 53.31
give leave *approve* 437.14
give life to *propagate* 21.15, *give birth to* 28.19
give light *light* 246.19
give money *donate* 491.13
give moral support 605.18
given 6.74, 472.8; *supplied* 89.7, *supposed* 359.6, *habituated* 397.14, *receiving* 473.9, *free of charge* 497.12, *circumstantial* 726.8, *certain* 840.7
given a bad press *criticized* 438.14
given a blessing *approved* 437.8
given away *given* 472.8, *free of charge* 497.12
given consideration 423.4
give new life to *support* 825.24
given free *free of charge* 497.12
given leave *approved* 437.8
given name *name* 202.8
given new life 28.15
give no clue *be unexplained* 364.15
give no credit *be ungrateful* 311.5
give no quarter *slaughter* 30.21, *have no mercy* 309.6, *be severe* 424.8

give nothing away *keep secret* 182.11
give notice *communicate* 176.10, *caution* 287.15, *predict* 358.14, *warn* 814.8, *resign* 835.5
give no trouble *be easy* 823.14
given out *dispersed* 776.6
given permission *given consideration* 423.4
given that *under the circumstances* 726.16
given the bum's rush [Inf] *rejected* 383.6
given the heave-ho [Inf] *rejected* 383.6
given the red light *refused* 506.5
given the rough edge of one's tongue *criticized* 438.14
given the third degree *questioned* 333.15
given the thumbs down *refused* 506.5
given to drink *drunken* 121.28
given up *relinquished* 392.2
give occasion for *cause* 675.8
give off 556.25; *secrete* 24.7, *excrete* 25.20
give one a hard *or* bad time *cause difficulties* 824.22
give one a knuckle sandwich [Inf] *fight* 422.23
give one a loan *lend* 475.6
give one a refill *provide drink* 93.21
give one a run for one's money *elude* 816.10
give one's all *exert oneself* 122.11
give one's best regards *or* best wishes *be courteous* 410.9
give one's blessing *be benevolent* 305.10, *approve* 437.14, *permit* 502.6, *consent* 735.28
give one's blessing to *agree with* 462.10
give oneself airs *be vain* 402.14, *put on airs* 404.27
give oneself a pat on the back *be vain* 402.14
give oneself up *capitulate* 421.6
give one's IOU *guarantee* 458.13, *contract* 462.11, *promise* 464.10, *borrow* 476.10
give one's money back *compensate* 478.6
give one's word *promise* 458.11, 464.10
give one's (solemn) word *or* oath *vow* 189.23
give one's word of honor *vow* 189.23
give one the benefit of the doubt *show mercy* 312.11
give one the giggles *make someone laugh* 368.7
give one the slip *evade* 386.19, *elude* 816.10
give one trouble *be difficult* 824.16
give one what for *berate* 438.20, *exact retribution* 454.27
give or take *nearly* 586.18
give out 472.12; *divulge* 180.9, *fatigue* 820.6
give out *or* off *let out* 709.26
give over *give* 472.10
give over! *cease!* 668.14
give peace to *pacify* 74.9
give permission *authorize* 52.14, 833.10, *agree with* 462.10, *permit* 502.6
give personal recognizance *promise* 464.10
give personal reward *reward* 453.13

give place *retreat* 680.17
give pleasure 214.13; *make pleasant* 271.10
give points to *be unequal* 741.7
give power *empower* 514.20
give praise to 472.13
give priority 769.15
give quarter *show pity* 308.8, *be lenient* 423.5
giver 472.7; *provisioner* 89.4
give recognition *recognize* 487.13
give refuge to 708.15
give rein to one's imagination *imagine* 360.14
give relief *philanthropize* 307.8
give relief to *support* 825.24
give respects *defer to* 410.12
give respite *show pity* 308.8
give responsibility *commission* 833.8
give rise to *cause* 675.8
give sanctuary to *be hospitable* 477.21, *give refuge to* 708.15
give satisfaction *atone* 313.7, *fight* 422.23, *put right* 429.14, *offer reparation* 504.15
give scope *make easy* 823.15, *set free* 829.17
give security *certify* 464.11
give shelter to *be hospitable* 477.21
give someone a bad time *inflict pain* 215.10
give someone a black *or* dirty look 242.21
give someone a buzz *or* tinkle *or* jingle [Inf] *telephone* 169.20
give someone a call *telephone* 169.20
give someone a chance *be permissive* 502.7
give someone a free hand *be permissive* 502.7
give someone a fright *frighten* 283.17, *surprise* 292.9
give someone a good send-off *part* 705.13
give someone an inferiority complex *arouse jealousy* 314.10
give someone a secret sign *sign* 183.19
give someone carte blanche *or a blank check* *set free* 829.17
give someone his *or* her head *be permissive* 502.7, *set free* 829.17
give someone his *or* her walking papers *or* marching orders [Inf] *relegate* 574.18, *eject* 701.8, *dismiss* 709.15, *terminate* 834.7
give someone his money's worth *make cheap* 497.14
give someone leeway *set free* 829.17
give someone lip [Inf] *be discourteous* 411.7
give someone some lip [Inf] *defy* 416.7
give someone the ax [Inf] *terminate* 834.7
give someone the bird [Inf] *repel* 701.7
give someone the blues *make sullen* 304.13
give someone the boot [Inf] *eject* 701.8
give someone the (glad *or* evil) eye [Inf] *look* 242.21
give someone the finger [Inf] *complain* 507.8
give someone the golden handshake *terminate* 834.7
give someone the heave-ho [Inf] *terminate* 834.7

give someone *or* something the once-over [Inf] *inspect* 242.22
give someone the slip *lose someone* 468.20, *quit* 705.10
give strength to *strengthen* 516.15
give stripes *hit* 454.28
give strokes *hit* 454.28
give suck *feed* 90.41, *provide drink* 93.21
give support *advise* 825.27
give supportive evidence *justify* 441.12
give sworn testimony *attest* 189.22
give temporarily *lend* 475.6
give terms *conciliate* 74.10
give thanks 310.7; *worship* 83.15, *follow rites* 85.19
give the alarm *give warning* 814.10
give the appearance of truth *seem true* 721.26
give the ax to [Inf] *dismiss* 709.15
give the battle cry *be insubordinate* 416.8
give the benefit of the doubt *acquit* 54.32
give the bird [Inf] *complain* 507.8
give the bum's rush [Inf] *expel* 709.14
give the bum's rush to [Inf] *exclude* 383.11
give the cold shoulder *insult* 436.21, *ostracize* 709.17
give the devil his due *be right* 429.12
give the elbow *relegate* 574.18, *eject* 764.8
give the evil eye to *curse* 301.13
give the freedom of *set free* 829.17
give the game away [Inf] *tell on* 180.10
give the go-ahead *approve* 437.14, *permit* 502.6, 735.29
give the go-by [Inf] *shun* 386.14, *insult* 436.21
give the green light *assent* 346.6, *approve* 437.14, *vindicate* 441.11, *agree with* 462.10, *permit* 502.6, 735.29
give the heave-ho [Inf] *discard* 383.12, *relegate* 574.18, *expel* 709.14, *eject* 764.8
give the impression *appear outwardly* 610.14
give the kiss of life *treat* 115.17
give the lie to *negate* 190.16
give the nod to [Inf] *agree with* 462.10, *permit* 502.6, 735.29
give the OK *or* O.K. *or* okay *assent* 346.6, *approve* 437.14, *vindicate* 441.11, *agree with* 462.10, *permit* 502.6, 735.29
give the red light *refuse* 347.9, 506.8, *withhold approval* 438.17, *veto* 503.9
give the rough edge of one's tongue *berate* 438.20
give the run of *set free* 829.17
give the sack [Inf] *dismiss* 709.15
give the seal of approval to *give moral support* 605.18
give the silent treatment *ostracize* 709.17
give the stamp *or* seal *or* nod of approval *approve* 437.14
give the third degree *torture* 454.29
give the true story *be truthful* 191.7, *be literal* 721.25
give the works [Inf] *torture* 454.29

give the wrong answer *be wrong* 430.18

give the wrong idea *or* **impression** *delude* 720.16

give three cheers *cheer* 239.15, *be grateful* 310.6, *acclaim* 437.18

give thumbs down *refuse* 347.9, 506.8, *withhold approval* 438.17, *veto* 503.9

give thumbs up *assent* 346.6, *approve* 437.14, *agree with* 462.10, *permit* 502.6, 735.29

give tidings of *report* 171.9

give tit for tat *retaliate* 489.23, *exchange* 673.5, *reciprocate* 729.7

give to *commission* 833.8

give to charity 472.16; *donate* 491.13

give to eat *feed* 90.41

give tongue *make an animal sound* 240.7

give trouble *cause trouble* 824.21

give two cheers *disparage* 195.15

give umbrage *offend* 302.15

give undivided attention to *take note of* 323.10

give up *secrete* 24.7, *be persuaded* 178.20, *be hopeless* 282.11, *be ignorant* 349.8, *discard* 383.12, *relinquish* 392.3, *withdraw* 392.5, *stop using* 394.10, *disaccustom* 398.6, *capitulate* 421.6, *be self-restrained* 455.10, *give out* 472.12, *stop* 668.10, *not complete* 762.9, *exclude* 764.7, *discontinue* 775.10, *resign* 835.5

give up alcohol 120.6

give up arms *be moderate* 521.6

give up drinking *give up alcohol* 120.6

give up eating *fast* 118.8

give up hope *be hopeless* 282.11

give up one's friends *be unsocial* 409.10

give up one's social life *be unsocial* 409.10

give up the crown *resign* 835.5

give up the ghost *die* 29.17, 773.21

give up work *have leisure time* 125.5

give utterance to *speak* 205.17

give vent to *divulge* 180.9, *let out* 709.26

give vows *assure* 810.23

give warning 814.10; *predict* 358.14

give way *capitulate* 421.6, *be weak* 517.12, *yield* 543.17, *be brittle* 548.4, *retreat* 680.17, *droop* 714.14

give weight to *make important* 799.14

give what is coming to him *or* **her** *exact retribution* 454.27

give what is due *pay* 453.15

give with both hands *be generous* 498.10

give written authority *authorize* 833.10

giving 453.12, 472.1, 472.9; *charitable* 305.9, *lending* 475.1, *donation* 491.6, *generous* 498.6, *pliant* 543.7, *elastic* 546.5

giving away *signifying* 183.11

giving back 478.1; *restoration* 671.2, 809.2

giving credit *thanking* 310.5, *lending* 475.1

giving in *submission* 421.1

giving light *lightening* 246.3

giving notice *resignation* 835.1

giving out *dispersion* 776.1

giving temporarily *lending* 475.1

giving up *relinquishment* 392.1

giving up the fort *submission* 421.1

giving way *submission* 421.1

gizzard *avian characteristic* 36.6

glabrous *or* **glabrate** *smooth* 545.4, *bald* 614.16

glacé *lustrous* 246.15, *polished* 545.7, *smooth* 545.10

glacé fruit *sweetener* 222.2

glacial *glaciated* 8.62, *cold* 218.9, *primal* 653.14

glacial advance *glaciation* 8.46

glacial budget *glaciation* 8.46

glacial deposit *sediment* 8.29

glacial ice *erosion* 8.41

glacial lake *lake* 568.1

glacial maximum *glaciation* 8.46

glacial period *glaciation* 8.46, *geological past* 651.5

glacial recession *or* **retreat** *glaciation* 8.46

glacial surge *glaciation* 8.46

glacial valley *landform* 8.9

glaciate *make cold* 218.15, *be dense* 540.8, *solidify* 542.10

glaciated 8.62

glaciation 8.46; *climatic change* 9.37, *concentration* 540.2, *hardening* 542.2

glacier 8.44; *rock face* 161.6, *ice* 218.5

glacier flour *glacier* 8.44

glacier milk *glacier* 8.44

glaciological *geologic* 8.50

glaciologist *geologist* 8.4

glaciology *geology* 8.1

glacis *fort* 419.13

glad *joyful* 269.6

gladden *give pleasure* 214.13, *cause joy* 269.11

glade *trees* 43.4, *geographical space* 563.3, *open space* 583.6

glad eye [Inf] *look* 242.7

glad-hand [Inf] *welcome* 408.18

gladiator *fighter* 422.14

gladiatorial *military* 58.10, *contentious* 422.20

gladiatorial combat *slaughter* 30.5, *duel* 422.12

gladiolus *or* **gladiola** *Flowers* 42

gladly *joyfully* 269.13, *willingly* 373.15

gladness *joy* 269.1

glad rags [Inf] *finery* 100.6

gladsome *joyful* 269.6

Gladstone bag *baggage* 578.8

glad tidings *news* 171.1

glair *paste* 561.4

glaive [Arch] *sharp weapon* 78.6

glamorize *beautify* 530.14

glamorous *beautiful* 529.7, *fashionable* 536.5

glamorously *dressily* 100.47, *beautifully* 529.13, 530.16, *fashionably* 536.9

glamour *spell* 86.8, *beauty* 529.1

glamour girl *attractive female* 529.5

glance *gesture* 183.5, 183.17, *look* 242.7, 242.21, *light up* 246.20, *meet* 586.15, *divert* 698.16, *change direction* 703.15

glancing *gestural* 183.13, *contiguous* 216.8, *meeting* 586.16

glancing light *variegated thing* 263.5

glancingly *watchfully* 242.29

gland *internal organ* 19.13, *secretory mechanism* 24.3

glanders *animal disease* 34.10

glandular *secretory* 24.4, *of a secretion* 24.5

glandular fever *infection* 114.7

glandularly 24.8

glandulous *of a secretion* 24.5

glandulously *glandularly* 24.8

glans penis *organs of reproduction* 21.9

glare *shine* 9.56, *look* 242.7, 242.21, *quality of light* 246.2, *light up* 246.20, *be serious* 278.7, *be angry* 302.19, *sign of irascibility* 303.6, *frown* 303.15, *sign of irritability* 304.4, *be irritable* 304.14, *show of disapproval* 438.6

glaring *publicized* 173.14, *seeing* 242.17, *clear* 244.6, *bright* 246.14, *gaudy* 251.12, *frowning* 304.10, *strong to the senses* 516.12, *accentuated* 843.11

glaring error *blunder* 351.9

glaring lights Phobias 283

glaringly *frowningly* 304.18

Glasgow *major British cities* 567.7

Glasgow school Western Art Styles 133

glasnost [Russ] *openness* 180.3

glass 249.5; *weather instrument* 9.7, *crystal* 11.14, *size of drink* 93.3, *drink container* 93.13, *building materials* 104.2, *ceramics* 129.1, *industrial ceramics* 129.6, *make ceramics* 129.10, *window* 134.10, *reflector* 242.10, *transparent thing* 249.4, Phobias 283, *weak thing* 517.5, *brittle thing* 548.2, *drinking vessel* 578.13

glassblower *artisan* 123.13, *ceramist* 129.7

glassblowing *ceramic process* 129.5

glass electrode *electrochemistry* 11.19

glass engraving Hobbies and Pastimes 167

glasses *optical element* 10.20, *visual aid* 242.14, *aid for poor sight* 243.5, *transparent thing* 249.4

glass eye *substitute* 672.2

glass fiber *industrial ceramics* 129.6

glass(ful) *container(ful)* 738.2

glassful *size of drink* 93.3

glass harmonica Musical Instruments 142

glasshouse [Brit] *nursery* 17.4

glasshouse [Brit inf] *the inside* 55.2

glassiness *quality of light* 246.2, *transparency* 249.1, *smoothness* 545.1

glasslike *transparent* 249.7

glassmaking *craft* 133.2

glass-reinforced plastic (GRP) board *sailboard parts* 150.20

glass sculpture *sculpture* 144.1

glass snake *lizard* 37.5

glassware *tableware* 92.13, Ceramics 129, *glass* 249.5, *crockery* 578.16

glassworker *ceramist* 129.7

glassworking *ceramic process* 129.5

glassy *types of igneous texture* 8.33, *lustrous* 246.15, *transparent* 249.7, *drained of color* 252.6, *hard* 542.5, *polished* 545.7

glaucoma *tropical disease* 114.10, *blindness* 243.3

glaucomatous *blind* 243.11

glaucous *green* 260.7

glaze 129.3, 246.22; *frost* 9.25, *ice* 218.5, *sweeten* 222.7, *make dim* 248.8, *coloring agent* 251.5, *polish* 545.3, *smooth* 545.10, *paste* 561.4, *coating* 613.8, *coat* 613.28

glazed *ceramic* 129.9, *frozen* 218.10, *sweet* 222.5, *polished* 545.7, *covered* 613.19

glazed ware Ceramics 129

glaze-fire *make ceramics* 129.10

glaze firing *ceramic process* 129.5

glaze frost *frost* 9.25

glaze kiln *ceramic workshop and tools* 129.8

glaze over *be dim* 248.7

glazer *ceramist* 129.7

glazing *ceramic process* 129.5

gleam *quality of light* 246.2, *light up* 246.20

gleaming *lustrous* 246.15, *polished* 545.7

gleamingly *lightly* 246.23

glean *farm* 16.19, Collective Names 59, *store* 105.17, *choose* 382.14, *acquire* 467.19, *draw out* 711.17

gleaner *collector* 59.17, *cleaner* 111.12, *gainer* 467.9

gleaning *acquisition* 467.4

gleanings *chosen thing* 382.8, *earnings* 467.5, *yield* 467.8, *takings* 477.8, *stolen goods* 479.4

glee *song* 140.11, *gaiety* 269.3

glee club *singing group* 141.6

gleeful *cheerful* 269.7

gleefully *cheerfully* 269.14

gleefulness *gaiety* 269.3

gleet *pus* 25.7, *body fluid* 555.3

glen *valley* 572.8, *concave land* 635.2

glengarry *cap* 100.33

glib *talkative* 207.5, *deferential* 410.8, *smooth-mannered* 545.9, *easy* 823.9

glibly *talkatively* 207.9, *deferentially* 410.15, *suavely* 545.15

glibness *talkativeness* 207.1, *deference* 410.4, *simplicity* 823.2

glib talk *empty talk* 362.5

glib tongue *cunning person* 822.3

glide *mass movement* 8.28, *fencing movements* 153.3, *fence* 153.7, *swim* 164.14, *conceal oneself* 181.15, *not act* 413.11, *be light* 539.8, *go smoothly* 545.11, *flow* 570.10, *fly* 689.13, *fall* 714.4, *slide* 714.17, *go easily* 823.18

glide path *flight* 689.5

glide plane *operation of symmetry* 626.2

glider *aircraft* 689.3

glide reflection *transformation* 6.46

glider pilot *aircraft personnel* 689.8

gliding Sporting Activities 145, *aviation* 689.1, *flying* 689.11, *falling* 714.11

glimmer *shine* 9.56, *light up* 246.20

glimmering *lucent* 246.13

glimmer of hope *hope* 281.1

glimpse *look* 242.7, *see* 242.20, *discovery* 345.1, *discover* 345.11

glint *quality of light* 246.2, *light up* 246.20

glinting *bright* 246.14

glissade *mountaineer* 161.10, *fall* 714.4, *slide* 714.17

glissading *climbing techniques* 161.3

glissando Musical Terms and Expression Marks 140

glisten *light up* 246.20

glistening *quality of light* 246.2, *lustrous* 246.15

glister *quality of light* 246.2

glitch [Inf] *technical problem* 826.3

glitter *quality of light* 246.2, *light up* 246.20, *flashiness* 404.4, *put on a show* 404.28

glitterati *the rich* 485.7, *fashionable elite* 536.4

glittering *bright* 246.14, *flashy* 404.17, *opulent* 485.10

glitteringly *flashily* 404.32
glittery *bright* 246.14
glitz [Inf] *vulgarity* 535.1
glitzily [Inf] *grandly* 404.37
glitzy [Inf] *clear* 244.6, *grand* 404.22, *opulent* 485.10, *vulgar* 535.6
gloaming *dimness* 248.1, *evening* 656.2
gloating *malice* 306.2, *cruel* 306.10
glob *mass* 579.7
global *terrestrial* 8.52, *extensive* 563.12, *whole* 759.6, *including* 763.3, *universal* 778.10
global approach *inclusion* 763.1
globalism *generality* 778.1
globality *generality* 778.1
globalize *generalize* 778.14
globally *extensively* 563.18, *inclusively* 763.8, *universally* 778.23
global outlook *internationalism* 566.5
global war *world war* 76.2
global warming *climatic change* 9.37, *hot weather* 217.6
globe *Earth* 8.6, *map* 187.5, *round thing* 633.3, *whole thing* 759.2
globeflower Flowers 42
globe thistle Flowers 42
globose *round* 633.7
globosely *roundly* 633.11
globosity *roundness* 633.1
globous *round* 633.7
globular *round* 633.7
globular cloud *cloud appearance* 9.19
globular cluster *star* 7.8
globularity *roundness* 633.1
globularly *roundly* 633.11
globular protein *protein* 12.9
globule *round thing* 633.3
globulin *protein* 12.9, *blood* 555.4
glockenspiel Musical Instruments 142
glomerate *cumulate* 59.20
Glomma Rivers 570
glom onto [Inf] *gain* 467.15
gloom *darkness* 247.1, *depression* 270.2, *seriousness* 278.1, *lack of hope* 282.2
gloom and doom *lack of hope* 282.2, *adversity* 848.1
gloomily *darkly* 247.11, *blackly* 254.12, *grayly* 255.10, *bluely* 261.11, *sorrowfully* 270.10, *unhopefully* 282.14, *sullenly* 304.16, *dismally* 304.19
gloominess *darkness* 247.1, *dullness* 255.5, *depression* 270.2, *lack of hope* 282.2, *sullenness* 304.1, *overcast* 304.6
gloomy *cloudy* 9.44, *dark* 247.5, *dimmed* 248.6, *sad* 254.10, *dull* 255.8, *depressed* 261.7, 270.5, *without hope* 282.7, *sullen* 304.8, *overcast* 304.11, *adverse* 848.10
gloomy places Phobias 283
glop [Inf] *mud* 561.8
Gloria *Eucharist* 85.7
Gloria *or* **Gloria Patri** *prayer* 85.10
Gloria in excelsis *prayer* 85.10
glorification *deification* 82.13, *worship* 83.1, *praise* 437.3, *intensification* 746.2
glorified *deified* 82.20, *worshiped* 83.14, *ritualistic* 85.15
glorify *deify* 82.23, *worship* 83.15, *publicize* 173.18, *praise* 435.15, 437.16, *exalt* 596.19, *intensify* 746.8, *make important* 799.14
glorifying *worshipful* 83.12
gloriole *highlight* 246.12

glorious *ritualistic* 85.15, *rejoicing* 279.4, *grand* 404.22, *beautiful* 529.7
Glorious Koran, the *Islamic text* 81.18
gloriously *grandly* 404.37
gloriously drunk *drunk* 121.25
gloriousness *beauty* 529.1
glory *applause* 279.2, *rejoice* 279.5, *grandeur* 404.10, *praise* 437.3, *prosperity* 847.1
glory hole *room* 60.9
glory of war 76.17
glory to God in the highest! *hallelujah!* 83.18
gloss *word book* 5.27, *dissertation* 203.1, *dissertate* 203.5, *quality of light* 246.2, *practice sophistry* 330.11, *annotation* 365.2, *annotate* 365.14, *polish* 545.3, *smooth* 545.10, *make easy* 823.15
glossarial *worded* 5.38, *dissertational* 203.4, *annotative* 365.10, *of a list* 785.10
glossarially *lexically* 5.46, *inventorially* 785.13
glossarist *dissertator* 203.3, *interpreter* 365.6
glossary *word book* 5.27, *book part* 174.5, *division* 577.6, *book of lists* 785.3
glossator *interpreter* 365.6
glossed *interpreted* 365.9
glossematics Linguistic Studies 5
gloss finish *darkroom equipment* 132.21
glossiness *smoothness* 545.1
glossolalia *nonstandard language* 5.7, *religiousness* 81.2, *occult and psychic phenomena* 86.7, *power of speech* 205.5
glossological [Arch] *linguistic* 5.34
glossology [Arch] *linguistics* 5.1
glossophobia Phobias 283
gloss over *conceal* 181.12
glossy *portrait* 132.5, *lustrous* 246.15, *polished* 545.7
glossy magazine *magazine* 175.3
glossy paper *paper* 104.5
glottal stop *spoken letter* 5.15
glottis *throat* 19.12, *speech organ* 205.4
glottochronology Linguistic Studies 5
Gloucester Old Spots Breeds of Pigs 16
glove *accessory* 100.28, *clothe* 100.43
gloved *dressed* 100.38
glove puppet *figure* 187.4
gloves *hockey clothing* 158.6, *ski equipment* 162.10, *soccer uniform* 163.3, *protective clothing* 419.6
glow *sweat* 25.24, *emphasis* 200.1, *emphasize* 200.6, *fire* 217.8, 246.9, *heat* 217.17, *quality of light* 246.2, *light up* 246.20, *face color* 251.9, *redness* 257.1, *redden* 257.9, *appeal* 529.4, *be beautiful* 529.11
glower *look* 242.7, 242.21, *be serious* 278.7, *be angry* 302.19, *sign of irascibility* 303.6, *frown* 303.15, *sign of irritability* 304.4, *be irritable* 304.14
glowering *frowning* 303.12, 304.10, *overcast* 304.11
gloweringly *frowningly* 304.18
glowing *sweaty* 25.17, *healthy* 113.4, *emphatic* 200.3, *hot* 217.11, *lucent* 246.13, *colorful* 251.11, *red-faced* 257.6
glowing health *health* 113.1

glowingly *lightly* 246.23, *gorgeously* 529.14
glowing terms *bombast* 194.4, *compliment* 437.4
glow lamp *electron tube* 14.40
glowworm *worm* 39.14, *larva* 40.9, *flickering light* 246.10
gloxinia Flowers 42
glucagon Human Hormones 12
glucocorticoid *hormone* 12.16
gluconeogenesis *bioenergetics* 12.23
gluconeogenic *biochemical* 12.25
glucose Common Sugars 12, *food content* 90.3
glucoside *saccharide* 12.4
glue *retainer* 471.3, *retain* 471.7, *adhesive* 561.3, 755.3, *stick* 561.20, *intertwine* 752.19, *connect* 754.13, *cause to adhere* 755.10
glued *retained* 471.6, *tied* 752.13, *connected* 754.11, *adhering* 755.7
glue-laminated (glulam) lumber *construction material* 14.21
gluelike *retentive* 471.5, *mucilaginous* 561.15
glue onto *add* 748.11
glue sniffing *drug use* 121.9
glue together *add* 748.11, *repair* 809.10
gluey *retentive* 471.5, *mucilaginous* 561.15, *adhesive* 755.5
glueyness *viscosity* 561.1
glum *depressed* 261.7, 270.5, *serious* 278.4, *sullen* 304.8
glume *grass plant* 45.3
glumly *sorrowfully* 270.10, *solemnly* 278.9, *sullenly* 304.16
glumness *depression* 270.2, *sullenness* 304.1
glut *fertility* 22.1, *excess* 99.1, *overindulge* 99.10, *be greedy* 119.4, *bore* 296.8, *surplus* 750.4
glutamic acid Amino Acids 12
glutamine Amino Acids 12
gluteal *back* 622.6
gluten *protein* 12.9, *adhesive* 561.3, *paste* 561.4
glutenous *viscous* 561.14
gluteus maximus *rear end* 622.4
glutinosity *viscosity* 561.1
glutinous *mucilaginous* 561.15
glutinousness *viscosity* 561.1
glut oneself *be greedy* 119.4
glut the market *make cheap* 497.14
glutting *gluttonous* 119.3
glutton 119.2; *eater* 92.15, *desirer* 288.9, *self-indulgent person* 456.5
glutton for work *or* **punishment** *hard worker* 414.11
gluttonize *eat well* 92.23, *be greedy* 119.4
gluttonizing *gluttonous* 119.3
gluttonous 119.3; *eating* 92.18, *covetous* 288.14, *impious* 448.11, *overindulgent* 456.8
gluttonously 119.5; *carnivorously* 92.27, *covetously* 288.28
gluttony 119.1; *appetite* 92.2, *immoderation* 99.2, *iniquity* 448.3, *overindulgence* 456.3
glycan *polysaccharide* 12.5
glyceride *fat* 12.7
glycerin *or* **glycerine** *lubricant* 562.7
glycerinate *lubricate* 562.15
glycerol *sweetener* 222.2, *oil* 562.3
glycerophosphatide *fat* 12.7
glycine Amino Acids 12
glycogen *carbohydrate* 12.3, *polysaccharide* 12.5
glycolipid *fat* 12.7

glycolysis *bioenergetics* 12.23, *respiration* 12.24, *cell biology* 13.14
glycolytic *biochemical* 12.25
glycoprotein *protein* 12.9
glycosaminoglycan (GAG) *polysaccharide* 12.5
glycoside *saccharide* 12.4
glyph *relief carving* 144.2
glyptic *sculptural* 144.7
glyptics *engraving* 144.3
glyptography *engraving* 144.3
gnarl *tree part* 43.2, *make rough* 544.11, *coarsen* 552.12
gnarled *treelike* 43.10, *condensed* 540.7, *coarse* 544.6
gnarly *coarse* 544.6
gnash *chew* 92.22
gnashing *eating* 92.1, *violent* 520.5
gnashing one's teeth *burst of anger* 302.6
gnash one's teeth *gesture* 183.17, *vent one's anger* 302.21
gnat *insect* 40.1
gnaw *chew* 92.22, *be painful* 215.9, *abrade* 554.13, *take apart* 753.16, *eat away* 808.19
gnaw at the roots *eat away* 808.19
gnaw away *abrade* 554.13
gnawing *rodentlike* 35.28, *painful* 215.4, *frictional* 554.10
gnawing mammal 35.13
gneissic *chalky* 8.59
gneissic banding *metamorphic rock* 8.36
gneissoid *chalky* 8.59
gneissose *chalky* 8.59
gnome *sprite* 86.12, *maxim* 177.1, *evil spirit* 446.4, *little person* 580.5
gnomic *proverbial* 177.2
gnomic formula *maxim* 177.1
gnomon *face* 646.8
gnosis *mystery* 182.4, *knowledge* 348.1
gnostic Philosophical Schools of Thought 4, *educated* 48.19, *unintelligible* 364.4, *mysterious* 844.11
gnosticism Philosophical Schools of Thought 4
gnotobiotic *biological* 13.27, *agricultural* 16.16
gnotobiotically *agriculturally* 16.21
gnotobiotics *livestock farming* 16.10
go Board and Table Games 167, *depart* 265.6, 705.8, *experiment* 335.1, *attempt* 390.1, *energy* 414.4, *be operational* 509.10, *vigor* 518.1, *reach out* 585.10, *period of activity* 641.4, *cycle* 663.3, *be in motion* 677.14, *proceed* 692.16, *aim* 697.14, *exit* 707.13, *be in order* 765.23, *be effective* 845.15
go [Inf] *excrete* 25.20
go! 709.30
go aboard *enter* 706.11, *mount* 713.24
go aboard *or* **on board** *set out* 705.12
go about *undertake* 391.7, *turn around* 680.22
go about it the wrong way *be unskillful* 128.8
go absent without leave (AWOL) *disobey* 427.12, *escape* 816.8
go across *cross* 692.17
goad *incentive* 178.4, *motivate* 178.17, *stimulus* 212.3, *be piquant* 221.9, *annoy* 276.7, *make angry* 302.18, *offer* 504.11, *negative stimulus* 508.4, *manipulate*

508.12, *make violent* 520.10, *sharp-pointed thing* 549.4, *use a sharp tool* 549.17, *impel* 695.9, *haste* 818.1, *hasten* 818.4
goaded *motivated* 508.8
go adrift *go astray* 698.17
go after *pursue* 385.11, *bring* 685.11, *follow* 770.10
go against *counteract* 510.7, *be contrary* 828.16
go against one's word *be dishonorable* 192.21
go against the grain *be different* 463.11, *make rough* 544.11, *be independent* 782.20
go ahead *press on* 679.9, *maintain progress* 679.14, *make a beginning* 771.26
go-ahead *approval* 437.1, *tolerance* 502.2, *vigorous* 518.2, *course* 679.2, *forward* 679.6, *permission* 735.9
go ahead of *precede* 769.13
goal *hockey areas* 158.2, *ice hockey tactics* 158.4, *stadium* 163.2, *motive* 178.5, *aspiration* 281.3, *wish* 288.2, *purpose* 327.4, *future intention* 374.3, *objective* 374.5, *venture* 390.2, *motivation* 508.1, *direction* 697.1, *destination* 704.6, *aim* 773.12, *successful thing* 845.5
goal area *stadium* 163.2
goal crease *hockey areas* 158.2
goal-directed *purposive* 327.11
goalie *hockey player* 158.8
goalkeeper *hockey player* 158.8, *protector* 419.16
goalkeeper or **goalie** *soccer participant* 163.4
goalkeeper's or **goalie stick** *hockey equipment* 158.3
goalkeeper's protective clothing *hockey clothing* 158.6
goal kick *soccer play* 163.5
goal line *stadium* 155.3, 163.2, *hockey areas* 158.2
go all out *exert oneself* 122.11, *try hard* 390.7, *travel at maximum speed* 694.11, *lack restraint* 829.21
go all out for *aim* 327.17
go all the way [Inf] *have sex* 20.21
go all the way with *assent* 346.6
goalminder *hockey player* 158.8
go along *depart* 705.8
go along with *assent* 346.6, *be willing* 373.12, *acquiesce* 421.5, *obey* 426.7, *conform* 781.11, *concur* 827.16
goal-oriented *motivated* 508.8
goalpost *hockey areas* 158.2, *stadium* 163.2
goalposts *stadium* 155.3
goal setting *personnel management* 126.4
goaltend *play basketball* 148.7
goaltender *hockey player* 158.8
goaltending *violations* 148.5
go amiss *be inconvenient* 804.9, *miscarry* 846.19
go and get *bring* 685.11
go and return *be cyclic* 663.11
Goa powder *Tree Products* 43
go around *surround* 615.7, *circle* 631.6, *be in motion* 677.14, *orbit* 681.8, *rotate* 682.14, *find one's way* 691.15
go around in circles *be irresolute* 378.9, *orbit* 681.8, *waste effort* 802.13
go around with *befriend* 62.10
go as *act* 187.13
go ashore *land* 704.16
go askew *go wrong* 430.23

go astern *sail* 150.29, *navigate* 690.15
go as the crow flies *short-cut* 591.11
go astray 698.17; *sin* 430.22, *be immoral* 432.13, *be in danger* 811.11
Goat *Constellations* 7
goat *livestock* 16.11, *laughingstock* 369.4
go at a snail's pace *move slowly* 693.11
goatee *body covering* 19.4
goatherd *farm worker* 16.15
goatish *desirous* 20.18, *unchaste* 432.10
goatishness *sexual longing* 20.6
go at it *make a beginning* 771.26
go at it nineteen to the dozen *be active* 414.18
go at liberty *be liberated* 831.7
goatlike *ungulate* 35.31
goats *Collective Names* 59
goatsbeard *Flowers* 42
goatskin *leather* 104.7
goat's milk *milk* 93.5
go away *depart* 265.6, 705.8, *exit* 707.13, *diverge* 753.20
go away! *go!* 709.30
go AWOL *depart* 265.6
go awry *go wrong* 430.23, *miscarry* 846.19
gob *mass* 579.7
gob [Inf] *naval person* 77.25, *nautical person* 690.12
go back *be in the rear* 622.7, *reverse* 671.9, *680.18, *turn around* 698.25, *return to* 797.18
go back a long way *be old* 653.15
go back and forth *vacillate* 378.8, *be regular* 663.10
go back in time *be old* 653.15
go back on *not observe* 466.9
go back on one's word *withdraw* 392.5
go back to square one *begin again* 771.36, *reconsider* 807.23
go back to the beginning *restore* 671.10, *renew* 797.19
go back to the drawing board *reverse* 680.18, *begin again* 771.36
go back to the past *look back* 651.18
go backward 680.16
go bad *be dirty* 112.10, *sour* 223.8, *decay* 808.16
go bail for *be in debt* 488.9, *protect* 810.21, *liberate* 831.6
go bald *shed* 614.21
go bankrupt *lose one's money* 486.15, *be unable to pay* 490.11, *become insolvent* 846.17, *need money* 848.14
gobbet *bite* 92.10, *particle* 760.4
gobble *eat well* 92.23, *be greedy* 119.4, *golf shots* 156.4, *make a bird sound* 240.8, *ingest* 708.17
gobbledegook *nonstandard language* 5.7, *obscurity* 197.1, *vernacular* 205.8, *senseless talk* 362.4, *equivocation* 380.1
gobbler *eater* 92.15, *glutton* 119.2
gobbler [Inf] *male bird* 36.15
gobble up *consume* 523.16
gobbling *appetite* 92.2, *gluttonous* 119.3
go before *predict* 358.14, *prepare the way* 388.15, *precede* 657.13, *769.13, *show in* 708.13
go begging *be useless* 802.11
go belly up [Inf] *die* 29.17, *lose money* 468.15, *lose one's money* 486.15, *be unable to pay* 490.11,

become insolvent 846.17, *need money* 848.14
go below *underlie* 597.23, 601.11
go below the surface *hide* 844.13
go berserk *become angry* 302.20, *strike* 418.21, *be violent* 520.8
go-between *matchmaker* 64.13, *mediator* 75.2, *agent* 80.3, 123.15, *negotiator* 460.4, *assistant* 511.3, *person who joins* 752.9, *middleman* 772.7
go beyond *overstep* 712.12
go beyond belief *be improbable* 839.7
go beyond the bounds of reason or **probability** *be improbable* 839.7
Gobi *hot place* 217.5, *Deserts* 572
go blank *underact* 136.36
goblet *drink container* 93.13
goblin *sprite* 86.12, *frightener* 283.7, *evil spirit* 446.4
go blind *be blind* 243.18
go bond for *guarantee* 458.13
go broke *lose money* 468.15, *lose one's money* 486.15
gobs [Inf] *mass* 579.7, *certain amount* 738.3
go bust [Inf] *lose money* 468.15, *speculate* 480.19, *lose one's money* 486.15, *be unable to pay* 490.11, *close* 637.10, *become insolvent* 846.17
go busted [Inf] *lose one's money* 486.15
go by *abide by* 781.12
go-by [Inf] *insult* 436.5
go by fits and starts *be irregular* 664.5
go by the board *miscarry* 846.19
go by the book *be accurate* 350.5, *follow the rules* 780.17
go by the card *navigate* 690.15
go by the rule book *have no mercy* 309.6
go cap in hand *request* 505.10
go cap in hand to *appeal to* 209.9
go chase yourself! [Inf] *go!* 709.30
go cold turkey [Inf] *drug oneself* 121.37
go contemporary *be trendy* 652.18
go contrary to *be opposite* 731.4
go counter to *negate* 190.16
go courting *court* 299.26
God 82.6; *deity* 82.1, *idol* 83.5, *Phobias* 283, *first cause* 675.6
God! *miscellaneous swearwords* 301.20
God Almighty! *miscellaneous swearwords* 301.20
go dancing *dance* 135.7
Godavari *Rivers* 570
God bless! *hallelujah!* 83.18
goddammit! [Inf] *miscellaneous swearwords* 301.20
goddamn it! [Inf] *miscellaneous swearwords* 301.20
goddaughter *woman in the family* 33.13, *family circle* 65.4
goddess *deity* 82.1
goddesses and gods of love 299.14
goddesslike *attractive* 529.8
go dead slow *move slowly* 693.11
go deaf *be deaf* 229.8
Gödel numbers *Mathematical Concepts* 6
godfather *man in the family* 32.12, *family circle* 65.4
God-fearing *religious* 81.21
godforsaken *lonely* 409.8, *impious*

448.11, *unoccupied* 576.13, *distant* 585.5
godforsaken hole *solitary place* 409.4
godforsaken place *distant place* 585.3
God-given *given* 472.8
godhead *deity* 82.1
God Incarnate *God the Son* 82.9
God in Heaven! *miscellaneous swearwords* 301.20
go directly *aim* 697.14
go dirt-cheap *be cheap* 497.13
go displacement sailing *windsurf* 150.33
God knows where *distant place* 585.3
godless *impious* 448.11
godlessness *impiety* 448.4
godlike *divine* 82.16, *attractive* 529.8, *self-existent* 717.15
godliness *rightfulness* 429.1, *virtue* 447.1
godly *religious* 81.21, *divine* 82.16, *right* 429.7, *virtuous* 447.5, *blameless* 805.12
godmother *woman in the family* 33.13, *family circle* 65.4
go down *be destroyed* 523.17, *become smaller* 582.14, *descend* 714.12, *decrease* 747.7
go downhill *be destroyed* 523.17, *descend* 714.12, *deteriorate* 808.14, *be in trouble* 848.13
go downhill fast *be destroyed* 523.17
go down in the world *be in trouble* 848.13
go down on [Inf] *stimulate* 20.22
go down on bended knee *propose (marriage)* 299.28, *offer* 504.11
go down on one's knees to *petition* 505.11
go down the drain *be wasted* 96.22, *go to waste* 468.19
go down the tube [Inf] *go to waste* 468.19
go down the tubes or **chute** or **drain** [Inf] *go backward* 680.16
go down with one's ship *hold out* 377.13, *do one's duty* 434.17
godparent *family circle* 65.4
godroon *Architectural Elements* 134
gods *place for viewing* 242.13
gods, the *auditorium* 136.17
God's acre *burial place* 31.7
gods and goddesses of marriage 64.14
God save! *hallelujah!* 83.18
God's country *native country* 566.6
God's creation *person* 18.8
godsend *good thing* 445.9
God's image *person* 18.8
godson *man in the family* 32.12, *family circle* 65.4
God's peace! *peace!* 73.13
Godspeed! *goodbye!* 705.14
God's plenty *plenty* 97.2
God's will *inevitability* 95.6
God the Father 82.8; *trinitarian god* 82.7
God the Holy Ghost 82.10
God the Holy Ghost or **Holy Spirit** *trinitarian god* 82.7
God the Son 82.9; *trinitarian god* 82.7
go Dutch *participate* 408.15, *pay one's way* 489.19, *be equal* 740.11, *go halves* 789.16
Godwin Austen *Mountains and Hills* 569

Godzilla Legendary Creatures 360
go easily 823.18
go easy *be moderate* 521.6
go easy! [Inf] *be careful!* 287.20, *do easily* 823.16
go easy on *show pity* 308.8, *be lenient* 423.5
goer *racehorse* 159.2, *outgoer* 707.9
go far *be prosperous* 847.6
go farther and fare worse *deteriorate* 808.14
go fast *maintain progress* 679.14, *make haste* 818.5
go faster *make haste* 818.5
gofer [Inf] *office assistant* 69.6, *hard worker* 414.11, *submitter* 421.2, *inferior* 745.4, *helper* 825.12, *subordinate* 832.3
go fifty-fifty *compromise* 461.7, *be equal* 740.11, *go halves* 789.16
go first *precede* 769.13
go fish Card Games 168
go flat *decay* 808.16
go flat out [Inf] *try hard* 390.7, *lack restraint* 829.21
go for *aim* 374.10, 697.14, *attack* 418.17, *strike* 418.21, *fight* 422.23, *bring* 685.11
go for a good price *be sold* 482.22
go for a song *be cheap* 497.13
go for broke *aim* 374.10, *brace oneself* 376.13, *try hard* 390.7
go for help *help* 825.23
go for it [Inf] *aim* 374.10, *brace oneself* 376.13
go for it! [Inf] *here goes!* 376.18, 390.11
go forth *set out* 705.12
go for the jack *bowl* 151.8
go forward 679.8
go free *be free* 829.16, *be liberated* 831.7
go freestyle sailing *windsurf* 150.33
go from bad to worse *become aggravated* 276.6, *become inferior* 745.11, *deteriorate* 808.14
go from door to door *solicit money* 505.13
go from the sublime to the ridiculous *be ridiculous* 368.6
go full bat [Brit inf] *travel at maximum speed* 694.11
go full belt *attack* 418.17
go full tilt *or* **full pelt** *or* **full steam** *travel at maximum speed* 694.11
go-getter [Inf] *person who undertakes* 391.3, *doer* 412.3, *hard worker* 414.11
go-getting [Inf] *active* 414.13, *vigorous* 518.2, *forward* 679.6
goggle *look* 242.21
goggle at *wonder* 294.12
goggle-eyed *seeing* 242.17
goggles *climbing equipment* 161.4, *ski equipment* 162.10, *swimming equipment* 164.8, *visual aid* 242.14, *protective clothing* 419.6, *protection from the weather* 810.9
go-go [Inf] *swift* 694.6
go-go boots [Inf] *boots* 100.31
go-go dancer *dancer* 135.4
go-go dancing Dancing Types 135
go gray *age* 27.16, *gray* 255.9
go great guns [Inf] *attain one's goal* 845.13
go half and half *compromise* 461.7
go halfway *stand in the middle* 772.17
go halves 789.16; *get one's allotment* 474.6, *be equal* 740.11
go hand in glove with *accompany* 794.16

go hand in hand *synchronize* 649.7, *accompany* 794.16
go hatless *uncover* 614.17
go home *reverse* 680.18
go hungry *fast* 118.8
go hunting *hunt* 160.12, 385.14
go in *or* **into** *enter* 706.11
go in cahoots [Inf] *concur* 827.16
go indoors *go inside* 611.15
go in for *address oneself to* 209.13, *undertake* 391.7, *have a habit* 397.16
going *dying* 29.12, *disappearance* 265.1, *disappearing* 265.3, *active* 414.13, *operational* 509.7, *motion* 677.1, *moving* 677.12, *departure* 705.1, *outgoing* 707.10
going after *pursuit* 385.1, *sequence* 770.1
going all the way [Inf] *sexual intercourse* 20.9
going apart *parting* 703.2
going ashore *landing* 704.2
going away *disappearance* 265.1, *departure* 705.1
going back *equivocating* 380.6, *reversion* 671.1, *backward motion* 680.1
going back and forth *inconstancy* 378.2
going before *precedence* 769.1
going belly up [Inf] *financial loss* 468.4
going blind *blindness* 243.3
going both ways [Inf] *sexual nature* 20.4
going cheap *or* **cheaply** *bargain* 497.10
going down *descent* 714.1, *decreasing* 747.5
going down fighting *enduring* 377.9
going downhill *deteriorated* 808.8
going down the tubes *or* **chute** *or* **drain** [Inf] *backsliding* 680.8
going down with guns blazing *enduring* 377.9
going Dutch *equality* 740.1
going for a song *bargain* 497.10
going forward *forward motion* 679.1
going gray *aging* 27.13
going halves *equality* 740.1
going on *in progress* 679.16, *incomplete* 762.5
going on and on *diffuse* 199.3, *continuing forever* 664.6
going on a rampage *burst of anger* 302.6
going on board *start* 705.2
going out *exit* 707.1
going out of business *closure* 637.4, *unsuccessful thing* 846.8
going-out-of-business sale *sale* 482.2, *bargain* 495.2
going over again *iteration* 797.2
going rate *fee* 494.3
goings-on [Inf] *matter of interest* 328.3
going steady [Inf] *courtship* 299.10
going the rounds *newsworthy* 171.8
going through the roof *costly* 496.7, 500.6
going to bed with *sexual intercourse* 20.9
going to extremes *extravagance* 194.3
going together [Inf] *courtship* 299.10
going to hell in a handbasket *deterioration* 808.1
going to law *litigation* 54.1

going too far *extravagance* 194.3
going to pot *deteriorated* 808.8
going to seed *aging* 27.13
going to the head *intoxicating* 121.29
going to the root *essential* 799.10
going to the wall *financial loss* 468.4
going under *closure* 637.4
going up *mounting* 713.8
going with *or* **going out with** [Inf] *courtship* 299.10
going without *fasting* 118.5, *abstaining* 386.11
go in one ear and out the other *be unheard* 229.12, *be forgotten* 355.12
go in opposition *oppose* 828.15
go inside 611.15
go in the red *lose money* 468.15
go into *dissertate* 203.5
go into a brown study *fantasize* 360.15
go into a decline *be unhealthy* 114.29
go into a frenzy *become angry* 302.20
go into a huddle *chat* 210.12
go into a partnership *contract* 459.8
go into a rage *become angry* 302.20
go into a tailspin *decrease* 747.7
go into a trance *experience psychic phenomena* 86.23
go into debt *lose one's money* 486.15
go into detail *be diffuse* 199.5, *circumstantiate* 726.12, *particularize* 779.17
go into details *be accurate* 350.5
go into ecstasies *rejoice* 279.5
go into hiding *become invisible* 245.6
go into league with *contract* 459.8
go into liquidation *be unable to pay* 490.11
go into mourning *lament* 280.7
go into orbit *circle* 631.6, *orbit* 681.8, *rotate* 682.14
go into overdrive [Inf] *make haste* 818.5
go into particulars *be accurate* 350.5
go into partnership with *come together* 757.10, *join with* 827.15
go into politics *run for office* 50.10
go into purdah *become invisible* 245.6
go into recession *decrease* 747.7
go into retirement *have leisure time* 125.5, *depart* 265.6, *be unsocial* 409.10, *resign* 835.5
go into retreat *depart* 265.6
go into reverse *reverse* 680.18
go into seclusion *be unsocial* 409.10, *be aloof* 756.8
go into stocks *or* **bonds** *finance* 457.7
go into the red *acquire credit* 487.11, *be in debt* 488.9, *overpay* 496.11
go into training *learn* 48.23
go in with *join with* 827.15
go it alone *be one* 788.17, *be independent* 829.18
go jump in the lake! [Inf] *go!* 709.30
go kaput [Inf] *go wrong* 430.23, *malfunction* 846.20
go-kart *racing* 146.9
go-karting Sporting Activities 145, *automobile racing* 146.1

go lame *be weak* 517.12, *hesitate* 693.12
Golan Heights Mountains and Hills 569
golconda *wealth* 485.1
gold Chemical Elements and Common Allotropes 11, *track and field* 166.20, *yellow thing* 259.4, *yellow* 259.7, Phobias 283, *money* 484.1, *bullion* 484.16
gold and silver standard *currency market* 484.8
goldarn [Inf] *or* **goldarned** [Inf] *miscellaneous euphemisms* 301.12
Goldbach conjecture Mathematical Concepts 6
gold bar *bullion* 484.16
gold-based *monetary* 484.22
goldbrick [Inf] *neglector* 326.3, *shirk* 386.18, *plodder* 693.6
goldbricker [Inf] *schemer* 193.10, *avoider* 386.8
goldbricking [Inf] *shirking* 386.4
gold coinage *coinage* 484.13
gold decoration *decoration* 129.4
gold digger [Inf] *lover* 299.11, *gainer* 467.9
gold-digging [Inf] *gain-seeking* 467.11
gold dust Flowers 42
golden *orange* 258.5, *yellow* 259.7, *cheering* 281.9, *seasonal* 654.7, *prosperous* 847.5
Golden Age Ages, Decades, Eras 641
golden age *symbol of peace* 73.6, *naiveté* 449.4, *historical past* 651.6, *comfortable circumstances* 726.5, *time of plenty* 847.3
golden ager *older person* 27.7
golden bell Flowers 42
golden-brown algae *algae* 47.11
golden calf *idol* 83.5
golden days *time of plenty* 847.3
Golden Delicious Apple Varieties 44
golden dream *reverie* 360.6
golden goose *wealth* 485.1
golden hair *yellow thing* 259.4
golden-haired *yellow-haired* 259.9
golden handshake *acknowledgment* 310.3, *reward for service* 453.5, *profit* 467.6, *reward* 472.4, *pay* 489.6, *inducement* 508.2, *parting* 705.3, *compensation* 743.1, *extra* 748.6, *termination* 834.2
golden jubilee *anniversary* 405.5
goldenly *yellowly* 259.13
golden mean *rule* 6.42, *treatment* 143.6, *moderation* 455.3, 521.1, *medium* 742.2, *middle way* 772.3
goldenness *yellowness* 259.1
golden opportunity *tentative offer* 504.2, *opportunity* 583.8, 659.2
golden parachute *reward for service* 453.5, *profit* 467.6, *pay* 489.6, *compensation* 743.1
golden rectangle *polygon* 6.42
golden retriever Breeds of Dogs 35
goldenrod Flowers 42
golden rule *line of action* 399.4
golden section *polygon* 6.42, *treatment* 143.6
golden time *time of plenty* 847.3
golden touch *wealth* 485.1
golden wedding anniversary *anniversary* 405.5
golden years *old age* 27.5
golden-yellow *yellow* 259.7
goldfish *orange thing* 258.3
goldflower Flowers 42

Gold Gloves *boxing associations* 152.7
gold leaf *decorative method* 532.3
gold medal *competition* 166.18, *insignia* 184.5
gold-medal *unbeatable* 744.13, *best* 805.9
gold mine *wealth* 485.1
gold plate *coating* 613.8
gold reserves *funds* 484.6
gold-rimmed glasses *visual aid* 242.14
goldsmith *artisan* 123.13
gold standard *international finance* 457.2, *currency market* 484.8
gold star *military honor* 58.9
Goldstein-Sheerer test Intelligence Tests 108
gold tooth *teeth* 19.8
gold watch *acknowledgment* 310.3
Goldwynism *language error* 351.10
golem Legendary Creatures 360
golf 156.1, Sporting Activities 145, *athletics* 422.7
golf bag *golf equipment* 156.5, *bag* 578.7
golf ball *golf equipment* 156.5
golf club *golf equipment* 156.5, *golfing associations and tournaments* 156.6, *impeller* 695.7
golf club part *golf equipment* 156.5
golf course 156.2
golf equipment 156.5
golfer 156.7
golf game *golf* 156.1
golf glove *golf equipment* 156.5
golfing *golf* 156.1
golfing associations and tournaments 156.6
golfing terms 156.3
golf match *golf* 156.1
golf rules *golfing terms* 156.3
golf shoes *shoes* 100.30
golf shots 156.4
Golgi body *cell structure* 13.16
golgotha *burial place* 31.7
Goliardic verse Western Literary Groups 139
Goliath *person of strength* 516.8, *tall person* 596.6
goliath *big person* 579.10
go like a bat out of hell [Inf] *be full of vigor* 518.4, *make haste* 818.5
go like a rocket *make haste* 818.5
go like clockwork *be in order* 765.23, *go easily* 823.18
golly! [Inf] *miscellaneous euphemisms* 301.21
golly gee! [Inf] *miscellaneous euphemisms* 301.21
go looking for trouble *pick a fight* 463.10
go lower *deepen* 598.21
go mad *become insane* 110.12, *feel deeply* 266.16, *be foolish* 353.6
gombroon Ceramics 129
go missing *abscond* 576.16
go modern *be trendy* 652.18
go moldy *sour* 223.8
go mountaineering *mountaineer* 161.10
gomuti Trees and Shrubs 43
gonadotrophin *hormone* 12.16
gonadotropic hormone *hormone* 12.16
gonadotropin-releasing hormone Human Hormones 12
gonads *internal organ* 19.13, *sexual organs* 20.2
gondola *railroad car* 688.5, Ships and Boats 690, *cableway* 691.11
gondolier *transferrer* 685.4,

transporter 686.4, *nautical person* 690.12
Gondwana *plate tectonics* 8.19
gone dead 29.11, *dead drunk* 121.27, *disappeared* 265.4, *forgotten* 355.7, *inactive* 413.9, *away* 576.8, *over* 651.12, *departed* 705.6, *zero* 786.5, *hopeless* 837.6
gone [Inf] *dead drunk* 121.27
gone away *disappeared* 265.4, *departed* 705.6
gone bad *unhygienic* 114.27, *spoiled* 808.9
gone before *dead* 29.11
gone but not forgotten *dead* 29.11
gone by the board *losing* 468.9
gone down the drain *losing* 468.9
gone forever *losing* 468.9, *over* 651.12
gone for good *losing* 468.9, *over* 651.12
gone from bad to worse *deteriorated* 808.8
gone missing *or* **astray** *losing* 468.9, *misplaced* 574.13
gone off *departed* 705.6, *spoiled* 808.9
gone on [Inf] *in love* 299.16
goner [Inf] *dying person* 29.6, *hopeless person* 282.5
gone to ground *disappeared* 265.4
gone to join one's ancestors *dead* 29.11
gone to pot *middle-aged* 27.14, *beggarly* 486.12
gone to ruin *beggarly* 486.12
gone to seed *botanical* 17.15, *plantlike* 41.13
gone wrong 430.17
gonfalon *flag* 184.8
gong Musical Instruments 142, *source of resonance* 236.4, *signal* 646.9, *sea marker* 690.7
Gongga Shan Mountains and Hills 569
Gongorism Western Literary Groups 139
gonidium *reproductive body* 47.14
go nightclubbing *participate* 408.15
goniometer Fields of Measurement 589, *angular measurement* 628.4, *position finder* 690.8
goniometry Fields of Measurement 589, *angular measurement* 628.4
gonion *angle* 628.1
gonorrhea *sexually transmitted disease (STD)* 114.17
gonorrheic *infectious person* 114.9
goo [Inf] *dirt* 112.5, *mud* 561.8
good 445.1, 445.10; *edible* 92.20, *skillful* 127.10, *desirable* 288.11, *benevolent* 305.7, *usefulness* 393.2, 801.1, *well-behaved* 399.15, *obedient* 426.4, *right* 429.7, *moral* 431.9, *virtuous* 447.5, *innocent* 449.6, *auspicious* 458.10, *usability* 801.2, *usable* 801.6, *profitable* 801.8, *trustworthy* 810.17, *beneficial* 825.20
good and bad *imperfect* 806.5
good and early *early* 657.8, 657.17
good and tired [Inf] *bored* 296.5, *tiredly* 820.7
good as gold *virtuous* 447.5
good as new *renewed* 652.14
good at *excellent* 68.16, *skillful* 127.10, *knowledgeable* 348.7
good behavior *good conduct* 399.5,

good manners 410.2, *loyalty* 426.2, *kindness* 445.3, *virtues* 447.2
good bone structure *attractiveness* 529.2
Good Book, the *Christian text* 81.16
good books *admiration* 437.2
good break [Inf] *good fortune* 847.2
good breeding *nobleness* 70.3, *good manners* 410.2, *refinement* 534.1
good build *attractiveness* 529.2
good buy *purchase* 481.1
goodbye *parting* 705.3
goodbye! 705.14
good chance 842.6; *opportunity* 659.2, *strong possibility* 836.3, *chance* 838.4
good cheer *food* 90.1, *cheerfulness* 269.2, *sociability* 408.1
good child *well-behaved person* 399.6
good citizen *philanthropist* 307.5
good citizenship *public-spiritedness* 307.2
good clip *swiftness* 694.1
good color *repute* 370.1
good companion *social person* 408.7
good company 408.9; *amiability* 271.3, *social person* 408.7
good condition *health* 113.1, *orderliness* 765.5
good condition *or* **shape** *physical state* 725.6
good conduct 399.5
good conscience *morality* 431.1, *virtue* 447.1
good constitution *health* 113.1
good credit risk *solvent* 485.9, *credit* 487.1
good debt *debt* 488.1
good deed *benevolent act* 305.5, *support* 825.2
good deportment *good manners* 410.2
good diet *health improvement* 113.3
good ear *hearing* 228.1
good eater *glutton* 119.2
good English *standard language* 5.6, *grammar* 5.28
good enough *satisfactory* 273.6
good excuse *defense* 441.2
good eyesight *visual acuity* 242.2
good faith *loyalty* 426.2, *morals* 431.2
good family [Brit] *family tree* 65.3
good features *attractiveness* 529.2
good feeling 266.4; *pleasure* 214.2
good fellow *social person* 408.7
good-fellowed *compassionate* 305.8
good fellowship *good company* 408.9
good few, a *many* 795.6
good fit *compatibility* 462.3
good for *beneficial* 445.11, *usable* 801.6
good for it *solvent* 485.9
good form *formality* 406.1, *etiquette* 406.3, 534.3
good-for-nothing *miscreant* 448.6, *loser* 468.8, *powerless* 515.6, *unimportant* 800.10, *useless* 802.7
good for one *healthful* 113.7
good fortune 847.2; *good thing* 445.9, *comfortable circumstances* 726.5, *luck* 842.3
Good Friday Christian Holy Days and Seasons 85, *fast* 118.4
good giver *giver* 472.7

good God! *miscellaneous swearwords* 301.20
good God Almighty! *miscellaneous swearwords* 301.20
good graces *admiration* 437.2
good grammar *grammar* 5.28
good grounds *defense* 441.2
good habit *habit* 397.1
good head for *aptitude* 127.4
good health *health* 113.1
good-hearted *kind* 445.12
good-heartedness *kindness* 445.3
good heavens! 292.15; *wonderful!* 294.20
good host *or* **hostess** *social person* 408.7
good housekeeping *thrift* 499.1
good humor *cheerfulness* 269.2, *courtesy* 410.1, *state of mind* 725.5
good-humored *cheerful* 269.7, *courteous* 410.6, *conditional* 725.7
good-humoredly *cheerfully* 269.14, *courteously* 410.13, *in good form* 725.11
good husbandry *thrift* 499.1
good idea *creative thought* 317.3, *plan* 327.3
good influence *improvement* 807.1
good in parts *imperfect* 806.5
good intention *intention* 374.1
good intentions *conduct* 399.1
good judgment *legal justice* 53.4
good lady *married woman* 64.11
good life, the *pleasure* 214.2, *opulence* 485.3, *comfortable circumstances* 726.5, *prosperity* 847.1
goodliness *kindness* 445.3, *excellence* 445.4, *virtue* 447.1
good-looking *attractive* 529.8, 700.10
good looks *attractiveness* 529.2
good luck *good thing* 445.9, *opportunity* 659.2, *luck* 842.3, *good fortune* 847.2
good luck! 842.19
good-luck charm *talisman* 86.9, *good-luck sign* 358.6, *preserver* 815.9
good-luck sign 358.6
goodly *good* 445.10, *kind* 445.12, *great* 445.14, *virtuous* 447.5, *big* 579.13
goodman [Arch] *male title of address* 32.3, *married man* 64.10
good management *thrift* 499.1
good-mannered 410.7
good manners 410.2; *good conduct* 399.5, *etiquette* 406.3, 534.3, *social success* 408.3, *kindness* 445.3, *refinement* 534.1
good many *many* 795.6
good match *marriageability* 64.4
good memory *memory* 354.1
good mixer *social person* 408.7
good move *successful thing* 845.5
good nature *benevolence* 305.1
good-natured *harmless* 73.9, *cheerful* 269.7, *likable* 271.6, *benevolent* 305.7, *kind* 445.12
good-naturedly *cheerfully* 269.14, *benevolently* 305.13, *kindly* 445.20
good-naturedness *kindness* 445.3
good neighbor *benevolent person* 305.6, *philanthropist* 307.5, *social person* 408.7, *good person* 445.6, *supporter* 825.13
goodness *healthfulness* 113.2, *skill* 127.1, *benevolence* 305.1, *good conduct* 399.5, *obedience* 426.1, *rightfulness* 429.1, *morality* 431.1, *morals* 431.2, *good* 445.1, *virtue* 447.1, *innocence* 449.1

goodness! *miscellaneous euphemisms* 301.21

goodness and mercy *compassion* 305.2

goodness gracious! *wonderful!* 294.20, *miscellaneous euphemisms* 301.21

goodness-of-fit test *hypothesis testing* 6.52

good news *news* 171.1, Phobias 283

goodnight *parting* 705.3

goodnight! *goodbye!* 705.14

good notice *compliment* 437.4

good nutrition *health improvement* 113.3

good occasion *timeliness* 659.1

good odds *good chance* 842.6

good odor *reputation* 224.4

good offices *pacification* 74.1, *mediation* 75.1, *patronage* 810.7, *support* 825.2

good old days *past time* 3.6, 651.1

good omen *omen* 358.5, *potential* 458.4

good opinion *respect* 435.1, *admiration* 437.2

good opportunity *opportunity* 659.2, *strong possibility* 836.3

good part *role* 136.23

good person 445.6; *innocent person* 449.5

good policy *convenience* 803.1

good possibility *good chance* 842.6

good press *compliment* 437.4

good prospects *potential* 458.4

good quality *excellence* 445.4

good reason *defense* 441.2

good reference *repute* 370.1

good report *repute* 370.1

good review *criticism* 365.3

good riddance *deliverance* 817.1

good role model *doer* 412.3

goods *possessions* 470.5, *personal estate* 470.6, *merchandise* 482.6, 522.6, *transferred thing* 685.6, *freightage* 686.3

good sales *sales* 482.3

good Samaritan *benevolent person* 305.6, *philanthropist* 307.5, *good person* 445.6, *giver* 472.7, *generous person* 498.5, *volunteer* 504.7, *supporter* 825.1

goods and chattels *possession of property* 469.3

goods and services *produce* 522.5

good sense *rationality* 109.2, *intelligence* 352.2

good-sheet inlay *decorative woodwork* 131.2

Good Shepherd *God the Son* 82.9

good shot *hunter* 382.6, *shooter* 696.11, *successful thing* 845.5

good-size *big* 579.13

goods on approval *merchandise* 482.6

goods on assignment *merchandise* 482.6

good spirits *cheerfulness* 269.2, *state of mind* 725.5

good stead *usefulness* 801.1

goods train [Brit] *train* 688.4

good taste *subtlety* 195.3, *judiciousness* 337.2, *elegance* 527.1, *refinement* 534.1

good-tempered *detached* 4.18

good terms *friendly relations* 62.3

good thing 445.9

good things to come *potential* 458.4

good time 214.3; *fun* 269.4

good times *opulence* 485.3, *time of plenty* 847.3

good times coming *idealism* 360.7

good trim *orderliness* 765.5

good try *attempt* 390.1

good turn *benevolent act* 305.5, *kindness* 445.3, *support* 825.2

good use *use* 393.1

good vibes [Inf] *agreement* 462.1

good vibrations [Inf] *agreement* 462.1

good way *great distance* 585.2

goodwife [Arch] *female title of address* 33.3, *married woman* 64.11

goodwill 373.4; *friendship* 62.1, *benevolence* 305.1, *philanthropy* 307.1, *kindness* 445.3, *agreement* 462.1, *helpfulness* 825.10

goodwilled 373.10; *benevolent* 305.7

good wishes *greeting* 435.5

good with money *thrifty* 499.4

good word *news* 171.1, *compliment* 437.4

good work *benevolent act* 305.5

good works *charity* 305.3, 307.3

goody [Arch] *female title of address* 33.3, *married woman* 64.11

goody-goody 445.8; *effeminate male* 32.8, *innocent person* 449.5, *innocent* 449.6

goody two shoes *goody-goody* 445.8, *innocent person* 449.5

gooey *retentive* 471.5

gooey [Inf] *viscous* 561.14

gooeyness [Inf] *doughiness* 561.2

goof [Inf] *blunder* 351.9, *be wrong* 430.18

goofball [Inf] *sedatives* 121.19

go off *be dirty* 112.10, *sour* 223.8, *burst* 232.9, *sidestep* 698.22, *decay* 808.16

go off *or* **away** *move apart* 703.11

go off at a tangent *deviate* 698.15, *digress* 775.13

go off at the drop of a hat *be eager* 373.13

go off half-cocked *be unprepared* 389.14, *hasten* 657.15, *be untimely* 660.8

go off like a shot *be eager* 373.13

go off on a tangent *be extraneous* 724.12, *be unrelated* 728.12

go off on *or* **at a tangent** *be circuitous* 199.6, *angle* 628.11

go off one's head [Inf] *become insane* 110.12

go offside *play soccer* 163.8

go off the air *be unheard* 229.12, *disappear* 265.5

go off the beaten track *be independent* 782.20

go off the gold standard *devalue the currency* 490.14

go off the point *digress* 775.13

goofing off [Inf] *shirking* 386.4, *lingering* 693.4

goof off [Inf] *hesitate* 693.12

goof-off [Inf] *avoider* 386.8, *plodder* 693.6

goof up [Inf] *be clumsy* 128.9, *be wrong* 430.18

googol *large number* 783.3, *million* 792.11

googolplex *large number* 783.3, *million* 792.11

goo-goo eyes [Inf] *communication of love* 299.6

gook Nicknames for Inhabitants 61

gook [Inf] *mud* 561.8

goombah [Inf] *friend* 62.2

go on 642.7; *maintain* 377.12, *be frequent* 661.5, *continue* 669.8, *be in motion* 677.14, *depart* 705.8, *go on!* 57.8, 294.20

go on! *57.8, 294.20*

go on a bender [Inf] *get drunk* 121.35, *overindulge* 456.11

go on a binge [Inf] *be greedy* 119.4, *rejoice* 279.5

go on a blind [Inf] *get drunk* 121.35

go on about *moralize* 431.14, *harp* 797.17

go on a crash diet *eat less* 118.9

go on active service *be at war* 76.32

go on a diet *eat less* 118.9, *abstain* 455.11

go on a fool's errand *figurative expressions* 128.11, *be wasteful* 468.16

go on a furlough *have leisure time* 125.5, *take it easy* 819.3

go on a honeymoon *marry* 64.19

go on a hunger strike *fast* 118.8, *lose weight* 468.14

go on a liquid diet *eat less* 118.9

go on a mission *engage* 833.9

go on a pilgrimage *revere* 81.26, *worship* 83.15

go on a protest march *cause mischief* 507.9

go on a rampage *shatter the peace* 232.10, *vent one's anger* 302.21

go on a spending spree *expend* 491.11, *overspend* 500.8

go on a spree *get drunk* 121.35, *participate* 408.15

go on a starvation diet *eat less* 118.9

go on at *harp* 797.17

go on a wild-goose chase *figurative expressions* 128.11, *be wasteful* 468.16, *waste effort* 802.13

go on board *mount* 713.24

go one better *outdo* 744.18

go one better [Inf] *be cunning* 822.5

go one's own way *follow one's own will* 372.13, *be independent* 782.20, 829.18, *be one* 788.17

go one's separate ways *disband* 776.13

go on for a long time *protract* 669.9

go on forever *bore* 296.8

go on furlough *absent oneself* 576.15

go on hind legs *arise* 715.15

go on holiday *absent oneself* 576.15

go on leave *be refreshed* 94.8, *exempt oneself* 434.12, *absent oneself* 576.15, *take it easy* 819.3

go on oiled wheels *go easily* 823.18

go on one's feelings *be intuitive* 320.9

go on relief *be poor* 486.14

go on sabbatical *absent oneself* 576.15

go onside *play soccer* 163.8

go on strike *refuse* 506.8, *cause mischief* 507.9

go *or* **go out on strike** *stop work* 668.11

go on the attack *attack* 418.17

go on the blink *go wrong* 430.23

go on the lam [Inf] *conceal oneself* 181.15, *run away* 386.21, *be safe*

810.20, *shelter* 812.8, *be liberated* 831.7, *hide* 844.13

go on the rampage *attack successfully* 418.25, *be violent* 520.8, *be disorderly* 766.22

go on the road *entertain* 138.16

go on the rocks *be destroyed* 523.17, *become insolvent* 846.17, *be in trouble* 848.13

go on the stock exchange *speculate* 480.19

go on the wagon [Inf] *give up alcohol* 120.6, *abstain* 386.16, 455.11, *restrain oneself* 830.15

go on the warpath *be at war* 76.32, *pick a fight* 463.10, *be violent* 520.8

go onto the offensive *attack* 418.17

go on tour *entertain* 138.16

go on trial *be accused* 442.10

go on vacation *absent oneself* 576.15, *take it easy* 819.3

go on welfare *be poor* 486.14

goose *livestock* 16.11, *water bird* 36.9, *female bird* 36.16, *meat* 90.22, *game* 160.6, Board and Table Games 167

goose, Aleutian Canada Endangered US Birds 36

goose [Inf] *touch* 216.9

goose barnacle *crustacean* 39.10

gooseboy *farm worker* 16.15

goose bumps *symptoms of fear* 283.3, *rough skin* 544.3

goose egg [Inf] *zero* 786.1

goose fair *market* 483.1

goose flesh *stimulus* 212.3, *symptoms of fear* 283.3, *rough skin* 544.3

goosefoot family *seed plant* 41.3

goosegirl *farm worker* 16.15

gooselike *avian* 36.19

gooseneck *sailboat parts and accessories* 150.4

goosenecked *sailing* 150.25

goose pimples *stimulus* 212.3, *symptoms of fear* 283.3, *rough skin* 544.3

goose step *bodily movement* 677.11

goosing [Inf] *touching* 216.2

goosy *avian* 36.19

go out *become dark* 247.9, *participate* 408.15, *exit* 707.13, *come to an end* 773.23

go out for trade *trade* 480.18

go out like a lamb *be moderate* 521.6

go out of business *close* 637.10, *stop work* 668.11, *become insolvent* 846.17

go out of commission *go wrong* 430.23

go out of one's way to *be eager* 373.13

go out of print *disappear* 265.5

go out of style *grow old* 653.16

go out of use *disappear* 265.5

go out on a limb *take a chance* 842.14

go out on a limb [Inf] *be rash* 286.8

go out on the town *participate* 408.15

go out with *seek friendship* 62.11, *unify* 752.15, *keep company with* 794.17

go over *be irresolute* 378.9, *attain one's goal* 845.13

go over again *iterate* 797.16

go over again and again *harp* 797.17

go over big [Inf] *attain one's goal* 845.13

go overboard *overdo* 99.11

go over one's head *be unintelligible* 364.11

go over the hill [Inf] *be liberated* 831.7

go over the limit *exaggerate* 712.16

go over the same ground *iterate* 797.16, *return to* 797.18

go over the top *battle* 76.33, *attack* 418.17, *climb* 713.21

go over the wall [Inf] *escape* 816.8, *be liberated* 831.7

GOP *Political Parties* 50

gopak *Dances* 135

go partners *join with* 827.15

go partying *participate* 408.15

go pitapat *vibrate* 683.13, *shake* 684.24

go public *publish* 173.15, *divulge* 180.9

go quietly *be moderate* 521.6

go rafting *raft* 150.34

Gorbatov Red *Breeds of Cattle* 16

Gordian knot *puzzle* 182.5, *problem* 824.4

Gordon setter *Breeds of Dogs* 35

gore *part of garment* 100.27, *red thing* 257.3, *be sharp* 549.15, *blood* 555.4, *mucus* 561.6

gored skirt *skirt* 100.12

go regularly *have a habit* 397.16

gorge *landform* 8.9, *overindulge* 99.10, 456.11, *be greedy* 119.4, *valley* 572.8, *gulf* 587.3, *lowlands* 597.6, *concave land* 635.2

gorged *immoderate* 99.6, *gluttonous* 119.3, *full* 761.8

gorge oneself *eat well* 92.23

gorgeous *delightful* 271.7, *grand* 404.22, *beautiful* 529.7

gorgeously 529.14

gorgeousness *grandeur* 404.10, *beauty* 529.1

gorger *glutton* 119.2

gorgerin *Architectural Elements* 134

gorget *historic armor* 419.8

gorging *appetite* 92.2, *gluttonous* 119.3

Gorgon *Legendary Creatures* 360

go right through one *be strident* 238.7

goriness *fluidity* 555.5

goring *hit* 418.9

gormandize *eat well* 92.23, *be greedy* 119.4

gormandizing *appetite* 92.2, *overindulgence* 456.3, *overindulgent* 456.8

go rusty *be unskillful* 128.8

gory *murderous* 30.18, *bloody* 257.8, 555.18, *viscous* 561.14

Gosain *priest* 84.8

Gosainthan *Mountains and Hills* 569

go scot-free *get a reprieve* 816.9, *be liberated* 831.7

go separate or **different ways** *diverge* 753.20

go separate ways *separate* 703.12

go septic *decay* 808.16

gosh! *miscellaneous euphemisms* 301.21

go shares *be equal* 740.11

goshawk *bird of prey* 36.11

goshawks *Collective Names* 59

go shooting *hunt* 160.12, 385.14

go shopping *shop* 481.15

go short and wide *bowl* 151.24

go sideways *move sideways* 623.9

go sideways or **sidewise** *be in motion* 677.14

gosling *livestock* 16.11, *young bird* 36.17

go slow or **slowly** *move slowly* 693.11

go-slow [Brit] *hesitation* 693.5

go small-game or **big-game hunting** *hunt* 160.12

go smoothly 545.11; *go easily* 823.18

go so far but no further *compromise* 461.7

go solo *be one* 788.17

go sour *sour* 223.8, *decay* 808.16

Gospel *Eucharist* 85.7

gospel music *sacred music* 140.3

Gospels *Christian text* 81.16

Gospel side *laterality* 623.3

gospel song *ritual music* 85.9

gospel truth *the truth* 721.3

gossamer *Fabrics and Fibers* 130, *transparent thing* 249.4, *weak thing* 517.5, *delicate* 552.10, *fineness* 595.5, *fine* 595.12, *little bit* 800.4

gossameriness *grain* 552.2

gossamery *insubstantial* 539.5, *delicate* 552.10

gossip 192.11, *Children's and Party Games* 167, *inside information* 170.4, *informer* 170.8, *news source* 171.4, *report* 171.9, *publishing* 173.2, *publish* 173.15, *adviser* 176.5, *partial truth* 192.7, *distort the truth* 192.25, *speaker* 205.12, *talk* 207.3, *talker* 207.4, *chat* 210.2, 210.12, *chatterer* 210.7, *prying* 321.2, *meddler* 321.4, *meddle* 321.8, *matter of interest* 328.3, *defamation* 440.3, *disparager* 440.7, *vilify* 440.14

gossip column *news story* 171.3

gossip columnist *print journalist* 175.5, *disparager* 440.7

gossiper *gossip* 192.11, *speaker* 205.12, *disparager* 440.7

gossiping *defamatory* 440.9

gossipmonger *gossip* 192.11, *meddler* 321.4

gossipy *communicative* 169.16, *informative* 170.10, *newsworthy* 171.8, *effusive* 207.6, *conversational* 210.10, *prying* 321.6, *local* 328.8

gossypose *Common Sugars* 12

go stale *decay* 808.16

go steady [Inf] *court* 299.26

go steady with *unify* 752.15

go straight *be virtuous* 447.8, *aim* 697.14

go supersonic *fly* 689.13

Gotham *New York* 567.6

go the limit *pursue* 377.11

go the round *ring* 681.9

go the rounds *be published* 173.19

go the whole hog *be resolute* 376.11, *pursue* 377.11, *try* 414.21

Gothic *Furniture Styles* 101, *historic* 653.13

Gothic architecture *Architectural Styles* 134

Gothic art *Western Art Styles* 133

gothic novel *novel* 139.3

Gothic Revival *Architectural Styles* 134

Gothic type *type* 173.5

go through *feel* 266.14, *use up* 393.12, *behave toward* 399.20, *consume* 491.12, *waste* 500.7, *infiltrate* 706.13

go through fire and water *be resolute* 376.11

go through hell *feel pain* 215.8

go through phases *be changeable* 666.5

go through the bankruptcy court *be unable to pay* 490.11

go through the books *audit* 493.10

go through the ceiling or **roof** *cost a lot* 496.9

go through the roof or **ceiling** *increase* 746.6

Gotland *Islands* 572

Gotland pony *Horse and Pony Breeds* 159

goto *programming concepts* 15.24

go to *reach out* 585.10

go to a concert or **the opera** *enjoy music* 141.19

go to a funeral *pay one's last respects* 31.12

go to all lengths *be resolute* 376.11

go to-and-fro *vacillate* 378.8, *be regular* 663.10

go to any length 590.13; *be resolute* 376.11

go to any lengths *exert oneself* 122.11, *pursue* 377.11, *go to any length* 590.13

go to arbitration *compromise* 461.7

go to bat for *back* 825.28

go to bed *sleep* 415.14, *take it easy* 819.3

go to bed late *be busy* 414.19

go to bed with *have sex* 20.21

go to blazes! [Inf] *miscellaneous swearwords* 301.20, *be destroyed* 523.17

go to church *be religious* 81.25

go to confession *confess* 451.8

go to court *dispute* 463.9

go to earth *conceal oneself* 181.15

go to exaggerated lengths *exaggerate* 194.11

go to extremes *be extravagant* 194.13

go together *accompany* 794.16

go together [Inf] *court* 299.26

go together with *accompany* 794.16

go to ground *disappear* 265.5

go to hell *sin* 430.22, *be destroyed* 523.17

go to hell! [Inf] *miscellaneous swearwords* 301.20

go to hell in a handbasket *sin* 430.22

go to it [Inf] *make a beginning* 771.26

go to meet *meet* 704.20

go too far *be extravagant* 194.13, *overstep* 712.12, *lack restraint* 829.21

go to one's corner *box* 152.19

go to one's eternal rest *be motionless* 678.7

go to one's head *be intoxicating* 121.36

go to parties *participate* 408.15

go to pieces *be destroyed* 523.17, *disintegrate* 758.6, *deteriorate* 808.14

go topless *undress* 614.18

go to pot *age* 27.16, *be wasted* 96.22, *be immoral* 432.13, *go to waste* 468.19, *lose one's money* 486.15, *be destroyed* 523.17, *deteriorate* 808.14, *be in trouble* 848.13

go to press *report* 175.9

go to prison or **jail** *be punished* 454.31

go to rack and ruin *be immoral* 432.13, *be destroyed* 523.17, *deteriorate* 808.14, *be in trouble* 848.13

go to ruin *be wasted* 96.22, *lose one's money* 486.15, *disintegrate* 808.15

go to school *learn* 48.23

go to sea in a sieve *be rash* 286.8

go to seed *age* 27.16, *go to waste* 468.19, *disintegrate* 808.15

go to sleep *be insensible* 213.7, *take it easy* 819.3

go to the bad *sin* 430.22, *be immoral* 432.13, *be wicked* 448.13, *deteriorate* 808.14

go to the bathroom or **toilet** *excrete* 25.20

go to or **on the block** *be sold* 482.22

go to the devil *deteriorate* 808.14

go to the dogs [Inf] *sin* 430.22, *be immoral* 432.13, *be wicked* 448.13, *go to waste* 468.19, *be destroyed* 523.17, *deteriorate* 808.14, *decline* 846.16, *be in trouble* 848.13

go to the gallows *be executed* 454.32

go to the happy hunting ground *be motionless* 678.7

go to the hospital *be unhealthy* 114.29

go to the law *litigate* 54.27

go to the other extreme *be opposite* 731.4

go to the polls *vote* 382.16

go to the relief of *help* 825.23

go to the starting grid *be on the track* 146.11

go to the wall *lose money* 468.15, *lose one's money* 486.15, *be unable to pay* 490.11, *be destroyed* 523.17, *close* 637.10, *be in difficulty* 824.19, *become insolvent* 846.17

go to war 76.29; *declare war* 422.25

go to waste 468.19; *be wasted* 96.22, *be destroyed* 523.17, *be useless* 802.11

gotten *received* 492.6

Götterdämmerung *end of time* 773.5

gouache *painting* 143.3, *material* 143.9, *paint* 251.6

gouge *erosion* 8.41, *erode* 8.67, *material* 144.6, *wrestling terms* 152.10, *wrestle* 152.20, *overcharge* 496.10, *notch* 636.1, 636.5

gouged *weathered* 8.61

gouge out *make concave* 635.7, *dig out* 711.15

gouge someone's eyes out *blind* 243.17

gouging *extortion* 496.4, *costly* 496.7

goulash *meat dish* 90.21, *mixed thing* 751.2

go under *be destroyed* 523.17, *close* 637.10, *descend* 714.12, *be in difficulty* 824.19

go underground *conceal oneself* 181.15, *be safe* 810.20, *hide* 844.13

go underwater *descend* 714.12

go unnoticed *be average* 742.8

go unpunished *get a reprieve* 816.9

go up 713.23; *ascend* 713.19

go up in a puff of smoke *cease to exist* 718.13

go up in flames *burn* 217.18

go up in smoke *miscarry* 846.19

go up in the world *be prosperous* 847.6

go up up in smoke *go to waste* 468.19

gourd *bottle* 578.14

gourmand *eater* 92.15, *pleasure-*

seeker 214.4, *self-indulgent person* 456.5, *refined person* 534.4

gourmandism *appetite* 92.2

gourmandize *feel pleasure* 214.12

gourmandizing *pleasure* 214.2

gourmet *eater* 92.15, *pleasure-seeker* 214.4, *discriminator* 337.6, *self-indulgent person* 456.5, *refined person* 534.4

gourmet eating *delicate eating* 92.3

gout *joint disease* 114.19

gouty *of disease* 114.25

govern 49.26; *have authority* 52.13, *wield authority* 52.16, *master* 68.17, *manage* 126.10, *have authority over* 425.12, *be powerful* 514.18, *moderate* 521.7, *regionalize* 564.15, *restore order* 765.22, *rule over* 780.13

governance 49.18, 52.6; *government* 49.1, *authority* 52.1, 514.5, *management* 126.1, *tactics* 399.12

governess *educator* 48.4, *personal attendant* 69.5, *protector* 810.11

governing 49.25; *authoritative* 52.9, *managerial* 126.9, *dominant* 744.9

governing board *management board* 126.2

governing body 49.19; *management board* 126.2

government 49.1; *political science* 50.2, *governance* 52.6, *authority* 425.3, 780.6

government, the *governing body* 49.19, *the power structure* 68.12

governmental 49.24; *communal* 2.12, *national* 18.16, *political* 50.9, *architectural types* 134.2, *behaving* 399.14, *commanding* 425.7, *administrative* 564.13

governmental authority *governance* 52.6

governmental committee *advisory body* 176.6

governmental funds *treasury* 484.19

governmentally 49.27; *sociologically* 2.15, *politically* 50.11, *commandingly* 425.15

governmental power *governance* 49.18

government by estates *feudalism* 49.5

government by women 49.3

government circles *governing body* 49.19

government debt *national debt* 488.2

government institution *social institution* 2.8

government office 124.13

government official *summit meeting* 600.3

government papers *record* 185.1

government post *position of authority* 52.4

governor 49.23; *person in authority* 52.7, *master* 68.1, *leader* 68.3, *educational leader* 68.11, *means of restraint* 830.6, *commissioner* 833.5

governor general [Brit] *leader* 68.3

governor (of speed) *restraint* 826.8

governorship *position of authority* 52.4, *council* 833.4

governor's mansion *official residence* 60.6

Governor Winthrop *type of desk* 101.6

go way back *be friends* 62.9

go west [Inf] *die* 29.17, *be destroyed* 523.17

go where the wind blows *be irresolute* 378.9

go whitewater canoeing *canoe* 150.31

go with *unify* 752.15, *accompany* 794.16

go with *or* **go out with** [Inf] *court* 299.26

go with [Inf] *stay near* 586.13

go without *fast* 118.8, *refuse oneself* 506.10

go or do without *abstain* 386.16

go without food *fast* 118.8

go with the crowd *be average* 742.8

go with the flow [Inf] *follow* 401.14, *conform* 735.27, *abide by* 781.12

go or move with the stream *march on* 679.11

go with the tide *or* **flow** *do easily* 823.16

gown *vestment* 84.11, *dress* 100.11, *clothe* 100.43

gowned *dressed* 100.38

go wrong 430.23; *disappoint* 293.9, *be immoral* 432.13, *miscarry* 846.19, *malfunction* 846.20

grab *touch* 216.9, *retain* 471.7, *take* 477.14, *take away forcefully* 477.19, *miscellaneous automotive terms* 687.14

grab away *chase* 385.13

grab bag *winnings* 492.5, *miscellany* 751.3, *game of chance* 842.5

grabber *taker* 477.9

grabbing *retention* 471.1, *taking* 477.1, *stealing* 479.1

grab bucket *construction equipment* 14.23

grabby *gain-seeking* 467.11

graben *landform* 8.9

grab one [Inf] *have an idea* 327.13

grab some z's [Inf] *take it easy* 819.13

grab the brass ring [Inf] *chase* 385.13

grab the limelight *show off* 404.26

grab the opportunity *take the opportunity* 659.7

grab the wheel *manage* 126.10

grab turn *competitive swimming* 164.3

grace 527.2; *prayer* 85.10, *social skill* 127.3, *philanthropy* 307.1, *mercy* 308.3, *thanks* 310.2, *forgiveness* 312.1, *kindness* 445.3, *virtues* 447.2, *reward* 472.4, *elegance* 527.1, *beauty* 529.1, *beautify* 529.12, 530.14, *ornament* 532.12, *refinement* 534.1, *stylishness* 537.2

grace before meals *thanks* 310.2

graceful 527.4; *courteous* 410.6, *kind* 445.12, *principled* 447.6, *elegant* 527.3, *beautiful* 529.7, *refined* 534.5, *stylish* 537.7

graceful gesture *sign of courtesy* 410.5

gracefully 527.8; *divinely* 82.24, *dancingly* 135.8, *courteously* 410.13, *elegantly* 527.7, 529.15, 534.8, *stylishly* 537.11

gracefulness *courtesy* 410.1, *grace* 527.2, *beauty* 529.1

Grace Gospel Fellowship *Christian Groups* 81

graceless 528.7; *clumsy* 128.6, *ugly* 531.3

gracelessly *inelegantly* 528.11, 531.7

gracelessness *inelegance* 528.1, *ugliness* 531.1

grace note *musical ornament* 140.19

grace period *delay* 658.3

Graces, the *Deities* 82

graces *courtesies* 410.3

grace the occasion *appear* 575.16

gracile *graceful* 527.4, *beautiful* 529.7, *thin* 595.9

gracility *thinness* 595.1

gracious *friendly* 62.5, *benevolent* 305.7, *philanthropic* 307.6, *pitying* 308.4, *goodwilled* 373.10, *well-behaved* 399.15, *sociable* 407.7, *courteous* 410.6, *showing respect* 435.7, *kind* 445.12

gracious host *or* **hostess** *well-behaved person* 399.6

gracious living *refinement* 534.1

graciously *amicably* 62.13, *benevolently* 305.13, *philanthropically* 307.9, *pityingly* 308.11, *well* 399.22, *courteously* 410.13, *leniently* 423.6, *respectfully* 435.19, *kindly* 445.20, *elegantly* 534.8

gracious manners *good conduct* 399.5

graciousness *benevolence* 305.1, *goodwill* 373.4, *good conduct* 399.5, *sociability* 407.2, *courtesy* 410.1, *leniency* 423.1, *kindness* 445.3

gradation 739.3; *syntax* 5.32, *rung* 636.3, *hierarchy* 765.3, *categorization* 767.5

gradational 739.5; *hierarchical* 765.12

grade *engineer* 14.48, *discriminate* 337.12, *size* 579.17, *measure* 589.20, 739.7, *descent* 597.4, *make horizontal* 603.10, *obliqueness* 607.1, *be oblique* 607.10, *rung* 636.3, *track* 688.2, *relative position* 725.5, *rank* 739.2, *position* 765.4, *systematize* 765.19, *category* 767.6, *categorize* 767.21, *social class* 777.5, *students* 777.6, *sort* 777.13

grade A *excellence* 445.4, *excellent* 445.13

grade crossing *track* 688.2, *junction* 691.9

graded *judged* 337.10, *leveled* 603.8, *oblique* 607.6, *gradational* 739.5, *hierarchical* 765.12, *categorized* 767.15, *classed* 777.11

grade school *school* 48.11

gradient *line* 6.35, *vector* 6.48, *incline* 713.3

gradient post *track* 688.2

gradient wind *wind* 9.12

grading *rank* 739.2, *gradation* 739.3, *categorization* 767.5, *classification* 777.2

Gradual *Eucharist* 85.7

gradual *ritual music* 85.9, *unhurried* 693.8, *gradational* 739.5

gradualism *slowness* 693.1, *degree* 739.1

gradually *slowly* 693.14, *by degrees* 739.10, *partly* 760.17

gradualness *degree* 739.1

graduate *curricular* 48.21, *expert* 68.13, *skilled person* 127.7, *discriminate* 337.12, *launch* 405.14, *size* 579.17, *measure* 589.20, 739.7, *get better* 807.21, *successful person* 845.6, *do well* 845.12

graduated *judged* 337.10, *measured* 589.16, *gradational* 739.5

graduated length method (GLM) *skiing* 162.1

graduated reciprocation in tension reduction *Psychological Tests* 108

graduated scale *measuring instrument* 589.12

graduate school *school* 48.11, *type of school* 48.12

graduation *discrimination* 337.1, *ceremony* 405.3, *formal occasion* 406.4, *gradation* 739.3, *categorization* 767.5, *promotion* 807.5

gradus *word book* 5.27

graffiti *inscription* 185.4

graffiti art *Western Art Styles* 133

graffito *drawing* 143.4

graft *plant breeding* 17.6, *cultivate* 17.19, *propagate* 21.15, *immorality* 432.1, *stolen goods* 479.4, *dishonesty* 479.7, *insertion* 710.1, *plant* 710.14, *extra* 748.6, *connection* 754.1, *connect* 754.13

grafted *ornamental* 17.17, *inserted* 710.5

graft hybrid *plant breeding* 17.6

grafting *gardening* 17.5, *surgery* 107.15, *insertion* 710.1

graft union *plant breeding* 17.6

graham cracker *bread* 90.10

grain 552.2, 553.6; *animal feed* 16.12, *seed* 41.9, *fruits* 44.1, *fruit structure* 44.3, *cereal grass* 45.4, *animal food* 90.2, *attitude* 513.2, *coarsen* 552.12, *grind* 553.23, *little thing* 580.3, *General Units* 589, *weaving* 609.2, *type* 777.4

grain [Arch] *color* 251.1

grain bin *farm building* 16.4, *storehouse* 105.8

grained *rough* 552.8

grain elevator *farm building* 16.4, *storehouse* 105.8

grain farm *farm* 16.2

grain farming *arable farming* 16.6

graininess 553.2; *exposure* 132.15, *grain* 552.2

grain of sand *little thing* 580.3

Grain scan *diagnostic radiology* 107.12

grainy 553.17; *exposed* 132.25, *coarse* 544.6, *rough* 552.8

gram *weight measurement* 538.6, *Scientific and Technical Units* 589

gram atom *or* **gram-atomic weight** *Scientific and Technical Units* 589

graminaceous *grasslike* 45.7

graminaceous plant *grass* 45.1

Gramineae *grass* 45.1

gramineous *grasslike* 45.7

graminiferous *grasslike* 45.7

graminivore *grass eater* 45.6

graminivorous *grass-eating* 45.9, *eating* 92.18

graminivorousness *eating habit* 92.7

grammar 5.28; *Linguistic Studies* 5, *language* 5.4, *language element* 5.13, *schoolbook* 48.15, *type of book* 174.3, *part of speech* 760.7

grammar book *schoolbook* 48.15

grammarian *linguist* 5.3

grammar school *school* 48.11

grammatical *of grammar* 5.41

grammatical analysis *syntax* 5.32

grammatical error *language error* 351.10

grammatically 5.48; *linguistically* 5.44

grammatical meaning *type of meaning* 361.4

grammaticalness *grammar* 5.28

grammatical rules *grammar* 5.28

grammatical studies *syntax* 5.32

grammatical term 5.29

grammaticize *use language* 5.42

grammatist *linguist* 5.3

grammatology Linguistic Studies 5

gram molecule *or* **grammolecular weight** Scientific and Technical Units 589

gramophone record *recording* 185.6

Grampian Mountains Mountains and Hills 569

gramps [Inf] *male title of address* 32.3, *man in the family* 32.12

granadilla Flowers 42

granary *farm building* 16.4, *storehouse* 105.8

Gran Canaria Islands 572

grand 404.22; *manorial* 60.21, *serious* 200.5, *majestic* 297.12, 404.21, *elegant* 527.3, *huge* 579.14, *exalted* 596.10, *important* 799.7

grand [Inf] *fortune* 484.4, US *coinage* 484.10, *thousand* 792.10

grandaunt *family member* 65.2

grand-champion *best* 805.9

grandchild *family member* 65.2

granddad [Inf] *family member* 65.2

granddaddy [Inf] *family member* 65.2

granddaughter *woman in the family* 33.13, *family member* 65.2

grand design *whole situation* 759.3

grand duchy *dominion* 566.3

grand duke *nobleman* 70.1

Grande, Rio Rivers 570

grande dame *proud person* 297.7

grandee *important person* 799.5

grandeur 404.10; *seriousness* 200.2, *majesty* 297.5, *elegance* 527.1, *largeness* 579.2

grandfather *man* 27.8, *man in the family* 32.12, *family member* 65.2

grandfather's clock *or* **grandmother's clock** Timepieces and Timers 646

grand finale *show* 404.12

Grand Guignol *dramatic style* 136.3

grandiloquence *bombast* 194.4, *seriousness* 200.2, *power of speech* 205.5, *pomposity* 404.5, *inelegance of expression* 528.4

grandiloquent *bombastic* 194.10, *serious* 200.5, *articulate* 205.16, *pompous* 404.18, *inelegant* 528.6, *ornate* 532.10, *exaggerated* 712.9

grandiloquently *exaggeratedly* 194.16, *emphatically* 200.7, *orally* 205.21, *pompously* 404.33

grandiose *extravagant* 194.9, *arrogant* 297.9, *grand* 404.22, *inelegant* 528.6, *ornate* 532.10, *exaggerated* 712.9

grandiosely *arrogantly* 297.18, *grandly* 404.37

grandiose-type delusional disorder *psychosis* 108.10

grandiosity *arrogance* 297.2, *grandeur* 404.10

grand jury *jury* 54.11, 341.6, *pretrial proceedings* 54.13

Grand Lama *priest* 84.8

grand larceny *theft* 479.2

grandly 404.37; *majestically* 297.21, 404.36, *exaltedly* 596.22

grandma [Inf] *woman in the family* 33.13, *family member* 65.2

grand mal *neurological disease* 114.20

grandmama [Inf] *woman in the family* 33.13

grand master *expert* 68.13

grandmommy [Inf] *family member* 65.2

grandmother *woman* 27.9, *woman in the family* 33.13, *family member* 65.2

grandmother's tea Children's and Party Games 167

Grand National [Brit] *famous horse races* 159.13

grandnephew *family member* 65.2

grandness *grandeur* 404.10, *largeness* 579.2

grandniece *family member* 65.2

grand opening *beginning* 652.4

grand opening sale *sale* 482.2, *bargain* 495.2

grand opera *opera* 140.8

grandpa [Inf] *man in the family* 32.12, *family member* 65.2

grand parade *ceremonial* 404.11

grandparent *family member* 65.2

grandparents *old people* 653.6

grand piano Musical Instruments 142

Grand Prix *racing* 146.9

Grand Prix (GP) *Formula 1 World Championship races* 146.5

Grand Prix (GP) races *races* 146.4

Grand Prix racer *driver* 146.8

grand scheme, the *final intention* 374.4

grandsire *family member* 65.2

Grand Slam *golfing associations and tournaments* 156.6

grand slam *bridge* 168.4, *successful thing* 845.5

grand-slam home run *batting terms* 147.6

grand-slammer *batting terms* 147.6

grandson *man in the family* 32.12, *family member* 65.2

grandstand *baseball field* 147.3, *place for viewing* 242.13

grandstander *show-off* 404.13

grand strategy *military affairs* 58.1, *art of war* 76.16

grand style, the *literary device* 139.12

grand style *or* **grand manner** Western Art Styles 133

Grand Teton Mountains and Hills 569

grand theft *theft* 479.2

granduncle *family member* 65.2

grand unification theory *fundamental interaction* 10.65, *whole situation* 759.3

grand view *whole situation* 759.3

grange *farm* 16.2, *farm building* 16.4, *mansion* 60.5

granger *agriculturist* 16.14

Grani Notable Horses 159

granite *masonry* 14.22, *building materials* 104.2, *material* 144.6, *hard substance* 542.3, *hard* 542.5

Granite Peak Mountains and Hills 569

granitic *chalky* 8.59, *hard* 542.5

granny *woman* 27.9

granny glasses *visual aid* 242.14

granny knot Knots, Bends, Hitches, Splices 754

Granny Smith Apple Varieties 44

Gran Paradiso Mountains and Hills 569

grant 453.4, 453.14, 489.7, 735.10, 735.30; *acquisition of authority* 52.5, *gain authority* 52.15, *admit* 180.11, *assent* 346.6, *acquiesce* 421.5, *profit* 467.6, *own property* 470.11, *giving* 472.1, *gift* 472.2, *give* 472.10, *lending* 475.1, *lend* 475.6, *credit* 487.10, *income* 492.3, *permit* 502.3, *financial support* 605.8, *support financially* 605.19, *adoption* 692.2, *adopt* 692.14, *financial assistance* 825.6

grant absolution *forgive* 312.8, *acquit* 434.10

grant a loan *credit* 487.10

grant amnesty *forgive* 312.8, *be lenient* 423.5

grant amnesty to *acquit* 434.10

grant an armistice *conciliate* 74.10

grant a pardon *show pity* 308.8

grant a respite *acquit* 54.32

grant asylum *give refuge to* 708.15, *protect* 810.21

grant a truce *conciliate* 74.10

grant a visa to *be hospitable* 477.21

grant bail to *liberate* 831.6

grant clemency *conciliate* 74.10, *be compassionate* 305.11

granted 735.20; *authorized* 52.11, *supposed* 359.6, *given* 472.8, *received* 492.6, *adopted* 692.10

granted amnesty *forgiven* 312.5, *given consideration* 423.4

granted for the sake of argument *supposed* 359.6

grantee [Form] *recipient* 473.5

grant equality to *treat equally* 831.8

grant equal rights to *treat equally* 831.8

grant forgiveness *forgive* 312.8

Granth *other text* 81.19

grant immunity *forgive* 312.8, *permit* 502.6, *set free* 829.17

grant immunity *or* **impunity** *exempt* 430.14

grant-in-aid *gift* 472.2, *grant* 489.7

granting *giving* 472.1, 472.9, *under the circumstances* 726.16

granting a visa *taking in* 477.7

grant lawful *or* **legal authority** *authorize* 52.14

grant leave *permit* 735.29

grantor *giver* 472.7

grant peace *conciliate* 74.10

grant permission *authorize* 52.14

grant power of attorney *commission* 833.8

grant remission *vindicate* 441.11

granular *rough* 552.8, *grainy* 553.17, *tiny* 560.9

granularity *graininess* 553.2

granularly *flakily* 553.30

granular snow *snow* 9.30, 218.6

granular texture *grain* 552.2

granulate *solidify* 542.10, *make rough* 544.11, *coarsen* 552.12, *grind* 553.23, *come to dust* 553.28

granulated *hardened* 542.7, *coarse* 544.6, *rough* 552.8, *pulverized* 553.20

granulated sugar *basic cooking ingredient* 91.8, *sweetener* 222.2

granulation *hardening* 542.2, *roughness* 544.1, *grain* 552.2, *graininess* 553.2, *pulverization* 553.4

granule *sun* 7.15, *fertilizer* 16.9, *grain* 553.6, *little thing* 580.3

granules *sediment* 8.29

granulet *grain* 553.6

granulization *pulverization* 553.4

granulize *grind* 553.23

granulocyte *blood* 555.4

grape *missile* 696.7

grape, the *wine* 93.11

grape hyacinth Flowers 42

grapeshot *historical ammunition* 78.12, *missile* 696.7

grape sugar Common Sugars 12

grapevine *figurative usage* 44.4, *information source* 170.6

graph 6.30; *combinatorics* 6.63, *represent* 6.91, *drawing* 143.4, *illustration* 187.2, *map* 387.7, *outline* 617.1, 617.5, *chart* 767.8

graph coloring *combinatorics* 6.63

grapheme *language element* 5.13, *written letter* 5.14

graphemics Linguistic Studies 5

graphic *pictorial* 6.75, 133.8, *descriptive* 139.17, 202.11, *representational* 187.8, *emphatic* 200.3, *intelligible* 363.5, *realistic* 719.7, *diagrammatic* 767.17

graphical *written* 5.36

graphically *linguistically* 5.44, *pictorially* 133.11, *representationally* 187.15, *descriptively* 202.18

graphical user interface (GUI) *programming concepts* 15.24

graphic artist *visual artist* 133.6

graphic arts *visual arts* 133.1

graphic character *character* 15.18

graphic equalizer *sound quality* 230.4

graphicness *intelligibility* 363.1

graphic representation *graph* 6.30

graphics *programming concepts* 15.24, *illustration* 187.2

graphics adaptor *card* 15.7

graphics card *card* 15.7

graphite Chemical Elements and Common Allotropes 11, *lubricant* 562.7

graphology *divination* 358.2

graphophobia Phobias 283

grapnel *retainer* 471.3, *safety device* 810.15

grapple *fight* 77.35, 422.23, *wrestle* 152.20, *attack* 418.17, *contend* 422.22, *retain* 471.7, *unify* 752.15, *intertwine* 752.19, *yoke* 754.8

grappler *wrestler* 152.12

grapple with *strike* 418.21, *contend* 422.22, *adhere* 755.8, *confront* 828.19

grappling *contending* 422.19

grappling iron *retainer* 471.3, *yoke* 754.8, *safety device* 810.15

Grasmere Lakes 568

grasp *rationalize* 4.20, *learn* 68.18, *touch* 216.9, *have an idea* 327.13, *knowledge* 348.1, *get to know* 348.12, *be wise* 352.6, *understanding* 363.4, *understand* 363.9, *possession* 469.1, *retention* 471.1, *retain* 471.7, *take* 477.14, *range* 563.7, *adhere* 755.8, *safekeeping* 810.6, *preserve* 815.14

grasped *retained* 471.6

grasping *touching* 216.2, *gain-seeking* 467.11, *retentive* 471.5, *taking* 477.1, 477.12

graspingly *avariciously* 477.22

grasping nature *taking* 477.1

grasp the meaning *understand* 363.9

grasp the nettle [Aus] *undertake* 391.7

grass 45.1; *animal feed* 16.12, *graze* 35.35, *grassland* 45.2, *manage grassland* 45.10, *animal food* 90.2, *grip* 151.4, *green thing* 260.4

grass [Brit inf] *inform on* 170.13, *testify* 336.10

grass [Inf] *hemp derivatives* 121.16

grass court *tennis court* 165.3

grass-covered *grassy* 45.8

grasscutter 45.5; *sharp-edged thing* 549.6

grass eater 45.6

grass-eating 45.9

grasses *seed plant* 41.3

grass family *grass* 45.1

grass flower *grass plant* 45.3

grass-green *grassy* 45.8, *green* 260.7

grasshopper *insect* 40.1

grasshoppers Collective Names 59

grassland 45.2; *farm* 16.2, *farmland* 16.3, *plants* 41.1, *green place* 260.2, *geographical space* 563.3, *lowland* 572.6

grassless *desert* 560.12

grasslike 45.7

grasslike plant *grass* 45.1

grass of Parnassus Flowers 42

grass over *manage grassland* 45.10

grass plant 45.3

grass roots *common people* 71.2, *countryside* 564.3, *general public* 778.6, *chief thing* 799.3

grass-roots *local* 564.14, *essential* 799.10

grass-skiing *skiing* 162.1

grass skirt *skirt* 100.12

grasstrack *racing* 146.9

grasstrack racing *automobile racing* 146.1

grass widow *divorced person* 66.4, *surviving spouse* 66.6

grass widower *divorced person* 66.4, *surviving spouse* 66.6

grass widowerhood *divorce* 66.1

grass widowhood *divorce* 66.1

grassy 45.8; *botanical* 17.15, *plantlike* 41.13, *verdant* 260.8, *compressible* 543.9, *of landmasses* 572.12

grate 553.24; *cook* 91.10, *place for fire* 217.9, *sound hoarse* 238.8, *make an insect sound* 240.9, *be dissonant* 241.6, *cause dislike* 291.16, *make rough* 544.11, *grind* 554.15, *porosity* 583.5

grated *coarse* 544.6, *pulverized* 553.20

grateful 310.4

gratefully 310.8

gratefulness *gratitude* 310.1

grateful thanks *thanks* 310.2

grate on one's ears *be strident* 238.7

grater 553.12; *cooking equipment* 91.6, *rough thing* 544.2

gratification *physical pleasure* 214.1, *pleasure* 271.2, *satisfaction* 273.1, *leniency* 423.1

gratified *pleased* 214.9, *satisfied* 273.4, *given consideration* 423.4

gratify *give pleasure* 214.13, *make pleasant* 271.10, *satisfy* 273.7, *be lenient* 423.5

gratifying *pleasant* 214.7, 271.5, *satisfying* 273.5

gratifyingly *leniently* 423.6

grating *strident* 238.4, *hoarse* 238.5, *dissonant* 241.4, *disliked* 291.10, *inelegant* 528.6, *pulverization* 553.4, *irritation* 554.9, *rough* 554.11

gratis *given* 472.8, *as a gift* 472.17, *free of charge* 497.12

gratitude 310.1; *reward* 453.1

gratuitous *suppositional* 359.5, *gainful* 467.10, *given* 472.8, *free of charge* 497.12

gratuitously *gainfully* 467.24, *as a gift* 472.17

gratuitousness *absence of charge* 497.6

gratuity *acknowledgment* 310.3, *bounty* 453.8, *gift* 472.2, *pay* 489.6, *absence of charge* 497.6, *positive stimulus* 508.5, *extra* 748.6

graupel *hail* 9.29

gravamen *accusation* 442.1, *essential content* 723.2

grave *death* 29.1, *burial place* 31.7

grave Musical Terms and Expression Marks 140

grave *important* 144.11, *serious* 200.5, 278.4, 799.8, *dignified* 297.11, *formal* 406.6, *moralistic* 431.12, *closed place* 584.4, *deep-seated* 598.17, *enclosed area* 619.2, *concave land* 635.2, *resting place* 668.5

grave accent Accents and Diacritical Marks 5

grave affair *important matter* 799.2

graveclothes 100.25; *funeral object* 31.6

gravedigger *funeral person* 31.5, *digger* 635.4

gravel *sediment* 8.29, *soil* 8.42, *masonry* 14.22, *building materials* 104.2, *grit* 553.8, *paving* 613.14, *pave* 613.32

gravelliness *graininess* 553.2

gravelly *earthy* 8.60, *nonresonant* 233.7, *hoarse* 238.5, *coarse* 544.6, *grainy* 553.17

gravely *emphatically* 200.7, *solemnly* 278.9, *with dignity* 297.20, *moralistically* 431.16, *with deep feeling* 598.29

graveness *self-righteousness* 431.7

graven image *idol* 83.5, *image* 187.3

grave note *deepness* 236.3

Gravenstein Apple Varieties 44

grave pit *burial place* 31.7

graver *woodworking tool* 131.6, *material* 144.6

graverobber *plunderer* 479.9

graverobbing *plundering* 479.5, *stolen* 479.12

grave-robbing *digging out* 711.3

graveside service *funeral* 31.4

gravestone *funeral object* 31.6, *monument* 185.10, *cover* 613.2

graveyard *burial place* 31.7, *resting place* 668.5

graveyard school Western Literary Groups 139

gravid *pregnant* 21.12

gravimetric *geophysical* 8.51, *analytic* 11.32

gravimetric analysis 11.18

gravimetry *geophysics* 8.2, *gravimetric analysis* 11.18

gravitate *be heavy* 538.12, *descend* 714.12

gravitate toward *tend* 513.5

gravitation *attitude* 513.2, *gravity* 538.2, *sinkage* 714.2

gravitational *magnetic* 700.9

gravitational collapse *stellar evolution* 7.10

gravitational constant *universe* 7.3, *fundamental constant* 10.69

gravitational force *universe* 7.3, *force* 10.9

gravitational interaction *fundamental interaction* 10.65

gravitational pull *gravity* 538.2

gravitational redshift *galaxy* 7.5

gravity 538.2; *seriousness* 200.2, 278.1, *importance* 278.3, 799.1, Phobias 283, *dignity* 297.4, *formality* 406.1, *self-righteousness* 431.7, *influence* 512.1, *material world* 524.1, *depth of feeling* 598.7, *pulling power* 700.2, *quantity* 738.1

gravity dam *dam* 551.12

gravity-defying *ascending* 713.13

gravity geophysics *geophysics* 8.2

gravlax or **gravlaks** *fish dish* 90.19

gravy *side dish* 90.15, 794.11, *juice* 555.2, *semiliquid* 561.7, *cash* 484.2

gravy [Inf] *profit* 467.6, *giveaway* 472.5

gravy boat *tableware* 92.13, *crockery* 578.16

gray 255.6, 255.9; *cloudy* 9.44, *age* 27.16, *horse by color* 159.7, *dim* 248.4, *colorless* 252.5, *gray-haired* 255.7, Scientific and Technical Units 589, *old* 653.10, *mediocre* 742.7, *irresolute* 772.13

gray area *figurative usage* 255.4, *middle ground* 772.4

gray arsenic Chemical Elements and Common Allotropes 11

graybeard *man* 27.8, *figurative usage* 255.4

gray-black *black* 254.5

gray-blue *blue* 261.5

gray color *grayness* 255.1

gray eminence *deputy* 80.1, *one who conceals* 181.7, *figurative usage* 255.4, *indirect influence* 512.4, *backstage manipulator* 844.3

Gray Friar *figurative usage* 255.4

gray-green *green* 260.7

gray hair *gray thing* 255.3

gray-haired 255.7; *aged* 27.15, *old* 653.10

gray-headed *gray-haired* 255.7

grayhen *female bird* 36.16

gray hen *gray thing* 255.3

graying *aging* 27.13, *gray-haired* 255.7

grayish *gray* 255.6

grayishness *grayness* 255.1

gray knight *figurative usage* 255.4

Gray Lady *figurative usage* 255.4

graylag *gray thing* 255.3

grayling *food fish and shellfish* 90.20

grayly 255.10

gray market *figurative usage* 255.4, *seller's market* 833.3

gray matter *figurative usage* 255.4, *brain* 315.6

gray matter [Inf] *intelligence* 352.2

gray mold *pests and diseases* 17.12

grayness 255.1; *old age* 27.5, *murk* 248.2

Gray Panther *older person* 27.7, *figurative usage* 255.4

gray pigment 255.2

gray population *figurative usage* 255.4

gray scale *composition* 132.17

gray squirrel *gray thing* 255.3

gray thing 255.3

graywacke *gray thing* 255.3

gray whale *gray thing* 255.3

gray wolf *gray thing* 255.3

graze 35.35; *practice livestock farming* 16.20, *eat grass* 45.11, *feed* 90.41, *eat* 92.21, *painful injury* 215.3, *inflict pain* 215.10, *type of touch* 216.3, *touch* 216.9,

abrade 554.13, *meeting* 586.5, *meet* 586.15

graze [Inf] *have a meal* 92.25

grazed *farmable* 16.17, *injured* 215.5

grazer *type of animal* 34.5, *grass eater* 45.6

graze the surface *be superficial* 599.6

grazier [Brit] *agriculturist* 16.14, *producer* 522.10

grazing *farmland* 16.3, *livestock farming* 16.10, *grassland* 45.2, *grass-eating* 45.9, *eating habit* 92.7, *eating* 92.18, *touching* 216.6, *scraping* 554.4, *meeting* 586.10

grazing [Inf] *eating meals* 92.4

grazing-incidence telescope *radio telescope* 7.26

grease *basic cooking ingredient* 91.8, *dirty* 112.11, *sound reducer* 233.5, *soften* 543.14, *polish* 545.3, *smooth* 545.10, *lubricant* 562.7, *lubricate* 562.15, *make easy* 823.15

grease [Inf] *bribe* 178.18, 472.3

greaseball Nicknames for Inhabitants 61

greased *polished* 545.7, *lubricated* 562.14

greased palm *incentive* 178.4

grease gun *lubricator* 562.10

grease monkey [Inf] *artisan* 123.13

grease one's palm *remunerate* 489.21

greasepaint *costume* 100.10, *stage requisite* 136.21, *cosmetics* 530.4

greaseproof paper *paper* 104.5

greaser Nicknames for Inhabitants 61

grease the palm *bribe* 178.18

grease the way *make easy* 823.15

grease the wheels *see* 562.18, *make easy* 823.15, *further* 825.30

greasewood Trees and Shrubs 43

greasily *oilily* 562.19

greasiness *smoothness* 545.1, *oiliness* 562.1

greasing *lubrication* 562.2

greasy *dirty* 112.7, *unctuous* 439.10, *polished* 545.7, *oily* 562.11, *lubricated* 562.14

greasy spoon [Inf] *eating place* 92.17

great 445.14; *masterful* 68.15, *plentiful* 97.4, *wondrous* 294.9, *excellent* 445.13, *influential* 512.8, *powerful* 514.15, *strong* 516.9, *heavy* 538.9, *spacious* 563.13, *big* 579.13, *exalted* 596.10, *deep* 598.9, *important* 799.7

great! *wonderful!* 294.20, 445.24

great American game, the *baseball* 147.1

great auk *extinct bird* 36.14

great-aunt *family member* 65.2

Great Basin Deserts 572

Great Bear Constellations 7, Lakes 568

great big *huge* 579.14

great bloodshed *slaughter* 30.5

Great Britain Islands 572

great catch *celebrity* 799.6

great circle *circle* 6.40, *half* 789.7

great-circle sailing *navigation* 690.5

greatcoat [Brit] *coat* 100.19

Great Dane Breeds of Dogs 35

great day *rejoicing* 279.1, *anniversary* 405.5, *important matter* 799.2

great distance 585.2

Great Divide, the *distant place* 585.3

great divide, the *death* 29.1
Great Dividing Range
  Mountains and Hills 569
Great Dog Constellations 7
great doings *activity* 414.1,
  important matter 799.2
greaten *grow* 581.17
greater *ranked* 6.72, *quantitative*
  738.6, *superior* 744.8
greater and greater *increasingly*
  746.9
greater city *city* 567.1
greater good *choice* 382.3
Greater London *London* 567.8
Greater New York *New York*
  567.6
greater number *majority* 793.3
greater number, a *plurality* 793.1
greater part *large part* 579.3,
  majority 793.3
greater proportion *majority*
  793.3
greater trumps *cards* 168.2
greatest *ranked* 6.72, *best* 744.10
greatest, the *paragon* 744.6,
  important person 799.5
greatest common divisor
  (GCD) *multiplication* 6.15
greatest common factor (GCF)
  [Brit] *multiplication* 6.15
greatest number *majority* 793.3
great expectations *aspiration*
  281.3, *looking to the future* 650.4
great-grandchild *family member*
  65.2
great-granddaughter *family*
  member 65.2
great-grandfather *family member*
  65.2
great-grandmother *family*
  member 65.2
great-grandparent *family member*
  65.2
great-grandson *family member*
  65.2
great-great-grandparent *person*
  of the past 651.7
great hundred *hundreds* 792.9
Great Indian Deserts 572
Great Lakes 568
Great Lakes Lakes 568
great leveler *personifications and*
  symbols 29.4
greatly *excellently* 445.21, *heavily*
  538.16, *largely* 579.19, *exaltedly*
  596.22
great man *or* woman *important*
  person 799.5
Great Mogul *sovereign* 68.2
Great Mother *world soul* 82.3
Great Nebula in Orion *nebula*
  7.6
greatness *excellence* 445.4, *influence*
  512.1, *authority* 516.5, *largeness*
  579.2, *exaltation* 596.3, *superiority*
  744.1, *importance* 799.1
great news *important matter* 799.2
great number *multitude* 795.1
Great Ouse Rivers 570
great outdoors, the *open air*
  558.5, *outside* 610.3
Great Plains *regions of the United*
  States 564.7
great price *costliness* 496.1
Great Pyrenees Breeds of Dogs
  35
great quantity *plenty* 97.2, *excess*
  99.1, *certain amount* 738.3
great respect *admiration* 435.2
Great Salt Lake Lakes 568,
  Deserts 572
Great Sandy Deserts 572
great Scott! *good heavens!* 292.15

great seal *means of identification*
  184.3
Great Slave Lakes 568
Great Smoky Mountains
  Mountains and Hills 569
great speed *swiftness* 694.1
Great Spirit *God* 82.6
Great Square of Pegasus
  constellation 7.13
great thing *chief thing* 799.3
great-uncle *family member* 65.2
great unwashed *common people*
  71.2, *vulgar group* 535.5
Great Victoria Deserts 572
Great Vowel Shift *linguistic theory*
  5.2
Great Wall of China *separator*
  753.5
Great War, the *world war* 76.2
great waters [Inf] *sea* 571.1
great way *great distance* 585.2
Great Wen, the *London* 567.8
great work *masterpiece* 127.5
great worth *value* 496.6
greave *historic armor* 419.8
grebe *water bird* 36.9
Grecian couch *couch* 101.7
Greco-Latin square *combinatorics*
  6.63
Greco-Roman *type of wrestling*
  152.9, *wrestling* 152.18
Greco-Roman wrestler *wrestler*
  152.12
Greece Countries 566
greed *appetite* 92.2, *gluttony* 119.1,
  covetousness 288.4, *jealousy* 314.2,
  immorality 432.1, *selfishness*
  444.1, *overindulgence* 456.3, *gain*
  467.1, *taking* 477.1, *excessiveness*
  712.4
greedily *carnivorously* 92.27,
  gluttonously 119.5, *covetously*
  288.28, *jealously* 314.12,
  immorally 432.18, *selfishly* 444.8,
  gainfully 467.24, *avariciously*
  477.22, *excessively* 712.17
greediness *gluttony* 119.1,
  covetousness 288.4
greedy *eating* 92.18, *unprovided*
  98.6, *gluttonous* 119.5, *covetous*
  288.14, *jealous* 314.5, *selfish*
  444.4, *overindulgent* 456.8, *gain-*
  seeking 467.11, *taking* 477.12
greedy person **477.11;** *glutton*
  119.2
greedy pig *desirer* 288.9
Greek [Inf] *senseless talk* 362.4
Greek architecture Architectural
  Styles 134
Greek chorus *role* 136.23
Greek cross plan *church*
  architecture 134.11
Greek drama *dramatic style* 136.3
Greek fire *propellant* 78.14, *cause*
  of fire 217.10
Greek mode *mode* 140.17
Greek terms Phobias 283
Greek theater *theater* 136.16
Greek tragedy *tragedy* 136.10
Green Rivers 570
green **260.7, 260.14;** *immature*
  26.12, 389.9, 652.12, *plantlike*
  41.13, *of plants* 41.14, *grassland*
  45.2, *grassy* 45.8, *believing* 87.6,
  Bean Varieties 90, *unhealthy*
  114.23, *unskilled* 128.5, *sports*
  ground 145.2, *green bowling*
  151.3, *grip* 151.4, *golf course*
  156.2, *ski* 162.27, *acid* 223.5,
  spectrum 251.3, *green place* 260.2,
  verdant 260.8, *raw* 260.9, *sick*
  260.12, *environmental* 260.13,
  jealous 314.5, *ignorant* 349.5,
  unaccustomed 398.3, *naive* 449.9,

821.3, *nautical* 690.14, *embryonic*
  771.19, *preserving* 815.11
green [Inf] *cash* 484.2
green algae *algae* 47.11
green apple *sour thing* 223.3
green around the gills [Inf] *sick*
  114.24, 260.12
greenback *figurative usage* 260.5,
  US coinage 484.10
Green Bay *figurative usage* 260.5
green bean *green thing* 260.4
green belt *karate* 152.14, *tae kwon*
  do 152.15, *aikido* 152.16
greenbelt *green place* 260.2,
  geographical space 563.3, *regions*
  564.2, *suburb* 567.11
Green Berets *figurative usage*
  260.5
green-blue *blue* 261.5
green bowling 151.3, Sporting
  Activities 145, *bowling* 151.1
green card *green thing* 260.4,
  permit 502.3
green color *greenness* 260.1
greenery *plants* 41.1, *leaf* 41.6,
  green place 260.2
green-eyed **260.11;** *hostile* 63.6,
  hating 300.7, *resentful* 302.8,
  jealous 314.5
green-eyed monster *figurative*
  usage 260.5, *resentment* 302.1,
  jealousy 314.2
green-eyed monster, the
  personal conflict 63.2
greenfinch *green thing* 260.4
green flash *green thing* 260.4
greenflies *pests and diseases* 17.12
greenfly *green thing* 260.4
greengage plum *green thing* 260.4
greengrocer [Brit] *food provider*
  90.6, *retailer* 482.11
greenheart Trees and Shrubs 43,
  green thing 260.4
greenhorn *unskilled person* 128.3,
  figurative usage 260.5, *ignorant*
  person 349.4, *innocent person*
  449.5, *new arrival* 652.7, 724.6,
  beginner 771.14, *naive person*
  821.2
greenhorn [Inf] *beginner* 398.2
greenhouse *nursery* 17.4,
  transparent thing 249.4, *figurative*
  usage 260.5
greenhouse effect *climatic change*
  9.37, *lack of hygiene* 112.3,
  pollution 117.8, *hot weather* 217.6,
  figurative usage 260.5
greenhouse gardening Hobbies
  and Pastimes 167
greenhouse plant *plant* 41.2
greenie [Inf] *stimulants* 121.18,
  green thing 260.4
greenish *green* 260.7
greenish-yellow *yellow* 259.7
Greenland *cold place* 218.7,
  figurative usage 260.5, Islands
  572, *landmass* 572.1
Greenland Sea *figurative usage*
  260.5, Oceans and Seas 571
green leaf *green thing* 260.4
green light *safety light* 246.7, *green*
  thing 260.4, *yes* 346.2, *approval*
  437.1, *vindication* 441.1, *tolerance*
  502.2, *permission* 735.9
greenly **260.15;** *youthfully* 26.14
greenmail *figurative usage* 260.5,
  bargaining 480.10, *purchasing*
  481.2
green manure *crop* 16.8, *fertilizer*
  16.9
green monkey disease *tropical*
  disease 114.10
Green Mountains *figurative usage*
  260.5, Mountains and Hills 569

green movement *ecology* 815.3
greenness **260.1;** *immaturity* 26.3,
  389.3, 652.3, *unskillfulness* 128.1,
  sourness 223.1, *naiveté* 449.4,
  821.1
green olive *green thing* 260.4
Green Paper [Brit] *green thing*
  260.4
Green party *green politics* 260.6,
  Political Parties 50
green pea *green thing* 260.4
Greenpeace *green politics* 260.6
green pepper *green thing* 260.4
green pigment **260.3**
green place **260.2**
green plant *plant* 41.2
green plants *plants* 41.1
green politics **260.6**
green porphyry *green thing* 260.4
green pound [Brit] *figurative usage*
  260.5
green revolution *agriculture* 16.1
Green River ordinance *figurative*
  usage 260.5
greenroom *stage* 136.18, *figurative*
  usage 260.5
green run *ski run* 162.2
Greens *green politics* 260.6
greens *salad* 90.16, *green thing*
  260.4
greensand *green thing* 260.4
greensick *sick* 260.12
greenskeeper *or* greenkeeper
  green place 260.2
green snake *green thing* 260.4
Green's theorem Mathematical
  Concepts 6
greenstick fracture *figurative*
  usage 260.5
greenstone *green thing* 260.4
green stuff [Inf] *figurative usage*
  260.5, *cash* 484.2
greensward *grassland* 45.2
green tea *tea* 93.7, *figurative usage*
  260.5
green thing **260.4**
green thumb *horticulturist* 17.13,
  figurative usage 260.5, *ability*
  340.2
green turtle *green thing* 260.4
green vegetable *vegetable* 17.11
green vegetables *fruits* 44.1
Greenwich Time *or* **Greenwich**
  Mean Time (GMT) *or*
  Universal Time (UT) *time zone*
  646.5
Greenwich Village *New York*
  567.6
green with envy *hostile* 63.6,
  green-eyed 260.11, *resentful* 302.8,
  envious 314.4
greenwood *trees* 43.4, *green place*
  260.2
greet 410.11; *gesture* 183.17,
  approach 209.10, *welcome* 408.18,
  salute 435.17, *receive someone*
  473.14
greeting 435.5, 435.8; *utterance*
  205.10, *salutation* 209.2,
  salutatory 209.7, *welcome* 408.10,
  sign of courtesy 410.5, *reception*
  473.4, 704.3
greetings *cry of greeting* 239.4,
  greeting 435.5
greetings! *welcome!* 704.24
greet the day *arise* 655.7
gregale *Notable Winds* 9
gregarious *sociable* 408.11
gregariously *sociably* 408.19
gregariousness *sociability* 408.1
Gregorian calendar *calendar*
  646.3
Gregorian chant *ritual music* 85.9,
  sacred music 140.3

Gregorian mode *mode* 140.17
Gregory's series Mathematical
 Concepts 6
greige *white* 253.7, *grayness* 255.1,
 gray 255.6
gremlin *sprite* 86.12, Legendary
 Creatures 360, *evil spirit* 446.4,
 miscellaneous aviation terms 689.9,
 technical problem 826.3, *hinderer*
 826.11
Grenada Countries 566, Islands
 572
grenade *bomb* 78.15, *banger* 234.3
grenade launcher *firearm* 78.7
grenadier *historical soldier* 77.8
grenadine Fabrics and Fibers 130
Grenadines Islands 572
Gresham's law *economic
 deterioration* 808.2
Gretna Green wedding *or
 marriage* [Brit inf] *wedding* 64.5
greyhound Breeds of Dogs 35,
 gray thing 255.5
greyhound racing Sporting
 Activities 145, *race* 422.8
greyhounds Collective Names 59
gribble *crustacean* 39.10
grid *electron tube* 14.40, *stage*
 136.18, *automobile racing terms*
 146.3, *power supplier* 514.14,
 braid 609.3
griddle *cooker* 91.5, *cooking
 equipment* 91.6, *cook* 91.10,
 burner 217.4
griddlecake *pancake* 90.11
gridiron *stage* 136.18, *stadium*
 155.3
gridlock *obstruction* 584.2, *stop*
 668.2, *lack of motion* 678.1,
 miscellaneous automotive terms
 687.14, *roadblock* 826.4
gridlocked *obstructed* 584.8
grid reference *exact location* 565.2
grid start *automobile racing terms*
 146.3
grief *adversity* 117.2, *sorrow* 270.1,
 lamentation 280.1
grief-stricken *sorrowful* 270.4
grievance *industrial dispute* 57.7,
 fault 430.2
grievance procedure *strike* 57.8
grieve 270.7, 308.7; *lament* 280.7,
 offend 302.15
grieved for *lamented* 280.5
grieve for *feel for* 266.17, *grieve*
 308.7
griever *lamenter* 280.3
grieving *lamentation* 280.1,
 lamenting 280.4
grievous *distressing* 270.6, *pitiful*
 308.5
grievous bodily harm *assault*
 695.4
grievously *destructively* 446.13,
 adversely 848.16
griffin Heraldic Terms 184,
 Legendary Creatures 360
griffon Breeds of Dogs 35,
 Legendary Creatures 360
grill *meat dish* 90.21, *cooker* 91.5,
 eating place 92.17, *burner* 217.4,
 brown 256.7, *interrogate* 333.17
grille *porosity* 583.5
grilled *browned* 256.6, *questioned*
 333.15
grilling *cooking technique* 91.2,
 questioning 333.2
grilse *young fish* 38.6
grim *serious* 278.4, *frightening*
 283.12, *sullen* 304.8, *strong-willed*
 376.10, *determined* 379.7,
 discourteous 411.5
grimace *gesture* 183.5, 183.17, *look*
 242.7, 242.21, *react against*

291.15, *sign of irascibility* 303.6,
 frown 303.15, *sign of irritability*
 304.4, *be irritable* 304.14,
 distortion of face 627.2, *make faces*
 627.10
grimacing *gestural* 183.13,
 frowning 303.12
Grimaldi man *primitive humanity*
 18.4
grim determination *resolution*
 376.1
grime *dirt* 112.5, *dirty* 112.11
Grimes Golden Apple Varieties
 44
griminess *dirtiness* 112.1
grimly *sullenly* 304.16,
 discourteously 411.8
Grimm's law *linguistic theory* 5.2
grimness *seriousness* 278.1,
 sullenness 304.1, *determination*
 379.2
Grim Reaper *personifications and
 symbols* 29.4
grim reaper *destroyer* 523.6
grimy *dirty* 112.7, *shady* 250.4
grin *show joy* 269.10, *distortion of
 face* 627.2, *make faces* 627.10
grin and bear it *take courage*
 284.15, *succumb* 421.7
grind 553.23, 554.15; *cook* 91.11,
 chew 92.22, *work* 122.1, 122.8,
 make ceramics 129.10, *be painful*
 215.9, *sound hoarse* 238.8,
 persevere 377.10, *demolish* 523.12,
 sharpen 549.16, *contract* 582.12,
 take apart 753.16
grinder *machine tool* 14.9, *teeth*
 19.8, *sandwich* 90.9, *cooking
 equipment* 91.6, *pulverizer* 553.11,
 contractor 582.6
grinding 554.3; *working* 122.6,
 ceramic process 129.5, *painful*
 215.4, *destroying* 523.2,
 pulverization 553.4, *rough* 554.11,
 shortening 582.2
grind into the dust *knock down*
 523.13
grindstone *work* 122.1, *boring
 thing* 296.3, *sharpener* 549.8,
 pulverizer 553.11
grind to a halt *stop* 668.10
grind to dust *demolish* 523.12
grind to powder *demolish* 523.12
grind underfoot *knock down*
 523.13
grind under one's heel *knock
 down* 523.13
gringo Nicknames for Inhabitants
 61
grinner *joyful person* 269.5
grinning *cheerful* 269.7
grip 151.4; *governance* 52.6, *hand
 tool* 103.3, *skill* 127.1, *golf
 equipment* 156.5, *horizontal bar*
 157.5, *gesture* 183.5, *pain* 215.1,
 be painful 215.9, *touch* 216.9,
 possession 469.1, *retention* 471.1,
 retainer 471.3, *retain* 471.7,
 influence 512.1, *bag* 578.7,
 baggage 578.8, *spasm* 684.8,
 friction 699.4, *unify* 752.15,
 intertwine 752.19, *bind* 754.14,
 adhere 755.8, *safekeeping* 810.6
gripe *show tenaciousness* 471.8,
 complain 507.8, *object* 828.18
gripe [Inf] *expression of
 dissatisfaction* 274.2, *be dissatisfied*
 274.7, *fault* 430.2
griper [Inf] *dissatisfied person* 274.3
gripes *gastroenterological disease*
 114.11
grip of steel *retention* 471.1

gripped *retained* 471.6, *bound*
 754.12
gripping *painful* 215.4, *touching*
 216.2, *retentive* 471.5, *appealing*
 512.9
grisaille *painting* 143.3, *grayness*
 255.1
griseous *gray* 255.6
grisly *frightening* 283.12, *ugly*
 531.3
grist *materials* 104.1, *meal* 553.7
gristle *solid body* 540.4, *hard
 substance* 542.3
gristly *hard* 542.5, *chewy* 547.9
grist to one's mill *gain* 467.1
grit 553.8; *steadfastness* 284.3, *will*
 376.5, *stamina* 377.4, *endurance*
 516.4, *hard substance* 542.3, *grain*
 552.2
grit one's teeth *gesture* 183.17,
 brace oneself 376.13, *hold out*
 377.13
gritted teeth *will* 376.5
grittily *toughly* 542.12, *flakily*
 553.30
grittiness *hardness* 542.1, *grain*
 552.2, *graininess* 553.2
gritty *enduring* 377.9, *hard* 542.5,
 rough 552.8, *grainy* 553.17
grizzle *whiten* 253.12, *variegate*
 263.11
grizzled *gray-haired* 255.7, *mottled*
 263.10, *old* 653.10
grizzly *gray-haired* 255.7
groan *express pain* 215.11, *cry of
 pain* 239.5, *cry* 239.16, *lament*
 280.2, *gesture of protest* 507.3,
 complain 507.8
groaner *lamenter* 280.3
groaning *crying* 239.11
groaning board *plenty* 90.4
groats *meal* 553.7
grocer *provisioner* 89.4, *food
 provider* 90.6, *retailer* 482.11
groceries *food* 90.1
groceryman *retailer* 482.11
grocery store *food provider* 90.6,
 store 124.4, 483.8
Groenendael Breeds of Dogs 35
grog *alcohol* 121.5
groggy *ill* 517.8, *sedentary* 678.5
grogram Fabrics and Fibers 130
groin Architectural Elements 134,
 vault 134.8, *water system* 551.13,
 fork 703.5, *safety device* 810.15
grommet *flag* 184.8
Groningen Horse and Pony
 Breeds 159
Groningen Whiteheaded Breeds
 of Cattle 16
groom *farm worker* 16.15, *practice
 livestock farming* 16.20, *boyfriend*
 32.4, *wedding party* 64.7, *spouse*
 64.8, *domestic servant* 69.7, *dress
 up* 100.45, *clean* 111.17, *horse
 person* 159.14, *ride* 159.16, *brief*
 388.20, *tidy* 765.21
groomed *dressed up* 100.39,
 equipped 388.10, *smooth* 545.4,
 orderly 765.13
grooming *elegance* 527.1
grooming kit *riding equipment*
 159.9
groomsman *wedding party* 64.7
groove *automobile racing terms*
 146.3, *way* 397.3, *crack* 587.2,
 587.7, *round* 633.6, *notch* 636.1,
 furrow 638.1, 638.5, *passage*
 691.5, *custom* 780.5
grooved *cracked* 587.5, *furrowed*
 638.3
groovy [Inf] *fashionable* 536.5
grope *be clumsy* 128.9, *touch* 216.9
grope [Inf] *type of touch* 216.3,

touch 216.9, *communicate love*
 299.25
grope one's way *hesitate* 693.12
groping *clumsy* 128.6, *hesitant*
 693.9
groping [Inf] *touching* 216.2,
 communication of love 299.6
groschen *national coins* 484.11
grosgrain Fabrics and Fibers 130
gross *bad-mannered* 411.6, *profit*
 467.6, *gainful* 467.10, *receive*
 473.13, 492.7, *indecorous* 528.8,
 ugly 531.3, *vulgar* 535.6, *fat*
 579.15, *whole* 759.6, *hundreds*
 792.9
gross amount, the *all* 759.4
gross behavior *bad manners* 411.2
gross domestic product (GDP)
 produce 522.5
Grossglockner Mountains and
 Hills 569
gross income *economic factor* 56.8
gross indecency *sexual offense*
 432.6
grossly *rudely* 411.9, *at great cost*
 496.12, *inelegantly* 528.11, 531.7,
 vulgarly 535.10
gross national product (GNP)
 economic indicator 56.4, *earnings*
 467.5, *produce* 522.5
grossness 535.3; *bad manners*
 411.2, *impropriety* 528.2, *fatness*
 579.5
gross out [Inf] *cause dislike* 291.16
gross profit *return* 453.6, *profit*
 467.6
gross profits *money received* 492.2
gross receipts *earnings* 467.5,
 something received 473.2, *money
 received* 492.2
gross return *earnings* 467.5
gross revenue *earnings* 467.5
gross score *golfing terms* 156.3
gross structure *anatomy* 13.12
gross ton [Brit] General Units 589
gross (total) *total* 738.4
gross weight *weighing* 538.4
grotesque *misrepresented* 188.4,
 astonishing 294.10, *fantastic*
 360.11, *inelegant* 528.6, *deformed*
 627.7
grotesquely *astonishingly* 294.19,
 asymmetrically 627.13
grotesquerie *misrepresentation*
 188.1, *distortion of body* 627.3
grotto *ornamental garden* 17.3
grotty [Inf] *unclean* 112.8, *ugly*
 531.3
grouch *irascible person* 303.7, *sullen
 person* 304.7, *be irritable* 304.14,
 discourteous person 411.4
grouchily *crossly* 303.20, *irritably*
 304.17
grouchiness *crossness* 303.4,
 irritableness 304.3
grouchy *cross* 303.11, *irritable*
 304.9, *argumentative* 329.7
ground *continent* 8.8, *electric
 potential* 10.40, *conduct* 14.51,
 educate 48.22, *claim* 72.2, *culinary*
 91.9, *material* 143.9, *sports ground*
 145.2, *play baseball* 147.9, *fishing*
 154.13, *imprison* 454.23, *destroyed*
 523.9, *pulverized* 553.20, *region*
 564.1, *circumstances* 573.2, *base*
 601.1, 601.10, *basis* 601.3, *bottom*
 601.6, *reason* 675.4, *sail* 690.16,
 land 704.16, *link* 752.18, *partial*
 760.11, *safety device* 810.15, *make
 certain* 840.14
ground *or grounds* *motive* 178.5
ground-attack aircraft *military
 aircraft* 77.30
ground bait *bait* 154.6

ground ball *batting terms* 147.6
ground-based observatory *observatory* 7.24
ground bass *harmonic element* 140.14
ground beef *beef* 90.24
groundbreaker *precursor* 769.7
ground-breaking *preparatory* 769.11
ground cloth *floor covering* 613.13
ground control *flight control* 689.7
ground-controlled approach (GCA) *flight control* 689.7
ground cover *garden plant* 17.10
ground covering *base* 601.1
ground crew *air force person* 77.31, *aircraft personnel* 689.8
ground drive *tennis strokes* 165.2
grounded *circumstantial* 573.7, *stabilized* 674.4, *lowered* 716.7
grounded [Inf] *punished* 454.19
ground engineer *aircraft personnel* 689.8
grounder *batting terms* 147.6
ground floor *base* 601.1
ground fog *fog* 9.32
ground-force attack *land attack* 418.3
ground frost *frost* 9.25
ground gained *advance* 467.3, 679.3
ground game *play* 155.8
ground glass *glass* 249.5
grounding *downthrow* 716.2
grounding [Inf] *punishment* 454.1
ground intentionally *exhibit penalty behavior* 155.21
groundless *sophistic* 330.7, *untrue* 722.6, *causeless* 842.11
groundlessly *sophistically* 330.14
ground-level *bottom* 601.6
groundling *theatergoer* 136.30
groundnuts *crop* 16.8
ground pine *fern* 46.1
ground plan *map* 387.7, *outline* 617.1
ground round *beef* 90.24
grounds *dirt* 112.5, *explanation* 319.4, *line of argument* 329.3, *evidence* 339.1, *specification* 340.6, *defense* 441.2, *property* 470.1, *motivation* 508.1, *mud* 561.8, *basis* 601.3, 605.4, *reason* 674.5, *residue* 750.2, *confirmation* 840.3
grounds for dismissal *bargaining terms* 57.10
grounds for divorce *divorce court* 66.3
groundsheet *floor covering* 613.13
groundskeeper *domestic servant* 69.7
groundskeeping *horticulture* 17.1
groundspeed *flight* 689.5, *speed* 694.2
ground state *excited atom* 10.55
ground station *weather station* 9.5
ground stroke *tennis strokes* 165.2
groundswell *atmospheric agitation* 684.13
ground to dust *pulverized* 553.20
ground under repair *golf course* 156.2
groundwater 8.11; *erosion* 8.41
groundwork *preparations* 388.2, *basis* 601.3, *arrangements* 767.10, *preparation* 769.3, *rudiments* 771.7
group 18.13, 59.8, 59.24, 623.5; *social organization* 2.5, *set* 6.19, *chemical element* 11.3, *assembly* 59.1, *party* 59.3, *assemble* 59.23, *come together* 59.25, 757.10, *air force unit* 77.29, *design* 133.9, *sculpture* 144.1, *calling* 178.6, *size*

579.17, *alliance* 735.5, *association* 752.2, *collection* 757.3, *part* 760.1, *systematize* 765.19, *category* 767.6, *arrange* 767.18, *categorize* 767.21, *class* 777.1, 777.12, *social class* 777.5
Group 47 Western Literary Groups 139
group activity *sociability* 408.1, *social activity* 414.2
group behavior *social organization* 2.5
grouped 59.21, 765.11; *partial* 760.11, *arranged* 767.11, *categorized* 767.15, *classed* 777.11
Groupe de Recherche d'Art Visuel Western Art Styles 133
group grope [Inf] *sex act* 20.10
group home *haven* 810.3, *safe house* 812.5
groupie [Inf] *idolater* 83.7, *adherent* 755.4, *follower* 794.10
group influence 512.6
grouping 765.2; *collection* 59.2, *group* 59.8, *treatment* 143.6, *arrangement* 767.1, *categorization* 767.5, *class* 777.1, *classification* 777.2
group interaction *social organization* 2.5
Group of Seven (G7) *economic organization* 56.6
group photograph *portrait* 132.5
group practice *medical practice* 107.3
group psychology Psychological Theories, Schools 108
group psychotherapy *psychotherapy* 108.4
group sex *sex act* 20.10
group shot *portrait* 132.5
group solidarity *social organization* 2.5
group test Psychological Tests 108
group theory Branches of Mathematics 6
group therapy *therapy* 115.12
group together *assemble* 59.23, *come together* 757.10
Group Zero Western Art Styles 133
grouse *table bird* 36.10, Collective Names 59, *meat* 90.22, *game* 160.6, *complain* 507.8, *object* 828.18
grouse [Inf] *expression of dissatisfaction* 274.2, *be dissatisfied* 274.7, *complaint* 304.5, *be irritable* 304.14, *fault* 430.2
grouser [Inf] *dissatisfied person* 274.3, *sullen person* 304.7, *discourteous person* 411.4, *protester* 507.4
grout *masonry* 14.22, *material* 129.2, *wall covering* 613.12, *face* 613.31, *adhesive* 755.3
grouts *dirt* 112.5
grove *trees* 43.4
grovel *humble oneself* 298.18, *be solicitous* 323.13, *fawn* 401.9, *succumb* 421.7, *show obeisance to* 426.8, *show respect* 435.16, *be low* 597.20, *be horizontal* 603.9, *bow* 716.22, *be subject to* 832.12
groveler *humble person* 298.7, *sycophant* 401.3, *submitter* 421.2
groveling *sycophancy* 401.2, *sycophant* 401.7, *submission* 421.1, *obeisance* 426.3, *debasement* 716.5, *degraded* 716.10
grovelingly *sycophantically* 401.16
groves of academe *academia* 348.6
grow 43.15, 581.17, 676.10; *farm*

16.19, *practice livestock farming* 16.20, *age* 27.16, *vegetate* 41.21, *increase* 467.17, 746.6, *bring into existence* 522.14, *be tall* 596.16, *be converted* 670.12, *further* 679.13, *rear* 715.10, *come to be* 717.19, *change by degrees* 739.8, *make bigger* 746.7
grow better *get better* 807.21
grow by leaps and bounds *increase* 746.6
grow dark *cloud* 9.54, *become dark* 247.9
grow dim *be dim* 248.7, *decrease* 747.7
grower *agriculturist* 16.14, *horticulturist* 17.13, *producer* 522.10
grow fat *be prosperous* 847.6
grow from *grow* 676.10
grow fruit *garden* 17.18
growing 581.12, 676.6; *maturing* 27.12, *plantlike* 41.13, *vigorous* 518.2, *manufacture* 892.5, *converting* 670.8, *rearing* 715.2, *gradational* 739.5, *increasing* 746.4
growing apart *separation* 753.1
growing old *aging* 27.13, Phobias 283
growing pains *youthfulness* 26.2
growing plants *gardening* 17.5
growing season *summer* 654.4
growing soft *decrease* 747.1
growing together *combination* 757.1
growing up *bodily development* 19.17, *growth* 581.4, *growing* 581.12
grow in profusion *abound* 97.8
growl *speak in a particular way* 205.18, *animal sound* 240.1, *make an animal sound* 240.7, *be angry* 302.19, *sign of irascibility* 303.6, *frown* 303.15, *sign of irritability* 304.4, *be irritable* 304.14
grow larger *increase* 746.6
growler *iceberg* 8.45
grow less *decrease* 747.7
grow light 246.21
grow like a weed *grow* 581.17
growling *ululant* 240.4, *frowning* 303.12, 304.10, *discourteous* 411.5, *bad-mannered* 411.6
growlingly *frowningly* 304.18
growly *irritable* 304.9
grow moss *decay* 808.16
grown 581.11; *produced* 522.12, *reared* 715.7
grown gall *pests and diseases* 17.12
grown old *aged* 27.15
grownup *older person* 27.7
grown up *grown* 581.11
grown-up *adult* 27.11
grow old 653.16; *age* 27.16, *disintegrate* 808.15
grow on one *become a habit* 397.17
grow pale *or* **faint** *be dim* 248.7
grow rank *be dirty* 112.10
grow rich *increase* 746.6, *be prosperous* 847.6
grow rusty *be unaccustomed* 398.5
grow smaller *decrease* 747.7
grow soft *decrease* 747.7
grow stale *decay* 808.16
grow tall *be tall* 596.16
growth 581.4, 676.3; *crystal* 11.14, *physiology* 13.13, *body process* 19.15, *bodily development* 19.17, *life function* 28.6, *plants* 41.1, *cancer* 114.15, *augmentation* 467.2, *manufacture* 522.2,

evolution 670.3, *development* 679.4, *increase* 746.1
growth hormone Human Hormones 12
growth ring *tree part* 43.2
growth study *measurement* 1.9
growth substance *plant hormone* 12.17
grow together *adhere* 755.8, *combine* 757.9
grow up *age* 27.16, *grow* 581.17, *ascend* 713.19, *increase* 746.6, *be complete* 761.10
grow vegetables *garden* 17.18
grow weak *be unhealthy* 114.29, *be weak* 517.12
groyne *water system* 551.13
Grozny Breeds of Sheep 16
grub *young animal* 26.4, *larva* 40.9, *manage trees* 43.14, *persevere* 377.10
grub [Inf] *food* 90.1
grubbily *dirtily* 112.12
grubbiness *dirtiness* 112.1, *untidiness* 766.3
grubby *verminous* 40.13, *dirty* 112.7, *untidy* 766.11
grub out *extract* 711.13
grub's on! *come and get it!* 92.28
grudge 375.15, 501.7; *ill feeling* 63.3, *be hostile* 63.10, *bad feeling* 266.5, *hate* 300.1, *resentment* 302.1, *bitterness* 306.3, *be malevolent* 306.12, *jealousy* 314.2, *be jealous* 314.8
grudge match *contest* 422.4
grudging *hostile* 63.6, *resentful* 302.8, *bitter* 306.9, *jealous* 314.5, *mean* 501.4, *troublesome* 824.13
grudging apology *confession* 451.2
grudging consent *unwillingness* 375.1
grudgingly *hostilely* 63.13, *malevolently* 306.14, *bitterly* 306.16, *jealously* 314.12, *unwillingly* 375.17, *meanly* 501.8
grudgingness *jealousy* 314.2, *unwillingness* 375.1
grudging service *disobedience* 375.5
grudging thanks *ingratitude* 311.1
gruel *cereal* 90.12, *semiliquid* 561.7
grueling *laborious* 122.7, *punishing* 454.20, *fatiguing* 820.4, *difficult* 824.9
gruesome *frightening* 283.12, *ugly* 531.3
gruff *sparing with words* 208.6, *hoarse* 238.5, *ill-natured* 303.9, *irritable* 304.9, *discourteous* 411.5, *abrupt* 591.8
gruffly *ill-naturedly* 303.18, *irritably* 304.17, *discourteously* 411.8, *abruptly* 591.13
gruffness *hoarseness* 238.2, *ill nature* 303.2, *irritableness* 304.3, *discourtesy* 411.1, *abruptness* 591.4
gru-gru palm Trees and Shrubs 43
grum *sullen* 304.8
Grumbacher red *red pigment* 257.2
grumble *drumming* 235.1, *drum* 235.10, *be dissatisfied* 274.7, *complaint* 305.5, *be irritable* 304.14, *complain* 507.8
grumbler *dissatisfied person* 274.3, *sullen person* 304.7, *protester* 507.4
grumbling *drumming* 235.1, *bad-mannered* 411.6
grumblingly *irritably* 304.17
grumbly *irritable* 304.9
grume *mucus* 561.6
grumly *sullenly* 304.16

---

grumness *sullenness* 304.1

grump *irascible person* 303.7, *sullen person* 304.7, *be irritable* 304.14

grumpily *splenetically* 223.10, *crossly* 303.20, *irritably* 304.17

grumpiness *crossness* 303.4, *irritableness* 304.3

grumpish *irritable* 304.9

grumpishly *irritably* 304.17

grumpishness *irritableness* 304.3

grumps, the [Inf] *sign of irritability* 304.4

grumpy *splenetic* 223.7, *cross* 303.11, *irritable* 304.9

Grundyism *self-righteousness* 431.7

grunge *rock music* 140.6

grunge [Inf] *dirt* 112.5

grunt *hoarseness* 238.2, *sound hoarse* 238.8, *animal sound* 240.1, *make an animal sound* 240.7, *be fatigued* 820.5

grunt [Inf] *soldier* 77.4, *submitter* 421.2, *subordinate* 832.3

grunt-and-groan [Inf] *wrestling* 152.18

grunt-and-groaner [Inf] *wrestler* 152.18

grunting *hoarse* 238.5, *ululant* 240.4

Grus Constellations 7

grylloblatodean *insectile* 40.11

gryphon Legendary Creatures 360

G string *part of stringed instrument* 142.2

G-string *underwear* 100.22

G-suit *suit* 100.16

guacamole *sauce* 90.17

Guadalcanal Islands 572

Guadalquivir Rivers 570

Guadeloupe Islands 572

Guadiana Rivers 570

guaiacum Trees and Shrubs 43

Guam American States 564, Islands 572

guanine *nucleotide* 12.10

guano *fertilizer* 22.6, *feces* 25.5, *dirt* 112.5

guarantee 458.3, 458.13, 840.4; *vow* 189.3, 189.23, *verify* 336.8, *contract* 391.2, *promise* 464.2, 464.10, *safety* 810.1, *assure* 810.23, *finance* 825.31, *make certain* 840.14

guaranteed 464.6, 840.10; *vowed* 189.14, *guaranteeing* 458.9, *guaranteed* 464.6, *trustworthy* 810.17

guaranteed annual income *social assistance* 825.4

guaranteed loan *loan* 488.3

guaranteed wage *or* **payments** *bargaining terms* 57.10

guaranteeing 458.9

guarantor *affirmer* 189.9, *promise maker* 458.6, *debtor* 488.6

guaranty *loan* 488.3

guard 419.15; *defend* 77.37, 419.20, *basketball team* 148.2, *play basketball* 148.7, *fencing movements* 153.3, *fence* 153.7, *offense* 155.6, *observer* 242.15, *suspect* 314.9, *watchfulness* 325.5, *care for* 325.12, *secure* 464.9, *give moral support* 605.18, *protective covering* 613.5, *protect* 613.26, 810.21, *accompanier* 794.6, *escort* 794.18, *protection* 810.2, *surveillant* 810.12, *warner* 814.5, *preserve* 815.14, *detain* 830.16

guard against *take note of* 323.10, *have foresight* 357.8, *be prepared* 388.17

guard boat Ships and Boats 690

guard cell *leaf* 41.6

guard dog *dog* 35.10, *self-defense* 419.5, *watchdog* 810.14

guard duty *watchfulness* 325.5

guarded *sparing with words* 208.6, *cautious* 287.6, *suspicious* 314.6, *protected* 613.20, *accompanied* 794.15, *safe* 810.16

guardedly *cautiously* 287.16, *suspiciously* 314.13

guardedness *caution* 287.1, *suspicion* 314.3, *watchfulness* 325.5

guarded speech 208.3

guardhouse *prison* 55.1

guardian *prison officer* 55.8, *protector* 419.16, 810.11, *supporter* 605.9, *supportive* 605.11, *tutelary* 810.19

guardian angel *angel* 82.11, *supporter* 605.9, *protector* 810.11, *benefactor* 825.15

Guardian Angels *surveillant* 810.12

guardian of morality *moralist* 431.8

guardianship *patronage* 810.7

guarding *playing terms* 148.4, *watchfulness* 325.5, *watchful* 325.10, *supportive* 605.11, *tutelary* 810.19, *detention* 830.5

guard of honor *mark of respect* 435.4

guard one's pride 297.16

guardrail *safety device* 810.15

guar gum *adhesive* 561.3

Guatemala Countries 566

Guatemala City Countries 566

guayule Trees and Shrubs 43

gubernatorial *governmental* 49.24, *commissioned* 833.6

guck [Inf] *mud* 561.8

guddle [Scot] *hunt* 385.14

guddler [Scot] *hunter* 385.6

guelder rose Flowers 42

guerdon *reward* 453.1, 453.13, *compensation* 743.1, *compensate* 743.7

Guernsey Breeds of Cattle 16, Islands 572

guernsey *sweater* 100.17

guerrilla 77.7; *killer* 30.11, *attacker* 418.10, *revenger* 420.2, *seditionist* 427.7

guerrilla attack *terrorist attack* 418.7

guerrilla warfare *offensive warfare* 76.1, *resistance movement* 417.3, *revolution* 427.4

guess *be of the opinion* 87.10, *speculate* 294.13, *theory* 327.2, 359.3, *theorize* 327.16, 720.14, *doubt* 333.19, *experiment* 335.11, *judgment* 341.1, *estimate* 341.11, *predict* 358.14, *conjecture* 359.3, *suppose* 359.8, *uncertainty* 841.1

guess at *feel instinctively* 266.15, *speculate* 294.13

guessed *supposed* 359.6

guesser *theorist* 359.4

guessing *skeptical* 333.14, *conjecture* 359.3, *suppositional* 359.5

guesstimate [Inf] *theorize* 327.16, *predict* 358.14, *conjecture* 359.3, *suppose* 359.8, *calculate* 784.10

guesstimated [Inf] *theoretical* 327.10

guesstimating [Inf] *suppositional* 359.5

guesswork *uncertainty* 333.6, 841.1, *experimentation* 335.3, *judgment* 341.1, *unknown thing* 349.3, *inaccuracy* 351.3, *divination*

358.2, *conjecture* 359.3, *theory* 720.4

guest *resident* 61.6, *social person* 408.7, *transient* 643.2, *entrant* 706.7

guesthouse *hotel* 60.12

guest soap *cleaning agent* 111.9

guest ticket *or* **pass** *absence of charge* 497.6

guest worker *new arrival* 724.6

guff [Inf] *nonsense* 192.8, *talk* 207.3, *empty talk* 362.5

guffaw *cry of amusement* 239.2, *laugh* 239.14, 277.12, *laughter* 277.8

guidable *directable* 697.10

guidance *education* 48.1, *directorship* 126.5, *advice* 176.1, *treatment* 399.11, *welfare* 445.2, *directions* 697.7, *support* 825.2

guidance counselor *educator* 48.4, *adviser* 176.5

guide 126.6, 697.4, 780.4; *educate* 48.22, *expert* 52.8, 68.13, *leader* 126.8, *direct* 126.11, 697.13, 780.14, *mountaineer* 161.8, *adviser* 176.5, 825.14, *advise* 176.9, 825.27, *indicator* 183.7, *sign* 183.19, *conductor* 399.13, *conduct* 399.21, *influence* 512.11, *baseline* 601.4, *precursor* 769.7, *precede* 769.13, *pioneer* 771.29, *usher* 794.4, *escort* 794.18

guidebook *climbing equipment* 161.4, *type of book* 174.3, *book of lists* 785.3

guided *strategic* 78.16, *directed* 697.9, *accompanied* 794.15

guided missile *modern missile weapon* 78.4, *missile* 696.7

guide dog *dog* 35.10, *aid for poor sight* 243.5

guided wave *wave* 683.4

guideless *vulnerable* 811.9

guideline *baseline* 601.4, *guide* 780.4

guide number *lighting* 132.16

guidepost *indicator* 183.7

guiding *educational* 48.17, *managerial* 126.9, *advisory* 176.7, *influential* 512.8, *directions* 697.7, *directing* 697.12, *preparatory* 769.11

guiding light *motive* 178.5, *motivation* 508.1

guiding principle *motive* 178.5, *motivation* 508.1

guiding spirit *minor deity* 82.2

guiding star *indicator* 183.7, *motivation* 508.1

guidon *flag* 184.8

guild *organized labor* 57.5, *association* 59.4, *alliance* 735.5

guilder *national coins* 484.11

guile 193.3; *hypocrisy* 330.5, *cunning* 822.1

guileful *artful* 193.13, *cunning* 822.4

guilefully *deceptively* 193.21

guileless *ingenuous* 191.6, *easily seen through* 249.10, *naive* 449.9, 821.3, *natural* 526.10

guilelessly *ingenuously* 191.11, *naively* 449.15

guilelessness *ingenuousness* 191.3, *openness* 249.6, *naiveté* 449.4, 821.1, *naturalness* 526.4

guillemets Punctuation Marks 5

guilloche Architectural Elements 134

guillotine *execute* 30.22, 454.30, *instrument of execution* 454.15

guillotining *capital punishment* 454.12

guilt 450.1; *lawbreaking* 53.14, *penitence* 451.1

guilt complex *sign of guilt* 450.2

guilt feelings *penitence* 451.1

guiltily 53.38, 450.12; *villainously* 448.18, *penitently* 451.10

guiltiness *errancy* 351.7, *guilt* 450.1

guiltless *acquitted* 54.25, *virtuous* 447.5, *incorrupt* 449.7, *blameless* 805.12

guiltlessly *forgivingly* 53.37, *virtuously* 447.9, *faultlessly* 449.14

guiltlessness *virtue* 447.1, *incorruption* 449.2, *immaculateness* 805.2

guilt offering *substitute* 672.2

guilty 450.6; *offending* 53.25, *convicted* 54.26, *errant* 351.12, *immoral* 430.11, *unsatisfactory* 438.15, *villainous* 448.12, *penitent* 451.5

guilty act *wrongdoing* 430.7, *wicked act* 448.7, *sin* 450.3

guilty behavior *sign of guilt* 450.2

guilty conscience *sign of guilt* 450.2, *penitence* 451.1

guilty feelings *sign of guilt* 450.2

guilty love *fornication* 432.3

guilty party *accused person* 442.4, *guilty person* 450.5

guilty person 450.5

guimpe *neckwear* 100.29

Guinea Countries 566

guinea Nicknames for Inhabitants 61

Guinea-Bissau Countries 566

guinea cock *male bird* 36.15

guinea fowl *table bird* 36.10

guinea pig *experimental subject* 335.7

guinea worm *parasite* 39.18

Guinevere Famous Lovers 299

guisarme *sharp weapon* 78.6

guise *ungenuineness* 192.2, *spectacle* 264.6, *mode of behavior* 399.2, *style* 537.1, *appearance* 610.4, *way* 691.1, *state* 725.1

guitar Musical Instruments 142

guitarist *player* 141.2

Gujarati Breeds of Sheep 16

Gulag *imprisonment* 454.2

gulag *prison* 55.1

gulch *gulf* 587.3, *lowlands* 597.6

gules Heraldic Terms 184, *red* 257.5

gulf 587.3; *inlet* 572.9, *the depths* 598.2, *concave land* 635.2

Gulf Coast *regions of the United States* 564.7

gull *water bird* 36.9, *deceive* 193.16

gullet *eating organ* 92.14

gullibility *believing* 87.2, *incuriosity* 322.1, *misjudgment* 342.1, *naiveté* 821.1

gullible *believing* 87.6, *raw* 260.9, *incurious* 322.3, *misjudging* 342.6, *naive* 821.3

gullibly *believingly* 87.12, *incuriously* 322.6, *misguidedly* 342.12, *naively* 821.5

gully *rock face* 161.6, *valley* 572.8, *gulf* 587.3, *narrow place* 593.2, *lowlands* 597.6, *concave land* 635.2

gullywasher *rain* 9.27, *natural violence* 520.3

gulp Collective Names 59, *eat* 92.21, *size of drink* 88.7, *drink* 93.19, *be greedy* 119.4, *intake* 708.5, *ingest* 708.17

gulp down *eat* 92.21, *drink* 93.19, *ingest* 708.17

gulping *eating* 92.1, *drinking* 93.1, *gluttonous* 119.3, *intake* 708.5

gum *secreted substance* 24.2, *retainer* 471.3, *retain* 471.7, *adhesive* 561.3, 755.3, *stick* 561.20, *cause to adhere* 755.10

gum *or* **gum tree** Trees and Shrubs 43

gum arabic *polysaccharide* 12.5

gumbo *soup* 90.14, *semiliquid* 561.7, *viscous* 561.14, *mixed thing* 751.2

gumbolike *viscous* 561.14

gumdrop *sweets* 90.39

gum elastic *rubber* 546.3

gumlike *viscous* 561.14, *resinous* 562.13

gummed *retained* 471.6

gumminess *viscosity* 561.1

gummous *viscous* 561.14, *resinous* 562.13

gummy *retentive* 471.5, *viscous* 561.14, *resinous* 562.13, *adhesive* 755.5

gum print *printing* 132.20

gum resin *resin* 562.6

gum rosin *resin* 562.6

gums *mouth* 19.7

gum(s) *resin* 562.6

gumshoe [Inf] *discoverer* 345.7

gumshoes *boots* 100.31

gum up *stick* 561.20

gum up [Inf] *block* 826.17

gum up the works [Inf] *block* 826.17

gun *murder weapon* 30.3, Historical Missile Weapons 78, *firearm* 78.7, *sailboard parts* 150.20, *banger* 234.3, *hunter* 385.6, *agent of destruction* 523.7, *shoot* 696.18

gun [Inf] *shooter* 696.11

gun bearer *transferrer* 685.4, *transporter* 686.4

gunboat *warship* 77.21, Ships and Boats 690

gunboat diplomacy *psychological warfare* 76.13, *navy* 77.18

guncarriage *guns* 78.9

guncotton *propellant* 78.14, 696.9

gundog *dog* 35.10

gun dog *hunting dog* 160.7

gun down *murder* 30.20, *slaughter* 30.21, *fight* 77.35, *shoot* 696.18

gun emplacement *guns* 78.9, *fortification* 419.12

gunfire *burst of sound* 232.4, *firing* 418.6, *shot* 696.6

gung-ho [Inf] *military* 58.10, *warlike* 76.27, *combative* 77.32, *eager* 373.8, *national* 566.10

gung-ho attitude [Inf] *assiduity* 414.8

gunk [Inf] *dirt* 112.5, *mud* 561.8

gunky [Inf] *viscous* 561.14

gunman *murderer* 30.12, *combatant* 77.1, *coercer* 428.4, *dishonest person* 479.11, *shooter* 696.11

gunmetal *gray thing* 255.3

gunnel *canoe parts* 150.10, *rowboat parts* 150.15, *edge* 618.1

gunner *air force person* 77.31, *shooter* 696.11

gunnery *military training* 76.19, *firing* 418.6, *shooting* 696.5

Gunnery Sergeant US Military Ranks 58

gunning *hunting* 160.2, *hunt* 385.3

gunny Fabrics and Fibers 130

gun park *guns* 78.9

gunpowder *propellant* 78.14, 696.9

gun room *arsenal* 78.3, *storehouse* 105.8

gunrunning *arms race* 78.2

guns **78.9**

---

gunshot *shot* 696.6, *danger signal* 811.5

gun sight *visual aid* 242.14

gunsmith *artisan* 123.13

Gunter's chain General Units 589, *measuring instrument* 589.12

gunwale *canoe parts* 150.10, *rowboat parts* 150.15, *edge* 618.1

Gurez Breeds of Sheep 16

gurge *vortex* 682.6, *swirl* 682.16

gurgle *small sound* 233.4, *sound faint* 233.8, *bubble* 558.24, *flow* 570.10

gurgling *nonresonant* 233.7

guru *sage* 4.11, *educator* 48.4, *expert* 52.8, 127.9, *religious leader* 68.9, *educational leader* 68.11, *priest* 84.8, *intellectual* 315.7, *wise person* 352.3

gush *diffuseness* 199.1, *be diffuse* 199.5, *effusiveness* 207.2, *be talkative* 207.7, *talk nonsense* 362.12, *flow* 555.25, 570.4, 570.10, *outflow* 707.4, *run out* 707.15, *upturn* 713.2, *spring up* 713.22, *spread* 746.3, *leak* 816.11

gusher *outflow* 707.4

gushiness *effusiveness* 207.2

gushing *overdone* 99.7, *diffuse* 199.3, *effusive* 207.6, *flowing* 570.7, *outflow* 707.4, *ascending* 713.13

gushingly *effusively* 207.10

gush out *run out* 707.15

gusla *or* **gusle** Musical Instruments 142

gusli Musical Instruments 142

gusset *part of garment* 100.27

gussied up [Inf] *dressed up* 100.39, *beautified* 530.12

gussy up [Inf] *dress up* 100.45, *beautify* 530.14

gust *wind* 9.12, *blow* 9.53, 558.22, *air flow* 558.4

gustation *appetizer* 219.2

gusto *emphasis* 200.1, *flavor* 219.3, *joy* 269.1, *vigor* 518.1

gusty *windy* 9.42, *breezy* 558.15

gut *cook* 91.10, *lay waste* 523.14, *inlet* 572.9, *void* 709.23, *draw out* 711.17

gut [Inf] *intuitive* 266.10

Gutai group Western Art Styles 133

gut feeling *or* **reaction** [Inf] *intuition* 320.1

gutless [Inf] *cowardly* 285.4, *weak-willed* 517.10, *inert* 519.2

gutlessly [Inf] *cowardly* 285.9

gutlessness [Inf] *cowardice* 285.1, *indecisiveness* 517.2, *inertness* 519.1

gut reaction [Inf] *impression* 266.2, *instinct* 318.3, 320.4

guts *internal organ* 19.13, *eating organ* 92.14, *seat of feelings* 266.7, *insides* 577.3, *internals* 611.3, *component* 760.3

guts [Inf] *courage* 284.1, *stamina* 377.4, *endurance* 516.4

guts [Inf] *vigor* 518.1

gutsiness [Inf] *courage* 284.1, *stamina* 377.4

gutsy [Inf] *courageous* 284.9, *enduring* 377.9, *vigorous* 518.2

gutta Architectural Elements 134

gutta-percha Tree Products 43, *rubber* 546.3

gutta-percha ball *or* **guttie** *golf equipment* 156.5

guttation *physiology* 13.13, *secretion* 24.1, *dew* 559.6

gutter *bowling* 151.1, 151.6, *be dim* 248.7, *wicked place* 448.8, *furrow*

638.1, 638.5, *be changeable* 666.5, *flicker* 684.26, *outlet* 707.8

gutter ball *bowling delivery* 151.2

guttering *flickering* 684.20

gutter shot *bowling delivery* 151.2

gutting *drawing off* 711.4

guttural *spoken letter* 5.15, *voiced* 5.37, *phonetic* 205.14, *hoarse* 238.5

guttural accent *regional pronunciation* 205.7

guttural consonant *spoken letter* 5.15

gutturalize *sound hoarse* 238.8

gutturally *stridently* 238.10

gutturalness *hoarseness* 238.2

guttural sound *hoarseness* 238.2

guv [Brit inf] *master* 68.1

guy *deride* 369.7, *disdain* 400.16, *ridicule* 440.15, *line* 754.5, *tackle* 754.6

guy [Inf] *average person* 18.9, *male* 32.1

Guyana Countries 566

guy derrick *construction equipment* 14.23

guyot *ocean floor* 8.18

guy rope *line* 754.5

guy wires *horizontal bar* 157.5

guzzle *eat well* 92.23, *be greedy* 119.4, *get drunk* 121.35

guzzler *drinker* 93.16, *glutton* 119.2

guzzling *appetite* 92.2, *eating* 92.18, *gluttonous* 119.3, *drunken* 121.28

gym *sports ground* 145.2

gymkhana Sporting Activities 145, *equestrianism* 159.8, *sporting event* 422.6

gymnasium *school place* 48.16, *sports ground* 145.2

gymnast 157.10; *athlete* 422.15

gymnastic 157.11; *keeping fit* 113.10, *sporting* 145.5

gymnastically 157.13; *sportingly* 145.7

gymnastics 157.1; *health improvement* 113.3, *athletics* 422.7, *bodily movement* 677.11

gymnastics association *gymnastics organizations* 157.9

gymnastics club *gymnastics organizations* 157.9

gymnastics coach *gymnast* 157.10

gymnastic scoring *gymnastics* 157.1

gymnastics equipment **157.2**

gymnastics judge *gymnast* 157.10

gymnastics organizations **157.9**

gymnastics routine *gymnastics* 157.1

Gymnophiona *amphibian* 37.10

gymnophobia Phobias 283

gymnosophical *naked* 614.12

gymnosophist *nude person* 614.5

gymnosophy *nudism* 614.4

gymnosperm *seed plant* 41.3

Gymnospermae *seed plant* 41.3

gym shoes *shoes* 100.30, *basketball court* 148.3, *gymnastics equipment* 157.2

gym shorts *shorts* 100.15

gym suit *gymnastics equipment* 157.2

gynandromorph *sexual nature* 20.4

gynandromorphic *of sexual nature* 20.17

gynandromorphism *sexual nature* 20.4

gynandry *sexual nature* 20.4

gynarchy *femaleness* 33.2, *government by women* 49.3

---

gynecocracy *government by women* 49.3

gynecological *medical* 107.28

gynecologist *medical specialist* 107.20

gynecology *femaleness* 33.2

gynephobia Phobias 283

gynoecium *organs of reproduction* 21.9, *flower part* 42.3

gyp *foul play* 193.6, *swindle* 193.19

gypper *or* **gypster** *schemer* 193.19

gyppo Nicknames for Inhabitants 61

gypsophila Flowers 42

gypsum *material* 129.2

gypsy *diviner* 86.14, *peddler* 482.9, *foreign* 724.9

Gypsy sign *symbol* 183.3

gyrate *be in motion* 677.14, *rotate* 682.14

gyrating *directional* 677.13, *orbiting* 681.7, *rotating* 682.11

gyration *movement* 677.3, *rotation* 682.1

gyrational *directional* 677.13, *rotary* 682.12

gyratory *directional* 677.13, *circular* 681.6, *rotary* 682.12

gyre *ocean current* 8.15, *orbital motion* 681.1, *rotate* 682.14

gyrene [Inf] *marines* 77.26

gyro *rotator* 682.8

gyrocompass *rotator* 682.8, *navigational aid* 690.6

gyron Heraldic Terms 184

gyroplane *rotator* 682.8

gyroscope *rotator* 682.8

gyroscopic *rotary* 682.12

gyroscopic compass *navigational aid* 690.6

gyrostabilizer *rotator* 682.8

gyrostatic *rotary* 682.12

gyrostatics *science of rotation* 682.10

H

H [Inf] *opiates* 121.17

H₂O *water* 557.1

haar [Scot] *murk* 248.2

habanera Dances 135

habeas corpus *pretrial proceedings* 54.13, *demand* 425.2

haberdasher *clothier* 100.37, *retailer* 482.11

habergeon *historic armor* 419.8

habilimentation *the clothing business* 100.36

habilimented *dressed* 100.38

habiliments *clothing* 100.1

habit 397.1; *tradition* 1.7, *crystal* 11.14, *vestment* 84.11, *drug use* 121.9, *expected thing* 356.3, *regularity* 730.6, *method* 765.7, *custom* 780.5, *repetitiveness* 797.3

habitant *inhabitant* 61.1

habitat 60.1; *place of residence* 209.4, *location* 565.1

habitation 60.2; *place of residence* 209.4, *residence* 575.2

habited *dressed* 100.38

habit-forming 397.15; *intoxicating* 121.29, *addictive* 121.32, *enticing* 178.13, *appealing* 512.9

habits *way of life* 399.9

habitual 397.9, 765.15; *frequent* 661.4, *regular* 730.12, *common* 778.13, *customary* 780.9, *monotonous* 797.12

habitual action *habit* 397.1

habitual drunkard *drunkard* 121.8

habitual liar *liar* 192.10

---

habitually 397.20; *in a trance*
121.40, *frequently* 661.7, *regularly*
730.21, *prevailingly* 742.11,
usually 778.21, *as a rule* 780.18
habitual lying *lying* 192.5
habitually lie *lie* 192.23
habitualness *frequency* 661.1,
average 778.4
habituate *have a habit* 397.16
habituated 397.14; *attending*
575.9
habituation 397.7
habitude *tendency* 397.2
habitué *creature of habit* 397.8,
social person 408.7, *attender* 575.6
haboob Notable Winds 9
háček Accents and Diacritical
Marks 5
hacienda *farm* 16.2, *mansion* 60.5,
property 470.1
hack *unskilled person* 128.3, *play*
basketball 148.7, *horse* 159.1,
saddle horse 159.5, *ride* 159.16,
print journalist 175.5, *descriptive*
writer 202.10, *make rough* 544.11,
open 583.15, *notch* 636.1, 636.5,
take apart 753.16
hack [Inf] *automobile* 687.6
hackamore *riding equipment* 159.9
hackbrett Musical Instruments
142
hackbut *historical handgun* 78.8
hacked *barbed* 544.7, *open* 583.10
hacker *dishonest person* 479.11
hacker [Inf] *computer user* 15.3,
golfer 156.7
hacking *violations* 148.5, *dishonesty*
479.7
Hackney Horse and Pony Breeds
159
hackney *workhorse* 159.3,
automobile 687.6
hackney cab *automobile* 687.6
hackneyed *worded* 5.38, *proverbial*
177.2, *unemphatic* 201.2,
meaningless 362.7, *familiar*
397.10, *common* 778.13,
monotonous 797.12
hackneyed expression *catchword*
5.22, *generalization* 778.5
hackneyed phrase *maxim* 177.1
Hackney pony Horse and Pony
Breeds 159
hack work *work* 122.1
hadal *oceanic* 8.53
Hadamard matrix *combinatorics*
6.63
had best *be the duty of* 433.16
had better *be the duty of* 433.16
haddock *food fish and shellfish*
90.20
hadephobia Phobias 283
Hades Deities 82, *evil place* 446.6
Hadith *Islamic text* 81.18
hadron *elementary particle* 10.53
haematoxylon Trees and Shrubs
43
Haflinger pony Horse and Pony
Breeds 159
hafnium Chemical Elements and
Common Allotropes 11
hag *ugly thing* 531.2
hagbut *historical handgun* 78.8
haggard *emaciated* 595.10, *fatigued*
820.2
haggardly *thin* 595.18
haggardness *emaciation* 595.2
haggis [Scot] *sausage* 90.29
haggle *negotiate* 460.6, *bargain*
480.20, *buy cheaply* 497.15, *offer*
to buy 504.12
haggler *trader* 480.11, *purchaser*
481.7
haggling *negotiation* 460.1,

negotiated 460.5, *bargaining*
480.10, *buying* 481.9
hagiographer *descriptive writer*
202.10
hagiographical *theological* 81.24
hagiography Theologies 81,
deified person 82.14, *nonfiction*
139.6, *flattery* 439.1
hagiolatry *deified person* 82.14
hagiological *theological* 81.24
hagiology Theologies 81, *deified*
person 82.14
hagiophobia Phobias 283
hagioscope *place for viewing*
242.13
hagridden *bewitched* 86.21
ha-ha *ornamental garden* 17.3, *crack*
587.2, *enclosing thing* 619.3,
separator 753.5
haiku Poem or Verse Forms 139
hail 9.29; *precipitation* 9.26, *snow*
9.58, 218.6, *proclamation* 183.8,
signal 183.18, *salutation* 209.2,
approach 209.10, *cry of greeting*
239.4, *greet* 410.11, *acclaim*
437.18, *throng* 795.4
hail! *hello!* 704.23
hail-fellow well met *sociable*
408.11
hailing *signaling* 183.14, *salutatory*
209.7
Hail Mary *prayer* 85.10
hail-Mary *play* 155.8
hailstone *precipitation* 9.26, *hail*
9.29, *snow* 218.6
hailstorm *snow* 218.6, *natural*
violence 520.3
Hainan Islands 572
hair *body covering* 19.4, *mammalian*
characteristic 35.3, Phobias 283,
fineness 595.5, *animal covering*
613.15
hair band *hairdressing tool* 530.9,
circular thing 631.3
hairbreadth escape *narrow escape*
811.4, 816.3
hairbrush *cleaning tool* 111.10,
instrument of punishment 454.13,
smoother 545.2
hair clip *hairdressing tool* 530.9
haircloth Fabrics and Fibers 130
hair coloring *hairdressing* 530.7
hair conditioner *pomade* 562.9
haircut *coiffure* 530.8, *depilation*
614.8
hair cutting *hairdressing* 530.7
hair disease Phobias 283
hairdo *coiffure* 530.8
hairdresser *personal attendant*
69.5, *cleaner* 111.12, *beautician*
530.11
hairdresser's *hairdressing salon*
530.10
hairdressing 530.7
hairdressing salon 530.10
hairdressing tool 530.9
hair dryer *hairdressing tool* 530.9,
dryer 500.5
hair dyeing *hairdressing* 530.7
hairiness *roughness* 544.1
hairless *smooth* 545.4, *bald* 614.16
hairlessness *baldness* 614.9
hairlike *fine* 595.12
hairline crack *opening* 583.1, *crack*
587.2
hair loss *baldness* 614.9
hair net *headdress* 100.35,
hairdressing tool 530.9
hair of the dog [Inf] *drink* 121.6
hair oil *pomade* 562.9
hair on end *warning signal* 814.3
hair ornament *jewelry* 532.6
hairpiece *hairdressing* 530.7, *body*
covering 613.3

hairpin *automobile racing terms*
146.3, *ski race* 162.4, *snowplow*
162.29, *hairdressing tool* 530.9,
fastener 754.7
hairpin bend *road attribute* 687.3,
deviating course 698.2
hairpin turn *divergence* 607.2
hair-pulling *wrestling terms* 152.10
hair-raising *exciting* 212.8,
frightening 283.12
hair removal *hairdressing* 530.7,
depilation 614.8
hair remover *depilation* 614.8
hair-removing *depilatory* 614.15
hair replacement *hairdressing*
530.7
hair salon *hairdressing salon*
530.10
hairsbreadth *closeness* 593.4, *close*
593.10, *short distance* 586.2
hair shirt *penitence* 313.3
hairsplitter *sophist* 330.6,
discriminator 337.6
hairsplitting *quibbling* 330.4,
330.9, *judiciousness* 337.2,
discriminating 337.9, *accuracy*
350.1, *accurate* 350.3
hair spray *hairdressing tool* 530.9
hairspring *spring* 546.4
hair standing on end *symptoms of*
fear 283.3
hairstyle *coiffure* 530.8
hair styling *hairdressing* 530.7
hair stylist *filmmaker* 137.14
hairstylist *beautician* 530.11
hairstylist's tool *hairdressing tool*
530.9
hair-trigger *swift* 694.6
hair weaving *hairdressing* 530.7
hairy 19.20; *barbed* 544.7, *rough*
552.8
hairy [Inf] *dangerous* 811.7, *difficult*
824.9
Haiti Countries 566
hajj *act of worship* 83.2
hajji *religious person* 81.9
hake *food fish and shellfish* 90.20
hakea Trees and Shrubs 43
hakham *priest* 84.8
hakim *healer* 107.22
halberd *sharp weapon* 78.6
halberdier *historical soldier* 77.8
halcyon *peaceful* 73.8, *quiescent*
678.6, *prosperous* 847.5
halcyon days *weather* 9.3, *good*
thing 445.9, *comfortable*
circumstances 726.5, *time of plenty*
847.3
hale *healthy* 113.4, *physically strong*
516.10, *vigorous* 518.2, *in form*
624.8, *pull* 699.10, *sound* 759.8
hale and hearty *healthy* 113.4,
physically strong 516.10, *vigorous*
518.2, *sound* 759.8
haleness *health* 113.1
half 789.7, 789.12; *basketball*
148.1, *game time* 155.4, *partly*
760.17, *incompletely* 762.10, *less*
than one 787.4, *fractional* 787.5,
in half 789.21
half [Brit] *size of drink* 93.3
half a chance *poor chance* 842.8
half a gale *wind strength* 9.13
half a hundred *twenty and over*
792.8
half a jiffy [Inf] *instant* 645.3
half a mind *will* 372.1
half a mo [Inf] *short duration*
643.3, *instant* 645.3
half-and-half *on equal terms*
740.9, *medium* 742.6, *medianly*
742.12, *diluted* 751.9, *partly*
760.17, *irresolute* 772.13,
irresolutely 772.23, *in half* 789.21

half a sec [Inf] *instant* 645.3
half-asleep *not awake* 415.12
half-assed [Inf] *bungled* 128.7
half a tick [Brit inf] *instant* 645.3
halfback *offense* 155.6, *hockey*
player 158.8
half-bagged [Inf] *slightly drunk*
121.26
half-baked *bungled* 128.7,
semiskilled 349.6, *unpremeditated*
389.7, *uncooked* 389.12,
uncompleted 762.7
half-ball *billiard* 149.6
half-ball stroke *billiards play*
149.2
half-begin *not complete* 762.9
half-begun *incomplete* 762.7
half-believe *disbelieve* 88.8
half-breed *race* 1.5
half brother *family member* 65.2
half-caste *race* 1.5
half cell *electrochemistry* 11.19
half century *twenty and over* 792.8
half circle *circle* 631.2
half-clothed *in dishabille* 100.40
half-cocked *immature* 389.9
half-cooked *uncooked* 389.12
halfcourt line *basketball court*
148.3
half-dark *dim* 248.4
half-dead *dying* 29.12, *inactive*
413.9, *fatigued* 820.2
half-developed *immature* 389.9
half-do *not complete* 762.9
half-dollar *US coinage* 484.10
half-done *neglected* 326.6,
incomplete 762.5, *uncompleted*
762.7
half-dozen *or* **half a dozen** *six*
792.2
half-dressed *in dishabille* 100.40
half fare *bargain* 497.4
half-fed *underfed* 98.7
half-filled *incomplete* 806.6
half-finish *not complete* 762.9
half-finished *unformed* 389.11,
partial 760.11, *incomplete* 762.5,
806.6, *uncompleted* 762.7
half-formed *unformed* 389.11
half-furnished *unequipped* 389.13
half-gone *inactive* 413.9
half-grown *immature* 389.9
half-hardy *botanical* 17.15, *wild*
41.15
half-heard *faint* 233.6
halfhearted *indifferent* 289.7,
unenthusiastic 375.10, *weak-willed*
517.10, *incomplete* 762.5
half-hearted attempt *attempt*
390.1
halfheartedly *indifferently* 289.17,
unwillingly 375.17, *weakly*
517.14, *moderately* 521.10
halfheartedness *indifference*
289.1, *unenthusiasm* 375.3,
incompleteness 762.1
halfhearted thanks *ingratitude*
311.1
half hitch Knots, Bends, Hitches,
Splices 754
half-holiday *time off* 125.2
half-hunter watch Timepieces
and Timers 646
half knot Knots, Bends, Hitches,
Splices 754
half-length portrait *type of*
painting 143.5
half-life *dating* 8.48, *radioactivity*
10.58
half-light *dimness* 248.1, *hue* 251.4
half line *part of poem* 139.9
half-lit *dim* 248.4
half-mast *lower the flag* 716.23
half measure *mediocrity* 742.3

half-measure 461.2, 461.5
half measures *bungling* 128.2, *waste of effort* 802.4
half-moon *moon* 7.18, *curved thing* 629.3
half-moon glasses *visual aid* 242.14
half nelson *wrestling terms* 152.10, *retention* 471.1
half note *notation* 140.20
half pay *income* 492.3
half pint [Inf] *little person* 580.5
half-point *compass direction* 697.5
half-price *bargain* 497.10
half rations *incompleteness* 98.2
half relief *relief carving* 144.2
half-remembered *forgotten* 355.7
half rhyme *rhyme* 139.11
half-ripe *immature* 389.9
half round Architectural Elements 134
half-seas over [Inf] *drunk* 121.25
half-seen *difficult to see* 245.4
half-shot [Inf] *slightly drunk* 121.26
half sister *family member* 65.2
half-skilled *unskilled* 128.5
half-slip *underwear* 100.22
half starve *eat less* 118.9, *abstain* 455.11
half-starved *underfed* 98.7, 118.7, *hungry* 288.16
half the battle *gist* 799.4
half-timbering *construction* 522.9
halftime *basketball* 148.1, *game time* 155.4, *period of activity* 641.4
half title *book part* 174.5
halftone *photograph* 132.3, *hue* 251.4
half-true *partially true* 192.18
half-truth *partial truth* 192.7
half-turn *floor exercise* 157.4
half volley *tennis strokes* 165.2
halfway *soccer* 163.7, *compromise* 461.1, *compromising* 461.4, *compromisingly* 461.9, *central* 612.6, *centrally* 612.12, *medium* 742.6, *medianly* 742.12, *middle way* 772.3, *midway* 772.10, 772.22, *stand in the middle* 772.17, *half* 789.12
halfway house *prison* 55.1, *retreat* 60.13, *moderation* 521.1, *medium* 742.2, *middle way* 772.3, *haven* 810.3, *safe house* 812.5
halfway line *stadium* 163.2
halfway measures *middle ground* 772.4
halfway point *medium* 742.2, *middle way* 772.3
half-white *white* 253.7
half-wit *unintelligent person* 316.4
half-witted *unintelligent* 316.6, *simpleminded* 526.11
halfword *computer information* 15.17
halibut *food fish and shellfish* 90.20
Halifax Canadian Provinces 564
halitosis *unpleasant-smelling thing* 227.2
hall *school place* 48.16, *room* 60.9, *theater* 136.16, *club* 138.7, *showplace* 843.4
hall church *church architecture* 134.11
Hall effect Classical Physical Laws 10
hallelujah *cry of praise* 239.3, *applause* 279.2, *rejoicing* 405.8
hallelujah! *hurrah!* 279.8
Halley's comet *comet* 7.20
hallmark *sign* 183.1, *means of identification* 184.3, *identify*

184.11, *name* 202.8, *special feature* 779.4
hallmarked *identified* 184.9
hall of mirrors *visual distortion* 243.6
halloo *chase* 385.13
halloo! *after him!* 385.19
hallow *deify* 82.23, *commemorate* 405.11
hallowed *holy* 82.19
hallowed by custom *established* 397.12
hallowedness *divine attribute* 82.4
Halloween Christian Holy Days and Seasons 85, *witchcraft* 86.6
halls of Ivy *university* 48.14
hallucinate *experience psychic phenomena* 86.23, *imagine* 360.14, 720.13
hallucinating *manic* 110.10
hallucination *occult and psychic phenomena* 86.7, *delusion* 110.2, *spectacle* 264.6, *fallibility* 351.6, *fantasy* 360.5, *illusion* 720.2
hallucinatory *seeming* 264.11, *illusory* 720.9
hallucinogenic *addictive* 121.32
hallucinogens 121.20
hallux Human Bones 19, *appendage* 19.5
hallway *room* 60.9
halma Board and Table Games 167
halo *galaxy* 7.5, *highlight* 246.12, *circular thing* 631.3
haloed *deified* 82.20, *lustrous* 246.15
halogen *chemical element* 11.3
halogenate *react* 11.38
halogen light *electric light* 246.6
halon *pollution* 117.8
halothane *anesthetic* 213.3
halt *pause* 415.15, *be weak* 517.12, *delay* 658.3, 658.13, *stop* 668.2, 668.10, *lack of motion* 678.1, *hesitate* 693.12, *stopover* 704.7, *cessation* 773.2, *cease* 773.20, *discontinue* 775.10, *snag* 824.8, *discontinuance* 846.4
halted *held up* 658.6, *stopped* 668.7, *discontinued* 775.8
halter *shirt* 100.13, *riding equipment* 159.9, *instrument of execution* 454.15, *yoke* 754.8, *means of restraint* 830.6
halter-break *ride* 159.16
halt hostilities *pacify* 74.11
halting *irregular* 664.3, *slow* 693.7
haltingly *irregularly* 664.6, *slowly* 693.14
halt one's progress *deter* 179.8
halt the arms race *pacify* 74.9
halve 789.15; *divide* 753.18, *split down the middle* 772.20
halved *separate* 753.7, *half* 789.12
halved hole *golfing terms* 156.3
halving 789.6
halyard *sailboat parts and accessories* 150.4, *flag* 184.8, *tackle* 754.6
ham *unskilled person* 128.3, *actor* 136.25, *overact* 136.35, *exaggerate* 194.11
ham acting *or* **hamming** *or* **hamming it up** *acting* 136.22
hamadryad *figurative usage* 43.9, *minor deity* 82.2
hamartia *tragedy* 136.10
hamartophobia Phobias 283
Hamburg Breeds of Fowl 16
hamburger *sandwich* 90.9, *beef* 90.24
hamburger place *eating place* 92.17

ham-handed *clumsy* 128.6, *graceless* 528.7
ham-handedness *unskillfulness* 128.1, *awkwardness* 824.2
Hamiltonian circuit *combinatorics* 6.63
Hamilton's principle Mathematical Concepts 6
Hamito-Semitic *language family* 5.12
ham it up *be unskillful* 128.8, *overact* 136.35, *exaggerate* 194.11, *show off* 404.26
hamlet *village* 567.3
hammed-up *dramatized* 136.32
hammer 553.13; Human Bones 19, *ear* 19.10, 228.2, *blunt weapon* 78.5, *hand tool* 103.3, *sound* 141.15, *part of keyboard instrument* 142.6, *hammer throwing* 166.14, *burst* 232.9, *strike* 418.21, *beat* 553.27, 695.12, *impeller* 695.7, *collide* 695.10, *resound* 797.21
hammer and tongs *laboriously* 122.13, *with vigor* 518.6, *violently* 520.11
hammer at *exert oneself* 122.11
hammer away *persevere* 377.10
hammer away at *harp* 797.17
hammer-beam *roof* 134.7
hammer glove *hammer throwing* 166.14
hammerhead *impeller* 695.7
hammer home *emphasize* 200.6
hammer in *impact* 710.11, *link* 752.18
hammering *ramming* 695.3, *reverberation* 797.6, *reverberatory* 797.14
hammer into *harp* 797.17
hammerlock *retention* 471.1
hammer out *fashion* 536.7, *form* 624.9
hammer throw *hammer throwing* 166.14
hammer throwing 166.14; Sporting Activities 145, *field event* 166.10
hamming *exaggeration* 194.1
hammock *type of bed* 101.9
hammy *dramatized* 136.32
hamper *thwart* 293.10, *make heavy* 538.14, *basket* 578.6, *limit* 620.7, *cause difficulties* 824.22, *hinder* 826.15
hampered *dissuaded* 179.5, *frustrated* 293.5
hampering *frustrating* 293.7, *hindrance* 826.1
Hampshire Breeds of Pigs 16, Breeds of Sheep 16
Hampshire Down Breeds of Sheep 16
Hampstead *London* 567.8
ham radio *radio broadcasting* 172.4
hamstring *ruin* 523.15
Han Rivers 570
hand *average person* 18.9, *appendage* 19.5, *worker* 123.1, 412.8, *stationary rings* 157.8, *cards* 168.2, *sense organ* 212.4, *acclaim* 437.5, *retainer* 471.3, *operative* 509.6, *assistant* 511.3, *nautical person* 690.12, *help* 825.1
hand and *or* **in glove** *intimately* 62.14, *contiguous* 216.8, *associated* 794.14, *hand in hand* 794.21, *associating* 827.11, *cooperatively* 827.18
hand back *give back* 478.5, *restore* 809.12
handbag *money storage* 484.20, *bag* 578.7, *transferred thing* 685.6

handball Sporting Activities 145, *soccer play* 163.5
handbarrow *wagon* 687.5
hand beater *cooking equipment* 91.6
hand bell *source of resonance* 236.4
hand bells Musical Instruments 142, *percussion instrument* 142.5
handbill *advertisement* 173.9
handbook *schoolbook* 48.15, *type of book* 174.3
hand brake *bicycle part* 687.11
handbreadth *breadth* 592.1
H and C *stimulants* 121.18
handcart *cart* 578.9, *wagon* 687.5
handclap *acclaim* 437.5
handclapping *acclaim* 437.5
handclasp *welcome* 408.10, *sign of courtesy* 410.5
hand cream *or* **lotion** *toiletries* 530.6, *pomade* 562.9
handcuff *intertwine* 752.19, *bind* 754.14, *restrain someone* 830.17
handcuffed *bound* 754.12
handcuffs *fastener* 754.7, *means of restraint* 830.6
hand down *bequeath* 372.15, *transfer property* 470.12
hand down a judgment *rule* 780.12
handed *sided* 623.7
handed down *societal* 1.13, *bequeathed* 372.10
handedness *laterality* 623.3
hand-feed *practice livestock farming* 16.20
handful *container(ful)* 738.2, *few* 796.1
handful, a *plurality* 793.1
handful [Inf] *troublemaker* 427.5, *difficult task* 824.3
hand grenade Historical Missile Weapons 78, *bomb* 78.15
handgrip *fishing tackle* 154.7
handgun *firearm* 78.7
handheld computer *computer* 15.1
handhold *rock face* 161.6, *retention* 471.1
hand horn Musical Instruments 142
handicap *illness* 114.2, *golfing terms* 156.3, *horse racing* 159.10, *prize competition* 422.5, *disability* 515.4, *weighing down* 538.5, *make heavy* 538.14, *inequality* 741.1, *unbalance* 741.8, *advantage* 744.3, *deficiency* 745.2, *be inconvenient* 804.9, *burden* 826.10, 826.21
handicapped *ponderous* 538.11, *blocked* 826.13
handicap racing *competitive sailing* 150.6
handicap score *golfing terms* 156.3
handicap stroke *golf shots* 156.4
handicraft *craft* 133.2
handicraftsman *artisan* 123.13, *worker* 412.8
handicraftswoman *artisan* 123.13, *worker* 412.8
handicraft worker *worker* 412.8
handily *skillfully* 127.16, *proficiently* 445.22, *instrumentally* 511.9, *usefully* 801.12, *conveniently* 803.6
hand in *squash terms* 165.10
handiness *manual skill* 127.2, *proficiency* 445.5, *instrumentality* 511.1, *availability* 575.5, *littleness* 580.1, *nearness* 586.1, *usefulness* 801.1, *convenience* 803.1, *wieldiness* 823.3
handing back *giving back* 478.1

handing in one's notice
resignation 835.1
hand in hand 794.21; *intimately*
62.14, *contiguous* 216.8, *sociably*
408.19, *near* 586.6, *laterally*
623.11, *united* 752.10
hand in one's notice *resign* 835.5
hand in one's resignation *resign*
835.5
hand it to *compliment* 437.17
handiwork *production* 522.1,
visible effect 676.2
hand job [Inf] *sex act* 20.10
handkerchief *accessory* 100.28,
cleaning cloth 111.11
hand-knit *or* **hand-knitted
sweater** *sweater* 100.17
handle *hand* 103.3, *manage*
126.10, *rowboat parts* 150.15,
touch 216.9, *use up* 393.12, *behave
toward* 399.20, *trade* 480.18,
merchandise 482.17, *take action*
509.12, *include* 613.33
handle [Inf] *name* 202.8
handle a consignment *transport*
686.10
handlebars *bicycle part* 687.11
handle cargo *transport* 686.10
handled *soccer* 163.7
handler *operator* 509.5, *coverer*
613.18
**handle sailboat equipment
150.30**
handle tenderly *be lenient* 423.5
handle with kid *or* **velvet
gloves** *be lenient* 423.5
handling 216.7; *management*
126.1, 509.4, *soccer play* 163.5,
touching 216.2, *use* 393.1,
treatment 399.11, *action* 412.1,
coverage 613.16
hand loom *fabric-handling tool*
130.12, *weaving* 609.2
handmaid *domestic servant* 69.7
handmaiden *domestic servant* 69.7
hand-me-down *used* 393.5
hand-me-downs *old clothes* 100.8
hand-milk *practice livestock farming*
16.20
hand mirror *reflector* 242.10
hand of death *personifications and
symbols* 29.4
hand off *play offense* 155.18
hand-off *play* 155.8
hand of friendship *peace offering*
74.5
hand on *transfer property* 470.12
hand on *or* **down** *bring* 685.11
hand-operated *handling* 216.7,
practical 511.6
handout *positive stimulus* 508.5
handout [Inf] *news story* 171.3,
advertisement 173.9, *charity* 307.3,
offering 472.6, *gift* 498.3, *social
assistance* 825.4
hand out *provision* 89.9, *squash
terms* 165.10
hand out a sample *offer* 504.11
hand out bouquets *reward*
453.13
hand out brickbats *berate*
438.20
handover *transfer of property*
470.4, *conveyance* 685.2
hand over *relinquish* 392.3,
transfer property 470.4, *give*
472.10, *transfer* 685.8, *convey*
685.9, *cross* 692.17
hand over fist *up* 713.25
hand over one's sword *capitulate*
421.6
hand over the baton *participate*
166.22

hand paddle *swimming equipment*
164.8
hand-paint *make ceramics* 129.10
hand-painted *ceramic* 129.9
hand-painted decoration
decoration 129.4
handpick *choose* 382.14, *subtract*
749.6
handpicked *selected* 382.11
handpicking *selecting* 382.4
handprop *stage requisite* 136.21
hands *personnel* 123.16, *face* 646.8
hands across the sea *friendly
relations* 62.3
hand's breadth *breadth* 592.1
hands-down *easy* 823.9
handsel *giveaway* 472.5, *type of
payment* 489.3
handset *telephone* 169.10
handshake *computer
communications* 15.25, *gesture*
183.5, *welcome* 408.10, *sign of
courtesy* 410.5, *promise* 458.1,
reception 704.3
hand signal *gesture* 183.5
hands in pockets *gesture* 183.5
hands off *do-nothing* 413.6
hands off! 386.26
hands-off *inactive* 413.9
handsome *generous* 498.6,
attractive 529.8
handsome fortune *wealth* 485.1
handsomely *beautifully* 529.13,
530.16
handsomeness *attractiveness* 529.2
hands-on *handling* 216.7
hands on hips *gesture* 183.5
handspike *hand tool* 103.3
handspring *floor exercise* 157.4,
pommel horse 157.7, *act of
inversion* 608.3, *become inverted*
608.8
handstand *horizontal bar* 157.5,
stationary rings 157.8, *competitive
diving* 164.7, *diving* 164.13, *act of
inversion* 608.3, *become inverted*
608.8
handstrap *gymnastics equipment*
157.2
hand technique *jumping* 166.11
hand to hand *manually* 216.13,
contentious 422.20, *near* 586.6,
commercially 686.12
hand-to-hand fight *duel* 422.12
hand-to-mouth *sufficient* 97.3,
poor 486.8
hand-to-mouth existence
poverty 486.1
hand tool 103.3; *tool* 103.1
hand to on a plate *follow* 745.12
hand towel *cleaning cloth* 111.11
hand-turn *make ceramics* 129.10
hand-turned *ceramic* 129.9
hand-turned wheel *ceramic
workshop and tools* 129.8
handwoven *interwoven* 609.6
hand-wringing *agitation* 684.1
handwrite *word* 5.43
handwriting *written letter* 5.14
handwritten *written* 5.36
handy *skillful* 127.10, *touchable*
216.5, *usable* 393.6, *proficient*
445.15, *instrumental* 511.4, *light*
539.4, *available* 575.11,
undersized 580.8, *next* 586.8,
useful 801.5, *convenient* 803.3,
wieldy 823.12, *helpful* 825.19
handyman *servant* 69.1, *repair
worker* 123.8, *skilled person* 127.7,
hard worker 414.11, *repairer*
809.5
hang *execute* 30.22, 454.30, *exercise*
157.12, *suspend* 604.13
hang about *wait* 658.12

hangar *airport* 689.4
hang around *wait* 658.12
hang around [Inf] *appear* 575.16
hang around *or* **about** [Inf] *be
inactive* 415.13, *stay near* 586.13
hang around *or* **out with** [Inf]
fraternize 408.17
hang around with [Inf] *keep
company with* 794.17
hang back *doubt* 287.13, *delay*
375.16, *shy* 386.17, *escape notice*
403.14, *wait* 658.12, *be inhibited*
826.20, *hesitate* 841.18
hang by a thread *be in danger*
811.11
hang by the neck *execute* 454.30
hangdog *humiliated* 298.12,
sycophantic 401.7, *appearing guilty*
450.7
hangdog look *sign of sullenness*
304.2
hangdog look *or* **expression**
humiliation 298.5
hang down *suspend* 604.13, *droop*
714.14
hang, draw, and quarter *execute*
454.30
hanger *sharp weapon* 78.6, *hand
tool* 103.3
hanger [Inf] *playing terms* 148.4
hanger-on *adherent* 401.5, 755.4,
flatterer 439.6, *beggar* 505.6,
follower 794.10, *dependent* 832.4
hangfire *delay* 375.6
hang fire *delay* 375.16,
procrastinate 413.12, *wait* 658.12,
pause 668.13, *be motionless* 678.7
hang fire [Inf] *be infertile* 23.8
hang glider *aircraft* 689.3
hang gliding *Sporting Activities*
145
hang in [Inf] *insist* 376.14
hanging *murder* 30.2, *execution*
30.6, *stage set* 136.19, *weak* 517.6,
suspension 604.1, *suspended* 604.7,
wall covering 613.12, *nonadhesive*
756.4
hanging back *inhibition* 826.9,
irresolute 841.10
hanging ball *golfing terms* 156.3
hanging basket *ornamental garden*
17.3
hanging by a thread *dying* 29.12,
unsafe 811.8
hanging by the wrists *corporal
punishment* 454.11
**hanging, drawing, and
quartering** *capital punishment*
454.12
hanging garden *garden* 17.2
Hanging Gardens of Babylon
garden 17.2, *Seven Wonders of
the Ancient World* 294
hanging in there *enduring* 377.9
hanging judge *judge* 54.10, *strict
person* 424.4, *punisher* 454.16
hanging offense *wicked act* 448.7
hanging on *retention* 471.1
hanging oneself *suicide* 30.8
hanging out [Inf] *frequenting*
661.2
hanging rope *instrument of
execution* 454.15
hanging up *stop* 668.2
hanging valley *landform* 8.9
hang in there [Inf] *take courage*
284.15, *insist* 376.14, *last* 642.6,
protract 669.9
hang it up [Inf] *stop work* 394.12,
acquiesce 421.5
hang like a millstone *weigh on*
538.13
hang loose [Inf] *ease* 543.15
hangman *killer* 30.11, *executioner*

30.13, *Children's and Party
Games* 167, *punisher* 454.16,
violent animal 520.4, *destroyer*
523.6
hangman's knot *Knots, Bends,
Hitches, Splices* 754
hang on *hold out* 377.13, *follow*
401.14, *last* 642.6, *delay* 658.13,
protract 669.9, *show determination*
674.8, *link* 752.18, *be tenacious*
755.9
hang on by one's teeth *hold out*
377.13
hang oneself *commit suicide* 30.24
hang one's head in shame *be
penitent* 451.7
hang one's lip *be sullen* 304.12
hang on for dear life *hold out*
377.13, *show tenaciousness* 471.8
hang on like grim death *hold out*
377.13
hang on someone's words *or*
lips *hear* 228.13
hang on the skirts *or* **sleeve of**
follow 401.14
hang on to save 105.20, *be selfish*
444.6, *retain* 471.7
hang on with all one's might
show tenaciousness 471.8
hangout [Inf] *habitat* 60.1
hang out *dry* 560.17
hang out [Inf] *appear* 575.16
hang out at [Inf] *frequent* 60.25,
661.6
hang out the flags *or* **bunting**
salute 405.13
hang out to dry *dry* 560.17
hang out with [Inf] *keep company
with* 794.17
hangover *drunken behavior* 121.4
hang over *overhang* 604.14,
hesitate 693.12
hang time *kick* 155.12
hang together *conform* 735.27,
unify 752.15, *adhere* 755.8, *work
together* 827.14
hang tough [Inf] *take courage*
284.15, *insist* 376.14, *be tough*
547.13
hang up *stop using* 394.10, *suspend*
604.13, *stop* 668.10
hang-up [Inf] *diligence* 323.4, *delay*
658.13, *defect* 806.4, *obstacle* 826.2
hang upon *follow from* 676.9
hang up one's hat *take up
residence* 60.24
hang up one's spikes [Inf] *stop
work* 394.12
hang weights on *make heavy*
538.14
hank *handle sailboat equipment*
150.30, *General Units* 589
Hanka *Lakes* 568
hanker *envy* 314.7
hanker after *like* 290.8
hankerer *desirer* 288.9
hankering *desire* 288.1, *desirous*
288.13, *liking* 290.1, 290.4
hanky-panky [Inf] *sexual
intercourse* 20.9, *foul play* 193.6,
disreputable action 371.3
Hanoi *Countries* 566
Hanoi, tower of *Mathematical
Concepts* 6
Hanoverian *Horse and Pony
Breeds* 159, *historic* 653.13
hanse *arch* 134.5
Hansen's disease *tropical disease*
114.10
Hanukkah *Jewish Holy Days and
Seasons* 85
hap *chance* 842.12
haphazard *clumsy* 128.6,
indiscriminate 338.8, *irregular*

664.3, 766.10, *inconsistent* 732.7,
hasty 818.3, *capricious* 841.16,
causeless 842.11
haphazardly *indiscriminately*
338.15, *irregularly* 664.6,
inconsistently 732.16, *in disorder*
766.24, *randomly* 842.16
haphazardness *inaccuracy* 351.3,
irregularity 664.1, *inconsistency*
732.3, *irregular order* 766.2, *lack
of motive* 842.2
haphido Sporting Activities 145
hapless *unlucky* 848.12
haply *possibly* 836.9
hapnophobia Phobias 283
happen *occur* 264.14, *act* 412.11,
react 676.8, *take effect* 676.11, *be
real* 719.10, *chance* 842.12
happen again *be repeated* 797.20
happen at the same time *be
simultaneous* 649.6, *be the same*
730.13
happen every day *be frequent*
661.5
happening *dramatic style* 136.3,
visibility 264.4, *topical* 328.5,
action 412.1, *acting* 412.9, *present*
647.4, *effect* 676.1, *thing* 717.3,
occurrence 726.2
happenings *news* 171.1, *matter of
interest* 328.3
happen now and then *be
infrequent* 662.3
happen often *be frequent* 661.5
happenstance *chance* 842.1
happen upon *chance upon* 842.13
happen upon *or on* *discover*
345.11
happen yearly *be cyclic* 663.11
happiest days of one's life *youth*
26.1
happily *pleasingly* 214.15, *joyfully*
269.13, *with satisfaction* 273.13,
opportunely 659.8, *prosperously*
847.9
happiness *pleasure* 214.2, *joy*
269.1, *satisfaction* 273.1, *rejoicing*
279.1, Phobias 283, *welfare*
445.2, *prosperity* 847.1
happy *pacificatory* 74.8, *joyful*
269.6, *satisfied* 273.4, *rejoicing*
279.4, *timely* 659.4
happy chance *opportunity* 659.2
happy coincidence *timeliness*
659.1
happy couple *married couple* 64.9
happy days *or* **ending** *good thing*
445.9
happy dreams *ease* 819.1
happy ending *successfulness* 845.3
happy few *best people* 744.7
happy fortune *good fortune* 847.2
happy-go-lucky *unskillful* 128.4,
imprudent 286.7, *thoughtless* 318.7
happy hour *drink occasion* 93.14,
good time 214.3
happy hunting ground *after
death* 29.9, *heaven* 82.15
happy land *heaven* 82.15
happy medium *moderation* 455.3,
521.1, *compromise* 461.1, *medium*
742.2, *middle way* 777.3
Happy Valley *dreamland* 360.8
hapteron *plant body* 47.13
haptophobia *or* **hapnophobia**
Phobias 283
hara-kiri *suicide* 30.8, *non-
Christian ritual* 85.8, *self-
punishment* 454.10
harangue *be diffuse* 199.5,
dissertation 203.1, *public speaking*
205.11, *speak to* 205.19, *address*
209.1, 209.8, *moralize* 431.1
haranguer *speaker* 205.12

Harare Countries 566
harass *irritate* 302.16, *harm*
306.13, *discriminate against*
337.14, *pursue* 385.11, *meddle*
414.23, *suppress* 428.9, *be evil*
446.10, *disturb* 768.10
harassed *worried* 283.11,
suppressed 428.6, *troubled* 824.15
harassing *malign* 306.11
harassment *annoyance* 276.2,
malignity 306.5, *attack* 418.1,
suppression 428.2
harbinger *omen* 358.5, *predict*
358.14, *precursor* 769.7
harbor 812.6; *water system* 551.13,
shelter 613.6, *enclosed area* 619.2,
stopping place 668.4, *destination*
704.6, *protect* 810.21
harbor a design *intend* 374.8
harborage *harbor* 812.6
harbored *sheltered* 812.7
harbor resentment *resent* 302.13
hard 542.5, 547.8; *drinkable* 93.18,
intoxicating 121.29, *laborious*
122.7, *ceramic* 129.9, *obscure*
197.2, *acid* 223.5, *pitiless* 309.3,
tenacious 376.9, *determined* 379.7,
674.5, *obstinate* 417.7, *severe*
424.5, *impenitent* 452.2, *punishing*
454.20, *with vigor* 518.6, *thick-
skinned* 594.8, *stable* 674.3,
difficult 824.9, *adverse* 848.10
hard-and-fast *legal* 780.8
hard as iron *strong-willed* 376.10
hard as nails [Inf] *determined*
379.7, *mentally hard* 542.8, *hard*
547.8
hard-ass [Inf] *obstinate person*
379.4
hard at it *working* 122.6, *busy*
414.15
hard at work *busy* 414.15
hardball *baseball* 147.1
hard bargain *negotiate* 460.6
hard bargaining *negotiation* 460.1,
bargaining 480.10
hard blow *misadventure* 848.2
hardboard *wood* 131.3
hard-boil *harden* 542.9
hard-boiled [Inf] *mentally tough*
547.12
hard-boiled egg *egg dish* 90.18
hard breathing *fatigue* 820.1
hard by *nearby* 586.17
hard candy *sweets* 90.39
hard cash *cash* 484.2
hard center *hardness* 542.1
hard cider *alcoholic drink* 93.9
hard coal *coal* 106.4
hardcopy device 15.10;
peripheral 15.8
hard core *rock music* 140.6, *solid
body* 540.4, *hardness* 542.1
hard-core *determined* 379.7,
resistant 417.6
hard-core pornography
pornography 432.7
hard-core supporter *tenacious
person* 377.5
hard corn *ulcer* 114.18
hard court *tennis court* 165.3
hardcover *book* 174.1
hard currency *money* 484.1
hard disk *magnetic recording* 10.51,
disk 15.5
hard dose *affliction* 454.9
hard drink *alcohol* 121.5
hard drinker *drinker* 93.16,
drunkard 121.8
hard drinking *drinking* 121.2
hard-drinking *drunken* 121.28
hard driving *swiftness* 694.1
hard drug *drug* 121.14
harden 542.9; *handle sailboat*

equipment 150.30, *be indifferent*
289.12, *accustom* 397.18, *cost a lot*
496.9, *strengthen* 516.15, *be dense*
540.8, *make tough* 547.15, *thicken*
594.9, *season* 654.11, *be stable*
674.6
hardened 542.7; *insensible* 213.4,
insensitive 268.4, *determined*
379.7, *habituated* 397.14,
impenitent 452.2, *toughened* 547.7,
seasoned 654.9
hardening 542.2; *habituation*
397.7, *strengthening* 516.7, *density*
540.1, *stability* 674.1
hardening of the arteries
cardiovascular disease 114.13,
hardening 542.2, *physical
deterioration* 808.4
harden one's heart *be hostile*
63.10, *be indifferent* 289.12, *be
impenitent* 452.4
harden one's heart to *refuse*
506.8
hard facts *chief thing* 799.3
hard fate *bad fortune* 848.7
hard feelings *ill feeling* 63.3, *bad
feeling* 266.5, *hate* 300.1,
resentment 302.1
hard-fire *make ceramics* 129.10
hard firing *ceramic process* 129.5
hard-fought *laborious* 122.7
hard freeze *cold weather* 9.24
hard frost *frost* 9.25, *ice* 218.5
hard furrow to plow *difficult task*
824.3
hard going *difficult task* 824.3
hard goods *merchandise* 522.6
hard-grained *woody* 43.11
hard hand *severity* 424.1
hard hat *helmet* 100.34, *protective
covering* 613.5
hardhead *obstinate person* 379.4
hardheaded *willful* 372.8,
obstinate 379.5, *resistant* 417.6,
severe 424.5
hardheadedly *resistingly* 417.14
hardheadedness *willfulness*
372.3, *obstinacy* 417.2
hardhearted *pitiless* 309.3, *severe*
424.5, *impenitent* 452.2, *mentally
hard* 542.8, *mentally tough* 547.12
hardheartedly *pitilessly* 309.7,
severely 424.11, *impenitently*
452.5, *inflexibly* 542.13, *single-
mindedly* 547.19
hardheartedness *heedlessness*
268.2, *pitilessness* 309.1,
impenitence 452.1, *mental hardness*
542.4, *mental toughness* 547.5
hard-hitting *tenacious* 376.9
hardihood *courage* 284.1
hardily *strongly* 516.17, *stalwartly*
547.17
hardiness *courage* 284.1,
stalwartness 547.3
hard knocks *fight* 422.9
hard labor *work* 122.1,
imprisonment 454.2
hard landing *rocketry* 7.32
hard *or* **soft** *or* **gas-permeable
lenses** *visual aid* 242.14
hard life *critical situation* 824.6,
adversity 848.1
hard light *lighting* 132.16
hard line *determination* 379.2
hard-line *combative* 77.32,
determined 379.7, *obstinate* 417.7
hard-liner *political party member*
50.6, *militarist* 77.3, *obstinate
person* 379.4, *resister* 417.5, *strict
person* 424.4
hard liquor *alcohol* 121.5
hard luck *lost chance* 660.3, *bad
fortune* 848.7

hard luck! *good luck!* 842.19
hardly *barely* 593.18, *infrequently*
662.4, *sparsely* 796.11, *difficultly*
824.23
hardly a chance *improbability*
839.1
hardly alike *incomparably* 734.12
hardly any *few* 796.5
hardly breathing *inactive* 413.9
hardly ever *seldom* 640.9, *rarely*
839.10
hard master *strict person* 424.4
hard-mouthed *refractory* 379.6
hardness 542.1; *heedlessness* 268.2,
pitilessness 309.1, *tenacity* 376.4,
determination 379.2, 674.2,
obstinacy 417.2, *severity* 424.1,
impenitence 452.1, *density* 540.1,
toughness 547.1, *grain* 552.2,
callousness 594.4, *difficulty* 824.1
hardness of heart *impenitence*
452.1, *mental hardness* 542.4
hard news *news* 171.1
hard-nose [Inf] *obstinate person*
379.4
hard-nosed [Inf] *resistant* 417.6,
mentally tough 547.12
hard nut to crack *puzzle* 182.5,
unintelligible thing 364.3, *problem*
824.4
hard of hearing *deaf* 229.4
hard on the eyes *ugly* 531.3
hard-packed *snow* 162.28
hard-packed snow *skiing snow*
162.3
hard pad *animal disease* 34.10
hard palate *speech organ* 205.4
hardpan *solid body* 540.4, *base*
601.1
hard-paste *ceramic* 129.9
hard paste porcelain Ceramics
129
hard pitch *pitching terms* 147.5
hard porn [Inf] *pornography* 432.7
hard-pressed *insolvent* 486.10,
hasty 818.3
hard pruning *gardening* 17.5
hard pull *difficult task* 824.3
hard put to it *insolvent* 486.10
hard resin *resin* 562.6
hard-right *conservative* 815.13
hard road to travel *difficult task*
824.3
hard rock *rock music* 140.6
hard roe *fish characteristic* 38.8
hard row of stumps *difficult task*
824.3
hard row (to hoe) *affliction* 454.9
hard row to hoe *difficult task*
824.3
hard rubber *rubber* 546.3
hard sell *publicity* 178.7,
salesmanship 482.4, *inducement*
508.2
hard-sell *publicize* 178.19
hard selling *publicity* 178.7
hard-selling *persuasive* 178.12
hard-shell *determined* 379.7,
resistant 417.6
hardship *neediness* 95.3, *poverty*
486.1, *critical situation* 824.6,
adversity 848.1
hard shoulder *edge* 618.1
hard snowboard boots
snowboarding equipment 162.12
hardstand *miscellaneous automotive
terms* 687.14, *airport* 689.4
hard stuff [Inf] *alcoholic drink* 93.9
hard substance 542.3
hard task *undertaking* 391.1,
difficult task 824.3
hard thinking *thought* 317.1
hard tick *arachnid* 40.4
hard times *insolvency* 486.2, *critical*

situation 824.6, awkward situation 824.7, time of adversity 848.8
hard to believe disbelieved 88.7, questionable 839.5
hard to catch avoiding 386.9
hard to decode unintelligible 364.4
hard to find not enough 98.5
hard to pin down suppositional 359.5
hard to please troublesome 824.13
hard to satisfy troublesome 824.13
hard to swallow [Inf] questionable 839.5
hard to understand difficult 364.8
hard up [Inf] needy 95.12, unprovided 98.6, poor 486.8, insolvent 486.10, unprosperous 848.11
hard use use 393.1
hard vacuum surface chemistry 11.20
hardware merchandise 522.6, hard substance 542.3
hard water water 557.1
hard way, the exertion 122.4, laboriously 122.13, difficult task 824.3, difficultly 824.23, in the way 826.23
hard-wearing strengthened 516.13, tough 547.6
hard winter cold weather 9.24
hardwire program 15.29
hard-won laborious 122.7
hardwood woody 43.11, wood 131.3, canoeing 150.26, hard substance 542.3
hardwood (tree) tree 43.1
hardwood flooring floor covering 613.13
hard word word 5.17
hard words obscurity 197.1, berating 438.5
hard work work 122.1, commitment 377.2, assiduity 414.8, difficult task 824.3
hard worker 414.11; person who undertakes 391.3
hardworking working 122.6, industrious 414.16
hardy botanical 17.15, wild 41.15, of good constitution 113.5, courageous 284.9, physically strong 516.10, vigorous 518.2, stalwart 547.10
Hare Constellations 7
hare gnawing mammal 35.13, meat 90.22, game 160.6
harebell Flowers 42
harebrained reckless 286.6, foolish 353.5
harelike rabbitlike 35.29
harem womenfolk 33.14
hares Collective Names 59
hare's fur glaze glaze 129.3
harissa notable international dishes 90.40
hark hear 228.13, chase 385.13
hark back recollect 3.16, remember 354.12, look back 651.18, reverse 671.9
harking back recollection 3.8
Harlem New York 567.6
Harlem Renaissance Western Art Styles 133, Western Literary Groups 139
Harlequin stock part 136.24, clown 138.10, variegated thing 263.5, Famous Lovers 299
harlequinade dramatic style 136.3
harlot loose woman 33.6, sexually immoral person 432.8
harlotry prostitution 432.4

harlot's trade prostitution 432.4
harm 306.13; affliction 117.1, afflict 117.16, malignity 306.5, ill-use 395.2, 395.7, wrongdoing 430.7, wrong 430.19, be evil 446.10, loss 468.1, destroy 468.18, weaken 517.13, inconvenience 804.1, be inconvenient 804.9
harmattan Notable Winds 9
harmful unhygienic 114.27, afflicting 117.11, malign 306.11, abusive 395.5, unlawful 430.15, detrimental 446.8, destructive 523.8, inconvenient 804.5, dangerous 811.7, adverse 848.10
harmfully banefully 117.19, malignly 306.18, offensively 395.9, destructively 446.13, adversely 848.16
harmfulness malice 306.2
harmless 73.9; health-giving 113.6, humble 298.8, innocent 449.6, moderate 521.3, trustworthy 810.17
harmlessly innocently 449.13, powerlessly 515.16
harmlessness humility 298.1, innocence 449.1, safety 810.1
Harmodius Notable Friendships 62
harmonic 140.27; cyclic 6.82, musical note 140.15, tone 140.24, 230.2, musical 140.25, oscillating 683.8, harmonizing 735.12
harmonica Musical Instruments 142
harmonically tunefully 140.30, in harmony 735.32
harmonic analysis Branches of Mathematics 6
harmonic element 140.14
harmonic minor scale scale 140.16
harmonic motion frequency 663.2, oscillation 683.1
harmonic progression sequence 6.18, harmonics 140.13
harmonics 140.13
harmonic scale scale 140.16
harmonious 735.11, 765.16; friendly 62.5, peaceful 73.8, melodious 140.26, colorful 251.11, agreeing 462.6, 730.8, corresponding 606.6, symmetrical 626.4, even 626.5, harmonizing 735.12, agreeable 752.11, collaborative 777.7, uniform 780.10, conforming 781.8, associating 827.11
harmoniously 735.31; amicably 62.13, tunefully 140.30, agreeably 462.14, 752.22, gracefully 527.8, synchronously 649.9, agreeingly 730.19, in harmony 735.32, in combination 757.11, conformingly 781.16, cooperatively 827.18
harmoniousness melodiousness 140.12
harmonistically in harmony 735.32
harmonium Musical Instruments 142
harmonization 735.2; harmonics 140.13, agreement 462.1, mixture 751.1
harmonize 140.28, 735.22, 765.20; conciliate 74.10, sing 141.16, agree with 462.10, correspond 606.8, symmetrize 626.6, synchronize 649.7, agree 730.14, mix 751.12, come together 757.10, conform 781.11, concur 827.16

harmonized mixed 751.8, combinatory 757.6
harmonizing 735.12
harmonograph measuring instrument 683.6
harmony 765.8; friendship 62.1, friendly relations 62.3, peace 73.1, music 140.1, melodiousness 140.12, harmonics 140.13, floor exercise 157.4, assent 346.1, agreement 462.1, 730.2, 752.4, grace 527.2, beauty 529.1, correspondence 606.2, symmetry 626.1, evenness 626.3, accord 735.1, harmonization 735.2, mixed thing 751.2, collaboration 757.2, completeness 761.1, conformity 781.1, fellowship 827.2
harness practice livestock farming 16.20, equipment 103.6, sailboard parts 150.20, fighting chair 154.8, riding equipment 159.9, climbing equipment 161.4, historic armor 419.8, link 752.18, tackle 754.6, yoke 754.8, bind 754.14, means of restraint 830.6, restrain someone 830.17
harnessed bound 754.12
harness hitch Knots, Bends, Hitches, Splices 754
harness line sailboard parts 150.20
harness maker horse person 159.14
harness race horse racing 159.10
harness racing Sporting Activities 145
harness together unite 752.14
harp 797.17, Musical Instruments 142
harpaxophobia Phobias 283
Harpies, the Deities 82
harping repetitious 797.11
harpist player 141.2
harp on continue 669.8, harp 797.17
harpoon Historical Missile Weapons 78, sharp weapon 78.6, sharp-pointed thing 549.4, use a sharp tool 549.17
harpsichord Musical Instruments 142
harpsichordist player 141.2
Harpy Legendary Creatures 360
harpy unpleasant woman 33.7, evil spirit 446.4
harquebus historical handgun 78.8
harquebusier historical soldier 77.8
harras Collective Names 59
harridan irascible person 303.7
harrier Breeds of Dogs 35, bird of prey 36.11, speeder 694.5
Harrisburg American States 564
Harris tweed Fabrics and Fibers 130
harrow farm tool 16.5, farm 16.19, inflict pain 215.10, smoother 545.2, smooth 545.10, sharp-pointed thing 549.4, use a sharp tool 549.17
harrowed uniform 545.5
harrowing cultivation 16.7, painful 215.4, distressing 270.6
harry harm 306.13, attack 418.17
harrying attacking 418.14
harsh unpalatable 223.6, splenetic 223.7, hearable 228.12, strident 238.4, dissonant 241.4, gaudy 251.12, off-color 251.15, cruel 306.10, pitiless 309.3, discourteous 411.5, severe 424.5, critical 438.13, violent 520.5
harsh criticism criticism 438.4
harshly sourly 223.9, splenetically 223.10, stridently 238.10,

dissonantly 241.7, cruelly 306.17, pitilessly 309.7, discourteously 411.8, severely 424.11
harshness stimulation 221.4, harsh sound 238.1, dissonance 241.1, cruelty 306.4, pitilessness 309.1, discourtesy 411.1, severity 424.1, violence 520.1
harsh sound 238.1
harsh treatment severity 424.1
harsh voice speech difficulty 206.1
harsh words berating 438.5
hart male animal 32.15, male mammal 35.18
Hartford American States 564
hartshorn tonic 115.8
harum-scarum inconsistently 732.16, disorderly 766.15, anyhow 766.25
haruspex imam 84.7, diviner 86.14
haruspical divinatory 86.18, presageful 358.13
haruspicate look ahead 650.11
haruspicy divination 358.2
haruspicy or **haruspication** divination 86.5
Harvard–Yale race rowing competitions 150.18
harvest farm 16.19, store 105.1, 105.17, yield 467.8, acquire 467.19, plant products 522.8, fall 654.5, growth 676.3, grow 676.10
harvested yielding 467.14
harvester farm tool 16.5, collector 59.17
harvest home feast 92.9
harvesting cultivation 16.7
harvestman arachnid 40.4
harvest moon moon 7.18, natural light 246.4, fall 654.5
harvest supper feast 92.9
harvest time fall 654.5
Harz Mountains Mountains and Hills 569
has-been loser 846.9
hash meat dish 90.21, mixed thing 751.2, miscellany 751.3, confusion 766.4, mix-up 766.5, confuse 766.19
hash [Inf] hemp derivatives 121.16
hash browns vegetable 90.33
Hashem God 82.6
hashing programming concepts 15.24
hashish hemp derivatives 121.16
hash mark stadium 155.3
hash mark [Inf] insignia 184.5
hash table data-related concepts 15.23
Hasid Jew 81.11
Hasidic denominational 81.23
Hasidism Judaism 81.6
hasp joint 752.7, fastener 754.7
hassle exertion 122.4, contention 422.1, be severe 424.8, discompose 766.18, haste 818.1
hassle [Inf] annoyance 276.2, annoy 276.7, 804.10, alacrity 414.3, meddle 414.23, dispute 463.3, 463.9, disturb 768.10, be difficult 824.16, bother 826.16
hassled [Inf] disturbed 768.6
hassock grassland 45.2
hastate of leaves 41.18, sharp 549.10
haste 818.1; rashness 286.1, alacrity 414.3, prematurity 657.6, swiftness 694.1
hasten 657.15, 818.4; be active 414.18, start early 657.12, awaken 675.9, further 679.13, 825.30, scamper 694.12, hurry someone up 694.15, make haste 818.5, make easy 823.15

hasten away *make haste* 818.5
hastening *haste* 818.1, *hasty* 818.3, *easing* 823.7
hasten off *hurry off* 705.11
hasten someone's end *kill* 30.19
hastily 818.7; *rashly* 286.9, *unreadily* 389.16, *superficially* 599.8, *early* 657.17, *prematurely* 657.20, *hurryingly* 694.18
hastiness 818.2; *rashness* 286.1, *unpremeditation* 389.2, *superficiality* 599.2, *prematurity* 657.6, *swiftness* 694.1
hasty 818.3; *clumsy* 128.6, *rash* 286.5, *unpremeditated* 389.7, *superficial* 599.4, *premature* 657.10, *swift* 694.6
hasty retreat *escape* 816.1
hat 100.32; *body covering* 613.3
hatch *propagate* 21.15, *have young* 21.16, *eggs* 36.5, *young bird* 36.17, *nest* 36.22, *develop* 40.18, *draw* 143.13, *sailboat parts and accessories* 150.4, *make dark* 247.10, *imagine* 360.14, *bring into existence* 522.14, *means of entry* 706.6, *fabricate* 720.17
hatch a plot *plot* 387.15
hatchback *automobile* 687.6
hatcheck girl *attendant* 69.4
hatched *produced* 522.12
hatcher *planner* 387.9
hatchery *dwelling* 36.4, *source* 675.2
hatchet *sharp weapon* 78.6, *sharp-edged thing* 549.6
hatchet face *thinness* 595.1
hatchet-faced *thin* 595.9
hatchet job *criticism* 440.2, *destroying* 523.2
hatchet man *murderer* 30.12, *disparager* 440.7, *villain* 448.5, *punisher* 454.16, *destroyer* 523.6
hatching *genesis* 21.5, *darkening* 247.2
hatchment *funeral object* 31.6, *Heraldic Terms* 184
hatchway *means of entry* 706.6
hate 300.1, 300.11; *be hostile* 63.10, *antipathy* 291.2, *detest* 291.13, *malevolence* 306.1, *be malevolent* 306.12, *opposition* 828.1, *be against* 828.17
hateable *hateful* 300.10
hated 300.9; *detested* 291.11
hated thing 300.5
hate evil *be virtuous* 447.8
hate-filled *malevolent* 306.7
hateful 300.10; *unpleasant* 272.6, *antipathetic* 291.7, *hating* 300.7, *malevolent* 306.7, *evil* 446.7
hatefully 300.14; *aggressively* 63.14, *discontentedly* 291.17, *malevolently* 306.14, *evilly* 446.12
hatefulness 300.4; *malevolence* 306.1, *evil* 446.1
hater 300.6; *feeling person* 266.8
hater of humankind *misanthrope* 291.5
hate someone's guts [Inf] *hate* 300.11
hate the world *detest* 291.13
Hathor *Deities* 82
hating 300.7; *malevolent* 306.7
hatless *uncovered* 614.10
hatmaking *the clothing business* 100.36
hatpin *jewelry* 532.6, *fastener* 754.7
hatred *bad feeling* 266.5, *antipathy* 291.2, *hate* 300.1, *malevolence* 306.1, *opposition* 828.1
hatred of humankind *misanthropy* 291.4
hatted *dressed* 100.38

hatter *clothier* 100.37
hatting *the clothing business* 100.36
hat trick *batting terms* 147.6, *triple thing* 790.3, *successful thing* 845.5
hauberk *historic armor* 419.8
haughtily *arrogantly* 297.18, 400.21, *unsocially* 409.13
haughtiness *arrogance* 297.2, 400.4, *unsociability* 409.1
haughty *arrogant* 297.9, 400.11, *unsociable* 409.6, *contemptuous* 436.12
haul *engineer* 14.48, *work* 122.8, *mountaineer* 161.10, *acquisition* 467.4, *takings* 477.8, *set in motion* 677.16, *convey* 685.9, *transport* 686.10, *pull* 699.2, 699.10
haulage *conveyance* 685.2, *transportation* 686.1, *traction* 699.1
haul ass [Inf] *be swift* 694.10
haul before the court or **judge** *litigate* 54.27
haul down *lower the flag* 716.23
haul down the flag *capitulate* 421.6
hauled up *accused* 442.5
hauler *construction equipment* 14.23, *transferrer* 685.4, *transporter* 686.10, *towline* 699.5
haulier [Brit] *towline* 699.5
haul in *fish* 154.14, *detain* 830.16
hauling *conveyance* 685.2, *traction* 699.1, *tractional* 699.7
hauling over the coals *condemnation* 438.2
haulm *grass plant* 45.3
haul over the coals *condemn* 438.18
haul up *accuse* 442.8, *gather up* 715.14
haunch *arch* 134.5
haunch bone *Human Bones* 19
haunches *rear end* 622.4
haunt *habitat* 60.1, *frequent* 60.25, 661.6, *remind* 354.13, *have a habit* 397.16, *plot* 564.9, *location* 565.1, *appear* 575.16, *protract* 669.9
haunted *bewitched* 86.21, *worried* 283.11, *omnipresent* 575.10
haunter *attender* 575.6
haunting *memorable* 354.7, *habit-forming* 397.15, *frequenting* 661.2, *frequent* 661.4, *recurrent* 797.13
hauntingly *frequently* 661.7
hausfrau *domestic worker* 123.4
haustorium *fungal body* 47.4
hautboy or **hautbois** *Musical Instruments* 142
haute couture *dressing* 100.2, *fashion* 536.1
haute cuisine *cooking* 91.1
haute école *equestrianism* 159.8
hauteur *arrogance* 297.2
haut monde *fashionable elite* 536.4
Havana *tobacco* 121.23, *Countries* 566
Havana brown *Breeds of Cats* 35
have *understand* 363.9, *possess* 469.14, *include* 763.5
have a baby *have young* 21.16
have a bad attitude *be negative* 190.21
have a bad conscience *appear guilty* 450.10
have a bad or **hard time** *be in trouble* 848.13
have a bad outcome or **result** *be disappointed* 293.8
have a bad temper *be irascible* 303.13

have a ball [Inf] *feel pleasure* 214.12, *rejoice* 279.5
have a bath *bathe* 111.18
have a bearing on *relate to* 727.9
have a bent *tend* 513.5
have a bias *prefer* 382.13
have a big appetite *be greedy* 119.4
have a big heart *be unselfish* 443.7
have a big mouth *be talkative* 207.7
have a birthday *commemorate* 663.12
have a bite *fish* 154.14
have a blank check *lack restraint* 829.21
have a bleak outlook *be negative* 190.21
have a blind spot *be blind to* 243.19, *find unintelligible* 364.14
have a body wave *coif* 530.15
have a bone to pick *disagree* 463.8, *pick a fight* 463.10
have a bowel movement (BM) *defecate* 25.21
have a brainstorm or **brain wave** [Inf] *have an idea* 317.12, *improvise* 396.6
have a break *be refreshed* 94.8
have a breakdown *have a mishap* 826.18
have a bright future *show potential* 458.14
have a brush with *fight* 422.23
have a bumper crop *acquire* 467.19
have a bumpy face *be rough* 544.10
have a burst of energy *accelerate* 694.14
have a burst of speed *accelerate* 694.14
have a buyer *be sold* 482.22
have a cameo role *underact* 136.36, *act* 137.20
have a card up one's sleeve *be cunning* 822.5
have a cash-flow crisis *be unable to pay* 490.11
have a cast of mind *be inclined toward* 290.10
have a catnap *take it easy* 819.3
have a chance *take a chance* 842.14
have a change of pace *be refreshed* 94.8
have a chat *chat* 210.12
have a check bounce *need money* 848.14
have a chink in one's armor *be imperfect* 806.8
have a chip on one's shoulder *pick a fight* 463.10
have a clean bill of health *be healthy* 113.11
have a clear conscience *be innocent* 449.10
have a clear head *be sober* 120.8
have a close call *escape* 816.8
have a closed mind *be obstinate* 379.10, *be narrow-minded* 593.16
have a close shave [Inf] *escape* 816.8
have acne *be rough* 544.10
have a cold in the nose *have no smell* 225.7
have a comedown *be in trouble* 848.13
have a common resolve *agree* 730.14
have a complaint *be unhealthy* 114.29
have a connection with *relate to* 727.9

have a conniption fit [Inf] *become angry* 302.20
have a conservative outlook *be inhibited* 826.20
have a crack *be imperfect* 806.8
have a credibility gap *be different* 463.11
have a crisis of faith *recant* 81.27
have a cross to bear *burden* 826.21
have a crush on [Inf] *like* 290.8, *be in love* 299.23
have a cut at *stab* 418.22
have a discussion *negotiate* 460.6
have a disliking for *disapprove* 438.16
have a distinctive appearance *be recognizable* 863.12
have a donnybrook *dispute* 463.9
have a double meaning *be equivocal* 380.7
have (a drop) too much *get drunk* 121.35
have a drink *drink* 93.19
have a dustup *dispute* 463.9
have advance knowledge *foresee* 357.9
have a falling-out *quarrel* 302.17, *disagree* 463.8
have a fault *be imperfect* 806.8
have a feed *have a meal* 92.25
have a feeling about *be intuitive* 320.9
have a fencing bout *fence* 153.7
have a fight *fight* 422.23
have a financial loss *lose money* 468.15
have a financial reverse *need money* 848.14
have a financial setback *need money* 848.14
have a finger in *be active in* 412.17
have a finger in every pie *meddle* 414.23
have a fit *become angry* 302.20
have a flair for *be skillful* 127.14
have a flat *have a mishap* 826.18
have a flight of fancy *tell a tall story* 194.15, *be capricious* 364.8
have a fling *overindulge* 456.11
have a fling at *strike* 418.21
have a flying or **running start** *have an advantage* 618.10
have a fly in the ointment *have a mishap* 826.18
have a fondness for *like* 299.22
have a free hand *be permitted* 502.8, *lack restraint* 829.21
have a free kick *play soccer* 163.8
have a free mind *be free* 829.16
have a free shot *play soccer* 163.8
have a frog in one's throat *sound hoarse* 238.8
have a full nelson on *wrestle* 152.20
have a funny feeling about *be intuitive* 320.9
have a gainful occupation *get paid* 453.17
have a gander (at) [Inf] *inspect* 242.22
have a generous or **a big heart** *be benevolent* 305.10
have a generous nature *give* 472.10
have a genius for *tend* 513.5
have a gift *tend* 513.5
have a gift for *be skillful* 127.14
have a go *experiment* 335.11, *attempt* 390.6
have a go! *here goes!* 390.11
have a goal kick *play soccer* 163.8
have a go at *contend* 422.22

have a good appetite *eat well* 92.23

have a good ear *have an ear for* 228.14

have a good head for *be skillful* 127.14

have a good head on one's shoulders [Inf] *be intelligent* 315.11

have a good idea *have an idea* 317.12

have a good influence on *improve* 807.15

have a good mind to *be willing* 373.12

have a good reputation 370.5

have a good time *enjoy* 269.9

have a good time of it *be prosperous* 847.6

have a grasping nature *take* 477.14

have a green thumb *garden* 17.18

have a grip of iron *show tenaciousness* 471.8

have a grip of steel *show tenaciousness* 471.8

have a grudge against *detest* 291.13

have a gut feeling *or* **reaction** [Inf] *be intuitive* 320.9

have a habit 397.16

have a hairbreadth escape *escape* 816.8

have a hand in *be active in* 412.17, *be an instrument* 511.7, *determine* 675.11, *further* 825.30

have a hard time of it *be in difficulty* 824.19

have a head start *have an advantage* 618.10

have a heart! *have pity!* 308.13

have a heart attack *be unhealthy* 114.29

have a heart of gold *be benevolent* 305.10

have a heart of stone *be indifferent* 289.12

have a heart-to-heart [Inf] *chat* 210.12

have a hiccup [Inf] *have a mishap* 826.18

have a high opinion of *respect* 435.13

have a high opinion of oneself *be vain* 402.14

have a high profile *be visible* 244.7

have a hobby *make merry* 167.13

have a hold over *or* **on** *be an influence* 512.13

have a hollow leg *be greedy* 119.4

have a honeymoon period *agree with* 462.10

have a hopeless case *be powerless* 515.11

have a hunch *feel instinctively* 266.15, *be intuitive* 320.9, *theorize* 327.16, *suppose* 359.8

have a jagged edge *be sharp* 549.15

have a knack for *be skillful* 127.14

have a knee-jerk reaction [Inf] *be instinctive* 320.10

have a knock-down-drag-out fight *dispute* 463.9

have a large part in *determine* 675.11

have a leaning *tend* 513.5

have a liaison *fornicate* 432.14

have a liberated mind *be free* 829.16

have all one could ask for *be satisfied* 273.8

have all the appearances *or* **features of** *seem like* 733.14

have all the earmarks of *seem like* 733.14

have all the fight knocked out of one *capitulate* 421.6

have all the hallmarks of *seem like* 733.14

have all the luck *be fortunate* 847.7

have all the signs of *seem like* 733.14

have all the time in the world *have leisure time* 125.5

have all the virtues *be virtuous* 447.8

have all to oneself *possess* 469.14

have a long face *be sullen* 304.12

have a look at *inspect* 242.22

have a look of *appear* 264.12

have a look-see [Inf] *inspect* 242.22

have a lot of get-up-and-go *be full of vigor* 518.4

have a lot of pizazz [Inf] *be full of vigor* 518.4

have a lot to learn *be ignorant* 349.8

have a low *or* **poor opinion of** *disapprove* 438.16

have a low IQ (intelligence quotient) *lack intellect* 316.8

have a low opinion of *disrespect* 436.18

have a lucky break *be fortunate* 847.7

have a market *be sold* 482.22

have a meal 92.25

have a meaning *mean* 361.13

have a mental block *forget* 186.11

have a method *find a way* 691.14

have a millstone around one's neck *burden* 826.21

have a mind *or* **brain like a sieve** *be forgetful* 355.11

have a mind of one's own *follow one's own will* 372.13

have a mind to *resolve* 374.9

have a misadventure *have a mishap* 660.11

have a misfortune *lose one's chance* 660.10

have a mishap 660.11, 826.18; *be in trouble* 848.13

have a monkey on one's back [Inf] *burden* 826.21

have a monotonous job *be bored* 296.7

have a moral attitude *moralize* 431.14

have a moral sense *or* **conscience** *have a sense of duty* 433.13

have a motive *resolve* 374.9

have a mutual relationship *correspond to* 727.10

have an accident *have a mishap* 660.11, 826.18, *be in trouble* 848.13

have an account with *acquire credit* 487.11, *be in debt* 488.9

have an ace in the hole *have an advantage* 618.10

have an ace up one's sleeve *be ahead* 744.17

have an active interest *be sociable* 414.22

have an advantage 618.10; *gain* 467.15, *be ahead* 744.17

have an affinity *combine* 757.9

have an affinity for *like* 290.8, *agree with* 462.10

have an affliction *be unhealthy* 114.29

have an ague *shake* 684.24

have an albatross around one's neck *burden* 826.21

have an anniversary *commemorate* 663.12

have an aptitude *tend* 513.5

have a narrow escape *escape* 816.8

have a narrow squeak *escape* 816.8

have an athletic build *be tough* 547.13

have an attachment to *like* 290.8

have an attack *be unhealthy* 114.29

have an attraction *attract* 700.11

have an audience of one *soliloquize* 211.4

have an aversion to *dislike* 291.12

have an avocation *make merry* 167.13

have an ax to grind *be selfish* 444.6, *be cunning* 822.5

have and hold *possess* 469.14

have an ear for 228.14; *be skillful* 127.14

have an edge *be sharp* 549.15

have an edge on *have an advantage* 618.10

have a need for *request* 505.10

have an effect *determine* 675.11, *affect* 676.7

have an emergency *be in difficulties* 726.14

have an empty stomach *fast* 118.8

have (a) nerve *defy* 416.7

have an estate *own property* 470.11

have a new lease on life *revive* 809.14

have a new look *become new* 652.19

have an excess of *be excessive* 99.9

have an expense account *profit* 467.22

have an eye for *be skillful* 127.14

have an eye for *or* **to business** *trade* 480.18

have an eye to *intend* 374.8, 650.10

have an eye to the future *or* **the main chance** *have foresight* 357.8

have a nice day! *goodbye!* 705.14

have an idea 317.12, 327.13; *invent* 345.14, *suppose* 359.8

have an illness *be in trouble* 848.13

have an impact on *influence* 508.11

have an in *infiltrate* 706.13

have an income *earn* 467.20, *receive* 473.13

have an independent mind *liberate* 831.6

have an industrial dispute 57.20

have an inkling *suppose* 359.8

have an inspiration *imagine* 360.14

have an instinct *tend* 513.5

have an iron grip *show tenaciousness* 471.8

have an obligation *be grateful* 310.6

have an open mind *be broad-minded* 592.13

have a notion *suppose* 359.8

have an overdraft *borrow* 476.10

have an oversight *not observe* 466.9

have ants in one's pants [Inf] *shake* 684.24

have an ulterior motive *be cunning* 822.5

have an uncontrollable temper *be irascible* 303.13

have a part to play *influence* 512.11

have a party *rejoice* 279.5

have a passion for *enjoy* 290.9

have a penchant for *be inclined toward* 290.10

have a permanent *or* **a perm** *coif* 530.15

have a piece of luck *win an award* 467.23

have a point *be sharp* 549.15

have a point of view *have an idea* 317.12

have a policy *plan ahead* 387.13

have a poor appetite *taste* 92.24

have a poor ear *have an ear for* 228.14

have a poor return *lose money* 468.15

have a portfolio *own property* 470.11

have a powwow with [Inf] *consult* 176.11

have a predicament *or* **a problem** *or* **a dilemma** *be in a predicament* 725.9

have a predisposition *tend* 513.5

have a preference *prefer* 382.13

have a preference for *be inclined toward* 290.10

have a premonition *look ahead* 650.11

have a price war *sell at a loss* 482.19

have a prizefight *box* 152.19

have a problem *be in difficulty* 824.19

have a propensity *tend* 513.5

have a propensity for *be inclined toward* 290.10

have a punch-up [Inf] *fight* 422.23

have a purpose *resolve* 374.9

have a quick word with *converse* 210.11

have a rapport with 735.24

have a regular heartbeat *be regular* 663.10

have a relationship *relate to* 727.9

have a responsible position *direct* 126.11

have a rest *be refreshed* 94.8, *take it easy* 819.3

have a reversal *lose* 468.12

have a rightful claim to *have rights* 429.13

have a role in *participate* 760.16

have a roof over one's head *be safe* 810.20

have a rough surface *or* **texture** *be rough* 544.10

have a route *find one's way* 691.15

have artistic license *be free* 829.16

have a run-in *dispute* 463.9

have a running start *be ahead* 744.17

have a run of good luck *be fortunate* 847.7

have a sale *sell off* 482.20

have a say in *influence* 512.11

have a screen test *act* 137.20

have a screw loose [Inf] *become insane* 110.12

have a seat! *welcome!* 704.24

have a second meaning *be equivocal* 380.7

have a seizure *be unhealthy* 114.29

have a sense *mean* 361.13

have a sense of community *socialize* 2.14

have a sense of duty 433.13

have a sense of loyalty *observe* 465.4

have a sense of responsibility *observe* 465.4

have a setback *lose* 468.12

have a set-to *argue* 329.11, *dispute* 463.9

have a sharp tongue *be irascible* 303.13

have a shit [Inf] *defecate* 25.21

have a shopping list *shop* 481.15

have a shortcoming *not perform* 466.10

have a short fuse [Inf] *be irascible* 303.13

have a short memory *be forgetful* 355.11

have a short or **quick temper** *be irascible* 303.13, *be short* 591.10

have a shower *bathe* 111.18

have a show of force *suppress* 424.9

have a side effect *affect* 676.7

have a simple answer *be easy* 823.14

have a sister city *unite* 752.14

have a sit-down strike *refuse* 506.8

have a small chance *take a chance* 842.14

have as many phases as the moon *be changeable* 666.5

have a smattering of knowledge *know little* 349.9

have a social conscience *philanthropize* 307.8

have a stake in *have joint possession* 469.15

have a stroke *be unhealthy* 114.29

have a stroke of luck *be fortunate* 847.7

have a summit meeting *negotiate* 460.6

have a suspicion *speculate* 294.13

have a suspicion about *be uncertain* 841.17

have at *fight* 422.23

have a talk *converse* 210.11

have a temper *be irascible* 303.13

have a temper tantrum *become angry* 302.20

have a tendency *have a habit* 397.16, *tend* 513.5

have a tête-à-tête with *consult* 176.11

have a theory *suppose* 359.8

have a thick skin *be indifferent* 289.12

have a tiff *quarrel* 302.17

have a tiger by the tail [Inf] *cause trouble* 824.21

have a tin ear *have an ear for* 228.14

have a title 72.12

have at one's beck and call *be available to one* 425.13

have at one's command *have at one's disposal* 393.14, *be available to one* 425.13

have at one's disposal 393.14; *be available to one* 425.13, *possess* 469.14

have at one's elbow *consult* 176.11

have at one's mercy *subject* 832.10

have a touchback *kick* 155.20

have a use for *find useful* 801.11

have authority 52.13; *govern* 49.26, *be powerful* 514.18, *be independent* 829.18

have authority over 425.12; *have jurisdiction over* 54.30

have authorization *be permitted* 502.8

have a vantage point *be ahead* 744.17

have a viselike grip *show tenaciousness* 471.8

have a visible effect *affect* 676.7

have a voice *influence* 512.11

have a walkover *do easily* 823.16

have a way with *manage* 126.10

have a weakness for *be inclined toward* 290.10, *like* 299.22

have a weight on one's shoulders *burden* 826.21

have a will of one's own *be independent* 829.18

have a word with *converse* 210.11

have bad breath *stink* 227.5

have bad luck *lose one's chance* 660.10, *fail* 846.12

have balls [Inf] *be courageous* 284.14, *be full of vigor* 518.4

have barefaced cheek *defy* 416.7

have bats in one's belfry [Inf] *become insane* 110.12

have before the court or **judge** *litigate* 54.27

have being *live* 28.17

have belongings *own property* 470.11

have bills to pay *be in debt* 488.9

have blood on one's hands *be guilty* 450.9

have body odor or **BO** *stink* 227.5

have bought it [Inf] *be destroyed* 523.17

have bought the farm [Inf] *be destroyed* 523.17

have brains *be intelligent* 352.7

have buoyancy *be adaptable* 546.9

have by the throat *retain* 471.7

have capital gains *profit* 467.22

have carte blanche *lack restraint* 829.21

have charge of *manage* 126.10, *protect* 810.21

have charges brought against one *be accused* 442.10

have charisma *influence* 512.11, *be powerful* 514.18

have cheek *defy* 416.7

have children *have young* 21.16

have chutzpa [Inf] *defy* 416.7

have clairvoyance *foresee* 357.9

have clean hands *be innocent* 449.10

have clearance *be permitted* 502.8

have clout [Inf] *have authority* 52.13, *influence* 512.11

have coming *have rights* 429.13

have command *direct* 126.11

have compassion *be lenient* 423.5, *be kind* 543.16

have conformity *be compatible* 462.12

have consequence *affect* 676.7

have continuity *be frequent* 661.5

have crimes to answer for *be guilty* 450.9

have currency *prevail* 778.19

have dealings with *befriend* 62.10, *trade* 480.18

have debts *burden* 826.21

have deep understanding *be profound* 598.23

have defective sight *see badly* 243.16

have dependents to support *burden* 826.21

have designs *plot* 387.15

have designs on *like* 290.8, *aim* 374.10, *promise oneself* 458.15

have differences with *quarrel* 272.9, *dissent* 347.8, *disagree* 463.8

have different opinions *dissent* 732.13

have difficulties *be in a predicament* 725.9, *be in trouble* 848.13

have difficulty 824.18

have difficulty speaking 206.9

have diminishing returns *lose money* 468.15

have diplomatic immunity *be exempt* 434.11

have discord *dissent* 732.13

have done with *stop using* 394.10

have doubts about *disbelieve* 88.8

have egg on one's face [Inf] *figurative expressions* 128.11

have elbowroom *have scope* 829.20

have enough 97.7; *be complete* 761.10

have enough rope to hang oneself *have scope* 829.20

have equity or **interest** or **a stake in** *have rights* 429.13

have every intention *resolve* 374.9

have every intention to *intend* 650.10

have everything *be complete* 761.10

have everything going one's way *be prosperous* 847.6

have exclusive possession of *possess* 469.14

have exclusive rights to *possess* 469.14

have experience *be expert* 127.15

have expertise *be an authority on* 52.17

have expired *be past* 651.16

have extra money *profit* 467.22

have extrasensory perception (ESP) *divine* 358.15

have eyes bigger than one's stomach *be greedy* 119.4

have eyes in the back of one's head *see* 242.20

have faith *be religious* 81.25, *expect* 281.12

have faith in *believe* 87.9, *be certain* 840.13

have family responsibilities *burden* 826.21

have feet of clay *be imperfect* 806.8

have fine qualities *be virtuous* 447.8

have fish to fry *take charge of* 391.8

have flexibility *be elastic* 546.7

have fond illusions *deceive* 193.16

have foreplay *stimulate* 20.22

have foresight 357.8

have for sale *sell* 482.15

have freedom of choice *be free* 829.16

have free time 413.15; *have leisure time* 125.5

have free will *be free* 829.16

have friends *be friends* 62.9, *fraternize* 408.17

have friends in high places *influence* 512.11

have from *receive* 473.13

have fun *feel pleasure* 214.12, *enjoy* 269.9

have fun with *fraternize* 408.17

have gangrene *be dirty* 112.10

have or **pass gas** *belch* 709.28

have G-force loading *be on the track* 146.11

have good breeding *have good manners* 410.10

have good hang time *kick* 155.20

have good manners 410.10; *better* 445.17

have good prospects *show potential* 458.14

have good vibes [Inf] *agree with* 462.10

have good vibrations [Inf] *agree with* 462.10

have goose flesh or **goose pimples** *sense* 212.9, *be cold* 218.13

have ground clearance *be on the track* 146.11

have grounds for *be right* 429.12

have guilt feelings *be penitent* 451.7

have guts [Inf] *be courageous* 284.14

have had (a drop) too much *be drunk* 121.34

have had enough *capitulate* 421.6

have had it up to here *have enough* 97.7

have had one's day *be past* 651.16

have had one's lesson *serve one right* 420.5

have had one too many *be drunk* 121.34

have halitosis *stink* 227.5

have high hopes *aspire* 281.13

have high regard for *like* 290.8, *love* 299.21

have histrionics *exaggerate* 194.11

have hoped for better *be disappointed* 293.8

have horns *be sharp* 549.15

have hutzpa [Inf] *defy* 416.7

have hysterics *feel deeply* 266.16

have immunity *be exempt* 434.11

have impact *affect* 676.7

have importance *influence* 512.11

have independent means *be independent* 829.18

have inferior rank *be subject to* 832.12

have influence *influence* 512.11

have in hand *possess* 469.14, *detain* 471.9

have in mind *be of the opinion* 87.10, *mean* 361.13, *intend* 374.8

have in mind to *intend* 650.10

have in one's book *behave toward* 399.20

have in one's grip or **one's grasp** *possess* 469.14

have in one's name *possess* 469.14

have in one's possession *possess* 469.14

have in one's power *be an influence* 512.13

have in prospect *expect* 356.6

have in reserve *not use* 394.9

have insight 360.16; *understand* 363.9

have intercourse *have sex* 20.21

have in the bag [Inf] *secure one's objective* 464.12

have in view *intend* 374.8

have irons in the fire *take charge of* 391.8

have it all *be complete* 761.10

have it all one's own way *impose one's will* 372.14, *do easily* 823.16

have it all one's way *defeat* 845.17

have it bad *be in love* 299.23

have it both ways **789.17**

have it coming to one *be punished* 454.31

have it easy *do easily* 823.16, *be prosperous* 847.6

have it from *be informed* 170.15

have it in for *hate* 300.11, *be malevolent* 306.12

have it in the bag *do easily* 823.16

have it made [Inf] *be prosperous* 847.6

have it one's own way *be independent* 829.18

have it on good authority *be informed* 170.15

have it over one *overtake* 744.16

have it soft *do easily* 823.16

have its roots in *follow from* 676.9

have joint possession **469.15**

have jurisdiction *regionalize* 564.15

have jurisdiction over **54.30**

have (just) the right touch *be skillful* 127.14

Havel *Rivers* 570

have leisure time **125.5**

have life *live* 28.17

have little *or* nothing in common *diverge* 734.8

have little to say *be taciturn* 208.7

have little weight *be light* 539.8

have long ears *hear* 228.13

have losses *lose money* 468.15

have luck *take a chance* 842.14, *be fortunate* 847.7

have many irons in the fire *diversify* 732.11

have many strings to one's bow *diversify* 732.11

have marital relations *have sex* 20.21

have mercy! *have pity!* 308.13

have mercy on *show pity* 308.8

have method in one's madness *be cunning* 822.5

have misgivings *be fearful* 283.15, *doubt* 333.19

have mobility *be in motion* 677.14

have money *be rich* 485.12

have money coming in *earn* 467.20

have money coming out of one's ears [Inf] *be rich* 485.12

have money to burn *be rich* 485.12

have more than enough *have enough* 97.7, *be in difficulty* 824.19

haven **810.3**; *retreat* 60.13, *shelter* 613.6, *destination* 704.6, *harbor* 812.6

have natural talent *tend* 513.5

have never felt better *be healthy* 113.11

have nine lives *live* 28.17, *be safe* 810.20

have no affectations *be naive* 821.4

have no alibi *be guilty* 450.9

have no aspirations *be mediocre* 289.16

have no bearing *mean nothing* 362.10

have no bearing on *be unrelated* 728.12

have no bounds *have no limit* 798.8

have no chance *be powerless* 515.11, *be useless* 802.11

have no choice *be compelled* 428.11

have no clout *be unimportant* 800.18

have no common ground *disagree* 753.19

have no conscience *be impenitent* 452.4

have no control *lack authority* 515.12

have no cure *be hopeless* 282.11

have no depth *be superficial* 599.6

have no desire for *be disinclined* 291.14

have no desires *be indifferent* 289.12

have no difference *be the same* 730.13

have no doubt *be certain* 840.13

have no doubts about *believe* 87.9

have no ear for *fail to hear* 229.9

have no end *be eternal* 644.7

have no excuse *be guilty* 450.9

have no existence *be nothing* 190.20

have no fault to find *admire* 437.15

have no feelings *be tough* 547.13

have no fight left *capitulate* 421.6

have no function *have free time* 413.15

have no grasp of *find unintelligible* 364.14

have no guile *be naive* 449.12, 821.4

have no guilt *be innocent* 449.10

have no guts [Inf] *be a coward* 285.7

have no hand in *shun* 386.14

have no hang-ups [Inf] *be naive* 821.4

have no heart *be pitiless* 309.5

have no inclination for *be disinclined* 291.14

have no influence *lack authority* 515.12

have no issue *be infertile* 23.8

have no law *be illegal* 53.30

have no liability *be exempt* 434.11

have no life *not act* 413.11

have no limit **798.8**

have no love for *hate* 300.11

have no luck *be in trouble* 848.13

have no manners *be discourteous* 411.7

have no meaning *mean nothing* 362.10

have no meaning for *not understand* 362.11

have no mercy **309.6**

have no money *need money* 848.14

have no morals *be careless* 289.14, *be immoral* 432.13

have no more *lose* 468.12

have no objection *agree* 735.23

have no objection to *agree with* 462.10

have no offers *be celibate* 67.9

have no offspring *be infertile* 23.8

have no option *be compelled* 428.11

have no passion *be indifferent* 289.12

have no patience *be irascible* 303.13

have no plans *be unprepared* 389.14

have no point *be extraneous* 724.12

have no point *or* meaning *be unrelated* 728.12

have no power *lack authority* 515.12

have no prejudice *be impartial* 289.15

have no prospects *be poor* 486.14

have no pull *be unimportant* 800.18

have no purpose *be useless* 802.11

have no questions *or* doubts about *understand* 295.6

have no ready cash *be unable to pay* 490.11

have no recollection of *forget* 355.10

have no regard for *disapprove* 438.16

have no regrets *be impenitent* 452.4

have no relation to *be extraneous* 724.12

have no relevance *be extraneous* 724.12

have no remedy *be hopeless* 282.11

have no remorse *be impenitent* 452.4

have no resistance *be powerless* 515.11

have no respect for *disapprove* 438.16

have no respect *or* regard for *disrespect* 436.18

have no responsibility *be exempt* 434.11

have no say *lack authority* 515.12

have no secrets *be intelligible* 363.10, *show oneself* 843.15

have no self-doubt *be vain* 402.14

have no sense of pride *be humble* 298.16

have no sex *be continent* 67.10

have no shame *show oneself* 843.15

have no significance *be superficial* 599.6

have no smell **225.7**

have no solution *be unexplained* 364.15

have no stomach for *be a coward* 285.7, *be disinclined* 291.14, *be unwilling* 375.12

have no strength left *be fatigued* 820.5

have no substance *be unreal* 722.12

have no taste *be tasteless* 220.6

have nothing left to give *be fatigued* 820.5

have nothing on *be inferior* 745.10

have nothing to add *complete* 761.9

have nothing to be ashamed of *be innocent* 449.10

have nothing to complain about *be satisfied* 273.8

have nothing to confess *be innocent* 449.10

have nothing to declare *be innocent* 449.10

have nothing to do *have free time* 413.15

have nothing to do with *shun* 386.14, *ignore* 409.11, *disagree* 463.8, *not connect* 728.13

have nothing to eat *fast* 118.8

have nothing to go on *be ignorant* 349.8

have nothing to grumble about *be satisfied* 273.8

have nothing to hide *be innocent* 449.10

have nothing to it *not cause wonder* 295.7

have nothing to say for oneself *be guilty* 450.9

have nothing to show for *lose money* 468.15

have no thought for others *be egotistic* 444.7

have no thought for the consequences *be foolish* 353.6

have no time for *be disinclined* 291.14, *be discourteous* 411.7, *disrespect* 436.18

have no time to lose *be active* 414.18, *have no time to spare* 818.6

have no time to spare **818.6**

have no tricks *be naive* 821.4

have no truck with [Inf] *dissociate* 375.14

have-nots, the *common people* 71.2, *the poor* 486.7

have no use *be superfluous* 99.12, *be useless* 802.11

have no use for *be disinclined* 291.14, *not use* 394.9

have no weight *be unimportant* 800.18

have no words to express wonder 294.12

have no work *have leisure time* 125.5

have odor **224.8**

have offspring *have young* 21.16

have on *wear* 100.46

have one foot in the grave *age* 27.16

have one for the road *part* 705.13

have one hand tied behind one's back *have difficulty* 824.18

have one's back to the wall *face danger* 811.12, *be in difficulty* 824.19

have one's cake and eat it too *have it both ways* 789.17

have one's conviction overturned *get a reprieve* 816.9

have one's doubts *doubt* 333.19, *be uncertain* 841.17

have one's eye on *covet* 288.18

have one's eyes opened *understand* 363.9

have one's fill *be full* 761.12

have one's fling *be active* 414.18, *lack restraint* 829.21

have one's foibles *be wicked* 448.13

have one's friend [Inf] *bleed* 25.26

have one's hand in *be skillful* 127.14

have one's hands full *be busy* 414.19, *be in difficulty* 824.19

have one's head *have scope* 829.20

have one's head for *punish* 454.22

have one's head in the clouds *lack thought* 318.12

have one's head screwed on the right way [Inf] *be intelligent* 315.11, 352.7

have one's head turned *become conceited* 402.16

have one's heart in one's mouth *be fearful* 283.15

have one's heart in one's work *exert oneself* 122.11

have one's heart in the right place *be benevolent* 305.10

have one's heart's desire *be satisfied* 273.8

have one's heart skip *or* miss a beat *be afraid* 283.14

have one's heart stand still *be afraid* 283.14

have one's marriage annulled *divorce* 66.9

have one's nose out of joint *be offended* 302.14

have one's nose to the grindstone *be bored* 296.7

have one's own way *impose one's will* 372.14

have one's period *bleed* 25.26, *be cyclic* 663.11

have one's plans ruined *be disappointed* 293.8

have one's plate full [Inf] *be busy* 414.19

have one's pound of flesh *be severe* 424.8

have one's pride *be proud* 297.15

have one's reward *be rewarded* 453.16

have one's say *be assertive* 189.28, *speak* 205.17

have one's self-respect *be proud* 297.15

have one's ship come in *or home get rich* 485.13

have one's way *be independent* 829.18

have one's way with *seduce* 432.16

have one's weak side *be wicked* 448.15

have one's wits about one *be sane* 109.5, *be skillful* 127.14, *awake* 212.10, *be intelligent* 315.11, *be wise* 352.6

have one's work cut out *have difficulty* 824.18

have one too many *get drunk* 121.35

have on offer *trade in* 457.8, *sell* 482.15

have on one's plate *behave toward* 399.20

have on the carpet *punish* 454.22

have on the side *not use* 394.9

have other fish to fry *be active* 414.18

have other *or bigger fish to fry renounce* 392.4

have other things to do *be active* 414.18

have over a barrel [Inf] *have authority* 52.13

have overall responsibility *direct* 126.11

have perfect *or absolute pitch have an ear for* 228.14

have permission *be permitted* 502.8

have persistence *show tenaciousness* 471.8

have personal motives *be selfish* 444.6

have pertinence *be suitable* 462.13

have physical strength *be tough* 547.13

have pity *show pity* 308.8, *be lenient* 423.5

have pity! 308.13

have pity for *pity* 308.6

have play *have scope* 829.20

have plenty of rope *have scope* 829.20

have plenty of time *have leisure time* 125.5

have possession *play offense* 155.18

have possibilities *show potential* 458.14

have power *govern* 49.26, *be powerful* 514.18

have power over *have jurisdiction over* 54.30, *be an influence* 512.13

have power *or sway or rule over have authority over* 425.12

have precedence *take precedence* 769.14

have prior information *foresee* 357.9

have priority *take precedence* 769.14, *be important* 799.13

have progeny *have young* 21.16

have prongs *be sharp* 549.15

have prospects *expect* 650.12

have pull [Inf] *influence* 512.11

have pulling power [Inf] *influence* 512.11

have qualms *be fearful* 283.15

have quick wits *be mentally sharp* 549.18

have ready *prepare for action* 388.18

have recourse to *resort to* 393.13

have regard for *be benevolent* 305.12, *observe* 465.4

have regrets *be penitent* 451.7

have regular wages *earn* 467.20

have relevance *be suitable* 462.13, *relate to* 727.9

have reservations *disbelieve* 88.8, *doubt* 287.13

have resilience *be adaptable* 546.9

have resources *own property* 470.11

have respect for *respect* 435.13

have responsibility *direct* 126.11

have right on one's side *be right* 429.12

have rights 429.13

have room to breathe *have scope* 829.20

haversack *baggage* 578.8

haversine (hav) *trigonometric function* 6.50

haves, the *the rich* 485.7, *prosperous person* 847.4

have saving graces *be virtuous* 447.8

have scope 829.20

have scruples *be unwilling* 375.12

have second sight *foresee* 357.9

have second thoughts 317.11; *doubt* 287.13, *hesitate* 378.10, *equivocate* 380.8, *confess* 451.8, *reconsider* 807.23

have seen better days *deteriorate* 808.14, *be in trouble* 848.13

have seen it all before *understand* 295.6

have self-control *limit* 620.7

have self-motivation *be motivated* 508.10

have self-reliance *be independent* 829.18

have self-restraint *limit* 620.7

have several irons in the fire *be busy* 414.19

have sex 20.21

have sexual relations *have sex* 20.21, *unite sexually* 752.20

have sharp wits *be mentally sharp* 549.18

have someone on the ropes *box* 152.19

have someone's blessing *be permitted* 502.8

have someone's ear *hear* 228.13

have something extra *be ahead* 744.17

have something in hand *be ahead* 744.17

have something in one's eye *see badly* 243.16

have something in reserve *be ahead* 744.17

have some use *be useful* 801.9

have sovereignty *become a nation* 566.11

have spare time *have leisure time* 125.5

have spots in front of one's eyes *see badly* 243.16

have stamina *be powerful* 514.18

have sticky fingers [Inf] *steal* 479.14

have substance *own property* 470.11, *be real* 721.21

have success *gain* 467.15, *be successful* 845.11

have survivability *be tough* 547.13

have sway *be an influence* 512.13

have taste *be elegant* 527.6

have tea *have a meal* 92.25

have temerity *defy* 416.7

have tenacity *show tenaciousness* 471.8, *be tough* 547.13

have tenure of *possess* 469.14

have that little extra something *have an advantage* 618.10

have the advantage *be unequal* 741.7

have the appearance of *appear* 264.12

have the audacity 400.15

have the best intentions *be charitable* 305.12, *be innocent* 449.10

have the best of both worlds *have it both ways* 789.17

have the best of it *be victorious* 845.16

have the blues *be sullen* 304.12

have the casting vote *be an influence* 512.13, *determine* 675.11

have the courage of one's convictions *be courageous* 284.14

have the curse [Inf] *bleed* 25.26

have the deck *or cards stacked against one face danger* 811.12

have the deed for *possess* 469.14

have the desired effect *be convenient* 803.5

have the ear of *influence* 512.11

have the edge on *or over be ahead* 744.17

have the effect of *cause* 675.8

have the final say *answer back* 334.19, *be an influence* 512.13

have the freedom of *have scope* 829.20

have the game in one's hands *do easily* 823.16

have the golden touch *be rich* 485.12

have the habit of *have a habit* 397.16

have the hots for [Inf] *lust after* 288.20

have the innocence of a child *be naive* 449.12

have the inside track *have an advantage* 618.10, *be ahead* 744.17

have the jitters *be sensitive* 267.5

have the jump on *have an advantage* 618.10

have the jump on someone *be ahead* 744.17

have the knack *be skillful* 127.14, *qualify* 340.11

have the knack *or gift for be good at* 445.18

have the know-how *be an authority on* 52.17, *be expert* 127.15

have the knowledge *be expert* 127.15

have the last laugh *overtake* 744.16

have the last word *be assertive* 189.28, *refute* 332.7, *answer back* 334.19

have the lead *lead* 744.19

have the look of power *have authority over* 425.12

have the makings of *be probable* 838.8

have the means *have enough* 97.7, *find means* 102.6

have the measure of *manage* 126.10

have the Midas touch *profit* 467.22

have them rolling in the aisles *make someone laugh* 368.7

have the munchies [Inf] *eat well* 92.23

have the nerve *or gall or cheek have the audacity* 400.15

have the odds (stacked) against one *face danger* 811.12

have the opinion *be of the opinion* 87.10

have the pole position *be on the track* 146.11, *be ahead* 744.17

have the right *have rights* 429.13

have the right connections *influence* 512.11

have the ring of truth *seem true* 721.26

have the run of *have scope* 829.20

have the runs *or trots or shits or squits* [Inf] *defecate* 25.21

have the same meaning *mean* 361.13

have the say-so *have authority* 52.13

have the shivers *be cold* 218.13

have the spotlight on one *be visible* 843.16

have the trick of *be skillful* 127.14

have the upper hand *be an influence* 512.13

have the use of *have at one's disposal* 393.14

have the verdict read *try a case* 54.28

have the wolf at one's door *need money* 848.14

have the words taken out of one's mouth *lapse into silence* 208.8

have the world at one's feet *attain one's goal* 845.13

have thoughts above one's station *aim* 327.17

have time on one's hands *have leisure time* 125.5, *be bored* 296.7

have time to kill *be bored* 296.7

have time to spare *start early* 657.12

have title to *possess* 469.14

have to *be compelled* 428.11

have to dinner *feed* 90.41

have to do with *behave toward* 399.20, *be active in* 412.17, *relate to* 727.9

have to hand it to *follow* 745.12

have tone *be elastic* 546.7

have too many irons in the fire *overdo* 99.11, *figurative expressions* 128.11, *take on too much* 391.9

have too much on one's plate [Inf] *overdo* 99.11, *take on too much* 391.9

have to one's name *own property* 470.11

have to repay *be in debt* 488.9

have to run for it *be in danger* 811.11

have trouble *have difficulty* 824.18, *be in trouble* 848.13

have tunnel vision *prejudge* 337.13

have two meanings *be equivocal* 380.7

have under one's belt [Inf] *secure one's objective* 464.12

have under one's thumb *have authority* 52.13, *be an influence* 512.13

have understanding *have insight* 360.16, *understand* 363.9

have vitality *be powerful* 514.18

have wealth *earn* 467.20, *be rich* 485.12

have weight *be heavy* 538.12

have what it takes *endure* 377.14, *be strong* 516.14

have withdrawal symptoms *drug oneself* 121.37

have words *argue* 329.11

have X-ray eyes *see* 242.20

have young 21.16

have zest *be full of vigor* 518.4

having *possessing* 469.11, *including* 763.3

having a light touch *light* 539.4

having and holding *possessing* 469.11

having an excuse *vindicable* 441.9

having a part *joint possession* 469.6

having a share *joint possession* 469.6

having ears *eared* 228.10

having full play *free-ranging* 829.13

having had (a drop) too much *drunk* 121.25

having had one too many *drunk* 121.25

having it good *prosperity* 847.1

having life *life* 28.1

having merits *good* 445.10

having motion *moving* 677.12

having no case *convicted* 54.26

having no legal protection *unlawful* 53.23

having no regrets *impenitent* 452.2

having poor sight *or* **vision** *visually impaired* 243.9

having possessions *possessing* 469.11

having sex *sexual intercourse* 20.9

having tea *eating meals* 92.4

having two left feet *graceless* 528.7

having weight *heavy* 538.9

havoc 523.5; *devastation* 96.5, *military attack* 418.2, *impairment* 808.7

haw *sidestep* 698.22

Hawaii *American States* 564, *Islands* 572

Hawaiian guitar *Musical Instruments* 142

Hawaiian Islands *Islands* 572

Hawes Water *Lakes* 568

hawk *salivate* 25.25, *bird of prey* 36.11, *militarist* 77.3, *publish* 173.15, *sound hoarse* 238.8, *sell* 482.15, *petition* 505.11

hawk [Inf] *strict person* 424.4

hawker *crier* 239.8, *peddler* 482.9

Hawkesbury *Rivers* 570

hawk-eyed *seeing* 242.17

hawkish *avian* 36.19, *warlike* 76.27, *militant* 418.13, *contentious* 422.20

hawkishness *bellicosity* 76.15

hawks *Collective Names* 59

hawkweed *Flowers* 42

hawser *towline* 699.5, *line* 754.5

hawser bend *Knots, Bends, Hitches, Splices* 754

hawthorn *Trees and Shrubs* 43

hay *farmland* 16.3, *animal feed* 16.12, *animal food* 90.2

haybarn *farm building* 16.4

haycock *farmland* 16.3

hayfield *farmland* 16.3

hayfork *farm tool* 16.5

haylage *animal feed* 16.12

hayloft *farm building* 16.4

haymaker *farm tool* 16.5

haymaker [Inf] *boxing* 152.2

haymaking *summer* 654.4

hay-making *cultivation* 16.7

haymow *farm building* 16.4

hayrack *farm building* 16.4

hay rake *farm tool* 16.5

hayrick [Brit] *farmland* 16.3

hayseed *countryman* 61.8, *naive person* 921.2

haystack *farmland* 16.3

hay turner *farm tool* 16.5

hay wain *farm tool* 16.5

haywire [Inf] *muddled* 766.13

hazan *rabbi* 84.6

hazard *billiards play* 149.2, *golf course* 156.2, *be courageous* 284.14, *speculate* 294.13, *danger* 811.1, *face danger* 811.12, *endanger* 811.13, *trap* 813.1, *obstacle* 826.2, *unreliability* 841.7, *risk* 841.21, *chance* 842.1, *take a chance* 842.14

hazard a guess *speculate* 294.13, *suppose* 359.8

hazarding *endangerment* 811.2

hazardous *dangerous* 811.7, *trapped* 813.5, *blocked* 826.13, *unreliable* 841.15

hazardously *dangerously* 811.14, *in the way* 826.23, *unreliably* 841.25

hazardousness *danger* 811.1

hazardous waste *nuclear problem* 10.62

haze *mist* 9.33, *fog* 9.59, *invisibility* 245.1, *that which makes invisible* 245.2, *murk* 248.2, *transparent thing* 249.4, *wateriness* 557.3, *make uncertain* 841.19

haze filter *filter* 132.14

hazel *Trees and Shrubs* 43, *brown* 256.5

hazily *meteorologically* 9.60, *invisibly* 245.8, *dimly* 248.10, *shapelessly* 625.5, *indeterminately* 841.24

haziness *invisibility* 245.1, *murk* 248.2, *opaqueness* 250.1, *shapelessness* 625.1, *indeterminacy* 841.6

hazy *foggy* 9.51, *difficult to see* 245.4, *murky* 248.5, *shady* 250.4, *mottled* 263.10, *difficult* 364.8, *shapeless* 625.2, *unreal* 720.8, *indeterminate* 841.14

hazy recollection *poor memory* 355.2

H-beam *superstructure* 551.7

H-bomb *bomb* 78.15

he *male* 32.1

head 19.6, 600.7; *important person* 18.11, 799.5, *place for excretion* 25.11, *person in authority* 52.7, *company leader* 68.8, *educational leader* 68.11, *masterful* 68.15, *master* 68.17, *lead* 126.12, 744.19, *type of painting* 143.5, *sculpture* 144.1, *grip* 151.4, *bowling* 151.6, *golf equipment* 156.5, *soccer play* 163.5, *play soccer* 163.8, *brain* 315.6, *means of prediction* 358.10, *force* 514.8, *plant products* 522.8, *water cycle* 557.17, *river parts* 570.3, *peninsula* 572.5, *Fields of Measurement* 589, *summit* 600.1, *architectural summit* 600.4, *focus* 612.3, *focal* 612.8, *be in front* 621.15, *aim* 697.14, *category* 767.6, *precede* 769.13, *front* 771.17, *pioneer* 771.29, *class* 777.1

head [Inf] *drug taker* 121.12

headache *symptom* 114.3, *painful condition* 215.2, *problem* 824.4

headachy *sick* 114.24

head and shoulders above *superior* 744.8

head an institution *master* 68.17

head a school *master* 68.17

headband *headdress* 100.35, *hairdressing tool* 530.9, *band* 754.9

headboard *type of bed* 101.9

headcase [Inf] *insane person* 110.5

headcloth *headdress* 100.35

head coach *basketball team* 148.2, *football player* 155.15

head cold *respiratory disease* 114.12, *lack of sense of smell* 225.2

head count *count* 784.3, *list of names* 785.7

headdress 100.35; *vestment* 84.11

headed *titled* 72.9, *soccer* 163.7

headed for *directed* 697.9, *inevitable* 840.11

header *masonry* 14.22, *data-related concepts* 15.23, *soccer play* 163.5

header [Inf] *fall* 714.4

headfirst *rashly* 286.9

head for *aim* 327.17, 697.14, *navigate* 690.15

headgear *hat* 100.32

head guard *protective clothing* 419.6

head honcho [Inf] *company leader* 68.8, *manager* 126.7, *superior* 744.5

headhunter *killer* 30.11, *pursuer* 385.5

headhunting *murderous* 30.18

headily *odorously* 224.10

heading *title* 72.1, *soccer play* 163.5, *soccer* 163.7, *flag* 184.8, *brief description* 202.2, *flight* 689.9, *bearing* 697.2, *category* 767.6, *class* 777.1

heading for *in the future* 650.13

heading for the scrap heap *destroyed* 523.9

heading up *managerial* 126.9, *sailing terms* 150.5

head in the clouds *lack of thought* 318.1, *absent-mindedness* 324.2, *oblivious* 355.9, *reverie* 360.6

head in the sand *defeatism* 413.7

head into *make a beginning* 771.26

head into the wind *navigate* 690.15

headland *farmland* 16.3, *mountain* 569.1, *peninsula* 572.5, *heights* 596.4

headless *reduced* 749.5

headlight *safety light* 246.7

headline *print news* 171.7, *publicize* 173.18, *newsworthy* 175.7, *make important* 799.14, *display* 843.13

headlined *publicized* 173.14

head linesman *football player* 155.15

headlock *wrestling terms* 152.10, *retention* 471.1

headlong *rash* 286.5, *rashly* 286.9, *impulsively* 318.16, *swift* 694.6, *swiftly* 694.16, *hasty* 818.3

headlong plunge *acceleration* 694.3

headlong rush *acceleration* 694.3

headman *leader* 68.3

headmanning the puck *ice hockey tactics* 158.4

headmaster *educator* 48.4, *person in authority* 52.7, *educational leader* 68.11

headmistress *educator* 48.4, *person in authority* 52.7, *educational leader* 68.11

headmost *elite* 744.12, *primary* 769.10

head nurse *nurse* 107.23

head (of coin) *front* 621.1

head off *deter* 179.8, *repel* 701.7, *fend off* 701.9

head office *office* 124.2

head of hair *body covering* 19.4

head of pressure *water cycle* 557.17

head of state *leader* 68.3, *person in command* 425.5

head of the class *excellence* 445.4

head of the department *employer* 57.3

head of the family *or* **house** *family member* 65.2

head of the household *householder* 61.5

head of the line *priority* 769.2

head-on *front-running* 621.10, *discordant* 828.12

head-on collision *collision* 695.2

head over heels *inverted* 608.5, *inversely* 608.9, *around* 682.17, *completely* 759.14, *muddled* 766.13

head over heels in love *in love* 299.10

headphone *dial* 169.12

headphones *receiver* 473.8

headquarter *centralize* 612.11

headquarters *administrative headquarters* 564.5

headquarters (HQ) *military affairs* 58.1, *center of activity* 612.4

headroom *sailboat parts and accessories* 150.4, *available space* 563.6, *interval* 587.1

headsail *sailboat parts and accessories* 150.4

head scarf *headdress* 100.35

headset *dial* 169.12, *receiver* 473.8

headshrinker [Inf] *psychiatrist* 108.34, 110.8

headsman *punisher* 454.16

headsman's ax *instrument of execution* 454.15

headstall *riding equipment* 159.9

headstand *act of inversion* 608.3, *become inverted* 608.8

head start *advantage* 618.4, 744.3, *earliness* 657.1, *priority* 769.2

headstock *axle* 682.7

headstone *funeral object* 31.6

head straight on *aim* 697.14

headstream *river parts* 570.3

headstrong *foolish* 353.5, *willful* 372.8, *obstinate* 379.5, *troublesome* 824.13

headstrongness *tenacity* 755.2

head teacher *educator* 48.4

head-to-head *contentious* 422.20, *opposite* 731.3

head-to-head contest *duel* 422.12

head-to-wind *sailing* 150.25

head up *lead* 126.12, *sail* 150.29, *precede* 769.13

head waiter *attendant* 69.4

headwaters *tributary* 570.2, *river parts* 570.3, *source* 675.2

headway *advance* 467.3, *available space* 563.6, *forward motion* 677.4, 679.1, *promotion* 807.5
headwind *wind* 9.12, *opposing force* 510.2, *flight* 689.5
headwork *Architectural Elements* 134, *thought* 317.1
heady *intoxicating* 121.29, *odorous* 224.5, *fragrant* 226.4, *strong to the senses* 516.12
heady scent *odor* 224.1
heal *conciliate* 74.10, *practice medicine* 107.32, *make healthy* 113.13, *remedy* 115.16, *treat* 115.17, *put right* 429.14, *cure* 809.15
heal-all *remedy* 115.1
healed *getting well* 113.9, *cured* 809.8
healer 107.22; *repairer* 809.5
healing *therapeutic* 107.30, *healing art* 115.13, *remedial* 115.14, *recuperation* 809.4, *restorative* 809.9
healing art 115.13; *therapy* 115.12
healing gift *remedy* 115.1
healing quality or **property** *remedy* 115.1
healing touch *healing art* 115.13
heal over or **up** *intertwine* 752.19
health 113.1; *drink* 93.2, *tribute* 405.6, *vigor* 518.1, *nature* 624.5
health and safety representative *union member* 57.6
health and strength *health* 113.1
health and wealth *prosperity* 847.1
health care 107.7; *navy specialties* 77.24, *medicine* 107.1
health center *hospital* 107.16
health club *health improvement* 113.3
health diet *dieting* 118.2
health education *health care* 107.7
health farm *health improvement* 113.3
health food *food* 90.1
health food restaurant *eating place* 92.17
health food shop *food provider* 90.6
healthful 113.7; *hygienic* 116.3
healthfully *healthily* 113.14, *remedially* 115.19, *hygienically* 116.5
healthfulness 113.2
health-giving 113.6; *healthful* 113.7, *hygienic* 116.3
healthily 113.14; *hygienically* 116.5, *well* 445.19, *formatively* 624.10, *in good form* 725.11
health improvement 113.3
healthiness *health* 113.1, *good* 445.1
health inspector *hygienist* 116.2
health insurance *benefits* 57.11, *security* 464.1, *social assistance* 825.4
health maintenance organization (HMO) *medical practice* 107.3
health officer *doctor* 107.19
health promotion *health care* 107.7
health resort *health improvement* 113.3
health salts *purgative* 115.7
health services *army commands* 77.13
health spa *health improvement* 113.3
healthy 113.4; *hygienic* 116.3, *good*

445.10, *physically strong* 516.10, *vigorous* 518.2, *invigorating* 518.3, *in form* 624.8, *conditional* 725.7, *sound* 759.8, *cured* 809.8
healthy [Inf] *big* 579.13
healthy eating *diet* 92.5
healthy economy *economy* 56.3
healthy food *food* 90.1
healthy hue *face color* 251.9
healthy state *health* 113.1
heap 105.19; *assemblage* 59.13, *assemble* 59.23, *store* 105.1, *indiscrimination* 338.4, *be indiscriminate* 338.10, *acquisition* 467.4, *acquire* 467.19, *mass* 579.7, *particle* 796.4
heap [Inf] *automobile* 687.6, *certain amount* 738.3, *profuseness* 795.3
heap abuse on *vilify* 301.15
heaped *collected* 59.19, *stored* 105.14
heaped cloud *cloud appearance* 9.19
heaped up *collected* 757.8
heaping coals of fire *retaliation* 420.1
heap on *augment* 748.13
heaps of money [Inf] *money* 485.2
heap up *combine* 757.9
hear 228.13; *be informed* 170.15, *sense* 212.9, *question* 333.16, *judge* 341.10
hearable 228.12; *sounding* 230.7
hearably *aurally* 228.16
hear a case *try a case* 54.28, *judge* 54.31
hear a cause of action *judge* 54.31
hear a complaint *judge* 54.31
hear both sides *be right* 429.12
heard *communicated* 169.15, *broadcast* 172.12, *sounding* 230.7, *received* 473.11
heard of *known* 348.9
hearer 228.7; *recipient* 473.5
hear from *hear* 228.13
hear hear! *bravo!* 437.23
hearing 228.1, 228.9; *sensory* 19.22, *life function* 28.6, *legal process* 54.3, *pretrial proceedings* 54.13, *sensation* 212.1, *audition* 228.6, *questionnaire* 335.2, *rehearsal* 335.2, *Fields of Measurement* 589
hearing aid *aid to the deaf* 229.3
hearing distance *hearing* 228.1
hearing-impaired *deaf* 229.4
hearing impairment *deafness* 229.1
hearing loss *deafness* 229.1
hearing officer *judge* 54.10
hearing organ *ear* 19.10, 228.2
hearing specialist *ear doctor* 228.5
hearing test *test* 107.10
hearken *hear* 228.13
hearkener *hearer* 228.7
hear no evil *be virtuous* 447.8
hear of *hear* 228.13
hear one's confession *perform rites* 85.18
hear on the grapevine *hear* 228.13
hear out *hear* 228.13
hearsay *publishing* 173.2, *circumstantial* 726.8
hearsay evidence *evidence* 54.15, *legal evidence* 339.4
hearse *funeral object* 31.6
heart *internal organ* 19.13, *variety meat* 90.30, *seat of feelings* 266.7, *plant products* 522.8, *insides* 577.3, *depth of feeling* 598.7, *inner nature*

611.4, *core* 612.2, *essential content* 723.2, *middle* 772.1, *gist* 799.4
heartache *sorrow* 270.1
heart and soul *wholly* 759.11, *completely* 759.14
heart attack *cardiovascular disease* 114.13
heartbeat *computer communications* 15.25, *vibration* 683.2
heartbreak *sorrow* 270.1
heartbreaker *libertine* 32.7, *lover* 299.11
heartbreaking *distressing* 270.6, *lamentable* 280.6, *pitiful* 308.5
heartbreakingly *pitifully* 308.12
heartbroken *sorrowful* 270.4, *disappointed* 293.4
heartburn *gastroenterological disease* 114.11, *jealousy* 314.2
heartburning *resentment* 302.1, *jealousy* 314.2
heart condition *cardiovascular disease* 114.13
heart disease *disease* 114.4, *cardiovascular disease* 114.13, *Phobias* 283
hear tell *hear* 228.13
hearten *bring cheer* 269.12, *give courage* 284.16, *invigorate* 518.5, *give moral support* 605.18, *support* 825.24
heartening *cheering* 281.9, *encouraging* 284.13, *moral support* 605.7, *supportive* 605.11, 825.18
hearteningly *encouragingly* 284.21
heart failure *cardiovascular disease* 114.13
heartfelt *emotive* 266.13, *deep-seated* 598.17
heartfelt apology *confession* 451.2
hearth *home* 60.3, *place for fire* 217.9, *private space* 812.2
hearth and home *home* 60.3
hear the call *be persuaded* 178.20
hear the case *judge* 341.10
hear things *hear* 228.13, *imagine* 720.13
hearth rug *floor covering* 613.13
hearthstone *cleaning agent* 111.9, *place for fire* 217.9
heartily *amicably* 62.13, *healthily* 113.14, *laboriously* 122.13, *sociably* 408.19, *acutely* 516.18, *formatively* 624.10
heartiness *friendship* 62.1, *health* 113.1
heartland *region* 564.1, *regions* 564.2, *regions of the United States* 564.7, *inland* 611.2, *middle* 772.1
heartless *heedless* 268.5, *cruel* 306.10, *pitiless* 309.3, *impenitent* 452.2, *mentally hard* 542.8
heartlessly *insensitively* 268.7, *cruelly* 306.17, *pitilessly* 309.7
heartlessness *heedlessness* 268.2, *cruelty* 306.4, *pitilessness* 309.1
heart of gold *benevolence* 305.1
heart of oak *will* 376.5
heart of stone *pitilessness* 309.1, *impenitence* 452.1
heart of the matter *conciseness* 198.1, *topic* 328.1, *middle* 772.1, *gist* 799.4
heart pain *painful condition* 215.2, *fatigue* 820.1
heart problems *Phobias* 283
heartrending *pitiful* 308.5
heart-rendingly *pitifully* 308.12
hearts *Card Games* 168, *cards* 168.2
heart's desire *object of desire* 288.8, *objective* 374.5
heart-stopping *unsafe* 811.8

heartthrob *loved one* 299.13, *vibration* 683.2
heart-to-heart [Inf] *chat* 210.2
heart trouble *cardiovascular disease* 114.13
heart urchin *echinoderm* 39.5
heart-warming *cheering* 269.8
heartwood *timber* 43.3, *wood* 131.3, *hard substance* 542.3
hearty *friendly* 62.5, *healthy* 113.4, *sociable* 408.11, *in form* 624.8, *nautical person* 690.12
hearty assent *consent* 735.8
hearty eater *eater* 92.15, *glutton* 119.2
hearty thanks *thanks* 310.2
hearty welcome *welcome* 408.10
hear voices *hear* 228.13
heat 10.25, 10.74, 217.1, 217.17; *hot weather* 9.22, *classical physics* 10.2, *sexual desire* 20.5, *cook* 91.10, *track event* 166.1, *emotion* 266.3, *Phobias* 283, *anger* 302.4, *prize competition* 422.5, *energy* 514.7, *generate power* 514.19, *harden* 542.9, *Fields of Measurement* 589, *seasons* 654.2, *part* 760.1
heat [Inf] *law enforcement agency* 53.7
heat capacity *heat flow* 10.27
heated 217.15; *passionate* 266.12, *angry* 302.11, *violent* 520.5
heatedly *angrily* 302.24
heated pool *swimming place* 164.9
heated shot *historical ammunition* 78.12
heated up *heated* 217.15
heat-engine cycle *engine cycle* 14.13
heat engines *industrial processes* 14.27
heater 217.3
heat exchange *heat flow* 10.27
heat exchanger *power supplier* 514.14
heat exhaustion *effects of hot weather* 217.7
heat flow 10.27
heat flow rate *heat flow* 10.27
heath *grassland* 45.2, *lowland* 572.6
heat haze *mist* 9.33
Heathcliff *Famous Lovers* 299
heath cock *male bird* 36.15
heathen *disbeliever* 88.5, *disbelieving* 88.6
heathenism *unbelief* 88.4
heather *Flowers* 42, *purple thing* 262.3
heath hen *female bird* 36.16
heat index *weather data* 9.6
heating 217.12
heating device *heat* 10.25
heating effect 10.28
heating element *heater* 217.3
heat lamp *place for fire* 217.9
heat lightning *natural light* 246.4
heat measurement 217.2
heat rash *skin disease* 114.16, *effects of hot weather* 217.7
heat-resistant suit *modern armor* 419.7
heat retention *preservation of provisions* 815.6
heat-seeking missile *missile* 696.7
heat source *fuel* 106.1
heatstroke *effects of hot weather* 217.7
heat the boiler *prepare for action* 388.18
heat through *heat* 217.17

---

heat transfer *atmospheric process* 9.9, *heat flow* 10.27

heat transport *atmospheric process* 9.9

heat-treat *harden* 542.9

heat-treated *hardened* 542.7

heat treatment *therapy* 115.12

heat unit *heat measurement* 217.2

heat up *antagonize* 63.12, *cook* 91.10, *heat* 217.17, *intensify* 746.8

heat wave *hot weather* 9.22, 217.6, *wave* 683.4

heave *exertion* 122.4, *work* 122.8, *handle sailboat equipment* 150.30, *wave* 571.3, *billow* 571.9, *vibrate* 683.13, *convey* 685.9, *maneuver* 689.14, *blow* 695.5, *impel* 695.9, *throw* 696.4, 696.17, *pull* 699.2, 699.10, *vomit* 709.27, *raising* 715.1, *raise* 715.9

heave a brick *stone* 418.23

heaved *raised* 715.6

heave-ho [Inf] *rejection* 383.1, *relegation* 574.4, *expulsion* 709.1, *ejection* 764.2, *termination* 834.2

heave in sight *appear* 244.8, *become visible* 264.13

heaven 82.15; *after death* 29.9, *idealized pleasure* 214.5, *joy* 269.1, *pleasantness* 271.1, *Phobias* 283, *occult influence* 512.2, *nonmaterial world* 525.1, *top of the world* 600.2, *life without end* 644.2, *future condition* 650.3

heavenly 82.22; *astronomical* 7.33, *idyllic* 214.11, *pleasant* 271.5, *delightful* 271.7, *nonmaterial* 525.8, *beautiful* 529.7

heavenly being *angel* 82.11

heavenly body *star* 7.8

heavenly host *angel* 82.11

heaven on earth *idealized pleasure* 214.5

heavens *universe* 7.3, *empty space* 563.2, *top of the world* 600.2

heavens, the *air* 558.1

heaven-sent *great* 445.14, *timely* 659.4

heavenward *higher* 596.21, *toward* 697.18, *up* 713.25

heave out *expel* 709.14

heaver *thrower* 696.10

heave the lead *measure depth* 598.22, *navigate* 690.15

heave to *sail* 150.29, 690.16

heavier-than-air *flyable* 689.12

heavily 538.16; *boringly* 296.10, *densely* 540.10, *thick* 594.11, *motionlessly* 678.9, *wholely* 738.9

heavily built *stocky* 579.16

heaviness 538.1; *boringness* 296.2, *sleep* 415.5, *inelegance* 528.1, *pulpiness* 561.9, *squatness* 579.6, *thickness* 594.1, *quantity* 738.1

heaving *sailing* 150.25, *flight maneuver* 689.6, *throwing* 696.3, *traction* 699.1, *vomiting* 709.7

heaving line *sailboat parts and accessories* 150.4

heaving line bend *Knots, Bends, Hitches, Splices* 754

heavy 538.9; *cloudy* 9.44, *humid* 9.48, *rainy* 9.50, *laborious* 122.7, *stock part* 136.24, *serious* 200.5, 799.8, *nonresonant* 233.7, *boring* 296.6, *inert* 519.2, *heavily* 538.16, *dense* 540.6, *thick* 561.17, 594.5, *oceanic* 571.7, *stocky* 579.16, *sedentary* 678.5, *quantitative* 738.6, *difficult* 824.9

heavy [Inf] *role* 136.23

heavy-armed *defended* 419.18

heavy artillery *guns* 78.9

heavy as a horse *heavy* 538.9

heavy as lead *heavy* 538.9

heavy bombardment *combined attack* 418.5

heavy bomber *military aircraft* 77.30

heavy build *squatness* 579.6

heavy cream *fat* 562.4

heavy cruiser *warship* 77.21

heavy drinker *drinker* 93.16

heavy-duty *strengthened* 516.13

heavy eater *eater* 92.15, *glutton* 119.2

heavy-eyed *not awake* 415.12, *fatigued* 820.2

heavy food *food* 90.1

heavy-footed *clumsy* 128.6, *graceless* 528.7

heavy-going *rough* 824.10

heavy-handed *clumsy* 128.6, *insensible* 213.4, *handling* 216.7, *severe* 424.5, *violent* 520.5, *graceless* 528.7, *ponderous* 538.11

heavy-handedly *severely* 424.11

heavy-handedness *unskillfulness* 128.1, *insensibility* 213.1, *inelegance* 528.1

heavy-hearted *sorrowful* 270.4

heavy-heartedness *sorrow* 270.1

heavy industry *manufacture* 522.2

heavy-laden *blocked* 826.13

heavy-lidded *fatigued* 820.2

heavy metal *chemical element* 11.3, *rock music* 140.6

heavy scene [Inf] *important matter* 799.2

heavy sea *wave* 571.3, *atmospheric agitation* 684.13

heavyset *stocky* 579.16

heavy sledding *difficult task* 824.3

heavy sleep *sleep* 415.5

heavy sound *dull sound* 233.2

heavy swell *wave* 571.3

heavy water (D₂O) *water* 557.1

heavy-water reactor (HWR) *nuclear power production* 1014.10

heavyweight *boxing weight divisions* 152.6, *combat* 152.17, *weighing* 538.4, *heavy* 538.9, *big person* 579.10, *big* 579.13, *important person* 799.5

heavyweight champion *boxer* 152.8

heavy weight or **object** *weight* 538.8

heavy wet snow *skiing snow* 162.3

heavy with *pregnant* 21.12

heavy work *work* 122.1

hebdomad *seven* 792.3

hebdomadal *cyclic* 663.7

hebdomadary *cyclic* 663.7

hebdomal *seventh* 792.14

Hebe *Planets and Their Satellites* 7, *Deities* 82

hebephrenia *psychosis* 110.3

hebetude *ignorance* 316.3, *dullness* 550.3

hebetudinous *dull* 550.7

Hebraism *Judaism* 81.6

Hebrew *denominational* 81.23

Hebrew school *religious school* 48.13

Hebrides *regions of the British Isles* 564.8, *Islands* 572

Hecate *Deities* 82, *witch* 86.15

hecatomb *offering* 504.5, *havoc* 523.5, *hundreds* 792.9

heck! *miscellaneous euphemisms* 301.21

heckelclarina *Musical Instruments* 142

heckelphone *Musical Instruments* 142

heckle *taunt* 436.23, *show disapproval* 438.21, *bother* 826.16

heckler *dissenter* 347.5, *hinderer* 826.11, *opposer* 828.9

heck of a lot [Inf] *profuseness* 795.3

hectic *red-faced* 257.6, *busy* 414.15

hectic flush *redness* 257.1

hecto *Decimal Prefixes* 589

hector *exaggerator* 194.6, *intimidate* 283.18

hectoring *intimidation* 283.6

hedge *farmland* 16.3, *ornamental garden* 17.3, *evade* 181.17, *proceed with caution* 287.12, *quibble* 330.13, *be equivocal* 380.7, *be evasive* 386.20, *fence* 419.21, *circumlocute* 607.12, *enclosing thing* 619.3, *limit marker* 620.4, *separator* 753.5, *shelter* 812.4

hedge clipper *garden tool* 103.4

hedgecutter *farm tool* 16.5

hedgehog cactus *Flowers* 42

hedgehopping *flight maneuver* 689.6

hedge one's bets *proceed with caution* 287.12, *make conditions* 460.7, *stand in the middle* 772.17, *be safe* 810.20

hedgerow *farmland* 16.3, *enclosing thing* 619.3

hedgerow tree *tree* 43.1

hedge trimmer *garden tool* 17.7

hedging *cultivation* 16.7, *quibbling* 330.4, 330.9, *evasion* 380.2, *indirectness* 607.3, *indirect* 607.8

hedonic *pleasure-loving* 271.9

hedonism *Philosophical Schools of Thought* 4, *physical pleasure* 214.1, *pleasure* 271.2, *self-indulgence* 456.1

hedonist *Philosophical Schools of Thought* 4, *pleasure-seeker* 214.4, *self-indulgent person* 456.5

hedonistic *gluttonous* 119.3, *pleasure-seeking* 214.10, *pleasure-loving* 271.9, *self-indulgent* 456.6

hedonize *be greedy* 119.4

hedonophobia *Phobias* 283

heebie-jeebies [Inf] *drunken behavior* 121.4, *stimulus* 212.3, *symptoms of fear* 283.3, *agitation* 684.1

heed *hearing* 228.1, *hear* 228.13, *prudence* 287.2, *carefulness* 323.3, 325.1, *scrutinize* 323.11, *be careful* 325.11, *obey* 426.7, *show respect* 435.16, *observance* 465.1, *observe* 465.4

heeded *observant* 465.3

heedful *prudent* 287.7, *watchful* 323.6, *careful* 325.6, *observant* 465.3

heedfully *prudently* 287.17, *attentively* 323.14, *observantly* 465.6

heedfulness *prudence* 287.2, *observance* 465.1

heeding *hearing* 228.1, *observance* 465.1, *observant* 465.3

heedless 268.5; *unhearing* 229.5, *reckless* 286.6, *careless* 289.8, *ungrateful* 311.2, *inconsiderate* 318.9, *incurious* 322.3, *inattentive* 324.5, *negligent* 326.4, *foolish* 353.5, *unthinking* 355.8, *nonobservant* 466.5, *hasty* 818.3

heedlessly *recklessly* 286.10, *carelessly* 289.18, *ungratefully* 311.6, *apathetically* 322.7, *inattentively* 324.12, 466.13, *forgetfully* 355.14, *rashly* 818.8

heedlessness 268.2; *inattention* 229.2, 324.1, *insensitivity* 268.1,

recklessness 286.2, *carelessness* 289.2, *negligence* 326.1, *folly* 353.1, *unthinkingness* 355.3, *nonobservance* 466.1

heed the call *be motivated* 508.10

hee-haw *animal sound* 240.1

heel *plant breeding* 17.6, *sail* 150.29, *golf equipment* 156.5, *ski equipment* 162.10, *back* 622.1, *deviate* 698.15, *unbalance* 741.8, *repair* 809.10

heel bone *Human Bones* 19

heel in *cultivate* 17.19

heeling *unbalanced* 741.5, *repair* 809.1

heel over *sail* 690.16

heelside turn *snowboarding* 162.11

heeltap *size of drink* 93.3, *residue* 750.2, *tail* 773.8

heft *heaviness* 538.1, *weigh* 538.15, *raise* 715.9

heftiness *heaviness* 538.1, *squatness* 579.6

hefting *weighing* 538.4

hefty *heavy* 538.9, *stocky* 579.16, *difficult* 824.9

Hegelian *Philosophical Schools of Thought* 4, *nonmaterialist* 525.7, *idealistic* 525.10

Hegelianism *Philosophical Schools of Thought* 4, *idealism* 525.5

hegemonic *authoritative* 52.9, *managerial* 126.9, *powerful* 514.15, *unbeatable* 744.13

hegemonistic *authoritative* 52.9

hegemony *authority* 52.1, 514.5, *personal influence* 512.3, *leadership* 744.2

hegira *departure* 705.1

Heidelberg man *prehistoric human* 653.7

heifer *livestock* 16.11, *female animal* 33.15, *female mammal* 35.19

height 596.1, 715.4; *line* 6.35, *dimension* 10.5, *competitive diving* 164.7, *space* 563.1, *size* 579.1, *measurability* 589.2, *measuring instrument* 589.12, *longness* 590.3, *quantity* 738.1, *degree* 739.1, *summit* 744.4

heighten 596.14; *enlarge* 194.12, *aggravate* 276.5, *increase* 581.16, *promote* 715.13, *intensify* 746.8

heighten awareness *arouse sensation* 212.11

heightened *enlarged* 194.8, *aggravated* 276.3, *swelled* 581.10, *increased* 746.5

heightener *stimulus* 212.3

heightening *enlargement* 194.2, *aggravation* 276.1, *increase* 581.3, *growing* 581.12, *intensification* 746.2

height measurement 596.5

height of perfection *peak* 805.5

heights 596.4, *Phobias* 283, *mountain* 569.1, *upland* 572.7

heights, the *summit* 744.4

height-weight ratio *measurement* 1.9

Heimdall *Deities* 82

heinous *offending* 53.25, *black-hearted* 254.9, *cruel* 306.10, *evil* 446.7, *wicked* 448.9, *sinful* 450.8

heinously *cruelly* 306.17, *disgracefully* 371.8, *evilly* 446.12, *wickedly* 448.15

heinousness *cruelty* 306.4, *evil* 446.1, *wickedness* 448.1

heir *gainer* 467.9, *beneficiary* 473.6, *wealthy person* 485.6, *person remaining* 750.6, *successor* 770.6

heir apparent *beneficiary* 473.6
heir-at-law *beneficiary* 473.6
heirdom *inheritance* 469.5
heiress *gainer* 467.9, *beneficiary* 473.6, *wealthy person* 485.6
heirloom *personal estate* 470.6, *receiving* 473.1, *antiquity* 653.4
heir presumptive *beneficiary* 473.6
heirs *future generation* 650.2
heirship *inheritance* 469.5, *receiving* 473.1
heir to a fortune *wealthy person* 485.6
Heisenberg uncertainty principle *Classical Physical Laws* 10, *causality* 10.66
heist *raise* 715.9
heist [Inf] *taking away* 477.5, *take money away* 477.20, *theft* 479.2, *steal* 479.14
hejira *departure* 705.1
Hel *Deities* 82, *evil place* 446.6
held *imprisoned* 55.9, *saved* 105.15, *soccer* 163.7, *possessed* 469.13, *retained* 471.6, *containing* 578.18, *stable* 674.3
held back *limited* 620.5, *hindering* 826.12, *restrained* 830.9
held ball *playing terms* 148.4
held in *retained* 471.6
held in contempt *hated* 300.9
held in low esteem *disrespected* 436.16
held in respect *respected* 435.10
held position *balance beam* 157.3
held up 658.6; *deferred* 604.9, *stopped* 668.7, *delayed* 693.10, *hindering* 826.12
Helen *Famous Lovers* 299
Helena *American States* 564
Helene *Planets and Their Satellites* 7
Helgoland *Islands* 572
heliacal *astronomical* 7.33
helical *curvilinear* 6.78, *convolutional* 632.4, *circular* 681.6
helical gear *gear* 14.7
helically *circularly* 632.8
Helicon *Mountains and Hills* 569
helicon *Musical Instruments* 142
helicopter *military aircraft* 77.30, *aircraft* 689.3
helicopter gunship *military aircraft* 77.30
helicopter pilot *aircraft personnel* 689.8
helicopter skiing *skiing* 162.1
heliocentric *astronomical* 7.33, *central* 612.6
heliocentrically *astronomically* 7.36
heliographic *signaling* 183.14
heliolater *idolater* 83.7
heliolatrous *idolatrous* 83.13
heliolatry *idolatry* 83.4
heliophobia *Phobias* 283
Helios *sun* 7.15, *Deities* 82
heliostat *telescope* 7.25
heliotrope *Flowers* 42, *purple thing* 262.3, *purple* 262.6
helipad *destination* 704.6
heliport *destination* 704.6
heli-skiing *skiing* 162.1
helium *Chemical Elements and Common Allotropes* 11, *propellant* 696.9
helium balloon *aircraft* 689.3, *lifter* 715.5
helium-neon laser *laser (light amplification by stimulated emission of radiation)* 10.18
helix *curve* 6.38, *ear* 19.10,

Architectural Elements 134, *orbital motion* 681.1
hell *after death* 29.9, *hot place* 217.5, *Phobias* 283, *evil place* 446.6, *wicked place* 448.8, *nonmaterial world* 525.1, *future condition* 650.3, *adversity* 848.1
hell! *miscellaneous swearwords* 301.20
Helladic *historic* 653.13
hellbent *foolish* 353.5, *intending* 374.6, *resolute* 376.7
hellborn *demonic* 446.9
hellcat *violent animal* 520.4
hellebore *Flowers* 42
Hellenic *language family* 5.12, *historic* 653.13
Hellenistic *historic* 653.13
Hellenistic art *Western Art Styles* 133
Hellenologophobia *Phobias* 283
hellfire *future condition* 650.3
hell-for-leather [Inf] *swiftly* 694.16
hellhole *wicked place* 448.8
hellhound *evil person* 446.3, *violent animal* 520.4
hellish *witchlike* 86.19, *demonic* 446.9
hellishly *devilishly* 446.14
hello *cry of greeting* 239.4
hello! 704.23
hell of a lot [Inf] *profuseness* 795.3
hell on earth *pain* 215.1
hell-raiser [Inf] *violent animal* 520.4
hell-raising *disorderly* 766.15
Hell's Kitchen *New York* 567.6
hell *or* the devil to pay *reckoning* 454.8
helm *guide* 126.6, *sailboat parts and accessories* 150.4, *historic armor* 419.8, *ship's steering* 690.9
Helmand *Rivers* 570
helmet 100.34; *football uniform* 155.2, *hockey clothing* 158.6, *climbing equipment* 161.4, *Heraldic Terms* 184, *protective clothing* 419.6, *historic armor* 419.8, *protective covering* 613.5
Helmholtz function *Classical Physical Laws* 10
helminth *worm* 39.14, *parasite* 39.18, *disease-causing agent* 114.5
helminthic *wormlike* 39.24
helminthoid *wormlike* 39.24
helminthologic(al) *wormlike* 39.24
helminthologist *animal scientist* 34.7, *invertebrate zoologist* 39.3
helminthology *animal science* 34.6, *invertebrate zoology* 39.2
helminthophobia *Phobias* 283
helmsman *boating person* 150.24, *nautical person* 690.12
helmsmanship *navigation* 690.5, *direction* 697.1
Héloïse *Famous Lovers* 299
helotism *servility* 401.1
help 825.1, 825.23; *be favorable* 62.12, *servant* 69.1, *serve* 69.11, *represent* 80.6, *remedy* 115.1, 115.16, *domestic worker* 123.4, *aid* 275.2, 275.10, *be compassionate* 305.11, *philanthropize* 307.8, *be eager* 373.13, *courtesy* 410.1, *motivate* 447.12, *better* 445.17, *gift* 472.2, *fund* 472.15, *instrumentality* 511.1, *assistant* 511.3, *be an instrument* 511.7, *moral support* 605.7, *give moral support* 605.18, *determine* 675.11, *usefulness* 801.1, *be useful* 801.9, *be convenient* 803.5, *smoothness*

823.5, *make easy* 823.15, *cooperation* 827.1, *cooperate* 827.12
help a lame dog over a stile *improve* 825.26
help a lame duck *improve* 825.26
help along *further* 825.30
help decide *determine* 675.11
helper 275.5, 825.12; *philanthropist* 307.5, *good person* 445.6, *giver* 472.7, *volunteer* 504.7, *assistant* 511.3, *ancillary* 605.5, *supporter* 605.9, *cooperator* 827.8, *subordinate* 832.3
helpful 825.19; *educational* 48.17, *favorable* 62.8, *remedial* 115.14, *relieving* 275.7, *compassionate* 305.8, *philanthropic* 307.6, *goodwilled* 373.10, *beneficial* 445.11, *kind* 445.12, *instrumental* 511.4, *supportive* 605.11, *important* 799.7, *useful* 801.5, *convenient* 803.7, *feasible* 823.10, *cooperative* 827.9
helpful act *benevolent act* 305.5
helpfully 825.32; *educationally* 48.25, *favorably* 62.15, *comfortingly* 275.14, *compassionately* 305.14, *philanthropically* 307.9, *kindly* 445.20, *instrumentally* 511.9, *supportively* 605.20, *usefully* 801.12
helpfulness 825.10; *compassion* 305.2, *philanthropy* 307.1, *goodwill* 373.4, *kindness* 445.3, *usefulness* 801.1, *convenience* 803.1, *cooperation* 827.1
helping 92.11, 825.16; *serving* 69.9, *relieving* 275.7, *portion* 474.2, *instrumental* 511.4, *supportive* 605.11, *particle* 760.4
helping hand *aid* 275.2, *charity* 307.3, *willing worker* 373.6, *moral support* 605.7, *supporter* 605.9, *help* 825.1, *helper* 825.12
helpless 515.9; *weak* 517.6, *vulnerable* 811.9
helplessly *powerlessly* 515.16, *weakly* 517.14, *dangerously* 811.14
helplessness 515.3; *weakness* 517.1, *vulnerability* 811.6
helpmate *spouse* 64.8, *helper* 275.5, *supporter* 605.9, 825.13
helpmeet *spouse* 64.8, *helper* 275.5, *supporter* 605.9, 825.13
help on *or* along *make easy* 823.15
help oneself to *take away* 477.18
help out *help* 825.23, *finance* 825.31
help up *raise* 715.9
help with money *fund* 472.15
help yourself! *welcome!* 704.24
Helsinki *Countries* 566
helter-skelter *inconsistently* 732.16, *anyhow* 766.25, *hastily* 818.7
Helvellyn *Mountains and Hills* 569
hem *make clothing* 100.44, *shorten* 591.9, *edging* 618.2, *edge* 618.8
hemal *or* hematal *bloody* 555.18
he-man [Inf] *macho man* 32.6, *courageous person* 284.8, *person of strength* 516.8
hem and haw *balance* 378.11
hemangioma *mark* 533.2
hemaphobia *Phobias* 283
hematemesis *bleeding* 25.10
hematic *bloody* 555.18
hematology *Medical Specialties* 107
hematophobia *or* hemophobia *Phobias* 283

hematopoietic disease *disease* 114.4
hematoxylin *Tree Products* 43
hematuria *bleeding* 25.10
heme *respiration* 12.24
hemeralopia *faulty vision* 243.1
hemeralopic *visually impaired* 243.9
hemiacetal *saccharide* 12.4
hemic *bloody* 555.18
hemicellulose *polysaccharide* 12.5
Hemichordata *protochordate* 39.4
hemichordate *protochordate* 39.4, *invertebrate* 39.20
hemidemisemiquaver *notation* 140.20
hemihydrate *salt* 11.12
hemiketal *saccharide* 12.4
hem in *besiege* 418.20, *enclose* 619.6, *limit* 830.13
hemiplegia *neurological disease* 114.20
hemiplegic *sick person* 114.22
hemipteran *or* hemipterous *insectile* 40.11
hemisphere *region* 564.1, *round thing* 633.3, *part* 760.1, *half* 789.7
hemispherical *round* 633.7
hemistich *part of poem* 139.9
hemline *part of garment* 100.27, *edging* 618.2
hemlock *poison* 117.7, *instrument of execution* 454.15
hemlock *or* hemlock spruce *Trees and Shrubs* 43
hemmed *edged* 618.6
hemmed-in *surrounded* 615.5, *enclosed* 619.4
hemming *sewing* 130.5
hemogenic *bloody* 555.18
hemoglobin *protein* 12.9, *pigment* 12.18, *respiration* 12.24, *blood* 555.4
hemolytic anemia *blood disease* 114.14
hemophilia *bleeding* 25.10, *blood disease* 114.14, *fluidity* 555.5
hemophiliac *sick person* 114.22
hemophilic *of disease* 114.25, *bloody* 555.18
hemoprotein *protein* 12.9
hemoptysis *bleeding* 25.10
hemorrhage *bleeding* 25.10, *bleed* 25.26, *symptom* 114.3, *lessening* 468.6, *lessen* 468.17, *flow* 555.6, *outflow* 707.4
hemorrhagic anemia *blood disease* 114.14
hemorrhaging *bleeding* 25.19
hemorrhea *bleeding* 25.10
hemostasis *concentration* 540.2
hemostatic *dense* 540.6
hemp *hemp derivatives* 121.16
hemp derivatives 121.16
hempen collar *instrument of execution* 454.15
hen *livestock* 16.11, *female animal* 33.15, *female bird* 36.16
hence *with the effect of* 676.12, *accordingly* 735.39
henceforth *after* 650.14
henceforward *after* 650.14
henchman *servant* 69.1, *personal attendant* 69.5, *defender* 419.14, *helper* 825.12
hencoop *farm building* 16.4, *cage* 60.15
hencote *farm building* 16.4
hendecagon *eleven to nineteen* 792.7
hendecagonal *eleventh and above* 792.18
hendecahedron *eleven to nineteen* 792.7

hendecasyllabic *metrical* 139.20
henhouse *farm building* 16.4, *cage* 60.15
Henley Royal Regatta *rowing competitions* 150.18
henna *Tree Products* 43, *red pigment* 257.2, *orange pigment* 258.2
hennery *farm building* 16.4, *cage* 60.15
hen party [Inf] *womenfolk* 33.14, *social gathering* 59.7, *party* 408.6
henpeck *subject* 832.10
henpecked *subject* 832.6
henpecked husband *married man* 64.10
Henri Deux style Architectural Styles 134
Henri Quatre style Architectural Styles 134
hen run *farm building* 16.4
henry Scientific and Technical Units 589
hepatic *mosslike* 46.7
Hepaticae *moss* 46.4
Hepaticopsida *moss* 46.4
Hephaestus Deities 82
Hepplewhite Furniture Styles 101
heptad *seven* 792.3
heptadic *seventh* 792.14
heptagon *polygon* 6.42, *angled figure* 628.3, *seven* 792.3
heptagonal *polygonal* 6.79, *angled* 628.9, *seventh* 792.14
heptahedral *seventh* 792.14
heptahedron *seven* 792.3
heptameter *meter* 139.10, *seven* 792.3
heptane *fuels* 106.2
heptangular *seventh* 792.14
heptastich *part of poem* 139.9
Heptateuch *seven* 792.3
heptathlon Sporting Activities 145, *multi-event contest* 166.16
heptatonic *seventh* 792.14
heptavalent *chemical compound* 11.4
heptose *saccharide* 12.4
her *female* 33.1
Hera *gods and goddesses of marriage* 64.14, Deities 82
Heraclitean Philosophical Schools of Thought 4
Heracliteanism Philosophical Schools of Thought 4
Heraclitus Notable Friendships 62
herald *informer* 170.8, *publicizer* 173.11, *proclaim* 173.16, *signal* 183.18, *discoverer* 345.7, *invent* 345.14, *omen* 358.5, *predict* 358.14, *precursor* 769.7, *forecast* 769.17
heraldic 184.10
heraldically *identifiably* 184.13
heraldic color 251.1
heraldic sign *insignia* 184.5
heraldic tincture Heraldic Terms 184
heralding *predicting* 358.11
heraldry *insignia* 184.5
herb *garden plant* 17.10, *vegetable* 17.11, *plant* 41.2, *medicine* 115.2, *seasoning* 221.2, *source of fragrance* 226.2, *admixture* 751.5
herbaceous *horticultural* 17.14, *plantlike* 41.13, *of plants* 41.14
herbaceous border *ornamental garden* 17.3
herbaceously 41.24
herbaceous perennial *plant* 41.2
herbaceous plant *plant* 41.2
herbage *plants* 41.1, *grassland* 45.2

herbal *horticultural* 17.14, *herbarium* 41.12, *plantlike* 41.13
herbalism *alternative medicine* 107.4, *treatment* 107.14
herbalist *plant scientist* 41.11, *healer* 107.7
herbal remedy *medicine* 115.2
herbal tea *tea* 93.7
herbarium 41.12
herb garden *garden* 17.2
herbicidal 17.16
herbicide *pest control* 16.13, *pest killer* 17.9, *killing agent* 30.15, *poison* 117.7
herbivore *type of animal* 34.5, *grass eater* 45.6, *eater* 92.15
herbivority *eating habit* 92.7
herbivorous *of animals* 34.13, *fruit-eating* 44.7, *grass-eating* 45.9, *eating* 92.18
herbivorously 45.12; *carnivorously* 92.27
herb Robert Flowers 42
herbs *basic cooking ingredient* 91.8
herb sausage *sausage* 90.29
herb tea *tonic* 115.8
herby *piquant* 221.6, *odorous* 224.5
herculean *laborious* 122.7, *physically strong* 516.10, *difficult* 824.9
herculean task *difficult task* 824.3
Hercules Constellations 7, Notable Friendships 62, *person of strength* 516.8
Hercules-club Trees and Shrubs 43
herd 59.29; *practice livestock farming* 16.20, *assemblage of mammals* 35.22, Collective Names 59, *assembly* 59.1, *assembling* 59.12
herded *assembled* 59.18
herder *farm worker* 16.15
herding *livestock farming* 16.10
herd manager *farm worker* 16.15
Herdsman Constellations 7
herdsman *farm worker* 16.15
Herdwick Breeds of Sheep 16
here 575.19; *where* 565.12, *available* 647.6, *on arrival* 704.22
hereabouts *where* 565.12, *nearby* 586.17
hereafter *after death* 29.9, *judgment day* 341.4, *nonmaterial world* 525.1, *future condition* 650.3, *after* 650.14, *life without end* 644.2
here and now *present time* 647.1
here and now, the *reality* 719.1
here and there *where* 565.12, *sometimes* 662.5, *via* 691.17, *discontinuously* 775.15, *diffusely* 776.18, *in ones and twos* 796.10
hereat *where* 565.12
hereditament *legal property terms* 470.2, *receiving* 473.1, *visible effect* 676.2, *estate* 471.4
hereditarily *proprietarily* 470.14, *receptively* 473.15
hereditary *genetic* 13.32, *propertied* 470.9, *receivable* 473.12, *received* 492.6, *caused* 676.5, *remaining* 750.7
hereditary character *genetics* 13.19
heredity *genetics* 13.19, Phobias 283
Hereford Breeds of Cattle 16, Breeds of Pigs 16
here goes! 376.18, 390.11
hereinafter *after* 650.14
here lies *funeral object* 31.6
hereness *presence* 575.1
Herens Breeds of Cattle 16

here's looking at you! *cheers!* 93.22
here's mud in your eye! *cheers!* 93.22
here's to you! *cheers!* 93.22
heresy *errancy* 351.7, *nonconformism* 782.3
heresy-hunting *social discrimination* 337.4
here, there, and everywhere *extensively* 563.18
heretic *disbeliever* 88.5, *deviant* 698.7, *dissenter* 782.8
heretical *dissenting* 347.7, *errant* 351.12, *nonobservant* 466.5, *nonconformist* 782.13
heretically *defiantly* 466.14
here today gone tomorrow *disappearing* 265.3, *transient* 643.4
heretofore *before now* 651.21
herewith [Form] *instrumentally* 511.9
Her Highness [Brit] *important person* 799.5
heritability *transfer of property* 470.4
heritable *propertied* 470.9
heritably *proprietarily* 470.9
heritage *inheritance* 469.5, *receiving* 473.1, *legacy* 492.4
heritor *beneficiary* 473.6
herky-jerky *irregular* 664.3
Herlen Rivers 570
herm *sculpture* 144.1
hermaphrodite *sexual nature* 20.4, *of sexual nature* 20.17
hermaphrodite brig or **brigantine** Sailing Ships and Boats 690
hermaphroditic *of sexual nature* 20.17
hermaphroditism *sexual nature* 20.4
hermeneutic *logical* 329.9, *interpretive* 365.8
hermeneutically *linguistically* 5.44
hermeneutics Theologies 81, *interpretation* 365.1, *science of interpretation* 365.5
Hermes Planets and Their Satellites 7, Deities 82, *messenger* 685.5
hermetic *occult* 86.16
hermetically *impermeably* 584.17
hermetically sealed *closed* 584.7, *invulnerable* 810.18
Hermeticism Western Literary Groups 139
hermeticism *occultism* 86.1
hermetics *occultism* 86.1
hermit 782.9; *celibate* 67.4, *religious* 84.9, *one who conceals* 181.7, *unsocial person* 409.5, *deviant* 698.7, *individualist* 756.3, *loner* 788.8
hermitage *clerical dwelling* 84.10, *private space* 812.2
hermit crab *crustacean* 39.10
hermitlike *religious* 81.21
Hermoder Deities 82
Hermon, Mount Mountains and Hills 569
her nibs [Inf] *proud person* 297.7
Hero Famous Lovers 299
hero *idol* 83.5, *sandwich* 90.9, *role* 136.23, *courageous person* 284.8, *wonderful person* 294.6, *doer* 412.3, *successful person* 845.6
heroic 284.10; *societal* 1.13, *martial* 77.33, *laborious* 122.7, *poetic* 139.19, *narrative* 202.12, *tenacious* 376.9, *swaggering*

404.20, *acting* 412.9, *principled* 447.6, *historic* 653.13
heroic age *historical past* 651.6
heroically 284.18; *martially* 77.39, *swaggeringly* 404.35, *ethically* 447.10
heroic couplet *meter* 139.10
heroic drama *dramatic style* 136.3
heroic poetry *poetry* 139.8
heroic qualities *virtues* 447.2
heroics *courageous act* 284.7
heroin [Inf] *opiates* 121.17
heroine *idol* 83.5, *role* 136.23, *courageous person* 284.8, *wonderful person* 294.6, *doer* 412.3, *successful person* 845.6
heroism 284.2; *tenacity* 376.4, *virtues* 447.2
heron *water bird* 36.9
herons Collective Names 59
Heron's formula Mathematical Concepts 6
Hero's formula Mathematical Concepts 6
hero's welcome *reception* 405.4
hero worship *idolatry* 83.4, *wonder* 294.1, *love* 299.1, *praise* 437.3
hero-worship *idolize* 83.16, *wonder* 294.12, *love* 299.21, *admiration* 435.2, *revere* 435.14, *praise* 437.16
hero-worshiper *idolater* 83.7, *approver* 437.7
hero-worshiping *idolatrous* 83.13, *reverent* 435.9, *approving* 437.9
herpes *skin disease* 114.16, *sexually transmitted disease (STD)* 114.17
herpes simplex *sexually transmitted disease (STD)* 114.17
herpes zoster *skin disease* 114.16
herpetologist 37.15
herpetologist 37.3; *animal scientist* 34.7
herpetology 37.2; *animal science* 34.6
herpetophobia Phobias 283
Herr [Ger] *male title of address* 32.3
herring Collective Names 59, *food fish and shellfish* 90.20
herringbone Fabrics and Fibers 130, *joined* 131.8, *skiing techniques* 162.5, *cross-country techniques* 162.8
herringbone strutting *carpenter's term* 131.5
herringlike *fishlike* 38.10
herring pond, the [Brit inf] *sea* 571.1
herring roe *fish product* 38.9
herself *female* 33.1
Hershey bar [Inf] *insignia* 184.5
hertz Scientific and Technical Units 589
hertz (Hz) *radio frequency* 661.3
Hertzsprung–Russell diagram *star luminosity* 7.12
hesitance *reticence* 287.3, *indecisiveness* 517.2
hesitancy *disbelief* 88.1, *reticence* 287.3, *vacillation* 378.1
hesitant 693.9; *disbelieving* 88.6, *reticent* 287.8, *unenthusiastic* 375.10, *vacillating* 378.5, 683.10, *weak-willed* 517.10, *irresolute* 841.11
hesitantly *disbelievingly* 88.10, *reticently* 287.8, *unwillingly* 375.17, *ambivalently* 378.14, *shyly* 386.25, *uncertainly* 841.22
hesitate 378.10, 693.12, 841.18; *disbelieve* 88.8, *doubt* 287.13, *333.19, delay* 375.16, *escape notice*

403.14, *be irresolute* 666.6, *vacillate* 683.14
hesitating *skeptical* 333.14, *irresolute* 666.4, 841.10
hesitatingly *questionably* 333.22
hesitation 693.5; *disbelief* 88.1, *uncertainty* 333.6, *unenthusiasm* 375.3, *vacillation* 378.1, 683.3, *irresolution* 461.3, 666.2, 841.3
hesitator *inactive person* 413.8
Hesperides *heaven* 82.15
hesperidium *botanical fruit* 44.2
Hesperus *star* 7.8, *evening* 656.2
hessian Fabrics and Fibers 130
Hestia Deities 82
hetaera *or* **hetaira** *girlfriend* 33.4
heterochromosome *chromosome* 13.21
heteroclite *or* **heteroclitic** *of grammar* 5.41
heterocyclic *chemical compound* 11.4
heterodox *dissenting* 347.7, *nonconformist* 782.13
heterodoxy *errancy* 351.7, *nonconformism* 782.3
heterogeneity *disparity* 728.3, *variety* 732.2, *nonuniformity* 734.2, *inequality* 741.1, *mixture* 751.1
heterogeneous *chemical* 14.46, *disparate* 728.9, *varied* 732.6, *nonuniform* 734.5, *mixed* 751.8
heterogeneous catalysis *catalysis* 11.16
heterogeneously *sociologically* 2.15, *disparately* 728.19, *variously* 732.15, *nonuniformly* 734.11, *mixedly* 751.16
heterogeneous reactors *chemical reaction thermodynamics* 14.29
heterogenous *general* 778.9
heterolysis *chemical reaction* 11.8
heterolytic *reactive* 11.29
heterolytic fission *chemical reaction* 11.8
heterolyze *react* 11.38
heterophobia Phobias 283
heterophony *harmonic element* 140.14
heteropolar bond *chemical bond* 11.6
heteropolysaccharide *polysaccharide* 12.5
heteropteran *insectile* 40.11
heterosexual *sexual nature* 20.4, *of sexual nature* 20.17, *straight person* 630.7, *traditional* 630.13
heterosexuality *sexual nature* 20.4, *traditionality* 630.6
heterosome *chromosome* 13.21
heterothallic *of fungi* 47.19
het up [Inf] *angry* 302.11
heuristic *philosophical investigation* 4.4, *dialectical* 4.16, *theoretic(al)* 6.66, *logical argument* 329.2, *logical* 329.9, *finding out* 345.3, *discoverable* 345.10
heuristic solution *reasoning* 6.61
hevea Trees and Shrubs 43
hew *fashion* 536.7, *open* 583.15, *form* 624.9, *take apart* 753.16
hew down *flatten* 716.15
hewn *open* 583.10
hex *spell* 86.8, *bewitch* 86.25, *curse* 301.1, 301.13, *make evil* 446.11, *cause adversity* 848.15
hexacanth *invertebrate larva* 39.19
hexachord *six* 792.2
hexad *six* 792.2
hexadecimal *computer information* 15.17, *eleven to nineteen* 792.7, *eleventh and above* 792.18

hexadecimal *or* **hex notation** *number system* 6.7
hexadic *sixth* 792.13
hexagon *polygon* 6.42, *angled figure* 628.3, *six* 792.2
hexagonal *polygonal* 6.79, *status adjectives* 11.25, *angled* 628.9, *sixth* 792.13
hexagonal close-packed *status adjectives* 11.25
hexagonal close packing *crystal* 11.14
hexagonal crystal *crystal* 8.39, 11.14
hexagram *polygon* 6.42, *angled figure* 628.3, *six* 792.2
hexagrammoid *angled* 628.9
hexahedral *cubic* 6.81, *sixth* 792.13
hexahedron *polyhedron* 6.44, *six* 792.2
hexameter *meter* 139.10, *six* 792.2
hexane *fuels* 106.2
hexangular *sixth* 792.13
hexapod *six* 792.2
Hexapoda *insect* 40.1
hexastich *part of poem* 139.9
Hexateuch *six* 792.2
hexatonic *sixth* 792.13
hexavalent *chemical compound* 11.4
hexed *bewitched* 86.21, *cursed* 301.8
hexentric nut (hex) *climbing equipment* 161.4
hexose *saccharide* 12.4
heyday *youth* 26.1, *time of plenty* 847.3
hi *cry of greeting* 239.4
hi! *hello!* 704.23
hiatus *intervening space* 563.8, *interval* 587.1, *omission* 762.4, *gap* 775.4
hibachi *cooker* 91.5
hibernal *seasonal* 654.7
hibernate *sleep* 415.14, *spend the season* 654.10, *be latent* 844.12
hibernating *not awake* 415.12, *inert* 519.2, *latent* 844.6
hibernation *sleep* 415.5, *inertness* 519.1, *winter* 654.6, *latency* 844.1
hibernator *sleeper* 415.7
Hibernicism *regional pronunciation* 205.7
hibiscus Flowers 42
hiccup *be drunk* 121.34, *belch* 556.5, 709.8, *eructate* 709.28
hiccup [Inf] *technical problem* 826.3
hiccupping *slightly drunk* 121.26, *eructative* 709.13
hiccups *drunken behavior* 121.4
hic jacet [L] *funeral object* 31.6
hick *countryman* 61.8, *commoner* 71.1, *unskilled person* 128.3, *urban* 567.14, *insignificant* 745.6, *naive person* 821.2
hickey [Inf] *mark* 533.2
hickory Trees and Shrubs 43
hick town *village* 567.3
Hidalgo Planets and Their Satellites 7
hidden 243.15; *concealed* 181.8, 844.7, *mysterious* 182.10, *private* 245.5, *disappeared* 265.4, *unintelligible* 364.4, *unrecognizable* 364.7, *fugitive* 386.10, *secluded* 409.9, *secret* 611.13, *protected* 613.20
hidden away *concealed* 844.7
hidden cause *contributory cause* 675.3
hidden cost(s) *cost(s)* 491.3

hidden crevasse *climbing dangers* 161.5
hidden danger 813.3
hidden depths *latency* 844.1
hidden fires *latency* 844.1
hidden hand *indirect influence* 512.4, *backstage manipulator* 844.3
hidden income *reward for service* 453.5
hidden influence *indirect influence* 512.4
hidden meaning *type of meaning* 361.4, *mysteriousness* 844.5
hidden panel *means of escape* 816.4
hidden power *authority* 52.1
hidden treasure Children's and Party Games 167
hide 613.27, 844.13; *occult* 86.22, *leather* 104.7, *bury* 105.22, *conceal* 181.12, *conceal oneself* 181.15, *keep secret* 182.11, *become invisible* 245.6, *make invisible* 245.7, *disappear* 265.5, *cause to disappear* 265.7, *evade* 386.19, *animal products* 522.7, *keep inside* 611.17, *animal covering* 613.15, *be aloof* 756.8, *be safe* 810.20, *protect* 810.21, *preserve* 815.4, *elude* 816.10, *be cunning* 822.5
hide [Inf] *hit* 454.28
hide-and-seek Children's and Party Games 167
hideaway *retreat* 60.13, *hiding place* 181.2, *shelter* 613.6
hide away *conceal* 181.12, *make invisible* 245.7, *protect* 810.21
hide behind the skirts of *shelter* 812.8
hidebound *unjust* 342.7, *unyielding* 379.8
hideboundness *formality* 406.1
hide in sight Children's and Party Games 167
hide one's abilities *be infertile* 23.8
hide one's light under a bushel *be infertile* 23.8, *escape notice* 403.14
hideosity *ugliness* 531.1
hideous *frightening* 283.12, *ugly* 531.3, *deformed* 627.7, *repulsive* 701.4
hideously 531.6; *frighteningly* 283.20, *asymmetrically* 627.13, *repulsively* 701.11
hideousness *ugliness* 531.1, *distortion of body* 627.3
hideout *hiding place* 181.2, *solitary place* 409.4, *shelter* 613.6, 812.4
hide out *conceal oneself* 181.15
hider *one who conceals* 181.7, *cunning person* 822.3
hide the thimble Children's and Party Games 167
hide under a bushel *make invisible* 245.7
hidey-hole [Inf] *hiding place* 181.2, *that which makes invisible* 245.2, *shelter* 812.4
hiding *concealment* 181.1, 844.2, *secrecy* 182.1, *blinding* 243.13, *invisibility* 245.1, *blacking out* 265.2, *disappearing* 265.3, *evasion* 386.5, *fugitive* 386.10, *covering* 613.1, *ramming* 695.3, *concealed* 844.7, *victory* 845.4, *defeat* 846.7
hiding [Inf] *corporal punishment* 454.11
hiding place 181.2; *that which makes invisible* 245.2, *solitary place* 409.4, *shelter* 613.6, 812.4
hie *be swift* 694.10

hierarch *priest* 84.8
hierarchic *ranked* 739.6
hierarchical 765.12; *priestly* 84.12, *ranked* 739.6, *categorical* 767.16, *sequential* 770.7, *classificatory* 777.9
hierarchical database *database* 15.15
hierarchically *differentially* 739.9, *in order* 765.26, *taxonomically* 777.15
hierarchy 765.3; *theocracy* 49.4, *rank* 739.2, *categorization* 767.5, *sequence* 770.1, *classification* 777.2
hierarchy of authority *social stratification* 2.7
hieratic *priestly* 84.12
hierocracy *theocracy* 49.4, *priesthood* 84.2
hierocratic *priestly* 84.12
hierocratically *clerically* 84.17
hieroglyphic *or* **hieroglyph** *written letter* 5.14, *symbol* 183.3, *representation* 187.1
hieroglyphical *written* 5.36, *representational* 187.8
hieroglyphically *linguistically* 5.44
hieroglyphics *puzzle* 182.5
hierographical *theological* 81.24
hierography Theologies 81
hierological *theological* 81.24
hierology Theologies 81
hieromancer *diviner* 86.14
hieromonach *religious* 84.9
hierophant *priest* 84.8, *ritualist* 85.14
hierophantic *priestly* 84.12
hierophantically *clerically* 84.17
hierophobia Phobias 283
hifalutin [Inf] *arrogant* 297.9, *lofty* 404.15
hifalutin ways [Inf] *airs* 404.2
hi-fi system *radio reception* 172.2
higgle *bargain* 480.20
higgledy-piggledy *indiscriminate* 338.8, *inconsistently* 732.16, *mixed up* 751.11, *mixedly* 751.16, *muddled* 766.13, *anyhow* 766.25
higgling *bargaining* 480.10
high 596.7, 596.20; *weather system* 9.10, *windy* 9.42, *fast* 166.23, *unpalatable* 223.6, *putrid* 227.4, *shrill* 238.6, *rejoicing* 279.4, *spacious* 563.13, *mountainous* 569.5, *of landmasses* 572.12, *long* 590.6, *quantitative* 738.6, *important* 799.7
high [Inf] *wasted* 96.14, *drunk* 121.25, *drugged* 121.30, *pleased* 214.9, *cheerful* 269.7
high achiever *doer* 412.3
high-altitude *mountaineering* 161.9
high-altitude wind *wind* 9.12
high and dry *dry* 560.7, *stable* 674.3
high and low *extensively* 563.18, *completely* 759.14
high-and-mightiness *airs* 404.2
high-and-mighty *arrogant* 297.9, *lofty* 404.15
high approval *importance* 799.1
high as a kite [Inf] *drugged* 121.30, *joyful* 269.6
high as a steeple *high* 596.7
highball *mixed drink* 93.12, *drink* 121.6, *track* 688.2
highball it [Inf] *run* 694.13
high-beam headlight *safety light* 246.7
high birthrate *productiveness* 22.3
high blood pressure *symptom* 114.3, *cardiovascular disease* 114.13

high boots *boots* 100.31
high-born *aristocratic* 70.4
highboy *cabinet* 101.8
highbrow *sage* 4.11, *educated* 48.19, *educational leader* 68.11, *intellectual* 315.7, *knowledgeable person* 348.5, *literate* 348.8, *wise* 352.4
high buildings Phobias 283
high caliber *superiority* 744.1
high-calorie *edible* 92.20
high camp *comedy* 136.11
high-caste *aristocratic* 70.4
high casualties *slaughter* 30.5
highchair *type of chair* 101.4
High Church *Christianity* 81.5
High-Church *denominational* 81.23
high-class *aristocratic* 70.4, *excellent* 445.1
high cloud *cloud* 9.17
high collar *neckwear* 100.29
high color *redness* 257.1
high-colored *colorful* 251.11
high comedy *comedy* 136.11
high command, the *governance* 52.6
high commissioner [Brit] *leader* 68.3
high-cost *costly* 496.7
high country *mountain* 569.1, *upland* 572.7
high court *law court* 54.8
high-definition *clear* 244.6
high-definition television (HDTV) *television (TV)* 172.5
high-density *crowded* 795.10
high dive *diving* 164.6
high dudgeon *resentment* 302.1
high endeavor *venture* 390.2
high-energy physics Fields of Modern Physics 10
high-energy radiation *radioactivity* 10.58
higher 596.8, 596.21; *ranked* 6.72, *superior* 744.8
higher criticism *criticism* 365.3
higher education *educational system* 48.8
higher jump *advance* 467.3
higher mathematics *mathematics* 6.1
higher position *priority* 769.2
higher rank *priority* 769.2
higher-ups [Inf] *governance* 52.6, *the power structure* 68.12, *management board* 126.2
highest *ranked* 6.72, *higher* 596.8, *top* 600.6, *unique* 744.11
highest bidder *purchaser* 481.7
highest common factor (HCF) *multiplication* 6.15
highest degree or **level** *summit* 600.1
highest point *summit* 600.1
highest point or **degree** *limit* 761.4
highest state *summit* 600.1
high executioner *punisher* 454.16
high explosive *explosive* 78.13
highfalutin [Inf] *arrogant* 297.9, *lofty* 404.15
highfalutin ways [Inf] *airs* 404.2
high fashion *dressing* 100.2, *fashion* 536.1, *trendiness* 652.2
high-fiber *health-giving* 113.6
high-fiber food *food* 90.1
high-fidelity or **hi-fi** *sounding* 230.7
high-fidelity or **hi-fi system** *sound reproduction* 230.6
high finance *finance* 457.1
high-five *applause* 279.2, *fete* 279.6

highflier *doer* 412.3, *superior person* 445.7, *paragon* 744.6
high-flown *arrogant* 297.9, *imaginative* 360.10, *promoted* 715.8
highflying *arrogant* 297.9
Highgate London 567.8
high-geared *swift* 694.6
high-grade rock *metamorphic rock* 8.36
high ground *summit* 744.4
high-handed *authoritative* 52.9, 425.8, *arrogant* 297.9, *severe* 424.5
high-handedly *authoritatively* 52.18, *arrogantly* 297.18, *severely* 424.11, *commandingly* 425.15
high hat *hat* 100.32
high-hat cymbals Musical Instruments 142
high-hatter *proud person* 297.7
high heels *shoes* 100.30
High Holy Days Jewish Holy Days and Seasons 85
high hopes *aspiration* 281.3
high income *wealth* 485.1
high-inside *fencing movements* 153.3, *fencing* 153.6, *on guard* 153.8
high interest *interest* 488.4
high IQ (intelligence quotient) *intelligence* 352.2
high jinks *celebration* 405.1
high jump or **jumping** *jumping* 166.11
high jumping Sporting Activities 145
high key *composition* 132.17
high-kicker *dancer* 135.4
Highland Breeds of Cattle 16
highland 596.11; *regional* 564.12, *upland* 572.7, *of landmasses* 572.12, *heights* 596.4, *incline* 713.3
Highland fling Dances 135
Highland pony Horse and Pony Breeds 159
Highlands *regions of the British Isles* 564.8, Mountains and Hills 569
highlands *moon* 7.18, *regions* 564.2, *mountain* 569.1, *heights* 596.4
high level *managerial* 126.9
high-level *head* 600.7, *important* 799.7
high-level bombing *air attack* 418.4
high-level language *programming language* 15.16
high-level talks *debate* 210.3, *discussion* 460.2
high-level waste *nuclear problem* 10.62
highlife *self-indulgence* 456.1
highlight 246.12; *publicize* 173.18, *signify* 183.16, *emphasize* 200.6, *make visible* 244.9, *light* 246.19, *present* 264.15, *choose* 382.14, *coif* 530.15, *essential content* 723.2, *chief thing* 799.3, *make important* 799.14, *manifestation* 843.2, *reveal* 843.14
highlighted *emphasized* 200.4, *clear* 244.6, *lit* 246.16, *beautified* 530.12, *accentuated* 843.11
highlighter *that which makes visible* 244.4
highlights *composition* 132.17
high liver [Inf] *self-indulgent person* 456.5
high-living *self-indulgent* 456.6
high-low-jack Card Games 168
highly 715.16; *wholely* 738.9
highly colored *exaggerated* 194.7,

descriptive 202.11, *intelligible* 363.5
highly considered *respected* 435.10
highly flavored *piquant* 221.6, *strong to the senses* 516.12
highly qualified *skillful* 127.10, *expert* 127.12
highly regarded *respected* 435.10
highly seasoned *piquant* 221.6, *strong to the senses* 516.12
highly strung *oversensitive* 267.4, *fearful* 283.10
highly thought of *reputable* 370.3, *respected* 435.10
High Mass Eucharist 85.7
high-minded *dignified* 297.11, *moral* 431.9, *unselfish* 443.5
high-mindedly *with dignity* 297.20, *unselfishly* 443.9
high-mindedness *unselfishness* 443.2
high-muck-a-muck *celebrity* 799.5
high-muck-a-mucks *management board* 126.2
highness *longness* 590.3, *height* 596.1
high noon *noon* 655.4
high-noon *daily* 655.6
high note *tone* 140.24, *shrillness* 238.7
high-octane *gas* 106.14
high-octane gas *petroleum* 562.5
high office *position of authority* 52.4
high off or **on the hog** *wealthily* 485.16
high opinion *respect* 435.1
high-outside *fencing movements* 153.3, *fencing* 153.6, *on guard* 153.8
high-performance liquid chromatography (HPLC) *analysis* 11.17
high pitch *tone* 140.24, *shrillness* 238.7
high-pitched *shrill* 238.6
high places Phobias 283
highpockets [Inf] *big person* 579.10, *tall person* 596.6
high point *essential content* 723.2, *chief thing* 799.3
high post *playing terms* 148.4
high-powered *hunting* 160.11, *strong* 516.9
high-powered rifle *hunting equipment* 160.4
high-pressure *authoritative* 52.9, *compelling* 428.6
high-pressure area *weather system* 9.10
high-pressure worker *hard worker* 414.11
high price *costliness* 496.1
high-price *costly* 496.7
high-priced *costly* 496.7, 500.6
high priest *religious leader* 68.9, *priest* 84.8, *leader* 126.8
high-principled *right* 429.7, *principled* 447.6
high principles *virtues* 447.2
high priority *important* 799.7
high productivity *productiveness* 22.3
high profile *clarity* 244.2
high-profile *clear* 244.6
high quality *excellence* 445.4
high ranking *notable* 799.11
high rate *fee* 494.3
high regard *admiration* 435.2
high relief *relief carving* 144.2, *that which makes visible* 244.4

High Renaissance style Architectural Styles 134
high resolution *separation* 753.1
high-resolution *separable* 753.11
high-rise *manorial* 60.21, *architectural structure* 134.4, *high* 596.7
high-rise apartments or **flats** [Brit] *apartment house* 60.8
high-rise building *building* 551.9
high road, the *easy thing* 823.6
high roller [Inf] *gambler* 167.6, *spendthrift* 500.3
high school *school* 48.11
high school football *football* 155.1
high seas *sea* 571.1
high sign *symbol* 183.3
high society *aristocracy* 70.2, *society* 408.8, *fashionable elite* 536.4
high-sounding *loud* 232.6
high-speed *swift* 694.6
high-speed chairlift *ski run* 162.2
high-speed steel *machine tool* 14.9
high-spirited *proud* 297.10, *conditional* 725.7
high spirits *joy* 269.1, *energy* 414.4, *state of mind* 725.5
high standard of living *prosperity* 847.1
high standing *respect* 435.1, *importance* 799.1
high-stepper *racehorse* 159.2
highstick *play field hockey* 158.10
highsticking *ice hockey tactics* 158.4, *field hockey tactics* 158.5
high street [Brit] *urban area* 567.10
high-street [Brit] *urban* 567.14
high-strung *touchy* 303.10
high summer *summer* 654.4
hightail [Inf] *hurry off* 705.11
high tar *tobacco* 121.23
high-tar *tobacco* 121.33
high tax bracket *wealth* 485.1
high tea *social gathering* 408.4
high tea [Brit] *meal* 92.8
high tech *means* 102.1
high-tech *productive* 522.11
high technology *means* 102.1, *manufacture* 522.2
high-technology *productive* 522.11
high-tech war *warfare* 76.3
high temperature *symptom* 114.3, *heat* 217.1
high temperatures Fields of Measurement 589
high-temperature superconductor *superconductivity* 10.35
high-tensile steel *shipbuilding* 690.4
high-test gas *petroleum* 562.5
high tide *tide* 8.17, 571.2
high-top fade *coiffure* 530.8
high tragedy *tragedy* 136.10
high treason *subversion* 427.3
high turnout *throng* 795.4
high up *high* 596.7, 596.20
high vacuum *surface chemistry* 11.20
high value *value* 496.6
high-value *valuable* 496.8
high-velocity *swift* 694.6
high volume *loudness* 232.1
high water *tide* 571.2
high-water mark *measuring instrument* 589.12, *limit marker* 620.4
highway *road* 687.2, 691.4, *thoroughfare* 692.6, *means of connection* 754.4

highway bridge *bridge* 551.10
highwayman *thief* 479.8
highway patrol *law enforcement agency* 53.7
highway restaurant *eating place* 92.17, *stopping place* 668.4
highway robber *thief* 479.8
highway robbery [Inf] *overpricing* 496.2
highway sign *sign* 183.1, *indicator* 183.7
high wind *wind strength* 9.13
high-wire artist *circus performer* 138.9
high-yielding *productive* 22.9, 522.11
HII region *interstellar matter* 7.7
hijack *take away forcefully* 477.19, *steal* 479.14
hijacked *stolen* 479.12
hijacker *coercer* 428.4, *raider* 477.10, *thief* 479.8
hijacking *stealing* 479.1, *stolen* 479.12
hike *increase* 581.16, *raise* 715.9
hiked *increased* 746.5
hiked up *raised* 715.6
hike up *increase* 581.16, *erect* 715.11, *intensify* 746.8
hiking Sporting Activities 145, Hobbies and Pastimes 167, *increase* 581.3
hiking boots *boots* 100.31
hiking trail *passage* 691.5
hiking up *raising* 715.1
hilarious *humorous* 277.9, *ridiculous* 368.5
hilariously *humorously* 277.13, *funnily* 368.10
hilarity *amusement* 277.2, *laughter* 277.8
Hilbert space Mathematical Concepts 6
Hilbert's problems Mathematical Concepts 6
Hill, the *the power structure* 68.12
hill 569.2; *landform* 8.9, Collective Names 59, *obliquity* 628.2, *dome* 634.4, *incline* 713.3, *inclination* 714.6
hillbilly [Off] *countryman* 61.8, *commoner* 71.1, *naive person* 821.2
hillbilly music *folk music* 140.7
hill climbing *automobile racing* 146.1
hill farm *farm* 16.2
hill farmer *agriculturist* 16.14
hill fog *fog* 9.32
hill mist *mist* 9.33
hillock *hill* 569.2, *lowlands* 597.6, *dome* 634.4
hillside *hill* 569.2, *heights* 596.4, *side* 623.1
hilltop *hill* 569.2, *heights* 596.4, *summit* 600.1
hilly 569.6; *oblique* 628.8
hilum *seed* 41.9
him *male* 32.1
Himalayan colorpoint Breeds of Cats 35
Himalayan hybrids Breeds of Cats 35
Himalayas Mountains and Hills 569
Himalia Planets and Their Satellites 7
himation [Arch] *robe* 100.20
himself *male* 32.1
hind *female animal* 33.15, *female mammal* 35.19, *back* 622.6
hind end [Inf] *rear end* 622.4
hinder 826.15; *be insufficient* 98.9, *thwart* 293.10, *oppose* 375.13, *avert* 386.15, *resist* 417.10, *disobey*

427.12, *counteract* 510.7, *make heavy* 538.14, *obstruct* 584.13, *debar* 604.17, *limit* 620.7, *delay* 658.13, *cause to cease* 668.12, *slow down* 693.13, *disrupt* 768.12, *be useless* 802.11, *be inconvenient* 804.9, *cause difficulties* 824.22, *withstand* 828.20, *restrain* 830.12
hindered *unprovided* 98.6, *dissuaded* 179.5, *frustrated* 293.5, *excluded* 604.11, *held up* 658.6, *stopped* 668.7, *disrupted* 768.8, *hindering* 826.12
hinderer 826.11
hindering 826.12; *frustrating* 293.7, *fugitive* 386.10, *excluded* 604.11, *delaying* 658.8, *inconvenient* 804.5, *hindrance* 826.1, *uncooperative* 828.14
hindmost 773.18; *back* 622.6
hindquarters *rear end* 622.4
hindrance 826.1; *deterrence* 179.2, *frustration* 293.2, *opposition* 375.2, 828.1, *avoidance* 386.1, *obstruction* 510.3, 584.2, *debarment* 604.5, *limit* 620.1, *delay* 658.3, *stop* 668.2, *disruption* 768.4, *inconvenience* 804.1, *defect* 806.4, *snag* 824.8, *hinderer* 826.11, *restraint* 830.1
hindsight *memory* 354.1
Hindu *other religious member* 81.13, *denominational* 81.23
Hinduism *other religions* 81.8
Hindu Kush Mountains and Hills 569
Hindu text *other text* 81.19
hindward *behind* 622.8, *backward* 680.23
hinge *axle* 682.7, *joint* 752.7, *means of connection* 754.4, *fastener* 754.7, *connect* 754.13
hinged *connected* 754.11
hint *inside information* 170.4, *tip* 170.14, *communication* 176.3, *communicate* 176.10, *divulgence* 180.2, *divulge* 180.9, *impression* 266.2, *theory* 327.2, *notice* 358.3, *predict* 358.14, *basis of supposition* 359.2, *propound* 359.9, *manipulate* 508.12, *little piece* 580.4, *few* 796.1, *warning* 814.1, *warn* 814.8, *quietness* 844.4, *imply* 844.14
hint at *signify* 183.16, *mean* 361.13
hinted *tacit* 844.10
hinterland *geographical space* 563.3, *region* 564.1, *countryside* 564.3, *back* 622.1
hinterland or **hinterlands** *outside* 610.3, *inland* 611.2
hinting *suppositional* 359.5, *warning* 814.6
hip *roof* 134.7, *joint* 752.7
hip [Inf] *educated* 48.19, *fashionable* 536.5
hip bath *basin* 578.12
hipbone Human Bones 19
hip boots *boots* 100.31
hip flask *drink container* 93.13, *bottle* 578.14
hip, hip, hooray *cry of praise* 239.3, *hurrah!* 279.8
hip-hop *rock music* 140.6
hiphuggers *pants* 100.14
hipped *roof* 134.7
hippie *dissenter* 347.5, *protester* 507.4, *nonconformist* 782.7, *unconventional* 782.14, *freethinker* 829.10
hippo [Inf] *big person* 579.10
Hippocratic *medical* 107.28
Hippocratic oath *medical ethics* 107.2

hippodrome *theater* 136.16
hippogriff or **hippogryph** Legendary Creatures 360
hippophobia Phobias 283
hippopotami Collective Names 59
hippopotamus *pachyderm* 35.15, *hoofed mammal* 35.16, *big thing* 579.9
hippy *fat* 579.15
hips *side* 623.1
Hirado ware Ceramics 129
hircine *ungulate* 35.31
hire *employ* 57.18, *transfer of property* 470.4, *transfer property* 470.12, *fee* 494.3, *engage* 833.9
hired 57.17; *receiving pay* 489.14
hired gun *murderer* 30.12
hired hand *servant* 69.1
hired help *servant* 69.1
hired killer *murderer* 30.12, *villain* 448.5
hired mourner *funeral person* 31.5
HI region *interstellar matter* 7.7
hireling *servant* 69.1, *inferior* 745.4
hire personnel *find means* 102.6
hire-purchase [Brit] *credit* 476.4
hirer *person transferring property* 470.8
hiring *hired* 57.17
hiring practices *bargaining terms* 57.10
hirsute *hairy* 19.20, *barbed* 544.7
hirudinean *wormlike* 39.24
hirundine *avian* 36.19
His Highness [Brit] *important person* 799.5
His Holiness *professional title* 72.6
his or **her honor** *judge* 54.10
his or **her nibs** [Inf] *proud person* 297.7, *celebrity* 799.6
Hispaniola Islands 572
Hispano Arab Horse and Pony Breeds 159
Hispano-Moresque architecture Architectural Styles 134
Hispano-Moresque art Western Art Styles 133
Hispano-Moresque ware Ceramics 129
hispid *coarse* 544.6, *barbed* 544.7, *spiked* 549.11
hispidity *roughness* 544.1
hiss 237.1, 237.3, 239.17; *radio reception* 172.2, *gesture* 183.5, 183.17, *have difficulty speaking* 206.9, *cry of disapproval* 239.7, *animal sound* 240.1, *bird sound* 240.2, *make an animal sound* 240.7, *make a bird sound* 240.8, *broadcast dissonance* 241.3, *expression of dissatisfaction* 274.2, *be dissatisfied* 274.7, *taunt* 436.6, 436.23, *show of disapproval* 438.6, *show disapproval* 438.21, *gesture of protest* 507.3, *complain* 507.8
His Satanic Majesty *devil* 446.5
hissed *criticized* 438.14
hissing 237.2, 239.12; *snakelike* 37.13, *inarticulate* 206.6, *hiss* 237.1, *ululant* 240.4, *taunting* 436.14, *protesting* 507.5
histidine Amino Acids 12
histochemistry *cell biology* 13.14
histogram *graph* 6.30, *probability distribution* 6.56
histological *biological* 13.27
histologically *biologically* 13.36
histologist *life scientist* 13.26, *anatomist* 551.16
histology 13.4; *cell biology* 13.14, *science of structure* 551.15
histone *protein* 12.9

histoplasmosis *fungal disease* 47.6
historian 3.3, 651.10; *author* 139.13, *record keeper* 185.8, *descriptive writer* 202.10, *keeper of time* 646.10
historic 3.11, 653.13; *historical* 3.10, *past* 651.11
historical 3.10; *dramatic* 137.16, *past* 651.11, *historic* 653.13, *real* 717.14, 719.6, *certain* 840.7
historical ammunition 78.12
historical documents *record* 185.1
historical event *type of painting* 143.5
historical film *movie type* 137.3
historical geology *geology* 8.1
historical gun 78.10
historical handgun 78.8
historical linguistics Linguistic Studies 5
historically 3.17; *archaically* 653.20
historical map *map* 187.5
historical materialism *types of history* 3.2
historical method *historicism* 3.7
historical methodology *history* 3.1
historical monument *conservation* 815.2
historicalness 3.9
historical novel *novel* 139.3
historical painter *painter* 143.7
historical past 651.6
historical present *grammatical term* 5.29, *present time* 647.1, *past tense* 651.2
historical preservation *conservation* 815.2
historical property terms 470.3
historical record *record* 185.1
historical soldier 77.8
historical tax 494.8
historical warships 77.22
historic armor 419.8
historic building *antiquity* 653.4
historic comedy 136.12
historic fencing *fencing* 153.1
historicism 3.7
historicity *historicalness* 3.9, *demonstrable existence* 717.5, *realism* 719.3, *certainty* 840.1
historiographer *historian* 3.3, *author* 139.13, *descriptive writer* 202.10, *keeper of time* 646.10
historiographical *historical* 3.10, *narrative* 139.18
historiography *history* 3.1, *nonfiction* 139.6
history 3.1; *chronicle* 3.4, *past time* 3.6, 651.1, *life story* 28.11, *nonfiction* 139.6, *record* 185.1, *authorization* 340.4, *retrospect* 354.2, *conduct* 399.1, *chronology* 646.2, *study of the past* 651.9
history of ideas *types of history* 3.2
history of illness 114.2
history of mathematics *types of history* 3.2
history of science *types of history* 3.2
history painting Western Art Styles 133
histricomorph *gnawing mammal* 35.13
histrionic *dramatic* 136.31, 404.16, *exaggerated* 194.7, *demonstrative* 331.10, *affected* 367.3
histrionically *dramatically* 136.38, 404.31, *exaggeratedly* 194.16, *demonstratively* 331.21, *showily* 367.6

histrionic art *drama* 136.1
histrionic personality disorder *personality disorder* 108.7
histrionics *drama* 136.1, *dramaturgy* 136.6, *acting* 136.22, *exaggeration* 194.1, *demonstrativeness* 331.2, *affectation* 367.1, *dramatics* 404.3
hit 418.9, 454.28, 695.11; *fight* 77.35, *workmanlike job* 127.6, *theatrical performance* 136.13, *popular music* 140.4, *batting terms* 147.6, *play baseball* 147.9, *grip* 151.4, *combat* 152.17, *fencing movements* 153.3, *fence* 153.7, *play* 156.8, *play ice hockey* 158.9, *painful injury* 215.3, *inflict pain* 215.10, *type of touch* 216.3, *touch* 216.9, *react against* 291.15, *strike* 418.21, *good thing* 445.9, *corporal punishment* 454.11, *use violence* 520.9, *meet* 586.15, *blow* 695.5, *shoot* 696.18, *arrive* 704.13, *successfulness* 845.3, *successful thing* 845.5, *successful person* 845.6
hit [Inf] *drug dose* 121.15
hit a double *play baseball* 147.9
hit a fly *play baseball* 147.9
hit a grand-slam home run *play baseball* 147.9
hit a grand-slammer *play baseball* 147.9
hit a grounder *play baseball* 147.9
hit a home run or **homer** *play baseball* 147.9
hit a line drive *play baseball* 147.9
hit a mental block *lack thought* 318.12
hit-and-run accident *miscellaneous automotive terms* 687.14
hit-and-run play *batting terms* 147.6
hit a receiver *play offense* 155.18
hit a shot *play basketball* 148.7
hit a single *play baseball* 147.9
hit a slalom pole *ski* 162.35
hit a snag *have a mishap* 826.18
hit a straight *be on the track* 146.11
hit a streak of luck *be fortunate* 847.7
hit a triple *play baseball* 147.9
hit a wrong or **sour note** or **clinker** [Inf] *be dissonant* 241.6
hit back *retaliate* 420.4
hit below the belt *box* 152.19, *do wrong* 430.20
hit bottom *despair* 270.8, *underlie* 597.23, 601.11
hitch *practice livestock farming* 16.20, *frustration* 293.2, *stop* 668.2, *jerk* 699.3, *pull at* 699.12, *joint* 752.7, *link* 752.18, *snag* 824.8, *obstacle* 826.2
hitch and hike *oscillate* 683.12
hitched *tied* 752.13
hitched [Inf] *married* 64.16
hitchhiker *miscellaneous automotive terms* 687.14
hitchkick technique *jumping* 166.11
hitch to *add* 748.11
hitch up to *add* 748.11
hit hard *be full of vigor* 518.4
hit hard times *be in difficulty* 824.19
hitherto *historically* 3.17, *before now* 651.21
hit-in *field hockey tactics* 158.5
hit into a double play *play baseball* 147.9
hit it *attain one's goal* 845.13
hit it big *be important* 799.13

hit it off *attain one's goal* 845.13
hit it off [Inf] *agree with* 462.10
hit man [Inf] *murderer* 30.12, *combatant* 77.1, *villain* 448.5, *punisher* 454.16, *destroyer* 523.6
hit one *have an idea* 327.13
hit one in the eye *be visible* 244.7
hit or miss *inaccuracy* 351.3
hit-or-miss *imprudent* 286.7, *careless* 324.8, *irregular* 766.10, *chance* 842.10
hit over the head *club* 695.15
hit rock bottom *not exist* 786.6, *be in trouble* 848.13
hit someone up [Inf] *borrow* 476.10
hitter *baseball team* 147.2
hit the batter *play baseball* 147.9
hit the big time [Inf] *be prosperous* 847.6
hit the bottle *get drunk* 121.35
hit the crossbar *kick* 155.20
hit the groove *be on the track* 146.11
hit the headlines *be published* 173.19
hit the jackpot *get rich* 485.13
hit the jackpot [Inf] *win an award* 467.23, *attain one's goal* 845.13
hit the mark *attain one's goal* 845.13
hit the nail on the head *be accurate* 350.5, 721.22
hit the news *be published* 173.19
hit the road [Inf] *conceal oneself* 181.15, *set out* 705.12, *start off* 771.27
hit the roof or **ceiling** [Inf] *feel deeply* 266.16, *become angry* 302.20
hit the shops [Inf] *shop* 481.15
hit the skids [Inf] *become inferior* 745.11, *deteriorate* 808.14, *be in trouble* 848.13
hit the spot [Inf] *be convenient* 803.5
hit the streets *be published* 173.19
hit the target *bomb* 418.19, *reach* 704.14
hitting *combat* 152.17, *field hockey tactics* 158.5, *corporal punishment* 454.11
hitting below the belt *boxing techniques* 152.5
hitting on *locating* 565.3
hitting the bottle [Inf] *substance abuse* 121.1
hitting up [Inf] *drug use* 121.9, *borrowing* 476.1, *taking* 477.1
Hittite architecture *Architectural Styles* 134
hit tune *popular music* 140.4
hit up [Inf] *take* 477.14
hit upon *discover* 345.11, *reach* 704.14, *chance upon* 842.13
hit upon or *on* *find* 565.11
HIV-carrier *infectious person* 114.9
hive *dwelling* 40.7, *Collective Names* 59, *business* 414.6, *throng* 795.4, *shelter* 812.4
hive of activity *business* 414.6
hive off [Brit] *disperse* 776.12
hive of industry *industrial area* 124.14, *business* 414.6
hives *skin disease* 114.16
hiya! [Inf] *hello!* 704.23
Hizen porcelain *Ceramics* 129
hoagie *sandwich* 90.9
hoar *frost* 9.25, *frozen* 218.10, *white thing* 253.4, *gray-haired* 255.7
hoard 501.6; *assemblage* 59.13, *assemble* 59.23, *store* 105.1, 105.17, *acquisition* 467.4, *acquire*

467.19, *buy in* 481.13, *protect* 810.21
hoarded *collected* 59.19, *stored* 105.14
hoarder *collector* 59.17, *gainer* 467.9, *purchaser* 481.7, *miser* 501.3
hoar frost *frost* 9.25, *ice* 218.5
hoarily *maturely* 27.18
hoariness *old age* 27.5, *whiteness* 253.1, *elderliness* 653.2
hoarse 238.5; *voiceless* 206.5, *nonresonant* 233.7, *dissonant* 241.4
hoarsely *voicelessly* 206.11, *dissonantly* 241.7
hoarseness 238.2; *symptom* 114.3, *speech difficulty* 206.1, *undercurrent of sound* 233.3, *dissonance* 241.1
hoary *aged* 27.15, *whitened* 253.8, *gray-haired* 255.7, *old* 653.10
hoax 193.7, 193.20; *false alarm* 814.4
hoaxer 193.11
Hobbesean *Philosophical Schools of Thought* 4
Hobbism *Philosophical Schools of Thought* 4, *political and economic philosophy* 4.6
hobbit *Legendary Creatures* 360, *little person* 580.5
hobble *ruin* 523.15, *slow motion* 693.3, *move slowly* 693.11, *intertwine* 752.19, *hinder* 826.15, *means of restraint* 830.6, *restrain someone* 830.17
hobble [Arch] *predicament* 824.5
hobble skirt *skirt* 100.12
hobbling *ill* 517.8, *slow* 693.7, *physical deterioration* 808.4
hobby *amusement* 167.7, *likes* 290.3, *activity* 385.4, *social activity* 414.2
hobbyhorse *oscillator* 683.7
hobgoblin *sprite* 86.12, *frightener* 283.7
hobnail boots *boots* 100.31
hobnob *keep company with* 794.17
hobnobbing *sociability* 408.1
hobnob with *be friends* 62.9
hobo *nonworker* 415.4, *poor person* 486.6, *beggar* 505.6
Hobson's choice *necessitation* 95.5, *difficult question* 333.4, *choice* 382.3, *compulsion* 428.1
hock *pork* 90.26, *borrow* 476.10
hocked *guaranteed* 464.6
hockey 158.1; *athletics* 422.7
hockey areas 158.2
hockey ball *hockey equipment* 158.3
hockey clothing 158.6
hockey equipment 158.3
hockey organizations 158.7
hockey player 158.8
hockey season *seasons* 654.2
hockey skates *hockey clothing* 158.6
hockey stick *hockey equipment* 158.3, *impeller* 695.7
hockey stop *skiing techniques* 162.5
hockey team *hockey player* 158.8
hocking *lending* 475.1, *borrowing* 476.1
hockshop *lending institution* 475.4
hocus-pocus *spell* 86.8, *nonsense* 362.2
Hoder *Deities* 82
hodgepodge *miscellany* 59.15, 751.3, *variety* 732.2, *confusion* 766.4

Hodgkin's disease *blood disease* 114.14
hodophobia *Phobias* 283
hoe *farm* 16.19, *garden tool* 17.7, 103.4, *cultivate* 17.19, *cleaning tool* 111.10
hoed *ornamental* 17.17
hoedown *dance* 135.1, *party* 408.6
hoeing *cultivation* 16.7
Hoenir *Deities* 82
hoe one's own row *be one* 788.17
hog *livestock* 16.11, *male animal* 32.15, *eater* 92.15, *glutton* 119.2, *selfish person* 444.3, *be selfish* 444.6, *possess* 469.14
hogan *house* 60.4
hogback *mountain range* 569.3
hog cholera *animal disease* 34.10
Hoggar Mountains *Mountains and Hills* 569
hoggish *ungulate* 35.31, *unclean* 112.8, *gluttonous* 119.3, *selfish* 444.4
hoggishly *gluttonously* 119.5
hoggishness *gluttony* 119.1
hogherd *farm worker* 16.15
hogs *Collective Names* 59
hogshead *vessel* 578.11, *General Units* 589
hog the limelight *show off* 404.26
hog wallow *swill* 112.6
hogwash *swill* 112.6, *nonsense* 192.8
ho-hum *boring* 296.6
hoi polloi *group* 18.13, *common people* 71.2, *business* 414.6, *vulgar group* 535.5, *inferior* 745.4, *general public* 778.6
hoist *construction equipment* 14.23, *engineer* 14.48, *handle sailboat equipment* 150.30, *flag* 184.8, *heighten* 596.14, *raising* 715.1, *lifter* 715.5, *raise* 715.9
hoisted *raised* 715.6
hoisting one's flag over *claiming* 469.2
hoist the blue peter *set out* 705.12
hoity-toity *arrogant* 297.9
hoke *talk nonsense* 192.26
hokey *unauthentic* 722.9, *imitation* 736.8
hokeyness *unauthenticity* 722.4
hokiness *unauthenticity* 722.4
Hokkaido *Islands* 572
hokum *nonsense* 192.8, *senseless talk* 362.4
Holando-Argentina *Breeds of Cattle* 16
Holborn *London* 567.8
hold *governance* 52.6, *arrest* 55.12, *believe* 87.9, *storeroom* 105.7, *drug oneself* 121.37, *exhibit penalty behavior* 155.21, *exercise* 157.12, *field hockey tactics* 158.5, *play field hockey* 158.10, *rock face* 161.6, *ice-dancing move* 162.19, *play soccer* 163.8, *touch* 216.9, *feel* 266.14, *state* 329.13, *understand* 363.9, *possession* 469.1, *possess* 469.14, *retention* 471.1, *take away forcefully* 477.19, *influence* 512.1, *indirect influence* 512.4, *extend* 563.14, *contain* 577.10, *support* 605.16, *delay* 658.13, *cause to cease* 668.12, *be stable* 674.6, *pilot* 689.15, *continue to be* 717.20, *adhere* 755.8, *include* 770.3, *preserve* 815.14, *detain* 830.16
hold [Inf] *drug oneself* 121.37
hold a boxing match *box* 152.19
hold a brief for *plead for* 419.25, *advise* 825.27

hold a charity event *solicit money* 505.13

hold a clearance sale *sell off* 482.20

hold a conference *confer* 210.13, *negotiate* 460.6

hold a conversation *converse* 210.11

hold a council *confer* 210.13

hold a course *navigate* 690.15

hold a court case *accuse* 442.8

hold a demonstration *be insubordinate* 416.8

hold a dialogue *summit* 600.11

hold a directorship *master* 68.17

hold a finger to the wind *test* 390.9

hold a fire sale *sell off* 482.20

hold against one's will *arrest* 55.12

hold a going-out-of-business sale *sell off* 482.20

hold a grudge *hate* 300.11, *resent* 302.13

hold a heading *aim* 697.14

hold a high opinion of *respect* 435.13

holdall *baggage* 578.8

hold all the aces *be an influence* 512.13, *overtake* 744.16

hold all the cards *be an influence* 512.13, *overtake* 744.16

hold all the trumps *do easily* 823.16

hold a meeting *call together* 59.28

hold an advantage *be ahead* 744.17

hold an open house *be sociable* 408.14

hold an opinion *propound a philosophy* 4.21

hold apart *divide* 753.18, *come between* 753.21

hold a point of view *have an idea* 317.12

hold a position *exercise* 157.12

hold a protest meeting *cause mischief* 507.9

hold a responsible position *direct* 126.11

hold a sale *sell off* 482.20

hold a séance *or* sitting *conjure* 86.26

hold a sit-in *be insubordinate* 416.8

hold a subordinate position *be subject to* 832.12

hold a summit *confer* 210.13, *negotiate* 460.6

hold a summit meeting *summit* 600.11

hold a symposium *dissertate* 203.5

hold at bay *parry* 419.27, *limit* 830.13

hold a trial *accuse* 442.8

hold a wake *pay one's last respects* 31.12

hold a wrestling match *wrestle* 152.20

hold back *deter* 179.8, *doubt* 287.13, *delay* 375.16, 658.13, *abstain* 386.16, *compel* 428.8, *be self-restrained* 455.10, *detain* 471.9, *defer* 604.15, *limit* 620.7, *pause* 668.13, *slow down* 693.13, *hinder* 826.15, *restrain* 830.12, *restrain oneself* 830.15, *hesitate* 841.18

hold captive *or* hostage *arrest* 55.12

hold center stage *be visible* 843.16

hold cheap *underestimate* 344.5,

disrespect 436.18, *think unimportant* 800.19

hold court *judge* 54.31

hold dear *like* 290.8, *love* 299.21, *respect* 435.13

hold down *detain* 471.9, *bear down on* 716.18, *restrain* 830.12, *subject* 832.10

holder *titleholder* 72.4, *receptacle* 105.11, *special team* 155.11, *possessor* 469.10, *property owner* 470.7, *recipient* 473.5, *container* 578.1

hold exclusive rights *limit* 830.13

holdfast *plant body* 47.13, *fastener* 754.7

hold fast *touch* 216.9, *insist* 376.14, *hold out* 377.13, *adhere* 755.8

hold for *intend for* 374.11

hold for questioning *interrogate* 333.17

hold for ransom *kidnap* 479.15

hold forth *speak to* 205.19, *be talkative* 207.7, *address* 209.8, *moralize* 431.14

hold forth without interruption *monopolize the conversation* 211.5

hold hands *communicate love* 299.25, *unify* 752.15

hold in *detain* 471.9, *limit* 620.7

hold in abeyance *not use* 394.9

hold in captivity *detain* 830.16

hold in check *slow down* 693.13, *restrain* 830.12

hold in common *have joint possession* 469.15, *interface* 616.5

hold incommunicado *detain* 830.16

hold in contempt *hate* 300.11, *disdain* 400.16, *disrespect* 436.18, *scorn* 436.19, *disapprove* 438.16

hold in detention *arrest* 55.12

holding *farm* 16.2, *playing terms* 148.4, *penalty* 155.13, *ice hockey tactics* 158.4, *soccer* 163.7, *touching* 216.2, *claim* 429.3, *possession* 469.1, *possessing* 469.11, *property* 470.1, *corporate* 480.17, *plot* 564.9, *loaded* 577.8, *containing* 578.18, *flight control* 689.7, *including* 763.3

holding [Inf] *drug pushing* 121.10

holding back *detention* 471.2, *irresolute* 841.10

holding cell *prison cell* 55.3

holding company *company* 480.7

holding in *detention* 471.2

holding offside *soccer play* 163.5

holding on *retention* 471.1

holding one's own *getting well* 113.9

holdings *stock in trade* 105.2

holding splits *floor exercise* 157.4

holding the faith *religious* 81.21

holding the reins *managerial* 126.9

holding together *adhesion* 755.1

holding up *support* 605.1

hold in high esteem *respect* 435.13

hold in high regard *respect* 435.13, *admire* 437.15

hold in low esteem *disrespect* 436.18, *disapprove* 438.16

hold in low estimation *disapprove* 438.16

hold in low regard *dislike* 291.12

hold in one's arms *communicate love* 299.25

hold in one's mind *memorize* 354.11, *remember* 471.10

hold in perpetuity *perpetuate* 640.5

hold in reverence *revere* 435.14

hold in solution *dissolve* 555.23

hold in the palm of one's hand *have authority* 52.13

hold in trust *represent* 80.6

hold it against *be hostile* 63.10

hold jurisdiction over *wield authority* 52.16

hold mass executions *execute* 454.30

hold no brief for *leave alone* 413.13

hold off *avoid* 386.13, *not use* 394.9, *resist* 417.10, *parry* 419.27

hold office *govern* 49.26, *run for office* 50.10, *wield authority* 52.16, *direct* 126.11

hold off the wet *keep dry* 560.22

hold on *touch* 216.9, *retain* 471.7, *delay* 658.13, *be tenacious* 755.9

hold one back *hinder* 826.15

hold one's breath *be silent* 231.3, *be motionless* 678.7

hold oneself back *restrain oneself* 830.15

hold oneself in readiness *be prepared* 388.17

hold oneself straight *be vertical* 602.8

hold oneself up *arise* 715.15

hold one's ground *be at war* 76.32, *insist* 376.14, *show determination* 674.8

hold one's head high *be proud* 297.15

hold one's head up *arise* 715.15

hold one's horses *delay* 658.13

hold one's lead *maintain progress* 679.14

hold one's liquor *be sober* 120.8

hold one's nose *have no smell* 225.7

hold one's own *survive* 419.31, *be equal* 740.11, *withstand* 828.20

hold one's tongue *be silent* 181.16, 231.3, *keep secret* 182.11, *be voiceless* 206.8, *be taciturn* 208.7, *doubt* 287.13

hold on life *life cycle* 28.7

hold on like a bulldog *show tenaciousness* 471.8, *be tenacious* 755.9

hold on like a snapping turtle *or* snapper *show tenaciousness* 471.8

hold on to *save* 105.20, *detain* 471.9

hold opposite opinions *dissent* 732.13

hold opposite views *disagree* 463.8

hold out 377.13; *be strong* 516.14, *last* 642.6, *show determination* 674.8, *withstand* 828.20

hold out *or* fast *insist* 376.14

hold out a carrot *entice* 178.16, *influence* 508.11

hold out a hand to *advise* 825.27

hold out an incentive *offer* 504.11

hold out for *hold out* 377.13, *contend* 422.22, *bargain* 480.20

hold out hope *inspire hope* 281.14

hold out hopes *predict* 358.14

hold out hopes for *show potential* 458.14

hold out one's hand *pacify* 74.9, *gesture* 183.17, *solicit money* 505.13

hold out one's hand to *receive someone* 473.14

hold out the olive branch *pacify* 74.9

hold out the peace pipe *pacify* 74.9

hold out to the bitter end *show determination* 674.8

hold out to the last *hold out* 377.13

hold over *delay* 658.13

hold over one's head *endanger* 811.13

hold position *be on the track* 146.11

hold power *direct* 126.11

hold someone's hand *sustain* 825.25

hold someone up *steal* 479.14

hold steady *aim* 697.14

hold surgery *practice medicine* 107.32

hold sway *govern* 49.26, *have authority* 52.13, *be powerful* 514.18, *be the rule* 780.16

hold sway over *rule over* 780.13

hold talks *confer* 210.13, *negotiate* 460.6

hold the ball *play basketball* 148.7

hold the faith *be religious* 81.25

hold the fort *be a substitute* 672.6

hold the helm *navigate* 690.15

hold the lead *lead* 744.19

hold the line *delay* 658.13, *aim* 697.14

hold the purse strings *manage* 126.10, *finance* 457.7

hold the reins *govern* 49.26, *manage* 126.10, *lead* 126.12

hold the reins of government *wield authority* 52.16

hold the road *show determination* 674.8, *equalize* 740.12

hold the tiller *lead* 126.12

hold the trump hand *be ahead* 744.17

hold the upper hand *be ahead* 744.17

hold the whip hand *be an influence* 512.13

hold tight *or* fast *retain* 471.7

hold to *or* by *observe* 465.4

hold together *conform* 735.27, *unify* 752.15, *adhere* 755.8, *cause to adhere* 755.10, *work together* 827.14

hold to ransom *force* 428.10

hold true *be true* 721.20

holdup *deferment* 604.3, *delay* 658.3, *stop* 668.2, *hesitation* 693.5

hold up *bolster* 377.15, *detain* 471.9, *overcharge* 496.10, *be strong* 516.14, *lighten* 539.9, *heighten* 596.14, *defer* 604.15, *support* 605.16, *delay* 658.13, *stop* 668.10, *cause to cease* 668.12, *pause* 668.13, *be stable* 674.6, *erect* 715.11, *be true* 721.20

hold up in the wash [Inf] *be true* 721.20

holdup man *dishonest person* 479.11

hold up one's hands *capitulate* 421.6

hold up to view *disclose* 180.8

hold water *be reasonable* 319.12, *be true* 721.20

hold with *approve* 437.14

hold within *keep inside* 611.17

hold your tongue! *hush!* 231.6

hole 583.4, 583.17; *semiconductor* 10.34, *prison* 55.1, *shack* 60.10, *natural habitat* 60.16, *golf course* 156.2, *play* 156.8, *wicked place* 448.8, *little space* 580.6, *opening* 583.1, *crack* 587.2, *concave land*

635.2, *insert* 710.9, *emptiness* 718.4, *predicament* 725.3, 824.5, *separateness* 753.3, *shelter* 812.4

hole [Inf] *location* 565.1

hole conduction *semiconductor* 10.34

holed 583.12

hole-high ball *golfing terms* 156.3

hole in one *golfing terms* 156.3, *golf shots* 156.4, *successful thing* 845.5

hole-in-the-wall *little space* 580.6

hole out *golf shots* 156.4

holey *worn* 808.13

Holi *religious festival* 85.13

holiday *holy day* 85.12, *refresher* 94.2, *time off* 125.2, *pleasant thing* 271.4, *rejoicing* 279.1, *day to remember* 354.5, *celebration* 405.1, *leave of absence* 576.4, *pause* 668.3, *ease* 819.1, *time of plenty* 847.3

holidays *benefits* 57.11

holiday sale *sale* 482.2

holier than thou *innocent* 449.6

holier-than-thou *zealous* 81.22, *prideful* 297.8, *moralistic* 431.12

Holiness *professional title* 72.6

holiness *divine attribute* 82.4, *virtue* 447.1

holism Philosophical Schools of Thought 4, *whole* 759.1

holist Philosophical Schools of Thought 4

holistic *whole* 759.6

holistically *wholly* 759.11

holistic medicine *alternative medicine* 107.4, *healing art* 115.13

Holland Breeds of Fowl 16

hollandaise *sauce* 90.17

holler *cry* 239.1, *cry out* 239.13

hollow *ungenuine* 192.13, *resonant* 236.6, *meaningless* 362.7, *insufficient* 517.11, *vacant* 576.12, *opening* 583.1, *hole* 583.17, *lowlands* 597.6, *deep-sounding* 598.19, *concave land* 635.2, *concave* 635.5, *make concave* 635.7, *depression* 716.4, *unreal* 720.8, *completely* 759.14, *incomplete* 762.5

hollow-cheeked *emaciated* 595.10

hollow cheeks *emaciation* 595.2

hollow-chisel mortiser *woodworking tool* 131.6

hollowed *holed* 583.12

hollow-eyed *emaciated* 595.10, *fatigued* 820.2

hollow eyes *emaciation* 595.2

hollowly *absently* 576.18, *concavely* 635.8

hollow man *insubstantial person* 720.5

hollowness *ungenuineness* 192.2, *resonance* 236.1, *emptiness* 576.2, *concavity* 635.1, *incompleteness* 762.1

hollow out *make concave* 635.7

hollow tile *industrial ceramics* 129.6

hollow tree *hiding place* 181.2

holly Trees and Shrubs 43, *green thing* 260.4

hollyhock Flowers 42

Hollywood *motion pictures* 137.1

holm [Brit] *island* 572.2

holmium Chemical Elements and Common Allotropes 11

holm oak *or* **holly oak** Trees and Shrubs 43

Holocaust, the *slaughter* 30.5

holocaust *slaughter* 30.5, *fire* 217.8, *violence by person* 520.2, *havoc* 523.5

Holocene Epoch Geologic Time Intervals 8

holocephalan *fish* 38.5

holocrine *secretory* 24.4

holocrine gland *secretory mechanism* 24.3

holocrine secretion *secretion* 24.1

holoenzyme *enzyme* 12.11

hologram *optical element* 10.20, *image* 187.3, *highlight* 246.12, *spectacle* 264.6

hologram *or* **holograph** *stereoscopic image* 132.7

holograph *optical element* 10.20, *original* 737.2

holographic image *stereoscopic image* 132.7

holographic optical element *optical element* 10.20

holography *optical characteristic* 10.21, *photographic specialties* 132.2, *highlight* 246.12

holophrase *word* 5.17

holophrastic *of language* 5.35

holothurian *echinoderm* 39.5, *echinodermal* 39.21

holothurioid *echinodermal* 39.21

Holstein Horse and Pony Breeds 159

Holstein-Friesian *or* **Holstein** Breeds of Cattle 16

holster *ammunition* 78.11

holt [Arch] *trees* 43.4

Holtzman inkblot technique Psychological Tests 108

holy 82.19; *religious* 81.21, *virtuous* 447.5

Holy Ark *sacred object* 83.11

Holy Bible *Christian text* 81.16

Holy City *heaven* 82.15

Holy Communion *Eucharist* 85.7

holy cow! [Inf] *wonderful!* 294.20

holy day 85.12; *anniversary* 405.5

Holy Grail *objective* 374.5

Holy Joe [Inf] *member of the clergy* 84.5

holy mackerel! [Inf] *wonderful!* 294.20

holy man *religious person* 81.9

Holy Mary *deified person* 82.14

holy matrimony *marriage* 64.1

holy moly! [Inf] *wonderful!* 294.20

Holy Moses! [Inf] *wonderful!* 294.20

Holy Name Day Christian Holy Days and Seasons 85

holy of holies *shrine* 83.10, *enclosed area* 619.2, *private space* 812.2

holy orders *monasticism* 67.3, *clergy* 84.1, *Christian rite* 85.5

holy place *shrine* 83.10, *center of activity* 614.2

holy rite *Christian rite* 85.5

Holy Roller [Inf *and* Off] *religionist* 81.14

Holy Saturday Christian Holy Days and Seasons 85

holy shit! [Inf] *wonderful!* 294.20

holy smoke! [Inf] *wonderful!* 294.20

Holy Spirit *God the Holy Ghost* 82.10

holystone *cleaning agent* 111.9, *clean* 111.17

holy terror [Inf] *malefactor* 306.6, *evil person* 446.3

holy things Phobias 283

Holy Thursday Christian Holy Days and Seasons 85

Holy Trinity *trinitarian god* 82.7

holy war 76.8

holy warrior *attacker* 418.10

holy water 557.15; *sacred object* 83.11

holy wedlock *marriage* 64.1

Holy Week Christian Holy Days and Seasons 85

homage *worship* 83.1, *submission* 421.1, *obeisance* 426.3, *deference* 433.4, *admiration* 435.2, *praise* 437.3

homburg *hat* 100.32

home 60.3; *habitation* 60.2, *domestic* 60.20, *place of residence* 209.4, *charitable organization* 305.4, *native country* 566.6, *station* 601.5, *internal* 611.9, *source* 675.2, *destination* 704.6, *on arrival* 704.16, *on arrival* 704.22, *private space* 812.2, *shelter* 812.4

home again *on arrival* 704.22

home base *station* 601.5

homebody *unsocial person* 409.5

home-brew *beer* 93.10, *alcohol* 121.5

home circle *society* 408.8

homecoming *return* 680.9, 704.4

home computer *computer* 15.1

Home Counties *regions of the British Isles* 564.8

home decoration *interior decoration* 532.4

home economics 56.2; *cooking* 91.1, *management* 126.1

home farm *farm* 16.2

home free *safe* 810.16, *successful* 845.8

home furnishings *furniture* 101.1

home ground *habitat* 60.1, *native country* 566.6

homegrown food *food* 90.1

home help *domestic worker* 123.4

home in *focus* 702.11

home in on *find* 565.11, *centralize* 612.11

homeland *home* 60.3, *native country* 566.6

homeless *beggarly* 486.12, *stateless* 574.14, *changeable* 666.3, *unprosperous* 848.11

homelessness *beggary* 486.3, *adversity* 848.1

homeless person *poor person* 486.6, *displaced person* 574.7, *person in adversity* 848.9

homeless shelter *charitable organization* 305.4

homelike *fit for habitation* 60.19

homeliness *humility* 298.1, *familiarity* 407.3, *ugliness* 531.1

homeliness [Brit] *simplicity* 526.1

home-loving *housebound* 415.9

homely *fit for habitation* 60.19, *humble* 298.8, *familiar* 407.8, *ugly* 531.3

homely [Brit] *simple* 526.7

homely as a mud fence *ugly* 531.3

homemade *bungled* 128.7, *produced* 522.12, *naive* 821.3

home management *home economics* 56.2

home nurse *nurse* 107.23

Home Office [Brit] *law enforcement agency* 53.7

homeopathic *medical* 107.28

homeopathist *healer* 107.22

homeopathy *alternative medicine* 107.4, *treatment* 107.14, *healing art* 115.13

homeostasis *stability* 674.1, *regularity* 730.6, *equilibrium* 740.2

homeostatic *stable* 674.3, *regular* 730.12, *equal* 740.8

homeostatically *regularly* 730.21

homeotherm *mammal* 35.1

homeowner *householder* 61.5

home permanent *coiffure* 530.8

home plate *baseball field* 147.3

homer *successful thing* 845.5

Homeric *poetic* 139.19, *huge* 579.14

Homeric epithet *literary device* 139.12

Homeric simile *literary device* 139.12

home rule *self-government* 49.9, *independence* 829.5

home run *batting terms* 147.6, *successful thing* 845.5

home-run hitter *baseball team* 147.2

home-run leader *baseball team* 147.2

home schooling *educational system* 48.2

homesick *desirous* 288.13

homesickness *desire* 288.1

home side *group* 623.5

homespun Fabrics and Fibers 130, *produced* 522.12, *simple* 526.7, *rough thing* 544.2, *rough* 552.8, *naive* 821.3

homestead *farm* 16.2, *home* 60.3, *property* 470.1

homesteader *settler* 61.4

home stretch *racetrack* 159.12, *close* 773.9

home surroundings Phobias 283

home sweet home *home* 60.3

hometown *home* 60.3

home trade *commercial trade* 480.2

home truth *condemnation* 438.2, *the truth* 721.3

home truths *realities* 719.5

home tutor *educator* 48.4

homeward *toward* 697.18, *approaching* 704.10

homeward bound *returning* 680.15, *approaching* 704.10

homeward journey *return* 680.9

homework *work* 122.1, *preparations* 388.2

home workplace 124.3

homey *fit for habitation* 60.19, *simple* 526.7

homeyness *familiarity* 407.3, *simplicity* 526.1

homichlophobia Phobias 283

homicidal *murderous* 30.18, *malign* 306.11

homicidally *deadly* 30.26

homicidal maniac *murderer* 30.12, *violent animal* 520.4

homicide 30.4; *malignity* 306.5, *violation of the law* 427.2, *violence by person* 520.2

homilist *educator* 48.4

homilize *moralize* 431.14

homilophobia Phobias 283

homily *dissertation* 203.1, *public speaking* 205.11, *address* 209.1, *moral* 431.5

hominess *simplicity* 526.1

homing *returning* 680.15, *entering* 706.9

homing in on *locating* 565.3

homing pigeon *messenger* 685.5

hominid *humankind* 18.1, *primate* 35.17, 35.32, *prehistoric human* 653.7

Hominidae *primate* 35.17

hominoid *human* 18.15

homo [Inf *and* Off] *homosexual* 32.9

homocentric *or* **homocentrical** *centered* 612.9

homocentrically *centrally* 612.12

homocentricity *centrality* 612.5

homocyclic *chemical compound* 11.4

Homo erectus *human ancestor* 18.3, *prehistoric human* 653.7

homoerotic *of sexual nature* 20.17

homoeroticism *sexual nature* 20.4

homogeneity *society* 2.6, *sameness* 730.1

homogeneous *chemical* 14.46, *same* 730.7, *similar* 733.7

homogeneous catalysis *catalysis* 11.16

homogeneously *identically* 730.18, *similarly* 733.17

homogeneous reactors *chemical reaction thermodynamics* 14.29

homogenize *make the same* 730.16, *make similar* 733.15

homogenized milk *milk* 93.5

homogenous *related* 727.6

homogenously *relevantly* 727.12

homogeny *relatedness* 727.1

homograph *word* 5.17, *equivalence* 730.3

homographic *worded* 5.38, *equivalent* 730.9

homoiotherm *mammal* 35.1

homoiothermal *warm-blooded* 217.14

homoiothermic *mammalian* 35.23

homological *equivalent* 730.9

homological algebra Branches of Mathematics 6

homologically *equivalently* 730.20

homologize *be equivalent* 730.15

homologous *related* 727.6, *equivalent* 730.9, *equal* 740.8

homologous chromosome *chromosome* 13.21

homologously *relevantly* 727.12, *equivalently* 730.20

homologue *equivalence* 730.3

homology *transformation* 6.46, *relatedness* 727.1, *equivalence* 730.3

homolysis *chemical reaction* 11.8

homolytic *reactive* 11.29

homolytic fission *chemical reaction* 11.8

Homo neanderthalensis *primitive humanity* 18.4

homonym *word* 5.17, *equivalence* 730.3

homonymic or **homonymous** *worded* 5.38, *equivalent* 730.9

homonymous *linguistic* 361.9, *equivocal* 380.5

homonymously *equivalently* 730.20

homophilia *sexual nature* 20.4

homophobe *bigot* 337.7

homophobia Phobias 283, *social discrimination* 337.4, *unfair treatment* 342.4

homophobic *discriminatory* 337.11, *unjust* 342.7

homophobically *prejudicially* 337.17

homophone *word* 5.17, *equivalence* 730.3

homophonic *worded* 5.38, *melodious* 140.26, *harmonic* 140.27, *harmonizing* 735.12

homophonic or **homophonous** *equivalent* 730.9

homophonically *equivalently* 730.20, *in harmony* 735.32

homophony *harmonic element* 140.14, *harmonization* 735.2

homopolar bond *chemical bond* 11.6

homopolymer(ization) *polymer* 11.9

homopolysaccharide *polysaccharide* 12.5

homopteran *insectile* 40.11

Homo sapiens *humankind* 18.1, *primate* 35.17

homosexual 32.9, 33.10; *sexual nature* 20.4, *of sexual nature* 20.17, *male* 32.16

homosexuality *sexual nature* 20.4, Phobias 283

homosexual marriage *type of marriage* 64.3

homothallic *of fungi* 47.19

homothety *transformation* 6.46

homunculus *little person* 580.5

homy *fit for habitation* 60.19, *simple* 526.7

hon [Inf] *term of endearment* 299.7

honan Fabrics and Fibers 130

Honduras Countries 566

hone *be accurate* 350.5, *sharpener* 549.8, *sharpen* 549.16

honed *sharp-edged* 549.12

honest 630.11; *law-abiding* 53.20, *truthful* 191.4, *right* 429.7, *moral* 431.9, *unselfish* 443.5, *principled* 447.6, *natural* 526.10, *open* 583.13, *naive* 821.3

honest! *that's for sure!* 721.34

honestly 630.18; *truthfully* 191.9, *earnestly* 278.10, *right* 429.15, *morally* 431.15, *unselfishly* 443.9, *ethically* 447.10, *naturally* 526.16, *candidly* 583.23, *certainly* 719.14, *frankly* 843.18

honest money *money* 484.1

honest sweat *sweat* 25.8

honest to God! *yes!* 189.36

honest-to-God *really* 719.13

honest-to-goodness or **honest-to-God** *authentic* 721.16

honest truth, the or **honest-to-goodness** or **honest-to-God truth** *the truth* 721.3

honesty 630.4, Flowers 42, *openness* 180.3, 583.7, *truthfulness* 191.1, *rightfulness* 429.1, *morals* 431.2, *unselfishness* 443.2, *virtues* 447.2, *naturalness* 526.4, *naiveté* 821.1

honey *woman considered as a sex object* [Inf and Off] 33.8, *dwelling* 40.7, *sweetener* 222.2, *sweeten* 222.7, *yellow thing* 259.4, *term of endearment* 299.7, *semiliquid* 561.7

honey [Inf] *term of endearment* 299.7

honeybee *social insect* 40.6

honey-blond *yellow-haired* 259.9

honey bun [Inf] *term of endearment* 299.7

honeybunch [Inf] *term of endearment* 299.7

honey child [Inf] *term of endearment* 299.7

honey-colored *yellow* 259.7

honeycomb *sweetener* 222.2, *porosity* 583.5, *hole* 583.17, *cavity* 635.3, *make concave* 635.7, *eat away* 808.19

honeycombed *holed* 583.12, *spoiled* 808.9

honeydew *secreted substance* 24.2, *sweetener* 222.2

honeyed 439.8; *sweet* 222.5

honeyed phrases *blarney* 439.2

honeyed words *persuasion* 178.1, *blarney* 439.2

honey locust Trees and Shrubs 43

honeymoon *general wedding terms* 64.6, *marry* 64.19, *pleasant thing* 271.4

honeymooners *married couple* 64.9, *lovers* 299.12

honeymoon period *agreement* 462.1, *time of plenty* 847.3

honeymoon suite *general wedding terms* 64.6

honeypot *pot* 578.15

honeysuckle Flowers 42

honey-tongued *honeyed* 439.8

Hong Kong *other famous world cities* 567.9, Islands 572

Honiara Countries 566

honk *signal* 183.18, *burst of sound* 232.4, *bird sound* 240.2, *make a bird sound* 240.8, *warning signal* 814.3, *give warning* 814.10

Honolulu American States 564

honor 58.14, 72.3; *religiousness* 81.2, *revere* 81.26, 435.14, *worship* 83.1, 83.15, *calling* 178.6, *pleasant thing* 271.4, *fete* 279.6, *dignity* 297.4, *commemorate* 354.14, 405.11, *greet* 410.11, *rightfulness* 429.1, *morals* 431.2, *respect* 435.1, *admiration* 437.2, *praise* 437.3, 437.16, *admire* 437.15, *virtue* 447.1, *reward* 453.1, 453.13, *pay off* 489.17, *decoration* 532.1, *decorate* 532.11, *make important* 799.14

honor a bill *pay off* 489.17

honorable *honored* 58.12, *truthful* 191.4, *dignified* 297.11, *reputable* 370.3, *celebrative* 405.9, *right* 429.7, *moral* 431.9, *unselfish* 443.5, *virtuous* 447.5, *observant* 465.3, *honest* 630.11, *naive* 821.3

honorable discharge *military honor* 58.9, *termination* 834.2

honorable mention *compliment* 437.4

honorableness *truthfulness* 191.1, *unselfishness* 443.2, *honesty* 630.4

honorably *with honor* 58.16, *aristocratically* 70.6, *worshipfully* 83.17, *truthfully* 191.9, *with dignity* 297.20, *reputably* 370.6, *right* 429.15, *morally* 431.15, *dutifully* 433.19, *unselfishly* 443.9, *virtuously* 447.9, *observantly* 465.6, *honestly* 630.18

honor and glory *prosperity* 847.1

honorarily *worthily* 72.14

honorarium *reward for service* 453.5, *profit* 467.6, *gift* 472.2, *pay* 489.6

honorary *titular* 72.10, *free of charge* 497.12

honorary degree *reward* 453.1

honorary title *reward* 453.1

honorary treasurer *treasurer* 484.18

honored 58.12, 72.11; *worshiped* 83.14, *reputable* 370.3, *respected* 435.10, *decorated* 532.9

honorific 72.5; *title* 72.1, *professional title* 72.6, *respectful* 435.6

honorifically *worshipfully* 83.17

honoring *worshipful* 83.12, *commemoration* 405.2

honor one's obligations *perform* 465.5

honor point Heraldic Terms 184

honors *military honor* 58.9, *honor* 72.3, *golf shots* 156.4, *reward* 453.1

honors or **honor cards** *bridge* 168.4

honors graduate *successful person* 845.6

honor system *golfing terms* 156.3

honor with *give* 472.10

honor with a title *reward* 453.13

honor with one's presence *appear* 575.16

Honshu Islands 572

hooch or **hootch** [Inf] *alcoholic drink* 93.9, *alcohol* 121.5

Hood, Mount Mountains and Hills 569

hood *vestment* 84.11, *formal clothes* 100.5, *headdress* 100.35, *clothe* 100.43, *toboggan parts* 162.24, *shade maker* 247.4, *make dark* 247.10, *body covering* 613.3, *protective covering* 613.5, *hide* 613.27

hood [Inf] *criminal* 427.6, *villain* 448.5

hooded *dressed* 100.38, *concealed* 181.8, *protected* 613.20

hoodlum *combatant* 77.1, *criminal* 427.6, *villain* 448.5, *dishonest person* 479.11, *vulgar person* 535.4

hood mold Architectural Elements 134

hoodoo *witchcraft* 86.6, *occult influence* 512.2

hoodwink *deceive* 181.14, 193.16, *blind* 243.17

hoodwinked *deceived* 193.15

hooey [Inf] *nonsense* 192.8, *empty talk* 362.5

hooey! [Inf] *nonsense!* 362.14

hoof [Inf] *dance* 135.7

hoof-and-mouth disease *animal disease* 34.10

hoofed *ungulate* 35.31

hoofed mammal 35.16

hoofer *dancer* 135.4

hoof it [Inf] *dance* 135.7

hoofpick *riding equipment* 159.9

Hooghly Rivers 570

hook *hand tool* 103.3, *knit* 130.19, *bowling delivery* 151.2, *fishing tackle* 154.7, *fish* 154.14, *golf shots* 156.4, *play* 156.8, *field hockey tactics* 158.5, *play field hockey* 158.10, *retainer* 471.3, *sharp-pointed thing* 549.4, *use a sharp tool* 549.17, *peninsula* 572.5, *sporting hit* 695.6, *divert* 698.16, *joint* 752.7, *fastener* 754.7, *yoke* 754.8, *connect* 754.13

hook [Inf] *prostitute* 432.17

hookah *tobacco implements* 121.24

hook and eye *part of garment* 100.27, *fastener* 754.7

hooked *woven* 130.15, *bowling* 151.6, *angular* 628.7, *connected* 754.11

hooked [Inf] *married* 64.16, *addicted* 121.31

hooked-in *windsurfing* 150.28

hooked rug *floor covering* 613.13

hooker [Inf] *sexually immoral person* 432.8

Hooker's green *green pigment* 260.3

Hooke's law Classical Physical Laws 10

hookey *desertion* 386.7, *absenteeism* 576.3

hook in *windsurf* 150.33

hooking *weaving* 130.6, *ice hockey tactics* 158.4

hook, line, and sinker [Inf] *wholly* 759.11

hook on *link* 752.18

hook over *angle* 628.11

hook pass *playing terms* 148.4, *play* 155.8

hooks [Inf] *retainer* 471.3

hook shot *playing terms* 148.4

hookup *miscellaneous aviation terms* 689.9, *linkage* 752.3, *association* 827.6

hookup [Inf] alliance 64.2
hook up suspend 604.13, service 689.16, join 827.17,
hook up to add 748.11
hook up with [Inf] merge 64.21, fraternize 408.17, link 752.18
hookworm parasite 39.18
hookworm disease tropical disease 114.10
hooky desertion 386.7, absenteeism 576.3, escape 816.1
hooligan combatant 77.1, unpleasant person 272.5, criminal 427.6, villain 448.5, vulgar person 535.4, distorter 627.5
hooliganism violence by person 520.2, vulgarity 535.1, lawlessness 766.6
hoop underwear 100.22, toy 167.9, circular thing 631.3, means of connection 754.4
hoopla [Inf] public relations (PR) 173.8, publicity 178.7, exaggeration 194.1
hoop pine Trees and Shrubs 43
hoop skirt skirt 100.12
hoorah cry of praise 239.3, cheer 239.15
hooray cry of praise 239.3, cheer 239.15
hoosegow [Inf] the inside 55.2
hoot gesture 183.5, 183.17, cry of disapproval 239.7, hiss 239.17, bird sound 240.2, make a bird sound 240.8, taunt 436.6, 436.23
hoot [Inf] joke 277.6
hootchy-kootchy Dances 135
hootchy-kootchy show show 138.4
hooter crier 239.8, signal 646.9
hooter [Brit inf] nose 19.11
hooting tumult 232.5, hissing 239.12, taunting 436.14
hoot owl bird of prey 36.11
hop dance 135.7, jumping 166.11, bodily movement 677.11, jump 713.7, spring up 713.22
hop [Inf] dance 135.1, party 408.6
hop aboard mount 713.24
hop about be agitated 684.21
hopak Dances 135
HOPE Programming Languages 15
hope 281.1, 281.10; believing 87.2, wish 288.2, object of desire 288.8, expectation 356.1, expect 356.6, objective 374.5, virtues 447.2, show potential 458.14, security 464.1, motivation 508.1, make possible 836.7
hope against hope hope 281.10
hope and a prayer hope 281.1
hope and pray hope 281.10
hope chest cabinet 101.8, reserve 105.3, preparations 388.2
hoped for expected 356.5, foreseen 650.8
hope for aspire to 288.19, expect 356.6, look ahead 610.11
hope for the best hope 281.10
hopeful 281.6; hoper 281.5, desirous 288.13, overestimator 343.2, expecting 356.4, intending 374.6, candidate 422.18, principled 447.6
hopefully 281.15; desirously 288.26, expectantly 356.10, prospectively 374.12, ethically 447.10
hopefulness hope 281.1, expectation 356.1
hopeless 282.6, 837.6; dying 29.12, without skill 282.10, disappointed 293.4, inactive 413.9, impenitent 452.2, losing 468.9,

unfashionable 528.10, futile 802.10, failed 846.10
hopeless case dying person 29.6, futility 282.3, loser 846.9
hopeless failure failure 846.1
hopeless loss loss 468.1
hopelessly 282.13, 837.12; unskillfully 282.17, disappointedly 293.11, irrecoverably 468.21, unsuccessfully 846.21
hopelessness 282.1, 837.2; lack of skill 282.4, disappointment 293.1, defeatism 413.7, futility 802.3
hopeless person 282.5
hopeless situation futility 282.3
hoper 281.5; desirer 288.9
hopes expectations 356.2
hopes unrealized frustration 293.2
hope to God hope 281.10
hophead [Inf] drug taker 121.12
hop in mount 713.24
hoping hope 281.1, hopeful 281.6, desirous 288.13
hopingly hopefully 281.15, desirously 288.26
hop-o'-my-thumb little person 580.5
hop on set out 705.12
hopped-up [Inf] swift 694.6
hopper insect 40.1, batting terms 147.6, vessel 578.11
hopper car railroad car 688.5
hopping jumping 166.11, restlessness 684.5, agitated 684.15, leaping 713.17
hopping mad angry 302.11
hopsack Fabrics and Fibers 130
hopscotch Children's and Party Games 167
hop, skip, and jump jump 713.7
hop, step, and jump jumping 166.11
hop to it [Inf] hasten 657.15
hoptree Trees and Shrubs 43
hora Dances 135
Horae, the Deities 82
Horatian Poem or Verse Forms 139, poetic 139.19
horde crowd 59.11, 59.26, throng 795.4
horehound Herbs and Spices 91
horizon celestial sphere 7.4, visibility 244.1, that which makes invisible 245.2, disappearance 265.1, distant place 585.3, horizontal surface 603.3, edge 617.3, curved thing 629.3
horizontal 603.6; linear 6.77, uniform 545.5, horizontal surface 603.3, straight 630.8
horizontal angle horizontal surface 603.3
horizontal axis horizontal surface 603.3
horizontal bar 157.5, Sporting Activities 145, gymnastics equipment 157.2
horizontality 603.1; smoothness 545.1, straightness 630.1
horizontal line horizontal surface 603.3, straight line 630.2
horizontally 603.11; smoothly 545.13, straight 630.16
horizontal machine machine tool 14.9
horizontal member superstructure 551.7
horizontalness horizontality 603.1
horizontal scale balance beam 157.3
horizontal surface 603.3
horizontal tab (HT) character 15.18

hormephobia Phobias 283
hormic psychology Psychological Theories, Schools 108
hormonal biochemical 12.25, fluid 19.25, of a secretion 24.5
hormonally biochemically 12.27
hormone 12.16; body fluid 19.16, secreted substance 24.2
hormonelike substance hormone 12.16
hormone replacement therapy (HRT) treatment 107.14, therapy 115.12
hormone therapy therapy 115.12
horn Musical Instruments 142, brass instrument 142.3, signal 183.6, source of resonance 54.7, hard substance 542.3, sharp-pointed growth 549.5, skeleton 551.14, cone 633.5, warning signal 814.3
horn [Inf] telephone 169.10
hornbeam Trees and Shrubs 43
horned toothed 549.13
horned moon moon 7.18
horned owl bird of prey 36.11
hornet's nest natural habitat 60.16
Horney psychologist 108.33
Horneyan psychology Psychological Theories, Schools 108
hornified hardened 542.7
hornily [Inf] lustfully 288.29
horn in invade 706.12
horniness [Inf] sexual longing 20.6, sexual desire 288.5, sexual love 299.3
horn inlay decorative woodwork 131.2
hornlike toothed 549.13
horn of plenty fertility 22.1, plenty 97.2
hornpipe Dances 135
horn player player 141.2
horn-rimmed glasses visual aid 242.14
horns of a dilemma irresolution 841.3
hornswoggle [Inf] swindle 193.19
hornwort moss 46.4
horny hard 542.5
horny [Inf] desirous 20.18, lustful 288.15, unchaste 432.10
horny-handed working 122.6
horologe timekeeper 646.7
horological timekeeping 646.11
horologically 646.15
horologist horology 646.6
Horologium Constellations 7
horology 646.6; time measurement 639.5
horoscope divination 86.5, prediction 358.1, occult influence 512.2, looking to the future 650.4
horoscopy divination 86.5, 358.2
horrendous frightening 283.12
horrendously frighteningly 283.20
horrible unpleasant 272.6, frightening 283.12, evil 446.7, repulsive 701.4
horribleness evil 446.1
horribly frighteningly 283.20, evilly 446.12, hideously 531.6, repulsively 701.11
horrid unpleasant 272.6, frightening 283.12, ugly 531.3
horridly hideously 531.6
horrific frightening 283.12
horrifically frighteningly 283.20
horrification terrorization 283.5
horrified frightened 283.9
horrify displease 272.8, frighten 283.17, cause dislike 291.16

horrifying frightening 283.12
horrifyingly frighteningly 283.20
horripilate sense 212.9, be rough 544.10
horripilation stimulus 212.3, roughness 544.1
horror fear 283.1, antipathy 291.2, evil thing 446.2, ugly thing 531.2
horrors [Inf] drunken behavior 121.4
horror story story 139.4
horror-struck frightened 283.9
hors de combat [Fr] disabled 515.10, broken down 802.8
hors d'oeuvre 90.13; dish 90.7, bite 92.10, appetizer 219.2, preface 769.5
horse 159.1
horse [Inf] opiates 121.17
horse around [Inf] play the fool 353.7
horse artillery historical gun 78.10, horse person 159.14
horseback riding Sporting Activities 145, equestrianism 159.8
horseback-riding equine 159.15
horsebean Bean Varieties 90
horse by color 159.7
horse chestnut Trees and Shrubs 43
horse doctor horse person 159.14
horse-drawn tractional 699.7
horse fair market 483.1
horseflesh horse 159.1
horsehair Fabrics and Fibers 130
horsehide leather 104.7
horsehide [Inf] baseball equipment 147.4
horse latitudes wind system 9.15, world region 564.6, repose 678.2
horselaugh cry of amusement 239.2
horselike ungulate 35.31
horseman horse person 159.14
horsemanship equestrianism 159.8
horse marine unskilled person 128.3
horse of a different or another color incomparability 734.3
horse person 159.14
horse pistol historical handgun 78.8
horsepower exertion 122.4, type of power 514.6, General Units 589
horsepower-hour General Units 589
horse race horse racing 159.10
horse racing 159.10; Sporting Activities 145, race 422.8
horse-racing equine 159.15
horse-racing betting terms 159.11
horseradish sauce 90.17, Herbs and Spices 91
horseradish tree Trees and Shrubs 43
horse rider horse person 159.14
horses Collective Names 59, Phobias 283
horse sense common sense 315.4, intelligence 352.2
horseshoe talisman 86.9, arch 134.5, good-luck sign 358.6, curved thing 629.3
horseshoe crab extinct arthropod 39.7
horseshoe magnet magnet 10.47, 700.3
horseshoe pitching Sporting Activities 145
horseshoes Children's and Party Games 167

horse show *equestrianism* 159.8, *sporting event* 422.6
horse soldier *horse person* 159.14
horsetail *fern* 46.1
horse-trade *negotiate* 460.6
horse trader *trader* 480.11
horse trading *negotiation* 460.1
horse-trading *bargaining* 480.10
horse trials *equestrianism* 159.8
horsewhip *instrument of punishment* 454.13, *hit* 454.28
horsewhipping *corporal punishment* 454.11
horsewoman *horse person* 159.14
horsewomanship *equestrianism* 159.8
horst *landform* 8.9
horsy or **horsey** *ungulate* 35.31
hortative *motivational* 508.7
hortatively *influentially* 508.13
hortatorily *advisory* 176.12, *influentially* 508.13
hortatory *motivational* 508.7
hortatory or **hortative** *advisory* 176.7, *persuasive* 178.12
horticultural 17.14, Bean Varieties 90
horticulturally 17.20; *botanically* 41.25
horticulture 17.1; *plant science* 41.10
horticulturist 17.13
hortus siccus *herbarium* 41.12
Horus Deities 82
hosanna *cry of praise* 239.3, *applause* 279.2, *rejoicing* 405.8
hosanna! *hallelujah!* 83.18, *hurrah!* 279.8
hose 557.33; *garden tool* 17.7, *legwear* 100.26, *sprinkle* 559.14
hose down *hose* 557.33
hosel *golf equipment* 156.5
hosier *clothier* 100.37
hosiery *legwear* 100.26, *the clothing business* 100.36, *merchandise* 522.6
hosing *watering* 557.8, *sprinkle* 559.5
hosing down *watering* 557.8
hospice *retreat* 60.13, *nursing home* 107.18, *haven* 810.3, *safe house* 812.5
hospitable *friendly* 62.5, *charitable* 305.9, *sociable* 408.11, *generous* 498.6, *welcoming* 704.12, *receptive* 708.9
hospitably *amicably* 62.13, *charitably* 305.15, *sociably* 408.19, *receptively* 708.20
hospital 107.16; *service workplace* 124.5, *building* 551.9, *resting place* 668.5
hospital administrator *paramedic* 107.24
hospital case *sick person* 114.22
hospital doctor *doctor* 107.19
hospitality *friendship* 62.1, *eating meals* 92.4, *charity* 305.3, *sociability* 408.1, *good company* 408.9, *taking in* 477.7, *generosity* 498.1, *reception* 704.3, *receptivity* 708.2
hospitalization *therapy* 115.12
hospitalize *treat* 115.17
hospitalized *sick* 114.24
hospital patient *sick person* 114.22
hospitals Phobias 283
hospital ship *warship* 77.21
hospital social worker *paramedic* 107.24
hospital ward *hospital* 107.16
Host Eucharist 85.7
host *ecology* 13.25, Collective

Names 59, *crowd* 59.11, *disease-causing agent* 114.5, *lead* 126.12, *broadcasting personnel* 172.11, *social person* 408.7, *be sociable* 408.14, *receive someone* 473.14, *throng* 795.4
hostage *prisoner* 55.7, *subjected person* 832.5
hostage taking *terrorist attack* 418.7
hostelry *hotel* 60.12
hostess *attendant* 69.4, *social person* 408.7
hostile 63.6; *combative* 77.32, *antipathetic* 291.7, *hating* 300.7, *malicious* 306.8, *jealous* 314.5, *censuring* 438.12, *disagreeing* 463.6, *protesting* 507.5, *counteracting* 510.6, *defensive* 701.6, *disunited* 753.10, *oppositional* 828.11, *adverse* 848.10
hostile attack *military attack* 418.2
hostile critic *disparager* 440.7
hostile criticism *criticism* 438.4, 440.2
hostile jury *unfavorable verdict* 54.20
hostilely *discontentedly* 291.17, *with hate* 300.13, *maliciously* 306.15, *jealously* 314.12, *in disagreement* 463.12, *disapprovingly* 507.10, *counter* 510.8, *disunitedly* 753.25
hostile person 63.5
hostile takeover *deal* 457.9
hostile verdict *unfavorable verdict* 54.20
hostile witness *accuser* 442.3
hostilities *act of hostility* 63.4, *belligerency* 76.14
hostility 63.1; *antipathy* 291.2, *hate* 300.1, *malice* 306.2, *jealousy* 314.2, *attack* 418.1, *censure* 438.3, *divisiveness* 463.2, *protest* 507.1, *opposing force* 510.2, *disunity* 753.4, *opposition* 828.1
hostler *horse person* 159.14
hot 9.47, 217.11; *desirous* 20.18, *piquant* 221.6, *strong to the senses* 516.12, *rainless* 560.11, *near* 586.6
hot [Inf] *stolen* 479.12
hot air *theory* 720.4
hot air [Inf] *bombast* 194.4, *talk* 207.3, *figurative overestimation* 343.3, *empty talk* 362.5
hot-air *flyable* 689.12
hot-air balloon *aircraft* 689.3, *lifter* 715.5
hot-air vent or *duct* *heater* 217.3
hot and bothered [Inf] *desirous* 20.18, *restless* 684.16
hot as hell *hot* 217.11
hot bath *bath* 111.6
hotbed *nursery* 17.4, *fertile land* 22.2, *infection* 114.7, *center of activity* 612.4, *source* 675.2
hot blood *sexual longing* 20.6
hot-blooded *desirous* 20.18, *susceptible* 212.7, *touchy* 303.10
hot-bloodedness *touchiness* 303.3
hot body *heat* 10.25
hot cake *pancake* 90.11
hot chocolate *milk* 93.5, *sweet drink* 222.4
hot climate *climate* 9.35
hot corner *other game terms* 147.7
hot day *hot weather* 217.6
hot dog *sandwich* 90.9, *ski* 162.35
hotdogging *skiing* 161.2
hot dogging *ski* 162.27
hot dog stand *eating place* 92.17
hotel 60.12; *service workplace*

124.5, *building* 551.9, *resting place* 668.5
hotelier *caterer* 89.5
hotel manager *caterer* 89.5
hot enough to fry an egg on *hot* 217.11
hot flush *heat* 217.1
hotfoot *hasty* 818.3, *hastily* 818.7
hotfoot it [Inf] *be swift* 694.10
hot for [Inf] *lustful* 288.15
hot goods [Inf] *takings* 477.8, *stolen goods* 479.4
hothead *feeling person* 266.8, *rash move* 286.4, *irascible person* 303.7, *rash person* 353.4
hotheaded *passionate* 266.12, *rash* 286.5, *irritable* 302.10, *irascible* 303.8, *foolish* 353.5, *murderous* 520.7, *hasty* 818.3
hotheadedly *irritably* 302.23, *irascibly* 303.17
hotheadedness *rashness* 286.1, *anger* 302.4, *irascibility* 303.1
hothouse *nursery* 17.4
hothouse plant *plant* 41.2
hot line *telephone* 169.10, *information source* 170.6
hotly *meteorologically* 9.60, *warmly* 217.20
hotly contested *competitive* 422.21
hot-metal printing *book printing* 174.10
hot-metal typesetting *typesetting* 173.4
hot money *funds* 484.6
hotness *heat* 10.25, 217.1
hot news *news* 171.1
hot off the press *newsworthy* 171.8, *published* 173.12, *topical* 328.5, *new* 652.9
hot on the trail *on the trail* 160.13, 385.18
hot or cold Children's and Party Games 167
hot pad *cooking equipment* 91.6
hot pants *shorts* 100.15
hot pants [Inf] *sexual desire* 288.5
hot pants or *rocks* or *nuts* [Inf] *sexual longing* 20.6
hot place 217.5
hot plate *cooker* 91.5, *cooking equipment* 91.6, *burner* 217.4
hot potato Children's and Party Games 167
hot press *smoother* 545.2
hot-press *smooth* 545.10
hot property [Inf] *takings* 477.8, *stolen goods* 479.4
hot pursuit *chase* 385.2
hot-rod racing *automobile racing* 146.1
hots, the [Inf] *sexual longing* 20.6, *sexual desire* 288.5
hot seat [Inf] *instrument of execution* 454.15
hot shoe *flash* 132.13
hot shot *drug dose* 121.15
hot shot [Inf] *show-off* 404.13
hot shower *bath* 111.6
hot spell *hot weather* 9.22, 217.6
hot spring 572.11; *eruption* 8.27
hot springs *health improvement* 113.3
hot substance *heat* 10.25
hot temper *short temper* 303.5
hot-tempered *irascible* 303.8
hotter *warm* 9.46
hot tip [Inf] *inside information* 170.4
hot toddy *sweet drink* 222.4
hot to trot [Inf] *desirous* 20.18
hot tub *bath* 111.6, *basin* 578.12
hot-tubbing *washing* 557.11

hot under the collar [Inf] *angry* 302.11
hot war *war* 76.1
hot water *cleaning agent* 111.9
hot water [Inf] *predicament* 725.3, 824.5
hot-water bottle *heater* 217.3, *bottle* 578.14
hot-water pipe *heater* 217.3
hot-water tank *heater* 217.3
hot weather 9.22, 217.6
hot-wiring *miscellaneous automotive terms* 687.14
Houdan Breeds of Fowl 16
Houdini *escaper* 816.5
hound *dog* 35.10, *oppose* 63.11, *hunting dog* 160.7, *harm* 306.13, *pursue* 385.11
hounded *pursued* 385.10
hounding *pursuit* 385.1
hounds Collective Names 59
hound's tooth or **hound's tooth check** *check* 263.2
houngan *imam* 84.7, *occultist* 86.13
hour *time period* 641.2, *chronology* 646.2, *occurrence* 726.2
hour angle *celestial sphere* 7.4
hour by hour *cyclically* 663.15
hourglass *contracted thing* 582.5, Timepieces and Timers 646
hourglass figure *contracted thing* 582.5, *thinness* 595.1
hour hand *indicator* 183.7
hourly *for specified periods* 641.12, *frequently* 661.7, *cyclic* 663.7, *cyclically* 663.15, *regular* 730.12, *regularly* 730.21
hourly worker *employee* 57.4
hour of decision *critical moment* 726.7
hours worked *bargaining terms* 57.10
Housatonic Rivers 570
House *United States government* 49.21
house 60.4; *association* 59.4, *habitation* 60.2, *family tree* 65.3, *architectural structure* 134.4, *theater* 136.1, *theatergoer* 136.30, *club* 138.7, *place of residence* 209.4, *hearer* 228.7, *property* 470.1, *store* 483.8, *building* 551.9, *protect* 613.26, 810.21, *entrant* 706.7
house arrest *arrest* 55.5, *imprisonment* 454.2, *detention* 830.5
houseboat *mobile home* 60.11, Ships and Boats 690
housebound 415.9; *detained* 830.11
houseboy *domestic servant* 69.7
housebreak *steal* 479.14
housebreaker *lawbreaker* 53.15, *criminal* 427.6, *thief* 479.8, *intruder* 706.8
housebreaking *stealing* 479.1, *inroad* 706.3
housebroken *excremental* 25.13
house built on sand *weak thing* 517.5
house cat *cat* 35.11
housecleaner *cleaner* 111.12
housecleaning *cleaning* 111.2
housecoat *robe* 100.20
house curtain *stage set* 136.19
housed *inhabiting* 60.18, *joined* 131.8, *sheltered* 812.7
house divided against itself *divisiveness* 463.2
housed joint *carpenter's term* 131.5
housedress *dress* 100.11
house fire *fire* 217.8

house furnishings *furniture* 101.1
household *group* 59.8, *home* 60.3, *domestic* 60.20, *inhabitants* 61.2, *family* 65.1, *familiar* 397.10, *average* 742.5
household effects *furniture* 101.1
householder 61.5; *possessor* 469.10, *property owner* 470.7
household god *minor deity* 82.2
household goods *furniture* 101.1
household insurance *insurance* 810.10
household management *management* 126.1
household servant *servant* 69.1
household words *unpretentiousness* 526.2
househusband *man in the family* 32.12, *married man* 64.10
housekeep 60.23
housekeeper *domestic servant* 69.7, *domestic worker* 123.4
housekeeping *management* 126.1
houseless *stateless* 574.14
houselights *stage lighting* 136.20
house lights *electric light* 246.6
house magazine *magazine* 175.3
housemaid *domestic servant* 69.7, *cleaner* 111.12
housemaid's knee *joint disease* 114.19
House majority leader *elected official* 50.8
houseman *domestic servant* 69.7
housemaster *educational leader* 68.11
House minority leader *elected official* 50.8
housemother *educational leader* 68.11
house number *place of residence* 209.4
house of cards *weak thing* 517.5
House of Commons *British government* 49.22
house of detention *or correction* *prison* 55.1
house of God *place of worship* 83.8
house of ill repute *or ill fame or assignation* *brothel* 432.5
House of Lords *British government* 49.22
House of Peers *British government* 49.22
house of prayer *place of worship* 83.8
house of prostitution *wicked place* 448.8
House of Representatives *United States government* 49.21, *representative body* 79.2
house of worship *place of worship* 83.8
house organ *magazine* 175.3
house party *party* 408.6
house pet *domestic animal* 34.3
houseplant *plant* 41.2
house-proud *arrogant* 297.9
house rent *fee* 494.3
house rules *tradition* 397.5
House seat *position of authority* 52.4
house-sharing *jointly possessing* 469.12
house steward *domestic servant* 69.7
housetop *architectural summit* 600.4, *overhead covering* 613.11
house-trained [Brit] *excremental* 25.13
House-Tree-Person (HTP) Projective Test *Psychological Tests* 108

housewarming *social gathering* 59.7, *party* 408.6, *beginning* 652.4
House whip *person in authority* 52.7
housewife *woman in the family* 33.13, *married woman* 64.11, *domestic worker* 123.4
housewifery *management* 126.1
housework *work* 122.1
housing *protective covering* 613.5, *casing* 613.9
Houston *major US cities* 567.5
Houyhnhnm Land *Imaginary Places* 360
Houyhnhnm *Legendary Creatures* 360
hovel *shack* 60.10
hover *fly* 36.23, 689.13, *Collective Names* 59, *be light* 539.8, *suspend* 604.13, *defer* 604.15, *be irresolute* 666.6, *hesitate* 693.12
hovercraft *Ships and Boats* 690
hovering *suspension* 604.1, *deferred* 604.9, *flying* 689.13
hover on the brink *be in danger* 811.11
hover over *be solicitous* 323.13, *stay near* 586.13, *overhang* 604.14
how 691.16; *by means of* 102.7
how about that! *wonderful!* 294.20
how are you? *hello!* 704.23
how do you do? *hello!* 704.23
how-do-you-do [Inf] *predicament* 824.5
however *how* 691.16
however little *by degrees* 739.10
however much *by degrees* 739.10
how it is *circumstances* 573.2, *state of affairs* 725.4
howitzer *guns* 78.9
howl *blow* 9.53, *express pain* 215.11, *tumult* 232.5, *be loud* 232.8, *harsh sound* 238.1, *be strident* 238.7, *cry* 239.1, 239.16, *cry of sorrow* 239.6, *cry out* 239.13, *animal sound* 240.1, *make an animal sound* 240.7, *grieve* 270.7, *laugh* 277.12, *lament* 280.2, *weep* 280.8, *gesture of protest* 507.3, *complain* 507.8
howler *mistake* 342.2, *blunder* 351.9, 528.5, *joke* 368.4
howling *strident* 238.4, *crying* 239.11, *ululant* 240.4, *violent* 520.5
howling gale *wind strength* 9.13
howling success [Inf] *successfulness* 845.3
how things stack up [Inf] *state of affairs* 725.4
how things stand *circumstances* 573.2, *state of affairs* 725.4
how-to book *type of book* 174.3
hoy *Sailing Ships and Boats* 690, *Ships and Boats* 690
hoya *Flowers* 42
hoyden *young woman* 26.9, *mannish female* 33.9
hoydenish *female* 33.16
Hsi Chiang *Rivers* 570
Huçul pony *Horse and Pony Breeds* 159
Huang He *Rivers* 570
Huascaran *Mountains and Hills* 569
hub *machine element* 14.8, *core* 612.2, *center of activity* 612.4, *axle* 682.7, *focus* 702.5, *gist* 799.4
hubble-bubble *tobacco implements* 121.24
Hubble classification *galaxy* 7.5
Hubble constant *galaxy* 7.5

Hubble Space Telescope *telescope* 7.25
hubbub *tumult* 232.5, 684.2, *cry* 239.1, *dissonance* 241.1, *confusion* 766.4, *commotion* 768.5
hubby [Inf] *married man* 64.10
hub gear *bicycle part* 687.11
hubris *tragedy* 136.10, *pride* 297.1, *overestimation* 343.1, *boastfulness* 402.6
hubristic *prideful* 297.8, *overestimating* 343.4, *boastful* 402.13
huckaback *or huck* *Fabrics and Fibers* 130
Huckleberry Finn *Notable Friendships* 62
huckster *publicizer* 173.11, *boast* 194.14, *bargain* 480.20, *peddler* 482.9
huckstering *bombast* 194.4
huddle 155.7; *come together* 59.25, *advisory body* 176.6, *consult* 176.11, *place for conversation* 210.5, *become smaller* 582.14
huddled *squeezed* 582.9
huddled masses *vulgar group* 535.5
Hudibrastic verse *poetry* 139.8
Hudson *Rivers* 570
Hudson River school *Western Art Styles* 133
hue 251.4; *color* 251.1, *nature* 723.4, *admixture* 751.5, *type* 777.4
hue and cry *proclamation* 183.8, *hunt* 385.3
hued *colored* 251.10
hueless *colorless* 252.5
huff *burst of anger* 302.6, *offend* 302.15, *blow* 558.22
huffed *resentful* 302.8
huffily *touchily* 303.19
huffiness *touchiness* 303.3
huffy *touchy* 303.10
hug *gesture* 183.5, 183.17, *give pleasure* 214.13, *comfort* 214.14, *communication of love* 299.6, *communicate love* 299.25, *welcome* 408.10, 408.18, *be sociable* 408.14, *sign of courtesy* 410.5, *greet* 410.11, *retention* 471.1, *retain* 471.7, *stay near* 586.13, *enfoldment* 637.3, *enfold* 637.9, *adhere* 755.8, *preserve* 815.14
huge 579.14
hugely 579.21; *wholly* 738.9
hugeness *largeness* 579.2
huggable *lovable* 299.20
hugger-mugger *secretiveness* 182.3, *secret* 182.8
hugging *communication of love* 299.6
hug oneself *show off* 402.15
hug to the figure *adhere* 755.8
hula-hula *or hula* *Dances* 135
hulk *unskilled person* 128.3, *be clumsy* 128.9, *big person* 579.10
hulkiness *squatness* 579.6
hulking *clumsy* 128.6, 824.14, *stocky* 579.16, *awkward* 804.6
hulky *stocky* 579.16
hull *seed* 41.9, *sailboat parts and accessories* 150.4, *sailboat parts* 150.20, *exteriority* 610.2, *casing* 613.9
hullabaloo *tumult* 232.5, *cry* 239.1, *dissonance* 241.1, *confusion* 766.4, *commotion* 768.5
hum 235.11; *blow* 9.53, *sing* 141.16, *radio reception* 172.2, *undercurrent of sound* 233.3, *sound faint* 233.8, *humming* 235.2, *resonate* 236.9, *insect sound* 240.3,

make an insect sound 240.9, *business* 414.6, *be busy* 414.19, *crowd* 795.11
human 18.15; *person* 18.8, *object* 524.6
human ancestor 18.3
human being *person* 18.8, *living being* 28.3
human body size *Fields of Measurement* 589
human cannonball *circus performer* 138.9
human communications *social environment* 2.4
human development *social change* 2.9
human dynamo *busy person* 414.10
humane *compassionate* 305.8, *philanthropic* 307.6, *pitying* 308.4, *lenient* 423.3, *kind* 445.12
human ecologist *anthropologist* 1.3
human ecology *anthropology* 1.1, *sociology* 2.1
humanely *compassionately* 305.14, *philanthropically* 307.9, *pityingly* 308.11, *leniently* 423.6, *kindly* 445.20
humaneness *philanthropy* 307.1, *leniency* 423.1
human error *fallibility* 351.6
human existence *life* 28.1
human failing *human fallibility* 18.2, *vulnerability* 811.6
human fallibility 18.2
human family 65.5; *humankind* 18.1
human family, the *group* 18.13
human frailty *human fallibility* 18.2
Human Genome Project *biochemistry* 12.1
human geography *anthropology* 1.1
human interaction *social environment* 2.4
humanism *Philosophical Schools of Thought* 4, *study of humankind* 18.6
humanist *Philosophical Schools of Thought* 4, *studier of humankind* 18.7, *materialist* 524.3, *freethinker* 829.10, *independent* 829.12
humanistic *human* 18.15, *literary* 139.15, *independent* 829.12
humanistically *humanly* 18.18
humanistic psychology *Psychological Theories, Schools* 108
humanitarian *benevolent person* 305.6, *philanthropist* 307.5, *philanthropic* 307.6, *public-spirited* 307.7, *good person* 445.6, *generous person* 498.5, *magnanimous* 498.7, *volunteer* 504.7, *voluntary* 504.9
humanitarianism *study of humankind* 18.6, *compassion* 305.2, *philanthropy* 307.1, *public-spiritedness* 307.2
humanities *study of life* 28.9, *subject* 48.3, *learning* 348.3
humanities, the *literature* 139.1
humanity *humankind* 18.1, *human family* 65.5, *compassion* 305.2, *philanthropy* 307.1, *pity* 308.1, *leniency* 423.1, *kindness* 445.3
humanize *make human* 18.17, *refine* 534.7
humankind 18.1; *life* 28.1, *human family* 65.5
human life *life* 28.1
humanlike *human* 18.15

humanlike machine 18.12
humanly 18.18; *sociologically* 2.15
human nature *human fallibility* 18.2
humanness *compassion* 305.2
humanoid *humanlike machine* 18.12, *human* 18.15, Legendary Creatures 360, *prehistoric human* 653.7
human race *humankind* 18.1, *human family* 65.5
human resources *personnel management* 126.4
human rights *rights* 429.4, *free rights* 829.4
human sacrifice *martyr* 504.6
human scientist *anthropologist* 1.3
human social behavior *social environment* 2.4
human species *humankind* 18.1
human studies *anthropology* 1.1
human weakness *human fallibility* 18.2
humble 298.8, 597.25; *religious* 81.21, *humiliate* 298.19, *underestimating* 344.3, *modest* 403.6, *courteous* 410.6, *submitting* 421.3, *obeisant* 426.6, *showing respect* 435.7, *unselfish* 443.5, *simple* 526.7, *lowly* 597.17, *debase* 716.16, *insignificant* 745.6, *subordinate* 745.8, *subject* 832.10
humble apology *confession* 451.2
humble confession *confession* 451.2
humbled *humiliated* 298.12, *lowered* 597.18, *outclassed* 745.9
humbleness *humility* 298.1, *respectfulness* 435.3, *simplicity* 526.1, *lowliness* 597.8, *inferiority* 745.1
humble oneself 298.18; *revere* 81.26, *worship* 83.15
humble person 298.7
humble servant *servant* 69.1
humble submission *submission* 421.1
humbling 597.9; *humiliating* 298.14
humbly 298.22, 597.27, 716.26; *commonly* 71.4, *religiously* 81.29, *worshipfully* 83.17, *pessimistically* 344.6, *modestly* 403.15, *courteously* 410.13, *with humility* 421.8, *respectfully* 435.19, *unselfishly* 443.9, *basely* 745.16
Humbolt Rivers 570
humbug *nonsense* 192.8, *hoax* 193.7, 193.20, *deceiver* 193.8, *deceive* 193.16, *hypocrisy* 330.5, *empty talk* 362.5, *pretender* 367.2
humbug! *nonsense!* 362.14
humbugger *hoaxer* 193.11
humbuggery *deception* 193.1
humdinger [Inf] *good thing* 445.9
humdrum *tasteless* 220.4, *boring* 296.6, *repetitiveness* 797.3, *monotonous* 797.12
humdrumness *boringness* 296.2
humectant *wetting* 557.26, *moist* 559.9
humerus Human Bones 19
Hume's Law *philosophical term* 4.7
humid 9.48; *unhygienic* 114.27, *warm* 217.13, *moist* 559.9
humid climate *climate* 9.35
humidify *moisten* 559.13
humidity 559.3; *weather data* 9.6, *moisture* 9.31, Fields of Measurement 589
humidly *meteorologically* 9.60, *moistly* 559.17
humidness *moisture* 9.31, *humidity* 559.3

humidor *tobacco implements* 121.24
humilative *humiliating* 298.14
humilatory *humiliating* 298.14
humiliate 298.19; *demoralize* 432.15, *desecrate* 436.24, *humble* 597.25, *debase* 716.16, *make unimportant* 800.20, *subject* 832.10, *cause adversity* 848.15
humiliated 298.12; *penitential* 451.6, *lowered* 597.18, *degraded* 716.10, *insignificant* 745.6, *outclassed* 745.9
humiliate oneself *be disreputable* 371.5, *do penance* 451.9
humiliating 298.14, 436.15; *penitential* 451.6, *degraded* 716.10
humiliatingly 298.25; *penitently* 451.10
humiliation 298.5; *indignity* 436.7, *humbling* 597.9, *downfall* 714.7, 848.4, *debasement* 716.5
humility 298.1; *religiousness* 81.2, *underestimation* 344.1, *modesty* 403.1, *courtesy* 410.1, *submission* 421.1, *obeisance* 426.3, *respectfulness* 435.3, *unselfishness* 443.2, *inferiority* 745.1
Humism Philosophical Schools of Thought 4
Humist Philosophical Schools of Thought 4
hummer *singer* 141.4
humming 235.2, 235.7, 240.6; *nonresonant* 233.7, *resonance* 236.1, *resonant* 236.6, *busy* 414.15
hummingbirds Collective Names 59
humming top *rotator* 682.8
hummock *hill* 569.2, *lowlands* 597.6, *dome* 634.4
hummus *notable international dishes* 90.40
hum of activity *business* 414.6
humor [Arch] *personality type* 108.6, *caprice* 381.1, *be lenient* 423.5, *attitude* 513.2, *body fluid* 555.3, *nature* 723.4, *state of mind* 725.5
humor [Arch] *body fluid* 19.16
humoral *rheumy* 555.16
humor column *news story* 171.3
humoresque Musical Forms 140
humoring *leniency* 423.1
humorist 277.7; *entertainer* 138.8
humorless *serious* 278.4
humorlessness *seriousness* 278.1
humorous 277.9; *ridiculous* 368.5
humorously 277.13
humorousness *humor* 277.1
hump *bulge* 634.2, *be convex* 634.7
hump [Inf] *work* 122.8
humpback bridge *bridge* 691.7
humped *convex* 634.5
Humphreys Peak Mountains and Hills 569
humus *fertilizer* 22.6
Hun Nicknames for Inhabitants 61
hun *destroyer* 523.6
hunch *impression* 266.2, *insight* 320.3, *theory* 327.2, *prediction* 358.1, *basis of supposition* 359.2, *spontaneity* 396.2, *bow* 716.6
hunchback *distortion of body* 627.3
hunchbacked *deformed* 627.7
hunch down *sit* 716.20
hunched *sedentary* 716.11
hundred *hundreds* 792.9, *myriad* 795.7
hundred and one, a *myriad* 795.7
Hundred Days *hundreds* 792.9
hundredfold *hundredth* 792.20, *fivefold* 792.26
hundred percent *hundreds* 792.9

hundreds 792.9; *multitude* 795.1
hundreds and hundreds *hundreds* 792.9
hundreds and thousands *hundreds* 792.9, *multitude* 795.1
hundreds of thousands *multitude* 795.1
hundreds place *number system* 6.7
hundredth 792.20
hundred thousand *thousand* 792.10
hundred-to-one or **million-to-one chance** or **shot** *improbability* 839.1
hundredweight *weight measurement* 538.6, General Units 589, *hundreds* 792.9
Hundred Years War Major Wars 76
hung *suspended* 604.7
Hungarian Combing Wool Merino Breeds of Sheep 16
Hungarian GP at Hungaroring Formula 1 World Championship races 146.5
Hungarian Pied Breeds of Cattle 16
Hungarian pointer Breeds of Dogs 35
Hungarian Simmental Breeds of Cattle 16
Hungarian White Breeds of Pigs 16
Hungary Countries 566
hunger *appetite* 92.2, 288.6, *eat well* 92.23, *short rations* 118.3, *fast* 118.8, *be hungry* 288.21, *beggary* 486.3
hunger for *eat well* 92.23, *aspire to* 288.19
hunger pain or **pang** *painful condition* 215.2
hunger strike *fasting* 118.1, *gesture of protest* 507.3
hunger striking *short rations* 118.3
hung jury *stalemate* 740.3
hung over *drunk* 121.25
hungrily *carnivorously* 92.27, *abstemiously* 118.11, *gluttonously* 119.5, *eagerly* 288.27
hungriness *appetite* 288.6
hungry 288.16; *eating* 92.18, *underfed* 98.7, 118.7, *beggarly* 486.12
hungry as a bear *underfed* 98.7
hungry enough to eat a horse *underfed* 118.7
hungry for knowledge *educatable* 48.18
hung-up [Inf] *diligent* 323.7
hunk *mass* 579.7, *certain amount* 738.3, *particle* 760.4
hunk [Inf] *sex object* 20.8, *macho man* 32.6, *person of strength* 516.8, *attractive male* 529.6, *charmer* 700.6
hunker down *sit* 716.20, *hide* 844.13
hunkered down *sedentary* 716.11
hunkers *rear end* 622.4
Hunky or **Hunkie** Nicknames for Inhabitants 61
hunky [Inf] *attractive* 700.10
hunky-dory [Inf] *great* 445.14
hunt 160.12, 385.3, 385.14; *kill animals* 30.25, *ride* 159.16, *hunting* 160.2, *question* 333.16, *pursue* 385.11, *attack* 418.17, *maneuver* 689.14
hunt down *oppose* 63.11, *hunt* 385.14, *suppress* 424.9
hunted *pursued* 385.10, *fugitive* 386.10

Hunter Rivers 570
hunter 160.9, 385.6; *animal killer* 30.14, *horse* 159.1, *shooter* 696.11
hunter or **hunting watch** Timepieces and Timers 646
hunter pace *equestrianism* 159.8
hunter's moon *moon* 7.18
hunter trials *equestrianism* 159.8
hunt for *hunt* 160.12
hunting 160.2, 160.11, 385.9; *animal killing* 30.10, Sporting Activities 145, *pursuit* 385.1, *hunt* 385.3, *flight maneuver* 689.6
hunting accessories 160.5
hunting and shooting *hunt* 385.3
hunting associations 160.8
hunting blind *that which makes invisible* 245.2
hunting boots *hunting accessories* 160.5
hunting clothes *hunting accessories* 160.5
hunting dog 160.7; *dog* 35.10
Hunting Dogs Constellations 7
hunting equipment 160.4
hunting jacket *hunting accessories* 160.5
hunting license *game laws* 160.3, *permit* 503.2
hunting limit *game laws* 160.3
hunting lodge *hunting associations* 160.8
hunting party *hunting associations* 160.8
hunting rifle *hunting equipment* 160.4
hunting season *game laws* 160.3, *seasons* 654.2
Huntington's chorea *neurological disease* 114.20
hunt out *drive out* 709.19
huntress *hunter* 385.6
huntsman *animal killer* 30.14, *hunter* 385.6
hunt the facts *question* 333.16
Huon pine Trees and Shrubs 43
hurdle *competitive diving* 164.7, *hurdles* 166.6, *participate* 166.22, *climb* 713.21, *spring up* 713.22, *snag* 824.8, *obstacle* 826.2
hurdle [Brit] *farm building* 16.4
hurdler *track and field eventer* 166.19
hurdle race *horse racing* 159.10
hurdles 166.6
hurdling Sporting Activities 145, *track and field* 166.20
hurdy-gurdy Musical Instruments 142
hurl *throw* 696.4, 696.17
hurl at *stone* 418.23
hurl a volley of abuse at *vilify* 301.15
hurl defiance at *defy* 416.7
hurler *thrower* 696.10
hurling Sporting Activities 145, *throwing* 696.3
hurling [Brit] *hockey* 158.1
hurl oneself *be violent* 520.8
hurly-burly *tumult* 684.2, *disruption* 766.7, *commotion* 768.5
Huron Lakes 568
hurrah *cry of praise* 239.3, *cheer* 239.15, *applause* 279.2
hurrah! *bravo!* 279.8, 437.23
hurray! *bravo!* 437.23
hurricane *wind vortex* 9.14, *natural violence* 520.3, *rough thing* 544.2, *atmospheric agitation* 684.13, *natural hazard* 813.4
hurricane-force *windy* 9.42
hurricanes Phobias 283

hurricane warning *warning*
814.1

hurricane watch *or* **warning**
weather forecast 9.4

hurried *swift* 694.6, *hasty* 818.3

hurriedly *early* 657.17, *hastily*
818.7

hurry *alacrity* 414.3, *be active*
414.18, *motivate* 508.9, *start early*
657.12, *swiftness* 694.1, *scamper*
694.12, *haste* 818.1, *hasten* 818.4,
make haste 818.5

hurrying *speeding* 694.7

hurryingly 694.18

hurry off 705.11

hurry-scurry *alacrity* 414.3, *haste*
818.1

hurry someone up 694.15

hurry up! 818.9

hurry-up offense *offense* 155.6

hurt *pain* 117.5, 215.1, *miserable*
117.12, *feeling pain* 215.6, *feel
pain* 215.8, *be painful* 215.9,
inflict pain 215.10, *offense* 302.2,
offended 302.9, *offend* 302.15,
malignity 306.5, *harm* 306.13,
wrongdoing 430.7, *wrong* 430.19,
be evil 446.10, *punish* 454.22,
weaken 517.13, *inconvenience*
804.1, *be inconvenient* 804.9

Hurter-Driffield (H-D) curve
exposure 132.15

hurtful *inflicting pain* 215.7, *malign*
306.11, *unlawful* 430.15,
detrimental 446.8, *unpleasant*
501.5, *inconvenient* 804.5

hurtfully *painfully* 215.12,
destructively 446.13

hurtfulness *pain* 215.1,
unpleasantness 501.2

hurting *painful* 215.4, *feeling pain*
215.6, *inflicting pain* 215.7,
insolvent 486.10

hurtle *be violent* 520.8, *be swift*
694.10

hurtle [Arch] *collide* 695.10

hurtling *speeding* 694.7

hurt one's pocket *cost a lot* 496.9

hurt pride *humiliation* 298.5

hurt the ears *be dissonant* 241.6

husband *man* 27.8, *man in the
family* 32.12, *economize* 56.11,
married man 64.10, *family member*
65.2, *master* 68.1, *deposit* 105.21,
loved one 299.13, *be thrifty* 499.5,
partner 794.2

husband and wife *married couple*
64.9

husbandhood *marriage* 64.1

husbandless *widowed* 66.8, *celibate*
67.6

husbandly *matrimonial* 64.15

husbandman *agriculturist* 16.14

husband one's resources *be
thrifty* 499.5

husbandry *agriculture* 16.1, *home
economics* 56.2, *management*
126.1, *conservation* 815.2

husband swapping *sexual
intercourse* 20.9

hush *strike dumb* 206.10, *silence*
231.1, 231.4, *mute* 233.9, *hiss*
237.1, 237.3, *calm* 521.8, *repose*
678.2, *make smaller* 747.8

hush! 231.6

hushed *silent* 231.2, *faint* 233.6,
quiescent 678.6

hushed tone *undercurrent of sound*
233.3

hush-hush *secret* 182.8, *important*
799.7, *concealed* 844.7

hush money *bribe* 472.3, *levy*
494.7, *positive stimulus* 508.5

hush puppy *bread* 90.10

hush up *keep secret* 182.11

husk *seed* 41.9, *fruit structure* 44.3,
cereal grass 45.4, Collective
Names 59, *emptiness* 576.2,
exteriority 610.2, *casing* 613.9,
depilate 614.20, *remainder* 750.1,
residue 750.2

husked *shed* 614.14

huskily *voicelessly* 206.11, *strongly*
516.17

huskiness *speech difficulty* 206.1,
hoarseness 238.2

husking *peeling* 614.6

husks *refuse* 802.5

husky Breeds of Dogs 35, *voiceless*
206.5, *nonresonant* 233.7, *hoarse*
238.5, *physically strong* 516.10

hussar *horse person* 159.14

hussy *young woman* 26.9, *loose
woman* 33.6, *insolent person* 400.7,
sexually immoral person 432.8

hustings *publicity* 173.7

hustle *alacrity* 414.3, *be active*
414.18, *request* 505.10, *motivate*
508.9, *set in motion* 677.16, *jolt*
684.23, *be swift* 694.10, *blow*
695.5, *impel* 695.9, *propel* 696.15,
haste 818.1, *hasten* 818.4, *make
haste* 818.5

hustle [Inf] *prostitute* 432.17, *steal*
479.14

hustle and bustle *alacrity* 414.3

hustle away *hasten* 818.4

hustle out *expel* 709.14

hustler *busy person* 414.10,
requester 505.5, *speeder* 694.5

hustler [Inf] *sexually immoral
person* 432.8

hustling *busy* 414.15, *speeding*
694.7

hustling [Inf] *stealing* 479.1

hut *shack* 60.10

hutch *farm building* 16.4, *mammal
dwelling* 35.21, *shack* 60.10, *cage*
60.15, *cabinet* 101.8, *receptacle*
105.11, *closed place* 584.4, *enclose*
584.16, *enclosed area* 619.2,
shelter 812.4

hutzpa [Inf] *audacity* 400.3,
defiance 416.1, *assurance*
621.8

Hu-Yang Breeds of Sheep 16

Huygens' principle *wavelength*
683.5

huzzah *cry of praise* 239.3, *cheer*
239.15, *applause* 279.2, *acclaim*
437.5, 437.18

hyacinth Flowers 42

hyacinthine *blue* 261.5, *purple*
262.6

Hyaenidae *flesh-eating mammal*
35.9

hyaline *transparent thing* 249.4,
transparent 249.7

hyalite *transparent thing* 249.4

hyalophobia *or* **hyelophobia**
Phobias 283

hyancinth *purple thing* 262.3

hybrid 751.6; *new word* 5.18, *plant
breeding* 17.6, *mixed* 751.8,
compound 757.4

hybrid bike *bicycle* 687.10

hybrid computer *computer* 15.1

hybrid flower *hybrid* 751.6

hybridization *chemical bond* 11.6,
mixture 751.1

hybridize *mix* 751.12

hybrid language *regional
pronunciation* 205.7

hybrid orbital *chemical bond* 11.6

hybrid word *or* **expression** *new
word* 5.18

hydathode *secretory mechanism*
24.3

hydatid *invertebrate larva* 39.19

Hyde Park *London* 567.8

hydra Legendary Creatures 360

hydragogue *solvent* 555.9

hydrangea Flowers 42

hydrant *irrigator* 557.13

hydrate 557.6; *salt* 11.12, *react*
11.38, *water* 557.29

hydrated *acid* 11.27, *watery*
557.21

hydration *weathering* 8.40, *hydrate*
557.6

hydraulic *mechanical* 103.7, *watery*
557.21

hydraulically *instrumentally*
103.9, *hydrodynamically* 557.35

hydraulic cement *industrial
ceramics* 129.6

hydraulic engineer *civil engineer*
14.19

hydraulic engineering *civil
engineering* 14.17

hydraulic lift *lifter* 715.5

hydraulic power *type of power*
514.6

hydraulics *fluid mechanics* 555.13,
hydrography 557.18

hydraulic tailgate *lifter* 715.5

hydraulis *or* **hydraulos** Musical
Instruments 142

hydrocephalic *of disease* 114.25

hydrocephalous *of disease* 114.25

**hydrochlorofluorocarbon
(HCFC)** *pollution* 117.8

hydrocortisone Human
Hormones 12

hydrodynamic *physical* 10.70,
watery 557.21

hydrodynamically 557.35;
physically 10.78

hydrodynamics *classical physics*
10.2, *fluid mechanics* 555.13,
hydrography 557.18

hydroelectric *electric* 14.47, *gas*
106.14

hydroelectrically *powerfully*
106.19

hydroelectrical power *power
source* 514.13

hydroelectricity *electricity* 106.5

hydroelectric plant *power
supplier* 514.14

hydroelectric power *renewable
energy* 106.9, *type of power* 514.6

hydrofoil Ships and Boats 690

hydrogen Chemical Elements and
Common Allotropes 11, *essential
element* 12.15, *propellant* 696.9

hydrogenate *react* 11.38, *aerate*
556.24

hydrogenated fat *fat* 562.4

hydrogen balloon *lifter* 715.5

hydrogen bomb *bomb* 78.15,
nuclear power production 514.10

hydrogen bond *chemical bond*
11.6

hydrogen cyanide *poison* 117.7

hydrogen electrode
electrochemistry 11.19

hydrogen peroxide *prophylaxis*
115.4, *color remover* 252.4

hydrogen sulfide *unpleasant-
smelling thing* 227.2

hydrogeologist *geologist* 8.4

hydrogeology *geology* 8.1, *fluid
mechanics* 555.13

hydrograph *measuring instrument*
557.19

hydrographer *hydrologist* 557.20,
oceanographer 571.6

hydrographic *geophysical* 8.51,
oceanographic 571.8

hydrographically
oceanographically 571.11

hydrography 557.18;
oceanography 571.5

hydroid *coelenterate* 39.25

hydrokinetics *fluid mechanics*
555.13, *hydrography* 557.18

hydrolase *enzyme* 12.11

hydrolized *disintegrating* 758.5

hydrological 570.9; *geologic* 8.50

hydrological cycle *water cycle*
8.12

hydrologically *geologically* 8.68,
fluently 570.13

hydrologic cycle *water cycle*
557.17

hydrologist 557.20

hydrology *fluid mechanics* 555.13,
hydrography 557.18

hydrolysis *hydrate* 557.6,
deconstruction 758.2

hydrolytically *to pieces* 758.8

hydrolyze *react* 11.38, *deconstruct*
758.7

hydromancy *divination* 86.5, *holy
water* 557.15

hydromechanics *fluid mechanics*
555.13, *hydrography* 557.18

hydrometeor *precipitation* 9.26,
water cycle 557.17

hydrometeorologic(al) *rainy*
9.50

hydrometeorology *meteorology*
9.1

hydrometer *relative density* 540.3,
flowmeter 555.12, Fields of
Measurement 589

hydrometric *watery* 557.21

hydrometrically *hydrodynamically*
557.35

hydrometry *hydrography* 557.18,
Fields of Measurement 589

hydropathy *hydrotherapy* 557.7

hydrophilic *status adjectives* 11.25

hydrophobia *infection* 114.7,
Phobias 283

hydrophobic *status adjectives* 11.25

hydrophobophobia Phobias 283

hydrophyte *plant* 41.2

hydrophytic *of plants* 41.14

hydroponic *agricultural* 16.16,
horticultural 17.14

hydroponically *agriculturally*
16.21, *horticulturally* 17.20

hydroponic food *food* 90.1

hydroponics *arable farming* 16.6,
gardening 17.5, *hydrography*
557.18

hydroscopically *hydrodynamically*
557.35

hydrosol *phase* 11.13

hydrosphere Earth 8.6, *water cycle*
557.17

hydrospheric *terrestrial* 8.52,
hydrological 570.9

hydrostat *measuring instrument*
557.19

hydrostatic *watery* 557.21,
hydrological 570.9

hydrostatically *hydrodynamically*
557.35

hydrostatic head *water cycle*
557.17

hydrostatics *fluid mechanics*
555.13, *hydrography* 557.18

hydrotherapeutic *cleansing*
557.27

hydrotherapeutics *hydrotherapy*
557.7

hydrotherapy 557.7; *therapy*
115.12

hydrothermal water *water* 557.1

hydrous *watery* 557.21

Hydrozoa *coelenterate* 39.15

hydrozoan *coelenterate* 39.15,
39.25

Hydrus Constellations 7
hyetographic(al) *rainy* 9.50
hyetography *meteorology* 9.1
Hygiea Planets and Their Satellites 7
hygiene 116.1; *health care* 107.7, *cleaning* 111.2, *ablutions* 111.4, *healthfulness* 113.2, *prophylaxis* 115.4, *sanitary precaution* 810.8
hygienic 116.13; *clean* 111.13, *cleansing* 111.16, *healthful* 113.7, *remedial* 115.14, *safe* 810.16, *tutelary* 810.19, *preserving* 815.11
hygienically 116.5; *cleanly* 111.20, *healthily* 113.14, *safely* 810.24
hygienics *health improvement* 113.3
hygienist 116.2; *paramedic* 107.24
hygric 557.28
hygrograph *weather instrument* 9.7, *measuring instrument* 557.19
hygrographic *barometric* 9.39
hygrometer *weather instrument* 9.7, *measuring instrument* 557.19, Fields of Measurement 589
hygrometric *barometric* 9.39, *hygric* 557.28
hygrometry *hydrography* 557.18, Fields of Measurement 589
hygrophilous *hygric* 557.28
hygrophobia Phobias 283
hygroscope *measuring instrument* 557.19
hygroscopic *hygric* 557.28
hygrothermal *hygric* 557.28
hygrothermograph *measuring instrument* 557.19
hylomorphism Philosophical Schools of Thought 4
hylomorphist Philosophical Schools of Thought 4
hylotheism Philosophical Schools of Thought 4
hylotheist Philosophical Schools of Thought 4
hylozoism Philosophical Schools of Thought 4
hylozoist Philosophical Schools of Thought 4
Hymen *gods and goddesses of marriage* 64.14
hymen *body covering* 19.4
hymeneal *general wedding terms* 64.6, *matrimonial* 64.15
hymeneal rites *wedding* 64.5
hymenium *fungal body* 47.4
hymenopteran *or* **hymenopterous** *insectile* 40.11
Hymettus Mountains and Hills 569
hymn *ritual music* 85.9, Poem or Verse Forms 139, Musical Forms 140, *sacred music* 140.3, *song* 140.11, *applause* 279.2, *thanks* 310.2
hymnal *ritual music* 85.9
hymnody *sacred music* 140.3
hymnography *ritual music* 85.9
hymnographical *singing* 85.16
hymnological *singing* 85.16
hymnology *ritual music* 85.9, *sacred music* 140.3
hymn singer *worshiper* 83.6
hymn singing *act of worship* 83.2, *ritual music* 85.9
hymn-singing *singing* 85.16
hymn writer *composer* 141.9
hyoid bone Human Bones 19
hypabyssal intrusion *igneous rock* 8.32
hype [Inf] *drug taker* 121.12, *drug dose* 121.15, *public relations (PR)*

173.8, *publicize* 173.18, 178.19, *publicity* 178.7, *exaggeration* 194.1, *exaggerate* 194.11, *overestimation* 343.1, *overestimate* 343.6, *compliment* 437.17, *flattery* 439.1, *flatter* 439.12, *promote* 807.18
hyped [Inf] *exaggerated* 194.7
hyped-up [Inf] *susceptible* 212.7
hypegiaphobia Phobias 283
hyper [Inf] *fidgety* 414.14
hyperacidity *gastroenterological disease* 114.11
hyperactive *susceptible* 212.7, *fidgety* 414.14
hyperactive child *busy person* 414.10
hyperactivity *overactivity* 414.9
hyperbola *curve* 6.38, 629.1
hyperbole *exaggeration* 194.1, *overestimation* 343.1, *unrestrainedness* 500.2, *excessiveness* 712.4
hyperbolic *curvilinear* 6.78, *exaggerated* 194.7, 712.9, *unrestrained* 500.5, *ornate* 532.10, *curved* 629.4
hyperbolically *exaggeratedly* 194.16, *overoptimistically* 343.7, *ornately* 532.14, *curvedly* 629.7, *excessively* 712.17
hyperbolic cosine (cosh) *trigonometric function* 6.50
hyperbolic function *trigonometric function* 6.50
hyperbolic geometry *geometry* 6.32
hyperbolic orbit *orbit* 7.22
hyperbolic sine (sinh) *trigonometric function* 6.50
hyperbolic spiral *curve* 6.38
hyperbolic tangent (tanh) *trigonometric function* 6.50
hyperbolism *exaggeration* 194.1
hyperbolize *exaggerate* 194.11
hyperboloid *curved surface* 6.43
hyperboloid(al) *spherical* 6.80
hyperborean *distant* 585.5, *directional* 697.8
hypercathexis *cathexis* 108.32
hypercritical *critical* 438.13, *troublesome* 824.13
hypercriticalness *criticism* 438.4
hypercriticism *criticism* 438.4
hypercube *space* 6.33
hyperesthesia *sensitivity* 212.2
hyperfocal distance *composition* 132.17
hypericum Flowers 42
Hyperion Planets and Their Satellites 7, *sun* 7.15, Deities 82
hyperopia *sight defect* 243.2
hyperopic *weak-sighted* 243.10
hyperphysical *psychic* 86.17
hyperphysics *supernaturalism* 86.3
hyperplasia *gigantism* 579.4
hyperpyrexia *symptom* 114.3
hypersensitive *oversensitive* 267.4, *touchy* 303.10
hypersensitively *touchily* 303.19
hypersensitivity *oversensitivity* 267.2, *touchiness* 303.3
hypersensitization *exposure* 132.15
hypersonic *flyable* 689.12, *swift* 694.6
hypersonically *swiftly* 694.16
hypersonic speed *speed* 694.2
hyperspace *space* 6.33
hypersphere *space* 6.33
hypertension *symptom* 114.3, *cardiovascular disease* 114.13
hyperthermia *symptom* 114.3

hyperthyroidism *overactivity* 414.9
hypertrophied *grown* 581.11
hypertrophy *gigantism* 579.4, *growth* 581.4, *increase* 581.16
hypha *fungal body* 47.4
hyphal *of fungi* 47.19
hyphen Accents and Diacritical Marks 5, *joint* 752.7, *separator* 753.5, *means of connection* 754.4
hyphenate *punctuate* 183.20, *unite* 752.14
hyphenated *punctuated* 183.15, *connected* 754.11
hyphenation *linkage* 752.3
hyping [Inf] *bombastic* 194.10
hypnophobia Phobias 283
hypnosis *occult and psychic phenomena* 86.7, *analgesic* 115.6, *desensitization* 213.2, *anesthetic* 213.3, Phobias 283, *oblivion* 355.4, *sleep* 415.5
hypnospore *reproductive body* 47.14
hypnotherapeutic *psychological* 108.36
hypnotherapist *psychologist* 108.33
hypnotherapy *psychotherapy* 108.4, *therapy* 115.12
hypnotic *witchlike* 86.19, *medicinal* 115.15, *anesthetic* 213.6, *reliever* 275.4, *relieving* 275.7, *compelling* 428.6, *motivational* 508.7, *appealing* 512.9, *moderating* 521.5
hypnotically *occultly* 86.27, *forgetfully* 355.14, *compellingly* 428.12, *influentially* 508.13, 512.14, *attractionally* 700.13
hypnotic trance *occult and psychic phenomena* 86.7, *trance* 108.18
hypnotism *occultism* 86.1, *magic* 138.3, *occult influence* 512.2, *pulling power* 700.2
hypnotist *occultist* 86.13, *magician* 138.11, *motivator* 508.6
hypnotize *bewitch* 86.25, *entertain* 138.16, *anesthetize* 213.8, *make inactive* 415.16, *be irresistible* 428.9, *manipulate* 508.12, *be an influence* 512.13, *lure* 700.12
hypnotized *bewitched* 86.21, *desensitized* 213.5, *oblivious* 355.9, *not awake* 415.12, *motivated* 508.8
hypnotizer *motivator* 508.6
Hypnus Deities 82
hypo *darkroom equipment* 132.21
hypoaeolian mode *mode* 140.17
hypocaust *heater* 217.3
hypocenter (focus) *seismic activity* 8.24
hypochondria *delusion* 110.2, *ill health* 114.1
hypochondriac *insane person* 110.5, *sick person* 114.22, *unhealthy* 114.23, *weak person* 517.4
hypochondriacal *psychologically disturbed* 108.39
hypochondriasis *somatoform disorder* 108.19
hypocrisy 330.5; *ungenuineness* 192.2, *flattery* 439.1, *cunning* 822.1
hypocrite 192.9; *assenter* 346.3, *pretender* 367.2, *distorter* 627.5, *cunning person* 822.3
hypocritical 330.10; *ungenuine* 192.13, *flattering* 439.7, *double-edged* 789.10, *cunning* 822.4
hypocritically 330.15; *untruthfully* 192.27, *distortedly* 627.14

hypocriticalness *ungenuineness* 192.2
hypocycloid *curve* 6.38
hypodermic needle *sharp-pointed thing* 549.4, *opener* 583.2
hypodorian mode *mode* 140.17
hypogeal *or* **hypogaeal** *under* 598.13
hypogeous *or* **hypogaeous** *under* 598.13
hypogynous *of flowers* 42.11
hypoid gear *gear* 14.7
hypoionian mode *mode* 140.17
hypolydian mode *mode* 140.17
hypomania *delusion* 110.2
hypomaniac *insane person* 110.5
hypomanic episode *mood disorder* 108.12
hypomenorrhea *bleeding* 25.10
hypomixolydian mode *mode* 140.17
hypophyge Architectural Elements 134
hypotaxis *syntax* 5.32
hypotension *symptom* 114.3, *cardiovascular disease* 114.13
hypotenuse *triangle* 6.41
hypotheca *plant body* 47.13
hypothermia *symptom* 114.3, *climbing dangers* 161.5
hypothesis *philosophy* 4.1, *philosophical term* 4.7, *theory* 6.62, 327.2, 720.4, *physical law* 10.4, *belief* 87.1, *contention* 189.4, *explanation* 319.4, *line of argument* 329.3, *supposition* 359.1
hypothesist *theorist* 359.4
hypothesis testing 6.52
hypothesize *philosophize* 4.19, *theorize* 6.84, 327.16, 720.14, *contend* 189.24, *have an idea* 317.12, *state* 329.13, *suppose* 359.8
hypothesized *contended* 189.15, *supposed* 359.6
hypothesizer *philosopher* 4.9
hypothetical *philosophical* 4.12, *theoretical* 6.66, 10.71, 327.10, 720.10, *believed* 87.8, *contended* 189.15, *logical* 329.9, *suppositional* 359.5, *imaginary* 360.12, *uncertain* 841.9
hypothetical argument *supposition* 359.1
hypothetically *theoretically* 4.24, 327.19, *believably* 87.13, *allegedly* 189.31, *arguably* 329.16, *supposedly* 359.10, *ideally* 720.18
hypsographic *or* **hypsographical** *altimetrical* 596.13
hypsography *height measurement* 596.5
hypsometer *height measurement* 596.5
hypsometric *or* **hypsometrical** *altimetrical* 596.13
hypsometrically *altimetrically* 596.23
hypsometry Fields of Measurement 589, *height measurement* 596.5
hypsophobia *or* **hypsiphobia** Phobias 283
hyracoid *ungulate* 35.31
Hyracoidea *hoofed mammal* 35.16
hyraxlike *ungulate* 35.31
hyssop Flowers 42, Herbs and Spices 91
hysterectomy *that which makes infertile* 23.4
hysteresis *magnetic phenomenon* 10.50, *hesitation* 693.5

hysteretic *delayed* 693.10
hysteria *anxiety disorder* 108.11, *somatoform disorder* 108.19, *delusion* 110.2, *mental breakdown* 110.4
hysteric *insane person* 110.5
hysterical *manic* 110.10, *passionate* 266.12, *humorous* 277.9, *violent* 520.5
hysterically *psychologically* 108.42, *with feeling* 266.18
hysterical trance *trance* 108.18
hysteron proteron *inverted thing* 608.4
hysteroscope *diagnostic instrument* 107.13

I

I *someone* 18.10, *one* 788.1
IAL *Programming Languages* 15
iamb *meter* 139.10
iambic *metrical* 139.20
iambic pentameter *meter* 139.10
Iapetus *Planets and Their Satellites* 7
iatric *medical* 107.28
iatrogenic *of disease* 114.25
iatrophobia *Phobias* 283
I-beam *superstructure* 551.7
ibid *identically* 730.18
ibidem [L] *identically* 730.18
ibis *water bird* 36.9
Ibiza *Islands* 572
Ibizan hound *Breeds of Dogs* 35
Iblis *Legendary Creatures* 360, *devil* 446.5
ibuprofen *analgesic* 115.6
Icarus *Planets and Their Satellites* 7
ice 218.5; *frost* 9.25, *snow* 9.58, *dessert* 90.35, *climbing dangers* 161.5, *mountaineering* 161.9, *skiing snow* 162.3, *sweeten* 222.7, *transparent thing* 249.4, *Phobias* 283, *brittle thing* 548.2, *water* 557.1, *top* 600.10, *coat* 613.28, *preserver* 815.9
ice! *danger!* 162.39
Ice Age *Ages, Decades, Eras* 641
ice age *glaciation* 8.46, *climatic change* 9.37, *cold weather* 218.8, *geological past* 651.5
ice ax *climbing equipment* 161.4
ice bag *cooler* 218.4
ice bar *ice fishing* 154.4
iceberg 8.45; *island* 572.2
iceberg [Inf] *insensitive person* 268.3, *unsocial person* 409.5
ice-blue *blue* 261.5
iceboat *Ships and Boats* 690
iceboating *Sporting Activities* 145
icebound *cold* 218.9
icebox *kitchen container* 91.7, *refrigerator* 105.10, *cooler* 218.4
icebox [Inf] *prison cell* 55.3
icebreaker *warship* 77.21
icebreaker *or* **iceboat** *Ships and Boats* 690
ice bucket *cooler* 218.4
icecap *glacier* 8.44, *ice* 218.5
ice climbing *Sporting Activities* 145, *mountaineering* 161.1
ice cloud *cloud* 9.17
ice-cold *cold* 218.9
ice cream *dessert* 90.35, *confectionery* 222.3
ice-cream cone *dessert* 90.35
ice-cream parlor *eating place* 92.17
ice-cream social *party* 408.6
ice-cream soda *soft drink* 93.8, *sweet drink* 222.4

ice crystal *precipitation* 9.26
ice cube *ice* 218.5
iced *frozen* 218.10, *sweet* 222.5, *preserved* 815.12
ice-dance *ice-skating* 162.32
ice-dance music *ice-dancing move* 162.19
ice dancer *ice skater* 162.22
ice dancing 162.18; *Sporting Activities* 145
ice-dancing move 162.19
iced coffee *coffee* 93.6
iced up *cold* 218.9
icefall *glacier* 8.44
ice field *glacier* 8.44, *ice* 218.5
ice fish *fish* 154.14
ice fishing 154.4; *Sporting Activities* 145
ice floe *iceberg* 8.45, *ice* 218.5, *island* 572.2
ice hockey *Sporting Activities* 145, *hockey* 158.1
ice hockey stick *hockey equipment* 158.3
ice hockey tactics 158.4
ice hole *ice fishing* 154.4
ice house *cooler* 218.4
Iceland *cold place* 218.7, *Countries* 566, *Islands* 572
Icelandic *Breeds of Cattle* 16, *Breeds of Sheep* 16
Iceland pony *Horse and Pony Breeds* 159
ice machine *cooler* 218.4
Iceman *Legendary Creatures* 360
ice milk *milk* 93.5
ice over *snow* 9.58, *become cold* 218.14
ice pack *iceberg* 8.45, *cooler* 218.4
icepick *sharp-pointed thing* 549.4
ice queen [Inf] *insensitive person* 268.3
ice raft *iceberg* 8.45
ice rink *hockey areas* 158.2
ice screws *climbing equipment* 161.4
ice sheet *glacier* 8.44, *ice* 218.5
ice shelf *glacier* 8.44
ice show *circus* 138.2
ice-skate 162.36
ice skater 162.22
ice skates *means of transportation* 686.2
ice skating 162.15
ice-skating 162.32
ice-skating association 162.21
ice-skating techniques 162.16
ice spoon *ice fishing* 154.4
ice surfing *windsurfing* 150.19
ice the puck *play ice hockey* 158.9
ice tongue *glacier* 8.44
ice up *become cold* 218.14
ice water *water* 93.4
I Ching *other text* 81.19, *divination* 86.5
ichor *pus* 25.7, *body fluid* 555.3
ichorous *rheumy* 555.16
ichthyic *fishlike* 38.10
ichthyoid(al) *fishlike* 38.10
ichthyolite *fossil fish* 38.7
ichthyological 38.11
ichthyologist 38.3; *animal scientist* 34.7
ichthyology *animal science* 34.6, *study of fish* 38.2
ichthyomancy *divination* 86.5
ichthyomorphic *fishlike* 38.10
ichthyophagy *eating habit* 92.7
ichthyophile *ichthyologist* 38.3
ichthyophobia *Phobias* 283
ichthyopterygian *extinct reptile* 37.9
ichthyosaur *extinct reptile* 37.9

ichthyosaurus *prehistoric animal* 653.8
ichthyosis *dry skin* 560.6
icicle *ice* 218.5, *insensitive person* 268.3, *brittle thing* 548.2
icily *coldly* 218.16, *unsocially* 409.13, *toughly* 542.12
iciness *hostility* 63.1, *freezing* 218.2, *unsociability* 409.1
icing *ice hockey tactics* 158.4, *freezing* 218.2, *confectionery* 222.3, *top layer* 600.5, *coating* 613.8, *miscellaneous aviation terms* 689.9
icing on the cake *ornamentation* 748.5
icing sugar *sweetener* 222.2
ICON *Programming Languages* 15
icon *computing terms* 15.22, *idol* 83.5, *sacred object* 83.11, *actor* 137.13, *painting* 143.3, *image* 187.3
iconic *pictorial* 133.8, *representational* 187.8, *representing* 202.14
iconoclasm *destructiveness* 523.3, *nonconformism* 782.3
iconoclast *religionist* 81.14, *destroyer* 523.6, *dissenter* 782.8
iconoclastic *nonconformist* 782.13
iconography *symbolism* 183.4
iconolater *idolater* 83.7
iconolatrous *idolatrous* 83.13
iconolatry *idolatry* 83.4
iconology *symbolism* 183.4
icon painter *painter* 143.7
icosahedron *polyhedron* 6.44
icterus *yellow skin* 259.3
icthyomancer *diviner* 86.14
icy *windy* 9.42, *cool* 9.49, *hostile* 63.6, *cold* 218.9, *strong-willed* 376.10, *unsociable* 409.6, *hardened* 542.7, *seasonal* 654.7
ID *means of identification* 184.3, *documentation* 339.6
id *psyche* 108.25, *libido* 108.26, *internal world* 525.6
Ida *Mountains and Hills* 569
Idaho *American States* 564
Idared *Apple Varieties* 44
ID card *personal identification* 184.4
idea 327.1; *philosophy* 4.1, *belief* 87.1, *image* 187.3, *impression* 266.2, *creative thought* 317.3, *theory* 327.2, *topic* 328.1, *gist* 329.4, *invention* 345.4, *supposition* 359.1, *conception* 360.4, *meaning* 361.1, *point* 361.5, *caprice* 381.1, *method* 387.4, *spontaneity* 396.2, *work of art* 522.4, *form* 624.1, *reason* 675.4
idea behind *reason* 675.4
idea conveyed *meaning* 361.1
ideal 327.6, 327.12, 805.6, **805.17**; *philosophical* 4.12, *motive* 178.5, *object of desire* 288.8, *conception* 360.4, *imaginary* 360.12, *good* 445.1, *motivation* 508.1, *undertaking* 675.5, *theoretical* 720.10, *limit* 761.4
ideal, the *perfection* 805.1
idealism 327.7, 360.7, 525.5; *Philosophical Schools of Thought* 4, *overestimation* 343.1, *unselfishness* 443.2, *virtue* 447.1, *theory* 720.4
idealist *Philosophical Schools of Thought* 4, *philosopher* 4.9, *hoper* 281.5, *discriminator* 337.6, *overestimator* 343.2, *visionary* 360.9, *attempter* 390.3, *nonmaterialist* 525.7, *idealistic* 525.10, *unrealistic person* 720.6
idealistic 525.10; *hopeful* 281.6, *ideal* 327.12, *imaginative* 360.10,

unselfish 443.5, *virtuous* 447.5, *unrealistic* 720.11, *improving* 807.14
idealistically *theoretically* 4.24, *imaginatively* 327.21, 360.17, *overoptimistically* 343.7, *unselfishly* 443.9, *virtuously* 447.9, *subjectively* 525.14
ideality *idealism* 327.7, *supposition* 359.1, *conception* 360.4
idealization *theory* 6.62, *idealism* 327.7, *conception* 360.4
idealize 720.15; *idolize* 83.16, *imagine* 327.14, *fantasize* 360.15
idealized *ideal* 327.12, *good* 445.10
idealized pleasure 214.5
ideally 327.22, 720.18; *theoretically* 4.24, *well* 445.19
idealness *idealism* 327.7, *perfection* 805.1
ideals *ideology* 327.5, *way of life* 399.9, *morals* 431.2, *virtues* 447.2
idea of, the *supposition* 359.1
ideas *materials* 104.1, *Phobias* 283
ideate *think* 315.12, *have an idea* 317.12, *imagine* 327.14
ideation *thought* 317.1, *conception* 360.4
ideational 327.9; *philosophical* 4.12
ideatum *idea* 327.1
I declare! *wonderful!* 294.20
idée fixe [Fr] *prejudgment* 342.5, *opinionatedness* 379.3
idem *same* 730.7
identical *ranked* 6.72, *similar* 361.7, *same* 730.7, *look-alike* 730.10, *equal* 790.7
identically 730.18; *equally* 790.13
identicalness *sameness* 730.1
identical twin *look-alike* 730.4
identical twins *twin* 789.5
identifiability *visibility* 244.1
identifiable 843.10; *identified* 184.9, *visible* 244.5, *discoverable* 345.10, *recognizable* 363.7
identifiably 184.13; *originally* 345.16
identification 184.1; *defense mechanism* 108.23, *nomenclature* 202.7, *discovery* 345.1, *memory* 354.1
identification (ID) *certificate* 185.2
identification papers *personal identification* 184.4
identification sign *sign* 183.1
identified 184.9; *named* 202.13
identify 184.11; *discover* 345.11, *know* 348.10, *remember* 354.12, *recognize* 363.11, *choose* 382.14, *characterize* 723.11, 779.15
identifying *signifying* 183.11
identifying sign *sign* 183.1
identify oneself 184.12
identify with *have a rapport with* 735.24
Identikit™ *means of identification* 184.3
identity 184.2; *philosophical term* 4.7, *set* 6.19, *equality* 6.24, *type of meaning* 361.4, *sameness* 730.1, *compatibility* 735.4, *singularity* 788.4
identity card *personal identification* 184.4, *documentation* 339.6
identity element *set* 6.19
identity matrix *matrix* 6.20
ideogram *or* **ideograph** *written letter* 5.14
ideographic *written* 5.36
ideological *philosophical* 4.12, *reasoning* 317.6, *ideal* 327.12

ideologically 327.23; *theoretically* 4.24

ideological war *war of independence* 76.9

ideologue *philosopher* 4.9

ideology 327.5; *philosophical system* 4.2, *belief system* 87.3

ideophobia Phobias 283

ides *day* 646.4

id est [L] *demonstrably* 331.22

idiochromosome *chromosome* 13.21

idiocrasy *caprice* 381.1

idiocy *lack of intellect* 316.1, *folly* 353.1

idiographic *philosophical* 4.12

idiolect *nonstandard language* 5.7, *vernacular* 205.8, *mode of expression* 537.3

idiom *dialect* 5.24, *vernacular* 205.8, *type of meaning* 361.4, *unpretentiousness* 526.2, *style* 537.1

idiomatic *of language* 5.35, *symbolic* 361.8, *characteristic* 779.12

idiomatically *colloquially* 5.45, *stylistically* 537.11

idiomatic speech *vernacular* 205.8

idiophone *musical instrument* 142.1

idioplasm *cell structure* 13.16

idiosyncrasy 782.5; *caprice* 381.1, *tendency* 397.2, *attitude* 513.2, *style* 537.1, *originality* 737.1, *characteristic* 779.5, *defect* 806.4

idiosyncratic *capricious* 381.4, *characteristic* 723.9, 779.12, *unusual* 782.15

idiosyncratically *stylistically* 537.11

idiot *unintelligent person* 316.4, *foolish person* 353.3, *object of ridicule* 368.3

idiot box [Inf] *television set* 172.6

idiotic *intellectually subnormal* 316.7, *foolish* 353.5, *meaningless* 362.7

idiotically *unintelligently* 316.9, *foolishly* 353.8, *ridiculously* 368.8

idiot savant *wonderful person* 294.6

idle 394.6; *leisurely* 125.4, *apathetic* 322.4, *inactive* 413.9, *have free time* 413.15, *not working* 415.10, *not participating* 415.11, *be inactive* 415.13, *inert* 519.2, *be motionless* 678.7, *unhurried* 693.8, *move slowly* 693.11, *futile* 802.10, *at ease* 819.2

idle fancy *idealism* 360.7

idle gossip *talk* 207.3, *chat* 210.2

idle hours *leisure* 413.4

idle moments *leisure* 125.1

idleness 415.3; *leisure* 125.1, 413.4, *apathy* 322.2, *disuse* 394.3, *inertness* 519.1, *futility* 802.3, *ease* 819.1

idler *neglector* 326.3, *avoider* 386.8, *inactive person* 413.8, *nonworker* 415.4, *latecomer* 658.4, *plodder* 693.6

idle rich *inactive person* 413.8, *nonworker* 415.4

idler wheel *wheel* 682.9

idle speech *empty talk* 362.5

idle talk *chat* 210.2

idly *apathetically* 322.7, *out of use* 394.13, *inactively* 413.16, *inertly* 519.5, *slowly* 693.14

idol 83.5; *minor deity* 82.2, *actor* 137.13, *image* 187.3, *wonderful person* 294.6

idolater 83.7

idolatrize *idolize* 83.16

idolatrous 83.13

idolatrously *worshipfully* 83.17

idolatry 83.4; *worship* 83.1, *love* 299.1, *praise* 437.3, *impiety* 448.4

idolism *idolatry* 83.4

idolization *deification* 82.13, *idolatry* 83.4, *love* 299.1, *admiration* 435.2

idolize 83.16; *deify* 82.23, *wonder* 294.12, *love* 299.21, *revere* 435.14, *praise* 437.16

idolized *deified* 82.20, *worshiped* 83.14, *beloved* 299.19

idolizer *idolater* 83.7

idolizing *idolatrous* 83.13, *loving* 299.15, *reverent* 435.9, *praise* 437.3

I don't believe it! *good heavens!* 292.15, *wonderful!* 294.20

I doubt it Card Games 168

idyll Poem or Verse Forms 139

idyllic 214.11; *poetic* 139.19, *pleasant* 271.5

i.e. *demonstrably* 331.22, *in other words* 365.18, *particularly* 779.21

iffy [Inf] *disreputable* 371.4, *dangerous* 811.7, *chance* 842.10

if not *under the circumstances* 726.16

if one can trust one's ears *reportedly* 170.16

I-formation *offense* 155.6

if possible *possibly* 836.9

if so *under the circumstances* 726.16

if worst comes to worst *adversely* 848.16

IgD *blood* 555.4

IgE *blood* 555.4

IgG *blood* 555.4

igloo *house* 60.4, *cold place* 218.7

IgM *blood* 555.4

igneous *petrographic* 8.58, *on fire* 217.16

igneous rock 8.32; *rock* 8.30

ignis fatuus *flickering light* 246.10, *illusion* 720.2

ignite *fuel* 106.16, *burn* 217.18, *light* 246.19

igniter *fuel starter* 106.3, *fire* 246.9

ignition *fire* 217.8

ignition system *fuel starter* 106.3

ignoble *lowered* 597.18

ignobly *disreputably* 371.7

ignominious *vilifying* 301.9, *disreputable* 371.4

ignominiously *vilifyingly* 301.18, *disreputably* 371.7

ignominy *disrepute* 371.1, *humbling* 597.9

ignomious *lowered* 597.18

ignomiously *disgracefully* 597.28

ignoramus *unintelligent person* 316.4, *ignorant person* 349.4

ignorance 316.3, 318.2, 349.1; *unskillfulness* 128.1, *figurative blindness* 243.8, *unaccustomedness* 398.1, *naiveté* 821.1

ignorant 349.5; *unskilled* 128.5, *blind to* 243.14, *unintelligent* 316.6, *thoughtless* 318.7, *untrained* 389.8, *naive* 821.3

ignorantly 349.11; *unintelligently* 316.9, *unaccustomedly* 398.7

ignorant of *unaccustomed* 398.3

ignorant person 349.4

ignore 409.11, 413.14; *be insensible* 213.7, *fail to hear* 229.9, *be blind to* 243.19, *be ungrateful* 311.5, *show mercy* 312.11, *be inattentive* 324.10, *be thoughtless* 324.11, *be neglectful* 326.7, *shun*

386.14, *not use* 394.9, *be discourteous* 411.7, *be insubordinate* 416.8, *dishonor* 436.20, *not observe* 466.9, *exclude* 764.7

ignored *unthanked* 311.3, *overlooked* 312.6, *neglected* 326.6, *undervalued* 436.17

ignore formalities *have no time to spare* 818.6

ignore instructions *disobey* 427.12

ignorer *neglector* 326.3

ignore the consequences *be rash* 286.8, *lack thought* 318.12

ignoring *thoughtlessness* 324.3, *rejecting* 383.2, *exclusively* 764.10

iguana *lizard* 37.5

II *two* 789.1

III *three* 790.1

IIII *four* 791.1

Ijsselmeer *or* **Ijssel** Lakes 568

ikat *dyeing* 130.9

ikat-weave *woven* 130.15

Ile-de-France Breeds of Sheep 16

Ili Rivers 570

Iliamna Lakes 568

ilingophobia Phobias 283

ilium Human Bones 19

ilk *family tree* 65.3, *sort* 202.6, *type* 777.4

ill 517.8; *unhealthy* 114.23, *sick* 114.24, *evilly* 446.12, *difficultly* 824.23, *adverse* 848.10

ill-advised *bungled* 128.7, *imprudent* 286.7, *misjudged* 342.8, *foolish* 353.5, *inconvenient* 804.5

ill-balanced *unbalanced* 741.5

ill-behaved *troublesome* 824.13

ill-bred *badly behaved* 399.16, *bad-mannered* 411.6, *vulgar* 535.6

ill-breeding *bad conduct* 399.7, *grossness* 535.3

ill-considered *unskillful* 128.4, *bungled* 128.7, *imprudent* 286.7, *foolish* 353.5, *inconvenient* 804.5, *hasty* 818.3

ill-contrived *bungled* 128.7, *inconvenient* 804.5

ill-defined *bungled* 128.7, *difficult to see* 245.4, *murky* 248.5, *vague* 338.9, *shapeless* 625.2, *generalized* 778.12

ill-devised *bungled* 128.7

ill-disposed *hostile* 63.6, *malevolent* 306.7

ill disposition *malevolence* 306.1

illegal *unlawful* 53.23, 430.15, *immoral* 432.9, *villainous* 448.12, *sinful* 450.8, *violating* 466.8, *prohibited* 503.5, *unauthorized* 515.7

illegal borrowing 476.3; *infringement* 479.6

illegal drug *drug* 115.9, 121.14

illegal entry *inroad* 706.3

illegal execution *capital punishment* 454.12

illegal hold *wrestling terms* 152.10

illegal immigrant *illegal occupant* 61.9

illegality 53.10, 450.4; *unlawfulness* 430.6, *guilt* 450.1, *infraction* 466.4, *prohibition* 503.1

illegalize *make illegal* 53.29

illegally 53.34; *guiltily* 53.38, *villainously* 448.18, *defiantly* 466.14, *prohibitively* 503.11, *powerlessly* 515.16

illegally ground the ball *exhibit penalty behavior* 155.21

illegal motion *penalty* 155.13

illegal occupant 61.9

illegal offer 504.4

illegal speed *speed* 694.2

illegal use of hands *penalty* 155.13

illegibility *obliteration* 186.1, *nonsense* 362.2, *unintelligibility* 364.1

illegible *obliterated* 186.4, *meaningless* 362.7, *unintelligible* 364.4, *problematic* 824.11

illegibly *forgetfully* 186.12, *unintelligibly* 364.16

illegitimacy *illegality* 53.10, *deception* 193.1, *unlawfulness* 430.6, *prohibition* 503.1, *unauthenticity* 722.4

illegitimate *deceptive* 193.12, *unlawful* 430.15, *prohibited* 503.5, *unauthentic* 722.9

illegitimate child *family member* 65.2

illegitimately *deceptively* 193.21, *prohibitively* 503.11, *unauthentically* 722.17

illegitimize *make illegal* 53.29

ill-equipped *unprovided* 98.6

ill-fated *unlucky* 848.12

ill-favored *ugly* 531.3

ill feeling 63.3

ill feelings *resentment* 302.1

ill fortune *lost chance* 660.3, *luck* 842.3, *bad fortune* 848.7

ill-furnished *unprovided* 98.6

ill-gotten *stolen* 479.12

ill-gotten gains *something received* 473.2, *takings* 477.8, *stolen goods* 479.4

ill health 114.1; *imperfection* 806.1

ill humor *resentment* 302.1, *short temper* 303.5, *irritableness* 304.3

ill-humored *resentful* 302.8, *cross* 303.11, *irritable* 304.9

ill-humoredly *crossly* 303.20, *irritably* 304.17

ill-humoredness *crossness* 303.4, *irritableness* 304.3

illiberal *opinionated* 379.9, *narrow-minded* 593.13

illiberality *opinionatedness* 379.3, *narrow-mindedness* 593.7

illiberally *narrow-mindedly* 593.20

illicit *unlawful* 430.15, *prohibited* 503.5

illicit love *fornication* 432.3, *liberality* 829.8

illicitly *illegally* 53.34, *immorally* 430.27, *prohibitively* 503.11

illicitness *illegality* 53.10, *unlawfulness* 430.6, *prohibition* 503.1

Illimani Mountains and Hills 569

illimitability *infinity* 798.1

illimitable *infinite* 798.5

illimitably *infinitely* 798.10

Illinois American States 564, Rivers 570

ill-intentioned *malicious* 306.8

illiteracy *ignorance* 349.1

illiterate *of language* 5.35, *ignorant person* 349.4, *ignorant* 349.5

illiterately *colloquially* 5.45

ill-judged *bungled* 128.7

ill-lit *dark* 247.5, *dim* 248.4

ill luck *lost chance* 660.3

ill-mannered *clumsy* 128.6, *ungrateful* 311.2, *badly behaved* 399.16, *bad-mannered* 411.6

ill-mannered person *badly behaved person* 399.8

ill-matched *married* 64.16, *unequal* 741.4

ill nature 303.2; *irritableness* 304.3, *malevolence* 306.1

ill-natured 303.9; *irritable* 304.9, *malevolent* 306.7
ill-naturedly 303.18; *irritably* 304.17
ill-naturedness *ill nature* 303.2, *irritableness* 304.3
illness 114.2; *ill health* 114.1, *affliction* 117.1, Phobias 283, *disability* 515.4, *physical deterioration* 808.4, *adverse health* 848.5
illogic *faulty reasoning* 351.4
illogical 728.7; *unintelligent* 316.6, *sophistic* 330.7, *erroneous* 351.11, *meaningless* 362.7, *impossible* 837.4
illogicality *ignorance* 316.3, *sophistry* 330.1, *nonsense* 362.2, *unrelatedness* 728.1, *impossibility* 837.1, *lack of motive* 842.2
illogically 728.17; *unintelligently* 316.9, *sophistically* 330.14, *meaninglessly* 362.13, *impossibly* 837.11
illogicalness *sophistry* 330.1
ill-omened *inauspicious* 282.8, *presageful* 358.13, *untimely* 660.5, *warning* 814.6
ill person *infectious person* 114.9
ill-planned *inconvenient* 804.5
ill-prepared *bungled* 128.7
ill-proportioned *graceless* 528.7
ill-provided *unequipped* 389.13
ill repute *disrepute* 371.1
ill service *malignity* 306.5
ill-sorted *unequal* 741.4
ill-sounding *inelegant* 528.6
ill-spent *futile* 802.10
ill-starred *presageful* 358.13, *untimely* 660.5, *unlucky* 848.12
ill-supplied *unprovided* 98.6
ill temper *ill nature* 303.2, *short temper* 303.5, *irritableness* 304.3
ill-tempered *ill-natured* 303.9, *irritable* 304.9
ill-temperedly *irritably* 304.17
ill-temperedness *ill nature* 303.2, *irritableness* 304.3
ill-timed *bungled* 128.7, *misjudged* 342.8, *untimely* 660.5, *inconvenient* 804.5
ill-treat *harm* 306.13, *ill-use* 395.7, *wrong* 430.19
ill-treated *ill-used* 395.4
ill-treatment *malignity* 306.5, *ill-use* 395.2
ill turn *malignity* 306.5
illuminance *light* 10.17
illuminate *rationalize* 4.20, *educate* 48.22, *paint* 143.12, *clarify* 196.3, *make visible* 244.9, *light* 246.19, *color* 251.16, *explain* 331.16, *interpret* 365.12, *decorate* 532.11, *display* 843.13, *reveal* 843.14
illuminated *painted* 143.10, *clear* 244.6, *lit* 246.16, *explanatory* 331.11
illuminated sign *electric light* 246.6
illuminati *intellectual* 315.7, *academia* 348.6
illuminating *educational* 48.17, *armor-piercing* 78.18, *informative* 170.10, *descriptive* 202.11, *dissertational* 203.4, *lucent* 246.13, *explanatory* 331.11, *interpretive* 365.8
illuminating ammunition *ammunition* 78.11
illuminatingly *educationally* 48.25, *discursively* 203.6, *lightly* 246.23, *demonstrably* 331.22
illumination *light* 10.17, 246.1, *education* 48.1, *picture* 133.5, (*act*

of) *painting* 143.1, *illustration* 187.2, *that which makes visible* 244.4, *lightening* 246.3, *explanation* 331.3, *finding out* 345.3, *knowledge* 348.1, *interpretation* 365.1, *decorative method* 532.3
illuminations *salute* 405.7
illuminator *visual artist* 133.6, *decorator* 532.8
illumine *light* 246.19
ill-use 395.2, 395.7; *wrong* 430.19
ill-used 395.4
illusion 720.2; *occult and psychic phenomena* 86.7, *delusion* 110.2, *spectacle* 264.6, *fallibility* 351.6, *fantasy* 360.5, *unreality* 722.2
illusionary *imaginary* 360.12
illusionism *treatment* 143.6, *delusion* 720.3
illusionist *magician* 138.11, *imitator* 736.6
illusionistic *pictorial* 133.8
illusive *imaginary* 360.12, *unreal* 722.7
illusively *unreally* 722.15
illusorily *unreally* 722.15
illusoriness *unreality* 722.2
illusory 720.9; *seeming* 264.11, *sophistic* 330.7, *imaginary* 360.12, *nonmaterial* 525.8, *unreal* 718.10, 722.7
illustrate 187.11; *rationalize* 4.20, *draw* 143.13, *describe* 202.15, *make visible* 244.9, *explain* 331.16, *prove* 336.9, *interpret* 365.12, *decorate* 532.11, *outline* 617.5
illustrated *explanatory* 331.11, *interpreted* 365.9
illustrating (*act of*) *drawing* 143.2
illustration 187.2; *craft* 133.2, *picture* 133.5, *drawing* 143.4, *explanation* 331.3, *proof* 336.2, *interpretation* 365.1, *decorative method* 532.3, *outline* 617.1
illustrative *artistic* 133.7, *representational* 187.8, *descriptive* 202.11, *explanatory* 331.11, *verificatory* 336.6, *intelligible* 363.5, *interpretive* 365.8
illustratively *artistically* 133.10, *representationally* 187.15, *descriptively* 202.18, *demonstrably* 331.22, *verifiably* 336.11, *in other words* 365.18
illustrator *visual artist* 133.6, *demonstrator* 331.6, *decorator* 532.8
illustriously *aristocratically* 70.6, *eminently* 370.7
ill will *ill feeling* 63.3, *bad feeling* 266.5, *antipathy* 291.2, *hate* 300.1, *resentment* 302.1, *malevolence* 306.1, *jealousy* 314.2, *evil* 446.1
ill-willed *malevolent* 306.7, *jealous* 314.5, *evil* 446.7
ill wind *evil thing* 446.2, *threat* 848.3
ill-wisher *hostile person* 63.5
ill wishes *curse* 301.1
ill-wishing *malevolent* 306.7
image 187.3; *mathematical function* 6.27, *idol* 83.5, *symbol* 108.28, *photograph* 132.3, *picture* 133.5, *sign* 183.1, *represent* 187.10, *reflection* 242.9, *appearance* 264.1, 610.4, *spectacle* 264.6, *conception* 360.4, *type of meaning* 361.4, *artificiality* 720.7, *look-alike* 730.4, *counterpart* 733.5, *copy* 736.2
image blur *composition* 132.17
image-building *imagination* 360.1
image distance *lens system* 10.22

imagemaker *publicizer* 173.11
image of God *humankind* 18.1
imagery *literary device* 139.12, *imagination* 360.1
imaginable 360.13; *supposed* 359.6, *possible* 836.5
imaginably *potentially* 836.11
imaginarily *unreally* 722.15
imaginariness *unreality* 722.2
imaginary 360.12; *complex* 6.69, *seeming* 264.11, *supposed* 359.6, *nonmaterial* 525.8, *unreal* 718.10, 722.7, *theoretical* 720.10, *numerical* 783.7
imaginary number *real number* 6.5, *kind of number* 783.2
imaginary part *complex number* 6.6
imaginary world *conception* 360.4, *nonmaterial world* 525.1
imagination 327.8, 360.1; *enrichment* 22.5, *visualization* 242.6, *creative thought* 317.3, *nonreality* 718.5, *unreality* 722.2, *originality* 737.1, *cunning* 822.1
imaginative 360.10; *enriching* 22.11, *artistic* 133.7, *narrative* 202.12, *ideational* 327.9, *original* 737.4, *cunning* 822.4
imaginative exercise *conception* 360.4
imaginative journalism *distortion of truth* 627.4
imaginatively 327.21, 360.17; *artistically* 133.10, *descriptively* 202.18, *thoughtfully* 317.13, *originally* 737.8
imaginativeness *enrichment* 22.5, *imagination* 327.8, 360.1
imagine 327.14, 360.14, 720.13; *be of the opinion* 87.10, *recount* 202.16, *visualize* 242.24, *think* 317.9, *have an idea* 317.12, *suppose* 359.8, *dream up* 522.15, *be unreal* 722.12, *originate* 737.7
imagined *ideational* 327.9, *supposed* 359.6, *imaginary* 360.12, *produced* 522.12, *unreal* 722.7
imagine that! *wonderful!* 294.20
imaging device 242.11
imaging processes *industrial processes* 14.27
imagism Western Literary Groups 139
imago *insect metamorphal stage* 40.8, *symbol* 108.28, *idea* 327.1
imam 84.7; *religious leader* 68.9
Imari ware Ceramics 129
imbalance 741.2; *distortion* 627.1, *distort* 627.9, *changeableness* 666.1, *disparity* 728.3, *dissimilarity* 734.1
imbalanced *changeable* 666.3, *disparate* 728.9, *dissimilar* 734.4
imbecile *unintelligent person* 316.4
imbecilic *intellectually subnormal* 316.7
imbecility *lack of intellect* 316.1
imbibe *drink* 93.19, *ingest* 708.17
imbiber *drinker* 93.16
imbibing *drinking* 93.1, 93.17
imbibition *drinking* 93.1, *intake* 708.5
imbibitory *absorbent* 708.11
imbrex Architectural Elements 134
imbricate *overlay* 613.25
imbricated *or* **imbricate** *roof* 134.7
imbrication *covering* 613.1
imbroglio *variety* 751.4, *problem* 824.4
imbrue *color* 251.16, *water* 557.29
imbruement *soaking* 557.9

imbue *color* 251.16, *accustom* 397.18, *steep* 557.31, *be present* 575.13, *inject* 710.10, *mix* 751.12, *assimilate* 781.14
imbued *fixed* 397.13, *omnipresent* 575.10
imbuement *omnipresence* 575.4
imino acid *amino acid* 12.8
imitate 736.9; *act* 136.34, *entertain* 138.16, *gesture* 183.17, *represent* 187.10, *appear* 264.12, *ridicule* 436.22, *borrow illegally* 476.12, *take away* 477.18, *infringe* 479.17, *be a substitute* 672.6, *fabricate* 720.17, *copy* 730.17, *simulate* 733.16, *abide by* 781.12, *repeat* 797.15
imitated *imaginary* 360.12, *borrowed* 476.8, *unauthentic* 722.9, *duplicate* 730.11, *simulated* 733.11, *imitative* 736.7
imitating *ridiculing* 436.13, *illegal borrowing* 476.3, *infringement* 479.6
imitation 736.1, 736.8; *deputizing* 80.4, *representation* 187.1, 202.9, *impression* 264.7, *ridicule* 436.4, *illegal borrowing* 476.3, *taking away* 477.5, *infringement* 479.6, *artificiality* 720.7, *artificial* 720.12, *unauthenticity* 722.4, *unauthentic* 722.9, *copy* 730.5, 736.2, *simulation* 733.4, *simulated* 733.11, *conformity* 781.1, *repetition* 797.1
imitative 736.7; *deputizing* 80.4, *representational* 187.8, *repeated* 797.8
imitatively 733.20, 736.12; *indirectly* 80.8
imitator 736.6; *borrower* 476.7, *infringer* 479.10, *conformist* 781.6
immaculacy *innocence* 449.1, *immaculateness* 805.2
immaculate 805.11; *clean* 111.13, *pure* 253.11, 431.11, *virtuous* 447.5, *innocent* 449.6
Immaculate Conception Christian Holy Days and Seasons 85
immaculately *virtuously* 447.9, *innocently* 449.13, *perfectly* 805.21
immaculateness 805.2; *cleanliness* 111.1
immanence *omnipresence* 575.4
immanent *omnipresent* 575.10, *intrinsic* 723.6
immaterial *spiritual* 86.20, *invisible* 245.3, *insignificant* 289.10, *nonmaterial* 525.8, *sparse* 541.3, *extraneous* 724.8, *unrelated* 728.6, *unimportant* 800.10
immaterialism Philosophical Schools of Thought 4, *immateriality* 525.2, *unreality* 720.1
immaterialist Philosophical Schools of Thought 4, *nonmaterial* 525.8
immaterialistic *nonmaterial* 525.8
immateriality 525.2; *insignificance* 289.4, *sparseness* 541.1, *unreality* 720.1, *extraneousness* 724.1, *unrelatedness* 728.1, *unimportance* 800.1
immaterialize *occult* 86.22, *dematerialize* 525.12
immaterially *unexceptionally* 289.20, *metaphysically* 525.13, *extraneously* 724.16, *irrelatively* 728.16
immaterialness *immateriality* 525.2
immature 26.12, 40.14, 389.9,

652.12; *unskilled* 128.5, *acid* 223.5, *raw* 260.9, *unintelligent* 316.6, *unaccustomed* 398.3, *naive* 449.9, 821.3, *untimely* 660.5, *incomplete* 762.5, 806.6, *uncompleted* 762.7

immature amphibian *young amphibian* 37.11

immaturely 389.18, 652.23; *youthfully* 26.14, *greenly* 260.15, *unaccustomedly* 398.7, *naively* 449.15, *at the wrong time* 660.12

immaturity 26.3, 389.3, 652.3; *youth* 26.1, *unskillfulness* 128.1, *ignorance* 316.3, *naiveté* 449.4, 821.1, *helplessness* 515.3, *untimeliness* 660.1, *incompleteness* 762.1, 806.2, *nonachievement* 762.3

immeasurability 798.2

immeasurable 798.6; *divine* 82.16, *deep* 598.9, *numberless* 795.8

immeasurably 798.11; *deep* 598.25, *numerously* 795.13

immediacy 645.1; *availability* 575.5, *nearness* 586.1, *earliness* 657.1, *haste* 818.1

immediate 645.5; *topical* 328.5, *available* 575.11, *next* 586.8, *present* 647.4, *early* 657.8, *swift* 694.6, *direct* 697.11, *hasty* 818.3

immediate area *availability* 575.5

immediate constituent *grammatical term* 5.29

immediate family *family circle* 65.4

immediately 645.8; *right away* 429.20, *early* 657.17, *hurryingly* 694.18, *hastily* 818.7

immediateness *immediacy* 645.1

immediate purpose *usefulness* 393.2

Immelmann *or* **Immelmann turn** *flight maneuver* 689.6

immemorial *societal* 1.13, *lasting* 639.9, *agelong* 644.5, *olden* 653.11

immemorially *archaically* 653.20

immemorial wisdom *tradition* 1.7

immense *spacious* 563.13, *huge* 579.14, *immeasurable* 798.6

immensely *spaciously* 563.17, *hugely* 579.21, *immeasurably* 798.11

immenseness *largeness* 579.2, *vastness* 798.3

immensity *spaciousness* 563.4, *largeness* 579.2, *vastness* 798.3

immerge [Arch] *immerse* 710.12

immerse 598.24, 710.12; *water* 557.29, *deepen* 598.21

immersed 710.7; *flooded* 557.24, *under* 598.13, *in deep* 598.18

immerse oneself in *immerse* 710.12

immersion 598.8, 710.3; *baptism* 85.6, *soaking* 557.9, *holy water* 557.15, *sinkage* 714.2

immersion heater *heater* 217.3

immigrant *settler* 61.4, *resident* 61.11, *new arrival* 652.7, 724.6, *arriving* 704.9, *entrant* 706.7, *entering* 706.9

immigrate *settle* 61.14, *enroll* 706.16, *be foreign* 724.13

immigration *right of entry* 706.4

imminent 657.9; *expected* 356.5, *future* 650.6, *approaching* 704.10

imminently *in the future* 650.13, *soon* 657.18

immiscibility *separateness* 753.3, *nonadhesion* 756.1

immiscible *unjoined* 753.9, *nonadhesive* 756.4

immiscibly *noncohesively* 756.9

immission *admittance* 708.1

immix *mix* 751.12

immixture *mixture* 796.1

immobile *inactive* 413.9, 415.8, *inert* 519.2, *permanent* 667.2, *stable* 674.3, *motionless* 678.4

immobility 413.2; *inactivity* 415.1, *inertness* 519.1, *permanence* 667.1, *stability* 674.1, *lack of motion* 678.1

immobilization *stability* 674.1

immobilize *do martial arts* 152.21, *make inactive* 415.16, *make permanent* 667.5, *make motionless* 678.8

immobilized *wrestling* 152.18

immoderate 99.6; *overindulgent* 456.8, *unrestrained* 500.5, *violent* 520.5, *unconditional* 829.14

immoderately 99.14; *self-indulgently* 456.12, *extravagantly* 500.9, *excessively* 829.23

immoderation 99.2; *overindulgence* 456.3, *unrestrainedness* 500.2, *liberality* 829.8

immodest *vain* 402.8, *unchaste* 432.10, *open* 843.12

immodestly *vainly* 402.17, *promiscuously* 432.19

immodesty *vanity* 402.1, *sexual immorality* 432.2, *openness* 843.6

immolate *kill ritually* 30.23

immolation *ritual killing* 30.7

immoral 430.11, 432.9; *disreputable* 371.4, *disobedient* 427.10, *wrongful* 430.10, *evil* 446.7, *depraved* 448.10, *ribald* 535.8, *devious* 607.9

immorality 432.1; *disobedience* 427.1, *wrong* 430.1, *evil* 446.1, *depravity* 448.2, *deviousness* 607.4, *moral deterioration* 803.3

immorally 430.27, 432.18; *disobediently* 427.14, *wrongly* 430.24, *evilly* 446.12, *unvirtuously* 448.16, *deviously* 607.16

immoral ways *wickedness* 448.1

immortal *deity* 82.1, *divine* 82.16, *timeless* 640.3, *permanent* 642.5, 667.2, *eternal* 644.4, 798.7

immortality *new life* 28.8, *divine attribute* 82.4, *timelessness* 640.1, *life without end* 644.2, *permanence* 667.1

immortalization *deification* 82.13

immortalize *deify* 82.23, *perpetuate* 640.5, *make eternal* 644.8, *make permanent* 667.5

immortalized *deified* 82.20

immortal life *new life* 28.8

immortally *permanently* 667.6, *eternally* 798.12

immotile *motionless* 678.4

immovability *determination* 379.2, *mental hardness* 542.4, *stability* 674.1

immovable *tenacious* 376.9, *determined* 379.7, *fast* 464.8, *propertied* 470.9, *permanent* 667.2, *stable* 674.3, *motionless* 678.4, *tied* 752.13

immovables *legal property terms* 470.2

immovably *fastly* 464.16, *inextricably* 752.23

immune *acquitted* 54.25, *health-giving* 113.6, *insensitive* 268.4, *exempt* 434.5, *secure* 464.5, *invulnerable* 810.18, *escaping* 816.7, *free* 829.11

immunity *hygiene* 116.1,

immunization *health care* 107.7, *prophylaxis* 115.4, *hygiene* 116.1, *sanitary precaution* 810.8

immunize 810.22; *practice medicine* 107.32, *treat* 115.17, *practice hygiene* 116.4

immunized *health-giving* 113.6, *safe* 810.16

immunizing *hygienic* 116.3

immunoglobulin *protein* 12.9

immunoglobulin A (IgA) *blood* 555.4

immunological *biological* 13.27

immunologically *biologically* 13.36

immunologist *life scientist* 13.26, *medical specialist* 107.20

immunology *biochemistry* 13.3, *Medical Specialties* 107, *medical science* 107.5

immunosuppressive *medicine* 115.2

immunotherapy *treatment* 107.14, *therapy* 115.12

immure *imprison* 55.11, *enclose* 584.16

immured *imprisoned* 55.9

immurement *detention* 830.5

immurement *or* **immuration** *imprisonment* 55.4

immutability 640.2; *permanence* 667.1, *stability* 674.1

immutable *mentally hard* 542.8, *changeless* 640.4, *eternal* 644.4, *permanent* 667.2, *stable* 674.3

immutably *inflexibly* 542.13, *permanently* 667.6, *stably* 674.9

imp *sprite* 86.12, *capricious person* 381.3, *troublemaker* 427.5, *evil spirit* 446.4

imp [Arch] *plant* 710.14

impact 710.11; *impression* 264.7, *influence* 512.1, *effect* 676.1, *collision* 695.2, *collide* 695.10, *unite closely* 752.16

impacted *inserted* 710.5

impaction *insertion* 710.1

impactment *insertion* 710.1

impact printer *hardcopy device* 15.10

impact upon *affect* 676.7

impair 808.18; *be clumsy* 128.9, *ill-use* 395.7, *meddle* 414.23, *be evil* 446.10, *destroy* 468.18, *change* 512.12, *weaken* 517.13, *make ugly* 531.4, *blemish* 533.7, *deform* 627.11, *change for the worse* 665.18, *transgress* 712.14, *make useless* 802.12, *hinder* 826.15

impair [Fr] *numerical* 783.7

impaired *spoiled* 808.9

impaired visibility *murk* 248.2

impaired vision *faulty vision* 243.1

impairment 808.7; *loss* 468.1, *weakness* 517.1, *deficiency* 745.2, *noncompletion* 762.2, *deterioration* 808.1

impale *identify* 184.11, *inflict pain* 215.10, *stab* 418.22, *execute* 454.30

impalement *Heraldic Terms* 184, *hit* 418.9, *capital punishment* 454.12

impaling *Heraldic Terms* 184

impalpability *immateriality* 525.2, *littleness* 580.1, *unreality* 720.1, 722.2

impalpable *nonmaterial* 525.8, *little* 580.7, *unreal* 720.8, 722.7

impalpably *metaphysically* 525.13,

infinitesimally 580.13, *unreally* 722.15

impanation *Eucharist* 85.7

impanel a jury *try a case* 54.28

impaneling a jury *jury selection* 54.14

imparity *inequality* 741.1

impart *educate* 48.22, *communicate* 169.18, 170.12, *speak* 205.17, *bequeath* 372.15, *give* 472.10

impartable *communicational* 169.17, *given* 472.8

impartation *giving* 472.1

imparter *giver* 472.7

impartial 289.9, 338.6; *rational* 4.15, *wise* 352.4, *right* 429.7, *disinterested* 443.4, *broad-minded* 592.9, *equal* 740.8, *mediatory* 772.11

impartiality 289.3, 338.2; *legal justice* 53.4, *rightfulness* 429.1, *disinterestedness* 443.1, *moderation* 521.1, *broad-mindedness* 592.3, *middle ground* 772.4

impartially 289.19, 338.13; *rationally* 4.25, *right* 429.15, *disinterestedly* 443.8, *broad-mindedly* 592.17, *equitably* 740.15, *midway* 772.22

impartial person 443.3

imparting *giving* 472.1, 472.9

impart life *give birth to* 28.19

impart momentum *accelerate* 694.14, *impel* 695.9

impart odor to 224.9

impassability *closure* 584.1

impassable *obstructed* 584.8, *rough* 824.10

impasse *obstruction* 584.2, *snag* 824.8, *obstacle* 826.2, 837.3

impassibly *impermeably* 584.17

impassioned *emphatic* 200.3, *passionate* 266.12

impassive *insensible* 213.4, *insensitive* 268.4, *heedless* 268.5, *indifferent* 289.7, *wonderless* 295.3, *incurious* 322.3, *unintelligible* 364.4, *inactive* 413.9, *not participating* 415.11, *inert* 519.2, *quiescent* 678.6

impassively 415.18; *indifferently* 289.17, *without wonder* 295.8, *apathetically* 322.7, *unintelligibly* 364.16, *inactively* 413.16, *inertly* 519.5, *motionlessly* 678.9

impassivity *heedlessness* 268.2, *lack of wonder* 295.1, *incuriosity* 322.1, *unintelligibility* 364.1, *immobility* 413.2, *idleness* 415.3, *inertness* 519.1

impatience *recklessness* 286.2, *irascibility* 303.1, *bad manners* 411.2, *hastiness* 818.2

impatiens *Flowers* 42

impatient *reckless* 286.6, *irascible* 303.8, *discourteous* 411.5, *hasty* 818.3

impatiently *recklessly* 286.10, *irascibly* 303.17, *discourteously* 411.8, *rashly* 818.8

impeach *litigate* 54.27, *condemn* 438.18, *accuse* 442.8, *remove power from* 515.13

impeachability *guilt* 450.1

impeachable *unsatisfactory* 438.15, *accusatory* 442.6, *guilty* 450.6

impeached *discarded* 383.8, *condemned* 438.11, *accused* 442.5

impeacher *accuser* 442.3

impeaching *condemning* 438.10

impeachment *condemnation* 438.2, *accusation* 442.1

impeccability *virtue* 447.1,

incorruption 449.2, perfection
805.1
impeccable *virtuous* 447.5,
incorrupt 449.7, *infallible* 805.10,
blameless 805.1
impeccably *virtuously* 447.9,
faultlessly 449.14, *perfectly* 805.21
impecuniosity *poverty* 486.1
impecunious *poor* 486.8,
unprosperous 848.11
impecuniously *poorly* 486.17
impecuniousness *poverty* 486.1
impedance *resistance* 10.41
impede *prohibit* 503.8, *slow down*
693.13, *hinder* 826.15, *block*
826.17, *restrain* 830.12
impeded *delayed* 693.10, *hindering*
826.12
impeder *hinderer* 826.11
impediment *frustration* 293.2,
prohibition 503.1, *inconvenience*
804.1, *hindrance* 826.1, *obstacle*
826.2, *restraint* 830.1
impediment [Form] *separation*
66.2
impedimenta *possessions* 470.5,
transferred thing 685.6
impeding *hindering* 826.12
impel 695.9; *necessitate* 95.17,
persuade 178.15, *direct* 384.10,
push 414.20, *compel* 428.6,
motivate 508.9, *awaken* 675.9, *set
in motion* 677.16, *propel* 696.15,
hasten 818.4
impelled *directed* 384.7, *motivated*
508.8
impellent *impulsion* 695.1,
impelling 695.8
impeller 695.7; *rotator* 682.8,
propeller 696.8
impelling 695.8; *causal* 675.7,
moving 677.12
impelling force *impulsion* 695.1
impend *be probable* 838.8
impending *expected* 356.5, *in
preparation* 388.8, *future* 650.6,
imminent 657.9, *approaching*
704.10
impending disaster *danger* 811.1
impenetrability *opaqueness* 250.1,
unintelligibility 364.1, *strength*
516.1, *density* 540.1, *hardness*
542.1, *closure* 584.1, *denseness*
594.2, *hopelessness* 837.2
impenetrable *opaque* 250.3,
unintelligible 364.4, *unyielding*
379.8, *strong* 516.9, *dense* 540.6,
594.6, *obstructed* 584.8, *rough*
824.10, *problematic* 824.11,
hopeless 837.6, *concealed* 844.7
impenetrableness *determination*
379.2
impenetrably *opaquely* 250.9,
unintelligibly 364.16, *impermeably*
584.17, *densely* 594.12
impenitence 452.1
impenitent 452.2
impenitently 452.5
impenitentness *impenitence* 452.1
imperative *philosophical term* 4.7,
grammatical term 5.29,
authoritative 52.9, *necessity* 95.1,
necessary 95.10, *necessitative*
95.11, *commanding* 425.7,
compelling 428.6, *duty-bound*
433.8, *allowing no delay* 645.7,
essential 723.5, *important* 799.7
imperatively *necessarily* 95.22,
commandingly 425.15, *compellingly*
428.12
imperceptibility *invisibility* 245.1,
littleness 580.1, *concealment* 844.2
imperceptible *invisible* 245.3,

insufficient 517.11, little 580.7,
unhurried 693.8
imperceptibly *insensibly* 213.9,
invisibly 245.8, *weakly* 517.14,
infinitesimally 580.13
imperceptive *blind to* 243.14,
insensitive 268.4, *unintelligent*
316.6
imperceptively *unintelligently*
316.9, *unselectively* 338.12,
obtusely 550.12
imperceptiveness *ignorance* 316.3
impercipience *dullness* 550.3
impercipient *insensitive* 268.4
imperfect 806.5; *grammatical term*
5.29, *of flowers* 42.11, *bungled*
128.7, *unformed* 389.11,
blemished 533.5, *deformed* 627.7,
incorrect 722.8, *low quality* 745.7,
partial 760.11, *shortened* 762.6,
uncompleted 762.7
imperfect fungi *fungi* 47.3
imperfection 806.1; *insufficiency*
98.1, *Phobias* 283, *immaturity*
389.3, *blemish* 533.1, *distortion of
body* 627.3, *untrueness* 722.3,
deficiency 795.2, *incompleteness*
762.1, *nonachievement* 762.3,
vulnerability 811.6
imperfect item 806.3
imperfectly 806.10; *unskillfully*
128.12, *immaturely* 389.18,
asymmetrically 627.13, *incorrectly*
722.16, *badly* 745.15, *incompletely*
762.10
imperfectness *imperfection* 806.1
imperial *governing* 49.25, *dominant*
744.9
imperial [Brit] *metrical* 589.15
Imperial Defence College [Brit]
military training 58.3
imperialism *governance* 49.18,
dominion 566.3, *expansionism*
712.5
imperialist *militarist* 77.3
imperialistic *national* 566.10
imperialistically *nationally*
566.13
imperialist war *war* 76.1
imperial purple *figurative usage*
262.4
imperial system [Brit] *measuring
system* 589.4
imperil *endanger* 811.13
imperilment *endangerment* 811.2
imperious *authoritative* 52.9,
425.8, *masterful* 68.15, *arrogant*
297.9
imperiously *masterfully* 68.19,
arrogantly 297.18, *commandingly*
425.15
imperiousness *authority* 52.1
imperishability *eternity* 644.1,
permanence 667.1
imperishable *changeless* 640.4,
eternal 644.4, *permanent* 667.2,
stable 674.3
imperishably *permanently* 667.6,
stably 674.9
imperium *leadership* 744.2
impermanence *transience* 643.1,
changeableness 666.1
impermanent 643.5; *changeable*
666.3
impermanently *transiently* 643.8,
changeably 666.7
impermeability *opaqueness* 250.1,
density 540.1, *closure* 584.1
impermeable *opaque* 250.3, *dense*
540.6, *closed* 584.7
impermeably 584.17; *opaquely*
250.9
impermissibility *illegality* 53.10,
prohibition 503.1

impermissible *prohibited* 503.5
impermissibly *prohibitively*
503.11
impersonal *indifferent* 289.7,
disinterested 443.4, *material* 524.7
impersonally *indifferently* 289.17,
disinterestedly 443.8, *materially*
524.9
impersonate *act* 136.34, 187.13,
entertain 138.16, *represent* 187.10,
be untruthful 192.20, *imitate*
736.9
impersonating *acting* 187.6,
187.9, *imitative* 736.7
impersonation *acting* 136.22,
187.6, *ridicule* 436.4, *imitation*
736.1, *mimicry* 736.3
impersonator *entertainer* 138.8,
hoaxer 193.11, *imitator* 736.6
impertinence *objectionability*
272.2, *insolence* 400.1, *insolent
person* 400.7, *defiance* 416.1,
disrespect 436.1, *unrelatedness*
728.1
impertinent *objectionable* 272.7,
insolent 400.8, *bad-mannered*
411.6, *defiant* 416.5, *disrespectful*
436.9, *unrelated* 728.6
impertinently *insolently* 400.18,
rudely 411.9, *defiantly* 416.9,
disrespectfully 436.25, *irrelatively*
728.16
imperturbability *philosophical
attitude* 4.3, *lack of wonder* 295.1,
incuriosity 322.1, *determination*
674.2, *repose* 678.2
imperturbable *detached* 4.18,
wonderless 295.3, *incurious* 322.3,
determined 674.5, *quiescent* 678.6
imperturbably *stoically* 4.26,
without wonder 295.8,
apathetically 322.7, *determinedly*
674.10
impervious *insensible* 213.4,
opaque 250.3, *insensitive* 268.4,
unyielding 379.8, *dense* 540.6,
closed 584.7, *hopeless* 837.6
imperviously *opaquely* 250.9,
densely 540.10, *impermeably*
584.17
imperviousness *opaqueness* 250.1,
determination 379.2, *density* 540.1,
closure 584.1, *hopelessness* 837.2
impetigo *skin disease* 114.16
impetrate *pray* 85.20
impetration *prayer* 85.10
impetrational *prayerful* 85.17
impetuosity *rashness* 286.1,
impulsiveness 318.6, *spontaneity*
396.2, *violence* 520.1, *hastiness*
818.2
impetuous *passionate* 266.12,
adventurous 284.12, *rash* 286.5,
impulsive 318.11, *spontaneous*
396.5, *premature* 657.10, *hasty*
818.3
impetuously *adventurously*
284.20, *rashly* 286.9, 818.8,
impulsively 318.16, *inattentively*
324.12, *unreadily* 389.16,
spontaneously 396.8, *prematurely*
657.20
impetuousness *adventurousness*
284.4, *rashness* 286.1,
unpremeditation 389.2, *spontaneity*
396.2, *hastiness* 818.2
impetus *motive* 178.5, *motivation*
508.1, *type of power* 514.6, *vigor*
518.1, *momentum* 677.2,
acceleration 694.3, *impulsion*
695.1, *propulsion* 696.1
impiety 448.4; *misuse* 395.1
impinge *meet* 586.15, *transgress*
712.14

impermissible *prohibited* 503.5
impingement *meeting* 586.5
impinge upon *collide* 695.10
impinging *meeting* 586.10
impious 448.11; *abusive* 395.5
impiously 448.17; *abusively* 395.8
implacability *relentlessness* 309.2,
tenacity 376.4
implacable *relentless* 309.4,
tenacious 376.9, *strong-willed*
376.10, *unyielding* 379.8
implacably *relentlessly* 309.8
implant *accustom* 397.18, *inject*
710.10, *plant* 710.14, *assimilate*
781.14
implantation *insertion* 710.1,
injection 710.2
implanted *fixed* 397.13, *injected*
710.6
implausibility 839.3;
unbelievability 88.2,
questionableness 333.7
implausible *disbelieved* 88.7,
questionable 333.13, 839.5
implausibly *unbelievably* 88.11,
questionably 333.22
implead *litigate* 54.27
implement *tool* 103.1, *do
something* 412.13, *take action*
509.12, *instrument* 511.2, *be an
instrument* 511.7
implementation *action* 412.1,
operation 509.1
implicate *accuse* 442.8, *include*
763.5
implicated *accused* 442.5, *guilty*
450.6, *related* 727.6
implication *mathematical logic*
6.60, *meaning* 361.1, *accusation*
442.1, *guilt* 450.1, *relatedness*
727.1, *inclusion* 763.1, *quietness*
844.4
implication sign *mathematical
symbol* 6.11
implicative *symbolic* 183.12, *tacit*
844.10
implicit *given* 6.74, *similar* 361.7,
tacit 844.10
implicitly *latently* 844.15, *tacitly*
844.16
implied *similar* 361.7, *meant*
361.12, *circumstantial* 726.8, *tacit*
844.10
implied consent *permission* 502.1
implied sense *type of meaning*
361.4
implode *squeeze* 582.13
implore *pray* 85.20, *request* 505.10
imploring *request* 505.1
implosion *squeeze* 582.3
implosive *contracting* 582.10
imply 844.14; *tip* 170.14, *signify*
183.16, *state* 329.13, *make evident*
339.11, *mean* 361.13
impolite *objectionable* 272.7, *badly
behaved* 399.16, *rude* 400.9,
discourteous 411.5, *disrespectful*
436.9, *indecorous* 528.8
impolitely *badly* 399.23, *rudely*
400.19, *unsocially* 409.13,
discourteously 411.8
impoliteness *objectionability*
272.2, *rudeness* 400.2, *discourtesy*
411.1, *disrespect* 436.1
impolitic *unskillful* 128.4,
inconvenient 804.5
imponderability *immateriality*
525.2, *lightness* 539.1, *littleness*
580.1
imponderable *nonmaterial* 525.8,
light 539.4, *little* 580.7
imponderableness *lightness* 539.1
imponderably *metaphysically*
525.13, *lightly* 539.10,
infinitesimally 580.13

---

impeccable — imponderably

imponderous *light* 539.4

import *international trade* 56.7, *economic* 56.10, *trade* 56.12, *importance* 278.3, *799.1, meaning* 361.1, *significance* 361.2, 676.4, *mean* 361.13, *trade in* 457.8, *conveyance* 685.2, *convey* 685.9, *entry* 706.1, *admittance* 708.1, *admit* 708.12, *insertion* 710.1, *insert* 710.9, *be external* 724.15, *be important* 799.13

importable *transferable* 685.7

importance 278.3, *799.1; seriousness* 200.2, 278.1, *significance* 361.2, *influence* 512.1, *exaltation* 596.3, *priority* 769.2, *haste* 818.1

important 278.6, *799.7; managerial* 126.9, *serious* 200.5, 278.4, *significant* 361.11, *awe-inspiring* 435.12, *operative* 509.9, *influential* 512.8, *exalted* 596.10, *best* 805.9

importantly 799.15; *earnestly* 278.10, *operationally* 509.13, *influentially* 512.14, *exaltedly* 596.22, *superbly* 744.22

important matter 799.2

important occasion *important matter* 799.2

important person 18.11, *799.5*

importation *conveyance* 685.2, *right of entry* 706.4, *admittance* 708.1, *insertion* 710.1, *externality* 724.4

imported *entering* 706.9, *inserted* 710.5, *external* 724.11

imported word *new word* 5.18

importer *trader* 480.11, *merchant* 482.10, *transferrer* 685.4, *transporter* 686.4

importing *symbolic* 361.8, *right of entry* 706.4, *admittance* 708.1, *external* 724.11

importunate *allowing no delay* 645.7

importune *meddle* 414.23, *prostitute* 432.17

importuning *prostitution* 432.4

importunity *exhortation* 178.2, *request* 505.1

impose *necessitate* 95.17, *print* 173.17, *demand* 425.11, *have authority over* 425.12, *compel* 428.8, *command respect* 435.18, *punish* 454.22, *augment* 748.13

impose a ban *command* 425.10, *prohibit* 503.8

impose a curfew *detain* 830.16

impose a duty 433.14; *compel* 428.8

impose a fine *restrain* 830.12

impose an embargo *command* 425.10, *restrain commerce* 830.14

impose a penalty *penalize* 454.26

impose a tariff *restrain commerce* 830.14

impose conditions *make conditions* 460.7

imposed peace *peace* 73.1, *treaty* 74.2

impose martial law *be severe* 424.8

impose on *resort to* 393.13

impose one's will *372.14*

impose order upon *make regular* 663.9

impose peace *pacify* 74.9

impose upon *wrong* 430.19

imposing *majestic* 297.12, *grand* 404.22, *awe-inspiring* 435.12, *huge* 579.14, *notable* 799.11

imposingly *majestically* 297.21

imposition *burden* 117.3,

---

typesetting 173.4, *affliction* 454.9, *levy* 494.7, *addition* 748.1

imposition on one's time *business* 414.6

impossibility 837.1; *probability* 6.59, *unbelievability* 88.2, *futility* 282.3, *hopelessness* 837.2, *poor chance* 842.8

impossibility of discovery *unintelligibility* 364.1

impossible 837.4; *disbelieved* 88.7, *futile* 282.9, *difficult* 824.9

impossible! *no!* 506.12

impossibleness *impossibility* 837.1

impossible to explain *unintelligible* 364.4

impossibly 837.11; *futilely* 282.16

impost Architectural Elements 134, *payment* 433.5, *levy* 494.7

imposter *unskilled person* 128.3, *substitute* 672.2, *imitator* 736.6

impostor or **imposter** *hoaxer* 193.11

impostrous or **imposturous** *deceptive* 193.12

imposture *deception* 193.1, *hoax* 193.7, *copy* 736.2, *cunning* 822.1

impotence *infertility* 23.1, *unskillfulness* 128.1, *inaction* 413.1, *powerlessness* 515.1, *disability* 515.4, *weakness* 517.1, *uselessness* 802.1

impotency *sexlessness* 20.13

impotent *undersexed* 20.20, *infertile* 23.7, *unskillful* 128.4, *inactive* 413.9, *disabled* 515.10, *weak* 517.6, *useless* 802.7

impotently *unproductively* 23.12, *powerlessly* 515.16, *weakly* 517.14

impound *arrest* 55.12, *take back* 477.17, *enclose* 584.16, *detain* 830.16

impounding *taking back* 477.4

impoundment *dam* 551.12, *detention* 830.5

impoverish 486.16; *expend* 96.16, *lessen* 468.17, *weaken* 517.13, *make smaller* 747.8

impoverished 486.11; *unprofitable* 468.10, *weakened* 517.9, *meager* 593.12, *spoiled* 808.9

impoverishment *lessening* 468.6, *poverty* 486.1, *weakness* 517.1, *meagerness* 593.6, *decrease* 747.1, *economic deterioration* 808.2

impracticability *uselessness* 802.1, *hopelessness* 837.2

impracticable *useless* 802.7, *difficult* 824.9

impractical *philosophical* 4.12, *ideal* 327.12, *fantastic* 360.11, *unused* 394.5, *useless* 802.7, *hopeless* 837.6

impracticality *idealism* 327.7, *uselessness* 802.1, *hopelessness* 837.2

impractically *imaginatively* 327.21, *out of use* 394.13, *uselessly* 802.14, *hopelessly* 837.12

imprecate *curse* 301.13

imprecated *cursed* 301.8

imprecation *curse* 301.1

imprecatory *cursing* 301.7

imprecise *obscure* 197.2, *wrong* 430.12, *incorrect* 722.8, *generalized* 778.12, *indeterminate* 841.14

imprecisely *obscurely* 197.4, *wrongly* 351.18, *wrongfully* 430.25, *incorrectly* 722.16, *indeterminately* 841.24

impreciseness *obscurity* 197.1,

---

incorrectness 430.3, *untrueness* 722.3

imprecision *obscurity* 197.1, *inaccuracy* 351.3, *incorrectness* 430.3, *untrueness* 722.3, *nonspecificness* 778.2, *indeterminacy* 841.6

impregnability *security* 464.1, *strength* 516.1, *safety* 810.1

impregnable *secure* 464.5, *strong* 516.9, *invulnerable* 810.18

impregnably *surely* 464.15, *safely* 810.24

impregnate *reproduce oneself* 21.14, *propagate* 21.15, *fertilize* 22.12, *water* 557.29, *be present* 575.13, *inject* 710.10, *mix* 751.12

impregnated *pregnant* 21.12, *injected* 710.6

impregnation *fertilization* 21.6, *procreation* 22.4, *soaking* 557.9, *injection* 710.2, *mixture* 751.1

impregnator *propagator* 21.7

impresario *producer* 136.28, *displayer* 843.7

impress *enlist* 58.13, *engrave* 144.11, *print* 173.17, *persuade* 178.15, *identify* 184.11, *arouse sensation* 212.11, *be wondrous* 294.14, *force* 428.10, *command respect* 435.18, *kidnap* 479.15, *motivate* 508.9, *influence* 512.11, *soften* 543.14, *make concave* 635.7, *visible effect* 676.2

impress or **impression** *means of identification* 184.3

impressed *engraved* 144.9, *persuadable* 178.14, *wondering* 294.7

impressed with oneself *self-admiring* 402.10

impressibility *persuadability* 178.8, *softness* 543.1

impressible *persuadable* 178.14, *pliant* 543.7

impression 264.7, *266.2; belief* 87.1, *printing* 173.3, *representation* 187.1, 202.9, *sensation* 212.1, *touch* 216.1, *insight* 320.3, *conception* 360.4, *influence* 512.1, *appearance* 610.4, *viewpoint* 628.5, *concavity* 635.1

impressionability *persuadability* 178.8, *sensitivity* 267.1

impressionable 543.12; *educatable* 48.18, *persuadable* 178.14, *susceptible* 212.7, *feeling* 266.9, *irresolute* 666.4, *convertible* 670.9

impressionably *soft-heartedly* 543.19, *changeably* 666.7

impressional *apparent* 610.10

impressionism Western Art Styles 133

impressionist *entertainer* 138.8

impressionistic *descriptive* 202.11, *representing* 202.14, *outlined* 617.4

impressionist music *classical music* 140.2

impressive *believable* 87.7, *persuasive* 178.12, *serious* 200.5, *exciting* 212.8, *appearing* 264.9, *wondrous* 294.9, *grand* 404.22, *awe-inspiring* 435.12, *excellent* 445.13, *influential* 512.8, *notable* 799.11

impressive effort *exertion* 124.4

impressively *persuasively* 178.21, *wondrously* 294.18, *influentially* 512.14

impressiveness *seriousness* 200.2

impressment *military affairs* 58.1, *coercive method* 428.3, *kidnapping* 479.3

---

impress on *emphasize* 200.6

impress upon *affect* 676.7

imprimatur *book part* 174.5, *approval* 437.1, *permit* 502.3

imprint *printing* 173.3, *print* 173.17, *sign* 183.1, *means of identification* 184.3, *identify* 184.11, *make concave* 635.7, *visible effect* 676.2, *affect* 676.7

imprinted *identified* 184.9

imprison 55.11, *454.23; exclude* 409.12, *detain* 471.9, 830.16, *enclose* 584.16, 619.6

imprisoned 55.9; *punished* 454.19, *retained* 471.6, *enclosed* 584.11, 619.4, *detained* 830.11

imprisoning *detention* 471.2

imprisonment 55.4, *454.2; detention* 830.5

improbability 839.1; *unbelievability* 88.2, *questionableness* 333.7, *indemonstrability* 841.5, *poor chance* 842.8

improbable 839.4; *disbelieved* 88.7, *questionable* 333.13, *indemonstrable* 841.12

improbably 839.8; *questionably* 333.22, *unreliably* 841.25

improbity *lawbreaking* 53.14, *iniquity* 448.3, *cunning* 822.1

impromptu Musical Forms 140, *unpremeditation* 389.2, *spontaneous* 389.6, *spontaneously* 389.17, *improvised* 396.4, *extempore* 396.7

impromptu talk *improvisation* 396.1

improper 430.14; *indecorous* 528.8, *inconvenient* 804.5

improper fraction *fraction* 787.1

improperly 430.26; *vulgarly* 535.10, *incompletely* 762.10, *inconveniently* 804.11

impropriety 430.5, 528.2; *sin* 450.3, *grossness* 535.3, *inconvenience* 804.1

improvable 807.13; *acquisitive* 467.13, *convertible* 670.9

improvably *better* 807.24

improve 467.18, *807.15, 825.26; educate* 48.22, *modify* 340.13, *better* 445.17, *show potential* 458.14, *make rich* 485.15, *change* 512.12, *refine* 534.7, *change for the better* 665.17, *be converted* 670.12, *further* 679.13, *upturn* 713.20, *increase* 746.6, *perfect* 805.19, *get better* 807.21, *refurbish* 809.11

improved 807.12; *modified* 340.9, *acquisitive* 467.13, *beautified* 530.12, *changed* 665.10, *converted* 670.7, *advanced* 713.16, *repaired* 809.6

improved productivity *economic development* 56.5

improved relations *pacification* 74.1

improved technology *economic development* 56.5

improved version *reconsideration* 807.9

improve living conditions *socialize* 2.14

improvement 679.5, 807.1; *modification* 340.5, *righting wrong* 429.6, *welfare* 445.2, *international finance* 457.2, *advance* 467.3, *beautification* 530.1, *change for the better* 665.4, *evolution* 670.3, *ascendancy* 713.5, *increase* 746.1, *help* 825.1

improve on *be superior* 744.15

improve oneself *get better* 807.21
improve on nature *beautify* 807.20
improver 807.11; *changer* 665.9, *converter* 670.5
improve the occasion *take the opportunity* 659.7
improve upon *improve* 807.15
improvidence *waste* 96.1, *imprudence* 286.3, *unpremeditation* 389.2, *extravagance* 500.1
improvident *wasteful* 96.9, *imprudent* 286.7, *unpremeditated* 389.7, *extravagant* 500.4
improvidently *wastefully* 96.23, *unreadily* 389.16
improving 807.14; *educational* 48.17, *beneficial* 445.11, *converting* 670.8
improvingly *educationally* 48.25
improvisation 396.1; *dramatic style* 136.3, *acting* 136.22, *show business* 138.1, *fantasy* 360.5, *method* 387.4, *unpremeditation* 389.2
improvisatorily *entertainingly* 138.17
improvisatory *variety* 138.13
improvise 389.15, 396.6; *act* 136.34, *entertain* 138.16, *play* 141.14, *compose* 141.18, *imagine* 360.14
improvised 396.4; *dramatized* 136.32, *composed* 141.13, *spontaneous* 389.6
improvised drama *dramatic style* 136.3
improviser 396.3; *actor* 136.25, *entertainer* 138.8, *composer* 141.9
improvising *acting* 136.22
improvvisatore [It] *improviser* 396.3
imprudence 286.3; *folly* 353.1, *inconvenience* 804.1
imprudent 286.7; *foolish* 353.5, *inconvenient* 804.5
imprudently 286.11; *foolishly* 353.8
impudence *insolence* 400.1, *bad manners* 411.2, *defiance* 416.1, *disrespect* 436.1, *openness* 843.6
impudent *insolent* 400.8, *bad-mannered* 411.6, *defiant* 416.5, *disrespectful* 436.9, *open* 843.12
impudently *insolently* 400.18, *rudely* 411.9, *defiantly* 416.9, *disrespectfully* 436.25
impudent talk *act of defiance* 416.3
impugn *negate* 190.16, *doubt* 333.19, *object* 828.18
impugned *negated* 190.10
impugning *negational* 190.9
impugnment *negation* 190.1, *objection* 828.2
impulse *turbine type* 14.12, *involuntariness* 95.9, *motive* 178.5, *impression* 266.2, *instinct* 318.3, *insight* 320.3, *caprice* 381.1, *spontaneity* 396.2, *motivation* 508.1, *influence* 512.1, *type of power* 514.6, *acceleration* 694.3, *impulsion* 695.1
impulse-control disorder 108.16
impulse-control disorders *mental disorder* 108.8
impulse-reaction *turbine type* 14.12
impulsion 695.1; *compulsion* 108.13, *type of power* 514.6, *cause* 675.1, *momentum* 677.2, *propulsion* 696.1, *haste* 818.1
impulsive 318.11; *involuntary* 95.15, *unskillful* 128.4, *intuitive*

266.10, *rash* 286.5, *capricious* 381.4, *spontaneous* 396.5, *impelling* 695.8, *hasty* 818.3
impulsively 318.16; *involuntarily* 95.23, *rashly* 286.9, 818.8, *spontaneously* 396.8, *dynamically* 695.16, *propulsively* 696.21
impulsiveness 318.6; *rashness* 286.1, *spontaneity* 396.2, *hastiness* 818.2
impunity *favorable verdict* 54.19, *exemption* 434.1, *escape* 816.1
impure *unclean* 112.8, *polluting* 117.15, *unchaste* 432.10, *depraved* 448.10, *unauthentic* 722.9, *unconditional* 829.14
impurely *promiscuously* 432.19, *unvirtuously* 448.16, *excessively* 829.23
impureness *moral deterioration* 808.3
impure thoughts *sexual immorality* 432.2
impurities reduction *systems and process control* 14.28
impurity *uncleanness* 112.2, *depravity* 448.2, *unauthenticity* 722.4, *moral deterioration* 808.3
impurity atom *semiconductor* 10.34
imputation *accusation* 442.1
imputative *accusatory* 442.6
impute *accuse* 442.8
in 706.17, 710.16; *tennis terms* 165.5, *readily available* 575.21
in [Inf] *fashionable* 536.5, *trendy* 652.11
in a bad humor *irritable* 304.9
in a bad mood *irritable* 304.9
in a bad way *sick* 114.24, *deteriorated* 808.8, *endangered* 811.10, *adverse* 848.10
in a beeline *directly* 697.16
in a belligerent way *in defiance* 416.10
in abeyance *idle* 394.6, *inactive* 413.9, *inoperative* 515.8, *suspended* 519.3, *inertly* 519.5, *latent* 844.6
in a big way *hugely* 579.21
inability *unskillfulness* 128.1, *powerlessness* 515.1, *limitation* 620.2, *uselessness* 802.1, *failure* 846.1
inability to act *inaction* 413.1
inability to pay *amount owing* 488.5, *insolvency* 490.5, 846.6
inability to see *figurative blindness* 243.8
inability to wait *hastiness* 818.2
in a bind *endangered* 811.10
in a blissful manner *prosperously* 847.9
in a body *together* 59.31, 794.20
in a bored manner 296.9
in a boring manner *boringly* 296.10
in Abraham's bosom *dead* 29.11
in a brown study *thoughtful* 4.17, *speculative* 317.8, *absent-minded* 324.6, *imaginative* 360.10
in absentia *absently* 576.18
in abundance *ample* 795.9
in a carefree manner *easily* 819.5
inaccessibility *unsociability* 409.1, *distance* 585.1, 804.4, *hopelessness* 837.2
inaccessible *unsociable* 409.6, *distant* 585.5, *hopeless* 837.6
inaccessibly *unsocially* 409.13
in accord 735.33; *conforming* 781.8, *conformingly* 781.16
in accordance *harmoniously* 735.31, *conformingly* 781.16

in accord with *agreeing* 462.6
inaccuracy 351.3; *obscurity* 197.1, *tastelessness* 338.3, *incorrectness* 430.3, *untrueness* 722.3, *indeterminacy* 841.6
inaccurate *misrepresented* 188.4, *obscure* 197.2, *unrefined* 338.7, *erroneous* 351.11, *wrong* 430.12, *incorrect* 722.8, *indeterminate* 841.14
inaccurately *unrepresentatively* 188.8, *obscurely* 197.4, *indiscriminately* 338.15, *wrongly* 351.18, *wrongfully* 430.25, *incorrectly* 722.16, *indeterminately* 841.24
inaccurateness *untrueness* 722.3
in accusation *accusingly* 442.11
in a circle *around* 682.17
in a clear style *intelligibly* 363.13
in a cold sweat *frightened* 283.9
in a coma *sick* 114.24
in a controversial way *in disagreement* 463.12, *uncooperatively* 506.11
in a corner *troubled* 824.15, *blocked* 826.13, *in the way* 826.23
in a courageous way *defiantly* 416.9
in a cowardly way *weakly* 517.14
in a critical condition *dying* 29.12
in a critical way *disapprovingly* 507.10
inaction 413.1; *shirking* 386.4, *inactivity* 415.1, *inertness* 519.1, *lack of motion* 678.1
in action *acting* 412.9, *active* 414.13
inactivate *make inactive* 415.16
inactive 413.9, 415.8; *reactive* 11.29, *leisurely* 125.4, *indifferent* 289.7, *apathetic* 322.11, *avoiding* 386.9, *obedient* 426.4, *inert* 519.2, *motionless* 678.4, *latent* 844.6
inactively 413.16, 415.17; *indifferently* 289.17, *obediently* 426.9, *inertly* 519.5, *motionlessly* 678.9
inactive person 413.8
inactive volcano *volcanic activity* 8.26
inactivity 415.1; *leisure* 125.1, *indifference* 289.1, *apathy* 322.2, *shirking* 386.4, *disuse* 394.3, *inaction* 413.1, *submission* 421.1, *obedience* 426.1, *inertness* 519.1, *lack of motion* 678.1, *ease* 819.1, *latency* 844.1
in actuality *really* 719.13
in a daze *wonderingly* 294.16
in addition *increasingly* 746.9
in addition (to) *additionally* 748.15
in a decline *sick* 114.24
in a delicate condition *pregnant* 21.12
inadequacy 486.5; *insufficiency* 98.1, *lack of skill* 282.4, *meagerness* 593.6, *inequality* 741.1, *deficiency* 745.2, *incompleteness* 762.1, 806.2, *uselessness* 802.1
inadequate 486.13; *insufficient* 98.4, 517.11, *unskillful* 128.4, *without skill* 282.10, *disappointing* 293.6, *unpremeditated* 389.7, *unsatisfactory* 438.15, *undersized* 580.8, *meager* 593.12, *unequal* 741.4, *partial* 760.11, *incomplete* 762.5, 806.6, *useless* 802.7
inadequately 486.19; *insufficiently* 98.11, *unskillfully* 282.17, 398.8, *disappointingly* 293.12, *weakly*

517.14, *meagerly* 593.19, *unequally* 741.10, *partly* 760.17, *incompletely* 762.10
in a different ballpark [Inf] *incomparably* 734.12
in a different class *superior* 744.8
in a different direction *nonuniformly* 734.11
in a different realm *incomparably* 734.12
in a different way *differently* 463.13
in a dilemma *questionably* 333.22, *troubled* 824.15
in a direct *or* **straight line** *directly* 697.16
in a dishonest way *thievishly* 479.19
in a disorderly manner *irregularly* 664.6
in a dither *agitatedly* 684.27
inadmissibility *exclusion* 764.1
inadmissible *excluded* 764.6, *inconvenient* 804.5
inadmissible evidence *legal evidence* 339.4
in a downward curve *or* **spiral** *decreasingly* 749.9
in a dream *forgetfully* 355.14
in a drunken stupor *dead drunk* 121.27, *drunkenly* 121.39
in advance *on loan* 475.7, *cash down* 489.25, *before* 621.14, *early* 657.17, *first* 769.19
in adverse circumstances *unprosperous* 848.11, *adversely* 848.16
in adversity *adversely* 848.16
inadvertent *causeless* 842.11
inadvertently *by chance* 842.15
inadvisability *inconvenience* 804.1
inadvisable *inconvenient* 804.5
inadvisably *inconveniently* 804.11
in a fair way *equitably* 740.15
in a false light *unrepresentatively* 188.8
in a few words *summarily* 204.10
in affiliation with *in alliance* 735.35
in a firm grip *tenaciously* 471.11
in a fix [Inf] *troubled* 824.15, *blocked* 826.13
in a fixed position *fastly* 464.16
in a flap [Inf] *restless* 684.16
in a flash *in the shortest possible time* 645.9, *hastily* 818.7
in a flight of fancy *imaginatively* 360.17
in a foreign country *strangely* 724.17
in a friendly fashion *sociably* 408.19
in a friendly way *or* **spirit** *amicably* 62.13
in a funk *frightened* 283.9
in a generous-hearted manner *receptively* 473.15
in a gentlemanly *or* **ladylike manner** *well* 399.22
in agony *feeling pain* 215.6
in a gracious manner *leniently* 423.6
in a greedy fashion *avariciously* 477.22
in agreement *pacifically* 74.12, *assenting* 346.4, *collaborative* 757.7, *conforming* 781.8
in a harmless way *innocently* 449.13
in a heap *indiscriminately* 338.15
in a helpful way *compassionately* 305.14
in a high-handed manner *severely* 424.11

in a huff *angry* 302.11
in a humble manner *unselfishly* 443.9
in a hurry *hasty* 818.3
in aid of 825.33
in a jam [Inf] *endangered* 811.10, *troubled* 824.15
in a jumble *in disorder* 766.24
in a lather [Inf] *agitatedly* 684.27
inalienable *rightful* 429.9, *essential* 723.5, *free* 829.11
inalienable rights *rights* 429.4, *free rights* 829.4
in a line 774.17; *lengthwise* 590.14
in all *completely* 759.14
in all areas *extensively* 563.18
in all conscience *assuredly* 189.30, *earnestly* 278.10
in all directions 697.19; *unprepared* 389.5, *everywhere* 776.19
in all haste *hasty* 818.3
in alliance 735.35
in all innocence *virtuously* 447.9, *innocently* 449.13
in all lands *extensively* 563.18
in all likelihood *demonstrably* 331.22, *really* 719.13, *potentially* 836.11, *probably* 838.11
in all manner of ways *in all directions* 697.19
in all places *extensively* 563.18
in all probability *probably* 838.11
in all quarters *everywhere* 776.19
in all respects *completely* 759.14
in all seriousness *earnestly* 278.10
in all truth *on the whole* 759.13
in a loose manner *noncohesively* 756.9
in a low-key manner *understatedly* 195.18
inalterability *permanence* 667.1
inalterable *stable* 674.3
in a mass *together* 59.31
in amazement *wonderingly* 294.16
in ambush *invisible* 245.3
in amends *redemptively* 478.7
in a mess *indiscriminately* 338.15, *in disorder* 766.24, *troubled* 824.15
in a minority *fewer* 796.7
in a moment *transiently* 643.8
inamorata *or* inamorato *loved one* 299.13
in a muddle *indiscriminately* 338.15, *in disorder* 766.24
in an accommodating manner *compromisingly* 461.9
in an active manner *operationally* 509.13
in an affectionate way *lovingly* 299.29
in an aggressive way *in disagreement* 463.12
in an alien way *in isolation* 753.24
in a natural state *unprocessed* 389.10
in a natural way *materially* 524.9
in ancient times *anciently* 653.18
in and out *changeably* 666.7, *to and fro* 683.16
inane *unemphatic* 201.2, *unintelligent* 316.6, *thoughtless* 318.7, *foolish* 353.5, *meaningless* 362.7
in a negative manner *inhibitively* 826.24
inanely *unintelligently* 316.9
in an evasive manner *irresolutely* 461.10
in an everyday manner *orderly* 663.19
in an excellent manner *worthily* 447.11

in an expert manner *expertly* 52.21
in anger *angrily* 302.24
in an ill humor *irritably* 304.17
inanimate *dead* 29.11, *inactive* 415.8
inanimately *fatally* 29.18, *inactively* 415.17
inanimate object *object* 524.6
in an inferior state *or* place *inferiorly* 745.13
in an informal way *informally* 829.24
in an inhibited way *inhibitively* 826.24
in an instant *transiently* 643.8, *in the shortest possible time* 645.9
in an interesting condition *pregnant* 21.12
in an intimate fashion *intimately* 62.14
in an intrusive manner *with delay* 826.22
inanity *ignorance* 316.3, *lack of thought* 318.1, *folly* 353.1, *nonsense* 362.2
in a noble manner *masterfully* 68.17
in an obscene manner *unvirtuously* 448.16
in an open-minded way *receptively* 473.15
in an optimistic way *auspiciously* 458.17
in answer 334.25; *apologetically* 329.18, *in reply* 332.10
in anticipation 769.20; *in preparation* 388.22, *probably* 838.11
in an uncompromising way *obstinately* 379.11
in an undertone *faintly* 233.11
in an ungentlemanly *or* unladylike manner *badly* 399.23
in a nutshell *proverbially* 177.4, *concisely* 198.6, *summarily* 204.10, *little* 580.12, *shortly* 591.12
in any case *how* 691.16
in any event *how* 691.16, *perchance* 842.18
in A one *or* A number one *or* A 1 condition [Inf] *healthy* 113.4
in a peaceful manner *agreeably* 462.14
in a peaceful way *peacefully* 73.12
in a perfect way *innocently* 449.13, *supremely* 744.23
in a perfect world *ideally* 327.22
in a permissive fashion *with permission* 502.10
in a persuasive manner *persuasively* 504.18
in a pickle [Inf] *troubled* 824.15, *blocked* 826.13
in a pinch *in need* 95.21
in a polite manner *courteously* 410.13
inappetence *or* inappetency *indifference* 289.1
inappetent *indifferent* 289.7
in apple-pie order *orderly* 765.13
inapplicability *extraneousness* 724.1, *unrelatedness* 728.1, *uselessness* 802.1
inapplicable *extraneous* 724.8, *unrelated* 728.6, *useless* 802.7
inapplicably *extraneously* 724.16, *irrelatively* 728.16
inapposite *unrelated* 728.6
inappositely *irrelatively* 728.16
inappositeness *unrelatedness* 728.1
inappreciability *littleness* 580.1

inappreciable *invisible* 245.3, *little* 580.7, *unimportant* 800.10
inappreciably *infinitesimally* 580.13
inapprehensibility *unintelligibility* 364.1
inapprehensible *unintelligible* 364.4
inappropriate *improper* 430.14, *untimely* 660.5, *unrelated* 728.6, *inconvenient* 804.5
inappropriately *improperly* 430.26, *at the wrong time* 660.12, *irrelatively* 728.16
inappropriateness *impropriety* 430.5, *untimeliness* 660.1, *unrelatedness* 728.1, *inconvenience* 804.1
in a predicament *troubled* 824.15
inapt *unskillful* 128.4, *improper* 430.14, *untimely* 660.5, *unrelated* 728.6, *useless* 802.7
inaptitude *unrelatedness* 728.1, *uselessness* 802.1, *inconvenience* 804.1
inaptly *irrelatively* 728.16
inaptness *unskillfulness* 128.1, *impropriety* 430.5, *unrelatedness* 728.1
in a quandary *troubled* 824.15, *confused* 841.11, *confusingly* 841.23
in a rage *angry* 302.11
in a receptive way *receptively* 473.15
in a repressive way *prohibitively* 503.11
in a resolute manner *determinedly* 674.10
Inari Lakes 568
in armor *equipped* 388.10
in a roundabout way *circuitously* 199.8, *circularly* 681.10
in a row *sequential* 770.7
in a row *or* queue *in a line* 774.17
in arrears *insolvently* 488.11, *nonpaying* 490.7, *without paying* 490.15, *with a remainder* 750.12, *incomplete* 762.5, *incompletely* 762.10
inarticulate 206.6; *voiceless* 206.5, *silent* 208.5, *wondering* 294.7, *unintelligible* 364.4, *shy* 403.8, *naive* 821.3
inarticulately *unintelligibly* 364.16
inarticulateness *speech difficulty* 206.1, *silence* 208.2
inarticulation *speech difficulty* 206.1
inartistic *bungled* 128.7
in a rush *hasty* 818.3
in a rut *boringly* 296.10
in a safe manner *surely* 464.15
in ascendancy *superior* 744.8
in a scrape *troubled* 824.15
in a secret manner *under censorship* 503.13
in a seductive manner *influentially* 508.13
in a sense *meaningfully* 361.16
in a series *consecutively* 774.15
in a sharp tone *ill-naturedly* 303.18
in a short time *soon* 657.18
in a short while *soon* 657.18
in a shy manner *unsocially* 409.13
in a small way *little* 580.12
in a snit *resentful* 302.8
in a spin *around* 682.17, *restless* 684.14
in a spiteful manner *vindictively* 441.16

in a spiteful way *aggressively* 63.14
in association *cliquishly* 59.32, *collaborative* 757.7
in association with *in alliance* 735.35
in a standoffish mood *reservedly* 585.15
in a state of *conditionally* 725.10
in a state of flux *changeable* 666.3
in a state of nature *naive* 821.3
in a state of war *warring* 76.26
in a straight line *horizontally* 603.11
in a stubborn manner *inflexibly* 542.13
in a swinging motion *regularly* 663.14
in a tangle *troubled* 824.15
in a temporary manner *compromisingly* 461.9
in a tense manner *toughly* 542.12
in a tight corner *endangered* 811.10
in a tight spot *troubled* 824.15
in a tizzy [Inf] *agitatedly* 684.27
in a trance 121.40; *oblivious* 355.9, *forgetfully* 355.14, *imaginative* 360.10
in a trice *transiently* 643.8, *in the shortest possible time* 645.9
in a trickle *in ones and twos* 796.10
in a true manner *truly* 721.27
in attendance *attending* 575.9, *available* 647.6
inattention 229.2, 324.1; *bungling* 128.2, *imprudence* 286.3, *carelessness* 289.2, *inconsideration* 318.4, *negligence* 326.1, *unthinkingness* 355.3, *discourtesy* 411.1, *restlessness* 414.7, *nonobservance* 466.1, *nonachievement* 762.3
inattentive 324.5; *unskillful* 128.4, *unhearing* 229.5, *imprudent* 286.7, *careless* 289.8, *inconsiderate* 318.9, *negligent* 326.4, *foolish* 353.5, *unthinking* 355.8, *discourteous* 411.5, *nonobservant* 466.5, *wandering* 698.13, *uncompleted* 762.7
inattentively 324.12, 466.13; *imprudently* 286.11, *carelessly* 289.18, *forgetfully* 355.14, *discourteously* 411.8
inattentiveness *inattention* 324.1
in a twinkling *transiently* 643.8, *in the shortest possible time* 645.9
inaudibility *sound* 10.15, *silence* 231.1, *faintness of sound* 233.1, *unintelligibility* 364.1
inaudible *voiceless* 206.5, *unheard* 229.7, *silent* 231.2, *unintelligible* 364.4, *insufficient* 517.11
inaudibly *deafly* 229.13, *silently* 231.5, *unintelligibly* 364.16, *weakly* 517.14
inaugural 771.21; *beginning* 583.14, *precursory* 769.12, *premiere* 771.9, *commissioned* 833.6
inaugural address *salutation* 209.2
inaugurate 675.10, 771.31; *launch* 405.14, *begin* 583.21, *be new* 652.17, *introduce* 708.16, *install* 710.15, *forerun* 769.16, *commission* 833.8
inaugurated 652.13; *enrolled* 771.24
inauguration 771.6; *ceremony* 405.3, *formal occasion* 406.4, *beginning* 583.9, 652.4, *bringing in* 708.4, *commission* 833.1

inauguratory *inaugural* 771.21
inauspicious **282.8;** *presageful* 358.13, *untimely* 660.5, *improbable* 839.4, *adverse* 848.10
inauspiciously **282.15;** *predictively* 358.16, *at the wrong time* 660.12, *adversely* 848.16
inauspiciousness *lack of hope* 282.2, *untimeliness* 660.1
inauthentic *unauthentic* 722.9
inauthentically *unauthentically* 722.17
inauthenticity *unauthenticity* 722.4
in authority **52.20;** *influential* 512.8, *dominant* 744.9
in autumn *seasonally* 654.12
in a vindictive way *evilly* 446.12
in a way *to a degree* 739.11
in awe *wonderingly* 294.16, *reverent* 435.9
in a while *soon* 657.18, *later* 658.16
in a whirl *around* 682.17
in a whisper *secretly* 182.14, *faintly* 233.11
in a wicked way *disobediently* 427.14
in a word *concisely* 198.6, *summarily* 204.10, *shortly* 591.12
in a world of one's own *speculative* 317.8, *absent-minded* 324.6, *oblivious* 355.9
in bad form *in good form* 725.11
in bad health *sick* 114.24
in bad spirits *in good form* 725.11
in bad taste *indecorous* 528.8, *vulgar* 535.6, *discourteously* 535.11
in bad with [Inf] *estranged* 63.8
in balance *correlatively* 729.12, *harmoniously* 735.31
in balk *billiard* 149.6
in battle *warring* 76.26
in bed *sick* 114.24
in behalf of *indirectly* 80.8, *alternatively* 613.36
in between *medianly* 742.12, *in the middle* 772.21
in bits *separately* 753.22, *apart* 753.23, *to pieces* 758.8
in bits and pieces *partly* 760.17, *dilapidated* 808.11
in black *lamentingly* 280.9
in black and white *recorded* 185.12, *on record* 185.16
in bliss *prosperous* 847.5
in bloom *horticultural* 17.14, *flowering* 42.10
in blossom *flowering* 42.10
in blue water *nautically* 571.10
inboard *offshore* 150.35, Ships and Boats 690
in bold relief *clear* 244.6
in bold *or* **high relief** *accentuated* 843.11
in bondage *captive* 832.9
in bonds *obediently* 69.12, *detained* 830.11, *captive* 832.9
inborn *intrinsic* 723.6
inborn aptitude *aptitude* 127.4
inbound *approaching* 704.10, *entering* 706.9
in brackets *in* 710.16
inbred *domesticated* 16.18, *intrinsic* 723.6, *combinatory* 757.6
in brief *concisely* 198.6, *shortly* 591.12, *essentially* 617.6
in broad daylight *manifestly* 331.20, 843.17, *evidently* 339.16
in bulk *one and all* 759.12
in business *in trade* 480.22
in cahoots [Inf] *as one* 752.21, *associating* 827.11

incalculability *immeasurability* 798.2
incalculable *numberless* 795.8, *immeasurable* 798.6, *chance* 842.10
incalculably *numerously* 795.13, *immeasurably* 798.11
in camera *secretly* 182.14, *private* 245.5, *invisibly* 245.8
Incan architecture Architectural Styles 134
incandesce *light up* 246.20
incandescence *light* 10.17, 246.1, *heating effect* 10.28, *heat* 217.1
incandescent *hot* 217.11, *lucent* 246.13
incandescent light **246.5**
incandescently *lightly* 246.23
incant *bewitch* 86.25
incantation *spell* 86.8, *petition* 505.2
incantational *witchlike* 86.19, *requesting* 505.7
incantatory *witchlike* 86.19
incapability *powerlessness* 515.1
incapable *insufficient* 98.4, *unskillful* 128.4, *powerless* 515.6
incapable of thought *thoughtless* 318.7
incapably *unskillfully* 398.8
incapacitate *make inactive* 415.16, *remove power from* 515.13, *hinder* 826.15
incapacitated *drugged* 121.30, *disabled* 515.10
incapacity *unskillfulness* 128.1, *powerlessness* 515.1, *decline* 846.5
in captivity *imprisoned* 55.9, *obediently* 69.12, *detained* 830.11, *captive* 832.9, *dependently* 833.13
incarcerate *imprison* 55.11, 454.23, *enclose* 584.16, *detain* 830.16
incarcerated *imprisoned* 55.9, *detained* 830.11
incarceration *imprisonment* 55.4, 454.2, *detention* 830.5
incarnadine *bloody* 257.8, *redden* 257.9
incarnate *alive* 28.13, *Christlike* 82.18, *represent* 187.10, *appearing* 264.9, *material* 524.7, *be material* 524.8, *quintessential* 723.8, *embody* 723.12
incarnated *material* 524.7
incarnation *body* 19.1, *divine manifestation* 82.5, *representation* 187.1, *appearance* 264.1, *materialization* 524.2, *quintessence* 723.3, *manifestation* 843.2
Incarnation, the God the Son 82.9
in cash *solvent* 485.9
incautious *imprudent* 286.7, *foolish* 353.5, *spontaneous* 396.5
incautiously *imprudently* 286.11
incautiousness *imprudence* 286.3
incendiary *armor-piercing* 78.18, *combustible* 106.12, *cause of fire* 217.10, *on fire* 217.16, *destructive* 523.8
incendiary ammunition *ammunition* 78.11
incendiary bomb *bomb* 78.15, *cause of fire* 217.10
incense **226.3;** *sacred object* 83.11, *source of fragrance* 226.2, *cause dislike* 291.16, *cause hate* 300.12, *make angry* 302.18
incense cedar Trees and Shrubs 43
incensed *angry* 302.11
incenter *triangle* 6.41
incentive **178.4;** *personnel management* 126.4, *persuasive*

178.12, *reward for service* 453.5, *bargain* 495.2, *inducement* 508.2, *positive stimulus* 508.5, *motivational* 508.7, *impulsion* 695.1
incentive pay *gift* 472.2
inception *beginning* 583.9, 652.4, *inauguration* 771.6
inceptive *beginning* 583.14, *causal* 675.7, *inaugural* 771.21
inceptively *causally* 675.12
incertitude *vacillation* 378.1, *uncertainty* 841.1
incessancy *frequency* 661.1, *continuity* 774.4
incessant *drumming* 235.6, *active* 414.13, *permanent* 642.5, *continuing forever* 644.6, *frequent* 661.4, *continuous* 669.5, 774.9, *recurrent* 797.13
incessantly *repeatedly* 235.15, 797.22, *ever* 640.7, *everlastingly* 642.10, *frequently* 661.7, *continually* 669.10, *continuously* 774.16
incest *sexual perversion* 20.12, *sexual offense* 432.6
incestuous *perverted* 432.12
inch *short distance* 586.2, General Units 589
in chains *captive* 832.9
inch along *move slowly* 693.11
in character *customary* 397.11, *characteristic* 779.12
in charge *in authority* 52.20, *managerial* 126.9, *managerially* 126.13
inch by inch *slowly* 693.14, *by degrees* 739.10
in check *limited* 620.5
inch forward *make one's way* 679.12
inchmeal *by degrees* 739.10
inchoate *immature* 389.9, 652.12, *embryonic* 771.19, *inaugural* 771.21
inchoation *source* 771.3
inchoative *inaugural* 771.21
in chorus *agreeing* 462.6, *synchronously* 649.9
incident *aspect of fiction* 139.5, *occurrence* 726.2
incidental *extraneous* 724.8, *aspect* 726.4, *circumstantial* 726.8, *detailed* 726.9, *unrelated* 728.6, *accompanying* 794.12, *secondary* 800.15, *causeless* 842.11
incidentally *extraneously* 724.16, *relatively* 726.17, *meticulously* 726.18, *irrelatively* 776.16, *unimportantly* 800.21
incidentalness *extraneousness* 724.1
incinerate *cremate* 31.11, *burn* 217.18, *consume* 523.16
incineration *cremation* 31.2, *destroying* 523.2
incinerator *cause of fire* 217.10, *place for waste* 802.6
incipience *inauguration* 771.6
incipiency *inauguration* 771.6
incipient *tiny* 580.9, *inaugural* 771.21
incircle *circle* 6.40
in circles *around* 682.17
in circulation *newsworthy* 171.8, *published* 173.12, 174.18, 175.8
incise *practice surgery* 107.33, *engrave* 144.11, *inscribe* 185.14, *crack* 587.7, *notch* 636.5
incised *engraved* 144.9
incision *surgery* 107.17, *crack* 587.2, *notch* 636.1, *separateness* 753.3

incisive *assertive* 189.20, *concise* 198.4, *emphatic* 200.3, *bitter* 306.9, *advantaged* 618.7
incisively *concisely* 198.6, *emphatically* 200.7, *bitterly* 306.16
incisiveness *assertiveness* 189.8, *conciseness* 198.1, *emphasis* 200.1, *bitterness* 306.3, *cleverness* 315.3
incisor *teeth* 19.8
incisural *notched* 636.4
incisure *notch* 636.1
incitable *persuadable* 178.14
incitation *stimulus* 508.3
Incitatus Notable Horses 159
incite *motivate* 178.17, *give courage* 284.16, *manipulate* 508.12, *make violent* 520.10, *awaken* 675.9, *impel* 695.9, *hasten* 818.4
incited *persuadable* 178.14, *motivated* 508.8
incitement *exhortation* 178.2, *incentive* 178.4, *encouragement* 284.6, *inspiration* 360.2, *impulsion* 695.1
inciting *persuasive* 178.12, *encouraging* 284.13, *motivational* 508.7
incitive *motivational* 508.7
incivil *rude* 400.9
incivility *objectionability* 272.2, *rudeness* 400.2, *discourtesy* 411.1, *disrespect* 436.1, *grossness* 535.3
in clauses *phraseologically* 5.47
inclemency *cold weather* 218.8, *pitilessness* 309.1, *severity* 424.1
inclement *stormy* 9.45, *cold* 218.9, *pitiless* 309.3, *severe* 424.5
inclemently *pitilessly* 309.7
inclination **290.2, 714.6;** *orbit* 7.22, *geomagnetism* 8.3, *aptitude* 127.4, *will* 372.1, *preference* 382.2, *tendency* 397.2, *mark of respect* 435.4, *attitude* 513.2, *obliqueness* 607.1, *bearing* 697.2
inclinational *oblique* 607.6
incline **713.3;** *prefer* 382.13, *lay the foundations* 388.16, *influence* 508.11, *tend* 513.5, *mountain* 569.1, *heights* 596.4, *rise* 596.17, *obliqueness* 607.1, *be oblique* 607.10, *angle* 628.11, *aim* 697.14, *slide* 714.17, *lean* 716.19
inclined *willed* 372.6, *intending* 374.6, *preferential* 382.10, *oblique* 607.6, 628.8
inclined fold *fold* 8.22
inclined plane *surface* 6.36, *simple machine* 14.6
inclined railroad *railroad system* 688.1
inclined to forget *forgetful* 186.7
inclined toward **290.5;** *tending to* 513.4
incline one's head *show respect* 435.16, *bow* 716.22
incline toward *tend* 513.5
inclining *tending to* 513.4, *rising* 596.12, *oblique* 607.6
inclining toward *tending to* 513.4
in clover *wealthy* 485.8, *wealthily* 485.16, *prosperously* 847.9
include **613.33, 763.5;** *focus on* 328.9, *embody* 577.11, 723.12, *admit* 708.12, *insert* 710.9, *augment* 748.13, *unify* 752.15
included **763.4;** *inset* 710.8, *additional* 748.8
including **763.3;** *containing* 577.7, *additionally* 748.15
inclusion **763.1;** *coverage* 613.16, *admittance* 708.1, *insert* 710.4, *addition* 748.1
inclusion-exclusion (principle of) *combinatorics* 6.63

inclusive 613.22; *containing* 577.7, *additional* 748.8, *including* 763.3, *general* 778.9

inclusively 613.35, 763.8; *internally* 577.15

inclusiveness *whole* 759.1, *inclusion* 763.1, *generality* 778.1

inclusive of *additionally* 748.15

incognito *disguised* 181.9, *anonymity* 182.7, *mysterious* 182.10, *secretly* 182.14

incognito or **incognita** *ungenuine* 192.13

incognizable *unrecognizable* 364.7

incognizance *ignorance* 349.1

incognizant *ignorant* 349.5

incoherence *insanity* 110.1, *nonsense* 362.2, *nonadhesion* 756.1, *disintegration* 758.1, *disorder* 766.1, *discontinuity* 775.1, *indeterminacy* 841.6

incoherent *diffuse* 199.3, *meaningless* 362.7, *unintelligible* 364.4, *nonadhesive* 756.4, *confused* 766.12, *discontinuous* 775.7, *indeterminate* 841.14

incoherently *unintelligibly* 364.16, *noncohesively* 756.9, *indeterminately* 841.24

in cold blood *indifferently* 289.17, *pitilessly* 309.7

in cold storage *inertly* 519.5, *held up* 658.6

in collaboration *additionally* 748.15

in combat *aggressively* 418.27

in combination 757.11

income 492.3; *economic factor* 56.8, *resources* 102.4, *reward for service* 453.5, *earnings* 467.5, *personal estate* 470.6, *something received* 473.2, *pay* 489.6, *produce* 522.5

incomer *settler* 61.4, *new arrival* 652.7, *entrant* 706.7

income tax *tax* 494.5

income tax return *record* 185.1

in comfort *prosperously* 847.9

incoming *arriving* 704.9, *approaching* 704.10, *entry* 706.1, *entering* 706.9, *externality* 724.4, *external* 724.11

incomings *money received* 492.2

incoming tide *hidden danger* 813.3

in command *in authority* 52.20, *managerially* 126.13

in commemoration of *in honor of* 405.14

incommensurability *incomparability* 734.3

incommensurable *divisible* 6.71, *incomparable* 734.6

incommensurableness *incomparability* 734.3

incommensurably *incomparably* 734.12

incommensurate *incomparable* 734.6

incommensurately *incomparably* 734.12

incommensurateness *incomparability* 734.3

in commerce *in trade* 480.22

in commission *in use* 393.8

in committee *discussing* 210.9

incommode *be inconvenient* 804.9

incommodious *narrow* 593.8, *inconvenient* 804.5

incommodiously *narrowly* 593.17, *inconveniently* 804.11

incommodiousness *narrowness* 593.1, *inconvenience* 804.1

in common 469.17

in common parlance *simply* 526.14

incommunicability *unintelligibility* 364.1

incommunicable *unintelligible* 364.4

incommunicado *silent* 181.10

incommunicative *taciturn* 208.4

incommunicatively *taciturnly* 208.9

incommunicativeness *taciturnity* 208.1

incommutability *stability* 674.1

incommutable *stable* 674.3

in-company *unionized* 57.14

in-company union *organized labor* 57.5

incomparability 734.3; *superiority* 744.1

incomparable 734.6; *novel* 737.5, *best* 744.10, 805.9

incomparableness *incomparability* 734.3

incomparably 734.12; *originally* 737.8, *supremely* 744.23

in comparison *relevantly* 727.12

incompatibility *reasoning* 6.61, *personal conflict* 63.2, *divorce court* 66.3, *unsociability* 409.1, *divisiveness* 463.2, *difference* 463.4, *dissimilarity* 734.1, *nonconformity* 782.1

incompatible *logical* 6.83, *arguing* 329.6, *disagreeing* 463.6, *different* 463.7, *dissimilar* 734.4, *nonconforming* 782.11, *contrary* 828.13

incompatibly *argumentatively* 329.15, *unsocially* 409.13, *in disagreement* 463.12, *differently* 463.13, *dissimilarly* 734.10

in compensation 743.10; *rewardingly* 453.19, *redemptively* 478.7

incompetence *insufficiency* 98.1, *unskillfulness* 128.1, *lack of skill* 282.4, *powerlessness* 515.1, *uselessness* 802.1

incompetent *insufficient* 98.4, *unskilled person* 128.3, *unskillful* 128.4, *without skill* 282.10, *loser* 468.8, *powerless person* 515.5, *powerless* 515.6, *useless* 802.7

incompetently *insufficiently* 98.11, *unskillfully* 128.12, *282.17, 398.8, *powerlessly* 515.16, *uselessly* 802.14

incomplete 762.5, 806.6; *logical* 6.83, *insufficient* 98.4, *indifferent* 326.5, *neglected* 326.6, *unfinished* 544.9, *shapeless* 625.2, *partial* 760.11, *uncompleted* 762.7, *fractional* 787.5

incompletely 544.14, 762.10; *negligently* 326.8, *immaturely* 389.18, *partly* 760.17, *imperfectly* 806.10

incompleteness 98.2, 762.1, 806.2; *immaturity* 389.3, *rough idea* 544.4, *shapelessness* 625.1, *noncompletion* 762.2

incomplete pass *play* 155.8

incomplete set *imperfect item* 806.3

incomplete work *nonachievement* 762.3

incompletion *shapelessness* 625.1, *noncompletion* 762.2

in compliance with *obediently* 426.9

incomprehensibility *obscurity* 197.1, *unintelligibility* 364.1, *immeasurability* 798.2

incomprehensible *obscure* 197.2,

unintelligible 364.4, *immeasurable* 798.6

incomprehensibly *obscurely* 197.4, *unintelligibly* 364.16

incomprehension *ignorance* 316.3, 349.1

incompressibility *density* 540.1

incompressible *dense* 540.6

incompressible fluid *fluid* 555.1

inconceivability *unintelligibility* 364.1, *impossibility* 837.1

inconceivable *astonishing* 294.10, *unintelligible* 364.4, *impossible* 837.4

inconceivably *astonishingly* 294.19, *unintelligibly* 364.16, *impossibly* 837.11

in concert *synchronously* 649.9, *in harmony* 735.32, *in accord* 735.33, *agreeable* 752.11, *agreeably* 752.22, *in combination* 757.11

in conclusion *conclusively* 334.26, *finally* 773.24

inconclusive *insufficient* 517.11

inconclusively *weakly* 517.14

in condition *healthy* 113.4, *in good form* 725.11

in conference *discussing* 210.9

in confidence *secretly* 182.14

in confinement *punished* 454.19

in conflict *argumentatively* 329.15

in conflict with *disapprovingly* 507.10

in conformity *literally* 721.32

in conformity with *obediently* 426.9

in confrontation *at odds* 828.23

in confusion *in disorder* 766.24

incongruence *disparity* 728.3, *diversity* 732.1

incongruent *disparate* 728.9, *unequal* 741.4

incongruently *disparately* 728.19

incongruity *impropriety* 430.5, *difference* 463.4, *disparity* 728.3, *diversity* 732.1, *dissimilarity* 734.1, *nonconformity* 782.1

incongruous *improper* 430.14, *different* 463.7, *unusual* 664.4, *diverse* 732.5, *dissimilar* 734.4, *nonconforming* 782.11

incongruously *differently* 463.13, *unusually* 664.7, *diversely* 732.14, *dissimilarly* 734.10, *unconformably* 782.21

incongruousness *unusualness* 664.2

in conjunction with *additionally* 748.15, *as one* 752.21

in connection with 754.16

inconsequence *insignificance* 289.4, *unimportance* 800.1

in consequence *with the effect of* 676.12, *consequently* 770.15

inconsequential *insignificant* 289.10, 800.12, *sophistic* 330.7, *aimless* 362.8

inconsequentially *unexceptionally* 289.20, *unimportantly* 800.21

inconsiderable *little* 580.7, *superficial* 599.4, *insignificant* 745.6, *unimportant* 800.10

inconsiderably *infinitesimally* 580.13, *insignificantly* 745.14

inconsiderate 318.9; *blind to* 243.14, *imprudent* 286.7, *ungrateful* 311.2, *thoughtless* 324.7, *badly behaved* 399.16, *discourteous* 411.5

inconsiderately *imprudently* 286.11, *ungratefully* 311.6, *inattentively* 324.12, *badly* 399.23, *discourteously* 411.8

inconsiderateness *ingratitude* 311.1

inconsideration 318.4; *imprudence* 286.3, *thoughtlessness* 324.3, *discourtesy* 411.1

inconsistency 732.3; *reasoning* 6.61, *sophistry* 330.1, *faulty reasoning* 351.4, *vacillation* 380.3, *capriciousness* 381.2, *difference* 463.4, *irregularity* 664.1, *changeableness* 666.1, *unreliability* 722.5, 841.7, *disparity* 728.3, *dissimilarity* 734.1, *nonconformity* 782.1, *contrariety* 828.6, *lack of motive* 842.2

inconsistent 732.7; *logical* 6.83, *sophistic* 330.7, *erroneous* 351.11, *equivocating* 380.6, *erratic* 381.5, *different* 463.7, *irregular* 664.3, *changeable* 666.3, *unreliable* 722.10, 841.15, *disparate* 728.9, *dissimilar* 734.4, *nonconforming* 782.11, *contrary* 828.13

inconsistently 732.16; *sophistically* 330.14, *erratically* 381.8, *differently* 463.13, *irregularly* 664.6, *changeably* 666.7, *disparately* 728.19, *dissimilarly* 734.10, *unconformably* 782.21, *unreliably* 841.25

inconsolable *sorrowful* 270.4, *without hope* 282.7

inconsolably *unhopefully* 282.14

inconsonance *disparity* 728.3

inconsonant *disparate* 728.9

inconsonantly *disparately* 728.19

inconspicuous *difficult to see* 245.4

inconstancy 378.2; *capriciousness* 381.2, 841.8, *irregularity* 664.1, *changeableness* 666.1, *inconsistency* 732.3

inconstant 378.6; *erratic* 381.5, *irregular* 664.3, *changeable* 666.3, *inconsistent* 732.7, *capricious* 841.16

inconstantly *irregularly* 664.6, *changeably* 666.7, *inconsistently* 732.16, *capriciously* 841.26

in constant use *in use* 393.8

in contact *juxtaposed* 586.9, *beside* 586.20, *connective* 754.10

in contempt of *in disagreement* 463.12

incontestable *identifiable* 843.10

in context *relevantly* 727.12

incontinence *urination* 25.4, *sexual immorality* 432.2, *overindulgence* 456.3, *liberality* 829.8

incontinent *excremental* 25.13, *unchaste* 432.10, *overindulgent* 456.8, *unconditional* 829.14

incontinently *self-indulgently* 456.12, *excessively* 829.23

in contradiction *negatively* 190.22, *uncooperatively* 506.11

in contrast *counter* 510.8, *relevantly* 727.12

in control *in authority* 52.20, *managerial* 126.9, *managerially* 126.13

incontrovertible *stable* 674.3, *decided* 840.9

inconvenience 804.1; *untimeliness* 660.1, *disruption* 768.4, *disrupt* 768.12, *uselessness* 802.1, *be inconvenient* 804.9, *snag* 824.8, *cause difficulties* 824.22, *obstacle* 826.2, *burden* 826.10, 826.21, *block* 826.17

inconvenienced *disrupted* 768.8, *troubled* 824.15

inconvenient 804.5, 824.12;

misjudged 342.8, *untimely* 660.5, *useless* 802.7, *blocked* 826.13
inconveniently 804.11; *at the wrong time* 660.12, *disturbingly* 768.13, *uselessly* 802.14, *awkwardly* 824.26, *in the way* 826.23
in conversation *in answer* 334.25
in convoy *together* 794.20
incorporate *trade* 480.18, *federate* 480.21, *include* 613.33, 763.5, *absorb* 708.19, *embody* 723.12, *unify* 752.15, *combine* 757.9
incorporate [Arch] *nonmaterial* 525.8
incorporated *corporate* 480.17, *inclusive* 613.22, *united* 752.10, *combined* 757.5, *combinatory* 757.6
incorporated company (Inc.) *company* 480.7
incorporating *including* 763.3
incorporation *coverage* 613.16, *absorption* 708.6, *combination* 757.1, *inclusion* 763.1, *association* 827.6
incorporative *language type* 5.11, *including* 763.3
incorporator *coverer* 613.18
incorporeal *spiritual* 86.20, *nonmaterial* 525.8, *sparse* 541.3, *unreal* 720.8
incorporeality *immateriality* 525.2, *sparseness* 541.1, *unreality* 720.1
incorporeally *metaphysically* 525.13
incorporealness *immateriality* 525.2
incorporeity *immateriality* 525.2
incorrect 722.8; *logical* 6.83, *misrepresented* 188.4, *erroneous* 351.11, *wrong* 430.12, *inelegant* 528.6
incorrectly 722.16; *unrepresentatively* 188.8, *wrongly* 351.18, *wrongfully* 430.25
incorrectness 430.3; *erroneousness* 351.2, *inelegance of expression* 528.4, *grossness* 535.3, *untrueness* 722.3
incorrect spelling *spelling* 5.26
incorrect usage *grammar* 5.28, *language error* 351.10
incorrigibility *hopelessness* 282.1, *obstinacy* 379.1, *impenitence* 452.1
incorrigible *hopeless* 282.6, *obstinate* 379.5, *refractory* 379.6, *impenitent* 452.2, *losing* 468.9
incorrigibly *hopelessly* 282.13
incorrupt 449.7
incorruptedness *incorruption* 449.2
incorruptibility *health* 113.1, *incorruption* 449.2, *eternity* 644.1
incorruptible *incorrupt* 449.7, *changeless* 640.4, *eternal* 644.4
incorruption 449.2; *health* 113.1
in court *legally* 53.33, *in litigation* 54.34
incrassate *viscous* 561.14, *thicken* 561.21, *thick* 594.5
incrassated *swelled* 581.10
incrassation *viscosity* 561.1
increase 467.17, 581.3, 581.16, 746.1, 746.6; *excess* 99.1, *store* 105.17, *aggravate* 276.5, *augmentation* 467.2, *produce* 522.5, *growth* 676.3, *grow* 676.10, *incline* 713.3, *send up* 715.12, *quantify* 738.7, *change by degrees* 739.8, *make bigger* 746.7, *addition* 748.1, *multiplication*

793.4, *pluralize* 793.9, *uplift* 807.2, *get better* 807.21
increased 746.5; *aggravated* 276.3, *swelled* 581.10, *quantitative* 738.6, *multiplicative* 793.8
increased output *manufacture* 522.2
increase fourfold *quadruple* 791.11
increase in size *expansion* 581.1, *enlarge* 581.14
increase numbers *make bigger* 746.7
increase one's demands *be unsatisfied* 98.10
increaser *enlarger* 581.8
increase the chances *make probable* 838.9
increase the odds *make probable* 838.9
increase threefold *triple* 790.10
increase worth *or value be good* 445.16
increasing 746.4; *growing* 581.12, 676.6, *gradational* 739.5, *multiplicative* 793.8, *improving* 807.14
increasingly 746.9; *largely* 581.18, *by degrees* 739.10
incredibility *unbelievability* 88.2, *implausibility* 839.3
incredible *disbelieved* 88.7, *astonishing* 294.10, *unbelievable* 837.5, *questionable* 839.5
incredibly *unbelievably* 88.11, *astonishingly* 294.19, *impossibly* 837.11, *improbably* 839.8
in credit 487.8; *financially* 493.13
incredulity 88.3; *astonishment* 292.2, *suspicion* 841.2
incredulous *disbelieving* 88.6, *astonished* 292.6
incredulously *disbelievingly* 88.10, *with surprise* 292.13, *surprisingly* 292.14
increment *differentiation* 6.29, *reward for service* 453.5, *augmentation* 467.2, *increase* 746.1, *addition* 748.1
incremental *additional* 748.8
incriminate *accuse* 442.8
incriminated *accused* 442.5
incriminating evidence *legal evidence* 339.4
incrimination *accusation* 442.1
incriminator *accuser* 442.3
incriminatory *accusatory* 442.6
in-crowd *group* 59.8, *avant-garde* 652.6
in crowds 795.14
incrust *face* 613.31
incrustation *cover* 613.2, *wall covering* 613.12
incubate *propagate* 21.15, *rear* 715.10
incubation *genesis* 21.5
incubator *source* 675.2, *preserver* 815.9
incubus *evil spirit* 446.4, *weighing down* 538.5
inculcate *educate* 48.22, *moralize* 431.14
inculpability *incorruption* 449.2
inculpable *incorrupt* 449.7
inculpate *accuse* 442.8
inculpated *guilty* 450.6
inculpation *guilt* 450.1
incumbency *sense of duty* 433.2
incumbent *duteous* 433.7
incumbent on *duty-bound* 433.8, *ponderous* 538.11
incunabulum *rare book* 174.2
incurability *hopelessness* 282.1
incurable *killing* 30.17, *sick*

114.24, *hopeless* 282.6, *unyielding* 379.8
incurably *hopelessly* 282.13
incur a duty 433.15; *direct* 126.11
incur a penalty *forfeit* 468.13
incur a responsibility *incur a duty* 433.15
incur blame *cause dislike* 291.16
incur costs *expend* 491.11
incur expenses *expend* 491.11
incuriosity 322.1; *indifference* 289.1, *lack of wonder* 295.1, *inattention* 324.1
incurious 322.3; *indifferent* 289.7, *wonderless* 295.3, *inattentive* 324.5
incuriously 322.6; *indifferently* 289.17, *without wonder* 295.8, *inattentively* 324.12
incur liabilities *buy on credit* 476.13
incur losses *lose money* 468.15
incurred *undertaken* 391.4
incursion *offensive warfare* 76.11, *military attack* 418.2, *inroad* 706.3, *transgression* 712.3
incursive *invasive* 706.10
incursively *in* 706.17
incur upon *attack successfully* 418.25
incurvate *concave* 635.5
incurvation *concavity* 635.1
incurvature *curvature* 629.2
incus *Human Bones* 19, *ear* 19.10, 228.2
in custody *detained* 830.11
in danger *vulnerable* 811.9, *endangered* 811.10
in date order *chronological* 639.12
in days of yore *in the past* 651.20
in debt *indebted* 486.9, 488.7, *insolvently* 488.11, *without paying* 490.15, *financially* 493.13, *blocked* 826.13
indebted 486.9, 488.7; *grateful* 310.4, *nonpaying* 490.7, *blocked* 826.13
indebtedness *gratitude* 310.1, *insolvency* 486.2, *debt* 488.1
indecency *obscenity* 112.4, *profanity* 301.3, *immorality* 432.1, *depravity* 448.2, *grossness* 535.3
indecent 261.8; *obscene* 112.9, *profane* 301.10, *immoral* 432.9, *depraved* 448.10, *ribald* 535.8
indecent assault *personal attack* 418.8, *sexual offense* 432.6
indecent exposure *sexual offense* 432.6, *bareness* 614.3
indecently *dirtily* 112.12, *bluely* 261.11, *profanely* 301.19, *immorally* 432.18, *unvirtuously* 448.16, *ribaldly* 535.12
indecently assault *seduce* 432.16
indecipherable *problematic* 824.11
indecision *vacillation* 378.1, 683.3, *indecisiveness* 517.2, *inertness* 519.1, *deferment* 604.3, *irresolution* 841.3
indecisive *spineless* 285.5, *vacillating* 378.5, *weak-willed* 517.10, *inert* 519.2, *deferred* 604.9, *irresolute* 841.10
indecisively *irresolutely* 378.13, *weakly* 517.14, *interruptedly* 604.20, *uncertainly* 841.22
indecisiveness 517.2; *inertness* 519.1, *deferment* 604.3, *irresolution* 841.3
in decline *decreasingly* 747.9, *deteriorated* 808.8
indecorous 528.8; *improper* 430.14, *vulgar* 535.6
indecorously *improperly* 430.26,

inelegantly 528.11, *vulgarly* 535.10
indecorousness *impropriety* 430.5, *vulgarity* 535.1
indecorum *impropriety* 430.5, *vulgarity* 535.1
in deduction *by subtraction* 749.8
indeed *assuredly* 189.30, 336.12, *earnestly* 278.10, *certainly* 719.14, *in truth* 721.28
in deep 598.18; *intensely* 598.28
in deep water *troubled* 824.15
indefatigability *commitment* 377.2, *assiduity* 414.8
indefatigable *committed* 377.7, *industrious* 414.16, *stalwart* 547.10
in default *with a remainder* 750.12, *incomplete* 762.5
in default of *instead* 672.8
indefeasible *stable* 674.3
indefectibility *perfection* 805.1
indefectible *infallible* 805.10
in defense *apologetic* 329.10, *apologetically* 329.18, *in reply* 332.10, *in answer* 334.25, *defensively* 419.32
indefensible *helpless* 515.9
indefensibly *powerlessly* 515.16
in defiance 416.10
in defiance of *in disagreement* 463.12, *disapprovingly* 507.10
indefinable *unintelligible* 364.4
indefinableness *unintelligibility* 364.1
indefinite *of grammar* 5.41, *obscure* 197.2, *difficult to see* 245.4, *inscrutable* 250.5, *unrecognizable* 364.7, *equivocal* 380.5, *shapeless* 625.2, *unreal* 720.8, *generalized* 778.12, *indeterminate* 841.14
indefinite article *part of speech* 5.30
indefinite integral *differentiation* 6.29
indefinitely *obscurely* 197.4, *invisibly* 245.8, *shapelessly* 625.5, *infinitely* 798.10, *indeterminately* 841.24
indefiniteness *obscurity* 197.1, *equivocation* 380.1, *indeterminacy* 841.6
indehiscent *of a fruit* 44.8
indehiscent fruit *botanical fruit* 44.2
indelible *memorable* 354.7, *stable* 674.3
indelible ink *black pigment* 254.2
indelibly *stably* 674.9
indelicacy *tastelessness* 338.3, *impropriety* 528.2, *vulgarity* 535.1
indelicate *profane* 301.10, *unrefined* 338.7, *indecorous* 528.8, *ugly* 531.3, *vulgar* 535.6
indelicate language *offensive language* 301.5
indelicately *profanely* 301.19, *tastelessly* 338.14, *inelegantly* 528.11, 531.7, *vulgarly* 535.10
in demand *desired* 288.10, *praiseworthy* 437.12, *sold* 482.14
indemnification *atonement* 313.1, *compensation* 453.7, 478.2, 743.1
indemnificatory *atoning* 313.5, *compensatory* 453.11, 743.5, *restoring* 478.4
indemnified *compensated* 743.3
indemnifier *atoner* 313.4
indemnify *recompense* 273.11, *forgive* 312.8, *atone* 313.7, *pay* 453.15, *promise* 464.10, *compensate* 478.6, 743.7, *pay back* 489.20

indemnifying *restoring* 478.4, *compensatory* 743.5
indemnity *reparation* 273.2, *forgiveness* 312.1, *atonement* 313.1, *compensation* 453.7, 478.2, 743.1, *promise* 464.2, *repayment* 489.5, *damages* 489.8
indemonstrability 841.5
indemonstrable 841.12
indent *punctuate* 183.20, *make rough* 544.11, *make concave* 635.7, *notch* 636.5
indentation *nap* 552.3, *concavity* 635.1, *notch* 636.1, *depression* 716.4
indented *punctuated* 183.15, *concave* 635.5, *notched* 636.4
indention *concavity* 635.1
indenture *contract* 462.2, 462.11, *subject* 832.10
indentured *captive* 832.9
indentured servant *subjected person* 832.5
indentureship *subjection* 832.1
independence 829.5; *proudness* 297.3, *free will* 372.4, *freedom* 407.4, *acquittal* 434.2, *solvency* 485.4, *separateness* 724.3, *nonconformity* 728.4, *originality* 737.1, *aloofness* 756.2, *self-help* 825.11
independent 434.7, 829.12; *given* 6.74, *governmental* 49.24, *unionized* 57.14, *celibate* 67.6, *proud* 297.10, *free-willed* 372.9, *free* 407.9, *nonobservant* 466.5, *national* 566.10, *separate* 724.10, *nonconforming* 728.10, *individualist* 756.3, *aloof* 756.5, *nonconformist* 782.7, *unconventional* 782.14, *solo* 788.14, *self-helpful* 825.22, *free person* 829.9, *liberated* 831.4
independent clause *clause* 5.31
independent contractor *independent worker* 123.3
independent distributor *sales worker* 123.6
independently *industrially* 57.22, *celibately* 67.12, *proudly* 297.19, *defiantly* 466.14, *nationally* 566.13, *separately* 724.18, *individualistically* 728.20, *aloofly* 756.10, *out of step* 782.22, *alone* 788.20, *freely* 829.22
independent means *independence* 829.5
independent mind *liberation* 831.1
independent rule *independence* 829.5
independent state *country* 566.1
independent union *organized labor* 57.5
independent variable *mathematical function* 6.27
independent voter *free person* 829.9
independent worker 123.3
in depth *intensely* 598.28
in-depth reporting *print journalism* 175.4
in descending order *decreasingly* 747.9
indescribable *astonishing* 294.10
indescribably *astonishingly* 294.19
indestructibility *permanence* 667.1, *stability* 674.1
indestructible *tough* 542.6, 547.6, *changeless* 640.4, *permanent* 667.2, *unfailing* 667.3, *stable* 674.3
indestructibly *toughly* 547.16, *permanently* 667.6, *stably* 674.9

in detail *diffusely* 199.7, *carefully* 325.13, *intensely* 598.28, *partly* 760.17, *specifically* 779.22
in detention *imprisoned* 55.9
indeterminable *immeasurable* 798.6
indeterminableness *immeasurability* 798.2
indeterminably *immeasurably* 798.11
indeterminacy 841.6; *causality* 10.66, *chance* 842.1, *lack of motive* 842.2
indeterminant *causeless* 842.11
indeterminate 841.14; *unreal* 720.8, *generalized* 778.12, *chance* 842.10
indeterminately 841.24
indetermination *chance* 842.1
index *multiplication* 6.15, *type of book* 174.3, *book part* 174.5, Reference Signs 183, *indicator* 183.7, *record book* 185.5, *record* 185.13, *division* 577.6, *itemize* 577.13, *systematize* 765.19, *catalog* 767.7, *categorize* 767.21, *sort* 777.13, *power* 783.6, *table* 785.2, *list* 785.11
Index, the *censorship* 503.4
index card *record book* 185.5
indexed *identified* 184.9, *recorded* 185.12, *itemized* 577.9, *grouped* 765.11, *categorized* 767.15, *classed* 777.11, *listed* 785.9
indexes *statistics* 784.2
index finger *appendage* 19.5, *indicator* 183.7
index fossil *fossil* 8.49
indexical *grouped* 765.11, *classificatory* 777.9
indexically *thematically* 577.16, *in place* 767.24
indexing *recordkeeping* 185.7, *grouping* 765.2, *categorization* 767.5, *listing* 785.8
Index Librorum Prohibitorum [L] *censorship* 503.4
India Countries 566, *landmass* 572.1
India drugget *floor covering* 613.13
India ink *black pigment* 254.2
Indiaman Sailing Ships and Boats 690
Indian *race* 1.5, *racial* 1.12, Constellations 7, Deserts 572
Indiana American States 564
Indianapolis American States 564
Indianapolis 500 race *races* 146.4
Indianapolis Motor Speedway Association (IMSA) *racing governing bodies* 146.7
Indian architecture Architectural Styles 134
Indian mode *mode* 140.17
Indian mulberry Trees and Shrubs 43
Indian Ocean Oceans and Seas 571
Indian paintbrush Flowers 42
Indian pony *horse* 159.1
Indian red *red pigment* 257.2
Indian summer *weather* 9.3, *hot weather* 9.22, *fall* 654.5, *revival* 809.3
Indian tea *tea* 93.7
Indian yellow *yellow pigment* 259.2
India paper *paper* 104.5
in diapers *young* 26.11
India rubber *rubber* 546.3
indicate *direct* 126.11, 697.13, *tip* 170.14, *signify* 183.16, *sign* 183.19, *identify* 184.11, *make*

visible 244.9, *epitomize* 327.18, *state* 329.13, *explain* 331.16, *make evident* 339.11, *predict* 358.14, *mean* 361.13, *precede* 769.13, *display* 843.13, *reveal* 843.14, *imply* 844.14
indicated *tacit* 844.10
indicating *informative* 170.10, *identification* 184.1, *symbolic* 361.8
indication 339.3; *reasoning* 6.61, *symptom* 114.3, *sign* 183.1, *identification* 184.1, *representation* 187.1, *brief description* 202.2, *nomenclature* 202.7, *theory* 327.2, *explanation* 331.3, *omen* 358.5, *concomitant* 794.4, *forewarning* 814.2, *manifestation* 843.2
indicative *grammatical term* 5.29, *diagnostic* 107.29, *signifying* 183.11, *theoretical* 327.10, *explanatory* 331.11, *evidential* 339.8, *predicting* 358.11, *linguistic* 361.9, *identifiable* 843.10
indicatively 183.21; *identifiably* 184.13, *purposively* 327.20, *demonstrably* 331.22, *as evidence* 339.15
indicator 183.7; *gravimetric analysis* 11.18, *sign* 183.1, *indication* 339.3, *meter* 589.13, *forewarning* 814.2
indicatory *signifying* 183.11
indices *statistics* 784.2
indict *litigate* 54.27, *accuse* 442.8
indictability *guilt* 450.1
indictable *accusatory* 442.6
indicted *accused* 442.5
indicter *accuser* 442.3
indictment *pretrial proceedings* 54.13, *accusation* 442.1
indifference 289.1, 326.2; *coexistence* 73.3, *mood disorder* 108.12, *dilution* 220.2, *inattention* 229.2, 324.1, *heedlessness* 268.2, *lack of wonder* 295.1, *boredom* 296.1, *incuriosity* 322.1, *thoughtlessness* 324.3, *lack of discrimination* 338.1, *unthinkingness* 355.3, *unenthusiasm* 375.3, *informality* 407.1, *unsociability* 409.1, *defeatism* 413.7, *idleness* 415.3, *disinterestedness* 443.1, *nonobservance* 466.1, *inertness* 519.1, *lack of motion* 678.1, *mediocrity* 742.3, *resignedness* 835.2
indifferent 289.7, 326.5; *tasteless* 220.4, *unhearing* 229.5, *insensitive* 268.4, *indifferent person* 289.6, *wonderless* 295.3, *bored* 296.5, *incurious* 322.3, *undiscriminating* 338.5, *unthinking* 355.8, *informal* 407.6, *unsociable* 409.6, *inactive* 413.9, *not participating* 415.11, *disinterested* 443.4, *nonobservant* 466.5, *inert* 519.2, *moderate* 521.3, *sedentary* 678.5, *mediocre* 742.7, *irresolute* 772.13, *independent* 829.12, *resigned* 835.4
indifferentism *indifference* 289.1
indifferentist *indifferent person* 289.6
indifferently 289.17; *insensitively* 268.7, *without wonder* 295.8, *in a bored manner* 296.9, *apathetically* 322.7, *inattentively* 324.12, *unselectively* 338.12, *forgetfully* 355.14, *resignedly* 392.6, 835.7, *unsocially* 409.13, *inactively* 413.16, *impassively* 415.18,

disinterestedly 443.8, *inertly* 519.5, *freely* 829.22
indifferent person 289.6
in different ways *diversely* 732.14
in difficulties *insolvent* 486.10, *indebted* 488.7, *troubled* 824.15, *adverse* 848.10
indigence *neediness* 95.3, *poverty* 486.1
indigene *inhabitant* 61.1
indigeneity *national* 61.3
indigenous *racial* 1.12, *wild* 41.15, *native* 61.12
indigenously *beforehand* 657.19
indigenousness *national* 61.3
indigenous race *race* 1.5
indigent *needy* 95.12, *poor person* 486.6, *poor* 486.8
indigestible *chewiness* 547.2
indigestible *unhygienic* 114.27, *chewy* 547.9
indigestibly *toughly* 547.16
Indigirka Rivers 570
indignant *offended* 302.9, *bitter* 306.9, *disapproving* 438.8
indignantly *irritably* 302.23, *bitterly* 306.16
indignation *resentment* 302.1, *disapproval* 438.1
indignity 436.7; *humiliation* 298.5, *offense* 302.2
indigo *spectrum* 251.3, *blueness* 261.1, *blue* 261.5, *purple* 262.6
in diplomatic language *feasibly* 460.9
indirect 607.8, 698.9; *of grammar* 5.41, *soccer* 163.7, *uncandid* 192.15, *obscure* 197.2, *circumlocutory* 199.4, *divergent* 607.7, *circumstantial* 726.8, *mysterious* 844.11
indirect course *deviating course* 698.2
indirect free kick *soccer play* 163.5
indirect influence 512.4
indirection *divergence* 607.2, *deviation* 698.1
indirectly 80.8, 607.15, 698.28; *grammatically* 5.48, *uncandidly* 192.29, *obscurely* 197.4, *circuitously* 199.8, *divergently* 607.14, *relatively* 726.17, *mysteriously* 844.17
indirect motion *deviating motion* 698.3
indirectness 607.3; *lack of candor* 192.4, *obscurity* 197.1, *circumlocution* 199.2, *divergence* 607.2
indirect object *part of speech* 5.30
indirect proof *reasoning* 6.61
indirect question *clause* 5.31
indirect radiation *sun* 9.21
indirect tax *money received* 492.2, *tax* 494.5
in dire straits *indebted* 488.7, *unprosperous* 848.11
in disagreement 463.12
in disarray *disordered* 766.9, *in disorder* 766.24
indiscernibility *invisibility* 245.1
indiscernible *invisible* 245.3, *little* 580.7
indiscernibly *invisibly* 245.8, *infinitesimally* 580.13
indiscipline *anarchy* 51.1, *disobedience* 427.1
indiscreet *clumsy* 128.6, *informative* 170.10, *disclosing* 180.6, *imprudent* 286.7, *unrefined* 338.7
indiscreetly *openly* 180.13, *imprudently* 286.11

indiscreetness *imprudence* 286.3
indiscretion *bungling* 128.2, *divulgence* 180.2, *imprudence* 286.3, *tastelessness* 338.3, *folly* 353.1, *sin* 450.3
indiscriminate 338.8
indiscriminate bombing *air attack* 418.4
indiscriminately 338.15; *wrongly* 430.24, *in disorder* 766.24
indiscriminating *clumsy* 128.6
indiscrimination 338.4; *impartiality* 289.3, *lack of discrimination* 338.1
indiscriminative *impartial* 289.9
in disequilibrium *unbalanced* 741.5
in dishabille 100.40
in disorder 766.24; *disordered* 766.9
indispensability 95.2
indispensable *necessary* 95.10, *essential* 723.5, *important* 799.7
indispensableness *indispensability* 95.2
indispensably *with need* 95.20
indispose *put off* 179.10
indisposed *sick* 114.24, *dissuaded* 179.5, *unwilling* 375.8
indisposedness *unwillingness* 375.1
indisposition *ill health* 114.1, *illness* 114.2, *unwillingness* 375.1
indisputability *authenticity* 721.7, *certainty* 840.1
indisputability or indisputableness *definiteness* 189.6
indisputable *definite* 189.18, *demonstrable* 331.12, *stable* 674.3, *real* 717.14, *authentic* 721.16, *certain* 840.7
indisputable fact *truth* 721.1
indisputableness *authenticity* 721.7
indisputably *definitely* 189.33, *assuredly* 336.12, *stably* 674.9, *authentically* 721.31
in disrepair *in good form* 725.11, *dilapidated* 808.11
indissolubility *density* 540.1, *oneness* 788.3
indissoluble *retentive* 471.5, *condensed* 540.7, *stable* 674.3, *united* 752.10, *whole* 788.12
indissolubly *tenaciously* 471.11, *stably* 674.9, *as one* 752.21
indistinct *obscure* 197.2, *faint* 233.6, *hidden* 243.15, *difficult to see* 245.4, *murky* 248.5, *vague* 338.9, *unrecognizable* 364.7, *indeterminate* 841.14
indistinctive *vague* 338.9
indistinctly *obscurely* 197.4, *faintly* 233.11, *invisibly* 245.8, *dimly* 248.10, *indeterminately* 841.24
indistinctness *obscurity* 197.1, *faintness of sound* 233.1, *invisibility* 245.1, *murk* 248.2, *indeterminacy* 841.6
indistinguishability *invisibility* 245.1, *sameness* 730.1
indistinguishable *invisible* 245.3, *murky* 248.5, *unrecognizable* 364.7, *same* 730.7
indistinguishableness *sameness* 730.1
indistinguishably *invisibly* 245.8, *indiscriminately* 338.15, *identically* 730.18
in distress *poor* 486.8
indium Chemical Elements and Common Allotropes 11
individual *living organism* 13.10,

person 18.8, *someone* 18.10, *human* 18.15, *living being* 28.3, *symbolic* 183.12, *diverse* 732.5, *nonuniform* 734.5, *novel* 737.5, *whole* 759.6, *complete* 761.6, *special* 779.10, *unusual* 782.15, *one* 788.1, 788.10, *singular* 788.13, *independent* 829.12
individual, the *the special* 779.8
individual events *competitive swimming* 164.3
individualism Philosophical Schools of Thought 4, *selfishness* 444.1, *independence* 829.5
individualist 756.3, Philosophical Schools of Thought 4, *free person* 829.9
individualistic *selfish* 444.4, *nonconforming* 728.10, *special* 779.10, *unusual* 782.15, *independent* 829.12
individualistically 728.20; *selfishly* 444.8, *nonuniformly* 734.11, *freely* 829.22
individuality *identity* 184.2, *nonconformity* 728.4, *diversity* 732.1, *nonuniformity* 734.2, *originality* 737.1, *specialty* 779.1, *unusualness* 782.4, *singularity* 788.4, *independence* 829.5
individualize *characterize* 779.15
individualized *customized* 779.14
individually *humanly* 18.18, *indicatively* 183.21, *diversely* 732.14, *originally* 737.8, *one by one* 788.21, *freely* 829.22
individual medley race *competitive swimming* 164.3
individual project *educational topic* 328.4
individual psychology Psychological Theories, Schools 108
Individual Retirement Account (IRA) *personal finance* 457.5
indivisibility *density* 540.1, *adhesion* 755.1, *whole* 759.1, *oneness* 788.3
indivisible *divisible* 6.71, *dense* 540.6, *integral* 723.7, *united* 752.10, *adhesive* 755.5, *whole* 788.12
indivisibly *as one* 752.21, *cohesively* 755.11, *wholly* 788.22
Indo-Brazilian Breeds of Cattle 16
indocile *obstinate* 379.5
indocility *disobedience* 375.5, *obstinacy* 379.1
indoctrinate *educate* 48.22, *make someone believe* 87.11, *publicize* 178.19, *accustom* 397.18, *persuade* 670.14, *assimilate* 781.14
indoctrination *education* 48.1, *publicity* 178.7, *habituation* 397.7, *religious conversion* 670.4
indoctrinator *persuader* 178.9, *converter* 670.5
Indo-European *language family* 5.12
Indo-Iranian *language family* 5.12
indoleacetic acid (IAA) *plant hormone* 12.17
indolence *leisure* 413.4, *idleness* 415.3, *inertness* 519.1, *lack of motion* 678.1, *slowness* 693.1
indolent *inactive* 413.9, *not participating* 415.11, *inert* 519.2, *sedentary* 678.5, *unhurried* 693.8
indolently *impassively* 415.18, *inertly* 519.5, *slowly* 693.14
in (domestic) service *obediently* 69.12

indomitable *steadfast* 284.11, *persevering* 377.6
indomitably *steadfastly* 284.19
Indonesia Countries 566, Islands 572
indoor *swimming* 164.12, *internal* 611.9, *enclosed* 619.4
indoor game *type of game* 167.2
indoor garden *garden* 17.2
indoor gardening *horticulture* 17.1
indoor pool *swimming place* 164.9
indoors *internally* 611.18
indoor sport *sporting activity* 145.3
indoor tennis *tennis* 165.1
in double harness *married* 64.16, *matrimonially* 64.23
in double jeopardy *endangered* 811.10
in double-time *or* **double-quick time** *swiftly* 694.16
in doubt *questionable* 333.13, *questionably* 333.22
in draft *under discussion* 387.17
indraft *intake* 708.5
indraught *influx* 706.2
indrawal *influx* 706.2
indrawing *influx* 706.2
in dribs and drabs *partly* 760.17, *discontinuously* 775.15, *in ones and twos* 796.10
indubitability *authenticity* 721.7, *certainty* 840.1
indubitability or indubitableness *definiteness* 189.6
indubitable *definite* 189.18, *authentic* 721.16, *probable* 838.6, *certain* 840.7, *decided* 840.9
indubitableness *authenticity* 721.7
indubitably *definitely* 189.33, *certainly* 719.14, 840.15, *authentically* 721.31, *probably* 838.11
induce *practice surgery* 107.33, *persuade* 178.15, *think* 315.12, *reason* 319.11, *discuss* 329.12, *offer* 504.11, *motivate* 508.9, *awaken* 675.9, *attract* 700.11, *draw out* 711.17
induced *persuadable* 178.14, *motivated* 508.8
induced current *electric current* 10.39
induced sweat *sweat* 25.8
inducement 508.2; *persuasion* 178.1, *incentive* 178.4, *reward for service* 453.5, *bribe* 472.3, *positive stimulus* 508.5, *pulling power* 700.2
inducible *persuadable* 178.14
inducing *persuasive* 178.12
inducing secretion 24.6
induct *interact* 10.73, *launch* 405.14, *enroll* 706.16, 771.33, *install* 710.15, *inaugurate* 771.31, *commission* 833.8
inductance *resistance* 10.41, *electrical power* 514.12
induction *philosophical investigation* 4.4, *reasoning* 6.61, 319.2, *developmental biology* 13.22, *ordination* 84.3, *surgery* 107.15, *way of thinking* 317.4, *logical argument* 329.2, *basis of supposition* 359.2, *electrical power* 514.12, *entry* 706.1, *bringing in* 708.4, *enrollment* 771.8, *commission* 833.1
induction training *bargaining terms* 57.10
inductive *logical* 6.83, *electric* 14.47, *intellectual* 315.8, *rational*

319.8, *nuclear* 514.17, *magnetic* 700.9
inductively *logically* 329.17, *attractionally* 700.13
inductive reasoning *reasoning* 319.2
inductor *circuit* 10.43, *circuit element* 14.39
in due course *in the future* 650.13, *later* 658.16
in due form *formally* 406.12
indulge *give pleasure* 214.13, *satisfy* 273.7, *show pity* 308.8, *forgive* 312.8, *show mercy* 312.11, *be solicitous* 323.13, *be lenient* 423.5, *be permissive* 502.7, *improve* 825.26
indulged *overlooked* 312.6, *given consideration* 423.4
indulge in *conduct oneself* 399.17, *occupy oneself* 412.15, *indulge oneself* 456.10
indulge in wishful thinking *deceive* 193.16
indulgence *pleasure* 214.2, *mercy* 308.3, *forgiveness* 312.1, *forgivingness* 312.3, *solicitude* 323.5, *freedom* 407.4, *leniency* 423.1, *tolerance* 502.2, *moral deterioration* 808.3
indulgent *pitying* 308.4, *forgiving* 312.4, *solicitous* 323.8, *free* 407.9, *lenient* 423.3, *permitting* 502.5, *easygoing* 823.13, *benevolent* 825.21
indulgently *pleasingly* 214.15, *pityingly* 308.11, *forgivingly* 312.13, *freely* 407.12, *leniently* 423.6, *with permission* 502.10
indulge one's appetite *be greedy* 119.4
indulge oneself 456.10; *be greedy* 119.4, *feel pleasure* 214.12, *be selfish* 444.6
indulge one's fancy *choose* 382.14
indulger *lenient person* 423.2
indurate *be impenitent* 452.4, *hardened* 542.7
indurated *hardened* 542.7
induration *impenitence* 452.1
indurative *impenitent* 452.2
Indus Constellations 7, Rivers 570
indusium *fern plant* 46.2
industrial *communal* 2.12, *ceramic* 129.9, *architectural types* 134.2, *professional* 480.15, *productive* 522.11
industrial action *mass demonstration* 331.7
industrial architect *architect* 134.3
industrial area 124.14
industrial art *visual arts* 133.1
industrial artist *visual artist* 133.6
industrial building *building* 551.9
industrial ceramics 129.6
industrial chemistry 11.21, Branches of Chemistry 11
industrial city *city* 567.1
industrial conflict *industrial dispute* 57.7
industrial design *visual arts* 133.1
industrial designer *visual artist* 133.6
industrial dispute 57.7
industrial engineer *engineer* 14.2, *mechanical engineer* 14.4
industrial engineering *engineering* 14.1, *mechanical engineering* 14.3
industrial institution *social institution* 2.8
industrialist *producer* 522.10

industrialization *economic development* 56.5, *manufacture* 522.2

industrialize *socialize* 2.14, *produce* 522.13

industrialized *communal* 2.12, *productive* 522.11

industrialized society *society* 2.6

industrializing *communal* 2.12

industrial law *labor law* 57.12

industrially **57.22**; *sociology* 2.15

industrial medicine *medicine* 107.1

industrial organization *social organization* 2.5

industrial park *plant* 124.7

industrial processes **14.27**

industrial psychologist *psychologist* 108.33

industrial psychology Psychological Theories, Schools 108

industrial relations *labor relations* 57.1

Industrial Revolution Ages, Decades, Eras 641, *historical past* 651.6

industrial strife *industrial dispute* 57.7

industrial town *industrial area* 124.14

industrial tribunal *bargaining* 57.9

industrial union *organized labor* 57.5

industrial unionism *work practices* 57.2

industries fair *fair* 483.2

industrious **414.16**; *working* 122.6, *committed* 377.7, *acting* 412.9

industriously *actively* 414.24

industriousness *commitment* 377.2, *assiduity* 414.8

industry *work* 122.1, *business* 414.6, 480.6, *assiduity* 414.8, *manufacture* 522.2

industry-wide *disputed* 57.15

industry-wide strike *strike* 57.8

in Dutch *troubled* 824.15

indweller *inhabitant* 61.1

indwelt *inhabited* 61.10

Indy Car *racing automobile* 146.2

Indy Car racer *driver* 146.8

Indy Car races *races* 146.1

Indy Car racing *automobile racing* 146.1

Indy Racing League (IRL) *racing governing bodies* 146.7

in earnest *assuredly* 189.30, *earnestly* 376.16

in easy circumstances *wealthy* 485.8

inebriant *intoxicating* 121.29

inebriate *drunkard* 121.8, *drunken* 121.28, *be intoxicating* 121.36

inebriated *drunk* 121.25

inebriating *intoxicating* 121.29

inebriation *drunkenness* 121.3

inebriety *drunkenness* 121.3

inedibility *chewiness* 547.2

inedible *unhygienic* 114.27, *unpalatable* 223.6, *chewy* 547.9

inedibly *sourly* 223.9

ineffability *unintelligibility* 364.1

ineffable *divine* 82.16, *astonishing* 294.10, *unknown* 349.7, *unintelligible* 364.4, *unbelievable* 837.5

ineffably *divinely* 82.24, *astonishingly* 294.19

in effect *in use* 393.8, *existing* 717.11, *really* 719.13, *on the whole* 759.13

ineffective *unemphatic* 201.2, *meaningless* 362.7, *powerless* 515.6, *incomplete* 762.5, *useless* 802.7, *failed* 846.10

ineffectively *powerlessly* 515.16, *incompletely* 762.10, *uselessly* 802.14, *unsuccessfully* 846.21

ineffectiveness *lack of emphasis* 201.1, *lack of authority* 515.2, *incompleteness* 762.1, *uselessness* 802.1, *failure* 846.1

ineffectual *unskillful* 128.4, *meaningless* 362.7, *aimless* 362.8, *powerless* 515.6, *weak* 517.6, *incomplete* 762.5, *unimportant* 800.10, *useless* 802.7, *failed* 846.10

ineffectuality *unskillfulness* 128.1, *nonsense* 362.2, *aimlessness* 362.3, *lack of authority* 515.2, *indecisiveness* 517.2, *incompleteness* 762.1

ineffectually *powerlessly* 515.16, *weakly* 517.14, *incompletely* 762.10, *unimportantly* 800.21, *uselessly* 802.14, *unsuccessfully* 846.21

ineffectualness *uselessness* 802.1

inefficacious *powerless* 515.6, *failed* 846.10

inefficaciously *unsuccessfully* 846.21

inefficacy *uselessness* 802.1

inefficiency *unskillfulness* 128.1, *uselessness* 802.1, *failure* 846.1

inefficient *unskillful* 128.4, *powerless* 515.6, *useless* 802.7

inefficiently *unskillfully* 128.12, *powerlessly* 515.16

inelastic *unyielding* 379.8, *dense* 540.6, *tough* 542.6, *hard* 547.8, *brittle* 548.3

inelasticity *determination* 379.2, *obstinacy* 417.2, *hardness* 542.1, *brittleness* 548.1

inelastic scattering *nuclear reaction* 10.59

inelastic strain *load* 14.14

inelegance **528.1**; *ugliness* 531.1, *vulgarity* 535.1

inelegance of expression **528.4**

inelegancy *inelegance* 528.1

inelegant **528.6**; *clumsy* 128.6, *ugly* 531.3, *vulgar* 535.6

inelegantly **528.11, 531.7**; *vulgarly* 535.10

ineligible *unselected* 383.7, *inconvenient* 804.5

ineligible receiver *penalty* 155.13

ineluctability *inevitability* 95.6, 840.5

ineluctable *inevitable* 95.14, 840.11, *compulsory* 428.7

ineluctably *necessarily* 95.22, *inevitably* 840.17

in embryo *incomplete* 762.5, *in the bud* 771.39

in employment *obediently* 69.12

inept *unskillful* 128.4, *without skill* 282.10, *foolish* 353.5, *powerless* 515.6, *useless* 802.7, *inconvenient* 804.5

ineptitude *unskillfulness* 128.1, *lack of skill* 282.4, *folly* 353.1, *powerlessness* 515.1, *uselessness* 802.1

ineptly *unskillfully* 128.12, 282.17, *powerlessly* 515.16

ineptness *unskillfulness* 128.1

inequality **741.1**; *equality* 6.24, *injustice* 342.3, *difference* 463.4, *roughness* 544.1, *irregularity* 664.1, *disparity* 728.3, *dissimilarity* 734.1

in equal measure *compromisingly* 461.9

in equal parts *compromisingly* 461.9

in equal portions *compatibly* 462.16

inequilateral *dissimilar* 734.4

inequilaterally *dissimilarly* 734.10

in equilibrium *as good as* 740.14

inequitable *discriminatory* 337.11, *wrongful* 430.10, *unjust* 741.6

inequitably *prejudicially* 337.17, *wrongly* 430.24, *unjustly* 741.12

inequity *prejudice* 337.3, *wrong* 430.1, *injustice* 741.3

ineradicable *stable* 674.3, *integral* 723.7

inerrancy *right* 429.2

inerrant *correct* 429.8

inerrantist *religionist* 81.14

in error *misjudging* 342.6, *misguidedly* 342.12, *mistaken* 351.13, *erroneously* 351.17, *mistakenly* 366.6

inert **519.2**; *desensitized* 213.5, *indifferent* 289.7, *avoiding* 386.9, *inactive* 413.9, 415.8, *sedentary* 678.5, *unhurried* 693.8, *vegetating* 717.17, *latent* 844.6

inert gas *chemical element* 11.3, *gas* 556.1

inertia *mass* 10.8, *indifference* 289.1, *inaction* 413.1, *inactivity* 415.1, *inertness* 519.1, *lack of motion* 678.1, *slowness* 693.1, *mere existence* 717.10

inertial navigation *navigation* 690.5

inertly **519.5**; *indifferently* 289.17, *apathetically* 322.7, *inactively* 413.16, 415.17, *motionlessly* 678.9

inertness **519.1**; *inaction* 413.1, *inactivity* 415.1, *lack of motion* 678.1, *slowness* 693.1, *latency* 844.1

inescapable *inevitable* 95.14, 840.11, *duty-bound* 433.8

inescapableness *inevitability* 840.5

inescapably *inevitably* 840.17

in escrow *saved* 105.15

in essence **723.13**; *thematically* 328.13, *structurally* 577.14, *basically* 601.14, *on the whole* 759.13

inessential *extraneous* 724.8, *trifle* 800.3, *unimportant* 800.10

inessentiality *extraneousness* 724.1, *unimportance* 800.1

inestimable *valuable* 496.8, *immeasurable* 798.6

inestimably *immeasurably* 798.11

in estrangement *without one's spouse* 66.14

in everyday use *in use* 393.8

in every direction *in all directions* 697.19

in every nook and cranny *extensively* 563.18

in every place *extensively* 563.18

in every quarter *extensively* 563.18, *in all directions* 697.19

in every respect *wholly* 759.11

in every way *completely* 759.14

in evidence *demonstrably* 331.22, *as evidence* 339.15

inevitability **95.6, 840.5**

inevitable **95.14, 840.11**; *compelling* 428.6

inevitableness *inevitability* 840.5

inevitably **840.17**; *necessarily* 95.22, *compellingly* 428.12

inexact *clumsy* 128.6, *obscure* 197.2, *unemphatic* 201.2, *indifferent* 326.5, *vague* 338.9, *erroneous* 351.11, *incorrect* 722.8, *generalized* 778.12, *indeterminate* 841.14

inexactitude *lack of emphasis* 201.1, *indifference* 326.2, *indiscrimination* 338.4, *inaccuracy* 351.3, *incorrectness* 430.3, *untrueness* 722.3, *nonspecificness* 778.2

inexactly *obscurely* 197.4, *unemphatically* 201.4, *indiscriminately* 338.15, *wrongly* 351.18, *incorrectly* 722.16

in exactly the same words *literally* 721.32

inexactness *obscurity* 197.1, *misjudgment* 342.1, *inaccuracy* 351.3, *untrueness* 722.3, *indeterminacy* 841.6

in excess *self-indulgently* 456.12

in excess of requirements *excessively* 99.13

in exchange **673.3, 673.6**; *by transfer* 470.15

in exchange for *in exchange* 673.6

inexcitability *indifference* 289.1, *lack of wonder* 295.1, *inertness* 519.1

inexcitable *indifferent* 289.7, *wonderless* 295.3, *quiescent* 678.6

inexcitably *indifferently* 289.17, *without wonder* 295.8

inexcusable *unforgivable* 430.16, *guilty* 450.6

inexcusably *guiltily* 450.12

inexhaustibility *infinity* 798.1

inexhaustible *protracted* 669.7, *numberless* 795.8, *infinite* 798.5

inexhaustibly *extravagantly* 500.9, *continually* 669.10

in existence *in person* 575.18

inexistent *absent* 576.7, *unreal* 722.7

inexorability *inevitability* 95.6, 840.5, *relentlessness* 309.2, *tenacity* 376.4

inexorable *inevitable* 95.14, 840.11, *relentless* 309.4, *tenacious* 376.9, *strong-willed* 376.10, *unyielding* 379.8, *ongoing* 679.7

inexorably *necessarily* 95.22, *relentlessly* 309.8, *obstinately* 379.11, *inevitably* 840.17

inexpectant *unprepared* 389.5

in expectation *expecting* 356.4

inexpedience *untimeliness* 660.1, *uselessness* 802.1, *inconvenience* 804.1

inexpediency *uselessness* 802.1, *inconvenience* 804.1

inexpedient *untimely* 660.5, *useless* 802.7, *inconvenient* 804.5

inexpediently *at the wrong time* 660.12, *inconveniently* 804.11

inexpensive *cheap* 497.9

inexpensively *cheaply* 481.19, 497.16

inexperience *immaturity* 26.3, 652.3, *unskillfulness* 128.1, *lack of knowledge* 349.2, *unaccustomedness* 398.1, *naiveté* 449.4, 821.1

inexperienced *immature* 26.12, 652.12, *unskilled* 128.5, *raw* 260.9, *semiskilled* 349.6, *untrained* 389.8, *unaccustomed* 398.3, *naive* 449.9, 821.3

inexpert *unskilled* 128.5, *raw* 260.9, *semiskilled* 349.6

inexpertly *unskillfully* 128.12, 398.8

inexpertness *unskillfulness* 128.1, *lack of knowledge* 349.2

in explanation *in other words* 365.18, *justifyingly* 441.15

inexplicability *unintelligibility* 364.1, *chance* 842.1, *lack of motive* 842.2

inexplicable *unintelligible* 364.4, *causeless* 842.11

inexplicably *unintelligibly* 364.16, *randomly* 842.16

inexpressibility *unintelligibility* 364.1

inexpressible *astonishing* 294.10, *unintelligible* 364.4

inexpressibly *astonishingly* 294.19

inexpugnable *invulnerable* 810.18

inextensibility *hardness* 542.1

in extenso [L] *diffusely* 199.7, *lengthwise* 590.14

inextinguishable *violent* 520.5, *stable* 674.3

in extremis [L] *dying* 29.12

inextricable *united* 752.10, *adhesive* 755.5

inextricably *752.23; as one* 752.21, *cohesively* 755.11

in fact *really* 717.22, 719.13, *in truth* 721.28

in fair health *getting well* 113.9

in fairness *right* 429.15

infallibility *840.6; right* 429.2, *perfection* 805.1

infallible *805.10, 840.12; correct* 429.8

infallibly *correctly* 429.16

infamous *publicized* 173.14, *known* 348.9, *disreputable* 371.4, *immoral* 430.11, *wicked* 448.9, *accentuated* 843.11

infamously *disreputably* 371.7, *improperly* 430.26, *wickedly* 448.15

infamousness *wickedness* 448.1

infamy *publicity* 173.7, *disrepute* 371.1, *wickedness* 448.1

infancy *bodily development* 19.17, *youth* 26.1, *age* 27.1, *helplessness* 515.3, *conception* 771.4

infant *child* 26.6, *young* 26.11, *innocent person* 449.5, *weak person* 517.4, *beginner* 771.14, *embryonic* 771.19

infant exposure *homicide* 30.4

infanticide *homicide* 30.4

infantile *young* 26.11, *unintelligent* 316.6

infantile fixation *fixation* 108.21

infantile paralysis *infection* 114.7, *neurological disease* 114.20

infantry assault *land attack* 418.3

infantry engagement *battle* 76.23

infantryman *army combat specialist* 77.16, *army person* 77.17

infants' wear *baby clothes* 100.24, *dry goods* 130.3

infarct *stopper* 584.3

infarction *cardiovascular disease* 114.13

in fashion *established* 397.12, *fashionable* 536.5, *present* 647.4, *trendily* 652.24

infatuated *liking* 290.4

infatuated with *in love* 299.16

infatuating *likable* 290.7

infatuation *liking* 290.1, *likes* 290.3, *romantic love* 299.2

in favor *friendly with* 62.6, *reputable* 370.3, *willing* 373.7, *recommending* 437.11

in favor of *instead* 672.8

in fear and trembling *frightened* 283.9

in fear of *fearfully* 283.19

infect *dirty* 112.11, *cause ill health* 114.30, *poison* 117.18, *manipulate* 508.12, *change* 512.12, *transfer* 685.8, *convey* 685.9, *mix together* 751.14, *make worse* 808.17

infected *sick* 114.24, *contagious* 114.26

infection 114.7; *uncleanness* 112.2, *disease* 114.4, *plague* 114.6, *influence* 512.1, *transmission* 685.3, *mixture* 751.1, *physical deterioration* 808.4, *adverse health* 848.5

infectious *unclean* 112.8, *of disease* 114.25, *contagious* 114.26, *appealing* 512.9, *transferable* 685.7, *dangerous* 811.7

infectious disease *disease* 114.4, *transferred thing* 685.6

infectious hepatitis *infection* 114.7

infectiously *unhygienically* 114.32, *influentially* 512.14, *in transit* 685.13

infectious mononucleosis *infection* 114.7

infectiousness *lack of hygiene* 112.3, *infection* 114.7

infectious person 114.9

infective *contagious* 114.26

infector *transferrer* 685.4

infecund *infertile* 23.7

infecundity *infertility* 23.1

infelicitous *bungled* 128.7, *accidental* 660.7, *inconvenient* 804.5

infelicity *bungling* 128.2

infer 361.14; *rationalize* 4.20, *theorize* 6.84, *be informed* 170.15, *have an idea* 317.12, *reason* 319.11, *estimate* 341.11, *suppose* 359.8, *interpret* 365.12

inference *philosophical investigation* 4.4, *philosophical term* 4.7, *reasoning* 6.61, 319.2, *inside information* 170.4, *judgment* 341.1, *basis of supposition* 359.2, *effect* 676.1, *quietness* 844.4

inferential *logical* 6.83, *rational* 319.8, *circumstantial* 726.8, *tacit* 844.10

inferentially *relatively* 726.17

inferior 745.4, 745.5; *servant* 69.1, *insufficient* 98.4, *without skill* 282.10, *disappointing* 239.6, *shoddy* 497.11, *lowly* 597.17, *substandard* 597.19, *unequal* 741.4, *nonentity* 800.8, *cheap* 800.16, *imperfect* 806.5, *subordinate* 832.3, 832.8

inferior court *law court* 54.8

inferiority 745.1; *insufficiency* 98.1, *type of complex* 108.22, *lack of skill* 282.4, *lowliness* 597.8, *inequality* 741.1, *triviality* 800.2, *imperfection* 806.1, *subjection* 832.1

inferiorly 745.13

inferior planet *planet* 7.16

inferior rank *subjection* 832.1

inferior standing *inferiority* 745.1

inferior state 745.3

inferior status *inferiority* 745.1, *subjection* 832.1

inferior version *imperfect item* 806.3

infernal *demonic* 446.9

infernally *devilishly* 446.14

infernal machine *bomb* 78.15

inferno *evil place* 446.6, *confusion* 766.4

inferred *supposed* 359.6, *similar* 361.7, *tacit* 844.10

infertile 23.7; *disabled* 515.10

infertile land 23.2

infertile state 23.3

infertility 23.1; *scarcity* 98.3, *disability* 515.4

infest 40.17; *afflict* 117.16, *transgress* 712.14, *overcrowd* 795.12

infestation *lack of hygiene* 112.3, *affliction* 117.1, *transgression* 712.3

infested *verminous* 40.13, *unhygienic* 114.27, *overrun* 712.6

infidel *disbeliever* 88.5

infidelity *unbelief* 88.4, *dishonorableness* 192.3, *love affair* 299.9, *fornication* 432.3, *irresolution* 666.2, *unreliability* 722.5

infield *baseball field* 147.3, *racetrack* 159.12

infielder *baseball team* 147.2

infield fly *other game terms* 147.7

infield fly rule *other game terms* 147.7

infighting *fight* 422.9, *divisiveness* 463.2

in file *in a line* 774.17

infiltrate 706.13; *subvert* 427.13, *water* 557.29, *be present* 575.13, *enter* 692.18, *absorb* 708.19, *mix together* 751.14

infiltrating *penetrating* 692.12

infiltration *subversion* 427.3, *steeping* 557.10, *passage into* 692.4, *inroad* 706.3, *mixture* 751.1

infiltrator *seditionist* 427.7

in fine feather *dressed up* 100.39, *formally dressed* 406.8

in fine *or* **high feather** *healthy* 113.4

in fine fettle *healthy* 113.4, *in form* 624.8, *in good form* 725.11, *sound* 759.8, *orderly* 765.13

in fine form *healthy* 113.4

in fine trim *healthy* 113.4

infinite 798.5; *complex* 6.69, *astronomical* 7.33, *divine* 82.16, *extensive* 563.12, *omnipresent* 575.10, *huge* 579.11, *lengthy* 590.9, *deep* 598.9, *eternal* 644.4, *quantitative* 738.6, *fractional* 783.8, *numberless* 795.8

infinitely 798.10; *mathematically* 6.93, *astronomically* 7.36, *divinely* 82.24, *hugely* 579.21, *deep* 598.25, *wholly* 738.9, *numerously* 795.13

infiniteness *infinity* 798.1

infinite number *number* 6.4, *absolutes* 6.9

infinite set *set* 6.19

infinitesimal *complex* 6.69, *difficult to see* 245.4, *tiny* 580.9, *small* 787.6

infinitesimal calculus *calculus* 6.28

infinitesimally 580.13; *mathematically* 6.93

infinite space *empty space* 563.2, *vastness* 798.3

infinitive *grammatical term* 5.29

infinitude *absolutes* 6.9, *eternity* 644.1, *infinity* 798.1

infinity 798.1; *absolutes* 6.9, *divine attribute* 82.4, *composition* 132.17, *Phobias* 283, *empty space* 563.2, *distance* 585.1, *longness* 590.3, *the depths* 598.2, *eternity* 644.1, *eternally* 644.10, *numbers* 738.5,

large number 783.3, *multiplicity* 795.2

infirm *unhealthy* 114.23, *vacillating* 378.5, *impious* 448.11, *ill* 517.8, *unreliable* 841.15

infirmary *school place* 48.16, *hospital* 107.16

infirmity *old age* 27.5, *ill health* 114.1, *illness* 114.2, *iniquity* 448.3, *poor health* 517.3, *imperfection* 806.1, *unreliability* 841.7

infirmity of purpose *vacillation* 378.1

in fits *jerkily* 684.29

in fits and starts *inconsistently* 732.16

infix *part of speech* 5.30, *inset* 710.13, *additional item* 748.3, *insert* 748.12, *link* 752.18

infixed *inserted* 710.5

infixion *insertion* 710.1

inflame *aggravate* 276.5, *cause dislike* 291.16, *make angry* 302.18, *invigorate* 518.5, *make violent* 520.10

inflamed *of disease* 114.25, *passionate* 266.12, *angry* 302.11, *motivated* 375.30, *violent* 520.5

in flames *on fire* 217.16

inflaming *motivational* 508.7

inflammability *fire* 217.8

inflammable *combustible* 106.12, *on fire* 217.16, *dangerous* 811.7

inflammation *symptom* 114.3, *ulcer* 114.18, *heat* 217.1

inflammatory *motivational* 508.7

inflatable *enlargement* 581.7, *enlargeable* 581.13, *Ships and Boats* 690

inflate *enlarge* 194.12, *boast* 194.14, *become conceited* 402.16, *increase* 467.17, *demonetize* 484.25, *overcharge* 496.10, *swell* 581.15, *change by degrees* 739.8, *make bigger* 746.7

inflated *exaggerated* 194.7, *enlarged* 194.8, *misinterpreted* 366.3, *aerial* 558.14, *swelled* 581.10

inflatedness *bombast* 194.4

inflater *enlarger* 581.8

inflating *bombastic* 194.10

inflation 484.9; *economic factor* 56.8, *enlargement* 194.2, *augmentation* 467.2, *cost(s)* 491.3, *inflationary price* 496.3, *swelling* 581.2

inflationary *economic* 56.10, *financial* 457.6, *acquisitive* 467.13, *monetary* 484.22, *costly* 496.7, *500.6, *enlargeable* 581.13

inflationary pressure *inflationary price* 496.3

inflationary price 496.3

inflationary spiral *economic factor* 56.8, *inflation* 484.9, *inflationary price* 496.3

inflationary universe *universe* 7.3

inflect (a word) *cause change* 665.16

inflected *of language* 5.35, *of grammar* 5.41

inflection *spoken letter* 5.15, *grammatical term* 5.29, *part of speech* 5.30, *mode of speech* 205.6, *change* 665.1, *additional item* 748.3

inflectional *language type* 5.11, *worded* 5.38, *of grammar* 5.41

inflectionally *lexically* 5.46

inflexibility *relentlessness* 309.2, *tenacity* 376.4, *determination* 379.2, 674.2, *obstinacy* 417.2,

severity 424.1, *hardness* 542.1, *mental hardness* 542.4, *mental toughness* 547.5, *stability* 674.1
inflexible *relentless* 309.4, *tenacious* 376.9, *strong-willed* 376.10, *unyielding* 379.8, *obstinate* 417.7, *severe* 424.5, *tough* 542.6, *mentally hard* 542.8, *mentally tough* 547.12, *stable* 674.3, *determined* 674.5, *inevitable* 840.11
inflexibly 542.13; *relentlessly* 309.8, *resistingly* 417.14, *severely* 424.11, *single-mindedly* 547.19, *stably* 674.9, *determinedly* 674.10
inflict *force* 428.10, *punish* 454.22
inflicting pain 215.7
infliction *affliction* 454.9
inflict pain 215.10; *punish* 454.22, *torture* 454.29
inflict punishment *retaliate* 420.4, *punish* 454.22
in flight *aeronautically* 689.17, *fugitively* 816.12
in-flight magazine *magazine* 175.3
in flood *flooded* 570.8
in *or* **at flood** *fluently* 570.13
inflooding *influx* 706.2, *invasive* 706.10
inflorescence *flower head* 42.4
inflorescent *flowering* 42.10
inflow *flow* 570.4, *influx* 706.2, *flood in* 706.14
in flower *flowering* 42.10
inflowing *invasive* 706.10
influence 508.11, 512.1, 512.11; *run for office* 50.10, *authority* 52.1, 514.5, 780.6, *have authority* 52.13, *make someone believe* 87.11, *leader* 126.8, *manage* 126.10, *persuasion* 178.1, *motivator* 178.11, *persuade* 178.15, 670.14, *propound* 359.9, *action* 412.1, *motivate* 412.12, *be irresistible* 428.9, *inducement* 508.2, *operation* 509.1, *activate* 509.11, *instrumentality* 511.1, 801.3, *instrument* 511.2, *be an instrument* 511.7, *tendency* 513.1, *tend* 513.5, *be powerful* 514.18, *changer* 665.9, *cause change* 665.16, *contributory cause* 675.3, *awaken* 675.9, *attract* 700.11, *superiority* 744.1, *forerun* 769.16, *importance* 799.1, *be important* 799.13, *hide* 844.13
influenceable *convertible* 670.9
influenced 670.10; *motivated* 508.8
influence negatively *change* 512.12
influence peddler *influential person* 512.5
influence positively *change* 512.12
influencer *persuader* 178.9
influencing *motivational* 508.7
influential 512.8; *political* 50.9, *authoritative* 52.9, *persuasive* 178.12, *effective* 412.10, *compelling* 428.6, *motivational* 508.7, *operative* 509.9, *causal* 511.5, 675.7, *powerful* 514.15, *magnetic* 700.9, *ruling* 780.11, *notable* 799.11
influentially 508.13, 512.14; *persuasively* 178.21, *effectively* 412.19, *compellingly* 428.12, *operationally* 509.13, *instrumentally* 511.9, *powerfully* 514.21, *causally* 675.12, *attractively* 700.14
influential person 512.5; *important person* 799.5
influenza *respiratory disease* 114.12

influx 706.2
in flux *flowing* 570.7
info [Inf] *information* 170.1
in focus *visible* 244.5, *clear* 244.6
infomercial [Inf] *advertisement* 173.9
in force *in use* 393.8, *operative* 509.9, *strongly* 516.17, *existing* 717.11
in form 624.8
inform 170.11; *chronicle* 3.15, *educate* 48.22, *communicate* 169.18, 176.10, *report* 171.9, *broadcast* 172.13, *publish* 173.15, *divulge* 180.9, *signal* 183.18, *be dishonorable* 192.21, *testify* 336.10, *give evidence* 339.12, *cause to know* 348.13, *mean* 361.13, *interpret* 365.12, *brief* 388.20, *characterize* 723.11, *warn* 844.8
inform against *inform on* 170.13, *accuse* 442.8
informal 407.6, 829.15; *of language* 5.35, *unlawful* 53.23, *stylish* 100.42, *conversational* 210.10, *indifferent* 326.5, *agreements* 459.2, *nonobservant* 466.5
informal clothes 100.7
informal clothing 407.5
informal dress *dressing* 100.2
informality 407.1, 829.6; *indifference* 326.2, *nonobservance* 466.1
informal language *or* **speech** *spoken language* 205.2
informally 407.11, 829.24; *colloquially* 5.45, *dressily* 100.47, *conversationally* 210.14, *inattentively* 466.13
informally dressed *in dishabille* 100.40
informal meal *meal* 92.8
informalness *informality* 407.1
informant *informer* 170.8, *discloser* 180.4, *verifier* 336.4, *witness* 339.7, *warner* 814.5
information 170.1, 348.2; *news* 171.1, *communication* 176.3, *evidence* 339.1, *warning* 814.1
informational *educational* 48.17, *informative* 170.10
information center *information source* 170.6, *library* 174.14
information processing *information technology (IT)* 170.7, *computing* 784.4
information retrieval *information technology (IT)* 170.7, *computing* 784.4
information source 170.6
information superhighway *computer communications* 15.25
information systems *army commands* 77.13
information technology (IT) 170.7; *computing* 15.2, 784.4
information theory *information technology (IT)* 170.7
informative 170.10; *educational* 48.17, *newsworthy* 171.8, 175.7, *advisory* 176.7, *disclosing* 180.6, *descriptive* 202.11, *conversational* 210.10, *intelligible* 363.5, *warning* 814.6, *helpful* 825.11
informatively *educationally* 48.25, *newsworthily* 171.10, *journalistically* 175.10, *advisorily* 176.12
informativeness *intelligibility* 363.1
informatory *informative* 170.10
informed 170.9; *evidential* 339.8, *knowledgeable* 348.7

informedly *educationally* 48.25
informer 170.8; *news source* 171.4, *discloser* 180.4, *hypocrite* 192.9, *talker* 207.4, *verifier* 336.4, *witness* 339.7, *accuser* 442.3
inform on 170.13; *tell on* 180.10, *accuse* 442.8
in fours 791.14
infraction 466.4; *lawbreaking* 53.14, *violation of the law* 427.2, *wrongdoing* 430.7, *transgression* 712.3, *dissent* 782.2
infractor *wrongdoer* 430.8
infra dig *common* 71.3, *indecorous* 528.8, *vulgar* 535.6
infrangibility *toughness* 547.1
infrangible *dense* 540.6, *tough* 547.6, *adhesive* 755.5
infrangibly *toughly* 547.16
infrared (IR) radiation *electromagnetic radiation* 10.14
infrared (IR) spectrometry *analysis* 11.17
infrared astronomy *astronomy* 7.1
infrared film *film* 132.8
infrared observatory *observatory* 7.24
infrared photography *photographic specialties* 132.2
infrared radiation *light* 246.1
infrared spectrum *emission* 10.56
infrared telescope *telescope* 7.25
infrasonic *physical* 10.70
infrasonic frequency *sound propagation* 230.3
infrasound *sound* 10.15, 230.1
infrastructural *structural* 551.17, *foundational* 605.12
infrastructure *substructure* 551.8, *foundation* 601.2, *supporting structure* 605.2
infrequence *infrequency* 662.1
infrequency 662.1; *scarcity* 98.3, *irregularity* 664.1, *rarity* 796.4
infrequent 662.2; *scarce* 98.8, *valuable* 496.8, *periodic* 639.10, *irregular* 664.3, *dispersed* 776.6, *sparse* 796.6
infrequently 662.4; *not enough* 98.12, *sometimes* 639.10, *irregularly* 664.6, *discontinuously* 775.15, *diffusely* 776.18, *sparsely* 796.11
infrequent occurrence *infrequency* 662.1
in friendship *sociably* 408.19
infringe 479.17; *besiege* 418.20, *disobey* 427.12, *do wrong* 430.20, *transgress* 712.14, *be external* 724.15
infringe a copyright *borrow illegally* 476.12, *take over* 477.16
infringed *violating* 466.8, *borrowed* 476.8, *fraudulent* 479.13
infringement 479.6; *lawbreaking* 53.14, *military attack* 418.2, *violation of the law* 427.2, *wrongdoing* 430.7, *infraction* 466.4, *transgression* 712.3, *externality* 724.4, *dissent* 782.2
infringement of copyright *illegal borrowing* 476.3, *taking over* 477.3, *infringement* 479.6
infringe on *violate the law* 466.12
infringer 479.10; *taker* 477.9
infringe the law *break the law* 782.19
infringing *offending* 53.25, *unlawful* 430.15, *violating* 466.8, *external* 724.11
in front *at a distance* 585.13, *front-running* 621.10, *before* 621.14, *ahead* 712.18, *first* 769.19

in front of *before* 769.18
in front of one's face *or* **eyes** *clear* 244.6
in full *diffusely* 199.7, *meticulously* 726.18, *fully* 761.14
in full bloom *maturely* 27.18, *flowering* 42.10
in full blow *flowering* 42.10
in full career *at full speed* 694.17
in full cry *loudly* 232.11, *on the trail* 385.18
in full dress *formally dressed* 406.8
in full gallop *at full speed* 694.17
in full possession of one's faculties *sane* 109.3
in full sail *at full speed* 694.17
in full swing *busy* 414.15
in full view *publicly* 173.20, *visible* 244.5, *manifestly* 843.17
in full war paint [Inf] *equipped* 388.10
in fun *humorously* 277.13
in funds *solvent* 485.9
infuriate *antagonize* 63.12, *cause dislike* 291.16, *cause hate* 300.12, *make angry* 302.18, *make violent* 520.10
infuriated *angry* 302.11, *violent* 520.5
infuriating *maddening* 302.12
infuriatingly *maddeningly* 302.25
infuse *dissolve* 555.23, *steep* 557.31, *inject* 710.10, *obtain an extract* 711.19, *mix* 751.12
infused *injected* 710.6
infuse new *or* **fresh blood into** *restore* 807.17
infusible *condensed* 540.7
infusion *drink* 93.2, *dose of medicine* 115.3, *tonic* 115.8, *solution* 555.10, *steeping* 557.10, *injection* 710.2, *obtaining of an extract* 711.7, *extract* 711.8, *mixture* 751.1, *mixed thing* 751.2, *admixture* 751.5
in future *in the future* 650.13
ingathering *collection* 59.2
in general *on average* 742.10, *on the whole* 759.13, *generally* 778.20
ingenious *skillful* 127.10, *ideational* 327.9, *imaginative* 360.10, *planning* 387.11, *cunning* 822.4
ingeniously *expertly* 52.21, *skillfully* 127.16, *imaginatively* 327.21, 360.17, *conspiratorially* 387.18
ingenious plan *method* 387.4
ingenue *stock part* 136.24, *innocent person* 449.5, *naive person* 821.2
ingenuity *skill* 127.1, *imagination* 327.8, 360.1, *cunning* 822.1
ingenuous 191.6; *immature* 26.12, 652.12, *easily seen through* 249.10, *raw* 260.9, *naive* 449.9, 821.3, *natural* 526.10, *open* 583.13
ingenuously 191.11; *naively* 449.15, 821.5, *candidly* 583.23
ingenuousness 191.3; *immaturity* 26.3, 652.3, *openness* 249.6, 583.7, *naiveté* 449.4, 821.1
ingenuous person *naive person* 821.2
ingest 708.17; *eat* 92.21
ingesting *eating* 92.1
ingestion *body process* 19.15, *life function* 28.6, *eating* 92.1, *intake* 708.5
ingestive *absorbent* 708.11
inglenook *home* 60.3, *place for fire* 217.9, *compartment* 578.2

in glowing terms *emphatically* 200.7

ingoing *introverted* 108.37, *entry* 706.1, *entering* 706.9

ingoingness *personality type* 108.6

in good condition *healthy* 113.4, *in form* 624.8, *orderly* 765.13

in good conscience *morally* 431.15

in good fellowship *compassionately* 305.14

in good form 725.11

in good health *healthy* 113.4, *sound* 759.8

in good heart *healthy* 113.4

in goodness *virtuously* 447.9

in good odor *praiseworthy* 437.12

in good order *orderly* 765.13

in good shape *healthy* 113.4, *physically strong* 516.10

in good spirits *in good form* 725.11

in good taste *tastefully* 534.9

in good time *early* 657.17

in good trim *orderly* 765.13

ingot *bullion* 484.16

ingraft *accustom* 397.18, *plant* 710.14

ingrained *fixed* 397.13, *stabilized* 674.4, *intrinsic* 723.6, *combinatory* 757.6

ingrate *ingratitude* 311.1

ingratiate *smooth over* 545.12

ingratiate oneself *fawn* 401.9, *defer to* 410.12, *cajole* 439.14

ingratiating *servile* 401.6, *sycophantic* 401.7, *deferential* 410.8, *showing respect* 435.7, *cajoling* 439.9, *smooth-mannered* 545.9

ingratiatingly *sycophantically* 401.16, *deferentially* 410.15

ingratiation *sycophancy* 401.2, *deference* 410.4, *cajolery* 439.3

ingratitude 311.1; *unthinkingness* 355.3

ingredient *physical element* 524.5, *additional item* 748.3, *admixture* 751.5, *component* 760.3, *thing included* 763.2

ingredients *contents* 577.1

ingress *military attack* 418.2, *flow* 570.4, *forward motion* 677.4, *passage into* 692.4, *entry* 706.1, *entrance* 706.5, *injection* 710.2

ingression *entry* 706.1

ingressive *entering* 706.9

in-group *group* 59.8, *the power structure* 68.12, *avant-garde* 652.6

ingrowing *invasive* 706.10

inguen *fork* 703.5

ingurgitate *eat* 92.21, *ingest* 708.17

ingurgitation *eating* 92.1, *intake* 708.5

inhabit 60.22, 61.13; *settle* 565.10, *reside* 575.17, *exist* 717.18

inhabitable *fit for habitation* 60.19

inhabitance *residence* 575.2

inhabitant 61.1

inhabitants 61.2; *group* 18.13

inhabited 61.10

inhabiter *inhabitant* 61.1

inhabiting 60.18

inhalant *dose of medicine* 115.3

inhalation *sense of smell* 224.2, *respiration* 558.8, *influx* 706.2, *intake* 708.5

inhale *smoke* 121.38, *smell* 224.7, *respire* 558.21, *draw in* 708.18

inhalement *intake* 708.5

in half 789.21

inhaling *respiratory* 558.19

in halves *separately* 753.22, *in half* 789.21

in hand 388.11; *in preparation* 388.22, *in production* 551.25

in harbor *safe* 810.16

inharmonious *strident* 238.4, *dissonant* 241.4, *off-color* 251.15

in harmony 735.32; *tunefully* 140.30, *agreeably* 462.14, *collaborative* 757.7, *conformingly* 781.16

in harness *equipped* 388.10, *acting* 412.9, *busy* 414.15, *captive* 832.9

in haste *hasty* 818.3

in health *healthy* 113.4

in heaps *in crowds* 795.14

in heat *desirous* 20.18, *reproductive* 21.11, *in season* 654.8

in heaven *on top of the world* 600.14

in hell *devilishly* 446.14

in hellfire *devilishly* 446.14

inherent *basic* 601.8, *intrinsic* 611.11, 717.12, 723.6, *included* 763.4

inherent ability *aptitude* 127.4

inherent authority *legal power* 52.2

inherently *basically* 601.14, *intrinsically* 611.20, *really* 717.22, *inclusively* 763.8

inherit *be entitled to* 72.13, *profit* 467.22, *own property* 470.11, *transfer property* 470.12, *receive* 473.13, 492.7, *take* 477.14, *get rich* 485.13, *follow from* 676.9, *succeed* 770.11

inheritable *transferring property* 470.10

inheritance 469.5; *genetics* 13.19, *profit* 467.6, *transfer of property* 470.4, *personal estate* 470.6, *gift* 472.2, *receiving* 473.1, *taking* 477.1, *legacy* 492.4, *visible effect* 676.2, *estate* 750.5, *succession* 770.2

inheritance of acquired characteristics *evolution* 13.23

inheritance tax *tax* 494.5

inherited *received* 473.11, 492.6, *caused* 676.5

inheriting *gainful* 467.10, *taking* 477.12

inheriting from *caused* 676.5

inheritor *beneficiary* 473.6, *person remaining* 750.6, *successor* 770.6

inheritors *future generation* 650.2

inheritress *beneficiary* 473.6

inheritrix *beneficiary* 473.6

inhibit *react* 11.38, *prohibit* 503.8, *counteract* 510.7, *limit* 620.7

inhibited *unconscious* 108.40, *uncandid* 192.15, *self-restrained* 830.10

inhibitedly *psychologically* 108.42, *uncandidly* 192.29

inhibiting *catalytic* 11.30, *prohibited* 503.5, *limited* 620.5, *self-restrained* 830.10

inhibition 826.9; *enzyme* 12.11, *defense mechanism* 108.23, *lack of candor* 192.4, *limitation* 620.2, *self-restraint* 830.4

inhibitive 826.14

inhibitively 826.24

inhibitor *catalysis* 11.16, *opposing force* 510.2

in hiding *invisibly* 245.8, *fleetingly* 265.8, *fugitively* 816.12

in high dudgeon *offended* 302.9

in high esteem *praiseworthy* 437.12

in high gear *swiftly* 694.16, *at full speed* 694.17

in high hopes *expecting* 356.4

in high relief *clear* 244.6

in high spirits *cheerfully* 269.14

in hock *needy* 95.12, *guaranteed* 464.6, *indebted* 486.9, 488.7, *nonpaying* 490.7

in holes *worn* 808.13

in holy wedlock *matrimonially* 64.23

in honor of 405.15

inhospitable *hostile* 63.6

inhospitably *hostilely* 63.13, *unsocially* 409.13

inhospitality *unsociability* 409.1

in hot pursuit *on the trail* 160.13, *pursuant to* 385.17

in hot water [Inf] *troubled* 824.15

in-house *residing* 575.8, *internal* 611.9, *inland* 611.19

inhuman *cruel* 306.10, *wicked* 448.9

inhumane *cruel* 306.10, *pitiless* 309.3, *severe* 424.5

inhumanely *pitilessly* 309.7, *severely* 424.11, *wickedly* 448.15

inhumaneness *cruelty* 306.4

inhumanity *misanthropy* 291.4, *cruelty* 306.4, *pitilessness* 309.1, *severity* 424.1, *wickedness* 448.1

inhumanly *cruelly* 306.17

inhumation *burial* 311.1

inhume *bury* 31.10

inhumed *buried* 31.8

in hysterics *violent* 520.5

in ICU *sick* 114.24

in ignorance *ignorantly* 349.11

inimical *hostile* 63.6, *antipathetic* 291.7, *disagreeing* 463.6, *counteracting* 510.6, *disunited* 753.10, *oppositional* 828.11

inimicality *hostility* 63.1

inimically *hostilely* 63.13, *aggressively* 77.38, *argumentatively* 329.15, *in disagreement* 463.12, *counter* 510.8, *disunitedly* 753.25, *opposingly* 828.22

inimitability *superiority* 744.1

inimitable *novel* 737.5, *best* 744.10, *exceptional* 779.13

inimitably *originally* 737.8, *supremely* 744.23

in Indian file *in a line* 774.17

in infancy *in the bud* 771.39

in installments *on loan* 476.14, *cash down* 489.25, *partly* 760.17, *incompletely* 762.10

in intensive care *sick* 114.24

iniquitous *malicious* 306.8, *wrongful* 430.10, *evil* 446.7

iniquitously *maliciously* 306.15, *wrongly* 430.24, *evilly* 446.12, *unvirtuously* 448.16

iniquitousness *malice* 306.2

iniquity 448.3; *wrong* 430.1, *evil* 446.1, *sin* 450.3

initial *written letter* 5.14, *word* 5.43, *sign* 183.19, *identify oneself* 184.12, *beginning* 583.14, 771.16, *precursory* 769.12

initially *first* 771.37

initial rhyme *rhyme* 139.11

initials *personal identification* 184.4, *inscription* 185.4

Initial Teaching Alphabet *alphabet* 5.16

initiate *learner* 48.6, *undertake* 391.7, *behave toward* 399.20, *launch* 405.14, *motivate* 508.9, *begin* 583.21, 771.25, *be new* 652.17, *inaugurate* 675.10, 771.31, *enroll* 706.16, 771.33, *introduce* 708.16, *install* 710.15, *originate* 737.7, *forerun* 769.16, *beginner* 771.14

initiate a (leveraged) buyout *bargain* 480.20

initiated *inaugurated* 652.13, *enrolled* 771.24

initiation *non-Christian ritual* 85.8, *ceremony* 405.3, *reception* 473.4, *beginning* 583.9, 652.4, *cause* 675.1, *entry* 706.1, *bringing in* 708.4, *originality* 737.1, *enrollment* 771.8

initiation ceremony *enrollment* 771.8

initiative *energy* 414.4, *introductory* 708.10, *starting point* 771.11, *beginning* 771.16, *freedom* 829.1

initiator *originator* 771.15

initiatory *causal* 675.7, *introductory* 708.10, 771.23, *precursory* 769.12, *beginning* 771.16

in its own way *characteristically* 779.20

in jail *in prison* 55.14

inject 710.10; *practice medicine* 107.32, *medicate* 115.18, *hole* 583.17

injected 710.6; *holed* 583.12

injecting *drug use* 121.9

injection 710.2; *rocketry* 7.32, *dose of medicine* 115.3, *capital punishment* 454.12

injective *functional* 6.73

inject oneself *drug oneself* 121.37

in jeopardy *endangered* 811.10

injest *steep* 557.31

injudicial *unlawful* 53.23

injudicious *imprudent* 286.7, *foolish* 353.5, *inconvenient* 804.5

injudiciously *imprudently* 286.11, *inconveniently* 804.11

injudiciousness *imprudence* 286.3, *folly* 353.1

injunction *demand* 425.2, 505.3, *prohibition* 503.1, *rule* 780.1, *hindrance* 826.1, *restraint* 830.1

injunctive *disputed* 57.15, *commanding* 425.7, *vetoed* 503.6, *demanding* 505.8, *legal* 780.8, *restraining* 830.8

injunctively *by veto* 503.12

injure *inflict pain* 215.10, *harm* 306.13, *ill-use* 395.7, *wrong* 430.19, *be evil* 446.10, *destroy* 468.18, *weaken* 517.13, *cause adversity* 848.15

injured 215.5

injured husband *married man* 64.10, *stock part* 136.24

injured pride *humiliation* 298.5

injurious *unhygienic* 114.27, *malign* 306.11, *abusive* 395.5, *bad-mannered* 411.6, *unlawful* 430.15, *defamatory* 440.9, *detrimental* 446.8, *destructive* 523.8

injuriously *malignly* 306.18, *offensively* 395.9

injury *Phobias* 283, *ill-use* 395.2, *fault* 430.2, *wrongdoing* 430.7, *sin* 450.3, *affliction* 454.9, *loss* 468.1, *misadventure* 848.2

injury time *extra* 748.6

injustice 342.3, 741.3; *personal attack* 418.8, *wrong* 430.1, *fault* 430.2, *sin* 450.3

in juxtaposition *beside* 586.20

ink *material* 143.9, *dark thing*

247.3, *black thing* 254.3, *blacken* 254.11
inkberry Trees and Shrubs 43
inkblot test Psychological Tests 108
inked *drawn* 143.11
in keeping *conforming* 781.8, *conformingly* 781.16
in keeping with *agreeing* 462.6
in key *tunefully* 140.30
inkily *blackly* 254.12
ink in *paint* 143.12, *blacken* 254.11
in kind *in exchange* 673.6
inkiness *blackness* 254.1
ink-jet printer *hardcopy device* 15.10
inkling *impression* 266.2, *theory* 327.2, *information* 348.2, *basis of supposition* 359.2, *suggestion* 800.9
inky *black* 254.5
in labor *pregnant* 21.12
inlaid *type of furniture* 101.2, *checked* 263.8, *decorated* 532.9, *inset* 710.8
inland 611.2, 611.8, 611.19; *transportable* 686.7, *nautical* 690.14
inland navigation *water transportation* 690.1
inlands *inland* 611.2
Inland Sea Oceans and Seas 571
inland sea *lake* 568.1
inland waterway *waterway* 690.2
in-laws *family member* 65.2
inlay *work wood* 131.9, *check* 263.2, *variegate* 263.11, *insert* 710.4, *inset* 710.13
inlayer *furniture making* 101.3
in layers 588.11; *layered* 588.6
inlaying *furniture making* 101.3
in league *collaborative* 757.7
in league with *as one* 752.21, *in combination* 757.11
in length *lengthwise* 590.14
inlet 572.9; *concave land* 635.2, *channel* 691.10, *entrance* 706.5
in lieu *answerably* 334.28, *in place of* 574.21
in lieu of *instead* 672.8
in life *alive* 28.13
in like manner *similarly* 733.17
in limbo *disused* 394.8
in line *conforming* 781.8, *conformingly* 781.16
in-line skates *means of transportation* 686.2
in-line skating Sporting Activities 145
in line with *directly* 697.16
in liquidation *destroyed* 523.9
in liquor *drunk* 121.25
in litigation 54.34
in loads *in crowds* 795.14
in lock step *synchronized* 649.5
in loco [L] *where* 565.12, *convenient* 803.3
in loco parentis [L] *instead* 672.8, *under commission* 833.11
in lots *partly* 760.17
in love 299.16
in love with *in love* 299.16
in love with one's own voice *diffusely* 199.7
in low gear *in slow motion* 693.15
in luck *prosperous* 847.5
in luxury *prosperous* 847.5
in masses *in crowds* 795.14
inmate *prisoner* 55.7, *inhabitant* 61.1, *closed-in person* 584.6, *subjected person* 832.5
in medias res [L] *in the middle* 772.21
in memoriam *funereally* 31.13, *memorably* 354.16

in memory of *memorably* 354.16, *in honor of* 405.15
in midair *pendulously* 604.19
in midstream *in transit* 685.13
in-migrant *entrant* 706.7
in-migration *right of entry* 706.4
in miniature *little* 580.12
in mint condition *repaired* 809.6
in moderation *moderately* 521.10, *midway* 772.22, *self-restrainedly* 830.19
in modo di Musical Terms and Expression Marks 140
in more than one way *differently* 463.13
in mortal fear *frightened* 283.9
inmost *interior* 611.7, *secret* 611.13
in mothballs *saved* 105.15
in motion 677.19; *moving* 677.12
in mourning *lamentingly* 280.9
inn *hotel* 60.12
innaccessible *distant* 804.8
in name only *apparently* 720.19
innards *internal organ* 19.13, *insides* 577.3, *internals* 611.3, *component* 760.3
innate *instinctive* 320.8, *intrinsic* 611.11, 717.12, 723.6
innate ability *aptitude* 127.4, *ability* 340.2
innately *intrinsically* 611.20
innateness *nature* 717.4
innate reaction *instinct* 320.4
in need 95.21; *poor* 486.8, *poorly* 486.17
in need of *incomplete* 762.5
in need of repair *gone wrong* 430.17
in need of rest *fatigued* 820.2
inner *interior* 611.7, *included* 763.4, *middle* 772.9
inner being *spirit* 86.10
inner cabinet *management board* 126.2
inner circle *governance* 52.6, *the power structure* 68.12, *exclusiveness* 764.4
inner city *urban area* 567.10
inner-city *environmental* 60.17, *urban* 567.14
inner-city ghetto *dilapidation* 808.5
inner core *earth zone* 8.7
inner-directed *introverted* 108.37, *independent* 829.12
inner ear *ear* 19.10, 228.2
inner form *form* 624.1
inner layer *interior* 611.1
inner life *inner nature* 611.4
inner mind *spirit* 86.10
innermost *deeper* 598.10, *interior* 611.7
innermost part *the depths* 598.2
innermost recesses *quietness* 844.4
innermost thought *thoughtfulness* 317.2
inner nature 611.4
inner part *interior* 611.1
inner person *quietness* 844.4
inner personality *inner nature* 611.4
inner product *vector* 6.48
inner sense *psychic power* 86.4
inner side *interior* 611.1
inner strength *stamina* 377.4
inner surface *interior* 611.1
inner tube *survival swimming* 164.4
inner voice *sense of duty* 433.2
inner wall *interior* 611.1
inner workings *insides* 577.3
inning *other game terms* 147.7,

billiards play 149.2, *period of activity* 641.4, *part* 760.1
innkeeper *caterer* 89.5
innocence 449.1; *favorable verdict* 54.19, *ingenuousness* 191.3, *ignorance* 349.1, *unaccustomedness* 398.1, *chastity* 431.3, *virtue* 447.1, *weakness* 517.1, *naturalness* 526.4, *immaturity* 652.3, *immaculateness* 805.2, *vulnerability* 811.6, *naiveté* 821.1
innocent 449.6; *young* 26.11, *acquitted* 54.25, *virginal* 67.7, *harmless* 73.9, *believer* 87.5, *believing* 87.6, *ingenuous* 191.6, *raw* 260.9, *ignorant* 349.5, *unaccustomed* 398.3, *chaste* 431.10, *vindicated* 441.8, *virtuous* 447.5, *innocent person* 449.5, *helpless* 515.9, *natural* 526.10, *immature* 652.12, *blameless* 805.12, *trustworthy* 810.17, *naive person* 821.2, *naive* 821.3
innocent as a child *naive* 449.9
innocent as a dove *innocent* 449.6
innocent as a lamb *innocent* 449.6
innocent as a newborn babe *naive* 449.9
innocent intentions *incorruption* 449.2
innocently 449.13; *youthfully* 26.14, *forgivingly* 53.37, *ingenuously* 191.11, *unaccustomedly* 398.7, *virtuously* 447.9, *powerlessly* 515.16, *naturally* 526.16, *naively* 821.5
innocent party *innocent person* 449.5
innocent person 449.5
innocent tumor *cancer* 114.15
innocuous *health-giving* 113.6, *innocent* 449.6, *trustworthy* 810.17
innocuously *innocently* 449.13
innominate bone Human Bones 19
in no place *nowhere* 718.17
in nothing flat *swiftly* 694.16
in no time *in the shortest possible time* 645.9, *swiftly* 694.16
in no uncertain terms *emphatically* 200.7, *intelligibly* 363.13
innovate *invent* 335.13, 771.30, *produce* 522.13, *be trendy* 652.18, *cause change* 665.16, *originate* 737.7, *forerun* 769.16
innovation *production* 522.1, *newness* 652.1, *change for the better* 665.4, *originality* 737.1, *original* 737.2, *invention* 771.5
innovational *changeable* 665.11
innovative *imaginative* 360.10, *enterprising* 391.5, *productive* 522.11, *new* 652.9, *changeable* 665.11, *original* 737.4, *preparatory* 769.11, *inventive* 771.20
innovatively *inventively* 335.15, *enterprisingly* 391.11, *productively* 522.17, *newly* 652.21, *changeably* 665.22, *originally* 737.8
innovator *experimenter* 335.5, *person who undertakes* 391.3, *improviser* 396.3, *producer* 522.10, *changer* 665.9, *originator* 737.3, *precursor* 769.7
innovatory *preparatory* 769.11
in no way *negatively* 190.22, *not at all* 718.15, *none* 786.7
innoxious *health-giving* 113.6
Inns of Court, the London 567.8
innuendo *aspersion* 440.4, *quietness* 844.4

innumerability *multiplicity* 795.2, *immeasurability* 798.2
innumerable *numberless* 795.8, *immeasurable* 798.6
innumerably *numerously* 795.13, *immeasurably* 798.11
in numerical order *numerically* 783.11
in obedience to *obediently* 426.9
inobservance *nonobservance* 466.1
inobservant *nonobservant* 466.5
in occupation *residing* 575.8
inoculate *treat* 115.17, *practice hygiene* 116.4, *inject* 710.10, *immunize* 810.22
inoculated *health-giving* 113.6, *injected* 710.6, *safe* 810.16
inoculation *prophylaxis* 115.4, *hygiene* 116.1, Phobias 283, *injection* 710.2, *sanitary precaution* 810.8
inodorous *odorless* 225.4
inodorousness *odorlessness* 225.1
inoffensive *harmless* 73.9, *humble* 298.8, *innocent* 449.6
inoffensively *humbly* 298.22, *innocently* 449.13
inoffensiveness *innocence* 449.1
in olden days *anciently* 653.18
in olden times *historically* 3.17
in on *informed* 170.9
in one piece *whole* 759.6
in one's absence *absently* 576.18
in ones and twos 796.10
in one's behalf *instead* 672.8
in one's best bib and tucker *equipped* 388.10, *formally dressed* 406.8
in one's birthday suit *revealingly* 614.22
in one's control *subject* 832.6
in one's crystal ball *foresightedly* 357.10
in one's cups *drunk* 121.25
in one's grasp *possessed* 469.13
in one's hands *possessed* 469.13
in one's head *ideational* 327.9, *theoretically* 327.19
in one's name *possessed* 469.13, *possessively* 469.16
in one's opinion *ideologically* 327.23
in one's own backyard *nearby* 586.17
in one's own time *leisurely* 125.6
in one's place *instead* 672.8
in one's pocket *subject* 832.6
in one's power *subject* 832.6
in one's prime *maturely* 27.18
in one's right mind *sane* 109.3, *cured* 809.8
in one's shell *unsociable* 409.6
in one's shirtsleeves *in dishabille* 100.40, *at ease* 819.2
in one's shoes *instead* 672.8
in one's spare time *leisurely* 125.6
in one's stride *systematically* 397.22
in one's Sunday best *formally dressed* 406.8
in one's teens *young* 26.11
in one's thoughts *topically* 328.11
in one way or another *how* 691.16
in open court *publicly* 173.20, *manifestly* 843.17
in open rebellion *in defiance* 416.10
inoperability *hopelessness* 837.2
inoperable *killing* 30.17, *sick* 114.24, *hopeless* 282.6, 837.6
inoperably *hopelessly* 837.12
in operation *usable* 393.6, *in use*

393.8, *acting* 412.9, *operational*
509.7
inoperational *unused* 394.5
inoperative 515.8; *inactive* 413.9,
broken down 802.8
inopportune *untimely* 660.5,
inconvenient 804.5
inopportunely *at the wrong time*
660.12, *inconveniently* 804.11
inopportune moment
untimeliness 660.1
inopportuneness *untimeliness*
660.1, *inconvenience* 804.1
in opposition *negatively* 190.22,
protestingly 331.23, *disapprovingly*
507.10, *oppositional* 828.11,
opposingly 828.22, *adverse* 848.10
in opposition to *counter* 510.8
in orbit *high* 596.20
in order 765.26; *in good form*
725.11, *hierarchical* 765.12,
orderly 765.25, *arranged* 767.11,
in place 767.24, *sequentially*
770.13, *consecutive* 774.7,
consecutively 774.15, *inventorially*
785.13
in orderly fashion *orderly* 765.25
in order to *with the intention of*
374.14
in order to influence *influentially*
508.13
in order to oppress *masterfully*
68.19
in order to prevent *by veto*
503.12
in order to provoke *in*
disagreement 463.12
inordinate *excessive* 99.5,
exaggerated 194.7, *extravagant*
194.9, *overindulgent* 456.8,
unrestrained 500.5
inordinately *excessively* 99.13,
194.17, *extravagantly* 500.9
inordinateness *overindulgence*
456.3
inorganic *mineral types* 8.38,
chemical compound 11.4, *chemical*
11.24
inorganic base *base* 11.11
inorganic chemist *chemist* 11.2
inorganic chemistry Branches of
Chemistry 11
inorganic pigment *coloring agent*
251.5
inorganic sediment *sediment* 8.29
inosculation *linkage* 752.3
in other words 365.18;
demonstrably 331.22, *meaningfully*
361.16
in outline *concisely* 198.6,
apparently 264.16, *essentially*
617.6, *uncompleted* 762.7
in over one's head *insolvently*
488.11
in pairs *two* 789.8, *two by two*
789.19
in Paradise *dead* 29.11
in parallel 606.9; *electronically*
14.54, *correspondingly* 334.27
in parentheses *in* 710.16
in part *partly* 760.17, *incompletely*
762.10
in particular *specially* 779.19
in partnership *cliquishly* 59.32,
collaborative 757.7
in partnership with *in alliance*
735.35, *as one* 752.21, *in*
combination 757.11
in parts *to pieces* 758.8, *partly*
760.17
in passage to *via* 691.17
in passing *in transit* 685.13, *by the*
way 692.20
in past times *in the past* 651.20

inpatient *patient* 107.25, *sick*
person 114.22
inpatient pharmacy *hospital*
107.16
in peace *peacefully* 73.12
in peak condition *healthy* 113.4
in perfect condition *unbroken*
805.13
in perfect health *ideal* 805.17
in perfect order *orderly* 765.13
in peril *endangered* 811.10
in perpetuity *eternally* 798.12
in person 575.18
in personam jurisdiction
jurisdiction 54.2
in pieces *separately* 753.22, *apart*
753.23, *to pieces* 758.8
in pieces *apart* 753.8
in place 767.24; *answerably*
334.28, *where* 565.12,
geographically 573.11, *on the spot*
575.20, *conformingly* 781.16
in place of 574.21; *instead* 672.8
in places *where* 565.12, *diffusely*
776.18, *in ones and twos* 796.10
in plain English *intelligibly*
363.13, *in other words* 365.18
in plain English *or* **language**
made easy 823.11
in plain terms *intelligibly* 363.13
in plain view *visibly* 244.10
in plain words *meaningfully*
361.16, *in other words* 365.18,
simply 526.14, *candidly* 583.23
in play *operational* 509.7
in-play wall *squash terms* 165.10
in plenty *ample* 795.9
in point of fact *really* 717.22, *in*
truth 721.28
in poor condition *sick* 114.24
in poor health *sick* 114.24, *adverse*
848.10
in poor shape *sick* 114.24, *adverse*
848.10
in port *safe* 810.16
in position *geographically* 573.11
in possession *possessing* 469.11
in possession of one's faculties
aged 27.15
inpouring *invasive* 706.10
in practice *in use* 393.8, *really*
719.13
in preparation 388.8, 388.22;
incomplete 762.5, *in anticipation*
769.20
in principle *basically* 601.14,
605.21
in print *published* 173.12, 174.18,
175.8
in prison 55.14
in private *privately* 181.18,
invisibly 245.8, *unsocially* 409.13,
aloofly 756.10
in production 551.25
in profit *profitably* 492.8
in profusion *ample* 795.9
in progress 679.16; *continuous*
669.5, *incomplete* 762.5
in proof *demonstrably* 331.22, *as*
evidence 339.15
in proportion *divisible* 6.71
in proportion to *harmoniously*
735.31
in propria persona *in person*
575.18
in protest *protestingly* 331.23,
dissentiently 347.10
in public *visibly* 244.10, *manifestly*
331.20, 843.17
in pursuance of *pursuant to*
385.17
in pursuit *pursuant to* 385.17
input *conduct* 14.51, *computing*

terms 15.22, *program* 15.29, *record*
185.13, *influx* 706.2
input device 15.11; *peripheral*
15.8
in Queer Street *insolvent* 486.10
inquest *after death* 29.9, *legal*
process 54.3, *questioning* 333.2
in question *problematically* 328.12,
arguable 329.8, *arguably* 329.16,
questionable 333.13, *questionably*
333.22, *dangerous* 811.7,
uncertainly 841.22
in quest of *pursuing* 385.8,
pursuant to 385.17
in quick succession *frequently*
661.7
inquietude *irresolution* 666.2,
agitation 684.1
inquire *philosophize* 4.19, *be curious*
321.7, *raise the point* 328.10,
discuss 329.12, *question* 333.16,
experiment 335.11
inquire into *dissertate* 203.5
inquirer *philosopher* 4.9,
conversationalist 210.6, *curious*
person 321.3, *questioner* 333.9,
experimenter 335.5, *attempter*
390.3, *requester* 505.5
inquiring *curious* 321.5, *curiosity*
333.8, *questioning* 333.11,
experimental 335.8, *tentative* 390.5
inquiring mind *curiosity* 321.1
inquiry *philosophical investigation*
4.4, *dissertation* 203.1, *curiosity*
321.1, *logical argument* 329.2,
question 333.1, *questioning* 333.2,
experiment 335.1, *undertaking*
391.1
Inquisition *place of judgment*
341.3, *instrument of torture* 454.14
inquisition *tribunal* 54.6, *curiosity*
321.1, *questioning* 333.2, *place of*
judgment 341.3, *suppression* 424.2
inquisitional *judiciary* 53.19,
judicatory 54.24, *judging* 341.7
inquisitive *educatable* 48.18,
curious 321.5, *questioning* 333.11
inquisitively *curiously* 321.9,
questioningly 333.21
inquisitiveness *educatability* 48.9,
curiosity 321.1, 333.8
inquisitive person *meddler*
414.12
inquisitor *curious person* 321.3,
questioner 333.9, *strict person*
424.4, *punisher* 454.16
inquisitorial *curious* 321.5, *severe*
424.5
inquisitorially *curiously* 321.9
in rags *beggarly* 486.12, *untidy*
766.11, *worn* 808.13
in rapid succession *frequently*
661.7
in rapport with *agreeing* 462.6
in re *in litigation* 54.34
in readiness *prepared* 388.9, *in*
preparation 388.22
in reality *really* 719.13, *in truth*
721.28
in real life *in truth* 721.28
in rebellion *subversive* 427.11
in rebellion against
disapprovingly 507.10
in receipt *profitably* 492.8
in receivership *destroyed* 523.9
in recession *deteriorated* 808.8
in recognition of one's services
gratefully 310.8
in recompense *redemptively* 478.7
in redemption *redemptively* 478.7
in reduced circumstances *poor*
486.8, *poorly* 486.17
in regard to *relevantly* 727.12
in relation to *relevantly* 727.12

in relation to *or* **with** *in*
connection with 754.16
in relays *sequentially* 770.13
in relief *accentuated* 843.11
in remembrance of *in honor of*
405.15
in rem jurisdiction *jurisdiction*
54.2
in repair *in good form* 725.11
in repentance *apologetically*
313.11
in reply 332.10; *in answer* 334.25
in repose *motionlessly* 678.9
in reprisal *retaliatory* 420.3
in requital *with vengeance* 420.6,
redemptively 478.7
in reserve *saved* 105.15, *unused*
394.5, *suspended* 519.3, *inertly*
519.5
in residence *inhabiting* 60.18,
residing 575.8, *readily available*
575.21
in response *apologetically* 329.18,
in reply 332.10, *in answer* 334.25
in restitution *redemptively* 478.7
in retaliation *retaliatory* 420.3
in retirement *leisurely* 125.4,
resigning 835.3
in retreat *defeated* 846.11
in return *in exchange* 673.6
in return for *in exchange* 673.6
in reverse *inversely* 608.9,
backward 680.23
in rhyme *in harmony* 735.32
inroad 706.3; *military attack* 418.2
in round numbers *nearly* 586.18
in ruins *destroyed* 523.9, *dilapidated*
808.11
inrun *influx* 706.2
in running order *operational*
509.7
inrush *influx* 706.2, *flood in* 706.14
inrushing *invasive* 706.10
in rut *desirous* 20.18
in sackcloth and ashes
lamentingly 280.9, *penitently*
451.10
in safe hands *safe* 810.16
in safe keeping *safe* 810.16
in safety *safe* 810.16, *safely* 810.24
insalubrious *killing* 30.17, *unclean*
112.8, *of disease* 114.25,
unhygienic 114.27
insalubriously *unhygienically*
114.32
insalubrity *lack of hygiene* 112.3
in (domestic) service *obediently*
69.12
ins and outs *circumstances* 726.1,
specifications 779.6
ins-and-outs *windsurfing* 150.19
insane 110.9; *violent* 520.5,
deranged 766.16
insane asylum *mental hospital*
110.6
insanely 110.15
insane person 110.5
insanitary *unhygienic* 114.27
insanitation *lack of hygiene* 112.3
insanity 110.1; *mental disorder*
108.8, *psychosis* 108.10, *Phobias*
283, *folly* 353.1, *derangement*
766.8
insanity defense *insanity* 110.1
insatiability *gluttony* 119.1
insatiable *unprovided* 98.6,
gluttonous 119.3, *covetous* 288.14
insatiable curiosity *curiosity*
333.8
insatiably *covetously* 288.28
in scale *gradational* 159.5
inscribe 185.14; *word* 5.43, *align*
6.92, *identify oneself* 184.12, *record*

185.13, annotate 365.14, enroll 706.16, introduce 708.16

inscribed *phrased* 5.39, *recorded* 185.12

inscribed figure *geometric figure* 6.39

inscribing *recordkeeping* 185.7

inscription 185.4; *funeral object* 31.6, *annotation* 365.2

inscrutability *obscurity* 250.2, *unintelligibility* 364.1

inscrutable 250.5; *mysterious* 182.10, *unintelligible* 364.4, *difficult* 364.8

inscrutably *opaquely* 250.9, *unintelligibly* 364.16

in search of *pursuant to* 385.17

in season 654.8; *reproductive* 21.11, *seasonal* 654.7

in seclusion *aloofly* 756.10

in secret *privately* 181.18, *secretly* 182.14

insect 39.9, 40.1; *animal* 34.1, *type of animal* 34.5, *disease-causing agent* 114.5, *bait* 154.6

Insecta *insect* 39.9, 40.1

insect-eating mammal 35.7

insecticidal *herbicidal* 17.16

insecticide *pest control* 16.13, *pest killer* 17.9, *killing agent* 30.15, *prophylaxis* 115.4, *poison* 117.7

insectiform *insectile* 40.11

insectile 40.11; *arthropodal* 39.22

Insectivora *insect-eating mammal* 35.7

insectivore *type of animal* 34.5, *insect-eating mammal* 35.7, *eater* 92.15

insectivorous 35.24; *of animals* 34.13, *of plants* 41.14, *eating* 92.18

insectivorously *carnivorously* 92.27

insectivorousness *eating habit* 92.7

insect larva *worm* 39.14

insectlike *arthropodal* 39.22, *insectile* 40.11

insect metamorphal stage 40.8

insects *Phobias* 283

insect sound 240.3

insect stings *Phobias* 283

insecure *suspicious* 314.6, *unsafe* 811.8, *vulnerable* 811.9, *unreliable* 841.15

insecurely *suspiciously* 314.13, *unreliably* 841.25

insecurity *suspicion* 314.3, *danger* 811.1, *vulnerability* 811.6, *unreliability* 841.7

in security *safe* 810.16

inselberg *hill* 569.2

in self-defense *professionally* 152.22, *defensively* 419.32, *retaliatory* 420.3

in self-reproach *penitently* 451.10

inseminate *reproduce oneself* 21.14, *propagate* 21.15, *fertilize* 22.12

insemination *fertilization* 21.6, *procreation* 22.4

inseminator *propagator* 21.7

insensate *cruel* 306.10

insensate cruelty *cruelty* 306.4

insensibility 213.1; *mood disorder* 108.12, *symptom* 114.3, *neurological disease* 114.20, *insensitivity* 268.1, *indifference* 289.1, *apathy* 322.2, *ignorance* 349.1, *oblivion* 355.4, *reverie* 360.6, *immobility* 413.2, *sleep* 415.5, *inertness* 519.1, *repose* 678.2, *fatigue* 820.1

insensible 213.4; *drugged* 121.30, *desensitized* 213.5, *insensitive*

268.4, *indifferent* 289.7, *apathetic* 322.4, *oblivious* 355.9, *inactive* 413.9, *not awake* 415.12, *disabled* 515.10, *inert* 519.2, *quiescent* 678.6

insensible to *indifferent* 289.7

insensibly 213.9; *in a trance* 121.40, *indifferently* 289.17, *sleepily* 415.19, *inertly* 519.5

insensitive 268.4; *insensible* 213.4, *unhearing* 229.5, *indifferent* 289.7, *inconsiderate* 318.9, *thoughtless* 324.7, *unrefined* 338.7, *discourteous* 411.5, *mentally hard* 542.8, *dull* 550.7, *thick-skinned* 594.8

insensitively 268.7; *insensibly* 213.9, *indifferently* 289.17, *thoughtlessly* 318.15, *apathetically* 322.7, *unselectively* 338.12, *discourteously* 411.8, *obtusely* 550.12, *callously* 594.14

insensitiveness *insensibility* 213.1, *insensitivity* 268.1, *inconsideration* 318.4, *dullness* 550.3

insensitive person 268.3

insensitivity 268.1; *inattention* 229.2, *indifference* 289.1, *inconsideration* 318.4, *thoughtlessness* 324.3, *tastelessness* 338.3, *discourtesy* 411.1, *dullness* 550.3, *callousness* 594.4

in sentences *phraseologically* 5.47

insentient *insensible* 213.4

inseparability *intimacy* 62.4, *density* 540.1, *nearness* 586.1, *adhesion* 755.1

inseparable *friend* 62.2, *intimate* 62.7, *dense* 540.6, *integral* 723.7, *united* 752.10, *adhesive* 755.5, *whole* 788.12, *associated* 794.14

inseparably *intimately* 62.14, *as one* 752.21, *inextricably* 752.23, *cohesively* 755.11, *together* 794.20

in sequence *sequentially* 770.13, *inventorially* 785.13

in series *electronically* 14.54, *in order* 765.26, *inventorially* 785.13

insert 710.4, 710.9, 748.12; *stuff* 577.12, *infiltrate* 706.13, *admit* 708.12, *insertion* 710.1

insert *or* **insertion** *advertisement* 173.9

inserted 710.5; *additional* 748.8

insertion 710.1; *rocketry* 7.32, *inroad* 706.3, *admittance* 708.1, *insert* 710.4, *addition* 748.1, *piece* 760.2, *repair* 809.1

in service *in use* 393.8

in-service training *educational system* 48.2, *bargaining terms* 57.10

in servitude *obediently* 69.12

inset 710.8, 710.13; *map* 187.5, *insert* 710.4

in set form *formally* 406.12

in set phrases *phraseologically* 5.47

in set terms *phraseologically* 5.47

in seventh heaven *joyful* 269.6, *on top of the world* 600.14

in shallow water *endangered* 811.10

in shape *in form* 624.8, *in good form* 725.11

inshore *near* 586.6

in short *concisely* 198.6, *summarily* 204.10, *thematically* 328.13, *shortly* 591.12

in shreds *dilapidated* 808.11

inside *space* 6.33, *soccer* 163.7, *insides* 577.3, *internally* 577.15, 611.18, *interior* 611.1, 611.7, *internal* 611.9, *side direction* 623.2,

in 710.16, *inclusively* 763.8, *middle* 772.1, 772.9

inside, the [Inf] 55.2

in side *badminton terms* 165.11

inside agent *informer* 170.8

inside and out *extensively* 563.18

inside information 170.4

inside job *plot* 387.6

inside left *soccer participant* 163.4

inside out *inverted* 608.5, *inversely* 608.9, *reversibly* 671.14

inside out and back-to-front *inverted* 608.5, *inversely* 608.9

insider *thing included* 763.2

insider dealing *dishonesty* 479.7

insider dealing *or* **trading** *foul play* 193.6

inside right *soccer participant* 163.4

insider trading *dishonesty* 479.7

inside run *play* 155.8

insides 577.3; *internal organ* 19.13

insides [Inf] *internals* 611.3, *component* 760.3

inside sales worker *sales worker* 123.6

inside-the-park home run *batting terms* 147.6

inside track *advantage* 618.4, 744.3

insidious *artful* 193.13, *cunning* 330.8, 822.4, *destructive* 523.8, *mysterious* 844.11

insidiously *hypocritically* 330.15

insidiousness *guile* 193.3, *cunning* 330.3

insight 320.3, 360.3; *refinement* 48.10, *psychic power* 86.4, *visualization* 242.6, *impression* 266.2, *way of thinking* 317.4, *intuition* 320.1, *judiciousness* 337.2, *wisdom* 352.1, *foresight* 357.1, *interpretation* 365.1, *profundity* 598.5

in sight *visually* 242.27, *visible* 244.5, *visibly* 244.10, *appearing* 264.9

insightful *refined* 48.20, *intuitive* 320.6, *discriminating* 337.9, *interpretive* 365.8, *profound* 598.15

insightfully *discerningly* 48.27, *judiciously* 337.16, *profoundly* 598.27

insightfulness *profundity* 598.5

in sight of *in progress* 679.16

insignia 184.5; *sign* 183.1

insignificance 289.4; *lack of meaning* 362.1, *superficiality* 599.2, *extraneousness* 724.1, *inferiority* 745.1, *unimportance* 800.1

insignificant 289.10, 745.6, 800.12; *meaningless* 362.7, *little* 580.7, *superficial* 599.4, *extraneous* 724.8, *small* 787.6

insignificantly 745.14; *unexceptionally* 289.20, *meaninglessly* 362.13, *infinitesimally* 580.13, *superficially* 599.8, *extraneously* 724.16, *unimportantly* 800.21

insignificant matter *trifle* 800.3

in silence *silently* 231.5

insincere *ungenuine* 192.13, *hypocritical* 330.10, *unmeant* 362.9, *flattering* 439.7, *cunning* 822.4

insincerely *untruthfully* 192.27, *hypocritically* 330.15, *showily* 367.6

insincere praise *flattery* 439.1

insincerity *ungenuineness* 192.2, *hypocrisy* 330.5, *flattery* 439.1, *cunning* 822.1

in single file *in a line* 774.17

insinuate *tip* 170.14, *vilify* 440.14, *accuse* 442.8, *manipulate* 508.12, *infiltrate* 706.13, *insert* 710.9, *imply* 844.14

insinuated *inserted* 710.5, *tacit* 844.10

insinuate oneself *fawn* 401.9, *be sycophantic* 439.15

insinuating *informative* 170.10, *defamatory* 440.9, *motivational* 508.7, *tacit* 844.10

insinuatingly *influentially* 508.13

insinuation *inside information* 170.4, *aspersion* 440.4, *accusation* 442.1, *inroad* 706.3, *insertion* 710.1, *quietness* 844.4

insipid *unemphatic* 201.2, *tasteless* 220.4, *drained of color* 252.6, *boring* 296.6, *insufficient* 517.11

insipidity *lack of emphasis* 201.1, *tastelessness* 220.1, *boringness* 296.2

insipidly *without taste* 220.8, *boringly* 296.10, *weakly* 517.14

insipidness *tastelessness* 220.1

insist 376.14; *persuade* 178.15, *be assertive* 189.28, *emphasize* 200.6, *be obstinate* 359.10, *compel* 428.8, *request* 505.10

insistence *persuasion* 178.1, *emphasis* 200.1, *tenacity* 376.4, *perseverance* 377.1, *request* 505.1, *importance* 799.1

insistent *emphatic* 200.3, *drumming* 235.6, *tenacious* 376.9, *persevering* 377.6, *requesting* 505.7

insistently *emphatically* 200.7, *repeatedly* 235.15, *demandingly* 356.12, *by request* 505.14

insisting *persuasive* 178.12

insist on *demand* 356.9, 425.11, *contend* 422.22, *compel* 428.8

insist on *or* **claim one's pound of flesh** *have no mercy* 309.6

insist on one's rights *have rights* 429.13

in situ *where* 565.12, *geographically* 573.11, *on the spot* 575.20

in slavery *obediently* 69.12, *dependently* 832.13

in slight measure *by degrees* 739.10

in slow motion 693.15

insobriety *drunkenness* 121.3

insolate *bake* 560.19

insolated *baked* 560.14

insolation *drying* 560.3

insolence 400.1; *arrogance* 297.2, *answer* 334.1, *bad manners* 411.2, *defiance* 416.1, *disrespect* 436.1

insolent 400.8; *arrogant* 297.9, *answering* 334.11, *insolent person* 400.7, *bad-mannered* 411.6, *defiant* 416.5, *disrespectful* 436.9

insolently 400.18; *arrogantly* 297.18, *in answer* 334.25, *rudely* 411.9, *defiantly* 416.9, *disrespectfully* 436.25

insolent person 400.7; *discourteous person* 411.4

in solitary [Inf] *imprisoned* 55.9

insoluble *numerable* 6.70, *unexplained* 364.6, *condensed* 540.7

insolubly *densely* 540.10

in solution *liquefied* 555.19

insolvable *numerable* 6.70

insolvency 486.2, 490.5, 846.6; *incompleteness* 98.2, *financial loss* 468.4, *ruin* 523.4

insolvent 486.10; *unprofitable* 468.10, *poor person* 486.6, *debtor* 488.6, *unable to pay* 488.8,

nonpaying 490.7, loser 846.9, failed 846.10
insolvent debtor nonpayer 490.6
insolvently 488.11; without paying 490.15, unsuccessfully 846.21
in some degree to a degree 739.11
in some measure to a degree 739.11, partly 760.17
in someone's bad books estranged 63.8
in someone's black book estranged 63.8
in someone's employ obediently 69.12
in someone's pay obediently 69.12
in someone's wake together 794.20
in some sense meaningfully 361.16
in some way (or other) how 691.16
insomnia mood disorder 108.12, restlessness 414.7
insomniac sick person 114.22
insouciance indifference 289.1, lack of wonder 295.1, incuriosity 322.1, negligence 326.1, ease of manner 823.4
insouciant indifferent 289.7, wonderless 295.3, incurious 322.3, negligent 326.4
insouciantly indifferently 289.17, without wonder 295.8
in spasms jerkily 684.29
in spate flooded 570.8
inspect 242.22; care for 325.12, question 333.16, estimate 341.11
inspect accounts audit 493.10
inspected questioned 333.15
inspection observation 242.5, watchfulness 325.5, questioning 333.2, judgment 341.1
inspection of accounts accounting 493.1
inspection of books accounting 493.1
inspector manager 126.7, observer 242.15, questioner 333.9, judge 341.5
inspector of accounts accountant 493.6
inspectorship position of authority 52.4
inspiration 360.2; minor deity 82.2, emphasis 200.1, encouragement 284.6, creative thought 317.3, way of thinking 317.4, intuition 320.1, imagination 327.8, invention 345.4, intelligence 352.2, method 387.4, spontaneity 396.2, motivation 508.1, influence 512.1, vigor 518.1, production 522.1, respiration 558.8, cause 675.1, intake 708.5
inspirational intuitive 266.10, appealing 512.9, causal 675.7
inspirationally wisely 4.28, imaginatively 327.21, influentially 508.13, 512.14, causally 675.12
inspiration from the Muse inspiration 360.2
inspire 327.15; motivate 178.17, 508.9, give courage 284.16, be irresistible 428.9, invigorate 518.5, respire 558.21, awaken 675.9, draw in 708.18
inspire awe be wondrous 294.14
inspired persuadable 178.14, emphatic 200.3, intuitive 320.6, ideational 327.9, imaginative 360.10, spontaneous 396.5, motivated 508.8
inspire hope 281.14

inspirer motivator 178.11, first cause 675.6
inspire respect command respect 435.18
inspiring encouraging 284.13, compelling 428.6, appealing 512.9, invigorating 518.3, causal 675.7
inspiringly wisely 4.28, causally 675.12
inspirit give courage 284.16, inspire 327.15, motivate 508.9, give moral support 605.18
inspissate be dense 540.8, viscous 561.14, thicken 561.21
inspissation viscosity 561.1
in spite bitterly 306.16
in spite of in disagreement 463.12, counter 510.8, additionally 748.15, difficultly 824.23
in spite of oneself unwillingly 375.17
in spitting distance nearby 586.17
in spots where 565.12, irregularly 664.6, discontinuously 775.15, in ones and twos 796.10
in spring seasonally 654.12
instability deformation 14.16, capriciousness 381.2, weakness 517.1, transience 643.1, irregularity 664.1, changeableness 666.1, inconsistency 732.3, vulnerability 811.6, unreliability 841.7
install 710.15; launch 405.14, situate 573.10, introduce 708.16, inaugurate 771.31, enroll 771.33, commission 833.8
install or **instal** locate 565.9
installation plant 124.7, placing 565.4, bringing in 708.4, inauguration 771.6, enrollment 771.8, commission 833.1
installed located 565.6, enrolled 771.24
installment borrowed 476.8, type of payment 489.3, part of writing 760.6, commission 833.1
installment buying borrowing 476.1, credit 476.4, 487.1
installment loan loan 475.2
installment plan credit 476.4, 487.1
installment plan payment type of payment 489.3
Instamatic™ camera 132.10
instance occurrence 726.2, circumstantiate 726.12
instance of inversion act of inversion 608.3
instant 645.3; ready-made 388.13, active 414.13, time period 641.2, short duration 643.3, point in time 645.4, immediate 645.5, present 647.4
instantaneity immediacy 645.1, swiftness 694.1
instantaneous immediate 645.5, swift 694.6
instantaneously right away 429.20, immediately 645.8, hurryingly 694.18
instantaneousness immediacy 645.1, swiftness 694.1
instant coffee coffee 93.6
instant dislike dislike 291.1
instantly right away 429.20, immediately 645.8
instate install 710.15, commission 833.8
instatement bringing in 708.4, commission 833.1
in statu quo [L] permanently 667.6
instatutory unlawful 53.23

instead 672.8; answerably 334.28, in place of 574.21
instead of instead 672.8
in step agreeing 462.6, synchronized 649.5, synchronously 649.9, conforming 781.8
instigate motivate 178.17, 508.9, inaugurate 675.10, 771.31
instigate lawlessness be anarchic 51.8
instigating motivational 508.7
instigation cause 675.1, inauguration 771.6
instigative motivational 508.7, inaugural 771.21
instigator motivator 178.11, 508.6, producer 522.10, first cause 675.6
instigatory inaugural 771.21
instill educate 48.22, inject 710.10, mix 751.12, assimilate 781.14
instillation mixture 751.1
instinct 318.3, 320.4; aptitude 127.4, 513.3, impression 266.2, basis of supposition 359.2, spontaneity 396.2
instinctive 318.8, 320.8; involuntary 95.15, intuitive 266.10, spontaneous 396.5
instinctive dislike dislike 291.1
instinctive feeling impression 266.2
instinctively involuntarily 95.23, mentally 315.13, thoughtlessly 318.15, intuitively 320.11, spontaneously 396.8
instinctiveness involuntariness 95.9, instinct 318.3, spontaneity 396.2
instinctual instinctive 320.8
institute type of school 48.12, association 480.8, produce 522.13, inaugurate 675.10, 771.31, enroll 771.33
instituted established 397.12
institute legal proceedings litigate 54.27
institute of higher learning university 48.14
institution law 53.1, ordination 84.3, custom 397.4, association 480.8, inauguration 771.6
institutional building building 551.9
institutionalization habituation 397.7
institutionalized established 397.12
institutionally cliquishly 59.32
institutionary inaugural 771.21
in stock provisioning 89.6, available 105.16, on sale 482.24
in storage saved 105.15
in store in hand 388.11, possessed 469.13
in strips in layers 588.11
instruct educate 48.22, master 68.17, inform 70.11, communicate 176.10, explain 331.16, cause to know 348.13, brief 388.20, command 425.10, moralize 431.14, assimilate 781.14, display 843.13
instructable educatable 48.18
instructed expert 127.12, knowledgeable 348.7, prepared 388.9, directed 697.9
instructing directing 697.12
instruction education 48.1, information 170.1, communication 176.3, learning 348.3, briefing 388.4, command 425.1, directions 697.7, guide 780.4
instructional educational 48.17, informative 170.10

instructions explanation 331.3, directions 697.7
instructions to the jury closing arguments 54.17
instructive educational 48.17, informative 170.10, advisory 176.7, punitive 454.18, influential 512.8, warning 814.6
instructively educationally 48.25, advisorily 176.12, warningly 814.11
instructor educator 48.4, educational leader 68.11, air force person 77.31, informer 170.8, demonstrator 331.6
instructorship 48.5
instrument 511.2; instrumentality 102.2, tool 103.1, agent 123.15, sycophant 401.3, nonentity 800.8, help 825.1
instrumental 142.8, 511.4, 801.7; mechanical 103.7, musical 141.11, experimental 335.8, used 393.5, causal 511.5, helping 825.16
instrumental aid 142.7
instrumental group 141.3
instrumentalism Philosophical Schools of Thought 4, experimentation 335.3
instrumentalist Philosophical Schools of Thought 4, player 141.2
instrumentality 102.2, 511.1, 801.3
instrumentally 103.9, 511.9; musically 141.20, usefully 393.15
instrumental music making Hobbies and Pastimes 167
instrumentation harmonics 140.13, instrumentality 511.1
instrument landing system (ILS) flight control 689.7
instrument of execution 454.15
instrument of punishment 454.13
instrument of torture 454.14
in style liked 290.6, fashionable 536.5, in good form 725.11
in subjection subject 832.6
insubordinate anarchic 51.5, disobedient 427.10, disrespectful 436.9, defiant 466.7, disorderly 507.6, 766.15
insubordinately anarchically 51.10, disobediently 427.14, disapprovingly 507.10
insubordination anarchy 51.1, disobedience 416.2, 427.1, defiance 466.3
in substance at heart 723.14, on the whole 759.13
insubstantial 539.5; spiritual 86.20, not enough 98.5, invisible 245.3, translucent 249.8, imaginary 360.12, insufficient 517.11, nonmaterial 525.8, sparse 541.3, brittle 548.3, airy 558.12, thinned 595.13, superficial 599.4, unreal 720.8, 722.7, incomplete 762.5, insignificant 800.12, unreliable 841.15
insubstantiality invisibility 245.1, translucency 249.2, immateriality 525.2, sparseness 541.1, thinning 595.6, superficiality 599.2, unreality 722.2, incompleteness 762.1, unimportance 800.1, unreliability 841.7
insubstantialize dematerialize 525.12
insubstantially not enough 98.12, transparently 249.13, metaphysically 525.13, lightly

539.10, *sparsely* 541.6, *fragilely* 548.5, *superficially* 599.8, *unreally* 722.15, *incompletely* 762.10, *unreliably* 841.25

insubstantial person 720.5

insubstantial thing *weak thing* 517.5

in succession *sequentially* 770.13, *consecutively* 774.15

insufferable *detested* 291.11

insufferably *distastefully* 291.19

insufficience *inequality* 741.1

insufficiency 98.1; *reasoning* 6.61, *need* 95.4, *nonperformance* 466.2, *financial loss* 468.4, *inadequacy* 486.5, *absence* 576.1, *inequality* 741.1, *deficiency* 745.2, *omission* 762.4, *incompleteness* 806.2, *decline* 846.5

insufficient 98.4, 517.11; *unskillful* 128.4, *disappointing* 293.6, *unsatisfactory* 438.15, *nonperforming* 466.6, *unprofitable* 468.10, *inadequate* 486.13, *unequal* 741.4, *partial* 760.11, *incomplete* 762.5, 806.6, *failed* 846.10

insufficient diet *short rations* 118.3

insufficient evidence *evidence* 54.15

insufficient food *scarcity* 90.5

insufficient funds *insolvency* 486.2, *amount owing* 488.5

insufficient income *poverty* 486.1

insufficiently 98.11; *disappointingly* 293.12, *inattentively* 466.13, *at a loss* 468.22, *inadequately* 486.19, *weakly* 517.14, *unequally* 741.10, *incompletely* 762.10, *imperfectly* 806.10, *unsuccessfully* 846.21

insular *discriminatory* 337.11, *unjust* 342.7, *regional* 564.12, *local* 564.14, *of landmasses* 572.12, *nonconforming* 728.10, *unjoined* 753.9, *alone* 788.15

insularism *prejudice* 337.3

insularity *unfair treatment* 342.4, *separateness* 724.3, *nonconformity* 728.4, *setting apart* 753.2, *exclusiveness* 764.4, *aloneness* 788.5

insularly *continentally* 572.13, *individualistically* 728.20

insulate *conduct* 14.51, *make ceramics* 129.10, *heat* 217.17, *muffle* 229.11, *protect* 613.26, 810.21, *set apart* 753.17

insulated *heated* 217.15, *cooled* 218.11, *protected* 613.20

insulating material *nonconductor* 14.35

insulation 10.36; *nonconductor* 14.35, *heater* 217.3, *protective covering* 613.5, *preservation of provisions* 815.6

insulator *electrical conduction* 10.33, *insulation* 10.36, *nonconductor* 14.35

insulin *Human Hormones* 12

insulin shock therapy *psychiatric treatment* 108.3

insult 400.6, 436.5, 436.21; *quarrel* 272.9, *offense* 302.2, *offend* 302.15, *answer back* 334.19, *disdain* 400.16, *act of discourtesy* 411.3, *be discourteous* 411.7, *act of defiance* 416.3, *be insubordinate* 416.8, *wrong* 430.19, *scorn* 440.5, *impairment* 808.7

insulted *offended* 302.9

insulting 436.10; *maddening*

302.12, *derisive* 400.12, *defiant* 416.5, *defamatory* 440.9

insultingly *maddeningly* 302.25, *derisively* 400.22, *defiantly* 416.9

in sum *one and all* 759.12

in summary *shortly* 591.12

in summer *seasonally* 654.12

insuperability *hopelessness* 837.2

insuperable *hopeless* 837.6

insuperably *hopelessly* 837.12

in support *intimately* 62.14, *justifyingly* 441.15

insurable *given* 472.8

insurance 810.10; *precaution* 287.4, *promise* 464.2, *guarantee* 840.4

insurance agent *coverer* 613.18

insurance certificate *certificate* 185.2

insurance papers *certificate* 185.2

insurance policy *precaution* 287.4, *purchase contract* 459.3, *promise* 464.2

insurance spraying *cultivation* 16.7

insure *take precautions* 287.14, *be prepared* 388.17, *guarantee* 458.13, *promise* 464.10, *certify* 464.11, *make certain* 840.14

insured *guaranteed* 464.6, 840.10, *safe* 810.16

insured mail *postal service* 169.5

insurer *coverer* 613.18

insurgence *resistance movement* 417.3, *revolution* 427.4

insurgency *revolution* 427.4, *disorder* 507.2

insurgent *lawless* 53.26, *resisting* 417.8, *seditionist* 427.7, *subversive* 427.11, *disorderly* 507.6

insurmountability *hopelessness* 837.2

insurmountable *hopeless* 837.6

insurmountable debt *insolvency* 490.5

insurmountably *hopelessly* 837.12

insurrection *act of defiance* 416.3, *resistance movement* 417.3, *revolution* 427.4, *disorder* 507.2

insurrectional *subversive* 427.11

insurrectionary *subversive* 427.11, *disorderly* 507.6

insurrectionist *seditionist* 427.7

in suspense 604.12, 604.21; *fearful* 283.10, *expecting* 356.4, *expectantly* 356.10, *inertly* 519.5

in suspension *liquefied* 555.19

in swarms *in crowds* 795.14

in sworn testimony *assuredly* 189.30

in sympathy *pityingly* 308.11

in sync [Inf] *synchronized* 649.5, *synchronously* 649.9, *in harmony* 735.32

intact *virginal* 67.7, *uncut* 759.7, *complete* 761.6, 805.14, *safe* 810.16, *preserved* 815.12

intaglio *relief carving* 144.2

intake 708.5; *influx* 706.2, *entrant* 706.7

intangibility *immateriality* 525.2, *littleness* 580.1, *unreality* 720.1, 722.2

intangible *spiritual* 86.20, *propertied* 470.9, *nonmaterial* 525.8, *little* 580.7, *unreal* 720.8, 722.7

intangible assets *personal estate* 470.6

intangibleness *unreality* 722.2

intangibles *personal estate* 470.6

intangibly *metaphysically* 525.13, *infinitesimally* 580.13, *unreally* 722.15

intarsia *decorative woodwork* 131.2

in tatters *destroyed* 523.9, *worn* 808.13

in Technicolor™ *colorfully* 251.19

integer *real number* 6.5, *whole thing* 759.2, *kind of number* 783.2, *one* 788.1

integers *numbers* 738.5

integral 723.7; *differentiation* 6.29, *numerical* 6.68, *functional* 6.73, *whole* 759.6, 788.12, *complete* 761.6, *fractional* 783.8, *mathematical* 784.9

integral calculus *calculus* 6.28

integral equation *equation* 6.25, *differentiation* 6.29

integrality *whole* 759.1, *completeness* 761.1

integrally *wholly* 759.11, 788.22

integral part *component* 760.3

integral sign *mathematical symbol* 6.11

integrant *component* 760.3

integrate *evaluate* 6.90, *equalize* 740.12, *mix* 751.12, *mix together* 751.14, *combine* 757.9, *be whole* 759.9, *complete* 761.9, *include* 763.5, *add* 784.11, *become one* 788.18

integrated *integral* 723.7, *mixed* 751.8, *combined* 757.5, *whole* 759.6, *included* 763.4

integrated circuit *semiconductor* 10.34, *circuit* 14.37, *little thing* 580.3

integration *differentiation* 6.29, *mixture* 751.1, *combination* 757.1, *whole* 759.1, *inclusion* 763.1, *calculation* 784.1, *association* 827.6

integrative *combinatory* 757.6

integrity *truthfulness* 191.1, *rightfulness* 429.1, *morals* 431.2, *virtue* 447.1, *whole* 759.1, *completeness* 761.1, *oneness* 788.3

integument *body covering* 19.4, *exteriority* 610.2, *casing* 613.9

integumental *covering* 613.21

integumentary *covering* 610.8

intellect 315.1, 348.4; *intelligence* 315.2, 352.2, *intellectual* 315.7, *reason* 319.1, *internal* 525.6

intellectual 315.7, 315.8; *sage* 4.11, *educated* 48.19, *expert* 52.8, 52.12, 127.9, *educational leader* 68.11, *professional worker* 123.11, *skilled person* 127.7, *thoughtful* 317.5, *reasoning* 317.6, 319.7, *reasoner* 319.5, *educational* 327.9, *knowledgeable person* 348.5, *literate* 348.8, *wise person* 352.3, *wise* 352.4

intellectualism *intellect* 315.1, *intelligence* 352.2

intellectuality *learnedness* 48.8, *intellect* 315.1

intellectualize *rationalize* 4.20, *think* 317.9

intellectually *philosophically* 4.23, *studiously* 48.26, *expertly* 52.21, *mentally* 315.13, *knowledgeably* 348.14

intellectually subnormal 316.7

intellectually weak *lacking intellect* 316.5

intellectual weakness *lack of intellect* 316.1

intelligence 315.2, 352.2; *educatability* 48.9, *navy specialties* 77.24, *air force commands* 77.28, *rationality* 109.2, *information* 170.1, *news* 171.1, *communication* 176.3, *intellect* 315.1, 348.4, *reason* 319.1, *evidence* 339.1, *ability* 514.3, *mental sharpness*

549.9, *warning* 814.1, *cunning* 822.1

intelligence and security *army commands* 77.13

intelligence quotient or **IQ** *intelligence* 315.2, *ability* 514.3

intelligence quotient test Intelligence Tests 108

intelligence service *secretiveness* 182.3

intelligence staff *military staff* 58.5

intelligence testing *psychometrics* 108.5

intelligent 315.9, 352.5; *educatable* 48.18, *rational* 109.4, *skillful* 127.10, *reasoning* 317.6, 319.7, *mentally sharp* 549.14, *cunning* 822.4

intelligent anticipation *foresight* 357.1

intelligent character recognition (ICR) *character recognition* 15.20

intelligently 315.14, 352.9; *studiously* 48.26, *skillfully* 127.16, *sharply* 549.19

intelligentsia *academia* 348.6

intelligibility 363.1; *rationality* 109.2, *clarity* 196.1, *type of meaning* 361.4, *unpretentiousness* 526.2, *simplicity* 823.2

intelligible 363.5; *rational* 109.4, *clear* 196.2, *meaningful* 361.6, *well-ordered* 765.14, *easy* 823.9, *identifiable* 843.10

intelligibly 363.13; *clearly* 196.4, *meaningfully* 361.16, *simply* 526.14

intemperance *immoderation* 99.2, *gluttony* 119.1, *drinking* 121.2, *extravagance* 194.3, *overindulgence* 456.3, *excessiveness* 712.4, *liberality* 829.8

intemperate *gluttonous* 119.3, *drunken* 121.28, *extravagant* 194.9, *overindulgent* 456.8, *violent* 520.5, *unconditional* 829.14

intemperately *excessively* 194.17, *829.23, self-indulgently* 456.12

in tempo *tunefully* 140.30

intend 361.15, 374.8, 650.10; *be inclined toward* 290.10, *aim* 327.17, *expect* 356.6, *mean* 361.13, *will* 372.11, *resolve* 376.12, *predetermine* 384.8, *predestine* 384.9

intended *meant* 359.7, 361.12, *intentional* 374.7, *predetermined* 384.4, *predestined* 384.6, *planned* 387.10

intended [Inf] *loved one* 299.13, *someone promised* 458.7

intend for 374.11

intending 374.6; *tending to* 513.4

intending evil or **harm** *malicious* 306.8

intendment *intention* 374.1

intense 598.16; *serious* 200.5, *colorful* 251.11, *passionate* 266.12, *strong* 516.9, *vigorous* 518.2, *violent* 520.5

intensely 598.28; *with feeling* 266.18, *acutely* 516.18

intensification 746.2; *aggravation* 276.1, *denseness* 594.2

intensified *aggravated* 276.3, *dense* 594.6, *increased* 746.5

intensify 746.8; *aggravate* 276.5, *invigorate* 518.5, *thicken* 594.9, *deepen* 598.21

intensifying *deepening* 598.14

intensity *seismic activity* 8.24, *emphasis* 200.1, *hue* 251.4,

emotion 266.3, potency 516.6, vigor 518.1, violence 520.1, deepness 598.6, degree 739.1
intensive word 5.17, part of speech 5.30, worded 5.38, of grammar 5.41
intensive care unit (ICU) hospital 107.16
intensive farming agriculture 16.1
intensively lexically 5.46
intensive therapy or **care** treatment 107.14
intent earnest 278.5, point 361.5, will 372.1, intention 374.1, declaration 376.2, aim 773.12
intention 374.1; motive 178.5, aspiration 281.3, inclination 290.2, plan 327.3, 387.1, type of meaning 361.4, point 361.5, will 372.1, declaration 376.2, predetermination 384.1, predestination 384.2, venture 390.2, betrothal 458.2, motivation 508.1, aim 773.12
intentional 374.7; purposive 327.11, willed 372.6, deliberate 384.5, planned 387.10
intentional bias final intention 374.4
intentional grounding penalty 155.13
intentionality 374.2
intentionally 374.13; purposively 327.20, as planned 387.16
intentional untruth falsehood 192.6
intentional walk or **pass** pitching terms 147.5
intentions conduct 399.1
intently resolutely 376.15
intentness assiduity 414.8
intent on intending 374.6
intent upon resolute 376.7
inter bury 31.10, conceal 181.12, immerse 710.12
interact 10.73; socialize 2.14, react 334.20, be sociable 414.22, interface 616.5, correspond to 727.10, reciprocate 729.7, 827.13
interacting symmetrical 626.4, interrelated 727.7, reciprocity 729.1, reciprocal 729.4
interaction 616.2; social environment 2.4, question and answer 334.3, action 412.1, social activity 414.2, joint operation 509.2, symmetry 626.1, interrelatedness 727.3, reciprocity 729.1, mutual relationship 827.3
interactive sociological 2.11, reactive 334.12, acting 412.9, active 414.13, interfacial 616.4, joint 827.10
interactive film movie type 137.3
interactively sociologically 2.15, in answer 334.25, interfacially 616.7
interalliance interrelatedness 727.3
interallied interrelated 727.7
interassociate correspond to 727.10
interassociated interrelated 727.7
interassociation interrelatedness 727.3
interbraiding spinning 130.4
interbred mixed 751.8
interbreed mix 751.12, mix together 751.14
interbreeding mixture 751.1
INTERCAL Programming Languages 15
intercalary interim 639.11
intercalate react 11.38, insert 710.9
intercalated interim 639.11, inserted 710.5

intercalation chemical compound 11.4, insertion 710.1
intercalative inserted 710.5
intercaste marriage type of marriage 64.3
intercede mediate 75.6, 772.19, pray 85.20, protest 507.7, advise 825.27
intercede for be an instrument 511.7
interceder mediator 75.2
intercept graph 6.30, hinder 826.15
intercepted pass play 155.8
interception play 155.8, hindrance 826.1
interceptor military aircraft 77.30
intercession mediation 75.1, protest 507.1, instrumentality 511.1, support 825.2
intercession or **intercessory prayer** prayer 85.10
intercessional mediatory 75.5, causal 511.5
intercessor mediator 75.2, negotiator 460.4, middleman 772.7
intercessory mediatory 75.5
interchange question and answer 334.3, react 334.20, transfer of property 470.4, transfer property 470.12, crossroads 609.4, cross 609.9, exchange 665.8, 665.21, 673.1, 673.5, substitute 672.5, move 677.15, transfer 685.1, 685.8, interrelatedness 727.3, reciprocity 729.1, reciprocate 729.7, equalization 740.4, linkage 752.3
interchangeability equivalence 730.3, equalization 740.4
interchangeable vague 338.9, exchangeable 665.13, in exchange 673.3, transferable 685.7, equivalent 730.9
interchangeably in answer 334.25, interweavingly 609.11, in exchange 673.6, in transit 685.13, equivalently 730.20
interchanged exchanged 673.4, interrelated 727.7, reciprocal 729.4, correlative 729.6
interchanging crossing 609.7, reciprocal 729.4
intercollegiate rowing 150.27
intercollegiate rowing rowing 150.14
Intercollegiate Soccer Football Association of America soccer associations and awards 163.6
Intercollegiate Yacht Racing Association (IYRA) yacht racing associations 150.7
intercolumniation column 134.6
intercom dial 169.12
intercommunicate 754.15; negotiate 460.6, meet 586.15, link 752.18
intercommunicating meeting 586.10
intercommunication conversation 210.1, sociability 408.1, negotiation 460.1, meeting 586.5, interweaving 609.1, interrelatedness 727.3, linkage 752.3, association 754.2
intercommunicative negotiated 460.5
intercommunion sociability 408.1
interconnect join 609.10, correspond to 727.10, interrelate 729.8, link 752.18, connect 754.13
interconnected interrelated 727.7, 729.5, connected 754.11
interconnected circuits circuit 10.43

interconnectedness symmetry 626.1
interconnecting crossing 609.7
interconnection interaction 616.2, interrelatedness 727.3, interrelation 729.2, linkage 752.3, connection 754.1, means of connection 754.4
interconnective connective 754.10
intercontinental strategic 78.16
intercontinental ballistic missile (ICBM) modern missile weapon 78.4
intercourse social environment 2.4, conversation 210.1, interrelatedness 727.3, linkage 752.3, association 754.2
intercrop interweave 609.8
interdependence symmetry 626.1, interrelatedness 727.3, interrelation 729.2
interdependent symmetrical 626.4, interrelated 727.7, 729.5
interdependently relevantly 727.12, interrelatedly 729.11
interdict reject 383.10, command 425.1, 425.10, demand 425.11, prohibition 503.1, prohibit 503.8, dissent 506.2, 506.9, debar 604.17, exclude 764.7, restraint 830.1, restrain 830.12, restrain someone 830.17
interdict or **interdiction** demand 425.2
interdicted commanding 425.7, excluded 604.11
interdiction rejection 383.1, prohibition 503.1, dissent 506.2, debarment 604.5, exclusion 764.1, hindrance 826.1
interdictive prohibited 503.5, dissenting 506.6, restraining 830.8
interdictively prohibitively 503.11, uncooperatively 506.11, restrainedly 830.18
interdictory excluded 604.11, excluding 764.5
interdigitate interweave 609.8
interdigitated interwoven 609.6
interdigitation interweaving 609.1
interdisciplinary education subject 48.3
interest 488.4; be piquant 221.9, curiosity 321.1, topic 328.1, activity 385.4, social activity 414.2, claim 429.3, welfare 445.2, profit 467.6, money received 492.2, influence 508.11, 512.1, produce 522.5, relate to 727.9, extra 748.6, importance 799.1, be important 799.13
interest-bearing productive 522.11
interested curious 321.5
interesting stimulating 221.7, problematic 328.7
interestingly stimulatingly 221.11, problematically 328.12
interest oneself in be sociable 414.22
interest rate finance 457.1
interest rates economic factor 56.8
interface 616.1, 616.5; computing terms 15.22, program 15.29, adjoin 216.11, meeting 586.5, meet 586.15, layer 588.9, intercommunicate 754.15
interfaced coated 588.7, connected 754.11
interfacer 616.3
interfacial 616.4
interfacially 616.7
interfacing contiguous 216.8, meeting 586.10, coat 588.3
interfaith mixed 751.8

interfaith marriage type of marriage 64.3, mixed thing 751.2
interfere exhibit penalty behavior 155.21, play field hockey 158.10, be active in 412.17, meddle 414.23, prohibit 503.8, debar 604.17, disrupt 768.12, interrupt 775.14, hinder 826.15
interfered with disrupted 768.8
interference wave property 10.12, batting terms 147.6, ice hockey tactics 158.4, field hockey tactics 158.5, radio reception 172.2, broadcast dissonance 241.3, that which makes invisible 245.2, overactivity 414.9, prohibition 503.1, obstruction 510.3, debarment 604.5, wavelength 683.5, disruption 768.4, hindrance 826.1
interferer meddler 414.12, hinderer 826.11
interfere with counteract 510.7, change for the worse 665.18, mix 751.12
interfere with [Brit] seduce 432.16
interfering overactivity 414.9, meddling 414.17, counteracting 510.6, causal 511.5, excluded 604.11, hindering 826.12
interfering so-and-so hinderer 826.11
interferometer Fields of Measurement 589
interferometry microscopy 10.68, Fields of Measurement 589
interferon protein 12.9, medicine 115.2
interfile interweave 609.8
interfuse interweave 609.8
interfusion interweaving 609.1, mixture 751.1
intergalactic astronomical 7.33, extensive 563.12
intergalactically astronomically 7.36, extensively 563.18
intergalactic space empty space 563.2
interglacial glaciation 8.46, glaciated 8.62, climatic change 9.37, interim 639.11
interglaciation climatic change 9.37
interim 639.11; interval 639.4, 775.2, occasional 647.5, pause 668.3, ease 819.1
interim period pause 668.3
interior 611.1, 611.7; space 6.33, type of painting 143.5, inland 611.8, included 763.4, middle 772.1, 772.9
interior, the inland 611.2
interior angle angle 6.37
interior decorating interior decoration 532.4
interior decoration 532.4
interior decorator decorator 532.8
interior design interior decoration 532.4
interior designer decorator 532.8
interiority interior 611.1, quietness 844.4
interior light safety light 246.7
interior monologue aspect of fiction 139.5, soliloquy 211.1
interior part interior 611.1
interjacence admittance 708.1
interject speak 205.17, answer back 334.19, insert 710.9, 748.12, interrupt 775.14
interjected retaliatory 334.13
interjecting retaliatory 334.13
interjection part of speech 5.30,

760.7, *utterance* 205.10, *salutation* 209.2, *counterstatement* 334.5, *admittance* 708.1, *insertion* 710.1, *addition* 748.1, *intervention* 775.5

interjectional *or* **interjectory** *of grammar* 5.41

interlace *interweave* 609.8, *mix* 751.12, *intertwine* 752.19

interlaced *interwoven* 609.6, *mixed* 751.8

interlacedly *interweavingly* 609.11

interlaced scanning *television set* 172.6

interlacement *interweaving* 609.1

interlacing *weaving* 130.6, *interweaving* 609.1, *interrelatedness* 727.3

interlard *mix* 751.12

interlay *interweave* 609.8, *mix* 751.12

interleave *mix* 732.12, 751.12

interline *stuff* 577.12, *layer* 588.9, *interweave* 609.8

interlineally *interweavingly* 609.11

interlineate *stuff* 577.12

interlineation *interweaving* 609.1, *additional item* 748.3

interlined *coated* 588.7

interlining *stuffing* 577.4, *layer* 588.1

interlink *join* 609.10, *correspond to* 727.10, *interrelate* 729.8

interlinkage *interrelatedness* 727.3

interlinked *interrelated* 727.7, 729.5

interlock *interweave* 609.8, *correspond to* 727.10, *unify* 752.15, *intertwine* 752.19

interlocking *interweaving* 609.1, *linkage* 752.3

interlock stitch *knitting* 130.7

interlocute *react* 334.20

interlocution *philosophical argument* 4.5, *conversation* 210.1, *interview* 210.4, *question and answer* 334.3

interlocutor *speaker* 205.12, *conversationalist* 210.6, *questioner* 333.9, *answerer* 334.10

interlocutory *conversing* 210.8, *reactive* 334.12

interlope *be external* 724.15

interloper *intruder* 724.7

interloping *externality* 724.4, *external* 724.11

interlude *dramatic style* 136.3, *play part* 136.8, *historic comedy* 136.12, *interval* 639.4, *pause* 668.3, *additional item* 748.3

interlunar *interim* 639.11

intermarriage *type of marriage* 64.3, *mixture* 751.1

intermarried *mixed* 751.8

intermarry *marry* 64.19, *mix together* 751.14

intermeddle *meddle* 414.23

intermeddler *meddler* 414.12

intermediacy *instrumentality* 511.1

intermediary *pacifier* 73.7, *mediator* 75.2, *delegated* 79.4, *agent* 80.3, *deputizing* 80.4, *speaker* 205.12, *negotiator* 460.4, *assistant* 511.3, *interfacer* 616.3, *interfacial* 616.4, *medium* 742.6, *person who joins* 752.9, *middleman* 772.7, *mediatory* 772.11

intermediate *mediate* 75.6, 772.19, *ski* 162.27, *causal* 511.5, *be an instrument* 511.7, *central* 612.6, *interim* 639.11, *medium* 742.6, *mediatory* 772.11

intermediate bond *chemical bond* 11.6

intermediate-level waste *nuclear problem* 10.62

intermediately *mediatorially* 75.7, *centrally* 612.12, *medianly* 742.12, *midway* 772.22

intermediateness *instrumentality* 511.1

intermediate rock *igneous rock* 8.32

intermediate run *ski run* 162.2

intermediate technology *manufacture* 522.2

intermediation *mediation* 75.1

intermediator *mediator* 75.2

intermedin *Human Hormones* 12

interment *burial* 31.1, *destruction* 186.2, *immersion* 710.3

intermeshed *interrelated* 727.7

intermeshing *interrelatedness* 727.3

intermetallic *chemical compound* 11.4

intermezzo *play part* 136.8, *Musical Forms* 140, *additional item* 748.3

interminability *longness* 590.3, *infinity* 798.1

interminable *lengthy* 590.9, *continuing forever* 644.6, *protracted* 669.7, *continuous* 774.9, *infinite* 798.5

interminably *at length* 590.15, *continually* 669.10, *infinitely* 798.10

intermingle *socialize* 2.14, *interweave* 609.8, *mix* 751.12

intermingled *indiscriminate* 338.8, *mixed* 751.8

intermingling *mixture* 751.1

intermission *play part* 136.8, *intervening space* 563.8, *interval* 587.1, 639.4, 775.2, *interruption* 604.4, *pause* 668.3

intermissive *interrupted* 604.10

intermit *interrupt* 604.16, *be regular* 663.10, *be irregular* 664.5

intermitted *interrupted* 604.10

intermittence *infrequency* 662.1, *irregularity* 664.1, *discontinuity* 775.1, *rarity* 796.4

intermittence *or* **intermittency** *interruption* 604.4

intermittent *interrupted* 604.10, *periodic* 639.10, 641.8, *infrequent* 662.2, *irregular* 664.3, *discontinuous* 775.7, *sparse* 796.6

intermittent explosive disorder *impulse-control disorder* 108.16

intermittently *interruptedly* 604.20, *sometimes* 639.19, *infrequently* 662.4, *irregularly* 664.6, *discontinuously* 775.15, *capriciously* 841.26

intermittent showers *or* **rain** *rain* 9.27

intermittingly *interruptedly* 604.20

intermix *mix* 732.12, 751.12

intermixed *mixed* 751.8

intermixedly *mixedly* 751.16

intermixture *mixture* 751.1

intermodal transportation *transportation* 686.1

intern *educator* 48.4, *imprison* 55.11, 454.23, *doctor* 107.19, *enclose* 584.16, *detain* 830.16

internal 19.23, 525.11, 611.9; *medical* 107.28, *private* 245.5, *interior* 611.7, *visceral* 611.10, *intrinsic* 611.11, *middle* 772.9

internal bleeding *symptom* 114.3

internal-combustion *engine type* 14.11

internal energy *thermodynamics* 10.30, *energy* 514.7

internal examination *health care* 107.7

internal friction *friction* 554.1

internal gear *gear* 14.7

internality *interior* 611.1

internalize *think* 317.9, *keep inside* 611.17, *absorb* 708.19

internally 577.15, 611.18; *invisibly* 245.8, *subjectively* 525.14, *intrinsically* 611.20, *inwardly* 611.21

internal medicine *Medical Specialties* 107, *medicine* 107.1

internalness *interior* 611.1

internal organ 19.13

internal organs *internals* 611.3

internal reflection *optical element* 10.20

internal respiration *respiration* 12.24

Internal Revenue Service (IRS) *tax system* 494.6

internal rhyme *rhyme* 139.11

internals 611.3

internal world 525.6

international *racing* 146.9, *soccer* 163.7, *corporate* 480.17, *dominant* 512.10, *national* 566.10, *universal* 778.10

international 10-square-meter canoe *canoe* 150.9

international agreement *alliance* 459.5, *contract* 462.2, *settlement* 735.6

International Amateur Boxing Association (IABA) *boxing associations* 152.7

International Atomic Energy Agency (IAEA) *nuclear power agencies* 514.11

International Bank for Reconstruction and Development (IBRD) *economic organization* 56.6

International Boxing Federation *boxing associations* 152.7

international candle *Scientific and Technical Units* 589

International Canoe Federation (ICF) *canoe associations* 150.13

International Casting Federation *fishing associations* 154.11

International Challenge Cup *canoe associations* 150.13

International Confederation of Free Trade Unions (ICFTU) *organized labor* 57.5

international corporation *company* 480.7

international date line *limit marker* 620.4

International Date Line *time zone* 646.5

International Development Association *economic organization* 56.6

international economic cooperation agreements *economic zone* 480.4

Internationaler Deutscher Skimarathon in Hirschau *cross-country skiing championships* 162.9

international fair *fair* 483.2

International Federation of Christian Trade Unions (IFCTU) *organized labor* 57.5

international finance 457.2

International Finance

Corporation (IFC) *economic organization* 56.6, *finance* 484.7

International Gothic *or* **International** Furniture Styles 101

International Gothic *or* **International style** Western Art Styles 133, Architectural Styles 134

international government *government* 49.1

International Hockey Board *hockey organizations* 158.7

International Ice Hockey Federation *hockey organizations* 158.7

internationalism 566.5; *political and economic philosophy* 4.6, *generality* 778.1

internationalist 566.9; *political and economic philosopher* 4.10, *philanthropist* 307.5

internationality *internationalism* 566.5

internationalize *generalize* 778.14

international language 5.8

international law *law* 53.1

International Lawn Tennis Challenge Trophy *notable tennis competitions* 165.8

international loan *loan* 475.2

internationally *humanly* 18.18, *influentially* 512.14, *nationally* 566.13, *universally* 778.23

international mail *postal service* 169.5

international market *free market* 483.4

International Measurement System (IMS) racing *competitive sailing* 150.6

International Monetary Fund (IMF) *economic organization* 56.6, *lending institution* 475.4, *finance* 484.7

international nautical mile General Units 589

international pact *alliance* 459.5

international paper *newspaper* 175.2

International Phonetic Alphabet (IPA) *alphabet* 5.16

international police *law enforcement agency* 53.7

International Practical Temperature Scale (IPTS) *scale* 589.9

international racing *automobile racing* 146.1

International Red Cross *charitable organization* 305.4

international relations *political science* 50.2

international sailing *sailing* 150.2

International Shooting Union (ISU) *hunting associations* 160.8

International Skating Union *ice-skating association* 162.21

International Ski Federation (ISF) *skiing associations* 162.13

international society *group* 18.13

International Standard Book Number (ISBN) *book part* 174.5, *means of identification* 184.3

International Standards Organization (ISO) *standard* 589.10

International Standards Organization 7-bit code (ISO-7) *character* 15.18

International Swimming Federation *swimming associations* 164.10

International System of Units *measuring system* 589.4

International Tennis Federation (ITF) *tennis organizations* 165.7

international trade 56.7; *commercial trade* 480.2

international union organization *organized labor* 57.5

International Yacht Racing Union (IYRU) *yacht racing associations* 150.7

internecine *murderous* 30.18, *destructive* 523.8

internecine war *civil war* 76.6

interned *imprisoned* 55.9

internee *prisoner* 55.7, *closed-in person* 584.6

Internet *computer communications* 15.25, *telecommunication* 169.7, *linkage* 752.3

internist *medical specialist* 107.20

internment *imprisonment* 55.4, 454.2, *war measures* 76.18, *detention* 830.5

internment camp *prison* 55.1

internode *stem* 41.5

interpellant *questioning* 333.11

interpellate *question* 333.16

interpellation *salutation* 209.2, *questioning* 333.2

interpellator *conversationalist* 210.6, *questioner* 333.9

interpenetrate *interweave* 609.8, *cooperate* 616.6, *enter* 692.18, *infiltrate* 706.13, *correspond to* 727.10

interpenetration *interweaving* 609.1, *interaction* 616.2, *passage into* 692.4, *inroad* 706.3, *interrelatedness* 727.3

interpenetrative *interfacial* 616.4

interpenetratively *interweavingly* 609.11

interpersonal relations *social environment* 2.4

interphase *cell division* 13.17

interplanetary *astronomical* 7.33

interplanetary space *solar system* 7.14, *empty space* 563.2

interplay *exchange* 673.1, *correspond to* 727.10, *reciprocity* 729.1, *reciprocate* 729.7, 827.13, *mutual relationship* 827.3

interplaying *interrelatedness* 727.3, *reciprocal* 729.4

interplead *litigate* 54.27

Interpol *law enforcement agency* 53.7

interpolate *equate* 6.88, *insert* 710.9, 748.12, *place in the middle* 772.18, *interrupt* 775.14, *add* 784.11

interpolated *inserted* 710.5, *additional* 748.8

interpolation *reasoning* 6.61, *insertion* 710.1, *additional item* 748.3, *piece* 760.2, *intervention* 775.5, *calculation* 784.1

interpolative *inserted* 710.5

interpose *mediate* 75.6, *meddle* 414.23, *be an instrument* 511.7, *insert* 748.12, *come between* 753.21, *place in the middle* 772.18, *interrupt* 775.14, *hinder* 826.15

interposition *mediation* 75.1, *instrumentality* 511.1, *addition* 748.1, *hindrance* 826.1

interpret 365.12; *rationalize* 4.20, *act* 136.34, *play* 141.14, *clarify* 196.3, *name* 202.17, *dissertate*

203.5, *solve* 334.21, *discriminate* 337.12, *make comprehensible* 363.8, *translate* 365.16, *change* 665.14, *cause change* 665.16, *transform* 670.13, *make easy* 823.15, *reveal* 843.14

interpretability *intelligibility* 363.1

interpretable *intelligible* 363.5

interpretation 365.1; *acting* 136.22, *dissertation* 203.1, *solution* 334.6, *discrimination* 337.1, *type of meaning* 361.4, *clarity* 363.2, *alteration* 665.2, *conversion* 670.1

interpretational *solved* 334.15, *discriminating* 337.9, *interpretive* 365.8

interpretative *symbolic* 361.8, *intelligible* 363.5, *interpretive* 365.8

interpretatively *in other words* 365.18

interpret dreams *divine* 86.24, 358.15

interpreted 365.9; *dramatized* 136.32, *solved* 334.15, *judged* 337.10, *simple* 363.6

interpreted language *programming language* 15.16

interpreter 365.6; *system software* 15.13

interpreter of dreams *forecaster* 358.9

interpretive 365.8; *literary* 139.15, *revelatory* 180.7, *symbolic* 183.12, 361.8, *descriptive* 202.11, *intelligible* 363.5

interpretive *or* **interpretative** *dissertational* 203.4

interpretive dancing Dancing Types 135

interpretively *musically* 141.20, *indicatively* 183.21, *in other words* 365.18

interpretively *or* **interpretatively** *discursively* 203.6

interpretive reporting *print journalism* 175.4

interpret literally *be literal* 721.25

interpret news 365.17

interpret the part *rehearse* 136.37

interpret the scriptures *theologize* 81.28

interquartile range *parameter* 6.57

interracial *mixed* 751.8

interracial marriage *type of marriage* 64.3, *mixed thing* 751.2

interred *buried* 31.8, *immersed* 710.7

interregnum *caretaker government* 49.14, *interval* 639.4

interrelate 729.8; *reciprocate* 827.13

interrelated 727.7, 729.5

interrelatedly 729.11

interrelatedness 727.3

interrelating *joint* 827.10

interrelation 729.2; *symmetry* 626.1

interrelationship *interrelation* 729.2

interrogate 333.17; *be curious* 321.7

interrogated *questioned* 333.15

interrogation *interview* 210.4, *questioning* 333.2

interrogation mark Punctuation Marks 5

interrogation point Punctuation Marks 5

interrogative *questioning* 333.11

interrogator *conversationalist* 210.6, *questioner* 333.9

interrupt 604.16, 775.14; *speak* 205.17, *be discourteous* 411.7, *meddle* 414.23, *be untimely* 660.8, *cause to cease* 668.12, *pause* 668.13, *invade* 706.12, *disrupt* 768.12, *hinder* 826.15

interrupted 604.10, 775.9; *stopped* 668.7, *separate* 753.7, *incomplete* 762.5, *disrupted* 768.8

interruptedly 604.20

interrupter *hinderer* 826.11

interrupting *untimely* 660.5

interruption 604.4, 775.3; *bad manners* 411.2, *overactivity* 414.9, *intervening space* 563.8, *interval* 587.1, *untimeliness* 660.1, *stop* 668.2, *pause* 668.3, *disruption* 768.4, *intervention* 775.5, *hindrance* 826.1

intersect *align* 6.92, *adjoin* 216.11, *cross* 609.9, *angle* 628.11, *converge* 702.9

intersecting *linear* 6.77, *vault* 134.8, *contiguous* 216.8, *crossing* 609.7, *convergent* 702.7

intersecting lines *line* 6.35

intersection *set* 6.19, *crossroads* 609.4, *angle* 628.1, *road attribute* 687.3, *crossing point* 692.7, *meeting place* 702.4, *point of union* 752.8

intersectional *crossing* 609.7

interspace *interval* 587.1, *space* 587.6

interspaced *spaced* 587.4

interspatial *spaced* 587.4

interspatially *apart* 587.8, *interweavingly* 609.11

intersperse *mix* 732.12, 751.12

interspersed *mixed* 751.8

interstate *transportable* 686.7

interstate highway *road* 687.2, *means of connection* 754.4

interstellar *astronomical* 7.33, *extensive* 563.12

interstellar cloud *nebula* 7.6

interstellar dust *interstellar matter* 7.7

interstellar gas *interstellar matter* 7.7

interstellar matter 7.7

interstellar molecule *interstellar matter* 7.7

interstellar space *empty space* 563.2

interstice *crack* 587.2

interstitial *chemical compound* 11.4, *spaced* 587.4

interstitial-cell-stimulating hormone Human Hormones 12

interstitially *apart* 587.8

interstream divide *running water* 8.10

intertexture *texture* 552.1, *interweaving* 609.1

intertidal *coastal* 8.54, *oceanic* 571.7

intertidal zone *tide* 8.17

intertropical convergence zone (ITCZ) *wind system* 9.15

intertwine 752.19; *interweave* 609.8, *enfold* 637.9, *mix* 751.12, *combine* 757.9

intertwined *interwoven* 609.6, *mixed* 751.8, *combinatory* 757.6

intertwinement *interweaving* 609.1

intertwining *spinning* 130.4, *interrelatedness* 727.3, *interrelated* 727.7

intertwiningly *interweavingly* 609.11

intertwist *mix* 751.12

intertwisted *mixed* 751.8

interurban *urban* 567.14

interval 587.1, 639.4, 739.4, 775.2; *weather* 9.3, *frequency* 10.6, *chord* 140.18, *written music* 140.21, *intervening space* 563.8, *opening* 583.1, *time* 819.1, *period* 641.1, *season* 654.1, *pause* 668.3, *emptiness* 718.4, *omission* 762.4, *ease* 819.1

interval [Brit] *play part* 136.8

intervalic *interim* 639.11

intervallic *spaced* 587.4

interval scale *nonparametric methods* 6.54

intervene *mediate* 75.6, 772.19, *be active in* 412.17, *meddle* 414.23, *trade* 480.18, *be an instrument* 511.7, *pass* 639.13, *enter* 692.18, *disrupt* 768.12, *interrupt* 775.14, *hinder* 826.15, *block* 826.17, *restrain commerce* 830.14

intervening *causal* 511.5, *penetrating* 692.12, *hindering* 826.12

intervening space 563.8; *interval* 587.1

intervenor *litigant* 54.4

intervention 775.5; *international trade* 56.7, *mediation* 75.1, *war* 76.1, *protectionism* 480.3, *instrumentality* 511.1, *passage into* 692.4, *disruption* 768.4, *hindrance* 826.1, *obstacle* 826.2, *economic restraint* 830.3

interventional *causal* 511.5, *hindering* 826.12, *blocked* 826.13, *restrained* 830.9

interventionally *in the way* 826.23

interventionism *protectionism* 480.3, *economic restraint* 830.3

interventionist *middleman* 772.7, *one who restrains* 830.7

interview 210.4; *news story* 171.3, *report* 171.9, 175.9, *audition* 228.6, *questionnaire* 333.3, *question* 333.16, *question and answer* 334.3, *react* 334.20, *social gathering* 408.4

interviewee *person questioned* 333.10, *answerer* 334.10

interviewer *news reporting* 171.5, *conversationalist* 210.6, *questioner* 333.9

interwar *interim* 639.11

interweave 609.8; *weave* 130.20, *correspond to* 727.10, *mix* 751.12, *intertwine* 752.19, *connect* 754.13, *combine* 757.9

interweaving 609.1; *weaving* 130.6, *interrelatedness* 727.3, *interrelated* 727.7

interweavingly 609.11

interwork *interweaving* 609.1

interworking *interrelatedness* 727.3, *interrelated* 727.7, *reciprocity* 729.1, *reciprocal* 729.4

interwoven 609.6; *mixed* 751.8, *tied* 752.13, *connected* 754.11, *combinatory* 757.6

intestate *forgotten* 186.6

intestinal *visceral* 611.10

intestinal fortitude *stamina* 377.4

intestinal gland *secretory mechanism* 24.3

intestines *internal organ* 19.13, *eating organ* 92.14, *internals* 611.3, *convoluted thing* 632.3

in that case *under the circumstances* 726.16, *accordingly* 735.39
in that event *under the circumstances* 726.16
in that place *where* 565.12
in the (very) act *guiltily* 450.12
in the abstract *theoretically* 4.24
in the act *actively* 412.18
in the affirmative *unanimously* 346.8, *with consent* 735.38
in the aftermath *after* 770.14
in the afternoon *daily* 655.8
in the aggregate *one and all* 759.12
in the air *newsworthy* 171.8, *published* 173.12, *high* 596.20, *ambient* 615.6
in the army *or* **the military** *warring* 76.26
in the ascendant *influential* 512.8, *ascending* 713.13
in the back country *outside* 610.17
in the background *in the offing* 585.12, *behind* 622.8, *causally* 675.12, *concealed* 844.7
in the back o' beyond [Aus inf] *at a distance* 585.13
in the bag *storing* 578.19
in the bag [Inf] *secured* 464.7
in the bank *possessed* 469.13
in the bargain bin *at a discount* 495.7
in the best interest of *beneficial* 445.11
in the big house [Inf] *imprisoned* 55.9, *detained* 830.11
in the black 487.15; *well-off* 467.12, *gainfully* 467.24, *solvent* 485.9, *in credit* 487.8, *paid* 489.11
in the book *on record* 185.16
in the boondocks *at a distance* 585.13
in the boonies [Inf] *at a distance* 585.13
in the bud 771.39; *embryonic* 771.19
in the business *meddling* 414.17
in the cannon's mouth *at war* 76.34, *martially* 77.39
in the cards *expected* 356.5, *predetermined* 384.4, *probable* 838.6
in the case *under the circumstances* 726.16
in the center of *centrally* 612.12
in the chair *managerially* 126.13
in the chips [Inf] *wealthy* 485.8
in the circumstances *conditionally* 725.10
in the clear *acquitted* 54.25, *incorrupt* 449.7, *safe* 810.16
in the clouds *high* 596.20
in the clutches of *subordinate* 832.8
in the cooler [Inf] *imprisoned* 55.9
in the corner *combat* 152.17
in the course of *all the time* 639.16
in the cradle *young* 26.11
in the current mode *trendily* 652.24
in the dark *blind to* 243.14, *darkly* 247.11, *ignorant* 349.5
in the database *on record* 185.16
in the days *or* **time of** *one day* 639.20
in the deep freeze [Inf] *inertly* 519.5
in the dim and distant past *historically* 3.17
in the direction of *via* 691.17
in the dirt *on the ground* 716.25
in the distance *distantly* 585.11

in the doctor's hands *unhealthily* 114.31
in the doldrums *depressed* 270.5, *without hope* 282.7
in the dough [Inf] *wealthy* 485.8
in the driver's seat *in authority* 52.20, *managerial* 126.9, *managerially* 126.13, *dominant* 512.10
in the end *conclusively* 334.26, *finally* 584.18, 773.24, *inevitably* 840.17
in the eyes of the law *legally* 53.33
in the face of *defiantly* 416.9, *disapprovingly* 507.10, *on the spot* 575.20
in the face of death *at war* 76.34, *dangerously* 811.14
in the family way *pregnant* 21.12
in the fast lane [Inf] *self-indulgently* 456.12
in the file *on record* 185.16
in the final analysis *finally* 773.24
in the first place *first* 769.19, 771.37
in the flesh *alive* 28.13, *material* 524.7, *in person* 575.18
in the flower of youth *young* 26.11
in the forefront *before* 621.14
in the foreground *accentuated* 843.11
in the fourth place *fourth* 791.15
in the freezer *preserved* 815.12
in the fresh air *odorless* 225.4, *odorlessly* 225.8
in the fullness of time *in the future* 650.13
in the future 650.13; *later* 658.16
in the gaseous state *gaseous* 556.14
in the gloaming *dimly* 248.10
in the good books of *friendly with* 62.6
in the good grace of *friendly with* 62.6
in the good old days *historically* 3.17, *anciently* 653.18
in the grave *buried* 31.8
in the gravy [Inf] *wealthy* 485.8
in the grip of *retained* 471.6
in the habit *habituated* 397.14
in the hands of *possessed* 469.13, *subordinate* 832.8
in the hands of the receiver *unable to pay* 488.8, *destroyed* 523.9
in the headlines *publicized* 173.14
in the heat of the moment *angrily* 302.24
in the hospital *sick* 114.24, *unhealthily* 114.31
in the hot seat [Inf] *managerially* 126.13, *endangered* 811.10
in the index *on record* 185.16
in the interim *meanwhile* 639.18, *at present* 647.9
in the interior *inland* 611.19
in the know *educated* 48.19, *informed* 170.9, *knowledgeable* 348.7
in the land of the living *alive* 28.13
in the large *largely* 579.19
in the lead *before* 621.14, 769.18, *surpassing* 712.10, *ahead* 712.18
in the lee of *safely* 810.24
in the limelight *onstage* 136.39, *publicly* 173.20, *accentuated* 843.11
in the line of duty *dutifully* 433.19

in the lion's den *endangered* 811.10
in the long run *on average* 742.10, *overall* 778.22
in the lowest position *inferiorly* 745.13
in the main *in essence* 723.13, *predominantly* 744.21, *on the whole* 759.13, *overall* 778.22, *as a rule* 780.18, *importantly* 799.15
in the majority 793.11
in the marketplace *in trade* 480.22
in the mass *one and all* 759.12
in the matter of *in litigation* 54.34
in the meantime *meanwhile* 639.18, *at present* 647.9
in the melting pot *complicated* 751.10
in the middle 772.21; *medianly* 742.12
in the middle of *centrally* 612.12
in the midmost part *centrally* 612.12
in the midst of *actively* 412.18, *in the middle* 772.21
in the mind *ideational* 327.9, *theoretically* 327.19, *topically* 328.11
in the mind's eye *ideational* 327.9, *theoretically* 327.19, *imaginatively* 360.17
in the minutes *on record* 185.16
in the mists of time *in the past* 651.20
in the money *wealthy* 485.8
in the money [Inf] *prosperously* 847.9
in the morning *daily* 655.8
in the name of *authoritatively* 52.18, *in aid of* 825.33
in the negative *negatively* 190.22, *denyingly* 190.23
in the neighborhood *environmentally* 60.26, *near* 586.6, *nearby* 586.17, *around* 615.8
in the news *newsworthy* 171.8, *published* 173.12, 175.8, *topical* 328.5, *topically* 328.11
in the nick of time *critically* 659.9
in the night *darkly* 247.11
in the nude *revealingly* 614.22
in the offing 585.12; *in preparation* 388.8, *in the future* 650.13
in the open *published* 173.12, *openly* 180.13, 583.22, *out-of-doors* 558.26, *manifest* 843.9
in the open air *out-of-doors* 558.26, *outside* 610.17
in the opposite direction *opposite* 731.5
in theory *theoretically* 327.19, *supposedly* 359.10, *ideally* 720.18
in the outback [Aus] *outside* 610.17
in the outland *or* **outlands** *outside* 610.17
in the ownership of *possessed* 469.13
in the past 651.20
in the pay of *subordinate* 832.8
in the picture *knowledgeable* 348.7
in the pink *healthy* 113.4, *ruddily* 257.10, *in form* 624.8, *orderly* 765.13, *ideal* 805.17
in the pipeline *incomplete* 762.5
in the plural *plural* 793.6
in the possession of *possessed* 469.13, *possessively* 469.16
in the poverty trap *poor* 486.8, *poorly* 486.17

in the presence of *on the spot* 575.20
in the present case *conditionally* 725.10
in the public eye *publicized* 173.14, *publicly* 173.20, *clear* 244.6
in the raw *or* **buff** *or* **the altogether** [Inf] *revealingly* 614.22
in the real world *in truth* 721.28
in the rear *behind* 622.8
in the red *unprofitable* 468.10, *at a loss* 468.22, *indebted* 486.9, 488.7, *charged* 487.9, *in the black* 487.15, *insolvently* 488.11, *nonpaying* 490.7, *without paying* 490.15
in the refrigerator *preserved* 815.12
in the right 429.11; *by rights* 429.17
in the right place at the right time *conveniently* 803.6
in the ring *professionally* 152.22
in the rough *roughly* 544.13, *indirect* 698.9
in the running *contending* 422.19
in the saddle *in authority* 52.20, *managerially* 126.13, *equipped* 388.10
in the same breath *in the shortest possible time* 645.9
in the same breath as *as* 649.10
in the same class *included* 763.4
in the same league *included* 763.4
in the same manner *or* **way** *similarly* 733.17
in the same place *identically* 730.18
in the same way *compatibly* 462.16
in the second place *second* 789.20
in the sense that *or* **of** *meaningfully* 361.16
in the service of *in aid of* 825.33
in the shade *darkly* 247.11
in the shops *or* **stores** *on sale* 482.24
in the shortest possible time 645.9
in the singular *one by one* 788.21
in the small *or* **wee small hours** *nightly* 656.6
in the soup [Inf] *endangered* 811.10, *troubled* 842.8
in the spotlight *onstage* 136.39, *publicly* 173.20
in the stars *predictably* 650.15
in the sticks [Inf] *at a distance* 585.13
in the sun *out-of-doors* 558.26
in the teeth of *defiantly* 416.9, *difficultly* 824.23
in the thick of *actively* 412.18, *in the middle* 772.21
in the thick of the fray *at war* 76.34, *martially* 77.39
in the third place *third* 790.14
in the twilight *dimly* 248.10
in the twinkling of an eye *transiently* 643.8, *in the shortest possible time* 645.9
in the usual course *usually* 778.21
in the vanguard *before* 621.14
in the vernacular *simply* 526.14
in the very moment that *as* 649.10
in the vicinity *environmentally* 60.26, *readily available* 575.21, *near* 586.6, *nearby* 586.17, *around* 615.8
in the vicinity *or* **neighborhood** *where* 565.12, *nearby* 803.7

in the way 826.23; *blocked* 826.13
in the way of marriage *matrimonially* 64.23
in the wind *in the future* 650.13
in the wind's eye *directionally* 697.20
in the wings *onstage* 136.39
in the works *under discussion* 387.17
in the worst possible taste *ribaldly* 535.12
in the wrong *immoral* 430.11, *guilty* 450.6
in the wrong way *inversely* 608.9
in the year of our Lord *one day* 639.20
in thing, the [Inf] *fashion* 536.1, *trendiness* 652.2
in this way *how* 691.16, *under the circumstances* 726.16
in threes 790.13
intimacy 62.4; *sexual intercourse* 20.9, *liking* 290.1, *sexual love* 299.3, *sociability* 408.1, *nearness* 586.1, *secrecy* 611.6
intimate 62.7; *coupling* 20.19, *friend* 62.2, *tip* 170.14, *secret* 182.8, 611.13, *signify* 183.16, *liking* 290.4, *mean* 361.13, *near* 586.6, *united* 752.10, *imply* 844.14
intimate apparel *underwear* 100.22
intimated *tacit* 844.10
intimately 62.14; *admiringly* 290.11, *secretly* 611.22, *as one* 752.21, *inextricably* 752.23
intimation *inside information* 170.4, *impression* 266.2, *information* 348.2, *notice* 358.3, *basis of supposition* 359.2, *suggestion* 800.9
in time *tunefully* 140.30, *synchronized* 649.5, *synchronously* 649.9, *early* 657.17, *later* 658.16
in times gone by *in the past* 651.20
intimidate 283.18; *motivate* 178.17, *daunt* 179.9, *harm* 306.13, *be severe* 424.8, *force* 428.10, *endanger* 811.13, *defeat* 832.11
intimidated *dissuaded* 179.5
intimidating *dissuasive* 179.4, *fearsome* 283.13, *malign* 306.11, *dominating* 832.7
intimidatingly *dissuasively* 179.12, *fearsomely* 283.21
intimidation 283.6; *psychological warfare* 76.13, *incentive* 178.4, *deterrence* 179.2, *malignity* 306.5, *attack* 418.1, *coercion* 428.2, *domination* 832.2
intimidator *frightener* 283.7
intimism *Western Art Styles* 133
intinction *Eucharist* 85.7
in tiptop condition [Inf] *healthy* 113.4
in token of *indicatively* 183.21
intolerable *painful* 215.4, *detested* 291.11
intolerably *distastefully* 291.19
intolerance *hostility* 63.1, *bad feeling* 266.5, *malignity* 306.5, *prejudice* 337.3, *injustice* 342.3, *dissentience* 347.7, *opinionatedness* 379.3, *severity* 424.1, *obstruction* 510.3, *narrow-mindedness* 593.7
intolerant 63.7; *displeased* 291.6, *malign* 306.11, *discriminatory* 337.11, *unjust* 342.7, *dissenting* 347.7, *opinionated* 379.9, *severe* 424.5, *counteracting* 510.6, *narrow-minded* 593.13

intolerantly *hostilely* 63.13, *malignly* 306.18, *prejudicially* 337.17, *unjustly* 342.13, *severely* 424.11, *counter* 510.8, *narrow-mindedly* 593.20
intonation *mode of speech* 205.6
intone *follow rites* 85.19, *sing* 141.16
in torment *devilishly* 446.14
into sight *visibly* 244.10
into *or* **in the bargain** *additionally* 748.15
into the interior *internally* 611.18
in toto [L] *wholly* 759.11, *completely* 759.14
in touch *educated* 48.19, *informed* 170.9
into view *visibly* 244.10
in tow *together* 794.20
intoxicant *addictive drug* 117.10, *intoxicating* 121.29
intoxicate *invigorate* 518.5
intoxicated *wasted* 96.14, *drunk* 121.25
intoxicated person *drunkard* 121.8
intoxicating 121.29; *strong to the senses* 516.12
intoxicating drug *drug* 115.9
intoxicating liquor *alcohol* 121.5
intoxication *drunkenness* 121.3, *physical deterioration* 808.4
intractability *relentlessness* 309.2, *obstinacy* 379.1, 417.2, *determination* 379.2, *disobedience* 427.1, *mental hardness* 542.4
intractable *relentless* 309.4, *obstinate* 379.5, 417.7, *disobedient* 427.10, *counteracting* 510.6, *mentally hard* 542.8, *troublesome* 824.13
intractably *relentlessly* 309.8, *resistingly* 417.14, *disobediently* 427.14, *counter* 510.8, *inflexibly* 542.13
intractile *mentally hard* 542.8
in trade 480.22
intrados *Architectural Elements* 134
in training *unskilled* 128.5
intramural *curricular* 48.21
intransigence *willfulness* 372.3, *determination* 379.2, *mental hardness* 542.4
intransigent *willful* 372.8, *strong-willed* 376.10, *tenacious person* 377.5, *obstinate person* 379.4, *determined* 379.7, *mentally hard* 542.8, *opposer* 828.9
intransigently *obstinately* 379.11, *inflexibly* 542.13
in transit 685.13; *convertibly* 670.15, *in motion* 677.19, *in progress* 679.16, *passing* 692.11, *by the way* 692.20
in transition *convertibly* 670.15
in transit to *via* 691.17
intransmutable *stable* 674.3
intraocular pressure *Fields of Measurement* 589
intrauterine device (IUD) *contraceptive* 23.6
intravenous (IV) pyelogram *diagnostic radiology* 107.12
intravenous injection *therapy* 115.12
intrepid *courageous* 284.9
intrepidity *courage* 284.1
intrepidly *courageously* 284.17

intricacy *subtlety* 534.2, *convolution* 632.1, *coil* 632.2, *difficulty* 824.1
intricate *mysterious* 182.10, *convolutional* 632.4, *united* 752.10, *problematic* 824.11
intricately *circularly* 632.8, *as one* 752.21, *problematically* 824.25
intricateness *convolution* 632.1
intrigant *schemer* 193.10, *planner* 387.9
intrigue *secretiveness* 182.3, *artifice* 193.5, *be piquant* 221.9, *love affair* 299.9, *plot* 387.6, *overactivity* 414.9, *subversion* 447.3, *fornication* 432.3, *influence* 508.11, *cunning* 822.1, *be cunning* 822.5, *concealment* 844.2
intriguer *planner* 387.9, *meddler* 414.12, *cunning person* 822.3
intriguing *stimulating* 221.7, *meddling* 414.17, *cunning* 822.4
intriguingly *stimulatingly* 221.11, *conspiratorially* 387.18
in trim *healthy* 113.4
intrinsic 611.11, 717.12, 723.6; *causal* 675.7, *truistic* 721.15, *included* 763.4, *special* 779.10
intrinsically 611.20, 721.30; *causally* 675.12, *in essence* 723.13, *inclusively* 763.8
intrinsic truth *truism* 721.6
in triplicate *thrice* 790.12
in triumph *victoriously* 845.20
introduce 708.16; *direct* 126.11, *produce* 137.21, *begin* 583.21, *enroll* 706.16, *show in* 708.13, *insert* 710.9, 748.12, *inject* 710.10, *forecast* 769.17
introduced *wild* 41.15, *inserted* 710.5
introduce oneself *fraternize* 408.17
introducing *starring* 137.18
introduction 771.10; *play part* 136.8, *book part* 174.5, *birth* 264.2, *beginning* 583.9, *front matter* 621.4, *entry* 706.1, *bringing in* 708.4, *insertion* 710.1, *preface* 769.5
introductive *introductory* 708.10
introductorily *preparatorily* 388.23
introductory 708.10, 771.23; *preparatory* 388.7, *beginning* 583.14, *precursory* 769.12
Introit *prayer* 85.10
introit *Eucharist* 85.7, *sacred music* 140.3
introject *insert* 710.9
introjected *inserted* 710.5
intromission *admittance* 708.1, *insertion* 710.1
intromissive *admissive* 708.8
intromit *admit* 708.12, *insert* 710.9
intromittent *admissive* 708.8
intromittent organ *organs of reproduction* 21.9
intron *genetic material* 13.20
introspect 611.16; *philosophize* 4.19, *think* 317.9, *question* 333.16
introspection *philosophical investigation* 4.4, *thoughtfulness* 317.2, *oblivion* 355.4, *inwardness* 611.5
introspection psychology *Psychological Theories, Schools* 108
introspective *thoughtful* 4.17, *speculative* 317.8, *questioning* 333.11, *oblivious* 355.9, *inward* 611.12

introspectively *thoughtfully* 4.27, 317.13, *questioningly* 333.21, *inwardly* 611.21
introspectiveness *inwardness* 611.5
in trouble *troubled* 824.15, *adverse* 848.10
introversion *personality type* 108.6, *shyness* 409.2, *inversion* 608.1, *inwardness* 611.5, *inhibition* 826.9, *self-restraint* 830.4
introversive *introverted* 108.37, *inward* 611.12, *inhibitive* 826.14, *self-restrained* 830.10
introvert *personality type* 108.6, *introverted* 108.37, *invert* 608.7, *keep inside* 611.17
introverted 108.37; *shy* 409.7, *inverted* 608.5, *inward* 611.12
introvertedness *personality type* 108.6
introvertive *inward* 611.12
intrude *meddle* 414.23, *pick a fight* 463.10, *be external* 660.8, *transgress* 712.14, *be external* 724.15, *disrupt* 768.12
intruder 706.8, 724.7; *dissenter* 463.5, *hinderer* 826.11
intrusion *untimeliness* 660.1, *inroad* 706.3, *transgression* 712.3, *externality* 724.4, *disruption* 768.4
intrusive *petrographic* 8.58, *meddling* 414.17, *untimely* 660.5, *invasive* 706.10, *transgressing* 712.7, *external* 724.11, *hindering* 826.12
intrusively *at the wrong time* 660.12, *in* 706.17, *excessively* 712.17, *externally* 724.19, *disturbingly* 768.13, *with delay* 826.22
intrusiveness *overactivity* 414.9
intrusive rock *igneous rock* 8.32
in truth 721.28; *assuredly* 189.30, 336.12, *certainly* 719.14
intuit *divine* 86.24, *feel instinctively* 266.15, *be intuitive* 320.9, *have an idea* 327.13, *be wise* 352.6, *suppose* 359.8
intuition 320.1; *philosophical investigation* 4.4, *psychic power* 86.4, *belief* 87.1, *impression* 266.2, *way of thinking* 317.4, *instinct* 318.3, *theory* 327.2, *knowledge* 348.1, *wisdom* 352.1, *basis of supposition* 359.2, *conjecture* 359.3, *spontaneity* 396.2
intuitionism *Philosophical Schools of Thought* 4
intuitionist *Philosophical Schools of Thought* 4
intuitive 266.10, 320.6; *instinctive* 318.8, *foreseeing* 357.5, *suppositional* 359.5, *spontaneous* 396.5
intuitively 320.11; *thoughtfully* 317.13, *spontaneously* 396.8
intuitiveness *intuition* 320.1, *spontaneity* 396.2
intuitive person 320.5
intuitive reasoning *intuition* 320.1
intumesce *increase* 746.6
intumescence *swelling* 581.2, *spread* 746.3
in tune *melodious* 140.26, *tunefully* 140.30, *agreeing* 462.6, *in harmony* 735.32
in turmoil *disorderly* 51.6, *confusedly* 51.11
in turn *in order* 765.26, *sequentially* 770.13, *consecutively* 774.15, *specifically* 779.22

intussuscept *invert* 608.7
intussusception *inversion* 608.1
in twain *separately* 753.22, *in half* 789.21
intwine *interweave* 609.8
in two *separately* 753.22, *in half* 789.21
in two minds *vacillating* 378.5
in twos *two* 789.8, *two by two* 789.19
in twos and threes *in ones and twos* 796.10
in two shakes of a lamb's tail [Inf] *immediately* 645.8
inulin *polysaccharide* 12.5
inunction *ointment* 562.8
inundant *flowing* 570.7
inundate *be excessive* 99.9, *water* 557.29, *flow* 570.10, *run out* 707.15
inundated *flooded* 557.24, 570.8, *overrun* 712.6
inundation *excess* 99.1, *agent of destruction* 523.7, *soaking* 557.9, *flow* 570.4, *outflow* 707.4, *overstepping* 712.1
inundatorily *fluently* 570.13
inundatory *flowing* 570.7
in unfinished form *incompletely* 544.14
in union with *as one* 752.21
in unison *agreeing* 462.6, *synchronously* 649.9, *in harmony* 735.32, *cohesively* 755.11, *together* 794.20
inurbane *discourteous* 411.5
inurbanity *discourtesy* 411.1
inure *accustom* 397.18
inured *habituated* 397.14
inurement *habituation* 397.7
in use 393.8; *operational* 509.7
inutile *useless* 802.7
inutility *superfluity* 99.4, *lack of authority* 515.2, *triviality* 800.2, *uselessness* 802.1
invade 706.12; *infest* 40.17, *be at war* 76.32, *conquer* 77.36, *attack successfully* 418.25, *transgress* 712.14, *be external* 724.15, *eat away* 808.19
invader *hostile person* 63.5, *attacker* 418.10, *intruder* 706.8
invading *attacking* 418.14, *external* 724.11
invaginate *invert* 608.7
invaginated *inverted* 608.5
invagination *inversion* 608.1
in vain *futilely* 282.16, *futile* 802.10, *uselessly* 802.14, *unsuccessfully* 846.21
invalid *logical* 6.83, *patient* 107.25, *infectious person* 114.9, *sick person* 114.22, *unhealthy* 114.23, *sophistic* 330.7, *meaningless* 362.7, *wrong* 430.12, *powerless person* 515.5, *unauthorized* 515.7, *weak person* 517.4, *insufficient* 517.11, *unauthentic* 722.9, *useless* 802.7, *canceled* 834.5
invalid argument *reasoning* 6.61
invalidate *theorize* 6.84, *disavow* 190.18, *refute* 332.7, *counteract* 510.7, *remove power from* 515.13, *weaken* 517.13, *abolish* 523.11, *cause not to exist* 718.14, *cancel* 834.6
invalidated *disavowing* 190.12, *unauthorized* 515.7, *canceled* 834.5
invalidating *disavowing* 190.12, *refuting* 332.6, *counteracting* 510.6
invalidation *disavowal* 190.3, *refutation* 332.1, *neutralization* 510.4, *cancellation* 834.1
invalidator *negator* 190.8

invalided *sick* 114.24
invalidism *ill health* 114.1, *poor health* 517.3
invalidity *reasoning* 6.61, *nonentity* 190.5, *sophistry* 330.1, *nonsense* 362.2, *incorrectness* 430.3, *lack of authority* 515.2, *unauthenticity* 722.4
invalidly *wrongfully* 430.25, *unauthentically* 722.11
invaluable *valuable* 496.8, *profitable* 801.8
invaluableness *value* 496.6
invariability *permanence* 667.1, *stability* 674.1, *regularity* 730.6, *repetitiveness* 797.3
invariable *given* 6.74, *habitual* 397.9, *permanent* 667.2, *stable* 674.3, *regular* 730.12, *monotonous* 797.12
invariableness *regularity* 730.6
invariably *regularly* 397.21, 730.21, *permanently* 667.6, *usually* 778.21, *universally* 778.23
invariant *algebraic expression* 6.23, *regular* 730.12
invariantly *regularly* 730.21
invasion *offensive warfare* 76.11, *military attack* 418.2, *inroad* 706.3, *transgression* 712.3, *externality* 724.4
invasive 706.10; *transgressing* 712.7, *external* 724.11
invasively *in* 706.17, *excessively* 712.17
invective *public speaking* 205.11, *address* 209.1, *vilification* 301.2, *vilifying* 301.9, *berating* 438.5
invectively *vilifyingly* 301.18
inveigh against *vilify* 301.15, *criticize* 418.26
inveigle *persuade* 178.15, *cajole* 439.14, *manipulate* 508.12, *trap* 813.6
inveigled *trapped* 813.5
inveiglement *persuasion* 178.1, *cajolery* 439.3
inveigler *persuader* 178.9, *flatterer* 439.6
inveigling *cajoling* 439.9
invent 335.13, 345.4, 771.30; *fabricate* 192.24, 720.17, *have an idea* 317.12, *imagine* 327.14, 360.14, *improvise* 396.6, *produce* 522.13, *design* 536.8, *structure* 551.20, *be trendy* 652.18, *cause change* 665.16, *cause* 675.8, *come to be* 717.19, *be unreal* 722.12, *originate* 737.7, *forerun* 769.16, *reveal* 843.14
invented *fabricated* 192.17, *imaginary* 360.12, *produced* 522.12, *unreal* 722.7
invention *fabrication* 192.17, *falsehood* 192.6, *plan* 327.3, *imagination* 360.1, *method* 387.4, *improvisation* 396.4, *production* 522.1, *newness* 652.1, *change for the better* 665.4, *cause* 675.1, *unreality* 722.2, *original* 737.2
inventive 771.20; *enriching* 22.11, *speculative* 317.8, *ideational* 327.9, *original* 335.9, 737.4, *discovering* 345.8, *imaginative* 360.10, *improvised* 396.4, *productive* 522.11, *new* 652.9, *changeable* 665.11, *causal* 675.7, *cunning* 822.4
inventively 335.15; *fruitfully* 22.15, *thoughtfully* 317.13, *imaginatively* 327.21, 360.17, *originally* 345.16, 737.8, *productively* 522.17, *newly* 652.21,

changeably 665.22, *causally* 675.12
inventiveness *enrichment* 22.5, *creative thought* 317.3, *imagination* 327.8, 360.1, *originality* 335.4, 737.1, *cunning* 822.1
inventive power *creative thought* 317.3
inventor *experimenter* 335.5, *discoverer* 345.7, *planner* 387.9, *improviser* 396.3, *producer* 522.10, *first cause* 675.6, *originator* 737.3, 771.15, *precursor* 769.7
inventorial *accounting* 493.7, *of a list* 785.10
inventorially 785.13
inventoried *listed* 785.9
inventory *stock in trade* 105.2, *collection* 105.12, *record* 185.1, *description* 202.1, *name* 202.17, *audit* 493.10, *division* 577.6, *unit* 759.5, *catalog* 767.7, *categorize* 767.21, *count* 784.3, *number* 784.13, *list* 785.1, 785.11
inventory management *management system* 126.3
inveracity *untruthfulness* 192.1
inverse 608.2, 608.6; *division* 6.16, *set* 6.19, *matrix* 6.20, *divisible* 6.71, *inverted thing* 608.4, *invert* 608.7, *opposite* 731.2, 731.3
inverse cosine (arccosine) *trigonometric function* 6.50
inversed *inverted* 608.5
inverse function *mathematical function* 6.27, *inverted thing* 608.4
inverse image *inverted thing* 608.4
inversely 608.9; *reversely* 608.10, *diametrically* 731.6
inverse proportion *inverted thing* 608.4
inverse sine (arcsine) *trigonometric function* 6.50
inverse tangent (arctangent) *trigonometric function* 6.50
inverse trigonometric function *trigonometric function* 6.50
inversion 608.1; *structure* 11.7, *literary device* 139.12, *inverted thing* 608.4, *operation of symmetry* 626.2, *alteration* 665.2, *reversal* 680.3, *oppositeness* 731.1, *calculation* 784.1
invert 608.7; *react* 11.38, *sexual nature* 20.4, *homosexual* 32.9, 33.10, *knock down* 523.13, *inverted thing* 608.4, *cause change* 665.16, *opposite* 731.2, *be opposite* 731.4
invertebrate 39.1, 39.20; *type of animal* 34.5, *of animals* 34.13, *mollusk* 39.13
invertebrate chordate *invertebrate* 39.1
invertebrate larva 39.19
invertebrate zoologist 39.3
invertebrate zoology 39.2
inverted 608.5; *arch* 134.5, *opposite* 731.3
inverted arch *or vault inverted thing* 608.4
inverted breaststroke *swimming techniques* 164.2
invertedly *reversibly* 671.14
inverted order *inversion* 608.1
inverted thing 608.4
invest *be at war* 76.32, *ordain* 84.16, *clothe* 100.43, *deposit* 105.21, *permit* 340.12, *besiege* 418.20, *finance* 457.7, *speculate* 480.19, *expend* 491.11, *introduce* 708.16, *install* 710.15, *enroll* 771.33, *commission* 833.8
invest authority *authorize* 52.14

invested *dressed* 100.38, *saved* 105.15, *expended* 491.9
invested authority *legal power* 52.2
investigate *philosophize* 4.19, *report* 175.9, *be curious* 321.7, *question* 333.16, *experiment* 335.11, *estimate* 341.11
investigated *questioned* 333.15
investigation *philosophical investigation* 4.4, *questioning* 333.2, *experiment* 335.1, *experimentation* 335.3
investigative *questioning* 333.11, *experimental* 335.8
investigative journalist *print journalist* 175.5, *discloser* 180.4
investigatively *questioningly* 333.21, *experimentally* 335.14
investigative reporter *broadcasting personnel* 172.11
investigative reporting *print journalism* 175.4
investigator *philosopher* 4.9, *discloser* 180.4, *curious person* 321.3, *questioner* 333.9, *experimenter* 335.5
invest in *finance* 457.7, *buy in* 481.13
investing *buying* 481.9
investiture *ordination* 84.3, *dressing* 100.2, *giving* 472.1, *bringing in* 708.4, *grant* 735.10, *enrollment* 771.8, *commission* 833.1
investment *blockading* 76.22, *provision* 89.1, *dressing* 100.2, *stock in trade* 105.2, *permission* 340.3, *military attack* 418.2, *finance* 457.1, *giving* 472.1, *speculation* 480.9, *expense* 491.2
investment account *wealth* 485.1
investment capital *resources* 102.4
investment portfolio *resources* 102.4
investments *resources* 102.4, *wealth* 485.1
investment specialist *financial adviser* 457.4
investment strength *finance* 457.1
investor *financial adviser* 457.4, *person transferring property* 470.8, *purchaser* 481.7, *depositor* 487.6, *spender* 491.7
invest with *give out* 472.12, *grant* 735.30
invest with power *empower* 514.20
inveteracy *habit* 397.1
inveterate *habituated* 397.14, *impenitent* 452.2, *olden* 653.11
inveterately *archaically* 653.20
invidious *unpleasant* 272.6, *hateful* 300.10, *malicious* 306.8, *envious* 314.4
invidiously *hatefully* 300.14, *maliciously* 306.15, *enviously* 314.11
invidiousness *hatefulness* 300.4, *malice* 306.2, *envy* 314.1
in view *visible* 242.19, 244.5, *visibly* 244.10, *available* 575.11
in view of *by virtue of* 447.12
invigilate *manage* 126.10, *watch* 242.23
invigilator *observer* 242.15
invigorate 28.22, 518.5; *refresh* 94.6, *arouse sensation* 212.11, *strengthen* 516.15, *intensify* 746.8, *revive* 809.14
invigorated *refreshed* 94.5
invigorating 518.3; *fine* 9.43,

refreshing 94.4, *healthful* 113.7, *cold* 218.9, *strengthening* 516.7
invigoratingly *refreshingly* 94.9
invigoration *refreshment* 94.1, *strengthening* 516.7, *vigor* 518.1, *intensification* 746.2
invincibility *strength* 516.1
invincible *resisting* 417.8, *strong* 516.9, *unbeatable* 744.13, *victorious* 845.10
invincibly *resistingly* 417.14, *supremely* 744.23, *successfully* 845.19
in vindication *justifyingly* 441.15
inviolability *strength* 516.1
inviolable *rightful* 429.9, *unfailing* 667.3
inviolable place *private space* 812.2
inviolably *permanently* 667.6
inviolate *strong* 516.9, *uncut* 759.7
in virtue of one's authority *authoritatively* 52.18
invisibility 245.1; *concealment* 181.1, 844.2, *disappearance* 265.1, *unintelligibility* 364.1, *littleness* 580.1
invisible 245.3; *hidden* 243.15, *disappeared* 265.4, *unintelligible* 364.4, *insufficient* 517.11, *little* 580.7, *concealed* 844.7
invisible earnings *commercial trade* 480.2
invisible goods *commercial trade* 480.2
invisible hand *economics* 56.1
invisible man *or* **woman** *anonymity* 182.7
invisible mending *repair* 809.1
invisibles *commercial trade* 480.2
invisible trade *international trade* 56.7, *commercial trade* 480.2
invisible writing *concealment* 844.2
invisibly 245.8; *stealthily* 182.15, *fleetingly* 265.8, *infinitesimally* 580.13
invitation *enticement* 178.3, *proclamation* 183.8, *offer* 504.1, *request* 505.1, *inducement* 508.2, *admittance* 708.1
invitational *requesting* 505.7
invitatory *receptive* 708.9
invite *entice* 178.16, *be sociable* 408.14, *command* 425.10, *be hospitable* 477.21, *request* 505.10, *welcome* 708.14
invite difficulties *have difficulty* 824.18
invite offers *offer* 504.11
inviting *enticing* 178.13, *signaling* 183.14, *luscious* 214.8, *tasty* 219.4, *pleasant* 271.5, *desirable* 288.11, *sociable* 408.11, *offered* 504.8, *requesting* 505.7, *motivational* 508.7, *welcoming* 704.12, *receptive* 708.9
invitingly *desirably* 288.24, *influentially* 508.13, *receptively* 708.20
in vitro fertilization (IVF) *fertilization* 21.6
in vogue *dressily* 100.47, *liked* 290.6, *established* 397.12, *fashionable* 536.5
invoice *means of identification* 184.3, *record* 185.1, *statement*

493.2, *settle accounts* 493.11, *bill* 494.4, 785.4, *demand* 505.12, *list* 785.11
invoiced *accounted* 493.8
invoke *pray* 85.20, *conjure* 86.26, *speak to* 205.19, *appeal to* 209.9, *petition* 505.11
invoke a blessing *pray* 85.20
involucel *leaf* 41.6
involucre *leaf* 41.6, *exteriority* 610.2, *casing* 613.9
involucre *or* **involucrum** *flower part* 42.3
involucrum *exteriority* 610.2, *casing* 613.9
involuntarily 95.23; *spontaneously* 396.8, *compellingly* 428.12, *dependently* 832.13
involuntariness 95.9; *spontaneity* 396.2
involuntary 95.15; *instinctive* 318.8, *unmeant* 362.9, *spontaneous* 396.5, *compelling* 428.6, *captive* 832.9
involuntary saving *levy* 494.7
involuntary servitude *subjection* 832.1
involute *curve* 6.38
involution *convolution* 632.1, *calculation* 784.1
involutional *convolutional* 632.4
involutional melancholia *mood disorder* 108.12
involve *intend* 361.15, *immerse* 598.24, *intercommunicate* 754.15, *include* 763.5
involved *obscure* 197.2, *active* 414.13, *in deep* 598.18, *ambiguous* 632.5, *related* 727.6, *united* 752.10, *problematic* 824.11
involved in *complicated* 751.10, *participating* 760.13
involved style *obscurity* 197.1
involved with *sensitive* 266.11
involvement *good feeling* 266.4, *love affair* 299.9, *immersion* 598.8, *relatedness* 727.1, *mixture* 751.1, *linkage* 752.3, *connection* 754.1, *inclusion* 763.1
involving effort *laborious* 122.7
invulnerability *security* 464.1, *strength* 516.1, *safety* 810.1
invulnerable 419.19, 810.18; *health-giving* 113.6, *secure* 464.5, *stable* 674.3
invulnerably *surely* 464.15, *strongly* 516.17, *stably* 674.9, *safely* 810.24
in want *in need* 95.21, *poor* 486.8
inward 611.12; *diving* 164.13, *private* 245.5, *invisibly* 245.8, *interior* 611.7, *internal* 611.9, *secret* 611.13, *entering* 706.9, *in* 706.17
inward, the *interior* 611.1
inwardbound *approaching* 704.10
inward dive *competitive diving* 164.7
inwardly 611.21; *invisibly* 245.8, *fleetingly* 265.8, *secretly* 611.22, *in* 706.17
inward nature *inner nature* 611.4
inwardness 611.5; *interior* 611.1, *secrecy* 611.6
inwards *internals* 611.3, *internally* 611.18
in waves *sequentially* 770.13
inweave *interweave* 609.8
in white tie and tails *formally dressed* 406.8
in winter *seasonally* 654.12
in with *friendly with* 62.6
in with a chance *contending* 422.19

in wonder *wondrously* 294.18
in words of one syllable *concisely* 198.6, *intelligibly* 363.13
in words to that effect *in other words* 365.18
in working order *in hand* 388.11, *operational* 509.7, *practical* 719.8
Io *Planets and Their Satellites* 7
iodine *Chemical Elements and Common Allotropes* 11, *essential element* 12.15, *prophylaxis* 115.4, *Fields of Measurement* 589
iodometry *Fields of Measurement* 589
ion 10.54; *electric charge* 10.38, *little thing* 580.3
ion exchange chromatography *analysis* 11.17
Ionian mode *mode* 140.17
Ionian Sea *Oceans and Seas* 571
Ionic *column* 134.6
ionic *chemical compound* 11.4, *meter* 139.10
ionically *chemically* 11.42
ionic bond *chemical bond* 11.6
ionization *ion* 10.54, *chemical reaction* 11.8, *chemical reaction thermodynamics* 14.29
ionization energy *ion* 10.54
ionization gauge *surface chemistry* 11.20
ionization potential *ion* 10.54
ionize *react* 11.38
ionizing radiation *radioactivity* 10.58
ionographic printer *hardcopy device* 15.10
ionosphere *atmosphere* 9.8, *atmospheric layer* 558.3
ionospheric *atmospheric* 9.40
ion pump *surface chemistry* 11.20
iophobia *Phobias* 283
iota *little piece* 580.4, *fragment* 787.3, *little bit* 800.4, *suggestion* 800.9
IOU *guarantee* 458.3, *purchase contract* 459.3, *contract* 462.2, *promise* 464.2, *loan* 476.5, *paper money* 484.14
Iowa *American States* 564
ipecac *purgative* 115.7
IPL *Programming Languages* 15
ipse dixit [L] *affirmation* 189.1
ipsissima verba [L] *sameness* 730.1
ipso facto *really* 717.22
IQ *ability* 514.3
Iran *Countries* 566
Iran-Iraq War *Major Wars* 76
Iraq *Countries* 566
Iraq Kurdi *Breeds of Sheep* 16
irascibility 303.1; *oversensitivity* 267.2, *irritableness* 302.5, 304.3, *capriciousness* 381.2, *divisiveness* 463.2, *irritation* 554.9, *abruptness* 591.4
irascible 303.8; *oversensitive* 267.4, *irritable* 302.10, 304.9, *argumentative* 329.7, *refractory* 379.6, *erratic* 381.5, *bad-mannered* 411.6, *contentious* 422.20, *disagreeing* 463.6, *abrupt* 591.8
irascibleness *irascibility* 303.1
irascible person 303.7
irascibly 303.17; *irritably* 302.23, 304.17, *rudely* 411.9, *contentiously* 422.27, *in disagreement* 463.12, *abruptly* 591.13
irate *angry* 302.11
irately *angrily* 302.24
ire *anger* 302.4

ireful *angry* 302.11
irefully *angrily* 302.24
Ireland *Countries* 566, *Islands* 572
Irene *Deities* 82
irenic *or* **irenical** *pacificatory* 74.8
irenically *pacifically* 74.12
irenics *pacification* 74.1, *peace movement* 74.4
iridesce *light up* 246.20
iridescence *quality of light* 246.2, *variegation* 263.1, *changeableness* 666.1
iridescent 263.7; *lustrous* 246.15, *changeable* 666.3
iridescent cloud *cloud appearance* 9.19
iridescently *variedly* 263.12, *changeably* 666.7
iridium *Chemical Elements and Common Allotropes* 11
Iris *Planets and Their Satellites* 7, *Deities* 82, *messenger* 685.5
iris *eye* 19.9, 242.3, *Flowers* 42, *stage lighting* 136.20
iris diaphragm *exposure equipment* 132.12, *stage lighting* 136.20
Irish accent *regional pronunciation* 205.7
Irish Cob *Horse and Pony Breeds* 159
Irish coffee *coffee* 93.6
Irish Draught *Horse and Pony Breeds* 159
Irish Hunter *Horse and Pony Breeds* 159
Irishism *regional pronunciation* 205.7
Irish jig *Dances* 135
Irish moss *moss* 46.4
Irish Sea *Oceans and Seas* 571
Irish setter *Breeds of Dogs* 35
Irish shamrock *national emblem* 184.7
Irish terrier *Breeds of Dogs* 35
Irish wake *funeral* 31.4
Irish water spaniel *Breeds of Dogs* 35
Irish wolfhound *Breeds of Dogs* 35
irk *cause dislike* 291.16, *bore* 296.8, *disturb* 768.10, *annoy* 804.10, *cause trouble* 824.21
irked *bored* 296.5, *disturbed* 768.6
irksome *unpleasant* 272.6, *disliked* 291.10, *boring* 296.6, *annoying* 804.7, *inconvenient* 826.12
irksomely *boringly* 296.10
irksomeness *boringness* 296.2
iron *Chemical Elements and Common Allotropes* 11, *essential element* 12.15, *food content* 90.3, *clean* 111.17, *tonic* 115.8, *fabric-handling tool* 130.12, *golf equipment* 156.5, *heater* 217.3, *gray thing* 255.3, *strong-willed* 376.10, *hard substance* 542.3, *hard* 542.5, *smoother* 545.2, *smooth* 545.10, 552.13, *massage* 554.16, *flattener* 603.4, *make horizontal* 603.10
Iron Age *Ages, Decades, Eras* 641, *primal* 653.14
Iron Age man *prehistoric human* 653.7
iron boot *instrument of torture* 454.14
ironbound *coarse* 544.6
ironbound coast *572.4, *hidden danger* 813.3
ironclad *historical warships* 77.22, *Ships and Boats* 690
ironclad oath *vow* 189.3
iron constitution *health* 113.1

Iron Curtain *separator* 753.5
ironed *cleaned* 111.14, *uniform* 545.5, *leveled* 603.8
iron-gray *gray* 255.6
iron grip *retention* 471.1
iron hand *governance* 52.6, *treatment* 399.11, *suppression* 424.2
iron horse [Arch] *train* 688.4
ironic *humorous* 277.9, *affected* 367.3, *ridiculing* 436.13, *double-edged* 789.10
ironical *affected* 367.3
ironically *humorously* 277.13, *affectedly* 367.5
ironing *fabric treatment* 130.10
ironist *humorist* 277.7, *pretender* 367.2
iron lung *preserver* 815.9
iron maiden *instrument of torture* 454.14
iron meteorite *or* **iron** *meteor* 7.21
ironmonger [Brit] *retailer* 482.11
iron nerve *determination* 674.2
iron-nerved *determined* 674.5
iron out *smooth* 545.10, *straighten* 630.14, *tidy* 765.21, *make easy* 823.15
iron out problems *consult* 176.11
iron rations *incompleteness* 98.2
iron rule *suppression* 424.2
irons *instrument of punishment* 454.13, *means of restraint* 830.6
iron shot *golf shots* 156.4
Ironsides *horse person* 159.14
ironstone *or* **ironstone china** Ceramics 129
ironware *merchandise* 522.6
iron will *willpower* 372.2, *will* 376.5, *determination* 674.2
iron-willed 372.7; *strong-willed* 376.10, *determined* 674.5
ironwood Trees and Shrubs 43
irony *literary device* 139.12, *wit* 277.3, *affectation* 367.1, *ridicule* 436.4, *duality* 789.2
irradiate *react* 11.38, *light* 246.19, *preserve* 815.14
irradiation *preservation of provisions* 815.6
irrational *real number* 6.5, *complex* 6.69, *divisible* 6.71, *sophistic* 330.7, *numerical* 783.7, *impossible* 837.4
irrationality *insanity* 110.1, *sophistry* 330.1, *lack of motive* 842.2
irrationally *unintelligently* 316.9, *sophistically* 330.14, *impossibly* 837.11
irrational number *real number* 6.5, *kind of number* 783.2
Irrawaddy Rivers 570
irreclaimable *impenitent* 452.2, *losing* 468.9
irreclaimably *irrecoverably* 468.21
irreconcilability *divisiveness* 463.2
irreconcilable *estranged* 63.8, *tenacious person* 377.5, *disagreeing* 463.6, *contrary* 828.13
irreconcilably *in disagreement* 463.12
irrecoverable *hopeless* 282.6, 837.6, *losing* 468.9, *over* 651.12
irrecoverableness *hopelessness* 282.1
irrecoverably 468.21; *hopelessly* 282.13, 837.12
irredeemability *hopelessness* 282.1
irredeemable *hopeless* 282.6, *impenitent* 452.2, *losing* 468.9, *unpaid* 490.8

irredeemably *hopelessly* 282.13, *irrecoverably* 468.21
irreducible *summary* 204.5
irreflexive relation *mathematical logic* 6.60
irreformability *hopelessness* 282.1
irreformable *hopeless* 282.6
irrefutable *decided* 840.9
irregular 664.3, 766.10; *of grammar* 5.41, *spatial* 6.76, *status adjectives* 11.25, *of flowers* 42.11, *unlawful* 53.23, *enlisted* 58.11, *soldier* 77.4, *free* 407.9, *abnormal* 430.13, *discounted* 495.3, *rough* 544.5, *distorted* 627.6, *periodic* 641.8, *infrequent* 662.2, *unusual* 664.4, *changeable* 666.3, *directional* 677.13, *inconsistent* 732.7, *unequal* 741.4, *discontinuous* 775.7, *unconventional* 782.14, *imperfect* 806.5, *unreliable* 841.15
irregular galaxy *galaxy* 7.5
irregularity 664.1; *illegality* 53.10, *freedom* 407.4, *abnormality* 430.4, *roughness* 544.1, *distortion* 627.1, *infrequency* 662.1, *unusualness* 664.2, *changeableness* 666.1, *inconsistency* 732.3, *irregular order* 766.2, *discontinuity* 775.1, *special case* 779.7, *imperfection* 806.1, *unreliability* 841.7
irregularly 664.6; *grammatically* 5.48, *freely* 407.12, *roughly* 544.13, *asymmetrically* 627.13, 741.11, *for short periods* 641.13, *infrequently* 662.4, *unusually* 664.7, *changeably* 666.7, *inconsistently* 732.16, *in disorder* 766.24, *discontinuously* 775.15, *imperfectly* 806.10, *unreliably* 841.25
irregular motion *movement* 677.3
irregular order 766.2
irregular polyhedron *polyhedron* 6.44
irregular union *fornication* 432.3
irrelative *extraneous* 724.8, *unrelated* 728.6
irrelatively 728.16
irrelativeness *unrelatedness* 728.1
irrelevance *circumlocution* 199.2, *insignificance* 289.4, *lack of meaning* 362.1, *extraneousness* 724.1, *unimportance* 800.1
irrelevance *or* **irrelevancy** *unrelatedness* 728.1
irrelevancy *extraneousness* 724.1, *unimportance* 800.1
irrelevant *circumlocutory* 199.4, *insignificant* 289.10, *meaningless* 362.7, *extraneous* 724.8, *unrelated* 728.6, *unimportant* 800.10
irrelevantly *unexceptionally* 289.20, *meaninglessly* 362.13, *extraneously* 724.16, *irrelatively* 728.16, *unimportantly* 800.21
irreligion *unbelief* 88.4
irreligionist *disbeliever* 88.5
irreligious *disbelieving* 88.6, *impious* 448.11
irreligiously *impiously* 448.17
irremediable *hopeless* 282.6
irremissible *unforgivable* 430.16
irremovable *determined* 379.7, *fast* 464.8
irreparability *hopelessness* 282.1
irreparable *hopeless* 282.6, 837.6
irreparable loss *loss* 468.1
irreparably *hopelessly* 282.13, 837.12
irreplaceability *importance* 799.1
irreplaceable *important* 799.7
irreprehensible *incorrupt* 449.7

irrepressible *refractory* 379.6, *violent* 520.5
irreproachability *virtue* 447.1, *incorruption* 449.2, *perfection* 805.1
irreproachable *virtuous* 447.5, *virtuously* 447.9, *incorrupt* 449.7, *infallible* 805.10
irreproachably *faultlessly* 449.14, *perfectly* 805.21
irresistibility *compulsion* 428.1
irresistible *enticing* 178.13, *compelling* 428.6, *motivational* 508.7, *appealing* 512.9, *attractive* 700.10
irresistible force *compulsion* 428.1, *impulsion* 695.1
irresistible impulse *insanity* 110.1
irresistible progress *improvement* 679.5
irresistibly *enticingly* 178.22, *compellingly* 428.12, *influentially* 508.13, 512.14, *powerfully* 514.21, *attractionally* 700.13
irresolute 461.6, 666.4, 772.13, 841.10; *spineless* 285.5, *vacillating* 378.5, *equivocating* 380.6, *permitting* 502.5, *disabled* 515.10, *weak-willed* 517.10, *inert* 519.2
irresolutely 378.13, 461.10, 772.23; *cowardly* 285.9, *powerlessly* 515.16, *weakly* 517.14, *changeably* 666.7, *uncertainly* 841.22
irresoluteness *vacillation* 378.1, *irresolution* 841.3
irresolution 461.3, 666.2, 841.3; *vacillation* 378.1, 380.3, 683.3, *indecisiveness* 517.2, *inertness* 519.1
irresponsibility *imprudence* 286.3, *folly* 353.1, *inconstancy* 378.2, *capriciousness* 381.2
irresponsible *imprudent* 286.7, *inconstant* 378.6, *erratic* 381.5, *capricious* 841.16
irresponsibly *imprudently* 286.11, *capriciously* 841.26
irretrievability *hopelessness* 282.1
irretrievable *hopeless* 282.6, *losing* 468.9
irretrievable breakdown *ruin* 523.4
irretrievable loss *loss* 468.1
irretrievably *hopelessly* 282.13, *irrecoverably* 468.21
irreverence *lack of wonder* 295.1, *disrespect* 436.1
irreverent *wonderless* 295.3, *disrespectful* 436.9
irreverently *without wonder* 295.8, *disrespectfully* 436.25
irreversibility *hopelessness* 282.1, *determination* 379.2, *stability* 674.1, *improvement* 679.5
irreversible *reactive* 11.29, *hopeless* 282.6, *determined* 379.7, *stable* 674.3, *ongoing* 679.7, *direct* 697.11
irreversible reaction *chemical reaction* 11.8
irreversibly *hopelessly* 282.13, *stably* 674.9
irrevocability *hopelessness* 282.1, *inevitability* 840.5
irrevocable *hopeless* 282.6, 837.6, *stable* 674.3
irrevocably *hopelessly* 282.13, 837.12, *stably* 674.9, *inevitably* 840.17
irrigate *farm* 16.19, *water* 557.29, *cause to flow* 570.11

irrigation *cultivation* 16.7, *watering* 557.8
irrigational *wetting* 557.26
irrigation system *water system* 551.13
irrigator 557.13; *farm tool* 16.5
irriguous [Arch] *wetting* 557.26
irritability *sensitivity* 212.2, *oversensitivity* 267.2, *irritableness* 302.5, 304.3, *irascibility* 303.1
irritable 302.10, 304.9; *susceptible* 212.7, *oversensitive* 267.4, *irascible* 303.8, *argumentative* 329.7, *contentious* 422.20
irritableness 302.5, 304.3
irritably 302.23, 304.17; *oversensitively* 267.7, *irascibly* 303.17, *argumentatively* 329.15, *contentiously* 422.27
irritant *frictional* 554.10
irritate 302.16; *antagonize* 63.12, *annoy* 276.7, 804.10, *cause dislike* 291.16, *cause hate* 300.12, *make irascible* 303.16, *make irritable* 304.15, *meddle* 414.23, *motivate* 508.9, *grind* 554.15, *disturb* 768.10, *make worse* 808.17
irritated *susceptible* 212.7, *resentful* 302.8, *cross* 303.11, *motivated* 508.8, *disturbed* 768.6
irritating *aggravating* 276.4, *disliked* 291.10, *maddening* 302.12, *meddling* 414.17, *annoying* 804.7
irritatingly *annoyingly* 276.9, 804.12, *distastefully* 291.19, *maddeningly* 302.25, *abrasively* 554.17, *disturbingly* 768.13
irritation 554.9; *pain* 215.1, *annoyance* 276.2, 804.2, *resentment* 302.1, *provocation* 302.3, *negative stimulus* 508.4
irrupt *invade* 706.12, *overstep* 712.12
irruption *military attack* 418.2, *inroad* 706.3, *overstepping* 712.1
irruptive *invasive* 706.10
Irtysh Rivers 570
isangoma *witch* 86.15
Isar Rivers 570
ischium Human Bones 19
isidium *lichen* 47.16
isinglass *fish product* 38.9, *semiliquid* 561.7
Isis Deities 82
Islam 81.7
Islamabad Countries 566
Islamic *denominational* 81.23
Islamic architecture Architectural Styles 134
Islamic text 81.18
Islamize *proselytize* 84.15
island 572.2; *landmass* 572.1, *of landmasses* 572.12
island arc *plate tectonics* 8.19
island chain *island* 572.2
island continent *island* 572.2
island group *island* 572.2
Islandia Imaginary Places 360
Island Pramenka Breeds of Sheep 16
Islands of the Blessed *heaven* 82.15
island universe *galaxy* 7.5, *of the Blessed Islands* *heaven* 82.15
isle *island* 572.2
Isle of Dogs, the London 567.8
islet *island* 572.2
isleted *of landmasses* 572.12
isoantibody *blood* 555.4
isobar *weather forecast* 9.4
isobaric *barometric* 9.39
isochronal *synchronized* 649.5, *frequent* 663.6

isochronally *synchronously* 649.9
isochronism *synchronism* 649.2
isochronon Timepieces and Timers 646
isochronous *synchronized* 649.5, *frequent* 663.6
isochronously *synchronously* 649.9
isocracy 49.11
isoenzyme *enzyme* 12.11
isogamy *reproductive body* 47.14
isogloss *regional pronunciation* 205.7
isokont *algae* 47.11
isolate *practice hygiene* 116.4, *choose* 382.14, *exclude* 409.12, 764.7, *separate* 724.14, *set apart* 753.17, *single out* 788.19
isolated *introverted* 108.37, *secret* 182.8, *lonely* 409.8, *secluded* 409.9, *separate* 724.10, *nonconforming* 728.10, *unjoined* 753.9, *aloof* 756.5, *solitary* 782.17, *alone* 788.15, *vulnerable* 811.9
isolated case *item* 788.2
isolated instance *special case* 779.7, *item* 788.2
isolatedly *individualistically* 728.20
isolate oneself *be one* 788.17
isolating *language type* 5.11
isolation *defense mechanism* 108.23, *prophylaxis* 115.4, *hygiene* 116.1, *privacy* 181.6, *separation* 409.3, *separateness* 724.3, *nonconformity* 728.4, *setting apart* 753.2, *aloofness* 756.2, *exclusion zone* 764.3, *aloneness* 788.5, *sanitary precaution* 810.8
isolation block *play* 155.8
isolationism *political and economic philosophy* 4.6, *shyness* 386.3, *nationalism* 566.4, *nonconformity* 728.4, *separateness* 753.3, *aloneness* 788.5, *noninterference* 829.3
isolationist *political and economic philosopher* 4.10, *nationalist* 566.8, *nonconforming* 728.10, *individualist* 756.3, *hermit* 782.9, *loner* 788.8, *alone* 788.15, *free* 829.11
isolationistic *national* 566.10
isolationist nation *country* 566.1
isolation ward *hospital* 107.16
Isolde Famous Lovers 299
isoleucine Amino Acids 12
isolophobia Phobias 283
isomer *structure* 11.7
isomerase *enzyme* 12.11
isomeric *structural* 11.28
isomerism *structure* 11.7
isometric (cubic) crystal *crystal* 8.39
isometric drawing *illustration* 187.2
isometric projection *transformation* 6.46, *map* 187.5
isometrics *health improvement* 113.3
isomorphic *formed* 624.6
isomorphism *form* 624.1
isomorphous *formed* 624.6
isopod *crustacean* 39.10
isoprene rubber *polymer* 11.9
isoprene unit *terpene* 12.20
isopteran *insectile* 40.11
isopterophobia Phobias 283
ISO rating *exposure* 132.15
isosceles *symmetrical* 626.4
isosceles triangle *triangle* 6.41, *angled figure* 628.3
isospin *quantum* 10.63
isostasy *earth movement* 8.20
isostatic *solid-earth* 8.55

isostatic adjustment *earth movement* 8.20
isostatic anomaly *earth movement* 8.20
isotactic *polymeric* 11.35
isotactic polymer *polymer* 11.9
isotherm *weather forecast* 9.4
isothermal *barometric* 9.39, *atmospheric* 9.40
isothermal change *heating effect* 10.28
isotope 10.57; *physical element* 524.5
isotope effect *chemical reaction* 11.8
isotopic *same* 730.7
isotopically *identically* 730.18
isotopy *sameness* 730.1
isotropy *equalization* 740.4
I spy Children's and Party Games 167
Israel *promised land* 458.5, Countries 566
Israeli Friesian Breeds of Cattle 16
issuance *coming out* 707.3, *dispersion* 776.1
issue 328.2; *litigation* 54.1, *report* 171.9, 175.9, *print* 173.17, *publish* 174.19, *magazine* 175.3, *first appearance* 264.3, *become visible* 264.13, *present* 264.15, *line of argument* 329.3, *gist* 329.4, *question* 333.1, *solution* 334.6, *stock exchange* 457.3, *coinage* 484.13, *monetize* 484.24, *product* 522.3, *effect* 676.1, *react* 676.8, *set out* 705.12, *coming out* 707.3, *emerge* 707.14, 771.35, *essential content* 723.2, *part of writing* 760.6, *successor* 770.6, *result* 770.12, *disperse* 776.12, *chief thing* 799.3, *leak* 816.6, 816.11
issue a caveat *warn* 814.8
issue a command *command* 425.10
issue a counterorder *cancel out* 834.8
issue a diploma *authorize* 833.10
issue a flat denial *negate* 190.16
issue a manifesto *command* 425.10
issue an edict *command* 425.10
issue an injunction *demand* 425.11, *restrain* 830.12
issue an ultimatum *demand* 505.12
issue a passport *authorize* 833.10
issue a public warning *warn* 814.8
issue a statement *command* 425.10
issue a suit *petition* 505.11
issue a warning *demand* 425.11
issue a warrant *demand* 425.11
issue a writ *authorize* 833.10
issued *published* 173.12, 174.18, 175.8, *monetary* 484.22, *dispersed* 776.6
issue forth *set out* 705.12, *emerge* 707.14, 771.35
issue from *follow from* 676.9
issue price *stock exchange* 457.3
issuing *outgoing* 707.10
Issyk-Kul Lakes 568
isthmian *of landmasses* 572.12, *narrow* 593.8
isthmus *peninsula* 572.5, *contracted thing* 582.5, *narrow place* 593.2, *means of connection* 754.4
Istoben Breeds of Cattle 16
istoriato ware Ceramics 129
Istrian Milk Breeds of Sheep 16
it [Inf] *enticement* 178.3

Italian architecture Architectural Styles 134
Italianate architecture Architectural Styles 134
Italian Brown Breeds of Cattle 16
Italian Friesian Breeds of Cattle 16
Italian GP at Monza *Formula 1 World Championship races* 146.5
Italian greyhound Breeds of Dogs 35
Italian Heavy Draught Horse and Pony Breeds 159
Italian Open *notable tennis competitions* 165.8
Italian Renaissance Furniture Styles 101
Italian Renaissance style Architectural Styles 134
Italic *language family* 5.12
italic *printed* 173.13
italicize *punctuate* 183.20, *emphasize* 200.6
italicized *punctuated* 183.15
italics *emphasis* 200.1
italic type *type* 173.5
Italy Countries 566
itch *sexual longing* 20.6, *skin disease* 114.16, *stimulus* 212.3, *sense* 212.9, *be touched by* 216.10, *shake* 684.24, *attraction* 700.1
itch for *desire* 288.17
itchiness *restlessness* 684.5
itching *restlessness* 684.5
itchy *exciting* 212.8, *restless* 684.16
itchy foot *restlessness* 414.7
item 788.2; *play part* 136.8, *record* 185.1, *issue* 328.2, *accounts* 493.4, *product* 522.3, *object* 524.6, *division* 577.6, *thing* 717.3, *aspect* 726.4, *component* 760.3, *thing included* 763.2, *one* 788.1
itemization *list* 785.1, *listing* 785.8
itemize 577.13; *register* 185.15, *name* 202.17, *explain* 331.16, *circumstantial* 726.12, *particularize* 760.15, *specify* 779.18, *list* 785.11
itemized 577.9; *accounting* 493.7, *component* 760.12, *listed* 785.9
itemized account *bill* 785.4
items *extra* 748.6, *list* 785.1
iterate 797.16; *persevere* 377.10, *be periodical* 641.9, *be the same* 730.13
iterated 797.9; *constant* 377.8
iteration 797.2; *algorithm* 6.26, *emphasis* 200.1, *constancy* 377.3, *recurrent period* 641.5
iterative *emphatic* 200.3, *periodical* 641.7, *repetitious* 797.11
it follows that *with the effect of* 676.12
I think not! *no!* 190.28
itinerary *plan* 357.2, *route* 691.2, *list of dates* 785.6
it's a boy! *welcome!* 704.24
it's a girl! *welcome!* 704.24
it's all the same to me! *who cares?* 289.21
it serves you right! *revenge!* 420.7
itty-bitty or **itsy-bitsy** [Inf] *tiny* 580.9
IV *four* 791.1
ivories [Inf] *teeth* 19.8, *part of keyboard instrument* 142.6
ivory *white thing* 253.4, *white* 253.7, *hard substance* 542.3
ivory black *black pigment* 254.2
ivory carving *sculpture* 144.1
ivory palm Trees and Shrubs 43
ivory tower *privacy* 181.6, *solitary place* 409.4, *private space* 812.2

ivy *green thing* 260.4
I/we surrender! 421.9
Iwo Jima Islands 572
IX *nine* 792.5
Ixworth Breeds of Fowl 16

J

J *canoeing* 150.26
jab *box* 152.19, *painful injury* 215.3, *inflict pain* 215.10, *type of touch* 216.3, *touch* 216.9, *hit* 418.9, 695.11, *blow* 695.5, *sporting hit* 695.6
jabbed *combat* 152.17
jabber *nonstandard language* 5.7, *boxer* 152.8, *talk* 207.3, *be talkative* 207.7, *empty talk* 362.5, *talk nonsense* 362.12
jabberer *talker* 207.4
jabbering *talk* 207.3, *talkative* 207.5
jabbing *boxing* 152.2, *combat* 152.17
jabot *neckwear* 100.29
jacaranda Trees and Shrubs 43
Jack [Inf] *male title of address* 32.3
jack *male animal* 32.15, *male mammal* 35.18, *hand tool* 103.3, *part of keyboard instrument* 142.6, *green bowling* 151.3, *cards* 168.2, *miscellaneous automotive terms* 687.14, *lifter* 715.5
jack [Inf] *cash* 484.2
jackal *sycophant* 401.3
jackass *male mammal* 35.18, *foolish person* 353.3
jackass bark Sailing Ships and Boats 690
jackass brig Sailing Ships and Boats 690
jackboot *treatment* 399.11, *suppression* 428.2
jackboots *boots* 100.31
jackdaw *songbird* 36.12
jacket 100.18; *packet* 578.4, *body covering* 613.3, *casing* 613.9, *wrap* 613.29, *enclosing thing* 619.3
jacketed *wrapped* 619.5
Jackfield ware Ceramics 129
Jack Frost *ice* 218.5
jack-high *bowls* 151.7
jacking off [Inf] *sex act* 20.10
jack-in-the-pulpit Flowers 42
jackknife *competitive diving* 164.7
jack ladder 713.10
jack-of-all-trades *worker* 123.1, *skilled person* 127.7, *hard worker* 414.11
jack-of-all-trades and master of none *nonentity* 800.8
jack off [Inf] *stimulate* 20.22
jack-o'-lantern *flickering light* 246.10, *illusion* 720.2
jack pine Trees and Shrubs 43
jack plane *woodworking tool* 131.6
jackpot *poker* 168.5, *prize* 453.2, *windfall* 467.7
Jack Russell terrier Breeds of Dogs 35
jacks Children's and Party Games 167
jackscrew *lifter* 715.5
Jackson American States 564
jackstraw *insubstantial person* 720.5
jackstraws Children's and Party Games 167
jack-tar *nautical person* 690.12
jack up *erect* 715.11
jack up [Inf] *intensify* 746.8
Jacob Breeds of Sheep 16

Jacobean Furniture Styles 101, historic 653.13
Jacobean architecture Architectural Styles 134
Jacobean tragedy tragedy 136.10
Jacobin troublemaker 427.5
Jacob's ladder ladder 713.10
jacquard or **jacquard weave** Fabrics and Fibers 130
Jacquard loom fabric-handling tool 130.12
jactation restlessness 684.5
jactitation restlessness 684.5
jaculate throw 696.17
jaculation throwing 696.3
jaculatory projectile 696.13
Jacuzzi™ basin 578.12
jade unpleasant woman 33.7, horse 159.1, green thing 260.4, green 260.7, bore 296.8, fatigue 820.6
jaded bored 296.5, common 778.13, fatigued 820.6
jadedly in a bored manner 296.9
jadedness boredom 296.1, fatigue 820.1
jaeger water bird 36.9
Jaf Horse and Pony Breeds 159
jag drinking bout 121.7
Jagerhorn Mountains and Hills 569
jagged coarse 544.6, toothed 549.13, notched 636.4
jagged edge sharp edge 549.3
jaggedly 636.7; roughly 544.13
jaggedness roughness 544.1
jaggy coarse 544.6, notched 636.4
jaguar variegated thing 263.5
jai alai Sporting Activities 145
Jaidara Breeds of Sheep 16
jail prison 55.1, imprison 55.11, 454.23, exclude 409.14, coercive method 428.3, instrument of punishment 454.13, enclose 584.16, 619.6, enclosed area 619.2
jailbird lawbreaker 53.15, prisoner 55.7, guilty person 450.5
jailbreak escape 816.1
jailbreaker escaper 816.5
jail cell prison cell 55.3
jailed enclosed 584.11, 619.4
jailer prison officer 55.8, person in command 425.5, closer 584.5, one who restrains 830.7
jailhouse prison 55.1
jail sentence prison sentence 55.6, imprisonment 454.2
Jain or **Jaina** or **Jainist** other religious member 81.13
Jainism other religions 81.8
Jainist text other text 81.19
Jakarta Countries 566
jalopy [Inf] automobile 687.6
jam sweets 90.39, play 141.14, sailing 150.25, mountaineer 161.10, sweetener 222.2, muffle 229.11, improvise 396.6, semiliquid 561.7, stuff 577.12, squeeze 582.13, thicken 594.9, delay 658.3, 658.13, stop 668.10, make motionless 678.8, intertwine 752.19, fill 761.11, throng 795.4, crowd 795.11, preserved thing 815.10, roadblock 826.4, malfunction 846.20
jam [Inf] beat time 140.29, predicament 725.3, 824.5
Jamaica Countries 566, Islands 572
Jamaica Hope Breeds of Cattle 16
Jamaica shorts shorts 100.15
jamb Architectural Elements 134
jambalaya rice 90.32
jamboree celebration 405.1

jam cleat sailboat parts and accessories 150.4
James psychologist 108.33, Rivers 570
jam in flood in 706.14, impact 710.11
jam jar pot 578.15
jammed obstructed 584.8, dense 594.6, held up 658.6, accessible 691.13, tied 752.13, full 761.8, crowded 795.10
jamming canoeing 150.26, climbing techniques 161.3, that which makes invisible 245.2
jamming stroke canoeing techniques 150.11
jammy gelatinous 561.16
jam-packed crowded 59.22, 795.10, full 761.8
jam session performance 141.8, improvisation 396.1
jane [Inf] female 33.1
Jane Doe average person 18.9, everyone 778.7
Jane Eyre Famous Lovers 299
jangle be strident 238.7, dissonance 241.1, be dissonant 241.6
jangling dissonant 241.4
janglingly dissonantly 241.7
janissary militarist 77.3
janitor attendant 69.4, cleaner 111.12, laborer 123.9
jansky Scientific and Technical Units 589
January sale sale 482.2
Janus Planets and Their Satellites 7, equivocator 380.4, duality 789.2
Janus-faced equivocating 380.6
Janus-like two-sided 789.9
Jap Nicknames for Inhabitants 61
Japan Countries 566, Islands 572
Japan, Sea of Oceans and Seas 571
japan black pigment 254.2, blacken 254.11, resin 562.6, coating 613.8, coat 613.28
Japanese Breeds of Cattle 16, Furniture Styles 101
Japanese architecture Architectural Styles 134
Japanese beetle pests and diseases 17.12
Japanese bobtail Breeds of Cats 35
Japanese cedar Trees and Shrubs 43
Japanese Chin or **Japanese spaniel** Breeds of Dogs 35
Japanese garden garden 17.2
Japanese GP at Suzuka Formula 1 World Championship races 146.5
Japanese maple Trees and Shrubs 43
Japanese rising sun national emblem 184.7
japanned type of furniture 101.2, resinous 562.13
jape rort 277.6, 368.4
japery amusement 277.2
japonica Flowers 42
Japurá Rivers 570
jar kitchen container 91.7, be strident 238.7, be dissonant 241.6, shock 292.3, surprise 292.9, vessel 578.11, jolt 684.9, 684.23, preserver 815.9
jar(ful) container(ful) 738.2
jardiniere nursery 17.4
jargon 5.21; vernacular 205.8, type of meaning 361.4, nonsense 362.2
jargonal of language 5.35
jargonish of language 5.35
jargonistic of language 5.35, technical 361.10

jargonize use language 5.42
jarhead [Inf] marines 77.26
jarrah Trees and Shrubs 43
jarred surprised 292.5
jarring strident 238.4, dissonant 241.4, surprising 292.7, inelegant 528.6, convulsive 684.19
jarringly dissonantly 241.7
jasmine tea tea 93.7
jaspé striped 263.9
jasper variegated thing 263.5
jasper or **jasperware** Ceramics 129
Jataka other text 81.19
jaundice yellow skin 259.3, jealousy 314.2, prejudice 337.3, bias 342.11
jaundiced unhealthy 114.23, yellow-faced 259.10, jealous 314.5, discriminatory 337.11, unjust 342.7
jaundiced eye unfair treatment 342.4
jaundiced eye or **view** or **look** jealousy 314.2
jaunt travel 686.5
jauntily cheerfully 269.14, flashily 404.32, dashingly 536.10
jauntiness gaiety 269.3
jaunty cheerful 269.7, flashy 404.17
Java Breeds of Fowl 16, Islands 572
java [Inf] coffee 93.6
Java man human ancestor 18.3, prehistoric human 653.7
Javanese Breeds of Cats 35
Java pony Horse and Pony Breeds 159
Java Sea Oceans and Seas 571
javelin Historical Missile Weapons 78, sharp weapon 78.6, javelin throwing 166.15, missile 696.7
javelin carrying javelin throwing 166.15
javelin throw javelin throwing 166.15
javelin thrower thrower 696.10
javelin throwing 166.15, Sporting Activities 145, field event 166.10
jaw mouth 19.7, empty talk 362.5, talk nonsense 362.12, side 623.1
jaw [Inf] talk 207.3, be talkative 207.7
jawbone Human Bones 19
jawbreaker [Inf] word 5.17
jawbreaking [Inf] problematic 824.11
jaw jaw not war war be at peace 73.10
jawless fish fish 38.5
jaws eating organ 92.14
jaws of death personifications and symbols 29.4, danger 811.1
Jaws of Life™ miscellaneous automotive terms 687.14
jay talker 207.4
jay, Florida scrub Endangered US Birds 36
jays Collective Names 59
jazz 140.5; musical 140.25
jazz [Inf] empty talk 362.5
jazz band instrumental group 141.3
jazz dancing Dancing Types 135
jazzed up [Inf] increased 746.5
jazz-funk rock music 140.6
jazzily tunefully 140.30
jazzman composer 141.9
jazz up [Inf] intensify 746.8
JCL Programming Languages 15
jealous 314.5; hostile 63.6, green-eyed 260.11, passionate 266.12,

hating 300.7, resentful 302.8, envious 314.4, selfish 444.4
jealously 314.12; hostilely 63.13, bad feeling 266.5, with hate 300.13, resentfully 302.22, enviously 314.11, selfishly 444.8
jealousness jealousy 314.2
jealous-type delusional disorder psychosis 108.10
jealousy 314.2; personal conflict 63.2, Phobias 283, hate 300.1, resentment 302.1, envy 314.1, rivalry 422.2, selfishness 444.1
jean Fabrics and Fibers 130
jeans informal clothes 100.7, pants 100.14
Jebel Mountains and Hills 569
jeepers or **jeepers creepers!** miscellaneous euphemisms 301.21
jeer cry of disapproval 239.7, hiss 239.17, derision 400.5, act of discourtesy 411.3, taunt 436.6, 436.23, show of disapproval 438.6, show disapproval 438.21, gesture of protest 507.3, complain 507.8
jeer at deride 369.7, disdain 400.16
jeered criticized 438.14
jeerer crier 239.8
jeering hissing 239.12, derisive 400.12, discourtesy 411.1, taunting 436.14, protesting 507.5
jeeringly derisively 369.8, 400.22, rudely 411.9
Jefferson City American States 564
Jehovah God 82.6
Jehovah's Witnesses Christian Groups 81
Jehovan 82.17
Jehu speeder 694.5
jejune underfed 98.7, tasteless 220.4
jejuneness dilution 220.2
jell be dense 540.8, solidify 542.10, thicken 561.21
jelled condensed 540.7, gelatinous 561.16
jellied gelatinous 561.16
jellied eel fish dish 90.19
jellification viscosity 561.1
jellify be dense 540.8, thicken 561.21
jelling condensed 540.7
Jell-O™ dessert 90.35
jelly sweets 90.39, sweetener 222.2, semiliquid 561.7, thicken 561.21, preserver 815.9, preserved thing 815.10
jelly bean sweets 90.39
jellyfish Collective Names 59
jellyfish [Inf] coward 285.3, weak person 517.4
jelly fungi fungi 47.3
jellylike gelatinous 561.16
jellylikeness viscosity 561.1
jelly mold crockery 578.16
jelutong Trees and Shrubs 43
jenny female animal 33.15, female mammal 35.19
jeopardize endanger 811.13
jeopardy danger 811.1, chance 842.1
jeremiad address 209.1
jerk 699.3; be rough 544.10, be irregular 664.5, jolt 684.9, 684.23, be agitated 684.21, shake 684.24, impel 695.9, pull at 699.12
jerk [Inf] unskilled person 128.3, foolish person 353.3
jerkily 684.29; irregularly 664.6
jerkin jacket 100.18
jerkiness irregularity 664.1, agitation 684.1, discontinuity 775.1
jerking irregular 664.3

jerking off [Inf] *sex act* 20.10

jerks, the *spasm* 684.8

jerkwater [Inf] *urban* 567.14, *insignificant* 745.6, *commonplace* 800.17

jerkwater town [Inf] *village* 567.3

jerkwater train *train* 688.4

jerky *irregular* 664.3, *convulsive* 684.19, *discontinuous* 775.7

jeroboam *bottle* 578.14

Jerry Nicknames for Inhabitants 61

jerry [Brit Inf] *place for excretion* 25.11

jerry-built *bungled* 128.7, *unpremeditated* 389.7, *weak* 517.6, *brittle* 548.3, *cheap* 800.16, *unsafe* 811.8

jerrycan *miscellaneous automotive terms* 687.14

Jersey Breeds of Cattle 16, Islands 572

jersey *sweater* 100.17, Fabrics and Fibers 130, *fabric* 130.1, *basketball court* 148.3, *football uniform* 155.2

Jersey Black Giant Breeds of Fowl 16

Jerseymac Apple Varieties 44

Jerusalem Countries 566

Jerusalem Bible *Christian text* 81.16

jest *entertain* 138.16, *joke* 277.6, 368.4, *be humorous* 277.11, *butt* 436.8

jester *clown* 138.10, *humorist* 277.7

jesting *amusement* 277.2

Jesuit *sophist* 330.6

Jesuitical *sophistic* 330.7

jesuitically *sophistically* 330.14

Jesuitism or **Jesuitry** *sophistry* 330.1

jesuitism or **jesuitry** *lack of candor* 192.4

Jesus Notable Friendships 62

Jesus! *miscellaneous swearwords* 301.20

Jesus' acceptance of the cross Stations of the Cross 85

Jesus being stripped of his garments Stations of the Cross 85

Jesus Christ *God the Son* 82.9

Jesus Christ! *miscellaneous swearwords* 301.20

Jesus' death Stations of the Cross 85

Jesus' encounter with his mother Stations of the Cross 85

Jesus' encounter with the women of Jerusalem Stations of the Cross 85

Jesus' first fall Stations of the Cross 85

Jesus freak [Inf] *religionist* 81.14

Jesus' removal from the cross Stations of the Cross 85

Jesus' second fall Stations of the Cross 85

Jesus' third fall Stations of the Cross 85

jet *engine type* 14.11, *snowplow* 162.29, *dark thing* 247.3, *black thing* 254.3, *black* 254.5, *flyable* 689.12, *means of propulsion* 696.2, *propellant* 696.9, *outflow* 707.4, *run out* 707.4, *disgorgement* 709.6, *let out* 709.26, *upturn* 713.2, *spring up* 713.22

jet-black *black* 254.5

jet boat or **jetboat** Ships and Boats 690

jet fuel *fuels* 106.2

jet lag *miscellaneous aviation terms* 689.9

jet-lagged *fatigued* 820.2

jet plane or **jet airplane** *aircraft* 689.3

jet power *type of power* 514.6

jet-propelled *swift* 694.6, *propelled* 696.14

jetsam *transferred thing* 685.6

jet set *aristocracy* 70.2, *the rich* 485.7, *fashionable elite* 536.4, *avant-garde* 652.6, *prosperous person* 847.4

jet-setter *nobleman* 70.1, *pleasure-seeker* 744.4, *busy person* 414.10, *fashionable elite* 536.4

jet skiing Sporting Activities 145

jet stream *air movement* 9.11

jetstream *air flow* 558.4

jettison *discard* 383.12, *renounce* 392.4, *stop using* 394.10, *lighten* 539.9, *eviction* 709.4, *throw away* 709.25

jettisoned *relinquished* 392.2, *disused* 394.8

jet turn *skiing techniques* 162.5

jetty *black* 254.5, *water system* 551.13, *harbor* 812.6, *barrier* 826.7

jeune premier *role* 136.23, *actor* 136.25

jeune première *role* 136.23, *actor* 136.25

jeunesse dorée [Fr] *the rich* 485.7

Jew 81.11

jewel *good thing* 445.9, *attractive female* 529.5, *jewelry* 532.6, *axle* 682.7

jeweler *artisan* 123.13, *decorator* 532.8

jewel in the crown *object of pride* 297.6, *excellence* 445.4, *showpiece* 843.3

jewelry 532.6; *accessory* 100.28

jewelry box *box* 578.5

Jewish *denominational* 81.23

Jewish calendar *calendar* 646.3

Jewish text 81.17

Jew's harp Musical Instruments 142

jib *sailboat parts and accessories* 150.4, *ski* 162.35, *dissociate* 375.14, *hesitate* 378.10

jib [Brit] *shrink back* 680.20

jib at [Brit] *refuse* 506.8

jibe *sailing terms* 150.5, *sail* 150.29, *taunt* 436.6, 436.23, *navigate* 690.15

jibing *taunting* 436.14

jiffy or **jiff** [Inf] *instant* 645.3

jig Dances 135, *dance* 135.7, *bait* 154.6, *prototype* 624.2, *jolt* 684.9, *shake* 684.24, *jerk* 699.3, *pull at* 699.12

jig about *dance* 135.7

jigger *size of drink* 93.3, *ceramic workshop and tools* 129.8, *make ceramics* 129.10

jiggery-pokery [Brit inf] *foul play* 193.6

jiggle *shake* 684.24, *jerk* 699.3, *pull at* 699.12

jiggler *agitator* 684.14

jigsaw *hand tool* 103.3, *woodworking tool* 131.6, *collaboration* 757.2

jigsaw puzzles Hobbies and Pastimes 167

jihad *holy war* 76.8

jill *female mammal* 35.19

jillion [Inf] *large number* 783.3, *million* 792.11, *myriad* 795.7

jillions [Inf] *multitude* 795.1

jilt *dislike* 291.12, *thwart* 293.10, *withdraw* 392.5

jilted *disliked* 291.10, *frustrated* 293.5

jim-dandy [Inf] *good thing* 445.9, *great* 445.14

jimjams [Inf] *drunken behavior* 121.4, *symptoms of fear* 283.3

jimmy *hand tool* 103.3

jingle Poem or Verse Forms 139, *ringing* 236.2

jingle [Inf] *telephone call* 169.11

jingling Johnny Musical Instruments 142

jingo *bigot* 337.7

jingoism *bellicosity* 76.15, *social discrimination* 337.4, *nationalism* 566.4

jingoist *militarist* 77.3, *bigot* 337.7, *nationalist* 566.8

jingoistic *of language* 5.35, *discriminatory* 337.11, *national* 566.10

jingoistically *prejudicially* 337.17, *nationally* 566.13

jinn *ghost* 86.11, Legendary Creatures 360

jinx *spell* 86.8, *bewitch* 86.25, *curse* 301.1, 301.13, *make evil* 446.11, *cause adversity* 848.15

jinxed *bewitched* 86.21, *cursed* 301.8

jism [Inf] *body fluid* 555.3

jitterbug *dancer* 135.4, *dance* 135.7

jitterbugging Dancing Types 135

jitteriness *agitation* 684.1

jitters *symptoms of fear* 283.3, *agitation* 684.1

jittery *sensitive* 266.11, *oversensitive* 267.4, *fearful* 283.10, *agitated* 684.15

jive *jazz* 140.5

jive [Inf] *empty talk* 362.5

jiver *dancer* 135.4

jo [Scot] *loved one* 299.13

Job *poor person* 486.6

job 122.3; *computing terms* 15.22, *task* 122.2, *undertaking* 391.1, *deed* 412.2, *line of duty* 433.3, *business* 480.6, 509.3, *employment* 573.3, *opportunity* 583.8, *engagement* 833.2

job [Inf] *theft* 479.2

jobber *contractor* 459.6, *trader* 480.11

jobbery *cunning* 822.1

jobbing *trade* 480.1

job description *bargaining terms* 57.10

job due yesterday *haste* 818.1

job flexibility *bargaining terms* 57.10

jobless *unemployed* 413.10, *not working* 415.10

joblessness *unemployment* 413.5

job lot *miscellany* 751.3

job satisfaction *reward* 453.1

Job's comforter *hopeless person* 282.5

job sharing *delegation* 79.3

job training *educational system* 48.2

Jock Nicknames for Inhabitants 61

jock *macho man* [Inf] 32.6

jock [Inf] *sportsman* 145.4

jockey *horse person* 159.14, *conduct oneself* 399.17, *athlete* 422.15, *be cunning* 822.5

jockey cap *cap* 100.33

jockeying *tactics* 399.12

jockeying for position *tactics* 399.12

jockey's colors *clothing* 184.6

jockstrap *underwear* 100.22, *sports equipment* 166.17, *body support* 605.6

jocose *humorous* 277.9

jocular *humorous* 277.9

jodhpurs *pants* 100.14

Joe [Inf] *male* 32.1

joe [Inf] *average person* 18.9

Joe Blow [Inf] *average person* 18.9, *commoner* 71.1, *everyone* 778.7

Joe Doakes [Inf] *average person* 18.9, *commoner* 71.1, *everyone* 778.7

Joe Schmo [Inf] *average person* 18.9

Joe Six-Pack [Inf] *everyone* 778.7

joey *young mammal* 35.20

jog *be healthy* 113.11, *ride* 159.16, *gesture* 183.17, *motivate* 508.9, *bodily movement* 677.11, *walk* 677.17, *jolt* 684.9, 684.23, *slow motion* 693.3, *move slowly* 693.11, *blow* 695.5, *impel* 695.9, *jerk* 699.3, *pull at* 699.12

jogging *health improvement* 113.3, *bodily improvement* 807.10

jogging pants *pants* 100.14

jogging suit *suit* 100.16, *sports equipment* 166.17

joggle *jolt* 684.9, 684.23, *blow* 695.5, *impel* 695.9, *jerk* 699.3, *pull at* 699.12

joggling *shaky* 684.18

jog on *march on* 679.11

jog one's memory *remind* 354.13

jog trot *bodily movement* 677.11, *slow motion* 693.3

john [Inf] *place for excretion* 25.11

John Barleycorn *alcohol* 121.5

John Doe *average person* 18.9, *everyone* 778.7

johnnycake *bread* 90.10

Johnny-come-lately *new arrival* 652.7, *latecomer* 658.4

Johnny-on-the-spot [Inf] *early comer* 657.4

John Q. Public *average person* 18.9, 742.4, *everyone* 778.7

Johnsonese *obscurity* 197.1

Johnsonian *obscure* 197.1

joie de vivre [Fr] *pleasure* 214.2, *joy* 269.1

join 609.10, 827.17; *put together* 59.30, *join in marriage* 64.20, *juxtapose* 586.14, *meet* 704.20, *enroll* 706.16, *make the same* 730.16, *form an alliance* 735.25, *add* 748.11, *support* 748.14, *joint* 752.7, *unite* 752.14, *intertwine* 752.19, *connection* 754.1, *connect* 754.13, *cause to adhere* 755.10, *combine* 757.9, *complete* 761.9, *concatenate* 774.13, *become one* 788.18, *repair* 809.10

join (a group) *unify* 752.15

join a charmed circle *limit* 830.13

join a consortium *contract* 459.8

join a hunting party *hunt* 160.12

join battle *confront* 828.19

joined 131.8; *cumulate* 59.20, *married* 64.16, *juxtaposed* 586.9, *related* 727.6, *additional* 748.8, *united* 752.10, *connected* 754.11, *combined* 757.5, *included* 763.4, *whole* 788.12, *associated* 794.14

joiner *artisan* 123.13, *woodworker* 131.4, *social person* 408.7, *person who joins* 752.9

joinery *woodworking* 131.1

join forces *band together* 59.27, *join with* 827.15

join forces with *come together* 757.10

join hands *come together* 757.10
join hands with *join with* 827.15
join in *socialize* 2.14, *participate* 145.6, 408.15, *be sociable* 414.22, *attend* 575.14, *work together* 827.14
join in battle *battle* 76.33
joining *juxtaposition* 586.4, *junction* 609.5, *convergent* 702.7, *addition* 748.1, *union* 752.1, *connection* 754.1
joining of forces *joint operation* 827.4
joining together *collection* 59.2, *construction* 59.16, *unification* 752.5, *combination* 757.1
joining up *war measures* 76.18
join in holy wedlock *join in marriage* 64.20
join in marriage **64.20**
join in the melee *fight* 422.23
join issue with *conflict* 422.26
join one's fortunes to *join with* 827.15
joint **752.7, 827.10**; *rock* 8.30, *carpenter's term* 131.5, *jointly possessing* 469.12, *interaction* 616.2, *means of connection* 754.4, *connective* 754.10, *combinatory* 757.6
joint [Inf] *the inside* 55.2, *hotel* 60.12, *drug dose* 121.15, *gambling house* 167.5
Joint Academic Network (JANET) *computer communications* 15.25
joint action *joint operation* 827.4
joint bank account *joint possession* 469.6
joint bar *rail* 688.3
Joint Chiefs of Staff *military organization* 58.4, *military staff* 58.5
joint consultation *strike* 57.8
joint control **827.5**
joint disease **114.19**
jointed *arthropodal* 39.22, *joined* 131.8, *fishing* 154.13, *angular* 628.7, *united* 752.10
jointed plugs *bait* 154.6
joint effort *or* venture *joint operation* 827.4
jointer *woodworking tool* 131.6
join the army **76.31**
join the chain gang *be in prison* 55.13
join the chase *hunt* 385.14
joint heir *beneficiary* 473.6
join the rat race [Inf] *be busy* 414.19
join the service *enlist* 58.13
joint immobility *Phobias* 283
jointing *unification* 752.5
jointly *cliquishly* 59.32, *in common* 469.17, *additionally* 748.15, *as one* 752.21, *in connection with* 754.16, *in combination* 757.11, *cooperatively* 827.18
jointly possessed *jointly possessing* 469.12
jointly possessing **469.12**
join together *put together* 59.30, *combine* 757.9
joint operation **509.2, 827.4;** *offensive warfare* 76.11
joint owner *possessor* 469.10
joint ownership *joint possession* 469.6
joint possession **469.6**
joint regulations *work practices* 57.2
joint resolution *declaration* 376.2
joint tenancy *joint possession* 469.6
jointure *legal property terms* 470.2

joint venture *joint operation* 509.2
join up *enlist* 58.13, *band together* 59.27, *join the army* 76.31
join up with *join with* 827.15
join with **827.15;** *unify* 752.15
joist *wood* 131.3, *carpenter's term* 131.5, *carpenter* 131.10, *Architectural Elements* 134, *superstructure* 551.7, *supporting part* 605.3
joisted *joined* 131.8
jojoba *Trees and Shrubs* 43
joke **277.6, 368.4;** *unskilled person* 128.3, *entertain* 138.16, *hoax* 193.7, *humorist* 277.7, *be humorous* 277.11, *form of derision* 369.2, *butt* 436.8
joker *clown* 138.10, *cards* 168.2, *artifice* 193.5, *derider* 369.3, *obstacle* 826.2
joker [Inf] *male* 32.1
joke's *or* laugh's on you!, the *revenge!* 420.7
jokesmith *humorist* 277.7
joke writer *dramatist* 136.27
jokey *humorous* 277.9
jokiness *humor* 277.1
joking *amusement* 277.2, *humorous* 277.9
jokingly *humorously* 277.13, *derisively* 369.8
jollification *celebration* 405.1
jolliness *rejoicing* 279.1
jollity *gaiety* 269.3, *celebration* 405.1, *sociability* 408.1
jolly *cheerful* 269.7, *rejoicing* 279.4, *sociable* 408.11
jolly boat *Sailing Ships and Boats* 690, *Ships and Boats* 690
Jolly Roger *flag* 184.8
jolt **684.9, 684.23;** *shock* 292.3, *surprise* 292.9, *motivate* 508.9, *be rough* 544.10, *collision* 695.2, *blow* 695.5, *impel* 695.9, *jerk* 699.3, *pull at* 699.12
jolted *surprised* 292.5
joltiness *roughness* 544.1, *turbulence* 684.3, *discontinuity* 775.1
jolting *surprising* 292.7, *bumpy* 544.8, *convulsive* 684.19
jolty *convulsive* 684.19, *discontinuous* 775.7
Jonared *Apple Varieties* 44
Jonathan *Apple Varieties* 44, *Notable Friendships* 62
jones [Inf] *drug use* 121.9, *opiates* 121.17
jongleur *entertainer* 138.8, *author* 139.13
jonquil *Flowers* 42
Jonsonian comedy *historic comedy* 136.12
Jordan *Countries* 566, *Rivers* 570
Joséphine *Famous Lovers* 299
Joseph's coat *variegated thing* 263.5
josh *be humorous* 277.11
joshing *amusement* 277.2
Joshua tree *Trees and Shrubs* 43
joss stick *incense* 226.3
jostle *disrespect* 156.18, *meet* 586.15, *jolt* 684.9, 684.23, *blow* 695.5, *impel* 695.9
jostling crowd *business* 414.6
jot *inscribe* 185.14, *little piece* 580.4, *fragment* 787.3, *little bit* 800.4, *suggestion* 800.9
jot down *inscribe* 185.14
jotter *record book* 185.5
jottings *notes* 185.3
Jotunheimen *Mountains and Hills* 569
joule *heat measurement* 217.2,

Scientific and Technical Units 589
Joule–Kelvin effect *Classical Physical Laws* 10
Joule's laws *Classical Physical Laws* 10
Joule–Thomson effect *Classical Physical Laws* 10
jounce *jolt* 684.9, 684.23
journal *chronicle* 3.4, *machine element* 14.8, *collection* 105.12, *nonfiction* 139.6, *publication media* 173.6, *periodical* 175.1, *magazine* 175.3, *record book* 185.5, *account book* 493.3, *periodical publication* 641.6, *chronology* 646.2, *axle* 682.7, *bill* 785.3
journal box *axle* 682.7
journalese *jargon* 5.21, *news story* 171.3
journalism *news* 171.1, *news reporting* 171.5, *publication media* 173.6, *factual account* 202.4
journalist *professional worker* 123.11, *news reporting* 171.5, *record keeper* 185.8, *descriptive writer* 202.10, *curious person* 321.3, *questioner* 333.9, *news interpreter* 365.7, *coverer* 613.18
journalistic *of language* 5.35, *newsworthy* 171.8, 175.7, *skeptical* 333.14
journalistically **175.10;** *colloquially* 5.45, *newsworthily* 171.10
journalize *account* 493.9
journey *travel* 686.5, 686.11, *passing* 692.3, *proceed* 692.16
journeyer *traveler* 686.6
journeying *travel* 686.5, *traveling* 686.9
journeyman *artisan* 123.13, *skilled person* 127.7
journeyman watch *Timepieces and Timers* 646
journey's end *destination* 704.6, *end point* 773.6
journeywork *work* 122.1
joust *fight* 77.35, *duel* 422.12
jousting *duel* 422.12
jousting armor *historic armor* 419.8
joust with *contend* 422.22
Jove *Deities* 82
JOVIAL *Programming Languages* 15
jovial *cheerful* 269.7, *sociable* 408.11
joviality *gaiety* 269.3, *sociability* 408.1
Jovian *astronomical* 7.33
jowl *side* 623.1
joy **269.1;** *pleasant thing* 271.4, *rejoicing* 279.1
joyful **269.6;** *rejoicing* 279.4
joyfully **269.13;** *rejoicingly* 279.7
joyfulness *joy* 269.1, *rejoicing* 279.1
joyful person **269.5**
joyless *depressed* 270.5
joylessly *sorrowfully* 270.10
joylessness *depression* 270.2
joyous *joyful* 269.6, *celebrative* 405.9, *festive* 408.13
joyously *joyfully* 269.13, *sociably* 408.19
joyousness *joy* 269.1
joyride *borrow illegally* 476.12
joyriding *illegal borrowing* 476.3
joystick *input device* 15.11, *guide* 126.6
J stroke *canoeing techniques* 150.11
Juba *Rivers* 570
jubbah *robe* 100.20

jubilant *joyful* 269.6, *rejoicing* 279.4
jubilantly *rejoicingly* 279.7
jubilate *rejoice* 279.5, *celebrate* 405.10
jubilation *rejoicing* 279.1, 405.8, *celebration* 405.1
jubilatory *celebrative* 405.9
jubilee *rejoicing* 279.1, *celebration* 405.1, *commemoration* 405.2, *anniversary* 405.5, *twenty and over* 792.8
Júcar *Rivers* 570
Judaeo-Christian *denominational* 81.23
Judaic *denominational* 81.23
Judaical *denominational* 81.23
Judaism **81.6**
Judaize *proselytize* 84.15
Judas *hypocrite* 192.9, *malefactor* 306.6, *equivocator* 380.4, *villain* 448.5
Judas-like *villainous* 448.12
Judas tree *Trees and Shrubs* 43
judder [Brit] *shake* 684.7, *jolt* 684.23
juddering [Brit] *shaking* 684.6, *shaky* 684.18
judge **53.32, 54.10, 54.31, 68.4, 341.5, 341.10;** *propound a philosophy* 4.21, *know* 48.24, *person in authority* 52.7, *law officer* 53.6, *court officer* 54.7, *litigate* 54.27, *try a case* 54.28, *judge* 54.31, *mediator* 75.2, *mediate* 75.6, *karate* 152.14, *tae kwon do* 152.15, *track and field eventer* 166.19, *compete in track and field* 166.21, *adviser* 176.5, *advise* 176.9, *reason* 319.11, *discriminator* 337.6, *discriminate* 337.12, *estimate* 341.11, *be wise* 352.6, *interpret* 365.12, *person in command* 425.5, *have authority over* 425.12, *impartial person* 443.3, *punisher* 454.16, *moderator* 521.2, *moderate* 521.7, *rule* 780.12, *one who restrains* 830.7
judge advocate *law officer* 53.6
judge advocate general *judge* 54.10
judge and jury *place of judgment* 341.3
judge best *select* 382.12
judge by eye *estimate* 341.11
judged **337.10, 341.9**
judge fairly *be right* 429.12
Judge of all men *God the Father* 82.8
judgeship *position of authority* 52.4
judging **341.7;** *judgment* 341.1
judgment **341.5;** *philosophy* 4.1, *refinement* 48.10, *verdict* 54.18, 341.2, *unfavorable verdict* 54.20, *mediation* 75.1, *belief* 87.1, *personnel management* 126.4, *recommendation* 176.2, *intelligence* 315.2, *reason* 319.1, *judiciousness* 337.2, *wisdom* 352.1, *interpretation* 365.1, *intentionality* 374.2, *declaration* 376.2, *selection* 382.1, *reckoning* 454.8, *ruling* 780.2
judgmental *displeased* 291.6, *reasoning* 319.7, *judging* 341.7
judgmentally *wisely* 4.28, *discerningly* 48.27, *mediatorially* 75.7, *judiciously* 337.16, *judicially* 341.12
Judgment Day *place of judgment* 341.3, *future condition* 650.3
judgment day **341.4**
judgment seat *tribunal* 54.6, *place of judgment* 341.3

judicative *judiciary* 53.19, *judicatory* 54.24

judicatorial *jurisdictional* 53.18, *judicatory* 54.24

judicatory **54.24;** *jurisdictional* 53.18, *judiciary* 53.19, *judicious* 341.8

judicature *jurisdiction* 53.3

judicial *judiciary* 53.19, *judicatory* 54.24, *judicious* 341.8

judicial assembly *place of judgment* 341.3

judicial branch *United States government* 49.21

judicially 341.12; *legally* 53.33

judicial murder *execution* 30.6, *capital punishment* 454.12

judicial oath *vow* 189.3

judicial opinion *ruling* 780.2

judicial separation *separation* 66.2

judiciary 53.19; *United States government* 49.21, *jurisdictional* 53.18, *judge* 54.10, *place of judgment* 341.3

judicious 341.8; *rational* 4.15, *refined* 48.20, *judiciary* 53.19, *advisable* 176.8, *prudent* 287.7, *thoughtful* 315.10, *discriminating* 337.9, *wise* 352.4, *moderate* 521.3, *convenient* 803.3

judiciously 337.16; *wisely* 4.28, 352.8, *discerningly* 48.27, *advisably* 176.13, *prudently* 287.17, *intelligently* 315.14, *judicially* 341.12, *moderately* 521.10

judiciousness 337.2; *prudence* 287.2, *thought* 315.5, *wisdom* 352.1, *moderation* 521.1

judo 152.13, Sporting Activities 145, *combat sport* 152.1, *wrestling* 152.18, *self-defense* 419.5

judo club *judo* 152.13

judo grade *judo* 152.13

judoist *judo* 152.13

judoka (judo player) *judo* 152.13

judo kata *judo* 152.13

judo mat *judo* 152.13

judo match *judo* 152.13

judo referee *judo* 152.13

jug *drink container* 93.13, *water carrier* 557.16, *vessel* 578.11

jug [Inf] *the inside* 55.2, *imprison* 55.11

jug ear *ear* 228.2

jug-eared *eared* 228.10

Jugendstil Western Art Styles 133, Architectural Styles 134, Western Literary Groups 139

juggernaut *agent of destruction* 523.7

juggle *entertain* 138.16, *practice sophistry* 330.11, *be cunning* 822.5

juggler *entertainer* 138.8, *circus performer* 138.9, *cunning person* 822.3

jugglery *cunning* 822.1

juice 555.2; *mixed drink* 93.12, *extract* 711.8

juice [Inf] *electric current* 10.39, *alcoholic drink* 93.9, *alcohol* 121.5

juice bar *eating place* 92.17

juiced [Inf] *dead drunk* 121.27

juice extractor *liquidizer* 555.11

juiceless *dried-up* 560.9

juice of the grape *wine* 93.11

juicer *cooking equipment* 91.6

juice up *invigorate* 518.5

juicily *fluidly* 555.26

juiciness 555.7; *youthfulness* 26.2

juicy *compressible* 543.9, *flowing* 555.15, *seasonal* 654.7

juicy part [Inf] *role* 136.23

jujitsu Sporting Activities 145, *combat sport* 152.1

juju *sacred object* 83.11, *talisman* 86.9

juju house *brothel* 432.5

julep *mixed drink* 93.12

Julian calendar *calendar* 646.3

Julia set Mathematical Concepts 6

julienne *cook* 91.10

Juliet Planets and Their Satellites 7, Famous Lovers 299

Juliet cap *cap* 100.33

jumar *mountaineer* 161.10

jumaring *climbing techniques* 161.3

jumars *climbing equipment* 161.4

jumble *miscellany* 59.15, 751.3, *indiscrimination* 338.4, *be indiscriminate* 338.10, *disorder* 625.4, 766.17, *mix* 732.12, *mixture* 751.1, *mix up* 751.13, *confusion* 984.8, *impair* 808.18

jumbled *indiscriminate* 338.8, *complicated* 751.10, *mixed up* 751.11, *disordered* 766.9, *muddled* 766.13, *problematic* 824.11

jumble sale [Brit] *sale* 482.2, *bazaar* 483.10, *bargain* 495.2, *discounter* 497.7

jumbo [Inf] *big thing* 579.9, *huge* 579.14

jumbo jet *aircraft* 689.3

Jumna Rivers 570

jump 713.7; *fencing movements* 153.3, *balance beam* 157.3, *floor exercise* 157.4, *exercise* 157.12, *ride* 159.16, *skiing* 162.1, *ice-skating techniques* 162.16, *snowplow* 162.29, *ice-skate* 162.36, *jumping* 166.11, *participate* 166.22, *shock* 292.3, *be surprised* 292.12, *strike* 418.21, *interval* 587.1, *bodily movement* 677.11, *jolt* 684.9, 684.23, *be agitated* 684.21, *acceleration* 694.3, *be swift* 694.10, *crossing* 712.2, *overstep* 712.12, *spring up* 713.22, *advantage* 744.3, *spread* 746.3

jump, the *advantage* 618.4

jump about *be agitated* 684.21

jump ahead *accelerate* 694.14

jump at *be eager* 373.13, *chase* 385.13

jump at the bidding of *pander to* 401.11

jump at the chance *assent* 346.6, *get in early* 657.16

jump a wave *windsurf* 150.33

jump bail *run away* 386.21, *escape* 816.8

jump ball *playing terms* 148.4

jump down someone's throat [Inf] *vent one's anger* 302.21, *show impatience* 303.14

jumped at *selected* 382.11

jumper *dress* 100.11, *gymnast* 157.10, *track and field eventer* 166.19, *snow vehicle* 687.9

jumper [Brit] *sweater* 100.17

jumpers *baby clothes* 100.24

jump for joy *rejoice* 279.5

jump forward *fence* 153.7

jump from a high place *commit suicide* 30.24

jump higher *improve* 467.18

jump in *dive* 164.15, *mount* 713.24

jumpiness *fearfulness* 283.2, *restlessness* 414.7, *agitation* 684.1

jumping 166.11; *gymnastics* 157.1, *balance beam* 157.3, *floor exercise* 157.4, *equine* 159.15, *field event* 166.10, *track and field* 166.20, *convulsive* 684.19, *leaping* 713.17

jumping at the chance *getting ahead* 657.7

jumping from a high place *suicide* 30.8

jumping-off place *village* 567.3, *distant place* 585.3

jumping-off place *or* **point** *baseline* 601.4

jumping-off point *place of departure* 705.4

jump in the middle *mediate* 75.6

jump in time *interval* 775.2

jump jockey [Brit] *horse person* 159.14

jump on *set out* 705.12

jump on the bandwagon *assent to* 346.7, *follow* 401.14, *be the same* 730.13, *conform* 735.27, *emulate* 736.11, *abide by* 781.12

jump out *emerge* 707.14

jump out of one's skin *be afraid* 283.14, *be surprised* 292.12

jump overboard *commit suicide* 30.24

jump rope Children's and Party Games 167

jumps *diving* 164.6

jumps [Inf] *symptoms of fear* 283.3

jump ship *abscond* 576.16

jump shot *playing terms* 148.4

jump start *miscellaneous automotive terms* 687.14

jump-start *start* 696.20

jumpsuit *suit* 100.16

jump the gun *start early* 657.12

jump the wall *be liberated* 831.7

jump to it *push* 414.20, *be early* 657.11

jump to one's feet *arise* 715.15

jump turn *skiing techniques* 162.5

jump up *spring up* 713.22, *arise* 715.15

jumpy *susceptible* 212.7, *oversensitive* 267.4, *fearful* 283.10, *fidgety* 414.14, *convulsive* 684.19

juncaceous *taxonomic* 41.16

junction 609.5, 691.9; *collection* 59.2, *contiguity* 216.4, *juxtaposition* 586.4, *angle* 628.1, *crossing point* 692.7, *meeting place* 702.4, *destination* 704.6, *union* 752.1, *joint* 752.7, *point of union* 752.8, *means of connection* 754.4

junction box *point of union* 752.8

juncture *circumstances* 573.2, *nearness* 586.1, *junction* 609.5, *point in time* 645.4, *occurrence* 726.2, *interval* 739.4, *joint* 752.7, *point of union* 752.8

Juneau American States 564

juneberry Trees and Shrubs 43

Jung *psychologist* 108.33

Jungfrau Mountains and Hills 569

Jungian psychology Psychological Theories, Schools 108

jungle *plants* 41.1, *trees* 43.4, *mix-up* 766.5

jungle-green *green* 260.7

junglegym *amusement park and playground equipment* 167.8

jungle warfare *warfare* 76.3

junior *young person* 26.7, *young* 26.11, *learner* 48.6, *inferior* 745.4, *subordinate* 745.8, 832.8, *dependent* 832.4

junior chamber of commerce (Jaycees) *economic zone* 480.4

junior college *type of school* 48.12

junior high *school* 48.11

juniority *subjection* 832.1

junior judo *judo* 152.13

junior lightweight *boxing weight divisions* 152.6

junior-lightweight *combat* 152.17

junior minister *politician* 50.7

junior officer *military position* 58.6

junior rank *subjection* 832.1

junior varsity player *football player* 155.15

juniper Trees and Shrubs 43

juniper berries Herbs and Spices 91

junk *discard* 383.12, *renounce* 392.4, *cheap item* 497.5, Sailing Ships and Boats 690, *residue* 750.2, *refuse* 802.5

junk [Inf] *opiates* 121.17, *empty talk* 362.5, *throw away* 709.25

junk art Western Art Styles 133

junked *disused* 394.8

junket *feast* 92.9, *celebrate* 405.10, *semiliquid* 561.7, *travel* 686.5

junk food *food* 90.1

junkie [Inf] *drug taker* 121.12

junk mail *postal communication* 169.4

junkman *or* **junk dealer** *peddler* 482.9

junk room *room* 60.9

junk sale *sale* 482.2

junk shop *discounter* 497.7

Juno Planets and Their Satellites 7, *gods and goddesses of marriage* 64.14, Deities 82

Junoesque *attractive* 529.8

Jupiter Planets and Their Satellites 7, *planet* 7.16, Deities 82

jural *judicatory* 54.24

Jurassic Period Geologic Time Intervals 8

Jur. D. (J.D.) *lawyer* 54.5

juridical *jurisdictional* 53.18, *judicious* 341.8

jurisdiction 53.3, 54.2; *governance* 52.6, *pretrial proceedings* 54.13, *authority* 514.5, *sphere* 564.10, *leadership* 744.2

jurisdictional 53.18, 54.23

jurisdictionally *legally* 53.33

jurisdictive *jurisdictional* 53.18, 54.23

Juris Doctor *lawyer* 54.5

jurisprudence 53.13

jurisprudential *legislative* 53.17, *judicatory* 54.24

jurisprudentially *legally* 53.33

jurist *lawyer* 54.5, *arguer* 319.6, *judge* 341.5

juristically *legally* 53.33

juror *jury* 54.11, 341.6

Juruá Rivers 570

jury **54.11, 341.6;** *tae kwon do* 152.15

jury box *courtroom* 54.12

jury instructions *closing arguments* 54.17

jury list *jury* 54.11, *list of names* 785.7

juryman *jury* 54.11

jury mast *safety device* 810.15

jury member *impartial person* 443.3

jury of one's peers *jury* 54.11

jury panel *jury* 54.11

jury poll *electing* 382.5

jury rig *safety device* 810.15

jury-rig *handle sailboat equipment* 150.30, *improvise* 396.6

jury-rigged *improvised* 396.4

jury-rigging *improvisation* 396.1

jury selection **54.14**

jury service *jury selection* 54.14

jurywoman *jury* 54.11

jus civile *law* 53.1

jus gentium *law* 53.1

jussive *grammatical term* 5.29

just *legal* 53.16, *impartial* 289.9, *judicious* 341.8, *accurately* 350.6, *wise* 352.4, *right* 429.7, *rightful* 429.9, *moral* 431.9, *disinterested* 443.4, *principled* 447.6, *moderate* 521.1, *newly* 652.21, *equal* 740.8, *free* 829.11

just a bit *by degrees* 739.10

just about *nearly* 586.18

just a few *few* 796.1

just alike *same* 730.7

just a minute *short duration* 643.3

just around the corner *nearby* 586.17, *future* 650.6, *in the future* 650.13, *imminent* 657.9

just as *as* 649.10, *similarly* 733.17

just a second *short duration* 643.3

just as *or* **what one thought** *predictable* 295.4

just as one would wish *perfectly* 805.21

just a tick [Brit inf] *short duration* 643.3

just between ourselves *secretly* 182.14

just caught *faint* 233.6

just cause *defense* 441.2

just compensation *equalization* 740.4

just deserts *retaliation* 420.1, *reward* 453.1, *retribution* 454.7

just do *suffice* 97.6

juste-milieu [Fr] *medium* 742.2

just enough *enough* 97.10

just happen *chance* 842.12

just heard *faint* 233.6

just here *where* 565.12

justice *legality* 53.9, *judge* 54.10, 68.4, 341.5, Phobias 283, *impartiality* 289.3, 338.2, *retaliation* 420.1, *rightfulness* 429.1, *morals* 431.2, *disinterestedness* 443.1, *virtues* 447.2, *reward* 453.1, *retribution* 454.7, *moderation* 521.1, *equality* 740.1

Justice Department *law enforcement agency* 53.7

justice of the peace (JP) *law officer* 53.6, *judge* 54.10, *person in authority* 52.7, *judge* 68.4

justice seen to be done *legal process* 54.3

justice served *legal justice* 53.4

justiciable *jurisdictional* 53.18, 54.23, *unjust* 53.24, *litigated* 54.22

justiciar *judge* 54.10

justiciary *jurisdictional* 53.18, *judicatory* 54.24

justifiable *forgivable* 312.7, *apologetic* 329.10, *in the right* 429.11, *vindicable* 441.9, *basic* 605.13

justifiably *rationally* 4.25, *forgivably* 312.14, *apologetically* 329.18, *demonstrably* 331.22, *basically* 605.21

justification *philosophy* 4.1, *authorization* 52.3, *favorable verdict* 54.19, *typesetting* 173.4, *motive* 178.5, *absolution* 312.2, *apology* 313.2, *explanation* 319.4, *plea* 329.5, *proof* 331.4, *defense* 441.2, *basis* 605.4

justified *authorized* 52.11, *forgiven* 312.5, *causal* 319.9, *apologetic* 329.10, *proven* 331.13, *rightful* 429.9, *in the right* 429.11, *basic* 605.13

justifier *vindicator* 441.5

justify **441.12;** *rationalize* 4.20,

authorize 52.14, *acquit* 54.32, *print* 173.17, *motivate* 178.17, *absolve* 312.10, *apologize* 313.8, *premise* 319.14, *plead* 329.14, *prove* 331.17, *have rights* 429.13

justifying *vindicatory* 441.7

justifyingly **441.15;** *justifyingly* 441.15

just in time *critically* 659.9

just know *be intuitive* 320.9

just lie there *be inert* 519.4

just like that *easily* 823.19

justly *legally* 53.33, *impartially* 289.19, *judicially* 341.12, *right* 429.15, *morally* 431.15, *disinterestedly* 443.8, *ethically* 447.10, *equitably* 740.15, *freely* 829.22

just miss *be defeated* 846.18

justness *legal justice* 53.4, *morals* 431.2, *moderation* 521.1

just now *at present* 647.9, *newly* 652.21

just once *once* 788.23

just out *new* 652.9

just price *equalization* 740.4

just punishment *revenge* 441.4

just retribution *retribution* 454.7

just revenge *retaliation* 420.1

just reward *death* 29.1

just right *sufficient* 97.3, *correct* 429.8, *perfect* 805.8

just sit *or* **stand there** *be inert* 519.4

just so *accurately* 350.6, *meticulously* 726.18, *orderly* 765.25, *perfect* 805.8

just the thing *good thing* 445.9

just the ticket [Inf] *good time* 214.3

just the time *timeliness* 659.1

just this once *infrequently* 662.4, *once* 788.23

just what one would have expected *expected thing* 356.3

just what the doctor ordered [Inf] *good time* 214.3

just when *as* 649.10

just win *be victorious* 845.16

jut *overhanging* 604.2, *overlay* 613.25, *emerge* 707.14

jute Fabrics and Fibers 130

Jutland Horse and Pony Breeds 159

jut out *protrude* 634.8

jut over *overhang* 604.14

jutting *appearing* 264.9, *overhanging* 604.8

juttingly *convexly* 634.9

jutting out *protuberant* 634.6

juvenescence *youthfulness* 26.2

juvenescent *young* 26.11

juvenile *developmental biology* 13.22, *developmental* 13.33, *young person* 26.7, *young* 26.11

juvenile court *type of court* 54.9

juvenile delinquency *wicked act* 448.7

juvenile delinquent *wrongdoer* 430.8

juvenile lead *stock part* 136.24, *actor* 136.25

juvenilely *youthfully* 26.14

juvenilia *youthfulness* 26.2

juvenility *youthfulness* 26.2

Juventas Deities 82

juxtapose **586.14;** *relate to* 727.9

juxtaposed **586.9**

juxtaposition **586.4;** *nearness* 803.2

juxtapositional *juxtaposed* 586.9

juxtapositive *juxtaposed* 586.9

K

K2 Mountains and Hills 569

Kabardin Horse and Pony Breeds 159

kaboom! *bang!* 234.9

kabuki *dramatic style* 136.3

Kabul Countries 566, Rivers 570

Kaddish [Heb] *public worship* 83.3, *non-Christian ritual* 85.8

kaffiyeh *or* **keffiyeh** *headdress* 100.35

kaftan *robe* 100.20

kahika Trees and Shrubs 43

Kahoolawe Islands 572

Kailyard school Western Literary Groups 139

kaiser *sovereign* 68.2

Kakiemon ware Ceramics 129

kakorraphiophobia Phobias 283

kala-azar *tropical disease* 114.10

Kalahari *hot place* 217.5, Deserts 572

kalanchoe Flowers 42

kale [Inf] *cash* 484.2

kale *crop* 16.8

kaleidoscope *variegated thing* 263.5, *miscellany* 751.3

kaleidoscopic *colored* 251.10, *variegated* 263.6, *changeable* 666.3, *diversified* 732.8, *complicated* 751.10

kaleidoscopically *variedly* 263.12, *variously* 732.15, *mixedly* 751.16

Kalif *priest* 84.8

Kalimantan Islands 572

kalmia Trees and Shrubs 43

Kalmyk Breeds of Cattle 16

kalogeros *religious* 84.9

Kama *goddesses and gods of love* 299.14, Rivers 570

kamarupa *spirit* 86.10

kame *mountain range* 569.3

Kamet Mountains and Hills 569

kamikaze *suicide* 30.8

kamikaze bombing *air attack* 418.4

Kampala Countries 566

kamsin Notable Winds 9

Kan Rivers 570

Kanaga Islands 572

Kanchenjunga Mountains and Hills 569

kangaroo court *injustice* 342.3

kangaroos Collective Names 59

kanji *written letter* 5.14

Kankrej Breeds of Cattle 16

Kansas American States 564, Rivers 570

kantele Musical Instruments 142

Kantian Philosophical Schools of Thought 4, *nonmaterialist* 525.7, *idealist* 525.10

Kantianism Philosophical Schools of Thought 4, *idealism* 525.5

kaolin *material* 129.2

kaon *elementary particle* 10.53

Kapellmeister *musical director* 141.7

kapok Tree Products 43

kapow! *bang!* 234.9

kaput [Inf] *gone wrong* 430.17, *destroyed* 523.9, *no more* 718.11, *broken down* 802.8, *worn* 808.13, *failed* 846.10

Karabair Horse and Pony Breeds 159

Karabakh Horse and Pony Breeds 159

Karacabey Horse and Pony Breeds 159

Karachaev Breeds of Sheep 16

Karadagh Horse and Pony Breeds 159

Karakachan Breeds of Sheep 16

Karakoram Range Mountains and Hills 569

Karakul Breeds of Sheep 16

Kara Kum Deserts 572

karaoke *popular music* 140.4

Kara Sea Oceans and Seas 571

karate **152.14,** Sporting Activities 145, *combat sport* 152.1, *wrestling* 152.18, *self-defense* 419.5, *athletics* 422.7

karate club *karate* 152.14

karate combatant *karate* 152.14

karate expert *karate* 152.14

karate grade *karate* 152.14

karate mat *karate* 152.14

karate referee *karate* 152.14

Karayaka Breeds of Sheep 16

Kariba Lakes 568

karma *inevitability* 95.6, *predestination* 384.2

karmic *inevitable* 95.14

karmic body *spirit* 86.10

Karnobat Breeds of Sheep 16

karri tree Trees and Shrubs 43

karting *automobile racing* 146.1

karting *or* **go-karting** Sporting Activities 145

karyokinesis *cell division* 13.17

karyoplasm *cell structure* 13.16

karyosome *cell structure* 13.16

Kasai Rivers 570

kasha *notable international dishes* 90.40

Kashmir Breeds of Cats 35, Fabrics and Fibers 130

Kaskaskia Rivers 570

katabatic *descending* 714.9

katabatic wind *wind* 9.12

Kathiawari pony Horse and Pony Breeds 159

Kathmandu Countries 566

Katmai, Mount Mountains and Hills 569

Katrine Lakes 568

Kauai Islands 572

kauri *or* **kauri pine** Trees and Shrubs 43

kayak *or* **kaiak** Ships and Boats 690

kayak *canoe* 150.9

kayaking Sporting Activities 145, *canoeing* 150.26

kayo [Inf] *annihilate* 773.22

Kazakh Breeds of Cattle 16

Kazakh Fat-rumped Breeds of Sheep 16

Kazakh Finewool Breeds of Sheep 16

Kazakh pony Horse and Pony Breeds 159

Kazakhstan Countries 566

Kazakh Whiteheaded Breeds of Cattle 16

Kazbek Mountains and Hills 569

Kaz Dagi Mountains and Hills 569

kazoo Musical Instruments 142

kedge *pull* 699.10, *safety device* 810.15

keef *hemp derivatives* 121.16

Keel Constellations 7

keel *avian characteristic* 36.6, Architectural Elements 134, *sailboat* 150.3, *sailboat parts and accessories* 150.4, *canoe parts* 150.10, *foundation* 601.2, *supporting structure* 605.2

keelboat Sailing Ships and Boats 690, Ships and Boats 690

keelhaul *punish* 454.22

keelhauling *punishment* 454.1

keel over *sail* 690.16

keel-stepped *sailing* 150.25
keel-stepped mast *sailboat parts and accessories* 150.4
keen *windy* 9.42, *funeral* 31.4, *pay one's last respects* 31.12, *emphatic* 200.3, *exciting* 212.8, *cry* 239.16, *lament* 280.2, 280.7, *bitter* 306.9, *condolence* 308.2, *curious* 321.5, *eager* 373.8, *active* 414.13, *competitive* 422.21, *strong in spirit* 516.11, *vigorous* 518.2, *sharp-edged* 549.12, *mentally sharp* 549.14, *advantaged* 618.7
keen as a razor *sharp-edged* 549.12
keen-edged *sharp-edged* 549.12
keener *funeral person* 31.5, *lamenter* 280.3
keen eye *sharp eye* 242.4
keening *cry of sorrow* 239.6, *lamentation* 280.1, *lamenting* 280.4
keenly *bitterly* 306.16, *curiously* 321.9, *eagerly* 373.16, *acutely* 516.18, *sharply* 549.19
keen-minded *mentally sharp* 549.14
keenness *emphasis* 200.1, *bitterness* 306.3, *eagerness* 373.2, *vigor* 518.1, *subtlety* 534.2, *mental sharpness* 549.9
keen-scented *odorous* 224.5
keen-witted *intelligent* 315.9
keen-wittedness *cleverness* 315.3
keep *save* 105.20, *play offense* 155.18, *not use* 394.9, *commemorate* 405.11, *fort* 419.13, *defend* 419.20, *observe* 465.4, *retain* 471.7, *detain* 471.9, *support financially* 605.19, *make permanent* 667.5, *protect* 810.21, *fortification* 812.3, *saving* 815.4, *preserve* 815.14, *sustenance* 825.3, *sustain* 825.25
keep abreast of *be equal* 740.11
keep accounts *account* 493.9, *check* 784.14
keep a clear head *be sober* 120.8
keep a covenant *be dutiful* 433.12
keep a date *meet* 704.20
keep a diary *chronicle* 3.15
keep a firm hold on *detain* 471.9
keep afloat *sail* 690.16
keep a full observance *observe* 465.4
keep a happy medium *be moderate* 455.12
keep a journal *chronologize* 646.13
keep a light rein *be lenient* 423.5
keep alive *support life* 28.21, *perpetuate* 640.5, *continue* 669.8, *preserve* 815.14
keep a lookout for *watch* 242.23
keep a low profile *conceal oneself* 181.15, *become invisible* 245.6, *escape notice* 403.14
keep an eye on *be cautious* 287.11, *take note of* 323.10, *care for* 325.12, *protect* 810.21
keep an eye out for *or* **open for** *watch* 242.23
keep an open mind *be impartial* 338.11, *be disinterested* 443.6, *be broad-minded* 592.13, *be free* 829.16, *hesitate* 841.18
keep apart *keep away* 585.9, *space* 587.6, *separate* 724.14, *divide* 753.18, *come between* 753.21
keep a pledge *or* **vow** *or* **oath** *be dutiful* 433.12
keep a routine *perform* 465.5
keep a safe distance *be safe* 810.20

keep a safe distance from *keep away* 585.9
keep a sharp lookout *have foresight* 357.8
keep a stiff upper lip *take courage* 284.15, *not wonder about* 295.5, *be disinterested* 443.6, *be calm* 455.13, *restrain oneself* 830.15
keep a straight face *be silent* 181.16, *be serious* 278.7
keep at a distance *keep away* 585.9, *lengthen* 590.12
keep a tally *number* 784.13
keep at arm's length *avoid* 386.13, *exclude* 409.12, *resist* 417.10, *parry* 419.27, *keep away* 585.9, *lengthen* 590.12, *fend off* 701.9
keep at bay *resist* 417.10, *parry* 419.27, *fend off* 701.9
keep a tight hold *or* **rein on** *detain* 471.9
keep a tight rein *be severe* 424.8
keep a tight rein on *restrain someone* 830.17
keep at it *work* 122.8, *protract* 669.9
keep at one's beck and call *subject* 832.10
keep away 585.9; *refuse* 506.8, *be absent* 576.14
keep away from *avoid* 386.13, *keep away* 585.9
keep a whole skin *be safe* 810.20
keep back *deter* 179.8, *detain* 471.9, *slow down* 693.13
keep behind bars *detain* 830.16
keep body and soul together *support life* 28.21
keep busy *be busy* 414.19
keep calm *restrain oneself* 830.15
keep clean *clean* 111.17
keep clear *avoid* 386.13
keep clear of *keep away* 585.9
keep close *keep secret* 182.11
keep close to *stay near* 586.13
keep coming *be repeated* 797.20
keep company with 794.17; *befriend* 62.10, *fraternize* 408.17
keep cool *be disinterested* 443.6
keep costs down *economize* 499.6
keep count *number* 784.13
keep dark *make dark* 247.10
keep down *abolish* 523.11, *bear down on* 716.18, *subject* 832.10
keep dry 560.22
keeper *magnet* 10.47, *prison officer* 55.8, *leader* 126.8, *play* 155.8, *protector* 419.16, 810.11, *provider* 605.10, *accompanier* 794.6
keeper of the purse *treasurer* 484.18
keeper of time 646.10
keep faith with *observe* 465.4
keep fit *be healthy* 113.11
keep for *intend for* 374.11
keep for a rainy day *delay* 658.13
keep for later *delay* 658.13
keep for oneself *be selfish* 444.6, *possess* 469.14
keep fresh *preserve* 815.14
keep from *avoid* 386.13
keep from laughing *be serious* 278.7
keep from sleep *fatigue* 820.6
keep going *maintain* 377.12, *continue* 669.8, *be in motion* 677.14, *preserve* 815.14
keep going! *go on!* 669.11
keep hands off *set free* 829.17
keep holy *commemorate* 405.11
keep house *housekeep* 60.23
keep in *imprison* 454.23, *detain*

206.8, *ignore* 413.14, *be latent* 844.12
keepnet *fishing tackle* 154.7
keep off *parry* 419.27, *keep away* 585.9
keep off! *hands off!* 386.26
keep off liquor *be sober* 120.8
keep on *be busy* 414.19, *continue* 669.8, *protract* 669.9, *press on* 679.9
keep on *or* **at** *persevere* 377.10
keep one guessing *be unintelligible* 364.11
keep one's balance *be stable* 674.6
keep one's chin up *take courage* 284.15
keep one's cool *not wonder about* 295.5, *be stable* 674.6, *restrain oneself* 830.15
keep one's counsel *keep secret* 182.11, *be taciturn* 208.7
keep one's distance *avoid* 386.13, *be unsocial* 409.10, *keep away* 585.9
keep one's ears open *hear* 228.13
keep one's ear to the ground *hear* 228.13
keep oneself to oneself *shun* 386.14
keep one's eyes *or* **an eye on** *watch* 242.23
keep one's eyes open *be cautious* 287.11
keep one's eyes skinned *or* **peeled** *watch* 242.23
keep one's fingers crossed *be hopeful* 281.11
keep one's hand in *accustom oneself* 397.11
keep one's hands clean *shun* 386.14
keep one's hat on *disrespect* 436.18
keep one's head above water *be safe* 810.20
keep one's head down *become invisible* 245.6
keep (up) one's health *be healthy* 113.11
keep one's mouth shut *be silent* 181.16, *keep secret* 182.11, *be taciturn* 208.7
keep one's nose clean *follow the rules* 780.17
keep one's nose to the grindstone *be bored* 296.7
keep one's offer open *offer* 504.11
keep one's powder dry *prepare oneself* 388.21
keep one's promise *perform* 465.5
keep one's reputation intact *guard one's pride* 297.16
keep one's shirt on [Inf] *restrain oneself* 830.15
keep one's trap shut [Inf] *be taciturn* 208.7
keep one's wallet *or* **purse shut** *be parsimonious* 490.13
keep one's word *be dutiful* 433.12
keep on hand *save* 105.20
keep on ice *preserve* 815.14
keep on keeping on *maintain* 377.12
keep on the go *be busy* 414.19
keep open house *receive someone* 473.14, *be generous* 498.10
keep order *wield authority* 52.16, *manage* 126.10, *secure* 464.9,

471.9, *enclose* 584.16, *surround* 615.7
keep incomplete *make shapeless* 625.3
keeping *observance* 465.1, *retention* 471.1, *safekeeping* 810.6, *tutelary* 810.19, *preservation* 815.1
keeping a Spartan regimen *fasting* 118.5
keeping a stiff upper lip *disinterestedness* 443.1, *calmness* 455.4, *calm* 455.9
keeping clean *cleanliness* 111.1
keeping cool *disinterestedness* 443.1
keeping down *submergence* 716.3
keeping fit 113.10; *health improvement* 113.3, Hobbies and Pastimes 167
keeping for oneself *selfishness* 444.1
keeping fresh *preservation* 815.1
keeping healthy *health improvement* 113.3
keeping in *detention* 471.2
keeping in mind *remembering* 354.8
keeping Lent *fasting* 118.5
keeping long hours *industrious* 414.16
keeping one's fast *fasting* 118.5
keeping one's own company *unsociability* 409.1
keeping on the right side of the law *observance* 465.1
keep in good repair *preserve* 815.14
keeping the faith *religious* 81.21
keeping to a budget *personal finance* 457.5
keeping to one's budget *home economics* 56.2
keeping to oneself *unsociability* 409.1
keeping to one side *setting apart* 753.2
keeping under *submergence* 716.3
keeping up appearances *etiquette* 534.3
keeping up with the Joneses *social ambition* 408.2
keeping within the law *legality* 53.9
keep in hand *not use* 394.9, *detain* 471.9
keep in mind *memorize* 354.11
keep in one's own hands *detain* 471.9
keep in one's place *succumb* 421.7
keep in perpetuity *perpetuate* 640.5
keep in purdah *exclude* 409.12
keep in reserve *not use* 394.9
keep inside 611.17
keep in sight *make visible* 244.9
keep in step *synchronize* 649.7, *abide by* 781.12
keep in step with *synchronize* 649.7, *be equal* 740.11
keep in the background *conceal oneself* 181.15
keep in *or* **stay in the background** *escape notice* 403.14
keep in the dark *make ignorant* 349.10
keep in time *synchronize* 649.7
keep in view *make visible* 244.9
keep it up! *go on!* 669.11
keep late hours *be late* 658.11
keep moving *be busy* 414.19
keep moving! *go on!* 669.11
keep mum *be silent* 181.16, 231.3, *keep secret* 182.11, *be voiceless*

restore order 765.22, *protect*
810.21, *restrain* 830.12
keep out *exclude* 764.7, *limit*
830.13
keep out of *shun* 386.14, *leave
alone* 413.13
keep out of mischief *behave well*
399.18
keep out of the way of *keep
away* 585.9
keep out of trouble *be at peace*
73.10
keep out of war *be at peace* 73.10
keep pace with *synchronize* 649.7,
be equal 740.11
keep posted *inform* 170.11,
recount 202.16
keep private *exclude* 409.12
keep quiet *be voiceless* 206.8, *be
taciturn* 208.7, *be silent* 231.3,
ignore 413.14, *submit* 421.4, *be
motionless* 678.7, *restrain oneself*
830.15, *be latent* 844.12, *hide*
844.13
keep quiet! *hush!* 231.6
keep running *preserve* 815.14
keep safe *protect* 810.21, *preserve*
815.14
keep safe and sound *secure* 464.9
keepsake *memento* 354.3, *gift*
472.2
keep secret 182.11; *detain* 471.9
keep sight of *make visible* 244.9
keep silent *be silent* 231.3
keep smiling *be hopeful* 281.11
keep someone guessing *make
uncertain* 841.19
keep someone in the dark
mystify 182.12
keep stable *make stable* 674.7
keep still *be motionless* 678.7, *be
silent* 181.16
keep still! *hush!* 231.6
keep straight *be virtuous* 447.8
keep tabs on *identify* 184.11
keep tabs on [Inf] *be cautious*
287.11
keep tempo *beat time* 140.29
keep the ball in play *continue*
669.8
keep the ball rolling *maintain*
377.12, *continue* 669.8
keep the books *account* 493.9
keep the faith *be religious* 81.25,
show obeisance to 426.8
keep the field *be at war* 76.32
keep the golden mean *be
moderate* 455.12, *stand in the
middle* 772.17
keep the law *obey* 426.7
keep the lid on [Inf] *keep secret*
182.11
keep the peace *be at peace* 73.10,
pacify 74.9, *be moderate* 521.6
keep the peace! *peace!* 73.13
keep the pot boiling *be busy*
414.19, *continue* 669.8
keep the proper observance
observe 465.4
keep the same beat *synchronize*
649.7
keep the score *number* 784.13
keep things moving *continue*
669.8
keep time 646.12; *beat time*
140.29, *time* 639.15, *measure time*
646.14
keep time with *synchronize* 649.7,
accompany 794.16
keep to a happy medium *stand
in the middle* 772.17
keep to an agreement *be dutiful*
433.12

keep together *work together*
827.14
keep to midstream *be in the
middle* 772.16
keep to oneself *be taciturn* 208.7,
be unsocial 409.10, *detain* 471.9,
be aloof 756.8
keep to one side *detain* 471.9
keep to the middle *be in the
middle* 772.16
keep to the middle way *be
moderate* 455.12
keep to the point *talk straight*
630.15
keep to the spirit of *observe*
465.4
keep to or **on the straight and
narrow** *be virtuous* 447.8
keep under *bear down on* 716.18
keep under cover *hide* 613.27,
protect 810.21, *preserve* 815.14
keep under lock and key *secure*
464.9, *detain* 830.16
keep under observation *watch*
242.23
keep under one's hat *keep secret*
182.11, *lack candor* 192.22
keep under one's thumb *subject*
832.10
keep under wraps *conceal*
181.12, *keep secret* 182.11
keep undetermined *defer* 604.15
keep up *maintain* 377.12, *make
permanent* 667.5, *continue* 669.8,
preserve 815.14
keep up the good work! *go on!*
669.11
keep up with *be equal* 740.11
keep up or **in touch with** *visit*
408.16
keep up with the Joneses
participate 408.15, *abide by* 781.12
keep warm *feel hot* 217.19
keep watertight *keep dry* 560.22
keep well *be healthy* 113.11
keep within bounds *be moderate*
455.12, *moderate* 521.7, *limit*
830.13
keep within limits *moderate*
521.7
keep within one's means *be
thrifty* 499.5
keep within the law *be legal*
53.28
keep your distance! *hands off!*
386.26
keep your mouth shut! *hush!*
231.6
keep your trap shut! [Inf] *hush!*
231.6
keeshond *Breeds of Dogs* 35
kef *hemp derivatives* 121.16
keg *vessel* 578.11
keister [Inf] *rear end* 622.4
kelp *alga* 47.10
kelpie *Breeds of Dogs* 35,
Legendary Creatures 360
Kelso *Notable Horses* 159
kelvin *Scientific and Technical
Units* 589
Kelvin scale *scale* 589.9
Kemerovo *Breeds of Pigs* 16
Kemi *Rivers* 570
kempt *orderly* 765.13
ken *knowledge* 348.1
Kenana *Breeds of Cattle* 16
kendo *Sporting Activities* 145,
fencing 153.1, *duel* 422.12
kenipo *Sporting Activities* 145
kennel *Collective Names* 59, *cage*
60.15, *closed place* 584.4, *enclose*
584.16, *enclosed area* 619.2,
shelter 812.4
kenning *literary device* 139.12

Kensington *London* 567.8
Kent bugle *Musical Instruments*
142
Kent mental test *Intelligence
Tests* 108
Kentucky *American States* 564
Kentucky Derby *famous horse
races* 159.13
Kenya *Countries* 566, *Mountains
and Hills* 569
Keogh plan *personal finance* 457.5
kepi *cap* 100.33
Keplerian telescope *telescope* 7.25
Kepler's laws *solar system* 7.14,
Classical Physical Laws 10
kept *saved* 105.15, *preserved* 815.12
kept back *retained* 471.6, *refused*
506.5
kept in *retained* 471.6
kept in check *restrained* 830.9
kept quiet *concealed* 844.7
kept under constraint *restrained*
830.9
kept under one's thumb
restrained 830.9
kept woman *girlfriend* 33.4, *lover*
299.11, *sexually immoral person*
432.8
keratin *protein* 12.9
keraunophobia *Phobias* 283
kerchief *neckwear* 100.29
kerf *notch* 636.1, 636.5
Kerguélen Islands *Islands* 572
kermes *Tree Products* 43, *red
pigment* 257.2
kern *type* 173.5, *print* 173.17
kernal *core* 612.2
kernel *mathematical function* 6.27,
seed 41.9, *fruit structure* 44.3,
insides 577.3, *essential content*
723.2, *middle* 772.1, *gist* 799.4
kernels *fruits* 44.1
kerning *typesetting* 173.4
kernmantel rope *climbing
equipment* 161.4
kerosene *fuels* 106.2, *oil* 106.7, *gas*
106.14, *petroleum* 562.5
kerosene lamp *incandescent light*
246.5
kerosene stove *place for fire* 217.9
Kerr effect *Classical Physical
Laws* 10
Kerry *Breeds of Cattle* 16
Kerry blue terrier *Breeds of Dogs*
35
Kerry Hill *Breeds of Sheep* 16
Kerulen *Rivers* 570
kestrel *bird of prey* 36.11
ketch *sailboat* 150.3, *Sailing Ships
and Boats* 690
ketchup *sauce* 90.17, *red thing*
257.3
ketoheptose *saccharide* 12.4
ketohexose *saccharide* 12.4
ketone *carbohydrate* 12.3
ketooctose *saccharide* 12.4
ketopentose *saccharide* 12.4
ketose *saccharide* 12.4
ketotetrose *saccharide* 12.4
ketotriose *saccharide* 12.4
kettle *cooking equipment* 91.6, *pot*
578.15
kettledrummer *player* 141.2
kettledrums *Musical Instruments*
142
kettle hat *helmet* 100.34
kettle of fish [Inf] *predicament*
824.5
kettle of fish *circumstances* 573.2
kevlar helmet *modern armor*
419.7
kewpie doll *prize* 453.2
key 140.23; *data-related concepts*
15.23, *woodwind* 142.4, *basketball*

court 148.3, *signs* 183.2,
interpretation 365.1, *translation*
365.4, *operative* 509.9, *island*
572.2, *opener* 583.2, *basic* 601.8,
central 612.6, *focal* 612.8, *critical*
659.5, *reason* 675.4, *degree* 739.1,
important 799.7, *safety device*
810.15
key banding *Architectural
Elements* 134
keyboard *input device* 15.11, *part of
keyboard instrument* 142.6
keyboarder *record keeper* 185.8
keyboard instrument *musical
instrument* 142.1
key card *opener* 583.2
key center *tone* 140.24
keyed up *prepared* 388.9
key figure *focus* 612.3
key grip *filmmaker* 137.14
keyhole *hole* 583.4
Key Largo *Islands* 572
key man *expert* 127.9
keymarking *stage of book
production* 174.7
Keynesian *political and economic
philosopher* 4.10, *of a political
philosophy* 4.14
Keynesian economics *economics*
56.1
Keynesianism *political and
economic philosophy* 4.6
keynote *musical note* 140.15, *topic*
328.1, *guide* 780.4, *gist* 799.4
keypad *input device* 15.11
key person *manager* 126.7,
important person 799.5
key point *critical time* 659.3,
important matter 799.2
keys *part of keyboard instrument*
142.6, *insignia* 184.5
key signature *written music*
140.21
keystone *Architectural Elements*
134, *supporting part* 605.3,
essential content 723.2, *middle*
772.1
Key West *Islands* 572
khaddar or **khadi** *Fabrics and
Fibers* 130
khaki *Fabrics and Fibers* 130,
brown 256.5
khakis *uniform* 100.9
khaki uniform *uniform* 100.9
khamsin *Notable Winds* 9
khan *sovereign* 68.2
Khanka *Lakes* 568
Khartoum *Countries* 566
Khnemu or **Khnum** *Deities* 82
Kholmogor *Breeds of Cattle* 16
kibble *grind* 553.23
kibbutz *farm* 16.2
kibbutznik *agriculturist* 16.14
kibe [Arch] *ulcer* 114.18
kibitzer *adviser* 176.5, *meddler*
321.4
kibitzer [Inf] *meddler* 414.12
kick 155.12, 155.20, 695.14;
wrestling terms 152.10, *wrestle*
152.20, *snowplow* 162.29, *soccer
play* 163.5, *play soccer* 163.8,
swimming techniques 164.2, *swim*
164.14, *gesture* 183.5, 183.17,
stimulus 212.3, *type of touch* 216.3,
touch 216.9, *piquancy* 221.1, *hit*
418.9, *strike* 418.21, *fight* 422.23,
counteraction 510.1, *blow* 695.5,
propulsion 696.1, *propel* 696.15
kick [Inf] *pleasure* 214.2, *fun*
269.4, *activity* 414.1, *protest*
507.1, 507.7, *vigor* 518.1, *object*
828.18
kick a field goal *kick* 155.20

kick a habit [Inf] *disaccustom* 398.6

kick around *subject* 832.10

kick around [Inf] *be inactive* 415.13

kick ass [Inf] *be at war* 76.32, *strike* 418.21

kickback *incentive* 178.4, *response* 334.4, *bribe* 472.3, *discount* 495.1, *illegal offer* 504.4, *positive stimulus* 508.5, *counteraction* 510.1, *reflex* 680.7

kick back *react* 334.20, *retaliate* 420.4, *counteract* 510.7, *swing* 671.12

kick back [Inf] *take a discount* 495.5

kickball Children's and Party Games 167

kick boxing Sporting Activities 145

kick downstairs [Inf] *disbar* 709.16

kicked *soccer* 163.7

kicked around *subject* 832.6

kicked out [Inf] *rejected* 383.6

kicker *special team* 155.11

kicking *wrestling* 152.18, *varsity* 155.17, *soccer play* 163.5, *soccer* 163.7, *attacking* 418.14, *violent* 520.5, *propulsion* 696.1

kicking ass [Inf] *punishment* 454.1

kicking out [Inf] *expulsion* 709.1

kicking team *special team* 155.11

kicking tee *kick* 155.12

kicking the ball *violations* 148.5

kicking upstairs *relegation* 574.4

kick in the ass [Inf] *treatment* 399.11

kick in the pants *treatment* 399.11

kick in the teeth *dissent* 506.2

kickoff *kick* 155.12, *soccer play* 163.5, *starting point* 771.11

kick off *kick* 155.20, *play soccer* 163.8, *start* 696.20, *make a beginning* 771.26

kick out [Inf] *discard* 383.12, *relegate* 574.18, *expel* 709.14, *dismiss* 709.15, *eject* 764.8

kick over *knock down* 523.13

kick over the traces *subvert* 427.13, *not conform* 782.18

kick pleat *part of garment* 100.27

kicks *swimming techniques* 164.2

kickshaw *cheap item* 497.5

kick someone in the teeth *dissent* 506.9

kickstand *bicycle part* 687.11

kick-start *start* 696.20, *activate* 771.28

kick steps *mountaineer* 161.10

kick the ball *play basketball* 148.7

kick the bucket [Inf] *die* 29.17, *cease to exist* 718.13

kick the can Children's and Party Games 167

kick the habit *give up alcohol* 120.6

kick the habit [Inf] *abstain* 386.16

kick turn *skiing techniques* 162.5, *cross-country techniques* 162.8

kick under the table *warning* 814.1, *warn* 814.8

kick up *be disorderly* 766.22

kick up a fuss *complain* 507.8

kick up a row *or* **rumpus** *or* **shindy** [Inf] *shatter the peace* 232.10

kick up a shindy [Inf] *be active* 414.18, *dispute* 463.9

kick up one's heels *enjoy* 269.9

kick upstairs *discard* 383.12, *relegate* 574.18, *dismiss* 709.15, *make unimportant* 800.20

kick wheel *ceramic workshop and tools* 129.8

kid *livestock* 16.11, *young animal* 26.4, *young mammal* 35.20, *be humorous* 277.11

kid [Inf] *progeny* 21.8, *child* 26.6, *young person* 26.7, *young man* 26.8, *family member* 65.2, *hoax* 193.20

kiddie [Inf] *child* 26.6

kidding *amusement* 277.2

kid gloves *treatment* 399.11, *leniency* 423.1

kid-glove treatment *leniency* 423.1

kidnap 479.15; *force* 428.10, *sin* 450.11, *take away forcefully* 477.19, *detain* 830.16

kidnapped *stolen* 479.12, *detained* 830.11

kidnapper *criminal* 427.6, *coercer* 428.4, *raider* 477.10, *thief* 479.8, *one who restrains* 830.7

kidnapping 479.3; *terrorist attack* 418.7, *coercive method* 428.3, *conquest* 477.6, *stolen* 479.12, *detention* 830.5

kidney *variety meat* 90.30, *sort* 202.6, *type* 777.4

kidney disease Phobias 283

kidneys *internal organ* 19.13

kids [Inf] *the young* 26.10, *family member* 65.2

kid stuff [Inf] *easy thing* 823.6

kielbasa *sausage* 90.29

Kierkegaardian Philosophical Schools of Thought 4

Kierkegaardianism Philosophical Schools of Thought 4

Kiev Countries 566

Kigali Countries 566

Kilimanjaro Mountains and Hills 569

kill 30.19; *be at war* 76.32, *conquer* 77.36, *hunt* 160.12, *harm* 306.13, *the hunted* 385.7, *attack successfully* 418.25, *be evil* 446.10, *be wicked* 448.13, *execute* 454.30, *censor* 503.10, *destroy* 523.10, *river* 570.1, *cause to cease* 668.12, *cause not to exist* 718.14, *annihilate* 773.22, *cancel* 834.6

kill animals 30.25

Killarney, Lakes of Lakes 568

killed 29.13; *hunting* 160.11, *canceled* 834.5

killer 30.11; *murderer* 30.12, *combatant* 77.1, *malefactor* 306.6, *attacker* 418.10, *criminal* 427.6, *villain* 448.5, *destroyer* 523.6

killer [Inf] *good thing* 445.9

killer-diller [Inf] *good thing* 445.9

killian *ice-dancing move* 162.19, *ice-skating* 162.32

killian hold *ice-dancing move* 162.19

killick *safety device* 810.15

kill in cold blood *harm* 306.13

killing 30.1, 30.17; *laborious* 122.7, *hunting* 160.2, *malignity* 306.5, *profit* 467.6, *destroying* 523.2, *success* 845.1

killing agent 30.15

killing field *slaughterhouse* 30.16, *battleground* 76.24

killing fields *field of battle* 422.11

killing oneself *suicide* 30.8

killjoy *sad person* 270.3, *hopeless person* 282.5, *inactive person* 413.8, *moderator* 521.2, *hinderer* 826.11

killock *safety device* 810.15

kill off *cease* 773.20

kill oneself *commit suicide* 30.24

kill ritually 30.23

kill the fatted calf *salute* 405.13, *participate* 408.15

kill the fatted calf for *fete* 279.6

kill the goose that lays the golden eggs *figurative expressions* 128.11

kill time *have free time* 413.15, *be inactive* 415.13, *spend time* 639.14

kiln *ceramic workshop and tools* 129.8, *place for fire* 217.9, *bake* 560.19

kiln furniture *ceramic workshop and tools* 129.8

kilo *weight measurement* 538.6, Decimal Prefixes 589, *thousand* 792.10

kilobyte *data-related concepts* 15.23, *thousand* 792.10

kilocalorie *heat measurement* 217.2, Scientific and Technical Units 589

kilogram *weight measurement* 538.6, *thousand* 792.10

kilohertz (kHz) *radio frequency* 661.3

kilometer *thousand* 792.10

kilometers per hour (kph) *speed* 694.2

kilt *skirt* 100.12

kilter *physical state* 725.6

kimono *robe* 100.20

kin *family* 65.1, *associate* 754.3

Kinabalu *or* **Kinabulu** Mountains and Hills 569

kind 445.12, 624.3; *friendly* 62.5, *sort* 202.6, *likable* 271.6, *benevolent* 305.7, 825.21, *philanthropic* 307.6, *pitying* 308.4, *forgiving* 312.4, *courteous* 410.6, *lenient* 423.3, *unselfish* 443.5, *fashion* 536.1, *soft-hearted* 543.11, *type* 777.4

kind act *benevolent act* 305.5, *kindness* 445.3

kind deed *benevolent act* 305.5

kindergarten *school* 48.11

kindest regards *greeting* 435.5

kindhearted *benevolent* 305.7, *philanthropic* 307.6, *kind* 445.12

kind-hearted *pitying* 308.4, *soft-hearted* 543.11

kindheartedly *benevolently* 305.13, *philanthropically* 307.9, *kindly* 445.20

kind-heartedly *pityingly* 308.11

kindheartedness *benevolence* 305.1, *philanthropy* 307.1, *kindness* 445.3

kindle *give birth* 35.33, Collective Names 59, *fuel* 106.16, *burn* 217.18, *light* 246.19, *invigorate* 518.5, *awaken* 675.9

kindliness *friendship* 62.1, *amiability* 271.3, *benevolence* 305.1, *philanthropy* 307.1, *courtesy* 410.1, *leniency* 423.1, *kindness* 445.3

kindling *timber* 43.3, *fuel starter* 106.3

kindly 445.20; *friendly* 62.5, *amicably* 62.13, *likable* 271.6, *benevolent* 305.7, 825.21, *benevolently* 305.13, 825.34, *philanthropic* 307.6, *philanthropically* 307.9, *pityingly* 308.11, *forgivingly* 312.13, *courteous* 410.6, *lenient* 423.3, *leniently* 423.6, *unselfishly* 443.9, *supportive* 605.11

kindly disposed *benevolent* 305.7

kindly disposition *benevolence* 305.1

Kindly Ones, the Deities 82

kindness 445.3; *friendship* 62.1, *lovingness* 299.4, *benevolence* 305.1, *benevolent act* 305.5, *philanthropy* 307.1, *pity* 308.1, *forgivingness* 312.3, *sociability* 408.1, *courtesy* 410.1, *leniency* 423.1, *unselfishness* 443.2, *soft-heartedness* 543.4, *support* 825.2, *helpfulness* 825.10

kind of *to a degree* 739.11

kind offices *support* 825.2

kind of number 783.2

kind person *benevolent person* 305.6, *giver* 472.7

kindred *family* 65.6, *related* 727.6

kindred spirit *affinity* 733.3

kind regards *greeting* 435.5

kind remembrances *courtesies* 410.3

kinematic *physical* 10.70, *directional* 677.13

kinematically *physically* 10.78

kinematics *classical physics* 10.2, *motion* 677.1

kinesiatrics *motion* 677.1

kinesics *gesture* 183.5

kinesiology *motion* 677.1

kinesipathy *motion* 677.1

kinesis *motion* 677.1

kinesitherapy *motion* 677.1

kinetic *physical* 10.70, *chemical* 11.24, 14.46, *motivational* 508.7, *directional* 677.13

kinetically *physically* 10.78, *electrochemically* 14.53, *in motion* 677.19

kinetic art Western Art Styles 133, *visual arts* 133.1

kinetic energy *energy* 10.10, 514.7, *motion* 677.1

kineticist *biochemist* 12.2

kinetics *chemistry* 11.1, *chemical reaction* 11.8, *industrial processes* 14.27, *chemical reaction thermodynamics* 14.29, *motion* 677.1

kinetic sculpture *sculpture* 144.1

kinetic theory *theory* 10.3

kinetophobia Phobias 283

king (termite) *social insect* 40.6

king *person in authority* 52.7, *sovereign* 68.2, *board games* 167.3, *play* 167.12, *cards* 168.2, *important person* 799.5

King Charles spaniel Breeds of Dogs 35

king crab *extinct arthropod* 39.7

kingdom *nation* 18.14, *body politic* 50.3, *region* 564.1, *dominion* 566.3, *taxonomical classification* 777.3

kingdom come *heaven* 82.15, *future condition* 650.3

Kingdom of God *heaven* 82.15

kingfish *food fish and shellfish* 90.20

kingfish [Inf] *company leader* 68.8

kingfisher *water bird* 36.9, *descender* 714.8

kingfisher-blue *blue* 261.5

King James Version *Christian text* 81.16

King Kong Legendary Creatures 360, *big thing* 579.9

kinglike *governing* 49.25

kingliness *nobleness* 70.3

kingly *governing* 49.25, *aristocratic* 70.4, *aristocratically* 70.6, *majestic* 297.12

kingmaker *indirect influence* 512.4

King of Kings *God* 82.6
King of Light *God* 82.6
King of the Jews *God the Son* 82.9
kingpin *manager* 126.7
kingpin [Inf] *company leader* 68.8, *important person* 799.5
king post *supporting part* 605.3
king-post truss *carpenter's term* 131.5
king's *of language* 5.35
king's English *standard language* 5.6
king's evidence *divulgence* 180.2
kingship *monarchy* 49.6
king-size *type of bed* 101.9, *tobacco* 121.23, 121.33, *big* 579.13
Kings Peak Mountains and Hills 569
king's ransom *money* 485.2
Kingston Countries 566
Kingstown Countries 566
kingwood Trees and Shrubs 43
kinin *plant hormone* 12.17
kink *caprice* 381.1, *rough thing* 544.2, *make rough* 544.11, *coil* 632.2, *idiosyncrasy* 782.5, *defect* 806.4
Kinkozan ware Ceramics 129
kinky *capricious* 381.4
kinky [Inf] *perverted* 432.12
kinogram *optical element* 10.20
kino gum Tree Products 43
Kinshasa Countries 566
kinship 727.2; *agreement* 462.1, *affinity* 733.3, *compatibility* 735.4
kinship group *group* 18.13, *family* 65.1
kinsman *associate* 754.3
Kioga Lakes 568
kiosk *stall* 483.9
kip *national coins* 484.11, General Units 589
kipper Nicknames for Inhabitants 61, *season* 221.8, *dry* 560.17, *preserve* 815.14
kippered *piquant* 221.6
kippered fish *fish dish* 90.19
Kirchoff's laws Classical Physical Laws 10
Kiribati Countries 566
Kiritimati Islands 572
kirk [Scot] *place of worship* 83.8
kirk *place of worship* 83.8
Kirkpatrick, Mount Mountains and Hills 569
Kirlian photography *occult and psychic phenomena* 86.7
Kiska Islands 572
kismet *predestination* 384.2
kiss *type of touch* 216.3, *touch* 216.9, *communication of love* 299.6, *communicate love* 299.25, *welcome* 408.10, 408.18, *sign of courtesy* 410.5, *greet* 410.11, *meet* 586.15
kissable *lovable* 299.20
kiss and make up *pacify* 74.11, *forgive and forget* 312.9
kiss-and-tell confession *nonfiction* 139.6
kiss ass [Inf] *fawn* 401.9
kisser [Inf] *body orifice* 583.3, *face* 621.6
kiss hands *bow* 716.22
kissing Phobias 283, *communication of love* 299.6
kissing disease [Inf] *infection* 114.7
kissing someone's hand *deference* 410.4
kissing the hem *mark of respect* 435.4
kiss off [Inf] *lose* 468.12, *eject* 701.8, *termination* 834.2, *terminate* 834.7

kiss of life *swimming rescue* 164.5
kiss of peace *Christian rite* 85.5, *Eucharist* 85.7
kiss rings *bow* 716.22
kiss someone's hand *defer to* 410.12
kiss the Book *vow* 189.23
kiss the hand of *shelter* 812.8
kiss the hem of someone's garment *show respect* 435.16
kiss the ring of *show respect* 435.16
kiss the rod *succumb* 421.7
kit *cat* 35.11, *young mammal* 35.20, *equipment* 103.6, Musical Instruments 142, *fitting out* 388.3, *unit* 759.5
kit and caboodle [Inf] *total* 738.4
kit bag *bag* 578.7
kitchen *room* 60.9, *cooking place* 91.4, *eating place* 92.17, *type of table* 101.5, *home workplace* 124.3
kitchen boy *domestic servant* 69.7
kitchen cabinet *cabinet* 578.3
kitchen container 91.7
kitchenette *room* 60.9, *cooking place* 91.4
kitchen garden *garden* 17.2
kitchen maid *domestic servant* 69.7
kitchen range *burner* 217.4
kitchen-sink drama *dramatic style* 136.3, *theater movements* 136.9, Western Literary Groups 139, *realism* 719.3
kitchen tool *tool* 103.1
kitchenware *merchandise* 522.6
kitchen work *work* 122.1
kite *bird of prey* 36.11, *false money* 484.15, *go up* 713.23
kite, Everglade snail Endangered US Birds 36
kite a check *monetize* 484.24
kiteflying Hobbies and Pastimes 167
kith *associate* 754.3
kithara Musical Instruments 142
kiting Sporting Activities 145
kitsch Western Art Styles 133, *tawdriness* 535.2
kitschy *vulgar* 535.6
kitten *have young* 21.16, *young animal* 26.4, *cat* 35.11, *young mammal* 35.20, *give birth* 35.33, *weak thing* 517.5
kittenish *carnivorous* 35.26
kittens Collective Names 59
kitty *cat* 35.11, *reserve* 105.3, *green bowling* 151.3, *gambling* 167.4, *prize* 453.2, *joint possession* 469.6
kitty-corner or **kitty-cornered** *oblique* 607.6, *obliquely* 607.13
Kitty O'Shea Famous Lovers 299
Kivu Lakes 568
kiwi *flightless bird* 36.8
Kladruber Horse and Pony Breeds 159
Klamath Rivers 570
Klamath Lakes Lakes 568
klaxon *danger signal* 811.5
Klein bottle *topology* 6.45, *continuum* 774.5
Kleine *psychologist* 108.33
kleptomania *impulse-control disorder* 108.16, *theft* 479.2
kleptomaniac *compulsive person* 428.5, *thief* 479.8, *stolen* 479.12
kleptophobia Phobias 283
klieg light *stage lighting* 136.20, *electric light* 246.6
klister *cross-country* 162.31
klister wax *ski equipment* 162.10
Klondike Rivers 570
klondike Card Games 168

klutz [Inf] *unintelligent person* 316.4
klutziness [Inf] *inelegance* 528.1
klutzy [Inf] *unintelligent* 316.6, *graceless* 528.7
klystron *electron tube* 14.40
K meson *elementary particle* 10.53
Knabstrup Horse and Pony Breeds 159
knack *means* 102.1, *aptitude* 127.4, *ability* 340.2, *method* 387.4, *cunning* 822.1
knacker [Brit] *animal killer* 30.14
knacker's yard [Brit] *slaughterhouse* 30.16
knackery [Brit] *animal killing* 30.10
knackwurst or **knockwurst** *sausage* 90.29
knap *hill* 569.2, *heights* 596.4, *summit* 600.1
knapsack *baggage* 578.8, *transferred thing* 685.6
knapweed Flowers 42
knave *cards* 168.2, *deceiver* 193.8, *miscreant* 448.6, *cunning person* 822.3
knavery *deception* 193.1, *wickedness* 448.1
knavish *dishonorable* 192.14, *deceptive* 193.12, *wicked* 448.9, *cunning* 822.4
knavishly *dishonorably* 192.28, *wickedly* 448.15
knead *cook* 91.10, *touch* 216.9, *soften* 543.14, *massage* 554.16, *form* 624.9, *mix* 751.12
kneading *massage* 554.6
knee *appendage* 19.5, *kick* 695.14, *joint* 752.7
kneecap Human Bones 19, *torture* 454.29
knee-deep *deep* 598.9, *shallow* 599.3
knee guard *basketball court* 148.3
knee-high *young* 26.11, *high* 596.7, *low* 597.10
knee-high to a grasshopper [Inf] *undersized* 580.8, *low* 597.10
knee-hole *type of desk* 101.6
kneeing *ice hockey tactics* 158.4
knee-jerk [Inf] *instinctive* 318.8, 320.8, *customary* 397.11
knee-jerk reaction [Inf] *involuntariness* 95.9, *habit* 397.1
knee-jerk response [Inf] *instinct* 318.3, 320.4
knee joint *angle* 628.1
kneel *worship* 83.15, *follow rites* 85.19, *knuckle under* 401.10, *defer to* 410.12, *succumb* 421.7, *show obeisance to* 426.8, *show respect* 435.16, *bow* 716.22
knee-length *long* 590.6
kneeling *act of worship* 83.2, *hunting* 160.11, *submission* 421.1, *submitting* 421.3, *obeisance* 426.3, *obeisant* 426.6, *mark of respect* 435.4, *showing respect* 435.7, *bow* 716.6, *degraded* 716.10
kneeling dive *diving* 164.6
kneeling position *target shooting* 160.1
kneel on *kick* 695.14
kneel to *petition* 505.11
knee pad *hockey clothing* 158.6
kneepan Human Bones 19
knees Phobias 283
knee-socks *legwear* 100.26, *soccer uniform* 163.3
knees-up [Brit inf] *dance* 135.1
knell *death* 29.1, *funeral* 31.4, *signal* 183.6, *ringing* 236.2, *ring* 236.10, *lament* 280.2, *ruin* 523.4,

forewarning 814.2, *give warning* 814.10
knickerbockers *pants* 100.14
knickers [Brit] *underwear* 100.22
knickers *pants* 100.14
knickknack *cheap item* 497.5, *decorative article* 532.5, *cheap thing* 800.7
knife *murder weapon* 30.3, *murder* 30.20, *sharp weapon* 78.6, *tableware* 92.13, *hand tool* 103.3, *inflict pain* 215.10, *stab* 418.22, *sharp-edged thing* 549.6, *use a sharp tool* 549.17, *opener* 583.2, *hole* 583.17
knifed *holed* 583.12
knife edge *rock face* 161.6, *sharp edge* 549.3, *cutting edge* 618.3
knife-edged *sharp-edged* 549.12
knifelike *sharp-edged* 549.12
knife pleat *pleat* 637.2
knife point *sharp point* 549.2
knife sharpener *sharpener* 549.8
knife-thrower *thrower* 696.10
knifing *murder* 30.2, *hit* 418.9
knight *military honor* 58.9, *honor* 58.14, *nobleman* 70.1, *make noble* 70.5, *combatant* 77.1, *horse person* 159.14, *board games* 167.3, *courageous person* 284.8, *defender* 419.14, *decorate* 532.11
knighted *honored* 58.12
knight-errant *visionary* 360.9, *defender* 419.14
knight-errantry *conception* 360.4
knighthood *military honor* 58.9
knight in shining armor *courageous person* 284.8, *protector* 810.11
knightliness *heroism* 284.2
knightly *military* 76.28, *heroic* 284.10, *courteously* 410.13
Knightsbridge London 567.8
knight's move *deviating motion* 698.3
knit 130.19; *sweater* 100.17, *weaving* 130.6, *knitting* 130.7, *perform* 522.16, *contract* 582.12, *become smaller* 582.14, *form* 624.9, *wrinkle* 638.6, *intertwine* 752.19
knit one's brow *be irritable* 304.14
knitted *woven* 130.15, *shortened* 582.8, *wrinkly* 638.4
knitted brow *wrinkle* 638.2
knitted fabric *fabric* 130.1
knitted sweater *sweater* 100.17
knitter *weaving* 609.2
knitting 130.7, Hobbies and Pastimes 167, *shortening* 582.2, *braid* 609.3, *forming* 624.4, *unification* 752.5
knitting machine *fabric-handling tool* 130.12
knitting needle *fabric-handling tool* 130.12, *sharp-pointed thing* 549.4
knit together *intertwine* 752.19
knitwear *dry goods* 130.3
knob *coarsen* 552.12, *hill* 569.2, *bulge* 283.4
knobbiness *roughness* 544.1
knobbly *coarse* 544.6
knobby *coarse* 544.6
knobkerrie *blunt weapon* 78.5
knock 235.4, 235.13; *type of touch* 216.3, *touch* 216.9, *burst* 232.9, *crack* 234.2, *hit* 418.9, 695.11, *jolt* 684.9, *blow* 695.5
knock [Inf] *criticism* 438.4, *berate* 438.20, *criticize* 440.12
knockabout *variety* 138.13, *comedy* 368.2, *ridiculous* 368.5

knockabout *or* **knockabout comedy** *comedy* 136.11
knock about *ill-use* 395.7
knock at the door *approach* 704.15
knock back [Inf] *drink* 93.19
knock back a few [Inf] *get drunk* 121.35
knockdown *boxing techniques* 152.5, *combat* 152.17, *bargain* 497.10, *lowering* 597.3
knock down 523.13; *box* 152.19, *refute* 332.7, *strike* 418.21, *lower* 597.21, *make horizontal* 603.10
knock down [Inf] *discount* 495.4, *make cheap* 497.14
knock down a few rungs *make unimportant* 800.20
knockdown argument *refutation* 332.1
knock-down-drag-out *disagreeing* 463.6
knock-down-drag-out fight *contention* 422.1, *dispute* 463.3
knock down pins *bowl* 151.8
knockdown price *bargain* 495.2
knockdown punch *boxing techniques* 152.5
knock down to *auction* 482.16
knocked down *lowered* 597.12, *leveled* 603.8
knocked flat *lowered* 597.12, *leveled* 603.8
knocked out *combat* 152.17, *desensitized* 213.5, *defeated* 846.11
knocked over *lowered* 597.12
knocker *impeller* 695.7
knocker [Inf] *disparager* 440.7
knockers [Inf] *bulge* 634.2
knock flat *ruin* 523.15, *lower* 597.21, *make horizontal* 603.10
knock for a loop [Inf] *astonish* 292.10
knock hard *burst* 232.9
knock heads together *collide* 695.10
knock in *impact* 710.11, *link* 752.18
knocking *knock* 235.4, *rattling* 235.8, *miscellaneous automotive terms* 687.14
knocking [Inf] *criticism* 440.2, *disparaging* 440.8
knocking down *destroying* 523.2
knocking knees *symptoms of fear* 283.3
knocking off course *or* **out of place** *displacement* 574.1
knocking on wood *good-luck sign* 358.6
knock into *meet* 704.20
knock into shape *form* 624.9
knock it off [Inf] *be silent* 231.3, *cease!* 668.14
knock it off! [Inf] *hush!* 231.6
knock off *discount* 495.4, *unstick* 756.6
knock off [Inf] *steal* 479.14
knock off course *displace* 574.15
knock-on effect [Brit] *consequence* 774.3
knock one's head against a brick wall *figurative expressions* 128.11
knock one's socks off [Inf] *be wondrous* 294.14
knock on *or* **touch wood** *be hopeful* 281.11
knockout *boxing techniques* 152.5, *combat* 152.17, *attractive female* 529.5, *ender* 773.11, *victory* 845.4
knockout [Inf] *wonderful person* 294.6, *good thing* 445.9
knock out *box* 152.19, *anesthetize*

213.8, *make inactive* 415.16, *overpower* 515.14, *ruin* 523.15, *annihilate* 773.22, *defeat* 845.17
knock out [Inf] *perform* 522.16
knockout blow *ruin* 523.4, *ender* 773.11
knockout competition *prize competition* 422.5
knockout drops *anesthetic* 213.3
knock out of shape *make shapeless* 625.3
knock out of true alignment *distort* 627.9
knockout punch *boxing techniques* 152.5, *ruin* 523.4
knock over *knock down* 523.13, *lower* 597.21
knock poker *Card Games* 168
knock rummy *Card Games* 168
knock the bottom out [Inf] *play basketball* 148.7
knock the bottom out of the market *make cheap* 497.14
knock the shit out of [Inf] *defeat* 845.17
knock the stuffing out of *defeat* 845.17
knock up *send up* 715.12
knock up [Inf] *propagate* 21.15
knoll *hill* 569.2, *lowlands* 597.6
knot *topology* 6.45, *tree part* 43.2, Collective Names 59, *weaving* 130.6, *sew* 130.18, *solid body* 540.4, *rough thing* 544.2, *make rough* 544.11, General Units 589, *bulge* 634.2, *nautical speed* 690.11, *speed* 694.2, *joint* 752.7, *link* 752.18, *line* 754.5, *connect* 754.13, *restraint* 834.2
knot garden *garden* 17.2
knothole *hole* 583.4
knotmeter log *navigational aid* 690.6
knotted *sewn* 130.14, *condensed* 540.7, *coarse* 544.6, *tied* 752.13, *connected* 754.11
knotted score *stalemate* 740.3
knottiness *difficulty* 824.1
knotting *topology* 6.45, *sewing* 130.5, *braid* 609.3, *unification* 752.5
knotty *mysterious* 182.10, *problematic* 333.12, 824.11, *condensed* 540.7, *coarse* 544.6
knotty problem *puzzle* 182.5, *difficult question* 333.4, *unintelligible thing* 364.3, *problem* 824.4
knout *instrument of punishment* 454.13
know 48.24, 348.10; *believe* 87.9, *manage* 126.10, *be expert* 127.15, *be informed* 170.15, *be intelligent* 352.7, *understand* 363.9, *be certain* 840.13
know, the [Inf] *information* 170.1
knowability *intelligibility* 363.1
knowable *known* 348.9, *intelligible* 363.5, *recognizable* 363.7
know again *remember* 354.12
know-all *vain person* 402.7
knowall [Inf] *intellectual* 315.7
know all the answers *learn* 68.18, *be skillful* 127.14, *know by heart* 348.11, *be cunning* 822.5
know all the ins and outs *be expert* 127.15
know a trick or two *be cunning* 822.5
know back to front *be an authority on* 52.17
know backward *be expert* 127.15
know backward and forward *know* 48.24, *be expert* 127.15

know by heart 348.11; *know* 48.24
know by instinct *feel instinctively* 266.15
know for sure *be certain* 840.13
know from A to Z *know by heart* 348.11
know full well *know by heart* 348.11
know how *qualify* 340.11
know-how *means* 102.1, *aptitude* 127.4, *ability* 340.2, *information* 348.2, *way* 691.1, *cunning* 822.1
know how to *learn* 68.18
know how to mix *participate* 408.15
know in advance *foresee* 357.9
knowing *feeling* 266.9, *knowledge* 348.1, *knowledgeable* 348.7, *wise* 352.4, *cunning* 822.4
knowingly *knowledgeably* 348.14
knowing no better *naive* 449.9
knowing no wrong *naive* 449.9
knowing one's place *showing respect* 435.7
knowing person *expert* 127.9
know inside out *know* 48.24, *be an authority on* 52.17
know inside out *or* **backward** *or* **backward and forward** *know by heart* 348.11
know it all *not wonder about* 295.5
know-it-all *insolent person* 400.7, *vain person* 402.7, *boastful* 402.13
know-it-all [Inf] *intellectual* 315.7
know just when to stop *be skillful* 127.14
knowledge 348.1; *means* 102.1, *skill* 127.1, *information* 170.1, *feelings* 266.1, *intellect* 315.1, *wisdom* 352.1, *understanding* 363.4, *profundity* 598.5, *cunning* 822.1, *certainty* 840.1
knowledgeable 348.7; *educated* 48.19, *expert* 52.12, *intelligent* 315.9, *reasoning* 319.7, *wise* 352.4, *profound* 598.15, *specialized* 779.11, *cunning* 822.4
knowledgeableness *cleverness* 315.3, *profundity* 598.5
knowledgeable person 348.5
knowledgeably 348.14; *wisely* 4.28, *expertly* 52.21, *skillfully* 127.16, *intelligently* 315.14, *profoundly* 598.27
knowledge of law *jurisprudence* 53.13
knowledge of the enemy *art of war* 76.16
knowledge-seeking *questioning* 333.11
know like a book *know* 48.24
know like the back of one's hand *know* 48.24
know like the back of one's hand [Inf] *know by heart* 348.11
know little 349.9
known 348.9; *given* 6.74, *identified* 184.9, *familiar* 397.10, *certain* 840.7
known as *identified* 184.9
known attitudes *conduct* 399.1
known by *identified* 184.9
know no better *be naive* 449.12, 821.4
know no bounds *be excessive* 99.9
know no law *be illegal* 53.30
know no limit *or* **bounds** *or* **end** *have no limit* 798.8
know nothing *be ignorant* 349.8
know no wrong *be naive* 449.12
know one's job *qualify* 340.11
know one's onions [Inf] *be expert* 127.15

know one's own mind *follow one's own will* 372.13, *be resolute* 376.11
know one's place *be modest* 403.11, *succumb* 421.7
know one's stuff [Inf] *be expert* 127.15, *know by heart* 348.11
know one's stuff *be an authority on* 52.17
know the ins and outs *circumstantiate* 726.12
know the real world *be real* 721.21
know the right people *influence* 512.11
know the ropes [Inf] *be expert* 127.15, *know by heart* 348.11
know the ropes *know* 48.24
know the score [Inf] *understand* 295.6, *be wise* 352.6
know the score *know* 48.24
know what one is about *be skillful* 127.14
know what's what [Inf] *be skillful* 127.14, *be intelligent* 315.11, *be wise* 352.6
know what's what *know* 48.24
know when one has had enough *be self-restrained* 455.10
know when to stop *be self-restrained* 455.10, *restrain oneself* 830.15
knub *nap* 552.3
knuckle *joint* 752.7
knuckle ball *pitching terms* 147.5
knuckle-duster *blunt weapon* 78.5
knuckle under 401.10; *submit* 298.17, *succumb* 421.7, *follow* 745.12
knurled *coarse* 544.6
KO [Inf] *ruin* 523.15, *annihilate* 773.22, *victory* 845.4, *defeat* 845.17
koa Trees and Shrubs 43
kobold *sprite* 86.12, Legendary Creatures 360
KO'd [Inf] *defeated* 846.11
Kodiak Islands 572
Kohen *rabbi* 84.6
kohl *cosmetics* 530.4
Kohoutek *comet* 7.20
koine *international language* 5.8
koinoniphobia Phobias 283
koji *religious* 84.9
Koko Nor Lakes 568
Koksoak Rivers 570
kolkhoz *farm* 16.2
Kolyma Rivers 570
kombu [Jap] *algal product* 47.15
Komodo dragon *lizard* 37.5
Komondor Breeds of Dogs 35
Konik pony Horse and Pony Breeds 159
konimeter *koniology* 553.15
koniology 553.15
koniophobia Phobias 283
kontakion *ritual music* 85.9
kook [Inf] *insane person* 110.5
kooky [Inf] *eccentric* 782.16
Kootenai *or* **Kootenay** Rivers 570
kopek *national coins* 484.11
kopophobia Phobias 283
Koran The Law 53.2, *Islamic text* 81.18
Korat Breeds of Cats 35
Kore Deities 82
Korean War Major Wars 76
Korsakoff's psychosis *or* **syndrome** *psychosis* 110.3
Kosciusko, Mount Mountains and Hills 569
kosher *edible* 92.20, *clean* 111.13, *conformist* 781.10

kosher food *food* 90.1
kosher salt *basic cooking ingredient* 91.8
Kostroma Breeds of Cattle 16
koto Musical Instruments 142
koumis *milk* 93.5
kowhai Trees and Shrubs 43
kowtow *knuckle under* 401.10, *defer to* 410.12, *submission* 421.1, *succumb* 421.7, *obeisance* 426.3, *show obeisance to* 426.8, *mark of respect* 435.4, *show respect* 435.16, *be horizontal* 603.9, *bow* 716.6, 716.22
kowtower *sycophant* 401.3
kowtowing *sycophantic* 401.7, *deference* 410.4, *deferential* 410.8, *showing respect* 435.7, *degraded* 716.10
kraft recovery cycle *systems and process control* 14.28
kraken Legendary Creatures 360
Krasnoyarsk Breeds of Sheep 16
K rations *short rations* 18.3
Kraut Nicknames for Inhabitants 61
Krebs cycle *bioenergetics* 12.23, *respiration* 12.24, *cell biology* 13.14
Kreis [Ger] *administrative region* 564.4
Kremlin, the *the power structure* 68.12
kreplach *pasta* 90.31
Krishna Rivers 570
krona *or* **krone** *national coins* 484.11
krožek Accents and Diacritical Marks 5
krypton Chemical Elements and Common Allotropes 11
Kuala Lumpur Countries 566
Kubachi ware Ceramics 129
Kuban Rivers 570
kudos *compliment* 437.4
Kuibyshev Breeds of Sheep 16
kukri *sharp weapon* 78.6
kumiss *milk* 93.5
kung fu Sporting Activities 145
Kunlun Mountains Mountains and Hills 569
Kura Rivers 570
Kuril Islands Islands 572
kurrajong Trees and Shrubs 43
kurtosis *probability distribution* 6.56
Kustanair Horse and Pony Breeds 159
Kutani porcelain Ceramics 129
kuvasz Breeds of Dogs 35
Kuwait Countries 566
Kuwait City Countries 566
kvetch [Inf] *dissatisfied person* 274.3, *be dissatisfied* 274.7
Kwajalein Islands 572
kwashiorkor *tropical disease* 114.10
Kyloe Breeds of Cattle 16
kymograph *measuring instrument* 683.6
Kyoga Lakes 568
kyogen *dramatic style* 136.3
Kyrgyzstan Countries 566
Kyrie Eucharist 85.7
Kyrie Eleison *prayer* 85.10
Kyushu Islands 572
Kyzyl Kum Deserts 572

L

lab *plant* 124.7, *place of experimentation* 335.6
labarum *flag* 184.8
Labe Rivers 570

label Architectural Elements 134, Heraldic Terms 184, *means of identification* 184.3, *personal identification* 184.4, *identify* 184.11, *name* 202.8, *type* 777.4, *class* 777.12, *make a generalization* 778.18, *characterize* 779.15, *showplace* 843.4
labeled *identified* 184.9
labeling *identification* 184.1, *generalization* 778.5
labial *spoken letter* 5.15, *voiced* 5.37
labia majora *organs of reproduction* 21.9
labia minora *organs of reproduction* 21.9
labiate *taxonomic* 41.16
labile *changeable* 666.3
labiodental *spoken letter* 5.15
labionasal *spoken letter* 5.15
labor *industrial* 57.13, Collective Names 59, *work* 122.8, *personnel* 123.16, *persevere* 377.10, *try hard* 390.7, *action* 412.1, *occupy oneself* 412.15, *assiduity* 414.8, *pitch* 684.25, *harp* 797.17, *make important* 799.14, *difficult task* 824.3
laboratory *school place* 48.16, *plant* 124.7, *place of experimentation* 335.6
laboratory animal *experimental subject* 335.7
laboratory assistant *chemical engineer* 14.25
Laboratory for Particle Physics *nuclear power agencies* 514.11
laboratory technician *technical worker* 123.14
laboratory test *diagnosis* 107.8
labor camp *prison* 55.1, *coercive method* 428.3, *imprisonment* 454.2
labor dispute *industrial dispute* 57.7
labored *laborious* 122.7, *inelegant* 528.6
labored breathing *fatigue* 820.1
laborer 123.9; *employee* 57.4, *servant* 69.1, *operative* 509.6, *producer* 522.10
labor force *bargaining* 57.9, *personnel* 123.16
labor in behalf of *serve* 825.29
laboring *working* 122.6, *industrious* 414.16
labor in vain *misspend* 96.17, *act foolishly* 128.10, *be wasteful* 468.16, *waste effort* 802.13
laborious 122.7; *industrious* 414.16, *punishing* 454.20, *fatiguing* 820.4, *difficult* 824.9
laboriously 122.13; *tiringly* 820.8, *arduously* 824.24
laboriousness *assiduity* 414.8, *difficulty* 824.1
labor law 57.12
labor-management body *bargaining* 57.9
labor-management relations *labor relations* 57.1
labor negotiations *bargaining* 57.9
labor of love *work* 122.1, *benevolent act* 305.5, *voluntary work* 373.5, *undertaking* 391.1, *giving* 472.1, *absence of charge* 497.6
labor of Sisyphus *waste* 468.5, *waste of effort* 802.4
labor organizer *union member* 57.6
labor pain *painful condition* 215.2
labor pool *resources* 102.4, *personnel* 123.16

labor relations 57.1
labor resources *resources* 102.4
laborsaving *leisurely* 125.4, *feasible* 823.10
labor-saving *mechanical* 103.7, *thrifty* 499.4
labor-saving device *convenience* 825.7
labor the obvious *be superfluous* 99.12, *waste effort* 802.13
labor under *be in a predicament* 725.9
labor under a disadvantage *have difficulty* 824.18
labor under a false impression *be in error* 351.15
labor under difficulties *have difficulty* 824.18
labor union *organized labor* 57.5, *association* 752.2
labor union official *union member* 57.6
labor union trade union *association* 778.5
Labour party Political Parties 50
Labrador retriever Breeds of Dogs 35
lab rat *experimental subject* 335.7
laburnum Flowers 42
labyrinth *puzzle* 182.5, *ear* 228.2, *convoluted thing* 632.3
labyrinthine *mysterious* 182.10, *convolutional* 632.4, *indirect* 698.9, *muddled* 766.13, *problematic* 824.11
labyrinthitis *ear problem* 228.4
lac *resin* 562.6, *thousand* 792.10
Lacanian psychology Psychological Theories, Schools 108
Lacaune Breeds of Sheep 16
laccolith *igneous rock* 8.32
lace *wear* 100.46, *fabric* 130.1, *weaving* 130.6, *sew* 130.18, *weave* 130.20, *transparent thing* 249.4, *decorative method* 532.3, *fineness* 595.5, *braid* 609.3, *interweave* 609.8, *mix* 751.12, *intertwine* 752.19, *line* 754.5, *connect* 754.13
laced *sewn* 130.14, *interwoven* 609.6, *connected* 754.11
lace into *strike* 418.21
lace maker *fabric handler* 130.11
lacemaker *decorator* 532.8
lacemaking *sewing* 130.5, Hobbies and Pastimes 167
lacerate *take apart* 753.16
lacerated *injured* 215.5
laceration *painful injury* 215.3, *separateness* 753.3
Lacerta Constellations 7
Lacertilia *lizard* 37.5
lacertilian *reptilian* 37.12
lacertilian *or* **lacertian** *lizard* 37.5
lace up *intertwine* 752.19
lace-ups *boots* 100.31
lace up tightly *unite closely* 752.16
lacework *sewing* 130.5, *decorative method* 532.3
lachanophobia Phobias 283
laches [Form] *nonobservance* 466.1
Lachesis Deities 82
Lachlan Rivers 570
lachrymal *of a secretion* 24.5, *rheumy* 555.16
lachrymal gland *secretory mechanism* 24.3
lachrymation *rheumy* 555.16
lachrymose *lamenting* 280.4
lacily *finely* 595.19
laciness *fineness* 595.5
lacing *weaving* 130.6
lacing intertwining *interweaving* 609.1

lack *need* 95.4, 95.16, *scarcity* 98.3, *be insufficient* 98.9, *poverty* 486.1, *inadequacy* 486.5, *be poor* 486.14, *request* 505.10, *absence* 576.1, *be inferior* 745.10, *incompleteness* 762.1, 806.2, *nonachievement* 762.3, *omission* 762.4, *be incomplete* 762.8, *fewness* 796.3, *defect* 806.4
lackadaisical *indifferent* 289.7, 326.5, *apathetic* 322.4, *perfunctory* 324.9
lackadaisically *indifferently* 289.17, *apathetically* 322.7
lackadaisicalness *indifference* 289.1
lack amazement *not wonder about* 295.5
lack authority 515.12
lack bias *be disinterested* 443.6
lack bias *or* **prejudice** *be truthful* 191.7
lack candor 192.22
lack compassion *be pitiless* 309.5
lack conviction *be irresolute* 461.8
lack courage *be a coward* 285.7
lack courtesy *disrespect* 436.18
lack definition *make shapeless* 625.3
lack discipline *lack restraint* 829.21
lack emotion *be disinterested* 443.6, *be calm* 455.13
lack equality *be rough* 544.10
lack experience *be naive* 449.12
lackey *servant* 69.1, *sycophant* 401.3, *assistant* 511.3, *conformist* 781.6, *subordinate* 832.3
lack factuality *be untrue* 722.11
lack fairness *be unjust* 741.9
lack flavor *be tasteless* 220.6
lack harmony *be dissonant* 241.6, *disagree* 753.19
lack hope *be hopeless* 282.11
lack information *be ignorant* 349.8
lacking *needy* 95.12, *insufficient* 98.4, 517.11, *unprovided* 98.6, *losing* 468.9, *inadequate* 486.13, *missing* 576.11, *nonexistent* 718.9, *incomplete* 762.5, 806.6, *uncompleted* 762.7, *zero* 786.5
lacking application *unused* 394.5
lacking breadth *narrow* 593.8
lacking ceremony *nonobservant* 466.5
lacking definition *shapeless* 625.2
lacking emotion *calm* 455.9
lacking in morals *immoral* 432.9
lacking in taste *vulgar* 535.6
lacking integrity *dishonorable* 192.14
lacking intellect 316.5
lacking nothing *complete* 761.6
lacking sight *blind* 243.11
lacking strength *weak* 517.6
lacking substance *imaginary* 360.12
lack integrity *be dishonorable* 192.21
lack intellect 316.8
lack interest *be bored* 296.7
lack light *be dark* 247.8
lackluster *dimmed* 248.6, *colorless* 252.5, *drained of color* 252.6, *depressed* 270.5
lack maturity *be naive* 449.12
lack mercy *be severe* 424.8
lack nothing *be complete* 761.10
lack of ability *unskillfulness* 128.1
lack of action *inaction* 413.1
lack of admiration *lack of wonder* 295.1

lack of advantage *futility* 802.3
lack of amazement *lack of wonder* 295.1
lack of ambition *leisure* 413.4
lack of appetite *delicate eating* 92.3, *symptom* 114.3, *indifference* 289.1
lack of appreciation *ingratitude* 311.1
lack of astonishment *lack of wonder* 295.1
lack of attention *inattention* 229.2
lack of authenticity *unauthenticity* 722.4
lack of authority **515.2;** *anarchy* 51.1
lack of awareness *insensibility* 213.1
lack of awe *lack of wonder* 295.1
lack of benefit *futility* 802.3
lack of bias *truthfulness* 191.1, *disinterestedness* 443.1
lack of bite *toothlessness* 550.4
lack of brains *lack of intellect* 316.1
lack of candor **192.4**
lack of cause *lack of motive* 842.2
lack of censorship *free rights* 829.4
lack of ceremony *informality* 407.1, *nonobservance* 466.1
lack of change *permanence* 667.1
lack of choice *necessitation* 95.5
lack of clarity **364.2;** *obscurity* 197.1, *unintelligibility* 364.1
lack of color *colorlessness* 252.1, *unadornment* 526.3
lack of commitment *vacillation* 378.1, *irresolution* 461.3
lack of concealment *visibility* 244.1
lack of concentration *restlessness* 414.7
lack of confession *impenitence* 452.1
lack of confidence *suspicion* 314.3
lack of confinement *freedom* 829.1
lack of consent *refusal* 190.2, 506.1, *dissent* 506.2
lack of consideration *figurative blindness* 243.8, *discourtesy* 411.1
lack of continuity *discontinuity* 775.1
lack of contrition *impenitence* 452.1
lack of convention *informality* 407.1
lack of conviction *irresolution* 461.3
lack of courage *cowardice* 285.1
lack of curiosity *incuriosity* 322.1
lack of danger *safety* 810.1
lack of decoration *unadornment* 526.3
lack of definition *shapelessness* 625.1
lack of delay *immediacy* 645.1
lack of democracy *injustice* 741.3
lack of depth *shallowness* 599.1
lack of desire *indifference* 289.1
lack of deviation *regularity* 730.6
lack of difficulty *easiness* 823.1
lack of discernment *figurative blindness* 243.8
lack of discipline *lawlessness* 766.6, *liberality* 829.8
lack of discrimination **338.1**
lack of disguise *candor* 191.2
lack of ease *awkwardness* 824.2
lack of emotion *disinterestedness* 443.1, *calmness* 455.4
lack of emphasis **201.1**

lack of enjoyment *boredom* 296.1
lack of enlightenment *figurative blindness* 243.8
lack of enthusiasm *or zeal unenthusiasm* 375.3
lack of exaggeration *truthfulness* 191.1
lack of expression *unintelligibility* 364.1
lack of factuality *untruth* 722.1
lack of fairness *injustice* 741.3
lack of feeling *insensibility* 213.1, *insensitivity* 268.1
lack of finesse *or polish or style inelegance* 528.1
lack of fitness *ill health* 114.1
lack of food *scarcity* 90.5
lack of force *lack of emphasis* 201.1
lack of formality *informality* 407.1
lack of function *uselessness* 802.1
lack of grace *awkwardness* 824.2
lack of gratitude *ingratitude* 311.1
lack of harmony *disunity* 753.4
lack of haste *slowness* 693.1
lack of heat *cold* 218.1
lack of hindrance *smoothness* 823.5
lack of hope **282.2**
lack of hygiene **112.3**
lack of importance *extraneousness* 724.1
lack of incisiveness *toothlessness* 550.4
lack of inspiration *lack of emphasis* 201.1
lack of integrity *dishonorableness* 192.3
lack of intellect **316.1**
lack of intention *lack of motive* 842.2
lack of interest *indifference* 289.1, *lack of wonder* 295.1, *incuriosity* 322.1
lack of knowledge **349.2;** *ignorance* 316.3, 349.1
lack of light *darkness* 247.1
lack of maintenance *dilapidation* 808.5
lack of manners *bad manners* 411.2
lack of meaning **362.1;** *unintelligibility* 364.1
lack of memory *mental block* 318.5
lack of mercy *severity* 424.1
lack of moral fiber *dastardliness* 285.2
lack of morals *immorality* 432.1
lack of motion **678.1**
lack of motive **842.2**
lack of order *disintegration* 758.1
lack of ornamentation *unadornment* 526.3
lack of ostentation *modesty* 403.1
lack of passion *lack of emphasis* 201.1
lack of perception *figurative blindness* 243.8
lack of pigment *whiteness* 253.1
lack of pity *pitilessness* 309.1
lack of planning *inconvenience* 804.1
lack of politeness *bad manners* 411.2
lack of power *powerlessness* 515.1
lack of practice *unskillfulness* 128.1, *unaccustomedness* 398.1
lack of prejudice *truthfulness* 191.1, *disinterestedness* 443.1, *broad-mindedness* 592.3
lack of preparation **389.1**
lack of principle *depravity* 448.2

lack of principles *immorality* 432.1
lack of probity *dishonorableness* 192.3
lack of professionalism *unskillfulness* 128.1
lack of proficiency *unskillfulness* 128.1
lack of profit *financial loss* 468.4
lack of progress *inaction* 413.1
lack of protection *vulnerability* 811.6
lack of protocol *inconvenience* 804.1
lack of purpose *aimlessness* 362.3, 362.6, *futility* 802.3
lack of reason *nonsense* 362.2
lack of refinement *inelegance* 528.1, *vulgarity* 535.1
lack of repair *dilapidation* 808.5
lack of reserve *candor* 191.2
lack of resolution *vacillation* 378.1, *irresolution* 461.3
lack of respect *disrespect* 436.1
lack of restraint *candor* 191.2, *tastelessness* 338.3, *expansion* 592.2, *freedom* 829.1
lack of risk *safety* 810.1
lack of sanitation *lack of hygiene* 112.3
lack of scruples *dishonorableness* 192.3
lack of self-confidence *self-deprecation* 403.4
lack of sensation *insensibility* 213.1
lack of sense *unintelligibility* 364.1
lack of sense of smell **225.2**
lack of seriousness *triviality* 800.2
lack of sight *blindness* 243.3
lack of skill **282.4;** *unskillfulness* 128.1, *uselessness* 802.1, *awkwardness* 824.2
lack of smell *odorlessness* 225.1
lack of solidity *sparseness* 541.1
lack of sparkle *lack of emphasis* 201.1
lack of spirit *lack of emphasis* 201.1, *cowardice* 285.1, *lack of wonder* 295.1
lack of strength *ill health* 114.1, *weakness* 517.1
lack of style *lack of emphasis* 201.1
lack of substance *sparseness* 541.1, *unreality* 722.2, *unimportance* 800.1
lack of success *failure* 846.1
lack of surprise *predictability* 295.2
lack of sympathy *or compassion pitilessness* 309.1
lack of talent *unskillfulness* 128.1
lack of thoroughness *incompleteness* 806.2
lack of thought **318.1**
lack of training *lack of preparation* 389.1
lack of transparency *obscurity* 197.1
lack of understanding *ignorance* 316.3, *unintelligibility* 364.1
lack of unity *disunity* 753.4, *nonadhesion* 756.1
lack of use *nonuse* 394.1, *uselessness* 802.1
lack of variation *boringness* 296.2
lack of variety *or variation sameness* 730.1
lack of veneration *disrespect* 436.1
lack of ventilation *stench* 227.1

lack of veracity *untruthfulness* 192.1, *untruth* 722.1
lack of viscosity *nonadhesion* 756.1
lack of weight *lightness* 539.1
lack of wisdom *ignorance* 316.3
lack of wit *ignorance* 316.3
lack of wonder **295.1**
lack order *violate the law* 466.12
lack passion *de-emphasize* 201.3
lack planning *be unprepared* 389.14
lack prejudice *be disinterested* 443.6, *be broad-minded* 592.13
lack preparation *be unprepared* 389.14
lack reason *lack intellect* 316.8
lack regularity *be rough* 544.10, *be irregular* 664.5
lack resolution *be irresolute* 461.8
lack resolve *or commitment vacillate* 378.8
lack restraint **829.21;** *be free* 829.16
lack scruples *be dishonorable* 192.21
lack skill *be unskillful* 128.8
lack sophistication *be naive* 449.12
lack spirit *de-emphasize* 201.3
lack talent *be unskillful* 128.8
lack thought **318.12**
lack uniformity *be rough* 544.10
lack unity *disagree* 753.19
lack variation *bore* 296.8
lack weight *be light* 539.8
Lacombe *Breeds of Pigs* 16
laconic *concise* 198.4, *summary* 204.5, *sparing with words* 208.6
laconically *concisely* 198.6, *summarily* 204.10
laconism *or laconicism conciseness* 198.1, *summariness* 204.4, *guarded speech* 208.3
lacquer *work wood* 131.9, *color* 251.16, *coating* 613.8, *coat* 613.28
lacquered *type of furniture* 101.2, *polished* 545.7
lacquer tree *Trees and Shrubs* 43
lacrimal *fluid* 19.25, *of a secretion* 24.5
lacrimal bone *Human Bones* 19
lacrimal gland *secretory mechanism* 24.3
lacrimate *secrete* 24.7
lacrimation *secretion* 24.1
lacrimatory *secretory* 24.4, *of a secretion* 24.5, *inducing secretion* 24.6
lacrosse *Sporting Activities* 145
lactase *enzyme* 12.11
lactate **35.34;** *secrete* 24.7
lactating *secretory* 24.4
lactation *secretion* 24.1, *body fluid* 555.3, *juiciness* 555.7
lactational *secretory* 24.4
lactationally *glandularly* 24.8
lacteal *of a secretion* 24.5, *milky* 555.17
lacteally *glandularly* 24.8, *fluidly* 555.26
lacteous *[Arch] of a secretion* 24.5, *milky* 555.17
lactescence *whiteness* 253.1, *juiciness* 555.7
lactescent *secretory* 24.4, *milky* 555.17
lactic *Common Fatty Acids* 12, *drinkable* 93.18, *milky* 555.17
lactiferous *secretory* 24.4, *milky* 555.17
lactogenic *inducing secretion* 24.6
lactose *Common Sugars* 12, *food content* 90.3
lactovegetarian *eater* 92.15
lactovegetarian diet *diet* 92.5

lacuna *need* 95.4, *intervening space* 563.8, *interval* 587.1, *emptiness* 718.4, *omission* 762.4, *gap* 775.4, *defect* 806.4
lacustral *lakelike* 568.5
lacustrian *lake dweller* 568.4, *lakelike* 568.5
lacustrine *lakelike* 568.5
lacustrine dweller *lake dweller* 568.4
lacustrine dwelling *lake dwelling* 568.3
lacy *fine* 595.12, *interwoven* 609.6
lad *child* 26.6, *young man* 26.8, *male* 32.1, *male title of address* 32.3
lad [Brit inf] *horse person* 159.14
ladder 713.10; *access* 691.3, *means of connection* 754.4, *consecutiveness* 774.1, *means of escape* 816.4
ladder-back *type of chair* 101.4
ladderlike 713.18
laddie *young man* 26.8
lade *make heavy* 538.14, *contain* 577.10, *transport* 686.10, *fill* 761.11
laded *transportable* 686.7
laden *loaded* 538.10, 577.8, *full* 761.8
lader *transporter* 686.4
ladies', the [Inf] *place for excretion* 25.11
ladies and gentlemen of the chorus *cast* 136.26
ladies' man *libertine* 32.7, *lover* 299.11, *charmer* 700.6
Ladies' Professional Golfers' Association (LPGA) *golfing associations and tournaments* 156.6
ladies' room *place for excretion* 25.11
ladies' room attendant *cleaner* 111.12
ladies' wear *dry goods* 130.3
lading *displacement* 538.3, *load* 577.5, *freightage* 686.3, *transporting* 686.8
ladle 578.17; *cooking equipment* 91.6, *tableware* 92.13, *take away* 685.12
ladled *storing* 578.19
Ladoga *Lakes* 568
la dolce vita [Ital] *good time* 214.3
lads, the [Inf] *menfolk* 32.14
Lady *honorific* 72.5
Lady [Brit] *female title of address* 33.3
lady *female* 33.1, *female title of address* 33.3, *married woman* 64.11, *nobleman* 70.1, *well-behaved person* 399.6, *refined person* 534.4
Lady Bountiful *philanthropist* 307.5, *giver* 472.7, *generous person* 498.5
Lady chapel *place of worship* 83.8, *church architecture* 134.11
Lady Day *Christian Holy Days and Seasons* 85
lady fair *attractive female* 529.5
Lady Hamilton *Famous Lovers* 299
lady-in-waiting *domestic servant* 69.7
lady-killer [Inf] *lover* 299.11
ladylike *female* 33.16, *aristocratic* 70.4, *well-behaved person* 399.15, *good-mannered* 410.7, *cultured* 534.6
ladylike behavior *good conduct* 399.5
ladylikeness *good manners* 410.2
ladylove *lover* 299.11
lady luck *luck* 842.3
Lady Mayor [Brit] *leader* 68.3

lady of the bedchamber *domestic servant* 69.7
lady of the evening *loose woman* 33.6
lady of the house *family member* 65.2, *master* 68.1, *property owner* 470.7
lady of the manor *master* 68.1, *property owner* 470.7
lady's maid *domestic servant* 69.7
lady's man *charmer* 700.6
lady's-slipper *Flowers* 42
lady with the lamp *nurse* 107.23
La Fleche *Breeds of Fowl* 16
lag *prisoner* 55.7, *pool* 149.3, *heat* 217.17, *protect* 613.26, *lateness* 658.1, *be late* 658.11, *hesitate* 693.12, *be inferior* 745.10
lag [Brit inf] *lawbreaker* 53.15, *prison sentence* 55.6, *be in prison* 55.13, *prisoner* 56.7
lag behind *be late* 658.11
Lag b'Omer *Jewish Holy Days and Seasons* 85
lager *beer* 93.10
laggard *indifferent person* 289.6, *not participating* 415.11, *latecomer* 658.4, *plodder* 693.6
lagged *heated* 217.15
lagger [Brit inf] *prisoner* 55.7
lagging *heater* 217.3, *protective covering* 613.5, *lateness* 658.1, *delaying* 658.8, *lingering* 693.4, *hesitant* 693.9
lagging behind *delaying* 658.8
lagniappe *superfluity* 99.4, *gift* 472.2, 498.3, *positive stimulus* 508.5, *extra* 748.6
Lagomorpha *gnawing mammal* 35.13
lagomorphic *rabbitlike* 35.29
lagomorphous *rabbitlike* 35.29
lagoon *coast* 8.13, *lake* 568.1
Lagrange's theorem *Mathematical Concepts* 6
lahar *mass movement* 8.28
laid-back [Inf] *leisurely* 125.4, *soft-hearted* 543.11, *at ease* 819.2
laid bare *disclosed* 180.5, *dilapidated* 517.7, *uncovered* 614.10
laid into [Inf] *criticized* 438.14
laid low *weakened* 517.9, *lowered* 597.12, *leveled* 603.8
laid off *hired* 57.17, *discarded* 383.8, *unemployed* 413.10, *not working* 415.10, *relegated* 574.11, *canceled* 854.5
laid out [Inf] *expended* 491.9
laid to rest *buried* 31.8
laid up *disused* 394.8, *not working* 415.10
laid up [Inf] *sick* 114.24
laid up in lavender *preserved* 815.12
Laing *psychiatrist* 108.34
lair *mammal dwelling* 35.21, *natural habitat* 60.16, *privacy* 181.6, *shelter* 613.6, 812.4
laird [Scot] *master* 68.1
laisser faire *inaction* 413.1
laissez faire *economics* 56.1, *inaction* 413.1, *leniency* 423.1, *capitalism* 480.5, *noninterference* 829.3
laissez-faire *permitting* 502.5
laissez-faire attitude *tolerance* 502.2
laissez-passer *permit* 502.3, *passport* 692.8
lake 568.1; *swimming place* 164.9, *waterway* 690.2
Lake District *Lakes* 568

Lake District or **Country** *regions of the British Isles* 564.8
lake dweller 568.4
lake dwelling 568.3
lake-dwelling *lakelike* 568.5
lake fog *fog* 9.32
lake house *lake dwelling* 568.3
Lakeland terrier *Breeds of Dogs* 35
lakelet *small lake* 568.2
lakelike 568.5
lake lodge *lake dwelling* 568.3
Lakenvelder *Breeds of Fowl* 16
lake of fire and brimstone *evil place* 446.6
Lake of the Woods *Lakes* 568
Lake poet *author* 139.13
Lake poets *Western Literary Groups* 139
laker *lake dweller* 568.4
lakes *Phobias* 283
lake sediment *sediment* 8.29
lakeside *lakelike* 568.5
lakeside dweller *lake dweller* 568.4
lakeside house *lake dwelling* 568.3
lakeside village *lake dwelling* 568.3
lakh [India] *thousand* 792.10
lallation *speech defect* 206.2
lallygag [Inf] *communicate love* 299.25, *hesitate* 693.12
lallygagging [Inf] *communication of love* 299.6, *lingering* 693.4, *delayed* 693.10
lalophobia or **laliophobia** *Phobias* 283
lam [Inf] *hurry off* 705.11
lama *imam* 84.7
Lamarckian *evolutionary* 13.34
Lamarckism *evolution* 13.23
lamasery *clerical dwelling* 84.10
lamb 90.27; *livestock* 16.11, *practice livestock farming* 16.20, *have young* 21.16, *young animal* 26.4, *give birth* 35.33, *symbol of peace* 73.6, *meat* 90.22, *term of endearment* 299.7, *innocent person* 449.5, *naive person* 821.2
lamb or **lambkin** *young mammal* 35.20
lambaste *hit* 454.28
lambaste or **lambast** *berate* 438.20, *beat* 695.12
lambasted *criticized* 438.14
lambasting *berating* 438.5
lambent *lucent* 246.13
Lambert's law *Classical Physical Laws* 10
Lambeth *London* 567.8
Lambeth Palace *clerical dwelling* 84.10
Lambeth walk *Dances* 135
lambing house *farm building* 16.4
lambkin *young animal* 26.4, *term of endearment* 299.7
lamblike *innocent* 449.6
Lamb of God *God the Son* 82.9
lambrequin *Heraldic Terms* 184
lamb to the slaughter *believer* 87.5, *substitute* 672.2
lame *unemphatic* 201.2, *ill* 517.8, *weaken* 517.13, *make useless* 802.12
lamé *Fabrics and Fibers* 130
lamebrain [Inf] *unintelligent person* 316.4
lame dog *weak thing* 517.5
lame duck *loser* 468.8, *weak person* 517.4, *person in adversity* 848.9
lamella *fungal body* 47.4, *coat* 588.3

lamellar *chemical compound* 11.4, *platelike* 588.8
lamellate *platelike* 588.8
lamellated *platelike* 588.8
lamellation *layering* 588.5
lamellibranch *mollusk* 39.13
lamelliform *platelike* 588.8
lamely *unemphatically* 201.4
lameness *lack of emphasis* 201.1, *physical deterioration* 808.4
lament 280.2, 280.7; *funeral* 31.4, *pay one's last respects* 31.12, *cry* 239.16, *grieve* 270.7, 308.7, *condolence* 308.2
lamentable 280.6; *distressing* 270.6
lamentably 280.10
lamentation 280.1; *funeral* 31.4, *cry of sorrow* 239.6, *lament* 280.2, *condolence* 308.2
lamented 280.5; *dead* 29.11
lamenter 280.3
lamenting 280.4; *funeral* 31.9, *crying* 239.11, *lamentation* 280.1, *penitent* 451.5
lamentingly 280.9
lamia *ghost* 86.11, *Legendary Creatures* 360, *evil spirit* 446.4
lamina *surface* 6.36, *leaf* 41.6, *plant body* 47.13, *woodworking tool* 131.6, *brittle thing* 548.2, *coat* 588.3, *coating* 613.8
laminate *make ceramics* 129.10, *work wood* 131.9, *coat* 588.3, 613.28, *layered* 588.6, *layer* 588.9
laminated *type of furniture* 101.2, *snowplow* 162.9, *layered* 588.6, *coated* 588.7, *covered* 613.19
laminated glass *industrial ceramics* 129.6, *glass* 249.5
laminated paper *paper* 104.5
laminated ski *ski equipment* 162.10
lamination *layering* 588.5
Lammas *Christian Holy Days and Seasons* 85
Lammas Day *Christian Holy Days and Seasons* 85
Lammermuir Hills *Mountains and Hills* 569
Lamona *Breeds of Fowl* 16
lamp *incandescent light* 246.5
lampblack *black pigment* 254.2
lamplight *incandescent light* 246.5
lamplit *lit* 246.16
lampoon *entertainment* 277.4, *be humorous* 277.11, *form of derision* 369.2, *deride* 369.7, *ridicule* 436.4, 440.6, 440.15
lampooner *humorist* 277.7, *derider* 369.3, *disparager* 440.7
lampoonist *derider* 369.3, *disparager* 440.7
lampshade *protective covering* 613.5
lampshade making *Hobbies and Pastimes* 167
lampshell *mollusk* 39.13
Lanai *Islands* 572
lanate *barbed* 544.7
lance *murder* 30.20, *fight* 77.35, *weapon* 78.1, *sharp weapon* 78.6, *stab* 418.22, *sharp-pointed thing* 549.4, *opener* 583.2, *hole* 583.17
Lance Corporal *US Military Ranks* 58
lanced *holed* 583.12
lancelet *protochordate* 39.4
Lancelot *Famous Lovers* 299
lanceolate *of leaves* 41.18, *sharp* 549.10
lancer *historical soldier* 77.8, *horse person* 159.14
lance rest *historic armor* 419.8

lancers Dances 135
lance-shaped *sharp* 549.10
lancet *arch* 134.5, *window* 134.10, *opener* 583.2
lancewood Trees and Shrubs 43
lancination *pain* 215.1
Land [Ger] *administrative region* 564.4
land 704.16; *continent* 8.8, *of plants* 41.14, *participate* 166.22, *property* 470.1, *region* 564.1, *country* 566.1, *be motionless* 678.7, *fly* 689.13, *sail* 690.16, *drop* 714.15
land a blow *box* 152.19
Landais pony Horse and Pony Breeds 159
land a rabbit punch *box* 152.19
land attack 418.3
land breeze *wind* 9.12, *sailing terms* 150.5
land bridge *ocean floor* 8.18, *peninsula* 572.5
land court *type of court* 54.9
land crab *crustacean* 39.10
landed *possessing* 469.11, *propertied* 470.9
landed estate *possession of property* 469.3, *property* 470.1
landed gentry *aristocracy* 70.2
landed property *property* 470.1
lander *planetary probe* 7.31
landfall *landing* 704.2
landfill *place for waste* 802.6
landform 8.9; *landmass* 572.1
landholding *possession of property* 469.3
landing 704.2; *horizontal bar* 157.5, *jumping* 166.11, *level* 588.2, *flight* 689.5, *flying* 689.11, *stairway* 713.9, *fall* 714.4
landing area *jumping* 166.11
landing beam *flight control* 689.7
landing craft *warship* 77.21
landing field *airport* 689.4, *flight path* 691.12
landing force *armed force* 77.10
landing on one's feet *successfulness* 845.3
landing stage *stairway* 713.9
landing strip *airport* 689.4
land in the cooler [Inf] *be in prison* 55.13
landlady *master* 68.1, *title holder* 72.4, *possessor* 469.10
landlocked *lakelike* 568.5, *inland* 611.8
landlocked water *small lake* 568.2
landlord *master* 68.1, *titleholder* 72.4, *possessor* 469.10
landlubber *unskilled person* 128.3
landmark *indicator* 183.7, *essential content* 723.2, *important matter* 799.2
landmass 572.1; *continent* 8.8, *world region* 564.6
landmine *bomb* 78.15
land-office business *prosperity* 847.1
land of milk and honey *fertile land* 22.2, *idealized pleasure* 214.5, *dreamland* 360.8, *objective* 374.5, *promised land* 458.5
land of Nod *sleep* 415.5
land of our fathers *native country* 566.6
land of promise *promised land* 458.5
land of the gods *heaven* 82.15
land on one's feet *be safe* 810.20, *overcome obstacles* 845.14
land operations *offensive warfare* 76.11

Land o' the Leal [Scot] *heaven* 82.15
landowner *master* 68.1, *titleholder* 72.4, *possessor* 469.10, *property owner* 470.7
landownership *possession of property* 469.3
landowning *possession of property* 469.3, *possessing* 469.11
Landrace Breeds of Pigs 16
lands *property* 470.1
landscape *continent* 8.8, *garden* 17.18, *portrait* 132.5, *architectural types* 134.2, *type of painting* 143.5, *view* 242.8
landscape architect *horticulturist* 17.13
landscape architecture *horticulture* 17.1
landscaped *ornamental* 17.17
landscape gardener *horticulturist* 17.13
landscape gardening *horticulture* 17.1
landscape painter *painter* 143.7
landscape photography *photographic specialties* 132.2
landslide *mass movement* 8.28, *agent of destruction* 523.7, *downflow* 714.3
landslide victory *victory* 845.4
land station *weather station* 9.5
land tenure *possession of property* 469.3
land travel *motion* 677.1
landward *toward* 697.18
lane *track event* 166.1, *road attribute* 687.3, *route* 691.2, *road* 691.4, *thoroughfare* 692.6
Langhe Breeds of Sheep 16
langouste [Fr] *food fish and shellfish* 90.20
Langshan Breeds of Fowl 16
language 5.4; *programming language* 15.16, *subject* 48.3
language element 5.13
language error 351.10
language family 5.12
language group *language family* 5.12
language laboratory *school place* 48.16
language sign 5.33
language student *linguist* 5.3
language type 5.11
language universal *international language* 5.8
languid *unemphatic* 201.2, *bored* 296.5, *not participating* 415.11, *ill* 517.8, *inert* 519.2, *sedentary* 678.5, *unhurried* 693.8, *fatigued* 820.2
languidly *in a bored manner* 296.9, *impassively* 415.18, *weakly* 517.14, *inertly* 519.5, *motionlessly* 678.9, *slowly* 693.14
languish *be unhealthy* 114.29, *grieve* 270.7, *be weak* 517.12, *diminish* 597.24, *be fatigued* 820.5
languishing *sick* 114.24, *sorrowful* 270.4, *amorous* 299.18, *diminishing* 597.16
languishment *sorrow* 270.1, *lovingness* 299.4, *fatigue* 820.1
languor *boredom* 296.1, *idleness* 415.3, *inertness* 519.1, *lack of motion* 678.1, *slowness* 693.1, *fatigue* 820.1
languorous *sedentary* 678.5, *unhurried* 693.8, *fatigued* 820.2
languorously *in a bored manner* 296.9, *motionlessly* 678.9, *slowly* 693.14

lank *plain* 528.9, *thin* 595.9
lankily *high* 596.20
lankiness *thinness* 595.1, *height* 596.1
lanky *thin* 595.9, *tall* 596.9
lanolin *fat* 562.4, *pomade* 562.9
Lansing American States 564
lantern 246.8; *Architectural Elements* 134
lantern jaw *thinness* 595.1
lantern-jawed *thin* 595.9
lantern slide *printing* 132.20
lanthanide *or* lanthanon *or* lanthanoid *chemical element* 11.3
lanthanum Chemical Elements and Common Allotropes 11
lanyard *tackle* 754.6
lanyard knot Knots, Bends, Hitches, Splices 754
Laodicean *indifferent person* 289.6, *moderate person* 772.8
Laos Countries 566
lap *automobile racing terms* 146.3, *be on the track* 146.11, *sound faint* 233.8, *flow* 570.10, *layer* 588.1, *circle* 631.2, 631.6, *round* 633.6, *move around* 633.10, *fold* 637.7, *cycle* 663.3, *orbit* 681.3, *ring* 681.9, *accelerate* 694.14, *exceed* 712.15, *part* 760.1, *private space* 812.2
laparoscope *diagnostic instrument* 107.13
laparoscopy *diagnostic procedure* 107.11
La Paz Countries 566
lap dissolve *motion-picture editing* 137.8
lap dog *dog* 35.10, *sycophant* 401.3
lapel *part of garment* 100.27
lapel pin *clothing* 184.6
lapidary *phrased* 5.39, *funeral* 31.9, *engraver* 144.5
lapidate *stone* 418.23, *execute* 454.30, *throw* 696.17
lapidation *hit* 418.9, *capital punishment* 454.12
lapidification [Arch] *hardening* 542.2
lapis lazuli *blue thing* 261.3
lap joint *carpenter's term* 131.5
Laplace *or* Laplacian operator Mathematical Concepts 6
lap of luxury *comfortable circumstances* 726.5, *prosperity* 847.1
lapped *racing* 146.9
lapping *drinking* 93.1, *racing* 146.9, *acceleration* 694.3, *accelerating* 694.9
lap robe *body covering* 613.3
lapse *disbelieve* 88.8, *negligence* 324.4, *trivial error* 351.8, *err* 351.14, *transgress* 351.16, *be unaccustomed* 398.5, *sin* 430.22, 450.3, *be immoral* 432.13, *be wicked* 448.13, *intervening space* 563.8, *space* 563.15, *pass* 639.13, *backsliding* 680.8, *go backward* 680.16, *wandering* 698.4, *sinkage* 714.2, *deterioration* 808.1, *deteriorate* 808.14
lapsed *unimproved* 808.10
lapse into disorder *be disordered* 766.21
lapse into oblivion *follow* 745.12
lapse into silence 208.8
lapse of memory *poor memory* 355.2
lapse of time *passage of time* 639.3, *duration* 642.1
lapsing *receding* 680.11
lapsus calami [L] *trivial error* 351.8

lapsus linguae [L] *trivial error* 351.8
Laptev Sea Oceans and Seas 571
laptop computer *computer* 15.1
lap up *drink* 93.19, *ingest* 708.17
Laputa Imaginary Places 360
lapwing *water bird* 36.9
lapwings Collective Names 59
larboard *laterally* 623.11
larcenist *thief* 479.8
larcenous *stolen* 479.12
larcenously *thievishly* 479.19
larceny *theft* 479.2
larch Trees and Shrubs 43
lard *basic cooking ingredient* 91.8, *cook* 91.10, *lubricate* 562.15, *fat* 579.8
lardaceous *oily* 562.11
lardass [Inf] *big person* 579.10
larder *room* 60.9, *cooking place* 91.4, *kitchen container* 91.7, *storeroom* 105.7
larding needle *cooking equipment* 91.6
lardy *oily* 562.11
Lares *minor deity* 82.2
large *great* 445.14, *big* 498.9, *579.13, heavy* 538.9
large amount *certain amount* 738.3, *multitude* 795.1
large-animal practice *veterinary medicine* 107.26
large as life *big* 579.13
Large Black Breeds of Pigs 16
large-format camera *camera* 132.10
largehearted *benevolent* 305.7
largeheartedness *benevolence* 305.1
large inheritance *wealth* 485.1
large intestine *internal organ* 19.13
largely 579.19, 581.18; *heavily* 538.16, *on the whole* 759.13, *overall* 778.22, *importantly* 799.15
largeness 579.2; *excellence* 445.4, *size* 579.1
large number 783.3; *multitude* 795.1
large objects Phobias 283
large order *difficult task* 824.3
large part 579.3
large-print book *aid for poor sight* 243.5
larger *bigger* 581.9
larger than life *huge* 579.14
large-scale *big* 579.13
large-scale integration (LSI) *circuit* 14.37
large screen *television set* 172.6
large-size *big* 579.13
largess *benevolent act* 305.5, *giving* 472.1, *offering* 472.6
largest *ranked* 6.72
large turnout *throng* 795.4
Large White Breeds of Pigs 16
larghetto Musical Terms and Expression Marks 140
largo Musical Terms and Expression Marks 140
largo *slowly* 693.14
lariat *yoke* 754.8
lark *songbird* 36.12, *fun* 269.4, *joke* 277.6, *morning things* 655.3, *ascender* 713.12
lark around *occupy oneself* 412.15
larks Collective Names 59
lark's head Knots, Bends, Hitches, Splices 754
larkspur Flowers 42
larrup *hit* 454.28
larva 40.9; *developmental biology*

13.22, *young animal* 26.4, *insect metamorphal stage* 40.8
larval *developmental* 13.33, *immature* 40.14
laryngitis *respiratory disease* 114.12, *silence* 231.1
larynx *throat* 19.12, *speech organ* 205.4
lascivious *desirous* 20.18, *obscene* 112.9, *lustful* 288.15, *unchaste* 432.10
lasciviously *lustfully* 20.24, 288.29, *dirtily* 112.12, *promiscuously* 432.19
lasciviousness *sexual longing* 20.6, *obscenity* 112.4, *sexual desire* 288.5, *sexual love* 299.3, *sexual immorality* 432.2
laser 10.18; *highlight* 246.12
laser disk *recording* 185.6
laser printer *hardcopy device* 15.10
laser sailing Sporting Activities 145
laser show *show* 138.4, *highlight* 246.12
laser surgery *surgery* 107.15
laser targeting *air attack* 418.4
lash *berate* 438.20, *instrument of punishment* 454.13, *hit* 454.28, *negative stimulus* 508.4, *manipulate* 508.12, *make violent* 520.10, *blow* 695.5, *beat* 695.12, *link* 752.18, *connect* 754.13, *hasten* 818.4
lashed *tied* 752.13, *connected* 754.11
lashes *body covering* 19.4
lashing *line* 754.5
lashings [Brit inf] *plenty* 97.2
lash out at *strike* 418.21
lash up *intertwine* 752.19
lass *child* 26.6, *young woman* 26.9, *female* 33.1, *loved one* 299.13
Lassa fever *tropical disease* 114.10
Lassen Peak Mountains and Hills 569
lassie *young woman* 26.9, *female* 33.1
lassitude *fatigue* 820.1
lasso *circular thing* 631.3, *yoke* 754.8, *bind* 754.14
lassoed *bound* 754.12
lasso lift *ice-skating techniques* 162.16
last *642.6; live* 28.17, *be tough* 547.13, General Units 589, *be long* 590.11, *be permanent* 667.4, *protract* 669.9, *departing* 705.5, *continue to be* 717.20, *ending* 773.13, *hindmost* 773.18
last act *conclusion* 761.3, *ending* 773.10
last agony *dying* 29.3
last an eternity *be permanent* 667.4
last a round *wrestle* 152.20
last arriver *latecomer* 658.4
last ball *close* 773.9
last bid *attempt* 390.1
last breath *dying* 29.3, *cessation* 773.2
last cent *tail* 773.8
last challenge *attempt* 390.1
Last Day *judgment day* 341.4
last-ditcher *obstinate person* 379.4, *opposer* 828.9
last-ditch stand *delay* 658.3
last forever *be eternal* 644.7, *be permanent* 667.4, *be infinite* 798.9
last frontier *limit* 773.7
last gasp *dying* 29.3, *means* 102.1, *cessation* 773.2
last handshake *parting* 705.3
last hope *means* 102.1, *hope* 281.1

last hour *dying* 29.3
lasting 639.9, 642.4, 717.13; *pertaining to life* 28.14, *customary* 397.11, *tough* 547.16, *long-lasting* 590.7, *timeless* 640.3, *permanent* 667.2, *protracted* 669.7
lastingly *toughly* 547.16, *stalwartly* 547.17, *permanently* 667.6, *continually* 669.10
lastingness *toughness* 547.1
lasting peace *peace* 73.1
Last Judgment *judgment day* 341.4, *future condition* 650.3, *end of time* 773.5
last lap *destination* 704.6, *close* 773.9
last laugh *ending* 773.10
lastly *finally* 773.24
last minute *late hour* 658.2, *critical time* 659.3
last-minute *spontaneous* 396.5, *late in the day* 658.7, *critical* 659.5, *unsafe* 811.8, *hasty* 818.3
last-minute rescue *expedient* 387.5
last-minute rush *haste* 818.1
last moment *zero level* 786.3
last month *recent past* 651.4, *in the past* 651.20
last name *name* 202.8
last night *recent past* 651.4
last of the big spenders *waster* 96.8
last one out *person remaining* 750.6
last out *last* 642.6
last penny *tail* 773.8
last post *funeral* 31.4
last quarter *moon* 7.18
last resort *means* 102.1, *expedient* 387.5, *refuge* 812.1
last rites *dying* 29.3, *Christian rite* 85.5, *lamentation* 280.1
last round *close* 773.9
last roundup [Inf] *death* 29.1
last season *in the past* 651.20
last-second *unsafe* 811.8
last shot *attempt* 390.1
last stage *close* 773.9
last stop *destination* 704.6, *end point* 773.6
last straw *overdoing it* 99.3, *provocation* 302.3, *ender* 773.11, *burden* 826.10
last stroke *conclusion* 761.3
Last Summoner *personifications and symbols* 29.4
last thing one would expect, the *unexpectedness* 839.2
last things *final intention* 374.4, *future condition* 650.3
last throw *means* 102.1
last time of asking *demand* 505.3
last touch *conclusion* 761.3
last try *attempt* 390.1
last week *recent past* 651.4, *in the past* 651.20
last will and testament *final will* 372.5, *promise* 464.2, *giving* 472.1
last word *counterstatement* 334.5, *business offer* 504.3, *delay* 658.3, *ending* 773.10, *ideal* 805.6, *beautification* 807.7
last word, the [Inf] *trendiness* 652.2, *unbeatable* 744.13
last words *dying* 29.3, *parting* 705.3, *conclusion* 761.3, *cessation* 773.2
last year *recent past* 651.4, *in the past* 651.20
latch *joint* 752.7, *fastener* 754.7, *bind* 754.14
latched *obstructed* 584.8, *bound* 754.12

latchet hook *fabric-handling tool* 130.12
latch onto [Inf] *know* 48.24, *understand* 363.9, *follow* 401.14
late 658.5, 658.14; *dead* 29.11, 658.10, *unprepared* 389.5, *former* 651.14, *nightly* 656.6, *untimely* 660.5, *at the wrong time* 660.12, *delayed* 693.10, *preceding* 769.9, *resigning* 835.3
late *Homo sapiens primitive humanity* 18.4
late arriver *latecomer* 658.4
late bloomer *latecomer* 658.4
latecomer 658.4; *new arrival* 652.7
late developer *latecomer* 658.4
late edition *newspaper* 175.2
lateen Sailing Ships and Boats 690
late evening *dimness* 248.1
late extra *newspaper* 175.2
late hit [Inf] *penalty* 155.13
late hour 658.2
late in the day 658.7
late lamented *dead* 29.11, 658.10
late lamented, the *dead person* 29.7
lately *in the past* 651.20, *newly* 652.21, *late* 658.14, *formerly* 658.17
latency 844.1; *invisibility* 245.1, *type of meaning* 361.4, *plot* 387.6, *inertness* 519.1, *lack of motion* 678.1, *cunning* 822.1
lateness 658.1; *lack of preparation* 389.1, *untimeliness* 660.1, *haste* 818.1
late-night or **midnight supper** or **snack** *night* 656.3
latent 844.6; *occult* 86.16, *disguised* 181.9, *invisible* 245.3, *fugitive* 386.10, *inert* 519.2, *sedentary* 678.5
latent heat *thermodynamics* 10.30, *heat measurement* 217.2
latent image *emulsion* 132.9
latently 844.15; *inertly* 519.5, *motionlessly* 678.9
latent meaning *type of meaning* 361.4, *mysteriousness* 844.5
latentness *latency* 844.1
later 658.9, 658.16; *future* 650.6, *in the future* 650.13, *next* 770.8, *after* 770.14
lateral *play* 155.8, *play offense* 155.18, *side* 623.6
lateral bud *bud* 41.8
laterality 623.3; *side* 623.1
lateral line *fish characteristic* 38.8
laterally 623.11
lateral movement *ocean current* 8.15
lateral root *root* 41.7
laterals *muscles* 19.3
lateral thinking *basis of supposition* 359.2
later generation *successor* 770.6
late riser *latecomer* 658.4
lateritic soil *soil* 8.42
later on *in the future* 650.13, *later* 658.16
later time *different time* 648.1
late-running *delaying* 658.8
latest *present* 647.4, *new* 652.9
latest craze *trendiness* 652.2
latest fashion *trendiness* 652.2
latest fashion, the *dressing* 100.2
latest style, the *dressing* 100.2
latest thing *fashion* 536.1, *trendiness* 652.2
latest wrinkle [Inf] *newness* 652.1
late wood *timber* 43.3
latex *secreted substance* 24.2, Tree

Products 43, *plastics* 104.6, *rubber* 546.3, *juice* 555.2
lath *building materials* 104.2, *wood* 131.3, *carpenter's term* 131.5, *carpenter* 131.10, *slice* 588.4, *fineness* 595.5
lathe *machine tool* 14.9, *woodworking tool* 131.6, *carpenter* 131.10
lather *bathe* 111.18, *air bubble* 558.10, *lubricant* 562.7, *lubricate* 562.15
lather [Inf] *hit* 454.28
lathering *ablutions* 111.4
lathery *whitened* 253.8
lathi *blunt weapon* 78.5
lathing *wood* 131.3
lathwork *wood* 131.3
lathy *thin* 595.9
laticifer *secretory mechanism* 24.3
laticiferous *secretory* 24.4
Latin America *world region* 564.6
Latin American Integration Association (LAIA) *economic organization* 56.6
Latin cross plan *church architecture* 134.11
Latino *race* 1.5, 1.12
Latin square *combinatorics* 6.63
latitude *freedom* 407.4, *available space* 563.6, *exact location* 565.2, *situation* 573.1, *coordinates* 589.6, *breadth* 592.1, *broad-mindedness* 592.3, *scope* 829.7
latitudinal line *dividing line* 740.6
latitudinarian *lenient person* 423.2, *freethinker* 829.10, *independent* 829.12
latitudinarianism *freethinking* 829.2
latrine *place for excretion* 25.11, *unpleasant-smelling thing* 227.2
latter *back* 622.6, *next* 770.8
latter days *future condition* 650.3
Latter-Day Saints Christian Groups 81
latterly *newly* 652.21
lattice *combinatorics* 6.63, *crystal* 11.14, *framework* 551.4, *porosity* 583.5, *braid* 609.3
latticework *framework* 551.4
Latvia Countries 566
Latvian Brown Breeds of Cattle 16
Latvian Darkheaded Breeds of Sheep 16
Latvian Harness Horse Horse and Pony Breeds 159
laud *worship* 83.15, *applause* 279.2, *fete* 279.6, *praise* 435.15, 437.3, 437.16
laudable *desirable* 288.11, *respectable* 435.11, *praiseworthy* 437.12
laudably *desirably* 288.24
laudanum *analgesic* 115.6, *anesthetic* 213.3, *moderator* 521.2
laudation *worship* 83.1, *praise* 437.3
laudator *approver* 437.7
laudatory *ritualistic* 85.15, *approving* 437.9, *flattering* 439.7
lauded *worshiped* 83.14
lauder *rejoicer* 279.3
lauding *worshipful* 83.12
lauds *public worship* 83.3, *morning things* 655.3
laugh 239.14, 277.12; *gesture* 183.5, 183.17, *cry of amusement* 239.2, *show joy* 269.10
laugh [Inf] *joke* 277.6
laughable *humorous* 277.9, *ridiculous* 368.5
laughableness *ridiculousness* 368.1

laughably *humorously* 277.13
laugh all the way to the bank *profit* 467.22
laugh at *laugh* 277.12, *deride* 369.7, *exclude* 383.11, *disdain* 400.16, *taunt* 436.23
laugh at an offer *be unsatisfied* 98.10
laugh at danger *be courageous* 284.14
laughing *gestural* 183.13, *cheering* 239.10, *cheerful* 269.7
laughing gas *analgesic* 115.6
laughingstock 369.4; *object of ridicule* 368.3, *butt* 436.8
laugh in someone's face *be insubordinate* 416.8
laugh line [Inf] *wrinkle* 638.2
laugh one's head off *laugh* 277.12
laugh out of court *disdain* 400.16
laughter 277.8; *cry of amusement* 239.2, *gaiety* 269.3, *amusement* 277.2, Phobias 283
laugh till one cries *laugh* 277.12
launch 7.35, 405.14; *sail* 150.29, *first appearance* 264.3, *present* 264.15, *undertake* 391.7, *beginning* 583.9, 771.1, *begin* 583.21, *be new* 652.17, *inaugurate* 675.10, 771.31, Ships and Boats 690, *navigate* 696.15, *propel* 696.15, *start* 696.20, *inauguration* 771.6, *premiere* 771.9, *activate* 771.28
launch an appeal *gain* 467.15, *solicit money* 505.13
launch an attack *attack* 418.17
launch a trial balloon *publish* 173.15, *test* 390.9
launched *inaugurated* 652.13, *nautical* 690.14, *enrolled* 771.24
launched into eternity *dead* 29.11
launcher *rocketry* 7.32
launching *beginning* 652.4, *shipbuilding* 690.4, *premiere* 771.9
launching ceremony *shipbuilding* 690.4
launching pad *modern missile weapon* 78.4
launching site *flight path* 691.12
launch into *undertake* 391.7
launch into eternity *kill* 30.19
launch out at *strike* 418.21
launch vehicle *rocketry* 7.32
launder *clean* 111.17
laundered *cleaned* 111.14
launderer *cleaner* 111.12, *fabric handler* 130.11
launderette *washer* 111.7
laundering *fabric treatment* 130.10
laundress *fabric handler* 130.11
Laundromat™ *washer* 111.7
laundry 111.8; *cleaning* 111.2
laundry basket *basket* 578.6
laundry list [Inf] *list* 785.1
laundry maid *domestic servant* 69.7
laundry room *room* 60.9, *home workplace* 124.3
laundryman *cleaner* 111.12
laundrywoman *cleaner* 111.12
Laura Famous Lovers 299
Laurasia *plate tectonics* 8.19
laureate *paragon* 744.6
laurel Trees and Shrubs 43, *decoration* 532.1
laurels *honor* 72.3, *objective* 374.5
Laurentian Mountains Mountains and Hills 569
lauric Common Fatty Acids 12
Lausanne Countries 566
lav [Inf] *room* 60.9

lava *eruption* 8.27, *mud* 561.8
lavabo Eucharist 85.7
lava flow *eruption* 8.27
lavage *ablutions* 111.4
laval *volcanic* 8.57
lavation *ablutions* 111.4
lavatory *place for excretion* 25.11, *room* 60.9
lave *purify* 111.19, *refine* 534.7
lavender Flowers 42, Herbs and Spices 91, *purpleness* 262.1, *purple thing* 262.3, *purple* 262.6
lavender water 557.14
laver *algal product* 47.15
laverock [Scot] *ascender* 713.12
lavish *wasteful* 96.9, *waste* 96.15, 500.7, *plentiful* 97.4, *overdo* 99.11, *extravagant* 194.9, 500.4, *be extravagant* 194.13, *grand* 404.22, *opulent* 485.10, *generous* 498.6, *abundant* 498.8
lavishly *wastefully* 96.23, *excessively* 194.17, *grandly* 404.37, *wealthily* 485.16, *generously* 498.12, *extravagantly* 500.9
lavishness *waste* 96.1, *extravagance* 194.3, 500.1, *grandeur* 404.10, *opulence* 485.3
lavish upon *overdo* 99.11, *give* 472.10
law 53.1; *theory* 6.62, *legal power* 52.2, *law* 53.1, *maxim* 177.1, *tradition* 397.5, *command* 425.1, *permission* 502.1, *regularity* 663.1, *discipline* 765.9, *rule* 780.1
Law, the 53.2; *law* 53.1
law-abiding 53.20; *pacific* 74.7, *well-behaved* 399.15, *submitting* 421.3, *obedient* 426.4, *in the right* 429.11, *disciplined* 765.17, *conformist* 781.10
law-abiding citizen *well-behaved person* 399.6
law and equity *law* 53.1
law and order *peace* 73.1, *discipline* 765.9
lawbreaker 53.15; *criminal* 427.6, *wrongdoer* 430.8, *villain* 448.5
lawbreaking 53.14; *violation of the law* 427.2, *disobedient* 427.10, *wicked act* 448.7, *villainous* 448.12
law consultancy *jurisprudence* 53.13
law court 54.8; *courtroom* 54.12
law enforcement agency 53.7; *law enforcement agency* 53.7
law enforcement officer 53.8
law enforcer *law enforcement officer* 53.8
lawful *legitimate* 52.10, *legal* 53.16, *rightful* 429.9, *permitted* 502.4, *disciplined* 765.17
lawful authority *legal power* 52.2
lawfully *legitimately* 52.19, *legally* 53.33, *morally* 431.15, *with permission* 502.10
lawfulness *legal justice* 53.4, *legality* 53.9
lawful possession *possession* 469.1
lawgiver *lawmaker* 53.12
lawgiving *lawmaking* 53.11, *legislative* 53.17
lawless 53.26; *anarchic* 51.5, *disobedient* 427.10, *unlawful* 430.15, *disorderly* 766.15
lawlessly 53.35; *anarchically* 51.10, *disobediently* 427.14
lawlessness 766.6; *anarchy* 51.1, *violation of the law* 427.2, *unlawfulness* 430.6
lawmaker 53.12; *one who restrains* 830.7
lawmaking 53.11; *legislative* 53.17, *management* 126.1

lawn *ornamental garden* 17.3, *grassland* 45.2, Fabrics and Fibers 130, *green place* 260.2
lawn bowling *green bowling* 151.3
lawn grass *grass* 45.1
lawn mower *garden tool* 17.7, 103.4, *grasscutter* 45.5, *sharp-edged thing* 549.6
lawn party *party* 408.6
lawn rake *garden tool* 17.7
lawn tennis *tennis* 165.1
law of averages *formula* 780.7, *probability theory* 838.5, *calculation of chance* 842.9
law of commerce *law* 53.1
law of cosines *trigonometry* 6.49
law of diminishing returns *economic deterioration* 808.2
law officer 53.6
Law of Moses the Law 53.2
law of nations *law* 53.1
law of nature *formula* 780.7
law of physics *formula* 780.7
law of sines *trigonometry* 6.49
law of tangents *trigonometry* 6.49
law of the air *law* 53.1
law of the jungle *anarchism* 51.3, *formula* 780.7
law of the land *law* 53.1
law of the sea *law* 53.1
lawrencium Chemical Elements and Common Allotropes 11
law school *type of school* 48.12
laws of entropy Classical Physical Laws 10
laws of motion Classical Physical Laws 10, *motion* 677.1
laws of reflection Classical Physical Laws 10
laws of refraction Classical Physical Laws 10
laws of thermodynamics Classical Physical Laws 10
lawsuit *litigation* 54.1, *action* 412.1, *accusation* 442.1
lawsuits Phobias 283
lawyer 54.5; *law officer* 53.6, *agent* 80.3, *professional worker* 123.11, *arguer* 319.6, *curious person* 321.3, *questioner* 333.9, *negotiator* 460.4, *motivator* 508.6, *influential person* 512.5
lax *careless* 289.8, *indifferent* 326.5, *unrefined* 338.7, *free* 407.9, *not participating* 415.11, *lenient* 423.3, *unchaste* 432.10, *depraved* 448.10, *nonobservant* 466.5, *permitting* 502.5, *inert* 519.2, *soft* 543.6, *soft-hearted* 543.11, *nonadhesive* 756.4, *unconditional* 829.14, *indeterminate* 841.14
laxation *easiness* 543.5
laxative *fecal* 25.14, *cleaning agent* 111.9, *purgative* 115.7, *medicinal* 115.15, *ejector* 709.10, *expulsive* 709.11
laxity *carelessness* 289.2, *inaccuracy* 351.3, *freedom* 407.4, *leniency* 423.1, *sexual immorality* 432.2, *depravity* 448.2, *nonobservance* 466.1, *inertness* 519.1, *easiness* 543.5, *liberality* 829.8, *indeterminacy* 841.6
laxly *negligently* 326.8, *with permission* 502.10, *softly* 543.18, *soft-heartedly* 543.19, *noncohesively* 756.9
laxness *easiness* 543.5, *liberality* 829.8
lay *engineer* 14.48, *unskilled* 128.5, Poem or Verse Forms 139, *song* 140.11, *semiskilled* 349.6, *layer* 588.9, *bearing* 697.2
lay [Inf] *have sex* 20.21

lay a block *bowl* 151.8
lay aboard *attack* 418.17
layabout *inactive person* 413.8, *nonworker* 415.4
lay about one *strike* 418.21, *fight* 422.23
lay a false scent *or trail conceal oneself* 181.15
lay a hand on *be evil* 446.10
lay an embargo on *make motionless* 678.8
lay aside *discard* 383.12, *stop using* 394.10, *take away* 685.12, *exclude* 764.7
lay a trap for *plot* 387.15
lay at the feet of *give* 472.10
lay away *save* 105.20
layback *mountaineer* 161.10
laybacking *climbing techniques* 161.3
lay-back spin *ice-skating techniques* 162.16
lay bare *disclose* 180.8, *make visible* 244.9, *detect* 345.12, *uncover* 614.17, *reveal* 843.14
lay before *offer* 504.11
lay bricks *face* 613.31
lay-by [Brit] *track* 688.2
lay claim to *have rights* 429.13
lay disciple *religious* 84.9
lay down *propound a philosophy* 4.21, *suppose* 359.8, *layer* 588.9, *lower* 716.12, *rule* 780.12
lay down one's arms *capitulate* 421.6, *make peace* 73.11
lay down the law *govern* 49.26, *wield authority* 52.16, *command* 425.10, *rule* 780.12, *be certain* 840.13
lay eggs *have young* 21.6
lay eggs [Inf] *bomb* 418.19
layer 588.1, 588.9; *livestock* 16.11, *cultivate* 17.19, *propagate* 21.15, *atmospheric layer* 558.3, *base* 601.10, *be exterior* 610.13, *coating* 613.8, *coat* 613.28, *fold* 637.1, 637.7
layer cake *cake* 90.36
layer cloud *cloud appearance* 9.19
layered 588.6
layered cut *coiffure* 530.8
layering 588.5; *gardening* 17.5
layette *baby clothes* 100.24
lay eyes on [Inf] *see* 242.20
lay for [Inf] *aim* 697.14
lay hands on *touch* 216.9, *gain* 467.15
lay heads together *work together* 827.14
lay in ashes *lay waste* 523.14
laying bare *uncovering* 614.1
laying claim to *claiming* 469.2
laying hen *livestock* 16.11
laying into [Inf] *berating* 438.5
laying it on *deference* 410.4
laying off *bargaining terms* 57.10, *dismissal* 709.2
laying one's hands or fingers on *locating* 565.3
laying on of hands Christian rite 85.5, *healing art* 115.13, *touching* 216.2
laying open *manifestation* 843.2
laying the cornerstone *premiere* 771.9
laying waste *military attack* 418.2, *havoc* 523.5
lay in ruins *lay waste* 523.14
lay in the dust *knock down* 523.13
lay in the grave *bury* 31.10
lay into [Inf] *eat well* 92.23, *strike* 418.21, *berate* 438.20
lay it on *boast* 194.14, *defer to* 410.12, *flatter* 439.12

lay it on [Brit inf] *eat well* 92.23
lay it on thick *overdo* 99.11, *persuade* 178.15, *boast* 194.14, *flatter* 439.12
lay it on with a trowel *boast* 194.14, *flatter* 439.12
lay level *flatten* 716.15
lay low *strike* 418.21, *lower* 597.21, *make horizontal* 603.10
layoff *bargaining terms* 57.10, *soccer play* 163.5, *discarding* 383.3, *unemployment* 415.2, *relegation* 574.4, *stop* 668.2, *termination* 834.2
lay off *employ* 57.18, *play soccer* 163.8, *relieve from duty* 275.11, *discard* 383.12, *make inactive* 415.16, *relegate* 574.18, *stop work* 668.11, *dismiss* 709.15, *terminate* 834.7
lay off! *cease!* 668.14
layoff notice *rejection notice* 383.5
lay of the land *circumstances* 573.2, 726.1, *direction* 697.1, *state of affairs* 725.4
lay on *fight* 422.23, *augment* 748.13
lay one's back open *hit* 454.28
lay oneself open to *face danger* 811.12
lay one's hands on *take* 477.14
lay one's hands or **fingers on** *find* 565.11
lay one's head on the block *be executed* 454.32
lay on the lash *hit* 454.28
lay on the scales *weigh* 538.15
lay on the table *delay* 658.13
lay open *disclose* 180.8, *reveal* 843.14
layout *competitive diving* 164.7, *diving* 164.13, *stage of book production* 174.7, *map* 387.7, *circumstances* 573.2, *outline* 617.1, *order* 765.1, *array* 767.2
lay out *bury* 31.10, *design* 133.9, *sign* 183.13, *plan out* 387.14, *space* 563.15, *outline* 617.5, *form* 624.9, *bring down* 716.14, *order* 765.18, *arrange* 767.2
lay out [Inf] *pay* 489.16, *expend* 491.11
layover *interval* 775.2
lay over *overlay* 613.25, *pause* 775.11
layperson *ignorant person* 349.4
lay siege to *combat* 77.34, *besiege* 418.20
lay the blame on *accuse* 442.8
lay the cornerstone *plan out* 387.14
lay the first stone *open* 771.32
lay the foundation *plan out* 387.14
lay the foundations 388.16; *inaugurate* 675.10
lay the foundation stone *open* 771.32
lay to *sail* 690.16
lay together *unite* 752.14
lay to rest *bury* 31.10
lay traps *hunt* 385.14
lay under or **beneath** *underlie* 597.23, 601.11
lay up *save* 105.20, *stop using* 394.10, *make inactive* 415.16, *set apart* 753.17, *combine* 757.9, *make useless* 802.12
lay-up *playing terms* 148.4
lay up a sailboat *handle sailboat equipment* 150.30
lay up for a rainy day *have foresight* 357.8
lay up in lavender *perfume* 226.6

lay upon *demand* 425.11
lay waste 96.21, 523.14; *waste* 23.11, *be at war* 76.32, *attack successfully* 418.25, *lay waste* 523.14, *make useless* 802.12, *impair* 808.18
lazar *poor person* 486.6
Lazarus *poor person* 486.6
laze *be inactive* 415.13, *move slowly* 693.11, *take it easy* 819.3
lazily *negligently* 326.8, *inactively* 413.16, *impassively* 415.18, *inertly* 519.5, *slowly* 693.14
laziness *indifference* 326.2, *delay* 375.6, *leisure* 413.4, *idleness* 415.3, *inertness* 519.1, *slowness* 693.1
lazy *indifferent* 326.5, *procrastinating* 375.11, *inactive* 413.9, *not participating* 415.11, *impious* 448.11, *inert* 519.2, *unhurried* 693.8, *at ease* 819.2
lazybones [Inf] *reluctant person* 375.7
lazy jacks *sailboat parts and accessories* 150.4
l'chaim! [Hebrew] *cheers!* 93.22
lea *farmland* 16.3, *grassland* 45.2, *lowland* 572.6, *General Units* 589
leach *purify* 111.19, *dissolve* 555.23, *water* 557.29, *leak* 707.16
leaching *pollution* 117.8, *fluidization* 555.8, *soaking* 557.9, *leakage* 707.5
lead 126.12, 744.19, **Chemical Elements and Common Allotropes** 11, *govern* 49.26, *have authority* 52.13, *master* 68.17, *manage* 126.10, *role* 136.25, *actor* 136.25, *conduct* 141.17, 399.21, *fishing tackle* 154.7, *mountaineer* 161.10, *bridge* 168.4, *news source* 171.4, *newsworthy* 175.7, *signs* 183.2, *gray thing* 255.3, *the hunted* 385.7, *behave toward* 399.20, *motivate* 508.9, *influence* 512.11, *power supplier* 514.14, *weight* 538.8, *measuring instrument* 589.12, *bathymetry* 598.3, *be in front* 621.13, *navigational aid* 690.6, *direct* 697.13, 780.14, *aim* 697.14, *measure* 739.7, *advantage* 744.3, *yoke* 754.8, *priority* 769.2, *precedent* 769.4, *precede* 769.13, *pioneer* 771.29, *escort* 794.18, *safety device* 810.15, *restraint* 826.8, *means of restraint* 830.6, *restrain someone* 830.17
lead a bad life *behave badly* 399.19
leadable *directable* 697.10
lead a boring life *be bored* 296.7
lead a charmed life *be fortunate* 847.7
lead a cloistered life *be unsocial* 409.10
lead a coup *subvert* 427.13, *take over* 477.16
lead a coup d'état *gain authority* 52.15
lead actor or **actress** *actor* 137.13
lead a double life *be dishonorable* 192.21
lead a good life *behave well* 399.18
lead an uprising *cause mischief* 507.9
lead a putsch *cause mischief* 507.9
lead a rebellion *subvert* 427.13
lead article *article* 203.2
lead astray *demoralize* 432.15, *deprave* 448.14, *manipulate* 508.12

lead block *play* 155.8, *play offense* 155.18
lead by the nose *be an influence* 512.13, *subject* 832.10
lead captive *defeat* 832.11
lead crystal *ceramics* 129.1, *glass* 249.5
leaded gas *petroleum* 562.5
leaden *dark-colored* 247.7, *dim* 248.4, *colorless* 252.5, *gray* 255.6, *dull* 255.8, *boring* 296.6, *heavy* 538.9, *sedentary* 678.5
leaden hours *boring thing* 296.3
leadenly *heavily* 538.16
leadenness *darkness* 247.1
leader 68.3, 126.8; *computing terms* 15.22, *tree part* 43.3, *governor* 49.23, *person in authority* 52.7, *bowler* 151.5, *article* 203.2, *conductor* 399.13, *vanguard* 621.5, *superior* 744.5, *precursor* 769.7, *the special* 779.8, *usher* 794.7, *important person* 799.5
leader of the House of Commons *elected official* 50.8
leader of the opposition *elected official* 50.8, *defiant person* 416.4
leaders *Reference Signs* 183
leadership 744.2; *maturity* 27.3, *authority* 52.1, *directorship* 126.5, *treatment* 399.11, *personal influence* 512.3
lead-free gas *petroleum* 562.5
lead glass *glass* 249.5
lead-in *introduction* 771.10
leading *governing* 49.25, *authoritative* 52.9, *masterful* 68.15, *managerial* 126.9, *climbing techniques* 161.3, *card-playing* 168.6, *design and makeup* 174.8, *influential* 512.8, *tending to* 513.4, *head* 600.7, *focal* 612.8, *front-running* 621.10, *directions* 697.7, *directing* 697.12, *ranked* 739.6, *superior* 744.8, *primary* 769.10, *preparatory* 769.11, *front* 771.17, *important* 799.7, *notable* 799.11
leading edge *plate tectonics* 8.19
leading item *the special* 779.8
leading lady *actor* 136.25
leading light *celebrity* 799.6
leading man *actor* 136.25
leading man or **lady** *actor* 137.13
leading part *influence* 512.1
leading question *difficult question* 333.4
leading role *role* 136.23
leading sense *type of meaning* 361.4
leading to *tending to* 513.4
leading tone *musical note* 140.15
lead into temptation *entice* 178.16, *manipulate* 508.12
lead in triumph *defeat* 832.11
lead line *bathymetry* 598.3, *navigational aid* 690.6
leadoff man *baseball team* 147.2
lead on *lead* 126.12, *deceive* 193.16, *court* 299.26, *lure* 700.12
lead on a dance *evade* 386.19
lead on a merry dance *cause trouble* 824.21
lead one to expect *be probable* 838.8
lead over *lead* 126.12
lead-pipe cinch [Inf] *certainty* 840.1
lead role *role* 136.23
lead runner *precursor* 769.7
lead sinker *fishing tackle* 154.7
leadsman *nautical person* 690.12
lead story *news story* 171.3
lead the dance *lead* 744.19, *forerun* 769.16

lead the way *lead* 126.12, *invent* 345.14, *prepare the way* 388.15, *precede* 769.13, *pioneer* 771.29
lead through *lead* 126.12
lead to *tend* 513.5, *reach out* 585.10, *cause* 675.8
lead to the altar *marry* 64.19, *propose (marriage)* 299.28
lead up or **down the garden path** *deceive* 193.16, *distort the truth* 627.12
lead vocalist *singer* 141.4
lead worship *offer worship* 504.16
leaf 41.6; *vegetate* 41.21, *tree part* 43.2, *grass plant* 45.3, *fern plant* 46.2, *Architectural Elements* 134, *plant products* 522.8, *coat* 588.3, *notched thing* 636.2, *component* 760.3, *part of writing* 760.6
leaf blade *leaf* 41.6
leaf blower *garden tool* 17.7
leaf bud *bud* 41.8
leaf curl *pests and diseases* 17.12, *tree disease* 43.8
leaf cutting *plant breeding* 17.6
leaf-green *green* 260.7
leafhopper *pests and diseases* 17.12, *insect* 40.1
leafless *shed* 614.14
leaflet *leaf* 41.6, *fern plant* 46.2, *advertisement* 173.9
leaflike *platelike* 588.8
leaflike part *leaf* 41.6
leaf litter *trees* 43.4
leaf miner *pests and diseases* 17.12
leaf mold *pests and diseases* 17.12, *fertilizer* 22.6, *trees* 43.4
leaf out *grow* 43.15
leaf spot *pests and diseases* 17.12
leaf spring *spring* 546.4
leafstalk *stem* 41.5, *leaf* 41.6
leaf sweeper *garden tool* 17.7
leaf tissue *leaf* 41.6
leafy *plantlike* 41.13, *of plants* 41.14, *verdant* 260.8, *seasonal* 654.7
leafy liverwort *moss* 46.4
leafy vegetable *vegetable* 90.33
league *party* 59.3, *sportsman* 145.4, *alliance* 459.5, 735.5, *General Units* 589, *collaboration* 757.2, *type* 777.4, *social class* 777.5, *team* 827.7
leagued *collaborative* 757.7
League of Nations *world government* 49.17
league with *contract* 459.8, *come together* 757.10
leak 707.16, 816.6, 816.11; *waste away* 96.20, *inside information* 170.4, *news source* 171.4, *divulgence* 180.2, *divulge* 180.9, *lessen* 468.17, *seep* 559.16, *leakage* 707.5, *defect* 806.4, *be imperfect* 806.8
leak [Inf] *urination* 25.4, *urine* 25.6
leakage 707.5; *wasting away* 96.4, *lessening* 468.6, *inroad* 706.3, *reduction* 747.2, *leak* 816.6
leak air *leak* 816.11
leak away *leak* 816.11
leak detector *surface chemistry* 11.20
leaked *disclosed* 180.5
leak gas *leak* 816.11
leak in *infiltrate* 706.13
leaking *leakage* 707.5, *dilapidated* 808.11
leak out *be disclosed* 180.12, *leak* 707.16
leakproof *waterproof* 560.16, *invulnerable* 810.18

leaky 707.12; *holed* 583.12, *imperfect* 806.5, *unsafe* 811.8
lean 716.19; *underfed* 98.7, *prefer* 382.13, *tend* 513.5, *stalwart* 547.10, *thin* 595.9, *be low* 597.20, *be oblique* 607.10, *angle* 628.11, *unbalance* 741.8
lean clay *material* 129.2
Leander Famous Lovers 299
lean-faced *thin* 595.9
lean forward *lean* 716.19
leaning *inclination* 290.2, *inclined toward* 290.5, *preference* 382.2, *tendency* 397.2, *attitude* 513.2, *tending to* 513.4, *obliqueness* 607.1, *oblique* 607.6, *unbalanced* 741.5
leaning to one side *wrongful* 430.10
leaning toward *tending to* 513.4
leanly *stalwartly* 547.17
leanness *scarcity* 98.3, *stalwartness* 547.3, *thinness* 595.1
lean on [Inf] *compel* 428.8
lean on a broken reed *figurative expressions* 128.11
lean over backward *be eager* 373.13, *lean* 716.19
lean over backward [Inf] *be unselfish* 443.7
lean period *time of adversity* 848.8
lean-to *shack* 60.10, *roof* 134.7
lean to one side *discriminate* 430.21
lean toward *be inclined toward* 290.10, *discriminate* 430.21, *tend* 513.5
leap *assemblage of mammals* 35.22, Collective Names 59, *dance* 135.7, *participate* 166.22, *attempt* 390.1, *interval* 587.1, *bodily movement* 677.11, *walk* 677.17, *acceleration* 694.3, *be swift* 694.10, *jump* 713.7, *spring up* 713.22, *spread* 746.3, *preparation* 769.3
leap at *be eager* 373.13, *chase* 385.13
leapfrog Children's and Party Games 167, *oscillate* 683.12, *crossing* 712.5, *overstep* 712.12, *jump* 713.7
leaping 713.17; *agitated* 684.15
leap in the dark *rash move* 286.4, *endangerment* 811.2
leap out *be recognizable* 363.12
leaps and bounds *forward motion* 679.1
leap to one's feet *arise* 715.15
leap up *spring up* 713.22, *arise* 715.15
learn 48.23, 68.18; *be informed* 170.15, *hear* 228.13, *find out* 345.13, *get to know* 348.12, *memorize* 354.11, *understand* 363.9, *get better* 807.21
learn a habit *accustom oneself* 397.19
learn by experience *get better* 807.21
learn by heart *learn* 68.18, *memorize* 354.11
learn by rote *know by heart* 348.11, *memorize* 354.11
learned *educated* 48.19, *literary* 139.15, *intelligent* 315.9, *knowledgeable* 348.7, *wise* 352.4
learned by heart *memorized* 354.9
learned by rote *memorized* 354.9
learnedness 48.8
learned person *expert* 127.9
learner 48.6; *artisan* 123.13, *unskilled person* 128.3, *beginner* 771.14, *subordinate* 832.3

learn from (bitter) experience *confess* 451.8
learning 48.7, 348.3; *literature* 139.1, Phobias 283, *finding out* 345.3, *wisdom* 352.1, *understanding* 363.4, *in preparation* 388.8
learning by heart *memory* 354.1
learning by rote *memory* 354.1
learning center *library* 174.14
learn obedience *succumb* 421.7
learn one's lesson *confess* 451.8, *be warned* 814.9
learn one's lines *rehearse* 136.37, *act* 137.20
learn to live together *pacify* 74.11
lease *inhabit* 61.13, *purchase contract* 459.3, *possession of property* 469.3, *transfer of property* 470.4, *transfer property* 470.12
leaseback *transfer of property* 470.4
leased *inhabited* 61.10
leasehold *possession of property* 469.3, *property* 470.1, *propertied* 470.9
leaseholder *resident* 61.6, *possessor* 469.10, *property owner* 470.7
leaser *resident* 61.6
leash Collective Names 59, *link* 752.18, *yoke* 754.8, *bind* 754.14, *restraint* 826.8, *restrain* 826.19, *means of restraint* 830.6, *restrain someone* 830.17
leashed *bound* 754.12, *blocked* 826.13, *restrained* 830.9
leash the dogs of war *make peace* 73.11
leasing contract *purchase contract* 459.3
least 796.2; *ranked* 6.72, *quantitative* 738.6, *inferior* 745.5, *fewer* 796.7
least bit *little bit* 800.4
least common multiple (LCM) *multiplication* 6.15
least one can do *sufficiency* 97.1
leather 104.7; *type of furniture* 101.2, *type of chair* 101.4, *materials* 104.1, *cleaning cloth* 111.11, *hit* 454.28, *animal products* 522.7
leather [Inf] *beat* 695.12
leatherette Fabrics and Fibers 130
leather goods *dry goods* 130.3
leatheriness *chewiness* 547.2
leathering *ramming* 695.3
leatherjacket *larva* 40.9
leather jacket *jacket* 100.18
leather leg guard *hockey clothing* 158.6
leatherlike *hard* 547.8
leatherneck [Inf] *marines* 77.26
leather punch *opener* 583.2
leather shoes *shoes* 100.30
leatherware *dry goods* 130.3
leathery *hard* 542.5, 547.8
leave 750.10; *desert* 66.11, *save* 105.20, *time off* 125.2, *bequeath* 372.15, *shun* 386.14, *run away* 386.21, *relinquish* 392.3, *stop using* 394.10, *freedom* 407.4, *acquiesce* 421.5, *leniency* 423.1, *license* 434.4, *approval* 437.1, *will* 472.11, *permission* 502.1, 735.9, *permit* 502.3, *leave of absence* 576.4, *absent oneself* 576.15, *bring* 685.11, *parting* 705.3, *depart* 705.8, *exit* 707.13, *be dismissed* 707.18, *diverge* 753.20, *exclude* 764.7, *ease* 819.1, *resign* 835.5
leave a deposit *reserve* 464.14

leave a footprint *or* **fingerprint** *affect* 676.7
leave a gap *be insufficient* 98.9
leave ajar *open* 583.15
leave a loophole *make conditions* 460.7
leave a remainder *unbalance* 741.8
leave a runner stranded *play baseball* 147.9
leave a trace *affect* 676.7
leave at the starting post *accelerate* 694.14
leave behind *forget* 355.10, *improve* 467.18, *lose someone* 468.20, *accelerate* 694.14, *exceed* 712.15, *leave* 750.10
leave destitute *impoverish* 486.16
leave empty 576.17
leave half-done *be neglectful* 326.7
leave hanging *not complete* 762.9
leave home *quit* 705.10
leave imperfect 806.9
leave incomplete *be unfinished* 544.12, *not complete* 762.9
leave in high dudgeon *depart* 705.8
leave in suspense *be irresolute* 378.9
leave in the air *not complete* 762.9
leave in the lurch *disappoint* 293.9
leave it to *commission* 833.8
leave it to chance *take a chance* 842.14
leave it to fate *take a chance* 842.14
leave land behind *set out* 705.12
leaven *change* 512.12, *leavening* 539.3, *lighten* 539.9, *whisk* 558.23, *changer* 665.9, *cause change* 665.16, *chemical change* 670.2, *convert* 670.11, *transform* 670.13, *contributory cause* 675.3, *lifter* 715.5, *improve* 807.15
leavening 539.3, 539.7; *aeration* 558.11, *change* 665.1, *converting* 670.8
leavening agent *basic cooking ingredient* 91.8, *leavening* 539.3
leave no address *conceal oneself* 181.15
leave no choice *or* **alternative** *necessitate* 95.17, *compel* 428.8
leave no escape *compel* 428.8
leave no loose ends *complete* 759.10
leave no option *compel* 428.8
leave no remainder *equalize* 740.12
leave no room *or* **margin for error** *take precautions* 287.14
leave no space *or* **void** *be present* 575.13
leave no stone unturned *exert oneself* 122.11
leave no survivors *destroy* 186.10
leave nothing out *or* **undone** *complete* 761.9
leave nothing to be desired *be perfect* 805.20
leave nothing to chance *take precautions* 287.14, *complete* 761.9
leave no trace *destroy* 186.10, *quit* 705.10, *cease to exist* 718.13
leave of absence 576.4; *license* 434.4, *permit* 502.3
leave off *stop using* 394.10, *interrupt* 604.16, *stop* 668.10, *discontinue* 775.10
leave off! *cease!* 668.14

leave one's bills unpaid *not pay* 488.10
leave one's body *experience psychic phenomena* 86.23
leave one's card *visit* 408.16
leave one's husband a widower *widow* 66.12
leave one's post *resign* 835.5
leave one's wife a widow *widow* 66.12
leave on one side *pass* 692.15
leave on the cutting-room floor *obliterate* 186.8
leave out *lapse into silence* 208.8, *exempt* 434.9, *space* 563.15, *subtract* 749.6, *leave* 750.10, *not complete* 762.9, *exclude* 764.7
leave over *leave* 750.10
leaver *outgoer* 707.9
leaves *leaf* 41.6, *refuse* 802.5
leave speechless *astonish* 292.10
leave standing *accelerate* 694.14, *exceed* 712.15
leave-taking *parting* 705.3, *departing* 705.5
leave the country *quit* 705.10
leave the door open *offer* 504.11
leave the earth behind *go up* 713.23
leave the ground *go up* 713.23
leave the neighborhood *quit* 705.10
leave the nest *mature* 27.17, *quit* 705.10
leave the options open *make conditions* 460.7
leave the pocket *play offense* 155.18
leave the scene *absent oneself* 576.15
leave the stage *withdraw* 705.9
leave the straight and narrow *deviate* 698.15
leave time for *give* 472.10
leave to one's own devices *or* **choice** *set free* 829.17
leave undecided *be irresolute* 378.9
leave undeveloped *make shapeless* 625.3
leave undone *be neglectful* 326.7, *not complete* 762.9
leave unfinished *not complete* 762.9, *waste effort* 802.13, *leave imperfect* 806.9
leave work *withdraw* 705.9
leaving *giving* 472.1, *departure* 705.1, *departing* 705.5, *outgoing* 707.10
leaving behind *advance* 467.3
leaving ground *taking off* 713.6
leaving much to chance *chance* 842.10
leavings *dirt* 112.5, *product* 522.3, *residue* 750.2, *bits and pieces* 760.5, *refuse* 802.5
Lebanon Countries 566
Lebanon Mountains Mountains and Hills 569
Lebedin Breeds of Cattle 16
Lebensraum *available space* 563.6, *scope* 829.7
Lebesgue measure Mathematical Concepts 6
Lecce Breeds of Sheep 16
lech [Inf] *fornicate* 432.14
lecher *desirer* 288.9, *lover* 299.11, *sexually immoral person* 432.8, *miscreant* 448.6
lecherous *desirous* 20.18, *lustful* 288.15, *unchaste* 432.10
lecherously *lustfully* 20.24, 288.29, *promiscuously* 432.19

lecherousness *sexual desire* 288.5, *sexual immorality* 432.2

lechery *sexual desire* 288.5, *sexual immorality* 432.2

leching [Inf] *fornication* 432.3

lecithin *fat* 12.7

lectern *church interior* 83.9, *type of desk* 101.6

lection *interpretation* 365.1

lectionary *ritual manual* 85.11

lecture 777.7; *dissertation* 203.1, *public speaking* 205.11, *speak to* 205.19, *address* 209.1, 209.8, *explanation* 331.3, *explain* 331.16, *moralize* 431.14, *condemnation* 438.2

lecture hall *school place* 48.16

lecturer *educator* 48.4, *educational leader* 68.11, *persuader* 178.9, *dissertator* 203.3, *speaker* 205.12, *public speaker* 209.5, *demonstrator* 331.6

lectureship *instructorship* 48.5

LED *computer part* 15.4

led *directed* 697.9, *accompanied* 794.15

Leda *Planets and Their Satellites* 7

led by the nose *subject* 832.6

lederhosen *pants* 100.14

ledge *rock face* 161.6, *skiing snow* 162.3, *level* 588.2

ledged *snow* 162.28

ledger *record book* 185.5, *account book* 493.3, *bill* 785.4

ledger or **leger line** *written music* 140.21

ledgering *fishing* 154.1

ledger rod *fishing tackle* 154.7

lee *shelter* 812.4

leeboard *sailboat* 150.3

Leech *Lakes* 568

leech *parasite* 39.18, *sponger* 401.4, *nonworker* 415.4, *greedy person* 477.11, *adherent* 755.4

leech [Arch] *doctor* 107.19

leechlike *wormlike* 39.24

Leeds *major British cities* 567.7

Leeds pottery *Ceramics* 129

lee helm *sailing terms* 150.5

leek-green *green* 260.7

leer *gesture* 183.5, 183.17, *look* 242.7, 242.21, *distortion of face* 627.2, *make faces* 627.10

leerily *reticently* 287.18

leery *reticent* 287.8

lees *dirt* 112.5, *mud* 561.8, *residue* 750.2, *tail* 773.8

lee shore *hidden danger* 813.3

leeward *side direction* 623.2, *side* 623.6, *toward* 697.18

Leeward Islands *Islands* 572

lee-wave cloud *cloud appearance* 9.19

leeway *freedom* 407.4, *available space* 563.6, *distance* 585.1, *interval* 587.1, *deviating motion* 698.3, *scope* 829.7

left *political party* 50.5, *combat* 152.17, *soccer* 163.7, *bequeathed* 372.10, *side direction* 623.2, *side* 623.6, *sporting hit* 695.6, *departed* 705.6, *remaining* 750.7, *unjoined* 753.9

left, the *Phobias* 283

left behind *remaining* 750.7

left defense *hockey player* 158.8

left field *baseball field* 147.3, *laterality* 623.3

left fielder *baseball team* 147.2

left half *soccer participant* 163.4

left-hand *racing* 146.9, *side direction* 623.2, *sided* 623.7

left-handed *equivocal* 380.5, *insulting* 436.10

left-handed compliment *insult* 436.5

left-handed hitter *baseball team* 147.2

left-handed marriage *type of marriage* 64.3

left-handedness *laterality* 623.3

left-hand page *book part* 174.5

left-hand side *laterality* 623.3

left hanging *incomplete* 762.5, *uncompleted* 762.7

left high and dry *vulnerable* 811.9

left hook *boxing techniques* 152.5

left in the air *incomplete* 762.5, *uncompleted* 762.7

leftist *political party member* 50.6

left jab *boxing techniques* 152.5

left lateral detachment fault *fault* 8.21

left-luggage office [Brit] *railroad station* 688.6

left out *missing* 576.11, *excluded* 764.6

leftover *waste* 96.10, *superfluous* 99.8, *additional item* 748.3, *residue* 750.2

left over *surplus* 750.8

leftovers *waste product* 96.7, *superfluity* 99.4, *dirt* 112.5, *surplus* 750.4, *refuse* 802.5

left side *Phobias* 283, *laterality* 623.3

left stick *hockey equipment* 158.3

left to one's own devices *independent* 829.12

left to right *to and fro* 683.16

left to rot *idle* 394.6

left unfinished *uncompleted* 762.7

left uppercut *boxing techniques* 152.5

leftward *laterally* 623.11, *clockwise* 697.17

left wing *hockey player* 158.8, *laterality* 623.3

left-winger *political party member* 50.6

left without words *wondering* 294.7

lefty or **leftie** [Inf] *political party member* 50.6, *baseball team* 147.2

leg *appendage* 19.5, *veal* 90.25, *lamb* 90.27, *poultry* 90.28, *track event* 166.1, *part* 760.1, *component* 760.3

legacy 492.4; *final will* 372.5, *profit* 467.6, *personal estate* 470.6, *gift* 472.2, *receiving* 473.1, *visible effect* 676.2, *transferred thing* 685.6, *subsequence* 770.4

legal action *litigation* 54.1, *action* 412.1

legal administrator *law officer* 53.6

legal advice *jurisprudence* 53.13

legal adviser *adviser* 176.5

legal argument *debate* 319.3

legal authority *legal power* 52.2, *jurisdiction* 53.3, 54.2

legal case *litigation* 54.1

legal code *law* 53.1

legal costs *business expenses* 491.4

legal counsel *lawyer* 54.5

legal defense *defense* 441.2

legal dispute *litigation* 54.1

legal eagle [Inf] *lawyer* 54.5

legalese *jargon* 5.21

legal estate *property* 470.1

legal evidence 339.4

legal flaw *legal injustice* 53.5

legal force *coercion* 428.2

legal formality *jurisprudence* 53.13

legal heir *beneficiary* 473.6

legal imperative *duty* 433.1

legal injustice 53.5

legal innocence 449.3

legalism *legality* 53.9

legalistic 53.22; *formal* 406.6

legality 53.9; *legal power* 52.2, *legal justice* 53.4, *permission* 502.1

legalization *legality* 53.9

legalize *authorize* 52.14, *make legal* 53.27, *permit* 502.6

legalized *legitimate* 52.10, *legal* 53.16, *permitted* 502.4

legalized killing *execution* 30.6, *capital punishment* 454.12

legal justice 53.4

legal learning *jurisprudence* 53.13

legally 53.33; *dutifully* 433.19, *with permission* 502.10, *orderly* 663.13

legally blind *blind* 243.11

legally right *dutiful* 433.6

legally separated *divorced* 66.7

legal obligation *duty* 433.1

legal order *demand* 425.2

legal ownership 469.8

legal possession *possession* 469.1

legal power 52.2

legal practitioner *lawyer* 54.5

legal precedent *tradition* 397.5

legal procedure *legal process* 54.3

legal proceeding *action* 412.1

legal proceedings *legal process* 54.3

legal process 54.3

legal property terms 470.2

legal punishment *penalty* 454.5

legal remedy *litigation* 54.1

legal restraint *restraint* 830.1

legal right *claim* 429.3

legal rights *rights* 429.4, *free rights* 829.4

legal separation *separation* 66.2

legal tender *money* 484.1

legal trial *legal process* 54.3

legate *delegate* 79.1, *commissioner* 833.5

legatee *beneficiary* 473.6

legatine *delegated* 79.4

legation *representative body* 79.2, *council* 833.4

legationary *delegated* 79.4, *commissioned* 833.6

legato *Musical Terms and Expression Marks* 140

legator [Form] *giver* 472.7

legend *tradition* 1.7, 653.5, *chronicle* 3.4, *story* 139.4, *inscription* 185.4, *map* 187.5, *falsehood* 192.6, *brief description* 202.2, *annotation* 365.2

legendary *societal* 1.13, *chronicled* 3.12, *fictional* 139.16, *fabricated* 192.17, *imaginary* 360.12

legendary sea being 571.4

legendary strongman *person of strength* 516.8

Legendre polynomials *Mathematical Concepts* 6

Legendre symbol *Mathematical Concepts* 6

legerdemain *magic* 138.3

legerdemainist *magician* 138.11

leggiero *Musical Terms and Expression Marks* 140

legginess *height* 596.1

leggings *pants* 100.14, *legwear* 100.26

leggy *tall* 596.9

Leghorn *Breeds of Fowl* 16

legibility *clarity* 363.2

legible *simple* 363.6

legion *force* 59.10, *historical soldier* 77.8, *throng* 795.4, *multitudinous* 795.5

legionnaire's disease *respiratory disease* 114.12

Legion of Merit *US Military Medals* 58

legislate 53.31; *wield authority* 52.16, *act* 412.11, *command* 425.10

legislating *lawmaking* 53.11

legislation *lawmaking* 53.11, *management* 126.1, *command* 425.1

legislational *legislative* 53.17

legislative 53.17; *governmental* 49.24, *delegated* 79.4, *commanding* 425.7

legislative branch *United States government* 49.21

legislator *delegate* 79.1, *one who restrains* 830.7

legislator or **legislatrix** *lawmaker* 53.12

legislatorial *legislative* 53.17

legislature *United States government* 49.21, *British government* 49.22, *lawmaker* 53.12, *conference* 59.5, *representative body* 79.2

legit [Inf] *legal* 53.16, *drama* 136.1, *permitted* 502.4

legitimacy *legal power* 52.2, *legal justice* 53.4, *legality* 53.9, *right* 429.2, *authenticity* 721.7

legitimate 52.10, 53.21; *legal* 53.16, *correct* 429.8, *rightful* 429.9, *permitted* 502.4, *authentic* 721.16

legitimately 52.19; *legally* 53.33, *correctly* 429.16, *with permission* 502.10, *authentically* 721.31

legitimateness *legality* 53.9

legitimate succession *acquisition of authority* 52.5

legitimate theater *drama* 136.1

legitimatize *make legal* 53.27

legitimization *legality* 53.9

legitimize *authorize* 52.14, *make legal* 53.27, *permit* 502.6

legitimized *legal* 53.16

leg-of-mutton sleeve *part of garment* 100.27

leg-pull *joke* 277.6

legroom *available space* 563.6

legume *vegetable* 17.11, 90.33, *botanical fruit* 44.2

legumes *fruits* 44.1

leguminous *horticultural* 17.14, *taxonomic* 41.16, *fruiting* 44.5

leg up *advance* 679.3, *promotion* 715.3, *help* 825.1

leg warmers *legwear* 100.26

legwear 100.26

legwork *work* 122.1, *print journalism* 175.4

lei *flower* 42.1

Leibnizian *Philosophical Schools of Thought* 4

Leibnizianism *Philosophical Schools of Thought* 4

Leibniz's Law *philosophical term* 4.7

Leibniz's theorem *Mathematical Concepts* 6

Leicester *Breeds of Sheep* 16

leishmania *parasite* 39.18

leisure 125.1, 125.3, 413.4; *pause* 668.3, *directional* 677.13, *ease* 819.1

leisure class *the rich* 485.7, *social class* 777.5

leisured *leisurely* 125.4, *inactive*

413.9, *quiescent* 678.6, *at ease* 819.2
leisured classes *inactive person* 413.8, *nonworker* 415.4
leisureliness *slow motion* 677.9, *slowness* 693.1
leisurely 125.4, 125.6; *inactive* 413.9, *deliberate* 589.18, *late* 658.14, *unhurried* 693.8, *slowly* 693.14, *at ease* 819.2, *easygoing* 823.13
leisurely gait *slow motion* 693.3
leisurely progress *slowness* 693.1
leisure pool *swimming place* 164.9
leisure pursuit *activity* 385.4
leisure suit *suit* 100.16
leisure time *pause* 668.3
leisurewear *informal clothes* 100.7, *informal clothing* 407.5
leitmotiv *topic* 328.1
leitmotiv *or* **leitmotif** *aspect of fiction* 139.5, *melody* 140.10
lek *dwelling* 36.4, *national coins* 484.11
Leman Lakes 568
Le Mans 24-hour race *races* 146.4
Le Mans start *automobile racing terms* 146.3, *windsurfing terms* 150.21
lemma *theory* 6.62, *grass plant* 45.3
lemminglike *compliant* 781.9
lemniscate *curve* 6.38
Lemnos Islands 572
lemon Trees and Shrubs 43, *sour thing* 223.3, *yellow thing* 259.4
lemon [Inf] *figurative usage* 44.4, *unsuccessful thing* 846.8
lemonade *soft drink* 93.8, *sweet drink* 222.4
lemon grove *garden* 17.2
lemon mint Herbs and Spices 91
lemon squeezer *cooking equipment* 91.6
lemon tea *tea* 93.7
lemon verbena Herbs and Spices 91
lemony *acid* 223.5
lemon yellow *yellow pigment* 259.2
lemon-yellow *yellow* 259.7
lemures *ghost* 86.11
Lena Rivers 570
lend 475.6; *provision* 89.9, *transfer property* 470.12, *give* 472.10, *credit* 487.10, *finance* 825.31
lend a hand *be eager* 373.13, *help* 825.23
lend a helping hand *volunteer* 504.13, *give moral support* 605.18
lend an ear *hear* 228.13
lend at interest *lend* 475.6
lender 475.3, 487.5; *provisioner* 89.4, *merchant* 482.10
lend force to *strengthen* 516.15
lending 475.1; *loaned* 475.5, *loan* 488.3
lending at interest *lending* 475.1
lending institution 475.4
lending library [Brit] *library* 174.14
lending money *lending* 475.1
lending on collateral *lending* 475.1
lending on security *lending* 475.1
lend-lease *loan* 475.2
lend money *lend* 475.6
lend on collateral *lend* 475.6
lend oneself *advise* 825.27, *reciprocate* 827.13
lend oneself to *be an instrument* 511.7
lend on security *lend* 475.6
lend support *advise* 825.27
lend wings to *further* 825.30

length 590.1; *line* 6.35, *dimension* 10.5, 589.11, *space* 563.1, *size* 579.1, *measurability* 589.2, *measuring instrument* 589.12, *lengths* 590.5, *quantity* 738.1, *piece* 760.2
length and breadth *all* 759.4
lengthen 590.12; *be diffuse* 199.5, *extend* 563.14, *enlarge* 581.14, *make bigger* 744.7
lengthened 590.10; *bigger* 581.9, *protracted* 669.7
lengthener *enlarger* 581.8
lengthening 590.4; *expansion* 581.1, *growing* 581.12
lengthily *at length* 590.15
lengthiness *longness* 590.3
length of time *duration* 642.1
lengths 590.5, Fields of Measurement 589
lengthways *lengthwise* 590.8, 590.14, *horizontally* 603.11
lengthwise 590.8, 590.14; *horizontally* 603.11
lengthy 590.9; *diffuse* 199.3
lenience *leniency* 423.1
leniency 423.1; *peace offering* 74.5, *mercy* 308.3, *treatment* 399.11, *tolerance* 502.2, *easiness* 543.5
lenient 423.3; *pitying* 308.4, *forgiving* 312.4, *courteous* 410.6, *permitting* 502.5, *soft-hearted* 543.11, *easygoing* 823.13
leniently 423.6; *forgivingly* 53.37, 312.13, *pacifically* 74.12, *pityingly* 308.11, *courteously* 410.13, *with permission* 502.10, *soft-heartedly* 543.19
lenient person 423.2
Lenin Peak Mountains and Hills 569
lenitive *pacificatory* 74.8, *medicinal* 115.15, *moderator* 521.2, *moderating* 521.5, *ointment* 562.8, *lubricational* 562.12
lenity *mercy* 308.3, *forgivingness* 312.3, *leniency* 423.1
leno Fabrics and Fibers 130
leno weave *weaving* 130.6
lens 132.11; *optical element* 10.20, *eye* 19.9, 242.3, *industrial ceramics* 129.6, *transparent thing* 249.4, *bulge* 634.2
lens aperture *lens system* 10.22
lens attachment *lens* 132.11
lens cap *lens* 132.11
lens cover *lens* 132.11
lenses *visual aid* 242.14
lens filter *lens* 132.11, *filter* 132.14
lens hood *lens* 132.11
lensman [Inf] *photographer* 132.23
lens mount *lens* 132.11
lens system 10.22; *lens* 132.11
Lent Christian Holy Days and Seasons 85, *fast* 118.4, *penitence* 313.3, *seasons* 654.2
Lenten *fasting* 118.5
Lenten fare *incompleteness* 98.2, *short rations* 118.3
lenticular *curvilinear* 6.78, *convex* 634.5
lenticular cloud *cloud appearance* 9.19
lenticular galaxy *galaxy* 7.5
lentiform *convex* 634.5
lentigo *mark* 533.2
lentivirus *disease-causing agent* 114.5
lento Musical Terms and Expression Marks 140
Lenz's law Classical Physical Laws 10
Leo Constellations 7
Leo Minor Constellations 7

leonine *carnivorous* 35.26
leopard *male mammal* 35.18, *game* 160.6, *variegated thing* 263.5
leopardess *female mammal* 35.19
leopard lily Flowers 42
leopards Collective Names 59
leotard *legwear* 100.26, *gymnastics equipment* 157.2
lepidopteran *or* **lepidopterous** *insectile* 311.45
lepidopterist *entomologist* 40.3
lepidopterological *entomological* 40.15
lepidopterology *study of insects* 40.2
lepidoptery Hobbies and Pastimes 167
leporid *rabbitlike* 35.29
leporine *rabbitlike* 35.29
lepraphobia Phobias 283
leprechaun *sprite* 86.12, Legendary Creatures 360, *little person* 580.5
leprophobia Phobias 283
leprosy *tropical disease* 114.10, *skin disease* 114.16, Phobias 283
leprous *unclean* 112.8, *of disease* 114.25
leptodactylous *thin* 595.9
lepton *elementary particle* 10.53
leptosome *thin person* 595.4
leptosomic *thin* 595.9
Lepus Constellations 7
lesbian *sexual nature* 20.4, *of sexual nature* 20.17, *homosexual* 33.10, *female* 33.16
lesbianism *sexual nature* 20.4
lesbian marriage *type of marriage* 64.3
lesbo [Inf *and* Off] *homosexual* 33.10
Lesbos Islands 572
lese majesty *subversion* 427.3
Les Fauves Western Art Styles 133
lesion *painful injury* 215.3
Lesotho Countries 566
less *inferiorly* 745.13, *by subtraction* 749.8, *least* 796.2, *fewer* 796.7
less and less *by degrees* 739.10, *decreasingly* 747.9, 749.9
lessee *resident* 61.6, *possessor* 469.10, *property owner* 470.7, *recipient* 473.5
lessen 468.17; *relieve* 275.8, *weaken* 517.13, *mitigate* 521.9, *ease* 543.15, *contract* 582.12, *become smaller* 582.14, *diminish* 597.24, *decrease* 747.7
lessened *smaller* 582.7, *reduced* 749.5
lessening 468.6; *moderation* 521.1, *contraction* 582.2, *shortening* 582.2, *contracting* 582.10, *diminishment* 597.7, *decrease* 747.1
lesser *ranked* 6.72, *inferior* 745.5
lesser creation *inferior* 745.4
lesser evil *choice* 382.3
lesser of two evils *choice* 382.3, *substitution* 672.1
Lesson(s) Eucharist 85.7
lesson *dissertation* 203.1, *moral* 431.15, *condemnation* 438.2, *punishment* 454.1, *lecture* 777.7, *warning* 814.1
less so *decreasingly* 747.9
less sound *faintness of sound* 233.1
less than *inferiorly* 745.13
less than one 787.4
less than one's hopes *disappointing* 293.6
less than perfect *imperfect* 806.5

less than somewhat *not enough* 98.12
less than the going rate *at a discount* 495.7
less than the market rate *at a discount* 495.7
less than the truth *partial truth* 192.7
let *inhabited* 61.10, *tennis terms* 165.5, *badminton terms* 165.11, *suppose* 359.8, *possess* 469.14, *transfer of property* 470.4, *transfer property* 470.12, *permit* 502.6
let alone *shun* 386.14, *leave alone* 413.13, *continue* 669.8, *additionally* 748.15, *exclusively* 764.10
let an opportunity slip by *lose one's chance* 660.10
let be *continue* 669.8
let bygones be bygones *pacify* 74.11, *forgive and forget* 312.9, *forgive* 355.13
letch [Inf] *sexual longing* 20.6, *fornicate* 432.14
letch *or* **lech** [Inf] *desirer* 288.9
letching [Inf] *fornication* 432.3
letdown *lack of hope* 282.2, *disappointment* 293.1, *decline* 846.5
let down *disappointed* 293.4, *disappoint* 293.9, *lower* 716.12
let down the portcullis *shelter* 812.8
let drop *divulge* 180.9, *throw down* 716.13
let fall *be clumsy* 128.9, *divulge* 180.9, *throw down* 716.13
let fly *handle sailboat equipment* 150.30, *fire* 418.18, *shoot* 696.18
let go *acquitted* 54.25, *acquit* 54.32, 434.10, *relieve from duty* 275.11, *relinquished* 392.2, *relinquish* 392.3, *relegate* 574.18, *dismiss* 709.15, *throw down* 716.13, *deliver* 817.5, *set free* 829.17, *lack restraint* 829.21
let go for a song *make cheap* 497.14
let go free *liberate* 831.6
let go of *liberate* 831.6, *resign* 835.5
lethal *deadly* 29.14, *killing* 30.17, *toxic* 114.28, *destructive* 523.8
lethal injection *execution* 30.6, *instrument of execution* 454.17
lethally *deadly* 30.26, *destructively* 523.18
lethargic *indifferent* 289.7, *not participating* 415.11, *unhurried* 693.8
lethargically *indifferently* 289.17, *impassively* 415.18, *tiredly* 820.7
lethargy *mood disorder* 108.12, *indifference* 289.1, *idleness* 415.3, *submission* 421.1, *slowness* 693.1, *fatigue* 820.1
let have it [Inf] *hit* 695.11
Lethe *evil place* 446.6
let in *admit* 708.12, *insert* 748.12
let in daylight *disclose* 180.8
let it all hang out [Inf] *divulge* 180.9, *lack restraint* 829.21
let it be known *publish* 173.15
let it go no further *keep secret* 182.11
let it rip [Inf] *accelerate* 694.14
let judgment go by default *acquiesce* 421.5
let know *inform* 170.11
let loose *liberate* 831.6
let nature take its course *continue* 669.8
let off *acquitted* 54.25, 434.6, *acquit*

54.32, 434.10, *forgiven* 312.5, *absolve* 312.10, *shoot* 696.18, *deliver* 817.5, *set free* 829.17

let off scot-free *acquit* 434.10

let off steam *give off* 556.25

let off the hook *acquitted* 54.25, *acquit* 54.32, *be lenient* 423.5, *liberate* 831.6

let on *divulge* 180.9

let one in on *divulge* 180.9

let one's breath out *let out* 709.26

let oneself be walked all over *be servile* 401.8

let oneself go *be diffuse* 199.5, *deteriorate* 808.14, *lack restraint* 829.21

let oneself in *enter* 706.11

let oneself in for *take charge of* 391.8, *have difficulty* 824.18

let one's hair down *be informal* 407.10, 829.19, *lack restraint* 829.21

let one's imagination run riot *imagine* 360.14

let or hindrance *hindrance* 826.1

let out 709.26; *disclose* 180.8, *divulge* 180.9, *dismiss* 709.15, *deliver* 817.5, *liberate* 831.6

let-out [Brit] *legal injustice* 53.5

le tout ensemble [Fr] *all* 759.4

let out on bail *liberate* 831.6

let pass *show mercy* 312.11, *ignore* 413.14

let sleeping dogs lie *leave alone* 413.13, *continue* 669.8, *set free* 829.17

let slip *disclose* 180.8, *misjudge* 342.9, *throw down* 716.13

let slip through one's fingers *be wasteful* 468.16, *lose one's chance* 660.10

let some light in *disclose* 180.8

let someone down *not perform* 466.10, *discontinue* 846.14

let someone get away with it *be permissive* 502.7

let someone get away with murder [Inf] *be permissive* 502.7

let someone have it *strike* 418.21

letter *language element* 5.13, *word* 5.43, *correspondence* 169.2, *sign* 183.1, *identify* 184.11, *transferred thing* 685.6

letter bomb *bomb* 78.15

letter bombing *terrorist attack* 418.7

letter by letter *accurately* 350.6

letter carrier *postal worker* 169.6, *messenger* 685.5

lettered *written* 5.36, *literary* 139.15, *identified* 184.9

lettered player *prizewinner* 127.8

letter for letter *literally* 721.32, *imitatively* 736.12

letter-for-letter *linguistically* 5.44

letterhead *means of identification* 184.3

lettering *written letter* 5.14, *decorative method* 532.3

letter of credit *paper money* 484.14, *credit card* 487.2

letter of introduction *personal identification* 184.4, *recommendation* 437.6

letter of the law *jurisprudence* 53.13, *severity* 424.1

letter-perfect *correct* 350.4, 721.13

letterpress printing *book printing* 174.10

letterpress typography *printing* 173.3

letter-quality printer *hardcopy device* 15.10

letters *literature* 139.1, *learning* 348.3

letters a foot high *public relations (PR)* 173.8

letters after one's name *personal identification* 184.4

letters patent *authorization* 425.4, *permit* 502.3

letter to the editor *news story* 171.3

letter writer *correspondent* 169.3

letter writing *correspondence* 169.2

let the air out of *deflate* 195.16

let the ayes have it *assent to* 346.7

let the cat out of the bag *be clumsy* 128.9, *inform on* 170.13, *tell on* 180.10

let the world go by *have free time* 413.15

let things take care of themselves *leave alone* 413.13

let things take their course *leave alone* 413.13, *continue* 669.8

letting go *relinquishment* 392.1

letting the world go by *leisure* 413.4

let tomorrow take care of itself *be unprepared* 389.14

lettrism *Western Art Styles* 133

lettuce *green thing* 260.4

lettuce [Inf] *cash* 484.2

letup [Inf] *moderation* 521.1, *pause* 668.3, *interval* 775.2, *ease* 819.1

let up *stop* 668.10, *pause* 668.13, 775.11, *slow down* 693.13, *take it easy* 819.3

let up! *cease!* 668.14

let well enough alone *leave alone* 413.13

leucine *Amino Acids* 12

leucoderma *skin disease* 114.16

leukemia *blood disease* 114.14, *cancer* 114.15

leukemic *of disease* 114.25

leukocyte *blood* 555.4

leukoderma *whiteness* 253.1

leukophobia *Phobias* 283

leukorrhea *pus* 25.7

Levant *world region* 564.6

levanter *Notable Winds* 9

levee *retainer* 471.3, *dam* 551.12, *river parts* 570.3, *barrier* 826.7

level 588.2; *civil engineering tool* 14.18, *sound quality* 230.4, *fire* 418.18, *knock down* 523.13, *uniform* 545.5, *smooth* 545.10, *lowland* 572.6, 597.15, *low* 597.10, *baseline* 601.4, *horizontal surface* 603.3, *planimetry* 603.5, *horizontal* 603.6, *make horizontal* 603.10, *horizontally* 603.11, *rung* 636.3, *regular* 663.5, *frequent* 663.6, *make regular* 663.9, *flatten* 716.15, *correctly* 721.29, *relative position* 727.5, *make the same* 730.16, *rank* 739.2, *interval* 739.4, *gradational* 739.5, *on equal terms* 740.9, *equalize* 740.12, *make average* 742.9, *category* 767.6, *social class* 777.5

level crossing [Brit] *track* 688.2, *crossing point* 692.7

leveled 603.8; *lowered* 716.7

leveler *destroyer* 523.6, *flattener* 603.4

level-green *bowls* 151.7

level-green bowls *green bowling* 151.3

level ground *lowlands* 597.6, *horizontal surface* 603.3

levelheaded *detached* 4.18, *rational* 109.4, *wise* 352.4, *practical* 719.8

levelheadedness *philosophical attitude* 4.3, *wisdom* 352.1

leveling *downthrow* 716.2

leveling off *shortening* 582.2, *decline* 747.4

leveling out *decline* 747.4

leveling up or **down** *equalization* 740.4

levelly *smoothly* 545.13, *horizontally* 603.11, *correctly* 721.29, *differentially* 739.9

levelness *smoothness* 545.1, *lowness* 597.1, *horizontality* 603.1, *regularity* 663.1, *equality* 740.1

level off *become smaller* 582.14, *decrease* 747.7

level of meaning *type of meaning* 361.4

level out *make regular* 663.9, *decrease* 747.7

level up or **down** *equalize* 740.12, *make average* 742.9

level with *full* 761.8

Leven *Lakes* 568

lever *simple machine* 14.6, *hand tool* 103.3, *stationary rings* 157.8, *indirect influence* 512.4, *propeller* 696.8, *extractor* 711.9, *lifter* 715.5

leverage *loan* 488.3, *influence* 512.1, *superiority* 744.1, *scope* 829.7

leveraged *contractual* 480.16

leveret *young mammal* 35.20

lever out *displace* 711.14

Leviathan *Legendary Creatures* 360

leviathan *big thing* 579.9

levigate *smooth* 545.10, *pulverize* 553.26, *rub* 554.12

levigated *pulverized* 553.20

levigation *smoothness* 545.1, *pulverization* 553.4, *grinding* 554.3

levigator *pulverizer* 553.11

levirate *type of marriage* 64.3

levitate *experience psychic phenomena* 86.23, *be light* 539.8, *ascend* 713.19, *raise* 715.9

levitated *raised* 715.6

levitating *lightness* 539.1, *insubstantial* 539.5

levitation *occult and psychic phenomena* 86.7, *lightness* 539.1, *ascent* 713.1, *raising* 715.1

levitational *insubstantial* 539.5

levitative *insubstantial* 539.5

Levite *rabbi* 84.6

levity *gaiety* 269.3, *inconstancy* 378.2, *capriciousness* 381.2, *lightness* 539.1

levo form *structure* 11.7

levophobia *Phobias* 283

levulose *Common Sugars* 12

levy 494.7; *demand* 425.2, 425.11, 505.12, *payment* 433.5, *impose a duty* 433.14, *takings* 477.8, *take back* 477.17, *charge* 494.13

levying *taking back* 477.4

lewd *desirous* 20.18, *obscene* 112.9, *lustful* 288.15, *unchaste* 432.10, *ribald* 535.8

lewd gesture *gesture* 183.5, *act of discourtesy* 411.3, *indignity* 436.7

lewdly *lustfully* 20.24, 288.29, *dirtily* 112.12, *promiscuously* 432.19, *ribaldly* 535.12

lewdness *obscenity* 112.4, *sexual desire* 288.5, *sexual love* 299.3, *sexual immorality* 432.2

lewd talk *sexual offense* 432.6

Lewis acid *acid* 11.10

Lewis base *base* 11.11

Lewis dot structure *structure* 11.7

lexical *worded* 5.38, *linguistic* 361.9

lexically 5.46

lexical meaning *type of meaning* 361.4

lexicographer *linguist* 5.3, *interpreter* 365.6

lexicographically *linguistically* 5.44

lexicography *Linguistic Studies* 5, *language* 5.4, *word book* 5.27, *science of interpretation* 365.5

lexicologist *linguist* 5.3

lexicology *Linguistic Studies* 5

lexicon *word book* 5.27, *schoolbook* 48.15, *type of book* 174.3, *book of lists* 785.3

lexicostatistics *Linguistic Studies* 5

lexigraphy *written letter* 5.14

lex mercatoria *law* 53.1

lex scripta *law* 53.1

ley *grassland* 45.2

ley grass *grass* 45.1

Leyte *Islands* 572

lez [Inf and Offl] *homosexual* 33.10

L-form *structure* 11.7

l-form *structure* 11.7

Lhasa apso *Breeds of Dogs* 35

L'Hospital's rule *Mathematical Concepts* 6

Lhotse I *Mountains and Hills* 569

Lhotse II *Mountains and Hills* 569

liability 454.6; *answerability* 334.9, *sense of duty* 433.2, *guilt* 450.1, *debt* 488.1, *attitude* 513.2, *vulnerability* 811.6, *probability* 838.1

liable *convicted* 54.26, *answerable* 334.17, *duteous* 433.7, *punishable* 454.21, *indebted* 488.7, *vulnerable* 811.9, *probable* 838.6

liableness *probability* 838.1

liable to *tending to* 513.4

liable to illness *unhealthy* 114.23

liable to prosecution *accused* 442.5

liable to the law *jurisdictional* 53.18, 54.23

liaise *relate to* 727.9, *unify* 752.15, *intercommunicate* 754.15

liaising *connective* 754.10

liaison *mediator* 75.2, *love affair* 299.9, *fornication* 432.3, *relatedness* 727.1, *union* 752.1, *association* 754.2

liana or **liane** *plant* 41.2

liar 192.10; *exaggerator* 194.6, *equivocator* 380.4, *distorter* 627.5, *cunning person* 822.3

Liard *Rivers* 570

libation *drink* 93.2, 121.6, *alcohol* 121.5

libational *ritualistic* 85.15

libation to Bacchus *drink* 121.6

libeccio or **libeccio** *Notable Winds* 9

libel *misinformation* 188.3, *lying* 192.5, *lie* 192.23, *vilification* 301.2, *vilify* 301.15, *personal attack* 418.8, *criticize* 418.26, *defamation* 440.3, *defame* 440.13, *false accusation* 442.2, *accuse falsely* 442.9

libelant *litigant* 54.4, *liar* 192.10, *accuser* 442.3

libeled *perjurious* 442.7

libelee *litigant* 54.4

libeler *liar* 192.10, *disparager* 440.7, *accuser* 442.3

libelous *lying* 192.16, *vilifying* 301.9, *critical* 418.16, *defamatory* 440.9

libelous or **libellous** *perjurious* 442.7

libelously vilifyingly 301.18, disparagingly 440.16, accusingly 442.11

liberal curricular 48.21, plentiful 97.4, benevolent person 305.6, charitable 305.9, philanthropic 307.6, impartial 338.6, lenient person 423.2, giving 453.12, 472.9, expending 491.8, generous 498.6, broad-minded 592.9, general 778.9, free person 829.9, free 829.11

liberal arts subject 48.3

Liberal Democrat party Political Parties 50

liberalism freethinking 829.2

liberality 829.8; charity 305.3, philanthropy 307.1, giving 472.1, donation 491.6, generosity 498.1, broad-mindedness 592.3

liberalization liberation 831.1

liberalize be free 829.16, liberate 831.6

liberalized liberated 831.4

liberally charitably 305.15, as a gift 472.17, generously 491.14, 498.12, broad-mindedly 592.17

liberalness broad-mindedness 592.3

Liberal party Political Parties 50

liberal thinking liberation 831.1

liberate 831.6; secrete 24.7, acquit 54.32, 434.10, save 275.9, absolve 312.10, vindicate 441.11, extract 711.13, loosen 753.14, restore 809.12, deliver 817.5, disentangle 823.17, set free 829.17

liberated 831.4; acquitted 54.25, 434.6, dislodged 711.11, separate 753.7, escaping 816.7, delivered 817.4, free 829.11, unconditional 829.14

liberated man 32.13

liberated mind freethinking 829.2

liberated spirit liberation 831.1

liberated woman 33.12

liberating 831.5; separation 753.1

liberation 831.1; favorable verdict 54.19, aid 275.2, acquittal 434.2, extraction 711.1, escape 816.1, deliverance 817.1, freedom 829.1

liberation theology Theologies 81

liberator 831.3; deliverer 817.2

Liberia Countries 566

libertarian freethinker 829.10, free 829.11

libertarianism freethinking 829.2

Libertarian party Political Parties 50

libertinage sexual immorality 432.2

libertine 32.7; desirer 288.9, lover 299.11, sexually immoral person 432.8, unchaste 432.10, freethinker 829.10

libertinism sexual love 299.3, sexual immorality 432.2, liberality 829.8

Liberty Apple Varieties 44

liberty leisure 125.1, acquittal 434.2, permission 735.9, freedom 829.1

Liberty Island Islands 572

Liberty ship Ships and Boats 690

libidinal energy libido 108.26

libidinal object libido 108.26

libidinous desirous 20.18, lustful 288.15, unchaste 432.10

libidinously lustfully 20.24, 288.29, promiscuously 432.19

libidinousness sexual desire 288.5

libido 108.26; sexuality 20.3, sexual desire 288.5, sexual love 299.3, sexual immorality 432.2

libido analog libido 108.26

libido arrest fixation 108.21

libido fixation fixation 108.21

libido object libido 108.26

Libra Constellations 7

librarian library 174.14

librarianship library 174.14

library 174.14; school place 48.16, room 60.9, type of table 101.5, repository 105.13, studio 124.6, information source 170.6, privacy 181.6

library binding bookbinding 174.11

library furniture furniture 101.1

library school type of school 48.12

library science library 174.14

libration moon 7.18, oscillation 683.1

libratory oscillating 683.8

librettist dramatist 136.27, author 139.13, composer 141.9, descriptive writer 202.10

libretto script 136.7

Libreville Countries 566

Libya Countries 566

Libyan Deserts 572

Libyan Barb Horse and Pony Breeds 159

lice Collective Names 59, Phobias 283

license 434.4; authorization 52.3, 340.4, authorize 52.14, 833.10, legality 53.9, make legal 53.27, permit 340.12, 502.3, 502.6, 735.29, freedom 407.4, 829.1, approval 437.1, approve 437.14, tolerance 502.2, adoption 692.4, adopt 692.14, permission 735.9, liberality 829.8, authority 833.3

licensed authorized 52.11, 340.8, legal 53.16, law-abiding 53.20, approved 437.8, permitted 502.4, adopted 692.10, permitting 735.19

licensed practical nurse (LPN) nurse 107.23

licensee recipient 473.5, commissioner 833.5

license plate miscellaneous automotive terms 687.14

license plate number personal identification 184.4

licentiate authorization 340.4

licentious lawless 53.26, obscene 112.9, pleasure-seeking 214.10, immoral 432.8, unchaste 432.10, dissipated 456.7, unconditional 829.14

licentiously lustfully 20.24, excessively 829.23

licentiousness obscenity 112.4, sexual love 299.3, dissipation 456.2, liberality 829.8

lichen 47.16; lower plant 41.4, moss 46.4, fungal association 47.5, alga 47.10

lichened lichenoid 47.21

licheniform lichenoid 47.21

lichenized lichenoid 47.21

lichenoid 47.21

lichenological lichenoid 47.21

lichenologist plant scientist 41.11, study of lichens 47.17

lichenology plant science 41.10, study of lichens 47.17

lichenometry study of lichens 47.17

lichenose lichenoid 47.21

lichenous lichenoid 47.21

lich gate means of entry 706.6

Li Chi other text 81.19

licit legal 53.16, rightful 429.9, permitted 502.4

licitly legally 53.33

licitness legality 53.9

lick taste 92.24

lick [Inf] bodily movement 677.11, swiftness 694.1, beat 695.12, overtake 744.16, defeat 845.17

lick and a promise superficiality 599.2, incompleteness 762.1

licked [Inf] defeated 846.11

lickerish [Arch] desirous 20.18, unchaste 432.10

lickerishness [Arch] sexual immorality 432.2

lickety-split [Inf] swiftly 694.16, hastily 818.7

licking delicate eating 92.3, chewing 92.19

licking [Inf] ramming 695.3, victory 845.4, defeat 846.7

lick into shape [Inf] form 624.9, transform 670.13, tidy 765.21, make conform 781.13

lick one's lips be hungry 288.21

lickspittle sycophant 401.3

lick the dust humble oneself 298.18, knuckle under 401.10, succumb 421.7

lick the feet of fawn 401.9

lick the platter clean eat well 92.23

lick the shoes or boots of fawn 401.9

licorice root Herbs and Spices 91

lid shade maker 247.4, stopper 584.3, cover 613.2

lid [Inf] hat 100.32

lie 192.23; exercise 157.12, evasion 181.5, 380.2, misrepresentation 188.1, misrepresent 188.6, 366.5, falsehood 192.6, deceive 330.12, be equivocal 380.7, be situated 573.9, distortion of truth 627.4, distort the truth 627.12, stratagem 822.2

lie-abed sleeper 415.7

lie ahead be in the future 650.9

lie around be inactive 415.13, surround 615.7

lie at the bottom of cause 675.8

lie at the door of be the duty of 433.16

lieback mountaineer 161.10

lie back take it easy 819.3

liebacking climbing techniques 161.3

lie below the surface be interior 611.14, hide 844.13

lie beneath be interior 611.14, be latent 844.12

lie betwixt and between stand in the middle 772.17

Liechtenstein Countries 566

lied Musical Forms 140, song 140.11

lie dead not act 413.11

lie detector psychometrics 108.5, detector 345.6

lie doggo [Inf] conceal oneself 181.15

lie dormant sleep 415.14, be latent 844.12

lie down 716.21; be low 597.20, be horizontal 603.9, take it easy 819.3

lie facedown be low 597.20

lie fallow be infertile 23.8, be unused 394.11, have free time 413.15

lie flat be low 597.20, be horizontal 603.9

liege master 68.1, subjected person 832.5

liege lord master 68.1, protector 810.11

liegeman servant 69.1

Lie group Mathematical Concepts 6

lie heavy upon weigh on 538.13, make heavy 538.14

lie hidden hide 844.13

lie idle be unused 394.11, have free time 413.15, be inert 519.4

lie in ambush hide 844.13

lie in one's power be powerful 514.18

lie in one's throat or teeth lie 192.23

lie in the future be in the future 650.9

lie in the vicinity or neighborhood of be near 586.11

lie in wait trap 813.6

lie just around the corner be in the future 650.9

lie low conceal oneself 181.15, become invisible 34.6, disappear 265.5, be safe 810.20, elude 816.10, be cunning 822.5, hide 844.13

lien amount owing 488.5, insolvency 490.5

lientery defecation 25.3

lie of the ball golfing terms 156.3

lie opposite be opposite 731.4

lie out of the way be distant 585.8

lie parallel parallel 606.7

lierne vault 134.8

lierne rib Architectural Elements 134

lie still be inert 519.4

lie through one's teeth lie 192.23

lie to sail 690.16

lie under or beneath underlie 597.23, 601.11

lie under the surface be latent 844.12

Lieutenant US Military Ranks 58, military title 72.8

Lieutenant, junior grade US Military Ranks 58

lieutenant deputy 80.1, helper 825.12

Lieutenant Colonel US Military Ranks 58

Lieutenant Commander US Military Ranks 58

Lieutenant General US Military Ranks 58

lieutenant governor leader 68.3

lie with have sex 20.21

lie within be interior 611.14

life 28.1; activity 414.1, energy 414.4, vigor 518.1, existence 717.1

life activity life function 28.6

life after death new life 28.8, nonmaterial world 525.1, future condition 650.3

life-and-death important 278.6

life and soul of the party social person 408.7

life assurance [Brit] insurance 810.10

life belt survival swimming 164.4, protective covering 613.5, safety device 810.15, preserver 815.9

lifeblood life requirement 28.5, blood 555.4, essential content 723.2

lifeboat Ships and Boats 690, safety device 810.15, deliverer 817.2

lifeboat crew deliverer 817.2

life buoy survival swimming 164.4, safety device 810.15

life cycle 28.7; cycle 663.3, evolution 670.3

life everlasting life without end 644.2

life expectancy life cycle 28.7

life force 28.2; world soul 82.3

life function 28.6
life-giving *reproductive* 21.11, *alive* 28.13
lifeguard *swimmer* 164.11, *guard* 419.15, *security force* 464.3, *protector* 810.11
lifeguarding *swimming rescue* 164.5
life instinct *libido* 108.26
life insurance *benefits* 57.11, *insurance* 810.10
life jacket *survival swimming* 164.4, *protective covering* 613.5, *safety device* 810.15, *preserver* 815.9
lifeless *dead* 29.11, *tasteless* 220.4, *inactive* 415.8, *inert* 519.2, *sedentary* 678.5
lifelessly *fatally* 29.18, *inactively* 415.17, *inertly* 519.5, *motionlessly* 678.9
lifelessness *dilution* 220.2, *unenthusiasm* 375.3, *inactivity* 415.1, *inertness* 519.1
lifelike 721.19; *correct* 350.4, *realistic* 719.7
lifelikeness *verisimilitude* 721.10
lifeline *line* 754.5, *safety device* 810.15, *preserver* 815.9
lifelines *sailboat parts and accessories* 150.4
lifelong *pertaining to life* 28.14, *lasting* 642.4
lifelong dream *objective* 374.5
lifemanship *tactics* 399.12
life of ease *comfortable circumstances* 726.5, *prosperity* 847.1
life of Riley [Inf] *good time* 214.3, *opulence* 485.3, *prosperity* 847.1
life of the party *joyful person* 269.5
life on earth *living being* 28.3
life peer *nobleman* 70.1
life preserver *survival swimming* 164.4
life process *life function* 28.6
lifer [Inf] *prisoner* 55.7
life raft *safety device* 810.15
life requirement 28.5
life ring *survival swimming* 164.4
lifesaver *swimmer* 164.11, *protector* 810.11, *deliverer* 817.2
lifesaving *swimming rescue* 164.5, *deliverance* 817.1, *delivered* 817.4
life science 13.1; *study of life* 28.9
life scientist 13.26
life senses *life function* 28.6
life sentence *prison sentence* 55.6
life-size *big* 579.13
life span *age* 27.1, *life cycle* 28.7, *duration* 642.1
life story 28.11; *biography* 3.5, *nonfiction* 139.6, *factual account* 202.4
lifestyle *life story* 28.11, *way* 397.3, *way of life* 399.9, *mode* 725.2
life-support system *preserver* 815.9
life-threatening *deadly* 29.14, *killing* 30.17, *destructive* 523.8, *dangerous* 811.7
lifetime *age* 27.1, *life cycle* 28.7, *duration* 642.1
life to come *new life* 28.8, *future condition* 650.3
life vest *survival swimming* 164.4, *safety device* 810.15
life without end 644.2
Liffey *Rivers* 570
lift *exertion* 122.4, *work* 122.8, *ski run* 162.2, *ice-skating techniques* 162.16, *bobsled* 162.38, *hammer throwing* 166.14, *height* 596.1,

heighten 596.14, *advance* 679.3, *further* 679.13, *convey* 685.9, *miscellaneous aviation terms* 689.9, *drag* 699.11, *promotion* 715.3, *lifter* 715.5, *raise* 715.9, *uplift* 807.2, *support* 825.2, 825.24
lift [Brit] *means of transportation* 686.2, *lifter* 715.5
lift [Inf] *borrow illegally* 476.12, *theft* 479.2, *steal* 479.14, *infringe* 479.17
lift a finger *do something* 412.13
lift an oar *row* 150.32
lift bridge *bridge* 551.10
lift controls *liberate* 831.6
lifted *ice-skating* 162.32, *high* 596.7, *raised* 715.6
lifter 715.5
lifter [Inf] *thief* 479.8
lifting *toboggan race* 162.25, *ice-skating* 162.32, *bobsledding* 162.34, *leaping* 713.17, *raising* 715.1
lifting [Inf] *illegal borrowing* 476.3, *stealing* 479.1, *infringement* 479.6
liftoff *flight* 689.5, *start* 705.2, *taking off* 713.6
lift off *launch* 7.35, *fly* 689.13, *go up* 713.23
lift oneself *arise* 715.15
lift the ban on *permit* 502.6
lift the veil *disclose* 180.8, *detect* 345.12
lift up *heighten* 596.14, *raise* 715.9
ligament *muscles* 19.3, *skeleton* 551.14, *line* 754.5
ligand *chemical bond* 11.6
ligase *enzyme* 12.11
ligate *connect* 754.13
ligation *unification* 752.5
ligature *Accents and Diacritical Marks* 5, *linkage* 752.3, *line* 754.5
light 10.17, 246.1, 246.19, 539.4; *electromagnetic radiation* 10.14, *drinkable* 93.18, *fuel* 106.16, *exposed* 132.25, *compose a photograph* 132.27, *musical* 140.25, *that which makes visible* 244.4, *clear* 244.6, *lit* 246.16, *soft-hued* 251.13, *Phobias* 283, *interpretation* 365.1, *generate power* 514.19, *insufficient* 517.11, *design* 536.2, *sparse* 541.3, 796.6, *airy* 558.12, *Fields of Measurement* 589, *line* 595.12, *superficial* 599.4, *wave* 683.4, *quantitative* 738.6, *warning signal* 814.3, *easy* 823.9
light air *wind strength* 9.13
light artillery *guns* 78.9
light as a fairy *light* 539.4
light as a feather *or* **thistledown** *light* 539.4
light as air *light* 539.4
light as day *sunny* 246.17
light beam *light* 10.17
light-blue *blue* 261.5
lightboard *stage* 136.18, *stage lighting* 136.20
light bomber *military aircraft* 77.30
light breeze *wind strength* 9.13
light bulb *industrial ceramics* 129.6, *electric light* 246.6
light buoy *safety light* 246.7
light comedian *actor* 136.25
light comedy *comedy* 136.11
light-complexioned *white* 253.7
light cream *fat* 562.4
light cruiser *warship* 77.21
light drinker *drinker* 93.16
light eater *eater* 92.15
light emission *light* 10.17
light-emitting diode (LED)

photoelectricity 10.32, *photoemission* 246.11
lighten 539.9; *shine* 9.56, *light* 246.19, *grow light* 246.21, *bring cheer* 269.12, *mitigate* 521.9, *disentangle* 823.17
lightened *lit* 246.16
lightening 246.3, 539.2, 539.6; *lucent* 246.13
lighten ship *lighten* 539.9
lighter *fuel starter* 106.3, *cause of fire* 217.10, *fire* 246.9, *Ships and Boats* 690
lighterage *business expenses* 491.4, *conveyance* 685.2
lighter in one's purse *expending* 491.8
lighter-than-air *light* 539.4, *airy* 558.12, *flyable* 689.12
lighter-than-air craft *aircraft* 689.3
lightface *printed* 173.13
lightface type *type* 173.5
light fails *become dark* 247.9
light-fingered *stolen* 479.12, *light* 539.4
light-fingeredness *theft* 479.2
light-flyweight *boxing weight divisions* 152.6, *combat* 152.17
light-footed *active* 414.13, *light* 539.4, *swift* 694.6
light-gray *gray* 255.6
light hand *leniency* 423.1
light-handed *handling* 216.7, *light* 539.4
light-headed *irresolute* 666.4
lighthearted *cheerful* 269.7
lightheartedly *cheerfully* 269.14
lightheartedness *cheerfulness* 269.2
light heavyweight *boxing weight divisions* 152.6
light-heavyweight *combat* 152.17
light-horse cavalry *horse person* 159.14
light-horseman *horse person* 159.14
lighthouse *guide* 126.6, *indicator* 183.7, *safety light* 246.7, *sea marker* 690.7, *safety device* 810.15
lighthouse beacon *signal* 183.6
lighthouse keeper *warner* 814.5
light industry *manufacture* 522.2
lighting 132.16; *production* 137.6, *incandescent light* 246.5, *lucent* 246.13
lightless *dark* 247.5
light lunch *meal* 92.8
lightly 246.23, 539.10; *whitely* 253.13, *weakly* 517.14, *sparsely* 541.6, 796.11, *airily* 558.25, *finely* 595.19, *superficially* 599.8, *quantitatively* 738.8
lightly built *physical* 1.14
light machine gun *firearm* 78.7
light meal *meal* 92.8
light meter *exposure equipment* 132.12
light microscopy *cell biology* 13.14
light middleweight *boxing weight divisions* 152.6
light-middleweight *combat* 152.17
light-minded *unskillful* 128.4, *inconstant* 378.6, *capricious* 381.4, *irresolute* 666.4
light-mindedness *capriciousness* 381.2, *irresolution* 666.2
light music *popular music* 140.4
lightness 539.1; *paleness* 252.2, *subtlety* 534.2, *sparseness* 541.1, *airiness* 558.9, *fineness* 595.5, *superficiality* 599.2, *quantity* 738.1
lightning *thunderstorm* 9.20, *storm*

9.55, *climbing dangers* 161.5, *natural light* 246.4, *electrical power* 514.12
lightning conductor *thunderstorm* 9.20
lightning flash *or* **stroke** *thunderstorm* 9.20
lightning rod *safety device* 810.15
lightning sketch *drawing* 143.4
lightning speed *speed* 694.2
lightning strike [Brit] *strike* 57.8
light of one's life *loved one* 299.13
Light of the World *God the Son* 82.9
light on *insufficient* 98.4
light on one's feet *light* 539.4
light opera *opera* 140.8
light pen *input device* 15.11, *photoemission* 246.11
light pocket *insolvency* 486.2
light pollution *observatory* 7.24
lightproof *dark* 247.5, *opaque* 250.3, *closed* 584.7
light-rail rapid-transit system *railroad system* 688.1
light rain *rain* 9.27
light ray *light* 246.1
light reaction *photosynthesis* 12.22
light red oxide *red pigment* 257.2
light rein *leniency* 423.1
light relief *comedy* 136.11
lights *stage lighting* 136.20, *road attribute* 687.3, *track* 688.2
light-sensitive cell *eye* 242.3
light-sensitive material *photosensitivity* 10.23
lightship *indicator* 183.7, *safety light* 246.7, *Ships and Boats* 690, *sea marker* 690.7, *safety device* 810.15
light show *show* 138.4, *highlight* 246.12
light shower *rain* 9.27
light signal *safety light* 246.7
light-skinned *drained of color* 252.6
light sleep *sleep* 415.5
lightsome *active* 414.13
light source *lighting* 132.16, *incandescent light* 246.5
lights out *military call* 183.9, *darkening* 247.2, *night* 656.3
light station *sea marker* 690.7
light switch *electricity* 106.5
light the fuse *activate* 771.28
lighttight [Brit] *dark* 247.5, *opaque* 250.3
light up 246.20; *make visible* 244.9, *light* 246.19
light upon *win an award* 467.23, *reach* 704.14, *drop* 714.15, *chance upon* 842.13
light verse *poetry* 139.8
light vessel *Ships and Boats* 690
light-water reactor (LWR) *nuclear power production* 514.10
light wave *light* 246.1
lightweight *boxing weight divisions* 152.6, *combat* 152.17, *weak* 517.6, *light* 539.4, *little person* 580.5, *superficial* 599.4, *insignificant* 745.6, *nonentity* 800.8
lightweight [Inf] *weak person* 517.4
light welterweight *boxing weight divisions* 152.6
light-welterweight *combat* 152.17
light-year *astronomical unit* 7.23, *Scientific and Technical Units* 589
light years *distance* 585.1

---

ligneous *woody* 43.11, *combustible* 106.12, *chewy* 547.9
ligniform *woody* 43.11
lignin *polysaccharide* 12.5, *cell structure* 13.16, *timber* 43.3
lignite *brown thing* 256.3
lignite coal *coal* 106.4
lignitic *gas* 106.14
lignocaine *anesthetic* 213.3
lignography *woodworking* 131.1, *engraving* 144.3
lignum vitae Trees and Shrubs 43
ligule *leaf* 41.6, *grass plant* 45.3
Ligurian Sea Oceans and Seas 571
ligyrophobia Phobias 283
likability *lovability* 299.5
likable 271.6, **290.7**; *pleasant* 214.7, 271.5, *desirable* 288.11
likably 290.12
like 290.8, 299.22; *representational* 187.8, *take pleasure in* 271.11, *desire* 288.17, *love* 299.21, *will* 372.11, *admire* 437.15, *tend* 513.5, *corresponding* 606.6, *correspondingly* 606.10, *how* 691.16, *similar* 733.7, *comparable* 733.8, *comparably* 733.18, *conforming* 735.17, *conformingly* 735.37, *equal* 740.7, 740.8
like a bat cut of hell [Inf] *with vigor* 518.6, *hastily* 818.7
like a battering ram *violently* 520.11
like a bird *swift* 694.6
like a bolt from or **out of the blue** *surprisingly* 292.14
like a bull at a gate *violently* 520.11
like a bureaucracy *under commission* 833.11
like a cat on a hot tin roof *fidgety* 414.14
like a cat on hot bricks or **a hot tin roof** *jerkily* 684.29
like a diplomat *feasibly* 460.9
like a drowned rat *wet* 557.23
like a fish out of water *unskillful* 128.4
like a good Samaritan *voluntarily* 504.19
like a hog *gluttonously* 119.5
like a horse *gluttonously* 119.5, *heavily* 538.16
like a knight in shining armor *courteously* 410.13
like a leech *parasitically* 401.17
like all hell let loose *loudly* 232.11
like a lord *majestically* 297.21
like a machine *skillfully* 127.16
like a mad dog *violent* 520.5
like a man *persistently* 376.17
like a master *skillfully* 127.16
like a monk *celibately* 67.12
like a mule *obstinately* 379.11
like an acrobat *softly* 543.18
like an ape *imitatively* 736.12
like an athlete *softly* 543.18
like an eagle *swift* 694.6
like an expert *skillfully* 127.16
like a nun *celibately* 67.12
like a parrot *imitatively* 736.12
like a penitent *penitently* 451.10
like a phoenix from the ashes *repaired* 809.6
like a pig *gluttonously* 119.5
like a predator *avariciously* 477.22
like a puppet on a string *obedient* 426.4, *subordinate* 832.8
like a raging or **mad bull** *violent* 520.5
like a rocket *hastily* 818.7

like a sailor *nautical* 690.14, *nautically* 690.17
like a shot *voluntarily* 373.17, *immediately* 645.8
like a thief in the night *stealthily* 182.15
like a ton of bricks [Inf] *heavily* 538.16
like a vise *tenaciously* 471.11
like a wolf *gluttonously* 119.5
like best *prefer* 382.13
like better *prefer* 382.13
like cats and dogs *disagreeing* 463.6
like clockwork *regularly* 663.14, 730.21, *easily* 823.19
like crazy [Inf] *with vigor* 518.6
liked 290.6; *beloved* 299.19, *popular* 408.12
like death warmed over [Inf] *sick* 114.24
like for like *retaliation* 420.1, *retaliatory* 420.3
like friends *sociably* 408.19
like gangbusters [Inf] *with vigor* 518.6
like glue *tenaciously* 471.11
like gold dust *valuable* 496.8, *infrequent* 662.2
like greased lightning [Inf] *immediately* 645.8, *swift* 694.6, *hastily* 818.7
like hell [Inf] *with vigor* 518.6
like hell! [Inf] *no!* 506.12
like lead *heavily* 538.16
likelihood *probability* 6.59, 838.1, *demonstrability* 331.5, *expectation* 356.1, *looking to the future* 650.4, *possibility* 836.1, *good chance* 842.6
likeliness *probability* 838.1
likely *believable* 87.7, *demonstrably* 331.22, *expected* 356.5, *auspicious* 458.10, *tending to* 513.4, *predictable* 650.7, *predictably* 650.15, *realizable* 719.9, *possible* 836.5, *probable* 838.6, *probably* 838.11
like mad [Inf] *with vigor* 518.6
like man and wife *matrimonially* 64.23
like-minded *assenting* 346.4, *agreeing* 462.6, 735.13
like-mindedly *agreeably* 462.14, *in accord* 735.33
like-mindedness *agreement* 462.1, 735.3
liken *correspond* 606.8, *correspond to* 727.10, *compare* 733.13
likeness *picture* 133.5, *image* 187.3, *representation* 202.9, *reflection* 242.9, *impression* 264.7, *correspondence* 606.2, *similarity* 733.1, *conformity* 735.7, 781.1, *copy* 736.2, *equality* 740.1
like new *newly* 652.21, *repaired* 809.6, *cured* 809.8
likening *comparability* 733.2
like no other *characteristically* 779.20
like nothing *easily* 823.19
like or **likes of, the** *counterpart* 733.5, *type* 777.4
like putty in one's hands *used* 393.5, *obedient* 426.4, *irresolute* 666.4, *subject* 832.6
likes 290.3
like shooting fish in a barrel *easy* 823.9
like snow in August *infrequent* 662.2
like so [Inf] *under the circumstances* 726.16
like something the cat dragged in *untidy* 766.11

like stroke *golfing terms* 156.3
like taking candy from a baby *easy* 823.9
like the idea *assent* 346.6, *agree with* 462.10
like the rock of Gibraltar *steady* 376.8
like the sound of one's own voice *be talkative* 207.7
like to *enjoy* 290.9
like two peas in a pod *same* 730.7
likewise *agreeingly* 730.19, *similarly* 733.17, *conformingly* 735.37
liking 290.1, **290.4**; *good feeling* 266.4, *likes* 290.3, *love* 299.1, *will* 372.1, *preference* 382.2, *admiration* 437.2, *attitude* 513.2
lilac Flowers 42, *purpleness* 262.1, *purple thing* 262.3, *purple* 262.6
lilapsophobia Phobias 283
liliaceous *taxonomic* 41.16
Lilliput Imaginary Places 360
Lilliputian *undersized* 580.8
lilly-pilly Trees and Shrubs 43
Lilongwe Countries 569
lilt *song* 140.11, *unbalance* 741.8
lily *white thing* 253.4
lily family *seed plant* 41.3
lily-livered *cowardly* 285.4, *weak-willed* 517.10
lily-of-the-Nile Flowers 42
lily of the valley Flowers 42
lily pond *ornamental garden* 17.3
lily-white *white* 253.7
Lima Countries 566
lima Bean Varieties 90
limaçon *curve* 6.38
limb *sun* 7.15, *appendage* 19.5, *tree part* 43.2, *component* 760.3
limber *guns* 78.9, *pliant* 543.7
limberly *softly* 543.18
limberness *softness* 543.1
limber up *be healthy* 113.11, *prepare oneself* 388.21, *ease* 543.15
limbless *reduced* 749.5
limbless amphibian *amphibian* 37.10
limbo *disuse* 394.3, *evil place* 446.6, *emptiness* 718.4
lime *fertilizer* 16.9, 22.6, Trees and Shrubs 43, *sour thing* 223.3, *color remover* 252.4, *green thing* 260.4, *adhesive* 755.3
lime-green *green* 260.7
limekiln *ceramic workshop and tools* 129.8
limelight *stage lighting* 136.20, *publicity* 173.7, *electric light* 246.6
limen *sensitivity* 212.2
limerick Poem or Verse Forms 139
Limestone Breeds of Sheep 16
limestone *masonry* 14.22, *fertilizer* 16.9
limewater *water* 557.1
limey Nicknames for Inhabitants 61
limey [Brit inf] *naval person* 77.25
limey [Inf] *figurative usage* 44.4
liminal *interfacial* 616.4
limit 620.1, 620.7, 761.4, 773.7, **830.13**; *mathematical function* 6.27, *differentiation* 6.29, *stipulate* 89.11, *be insufficient* 998.9, *identify* 184.11, *specify* 340.14, *allocate* 474.5, *moderate* 521.7, *size* 579.1, *squeeze* 582.13, *narrow* 593.14, *summit* 600.1, *edge* 618.1, *border* 618.9, *limitation* 620.2, 830.2, *certain amount* 738.3, *quantify* 738.7, *make smaller* 747.8,

separator 753.5, *exclude* 764.7, *hinder* 826.15
limit, the *farthest point* 620.3
limitability *contractibility* 582.4
limitable *contractible* 582.11
limitation 620.2, 747.3, 830.2; *specification* 340.6, *legal property terms* 470.2, *squeeze* 582.3, *narrowness* 593.1, *degree* 739.1, *subtracted item* 749.2, *exclusion* 764.1, *defect* 806.4, *hindrance* 826.1
limitations *limitation* 830.2
limited 620.5; *provisional* 89.8, *not enough* 998.5, *conditional* 340.10, *temperate* 455.8, *propertied* 470.9, *corporate* 480.17, *moderate* 521.3, *local* 564.14, *undersized* 580.8, *squeezed* 582.9, *narrow* 593.8, *quantitative* 738.6, *gradational* 739.5, *excluding* 764.5, *commonplace* 800.17, *hindering* 826.12, *restrained* 830.9
limited-access highway *road attribute* 687.3
limited choice *choice* 382.3
limited company (Ltd) *company* 480.7
limitedly *narrowly* 593.17
limitedness *narrowness* 593.1
limited nuclear warfare *atomic warfare* 76.4
limited offer *positive stimulus* 508.5
limited options *choice* 382.3
limited partnership *company* 480.7
limited period *duration* 642.1
limited war *war* 76.1
limiting 773.17; *conditional* 340.10, *temperate* 455.8, *contracting* 582.10, *restraining* 830.8
limiting condition *specification* 340.6
limiting factor *limit* 620.1, *limitation* 830.2
limitless *huge* 579.14, *numberless* 795.8, *infinite* 798.5
limitlessly *hugely* 579.21, *infinitely* 798.10
limitlessness *infinity* 798.1
limitless resources *wealth* 485.1
limit marker 620.4
limit of endurance *fatigue* 820.1
limit oneself *be self-restrained* 455.10
limit one's speed *limit* 620.7
limits *edge* 618.1
limn *draw* 143.13, *describe* 202.15, *outline* 617.5
limner *visual artist* 133.6, *painter* 143.7, *drawer* 143.8
limnetic *lakelike* 568.5
limning (*act of*) *drawing* 143.2, *outline* 617.1
limnologic(al) *lakelike* 568.5
limnophilous *lakelike* 568.5
limnophobia Phobias 283
limo [Inf] *automobile* 687.6
Limoges or **Limoges ware** Ceramics 129
limonene *terpene* 12.20
Limousin Breeds of Cattle 16
limousine *automobile* 687.6
Limousin Half-bred Horse and Pony Breeds 159
limp *unemphatic* 201.2, *weak* 517.6, *be weak* 517.12, *inert* 519.2, *soft* 543.6, *slow motion* 693.3, *move slowly* 693.11
limpet *adherent* 755.4
limpet mine *bomb* 78.15

limpid *clear* 196.2, *transparent* 249.7, *simple* 363.6
limpidity *clarity* 196.1, 363.2, *transparency* 249.1
limpidly *clearly* 196.4, *transparently* 249.13
limpidness *transparency* 249.1
limping *ill* 517.8, *slow* 693.7
limply *inertly* 519.5, *softly* 543.18
limpness *lack of emphasis* 201.1, *weakness* 517.1, *softness* 543.1
Limpopo *Rivers* 570
limp-wristed [Inf] *of sexual nature* 20.17, *weak-willed* 517.10
limulus *extinct arthropod* 39.7
linchpin *supporting part* 605.3, *fastener* 754.7, *middle* 772.1, *gist* 799.4
Lincoln *Breeds of Sheep* 16, *American States* 564
Lincoln green *green* 260.7
Lincoln Longwool *Breeds of Sheep* 16
Lincoln Red *Breeds of Cattle* 16
lincture *or* **linctus** *dose of medicine* 115.3
linctus *mixed thing* 751.2
linden *Trees and Shrubs* 43
lindy *or* **Lindy Hop** *Dances* 135
line 6.35, 754.5, 774.2; *family tree* 65.3, *nobleness* 70.3, *armed force* 77.10, *part of poem* 139.9, *melody* 140.10, *written music* 140.21, *treatment* 143.6, *fishing tackle* 154.7, *golf shots* 156.4, *television set* 172.6, *approach* 209.3, *heat* 217.17, *stripe* 263.3, *tactics* 399.12, *merchandise* 482.6, *style* 537.1, *stuff* 577.12, *layer* 588.9, *Scientific and Technical Units* 589, *measuring instrument* 589.12, *piece* 590.2, *vertical* 602.3, *limit marker* 620.4, *wrinkle* 638.2, 638.6, *navigational aid* 690.6, *way* 691.1, *route* 691.2, *railroad* 691.8, *passage* 692.1, *direction* 697.1, *bearing* 697.2, *gradation* 739.3, *person remaining* 750.6, *part of writing* 760.6, *series* 770.3, *consecutiveness* 774.1, *procession* 774.6, *arrange* 774.14, *type* 777.4, *specialization* 779.3, *repair* 809.10
line [Inf] *empty talk* 362.5
lineage *family tree* 65.3, *nobleness* 70.3, *person of the past* 651.7, *person remaining* 750.6, *succession* 770.2, *line* 774.2
lineal *linear* 6.77, *family* 65.6, *consecutive* 774.7
lineaments *external appearance* 264.5, *nature* 624.5
linear 6.77; *functional* 6.73, *of leaves* 41.18, *pictorial* 133.8, *metrical* 589.15, *lengthwise* 590.8, *straight* 630.8, *consecutive* 774.7
linear algebra *algebra* 6.21
linear build *physical type* 1.8
linear circuit *circuit* 1.8.37
linear equation *equation* 6.25
linear extent *line* 6.35
linearity *line* 6.35, *straightness* 630.1
linearly *mathematically* 6.93
linear measure *line* 6.35, *measuring system* 589.4, *type of measurement* 589.8
linear motion *frequency* 10.6
linear perspective *treatment* 143.6
linear response *measurement* 10.67
linear scale *graph* 6.30, *scale* 589.9
linear strain *load* 14.14
linebacker *defense* 155.9
line call *huddle* 155.7

line cut *engraving* 144.3
lined *aged* 27.15, *heated* 217.15, *striped* 263.9, *loaded* 577.8, *coated* 588.7, *wrinkly* 638.4, *additional* 748.8
line dancing *Dancing Types* 135
line drawing *drawing* 143.4
line drive *batting terms* 147.6
line engraving *engraving* 144.3
linefeed (LF) *character* 15.18
line integral *differentiation* 6.29
line in the sand *limit marker* 620.4
line judge *football player* 155.15
lineman *telephone personnel* 169.14
line management *personnel management* 126.4
linen *Fabrics and Fibers* 130
linenfold *Architectural Elements* 134
linens *clothing* 100.1, *dry goods* 130.3
line of action 399.4; *way* 691.1
line of advance *route* 691.2
line of argument 329.3
line of attack *fencing movements* 153.3, *way* 691.1
line of battle *battle* 76.23
line of business *job* 122.3
line of credit *resources* 102.4, *credit* 487.1
line of direction *direction* 697.1
line of duty 433.3
line of least resistance *peace* 73.1, *submission* 421.1
line of reasoning *line of argument* 329.3
line of retreat *route* 691.2
line of sight *visibility* 244.1, *bearing* 697.2
line of succession *receiving* 473.1
line of symmetry *geometric figure* 6.39
line of type *typesetting* 173.4
line of work *job* 122.3, *line of duty* 433.3, *business* 480.6
line one's pocket *profit* 467.22, *get rich* 485.13
line printer *hardcopy device* 15.10
liner *coat* 588.3
lines *script* 136.7, 137.5, *sailboat parts and accessories* 150.4, *form* 624.1
line segment *line* 6.35
linesman *hockey player* 158.8, *soccer participant* 163.4, *tennis participant* 165.6
line spectrum *emission* 10.56
lineup *sportsman* 145.4, *baseball team* 147.2, *pool* 149.3, *order* 765.1, *arrangement* 767.1, *consecutiveness* 774.1, *list of names* 785.7
line up 765.24; *align* 6.92, *order* 765.18, *arrange* 767.18, 774.14
line up for *wait* 356.8
line up with *join with* 827.15
linewoman *telephone personnel* 169.14
linger *wait* 658.12, *hesitate* 693.12
lingerer *plodder* 693.6
lingerie *underwear* 100.22
lingering 693.4; *resonant* 236.6, *delayed* 693.10
lingeringly *slowly* 693.14
lingering note *resonance* 236.1
lingo *nonstandard language* 5.7, *jargon* 5.21, *vernacular* 205.8
lingua franca *international language* 5.8
lingual *linguistic* 5.34, *spoken* 205.13
linguine *pasta* 90.31
linguist 5.3; *interpreter* 365.6

linguistic 5.34, 361.9; *spoken* 205.13
linguistically 5.44; *orally* 205.21, *stylistically* 537.11
linguistic analysis *Philosophical Schools of Thought* 4, *Linguistic Studies* 5
linguistic analyst *Philosophical Schools of Thought* 4, *linguist* 5.3
linguistician *linguist* 5.3
linguistics 5.1; *meaning* 361.1, *science of interpretation* 365.5
linguistic scholar *linguist* 5.3
linguistic science *linguistics* 5.1
linguistic scientist *linguist* 5.3
linguistic sign 183.10
linguistic theory 5.2
linguistic time 639.6
linguistic universal *international language* 5.8
liniment *balm* 115.11, *ointment* 562.8
lining *stuffing* 577.4, *layer* 588.1, *additional item* 748.3
lining paper *coat* 588.3
link 752.18; *alliance* 64.2, *merge* 64.21, *incandescent light* 246.5, *meet* 586.15, *span* 592.12, *relatedness* 727.1, *relate to* 727.9, *linkage* 752.3, *joint* 752.7, *unite* 752.14, *connection* 754.1, *means of connection* 754.4, *connect* 754.13, *combine* 757.9, *component* 760.3, *concatenate* 774.13
linkage 752.3; *cell division* 13.17, *relatedness* 727.1, *adhesion* 755.1
linked *accessible* 691.13, *related* 727.6, *connected* 754.11, *adhesive* 755.5, *combinatory* 757.6, *included* 763.4
linked list *data-related concepts* 15.23, *programming concepts* 15.24
linked turn *snowboarding* 162.11
linker *system software* 15.13
linking *association of ideas* 108.31, *meeting* 586.10, *junction* 609.5, *connection* 754.1
links *sports ground* 145.2, *golf course* 156.2
linksman *golfer* 156.7
link together *link* 752.18
link up *band together* 59.27, *link* 752.18
link with *unify* 752.15
linocut *engraving* 144.3
linoleate *fat* 12.7
linoleic *Common Fatty Acids* 12
linolenate *fat* 12.7
linolenic *Common Fatty Acids* 12
linoleum *floor covering* 613.13
linoleum block *engraving* 144.3, *material* 144.6
linonophobia *Phobias* 283
linotyper *printer* 173.10
Linotype™ *typesetting* 173.4
linseed *crop* 16.8
linseed cake *or* **meal** *animal feed* 16.12
linsey-woolsey *Fabrics and Fibers* 130, *rough thing* 544.2, *rough* 552.8
linsey-woolsey [Arch] *miscellany* 751.3
lint *powder* 553.9
lintel *Architectural Elements* 134, *supporting part* 605.3, *means of entry* 706.6
lint remover *cleaning tool* 111.10
Lion *Constellations* 7
lion *male animal* 32.15, *male mammal* 35.18, *game* 160.6, *courageous person* 284.8, *violent animal* 520.4, *celebrity* 799.6
lioncel *Heraldic Terms* 184

lioness *female animal* 33.15, *female mammal* 35.19
lionhearted *courageous* 284.9
lionheartedness *courage* 284.1
lionization *praise* 437.3, *promotion* 715.3
lionize *idolize* 83.16, *fete* 279.6, *salute* 405.13, *revere* 435.14, *praise* 437.16, *promote* 715.13, *make important* 799.14
lionized *worshiped* 83.14, *promoted* 715.8
lionizer *idolater* 83.7
lionizing *idolatrous* 83.13, *approving* 437.9
lionlike *carnivorous* 35.26
lions *Collective Names* 59
lion's mouth *danger* 811.1
lion's share *excess* 99.1, *large part* 579.3, *majority* 793.3
lion tamer *circus performer* 138.9
lip *sound* 141.15, *edge* 618.1
lip [Inf] *rudeness* 400.2, *bad manners* 411.2, *defiance* 416.1
lipase *enzyme* 12.11
lip color *cosmetics* 530.4
lipid *fat* 12.7
lipoamide *coenzyme* 12.12
lip off [Inf] *answer back* 334.19, *be insolent* 400.14
lipoid acid *vitamin* 12.13
lipolysis *fat* 12.7
lipoprotein *fat* 12.7, *protein* 12.9
lipotropin *Human Hormones* 12
Lippizaner *Horse and Pony Breeds* 159
lippy [Inf] *effusive* 207.6, *bad-mannered* 411.6, *disrespectful* 436.9
lipread *be deaf* 229.8, *translate* 365.16
lipreader *interpreter* 365.6
lipreading *translation* 365.4, *aid to the deaf* 229.3
lip rouge *cosmetics* 530.4
lips *mouth* 19.7, *speech organ* 205.4
lip service *ungenuineness* 192.2
lipstick *costume* 100.10, *red pigment* 257.2, *cosmetics* 530.4
lipstick plant *Flowers* 42
liquate *make fluid* 555.22
liquefacient *solvent* 555.9, *liquefied* 555.19
liquefaction *temperature* 10.29, *fluidization* 555.8, *dilution* 776.3
liquefactive *liquefying* 555.20
liquefiable 555.21
liquefied 555.19; *diluted* 776.8
liquefier *solvent* 555.9
liquefy *heat* 10.74, *solidify* 11.37, *be transparent* 249.11, *soften* 543.14, *make fluid* 555.22, *come unstuck* 756.7, *dilute* 776.14
liquefying 555.20
liquescence *fluidization* 555.8
liquescent *liquefied* 555.19
liqueur *alcoholic drink* 93.9, *sweet drink* 222.4
liquid *spoken letter* 5.15, *voiced* 5.37, *phase* 11.13, *status adjectives* 11.25, *transparent* 249.7, *propertied* 470.9, *fluid* 555.1, 555.14, *water* 557.1, *watery* 557.21, *nonadhesion* 756.1, *nonadhesive* 756.4
liquidambar *Trees and Shrubs* 43
liquid assets *personal estate* 470.6, *funds* 484.6
liquidate *slaughter* 30.21, *destroy* 186.10, 523.10, *cause to disappear* 265.7, *bank* 484.26, *pay off* 489.17, *convert* 670.11, *exterminate* 709.22, *annihilate* 773.22

liquidated *destroyed* 186.5, *paid* 489.11, *converted* 670.7, *annihilated* 773.16

liquidation *slaughter* 30.5, *destruction* 186.2, 523.1, *payment* 489.1, *conversion* 670.1, *annihilation* 773.4

liquidator *collector* 473.7, *destroyer* 523.6, *converter* 670.5

liquid conductor *electrical conduction* 10.33, *electricity* 14.34

liquid crystal *crystal* 11.14

liquid-crystal display (LCD) *photoelectricity* 10.32, *display* 15.9 *photoemission* 246.11

liquid diet *diet* 92.5, *dieting* 118.2, 595.3

liquid fuel *rocketry* 7.32

liquidity *resources* 102.4, *funds* 484.6, *fluidity* 555.5, *nonadhesion* 756.1

liquidity ratio *credit* 487.1

liquidize *cook* 91.10, *make fluid* 555.22

liquidizer 555.11; *cooking equipment* 91.6

liquidly *fluidly* 555.26, *wetly* 557.34, *noncohesively* 756.9

liquidness *fluidity* 555.5

liquid oxygen *gas* 106.6, *cooler* 218.4

liquid state *fluid* 555.1

liquor *alcoholic drink* 93.9, *alcohol* 121.5, *fluid* 555.1

liquor cabinet *cabinet* 101.8

liquored up [Inf] *drunk* 121.25

liquor store *drink provider* 93.15

liquor up [Inf] *get drunk* 121.35

lira *national coins* 484.11

lira da braccio *Musical Instruments* 142

lira da gamba *Musical Instruments* 142

Lisbon *Countries* 566

Liski *Breeds of Sheep* 16

lisle *fiber* 130.2

lisle stockings *legwear* 100.26

L-isomer *amino acid* 12.8

LISP *Programming Languages* 15

lisp *speech defect* 206.2, *have difficulty speaking* 206.9, *hiss* 237.1, 237.3

lisping *mode of speech* 205.6, *speech defect* 206.2, *inarticulate* 206.6, *hiss* 237.1

lissome *pliant* 543.7

lissomely *softly* 543.18

list 785.1, 785.11; *Architectural Elements* 134, *record* 185.1, 185.13, *register* 185.15, *selection* 382.1, *audit* 493.10, *division* 577.6, *itemize* 577.13, *obliqueness* 607.1, *be oblique* 607.10, *chronology* 646.2, *sail* 690.16, *slide* 714.17, *imbalance* 741.2, *unbalance* 741.8, *subsume* 763.7, *catalog* 767.7, *categorize* 767.21, *series* 770.3, *class* 777.1, *specify* 779.18, *number* 784.13

listed 785.9; *recorded* 185.12, *itemized* 577.9, *included* 763.4, *grouped* 765.11, *categorized* 767.15

listed building [Brit] *preserved thing* 815.10

listel *Architectural Elements* 134

listen *enjoy music* 141.19, *hear* 228.13

listenability *sound quality* 230.4

listenable *hearable* 228.12

listener *hearer* 228.7, *recipient* 473.5

listen in *hear* 228.13

listening *hearing* 228.1, 228.9

listening in *hearing* 228.1

listen to *hear* 228.13

listen with deaf ears *prejudge* 337.13

listeriosis *gastroenterological disease* 114.11

listing 785.8; *recordkeeping* 185.7, *oblique* 607.6, *unbalanced* 741.5, *grouping* 765.2, *categorization* 767.5, *class* 777.1, *classification* 777.2, *list* 785.1

list of characters *group* 18.13

list of dates *or* **events** 785.6

list of illustrations *book part* 174.5

list of names 785.7

list of tables *book part* 174.5

list price *price* 494.1

list requirements *limit* 830.13

lit 246.16; *accessible* 691.13

litany *prayer* 85.10

liter *General Units* 589

literacy *learnedness* 48.8, *learning* 348.3

literal 721.18; *written* 5.36, *correct* 350.4, *meaningful* 361.6, *translational* 365.11, *observant* 465.3, *naive* 821.3

literal interpretation *literalness* 721.9

literalism *correctness* 350.2, *literalness* 721.9, *imitation* 736.1

literalistic *literal* 721.18

literalistically *literally* 721.32

literality *type of meaning* 361.4, *literalness* 721.9

literalize *be literal* 721.25

literally 721.32; *linguistically* 5.44, *accurately* 350.6, *meaningfully* 361.16, *observantly* 465.6, *imitatively* 736.12, *perfectly* 805.21

literal meaning *type of meaning* 361.4

literal meaning *or* **sense** *literalness* 721.9

literal-minded *naive* 821.3

literalness 721.9; *religiousness* 81.2, *correctness* 350.2

literal translation *translation* 365.4

literal truth, the *correctness* 350.2

literarily *linguistically* 5.44

literary 139.15; *of language* 5.35, *educated* 48.19

literary agent *agent* 80.3, *book publishing personnel* 174.12

literary composition *book* 174.1, *work of art* 522.4

literary conversion *translation* 365.4

literary critic *literary person* 139.14, *book review* 174.13, *interpreter* 365.6

literary device 139.12

literary language *standard language* 5.6

literary magazine *magazine* 175.3

literary person 139.14; *descriptive writer* 202.10

literary scholar *literary person* 139.14

literary style *mode of expression* 537.3

literary work *book* 174.1, *work of art* 522.4

literate 348.8; *educated* 48.19

literati *literary person* 139.14, *academia* 348.6

literatim *imitatively* 736.12

literature 139.1

lithe *graceful* 527.4, *pliant* 543.7

lithely *softly* 543.18

litheness *softness* 543.1

lithesome *pliant* 543.7

lithic *petrographic* 8.58, *hard* 542.5

lithification *petrogenesis* 8.31

lithified sediment *sedimentary rock* 8.34

lithify 8.66

lithium *Chemical Elements and Common Allotropes* 11

lithograph *engraving* 144.3, *illustration* 187.2, *representation* 202.9

lithographer *visual artist* 133.6, *printer* 173.10

lithography *reproduction* 21.1, *craft* 133.2, *printing* 173.3

lithoid *or* **lithoidal** *hard* 542.5

lithophone *Musical Instruments* 142

lithosphere *Earth* 8.6, *earth zone* 8.7

lithospheric *solid-earth* 8.55

lithospheric plate *plate tectonics* 8.19

Lithuania *Countries* 566

Lithuanian Blackheaded *Breeds of Sheep* 16

Lithuanian Heavy Draught *Horse and Pony Breeds* 159

Lithuanian Red *Breeds of Cattle* 16

litigable *litigated* 54.22

litigant 54.4; *litigating* 54.21, *accuser* 442.3, *opposer* 828.9

litigaphobia *Phobias* 283

litigate 54.27; *debate* 319.13, *accuse* 442.8, *object* 828.18

litigated 54.22

litigating 54.21

litigation 54.1; *Phobias* 283, *debate* 319.2, *accusation* 442.1

litigator *arguer* 319.6

litigious *legalistic* 53.22, *litigating* 54.21, *argumentative* 319.10, 329.7, *aggressive* 418.12, *accusatory* 442.6

litigiously *in litigation* 54.34, *aggressively* 77.38, *accusingly* 442.11

litotes *understatement* 195.1, *underestimation* 344.1

litter *progeny* 21.8, *have young* 21.16, *young animal* 26.4, *give birth* 35.33, *Collective Names* 59, *waste product* 96.7, *dirt* 112.5, *means of transportation* 686.2, *residue* 750.2, *sprinkle* 776.15, *refuse* 802.5

litterae humaniores *literature* 139.1

littérateur *intellectual* 315.7

litter basket *cleaning tool* 111.10

litter bearer *transferrer* 685.4, *transporter* 686.4

litter bin [Brit] *vessel* 578.11

littered *dirty* 112.7

little 580.7, 580.12; *incompleteness* 98.2, *insufficient* 517.11, *short* 591.6, *infrequently* 662.4, *few* 796.1, 796.5, *sparse* 796.6, *sparsely* 796.11

little, a *to a degree* 739.11, *partly* 760.17, *few* 796.1, 796.5

little angel *child* 26.6

little at a time, a *by degrees* 739.10, *partly* 760.17

Little Bear *Constellations* 7

Little Bighorn *Rivers* 570

little bit 800.4

little black dress *dark thing* 247.3

little boy *male* 32.1

little boys' room *place for excretion* 25.11

little by little *slowly* 693.14, *by degrees* 739.10, *partly* 760.17

little cherub *child* 26.6

Little Colorado *Rivers* 570

little creature *little person* 580.5

Little Dipper *Constellations* 7

Little Dog *Constellations* 7

little extra *extra* 748.6

little extra something *advantage* 618.4

little finger *appendage* 19.5

Little Fox *Constellations* 7

little game *tactics* 399.12

little girl *female* 33.1

little girls' room *place for excretion* 25.11

little green men *sprite* 86.12, *figurative usage* 260.5

Little Horse *Constellations* 7

little imp *child* 26.6

Little Italy *New York* 567.6

Little League *baseball leagues and championship games* 147.8

Little League baseball *baseball* 147.1

Little League World Series *baseball leagues and championship games* 147.8

Little Lion *Constellations* 7

little mama *woman considered as a sex object* [Inf *and* Off] 33.8

little man *commoner* 71.1, *everyone* 778.7

Little Missouri *Rivers* 570

little monkey *child* 26.6, *troublemaker* 427.5

littleness 580.1; *selfishness* 444.1, *shortness* 591.1

little one *child* 26.6

little piece 580.4

Little Rock *American States* 564

little shaver [Inf] *young man* 26.8

little something, a *gift* 472.2

little space 580.6

little theater *theater* 136.16

little thing 580.3

little toe *appendage* 19.5

little way *short distance* 586.2

little white lie *falsehood* 192.6

littoral *coastal* 8.54, *oceanic* 571.7, *of landmasses* 572.12, *edge* 618.1, *edging* 618.5

littoral zone *coast* 8.13

lit up *clear* 244.6, *lit* 246.16

lit up [Inf] *drunk* 121.25

liturgical *ritualistic* 85.15, *ceremonious* 406.7

liturgical drama *dramatic style* 136.3

liturgical east end *church architecture* 134.11

liturgical garment *vestment* 84.11

liturgically *ritually* 85.21

liturgical music *sacred music* 140.3

liturgics *ritualism* 85.2

liturgiology *ritualism* 85.2

liturgist *ritualist* 85.14

Liturgy *Eucharist* 85.7

liturgy *public worship* 83.3, *ritual* 85.1, *ceremony* 405.3

lituus *Musical Instruments* 142

livable *fit for habitation* 60.19

live 28.17; *electric potential* 10.40,

living 13.28, electric 14.47, alive 28.13, inhabit 60.22, entertaining 138.12, bowls 151.7, newsworthy 171.8, active 414.13, in person 575.18, be present 647.7, exist 717.18, be in a state of 725.8
live a bohemian life not observe 466.9
live a charmed life be safe 810.20
live a life of ease be in comfortable circumstances 726.13, be prosperous 847.6
live alone be celibate 67.9
live ammunition ammunition 78.11
live and let live leave alone 413.13, be lenient 427.5, be disinterested 443.6, set free 829.17
live animation movie type 137.3
live apart separate 66.10
live a simple life be naive 821.4
live as man and wife marry 64.19
live a Spartan life be unadorned 424.10
live at the same time be simultaneous 649.6
live ball playing terms 148.4
live-bearing pregnant 21.12
live beyond one's means overspend 500.8
live bowl grip 151.4
live by one's wits be skillful 127.14, be cunning 822.5
live coverage news reporting 171.5, broadcast news 171.6, broadcast material 172.9
lived in inhabited 61.10
live for today live in the present 647.8
live from day to day be unprepared 389.14
live from hand to mouth be needy 95.18, be poor 486.14
live frugally be self-restrained 455.10
live high off or on the hog indulge oneself 456.10
live high on the hog be prosperous 847.6
live immoderately lack restraint 829.21
live in inhabit 60.22, 61.13, serve 69.11, reside 575.17
live-in residing 575.8
live in a bohemian way be independent 829.18
live in a dream world fantasize 360.15
live in a fool's paradise deceive 193.16
live in an ivory tower deceive 193.16, be incurious 322.5
live in another land be foreign 724.13
live in a Spartan way restrain oneself 830.15
live in a state of grace be innocent 449.10
live in a state of nature be naive 821.4
live in a whirl be busy 414.19
live in cloud-cuckoo-land deceive 193.16
live in clover be prosperous 847.6
live in hope hope 281.10
live in ignorance be naive 821.4
live-in lover man in the family 32.12, woman in the family 33.13, common-law wife 64.12, partner 794.9
live-in maid domestic servant 69.7
live in one's own little world deceive 193.16

live in peace pacify 74.9
live in poverty be needy 95.18, be poor 486.14
live in single blessedness be celibate 67.9
live in the lap of luxury be in comfortable circumstances 726.13, be prosperous 847.6
live in the past look back 651.18
live in the present 647.8
live it up [Inf] indulge oneself 456.10
live jack grip 151.4
livelihood employment 573.3, sustenance 825.3
live like a hermit be monastic 67.11
live like a monk or nun be monastic 67.11, restrain oneself 830.15
liveliness 28.12; emphasis 200.1, stimulation 221.4, gaiety 269.3, energy 414.4, vigor 518.1, adaptability 546.2, quickness of mind 694.4
live load load 14.14, weighing 538.4
lively 28.16; vitally 28.23, emphatic 200.3, stimulating 221.7, cheerful 269.7, imaginative 360.10, sociable 408.11, active 414.13, busy 414.15, vigorous 518.2, adaptive 546.6, mentally quick 694.8
liven up invigorate 28.22
live off sponge 401.13
live off the fat of the land be prosperous 847.6
live on be remembered 354.15, protract 669.9, continue to be 717.20
live on a budget be thrifty 499.5
live on air fast 118.8
live on a pittance be needy 95.18, be poor 486.14
live on bread and water fast 118.8
live on or off capital expend 491.11
live on credit be in debt 488.9
live on easy street be rich 485.12, be prosperous 847.6
live one's life live 28.17
live on immoral earnings prostitute 432.17
live on rations fast 118.8
live on the road be foreign 724.13
live out one's time or life protract 669.9
live plainly be self-restrained 455.10
live poorly be poor 486.14
liver internal organ 19.13, variety meat 90.30
liver chestnut horse by color 159.7
liver-colored brown 256.5
live relay broadcast material 172.9
liver fluke animal disease 34.10, parasite 39.18
liveried dressed 100.38
liverishness gastroenterological disease 114.11
Liverpool major British cities 567.7
Liverpool poets Western Literary Groups 139
liver sausage sausage 90.29
liverwort moss 46.4
livery uniform 100.9, riding equipment 159.9, clothing 184.6, formal clothing 406.5
livery horse saddle horse 159.5
live separately separate 66.10
live show show 138.4
live side by side socialize 2.14

live simply be self-restrained 455.10, refuse oneself 506.10
livestock 16.11; domestic animal 34.3
livestock farm farm 16.2
livestock farmer agriculturist 16.14
livestock farming 16.10; agriculture 16.1
livestock market market 483.1
live theater drama 136.1
live the life of Riley [Inf] be rich 485.12, be prosperous 847.6
live through feel 266.14, be restored 809.13
live to a ripe old age age 27.16
live to eat be greedy 119.4
live to fight another day survive 419.31, be safe 810.20
live together keep company with 794.17
live well be prosperous 847.6
live wire [Inf] doer 412.3, busy person 414.10
live with be impartial 338.11, keep company with 794.17
live within one's means be thrifty 499.5
livid deathly 29.15, dark-colored 247.7, dim 248.4, drained of color 252.6, pale 253.10, bluish 261.6, angry 302.11
lividity blueness 261.1, lividness 262.5
lividly bluely 261.11, angrily 302.24
lividness 262.5; darkness 247.1, blueness 261.1
living 13.28; of language 5.35, life 28.1, alive 28.13, pertaining to life 28.14, inhabiting 60.18, property 470.1, existing 717.11, sustenance 825.3
living, the humankind 18.1, living being 28.3
living and breathing, the living being 28.3
living apart separation 66.2, divorced 66.7
living as man and wife marriage 64.1
living being 28.3; living organism 13.10, animal 34.1
living fossil fossil fish 38.7, extinct arthropod 39.7
living hell adversity 848.1
living high on the hog prosperous 847.5
living in resident 61.11
living in a fool's paradise self-deception 193.2
living in an ivory tower self-deception 193.2
living in cloud-cuckoo-land self-deception 193.2
living in clover prosperity 847.1
living in one's own little world self-deception 193.2
living language spoken language 205.2
living matter 28.4
living on or off capital expending 491.8
living on borrowed time aged 27.15
living on immoral earnings prostitution 432.4
living organism 13.10
living person living being 28.3
living quarters habitation 60.2
living room room 60.9, scope 829.7
living soul person 18.8, living being 28.3

living space available space 563.6, scope 829.7
living thing living being 28.3, animal 34.1
living tissue living matter 28.4
living wage sufficiency 97.1
living world 13.9
Livny Breeds of Pigs 16
lixiviate purify 111.19, dissolve 555.23, water 557.29, leak 707.16
lixiviation fluidization 555.8, soaking 557.9, leakage 707.5
lixivium solution 555.10
Lizard Constellations 7
lizard 37.5
lizardlike reptilian 37.12
lizardlike reptile lizard 37.5
Ljubljana Countries 566
llama means of transportation 686.2
llano grassland 45.2, lowland 572.6
load 14.14, 14.49, 577.5; running water 8.10, work 14.10, program 15.29, store 105.1, heap 105.19, merchandise 482.6, displacement 538.3, make heavy 538.14, contain 577.10, transferred thing 685.6, freightage 686.3, transport 686.10, service 689.16, certain amount 738.3, addition 748.1, augment 748.13, fill 761.11, adversity 848.1
load-bearing wall 134.9
load-bearing capacity mechanical strength 516.2
loaded 538.10, 577.8; mechanical 14.44, stored 105.17, predetermined 384.4, transportable 686.7, additional 748.8, full 761.18
loaded [Inf] dead drunk 121.27, drugged 121.30, well-off 467.12, wealthy 485.8
loaded dice predetermination 384.1, inequality 741.1
loaded table plenty 90.4
loader system software 15.13, transporter 686.4
load factor miscellaneous aviation terms 689.9
loading preparation 388.1, displacement 538.3, transportation 686.1, transporting 686.8, miscellaneous aviation terms 689.9
loading the bases pitching terms 147.5
load line indicator 183.7, measuring instrument 589.12
load of crap [Inf] falsehood 192.6
load off one's mind or shoulders [Inf], a ease 275.1
loads [Inf] profuseness 795.3
loadstar magnet 700.3
loadstone magnet 700.3
load the bases play baseball 147.9
load the dice predetermine 384.8
load the gun prepare for action 388.18
load tightly make dense 540.9
load with augment 748.13
load with ornament ornament 532.12
loaf bread 90.10, have free time 413.15, be inactive 415.13
loafer inactive person 413.8, nonworker 415.11
loafing leisure 413.4, not participating 415.11
loam soil 8.42, dirt 112.5
loamy earthy 8.60, compressible 543.9
loan 475.2, 476.5, 488.3; benevolent act 305.5, lend 475.6, credit 487.1, 487.10, financial assistance 825.6, finance 825.31
loan agreement borrowing 476.1

---

loan application *borrowing* 476.1
loan capital *loan* 488.3
loaned **475.5;** *borrowed* 476.8
loanee *debtor* 488.6
loaner *lender* 475.3
loaning *lending* 475.1
loan maker *lender* 487.5
loan office *lending institution* 475.4
loan officer *lender* 475.3
loan repayment *loan* 488.3
loan shark *lender* 475.3, 487.5, *overcharger* 496.5
loansharking *lending* 475.1, *extortion* 496.4
loanshift *new word* 5.18
loan transaction *borrowing* 476.1
loan translation *new word* 5.18
loanword *new word* 5.18
loath *unwilling* 375.8, *be unwilling* 375.12
loathe *detest* 291.13, *hate* 300.11, *be malevolent* 306.12
loathed *detested* 291.11, *hated* 300.9
loather *hater* 300.6
loathing *antipathy* 291.2, *hate* 300.1, *malevolence* 306.1, *malevolent* 306.7
loathingly *with hate* 300.13, *malevolently* 306.14
loathness *unwillingness* 375.1
loathsome *unpleasant* 272.6, *detested* 291.11, *hateful* 300.10, *repulsive* 701.4
loathsomely *hatefully* 300.14
loathsomeness *hatefulness* 300.4
loath to *disinclined* 291.9
lob *tennis strokes* 165.2, *play tennis* 165.13, *throw* 696.4, 696.17, *send up* 715.12
Lobachevskian geometry Mathematical Concepts 6
lobbed *raised* 715.6
lobbering *or* **loppering** [Dial] *viscosity* 561.1
lobbied *motivated* 508.8
lobbing *throwing* 696.3
lobby *political organization* 50.4, *run for office* 50.10, *room* 60.9, *motivator* 178.11, 508.6, *persuade* 178.15, *manipulate* 508.12, *group influence* 512.6, *influence* 512.11, *front entrance* 621.2, *means of entry* 706.6
lobbyer *motivator* 178.11
lobbying *persuasion* 178.1, *inducement* 508.2
lobbyist *motivator* 178.11, 508.6, *activist* 412.4, *requester* 505.5, *influential person* 512.5
lobed *of leaves* 41.18
lobe-finned fish *fish* 38.5
lobelia Flowers 42
loblolly *semiliquid* 561.7
loblolly pine Trees and Shrubs 43
lobster *crustacean* 39.10, *food fish and shellfish* 90.20
local **328.8, 564.14;** *types of history* 3.2, *governmental* 49.24, *environmental* 60.17, *inhabitant* 61.1, *native* 61.12, 566.7, *municipal resident* 567.12, *urban* 567.14, *situational* 573.6, *near* 586.6, *internal* 611.9, *rail* 688.8
local [Brit inf] *drink provider* 93.15
local aid society *charitable organization* 305.4
local anesthesia *analgesic* 115.6
local anesthetic *analgesic* 115.6
local area network (LAN) *computer communications* 15.25, *linkage* 752.3
local call *telephone call* 169.11
local climate *climate* 9.35

local color *aspect of fiction* 139.5, *treatment* 143.6
locale *habitat* 60.1, *motion-picture studio* 137.7, *plot* 564.9, *location* 565.1, *situation* 573.1, *surroundings* 615.1
local election *election* 382.6
local government *government* 49.1
Local Group, the *galaxy* 7.5
local-interest *local* 328.8
localism *regional pronunciation* 205.7
locality *habitat* 60.1, *plot* 564.9, *location* 565.1, *situation* 573.1, *near place* 586.3
localize *limit* 830.13
localized *local* 564.14
localized war *war* 76.1
locally *environmentally* 60.26, *topically* 328.11, *regionally* 564.16, *municipally* 567.16, *geographically* 573.11, *nearby* 586.17, *inland* 611.19
local paper *newspaper* 175.2
local pronunciation *regional pronunciation* 205.7
local radio *radio broadcasting* 172.4
local tax *tax* 494.5
local television *television (TV)* 172.5
local time *time zone* 646.5
local train *train* 688.4
local wind *wind* 9.12
local worthy *important person* 799.5
locatable *found* 565.7
locate **565.9;** *discover* 345.11, *settle* 560.10, *situate* 573.10, *station* 601.12, *centralize* 612.11, *arrange* 767.18
located **565.6;** *discovered* 345.9, *found* 565.7, *situated* 573.5, *based* 601.9
locating **565.3;** *placing* 565.4, *centrality* 612.5
location **565.1;** *point* 6.34, *motion-picture studio* 137.7, *place of residence* 209.4, *discovery* 345.1, *situation* 573.1, *station* 601.5, *direction* 697.1, *state* 725.1, *arrangement* 767.1
locational **565.8;** *socioeconomic* 2.13
locational theory *sociological research* 2.2
locative *grammatical term* 5.29
loch [Scot] *lake* 568.1
Loch Ness monster Legendary Creatures 360
Lochy Lakes 568
lock *body covering* 19.4, *retention* 471.1, *retain* 471.7, *water system* 551.13, *obstruction* 584.2, *obstruct* 584.13, *lack of motion* 678.1, *make motionless* 678.8, *miscellaneous automotive terms* 687.14, *channel* 691.10, *intertwine* 752.19, *fastener* 754.7, *bind* 754.14, *safety device* 810.15
lock and key *fastener* 754.7
lock away *secure* 464.9, *protect* 810.21
lockbox *safe* 464.4
lockdown *imprisonment* 55.4
locked *obstructed* 584.8, *bound* 754.12
locked away *secure* 464.5
locked up *secure* 464.5, *storing* 578.19
locker *receptacle* 105.11, *box* 578.5
lock horns *fight* 422.23, *dispute* 463.9
lock horns with *contend* 422.22

lock in *detain* 471.9
locking *canoeing techniques* 150.11
locking carabiner *climbing equipment* 161.4
locking in *detention* 471.2
lockjaw *infection* 114.7
lock oneself in *shelter* 812.8
lockout **826.6;** *refusal* 506.1, *stop* 668.2, *exclusion* 764.1
lock out *have an industrial dispute* 57.20, *refuse* 506.8, *stop work* 668.11, *block* 826.17
locksmith *artisan* 123.13
lock, stock, and barrel *wholly* 738.9, 759.11
lock the barn door after the horse is stolen *be untimely* 660.8
lock the blade *canoe* 150.31
lock together *intertwine* 752.19
lockup *prison* 55.1, *prison cell* 55.3
lock up *imprison* 55.11, 454.23, *conceal* 181.12, *defend* 419.20, *secure* 464.9, *intertwine* 752.19, *protect* 810.21
lock up *or in enclose* 584.16
loco [Inf] *insane* 110.9
locomotion *physiology* 13.13, *motion* 677.1
locomotive *moving* 677.12, *train* 688.4, *towline* 699.5
locomotory *physiological* 13.29
Locrian mode *mode* 140.17
locum *helper* 275.5
locum tenens [Brit] *helper* 275.5, *substitute* 672.2
locum tenens *or* **locum** [Brit] *substitute* 613.17
locus (of a point) *point* 6.34
locust *insect* 40.1, *pest* 40.5, Trees and Shrubs 43, *greedy person* 477.11
locusts Collective Names 59, *agent of destruction* 523.7
locution *language* 5.4, *phrasing* 5.25, *utterance* 205.10
locutionary *phrased* 5.39
lode *ore* 11.23, *source of supply* 105.4, *layer* 588.1
loden Fabrics and Fibers 130
loden green *green* 260.7
loden jacket *jacket* 100.18
lodestar *indicator* 183.7, *motivation* 508.1, *magnet* 700.3
lodestone *magnet* 10.47, 700.3
lodestuff *ore* 11.23
lodge *mammal dwelling* 35.21, *association* 59.4, *house* 60.4, *hotel* 60.12, *natural habitat* 60.16, *take up residence* 60.24, *inhabit* 61.13, *make motionless* 678.8, *shelter* 812.4
lodge a complaint *accuse* 442.8
lodged *inhabiting* 60.18
lodger *resident* 61.6, *possessor* 469.10
lodging *habitation* 60.2, *resting place* 668.5
lodgings *habitation* 60.2, *provisions* 89.3
Lodi Apple Varieties 44
lodicule *grass plant* 45.3
loess *sediment* 8.29, *transferred thing* 685.6, *residue* 750.2
loft *room* 60.9, *storeroom* 105.7, *studio* 124.6, *play* 156.8, *send up* 715.12
lofted shot *golf shots* 156.4
loftily **404.30;** *arrogantly* 297.18, 400.21, *unselfishly* 443.9
loftiness *seriousness* 200.2, *arrogance* 297.2, 400.4, *airs* 404.2, *contempt* 436.3,

unselfishness 443.2, *height* 596.1, 715.4, *superiority* 744.1
loft ladder *ladder* 713.10
lofty **404.15;** *serious* 200.5, *arrogant* 297.9, 400.11, *contemptuous* 436.12, *unselfish* 443.5, *spacious* 563.13, *mountainous* 569.5, *high* 596.7, *promoted* 715.8
lofty ground *summit* 744.4
log *chronicle* 3.4, 3.15, *logarithm* 6.17, *timber* 43.3, *manage trees* 43.14, *fuel starter* 106.3, *wood* 131.3, *record book* 185.5, *record* 185.13, *measuring instrument* 589.12, *navigational aid* 690.6, *power* 783.6
Logan, Mount Mountains and Hills 569
logan *oscillator* 683.7
logarithm **6.17;** *power* 783.6, *calculation* 784.1
logarithmic *functional* 6.73, *fractional* 783.8, *mathematical* 784.9
logarithmically *mathematically* 6.93, 784.15
logarithmic function *mathematical function* 6.27
logarithmic scale *logarithm* 6.17, *graph* 6.30, *scale* 589.9
logarithmic series *sequence* 6.18
logarithmic spiral *curve* 6.38
logarithm tables *logarithm* 6.17
logbook *chronicle* 3.4, *record book* 185.5
log cabin *house* 60.4
loge *auditorium* 136.17
loggan *oscillator* 683.7
logged *chronicled* 3.12, *joined* 131.8, *recorded* 185.12
logger *forester* 43.7, *woodworker* 131.4
loggia Architectural Elements 134, *passage* 691.5
logging *tree management* 43.6, *wood* 131.3
logging stone *oscillator* 683.7
logic Branches of Philosophy 4, *way of thinking* 317.4, *reasoning* 319.2, *logical argument* 329.2
logical **6.83, 329.9;** *rational* 4.15, 319.8, *intellectual* 315.8, *reasoning* 317.6
logical argument 329.2
logical connective *mathematical logic* 6.60
logical expression *mathematical logic* 6.60
logical formula *mathematical logic* 6.60
logical impossibility *impossibility* 837.1
logically **329.17;** *philosophically* 4.23, *rationally* 4.25, *mathematically* 6.93, *intelligently* 315.14, *thoughtfully* 317.13, *reasonably* 319.15
logical operation *operation* 6.12, *mathematical logic* 6.60
logical operator *mathematical symbol* 6.11, *mathematical logic* 6.60
logical order *hierarchy* 765.3
logical outcome *effect* 676.1
logical positivism Philosophical Schools of Thought 4
logical positivist Philosophical Schools of Thought 4
logical process *reasoning* 319.2
logical product *mathematical logic* 6.60
logical proposition *mathematical logic* 6.60

logical reasoning *reasoning* 6.61
logical sum *mathematical logic* 6.60
logical thought *reasoning* 319.2
logical value *mathematical logic* 6.60
logic chopper *sophist* 330.6
logic-chopping *sophistic* 330.7
logic circuit *circuit* 14.37
logician *philosopher* 4.9, *reasoner* 319.5
logicize *reason* 319.11, *discuss* 329.12
login *computing terms* 15.22
log in *program* 15.29
logistic *curve* 6.38
logistics *military affairs* 58.1, *art of war* 76.16, *naval commands* 77.19, *navy specialties* 77.24, *tactics* 399.12
logjam *delay* 658.3, *stop* 668.2, *stalemate* 740.3, *snag* 824.8
log jam *inaction* 413.1, *obstacle* 826.2
log-line knot *nautical speed* 690.11
Logo *Programming Languages* 15
logo *or* logotype *means of identification* 184.3
logoff *computing terms* 15.22
log off *program* 15.29
logomachize *discuss* 4.22, 329.12
logomachy *philosophical argument* 4.5
logomancy *divination* 86.5
logomania *talkativeness* 207.1
logometric *fractional* 783.8
logon *computing terms* 15.22
log on *program* 15.29
logophile *linguist* 5.3
logophobia *Phobias* 283
logorrhea *diffuseness* 199.1, *power of speech* 205.5, *talkativeness* 207.1
Logos *God the Son* 82.9
logout *computing terms* 15.22
log out *program* 15.29
logroll *exchange* 673.5
logroller *politician* 50.7
logrolling *exchange* 673.1, *mutual relationship* 827.3
log scale *scale* 589.9
log table *calculator* 784.5
log tables *logarithm* 6.17
logwood *Trees and Shrubs* 43
Lohi *Breeds of Sheep* 16
loin *veal* 90.25, *pork* 90.26, *lamb* 90.27
loincloth *underwear* 100.22
Loire *Rivers* 570
loiter *wait* 658.12, *hesitate* 693.12
loiterer *plodder* 693.6
loitering *lingering* 693.4, *delayed* 693.10
loiteringly *slowly* 693.14
Lokai *Horse and Pony Breeds* 159
Lokayata *Philosophical Schools of Thought* 4
Lokayatika *Philosophical Schools of Thought* 4
Loki *Deities* 82, *evil spirit* 446.4
loll *take it easy* 819.3
lollapalooza [Inf] *good thing* 445.9
lolling *not participating* 415.11
lollipop *sweets* 90.39
lollygag [Inf] *communicate love* 299.25, *hesitate* 693.12
lollygagging [Inf] *communication of love* 299.6, *lingering* 693.4, *delayed* 693.10
Lomami *Rivers* 570
Lomé *Countries* 566
loment *botanical fruit* 44.2
Lomond, Ben *Mountains and Hills* 569
Lomond, Loch *Lakes* 568

London 567.8, *Countries* 566, *major British cities* 567.7
London Bridge *Children's and Party Games* 167
lone *solitary* 782.17, *one* 788.10, *alone* 788.15
loneliness *Phobias* 283, *separation* 409.3, *setting apart* 753.2, *aloneness* 788.5
lonely 409.8; *unjoined* 753.9, *alone* 788.15
lonely hearts club *matchmaker* 64.13
lonely hearts column *matchmaker* 64.13
lonely pride *unsociability* 409.1
loneness *aloneness* 788.5
lone pair *chemical bond* 11.6
loner 788.8; *unsocial person* 409.5, *individualist* 756.3, *hermit* 782.9, *freethinker* 829.10
Lone Ranger *Notable Friendships* 62
lonesome *lonely* 409.8, *alone* 788.15
lonesomeness *aloneness* 788.5
lone wolf [Inf] *one who conceals* 181.7, *unsocial person* 409.5, *individualist* 756.3, *hermit* 782.9, *loner* 788.8, *freethinker* 829.10
lone woman *single person* 67.5
long 590.6; *snowplow* 162.29, *diffuse* 199.3, *spacious* 563.13, *lengthwise* 590.14, *quantitative* 738.6
long ago *past time* 3.6, *historically* 3.17, *in the past* 651.20
long ago and far away, the *past time* 651.1
long and the short of it, the *conciseness* 198.1
longanimity *forgivingness* 312.3
longanimous *forgiving* 312.4
long arm of the law *law* 53.1, *law enforcement agency* 53.7
long-awaited *expected* 356.5
longboat *Ships and Boats* 690
longbow *Historical Missile Weapons* 78, *agent of destruction* 523.7
long bread [Inf] *money* 485.2
long-case clock *Timepieces and Timers* 646
long chalk [Brit inf] *great distance* 585.2
longcloth *Fabrics and Fibers* 130
long-course *swimming* 164.12
long-course pool *swimming place* 164.9
long curls *coiffure* 530.8
long-distance *speed-skating* 162.33, *swimming* 164.12, *away* 585.6
long-distance call *telephone call* 169.11
long-distance communication *communications* 169.1
long-distance racing *speed skating* 162.20, *long-distance running* 166.4
long-distance riding *equestrianism* 159.8
long-distance running 166.4, *Sporting Activities* 145
long-distance swimmer *swimmer* 164.11
long-distance swimming *swimming* 164.1
long division *division* 6.16
long dozen *eleven to nineteen* 792.7
long-drawn-out *diffuse* 199.3, *pompous* 404.18, *lengthened* 590.10

long dress *formal clothing* 406.5
long drink *size of drink* 93.3, *drink* 121.6
long drink of water [Inf] *big person* 579.10, *thin person* 595.4, *tall person* 596.6
long duration 642.3; *continuance* 669.3
long-duration disordered personality *personality disorder* 108.7
long-eared *eared* 228.10
longed for *desired* 288.10, *liked* 290.6
longer *long* 590.6
longer endurance *advance* 467.3
longest *long* 590.6
longevity *age* 27.1, *life cycle* 28.7, *health* 113.1
long face *sign of sullenness* 304.2
long-faced *depressed* 270.5, *serious* 278.4, *sullen* 304.8
long fiber-reinforced polymers *chemical process industries* 14.26
long-focus lens *lens* 132.11
long for *be unsatisfied* 98.10, *aspire* 281.13, *desire* 288.17, 299.24, *like* 290.8, *envy* 314.7
long game *golf shots* 156.4
long gone *dead* 29.11
long-grain rice *rice* 90.32
long green [Inf] *money* 485.2
long habit *habit* 397.1
long haul *work* 122.1, *great distance* 585.2
long home *burial place* 31.7
Longhorn *Breeds of Cattle* 16
long horse *pommel horse* 157.7
long hot summer *hot weather* 217.6
long hundred *hundreds* 792.9
long hundredweight [Brit] *General Units* 589
longing *aspiration* 281.3, *aspiring* 281.8, *desire* 288.1, *desirous* 288.13, *liking* 290.1, 290.4, *sexual love* 299.3, *envious* 314.4
longing for *envy* 314.1
longingly *desirously* 288.26, *admiringly* 290.11, *enviously* 314.11
long in the tooth *middle-aged* 27.14
longish *long* 590.6
Long Island *Islands* 572
longitude *exact location* 565.2, *situation* 573.1, *coordinates* 589.6, *length* 590.1
longitudinal *lengthwise* 590.8
longitudinal dune *dune* 8.43
longitudinal line *dividing line* 740.6
longitudinally *lengthwise* 590.14
longitudinal strain *load* 14.14
longitudinal wave *wave* 10.11, 683.4
long johns [Inf] *underwear* 100.22
long jump *jumping* 166.11
long jumping *Sporting Activities* 145
long-lasting 590.7; *tough* 547.6, *lasting* 639.9, 642.4, *permanent* 667.2, *stable* 674.3
long-lastingness *continuation* 642.2
longleaf pine *Trees and Shrubs* 43
long-legged *long* 590.6, *tall* 596.9
long life *health* 113.1
long-life food *preserved thing* 815.10
long-limbed *tall* 596.9
longliner *Ships and Boats* 690

long-lived *pertaining to life* 28.14, *long-lasting* 590.7, *lasting* 642.4
long loser *billiards play* 149.2
long-lost *losing* 468.9
long moss *moss* 46.4
longness 590.3
long note *tempo* 140.22
long odds *gambling* 167.4, *remote possibility* 836.4, *improbability* 839.1, *poor chance* 842.8
long on looks *attractive* 529.8
long on-off *billiards play* 149.2
long pants *pants* 100.14
long pass *soccer play* 163.5
long past *antiquarian* 651.13
long period *chemical element* 11.3
long range *distance* 585.1
long-range *away* 585.6, *long-lasting* 590.7, *transportable* 686.7
long-range forecast *weather forecast* 9.4
long-range plan *plan* 357.2, 387.1
long row to hoe *difficult task* 824.3
long run *theatrical performance* 136.13, *great distance* 585.2, *future time* 650.1
longship *historical warships* 77.22, *Ships and Boats* 690
longshore current *ocean current* 8.15
long shot *composition* 132.17, *great distance* 585.2, *remote possibility* 836.4, *improbability* 839.1, *poor chance* 842.8
long-sighted *foreseeing* 357.5
long-sightedly *foresightedly* 357.10
long-sightedness *foresight* 357.1
long since *in the past* 651.20
long ski *ski equipment* 162.10
long sleeve *part of garment* 100.27
long-sleeved shirt *shirt* 100.13
long snapper *special team* 155.11
longsome *lengthened* 590.10
longsomely *at length* 590.15
longsomeness *lengthening* 590.4
long splice *Knots, Bends, Hitches, Splices* 754
longstanding *long-lasting* 590.7, *lasting* 642.4, *olden* 653.11, *unfailing* 667.3
longstanding client *creature of habit* 397.8
long story made short *outline* 617.1
long-suffering *forgivingness* 312.3, *forgiving* 312.4, *lenient* 423.3
long-sufferingly *forgivingly* 312.13
long term *future time* 650.1
long-term *long-lasting* 590.7, *lasting* 642.4
long-term forecast *weather forecast* 9.4
long-term loan *loan* 475.2
long-term plan *plan* 387.1
long-term soldier *soldier* 77.4
longtime *long-lasting* 590.7
long time *long duration* 642.3
long to *enjoy* 290.9
long ton *General Units* 589
long trail *great distance* 585.2
longueur *boring thing* 296.3
long underwear *underwear* 100.22
long-waisted *long* 590.6
long waits *Phobias* 283
long wave *radio transmission* 172.3
long wave (LW) *radio frequency* 661.3
long way *great distance* 585.2

long way around *deviating course* 698.2
long way off or **away, a** *distantly* 585.11
long while *long duration* 642.3
long-winded *diffuse* 199.3, *talkative* 207.5, *boring* 296.6, *lengthy* 590.9
long-windedly *diffusely* 199.7, *boringly* 296.10, *at length* 590.15
long-windedness *diffuseness* 199.1, *power of speech* 205.5, *talkativeness* 207.1, *boringness* 296.2, *inelegance of expression* 528.4, *longness* 590.3
long-winded person *boring person* 296.4
longwise or **longways** *lengthwise* 590.8, 590.14
long word *word* 5.17
Lonk *Breeds of Sheep* 16
loo *Card Games* 168
loo [*Brit inf*] *place for excretion* 25.11, *room* 60.9
looby *unskilled person* 128.3
loofah *cleaning tool* 111.10
look 242.7, 242.21; *inside information* 170.4, *gesture* 183.5, 183.17, *external appearance* 264.5, *appear* 264.12, *pursue* 385.11, *conduct* 399.1, *decoration* 532.1, *fashion* 536.1, *appear outwardly* 610.14, *nature* 624.5
look after *serve* 69.11, 825.29, *practice medicine* 107.32, *manage* 126.10, *protect* 810.21, *preserve* 815.14, *support* 825.24
look after oneself *be healthy* 113.11
look a gift horse in the mouth *be ungrateful* 311.5, *reject* 383.10
look ahead 650.11; *have foresight* 357.8, *plan ahead* 387.13
lookalike *substitute* 672.2, 672.3
look-alike 730.4, 730.10; *actor* 137.13, *image* 187.3, *impression* 264.7, *counterpart* 733.5, *twin* 789.5
look a mess *be ugly* 531.5
look ashamed *appear guilty* 450.10
look as if one had seen a ghost *be afraid* 283.14
look a sight or **a fright** *be ugly* 531.5
look askance *look* 242.21, *react against* 291.15
look askance at *be dissatisfied* 274.7
look at *look* 242.21, *expect* 356.6
look away *be blind to* 243.19
look back 651.18; *recollect* 3.16, *remember* 354.12, *reverse* 671.9
look bad *be ugly* 531.5
look before one leaps *proceed with caution* 287.12, *have foresight* 357.8
look big *put on airs* 404.27
look black *predict* 358.14
look blank *be silent* 181.16, *be unintelligible* 364.11
look closely at *inspect* 242.22
look daggers at *gesture* 183.17, *look* 242.21, *be angry* 302.19
look danger in the face *face danger* 811.12
look deadpan *be unintelligible* 364.11
look down a gun barrel *face danger* 811.12
look down on *dislike* 291.12, *disdain* 297.14, *scorn* 436.19, *disapprove* 438.16, *be high* 596.15
look down one's nose at *look*

242.21, *dislike* 291.12, *disdain* 297.14, *scorn* 436.19, *disapprove* 438.16
looked for *foreseen* 650.8
look embarrassed *appear guilty* 450.10
looker *observer* 242.15
looker [*Inf*] *attractive female* 529.5, *attractive male* 529.6
looker-on *observer* 242.15, *attender* 575.6
look expressionless *be unintelligible* 364.11
look favorably on *be benevolent* 305.10
look fit to kill [*Inf*] *be beautiful* 529.11
look for *expect* 356.6, *foresee* 357.9, *intend* 374.8, *be prepared* 388.17, *think likely* 838.10
look for a disagreement *pick a fight* 463.10
look for a needle in a haystack *attempt the impossible* 837.10
look for a short cut *do easily* 823.16
look for a welcome *approach* 704.15
look for the silver lining *hope* 281.10
look for trouble *pick a fight* 463.10
look forward to *expect* 281.12, 356.6, *promise oneself* 458.15, *look ahead* 650.11
look good *be beautiful* 529.11
look guilty *appear guilty* 450.10
look in *enter* 706.11
looking *gestural* 183.13, *seeing* 242.17
looking ahead *foreseeing* 357.5, *looking to the future* 650.4
looking back *recollection* 3.9, *retrospection* 651.3, *retrospective* 651.15, *reversion* 671.1
looking for *pursuit* 385.1
looking glass *reflector* 242.10
Looking-Glass Land *Imaginary Places* 360
looking guilty *appearing guilty* 450.7
looking out for number one *selfishness* 444.1, *egotistic* 444.5
looking to the future 650.4
looking up *improving* 807.14
look in on *visit* 585.16
look in one's eyes *conduct* 399.1
look into *philosophize* 4.19
look into a crystal *look ahead* 650.11
look in vain for *lose* 468.12
look kindly on *be auspicious* 847.8
look like *represent* 187.10, *appear* 264.12, *be similar* 733.12
look like hell or **the devil** *be ugly* 531.5
look like oneself again *get healthy* 113.12
look like rain *become dark* 247.9
look of power *authority* 425.3
look of reality *verisimilitude* 721.10
look ominous *predict* 358.14
look on *not act* 413.11, *lack authority* 515.12, *stand by* 575.15
look one in the face *be naive* 821.4
look one in the face or **eye** *be proud* 297.15
look one straight in the eyes *be naive* 821.4
look on the bright side *hope* 281.10
lookout *observer* 242.15,

watchfulness 325.5, *nautical person* 690.12, *surveillant* 810.12, *warner* 814.5
look out *be cautious* 287.11
look out! 814.12; *danger!* 162.39, *be careful!* 287.20
look out for *care for* 325.12, *wait* 356.8
look out for number one *be egotistic* 444.7, *indulge oneself* 456.10
look out the window *have free time* 413.15
look over *inspect* 242.22
look over one's shoulder *look back* 651.18
look real *seem true* 721.26
look right through *be discourteous* 411.7
looks *external appearance* 264.5
look-see [*Inf*] *observation* 242.5
look serious *be serious* 278.7
look sharp *be cautious* 287.11
look sheepish *appear guilty* 450.10
look sideways *look* 242.21
look someone in the face or **eye** *look* 242.21
look straight at *look* 242.21
look the other way *be blind to* 243.19, *be indifferent* 289.12, *shun* 386.14
look or **see through rose-colored glasses** *hope* 281.10
look to *impose a duty* 433.14
look to be *appear* 264.12
look to the future *have foresight* 357.8
look up *visit* 408.16
look up to *idolize* 83.16, *respect* 435.13, *revere* 435.14
look volumes *gesture* 183.17
look where you're going! *look out!* 814.12
look within oneself *introspect* 611.16
look young *be healthy* 113.11
loom *fabric-handling tool* 130.12, *rowboat parts* 150.15, *appear* 244.8, *become visible* 264.13, *be big* 579.18, *weaving* 609.2, *endanger* 811.13
loomed *interwoven* 609.6
looming *imminent* 657.9
loom large *be visible* 242.26, 843.16, *be big* 579.18, *be real* 719.10
loom up *be visible* 242.26
loon *water bird* 36.9
loon [*Inf*] *insane person* 110.5
loony [*Inf*] *insane person* 110.5
loony bin [*Inf*] *mental hospital* 110.6
loony tune [*Inf*] *insane person* 110.5
loop *programming concepts* 15.24, *program* 15.29, *contraceptive* 23.6, *ice-skating techniques* 162.16, *curve* 629.1, 629.6, *circle* 631.2, *circular thing* 631.3, *coil* 632.2, *convolute* 632.6, *orbit* 681.3, *ring* 681.9, *track* 688.2, *flight maneuver* 689.6, *maneuver* 689.14, *route* 691.2, *fastener* 754.7, *yoke* 754.8
looped *woven* 130.15, *curved* 629.4, *circular* 681.6
looper *larva* 40.9
loophole *legal injustice* 53.5, *expedient* 387.5, *fort* 419.13, *way out* 707.2, *defect* 806.4, *means of escape* 816.4
looping the loop *flight maneuver* 689.6

loop jump *ice-skating techniques* 162.16
loop knot *Knots, Bends, Hitches, Splices* 754
loopy [*Inf*] *insane* 110.9
loose *handle sailboat equipment* 150.30, *mountaineering* 161.9, *unemphatic* 201.2, *unrefined* 338.7, *erroneous* 351.11, *translational* 365.11, *free* 407.9, *unchaste* 432.10, *permitting* 502.5, *soft* 543.6, *changeable* 666.3, *wandering* 698.13, *separate* 753.7, *loosen* 753.14, *nonadhesive* 756.4, *unstick* 756.6, *divergent* 776.11, *generalized* 778.12, *escaping* 816.7, *make easy* 823.15, *unconditional* 829.14, *set free* 829.17, *liberate* 831.6, *indeterminate* 841.14
loose a line *handle sailboat equipment* 150.30
loose ball *playing terms* 148.4
loose bowels *defecation* 25.3
loose box *farm building* 16.4
loose cannon *destroyer* 523.6
loose end *nonachievement* 762.3
loose-fitting *nonadhesive* 756.4
loose-footed sail *sailboat parts and accessories* 150.4
loose impediments *golf course* 156.2
loose-knit *diffuse* 199.3
loose-limbed *pliant* 543.7
loosely *unemphatically* 201.4, *wrongly* 351.18, *freely* 407.12, *with permission* 502.10, *softly* 543.18, *separately* 753.22, *noncohesively* 756.9, *generally* 778.20, *excessively* 829.23, *indeterminately* 841.24
loosely packed *nonadhesive* 756.4
loose morals *sexual immorality* 432.2, *depravity* 448.2
loosen 753.14; *weaken* 517.13, *soften* 543.14, *ease* 543.15, 819.4, *unstick* 756.6, *liberate* 831.6
loosened *separate* 753.7
looseness *lack of emphasis* 201.1, *inaccuracy* 351.3, *freedom* 407.4, *weakness* 517.1, *softness* 543.1, *nonadhesion* 756.1, *nonspecificness* 778.2, *indeterminacy* 841.6
loosening *separation* 753.1
loosen one's grip *relinquish* 392.3
loosen up *ease* 543.15
loose off *shoot* 696.18
loose rocks *climbing dangers* 161.5
loose translation *translation* 365.4
loose woman 33.6; *sexually immoral person* 432.8
loosing *separation* 753.1, *liberation* 831.1
loot *take away forcefully* 477.19, *stolen goods* 479.4, *plunder* 479.16, *lay waste* 523.14
loot [*Inf*] *cash* 484.2
looter *raider* 477.10, *destroyer* 523.6
looting *plundering* 479.5, *stolen* 479.12, *havoc* 523.5
lop *cultivate* 17.19, *manage trees* 43.14, *shorten* 591.9, *take off* 749.7, *separate* 753.12
lope *ride* 159.16, *bodily movement* 677.11, *walk* 677.17, *be swift* 694.10
lop-eared *eared* 228.10
Lop Nur or **Lop Nor** *Lakes* 568
lopolith *igneous rock* 8.32
lopped *reduced* 749.5, *shortened* 762.6
lopper *garden tool* 17.7, 103.4, *thicken* 561.21

loppered *thick* 561.17

lopping *tree management* 43.6, *subtraction* 749.1

lopsided *clumsy* 128.6, *distorted* 627.6, *unbalanced* 741.5

lopsidedly *asymmetrically* 627.13

lopsidedness *distortion* 627.1, *imbalance* 741.2

loquacious *worded* 5.38, *informative* 170.10, *diffuse* 199.3, *speaking* 205.15, *talkative* 207.5, *conversing* 210.8

loquaciously *lexically* 5.46, *diffusely* 199.7, *talkatively* 207.9, *conversationally* 210.14

loquaciousness *talkativeness* 207.1

loquacity *wordiness* 5.23, *diffuseness* 199.1, *power of speech* 205.5, *talkativeness* 207.1

loran *flight control* 689.7, *position finder* 690.8

Lord *God* 82.6

Lord *or* **lord** *male title of address* 32.3

lord *master* 68.1, *nobleman* 70.1, *possessor* 469.10

Lord and Giver of Life *God the Holy Ghost* 82.10

lord and master *master* 68.1

lord and master [Arch] *married man* 64.10

Lord Fauntleroy *effeminate male* 32.8

lord-in-waiting *domestic servant* 69.7

lord it over *master* 68.17, *disdain* 297.14

lordliness *authority* 52.1, *majesty* 297.5

lordly *governing* 49.25, *authoritative* 52.9, 425.8, *masterful* 68.15, *aristocratic* 70.4, *aristocratically* 70.6, *majestic* 297.12

Lord Mayor [Brit] *leader* 68.3

Lord Nelson *Famous Lovers* 299

Lord of Lords *God* 82.6

lord of the bedchamber *domestic servant* 69.7

Lord of the Flies *devil* 446.5

lord of the manor *master* 68.1, *important person* 799.5

lord of the manor [Brit] *property owner* 470.7

Lord of Wisdom *God* 82.6

lord over *have authority* 52.13

lord paramount *master* 68.1

lords-and-ladies *Flowers* 42

Lord's day *holy day* 85.12, *ease* 819.1

lordship *aristocracy* 70.2, *possession* 469.1

Lord's Prayer *prayer* 85.10

Lord's Supper *Eucharist* 85.7

lore *tradition* 1.7, 653.5, *literature* 139.1, *learning* 348.3, *custom* 397.4, *cunning* 822.1

Lorelei *witch* 86.15, *tempter* 178.10

Lorentz–Fitzgerald contraction *Classical Physical Laws* 10

lorgnette *visual aid* 242.14

lorica *historic armor* 419.8, *animal covering* 613.15

lorimer *horse person* 159.14

lorn *lonely* 409.8

lorry [Brit] *truck* 578.10, 687.8, *means of transportation* 686.2

lorryload [Brit] *container(ful)* 738.2

Los Angeles *major US cities* 567.5

lose 468.12; *withdraw* 392.5, *sell at a loss* 482.19, *abolish* 523.11, *misplace* 574.20, *be inferior* 745.10, *decrease* 747.7, *be defeated* 846.18, *be in trouble* 848.13

lose a battle *be subject to* 832.12

lose a chance *lose* 468.12

lose an opportunity *lose one's chance* 660.10

lose badly *be defeated* 846.18

lose blood *bleed* 25.26

lose by a whisker *lose* 468.12, *be defeated* 846.18

lose color 252.7

lose consciousness *forfeit* 468.13, *be powerless* 515.11

lose contact with *lose* 468.12

lose control *be violent* 520.8, *deteriorate* 808.14

lose currency *grow old* 653.16

lose earnings *lose money* 468.15

lose everything *lose one's money* 486.15

lose face *act foolishly* 128.10, *become inferior* 745.11

lose faith in human nature *detest* 291.13

lose feathers *shed* 614.21

lose flavor *decay* 808.16

lose ground *go backward* 680.16, *slow down* 693.13, *deteriorate* 808.14

lose hands down *be defeated* 846.18

lose health *deteriorate* 808.14

lose heart *despair* 270.8, *be hopeless* 282.11

lose heat *become cold* 218.14

lose height *or* **altitude** *descend* 714.12

lose hope *despair* 270.8, *be hopeless* 282.11, *be disappointed* 293.8

lose interest *be indifferent* 289.12, *renounce* 392.4

lose interest in *lessen* 468.17

lose it *be unskillful* 128.8

lose its shine *tarnish* 248.9

lose leaves *grow* 43.15

lose momentum *slow down* 693.13

lose money 468.15

lose money on *sell at a loss* 482.19

lose not a moment *have no time to spare* 818.6

lose no time *hasten* 657.15, *have no time to spare* 818.6

lose one *be unintelligible* 364.11

lose one's bearings *go astray* 698.17

lose one's chance 660.10; *be late* 658.11

lose one's cunning *be unskillful* 128.8

lose one's feel *be unskillful* 128.8

lose one's fortune *need money* 848.14

lose one's freedom *forfeit* 468.13, *be subject to* 832.12

lose one's head *be foolish* 353.6

lose one's hearing *be deaf* 229.8

lose one's heart *be in love* 299.23

lose one's husband *or* **wife** *be widowed* 66.13

lose one's inheritance *need money* 848.14

lose one's life *die* 29.17

lose one's marbles [Inf] *become insane* 110.12, *lack intellect* 316.8

lose one's memory *lack thought* 318.12, *lose* 468.12

lose one's money 486.15

lose one's nerve *be a coward* 285.7

lose one's nerves *be unskillful* 128.8

lose one's powers of speech *have difficulty speaking* 206.9

lose one's rights *forfeit* 468.13, *be subject to* 832.12

lose one's sense of direction *go astray* 698.17

lose one's sense of smell *have no smell* 225.7

lose one's sight *be blind* 243.18

lose one's skill *be unskillful* 128.8

lose one's temper *become angry* 302.20

lose one's tongue *have difficulty speaking* 206.9

lose one's touch *be unskillful* 128.8

lose one's train of thought *digress* 775.13

lose one's voice *have difficulty speaking* 206.9, *lapse into silence* 208.8, *be silent* 231.3, *decrease* 747.7

lose one's way *go astray* 698.17

lose one's wits *become insane* 110.12

lose out *be unskillful* 128.8, *lose* 468.12, *fail* 846.12, *be defeated* 846.18

lose patience *become angry* 302.20

lose power *malfunction* 846.20

lose profits *lose money* 468.15

loser 468.8, 846.9; *unskilled person* 128.3, *hopeless person* 282.5, *subjected person* 832.5, *person in adversity* 848.9

lose repute *be disreputable* 371.5

lose sight of *lose* 468.12

lose someone 468.20; *accelerate* 694.14

lose someone's attention *make indifferent* 289.13

lose speed *slow down* 693.13

lose strength *be unhealthy* 114.29

lose taste *be tasteless* 220.6, *decay* 808.16

lose the baby *be infertile* 23.8

lose the battle *lose* 468.12, *lessen* 468.17, *be defeated* 846.18, *be in trouble* 848.13

lose the day *lose* 468.12

lose the election *lose* 468.12, *be defeated* 846.18

lose the game *lose* 468.12, *be defeated* 846.18

lose the match *be defeated* 846.18

lose the race *be defeated* 846.18

lose the scent *have no smell* 225.7

lose the thread *lose track of* 698.18, *be unrelated* 728.12

lose the upper hand *become inferior* 745.11

lose the vote *be defeated* 846.18

lose the war *be defeated* 846.18, *be in trouble* 848.13

lose time *be late* 658.11, *be untimely* 660.8

lose track of 698.18; *lose* 468.12, *misplace* 574.20

lose value *deteriorate* 808.14

lose water *leak* 816.11

lose weight 468.14; *eat less* 118.9, *abstain* 455.11, *lighten* 539.9, *become smaller* 582.14, *become thin* 595.15, *make smaller* 747.8

losing 468.9; *loss* 468.1, *misplacement* 574.6

losing balance *unbalanced* 741.5

losing battle *waste* 468.5

losing game *defeat* 846.7

losing general *loser* 846.9

losing ground *deterioration* 808.1

losing it *clumsy* 128.6

losing move *defeat* 846.7

losing one's feet *clumsy* 128.6

losing one's touch *clumsy* 128.6

losing person *loser* 846.9

losings *financial loss* 468.4

losing streak *loss* 468.1

losing the case *unfavorable verdict* 54.20

losing weight *dieting* 92.6, 118.2, *shortening* 582.2

loss 468.1; *wasting away* 96.4, *blacking out* 265.2, *affliction* 454.9, *ruin* 523.4, *absence* 576.1, *export* 707.7, *reduction* 747.2, *subtracted item* 749.2, *difference* 750.3, *omission* 762.4, *futility* 802.3, *impairment* 808.7, *leak* 816.6, *defeat* 846.7

losses *financial loss* 468.4

loss leader *enticement* 178.3, *financial loss* 468.4, *merchandise* 482.6, *bargain* 495.2, *positive stimulus* 508.5

loss-leading *unprofitable* 468.10

loss-making *unprofitable* 468.10, *decrescent* 747.6, *futile* 802.10

loss of battle *subjection* 832.1

loss of condition *ill health* 114.1

loss of consciousness *symptom* 114.3, *forfeiture* 468.2, *disability* 515.4, *fatigue* 820.1

loss of earnings *financial loss* 468.4

loss of face *indignity* 436.7

loss of faith *unbelief* 88.4

loss of fortune *insolvency* 486.2

loss of freedom *forfeiture* 468.2, *subjection* 832.1

loss of hope *lack of hope* 282.2

loss of innocence *depravity* 448.2

loss of interest *waste* 468.5

loss of life *death* 29.1

loss of memory *forgetfulness* 186.3, 355.1

loss of morale *moral deterioration* 808.3

loss of profit *financial loss* 468.4

loss of rights *forfeiture* 468.2, *subjection* 832.1

loss of strength *poor health* 517.3

loss of value *decrease* 747.1

loss of vision *blindness* 243.3

loss of voice *speech difficulty* 206.1

loss of weight 468.3

lost *disappeared* 265.4, *forgotten* 355.7, *impenitent* 452.2, *losing* 468.9, *misplaced* 574.13, *missing* 576.11, *indirect* 698.9, *incomplete* 762.5, *defeated* 846.11

lost and gone *over* 651.12

lost at sea *losing* 468.9

lost battle *defeat* 846.7, *downfall* 848.4

lost bet *unsuccessful thing* 846.8

lost cause *futility* 282.3, *defeat* 846.7

lost chance 660.3

lost child *the hunted* 385.7

lost connection *digression* 775.6

lost election *discarding* 383.3, *unsuccessful thing* 846.8

lost forever *over* 651.12

lost fortune *economic adversity* 848.6

lost from view *losing* 468.9

lost in amazement *at a loss* 468.11

lost inheritance *economic adversity* 848.6

lost in the distance *difficult to see* 245.4

lost in thought *thoughtful* 4.17, *concentrating* 317.7, *absent-minded* 324.6, *at a loss* 468.11

lost in wonder *wondering* 294.7

lost labor *overactivity* 414.9, *waste of effort* 802.4, *futility* 846.3

lost language *ancient language* 5.10

lost love *downfall* 848.4

lost melody *melody* 140.10
lost opportunity *lost chance* 660.3
lost sheep *loser* 468.8
lost soul *evil spirit* 446.4, *loser* 468.8
lost to sight *disappeared* 265.4
lost war *defeat* 846.7, *downfall* 848.4
lost-wax casting *sculpture* 144.1
lot *motion-picture studio* 137.7, *means of prediction* 358.10, *predestination* 384.2, *property* 470.1, *portion* 474.2, *limit* 620.1, *state* 725.1, *certain amount* 738.3, *luck* 842.3
lot, a *multitude* 795.1
lot acreage *plot* 564.9
Lothario *libertine* 32.7, *lover* 299.11, *charmer* 700.6
lotion *dose of medicine* 115.3, *balm* 115.11, *ointment* 562.8
lots *plenty* 97.2, *multitude* 795.1
lots of luck! *good luck!* 842.19
lottery *winnings* 492.5, *game of chance* 842.5
lotto *Board and Table Games* 167
lot to ask, a *undertaking* 391.1
lotus *Flowers* 42
lotus-eater *figurative usage* 44.4, *pleasure-seeker* 214.4, *visionary* 360.9, *nonworker* 415.4
lotus-eating *lack of motion* 678.1
Lotus of the True Law *other text* 81.19
loud 232.6; *hearable* 228.12, *strident* 238.4, *vociferous* 239.9, *gaudy* 251.12, *flashy* 404.17, *strong to the senses* 516.12, *indecorous* 528.8, *ornate* 532.10, *vulgar* 535.6, *accentuated* 843.11
loud breathing *loud sound* 232.2
loud cry *cry* 239.1
loud enough to wake the dead *hearable* 228.12
loud-hailer [Brit] *sound amplifier* 230.5
loud laughter *loud sound* 232.2
loudly 232.11; *stridently* 238.10, *vociferously* 239.18, *flashily* 404.32, *acutely* 516.18, *vulgarly* 535.10
loudmouth *discourteous person* 411.4
loudmouthed *shouting* 232.7, *vociferous* 239.9
loudness 232.1; *sound* 230.1, *hue* 251.4, *nonsense* 362.2, *flashiness* 404.4, *bad taste* 528.3
loudness level *sound propagation* 230.3
loud noise *loudness* 232.1
loud report *burst of sound* 232.4
loud sound 232.2
loudspeaker *sound amplifier* 230.5
loud-spoken *speaking* 205.15
loud tone 232.3
Lou Gehrig's disease *neurological disease* 114.20
lough [Irish] *lake* 568.1
Louisiana *American States* 564
Louis Quatorze *Furniture Styles* 101
Louis Quatorze style *Architectural Styles* 134
Louis Quinze *Furniture Styles* 101
Louis Quinze style *Architectural Styles* 134
Louis Seize *Furniture Styles* 101
Louis Seize style *Architectural Styles* 134
Louis Treize style *Architectural Styles* 134

Louisville slugger [Inf] *baseball equipment* 147.4
lounge *room* 60.9, *type of chair* 101.4, *be inactive* 415.13, *take it easy* 819.3
lounger *nonworker* 415.4
loungewear *informal clothes* 100.7, *informal clothing* 407.5
lounging pajamas *informal clothes* 100.7
lounging robe *informal clothes* 100.7
loupe *visual aid* 242.14
lour *become dark* 247.9, *be dim* 248.7, *sign of irascibility* 303.6, *frown* 303.15, *sign of irritability* 304.4, *be irritable* 304.14, *predict* 358.14
louring *dark* 247.5, *dim* 248.4, *frowning* 303.12, 304.10, *overcast* 304.11
louse *pest* 40.5, *dirt* 112.5
louse [Inf] *miscreant* 448.6
louse up [Inf] *be clumsy* 128.9, *blunder* 351.9, *err* 351.14, *hinder* 826.11
lousy *verminous* 40.13, *unclean* 112.8
lousy [Inf] *shoddy* 497.11
lousy with money [Inf] *wealthy* 485.8
lout *unskilled person* 128.3, *unpleasant person* 272.5, *malefactor* 306.6, *badly behaved person* 399.8, *discourteous person* 411.4, *vulgar person* 535.4
loutish *bad-mannered* 411.6
loutishly *rudely* 411.9
loutishness *bad manners* 411.2
louver *Architectural Elements* 134
lovability 299.5
lovable 299.20; *luscious* 214.8, *likable* 290.7
lovableness *lovability* 299.5
lovably 299.31; *likably* 290.12
lovage *Herbs and Spices* 91
love 299.1, 299.21; *divine attribute* 82.4, *tennis terms* 165.5, *good feeling* 266.4, *Phobias* 283, *desire* 288.17, *liking* 290.1, *like* 290.8, *term of endearment* 299.7, *loved one* 299.13, *be benevolent* 305.10, *courtesies* 410.3, *virtues* 447.2
love [Tennis] *zero* 786.1
love affair 299.9
love all [Tennis] *stalemate* 740.3
love and peace *agreement* 462.1
love a party *participate* 408.15
lovebirds *lovers* 299.12
love company *be sociable* 408.14
loved *beloved* 299.19
loved one 299.13
love food *be greedy* 119.4
love game *victory* 845.4
love good *be virtuous* 447.8
love-in-a-mist *Flowers* 42
love interest *stock part* 136.24
love letter *love token* 240.1
love-lies-bleeding *Flowers* 42
love life *sexuality* 20.3
loveliness *physical pleasure* 214.1, *pleasantness* 271.1, *beauty* 529.1
lovelorn *amorous* 299.18
lovelornness *lovingness* 299.4
lovely *luscious* 214.8, *pleasant* 271.5, *delightful* 271.7, *likable* 290.7, *lovable* 299.20, *attractive female* 529.5, *beautiful* 529.7
lovely build *attractiveness* 529.2
love lyric *love token* 299.8
lovely to behold *picturesque* 529.9
lovemaking *sexual intercourse* 20.9, *sexual love* 299.3, *courtship* 299.10

love match *type of marriage* 64.3, *courtship* 299.10
love music *enjoy music* 141.19
love nest *meeting place* 408.5
love of animals *feeling for animals* 34.11
love of language *language* 5.4
love of mankind *or* **humankind** *compassion* 305.2
love of one's country *love* 299.1
love of war *bellicosity* 76.15
love oneself *be egotistic* 444.7
love one's job *exert oneself* 122.11
love philter *eroticism* 20.7
love play *Phobias* 283
love poem *love token* 299.8
love potion *eroticism* 20.7
lover 299.11; *desirer* 288.9, *term of endearment* 299.7, *partner* 794.9
lover boy *boyfriend* 92.4
lover of language *linguist* 5.3
lovers 299.12
love scene *play part* 136.8
love seat *couch* 101.7
lovesick *amorous* 299.18
lovesickness *lovingness* 299.4
lovesome *lovable* 299.20
love song *song* 140.11, *love token* 299.8
love sonnet *love token* 299.8
love story *movie type* 137.3, *story* 139.4
love tap *communication of love* 299.6
love that dare not speak its name, the *sexual nature* 20.4
love the sound of one's own voice *be vain* 402.14
love to *enjoy* 290.9
love to distraction *be in love* 299.23
love to eat *be greedy* 119.4
love token 299.8
lovey [Brit inf] *term of endearment* 299.7
lovey-dovey [Inf] *amorous* 299.18
loving 299.15; *liking* 290.4, *benevolent* 305.7, *considerate* 325.7, *principled* 447.6
loving care *consideration* 325.2
loving couple *lovers* 299.12
loving cup *drink container* 93.13
loving-kindness *benevolence* 305.1
loving looks *communication of love* 299.6
lovingly 299.29; *admiringly* 290.11, *benevolently* 305.13, *ethically* 447.10
lovingness 299.4
loving touch *communication of love* 299.6
loving words *communication of love* 299.6
low 597.10, 597.26; *of language* 5.35, *weather system* 9.10, *faint* 233.6, *nonresonant* 233.7, *faintly* 233.11, *deep* 236.8, *hoarse* 238.5, *animal sound* 240.7, *make an animal sound* 240.7, *depressed* 270.5, *lowly* 298.9, *submitting* 421.3, *disregardful* 436.11, *cheap* 497.9, *shoddy* 497.11, *insufficient* 517.11, *ribald* 535.8, *short* 591.6, *lowered* 716.7, *inferior state* 745.3
low attendance *few* 796.1
low-beam headlight *safety light* 246.7
low birth rate *infertile state* 23.3
low blood pressure *symptom* 114.3, *cardiovascular disease* 114.13
lowborn *common* 71.3, *lowly* 298.9, 597.17
low bow *bow* 716.6

lowboy *cabinet* 101.8
lowbrow *ignorant* 349.5
low-budget *dramatic* 137.16, *cheap* 497.9
low-budget picture *movie type* 137.3
low-built *low* 597.10
low-calorie *edible* 92.20
low camp *comedy* 136.11
low-cholesterol diet *diet* 92.5
Low Church *Christianity* 81.5
Low-Church *denominational* 81.23
low-class *low quality* 745.7
low cloud *cloud* 9.17
low comedian *actor* 136.25
low comedy *comedy* 136.11
low-cut *stylish* 100.42, *low* 597.10
low definition *invisibility* 245.1, *murk* 248.2
low-definition *difficult to see* 245.4, *murky* 248.5
low-density *sparse* 796.6
lowdown [Inf] *inside information* 170.4, *evidence* 339.1, *the truth* 721.3
low down *villainous* 448.12, *low* 597.26
low ebb *lowest point* 597.5, *inferior state* 745.3
lower 597.14, 597.21, 716.12; *ranked* 6.72, *become dark* 247.9, *be dim* 248.7, *abase* 298.20, *be angry* 302.19, *sign of irascibility* 303.6, *frown* 303.15, *sign of irritability* 304.4, *be irritable* 304.14, *predict* 358.14, *desecrate* 436.24, *discount* 495.4, *vulgarize* 535.9, *deeper* 598.10, *deepen* 598.21, *make horizontal* 603.10, *descend* 714.12, *change by degrees* 739.8, *inferior* 745.5, *make smaller* 747.8, *pervert* 808.22, *warn* 814.8, *subordinate* 832.8, *subject* 832.10
lower animal *invertebrate* 39.1
lower atmosphere *atmospheric layer* 558.3
lower bound *set* 6.19
lower case *type* 173.5
lowercase *printed* 173.13
Lower Chamber *British government* 49.22
lower charges *make cheap* 497.14
lower class *social stratification* 2.7, *vulgar* 535.5, *inferiority* 745.1, *low quality* 745.7, *social class* 777.5
lower-class *socioeconomic* 2.13, *common* 71.3
lower classes, the *the poor* 486.7, *inferior* 745.4
lower criticism *criticism* 365.3
lowered 597.12, 597.18, 716.7; *abased* 298.13, *leveled* 603.8
Lower House *United States government* 49.21, *British government* 49.22
lowering 597.3, 716.1; *dark* 247.5, *dim* 248.4, *frowning* 303.12, 304.10, *overcast* 304.11, *deepening* 598.4, 598.14, *descent* 714.1, *sinkage* 714.2, *descending* 714.9, *lowered* 716.7
lowering the body *funeral* 31.4
lower jaw *mouth* 19.7
lower limit *differentiation* 6.29, *limit* 620.1, *certain amount* 738.3
lower middle class *middle class* 772.6
lowermost [Brit] *lower* 597.14, *bottom* 601.6
lower off *mountaineer* 161.10
lower oneself *humble oneself* 298.18, *be disreputable* 371.5

lower one's sights *relinquish* 392.3

lower one's voice *sound faint* 233.8

lower orders *common people* 71.2, *inferior* 745.4

lower plant **41.4**

lower standards *debase* 716.16

lower status *subjection* 832.1

lower than low *lowered* 597.18

lower the body *bury* 31.10

lower the flag **716.23**

lower the lights *make dim* 248.8

lower the official rate of exchange *devalue the currency* 490.14

lower the price *make cheap* 497.14

lower the standard *lower the flag* 716.23

lower the tone *vulgarize* 535.9

lower the volume *mute* 233.9

lower world *evil place* 446.6

lowest *ranked* 6.72, *lower* 597.14, *deeper* 598.10, *bottom* 601.6, *inferior* 745.5

lowest common denominator (LCD) *clarity* 363.2, *average* 778.4

lowest common multiple (LCM) *multiplication* 6.15

low esteem *contempt* 436.3

low estimation *disapproval* 438.1

lowest level *lowest point* 597.5, *base* 601.1

Lowestoft ware *Ceramics* 129

lowest point **597.5**; *base* 601.1, *inferior state* 745.3, *zero level* 786.3

lowest stratum *lowest point* 597.5, *base* 601.1

low-fat *edible* 92.20, *health-giving* 113.6

low-fat diet *diet* 92.5

low-fat food *food* 90.1

low-fat milk *milk* 93.5

low gear *slow motion* 693.3

low-grade *shoddy* 497.11, *substandard* 597.19, *low quality* 745.7

low-grade rock *metamorphic rock* 8.36

low income *poverty* 486.1

lowing *animal sound* 240.1, *ululant* 240.4

low-inside *fencing movements* 153.3, *fencing* 153.6, *on guard* 153.8

low in tone *dark* 254.6

low IQ *lack of intellect* 316.1

low key *composition* 132.17

low-key *understated* 195.8, *moderate* 521.3

lowland **572.6, 597.15**; *regional* 564.12

Lowlands *regions of the British Isles* 564.8

lowlands **597.6**; *regions* 564.2

low language *vulgarism* 5.20

low-level *secondary* 800.15

low-level bombing *air attack* 418.4

low-level cloud *cloud cover* 9.18

low-level flying *flight maneuver* 689.6

low-level language *programming language* 15.16

low-level radioactive waste *nuclear power production* 514.10

low-level waste *nuclear problem* 10.62

lowlife *miscreant* 448.6, *inferior* 745.4

lowlights *composition* 132.17

lowliness **298.2, 597.8**;

unpleasantness 501.2, *inferiority* 745.1

lowly **298.9, 597.17**; *common* 71.3, *submitting* 421.3, *unpleasant* 501.5, *inferior* 745.5

low-lying *low* 597.10, *lowland* 597.15

low man on the totem pole [Inf] *inferior* 745.4, *subordinate* 832.3

Low Mass *Eucharist* 85.7

low mental age *lack of intellect* 316.1

low-necked *stylish* 100.42, *low* 597.10

lowness **597.1**; *deepness* 236.3, *hoarseness* 238.2, *depression* 270.2, *tawdriness* 501.5, *shortness* 591.1, *inferior state* 745.3

low note *tone* 140.24, *deepness* 236.3

low on *insufficient* 98.4

low opinion *contempt* 436.3, *disapproval* 438.1

low-outside *fencing movements* 153.3, *fencing* 153.6, *on guard* 153.8

low-paid *poor* 486.8

low pay *incompleteness* 98.2, *poverty* 486.1

low pitch *tone* 140.24

low-pitched *deep-sounding* 598.19

low point *inferior state* 745.3

low post *playing terms* 148.4

low pressure *sparseness* 541.1

low-pressure *sparse* 541.3

low-pressure area *weather system* 9.10

low-priced *cheap* 497.9, 800.16

low profile *invisibility* 245.1

low-profile *reserved* 195.11, *difficult to see* 245.4

low quality **745.7**

low-quality *shoddy* 497.11, *substandard* 597.19

low rank *lowliness* 597.8

low-ranking *lowly* 597.17

low rate *fee* 494.3

low rating *disapproval* 438.1

low relief *relief carving* 144.2

low resolution *separation* 753.1

low-resolution *separable* 753.11

low-rise *low* 597.10

Lowry–Brønsted acid *acid* 11.10

Lowry–Brønsted base *base* 11.11

low-salt *health-giving* 113.6

low-salt *or* low-sodium food *food* 90.1

low-spirited *conditional* 725.7

low spirits *depression* 270.2, *state of mind* 725.5

low-standing *inferior* 745.5

low-statured *low* 597.10

low tar *tobacco* 121.23

low-tar *tobacco* 121.33

low-tech [Inf] *productive* 522.11

low technology *manufacture* 522.2

low-technology *productive* 522.11

low temperature *cold* 218.1, Fields of Measurement 589

low-temperature physics Fields of Modern Physics 10

low tide *tide* 8.17, 571.2

low-toned *dark* 254.6

low turnout *few* 796.1

low vacuum *surface chemistry* 11.20

low visibility *murk* 248.2

low voice *undercurrent of sound* 233.3, *deepness* 236.3

low voltages Fields of Measurement 589

low volume *faintness of sound* 233.1

low water *tide* 571.2

low-water mark *limit marker* 620.4

low-weight *light* 539.4

low yield *infertile state* 23.3

low-yield *infertile* 23.7

lox *fish dish* 90.19, *cooler* 218.4

lox *or* LOX *gas* 106.6

loyal **426.5**; *intimate* 62.7, *truthful* 191.4, *liking* 290.4, *loving* 299.15, *moral* 431.9, *deferential* 433.9, *observant* 465.6, *tenacious* 755.6, *naive* 821.3, *infallible* 840.12

loyal devotion *liking* 290.1

loyalist *conformist* 781.6

loyally *intimately* 62.14, *truthfully* 191.9, *admiringly* 290.11, *lovingly* 299.29, *obediently* 426.9, *morally* 431.15, *dutifully* 433.19, *observantly* 465.6, *tenaciously* 755.12

loyal supporter *tenacious person* 377.5

loyalty **426.2**; *truthfulness* 191.1, *love* 299.1, *morals* 431.2, *deference* 433.4, *respectfulness* 435.3, *observance* 465.1, *tenacity* 755.2, *infallibility* 840.6

loyalty oath *vow* 189.3

lozenge *polygon* 6.42, *dose of medicine* 115.3, Architectural Elements 134, Heraldic Terms 184, *angled figure* 628.3

LP (long-playing record) *recording* 50.12

LPGA Championship *golfing associations and tournaments* 156.6

L position *stationary rings* 157.8

Lualaba Rivers 570

Luanda Countries 566

Luapula Rivers 570

lubber *unskilled person* 128.3

lubber line *guide* 697.4

lubberliness *unskillfulness* 128.1

lubberly *clumsy* 128.6

lube [Inf] *lubrication* 562.2

lubricant **562.7**; *sound reducer* 233.5, *polish* 545.3

lubricate **562.15**; *soften* 543.14, *smooth* 545.10, *make easy* 823.15

lubricated **562.14**; *polished* 545.7, *wieldy* 823.12

lubricating *moderating* 521.5, *lubrication* 562.2, *lubricational* 562.12

lubricating agent *lubricant* 562.7

lubricating oil *lubricant* 562.7

lubrication **562.2**; *smoothness* 545.1

lubricational **562.12**

lubricative *lubricational* 562.12

lubricator **562.10**; *lubricant* 562.7

lubricatory *lubricational* 562.12

lubricious *unchaste* 432.10

lubricity *sexual immorality* 432.2, *smoothness* 545.1, *oiliness* 562.1, *lubrication* 562.2, *lubricational* 562.12

lubricous *polished* 545.7

lucency *light* 246.1

lucent **246.13**; *translucent* 249.8

Lucerne Lakes 568

lucid *rational* 4.15, 109.4, *clear* 196.2, 244.6, *easily seen through* 249.10, *meaningful* 361.6, *simple* 363.6

lucidity *philosophical attitude* 4.3, *rationality* 109.2, *clarity* 196.1, 363.2, *openness* 249.6, *simplicity* 823.2

lucidly *rationally* 4.25, *sanely*

109.6, *clearly* 196.4, *intelligibly* 363.13

Lucifer *star* 7.8, *angel* 82.11, *devil* 446.5

lucifer *fuel starter* 106.3, *fire* 246.9

luck **842.3**; *opportunity* 659.2, *comfortable circumstances* 726.5, *strong possibility* 836.3, *successfulness* 845.3, *good fortune* 847.2

luckily **842.17**; *opportunely* 659.8, *comfortably* 726.19, *prosperously* 847.9

luckiness *comfortable circumstances* 726.5

luckless *unlucky* 848.12

luck of the draw *potluck* 842.4, *good fortune* 847.2

luck on one's side *luck* 842.3

luck piece *talisman* 86.9

lucky *great* 445.14, *timely* 659.4, *comfortable* 726.10, *chance* 842.10, *successful* 845.8, *prosperous* 847.5

lucky bean *talisman* 86.9

lucky break [Inf] *opportunity* 583.8, 659.2, *luck* 842.3, *successfulness* 845.3, *good fortune* 847.2

lucky charm *talisman* 86.9

lucky devil *prosperous person* 847.4

lucky dog! *good luck!* 842.19

lucky draw *winnings* 492.5

lucky fellow *prosperous person* 847.4

lucky find *find* 345.5, *extra* 748.6

lucky man *someone promised* 458.7

lucky shot *unexpectedness* 839.2, *luck* 842.3, *good fortune* 847.2

lucky strike *luck* 842.3, *good fortune* 847.2

lucky stroke *successfulness* 845.3

lucrative *productive* 22.9, 522.11, *rewarding* 453.9, *gainful* 467.10, *profitable* 489.13, 801.8, *successful* 845.8

lucrative deal *gain* 467.1

lucratively *profitably* 453.20, *gainfully* 467.24, *successfully* 845.19

lucre *profit* 467.6, *cash* 484.2

lucubration *dissertation* 203.1

Lucullan banquet *feast* 92.9

Lucullus *eater* 92.15

ludicrous *foolish* 353.5, *meaningless* 362.7, *ridiculous* 368.5, *inelegant* 528.6

ludicrously *foolishly* 353.8, *ridiculously* 368.8

ludicrousness *folly* 353.1, *ridiculousness* 368.1

luff *sail* 150.29

luffa *cleaning tool* 111.10

luffing *sailing terms* 150.5, *sailing* 150.25

lug *hand tool* 103.3, *convey* 685.9, *pull* 699.2, 699.10

Lugano Lakes 568

luge Sporting Activities 145, *bobsledding* 162.23, *bobsled* 162.38

lugeing *toboggan race* 162.25, *bobsledding* 162.34

luge race *toboggan race* 162.25

luge techniques *toboggan race* 162.25

luggage *receptacle* 105.11, *possessions* 470.5, *baggage* 578.8, *transferred thing* 685.6, *freightage* 686.3

luggage label *personal identification* 184.4

luggage rack *compartment* 578.2

luggage van [Brit] *railroad car* 688.5

lugger Sailing Ships and Boats 690

lugubrious *depressed* 270.5

lugubriously *sorrowfully* 270.10

lukewarm *hot* 217.11, *indifferent* 289.7, *unenthusiastic* 375.10, *irresolute* 461.6, 772.13, *mediocre* 742.7

lukewarmly *indifferently* 289.17, *irresolutely* 461.10

lukewarmness *heat* 217.1, *indifference* 289.1, *irresolution* 461.3

lukewarm support *disparagement* 440.1

lull *silence* 231.1, 231.4, *comfort* 273.9, *ease* 275.1, 819.1, *inactivity* 415.1, *calm* 521.8, *interval* 639.4, 775.2, *delay* 658.3, *pause* 668.3, *lack of motion* 678.1, *repose* 678.2, *make motionless* 678.8

lullaby *song* 140.11, *moderator* 521.2

lull before the storm *repose* 678.2

lull in hostilities *truce* 73.2

lulu [Inf] *beautiful thing* 529.3

Luma *white* whitener 253.3

lumbago *joint disease* 114.19, *painful condition* 215.2

lumbar *back* 622.6

lumbar puncture *diagnostic procedure* 107.11

lumbar region *rear end* 622.4

lumber *construction material* 14.21, *timber* 43.3, *manage trees* 43.14, *be clumsy* 128.9, *wood* 131.3, *residue* 750.2

lumber [Inf] *baseball equipment* 147.4

lumberer *forester* 43.7

lumbering *tree management* 43.6, *clumsy* 128.6, 824.14, *stocky* 579.16, *slow motion* 693.3, *slow* 693.7, *awkward* 804.6

lumberjack *forester* 43.7, *power worker* 106.10, *woodworker* 131.4

lumber jacket *or* **lumberjack jacket** 100.18

lumbricoid *wormlike* 39.24

lumen Scientific and Technical Units 589

luminance *light* 10.17, 246.1

luminary *star* 7.8

luminesce *reflect* 10.76, *light up* 246.20

luminescence *light* 10.17, 246.1

luminescent *lucent* 246.13

luminiferous *lit* 246.16

luminism Western Art Styles 133

luminosity *light* 246.1, *hue* 251.4

luminosity class *star luminosity* 7.12

luminous *lucent* 246.13, *intelligible* 363.5

luminous efficacy *light* 10.17

luminous efficiency *light* 10.17

luminous energy *light* 246.1

luminous flux *light* 10.17

luminous intensity *light* 10.17

luminously *lightly* 246.23

luminousness *light* 246.1

lump *symptom* 114.3, *unskilled person* 128.3, *heaviness* 538.1, *solid body* 540.4, *hard substance* 542.3, *mass* 579.7, *particle* 760.4

lumpily *roughly* 544.13

lumpiness *heaviness* 538.1, *hardness* 542.1, *roughness* 544.1, *squatness* 579.6

lumpish *inert* 519.2, *heavy* 538.9, *stocky* 579.16

lumpishness *squatness* 579.6

lump it [Inf] *succumb* 421.7

lump sum *sum* 484.5

lump together *be indiscriminate* 338.10, *unite* 752.14, *combine* 757.9

lumpy *heavy* 538.9, *condensed* 540.7, *hard* 542.5, *coarse* 544.6, *thick* 561.17, *stocky* 579.16

lumpy cloud *cloud appearance* 9.19

lunacy *insanity* 110.1, *folly* 353.1

lunar *astronomical* 7.33, *oceanic* 571.7, *curved* 629.4

lunar base *space travel* 7.29

lunar eclipse *moon* 7.18, *darkness* 247.1

lunar landscape *infertile land* 23.2

lunar module *spacecraft* 7.28, *orbiting body* 681.4

lunar month *moon* 7.18, *time period* 641.2

lunar motion *oscillation* 683.1

lunar tide *tide* 571.2

lunate *curvilinear* 6.78

lunate bone Human Bones 19

lunatic *insane person* 110.5, *foolish* 353.5

lunatic asylum *mental hospital* 110.6

lunatic fringe *deviant* 698.7

lunch *social gathering* 59.7, *meal* 92.8, *have a meal* 92.25

lunch counter *eating place* 92.17

luncheon *meal* 92.8

luncheonette *eating place* 92.17

luncher *eater* 92.15

lunching *eating meals* 92.4

lunchroom *eating place* 92.17

lunchtime *noon* 655.4

lune *circle* 6.40

lunette Architectural Elements 134, *window* 134.10

lung *respiration* 558.8

lung cancer *respiratory disease* 114.12, *cancer* 114.15, *smoking* 121.22

lung capacity Fields of Measurement 589

lunge *wrestling* 152.18, *fencing movements* 153.3, *fence* 153.7, *stab* 418.22, *be swift* 694.10

lungi *accessory* 100.28

lunging *fencing* 153.6

lungs *internal organ* 19.13

lungwort Flowers 42

Luni Rivers 570

lunker *big thing* 579.9

Lupercalia *religious festival* 85.13

lupine *carnivorous* 35.26, Flowers 42

Lupus Constellations 7

lupus *skin disease* 114.16

lur Musical Instruments 142

lurch *be drunk* 121.34, *row* 150.32, *be ungraceful* 664.5, *stagger* 684.11, *pitch* 684.25, *victory* 845.4

lurcher *dog* 35.10

lurching *irregularity* 664.1, *irregular* 664.3

lure 700.5, 700.12; *bait* 154.6, *enticement* 178.3, *entice* 178.16, *desirability* 288.7, *cause desire* 288.22, *reward for service* 453.5, *offer* 504.1, 504.11, *inducement* 508.2, *positive stimulus* 508.5, *manipulate* 508.12, *influence* 512.11

lured *motivated* 508.8

lurer *tempter* 178.10

lurid *clear* 244.6, *gaudy* 251.12, *drained of color* 252.6, *blatant* 404.19

luridly *blatantly* 404.34

luridness *blatancy* 404.6

lurk *conceal oneself* 181.15, *become invisible* 245.6, *disappear* 265.5, *be cunning* 822.5, *hide* 844.13

lurker *cunning person* 822.3

lurking *invisible* 245.3, *concealment* 844.2, *concealed* 844.7

lurk in the shadows *be dark* 247.8

Lusaka Countries 566

Lüscher color test Psychological Tests 108

luscious 214.8

lush 485.11; *fertile* 22.8, *plantlike* 41.13, *plentiful* 97.4, *luscious* 214.8

lush [Inf] *drinking bout* 121.7, *drunkard* 121.8, *get drunk* 121.35

lushed [Inf] *dead drunk* 121.27

lushness *fertility* 22.1

Lusitano Horse and Pony Breeds 159

lust *sexual longing* 20.6, *desire* 288.1, *sexual desire* 288.5, *sexual love* 299.3, *envy* 314.7, *sexual immorality* 432.2, *depravity* 448.2, *iniquity* 448.3

lust after 288.20; *desire* 299.24, *deprave* 448.14

luster *mineral* 8.37, *light* 246.1, *quality of light* 246.2, *smoothness* 545.1

lusterless *dimmed* 248.6, *shady* 250.4, *colorless* 252.5

lusterware Ceramics 129

lustful 288.15; *desirous* 20.18, *unchaste* 432.10, *depraved* 448.10, *impious* 448.11

lustfully 20.24, 288.29; *promiscuously* 432.19, *unvirtuously* 448.16

lustfulness *sexual longing* 20.6, *sexual desire* 288.5, *sexual love* 299.3, *sexual immorality* 432.2

lustily *laboriously* 122.13, *loudly* 232.11, *acutely* 516.18, *with vigor* 518.6

lustiness *vigor* 518.1

lustral *cleansing* 111.16, *apologetic* 313.6

lustrate *purify* 111.19, *repent* 313.9

lustration Christian rite 85.5, *religious cleansing* 111.3, *penitence* 313.3

lustrative *apologetic* 313.6

lustrous 246.15

lusts of the flesh *sexual longing* 20.6

lusty *healthy* 113.4, *shouting* 232.7, *physically strong* 516.10, *vigorous* 518.2

lute *make ceramics* 129.10, Musical Instruments 142, *adhesive* 755.3, *cause to adhere* 755.10

luteal *of a secretion* 24.5

luteinizing hormone Human Hormones 12

lutenist *player* 141.2

luteolin *yellow pigment* 259.2

luteotropic hormone *or* **luteotropin** Human Hormones 12

luteous *yellowish* 259.8

lutetium Chemical Elements and Common Allotropes 11

Lutheranism Christian Groups 81

luting *ceramic process* 129.5, *adhesive* 755.3

lux Scientific and Technical Units 589

luxate *disconnect* 574.19

luxation *disconnection* 574.5

Luxembourg Countries 566

luxuriance *fertility* 22.1, *excess* 99.1

luxuriant *fertile* 22.8, *plantlike* 41.13, *plentiful* 97.4, *excessive* 99.5, *luscious* 214.8, *grand* 404.22, *ornate* 532.10, *dense* 540.6

luxuriantly *plentifully* 97.11, *grandly* 404.37

luxuriate *abound* 97.8, *be excessive* 99.9, *feel pleasure* 214.12

luxuriate in *indulge oneself* 456.10

luxuriating *plentiful* 97.4

luxurious *luscious* 214.8, *grand* 404.22, *opulent* 485.10, *prosperous* 847.5

luxuriously *pleasingly* 214.15, *grandly* 404.37, *wealthily* 485.16, *decoratively* 532.13, *prosperously* 847.9

luxuriousness *superfluity* 99.4, *grandeur* 404.10

luxury *superfluity* 99.4, *superfluous* 99.8, *pleasure* 214.2, 271.2, *grandeur* 404.10, *self-indulgence* 456.1, *opulence* 485.3, *costly* 496.7, *ornateness* 532.2, *successfulness* 845.3, *prosperity* 847.1

luxury coach *bus* 687.7

luxury price *costliness* 496.1

Luzon Islands 572

lyase *enzyme* 12.11

lycée [Fr] *type of school* 48.12

lyceum *type of school* 48.12

lych gate *means of entry* 706.6

lycine Amino Acids 12

lycopod *fern* 46.1

Lycopodium *fern* 46.1

lycopsid *fern* 46.1

lyddite *explosive* 78.13

Lydian mode *mode* 140.17

lye *solution* 555.10

lygophobia Phobias 283

lying 192.5, 192.16; *balance beam* 157.3, *hypocritical* 330.10, *misrepresentation* 366.2, *equivocating* 380.6, *misrepresented* 627.8

lying down *submitting* 421.3, *prostrate* 597.11, *recumbency* 603.2, *recumbent* 603.7

lying flat *prostrate* 597.11, *recumbency* 603.2, *recumbent* 603.7

lying-in-state *funeral* 31.4

lying low *concealed* 844.7

Lyman series Classical Physical Laws 10

lymph *body fluid* 19.16, 555.3

lymphatic *fluid* 19.25

lymphocyte *blood* 555.4

lymphogram *diagnostic radiology* 107.12

lymphogranuloma venereum *sexually transmitted disease (STD)* 114.17

lymphography *diagnostic radiology* 107.12

lymphoma *blood disease* 114.14

lynch *execute* 30.22, 454.30

lyncher *killer* 30.11, *punisher* 454.16

lynching *execution* 30.6, *murderous* 30.18, *capital punishment* 454.12

lynch law *injustice* 342.3

lynchpin *gist* 799.4

Lynx Constellations 7

lynx-eyed *jealous* 314.5

Lyonnesse Imaginary Places 360

lyophilic *status adjectives* 11.25

lyophobic *status adjectives* 11.25

Lyra Constellations 7

lyra viol Musical Instruments 142

Lyre Constellations 7

lyre Musical Instruments 142

lyric Poem or Verse Forms 139
lyric or **lyrical** *melodious* 140.26
lyrical *poetic* 139.19
lyrical abstraction Western Art Styles 133
lyrically *poetically* 139.23
lyricist *author* 139.13, *composer* 141.9
lyric poet *author* 139.13
lyric poetry *poetry* 139.8
lyric soprano *voice* 141.5
lyric tenor *voice* 141.5
Lysenkoism *evolution* 13.23
lysergic acid diethylamide (LSD) *hallucinogens* 121.20
Lysithea Planets and Their Satellites 7
lysosome *cell structure* 13.16
lysozyme *enzyme* 12.11
lyssophobia Phobias 283

M

M *thousand* 792.10
M [Inf] *opiates* 121.17
ma [Inf] *woman in the family* 33.13, *family member* 65.2
ma'am *female title of address* 33.3
Maariv [Heb] *public worship* 83.3
Maas Rivers 570
Maat Deities 82
Mab *sprite* 86.12
mac [Inf] *male title of address* 32.3
macabre *frightening* 283.12
macadam *building materials* 104.2, *paving* 613.14
macadamize *pave* 613.32
macaroni *pasta* 90.31
macaronic Poem or Verse Forms 139
Macassar oil *pomade* 562.9
Macdonnell Ranges Mountains and Hills 569
mace *blunt weapon* 78.5, Herbs and Spices 91, *insignia* 184.5
Macedonia Countries 566
macerate *soften* 543.14, *steep* 557.31
macerated *underfed* 98.7
maceration *steeping* 557.10, *pulping* 561.11
macerator *pulper* 561.13
Mace™ *chemical warfare* 117.9, *self-defense* 419.5
mach *speed* 694.2
mach or **mach number** Scientific and Technical Units 589
machete *sharp weapon* 78.6
Machiavelli *planner* 387.9, *cunning person* 822.3
Machiavellian *deceiver* 193.8, *artful* 193.13, *planning* 387.11, *cunning* 822.4
Machiavellianism *guile* 193.3, *cunning* 822.1
machicolation *fort* 419.13
machinate *scheme* 193.18, *practice sophistry* 330.11, *plot* 387.15
machination *artifice* 193.5, *cunning* 330.3, *plot* 387.6, *stratagem* 822.2
machinations *artifice* 193.5
machinator *politician* 50.7, *schemer* 193.10
machine *dynamic structure* 14.5, *apparatus* 103.2, *machinery* 103.5, *instrument* 511.2, *manufacture* 522.2, *perform* 522.16
machine code *programming language* 15.16
machine element 14.8
machine-groomed *snow* 162.28

machine-groomed snow *skiing snow* 162.3
machine gun *firearm* 78.7, *agent of destruction* 523.7
machine gunner *army combat specialist* 77.16
machine knitting *knitting* 130.7
machine loom *fabric-handling tool* 130.12
machine-made *produced* 522.12
machine-milk *practice livestock farming* 16.20
machine-minded *mechanical* 103.7
machine part *machine element* 14.8
machinery 103.5; *dynamic structure* 14.5, *supplies* 102.3, Phobias 283, *manufacture* 522.2, *component* 760.3
machine tool 14.9; *tool* 103.1
machine weapon *weapon* 78.1
machining *manufacture* 522.2
machinist *artisan* 123.13, *operative* 509.6
machismo *maleness* 32.2, *heroism* 284.2
Mach number Classical Physical Laws 10
mach number *speed* 694.2
macho *male* 32.16, *heroic* 284.10, *swaggering* 404.20
macho man 32.6
Macina Breeds of Sheep 16
Mackenzie Rivers 570
mackerel Collective Names 59, *food fish and shellfish* 90.20, *game fish* 154.10
mackerel sky *cloud appearance* 9.19, *variegated thing* 263.5
mackerel spinner *bait* 154.6
mackinaw Fabrics and Fibers 130
Mackinaw coat *jacket* 100.18
mackintosh *coat* 100.19, Fabrics and Fibers 130
Maclaurin series Mathematical Concepts 6, *sequence* 6.18
Macoun Apple Varieties 44
macramé *weaving* 130.6, Hobbies and Pastimes 167
macrobiotic diet *diet* 92.5
macroclimate *climate* 9.35
macrocosm *universe* 7.3, *whole thing* 759.2
macrocrystal *crystal* 8.39
macroeconomics *economics* 56.1
macro language *programming language* 15.16
macro lens *lens* 132.11
macrometeorology *meteorology* 9.1
macromolecular structure *molecular biology* 13.18
macromolecule *polymer* 11.9, *living matter* 28.4
macron Accents and Diacritical Marks 5
macronutrient *essential element* 12.15
macrophage *blood* 555.4
macrophobia Phobias 283
macrophotography *photographic specialties* 132.2
macroscopic *huge* 579.14
macroseism *seismic activity* 8.24
macrosociology *sociology* 2.1
macula *skin disease* 114.16, *maculation* 263.4, *mark* 533.2
macular *mottled* 263.10
maculate *mottled* 263.10, *variegate* 263.11, *mark* 533.8
maculate [Arch] *dirty* 112.11
maculation 263.4
mad *insane* 110.9, *angry* 302.11,

foolish 353.5, *meaningless* 362.7, *violent* 520.5, *deranged* 766.16
mad about *in love* 299.16
Madagascar Countries 566, Islands 572
Madam or **madam** *female title of address* 33.3
madam *title of respect* 72.7, *insolent person* 400.7, *sexually immoral person* 432.8
madame *title of respect* 72.7
madame [Fr] *female title of address* 33.3
mad as a hornet *angry* 302.11
mad as a march hare or **as a hatter** *insane* 110.9
madcap *rash move* 286.4, *reckless* 286.6, *rash person* 353.4, *foolish* 353.5
mad cow disease *animal disease* 34.10
mad dash *alacrity* 414.3
madden *antagonize* 63.12, *make insane* 110.13, *cause dislike* 291.16, *cause hate* 300.12, *make angry* 302.18, *make violent* 520.10
maddened *angry* 302.11, *violent* 520.5
maddening 302.12
maddeningly 302.25
madder *coloring agent* 251.5
madder lake *red pigment* 257.2
madding crowd *business* 414.6
maddish *angry* 302.11
mad dog *violent animal* 520.4
made *produced* 522.12, *designed* 536.6, *formed* 624.6, *created* 717.16
made beauteous *beautified* 530.12
made beautiful *beautified* 530.12
made easier *made easy* 823.11
made easy 823.11; *simple* 363.6
made-for-television *dramatic* 137.10
made-for-television or **TV movie** *movie type* 137.3, *program* 172.10
made in heaven *invulnerable* 810.18
Madeira Rivers 570, Islands 572
madeleine *cake* 90.36
made man and wife *married* 64.16
mademoiselle *female title of address* 33.3
made of money *wealthy* 485.8
made one *married* 64.16
made over *transferring property* 470.10
made public *published* 173.12, 175.8, *demonstrated* 331.9, *displayed* 843.8
made ready *prepared* 388.9
made simple *simple* 363.6
made to feel at home *popular* 408.12
made to grovel *subject* 832.6
made to measure *customized* 779.14
made-to-order *tailored* 100.41
made-to-order clothes *tailor-made clothes* 100.4
made unclean *misused* 395.3
made up *beautified* 530.12
made-up *culinary* 91.9, *fabricated* 192.17, *theoretical* 720.10, *united* 752.10
made up of *containing* 577.7, *including* 763.3
madhouse *mental hospital* 110.6, *confusion* 766.4
Madison Avenue *publicity* 178.7
madly *insanely* 110.15, *angrily* 302.24

madman *insane person* 110.5, *violent animal* 520.4
madness *insanity* 110.1, *burst of anger* 302.6, *folly* 353.1, *derangement* 766.8
Madonna *deified person* 82.14
Madonna lily Flowers 42
mad race *alacrity* 414.3
madras Fabrics and Fibers 130
madrasah *religious school* 48.13
Madrid Countries 566, *other famous world cities* 567.9
madrigal Poem or Verse Forms 139, Musical Forms 140, *song* 140.11
madrone Trees and Shrubs 43
mad scramble *alacrity* 414.3
Madura Islands 572
Madura foot *fungal disease* 47.6
Madurese Breeds of Cattle 16
madwoman *insane person* 110.5
maelstrom *activity* 414.1, *river turbulence* 570.5, *vortex* 682.6, *tumult* 684.2, *hidden danger* 813.3
maenad *drunkard* 121.8
maestoso Musical Terms and Expression Marks 140
maestro *educator* 48.4, *expert* 52.8, 68.13, *skilled person* 127.7, *musical director* 141.7
Mae West *survival swimming* 164.4, *safety device* 810.15
Mafia *villain* 448.5
Mafia member *criminal* 427.6
mafic rock *igneous rock* 8.32
mafioso *criminal* 427.6, *villain* 448.5
maftir *rabbi* 84.6
magazine 175.3; *ammunition* 78.11, *storehouse* 105.8, *publication media* 173.6, *periodical* 175.1, *periodical publication* 641.6
magazine-fed *bolt-action* 78.17
magazine-fed rifle *firearm* 78.7
magazine publishing *print journalism* 175.4
magazine section *newspaper* 175.2
magazine stand *cabinet* 101.8
magazinish *periodical* 175.6
magaziny *periodical* 175.6
Magdalena Rivers 570
mage [Arch] *witch* 86.15
magenta *red* 257.5, *purpleness* 262.1, *purple* 262.6
maggid *rabbi* 84.6
Maggiore Lakes 568
maggot *larva* 40.9, *bait* 154.6
maggot [Arch] *conception* 360.4, *caprice* 381.1
maggoty *verminous* 40.13, *unclean* 112.8
magic 138.3; *occultism* 86.1, *witchcraft* 86.6, *mystery* 182.4, *cause of wonder* 294.4, *wonder-working* 294.11, *occult influence* 512.2, *type of power* 514.6, *delusion* 720.3
magical 138.15; *witchlike* 86.19, *wonder-working* 294.11
magically 86.28; *wondrously* 294.18
magical power *type of power* 514.6
magic belt *talisman* 86.9
magic carpet *talisman* 86.9
magic circle *talisman* 86.9
magician 138.11; *witch* 86.15, *secret person* 182.6, *wonderful person* 294.6, *changer* 665.9
magic lantern *viewer* 132.22, *imaging device* 242.11
magic mushroom [Inf] *hallucinogens* 121.20

magic realism Western Art Styles 133, Western Literary Groups 139

magic ring talisman 86.9

magic show magic 138.3

magic spell spell 86.8, occult influence 512.2

magic sword talisman 86.9

magic symbol sign 183.1

magic word tolerance 502.2

magic words spell 86.8

magisterial governing 49.25, judiciary 53.19, judicatory 54.24, masterful 68.15, skillful 127.10, arrogant 297.9, dominant 744.9

magisterially arrogantly 297.18, superiorly 744.20

magisterialness authority 52.1

magistracy position of authority 52.4, jurisdiction 53.3, judge 54.10

magistral masterful 68.15

magistrality authority 52.1

magistrate person in authority 52.7, judge 54.10, 68.4, punisher 454.16

maglev magnetic phenomenon 10.50

magma volcanic activity 8.26, mixed thing 751.2

magma chamber volcanic activity 8.26

magmatic petrographic 8.58

magmatic rock igneous rock 8.32

magmatism petrogenesis 8.31

Magna Carta the Law 53.2, rights 429.4, free rights 829.4

magnanimity 498.2; charity 305.3, forgivingness 312.3, leniency 423.1, unselfishness 443.2, virtue 447.1

magnanimous 498.7; charitable 305.9, forgiving 312.4, lenient 423.3, unselfish 443.5, virtuous 447.5

magnanimously charitably 305.15, forgivingly 312.13, leniently 423.6, unselfishly 443.9, virtuously 447.9

magnate gainer 467.9, financier 484.17, wealthy person 485.6, important person 799.5

magnesium Chemical Elements and Common Allotropes 11, essential element 12.15

magnesium alloy construction material 14.21

magnet 10.47, 700.3; adherent 755.4

magnetic 700.9; physical 10.70, sensual 20.16, enticing 178.13, motivational 508.7, appealing 512.9, nuclear 514.17, attractive 699.9

magnetically 699.14; physically 10.78, energetically 514.22, attractionally 700.13

magnetic anomaly geomagnetism 8.3

magnetic attraction magnetism 10.45

magnetic card magnetic recording 10.51

magnetic compass navigational aid 690.6

magnetic constant magnetic quantity 10.48, fundamental constant 10.69

magnetic core memory memory 15.6

magnetic damping magnetic phenomenon 10.50

magnetic declination geomagnetism 10.46

magnetic deflection magnetic phenomenon 10.50

magnetic dip geomagnetism 10.46

magnetic dipole moment magnetic quantity 10.48

magnetic disk magnetic recording 10.51

magnetic epoch geomagnetism 10.46

magnetic equator geomagnetism 8.3, 10.46

magnetic field magnetic quantity 10.48, force 514.8, Fields of Measurement 589

magnetic field strength magnetic quantity 10.48

magnetic flux magnetic quantity 10.48

magnetic focusing magnetic phenomenon 10.50

magnetic force force 10.9, 514.8

magnetic hysteresis magnetic phenomenon 10.50

magnetic inclination geomagnetism 10.46

magnetic induction or **magnetic flux density** magnetic quantity 10.48

magnetic ink magnetic recording 10.51

magnetic ink character recognition (MICR) magnetic recording 10.51, character recognition 15.20

magnetic iron ore magnet 10.47

magnetic lens magnetic phenomenon 10.50

magnetic levitation magnetic phenomenon 10.50

magnetic memory magnetic recording 10.51

magnetic meridian geomagnetism 10.46

magnetic mine bomb 78.15

magnetic mirror magnetic phenomenon 10.50

magnetic moment magnetic quantity 10.48

magnetic monopole magnet 10.47

magnetic needle indicator 183.7, navigational aid 690.6, magnet 700.3

magnetic North geomagnetism 10.46

magnetic north compass direction 697.5

magnetic North Pole geomagnetism 10.46

magnetic personality inducement 508.2, personal influence 512.3

magnetic phenomenon 10.50

magnetic potential difference magnetic quantity 10.48

magnetic quantity 10.48

magnetic recording 10.51

magnetic repulsion magnetism 10.45, repulsion 701.1

magnetic resonance imaging (MRI) magnetic recording 10.51, analysis 11.17, diagnostic radiology 107.12

magnetic reversal geomagnetism 8.3, 10.46

magnetics classical physics 10.2

magnetic separating ceramic process 129.5

magnetic South geomagnetism 10.46

magnetic South Pole geomagnetism 10.46

magnetic storage magnetic recording 10.51

magnetic storm geomagnetism 8.3, atmospheric agitation 684.13

magnetic stripe magnetic recording 10.51

magnetic tape magnetic recording 10.51, record book 185.5, recording 185.6

magnetic tape drive peripheral 15.8

magnetic track magnetic recording 10.51

magnetic variable magnetic quantity 10.48

magnetic variation geomagnetism 10.46

magnetism 10.45; classical physics 10.2, enticement 178.3, inducement 508.2, influence 512.1, force 514.8, drawing power 699.6, pulling power 700.2, allurement 700.4, adhesion 755.1

magnetite magnet 10.47, 700.3

magnetization magnetic quantity 10.48, pulling power 700.2

magnetize interact 10.73, empower 514.20, draw in 699.13, attract 700.11

magnetized magnetic 700.9

magnetized iron magnet 700.3

magnetizing coil magnet 10.47

magneto generator 14.43, power supplier 514.14

magneto or **magnetoelectric generator** or **magneto-generator** electricity 106.5

magnetoelectric gas 106.14

magnetohydrodynamic physical 10.70

magnetohydrodynamically physically 10.78

magnetohydrodynamics Fields of Modern Physics 10

magnetometer Fields of Measurement 589

magnetometry Fields of Measurement 589

magnetomotive force magnetic quantity 10.48

magneton magnetic quantity 10.48, Scientific and Technical Units 589

magneto-optical disk disk 15.5

magneto-optical effect magnetic phenomenon 10.50

magnetosphere geomagnetism 8.3, 10.46, atmospheric layer 558.3

magnetostriction magnetic phenomenon 10.50

magnetron electron tube 14.40

magnifiable enlargeable 581.13

Magnificat prayer 85.10, Musical Forms 140

magnification worship 83.1, enlargement 194.2, visual aid 242.14, aggravation 276.1, increase 581.3, 746.1

magnificence majesty 297.5, grandeur 404.10, excellence 445.4, beauty 529.1

magnificent majestic 297.12, grand 404.22, excellent 445.13, beautiful 529.7

magnificently 529.16; majestically 297.21, grandly 404.37, excellently 445.21

magnified deified 82.20, worshiped 83.14, enlarged 194.8, aggravated 276.3, unrestrained 500.5, swelled 581.10, increased 746.5

magnifier visual aid 242.14

magnify deify 82.23, worship 83.15, enlarge 194.12, aggravate 276.5, praise 437.16, increase

581.16, make bigger 746.7, make important 799.14

magnifying glass visual aid 242.14

magnifying mirror reflector 242.10

magniloquence bombast 194.4, seriousness 200.2, power of speech 205.5, pomposity 404.5

magniloquent bombastic 194.10, diffuse 199.3, serious 200.5, articulate 205.16, ornate 532.10

magniloquently exaggeratedly 194.16, emphatically 200.7, orally 205.21, pompously 404.33

magnitude vector 6.48, star luminosity 7.12, influence 512.1, size 579.1, measurability 589.2, quantity 738.1, degree 739.1, importance 799.1

magnolia Flowers 42

magnum bottle 578.14

magnum opus masterpiece 68.14, 127.5, work of art 522.4

magnus hitch Knots, Bends, Hitches, Splices 754

magpie songbird 36.12, talker 207.4

magpies Collective Names 59

magus witch 86.15

maharajah sovereign 68.2

maharani or **maharanee** sovereign 68.2

mahatma occultist 86.13

Mahavastu other text 81.19

mahi-mahi food fish and shellfish 90.20

mah-jongg Board and Table Games 167

mahlstick material 143.9

mahogany Trees and Shrubs 43, brown 256.5

mahzor ritual manual 85.11

maid young woman 26.9, female 33.1, single person 67.5, attendant 69.4, domestic servant 69.7, cleaner 111.12, domestic worker 123.4

Maiden Constellations 7

maiden young woman 26.9, female 33.1, single woman 33.5, single person 67.5, celibate 67.6, horse racing 159.10, chaste person 431.6, immature 652.12, beginning 771.16

maiden aunt single person 67.5, 788.7

maidenhair tree Trees and Shrubs 43

maidenhead virginity 67.2

maidenhood virginity 67.2

maiden lady single person 67.5

maidenliness youthfulness 26.2

maidenly young 26.11, female 33.16, celibate 67.6, virginal 67.7, immaturely 652.23

maidenly or **maidenish** chaste 431.10

maiden name name 202.8

maiden race horse racing 159.10

maiden speech premiere 771.9

maiden voyage beginning 652.4, premiere 771.9

maid-in-waiting domestic servant 69.7

maid of honor wedding party 64.7

maidservant domestic servant 69.7

maieutic logical 329.9, causal 511.5

mail 685.10; postal communication 169.4, correspond 169.19, send 209.11, historic armor 419.8, protective covering 613.5, transferred thing 685.6, freightage 686.3, safety device 810.15

mailable *transferable* 685.7
mail a letter *correspond* 169.19
mailbag *postal communication* 169.4, *bag* 578.7
mailboat Ships and Boats 690
mail bomb *bomb* 78.15
mail bombing *terrorist attack* 418.7
mailbox *computer communications* 15.25, *postal communication* 169.4, *box* 578.5
mail car *railroad car* 688.5
mail carrier *postal worker* 169.6, *messenger* 685.5
mailed fist *suppression* 424.2
Mailgram™ *data transmission* 169.8
mailing *conveyance* 685.2
maillot *beachwear* 100.23
mailman Children's and Party Games 167, *postal worker* 169.6, *messenger* 685.5
mail-order selling *selling* 482.1
mail-order shopping *shopping* 481.3
mail pouch *postal communication* 169.4
mailwoman *postal worker* 169.6
maim *weaken* 517.13
maimed *defective* 806.7
Main Rivers 570
main *masterful* 68.15, *sea* 571.1, *focal* 612.8, *transportable* 686.7, *rail* 688.8, *accessible* 691.13, *elite* 744.12, *important* 799.7
main, the *large part* 579.3
main attraction *chief thing* 799.3
main body *armed force* 77.10, *large part* 579.3
main chain *protein* 12.9
main chance *gist* 799.4, *chance* 838.4, *good chance* 842.6
main course *dish* 90.7, *course* 92.12
main dish *dish* 90.7
Mai-Ndombe Lakes 568
Maine American States 564
Maine Anjou Breeds of Cattle 16
Maine coon Breeds of Cats 35
main entrance *front entrance* 621.2
main feature *the special* 779.8, *chief thing* 799.3
main force *coercion* 428.2
mainframe *computer* 15.1
main head *book part* 174.5
main ingredient *basis* 601.3
main interest *focus* 612.3
mainland *continent* 8.8
main line *railroad system* 688.1, *track* 688.2
mainline [Inf] *drug oneself* 121.37
mainliner [Inf] *drug taker* 121.12
main-line station *railroad station* 688.6
mainlining [Inf] *drug use* 121.9
mainly *focally* 612.14, *in essence* 723.11, *on average* 742.10, *predominantly* 744.21, *on the whole* 759.13, *overall* 778.22, *as a rule* 780.18, *importantly* 799.15
main man [Inf] *superior* 744.5
mainmast *sailboat parts and accessories* 150.4
main meaning *type of meaning* 361.4
main memory *memory* 15.6
main office *office* 124.2, *center of activity* 612.4
main part *excess* 99.1, *large part* 579.3, *gist* 799.4
main point *topic* 328.1, *gist* 799.4
main reaction *chemical reaction* 11.8

main road *means of connection* 754.4
mainsail *sailboat parts and accessories* 150.4
main sequence *stellar evolution* 7.10
main-sequence star *star luminosity* 7.12
main shock *seismic activity* 8.24
mainspring *motive* 178.5, *spring* 546.4, *source* 675.2
main squeeze [Inf] *loved one* 299.13
mainstay *security* 464.1, *supporter* 605.9, 825.13, *gist* 799.4, *refuge* 812.1
mainstream *musical* 140.25
mainstream jazz *jazz* 140.5
main street *business* 414.6, *urban area* 567.10
main-street *urban* 567.14
maintain 377.12; *propound a philosophy* 4.21, *believe* 87.9, *provision* 89.9, *practice surgery* 107.33, *contend* 189.24, *feel* 266.14, *state* 329.11, *conflict* 422.26, *detain* 471.9, *take action* 509.12, *support financially* 605.19, *perpetuate* 640.5, *continue* 669.8, *protract* 669.9, *repair* 809.10, *preserve* 815.14, *sustain* 825.25
maintain a household *housekeep* 60.23
maintain consistency *be compatible* 462.12
maintain control *be powerful* 514.18
maintain course *sail* 150.29
maintained *believed* 87.8, *contended* 189.15
maintainer *provider* 605.10
maintain firm control *be severe* 424.8
maintaining *constant* 377.8, *sustaining* 605.15
maintaining one's distance *unsociability* 409.1
maintain one's grip *hold out* 377.13
maintain one's ground *hold out* 377.13
maintain one's hold *retain* 471.7
maintain one's innocence *stand trial* 54.29
maintain progress 679.14
maintain the status quo *make permanent* 667.5
maintenance *divorce court* 66.3, *constancy* 377.3, *earnings* 467.5, *detention* 471.2, *something received* 473.2, *income* 492.3, *management* 509.4, *financial support* 605.8, *continuance* 669.3, *repair* 809.1, *preservation* 815.1, *saving* 815.4, *sustenance* 825.3, *social assistance* 825.4
main thing *chief thing* 799.3
main topic *chief thing* 799.3
maisonette *apartment* 60.7
maître d' *attendant* 69.4
maître d'hôtel *attendant* 69.4
maize *animal feed* 16.12, *cereal grass* 45.4
majestic 297.12, 404.21; *masterful* 68.15, *divine* 82.16, *serious* 200.5, *elegant* 527.3
majestically 297.21, 404.36; *divinely* 82.24, *emphatically* 200.7
majestic progress *improvement* 679.3
majesty 297.5; *divine attribute* 82.4, *pomp* 404.7, *elegance* 527.1
majolica Ceramics 129
majolica painter *ceramist* 129.7

Major US Military Ranks 58, *military title* 72.8
major *subject* 48.3, *masterful* 68.15, *skill* 127.1, *harmonic* 140.27, *focal* 612.8, *excellent* 744.14, *specialization* 779.3, *important* 799.7
major axis *curve* 6.38
major British cities 567.7
Majorca Islands 572
major depressive disorder *mood disorder* 108.12
major depressive episode *mood disorder* 108.12
major-domo *domestic servant* 69.7, *manager* 126.7
major earthquake *seismic activity* 8.24
major element *essential element* 12.15
Major General US Military Ranks 58, *military title* 72.8
major in *learn* 48.23, *specialize* 779.16
major interval *chord* 140.18
majority 793.3; *large part* 579.3, *certain amount* 738.3, *quantitative* 738.6, *gradational* 739.5, *superiority* 744.1, *part* 760.1, *plural* 793.6
majority leader *person in authority* 52.7, *party official* 68.5
majority rule *constitutional government* 49.8
majority verdict *verdict* 54.18
majority vote *electing* 382.5
majority whip *elected official* 50.8
major key *key* 140.23
major league baseball *baseball* 147.1
major part *large part* 579.3
major party *political party* 50.5
major planet *planet* 7.16
major poet *author* 139.13
major premise *or* term *philosophical term* 4.7
major scale *scale* 140.16
major subject *skill* 127.1
major suit *skill* 127.1, *bridge* 168.4
major surgery *surgery* 107.15
major third *third* 790.6
major US cities 567.5
major war *war* 76.1
Majuro Countries 566
majuscule *type* 173.5
Makalu Mountains and Hills 569
make *put together* 59.30, *compel* 428.8, *gain* 467.15, *produce* 522.13, *perform* 522.16, *fashion* 536.1, 536.7, 537.9, *shape* 551.21, *weaving* 609.2, *form* 624.9, *cause* 675.8, *awaken* 675.9, *come to be* 717.19, *type* 777.4, *total* 783.10, 784.12, *improve* 807.15
make *or* put in an appearance *become visible* 264.13, *arrive* 704.13
make a back pass *play soccer* 163.8
make a bad match *marry* 64.19
make a bad move *blunder* 846.13
make a bank shot *play basketball* 148.7, *play* 149.7
make a beeline *short-cut* 591.11
make a beeline for *aim* 697.14
make a beginning 771.26
make a bequest *transfer property* 470.12, *will* 472.11
make a bid *attempt* 390.6, *deal* 457.9, *bargain* 480.20
make a bid for *offer to buy* 504.12
make a bird sound 240.8
make a bloomer *be wrong* 430.18

make a bounce pass *play basketball* 148.7
make a bow *bow* 716.22
make a break *play* 149.7, *change* 665.14
make a break for *aim* 697.14
make abstruse *make obscure* 197.3
make a bundle [Inf] *get rich* 485.13
make a burnt offering *make an offering* 504.17
make a buy *bargain* 481.14
make a (leveraged) buyout *buy in* 481.13
make a call *telephone* 169.20
make a cat's-paw of *exploit* 393.11
make accurate *be accurate* 721.22
make a change *cause change* 665.16
make a charity appeal *solicit money* 505.13
make a choice *select* 382.12
make a circle *circle* 631.6
make a circuit *orbit* 681.8
make a clean breast of *talk straight* 630.15
make a clean breast of it *admit* 180.11, *be sincere* 191.8
make a clean sweep *clean* 111.17, *void* 709.23
make a comeback *be restored* 809.13
make a commotion *exaggerate* 194.11
make a compact *contract* 459.8, 462.11
make a compromise *compromise* 461.7
make a contract *guarantee* 458.13
make a copy of *reproduce* 21.13
make a corner in *buy in* 481.13
make acquaintance with *fraternize* 408.17
make a crossing *cross* 692.17
make a date *fraternize* 408.17
make addresses *court* 299.26
make a dead set at *attack* 418.17
make a deal *pacify* 74.11, *contract* 459.8, 462.11, *negotiate* 460.6, *compromise* 461.7, *bargain* 480.20, *come to an arrangement* 767.22
make a debut *emerge* 771.35
make a deposit *reserve* 464.14, *deposit* 487.12
make a deposition *attest* 189.22
make a detour *circle* 631.6
make a devil of a row *shatter the peace* 232.10
make a diagram *illustrate* 187.11
make a diagram of *describe* 202.15
make a disposition *transfer property* 470.12
make adjustments *compromise* 461.7
make a double play *play baseball* 147.9
make a downhill run *ski* 162.35
make a down payment *pay* 489.16
make a draft *blow* 558.22
make advances *seek friendship* 62.11, *desire* 299.24
make a face *react against* 291.15
make a fair catch *kick* 155.20
make a fair offer *offer* 504.11
make a false attack *fence* 153.7
make a false image *misrepresent* 188.6
make a faux pas *be clumsy* 128.9
make a film *produce* 137.21
make a final demand *demand* 505.12

make a find *buy cheaply* 481.11
make a fool of *humiliate* 298.19, *exploit* 393.11
make a fool of oneself *act foolishly* 128.10, *play the fool* 353.7
make a forced march *make haste* 818.5
make a fortune *profit* 467.22, *be prosperous* 847.6
make a free throw *play basketball* 148.7
make a fresh start *confess* 451.8, *begin again* 771.36
make a fresh *or* **new start** *become new* 652.19
make after *chase* 385.13
make a fuel stop *be on the track* 146.11
make a fuss *object* 828.18
make a fuss about *overestimate* 343.6, *make important* 799.14
make a generalization 778.18
make a gentleman's agreement *promise* 458.11
make a getaway *escape* 816.8
make a gift *give* 472.10
make a good buy *buy cheaply* 481.11
make a good fit *unify* 752.15
make a good guess *foresee* 357.9
make a good living *profit* 467.22
make a good match *marry* 64.19
make a good start *go forward* 679.8
make a go of *attain one's goal* 845.13
make a guess *suppose* 359.8
make a habit of *have a habit* 397.16
make a hash of *be clumsy* 128.9, *blunder* 846.13
make a hash *or* **mess of** *confuse* 766.19
make a hat trick *play ice hockey* 158.9, *play soccer* 163.8
make a hit *attain one's goal* 845.13
make a hockey stop *ski* 162.35
make a hole in one *play* 156.8
make a hole in one's pocket *cost a lot* 496.9
make a hook shot *play basketball* 148.7
make a house call *practice medicine* 107.32
make a jump shot *play basketball* 148.7
make a killing *profit* 467.22, *speculate* 480.19, *sell at a profit* 482.18, *get rich* 485.13, *buy at a discount* 495.6, *attain one's goal* 845.13
make a landfall *sail* 690.16, *land* 704.16
make a last-ditch stand *delay* 658.13
make a laughingstock of *ridicule* 436.22
make a legal defense *justify* 441.12
make a lewd *or* **rude gesture** *gesture* 183.17
make a lip *be sullen* 304.12
make a list *list* 785.11
make a little go a long way *starve* 118.10
make all clear for *make easy* 823.15
make allowances *modify* 340.13
make allowances for *show mercy* 312.11, *vindicate* 441.11
make a loan application *borrow* 476.10
make a long face *be serious* 278.7

make a long story short *outline* 617.5
make a maiden voyage *be new* 652.17
make a match *matchmake* 64.22
make amends *recompense* 273.11, *atone* 313.7, 489.24, *do penance* 451.9, *offer reparation* 504.15, *compensate* 743.7, *restore* 809.12
make amends for *atone* 313.7, *compensate* 478.6
make a mess (of) *dirty* 112.11
make a mess of *be clumsy* 128.9
make a mint *get rich* 485.13
make a mistake *be unskillful* 128.8, *err* 351.14, *be wrong* 430.18, *be incorrect* 722.13
make a mockery of *deride* 369.7
make a mountain out of a molehill *exaggerate* 194.11, *overestimate* 343.6
make a move *start off* 771.27
make an about-face *reverse* 671.9
make an addition to *support* 748.14
make a name for oneself *have a good reputation* 370.5
make an animal sound 240.7
make *or* **put in an appearance** *become visible* 264.13, *arrive* 704.13
make an arrest *detain* 830.16
make an ass of oneself *act foolishly* 128.10
make an attempt *attempt* 390.6
make an educated guess *predict* 358.14
make an effort *exert oneself* 122.11, *do something* 412.13, *try* 414.21
make an end to *cease* 773.20
make an entrance *act* 136.34, *appear* 244.8, *get in* 704.17, *enter* 706.11
make an error *play baseball* 147.9
make a nest egg *deposit* 105.21
make a net profit *profit* 467.22
make a new version *translate* 365.19
make an example of *punish* 454.22
make an exception *subtract* 749.6
make an exception (of) *exclude* 764.7
make an *or* **one's exit** *exit* 707.13
make angry 302.18; make irascible 303.16
make an honest woman of *marry* 64.19
make an idol of *idolize* 83.16
make an impression *be remembered* 354.15, *be full of vigor* 518.4, *be important* 799.13, *be visible* 843.16
make an impression in *soften* 543.14
make an incision *practice surgery* 107.33
make an insect sound 240.9
make an offer *bargain* 480.20, 481.14, *offer* 504.11
make an offer for *offer to buy* 504.12
make an offering 504.17; repent 313.9
make an off-the-lip turn *windsurf* 150.33
make a noise *sound* 230.8
make a note *remind* 354.13
make an overture *offer* 504.11
make a nuisance of oneself *annoy* 804.10

make an unlawful entry *steal* 479.14
make an unsecured loan *lend* 475.6
make a pact *or* **an alliance** *come together* 757.10
make a pact *or* **covenant** *settle* 735.26
make a pass *play soccer* 163.8
make a pass [Inf] *desire* 299.24
make a pass at *stab* 418.22
make a patsy of [Inf] *exploit* 393.11
make a pawn of *exploit* 393.11
make a payment *pay* 489.16
make a peace offering *make an offering* 504.17
make a pig *or* **hog of oneself** *be greedy* 119.4
make a pile [Inf] *get rich* 485.13
make a pilgrimage *worship* 83.15
make a pit stop *be on the track* 146.11
make a pit stop [Inf] *excrete* 25.20
make a plan *plan* 387.12
make a point *play tennis* 165.13, *raise the point* 328.10, *propound* 359.9
make a point (of) *contend* 422.22
make a point of *compel* 428.8
make a poor likeness *misrepresent* 188.6
make apparent *present* 264.15
make a prediction *predict* 358.14
make a preliminary sketch *be unfinished* 544.12
make a presentation *give* 472.10
make a present of *give* 472.10
make a prisoner *take away forcefully* 477.19
make a profit *trade in* 457.8, *gain* 467.15, *profit* 467.22, *sell at a profit* 482.18, *get rich* 485.13, *be prosperous* 847.6
make a prognosis *predict* 358.14
make a promise *promise* 458.11
make a public exhibition of oneself *show off* 404.26
make a purchase *purchase* 481.11
make a racket *be loud* 232.8
make a report on *estimate* 341.11
make a request *request* 505.10
make a reservation *reserve* 464.14
make a resolution *resolve* 376.12
make a rough copy *be unfinished* 544.12
make a rough sketch *lay the foundations* 388.16
make a round trip *circle* 631.6, *return* 671.11, *orbit* 681.8
make arrangements 767.23
make a rude remark *be insubordinate* 416.8
make a ruling *rule* 780.12
make a run *bobsled* 162.38
make a running attack *fence* 153.7
make a sacrifice *be unselfish* 443.7
make a sacrificial offering *make an offering* 504.17
make a sale *sell* 482.15
make a scene *become angry* 302.20
make a scissors turn *ski* 162.35
make a secured loan *lend* 475.6
make as good as new *restore* 809.12
make a show *put on a show* 404.28
make a show of *display* 843.13
make a side move *move sideways* 623.9
make a silk purse out of a

sow's ear *attempt the impossible* 837.10
make a sortie *counterattack* 418.24
make a space *space* 587.6
make a special request *request* 505.10
make a speech *run for office* 50.10
make a speech *or* **presentation** *address* 209.8
make a splash *put on a show* 404.28
make a stab at *experiment* 335.11
make a stand *battle* 76.33, *resist* 417.10, *entrench* 419.24, *contend* 422.22
make a start *make a beginning* 771.26
make a statement *recount* 202.16
make a stir *be important* 799.13, *make important* 799.14
make a strike *bowl* 151.8
make a success of *be successful* 845.11
make a suggestion *propound* 359.9
make a sweeping statement *make a generalization* 778.18
make a takeover bid *transfer property* 470.12, *bargain* 480.20
make a thumbnail sketch *outline* 617.5
make a to-do [Inf] *exaggerate* 194.11
make a tool *or* **handle of** *exploit* 393.11
make a trade-off *transfer property* 470.12
make a treaty *negotiate* 460.6
make a trial of *test* 390.9
make a truce *make peace* 73.11
make a U-turn *take back* 477.17, *change* 665.14, *reverse* 671.9, *turn around* 680.22
make available to all *make comprehensible* 363.8
make average 742.9
make a virtue of necessity *submit* 421.4, *compromise* 461.7
make a virtue out of necessity **95.19**
make a way *find a way* 691.14
make away with *kill* 30.19, *destroy* 523.10
make away with oneself *commit suicide* 30.24
make a weak effort *leave imperfect* 806.9
make a widow *widow* 66.12
make a widower *widow* 66.12
make a will *will* 472.11
make a wry face *be irritable* 304.14
make bad blood *cause dislike* 291.16
make barren *make impotent* 515.15, *make useless* 802.12
make basic plans *lay the foundations* 388.16
make believe *imagine* 360.14, *be unreal* 722.12
make-believe *fantasy* 360.5, *imaginary* 360.12, *nonreality* 718.5, *unreal* 718.10, 722.7, *theoretical* 720.10
make better *remedy* 115.16, *better* 445.17, *change* 512.12, *change for the better* 665.17, *improve* 807.15
make bigger 746.7; enlarge 581.14
make bitter *make irritable* 304.15
make blind *blind* 243.17
make bold *have the audacity* 400.15, *be discourteous* 411.7
make bold to *lack restraint* 829.21

make both ends meet *be thrifty* 499.5

make bright *smooth* 545.10

make by hand *perform* 522.16

make capital out of *profit* 467.22, *find useful* 801.11, *get better* 807.21

make captive *detain* 830.16

make ceramics 129.10

make certain 840.14; *verify* 336.8, *promise* 464.10, *assure* 810.23

make cheap 497.14

make circular 631.7

make claims upon *demand* 425.11

make clean *clean* 111.17

make clear *rationalize* 4.20, *clarify* 196.3, *explain* 331.16, *make comprehensible* 363.8, *interpret* 365.12, *make simple* 526.12, *rectify* 807.22, *make easy* 823.15

make clothing 100.44

make coarse *pervert* 808.22

make cold 218.15

make comfortable *comfort* 214.14

make common cause *work together* 827.14

make complete *complete* 761.9

make complex *be ambiguous* 632.7

make comprehensible 363.8

make compulsory *impose a duty* 433.14

make concave 635.7

make concessions *permit* 502.6

make concise *rectify* 807.22

make concrete *be material* 524.8

make conditions 460.7

make conform 781.13

make consistent *symmetrize* 626.6, *make regular* 663.9

make constant *make regular* 663.9

make contact *prepare the way* 388.15, *juxtapose* 586.14, *interface* 616.5, *link* 752.18

make continual *make regular* 663.9

make correct *be accurate* 721.22

make corrections *rectify* 807.22

make crystal-clear *make comprehensible* 363.8

make dark 247.10

make deaf *deafen* 229.10

make deeper *deepen* 598.21

make demands *demand* 425.11

make dense 540.9

make dependent *subject* 832.10

make different *cause change* 665.16

make difficulties *withstand* 828.20

make dim 248.8

make dirty *dirty* 112.11

make disappear *make transient* 643.7

make disorderly 766.20

make disproportionate *unbalance* 741.8

make dissimilar *misrepresent* 188.6

make diverse *be diverse* 732.10

make do *improvise* 396.6, *be thrifty* 499.5

make do with *have at one's disposal* 393.14, *take a substitute* 672.7

make drunk *be intoxicating* 121.36

make easier *make easy* 823.15

make easily understood *make comprehensible* 363.8

make easy 823.15; *make comprehensible* 363.8

make elastic 546.8

make ends meet *be parsimonious* 490.13

make enemies *antagonize* 63.12, *cause hate* 300.12, *divide* 753.18

make equal *cancel out* 834.8

make equivalent *correlate* 729.9

make eternal 644.8

make even *make regular* 663.9

make every second count *have no time to spare* 818.6

make evident 339.11

make evil 446.11

make exception *modify* 340.13

make excuses *shirk* 386.18

make excuses for *justify* 441.12

make exempt *acquit* 54.32

make exterior *externalize* 610.15

make external *externalize* 610.15

make extra demands *fatigue* 820.6

make eyes at *communicate love* 299.25

make faces 627.10

make faces at *taunt* 436.23

make famous *publicize* 173.18

make fast 464.13; *make stable* 674.7, *unite closely* 752.16

make fertile *fertilize* 22.12

make few demands *be lenient* 423.5

make fine adjustments *adjust* 721.23

make firm *make fast* 464.13, *unite closely* 752.16

make fluid 555.22

make for *further* 679.13, 825.30, *aim* 697.14

make fragrant *sweeten* 222.7

make free with *have the audacity* 400.15, *be discourteous* 411.7, *lack restraint* 829.21

make fresh *clean* 111.17

make friendly overtures to *seek friendship* 62.11

make friends *befriend* 62.10, *pacify* 74.11, *fraternize* 408.17

make friends with *come together* 757.10

make full *stuff* 577.12

make fun of *be humorous* 277.11, *disdain* 400.16, *ridicule* 436.22, 440.15

make glow *invigorate* 518.5

make good *atone* 313.7, *verify* 336.8, *retaliate* 420.4, *vindicate* 441.11, *perform* 465.5, *compensate* 478.6, 743.7, *achieve* 704.21, *equalize* 740.12, *get better* 807.21, *rectify* 807.22, *repair* 809.10, *do well* 845.12, *be prosperous* 847.6

make good *or* **right** *put right* 429.14

make good one's word *or* **promise** *perform* 465.5

make good progress *go forward* 679.8

make good time 679.10

make green *green* 260.14

make happen *activate* 509.11, *cause* 675.8

make happy *conciliate* 74.10

make hard *harden* 542.9

make haste 818.5

make hay of *exploit* 393.11

make hay while the sun shines *be skillful* 127.14, *be busy* 414.19, *take the opportunity* 659.7

make heads or tails of *know* 48.24

make headway *improve* 467.18, *go forward* 679.8, *get better* 807.21, *overcome obstacles* 845.14

make healthy 113.13; *restore* 807.17

make heavy 538.14

make heavy weather of *find difficult* 824.17

make hell freeze over *attempt the impossible* 837.10

make higher *heighten* 596.14

make history *be remembered* 354.15, *do great deeds* 412.14

make horizontal 603.10

make human 18.17

make hygienic *practice hygiene* 116.4

make ignorant 349.10

make ill *cause adversity* 848.15

make illegal 53.29; *prohibit* 503.8

make illegible *obliterate* 186.8

make immaculate *clean* 111.17

make immovable *make fast* 464.13

make immune *acquit* 54.32

make important 799.14; *reveal* 843.14

make impossible 837.8

make impotent 515.15

make improvements *improve* 807.15, *rectify* 807.22

make inactive 415.16; *make useless* 802.12, *impair* 808.18

make indifferent 289.13

make inferior *subject* 832.10

make infertile 23.9

make inoperative *or* **inoperable** *impair* 808.18

make inroads *transgress* 712.14

make insane 110.13

make insensitive *make indifferent* 289.13

make into *transform* 670.13

make invisible 245.7

make irascible 303.16

make irritable 304.15

make it [Inf] *have sex* 20.21, *get rich* 485.13, *reach* 704.14, *achieve* 704.21, *attain one's goal* 845.13, *be prosperous* 847.6

make it all square *be equal* 740.11

make it easy for *be permissive* 502.7

make it hard on oneself *have difficulty* 824.18

make it one's aim *attempt* 390.6

make it one's business to *aim at* 385.15

make it one's duty *incur a duty* 433.15, *guarantee* 458.13

make it to the top *be published* 173.19, *peak* 596.18, *be at the top* 600.9

make it tough for *cause difficulties* 824.22

make it up *pacify* 74.11, *compensate* 743.7

make it up as one goes along *improvise* 389.15

make jealous *arouse jealousy* 314.10

make known *communicate* 170.12, *publish* 173.15, *disclose* 180.8

make lame *make useless* 802.12

make larger *enlarge* 581.14

make law *command* 425.10

make laws *legislate* 53.31

make legal 53.27; *authorize* 52.14, *permit* 503.8

make less *make smaller* 747.8

make light *lighten* 539.9

make lighter *lighten* 539.9

make light of *play down* 195.17, *underestimate* 344.5, *do easily* 823.16

make light work of *do easily* 823.16

make likely *make probable* 838.9

make like new *restore* 809.12

make literal *be literal* 721.25

make little 580.10

make little of *underestimate* 344.5, *do easily* 823.16

make love *have sex* 20.21

make love not war *be at peace* 73.10

make lower *lower* 597.21

make mad *make violent* 520.10, *derange* 766.23

make mandatory *impose a duty* 433.14

make merry 167.13; *rejoice* 279.5, *celebrate* 405.10

make mincemeat of *demolish* 523.12, *ruin* 523.15

make mischief *disobey* 427.12

make money *be good* 445.16, *gain* 467.15, *earn* 467.20, *get rich* 485.13, *attain one's goal* 845.13, *be prosperous* 847.6

make more bigger 746.7

make motionless 678.8

make much ado *make important* 799.14

make much of *boast* 194.14, *salute* 405.13, *make important* 799.14

make music *play* 141.14

make mute *strike dumb* 206.10

make mutual concessions *compromise* 461.7

make mysterious 182.13

make narrow *or* **narrower** *narrow* 593.14

make neat *clean* 111.17, *tidy* 807.19

make neither head nor tail of *find unintelligible* 364.14

make neutral *cancel out* 834.8

make new 652.20

make no answer *be taciturn* 208.7

make noble 70.5

make no bones about *show oneself* 843.15

make no bones about it *be sincere* 191.8

make no comment *keep secret* 182.11

make no confession *be impenitent* 452.4

make no demands *be lenient* 423.5, *be easy* 823.14

make no difference *equalize* 740.12

make no distinction *be indiscriminate* 338.10

make no impact on *make indifferent* 289.13

make no impression *be unimportant* 800.18

make no mistake *recognize* 363.11

make no mystery *show oneself* 843.15

make no noise *be silent* 231.3

make nonsense of *mean nothing* 362.10

make no point *be circuitous* 199.6

make no preparations *be unprepared* 389.14

make no profit *lose money* 468.15

make no secret of *show oneself* 843.15

make no sense *mean nothing* 362.10

make no sign *keep secret* 182.11, *hide* 844.13

make notes *inscribe* 185.14

make nothing of *find unintelligible* 364.14

make no use of *not use* 96.18

make no waves *submit* 421.4

make nude **614.19**
make null and void *cancel* 834.6
make obeisance *knuckle under*
401.10, *defer to* 410.12, *show
respect* 435.16, *bow* 716.22
make objections *object* 828.18
make obligatory *demand* 425.11
make obscure **197.3**
make obvious *reveal* 843.14
make off *retreat* 386.22, *hurry off*
705.11
make off-limits *prohibit* 503.8
make off with *steal* 479.14
make one *join in marriage* 64.20,
unify 752.15, *become one* 788.18
make one feel small *or this high*
humiliate 298.19
make one more *support* 748.14
make one pause *daunt* 179.9
make one's adieus *part* 705.13
make one's apologies *apologize*
313.8
make one's bed and lie in it
serve one right 420.5
make one's blood boil *make
angry* 302.18
make one's contribution *insert*
748.12
make one's daily round *be cyclic*
663.11
make one's debut *launch* 405.14
make one's defense *stand trial*
54.29
make one's departure *depart*
705.8
make oneself *grudge* 375.15
make oneself at home *be
informal* 407.10, 829.19, *visit*
408.16
make oneself conspicuous *show
off* 404.26
make oneself felt *influence*
512.11
make oneself liable *incur a duty*
433.15
make oneself one of the family
visit 408.16
make oneself responsible *be in
debt* 488.9
make oneself scarce *retreat*
386.22, *absent oneself* 576.15,
hurry off 705.11, *escape* 816.8
make oneself useful *serve* 69.11,
be useful 801.9, *help* 825.23
make oneself welcome *visit*
408.16
make one's excuses *refuse* 506.8
make one's exit *withdraw* 705.9
make one's fortune *get rich*
485.13, *be prosperous* 847.6
make one's gorge rise *make
angry* 302.18, *be repulsive* 701.10
make one's head swim *be
intoxicating* 121.36, *be wondrous*
294.14
make one's head swim *or ache
be unintelligible* 364.11
make one's leave *depart* 705.8
make one's mark *do well* 845.12,
be prosperous 847.6
make one's money work for
one *speculate* 480.19
make one's mouth water *cause
desire* 288.22
make one's name (known)
publicize 173.18
make one's nest *take up residence*
60.24
make one's own *gain* 467.15,
characterize 779.15
make one's pile [Inf] *profit*
467.22
make one's point *influence*
508.11

make one's presence felt *attend*
575.14
make one's quarry *aim at* 385.15
make one's rounds *ring* 681.9
make one's submission *propound*
359.9
make one stop in one's tracks
daunt 179.9
make one's voice heard *influence*
512.11
make one's way **679.12;** *be in
motion* 677.14
make one yawn *bore* 296.8
make operate *activate* 509.11
make operational *prepare for
action* 388.18, *activate* 509.11
make ordinary *make regular*
663.9
make or mar *cause* 675.8
make out *know* 48.24, *see* 242.20,
recognize 363.11, *decipher* 365.13
make out [Inf] *have sex* 20.21,
communicate love 299.25
makeover *change for the better*
665.4
make over *transfer property*
470.12, *give* 472.10, *transfer*
685.8, *refurbish* 809.11
make overtures *befriend* 62.10,
desire 299.24, *negotiate* 460.6,
petition 505.11
make overweight *make heavy*
538.14
make parallel *parallel* 606.7
make peace **73.11;** *pacify* 74.9,
74.11, *forgive and forget* 312.9,
pause 668.13
make people stare *show off*
404.26
make periodical **641.10**
make permanent **644.9, 667.5**
make plain *make comprehensible*
363.8, *reveal* 843.14
make play with *exploit* 393.11
make pleasant **271.10;** *sweeten*
222.7
make plural *pluralize* 793.9
make pointed *sharpen* 549.16
make poo-poo [Inf] *defecate* 25.21
make poor *impoverish* 486.16
make porous *hole* 583.17
make port *sail* 690.16, *land*
704.16, *shelter* 812.8
make possible **836.7;** *permit*
502.6, *make easy* 823.9
make powerless *remove power
from* 515.13
make pregnant *propagate* 21.15
make preparations *prepare*
388.14
make probable **838.9**
make progress *be busy* 414.19,
continue 669.8, *go forward* 679.8,
get better 807.21
make prostrate *lower* 597.21,
make horizontal 603.10
make provision *prepare* 388.14
make provisions *have foresight*
357.8
make public *publish* 173.15
make purple *empurple* 262.7
Maker *God* 82.6
maker *producer* 522.10, *first cause*
675.6, *originator* 771.5
make rapid strides *improve*
467.18
make ready *educate* 48.22, *find
means* 102.6, *prepare* 388.14,
prepare for action 388.18
make-ready *printing* 173.3
make real **719.11;** *be material*
524.8
make red *redden* 257.9
make redress *compensate* 478.6

make redundant [Brit] *dismiss*
709.15, *eject* 764.8
make reference to *relate to* 727.9,
reveal 843.14
make regular **663.9**
make reparation *atone* 313.7, *put
right* 429.14
make reparations *compensate*
478.6
make restitution *atone* 313.7,
give back 478.5, *restore* 671.10,
compensate 743.7
make rich **485.15**
make right *atone* 313.7, *be accurate*
721.22
make rivers run uphill *attempt
the impossible* 837.10
Maker of all things *God the Father*
82.8
make room *space* 587.6
make room for *space* 563.15
make rough **544.11**
make round **633.9;** *make circular*
631.7
make rounds *proceed* 692.16
make routine *make regular* 663.9
make safe *secure* 464.9, *protect*
810.21
make sail *handle sailboat equipment*
150.30
make sane *be sane* 109.5
make sense *be reasonable* 319.12,
be intelligible 363.10
make sense of *interpret* 365.12
make shallow *shallow* 599.5
make shapeless **625.3**
make sharp *sharpen* 549.16
make (sheep's) eyes at *look*
242.21
makeshift *sufficient* 97.3, *means*
102.1, *method* 387.4,
unpremeditated 389.7, *improvised*
396.4, *substitute* 672.3, *imperfect
item* 806.3, *incomplete* 806.6
make shift to *attempt* 390.6
make shift with *have at one's
disposal* 393.14
make shipshape *straighten*
630.14, *tidy* 807.19
make short work of *eat well*
92.23, *work* 122.8, *try* 414.21,
ruin 523.15, *have no time to spare*
818.6, *do easily* 823.16
make similar **733.15**
make simple **526.12**
make smaller **747.8;** *make dense*
540.9, *contract* 582.12
make smooth *smooth* 552.13
make someone *publicize* 173.18
make someone believe **87.11**
make someone eat dust [Inf]
make haste 818.5
make someone jump *surprise*
292.9
make someone keep his *or her*
distance *repel* 701.7
make someone laugh **368.7**
make someone's ears burn *hear*
228.13
make someone sit up and take
notice *be important* 799.13
make someone's mouth water
influence 508.11
make something happen *insist*
376.14
make sound *make fast* 464.13
make sparse **541.5**
make special *characterize* 779.15
make speeches *speak to* 205.19
make spherical *make round* 633.9
make stable **674.7**
make steadfast *make fast* 464.13
make straight *straighten* 630.14
make strides *press on* 679.9

make strong *strengthen* 516.15
make sullen **304.13**
make superfluous *be superfluous*
99.12
make sure *make stable* 674.7, *make
certain* 840.14
make tangible *be real* 721.21
make taste **219.6**
make terms *contract* 459.8, 462.11
make terms *or proposals or a
bid or demands or concessions
make conditions* 460.7
make the best of a bad job
compromise 461.7
make the best of it *make a virtue
out of necessity* 95.19, *hope* 281.10,
improvise 396.6
make the big time [Inf] *attain
one's goal* 845.13
make the dust fly *be active*
414.18
make the effort *attempt* 390.6, *do
something* 412.13
make the first move *pioneer*
771.29
make the front page *be published*
173.19
make the grade *suffice* 97.6,
achieve 704.21, *get better* 807.21,
attain one's goal 845.13
make the leopard change its
spots *attempt the impossible* 837.10
make the lion lie down with
the lamb *make peace* 73.11
make the most of *overestimate*
343.6, *exploit* 393.11, *direct*
412.16, *promote* 807.18
make the most *or best of* have at
one's disposal 393.14
make the point *doubt* 333.19
make the rubble bounce *bomb*
418.19
make the running *accelerate*
694.14, *exceed* 712.15
make the same **730.16**
make the sign of the cross *follow
rites* 85.19
make the sparks fly *try* 414.21
make the welkin ring [Arch]
shatter the peace 232.10
make the world a safer place
make peace 73.11
make thin **595.17**
make things awkward *cause
difficulties* 824.22
make things difficult *cause
difficulties* 824.22, *make impossible*
837.8
make things easy for *influence*
508.11
make things hum *try* 414.21
make things worse *make worse*
808.17
make things *or matters* worse
cause difficulties 824.22
make tidy *clean* 111.17
make time for *give* 472.10
make time stand still *spend time*
639.14, *perpetuate* 640.5
make to order *make clothing*
100.44
make tough **547.15**
make tracks [Inf] *retreat* 386.22,
be swift 694.10, *depart* 705.8,
make haste 818.5
make transient **643.7**
make transparent **249.12**
make trouble *combat* 77.34, *pick a
fight* 463.10, *be disorderly* 766.22
make ugly **531.4;** *stain* 808.20
make unbreakable *make tough*
547.15
make uncertain **841.19**

make unclean *dirty* 112.11, *misuse* 395.6, *make worse* 808.17

make uniform *symmetrize* 626.6, *make regular* 663.9

make unimportant 800.20

make unintelligible 364.13

make unlike 734.9

make unpleasant *displease* 272.8

make unwelcome *exclude* 383.11, *be discourteous* 411.7, *fend off* 701.9, *ostracize* 709.17

makeup *costume* 100.10, *face color* 251.9, *cosmetics* 530.4, *form* 551.3, *contents* 577.1, *forming* 624.4, *nature* 723.4, *compound* 757.4, *inclusion* 763.1

make up *fabricate* 192.24, 720.17, *color* 251.16, *forgive and forget* 312.9, *imagine* 360.14, *produce* 522.13, *beautify* 530.14, 807.20, *design* 536.8, *embody* 577.11, *come to be* 717.19, *combine* 757.9, *complete* 761.9, *be included* 763.6

make up an account *account* 493.9

makeup artist *stagehand* 136.29, *filmmaker* 137.14, *beautician* 530.11

makeup bag *bag* 578.7

makeup brush *cosmetic tool* 530.5

makeup case *or* **box** *cosmetic tool* 530.5

make up for *atone* 313.7, *compensate* 743.7

make up for lost time *work* 122.8, *make good time* 679.10, *accelerate* 694.14, *make haste* 818.5

make up leeway *make good time* 679.10

make up one's mind *resolve* 376.12, *select* 382.12

makeup remover *cosmetic tool* 530.5

make up the numbers *support* 748.14

make up the shortfall *augment* 748.13

make up time *accelerate* 694.14

make up to [Inf] *seek friendship* 62.11, *fawn* 401.9, *cajole* 439.14

make useless 802.12

make use of *use* 393.9, *sponge* 401.13, *find useful* 801.11

make vertical 602.9

make violent 520.10

make visible 242.25, 244.9

make war *be at war* 76.32

make war on *oppose* 63.11

make water *urinate* 25.22

make waves [Inf] *not conform* 782.18, *be important* 799.13

make way *sail* 150.29, *navigate* 690.15

make way! *open up!* 583.24

make way for *avoid* 386.13, *acquiesce* 421.5, *sidestep* 698.22, *make easy* 823.15

make weak *weaken* 517.13

makeweight *weighing instrument* 538.7, *equalizer* 740.5, *counterbalance* 743.2, *fullness* 761.5

make welcome *be sociable* 408.14, *receive someone* 473.14

make well *conciliate* 74.10, *make healthy* 113.13, *cure* 809.15

make whole *complete* 761.9, *restore* 809.12

make whoopee [Inf] *rejoice* 279.5, *communicate love* 299.25, *celebrate* 405.10

make wicked *deprave* 448.14

make work *try* 414.21, *activate* 509.11

make-work rules *bargaining terms* 57.10

make worse 808.17; *aggravate* 276.5

make yellow 259.12

make young *be young* 26.13

make yourself at home! *welcome!* 704.24

making *production* 522.1, *manufacture* 522.2, *structuring* 551.5, *achievement* 704.8

making amends *compensation* 478.2

making a mountain out of a molehill *exaggeration* 194.1

making an end *dying* 29.3

making a profit *profitable* 801.8

making a run for it *desertion* 386.7

making as good as new *repair* 809.1

making a U-turn *taking back* 477.4

making dim *dimming* 248.3

making do *improvisation* 396.1

making ends meet *home economics* 56.2

making equal *canceling out* 834.3

making good *compensation* 478.2, *rectification* 807.8

making it [Inf] *sexual intercourse* 20.9

making light *lightening* 246.3

making light of *downplaying* 195.6

making like new *repair* 809.1

making love *sexual intercourse* 20.9, *sexual love* 299.3

making much of *bombast* 194.4

making of, the *improvement* 807.1

making one's own *claiming* 469.2

making out [Inf] *sexual intercourse* 20.9, *communication of love* 299.6

making ready *preparation* 388.1

making sense *intelligible* 363.5

making smooth *smoothness* 545.1

making terms *negotiation* 460.1

making the best of it *improvisation* 396.1

making tracks [Inf] *swiftness* 694.1

making up one's mind *selecting* 382.4

making use of *use* 393.1

making war *warfare* 76.3

making whoopee [Inf] *communication of love* 299.6, *celebration* 405.1

mako *food fish and shellfish* 90.20

Malabo Countries 566

malachite *green thing* 260.4

malacologist *animal scientist* 34.7, *invertebrate zoologist* 39.3

malacology *animal science* 34.6, *invertebrate zoology* 39.2

malacostracan *crustacean* 39.10

maladminister *be unskillful* 128.8, *misuse* 395.6

maladministered *bungled* 128.7

maladministration *bungling* 128.2, *misuse* 395.1

maladroit *clumsy* 128.6

malady *illness* 114.2, *affliction* 117.1

malaise *symptom* 114.3, *pain* 215.1, *depression* 270.2

Malaita Islands 572

malamute Breeds of Dogs 35

malapert [Arch] *insolent person* 400.7, *rude* 400.9

malapertly [Arch] *rudely* 400.19

Malapolski Horse and Pony Breeds 159

malapropism *word* 5.17, *language error* 351.10

malapropos *untimely* 660.5, *at the wrong time* 660.12, *inconvenient* 804.5

malar bone Human Bones 19

Mälaren *or* **Malar** Lakes 568

malaria *tropical disease* 114.10

malaria [Arch] *miasma* 556.3

malarial fever *tropical disease* 114.10

malarkey *or* **malarky** [Inf] *empty talk* 362.5

Malawi Countries 566, Lakes 568

malaxophobia Phobias 283

Malay Breeds of Fowl 16

Malaysia Countries 566

malcological *molluskan* 39.23

malcontent *dissatisfied person* 274.3, *dissatisfied* 274.4, *dissenter* 347.5, *troublemaker* 427.5, *protester* 507.4, *protesting* 507.5

malcontented *dissatisfied* 274.4, *envious* 314.8

malcontentedness *envy* 314.1

Maldives Countries 566, Islands 572

Male Countries 566

male 32.1, 32.16; *sex* 20.1, *sexual* 20.15, *of flowers* 42.11

male alto *voice* 141.5

male animal 32.15

male bird 36.15

male chauvinism *maleness* 32.2, *misanthropy* 291.4, *social discrimination* 337.4

male chauvinist *misanthrope* 291.5

male chauvinist pig [Inf *and* Off] *macho man* 32.6, *misanthrope* 291.5, *bigot* 337.7

maledict [Arch] *curse* 301.13

malediction *curse* 301.1, *evil thing* 446.2

maledictive *cursing* 301.7

maledictory *cursing* 301.7

male-dominated society *maleness* 32.2

malefactor 306.6; *lawbreaker* 53.15, *evildoer* 412.6, *wrongdoer* 430.8, *evil person* 446.3, *villain* 448.5, *guilty person* 450.5

male feminist *liberated man* 32.13

malefic *malicious* 306.8, *evil* 446.7

maleficence *malice* 306.2, *evil* 446.1

maleficent *malicious* 306.8, *evil* 446.7

maleic Common Fatty Acids 12

male mammal 35.18

male member *organs of reproduction* 21.9

male menopause *middle age* 27.4

maleness 32.2; *sex* 20.1

male person *male* 32.1

male pill *contraceptive* 23.6

male prostitute *libertine* 32.7, *sexually immoral person* 432.8

male sex organs *organs of reproduction* 21.9

male stripper *pornography* 432.7

male title of address 32.3

malevolence 306.1; *misanthropy* 291.4, *hate* 300.1, *evil* 446.1, *wickedness* 448.1, *occult influence* 512.2

malevolent 306.7; *hostile* 63.6, *poisonous* 117.14, *hating* 300.7, *pitiless* 309.3, *vindictive* 441.10, *evil* 446.7, *wicked* 448.9

malevolently 306.14; *banefully* 117.19, *with hate* 300.13, *pitilessly*

309.7, *vindictively* 441.16, *evilly* 446.12, *wickedly* 448.15

malfeasance *wrongdoing* 430.7

malfeasant *malefactor* 306.6, *unlawful* 430.15

malfeasor *malefactor* 306.6, *evil person* 446.3

malform *deform* 627.11

malformation *distortion of body* 627.3

malformed *deformed* 627.7

malfunction 846.20; *failure* 430.9, *go wrong* 430.23, *technical problem* 826.3, *have a mishap* 826.18

malfunctioning *gone wrong* 430.17, *blocked* 826.13

Mali Countries 566

malic Common Fatty Acids 12

malice 306.2; *legal injustice* 53.5, *hate* 300.1, *resentment* 302.1, *malevolence* 306.1, *evil* 446.1

malice aforethought *hate* 300.1

malice aforethought *or* **prepense** *malice* 306.2

malicious 306.8; *hating* 300.7, *resentful* 302.8, *malevolent* 306.7, *vindictive* 441.10, *evil* 446.7

malicious gossip *defamation* 440.3

maliciously 306.15; *with hate* 300.13, *resentfully* 302.22, *vindictively* 441.16, *evilly* 446.12, *destructively* 446.13

maliciousness *malice* 306.2

malign 306.11; *lie* 192.23, *hating* 300.7, *vilify* 301.15, *malicious* 306.8, *be malevolent* 306.12, *bring into disrepute* 371.6, *criticize* 418.26, *wrong* 430.19, *defame* 440.13

malignancy *or* **malignance** *malice* 306.2

malignant *killing* 30.17, *hating* 300.7, *malicious* 306.8, *evil* 446.7, *detrimental* 446.8

malignantly *deadly* 30.26, *with hate* 300.13

malignant tumor *cancer* 114.15

maligner *liar* 192.10

malign influence *evil thing* 446.2, *occult influence* 512.2, *bad fortune* 848.7

maligning *lying* 192.16, *critical* 418.16

malignity 306.5; *hate* 300.1, *malice* 306.2, *evil* 446.1

malignly 306.18; *with hate* 300.13

maline Fabrics and Fibers 130

malines Fabrics and Fibers 130

malinger *deceive* 193.16, *be neglectful* 326.7, *shirk* 386.18

malingerer *sick person* 114.22, *deceiver* 193.8, *neglector* 326.3, *avoider* 386.8

malingering *deceptive* 193.12, *indifferent* 326.5, *shirking* 386.4

malison [Arch] *curse* 301.1

mall *marketplace* 483.7, *building* 551.9, *urban area* 567.10, *center of activity* 612.4, *passage* 691.5

mallards Collective Names 59

malleability *educatability* 48.9, *persuadability* 178.8, *obedience* 426.1, *softness* 543.1, *pliancy* 781.3

malleable *educatable* 48.18, *persuadable* 178.14, *submitting* 421.3, *obedient* 426.4, *pliant* 543.7, *irresolute* 466.4, *conformable* 781.7, *wieldy* 823.12

malleably *studiously* 48.26, *adaptably* 781.15

mallee tree Trees and Shrubs 43

mallet *material* 144.6, *hammer* 553.13, *impeller* 695.7
malleus *Human Bones* 19, *ear* 19.10, 228.2
mallophagan *insectile* 40.11
Mallorca *Islands* 572
mallow *Flowers* 42
malnourished *unhealthy* 114.23, *emaciated* 595.10
malnutrition *emaciation* 595.2
malodor *stench* 227.1
malodorous *unclean* 112.8, *stinking* 227.3
malodorously *stinkingly* 227.6
malodorousness *stench* 227.1
malpractice *misuse* 395.1, *illegality* 450.4
Malta *Countries* 566, *Islands* 572
malt culms *animal feed* 16.12
malted milk *milk* 95.5
Maltese *Breeds of Dogs* 35, *Breeds of Cats* 35
Maltese cross *Flowers* 42
Malthusianism *economic deterioration* 808.2
maltose *Common Sugars* 12
maltreat *harm* 306.13, *ill-use* 395.7, *wrong* 430.19, *be evil* 446.10
maltreated *ill-used* 395.4
maltreatment *malignity* 306.5, *ill-use* 395.2
malt vinegar *basic cooking ingredient* 91.8
Malvi *Breeds of Cattle* 16
mama [Inf] *woman in the family* 33.13, *family member* 65.2
mama [Inf *and* Off] *sex object* 20.8
mamaloi *imam* 84.7
mama's boy *effeminate male* 32.8, *weak person* 517.4
mamba *snake* 37.6
mambo *Dances* 135
mamilla *bulge* 634.2
mamma *mammalian characteristic* 35.3
mammal 35.1; *type of animal* 34.5
mammal dwelling 35.21
Mammalia *mammal* 35.1
mammalian 35.23; *warm-blooded* 217.14
mammalian characteristic 35.3
mammal-like *mammalian* 35.23
mammal-like reptile *extinct reptile* 37.9
mammalogist 35.2; *animal scientist* 34.7
mammalogy *animal science* 34.6
mammary *of a secretion* 24.5
mammary gland *secretory mechanism* 24.3, *mammalian characteristic* 35.3
mammilla *mammalian characteristic* 35.3
mammogram *diagnostic radiology* 107.12
mammography *diagnostic radiology* 107.12
mammon *cash* 484.2
mammoth *big thing* 579.9, *huge* 579.14, *thing of the past* 651.8
mammothermography *diagnostic radiology* 107.12
Mamoré *Rivers* 570
man 27.8; *humankind* 18.1, *person* 18.8, *male* 32.1, *domestic servant* 69.7, *equip* 388.19, *adherent* 401.5, *take action* 509.12
man [Inf] *male title of address* 32.3
man, the [Inf] *governance* 52.6, *celebrity* 799.6
mana *minor deity* 82.2, *type of power* 514.6

man about the house *man in the family* 32.12
man about town *social person* 408.7
manacle *intertwine* 752.19, *bind* 754.14, *restrain someone* 830.17
manacled *bound* 754.12
manacles *fastener* 754.7, *means of restraint* 830.6
manage 126.10; *govern* 49.26, *wield authority* 52.16, *economize* 56.11, *master* 68.17, *represent* 80.6, *take charge of* 391.8, *behave toward* 399.20, *direct* 412.16, 780.14, *take action* 509.12, *be powerful* 514.18, *awaken* 675.9, *be in a state of* 725.8, *lead* 744.19, *order* 765.18, *make arrangements* 767.23, *overcome obstacles* 845.14
manageability *wieldiness* 823.3
manageable *obedient* 426.4, *cheap* 497.9, *workable* 509.8, *wieldy* 823.12
managed *industrial* 57.13, *financial* 457.6
managed currency *international finance* 457.2, *money* 484.1, *currency market* 484.8
manage grassland 45.10
management 126.1, 509.4; *government* 49.1, *governance* 52.6, *army commands* 77.13, *use* 393.1, *treatment* 399.11, *action* 412.1, *leadership* 744.2, *authority* 780.6
management accounting *accounts* 493.4
management board 126.2
management buyout *purchasing* 481.2
management by objectives *management system* 126.3, *plan* 387.1
management consultant *adviser* 176.5
management demands *bargaining* 57.9
management-employee relations *labor relations* 57.1
management information system (MIS) *computing* 15.2, *management system* 126.3
management lock-out *strike* 57.8
management practices *bargaining* 57.9
management review *planning* 387.8
management study *management system* 126.3
management system 126.3
management team *management board* 126.2
management theory *management system* 126.3
manager 126.7; *person in authority* 52.7, *employer* 57.3, *company leader* 68.8, *producer* 136.28, *baseball team* 147.2, *boxer* 152.8, *soccer participant* 163.4, *motivator* 178.11, 508.6, *planner* 387.9, *operator* 412.7, 509.5, *influential person* 512.5, *superior* 744.5
managerial 126.9; *authoritative* 52.9, *industrial* 57.13, *masterful* 68.15, *enterprising* 391.5, *effective* 412.10
managerial accounting *finance* 457.1
managerial control *directorship* 126.5
managerially 126.13; *legitimately* 52.19, *industrially* 57.22, *masterfully* 68.19
managers *management board* 126.2
managership *management* 126.1

manage the business of *represent* 80.6
manage the interests of *represent* 80.6
manage trees 43.14
managing *governing* 49.25, *industrial* 57.13, *management* 126.1, *managerial* 126.9, *directions* 697.7
managing director *employer* 57.3, *manager* 126.7, *operator* 412.7, *important person* 799.5
managing editor *book publishing personnel* 174.12, *print journalist* 175.5
Managra *Breeds of Pigs* 16
Managua *Countries* 566
Manama *Countries* 566
mañana [Sp] *future time* 650.1, *delay* 658.3
man and wife *married couple* 64.9
man a ship *navigate* 690.15
Manaslu *Mountains and Hills* 569
man-at-arms *combatant* 77.1, *soldier* 77.4, *army person* 77.17
man at the top *important person* 18.11
man at the wheel *nautical person* 690.12
Manawatu *Rivers* 570
mancala *Board and Table Games* 167
Mancha *Breeds of Sheep* 16
Manchester *major British cities* 567.7
Manchester terrier *Breeds of Dogs* 35
manchineel *Trees and Shrubs* 43
mandala *talisman* 86.9, *circle* 631.2
mandamus *legal process* 54.3
mandarin *leader* 68.3
mandarin collar *neckwear* 100.29
mandarin orange *orange thing* 258.3
mandatary *dominion* 566.3
mandate *acquisition of authority* 52.5, *gain authority* 52.15, *law* 53.1, *jurisdiction* 53.3, 54.2, *necessitate* 95.17, *specification* 340.6, *procedure* 387.2, *authorization* 425.4, *authorize* 425.14, 833.10, *coercion* 428.2, *compel* 428.8, *approval* 437.1, *approve* 437.14, *permission* 502.1, *region* 564.1, *exert sovereignty* 566.12, *authority* 833.3
mandate *or* **mandated territory** *dominion* 566.3
mandated *authorized* 52.11, 425.9, *approved* 437.8, *national* 566.10, *commissioned* 833.6
mandated territory *body politic* 50.3
mandatorially *advisorily* 176.12
mandatory *necessitative* 95.11, *conditional* 340.10, *commanding* 425.7, *compulsory* 428.7, *duty-bound* 433.8, *essential* 723.5, *legal* 780.8
Mandelbrot set *Mathematical Concepts* 6
mandible *Human Bones* 19, *mouth* 19.7
mandibles *eating organ* 92.14
mando-bass *Musical Instruments* 142
mando-cello *Musical Instruments* 142
mandola *Musical Instruments* 142
mandolin *Musical Instruments* 142
mandrel *axle* 682.7
manduce [Arch] *chew* 92.22

manducation [Arch] *eating* 92.1
Mandya *Breeds of Sheep* 16
man-eater *eater* 92.15
man-eater [Inf] *charmer* 700.6
man eating *eating habit* 92.7
man-eating *murderous* 30.18, *eating* 92.18
manège *equestrianism* 159.8
manes *ghost* 86.11
maneuver 677.18, 689.14; *be at war* 76.32, *manage* 126.10, *artifice* 193.5, *scheme* 193.18, *touch* 216.9, *plot* 387.15, *use* 393.9, *tactics* 399.12, *conduct oneself* 399.17, *deed* 412.2, *motivate* 412.12, *take action* 509.12, *stratagem* 822.2, *be cunning* 822.5
maneuverability *wieldiness* 823.3, *scope* 829.7
maneuverable *workable* 509.8, *wieldy* 823.12, *free-ranging* 829.13
maneuverer *motivator* 178.11, 508.6, *schemer* 193.10, *planner* 387.9, *cunning person* 822.3
maneuvering *artful* 193.13, *plot* 387.6, *tactics* 399.12, *management* 509.4
maneuvers *military training* 58.3, *art of war* 76.16, *tactics* 399.12
man Friday *office assistant* 69.6, *deputy* 80.1, *clerical worker* 123.5, *helper* 275.5
manful *heroic* 284.10
manfully *heroically* 284.18, *persistently* 376.17
manfulness *heroism* 284.2
Mangalarga *Horse and Pony Breeds* 159
Mangalitsa *Breeds of Pigs* 16
manganese *Chemical Elements and Common Allotropes* 11, *essential element* 12.15
mange *animal disease* 34.10, *skin disease* 114.16
mangel *animal feed* 16.12
mangle *fabric-handling tool* 130.12, *inflict pain* 215.10, *heater* 217.3, *smoother* 545.2, *smooth* 545.10, *contractor* 582.6, *flattener* 603.4
mangonel *Historical Missile Weapons* 78
mangrove *Trees and Shrubs* 43
mangy *unclean* 112.8, *shoddy* 497.11
manhandle *ill-use* 395.7, *convey* 685.9, *take away* 685.12
man-hater *hater* 300.6
man-hating *misanthropic* 291.8
Manhattan *New York* 567.6, *Islands* 572
manhood *sex* 20.1, *adulthood* 27.2, *maleness* 32.2
man-hour *General Units* 589, *period of activity* 641.4
man-hours *task* 122.2
manhunt *pursuit* 385.1
mania *neurosis* 108.9, *compulsion* 108.13, *delusion* 110.2, *psychiatric disease* 114.21, *emotion* 266.3, *likes* 290.3, *habit* 397.1
maniac *insane person* 110.5
maniacal *psychologically disturbed* 108.39
maniaphobia *Phobias* 283
manic 110.10; *passionate* 266.12, *fidgety* 414.14
manic-depressive *insane person* 110.5
manic-depressive psychosis *mood disorder* 108.12
manic episode *mood disorder* 108.12
Manicouagan *Rivers* 570

manicure *beauty treatment* 530.3, beautify 530.14

manicured *elegant* 527.3

manicure scissors *cosmetic tool* 530.5

manicure set *or* case *cosmetic tool* 530.5

manicurist *beautician* 530.11

manifest **843.9**; *publicized* 173.14, disclosed 180.5, disclose 180.8, represent 187.10, visible 242.19, 244.5, make visible 244.9, easily seen through 249.10, appearing 264.9, demonstrated 331.9, demonstrate 331.15, evident 339.9, show 404.24, statement 493.2, be material 524.8, present 575.7, opened up 583.11, existing 717.11, bill 785.4, display 843.13, reveal 843.14

manifestation **244.3, 843.2**; *ghost* 86.11, disclosure 180.1, signal 183.6, representation 187.1, appearance 264.1, demonstration 331.1, indication 339.3, show 404.12, materialization 524.2, presence 575.1, omnipresence 575.4, display 843.1

manifested *displayed* 843.8

manifestly **331.20, 843.17**; *visibly* 242.28, 244.10, apparently 264.16, evidently 339.16, originally 345.16, openly 583.22, really 717.22

manifestness *presence* 575.1, manifestation 843.2

manifesto *philosophical system* 4.2, law 53.1, belief system 87.3, publication 173.1, affirmation 189.1, prospectus 387.3, command 425.1

manifold *topology* 6.45, variety 732.2, varied 732.6, multiplicative 793.8, multitudinous 795.5

manifoldly *variously* 732.15

manikin *figure* 187.4, little person 580.5

Manila Countries 566

man in the family **32.12**

man in the moon *moon* 7.18

man in the street *average person* 18.9, everyone 778.7

man *or* woman in *or* on the street *average person* 742.4

man-in-the-street *commoner* 71.1

maniple *historical soldier* 77.8, vestment 84.11

manipulatable *workable* 509.8

manipulate **6.87, 508.12**; *have authority* 52.13, treat 115.17, manage 126.10, touch 216.9, practice sophistry 330.11, use 393.9, conduct oneself 399.17, behave toward 399.20, motivate 412.12, take action 509.12, be cunning 822.5

manipulated *misrepresentative* 193.14, misused 395.3

manipulate market prices *speculate* 480.19

manipulating *authoritative* 52.9, misrepresentative 193.14, touching 216.2, cunning 330.8

manipulation *evaluation* 6.22, sex act 20.10, authority 52.1, therapy 115.12, management 126.1, 509.4, cunning 330.3, plot 387.6, misuse 395.1, treatment 399.11, stratagem 822.2

manipulative *misrepresentative* 193.14

manipulatively *deceptively* 193.21

manipulative treatment *treatment* 107.14

manipulator *motivator* 178.11, 508.6, one who misrepresents 193.9, operator 412.7, influential person 512.5

Manipur pony Horse and Pony Breeds 159

Man, Isle of Islands 572

Manitoba Canadian Provinces 564, Lakes 568

manitou *God* 82.6

mankind *life* 28.1, human family 65.5

manlike *male* 32.16

manliness *maleness* 32.2, heroism 284.2

manly *sexual* 20.15, male 32.16, heroic 284.10, physically strong 516.10

man-made *produced* 522.12, artificial 720.12, imitation 736.8

man-made lake *lake* 568.1

manna *life requirement* 28.5, food 90.1, offering 472.6, sustenance 825.3

mannan *polysaccharide* 12.5

manned flight *space travel* 7.29

mannequin *fashion business* 536.3, displayer 843.7

manner *means* 102.1, external appearance 264.5, mode of behavior 399.2, fashion 536.1, style 537.1, way 691.1, mode 725.2, type 777.4

mannered *affected* 367.3, moral 431.9, inelegant 528.6

mannerism Western Art Styles 133, Architectural Styles 134, identification 184.1, tendency 397.2, style 537.1, characteristic 779.5, idiosyncrasy 782.5

mannerist Furniture Styles 101

mannerliness *good manners* 410.2

mannerly *disciplined* 765.17

manner of speaking *mode of expression* 537.3

manner of working *way* 691.1

manners *tradition* 397.5, mode of behavior 399.2, way of life 399.9, morals 431.2, etiquette 534.3

manners and customs *custom* 397.4

mannish *male* 32.16

mannish female **33.9**

mannishness *maleness* 32.2

mannitol *saccharide* 12.4

mannose Common Sugars 12

mano a mano *duel* 422.12, contentious 422.20

man of action *doer* 412.3, busy person 414.10

man of blood *killer* 30.11, violent animal 520.4

man of high standing *person of repute* 370.2

man of honor *person of repute* 370.2

man of impulse *capricious person* 381.3

man of letters *literary person* 139.14, descriptive writer 202.10

man of means *wealthy person* 485.6, prosperous person 847.4

man of peace *pacifier* 73.7

man of prayer *religious person* 81.9

man of property *possessor* 469.10, property owner 470.7, prosperous person 847.4

man of straw *nonentity* 800.8

man of straw [Brit] *insubstantial person* 720.5

man of substance *prosperous person* 847.4

man of the house *family member* 65.2, master 68.1, property owner 470.7

man of the world *man* 27.8, libertine 32.7

man of the year *successful person* 845.6

man-of-war *warship* 77.21

manometer *vaporimeter* 556.13, Fields of Measurement 589

manometry Fields of Measurement 589

manor *property* 470.1

manor house *mansion* 60.5

manorial **60.21**; *propertied* 470.9

Man o' War Notable Horses 159

manpower *force* 59.10, resources 102.4, exertion 122.4, personnel 123.16, type of power 514.6

manpower and training *naval commands* 77.19

man-powered weapon *weapon* 78.1

manqué *incomplete* 762.5

mansard *roof* 134.7

man's best friend *dog* 35.10

manse *official residence* 60.6, clerical dwelling 84.10

manservant *domestic servant* 69.7

man's evening dress *dark thing* 247.3

mansion **60.5**; *property* 470.1

man-size *big* 579.13

manslaughter *killing* 30.1, murder 30.2, accidental killing 30.9

mansuetude *courtesy* 410.1

mantel *rock face* 161.6, mountaineer 161.10

mantelet *historic armor* 419.8

mantel move *climbing techniques* 161.3

mantelpiece *supporting structure* 605.2

manteltree *figurative usage* 43.9

man the breach *entrench* 419.24

man the defenses *entrench* 419.24

man the fort *entrench* 419.24

man the guns *entrench* 419.24

mantic *divinatory* 86.18, predicting 358.11

manticore Legendary Creatures 360

mantilla *headdress* 100.35

mantis *insect* 40.1

mantissa *logarithm* 6.17, power 783.6

mantis shrimp *crustacean* 39.10

mantle *earth zone* 8.7, vestment 84.11, coat 100.19, clothe 100.43, redden 257.9

mantled *dressed* 100.38

mantle of snow *snow* 9.30

mantling *Heraldic Terms* 184

man-to-man assignment *ice hockey tactics* 158.4

man-to-man defense *playing terms* 148.4, defense 155.9

mantra *prayer* 85.10, maxim 177.1

mantua *dress* 100.11

manual *schoolbook* 48.15, industrial 57.13, part of keyboard instrument 142.6, type of book 174.3, handling 216.7, practical 511.6

manual labor *work* 122.1

manually **216.13**; *industrially* 57.22, laboriously 122.13, instrumentally 511.9

manual skill **127.2**

manual work *work* 122.1

manual worker *employee* 57.4, laborer 123.9, worker 412.8

manubrium *reproductive body* 47.14

manufacture **522.2**; *process* 14.50, construction 59.16, put together 59.30, publish 174.19, action 412.1, produce 522.13, shape 551.21, fabricate 720.17

manufactured *synthetic* 11.31, produced 522.12

manufactured item *product* 522.3

manufacturer *producer* 522.10

manufacturer's representative *or* rep [Inf] *sales worker* 123.6

manufacturing *industrial chemistry* 11.21, business 509.3, manufacture 522.2, productive 522.11

manufacturing plant *factory* 124.8

manufacturing town *industrial area* 124.14

manuka Trees and Shrubs 43

manumission *liberation* 831.1

manumit *set free* 829.17, liberate 831.6

manumitted *liberated* 831.4

manumitter *liberator* 831.3

manure *fertilizer* 16.9, 17.8, 22.6, cultivate 17.19, feces 25.5, dirt 112.5

manuring *cultivation* 16.7

manuscript *rare book* 174.2, original 737.2

manuscript editor *book publishing personnel* 174.12

manuscript preparation *stage of book production* 174.7

man without a country *displaced person* 574.7

Man/Woman of the Year *prizes* 453.3

Manx Breeds of Cats 35

many **795.6**; *frequent* 661.4, quantitative 738.6, plurality 793.1, plural 793.6, multitude 795.1, indeterminate 841.14

many a time *frequently* 661.7

many a time and oft [Arch] *frequently* 661.7

many-celled invertebrate *invertebrate* 39.1

many-colored *colored* 251.10, variegated 263.6

many-hued *variegated* 263.6

many irons in the fire *business* 414.6

many-one *functional* 6.73

many-sided *skillful* 127.10, side 623.6, various 793.7

many-sidedness *skill* 127.1, multiplicity 793.2

many thanks! [Inf] *thank you!* 310.9

many things Phobias 283

many times *frequently* 661.7

many times over *repeatedly* 797.22

many-tongued *shouting* 232.7

many voices *dissension* 732.4

Manzala Lakes 568

Mao jacket *jacket* 100.18

map **187.5, 187.12, 387.7**; *engineer* 14.48, climbing equipment 161.4, illustration 187.2, plan out 387.14, preparations 388.2, exact location 565.2, outline 617.1, 617.5, guide 697.4

map [Inf] *face* 621.6

map *or* mark out *or* shape a course *plan out* 387.14

maple Trees and Shrubs 43

maple sugar Tree Products 43

maple syrup *sweetener* 222.2

map of the heavens *map* 187.5

map out *forerun* 769.16

mapped *planned* 387.10, measured 589.16

mapper *planner* 387.9

mapping *mathematical function*

6.27, *civil engineering* 14.17, *map* 187.5

map reference *exact location* 565.2

Maputo *Countries* 566

maquette *sculpture* 144.1

maquis *guerrilla* 417.5

mar *afflict* 117.16, *be clumsy* 128.9, *change* 512.12, *weaken* 517.13, *make ugly* 531.4, *blemish* 533.7, *mix* 751.12, *impair* 808.18

Mara *devil* 446.5

marabout *religious person* 81.9, *unsocial person* 409.5, *hermit* 782.9, *loner* 788.8

Maracaibo *Lakes* 568

maracas *Musical Instruments* 142

Marajo *Islands* 572

maramus *emaciation* 595.2

marasmic *emaciated* 595.10

marasmus *shortening* 582.2, *physical deterioration* 808.4

marathon *cross-country skiing* 162.7, *long-distance running* 166.4, *great distance* 585.2

marathon dancing *Dancing Types* 135

marathoner *track and field eventer* 166.19

marathon racing *long-distance running* 166.4

marathon running *Sporting Activities* 145

maraud *conquer* 77.36

marauder *militarist* 77.3, *raider* 477.10, *plunderer* 479.9

marauding *stolen* 479.12

marble *masonry* 14.22, *building materials* 104.2, *sculpture* 144.1, *material* 144.6, *white thing* 253.4, *white* 253.7, *variegate* 263.11, *hard substance* 542.3, *hard* 542.5, *round thing* 633.3

marbled *striped* 263.9

marbled paper *variegated thing* 263.5

marbled ware *ceramics* 129.1

marbles *Children's and Party Games* 167

marblewood *Trees and Shrubs* 43

marbling *treatment* 143.6, *stripe* 263.3

marbly *striped* 263.9

Marburg-Ebola disease *tropical disease* 114.10

marcando *Musical Terms and Expression Marks* 140

marcato *Musical Terms and Expression Marks* 140

marcel *coiffure* 530.8

marcelled *beautified* 530.12

marcel waves *coiffure* 530.8

march *military training* 76.19, *be at war* 76.32, *Musical Forms* 140, *fencing movements* 153.3, *dance* 153.7, *mass demonstration* 331.7, *protest* 331.19, *show* 404.24, *act of defiance* 416.3, *be insubordinate* 416.8, *regions* 564.2, *bodily movement* 677.11, *walk* 677.17, *course* 679.2, *route* 691.2

march against *attack* 418.17

march away *set out* 705.12

Marche *Breeds of Cattle* 16

Märchen [Ger] *story* 139.4

marcher *defiant person* 416.4, *troublemaker* 427.5, *protester* 507.4

Marches, the *regions of the British Isles* 564.8

Marchigiana *Breeds of Cattle* 16

marching *demonstrating* 331.14, *motion* 677.1

marching band *instrumental group* 141.3

marching orders *command* 425.1, *relegation* 574.4

marching orders [Inf] *dismissal* 709.2, *termination* 834.2

march in lock step *synchronize* 649.7

march in slow time *move slowly* 693.11

March of Dimes *charitable organization* 305.4

march off *set out* 705.12

march of time *duration* 642.1

march *or* **passage** *or* **course of time** *course* 679.2

march on 679.11; *protract* 669.9

march out *quit* 705.10, *exit* 707.13

march past *show* 404.24

march-past *salute* 405.7

march to a different drummer *be different* 463.11, *be independent* 782.20

march to war *be at war* 76.32

marcia *Musical Terms and Expression Marks* 140

Marconi *sailing* 150.25

Marconi-rigged *sailing* 150.25

Marconi-rigged sailboat *sailboat* 150.3

Mardi Gras *Christian Holy Days and Seasons* 85

mare *female animal* 33.15, *female mammal* 35.19, *horse* 159.1

mare (pl. maria) *moon* 7.18

Maree *Lakes* 568

Maremma *Breeds of Cattle* 16

Maremmana *or* **Maremma** *Horse and Pony Breeds* 159

Marengo *Notable Horses* 159

mares *Collective Names* 59

mare's milk *milk* 93.5

mare's-tail *cloud appearance* 9.19

margarine *basic cooking ingredient* 91.8, *fat* 562.4

margin *superfluity* 99.4, *freedom* 407.4, *discount* 495.1, *available space* 563.6, *distance* 585.1, *interval* 587.1, *edge* 617.3, 618.1, *difference* 779.2

marginal *sailboard parts* 150.20, *windsurfing* 150.28, *outlined* 617.4, *edging* 618.5

marginalia *notes* 185.3, *annotation* 365.2, *appendage* 748.4

marginalize *edge* 618.8

marginally 618.11; *essentially* 617.6, *fractionally* 787.8

marginal note *appendage* 748.4

marginal notes *notes* 185.3

marginal tropics *climate zone* 9.36

margin of profit *return* 453.6

margrave *nobleman* 70.1

margravine *nobleman* 70.1

marguerite *Flowers* 42

mariage de convenance [Fr] *type of marriage* 64.3

Marianas *Islands* 572

Mariana Trench *the depths* 598.2

marigold *Flowers* 42, *orange thing* 258.3

marijuana *hemp derivatives* 121.16

marimba *Musical Instruments* 142

marina *enclosed area* 619.2, *harbor* 812.6

marinade *preserver* 815.9

marinate *season* 221.8, *soften* 543.14, *obtain an extract* 711.19, *preserve* 815.14

marinated *preserved* 815.12

marinating *obtaining of an extract* 711.7

marination *preservation of provisions* 815.6

marine *oceanic* 8.53, 571.7, *engine*

type 14.11, *of animals* 34.13, *warrior* 76.25, *marines* 77.26, *nautical* 690.14

marine biologist *life scientist* 13.26, *oceanographer* 571.6

marine biology *biology* 13.2, *oceanography* 571.5

marine chronometer *Timepieces and Timers* 646

marine engineer *mechanical engineer* 14.4

marine engineering *mechanical engineering* 14.3, *navy specialties* 77.24

marine fishes *fishes* 38.1

marine geology *geology* 8.1

marine mammal 35.12

marine painter *painter* 143.7

marine painting *type of painting* 143.5

marine park *zoo* 60.14

mariner *boating person* 150.24, *nautical person* 690.12

marine reptile *extinct reptile* 37.9

Mariner's Compass *Constellations* 7

marines 77.26; *the military* 58.2, *security force* 464.3

marine scientist 690.13

marine sextant *navigational aid* 690.6

marine terminal *building* 551.9

Mariolatry *deified person* 82.14

Mariology *Theologies* 81, *deified person* 82.14

marionette *toy* 167.9, *figure* 187.4

marionette show *show* 138.4

marital *matrimonial* 64.15

marital act *sexual intercourse* 20.9

maritally *matrimonially* 64.23

marital relations *sexual intercourse* 20.9

maritime *oceanic* 8.53, 571.7

maritime *or* **marine climate** *climate* 9.35

maritime meteorology *meteorology* 9.1

Maritsa *Rivers* 570

marjoram *Herbs and Spices* 91

mark 533.2, 533.8; *word* 5.43, *dirt* 112.5, *make ceramics* 129.10, *sign* 183.1, 183.19, *personal identification* 184.4, *identify* 184.11, *vestige* 185.11, *take note of* 323.10, *indication* 339.3, *repute* 370.1, *objective* 374.5, *commemorate* 405.11, *contract* 462.2, 462.11, *national coins* 484.11, *permit* 502.3, *blemish* 533.1, 533.7, *style* 537.1, *change for the worse* 665.18, *visible effect* 676.2, *affect* 676.7, *characterize* 723.11, 779.15, *gradation* 739.3, *measure* 739.7, *type* 777.4, *characteristic* 779.5, *importance* 799.1, *defect* 806.4, *stain* 808.20

mark as one's prey *aim at* 385.15

mark down *inscribe* 185.14, *choose* 382.14, *discount* 495.4

markdown *bargain* 497.10

mark down *make cheap* 497.14

marked 533.6; *identified* 184.9, *emphasized* 200.4, *strong* 516.9, *accessible* 691.13, *excellent* 744.14, *characteristic* 779.12, *imperfect* 806.5, *defective* 806.7, *manifest* 843.9

marked down *discounted* 495.3, *bargain* 497.10

markedly *characteristically* 779.20

marked man *accused person* 442.4

marked out for destruction *destroyed* 523.9

marked trail *ski run* 162.2

marker *player* 149.5, *bowler* 151.5, *golfer* 156.7, *signs* 183.2

market 482.5, 483.1; *economy* 56.3, *trade* 56.12, 480.18, *food provider* 90.6, *stock exchange* 457.3, *trade in* 457.8, *shop* 481.15, *sell* 482.15, *urban area* 567.10, *place of exchange* 673.2, *promote* 807.18, *display* 843.1

marketability *market* 482.5

marketable *mercantile* 480.13, *salable* 482.13

marketably 482.23

marketer *trader* 480.11, *merchant* 482.10

market expansion *economic development* 56.5

market garden [Brit] *farm* 16.2, *garden* 17.2, 17.18

market gardener [Brit] *horticulturist* 17.13

market gardening *manufacture* 522.2

market gardening [Brit] *arable farming* 16.6, *horticulture* 17.1

marketing *buying* 481.9, *selling* 482.1, 482.12

marketing management *management system* 126.3

marketplace 483.7; *business* 414.6, *urban area* 567.10, *center of activity* 612.4, *place of exchange* 673.2

market price *price* 494.1

market research *questioning* 333.2, *market* 482.5

market researcher *questioner* 333.9

market sector 483.5

market town *center of activity* 612.4

market town [Brit] *marketplace* 483.7, *town* 567.2

market trader *peddler* 482.9

market value *value* 494.2

marking *external appearance* 264.5

marking one's territory *claiming* 469.2

markings *insignia* 184.5, *name* 202.2

marking the occasion *commemoration* 405.2

markka *national coins* 484.11

mark of authority *insignia* 184.5

mark off *identify* 184.11, *measure* 589.20

mark of respect 435.4

mark out *sign* 183.19, *choose* 382.14, *set apart* 753.17

Markov chain *Mathematical Concepts* 6

Markov process *population* 6.55

mark paid *receive* 492.7

marksman *hunter* 385.6, *shooter* 696.11

marksman *or* **markswoman** *shooter* 160.10

marksmanship *target shooting* 160.1

markswoman *hunter* 385.6, *shooter* 696.11

mark the occasion *commemorate* 354.14, 405.11

mark the way *sign* 183.19

mark time *space* 563.15, *time* 639.15, *measure time* 646.14, *be motionless* 678.7

mark up *overcharge* 496.10

marl *fertilizer* 22.6, *fertilize* 22.12, *material* 129.2

marlin *game fish* 154.10

marlinespike *or* **marlinspike** *sharp-pointed thing* 549.4

marlinespike hitch Knots, Bends, Hitches, Splices 754
marling hitch Knots, Bends, Hitches, Splices 754
marm *female title of address* 33.3
marmalade *sweets* 90.39, *sweetener* 222.2, *preserved thing* 815.10
marmalade tree Trees and Shrubs 43
Marmara, Sea of Oceans and Seas 571
marmoreal *sculptural* 144.7
Marne Rivers 570
maroon *brown* 256.5, *red* 257.5, *divide* 753.18
marooned person *unsocial person* 409.7
marplot *unskilled person* 128.3, *hinderer* 826.11
marque *type* 777.4
marquee *overhead covering* 613.11
Marquesas Islands Islands 572
Marquess of Queensberry rules *boxing terms* 152.3
marquetried *type of furniture* 101.2
marquetry *decorative woodwork* 131.2, Hobbies and Pastimes 167, *check* 263.2
marquetry worker *woodworker* 131.4
marquis *nobleman* 70.1
marquise *nobleman* 70.1
marquisette Fabrics and Fibers 130
marred *blemished* 533.5, *low quality* 745.7
marriage 64.1; *social environment* 2.4, Phobias 283, *courtship* 299.10, *ceremony* 405.3, *sexual union* 752.6, *collaboration* 757.2, *companionship* 794.3
marriageability 64.4
marriageable 64.11
marriageable age *marriageability* 64.4
marriageableness *marriageability* 64.4
marriage adviser *matchmaker* 64.13, *mediator* 75.2
marriage banns *proclamation* 183.8
marriage bed *marriage* 64.1
marriage broker *matchmaker* 64.13, *mediator* 75.2
marriage bureau *matchmaker* 64.13
marriage by a justice of the peace *wedding* 64.5
marriage by proxy *type of marriage* 64.3
marriage certificate *personal identification* 184.4, *certificate* 185.2
marriage contract *betrothal* 458.2
marriage counselor *mediator* 75.2, *adviser* 176.5
marriage feast *general wedding terms* 64.6
marriage guidance counselor *matchmaker* 64.13, *mediator* 75.2
marriage license *general wedding terms* 64.6
marriage of convenience *type of marriage* 64.3
marriage on the rocks [Inf] *divorce* 566.1
marriage partner *spouse* 64.8
marriage procession *general wedding terms* 64.6
marriage relationship *relatedness* 727.1
marriages *news story* 171.3

marriage settlement *transfer of property* 470.4
marriage song *general wedding terms* 64.6
marriage tie *marriage* 64.1
marriage toast *general wedding terms* 64.6
marriage vows *wedding* 64.5
married 64.16; *related* 727.6, *united* 752.10, *collaborative* 757.7, *associated* 794.14
married couple 64.9
married man 64.10; *man in the family* 32.12
married name *name* 202.8
married status or **state** *marriage* 64.1
married woman 64.11; *woman in the family* 33.13
marrow *insides* 577.3, *core* 612.2, *essential content* 723.2, *middle* 772.1
marry 64.19; *perform rites* 85.18, *propose (marriage)* 299.28, *contract* 459.8, *unite* 752.14, *unite sexually* 752.20, *come together* 757.10, *enroll* 771.33
marry! [Arch] *good heavens!* 292.15
marry in haste *marry* 64.19
marry into money *marry* 64.19
marry off *join in marriage* 64.20
marry well *marry* 64.19
Mars Planets and Their Satellites 7, *planet* 7.16, Deities 82
marseilles Fabrics and Fibers 130
marsh 559.8, 572.3; *small lake* 568.2, *shallowness* 599.1, *hidden danger* 813.3
marshal *person in authority* 52.7, *call together* 59.28, *judge* 68.4, *driver* 146.8D, *identify* 184.11, *order* 765.18, *arrange* 767.18, *usher* 794.7, *escort* 794.18
marshaled *arranged* 767.11, *accompanied* 794.15
marshaling *assembling* 59.12, Heraldic Terms 184, *fitting out* 388.3, *arrangement* 767.1
Marshall Islands Countries 566, Islands 572
marsh bird *water bird* 36.9
marshiness *compressibility* 543.3, *bogginess* 559.7
marshland *marsh* 572.3, *shallowness* 599.1
marsh mallow Flowers 42
marshmallow *sweets* 90.39
marsh marigold Flowers 42
marshy 559.11; *unhygienic* 114.27, *compressible* 543.9, *sludgy* 561.18, *lakelike* 568.5, *of landmasses* 572.12
Mars orange *orange pigment* 258.2
marsupial *type of animal* 34.5, *pouched mammal* 35.5, *mammalian* 35.23
marsupial characteristic *pouched mammal* 35.5
Marsupialia *pouched mammal* 35.5
marsupium *pouched mammal* 35.5
mart *market* 483.1, *center of activity* 612.4
Martagon lily Flowers 42
martens Collective Names 59
Martha's Vineyard Islands 572
martial 77.33; *military* 58.10, 76.28, *heroic* 284.10
martial art *combat sport* 152.1
martial arts Sporting Activities 145, *self-defense* 419.5
martial law *military government* 49.16, *severity* 424.1
martially 77.39; *militarily* 58.15

martial music *glory of war* 76.17
Martian *astronomical* 7.33, *sprite* 86.12
Martin Lakes 568
martinet *absolute ruler* 68.7, *strict person* 424.4
martingale *riding equipment* 159.9
Martinique Islands 572
Martinmas Christian Holy Days and Seasons 85
martlet Heraldic Terms 184
martyr 504.6; *kill ritually* 30.23, *religious person* 81.9, *inflict pain* 215.10, *victim of discrimination* 337.8, *defiant person* 416.4, *torture* 454.29, *person in adversity* 848.9
martyrdom *way of dying* 29.5, *ritual killing* 30.7, *pain* 215.1, *unselfishness* 443.2, *capital punishment* 454.12, *offering* 504.5
martyred *killed* 29.13, *unselfish* 443.5, *sacrificial* 504.10
martyrization *ritual killing* 30.7, *capital punishment* 454.12
martyrize *kill ritually* 30.23, *torture* 454.29
martyrology *death count* 29.10
martyr to ill health *sick person* 114.22
marvel 294.3; *spectacle* 264.6, *wonderful person* 294.6, *wonder* 294.12
marveling *wondering* 294.7
marvel-of-Peru Flowers 42
marvelous *delightful* 271.7, *wondrous* 294.9
marvelous! *wonderful!* 294.20
marvelously *wondrously* 294.18, *successfully* 845.19
marvelousness *wonderfulness* 294.5
marvelous to relate *astonishingly* 294.19
Marwari pony Horse and Pony Breeds 159
Marxism *social stratification* 2.7, *political and economic philosophy* 4.6
Marxist *sociologist* 2.3, *socioeconomic* 2.13, *political and economic philosopher* 4.10, *of a political philosophy* 4.14, *materialist* 524.3
Marxist history *types of history* 3.2
Mary Ann [Inf] *hemp derivatives* 121.16
Mary Jane [Inf] *hemp derivatives* 121.16
Maryland American States 564
Maryland Hunt Cup *famous horse races* 159.13
Mary Warner [Inf] *hemp derivatives* 121.16
marzipan *sweets* 90.39
mascara *cosmetics* 530.4
mascon *moon* 7.18
mascot *talisman* 86.9, *good-luck sign* 358.6, *preserver* 815.9
masculine *grammatical term* 5.29, *of grammar* 5.41, *sexual* 20.15, *male* 32.16, *heroic* 284.10
masculine gender *maleness* 32.2
masculinely *heroically* 284.18
masculine rhyme *rhyme* 139.11
masculinity *sex* 20.1, *maleness* 32.2, *heroism* 284.2
maser *laser* 10.18
Maseru Countries 566
mash *animal feed* 16.12, *soften* 543.14, *beat* 553.27, *semiliquid* 561.7, *take apart* 753.16
mashed potatoes *vegetable* 90.33

masher *pulverizer* 553.11, *pulper* 561.13
masher [Inf] *lover* 299.11
mashie *golf equipment* 156.5
mashie niblick *golf equipment* 156.5
mashiness *pulpiness* 561.9
mashing *pulverization* 553.4
Mashona Breeds of Cattle 16
masjid [Arabic] *place of worship* 83.8
mask *costume* 100.10, *cover* 181.4, *disguise* 181.13, *ungenuineness* 192.2, *be untruthful* 192.20, *blind* 243.17, *that which makes invisible* 245.2, *make invisible* 245.7, *practice sophistry* 330.11, *party* 408.6, *circumlocute* 607.12, *body covering* 613.3, *hide* 613.27, *show* 621.7, *safety device* 810.15
masked *disguised* 181.9, *ungenuine* 192.13, *private* 245.5, *indirect* 607.8, *protected* 613.20, *concealed* 844.7
masked ball *dance* 135.1, *cover* 181.4, *party* 408.6
masker *coverer* 613.18
masking *blinding* 243.13
masking tape *that which makes invisible* 245.7, *adhesive* 755.3
Maslow's Hierarchy of Needs *management system* 126.3
masochism *sexual perversion* 20.12, *submission* 421.1
masochist *sexual perversion* 20.12, *submitter* 421.2
masochistic *submitting* 421.3
mason *artisan* 123.13
Mason-Dixon line *separator* 753.5
masonry 14.22; *building materials* 104.2
Masorah *Jewish text* 81.17
masque *dramatic style* 136.3, *party* 408.6
masquerade *costume* 100.10, *dance* 135.1, *deceive* 181.14, 330.12, *acting* 187.6, *act* 187.13, *party* 408.6, *body covering* 613.3, *hide* 613.27
masquerader *one who conceals* 181.7, *coverer* 613.18
Mass Eucharist 85.7
mass 10.8, 579.7; *crowd* 59.11, 59.26, 795.11, *assemblage* 59.13, *assemble* 59.23, *store* 105.1, Musical Forms 140, *sacred music* 140.3, *matter* 524.4, *heaviness* 538.1, *density* 540.1, *solid body* 540.4, *make dense* 540.9, *size* 579.1, *large part* 579.3, *dimension* 589.11, *thickness* 594.1, *quantity* 738.1, *certain amount* 738.3, *unite* 752.14, *particle* 760.4, *majority* 793.3, *throng* 795.4
Massa Breeds of Sheep 16
Massachusetts American States 564
massacre *slaughter* 30.5, 30.21, *conquer* 77.36, *malignity* 306.5, *harm* 306.13, *capital punishment* 454.12, *execute* 454.30, *violence by person* 520.2, *use violence* 520.9, *destroying* 523.2, *destroy* 523.10
massacred *killed* 29.13
Massacre of the Innocents *slaughter* 30.5
mass action *joint operation* 827.4
massage 554.6, 554.16; *therapy* 115.12, *treat* 791.15, *touch* 216.9, *soften* 543.14, *ease* 543.15
massage parlor *brothel* 432.5
massage the accounts *account* 493.9

massaging *touching* 216.2, *massage* 554.6
mass balances *chemical reaction thermodynamics* 14.29
mass book *ritual manual* 85.11
mass burial *burial* 31.1
mass communication *publication media* 173.6
mass communications *communications* 169.1
mass demonstration 331.7
mass destruction *destroying* 523.2
massed *collected* 59.19, *dense* 540.6, *crowded* 795.10
massed attack *combined attack* 418.5
masses *average person* 742.4, *general public* 778.6
masses, the *the group* 18.13, *common people* 71.2, *inferior* 745.4
massé shot *or* **massé** *billiards play* 149.2
masses of *throng* 795.4
masseur 554.8; *personal attendant* 69.5
masseuse *personal attendant* 69.5, *masseur* 554.8
mass execution *capital punishment* 454.12
mass grave *burial place* 31.7
massicot *yellow pigment* 259.2
massif *mountain* 569.1, *mountain range* 569.3
massive *material* 524.7, *heavy* 538.9, *dense* 540.6, *huge* 579.14, *thick* 594.5, *quantitative* 738.6
massively *heavily* 538.16, *densely* 540.10, *hugely* 579.21, *thick* 594.11, *wholly* 738.9
massiveness *heaviness* 538.1, *largeness* 579.2, *thickness* 594.1
mass media *communications* 169.1, *publication media* 173.6
mass meeting *rally* 59.6
mass movement 8.28; *activism* 414.5
mass murder *murder* 30.2, *malignity* 306.5, *capital punishment* 454.12, *destroying* 523.2
mass murderer *murderer* 30.12
mass number *isotope* 10.57
mass of *throng* 795.4
massotherapist *masseur* 554.8
massotherapy *massage* 554.6
mass-produce *reproduce* 21.13, *be fertile* 22.13, *produce* 522.13, *make the same* 730.16
mass-produced *produced* 522.12
mass production *reproduction* 21.1, *productiveness* 22.3, *manufacture* 522.2, *regularity* 730.6
mass screening *diagnosis* 107.8
mass spectrometry *analysis* 11.17
mass strike *strike* 57.8
mass suicide *suicide* 30.8
mass together *unite* 752.14
mass X ray *diagnostic radiology* 107.12
massy *material* 524.7, *heavy* 538.9, *dense* 540.6, *huge* 579.14
mast *sailboat parts and accessories* 150.4
mastaba *burial place* 31.7
master 68.1, 68.17; *male title of address* 32.3, *educator* 48.4, *know* 48.24, 348.10, *expert* 52.8, 68.13, *be an authority on* 52.17, *educational leader* 68.11, *excellent* 68.16, 744.14, *learn* 68.18, *artisan* 123.13, *manager* 126.7, *skilled person* 127.7, *visual artist* 133.6, *shooter* 160.10, *intellectual*

315.7, *understand* 363.9, *be good at* 445.18, *possessor* 469.10, *be an influence* 512.13, *nautical person* 690.12, *superior* 744.5, *specialist* 779.9, *perfectionist* 805.7, *defeat* 832.11, *overpower* 845.18
master bedroom *room* 60.9
master builder *architect* 134.3
Master Chief Petty Officer US Military Ranks 58
Master Chief Petty Officer of the Navy US Military Ranks 58
masterful 68.15; *authoritative* 52.9, *skillful* 127.10, *qualified* 340.7, *proficient* 445.15, *ruling* 780.11
masterfully 68.19; *expertly* 52.21, *capably* 340.15, *proficiently* 445.22
masterfulness *proficiency* 445.5
Master Gunnery Sergeant US Military Ranks 58
master key *opener* 583.2
masterliness *proficiency* 445.5
masterly *expert* 52.12, 805.16, *expertly* 52.21, *excellent* 68.16, *skillful* 127.10, *proficient* 445.15, *superbly* 744.22, *famous* 845.9
master mariner *nautical person* 690.12
master mason *artisan* 123.13
mastermind *manager* 126.7, *manage* 126.10, *skilled person* 127.7, *knowledgeable person* 348.5, *planner* 387.9, *conduct oneself* 399.17, *behave toward* 399.20, *paragon* 744.6
masterminding *treatment* 399.11
master of ceremonies *leader* 126.8, *entertainer* 138.8, *broadcasting personnel* 172.11, *displayer* 843.7
master of the house *master* 68.1
masterpiece 68.14, 127.5; *work of art* 133.4, 522.4, *marvel* 294.3, *good thing* 445.9, *beautiful thing* 529.3, *ideal* 805.6
master plan *plan* 387.1
Master Sergeant US Military Ranks 58
Masters Golf Tournament *golfing associations and tournaments* 156.6
mastership *skill* 127.1, *leadership* 744.2
Masters Tournament *notable tennis competitions* 165.8
masterstroke *masterpiece* 127.5, *marvel* 294.3, *method* 387.4, *good thing* 445.9
master stroke *stratagem* 822.2
masterwork *masterpiece* 68.14, 127.5, *work of art* 133.4, 522.4, *marvel* 294.3
mastery *authority* 52.1, 425.3, 780.6, *skill* 127.1, *artistry* 133.3, *ability* 340.2, *knowledge* 348.1, *learning* 348.3, *understanding* 363.4, *leadership* 744.2, *expertise* 805.4, *domination* 832.2, *success* 845.1
masthead *means of identification* 184.3, *punish* 454.22
masthead knot Knots, Bends, Hitches, Splices 754
masthead light *safety light* 246.7
mastic Tree Products 43, *adhesive* 561.3
masticate *chew* 92.22, *soften* 543.14
masticating *chewing* 92.19
mastication *eating* 92.1, *pulping* 561.11
masticatory *chewing* 92.19
mastic *resinous* 562.13

mastiff Breeds of Dogs 35
Mastigomycotina *fungi* 47.3
mastigophobia Phobias 283
Mastigophora *protozoan* 39.17
mastigophoran *protozoan* 39.17
mastodon *big thing* 579.9, *prehistoric animal* 653.8
mastoid bone Human Bones 19
mastoid process *ear* 19.10
masturbate *stimulate* 20.22
masturbation *sex act* 20.10, *physical pleasure* 214.1
Masuren Horse and Pony Breeds 159
mat *alga* 47.10, *weave* 130.20, *green bowling* 151.3, *gymnastics equipment* 157.2, *substructure* 551.8, *floor covering* 613.13
matador *animal killer* 30.14
matboard *paper* 104.5
match *marriage* 64.1, *matchmake* 64.22, *fuel starter* 106.3, *sports* 145.1, *tennis terms* 165.5, *cause of fire* 217.10, *fire* 246.9, *impression* 264.7, *appear* 264.12, *correspondence* 334.8, *answer to* 334.22, *prize competition* 422.5, *be compatible* 462.12, *size* 579.17, *correspondent* 606.3, *correspond* 606.8, *correspond to* 727.10, *look-alike* 730.4, *be equivalent* 730.15, *make the same* 730.16, *counterpart* 733.5, *be similar* 733.12, *conform* 735.27, 781.11, *equal* 740.7, *unite* 752.14, *intercommunicate* 754.15, *pair* 789.13, *counteract* 828.21
match against *confront* 828.19
matchbox *box* 578.5
matched 733.10; *married* 64.16, *look-alike* 730.10, *two* 789.8
matched in age *simultaneous* 649.4
matched pair *couple* 733.6
match fishing Sporting Activities 145
match in cunning *be cunning* 822.5
matching *stylish* 100.42, *colorful* 251.11, *correspondent* 334.16, *compatible* 462.8, *equivalent* 730.9, *look-alike* 730.10, *similar* 733.7
matching set *couple* 733.6
matchless *excellent* 445.13, *best* 744.10, 805.9
matchlessly *supremely* 744.23
matchlock *historical handgun* 78.8
matchlockman *historical soldier* 77.8
matchmake 64.22; *act as a go-between* 460.8, *pair* 789.13
matchmaker 64.13; *mediator* 75.2, *agent* 80.3, *negotiator* 460.4, *person who joins* 752.9
match oneself *contend* 422.22
match play *golf* 156.1
match point *tennis terms* 165.5, *critical moment* 726.7
match poorly *be different* 463.11
match race *horse racing* 159.10
matchstick *fuel starter* 106.3, *weak thing* 517.5
matchstick figure *outline* 617.1
match up with *be equal* 740.11
matchwood *weak thing* 517.5, *brittle thing* 548.2
mate *have sex* 20.21, *friend* 62.2, *matchmake* 64.22, *board games* 167.3, *play* 167.12, *social person* 408.7, *correspondent* 606.3, *nautical person* 690.12, *affinity* 733.3, *equal* 740.7, *unite sexually* 752.20, *come together* 757.10, *pair*

789.13, *companion* 794.8, *helper* 825.12
mate [Inf] *male title of address* 32.3
maté Trees and Shrubs 43, *tea* 93.7
mated *married* 64.16, *two* 789.8
mateless *celibate* 67.6
mater [Brit inf] *woman in the family* 33.13
materfamilias *woman in the family* 33.13, *family member* 65.2, *master* 68.1
material 104.8, 129.2, 524.7; *materials* 104.1, *fabric* 104.4, 130.1, *touchable* 216.5, *visible* 244.5, *appearing* 264.9, *matter* 524.4, *textile* 552.5, *present* 575.7, *substance* 577.2, *containing* 577.7, *intrinsic* 717.12, *real* 719.6, *essence* 723.1, *essential* 799.10
material balances *industrial processes* 14.27
material existence *material world* 524.1, *reality* 719.1
material implication *mathematical logic* 6.60
materialism Philosophical Schools of Thought 4, *materialization* 524.2
materialist 524.3, Philosophical Schools of Thought 4, *disbeliever* 88.5
materialistic *material* 524.7
materiality *material world* 524.1, *matter* 524.4, *presence* 575.1, *nature* 717.4, *reality* 719.1, *importance* 799.1
materialization 524.2; *divine manifestation* 82.5, *ghost* 86.11, *appearance* 264.1, *creation* 717.9, *manifestation* 843.2
materialize *appear* 244.8, 331.18, *become visible* 264.13, *be material* 524.8, *be present* 575.13, *come to be* 717.19, *make real* 719.11, *show oneself* 843.15
materialized *material* 524.7, *created* 717.16
materially 104.10, 524.9; *in person* 575.18, *structurally* 577.14, *in essence* 723.13, *importantly* 799.15
materialness *material world* 524.1, *presence* 575.1, *importance* 799.1
materials 104.1; *supplies* 102.3, *matter* 524.4, *fabric* 551.2
materials budget *budgeting* 493.5
materials engineer *chemical engineer* 14.25
materials engineering *chemical engineering* 14.24
material things *possessions* 470.5
material world 524.1; *real world* 719.2
materia medica *medicine* 115.2
matériel *army commands* 77.13, *naval commands* 77.19, *air force commands* 77.28, *stock in trade* 105.2
maternal *family* 65.6, *loving* 299.15
maternal/fetal medicine Medical Specialties 107
maternal love *love* 299.1
maternity *femaleness* 33.2
maternity allowance *social assistance* 825.4
maternity benefit *social assistance* 825.4
maternity clothes *clothing* 100.1
maternity dress *dress* 100.11
maternity grant *social assistance* 825.4

maternity hospital *hospital*
107.16
maternity leave *bargaining terms*
57.10
matey [Brit inf] *friendly* 62.5,
sociable 408.11
mateyness [Brit inf] *friendship*
62.1, *companionship* 794.3
math *mathematics* 6.1
mathematical **6.65, 784.9;**
linguistic 5.34, *theoretical* 10.71,
accounting 493.7
mathematical addition 748.2
mathematical biology *applied*
mathematics 6.3
mathematical biophysics *applied*
mathematics 6.3
mathematical computing
applied mathematics 6.3
mathematical ecology *applied*
mathematics 6.3
mathematical function 6.27
mathematical geography *applied*
mathematics 6.3
mathematical induction
reasoning 6.61
mathematical law *formula* 780.7
mathematical linguistics
Linguistic Studies 5
mathematical logic 6.60;
Branches of Mathematics 6
mathematically 6.93, 784.15;
quantitatively 738.8
mathematical model *theory* 6.62,
physical law 10.4
mathematical notation *symbol*
183.3, *representation* 187.1
mathematical physics *applied*
mathematics 6.3, Fields of Modern
Physics 10
mathematical precision *accuracy*
350.1
mathematical probability
probability 6.59, *probability theory*
838.5, *calculation of chance* 842.9
mathematical reasoning
reasoning 6.61
mathematical result 783.4
mathematical symbol 6.11
mathematical theorem
supposition 359.1
mathematician 6.2; *answerer*
334.10, *counter* 784.6
mathematics 6.1
maths [Brit] *mathematics* 6.1
matinée *theatrical performance*
136.13, *afternoon* 655.5
matinée idol *actor* 137.13
mating *sexual intercourse* 20.9,
coupling 20.19, *sexual union*
752.6
mating instinct *sexuality* 20.3,
sexual love 299.3
mating season *seasons* 654.2
matins *public worship* 83.3,
morning things 655.3
matriarch *woman* 27.9, *woman in*
the family 33.13, *master* 68.1
matriarchal *aged* 27.15,
governmental 49.24, *masterful*
68.15
matriarchally *maturely* 27.18
matriarchy *femaleness* 33.2,
government by women 49.3
matricide *homicide* 30.4
matriculate *enroll* 771.33, *be on a*
list 785.12
matriculated *enrolled* 771.24
matriculation *enrollment* 771.8
matrimonial 64.15; *ritualistic*
85.15, *contractual* 459.7
matrimonial agent *matchmaker*
64.13

matrimonial cause *divorce court*
66.3
matrimonially 64.23;
contractually 459.9
matrimony *marriage* 64.1,
Christian rite 85.5, Card Games
168
matrix 6.20; *prototype* 624.2
matrix mechanics Fields of
Modern Physics 10, *quantum*
theory 10.64
matrix structure *management*
system 126.3
matroid *combinatorics* 6.63
matron *woman* 27.9, *female* 33.1,
married woman 64.11, *master*
68.1
matronage *womenfolk* 33.14
matronliness *adulthood* 27.2
matronly *middle-aged* 27.14,
female 33.16, *matrimonial* 64.15,
masterful 68.15
matron of honor *wedding party*
64.7
matronymic *name* 202.8
Matsu Islands 572
matt *dimmed* 248.6, *shady* 250.4
matte *or* **matt** *ceramic* 129.9, *soft-*
hued 251.13
matte *or* **matt finish** *printing*
132.20
matted *dirty* 112.7, *condensed*
540.7, *barbed* 544.7, *textural*
552.7
matted hair *rough thing* 544.2
matter 524.4; *pus* 25.7, *fester*
25.23, *materials* 104.1, *dirt* 112.5,
ulcer 114.18, *topic* 328.1, *meaning*
361.1, *business* 509.3, *body fluid*
555.3, *mucus* 561.6, *substance*
577.2, *undertaking* 675.5, *real*
world 719.2, *essence* 723.1,
quantity 738.1, *importance* 799.1,
be important 799.13
matter at hand *undertaking* 391.1
matter for discussion *issue* 328.2
matter for judgment *litigation*
54.1
Matterhorn Mountains and Hills
569
mattering *pus* 25.7, *purulent*
25.16
matter of course *habit* 397.1,
custom 780.5
matter of fact *historicalness* 3.9,
indifferent 289.7, *fact* 717.6, *reality*
719.1
matter-of-fact *rational* 4.15,
unpretentious 526.8, *practical*
719.8, *naive* 821.3
matter-of-factly *indifferently*
289.17, *unpretentiously* 526.15,
naively 821.5
matter-of-factness
unpretentiousness 526.2, *naiveté*
821.1
matter of indifference *secondary*
matter 800.6
matter of interest 328.3
matter of life and death *necessity*
95.1, *important matter* 799.2
matter wave *wave* 683.4
matt finish *darkroom equipment*
132.21, *murk* 248.2
Matthew Walker Knots, Bends,
Hitches, Splices 754
matting Fabrics and Fibers 130,
floor covering 613.13
mattock *garden tool* 103.4, *sharp-*
edged thing 549.6
mattress *hiding place* 181.2, *money*
storage 484.20
mattress cover *bed covering* 613.7

maturation *bodily development*
19.17, *adulthood* 27.2, *growth*
581.4, *completion* 761.2
mature 27.17; *adult* 27.11, *middle-*
aged 27.14, *soften* 543.14, *grown*
581.11, *grow* 581.17, *old* 653.10,
season 654.11, *convert* 670.11, *be*
converted 670.12, *complete* 761.6,
perfect 805.8, 805.19, *promote*
807.18, *get better* 807.21
matured *expert* 127.12, *seasoned*
654.9, *perfect* 805.8
maturely 27.18; *venerably* 653.17
matureness *maturity* 27.3
maturing 27.12; *bodily development*
19.17, *habituation* 397.7, *growth*
581.4, *growing* 581.12, *converting*
670.8
maturity 27.3; *age* 27.1, *adulthood*
27.2, *preparedness* 388.5,
elderliness 653.2, *timeliness* 659.1,
completion 761.2, *perfection* 805.1
matutinal *daily* 655.6
matutinally *daily* 655.8
maudlin *slightly drunk* 121.26,
sensitive 267.3
Maui Islands 572
maul *inflict pain* 215.10, *type of*
touch 216.3, *touch* 216.9, *strike*
418.21, *impair* 808.18
maulstick *material* 143.9
mau-mau Card Games 168
Mauna Kea Mountains and Hills
569
Mauna Loa Mountains and Hills
569
maunder *be circuitous* 199.6
Maundy Thursday Christian
Holy Days and Seasons 85
Mauritania Countries 566
Mauritius Countries 566, Islands
572
mausoleum *burial place* 31.7,
monument 185.10
Mausoleum at Halicarnassus
Seven Wonders of the Ancient
World 294
mauvaise honte [Fr] *self-*
righteousness 431.7
mauve *purpleness* 262.1, *purple*
262.6
Mauve Decade Ages, Decades,
Eras 641
maven *specialist* 779.9
maverick *obstinate person* 379.4,
troublemaker 427.5, *individualist*
756.3, *nonconformist* 782.7,
unconventional 782.14, *freethinker*
829.10, *independent* 829.12
maw *eating organ* 92.14, *body orifice*
583.3
mawkish *sensitive* 267.3
mawkishly *with feeling* 266.18
mawkishness *emotionalism* 266.6
max [Inf] *unique* 744.11, *fullness*
761.5
maxidress *or* **maxi** *dress* 100.11
maxilla Human Bones 19
maxim 177.1; *philosophy* 4.1,
catchword 5.22, *advice* 176.1, *pithy*
saying 198.3, *moral* 431.5, *truism*
721.6, *guide* 780.4
maximal *ranked* 6.72, *top* 600.6,
unique 744.11
maximization *enlargement* 194.2
maximize *order* 6.89, *enlarge*
194.12, *overestimate* 343.6, *exploit*
393.11, *intensify* 746.8
maximized *enlarged* 194.8
maximum *summit* 600.1, *top*
600.6, *unique* 744.11, *fullness*
761.5
maximum-acceleration *racing*
146.9

maximum-acceleration event
automobile racing 146.1
maximum likelihood *probability*
6.59
maximum pressure *exertion*
122.4
maximum-security facility
prison 55.1
maximum-security
imprisonment *imprisonment*
55.4
maximum sentence *prison*
sentence 55.6
maximum speed *speed* 694.2
maximum-speed *racing* 146.9
maximum-speed event
automobile racing 146.1
maxiskirt *or* **maxi** *skirt* 100.12
maxwell Scientific and Technical
Units 589
Maxwell–Boltzmann statistics
Classical Physical Laws 10
Maxwell distribution Classical
Physical Laws 10
Maxwell's equation Classical
Physical Laws 10
maya *occult and psychic phenomena*
86.7
Mayan architecture
Architectural Styles 134
maybe *possibly* 836.9
May Day *spring* 654.3
Mayday *proclamation* 183.8, *danger*
signal 811.5
Mayfair *London* 567.8
mayflower Flowers 42
mayhem *havoc* 523.5
mayonnaise *sauce* 90.17
mayor *governor* 49.23, *person in*
authority 52.7, *leader* 68.3
mayoralty *position of authority* 52.4
mayoress *leader* 68.3
Maytide *spring* 654.3
Maytime *spring* 654.3
may tree [Brit] Trees and Shrubs
43
maze *puzzle* 182.5, *convoluted thing*
632.3, *mix-up* 766.5, *problem*
824.4
mazelike *convolutional* 632.4
mazurka Dances 135
mazy *indirect* 698.9
mazzard Trees and Shrubs 43
Mbabane Countries 566
M.C. *leader* 126.8, *entertainer*
138.8, *broadcasting personnel*
172.11, *displayer* 843.7
McCarthyism *social discrimination*
337.4, *pursuit* 385.1
McCoy, the *authenticity* 721.7
McIntosh Apple Varieties 44
McKinley, Mount *or* **Denali**
Mountains and Hills 569
McLeod gauge *surface chemistry*
11.20
me *internal world* 525.6
mea culpa [L] *apology* 313.2
Mead Lakes 568
mead *alcoholic drink* 93.9, *sweet*
drink 222.4
mead [Arch] *farmland* 16.3,
grassland 45.2, *lowland* 572.6
meadow *farmland* 16.3, *grassland*
45.2, *lowland* 572.6, *open space*
583.6
meadow grass *grass* 45.1
meadowland *grassland* 45.2
meadow mushroom [Brit]
mushroom 47.2
meadow rue Flowers 42
meadow saffron Flowers 42
meadowsweet Flowers 42
meadowy *grassy* 45.8
meager 593.12; *not enough* 98.5,

---

unemphatic 201.2, *inadequate* 486.13, *thrifty* 499.4, *little* 580.7, *sparse* 595.14, 796.6, *incomplete* 762.5

meager diet *scarcity* 90.5

meagerly 593.19; *not enough* 98.12, *inadequately* 486.19, *sparsely* 595.20, 796.11

meagerness 593.6; *incompleteness* 98.2, *lack of emphasis* 201.1, *inadequacy* 486.5, *littleness* 580.1, *sparseness* 595.8, *fewness* 796.3

meager resources *poverty* 486.1

meal 92.8, 553.7; *animal feed* 16.12, *basic cooking ingredient* 91.8

mealiness *graininess* 553.2

meals on wheels *charitable organization* 305.4

meal ticket *offering* 472.6

mealtime *culinary* 91.9

mealworm *larva* 40.9

mealy 553.18; *drained of color* 252.6

mealy bug *pests and diseases* 17.12

mealymouthed *sycophantic* 401.7

mealy-mouthed *ungenuine* 192.13, *moralistic* 431.12, *weak-willed* 517.10

mealy-mouthedly *untruthfully* 192.27

mealy-mouthedness *ungenuineness* 192.2, *self-righteousness* 431.7

mean 361.13, 501.4; *parameter* 6.57, *not enough* 98.5, *signify* 183.16, *stand for* 187.14, *objectionable* 272.7, *lowly* 298.9, *ill-natured* 303.9, *malicious* 306.8, *epitomize* 327.18, *intend* 374.8, *selfish* 444.4, *evil* 446.7, *beggarly* 486.12, *nonpaying* 490.7, *shoddy* 497.11, *ribald* 535.8, *lowered* 597.18, *center* 612.1, *central* 612.6, *numbers* 738.5, *medium* 742.2, 742.6, *include* 763.5, *middle way* 772.3, *middle* 772.9, *be important* 799.13, *imply* 844.14

mean business *be resolute* 376.11

meander *running water* 8.10, *flow* 570.10, *diverge* 607.11, *convolute* 632.6, *twist* 698.19

meandering *flowing* 570.7, *divergence* 607.2, *divergent* 607.7, *coil* 632.2, *convolutional* 632.4, *indirect* 698.9

meandering river *river* 570.1

mean deviation *parameter* 6.57

mean error *parameter* 6.57

meaning 361.1; *sign* 183.1, *purpose* 327.4, *interpretation* 365.1, *intention* 374.1, *significance* 676.4, *gist* 799.4

meaningful 361.6; *worded* 5.38, *symbolic* 183.12, *purposive* 327.11, *intelligible* 363.5, *profound* 598.15, *important* 799.7

meaningful look *articulation* 205.9, *voiceless speech* 206.4

meaningfully 361.16; *lexically* 5.46, *indicatively* 183.21, *purposively* 327.20, *profoundly* 598.27

meaningfulness *meaning* 361.1, *type of meaning* 361.4, *intelligibility* 363.1, *profundity* 598.5

meaning harm *malicious* 306.8

meaningless 362.7; *unintelligible* 364.4, *superficial* 599.4, *unrelated* 728.6

meaninglessly 362.13; *unintelligibly* 364.16, *irrelatively* 728.16

meaninglessness *lack of meaning* 362.1, *unintelligibility* 364.1,

superficiality 599.2, *unrelatedness* 728.1

meaningless noise *nonsense* 362.2

meaningly *meaningfully* 361.16

mean life *radioactivity* 10.58

mean little *be unimportant* 800.18

meanly 486.18, 501.8; *ill-naturedly* 303.18, *maliciously* 306.15, *deviously* 371.9, *selfishly* 444.8, *evilly* 446.12

mean-mindedness *selfishness* 444.1

meanness 501.1; *incompleteness* 98.2, *objectionability* 272.2, *lowliness* 298.2, *ill nature* 303.2, *malice* 306.2, *selfishness* 444.1, *evil* 446.1, *beggary* 486.3, *tawdriness* 535.2

mean no harm *be at peace* 73.10, *be innocent* 449.10

mean nothing 362.10; *be unintelligible* 364.11

means 102.1; *instrumentality* 102.2, 511.1, *personal estate* 470.6, *funds* 484.6, *instrument* 511.2, *way* 691.1, *circumstances* 726.1

means-ends analysis *artificial intelligence* 15.21

mean seriously *propound* 359.9

means of access *access* 691.3

means of connection 754.4

means of escape 816.4; *means* 102.1, *safety* 810.1, *safety device* 810.15

means of identification 184.3

means of prediction 358.10

means of propulsion 696.2

means of restraint 830.6

means of safety *protection* 810.2

means of transportation 686.2

mean something *mean* 361.13

mean something else *mean* 361.13

meanspirited *envious* 314.4, *selfish* 444.4

meanspiritedness *envy* 314.1, *selfishness* 444.1

means to an end *help* 825.1

meant 359.7, 361.12; *intentional* 374.7, *planned* 387.10, *tacit* 844.10

mean the opposite *mean* 361.13

mean the reverse *mean* 361.13

mean the same thing *mean* 361.13

meantime *interval* 639.4

mean to resolve 374.9, *intend* 650.10

mean to say *mean* 361.13

mean well *be charitable* 305.12

mean what one says *be definite* 189.26, *talk straight* 630.15

meanwhile 639.18; *at present* 647.9, *in the middle* 772.21

meany [Inf] *or* **meanie** [Inf] *miser* 501.3

measles *infection* 114.7

measly *nonpaying* 490.7, *sparse* 796.6

measurability 589.2

measurable 589.17; *numerable* 6.70, *calculable* 784.8

measurably 589.22; *mathematically* 784.15

measure 589.20, 739.7; *enumerate* 6.85, *experiment* 10.72, *process* 14.50, *make clothing* 100.44, *part of poem* 139.9, *meter* 139.12, *melody* 140.10, *written music* 140.21, *tempo* 140.22, *solution* 334.6, *solve* 334.21, *deed* 412.2, *portion* 474.2, *allocate* 474.5, *operation* 509.1, *weigh* 538.15,

space 563.1, *size* 579.1, 579.17, *measurement* 589.1, *unit of measurement* 589.5, *length* 590.1, *piece* 590.2, *be long* 590.11, *depth* 598.1, *be deep* 598.20, *limit* 620.1, *frequency* 663.2, *passage* 692.1, *quantity* 738.1, *quantify* 738.7, *degree* 739.1, *average* 742.1, *number* 784.13

measured 589.16; *sufficient* 97.3, *metrical* 139.20, *solved* 334.15, *deliberate* 384.5, *temperate* 455.8, *moderate* 521.3, *frequent* 663.6, *quantitative* 738.6, *gradational* 739.5

measure depth 598.22

measured quantity *quantity* 738.1

measure for measure *atonement* 313.1, *retaliation* 420.1, *exchange* 673.1, *reciprocity* 729.1, *compensatory* 743.5

measure-for-measure *reciprocal* 729.4

measureless *numberless* 795.8, *immeasurable* 798.6

measurelessly *immeasurably* 798.11

measurelessness *immeasurability* 798.2

measurement 1.9, 10.67, 589.1; *numeration* 6.10, *quantity* 738.1, *gradation* 739.3

measurements *size* 579.1

measurement ton Scientific and Technical Units 589

measure off *measure* 589.20

measure one's length *drop* 714.15

measure out 589.21; *give out* 472.12, *space* 563.15, *measure* 589.20, *limit* 620.7

measurer 589.14; *bowler* 151.5

measures *means* 102.1, *procedure* 387.2, *preparations* 388.2, *action* 412.1

measure theory Branches of Mathematics 6

measure time 646.14

measure up *measure* 589.20

measure up to *suffice* 97.6, *be equal* 740.11

measuring *measurement* 589.1, *metrical* 589.15, *quantity* 738.1, *quantitative* 738.6

measuring cup *cooking equipment* 91.6

measuring instrument 557.19, 589.12, 683.6; *indicator* 183.7

measuring rod *measuring instrument* 589.12

measuring spoon *cooking equipment* 91.6

measuring system 589.4

meat 90.22; *fruit structure* 44.3, *food* 90.1, Phobias 283, *topic* 328.1, *animal products* 522.7, *substance* 577.2, *essential content* 723.2

meat [Inf *and* Off] *sex object* 20.8

meat compartment *kitchen container* 91.7

meat dish 90.21

meat-eater *type of animal* 34.5, *eater* 92.15

meat eating *eating habit* 92.7

meat-eating *eating* 92.18

meathead [Inf] *foolish person* 353.3

meat hooks [Inf] *retainer* 471.3

meatiness *squatness* 579.6

meat juice *juice* 555.2

meatless day *fast* 118.4

meat market *food provider* 90.6, *market* 483.1

meat packer *laborer* 123.9

meat substitute 90.23

meat thermometer *cooking equipment* 91.6

meaty *emphatic* 200.3, *significant* 361.11, *stocky* 579.16

mecanopsis Flowers 42

Mecca *objective* 374.5

Mecca balsam Tree Products 43

mechanic *mechanical engineer* 14.4, *artisan* 123.13, *operator* 509.5, *miscellaneous automotive terms* 687.14, *repairer* 809.5

mechanical 14.44, 103.7; *physical* 10.70, *involuntary* 95.15, *mountaineering* 161.9, *stage of proof* 174.9, *practical* 511.6

mechanical advantage *work* 14.10

mechanical aid *apparatus* 103.2

mechanical belay *climbing techniques* 161.3

mechanical binding *bookbinding* 174.11

mechanical device *dynamic structure* 14.5, *apparatus* 103.2, *machinery* 103.5

mechanical digger *extractor* 711.9

mechanical drawing *drawing* 143.4, *illustration* 187.2, *representation* 202.9

mechanical editing *stage of book production* 174.7

mechanical energy *energy* 514.7

mechanical engineer 14.4; *engineer* 14.2, *professional worker* 123.11

mechanical engineering 14.3; *engineering* 14.1

mechanical force Fields of Measurement 589

mechanically *physically* 10.78, *structurally* 14.52, *involuntarily* 95.23, *instrumentally* 103.9, 511.9, *systematically* 397.22

mechanical malfunction *unsuccessful thing* 846.8

mechanical means *instrumentality* 511.1

mechanical oscillation *wave* 10.11

mechanical solidarity *society* 2.6

mechanical strength 516.2

mechanical wave *wave* 683.4

mechanical weathering *weathering* 8.40

mechanics *classical physics* 10.2, *impulsion* 695.1

mechanism Philosophical Schools of Thought 4, *chemical reaction* 11.8, *dynamic structure* 14.5, *instrumentality* 102.2, *machinery* 103.5, *instrument* 511.2, *component* 760.3

mechanist Philosophical Schools of Thought 4

mechanistic *mechanical* 103.7

mechanization *instrumentality* 511.1

mechanize *use tools* 103.8, *produce* 522.13

mechanized *mechanical* 103.7, *productive* 522.11

mechanophobia Phobias 283

Mecklenburg Horse and Pony Breeds 159

mecopteran *insectile* 40.11

medal *military honor* 58.9, *honor* 72.3, *relief carving* 144.2, *competition* 166.18, *insignia* 184.5, *monument* 185.10, *prize* 453.2, *decoration* 532.1

medalist *prizewinner* 127.8, *victor* 845.7

medallion *talisman* 86.9, Architectural Elements 134, *relief carving* 144.2, *jewelry* 532.6

Medal of Honor US Military Medals 58

medal play *golf* 156.1

meddle 321.8, 414.23; *be clumsy* 128.9, *be active in* 412.17, *change for the worse* 665.18, *impair* 808.18, *hinder* 826.15

meddler 321.4, 414.12; *adviser* 176.5, *hinderer* 826.11

meddlesome *prying* 321.6, *meddling* 414.17

meddlesomeness *overactivity* 414.9

meddle with *mix* 751.12

meddling 414.17; *prying* 321.2, 321.6, *overactivity* 414.9, *hindrance* 826.1, *hindering* 826.12

meddling person *meddler* 414.12

Medea *witch* 86.15

media, the *publication media* 173.6

media art Western Art Styles 133

media event *public relations (PR)* 173.8

media hype [Inf] *news story* 171.3

medial *central* 612.6, *medium* 742.6, *middle* 772.9

medially *centrally* 612.12, *medianly* 742.12, *in the middle* 772.21

median *triangle* 6.41, *parameter* 6.57, *center* 612.1, *central* 612.6, *medium* 742.2, 742.6, *middle way* 772.3, *middle* 772.9

medianly 742.12; *centrally* 612.12

mediant *musical note* 140.15

median triangle *triangle* 6.41

media personality *broadcasting personnel* 172.11

mediate 75.6, 772.19; *have an industrial dispute* 57.20, *make peace* 73.11, *conciliate* 74.10, *represent* 80.6, *negotiate* 460.6, *be an instrument* 511.7, *moderate* 521.7

mediated *disputed* 57.15, *negotiated* 460.5

mediately *mediatorially* 75.7

mediation 75.1; *strike* 57.8, *pacification* 74.1, *negotiation* 460.1, *instrumentality* 511.1, *middle ground* 772.4

mediative *causal* 511.5

mediator 75.2; *employer* 57.3, *matchmaker* 64.13, *pacifier* 73.7, *agent* 80.3, 123.15, *speaker* 205.12, *judge* 341.5, *negotiator* 460.4, *assistant* 511.3, *moderator* 521.2, *interfacer* 616.3, *middleman* 772.7

mediatorial *mediatory* 75.5

mediatorially 75.7; *pacifically* 74.12

mediatory 75.5, 772.11; *pacificatory* 74.8

medic *air force person* 77.31, *doctor* 107.19, *helper* 275.5

medicable *repairable* 809.7

Medicaid *medical practice* 107.3

medical 107.28; *health care* 107.7

medical adviser *adviser* 176.5

medical assistance 825.5

medical assistant *paramedic* 107.24

medical attendant *paramedic* 107.24

medical auxiliary *paramedic* 107.24

medical care *medicine* 107.1, *treatment* 107.14, *therapy* 115.12

medical center *center of activity* 612.4

medical covering 613.4

medical doctor (M.D.) *doctor* 107.19

medical ethics 107.2

medical examination *health care* 107.7

medical examiner *medical specialist* 107.20

medical history *health care* 107.7

medical home visit *health care* 107.7

medical insurance *medical practice* 107.3

medical intervention *treatment* 107.14

medical jurisprudence *medical ethics* 107.2

medically 107.35, 115.20

Medical Officer (M.O.) *doctor* 107.19

medical officer *hygienist* 116.2

medical physics Fields of Modern Physics 10

medical practice 107.3

medical practitioner *doctor* 107.19

medical profession *medicine* 107.1

medical school *type of school* 48.12

medical science 107.5

medical ship Ships and Boats 690

medical specialist 107.20; *psychiatrist* 108.34

medical student *doctor* 107.19

medical test *diagnosis* 107.8

medical treatment *treatment* 107.14, *therapy* 115.12

medicament *medicine* 115.2

Medicare *medical practice* 107.3, *security* 464.1

medicate 115.18; *practice medicine* 107.32, *cure* 809.15

medicated *restorative* 809.9

medication *treatment* 107.14, *medicine* 115.2

medicinal 115.15; *therapeutic* 107.30, *remedial* 115.14, *stimulating* 221.7, *restorative* 809.9

medicinal compound *mixed thing* 751.2

medicinal drink *stimulant* 221.5

medicinal herb *plant* 41.2, *medicine* 115.2

medicinally 115.21; *piquantly* 221.10

medicinal plant *plant* 41.2

medicinal value *remedy* 115.1

medicine 107.1, 115.2; *healing art* 115.13, *medical assistance* 825.5

medicine and surgery *naval commands* 77.19

medicine man *witch* 86.15, *warner* 814.5

medicine show *show* 138.4, *public relations (PR)* 173.8

medicine woman *witch* 86.15

medico [Inf] *doctor* 107.19

medicopsychology *psychiatry* 108.2

medieval *historic* 653.13

medieval architecture Architectural Styles 134

medievalism *historicism* 3.7, Western Literary Groups 139, *antiquarianism* 653.3

medievalist *antiquarian* 653.9

medieval ownership 469.9

Medina Rivers 570

mediocre 289.11, 742.7; *moderate* 521.3, *insignificant* 745.6, *middling* 772.14, *cheap* 800.16

mediocrity 289.5, 742.3; *deficiency*

745.2, *triviality* 800.2, *nonentity* 800.8

meditate *worship* 83.15, *speculate* 294.13, *think* 317.9, *intend* 374.8, *dematerialize* 525.12

meditation *act of worship* 83.2, *trance* 108.18, *thoughtfulness* 317.2

meditative *thoughtful* 4.17, *worshipful* 83.12, *speculative* 317.8

meditatively *thoughtfully* 4.27, *worshipfully* 83.17

meditativeness *thoughtfulness* 317.2

meditative trance *oblivion* 355.4

Mediterranean climate *climate* 9.35

Mediterranean Sea Oceans and Seas 571

medium 579.12, 742.2, 742.6; *occultist* 86.13, *culinary* 91.9, *instrumentality* 102.2, 511.1, *stage lighting* 136.20, *material* 143.9, *paint* 251.6, *intuitive person* 320.5, *interpreter* 365.6, *instrument* 511.2, *moderate* 521.3, *nonmaterialist* 525.7, *essence* 723.1, *middle way* 772.3, *middling* 772.14

medium artillery *guns* 78.9

medium bomber *military aircraft* 77.30

mediumism *occultism* 86.1

mediumistic *psychic* 86.17

mediumistic trance *occult and psychic phenomena* 86.7

medium of exchange *money* 484.1

medium-range *transportable* 686.7

medium shot *composition* 132.17

medium-size(d) *medium* 579.12

medium steel *shipbuilding* 690.4

medium-term forecast *weather forecast* 9.4

medium wave *radio transmission* 172.3

medium wave (MW) *radio frequency* 661.3

medley *miscellany* 59.15, 751.3, *swimming* 164.12, *variety* 732.2

medley of colors *variegation* 263.1

medley relay race *competitive swimming* 164.3, *relay racing* 166.5

medulla *stem* 41.5

medullary *compressible* 543.9

medullary sheath *nervous system* 19.14

Medusa *witch* 86.15, Legendary Creatures 360

medusa *coelenterate* 39.15

medusoid *coelenterate* 39.25

meed [Arch] *reward* 453.1, *compensation* 743.1

meed of praise *praise* 437.3

meek *humble* 298.8, *modest* 403.6, *submitting* 421.3, *obedient* 426.4, *helpless* 515.9

meekly *humbly* 298.22, *modestly* 403.15, *with humility* 421.8, *obediently* 426.9

meekness *humility* 298.1, *modesty* 403.1, *obedience* 426.1

meerschaum *tobacco implements* 121.24

meet 586.15, 704.20; *conference* 59.5, *come together* 59.25, 702.10, *adjoin* 216.11, *suffice* 273.10, *discover* 345.11, *prize competition* 422.5, *fight* 422.23, *perform* 465.5, *pay off* 489.17, *summit*

600.11, *cross* 609.9, *interface* 616.5, *collide* 695.10, *unify* 752.15, *intercommunicate* 754.15, *conform* 781.11

meet a deadline *have no time to spare* 818.6

meet a demand *be sold* 482.22

meet adversity *be in trouble* 848.13

meet around a conference table *confer* 210.13

meet by accident *or chance chance upon* 842.13

meet by chance *meet* 704.20

meet contractual obligations *employ* 57.18

meet God *be religious* 81.25

meet halfway *pacify* 74.11, *compromise* 461.7, *stand in the middle* 772.17

meet head on *confront* 828.19

meeting 586.5, 586.10, 704.5; *conference* 59.5, *religious group* 81.4, *sports* 145.1, *place for conversation* 210.5, *contiguity* 216.4, *contiguous* 216.8, *discovery* 345.1, *social gathering* 408.4, *interfacial* 616.4, *collision* 695.2, *convergence* 702.1, *convergent* 702.7, *union* 752.1, *connection* 754.1

meeting ground *interaction* 616.2

meeting halfway *compromise* 461.1

meeting house *place of worship* 83.8

meeting of minds *agreement* 735.3

meeting one's friends *social gathering* 408.4

meeting place 408.5, 702.4; *meeting* 704.5, *point of union* 752.8

meeting point *interface* 616.1, *meeting place* 702.4, *point of union* 752.8

meeting the cost *payment* 489.1

meeting with God *divine manifestation* 82.5

meet one at every turn *be excessive* 99.9, *be present* 575.13

meet one's maker *or death or end or fate die* 29.17

meet one's match *serve one right* 420.5

meet on the battlefield *battle* 76.33

meet requirements *suffice* 97.6

meet reward *retribution* 454.7

meet the cost *defray* 489.18, *expend* 491.11

meet the needs of *suffice* 273.10

meet with *discover* 345.11

meet with approbation *meet with approval* 437.20

meet with approval 437.20

meet with disapproval *be open to criticism* 438.22

meet with success *be successful* 845.11

mega Decimal Prefixes 589

mega [Inf] *huge* 579.14

megabucks [Inf] *money* 485.2

megabyte (meg or MB) *data-related concepts* 15.23

Megaera Deities 82

megahertz (MHz) *radio frequency* 661.3

megalith *monument* 185.10, *thing of the past* 651.8

megalithic *huge* 579.14

megalomania *compulsion* 108.13, *delusion* 110.2, *overestimation* 343.1, *vanity* 402.1

megalomaniac *insane person* 110.5, *overestimator* 343.2, *vain* 402.8, *compulsive person* 428.5
megalophobia Phobias 283
megalopolis *city* 567.1
megalopteran *insectile* 40.11
megaphone *sound amplifier* 230.5
megastar *idol* 83.5, *person of repute* 370.2
megaton bomb *bomb* 78.15
megrim *caprice* 381.1
megrims *animal disease* 34.10
meiosis *cell division* 13.17
meiotic *genetic* 13.32
Meissen ware Ceramics 129
Meissner effect Classical Physical Laws 10
Meistersinger *author* 139.13, *singer* 141.4
Mekong Rivers 570
melaleuca Trees and Shrubs 43
melancholia *mental breakdown* 110.4
melancholic *personality type* 108.6, *insane person* 110.5, *mentally ill* 110.11, *sad person* 270.3, *depressed* 270.5, *hopeless person* 282.5, *without hope* 282.7, *sullen* 304.8
melancholy *depressed* 261.7, *depression* 270.2, *lack of hope* 282.2, *boredom* 296.1, *bored* 296.5, *sullenness* 304.1, *sullen* 304.8
Melanesian *race* 1.5, *racial* 1.12
mélange *mixed thing* 751.2
melanin *pigment* 12.18, *black pigment* 254.2, *brownness* 256.1
melanism *blackness* 254.1
melanistic *dark-colored* 247.7, *dark* 254.6
melanocyte-stimulating hormone Human Hormones 12
melanoma *cancer* 114.15, *skin disease* 114.16
melanosis *blackness* 254.1
melatonin Human Hormones 12
meld *alliance* 64.2
melee *fight* 422.9, *confusion* 766.4
melinite *explosive* 78.13
meliorable *improvable* 807.13
meliorate *refine* 534.7, *improve* 807.15
melioration *education* 48.1, *improvement* 807.1
meliorative *improving* 807.14
Mélisande Famous Lovers 299
melissophobia Phobias 283
melitose Common Sugars 12
melitriose Common Sugars 12
melliferous *sweet* 222.5
mellifluent *melodious* 140.26, *sweet* 222.5
mellifluous *melodious* 140.26, *pleasurable* 214.6, *sweet* 222.5, *fluid* 527.5
mellifluously *tunefully* 140.30
mellophone Musical Instruments 142
mellow *adult* 27.11, *mature* 27.17, *melodious* 140.26, *deep* 236.8, *soft-hued* 251.13, *color* 251.16, *comfortable* 271.8, *soft-hearted* 543.11, *soften* 543.14, *ease* 543.15, *old* 653.10, *convert* 670.11, *be converted* 670.12, *get better* 807.21
mellowly *venerably* 653.17
mellowness *maturity* 27.3, *soft-heartedness* 543.4, *elderliness* 653.2
melodeon Musical Instruments 142
melodia Musical Instruments 142

melodic *musical* 140.25, *melodious* 140.26, *harmonizing* 735.12
melodically *tunefully* 140.30, *in harmony* 735.12
melodic line *melody* 140.10
melodic scale *scale* 140.16
melodious 140.26; *pleasant* 222.6, *harmonizing* 735.12
melodiously *tunefully* 140.30, *sweetly* 222.8, *in harmony* 735.32
melodiousness 140.12; *music* 140.1, *physical pleasure* 214.1, *sweetness* 222.1
melodize *harmonize* 140.28, 735.22
melodrama *dramatic style* 136.3, *tragedy* 136.10, *exaggeration* 194.1
melodramatic *dramatic* 136.31, 137.16, *exaggerated* 194.7, *passionate* 266.12
melodramatically *dramatically* 136.38, *exaggeratedly* 194.16
melodramatics *dramaturgy* 136.6
melodramatist *dramatist* 136.27
melodramatize *dramatize* 136.33
melody 140.10; *music* 140.1, *harmonization* 735.2
melon [Inf] *figurative usage* 44.4
melophobia Phobias 283
Melpomene Deities 82
melt 555.24; *volcanic activity* 8.26, *snow* 9.30, 9.58, *heat* 10.74, 217.17, *solidify* 11.37, *waste away* 96.20, *disappear* 265.5, *move to compassion* 308.9, *soften* 543.14, *be transient* 643.6, *convert* 670.11, *cease to exist* 718.13, *come unstuck* 756.7
meltable *liquefiable* 555.21
melt away *waste away* 96.20, *depart* 265.6, *cease to exist* 718.13, *change by degrees* 739.8, *decrease* 747.7
meltdown *nuclear problem* 10.62, *ruin* 523.4
melt down *heat* 217.17, *melt* 555.24, *obtain an extract* 711.19
melted *status adjectives* 11.25, *liquefied* 555.19
melting *temperature* 10.29, *phase* 11.13, *hot weather* 217.6, *disappearance* 265.1, *amorous* 299.18, *pliant* 543.7, *fluidization* 555.8, *liquefying* 555.20, *changeable* 666.3, *chemical change* 670.2, *converting* 670.8
melting look *look* 242.7
melting point *temperature* 10.29, *heat* 217.1
melting pot *nation* 18.14, *mixer* 751.7
melt into *change by degrees* 739.8
melton Fabrics and Fibers 130
melt on the air *sound faint* 233.8
melt the heart *move to compassion* 308.9
meltwater *glacier* 8.44, *snow* 9.30, *water* 557.1
Melville Islands 572
member 760.9; *set* 6.19, *rock* 8.30, *appendage* 19.5, *component* 760.3, *thing included* 763.2
member of *former servicewoman* 77.6
member of Congress *elected official* 50.8
member of one's generation *contemporary* 649.3
Member of Parliament (MP) [Brit] *elected official* 50.8, *person in authority* 52.7, *delegate* 79.1
member of the bar *lawyer* 54.5

member of the clergy 84.5; *professional worker* 123.11
member of the establishment *important person* 799.5
member of the resistance *revenger* 420.2
member of the staff *member* 760.9
member of the underground *revenger* 420.2
membership *sociability* 408.1, *inclusion* 763.1
members only *exclusiveness* 764.4
membrane *body covering* 19.4, *coat* 588.3
membrane filtration *biochemical applications* 14.30
membraneously *in layers* 588.11
membranophone *musical instrument* 142.1
membranous *internal* 19.23, *platelike* 588.8
memento 354.3; *monument* 185.10, *gift* 472.2
memento mori *personifications and symbols* 29.4
memo *record* 185.1, *reminder* 354.4
memoir *nonfiction* 139.6, *record* 185.1, *dissertation* 203.1
memoirs *biography* 3.5, *life story* 28.11, *retrospect* 354.2
memo pad *record book* 185.5
memorabilia *record* 185.1, *memento* 354.3, *remainder* 750.1
memorability *importance* 799.1
memorable 354.7; *historic* 3.11, *notable* 799.11
memorable date *day to remember* 354.5
memorably 354.16; *residually* 750.11, *importantly* 799.15
memorandum *reminder* 354.4
memorial 354.10; *funeral object* 31.6, *burial place* 31.7, *funeral* 31.9, *monument* 185.10, *memento* 354.3, *celebrative* 405.9
memorial arch *monument* 185.10
memorial inscription *monument* 185.10
memorialization *commemoration* 405.2, *eternalization* 644.3
memorialize *commemorate* 354.14, 405.11, *perpetuate* 640.5, *make eternal* 644.8
memorial service *funeral* 31.4, *commemoration* 405.2
memories *biography* 3.5, Phobias 283
memorization *memory* 354.1, *habituation* 397.7, *retentiveness* 471.4
memorize 354.11; *learn* 68.18, *rehearse* 136.37, *act* 137.20, *know by heart* 348.11, *remember* 471.10
memorized 354.9; *retained* 471.6
memorizing *retentiveness* 471.4
memory 15.6, 108.27, 354.1; *computer part* 15.4, *vault* 105.9, Card Games 168, *idea* 327.1, *commemoration* 405.2, *retentiveness* 471.4, *retrospection* 651.3, *remainder* 750.1
memory card *card* 15.7
memory game Children's and Party Games 167
memory gap *forgetfulness* 186.3
memory trace *memory* 108.27
memsahib [India] *female title of address* 33.3
men *menfolk* 32.14, *personnel* 123.16, Phobias 283
menace *intimidate* 283.18, *malignity* 306.5, *harm* 306.13, *predict* 358.14, *be evil* 446.10,

sense of danger 811.3, *endanger* 811.13, *forewarning* 814.2, *warn* 814.8
menacing *fearsome* 283.13, *overcast* 304.11, *malign* 306.11, *dangerous* 811.7, *warning* 814.6
menacingly *fearsomely* 283.21, *dismally* 304.19, *malignly* 306.18, *dangerously* 811.14
ménage *inhabitants* 61.2, *family* 65.1
ménage à trois *fornication* 432.3, *triple thing* 790.3
menagerie *zoo* 60.14, *repository* 105.13, *miscellany* 751.3
menarche *bleeding* 25.10
mend *get healthy* 113.12, *remedy* 115.16, *sew* 130.18, *put right* 429.14, *compensate* 743.7, *intertwine* 752.19, *restore* 807.17, *get better* 807.21, *rectify* 807.22, *repair* 809.1, 809.10
mendable *repairable* 809.7
mendacious *untruthful* 192.12, *hypocritical* 330.10, *misrepresented* 627.8
mendaciously *untruthfully* 192.27, *distortedly* 627.14
mendaciousness *untruthfulness* 192.1
mendacity *untruthfulness* 192.1, *hypocrisy* 330.5, *distortion of truth* 627.4
mended *repaired* 809.6
mendelevium Chemical Elements and Common Allotropes 11
Mendelian *genetic* 13.32
Mendelism or **Mendelian genetics** *genetics* 13.19
Mendel's law *genetics* 13.19
mender *improver* 807.11, *repairer* 809.5
Menderes Rivers 570
mendicancy *beggary* 486.3, *solicitation* 505.4
mendicant *religious* 84.9, *poor person* 486.6, *beggarly* 486.12, *beggar* 505.6, *begging* 505.9
mendicant friar *poor person* 486.6
mending *sewing* 130.5, *rectification* 807.8, *repair* 809.1, *recuperation* 809.4
Mendip Hills Mountains and Hills 569
Mendips, the *regions of the British Isles* 564.8
mend one's ways *get better* 807.21
menfolk 32.14
menhir *burial place* 31.7, *monument* 185.10, *thing of the past* 651.8
menial *servant* 69.1, *obedient* 69.10, *domestic worker* 123.4, *servile* 401.6, *submitter* 421.2, *submitting* 421.3
menially *obediently* 69.12, *servilely* 401.15
Menière's syndrome or **disease** *ear problem* 228.4
meningitis *infection* 114.7, *neurological disease* 114.20, Phobias 283
meningitophobia Phobias 283
meniscal *curved* 629.4
meniscoid *convex* 634.5
meniscus *circle* 6.40, *curve* 629.1, *convexity* 634.1
Mennecy ware Ceramics 129
Mennonite churches Christian Groups 81
meno Musical Terms and Expression Marks 140

men of today *contemporary* 649.3

meno mosso *Musical Terms and Expression Marks* 140

menopausal *bleeding* 25.19, *middle-aged* 27.14

menopause *infertile state* 23.3, *bleeding* 25.10, *middle age* 27.4

menophobia *Phobias* 283

menorah *sacred object* 83.11

Menorca *Islands* 572

menorrhagia *bleeding* 25.10

Mensa *Constellations* 7

mensal *culinary* 91.9

men's chorus *singing group* 141.6

men's clothing *clothing* 100.1

menses *bleeding* 25.10, *cycle* 663.3

men's magazine *magazine* 175.3

mens rea *intention* 374.1

men's room *place for excretion* 25.11

men's room attendant *cleaner* 111.12

mens sana [L] *sanity* 109.1

mens sana in corpore sano [L] *health* 113.1

menstrual *bleeding* 25.19, *cyclic* 663.7

menstrual cycle *recurrent period* 641.5, *cycle* 663.3

menstrual flow *body fluid* 555.3

menstrual flow *or* **flux** *or* **discharge** *bleeding* 25.10

menstruate *bleed* 25.26, *be cyclic* 663.11

menstruating *bleeding* 25.19

menstruation *bleeding* 25.10, *Phobias* 283, *cycle* 663.3

menstruum *solvent* 555.9

mensurability *measurability* 589.2

mensurable *numerable* 6.70, *measurable* 589.17, *calculable* 784.8

mensural *metrical* 589.15

mensuration *measurement* 10.67, *science of measurement* 589.3

mensurational *metrical* 589.15

mensurative *metrical* 589.15

men's wear *clothing* 100.1, *dry goods* 130.3

mental *thoughtful* 317.5, *ideational* 327.9, *internal* 525.11, *inward* 611.12

mental [Inf] *insane* 110.9

mental activity *thought* 317.1

mental agility *quickness of mind* 694.4

mental agitation *agitation* 684.1

mental and physical distress *fatigue* 820.1

mental arithmetic *numeration* 6.10

mental attitude *conduct* 399.1

mental block 318.5; *forgetfulness* 186.3, 355.1

mental body *spirit* 86.10

mental breakdown 110.4

mental case *insane person* 110.5, *sick person* 114.22

mental chemistry *psychology* 108.1

mental cruelty *divorce court* 66.3

mental deficiency 316.2

mental derangement *derangement* 766.8

mental disorder 108.8; *disease* 114.4, *derangement* 766.8

mental disorders specialist *psychiatrist* 108.34

mental entities *philosophical problem* 4.8

mental equilibrium *sanity* 109.1

mental fatigue *fatigue* 820.1

mental fluctuation *vacillation* 683.3

mental freedom *liberation* 831.1

mental handicap *mental deficiency* 316.2

mental hardness 542.4

mental health *sanity* 109.1

mental home *mental hospital* 110.6

mental hospital 110.6; *psychiatric hospital* 108.35, *safe house* 812.5

mental illness *mental disorder* 108.8, *psychosis* 108.10

mental illness *or* **disorder** *insanity* 110.1

mental image *image* 187.3, *idea* 327.1, *conception* 360.4

mental inertia *apathy* 322.2

mental instability *insanity* 110.1

mental institution *mental hospital* 110.6

mentalism *Philosophical Schools of Thought* 4

mentalist *Philosophical Schools of Thought* 4

mentality *intellect* 315.1, *intelligence* 315.2, *inner nature* 611.4

mentally 315.13; *theoretically* 327.19, *subjectively* 525.14, *inwardly* 611.21

mentally deficient *intellectually subnormal* 316.7

mentally deranged *deranged* 766.16

mentally handicapped *intellectually subnormal* 316.7

mentally hard 542.8

mentally ill 110.11

mentally quick 694.8

mentally sharp 549.14

mentally sound *sane* 109.3

mentally strong *mentally tough* 547.12

mentally subnormal *intellectually subnormal* 316.7

mentally tough 547.12

mentally weak *lacking intellect* 316.5

mental object *idea* 327.1

mental picture *idea* 327.1, *conception* 360.4

mental process *thought* 317.1

mental processes *psychology* 108.1

mental quickness *quickness of mind* 694.4

mental retardation *personality disorder* 108.7, *mental deficiency* 316.2

mental sharpness 549.9

mental shock *anxiety disorder* 108.11

mental state *psychology* 108.1

mental strength *mental toughness* 547.5

mental test *psychometrics* 108.5

mental toughness 547.5

mental traits *Fields of Measurement* 589

mental treatment *therapy* 115.12

mental weakness *lack of intellect* 316.1

menthol *terpene* 12.20, *tobacco* 121.23, 121.33

mention *publish* 173.15, *name* 202.17, *speak* 205.17, *specify* 779.18, *reveal* 843.14

mentioned *displayed* 843.8

mentor *sage* 4.11, *older person* 27.7, *educator* 48.4, *expert* 52.8, *educational leader* 68.11, *adviser* 176.5, 825.14, *protector* 810.11

menu *computing terms* 15.22, *dish* 90.7, *list* 785.1, *bill of fare* 785.5

meow *animal sound* 240.1, *make an animal sound* 240.7

meowing *ulular* 240.4

meperidine *analgesic* 115.6

Mephisto *devil* 446.5

Mephistophelean *demonic* 446.9

Mephistopheles *devil* 446.5

mephitic *toxic* 114.28, *stinking* 227.3, *miasmic* 556.16

mephitis *lack of hygiene* 112.3, *pollution* 117.8, *stench* 227.1, *miasma* 556.3

mercantile 480.13; *economic* 56.10

mercantilism *economic restraint* 830.3

mercantilist *one who restrains* 830.7

mercenary *military* 76.28, *militarist* 77.3, *martial* 77.33, *engaged* 83.7

mercenary army *army* 77.12

mercenary forces *the military* 58.2, *armed forces* 77.9

mercerize *make tough* 547.15

merchandisable *salable* 482.13

merchandise 482.6, 482.17, 522.6; *trade* 56.12, 480.18, *stock in trade* 105.2, *trade in* 457.8, *personal estate* 470.6, *sell* 482.15

merchandiser *trader* 480.11, *merchant* 482.10

merchandising *trade* 480.1, *selling* 482.1

merchant 482.10; *provisioner* 89.4, *trader* 480.11, *retailer* 482.11, *transportable* 686.7

merchantable *mercantile* 480.13, *salable* 482.13

merchant class *middle class* 772.6

merchant jack *flag* 184.8

merchantlike *mercantile* 480.13

merchantman *Sailing Ships and Boats* 690, *Ships and Boats* 690

merchant marine *navy* 77.18

merchant prince *merchant* 482.10

merchant ship *Sailing Ships and Boats* 690, *Ships and Boats* 690, *vessel* 690.3

merchant venturer *merchant* 482.10

merchant vessel *Ships and Boats* 690

merci! [Fr] *thank you!* 310.9

merciful *compassionate* 305.8, *pitying* 308.4, *forgiving* 312.4, *lenient* 423.3

mercifully *forgivingly* 53.37, 312.13, *pacifically* 74.12, *pityingly* 308.11, *leniently* 423.6

mercifulness *pity* 308.1, *mercy* 308.3, *forgivingness* 312.3, *leniency* 423.1

merciless *malicious* 306.8, *pitiless* 309.3, *relentless* 309.4, *unyielding* 379.8, *severe* 424.6

mercilessly *maliciously* 306.15, *pitilessly* 309.7, *relentlessly* 309.8, *severely* 424.11

mercilessness *malice* 306.2, *pitilessness* 309.1, *relentlessness* 309.2

mercurial *passionate* 266.12, *erratic* 381.5, *changeable* 666.3, *irresolute* 666.4, *moving* 677.12, *mentally quick* 694.8, *capricious* 841.16

mercurially *in motion* 677.19

Mercurian *astronomical* 7.33

Mercury *Planets and Their Satellites* 7, *planet* 7.16, *Deities* 82, *messenger* 685.5

mercury *Chemical Elements and Common Allotropes* 11

mercury barometer *weather instrument* 9.7

mercury-vapor lamp *electron tube* 14.40, *electric light* 246.6

mercy 308.3; *peace offering* 74.5, *divine attribute* 82.4, *compassion* 305.2, *pity* 308.1, *leniency* 423.1

mercy! *I/we surrender!* 421.9

mercy flight *aviation* 689.1

mercy killer *killer* 30.11

mercy killing *killing* 30.1

mere [Brit] *small lake* 568.2

mere detail *trifle* 800.3

mere existence 717.10; *poverty* 486.1

mere handful *few* 796.1

merely exist 717.21

merengue *folk music* 140.7

mere nothing *trifle* 800.3

mere notion *conjecture* 359.3

Mérens pony *Horse and Pony Breeds* 159

mere rhetoric *sophistry* 330.1

meretricious *ungenuine* 192.13, *affected* 367.3, *flashy* 404.17, *unchaste* 432.10, *indecorous* 528.8, *ornate* 532.10, *vulgar* 535.6

meretriciously *untruthfully* 192.27, *showily* 367.6, *flashily* 404.32

meretriciousness *ungenuineness* 192.2, *flashiness* 404.4

mere words *nonsense* 362.2

mere wreck *dilapidation* 808.5

merganser *descender* 714.8

merge 64.21; *deal* 457.9, *take over* 477.16, *convert* 670.11, *be the same* 730.13, *make the same* 730.16, *form an alliance* 735.25, *mix* 751.12, *unify* 752.15, *connect* 754.13, *combine* 757.9, *be included* 763.6, *become one* 788.18, *join* 827.17

merged *taking* 477.12, *corporate* 480.17, *related* 727.6, *same* 730.7, *allied* 735.15, *mixed* 751.8, *united* 752.10, *connected* 754.11, *combined* 757.5, *collected* 757.8, *included* 763.4

merge into in the background *escape notice* 403.14

mergence *sameness* 730.1

merger *alliance* 64.2, *taking over* 477.3, *bargaining* 480.10, *business offer* 504.3, *joint operation* 509.2, *relatedness* 727.1, *sameness* 730.1, *mixture* 751.1, *union* 752.1, *connection* 754.1, *combination* 757.1, *association* 827.6

merge with *join with* 827.15

merging *same* 730.7, *association* 827.6

meridian *celestial sphere* 7.4, *exact location* 565.2, *summit* 600.1, *top* 600.6, *daily* 655.6

méridienne *couch* 101.7

meridional *directional* 697.8

meringue *air bubble* 558.10

meringue pie *pie* 90.38

Merino *Breeds of Sheep* 16

merino *Fabrics and Fibers* 130

merit *title* 72.1, *be entitled to* 72.13, *qualify* 340.11, *claim* 429.3, *have rights* 429.13, *good* 445.1, *worth* 447.3, *distinction* 777.8, *importance* 799.1, *usability* 801.2

merited *qualified* 340.7

meritocracy *oligarchy* 49.10

meritocratic *governmental* 49.24

meritorious *worthily* 72.11, *desirable* 288.11, *praiseworthy* 437.12, *worthy* 447.7

meritoriously *worthily* 72.14, 447.11, *desirably* 288.24

meritoriousness *desirability* 288.7

Merlin *witch* 86.15

Merlin pony Horse and Pony Breeds 159
merlins Collective Names 59
merlon *fort* 419.13
mermaid *witch* 86.15, Legendary Creatures 360, *legendary sea being* 571.4
merman Legendary Creatures 360, *legendary sea being* 571.4
merrily *cheerfully* 269.14, *rejoicingly* 279.7, *sociably* 408.19
Merrimack Rivers 570
merriment *gaiety* 269.3, *fun* 269.4, *amusement* 277.2, *rejoicing* 279.1, *celebration* 405.1, *sociability* 408.1
merry *pleased* 214.9, *cheerful* 269.7, *humorous* 277.9, *rejoicing* 279.4, *celebrative* 405.9, *sociable* 408.11
merry-andrew *clown* 138.10
merrybells Flowers 42
merry-go-round *amusement park and playground equipment* 167.8, *reel* 682.4
merrymaker *joyful person* 269.5, *rejoicer* 279.3
merrymaking *amusement* 167.7, *gaiety* 269.3, *rejoicing* 279.1, *celebration* 405.1, *sociability* 408.1
merry men *army person* 77.17
merry widow *surviving spouse* 66.6, *stock part* 136.24
Mersenne numbers Mathematical Concepts 6
Mersenne prime Mathematical Concepts 6
mesa *landform* 8.9, *upland* 572.7, *heights* 596.4
mésalliance *type of marriage* 64.3, *no relation* 728.5
mescaline *hallucinogens* 121.20
mesh *braid* 609.3, *interweave* 609.8, *reciprocate* 827.13
meshing *unification* 752.5
Meshkenit Deities 82
mesh together *interweave* 609.8, *unify* 752.15
meshuga [Yiddish inf] *insane* 110.9
mesial *medium* 742.6, *middle* 772.9
mesmeric *compelling* 428.6, *motivational* 508.7, *appealing* 512.9, *moderating* 521.5
mesmerically *occultly* 86.27, *attractionally* 700.13
mesmerism *occultism* 86.1, *occult influence* 512.2, *pulling power* 700.2
mesmerize *bewitch* 86.25, *anesthetize* 213.8, *be irresistible* 428.9, *manipulate* 508.12, *be an influence* 512.13, *lure* 700.12
mesmerized *bewitched* 86.21, *motivated* 508.8
mesmerizer *motivator* 508.6
mesne profits *money received* 492.2
mesocarp *fruit structure* 44.3
meso form *structure* 11.7
Mesolithic *primal* 653.14
mesometeorology *meteorology* 9.1
mesomorph *physical type* 1.8, *personality type* 108.6, *nature* 624.5
mesomorphic *physical* 1.14
mesomorphism *personality type* 108.6
mesomorphy *physical type* 1.8, *personality type* 108.6
meson *elementary particle* 10.53, *little thing* 580.3
mesophyll *leaf* 41.6

Mesopotamian architecture Architectural Styles 134
mesosphere *atmospheric layer* 558.3
mesospheric *atmospheric* 558.13
mesozoan *invertebrate* 39.1, 39.20
Mesozoic *primal* 653.14
mesquite Trees and Shrubs 43
mess *eating place* 92.17, *have a meal* 92.25, *bungling* 128.2, *ugly thing* 531.2, *shapelessness* 625.1, *certain amount* 738.3, *miscellany* 751.3, *confusion* 766.4, *mix-up* 766.5, *predicament* 824.5, *error* 846.2
message *correspondence* 169.2, *communication* 170.2, *news event* 171.2, *advertisement* 173.9, *signal* 183.6, *topic* 328.1, *meaning* 361.1, *moral* 431.5, *transferred thing* 685.6
message conveyed *meaning* 361.1
message receiver *recipient* 473.5
messaline Fabrics and Fibers 130
messed up *bungled* 128.7, *mixed up* 766.14, *disarranged* 768.7
messenger 685.5; *office assistant* 69.6, *agent* 80.3, *postal worker* 169.6, *informer* 170.8, *publicizer* 173.11, *omen* 358.5, *speeder* 694.5, *precursor* 769.7, *commissioner* 833.5
messenger of God *angel* 82.11
messenger RNA (mRNA) *nucleotide* 12.10, *genetic material* 13.20
mess hall *room* 60.9, *eating place* 92.17
Messiah *God the Son* 82.9
messianic *Christlike* 82.18
messianically *divinely* 82.24
Messidor French Revolutionary Calendar 646
Messier Catalog *star catalog* 7.9
messily *dirtily* 112.12, *negligently* 326.8
messiness *dirtiness* 112.1, *indifference* 326.2, *untidiness* 766.3
messing *eating meals* 92.4
mess jacket *jacket* 100.18
mess kit *formal clothing* 406.5
messmate *friend* 62.2, *eater* 92.15
messroom *room* 60.9
messuage *legal property terms* 470.2
mess up *dirty* 112.11, *be clumsy* 128.9, *be wrong* 430.18, *mix up* 751.13, *confuse* 766.19, *make disorderly* 766.20, *disarrange* 768.11, *impair* 808.18
messy *dirty* 112.7, *bungled* 128.7, *indifferent* 326.5, *ugly* 531.3, *untidy* 766.11
Mesta Rivers 570
mesto Musical Terms and Expression Marks 140
metabolic 19.24; *biochemical* 12.25, *physiological* 13.29, *transformative* 665.12
metabolically *biochemically* 12.27
metabolic pathway *metabolism* 12.21
metabolism 12.21; *physiology* 13.13, *body process* 19.15, *transformation* 665.7
metabolite *metabolism* 12.21
metabolize 12.26; *transform* 665.20
metacarpal bones Human Bones 19
metacarpus Human Bones 19
metage *measurement* 589.1
metal *chemical element* 11.3, *metallurgy* 11.22, *ore* 11.23, *type of furniture* 101.2, *snowplow* 162.29,

Heraldic Terms 184, Phobias 283, *hard substance* 542.3
metal conductor *electrical conduction* 10.33
metal detector *detector* 345.6
metal engraver *engraver* 144.5
metal engraving *engraving* 144.3
metal fatigue *deformation* 14.16
metal inlay *decorative woodwork* 131.2
metallic *strident* 238.4
metallic bond *chemical bond* 11.6
metallic conductor *electricity* 14.34
metallic currency *coinage* 484.13
metallic pigment *coloring agent* 251.5
metallography *metallurgy* 11.22
metalloid *chemical element* 11.3, *metallurgy* 11.22
metallophobia Phobias 283
metallophone Musical Instruments 142
metalloprotein *protein* 12.9
metallurgic *metallurgical* 11.36
metallurgical 11.36; *chemical* 11.24
metallurgical engineer *engineer* 14.2
metallurgically *chemically* 11.42
metallurgy 11.22, Branches of Chemistry 11
metals *rail* 688.3
metal sculptor *sculptor* 144.4
metal sculpture *sculpture* 144.1
metal ski *ski equipment* 162.10
metalwork *craft* 133.2
metalworker *artisan* 123.13
metalworks *works* 124.9
metamathematics *mathematics* 6.1
metamorphic *petrographic* 8.58, *transformative* 665.12
metamorphic facies *metamorphism* 8.35
metamorphic grade *metamorphism* 8.35
metamorphic rock 8.36; *rock* 8.30
metamorphism 8.35
metamorphose *develop* 40.18, *transform* 665.20, 670.13, *be changeable* 666.5, *convert* 670.11
metamorphosed *converted* 670.7
metamorphosis *petrogenesis* 8.31, *developmental biology* 13.22, *transformation* 665.7, *changeableness* 666.1, *conversion* 670.1
metamorphous *transformative* 665.12
metanarrative *aspect of fiction* 139.5
metaphase *cell division* 13.17
metaphor *phrasing* 5.25, *literary device* 139.12, *type of meaning* 361.4, *interpretation* 365.1, *ornament* 532.7, *comparability* 733.2, *latency* 844.1, *mysteriousness* 844.5
metaphorical *or* **metaphoric** *phrased* 5.39, *symbolic* 361.8, *comparable* 733.8, *mysterious* 844.11
metaphorically *phraseologically* 5.47, *meaningfully* 361.16, *comparably* 733.18
metaphorical meaning *type of meaning* 361.4
metaphrastic *translational* 365.11
metaphysical *philosophical* 4.12, *theological* 81.24, *literary* 139.15, *nonmaterial* 525.8

metaphysical art Western Art Styles 133
metaphysical idealism *idealism* 525.5
metaphysically 525.13; *philosophically* 4.23, *occultly* 86.27
metaphysical poet *author* 139.13
metaphysical poetry *poetry* 139.8
Metaphysical poets Western Literary Groups 139
metaphysical world *nonmaterial world* 525.1
metaphysician *philosopher* 4.9, *occultist* 86.13
metaphysicist *occultist* 86.13
metaphysics Branches of Philosophy 4, *supernaturalism* 86.3, *philosophy of being* 717.2
metapsychic *psychic* 86.17
metapsychical *psychic* 86.17
metapsychist *occultist* 86.13
metapsychology *supernaturalism* 86.3, Psychological Theories, Schools 108
metastable *chemical compound* 11.4
metastable equilibrium *force* 10.9
metastable state *excited atom* 10.55
metastasis *transmission* 685.3
metastasize *transfer* 685.8
metastatic *transferable* 685.7
metastatically *in transit* 685.13
metatarsal bones Human Bones 19
metatarsus Human Bones 19
Metatheria *pouched mammal* 35.5
metatherian *pouched mammal* 35.5, *mammalian* 35.23
metathesis *inverted thing* 608.4, *transfer* 685.1
metathesize *transfer* 685.8
metathetic *transferable* 685.7
Metazoa *invertebrate* 39.1
metazoan *invertebrate* 39.1, 39.20
metempsychosis *materialization* 524.2, *transformation* 665.7, *transfer* 685.1
meteor 7.21; *natural light* 246.4, *transient* 643.2
meteoric *astronomical* 7.33, *transient* 643.4, *swift* 694.6
meteorically *astronomically* 7.36, *swiftly* 694.16
meteorite *meteor* 7.21
meteorite crater *meteor* 7.21
meteoritic *astronomical* 7.33
meteoroid *meteor* 7.21
meteorologic 9.38
meteorological *geophysical* 8.51, *meteorologic* 9.38
meteorologically 9.60; *geologically* 8.68
meteorological satellite *artificial satellite* 7.30
meteorologist 9.2; *geophysicist* 8.5, *forecaster* 358.9
meteorology 9.1; *geophysics* 8.2
meteorphobia Phobias 283
meteors Phobias 283
meteor shower *meteor* 7.21
meteor swarm *meteor* 7.21
mete out *give out* 472.12, *allocate* 474.5, *measure out* 589.21
meter 139.10, 589.13; *tempo* 140.22, Scientific and Technical Units 589, *measure* 589.20, *musical time* 639.7
meterable *measurable* 589.17
meter bar *measuring instrument* 589.12
metered *measured* 589.16
metered mail *postal service* 169.5

meter-kilogram-second (mks) system *measuring system* 589.4
meter-kilogram-second-ampere (mksa) system *measuring system* 589.4
meter reader *power worker* 106.10
methane *gas* 106.6
methanol *fuels* 106.2
methionine Amino Acids 12
Method, the *acting* 136.22
method 387.4, 765.7; *reasoning* 6.61, *means* 102.1, *approach* 209.3, *plan* 387.1, *way* 399.10, 691.1, *style* 537.1, *regularity* 730.6, *organization* 767.3, *formula* 780.7
Method acting *acting* 136.22
Method actor *actor* 136.25, 137.13
Method actress *actor* 136.25, 137.13
methodical *planned* 387.10, *formal* 406.6, *regular* 665.3, 730.12, *unhurried* 693.8, *well-ordered* 765.14, *organizational* 767.13, *uniform* 780.10
methodically 765.27; *as planned* 387.16, *in place* 767.24
methodicalness 765.6; *slowness* 693.1
Methodism Christian Groups 81
methodization *organization* 767.3
methodize *plan* 387.12, *systematize* 765.19, *organize* 767.19
methodized *organized* 767.12
method of operating *way* 399.10
method of operation (MO) *way* 691.1
method of payment *bargaining terms* 57.10
methodology *way* 691.1, *methodicalness* 765.6
Methuselah *older person* 27.7
methuselah *bottle* 578.14
methyl alcohol Tree Products 43
methylene blue *blue pigment* 261.2
methyl orange *gravimetric analysis* 11.18
methyl red *gravimetric analysis* 11.18
methyl violet *purple pigment* 262.2
methyphobia Phobias 283
meticulous *diligent* 323.7, *careful* 325.6, *discriminating* 337.9, *accurate* 350.3, *formal* 406.6, *severe* 424.5, *observant* 465.3, *unhurried* 693.8, *correct* 721.13, *detailed* 726.9, *well-ordered* 765.14, *perfectionistic* 805.18
meticulously 726.18; *attentively* 323.14, *judiciously* 337.16, *severely* 424.11, *observantly* 465.6, *correctly* 721.29
meticulousness *carefulness* 323.3, 325.1, *judiciousness* 337.2, *accuracy* 350.1, *severity* 424.1, *slowness* 693.1, *trueness* 721.4, *methodicalness* 765.6
métier *job* 122.3, *skill* 127.1, *information* 348.2, *business* 480.6, *sphere* 564.10, *special skill* 779.2
Metis Planets and Their Satellites 7
Métis Trotter Horse and Pony Breeds 159
Metonic *cyclic* 663.7
Metonic cycle *cycle* 663.3
metonym *word* 5.17
metonymy *literary device* 139.12
me-tooism [Inf] *imitation* 736.1
metope Architectural Elements 134

Metrazol™ shock therapy *psychiatric treatment* 108.3
metric 589.19; *metrical* 589.15
metrical 139.20, 589.15; *regular* 663.5
metrically *poetically* 139.23, *measurably* 589.22
metrical unit *meter* 139.10
metrication *measuring system* 589.4
metrics *meter* 139.10
metrological *metrical* 589.15
metrologically *measurably* 589.22
metrology *measurement* 10.67, *science of measurement* 589.3
metronome *instrumental aid* 142.7, Timepieces and Timers 646, *oscillator* 683.7
metrophobia Phobias 283
metropolis *city* 567.1
metropolitan *environmental* 60.17, *townsperson* 61.7, *native* 61.12, *administrative* 564.13, *urban* 567.14
metropolitan area *administrative region* 564.4, *city* 567.1, *urban area* 567.10
mettle *courage* 284.1, *proudness* 297.3, *will* 376.5, *stamina* 377.4, *vigor* 518.1
mettlesome *courageous* 284.9, *proud* 297.10, *active* 414.13, *vigorous* 518.2
Meuse Rivers 570
Meuse-Rhine-Yssel Breeds of Cattle 16
mew *dwelling* 36.4, *animal sound* 240.1, *make an animal sound* 240.7
mewl *cry* 239.16, *make an animal sound* 240.7
Mexican Civil War Major Wars 76
Mexican GP at Mexico City *Formula 1 World Championship races* 146.5
Mexican hairless Breeds of Dogs 35
Mexican War Major Wars 76
Mexico Countries 566
Mexico City Countries 566
mezuzah *sacred object* 83.11
mezza-majolica Ceramics 129
mezzanine *auditorium* 136.17
mezza voce Musical Terms and Expression Marks 140
mezzo Musical Terms and Expression Marks 140
mezzocerchio [Ital] *fencing movements* 153.3
mezzoforte or *mf* Musical Terms and Expression Marks 140
mezzo-relievo *relief carving* 144.2
mezzo-soprano *voice* 141.5
mezzotint *engraving* 144.3, *hue* 251.4
Mfumbiro Range Mountains and Hills 569
mho Scientific and Technical Units 589
Miami *major US cities* 567.5
miaow *animal sound* 240.1, *make an animal sound* 240.7
miasma 556.3; *lack of hygiene* 112.3, *infection* 114.7, *pollution* 117.8, *stench* 227.1, *murk* 248.2
miasmal *unhygienic* 114.27, *stinking* 227.3, *murky* 248.5, *miasmic* 556.16

miasmatic *miasmic* 556.16
miasmic 556.16; *killing* 30.17, *stinking* 227.3, *murky* 248.5
mice Phobias 283
Michael *angel* 82.11
Michaelmas Christian Holy Days and Seasons 85
Michaelmas daisy Flowers 42
Michaelmas Day Christian Holy Days and Seasons 85
Michelson–Morley experiment Classical Physical Laws 10
Michigan Card Games 168, American States 564, Lakes 568
Mick Nicknames for Inhabitants 61
Mickey or Mickey Finn [Inf] *anesthetic* 213.3
mickey mouse [Inf] *cheap* 800.16, *broken down* 802.8, *easy* 823.9
micro Decimal Prefixes 589
microbar Scientific and Technical Units 589
microbe *microorganism* 13.11, *disease-causing agent* 114.5, *little thing* 580.3
microbes; germs Phobias 283
microbial *living* 13.28, *tiny* 580.9
microbial genetics *genetics* 13.19
microbic *tiny* 580.9
microbiological *biological* 13.27
microbiologist *life scientist* 13.26, *medical specialist* 107.20
microbiology *biology* 13.2, *medical science* 107.5
microbiophobia Phobias 283
microburst *miscellaneous aviation terms* 689.9
microcard *record book* 185.5
microchip *circuit* 14.37, *little thing* 580.3
microcircuit *circuit* 14.37
microclimate *climate* 9.35
microcomputer *computer* 15.1
microcopy *photoreproduction* 132.6
microcosm *little thing* 580.3, *whole thing* 759.2
microcosmic *undersized* 580.8
microcosmically *microscopically* 580.14
microcrystal *crystal* 8.39, 11.14
microcrystalline *status adjectives* 11.25
microdot *little thing* 580.3
microeconomics *economics* 56.1
microelectronics *electronics* 14.33
microfibril *cell structure* 13.16
microfiche *photoreproduction* 132.6, *record book* 185.5, *little thing* 580.3
microfilaria *invertebrate larva* 39.19
microfilm *reproduce* 21.13, *photoreproduction* 132.6, *record book* 185.5, *little thing* 580.3
microfilming *photoreproduction* 21.1
microfilm reader *visual aid* 242.14
micrography *miniaturization* 580.2
microgravity *space travel* 7.29
microhabitat *habitat* 60.1
microlith *thing of the past* 651.8
micrometeorite *meteor* 7.21
micrometeorology *meteorology* 9.1
micrometer *miniaturization* 580.2, Fields of Measurement 589, *measuring instrument* 589.12
micrometer caliper Fields of Measurement 589
micrometer gauge Fields of Measurement 589

micrometry Fields of Measurement 589
microminiaturization *miniaturization* 580.2
micromorph *little person* 580.5
micron or micrometer Scientific and Technical Units 589
Micronesia Countries 566
micronization *pulverization* 553.4
micronize *pulverize* 553.26
micronutrient *essential element* 12.15
microorganism 13.11; *disease-causing agent* 114.5, *little thing* 580.3
microphobia Phobias 283
microphone *radio transmission* 172.3, *sound amplifier* 230.5
microphotograph *photoreproduction* 132.6, *little thing* 580.3
microphotography *photographic specialties* 132.2
microphyte *microorganism* 13.11, *little thing* 580.3
micropyle *seed* 41.9, *flower part* 42.3
microreader *visual aid* 242.14
Microscope or Microscopium Constellations 7
microscope *visual aid* 242.14, *that which makes visible* 244.4, *miniaturization* 580.2
microscopic *visual* 242.16, *difficult to see* 245.4, *tiny* 580.9
microscopical examination *cell biology* 13.14
microscopically 580.14
microscopy 10.68; *visual aid* 242.14, *miniaturization* 580.2
microsecond *time period* 641.2
microseism *seismic activity* 8.24
microskirt or micro *skirt* 100.12
microsome *cell structure* 13.16
microspore *spore* 553.10
microtubule *cell structure* 13.16
microvillus *cell structure* 13.16
microwave *electromagnetic radiation* 10.14, *cook* 91.10, *radio transmission* 172.3
microwave background *universe* 7.3
microwave cooking *cooking technique* 91.2
microwave generator *electron tube* 14.40
microwave oven *cooker* 91.5, *burner* 217.4
microwave spectroscopy *analysis* 11.17
microwave spectrum *emission* 10.56
micturate *urinate* 25.22
micturition *urination* 25.4
mid *medium* 742.6, *middle* 772.9, *half* 789.12
mid [Arch] *medium* 742.2
Midas *wealthy person* 485.6
Midas touch *wealth* 485.1, *good fortune* 847.2
Mid-Atlantic accent *regional pronunciation* 205.7
midchannel *river parts* 570.3
midcourse *midway* 772.10
midcourt *tennis court* 165.3
midday *noon* 655.4, *daily* 655.6, *midline* 772.2
midday sun *hot weather* 217.6
midden *fertilizer* 16.9, *place for waste* 802.6
middle 772.1, 772.9; *grammatical term* 5.29, *center* 612.1, *central* 612.6, *medium* 742.2, 742.6, *half* 789.12

middle age 27.4, 772.5; *bodily development* 19.17, *age* 27.1, *adulthood* 27.2

middle-aged 27.14, 772.15

Middle Ages Ages, Decades, Eras 641, *historical past* 651.6, *middle age* 772.5

Middle America *regions of the United States* 564.7

Middle American *conformist* 781.6

middle-brow *mediocre* 742.7

middle class 772.6; *social stratification* 2.7, *social class* 777.5

middle-class *socioeconomic* 2.13, *mediocre* 742.7, *middle-aged* 772.15

Middle Comedy *historic comedy* 136.12

middle course *compromise* 461.1, *medium* 742.2

middle course *or* **midcourse** *middle way* 772.3

middle distance *middle ground* 772.4

middle-distance *speed-skating* 162.33

middle-distance racing *speed skating* 162.20, *middle-distance running* 166.3

middle-distance running 166.3, Sporting Activities 145

middle ear *ear* 19.10, 228.2

Middle-Earth Imaginary Places 360

Middle East *world region* 564.6

middle finger *appendage* 19.5

middle ground 772.4; *compromise* 461.1, *medium* 742.2, *middle way* 772.3

middle-ground *medium* 742.6

middle life *middle age* 27.4, 772.5

middleman 772.7; *mediator* 75.2, *agent* 80.3, 123.15, *negotiator* 460.4, *merchant* 482.10, *retailer* 482.11, *interfacer* 616.3, *person who joins* 752.9

middle management *middle class* 772.6

middlemost *medium* 742.6, *medianly* 742.12

middle name *name* 202.8

middle of nowhere *distant place* 585.3

middle of the day *noon* 655.4

middle of the road *medium* 742.2, *middle way* 772.3

middle-of-the-road *politically moderate* 521.4, *medium* 742.6, *moderate* 772.12

middle-of-the-roader *moderate person* 772.8

middle point *center* 612.1

middle school *school* 48.11

middle term *medium* 742.2

middle way 772.3; *moderation* 455.3, 521.1, *compromise* 461.1

middleweight *boxing weight divisions* 152.6, *combat* 152.17

Middle West *regions of the United States* 564.7

Middle White Breeds of Pigs 16

middle years *middle age* 27.4, 772.5

middling 772.14; *mediocre* 289.11, 742.7, *moderate* 521.3, *medium* 742.6, *insignificant* 745.6

middlingly *unexceptionally* 289.20

middy blouse *shirt* 100.13

Mideast *world region* 564.6

midfield *soccer* 163.7, *middle way* 772.3, *midway* 772.10

midfield striker *soccer participant* 163.4

midfield stripe *stadium* 155.3

Midgard serpent Legendary Creatures 360

midge *insect* 40.1, *pest* 40.5, *little person* 580.5

midges *pests and diseases* 17.12

midget *little person* 580.5, *undersized* 580.8

midget-car racing *automobile racing* 146.1

Midget Ocean Racing Club (MORC) racing *competitive sailing* 150.6

midicoat *coat* 100.19

midiskirt *or* **midi skirt** 100.12

midland *inland* 611.8

Midlands *regions of the British Isles* 564.8, *inland* 611.2

midlife *middle-aged* 772.15

midlife crisis *middle age* 27.4, 772.5

midline 772.2; *tennis court* 165.3

midmost *central* 612.6, *centrally* 612.12, *medium* 742.6, *medianly* 742.12

mid- or middlemost *middle* 772.9

midnight *night* 656.3, *evening* 656.4, *midline* 772.2

midnight-blue *blue* 261.5

midnight hours *nighttime* 656.1

midnight supper *or* **snack** *meal* 92.8

midoceanic ridge *ocean floor* 8.18, *plate tectonics* 8.19

midpoint *point* 6.34, *center* 612.1, *medium* 742.2, *middle* 772.1

mid-range zoom *lens* 132.11

Midrash *Jewish text* 81.17

midriff *midline* 772.2

midsection *medium* 742.2

midst *middle* 772.1

midst of things *activity* 414.1

midstream *river parts* 570.3, *middle way* 772.3, *midway* 772.10, 772.22

midsummer *summer* 654.4, *seasonal* 654.7

Midsummer Day *summer* 654.4

midterm *medium* 742.2

midterm election *election* 382.6

midtown *urban area* 567.10, *urban* 567.14

midway 772.10, 772.22; *central* 612.6, *centrally* 612.12, *medium* 742.6, *medianly* 742.12, *middle way* 772.3, *half* 789.12

Midway Islands Islands 572

Midwest *regions of the United States* 564.7, *inland* 611.2

Midwestern accent *regional pronunciation* 205.7

midwife *nurse* 107.23

midwifery *health care* 107.7, *instrumentality* 511.1

midwinter *winter* 654.6, *seasonal* 654.7

mien *external appearance* 264.5, *conduct* 399.1, *appearance* 610.4, *nature* 624.5

miff *resentment* 302.1, *offend* 302.15

miffed *resentful* 302.8

might *authority* 52.1, *influence* 512.1, *power* 514.1, *strength* 516.1, *violence* 520.1

might and main *exertion* 122.4, *vigor* 514.1

might as well *prefer* 382.13

might be *be possible* 836.8

might do worse *prefer* 382.13

mightily *authoritatively* 52.18, *powerfully* 514.21, *hugely* 579.21

mightiness *influence* 512.1, *power* 514.1

might is right *bellicosity* 76.15

mighty *authoritative* 52.9, *influential* 512.8, *powerful* 514.15, *strong* 516.9

mighty effort *exertion* 122.4

mignonette Flowers 42, *green* 260.7

migraine *symptom* 114.3

migrant *birds* 36.1, *outgoer* 707.9, *foreign* 724.9

migrant worker *farm worker* 16.15, *agricultural laborer* 123.10, *new arrival* 724.6

migrate *emigrate* 707.17, *disband* 776.13

migrating dune *dune* 8.43

migration *motion* 677.1, *departure* 705.1, *emigration* 707.6, *disbandment* 776.2

migratory *outgoing* 705.7

migratory bird *birds* 36.1

mikado *sovereign* 68.2

mikvah [Hebrew] *non-Christian ritual* 85.8, *religious cleansing* 111.3

mil Scientific and Technical Units 589

milady *female title of address* 33.3

Milanese chant *ritual music* 85.9

milch cow *livestock* 16.11

mild *warm* 9.46, 217.13, *harmless* 73.9, *hot* 217.11, *tasteless* 220.4, *courteous* 410.6, *lenient* 423.3, *moderate* 521.3, *soft-hearted* 543.11

milder *warm* 9.46

mildew *pests and diseases* 17.12, *tree disease* 43.8, *fungus* 47.1, *mold* 47.22, *dirt* 112.10, *be dirty* 112.10, *afflict* 117.16, *agent of destruction* 523.7, *physical deterioration* 808.4, *decay* 808.16, *eat away* 808.19

mildewed *fungal* 47.18, *worn* 808.13

mildewy *botanical* 17.15, *fungal* 47.18

mildly *meteorologically* 9.60, *without taste* 220.8, *courteously* 410.13, *leniently* 423.6, *soft-heartedly* 543.19

mild manner *courtesy* 410.1

mild-mannered *harmless* 73.9, *courteous* 410.6

mildness *tastelessness* 220.1, *courtesy* 410.1, *leniency* 423.1, *moderation* 521.1, *soft-heartedness* 543.4

mile General Units 589

mileage *length* 590.1

mileage *or* **milage** *miscellaneous automotive terms* 687.14

mile long, a *at length* 590.15

milepost *indicator* 183.7

miles away *speculative* 317.8, *oblivious* 355.9, *great distance* 585.2

miles from nowhere *distant place* 585.3

miles per hour (mph) *speed* 694.2

milestone *indicator* 183.7, *measuring instrument* 589.12, *essential content* 723.2, *occurrence* 726.2, *interval* 739.4, *important matter* 799.2

milfoil Flowers 42

miliaria *skin disease* 114.16

miliary fever *tropical disease* 114.10

milieu *ambience* 615.3, *circumstances* 726.1

militancy *belligerency* 76.14, *heroism* 284.2, *action* 412.1, *activism* 414.5

militant 418.13; *military* 58.10, *aggressive* 63.9, *warring* 76.26, *warlike* 76.27, *militarist* 77.3, *combative* 77.32, *zealous* 81.22, *heroic* 284.10, *activist* 412.4, *acting* 412.9, *busy person* 414.10, *active* 414.13, *defiant person* 416.4, *defying* 416.6, *disagreeing* 463.6, *violent animal* 520.4

militant Christian *religionist* 81.14

militantly *at war* 76.34, *aggressively* 77.38, *heroically* 284.18, *in defiance* 416.10

militant scene *activism* 414.5

militarily 58.15; *sociologically* 2.15, *at war* 76.34

militarism *military custom* 58.8, *belligerency* 76.14, *suppression* 424.2

militarist 77.3; *combatant* 77.1, *strict person* 424.4

militaristic *warlike* 76.27, *combative* 77.32, *severe* 424.5

militaristically *at war* 76.34, *aggressively* 77.38

militarize *arm* 76.30

military 58.10, 76.28; *sociological* 2.11, *architectural types* 134.2

military, the 58.2

military academy *type of school* 48.12, *military training* 76.19

military action *warfare* 422.10

military affairs 58.1

military aircraft 77.30

military attack 418.2

military band *military custom* 58.8, *glory of war* 76.17, *instrumental group* 141.3

military bearing *military custom* 58.8

military branch *the military* 58.2

military burial *burial* 31.1

military call 183.9

military cap *cap* 100.33

military cemetery *burial place* 31.7

military conflict *war* 76.1, *contention* 422.1, *warfare* 422.10

military court *type of court* 54.9

military custom 58.8

military defeat *defeat* 846.7

military defenses 419.9

military discharge *truce* 73.2

military disgrace *military honor* 58.9

military dishonor *military honor* 58.9

military District of Washington *army commands* 77.13

military duty *war measures* 76.18

military encounter *warfare* 422.10

military equipment *military affairs* 58.1

military evolutions *art of war* 76.16

military experience *art of war* 76.16

military flag *flag* 184.8

military forces *the military* 58.2, *armed forces* 77.9

military government 49.16

military governor *person in authority* 52.7, *leader* 68.3

military headquarters staff *military staff* 58.5

military honor 58.9

military honors *military custom* 58.8

military insignia *insignia* 184.5

military installations *military affairs* 58.1

military intelligence *military staff* 58.5

military judge *judge* 54.10

military law 58.7; *law* 53.1

military leader 68.10

military leadership *art of war* 76.16

military man *soldier* 77.4

military music *military custom* 58.8

military officer *person in authority* 52.7, *military leader* 68.10

military operation *warfare* 76.3

military operations *military affairs* 58.1

military orders *word of command* 76.20

military organization 58.4

military police (MP) *law enforcement agency* 53.7

military position 58.6

military prison *prison* 55.1

military rank *position of authority* 52.4

military rations *short rations* 118.3

military salute *military custom* 58.8

military sanctions *economic warfare* 76.7

military science *military affairs* 58.1

military service *military affairs* 58.1

military service number *personal identification* 184.4

military spirit *military custom* 58.8, *bellicosity* 76.15

military staff 58.5

military strategy *military affairs* 58.1

military tactics *military affairs* 58.1

military title 72.8

military tradition *military custom* 58.8, *belligerency* 76.14

military training 58.3, 76.19

military uniform *uniform* 100.9, *clothing* 184.6

military victory *victory* 845.4

militate against *motivate* 412.12, *counteract* 510.7, *change* 512.12, *be inconvenient* 804.9, *be contrary* 828.16

militate for *motivate* 412.12

militia *the military* 58.2, *armed forces* 77.9, *reinforcements* 77.11, *army* 77.12, *security force* 810.13

militiaman *soldier* 77.4

Milk Rivers 570

milk 93.5; *practice livestock farming* 16.20, *body fluid* 19.16, 555.3, *secreted substance* 24.2, *mammalian characteristic* 35.3, *lactate* 35.34, *basic cooking ingredient* 91.8, *white thing* 253.4, *exploit* 393.11, *take away* 477.18, *juice* 555.2, *draw off* 711.16

milk and honey *plenty* 90.4, *prosperity* 847.1

milk and water *weak thing* 517.5

milk-and-water *tasteless* 220.4, *insufficient* 517.11

milk bar [Brit] *eating place* 92.17

milk cow *livestock* 16.11

milk dry *expend* 96.16

milked *domesticated* 16.18

milker *livestock* 16.11

milkiness *semitransparency* 249.3, *whiteness* 253.1, *juiciness* 555.7

milking *drawing off* 711.4

milking machine *farm tool* 16.5

milking parlor *farm building* 16.4

Milking Shorthorn Breeds of Cattle 16

milking stool *type of chair* 101.4

milk it *overact* 136.35

milk of human kindness *benevolence* 305.1

milk of magnesia *purgative* 115.7

milk shake *milk* 93.5

milksop *coward* 285.3, *weak person* 517.4

milksopping *spineless* 285.5

milksoppy *spineless* 285.5

milk sugar Common Sugars 12

milk tank *farm tool* 16.5

milk tooth *teeth* 19.8

milk train [Inf] *train* 688.4

milk-white *white* 253.7

milkwort Flowers 42

milky 555.17; *drinkable* 93.18, *murky* 248.5, *semitransparent* 249.9, *shady* 250.4, *colorless* 252.5, *white* 253.7, *oily* 562.11

Milky Way *galaxy* 7.5, *natural light* 246.4

mill *crowd* 59.26, 795.11, *factory* 124.8, *US coinage* 484.10, *perform* 522.16, *make rough* 544.11, *pulverizer* 553.11, *grind* 553.23

mill around *crowd* 59.26, *swirl* 682.16, *be agitated* 684.21

Mille Lacs Lakes 568

millenarian *thousand* 792.10, *thousandth* 792.21

millenary *thousand* 792.10, *thousandth* 792.21

millenary *or* **millenarian** *periodical* 641.7

millennial *periodical* 641.7, *agelong* 644.5, *anniversary* 663.8, *thousandth* 792.21

millennially *cyclically* 663.15

millennium *judgment day* 341.4, *idealism* 360.7, *time period* 641.2, *long duration* 642.3, *future condition* 650.3, *anniversary* 663.4, *thousand* 792.10

millet *crop* 16.8, *cereal grass* 45.4

milli Decimal Prefixes 589

milliard *million* 792.11

millibar Scientific and Technical Units 589

milligram *weight measurement* 538.6, *thousand* 792.10

milliliter *thousand* 792.10

millimeter *short distance* 586.2, *thousand* 792.10

milline General Units 589

milliner *clothier* 100.37, *retailer* 482.11

millinery *hat* 100.32, *the clothing business* 100.36

milling *crowded* 59.22, *pulverization* 553.4

milling machine *machine tool* 14.9

million 792.11; *myriad* 795.7

millionaire *gainer* 467.9, *wealthy person* 485.6, *prosperous person* 847.4

millionairess *wealthy person* 485.6

million instructions per second (MIPS) *computing terms* 15.22

million million *million* 792.11

millions *fortune* 484.4, *multitude* 795.1

millionth 792.22

millipede *thousand* 792.10

millisecond *time period* 641.2

millpond *small lake* 568.2

millstone *burden* 117.3, *weighing down* 538.5, *pulverizer* 553.11

millstone around one's neck *burden* 826.10

millstream *river* 570.1

mill wheel *wheel* 682.9

mill-wide process control *systems and process control* 14.28

milquetoast *frightened person* 283.8, *coward* 285.3

Miltonic *poetic* 139.19

Mimamsa Philosophical Schools of Thought 4

Mimamsan Philosophical Schools of Thought 4

Mimas Planets and Their Satellites 7

mime *dramatic style* 136.3, *actor* 136.25, *gesture* 183.17, *acting* 187.6, *act* 187.13, *show* 404.12, *mimicry* 736.3, *imitate* 736.9

mimeograph *duplicate* 736.4, *copy* 736.10

mimesis *acting* 136.22, *imitation* 736.1

mimetic *dramatic* 136.31, *imitative* 736.7

mimetically *dramatically* 136.38

mimic *act* 136.34, 187.13, *entertainer* 138.8, *entertain* 138.16, *gesture* 183.17, *derider* 369.3, *copy* 730.5, 730.17, *simulate* 733.16, *imitator* 736.6, *imitate* 736.9, *repeat* 797.15

mimicked *simulated* 733.11

mimicking *acting* 136.22, *simulation* 733.4

mimicry 736.3; *acting* 136.22, 187.6

miming *acting* 136.22

mimosa Flowers 42

Min Deities 82

minaccciando Musical Terms and Expression Marks 140

minatory *warning* 814.6

mince *cook* 91.10, *grind* 553.23, *walk* 677.17, *move slowly* 693.11, *take apart* 753.16

minced *culinary* 91.9, *partial* 760.11

mincer *cooking equipment* 91.6

mince words *be equivocal* 380.7

mincing steps *slow motion* 693.3

mind *spirit* 86.10, *psyche* 108.25, *hearing* 228.1, *hear* 228.13, *inclination* 290.2, *react against* 291.15, *be compassionate* 305.11, *intelligence* 315.2, 352.2, *reason* 319.1, *be careful* 325.11, *intellect* 348.4, *will* 372.1, *obey* 426.7, *internal world* 525.6, *protect* 810.21

Mind, the God 82.6

mind, the Phobias 283

Mindanao Islands 572

mind-blowing [Inf] *addictive* 121.32, *astonishing* 294.10

mind-body problem *philosophical problem* 4.8

mind-boggler [Inf] *difficult question* 333.4

mind-boggling [Inf] *astonishing* 294.10, *immeasurable* 798.6

mindful *prudent* 287.7, *compassionate* 305.8, *solicitous* 323.8, *careful* 325.6, *considerate* 325.7, *knowledgeable* 348.7, *remembering* 354.8

mindfully *prudently* 287.17, *compassionately* 305.14, *attentively* 323.14, *caringly* 325.14

mindfulness *prudence* 287.2, *compassion* 305.2, *attention* 323.1, *carefulness* 325.1, *consideration* 325.2

mindless *lacking intellect* 316.5, *thoughtless* 318.7

mindlessly *unintelligently* 316.9, *thoughtlessly* 318.15

mindlessness *lack of intellect* 316.1, *lack of thought* 318.1

mind like a sieve *poor memory* 355.2

mind made up *prejudgment* 342.5, *declaration* 376.2

mind of one's own *willfulness* 372.3, *obstinacy* 379.1

mind one's health *be healthy* 113.11

mind one's manners *be formal* 406.11, *have good manners* 410.10

mind one's own business *be indifferent* 289.12, *be incurious* 322.5, *be disinterested* 443.6, *be aloof* 756.8

mind one's p's and q's *behave well* 399.18, *be formal* 406.11, *have good manners* 410.10, *follow the rules* 780.17

Mindoro Islands 572

mind over matter *analgesic* 115.6, *willpower* 372.2

mind reader *occultist* 86.13, *magician* 138.11, *nonmaterialist* 525.7

mind reading *psychic power* 86.4, *magic* 138.3, *parapsychology* 525.4

mind-reading *magical* 138.15

mind-set *attitude* 513.2

mind's eye *visualization* 242.6, *memory* 354.1, *imagination* 360.1

mine *bomb* 78.15, *source of supply* 105.4, *works* 124.9, *military defenses* 419.9, *fence* 419.21, *take away* 477.18, *wealth* 485.1, *produce* 522.13, *knock down* 523.13, *hole* 583.4, *deepen* 598.21, *concave land* 635.2, *make concave* 635.7, *source* 675.2, *dig out* 711.15, *trap* 813.1

mine coal 106.18

minefield *trap* 813.1

mine host [Arch] *social person* 408.7

minelayer *warship* 77.21

mine of information *knowledgeable person* 348.5

miner *historical soldier* 77.8, *laborer* 123.9, *producer* 522.10, *closed-in person* 584.6, *digger* 635.4, *extractor* 711.9

mineral 8.37; *ore* 11.23, *materials* 104.1, *physical element* 524.5

mineral acid *acid* 11.10

mineral aggregate *rock* 8.30

mineral dye *dye* 130.8

mineralize *lithify* 8.66

mineralized *fossilized* 8.63

mineralocorticoid *hormone* 12.16

mineralogical *geologic* 8.50

mineralogically *geologically* 8.68

mineralogist *geologist* 8.4

mineralogy *geology* 8.1

mineraloid (amorphous) *mineral* 8.37

mineral oil *oil* 106.7, 562.3

mineral resources *mineral* 8.37

minerals *food content* 90.3

mineral types 8.38

mineral water *water* 93.4, *drinking water* 557.2

miner's lamp *lantern* 246.8

Minerva Deities 82

mineshaft *hole* 583.4

minesweeper *warship* 77.21

minginess *meanness* 501.1

mingle *socialize* 2.14, *be sociable* 414.22, *mix* 751.12, *combine* 757.9

mingled *mixed* 751.8, *combined* 757.5

mingle with *participate* 408.15

mingling *social activity* 414.2, *mixture* 751.1, *combination* 757.1

Ming ware Ceramics 129

mingy *mean* 501.4
Minhah or **Minchah** [Heb] *public worship* 83.3
Minho pony Horse and Pony Breeds 159
mini *little thing* 580.3, *undersized* 580.8
miniature *picture* 133.5, *painting* 143.3, *little thing* 580.3, *undersized* 580.8
miniature camera *camera* 132.10
miniature pinscher Breeds of Dogs 35
miniature poodle Breeds of Dogs 35
miniature schnauzer Breeds of Dogs 35
miniaturist *visual artist* 133.6
miniaturization 580.2; *contraction* 582.1
miniaturize *make little* 580.10, *contract* 582.12
miniaturized *undersized* 580.8, *smaller* 582.7
miniaturized version *little thing* 580.3
minibike *motorcycle* 687.12
minicab [Brit] *automobile* 687.6
minicomputer *computer* 15.1
minidress or **mini** *dress* 100.11
minim *notation* 140.20, *little piece* 580.4, General Units 589
minimal *ranked* 6.72, *simple* 195.10, *little* 580.7, *insignificant* 745.6, *sparse* 796.6, *fewer* 796.7
minimal art Western Art Styles 133
minimalism *simplicity* 195.4
minimalist *moderate person* 772.8
minimally *simply* 195.19, *little* 580.12, *inferiorly* 745.13
minimal sculpture *sculpture* 144.1
minimization *understatement* 195.1, *underestimation* 344.1
minimize *order* 6.89, *understate* 195.14, *underestimate* 344.5, *wrong* 430.19, *disparage* 440.11, *make little* 580.10, *make smaller* 747.8
minimized *understated* 195.8
minimizer *underestimator* 344.2
minimizing *underestimating* 344.3, *disparaging* 440.8
minimum *sufficiency* 97.1, *inferior state* 745.3, *insignificant* 745.6, *least* 796.2, *fewer* 796.7
minimum allowance *incompleteness* 98.2
minimum hours *bargaining terms* 57.10
minimum lending rate *finance* 457.1
minimum requirement *sufficiency* 97.1
minimum-security facility *prison* 55.1
minimum-security imprisonment *imprisonment* 55.4
minimum sentence *prison sentence* 55.6
minimum wage *incompleteness* 98.2
minimum wages *bargaining terms* 57.10
mining *deepening* 598.4, *digging out* 711.3
mining and metallurgical engineering *engineering* 14.1
mining engineer *engineer* 14.2, *professional worker* 123.11
minion *servant* 69.1, *sycophant* 401.3, *subordinate* 832.3

minipill *contraceptive* 23.6
miniseries *movie type* 137.3, *program* 172.10
miniskirt or **mini** *skirt* 100.12
minister *funeral person* 31.5, *politician* 50.7, *delegate* 79.1, *member of the clergy* 84.5, *ritualist* 85.14, *perform rites* 85.18, *agent* 123.15, *manage* 126.10, *offer worship* 504.16, *converter* 670.5, *adviser* 825.14
ministerial *governmental* 49.24, *delegated* 79.4, *priestly* 84.12
ministerially *governmentally* 49.27, *representatively* 79.8, *clerically* 84.17
ministering *serving* 69.9, *supportive* 825.18
ministering angel *nurse* 107.23, *supporter* 825.13
ministering spirit *angel* 82.11
minister of state [Brit] *person in authority* 52.7, *leader* 68.3
minister's cat Children's and Party Games 167
minister to *serve* 69.11, *practice medicine* 107.32, *treat* 115.17, *work for* 122.10, *obey* 426.7, *be an instrument* 511.7, *support* 825.24
ministrant *supportive* 825.18
ministration *support* 825.2
ministrative *supportive* 825.18
ministry *clergy* 84.1, *priesthood* 84.2, *support* 825.2
minium *red pigment* 257.2
mink farm *farm* 16.2
mink farming *livestock farming* 16.10
mink ranch *farm* 16.2
minnesinger *author* 139.13, *singer* 141.4
Minnesota American States 564, Rivers 570
Minnesota Multiphasic Personality Inventory Psychological Tests 108
Minnesota No. 1 Breeds of Pigs 16
Minnesota Preschool Scale Intelligence Tests 108
minnow *bait* 154.6, *little person* 580.5
Miño or **Minho** Rivers 570
Minoan architecture Architectural Styles 134
minor *young person* 26.7, *young* 26.11, *subject* 48.3, *harmonic* 140.27, *inferior* 745.4, *subordinate* 745.8, *secondary* 800.15
minor axis *curve* 6.38
Minorca Breeds of Fowl 16, Islands 572
minor deity 82.2
minor earthquake *seismic activity* 8.24
minor in *learn* 48.23
minor interval *chord* 140.18
minority *socioeconomic* 2.13, *youth* 26.1, *dissenters* 347.6, *helplessness* 515.3, *certain amount* 738.3, *gradational* 739.5, *part* 760.1, *least* 796.2, *fewer* 796.7
minority, the *least* 796.2
minority-group member *victim of discrimination* 337.8
minority leader *person in authority* 52.7, *party official* 68.5
minority party or **group** *the opposition* 828.8
minority rights *equal opportunity* 831.2
minority rule *oligarchy* 49.10
minority voice *protester* 331.8
minority whip *elected official* 50.8

minor key *key* 140.23
minor league baseball *baseball* 147.1
minor party *political party* 50.5
minor planet *planet* 7.16
Minor Planets or **Asteroids** Planets and Their Satellites 7
minor poet *author* 139.13
minor premise or **term** *philosophical term* 4.7
minor role *role* 136.23
minors, the *baseball leagues and championship games* 147.8
minor scale *scale* 140.16
minor suit *bridge* 168.4
minor surgery *surgery* 107.15
minor third *third* 790.6
Minotaur Legendary Creatures 360
minoxidil therapy *hairdressing* 530.7
Minsk Countries 566
minster *place of worship* 83.8
minstrel *entertainer* 138.8, *author* 139.13, *singer* 141.4
minstrel show *show* 138.4
mint Herbs and Spices 91, *works* 124.9, *monetize* 484.24, *money* 485.2, *perform* 522.16, *fashion* 536.7, *form* 624.9
mint condition *newness* 394.2, 652.1, *perfect condition* 805.3
minted *monetary* 484.22
minted coinage *coinage* 484.13
minter *financier* 484.17
mint family *seed plant* 41.3
minting *coinage* 484.13
mint master *financier* 484.17
mint money *get rich* 485.13
mint sauce *sauce* 90.17
minty *piquant* 221.6
minuend *subtraction* 6.14, *subtracted item* 749.2
minuet Dances 135, Musical Forms 140
minus *indebted* 488.7, *missing* 576.11, *nonexistent* 718.9, *inferiorly* 745.13, *subtraction* 749.1, *reduced* 749.5, *by subtraction* 749.8
minus acceleration *deceleration* 693.2
minuscule *type* 173.5, *tiny* 580.9
minus sign *mathematical symbol* 6.11, *symbol* 183.3
minute *chronicle* 3.15, *diffuse* 199.3, *little* 580.7, *tiny* 580.9, General Units 589, *careful* 593.11, *time period* 641.2, *detailed* 726.9
minute or two, a *short duration* 643.3
minute book *chronicle* 3.4, *record book* 185.5
minuted *chronicled* 3.12
minute distances Fields of Measurement 589
minute gun *signal* 183.6, 646.9
minute hand *indicator* 183.7
minutely *diffusely* 199.7, *little* 580.12, *meticulously* 726.18
minuteness *diffuseness* 199.1, *physical element* 524.5, *littleness* 580.1
minutes *chronicle* 3.4, *record* 185.1
minutia *little piece* 580.4, *aspect* 726.4
minutiae *specifications* 779.6, *trifle* 800.3
minx *young woman* 26.9, *female* 33.1, *unpleasant woman* 33.7, *insolent person* 400.7
Minya Konka Mountains and Hills 569

minyan [Hebrew] *worshiper* 83.6
Miocene Epoch Geologic Time Intervals 8
mirabile dictu [L] *astonishingly* 294.19
miracidium *invertebrate larva* 39.19
miracle *spectacle* 264.6, *marvel* 294.3, *unexpectedness* 839.2
miracle drug *drug* 115.9
miracle play *dramatic style* 136.3
miracle worker *wonderful person* 294.6
miracle working *cause of wonder* 294.4
miracle-working *wonder-working* 294.11
miraculous *wondrous* 294.9, *unbelievable* 837.5
miraculously *wondrously* 294.18
miraculousness *the occult* 86.2, *wonderfulness* 294.5, *unexpectedness* 839.2
mirador *place for viewing* 242.13
mirage *spectacle* 264.6, *fantasy* 360.5, *illusion* 720.2
MIRANDA Programming Languages 15
Miranda Planets and Their Satellites 7
Mira variable *variable star* 7.11
mire *dirt* 112.5, *marsh* 559.8, 572.3, *mud* 561.8
Mirgorod Breeds of Pigs 16
miriness *dirtiness* 112.1, *muddiness* 561.10
mirliton Musical Instruments 142
mirror *optical element* 10.20, *furniture* 101.1, *represent* 187.10, *reflector* 242.10, *make visible* 242.25, *appear* 264.12, *means of prediction* 358.10, *cosmetic tool* 530.5, *be similar* 733.12, *conform* 735.27, *imitate* 736.9, *double* 789.14, *repeat* 797.15
mirror aperture *lens system* 10.22
mirrored *outer* 264.10, *repeated* 797.8
mirror image *transformation* 6.46, *image* 187.3, *reflection* 242.9, *impression* 264.7, *twin* 789.5
mirroring *outer* 264.10, *imitation* 736.1
mirror lens *lens* 132.11
mirrorlike *visual* 242.16, *polished* 545.7
mirrors Phobias 283
mirror symmetry *geometric figure* 6.39
mirror system *lens system* 10.22
mirth *gaiety* 269.3, *amusement* 277.2
miru [Jap] *algal product* 47.15
miry *dirty* 112.7, *sludgy* 561.18, *of landmasses* 572.12
misaddress *misdirect* 698.21
misadventure 848.2; *mishap* 660.4
misaligning *difference* 463.4
misalliance *type of marriage* 64.3, *no relation* 728.1
misallied *misrelated* 728.11
misally *misrelate* 728.15
misandrist *misanthrope* 291.5, *hater* 300.6, *bigot* 337.7, *discriminatory* 337.11
misandrous *misanthropic* 291.8, *discriminatory* 337.11
misandry *misanthropy* 291.4, 300.3, *social discrimination* 337.4
misanthrope 291.5; *hater* 300.6, *miser* 501.3
misanthropic 291.8, 300.8
misanthropically 291.18

misanthropist *misanthrope* 291.5, *hater* 300.6

misanthropy 291.4, 300.3

misapplication *bungling* 128.2, *sophistry* 330.1, *misinterpretation* 366.1, *misuse* 395.1, *no relation* 728.5

misapplied *bungled* 128.7, *sophistic* 330.7, *misrelated* 728.11, *inconvenient* 804.5

misapply *misspend* 96.17, *be unskillful* 128.8, *practice sophistry* 330.11, *misuse* 395.6, *misrelate* 728.15

misapprehend *be in error* 351.15, *misinterpret* 366.4, *be incorrect* 722.13

misapprehension *error* 351.1, *misinterpretation* 366.1, *untrueness* 722.3

misappropriate *misuse* 395.6, *act dishonestly* 479.18, *misrelate* 728.15

misappropriated *misused* 395.3, *fraudulent* 479.13, *misrelated* 728.11

misappropriation *misuse* 395.1, *illegal borrowing* 476.3, *infringement* 479.6, *no relation* 728.5

misappropriation of funds *dishonesty* 479.7

misbegotten *ugly* 531.3

misbehave *behave badly* 399.19, *disobey* 427.12, *sin* 430.22

misbehaved *disobedient* 427.10

misbehavior *bad conduct* 399.7, *disobedience* 427.1, *sin* 450.3

misbelief *unbelief* 88.4, *mistake* 342.2

misbelieving *disbelieving* 88.6

miscalculate *misjudge* 342.9, *overestimate* 343.6, *underestimate* 344.5, *err* 351.14, *be wrong* 430.18

miscalculated *underestimated* 344.4

miscalculation *misjudgment* 342.1, *mistake* 342.2, *overestimation* 343.1, *underestimation* 344.1, *error* 351.1, *misinterpretation* 366.1

miscarriage *infertile state* 23.3, *mistake* 342.2, *unsuccessful thing* 846.8

miscarriage of justice *legal injustice* 53.5, *injustice* 342.3

miscarried *frustrating* 293.7, *failed* 846.10

miscarry 846.19; *be infertile* 23.8, *be clumsy* 128.9, *be wrong* 430.18, *cause not to exist* 718.14, *be in trouble* 848.13

miscarrying *failed* 846.10

miscast *dramatized* 136.32, *dramatize* 136.33

miscegenate *marry* 64.19

miscegenation *type of marriage* 64.3, *mixture* 751.1

miscegenetic *monogamous* 64.18, *mixed* 751.8

miscellanea *miscellany* 59.15, 751.3, *compendium* 204.3, *bits and pieces* 760.5

miscellaneous *indiscriminate* 338.8, *varied* 732.6, *complicated* 751.10, *general* 778.9

miscellaneous automotive terms 687.14

miscellaneous aviation terms 689.9

miscellaneous collection *miscellany* 751.3

miscellaneous euphemisms 301.12, 301.21

miscellaneous expenses *expense* 491.2

miscellaneously *variously* 732.15, *mixedly* 751.16

miscellaneousness *variety* 732.2

miscellaneous swearwords 301.20

miscellaneous terms 155.16

miscellanies *variety* 732.2

miscellany 59.15, 751.3; *compendium* 204.3, *variety* 732.2

mischance *lost chance* 660.3, *misadventure* 848.2, *bad fortune* 848.7

mischief *capriciousness* 381.2, *bad conduct* 399.7, *wrongdoing* 430.7, *evil* 446.1

mischief-maker *unpleasant person* 272.5, *troublemaker* 427.5, *evil person* 446.3, *protester* 507.4, *hinderer* 826.11

mischief-making *disobedience* 427.1, *disobedient* 427.10

mischievous *capricious* 381.4, *badly behaved* 399.16, *unlawful* 430.15, *evil* 446.7

mischievously *evilly* 446.12

mischievousness *evil* 446.1

miscibility *mixture* 751.1

miscible *mixed* 751.8

miscomputation *misinterpretation* 366.1

miscompute *misinterpret* 366.4

misconceive *misjudge* 342.9, *misinterpret* 366.4, *distort the truth* 627.12

misconceived *misinterpreted* 366.3, *incorrect* 722.8

misconception *misjudgment* 342.1, *mistake* 342.2, *error* 351.1, *misinterpretation* 366.1, *delusion* 720.3, *untrueness* 722.3

misconduct *bungling* 128.2, *be unskillful* 128.8, *bad conduct* 399.7, *bad manners* 411.2, *sin* 450.3

misconduct penalty *ice hockey tactics* 158.4

misconnect *misrelate* 728.15

misconnected *misrelated* 728.11

misconnection *no relation* 728.5

misconstruction *misjudgment* 342.1, *mistake* 342.2, *error* 351.1, *misinterpretation* 366.1, *distortion of truth* 627.4, *untrueness* 722.3

misconstrue *practice sophistry* 330.11, *misjudge* 342.9, *err* 351.14, *misinterpret* 366.4, *distort the truth* 627.12, *be incorrect* 722.13

misconstrued *misjudged* 342.8, *misinterpreted* 366.3, *incorrect* 722.8

miscount *be wrong* 430.18

miscreant 448.6; *lawbreaker* 53.15, *malefactor* 306.6, *wrongdoer* 430.8, *evil person* 446.3, *vulgar person* 535.4

miscue *billiards play* 149.2, *play* 149.7

miscue [Inf] *mistake* 342.2, *trivial error* 351.8

miscued *billiard* 149.6

misdate 660.9; *be in a different time* 648.3

misdated 660.6; *different in time* 648.2

misdating *wrong time* 660.2

misdeal *card playing* 168.1, *play cards* 168.7

misdealing *card playing* 168.1

misdeed *errancy* 351.7, *wrongdoing* 430.7, *sin* 450.3

misdemeanor *wicked act* 448.7, *illegality* 450.4

misdiagnose *misjudge* 342.9, *misinterpret* 366.4

misdiagnosis *mistake* 342.2, *misinterpretation* 366.1

misdirect 698.21; *be unskillful* 128.8, *misrepresent* 193.17, *misuse* 395.6, *manipulate* 508.12

misdirected *misrepresentative* 193.14, *misused* 395.3, *deviant* 698.8

misdirection *play* 155.8, *misinformation* 188.3, *misrepresentation* 193.4, *misuse* 395.1, *deviation* 698.1

misdo *misjudge* 342.9

misdoing *wrongdoing* 430.7, *sin* 450.3

misdoubt *suspicion* 314.3, *suspect* 314.9

misdoubtful *suspicious* 314.6

misdoubtfully *suspiciously* 314.13

mise *contract* 459.1

mise en scène [Fr] *stage set* 136.19

misemploy *misuse* 395.6

misemployed *misused* 395.3

misemployment *misuse* 395.1

mis en scène [Fr] *motion-picture studio* 137.7

miser 501.3; *nonpayer* 490.6, *bargain hunter* 497.8

miserable 117.12; *painful* 215.4, *sorrowful* 270.4, *lamenting* 280.4, *adverse* 848.10

miserably *sorrowfully* 270.10, *destructively* 446.13, *adversely* 848.16

Miserere *prayer* 85.10

misericord or **misericorde** *sharp weapon* 78.6

miserliness *selfishness* 444.1, *meanness* 501.1

miserly *not enough* 98.5, *selfish* 444.4, *nonpaying* 490.7, *mean* 501.4

misery *adversity* 117.2, 848.1, *sorrow* 270.1, *lamentation* 280.1

misestimate *misjudge* 342.9

misestimation *untrueness* 722.3

misevaluate *misinform* 188.7

misevaluation *misinformation* 188.3

misfire *bungling* 128.2, *malfunction* 846.20

misfiring *miscellaneous automotive terms* 687.14

misfit *unsocial person* 409.5, *dissenter* 463.5, *be different* 463.11, *loser* 846.9

misfitting *difference* 463.4, *different* 463.7

misform *make shapeless* 625.3

misfortune 301.6; *bad outcome* 293.3, *lost chance* 660.3, *deterioration* 808.1, *futility* 846.3, *adversity* 848.1, *bad fortune* 848.7

misgiving *disbelief* 88.1, *fearfulness* 283.2, *uncertainty* 333.6

misgovern *be unskillful* 128.8, *misuse* 395.6, *suppress* 424.9

misgovernment *bungling* 128.2

misguidance *misinformation* 188.3, *misrepresentation* 193.4

misguide *misrepresent* 193.17, *distort the truth* 627.12

misguided *bungled* 128.7, *misrepresentative* 193.14, *misjudging* 342.6, *misrepresented* 627.8

misguidedly 342.12

misguider *one who misrepresents* 193.9

mishandle *be unskillful* 128.8, *misuse* 395.6, *suppress* 424.9

mishandled *bungled* 128.7, *ill-used* 395.4

mishandling *bungling* 128.2, *misuse* 395.1

mishap 660.4; *negligence* 324.4, *obstacle* 826.2

mishit *bungling* 128.2, *be clumsy* 128.9

mishmash *miscellany* 751.3, *confusion* 766.4

Mishnah *Jewish text* 81.17

misimpression *mistake* 342.2, *untrueness* 722.3

misinform 188.7; *misrepresent* 193.17, *practice sophistry* 330.11, *make ignorant* 349.10, *distort the truth* 627.12, *misdirect* 698.21

misinformation 188.3; *evasion* 181.5, *misrepresentation* 193.4, *sophism* 330.2, *mistake* 342.2, *incorrectness* 430.3, *distortion of truth* 627.4

misinformed 188.5; *misrepresentative* 193.14, *sophistic* 330.7, *ignorant* 349.5, *wrong* 430.12, *misrepresented* 627.8

misinformer *one who misrepresents* 193.9

misinterpret 366.4; *misinform* 188.7, *misjudge* 342.9, *err* 351.14, *not understand* 362.11, *transform* 670.13, *be incorrect* 722.13

misinterpretation 366.1; *misjudgment* 342.1, *mistake* 342.2, *error* 351.1, *untrueness* 722.3

misinterpreted 366.3; *misinformed* 188.5, *misjudged* 342.8, *unmeant* 362.9, *incorrect* 722.8

misjudge 342.9; *overestimate* 343.6, *underestimate* 344.5, *err* 351.14, *find unintelligible* 364.14, *misinterpret* 366.4, *misuse* 395.6, *be wrong* 430.18, *be untimely* 660.8, *be incorrect* 722.13

misjudged 342.8; *overestimated* 343.5, *underestimated* 344.4, *incorrect* 722.8

misjudging 342.6

misjudgment 342.1; *legal injustice* 53.5, *bungling* 128.2, *overestimation* 343.1, *underestimation* 344.1, *error* 351.1, *act of folly* 353.2, *misinterpretation* 366.1, *misuse* 395.1, *untrueness* 722.3

mislaid *losing* 468.9, *misplaced* 574.13, *missing* 576.11

mislay *lose* 468.12, *misplace* 574.20

mislaying *loss* 468.1, *misplacement* 574.6

mislead *deceive* 181.14, 193.16, *practice sophistry* 330.11, *make ignorant* 349.10, *be equivocal* 380.7, *deprave* 448.14, *manipulate* 508.12, *circumlocute* 607.12, *distort the truth* 627.12, *misdirect* 698.21, *delude* 720.16

misleader *one who misrepresents* 193.9

misleading *deceptive* 193.12, *blinding* 243.13, *sophistic* 330.7, *equivocal* 380.5, *indirect* 607.8, *misrepresented* 627.8

misleadingness *deception* 193.1

misled *deceived* 193.15, *misjudging* 342.6, *ignorant* 349.5

mislike [Arch] *dislike* 291.12

misliked [Arch] *disliked* 291.10

mislocate *misplace* 574.20

mislocated *misplaced* 574.13
mislocation *misplacement* 574.6
mismanage *be unskillful* 128.8, *misuse* 395.6
mismanaged *bungled* 128.7
mismanagement *bungling* 128.2, *misuse* 395.1
mismanager *unskilled person* 128.3
mismarry *marry* 64.19
mismatch *no relation* 728.5
mismatched *misrelated* 728.11, *unequal* 741.4
mismatching *difference* 463.4
misnaming *nomenclature* 202.7
misogamic *celibate* 67.6, *misanthropic* 300.8
misogamist *single person* 67.5, *hater* 300.6
misogamy *celibacy* 67.1, *misanthropy* 300.3
misogynic *misanthropic* 300.8
misogynist *misanthrope* 291.5, *hater* 300.6, *bigot* 337.7, *discriminatory* 337.11
misogynous *misanthropic* 291.8, *discriminatory* 337.11
misogyny *misanthropy* 291.4, 300.3, *social discrimination* 337.4
misologist *hater* 300.6
misology *misanthropy* 300.3
misoneism *misanthropy* 300.3
misoneist *hater* 300.6
misoneistic *misanthropic* 300.8
misopedia *misanthropy* 300.3
misopedist *hater* 300.6
miso soup *notable international dishes* 90.40
misperception *bungling* 128.2
misplace **574.20;** *lose* 468.12
misplaced **574.13;** *losing* 468.9, *disordered* 766.9, *unconventional* 782.14
misplacement **574.6**
misplacing *loss* 468.1
misprint *err* 351.14
misprision *mistake* 342.2
misprize *underestimate* 344.5, *disrespect* 436.18
mispronounce *err* 351.14
mispronunciation *mode of speech* 205.6, *language error* 351.10, *blunder* 528.5
misput *misplaced* 574.13, *misplace* 574.20
misputting *misplacement* 574.6
misquotation *misinformation* 188.3, *misrepresentation* 351.5
misquote *misinform* 188.7, *practice sophistry* 330.11, *err* 351.14
misquoted *misinformed* 188.5, *misinterpreted* 366.3
misread *misjudge* 342.9, *unmeant* 362.9, *misinterpreted* 366.3, *misinterpret* 366.4
misreading *misinterpretation* 366.1
misreckon *misjudge* 342.9, *be wrong* 430.18
misrefer *misrelate* 728.15
misreference *no relation* 728.5
misrelate **728.15**
misrelated **728.11**
misremember *forget* 186.11, *be forgetful* 355.11
misrepresent **188.6, 193.17, 366.5;** *practice sophistry* 330.11, *err* 351.14, *accuse falsely* 442.9, *distort the truth* 627.12, *delude* 720.16
misrepresentation **188.1, 193.4, 351.5, 366.2;** *nonsense* 362.2, *false accusation* 442.2, *distortion of truth* 627.4
misrepresentative **193.14**
misrepresented **188.4, 627.8;**

misrepresentative 193.14, *unmeant* 362.9, *misinterpreted* 366.3, *perjurious* 442.7
misrepresentedly 366.7
misrepresenter *one who misrepresents* 193.9
misrepresenting *misrepresented* 188.4
misrule *bungling* 128.2, *be unskillful* 128.8, *misuse* 395.1, 395.6, *suppress* 424.9
Miss *title of respect* 72.7
Miss *or* **miss** *female title of address* 33.3
miss *young woman* 26.9, *be unsatisfied* 98.10, *bungling* 128.2, *billiards play* 149.2, *play* 149.7, *soccer play* 163.5, *play soccer* 163.8, *fail to hear* 229.9, *misjudge* 342.9, *be forgotten* 355.12, *be wrong* 430.18, *lose* 468.12, *unbalance* 741.8, *be incomplete* 762.8, *not complete* 762.9, *exclude* 764.7, *elude* 816.10, *error* 846.2, *fail* 846.12
missal *ritual manual* 85.11
miss an opportunity *lose* 468.12, *lose one's chance* 660.10, *fail* 846.12
Missa solemnis [L] *Eucharist* 85.7
missed *billiard* 149.6, *soccer* 163.7, *neglected* 326.6, *incomplete* 762.5
missed chance *bungling* 128.2, *bad fortune* 848.7
missed opportunity *lost chance* 660.3
missed out *excluded* 764.6
misshape *make ugly* 531.4, *blemish* 533.7, *make shapeless* 625.3, *distort* 627.9
misshapen *ugly* 531.3, *distorted* 627.6, *irregular* 766.10
misshapenly *asymmetrically* 627.13
misshapenness *distortion of body* 627.3, *irregular order* 766.2
missile **696.7;** *modern missile weapon* 78.4, *ammunition* 78.11, *projectile* 696.13
missiles *Phobias* 283
missile site *modern missile weapon* 78.4
missile strike *air attack* 418.4
missing **576.11;** *disappeared* 265.4, *losing* 468.9, *misplaced* 574.13, *nonexistent* 718.9, *incomplete* 762.5, *uncompleted* 762.7, *excluded* 764.6, *zero* 786.5
missing link *omission* 762.4, *digression* 775.6
missing part *omission* 762.4
missing person *the hunted* 385.7, *absentee* 576.5
mission *offensive warfare* 76.11, *representative body* 79.2, *place of worship* 83.8, *job* 122.3, *undertaking* 391.1, *line of duty* 433.3, *engagement* 833.2, *council* 833.4
mission architecture *Architectural Styles* 134
missionary *religious person* 81.9, *religionist* 81.14, *zealous* 81.22, *volunteer* 504.7, *converter* 670.5, *commissioner* 833.5
missis *or* **missus** [Arch] *married woman* 64.11
Mississippi *American States* 564, *Rivers* 570
miss nothing *take note of* 323.10
miss one's chance *be late* 658.11
miss one's cue *be unskillful* 128.8, *underact* 136.36
miss one's footing *drop* 714.15

miss one's way *go astray* 698.17
Missouri *American States* 564, *Rivers* 570
Missouri Fox Trotter *Horse and Pony Breeds* 159
miss out *exclude* 764.7
misspell *word* 5.43, *err* 351.14
misspelling *spelling* 5.26, *language error* 351.10
misspend **96.17;** *waste* 500.7
misstate *misinform* 188.7, *lie* 192.23, *err* 351.14
misstated *misinformed* 188.5
misstatement *misinformation* 188.3, *falsehood* 192.6, *misrepresentation* 351.5
misstep *impropriety* 430.5, *blunder* 528.5
miss the boat *be late* 658.11, *lose one's chance* 660.10, *fail* 846.12
miss the mark *be wrong* 430.18
miss the meaning of *not understand* 362.11
miss the point *lose track of* 698.18, *be extraneous* 724.12
miss the point of *not understand* 362.11
missus *female title of address* 33.3
missy [Inf] *young woman* 26.9, *female* 33.3
mist **9.33;** *moisture* 9.31, *fog* 9.59, *phase* 11.13, *invisibility* 245.1, *that which makes invisible* 245.2, *murk* 248.2, *make dim* 248.8, *transparent thing* 249.4, *be opaque* 250.6, *wateriness* 557.3, *sprinkle* 557.32, 559.14
mistake **342.2;** *bungling* 128.2, *negligence* 324.4, *misjudge* 342.9, *error* 351.1, 846.2, *act of folly* 353.2, *misinterpretation* 366.1, *misinterpret* 366.4, *incorrectness* 430.3, *be wrong* 430.18, *sin* 450.3, *untrueness* 722.3, *mix up* 751.13, *defect* 806.4
mistaken **351.13;** *misjudging* 342.6, *misjudged* 342.8, *unmeant* 362.9, *wrong* 430.12, *incorrect* 722.8, *mixed up* 751.11
mistakenly **366.6, 660.14;** *misguidedly* 342.12, *erroneously* 351.17, *wrongfully* 430.25, *incorrectly* 722.16
mistakenness *incorrectness* 430.3
mistake of law *legal injustice* 53.5
mistaught *misinformed* 188.5
mistbow *rainbow* 9.28
misteach *misinform* 188.7, *pervert* 808.22
misteaching *misinformation* 188.3
misted *shady* 250.4
mister *male title of address* 32.3
Mister Charlie [Inf] *male title of address* 32.3
Mister Fixit *servant* 69.1, *repair worker* 123.8
misthrow *bungling* 128.2, *be clumsy* 128.9
Misti, El *Mountains and Hills* 569
mistily *meteorologically* 9.60, *dimly* 248.10, *transparently* 249.13, *opaquely* 250.9, *grayly* 255.10, *shapelessly* 625.5, *indeterminately* 841.24
mistime *misjudge* 342.9, *be in a different time* 648.3, *be untimely* 660.8
mistimed *different in time* 648.2, *untimely* 660.5
mistiming *difference* 463.4, *untimeliness* 660.1
mistiness **559.2;** *invisibility* 245.1, *murk* 248.2, *semitransparency*

249.3, *shapelessness* 625.1, *indeterminacy* 841.6
mist over *be dim* 248.7
mistral *Notable Winds* 9
mistranslate *misinterpret* 366.4
mistranslated *unmeant* 362.9, *misinterpreted* 366.3
mistranslation *misinterpretation* 366.1
mistreat *harm* 306.13, *ill-use* 395.7, *wrong* 430.19, *be evil* 446.10
mistreated *ill-used* 395.4
mistreatment *ill-use* 395.2
mistress *female title of address* 33.3, *girlfriend* 33.4, *educator* 48.4, *master* 68.1, *title of respect* 72.7, *lover* 299.11, *possessor* 469.10
mistress of the house *master* 68.1
mistrial *injustice* 342.3
mistrust *disbelief* 88.1, *disbelieve* 88.8, *suspicion* 314.3, 841.2, *suspect* 314.9, *uncertainty* 333.6, *doubt* 333.19, *be uncertain* 841.17
mistrustful *disbelieving* 88.6, *suspicious* 314.6, *uncertain* 841.9
mistrustfully *disbelievingly* 88.10, *suspiciously* 314.13
mistrustfulness *suspicion* 314.3
misty **559.10;** *foggy* 9.51, *difficult to see* 245.4, *murky* 248.5, *semitransparent* 249.9, *shady* 250.4, *dull* 255.8, *difficult* 364.8, *shapeless* 625.2, *indeterminate* 841.14
Misty of Chincoteague *Notable Horses* 159
misunderstand *misjudge* 342.9, *be in error* 351.15, *find unintelligible* 364.14, *misinterpret* 366.4, *disagree* 463.8, *be mixed up* 751.15
misunderstanding *argument* 329.1, *misjudgment* 342.1, *error* 351.1, *misinterpretation* 366.1, *disagreement* 463.1
misunderstood *arguable* 329.8, *misjudged* 342.8, *unmeant* 362.9, *misinterpreted* 366.3
misusage *language error* 351.10, *misuse* 395.1
misuse **395.1, 395.6;** *expend* 96.16, *bungling* 128.2, *be unskillful* 128.8, *malignity* 306.5, *harm* 306.13, *use* 393.1, *exploit* 393.11, *wrong* 430.19, *waste* 468.5, *destroy* 468.18, *no relation* 728.5, *misrelate* 728.15, *pervert* 808.22
misused **395.3;** *misrelated* 728.11
misuse of power *ill-use* 395.2
misuse of words *misinformation* 188.3, *misuse* 395.1
misuse power *ill-use* 395.7
misuse words *misuse* 395.6
Mitchell, Mount *Mountains and Hills* 569
mite *child* 26.6, *arachnid* 40.4, *pest* 40.5, *incompleteness* 98.2, *little piece* 580.4
mitelike *arachnidan* 40.12
miter *vestment* 84.11, *carpenter's term* 131.5, *carpenter* 131.10, *angle* 628.11, *intertwine* 752.19
mitered *joined* 131.8, *angular* 628.7
miter joint *carpenter's term* 131.5, *angle* 628.11, *joint* 752.7
mites *Phobias* 283
mithridate *medicine* 115.2
mitigate **521.9;** *relieve* 275.8, *show pity* 308.8, *modify* 340.13, *justify* 441.12, *ease* 543.15, *smooth over* 545.12, *make smaller* 747.8
mitigated *modified* 340.9

mitigating *vindicatory* 441.7, *easing* 543.13
mitigating circumstances *defense* 441.2
mitigation *ease* 275.1, *mercy* 308.3, *modification* 340.5, *defense* 441.2, *moderation* 521.1, *easiness* 543.5, *limitation* 747.3
mitigative *vindicatory* 441.7
mitigatory *modified* 340.9
mitochondrial *cellular* 13.30
mitochondrion *cell structure* 13.16
mitosis *cell division* 13.17
mitotic *genetic* 13.32
mitrailleuse [Fr] *firearm* 78.7
mitral stenosis *cardiovascular disease* 114.13
mitt *accessory* 100.28
mitten *accessory* 100.28
mittens *climbing equipment* 161.4
mittimus [Form] *demand* 425.2
mitts [Inf] *retainer* 471.3
mitzvah *or* mitsvah [Hebrew] *benevolent act* 305.5
mix 732.12, 751.1; *cook* 91.10, *make ceramics* 129.10, *be indiscriminate* 338.10, *be sociable* 414.22, *swirl* 682.16, *agitate* 684.22, *variety* 732.2, *mixed thing* 751.2, *unite* 752.14, *combination* 757.1, *combine* 757.9
mix and match *mix* 751.12
mixed 751.8; *racial* 1.12, *mountaineering* 161.9, *indiscriminate* 338.8, *varied* 732.6, *combined* 757.5
mixed bag *miscellany* 59.15
mixed blessing *mediocrity* 742.3
mixed cloud *cloud* 9.17
mixed drink 93.12; *drink* 93.2
mixed economy *economics* 56.1
mixed episode *mood disorder* 108.12
mixed farm *farm* 16.2
mixed farming *agriculture* 16.1
mixed feelings *vacillation* 378.1
mixed foursome *golf* 156.1
mixed glyceride *fat* 12.7
mixed grill *meat dish* 90.21
mixed group *singing group* 141.6
mixed indicator *gravimetric analysis* 11.18
mixed lot *miscellany* 59.15
mixedly 751.16
mixed marriage *type of marriage* 64.3, *mixed thing* 751.2
mixed meeting *horse racing* 159.10
mixed metaphor *language error* 351.10
mixed number *real number* 6.5
mixed party *party* 408.6
mixed race *race* 1.5
mixed thing 751.2
mixed up 751.11, 766.14; *indiscriminate* 338.8
mixed-up *vacillating* 378.5
mixed vegetables *vegetable* 90.33
mixer 751.7; *soft drink* 93.8, *mixed drink* 93.12, *dance* 14.23, *filmmaker* 137.14, *social person* 408.7, *agitator* 684.14
mix in *augment* 748.13
mixing *social activity* 414.2, *mixture* 751.1, *combination* 757.1
mixing bowl *cooking equipment* 91.6, *crockery* 578.16, *mixer* 751.7
mixing it up [Inf] *combat* 152.17
mixing synthesis *process* 11.15
mixing tank *ceramic workshop and tools* 129.8
mix it (up) [Inf] *fight* 422.23
mixolydian mode *mode* 140.17

mix together 751.14; *combine* 757.9
mixture 751.1; *phase* 11.13, *miscellany* 59.15, *dose of medicine* 115.3, *indiscrimination* 338.4, *variety* 732.2, *mixed thing* 751.2, *combination* 757.1, *compound* 757.4, *impairment* 808.7
mixture of colors *variegation* 263.1
mix up 751.13; *make obscure* 197.3, *mix* 751.12, *disorder* 766.17, *confuse* 766.19, *hinder* 826.15
mix-up 766.5; *obstacle* 826.2
mix with *participate* 408.15, *augment* 748.13, *support* 748.14, *unify* 752.15
mizzen mast *sailboat parts and accessories* 150.4
mizzle *rain* 9.27, *mistiness* 559.2, *sprinkle* 559.14
mizzly *misty* 559.10
Mjøsa *Lakes* 568
ML *Programming Languages* 15
mm Hg *Scientific and Technical Units* 589
M'Naghten rule *insanity* 110.1
mnemonic *reminder* 354.4, *memorable* 354.7
mnemonically *memorably* 354.16
mnemophobia *Phobias* 283
mo [Inf] *instant* 645.3
moa *extinct bird* 36.14
moan *blow* 9.53, *gesture* 183.5, 183.17, *express pain* 215.11, *undercurrent of sound* 233.3, *sound faint* 233.8, *cry of pain* 239.5, *cry* 239.16, *grieve* 270.7, *be dissatisfied* 274.7, *lament* 280.2, *sign of sullenness* 304.2, *complaint* 304.5, *be sullen* 304.12, *be irritable* 304.14, *complain* 507.8, *object* 828.18
moaner *dissatisfied person* 274.3, *lamenter* 280.3, *protester* 507.4
moaning *gestural* 183.13, *crying* 239.11
moat *rock face* 161.6, *military defenses* 419.9, *fort* 419.13, *fence* 419.21, *crack* 587.2, *enclosing thing* 619.3, *concave land* 635.2, *protection* 810.2, *barrier* 826.7
mob *Collective Names* 59, *party* 59.3, *crowd* 59.11, 795.11, *excess* 99.1, *aim at* 385.15, *salute* 405.13, *association* 752.2, *be disorderly* 766.22, *throng* 795.4
Mob, the *villain* 448.5
mobbed *crowded* 795.10
mobcap *cap* 100.33
mobile *socioeconomic* 2.13, *analytic* 11.32, *sculpture* 144.1, *changeable* 666.3, *moving* 677.12, *capricious* 841.16
mobile belt *fold* 8.22
mobile camera *television recording* 172.7
mobile crane *construction equipment* 14.23
mobile home 60.11
mobile phase *analysis* 11.17
mobile phone *telephone* 169.10
mobile radio *radio* 172.1
mobile radio station *radio broadcasting* 172.4
mobile station *television broadcasting* 172.8
mobile unit *radio broadcasting* 172.4
mobile warfare *offensive warfare* 76.11
mobility *social stratification* 2.7,

changeableness 666.1, *motion* 677.1, *capriciousness* 841.8
mobilization *military affairs* 58.1, *collection* 59.2, *war measures* 76.18, *preparation* 388.1, *momentum* 677.2
mobilize *enlist* 58.13, *call together* 59.28, *arm* 76.30, *prepare for action* 388.18, *set in motion* 677.16, *unite* 752.14
mobilized *assembled* 59.18, *warring* 76.26, *prepared* 388.9
Möbius *or* Moebius strip *topology* 6.45, *continuum* 774.5
mob member *dishonest person* 479.11
mobocracy *mob rule* 49.12, *anarchism* 51.3
mobocratic *anarchistic* 51.7
mob rule 49.12; *anarchism* 51.3, *lawlessness* 766.6
mobs *Phobias* 283
mobster *criminal* 427.6, *villain* 448.5, *dishonest person* 479.11
Mobutu Sese Seko *Lakes* 568
moccasin flower *Flowers* 42
moccasins *shoes* 100.30
mocha *brown* 256.5
mock *disbelieve* 88.8, *be humorous* 277.11, *experimental* 335.8, *deride* 369.7, *exclude* 383.11, *disdain* 400.16, *wrong* 430.19, *taunt* 436.6, 436.23, *ridicule* 436.22, 440.15, *artificial* 720.12, *simulated* 733.11, *imitation* 736.8, *imitate* 736.9, *make unimportant* 800.20
mocker *disbeliever* 88.5, *disparager* 440.7
mockery *ungenuineness* 192.2, *joke* 368.4, *derision* 369.1, *form of derision* 369.2, *discourtesy* 411.1, *ridicule* 436.4, *mimicry* 736.3
mock-heroic *poetic* 139.19
mock-heroic poetry *poetry* 139.8
mocking *ungenuine* 192.13, *derisive* 369.5, *ridiculing* 436.13, *taunting* 436.14, *scornful* 440.10
mockingly 436.26; *untruthfully* 192.27, *derisively* 369.8, *rudely* 411.9, *imitatively* 736.12
mock orange *Flowers* 42
mock up *rehearse* 335.12, *be unfinished* 544.12
mock-up *rehearsal* 335.2, *rough idea* 544.4, *copy* 736.2, *showpiece* 843.3
mod [Inf] *fashionable* 536.5
modacrylic *fiber* 130.2
modal *harmonic* 140.27
modality *philosophical term* 4.7, *means* 102.1, *mode* 725.2
modal scale *scale* 140.16
mode 140.17, 725.2; *parameter* 6.57, *means* 102.1, *approach* 209.3, *likes* 290.3, *fashion* 536.1, *design* 536.2, *style* 537.1, *way* 691.1
model 358.4; *physical law* 10.4, *material* 143.9, *sculpture* 144.1, *sculpt* 144.10, *means of identification* 143.9, *figure* 187.4, *impression* 264.7, *ideal* 327.6, 327.12, 805.6, 805.17, *epitomize* 327.18, *explanation* 331.3, *rehearsal* 335.2, *experimental* 335.8, *rehearse* 335.12, *supposition* 359.1, *map* 387.7, *preparations* 388.2, *fashion business* 536.3, *design* 536.8, *little thing* 580.3, *undersized* 580.8, *standard* 589.7, *prototype* 624.2, *prototypical* 624.7, *form* 624.9, *copy* 736.2, *duplicate* 736.4, *original* 737.2, 737.4, *average* 742.1, *precedent* 769.4,

type 777.4, *guide* 780.4, *showpiece* 843.3, *displayer* 843.7, *display* 843.13
model after *imitate* 736.9
model builder *theorist* 359.4
modeled *sculpted* 144.8, *formed* 624.6
modeler *sculptor* 144.4
modeling *psychotherapy* 108.4, *sculpture* 144.1, *forming* 624.4
modeling clay *material* 144.6
modeling tool *material* 144.6
model making *Hobbies and Pastimes* 167
model oneself upon *imitate* 736.9
model railroading *Hobbies and Pastimes* 167
modem *communications device* 15.26, *data transmission* 169.8
Modena *Breeds of Cattle* 16
mode of behavior 399.2
mode of expression 537.3; *meaning* 361.1
mode of speech 205.6
moderate 521.3, 521.7, 772.12; *detached* 4.18, *warm* 9.46, *mediate* 75.6, *play down* 195.17, *relieve* 275.8, *modify* 340.13, *underestimating* 344.3, *abstaining* 386.11, *lenient* 423.3, *be lenient* 423.5, *chaste* 431.10, *temperate* 455.8, *cheap* 497.9, *thrifty* 499.4, *counteract* 510.7, *ease* 543.15, 819.4, *straight person* 630.7, *traditional* 630.13, *unhurried* 693.8, *slow down* 693.13, *medium* 742.6, *mediocre* 742.7, *decrease* 747.7, *moderate person* 772.8, *easy* 823.9, *free* 829.11, *self-restrained* 830.10
moderate breeze *wind strength* 9.13
moderate climate *climate* 9.35
moderated *downplayed* 195.13, *modified* 340.9
moderate drinker *sober person* 120.4
moderate frost *frost* 9.25
moderately 455.15, 521.10; *stoically* 4.26, *pacifically* 74.12, *understatedly* 195.18, *pessimistically* 344.6, *away* 386.23, *leniently* 423.6, *cheaply* 497.16, *economically* 499.7, *traditionally* 630.19, *slowly* 693.14, *medianly* 742.12, *partly* 760.17, *midway* 772.22, *freely* 829.22, *self-restrainedly* 830.19
moderateness *moderation* 455.3, 521.1, *traditionality* 630.6, *medium* 742.2, *middle ground* 772.4
moderate one's language *mitigate* 521.9
moderate person 772.8
moderating 521.5; *counteracting* 510.6, *easing* 543.13
moderating influence *mediator* 75.2
moderation 455.3, 521.1; *pacification* 74.1, *mediation* 75.1, *downplaying* 195.6, *abstinence* 386.2, *leniency* 423.1, *chastity* 431.3, *thrift* 499.1, *neutralization* 510.4, *traditionality* 630.6, *medium* 742.2, *decrease* 747.1, *decreasing* 747.5, *middle ground* 772.4, *recuperation* 809.4, *self-restraint* 830.4
moderato *Musical Terms and Expression Marks* 140
moderator 521.2; *mediator* 75.2, *impartial person* 443.3, *negotiator*

modern present 647.4, new 652.9
Modern Age Ages, Decades, Eras 641
modern armor 419.7
modern ballet ballet 135.2
modern dance dance 135.1
modern dance music popular music 140.4
modern dancer ballet dancer 135.5
modern dancing Dancing Types 135
modern day, the present day 647.2
modern-dress production production 136.14
Modernism Philosophical Schools of Thought 4
modernism Western Art Styles 133, Architectural Styles 134, Western Literary Groups 139, modernity 647.3, newness 652.1, trendiness 652.2
modernismo Western Literary Groups 139
modernist Philosophical Schools of Thought 4, Furniture Styles 101, author 139.13, modern person 652.8
modernistic new 652.9
modernistically newly 652.21
modernity 647.3; present day 647.2, newness 652.1
modernization bargaining terms 57.10, new start 652.5, change for the better 665.4, tidying 807.6
modernize employ 57.18, make new 652.20, change 665.14, further 679.13, beautify 807.20, refurbish 809.11
modernized hired 57.17, renewed 652.14, changed 665.10, improved 807.12
modernizing hired 57.17
modern jazz jazz 140.5
modern man modern person 652.8
modern master visual artist 133.6
modern missile weapon 78.4
modern music classical music 140.2
modern pentathlon Sporting Activities 145
modern person 652.8
modern poet author 139.13
modern production production 136.14
modern times present day 647.2
modern warfare warfare 76.3
modern woman liberated woman 33.12, modern person 652.8
modern world present day 647.2
modest 403.6; simple 195.10, reserved 195.11, humble 298.8, underestimating 344.3, unenthusiastic 375.10, chaste 431.10, unselfish 443.5, cheap 497.9, moderate 521.3, unpretentious 526.8, naive 821.3, self-restrained 830.10
modestly 403.15; reservedly 195.20, humbly 298.22, pessimistically 344.6, moralistically 431.16, unselfishly 443.9, cheaply 497.16, unpretentiously 526.15, self-restrainedly 830.19
modesty 403.1; simplicity 195.4, reserve 195.5, humility 298.1, underestimation 344.1, dissociation 375.4, shyness 409.2, chastity 431.3, unselfishness 443.2, unpretentiousness 526.2, naiveté 821.1, self-restraint 830.4

Modica Breeds of Cattle 16
modicum admixture 751.5
modification 340.5; change 665.1, conversion 670.1
modified 340.9; changed 665.10, converted 670.7
modified leaf leaf 41.6
modifier part of speech 5.30, changer 665.9
modify 340.13; change 665.14, cause change 665.16, transform 670.13, make unlike 734.9
modifying of grammar 5.41
modillion Architectural Elements 134
modish dressed up 100.39, fashionable 536.5, avant-garde 652.16
modishly dressily 100.47, fashionably 536.9, trendily 652.24
modishness stylishness 537.2
modiste clothier 100.37
Modula Programming Languages 15
modular house house 60.4
modulate modify 340.13, moderate 521.7, make periodical 641.10, change 665.14, harmonize 735.22
modulated broadcast 172.12, modified 340.9, harmonizing 735.12
modulating harmonizing 735.12
modulation mode of speech 205.6, modification 340.5, moderation 521.1, change 665.1, alteration 665.2, harmonization 735.2
modulator-demodulator communications device 15.26
module spacecraft 7.28, subject 48.3, Architectural Elements 134, piece 760.2, one 788.1
modulus complex number 6.6
modulus of elasticity strength of materials 14.15
modus operandi procedure 387.2, way 399.10, 691.1, mode 725.2
modus vivendi way of life 399.9, compromise 461.1, substitution 672.1, way 691.1, mode 725.2
Mogadishu Countries 566
Mogul sovereign 68.2
mogul skiing snow 162.3, ski 162.27, snowplow 162.29, important person 799.5
moguled ski 162.27
moguled trail ski run 162.2
mogul racer skier 162.14
mogul skiing skiing 162.1
mohair Fabrics and Fibers 130
Mohammedan Muslim 81.12
Mohammedanism Islam 81.7
Mohawk coiffure 530.8, Rivers 570
Mohorovičić discontinuity (Moho) earth zone 8.7
moiety piece 760.2, middle way 772.3, half 789.7
moil work 122.1, 122.8, persevere 377.10, swirl 682.16, tumult 684.2
moiler worker 123.1
Moira luck 842.3
moiré Fabrics and Fibers 130, variegation 263.1, variegated thing 263.5, iridescent 263.7
moist 559.9; flowing 555.15, watery 557.21
moist air atmosphere 9.8
moisten 559.13; water 557.29, lubricate 562.15
moistening wetting 557.26
moistful moist 559.9
moistly 559.17; meteorologically 9.60, fluidly 555.26, wetly 557.34, oilily 562.19

moistness wateriness 557.3, moisture 559.1
moisture 9.31, 559.1; weather data 9.6, juiciness 555.7, water 557.1
moistureless dry 560.7
moisture-proof waterproof 560.16
moisturizer balm 115.11
moisturizing lubricational 562.12
moisturizing cream or lotion toiletries 530.6
Mojave Deserts 572
mojo talisman 86.9
molar teeth 19.8
molar heat capacity heat flow 10.27
molasses animal feed 16.12, basic cooking ingredient 91.8, sweetener 222.2, brown thing 256.3, semiliquid 561.7, adherent 755.4
mold 47.22; fungus 47.1, educate 48.22, cooking equipment 91.6, lack of hygiene 112.3, dirt 112.5, afflict 117.16, make ceramics 129.10, sculpt 144.10, illustrate 187.11, unpalatability 223.2, perform 522.16, design 536.2, fashion 536.7, soften 543.14, form 551.3, 624.9, shape 551.21, wall covering 613.12, face 613.31, prototype 624.2, transform 670.13, nature 723.4, mode 725.2, original 737.2, disintegration 758.1, type 777.4, characteristic 779.5, make conform 781.13, physical deterioration 808.4
moldable pliant 543.7
mold and cast fossil 8.49
Moldau River 570
mold-breaking unfamiliar 652.10
mold clay make ceramics 129.10
molded sculptural 144.7, sculpted 144.8, formed 624.6
molded salad salad 90.16
molder mold 47.22, be dirty 112.10, sculptor 144.4, sour 223.8, grow old 653.16, disintegrate 758.6, decay 808.16
moldering olden 653.11, disintegration 758.1, disintegrated 758.3, worn 808.13
moldiness dirtiness 112.1, physical deterioration 808.4
molding Architectural Elements 134, sculpture 144.1, production 522.1, decorative method 532.3, structuring 551.5, wall covering 613.12, forming 624.4, adhesive 755.5
Moldova Countries 566
mold to the figure adhere 755.8
moldy botanical 17.15, fungal 47.18, dirty 112.7, unhygienic 114.27, unpalatable 223.6
mole insect-eating mammal 35.7, skin disease 114.16, informer 170.8, secret person 182.6, brownness 256.1, meddler 321.4, discoverer 345.7, mark 533.2, water system 551.13, Scientific and Technical Units 589, enclosing thing 619.3, safety device 810.15, warner 814.5, barrier 826.7
mole-catcher animal killer 30.14
molecular chemical compound 11.4, tiny 580.9, component 760.12
molecular biologist life scientist 13.26
molecular biology 13.18; histology 13.4, medical science 107.5
molecular cloud stellar evolution 7.10

molecular design systems and process control 14.28
molecular formula structure 11.7
molecular genetics molecular biology 13.18, genetics 13.19
molecular orbital chemical bond 11.6
molecular-orbital theory valence 11.5
molecular physics Fields of Modern Physics 10
molecular weight weight measurement 538.6
molecule physical element 524.5, little thing 580.3, piece 760.2
molehill lowlands 597.6
mole poblano notable international dishes 90.40
moles Collective Names 59
moleskin Fabrics and Fibers 130
molest harm 306.13, ill-use 395.7, be evil 446.10, disrupt 768.12
molestation sexual offense 20.11, ill-use 395.2, disruption 768.4
molested disrupted 768.8
Molisch's test sugar test 12.6
moll [Inf and Off] sex object 20.8, woman considered as a sex object 33.8
mollification pacification 74.1, ease 275.1, moderation 521.1, easiness 543.5
mollified relieved 275.6, easing 543.13
mollifier reliever 275.4, moderator 521.2
mollify conciliate 74.10, relieve 275.8, calm 521.8, ease 543.15
mollifying easiness 543.5, easing 543.13
Mollusca mollusk 39.13
mollusk 39.13; animal 34.1, type of animal 34.5
molluskan 39.23
mollusklike mollusk 39.13
mollycoddle effeminate male 32.8, comfort 214.14
mollycoddled pleased 214.9
Molokai Islands 572
Molotov cocktail bomb 78.15
molt peeling 614.6, shed 614.21
molted shed 614.14
molten volcanic 8.57, status adjectives 11.25, hot 217.11, heated 217.15, liquefied 555.19
molter shedder 614.7
molting peeling 614.6, 614.13
molto Musical Terms and Expression Marks 140
Moluccas Islands 572
molybdenum Chemical Elements and Common Allotropes 11, essential element 12.15
mom [Inf] woman in the family 33.13, family member 65.2
mom-and-pop store store 483.8
moment force 10.9, importance 278.3, 799.1, time period 641.2, short duration 643.3, instant 645.3, point in time 645.4, miscellaneous aviation terms 689.9, impulsion 695.1, occurrence 726.2
momentarily transiently 643.8
momentariness transience 643.1
momentary transient 643.4
momentary success success 845.1
moment of force impulsion 695.1
moment of inertia mass 10.8
moment of truth critical time 659.3
momentous important 278.6, influential 512.8, critical 659.5, serious 799.8

---

momentously *influentially* 512.14, *critically* 659.9

momentousness *importance* 278.3

momentum 677.2; *mass* 10.8, *impulsion* 695.1, *propulsion* 696.1

mommy [Inf] *family member* 65.2

monachal *monastic* 67.8, 84.13

Monaco Countries 566

Monaco GP at Monte Carlo *Formula 1 World Championship races* 146.5

monad *microorganism* 13.11, *physical element* 524.5, *little thing* 580.3, *thing* 717.3, *one* 788.1

monadic *dialectical* 4.16, *one* 788.10

monadism *existence* 717.1

monadnock *hill* 569.2

monandry *type of marriage* 64.3

monarch *person in authority* 52.7, *sovereign* 68.2, *important person* 799.5

monarchical *governmental* 49.24, *governing* 49.25

monarchical government *monarchy* 49.6

monarchist *reactionary* 427.9

Monarch Notes™ *schoolbook* 48.15

Monarch of Hell *devil* 446.5

monarchy 49.6; *British government* 49.22, *country* 566.1

monastery *monasticism* 67.3, *place of worship* 83.8, *clerical dwelling* 84.10, *privacy* 181.6, *enclosed area* 619.2, *private space* 812.2

monastic 67.8, 84.13; *celibate* 67.4, *religious* 81.21, 84.9, *enclosed* 619.4

monasticism 67.3

monastic order *monasticism* 67.3

monatomic *chemical compound* 11.4

monetarily 484.27; *financially* 457.11

monetarism *political and economic philosophy* 4.6

monetarist *political and economic philosopher* 4.10, *of a political philosophy* 4.14, *one who restrains* 830.7

monetary 484.22; *economic* 56.10, 480.14, *financial* 457.6

monetary aid *financial assistance* 825.6

monetary denomination *money* 484.1

monetary policy *economics* 56.1

monetary unit *money* 484.1

monetary value *value* 494.2

monetize 484.24

money 484.1, 485.2; *resources* 102.4, Phobias 283, *wealth* 485.1, *type of payment* 489.3, *positive stimulus* 508.5

moneybag *vault* 105.9, *money storage* 484.20

moneybags *wealthy person* 485.6

money belt *money storage* 484.20, *baggage* 578.8

money box *vault* 105.9, *money storage* 484.20, *box* 578.5

money broker *lender* 475.3

moneychanger *merchant* 482.10, *financier* 484.17

money coming in *money received* 492.2

money dealer *financier* 484.17

money dealings *finance* 457.1

money drawer *vault* 105.9

moneyed *wealthy* 485.8

moneyed class *the rich* 485.7

moneyer [Arch] *financier* 484.17

money for a rainy day *income* 492.3

moneygrubber [Inf] *selfish person* 444.3, *gainer* 467.9, *miser* 501.3

moneygrubbing [Inf] *selfish* 444.4, *gain* 467.1, *gain-seeking* 467.11, *mean* 501.4

money in the bank *funds* 484.6

moneylender *lender* 475.3, *merchant* 482.10, *financier* 484.17

moneylending *lending* 475.1

moneyless *poor* 486.8

moneymaker *gainer* 467.9, *wealthy person* 485.6

moneymaking *rewarding* 453.9, *gain* 467.1, *gainful* 467.10, *wealth* 485.1, *profitable* 489.13

moneyman *financier* 484.17

money management *finance* 457.1

money market *finance* 457.1

money of account *money* 484.1

money order *postal communication* 169.4, *paper money* 484.14

money power *finance* 457.1

money received 492.2; *something received* 473.2

money-saving *thrifty* 499.4

money storage 484.20

money supply *economic factor* 56.8

money's worth *value* 494.2

money to burn *superfluity* 99.4

moneywort Flowers 42

Mongolia Countries 566

Mongolian Breeds of Cattle 16, Breeds of Sheep 16

Mongolian Wild Horse Horse and Pony Breeds 159

Mongoloid *racial* 1.12

Mongoloid race *race* 1.5

mongrel *dog* 35.10, *hybrid* 751.6, *mixed* 751.8

mongrelism *mixture* 751.1

mongrelize *mix* 751.12

monies *funds* 484.6

moniker or **monicker** [Inf] *name* 202.8

moniliasis *fungal disease* 47.6

monism Philosophical Schools of Thought 4

monist Philosophical Schools of Thought 4

monition *warning* 814.1

monitor *display* 15.9, *lizard* 37.5, *adviser* 176.5, *hearer* 228.7, *observer* 242.15, *watch* 242.23, *keep time* 646.12, *protect* 810.21

monitorily *advisorily* 176.12, *dissuasively* 179.12, *warningly* 814.11

monitory *informative* 170.10, *dissuasive* 179.4, *predicting* 358.11, *censuring* 438.12, *punitive* 454.18, *warning* 814.6

monk *celibate* 67.4, *religious person* 81.9, *religious* 84.9, *unsocial person* 409.5, *chaste person* 431.6, *poor person* 486.6, *individualist* 756.3

monkey *primate* 35.17, *capricious person* 381.3, *butt* 436.8, *impeller* 695.7

monkey around or **about with** *be cunning* 822.5

monkey bars *amusement park and playground equipment* 167.8

monkey-bread tree Trees and Shrubs 43

monkey business *foul play* 193.6, *cunning* 822.1

monkey dog Breeds of Dogs 35

monkey flower Flowers 42

monkey jacket *jacket* 100.18

monkey on one's back [Inf] *burden* 826.10

monkey pinscher Breeds of Dogs 35

monkeypod Trees and Shrubs 43

monkey puzzle Trees and Shrubs 43

monkeys Collective Names 59

monkey's fist Knots, Bends, Hitches, Splices 754

monkey suit [Inf] *suit* 100.16

monkey wrench *hand tool* 103.3

monkey wrench in the works *obstacle* 826.2

monkfish *food fish and shellfish* 90.20

monkish *monastic* 67.8, 84.13

monkshood Flowers 42

mono *infection* 114.7, *one* 788.10

monoacidic *acid* 11.27

monoacidic base Base 11.11

monobasic *acid* 11.27

monobasic acid *acid* 11.10

monocarpellary *of a fruit* 44.8

monocarpic *of a fruit* 44.8

Monoceros Constellations 7

monochasial cyme *flower head* 42.4

monochasium *flower head* 42.4

monochromatic *colored* 251.10, *one-sided* 788.11

monochromatic light *light* 246.1

monochromatic radiation *laser (light amplification by stimulated emission of radiation)* 10.18

monochrome *physical* 10.70, *painting* 143.3, *color* 251.1

monochrome television *television (TV)* 172.5

monocle *visual aid* 242.14

monoclinic *status adjectives* 11.25

monoclinic crystal *crystal* 8.39, 11.14

monocotyledon or **monocot** or **monocotyl** *seed plant* 41.3

Monocotyledonae *seed plant* 41.3

monocotyledonous *taxonomic* 41.16

monocropping *arable farming* 16.6

monoculture *arable farming* 16.6

monocycle *bicycle* 687.10

monocyte *blood* 555.4

monodically *soliloquizingly* 211.6

monodist *soliloquist* 211.2

monodrama *play* 136.2, *soliloquy* 211.1

monodramatic *soliloquizing* 211.3

monody Poem or Verse Forms 139, *harmonic element* 140.14, *soliloquy* 211.1

monoecious *of flowers* 42.11

monofilament *fiber* 130.2

monogamist *married man* 64.10

monogamous 64.18

monogamously *matrimonially* 64.23

monogamy *type of marriage* 64.3

monoglottic *speaking* 205.15

monoglyceride *fat* 12.7

monogram *written letter* 5.14, *decoration* 129.4, *make ceramics* 129.10, *personal identification* 184.4

monograph *dissertation* 203.1

monogynist *married man* 64.10

monogyny *type of marriage* 64.3

monohull Sailing Ships and Boats 690

monokini *beachwear* 100.23, *swimming equipment* 164.8

monolingual *speaking* 205.15, *one-sided* 788.11

monolith *monument* 185.10

monolithic *dense* 540.6

monologic *soliloquizing* 211.3

monological *soliloquizing* 211.3

monologically *soliloquizingly* 211.6

monologist *speaker* 205.12, *soliloquist* 211.2, *soloist* 788.9

monologize *soliloquize* 211.4

monologue *play* 136.2, *dramaturgy* 136.6, *play part* 136.8, *public speaking* 205.11, *soliloquy* 211.1, *soloist* 788.9

monology *soliloquy* 211.1

monomania *compulsion* 108.13, *delusion* 110.2

monomaniac *insane person* 110.5, *compulsive person* 428.5

monomer *polymer* 11.9

monomeric *polymeric* 11.35

monometallism *currency market* 484.8

monometer *surface chemistry* 11.20, *meter* 139.10, 589.13

monomial term *algebraic expression* 6.23

monomolecular *reactive* 11.29

monophobia Phobias 283

monophonic *harmonic* 140.27

monophonic sound *sound quality* 230.4

monophony *harmonic element* 140.14

monopolist *selfish person* 444.3, *merchant* 482.10, *one who restrains* 830.7

monopolistic *selfish* 444.4, *possessing* 469.11, *dominant* 512.10, *restrained* 830.9

monopolistically *cliquishly* 59.32, *possessively* 469.16

monopolization *monopoly* 469.4

monopolize *be selfish* 444.6, *trade in* 457.8, *possess* 469.14, *detain* 471.9, *buy in* 481.13, *be an influence* 512.13, *limit* 620.7, *restrain commerce* 830.14

monopolized by *possessed* 469.13

monopolizer *possessor* 469.10

monopolize the conversation 211.5; *be talkative* 207.7

monopoly 469.4; *economic factor* 56.8, *association* 480.8, *selling* 482.1, *limit* 620.1, *exclusiveness* 764.4, *economic restraint* 830.3

Monopoly ™ Board and Table Games 167

monorail *transportable* 686.7, *railroad system* 688.1, *cableway* 691.11

monosaccharide *saccharide* 12.4

monosemous *linguistic* 361.9

monosemy *comprehensibility* 361.3

monostich *part of poem* 139.9

monosyllabic *language type* 5.11, *of language* 5.35, *concise* 198.4, *sparing with words* 208.6

monosyllabically *linguistically* 5.44

monosyllabism *conciseness* 198.1

monosyllable *word* 5.17

monoterpene *terpene* 12.20

monotone *photograph* 132.3, *tone* 140.24, *monotonous* 797.12

monotonic *sounding* 230.7

monotonous 797.12; *unemphatic* 201.2, *tasteless* 220.4, *humming* 235.7, *boring* 296.6, *equal* 740.8, *continuous* 774.9

monotonously *repeatedly* 235.15, 797.22, *boringly* 296.10

monotonousness *boringness* 296.2

monotonous work *assiduity* 414.8

monotony *lack of emphasis* 201.1, dilution 220.2, boringness 296.2, continuity 774.4, repetitiveness 797.3

Monotremata *egg-laying mammal* 35.4

monotrematous *mammalian* 35.23

monotreme *egg-laying mammal* 35.4

monounsaturated fat *fat* 12.7

monovalent *chemical compound* 11.4

Monroe Apple Varieties 44

Monrovia Countries 566

monsieur [Fr] *male title of address* 32.3

Monsignor *professional title* 72.6

monsignor *member of the clergy* 84.5

monsoon Notable Winds 9, *air flow* 558.4

monsoon season *rain* 9.27

monster *sprite* 86.12, *frightener* 283.7, *wonderful person* 294.6, *violent animal* 520.4, *ugly thing* 531.2, *big thing* 579.9, *huge* 579.14

monsters Phobias 283

monstrance *sacred object* 83.11

monstrosity *wonderful person* 294.6, *ugly thing* 531.2

monstrous *astonishing* 294.10, *cruel* 306.10, *ugly* 531.3, *huge* 579.14

monstrous lie *falsehood* 192.6

monstrously *astonishingly* 294.19, *cruelly* 306.17, *hugely* 579.21

monstrousness *cruelty* 306.4

montage *construction* 59.16, *picture* 133.5

Montana American States 564

montane *mountainous* 569.5

montbretia Flowers 42

mont-de-piété [Fr] *lending institution* 475.4

monte Card Games 168

Monte Carlo *automobile rallies* 146.6

Monte Carlo method Mathematical Concepts 6

Montedale Breeds of Sheep 16

Montessori system *educational system* 48.2

Montevideo Countries 566

Montezuma's revenge [Inf] *defecation* 25.3, *gastroenterological disease* 114.11

Montgomery American States 564

month *time period* 641.2

monthlies [Inf] *bleeding* 25.10

monthly *bleeding* 25.19, *magazine* 175.3, *habitual* 397.9, *periodical publication* 641.6, *periodical* 641.7, *for specified periods* 641.12, *cyclic* 663.7, *cyclically* 663.15, *regular* 730.12, *regularly* 730.21

monthly bills *cost(s)* 491.3

monthly discharge *bleeding* 25.10

month of Mayings *spring* 654.3

month of Sundays *long duration* 642.3

monticule *hill* 569.2

Montpelier American States 564

monument 185.10; *funeral object* 31.6, *indicator* 183.7, *memento* 354.1, *construction* 522.9, *antiquity* 653.4

monumental *historical* 3.10, *sculptural* 715.4, *mountainous* 569.5, *huge* 579.14

monumental sculptor *sculptor* 144.4

monumental sculpture *sculpture* 144.1

monument mason *funeral person* 31.5

Monza 1000-kilometer race races 146.4

moo *animal sound* 240.1, *make an animal sound* 240.7

mooch *be inactive* 415.13

mooch [Inf] *take* 477.14, *solicit money* 505.13

mooch around [Inf] *move slowly* 693.11

moocher [Inf] *beggar* 505.6

mooching *saltwater fishing* 154.3

mooching [Inf] *taking* 477.1, *solicitation* 505.4, *begging* 505.9

mood *grammatical term* 5.29, *aspect of fiction* 139.5, *emotion* 266.3, *caprice* 381.1, *conduct* 399.1, *attitude* 513.2, *nature* 723.4, *state of mind* 725.5

mood disorder 108.12

mood disorders *mental disorder* 108.8

mood episodes *mood disorder* 108.12

moodily *sullenly* 304.16, *changeably* 666.7

moodiness *sullenness* 304.1, *irresolution* 666.2

moody *sullen* 304.8, *erratic* 381.5, *irresolute* 666.4, *troublesome* 824.13

mooing *ululant* 240.4

moola *or* **moolah** [Inf] *cash* 484.2

Moon Planets and Their Satellites 7

moon 7.18; *satellite* 7.19, *natural light* 246.4, Phobias 283, *orbiting body* 681.4

moon [Inf] *taunt* 436.23, *undress* 614.18

moon, the *distant place* 585.3

moon base *space travel* 7.29

moonbeam *natural light* 246.4

moon boots *boots* 100.31

mooner [Inf] *nude person* 614.5

moon-faced *fat* 579.15

moonflower Flowers 42

moon goddess *minor deity* 82.2

Moonie *Christian* 81.10

mooning *amorous* 299.18

mooning [Inf] *sexual offense* 432.6, *undressing* 614.2

moonless *dark* 247.5

moonlight *work* 122.8, *natural light* 246.4

moonlighting *financial escape* 816.2

moonlit *lit* 246.16

moonrise *natural light* 246.4, *sunrise* 713.4

moonshine *nonsense* 192.8, *natural light* 246.4, *sophistry* 330.1, *empty talk* 362.5

moonshine [Inf] *alcoholic drink* 93.9, *alcohol* 121.5

moor *grassland* 45.2, *marsh* 572.3, *lowland* 572.6, *heights* 596.4, *sail* 690.16, *land* 704.16, *bind* 754.14

moored *stabilized* 674.4

mooring *sailing* 150.25, *landing* 704.2

mooring line *sailboat parts and accessories* 150.4, *line* 754.5

Moorish architecture Architectural Styles 134

moorland *grassland* 45.2, *geographical space* 563.3

moorland [Brit] *lowland* 572.6, *heights* 596.4

moor to *intertwine* 752.19

moory *of landmasses* 572.12

moose *game* 160.6

Moosehead Lakes 568

moot *problematic* 328.7, *arguable* 329.8, *discuss* 329.12, *questionable* 333.13, *doubt* 333.19, *suppositional* 359.5, *propound* 359.9, *uncertain* 841.9, *be uncertain* 841.17

mooted *problematic* 328.7, *supposed* 359.6

moot point *issue* 328.2, *difficult question* 333.4

mop *cleaning tool* 111.10, *clean* 111.17, *dryer* 560.5, *absorb* 560.20

mopboard *foundation* 601.2

mope *despair* 270.8, *be sullen* 304.12, *make sullen* 304.13

moped *motorcycle* 687.12

moper *sad person* 270.3, *dissatisfied person* 274.3, *hopeless person* 282.5, *sullen person* 304.7

mopes, the *sign of sullenness* 304.2

mopey *sullen* 304.8

mopiness *sullenness* 304.1

moping *depressed* 270.5, *amorous* 299.18

mopish *sullen* 304.8

mopishly *sullenly* 304.16

mopishness *sullenness* 304.1, *unsociability* 409.1

moppet *child* 26.6

mopping up *cleaning* 111.2

mop up *clean* 111.17, *absorb* 560.20

mop-up *conclusion* 761.3

mopy *sullen* 304.8, *unsociable* 409.6

moquette Fabrics and Fibers 130

morainal *glaciated* 8.62

moraine *glacier* 8.44, *hill* 569.2, *transferred thing* 685.6, *residue* 750.2

morainic *glaciated* 8.62

moral 431.5, 431.9; *philosophical* 4.12, *catchword* 5.22, *advisory* 176.7, *maxim* 177.1, *gist* 329.4, *right* 429.7, *duteous* 433.7, *good* 445.10, *virtuous* 447.5, *principled* 447.6

moral abandonment *immorality* 432.1

moral badness *immorality* 432.1

moral behavior *or* **conduct** *morality* 431.1

moral climate *morality* 431.1

moral code *philosophical system* 4.2, *religion* 81.1

moral corruption *immorality* 432.1

moral delinquency *immorality* 432.1

moral deterioration 808.3

moral dilemma *difficult question* 333.4

morale *military custom* 58.8, *state of mind* 725.5, *fellowship* 827.2

morale-boosting *supportive* 825.18

moral education *educational system* 48.2

moral error *errancy* 351.7

moral excellence *good* 445.1, *virtue* 447.1

moral fiber *willpower* 372.2, *will* 376.5, *rightfulness* 429.1, *morality* 431.1

moral imperative *duty* 433.7

moralist 431.8; *philosopher* 4.9, *well-behaved person* 399.6

moralistic 431.12; *proverbial* 177.2, *judging* 341.7, *right* 429.7

moralistically 431.16; *theoretically* 4.24, *judicially* 341.12

morality 431.1; *rightfulness* 429.1, *good* 445.1, *innocence* 449.1

morality play *dramatic style* 136.3

moralize 431.14; *propound a philosophy* 4.21, *advise* 176.9, *aphorize* 177.3

moralizing *advice* 176.1, *advisory* 176.7, *proverbial* 177.2, *moralistic* 431.12

moral law *code* 780.3

moral laws *virtues* 447.2

morally 431.15; *theoretically* 4.24, *advisorily* 176.12, *right* 429.15, *dutifully* 433.19, *well* 445.19, *virtuously* 447.9, *ethically* 447.10

morally bad *immoral* 432.9

morally corrupt *immoral* 432.9

morally right *dutiful* 433.6

morally weak *depraved* 448.10

morally wrong *immoral* 432.9

moral obligation *duty* 433.1

moral philosophy Branches of Philosophy 4

Moral Rearmament Christian Groups 81

moral rectitude *rightfulness* 429.1

moral relativism *philosophical problem* 4.8

morals 431.2; *philosophical system* 4.2, *religion* 81.1, *ideology* 327.5, *way of life* 399.9, *virtues* 447.2

moral sense *sense of duty* 433.2

moral sensibility *insight* 360.3

morals of an alley cat *sexual immorality* 432.2

moral standards *morality* 431.1

moral strength *morality* 431.1

moral support 605.7; *support* 825.2

moral tone *morality* 431.1

moral turpitude *immorality* 432.1, *depravity* 448.2

moral weakness *immorality* 432.1, *depravity* 448.2

morass *marsh* 572.3, *critical situation* 824.6

moratorium *disarmament* 74.3, *stoppage* 490.2, *interruption* 604.4, *delay* 658.3, *pause* 668.3

moratorium on nuclear testing *disarmament* 74.3

moratory *deferred* 604.9

Moravianism Christian Groups 81

morbid *deathly* 29.15, *of disease* 114.25

morbid curiosity *prying* 321.2

morbidity *ill health* 114.1

morbidly *unhealthily* 114.31, *unhygienically* 114.32

morbido Musical Terms and Expression Marks 140

morbid psychology Psychological Theories, Schools 108

morbific *of disease* 114.25, *contagious* 114.26

mordacious *bitter* 306.9

mordaciously *bitterly* 306.16

mordacity *bitterness* 306.3

mordancy *emphasis* 200.1, *bitterness* 306.3

mordant *dye* 130.8, *emphatic* 200.3, *coloring agent* 251.5, *bitter* 306.9, *strong to the senses* 516.12

mordent *musical ornament* 140.19

more *additional* 748.8, *additionally* 748.15, *plurality* 793.1, *majority* 793.3, *plural* 793.6, *in the majority* 793.11

more! *bravo!* 437.23

more and more *by degrees* 739.10, *increasingly* 746.9

more convenient time *different time* 648.1

more dead than alive *fatigued* 820.2

more often than not *frequently* 661.7, *as a rule* 780.18

more of the same *boring thing* 296.3

more or less *nearly* 586.18, *quantitative* 738.6, *quantitatively* 738.8, *on average* 742.10

moreover *additionally* 748.15

mores *tradition* 1.7, *social environment* 2.4, *custom* 397.4, *way of life* 399.9, *etiquette* 406.3, *morals* 431.2, *virtues* 447.2

more so *superior* 744.8, *increasingly* 746.9

more than a match for *superior* 744.8

more than enough *plenty* 97.2, *plentiful* 97.4, *enough* 97.10, *immoderation* 99.2, *abundant* 498.8

more than ever *supremely* 744.23

more than half *majority* 793.3

more than is fair *excess* 99.1

more than is needed *superfluity* 99.4

more than meets the eye *latency* 844.1

more than one *plurality* 793.1, *plural* 793.6

more than one bargained for *unexpectedness* 839.2

more than one can afford *costly* 496.7

more than one can shake a stick at [Inf] *numberless* 795.8

more than one's pocket can stand *costly* 496.7

more than the truth *partial truth* 192.7

more where it came from *plenty* 97.2

Morgan Horse and Pony Breeds 159

morganatic *monogamous* 64.18

morganatically *matrimonially* 64.23

morganatic marriage *type of marriage* 64.3

morgue *after death* 29.9, *mortuary* 31.3

moribund *aging* 27.13, *aged* 27.15, *dying* 29.12, *sick* 114.24

moribundity *dying* 29.3

moribundly *maturely* 27.18, *fatally* 29.18

morion *historic armor* 419.8

Mormon *married man* 64.10

Mormonism *type of marriage* 64.3, Christian Groups 81, Christianity 81.5

Mormon text *Christian text* 81.16

morn *morning* 655.2, *sunrise* 713.4

morning 655.2; *daytime* 655.1, *daily* 655.6, *sunrise* 713.4, *beginning* 771.1

morning-after pill *contraceptive* 23.6

morning coat *formal clothes* 100.5, *jacket* 100.18

morning coffee *drink occasion* 93.14

morning dress *formal clothes* 100.5, *formal clothing* 406.5

morning glory Flowers 42, *morning things* 655.3

morning light *morning* 655.2

morning, noon, and night *frequently* 661.7

morning paper *newspaper* 175.2

morning prayer *public worship* 83.3

morning service *public worship* 83.3

morning sickness *morning things* 655.3

morning star *star* 7.8, *morning things* 655.3

morning things 655.3

morningtide *morning* 655.2

morning time *morning* 655.2

Morocco Countries 566

moron *unintelligent person* 316.4

Moroni Countries 566

moronic *intellectually subnormal* 316.7

moronically *unintelligently* 316.9

morose *splenetic* 223.7, *depressed* 270.5, *sullen* 304.8, *unsociable* 409.6

morosely *splenetically* 223.10, *sullenly* 304.16, *unsocially* 409.13

moroseness *spleen* 223.4, *sullenness* 304.1, *unsociability* 409.1

morph [Inf] *opiates* 121.17

morpheme *language element* 5.13

morphemic *of grammar* 5.41

morphemically *grammatically* 5.48

Morpheus *sleep* 415.5

morphia *analgesic* 115.6

morphine *alkaloid* 12.19, *analgesic* 115.6, *opiates* 121.17, *soporific* 415.6

morphogenesis *forming* 624.4

morphogenic *or* **morphogenetic** *formed* 624.6

morphologic *or* **morphological** *formed* 624.6

morphological *worded* 5.38, *biological* 13.27, *organic* 551.18

morphologically *lexically* 5.46, *biologically* 13.36, *structurally* 551.24, *formatively* 624.10

morphologist *linguist* 5.3, *life scientist* 13.26, *anatomist* 551.16

morphology Linguistic Studies 5, *anatomy* 13.5, 13.12, *phonetics* 205.3, *form* 551.3, 624.1, *science of structure* 551.15

morphophonemics Linguistic Studies 5, *phonetics* 205.3

morphophonology Linguistic Studies 5, *phonetics* 205.3

Morris Furniture Styles 101

morris dancing Dancing Types 135

morrow [Arch] *future time* 650.1, *morning* 655.2

Mors Deities 82

Morse code *artificial language* 5.9, *data transmission* 169.8, *signaling* 169.9

morsel *bite* 92.10, *appetizer* 219.2, *little piece* 580.4, *particle* 760.4, *fragment* 787.3

mortal *person* 18.8, *human* 18.15, *deadly* 29.14, *killing* 30.17, *detrimental* 446.8, *sinful* 450.8, *destructive* 523.8, *impermanent* 643.5

mortal blow *ender* 773.11

mortal fear *fear* 283.1

mortality 29.2; *human fallibility* 18.2

mortality rate *death count* 29.10

mortality table *death count* 29.10

mortally *humanly* 18.18, *fatally* 29.18, *deadly* 30.26, *destructively* 446.13

mortally ill *dying* 29.12, *sick* 114.24

mortal remains *dead person* 29.7, *remainder* 750.1

mortals *humankind* 18.1

mortal sin *iniquity* 448.3, *sin* 450.3

mortar *construction material* 14.21, *masonry* 14.22, *historical gun* 78.10, *building materials* 104.2, *wall covering* 613.12, *face* 613.31, *missile* 696.7, *adhesive* 755.3

mortar and pestle *pulverizer* 553.11

mortar attack *combined attack* 418.5

mortarboard *formal clothes* 100.5, *cap* 100.33, *clothing* 184.6

mortar ketch Sailing Ships and Boats 690

mortarman *army combat specialist* 77.16

mortgage 476.6; *purchase contract* 459.3, *promise* 464.2, *certify* 464.11, *loan* 476.5, 488.3, *credit* 487.1, *acquire credit* 487.11, *burden* 826.10

mortgage company *lending institution* 475.4, *treasury* 484.19

mortgaged *guaranteed* 464.6, *borrowed* 476.8, *indebted* 488.7

mortgaged to the hilt *indebted* 488.7

mortgagee *possessor* 469.10, *lender* 475.3, 487.5

mortgage holder *lender* 475.3

mortgage one's house *borrow* 476.10, *burden* 826.21

mortgage repayment *loan* 488.3

mortgaging *borrowing* 476.1

mortgagor *debtor* 488.6

mortgagor *or* **mortgager** *borrower* 476.7

mortician *person dealing with the dead* 29.8, *funeral person* 31.5

mortification *humiliation* 298.5, *penitence* 313.3, *indignity* 436.7, *type of penance* 451.3

mortification of the flesh *type of penance* 451.3

mortified *humiliated* 298.12

mortify *be dirty* 112.10, *humiliate* 298.19

mortifying *humiliating* 298.14, 436.15, *apologetic* 313.6

mortifyingly *humiliatingly* 298.25, *apologetically* 313.11

mortify oneself *repent* 313.9

mortify one's flesh *do penance* 451.9

mortify the flesh *abstain* 455.11

mortise *carpenter's term* 131.5, *carpenter* 131.10, *intertwine* 752.19

mortise and tenon *carpenter's term* 131.5

mortise and tenon joint *joint* 752.7

mortised *joined* 131.8

mortise lock *fastener* 754.7

mortiser *woodworking tool* 131.6

mortmain *legal property terms* 470.2

mortuary 31.3; *after death* 29.9, *funeral* 31.9

mosaic *pests and diseases* 17.12, *tree disease* 43.8, *picture* 133.5, *pictorial* 133.8, *check* 263.2, *decorative method* 532.3, *miscellany* 751.3, *collaboration* 757.2

mosaics *craft* 133.2, Hobbies and Pastimes 167

mosan Western Art Styles 133

mosasaur *extinct reptile* 37.9

moschatel Flowers 42

Moscow Countries 566, *other famous world cities* 567.9

Moseley's law Classical Physical Laws 10

Moselle *or* **Mosel** Rivers 570

mosey along [Inf] *depart* 705.8

mosey along *or* **on** [Inf] *move slowly* 693.11

mosque *place of worship* 83.8, *architectural structure* 134.4

mosquito *insect* 40.1, *pest* 40.5

mosquito boat Ships and Boats 690

mosquito net *porosity* 583.5

mosquito netting *protective covering* 613.5

moss 46.4; *green thing* 260.4

moss ally *moss* 46.4

moss-covered *mosslike* 46.7

moss-grown *mosslike* 46.7

moss killer *pest killer* 17.9

mosslike 46.7

mosslike plant *moss* 46.4

mosso Musical Terms and Expression Marks 140

moss pink Flowers 42

moss plant 46.5

moss rose Flowers 42

moss stitch *knitting* 130.7

mosstrooper [Arch] *plunderer* 479.9

mossy *botanical* 17.15, *mosslike* 46.7, *compressible* 543.9

most *excess* 99.1, *quantitative* 738.6, *unique* 744.11, *majority* 793.3, *plural* 793.6, *in the majority* 793.11

most, the *paragon* 744.6, *supremely* 744.23

most certainly *assuredly* 336.12

most important *important* 799.7

most likely *probably* 838.11

mostly *in essence* 723.13, *on average* 742.10, *on the whole* 759.13, *overall* 778.22, *as a rule* 780.18

most recent *new* 840.13

Most Valuable Player (MVP) *prizewinner* 127.8, *baseball team* 147.2, *successful person* 845.6

mot *maxim* 977.1

mote *dirt* 112.5, *grain* 553.6, *little piece* 580.4

motel *hotel* 60.12, *service workplace* 124.5, *resting place* 668.5, *miscellaneous automotive terms* 687.14

motet *ritual music* 85.9, Musical Forms 140, *sacred music* 140.3

moth *insect* 40.1, *agent of destruction* 523.7

mothball *save* 105.20, *delay* 658.13, *preserver* 815.9

mothballed *saved* 105.15, *disused* 394.8, *inoperative* 515.8, *held up* 658.6, *preserved* 815.12

mothball fleet *navy* 77.18

mothballing *delay* 658.3

moth-eaten *verminous* 40.13, *antiquarian* 651.13, *olden* 653.11, *worn* 808.13

MO theory *valence* 11.5

Mother *professional title* 72.6

Mother, the *world soul* 82.3

mother *of language* 5.35, *propagator* 21.7, *woman* 27.9, *woman in the family* 33.13, *family member* 65.2, *type of complex* 108.22, *comfort* 214.14, *loved one* 299.13, *love* 299.21, *be compassionate* 305.11, *producer* 522.10, *first cause* 675.6, *produce* 771.34, *protect* 80.21, *preserve* 815.14, *sustain* 825.25

motherboard *computer part* 15.4

Mother Carey's chicken
forewarning 814.2

mother country *native country*
566.6

Mother Earth *Earth* 8.6

mother figure *substitute* 672.2

mother figure *or image or*
surrogate *surrogate* 108.29

mother fixation *fixation* 108.21

motherhood *femaleness* 33.2

Mother Hubbard *dress* 100.11

mother image *symbol* 108.28

mothering *sustenance* 825.3

mother-in-law *family member*
65.2, Phobias 283

motherland *home* 60.3, *native*
country 566.6

motherly *middle-aged* 27.14, *family*
65.6, *loving* 299.15

motherly eye *patronage* 810.7

Mother, may I? Children's and
Party Games 167

Mother Nature *world soul* 82.3

Mother of God *deified person*
82.14

Mother of God! *miscellaneous*
swearwords 301.20

Mother of Parliaments *British*
government 49.22

mother-of-pearl *variegated thing*
263.5

mother-of-pearl inlay *decorative*
woodwork 131.2

mother of the bride *wedding*
party 64.7

mother of the groom *wedding*
party 64.7

mother's boy *effeminate male* 32.8

mother's milk *milk* 93.5, *body*
fluid 555.3

mother's skirts *hiding place* 181.2

mother substitute *substitute*
672.2

mother superior *religious leader*
68.9, *religious* 84.9

mother symbol *symbol* 108.28

mother tongue *native language*
5.5, *spoken language* 205.2, *clarity*
363.2

mother wit *common sense* 315.4,
intelligence 352.2

mothproof *treat* 130.21,
invulnerable 810.18

mothproof *or* **mothproofed**
treated 130.16

mothproofing *fabric treatment*
130.10

mothy *verminous* 40.13

motif *aspect of fiction* 139.5, *melody*
140.10, *topic* 328.1

motile *algal* 47.20, *moving* 677.12

motility *motion* 677.1

motion 677.1; *frequency* 10.6,
recommendation 176.2, *gesture*
183.17, Phobias 283, *issue* 328.2,
conduct 399.1, *action* 412.1,
activity 414.1, *tentative offer* 504.2,
petition 505.2, *operation* 509.1,
move 677.15

motional *moving* 677.12

motion around *movement* 677.3

motion for summary judgment
pretrial proceedings 54.13

motion from *retreat* 680.2

motion into *forward motion* 677.4

motionless 678.4; *inactive* 413.9,
415.8, *inert* 519.2

motionlessly 678.9; *inactively*
415.17, *inertly* 519.5

motionlessness *immobility* 413.2,
inertness 519.1, *lack of motion*
678.1

motion out of *backward motion*
677.5

motion picture 137.2; *view*
242.8, *production* 843.5

motion-picture 137.15

motion-picture camera *camera*
132.10

motion-picture company
motion-picture studio 137.7

motion-picture editing 137.8

motion-picture film *recording*
185.6

motion-picture industry *motion*
pictures 137.1

motion-picture photography
137.9; *photographic specialties*
132.2

motion pictures 137.1

motion-picture studio 137.7

motion-picture theater 137.10

motion sickness *miscellaneous*
automotive terms 687.14

motion toward *forward motion*
679.1

motivate 178.17, 412.12, 508.9;
manage 126.10, *propound* 359.9,
have at one's disposal 393.14,
activate 509.11, *influence* 512.11,
awaken 675.9, *set in motion*
677.16, *impel* 695.9, *be important*
799.13

motivated 508.8; *educatable*
48.18, *persuadable* 178.14

motivating *persuasive* 178.12,
motivational 508.7, *appealing*
512.9

motivation 508.1; *educatability*
48.9, *personnel management*
126.4, *incentive* 178.4, *motive*
178.5, *influence* 512.1, *cause*
675.1, *momentum* 677.2

motivational 508.7; *moving*
677.12

motivationally *in motion* 677.19

motivator 178.11, 508.6; *leader*
126.8, *incentive* 178.4, *operator*
412.7, *first cause* 675.6

motive 178.5, 628.6; *explanation*
319.4, *intention* 374.1, *energy*
414.4, *motivation* 508.1, *influence*
512.1, *reason* 675.4, *moving*
677.12, *impelling* 695.8,
propulsive 696.12

motive force *libido* 108.26

motiveless *erratic* 381.5, *causeless*
842.11

motivelessness *capriciousness*
381.2

motive power *type of power* 514.6,
motion 677.1, *impulsion* 695.1,
propulsion 696.1

motivity *motion* 677.1

mot juste [Fr] *grace* 527.2

motley *costume* 100.10, *clown*
138.10, *variegation* 263.1,
variegated thing 263.5, *variegated*
263.6, *indiscriminate* 338.8, *varied*
732.6, *variety* 751.4, *complicated*
751.10

motley crew *variety* 751.4

moto Musical Terms and
Expression Marks 140

motocross racer *cyclist* 687.13

motor *dynamic structure* 14.5,
power supplier 514.14

motorbicycle *motorcycle* 687.12

motorbike *motorcycle* 687.12

motorbike and sidecar *motorcycle*
687.12

motorboat Ships and Boats 690

motorcade *miscellaneous*
automotive terms 687.14

motorcar [Brit] *automobile* 687.6

motor coach *bus* 687.7

motorcycle 687.12; *means of*

transportation 686.2, *road vehicle*
687.4

motorcycle courier *cyclist* 687.13

motorcycle racing Sporting
Activities 145, *race* 422.8

motorcyclist *cyclist* 687.13

motor drive *exposure equipment*
132.12

motor haulage *road transportation*
687.1

motor home *mobile home* 60.11

motor inn *or lodge* *hotel* 60.12

motorized *mechanical* 103.7

motorman *railroad worker* 688.7

motor-mouth [Inf] *talker* 207.4

motor neuron disease
neurological disease 114.20

motor oil *oil* 106.7, *petroleum*
562.5

motor racing Sporting Activities
145, *automobile racing* 146.1

motorscooter *motorcycle* 687.12

motor show *fair* 483.2, *display*
843.1

motor torpedo boat Ships and
Boats 690

motor transportation *road*
transportation 687.1

motorway [Brit] *road* 687.2,
thoroughfare 692.6

motor yacht Ships and Boats 690

motte *trees* 43.4

mottle *maculation* 263.4, *variegate*
263.11

mottled 263.10; *varied* 732.6,
complicated 751.10

mottled effect *variety* 751.4

mottlement *maculation* 263.4

mottling *maculation* 263.4

motto *catchword* 5.22, *maxim*
177.1, Heraldic Terms 184, *moral*
431.5

moue *gesture* 183.5, 183.17, *sign of*
sullenness 304.2, *distortion of face*
627.2

mound *burial place* 31.7,
assemblage 59.13, *monument*
185.10, *military defenses* 419.9,
hill 569.2, *dome* 634.4

mount 713.24; *have sex* 20.21,
exercise 157.12, *horse* 159.1, *saddle*
horse 159.5, *ride* 159.16, *cost a lot*
496.9, *mountain* 569.1, *rise*
596.17, *be in motion* 677.14, *set*
out 705.12, *enter* 706.11, *inset*
710.13, *mounting* 713.8, *climb*
713.21, *raise* 715.9, *increase* 746.6

mountain 569.1; *landform* 8.9,
racing 146.9, *ski* 162.27,
acquisition 467.4, *rough thing*
544.2, *mass* 579.7, *dome* 634.4

mountain artillery *guns* 78.9

mountain ash Trees and Shrubs
43

mountain bike *bicycle* 687.10

mountain biking Sporting
Activities 145

mountain building 8.23

mountain chain *mountain* 569.1

mountain climate *climate* 9.35

mountain-climb *mountaineer*
161.10

mountain climber *mountaineer*
161.8, *ascender* 713.12

mountain climbing
mountaineering 161.1

mountain-dwelling *mountainous*
569.5

mountaineer 161.8, 161.10;
ascender 713.12

mountaineering 161.1, 161.9,
Sporting Activities 145, *mounting*
713.8

mountaineering associations
161.7

Mountaineers, The
mountaineering associations 161.7

mountain lake *lake* 568.1

mountain lion *game* 160.6

mountain meteorology
meteorology 9.1

mountain mist *mist* 9.33

mountain of money *money* 485.2

mountainous 569.5; *acquisitive*
467.13, *huge* 579.14, *quantitative*
738.6

mountain out of a molehill
secondary matter 800.6

mountain oyster *variety meat*
90.30

mountain range 569.3; *mountain*
569.1

mountain running Sporting
Activities 145

mountain sickness *climbing*
dangers 161.5

mountainside *heights* 596.4

mountain skiing *skiing* 162.1

mountain ski touring *cross-*
country skiing 162.7

mountain stream *river* 570.1

Mountain Time *time zone* 646.5

mountaintop *rock face* 161.6,
privacy 181.6, *mountain* 569.1,
heights 596.4, *summit* 600.1

mountain warfare *warfare* 76.3

mountain wind *wind* 9.12

mountebank *unskilled person*
128.3, *deceiver* 193.8, *imitator*
736.6

mountebankery *deception* 193.1,
hypocrisy 330.5

mounted *equine* 159.15, *raised*
715.6

mounted crossbow Historical
Missile Weapons 78

mounted police *law enforcement*
agency 53.7, *horse person* 159.14

mounted rifles *horse person*
159.14

mounted troops *horse person*
159.14

mount guard *protect* 810.21

Mountie [Inf] *law enforcement*
officer 53.8

mounting 713.8; *production*
136.14, *costly* 496.7, *mountainous*
569.5, *rising* 596.12, 713.14,
ascending motion 677.7, *directional*
677.13

mounting costs *inflationary price*
496.3

Mount Olympus *heaven* 82.15

mount the barricades *subvert*
427.13

mount the throne *gain authority*
52.15

mourn *pay one's last respects* 31.12,
grieve 270.7, 308.7, *lament* 280.7

mourned *lamented* 280.5

Mourne Mountains Mountains
and Hills 569

mourner *funeral person* 31.5, *sad*
person 270.3, *lamenter* 280.3

mourn for *lament* 280.7, *grieve*
308.7

mournful *funeral* 31.9, *sad* 254.10,
sorrowful 270.4, *lamenting* 280.4

mournfully *sorrowfully* 270.10,
lamentingly 280.9

mournfulness *lamentation* 280.1

mourning *funeral* 31.4, 31.9, *sad*
254.10, *sorrow* 270.1, *sorrowful*
270.4, *lamentation* 280.1,
lamenting 280.4, *condolence* 308.2

mourning clothes *graveclothes*

100.25, *clothing* 184.6, *dark thing* 247.3, *black thing* 254.3

mourning color *purpleness* 262.1

mourning wear *formal clothing* 406.5

mouse *input device* 15.11, *frightened person* 283.8, *coward* 285.3, *humble person* 298.7, *submitter* 421.2

mouse-colored *gray* 255.6

mouselike *rodentlike* 35.28, *humble* 298.8

mouser *cat* 35.11

mousetrap *pest control* 16.13

moussaka *notable international dishes* 90.40

mousse *dessert* 90.35, *hairdressing tool* 530.9, *air bubble* 558.10, *semiliquid* 561.7

mousseline de laine [Fr] *Fabrics and Fibers* 130

mousseline de soie [Fr] *Fabrics and Fibers* 130

mousy *colorless* 252.5, *drained of color* 252.6, *gray* 255.6, *shy* 403.8, *plain* 528.9

mousy *or* **mousey** *rodentlike* 35.28

mouth 19.7; *head* 19.6, *eating organ* 92.14, *chew* 92.22, *speech organ* 205.4, *rudeness* 400.2, *river parts* 570.3, *inlet* 572.9, *body orifice* 583.3, *entrance* 706.5

mouthbreeder *fish* 38.5

mouthful *bite* 92.10, *public speaking* 205.11, *appetizer* 219.2, *container(ful)* 738.2

mouthful [Inf] *address* 209.1

mouthguard *football uniform* 155.2

mouth off [Inf] *be insolent* 400.14

mouth organ *Musical Instruments* 142

mouthpiece *representative* 75.3, *brass instrument* 142.3, *boxing equipment* 152.4, *telephone* 169.10, *news interpreter* 365.7

mouthpiece [Inf] *lawyer* 54.5

mouth-to-mouth *swimming* 164.12

mouth-to-mouth resuscitation *swimming rescue* 164.5

mouthwash *cleaning agent* 111.9, *prophylaxis* 115.4, *deodorant* 225.3

mouth-watering *edible* 92.20, *pleasurable* 214.6, *tasty* 219.4, *desirable* 288.11

mouth-wateringly *tastily* 219.7

mouthy *effusive* 207.6, *rude* 400.9

movability *motion* 677.1

movable *propertied* 470.9, *moving* 677.12, *transferable* 685.7, *transportable* 686.7

movable bridge *bridge* 551.10

movableness *motion* 677.1

movables *legal property terms* 470.2

movably *in motion* 677.19

move 677.15; *defecate* 25.21, *play* 167.12, *advise* 176.9, *motivate* 178.17, 412.12, 508.9, *move to compassion* 308.9, *propound* 359.9, *attempt* 390.1, *tactics* 399.12, *action* 412.1, *deed* 412.2, *be active* 414.18, *petition* 505.11, *take action* 509.12, *settle* 565.10, *displacement* 574.1, *displace* 574.15, *cause change* 665.16, *convert* 670.11, *be in motion* 677.14, *set in motion* 677.16, *agitate* 684.22, *take away* 685.12, *transport* 686.10, *travel* 686.11, *impel* 695.9, *propel* 696.15, *attract* 700.11, *quit* 705.10, *stratagem* 822.2, *change* 841.20

move across *cross* 692.17

move along *proceed* 692.16

move apart 703.11; *disband* 776.13

move around 633.10; *move* 677.15

move at the speed of light *be swift* 694.10

move at the speed of sound *be swift* 694.10

move back *retreat* 680.17

move close *near* 586.12

moved *motivated* 508.8, *displaced* 574.8

move down *descend* 597.22

move fast *be active* 414.18, *be swift* 694.10, *hurry off* 705.11, *make haste* 818.5

move forward *go forward* 679.8

move freely *be free* 829.16

move heaven and earth *exert oneself* 122.11, *pursue* 377.11

move house [Brit] *quit* 705.10

move illegally *exhibit penalty behavior* 155.21

move in *take up residence* 60.24, *settle* 61.14, 565.10

move into *possess* 469.14

move it! *hurry up!* 818.9

move lock, stock, and barrel *displace* 574.15

movement 677.3; *defecation* 25.3, *feces* 25.5, *religious group* 81.4, *dramaturgy* 136.6, *floor exercise* 157.4, *action* 412.1, *activity* 414.1, *operation* 509.1, *conversion* 670.1, *transfer* 685.1, *passing* 692.3, *musical part* 760.8

movement around *movement* 677.3

move off *set out* 705.12

move on *go on* 642.7

move one's bowels *defecate* 25.21

move out *withdraw* 392.5

move over *be in motion* 677.14

mover *motivator* 178.11

mover and shaker [Inf] *motivator* 178.11, *doer* 412.3, *influential person* 512.5

move sideways 623.9

move sidewise *move sideways* 623.9

move slowly 693.11; *have leisure time* 125.5

move through *pass* 692.15

move to and fro *oscillate* 683.12

move to compassion 308.9

move to tears *move to compassion* 308.9

move up *near* 586.12

move with the times *be trendy* 652.18, *get in early* 657.16, *change* 665.14

movie *motion picture* 137.2, 137.15, *work of art* 522.4

movie camera *camera* 132.10, *imaging device* 242.11

moviedom *motion pictures* 137.1

movie film *film* 132.8

moviegoer *attender* 575.6

movie house *motion-picture theater* 137.10

movieland *motion pictures* 137.1

moviemaker *filmmaker* 137.14

movie rating *censorship* 503.4

movies *motion pictures* 137.1

movies, the *motion pictures* 137.1

movie studio *motion-picture studio* 137.7

movie theater *motion-picture theater* 137.10

movie ticket *means of identification* 184.3

movie type 137.3

moving 677.12; *descriptive* 202.11,

emotive 266.13, *Phobias* 283, *pitiful* 308.5, *active* 414.13, *appealing* 512.9, *displaced* 574.8, *motion* 677.1, *ongoing* 679.7, *transfer* 685.1, *traveling* 686.9, *passing* 692.11, *impelling* 695.8

moving apart *parting* 703.2, *separation* 753.1

moving back and forth *swaying* 378.4

movingly *pitifully* 308.12

moving sidewalk *means of transportation* 686.2

moving spirit *motivator* 508.6

moving staircase *lifter* 715.5

moving target *objective* 374.5

moving target shooting *target shooting* 160.1

moving together *climbing techniques* 161.3

moving van *truck* 578.10

moving vehicles *Phobias* 283

moving with the times *getting ahead* 657.7

mow *farm* 16.19, *cultivate* 17.19, *manage grassland* 45.10, *storehouse* 105.8, *store* 105.17, *smooth* 545.10, *shorten* 591.9

mow [Arch] *sign of irritability* 304.4, *be irritable* 304.14

mow down *slaughter* 30.21, *be at war* 76.32, *knock down* 523.13, *flatten* 716.15

mowed *shortened* 591.7

mower *farm tool* 16.5

mowing *shortening* 591.7

mowing grass *grass* 45.1

mowing machine *farm tool* 16.5, *grasscutter* 45.5

mown *shortened* 591.7

moxie [Inf] *stamina* 377.4, *energy* 414.4

Mozambique *Countries* 566

Mozarabic style *Architectural Styles* 134

Mr. *male title of address* 32.3, *title of respect* 72.7

Mr. and Mrs. *married couple* 64.9

Mr. Average *everyone* 778.7

Mr. Big [Inf] *superior* 744.5, *celebrity* 799.6

Mr. Mom [Inf] *domestic worker* 123.4

Mr. Nobody *commoner* 71.1

Mrs. *female title of address* 33.3, *title of respect* 72.7

Mrs. Average *everyone* 778.7

Mrs. Grundy *moralist* 431.8, *conformist* 781.6

Mrs. Warren's profession *prostitution* 432.4

Mr. Universe *person of strength* 516.8

Ms. *female title of address* 33.3, *title of respect* 72.7

much ado *activity* 414.1

much ado about nothing *figurative overestimation* 343.3

much-married man *married man* 64.10

much obliged *grateful* 310.4

much obliged! *thank you!* 310.9

much the same *similar* 733.7, *equal* 740.8

mucilage *mucus* 561.6, *lubricant* 562.7, *adhesive* 755.3

mucilaginous 561.15

mucilaginously *viscously* 561.22

mucilaginousness *viscosity* 561.1

mucin *protein* 12.9

muck *fertilizer* 16.9, *farm* 16.19, *cultivate* 17.19, *feces* 25.5, *dirt* 112.5, *dirty* 112.11, *mud* 561.8, *refuse* 802.5

mucked up [Inf] *mixed up* 766.14

muckheap *fertilizer* 16.9

muckiness *dirtiness* 112.1

muck out *practice livestock farming* 16.20, *clean* 111.17

muckrake *farm tool* 16.5, *defame* 440.13

muckraker *print journalist* 175.5, *disparager* 440.7

muckraking *cultivation* 16.7, *print journalism* 175.4, *defamation* 440.3

muckspreading *cultivation* 16.7

muck up [Inf] *impair* 808.5

muck-up [Inf] *mix-up* 766.5

mucky *dirty* 112.7

mucoid *of a secretion* 24.5, *oily* 562.11

mucopolysaccharide *polysaccharide* 12.5

mucoprotein *protein* 12.9

mucous *fluid* 19.25, *thick* 561.17

mucous *or* **mucose** *of a secretion* 24.5

mucous membrane *body covering* 19.4

mucronate *sharp* 549.10

mucronation *sharpness* 549.1

mucus 561.6; *body fluid* 19.16, 555.3, *secreted substance* 24.2, *saliva* 25.9, *dirt* 112.5, *lubricant* 562.7

mud 561.8; *sediment* 8.29, *dirt* 112.5, *type of wrestling* 152.9, *marsh* 559.8, 572.3

mud brick *industrial ceramics* 129.6

mudder *horse racing* 159.10

muddied *shady* 250.4

muddily *continentally* 572.13

muddiness 561.10; *dirtiness* 112.1, *obscurity* 197.1, *opaqueness* 250.1, *boggiress* 559.7

muddle *disguise* 181.13, *obscurity* 197.1, *make obscure* 197.3, *indiscrimination* 338.4, *be indiscriminate* 338.10, *shapelessness* 625.1, *disorder* 625.4, 766.19, *tumult* 684.2, *mixture* 751.1, *variety* 751.4, *mix up* 751.13, *confusion* 766.4, *confuse* 766.19, *disarrangement* 768.2, *disarrange* 768.11, *predicament* 824.5

muddled 766.13; *slightly drunk* 121.26, *obscure* 197.2, *indiscriminate* 338.8, *misjudging* 342.6, *shapeless* 625.2, *mixed up* 751.11, *disordered* 766.9, *disarranged* 768.7

muddleheaded *confused* 766.12

muddle through *make one's way* 679.12, *overcome obstacles* 845.14

muddling *disturbing* 768.9

mud-dried *dirty* 112.7

muddy *dirty* 112.7, 112.11, *obscure* 197.2, *make obscure* 197.3, *tarnish* 248.9, *shady* 250.4, *opaque* 250.7, *difficult* 364.8, *compressible* 543.9, *marshy* 559.11, *sludgy* 561.18, *lakelike* 568.5, *of landmasses* 572.12

muddy pool *small lake* 568.2

muddy the waters *disguise* 181.13, *agitate* 684.22, *be cunning* 822.5

muddy waters *that which makes invisible* 245.2

Mudéjar style *Architectural Styles* 134

mud flap *bicycle part* 687.11

mud flat *marsh* 572.3, *shallowness* 599.1

mudflow *mass movement* 8.28

mudguard *bicycle part* 687.11
mud hen *water bird* 36.9
mudhole *marsh* 572.3
mudslinger *debater* 422.17, *disparager* 440.7
mudslinging *contention* 422.1, *defamation* 440.3, *defamatory* 440.9,
muesli *cereal* 90.12
muezzin *imam* 84.7
muezzin's call *proclamation* 183.8
muezzin's cry *public worship* 83.3
muff *accessory* 100.28, *bungling* 128.2, *unskilled person* 128.3, *be clumsy* 128.9, *blunder* 351.9, *err* 351.14
muffer *unskilled person* 128.3
muffin *bread* 90.10
muffin pan *or* **tin** *cooking equipment* 91.6
muffle **229.11;** *conceal* 181.12, *strike dumb* 206.10, *silence* 231.4, *mute* 233.9, *weaken* 517.13, *abolish* 523.11
muffled *nonresonant* 233.7, *insufficient* 517.11, *concealed* 844.7
muffled drum *funeral* 31.4, *signal* 183.6
muffled sound *faintness of sound* 233.1
muffled tone *or* **voice** *undercurrent of sound* 233.3
muffle kiln *ceramic workshop and tools* 129.8
muffler *neckwear* 100.29, *sound reducer* 233.5
mufti *informal clothes* 100.7, *informal clothing* 407.5
mug *drink container* 93.13, *take away* 275.13, *strike* 418.21, *steal* 479.14, *use violence* 520.9, *drinking vessel* 578.13
mug [Inf] *face* 621.6
mugger *lawbreaker* 53.15, *attacker* 418.10, *criminal* 427.6, *coercer* 428.4, *villain* 448.5, *raider* 477.10, *thief* 479.8, *violent animal* 520.4
mugginess *humidity* 559.3
mugging *personal attack* 418.8, *stealing* 479.1
muggy *humid* 9.48, *unhygienic* 114.27, *warm* 217.13, *moist* 559.9
mug shot [Inf] *portrait* 132.5
mug up *overact* 136.35
mugwump *moderate person* 772.8
mugwumpish *impartial* 338.6, *politically moderate* 521.4
mugwumpism *impartiality* 338.2
Muhammadan *Muslim* 81.12
Muhammadanism *Islam* 81.7
Muharram *religious festival* 85.13
mujtahid *imam* 84.7
mukdam *imam* 84.7
mulatto *race* 1.5, *racial* 1.12
mulberry *red thing* 257.3, *purple* 262.6
mulch *farm* 16.19, *fertilizer* 17.8, 22.6, *cultivate* 17.19, *fertilize* 22.12, *cover* 613.2
mulct *liability* 454.6, *confiscate* 454.25
mulctable *punishable* 454.21
mule *means of transportation* 686.2, *hybrid* 751.6
mule [Inf] *obstinate person* 379.4
muleheaded *obstinate* 379.5
muleheadedness *obstinacy* 379.1
mules *Collective Names* 59, *shoes* 100.30
mule train *means of transportation* 686.2
Mulhacén *Mountains and Hills* 569

mulish *ungulate* 35.31, *willful* 372.8, *obstinate* 379.5
mulishly *obstinately* 379.11
mulishness *willfulness* 372.3, *obstinacy* 379.1
Mull, Island of *Islands* 572
mull *sweeten* 222.7
mullah *educator* 48.4, *imam* 84.7
mullein Flowers 42
muller *pulverizer* 553.11
mullet *food fish and shellfish* 90.20, Heraldic Terms 184
mulligrubs *sign of irritability* 304.4
mullion Architectural Elements 134
mull over *concentrate* 317.10
multiangular *polygonal* 6.79
multicellular *cellular* 13.30
multicenter bond *chemical bond* 11.6
multicolor *spectrum* 251.3
multicolored *colored* 251.10, *variegated* 263.6, *varied* 732.6
multicultural *varied* 732.6, *mixed* 751.8
multiculturalism *variety* 732.2
multiemployer agreement *bargaining* 57.9
multiethnic *varied* 732.6
multi-event contest **166.16;** *field event* 166.10
multifaceted *side* 623.6, *diversified* 732.8, *various* 793.7
multifacial *cubic* 6.81
multifarious *varied* 732.6, *various* 793.7, *multitudinous* 795.5
multifariously *variously* 732.15, *plurally* 793.10, *numerously* 795.13
multifariousness *variety* 732.2, *multiplicity* 793.2
multiflagellate *algal* 47.20
multiflorous *horticultural* 17.14
multifold *multiplicative* 793.8, *multitudinous* 795.5
multifoldness *multiplicity* 795.2
multiform *varied* 732.6, *nonuniform* 734.5, *various* 793.7
multiformity *variety* 732.2, *nonuniformity* 734.2, *multiplicity* 793.2
multihull *sailing* 150.25, Sailing Ships and Boats 690
multilateral *contractual* 459.7, *side* 623.6, *various* 793.7
multilateralism *side* 623.1, *multiplicity* 793.2
multilateralist *pluralist* 793.5
multilaterally *contractually* 459.9, *plurally* 793.10
multilingual *linguist* 5.3, *linguistic* 5.34, *speaking* 205.15, *translational* 365.11, *various* 793.7
multilingually *linguistically* 5.44
multimillion *million* 792.11
multimillionaire *wealthy person* 485.6, *prosperous person* 847.4
multinational *corporate* 480.17, *dominant* 512.10, *various* 793.7
multinational company *group influence* 512.6
multinational corporation *company* 480.7
multinational market *free market* 483.4
multinomial *algebraic expression* 6.23, *functional* 6.73
multinucleate *nuclear* 13.31
multipartite *separate* 753.7
multiphase *chemical* 14.46
multiphase reactions *chemical reaction thermodynamics* 14.29
multipitch *mountaineering* 161.9
multiple *multiplication* 6.15,

793.4, *varied* 732.6, *plural* 793.6, *multiplicative* 793.8, *multitudinous* 795.5
multiple fruit *botanical fruit* 44.2
multiple image *portrait* 132.5
multiple independently targetable reentry vehicle (MIRV) *modern missile weapon* 78.4
multiple personality *multiplicity* 793.2
multiple personality disorder *dissociative disorder* 108.17
multiple sclerosis (MS) *neurological disease* 114.20, *hardening* 542.2
multiple span *bridge* 551.10
multiple star *star* 7.8
multiple store *or* **shop** *store* 483.8
multiplexer (mux) *communications device* 15.26
multipliable *enlargeable* 581.13
multiplicand *multiplication* 6.15, 793.4
multiplication **6.15, 793.4;** *reproduction* 21.1, *germination* 581.5, *increase* 746.1, *calculation* 784.1
multiplication sign *mathematical symbol* 6.11, *symbol* 183.3
multiplication table *calculator* 784.5, *multiplication* 793.4
multiplication tables *multiplication* 6.15
multiplicative **793.8**
multiplicity **793.2, 795.2;** *variety* 732.2
multiplied *reproduced* 21.10, *multiplicative* 793.8
multiplier *multiplication* 6.15, 793.4
multiplier reel *fishing tackle* 154.7
multiply *add* 6.86, 784.11, *procreate* 22.14, *mushroom* 47.23, *bring into existence* 522.14, *grow* 581.17, *increase* 746.6, *make bigger* 746.7, *pluralize* 793.9, *plurally* 793.10, *numerously* 795.13
multiply by five **792.24**
multiply by four *quadruple* 791.11
multiply by seven *multiply by five* 792.24
multiply by six *multiply by five* 792.24
multiply by three *triple* 790.10
multiply by two *double* 789.14
multiplying *growing* 581.12
multiplying by three *triplication* 790.4
multiply out *add* 6.86
multipoint tool *machine tool* 14.9
multipurpose *diversified* 732.8, *various* 793.7, *useful* 801.5
multiracial *mixed* 751.8, *various* 793.7
multiracial state *nation* 18.14
multirole *various* 793.7
multistage *layered* 588.6
multistage rocket *rocketry* 7.32
multistory *manorial* 60.21
multistory building *building* 551.9
multitasking *computing terms* 15.22
multitude **795.1;** *crowd* 59.11, *quantity* 738.1, *general public* 778.6, *multiplicity* 793.2, *throng* 795.4
multitudinal *multitudinous* 795.5
multitudinous **795.5;** *frequent* 661.4, *plural* 793.6
multitudinously *frequently* 661.7,

plurally 793.10, *numerously* 795.13
multitudinousness *frequency* 661.1, *multiplicity* 793.2, 795.2
multi-user dungeon (MUD) *computer communications* 15.25
multivariate analysis *statistical methods* 6.53
multivocal *meaningful* 361.6, *linguistic* 361.9
mum *taciturn* 208.4, *silent* 231.2
mum [Inf] *woman in the family* 33.13
mumble *speak in a particular way* 205.18, *undercurrent of sound* 233.3, *sound faint* 233.8
mumbled *nonresonant* 233.7
mumbledypeg Children's and Party Games 167
mumbling *nonresonant* 233.7, *unintelligibility* 364.1
mumbo jumbo *spell* 86.8, *obscurity* 197.1, *nonsense* 362.2
mummer *actor* 136.25
mummers' play *dramatic style* 136.3
mummery *acting* 136.22, *ceremony* 405.3
mummification *burial* 31.1, *drying* 560.3, *preservation of body* 815.7
mummified *posthumous* 29.16, *buried* 31.8, *dried-up* 560.9, *preserved* 815.12
mummify *bury* 31.10, *dry up* 560.21, *preserve* 815.14
mummy *dead person* 29.7, *preserved thing* 815.10
mummy [Inf] *woman in the family* 33.13
mummy chamber *burial place* 31.7
mummy wrapping *funeral object* 31.6
mump *be sullen* 304.12
MUMPS Programming Languages 15
mumps *infection* 114.7
mum's the word! *hush!* 231.6
munch *chew* 92.22
munchies [Inf] *snack* 90.8
munching *eating* 92.1
munchkin Breeds of Cats 35
mundane *unpretentious* 526.8, *monotonous* 797.12
mundaneness *unpretentiousness* 526.2
mundunugu *witch* 86.15
mung Bean Varieties 90
municipal *administrative* 564.13, *urban* 567.14
municipal building 567.13
municipal court *type of court* 54.9
municipal garden *garden* 17.2
municipal hospital *hospital* 107.16
municipality *body politic* 50.3, *city* 567.1
municipal library *library* 174.14
municipally **567.16;** *regionally* 564.16
municipal resident 567.12
municipal tax *tax* 494.5
munificence *charity* 305.3, *philanthropy* 307.1, *unselfishness* 443.2, *generosity* 498.1
munificent *philanthropic* 307.6, *unselfish* 443.5, *generous* 498.6
munificently *philanthropically* 307.9, *unselfishly* 443.9
munificentness *philanthropy* 307.1
muniments *certificate* 185.2
munitions *supplies* 102.3

Munt Deities 82

muon *elementary particle* 10.53, *little thing* 580.3

Muraköz Horse and Pony Breeds 159

mural *painting* 143.3, *interior decoration* 532.4

mural painter *painter* 143.7

murder 30.2, 30.20; *way of dying* 29.5, *killing* 30.1, *kill* 30.19, Collective Names 59, Children's and Party Games 167, *malignity* 306.5, *harm* 306.13, *violation of the law* 427.2, *disobey* 427.12, *evil thing* 446.2, *wicked act* 448.7, *be wicked* 448.13, *sin* 450.11, *execute* 454.30, *violence by person* 520.2, *use violence* 520.9, *destroying* 523.2, *destroy* 523.10, *cause to cease* 668.12, *cause not to exist* 718.14

murdered *killed* 29.13

murderer 30.12; *killer* 30.11, *lawbreaker* 53.15, *malefactor* 306.6, *attacker* 418.10, *criminal* 427.6, *evil person* 446.3, *villain* 448.5, *punisher* 454.16, *violent animal* 520.4, *destroyer* 523.6

murderess *murderer* 30.12

murder most foul *murder* 30.2

murder of the queen's *or* **king's English** [Inf] *language error* 351.10

murderous 30.18, 520.7; *deadly* 29.14, *malign* 306.11, *villainous* 448.12, *sinful* 450.8

murderously *deadly* 30.26, *malignly* 306.18, *villainously* 448.18, *violently* 520.11

murderousness *violence* 520.1

murder weapon 30.3

murex *red pigment* 257.2

Murgese Horse and Pony Breeds 159

muricate *or* **muricated** *rough* 544.5, *toothed* 549.13

murine *rodentlike* 35.28

murk 248.2; *darkness* 247.1, *dullness* 255.5

murkily *obscurely* 197.4, *grayly* 255.10

murkiness *obscurity* 197.1, *darkness* 247.1, *murk* 248.2, *opaqueness* 250.1

murky 248.5; *dirty* 112.7, *obscure* 197.2, *dark* 247.5, 254.6, *shady* 250.4, *dull* 255.8, *difficult* 364.8, *condensed* 540.7, *concealed* 844.7

murmur *blow* 9.53, *utterance* 205.10, *speak in a particular way* 205.18, *undercurrent of sound* 233.3, *sound faint* 233.8, *humming* 235.2, *hum* 235.11, *flow* 570.10

murmuration Collective Names 59, *undercurrent of sound* 233.3

murmured *nonresonant* 233.7

murmuring *nonresonant* 233.7

murmur of discontent *forewarning* 814.2

Murnau-Werdenfels Breeds of Cattle 16

murophobia *or* **musophobia** Phobias 283

Murphy *type of bed* 101.9

Murphy's law *formula* 780.7

murrain *animal disease* 34.10

Murray Rivers 570

Murray Grey Breeds of Cattle 16

murrelet, marbled Endangered US Birds 36

murrey Heraldic Terms 184

murrey [Arch] *red* 257.5, *purple* 262.6

Murrumbidgee Rivers 570

Musaf [Heb] *public worship* 83.3

Musca Constellations 7

Muscat Countries 566

Musci *moss* 46.4

muscle *exertion* 122.4, *incentive* 178.4, *bulge* 634.2, *line* 754.5

muscle [Inf] *accompanier* 794.6

musclebound *tough* 542.6

muscle cell *cell* 13.15

muscle in *invade* 706.12

muscle power *exertion* 122.4, *vigor* 514.2

muscle relaxant *medicine* 115.2

muscles 19.3; *stalwartness* 547.3

muscovado *brown thing* 256.3

muscular *bodily* 19.18, *male* 32.16, *physically strong* 516.10, *stalwart* 547.10

muscular dystrophy *neurological disease* 114.20

muscularity *physical strength* 516.3, *stalwartness* 547.3

muscularly *stalwartly* 547.17

muscular rheumatism *joint disease* 114.19

musculature *muscles* 19.3, *physical strength* 516.3

musculoskeletal disease *disease* 114.4

Muse *minor deity* 82.2, *inspiration* 360.2

muse *philosophize* 4.19, *speculate* 294.13, *fantasize* 360.15

Muses, the Deities 82

musette Musical Instruments 142

museum *repository* 105.13, *conservation* 815.2, *showplace* 843.4

museum going Hobbies and Pastimes 167

museum piece *work of art* 133.4, *thing of the past* 651.8, *antiquity* 653.4, *showpiece* 843.3

mush *cereal* 90.12, *semiliquid* 561.7

mush [Inf] *face* 621.6

mushiness *pulpiness* 561.9

mushroom 47.2, 47.23; *vegetable* 17.11, 90.33, *procreate* 22.14, *fungal body* 47.4, *white* 253.7, *brown* 256.5, *increase* 467.17, 746.6, *grow* 581.17

mushroom eating *study of fungi* 47.9

mushroom farm *farm* 16.2, *study of fungi* 47.9

mushroom farmer *study of fungi* 47.9

mushroom grower *study of fungi* 47.9

mushroom growing *horticulture* 17.1

mushrooming *growing* 581.12

mushy *amorous* 299.18, *pulpy* 561.19

music 140.1; *sound* 10.15, 230.1, Phobias 283

musica ficta *or* **musica falsa** *harmonic element* 140.14

musical 140.25, 141.11; *musical drama* 136.5, *dramatic* 136.31, 137.16, *movie type* 137.3, *opera* 140.8, *hearing* 228.9, *production* 843.5

musical chairs Children's and Party Games 167

musical comedy *musical drama* 136.5

musical composition 140.9; *work of art* 522.4

musical director 141.7

musical dissonance 241.2

musical drama 136.5; *opera* 140.8

musical ear *hearing* 228.1

musical form *kind* 624.3

musical glasses Musical Instruments 142

musical instrument 142.1

musical instrument digital interface (MIDI) program *application software* 15.14

musicality *music* 140.1, *melodiousness* 140.12, *hearing* 228.1

musically 141.20; *dramatically* 136.38

musicalness *music* 140.1, *melodiousness* 140.12

musical notation *symbol* 183.3, *representation* 187.1

musical note 140.15

musical ornament 140.19

musical part 760.8

musical quality *melodiousness* 140.12

musical saw Musical Instruments 142

musical score *production* 137.6

musical texture *melodiousness* 140.12

musical time 639.7

music box Musical Instruments 142

music director *filmmaker* 137.14

music drama *musical drama* 136.5

music hall *show business* 138.1, *club* 138.7, *performance* 141.8

musician 141.1; *artistic worker* 123.12, *skilled person* 127.7, *producer* 522.10

music lover 141.10

music maker *musician* 141.1

music-making *musical* 141.11

music master *music director* 141.7

musicography *harmonics* 140.13

musicology *harmonics* 140.13

musicophile *music lover* 141.10

musicophobia Phobias 283

music review *criticism* 365.3

music room *school place* 48.16

music school *type of school* 48.12

music stand *instrumental aid* 142.7, *supporting structure* 605.2

music teacher *musical director* 141.7

music theory *harmonics* 140.13

musing *philosophical investigation* 4.4, *thoughtful* 4.17, *thoughtfulness* 317.2, *speculative* 317.8

musk *secreted substance* 24.2, *fragrance* 226.1, *incense* 226.3

muskellunge *game fish* 154.10

musket *historical handgun* 78.8

musketeer *historical soldier* 77.8, *shooter* 696.11

musketry *firing* 418.6, *shooting* 696.5

musketry practice *military training* 76.19

musk gland *mammalian characteristic* 35.3

muskily *fragrantly* 226.7

muskiness *fragrance* 226.1

musk rose Flowers 42

musky *fragrant* 226.4

Muslim 81.12; *denominational* 81.23

Muslim architecture Architectural Styles 134

Muslim calendar *calendar* 646.3

Muslim fundamentalism Islam 81.7

Muslim fundamentalist *Muslim* 81.12

Muslimism Islam 81.7

muslin Fabrics and Fibers 130, *fineness* 595.5

mussel *food fish and shellfish* 90.20

mussel shrimp *crustacean* 39.10

Mussulman [Arch] *Muslim* 81.12

must *fungus* 47.1, *necessity* 95.1, *be compelled* 428.11, *be the duty of* 433.16

must, a *compulsion* 428.1

mustache *body covering* 19.4

mustached *hairy* 19.20

mustachioed *hairy* 19.20

Mustang Horse and Pony Breeds 159

mustang *horse* 159.1

mustard *crop* 16.8, Herbs and Spices 91, *yellow thing* 259.4, *yellow* 259.7

mustard family *seed plant* 41.3

mustard seed Herbs and Spices 91, *little thing* 580.3

mustard-yellow *yellow* 259.7

mustelid *flesh-eating mammal* 35.9

Mustelidae *flesh-eating mammal* 35.9

musteline *carnivorous* 35.26

muster Collective Names 59, *collection* 59.2, *call together* 59.28

mustered *assembled* 59.18

mustering Collective Names 59

muster out *disband* 776.13

muster roll *list of names* 785.7

muster *or* **summon up courage** *take courage* 284.15

must have *need* 95.16

mustily *dirtily* 112.12, *stinkingly* 227.6, *venerably* 653.17

mustiness *dirtiness* 112.1, *stench* 227.1

musty *fungal* 47.18, *dirty* 112.7, *unhygienic* 114.27, *stinking* 227.3, *olden* 653.11

mutability *change* 665.1, *changeableness* 666.1, *capriciousness* 841.8

mutable *changed* 665.10, *changeable* 665.11, 666.3, *capricious* 841.16

mutably *changeably* 665.22

mutant *genetic* 13.32

mutate *transform* 665.20, *convert* 670.11, *change* 841.20

mutated *changed* 665.10, *converted* 670.7

mutating *converting* 670.8

mutation Collective Names 59, *distortion of body* 627.3, *change* 665.1, *transformation* 665.7, *conversion* 670.1

mutational *genetic* 13.32

mutative *transformative* 665.12

mute 233.9; *funeral person* 31.5, Collective Names 59, *instrumental aid* 142.7, *speechless* 206.7, *strike dumb* 206.10, *silent* 208.5, 231.2, *muffle* 229.11, *silence* 231.4, *sound reducer* 233.5, *weaken* 517.13

mute button *sound reducer* 233.5

muted *unheard* 229.7, *silent* 231.2, *nonresonant* 233.7, *murky* 248.5, *soft-hued* 251.13, *unintelligible* 364.4, *insufficient* 517.11

mutedly *silently* 231.9

mutedness *silence* 231.1, *faintness of sound* 233.1

muted sound *faintness of sound* 233.1

muteness *mutism* 206.3, *silence* 208.2, 231.1, *unintelligibility* 364.1, *quietness* 844.4

mutilate *torture* 454.29, *ruin* 523.15, *make ugly* 531.4, *blemish* 533.7

mutilated ugly 531.3, reduced 749.5

mutilation ugliness 531.1, subtraction 749.1, noncompletion 762.2

mutineer rebel 427.8

mutineering disobedience 427.1

mutinous lawless 53.26, resisting 417.8, disobedient 427.10, subversive 427.11, defiant 466.7, disorderly 507.6, 766.15

mutinously resistingly 417.14, disobediently 427.14, subversively 427.15, defiantly 466.14, disapprovingly 507.10

mutinousness disobedience 427.1, revolution 427.4, defiance 466.3

mutiny resistance movement 417.3, revolt 417.12, disobedience 427.1, revolution 427.4, subvert 427.13, defiance 466.3, defy 466.11, protest 507.1, 507.7, disorder 507.2, cause mischief 507.9

mutism 206.3

Mutsu Apple Varieties 44

mutt [Inf] dog 35.10

mutter utterance 205.10, speak in a particular way 205.18, undercurrent of sound 233.3, sound faint 233.8, humming 235.2, hum 235.11, be irritable 304.14, quietness 844.4

muttered nonresonant 233.7

muttering nonresonant 233.7, forewarning 814.2

mutton meat 90.22

muttonchops body covering 19.4

mutual agreements 459.2, in exchange 673.3, reciprocal 729.4, joint 827.3

mutual affinity liking 290.1

mutual approach convergence 702.1

mutual assistance mutual relationship 827.3

Mutual Assured Destruction (MAD) atomic warfare 76.4

mutual attraction attraction 700.1

mutual concession compromise 461.1, moderation 521.1

mutual conductance resistance 10.41

mutual defense treaty alliance 459.5

mutual dependence interrelation 729.2

mutual exchange reciprocity 729.1

mutual friend friend 62.2

mutual fund finance 457.1

mutual inductance resistance 10.41

mutual induction magnetic phenomenon 10.50

mutualism ecology 13.25, interrelation 729.2, mutual relationship 827.3

mutualistic interrelated 729.5

mutuality exchange 673.1, relatedness 727.1, interrelation 729.2, compatibility 735.4, mutual relationship 827.3

mutualization interrelation 729.2

mutual love liking 290.1

mutually in exchange 673.6, convergently 702.12, relevantly 727.12, reciprocally 729.10

mutually approaching advancing 702.8

mutually dependent interrelated 729.5

mutualness mutual relationship 827.3

mutual pledge promise 458.1

mutual relation or **relationship** interrelation 729.2

mutual relationship 827.3

mutual repulsion repulsion 701.1

mutual support agreement 462.1

mutual support or **respect** or **regard** or **goodwill** friendly relations 62.3

mutual transfer transfer 685.1

mutual understanding agreement 462.1, compatibility 735.4

mutule Architectural Elements 134

muumuu dress 100.11

Muzzafarnagri Breeds of Sheep 16

muzzle silence 231.4, overpower 515.14, abolish 523.11, means of restraint 830.6, restrain someone 830.17

muzzled detained 830.11

muzzleloader historical handgun 78.8

Mweru Lakes 568

myalgia joint disease 114.19

Myanmar Countries 566

myasthenia neurological disease 114.20

myasthenia gravis neurological disease 114.20

mycelial of fungi 47.19

mycelium fungal body 47.4

Mycenaean architecture Architectural Styles 134

mycetoma fungal disease 47.6

mycobiont fungal association 47.5, lichen 47.16

mycological of fungi 47.19

mycologist plant scientist 41.11, study of fungi 47.9

mycology plant science 41.10, study of fungi 47.9

mycophagist study of fungi 47.9

mycophagy study of fungi 47.9

mycoplasma microorganism 13.11

mycorrhiza fungal association 47.5

mycosis fungal disease 47.6

mycostat antifungal agent 47.8

Mycota fungi 47.3

mycotic of fungi 47.19

my country right or wrong bellicosity 76.15

my dear man or **sir** male title of address 32.3

my dear woman or **lady** female title of address 33.3

myelin sheath nervous system 19.14

my good lady female title of address 33.3

my good man male title of address 32.3

my goodness! wonderful! 294.20

my gosh! wonderful! 294.20

my man [Inf] friend 62.2

myna or **mynah** cage bird 36.13

myocardial infarction (MI) cardiovascular disease 114.13

myocarditis cardiovascular disease 114.13

myoglobin protein 12.9, respiration 12.24

myomorph gnawing mammal 35.13

myopia sight defect 243.2

myopic weak-sighted 243.10

myriad 795.7; thousand 792.10, immeasurable 798.6

myriads multitude 795.1

myriapod 39.11

Myriapoda myriapod 39.11

myristic Common Fatty Acids 12

myrmecophobia Phobias 283

myrrh Tree Products 43, incense 226.3

myrrhic resinous 562.13

myrtle Trees and Shrubs 43

myself internal world 525.6

mysophobia Phobias 283

mystagogue occultist 86.13, leader 126.8

my stars! wonderful! 294.20

mysterious 182.10, 844.11; occult 86.16, obscure 197.2, astonishing 294.10, problematic 333.12, unknown 349.7, unintelligible 364.4, difficult 364.8, profound 598.15, unbelievable 837.5

mysteriously 844.17; occultly 86.27, obscurely 197.4, astonishingly 294.19, unintelligibly 364.16, profoundly 598.27

mysterious message unintelligible thing 364.3

mysteriousness 844.5; the occult 86.2, obscurity 197.1, wonderfulness 294.5, profundity 598.5

mysterious stranger anonymity 182.7

mystery 182.4; occultism 86.1, the occult 86.2, movie type 137.3, difficult question 333.4, unknown thing 349.3, unintelligibility 364.1, unintelligible thing 364.3, profundity 598.5, mysteriousness 844.5

mystery person latency 844.1

mystery play dramatic style 136.3

mystery story story 139.4

mystic Philosophical Schools of Thought 4, religious person 81.9, religious 81.21, occultist 86.13, unintelligible 364.4, mysterious 844.11

mystical divine 82.16, unintelligible 364.4, unbelievable 837.5

mystical experience divine manifestation 82.5

mystical intuition divine manifestation 82.5

mystically divinely 82.24, occultly 86.27, mysteriously 844.17

mysticism Philosophical Schools of Thought 4, religiousness 81.2, occultism 86.1, unintelligibility 364.1, mysteriousness 844.5

mystification occultism 86.1, evasion 181.5, mystery 182.4, cunning 330.3, unintelligibility 364.1

mystified confused 364.10, troubled 824.15

mystify 182.12; occult 86.22, obscure 250.8, practice sophistry 330.11, confuse 333.20, make ignorant 349.10, puzzle 364.12, cause difficulties 824.22, make uncertain 841.19

mystifying mysterious 182.10, inscrutable 250.5, cunning 330.8, meaningless 362.7

myth tradition 1.7, 653.5, chronicle 3.4, story 139.4, falsehood 192.6, idealism 360.7, unreality 722.2

mythical chronicled 3.12, fictional 139.16, fabricated 192.17, theoretical 720.10

mythical or **mythic** imaginary 360.12, unreal 722.7

mythically societally 1.17, unreally 722.15

mythicalness unreality 722.2

mythicize fabricate 192.24, be unreal 722.12

mythicized fabricated 192.17

mythmaker visionary 360.9

mythological societal 1.13, fictional 139.16, fabricated 192.17, narrative 202.12, imaginary 360.12

mythological or **mythologic** unreal 722.7

mythologically societally 1.17, unreally 722.15

mythologist studier of humankind 18.7, author 139.13

mythologize fabricate 192.24, recount 202.16, be unreal 722.12

mythologized fabricated 192.17

mythology tradition 1.7, 653.5, study of humankind 18.6, unreality 722.2

mythomane liar 192.10

mythomania lying 192.5

mythomaniac lying 192.16

mythophobia Phobias 283

Mytilene Islands 572

my word! wonderful! 294.20

myxomatosis animal disease 34.10

myxomycetes fungi 47.3

Myxomycota fungi 47.3

myxophobia Phobias 283

N

n. number 783.1

nab [Inf] imprison 55.12, take away forcefully 477.19, detain 830.16

Nabeshima ware Ceramics 129

Nabis Western Art Styles 133

nabla vector 6.48

nabob sovereign 68.2, wealthy person 485.6

nacre variegated thing 263.5

nacreous iridescent 263.7

nacreously variedly 263.12

nada [Sp] zero 786.1

nadir celestial sphere 7.4, orbit 7.22, lowest point 597.5, base 601.1, inferior state 745.3, zero level 786.3

nag unpleasant woman 33.7, horse 159.1, quarrel 272.9, irascible person 303.7, manipulate 508.12, harp 797.17

Nagari written letter 5.14

nagging criticism 438.4, critical 438.13

nag into motivate 178.17

Nagori Breeds of Cattle 16

nagual minor deity 82.2

Naiad Planets and Their Satellites 7

naiad minor deity 82.2

naïf believer 87.5, naive person 821.2, naive 821.3

nail body covering 19.4, sharp-pointed thing 549.4, link 752.18, fastener 754.7, connect 754.13

nail bomb bomb 78.15

nailbrush cleaning tool 111.10

nail clippers cosmetic tool 530.5

nail color cosmetics 530.4

nail down make fast 464.13, establish reality 719.12

nailed connected 754.11

nail enamel cosmetics 530.4

nail file cosmetic tool 530.5, smoother 545.2, abrasive 553.14, eraser 554.7

nail harmonica or **nail fiddle** Musical Instruments 142

nailhead Architectural Elements 134

nail in one's coffin defeat 846.7

nail one's colors to the mast brace oneself 376.13

nail polish red pigment 257.2, cosmetics 530.4

nail polish remover *cosmetic tool* 530.5

nails *weapon* 78.1, *retainer* 471.3

nail tips *cosmetics* 530.4

nail varnish *cosmetics* 530.4

nail wrapping *beauty treatment* 530.3

nainsook Fabrics and Fibers 130

Nairobi Countries 566

naive 449.9, 821.3; *immature* 26.12, 652.12, *believing* 87.6, *ingenuous* 191.6, *representing* 202.14, *raw* 260.9, *ignorant* 349.5, *unaccustomed* 398.3, *natural* 526.10, *open* 583.13, *vulnerable* 811.9

naive art Western Art Styles 133

naively 449.15, 821.5; *believingly* 87.12, *ingenuously* 191.11, *unaccustomedly* 398.7, *candidly* 583.23, *dangerously* 811.14

naiveness *ingenuousness* 191.3

naive person 821.2

naive realism Branches of Philosophy 4

naiveté 449.4, 821.1; *immaturity* 26.3, 652.3, *ingenuousness* 191.3, *ignorance* 349.1, *unaccustomedness* 398.1, *naturalness* 526.4, *openness* 583.7, *vulnerability* 811.6

naked 614.12; *clear* 244.6, *vulnerable* 811.9, *open* 843.12

naked ape, the *person* 18.8

naked as a jaybird *naked* 614.12

naked as the day one was born *naked* 614.12

naked eye *visibility* 244.1

naked force *suppression* 424.2

nakedly *revealingly* 614.22

nakedness *bareness* 614.3, *vulnerability* 811.6, *openness* 843.6

naked person *nude person* 614.5

naked truth, the *the truth* 721.3

Naknek Lakes 568

namby-pamby *coward* 285.3, *spineless* 285.5, *weak person* 517.4, *weak-willed* 517.10

Namcha Barwa Mountains and Hills 569

name 202.8, 202.17; *word* 5.17, *title* 72.1, *correspondence* 169.2, *personal identification* 184.4, *identify* 184.11, *specify* 779.18, *commission* 833.8, *fame* 845.2

name and address *personal identification* 184.4

name badge *personal identification* 184.4

name-calling *argument* 329.1

named 202.13; *worded* 5.38, *titled* 72.9, *identified* 184.9

name day *anniversary* 405.5, *day* 646.4

name in bright lights *public relations (PR)* 173.8

name in lights *fame* 845.2

namelessness *anonymity* 182.7

namely *in other words* 365.18, *particularly* 779.21

name names *tell on* 180.10, *specify* 779.18

name of the game [Inf] *essential content* 723.2

name part *role* 136.23

nameplate *personal identification* 184.4

names Phobias 283

namesake *name* 202.8

name tag *sign* 183.1

name tape *personal identification* 184.4

Namib Deserts 572

Namibia Countries 566

naming *identification* 184.1,

---

nomenclature 202.7, *named* 202.13

naming ceremony *nomenclature* 202.7

Namtar *evil spirit* 446.4

nana [Inf] *family member* 65.2

Nanda Devi Mountains and Hills 569

Nanfan pony Horse and Pony Breeds 159

Nanga Parbat Mountains and Hills 569

nankeen Fabrics and Fibers 130

Nanking ware Ceramics 129

Nanna Deities 82

nanny *personal attendant* 69.5, *domestic worker* 123.4, *protector* 810.11

nanny goat *livestock* 16.11, *female animal* 33.15, *female mammal* 35.19

nano Decimal Prefixes 589

nanosecond *time period* 641.2

Nantucket Islands 572

Naomi Notable Friendships 62

naos *shrine* 83.10, Architectural Elements 134

nap 552.3; *weaving* 130.6, 609.2, *weave* 130.20, Card Games 168, *desensitization* 213.2, *sleep* 415.5, 415.14, *afternoon* 655.5, *pause* 668.3, 668.13, *ease* 819.1, *take it easy* 819.3

napalm bomb *bomb* 78.15

nape *head* 19.6

napery *tableware* 92.13, *dry goods* 130.3

naphtha *oil* 106.7

Napierian logarithm *logarithm* 6.17

Napier's bones *calculator* 6.64, 784.5, *computer* 15.1

napkin *tableware* 92.13

Naples yellow *yellow pigment* 259.2

Napoleon Famous Lovers 299

napoleon Card Games 168

Napoleonic Code *the Law* 53.2

Napoleonic Wars Major Wars 76

napped *woven* 130.15

naproxen sodium *analgesic* 115.6

Naraka *evil place* 446.6

Narbada Rivers 570

narc [Inf] *law enforcement officer* 53.8

narcissism *eroticism* 20.7, *love* 299.1, *self-admiration* 402.4, *egotism* 444.2, *self-absorption* 456.4

narcissist *eroticism* 20.7, *selfish person* 444.3, *self-indulgent person* 456.5

narcissistic *loving* 299.15, *self-admiring* 402.10, *egotistic* 444.5, *self-absorbed* 456.9

narcissistic personality disorder *personality disorder* 108.7

Narcissus *vain person* 402.7

narcissus Flowers 42

narcolepsy *sleep disorder* 108.20

narcosis *oblivion* 355.4

narcotherapist *psychologist* 108.33

narcotic *drug* 115.9, 121.14, *medicinal* 115.15, *addictive drug* 117.10, *addictive* 121.32, *anesthetic* 213.3, 213.6, *soporific* 415.6, *moderating* 521.5

narcotically *in a trance* 121.40

narcotics *drug* 121.14

narcotics officer *law enforcement agency* 53.7

narcotization *desensitization* 213.2

---

narcotize *anesthetize* 213.8, *make inactive* 415.16

narcotized *not awake* 415.12

nard *ointment* 562.8

narghile *tobacco implements* 121.24

naris *nose* 19.11, *sense of smell* 224.2

nark [Brit inf] *informer* 170.8

Narnia Imaginary Places 360

Narragansett Breeds of Fowl 16

narrate *chronicle* 3.15, *write* 139.21, *communicate* 170.12, *record* 185.13, *recount* 202.16

narrated *chronicled* 3.12

narration 202.3; *chronicle* 3.4

narrative 139.18, 202.12; *chronicle* 3.4, *aspect of fiction* 139.5, *record* 185.1, *narration* 202.3

narrative art Western Art Styles 133

narrative fiction *fiction* 139.2

narratively 139.22

narrative poem Poem or Verse Forms 139

narrative poetry *poetry* 139.8

narrative voice *aspect of fiction* 139.5

narrative writing *narration* 202.3

narrator *actor* 136.25, *author* 139.13, *speaker* 205.12

narrow 593.8, 593.14; *unjust* 342.7, *shortened* 582.8, *contract* 582.12, *become smaller* 582.14, *narrow place* 593.2, *unite closely* 752.16, *excluding* 764.5, *restrained* 830.9

narrow-beaked *narrow* 593.8

narrow defeat *defeat* 846.7

narrow down *narrow* 593.14

narrowed 593.9; *shortened* 582.8

narrow escape 811.4, 816.3; *closeness* 593.4

narrow gauge *narrow place* 593.2, *rail* 688.3

narrow-gauge or **narrow-gauged** *narrow* 593.8

narrowing 593.3, 702.6; *simplification* 526.6, *shortening* 582.2, *contracting* 582.10, *narrowed* 593.9, *convergent* 702.7

narrowing gap *narrowing* 702.6

narrow-leaved *narrow* 593.8

narrowly 593.17; *exclusively* 764.10

narrow margin *closeness* 593.4

narrow means *poverty* 486.1

narrow mind *unfair treatment* 342.4

narrow-minded 593.13; *discriminatory* 337.11, *unjust* 342.7, *opinionated* 379.9, *moralistic* 431.12, *convinced* 840.8

narrow-mindedly 593.20; *prejudicially* 337.17, *unjustly* 342.13, *moralistically* 431.16

narrow-mindedness 593.7; *prejudice* 337.3, *unfair treatment* 342.4, *opinionatedness* 379.3, *self-righteousness* 431.7, *conviction* 840.2

narrowness 593.1, Phobias 283, *prejudice* 337.3

narrow-nosed *narrow* 593.8

narrow-petaled *narrow* 593.8

narrow place 593.2

narrows *narrow place* 593.2

narrow squeak *narrow escape* 816.3

narrow the gap *converge* 702.9

narrow thing *narrow place* 593.2

narrow victory *victory* 845.4

narrow waist *thinness* 595.1

narrow-waisted *thin* 595.9

---

narthex *church interior* 83.9, *church architecture* 134.11

nary a one *absence* 718.6

nasal *spoken letter* 5.15, *voiced* 5.37, *phonetic* 205.14, *olfactory* 224.6

nasal bone Human Bones 19

nasal cavity *nose* 19.11, *speech organ* 205.4, *sense of smell* 224.2, *body orifice* 583.3

nasal congestion *lack of sense of smell* 225.2

nasality *mode of speech* 205.6, *hoarseness* 238.2

nasally *odorously* 224.10

nasal mucus *dirt* 112.5

nasal organ *nose* 19.11

nasal tone *hoarseness* 238.2

nascence *conception* 771.4

nascency *conception* 771.4

nascent *embryonic* 771.19

nascent hydrogen Chemical Elements and Common Allotropes 11

Nashua Notable Horses 159

Nashville American States 564

Nassau Countries 566

Nassau scoring *golfing terms* 156.3

Nasser Lakes 568

nastily *unpleasantly* 272.10, *maliciously* 306.15, *discourteously* 411.8, *immorally* 432.18, *evilly* 446.12

nastiness *unpleasantness* 272.1, *malice* 306.2, *discourtesy* 411.1, *immorality* 432.1, *evil* 446.1

nasturtium Flowers 42

nasty *unclean* 112.8, *unhygienic* 114.27, *unpalatable* 220.5, 223.6, *unpleasant* 272.6, 501.5, *malicious* 306.8, *discourteous* 411.5, *offensive* 432.11, *evil* 446.7, *dangerous* 811.7

nasty look *show of disapproval* 438.6

nasty piece of work *malefactor* 306.6

nasty taste *bad taste* 220.3, *unpalatability* 223.2

nasty type *villain* 448.5

natal chart *divination* 86.5

natality *genesis* 21.5

natation *swimming* 164.1

natational *swimming* 164.12

natatorium *swimming place* 164.9

natatory or **natatorial** *swimming* 164.12

nation 18.14; *society* 1.6, *body politic* 50.3, *region* 564.1, *country* 566.1

national 18.16, 61.3, 566.10; *societal* 1.13, *of language* 5.35, *inhabitant* 61.1, *administrative* 564.13, *native* 566.7, *internal* 611.9, *universal* 778.10

National Association for Stock Car Auto Racing (NASCAR) *racing governing bodies* 146.7

National Association of Intercollegiate Athletics (NAIA) Tournament *basketball associations and tournaments* 148.6

National Association of Securities Dealers Automated Quotation System *stock exchange* 457.3

National Baseball Hall of Fame and Museum *baseball* 147.1

National Basketball Association (NBA) *basketball associations and tournaments* 148.6

National Bureau of Standards (NBS) *standard* 589.10

---

national chairperson *political party member* 50.6
national coins 484.11
National Collegiate Athletic Association (NCAA) *basketball associations and tournaments* 148.6, *soccer associations and awards* 163.6
National Collegiate Athletic Association (NCAA) baseball *baseball* 147.1
National Collegiate Athletic Association (NCAA) football *football* 155.1
National Collegiate Athletic Association (NCAA) swimming *swimming associations* 164.10
National Collegiate Athletic Association (NCAA) wrestler *wrestler* 152.12
national colors *flag* 184.8
national consciousness *nation* 18.14, *nationalism* 566.4
national credit *national debt* 488.2
national debt 488.2; *economic indicator* 56.4
national defense *security force* 464.3
national device *national emblem* 184.7
national economy *economy* 56.3
national election *election* 382.6
national emblem 184.7
national entity *nation* 18.14
national flag *flag* 184.8
National Football Conference (NFC) *football associations* 155.14
National Football League (NFL) *football associations* 155.14
national forest *trees* 43.4
National Front *Political Parties* 50
national government *government* 49.1
national grid *electricity* 106.5
National Guard *the military* 58.2, *reinforcements* 77.11, *army* 77.12, *security force* 464.3, 810.13
National Guardsman *security force* 810.13
National Health Service [Brit] *medical practice* 107.3
National Hockey League (NHL) *hockey organizations* 158.7
National Hot Rod Association (NHRA) *racing governing bodies* 146.7
National Hunt [Brit] *famous horse races* 159.13
national income *or* **earnings** *economy* 56.3
national income *income* 492.3
national insurance *social assistance* 825.4
National Invitational Tournament (NIT) *basketball associations and tournaments* 148.6
nationalism 566.4; *political and economic philosophy* 4.6, *nation* 18.14, *love* 299.1, *regionalism* 564.11, *separateness* 753.3
nationalist *or* **nationalistic** *loving* 299.15
nationalist 566.8; *political and economic philosopher* 4.10, *of a political philosophy* 4.14
nationalistic *of a political philosophy* 4.14, *national* 566.10
nationalistically *nationally* 566.13
nationality *society* 1.6, *nation*

18.14, *national* 61.3, *nationalism* 566.4
nationalization *economics* 56.1, *public ownership* 469.7, *transfer of property* 470.4, *taking over* 477.3, *market sector* 483.5
nationalize *economize* 56.11, *transfer property* 470.12, *take over* 477.16, *trade* 480.18
nationalized *economic* 56.10, *corporate* 480.17
National Labor Relations Act (NLRA) *labor law* 57.12
national language *native language* 5.5
National League *baseball leagues and championship games* 147.8
national library *library* 174.14
National Long White Lop-eared *Breeds of Pigs* 16
nationally 566.13; *societally* 1.17, *humanly* 18.18, *regionally* 564.16, *inland* 611.19, *universally* 778.23
national monument *monument* 185.10
National Ocean and Atmospheric Administration (NOAA) *chart* *navigational aid* 690.6
national official *union member* 57.6
national paper *newspaper* 175.2
national park *ecology* 815.3
National Physical Laboratory (NPL) [Brit] *standard* 589.10
national planning *plan* 387.1
National Rifle Association (NRA) *hunting associations* 160.8
national seashore *ecology* 815.3
national security *verbal concealment* 181.3
national service *war measures* 76.18
National Standard Race (NASTAR) *ski race* 162.4
national status *independence* 829.5
national union organization *organized labor* 57.5
National War College *military training* 58.3
nationhood *country* 566.1, *independence* 829.5
nation-state *nation* 18.14, *body politic* 50.3, *region* 564.1, *country* 566.1
nationwide *universal* 778.10
nationwide circulation *publicity* 173.7
native 61.12, 566.7; *race* 1.5, *racial* 1.12, *of language* 5.35, *elemental* 11.26, *wild* 41.15, *inhabitant* 61.1, *intrinsic* 611.11, *naive* 821.3
native accent *mode of speech* 205.6
Native American *race* 1.5, *racial* 1.12
native country 566.6
native custom *custom* 397.4
Native Dancer *Notable Horses* 159
native fashion *custom* 397.4
native land *home* 60.3, *native country* 566.6
native language 5.5
natively *intrinsically* 611.20
Native Mexican *Horse and Pony Breeds* 159
nativeness *national* 61.3
native population *inhabitants* 61.2
native soil *native country* 566.6
native state *natural state* 389.4
native tongue *native language* 5.5, *spoken language* 205.2

Native Turkish pony *Horse and Pony Breeds* 159
native wit *common sense* 315.4
nativity *genesis* 21.5, *type of painting* 143.5, *conception* 771.4
Natron *Lakes* 568
natter *vernacular* 205.8, *be talkative* 207.7, *chat* 210.2, 210.12
natterer *chatterer* 210.7
nattily *dressily* 100.47, *dashingly* 536.10
nattiness *stylishness* 537.2
natty *dressed up* 100.39, *stylish* 100.42, *clean* 111.13, *fashionable* 536.5
natural 526.10; *mineral types* 8.38, *living* 13.28, *musical note* 140.15, *fishing* 154.13, *mountaineering* 161.9, *unprocessed* 389.10, *spontaneous* 396.5, *customary* 397.11, *familiar* 407.8, *naive* 449.9, *821.3, *material* 524.7, *elegant* 527.3, *intrinsic* 611.11, *717.12, *realistic* 719.7, *authentic* 737.6, *eccentric* 782.10
natural bent *aptitude* 127.4
natural cement *industrial ceramics* 129.6
natural color *color* 251.1, *face color* 251.9
natural death *way of dying* 29.5
natural disaster *agent of destruction* 523.7, *misadventure* 848.2
natural dye *dye* 130.8, *coloring agent* 251.5
natural fabric *fabric* 130.1
natural feature *landform* 8.9
natural fiber *fiber* 130.2
natural fly *bait* 154.6
natural fly-fishing *fly-fishing* 154.2
natural food store *food provider* 90.6
natural gas *gas* 106.6, *power source* 514.13
natural habitat 60.16
natural harbor *inlet* 572.9
natural hazard 813.4
natural history *life science* 13.1
natural impulse *spontaneity* 396.2
naturalism *Philosophical Schools of Thought* 4, *Western Art Styles* 133, *theater movements* 136.9, *Western Literary Groups* 139, *realism* 719.3, *verisimilitude* 721.10
naturalist *Philosophical Schools of Thought* 4, *life scientist* 13.26, *plant scientist* 41.11, *materialist* 524.3, *lifelike* 721.19
naturalistic *literary* 139.15, *representational* 187.8, *descriptive* 202.11, *realistic* 719.7, *lifelike* 721.19
naturalistically *verisimilarly* 721.33
naturalization *habituation* 397.7, *evolution* 670.3, *bringing in* 708.4, *pliancy* 781.3
naturalize *accustom* 397.18, *make simple* 526.12, *be converted* 670.12, *give refuge to* 708.15, *assimilate* 781.14
naturalized *wild* 41.15, *resident* 61.11, *habituated* 397.14, *converted* 670.7
naturalized citizen *national* 61.3
natural lake *lake* 568.1
natural language *spoken language* 205.2
natural-language processing *artificial intelligence* 15.21
natural law *formula* 780.7

natural light 246.4; *lighting* 132.16
natural logarithm *logarithm* 6.17, *power* 783.6
naturally 526.16; *skillfully* 127.16, *on the water* 154.15, *spontaneously* 396.8, *informally* 407.11, *naively* 449.15, *materially* 524.9, *gracefully* 527.8, *intrinsically* 611.20, *with the effect of* 676.12
naturally! 295.10; *certainly!* 840.18
natural magic *witchcraft* 86.6
natural medicine *alternative medicine* 107.4
naturalness 526.4; *spontaneity* 396.2, *familiarity* 407.3, *naiveté* 449.4, 821.1, *elegance* 527.1
natural number *number* 6.4
natural philosophy *Branches of Philosophy* 4, *physics* 10.1
natural politeness *etiquette* 406.3
natural power *ability* 340.2
natural product chemistry *Branches of Chemistry* 11
natural resources *supplies* 102.3, *materials* 104.1, *source of supply* 105.4
natural rubber *rubber* 546.3
natural satellite *moon* 7.18, *satellite* 7.19
natural science *physics* 10.1
natural scientist *life scientist* 13.26
natural selection *evolution* 13.23
natural state 389.4
natural talent *aptitude* 127.4, 513.3
natural theology *Theologies* 81
natural trumpet *Musical Instruments* 142
natural violence 520.3
natural virtues *virtues* 447.2
natural weapon *weapon* 78.1
natural world *living world* 13.9, *material world* 524.1, *real world* 719.2
nature 624.5, 717.4, 723.4; *living world* 13.9, *sort* 202.6, *material world* 524.1, *type* 777.4, *characteristic* 779.5
nature cure *therapy* 115.12, *healing art* 115.13
nature of meaning *philosophical problem* 4.8
nature of the beast *nature* 723.4
nature of things *state of affairs* 725.4
nature of time *philosophical problem* 4.8
nature reserve *ecology* 815.3
naturism *nudism* 614.4
naturist *nude person* 614.5
naturistic *naked* 614.12
naturopath *healer* 107.22
naturopathy *alternative medicine* 107.4, *treatment* 107.14, *healing art* 115.13
naught *absolutes* 6.9, *nothingness* 718.2, *zero* 786.1
naughtily *badly* 399.23, *disobediently* 427.14, *immorally* 432.18
naughtiness *bad conduct* 399.7, *disobedience* 427.1, *immorality* 432.1, *sin* 450.3
naughty *badly behaved* 399.16, *disobedient* 427.10, *offensive* 432.11, *troublesome* 824.13
naughty child *badly behaved person* 399.8, *troublemaker* 427.5
naughty word *vulgarism* 5.20, *curse word* 301.4
nauplius *invertebrate larva* 39.19
Nauru *Countries* 566, *Islands* 572

nausea *symptom* 114.3, *gastroenterological disease* 114.11, *drunken behavior* 121.4, *vomiting* 709.7

nauseant *purgative* 115.7

nauseate *green* 260.14, *displease* 272.8, *cause dislike* 291.16, *cause hate* 300.12, *be repulsive* 701.10

nauseated *sick* 114.24, 260.12, *antipathetic* 291.7, *vomiting* 709.12

nauseating *immoderate* 99.6, *unclean* 112.8, *unpalatable* 223.6, *unpleasant* 272.6, *detested* 291.11, *repulsive* 701.4

nauseatingly *sourly* 223.9

nauseous *unclean* 112.8

nautch Dances 135

nautch dancer *dancer* 135.4

nautical **690.14;** *oceanic* 571.7

nautical almanac *type of book* 174.3, *navigational aid* 690.6

nautically 571.10, 690.17

nautical mile General Units 589

nautical mile per hour *nautical speed* 690.11

nautical person 690.12

nautical speed 690.11

nautilus *convoluted thing* 632.3

Nautilus ware Ceramics 129

Navajo Breeds of Sheep 16

Navajo-Churro Breeds of Sheep 16

naval *military* 58.10, 76.28, *nautical* 690.14

naval airman *naval person* 77.25

naval architect *marine scientist* 690.13

naval architecture *shipbuilding* 690.4

naval armament *navy* 77.18

naval commands 77.19

naval engagement *battle* 76.23

naval engineering *shipbuilding* 690.4

naval mine 77.23

naval officer *naval person* 77.25, *nautical person* 690.12

naval operations *offensive warfare* 76.11

naval person 77.25

naval unit 77.20

naval warfare 76.10

nave *church interior* 83.9, *church architecture* 134.11, *axle* 682.7

navel *center* 612.1

navicular bone Human Bones 19

navigable *transportable* 686.7

navigable river *river* 570.1, *channel* 691.10

navigable water *waterway* 690.2

navigate **690.15;** *lead* 126.12, *sail* 150.29, *mountaineer* 161.10, *conduct* 399.21, *find* 565.11, *pilot* 689.15, *aim* 697.14

navigated *transportable* 686.7

navigation **690.5;** *topography* 565.5, *water transportation* 690.1, *direction* 697.1

navigational *managerial* 126.9, *locational* 565.8, *transportable* 686.7

navigational aid **690.6**

navigational instrument *navigational aid* 690.6

navigational radar *position finder* 690.8

navigational satellite *artificial satellite* 7.30

navigational satellite *or* **NAVSAT** *position finder* 690.8

navigation laws **690.10**

navigation lights *safety light* 246.7

navigator *air force person* 77.31,

leader 126.8, *boating person* 150.24, *aircraft personnel* 689.8, *nautical person* 690.12

NAVSTAR Global Positioning System (GPS) *flight control* 689.7, *position finder* 690.8

navy **77.18;** *the military* 58.2, Bean Varieties 90, *blue* 261.5, *security force* 464.3

navy-blue *blue* 261.5

Navy Cross US Military Medals 58

navy specialties **77.24**

navy staff *military staff* 58.5

Naxos Islands 572

nay *refusal* 190.2, *disapproval* 347.2, *rejection* 383.1, *protest* 507.1

nay! *no!* 190.28

nays, the *dissenters* 347.6

naysay *refuse* 190.17, *deny* 332.8

naysayer *negator* 190.8, *opposer* 828.9

naysaying *disagreeing* 190.11, *refutation* 332.1

Nazarenes Western Art Styles 133

Nazism *suppression* 424.2

Nazi swastika *national emblem* 184.7

NBA Championship *basketball associations and tournaments* 148.6

NBA Most Valuable Player *basketball team* 148.2

NBA Playoffs *basketball associations and tournaments* 148.6

NBA Rookie of the Year *basketball team* 148.2

NC-17 *film-rating system* 137.4

NCAA Championship *basketball associations and tournaments* 148.6, *soccer associations and awards* 163.6

N'Dama Breeds of Cattle 16

n-dimensional space *space* 6.33

N'Djamena Countries 566

Neagh Lakes 568

Neanderthal man *primitive humanity* 18.4, *prehistoric human* 653.7

neap *oceanic* 571.7

neap tide *tide* 8.17

neap tide *or* **neap tide** 571.2

near **586.6, 586.12, 586.16;** *intimate* 62.7, *mean* 501.4, *available* 575.5, *close* 593.10, *side direction* 623.2, *future* 650.6, *imminent* 657.9, *approach* 704.15, *similar* 733.7, *next* 770.8

near and far *extensively* 563.18

near at hand *readily available* 575.21, *near* 586.16, *future* 650.6

nearby **586.17, 803.4, 803.7;** *local* 328.8, 564.14, *regionally* 564.16, *available* 575.11, 647.6, *near* 586.6

near death *sick* 114.24

near-death experience *dying* 29.3

near enough *nearly* 586.18

nearer **586.7**

nearest *available* 575.11, *next* 586.8, *close* 645.6

nearest the top *higher* 596.8

near future *future time* 650.1

near gale *wind strength* 9.13

near infrared *electromagnetic radiation* 10.14

nearing *nearer* 586.7, *approaching* 704.10

nearly **586.18;** *barely* 593.18, *comparably* 733.18, *quantitatively* 738.8, *on the whole* 759.13

nearly all *large part* 579.3

nearly the same *similar* 733.7

near miss *short distance* 586.2, *closeness* 593.4, *narrow escape* 811.4, 816.3, *error* 846.2

nearness **586.1, 803.2;** *intimacy* 62.4, *availability* 575.5, *closeness* 593.4, 645.2, *similarity* 733.1, *union* 752.1

near place **586.3**

near rhyme *rhyme* 139.11

near sea level *low* 597.26

nearside *miscellaneous automotive terms* 687.14

near sight *sight defect* 243.2

nearsighted *weak-sighted* 243.10

nearsightedness *visual acuity* 242.2, *sight defect* 243.2

near the ground *low* 597.26

near the surface *shallowly* 599.7

near the wind *directionally* 697.20

near thing *short distance* 586.2, *narrow escape* 811.4, 816.3

near tragedy *narrow escape* 811.4

near ultraviolet *electromagnetic radiation* 10.14

neat *clean* 111.13, *intoxicating* 121.29, *skillful* 127.10, *handling* 216.7, *fastidious* 325.9, *strong to the senses* 516.12, *simple* 526.7, *graceful* 527.4, *fluid* 527.5, *orderly* 765.13

neat and tidy *orderly* 765.13

neat as a pin *orderly* 765.13

neaten *clean* 111.17, *straighten* 630.14, *tidy* 765.21, 807.19

neath *or* **'neath** *low* 597.26

neatly *cleanly* 111.20, *skillfully* 127.16, *elegantly* 527.7, *dashingly* 536.10, *orderly* 765.25, *in place* 767.24

neatly put *graceful* 527.4, *fluid* 527.5

neatly wrought *graceful* 527.4, *fluid* 527.5

neatness *social skill* 127.3, *fastidiousness* 325.4, *simplicity* 526.1, *elegance* 527.1, *orderliness* 765.5

nebbish [Inf] *insubstantial person* 720.5

nebelung Breeds of Cats 35

Nebraska American States 564

nebula **7.6;** *interstellar matter* 7.7

nebulaphobia Phobias 283

nebular hypothesis *nebula* 7.6

nebulé *or* **nebuly** *molding* Architectural Elements 134

nebulosity *nebula* 7.6

nebulous *foggy* 9.51, *murky* 248.5, *difficult* 364.8, *unreal* 720.8, *generalized* 778.12

nebulous star *star* 7.8

necessarily **95.22;** *compellingly* 428.12, *with the effect of* 676.12, *really* 717.22, *in essence* 723.13

necessariness *necessity* 95.1

necessary **95.10;** *logical* 6.83, *necessity* 95.1, *desired* 288.10, *compelling* 428.6, *compulsory* 428.7, *existing* 717.11, *essential* 723.5, *important* 799.7, *certain* 840.7, *inevitable* 840.11

necessary and sufficient condition *reasoning* 6.61

necessary truth *philosophical term* 4.7

necessitarian **95.8;** *inevitable* 95.14

necessitarianism **95.7**

necessitate **95.17;** *compel* 428.8

necessitation **95.5**

necessitative **95.11**

necessitous *needy* 95.12, *poor* 486.8

necessitously *in need* 95.21

necessitousness *poverty* 486.1

necessitude [Arch] *necessity* 95.1

necessity **95.1;** *philosophical term* 4.7, *compulsion* 428.1, *poverty* 486.1, *demonstrable existence* 717.5, *certainty* 840.1, *inevitability* 840.5

Neches Rivers 570

neck *head* 19.6, *veal* 90.25, *part of garment* 100.27, Architectural Elements 134, *golf equipment* 156.5, *pommel horse* 157.7, *peninsula* 572.5, *contracted thing* 582.5, *narrow place* 593.2, *means of connection* 754.4

neck [Inf] *communicate love* 299.25

neck and crop *completely* 759.14

neck and neck *near* 586.6, *on equal terms* 740.9, *as good as* 740.14

neck-and-neck finish *contest* 422.4

neck-and-neck race *stalemate* 740.3

Neckar Rivers 570

neckband *neckwear* 100.29, *circular thing* 631.3, *band* 754.9

neckcloth *neckwear* 100.29

neckerchief *neckwear* 100.29

necking Architectural Elements 134

necking [Inf] *communication of love* 299.6

necklace *neckwear* 100.29, *jewelry* 532.6, *circular thing* 631.3

neck of the womb *organs of reproduction* 21.9

neck of the woods [Inf] *plot* 564.9, *location* 565.1

neckpiece *neckwear* 100.29

neck slice *lamb* 90.27

neckstrap *riding equipment* 159.9

necktie *neckwear* 100.29

neckwear **100.29**

necrolater *idolater* 83.7

necrolatrous *idolatrous* 83.13

necrolatry *idolatry* 83.4

necrological *funeral* 31.9

necrologist *funeral person* 31.5

necrology *biography* 3.5, *death count* 29.10

necromancer *diviner* 86.14, *witch* 86.15

necromancy *divination* 86.5, *witchcraft* 86.6

necromania *delusion* 110.2

necromantic *witchlike* 86.19

necromantically *magically* 86.28

necrophilia *sexual perversion* 20.12

necrophobia Phobias 283

necropolis *burial place* 31.7

necropsy *after death* 29.9

nectar *secreted substance* 24.2, *drink* 93.2, *sweetener* 222.2

nectared *sweet* 222.5

nectarine *orange thing* 258.3

nectarous *sweet* 222.5

nectary *secretory mechanism* 24.3, *flower part* 42.3

need **95.4, 95.16;** *necessity* 95.1, *be insufficient* 98.9, *wish* 288.2, *desire* 288.17, *demand* 356.9, *compulsion* 428.1, *poverty* 486.1, *be poor* 486.14, *incompleteness* 762.1, 806.2, *omission* 762.4, *be incomplete* 762.8, *economic adversity* 848.6

need a break *or* **holiday** *or* **vacation** *be fatigued* 820.5

need a change *be fatigued* 820.5

need an interpreter *be unintelligible* 364.11

need a rest *be fatigued* 820.5

needed *necessary* 95.10, *desired* 288.10
need few words *be concise* 198.5
needful *needy* 95.12
needfully *in need* 95.21
needfulness *indispensability* 95.2
need help *be in a predicament* 725.9
neediness 95.3; *poverty* 486.1, *meagerness* 593.6
needing *needy* 95.12, *unprovided* 98.6, *desirous* 288.13, *incomplete* 762.5
needing water *dry* 560.7
needle *leaf* 41.6, *tree part* 43.2, *fabric-handling tool* 130.12, *material* 144.6, *indicator* 183.7, *sharp-pointed thing* 549.4, *be sharp* 549.15, *opener* 583.2, *navigational aid* 690.6
needle [Inf] *irritate* 302.16, *manipulate* 508.12
needle aspirate *diagnostic procedure* 107.11
needle-flower tree Trees and Shrubs 43
needlelike *sharp* 549.10
needle marks [Inf] *drug use* 121.9
needle-pointed *sharp* 549.10
needles Phobias 283
needle-sharp *sharp* 549.10
needless *superfluous* 99.8
needlessly *superfluously* 99.15
needless risk *rash move* 286.4
needlewoman *artisan* 123.13
needlework *sewing* 130.5
needleworker *clothier* 100.37, *fabric handler* 130.11
need money 848.14
need repair *go wrong* 430.23
need training *be unprepared* 389.14
needy 95.12; *poor* 486.8, *meager* 593.12
needy, the *the poor* 486.7
needy person *poor person* 486.6
Néel temperature Classical Physical Laws 10
neem Trees and Shrubs 43
ne'er *never* 640.8
ne'er a one *absence* 718.6
ne'er-do-well *disreputable character* 371.2, *miscreant* 448.6, *loser* 468.8
nefarious *offending* 53.25, *black-hearted* 254.9, *disreputable* 371.4, *evil* 446.7, *wicked* 448.9
nefariously *disreputably* 371.7, *evilly* 446.12, *wickedly* 448.15
nefariousness *evil* 446.1, *wickedness* 448.1
Nefud Deserts 572
negate 190.16; *discuss* 4.22, *disbelieve* 88.8, *refute* 332.7, *refuse* 347.9, 506.8, *reject* 383.10, *renounce* 383.13, *counteract* 510.7, *abolish* 523.11, *cause not to exist* 718.14, *object* 828.18, *cancel* 834.6, *make impossible* 837.8
negated 190.10; *disavowing* 190.12, *rejected* 383.6, *renounced* 383.9, *canceled* 834.5
negating *disavowing* 190.12, *refuting* 332.6, *renunciation* 383.4, *refused* 506.5, *protesting* 507.5
negation 190.1; *philosophical term* 4.7, *mathematical logic* 6.60, *defense mechanism* 108.23, *refutation* 332.1, *denial* 332.2, *disapproval* 347.2, *rejection* 383.1, *refusal* 506.1, *protest* 507.1, *neutralization* 510.4, *negativeness* 718.3, *cancellation* 834.1

negational 190.9; *disavowing* 190.12, *nonexistent* 190.14
negationist *negator* 190.8
negative 190.15; *numerical* 6.68, 783.7, *electric* 14.47, *film* 132.8, *refusal* 190.2, *negational* 190.9, *disagreeing* 190.11, *denyingly* 190.23, *transparent thing* 249.4, *without hope* 282.7, *disapproval* 347.2, *resistant* 417.6, *critical* 438.13, *refused* 506.5, *protesting* 507.5, *nonexistent* 718.9, *duplicate* 736.4, *inhibitive* 826.14, *uncooperative* 828.14
negative acceleration *deceleration* 693.2
negative answer *refusal* 506.1
negative attitude *negativism* 190.7
negative balance of payments *national debt* 488.2
negative carrier *darkroom equipment* 132.21
negative charge *electric charge* 10.38
negative command *command* 425.1
negative correlation *correlation* 6.58
negative criticism *criticism* 438.4
negative equity *economic adversity* 848.6
negative feedback *circuit function* 14.38
negative ion *ion* 10.54
negatively 190.22; *mathematically* 6.93, *electronically* 14.54, *denyingly* 190.23, *pessimistically* 190.26, *unhopefully* 282.14, *in reply* 332.10, *resistingly* 417.14, *uncooperatively* 506.11, *disapprovingly* 507.10, *inhibitively* 826.24
negativeness 718.3; *negativism* 190.7, *resistance* 417.1, *uncooperativeness* 828.4
negative number *number* 6.4
negative outlook *underestimation* 344.1
negative reinforcement *conditioning* 108.24
negative resistance *circuit function* 14.38
negative result *failure* 846.1
negative review *criticism* 365.3
negative statement *negation* 190.1
negative stimulus 508.4
negative transference *association of ideas* 108.31
negative vote *rejection* 383.1
negativism 190.7; *defense mechanism* 108.23, *lack of hope* 282.2, *inhibition* 826.9
negativist *hopeless person* 282.5, *hinderer* 826.11, *opposer* 828.9
negativistic *without hope* 282.7
negativity *negativism* 190.7, *refutation* 332.1, *protest* 507.1, *negativeness* 718.3, *uncooperativeness* 828.4
negator 190.8
negatory *negational* 190.9
Negev Deserts 572
neglect 96.2; *imprudence* 286.3, *carelessness* 289.2, *be careless* 289.14, *be ungrateful* 311.5, *inconsideration* 318.4, *be neglectful* 326.7, *unthinkingness* 355.3, *forget* 355.10, *disobedience* 375.5, *dissociate* 375.14, *nonuse* 394.1, *not use* 394.9, *inaction* 413.1, *ignore* 413.14, *disesteem* 436.2, *dishonor* 436.20, *nonobservance*

466.1, *not observe* 466.9, *nonachievement* 762.3, *not complete* 762.9, *untidiness* 766.3, *dilapidation* 808.5
neglected 326.6; *bungled* 128.7, *unthanked* 311.3, *disused* 394.8, *undervalued* 436.17, *incomplete* 762.5, *uncompleted* 762.7, *obscure* 800.13
neglectful *imprudent* 286.7, *careless* 289.8, 324.8, *inconsiderate* 318.9, *negligent* 326.4, *unthinking* 355.8, *procrastinating* 375.11, *inactive* 413.9, *disregardful* 436.11, *nonobservant* 466.5, *uncompleted* 762.7, *untidy* 766.11
neglectfully *imprudently* 286.11, *carelessly* 289.18, *negligently* 326.8, *incompletely* 762.10, *unsuccessfully* 846.21
neglectfulness *negligence* 326.1, *nonobservance* 466.1
neglecting *rejecting* 383.2
neglect one's obligations *not observe* 466.9
neglect one's vows *not observe* 466.9
neglector 326.3
negligee *robe* 100.20, *nightwear* 100.21
negligence 324.4, 326.1; *imprudence* 286.3, *carelessness* 289.2, *inattention* 324.1, *tastelessness* 338.3, *inaccuracy* 351.3, *disobedience* 375.5, *nonuse* 394.1, *inaction* 413.1, *sin* 450.3, *nonobservance* 466.1, *incompleteness* 762.1, *nonachievement* 762.3, *untidiness* 766.3, *dilapidation* 808.5, *hastiness* 818.2
negligent 326.4; *clumsy* 128.6, *imprudent* 286.7, *careless* 289.8, 324.8, *unrefined* 338.7, *unthinking* 355.8, *procrastinating* 375.11, *unpremeditated* 389.7, *inactive* 413.9, *disregardful* 436.11, *nonobservant* 466.5, *untidy* 766.11, *hasty* 818.3
negligent dress *dressing* 100.2
negligently 326.8; *dressily* 100.47, *unskillfully* 128.12, *imprudently* 286.11, *carelessly* 289.18, *inattentively* 324.12, 466.13, *forgetfully* 355.14, *inactively* 413.16, *incompletely* 762.10, *unsuccessfully* 846.21
negligently dressed *in dishabille* 100.40
negligible *little* 580.7, *unimportant* 800.10
negligibly *infinitesimally* 580.13, *unimportantly* 800.21
negotiability *compromise* 461.1
negotiable *negotiated* 57.16, 460.5, *compromising* 461.4, *workable* 509.8, *transferable* 685.7
negotiable instrument *paper money* 484.14
negotiate 460.6; *trade* 56.12, *have an industrial dispute* 57.20, *unionize* 57.21, *mediate* 75.6, 772.19, *represent* 80.6, *consult* 176.11, *confer* 210.13, *deal* 457.9, *compromise* 461.7, *bargain* 480.20, *offer to buy* 504.12, *summit* 600.11, *cross* 692.17, *settle* 735.26
negotiate a contract *unionize* 57.21
negotiate a loan *lend* 475.6
negotiate a trade-off *pay* 489.16
negotiated 57.16, 460.5; *disputed* 57.15, *pacificatory* 74.8, *contractual* 480.16, *settled* 735.16

negotiated points *bargaining* 57.9
negotiated release *safety* 810.1
negotiate for *substitute for* 80.5
negotiating *bargaining* 57.9, *negotiated* 57.16, 460.5
negotiating body *representative body* 79.2
negotiating rights *bargaining* 57.9
negotiation 460.1; *mediation* 75.1, *consultation* 176.4, *compromise* 461.1, *bargaining* 480.10
negotiation points *bargaining terms* 57.10
negotiations *strike* 57.8, *bargaining* 57.9, *consultation* 176.4, *debate* 210.3, *negotiation* 460.1, *summit meeting* 600.3
negotiator 460.4; *mediator* 75.2, *delegate* 79.1, *agent* 80.3, *trader* 480.11, *summit meeting* 600.3, *interfacer* 616.3, *middleman* 772.7
Negrillo *race* 1.5
Negrito *race* 1.5
Negro *race* 1.5, Rivers 570
Negroid *racial* 1.12
Negroid race *race* 1.5
Negros Islands 572
Nehru jacket *jacket* 100.18
Neiderviller ware Ceramics 129
neigh *animal sound* 240.1, *make an animal sound* 240.7
neighbor *near place* 586.3, *juxtapose* 586.14
neighborhood *group* 18.13, *habitat* 60.1, *environmental* 60.17, *inhabitants* 61.2, *region* 564.1, *plot* 564.9, *availability* 575.5, *near place* 586.3, *surroundings* 615.1, *surrounding* 615.4
neighborhood store *store* 483.8
neighborhood watch *law enforcement officer* 53.8, *surveillant* 810.12
neighboring *local* 564.14, *near* 586.6, *surrounding* 615.4, *nearby* 803.4
neighborliness *friendship* 62.1, *sociability* 408.1
neighborly *friendly* 62.5, *sociable* 408.11, *benevolent* 825.21
neighing *ululant* 240.4
nein! [Ger] *no!* 190.28
Neisse Rivers 570
neither confirm nor deny *keep secret* 182.11, *be taciturn* 208.7
neither good nor bad *mediocre* 742.7
neither here nor there *away* 576.19, *nowhere* 718.17, *extraneously* 724.16, *irrelatively* 728.16, *medianly* 742.12, *irresolutely* 772.23
neither hide nor hair *not any* 718.7
neither hot nor cold *irresolute* 772.13
neither more nor less *equal* 740.8
neither one nor the other *compromising* 461.4
neither one thing nor the other *irresolute* 772.13, *indeterminacy* 841.6
Nejdi Breeds of Sheep 16
Nellore Breeds of Cattle 16, Breeds of Sheep 16
nelophobia Phobias 283
Nelson Rivers 570
Neman Rivers 570
nemesia Flowers 42

Nemesis Deities 82, *avenger* 441.6, *retribution* 454.7

nemesis *inevitability* 95.6, *retaliation* 420.1

Nemi Lakes 568

nemine contradicente or **nem. con.** [L] *in accord* 735.33

nemine dissentiente or **nem. diss.** [L] *in accord* 735.33

Neneh Deities 82

neo-Bechstein piano Musical Instruments 142

neoclassical Furniture Styles 101, *literary* 139.15

neoclassicism Western Art Styles 133, Architectural Styles 134, Western Literary Groups 139

neocolonial *governing* 49.25

neocolonialism *colonial government* 49.15

neo-Darwinian *evolutionary* 13.34

neo-Darwinism *evolution* 13.23

neo-Darwinist *life scientist* 13.26

neodymium Chemical Elements and Common Allotropes 11

neodymium-glass laser *laser* 10.18

neoexpressionism Western Art Styles 133

Neo-Gothic architecture Architectural Styles 134

neoimpressionism Western Art Styles 133

neo-Lamarckian *evolutionary* 13.34

neo-Lamarckism *evolution* 13.23

Neolithic *primal* 653.14

neological *worded* 5.38, *new* 652.9

neologically *newly* 652.21

neologism or **neology** *new word* 5.18

neologism *newness* 652.1

neologist *modern person* 652.8

neologistic *new* 652.9

neologistical *worded* 5.38, *new* 652.9

neologistically or **neologically** *lexically* 5.46

neologistically *newly* 652.21

neologize *word* 5.43

neology *newness* 652.1

neomycin *fungal antibiotic* 47.7

neon Chemical Elements and Common Allotropes 11

neonatal *embryonic* 771.19

neonate *beginner* 771.14

neonatology Medical Specialties 107

neon light *electron tube* 14.40, *electric light* 246.6

neon lighting *electric light* 246.6

neophilia *newness* 652.1

neophiliac *modern person* 652.8

neophobia Phobias 283

neophyte *learner* 48.6, *religious person* 81.9, *beginner* 398.2, 771.14, *new arrival* 652.7, *convert* 670.6

neophytic *new* 652.9

neoplasm *cancer* 114.15

neoplastic disease *disease* 114.4

neoplasticism Western Art Styles 133

Neoplatonic *idealistic* 525.10

Neoplatonically *subjectively* 525.14

Neoplatonism Philosophical Schools of Thought 4, *idealism* 525.5

Neoplatonist Philosophical Schools of Thought 4, *nonmaterialist* 525.7

neoprene *rubber* 546.3

neorealism Western Literary Groups 139

neoromanticism Western Art Styles 133

neotenous *developmental* 13.33, *amphibian* 37.14

neotenous amphibian *young amphibian* 37.11

neoteny *developmental biology* 13.22

neoteric *modern person* 652.8

Nepal Countries 566

nepenthe *analgesic* 115.6, *soporific* 415.6

neper Scientific and Technical Units 589

nephew *man in the family* 32.12, *family member* 65.2

nephological *cloudy* 9.44

nephology *meteorology* 9.1

nephophobia Phobias 283

nephrology Medical Specialties 107

Nephthys Deities 82

ne plus ultra [L] *limit* 761.4, *ideal* 805.6

nepotism *favoritism* 337.5, *injustice* 342.3

nepotistic *discriminatory* 337.11

Neptune Planets and Their Satellites 7, *planet* 7.16, Deities 82, *legendary sea being* 571.4

Neptunian *astronomical* 7.33

neptunium Chemical Elements and Common Allotropes 11

nerd [Inf] *unskilled person* 128.3, *boring person* 296.4

Nereid Planets and Their Satellites 7, *minor deity* 82.2, *legendary sea being* 571.4

Nereus *legendary sea being* 571.4

neritic *coastal* 8.54

neroli oil *figurative usage* 258.4

nerve *sense organ* 212.4, *courage* 284.1, *audacity* 400.3, *defiance* 416.1, *endurance* 516.4, *assurance* 621.8, *determination* 674.2

nerve cell *sense organ* 212.4

nerve center *sense organ* 212.4, *center of activity* 612.4

nerved *determined* 674.5

nerve end or **nerve ending** *sense organ* 212.4

nerve fiber *sense organ* 212.4

nerve gas *chemical warfare* 76.5

nerveless *insensible* 213.4, *weak-willed* 517.10

nervelessness *indecisiveness* 517.2

nerve oneself *strengthen oneself* 516.16

nerve-racking *in suspense* 604.12, *unsafe* 811.8

nerves *nervous system* 19.14, *ill health* 114.1, *symptoms of fear* 283.3, *restlessness* 414.7, *agitation* 684.1

nerves of steel *courage* 284.1, *determination* 674.2

nervily *audaciously* 400.20, *defiantly* 416.9

nerviness *defiance* 416.1

nervosity *agitation* 684.1

nervous *internal* 19.23, *fearful* 283.10, *fidgety* 414.14, *weak-willed* 517.10, *agitated* 684.15

nervous breakdown *mental disorder* 108.8, *mental breakdown* 110.4

nervously *fearfully* 283.19, *weakly* 517.14, *moderately* 521.10, *agitatedly* 684.27

nervous Nellie [Inf] *frightened person* 283.8

nervousness *fearfulness* 283.2,

restlessness 414.7, *defensiveness* 419.4, *indecisiveness* 517.2, *agitation* 684.1, *sense of danger* 811.3

nervous person *frightened person* 283.8

nervous system 19.14; *sense organ* 212.4

nervous tic *anxiety disorder* 108.11, *spasm* 684.8

nervous wreck *frightened person* 283.8

nervy *oversensitive* 267.4, *courageous* 284.9, *audacious* 400.10, *fidgety* 414.14, *defiant* 416.5

nescience *ignorance* 318.2, 349.1

nescient *ignorant* 349.5

Ness Lakes 568

ness *mountain* 569.1

nest 36.22; *dwelling* 36.4, 40.7, Collective Names 59, *home* 60.3, *natural habitat* 60.16, *take up residence* 60.24, *packet* 578.4, *source* 771.3, *throng* 795.4, *shelter* 812.4

nest building *dwelling* 36.4

nest egg *reserves* 102.5, *reserve* 105.3, *precaution* 287.4, *preparations* 388.2, *wealth* 485.1, *insurance* 810.10

nesting *programming concepts* 15.24

nestle *take up residence* 60.24, *feel pleasure* 214.12, *communicate love* 299.25

nestling *young animal* 26.4, *young bird* 36.17, *beginner* 771.14

Nestor *sage* 4.11

Net Constellations 7

nest site *dwelling* 36.4

net Fabrics and Fibers 130, *basketball court* 148.3, *fish* 154.14, *hockey areas* 158.2, *stadium* 163.2, *tennis court* 165.3, *transparent thing* 249.4, *profit* 467.6, *gainful* 467.10, *be profitable* 467.21, *propertied* 470.9, *receive* 473.13, 492.7, *braid* 609.3, *interweave* 609.8, *enclosing thing* 619.3, *surplus* 750.8, *trap* 813.6, *stratagem* 822.2

net [Inf] *linkage* 752.3

net assets *personal estate* 470.6

netball Sporting Activities 145, *tennis terms* 165.5

nether *lower* 597.14

Netherlands, The Countries 566

Netherlands Tulip Rally *automobile rallies* 146.6

nether world *evil place* 446.6

net income *economic factor* 56.8

net national product (NNP) *produce* 522.5

net player *tennis participant* 165.6

net position *tennis terms* 165.5

net posts *badminton terms* 165.11

net profit *return* 453.6, *profit* 467.6

net profit or **loss** *baseline* 601.4

net profits *money received* 492.2

net receipts *earnings* 467.5, *something received* 473.2, *money received* 492.2

net result *effect* 676.1

net return *earnings* 467.5

net revenue *earnings* 467.5

net score *golfing terms* 156.3

netted *woven* 130.15, *trapped* 813.5

Nettling Lakes 568

netting *farm building* 36.4, Fabrics and Fibers 130, *enclosing thing* 619.3

nettle *irritate* 302.16, *make irascible* 303.16, *sharp-pointed growth* 549.5

nettled *resentful* 302.8, *cross* 303.11

nettle family *seed plant* 41.3

nettle rash *skin disease* 114.16

net ton General Units 589

net (total) *total* 738.4

net weight *weighing* 538.4

network *combinatorics* 6.63, *circuit* 10.43, 14.37, *communications device* 15.26, *telecommunication* 169.7, *communicate* 169.18, *find means* 511.8, *weave* 552.4, *braid* 609.3, *linkage* 752.3, *link* 752.18, *association* 754.2, *intercommunicate* 754.15, *combine* 757.9

network adaptor *computer part* 15.4

network controller *computer part* 15.4

network database *database* 15.15

networked *combinatory* 757.6

networker *hearer* 228.7

networking *mutual relationship* 827.3

network television *television (TV)* 172.5

net worth *personal estate* 470.6

Neuchâtel Lakes 568

Neue Sachlichkeit Western Art Styles 133

Neumann's law Classical Physical Laws 10

neural *internal* 19.23

neuralgia *neurological disease* 114.20

neural net *artificial intelligence* 15.21

neurasthenia *mental breakdown* 110.4, *psychiatric disease* 114.21

neurilemmitis *neurological disease* 114.20

neurohormone *hormone* 12.16

neurological disease 114.20; *disease* 114.4

neurologically *medically* 107.35

neurology Medical Specialties 107

neuron *nervous system* 19.14, *sense organ* 212.4

neuropath *sick person* 114.22

neuropsychiatric *psychological* 108.36

neuropsychiatrist *psychiatrist* 108.34

neuropsychiatry *psychiatry* 108.2

neuropsychology Psychological Theories, Schools 108

neuropteran or **neuropterous** *insectile* 40.11

neuroscience *biochemistry* 13.3

neurosis 108.9; *mental disorder* 108.8, *mental breakdown* 110.4, *ill health* 114.1

neurosurgery Medical Specialties 107

neurotic *psychologically disturbed* 108.39, *insane person* 110.5, *mentally ill* 110.11

neurotically *psychologically* 108.42, *insanely* 110.15

neurotic-depressive reaction *neurosis* 108.9

neurotic disorder *neurosis* 108.9

neuroticism *neurosis* 108.9, *mental breakdown* 110.4

neurotic personality *personality disorder* 108.7

neurotransmitter biochemistry *biochemical applications* 14.30

neurotransmitter pharmacology *biochemical applications* 14.30

Neuse Rivers 570

Neusiedler Lakes 568

neuter *grammatical term* 5.29, *of grammar* 5.41, *sexlessness* 20.13, *undersexed* 20.20, *make infertile* 23.9, *make impotent* 515.15, *material* 524.7, *take off* 749.7

neutering *that which makes infertile* 23.4, *helplessness* 515.3

neutral *electric potential* 10.40, *acid* 11.27, *electric* 14.47, *pacific* 74.7, *colorless* 252.5, *gray* 255.6, *indifferent person* 289.6, *impartial* 289.9, 338.6, *avoiding* 386.9, *inactive* 413.9, *disinterested* 443.4, *irresolute* 461.6, *politically moderate* 521.4, *nonconforming* 728.10, *unjoined* 753.9, *mediatory* 772.11, *free person* 829.9, *free* 829.11

neutral color *color* 251.1

neutral-density (ND) filter *filter* 132.14

neutral ground *middle ground* 772.4

neutral hue *colorlessness* 252.1

neutralist *indifferent person* 289.6, *moderate person* 772.8

neutrality *coexistence* 73.3, *impartiality* 289.3, 338.2, *shyness* 386.3, *disinterestedness* 443.1, *irresolution* 461.3, *moderation* 521.1, *nonconformity* 728.4, *middle ground* 772.4, *noninterference* 829.3

neutralization 510.4; *chemical reaction* 11.8, *weakness* 517.1, *canceling out* 834.2

neutralize *react* 11.38, *remedy* 115.16, *make inactive* 415.16, *counteract* 510.7, *remove power from* 515.13, *mitigate* 521.9, *abolish* 523.11, *cancel out* 834.8

neutralized *analytic* 11.32, *canceled* 834.5

neutralizer *counteractant* 510.5

neutralizing *counteracting* 510.6, *canceling out* 834.3

neutrally *colorlessly* 252.9, *impartially* 289.19, 338.13, *disinterestedly* 443.8, *irresolutely* 461.10, *individualistically* 728.20, *in isolation* 753.24, *midway* 772.22, *freely* 829.22

neutral nation *country* 566.1

neutral person *moderate person* 772.8

neutral stick *hockey equipment* 158.3

neutral tint *colorlessness* 252.1, *grayness* 255.1

neutral zone *hockey areas* 158.2

neutrino *elementary particle* 10.53, *little thing* 580.3

neutron *atom* 10.52, *elementary particle* 10.53, *physical element* 524.5, *little thing* 580.3

neutron bomb *bomb* 78.15, *nuclear power production* 514.10

neutron number *isotope* 10.57

neutron star *stellar evolution* 7.10

neutrophil *blood* 555.4

Nevada American States 564

névé *snow* 9.30, *rock face* 161.6

never 640.8; *not ever* 718.16

never! *no!* 190.28, 506.12, *wonderful!* 294.20

never again *conclusively* 773.26, *once* 788.23

never a one *absence* 718.6

never cease *be eternal* 644.7, *be infinite* 798.9

never darken my door again! *go!* 709.30

never despair *hold out* 377.13

never despair! 281.18

never die *be infinite* 798.9

never end *be diffuse* 199.5, *bore* 296.8, *be infinite* 798.9

never-ending *diffuse* 199.3, *eternal* 644.4, *uncompleted* 762.7, *continuous* 774.9, *eternal* 798.7

never-ending story *nonachievement* 762.3

never-failing *successful* 845.8

never full *gluttonous* 119.3

never give up hope *hold out* 377.13

never hear the last of *harp* 797.17

never ill *of good constitution* 113.5

never in a million years *never* 640.8

never in a month of Sundays *never* 640.8, *unexpectedly* 839.9

Neverland Imaginary Places 360

never learn *be foolish* 353.1

never let go *show tenaciousness* 471.8

never let liquor pass one's lips *be sober* 120.8

never mind! *who cares?* 289.21, *no matter!* 800.22

nevermore *never* 640.8

never on time *late* 658.5

never out of date *timeless* 640.3

never out of fashion *timeless* 640.3

never say die *hold out* 377.13, *be strong* 516.14

never say die! *never despair!* 281.18, *go on!* 669.11

never say quit *hold out* 377.13

never solved *unexplained* 364.6

never stop *try* 414.21, *be full of vigor* 518.4

nevertheless *how* 691.16

never the same *changeable* 666.3

never touch *be self-restrained* 455.10

never touch a drop *be sober* 120.8

never vary *have a habit* 397.16

Nevis Islands 572

Nevis, Ben Mountains and Hills 569

nevus *mark* 533.2

new 394.7, 652.9; *fresh* 260.10, *unaccustomed* 398.3, *newly* 652.21, *novel* 737.5, *extra* 748.10, *embryonic* 771.19

New-Age Traveler *nonconformist* 782.7

New Alliance party Political Parties 50

new arrival 652.7, 724.6

new beginning 771.13; *restoration* 671.2

new birth *new life* 28.8, *revival* 809.3

newborn *beginning* 583.14, *new arrival* 652.7, *immature* 652.12, *beginner* 771.14, *embryonic* 771.19

newborn babe *innocent person* 449.5, *naive person* 821.2

new boy *entrant* 706.7, *beginner* 771.14

New Britain Islands 572

new broom *new arrival* 652.7, *abrogator* 834.4

New Brunswick Canadian Provinces 564

New Brutalism Architectural Styles 134

New Caledonia Islands 572

new chapter *new beginning* 771.13

new city *city* 567.1

New Comedy *historic comedy* 136.12

newcomer *beginner* 398.2, *innocent person* 449.5, *new arrival* 652.7, 724.6, *entrant* 706.7

new convert *new arrival* 652.7

New Criticism Western Literary Groups 139

new criticism *criticism* 365.3

New Delhi Countries 566

New Democratic party Political Parties 50

new departure *originality* 737.1

New Drama theater movements 136.9

new edition *reprint* 21.3, *repeat* 797.5, *reconsideration* 807.9

new energy *revival* 809.3

New England *regions of the United States* 564.7

New England accent *regional pronunciation* 205.7

New England colonial architecture Architectural Styles 134

New English Bible *Christian text* 81.16

new face *entrant* 706.7, *new arrival* 724.6

newfangled *worded* 5.38, *unfamiliar* 652.10

newfangled expression *new word* 5.18

newfangledness *newness* 652.1

Newfie Nicknames for Inhabitants 61

new flame [Inf] *loved one* 299.13

new-fledged *young* 26.11

New Forest pony Horse and Pony Breeds 159

Newfoundland Breeds of Dogs 35, Canadian Provinces 564, Islands 572

new franc *national coins* 484.11

new generation *the young* 26.10, *avant-garde* 652.6

New Georgia Group Islands 572

new girl *entrant* 706.7, *beginner* 771.14

New Guinea Islands 572

New Hampshire Breeds of Fowl 16, American States 564

New Hebrides Islands 572

new high *summit* 744.4

new hope *revival* 809.3

new humanism Western Literary Groups 139

new idea *reconsideration* 807.9

New Ireland Islands 572

New Jersey American States 564

New Jerusalem *heaven* 82.15

new kid on the block [Inf] *new arrival* 652.7, 724.6

New Kirgiz Horse and Pony Breeds 159

new leaf *new start* 652.5, *new beginning* 771.13, *improvement* 807.1

new lease on life *new start* 652.5

new life 28.8; *revival* 809.3

newline (NL) *character* 15.18

New Look *trendiness* 652.2

new look *fashion* 536.1, *new start* 652.5, *repair* 809.1

new-look *renewed* 652.14

newly 394.14, 652.21; *originally* 737.8

newly fledged *newly hatched* 36.20

newly hatched 36.20

newly opened *enrolled* 771.24

newly poor, the *the poor* 486.7

newly produced *new* 652.9

newly rich, the *the rich* 485.7

newlywed *married* 64.16

newlyweds *married couple* 64.9, *lovers* 299.12

new-made *new* 652.9

new man *liberated man* 32.13

new man or woman *modern person* 652.8, *convert* 670.6

Newmarket Card Games 167

new mathematics *mathematics* 6.1

new member *new arrival* 652.7, *entrant* 706.7

New Mexico American States 564

new-minted *new* 652.9

new money *money* 485.2

new moon *moon* 7.18

new morality *sexology* 20.14

new-mown lawn or field *source of fragrance* 226.2

newness 394.2, 652.1; Phobias 283, *immaturity* 389.3, *present day* 647.2, *originality* 737.1

new objectivity Western Art Styles 133

New Orleans jazz *jazz* 140.5

new page *new beginning* 771.13

new penny *national coins* 484.11

new production *production* 136.14, *newness* 652.1

new realism Western Art Styles 133

new resident *new arrival* 724.6

new resolution *improvement* 807.1

news 171.1; *information* 170.1, *public information* 170.5, *publication* 173.1, *communication* 176.3, *matter of interest* 328.3, *important matter* 799.2, *warning* 814.1

news agency *information source* 170.6, *news source* 171.4

news analysis *news story* 171.3

news article *news story* 171.3, *print news* 171.7

news blackout *censorship* 503.4

news brief *broadcast news* 171.6

news bulletin *broadcast news* 171.6

news bureau chief *print journalist* 175.5

news camera crew *broadcasting personnel* 172.11

news cameraman or camerawoman *broadcasting personnel* 172.11

newscast *broadcast news* 171.6

newscaster *professional worker* 123.11, *broadcasting personnel* 172.11

news commentator *broadcasting personnel* 172.11

news conference *news event* 171.2, *public relations (PR)* 173.8

news coverage *coverage* 613.16

news crew *broadcasting personnel* 172.11

newsdealer *retailer* 482.11

news dispatch *news story* 171.3

news event 171.2

news flash *broadcast news* 171.6

news gathering *news reporting* 171.5, *print journalism* 175.4

news happening *news event* 171.2

newshawk [Inf] *print journalist* 175.5

newshound [Inf] *print journalist* 175.5

news interpreter 365.7

news item *news story* 171.3

newsletter *news* 171.1, *publication* 173.1, *magazine* 175.3, *periodical publication* 641.6

newsmagazine *news* 171.1, *magazine* 175.3
newsmaker *celebrity* 799.6
newsman *professional worker* 123.11, *print journalist* 175.5
news media *news* 171.1
newsmonger *informer* 170.8, *news source* 171.4
newspaper 175.2; *news* 171.1, *publication media* 173.6, *periodical* 175.1
newspaperish *periodical* 175.6
newspaperman *print journalist* 175.5
newspaper publishing *print journalism* 175.4
newspaperwoman *print journalist* 175.5
newspapery *periodical* 175.6
newspeak *jargon* 5.21, *vernacular* 205.8, *equivocation* 380.1
news photographer *print journalist* 175.5
newsprint *paper* 104.5
newsprint ink *black pigment* 254.2
news program *broadcast news* 171.6
newsreader [Brit] *communications software* 15.27, *broadcasting personnel* 172.11
newsreel *broadcast news* 171.6
news release *news story* 171.3
news report *news story* 171.3, *broadcast news* 171.6
news reporter *news reporting* 171.5, *print journalist* 175.5
news reporting 171.5; *print journalism* 175.4
news source 171.4; *news interpreter* 365.7
newsstand *stall* 483.9
news story 171.3; *print news* 171.7
news syndicate *news source* 171.4
new start 652.5
news update *broadcast news* 171.6
new supply *revival* 809.3
newswoman *professional worker* 123.11, *print journalist* 175.5
newsworthily 171.10
newsworthy 171.8, 175.7, 799.12
newsy [Inf] *communicative* 169.16, *newsworthy* 171.8, 175.7, *conversational* 210.10
new tack *new beginning* 771.13
new technology *manufacture* 522.2
new term *new word* 5.18
New Testament *Christian text* 81.16
new things *Phobias* 283
New Thought *trendiness* 652.2
newtlike *amphibian* 37.14
new to *unaccustomed* 398.3
newton *Scientific and Technical Units* 589
Newtonian mechanics *classical physics* 10.2
Newtonian telescope *telescope* 7.25
Newton Pippin *Apple Varieties* 44
Newton's law of cooling *Classical Physical Laws* 10
Newton's law of gravitation *Classical Physical Laws* 10
Newton's laws of motion *Classical Physical Laws* 10
Newton's method *Mathematical Concepts* 6
Newton's rings *Classical Physical Laws* 10

new to the job *immature* 652.12
new town *town* 567.2
New Wave *Western Literary Groups* 139, *rock music* 140.6
new wave *trendiness* 652.2
new way *way* 399.10
new word 5.18
New World *world region* 564.6
New World monkey *primate* 35.17
new wrinkle [Inf] *newness* 652.1
New Year *Jewish Holy Days and Seasons* 85
New York 567.6; *American States* 564, *major US cities* 567.5
New York school *Western Art Styles* 133
New Zealand *Countries* 566, *Islands* 572
New Zealand Romney Marsh *Breeds of Sheep* 16
next 586.8, 770.8; *close* 645.6, *sequential* 770.7, *after* 770.14
next-door *local* 564.14, *near* 586.6, *nearby* 586.17, 803.4
next-door neighbor *near place* 586.3
next generation *avant-garde* 652.6
next-generation *caused* 676.5
next in line *beneficiary* 473.6
next installment *sequel* 770.5
next month *in the future* 650.13
next of kin *family* 65.1
next step *development* 679.4
next to *nearby* 803.7
next week *in the future* 650.13
next week *or* **month** *or* **year** *future time* 650.1
next world *after death* 29.9, *life without end* 644.2, *future condition* 650.3
next year *in the future* 650.13
nexus *critical time* 659.3, *association* 754.2, *means of connection* 754.4, *consecutiveness* 774.1, *gist* 799.4
Nguni *Breeds of Cattle* 16
Niamey *Countries* 566
nibble *bite* 92.10, *chew* 92.22, *taste* 92.24, 219.5, *appetizer* 219.2
nibbler *eater* 92.15
nibbles *snack* 90.8, *hors d'oeuvre* 90.13
nibbling *delicate eating* 92.3, *chewing* 92.19
Nibelung *little person* 580.5
niblick *golf equipment* 156.5
Nicaragua *Countries* 566, *Lakes* 568
nice *clean* 111.13, *pleasant* 214.7, 271.5, *benevolent* 305.7, *fastidious* 325.9, *accurate* 350.3, *courteous* 410.6, *kind* 445.12
nice body *attractiveness* 529.2
nicely *pleasantly* 271.12, *benevolently* 305.13, *courteously* 410.13, *kindly* 445.20
nice-nellyish *moralistic* 431.12
nice-nellyism *self-righteousness* 431.7
niceness *pleasantness* 271.1, *benevolence* 305.1, *fastidiousness* 325.4, *courtesy* 410.1, *kindness* 445.3
nice predicament *predicament* 824.5
nicety *accuracy* 350.1, *subtlety* 534.2
niche *ecology* 13.25, *hiding place* 181.2, *compartment* 578.2, *cavity* 635.3, *category* 767.6
nichts [Ger] *zero* 786.1
nick *crack* 587.2, 587.7, *notch* 636.1, 636.5

nick [Brit inf] *arrest* 55.12
nickel *Chemical Elements and Common Allotropes* 11, *US coinage* 484.10
nickel coinage *coinage* 484.13
nickel defense *defense* 155.9
nicker *animal sound* 240.1, *make an animal sound* 240.7
nicknack *cheap thing* 800.7
nickname *name* 202.8
nicknamed *named* 202.13
nicknaming *nomenclature* 202.7
nick of time *critical time* 659.3
Nicobar Islands *Islands* 572
Nicolette *Famous Lovers* 299
Nicosia *Countries* 566
nicotiana *Flowers* 42
nicotinamide adenine dinucleotide (NAD) *coenzyme* 12.12
nicotinamide adenine dinucleotide phosphate (NADP) *coenzyme* 12.12
nicotine *addictive drug* 117.10, *tobacco* 121.23
nicotinic acid *vitamin* 12.13
nictitation *faulty vision* 243.1
nidicolous *newly hatched* 36.20
nidification *dwelling* 36.4
nidifugous *newly hatched* 36.20
nidify *nest* 36.22
nidus *dwelling* 40.7
niece *woman in the family* 33.13, *family member* 65.2
niello *black pigment* 254.2, *blacken* 254.11
niente Musical Terms and Expression Marks 140
nierembergia *Flowers* 42
Nietzschean *Philosophical Schools of Thought* 4
Nietzscheanism *Philosophical Schools of Thought* 4
Nietzscheism *Philosophical Schools of Thought* 4
Niflheim *evil place* 446.6
nifty pace [Inf] *swiftness* 694.1
Niger *Countries* 566, *Rivers* 570
Nigeria *Countries* 566
niggard *miser* 501.3
niggardliness *selfishness* 444.1, *meanness* 501.1
niggardly *not enough* 98.5, *selfish* 444.4, *mean* 501.4, *meanly* 501.8, *sparse* 796.6
niggle *criticize* 438.19
niggling *criticism* 438.4, *critical* 438.13, *trivial* 800.14
nigh *near* 586.6, 586.16, *future* 650.6
night 656.3; *type of table* 101.5, *that which makes invisible* 245.2, *blackness* 254.1, *Phobias* 283, *nighttime* 656.1
night and day *frequently* 661.7, *oscillation* 683.1, *continuously* 774.16
night attack *military attack* 418.2
night blind *visually impaired* 243.9
night blindness *vitamin deficiency disease* 12.14, *faulty vision* 243.1, *darkness* 247.1
nightcap *nightwear* 100.21, *parting* 705.3
nightcap [Inf] *drink* 93.2, *soporific* 415.6, *moderator* 521.2,
nightclothes *nightwear* 100.21
nightclub *drink provider* 93.15, *dance hall* 135.3, *club* 138.7, *night* 656.3
night court *type of court* 54.9
night dew *dew* 559.6
nightdress *nightwear* 100.21
nightfall 714.5; *night* 656.3

night falls *become dark* 247.9
night fighter *military aircraft* 77.30
night glasses *visual aid* 242.14
nightgown *nightwear* 100.21
nighthawk [Inf] *night* 656.3
nightie [Inf] *nightwear* 100.21
nightingale *songbird* 36.12, *night* 656.3
nightingales Collective Names 59
nightjar *night* 656.3
nightlife *night* 656.3
night-light *lantern* 246.8, *night* 656.3
nightly 656.6; *evening* 656.4, *cyclic* 663.7, *cyclically* 663.15
nightmare *frightener* 283.7, *fantasy* 360.5, *night* 656.3, *illusion* 720.2, *false alarm* 814.4
nightmare disorder *sleep disorder* 108.20
night nurse *nurse* 107.23
Night of the Long Knives *slaughter* 30.5
night owl [Inf] *night* 656.3
night person *night* 656.3
night safe *vault* 105.9
night school *type of school* 48.12, *night* 656.3
night shift *night* 656.3
night-shift *negotiated* 57.16
night-shift work *bargaining terms* 57.10
nightshirt *nightwear* 100.21
night soil *feces* 25.5, *dirt* 112.5
night sounds *danger signal* 811.5
nightspot *club* 138.7
nightstand *type of table* 101.5
night things *night* 656.3
nighttime 656.1; *night* 656.3, *evening* 656.4, *late hour* 658.2
night vision *visual acuity* 242.2
night watch *guard* 419.15
night watchman *observer* 242.15, *guard* 419.15, *security force* 464.3, *closer* 584.5, *surveillant* 810.12
nightwear 100.21
nigrescence *blackness* 254.1
nigrescent *black* 254.5
nigritude *blackness* 254.1
nigrosine *black pigment* 254.2
nihil [L] *zero* 786.1
nihilism Philosophical Schools of Thought 4, *anarchism* 51.3, *defeatism* 413.7
nihilist Philosophical Schools of Thought 4, *anarchist* 51.4, *malefactor* 306.6, *inactive person* 413.8, *destroyer* 523.6
nihilistic *anarchistic* 51.7, *disorderly* 766.15
nihility *nothingness* 786.2
nihil obstat *permit* 502.3
Nihongi *other text* 81.19
Niihau Islands *Islands* 572
nikau *or* **nikau palm** Trees and Shrubs 43
Nikaya *other text* 81.19
Nike Deities 921
Nikkei Market *stock exchange* 457.7
nil *absolutes* 6.9, *nothingness* 718.2, *zero* 786.1, 786.5
nil desperandum! [L] *never despair!* 281.18
Nile Rivers 570
Nile green *green* 260.7
Nilgiri Hills Mountains and Hills 569
Nilo Breeds of Pigs 16
Nilotic *racial* 1.12
Nilotic type *race* 1.5
nimble *skillful* 127.10, *active* 414.13, *graceful* 527.4, *swift* 694.6

nimble-fingered *skillful* 127.10
nimble-footed *swift* 694.6
nimbleness *alacrity* 414.3, *swiftness* 694.1
nimble-witted *witty* 277.10, *mentally quick* 694.8
nimbly *actively* 414.24, *swiftly* 694.16
nimbostratous *cloudy* 9.44
nimbostratus *cloud* 9.17
nimbus *cloud* 9.17, *highlight* 246.12
nimby [Inf] *sedatives* 121.19
nimiety *excess* 99.1
Nimrod *hunter* 160.9, 385.6, *shooter* 696.11
Nina from Carolina [Inf] *nine* 792.5
nincompoop *unintelligent person* 316.4, *foolish person* 353.3
nine 792.5; *numeral* 6.8, *baseball team* 147.2, *ninth* 792.16
nine centuries *hundreds* 792.9
nine-days' wonder *marvel* 294.3, *transient* 643.2, *nine* 792.5
ninefold *ninth* 792.16
ninepins *bowling* 151.1
nine points of the law *possession* 469.1
niner [Inf] *nine* 792.5
nineteen *eleven to nineteen* 792.7
nineteenth *less than one* 787.4
Nineteenth Amendment *equal opportunity* 831.1
nineteenth hole [Inf] *eleven to nineteen* 792.7, *refreshments* 94.3, *golfing terms* 156.3
nine tenths of the law *possession* 469.1
ninetieth *twentieth* 792.19
ninety *twenty and over* 792.8
ninety-nine percent *large part* 579.3
ninety-pound weakling *weak person* 517.4
ninny *unintelligent person* 316.4, *foolish person* 353.3, *simpleton* 526.5, *naive person* 821.2
ninth 792.16; *ranked* 6.72, *chord* 140.18, *less than one* 787.4, *nine* 792.5
ninth inning *close* 773.9
Ninth of Av *Jewish Holy Days and Seasons* 85
ninth part *nine* 792.5
niobium *Chemical Elements and Common Allotropes* 11
Nip *Nicknames for Inhabitants* 61
nip *size of drink* 93.3, *drink* 93.19, 121.6, *inflict pain* 215.10, *type of touch* 216.3, *touch* 216.9, *appetizer* 219.2, *stimulant* 221.5, *converge* 702.9, *hurry off* 705.11
nipa *Trees and Shrubs* 43
nip and tuck *as good as* 740.14
Nipigon *Lakes* 568
nip in the air *cold weather* 9.24, 218.8
nip in the bud *deter* 179.8, *ruin* 523.15, *prepare* 657.14, *hinder* 826.15
nip off *hurry off* 705.11
nipper [Inf] *child* 26.6
nippers *hand tool* 103.3, *retainer* 471.3
nippiness *cold* 218.1, *cold weather* 218.8
nipping *drinking* 93.1
nipple *mammalian characteristic* 35.3, *bulge* 634.2
nippy *cool* 9.49, *cold* 218.9
nirvana *heaven* 82.15, *future condition* 650.3, *repose* 678.2, *ease* 819.1

nisi prius *legal process* 54.3
Nisus *Notable Friendships* 62
nit *pest* 40.5, *dirt* 112.5, *Scientific and Technical Units* 589
nitpick *scrutinize* 323.11, *quibble* 330.13, *criticize* 438.19, 440.12
nitpicker *sophist* 330.6, *disapprover* 438.7, *disparager* 440.7
nitpicking *laborious* 122.7, *carefulness* 323.3, *quibbling* 330.4, 330.9, *criticism* 438.4, *critical* 438.13, *disparagement* 440.1, *disparaging* 440.8, *detailed* 726.9, *trivial* 800.14, *troublesome* 824.13
nitrate *react* 11.38, *fertilizer* 16.9, 22.6
nitrile rubber *rubber* 546.3
nitrogen *Chemical Elements and Common Allotropes* 11, *essential element* 12.15, *fertilizer* 22.6, *air* 558.1
nitrogenous base *nucleotide* 12.10
nitroglycerine *explosive* 78.13, *agent of destruction* 523.7
nitrometer *meter* 589.13
nitrous oxide *analgesic* 115.6
nitty-gritty *meaning* 361.1, *fact* 717.6, *essential content* 723.2, *specifications* 779.6, *gist* 799.4
nitwit *unskilled person* 128.3, *unintelligent person* 316.4, *foolish person* 353.3
Nivôse *French Revolutionary Calendar* 646
nix [Inf] *nonentity* 190.5, *refuse* 190.17, *denyingly* 190.23, *withhold approval* 438.17, *veto* 503.9, *zero* 786.1
nix! [Inf] *no!* 190.28, 506.12
nixed [Inf] *disagreeing* 190.11
Njord *Deities* 82
Njorth *Deities* 82
no *refusal* 190.2, *refuse* 190.17, *denyingly* 190.23, *disapproval* 347.2, *rejection* 383.1, *veto* 503.3, *protest* 507.1, *zero* 786.5, *none* 786.7
no! 190.28, 506.12
no. *number* 783.1
no-account [Inf] *nonentity* 800.8, *unimportant* 800.10
no Adonis *ugly thing* 531.2
no allegiance *independence* 829.5
no answer *futility* 846.3
no apologies *impenitence* 452.1
no appeal *severity* 424.1
no association *no relation* 728.5
no attributable cause *lack of motive* 842.2
nob *bow* 716.22
nob [Brit inf] *nobleman* 70.1
no bearing *lack of meaning* 362.1
no beauty *ugly thing* 531.2
nobelium *Chemical Elements and Common Allotropes* 11
Nobel Prize *prizes* 453.3
nobile *Musical Terms and Expression Marks* 140
nobility *aristocracy* 70.2, *nobleness* 70.3, *dignity* 297.4, *rightfulness* 429.1, *morals* 431.2, *virtue* 447.1, *beauty* 529.1, *best people* 744.7
no bill *pretrial proceedings* 54.13
nobilmente *Musical Terms and Expression Marks* 140
noble *masterful* 68.15, *nobleman* 70.1, *aristocratic* 70.4, *dignified* 297.11, *right* 429.7, *moral* 431.9, *unselfish* 443.5, *virtuous* 447.5, *beautiful* 529.7, *cultured* 534.6, *elite* 744.12, *important person* 799.5, *important* 799.7
noble animal, the *person* 18.8

noble art of self-defense *boxing* 152.2
noble experiment, the *prohibition of alcohol* 120.2
noble family *nobleness* 70.3
noble gas *chemical element* 11.3, *gas* 556.1
nobleman 70.1
noble metal *chemical element* 11.3
nobleness 70.3; *unselfishness* 443.2
noble savage *naive person* 821.2
noblesse oblige *courtesy* 410.1
noblewoman *nobleman* 70.1
nobly *masterfully* 68.19, *aristocratically* 70.6, *with dignity* 297.20, *eminently* 370.7, *right* 429.15, *morally* 431.15, *unselfishly* 443.9, *virtuously* 447.9, *elegantly* 527.7, 529.15
nobody 576.6; *negator* 190.8, *absence* 718.6, *insubstantial person* 720.5, *zero* 786.1, *nonentity* 786.4, 800.8
nobody else *one* 788.1
nobody present *nobody* 576.6
nobody's fool *sage* 4.11
nobody there *nobody* 576.6
no break *business* 414.6
nobs [Brit inf] *best people* 744.7
no buts about it *certainly* 719.14
no buts or **question about it** *truly* 721.27
no case *favorable verdict* 54.19
no chance *uncooperatively* 506.11, *poor chance* 842.8
no choice *choice* 382.3, *compulsion* 428.1
nock *notch* 636.1, 636.5
no-claims bonus *miscellaneous automotive terms* 687.14
no common ground *incomparability* 734.3, *disunity* 753.4
no comparison *incomparability* 734.3
no compromise *determination* 379.2, *severity* 424.1
no connection *no relation* 728.5
no context *lack of meaning* 362.1
no-count [Inf] *unimportant* 800.10
no courage *defeatism* 413.7
noctilucent cloud *cloud* 9.17
nocturnal *of animals* 34.13, *dark* 247.5, *evening* 656.4
nocturnal enuresis *urination* 25.4
nocturnally *darkly* 247.11, *nightly* 656.6
nocturne *Musical Forms* 140, *type of painting* 143.5
nod *inside information* 170.4, *assent* 346.6, *mark of respect* 435.4, *show respect* 435.16, *approval* 437.1, *approve* 437.14, *tolerance* 502.2, *bow* 716.6
nod, the [Inf] *yes* 346.2, *agreement* 462.1
nodding *deference* 410.4, *deferential* 410.8, *showing respect* 435.7
nodding off *not awake* 415.12
node *angle* 6.37, *wave* 10.11, 683.4, *computer communications* 15.25, *stem* 41.5, *solid body* 540.4, *hard substance* 542.3, *joint* 752.7
no distance *short distance* 586.2
nod of approval *yes* 346.2, *approval* 437.1, *permission* 502.1
nod off *be insensible* 213.7, *sleep* 415.14
nod of the head *gesture* 183.5
nod one's head *gesture* 183.17
nodose or **nodous** *coarse* 544.6
nodosity *hardness* 542.1, *roughness* 544.1
nodular *coarse* 544.6

nodularity *hardness* 542.1
nodule *solid body* 540.4, *hard substance* 542.3
nodus *problem* 824.4
no easy task *difficult task* 824.3
no end [Inf] *extravagantly* 500.9, *numberless* 795.8, *numerously* 795.13
no end of or **to** *eternal* 798.7
no entry *exclusion* 764.1
noes, the *dissenters* 347.6
noetic *intellectual* 315.8
no exception *inclusion* 763.1
no-fault *divorce court* 66.3
no fear *uncooperatively* 506.11
no flies on [Inf] *cunning* 822.4
no friend *hostile person* 63.5
no frills *simplicity* 526.1
no-frills *practical* 719.8
no gentleman *discourteous person* 411.4
noggin *size of drink* 93.3
noggin [Inf] *head* 19.6
no gift for *unskillfulness* 128.1
no-go [Inf] *limited* 620.5, *broken down* 802.8
no-go area [Inf] *limit* 620.1
no going back *impenitence* 452.1
no good *without skill* 282.10, *useless* 802.7
no-good *loser* 468.8
no good reason *lack of motive* 842.2
no great matter *secondary matter* 800.6
no great shakes [Inf] *mediocre* 289.11, *mediocrity* 742.3, *secondary matter* 800.6, *commonplace* 800.17
no hangover *sobriety* 120.1
no harm done *unbroken* 805.13
no hassle *peace* 73.1
no holds barred *warfare* 76.3, *liberality* 829.8, *unconditional* 829.14
no-holds-barred *type of wrestling* 152.9, *wrestling* 152.18
no hope *hopelessness* 282.1
no hurry *leisure* 125.1, *slowness* 693.1
no ifs, ands, or buts *really* 717.22
no imitation *authenticity* 717.7
no inclination for *disinclination* 291.3
noise *sound* 10.15, 230.1, *radio reception* 172.2, *publish* 173.15, *loudness* 232.1, *dissonance* 241.1, *Phobias* 283, *commotion* 768.5
noise abatement *faintness of sound* 233.1
noiseless *silent* 231.2
noiselessly *silently* 231.5
noiselessness *silence* 231.1
noisily *loudly* 232.11, *vociferously* 239.18
noisiness *loudness* 232.1
noisome *unclean* 112.8, *poisonous* 117.14, *odorous* 224.5, *stinking* 227.3, *repulsive* 701.4
noisomely *repulsively* 701.11
noisy *sounding* 230.7, *loud* 232.6, *vociferous* 239.9
no joke *important matter* 799.2
no lady *discourteous person* 411.4
no laughing matter *important matter* 799.2
nolens volens [L] *necessarily* 95.22
no less *sufficiency* 97.1
no life *death* 29.1
nolle prosequi *termination* 834.2
no longer *before now* 651.21
no longer present *former* 651.14
no longer serving *former* 651.14
no longer with us *away* 576.8

no loss of time *swiftness* 694.1
no love lost *ill feeling* 63.3
no luck *futility* 846.3, *bad fortune* 848.7
nomadic *moving* 677.12, *foreign* 724.9
nomadically *in motion* 677.19, *strangely* 724.17
no man *nobody* 576.6
no manners *bad manners* 411.2
no-man's-land *exclusion zone* 764.3, *middle ground* 772.4
no marksman *unskilled person* 128.3
no marriage *divorce* 66.1
no matter *secondary matter* 800.6
no matter! 800.22
no matter how *how* 691.16
no matter what *or* **which** *whatever* 778.8
no matter who *everyone* 778.7
nombril point Heraldic Terms 184
nom de plume *anonymity* 182.7, *name* 202.8
no meaning *lack of meaning* 362.1
nomen *name* 202.8
nomenclature 202.7, Linguistic Studies 5, *language* 5.4
Nomex™ suit *modern armor* 419.7
nominal *symbolic* 183.12, *cheap* 497.9, *trivial* 800.14
nominalism Philosophical Schools of Thought 4, *form* 624.1
nominalist Philosophical Schools of Thought 4
nominally *cheaply* 497.16
nominal scale *nonparametric methods* 6.54
nominate *deputize* 80.7, *ordain* 84.16, *select* 382.12, *commission* 833.8
nominated *billiard* 149.6, *commissioned* 833.6
nominated ball *snooker* 149.4
nomination *delegation* 79.3, *ordination* 84.3, *selection* 382.1, *commission* 833.1
nominative *grammatical term* 5.29
nominee *chosen thing* 382.8, *commissioner* 833.5
nomological *legislative* 53.17
nomology *lawmaking* 53.11, *jurisprudence* 53.13
no money *economic adversity* 848.6
no morals *immorality* 432.1, *depravity* 448.2
no more 718.11; *dead* 29.11
nomothetic *or* **nomothetical** *managerial* 126.9
nomothetic *philosophical* 4.12, *legislative* 53.17
non! [Fr] *no!* 190.28
nonacceptance *rejection* 383.1, *disapproval* 438.1, *refusal* 506.1, *uncooperativeness* 828.4
nonacceptantly 190.25
nonaccepting *disapproving* 438.8, *refused* 506.5
nonaccomplishment *nonachievement* 762.3
nonachievement 762.3
nonaction *inaction* 413.1
nonactive *inactive* 413.9
nonactivist *reluctant person* 375.7
nonaddict *sober person* 120.4
nonadherence *nonobservance* 466.1, *nonadhesion* 756.1
nonadherent *nonobservant* 466.5, *nonadhesive* 756.4
nonadhering *nonadhesive* 756.4
nonadhesion 756.1
nonadhesive 756.4

nonadmission *exclusion* 764.1
nonage *youth* 26.1
nonagenarian *older person* 27.7, *twenty and over* 792.8
nonaggression *coexistence* 73.3
nonaggression pact *peace treaty* 73.5, *alliance* 459.5
nonaggressive *pacific* 74.7
nonagon *polygon* 6.42, *nine* 792.5
nonagonal *ninth* 792.16
nonalcoholic *drinkable* 93.18, *sober person* 120.4
nonalcoholic beverage *soft drink* 93.8
nonaligned *or* **unaligned** *national* 566.10
nonaligned *or* **unaligned country** *or* **nation** *country* 566.1
nonaligned *pacific* 74.7, *impartial* 338.6, *disinterested* 443.4, *unjoined* 753.9, *mediatory* 772.11, *free* 829.11
nonaligned nations *coexistence* 73.3
nonalignment *coexistence* 73.3, *impartiality* 338.2, *disinterestedness* 443.1, *setting apart* 753.2, *noninterference* 829.3
no name *latency* 844.1
no-name *anonymity* 182.7, *mysterious* 182.10
nonappearance *invisibility* 245.1, *disappearance* 265.1, *absenteeism* 576.3
nonapproval *rejection* 383.1, *disapproval* 438.1
nonapproving *disapproving* 438.8
nonary *nine* 792.5, *ninth* 792.16
nonassimilated *separate* 724.10
nonassimilation *separateness* 724.3
nonassociation *dissociation* 375.4
nonattached *unjoined* 753.9
nonattachment *setting apart* 753.2
nonattendance *absenteeism* 576.3
nonattendant *absent* 576.7
nonbearing *wall* 134.9
nonbeing *absence* 574.1, *nonexistence* 718.1, *nothingness* 786.2
nonbelief *incredulity* 88.3
nonbeliever *disbeliever* 88.5, *freethinker* 829.10
nonbelieving *nonobservant* 466.5, *independent* 829.12
nonbelligerent *pacifist* 74.6
nonbenzenoid aromatic *chemical compound* 11.4
nonbreakable *tough* 547.6
noncatalytic *chemical* 14.46
noncatalytically *electrochemically* 14.53
noncatalytic reactions *chemical reaction thermodynamics* 14.29
nonce *present time* 647.1
nonce word *new word* 5.18
nonchalance *indifference* 289.1, *lack of wonder* 295.1, *apathy* 322.2, *negligence* 326.1, *ease of manner* 823.4
nonchalant *indifferent* 289.7, *wonderless* 295.3, *incurious* 322.3, *negligent* 326.4
nonchalantly *indifferently* 289.17, *without wonder* 295.8
nonchordate invertebrate *invertebrate* 39.1
non-Christian ritual 85.8
nonclassical *physical* 10.70
nonclassically *physically* 10.78
nonclastic rock *sedimentary rock* 8.34
noncoagulation *fluidity* 555.5

noncoercion *freedom* 829.1
noncoherence *nonadhesion* 756.1
noncoherent *nonadhesive* 756.4
noncoherently *noncohesively* 756.9
noncohesion *nonadhesion* 756.1
noncohesive *nonadhesive* 756.4
noncohesively 756.9
noncombatant *enlisted* 58.11, *pacifist* 74.6, *pacific* 74.7
noncombination *nonadhesion* 756.1
noncommissioned *enlisted* 58.11
noncommissioned officer (NCO) *military position* 58.6
noncommittal 181.11; *silent* 181.10, *vacillating* 378.5, *avoiding* 386.9, *irresolute* 461.6, 772.13, *politically moderate* 521.4
noncommittally *privately* 181.18, *irresolutely* 378.13, 461.10
noncompetitive *associating* 827.11
noncompletion 762.2; *insufficiency* 98.1, *bungling* 128.2, *disappointment* 293.1, *nonperformance* 466.2, *failure* 846.1
noncompliance *disobedience* 375.5, 427.1, *nonobservance* 466.1, *refusal* 506.1, *protest* 507.1, *dissent* 782.2
noncompliant *disobedient* 427.10, *nonobservant* 466.5, *defiant* 466.7, *refused* 506.5, *protesting* 507.5, *dissident* 782.12
noncomplying *refused* 506.5
non compos mentis [L] *insane* 110.9
nonconcurrence *dissent* 782.2
nonconcurring *dissident* 782.12
nonconductor 14.35; *insulation* 10.36
nonconformance *nonobservance* 466.1, *nonconformity* 728.4, 782.1
nonconformant *nonobservant* 466.5
nonconformer *nonconformist* 782.7
nonconforming 728.10, 782.11; *nonobservant* 466.5, *unusual* 664.4, *unreliable* 722.10, *independent* 829.12
nonconformism 782.3; *dissentience* 347.3, *deviation* 698.1, *nonconformity* 782.1
Nonconformist Christian 81.10, *denominational* 81.23
nonconformist 782.7, 782.13; *disbeliever* 88.5, *dissenter* 347.5, *dissenting* 347.7, *uncustomary* 398.4, *informal* 407.6, *defiant person* 416.4, *troublemaker* 427.5, *nonobservant* 466.5, *protester* 507.4, *protesting* 507.5, *deviant* 698.7, 698.8, *nonconforming* 728.10, *individualist* 756.3, *freethinker* 829.10, *independent* 829.12
nonconformity 728.4, 782.1; *dissentience* 347.3, *unaccustomedness* 398.1, *informality* 407.1, *disobedience* 427.1, *difference* 463.4, *nonobservance* 466.1, *unusualness* 664.2, *unreliability* 722.5, *separateness* 724.3, *freethinking* 829.2
nonconsummation of marriage *divorce* 66.1
noncontinuation *nonachievement* 762.3
noncontinuous *universal* 6.67, *discontinuous* 775.7

noncontributory benefit *social assistance* 825.4
nonconvergence *parallelism* 606.1
nonconvergent *parallel* 606.5
nonconvergently *in parallel* 606.9
nonconverging *parallel* 606.5
nonconvertible *unused* 394.5
nonconvulsive electric treatment *psychiatric treatment* 108.3
noncooperation *dissentience* 347.3, *opposition* 375.2, *evasiveness* 386.6, *resistance* 417.1, *disobedience* 427.1, *disagreement* 463.1, *nonobservance* 466.1, *refusal* 506.1, *protest* 507.1, *uncooperativeness* 828.4
noncooperative *resistant* 417.6, *disobedient* 427.10, *disagreeing* 463.6, *nonobservant* 466.5, *refused* 506.5, *protesting* 507.5, *uncooperative* 828.14
noncooperatively *resistingly* 417.14
noncooperator *dissenter* 463.5
noncrystalline *status adjectives* 11.25
nondescript *tasteless* 220.4, *unimportant* 800.10
nondirective therapy *psychotherapy* 108.4
nondiscriminatory *including* 763.3
nondivergence *parallelism* 606.1
nondivergent *parallel* 606.5
nondivergently *in parallel* 606.9
nondiverging *parallel* 606.5
nondrinker *sober person* 120.4, *avoider* 386.8
nondrinking *sober* 120.5
nondrying oil *oil* 562.3
nondurable *impermanent* 643.5
nondutiable *chargeable* 494.11
none 786.7; *absence* 718.6, *zero* 786.1
nonelastic *hard* 547.8
nonelection *discarding* 383.3
nonemployment *unemployment* 413.5
nonentity 190.5, 786.4, 800.8; *negator* 190.8, *absence* 576.1, *nonexistence* 718.1, *insubstantial person* 720.5
nones *public worship* 83.3, *day* 646.4, *night* 656.3
nonessential *superfluity* 99.4, *superfluous* 99.8, *extraneous* 724.8, *unrelated* 728.6, *trifle* 800.3, *unimportant* 800.10
nonessential amino acid *amino acid* 12.8
nonessentially *irrelatively* 728.16
nonesuch *wonderful person* 294.6, *superior person* 445.7
nonet *instrumental group* 141.3, *nine* 792.5, *team* 827.7
nonetheless *how* 691.16
none the worse *cured* 809.8
none too soon *at a late hour* 658.15
none to spare *scarcity* 98.3
non-Euclidean geometry *geometry* 6.32
nonexclusive *including* 763.3, *general* 778.9
nonexistence 718.1; *nonentity* 190.5, *disappearance* 265.1, *absence* 576.1, *unreality* 720.1, 722.2, *nothingness* 786.2, *impossibility* 837.1
nonexistent 190.14, 718.9; *scarce* 98.8, *disappeared* 265.4, *imaginary* 360.12, *absent* 576.7, *unreal* 720.8, 722.7, *zero* 786.5

nonexistently *unreally* 722.15
nonexisting *nonexistent* 190.14, *unreal* 722.7
nonexternal *internal* 525.11
nonexternality *internal world* 525.6
nonexternally *subjectively* 525.14
nonextreme *politically moderate* 521.4, *moderate* 772.12
nonextremist *medium* 742.6, *moderate person* 772.8
nonfeasance *lawbreaking* 53.14, *nonperformance* 466.2
nonfiction 139.6; *factual account* 202.4
nonflammable *trustworthy* 810.17
nonfoliated rock *metamorphic rock* 8.36
nonfriction *lubrication* 562.2
nonfrictional *smooth* 545.4
nonfulfilling *nonperforming* 466.6
nonfulfillment *insufficiency* 98.1, *disappointment* 293.1, *nonperformance* 466.2, *noncompletion* 762.2
nonfunctional *decorated* 532.9, *useless* 802.7
nonfunctioning *broken down* 802.8
nonhappening *nonexistence* 718.1
nonillion *million* 792.11
nonimmunity *vulnerability* 811.6
noninclusion *exclusion* 764.1
nonindulgence *chastity* 431.3
nonindulgent *chaste* 431.10
nonindustrial *productive* 522.11
noninfectious *health-giving* 113.6
noninjurious *health-giving* 113.6
nonintention *lack of motive* 842.2
noninterference 829.3; *do-nothingism* 413.6
nonintervention *coexistence* 73.3, *shyness* 386.3, *do-nothingism* 413.6, *noninterference* 829.3
noninterventional *free* 829.11
noninterventionist *inactive person* 413.8
nonintimidation *freedom* 829.1
noninvolved *free* 829.11
noninvolvement *coexistence* 73.3, *indifference* 289.1, *shyness* 386.3, *disinterestedness* 443.1, *separateness* 724.3, *noninterference* 829.3
nonirritant *moderating* 521.5
Nonius Horse and Pony Breeds 159
nonjudgmental *impartial* 338.6
nonliability *exemption* 434.1, *tolerance* 502.2, *freedom* 829.1
nonliable *acquitted* 54.25, *exempt* 434.5, *free* 829.11
nonlinear *interrupted* 775.9
nonlinear circuit *circuit* 14.37
nonlinearity *digression* 775.6
nonlinear optics Fields of Modern Physics 10
nonmalignant *health-giving* 113.6
nonmanual *industrial* 57.13
nonmanual worker *employee* 57.4
nonmaterial 525.8; *spiritual* 86.20
nonmaterialist 525.7
nonmaterial world 525.1
nonmetal *chemical element* 11.3
nonnegative *numerical* 6.68
nonnegative number *number* 6.4
no-no [Inf] *obstacle* 837.3
nonobjective art Western Art Styles 133
nonobservance 466.1; *unacceptance* 190.4, *inattention* 324.1, *disobedience* 375.5, 427.1, *unaccustomedness* 398.1, *dissent* 782.2

nonobservant 466.5; *unaccustomed* 398.3, *disobedient* 427.10
nonobserving *dissident* 782.12
nonoccurrence *nonexistence* 718.1
nonoccurrent *absent* 576.7
no-nonsense *rational* 4.15, *practical* 719.8, *naive* 821.3
nonparametric methods 6.54
nonparametric statistics *statistics* 6.51
nonpareil *wonderful person* 294.6, *excellence* 445.4, *excellent* 445.13, *paragon* 744.6
nonpartisan *political* 50.9, *impartial* 338.6, *disinterested* 443.4, *moderate person* 772.8, *mediatory* 772.11, *free person* 829.9, *free* 829.11
nonpayer *debtor* 488.6
nonpaying 490.7; *unprofitable* 468.10, *unable to pay* 488.8
nonpaying person *loser* 846.9
nonpayment 490.1; *refusal* 506.1, *protest* 507.1, *financial escape* 816.2, *insolvency* 846.6
nonperformance 466.2; *failure* 846.1
nonperforming 466.6
nonperseverance *vacillation* 378.1
nonperson *insubstantial person* 720.5, *nonentity* 800.8
nonphysical *spiritual* 86.20, *nonmaterial* 525.8
nonphysical world *nonmaterial world* 525.1
nonplus *astonish* 292.10, *be wondrous* 294.14, *problem* 824.4, *cause difficulties* 824.22, *make uncertain* 841.19
nonplussed *wondering* 294.7, *confused* 364.10, 841.11, *troubled* 824.15
nonpolar *chemical compound* 11.4
nonpolar solvent *phase* 11.13
nonporous *closed* 584.7
nonporously *impermeably* 584.17
nonpractice *nonperformance* 466.2
nonpracticing *nonobservant* 466.5, *nonperforming* 466.6
nonpreparation *lack of preparation* 389.1
nonpresence *invisibility* 245.1, *absence* 576.1
nonprevalent *uncustomary* 398.4
nonprintable character *character* 15.18
nonprofit-making *unprofitable* 468.10
nonprosecution *favorable verdict* 54.19
nonprovision *unpremeditation* 389.2
nonradical *politically moderate* 521.4
nonreactionary *politically moderate* 521.4
nonrealism *misrepresentation* 188.1
nonrealist *avoider* 386.8
nonreality 718.5
nonrecognition *ingratitude* 311.1, *ignorance* 349.1
nonrecurrent *discontinued* 775.8
nonrecyclable *losing* 468.9
nonreflective *transparent* 249.7
nonrenewable *renewable* 106.15
nonrenewable energy source *fuel* 106.1
nonrepentance *impenitence* 452.1
nonrepresentational *misrepresented* 188.4
nonrepresentational art Western Art Styles 133

nonresident 576.9
nonresistance *submission* 421.1, *obedience* 426.1
nonresisting *submitting* 421.3, *obedient* 426.4
nonresistive *impressionable* 543.12
nonresistiveness *softness* 543.1
nonresonance *undercurrent of sound* 233.3
nonresonant 233.7; *hoarse* 238.5
nonresponsibility *exemption* 434.1
nonrestoration *loss* 468.1
nonrestriction *right of entry* 706.4
nonresumption *discontinuance* 846.4
nonrigid *soft* 543.6
nonrigidity *softness* 543.1
nonsaponifiable lipid *fat* 12.7
nonsatisfaction *insufficiency* 98.1, *noncompletion* 762.2
nonseed-bearing *taxonomic* 41.16
nonseed-bearing plant *lower plant* 41.4
nonsense 192.8, 362.2
nonsense *senseless talk* 362.4, *meaningless* 362.7, *unintelligibility* 364.1
nonsense! 362.14
nonsense poetry or **verse** *poetry* 139.8
nonsensical 192.19; *foolish* 353.5, *meaningless* 362.7, *unintelligible* 364.4
nonsensicality *nonsense* 362.2
nonsensically 192.30, 722.18; *foolishly* 353.8, *meaninglessly* 362.13
nonsensical talk *nonsense* 192.8
nonsensical writing or **verse** *nonsense* 362.2
nonsequential *interrupted* 775.9
non sequitur *philosophical term* 4.7, *sophism* 330.2, *unconnectedness* 728.2, *digression* 775.6
nonserial *interrupted* 775.9
nonseriality *digression* 775.6
nonsignificance *lack of meaning* 362.1
nonsignificant *meaningless* 362.7
nonsinusoidal wave *wave form* 10.13
nonsmoker *smoking* 121.22, *self-restrained person* 455.5
nonspecialist *unskilled* 128.5
nonspecific *generalized* 778.12
nonspecificness 778.2
nonspecific urethritis (NSU) *sexually transmitted disease (STD)* 114.17
nonspiritual *material* 524.7
nonstandard *of language* 5.35, *unconventional* 782.14
nonstandard language 5.7
nonstarter *unsuccessful thing* 846.8, *loser* 846.9
nonsterile *unclean* 112.8, *contagious* 114.26
nonsteroidal anti-inflammatory drug (NSAID) *analgesic* 115.6
nonstick *nonadhesive* 756.4
nonstoichiometric *chemical compound* 11.4
nonstop *diffuse* 199.3, *continuous* 630.10, 774.9, *continuing forever* 644.6, *frequent* 661.4, *continually* 669.10, *continuously* 774.16, *recurrent* 797.13
nonstop talker *talker* 207.4
nonstop talking *diffuseness* 199.1
nonstress test *prenatal diagnosis* 107.9

nonstriker *reactionary* 427.9, *protester* 507.4
nonsubsistence *nonexistence* 718.1
nonsuccess *failure* 430.9
nonsuch *superior person* 445.7
nonsuit *favorable verdict* 54.19
nonsuited *convicted* 54.26
nonsymmetrical *irregular* 766.10
nonsymmetry *irregular order* 766.2
nontaxable *chargeable* 494.11
nontoxic *trustworthy* 810.17
nontraditional *unfamiliar* 652.10
nontraditionally *newly* 652.21
nontranslucent *opaque* 250.3
nontransparent *opaque* 250.3
non-U [Inf] *common* 71.3, *uncustomary* 398.4
nonuniform 734.5; *rough* 544.5, *irregular* 664.3, 766.10, *disparate* 728.9, *varied* 732.6, *unequal* 741.4, *complicated* 751.10, *discontinuous* 775.7
nonuniformally *mixedly* 751.16
nonuniformity 734.2; *roughness* 544.1, *irregularity* 664.1, *disparity* 728.3, *variety* 732.2, *inconsistency* 732.3, *inequality* 741.1, *mixture* 751.1, *nonadhesion* 756.1, *irregular order* 766.2, *discontinuity* 775.1
nonuniformly 734.11; *disparately* 728.19, *variously* 732.15, *unequally* 741.10
nonuple *ninth* 792.16
nonuplet *nine* 792.5
nonuse 394.1; *unskillfulness* 128.1, *discarding* 383.3, *relinquishment* 392.1, *inaction* 413.1
nonuser (of drugs) *straight person* 630.7
nonutilization *neglect* 96.2
nonvenomous snake *snake* 37.6
nonviolence *pacification* 74.1, *moderation* 521.1
nonviolent *pacific* 74.7, *moderate* 521.3
nonviolent resistance *resistance movement* 417.3
nonviscosity *fluidity* 555.5
nonvolatile memory *memory* 15.6
nonvolatile oil *oil* 562.3
nonwage demands *bargaining terms* 57.10
nonwilling *refused* 506.5
nonwillingness *refusal* 506.1
nonworker 415.4
noodle *foolish person* 353.3
noodles *pasta* 90.31
nook *hiding place* 181.2, *compartment* 578.2, *cavity* 635.3, *private space* 812.2
nookie or **nooky** [Inf] *sexual intercourse* 20.9
nookie or **nooky** [Inf and Off] *sex object* 20.8
no omission *inclusion* 763.1
noon 655.4; *daytime* 655.1
noonday *noon* 655.4
no one *nobody* 576.6, *absence* 718.6, *zero* 786.1
noontide *noon* 655.4
noontime *noon* 655.4
noon whistle *noon* 655.4
noose *instrument of execution* 454.15, *circular thing* 631.3, *yoke* 754.8
nooseknot Knots, Bends, Hitches, Splices 754
noosphere *aerosphere* 558.2
no other *one* 788.1
no pattern *irregular order* 766.2
nope! [Inf] *no!* 190.28

no picnic [Inf] *difficult task* 824.3
no place *away* 576.19
Nō play *dramatic style* 136.3
no prisoners taken *warfare* 76.3
no problem *easily* 823.19
no progress *futility* 846.3
no question about it! *certainly!* 840.18
no quorum *incompleteness* 98.2
Nordic *racial* 1.12, *ski* 162.27
Nordic combined event Sporting Activities 145
Nordic skiing Sporting Activities 145, *skiing* 162.1, *cross-country skiing* 162.7
Nordic type *race* 1.5
no real alternative *choice* 382.3
no reason *lack of motive* 842.2
nor'easter Notable Winds 9
no regrets *impenitence* 452.1
no relation 728.5
no remorse *impenitence* 452.1
norepinephrine *hormone* 12.16
no resemblance *incomparability* 734.3
no rest for the wicked *business* 414.6
no result *futility* 846.3
no reward *ingratitude* 311.1
Norfolk Island pine Trees and Shrubs 43
Norfolk jacket *jacket* 100.18
Norfolk Red Polled Breeds of Cattle 16
Norfolk terrier Breeds of Dogs 35
Norfolk Trotter Horse and Pony Breeds 159
no rhyme or reason *irregular order* 766.2
norm *standard* 589.7, *average* 742.1, *guide* 780.4
Norma Constellations 7
normal *line* 6.35, *universal* 6.67, *linear* 6.77, *sane* 109.3, *customary* 397.11, *780.9*, *vertical* 602.3, *perpendicular* 602.6, *regular* 663.5, *average* 742.5, *common* 778.13
normal, the *expected thing* 356.3
normal behavior *expected thing* 356.3
normalcy *average* 742.1
normal distribution *probability distribution* 6.56
normal fault *fault* 8.21
normality *sanity* 109.1, *regularity* 663.1, *average* 742.1, 778.4
normalize *order* 6.89, *make regular* 663.9, *make average* 742.9, *organize* 767.19, *regulate* 780.15
normal lens *lens* 132.11
normally *orderly* 663.13, *prevailingly* 742.11, *usually* 778.21, *as a rule* 780.18
normalness *average* 778.4
normal sight *visual acuity* 242.2
normal stress *load* 14.14
normal temperature and pressure (NTP) *thermodynamics* 10.30
normal use *use* 393.1
normal vision *visual acuity* 242.2
Norman *arch* 134.5, Horse and Pony Breeds 159, *historic* 653.13
Norman architecture Architectural Styles 134
Normandy Breeds of Cattle 16
normative *philosophical* 4.12, *customary* 397.11, *average* 742.5
Norn *minor deity* 82.2
Norns, the the Deities 82
no room to spare *full* 761.8
no room to swing a cat in *little space* 580.6, *full* 761.8

no room to turn around *full* 761.8
North *bridge* 168.4, Islands 572
north *side direction* 623.2, *directional* 697.8, *directionally* 697.20
North America *world region* 564.6, *landmass* 572.1
North American Free Trade Association (NAFTA) *economic organization* 56.6
northbound *directional* 697.8
North Carolina American States 564
North Caucasus Breeds of Pigs 16
North Caucasus Mutton-Wool Breeds of Sheep 16
North Country Cheviot Breeds of Sheep 16
North Dakota American States 564
Northeast *regions of the United States* 564.7
northeast *compass direction* 697.5, *directional* 697.8, *directionally* 697.20
northeasterly *windy* 9.42, *directional* 697.8, *directionally* 697.20
northeastern *directional* 697.8
northeast trades *wind system* 9.15
northeastward *directionally* 697.20
northeastwardly *directionally* 697.20
northerly *windy* 9.42, *directional* 697.8, *directionally* 697.20
northern *regional* 564.12, *side* 623.6, *directional* 697.8
Northern Crown Constellations 7
Northern Hemisphere *world region* 564.6
northern lights Earth 7.17, *natural light* 246.4
Northern Mariana Islands, Commonwealth of the American States 564
northernmost *directional* 697.8
Northern Renaissance art Western Art Styles 133
Northern Spy Apple Varieties 44
northing *compass direction* 697.5
North Korea Countries 566
north magnetic pole *geomagnetism* 8.3
north-northeast *directionally* 697.20
north-northwest *directionally* 697.20
North Pole *cold place* 218.7, *distant place* 585.3
North Sea Oceans and Seas 571
North Siberian Breeds of Pigs 16
North Swedish Horse and Pony Breeds 159
North Swedish Trotter Horse and Pony Breeds 159
northward *compass direction* 697.5, *directional* 697.8, *directionally* 697.20
northwardly *directionally* 697.20
Northwest *regions of the United States* 564.7
northwest *compass direction* 697.5, *directional* 697.8, *directionally* 697.20
northwesterly *windy* 9.42, *directional* 697.8, *directionally* 697.20
northwestern *directional* 697.8
Northwest Territories Canadian Provinces 564
northwestward *directionally* 697.20

northwestwardly *directionally* 697.20
North Yemen Countries 566
Norway Countries 566
Norway maple Trees and Shrubs 43
Norway spruce Trees and Shrubs 43
Norwegian elkhound Breeds of Dogs 35
Norwegian forest Breeds of Cats 35
Norwegian Landrace Breeds of Pigs 16
Norwegian Racing Trotter Horse and Pony Breeds 159
Norwegian Red Breeds of Cattle 16
nor'wester Notable Winds 9
Norwich terrier Breeds of Dogs 35
no score *zero* 786.1
nose 19.11; *head* 19.6, *racing automobile* 146.2, *rock face* 161.6, *sense organ* 212.4, *taste* 219.1, *odor* 224.1, *sense of smell* 224.2, *smell* 224.7, *meddle* 321.8, *body orifice* 583.3, *bulge* 634.2, *protuberance* 634.3
nose bag *bag* 578.7
noseband *riding equipment* 159.9
nosebleeds *bleeding* 25.10, Phobias 283
nose candy [Inf] *stimulants* 121.18
no secret *known* 348.9
nosedive *flight maneuver* 689.6, *maneuver* 689.14, *fall* 714.4, *drop* 714.15, *decline* 747.4
nosediving *falling* 714.11
nose down *maneuver* 689.14
nosegay *flower* 42.1, *assemblage* 59.13
nose guard *defense* 155.9
nose job [Inf] *cosmetic surgery* 530.2
nosemaphobia or **nosophobia** Phobias 283
nose out *smell* 224.7
nose ring *jewelry* 532.6
nose to nose *contentious* 422.20, *near* 586.6, *beside* 586.20, *opposite* 731.3, *in a line* 774.17
nose-to-nose confrontation *duel* 422.12,
nose to tail *beside* 586.20
nose up *maneuver* 689.14
nosh [Inf] *food* 90.1, *snack* 90.8, *have a meal* 92.25
noshing [Inf] *eating meals* 92.4
no shining knight *discourteous person* 411.4
no-show *absentee* 576.5
nosily *officiously* 321.10
no sinecure *business* 414.6
nosiness *prying* 321.2
nosing *sense of smell* 224.2
no sir! [Inf] *no!* 190.28
no sirree! [Inf] *no!* 190.28
no sirree Bob! [Inf] *no!* 190.28
no slave *free person* 829.9
no slouch [Inf] *busy person* 414.10
no-smoking area *odorlessness* 225.1
nosocomephobia Phobias 283
nosology *medical science* 107.5
no sooner said than done *easy* 823.9
no spring chicken [Inf] *older person* 27.7
nostalgia *recollection* 3.8, *emotionalism* 266.6, *desire* 288.1, *memory* 354.1
nostalgic *desirous* 288.13,

memorable 354.7, *retroactive* 680.12
nostalgically *biographically* 3.18, *desirously* 288.26
no stomach for *disinclination* 291.3, *dissociation* 375.4
nostophobia Phobias 283
Nostradamus *diviner* 86.14, *warner* 814.5
no stranger to *knowledgeable* 348.7
no strike–no lockout agreement *bargaining* 57.9
nostril *nose* 19.11, *sense of smell* 224.2, *body orifice* 583.3
no strings attached *unconditional* 829.14
nostrum *remedy* 115.1, *expedient* 387.5
no success *bad fortune* 848.7
no such thing *nothingness* 718.2
no surplus *sufficiency* 97.1
no surrender! *fight on!* 417.16
no sweat [Inf] *easy thing* 823.6, *easily* 823.19
nosy *prying* 321.6, *meddling* 414.17
Nosy Parker [Inf] *observer* 242.15, *meddler* 321.4, 414.12
not *none* 786.7
not abide *be against* 828.17
notability *importance* 799.1
not a bit *not any* 718.7
not a bit alike *incomparably* 734.12
notable 799.11; *historic* 3.11, *wondrous* 294.9, *memorable* 354.7, *person of repute* 370.2, *reputable* 370.3, *exalted* 596.10, *exceptional* 779.13, *important person* 799.5, *manifest* 843.9
not able *powerless* 515.6
notable international dishes 90.40
notableness *exaltation* 596.3
notable point *important matter* 799.2
notable psychiatrists *psychiatrist* 108.34
notable psychologists *psychologist* 108.33
not a blessed one [Inf] *absence* 718.6, *zero* 786.1
notable tennis competitions 165.8
notably *aristocratically* 70.6, *wondrously* 294.18, *eminently* 370.7, *exaltedly* 596.22, *importantly* 799.15
not a breath of air *repose* 678.2
not accept 190.19; *not use* 394.9, *not observe* 466.9, *refuse* 506.8
not accepted *rejected* 383.6
not accomplish *not complete* 762.9
not accomplished *uncompleted* 762.7
not accountable *exempt* 434.5
not achieve *not complete* 762.9
not acknowledge *ignore* 409.11
not act 413.11
not activate *not use* 394.9
not activated *unused* 394.5
not adhere *not observe* 466.9
not admire *not wonder about* 295.5, *disapprove* 438.16
not a fake *authenticity* 721.7
not a few *many* 795.6
not affordable *costly* 496.7
not a full deck *incompleteness* 98.2
not a full team *incompleteness* 98.2
not a ghost of a chance *futility* 282.3
not a hair out of place *orderly* 765.13

not a hint *not any* 718.7
not a jot *not any* 718.7
not a jot or tittle *zero* 786.1
not a lick [Inf] *not any* 718.7, *zero* 786.1
not a living soul *or* thing *nobody* 576.6
not all it's cracked up to be [Inf] *overestimated* 343.5
not allow *dissent* 506.9
not allowed *prohibited* 503.5, *dissenting* 506.6
not allowed visitors *sick* 114.24
not allow out of one's sight *suspect* 314.9
not allow to forget *remind* 354.13
not all there *incomplete* 762.5
not all there [Inf] *unintelligent* 316.6
not alter *be stubborn* 542.11
not a mite *not any* 718.7, *zero* 786.1
not a mouse stirring *repose* 678.2
not an iota *not any* 718.7, *zero* 786.1
not answerable *exempt* 434.5
not anxious to please *discourteous* 411.5
not any 718.7; *zero* 786.1
not any more *before now* 651.21
not a one *absence* 718.6, *zero* 786.1
not a particle *not any* 718.7
not apparent *invisible* 245.3
not appear *depart* 265.6
not apply *be extraneous* 724.12
not approve *disapprove* 438.16
not a prayer *poor chance* 842.8
not apropos *unimportant* 800.10
notarized statement *certificate* 185.2
not arouse *not cause wonder* 295.7
notary *record keeper* 185.8
not a sausage [Brit inf] *zero* 786.1
not a scrap *not any* 718.7
not a shadow of a suspicion *or* doubt *not any* 718.7
not a single person *nobody* 576.6
not ask *be incurious* 322.5
not a smidgen *not any* 718.7
not a snowball's chance in hell [Inf] *poor chance* 842.8
not a soul *nobody* 576.6, *zero* 786.1
not a sound *silence* 231.1
not a speck *not any* 718.7
not a squeak *silence* 231.1
no taste *vulgarity* 535.1
not a suspicion *not any* 718.7
not as young as one was *middle-aged* 27.14
not at all 718.15; *negatively* 190.22, *to the contrary* 190.27, *uncooperatively* 506.11, *none* 786.7
not at any time *not ever* 718.16
not at home *nonresident* 576.9
notation 140.20; *written music* 140.21, *representation* 187.1, *gradation* 739.3, *number* 783.1
not a trace *not any* 718.7
not at risk *safe* 810.16
not attempt *shy* 386.17
not at the moment *another time* 648.4
not at war *harmless* 73.9
not at work *nonresident* 576.9
not available *unused* 394.5
not awake 415.12
not a whit *not any* 718.7, *zero* 786.1
not bad *getting well* 113.9, *satisfactory* 273.6, *mediocre* 742.7
not balance *be unequal* 741.7

not bat an eye *ignore* 413.14
not be *be nothing* 190.20, *not exist* 718.12, 786.6
not be able to find *lose* 468.12
not be affected by *be indifferent* 289.12
not bear inspection *be imperfect* 806.8
not beat about the bush *be concise* 198.5
not be conducive to *counteract* 510.7
not be frank *lack candor* 192.22
not believe *not observe* 466.9
not believe one's eyes *or* ears *wonder* 294.12
not belong *be excluded* 764.9
not belonging *unjoined* 753.9
not bend *be obstinate* 417.11, *be stubborn* 542.11
not bending *obstinacy* 417.2
not be tempted by *resist* 417.10
not be up to it *be inferior* 745.10
not be used to *be unaccustomed* 398.5
not be willing to *refuse* 506.8
not blessed with this world's goods *poor* 486.8
not blink an eye *not wonder about* 295.5
not blow one's own horn [Inf] *be modest* 403.11
not born yesterday *cunning* 822.4
not bothered *disinterested* 443.4
not breathe *be motionless* 678.7
not breathe a word *keep secret* 182.11, *be voiceless* 206.8
not broken *unaccustomed* 398.3
not budge *insist* 376.14, *hold out* 377.13, *be obstinate* 379.10, *ignore* 413.14, *show determination* 674.8, *be motionless* 678.7
not butt in *set free* 829.17
not buy [Inf] *refuse* 506.8
not by a long shot *to the contrary* 190.27
not by any stretch of the imagination *not at all* 718.15
not care *be indifferent* 289.12, *be incurious* 322.5
not care a straw about *be indifferent* 289.12
not care for *dislike* 291.12, *be neglectful* 326.7
not cater to *or* for *exclude* 383.11
not cause a stir *be average* 742.8
not cause wonder 295.7
notch 636.1, 636.5; *rowboat parts* 150.15, *identify* 184.11, *register* 185.15, *make rough* 544.11, *sharp point* 549.2, *sharpen* 549.16, *crack* 587.2, 587.7, *angle* 628.1, *gradation* 739.3
notch [Inf] *rung* 636.3
not change *be stable* 674.6
not charge *give* 472.10
not charged for *free of charge* 497.12
not charmed *displeased* 291.6
notched 636.4; *barbed* 544.7, *toothed* 549.13, *angular* 628.7
notched collar *or* lapel *notched thing* 636.2
notched thing 636.2
notched wood *rough thing* 544.2
not chicken feed [Inf] *important matter* 799.2
not choose *react against* 291.15, *hate* 300.11, *leave* 750.10
notch up 636.6; *number* 783.9
notchy *notched* 636.4
not cleared up *uncompleted* 762.7
not clear up *not complete* 762.9

not come *be absent* 576.14
not come amiss *be convenient* 803.5
not come off [Inf] *fail* 846.12, *miscarry* 846.19
not come to the point *be circuitous* 199.6, *be extraneous* 724.12
not come up to *be inferior* 745.10
not come up to *or* meet expectations *disappoint* 846.15
not come up to scratch *be inferior* 745.10, *disappoint* 846.15
not come up to standard *be inferior* 745.10
not come up to the mark *be inferior* 745.10
not come up with the goods [Inf] *fail* 846.12
not compare with *diverge* 734.8
not complete 762.9; *be unskillful* 128.8, *be neglectful* 326.7, *not perform* 466.10
not comply *not observe* 466.9, *refuse* 506.8, *protest* 507.7
not comply with *disobey* 427.12, *dissent* 506.9
not compromise *insist* 376.14
not concentrating *inattentive* 324.5
not confess *be impenitent* 452.4
not confessing *impenitent* 452.2
not conform 782.18; *disobey* 427.12, *not observe* 466.9
not conform to the facts *be untrue* 722.11
not connect 728.13
not consider *reject* 383.10
not considered *excluded* 764.6, *obscure* 800.13
not contemporary *different in time* 648.2
not contest *acquiesce* 421.5
not cooperate *dissociate* 375.14, *resist* 417.10, *disobey* 427.12, *disagree* 463.8, *not observe* 466.9, *refuse* 506.8, *protest* 507.7
not count *exclude* 383.11, *be unimportant* 800.18
not counted *excluded* 764.6
not counting *exclusively* 764.10
not covered by law *unlawful* 53.23
not cramp someone's style [Inf] *be permissive* 502.7, *set free* 829.17
not cricket *wrongful* 430.10
not current *uncustomary* 398.4
not customarily done *uncustomary* 398.4
not customary *unaccustomed* 398.3
not dangerous *trustworthy* 810.10
not deep *shallow* 599.3
not despised *important* 799.7
not deviate *talk straight* 630.15
not die *live* 28.17
not difficult *easy* 823.9
not discriminate *be indiscriminate* 338.10
not dispose of *detain* 471.9
not dispute *be definite* 189.26
not do *be powerless* 515.11, *be inconvenient* 804.9
not do as one is told *disobey* 427.12, *defy* 466.11
not doing well *adverse* 848.10
not do justice to *underestimate* 344.5
not done *uncustomary* 398.4, *improper* 430.14, *unconventional* 782.14
not do one's part *dissociate* 375.14
not doubt *be definite* 189.26

not drink *be sober* 120.8
not drunk *sober* 120.5
not dry behind the ears *unskilled* 128.5, *naive* 821.3
note *correspondence* 169.2, *identify* 184.11, *record* 185.1, *inscribe* 185.14, *bird sound* 240.2, *be attentive* 323.9, *reminder* 354.4, *annotation* 365.2, *paper money* 484.14, *outline* 617.5, *part of writing* 760.6, *list* 785.11, *importance* 799.1
not easy *difficult* 824.9, *blocked* 826.13
not eating *fasting* 118.5
notebook *schoolbook* 48.15, *record book* 185.5
notebook computer *computer* 15.1
noted *recorded* 185.12, *included* 763.4, *listed* 785.9
notedly *eminently* 370.7
note down *inscribe* 185.14
not empowered *unauthorized* 515.7
not enabled *powerless* 515.6
not enclose *open up* 583.16
not enough 98.5, 98.12
not enough to count *or* matter *few* 796.1
not enough work *leisure* 125.1
not entertain (the possibility of) *exclude* 764.7
not entire *incomplete* 806.6
note of explanation *annotation* 365.2
note of hand *paper money* 484.14
note of warning *forewarning* 814.2
notepad *record book* 185.5
notepaper *paper* 104.5
not equate *be unequal* 741.7
not equivocate *be definite* 189.26
notes 185.3; *chronicle* 3.4, *book part* 174.5, *outline* 617.1
not ever 718.16; *never* 640.8
noteworthiness *importance* 799.1
noteworthy *wondrous* 294.9, *memorable* 354.7, *exceptional* 779.13, *notable* 799.11
note writer *correspondent* 169.3
not excessive *temperate* 455.8, *moderate* 521.3
not exist 718.12, 786.6; *be nothing* 190.20, *be unreal* 722.12
not expect *be surprised* 292.12
not extreme *moderate* 521.3
not face *dissociate* 375.14
not fall from grace *be innocent* 449.10
not far *near* 586.16
not feeling like *unwilling* 375.8
not feel well *be unhealthy* 114.29
not finalize *not complete* 762.9
not finalized *uncompleted* 762.7
not find *lose* 468.12
not find one's way to first base [Inf] *lack intellect* 316.8
not finish *not complete* 762.9
not finished *incomplete* 762.5, *uncompleted* 762.7
not finish the job *be unskillful* 128.8
not fit *be extraneous* 724.12, *be inconvenient* 804.9
not fit in with *be different* 463.11, *be independent* 782.20
not fit to be seen *ugly* 531.3
not fit to hold a candle to *outclassed* 745.9
not follow *not observe* 466.9
not follow through *not complete* 762.9
not follow up *not complete* 762.9

not for all the tea in China!
[Inf] *no!* 506.12
not forget *remember* 471.10
not forgetting *additionally* 748.15
not for long *at present* 647.9
not for love nor money! *no!*
190.28
not for the life of me! *no!* 190.28
not for the world! *no!* 190.28
not free *servile* 401.6
not fresh *unhygienic* 114.27
not fulfill *not perform* 466.10, *not
complete* 762.9
not fully *partly* 760.17
not function *be useless* 802.11
not functioning *decrepit* 808.12
not get along *disagree* 463.8
not get it [Inf] *find unintelligible*
364.14
not get started *hesitate* 693.12
not getting it [Inf] *confused*
364.10
not give *be stubborn* 542.11
not give a damn [Inf] *be
indifferent* 289.12
not give a fig *be indifferent* 289.12
not give a hoot [Inf] *be indifferent*
289.12
not give an inch *insist* 376.14
not give another thought to
forget 355.10
not give the time of day *shun*
386.14
not give way *resist* 417.10
not go *be useless* 802.11
not go amiss *be convenient* 803.5
not good enough *unsatisfactory*
438.15, *imperfect* 806.5
not go out *pause* 415.15
not go well *miscarry* 846.19
not granted *dissenting* 506.6
not grasp it *find unintelligible*
364.14
not grow *decrease* 747.7
not guilty *acquitted* 54.25,
vindicated 441.8, *incorrupt* 449.7
not handle it *be inferior* 745.10
no thanks *ingratitude* 311.1
not hard *easy* 823.9
not have *or* **stand a chance** *take
a chance* 842.14
not have a clue [Inf] *be ignorant*
349.8, *be unskillful* 128.8
not have a dry thread *or* **stitch**
be moist 559.15
not have a moment to spare *or*
to call one's own *be busy*
414.19
not have anything to do with
be against 828.17
not have a penny *be poor* 486.14
**not have brains enough to
come in out of the rain** [Inf]
lack intellect 316.8
not have one's heart in it *be
indifferent* 289.12
not have one's marbles [Inf] *lack
intellect* 316.8
not have the foggiest idea *be
ignorant* 349.8
not have the heart to *be
unwilling* 375.12
**not have the sense one was
born with** *be foolish* 353.6
not have the skills *be unskillful*
128.8
not have the slightest idea *find
unintelligible* 364.14
**not have two pennies to rub
together** *be poor* 486.14
not hear of *withhold approval*
438.17
not heed *be neglectful* 326.7

not held against one *overlooked*
312.6
not held together *nonadhesive*
756.4
not help *be useless* 802.11, *be
inconvenient* 804.9
not here *away* 576.19
nothing *absolutes* 6.9, *nonentity*
190.5, 786.4, 800.8, *emptiness*
576.2, *nothingness* 718.2,
insubstantial person 720.5, *zero*
786.1, *trifle* 800.3
nothing alike *incomparably*
734.12
nothing at all *nothingness* 718.2,
zero 786.1
nothing daunted *attempting*
390.4
nothing doing! [Inf] *no!* 190.28,
506.12
nothing else *one* 788.1
nothing else but *certainly* 719.14
nothing happening *inaction*
413.1
nothing in common
incomparability 734.3
nothing in excess *moderation*
455.3
nothing in one's way *liberality*
829.8
nothing in particular *secondary
matter* 800.6
nothing in the kitty *insolvency*
490.5
nothing left out *inclusion* 763.1
nothing like it *best* 805.9
nothingness 718.2, 786.2;
nonentity 190.5, *empty space*
563.2, *emptiness* 576.2,
unimportance 800.1
nothing of note *secondary matter*
800.6
nothing of the kind *to the
contrary* 190.27
nothing of the sort *to the contrary*
190.27
nothing on earth *nothingness*
718.2
nothing out of the ordinary
inferior 745.5
nothing special *mediocrity* 742.3,
inferior 745.5
nothing stirring *repose* 678.2
nothing to boast *or* **brag about**
mediocrity 742.3
nothing to boast of *secondary
matter* 800.6
nothing to choose between
equality 740.1
nothing to confess *incorruption*
449.2
nothing to declare *incorruption*
449.2
nothing to it *predictable* 295.4,
secondary matter 800.6, *easy* 823.9
nothing to it! *naturally!* 295.10
nothing to shout about *inferior*
745.5
nothing to sneeze at [Inf]
important matter 799.2
nothing to spare *scarcity* 98.3
nothing to speak of *secondary
matter* 800.6
nothing to wonder about
predictable 295.4
nothing to worry about
secondary matter 800.6
nothing to write home about
predictable 295.4, *mediocrity*
742.3, *inferior* 745.5, *secondary
matter* 800.6
nothing under the sun
nothingness 718.2

**nothing ventured, nothing
gained!** *here goes!* 390.11
nothing whatever *nothingness*
718.2
not hold a candle to *be inferior*
745.10
not hold against one *show mercy*
312.11
not hold one's liquor *be drunk*
121.34
not hold up *be untrue* 722.11
not hold up in the wash [Inf] *be
untrue* 722.11
not hold water *be untrue* 722.11,
be imperfect 806.8
not hold with *be dissatisfied* 274.7,
be against 828.17
nothosaur *extinct reptile* 37.9
no thought for others *egotism*
444.2
notice 358.3; *publication* 173.1,
advertisement 173.9,
communication 176.3, *gesture*
183.17, *article* 203.2, *see* 242.20,
warning 287.5, 814.1, *attention*
323.1, *be attentive* 323.9, *judgment*
341.1, *discover* 345.11, *criticism*
365.3, *demand* 505.3
noticeable *sensate* 212.5, *visible*
242.19, 244.5, *manifest* 843.8
noticeably *visibly* 242.28, 244.10,
measurably 589.22
notice board *showplace* 843.4
notice of resignation *resignation*
835.1
noticing *seeing* 242.17
notifiable disease *disease* 114.4
not if I can help it! *no!* 190.28
notification *communication* 170.2,
176.3, *publication* 173.1, *warning*
814.1
notified *informed* 170.9
notifier *publicizer* 173.11
notify *educate* 48.22, *inform*
170.11, *proclaim* 173.16,
communicate 176.10, *predict*
358.14, *warn* 814.8
notifying *warning* 814.6
not imbibe *be sober* 120.8
no time to lose *haste* 818.1
not immune *vulnerable* 811.9
not impress *be imperfect* 806.8
not in a million years *never*
640.8, *not ever* 718.16
not in a month of Sundays *never*
640.8
not include *exclude* 764.7
not included *missing* 576.11,
excluded 764.6
not in contention *excluded* 764.6
not increase *decrease* 747.7
not in danger *safe* 810.16
not independent *captive* 832.9
not indulge *be sober* 120.8, *abstain*
386.16
not indulging *sober* 120.5
not in good health *sick* 114.24
not in proper condition *decrepit*
808.12
not in residence *nonresident* 576.9
not insist *be informal* 407.10,
submit 421.4
not interest *not cause wonder*
295.7
not interfere *continue* 669.8, *set
free* 829.17
not in the cards *improbable* 839.4
not in the habit of *unaccustomed*
398.3
not in the least *to the contrary*
190.27
not in the mood *unwilling* 375.8
not in the pink *imperfect* 806.5

not in the same league *outclassed*
745.9, *excluded* 764.6
not in time *untimely* 660.5
not involved *avoiding* 386.9
notion *philosophy* 4.1, *belief* 87.1,
impression 266.2, *idea* 327.1,
supposition 359.1, *conception*
360.4, *will* 372.1, *caprice* 381.1,
method 387.4
notional *philosophical* 4.12,
speculative 317.8, *theoretical*
327.10, *suppositional* 359.5,
imaginary 360.12
notionally *theoretically* 4.24,
327.19
not just stand there *attempt*
390.6
not just this minute *another time*
648.4
not know *be unskillful* 128.8, *be
ignorant* 349.8, *find unintelligible*
364.14
not know how *be unskillful* 128.8
**not knowing which way to
turn** *insolvent* 486.10
not know oneself *be converted*
670.12
not know one's own business
act foolishly 128.10
**not know the meaning of
failure** *overcome obstacles* 845.14
not know what one is about *act
foolishly* 128.10, *find unintelligible*
364.14
not know what to make of *find
unintelligible* 364.14
not know what to say *wonder*
294.12
not know when one is beaten
overcome obstacles 845.14
not know when to stop *be
extravagant* 194.13, *overindulge*
456.11
not know which way is up *be
busy* 414.19
not know which way to turn *be
busy* 414.19, *be in difficulty*
824.19, *be in trouble* 848.13
not lawful *unauthorized* 515.7
not leave a leg to stand on *refute*
332.7
**not let anyone get a word in
edgeways** *be talkative* 207.7
not let go *hold out* 377.13, *retain*
471.7, *preserve* 815.14
not let out of one's sight *make
visible* 244.9
**not let the grass grow under
one's feet** *attempt* 390.6, *be busy*
414.19
not liable *exempt* 434.5
not likely! *no!* 506.12
not like the look of *dislike*
291.12
not like the rest *excellent* 744.14
not listen *fail to hear* 229.9, *be
inattentive* 324.10, *be obstinate*
379.10
not listen to *disobey* 427.12
not live to eat *abstain* 455.11
not live up to expectations *be
imperfect* 806.8
not long *transiently* 643.8
not long ago *newly* 652.21
not long for this world *aged*
27.15, *dying* 29.12, *destroyed*
523.9
not long in the telling *concise*
198.4
not look for praise *be modest*
403.11
not look like *be dissimilar* 734.7
not look where one is going *be
clumsy* 128.9

not lose any sleep over *be indifferent* 289.12
not lucky *unlucky* 848.12
not mad *sane* 109.3
not maintain one's position *deteriorate* 808.14
not make a peep *be silent* 231.3
not make a sound *be silent* 231.3
not make ends meet *lose money* 468.15
not make or **hack it** [Inf] *be inferior* 745.10
not make out *find unintelligible* 364.14
not make sense *be unintelligible* 364.11
not make the grade *be inferior* 745.10, *be imperfect* 806.8, *fail* 846.12
not make the grade or **cut** *be inferior* 745.10
not many *few* 796.1, 796.5
not match *be unequal* 741.7
not matter *be unimportant* 800.18
not mean what one says *talk nonsense* 362.12
not measure up *be inferior* 745.10
not meddle *set free* 829.17
not meet expectations *be insufficient* 98.9, *disappoint* 293.9
not meet requirements *be insufficient* 98.9
not mention *lapse into silence* 208.8
not mince words or **matters** *be sincere* 191.8, *be naive* 821.4
not mind *be indifferent* 289.12, *be incurious* 322.5, *agree with* 462.10
not mind one's own business *meddle* 414.23
not missed *forgotten* 355.7
not modern *different in time* 648.2
not move *ignore* 413.14
not much *few* 796.5
not needed *redundant* 802.9
not notice *be inattentive* 324.10
not now *another time* 648.4, *in the future* 650.13
not observe 466.9; *not accept* 190.19
not obstruct *open up* 583.16
not occur *not exist* 786.6
not offered *refused* 506.5
not often *infrequently* 662.4
not of this world *imaginary* 360.12, *external* 724.11
not one *nobody* 576.6
not one's best *imperfect item* 806.3
not one's cup of tea *disliked* 291.10
not on guard *vulnerable* 811.9, *naive* 821.3
not on speaking terms *estranged* 63.8
not on the level [Inf] *disreputable* 371.4
not on this earth *nowhere* 718.17
not on time *late* 658.5
not on your life! [Inf] *no!* 506.12
not open one's mouth *be silent* 231.3
not operate *be powerless* 515.11
not operating *not working* 415.10
not oppose *agree with* 462.10
notoriety *publicity* 173.7, *disrepute* 371.1, *wickedness* 448.1
notorious *publicized* 173.14, *known* 348.9, *disreputable* 371.4, *wicked* 448.9, *accentuated* 843.11
notoriously *eminently* 370.7, *disreputably* 371.7, *wickedly* 448.15, *manifestly* 843.17
notoriousness *wickedness* 448.1
notornis *flightless bird* 36.8

not out of the woods *endangered* 811.10
not overdoing *temperate* 455.8
not overlooked *important* 799.7
not participating 415.11
not part with *detain* 471.9
not pass *be inferior* 745.10, *fail* 846.12
not pass muster *be imperfect* 806.8
not pass the test *be inferior* 745.10
not pay 488.10, 490.9
not paying *futile* 802.10
not peanuts [Inf] *important matter* 799.2
not perfect *imperfect* 806.5
not perform 466.10
not permitted *dissenting* 506.6
not plain sailing *obstacle* 826.2
not play *dissociate* 375.14
not play ball *dissociate* 375.14, *disagree* 463.8
not play by the rules *do wrong* 430.20
not playing the game [Inf] *wrongful* 430.10
not playing with a full deck [Inf] *unintelligent* 316.6
not play the game [Inf] *do wrong* 430.20
not possible *impossible* 837.4
not practice *not perform* 466.10
not prepared *unwilling* 375.8
not present *disappeared* 265.4, *absent* 576.7
not press *be lenient* 423.5
not press charges *acquit* 54.32
not proceed with *not use* 394.9
not prosecute *acquit* 54.32
not proud *humble* 298.8
not proven *acquitted* 54.25
not public *concealed* 844.7
not pull one's weight *dissociate* 375.14
not push oneself forward *be modest* 403.11
not put a foot wrong *be skillful* 127.14, *attain one's goal* 845.13
not put up with *be against* 828.17
not question *be definite* 189.26, *be incurious* 322.5
not quite *nearly* 586.18, *imperfectly* 806.10
not quite right *imperfect* 806.5
not raise or **lift a finger** *not act* 413.17
not raise an eyebrow *not wonder about* 295.5
not react *ignore* 413.14
not ready *unwilling* 375.8, *unprepared* 389.5
not real *supposed* 359.6, *imaginary* 360.12
not realize one's expectations *be disappointed* 293.8
not really *to the contrary* 190.27
not recommended *inconvenient* 804.5
not redeemable *impenitent* 452.2
not redeemed *impenitent* 452.2
not reform *be impenitent* 452.4
not register *find unintelligible* 364.14
not relate *be extraneous* 724.12
not related *unimportant* 800.10
not relate to *be unrelated* 728.12
not remember *forget* 355.10
not remembered *forgotten* 355.7
not representative *misrepresented* 188.4
not resemble *be dissimilar* 734.7
not resident *nonresident* 576.9
not resist *submit* 421.4, *obey* 426.7

not respect *be discourteous* 411.7
not respond *be indifferent* 289.12
not responsible *exempt* 434.5
not right *wrong* 430.12, *inconvenient* 804.5
no trouble *easy thing* 823.6
no-trump bid *bridge* 168.4
not safe *unsafe* 811.8
not say a word *be silent* 231.3
not see *be blind* 243.18
not see beyond one's nose *lack intellect* 316.8, *prejudge* 337.13
not seen before *unfamiliar* 652.10
not see the woods for the trees *find difficult* 824.17
not select *reject* 383.10
not serious 800.11
not set the world on fire *be mediocre* 289.16
not show up *be absent* 576.14
not signposted *invisible* 245.3
not singular *plural* 793.6
not sixteen ounces to the pound [Inf] *unintelligent* 316.6
not sleep *push* 414.20
not so *to the contrary* 190.27
not so minded *unwilling* 375.8
not sorry *impenitent* 452.2
not speak *be voiceless* 206.8, *be silent* 231.3
not square with the facts *be untrue* 722.11
not stand a chance *be impossible* 837.9, *take a chance* 872.14
not stand for *dissent* 506.9
not stand in the way of *permit* 502.6, *be permissive* 502.7, *make easy* 823.15
not stand on ceremony *be informal* 407.10
not start *malfunction* 846.20
not sticky *nonadhesive* 756.4
not stir (a step) *be motionless* 678.7
not stir *ignore* 413.14, *be inert* 519.4
not stirring *inactive* 413.9
not stop *continue* 669.8, 774.12
not stop and think *lack thought* 318.12
not strong *weak* 517.6
not subject to *exempt* 434.5
not succeed *fail* 846.12
not suffice *be insufficient* 98.9, *be unequal* 741.7, *be imperfect* 806.8
not sufficient *insufficient* 98.4
not support *be against* 828.17
not take a joke *be offended* 302.14
not take it lying down *push* 414.20, *revolt* 417.12, *retaliate* 420.4
not take no for an answer *hold out* 377.13, *be obstinate* 379.10, *compel* 428.8
not take sides *be impartial* 289.15
not tamper *set free* 829.17
not tell *keep secret* 182.11
not tell the truth *be untruthful* 192.20
not the end of the world *secondary matter* 800.6
not there *away* 576.19
not think much of *be dissatisfied* 274.7
not think twice about *be indifferent* 289.12
not thought through *uncompleted* 762.7
not to be caught napping *cunning* 822.4
not to be drawn *cunning* 822.4
not to be drawn out *taciturn* 208.4

not to be had for love or money *valuable* 496.8
not to be pinned down *inconstant* 378.6
not to be recommended *unsatisfactory* 438.15
not to be sneezed at [Inf] *important* 799.7
not to be sniffed or **sneezed at** [Inf] *preferential* 382.10
not to be thought of *unselected* 383.7, *impossible* 837.4
not today *another time* 648.4
not tolerate *be severe* 424.8, *prohibit* 503.8, *be against* 828.17
not to mention *additionally* 748.15
not too little *sufficient* 97.3
not too much *sufficient* 97.3
not to one's taste *disliked* 291.10
not toot one's own horn [Inf] *be modest* 403.11
not touch *abstain* 386.16, *not use* 394.9, *desist* 417.13
not touching *desisting* 417.4
not touch with a ten-foot pole *shun* 386.14
not transparent *obscure* 197.2
not trouble oneself *be incurious* 322.5
not trustworthy *untruthful* 192.12
not try *shy* 386.17
not try to hide *show oneself* 843.15
not turn a hair *be indifferent* 289.12, *not wonder about* 295.5
not turn up *be absent* 576.14
not understand 361.11; *find unintelligible* 364.14, *be mixed up* 751.15
not understandable *unintelligible* 364.4
not unlike *similar* 733.7
not up to date *incomplete* 762.5
not up to expectations *disappointing* 293.6, *imperfect* 806.5
not up to it *insufficient* 98.4
not up to much *inferior* 745.5
not up to scratch *unskillful* 128.4, *disappointing* 293.6
not up to snuff [Inf] *insufficient* 98.4, *unsatisfactory* 274.5
not up to snuff or **scratch** [Inf] *low quality* 745.7
not up to the mark *imperfect* 806.5
Notus *wind god* 9.16
not use 96.18, 394.9
not used *unused* 394.5
not used to *unaccustomed* 398.3
not useful *useless* 802.7
not using (drugs) *traditional* 630.13
not utilize *not use* 394.9
not utilized *unused* 394.5
not utter a squeak *be silent* 231.3
not vital *unimportant* 800.10
not wait to be asked *volunteer* 504.13
not walk straight *be drunk* 121.34
not want *exclude* 383.11
not want anything to do with *refuse* 506.8
not weaken *be strong* 516.14
not weigh *be unimportant* 800.18
not well *sick* 114.24
not well inclined *estranged* 63.8
not what one had expected or **hoped for** *bad outcome* 293.3
not wholly *partly* 760.17

not willing to hear of *refused* 506.5

not with it [Inf] *absent-minded* 324.6

notwithstanding *counter* 510.8

not wonder *be indifferent* 289.12

not wonder about 295.5

not work *be powerless* 515.11, *be useless* 802.11, *malfunction* 846.20

not worked out *uncompleted* 762.7

not working 415.10; *gone wrong* 430.17, *inoperative* 515.8, *broken down* 802.8, *decrepit* 808.12

not worth a second thought *trivial* 800.14

not worth considering *unimportant* 800.10

not worth the effort *futile* 802.10

not worth the paper it's written on *useless* 802.7

not worthwhile *futile* 802.10

not worth worrying about *unimportant* 800.10

no two ways about it *assuredly* 336.12

not yield *insist* 376.14, *be obstinate* 417.11, *be stubborn* 542.11

not yielding *obstinacy* 417.2

Nouakchott Countries 566

noumenalism Philosophical Schools of Thought 4

noumenalist Philosophical Schools of Thought 4

noumenon *philosophical term* 4.7, *idea* 327.1

noun *part of speech* 5.30, 760.7, *name* 202.8

noun clause *or* **phrase** *clause* 5.31

nourish *support life* 28.21, *feed* 90.41, *sustain* 825.25

nourishing *edible* 92.20, *health-giving* 113.6, *healthful* 113.7

nourishment *life requirement* 28.5, *food* 90.1, *sustenance* 825.3

nous *learnedness* 48.8, *intelligence* 315.2

nous [Brit inf] *common sense* 315.4

nouveau realisme Western Art Styles 133

nouveau riche *discourteous* 535.7, *new arrival* 652.7, *prosperous person* 847.4

nouveau roman Western Literary Groups 139

nouveaux riches *the rich* 485.7

nouvelle [Fr] *novel* 139.3

nouvelle cuisine [Fr] *cooking* 91.1, *trendiness* 652.2

nouvelle vague [Fr] *trendiness* 652.2

nouvelle vague Western Literary Groups 139

nova *stellar evolution* 7.10, *natural light* 246.4

Nova Scotia Canadian Provinces 564

Novaya Zemlya Islands 572

novel 139.3, 737.5; *fiction* 139.2, *conception* 360.4, *work of art* 522.4, *unfamiliar* 652.10

novelette *novel* 139.3

novelettist *author* 139.13

novel idea *creative thought* 317.3

novelist *author* 139.13, *book publishing personnel* 174.12, *descriptive writer* 202.10

novella *novel* 139.3, *work of art* 522.4

novel of ideas *novel* 139.3

novel of sensibility *novel* 139.3

novelty Phobias 283, *cheap item* 497.5, *newness* 652.1, *originality* 737.1, *cheap thing* 800.7

Novembergruppe Western Art Styles 133

novemdecillion *million* 792.11

novena Christian rite 85.5, *nine* 792.5

novenary *ninth* 792.16

novice *learner* 48.6, *religious* 84.9, *unskilled person* 128.3, *ski* 162.27, *ignorant person* 349.4, *beginner* 398.2, 771.14, *new arrival* 652.7, *immature* 652.12, *naive person* 821.2

novice run *ski run* 162.2

novitiate *briefing* 388.4

novocaine *anesthetic* 213.3

no voice *speech difficulty* 206.1

Novokirghiz Horse and Pony Breeds 159

now *at what time* 639.17, *immediately* 645.8, *at present* 647.9

nowadays *at present* 647.9

now and again *apart* 587.8, *sometimes* 639.19, 662.5, *for short periods* 641.13

now and then *apart* 587.8, *sometimes* 639.19, 662.5, *for short periods* 641.13, *infrequently* 662.4, *irregularly* 664.6, *discontinuously* 775.15

no way [Inf] *denyingly* 190.23, *uncooperatively* 506.11, *not at all* 718.15

no way! [Inf] *no!* 190.28, 506.12

no way José! [Inf] *no!* 190.28

no way out *futility* 282.3

noways [Inf] *denyingly* 190.23

nowhere 718.17; *away* 576.19

now here, now there *changeably* 666.7

nowhere to be found *losing* 468.9, *missing* 576.11

nowhere to turn *critical situation* 824.6

no-win situation [Inf] *predicament* 824.5

nowise [Inf] *denyingly* 190.23

no woman *nobody* 576.6

no words wasted *conciseness* 198.1

no work *leisure* 125.1, *unemployment* 413.5

no worse *getting well* 113.9

now that *changeably* 666.7

now this *changeably* 666.7

now you see it now you don't *disappearing* 265.3

noxious *unhygienic* 114.27, *poisonous* 117.14, *odorous* 224.5, *evil* 446.7, *destructive* 523.8

noxiously *unhygienically* 114.32, *banefully* 117.19, *evilly* 446.12

noxiousness *evil* 446.1

noyade *slaughter* 30.5, *capital punishment* 454.12

nozzle *garden tool* 17.7, *sprinkler* 557.12

n-space *space* 6.33

n-tuple *set* 6.19

n-type conductivity *semiconductor* 10.34

n-type semiconductor *semiconductor* 10.34

nuance *impression* 266.2, *interval* 739.4, *quietness* 844.4

nub *gist* 329.4, 799.4, *nap* 552.3, *substance* 577.2, *core* 612.2, *essential content* 723.2, *middle* 772.1

nubbiness *roughness* 544.1

nubbliness *roughness* 544.1

nubby *coarse* 544.6

Nubian Deserts 572

nubile *marriageable* 64.17

nubility *marriageability* 64.4

nucleal *nuclear* 13.31

nuclear 13.31, 514.17; *gas* 106.14, *core* 612.7, *middle* 772.9

nuclear accident *nuclear problem* 10.62

nuclear blast *havoc* 523.5

nuclear bomb *bomb* 78.15

nuclear carrier *warship* 77.21

nuclear chemistry Branches of Chemistry 11

nuclear contamination *nuclear problem* 10.62

nuclear energy *energy* 10.10, 514.7, *nuclear fusion* 10.61, *nuclear power* 106.8

nuclear energy industries *chemical process industries* 14.26

nuclear engineering *nuclear fusion* 10.61

nuclear fallout *agent of destruction* 523.7

nuclear family *family circle* 65.4

nuclear fission 10.60; *nuclear power* 106.8, *power source* 514.13, *separation* 753.1, *deconstruction* 758.2

nuclear force *force* 10.9

nuclear-free zone *peace movement* 74.4

nuclear fuel *nuclear power* 106.8, *propellant* 696.9

nuclear fusion 10.61; *nuclear power* 106.8, *power source* 514.13

nuclear generating station *nuclear power* 106.8

nuclear interaction *fundamental interaction* 10.65

nuclear magnetic resonance (NMR) *analysis* 11.17

nuclear magnetic resonance (NMR) scan *diagnostic radiology* 107.12

nuclear membrane *or* **nuclear envelope** *cell structure* 13.16H

nuclear missile *nuclear power production* 514.10, *agent of destruction* 523.7

nuclear particle *little thing* 580.3

nuclear physics Fields of Modern Physics 10

nuclear power 106.8, 514.9; *nuclear fusion* 10.61, *fuels* 106.2, *type of power* 514.6

nuclear power agencies 514.11

nuclear-powered *fired* 106.13

nuclear-powered aircraft carrier *nuclear power production* 514.10

nuclear-powered guided-missile cruiser *nuclear power production* 514.10

nuclear-powered submarine *nuclear power production* 514.10

nuclear power production 514.10

nuclear power research *nuclear power agencies* 514.11

nuclear problem 10.62

nuclear reaction 10.59

nuclear reactor *nuclear power production* 514.10

nuclear reactor *or* **nuclear pile** *nuclear power* 106.8

Nuclear Regulatory Commission (NRC) *nuclear power agencies* 514.11

nuclear submarine *warship* 77.21

nuclear war *warfare* 76.3

nuclear warfare *atomic warfare* 76.4

nuclear warhead *nuclear power production* 514.10, *agent of destruction* 523.7

nuclear waste *nuclear problem* 10.62

nuclear weapon *weapon* 78.1, *nuclear power production* 514.10, *agent of destruction* 523.7

nuclear weapons Phobias 283

nuclear winter *havoc* 523.5

nucleate *nuclear* 13.31, *be dense* 540.8, *core* 612.7, *centered* 612.9, *centralize* 612.11

nucleation *centrality* 612.5

nucleic *nuclear* 13.31

nucleic acid *nucleotide* 12.10, *cell structure* 13.16

nucleic-acid structure *molecular biology* 13.18

nucleolar *nuclear* 13.31

nucleolate(d) *nuclear* 13.31

nucleolus *cell structure* 13.16

nucleomitophobia Phobias 283

nucleon *atom* 10.52, *elementary particle* 10.53

nucleonics *nuclear fusion* 10.61, *nuclear power* 514.9

nucleon number *isotope* 10.57

nucleophile *chemical reaction* 11.8

nucleophilic *reactive* 11.29

nucleophilic reaction *chemical reaction* 11.8

nucleophilic substitution *chemical reaction* 11.8

nucleoplasm *cell structure* 13.16

nucleoprotein *protein* 12.9, *cell structure* 13.16

nucleoside *nucleotide* 12.10

nucleosome *cell structure* 13.16

nucleotide 12.10; *cell structure* 13.16

nucleus *galaxy* 7.5, *atom* 10.52, *personnel* 123.16, *solid body* 540.4, *little thing* 580.3, *core* 612.2, *source* 675.2, 771.3, *essential content* 723.2, *middle* 772.1, *gist* 799.4

nuclide *isotope* 10.57

nude *type of painting* 143.5, *nude person* 614.5, *naked* 614.12

nude, the *bareness* 614.3

nude figure *nude person* 614.5

nude model *nude person* 614.5

nude person 614.5

nudge *inside information* 170.4, *tip* 170.14, *incentive* 178.4, *motivate* 178.17, *gesture* 183.5, 183.17, *type of touch* 216.3, *touch* 216.9, *meeting* 586.5, *meet* 586.15, *set in motion* 677.16, *jolt* 684.9, *collision* 695.2, *blow* 695.5, *collide* 695.10, *warning* 814.1, *warn* 814.8

nudie [Inf] *nude person* 614.5

nudie show [Inf] *show* 138.4

nudism 614.4

nudist *nude person* 614.5, *naked* 614.12

nudity Phobias 283, *bareness* 614.3

nudophobia Phobias 283

Nueces Rivers 570

nugatory *trivial* 800.14

nugget *bullion* 484.16, *solid body* 540.4

nuisance *unpleasant person* 272.5, *annoyance* 276.2, 804.2, *boring person* 296.4, *alacrity* 414.3, *meddler* 414.12, *disturbance* 768.1

nuisance call *telephone call* 169.11

nuke [Inf] *be at war* 76.32, *bomb* 418.19, *cause not to exist* 718.14

Nuku'alofa Countries 566

null *nonexistent* 190.14, 718.9, *meaningless* 362.7, *absent* 576.7, *zero* 786.5, *useless* 802.7

null and void *nonexistent* 190.14, *vetoed* 503.6, *unauthorized* 515.7, *useless* 802.7, *canceled* 834.5

null character (NC) *character* 15.18

null hypothesis *hypothesis testing* 6.52

nullification *disavowal* 190.3, *refutation* 332.1, *neutralization* 510.4, *destruction* 523.1, *cancellation* 834.1

nullificationist *or* **nullificator** *negator* 190.8

nullified *disavowing* 190.12, *canceled* 834.5

nullifier *negator* 190.8, *counteractant* 510.5

nullify *disavow* 190.18, *refute* 332.7, *dissent* 506.9, *counteract* 510.7, *abolish* 523.11, *not exist* 786.6, *cancel* 834.6

nullifying *disavowing* 190.12, *counteracting* 510.6

nulli secundus [L] *best* 744.10, *supremely* 744.23

nullity *nonentity* 190.5, *negator* 190.8, *nonsense* 362.2, *nothingness* 718.2, 786.2, *unimportance* 800.1

null matrix *matrix* 6.20

null set *set* 6.19

numb *desensitized* 213.5, *indifferent* 289.7, *make indifferent* 289.13, *apathetic* 322.4, *overpower* 515.14, *inert* 519.2, *dull* 550.7, *sedentary* 678.5

number 6.4, 138.5, 783.1, 783.9, 784.13; *grammatical term* 5.29, *enumerate* 6.85, *identify* 184.11, *place of residence* 209.4, *total* 738.4, *quantify* 738.7, *be whole* 759.9, *part of writing* 760.6, *include* 763.5

number, a *plurality* 793.1

number [Inf] *clothing* 100.1

numberable *calculable* 784.8

number among one's possessions *possess* 469.14

number-cruncher [Inf] *calculator* 784.5

number-crunching [Inf] *computing* 784.4

numbered *billiard* 149.6, *identified* 184.9, *quantitative* 738.6

numbered ball *billiards* 149.1

numbering *numeration* 6.10, *count* 784.3

numberless 795.8; *immeasurable* 798.6

numberlessness *immeasurability* 798.2

number one *superior person* 445.7, *paragon* 744.6, *successful thing* 845.5, *successful person* 845.6

number one [Inf] *urine* 25.6

number-one *unbeatable* 744.13, *best* 805.9

number-one driver *driver* 146.8

number-one ranking *or* **rating** *successful thing* 845.5

numbers 738.5; *mathematics* 6.1, *Phobias* 283

numbers [Arch] *poetry* 139.8

number system 6.7

number theory *Branches of Mathematics* 6

number two *deputy* 80.1

number two [Inf] *feces* 25.5

number-two driver *driver* 146.8

number with *subsume* 763.7

number work *calculation* 784.1

numbing *anesthetic* 213.6

numbly *indifferently* 289.17, *apathetically* 322.7, *inertly* 519.5, *obtusely* 550.12

numbness *symptom* 114.3, *neurological disease* 114.20, *desensitization* 213.2, *indifference*

289.1, *apathy* 322.2, *inertness* 519.1, *dullness* 550.3, *lack of motion* 678.1

numbskull *unintelligent person* 316.4

numen *minor deity* 82.2

numerable 6.70; *calculable* 784.8

numeracy *mathematics* 6.1, *learning* 348.3

numeral 6.8; *number* 783.1

numerary *numerical* 783.7

numerate *educated* 48.19, *literate* 348.8, *numerical* 783.7, *number* 784.13

numeration 6.10; *calculation* 784.1

numerative *numerical* 783.7, *calculative* 784.7

numerator *division* 6.16, *ratio* 783.5

numeric *numerical* 783.7

numerical 6.68, 783.7; *hierarchical* 765.12, *calculative* 784.7

numerical analysis *Branches of Mathematics* 6

numerical answer 334.7

numerical coefficient *algebraic expression* 6.23

numerical forecast *weather forecast* 9.4

numerically 783.11; *mathematically* 6.93, 784.15, *in order* 765.26, *inventorially* 785.13

numerical meteorology *meteorology* 9.1

numerical order *hierarchy* 765.3

numerical taxonomy *taxonomy* 13.24

numerologist *diviner* 86.14

numerology *divination* 86.5

numerophobia *Phobias* 283

numero uno *superior person* 445.7, *paragon* 744.6

numerous *frequent* 661.4, *plural* 793.6, *multitudinous* 795.5

numerously 795.13; *frequently* 661.7

numerousness *frequency* 661.1, *multiplicity* 793.2, 795.2

numinous *holy* 82.19

numinously *divinely* 82.24

numinousness *the occult* 86.2

numismatic *monetary* 484.22

numismatically *monetarily* 484.27

numismatics *Hobbies and Pastimes* 167, *coinage* 484.13

numismatist *financier* 484.17

numismatology *coinage* 484.13

nummary *monetary* 484.22

nummular *monetary* 484.22

numskull *unintelligent person* 316.4, *simpleton* 526.5

nun *celibate* 67.4, *religious person* 81.9, *religious* 84.9, *chaste person* 431.6, *poor person* 486.6, *sea marker* 690.7, *individualist* 756.3

Nunc Dimittis *prayer* 85.10

nuncio *delegate* 79.1

nuncupative *spoken* 205.13

nunnery *monasticism* 67.3, *clerical dwelling* 84.10, *privacy* 181.6, *private space* 812.2

nunnish *monastic* 67.8

nun's habit *uniform* 100.9

nuptial *matrimonial* 64.15, *ritualistic* 85.15, *contractual* 459.7

nuptial benediction *wedding* 64.5

nuptial bond *marriage* 64.1

nuptially *matrimonially* 64.23, *contractually* 459.9

nuptial mass *wedding* 64.5

nuptial ode *general wedding terms* 64.6

nuptials *wedding* 64.5

nuptial song *general wedding terms* 64.6

nuptial vows *wedding* 64.5

nurse 107.23; *lactate* 35.34, *personal attendant* 69.5, *feed* 90.41, *provide drink* 93.21, *practice medicine* 107.32, *treat* 115.17, *professional worker* 123.11, *manage* 126.10, *helper* 275.5, *be compassionate* 305.11, *cure* 809.15, *protector* 810.11, *protect* 810.21, *preserve* 815.14, *support* 825.24

nurse cow *livestock* 16.11

nursemaid *personal attendant* 69.5, *protector* 810.11

nurse practitioner *nurse* 107.23

nurse resentment *resent* 302.13

nursery 17.4; *room* 60.9, *farm* 124.11, *source* 675.2

nursery education *educational system* 48.2

nurseryman *horticulturist* 17.13

nursery rhyme *Poem or Verse Forms* 139

nursery school *school* 48.11

nurserywoman *horticulturist* 17.13

nurse's aide *technical worker* 123.14

nurse's cap *cap* 100.33

nurse's uniform *uniform* 100.9, *clothing* 184.6

nurse through *cure* 809.15

nursing *treatment* 107.14, *therapeutic* 107.30, *therapy* 115.12

nursing assistant *technical worker* 123.14

nursing auxiliary *paramedic* 107.24

nursing care *treatment* 107.14

nursing home 107.18; *service workplace* 124.5, *resting place* 668.5, *haven* 810.3, *safe house* 812.5

nursing home patient *sick person* 114.22

nursling *child* 26.6

nurture *practice livestock farming* 16.20, *education* 48.1, *educate* 48.22, *food* 90.1, *feed* 90.41, *rear* 715.10, *sustenance* 825.3, *sustain* 825.25

nurtured *reared* 715.7

nurturing *rearing* 715.2, *supportive* 825.18

Nut *Deities* 82

nut *seed* 41.9, *botanical fruit* 44.2, *climbing equipment* 161.4, *fastener* 754.7

nut [Inf] *insane person* 110.5, *object of ridicule* 368.3, *eccentric* 782.10

nutate *oscillate* 683.12

nutation *oscillation* 683.1

nutational *oscillating* 683.8

nut bread *bread* 90.10

nutbrown *brown* 256.5

nut case [Inf] *insane person* 110.5

nut house *or* **nuthouse** [Inf] *mental hospital* 110.6

nutlet *fruit structure* 44.3

nutmeg *Herbs and Spices* 91

nutmeg grater *grater* 553.12

nut pine *Trees and Shrubs* 43

nutriment *food* 90.1

nutrition *physiology* 13.13, *food* 90.1, *cooking* 91.1, *diet* 92.5, *health care* 107.7

nutritional *edible* 92.20

nutrition expert *dietitian* 92.16

nutritionist *dietitian* 92.16, *paramedic* 107.24, *hygienist* 116.2

nutritious *edible* 92.20, *health-giving* 113.6, *healthful* 113.7

nutritiously *culinarily* 91.11, *edibly* 92.26, *healthily* 113.14

nutritiousness *healthfulness* 113.2

nutritive *edible* 92.20

nuts *Tree Products* 43, *fruits* 44.1, *snack* 90.8

nuts [Inf] *organs of reproduction* 21.9, *insane* 110.9

nuts and bolts *supplies* 102.3, *machinery* 103.5, *meaning* 361.1, *fact* 717.6, *essential content* 723.2, *rudiments* 771.7, *specifications* 779.6, *gist* 799.4

nutshell *casing* 613.9

nuttiness [Inf] *insanity* 110.1, *ridiculousness* 368.1

nutty [Inf] *insane* 110.9, *foolish* 353.5, *ridiculous* 368.5

nutty as a fruitcake [Inf] *insane* 110.9

nux vomica *Trees and Shrubs* 43

nuzzle *type of touch* 216.3, *touch* 216.9, *communicate love* 299.25

nuzzling *communication of love* 299.6

Nyasa *Lakes* 568

Nyaya *Philosophical Schools of Thought* 4

Nyayan *Philosophical Schools of Thought* 4

nybble *computer information* 15.17

nyckelharpa *Musical Instruments* 142

nyctalopia *faulty vision* 243.1

nyctalopic *visually impaired* 243.9

nyctophobia *Phobias* 283

nye *Collective Names* 59

nyet! [Russ] *no!* 190.28

nylon *polymer* 11.9, *plastics* 104.6, *fiber* 130.2

nylon line *fishing tackle* 154.7

nylons *legwear* 100.26

nylon stockings *porosity* 583.5

nylon webbing *climbing equipment* 161.4

nymph *developmental biology* 13.22, *young animal* 26.4, *young woman* 26.9, *female* 33.1, *larva* 40.9, *minor deity* 82.2

nymphet *young woman* 26.9, *loose woman* 33.6, *sexually immoral person* 432.8

nympho [Inf] *sexual perversion* 20.12, *loose woman* 33.6, *desirer* 288.9, *sexually immoral person* 432.8

nymphomania *sexual perversion* 20.12, *compulsion* 108.13, *sexual desire* 288.5, *sexual immorality* 432.2

nymphomaniac *sexual perversion* 20.12, *loose woman* 33.6, *desirer* 288.9, *sexually immoral person* 432.8, *perverted* 432.12

nymphomaniacal *lustful* 288.15

nystagmatic *weak-sighted* 243.9

nystagmus *faulty vision* 243.1

O

oaf *unskilled person* 128.3, *unpleasant person* 272.5, *unintelligent person* 316.4

oafish *unintelligent* 316.6

oafishness *ignorance* 316.3

Oahu *Islands* 572

oak *Trees and Shrubs* 43

oak apple *tree disease* 43.8

oak gall *tree disease* 43.8

Oak Leaf Cluster *US Military Medals* 58

oakmoss moss 46.4, lichen 47.16

Oaks [Brit] famous horse races 159.13

oar rowboat parts 150.15, boating person 150.24, nautical person 690.12, propeller 696.8

oarlock axle 682.7

oarsman boating person 150.24, nautical person 690.12

oasis irrigator 557.13, lake 568.1

oast-house [Brit] farm building 16.4

oast-house or **oast** [Brit] place for fire 217.9

oath witness 54.16, vow 189.3, curse word 301.4, duty 433.1, promise 458.1

oath of allegiance vow 189.3

oath of office vow 189.3

oatmeal cereal 90.12, brown 256.5

oats crop 16.8, animal feed 16.12, cereal grass 45.4, animal food 90.2

Ob Rivers 570

obbligato Musical Terms and Expression Marks 140

obduracy willfulness 372.3, obstinacy 379.1, 417.2, impenitence 452.1, mental hardness 542.4, determination 674.2

obdurate relentless 309.4, willful 372.8, obstinate 379.5, 417.7, impenitent 452.2, mentally hard 542.8, mentally tough 547.12, determined 674.5, troublesome 824.13

obdurately relentlessly 309.8, obstinately 379.11, single-mindedly 547.19, determinedly 674.10

obdurateness relentlessness 309.2, obstinacy 379.1, mental toughness 547.5

obeah idolatry 83.4, witchcraft 86.6, talisman 86.9

obeah doctor witch 86.15

obedience 426.1; submissiveness 298.3, acquiescence 373.3, submission 421.1, deference 433.4, kindness 445.3, virtues 447.2, observance 465.1, easiness 543.5, compliance 781.2, subjection 832.1

obedient 69.10, 426.4; law-abiding 53.20, submissive 298.10, acquiescent 373.9, submitting 421.3, deferential 433.9, kind 445.12, principled 447.6, observant 465.3, disciplined 765.17, compliant 781.9, subordinate 832.8

obediently 69.12, 426.9; submissively 298.23, with humility 421.8, kindly 445.20, ethically 447.10, observantly 465.6, adaptably 781.15

obeisance 426.3; sycophancy 401.2, deference 410.4, submission 421.1, admiration 435.2, mark of respect 435.4, greeting 435.5, bow 916.6

obeisant 426.6; sycophantic 401.7, deferential 410.8, showing respect 435.7

obeisantly deferentially 410.15

obelisk Reference Signs 183, monument 185.10

obelus Reference Signs 183

Oberammergau dramatic style 136.3

Oberinntal Grey Breeds of Cattle 16

Oberland Range Mountains and Hills 569

OBERON Programming Languages 15

Oberon Planets and Their Satellites 7

obese heavy 538.9, fat 579.15, thick 594.5, well-rounded 633.8

obesely fatly 579.22

obesity immoderation 99.2, heaviness 538.1, fatness 579.5, thickness 594.1, round body 633.2

obesophobia Phobias 283

obey 426.7; serve 69.11, revere 81.26, worship 83.15, follow rites 85.19, submit 298.17, 421.4, be willing 373.12, do one's duty 433.17, show respect 435.16, better 445.17, be virtuous 447.8, yield 543.17, abide by 781.12, be subject to 832.12

obeying the law observance 465.1

obey one's conscience be motivated 508.10

obey one's instincts be motivated 508.10

obey orders obey 426.7, follow the rules 780.17

obey regulations abide by 781.12

obey the law be moral 431.13, observe 465.4

obfuscate disguise 181.13, make mysterious 182.13, make obscure 197.3, make dim 248.8, opaque 250.7, practice sophistry 330.11, disorder 625.4

obfuscated shady 250.4, cunning 330.8

obfuscating problematic 824.11

obfuscation evasion 181.5, obscurity 197.1, darkening 247.2, opaqueness 250.1, cunning 330.3

obfuscatory obscure 197.2

obi talisman 86.9, accessory 100.28

Obie prizes 453.3

obituaries news story 171.3

obituarist funeral person 31.5

obituary biography 3.5, funeral 31.4, 31.9, record 185.1, parting 705.3

obituary or **obit** death count 29.10

obituary writer funeral person 31.5

object 524.6, 828.18; part of speech 5.30, try a case 54.28, negate 190.16, purpose 327.4, protest 331.19, 507.7, countercharge 332.9, doubt 333.19, answer back 334.19, refuse 347.9, point 361.5, objective 374.5, oppose 375.13, dissent 506.9, motivation 508.1, product 522.3, weight 538.8, reason 675.4, thing 717.3, aim 773.12

object code programming language 15.16

object distance lens system 10.22

objected to negated 190.10

objectification imagination 360.1

objectify imagine 360.14, be material 524.8

objecting litigating 54.21, demonstrating 331.14, retaliatory 334.13, resistant 417.6, censuring 438.12, dissenting 506.6

objection 828.2; horse racing 159.10, dissuasion 179.1, negation 190.1, dislike 300.2, countercharge 332.3, question 333.1, counterstatement 334.5, disapproval 347.2, opposition 375.2, resistance 417.1, censure 438.1, dissent 506.2, protest 507.1

objectionability 272.2

objectionable 272.7; detested 291.11, hateful 300.10, retaliatory 334.13, unforgivable 430.16, unsatisfactory 438.15, inconvenient 804.5

objection overruled witness 54.16

objection sustained witness 54.16

objective 374.5; rational 4.15, grammatical term 5.29, of grammar 5.41, lens system 10.22, motive 178.5, truthful 191.4, aspiration 281.3, wish 288.2, impartial 289.9, purpose 327.4, wise 352.4, future intention 374.3, declaration 376.2, venture 390.2, disinterested 443.4, motivation 508.1, material 524.7, direction 697.1, destination 704.6, aim 773.12

objective existence reality 719.1

objectively rationally 4.25, grammatically 5.48, truthfully 191.9, impartially 289.19, wisely 352.8, disinterestedly 443.8, materially 524.9

objective psychology Psychological Theories, Schools 108

objective reporting print journalism 175.4

objectivism Philosophical Schools of Thought 4

objectivist Philosophical Schools of Thought 4

objectivity philosophical attitude 4.3, truthfulness 191.1, impartiality 289.3, wisdom 352.1, disinterestedness 443.1

object lesson warning 814.1

object of admiration marvel 294.3

object of charity recipient 473.5

object of desire 288.8

object of one's affections loved one 299.13

object of pride 297.6

object of ridicule 368.3

object of scorn nonentity 800.8

object of wonder marvel 294.3

object of worship minor deity 82.2

objector negator 190.8, protester 331.8, 507.4, answerer 334.10, reluctant person 375.7, disapprover 438.7, dissenter 463.5, opposer 828.9

object-oriented programming (OOP) programming concepts 15.24

object to be dissatisfied 274.7, react against 291.15, hate 300.11, resist 417.10, disagree 463.8, be against 828.17

objet d'art work of art 133.4

objet trouvé [Fr] sculpture 144.1

objurgate condemn 438.18

objurgation condemnation 438.2

objurgative condemning 438.10

objurgatory condemning 438.10

oblast administrative region 564.4

oblate spherical 6.80

oblation act of worship 83.2, Eucharist 85.7, drink 93.2, penitence 313.3, offering 472.6, 504.5

oblational ritualistic 85.15, apologetic 313.6, sacrificial 504.10

oblatorily as a gift 472.17

oblatory apologetic 313.6, given 472.8, sacrificial 504.10

obligate impose a duty 433.14, contract 462.11

obligated grateful 310.4, duty-bound 433.8, guaranteeing 458.9, contractual 459.7

obligation necessitation 95.5, gratitude 310.1, answerability 334.9, specification 340.6, direction 384.3, contract 391.2, 459.1,

462.2, compulsion 428.1, duty 433.1, promise 458.1, 464.2, debt 488.1

obligatorily commandingly 425.15, compellingly 428.12, contractually 462.15

obligatory necessitative 95.11, answerable 334.17, conditional 340.10, commanding 425.7, compulsory 428.7, dutiful 433.6, contractual 459.7, 462.7, essential 723.5, legal 780.8

oblige serve 69.11, necessitate 95.17, be benevolent 305.10, answer to 334.22, specify 340.14, direct 384.10, be lenient 423.5, compel 428.8, impose a duty 433.14, improve 825.26

obliged grateful 310.4, answerable 334.17, meant 359.7, directed 384.7, duty-bound 433.8, indebted 488.7

obliging courteous 410.6, benevolent 825.21, cooperative 827.9

obligingly courteously 410.13, benevolently 825.34

obligingness courtesy 410.1

obligor promise maker 458.6, debtor 488.6

oblique 607.6, 628.8, 698.11; linear 6.77, circumlocutory 199.4, oblique line 607.5, diverge 607.11, side 623.6, directional 677.13, 697.8, mysterious 844.11

oblique angle angle 6.37, 628.1, oblique line 607.5

oblique-angled angled 628.9

oblique light dimness 248.1

oblique line 607.5

obliquely 607.13; circuitously 199.8, laterally 623.11, askew 628.12, indirectly 698.28, mysteriously 844.17

oblique motion movement 677.3

obliqueness 607.1; deviation 698.1

oblique triangle oblique line 607.5

obliquitous oblique 607.6

obliquity 628.2; obliqueness 607.1, deviation 698.1, imbalance 741.2

obliterate 186.8; clean 111.17, cause to disappear 265.7, destroy 523.10, erode 554.14, exterminate 709.22, subtract 749.6, eject 764.8, make useless 802.12, cancel 834.6

obliterated 186.4; no more 718.11, subtracted 749.3

obliteration 186.1; blacking out 265.2, destruction 523.1, wearing away 554.2, extinction 718.8, subtraction 749.1, ejection 764.2, cancellation 834.1

oblivion 355.4; destruction 186.2, inattention 229.2, lack of thought 318.1, negligence 326.1, sleep 415.5, extinction 718.8

oblivious 355.9; forgetful 186.7, insensible 213.4, unhearing 229.5, blind to 243.14, indifferent 289.7, thoughtless 318.7, inconsiderate 318.9, inattentive 324.5, negligent 326.4, ignorant 349.5, nonobservant 466.5

obliviously forgetfully 186.12, 355.14, insensibly 213.9, indifferently 289.17, thoughtlessly 318.15, inattentively 324.12, 466.13, ignorantly 349.11

obliviousness figurative blindness 243.8, inattention 324.1, oblivion 355.4, nonobservance 466.1

oblong polygon 6.42, polygonal 6.79, cubic 6.81, quadrilateral 791.2

O blood group blood 555.4
obloquial censuring 438.12
obloquy public speaking 205.11, vilification 301.2, disrespect 436.1, censure 438.3, defamation 440.3
obnoxious objectionable 272.7, hateful 300.10, badly behaved 399.16, repulsive 701.4
obnoxiously hatefully 300.14, badly 399.23, repulsively 701.11
obnoxiousness hatefulness 300.4
obnoxious person badly behaved person 399.8
oboe Musical Instruments 142
oboe da caccia Musical Instruments 142
oboe d'amore Musical Instruments 142
oboist player 141.2
obolus ancient coins 484.12
obscene 112.9; of language 5.35, indecent 261.8, profane 301.10, offensive 432.11, depraved 448.10, ribald 535.8, repulsive 701.4
obscene language vulgarism 5.20, offensive language 301.5
obscenely colloquially 5.45, dirtily 112.12, profanely 301.19, promiscuously 432.19, unvirtuously 448.16, ribaldly 535.12, repulsively 701.11
obscenity 112.4; nonstandard language 5.7, vulgarism 5.20, profanity 301.3, curse word 301.4, sexual immorality 432.2, depravity 448.2, grossness 535.3
obscurantism opinionatedness 379.3
obscurantist obstinate person 379.4
obscuration obscurity 197.1, darkening 247.2, blackness 254.1, blacking out 265.2
obscure 197.2, 250.8, 800.13; occult 86.16, 86.22, disguise 181.13, make mysterious 182.13, make obscure 197.3, hidden 243.15, blind 243.17, private 245.5, make invisible 245.7, murky 248.5, make dim 248.8, shady 250.4, opaque 250.7, cause to disappear 265.7, unknown 349.7, unintelligible 364.4, unclear 364.5, difficult 364.8, make unintelligible 364.13, lowly 597.17, profound 598.15, indirect 607.8, circumlocute 607.12, hide 613.27, shapeless 625.2, make shapeless 625.3, unreal 720.8, inferior 745.5, problematic 824.11, indeterminate 841.14, make uncertain 841.19, concealed 844.7
obscured concealed 181.8, difficult to see 245.4, private 245.5, murky 248.5, indirect 607.8, protected 613.20
obscurely 197.4; occultly 86.27, darkly 247.11, dimly 248.10, opaquely 250.9, blackly 254.12, humbly 597.27, profoundly 598.27, shapelessly 625.5, unimportantly 800.21, problematically 824.25, indeterminately 841.24
obscureness indirectness 607.3, shapelessness 625.1
obscure person nonentity 800.8
obscure point unintelligible thing 364.3
obscuring blinding 243.13, darkening 247.6, blacking out 265.2, covering 613.1
obscurity 197.1, 250.2; the occult 86.2, evasion 181.5, mystery 182.4, invisibility 245.1, darkness

247.1, murk 248.2, opaqueness 250.1, unintelligibility 364.1, lowliness 597.8, profundity 598.5, shapelessness 625.1, inferiority 745.1, unimportance 800.1, difficulty 824.1, indeterminacy 841.6, concealment 844.2
obsequial funeral 31.9
obsequies after death 29.9, funeral 31.4, public speaking 205.11
obsequious submissive 298.10, sycophantic 401.7, 439.11, obedient 426.4, showing respect 435.7
obsequiously phraseologically 5.47, submissively 298.23, sycophantically 401.16, obediently 426.9, respectfully 435.19, flatteringly 439.16
obsequiousness submissiveness 298.3, sycophancy 401.2, 439.5, obedience 426.1
obsequy lament 280.2
observability visibility 244.1
observable visible 242.19, 244.5
observably visibly 242.28
observance 465.1; religiousness 81.2, ritual 85.1, custom 397.4, line of action 399.4, celebration 405.1, commemoration 405.2, obedience 426.1, compliance 781.2
observant 465.3; prayerful 85.17, seeing 242.17, watchful 323.6, circumspect 325.8, obedient 426.4, mentally sharp 549.14
observantly 465.6; ritually 85.21, watchfully 242.29, attentively 323.14, obediently 426.9
observation 242.5; observatory 7.24, Children's and Party Games 167, maxim 177.1, utterance 205.10, idea 327.1, discovery 345.1, observance 465.1
observational theoretical 6.66
observational astronomy astronomy 7.1
observational error measurement 10.67
observation car place for viewing 242.13, railroad car 688.5
observation point place for viewing 242.13
observation post overview 425.6
observatory 7.24; place for viewing 242.13
observe 7.34, 465.4; philosophize 4.19, experiment 10.72, revere 81.26, follow rites 85.19, aphorize 177.3, watch 242.23, take note of 323.10, discover 345.11, commemorate 354.14, 405.11, do something 412.13, stand by 575.15, abide by 781.12
observe a ceremony or **ritual** perform 465.5
observe a limit be moderate 455.12
observe a practice perform 465.5
observe etiquette have good manners 410.10
observe neutrality be at peace 73.10
observe protocol have good manners 410.10
observer 242.15; astronomer 7.2, air force person 77.31, golfer 156.7, discoverer 345.7, attender 575.6, aircraft personnel 689.8
observe routine have a habit 397.16
observe the formalities put on a show 404.28, be formal 406.11
observe the rule of business perform 465.5

observe the rules obey 426.7
observe tradition have a habit 397.16
observing observant 465.3, watching 575.12
obsessed bewitched 86.21, passionate 266.12, diligent 323.7, resolute 376.7, opinionated 379.9
obsession compulsion 108.13, 428.1, delusion 110.2, emotion 266.3, diligence 323.4, prejudgment 342.5, opinionatedness 379.3, habit 397.1
obsessional neurosis neurosis 108.9
obsessive insane person 110.5, habit-forming 397.15
obsessive behavior delusion 110.2
obsessive-compulsive disorder anxiety disorder 108.11
obsessive-compulsive neurosis or **reaction** neurosis 108.9
obsessive-compulsive personality disorder personality disorder 108.7
obsessive dieter compulsive person 428.5
obsessive need compulsion 428.1
obsessiveness compulsion 428.1
obsidian dark thing 247.3, black thing 254.3
obsolescence disuse 394.3, extinction 718.8
obsolescent disappearing 265.3, former 651.14
obsolescently out of use 394.13
obsolete worded 5.38, disappeared 265.4, disused 394.8, unfashionable 528.10, antiquarian 651.13, no more 718.11, redundant 802.9
obsolete coinage false money 484.15
obsoletely lexically 5.46, out of use 394.13
obsoleteness disuse 394.3
obstacle 826.2, 837.3; hurdles 166.6, frustration 293.2, prohibition 503.1, obstruction 510.3, solid body 540.4, inconvenience 804.1, defect 806.4, trap 813.1, snag 824.8, restraint 830.1
obstacle course military training 76.19
obstetric medical 107.28
obstetrician medical specialist 107.20
obstetrics femaleness 33.2
obstetrics and gynecology Medical Specialties 107
obstinacy 379.1, 417.2; Collective Names 59, arrogance 297.2, willfulness 372.3, tenacity 376.4, 755.2, perseverance 377.1, severity 424.1, disobedience 427.1, impenitence 452.1, mental hardness 542.4, mental toughness 547.5, determination 674.2, preservation of status quo 815.8, contrariness 828.5, conviction 840.2
obstinate 379.5, 417.7; arrogant 297.9, willful 372.8, tenacious 376.9, 755.6, strong-willed 376.10, persevering 377.6, defiant 416.5, defying 416.6, severe 424.5, disobedient 427.10, impenitent 452.2, mentally hard 542.8, mentally tough 547.12, determined 674.5, conservative 815.3, troublesome 824.13, uncooperative 828.14, convinced 840.8
obstinately 379.11; arrogantly 297.18, defiantly 416.9, in defiance

416.10, resistingly 417.14, severely 424.11, disobediently 427.14, single-mindedly 547.19, determinedly 674.10, tenaciously 755.12, perversely 824.27, with certainty 840.16
obstinate person 379.4
obstreperous bad-mannered 411.6, disobedient 427.10, disorderly 766.15, troublesome 824.13
obstreperously vociferously 239.18, rudely 411.9, disobediently 427.14
obstreperousness disobedience 427.1
obstruct 584.13; thwart 293.10, dissociate 375.14, avert 386.15, resist 417.10, fence 419.21, stall 419.28, disobey 427.12, prohibit 503.8, counteract 510.7, stop the flow 570.12, delay 658.13, slow down 693.13, disrupt 768.12, make useless 802.12, be inconvenient 804.9, cause difficulties 824.22, hinder 826.15, withstand 828.20
obstructed 584.8; private 245.5, frustrated 293.5, held up 658.6, delayed 693.10, disrupted 768.8
obstructer hinderer 826.11, opposer 828.9
obstructing delaying 658.8
obstruction 510.3, 584.2; golf course 156.2, soccer play 163.5, frustration 293.2, avoidance 386.1, prohibition 503.1, delay 658.3, hesitation 693.5, disruption 768.4, snag 824.8, hindrance 826.1, uncooperativeness 828.4
obstructionism disobedience 427.1
obstructionist hinderer 826.11, opposer 828.9
obstructive negational 190.9, fugitive 386.10, resistant 417.6, disobedient 427.10, prohibited 503.5, counteracting 510.6, delaying 658.8, hindering 826.12, uncooperative 828.14
obstructively negatively 190.22, evasively 386.24, by veto 503.12, late 658.14, disturbingly 768.13, with delay 826.22
obstructiveness hindrance 826.1, uncooperativeness 828.4
obtain become a habit 397.17, gain 467.15, receive 473.13, take 477.14, purchase 481.10, bring 685.11, draw out 711.17, prevail 778.19
obtainable gainful 467.10
obtain a divorce divorce 66.9
obtain an extract 711.19
obtain assistance find means 511.8
obtainer recipient 473.5
obtaining familiar 397.10, taking 477.1, drawing out 711.5
obtaining of an extract 711.7
obtainment gain 467.1
obtain one's objective attain one's goal 845.13
obtrude let out 709.26
obtrusion disgorgement 709.6
obtrusive audacious 400.10, cocky 402.11, blatant 404.19, manifest 843.9
obtrusively audaciously 400.20, cockily 402.19, blatantly 404.34
obtrusiveness audacity 400.3, cockiness 402.4, manifest 404.6
obtund mitigate 521.9, blunt 550.9
obtundity dullness 550.3
obtuse unintelligent 316.6, dull 550.7, thick-witted 594.7

obtuse angle *angle* 6.37, 628.1
obtuse-angled *angled* 628.9
obtusely 550.12; *unintelligently* 316.9, *thick-wittedly* 594.13
obtuseness *ignorance* 316.3, *dullness* 550.3, *thick-wittedness* 594.3
obtuse *or* **obtuse-angled triangle** *triangle* 6.41
obverse *front* 621.1, 621.9, *opposite* 731.3
obversely *diametrically* 731.6
obversion *oppositeness* 731.1
obvert *be opposite* 731.4
obviate *counteract* 510.7, *disentangle* 823.17, *hinder* 826.15
obviation *hindrance* 826.1
obvious *theoretical* 6.66, *disclosed* 180.5, *clear* 196.2, *visible* 242.19, 244.5, *easily seen through* 249.10, *appearing* 264.9, *demonstrated* 331.9, *demonstrable* 331.12, *evident* 339.9, *simple* 363.6, *opened up* 583.11, *superficial* 599.4, *certain* 840.7, *manifest* 843.9
obviously *mathematically* 6.93, *clearly* 196.4, *visibly* 242.28, 244.10, *transparently* 249.13, *apparently* 264.16, *manifestly* 331.20, 843.17, *evidently* 339.16, *originally* 345.16, *openly* 583.22, *superficially* 599.8
obviousness *clarity* 196.1, 244.2, 363.2, *openness* 249.6, 843.6, *indication* 339.3, *unpretentiousness* 526.2, *superficiality* 599.2, *certainty* 840.1
ocarina Musical Instruments 142
occasion *celebration* 405.1, *opportunity* 583.8, *point in time* 645.4, *cause* 675.1, 675.8, *reason* 675.4, *occurrence* 726.2, *good chance* 842.6
occasional 647.5; *periodic* 639.10, *infrequent* 662.2, *sometimes* 662.5, *sparse* 796.6
occasional help *servant* 69.1
occasionalism Philosophical Schools of Thought 4
occasionalist Philosophical Schools of Thought 4
occasionally *sometimes* 639.19, *for short periods* 641.13, *infrequently* 662.4, *discontinuously* 775.15, *sparsely* 796.11
occasional showers *or* **rain** *rain* 9.27
occasional verse *poetry* 139.8
Occident *world region* 564.6, *compass direction* 697.5
Occidental *regional* 564.12, *directional* 697.8
occipital bone Human Bones 19
occlude *obstruct* 584.13
occluded *obstructed* 584.8
occluded front *air movement* 9.11
occlusion *air movement* 9.11, *obstruction* 584.2
occult 86.16, 86.22; *disguised* 181.9, *mysterious* 182.10, 844.11, *make dark* 247.10, *unintelligible* 364.4, *difficult* 364.8, *parapsychological* 525.9
occult, the 86.2; *spiritual world* 525.3
occult and psychic phenomena 86.7
occultation *orbit* 7.22, *concealment* 181.1, *darkening* 247.2, *blacking out* 265.2
occulted *disappeared* 265.4
occult influence 512.2
occulting *lucent* 246.13

occulting light *safety light* 246.7
occultism 86.1; *mystery* 182.4, *divination* 358.2, *unintelligibility* 364.1, *mysteriousness* 844.5
occultist 86.13; *nonmaterialist* 525.7
occultly 86.27; *metaphysically* 525.13
occult meaning *mysteriousness* 844.5
occultness *the occult* 86.2, *mysteriousness* 844.5
occult phenomena *spiritual world* 525.3
occult power *type of power* 514.6
occupancy *claiming* 469.2, *residence* 575.2
occupant *inhabitant* 61.1, *possessor* 469.10
occupation *job* 122.3, *mass demonstration* 331.7, *future intention* 374.3, *activity* 385.4, *undertaking* 391.1, *action* 412.1, *social activity* 414.2, *military attack* 418.2, *line of duty* 433.3, *claiming* 469.2, *business* 480.6, *employment* 573.3
occupational *socioeconomic* 2.13, *acting* 412.9, *professional* 480.15, *employed* 573.8
occupational disease *disease* 114.4
occupational medicine *medicine* 107.1
occupational therapist *paramedic* 107.24
occupational therapy *treatment* 107.14, *therapy* 115.12
occupied *inhabited* 61.10, *used* 393.5, *busy* 414.15, *on-duty* 433.10
occupied country *dominion* 566.3
occupier *inhabitant* 61.1, *householder* 61.5, *possessor* 469.10
occupy *inhabit* 60.22, 61.13, *protest* 331.19, *possess* 469.14, *exert sovereignty* 566.12, *reside* 575.17, *fill* 761.11
occupy a freehold *own property* 470.11
occupy a post *govern* 49.26
occupying *claiming* 469.2, *possessing* 469.11, *residing* 575.8
occupy oneself 412.15
occupy the center (ground) *stand in the middle* 772.17
occur 264.14; *be present* 575.13, *take effect* 676.11, *exist* 717.18, *be real* 719.10
occur annually *be cyclic* 663.11
occur infrequently *be infrequent* 662.3
occur monthly *be cyclic* 663.11
occur periodically *be frequent* 661.5
occur regularly *be frequent* 661.5
occurrence 726.2; *probability* 6.59, *visibility* 264.4, *existence* 717.1, *reality* 719.1
occurring *existing* 717.11, *real* 719.6
occur to one *have an idea* 327.13
ocean 8.14; *sea* 571.1, *the depths* 598.2, *transportable* 686.7, *nautical* 690.14
ocean basin *ocean floor* 8.18
ocean blue *sea* 571.1
ocean bottom *base* 601.1
ocean cruiser *sailboat* 150.3
ocean-cruising *sailing* 150.25
ocean current 8.15
ocean depths *cold place* 218.7, *sea* 571.1, *the depths* 598.2

ocean floor 8.18; *sea* 571.1, *the depths* 598.2, *base* 601.1
ocean-going *oceanic* 571.7, *transportable* 686.7, *nautical* 690.14
Oceania *world region* 564.6, *landmass* 572.1
oceanic 8.53, 571.7; *deep-sea* 598.11
oceanic bird *water bird* 36.9
oceanic climate *climate* 9.35
oceanic crust *earth zone* 8.7
oceanic ridge *ocean floor* 8.18, *mountain building* 8.23
oceanic rise *mountain building* 8.23
oceanic sediment *sediment* 8.29
oceanic trench *ocean floor* 8.18, *plate tectonics* 8.19
Oceanid *legendary sea being* 571.4
ocean liner Ships and Boats 690
oceanographer 571.6; *measurer* 589.14
oceanographic 571.8; *geophysical* 8.51, *metrical* 589.15
oceanographically 571.11; *measurably* 589.22
oceanography 571.5; *measurement* 589.1
ocean racer *sailboat* 150.3
ocean racing *competitive sailing* 150.6
ocean-racing *sailing* 150.25
ocean sailing *sailing* 150.2
ocean shore *coast* 572.4
ocean track *waterway* 690.2
Oceanus *legendary sea being* 571.4
oceanward *nautically* 571.10
ocean water *ocean* 8.14
ocean wave *wave* 8.16
ocher *orange pigment* 258.2
ocher *or* **ochre** *brown pigment* 256.2
ochlocracy *mob rule* 49.12, *anarchism* 51.3
ochlocratic *anarchistic* 51.7
ochlophobia Phobias 283
ochophobia Phobias 283
ochreous *orange* 258.5
ocicat Breeds of Cats 35
Ockham's *or* **Occam's razor** *philosophical term* 4.7
o'clock *horologically* 646.15
ocotillo Trees and Shrubs 43
octad *eight* 792.4
octadic *eighth* 792.15
octagon *polygon* 6.42, *angled figure* 628.3, *eight* 792.4
octagonal *polygonal* 6.79, *angled* 628.9, *eighth* 792.15
octagon style Architectural Styles 134
octahedral *cubic* 6.81, *eighth* 792.15
octahedron *polyhedron* 6.44, *eight* 792.4
octal *computer information* 15.17
octal notation *number system* 6.7
octameter *meter* 139.10
octane number *or* **rating** *gas* 106.6
octangular *eighth* 792.15
Octant *or* **Octans** Constellations 7
octant *measuring instrument* 589.12
octarchy *eight* 792.4
octastich *part of poem* 139.9
octateuch *eight* 792.4
octatonic *eighth* 792.15
octavalent *chemical compound* 11.4
octave *part of poem* 139.9, *chord* 140.18, *eight* 792.4
octavo (8vo) *eight* 792.4
octennial *eighth* 792.15
octet *part of poem* 139.9,

instrumental group 141.3, *eight* 792.4, *team* 827.7
octillion *million* 792.11
octo-basse Musical Instruments 142
octocentenary *hundreds* 792.9
octodecillion *million* 792.11
octogenarian *older person* 27.7, *twenty and over* 792.8
octonary *eight* 792.4, *eighth* 792.15
octopod *molluskan* 39.23
octopus *food fish and shellfish* 90.20, *eight fish* 792.4
octoroon *race* 1.5, *racial* 1.12
octose *saccharide* 12.4
octosyllabic *metrical* 139.20
octroi *tax* 494.5
octuple *eight* 792.4, *eighth* 792.15, *quintuple* 792.23
octuplet *eight* 792.4
ocular *visual* 242.16
OD *immoderation* 99.2, *overindulge* 99.10
odd *numerical* 6.68, 783.7, *insane* 110.9, *golfing terms* 156.3, *astonishing* 294.10, *strange* 364.9, *capricious* 381.4, *uncustomary* 398.4, *abnormal* 430.13, *different* 463.7, *unusual* 664.4, 782.15, *unequal* 741.4, *surplus* 750.8, *eccentric* 782.16
oddball [Inf] *strange* 364.9, *capricious person* 381.3, *capricious* 381.4, *deviant* 698.7, *eccentric* 782.10, 782.16
odd customer *eccentric* 782.10
odd fellow *eccentric* 782.10
odd items *extra* 748.6
oddity *wonderful person* 294.6, *caprice* 381.1, *unsocial person* 409.5, *abnormality* 430.4, *unusualness* 782.4, *eccentric* 782.10, *unexpectedness* 839.2
odd-job man *servant* 69.1
oddly *astonishingly* 294.19, *unusually* 398.9, 664.7, *erratically* 698.29, *unconformably* 782.21
odd man out *dissenter* 347.5
oddments *miscellany* 59.15, *extra* 748.6, *residue* 750.2, *bits and pieces* 760.5
odd moments *leisure* 125.1
oddness *insanity* 110.1, *abnormality* 430.4, *unusualness* 664.2, *imbalance* 741.2
odd number *number* 6.4, *imbalance* 741.2, *kind of number* 783.2
odds *horse-racing betting terms* 159.11, *gambling* 167.4, *inequality* 741.1, *advantage* 744.3, *possibility* 836.1, *probability* 838.1
odds and ends *miscellany* 59.15, *variety* 732.2, *extra* 748.6, *residue* 750.2, *bits and pieces* 760.5, *refuse* 802.5
oddsmaker *forecaster* 358.9
odds-on *strong possibility* 836.3, *good chance* 842.6
odds-on bet *horse racing* 159.10
odds-on chance *chance* 838.4
odds-on favorite *finalist* 422.16
odd stick [Inf] *eccentric* 782.10
odd-toed *ungulate* 35.31
odd-toed ungulate *hoofed mammal* 35.16
ode Poem *or* Verse Forms 139
odeon *theater* 136.16
Oder Rivers 570
odeum *theater* 136.16
Odin Deities 82
odious *unpleasant* 272.6, *hateful* 300.10, *evil* 446.7

odiously *hatefully* 300.14, *evilly* 446.12

odiousness *hatefulness* 300.4

odium *hate* 300.1

Odmir *Deities* 82

odometer *indicator* 183.7, *Fields of Measurement* 589, *measuring instrument* 589.12

odometry *Fields of Measurement* 589

odontoid *toothed* 549.13

odontophobia *Phobias* 283

odor 224.1; *characteristic* 779.5

odor-free *odorless* 225.4

odoriferous *odorous* 224.5

odoriferously *odorously* 224.10

odorimetry *odor* 224.1

odorless 225.4

odorlessly 225.8

odorlessness 225.1

odor of sanctity *reputation* 224.4

odorous 224.5

odorously 224.10

odorousness *odor* 224.1

odynesphobia *or* **odynephobia** *or* **odynophobia** *Phobias* 283

odyssey *travel* 686.5

Oedipus *type of complex* 108.22

oenophobia *Phobias* 283

oersted *Scientific and Technical Units* 589

oeuvre [Fr] *work of art* 522.4

oeuvres [Fr] *compilation* 174.4

of academic interest *suppositional* 359.1

of advanced years *old* 653.10

of a fruit 44.8

of age *grown* 581.11

of a list 785.10

of all work *useful* 801.5

of animals 34.13

of another age *different in time* 648.2

of another opinion *dissenting* 347.7

of another time *different in time* 648.2

of another world *imaginary* 360.12

of a philosophy 4.13

of a political philosophy 4.14

of a secretion 24.5

of assistance *helping* 825.16

of authority *influential* 512.8

of choice *excellent* 744.14

of common occurrence *frequent* 661.4

of concern *significant* 799.9

of consequence *important* 278.6, *serious* 799.8

of consideration *significant* 799.9

of course *with the effect of* 676.12, *as usual* 781.17

of course! *naturally!* 295.10, *certainly!* 840.18

of different opinions *dissenting* 732.9

of disease 114.25

of doubtful meaning *difficult* 364.8

off *unhygienic* 114.27, *putrid* 227.4, *unmelodious* 241.5, *not working* 415.10, *off-duty* 433.11, *away* 576.8, *at a distance* 585.13, *canceled* 773.15, *imperfect* 806.5, *spoiled* 808.9

off [Brit] *unpalatable* 223.6

off-again, on-again *irregular* 664.3, *irregularly* 664.6, *discontinuous* 775.7

off-air *unheard* 229.7

offal *variety meat* 90.30, *dirt* 112.5, *insides* 577.3, *refuse* 802.5

off and on *apart* 587.8, *for short*

---

periods 641.13, *irregularly* 664.6, *changeably* 666.7, *discontinuously* 775.15

off-balance *displaced* 574.8, *unbalanced* 741.5

off base [Inf] *wrong* 430.12

offbeat *capricious* 381.4, *uncustomary* 398.4, *novel* 737.5, *eccentric* 782.16

off Broadway *drama* 136.1

off-camber *racing* 146.9

off-center *distorted* 627.6, *deviant* 698.8, *unbalanced* 741.5

off chance *remote possibility* 836.4, *poor chance* 842.8

off-color 251.15; *obscene* 112.9, *sick* 114.24, *improper* 430.14, *discourteous* 535.7, *imperfect* 806.5

off course *at a loss* 468.11, *displaced* 574.8, *wrong* 430.12, *divergent* 607.7, *divergently* 607.14, *indirect* 698.9, *disturbingly* 768.13

off day *bungling* 128.2

off drink *sober* 120.5

off-duty 433.11; *leisurely* 125.4, *not working* 415.10

offend 302.15; *be illegal* 53.30, *displease* 272.8, *quarrel* 272.9, *cause dislike* 291.16, *make irascible* 303.16, *make irritable* 304.15, *disdain* 400.16, *wrong* 430.19, *do wrong* 430.20, *demoralize* 432.15, *insult* 436.21, *be wicked* 448.13, *violate the law* 466.12, *be ugly* 531.5, *be repulsive* 701.10

offended 302.9; *cross* 303.11

offender *lawbreaker* 53.15, *malefactor* 306.6, *evildoer* 412.6, *wrongdoer* 430.8, *villain* 448.5, *guilty person* 450.5

offending 53.25

offend the eye *be ugly* 531.5

offense 155.6, 302.2; *lawbreaking* 53.14, *bad feeling* 266.5, *errancy* 351.7, *insult* 400.6, *wrongdoing* 430.7, *illegality* 450.4, *infraction* 466.4

offensive 432.11; *military* 58.10, *battle* 76.23, *unclean* 112.8, *varsity* 155.17, *stinking* 227.3, *objectionable* 272.7, *detested* 291.11, *hateful* 300.10, *profane* 301.10, *maddening* 302.12, *abusive* 395.5, *derisive* 400.12, *bad-mannered* 411.6, *defiant* 416.5, *military attack* 418.2, *militant* 418.13, *unlawful* 430.15, *insulting* 436.10, *villainous* 448.12, *ribald* 535.8, *repulsive* 701.4, *inconvenient* 804.5

offensive back *offense* 155.6

offensive backfield *offense* 155.6

offensive campaign *military attack* 418.2

offensive coordinator *football player* 155.15

offensive drive *offense* 155.6

offensive formation *offense* 155.6

offensive foul *playing terms* 148.4, *penalty* 155.13

offensive halfback *soccer participant* 163.4

offensive language 301.5

offensive line *offense* 155.6

offensive lineman *offense* 155.6

offensively 395.9; *dirtily* 112.12, *unpleasantly* 272.10, *distastefully* 291.19, *hatefully* 300.14, *profanely* 301.19, *maddeningly* 302.25, *derisively* 400.22, *rudely* 411.9, *defiantly* 416.9, *aggressively* 418.27, *villainously* 448.18,

---

discourteously 535.11, *repulsively* 701.11

offensiveness *objectionability* 272.2, *hatefulness* 300.4, *bad manners* 411.2

offensive operations *military attack* 418.2

offensive talk *sexual offense* 432.6

offensive team *offense* 155.6

offensive warfare 76.1

offer 504.1, 504.11; *worship* 83.15, *provision* 89.9, *supposition* 359.1, *propound* 359.9, *volunteer* 373.14, *attempt* 390.6, *reward for service* 453.5, *basis for negotiations* 460.2, *give praise to* 472.13, *bargaining* 480.10, *bargain* 480.20, 481.14, *purchasing* 481.2, *petition* 505.2, 505.11

offer a bargain *discount* 495.4

offer a bribe *bribe* 178.18

offer a defense *be accused* 442.10

offer a discount *discount* 495.4

offer advice *advise* 176.9

offer a fair price for *offer to buy* 504.12

offer a gift *make an offering* 504.17

offer a good living *be profitable* 467.21

offer amnesty to *cancel* 834.6

offer an easy read *make comprehensible* 363.8

offer an excuse *or* **explanation** *apologize* 313.8

offer an inducement *bribe* 178.18

offer an interpretation *translate* 365.16

offer an opportunity *be timely* 659.6

offer a prayer *pray* 85.20

offer a prize *reward* 453.13

offer a reward *reward* 453.13

offer a sacrifice *repent* 313.9, *make an offering* 504.17

offer a sacrificial lamb *make an offering* 504.17

offer a solution *negotiate* 460.6

offer assurance *or* **understanding** *be dutiful* 433.12

offer battle *battle* 76.33

offer collateral *certify* 464.11

offer constructive criticism *criticize* 365.15

offer counsel *advise* 176.9

offer criticism *criticize* 365.15

offer easy terms *make cheap* 497.14

offered 504.8; *voluntary* 373.11, *requesting* 505.7

offered for arbitration *litigated* 54.22

offer employment *employ* 57.18

offerer *purchaser* 481.7

offer for approval *display* 843.13

offer for sale *trade in* 457.8, *sell* 482.15, *offer* 504.11

offer help *or* **assistance** *volunteer* 504.13

offer homage *show obeisance to* 426.8

offer hospitality *volunteer* 504.13

offer in defense *countercharge* 332.9

offering 472.6, 504.5; *act of worship* 83.2, *benevolent act* 305.5, *penitence* 313.3, *voluntary* 373.11, *giving* 453.12, 472.1, *voluntary payment* 489.4, *grant* 489.7, *offered* 504.8

offering homage *obeisant* 426.6

offering no advantage *futile* 802.10

offering no benefit *futile* 802.10

---

offer no apologies *be impenitent* 452.4

offer no compromise *be severe* 424.8

offer no surprises *not cause wonder* 295.7

offer of one's hand in marriage *courtship* 299.10, *tentative offer* 504.2

offer one cannot refuse *incentive* 178.4, *negotiation* 460.1, *positive stimulus* 508.5

offer one's apologies *ask forgiveness* 312.12, *apologize* 313.8, *offer reparation* 504.15

offer *or* **request** *or* **ask for one's hand** *propose (marriage)* 299.28

offer one's hand in marriage *offer* 504.11

offer one's intercession *mediate* 75.6

offer one's life *sacrifice* 504.14

offer one's resignation *resign* 835.5

offer price *price* 494.1

offer readability *be intelligible* 363.10

offer refuge *or* **shelter** *secure* 464.9

offer reparation 504.15

offer resistance *resist* 417.10

offer satisfaction *offer reparation* 504.15

offer sympathy to *comfort* 214.14

offer to buy 504.12

offertory *Eucharist* 85.7, *offering* 472.6, 504.5

offer up *kill ritually* 30.23, *give praise to* 472.13

offer value for money *make cheap* 497.14

offer worship 504.16

off familiar territory *at a loss* 468.11

off food *fasting* 118.5

off form *clumsy* 128.6, *imperfect* 806.5

off guard *surprised* 292.5

offhand *imprudent* 286.7, *spontaneously* 389.17, *improvised* 396.4, *extempore* 396.7, *informal* 407.6, *informally* 407.11

offhanded *indifferent* 326.5, *improvised* 396.4

offhandedly *extempore* 396.7, *informally* 407.11, *discourteously* 411.8

offhandedness *indifference* 326.2, *improvisation* 396.1, *informality* 407.1

office 124.2; *room* 60.9, *ritual* 85.1, *home workplace* 124.3, *ceremony* 405.3, *line of duty* 433.3, *business* 509.3, *employment* 573.3, *duration* 642.1, *engagement* 833.2

office assistant 69.6

office automation program *application software* 15.14

office automation tools 15.19

office building *building* 551.9

office decoration *interior decoration* 532.4

office furniture *furniture* 101.1

officeholder *elected official* 50.8

office management *management system* 126.3

office manager *manager* 126.7

office memorandum *record* 185.1

office of power *position of authority* 52.4

officer *official* 68.6, *soldier* 77.4, *agent* 123.15, *commissioner* 833.5

officer of the court *law officer* 53.6

Officers *US Military Ranks 58*

officer training *military training* 58.3

officer-training school *type of school* 48.12

offices *support* 825.2

office supplies *business expenses* 491.4

office worker *office assistant* 69.6, *clerical worker* 123.5

official 68.6; *of language* 5.35, *governmental* 49.24, *person in authority* 52.7, *legitimate* 52.10, *disputed* 57.15, *ritualistic* 85.15, *agent* 123.15, *managerial* 126.9, *basketball team* 148.2, *recorded* 185.12, *established* 397.12, *formal* 406.6, *legal* 780.8, *commissioner* 833.5, *commissioned* 833.6

official body *representative body* 79.2

officialdom 49.20; *governance* 52.6, *the power structure* 68.12

officialese *jargon* 5.21

officialism *officialdom* 49.20, *governance* 52.6

officialize *wield authority* 52.16

official language *standard language* 5.6

officially *legitimately* 52.19, *industrially* 57.22, *ritually* 85.21, *managerially* 126.13, *on record* 185.16, *formally* 406.12, *under commission* 833.11

official procedure *standard procedure* 397.6

official publication *record* 185.1

official punishment *penalty* 454.5

official receiver *collector* 473.7

official record *record* 185.1

official reply *acknowledgment* 334.2

official report *record* 185.1

official representative *delegate* 79.1, *commissioner* 833.5

official residence 60.6

official scorer *baseball team* 147.2

official stamp *means of identification* 184.3

official's time-out *game time* 155.4

official strike *strike* 57.8

official visit *social gathering* 408.4

officiate *mediate* 75.6, *perform rites* 85.18, *direct* 412.16, *offer worship* 504.16

officious *authoritative* 52.9, *managerial* 126.9, *prying* 321.6, *meddling* 414.17

officiously 321.10

officiousness *overdoing it* 99.3, *prying* 321.2, *overactivity* 414.9

officious person *meddler* 414.12

offing *distant place* 585.3

off-key *unmelodious* 241.5

of flesh and blood *material* 524.7

off-limits *prohibited* 503.5, *limited* 620.5, *within limits* 620.8

off-limits area *limit* 620.1, *setting apart* 753.2, *limitation* 830.2

off-line *computerized* 15.28

off-load *lighten* 539.9, *transport* 686.10, *unload* 709.24

off-loaded *lightening* 539.6

off-loading *transportation* 686.1, *eviction* 709.4

of flowers 42.11

off note *musical dissonance* 241.2

off off Broadway *drama* 136.1

off on a tangent *irrelatively* 728.16

off oneself [Inf] *commit suicide* 30.24

off one's food *sick* 114.24

off one's guard *vulnerable* 811.9

off one's nut *or* **noodle** *or* **onion** *or* **rocker** [Inf] *insane* 110.9

off one's stride *clumsy* 128.6

off one's timing *clumsy* 128.6

off-peak *bargain* 497.10

off-peak fare *bargain* 497.4

off-piste skiing Sporting Activities 145

off-pitch *unmelodious* 241.5

offprint *reprint* 21.3, *printing* 173.3, *duplicate* 736.4, *repeat* 797.5

off-putting *dissuasive* 179.4, *repulsive* 701.4, *disturbing* 768.9

off-road bike *bicycle* 687.10

offscourings *dirt* 112.5, *residue* 750.2, *refuse* 802.5

off-season *bargain* 497.10, *seasonal* 654.7

off-season fare *bargain* 497.4

off-season traveler *bargain hunter* 497.8

offset *plant breeding* 17.6, *printing* 173.3, *neutralization* 510.4, *make the same* 730.16, *equalization* 740.4, *equalize* 740.12, *counterbalance* 743.2, 743.8, *counterbalanced* 743.6, *subtraction* 749.1, *subtract* 749.6, *counteract* 828.21, *cancel out* 834.8

offset lithography *printing* 173.3, *book printing* 174.10

offset printing *book printing* 174.10

offsetting *counteracting* 510.6, *counterbalanced* 743.6

offshoot *young plant* 26.5, *stem* 41.5, *product* 522.3, *fork* 703.5, *component* 760.3

offshore 150.35; *sailing* 150.25, *nautically* 571.10, *distant* 585.5, *nautical* 690.14

offshore boat *sailboat* 150.3

offshore racing *competitive sailing* 150.6

offshore rig *oil* 106.7

offshore wind *wind* 9.12

offshore yacht racing Sporting Activities 145

offside *penalty* 155.13, *soccer* 163.7, *side direction* 623.2

offside pass *ice hockey tactics* 158.4

offsides *ice hockey tactics* 158.4

off soundings *nautically* 571.10

offspring *progeny* 21.8, *family member* 65.2, *loved one* 299.13, *produce* 522.5, *person remaining* 750.6, *successor* 770.6

offstage *onstage* 136.39

off stride *imperfect* 806.5

off-target *wrong* 430.12, *divergent* 607.7, *divergently* 607.14, *distorted* 627.6, *indirect* 698.9

off the active list *suspended* 519.3

off the air *unheard* 229.7

off the beam *indirect* 698.9

off the beam [Inf] *wrong* 430.12

off the beaten track *secluded* 409.9, *out of step* 782.22

off the bottle *sober* 120.5

off the cuff *extempore* 396.7, *spontaneous* 389.6, *spontaneously* 389.17, *improvised* 396.4

off the fairway *indirect* 698.9

off the hard stuff *sober* 120.5

off the hook *acquitted* 434.6

off-the-lip *windsurfing* 150.28

off-the-lip turn *windsurfing terms* 150.21

off the mark *indirect* 698.9, *astray* 698.27

off the point *wandering* 698.13, *unimportant* 800.10

off the premises *away* 576.19

off-the-rack *tailored* 100.41, *ready-made* 388.13, *prototypical* 624.7, *immediate* 645.5

off-the-rack clothes *store-bought clothes* 100.3

off the record *secretly* 182.14, *conversationally* 210.14

off-the-record *secret* 182.8, *concealed* 844.7

off-the-shoulder *stylish* 100.42

off the subject *wandering* 698.13, *irrelatively* 728.16

off the top of one's head *spontaneous* 389.6, *extempore* 396.7

off the wagon [Inf] *drinking* 93.17

off the wall [Inf] *insane* 110.9, *unconventional* 782.14

off-track *cross-country* 162.31

off-track touring *cross-country skiing* 162.7

off-trail *ski* 162.27

off-trail skiing *skiing* 162.1

of fungi 47.19

off-white *white* 253.7

off-whiteness *whiteness* 253.1

offwidth *mountaineering* 161.9

offwidth crack *rock face* 161.6

offwind *sailing* 150.25

off with you! *go!* 709.30

off work *not working* 415.10, *off-duty* 433.11

off you go! *go!* 709.30

of good conscience *moral* 431.9

of good constitution 113.5

of good family *aristocratic* 70.4

of good omen *presageful* 358.13

of grammar 5.41

of help *useful* 801.5, *helping* 825.16

of historical interest *historic* 653.13

of humble birth *common* 71.3

of importance *serious* 799.8

of inferior quality 597.29

of known date *chronological* 639.12

of landmasses 572.12

of language 5.35

of late *newly* 652.21

of leaves 41.18

of like mind *agreeing* 462.6

of little value *unimportant* 800.10

of low quality *of inferior quality* 597.29

of many parts *gifted* 127.11

of mark *notable* 799.11

of marriageable age *marriageable* 64.17

of material *materially* 524.9

of mature years *middle-aged* 27.14

of mixed blood *mixed* 751.8

of moment *significant* 361.11

of necessity *necessarily* 95.22, *compelling* 428.6, *compellingly* 428.12

of no account *disrespected* 436.16

of no consequence *insignificant* 800.12

of no effect *failed* 846.10

of no fixed abode *stateless* 574.14, *changeable* 666.3

of no fixed address *stateless* 574.14

of no great weight *insignificant* 800.12

of no use *useless* 802.7

of no value *disrespected* 436.16

of old *historically* 3.17, *in the past* 651.20, *anciently* 653.18

of one mind *agreeing* 462.6

of one *or* **the same mind** *in accord* 735.33

of one resolve *agreeing* 730.8

of one's own accord *voluntarily* 373.17, *with consent* 735.38, *freely* 829.22

of one's own free will *voluntarily* 373.17, *voluntary* 504.9, *freely* 829.22

of one's own volition *freely* 829.22

of opposite polarity *abducent* 701.5

of plants 41.14

of repute *reputable* 370.3

of roots 41.19

of second rank *secondary* 800.15

of service *useful* 801.5, *helping* 825.16

of sexual nature 20.17

of sound mind *sane* 109.3

of stems 41.17

oft [Arch] *frequently* 661.7

often *sometimes* 639.19, *frequently* 661.7, *differentially* 739.9, *repeatedly* 797.22

often encountered *frequent* 661.4

oftenness *frequency* 661.1

oftentimes *frequently* 661.7

of that ilk *same* 730.7

of that order *this size* 579.11

of the deepest dye *dark* 254.6

of the essence *essential* 723.5

of the people *common* 71.3

of the same generation *or* **year** *or* **age** *simultaneous* 649.4

of the same kidney *same* 730.7

of the same mind *agreeing* 730.8

of the same vintage *simultaneous* 649.4

of this date *present* 647.4

of today *present* 647.4

of today's date *present* 647.4

of two minds *vacillating* 378.5

of unsound mind *insane* 110.9

of use *usable* 393.6, *useful* 801.5

of weak constitution *unhealthy* 114.23

of weight *serious* 799.8

of yore *historically* 3.17, *anciently* 653.18

ogdoad *eight* 792.4

ogee Architectural Elements 134, *arch* 134.5

ogham *or* **ogam alphabet** *alphabet* 5.16

ogive Architectural Elements 134, *arch* 134.5

ogle *gesture* 183.5, 183.17, *look* 242.7, 242.21, *communication of love* 299.6, *communicate love* 299.25, *be discourteous* 411.7

ogre *frightener* 283.7, *evil spirit* 446.4, *villain* 448.5, *big person* 579.10

ogress *big person* 579.10

Ohio American States 564, Rivers 570

Ohio Improved Chester Breeds of Pigs 16

ohm Scientific and Technical Units 589

Ohm's law Classical Physical Laws 10

oikophobia Phobias 283

oil 106.7, 562.3; *fat* 12.7, *food content* 90.3, *basic cooking*

---

ingredient 91.8, *fuels* 106.2, *gas* 106.14, *dose of medicine* 115.3, *balm* 115.11, *painting* 143.3, *bribe* 178.18, *illustration* 187.2, *sound reducer* 233.5, *blarney* 439.13, *power source* 514.13, *soften* 543.14, *polish* 545.3, *smooth* 545.10, *lubricate* 562.15, *transportable* 686.7, *propellant* 696.9, *make easy* 823.15

oil and water *separateness* 753.3
oilcan *oil* 106.7, *lubricator* 562.10
oil derrick *oil* 106.7
oil drum *oil* 106.7
oiled *polished* 545.7, *lubricated* 562.14
oiler Ships and Boats 690
oil field *source of supply* 105.4, *oil* 106.7
oil filter *cleaning tool* 111.10
oil-fired *fired* 106.13, *heated* 217.15
oil gland *secretory mechanism* 24.3
oilily 562.19
oiliness 562.1; *unctuousness* 439.4, *smoothness* 545.1
oiling *lubrication* 562.2
oil lamp *incandescent light* 246.5
oilman *power worker* 106.10
oil one's tongue *be talkative* 207.7
oil on troubled waters *remedy* 115.1, *moderator* 521.2
oil paint *material* 143.9, *paint* 251.6
oil painter *painter* 143.7
oil painting *illustration* 187.2
oil palm Trees and Shrubs 43
oil pipeline *oil* 106.7
oil-powered *fired* 106.13
oil refinery *oil* 106.7
oil refining *industrial chemistry* 11.21
oil reserves *oil* 106.7
oil rig *oil* 106.7
oils *material* 143.9
oil shale *oil* 106.7
oilskin Fabrics and Fibers 130
oilskins *coat* 100.19, *protection from the weather* 810.9
oil slick *oil* 106.7
oilstone *sharpener* 549.8
oil tanker *oil* 106.7, Ships and Boats 690
oil-tempered *hardened* 542.7
oil the tongue *blarney* 439.13
oil the wheels *ease* 562.18
oil well *oil* 106.7
oil worker *power worker* 106.10
oily 562.11; *dirty* 112.7, *sycophantic* 401.7, *unctuous* 439.10, *polished* 545.7, *lubricated* 562.14
oink *animal sound* 240.1, *make an animal sound* 240.1
ointment 562.8; *dose of medicine* 115.3, *balm* 115.11
Oise Rivers 570
Ojos del Salado Mountains and Hills 569
OK *satisfactory* 273.6, *yes* 346.2, *proper* 429.10
OK or **O.K.** or **okay** *approve* 437.14, *permission* 735.9, *mediocre* 742.7
OK or **O.K.** or **okay, the** *approval* 437.1 *vindication* 441.1, *agreement* 462.1, *tolerance* 502.2
OK! or **O.K.!** or **okay!** *yes!* 189.36
Oka Rivers 570
okapi *hoofed mammal* 35.16
okay *permission* 735.9
OK'd *authorized* 52.11, *permitting* 735.19
Okeechobee Lakes 568

Okhotsk, Sea of Oceans and Seas 571
Okinawa Islands 572
Oklahoma American States 564
Oklahoma City American States 564
okra *crop* 16.8
old, the *old people* 27.10
old 653.10; *historical* 3.10, *aged* 27.15, *customary* 397.11, *past* 651.11, *dead* 658.10
old age 27.5; *bodily development* 19.17, *age* 27.1, *adulthood* 27.2, *elderliness* 653.2, *physical deterioration* 808.4
old-age pension *social assistance* 825.4
old and gray *aged* 27.15, *old* 653.10
old as Methuselah *aged* 27.15
old as the hills *aged* 27.15
old bachelor *man* 27.8
old bag [Inf *and* Off] *woman* 27.9, *ugly thing* 531.4
old bat [Inf *and* Off] *woman* 27.9
old bone *brittle thing* 548.2
old boy *man* 27.8
old-boy network *cunning* 822.1, *backstage manipulator* 844.3
old campaigner *former soldier* 77.5
old chestnut *joke* 277.6
Old Clootie [Brit] *devil* 446.5
old clothes 100.8
old codger *man* 27.8
old college try *attempt* 390.1
Old Comedy *historic comedy* 136.12
old country, the *native country* 566.6
old dog [Inf] *man* 27.8
olden 653.11; *past* 651.11
Oldenburg Horse and Pony Breeds 159
olden days *past time* 3.6, 651.1, *oldness* 653.1
Old English sheepdog Breeds of Dogs 35
Old English type *type* 173.5
olden times *past time* 651.1, *oldness* 653.1
older *old* 653.10
older generation *old people* 27.10, 653.6
older man *man* 27.8
older person 27.7
older photograph 132.4
older woman *woman* 27.9
oldest profession *prostitution* 432.4
old-fashioned *disused* 394.8, *customary* 397.11, *uncustomary* 398.4, *courteous* 410.6, *traditional* 630.13, *antiquarian* 651.13, *conformist* 781.10, *redundant* 802.9, *unimproved* 808.10, *conservative* 815.13
old flame [Inf] *loved one* 299.13
old fogy *older person* 27.7, *boring person* 296.4, *obstinate person* 379.4, *creature of habit* 397.8, *conformist* 781.6
old gal [Inf *and* Off] *woman* 27.9
old geezer [Inf] *man* 27.8
Old Glory *flag* 184.8
old-gold *orange* 258.5, *yellow* 259.7
old guard *creature of habit* 397.8
old guy [Inf] *man* 27.8
old hand *expert* 52.8, 68.13, 127.9
Old Harry [Arch] *devil* 446.5
old hat *uncustomary* 398.4, *unfashionable* 528.10, *antiquarian* 651.13

Old Horny [Inf] *devil* 446.5
old horse *horse* 159.1
old ivory *yellow thing* 259.4
old joke *repetitiveness* 797.3
old lady [Inf] *woman in the family* 33.13, *married woman* 64.11, *loved one* 299.13
old-line *customary* 397.11
old maid Card Games 167
old maid [Off] *single person* 67.5, *single woman* 33.5
old-maidish *celibate* 67.6, *moralistic* 431.12
old man *man* 27.8, *male* 32.1
old man [Inf] *male title of address* 32.3, *man in the family* 33.12, *married man* 64.10, *manager* 126.7, *loved one* 299.13
Old Man, the [Inf] *military leader* 68.10
old-man cactus Flowers 42
old-man's-beard Flowers 42
old man's bundle Card Games 167
old master *expert* 52.8, *work of art* 133.4, *visual artist* 133.6
old money *money* 485.2
oldness 653.1; *adulthood* 27.2
Old Nick [Inf] *devil* 446.5
old paper *brittle thing* 548.2
old people 27.10, 653.6, Phobias 283
old people's home *safe house* 812.5
old person *older person* 27.7
old salt *nautical person* 690.12
old-school *opinionated* 379.9
old school tie [Brit] *clothing* 184.6
Old Scratch [Inf] *devil* 446.5
old sledge Card Games 167
old softy [Inf] *lenient person* 423.2
old soldier *former soldier* 77.5, *expert* 127.9
Old South, the *regions of the United States* 564.7
old stager *expert* 127.9
oldster *older person* 27.7
Old Testament *Christian text* 81.16
old-timer [Inf] *man* 27.8
old times *past time* 3.6
old trick *stratagem* 822.2
old trooper *former soldier* 77.5
old way, the *custom* 397.4
old witch *woman* 27.9, *ugly thing* 531.4
old wives' medicine *alternative medicine* 107.4
old wives' tale *falsehood* 192.6, *fallibility* 351.6
old woman [Inf] *woman in the family* 33.13
old woman *woman* 27.9, *female* 33.1
Old Worcester ware Ceramics 129
Old World *world region* 564.6
old-world *customary* 397.11, *courteous* 410.6, *olden* 653.11
old-worldly *courteously* 410.13, *archaically* 653.20
Old World monkey *primate* 35.17
olé! *bravo!* 437.23
oleaginous *oily* 562.11
oleander Flowers 42
olefin *fiber* 130.2
oleic Common Fatty Acids 12, *oily* 562.11
olent *odorous* 224.5
oleoresin *resin* 562.6
olericulture *horticulture* 17.1
oleum *oil* 562.3
olfaction *sense of smell* 224.2
olfactive *olfactory* 224.6

olfactologist *odor* 224.1
olfactology *odor* 224.1
olfactometry *odor* 224.1
olfactophobia Phobias 283
olfactorily *odorously* 224.10
olfactory 224.6
olfactory nerve *nose* 19.11, *sense of smell* 224.2
olfactronics *odor* 224.1
olibanum *incense* 226.3
oligarch *company leader* 68.8
oligarchic *governmental* 49.24, *masterful* 68.15
oligarchical *national* 18.16
oligarchy 49.10; *country* 566.1
Oligocene Epoch Geologic Time Intervals 8
oligochaetous *wormlike* 39.24
oligomenorrhea *bleeding* 25.10
oligomeric protein *protein* 12.9
oligopeptide *amino acid* 12.8
oligopolist *merchant* 482.10
oligopoly *selling* 482.1
oligosaccharide *saccharide* 12.4
oliphant Musical Instruments 142
olive branch *figurative usage* 43.9, *symbol of peace* 73.6, *peace offering* 74.5
olive-drabs *uniform* 100.9
olive-green *green* 260.7
olive grove *garden* 17.2
olive oil Tree Products 43, *basic cooking ingredient* 91.8
Olives, Mount of Mountains and Hills 569
olives *side dish* 90.15
olivine *green thing* 260.4
olla podrida *mixed thing* 751.2
Olympia American States 564
Olympian *deity* 82.1, *unsociable* 409.6
Olympic *sailing* 150.25, *type of wrestling* 152.9, *combat* 152.17, *gymnastic* 157.11, *ski* 162.27, *track and field* 166.20
Olympic boxer *boxer* 152.8
Olympic canoeing *canoe racing* 150.12
Olympic champion *victor* 845.7
Olympic-class racing *competitive sailing* 150.6
Olympic Games *boxing associations* 152.7, *notable tennis competitions* 165.8, *competition* 166.18, *prize competition* 422.5
Olympic Gold or **Silver** or **Bronze Medal** *prizes* 453.3
Olympic gymnastics *gymnastics* 157.1
Olympic hockey *hockey* 158.1
Olympic ice dancing *ice dancing* 162.18
Olympic lugeing *toboggan race* 162.25
Olympic Mountains Mountains and Hills 569
Olympic regatta *rowing* 150.14, *rowing competitions* 150.18
Olympic rowing *rowing* 150.14
Olympics *hockey organizations* 158.7, *prize competition* 422.5
Olympic-size(d) *swimming* 164.12
Olympic-size(d) pool *swimming place* 164.9
Olympic skating *ice skating* 162.15
Olympic skiing *skiing* 162.1
Olympic swimming *competitive swimming* 164.3
Olympic target shooting *target shooting* 160.1
Olympic wrestler *wrestler* 152.12
Olympus, Mount Mountains and Hills 569

Olympus *heaven* 82.15, Imaginary Places 360
Om *God* 82.6, *prayer* 85.10
Omaha Notable Horses 159
Oman Countries 566
ombre Card Games 168
ombrophobia Phobias 283
ombudsman *representative* 75.3
ombudsperson *middleman* 772.7
Omdurman Countries 566
omelette *or* omelet *egg dish* 90.18
omelette pan *cooking equipment* 91.6
omen 358.5; *sign* 183.1, *expectations* 356.2, *preview* 769.6, *forewarning* 814.2, *manifestation* 843.2
ominous *symbolic* 183.12, *inauspicious* 282.8, *presageful* 358.13, *untimely* 660.5, *dangerous* 811.7, *warning* 814.6, *adverse* 848.10
ominously *indicatively* 183.21, *inauspiciously* 282.15, *predictively* 358.16, *at the wrong time* 660.12, *dangerously* 811.14, *warningly* 814.11, *adversely* 848.16
ominousness *omen* 358.5, *untimeliness* 660.1
omission 762.4; *negligence* 326.1, *trivial error* 351.8, *nonperformance* 466.2, *exclusion* 764.1, *error* 846.2
omissive *nonperforming* 466.6
omit *err* 351.14, *forget* 355.10, *not perform* 466.10, *space* 563.15, *subtract* 749.6, *not complete* 762.9, *exclude* 764.7
omitted *missing* 576.11, *incomplete* 762.5, *excluded* 764.6
omitting *incomplete* 762.5, *exclusively* 764.10
Om padme hum [Buddhism] *prayer* 85.10
ommataphobia Phobias 283
omnibus *bus* 687.7
omnifarious *varied* 732.6
omnifariously *variously* 732.15
omnifariousness *variety* 732.2
omnipotence *divine attribute* 82.4, *powerfulness* 514.4
omnipotent *divine* 82.16, *powerful* 514.15
omnipotently *divinely* 82.24, *powerfully* 514.21
omnipresence 575.4; *divine attribute* 82.4, *widespreadness* 778.3
omnipresent 575.10; *divine* 82.16, *universal* 778.10
omniscience *divine attribute* 82.4, *learning* 348.3
omniscient *divine* 82.16, *knowledgeable* 348.7
omnisciently *divinely* 82.24
omniscient narrator *aspect of fiction* 139.5
omnium-gatherum *variety* 751.4
omnivore *type of animal* 34.5, *eater* 92.15, *glutton* 119.2
omnivorous *of animals* 34.13, *eating* 92.18, *gluttonous* 119.3, *undiscriminating* 338.5
omnivorously *carnivorously* 92.27
omnivorousness *eating habit* 92.7
omophagia *eating habit* 92.7
omophagic *eating* 92.18
omophagically *carnivorously* 92.27
omophagous *eating* 92.18
omophagously *carnivorously* 92.27
omphalos *center* 612.1
on *forward* 679.15, *via* 691.17, *displayed* 843.8

on account 493.12; *on credit* 487.14
on account of *by virtue of* 447.12
on a crash diet *on a diet* 118.6
on active duty *warring* 76.26
on a declining scale *decreasingly* 747.9
on a diet 118.6
on a downer [Inf] *decreasing* 747.5
on advance *on loan* 475.7
on a fact-finding mission *questioningly* 333.21
on a firm basis *stably* 674.9
on a firm footing *strengthened* 516.13, *stably* 674.9
on a firm foundation *strengthened* 516.13
on a first-name basis with *friendly with* 62.6
onager Historical Missile Weapons 78
on a good footing *friendly with* 62.6
on a high [Inf] *pleased* 214.9
on a hunch *spontaneous* 365.11
on a hunger strike *on a diet* 118.6
on a large scale *largely* 579.19
on a leash *or* lead *obedient* 426.4
on a level *horizontally* 603.11
on a liquid diet *on a diet* 118.6
on all counts *completely* 759.14
on all cylinders *laboriously* 122.13, *actively* 414.24
on all fours *in fours* 791.14
on all sides *inclusively* 613.35, *surrounded* 615.5, *around* 615.8
on a mission *questioningly* 333.21
on analysis *to pieces* 758.8
on and off *sometimes* 639.19, *for short periods* 641.13, *irregularly* 664.6, *changeably* 666.7
on and on *diffusely* 199.7, *eternally* 644.10, *continually* 669.10
on an ego trip [Inf] *egoistically* 444.9
on an even keel *smoothly* 545.13, *equal* 740.8, *as good as* 740.14
onanism *sex act* 20.10
on a par *on equal terms* 740.9
on approval *tentative* 390.5
on a quest *questioningly* 333.21
on arrival 704.22
on a shoestring *meanly* 501.8
on a small scale *little* 580.12
on a starvation diet *on a diet* 118.6
on a string *pendulously* 604.19
on a strong foundation *stably* 674.9
on a tangent *circuitously* 199.8
on a tightrope *troubled* 824.15
on a treadmill *boringly* 296.10
on auction *offered* 504.8
on average 742.10; *overall* 778.22, *probably* 838.11
on a whim *capriciously* 841.26
on a wild-goose chase *uselessly* 802.14
on bad terms *estranged* 63.8
on balance *on average* 742.10, *overall* 778.22
on behalf of *indirectly* 80.8, *beneficial* 445.11, *alternatively* 613.36, *instead* 672.8, *in aid of* 825.33
on bended knee *submissively* 298.23, *sycophantic* 401.7, *submitting* 421.3, *showing respect* 435.7
on board *nautical* 690.14, *nautically* 690.17
on bread and water *on a diet* 118.6, *abstemiously* 118.11

on call *prepared* 388.9, *on-duty* 433.10, *readily available* 575.21, *useful* 801.5, *supplementary* 825.17
once 788.23; *historically* 3.17, *infrequently* 662.4
once again *again* 797.23
once and for all *persistently* 376.17, *infrequently* 662.4, *permanently* 667.6, *conclusively* 773.26, *once* 788.23
once bitten twice shy *warned* 814.7
once in a blue moon *seldom* 640.9, *infrequently* 662.4, *rarely* 839.10
once in a coon's age [Inf] *infrequently* 662.4
once in a lifetime *rarely* 839.10
once-in-a-lifetime *singular* 788.13
once in a month of Sundays *infrequently* 662.4
once in a while *sometimes* 639.19, 662.5, *irregularly* 664.6, *discontinuously* 775.15
once more *again* 652.22, 797.23, *twice* 789.18
once more unto the breach! *here goes!* 378.18
once only *once* 788.23
once or twice *infrequently* 662.4
once-over [Inf] *observation* 242.5, *superficiality* 599.2
once-over-lightly [Inf] *superficiality* 599.2
once removed *diverging* 698.12
once upon a time *one day* 639.20, *in the past* 651.20
onchocerciasis *tropical disease* 114.10, *blindness* 243.3
onchosphere *invertebrate larva* 39.19
on cloud nine [Inf] *joyful* 269.6, *on top of the world* 600.14
oncogenic *of disease* 114.25
oncogenous *of disease* 114.25
on collateral *loaned* 475.5, *on loan* 475.7
oncology Medical Specialties 107
oncoming *future* 650.6, *ongoing* 679.7, *advancing* 702.8, *approaching* 704.10
on compulsion *compellingly* 428.12
on course *directly* 697.16
on credit 487.14; *loaned* 475.5, *on loan* 475.7, *insolvently* 488.11, *on account* 493.12
on dangerous ground *endangered* 811.10
on death row *in prison* 55.14, *endangered* 811.10
on deck *usable* 393.6, *nautically* 690.17
on-deck circle *baseball field* 147.3
on demand *enough* 97.10, *cash down* 489.25
ondes martenot Musical Instruments 142
on display *clear* 244.6, *evidently* 339.16, *displayed* 843.8
on double time *laboriously* 122.13
on-duty 433.10
one 788.1, 788.10; *numeral* 6.8, *someone* 18.10, *married* 64.16, *agreeing* 730.8, *whole* 759.6
one-act play *play* 136.2
one after another *consecutively* 774.15
one after the other *sequentially* 770.13, *consecutively* 774.15
on eagle's wings *swiftly* 694.16

one and all 759.12; *all* 759.4, *everyone* 778.7
one and only, the *originality* 737.1
one and only *novel* 737.5, *one* 788.1, *singular* 788.13
one and the same *sameness* 730.1, *same* 730.7, *one* 788.10
on easy street *wealthy* 485.8, *prosperously* 847.9
one at a time *separately* 753.22, *one by one* 788.21
one at the receiving end *recipient* 473.5
one behind the other *consecutively* 774.15
one bone and one flesh *married* 64.16
one by one 788.21; *separately* 753.22, *specifically* 779.22
one cent US coinage 484.10
one chance in a million *poor chance* 842.8
one day 639.20
one-design *sailing* 150.25
one-design boat *sailboat* 150.3
one-design racing *competitive sailing* 150.6, *windsurfing* 150.19
on edge *fearful* 283.10
one-dimensional *superficial* 599.4
one-dimensionally *superficially* 599.8
one-dimensional wave *wave* 683.4
one-dollar bill US coinage 484.10
one eighth *eight* 792.4
one-eyed *visually impaired* 243.9
one fifth *five* 792.1
one fine day *in the future* 650.13
one flesh *marriage* 64.1, *married couple* 64.9
one foot in the grave *physical deterioration* 808.4
one-foot upright spin *ice-skating techniques* 162.16
one for the book *or* books *marvel* 294.3
one for the road *refreshments* 94.3, *drink* 121.6, *parting* 705.3
one fourth *quarter* 791.6
Onega Lakes 568, Rivers 570
one-handed *clumsy* 128.6
one-hop [Inf] *continuous* 630.10
one-horse *insignificant* 745.6, *commonplace* 800.17
one-horse town *village* 567.3
one hundred *hundreds* 792.9
one hundred fifty *hundreds* 792.9
one hundredfold *hundreds* 792.9
one hundred forty-four *hundreds* 792.9
one hundred percent *all* 759.4, *wholly* 759.11, *ideal* 805.6, *complete* 805.14
one hundred twenty *hundreds* 792.9
one in a thousand *or* million *marvel* 294.3
oneirocritic *interpreter* 365.6
oneirocritical *interpretive* 365.8
oneirocriticism *science of interpretation* 365.5
oneiromancer *diviner* 86.14
oneiromancy *divination* 86.5
oneirophobia Phobias 283
one-liner *joke* 277.6
one-man solo 788.14
one-man band *instrumental group* 141.3, *soloist* 788.9
one-man (C-1) canoe race *canoe racing* 150.12
one-man show *soliloquy* 211.1, *soloist* 788.9

one-many *functional* 6.73
on end *vertically* 602.11
oneness **788.3;** *agreement* 730.2, *whole* 759.1
oneness with *agreement* 730.2
one-night stand *sexual intercourse* 20.9, *engagement* 136.15, 138.6
one ninth *nine* 792.5
one of a kind *infrequent* 662.2, *novel* 737.5, *exceptional* 779.13
one-off *impermanent* 643.5
one of the boys *or* girls *or* lads *or* lasses *contemporary* 649.3
one of the family *social person* 408.7
one of the gang *contemporary* 649.3
one of these days *another time* 648.4
one of those days *bungling* 128.2
one-one *functional* 6.73
one-on-one *duel* 422.12
one or two *few* 796.1
one pair *poker* 168.5
one-person show *play* 136.2
one-piece *tailored* 100.41, *swimming* 164.12, *one-sided* 788.11
one-piece suit *suit* 100.16, *beachwear* 100.23
one-piece swimsuit *swimming equipment* 164.8
on equal terms **740.9;** *equally* 740.13
onerous *ponderous* 538.11, *awkward* 804.6, *difficult* 824.9
onerously *burdensomely* 538.11
onerousness *weighing down* 538.5
one's age *age* 27.1
one's all *possessions* 470.5
one's betrothed *spouse* 64.8
one's (elders and) betters *best people* 744.7
one's born days *life cycle* 28.7
one's cut *discount* 495.1
one's day in court *litigation* 54.1
one's despair *unskilled person* 128.3
one's duty *duty* 433.1
one-seater toboggan *bobsledding* 162.23
oneself again *cured* 809.8
one seventh *seven* 792.3
one's fault *guilt* 450.1
one's fill *plenty* 97.2
one's fortune *personal estate* 470.6
one's friend [Inf] *bleeding* 25.10
one-sided **788.11;** *discriminatory* 337.11, *unjust* 342.7, *wrongful* 430.10
one-sidedly *wrongly* 430.24
one-sidedness *prejudice* 337.3, *injustice* 342.3
one sixth *six* 792.2
one-size *one-sided* 788.11
one's level best *attempt* 390.1
one's lot *inevitability* 95.6, *luck* 842.3
one's money *personal estate* 470.6
one's money's worth *purchase* 481.1
one's native ground *native country* 566.6
one's own *possessed* 469.13
one's own boss *free person* 829.9
one's own devices *liberality* 829.8
one's own hand *original* 737.2
one's own man *or* woman *free person* 829.9
one's own master *independent* 829.12
one's own person *individualist* 756.3

one's own sweet will *willfulness* 372.3
one's own way *liberality* 829.8
one's prime *middle age* 27.4
one's promised *spouse* 64.8
one-step *Dances* 135
one step ahead *superior* 744.8
one's time of life *age* 27.1
one's word *promise* 458.1
one-syllable word *word* 5.17
one-tailed test *hypothesis testing* 6.52
one tenth *ten* 792.6
one thing *Phobias* 283
one thing after another *consecutiveness* 774.1
one third *third* 790.6
one-time *former* 653.12, *preceding* 769.9, *resigning* 835.3
one-time offer *infrequency* 662.1
one too many *immoderation* 99.2
one-to-one *functional* 6.73, *on equal terms* 740.9
one-upmanship *tactics* 399.12, *advantage* 744.3
one up on *surpassing* 712.10, *superior* 744.8
on everyone's lips *publicized* 173.14
on every side *in all directions* 697.19
one voice *agreement* 735.3
one- wave *wave* 683.4
one-way *direct* 697.11, *one-sided* 788.11
one-way communication *telecommunication* 169.7
one-way system *road attribute* 687.3
one who conceals **181.7**
one who misrepresents **193.9**
one who restrains **830.7**
one-woman *solo* 788.14
one-woman show *soliloquy* 211.1, *soloist* 788.9
on exhibition *manifestly* 843.17
one you can hang the wash on [Inf] *batting terms* 147.6
on film *on record* 185.16
on fire **217.16**
on foot *in preparation* 388.8
on foreign soil *strangely* 724.17
ongoing **679.7;** *alive* 28.13, *continuous* 669.5, *consecutive* 774.7
Ongole *Breeds of Cattle* 16
on good grounds *as evidence* 339.15
on good terms *friendly with* 62.6, *agreeing* 462.6, *agreeably* 462.14
on guard **153.8;** *fencing movements* 153.3, *cautious* 287.6, *watchful* 323.6, 325.10, *defending* 419.17, *defensively* 419.32,
on hand *usable* 393.6, *possessed* 469.13, *attending* 575.9
on high *heavenly* 82.22, *high* 596.20, *highly* 715.16
on hold *suspended* 519.3, *inertly* 519.5, *interruptedly* 604.20, *held up* 658.6, *recessed* 668.8
on holiday *leisurely* 125.4, *nonresident* 576.9, *away* 576.19, *easily* 819.5
on home ground *safe* 810.16
oni *Legendary Creatures* 360
on ice *frozen* 218.10, *preserved* 815.12
on ice [Inf] *imprisoned* 55.9, *suspended* 519.3, *inertly* 519.5, *held up* 658.6
on impulse *capriciously* 381.7

on information given *reportedly* 170.16
on instinct *intuitively* 320.11
on instruments *aeronautically* 689.17
on intimate terms *intimate* 62.7
onion *Herbs and Spices* 91
onion flakes *Herbs and Spices* 91
onion salt *Herbs and Spices* 91
onionskin *paper* 104.5
on its last legs *dilapidated* 517.7, *worn* 808.13
on its own *alone* 788.20
on land *continentally* 572.13
on leave *leisurely* 125.4, *nonresident* 576.9, *away* 576.19, *easily* 819.5
on-line *computerized* 15.28, *useful* 801.5
on loan 475.7, 476.14; *loaned* 475.5, *insolvently* 488.11
on location *where* 565.12, *geographically* 573.11, *on the spot* 575.20, *nonresident* 576.9, *away* 576.19
onlooker *observer* 242.15, *attender* 575.6
only *one* 788.10, *once* 788.23
only a few *few* 796.1
only a step *nearby* 586.17
only begetter *first cause* 675.6
only-begotten *singular* 788.13
only chance *opportunity* 659.2
only child *single person* 788.7
only choice *choice* 382.3
only exception *item* 788.2
only for oneself *selfishly* 444.8
only just *barely* 593.18
only just enough *sufficient* 97.3
only once *infrequently* 662.4
only yesterday *in the past* 651.20, *newly* 652.21
on meager rations *on a diet* 118.6
on mortgage *guaranteed* 464.6
on my word of honor! *yes!* 189.36
on no account *uncooperatively* 506.11, *not at all* 718.15
on oath *assuredly* 189.30, *promised* 458.8, *as promised* 458.16
on occasion *for short periods* 641.13
on offer *offered* 504.8
onomasiology *Linguistic Studies* 5
onomastics *Linguistic Studies* 5, *nomenclature* 202.7
onomatology *Linguistic Studies* 5, *nomenclature* 202.7
onomatophobia *Phobias* 283
onomatopoeia *literary device* 139.12, *imitation* 736.1
onomatopoeic *worded* 5.38, *metrical* 139.20, *imitative* 736.7
onomatopoeic word *word* 5.17
onomatopoetically *imitatively* 736.12
on one *as a gift* 472.17
on one's back *inactive* 415.8, *disabled* 515.10, *humbly* 716.26
on one's beam-ends [Inf] *insolvent* 486.10, *failed* 846.10, *unprosperous* 848.11
on one's best behavior *well-behaved* 399.15
on one's credit account *on loan* 476.14
on one's deathbed *dying* 29.12
on one's doorstep *nearby* 586.17
on one's feet *showing respect* 435.7
on one's hind legs *highly* 715.16
on one's knees *sycophantic* 401.7, *sycophantically* 401.16, *showing respect* 435.7, *humbly* 716.26

on one's last legs *weakened* 517.9, *weakly* 517.14, *adverse* 848.10
on one's legs *getting well* 113.9
on one's lonesome [Inf] *alone* 788.20
on one's marks *prepared* 388.9
on one's own *voluntarily* 373.17, *lonely* 409.8, *solo* 788.14, *alone* 788.20
on one's own accord *voluntary* 504.9
on one's own account *freely* 829.22
on one's own initiative *freely* 829.22
on one's own initiative *or* volition *voluntarily* 373.17
on one's own responsibility *freely* 829.22
on one's own say-so *freely* 829.22
on one's toes *active* 414.13, *actively* 414.24
on one's uppers [Inf] *insolvent* 486.10, *poorly* 486.17
on one's way *forward* 679.15
on one's word *promised* 458.8
on opposite sides *opposite* 731.5
on overtime *laboriously* 122.13
on paper *recorded* 185.12, *on record* 185.16
on parade *demonstrating* 331.14
on parole *liberated* 831.4
on pins and needles *fearful* 283.10, *in suspense* 604.21
on pitch *tunefully* 140.30
on press *published* 173.12
on probation *experimentally* 335.14
on purpose *purposively* 327.20, *intentionally* 374.13
on Queer Street *troubled* 824.15
on reconsideration *thoughtfully* 317.13
on record **185.16**
on remand *arrested* 55.10, *detained* 830.11
on route to *via* 691.17
onrush *flow* 570.4, *momentum* 677.2
on sabbatical *leisurely* 125.4, *nonresident* 576.9, *away* 576.19, *easily* 819.5
on sale **482.24;** *discounted* 495.3, *bargain* 497.10
on schedule *early* 657.17
on second thought *thoughtfully* 317.13
on security *on loan* 475.7
onset *birth* 264.2, *military attack* 418.2, *arrival* 704.1, *beginning* 771.1
on several levels *in layers* 588.11
on shaky foundations *unsafe* 811.8
onshore *offshore* 150.35
onshore wind 9.12
onshot *grip* 151.4
on show *clear* 244.6, *appearing* 264.9, *displayed* 843.8, *manifestly* 843.17
onside *soccer play* 163.5, *soccer* 163.7
onside kick *kick* 155.12
on sight *apparently* 264.16
on site *where* 565.12, *geographically* 573.11, *on the spot* 575.20
on-site broadcast *broadcast material* 172.9
onslaught *vilification* 301.2, *military attack* 418.2, *berating* 438.5
on slippery ground *endangered* 811.10

on someone's authority *with consent* 735.38

on spec *experimentally* 335.14

on special offer *at a discount* 495.7, *offered* 504.8

onstage **136.39**

on stage *publicly* 173.20

on standby *expecting* 356.4

on stilts *high* 596.20, *highly* 715.16

on-stream *useful* 801.5

on strike *not working* 415.10

on sure ground *safe* 810.16

Ont *Deities* 82

on tap [Inf] *enough* 97.10, *usable* 393.6, *available* 575.11, *readily available* 575.21, *useful* 801.5

on tape *on record* 185.16

Ontario *Canadian Provinces* 564, *Lakes* 568

on tenterhooks *fearful* 283.10, *expecting* 356.4, *expectantly* 356.10

on terra firma *safe* 810.16

on that ground *accordingly* 735.39

on the active list *operational* 509.7

on the agenda *problematic* 328.7, *problematically* 328.12

on the alert *active* 414.13

on the anvil *in preparation* 388.8

on the assumption that *theoretically* 4.24

on the attack *aggressively* 418.27

on the back burner *held up* 658.6

on the ball *intelligent* 352.5

on the beam *straight* 630.16, *aeronautically* 689.17

on the beat *synchronized* 649.5, *synchronously* 649.9

on the bias *obliquely* 607.13, *askew* 628.12

on the Bible *assuredly* 189.30

on the bill *on account* 493.12

on the blind side *invisibly* 245.8

on the blink *gone wrong* 430.17

on the block *on sale* 482.24

on the boil *heating* 217.12

on the books *on record* 185.16

on the border *marginally* 618.11

on the borderline *questionably* 333.22

on the bottle *drunken* 121.28

on the bottom *on the ground* 716.25

on the bounce *in answer* 334.25

on the brain *topically* 328.11

on the breadline *poor* 486.8, *poorly* 486.17

on the bridge *nautically* 690.17

on the brink *verging on* 586.19, *farthest* 620.6, *unsafe* 811.8, *dangerously* 811.14

on the button [Inf] *accurate* 350.1, *correctly* 429.16, 721.29

on the cards *expected* 356.5

on the cheap [Inf] *cheaply* 497.16

on the chin *professionally* 152.22

on the contrary *arguably* 329.16, *to the contrary* 339.17

on the credit side *gainful* 467.10

on the crest *supremely* 744.23

on the crest of the wave *at the summit* 600.12

on the cuff [Inf] *on credit* 487.14, *insolvently* 488.11

on the cutting edge *managerially* 126.13

on the danger list *dying* 29.12, *sick* 114.24

on the decline *deteriorated* 808.8

on the defensive *warring* 76.26, *defending* 419.17, *defensively* 419.32

on the descendant *descending* 714.9

on the dole *unemployed* 413.10, *poor* 486.8, *poorly* 486.17

on the doorstep *or* threshold *on arrival* 704.22

on the dot [Inf] *immediately* 645.8

on the dot *or* button [Inf] *early* 657.17

on the double *swiftly* 694.16

on the double! *hurry up!* 818.9

on the downgrade *drooping* 714.10, *spoiled* 808.9, *adverse* 848.10

on the downward path *spoiled* 808.9

on the drawing board *under discussion* 387.17, *in preparation* 388.8

on the edge *marginally* 618.11, *unsafe* 811.8

on the edge of a cliff *fearful* 283.10

on the face of it *apparently* 264.16, 610.18, *manifestly* 843.17

on the face of the earth *extensively* 563.18

on the floor *on the ground* 716.25

on the fritz [Inf] *worn* 808.13

on the front line *martially* 77.39

on the go *working* 122.6, *busy* 414.15, *actively* 414.24, *in motion* 677.19

on the gravy train [Inf] *wealthily* 485.16

on the ground **716.25**; *on the spot* 575.20

on the heavy side *asymmetrically* 741.11

on the high seas *nautically* 571.10, 690.17, *in transit* 685.13, *nautical* 690.14

on the home stretch *safe* 810.16

on the hop *in motion* 677.19

on the horizon *in the offing* 585.12, *horizontally* 603.11, *in the future* 650.13

on the horns of a dilemma *questionably* 333.22, *troubled* 824.15, *confusingly* 841.23

on the house *as a gift* 472.17, *free of charge* 497.12, *cheaply* 497.16

on the increase *increasing* 746.4

on the inside [Inf] *imprisoned* 55.9, *in prison* 55.14

on the instant *in the shortest possible time* 645.9

on the job *industrially* 57.22, *on-duty* 433.10

on-the-job relations *labor relations* 57.1

on-the-job training *educational system* 48.2, *bargaining terms* 57.10

on the lam [Inf] *fugitive* 386.10

on the level [Inf] *naive* 821.3

on the light side *asymmetrically* 741.11

on the lines of *how* 691.16

on the list *on record* 185.16, *included* 763.4

on the lookout *seeing* 242.17, *expecting* 356.4

on the lookout for *pursuant to* 385.17

on the loose *free* 829.11

on the losing team *or* side *defeated* 846.11

on the make [Inf] *ambitiously* 390.10, *busy* 414.15

on the march *in motion* 677.19

on the mark *accurately* 350.6, *directed* 697.9

on the market *on sale* 482.24, *offered* 504.8

on the mend *getting well* 113.9, *improving* 807.14, *cured* 809.8

on the menu *provisioning* 89.6

on the money [Inf] *directed* 697.9

on the morrow [Arch] *in the future* 650.13

on the move *busy* 414.15, *in motion* 677.19

on the nose *offshore* 150.35, *professionally* 152.22

on the nose [Inf] *enough* 97.10, *correctly* 429.16, 721.29, *directed* 697.9

on the occasion of *in honor of* 405.15

on the off chance *possibly* 836.9

on the offensive *warring* 76.26, *militant* 418.13, *aggressively* 418.27

on the one hand and on the other *equally* 626.8

on the opposite side *opposite* 731.5

on the other hand *arguably* 329.16, *to the contrary* 339.17

on the other side *dead* 29.11, *ahead* 712.18, *opposite* 731.5, *opposingly* 828.22

on the other side of the fence *opposite* 731.5

on the outside *exteriorly* 610.16, *externally* 724.19

on the outskirt *or* outskirts *outside* 610.17

on the payroll *obediently* 69.12

on the poverty line *poorly* 486.17

on the premises *residing* 575.8, *readily available* 575.21

on the q.t. [Inf] *stealthily* 182.15

on the quarter *offshore* 150.35

on the quarterdeck *nautically* 690.17

on the quiet *stealthily* 182.15

on the qui vive *active* 414.13

on the rag [Inf] *bleeding* 25.19

on the rail *offshore* 150.35

on the rampage *violent* 520.5, *disruptively* 766.26

on the razor's edge *endangered* 811.10

on the rebound *in answer* 334.25

on the receiving end *receiving* 473.9

on the right side of *friendly with* 62.6

on the right track *discovering* 345.8, *directly* 697.16

on the road *nonresident* 576.9, *in motion* 677.19, *forward* 679.15, *in transit* 685.13, *via* 914.17

on the road to ruin *unprosperous* 848.11

on the rocks *frozen* 218.10, *endangered* 811.10

on the rocks [Inf] *divorced* 66.7, *poorly* 486.17, *failed* 846.10

on the ropes *combat* 152.17

on the run *spontaneously* 396.8, *in motion* 677.19, *endangered* 811.10

on the safe side *prudent* 287.7, *prudently* 287.17, *safe* 810.16

on the same footing *on equal terms* 740.9

on the same level *horizontally* 603.11, *on equal terms* 740.9

on the same plane *on equal terms* 740.9

on the same wavelength *agreeably* 462.14, *collaborative* 757.7

on the scent *on the trail* 160.13, 385.18

on the sea *nautically* 571.10

on the shelf [Inf] *celibate* 67.6, *clumsy* 128.6, *disused* 394.8, *interruptedly* 604.20, *surplus* 750.8

on the shelves *on sale* 482.24

on the shoulders of *highly* 715.16

on the sick list *sick* 114.24, *unhealthily* 114.31

on the side *additionally* 748.15

on the side of the angels *in the right* 429.11, *virtuous* 447.5

on the slide *decreasing* 747.5

on the slippery slope *adverse* 848.10

on the sly *stealthily* 182.15, *hypocritically* 330.15, *cunningly* 822.6

on the spot **575.20**; *where* 565.12, *available* 575.11, *next* 586.8, *immediately* 645.8, *troubled* 824.15

on-the-spot *immediate* 645.5

on-the-spot purchase *purchasing* 481.2

on the spur of the moment *spontaneous* 389.6, *spontaneously* 389.17, 396.8, *hastily* 818.7

on the staff *obediently* 69.12

on the stage *manifestly* 843.17

on the stocks *in preparation* 388.8, 388.22

on the street *beggarly* 486.12, *poorly* 486.17

on the surface *on the water* 154.15, *visibly* 244.10, *apparently* 264.16, 610.18, *texturally* 552.15, *shallowly* 599.7, *superficially* 599.8, *exteriorly* 610.16, *externally* 724.19, *manifest* 843.9, *manifestly* 843.17

on the tab [Inf] *on account* 493.12

on the table *problematically* 328.12

on the tail *offshore* 150.35

on the threshold *interfacially* 616.7, *marginally* 618.11

on the tip of one's tongue *forgotten* 355.7, *verging on* 586.19, *nearby* 803.7

on the top 600.13

on the track *on the trail* 160.13, 385.18

on the trail **160.13, 385.18**; *discovering* 345.8

on the treadmill *laboriously* 122.13

on the trot *busy* 414.15

on the turn *unpalatable* 223.6

on the up and up [Inf] *naive* 821.3

on the upgrade *getting well* 113.9

on the verge *unsafe* 811.8

on the verge of *verging on* 586.19

on the wagon [Inf] *sober* 120.5, *abstaining* 386.11, *abstinent* 455.7

on the waiting list *on record* 185.16, *expecting* 356.4

on the wane *aging* 27.13, *weakened* 517.9, *decreasingly* 747.9, *adverse* 848.10

on the warpath *warring* 76.26, *militant* 418.13, *aggressively* 418.27, *violent* 520.5

on the water **154.15**

on the way *in transit* 685.13, *via* 691.17

on the way out *deteriorated* 808.8

on the way to *convertibly* 670.15, *forward* 679.15

on the whole **759.13**; *broadly* 592.15, *on average* 742.10, *overall* 778.22, *as a rule* 780.15

on the wing *in motion* 677.19, *in transit* 685.13
on the wrong track *disturbingly* 768.13
on thin ice *endangered* 811.10
on this side of the grave *alive* 28.13
on this spot *where* 565.12
on time *early* 657.17
on tiptoe *high* 596.20, *highly* 715.16
ontogenic *or* **ontogenetic** *developmental* 13.33
ontogeny *developmental biology* 13.22
ontological *intrinsic* 717.12
ontologically *philosophically* 4.23
ontological time *time* 639.1
ontologism Philosophical Schools of Thought 4
ontologist Philosophical Schools of Thought 4
ontology Branches of Philosophy 4, *philosophy of being* 717.2
on top *high* 596.20, *on the top* 600.13, *victorious* 845.10
on top of *on the top* 600.13, *additionally* 748.15
on top of the heap *victoriously* 845.20
on top of the world 600.14
ontotheological *theological* 81.24
ontotheology Theologies 81
on tour *nonresident* 576.9, *away* 576.19
on trial *litigated* 54.22, *experimentally* 335.14, *judged* 341.9
onus of guilt *sign of guilt* 450.2
on vacation *leisurely* 125.4, *off-duty* 433.11, *nonresident* 576.9, *away* 576.19, *easily* 819.5
on velvet [Inf] *prosperously* 847.9
on view *appearing* 264.9, *displayed* 843.8
onward *forward* 679.6, 679.15, *propulsively* 696.21
onward and upward *up* 713.25
onward and upward! *go on!* 669.11
onward course *course* 679.2
on welfare *poor* 486.8, *poorly* 486.17
Onychophora *arthropodlike invertebrate* 39.12
onychophoran *arthropodlike invertebrate* 39.12
on your left! *danger!* 162.39
on your right! *danger!* 162.39
on your way! *go!* 709.30
oodles [Inf] *plenty* 97.2, *large number* 783.3, *profuseness* 795.3
oogamy *reproductive body* 47.14
oogonium *reproductive body* 47.14
oomph [Inf] *emphasis* 200.1, *vigor* 518.1
Oort cloud *comet* 7.20
oosphere *reproductive body* 47.14
ooze *sediment* 8.29, *drain* 8.64, *dirt* 112.5, *flow* 555.25, *marsh* 559.8, 572.3, *seep* 559.16, *mud* 561.8, *move slowly* 693.11, *leakage* 707.5, *leak* 707.16
ooze at every pore *be excessive* 99.9
ooze out *leak* 707.16
oozily *fluidly* 555.26, *wetly* 557.34, *moistly* 559.17, *slimily* 561.23
ooziness *muddiness* 561.10
oozing *seeping* 557.25, *leakage* 707.5
oozy *marshy* 559.11, *sludgy* 561.18, *leaky* 707.12
op. *surgery* 107.15

opacity *exposure* 132.15, *obscurity* 197.1, 250.2, *opaqueness* 250.1
opal *variegated thing* 263.5
opalescence *quality of light* 246.2, *semitransparency* 249.3, *variegation* 263.1
opalescent *lustrous* 246.15, *semitransparent* 249.9, *iridescent* 263.7
opal glass *glass* 249.5
opaline *semitransparent* 249.9, *shady* 250.4, *iridescent* 263.7
opaque 250.3, 250.7; *ceramic* 129.9, *obscure* 197.2, *murky* 248.5
opaquely 250.9; *ornamentally* 129.11
opaqueness 250.1; *murk* 248.2
opaque pigment *coloring agent* 251.5
opaque white glaze *glaze* 129.3
op art Western Art Styles 133
Op-Ed column *article* 203.2
Op-Ed page *news story* 171.3
open 583.10, 583.13, 583.15, 771.32, 843.12; *unionized* 57.14, *dramatize* 136.33, *canoeing* 150.26, *humiliation* 160.11, *snowplow* 162.29, *play* 167.12, *communicative* 169.16, *published* 173.12, *disclosed* 180.5, *disclosing* 180.6, *disclose* 180.8, *candid* 191.5, *visible* 244.5, *clear* 244.6, *easily seen through* 249.10, *make transparent* 249.12, *demonstrative* 331.10, *disinterested* 443.4, *receptive* 473.10, 708.9, *natural* 526.10, *of landmasses* 572.12, *bigger* 581.9, *cracked* 587.5, *crack* 587.7, *broad* 592.5, *broaden* 592.11, *externalized* 610.11, *uncover* 614.17, *direct* 630.12, *be new* 652.17, *inaugurate* 675.10, *separate* 753.7, *begin* 771.25, *naive* 821.3, *independent* 829.12, *informal* 829.15, *manifest* 843.9
open, the *outside* 610.3
open a campaign *be at war* 76.32
open a charge *or* **credit account** *acquire credit* 487.11
open a credit account *buy on credit* 476.13
open air 558.5; *outside* 610.3
open-air 558.16; *outside* 610.9
open-air theater *theater* 136.16
open an account *budget* 457.10
open an account with *trade* 480.18
open and aboveboard *manifestly* 843.17
open-and-shut *predetermined* 384.4, *decided* 840.9, *manifest* 843.9
open-and-shut case *predetermination* 384.1, *certainty* 840.1, *openness* 843.6
open a trade *trade* 56.12, 480.18, *trade in* 457.8
open a way *enter* 692.18
open a window *deodorize* 225.6
open book *rock face* 161.6
open canoe *canoe* 150.9
open circuit *circuit* 14.37
open-class racing *windsurfing* 150.19
open classroom school *type of school* 48.12
open cluster *star* 7.8
open competition *prize competition* 422.5
open conflict *dispute* 463.3
open country *geographical space* 563.3, *lowland* 572.6, *open space* 583.6
open court *law court* 54.8

open cruising race *canoe racing* 150.12
open door *opportunity* 583.8, *refuge* 708.3
open-door *opened up* 583.11
open-door policy *free market* 483.4, *right of entry* 706.4
opened *broadened* 592.7, *uncovered* 614.10, *inaugurated* 652.13, *enrolled* 771.24
opened up 583.11
open-ended *eternal* 798.7
opener 583.2; *preface* 769.5, *introduction* 771.10
open exchange *consultation* 176.4
open face *fishing* 154.13, *openness* 583.7
open-faced *open* 583.13
open-face reel *fishing tackle* 154.7
open-field *hunting* 160.11
open fire *battle* 76.33, *place for fire* 217.9, *declare war* 422.25, *shoot* 696.18
open fire (on) *fire* 418.18
open for bid *offered* 504.8
open for use *or* **service** *in use* 393.8
open forum *place for conversation* 210.5
open gate *ski race* 162.4
open grave *burial place* 31.7
open hand *instrument of punishment* 454.13
openhanded *plentiful* 97.4, *charitable* 305.9, *philanthropic* 307.6, *unselfish* 443.5, *giving* 453.12, 472.9, *generous* 498.6
openhandedly *charitably* 305.15, *philanthropically* 307.9, *unselfishly* 443.9
openhandedness *charity* 305.3, *philanthropy* 307.1, *unselfishness* 443.2, *generosity* 498.1
open heart *openness* 583.7
open-hearted *candid* 191.5, *easily seen through* 249.10, *benevolent* 305.7, *open* 583.13
open-heartedly *candidly* 191.10
open-heartedness *candor* 191.2, *openness* 249.6, *benevolence* 305.1
open hearth *ceramic workshop and tools* 129.8
open hostilities *go to war* 76.29
open house *social gathering* 59.7, *party* 408.6
open information *public information* 170.5
opening 583.1; *part of garment* 100.27, *window* 134.10, *board games* 167.3, *card-playing* 168.6, *first appearance* 264.3, *tentative offer* 504.2, *expansion* 581.1, 592.2, *growing* 581.12, *opportunity* 583.8, 659.2, *crack* 587.2, *uncovering* 614.1, *beginning* 652.4, 771.1, 771.16, *entrance* 706.5, *outlet* 707.8, *separateness* 753.3, *preface* 769.5, *premiere* 771.9, *starting point* 771.11, *strong possibility* 836.3
opening an umbrella indoors *bad-luck sign* 358.7
opening bid *bridge* 168.4
opening ceremony *premiere* 771.9
opening eyes Phobias 283
opening gambit *first move* 771.12
opening line *introduction* 771.10
opening move *first move* 771.12
opening night *theatrical performance* 136.13
opening one's doors *taking in* 477.7
opening scene *play part* 136.8

opening up *first appearance* 264.3, *openness* 583.7
openly 180.13, 583.22; *publicly* 173.20, *candidly* 191.10, 583.23, *visibly* 244.10, *transparently* 249.13, *demonstratively* 331.21, *disinterestedly* 443.8, *unpretentiously* 526.15, *naturally* 526.16, *continentally* 572.13, *broadly* 592.15, *honestly* 630.18, *naively* 821.5, *informally* 829.24, *manifestly* 843.17
openly happen *be visible* 843.16
open market *economic zone* 480.4, *market* 483.1, *free market* 483.4, *noninterference* 829.3
open mind *impartiality* 289.3, *uncertainty* 841.1
open-minded *impartial* 289.9, *disinterested* 443.4, *receptive* 473.10, *broad-minded* 592.9, *free* 829.11, *uncertain* 841.9
open-mindedly *impartially* 289.19, *disinterestedly* 443.8, *broad-mindedly* 592.17, *freely* 829.22
open-mindedness *disinterestedness* 443.1, *broad-mindedness* 592.3, *freethinking* 829.2
open mouth *warning signal* 814.3
open-mouthed *wondering* 294.7, *open* 583.10
openness 180.3, 249.6, 583.7, 843.6; *publicity* 173.7, *candor* 191.2, *effusiveness* 207.2, *demonstrativeness* 331.2, *naturalness* 526.4, *breadth* 592.1, *externalization* 610.5, *directness* 630.5, *receptivity* 708.2, *vulnerability* 811.6, *naiveté* 821.1, *informality* 829.6
open one's doors to *receive someone* 473.14, *be hospitable* 477.21
open one's eyes *be intelligible* 363.10
open one's heart *be sincere* 191.8, *be open* 583.19
open one's heart to *admit* 180.11
open one's mind to *be disinterested* 443.6
open one's pocket *expend* 491.11
open one's purse *give to charity* 472.16
open one's wallet *or* **purse** *pay* 489.16
open out *appear* 244.8, *make transparent* 249.12, *open* 583.15
open Pandora's box *cause trouble* 824.21
open places Phobias 283
open-plan *opened up* 583.11
open primary *election* 382.6
open quarrel *contention* 422.1
open sandwich *sandwich* 90.9
open sea *open space* 583.6
open season *game laws* 160.3, *seasons* 654.2
open sesame *spell* 86.8, *means of identification* 184.3, *tolerance* 502.2, *opener* 583.2
open sesame! *open up!* 583.24
open sewer *lack of hygiene* 112.3
open shop *organized labor* 57.5
open space 583.6; *geographical space* 563.3, *opening* 583.1
open table *pool* 149.3
open texture *translucency* 249.2
open-textured *translucent* 249.8
open the bidding *offer* 504.11
open the books *divulge* 180.9
open the door *enter* 706.11
open the door to *inaugurate*

675.10, *admit* 708.12, *make easy* 823.15
open the floodgates *be permissive* 502.7, *let out* 709.26
open the hatches *admit* 708.12
open the sluice gates *cause to flow* 570.11, *let out* 709.26
open the throttle *accelerate* 694.14
open to *vulnerable* 811.9
open to criticism *unsatisfactory* 438.15
open to debate *questionable* 333.13
open to offers *offered* 504.8
open to question *arguable* 329.8, *questionable* 333.13
open to solution *solvable* 334.14
open to suggestion *persuadable* 178.14
open to the public *clear* 244.6
open to view *clear* 244.6
open universe *universe* 7.3
open up 583.16; *compose a photograph* 132.27, *disclose* 180.8, *be sincere* 191.8, *make visible* 244.9, *open* 583.15, *be open* 583.19, *uncover* 614.17, *pioneer* 771.29, *promote* 807.18, *make easy* 823.15, *reveal* 843.14
open up [Inf] *accelerate* 694.14
open up! 583.24
open verdict *uncertainty* 841.1
open vote *electing* 382.5
open war *warfare* 76.3
open-water *swimming* 164.12
open-water swimming *swimming* 164.1
open-weave *woven* 130.15
open windows *air* 94.7
opera 140.8; *musical drama* 136.5, Musical Forms 140, *performance* 141.8, *show* 404.12
operability *possibleness* 836.2
operable *workable* 509.8, *repairable* 809.7, *possible* 836.5
opera buff *theatergoer* 136.30
opera buffa *musical drama* 136.5
opera glasses *visual aid* 242.14
operagoer *theatergoer* 136.30, *music lover* 141.10
opera hat *hat* 100.32
opera house *performance* 141.8
opera lover *music lover* 141.10
operand *mathematical symbol* 6.11
operant conditioning *conditioning* 108.24
opera seria *musical drama* 136.5
opera singer *actor* 136.25, *singer* 141.4
operate *practice surgery* 107.33, *use* 393.9, *behave toward* 399.20, *act* 412.11, *speculate* 480.19, *be operational* 509.10, *be an instrument* 511.7, *find a way* 691.14, *be in order* 765.23, *be useful* 801.9, *cure* 809.15
operate a closed shop *restrain commerce* 830.14
operate at a loss *lose money* 468.15
operate in the corridors of power *master* 68.17
operate on or **upon** *manipulate* 508.12
operate on the black market *trade* 480.18
operatic *dramatic* 136.31, *musical* 140.25, 141.11
operatically *dramatically* 136.38
operatic music *classical music* 140.2
operatic tenor *voice* 141.5

operating *operational* 509.7, *practical* 511.6
operating forces *naval commands* 77.19
operating room *hospital* 107.16
operating system (OS) *software* 15.12
operation 6.12, 509.1; *offensive warfare* 76.11, *surgery* 107.15, *task* 122.2, *venture* 390.2, *undertaking* 391.1, *treatment* 399.11, *action* 412.1, *deed* 412.2, *instrumentality* 511.1, *way* 691.1
operational 509.7; *military* 76.28, *in hand* 388.11, *effective* 412.10, *practical* 511.6
operational calculus Branches of Mathematics 6
operational command *military organization* 58.4
operational fleet *military organization* 58.4
operationally 509.13
operational research *planning* 387.8
operation of symmetry 626.2
operations *offensive warfare* 76.11
operations research *applied mathematics* 6.3
operations room *planning* 387.8
operative 509.6, 509.9; *worker* 123.1, 412.8, *acting* 412.9, *active* 414.13, *practical* 511.6, 719.8, *useful* 801.5
operator 412.7, 509.5; *philosophical term* 4.7, *mathematical symbol* 6.11, *mathematical logic* 6.60, *agent* 123.15, *telephone personnel* 169.14, *user* 393.4, *merchant* 482.10
operator gene *genetic material* 13.20
operculum *fish characteristic* 38.8, *animal covering* 613.15
operetta *musical drama* 136.5, Musical Forms 140, *opera* 140.8
operon *genetic material* 13.20
operoseness *exertion* 122.4
Ophelia Planets and Their Satellites 7
ophicleide Musical Instruments 142
Ophidia *snake* 37.6
ophidian *snake* 37.6, *reptilian* 37.12, *snakelike* 37.13
ophidiophobia or **ophiophobia** Phobias 283
ophiolater *idolater* 83.7
ophiolatrous *idolatrous* 83.13
ophiolatry *idolatry* 83.4
ophiological *herpetological* 37.15
ophiologist *herpetologist* 37.3
ophiology *herpetology* 37.2
ophiomancer *diviner* 86.14
ophiomancy *divination* 86.5
ophiomorphic *snakelike* 37.13
Ophiuchus Constellations 7
ophiuroid *echinoderm* 39.5, *echinodermal* 39.21
ophresiophobia Phobias 283
ophthalmia or **ophthalmitis** *eye disease* 243.4
ophthalmic *sensory* 19.22, *visual* 242.16
ophthalmological *medical* 107.28
ophthalmologist *medical specialist* 107.20, *aid for poor sight* 243.5
ophthalmology Medical Specialties 107, *aid for poor sight* 243.5
ophthalmoscope *diagnostic instrument* 107.13

opiate *reliever* 275.4, *soporific* 415.6, *moderator* 521.2
opiates 121.17
opilionid *arachnid* 40.4
opine *propound a philosophy* 4.21, *be of the opinion* 87.10, *feel* 266.14, *theorize* 327.16, *suppose* 359.8
opinion *philosophy* 4.1, *belief* 87.1, *recommendation* 176.2, *utterance* 205.10, *feelings* 266.1, *theory* 327.2, *line of argument* 329.3, *judgment* 341.1, *supposition* 359.1, *conduct* 399.1, *ruling* 780.2
opinionated 379.9; *believing* 87.6, *boastful* 402.13, *convinced* 840.8
opinionatedness 379.3
opinion column *news story* 171.3
opinion poll *count* 784.3
opinions Phobias 283
opium *opiates* 121.17, *anesthetic* 213.3, *soporific* 415.6, *moderator* 521.2
opium den *wicked place* 448.8
opium poppy Flowers 42
Opium Wars Major Wars 76
opossum shrimp *crustacean* 39.10
oppidan *townsperson* 61.7, *municipal resident* 567.12, *urban* 567.14
opponent 828.10; *hostile person* 63.5, *combatant* 77.1, *sportsman* 145.4, *dissenter* 347.5, *defiant person* 416.4, *resister* 417.5, *contender* 422.13, *troublemaker* 427.5, *disapprover* 438.7
opportune *timely* 659.4, *comfortable* 726.10, *convenient* 803.3
opportunely 659.8; *comfortably* 726.19, *conveniently* 803.6
opportuneness *timeliness* 659.1
opportunism *tactics* 399.12, *selfishness* 444.1
opportunist *equivocator* 380.4, *selfish person* 443.3
opportunistic *enterprising* 391.5, *selfish* 444.4
opportunity 583.8, 659.2; *leisure* 125.1, *tentative offer* 504.2, *reason* 675.4, *time* 726.3, *convenience* 803.1, *possibility* 836.1, *good chance* 842.6
oppose 63.11, 375.13, 828.15; *defend* 77.37, *negate* 190.16, *argue* 329.11, *protest* 331.19, 507.7, *deny* 332.8, *refuse* 347.9, *defy* 416.7, *be insubordinate* 416.8, *resist* 417.10, *counterattack* 418.24, *contend* 422.22, *disobey* 427.12, *dissent* 506.9, *counteract* 510.7, *invert* 608.7, *disagree* 753.19, *hinder* 826.15
oppose change *make permanent* 667.5
opposed *aggressive* 63.9, *negated* 190.10, *refusing* 375.9, *resistant* 417.6, *disunited* 753.10, *oppositional* 828.11, *adverse* 848.10
opposed to *counteracting* 510.6
opposer 828.9; *negator* 190.8, *resister* 417.5, *disapprover* 438.7
opposing *aggressive* 63.9, *combative* 77.32, *dissuasive* 179.4, *negational* 190.9, *demonstrating* 331.14, *dissenting* 347.7, 506.6, *refusing* 375.9, *resistant* 417.6, *counterattacking* 418.15, *disobedient* 427.10, *censuring* 438.12, *protesting* 507.5, *counteracting* 510.6, *opposite* 731.3, *oppositional* 828.11, *adverse* 848.10

opposing action or **cause** *counteraction* 510.1
opposing force 510.2; *the opposition* 828.8
opposingly 828.22; *negatively* 190.22, *diametrically* 731.6
opposing party *the opposition* 828.8
opposing side *group* 623.5
opposite 731.2, 731.3, 731.5; *triangle* 6.41, *oppositeness* 190.6, *negational* 190.9, *type of meaning* 361.4, *dissenting* 506.6, *inverse* 608.2, 608.6, *disunited* 753.10, *contrary* 828.13
opposite angles *angle* 6.37
opposite camp *the opposition* 828.8
oppositely *negatively* 190.22, *uncooperatively* 506.11, *reversely* 608.10, *relevantly* 727.12, *opposite* 731.5, *disunitedly* 753.25
opposite meaning *type of meaning* 361.4
oppositeness 190.6, 731.1; *contrariety* 828.6
opposite number *equal* 740.7
opposite pole *opposite* 731.2
opposite sex Phobias 283
opposite side *group* 623.5, *opposite* 731.2
opposite tide *tide* 571.2
opposition 375.2, 828.1; *hostility* 63.1, *dissuasion* 179.1, *negation* 190.1, *dissentience* 347.3, *disobedience* 416.2, 427.1, *resistance* 417.1, *censure* 438.3, *dissent* 506.2, *protest* 507.1, *counteraction* 510.1, *angular measurement* 628.4, *oppositeness* 731.1, *disunity* 753.4, *hindrance* 826.1, *adversity* 848.1
opposition, the *the dissenters* 347.6
oppositional 828.11; *counteracting* 510.6, *opposite* 731.3
oppositionary *opposite* 731.3
oppositionist *opposer* 828.9
opposition party *the opposition* 828.8
opposition rally *act of defiance* 416.3
oppress *govern* 49.26, *oppose* 63.11, *master* 68.17, *harm* 306.13, *discriminate against* 337.14, *pursue* 385.11, *ill-use* 395.7, *meddle* 414.23, *suppress* 424.6, *compel* 428.8, *wrong* 430.19, *weigh on* 538.13, *make heavy* 538.14, *restrain* 830.12, *defeat* 832.11, *cause adversity* 848.15
oppressed *judged* 337.10, *ill-used* 395.4, *suppressed* 424.6, *ponderous* 538.11
oppressed, the *the victim of discrimination* 337.8
oppressing *dominating* 832.7
oppression *ill-use* 395.2, *suppression* 424.2, *weighing down* 538.5, *submergence* 716.3, *domination* 832.2
oppressive *humid* 9.48, *lawless* 53.26, *intolerant* 63.7, *masterful* 68.15, *abusive* 395.5, *severe* 424.5, *compelling* 428.6, *ponderous* 538.11, *difficult* 824.9, *restraining* 830.8, *dominating* 832.7
oppressively *hostilely* 63.13, *masterfully* 68.19, *offensively* 395.9, *severely* 424.11, *compellingly* 428.12, *burdensomely* 538.17, *down* 716.24
oppressiveness *weighing down* 538.5

oppressive person *strict person* 424.4

oppressor *absolute ruler* 68.7, *strict person* 424.4

opprobrious *vilifying* 301.9, *insulting* 436.10

opprobriously *vilifyingly* 301.18

opprobrium *vilification* 301.2, *disrespect* 436.1

oppugn *object* 828.18

oppugnancy *contrariness* 828.5

oppugnant *uncooperative* 828.14

opsonin *blood* 555.4

opt *choose* 382.14

optative *grammatical term* 5.29

opted for *willed* 372.6, *selected* 382.11

opt for *will* 372.11, *choose* 382.14

optic *physical* 10.70, *sensory* 19.22, *eye* 242.3, *visual* 242.16

optical *physical* 10.70, *ceramic* 129.9, *pictorial* 133.8, *visual* 242.16

optical activity *photosensitivity* 10.23, *structure* 11.7, *amino acid* 12.8

optical astronomy *astronomy* 7.1

optical characteristic 10.21

optical character recognition (OCR) *character recognition* 15.20

optical disk *disk* 15.5, *recording* 185.6

optical double *star* 7.8

optical element 10.20

optical fiber *optical element* 10.20

optical glass *industrial ceramics* 129.6

optical illusion *visual distortion* 243.6, *fantasy* 360.5, *delusion* 720.3

optical instrument *visual aid* 242.14, *that which makes visible* 244.4

optical isomer(ism) *structure* 11.7

optically *physically* 10.78, *ornamentally* 129.11, *pictorially* 133.11, *visually* 242.27

optical observatory *observatory* 7.24

optical perspective *treatment* 143.6

optical rotary dispersion (ORD) *structure* 11.7

optical rotation *photosensitivity* 10.23, *structure* 11.7

optical spectrum *emission* 10.56

optical telescope *telescope* 7.25

optic axis *lens system* 10.22

optician *aid for poor sight* 243.5

optic nerve *eye* 19.9, 242.3

optics *classical physics* 10.2, *visual aid* 242.14

optimism Philosophical Schools of Thought 4, *cheerfulness* 269.2, *hope* 281.1, *idealism* 327.7, *expectation* 356.1

optimist Philosophical Schools of Thought 4, *joyful person* 269.5, *hoper* 281.5, *overestimator* 343.2

optimistic *cheerful* 269.7, *hopeful* 281.6, *ideal* 327.12, *expecting* 356.4, *auspicious* 458.10

optimistically *cheerfully* 269.14, *hopefully* 281.15, *imaginatively* 327.21, *expectantly* 356.10, *auspiciously* 458.17

optimum *best* 805.9

opting *preferential* 382.10

opting for *or* **against** *selecting* 382.4

opting out *refusing* 375.9

option *play offense* 155.18, *will* 372.1, *choice* 382.3, *freedom* 829.1

optional *gymnastic* 157.11, *selected* 382.11

optional exercise *gymnastics* 157.1

optionally *by choice* 382.18

option pass *play* 155.8

option run *play* 155.8

optoelectronics *photosensitivity* 10.23, *electronics* 14.33

optometer Fields of Measurement 589

optometrist *aid for poor sight* 243.5

optometry *aid for poor sight* 243.5, Fields of Measurement 589

optophobia Phobias 283

opt out *oppose* 375.13, *be independent* 782.20

opt-out clause *safety* 810.1

opulence 485.3; *pleasure* 214.2

opulent 485.10; *luscious* 214.8, *prosperous* 847.5

opulently *wealthily* 485.16, *prosperously* 847.9

opuntia Flowers 42

opus *musical composition* 140.9, *book* 174.1

or Heraldic Terms 184, *orange* 258.5, *yellow* 259.7

oracle 358.8; *diviner* 86.14, *maxim* 177.1, *intellectual* 315.7, *wise person* 352.3, *equivocation* 380.1, *predictor* 650.5, *mysteriousness* 844.5

oracular *divine* 82.16, *divinatory* 86.18, *proverbial* 177.2, *wise* 352.4, *predicting* 358.11, *unintelligible* 364.4, *difficult* 364.8, *equivocal* 380.5

oral *societal* 1.13, *dental* 107.31, *communicational* 169.17, *spoken* 205.13

oral cavity *mouth* 19.7, *speech organ* 205.4, *body orifice* 583.3

oral communication *speech* 205.1

oral contraceptive *hormone* 12.16, *contraceptive* 23.6

oral examination *audition* 228.6, *questionnaire* 333.3

oral-genital stimulation *sex act* 20.10

oral history *chronicle* 3.4, *literature* 139.1

oral hygiene *ablutions* 111.4

oral hygienist *paramedic* 107.24

orally 205.21

oral pathologist *dentist* 107.21

oral pathology *dentistry* 107.6

oral sex *sex act* 20.10

oral surgeon *dentist* 107.21

oral surgery *dentistry* 107.6

oral tobacco *tobacco* 121.23

oral tradition *tradition* 1.7

Orange Rivers 570

orange 258.5; *spectrum* 251.3, *orange thing* 258.3

orangeade *soft drink* 93.8, *sweet drink* 222.4, *orange thing* 258.3

orange belt *karate* 152.14, *aikido* 152.16

orange blossom cocktail *figurative usage* 258.4

Orange Bowl *football* 155.1

orange-brown *brown* 256.5

orange color *orangeness* 258.1

orange flower oil *figurative usage* 258.4

Orange Free State *figurative usage* 258.4

orange grove *garden* 17.2

orange hawkweed *orange thing* 258.3

orange juice *orange thing* 258.3

Orangeman *figurative usage* 258.4

Orangeman's Day *figurative usage* 258.4

orange marmalade *orange thing* 258.3

orangeness 258.1

orange pekoe *tea* 93.7, *figurative usage* 258.4

orange pigment 258.2

orange-pink *red* 257.5

orange roughy *food fish and shellfish* 90.20

orangery *nursery* 17.4, *trees* 43.4, *figurative usage* 258.4

orange squash [Brit] *orange thing* 258.3

orange stick *figurative usage* 258.4, *cosmetic tool* 530.5

orange sunshine [Inf] *hallucinogens* 121.20

orange thing 258.3

orangewood *figurative usage* 258.4

orate *dissertate* 203.5, *speak to* 205.19, *address* 209.8

oration *dissertation* 203.1, *public speaking* 205.11, *address* 209.1

orator *persuader* 178.9, *dissertator* 203.3, *speaker* 205.12, *public speaker* 209.5, *motivator* 508.6, *stylist* 537.4

oratorical *addressing* 209.6

oratorically 209.14

oratorio Musical Forms 140, *sacred music* 140.3

oratory *place of worship* 83.8, *public speaking* 205.11, *mode of expression* 537.3

orb *star* 7.8, *eye* 19.9, 242.3, *insignia* 184.5, *round thing* 633.3

orbicular *of leaves* 41.18, *circular* 631.5, *round* 633.7

orbicularity *circularity* 631.1, *roundness* 633.1

orbicularly *circularly* 631.8, *roundly* 633.11

orbit 7.22, 681.3, 681.8; *rocketry* 7.32, *observe* 7.34, *eye* 242.3, *sphere of influence* 512.7, *region* 564.1, *sphere* 564.10, *circle* 631.2, 631.6, *round thing* 633.3, *round* 633.6, *move around* 633.10, *cycle* 663.3, *be cyclic* 663.11, *rotation* 682.1, *rotate* 682.14, *route* 691.2, *flight path* 691.12, *find one's way* 691.15

orbital 681.5; *chemical bond* 11.6, *circular* 631.5, *cyclic* 663.7, *rotary* 682.12

orbital [Brit] *rotary* 682.5

orbitally *circularly* 631.8, *cyclically* 663.15

orbital motion 681.1; *cycle* 663.3, *rotation* 682.1

orbital period *orbit* 7.22

orbitary *orbital* 681.5

orbiter *planetary probe* 7.31

orbiting 681.7; *orbital motion* 681.1, *rotation* 682.1, *rotating* 682.11

orbiting body 681.4

orbiting observatory *artificial satellite* 7.30

orc *sprite* 86.12, Legendary Creatures 360

orchard *garden* 17.2, *trees* 43.4

orchardist *horticulturist* 17.13

orchestra *team* 59.9, *stage* 136.18, *instrumental group* 141.3, *collection* 757.3

orchestra circle *auditorium* 136.17

orchestra conductor *artistic worker* 123.12

orchestra director *artistic worker* 123.12

orchestral music *classical music* 140.2

orchestra pit *stage* 136.18

orchestra player *player* 141.2

orchestrate *manage* 126.10, *compose* 141.18, *behave toward* 399.20, *harmonize* 735.22

orchestrated *composed* 141.13, *harmonizing* 735.12, *collaborative* 757.7

orchestration *management* 126.1, *harmonics* 140.13, *treatment* 399.11, *harmonization* 735.2, *collaboration* 757.2

orchestrator *composer* 141.9

orchid Flowers 42, *purple* 262.6

orchidaceous *taxonomic* 41.16

orchids *seed plant* 41.3

Orcus *evil place* 446.6

Ord Rivers 570

ordain 84.16; *gain authority* 52.15, *legislate* 53.31, *impose one's will* 372.14, *introduce* 708.16, *install* 710.15, *order* 765.18, *enroll* 771.33, *rule* 780.12, *commission* 833.8

ordained *authorized* 52.11, *priestly* 84.12, *ritualistic* 85.15, *inevitable* 95.14, *predestined* 384.6, *ordered* 765.10

ordainment *ordination* 84.3, *commission* 833.1

ordeal *pain* 215.1

order 6.89, 765.1, 765.18; *matrix* 6.20, *law* 53.1, *legislate* 53.31, *legal process* 54.3, *military honor* 58.9, *association* 59.4, *peace* 73.1, *word of command* 76.20, *religious group* 81.4, *ritual* 85.1, *information* 170.1, *maxim* 177.1, *verdict* 341.2, *impose one's will* 372.14, *planning* 387.8, *plan* 387.12, *prepare for action* 388.18, *command* 425.1, 425.10, *coercion* 428.2, *compel* 428.8, *impose a duty* 433.14, *reserve* 464.14, *buy on credit* 481.12, *paper money* 484.14, *demand* 505.3, 505.12, *space* 563.15, *form* 624.1, 624.9, *kind* 624.3, *prepare* 657.14, *regularity* 663.1, 730.6, *make regular* 663.9, *way* 691.1, *state* 725.1, *relative position* 727.5, *rank* 727.11, 739.2, *measure* 739.7, *part* 760.1, *arrangement* 767.1, *category* 767.6, *arrange* 767.18, *sequence* 770.1, *consecutiveness* 774.1, *class* 777.1, *taxonomical classification* 777.3, *social class* 777.5, *sort* 777.13, *rule* 780.1, *regulate* 780.15

order by telephone *buy on credit* 481.12

ordered 765.10; *ranked* 6.72, 727.8, *regular* 730.12, *arranged* 767.11, *classed* 777.11

ordered arrangement *set* 6.19

ordered set *set* 6.19

ordering *nonparametric methods* 6.54, *commanding* 425.7, *dominant* 744.9, *arrangement* 767.1, *classification* 777.2

ordering relation *mathematical logic* 6.60

orderless *complicated* 751.10, *disordered* 766.9

orderliness 765.5; *fastidiousness* 325.4, *regularity* 663.1, 730.6

orderly 663.13, 765.13, 765.25; *servant* 69.1, *paramedic* 107.24, *clean* 111.13, *fastidious* 325.9, *planned* 387.10, *formal* 406.6, *formed* 624.6, *regular* 663.5,

730.12, *arranged* 767.11, *uniform* 780.10

order number *nonparametric methods* 6.54

order of battle *battle* 76.23

order of business *list of dates* 785.6

order off *or* **away** *send away* 709.18

order of magnitude *size* 579.1

order of service *chronology* 646.2

order of the day *predetermination* 384.1, *plan* 387.1, *tradition* 397.5, *command* 425.1, *chronology* 646.2, *convention* 781.5

order of the Mass *Eucharist* 85.7

order of things *custom* 780.5

order of worship *ritual* 85.1

order one's life *prepare oneself* 388.21

order through a catalog *buy on credit* 481.12

ordinal *number* 6.4, *ranked* 6.72, *consecutive* 774.7, *numerical* 783.7

ordinal number *number* 6.4, *kind of number* 783.2

ordinal scale *nonparametric methods* 6.54

ordinance *law* 53.1, *ritual* 85.1, *command* 425.1, *rule* 780.1

ordinand *member of the clergy* 84.5

ordinarily *predictably* 295.9, *simply* 526.14, *frequently* 661.7, *orderly* 663.13, *prevailingly* 742.11, *insignificantly* 745.14, *usually* 778.21, *as a rule* 780.18

ordinariness *mediocrity* 289.5, *predictability* 295.2, *simplicity* 526.1, *regularity* 663.1, *average* 742.1, *778.4, *inferiority* 745.1

ordinary *Heraldic Terms* 184, *mediocre* 289.11, *742.7, *predictable* 295.4, *familiar* 397.10, *moderate* 521.3, *simple* 526.7, *regular* 663.5, *average* 742.5, *inferior* 745.5, *insignificant* 745.6, *middling* 772.14, *common* 778.13, *commonplace* 800.17

ordinary, the *average* 742.1

ordinary differential equation *differentiation* 6.29

ordinary guy [Inf] *average person* 742.4

ordinary Joe [Inf] *everyone* 778.7

ordinary-language philosophy Philosophical Schools of Thought 4, Linguistic Studies 5

ordinary matter *secondary matter* 800.6

ordinary person *average person* 18.9

ordinary run *average* 778.4

ordinate *coordinates* 6.31, 589.6

ordination 84.3; *bringing in* 708.4, *enrollment* 771.8, *commission* 833.1

ordnance *guns* 78.9

ordo calendar *calendar* 646.3

Ordovician Period Geologic Time Intervals 8

ordure *feces* 25.5, *dirt* 112.5

ore 11.23; *materials* 104.1

oread *minor deity* 82.2

oregano Herbs and Spices 91

Oregon American States 564

ore roaster *ceramic workshop and tools* 129.8

Orestes Notable Friendships 62

organ Musical Instruments 142, *magazine* 175.3, *instrument* 511.2, *component* 760.3

organdie Fabrics and Fibers 130

organ donor *giver* 472.7

organdy Fabrics and Fibers 130, *transparent thing* 249.4

organelles *cell structure* 13.16

organic 551.18; *communal* 2.12, *chemical compound* 11.4, *chemical* 11.24, *living* 13.28, *quintessential* 723.8

organic acid *acid* 11.10

organically *agriculturally* 16.21, *structurally* 551.24

organic base *base* 11.11

organic being *living organism* 13.10

organic chemist *chemist* 11.2

organic chemistry Branches of Chemistry 11

organic disease *disease* 114.4

organic farm *farm* 16.2

organic farming *agriculture* 16.1

organic food *food* 90.1

organic food store *food provider* 90.6

organicism Philosophical Schools of Thought 4

organicist Philosophical Schools of Thought 4

organic manure *fertilizer* 16.9

organic matter *matter* 524.4

organic pigment *coloring agent* 251.5

organic sediment *sediment* 8.29

organic solidarity *society* 2.6

organic structure *structure* 551.1

organism *living organism* 13.10, *living matter* 28.4, *matter* 524.4

organismal *organic* 551.18

organismic *organic* 551.18

organist *player* 141.2

organization 767.3; *association* 59.4, *personnel* 123.16, *management* 126.1, *planning* 387.8, *preparation* 388.1, *treatment* 399.11, *production* 522.1, *structure* 551.1, *unification* 752.5, *order* 765.1, *method* 765.7

organizational 767.13; *managerial* 126.9, *structural* 551.17

organizational behavior *personnel management* 126.4

organizational management *management system* 126.3, *personnel management* 126.4

organization man *conformist* 781.6

Organization of Petroleum-Exporting Countries (OPEC) *economic organization* 56.6

organize 767.19; *socialize* 2.14, *unionize* 57.21, *manage* 126.10, *plan* 387.12, *lay the foundations* 388.16, *behave toward* 399.20, *produce* 522.13, *structure* 551.20, *space* 563.15, *regionalize* 564.15, *order* 765.18, *make arrangements* 767.23, *sort* 777.13, *regulate* 780.15

organize a dragnet *pursue* 385.11

organize a search party *pursue* 385.11

organize a vigilante committee *pursue* 385.11

organized 767.12; *unionized* 57.14, *planned* 387.10, *ordered* 765.10

organized boycott *strike* 57.8

organized crime *villain* 448.5

organized labor 57.5

organized society *group* 18.13

organized strike *strike* 57.8

organizer *union member* 57.6, *planner* 387.9, *person who joins* 752.9

organ meat *variety meat* 90.30

organ music *classical music* 140.2

organ of sight *eye* 19.9

organ of taste *mouth* 19.7

organometallic *chemical compound* 11.4

organ-pipe cactus Flowers 42

organ player *player* 141.2

organs of reproduction 21.9

organza Fabrics and Fibers 130, *transparent thing* 249.4

orgasm *sex act* 20.10, *physical pleasure* 214.1, *spasm* 684.8

orgasmic *coupling* 20.19, *convulsive* 684.19

orgastic *coupling* 20.19

orgy *feast* 92.9, *celebration* 405.1, *dissipation* 456.2

orgy of drinking *drinking bout* 121.7

oriel *window* 134.10

Orient *world region* 564.6, *compass direction* 697.5

orient 697.15; *accustom* 397.18, *direct* 697.13

Oriental *race* 1.5, *racial* 1.12, *regional* 564.12, *directional* 697.8

Oriental rug *or* **carpet** *floor covering* 613.13

oriental shorthair Breeds of Cats 35

orientate *accustom* 397.18, *situate* 573.10, *orient* 697.15

orientated *habituated* 397.14, *situated* 573.5

orientation 697.3; *line* 6.35, *supposition* 359.1, *habituation* 397.7, *situation* 573.1

oriented *habituated* 397.14, *directed* 697.9

orienteering Sporting Activities 145, *sporting event* 422.6, *topography* 565.5

orient oneself *orient* 697.15

orifice *opening* 583.1, *crack* 587.2, *entrance* 706.5, *outlet* 707.8

oriflamme *flag* 184.8

origami Hobbies and Pastimes 167, *pleat* 637.2

origin *graph* 6.30, *matter* 524.4, *creation* 771.2, *source* 771.3, *invention* 771.5

original 335.9, 737.2, 737.4; *ice-skating* 162.32, *ideational* 327.9, *imaginative* 360.10, *uncustomary* 398.4, *productive* 522.11, *prototypical* 624.7, *new* 652.9, *causal* 675.7, *prime* 771.18, *inventive* 771.20, *special* 779.10, *eccentric* 782.10, *unusual* 782.15

original jurisdiction *jurisdiction* 54.2

originally 345.16, 737.8; *imaginatively* 327.21, *unusually* 398.9, *formatively* 624.10, *newly* 652.21, *archaically* 653.20, *causally* 675.12, *first* 771.37

original meaning *type of meaning* 361.4

original screenplay *script* 137.5

original sin *iniquity* 448.3, *sin* 450.3

original thought *originality* 737.1

original work *production* 522.1

originate 737.7; *have an idea* 317.12, *imagine* 327.14, 360.14, *invent* 345.14, 771.30, *produce* 522.13, *design* 536.8, *be trendy* 652.18, *cause* 675.8, *begin* 771.25, *emerge* 771.35

originate in *or* **from** *follow from* 676.9

origination *invention* 345.4, 771.5, *production* 522.1, *cause* 675.1, *creation* 771.2

originative *reproductive* 21.11

originator 737.3, 771.15; *discoverer* 345.7, *planner* 387.9, *producer* 522.10, *first cause* 675.6

Orinoco Rivers 570

oriole *songbird* 36.12

Orion Constellations 7

Orion's Belt *constellation* 7.13

Orion's Sword *constellation* 7.13

orismology *nomenclature* 202.7

orison *prayer* 85.10

Orizaba Mountains and Hills 569

Orkney Islands Islands 572

Orlando Famous Lovers 299

Orlon™ *fiber* 130.2

Orlov Trotter Horse and Pony Breeds 159

Ormazd *God* 82.6

ormolu *decorative method* 532.3

ornament 532.7, 532.12; *be an architect* 134.13, *grace* 527.2, *be elegant* 527.6, *beautify* 530.14, 807.20, *decorate* 532.11, *augment* 748.13, *concomitant* 794.4, *beautification* 807.7

ornamental 17.17, 748.9; *ceramic* 129.9, *artistic* 133.7, *architectural* 134.12, *variegated* 263.6, *appealing* 529.10, *ornate* 532.10, *useless* 802.7

ornamental garden 17.3; *garden* 17.2

ornamental grass *grass* 45.1

ornamentally 129.11; *horticulturally* 17.20, *architecturally* 134.14, *variedly* 263.12, *decoratively* 532.13

ornamental tree *tree* 43.1

ornamental ware *ceramics* 129.1

ornamentation 748.5; *decoration* 532.1, *ornateness* 532.2, *ornament* 532.7, *beautification* 807.7

ornamented *architectural* 134.12, *ornate* 532.10

ornate 532.10; *floral* 42.9, *diffuse* 199.3, *decorated* 532.9

ornately 532.14; *stylistically* 537.11

ornateness 532.2; *decoration* 532.1

orneriness *ill nature* 303.2, *obstinacy* 379.1, *disobedience* 427.1

ornery *ill-natured* 303.9, *obstinate* 379.5, *disobedient* 427.10

ornithine Amino Acids 12

ornithischian *extinct reptile* 37.9

ornithological 36.21

ornithologist 36.3; *animal scientist* 34.7

ornithology 36.2; *animal science* 34.6

ornithophobia Phobias 283

ornithopod *extinct reptile* 37.9

orogenesis *mountain building* 8.23

orogenic *tectonic* 8.56, *mountainous* 569.5

orogeny *earth movement* 8.20, *mountain building* 8.23

orographic *mountainous* 569.5

orography *study of mountains* 569.4

orological *mountainous* 569.5

orologist *study of mountains* 569.4

orology *study of mountains* 569.4

orometer *study of mountains* 569.4, *height measurement* 596.5

orometric *mountainous* 569.5

Orontes Rivers 570

orotund *deep* 236.8, *ornate* 532.10

orotundity *power of speech* 205.5

orphan *person remaining* 750.6, *remaining* 750.7, *dependent* 832.4
orphanage *haven* 810.3, *safe house* 812.5
orphan drug *drug* 115.9
orphaned *helpless* 515.9, *remaining* 750.7
orpharion Musical Instruments 142
orphism *or* **Orphic cubism** Western Art Styles 133
orphrey *vestment* 84.11
orpiment *yellow pigment* 259.2
Orpington Breeds of Fowl 16
orrery *observatory* 7.24
orthocenter *triangle* 6.41
orthodontic *dental* 107.31
orthodontics *dentistry* 107.6
orthodontist *dentist* 107.21
Orthodox *denominational* 81.23
orthodox *religious* 81.21, *believing* 87.6, *customary* 397.11, *severe* 424.5, *observant* 465.3, *average* 742.5, *conformist* 781.10, *convinced* 840.8
Orthodox Jew *Jew* 81.11
Orthodox Judaism *Judaism* 81.6
orthodoxly *observantly* 465.6
orthodox medicine *medicine* 107.1
orthodoxy *severity* 424.1, *conventionalism* 781.4, *conviction* 840.2
orthoepy Linguistic Studies 5, *phonetics* 205.3
orthogonal *linear* 6.77, *perpendicular* 602.6
orthogonality *perpendicularity* 602.2
orthogonally *perpendicularly* 602.12
orthogonal projection *transformation* 6.46
orthographer *linguist* 5.3
orthographic **5.40;** *linear* 6.77
orthographically *linguistically* 5.44
orthographic convention *spelling* 5.26
orthographic *or* **orthogonal projection** *map* 187.5
orthography *language* 5.4, *spelling* 5.26
orthohydrogen Chemical Elements and Common Allotropes 11
orthopedics Medical Specialties 107, *therapy* 115.12
orthophobia Phobias 283
orthopsychiatry *psychiatry* 108.2
orthopteran *or* **orthopterous** *insectile* 40.11
orthorhombic *status adjectives* 11.25
orthorhombic crystal *crystal* 8.39, 11.14
Ortley Apple Varieties 44
os *mountain range* 569.3
Osage Rivers 570
Oscar *motion pictures* 137.1, *prizes* 453.3
oscillate **683.12;** *wave* 10.77, *conduct* 14.51, *resonate* 236.9, *vacillate* 378.8, *suspend* 604.13, *be regular* 663.10, *be changeable* 666.5, *be in motion* 677.14, *slide* 698.24, *resound* 797.21
oscillating current *wave* 10.11
oscillating universe *universe* 7.3
oscillation **683.1;** *wave* 10.11,

circuit function 14.38, *resonance* 236.1, *inconstancy* 378.2, *electrical power* 514.12, *suspension* 604.1, *frequency* 661.1, 663.2, *changeableness* 666.1, *movement* 677.3, *regular movement* 677.10, *reverberation* 797.6
oscillator **683.7;** *circuit* 10.43, *generator* 14.43
oscillatory *suspended* 604.7, *frequent* 663.6, *oscillating* 683.8, *reverberatory* 797.14
oscillograph *measuring instrument* 683.6
oscillometer *measuring instrument* 683.6
oscilloscope *electrical instrument* 14.41, *measuring instrument* 683.6
oscine *avian* 36.19
oscine bird *songbird* 36.12
oscitancy *sleep* 415.5
oscitancy *or* **oscitance** *carelessness* 289.2
oscitant *careless* 289.8
osculate *communicate love* 299.25
osculation *communication of love* 299.6
Oseretsky test Psychological Tests 108
O-shaped *circular* 681.6
osier Trees and Shrubs 43, *line* 754.5
Osiris Deities 82
Oslo Countries 566
osmidrosis *stench* 227.1
osmium Chemical Elements and Common Allotropes 11
osmophobia Phobias 283
osmoregulation *physiology* 13.13
osmose *enter* 692.18, *absorb* 708.19
osmosis *force* 10.9, *transmission* 685.3, *passage into* 692.4, *absorption* 708.6
osmotic *penetrating* 692.12, *absorbent* 708.11
osprey *bird of prey* 36.11
Ossa, Mount Mountains and Hills 569
osseous *hard* 542.5
ossia Musical Terms and Expression Marks 140
ossicle *solid body* 540.4
ossific *hard* 542.5
ossification *concentration* 540.2, *hardening* 542.2
ossified *hardened* 542.7
ossify *be dense* 540.8, *solidify* 542.10
ossuary *funeral object* 31.6
ostensible *outer* 264.10, *evident* 339.9, *apparent* 610.10, *probable* 838.6, *certain* 840.7, *manifest* 843.9
ostensibly *visibly* 244.10, *apparently* 264.16, 610.18, 720.19, *evidently* 339.16, *seemingly* 733.19, *probably* 838.11
ostensory *or* **ostensorium** *sacred object* 83.11
ostentation Collective Names 59, *public relations (PR)* 173.8, *extravagance* 194.3, *arrogance* 297.2, *demonstrativeness* 331.2, *boastfulness* 402.6, *showiness* 404.1, *ornateness* 532.2, *manifestation* 843.2
ostentatious *extravagant* 194.9, *arrogant* 297.9, *demonstrative* 331.10, *boastful* 402.13, *showy* 404.14, *unrestrained* 500.5, *inelegant* 528.6, *ornate* 532.10, *vulgar* 535.6, *accentuated* 843.11
ostentatiously *excessively* 194.17,

arrogantly 297.18, *demonstratively* 331.21, *boastfully* 402.21, *showily* 404.29, *decoratively* 532.13, *ornately* 532.14, *vulgarly* 535.10
ostentatiousness *arrogance* 297.2, *showiness* 404.1
osteoarthritis *joint disease* 114.19
osteography *science of structure* 551.15
Osteolepis *fossil fish* 38.7
osteology *measurement* 1.9, *science of structure* 551.15
osteomalacia *vitamin deficiency disease* 12.14
osteometric *anthropological* 1.10
osteometry *measurement* 1.9
osteopath *healer* 107.22
osteopathic *medical* 107.28
osteopathic medicine *medicine* 107.1
osteopathy *treatment* 107.14, *therapy* 115.12, *touching* 216.2
ostracism **709.3;** *separation* 409.3, *disapproval* 438.1, *exile* 454.3, *prohibition* 503.1, *ejection* 764.2
ostracization *ostracism* 709.3
ostracize **709.17;** *exclude* 409.12, 764.7, *withhold approval* 438.17, *exile* 454.24, *prohibit* 503.8, *replace* 574.17, *set apart* 753.17
ostracized *lonely* 409.8, *disapproved* 438.9, *replaced* 574.10
ostracod *crustacean* 39.10
ostracoderm *fossil fish* 38.7
ostraconophobia Phobias 283
ostrich *flightless bird* 36.8, *visionary* 360.9, *avoider* 386.8
ostrich feathers *finery* 100.6
ostrichlike *avian* 36.19, *inactive* 413.9
otalgia *ear problem* 228.4
otalgic *otological* 228.11
other *side direction* 623.2, *foreign* 724.9
other day, the *in the past* 651.20
other-directed *externalized* 610.11
other-directedness *personality type* 108.6, *externalization* 610.5
other end of the spectrum *opposite* 731.2
other extreme *opposite* 731.2
other famous world cities **567.9**
other game terms **147.7**
other minds *philosophical problem* 4.8
otherness *foreignness* 724.2
other religions **81.8**
other religious member **81.13**
other self *look-alike* 730.4
other side *opposite* 731.2
other side, the *death* 29.1, *extraneousness* 610.6, *the opposition* 828.8
other side of the coin *inverted thing* 608.4, *opposite* 731.2
other side of the fence *opposite* 731.2
other text **81.19**
other things being equal *as good as* 740.14
other time *different time* 648.1
otherwise engaged *oblivious* 355.9
other woman, the *lover* 299.11
other world *nonmaterial world* 525.1
otherworldliness *the occult* 86.2, *immateriality* 525.2, *extraneousness* 610.6
otherworldly *religious* 81.21, *spiritual* 86.20, *fantastic* 360.11, *nonmaterial* 525.8, *extraneous* 610.12
otic *sensory* 19.22, *aural* 228.8

otiose *superfluous* 99.8, *surplus* 750.8, *repetitious* 797.11
otitis *ear problem* 228.4
otolaryngological *otological* 228.11
otolaryngologist *ear doctor* 228.5
otolaryngology Medical Specialties 107, *study of hearing* 228.3
otological **228.11**
otologist *ear doctor* 228.5
otology *study of hearing* 228.3
otorhinolaryngological *otological* 228.11
otorhinolaryngologist *ear doctor* 228.5
otorhinolaryngology *study of hearing* 228.3
otosclerosis *ear problem* 228.4
otoscope *diagnostic instrument* 107.13
otoscopic *otological* 228.11
otoscopy *study of hearing* 228.3
ottar *or* **otto** *incense* 226.3
ottava rima *rhyme* 139.11
Ottawa Countries 566, Rivers 570
otterhound Breeds of Dogs 35
Otto cycle Classical Physical Laws 10, *engine cycle* 14.13
Ottoman *historic* 653.13
Ottonian architecture Architectural Styles 134
ouabain Tree Products 43
Ouachita Rivers 570
Ouachita Mountains Mountains and Hills 569
Ouagadougou Countries 566
Oubangui Rivers 570
oubliette *prison* 55.1
ouch *cry of pain* 239.5
oud Musical Instruments 142
ought to *be the duty of* 433.16
Ouija ™ Board and Table Games 167
Ouija™ board *occult and psychic phenomena* 86.7, *means of prediction* 358.10
ounce *weight measurement* 538.6, General Units 589
Our Father *Christian rite* 85.5, *prayer* 85.10
Our Lady *deified person* 82.14
ourselves *humankind* 18.1
our side *group* 623.5
our times *present day* 647.2
oust *discard* 383.12, *replace* 574.17, *be a substitute* 672.6, *evict* 709.20, *eject* 764.8, *terminate* 834.7
ousted *discarded* 383.9
ouster *discarding* 383.3, *ejector* 709.10
ousting *eviction* 709.4
out *other game terms* 147.7, *tennis terms* 165.5, *not working* 415.10, *defense* 441.2, *unprofitable* 468.10, *unfashionable* 528.10, *away* 576.8, *forth* 707.19, *hopeless* 837.6
out-and-out *complete* 761.6
Outaouais Rivers 570
out at (the) elbows *beggarly* 486.12
outback [Aus] *geographical space* 563.3, *countryside* 564.3, *distant place* 585.3, *outside* 610.3, 610.9, 610.17
outbalance *be heavy* 538.12
outbid *bargain* 480.20, *surpassing* 712.10, *exceed* 712.15, *outdo* 744.18
outboard *offshore* 150.35, Ships and Boats 690
outbound *outgoing* 707.10
out brake *be on the track* 146.11

outbrave *be courageous* 284.14
outbreak *coming out* 707.3, *beginning* 771.1
outbreaking *automobile racing terms* 146.3
outbreak of war *belligerency* 76.14
outbuilding *additional item* 748.3
outburst *cry* 239.1, *burst of anger* 302.6, *coming out* 707.3, *disgorgement* 709.6, *commotion* 768.5
outcast *displaced person* 574.7, *stateless* 574.14, *deviant* 698.7, *new arrival* 724.6, *surplus* 750.8, *excluded* 764.6
outclass *accelerate* 694.14, *exceed* 712.15, *be unequal* 741.7, *overpower* 845.18
outclassed 745.9; *surpassing* 712.10, *excluded* 764.6, *defeated* 846.11
outclassing *superior* 744.8
out cold [Inf] *dead drunk* 121.27, *desensitized* 213.5, *not awake* 415.12
outcome *solution* 334.6, 376.6, *product* 522.3, *baseline* 601.4, *effect* 676.1, *coming out* 707.3, *sequel* 770.5, *ruling* 780.2
outcoming *coming out* 707.3
outcrop *rock face* 161.6
outcry *loudness* 232.1, *cry* 239.1, *show of disapproval* 438.6, *protest* 507.1, *commotion* 768.5
outdated *unfashionable* 528.10, *antiquarian* 651.13, *olden* 653.11, *unimproved* 808.10
outdistance *be distant* 585.8, *accelerate* 694.14, *exceed* 712.15, *overtake* 744.16, *outdo* 744.18
outdo 744.18; *contend* 422.22, *accelerate* 694.14, *exceed* 712.15, *be unequal* 741.7, *be cunning* 822.5
outdoing *contending* 422.19
outdone *surpassing* 712.10
outdoor *swimming* 164.12, *open-air* 558.16, *outside* 610.9
outdoor game *type of game* 167.2
outdoor pool *swimming place* 164.9
outdoors *open air* 558.5, *outside* 610.3, 610.9, 610.17
outdoor sport *sporting activity* 145.3
outdoor tennis *tennis* 165.1
outdoor theater *theater* 136.16
outdrive *accelerate* 694.14
outer 264.10; *exterior* 610.7, *external* 724.11
outer atmosphere *atmospheric layer* 558.3
outer core *earth zone* 8.7
outer darkness *exclusion zone* 764.3
outer-directed *extroverted* 108.38
outer ear *ear* 19.10, 228.2
outer face *superficiality* 599.2, *exterior* 610.1, *appearance* 610.4
outer layer *exteriority* 610.2
Outer Mongolia *distant place* 585.3
outermost *exterior* 610.7
outer product *vector* 6.48
outer side *exterior* 610.1
outer space *universe* 7.3, *empty space* 563.2, *distant place* 585.3, *vastness* 798.3
outer surface *exterior* 610.1
outer wall *exteriority* 610.2
outerwear *dry goods* 130.3
outface *be courageous* 284.14, *brace oneself* 376.13

outfall *outflow* 707.4, *outlet* 707.8
outfield *baseball field* 147.3
outfielder *baseball team* 147.2
outfield fence *baseball field* 147.3
outfit *military organization* 58.4, *party* 59.3, *team* 59.9, *provision* 89.9, *clothing* 100.1, *costume* 100.10, *suit* 100.16, *make clothing* 100.44, *equipment* 103.6, *cast* 136.26, *fitting out* 388.3, *equip* 388.19, *circumstances* 573.2, *unit* 759.5
outfitter *clothier* 100.37
outfitting *provisioning* 89.2
outflank *exceed* 712.15, *overpower* 845.18
outflanking *tactics* 399.12
outflow 707.4; *wasting away* 96.4, *excess* 99.1, *lessening* 468.6, *flow* 570.4, *run out* 707.15, *leak* 816.6
outflowing 707.11; *outflow* 707.4
outflux *outflow* 707.4
out for *intending* 374.6
out for *or* **to** *ambitiously* 390.10
out for the count *desensitized* 213.5
out front *publicly* 173.20
outgas *absorb* 11.40
outgassed *absorbed* 11.34
outgassing *surface chemistry* 11.20
outgo *exit* 707.1, *outdo* 744.18
outgoer 707.9
outgoing 705.7, 707.10; *extroverted* 108.38, *sociable* 408.11, *vigorous* 518.2, *externalized* 610.11, *exit* 707.1, *resigning* 835.3
outgoingness *personality type* 108.6
outgoings *export* 707.7
outgrow *grow* 581.17
outgrown *uncustomary* 398.4
outgrowth *growth* 676.3
outgunned *defeated* 846.11
outhaul *sailboat parts and accessories* 150.4
out-Herod Herod *boast* 194.14, *overtake* 744.16
outhouse *place for excretion* 25.11, *shack* 60.10, *additional item* 748.3
out in front *unequally* 741.10
outing *travel* 686.5
out in the cold *excluded* 764.6
out in the open *publicly* 173.20, *naive* 821.3, *manifestly* 843.17
outjump *outdo* 744.18
outland *outside* 610.9
outland *or* **outlands** *outside* 610.3
outlander *foreigner* 724.5
outlandish *astonishing* 294.10, *fantastic* 360.11, *foreign* 724.9, *unusual* 782.15, *eccentric* 782.16
outlandishly *astonishingly* 294.19, *strangely* 724.17, *unconformably* 782.21
outlandishness *unusualness* 782.4
outlandish notion *caprice* 381.1
outlast *be tough* 547.13, *last* 642.6, *be eternal* 644.7
outlaw *make illegal* 53.29, *horse* 159.1, *exclude* 409.12, *evil person* 446.3, *villain* 448.5, *villainous* 448.12, *exile* 454.24, *dishonest person* 479.11, *prohibit* 503.8, *deviant* 698.7, *ostracize* 709.17, *eject* 764.8, *dissenter* 782.8
outlawing *exile* 454.3, *ostracism* 709.3
outlawry *plundering* 479.5, *ostracism* 709.3
outlay *payment* 489.1, *cost(s)* 491.3, *export* 707.7
outleap *outdo* 744.18

outlet 707.8; *inlet* 572.9, *channel* 691.10
outlie *be distant* 585.8, *surround* 615.7
outline 198.2, 204.2, 617.1, **617.5**; *drawing* 143.4, *draw* 143.13, *identification* 184.1, *representation* 187.1, *illustrate* 187.11, *map* 187.12, 387.7, *be concise* 198.5, *brief description* 202.2, *describe* 202.15, *summarize* 204.7, *external appearance* 264.5, *present* 264.15, *gist* 329.4, *suppose* 359.8, *propound* 359.9, *preparations* 388.2, *lay the foundations* 388.16, *shortened version* 591.3, *exteriority* 610.2, *be exterior* 610.13, *form* 624.1, 624.9, *not complete* 762.9, *rudiments* 771.7
outlined 617.4; *drawn* 143.11, *concise* 198.4
outliner *drawer* 143.8
outlining *(act of) drawing* 143.2
outlive *last* 642.6, *be eternal* 644.7, *be permanent* 667.4
outlive one's spouse *be widowed* 66.13
outlook *philosophy* 4.1, *weather forecast* 9.4, *religion* 81.1, *window* 134.10, *view* 242.8, *expectations* 356.2, *conduct* 399.1, *future condition* 650.3, *looking to the future* 650.4, *probability* 838.1
out loud *aurally* 228.16
outlying *distant* 585.5, *outside* 610.9, *surrounding* 615.4
outmaneuver *deceive* 193.16, *have an advantage* 618.10, *navigate* 690.15, *exceed* 712.15, *outdo* 744.18, *overpower* 845.18
outmaneuvered *surpassing* 712.10, *defeated* 846.11
outmarch *accelerate* 694.14, *outdo* 744.18
outmatch *be strong* 516.14
outmatched *defeated* 846.11
out-migrant *outgoer* 707.9
out-migrate *emigrate* 707.17
out-migration *emigration* 707.6
outmoded *unfashionable* 528.10, *antiquarian* 651.13, *olden* 653.11, *redundant* 802.9
outnumber *be excessive* 99.9, *overcrowd* 795.12
outnumbered *excessive* 99.5
out of *caused* 676.5
out of account *excluded* 764.6
out of action *not working* 415.10, *inoperative* 515.8, *broken down* 802.8
out of a job *relegated* 574.11
out of alignment *distorted* 627.6
out of balance *distorted* 627.6
out-of-body experience *occult and psychic phenomena* 86.7
out of bounds *golf course* 156.2, *prohibited* 503.5, *in the offing* 585.12, *within limits* 620.8, *out of reach* 712.11
out of breath *or* **wind** *panting* 820.3
out of circulation *inoperative* 515.8
out of commission *disused* 394.8, *not working* 415.10, *gone wrong* 430.17, *in good form* 725.11
out of context *distorted* 627.6
out of control *disobedient* 427.10, *helpless* 515.9, *violent* 520.5, *disorderly* 766.15
out of countenance *humiliated* 298.12

out of danger *safe* 810.16, *safely* 810.24
out-of-date *unfashionable* 528.10, *different in time* 648.2, *antiquarian* 651.13
out of debt *solvent* 485.9, *paid* 489.11
out-of-door *open-air* 558.16
out-of-doors 558.26; *outside* 610.3, 610.9, 610.17
out of earshot *unheard* 229.7, *deafly* 229.13, *faintly* 233.11, *in the offing* 585.12
out of fashion *shoddy* 497.11, *unfashionable* 528.10
out of favor *disliked* 291.10
out-of-focus *difficult to see* 245.4
out of hand *troublesome* 824.13
out of harm's way *safe* 810.16, *safely* 810.24
out of harness *informal* 829.15
out of hearing *in the offing* 585.12
out of hiding *visibly* 244.10
out of house and home *gluttonously* 119.5
out of humor *irritable* 304.9
out of it [Inf] *dead drunk* 121.27, *confused* 364.10
out of joint *disconnected* 574.12, *disordered* 766.9
out of keeping *out of step* 782.22
out of kilter *sick* 114.24, *clumsy* 128.6, *distorted* 627.6, *in good form* 725.11, *decrepit* 808.12
out of kindness *benevolently* 305.13
out of line *wrongful* 430.10, *unconventional* 782.14, *out of step* 782.22
out of luck *unlucky* 848.12
out of mind *forgotten* 355.7, *losing* 468.9
out of one's depth *confused* 364.10, *at a loss* 468.11, *troubled* 824.15
out of *or* **beyond one's depth** *deep* 598.25
out of one's element *at a loss* 468.11, *unconventional* 782.14
out of one's head *insane* 110.9
out of one's mind *or* **senses** *insane* 110.9
out of one's skull [Inf] *insane* 110.9
out of operation *out of use* 394.13
out of order *unused* 394.5, *gone wrong* 430.17, *inoperative* 515.8, *untimely* 660.5, *in good form* 725.11, *complicated* 751.10, *disordered* 766.9, *broken down* 802.8, *decrepit* 808.12
out of place *at a loss* 468.11, *displaced* 574.8, *disordered* 766.9, *unconventional* 782.14, *inconvenient* 804.5
out-of-play wall *squash terms* 165.10
out-of-pocket *unprofitable* 468.10, *at a loss* 468.22, *impoverished* 486.11, *expending* 491.8
out-of-pocket expenses *expense* 491.2
out of practice *clumsy* 128.6
out of print *obliterated* 186.4
out of proportion *disparately* 728.19
out of range *unheard* 229.7, *deafly* 229.13, *invisible* 245.3, *invisibly* 245.8, *disappeared* 265.4, *away* 585.6, *in the offing* 585.12, *fugitively* 816.12

---

out of reach 712.11; *away* 585.6, *in the offing* 585.12

out of season *seasonal* 654.7, *untimely* 660.5

out of service *unused* 394.5

out of shape *distorted* 627.6

out of sight *invisible* 245.3, *invisibly* 245.8, *disappeared* 265.4, *forgotten* 355.7, *losing* 468.9, *away* 576.8, 585.6, *in the offing* 585.13, *fugitively* 816.12

out of sight [Inf] *at great cost* 496.12

out-of-sight *costly* 496.7

out of sorts *sick* 114.24, *sullen* 304.8

out of soundings *nautically* 571.10

out of spite *bitterly* 306.16

out of step 782.22; *inconsistently* 732.16, *unconventional* 782.14

out of step *or* **fashion** *uncustomary* 398.4

out of stock *not enough* 98.5

out of style *unfashionable* 528.10

out of sync [Inf] *clumsy* 128.6, *different in time* 648.2, *deviant* 698.8

out of the Ark *olden* 653.11

out of the black *in the black* 487.15

out of the blue *surprisingly* 292.14, *unexpectedly* 839.9

out of the common run *superbly* 744.22

out of the corner of one's eye *watchfully* 242.29

out of the frying pan into the fire *from bad to worse* 276.8, *worse* 808.23, *adversely* 848.16

out of the habit *unaccustomed* 398.3

out of the house *away* 576.19

out of the ordinary *uncustomary* 398.4, *unfamiliar* 652.10, *characteristic* 779.12, *unusual* 782.15

out of the picture *disappeared* 265.4

out of the question *unselected* 383.7, *impossible* 837.4

out of the question! *no!* 190.28

out of the red *in the black* 487.15, *paid* 489.11

out of the running *powerless* 515.6, *unimportant* 800.10, *defeated* 846.11

out of the top drawer *superbly* 744.22

out of the way *at a distance* 585.13, *out of step* 782.22

out-of-the-way *secluded* 409.9, *distant* 585.5, 804.8, *indirect* 698.9

out of the woods *safe* 810.16

out of thin air *extempore* 396.7

out of this world *pleasant* 271.5, *away* 585.6, *distantly* 585.11, *unbeatable* 744.13, *supremely* 744.23, *eccentric* 782.16

out of time *beyond time* 640.6

out of touch *clumsy* 128.6, *silent* 181.10, *uncustomary* 398.4, *unfashionable* 528.10

out of town *nonresident* 576.9, *away* 576.19

out of training *clumsy* 128.6

out of true *wrongly* 351.18

out of tune *unmelodious* 241.5, *unconventional* 782.14

out of turn *untimely* 660.5

out of use 394.13; *disused* 394.8

out of view *invisibly* 245.8, *losing* 468.9

out of whack [Inf] *in good form* 725.11, *worn* 808.13

out of work *unemployed* 413.10, *not working* 415.10

out on a limb *out of step* 782.22, *vulnerable* 811.9, *troubled* 824.15

out on bail *liberated* 831.4

outpace *accelerate* 694.14, *outdo* 744.18

outpatient *patient* 107.25, *sick person* 114.22

outpatient clinic *hospital* 107.16

outperform *outdo* 744.18

outplay *outdo* 744.18, *overpower* 845.18

outplayed *defeated* 846.11

outpoint *overpower* 845.18

outpost *privacy* 181.6, *regions* 564.2, *distant place* 585.3, *farthest point* 620.3

outposts *surroundings* 615.1

outpour *outflow* 707.4, *run out* 707.15, *disgorgement* 709.6, *let out* 709.26

outpouring *diffuseness* 199.1, *outflow* 707.4, *outflowing* 707.11

output *conduct* 14.51, *computing terms* 15.22, *program* 15.29, *yield* 467.8, *production* 522.1, *product* 522.3, *produce* 522.13

outrace *outdo* 744.18

outrage *offense* 302.2, *offend* 302.15, *malignity* 306.5, *insult* 400.6, *be discourteous* 411.7, *severity* 424.1, *illegality* 450.4, *impairment* 808.7

outraged *offended* 302.9

outrageous *extravagant* 194.9, *abusive* 395.5, *derisive* 400.12, *insulting* 436.10, *unrestrained* 500.5, *violent* 520.5

outrageously *excessively* 194.17, *malignly* 306.18, *disgracefully* 371.8, *abusively* 395.8, *derisively* 400.22, *at great cost* 496.12

outrageousness *excess* 99.1, *extravagance* 194.3

outraging *maddening* 302.12

outrange *be distant* 585.8, *outdo* 744.18

outrank *be unequal* 741.7, *outdo* 744.18, *take precedence* 769.14

outré *astonishing* 294.10

outreach *reach out* 585.10, *outdo* 744.18

outride *exceed* 712.15, *outdo* 744.18

outrider *accompanier* 794.6

outrigger *canoe* 150.9, *Ships and Boats* 690

outright *openly* 180.13, *completely* 759.14

outright gift *giveaway* 472.5

outright purchase *purchasing* 481.2

outrival *contend* 422.22, *exceed* 712.15

outrun *lose someone* 468.20, *accelerate* 694.14, *exceed* 712.15, *outdo* 744.18, *make haste* 818.5

outrun the constable *not pay* 488.10, 490.9

outsail *accelerate* 694.14

outset *start* 705.2, *place of departure* 705.4, *beginning* 771.1

outshine *have an advantage* 618.10, *outdo* 744.18

outshone *outclassed* 745.9, *defeated* 846.11

outside 610.3, 610.9, 610.17; *space* 6.33, *soccer* 163.7, *external appearance* 264.5, *out-of-doors* 558.26, *exterior* 610.1, 610.7, *exteriorly* 610.16, *side direction* 623.2, *externality* 724.4, *external* 724.11, *exclusively* 764.10

out side *badminton terms* 165.11

outside, the *exclusion zone* 764.3

outside agency *golfer* 156.7

outside chance *remote possibility* 836.4, *improbability* 839.1

outside edge *edge* 617.3, *farthest point* 620.3

outside left *soccer participant* 163.4

outside of *exclusively* 764.10

outsider *horse racing* 159.10, *unsocial person* 409.5, *dissenter* 463.5, *foreigner* 724.5

outside right *soccer participant* 163.4

outside run *play* 155.8

outside sales worker *sales worker* 123.6

outside time *beyond time* 640.6

outsize *largeness* 579.2, *huge* 579.14

outsized *spacious* 563.13

outskirt *or* **outskirts** *outside* 610.3

outskirts *suburb* 567.11, *distant place* 585.3, *surroundings* 615.1

outsmart *deceive* 193.16, *refute* 332.7, *be cunning* 822.5

outspoken 550.6; *disclosing* 180.6, *assertive* 189.20, *candid* 191.5, *speaking* 205.15, *defiant* 416.5, *naive* 821.3

outspokenly *assertively* 189.35, *candidly* 191.10

outspokenness 550.2; *openness* 180.3, *assertiveness* 189.8, *candor* 191.2, *naïveté* 821.1

outspread *bigger* 581.9, *enlarge* 581.14, *move apart* 703.11

outspreading *expansion* 581.1

outstanding *clear* 244.6, *borrowed* 476.8, *excellent* 744.14, *surplus* 750.8, *notable* 799.11

outstanding balance *loan* 476.5, *credit* 487.1

outstandingly *eminently* 370.7, *superbly* 744.22, *with a remainder* 750.12

outstare *defy* 416.7

outstay one's welcome *invade* 706.12

outstep *outdo* 744.18

outstretch *enlarge* 581.14, *reach out* 585.10

outstretched *bigger* 581.9

outstretched hand *peace offering* 74.5

outstretching *expansion* 581.1

outstrip *improve* 467.18, *lose someone* 468.20, *have an advantage* 618.10, *accelerate* 694.14, *exceed* 712.15, *be unequal* 741.7, *outdo* 744.18, *make haste* 818.5

outtake *news event* 171.2

outtalk 207.8

outthink *have an advantage* 618.10

out to *intending* 374.6

out to lunch [Inf] *unintelligent* 316.6, *absent-minded* 324.6, *oblivious* 355.9

outvie *outdo* 744.18

outvote *be unequal* 741.7

outvoted *defeated* 846.11

outward 621.11; *visible* 244.5, *outer* 264.10, *superficial* 599.4, *exterior* 610.7, *apparent* 610.10, *forth* 707.19, *external* 724.11

outward appearance *superficiality* 599.2, *appearance* 610.4, *show* 621.7, *outward-bound* *outgoing* 705.7, 707.10

outward feature *exteriority* 610.2

outward form *or* **appearance** *external appearance* 264.5

outwardly *visibly* 244.10, *apparently* 264.16, 610.18, *superficially* 599.8, *forth* 707.19, *externally* 724.19

outwardness *superficiality* 599.2, *appearance* 610.4, *externality* 724.4

outwards *visibly* 244.10

outweigh *be an influence* 512.13, *be heavy* 538.12, *be unequal* 741.7

outwit *deceive* 193.16, *refute* 332.7, *have an advantage* 618.10, *outdo* 744.18, *be cunning* 822.5

outwitted *defeated* 846.11

outwork *fortification* 419.12

outworn *antiquarian* 651.13

ouzo *alcoholic drink* 93.9

ova and parasite screen *diagnostic procedure* 107.11

oval *curve* 6.38, 629.1, *curvilinear* 6.78, *spherical* 6.80, *automobile racing terms* 146.3, *racetrack* 159.12, *curved* 629.4, *circle* 631.2, *circular* 631.5

ovally *circularly* 631.8

ovarian *reproductive* 21.11, *of a secretion* 24.5

ovary *organs of reproduction* 21.9, *flower part* 42.3

ovate *of leaves* 41.18, *circular* 631.5

ovately *circularly* 631.8

ovation *play part* 136.8, *applause* 279.2, *ceremony* 405.3, *tribute* 405.6, *acclaim* 437.5

Ovce Polje *Breeds of Sheep* 16

oven *cooker* 91.5, *ceramic workshop and tools* 129.8, *burner* 217.4, *hot place* 217.5

oven-fresh *new* 652.9

oven glove *cooking equipment* 91.6

oven mitt *cooking equipment* 91.6

oven-ready *culinary* 91.9, *ready-made* 388.13

oven-roasting *cooking technique* 91.2

ovenware *Ceramics* 129

over 651.12; *historical* 3.10, *finally* 584.18, *high* 596.20, *via* 691.17, *superior* 744.8, *surplus* 750.8, *completed* 761.7, *ended* 773.14, *hopeless* 837.6

overabundance *fertility* 22.1, *excess* 99.1, *surplus* 750.4

overabundant *fertile* 22.8, *surplus* 750.8

overabundantly *residually* 750.11

overachieve *overdo* 99.11

overachievement *overdoing it* 99.3

overact 136.35; *overdo* 99.11, *be unskillful* 128.8, *exaggerate* 194.11, 712.16

overacted *overdone* 99.7, *dramatized* 136.32, *exaggerated* 194.7

overacting *acting* 136.22, *exaggeration* 194.1, *excessiveness* 712.4

overactive *overdone* 99.7, *fidgety* 414.14

overactivity 414.9; *overdoing it* 99.3, *exertion* 122.4

over again *twice* 789.18

over against *via* 691.17

overage *superfluity* 99.4

overall 778.22; *on average* 742.10, *including* 763.3, *general* 778.9

overall design *final intention* 374.4

overall length *length* 590.1

overall plan *plan* 387.1

overalls *pants* 100.14
overambition *overactivity* 414.9
overambitious **391.6;** *exaggerated* 712.9
overambitiously *rashly* 391.12
over and above *excessively* 99.13, *additionally* 748.15
over and done with *finally* 584.18, *over* 651.12, *no more* 718.11, *ended* 773.14
over and over *repeatedly* 235.15, 797.22, *frequently* 661.7
over-and-under *hunting* 160.11
over-and-under double-barreled shotgun *hunting equipment* 160.4
overappreciative *approving* 437.9
overarch *top* 600.10, *overlay* 613.25
overarched *topped* 600.8
overarching *topped* 600.8, *covering* 613.1, 613.21
overattentive *sycophantic* 401.7
overawe *intimidate* 283.18, *command respect* 435.18, *be an influence* 512.13
overbalance *weighing down* 538.5, *be heavy* 538.12, *trip* 714.16, *imbalance* 741.2, *unbalance* 741.8
overbalanced *ponderous* 538.11, *unbalanced* 741.5
overbear *be an influence* 512.13
overbearance *authority* 52.1
overbearing *authoritative* 52.9, *arrogant* 297.9, *severe* 424.5
overbearingly *arrogantly* 297.18
overbid *bargain* 480.20, *exceed* 712.15, *exaggerate* 712.16
overblouse *shirt* 100.13
overblown *middle-aged* 27.14
overbold *reckless* 286.6
overboldly *recklessly* 286.10
overboldness *recklessness* 286.2
overburden *overdo* 99.11, *make heavy* 538.14, *fatigue* 820.6, *cause adversity* 848.15
overburdened *overdone* 99.7, *ponderous* 538.11, *blocked* 826.13
overburdening *weighing down* 538.5
overbusy *meddling* 414.17
overcall one's hand *exaggerate* 712.16
overcast **304.6, 304.11;** *cloudy* 9.44, *dark* 247.5, *dim* 248.4, *dull* 255.8
overcast sky *cloud cover* 9.18
overcaution *cowardice* 285.1, *reticence* 287.3
overcautious *cowardly* 285.4, *reticent* 287.8
overcautiously *cowardly* 285.9, *reticently* 287.18
overcautiousness *reticence* 287.3
overcharge **496.10;** *overdo* 99.11, *cathexis* 108.32, *overestimate* 343.6, *settle accounts* 493.11, *fee* 494.3, *overpricing* 496.2
overcharged *overdone* 99.7, *costly* 496.7
overcharger **496.5**
overcharging *overpricing* 496.2, *costly* 496.7
overclouded *cloudy* 9.44
overcoat *coat* 100.19
overcolor *exaggerate* 194.11
overcolored *exaggerated* 194.7
overcoloring *exaggeration* 194.1
overcome *master* 68.17, *conquer* 77.36, *oversensitive* 267.4, *attack successfully* 418.25, *be an influence* 512.13, *lowered* 597.12, *lower* 597.21, *be superior* 744.15, *defeat* 832.11, *overpower* 845.18

overcome difficulties *overcome obstacles* 845.14
overcome obstacles **845.14**
overcoming *domination* 832.2, *dominating* 832.7
overcommend *flatter* 439.12
overcommunicative *informative* 170.10
overcompensate *unbalance* 741.8
overcompensation *defense mechanism* 108.23, *exaggeration* 194.1, *imbalance* 741.2
overcompressed *obscure* 197.2
overcompression *obscurity* 197.1
overconfidence *recklessness* 286.2, *pride* 297.1, *overestimation* 343.1, *conviction* 840.2
overconfident *reckless* 286.6, *prideful* 297.8, *overestimating* 343.4, *assured* 621.12, *convinced* 840.8
overconfidently *recklessly* 286.10, *pridefully* 297.17, *overoptimistically* 343.7
overcooked *culinary* 91.9
overcritical *critical* 438.13, *troublesome* 824.13
overcriticalness *criticism* 438.4
overcrop *expend* 96.16
overcrowd **795.12**
overcrowded *accessible* 691.13, *crowded* 795.10
overdaring *endangerment* 811.2
overdecorated *decorated* 532.9
overdevelop *increase* 581.16
overdeveloped *grown* 581.11
overdevelopment *growth* 581.4
overdevout *zealous* 81.22
overdiversification *overactivity* 414.9
overdo **99.11;** *exaggerate* 194.11, 712.16, *be extravagant* 194.13, *overindulge* 456.11
overdoing *exaggeration* 194.1, *overindulgence* 456.3
overdoing it **99.3;** *exertion* 122.4, *extravagance* 194.3, *fatigue* 820.1
overdo it *overwork* 122.9, *be extravagant* 194.13, *try* 414.21, *flatter* 439.12, *be fatigued* 820.5
overdone **99.7;** *exaggerated* 194.7, 712.9, *extravagant* 194.9, *designed* 536.6, *styled* 537.6, *chewy* 547.9
overdose *commit suicide* 30.24, *immoderation* 99.2, *overindulge* 99.10
overdraft *resources* 102.4, *financial loss* 468.4, *loan* 476.5, *credit* 487.1, *debt* 488.1, *amount owing* 488.5, *insolvency* 490.5
overdramatization *misrepresentation* 188.1
overdramatize *misrepresent* 188.6
overdraw *misrepresent* 188.6, *exaggerate* 194.11, *lose money* 468.15, *acquire credit* 487.11, *be in debt* 488.9, *overspend* 500.8
overdrawing *exaggeration* 194.1
overdrawn *exaggerated* 194.7, *unprofitable* 468.10, *charged* 487.9, *indebted* 488.7
overdrawn account *insolvency* 490.5
overdress *dress* 100.11
overdressed *dressed up* 100.39, *indecorous* 528.8
overdressing *dressing* 100.2
overdrink *overindulge* 99.10
overdrinking *immoderation* 99.2
overdrive *miscellaneous automotive terms* 687.14, *fatigue* 820.6
overdue *late* 658.5
overdue account *credit* 487.1

overdue amount *amount owing* 488.5
overdue payment *amount owing* 488.5, *type of payment* 489.3
overeat *eat well* 92.23, *overindulge* 99.10, *be greedy* 119.4
overeater *eater* 92.15
overeating *appetite* 92.2, *immoderation* 99.2, *gluttony* 119.1, *gluttonous* 119.3, *overindulgence* 456.3
overemotional *oversensitive* 267.4
overemotionalism *emotionalism* 266.6, *demonstrativeness* 331.2
overemotionally *oversensitively* 267.7
overemphasis *overdoing it* 99.3, *misrepresentation* 188.1, *exaggeration* 194.1
overemphasize *misrepresent* 188.6, *exaggerate* 194.11
overemphasized *exaggerated* 194.7
overemphatically *exaggeratedly* 194.16
overemployed *busy* 414.15
overenlargement *increase* 746.1
overenthusiasm *recklessness* 286.2
overenthusiastic *reckless* 286.6, *overestimating* 343.4
overenthusiastically *exaggeratedly* 194.16, *recklessly* 286.10, *overoptimistically* 343.7
overesteem *flatter* 439.12
overestimate **343.6;** *exaggerate* 194.11, 712.16, *misjudge* 342.9, *misrepresent* 366.5, *praise* 437.16, *flatter* 439.12, *be incorrect* 722.13, *make important* 799.14
overestimated **343.5;** *exaggerated* 194.7, *misjudged* 342.8, *incorrect* 722.8
overestimating **343.4;** *approving* 437.9
overestimation **343.1;** *overdoing it* 99.3, *misinformation* 188.3, *exaggeration* 194.1, *misjudgment* 342.1, *misrepresentation* 366.2, *praise* 437.3, *excessiveness* 712.4, *untrueness* 722.3
overestimator **343.2**
overexcited *overdone* 99.7, *susceptible* 212.7
overexert *overdo* 99.11, *be fatigued* 820.5
overexertion *overdoing it* 99.3, *exertion* 122.4, *overactivity* 414.9, *fatigue* 820.1
overexpand *overdo* 99.11
overexpansion *overdoing it* 99.3, *overactivity* 414.9
overexpose *exaggerate* 194.11
overexposed *exposed* 132.25, *exaggerated* 194.7, *colorless* 252.5
overexposed photograph *or negative* *pen-and-ink sketch* 252.3
overexposure *composition* 132.17, *exaggeration* 194.1, *lightening* 246.3, *pen-and-ink sketch* 252.3
overexpression *overdoing it* 99.3
overextend *overdo* 99.11
overextended *overdone* 99.7, *overambitious* 391.6, *unprofitable* 468.10, *surpassing* 712.10
overextension *overdoing it* 99.3, *overactivity* 414.9, *expansionism* 712.5
overfall *wave* 571.3
overfatigued *fatigued* 820.2
overfed *immoderate* 99.6, *fat* 579.15
overfeed *overindulge* 99.10
overfeeding *immoderation* 99.2

overfill *fill* 761.11
overfilled *full* 761.8
overfish *expend* 96.16
overflight *flight* 689.5
overflow *abound* 97.8, *excess* 99.1, *be excessive* 99.9, *be diffuse* 199.5, *flow* 570.4, 570.10, *outlet* 707.8, *run out* 707.15, *overstep* 712.12, *be full* 761.12, *crowd* 795.11
overflowed *flooded* 557.24
overflowing *excessive* 99.5, *diffuse* 199.3, *abundant* 498.8, *flowing* 570.7, *overstepping* 712.1, *overrun* 712.6, *full* 761.8
overfly *maneuver* 689.14
overfrank *discourteous* 411.5
overfulfill *overindulge* 99.10
overfulfilled *immoderate* 99.6
overfulfilling *immoderate* 99.6
overfulfillment *immoderation* 99.2, *excessiveness* 712.4
overfull *excessive* 99.5, *full* 761.8
overglaze *glaze* 129.3, *make ceramics* 129.10
overglazed *ceramic* 129.9
overglaze decoration *glaze* 129.3
overgorged *gluttonous* 119.3
overgorging *gluttonous* 119.3
overgraze *waste* 23.11, *expend* 96.16
overgrow *vegetate* 41.21, *grow* 581.17, *overstep* 712.12
overgrown *plantlike* 41.13, *huge* 579.14, *grown* 581.11, *overrun* 712.6
overgrowth *rough thing* 544.2, *largeness* 579.2, *growth* 581.4, *overstepping* 712.1, *surplus* 750.2
overhand *rock face* 161.6, *forehand* 165.12
overhand knot *Knots, Bends, Hitches, Splices* 754
overhang **604.14;** *be high* 596.15, *overhanging* 604.2, *overlay* 613.25, *be in the future* 650.9
overhanging **604.2, 604.8;** *highland* 596.11, *future* 650.6
overhastily *rashly* 286.9, 818.8, *prematurely* 657.20
overhastiness *rashness* 286.1, *alacrity* 414.3
overhasty *rash* 286.5, *hasty* 818.3
overhaul *accelerate* 694.14, *repair* 809.1, 809.10, *restore* 809.12
overhauling *repair* 809.1
overhead *business expenses* 491.4, *high* 596.20
overhead covering **613.11**
overhead projector *viewer* 132.22
overhead rack *or locker compartment* 578.2
overhead smash *tennis strokes* 165.2
overhear *be informed* 170.15, *hear* 228.13
overhearing *hearing* 228.1
overheat *malfunction* 846.20
overheated *unhygienic* 114.27, *heating* 217.12
overheating *heat* 217.1
overindulge **99.10, 456.11;** *eat well* 92.23, *be greedy* 119.4, *be extravagant* 194.13, *exaggerate* 712.16
overindulgence **456.3;** *appetite* 92.2, *immoderation* 99.2, *gluttony* 119.1, *extravagance* 194.3, *excessiveness* 712.4
overindulgent **456.8;** *immoderate* 99.6, *gluttonous* 119.3, *extravagant* 194.9, *permitting* 502.5, *exaggerated* 712.9

overindulgently *immoderately* 99.14, *excessively* 712.17
overindulging *gluttony* 119.1
overjoyed *joyful* 269.6
overkill *immoderation* 99.2, *overdoing it* 99.3, *exaggeration* 194.1, *exaggerate* 194.11, *imbalance* 741.2
overladen *loaded* 538.10, *ponderous* 538.11
overlaid *coated* 588.7
overlap *superfluity* 99.4, *adjoin* 216.11, *layer* 588.1, *588.9, *overlay* 613.25, *fold* 637.1, 637.7
overlap integral *chemical bond* 11.6
overlapped *coated* 588.7
overlapping *contiguous* 216.8, *coated* 588.7, *covering* 613.1, 613.21
over-large *huge* 579.14
overlaudation *flattery* 439.1
overlay 613.25; *conceal* 181.12, *ornament* 532.12, *smooth* 545.10, *coat* 588.3, *layer* 588.9, *covering* 613.1, *coating* 613.8, *augment* 748.13
overlayer *layer* 588.1
overlaying *coated* 588.7, *covering* 613.1, 613.21
overleap *overstep* 712.12, *overtake* 744.16
overlie *be exterior* 610.13
overload *overdoing it* 99.3, *overdo* 99.11, *ornament* 532.12, *displacement* 538.3, *make heavy* 538.14, *imbalance* 741.2, *augment* 748.13, *surplus* 750.4, *fatigue* 820.6, *burden* 826.10, 826.21, *cause adversity* 848.15
overloaded *overdone* 99.7, *overambitious* 391.6, *loaded* 538.10, *ponderous* 538.11, *unbalanced* 741.5, *surplus* 750.8, *full* 761.8, *blocked* 826.13
overloading *displacement* 538.3
overlong *boring* 296.6, *lengthy* 590.9, *surpassing* 712.10
overlook *be blind to* 243.19, *show mercy* 312.11, *be inattentive* 324.10, *err* 351.14, *forget* 355.10, *not use* 394.9, *not observe* 466.9, *be high* 596.15, *overtake* 744.16, *think unimportant* 800.19
overlooked 312.6; *neglected* 326.6, *nonobservant* 466.5, *obscure* 800.13
overlooking *forgivingness* 312.3, *forgiving* 312.4, *nonobservance* 466.1, *nonobservant* 466.5, *highland* 596.11
overlord *master* 68.1, *possessor* 469.10
overlordship *governance* 49.18
overly *excessively* 99.13
overlying *covering* 613.21
overlying layer *exteriority* 610.2
overman *overcrowd* 795.12
overmanned *crowded* 795.10
overmaster *attack successfully* 418.25, *be an influence* 512.13, *be strong* 516.14, *overpower* 845.18
overmeasurement *superfluity* 99.4
overmighty *lawless* 53.26
overmodest *moralistic* 431.12
overmodesty *self-righteousness* 431.7
overmuch *excessive* 99.5, *excessively* 99.13
over my dead body! *no!* 190.28, 506.12
overnight *nightly* 656.6

overnight bag *bag* 578.7, *baggage* 578.8
overnight sensation *success* 845.1
over one's head *difficult* 1022.10
over one's head in debt *indebted* 488.7, *nonpaying* 490.7
overoptimism *overdoing it* 99.3, *overestimation* 343.1
overoptimistic *overdone* 99.7, *overestimating* 343.4
overoptimistically 343.7
overornamentally *obscurely* 197.4
overornamentation *obscurity* 197.1
overornamented *obscure* 197.2
overpaint *paint* 143.12
overpainting *(act of) painting* 143.1
overpass *bridge* 551.10, 691.7, *crossroads* 609.4, *crossing point* 692.7, *overstep* 712.12
overpassing *overstepping* 712.1
overpay 496.11
overpayment *overdoing it* 99.3
overplay *overdo* 99.11, *overact* 136.35, *exaggerate* 712.16, *overtake* 744.16
overplayed *overdone* 99.7, *dramatized* 136.32
overplaying *excessiveness* 712.4
overplus *superfluity* 99.4
overpolarization *electrochemistry* 11.19
overpolite *overdone* 99.7
overpoliteness *overdoing it* 99.3
overpopulate *be excessive* 99.9, *overcrowd* 795.12
overpopulated *excessive* 99.5, *crowded* 795.10
overpopulation *excess* 99.1, *economic deterioration* 808.2
overpossessive *jealous* 314.5
overpower 515.14, 845.18; *master* 68.17, *attack successfully* 418.25, *be strong* 516.14, *lower* 597.21, *defeat* 832.11
overpowering *stinking* 227.3, *attacking* 418.14, *strong* 516.9, *domination* 832.2, *dominating* 832.7
overpraise *overdoing it* 99.3, *overdo* 99.11, *bombast* 194.4, *boast* 194.14, *overestimate* 343.6, *praise* 437.3, 437.16, *flattery* 439.1, *flatter* 439.12
overpraised *exaggerated* 194.7, *overestimated* 343.5
overpraising *approving* 437.9
overpreciseness *formalism* 406.2
overprice *overestimate* 343.6, *overcharge* 496.10
overpriced *overestimated* 343.5, *costly* 496.7, 500.6
overpricing 496.2
overprint *identify* 184.11, *obliterate* 186.8
overprinted *concealed* 181.8
overprinting *obliteration* 186.1
overprize *overestimate* 343.6
overproduce *be excessive* 99.9
overproduction *waste* 96.1
overproof *intoxicating* 121.29
overproud *vain* 402.8
overrate *boast* 194.14, *misjudge* 342.9, *overestimate* 343.6, *exaggerate* 712.16, *intensify* 746.8, *make important* 799.14
overrated *exaggerated* 194.7, 712.9, *misjudged* 342.8, *overestimated* 343.5
overrating *bombast* 194.4, *overestimation* 343.1, *excessiveness* 712.4

overreach *aim* 327.17, *overstep* 712.12, *be cunning* 822.5
overreaching *excessive* 712.8
overreact *exaggerate* 194.11, *be sensitive* 267.5, *misuse* 395.6
overreaction *overdoing it* 99.3, *exaggeration* 194.1, *misuse* 395.1
overrefinement *formalism* 406.2
overreligious *zealous* 81.22
over-rev [Inf] *be on the track* 146.11
override *manipulate* 508.12, *be an influence* 512.13, *overtake* 744.16, *overpower* 845.18
overriding *compelling* 428.6, *dominant* 744.9, *important* 799.7
overrighteous *zealous* 81.22
overripe *unpalatable* 223.6, *compressible* 543.9, *pulpy* 561.19, *imperfect* 806.5
overripen *soften* 543.14
overripeness *pulpiness* 561.9, *imperfection* 806.1
overrule *cancel* 834.6
overruled verdict *legal injustice* 53.5
overruling *authoritative* 52.9, *dominant* 744.9, *important* 799.7
overrun 712.6; *vegetate* 41.23, *superfluity* 99.4, *be superfluous* 99.12, *attack successfully* 418.25, *take over* 477.16, *flow* 570.4, 570.10, *be present* 575.13, *overstepping* 712.1, *overstep* 712.12, *transgress* 712.14, *full* 761.8, *fill* 761.11, *crowded* 795.10, *overcrowd* 795.12, *eat away* 808.19
overrunning *military attack* 418.2, *overstepping* 712.1, *victory* 845.4
oversatisfy *overindulge* 99.10
oversea *nautically* 571.10
overseas *nautically* 571.10, *distant* 585.5, *distantly* 585.11, *foreign* 724.9, *strangely* 724.17
overseas call *telephone call* 169.11
overseas mail *postal service* 169.5
oversee *manage* 126.10, *watch* 242.23, *direct* 780.14
overseer *employer* 57.3, *manager* 126.7, *observer* 242.15
oversell *overdo* 99.11, *boast* 194.14, *overcharge* 496.10
overselling *exaggeration* 194.1
oversensitive 267.4; *susceptible* 212.7, *touchy* 303.10
oversensitively 267.7; *touchily* 303.19
oversensitivity 267.2; *sensitivity* 212.2, *touchiness* 303.3
overset *downthrow* 716.2, *overthrown* 716.9, *bring down* 716.14
oversexed *desirous* 20.18
overshadow *make dark* 247.10, *hide* 613.27, *overtake* 744.16
overshadowing *dimming* 248.3, *covering* 613.1
overshift *defense* 155.9, *play defense* 155.19
overshoes *boots* 100.31
overshoot *be clumsy* 128.9, *be extravagant* 194.13, *flight* 689.5, *maneuver* 689.14, *unbalance* 741.8
overshooting *extravagance* 194.3
overshot *extravagant* 194.9
oversight *negligence* 324.4, 326.1, *trivial error* 351.8, *nonobservance* 466.1, *nonachievement* 762.3
oversize *largeness* 579.2
oversized *spacious* 563.13, *huge* 579.14
overskirt *skirt* 100.12

oversleep *be late* 658.11
oversold *exaggerated* 194.7
oversoul *world soul* 82.3
overspecialized *problematic* 824.11
overspend 500.8; *waste* 96.15, *overdo* 99.11, *be extravagant* 194.13, *lose money* 468.15, *be in debt* 488.9, *expend* 491.11, *overpay* 496.11
overspender *loser* 468.8
overspending *waste* 96.1, *extravagance* 194.3, *extravagant* 194.9, *financial loss* 468.4
overspent *unprofitable* 468.10
overspill *excess* 99.1, *be excessive* 99.9
overspread *overrun* 712.6, *overstep* 712.12
overspreading *overstepping* 712.1
overstaff *overcrowd* 795.12
overstaffed *crowded* 795.10
overstate *affirm* 189.21, *distort the truth* 192.25, *exaggerate* 194.11, *overestimate* 343.6
overstated *affirmed* 189.11, *partially true* 192.18, *exaggerated* 194.7, *gaudy* 251.12, *ornate* 532.10
overstatement *affirmation* 189.1, *partial truth* 192.7, *exaggeration* 194.1, *overestimation* 343.1, *ornateness* 532.2
oversteer *miscellaneous automotive terms* 687.14
overstep 712.12; *be clumsy* 128.9, *overtake* 744.16
overstep oneself *aim* 327.17
overstepping 712.1; *lawbreaking* 53.14, *extravagant* 194.9, *improvement* 679.5
overstepping the mark *extravagance* 194.3
overstep the bounds *overstep* 712.12
overstep the mark *overdo* 99.11, *be extravagant* 194.13, *overstep* 712.12
overstock *superfluity* 99.4, *be superfluous* 99.12
overstrain *fatigue* 820.6
overstrained *fatigued* 820.2
overstress *exaggeration* 194.1, *exaggerate* 194.11
overstressed *exaggerated* 194.7
overstretched *overdone* 99.7
overstretching oneself *overdoing it* 99.3
overstrict *zealous* 81.22
overstride *overstep* 712.12
oversubscribe *overdo* 99.11
oversubtlety *quibbling* 330.4
oversupplied *bargain* 497.10
oversupply *plenty* 90.4, *superfluity* 99.4, *be superfluous* 99.12, *overactivity* 414.9, *declining prices* 497.2, *surplus* 750.4
oversweetness *sweetness* 222.1
overt *visible* 244.5, *manifest* 843.9
overt act *deed* 412.2
overtake 744.16; *improve* 467.18, *maintain progress* 679.14, *pass* 692.15, *accelerate* 694.14, *exceed* 712.15, *make haste* 818.5
overtaken *overrun* 712.6
overtaking *advance* 467.3, *improvement* 679.5, *miscellaneous automotive terms* 687.14, *passing* 692.11, *acceleration* 694.3, *accelerating* 694.9, *overstepping* 712.1, *surpassing* 712.10
overtask *ill-use* 395.7
overtax *overdo* 99.11, *ill-use* 395.7, *take back* 477.17, *make heavy* 538.14, *fatigue* 820.6

overtaxation *overdoing it* 99.3
overtaxed *overdone* 99.7, *ponderous* 538.11
overtaxing *weighing down* 538.5, *ponderous* 538.11
overtax one's strength *be fatigued* 820.5
overtechnical *problematic* 824.11
over the border *ahead* 712.18
over-the-counter drug *drug* 115.9
over-the-counter market *seller's market* 483.3
over-the-counter medication *medicine* 115.2
over the hill *aged* 27.15, *old* 653.10
over-the-hill gang [Inf] *old people* 27.10
over the hills and far away *distantly* 585.11, *ahead* 712.18, *fugitively* 816.12
over the horizon *invisible* 245.3
over the moon [Inf] *overdone* 99.7, *joyful* 269.6
over the top *fully* 761.14
over the water *nautically* 571.10
overthrow *anarchy* 51.1, *be anarchic* 51.8, *gain authority* 52.15, *go to war* 76.29, *bungling* 128.2, *be clumsy* 128.9, *refutation* 332.1, *refute* 332.7, *deed* 412.2, *subvert* 427.13, *destruction* 523.1, *abolish* 523.11, *knock down* 523.13, *replacement* 574.3, *replace* 574.17, *lowering* 597.3, *lower* 597.21, *sudden change* 665.3, *downthrow* 716.2, *bring down* 716.14, *impair* 808.18, *overpower* 845.18
overthrowing *acquisition of authority* 52.5
overthrown 716.9; *replaced* 574.10, *lowered* 597.12, *changed* 665.10, *defeated* 846.11
overtime *negotiated* 57.16, *task* 122.2, *basketball* 148.1, *game time* 155.4, *period of activity* 641.4
overtime ban *strike* 57.8
overtime pay *reward for service* 453.5, *pay* 489.6
overtime victory *victory* 845.4
overtime work *bargaining terms* 57.10
overtired *spoiled* 808.9, *fatigued* 820.2
overtiredness *fatigue* 820.1
overtly *actively* 412.18, *manifestly* 843.17
overtness *visibility* 244.1
overtone *musical note* 140.15, *tone* 140.24, 230.2, *ambience* 615.3
overtop *tower over* 569.7, *be high* 596.15, *top* 600.10, *overtake* 744.16
overtopped *topped* 600.8
overtopping *highland* 596.11, *topped* 600.8, *superior* 744.8
overtrump *overtake* 744.16
overture *play part* 136.8, *Musical Forms* 140, *tentative offer* 504.2, *preface* 769.5
overturn *refute* 332.7, *abolish* 523.11, *knock down* 523.13, *act of inversion* 608.3, *become inverted* 608.8, *sail* 690.16, *trip* 714.16, *downthrow* 716.2, *bring down* 716.14, *overpower* 845.18
overturned *overthrown* 716.9
overturned fold *fold* 8.22
overturned verdict *legal injustice* 53.5
overturning *refuting* 332.6,

destruction 523.1, *fall* 714.4, *downthrow* 716.2
overuse *ill-use* 395.2, 395.7
overused *common* 778.13
overvaluation *exaggeration* 194.1, *misjudgment* 342.1, *overestimation* 343.1
overvalue *exaggerate* 194.11, *misjudge* 342.9, *overestimate* 343.6
overvalued *exaggerated* 194.7, *misjudged* 342.8, *overestimated* 343.5
overview 425.6; *management* 126.1, *summary* 204.1, *whole situation* 759.3
overween [Arch] *pride oneself* 297.13
overweening *audacious* 400.10
overweeningly *audaciously* 400.20
overweening pride *pride* 297.1, *overestimation* 343.1
overweigh *be heavy* 538.12, *make heavy* 538.14
overweighed *loaded* 538.10
overweight *weighing* 538.4, *heavy* 538.9, *fat* 579.15, *swelled* 581.10, *thick* 594.5, *well-rounded* 633.8
overweighted *loaded* 538.10
overweighting *displacement* 538.3
overwhelm *be excessive* 99.9, *attack successfully* 418.25, *command respect* 435.18, *be strong* 516.14, *consume* 523.16, *fill* 761.11, *overcrowd* 795.12, *defeat* 845.17
overwhelmed *excessive* 99.5, *oversensitive* 267.4
overwhelming *excessive* 99.5, *emotive* 266.13, *astonishing* 294.10, *attacking* 418.14, *strong* 516.9, *explosive* 520.6, *destructive* 523.8
overwhelmingly *excessively* 99.13
overwinter *be dormant* 41.22, *spend the season* 654.10
overwork 122.9; *waste* 96.1, *expend* 96.16, *overdoing it* 99.3, *overdo* 99.11, *exertion* 122.4, *overwork* 122.9, *use up* 393.12, *ill-use* 395.2, 395.7, *try* 414.21, *make useless* 802.12, *fatigue* 820.1, 820.6, *be fatigued* 820.5
overworked *overdone* 99.7, *busy* 414.15, *common* 778.13, *fatigued* 820.2
overwrite *exaggerate* 194.11
overwriting *exaggeration* 194.1
overwritten *exaggerated* 194.7
overwrought *oversensitive* 267.4, *fidgety* 414.14, *fatigued* 820.2
overzealous *reckless* 286.6
overzealously *recklessly* 286.10
overzealousness *recklessness* 286.2
ovine *ungulate* 35.31
oviparous *pregnant* 21.12
ovipositor *organs of reproduction* 21.9
ovoid *spherical* 6.80, *circular* 631.5, *round* 633.7
ovolo *Architectural Elements* 134
ovule *seed* 41.9, *flower part* 42.3
ovum *organs of reproduction* 21.9
ow *cry of pain* 239.5
owe *be in debt* 488.9, *leave* 750.10
owed *payable* 489.12, *surplus* 750.8
owe everything to *follow from* 676.9
owe loyalty to *be subject to* 832.12
owe money *be in debt* 488.9
ower *borrower* 476.7
owing *indebted* 486.9, 488.7, *debt* 488.1, *payable* 489.12, *convenient* 803.3

owing nothing *paid* 489.11
owing to *by virtue of* 447.12, *caused* 676.5
owl, Mexican spotted Endangered US Birds 36
owl, northern spotted Endangered US Birds 36
owl *bird of prey* 36.11, *night* 656.3
owlet *young bird* 36.17
owlish *avian* 36.19
owl-like *avian* 36.19
owls Collective Names 59
own *admit* 180.11, *avow* 189.27, *possess* 469.14
own account *freedom* 829.1
own assets *own property* 470.11
own authority *independence* 829.5
own backyard *habitat* 60.1
own bonds *own property* 470.11
owned *avowed* 189.19, *possessed* 469.13
owned by *possessed* 469.13
owned property *possession of property* 469.3
owner *master* 68.1, *titleholder* 72.4, *horse person* 159.14, *user* 393.4, *possessor* 469.10, *property owner* 470.7
owner-occupier *householder* 61.5, *possessor* 469.10
owners *management board* 126.2
ownership *claim* 429.3, *possession* 469.1
ownership papers *certificate* 185.2
own free will *freedom* 829.1
owning *possession* 469.1, *possessing* 469.11
own initiative *freedom* 829.1
own personal effects *own property* 470.11
own property 470.11
own responsibility *freedom* 829.1
own shares of stocks *own property* 470.11
own up *admit* 180.11
own up to *avow* 189.27
own volition *freedom* 829.1
own way *independence* 829.5
Owyhee Rivers 570
ox *male animal* 32.15, *means of transportation* 686.2
oxalic Common Fatty Acids 12
oxalis Flowers 42
oxblood *red* 257.5
oxbow lake *lake* 568.1
Oxbridge [Brit] *university* 48.14
ox cheek *variety meat* 90.30
oxen Collective Names 59
oxeye daisy Flowers 42
Oxfam *charitable organization* 305.4
Oxford accent *regional pronunciation* 205.7
Oxford–Cambridge race *rowing competitions* 150.18
Oxford Down Breeds of Sheep 16
oxfords or **Oxford shoes** *shoes* 100.30
oxidation *weathering* 8.40
oxide *mineral types* 8.38
oxidization *decay* 808.6
oxidize *react* 11.38
oxidoreductase *enzyme* 12.11
oxlike *ungulate* 35.31
oxlip Flowers 42
oxyacetylene torch *cause of fire* 217.10
oxygen Chemical Elements and Common Allotropes 11, *essential element* 12.15, *life requirement* 28.5, *refresher* 94.2, *air* 558.1
oxygenate *aerate* 556.24, 558.20
oxygenation *ventilation* 558.6

oxygen depletion *pollution* 117.8
oxygenic *oxygenous* 556.22
oxygenization *ventilation* 558.6
oxygenous 556.22
oxygen tent *safety device* 810.15
oxytocin Human Hormones 12
oyster *food fish and shellfish* 90.20, *grayness* 255.1
oystercatcher *water bird* 36.9
oyster fork *tableware* 92.13
oysterlike *molluskan* 39.23
oyster pieces *decorative woodwork* 131.2
oyster-white *white* 253.7
oysterwood marquetry *decorative woodwork* 131.2
Oz Imaginary Places 360
Ozark Mountains Mountains and Hills 569
ozone Chemical Elements and Common Allotropes 11, *air* 558.1, *open air* 558.5
ozone depletion *pollution* 117.8
ozone layer *atmosphere* 9.8
ozonic *oxygenous* 556.22
ozoniferous *oxygenous* 556.22
ozonize *react* 11.38
ozonosphere *atmosphere* 9.8, *atmospheric layer* 558.3
ozonous *oxygenous* 556.22

P

pa [Inf] *man in the family* 32.12, *family member* 65.2
pabulum *food* 90.1
pace Collective Names 59, Architectural Elements 134, *bodily movement* 677.11, *slow motion* 693.3
paced start *automobile racing terms* 146.3
pacemaker *horse racing* 159.10, *substitute* 672.2
pace off *measure* 589.20
pacer *racehorse* 159.2
pacesetter *leader* 126.8
pachyderm 35.15
pachydermatous *elephantlike* 35.30, *thick* 594.5
pacifiable *pacificatory* 74.8
pacific 74.7; *detached* 4.18, *moderate* 521.3, *quiescent* 678.6
Pacific Air Forces *air force commands* 77.28
pacifically 74.12; *peacefully* 73.12
pacification 74.1; *pacifism* 73.4, *mediation* 75.1, *atonement* 313.1
pacificatory 74.8; *mediatory* 75.5, *moderating* 521.5
Pacific Northwest *regions of the United States* 56.7
Pacific Ocean Oceans and Seas 571
Pacific Rim *international trade* 56.7
Pacific Time *time zone* 646.5
pacified *pacificatory* 74.8
pacifier 73.7; *mediator* 75.2, *atoner* 313.4, *moderator* 521.2
pacifism 73.4
pacifist 74.6; *political and economic philosopher* 4.10, *of a political philosophy* 4.14, *pacifier* 73.7, *pacific* 74.7, *resister* 417.5
pacify 74.9, 74.11; *make peace* 73.11, *mediate* 75.6, *comfort* 273.9, *relieve* 275.8, *atone* 313.7, *offer reparation* 504.15, *mitigate* 521.9, *smooth over* 545.12, *make motionless* 678.8, *restore order* 765.22

pacifying *pacification* 74.1, *pacificatory* 74.8, *satisfying* 273.5, *atoning* 313.5
pacifyingly *atoningly* 313.10
pacing *horse racing* 159.10, *agitation* 684.1
pack *assemblage of mammals* 35.22, Collective Names 59, *group* 59.8, *crowd* 59.26, 795.11, *save* 105.20, *cards* 168.2, *make dense* 540.9, *stuff* 577.12, *packet* 578.4, *contain* 578.20, *thicken* 594.9, *wrap* 613.29, *transferred thing* 685.6, *convey* 685.9, *transportable* 686.7, *certain amount* 738.3, *quantify* 738.7, *unite closely* 752.16, *unit* 759.5, *fill* 761.11, *throng* 795.4
package *group* 59.24, *heap* 105.19, *be an architect* 134.13, *postal communication* 553.3, *contain* 577.10, 578.20, *stuff* 577.12, *wrap* 613.29, 619.7, *enclosing thing* 619.3, *inclusion* 763.1
packaged *grouped* 59.21, *stored* 105.14, *protected* 613.20, *wrapped* 619.5
package deal *inclusion* 763.1
packaged food *food* 90.1
packager *coverer* 613.18
package store *drink provider* 93.15
packaging *packet* 578.4, *wrapping* 613.10, *preservation of provisions* 815.6
pack a jury *predetermine* 384.8
pack animal *means of transportation* 686.2
pack a punch [Inf] *be strong* 516.14
pack away *save* 105.20, *stop using* 394.10
packed *crowded* 59.22, 795.10, *predetermined* 384.4, *loaded* 577.8, *storing* 578.19, *obstructed* 584.8, *dense* 594.6, *quantitative* 738.6, *full* 761.8
packed away *saved* 105.15
packed house *theatergoer* 136.30
packed jury *injustice* 342.3, *predetermination* 384.1
packed lunch *meal* 92.8
packed-powder *snow* 162.28
packed-powder snow *skiing snow* 162.3
packer *laborer* 123.9
packet 578.4; *computer communications* 15.25, *tobacco implements* 121.24, *certain amount* 738.3
packet boat *or* **packet ship** Ships and Boats 690
packet switch *communications device* 15.26
packhorse *workhorse* 159.3, *means of transportation* 686.2
pack ice *iceberg* 8.45, *ice* 218.5
pack in *flood in* 706.14, *impact* 710.11, *fill* 761.11
packing *stuffing* 577.4, *storing* 578.19, *preservation of provisions* 815.6
packing box *or* **case** *box* 578.5
packing case *receptacle* 105.11
pack it in *relinquish* 392.3, *resign* 835.5
pack it in! *cease!* 668.14
pack off *eject* 701.8, *send away* 709.18
pack of lies *falsehood* 192.6
pack rat *collector* 59.17
pack together *make dense* 540.9
pact *contract* 459.1, 462.2, *settlement* 735.6
pad *be diffuse* 199.5, *heat* 217.17, *small sound* 233.4, *buffer* 419.22,

soften 543.14, *stuff* 577.12, *swell* 581.15, *fatten* 594.10
padded *fencing* 153.6, *diffuse* 199.3, *heated* 217.15, *compressible* 543.9, *loaded* 577.8, *swelled* 581.10, *thick* 594.5, *ornamental* 748.9
padded cell *mental hospital* 110.6
padded glove *fencing equipment* 153.2
padding *superfluity* 99.4, *diffuseness* 199.1, *stuffing* 577.4, *enlarger* 581.8, *thickness* 594.1, *additional item* 748.3, *iteration* 797.2
Paddington *London* 567.8
paddle *canoe parts* 150.10, *canoe* 150.31, *row* 150.32, *hit* 454.28, *agitator* 684.14, *agitate* 684.22
paddleboat Ships and Boats 690
paddled *canoeing* 150.26
paddle one's own canoe [Inf] *conduct oneself* 399.17, *be one* 788.17, *be independent* 829.18
paddler *boating person* 150.24, *nautical person* 690.12
paddle steamer Ships and Boats 690
paddle wheel *wheel* 682.9, *propeller* 696.8
paddling Collective Names 59, *canoeing* 150.8, 150.26, *rowing techniques* 150.16, *rowing* 150.27, *corporal punishment* 454.11, *ramming* 695.3
paddling canoe *canoe* 150.9
paddock *farmland* 16.3, *racetrack* 159.12, *enclosed area* 619.2
paddock [Arch] *amphibian* 37.10
paddock grazing *livestock farming* 16.10
Paddy Nicknames for Inhabitants 61
paddy *farmland* 16.3
paddy field *farmland* 16.3
paddy wagon [Inf] *automobile* 687.6
padlock *obstruction* 584.2, *obstruct* 584.13, *fastener* 754.7, *bind* 754.14
padlocked *obstructed* 584.8, *bound* 754.12
pad out *make bigger* 746.7
padre *member of the clergy* 84.5
pads *football uniform* 155.2
paean *ritual music* 85.9, *sacred music* 140.3, *cry of praise* 239.3, *thanks* 310.2, *compliment* 437.4
paeon *meter* 139.10
pagan *disbeliever* 88.5, *disbelieving* 88.6
paganism *unbelief* 88.4
page *wedding party* 64.7, *attendant* 69.4, *book part* 174.5, *identify* 184.11, *transferrer* 685.4, *transporter* 686.4, *part of writing* 760.6
pageant *circus* 138.2, *view* 242.8, *mass demonstration* 331.7, *show* 404.12, *formal occasion* 406.4, *procession* 774.6, *manifestation* 843.2
pageantry *pomp* 404.7, *manifestation* 843.2
pageboy *wedding party* 64.7, *coiffure* 530.8
page number *book part* 174.5
page proof *stage of proof* 174.9
pager *radio* 172.1
paginate *publish* 174.19, *identify* 184.11
pagoda *place of worship* 83.8
pagoda tree Trees and Shrubs 43
Pago Pago American States 564, *distant place* 585.3

pagophobia Phobias 283
Pahlavan Horse and Pony Breeds 159
pahoehoe *eruption* 8.27
paid 489.11; *gainful* 467.10, *receiving* 473.9, *expended* 491.9, *received* 492.6, *engaged* 833.7
paid back *compensated* 743.3
paid for *bought* 481.8
paid helper *servant* 69.1
paid in advance *receiving pay* 489.14
paid in full *paid* 489.11
paid out *expended* 491.9
Päijänne Lakes 568
pail *vessel* 578.11
pain 117.5, 215.1; *symptom* 114.3, *inflict pain* 215.10, *sorrow* 270.1, *unpleasantness* 272.1, Phobias 283, *inconvenience* 804.1, *adverse health* 848.5
pain [Inf] *unpleasant person* 272.5, *boring person* 296.4
pain disorder *somatoform disorder* 108.19
pained *miserable* 117.12, *feeling pain* 215.6, *offended* 302.9
pain-free *easygoing* 823.13
painful 215.4; *of disease* 114.25, *miserable* 117.12, *laborious* 122.7, *inflicting pain* 215.7, *distressing* 270.6, *unpleasant* 272.6, *detrimental* 446.8, *punishing* 454.20
painful condition 215.2
painful injury 215.3
painfully 215.12; *destructively* 446.13
painfulness *pain* 215.1
pain in the neck *or* **ass** [Inf] *unpleasant person* 272.5, *boring person* 296.4, *troublemaker* 427.5
painkiller *analgesic* 115.6, *anesthetic* 213.3, *reliever* 275.4, *moderator* 521.2
painkilling *moderating* 521.5
painless *simple* 526.7, *easy* 823.9
painlessly *pleasingly* 214.15, *simply* 526.14
painlessness *simplicity* 526.1
pain relief *analgesic* 115.6
pain-relieving *medicinal* 115.15
pains *exertion* 122.4
pains and penalties *penalty* 454.5
painstaking *laborious* 122.7, *diligent* 323.7, *fastidious* 325.9, *assiduity* 414.8, *careful* 593.11
painstakingness *fastidiousness* 325.4
paint 143.12, 251.6; *cleaning agent* 111.9, *dose of medicine* 115.3, *make ceramics* 129.10, *work wood* 131.9, *design* 133.9, *record* 185.13, *illustrate* 187.11, *describe* 202.15, *coloring agent* 251.5, *color* 251.16, *imagine* 360.14, *dream up* 522.15, *cosmetics* 530.4, *beautify* 530.14, *decorate* 532.11, *smooth* 545.10, *coating* 613.8, *wall covering* 613.12, *coat* 613.28, *face* 613.31, *augment* 748.13, *preserver* 815.9, *preserve* 815.14
paintable *representational* 187.8
paint and decorate *decorate* 532.11
paint box *cosmetic tool* 530.5
paintbrush *material* 143.9
Painted Deserts 572
painted 143.10; *type of furniture* 101.2, *colored* 251.10, *flashy* 404.17, *covered* 613.19
painted image *image* 187.3
painted tongue Flowers 42

Painter Constellations 7
painter 143.7; *artisan* 123.13, *visual artist* 133.6, *sailboat parts and accessories* 150.4, *producer* 522.10, *decorator* 532.8, *coverer* 613.18, *line* 754.5
painterliness *treatment* 143.6
painterly *artistic* 133.7, *representational* 187.8
painterly values *treatment* 143.6
Painters Eleven Western Art Styles 133
painting 143.3; *craft* 133.2, *picture* 133.5, Hobbies and Pastimes 167, *illustration* 187.2, *view* 242.8, *work of art* 522.4, *decorative method* 532.3, *interior decoration* 532.4, *upkeep* 815.5
painting over *obliteration* 186.1
painting the lily *exaggeration* 194.1
paint in words *imagine* 360.14
paint manufacturing *chemical process industries* 14.26
paint oneself into a corner *figurative expressions* 128.11, *be in difficulty* 824.19
paint over *conceal* 181.12, *obliterate* 186.8, *transform* 670.13, *augment* 748.13
paints *material* 143.9
paint the lily *be superfluous* 99.12, *exaggerate* 194.11, *ornament* 532.12
paint the town red [Inf] *rejoice* 279.5, *participate* 408.15
paint tube *material* 143.9
paint with a broad brush *make a generalization* 778.18
pair 789.13; *have sex* 20.21, *ice-skating* 162.32, *look-alike* 730.4, *make the same* 730.16, *couple* 733.6, *unite* 752.14, *numerical* 783.7, *two* 789.1, *twosome* 789.3
paired *married* 64.16, *related* 727.6, *look-alike* 730.10, *matched* 733.10, *two* 789.8, *associated* 794.14
pairing *sexual intercourse* 20.9, *coupling* 20.19, *doubling* 789.4
pair of compasses *geometric construction* 6.47
pair off *unite* 752.14, *pair* 789.13
pair of spectacles *visual aid* 242.14
pairs *bowls* 151.7, *ice skating* 162.15
pair skating *ice skating* 162.15
pair-skating *ice-skating* 162.32
pair-skating movement *ice-skating techniques* 162.16
pairs match *or* **pairs** *green bowling* 151.3
pairs sit spin *ice-skating techniques* 162.16
pair up *relate to* 727.9, *unite* 752.14, *intercommunicate* 754.15, *keep company with* 794.17
paisa *national coins* 484.11
paisley Fabrics and Fibers 130
pajama party *night* 656.3
pajamas *nightwear* 100.21
Paki Nicknames for Inhabitants 61
Pakistan Countries 566
pal [Inf] *male title of address* 32.3, *friend* 62.2, *social person* 408.7
palace *mansion* 60.5
paladin *combatant* 77.1, *defender* 419.14
pal around with [Inf] *fraternize* 408.17
Palas Merino Breeds of Sheep 16
palatability *taste* 219.1

palatable *edible* 92.20, *pleasurable* 214.6, *tasty* 219.4
palatably *culinarily* 91.11, *tastily* 219.7
palate *taste* 219.1, *judiciousness* 337.2
palate bone Human Bones 19
palate-tickling *delicate eating* 92.3, *edible* 92.20
palatial *manorial* 60.21, *majestic* 404.21, *opulent* 485.10
palatinate *body politic* 50.3, *dominion* 566.3
Palau Islands 572
palaver *talk* 207.3
Palawan Islands 572
pale 253.10; *unhealthy* 114.23, Heraldic Terms 184, *difficult to see* 245.4, *be dim* 248.7, *soft-hued* 251.13, *drained of color* 252.6, *lose color* 252.7, *decolor* 252.8, *whiten* 253.12, *ill* 517.8, *region* 564.1, *enclosed area* 619.2, *enclosing thing* 619.3, *enclose* 619.6, *fastener* 754.7, *exclusion zone* 764.3, *fatigued* 820.2
palea *grass plant* 45.3
pale as a ghost *unhealthy* 114.23, *frightened* 283.9
pale-blue *blue* 261.5
pale-brown *brown* 256.5
pale-gray *gray* 255.6
pale horse *personifications and symbols* 29.4
pale imitation *bungling* 128.2
palely *whitely* 253.13
paleness 252.2; *invisibility* 245.1, *dimness* 248.1, *hue* 251.4, *face color* 251.9, *whiteness* 253.1, *warning signal* 814.3
paleoanthropographic *paleoanthropological* 1.11
paleoanthropographically *paleoanthropologically* 1.16
paleoanthropography *prehistoric anthropology* 1.2
paleoanthropological 1.11
paleoanthropologically 1.16
paleoanthropologist 1.4; *historian* 651.10
paleoanthropology *prehistoric anthropology* 1.2, *study of the past* 651.9
paleobotanist *plant scientist* 41.11
paleobotany *botany* 13.7, *plant science* 41.10
Paleocene Epoch Geologic Time Intervals 8
paleoclimatologist *geologist* 8.4, *historian* 651.10
paleoclimatology *geology* 8.1, *study of the past* 651.9
paleoethnographer *paleoanthropologist* 1.4
paleoethnographic *paleoanthropological* 1.11
paleoethnographically *paleoanthropologically* 1.16
paleoethnography *prehistoric anthropology* 1.2
paleoethnological *paleoanthropological* 1.11
paleoethnologically *paleoanthropologically* 1.16
paleoethnologist *paleoanthropologist* 1.4, *historian* 651.10
paleoethnology *prehistoric anthropology* 1.2, *study of the past* 651.9
paleogeographer *geologist* 8.4, *historian* 651.10
paleogeographically *geologically* 8.68

paleogeography *geology* 8.1, *study of the past* 651.9
paleogeologically *geologically* 8.68
paleographer *linguist* 5.3, *interpreter* 365.6, *historian* 651.10
paleography Linguistic Studies 5, *science of interpretation* 365.5, *study of the past* 651.9
Paleolithic *primal* 653.14
paleomagnetic *geophysical* 8.51
paleomagnetism *geomagnetism* 8.3, 10.46
paleometeorologist *historian* 651.10
paleometeorology *study of the past* 651.9
paleontographer *historian* 651.10
paleontography *study of the past* 651.9
paleontological *geologic* 8.50, *biological* 13.27
paleontologist *geologist* 8.4, *life scientist* 13.26, *animal scientist* 34.7, *historian* 651.10
paleontology *geology* 8.1, *life science* 13.1, *evolution* 13.23, *animal science* 34.6, *study of the past* 651.9
paleopsychological *paleoanthropological* 1.11
paleopsychologically *paleoanthropologically* 1.16
paleopsychologist *paleoanthropologist* 1.4
Paleozoic *primal* 653.14
paleozoological *of animals* 34.13
paleozoologist *historian* 651.10
paleozoology *study of the past* 651.9
pale-purple *purple* 262.6
pale rider *personifications and symbols* 29.4
pales *barrier* 419.10
paletot *coat* 100.19
palette *material* 143.9, *paint* 251.6
palette knife *material* 143.9
pale-yellow *yellow* 259.7
palfrey *saddle horse* 159.5
Pali Canon *other text* 81.19
Palikir Countries 566
palimony *earnings* 467.5, *gift* 472.2, *something received* 473.2, *income* 492.3
palimpsest *obliteration* 186.1
palindrome *word* 5.17, *inverted thing* 608.4
palindromic *worded* 5.38
paling *barrier* 419.10, *enclosing thing* 619.3
palingenesis *revival* 809.3
palinode Poem or Verse Forms 139
palisade *leaf* 41.6, *barrier* 419.10, *fence* 419.21, *protection* 810.2
Palissy ware Ceramics 129
pall *funeral object* 31.6, *bore* 296.8, *cover* 613.2
Palladian Furniture Styles 101, *window* 134.10
Palladianism Architectural Styles 134
Palladian Revival Architectural Styles 134
palladium Chemical Elements and Common Allotropes 11
Pallas Planets and Their Satellites 7
pallbearer *funeral person* 31.5, *transferrer* 685.4, *transporter* 686.4
pallet *box* 578.5, *freightage* 686.3
palletization *transportation* 686.1
palliate *practice medicine* 107.32, *remedy* 115.16, *relieve* 275.8,

modify 340.13, *justify* 441.12, *mitigate* 521.9
palliated *modified* 340.9
palliation *ease* 275.1, *modification* 340.5, *defense* 441.2
palliative *analgesic* 115.6, *medicinal* 115.15, *reliever* 275.4, *relieving* 275.7, *modified* 340.9, *vindicatory* 441.7, *moderator* 521.2
palliatively *justifyingly* 441.15
palliative treatment *treatment* 107.14
palliator *vindicator* 441.5
pallid *deathly* 29.15, *drained of color* 252.6, *pale* 253.10, *ill* 517.8
pallidity *paleness* 252.2
pallidly *whitely* 253.13
pallium *vestment* 84.11
pallor *face color* 251.9, *paleness* 252.2, *whiteness* 253.1
pally [Inf] *friendly* 62.5, *sociable* 408.11
palm *honor* 72.3, *means of prediction* 358.10
palm, the *grip* 151.4
palmaceous *treelike* 43.10
palmate *of leaves* 41.18, *treelike* 43.10, *fanlike* 703.8
palmelloid *algal* 47.20
palmer *religious person* 81.9, *religious* 84.9
palm frond *tree part* 43.2
palm grease [Inf] *cash* 484.2
palmist *diviner* 86.14
palmistry *divination* 86.5
palmitic Common Fatty Acids 12
palm leaf *tree part* 43.2
palm off *substitute* 672.5
palm oil Tree Products 43
palm oil [Inf] *cash* 484.2
palm reader *diviner* 86.14
palm reading *divination* 86.5
palms *seed plant* 41.3, *honor* 72.3
Palm Sunday Christian Holy Days and Seasons 85
palm tree *tree* 43.1
palmy *prosperous* 847.5
palmy days *time of plenty* 847.3
palmyra Trees and Shrubs 43
Palomar, Mount Mountains and Hills 569
Palomino Horse and Pony Breeds 159
palomino *horse by color* 159.7
palpability *touch* 216.1, *material world* 524.1
palpable *sensate* 212.5, *touchable* 216.5, *visible* 244.5, *material* 524.7, *manifest* 843.9
palpably 216.12; *materially* 524.9, *manifestly* 843.17
palpate *touch* 216.9
palpating *touching* 216.2
palpitant *vibrating* 683.9
palpitate *be fearful* 283.15, *vibrate* 683.13, *shake* 684.24
palpitating *vibrating* 683.9
palpitation *cardiovascular disease* 114.13, *drumming* 235.1, *vibration* 683.2, *beat* 684.10
palpitations *symptoms of fear* 283.3, *fatigue* 820.1
palsied *of disease* 114.25, *convulsive* 684.19
palsy *neurological disease* 114.20, *shake* 684.7
palsy-walsy [Inf] *friendly* 62.5
palter *quibble* 330.13
paltering *quibbling* 330.4
paltriness *littleness* 580.1
paltry *shoddy* 497.11, *little* 580.7
paltry sum *change* 484.3
paludal *of landmasses* 572.12
palynology *plant science* 41.10

Pamirs Range Mountains and Hills 569
pampas *plants* 41.1, *grassland* 45.2, *lowland* 572.6, *horizontal surface* 603.3
pamper *overindulge* 99.10, *comfort* 214.14, *love* 299.21, *be permissive* 502.7, *sustain* 825.25
pampered *pleased* 214.9, *beloved* 299.19
pampero Notable Winds 9
pamphlet *advertisement* 173.9, *publicize* 173.18, *magazine* 175.3, *work of art* 522.4
pamphleteer *publicizer* 173.11, *publicize* 178.19, *dissertator* 203.3
pamphleteering *publicity* 178.7
Pan Planets and Their Satellites 7, Deities 82
pan *cooking equipment* 91.6, *compose a photograph* 132.27, *exclude* 383.11, *pot* 578.15
pan [Inf] *berate* 438.20, *criticize* 365.15, 440.12, *face* 621.6
panacea *remedy* 115.1
panacean *medicinal* 115.15
panache *emphasis* 200.1, *flashiness* 404.4, *stylishness* 537.2
Panama Breeds of Sheep 16, Countries 566
Panama City Countries 566
Panama hat or **Panama** *hat* 100.32
Pan-American Games *competition* 166.18
panatella *tobacco* 121.23
Panathenaea *religious festival* 85.13
Panay Islands 572
pan-broiling *cooking technique* 91.2
pancake 90.11; *cosmetics* 530.4
Pancake Day Christian Holy Days and Seasons 85
pancake house *eating place* 92.17
pancake landing *flight* 689.9
pancake race *sporting event* 422.6
Panchen Lama *priest* 84.8
panchromatic film *film* 132.8
pancreas *internal organ* 19.13
pancreatic *of a secretion* 24.5
pancreatic cancer *cancer* 114.15
pancreatic juice *secreted substance* 24.2
panda car [Brit] *automobile* 687.6
pandect *law* 53.1
Pandects of Justinian The Law 53.2
pandemic *plague* 114.6, *contagious* 114.26, *universal* 778.10
pandemoniacal *demonic* 446.9
pandemonic *demonic* 446.9
Pandemonium *evil place* 446.6
pandemonium Collective Names 59, *tumult* 232.5, *dissonance* 241.1, *variety* 751.4, *confusion* 766.4
pander *provision* 89.9, *sexually immoral person* 432.8, *prostitute* 432.17
pander or **panderer** *agent* 80.3, *provisioner* 89.4, *person who joins* 752.9
pandering *prostitution* 432.4
pander to 401.11; *serve* 69.11, 825.29
pandit *educator* 48.4
Pandora Planets and Their Satellites 7
pandora Musical Instruments 142
Pandora's Box *evil thing* 446.2
pane *glass* 249.5, *slice* 588.4
paned *striped* 263.9
panegyric *public speaking* 205.11,

praise 437.3, approving 437.9, flattery 439.1

panegyrist approver 437.7

panegyrize praise 437.16

panel party 59.3, carpenter 131.10, slice 588.4, face 613.31, list of names 785.7

panel-back type of chair 101.4

panelboard wood 131.3

paneled type of bed 101.9, striped 263.9, covered 613.19

paneling wood 131.3, wall covering 613.12

panel of judges place of judgment 341.3

panel saw woodworking tool 131.6

panel show program 172.10

panel truck truck 687.8

panelwork wood 131.3

pan-fry cook 91.10

pan-frying cooking technique 91.2

pang pain 117.5, 215.1, spasm 684.8

panga sharp weapon 78.6

Pangaea plate tectonics 8.19

pangolin insect-eating mammal 35.7

pangs pain 215.1, penitence 451.1

pangs of conscience penitence 451.1

panhandle regions 564.2

panhandle [Inf] solicit money 505.13

panhandler [Inf] recipient 473.5, beggar 505.6

panhandling [Inf] solicitation 505.4

panic fear 283.1, be afraid 283.14, frighten 283.17, haste 818.1

panic attack anxiety disorder 108.11

panic button danger signal 811.5

panicky fearful 283.10

panicle flower head 42.4, grass plant 45.3

panic-stricken frightened 283.9

panjandrum exaggerator 194.6, overestimator 343.2

panlogism Philosophical Schools of Thought 4

panlogist Philosophical Schools of Thought 4

panned [Inf] criticized 438.14

panne velvet Fabrics and Fibers 130

pannier underwear 100.22, basket 578.6, bicycle part 687.11

panning framing 132.18, criticism 365.3, 438.4, 440.2

panoplied invulnerable 810.18

panoply finery 100.6, protection 810.2

panoply of war glory of war 76.17

panorama type of painting 143.5, view 242.8, whole situation 759.3

panoramic visual 242.16, general 778.9

pan out [Inf] take effect 676.11

panphobia Phobias 283

panpipe Musical Instruments 142

panpsychic psychic 86.17

panpsychist occultist 86.13

pansy Flowers 42, purple thing 262.3

pansy [Inf] weak person 517.4

pansy [Inf and Off] homosexual 32.9

pant speak in a particular way 205.18, vibrate 683.13, be fatigued 820.5

Pantagruel big person 579.10

pantalets or **pantalettes** underwear 100.22

Pantaloon or **Pantalone** stock part 136.24, clown 138.10

pantaloon man 27.8

pantaloons pants 100.14

pant for lust after 288.20

pantheism Philosophical Schools of Thought 4

pantheist Philosophical Schools of Thought 4

pantheon place of worship 83.8

panties underwear 100.22

pantile industrial ceramics 129.6

panting 820.3; restless 684.16, fatigue 820.1

pantograph duplicate 736.4

pantomime dramatic style 136.3, Children's and Party Games 167, gesture 183.17, mimicry 736.3

pantomimic gestural 183.13

pantomiming acting 136.22

pantomimist actor 136.25

pantothenic acid vitamin 12.13

pantry room 60.9, cooking place 91.4, kitchen container 91.7, storeroom 105.7

pants 100.14; informal clothes 100.7

pantsuit informal clothes 100.7, suit 100.16

panty girdle underwear 100.22

pantyhose legwear 100.26

pantywaist [Inf] effeminate male 32.8

Paolo Famous Lovers 299

pap mammalian characteristic 35.3, food 90.1, semiliquid 561.7

papa [Inf] man in the family 32.12, family member 65.2, priest 88.4

papacy priesthood 84.2

papagayo Notable Winds 9

papain enzyme 12.11

papal masterful 68.15, priestly 84.12, commanding 425.7

papal decree command 425.1

papalism Christianity 81.5

papaloi imam 84.7

papal rule theocracy 49.4

paparazzo photographer 132.23, print journalist 175.5

papaverine alkaloid 12.19

paper 104.5; materials 104.1, material 143.9, document 170.3, newspaper 175.2, dissertation 203.1, Phobias 283, weak thing 517.5, fineness 595.5, face 613.31

paper [Inf] written music 140.21, absence of charge 497.6

paperback book 174.1

paper bag bag 578.7

paper binding bookbinding 174.11

paper chase chase 385.2

paper chromatography analysis 11.17

paper clip retainer 471.3, joint 752.7

paper-clip fishing Children's and Party Games 167

paper doll toy 167.9

papered covered 613.19

paper folding pleat 637.2

paper handkerchief cleaning cloth 111.11

paperiness fineness 595.5

paper mill factory 124.8

paper money 484.14; money 484.1, cash 484.2

paper mulberry Trees and Shrubs 43

paper over conceal 181.12, transform 670.13, repair 809.10

paper over the cracks be insufficient 98.9, be unskillful 128.8, put on a show 404.28, transform 670.13, not complete 762.9

paper-plate throw Children's and Party Games 167

papers record 185.1, documentation 339.6

paper sculpture sculpture 144.1

paper tape punch peripheral 15.8

paper tape reader peripheral 15.8

paper tiger insubstantial person 720.5

paper towel paper 104.5

paper war psychological warfare 76.13

paper warfare contention 422.1

paper-white narcissus Flowers 42

papery brittle 548.3, fine 595.12

paphiopedilum Flowers 42

papier-mâché paper 104.5, material 144.6

papilla mammalian characteristic 35.3, bulge 634.2

papillon Breeds of Dogs 35

papish denominational 81.23

papism [Off] Christianity 81.5

papist [Off] Christian 81.10, denominational 81.23

paprika, hot Herbs and Spices 91

paprika, sweet Herbs and Spices 91

pap smear diagnostic procedure 107.11

Papua New Guinea Countries 566

papyrophobia Phobias 283

papyrus grass 45.1

par golfing terms 156.3, international finance 457.2, currency market 484.8, equality 740.1, on equal terms 740.9, average 742.1, 742.5

parable story 139.4, equivocation 380.1, comparability 733.2

parabola curve 6.38, 629.1

parabolic curvilinear 6.78, arch 134.5, vault 134.8, curved 629.4

parabolically curvedly 629.7

parabolic orbit orbit 7.22

paraboloid curved surface 6.43

paraboloid(al) spherical 6.80

paracentesis disgorgement 709.6

parachronism wrong time 660.2

parachronistic misdated 660.6

parachronistically anachronistically 660.13

parachute drop 714.15, safety device 810.15

parachuting Sporting Activities 145

parachutist descender 714.8

Paraclete God the Holy Ghost 82.10

parade Collective Names 59, visibility 264.4, mass demonstration 331.7, protest 331.19, pomp 404.7, show 404.12, 404.24, reception 405.4, formal occasion 406.4, greet 410.11, passage 691.5, procession 774.6, display 843.1, 843.13

paraded displayed 843.8

parade of honor mark of respect 435.4

parade one's wares put on a show 404.28

paradigm syntax 5.32, ideal 327.6, prototype 624.2, original 737.2, precedent 769.4

paradigmatic or **paradigmatical** ideal 327.6, prototypical 624.7

paradigmatically ideologically 327.23, formatively 624.10

parading demonstrating 331.14

paradisaical heavenly 82.22

paradisal heavenly 82.22

paradise after death 29.9, heaven 82.15, life without end 644.2, future condition 650.3

paradisiac heavenly 82.22

paradisiacal heavenly 82.22

paradisiacal or **paradisiac** idyllic 214.11

parados military defenses 419.9

paradox philosophical term 4.7, reasoning 6.61, sophism 330.2, unintelligible thing 364.3, impossibility 837.1

paradoxical logical 6.83, sophistic 330.7, difficult 364.8, impossible 837.4

paradoxically sophistically 330.14, impossibly 837.11

paradox of the unexpected hanging philosophical problem 4.8

paradrop aviation 689.1

paraffin petroleum 562.5

paraffinic oily 562.11

paraffin lamp incandescent light 246.5

paragliding Sporting Activities 145

paragon 744.6; skilled person 127.7, wonderful person 294.6, ideal 327.6, 805.6, excellence 445.4

paragon of beauty attractive female 529.5

paragraph ice-skating 162.32, Reference Signs 183, passage 692.1, part of writing 760.6

paragraph bracket ice-skating techniques 162.16

paragraph double three ice-skating techniques 162.16

paragraphed punctuated 183.15

paragraph loop ice-skating techniques 162.16

Paraguay Countries 566, Rivers 570

parahydrogen Chemical Elements and Common Allotropes 11

parakeet cage bird 36.13

parallax star luminosity 7.12

parallel 606.4, 606.5, 606.7; linear 6.77, snowplow 162.29, correspondent 334.16, answer to 334.22, compatible 462.8, exact location 565.2, correspondence 606.2, corresponding 606.6, correspond 606.8, directional 697.8, relatedness 774.6, related 727.6, correspond to 727.10, correlation 729.3, correlative 729.6, correlate 729.9, similarity 733.1, similar 733.7, comparable 733.8, be similar 733.12, conforming 735.17, conform 735.27, equal 740.7, 740.8, on equal terms 740.9, be equal 740.11, concurrent 794.13

parallel bars Sporting Activities 145, gymnastics equipment 157.2, parallel 606.4

parallel christie skiing techniques 162.5

parallel connection circuit element 14.39

parallelepiped polyhedron 6.44

parallelepiped or **parallelepipedon** parallel 606.4

parallel evolution evolution 13.23

parallelism 606.1; literary device 139.12, correspondence 334.8, compatibility 462.3, symmetry 626.1, correlation 729.3, comparability 733.2, conformity 735.7, equality 740.1

parallelistic parallel 606.5

parallelization parallelism 606.1

---

parallelize *parallel* 606.7, *correlate* 729.9
parallel line *parallel* 606.4
parallel lines *line* 6.35
parallelly *correspondingly* 606.10, *correlatively* 729.12
parallel of latitude *parallel* 606.4
parallelogram *polygon* 6.42, *parallel* 606.4, *angled figure* 628.3, *quadrilateral* 791.2
parallelogram of forces *vector* 6.48
parallel port *computer part* 15.4
parallel processor *computer* 15.1
parallels Reference Signs 183
parallel sailing *navigation* 690.5
parallel swing *skiing techniques* 162.5
parallel turn *cross-country techniques* 162.8, *ski* 162.35
parallepiped *angled figure* 628.3
paralogism *sophism* 330.2
paralogist *sophist* 330.6
paralogistic *sophistic* 330.7
paralysis *symptom* 114.3, *neurological disease* 114.20, *insensibility* 213.1, *desensitization* 213.2, *immobility* 413.2, *disability* 515.4, *inertness* 519.1
paralytic *sick person* 114.22, *of disease* 114.25, *disabled* 515.10
paralyze *overpower* 515.14
paralyzed *of disease* 114.25, *desensitized* 213.5, *inactive* 413.9, *disabled* 515.10, *inert* 519.2, *motionless* 678.4
paralyzed [Inf] *dead drunk* 121.27
paralyzed with fear *frightened* 283.9
paramagnet *magnet* 700.3
paramagnetism *magnetism* 10.45
Paramaribo Countries 566
paramedic 107.24; *helper* 275.5
parameter 6.57; *algebraic expression* 6.23
parameters *specification* 340.6
parametric *given* 6.74, *conditional* 340.10
parametric statistics *statistics* 6.51
paramilitary *military* 76.28
paramount *head* 600.7, *essential* 723.5, *elite* 744.14, *important* 799.7
paramountcy *importance* 799.1
paramountly *predominantly* 744.21
paramour *lover* 299.11
Paraná Rivers 570
Paraná pine Trees and Shrubs 43
parang *sharp weapon* 78.6
paranoia *compulsion* 108.13, *dissociative disorder* 108.17, *delusion* 110.2, *suspicion* 314.3
paranoid *psychologically disturbed* 108.39, *suspicious* 314.6
paranoid *or* **paranoiac** *insane person* 110.5, *mentally ill* 110.11
paranoid personality *dissociative disorder* 108.17
paranoid personality disorder *personality disorder* 108.7
paranoid-type schizophrenia *psychosis* 108.10
paranormal *occult* 86.16, *extraneous* 610.12, *external* 724.11
paranormal, the *the occult* 86.2, *extraneousness* 610.6, *externality* 724.4
paranormally *occultly* 86.27
parapet Architectural Elements 134, *fort* 419.13, *fortification* 812.3, *barrier* 826.7

paraph *personal identification* 184.4, *identify oneself* 184.12
paraphernalia *accessory* 100.28, *equipment* 103.6, *possessions* 470.5
paraphilia *sexual perversion* 20.12
paraphiliac *sexual perversion* 20.12
paraphilias *sexual disorder* 108.14
paraphobia Phobias 283
paraphrase *phrasing* 5.25, *type of meaning* 361.4, *mean* 361.13, *translation* 365.4, *translate* 365.16
paraphrased *phrased* 5.39
paraphraser *interpreter* 365.6
paraphrasing *phrased* 5.39
paraphrast *interpreter* 365.6
paraphrastic *phrased* 5.39, *similar* 361.7, *translational* 365.11
paraphrenia *delusion* 110.2
paraplegia *neurological disease* 114.20
paraplegic *sick person* 114.22
paraprofessional *technical worker* 123.14
parapsychological 525.9; *psychic* 86.17
parapsychologically *occultly* 86.27
parapsychologist *occultist* 86.13, *nonmaterialist* 525.7
parapsychology 525.4; *supernaturalism* 86.3, Psychological Theories, Schools 108
paraquat *pest control* 16.13, *poison* 117.7
pararhyme *rhyme* 139.11
parascending Sporting Activities 145
parasite 39.18; *ecology* 13.25, *type of animal* 34.5, *pest* 40.5, *plant* 41.2, *lower plant* 41.4, *fungal association* 47.5, *superfluity* 99.4, *disease-causing agent* 114.5, *sponger* 401.4, *nonworker* 415.4, *greedy person* 477.11, *adherent* 755.4, *follower* 794.10, *dependent* 832.4
parasites Phobias 283
parasitic *of animals* 34.13, *of plants* 41.14, *of fungi* 47.19, *sycophantic* 401.7, *not participating* 415.11, *tenacious* 755.6
parasitically 401.17; *saprophytically* 47.24, *tenaciously* 755.12
parasitic fungus *fungal association* 47.5
parasitic worm *worm* 39.14
parasitism *ecology* 13.25, *fungal association* 47.5, *sycophancy* 401.2
parasitize *infest* 40.17, *sponge* 401.13
parasitological *biological* 13.27
parasitologist *life scientist* 13.26, *invertebrate zoologist* 39.3, *medical specialist* 107.20
parasitology *biology* 13.2, *invertebrate zoology* 39.2, *medical science* 107.9
parasitophobia Phobias 283
parasol *shade maker* 247.4, *protective covering* 613.5, *protection from the weather* 810.9
parasomnia *sleep disorder* 108.20
parataxis *syntax* 5.32
parathion *pest control* 16.13
parathormone Human Hormones 12
parathyroid hormone Human Hormones 12
paratrooper *army combat specialist* 77.16, *descender* 714.8
paratrooper boots *boots* 100.31
paratyphoid *infection* 114.7

paraxial ray *lens system* 10.22
Parazoa *sponge* 39.16
parazoan *invertebrate* 39.1, *sponge* 39.16
parboil *cook* 91.10, *heat* 217.17
parboiling *cooking technique* 91.2
parcel *farmland* 16.3, Collective Names 59, *group* 59.24, *postal communication* 169.4, *property* 470.1, *plot* 564.9, *contain* 577.10, *packet* 578.4, *certain amount* 738.3, *quantify* 738.7, *piece* 760.2
parceled *grouped* 59.21
parceling out *allocation* 474.1
parcel out *allocate* 474.5
parcel post *postal service* 169.5
parch *heat* 217.17, *thirst* 560.18, *dry up* 560.21
parched *hungry* 288.16, *thirsty* 560.8, *baked* 560.14
parchedness *dryness* 560.1
Parcheesi ™ Board and Table Games 167
parchment *leather* 104.7, *brittle thing* 548.2
parchmentlike *dried-up* 560.9
pardon *favorable verdict* 54.19, *acquit* 54.32, *434.10, *peace treaty* 73.5, *peace offering* 74.5, *mercy* 308.3, *show pity* 308.8, *forgiveness* 312.1, *forgive* 312.8, *amnesty* 355.5, *leniency* 423.1, *be lenient* 423.5, *acquittal* 434.2, *vindication* 441.1, *vindicate* 441.11, *liberate* 831.6
pardonable *forgivable* 312.7, *vindicable* 441.9
pardonably *forgivingly* 53.37, *forgivably* 312.14
pardoned *acquitted* 54.25, *434.6, *forgiven* 312.5, *given consideration* 423.4, *vindicated* 441.8
pardoning *liberation* 831.1
pare *cook* 91.10, *play down* 195.17, *depilate* 614.20, *change by degrees* 739.8, *separate* 753.12
pared *downplayed* 195.13
pared down *downplayed* 195.13
pare down *play down* 195.17, *make smaller* 747.8, *reduce* 796.8
paregoric *analgesic* 115.6
paregoric [Arch] *medicinal* 115.15
parenchymatous *algal* 47.20
parens [Inf] Punctuation Marks 5
parent *of language* 5.35, *propagator* 21.7, *family member* 65.2, *type of complex* 108.22, *loved one* 299.13, *corporate* 480.17, *influential person* 512.5, *producer* 522.10, *first cause* 675.6
parental *family* 65.6
parental love *love* 299.1
parent-daughter relationship *dating* 8.48
parent fixation *fixation* 108.21
parentheses Punctuation Marks 5, *mathematical symbol* 6.11, *enclosing thing* 619.3, *insertion* 710.1
parenthesis *deviation* 698.1, *means of connection* 754.4, *digression* 775.6
parenthesize *punctuate* 183.20
parenthetic *interrupted* 775.9
parenthetical *inserted* 710.5
parenthetically in 710.16
parent language *native language* 5.5
parent nuclide *radioactivity* 10.58
parent rock *metamorphic rock* 8.36
parents-in-law Phobias 283
paresis *neurological disease* 114.20
par excellence *supremely* 744.23, *importantly* 799.15

parfum [Fr] *fragrance* 226.1
parget *face* 613.31
parget *or* **pargeting** *wall covering* 613.12
pariah dog *dog* 35.10
Parian porcelain Ceramics 129
parietal bone Human Bones 19
parimutuel *horse-racing betting terms* 159.11
paring *slice* 588.4
paring down *downplaying* 195.6, *simplification* 526.6
parings *bits and pieces* 760.5
pari passu [L] *synchronously* 649.9, *as good as* 740.14
Paris Famous Lovers 299, Countries 566, *other famous world cities* 567.9
Paris, school of Western Art Styles 133
Paris fashion *dressing* 100.2
Paris green *green pigment* 260.3
parish *clerical venue* 84.4, *administrative region* 564.4, *part* 760.1
parishioner *worshiper* 83.6
parishioner [Brit] *municipal resident* 567.12
Paris white *whitener* 253.3
parity *quantum* 10.63, *computing terms* 15.22, *international finance* 457.2, *currency market* 484.8, *similarity* 733.1, *equality* 740.1
park *grassland* 45.2, *sports ground* 145.2, *green place* 260.2, *enclosed area* 619.2, *fly* 689.13
parka *jacket* 100.18, *climbing equipment* 161.4
parking *miscellaneous automotive terms* 687.14, *flying* 689.11
parking brake *miscellaneous automotive terms* 687.14
parking light *safety light* 246.5
parking lot *miscellaneous automotive terms* 687.14
parking meter *miscellaneous automotive terms* 687.14
parking orbit *rocketry* 7.32, *flight path* 691.12
parking space *reserved space* 563.5, *miscellaneous automotive terms* 687.14
parkinsonism *or* **Parkinson's disease** *neurological disease* 114.20, *shake* 684.7
Parkinson's law *overactivity* 414.9, *formula* 780.7
park keeper *protector* 419.16, 810.11
parkland *grassland* 45.2
park one's carcass [Inf] *take up residence* 60.24
park oneself [Inf] *sit* 716.20
parlance *spoken language* 205.2, *vernacular* 205.8
parlando Musical Terms and Expression Marks 140
parley *conference* 75.4, *consultation* 176.4, *consult* 176.11, *place for conversation* 210.5, *converse* 210.11, *confer* 210.13
parley with *approach* 209.10
parliament Collective Names 59, *representative body* 79.2
parliamentarian *elected official* 50.8
parliamentarian [Brit] *delegate* 79.1
parliamentarily *representatively* 79.8
parliamentary *governmental* 49.24, *delegated* 79.4
parliamentary committee [Brit] *advisory body* 176.6

parliamentary democracy *constitutional government* 49.8
parliamentary offices [Brit] *government office* 124.13
PARLOG Programming Languages 15
parlor *room* 60.9
parlor car *railroad car* 688.5
parlormaid *domestic servant* 69.7
parlor palm Trees and Shrubs 43
parlous state *danger* 811.1
parlous straits *critical situation* 824.6
Parma violet *purple pigment* 262.2
Parnaíba Rivers 570
Parnassian *poetic* 139.19
Parnassians Western Literary Groups 139
Parnassus, Mount Mountains and Hills 569
parochial *priestly* 84.12, *discriminatory* 337.11, *unjust* 342.7, *administrative* 564.13, *commonplace* 800.17
parochialism *prejudice* 337.3, *unfair treatment* 342.4, *regionalism* 564.11
parochially *clerically* 84.17, *prejudicially* 337.17, *unjustly* 342.13
parochial school *religious school* 48.13
parodic *ridiculing* 436.13
parodied *misrepresented* 188.4, 627.8, *imitative* 736.7
parody *misrepresentation* 188.1, *misrepresent* 188.6, *entertainment* 277.4, *be humorous* 277.11, *form of derision* 369.2, *ridicule* 436.4, *adopt* 476.11, *distortion of truth* 627.4, *imitation* 736.1, *mimicry* 736.3, *imitate* 736.9
parol *spoken* 205.13
parole *permit* 502.3, *liberation* 831.1, *liberate* 831.6
parole [Fr] *vernacular* 205.8
paroled *liberated* 831.4
parolee *free person* 829.9
paronomasia *literary device* 139.12, *equivocation* 380.1
paronym *word* 5.17
paronymic *or* **paronymous** *worded* 5.38
parotid *of a secretion* 24.5
paroxysm *burst of anger* 302.6, *seizure* 418.11, *violence by person* 520.2, *spasm* 684.8
paroxysmally *angrily* 302.24
paroxysmic *angry* 302.11, *convulsive* 684.19
parquet *variegated thing* 263.5, *floor covering* 613.13
parquet circle *auditorium* 136.17
parquetry *decorative woodwork* 131.2, Architectural Elements 134, *check* 263.2
parr *young fish* 38.6
parricide *homicide* 30.4
parried *fencing* 153.6
parrot *cage bird* 36.13, *imitator* 736.6, *imitate* 736.9, *conformist* 781.6, *repeat* 797.15
parrot fever *animal disease* 34.10
parroting *imitative* 736.7, *repetition* 797.1
parrotlike *avian* 36.19, *imitative* 736.7, *repeated* 797.8
parrotry *mimicry* 736.3, *conformity* 781.1
parrots Collective Names 59
parry 419.27; *boxing techniques* 152.5, *box* 152.19, *fencing movements* 153.3, *fence* 153.7, *play soccer* 163.8, *countercharge* 332.9,

evasion 386.5, *evade* 386.19, *defense* 419.1, *retaliate* 420.4, *deflection* 701.3, *fend off* 701.9
parrying *combat* 152.17, *fencing* 153.6, *soccer play* 163.5
Parry Islands Islands 572
parse *use language* 5.42
parsec *astronomical unit* 7.23, Scientific and Technical Units 589
Parsee *or* **Parsi** *other religious member* 81.13
parser *system software* 15.13
parsimonious *not enough* 98.5, *selfish* 444.4, *self-restrained* 455.6, *retentive* 471.5, *mean* 501.4
parsimoniously *not enough* 98.12, *selfishly* 444.8, *with self-restraint* 455.14, *tenaciously* 471.11, *meanly* 501.8
parsimoniousness *meanness* 501.1
parsimony *incompleteness* 98.2, *selfishness* 444.1, *self-restraint* 455.1, *meanness* 501.1
parsing *syntax* 5.32, *programming concepts* 15.24
parsley Herbs and Spices 91, *green thing* 260.4
parsley family *seed plant* 41.3
parson *member of the clergy* 84.5
parsonage *official residence* 60.6, *clerical dwelling* 84.10
part 705.13, 760.1, 760.14; *separate* 66.10, 753.12, *machinery* 103.5, *role* 136.23, *book part* 174.5, *claim* 429.3, *coiffure* 530.8, *space* 587.6, *move apart* 703.11, *certain amount* 738.3, *interval* 739.4, *diverge* 753.20, *piece* 760.2, *component* 760.3, *musical part* 760.8, *thing included* 763.2, *disperse* 776.12, *disband* 776.13, *fractional part* 787.2, *fractional* 787.5, *divide* 787.7
partake *have a meal* 92.25
partaker *eater* 92.15
partaking *eating meals* 92.4, *sociability* 408.1
part and parcel *total* 738.4, *component* 760.3
part and parcel of *included* 763.4
part by part *partly* 760.17
part company *retreat* 386.22, *separate* 703.12, *part* 705.13, *diverge* 753.20, *disband* 776.13
part company with *disagree* 463.8
parted *spaced* 587.4, *partial* 760.11
parterre *garden* 17.2, *auditorium* 136.17
part for part *partly* 760.17
parthenocarpic *of a fruit* 44.8
parthenogenesis *genesis* 21.5
parthenogenetic *pregnant* 21.12
parthenophobia Phobias 283
Parthian architecture Architectural Styles 134
Parthian shot *parting* 705.3, *ending* 773.10, *stratagem* 822.2
partial 760.11; *discriminatory* 337.11, *unjust* 342.7, 741.6, *preferential* 382.10, *wrongful* 430.10, *tending to* 513.4, *narrow-minded* 593.13, *incomplete* 762.5, 806.6, *fractional* 787.5
partial deafness *deafness* 229.1
partial derivative *differentiation* 6.29
partial differential equation *differentiation* 6.29
partial eclipse *sun* 7.15, *dimness* 248.1
partial excuse *defense* 441.2

partial fraction *division* 6.16
partiality *friendship* 62.1, *inclination* 290.2, *love* 299.1, *injustice* 342.3, 741.3, *preference* 382.2, *wrong* 430.1, *attitude* 513.2, *narrow-mindedness* 593.7, *incompleteness* 762.1
partial knowledge *information* 348.2
partially *unjustly* 342.13, *partly* 760.17, *incompletely* 762.10, *fractionally* 787.8
partially deaf *deaf* 229.4
partially ordered *ranked* 6.72
partially ordered set (poset) *set* 6.19
partially sighted *visually impaired* 243.9
partially true 192.18
partialness *incompleteness* 762.1
partial paralysis *neurological disease* 114.20
partial payment *type of payment* 489.3
partial to *desirous* 288.13, *inclined toward* 290.5
partial truth 192.7
partible *separable* 753.11
participant *contender* 422.13, *attender* 575.6, *thing included* 763.2
participate 145.6, 166.22, 408.15, 760.16; *socialize* 2.14, *conduct oneself* 399.17, *be active in* 412.17, *be sociable* 414.22, *attend* 575.14, *be included* 763.6, *work together* 827.14
participate actively *be sociable* 414.22
participating 760.13; *meddling* 414.17, *attending* 575.9
participation 760.10; *sociability* 408.1, *social activity* 414.2, *attendance* 575.3, *inclusion* 763.1, *mutual relationship* 827.3
participator *agent* 123.15, *busy person* 414.10
participator sport *sporting activity* 145.3
participatory *cooperative* 827.9
participial *of grammar* 5.41
participially *grammatically* 5.48
participle *part of speech* 5.13
particle 760.4; *part of speech* 5.30, *elementary particle* 10.53, *grain* 553.6, *little thing* 580.3, *fragment* 787.3
particle physics Fields of Modern Physics 10
parti-colored *variegated* 263.6
particular *fastidious* 325.9, *selecting* 382.9, *characteristic* 723.9, *aspect* 726.4, *detailed* 726.9, *component* 760.3, 760.12, *typical* 777.10, *special* 779.10, *singular* 788.13, *perfectionistic* 805.18, *troublesome* 824.13
particular, the *the special* 779.8
particular instance *probability* 6.59
particular interpretation *interpretation* 365.1
particularity *identity* 184.2, *fastidiousness* 325.4, *specialty* 779.1, *singularity* 788.4
particularization *specialization* 779.3
particularize 760.15, 779.17; *be diffuse* 199.5, *name* 202.17, *explain* 331.16, *be accurate* 350.5, *circumstantiate* 726.12
particularly 779.21; *meticulously* 726.18
particulars *description* 202.1,

circumstances 726.1, *specifications* 779.6
particulate radiation *radioactivity* 10.58
parting 703.2, 705.3; *departing* 705.5, *separation* 753.1, *divergence* 776.5
parting gift *acknowledgment* 310.3
parting of the ways *faction* 347.4, *disagreement* 463.1, *parting* 703.2
parting shot *counterstatement* 334.5, *parting* 705.3, *ending* 773.10
parti pris [Fr] *prejudgment* 342.5, *predetermination* 384.1
partisan *political* 50.9, *guerrilla* 77.7, *sharp weapon* 78.6, *bigot* 337.7, *discriminatory* 337.11, *unjust* 342.7, *dissenter* 347.5, *dissenting* 347.7, *seditionist* 427.7, *wrongful* 430.10, *convinced* 840.8
partisanly *politically* 50.11
partisan politics *politics* 50.1
partisanship *friendship* 62.1, *prejudice* 337.3, *favoritism* 337.5, *injustice* 342.3, *wrong* 430.1, *conviction* 840.2
partita Musical Forms 140
partition *combinatorics* 6.63, *that which makes invisible* 245.2, *allocation* 474.1, *separateness* 753.3, *separator* 753.5, *divide* 753.18, *part* 760.1, 760.14
partitioned *separate* 753.7, *partial* 760.11
partitive *partial* 760.11
partitively *to pieces* 758.8
partly 760.17; *incompletely* 762.10, *fractionally* 787.8
partly visible *difficult to see* 245.4
partner 794.9; *spouse* 64.8, *common-law wife* 64.12, *coworker* 123.17, *tennis terms* 165.5, *bridge* 168.4, *possessor* 469.10, *interrelate* 729.8, *form an alliance* 735.25, *unify* 752.15, *come together* 757.10, *companion* 794.8, *keep company with* 794.17, *helper* 825.12, *cooperator* 827.8
partnered *married* 64.16, *allied* 735.15, *united* 752.10, *associated* 794.14
partners *team* 827.7
partnership *alliance* 64.2, 735.5, *contract* 459.1, *joint possession* 469.6, *company* 480.7, *association* 480.8, *relatedness* 727.1, *interrelation* 729.2, *companionship* 794.3, *joint control* 827.5
part of *participating* 760.13, *included* 763.4
part of brass instrument *brass instrument* 142.3
part of garment 100.27
part of keyboard instrument 142.6
part of percussion instrument *percussion instrument* 142.5
part of poem 139.9
part of speech 5.30, 760.7; *language element* 5.13
part of stringed instrument 142.2
part of the bargain *basis for negotiations* 460.2
part of woodwind instrument *woodwind* 142.4
part of writing 760.6
parton *little thing* 580.3
part ownership *joint possession* 469.6
part payment *part* 760.1
partridge *table bird* 36.10, *meat* 90.22, *game* 160.6

partridges Collective Names 59
parts location 565.1, contents 577.1
parts of a circle 631.4
part song song 140.11
part-time worker employee 57.4
parturient pregnant 21.12, embryonic 771.19
parturition genesis 21.5, conception 771.4
part with give out 472.12
party 59.3, 408.6; someone 18.10, litigant 54.4, military organization 58.4, Collective Names 59, assembly 59.1, social gathering 59.7, 408.4, group 59.8, army unit 77.14, feast 92.9, make merry 167.13, telephone personnel 169.14, place for conversation 210.5, rejoicing 279.1, celebration 405.1, celebrate 405.10, promise maker 458.6, association 480.8, collection 757.3, part 760.1
party [Inf] rejoice 279.5
party boss political party member 50.6
party chairperson political party member 50.6
party dress formal clothes 100.5, dress 100.11
partyer rejoicer 279.3
partygoer joyful person 269.5
party hack political party member 50.6
party in divorce case divorce court 66.3
party leader political party member 50.6
party line telephone 169.10, prospectus 387.3, tactics 399.12, convention 781.5
party manager elected official 50.8
party member political party member 50.6
party-minded dissenting 347.7, sociable 408.11
party official 68.5; person in authority 52.7
party politics politics 50.1
party pooper [Inf] inactive person 413.8, hinderer 826.11
party ticket prospectus 387.3
party to a suit litigant 54.4, accuser 442.3
par value value 494.2
parvenu common 71.3, gainer 467.9, wealthy person 485.6, discourteous 535.7, new arrival 652.7, prosperous person 847.4
Pascal Programming Languages 15
pascal Scientific and Technical Units 589
Pascal's theorem Mathematical Concepts 6
Pascal's triangle Mathematical Concepts 6
paschal candle sacred object 83.11
Paschen series Classical Physical Laws 10
pasha leader 68.3
Pasiphaë Planets and Their Satellites 7
paso doble Dances 135, ice-dancing move 162.19
Paso Fino Horse and Pony Breeds 159
pasquinade ridicule 440.6
pass 639.13, 651.17, 692.15; excrete 25.20, defecate 25.21, die 29.17, legislate 53.31, Collective Names 59, sufficiency 97.1, suffice 97.6, have leisure time 125.5, playing terms 148.4, play basketball 148.7, play 155.8, play offense

155.18, ice hockey tactics 158.4, field hockey tactics 158.5, play ice hockey 158.9, play field hockey 158.10, soccer play 163.5, play soccer 163.8, bridge 168.4, play cards 168.7, disappear 265.5, be mediocre 289.16, documentation 339.6, qualify 340.11, select 382.12, approve 437.14, monetize 484.24, permit 502.3, opening 583.1, gulf 587.3, narrow place 593.2, concave land 635.2, go on 642.7, be transient 643.6, convert 670.11, thoroughfare 692.6, passport 692.8, adopt 692.14, accelerate 694.14, throw 696.4, right of entry 706.4, overtake 744.16, safe conduct 810.4, do well 845.12
pass a bad check monetize 484.24
passable satisfactory 273.6, mediocre 289.11, 742.7, approvable 437.13, moderate 521.3
passableness mediocrity 289.5, 742.3
passably 692.19; unexceptionally 289.20, approvably 437.22
passacaglia Musical Forms 140
pass a decree command 420.8
passage 691.5, 692.1; harmonic element 140.14, sailing 150.2, opening 583.1, interval 587.1, narrow place 593.2, alteration 665.2, momentum 677.2, course 679.2, conveyance 685.2, water transportation 690.1, access 691.3, adoption 692.2, passing 692.3, entrance 706.5, part of writing 760.6
passage into 692.4
passage of arms warfare 422.10
passage of time 639.3; duration 642.1
passage rite non-Christian ritual 85.8
passageway opening 583.1, passage 691.5, thoroughfare 692.6
pass and repass oscillate 683.12
passant Heraldic Terms 184
pass around publish 173.15, be published 173.19
pass around the hat fund 472.15, solicit money 505.13
pass as stand for 187.14
pass away die 29.17, 773.21, disappear 265.5, be transient 643.6, pass 651.17, withdraw 705.9, exit 707.13, cease to exist 718.13, decrease 747.7
pass-back field hockey tactics 158.5
passbook account book 493.3
pass by pass 639.13, 692.15, be transient 643.6
passé unfashionable 528.10, antiquarian 651.13, olden 653.11
passé composé [Fr] grammatical term 5.29
passed dead 29.11, expert 127.12, soccer 163.7, approved 437.8, permitted 502.4, adopted 692.10
passed away dead 29.11, no more 718.11
passed on bequeathed 372.10
passed over dead 29.11, surplus 750.8
passel certain amount 738.3
passenger nonworker 415.4, transferred thing 685.6, traveler 686.6, transportable 686.7
passenger pigeon extinct bird 36.14
passenger ship vessel 690.3
passenger train train 688.4

passenger transportation transportation 686.1
passer basketball team 148.2, offense 155.6
passerby verifier 336.4, witness 339.7, attender 575.6, transient 643.2
passeriform avian 36.19
passerine avian 36.19
passerine bird songbird 36.12
pass for stand for 187.14
pass from hand to hand be transferred 470.13
pass gas belch 709.28
pass holder bargain hunter 497.8
passim [L] where 565.12, sometimes 662.5, discontinuously 775.15
passing 692.3, 692.11; dying 29.3, playing terms 148.4, soccer play 163.5, soccer 163.7, disappearance 265.1, disappearing 265.3, transient 643.4, occasional 647.5, moving 677.12, acceleration 694.3, accelerating 694.9, cessation 773.2
passing along 692.5
passing away dying 29.3, disappearance 265.1
passing bell after death 29.9, funeral 31.4
passing fancy romantic love 299.2, caprice 381.1, transient 643.2
passing game play 155.8
passing gas flatulence 709.9
passing grade sufficiency 97.1
passing into law lawmaking 53.11
passing lane road attribute 687.3, thoroughfare 692.6
passing of the buck self-exemption 434.3
passing over dying 29.3
passing the buck shirking 386.4
passing through forward motion 677.4
passing up self-restraint 455.1
pass interference penalty 155.13
pass into history pass 651.17, decrease 747.7
pass into oblivion decrease 747.7
pass into one's hand receive 473.13
passion sexual longing 20.6, compulsion 108.13, delusion 110.2, Musical Forms 140, sacred music 140.3, emphasis 200.1, emotion 266.3, desire 288.1, eagerness 288.3, sexual desire 288.5, liking 290.1, romantic love 299.2, sexual love 299.3, anger 302.4, violence 520.1
passionate 266.12; desirous 20.18, 288.13, emphatic 200.3, lustful 288.15, liking 290.4, amorous 299.18, angry 302.11
passionate friendship intimacy 62.4
passionately lustfully 20.24, 288.29, emphatically 200.7, with feeling 266.18, eagerly 288.27, admiringly 290.11, amorously 299.30, angrily 302.24
passionflower Flowers 42
passionless indifferent 289.7
passion play dramatic style 136.3
passive grammatical term 5.29, reactive 11.29, pacific 74.7, avoiding 386.9, inactive 413.9, 415.8, obedient 326.4, inert 519.2, sedentary 678.5, compliant 781.9, latent 844.6
passively stoically 4.26, shyly 386.25, inactively 415.17, obediently 426.9, inertly 519.5,

motionlessly 678.9, adaptably 781.15, latently 844.15
passiveness submission 421.1, obedience 426.1, inertness 519.1, lack of motion 678.1
passive resistance inaction 413.1, resistance movement 417.3, defense 419.1, disobedience 427.1
passive resister pacifist 74.6, dissenter 347.5
passive sex submission 421.1
passive smoking smoking 121.22
passivity shirking 386.4, immobility 413.2, inactivity 415.1, submission 421.1, obedience 426.1, inertness 519.1, lack of motion 678.1, latency 844.1
passivity or passiveness indifference 289.1
pass judgment judge 54.31, 341.10, have authority over 425.12
passkey opener 583.2
pass mark sufficiency 97.1
pass muster suffice 97.6, meet with approval 437.20
pass on bequeath 372.15, transfer property 470.12, be transferred 470.13, go forward 679.8, bring 685.11, die 773.21
pass oneself off as be untruthful 192.20
pass one's prime age 27.16
pass on the information recount 202.16
pass out be drunk 121.34, be insensible 213.7, be powerless 515.11, exit 707.13
pass out of the picture [Inf] cease to exist 718.13
Passover Jewish Holy Days and Seasons 85
pass over die 29.17, lapse into silence 208.8, reject 383.10, not observe 466.9, withdraw 705.9, exit 707.13, exclude 764.7, think unimportant 800.19
pass over one's head not understand 362.11
passport 692.8; personal identification 184.4, certificate 185.2, verification 336.1, documentation 339.6, promise 464.2, permit 502.3, right of entry 706.4, safe conduct 810.4, authority 833.3
passport photograph personal identification 184.4
pass reception play 155.8
pass rush defensive huddle 155.10, play defense 155.19
pass sentence judge 53.32, 54.31
pass the buck shirk 386.18, leave alone 413.13, exempt oneself 434.12
pass the crisis change for the better 665.17, get better 807.21
pass the point of no return cross 712.13
pass the summer spend the season 654.10
pass the test meet with approval 437.20
pass the time of day converse 210.11
pass the time of day with approach 209.10
pass the winter spend the season 654.10
pass through pass 692.15, infiltrate 706.13
pass time spend time 639.14
pass to another be transferred 470.13
pass up abstain 386.16, not act

413.11, *acquiesce* 421.5, *be self-restrained* 455.10, *refuse* 506.8
pass water *urinate* 25.22
pass with flying colors *overpower* 845.18
password *computing terms* 15.22, *word of command* 76.20, *symbol* 183.3, *means of identification* 184.3, *name* 202.8, *opener* 583.2
past 651.11; *biography* 3.5, *historical* 3.10, *grammatical term* 5.29, *disappeared* 265.4, *forgotten* 355.7, *uncustomary* 398.4, *time* 639.1, *dead* 658.10, *no more* 718.11, *resigning* 835.3
past, the *past time* 3.6, 651.1
pasta 90.31
past age *history* 3.1, *past time* 3.6
past and gone *disappeared* 265.4, *over* 651.12
past behavior *conduct* 399.1
paste 561.4; *retainer* 471.3, *retain* 471.7, *semiliquid* 561.7, *stick* 561.20, *mixed thing* 751.2, *adhesive* 755.3, *cause to adhere* 755.10
paste [Inf] *hit* 695.11
pasteboard *paper* 104.5
pasted *adhering* 755.7
pastel *material* 143.9, *subtle* 195.9, *soft-hued* 251.13
pastel drawing *drawing* 143.4
pastelist *painter* 143.7
pasteurization *cleaning* 111.2, *hygiene* 116.1
pasteurize *purify* 111.19, *practice hygiene* 116.4, *immunize* 810.22
pasteurized *cleaned* 111.14, *hygienic* 116.3
pasteurized milk *milk* 93.5
past historic *grammatical term* 5.29
past hope *hopeless* 282.6
pasticcio *illegal borrowing* 476.3, *copy* 736.2, *mixed thing* 751.2
pastiche *Poem or Verse Forms* 139, *illegal borrowing* 476.3, *copy* 736.2, *mixed thing* 751.2
pastille *dose of medicine* 115.3
pastime *game* 167.1, *activity* 385.4, *social activity* 414.2
pastiness *doughiness* 561.2
past it [Inf] *broken down* 802.8
past its date *antiquarian* 651.13
past its prime *imperfect* 806.5
past its sell-by date *shoddy* 497.11
past its sell date *imperfect* 806.5
past master *expert* 68.13, *skilled person* 127.7
past one's best or **prime** *deteriorated* 808.8
past one's prime *aged* 27.15, *old* 653.10
pastor *member of the clergy* 84.5, *ritualist* 85.14, *adviser* 825.14
pastorage *priesthood* 84.2
pastoral *agricultural* 16.16, *priestly* 84.12, *dramatic style* 136.3, *Poem or Verse Forms* 139, *poetic* 139.19, *type of painting* 143.5
pastoral care *priesthood* 84.2
pastorally *agriculturally* 16.21
pastoral poet *author* 139.13
pastoral poetry *poetry* 139.8
pastoral staff *insignia* 184.5
pastoral theology *Theologies* 81
pastorate *priesthood* 84.2
pastorship *priesthood* 84.2
past participle *part of speech* 5.30, *past tense* 651.2
past perfect *grammatical term* 5.29
past perfect tense *past tense* 651.2

pastrami *beef* 90.24
pastry 90.37; *confectionery* 222.3, *brittle thing* 548.2
pastry bag *cooking equipment* 91.6
pastry chef *cook* 91.3
pastry shell *casing* 613.9
pastry shop *confectionery* 222.3
past tense 651.2; *linguistic time* 639.6
past time 3.6, 651.1; *history* 3.1, *different time* 648.1
past times *past time* 651.1
pasturage *grassland* 45.2, *animal food* 90.2
pasture *farm* 16.2, *farmland* 16.3, *eat grass* 45.11, *animal food* 90.2, *feed* 90.41, *eat* 92.21, *green place* 260.2
pasture grass *grass* 45.1
pastureland *grassland* 45.2
pastures new *new beginning* 771.13
pasturing *eating habit* 92.7
pasty *drained of color* 252.6, *pliant* 543.7, *mucilaginous* 561.15, *pulpy* 561.19
pasty [Brit] *meat dish* 90.21
pat *gesture* 183.5, 183.17, *touch* 216.9, *communication of love* 299.6, *communicate love* 299.25, *blow* 695.5, *tap* 695.13
patch *programming concepts* 15.24, *program* 15.29, *farmland* 16.3, *dirt* 112.5, *dirty* 112.11, *blinder* 243.7, *check* 263.2, *maculation* 263.4, *variegate* 263.11, *region* 564.1, *plot* 564.9, *location* 565.1, *additional item* 748.3, *intertwine* 752.19, *piece* 760.2, *rectify* 807.22, *repair* 809.1, 809.10
patched *checked* 263.8, *beggarly* 486.12, *complicated* 751.10, *united* 752.10
patched up *repaired* 809.6
patchily *variedly* 263.12, *mixedly* 751.16
patchiness *check* 263.2, *maculation* 263.4, *irregularity* 664.1, *inequality* 741.1, *mixture* 751.1, *imperfection* 806.1
patching *repair* 809.1
patching up *repair* 809.1
patch of cloud *cloud appearance* 9.19
patchouli *incense* 226.3
patch pocket *part of garment* 100.27
patch through *link* 752.18
patch together *assemble* 551.23
patch up *restore* 807.17, *repair* 809.10
patch up a quarrel *pacify* 74.11
patchwork *check* 263.2, *decorative method* 532.3, *miscellany* 751.3, *collaboration* 757.2
patchworking *Hobbies and Pastimes* 167
patchwork quilt *variegated thing* 263.5, *bed covering* 613.7
patchy *checked* 263.8, *irregular* 664.3, *unequal* 741.4, *complicated* 751.10, *discontinuous* 775.7, *imperfect* 806.5
patchy cloud *cloud cover* 9.18
pâté *hors d'oeuvre* 90.13, *sausage* 90.29
pâté de foie gras [Fr] *sausage* 90.29
patella *Human Bones* 19
patent *visible* 242.19, 244.5, *easily seen through* 249.10, *appearing* 264.9, *license* 434.4, *property* 470.1, *permit* 502.3, 735.29, *permitted* 502.4, *opened up* 583.11, *limit* 620.1, 620.7, *permission*

735.9, *originate* 737.7, *manifest* 843.9
patented *propertied* 470.9, *limited* 620.5, *permitting* 735.19, *authentic* 737.6
patented invention *original* 737.2
patent leather shoes *shoes* 100.30
patently *visibly* 242.28, 244.10, *openly* 583.22
patent medicine *remedy* 115.1, *medicine* 115.2, *mixed thing* 751.2
pater [Brit inf] *man in the family* 32.12
patera *Architectural Elements* 134
paterfamilias *man in the family* 32.12, *family member* 65.2, *master* 68.1
paternal *family* 65.6, *loving* 299.15
paternal love *love* 299.1
paternity *maleness* 32.2
paternity leave *bargaining terms* 57.10
Paternoster *prayer* 85.10
paternoster *Christian rite* 85.5, *spell* 86.8, *means of transportation* 686.2
path *point* 6.34, *combinatorics* 6.63, *grip* 151.4, *access* 691.3, *passage* 691.5, *thoroughfare* 692.6, *bearing* 697.2, *way out* 707.2
pathetic *without skill* 282.10, *pitiful* 308.5, *insufficient* 517.11
pathetically *unskillfully* 282.17, *pitifully* 308.12, *weakly* 517.14
pathetic fallacy *literary device* 139.12
pathfinder *discoverer* 345.7, *precursor* 769.7
path of least resistance *route* 691.2
pathogen *disease-causing agent* 114.5
pathogenic *of disease* 114.25, *contagious* 114.26
pathological *murderous* 30.18, *medical* 107.28, *of disease* 114.25, *lying* 192.16
pathological gambling *impulse-control disorder* 108.16
pathological killer *murderer* 30.12
pathological liar *liar* 192.10
pathologically *medically* 107.35, 115.20, *unhealthily* 114.31
pathological lying *lying* 192.5
pathologically lie *lie* 192.23
pathologic specimen *postmortem (examination) (PM)* 107.17
pathologist *person dealing with the dead* 29.8, *medical specialist* 107.20
pathology *life science* 13.1, *study of life* 28.9, *Medical Specialties* 107, *medical science* 107.5
pathology report *postmortem (examination) (PM)* 107.17
pathophobia *Phobias* 283
pathos *pity* 308.1
pathway *passage* 691.5, *thoroughfare* 692.6
patience *Card Games* 168, *forgivingness* 312.3, *constancy* 377.3, *leniency* 423.1, *slowness* 693.1
patient 107.25; *detached* 4.18, *infectious person* 114.9, *sick person* 114.22, *forgiving* 312.4, *experimental subject* 335.7, *constant* 377.8, *lenient* 423.3, *unhurried* 693.8
patiently *stoically* 4.26, *forgivingly* 312.13, *perseveringly* 377.16, *leniently* 423.6, *slowly* 693.14

patina *quality of light* 246.2, *hue* 251.4, *green thing* 260.4, *polish* 545.3, *coat* 588.3, *decay* 808.6
patinate *green* 260.14
patinated *soft-hued* 251.13
patine *green* 260.14
patinous *green* 260.7
patio *ornamental garden* 17.3, *Architectural Elements* 134, *enclosed area* 619.2
patio door *Architectural Elements* 134, *means of entry* 706.6
patio set *ornamental garden* 17.3
pato *Sporting Activities* 145
patois *native language* 5.5, *dialect* 5.24, *regional pronunciation* 205.7, *vernacular* 205.8
pat oneself on the back *pride oneself* 297.13
pat on the back *compliment* 437.4, 437.17, *reward* 453.13
pat on the head *communicate love* 299.25
Patos *Lakes* 568
patria [L] *native country* 566.6
patriarch *man* 27.8, *man in the family* 32.12, *master* 68.1, *priest* 84.8
patriarchal *aged* 27.15, *governmental* 49.24, *masterful* 68.15, *old* 653.10
patriarchally *maturely* 27.18, *venerably* 653.17
patriarchy *maleness* 32.2, *tribalism* 49.2
patrician *nobleman* 70.1, *aristocratic* 70.4
patricide *homicide* 30.4
patrimonial *propertied* 470.9, *received* 492.6, *remaining* 750.7
patrimonially *proprietarily* 470.14, *profitably* 492.8
patrimony *inheritance* 469.5, *receiving* 473.1, *legacy* 492.4, *estate* 750.5
patriophobia *Phobias* 283
patriot *nationalist* 566.8
patriotic *loving* 299.15
patriotically *lovingly* 299.29, *nationally* 566.13
patriotism *bellicosity* 76.15, *love* 299.1, *nationalism* 566.4
patristic *theological* 81.24
patristics *Theologies* 81
patristic theology *Theologies* 81
Patroclus *Notable Friendships* 62
patrol *guard* 419.15, *secure* 464.9, *passing along* 692.5, *proceed* 692.16, *protect* 810.21, *restrain* 830.12
patrol boat *Ships and Boats* 690
patrol boat or **PT boat** or **motor torpedo boat** *warship* 77.21
patrol car *automobile* 687.6
patrolman *law enforcement officer* 53.8, *observer* 242.15, *guard* 419.15, *security force* 810.13
patrol plane *military aircraft* 77.30
patrol torpedo boat *Ships and Boats* 690
patrol wagon *automobile* 687.6
patrolwoman *law enforcement officer* 53.8, *guard* 419.15
patron *man* 27.8, *producer* 136.28, *benevolent person* 305.6, *defender* 419.14, *approver* 437.7, *giver* 472.7, *purchaser* 481.7, *attender* 575.6, *provider* 605.10, *protector* 810.11, *benefactor* 825.15
patronage 810.7, 825.9; *authority* 52.1, *management* 126.1, *charity* 305.3, *authorization* 425.4, *approval* 437.1, *custom* 480.12,

481.6, *indirect influence* 512.4, *financial support* 605.8, *commission* 833.1

patronal *sustaining* 605.15

patroness *giver* 472.7, *protector* 810.11

patronize *have authority* 52.13, *disdain* 297.14, *approve* 437.14, *support financially* 605.19, *frequent* 661.6, *grant* 735.30, *protect* 810.21, *advise* 825.27, *commission* 833.8

patronized *approved* 437.8, *safe* 810.16

patronizing *arrogant* 297.9, *frequenting* 661.2

patronizingly *arrogantly* 297.18

patronly *sustaining* 605.15

patrons *custom* 480.12

patron saint *supporter* 605.9, *protector* 810.11, *benefactor* 825.15

patronymic *name* 202.8

patsy [Inf] *powerless person* 515.5, *weak person* 517.4, *substitute* 672.2, *loser* 846.9

pattens *shoes* 100.30

patter *jargon* 5.21, *use language* 5.42, *rain* 9.57, *vernacular* 205.8, *small sound* 233.4, *sound faint* 233.8, *knock* 235.13, *empty talk* 362.5, *inducement* 508.2, *walk* 677.17, *drip* 714.13

pattering *nonresonant* 233.7

pattern *perceptual concept* 108.30, *weaving* 130.6, *fabric-handling tool* 130.12, *variegate* 263.11, *ideal* 327.6, 805.6, *epitomize* 327.18, *map* 387.7, *habit* 397.1, *design* 536.8, *style* 537.1, *fashion* 537.9, *structure* 551.1, 551.20, *standard* 589.7, *baseline* 601.4, *form* 624.1, *prototype* 624.2, *frequency* 663.2, *nature* 723.4, *regularity* 730.6, *original* 737.2, *order* 765.1, *method* 765.7, *array* 767.2, *precedent* 769.4, *guide* 780.4

pattern after *imitate* 736.9

patterned *identified* 184.9, *variegated* 263.6, *decorated* 532.9, *designed* 537.5, *regular* 730.12

patterning *dyeing* 130.9, *decoration* 532.1, *structuring* 551.5, *form* 624.1

pattern poetry *poetry* 139.8

pattern settlement *strike* 57.8

patting *gestural* 183.13

patulous *growing* 581.12, *broad* 592.5

paucity *scarcity* 98.3, *inadequacy* 486.5, *absence* 576.1, *sparseness* 595.8, *infrequency* 662.1, *fewness* 796.3

paulownia Trees and Shrubs 43

Paul Pry *meddler* 321.4

paunch *eating organ* 92.14, *fat* 579.8

paunchiness *fatness* 579.5, *round body* 633.2

paunchy *fat* 579.15, *well-rounded* 633.8

pauper *poor person* 486.6

pauperism *poverty* 486.1

pauperize *impoverish* 486.16

pauperized *impoverished* 486.11

pauropod *myriapod* 39.11

pause **415.15, 668.3, 668.13, 775.11;** *written music* 140.21, *not act* 413.11, *intervening space* 563.8, *space* 563.15, *interruption* 604.4, *interrupt* 604.16, *interval* 639.4, 775.2, *period* 641.1, *delay* 658.3, *wait* 658.12, *lack of motion* 678.1, *hesitate* 693.12, *stop at* 704.18, *gap* 775.4, *ease* 819.1

pause for breath *interval* 639.4, *pause* 668.13

pause for thought *interval* 775.2, *pause* 775.11

pavane Dances 135, Musical Forms 140

pave **613.32;** *engineer* 14.48, *smooth* 545.10, *base* 601.10

paved *accessible* 691.13

pavement *base* 601.1, *paving* 613.14

paver *preparer* 388.6, *coverer* 613.18

pave the way *prepare the way* 388.15, *forerun* 769.16, *make easy* 823.15

pavilion Architectural Elements 134, *club* 138.7

paving **613.14;** *ornamental garden* 17.3, *building materials* 104.2, *base* 601.1, *covering* 613.1

pavior *masonry* 14.22, *preparer* 388.6

pavis *historic armor* 419.8

Pavlov *psychologist* 108.33

Pavlovian *instinctive* 320.8

Pavlovian conditioning *conditioning* 108.24

Pavlovian psychology Psychological Theories, Schools 108

Pavlovian reaction *involuntariness* 95.9, *instinct* 318.3

Pavlovian response *instinct* 320.4

Pavo Constellations 7

pavonine *iridescent* 263.7

paw *sense organ* 212.4, *type of touch* 216.3, *touch* 216.9, *retainer* 471.3

pawn *board games* 167.3, *borrow* 476.10, *assistant* 511.3, *exchange* 673.5, *inferior* 745.4, *nonentity* 800.8

pawnbroker *person transferring property* 470.8, *lender* 475.3, 487.5

pawnbroker's shop *lending institution* 475.4

pawnbroking *lending* 475.1

pawned *guaranteed* 464.6, *borrowed* 476.8, *exchanged* 673.4

pawner *borrower* 476.7

pawning *borrowing* 476.1, *exchange* 673.1

pawnshop *place of exchange* 673.2

pawn ticket *guarantee* 458.3, *promise* 436.2

paw the ground *gesture* 183.17

Pax *prayer* 85.10

Pax Britannica *peace* 73.1

Pax Romana *peace* 73.1

pay **453.15, 489.6, 489.16;** *handle sailboat equipment* 150.30, *atone* 313.7, *reward for service* 453.5, *earnings* 467.5, *be profitable* 467.21, *fund* 472.15, *something received* 473.2, *bank* 484.26, *expend* 491.11, *income* 492.3, *positive stimulus* 508.5, *benefit* 801.10

payable **489.12**

payable on demand *payable* 489.12

pay a call [Inf] *excrete* 25.20

pay a compliment *compliment* 437.17

pay a dividend *be profitable* 467.21

pay an exorbitant price *pay* 489.16

pay a penalty *be punished* 454.31

pay a pretty penny [Inf] *overpay* 496.11

pay a salary *remunerate* 489.21

pay attention *hear* 228.13, *be attentive* 323.9

pay attention to *be solicitous* 323.13, *be careful* 325.11

pay attention to detail *be careful* 593.15

pay a visit *visit* 408.16

pay back **489.20;** *atone* 313.7, *exact retribution* 454.27, *compensate* 478.6, 743.7, *retaliate* 489.23, *restore* 809.12

pay back taxes *compensate* 478.6

pay by cashier's check *pay* 489.16

pay by check *buy on credit* 481.12, *pay* 489.16

pay by credit *or* **charge card** *buy on credit* 481.12

pay by standing order *or* **direct debit** *pay* 489.16

pay cash *pay* 489.16

pay cash for *purchase* 481.10

paycheck *earnings* 467.5

pay check *pay* 489.6

pay commission *remunerate* 489.21

pay conscience money *compensate* 478.6

pay court *seek friendship* 62.11

pay court to *court* 299.26, *fawn* 401.9

pay damages *compensate* 478.6

pay dearly *pay* 489.16, *overpay* 496.11

pay differential *bargaining terms* 57.10

pay dividends *profit* 467.22, *be effective* 845.15

pay duty on 433.18

payee *recipient* 473.5

pay envelope *pay* 489.6

payer **489.9;** *treasurer* 484.18

pay for *fund* 472.15, *purchase* 481.10, *defray* 481.18, 489.18, *pay* 489.16, *donate* 491.13, *support financially* 605.19

pay for it with one's head *be executed* 454.32

pay freeze *economic restraint* 830.3

pay heed *be attentive* 323.9

pay homage *defer to* 410.12, *show obeisance to* 426.8, *praise* 437.16, *observe* 465.4, *be subject to* 832.12

pay in advance *reserve* 464.14, *pay* 489.16

pay increase *augmentation* 467.2, *positive stimulus* 508.5

pay increases *economic factor* 56.8

pay indemnity *compensate* 478.6

pay in full *pay off* 489.17

paying **489.10;** *productive* 22.9, *522.11, rewarding* 453.9, *gainful* 467.10, *payment* 489.1, *profitable* 801.8, *successful* 845.8

paying back *compensation* 478.2

paying for *payment* 489.1

paying guest *resident* 61.6, *possessor* 469.10

paying in return **489.15**

paying off *credit* 487.1, *payment* 489.1

paying out *payment* 489.1

paying respect to *observance* 465.1

pay in kind *pay* 489.16, *exchange* 673.5, *reciprocate* 729.7

pay interest *be profitable* 467.21, *be in debt* 488.9

pay lip service to *be untruthful* 192.20

payload *rocketry* 7.32, *load* 577.5, *transferred thing* 685.6, *freightage* 686.3, *aviation* 689.1

paymaster *treasurer* 484.18, *payer* 489.9, *accountant* 493.6

payment **433.5, 489.1;** *atonement* 313.1, *reward for service* 453.5, *liability* 454.6, *funds* 484.6, *expenditure* 491.1, *positive stimulus* 508.5, *financial support* 605.8

payment in kind *reward for service* 453.5, *trade* 480.1, *type of payment* 489.3, *reciprocity* 729.1

payment in lieu *repayment* 489.5, *pay* 489.6

payment of damages *unfavorable verdict* 54.20

payment refused *amount owing* 488.5

payments and receipts *accounts* 493.4

pay more than it's worth *overpay* 496.11

Payne's gray *gray pigment* 255.2

pay no attention *be inattentive* 324.10

pay no heed to *be inattentive* 324.10, *disobey* 427.12, *not observe* 466.9

pay no regard to *not observe* 466.9

payoff *horse-racing betting terms* 159.11, *reward for service* 453.5, *payment* 489.1, *pay* 489.6, *damages* 489.8, *effect* 676.1, *compensation* 743.1, *conclusion* 761.3, *sequel* 770.5

payoff [Inf] *incentive* 178.4

pay off **489.17;** *serve one right* 420.5, *pay* 453.15, *buy off* 481.17, *retaliate* 489.23, *react* 676.8, *compensate* 743.7, *benefit* 801.10, *be effective* 845.15

pay off [Inf] *bribe* 178.18, *buy off* 481.17, *remunerate* 489.21

pay off a debt *be liberated* 831.7

pay off a loan *compensate* 478.6

pay off a mortgage *be liberated* 831.7

pay off old scores *retaliate* 420.4, 489.23

payola [Inf] *incentive* 178.4, *damages* 489.8

pay on call *pay* 489.16

pay on delivery *pay* 489.16

pay on demand *pay* 489.16

pay one back *retaliate* 420.4

pay one in his own coin *retaliate* 420.4

pay one's last respects 31.12

pay one's respects *fete* 279.6, *grieve* 308.7, *commemorate* 405.11, *defer to* 410.12, *show respect* 435.16, *observe* 465.4, *bow* 716.22

pay one's share *fund* 472.15, *pay one's way* 489.19

pay one's way **489.19**

pay on sight *pay* 489.16

pay on the dot *pay* 489.16

pay on the spot *purchase* 481.10

payout *payment* 489.1, *pay* 489.6

pay out *pay* 489.16, *expend* 491.11

pay packet *earnings* 467.5

pay-per-view movie *movie type* 137.3

pay phone *telephone* 169.10

pay reparations *put right* 429.14

payroll *personnel* 123.16, *pay* 489.6, *list of names* 785.7

pay slip *pay* 489.6

pay television *television (TV)* 172.5

pay the freight [Inf] *defray* 489.18

pay the piper *defray* 489.18

pay the ultimate price *be executed* 454.32

---

pay through the nose *pay* 489.16, *overpay* 496.11

pay too much *overpay* 496.11

pay tribute *be grateful* 310.6, *commemorate* 354.14, *congratulate* 405.12, *show obeisance to* 426.8, *show respect* 435.16, *praise* 437.16, *reward* 453.13, *be subject to* 832.12

pay tribute to mammon *seek riches* 485.14

pay under the table *bribe* 178.18

pay up *pay off* 489.17, *settle accounts* 493.11, *compensate* 743.7

pay wages *remunerate* 489.21

pay well *be profitable* 467.21

p-block *chemical element* 11.3

pea *round thing* 633.3

peabrain [Inf] *unintelligent person* 316.4

Peace Rivers 570

peace 73.1; *time off* 125.2, *silence* 231.1, *agreement* 421.4, 752.4, *repose* 678.2, *harmony* 765.8, *ease* 819.1

peace! *hush!* 231.6

peaceable *friendly* 62.5, *harmless* 73.9, *moderate* 521.3, *disciplined* 765.17

peaceable kingdom *peace* 73.1

peaceableness *friendship* 62.1, *coexistence* 73.3

peaceably *peacefully* 73.12

peace agreement *peace treaty* 73.5

peace and quiet *peace* 73.1, *harmony* 765.8, *ease* 819.1

peace at any price *pacification* 74.1, *submission* 421.1

peace be with you! *peace!* 73.13

peace camp *peace movement* 74.4

peace conference *conference* 75.4

peaceful 73.8; *silent* 231.2, *submitting* 421.3, *agreeing* 462.6, *inert* 519.2, *moderate* 521.3, *soothing* 545.6, *quiescent* 678.6, *agreeable* 752.11, *harmonious* 765.16, *at ease* 819.2

peaceful approach *peace offering* 74.5

peaceful death *way of dying* 29.5

peacefully 73.12; *pacifically* 74.12, *silently* 231.5, *agreeably* 462.14, *752.22, inertly* 519.5, *soothingly* 545.14, *motionlessly* 678.9, *easily* 819.5

peacefulness *peace* 73.1, *inertness* 519.1, *smoothness* 545.1, *repose* 678.2

peaceful protest *gesture of protest* 507.3

peacekeeper *pacifier* 73.7

peacelike *peaceful* 73.8

peace lover *pacifier* 73.7

peace-loving *pacific* 74.7, *pacificatory* 74.8

peacemaker *pacifier* 73.7, *mediator* 75.2, *representative* 75.3, *negotiator* 460.4, *assenter* 462.5, *moderator* 521.2

peacemaking *pacification* 74.1, *peace movement* 74.4, *pacificatory* 74.8

peace movement 74.4; *pacifism* 73.4

peace negotiator *pacifier* 73.7

peacenik [Inf] *pacifist* 74.6

peace offer *peace offering* 74.5

peace offering 74.5; *penitence* 313.3, *offering* 472.6, 504.5

peace of mind *peace* 73.1, *satisfaction* 273.1

peace overture *peace offering* 74.5

peace party *peace movement* 74.4

peace pipe *symbol of peace* 73.6, *peace offering* 74.5

peace process *peace movement* 74.4

peace sign *symbol of peace* 73.6

peace that passeth all understanding *peace* 73.1, *ease* 819.1

peacetime *peace* 73.1, *harmless* 73.9

peace treaty 73.5; *treaty* 74.2, *alliance* 459.5, *contract* 462.2

peach *red thing* 257.3, *orange thing* 258.3, *orange* 258.5

peach [Inf] *good thing* 445.9

peach-colored *red* 257.5

peachiness *grain* 552.2

peachlike *smooth* 545.4

peachy *appealing* 529.10

peacoat *or* **pea jacket** *coat* 100.19

Peacock Constellations 7

peacock *male bird* 36.15, *proud person* 297.7, *vain person* 402.7, *show-off* 404.13, *show off* 404.26, *displayer* 843.7

peacock-blue *blue* 261.5

peacockery *exhibitionism* 404.9

peacockish *boastful* 402.13

peacocks Collective Names 59

peacock's tail *variegated thing* 263.5

pea crab *crustacean* 39.10

pea family *seed plant* 41.3

pea-green *green* 260.7

peahen *female bird* 36.16

peak 596.18, 805.5; *be unhealthy* 114.29, *rock face* 161.6, *sharp-pointed thing* 549.4, *be sharp* 549.15, *mountain* 569.1, *wave* 571.3, *billow* 571.9, *pinnacle* 596.2, *heights* 596.4, *summit* 600.1, 744.4, *top* 600.6, *be at the top* 600.9, *be superior* 744.15, *limit* 761.4, 773.7

peakbag *mountaineer* 161.10

Peak District, the *regions of the British Isles* 564.8

peaked *unhealthy* 114.23, *drained of color* 252.6, *emaciated* 595.10, *topped* 600.8

peak of perfection *peak* 805.5

peaky *unhealthy* 114.23, *sick* 114.24, *drained of color* 252.6

peal *percussion instrument* 142.5, *loud tone* 232.3, *be loud* 232.8, *bang* 234.1, 234.6, *ring* 235.14, 236.10, *ringing* 236.2

pealing 235.9; *loud* 232.6, *ringing* 235.5, 236.7

pean Heraldic Terms 184

Peano's axioms Mathematical Concepts 6

peanut brittle *brittle thing* 548.2

peanut gallery [Inf] *auditorium* 136.17

peanuts *crop* 16.8

peanuts [Inf] *figurative usage* 44.4, *change* 484.3, *little bit* 800.4

peardrop Architectural Elements 134

Pearl Rivers 570

pearl *white thing* 253.4, *attractive female* 529.5

pearl-gray *gray* 255.6

pearliness *semitransparency* 249.3, *whiteness* 253.1, *variegation* 263.1

pearlized *lustrous* 246.15

pearl molding Architectural Elements 134

pearls of wisdom *advice* 176.1

pearly *lustrous* 246.15, *semitransparent* 249.9, *soft-hued* 251.13, *white* 253.7, *gray* 255.6, *iridescent* 263.7

pearly whites [Inf] *teeth* 19.8

pear shape *round body* 633.2

pear-shaped *rounded* 629.5, *well-rounded* 633.8

peas *crop* 16.8

peasant *agricultural* 16.16, *countryman* 61.8, *commoner* 71.1, *lowly* 597.17

peasant blouse *shirt* 100.13

peasant farmer *agriculturist* 16.14

peasantry *common people* 71.2, *lowliness* 597.8

peasants *vulgar group* 535.5

peasant skirt *skirt* 100.12

pea soup [Inf] *fog* 9.32, *that which makes invisible* 245.2, *murk* 248.2

peasouper [Brit inf] *fog* 9.32

peat *fertilizer* 17.8, *fuels* 106.2, *propellant* 696.9

peat bog *marsh* 572.3

peat-brown *brown* 256.5

peat cutter *power worker* 106.10

peatland *marsh* 572.3

peat moss *fertilizer* 22.6, *moss* 46.4

pebble *hard substance* 542.3

pebbled *grainy* 553.17, *of landmasses* 572.12

pebble dash *wall covering* 613.12

pebble-dashed *covered* 613.19

pebble glasses *visual aid* 242.14

pebbles *sediment* 8.29, *coast* 572.4

pebbly *earthy* 8.60, *grainy* 553.17

peccability *iniquity* 448.3, *imperfection* 806.1

peccable *imperfect* 806.5

peccadillo *sin* 450.3, *trifling fault* 800.5, *imperfection* 806.1

peccancy *evil* 446.1, *guilt* 450.1

peccant *evil* 446.7, *guilty* 450.6

peccantly *evilly* 446.12

peccatiphobia Phobias 283

Pechora Rivers 570

peck *nest* 36.22, *chew* 92.22, *communication of love* 299.6, *General Units* 589, *blow* 695.5, *tap* 695.13

peck at *taste* 92.24

pecker *eater* 92.15

pecker [Inf] *organs of reproduction* 21.9

pecking *delicate eating* 92.3

pecking *or* **peck order** *social stratification* 2.7

pecking order *hierarchy* 765.3, *social class* 777.5

peckings [Inf] *food* 90.1

peckish [Brit inf] *hungry* 288.16

peck on the cheek *communication of love* 299.6, *welcome* 408.10

Pecos Rivers 570

pecs [Inf] *bulge* 634.2

pectic substance *polysaccharide* 12.5

pectin *polysaccharide* 12.5, *preserver* 815.9

pectinate *or* **pectinated** *toothed* 549.13

pectoral fin *fish characteristic* 38.8

pectorals *muscles* 19.3, *bulge* 634.2

peculation *misuse* 395.1

peculator *dishonest person* 479.11

peculiar *insane* 110.9, *astonishing* 294.10, *capricious* 381.4, *unusual* 664.4, 782.15, *characteristic* 723.9, 779.12, *typical* 777.10, *eccentric* 782.16

peculiarity *caprice* 381.1, *style* 537.1, *unusualness* 664.2, 782.4, *characteristic* 779.5, *special case* 779.7, *idiosyncrasy* 782.5

peculiarly *astonishingly* 294.19,

unusually 664.7, *characteristically* 779.20, *unconformably* 782.21

peculiar trait *idiosyncrasy* 782.5

pecuniarily *financially* 457.11

pecuniary *economic* 56.10, *financial* 457.6, *monetary* 484.22

pecuniary assistance *financial support* 605.8

pecuniously *monetarily* 484.27

pedagogical *educational* 48.17

pedagogically *educationally* 48.25

pedagogue *educator* 48.4, *educational leader* 68.11

pedagogy *education* 48.1

pedal *hand tool* 103.3, *sound* 141.15, *part of keyboard instrument* 142.6, *bicycle part* 687.11, *propeller* 696.8, *propel* 696.15

pedalfer *soil* 8.42

pedal note *deepness* 236.3

pedal power *type of power* 514.6

pedal pushers *pants* 100.14

pedal wheel *ceramic workshop and tools* 129.8

pedant *discriminator* 337.6, *knowledgeable person* 348.5, *obstinate person* 379.4, *strict person* 424.4, *conformist* 781.6, *perfectionist* 805.7

pedantic *diligent* 323.7, *fastidious* 325.9, *discriminating* 337.9, *literate* 348.8, *accurate* 350.3, *formal* 406.6, *severe* 424.5, *observant* 465.3, *conformist* 781.10, *perfectionistic* 805.18, *troublesome* 824.13

pedantically *attentively* 323.14, *judiciously* 337.16, *knowledgeably* 348.14, *severely* 424.11, *observantly* 465.6

pedantry *diligence* 323.4, *fastidiousness* 325.4, *accuracy* 350.1, *formalism* 406.2, *severity* 424.1

peddle *trade* 480.18, *sell* 482.15

peddler 482.9

peddling *selling* 482.1, *trivial* 800.14

pederast *sexual perversion* 20.12, *sexually immoral person* 432.8

pederasty *sexual perversion* 20.12, *sexual offense* 432.6

pedestal *type of table* 101.5, *foundation* 601.2, *supporting structure* 605.2

pedestrian *boring* 296.6, *mediocre* 742.7

pedestrian bridge *bridge* 551.10

pedestrian crossing *road attribute* 687.3, *crossing point* 692.7

pedestrianism *motion* 677.1

pedestrian light *safety light* 246.7

pedestrian precinct *marketplace* 483.7

pediaphobia Phobias 283

pediatric *medical* 107.28

pediatrician *medical specialist* 107.20

pediatric patient *sick person* 114.22

pediatrics Medical Specialties 107

pediatric surgery Medical Specialties 107

pedicab *bicycle* 687.10

pedicel *stem* 41.5

pediculophobia Phobias 283

pediculosis *uncleanness* 112.2

pediculous *unclean* 112.8

pedicure *beauty treatment* 530.3

pedicurist *beautician* 530.11

pedigree *family tree* 65.3, *nobleness* 70.3, *line* 774.2

pediment Architectural Elements 134
pedocal *soil* 8.42
pedogenesis *developmental biology* 13.22
pedogenetic *or* **pedogenic** *developmental* 13.33
pedological *geologic* 8.50
pedologist *geologist* 8.4
pedology *geology* 8.1
pedometer *measuring instrument* 589.12
pedophile *sexually immoral person* 432.8, *villain* 448.5
pedophilia *sexual perversion* 20.12, *sexual disorder* 108.14
pedophobia Phobias 283
peduncle *stem* 41.5
pee [Inf] *urine* 25.6, *urinate* 25.22, *body fluid* 555.3
peek *look* 242.7, 242.21
Peel Rivers 570
peel *fruit structure* 44.3, *cook* 91.10, *feel hot* 217.19, *coat* 588.3, *scale* 588.10, *casing* 613.9, *depilate* 614.20, *shed* 614.21, *take off* 749.7, *residue* 750.2, *separate* 753.12, *refuse* 802.5
peeled *shed* 614.14
peeler [Inf] *nude person* 614.5
peeling 614.6, 614.13; *effects of hot weather* 217.7, *residue* 750.2
peeling off *automobile racing terms* 146.3, *nonadhesive* 756.4
peelings *bits and pieces* 760.5
peel off *be on the track* 146.11, *scale* 588.10, *undress* 614.18, *unstick* 756.6, *come unstuck* 756.7
peel-off *ice hockey tactics* 158.4
peen *impeller* 695.7
peep Collective Names 59, *bird sound* 240.2, *make a bird sound* 240.8, *look* 242.7, 242.21, *become visible* 264.13
peepee [Inf] *urine* 25.6, *urinate* 25.22
peepers [Inf] *eye* 19.9, 242.3
peephole *place for viewing* 242.13, *hole* 583.4
peeping *singing* 240.5
Peeping Tom *eroticism* 20.7, *observer* 242.15, *meddler* 321.4
peep into the future *foresee* 357.9
peep out *become visible* 264.13
peep show *show* 138.4, *view* 242.8, *pornography* 432.7
peep sight *place for viewing* 242.13
peer *elected official* 50.8, *nobleman* 70.1, *contemporary* 649.3, *equal* 740.7
peerage *aristocracy* 70.2
peerer *observer* 242.15
peer group *social organization* 2.5, *group* 59.8, *family* 65.1, *society* 408.8, *contemporary* 649.3
peering *observation* 242.5
peerless *excellent* 445.13, *quintessential* 723.8, *best* 744.10, 805.9
peerlessly *excellently* 445.21, *supremely* 744.23
peeve *annoy* 276.7, *hated thing* 300.5, *make irascible* 303.16, *sign of irritability* 304.4, *make irritable* 304.15
peeved *resentful* 302.8
peevish *hostile* 63.6, *resentful* 302.8, *irascible* 303.8, *irritable* 304.9, *argumentative* 329.7, *discourteous* 411.5
peevishly *hostilely* 63.13, *resentfully* 302.22, *irascibly*

303.17, *irritably* 304.17, *discourteously* 411.8
peevishness *ill feeling* 63.3, *resentment* 302.1, *irascibility* 303.1, *irritableness* 304.3
peewee [Inf] *child* 26.6, *little person* 580.5
peg *hand tool* 103.3, *stopper* 584.3, *rung* 636.3, *gradation* 739.3, *measure* 739.7, *fastener* 754.7, *connect* 754.13
peg [Inf] *throw* 696.4, 696.17
Pegasus Constellations 7, Notable Horses 159, Legendary Creatures 360
peg away *work* 122.8, *persevere* 377.10, *protract* 669.9
pegboard *showplace* 843.4
pegged *connected* 754.11
pegged pants *or* **trousers** *pants* 100.14
pegmatite *material* 129.2
pegmatitic *types of igneous texture* 8.33
peg top *rotator* 682.8
peignoir *robe* 100.20
peine forte et dure [Fr] *punishment* 454.1
Peipus Lakes 568
pejorative *word* 5.17, *worded* 5.38, *dissatisfied* 274.4, *insulting* 436.10, *contemptuous* 436.12, *disparaging* 440.8
pejoratively *lexically* 5.46, *disparagingly* 440.16
peke-faced Persian Breeds of Cats 35
Peking duck *notable international dishes* 90.40
Pekingese Breeds of Dogs 35
Peking man *human ancestor* 18.3, *prehistoric human* 653.7
pekoe *tea* 93.7
pelage *mammalian characteristic* 35.3
pelagian *oceanic* 571.7
pelagic *oceanic* 8.53, 571.7, *of animals* 34.13
pelagic ooze *sediment* 8.29
pelargonic Common Fatty Acids 12
pelargonium Flowers 42
p-electron *atom* 10.52
pelf *profit* 467.6, *cash* 484.2
pelican *water bird* 36.9
pelican, brown Endangered US Birds 36
pellagra *vitamin deficiency disease* 12.14
Pelléas Famous Lovers 299
pellet *ammunition* 78.11, *hunting equipment* 160.4, *round thing* 633.3, *missile* 696.7
pellicle *body covering* 19.4, *coat* 588.3
pellicular *platelike* 588.8
pell-mell *anyhow* 766.25, *hastily* 818.7
Pell's equation Mathematical Concepts 6
pellucid *clear* 196.2, *transparent* 249.7, *simple* 363.6
pellucidity *transparency* 249.1, *clarity* 363.2
pellucidity *or* **pellucidness** *clarity* 196.1
pellucidly *clearly* 196.4, *transparently* 249.13
pellucidness *transparency* 249.1
Pelopidas Notable Friendships 62
Peloponnesian Wars Major Wars 76
pelota Sporting Activities 145
pelt *rain* 9.57, *stone* 418.23, *animal*

covering 613.15, *blow* 695.5, *hit* 695.11, *throw* 696.17, *shoot* 696.18
peltate *of leaves* 41.18
Peltier effect Classical Physical Laws 10
pelting *rainy* 9.50, *speeding* 694.7, *throwing* 696.3
pelt with rotten eggs *show disapproval* 438.21
pelvic fin *fish characteristic* 38.8
pelvic inflammatory disease (PID) *sexually transmitted disease (STD)* 114.17
pelvis Human Bones 19
Pemba Islands 572
pen *farm building* 16.4, *practice livestock farming* 16.20, *female animal* 33.15, *mammal dwelling* 35.21, *female bird* 36.16, *the inside* [Inf] 55.2, *write* 139.21, *material* 143.9, *enclose* 584.16, 619.6, *enclosed area* 619.2, *shelter* 812.4
pen *or* **pencil pusher** [Inf] *descriptive writer* 202.10
penal *punitive* 454.18
penal code *law* 53.1, *penology* 454.17
penal colony *imprisonment* 454.2
penal institution *prison* 55.1
penalization *punishment* 454.1
penalize 454.26; *be inconvenient* 804.9
penalizing *punitive* 454.18
penally *punitively* 454.33
penal servitude *imprisonment* 454.2
penalty 155.13, 454.5; *work* 122.1, *horse racing* 159.10, *soccer play* 163.5, *forfeiture* 468.2, *compensation* 478.2, 743.1, *damages* 489.8, *levy* 494.7, *ruling* 780.2, *restraint* 830.1
penalty area *stadium* 163.2
penalty award *ice hockey tactics* 158.4, *field hockey tactics* 158.5
penalty box *ice hockey tactics* 158.4
penalty clause *coercive method* 428.3
penalty corner *field hockey tactics* 158.5
penalty flag *penalty* 155.13
penalty kick *soccer play* 163.5
penalty marker *penalty* 155.13
penalty plays *ice hockey tactics* 158.4, *field hockey tactics* 158.5
penalty shot *playing terms* 148.4, *ice hockey tactics* 158.4
penalty spot *hockey areas* 158.2, *stadium* 163.2
penalty stroke *golf shots* 156.4, *field hockey tactics* 158.5
penal work *work* 122.1
penance Christian rite 85.5, *penitence* 313.3, *self-punishment* 454.10, *compensation* 743.1
pen-and-ink *drawing* 143.4
pen-and-ink sketch 252.3
Penates *minor deity* 82.2
pence *national coins* 484.11
penchant *inclination* 290.2, *tendency* 397.2, *attitude* 513.2
pencil *(act of) drawing* 143.2, *material* 143.9, *draw* 143.13, *cosmetic tool* 530.5
pencil beam of light *light* 10.17
pencil cedar Trees and Shrubs 43
pencil drawing *drawing* 143.4
pencil point *sharp point* 549.2
pendant Architectural Elements 134, *vault* 134.8, *jewelry* 532.6, *counterpart* 733.5
pendency *deferment* 604.3

pendent *suspended* 604.7, *overhanging* 604.8
pendente lite *in litigation* 54.34
pendentive *or* **pendentive dome** *roof* 134.7
pendently *pendulously* 604.19
pending *suspended* 519.3, *deferred* 604.9, *temporal* 639.8, *future* 650.6, *recessed* 668.8
pendular motion *oscillation* 683.1
pendulate *oscillate* 683.12
pendulation *oscillation* 683.1
pendulous *suspended* 604.7, *nonadhesive* 756.4
pendulously 604.19; *noncohesively* 756.9
pendulousness *suspension* 604.1
pendulum *climbing techniques* 161.3, *mountaineer* 161.10, *oscillator* 683.7
pendulum clock Timepieces and Timers 646
pendulumlike *suspended* 604.7
pendulum movement *frequency* 663.2
pendulum wheel *oscillator* 683.7
Peneia pony Horse and Pony Breeds 159
penetrability *intelligibility* 363.1
penetrable *intelligible* 363.5
penetrate *play defense* 155.19, *emphasize* 200.6, *understand* 363.9, *be intelligible* 363.10, *be present* 575.13, *hole* 583.17, *be profound* 598.23, *enter* 692.18, *infiltrate* 706.13, *inject* 710.10, *mix together* 751.14
penetrated *holed* 583.12
penetrating 692.12; *emphatic* 200.3, *strident* 238.4, *omnipresent* 575.10, *profound* 598.15, *invasive* 706.10
penetrating eye *sharp eye* 242.4
penetratingly *profoundly* 598.27
penetration *defense* 155.9, *emphasis* 200.1, *wisdom* 352.1, *profundity* 598.5, *passage into* 692.4, *inroad* 706.3, *injection* 710.2, *mixture* 751.1
penguin *flightless bird* 36.8
penguins Collective Names 59
peniaphobia Phobias 283
penicillin *fungal antibiotic* 47.7
penile *reproductive* 21.11
pen in *arrest* 55.12
peninsula 572.5; *coast* 8.13, *narrow place* 593.2
peninsular *regional* 564.12, *of landmasses* 572.12
penis *organs of reproduction* 21.9
Penistone Breeds of Sheep 16
penitence 313.3, 451.1; *act of worship* 83.2, *Christian rite* 85.5, *sign of guilt* 450.2, *improvement* 807.1
penitent 451.5; *worshiper* 83.6, *worshipful* 83.12, *atoner* 313.4, *apologetic* 313.6, *penitent person* 451.4
penitential 451.6; *ritualistic* 85.15, *apologetic* 313.6, *compensatory* 743.5
penitential act *or* **exercise** *penitence* 313.3
penitentially *worshipfully* 83.17, *ritually* 85.21, *apologetically* 313.11, *penitently* 451.10, *correctively* 743.11
penitentiary *prison* 55.1, *penitential* 451.6, *building* 551.9, *compensatory* 743.5
penitently 451.10; *apologetically* 313.11
penitent person 451.4

penman *author* 139.13
penmanship *written letter* 5.14
pen name *anonymity* 182.7, *name* 202.8
pennant *sailboat parts and accessories* 150.4, *flag* 184.8
pennant winner *baseball leagues and championship games* 147.8
penned *retained* 471.6, *enclosed* 619.4, *sheltered* 812.7
penned in *imprisoned* 55.9
penniless *poor* 486.8, *unprosperous* 848.11
pennilessness *poverty* 486.1
Pennine Chain *Mountains and Hills* 569
Pennines, the *regions of the British Isles* 564.8
penning in *arrest* 55.5
pennon *flag* 184.8
Pennsylvania *American States* 564
Pennsylvania Dutch *Furniture Styles* 101
Pennsylvania Dutch *or German regional pronunciation* 205.7
Pennsylvania Dutch *or German ware* *Ceramics* 129
penny *US coinage* 484.10, *little bit* 800.4
penny-ante [Inf] *insignificant* 745.6
penny broker *financial adviser* 457.4
penny dreadful [Brit] *novel* 139.3
penny loafers *shoes* 100.30
penny pincher *bargain hunter* 497.8, *miser* 501.3
penny-pinching *mean* 501.4
penny post [Arch] *postal service* 169.5
pennyroyal *Flowers* 42
pennyweight *weight measurement* 538.6, *General Units* 589
penny whistle *Musical Instruments* 142, *shrillness* 238.3
penny wise and pound foolish *wasteful* 96.9
Penobscot *Rivers* 570
penological *punitive* 454.18
penologically *punitively* 454.33
penologist *penology* 454.17
penology 454.17
penology *or poenology jurisprudence* 53.13
penorcon *Musical Instruments* 142
pen pal *correspondent* 169.3
pen *or pencil pusher* [Inf] *descriptive writer* 202.10
pensile *suspended* 604.7
pension *hotel* 60.12, *reward for service* 453.5, *personal finance* 457.5, *earnings* 467.5, *something received* 473.2, *pay* 489.6, *income* 492.3, *financial support* 605.8, *support financially* 605.19, *social assistance* 825.4
pensionable age *old age* 27.5
pensionary *given* 472.8, *receivable* 473.12, *sustaining* 605.15
pensioned *receiving* 473.9, *resigning* 835.3
pensioned off *resigning* 835.3
pensioned-off *receiving* 473.9
pensioner *older person* 27.7, *recipient* 473.5
pensioners *old people* 653.6
pension fund *income* 492.3
pension off *dismiss* 709.15
pension program *benefits* 57.11
pensive *thoughtful* 4.17, *serious* 278.4, *concentrating* 317.7

pensively *thoughtfully* 4.27, *solemnly* 278.9
pensiveness *thoughtfulness* 317.2
pent *narrow* 593.8
pentachord *five* 792.1
pentacle *polygon* 6.42, *spell* 86.8, *five* 792.1
pentad *five* 792.1
pentadic *fifth* 792.12
Pentagon *the military* 58.2, *the power structure* 68.12
pentagon *polygon* 6.42, *angled figure* 628.3, *five* 792.1
pentagonal *polygonal* 6.79, *angled* 628.9, *fifth* 792.12
Pentagonese *equivocation* 380.1
pentagram *polygon* 6.42, *spell* 86.8, *five* 792.1
pentahedral *fifth* 792.12
pentahedron *polyhedron* 6.44, *five* 792.1
pentameter *meter* 139.10, *five* 792.1
pentane *fuels* 106.2
pentangle *polygon* 6.42
pentangular *fifth* 792.12
pentaprism *lens* 132.11
pentarchy *five* 792.1
pentastich *part of poem* 139.9, *five* 792.1
pentastomid *arthropodlike invertebrate* 39.12
Pentastomida *arthropodlike invertebrate* 39.12
Pentateuch *the Law* 53.2, *five* 792.1
pentathlon *multi-event contest* 166.16, *five* 792.1
pentatonic *fifth* 792.12
pentavalent *chemical compound* 11.4
Pentecost *Christian Holy Days and Seasons* 85, *Jewish Holy Days and Seasons* 85
Pentecostal churches *Christian Groups* 81
Pentecost season *Christian Holy Days and Seasons* 85
pentheraphobia *Phobias* 283
penthouse *apartment* 60.7, *property* 470.1
pentode *electron tube* 14.40
pentose *Common Sugars* 12, *saccharide* 12.4
pent up *self-restrained* 830.10
pent-up *narrow* 593.8, *enclosed* 619.4
penumbra *dimness* 248.1
pen up *enclose* 619.6
penurious *poor* 486.8, *mean* 501.4, *unprosperous* 848.11
penuriously *poorly* 486.17
penury *neediness* 95.3, *poverty* 486.1
peon *office assistant* 69.6, *army person* 77.17, *subjected person* 832.5
peonage *servility* 401.1, *subjection* 832.1
peony *Flowers* 42, *red thing* 257.3
people *society* 1.6, *humankind* 18.1, *group* 18.13, 59.8, *nation* 18.14, *inhabitants* 61.2, *settle* 61.14, *family* 65.1, *human family* 65.5, *Phobias* 283
people, the *common people* 71.2
people at large *inhabitants* 61.2
people mover *means of transportation* 686.2
people of today *contemporary* 649.3
people's mandate *acquisition of authority* 52.5

peoples of the earth *humankind* 18.1
pep [Inf] *energy* 414.4, *vigor* 518.1
peplum *part of garment* 100.27
pepo *botanical fruit* 44.2
pepper *basic cooking ingredient* 91.8, *seasoning* 221.2, *season* 221.8, *variegate* 263.11, *fire* 418.18, *shoot* 696.18, *sprinkle* 776.15
pepper-and-salt *gray-haired* 255.7, *mottled* 263.10
peppercorn *seasoning* 221.2
peppercorns *Herbs and Spices* 91
peppered *mottled* 263.10, *sprinkled* 776.9
peppered with shot *holed* 583.12
pepperiness *irascibility* 303.1
peppering *sprinkling* 776.4
pepper mill *pulverizer* 553.11
peppermint *sweets* 90.39, *Herbs and Spices* 91
peppermint tea *tea* 93.7
pepper spray *self-defense* 419.5
pepper tree *Trees and Shrubs* 43
pepper with shot *hole* 583.17
peppery *piquant* 221.6, *irascible* 303.8
pep pill *stimulants* 121.18, *tonic* 115.8
peppy [Inf] *emphatic* 200.3, *vigorous* 518.2
pep rally *miscellaneous terms* 155.16, *exhortation* 178.2
Pepsi *Nicknames for Inhabitants* 61
Pepsi™ *soft drink* 93.8
pepsin *enzyme* 12.11
pep squad *miscellaneous terms* 155.16
pep talk *exhortation* 178.2, *salutation* 209.2
peptic *medicinal* 115.15
peptic ulcer *gastroenterological disease* 114.11
peptidase *enzyme* 12.11
peptide *amino acid* 12.8
peptide bond *amino acid* 12.8
peptidoglycan *protein* 12.9
pep up [Inf] *invigorate* 518.5, *mix* 751.12
per *instrumentally* 511.9
peradventure [Arch] *possibly* 836.9
perambulate *proceed* 692.16
perambulation *motion* 677.1, *passing along* 692.5
perambulator *means of transportation* 686.2
per annum *cyclically* 663.15
percale *Fabrics and Fibers* 130
percaline *Fabrics and Fibers* 130
per capita *proportionately* 474.7
perceivability *visibility* 244.1
perceivable *visible* 242.19, 244.5
perceive *know* 48.24, 348.10, *sense* 212.9, *hear* 228.13, *see* 242.20, *visualize* 242.24, *feel* 266.14, *think* 315.12, *reason* 319.11, *be intuitive* 320.9, *have an idea* 327.13, *discover* 345.11, *imagine* 360.14, *recognize* 363.11
perceived *known* 348.9
percent *mathematically* 6.93, *ratio* 783.5
percentage *division* 6.16, *profit* 467.6, *discount* 495.1, *part* 760.1, *ratio* 783.5, *fractional part* 787.2
percentile *parameter* 6.57, *divisible* 6.71
perceptibility *visibility* 244.1
perceptible *sensate* 212.5, *touchable* 216.5, *visible* 242.19,

244.5, *discoverable* 345.10, *measurable* 589.17
perceptibly *visibly* 242.28, 244.10, *measurably* 589.22
perception *refinement* 48.10, *sensation* 212.1, *visualization* 242.6, *feelings* 266.1, *intellect* 315.1, *reason* 319.1, *intuition* 320.1, *idea* 327.1, *imagination* 327.8, 360.1, *judiciousness* 337.2, *discovery* 345.1, *knowledge* 348.1, *wisdom* 352.1, *understanding* 363.4
perceptive *refined* 48.20, *susceptible* 212.7, *seeing* 242.17, *feeling* 266.9, *sensitive* 267.3, *reasoning* 319.7, *intuitive* 320.6, *discriminating* 337.9, *knowledgeable* 348.7, *wise* 352.4, *foreseeing* 357.5, *imaginative* 360.10, *mentally sharp* 549.14
perceptively *discerningly* 48.27, *sensitively* 267.6, *imaginatively* 327.21, *judiciously* 337.16, *foresightedly* 357.10
perceptiveness *refinement* 48.10, *sensitivity* 267.1, *intellect* 315.1
perceptual *theoretical* 327.10
perceptual abstraction *Western Art Styles* 133
perceptual computing *artificial intelligence* 15.21
perceptual concept 108.30
perch *dwelling* 36.4, *nest* 36.22, *natural habitat* 60.16, *take up residence* 60.24, *food fish and shellfish* 90.20, *game fish* 154.10, *be motionless* 678.7, *land* 704.16, *sit* 716.20, *take it easy* 819.3
perchance 842.18; *possibly* 836.9
Percheron *Horse and Pony Breeds* 159
perching *avian* 36.19
perching bird *songbird* 36.12
perching duck *water bird* 36.9
perchlike *fishlike* 38.10
percipience *intellect* 315.1
percipient *sensible* 212.6
percoid *fishlike* 38.10
percolate *drain* 8.64, *purify* 111.19, *dissolve* 555.23, *water* 557.29, *seep* 559.16, *enter* 692.18, *infiltrate* 706.13, *leak* 707.16, *absorb* 708.19
percolating *seeping* 559.12, *penetrating* 692.12, *leakage* 707.5
percolation *water cycle* 8.12, *cleaning* 111.2, *fluidization* 555.8, *soaking* 557.9, *seepage* 559.4, *passage into* 692.4, *inroad* 706.3, *leakage* 707.5, *absorption* 708.6
percolator *pot* 578.15
percuss *collide* 695.10
percussion *collision* 695.2
percussion cap *fuel starter* 106.3
percussion instrument 142.5; *musical instrument* 142.1
percussionist *player* 141.2
percussively *dynamically* 695.16
perdendo *Musical Terms and Expression Marks* 140
per diem *cyclically* 663.15
perdition *evil place* 446.6, *forfeiture* 468.2, *ruin* 523.4
perdurability *continuation* 642.2
peregrinate *travel* 686.11
peregrinating *traveling* 686.9
peregrination *travel* 686.5
peregrinator *traveler* 686.6
pereira bark *Tree Products* 43
peremptory *authoritative* 52.9, *duty-bound* 433.8
peremptory challenge *jury selection* 54.14

perennate *be dormant* 41.22
perennial *garden plant* 17.10,
  botanical 17.15, *plant* 41.2, *of
  plants* 41.14, *flowering plant* 42.2,
  permanent 642.5, *cyclic* 663.7,
  unfailing 667.3, *stable* 674.3
perennially *horticulturally* 17.20,
  herbaceously 41.24, *chronologically*
  639.21, *everlastingly* 642.10,
  cyclically 663.15, *permanently*
  667.6, *stably* 674.9
perfect 805.8, 805.19; *of flowers*
  42.11, *divine* 82.16, *clean* 111.13,
  skillful 127.10, *accurate* 350.3,
  correct 429.8, 721.13, *pure*
  431.11, *excellent* 445.13, *virtuous*
  447.5, *innocent* 449.6, *be elegant*
  527.6, *be accurate* 721.22, *unique*
  744.11, *uncut* 759.7, *complete*
  759.10, 761.6, 761.9, *best* 805.9,
  improve 807.15, *preserved* 815.12
perfecta *horse-racing betting terms*
  159.11
perfect binding *bookbinding*
  174.11
perfect cadence *harmonic element*
  140.14
perfect candidate *assenter* 462.5
perfect condition 805.3
perfected *complete* 761.6, *perfect*
  805.8
perfecter *perfectionist* 805.7
perfect fit *compatibility* 462.3
perfect game *pitching terms* 147.5
perfectibility *improvement* 679.5,
  imperfection 806.1
perfectible *imperfect* 806.5,
  improvable 807.13
perfection 805.1; *masterpiece*
  68.14, *divine attribute* 82.4,
  manual skill 127.2, *fastidiousness*
  325.4, *right* 429.2, *purity* 431.4,
  excellence 445.4, *virtue* 447.1,
  innocence 449.1, *trueness* 721.4,
  superiority 744.1, *completeness*
  761.1, *limit* 761.4, *improvement*
  807.1
perfectionism *fastidiousness* 325.4,
  judiciousness 337.2, *assiduity* 414.8
perfectionist 805.7; *discriminator*
  337.6, *discriminating* 337.9
perfectionistic 805.18; *fastidious*
  325.9
perfectly 805.21; *divinely* 82.24,
  carefully 325.13, *ideally* 327.22,
  720.18, *correctly* 429.16, 721.29,
  excellently 445.21, *virtuously*
  447.9, *innocently* 449.13,
  supremely 744.23, *completely*
  759.14, 761.13
perfect moment *timeliness* 659.1
perfectness *perfection* 805.1
perfect number *number* 6.4
perfect participle *part of speech*
  5.30
perfect pitch *tone* 140.24, *hearing*
  228.1, *accuracy* 350.1
perfect radiator *heating effect*
  10.28
perfect sacrifice *batting terms*
  147.6
perfect silence *silence* 231.1
perfect tense *past tense* 651.2
perfect touch *stylishness* 537.2
perfect vision *visual acuity* 242.2
perfect wreck *dilapidation* 808.5
perfervid *active* 414.13
perfidious *dishonorable* 192.14,
  cunning 330.8, 822.4, *disobedient*
  427.10, *misrepresented* 627.8,
  unreliable 841.15, *mysterious*
  844.11
perfidiously *hypocritically* 330.15,

disobediently 427.14, *distortedly*
  627.14
perfidiousness *disobedience* 427.1
perfidy *dishonorableness* 192.3,
  disobedience 427.1, *distortion of
  truth* 627.4
perforate *use a sharp tool* 549.17,
  hole 583.17
perforated *holed* 583.12
perforation *opening* 583.1
perforator *sharp-pointed thing*
  549.4
perforce *necessarily* 95.22,
  compellingly 428.12
perform 465.5, 522.16; *act*
  136.34, 137.20, 187.13, 412.11,
  entertain 138.16, *play* 141.14,
  occur 264.14, *demonstrate* 331.15,
  appear 331.18, *follow up* 385.16,
  show 404.24, *commemorate*
  405.11, *obey* 426.7, *be operational*
  509.10, *be an instrument* 511.7,
  complete 761.9, *be useful* 801.9,
  display 843.13
performable *possible* 836.5
perform a function *be useful*
  801.9
perform a miracle *cure* 809.15
performance 141.8, 465.2;
  theatrical performance 136.13,
  acting 136.22, 187.6, *number*
  138.5, *view* 242.8, *manifestation*
  244.3, *visibility* 264.4,
  demonstration 331.1, *celebration*
  405.1, *action* 412.1, *operation*
  509.1, *instrumentality* 511.1,
  production 522.1, 843.5, *work of
  art* 522.4
performance art *Western Art
  Styles* 133
performance gain *advance* 467.3
performance-oriented
  instrumental 511.4
performance poetry *poetry* 139.8
**Performance Racing Handicap
  Factor (PRHF) racing**
  competitive sailing 150.6
perform a stunt *do great deeds*
  412.14
perform better *improve* 467.18
performed *dramatized* 136.32,
  directed 141.12
performer 412.5; *artistic worker*
  123.12, *entertainer* 138.8,
  musician 141.1, *demonstrator*
  331.6
performing *acting* 136.22, 187.6,
  187.9, 412.9, *musical* 141.11
performing area *stage* 136.18
perform magic *entertain* 138.16,
  do wonders 294.15, *transform*
  665.20
perform rites 85.18; *perform*
  465.5
perform skillfully *be good at*
  445.18
perform the act of love *have sex*
  20.21
perform the hajj *revere* 81.26
perfume 226.6; *odor* 224.1, *impart
  odor to* 224.9, *fragrance* 226.1,
  source of fragrance 226.2, *toiletries*
  530.6, *beautify* 530.14, *give off*
  556.25
perfumed *pleasurable* 214.6,
  odorous 224.5, *fragrant* 226.4
perfume dynamics *fragrance*
  226.1
perfume oil *toiletries* 530.6
perfunctorily *indifferently* 289.17,
  incompletely 762.10
perfunctoriness *indifference*
  289.1, *disobedience* 375.5,
  nonobservance 466.1,

incompleteness 762.1, 806.2,
  nonachievement 762.3
perfunctory 324.9; *bungled* 128.7,
  indifferent 289.7, *unrefined* 338.7,
  nonobservant 466.5, *incomplete*
  762.5, 806.6, *uncompleted* 762.7,
  hasty 818.3
perfuse *practice surgery* 107.33,
  treat 115.17, *transfer* 685.8, *inject*
  710.10
perfused *injected* 710.6
perfusion *surgery* 107.15,
  transmission 685.3, *injection* 710.2
pergola *ornamental garden* 17.3
perhaps *possibly* 836.9, *perchance*
  842.18
per head *proportionately* 474.7
perianth *flower part* 42.3
periapt *talisman* 86.9
pericarditis *cardiovascular disease*
  114.13
pericardium *body covering* 19.4
pericarp *seed* 41.9, *fruit structure*
  44.3
perigee *rocketry* 7.32, *nearness*
  586.1
perigon *angle* 6.37
perigynous *of flowers* 42.11
perihelion *orbit* 7.22, *nearness*
  586.1
peril *danger* 811.1
perilous *dangerous* 811.7,
  unreliable 841.15
perilously *dangerously* 811.14,
  unreliably 841.25
perilousness *danger* 811.1
perilous state *danger* 811.1
perimeter *line* 6.35, *stadium*
  163.2, *surroundings* 615.1, *edge*
  617.3
perimetric or **perimetrical**
  surrounding 615.4
perinatal *pregnant* 21.12
period 641.1; *Punctuation Marks*
  5, *geological time* 8.47, *weather*
  9.3, *frequency* 10.6, *chemical
  element* 11.3, *bleeding* 25.10,
  allotted task 474.3, *intervening
  space* 563.8, *time* 639.1, *duration*
  642.1, *season* 654.1, *cycle* 663.3,
  wavelength 683.5, *interval* 739.4,
  separator 753.5, *ender* 773.11
periodic 639.10, 641.8; *cyclic* 6.82,
  seasonal 654.7, *frequent* 661.4,
  663.6, *directional* 677.13, *cyclical*
  774.10, *recurrent* 797.13
periodical 175.1, 175.6, 641.7;
  publication 173.1, *publication
  media* 173.6, *magazine* 175.3,
  periodic 639.10, *periodical
  publication* 641.6, *frequent* 663.6,
  oscillating 683.8
periodically 641.11; *frequently*
  661.7, *regularly* 663.14,
  discontinuously 775.15
periodical publication 641.6
periodic function *mathematical
  function* 6.27, *recurrent period*
  641.5
periodicity *recurrent period* 641.5,
  season 654.1, *frequency* 661.1,
  663.2, *oscillation* 683.1, *continuum*
  774.5
periodic table of elements
  chemical element 11.3
period of activity 641.4
period of detention *prison
  sentence* 55.6
period of work *task* 122.2
periodontal *dental* 107.31
periodontal tissue *mouth* 19.7
periodontic *dental* 107.31
periodontics *dentistry* 107.6
periodontist *dentist* 107.21

periodontologist *dentist* 107.21
periodontology *dentistry* 107.6
Peripatetic *Philosophical Schools
  of Thought* 4
peripatetic *moving* 677.12
peripatetically *in motion* 677.19
Peripateticism *Philosophical
  Schools of Thought* 4
peripeteia *literary device* 139.12
peripheral 15.8; *computer part*
  15.4, *away* 585.6, *covering* 610.8,
  surrounding 615.4, *outlined* 617.4,
  edging 618.5, *external* 724.11,
  extra 748.6, *excluded* 764.6,
  secondary 800.15
peripherally *exteriorly* 610.16,
  essentially 617.6, *marginally*
  618.11, *externally* 724.19
peripherals *separates* 753.6
périphérique [Fr] *rotary* 682.5
periphery *distant place* 585.3,
  exteriority 610.2, *surroundings*
  615.1, *edge* 618.1, *externality*
  724.4
periphrasis *phrasing* 5.25, *literary
  device* 139.12, *circumlocution*
  199.2, *indirectness* 607.3
periphrastic *phrased* 5.39,
  circumlocutory 199.4, *indirect*
  607.8
periphrastically *phraseologically*
  5.47, *circuitously* 199.8, *indirectly*
  607.15
perish *die* 29.17, *waste away* 96.20,
  disappear 265.5, *be destroyed*
  523.17, *disintegrate* 808.15
perishability *mortality* 29.2
perishable *transient* 643.4
perishable goods *merchandise*
  482.6
perishables *merchandise* 482.6
perishing *cool* 9.49, *dying* 29.3,
  29.12
perissodactyl *hoofed mammal*
  35.16, *ungulate* 35.31
Perissodactyla *hoofed mammal*
  35.16
peristyle *Architectural Elements*
  134, *column* 134.6
peritoneum *body covering* 19.4
periwig *body covering* 613.3
periwinkle *Flowers* 42
perjure *lie* 192.23
perjured *perjurious* 442.7
perjured testimony *false
  accusation* 442.2
perjure oneself *accuse falsely*
  442.9
perjurer *liar* 192.10, *accuser* 442.3
perjurious 442.7; *lying* 192.16
perjuriously *accusingly* 442.11
perjury *witness* 54.16, *evasion*
  181.5, *lying* 192.5, *false accusation*
  442.2
perk [Inf] *reward for service* 453.5,
  profit 467.6, *reward* 472.4,
  something received 473.2, *absence of
  charge* 497.6, *positive stimulus*
  508.5, *extra* 748.6
perked up *refreshed* 94.5
perkily *cheerfully* 269.14
perking up *refreshment* 94.1,
  recuperation 809.4
perk up *be refreshed* 94.8, *bring
  cheer* 269.12, *raise* 715.9
perky *cheerful* 269.7
perm [Inf] *coiffure* 530.8, *coif*
  530.15
permafrost *frost* 9.25
Permain *Apple Varieties* 44
permanence 667.1; *constancy*
  377.3, *immutability* 640.2,
  continuation 642.2, *eternity* 644.1,
  stability 674.1, *conservation* 815.2

permanency *continuation* 642.2, *permanence* 667.1
permanent 642.5, 667.2; *combinatorics* 6.63, *constant* 377.8, *customary* 397.11, *changeless* 640.4, *eternal* 644.4, *stable* 674.3
permanently 667.6; *for good* 445.23, *everlastingly* 642.10, *stably* 674.9
permanent magenta *purple pigment* 262.2
permanent magnet *magnet* 10.47
permanent post *safety* 810.1
permanent stoppage *stop* 668.2
permanent tooth *teeth* 19.8
permanent wave *coiffure* 530.8
permanent way *rail* 688.3
permeability *magnetic quantity* 10.48
permeability of vacuum *fundamental constant* 10.69
permeable *leaky* 707.12
permeate *be an influence* 512.13, *water* 557.29, *be present* 575.13, *hole* 583.17, *cooperate* 616.6, *enter* 692.18, *infiltrate* 706.13, *absorb* 708.19, *mix together* 751.14
permeated *fixed* 397.13, *holed* 583.12, *interfacial* 616.4
permeating *omnipresent* 575.10, *penetrating* 692.12
permeation *soaking* 557.9, *seepage* 559.4, *omnipresence* 575.4, *interaction* 616.2, *passage into* 692.4, *mixture* 751.1
permeative *omnipresent* 575.10
Permian Period Geologic Time Intervals 8
permineralization *fossil* 8.49
permissible *legal* 53.16, *approvable* 437.13, *permitting* 502.5
permissibly *with permission* 502.10
permission 340.3, 502.1, 735.9; *authorization* 52.3, *legality* 53.9, *assent* 346.1, *leniency* 423.1, *license* 434.4, *approval* 437.1, *agreement* 462.1, *adoption* 692.2, *right of entry* 706.4, *authority* 833.3
permissions notice *book part* 174.5
permission to enter upon land or other property *pretrial proceedings* 54.13
permissive *free* 407.9, *lenient* 423.3, *permitting* 502.5, *easygoing* 823.13, *unconditional* 829.14
permissively *freely* 407.12, *leniently* 423.6, *with permission* 502.10, *excessively* 829.23
permissiveness *freedom* 407.4, *leniency* 423.1, *tolerance* 502.2, *liberality* 829.8
permissive parent *lenient person* 423.2
permissive society *freedom* 407.4, *fornication* 432.3, *tolerance* 502.2, *liberality* 829.8
permit 340.12, 502.3, 502.6, 735.29; *authorization* 52.3, 340.4, 425.4, *authorize* 52.14, 425.14, 833.10, *make legal* 53.27, *personal identification* 184.4, *verification* 336.1, *documentation* 339.6, *assent* 346.6, *be lenient* 423.5, *license* 434.4, *approve* 437.14, *promise* 464.2, *passport* 692.8, *adopt* 692.14, *right of entry* 706.4, *permission* 735.9, *safe conduct* 810.4, *make easy* 823.15, *authority* 833.3, *make possible* 836.7
permit oneself *lack restraint* 829.21

permitted 502.4; *authorized* 52.11, 340.8, *legal* 53.16, *given consideration* 423.4, *rightful* 429.9, *approved* 437.8, *adopted* 692.10, *permitting* 735.19
permitter *lenient person* 423.2
permitting 502.5, 735.19
permittivity *electric field* 10.42
permittivity of vacuum *fundamental constant* 10.69
permutation *set* 6.19, *exchange* 673.1, *calculation* 784.1
Pern Imaginary Places 360
pernicious *malicious* 306.8, *detrimental* 446.8, *destructive* 523.8
pernicious anemia *vitamin deficiency disease* 12.14, *blood disease* 114.14
perniciously *maliciously* 306.15, *destructively* 446.13
perniciousness *malice* 306.2
perorate *dissertate* 203.5, *speak to* 205.19, *address* 209.8, *iterate* 797.16
peroration *dissertation* 203.1, *public speaking* 205.11, *salutation* 209.2, *iteration* 797.2
peroxide *lightening* 246.3, *color remover* 252.4, *decolor* 252.8
peroxide blond *white-haired* 253.9
perpendicular 602.6; *line* 6.35, *linear* 6.77, *vertical* 602.3, *angle* 628.1, *angled* 628.9, *straight line* 630.2, *straight* 630.8
perpendicularity 602.2; *measuring instrument* 589.12, *straightness* 630.1
perpendicular lines *line* 6.35
perpendicularly 602.12; *straight* 630.16
perpendicular style Architectural Styles 134
perpetrate *do something* 412.13
perpetration *action* 412.1
perpetrator *agent* 123.15, *doer* 412.3
perpetual *habitual* 397.9, *nonmaterial* 525.8, *lasting* 639.9, 717.13, *timeless* 640.3, *permanent* 642.5, 667.2, *eternal* 644.4, 798.7, *protracted* 669.7, *stable* 674.3, *continuous* 774.9
perpetual calendar *calendar* 646.3
perpetually *metaphysically* 525.13, *chronologically* 639.21, *frequently* 661.7, *permanently* 667.6, *continually* 669.10, *stably* 674.9, *continuously* 774.16, *eternally* 798.12
perpetual motion *eternity* 798.4
perpetuate 640.5; *make eternal* 644.8, *make permanent* 667.5, *protract* 669.9, *be infinite* 798.9, *preserve* 815.14
perpetuation *immutability* 640.2, *eternalization* 644.3, *protraction* 669.4, *conservation* 815.2
perpetuity *nonmaterial world* 525.1, *immutability* 640.2, *eternity* 644.1, 798.4, *permanence* 667.1, *protraction* 669.4, *continuing existence* 717.7
perplex *mystify* 182.12, *obscure* 250.8, *be wondrous* 294.14, *puzzle* 364.12, *cause difficulties* 824.22, *make uncertain* 841.19
perplexed *wondering* 294.7, *confused* 364.10, 841.11, *troubled* 824.15
perplexedly *speculatively* 294.17
perplexing *mysterious* 182.10,

astonishing 294.10, *difficult* 364.8, *problematic* 824.11, *confused* 841.11
perplexingly *astonishingly* 294.19
perplexing question *unintelligible thing* 364.3
perplexity *incredulity* 88.3, *unintelligibility* 364.1, *problem* 824.4, *confusion* 841.4
per procurationem or **per pro.** *alternatively* 613.36, *under commission* 833.11
perquisite *superfluity* 99.4, *claim* 429.3, *reward for service* 453.5, *profit* 467.6, *reward* 472.4, *something received* 473.2, *absence of charge* 497.6, *extra* 748.6
perron Architectural Elements 134, *stairway* 713.9
perse *blue* 261.5
per se *in essence* 723.13, *alone* 788.20
persecute *oppose* 63.11, *harm* 306.13, *discriminate against* 337.14, *pursue* 385.11, *meddle* 414.23, *suppress* 424.9, *wrong* 430.19, *be evil* 446.10, *punish* 454.22, *torture* 454.29, *counteract* 510.7
persecuted *judged* 337.10, *suppressed* 424.6
persecuted, the *victim of discrimination* 337.8
persecuting *intolerant* 63.7, *malign* 306.11
persecution *hostility* 63.1, *type of complex* 108.22, *malignity* 306.5, *pursuit* 385.1, *ill-use* 395.2, *suppression* 424.2, *punishment* 454.1, *obstruction* 510.3
persecution mania *delusion* 110.2
persecution to the death *capital punishment* 454.12
persecutor *bigot* 337.7, *strict person* 424.4, *punisher* 454.16
persecutory-type delusional disorder *psychosis* 108.10
Persephone Deities 82
Perseus Constellations 7
perseverance 377.1; *steadfastness* 284.3, *tenacity* 376.4, 755.2, *determination* 379.2, *pursuit* 385.1, *assiduity* 414.8, *permanence* 667.1, *continuance* 669.3, *protraction* 669.4
perseverate *persevere* 377.10
persevere 377.10; *work* 122.8, *exert oneself* 122.11, *take courage* 284.15, *be obstinate* 379.10, *pursue* 385.11, *try* 414.21, *last* 642.6, *be permanent* 667.4, *protract* 669.9, *show determination* 674.8, *be tenacious* 755.9, *overcome obstacles* 845.14
persevering 377.6; *working* 122.6, *steadfast* 284.11, *tenacious* 376.9, 755.6, *determined* 379.7, *pursuit* 385.1, *industrious* 414.16, *permanent* 667.2
perseveringly 377.16; *permanently* 667.6
Persian Breeds of Cats 35, *historic* 653.13
Persian architecture Architectural Styles 134
Persian Gulf War Major Wars 76
Persian rug or **carpet** *floor covering* 613.13
Persian wheel *extractor* 711.9
persist *live* 28.17, *take courage* 284.15, *insist* 376.14, *persevere* 377.10, *be obstinate* 379.10, *pursue* 385.11, *try* 414.21, *be permanent* 667.4, *protract* 669.9,

show determination 674.8, *continue to be* 717.20
persistence *tenacity* 376.4, 755.2, *perseverance* 377.1, *determination* 379.2, *pursuit* 385.1, *retention* 471.1, *frequency* 661.1, *permanence* 667.1, *protraction* 669.4, *continuing existence* 717.7
persistent *rainy* 9.50, *drumming* 235.6, *resonant* 236.6, *tenacious* 376.9, 755.6, *persevering* 377.6, *determined* 379.7, *frequent* 661.4, *permanent* 667.2, *protracted* 669.7, *lasting* 717.13
persistently 376.17; *repeatedly* 235.15, *perseveringly* 377.16, *frequently* 661.7, *permanently* 667.6, *continually* 669.10, *tenaciously* 755.12
persistent rain *rain* 9.27
persistent vegetative state or **syndrome** *mere existence* 717.10
persist in *protract* 669.9
persisting *resonant* 236.6, *pursuit* 385.1, *lasting* 717.13
persnicketiness [Inf] *fastidiousness* 325.4
persnickety [Inf] *fastidious* 325.9, *detailed* 726.9, *troublesome* 824.13
person 18.8; *living being* 28.3, *role* 136.23, *one* 788.1
persona *psyche* 108.25, *show* 621.7, *one* 788.1
personable *appealing* 529.10
personableness *appeal* 529.4
personage *important person* 18.11, 799.5, *role* 136.23
personal *of language* 5.35, *human* 18.15, *internal* 525.11, *secret* 611.13, *novel* 737.5, *characteristic* 779.12
personal adviser *adviser* 176.5
personal aims *selfishness* 444.1
personal alarm *self-defense* 419.5
personal assistant *clerical worker* 123.5
personal attack 418.8
personal attendance *attendance* 575.3
personal attendant 69.5
personal bearing *conduct* 399.1
personal belongings *transferred thing* 685.6
personal benefit *gain* 467.1
personal borrower *debtor* 488.6
personal call *telephone call* 169.11
personal code or **standards** *code* 780.3
personal computer (PC) *computer* 15.1
personal conflict 63.2
personal correspondence *correspondence* 169.2
personal desires *selfishness* 444.1
personal digital assistant (PDA) *computer* 15.1
personal effects *visible effect* 676.2
personal error *measurement* 10.67
personal estate 470.6
personal feeling *interpretation* 365.1
personal file *record* 185.1
personal finance 457.5
personal foul *playing terms* 148.4, *penalty* 155.13
personal freedom *free will* 372.4
personal history *record* 185.1
personal honor *virtue* 447.1
personal identification 184.4
personal identification number or **PIN** *personal identification* 184.4, *till* 484.21

personal identity *philosophical problem* 4.8
personal influence 512.3
personal initiative *freedom* 829.1
personalism Philosophical Schools of Thought 4
personalist Philosophical Schools of Thought 4
personality *psyche* 108.25, *identity* 184.2, *personal influence* 512.3, *focus* 612.3, *important person* 799.5
personality adjustment test Psychological Tests 108
personality disorder 108.7
personality inventory Psychological Tests 108
personality research form Psychological Tests 108
personality tendency *personality type* 108.6
personality test Psychological Tests 108
personality type 108.6
personality-type disorder *psychiatric disease* 114.21
personalize *characterize* 779.15
personalized *customized* 779.14
personal language *nonstandard language* 5.7
personal liberty *freedom* 829.1
personal loan *loan* 475.2, 476.5, 488.3
personally *humanly* 18.18, *subjectively* 525.14, *in person* 575.18, *secretly* 611.22, *originally* 737.8
personal motive *motive* 628.6
personal note *inscription* 185.4
personal organizer *computer* 15.1
personal property *possession of property* 469.3, *possessions* 470.5
personal question *difficult question* 333.4
personal reasons *calling* 178.6
personal recognizance *pretrial proceedings* 54.13
personal reward *reward* 453.1
personals *news story* 171.3
personal section *newspaper* 175.2
personal sector *economy* 56.3
personal servant *personal attendant* 69.5
personal style *style* 537.1, *mode of expression* 537.3
personal transportation *transportation* 686.1
personalty *legal property terms* 470.2
personal violence *malignity* 306.5
personate *represent* 187.10
personation *acting* 136.22
person dealing with the dead 29.8
personhood *singularity* 788.4
personification *literary device* 139.12, *representation* 187.1, *quintessence* 723.3, *manifestation* 843.2
personifications and symbols 29.4
personified *identifiable* 843.10
personify *act* 136.34, *represent* 187.10, *be material* 524.8, *embody* 723.12
person in adversity 848.9
person in authority 52.7; *official* 68.6
person in charge *manager* 126.7
person included *thing included* 763.2
person in command 425.5
person in holy orders *member of the clergy* 84.5

person in office *official* 68.6
person left *person remaining* 750.6
personnel 123.16; *force* 59.10, *naval commands* 77.19, *resources* 102.4, *personnel management* 126.4
personnel management 126.4
personnel manager *employer* 57.3
personnel office *employer* 57.3
personnel staff *military staff* 58.5
person of active habits *busy person* 414.10
person of antiquity *person of the past* 651.7
person of goodwill *good person* 445.6
person of many parts *skilled person* 127.7
person of note *important person* 18.11
person of repute 370.2; *prosperous person* 847.4
person of strength 516.8
person of taste *refined person* 534.4
person of the cloth *member of the clergy* 84.5
person of the past 651.7
person on the lam [Inf] *the hunted* 385.7
person questioned 333.10
person remaining 750.6
persons *humankind* 18.1
persons of the drama *cast* 136.26
person-to-person call *telephone call* 169.11
person-to-person interaction *social activity* 414.2
person transferring property 470.8
person who brings home the bacon *breadwinner* 123.2
person who joins 752.9
person who undertakes 391.3
perspective *religion* 81.1, *composition* 132.17, *architecture* 134.1, *treatment* 143.6, *viewpoint* 242.12, *distance* 585.1, *convergent view* 702.3
perspective projection *transformation* 6.46
perspicacious *wise* 352.4, *foreseeing* 357.5, *mentally sharp* 549.14, *profound* 598.15
perspicaciously *wisely* 352.8, *sharply* 549.19, *profoundly* 598.27
perspicaciousness *mental sharpness* 549.9
perspicacity *visualization* 242.6, *wisdom* 352.1, *foresight* 357.1, *mental sharpness* 549.9, *profundity* 598.5
perspicuity *clarity* 196.1, 363.2
perspicuous *clear* 196.2, *demonstrable* 331.12, *meaningful* 361.6, *simple* 363.6
perspicuously *clearly* 196.4
perspicuousness *clarity* 196.1
perspiration *body fluid* 19.16, 555.3, *secretion* 24.1, *sweat* 25.8, *heat* 217.1, *exudate* 557.4, *outflow* 707.4
perspire *secrete* 24.7, *sweat* 25.24, *feel hot* 217.19, *seep* 559.16, *leak* 707.16
perspiring *fluid* 19.25, *sweat* 25.8, *sweaty* 25.17, *seeping* 559.12
persuadability 178.8; *acquiescence* 373.3
persuadable 178.14; *acquiescent* 373.9, *convertible* 670.9
persuade 178.15, 670.14; *make someone believe* 87.11, *advise* 176.9, *comfort* 273.9, *plead*

329.14, *propound* 359.9, *be irresistible* 428.9, *offer* 504.11, *petition* 505.11, *influence* 508.11, 512.11, *attract* 700.11
persuaded *persuadable* 178.14, *motivated* 508.8, *influenced* 670.10, *convinced* 840.8
persuaded against *dissuaded* 179.5
persuade oneself *suppose* 359.8
persuader 178.9; *publicizer* 173.11, *motivator* 508.6
persuasibility *persuadability* 178.8
persuasible *persuadable* 178.14
persuasion 178.1; *religion* 81.1, *belief* 87.1, *belief system* 87.3, *communication* 176.3, *request* 505.1, *inducement* 508.2, *influence* 512.1, *authority* 514.5, *religious conversion* 670.4, *type* 777.4
persuasive 178.12; *believable* 87.7, *advisory* 176.7, *compelling* 428.6, *offered* 504.8, *motivational* 508.7, *influential* 512.8, *strong* 516.9, *plausible* 838.7
persuasively 178.21, 504.18; *believably* 87.13, *advisorily* 176.12, *compellingly* 428.12, *influentially* 508.13, 512.14, *acutely* 516.18
persuasiveness *persuasion* 178.1, *inducement* 508.2, *potency* 516.6
pert *rude* 400.9, *cocky* 402.11, *defiant* 416.5, *disrespectful* 436.9
pertain *be the answer* 334.23, *relate to* 727.9
pertaining *included* 763.4
pertaining to life 28.14
pertain to *be included* 763.6
pertinacious *persevering* 377.6, *obstinate* 379.5, *tenacious* 755.6
pertinaciously *tenaciously* 755.12
pertinaciousness *perseverance* 377.1, *obstinacy* 379.1
pertinacity *perseverance* 377.1, *obstinacy* 379.1, *tenacity* 755.2
pertinence *suitability* 462.4, *relatedness* 727.1
pertinent *suitable* 462.9, *related* 727.6, *included* 763.4
pertinently *suitably* 462.17, *relevantly* 727.12, *inclusively* 763.8
pertly *rudely* 400.19, *cockily* 402.19, *defiantly* 416.9
pertness *rudeness* 400.2, *cockiness* 402.3, *defiance* 416.1
perturb *displace* 574.15, *agitate* 684.22, *discompose* 766.18, *disturb* 768.10, *cause difficulties* 824.22
perturbation *fearfulness* 283.2, *displacement* 574.1, *agitation* 684.1, *disturbance* 768.1
perturbed *fearful* 283.10, *agitated* 684.15, *confused* 766.12, *disturbed* 768.6, *troubled* 824.15
perturbedness *agitation* 684.1
perturbing *displaced* 574.8
pertussis *infection* 114.7, *respiratory disease* 114.12
Peru Countries 566
peruke *body covering* 613.3
perusal *learning* 48.7, *observation* 242.5
peruse *learn* 48.23, *inspect* 242.22
Peruvian marching powder [Inf] *stimulants* 121.18
Peruvian Stepping Horse *or* Peruvian Paso Horse and Pony Breeds 159
pervade *be an influence* 512.13, *be present* 575.13, *mix together* 751.14, *fill* 761.11
pervading *omnipresent* 575.10

pervasion *omnipresence* 575.4, *mixture* 751.1
pervasive *dominant* 512.10, *omnipresent* 575.10, *broad* 592.5, *intense* 598.16, *complicated* 751.10, *universal* 778.10
pervasively *influentially* 512.14, *intensely* 598.28, *mixedly* 751.16
pervasiveness *omnipresence* 575.4, *breadth* 592.1, *deepness* 598.6, *widespreadness* 778.3
perverse *errant* 351.12, *obstinate* 379.5, *refractory* 379.6, *depraved* 448.10, *devious* 607.9, *changed* 665.10, *troublesome* 824.13, *uncooperative* 828.14
perversely 824.27; *deviously* 607.16, *distortedly* 627.14, *disturbingly* 768.13, *opposingly* 828.22
perverseness *obstinacy* 379.1, *deviousness* 607.4, *contrariness* 828.5
perversion *sexual perversion* 20.12, *misrepresentation* 188.1, 193.4, 366.2, *errancy* 351.7, *misuse* 395.1, *abnormality* 430.4, *depravity* 448.2, *distortion of truth* 627.4, *change for the worse* 665.5, *evolution* 670.3, *moral deterioration* 808.3
perversity *obstinacy* 379.1, *deviousness* 607.4, *contrariness* 828.5
perversive *misrepresentative* 193.14
pervert 808.22; *sexual perversion* 20.12, *misrepresent* 188.6, 193.17, 366.5, *misuse* 395.6, *sexually immoral person* 432.8, *demoralize* 432.15, *be evil* 446.10, *miscreant* 448.6, *deprave* 448.14, *distorter* 627.5, *distort the truth* 627.12, *change for the worse* 665.18, *transform* 670.13, *deviant* 698.7, *delude* 720.16
perverted 432.12; *misrepresented* 188.4, 627.8, *misrepresentative* 193.14, *errant* 351.12, *misused* 395.3, *abnormal* 430.13, *depraved* 448.10, *changed* 665.10
pervertedly *abusively* 395.8
perverter *one who misrepresents* 193.9
perverting *depraved* 448.10
pervertly *unvirtuously* 448.16
Pesach Jewish Holy Days and Seasons 85
pesante Musical Terms and Expression Marks 140
peseta *national coins* 484.11
peso *national coins* 484.11
pessimism Philosophical Schools of Thought 4, *negativism* 190.7, *lack of hope* 282.2, *underestimation* 344.1, *expectation* 356.1, *defeatism* 413.7
pessimist Philosophical Schools of Thought 4, *negator* 190.8, *hopeless person* 282.5, *underestimator* 344.2, *inactive person* 413.8
pessimistic *negative* 190.15, *without hope* 282.7, *underestimating* 344.3, *expecting* 356.4
pessimistically 190.26, 344.6; *unhopefully* 282.14, *expectantly* 356.10
pest 40.5; *plague* 114.6, *affliction* 117.1, *unpleasant person* 272.5, *boring person* 296.4
pest control 16.13
pester *bore* 296.8, *irritate* 302.16, *be inconsiderate* 318.13, *meddle* 414.23, *criticize* 438.19, *petition*

505.11, *discompose* 766.18, *disturb* 768.10, *annoy* 804.10, *be difficult* 824.16

pestering *inconsiderate* 318.9, *criticism* 438.4, *critical* 438.13, *petition* 505.2

pest exterminator *animal killer* 30.14

pesticidal *herbicidal* 17.16

pesticide *pest control* 16.13, *pest killer* 17.9, *killing agent* 30.15, *agent of destruction* 523.7

pestiferous *contagious* 114.26

pestilence *plague* 114.6, *affliction* 117.1, *evil thing* 446.2, *agent of destruction* 523.7

pestilent *contagious* 114.26, *toxic* 114.28, *afflicting* 117.11, *polluting* 117.15

pestilential *toxic* 114.28

pestilentially *unhygienically* 114.32

pest killer 17.9

pestle *pulverizer* 553.11, *pulverize* 553.26

pestled *pulverized* 553.20

pesto *sauce* 90.17

pests and diseases 17.12

pet *domestic animal* 34.3, *idol* 83.5, *give pleasure* 95.7, *comfort* 214.14, *term of endearment* 299.7, *communicate love* 299.25, *preferential* 382.10, *massage* 554.16

pet [Inf] *type of touch* 216.3, *touch* 216.9

peta Decimal Prefixes 589

petal *leaf* 41.6, *flower part* 42.3

pet aversion *hated thing* 300.5

pet cemetery *burial place* 31.7

petechia *bleeding* 25.10

peterman [Inf] *thief* 479.8

peter out *disappear* 265.5, *stop* 668.10, *cease to exist* 718.13, *decrease* 747.7, *come to an end* 773.23

Peter Pan collar *neckwear* 100.29

Peter's pence or **Peter pence** *offering* 472.6

pet food *animal food* 90.2

pet hate *hated thing* 300.5

pethidine *anesthetic* 213.3

pétillant [Fr] *insubstantial* 539.5

petiole *stem* 41.5, *leaf* 41.6

petit déjeuner [Fr] *meal* 92.8

petit four *cake* 90.36

petite *little* 580.7

petiteness *littleness* 580.1

petit four *cake* 90.36

petition 505.2, 505.11; *litigate* 54.27, *act of worship* 83.2, *worship* 83.15, *prayer* 85.10, *pray* 85.20, *appeal to* 209.9, *ask permission* 502.9

petitionary *prayerful* 85.17

petitionary prayer *prayer* 85.10

petitioned *requesting* 505.7

petitioner *litigant* 54.4, *worshiper* 83.6, *record keeper* 185.8, *accuser* 442.3, *requester* 505.5

petit jury *jury* 54.11, 341.6

petit mal *neurological disease* 114.20

pet name *name* 202.8

pet names *communication of love* 299.6

pet owner *animal welfarist* 34.9

pet peeve *hated thing* 300.5

Petrarch Famous Lovers 299

Petrarchan Poem or Verse Forms 139, *poetic* 139.19

petrel *water bird* 36.9

petrifaction *concentration* 540.2, *hardening* 542.2

petrifactive *hard* 542.5

---

petrification *hardening* 542.2

petrification (replacement) *fossil* 8.49

petrified *fossilized* 8.63, *frightened* 283.9, *wondering* 294.7, *hardened* 542.7, *motionless* 678.4

petrified forest *thing of the past* 651.8

petrified wood *antiquity* 653.4

petrify *lithify* 8.66, *frighten* 283.17, *be wondrous* 294.14, *be dense* 540.8, *solidify* 542.10

petrifying *frightening* 283.12, *astonishing* 294.10, *hard* 542.5

petrochemicals *industrial chemistry* 11.21

petrogenesis 8.31

petrogenic *petrographic* 8.58

petroglyph *sculpture* 144.1

petrographic 8.58

petrographical *petrographic* 8.58

petrographically *geologically* 8.68

petrol [Brit] *oil* 106.7

petrolatum *balm* 115.11

petroleous *gas* 106.14

petroleum 562.5; *oil* 106.7

petroleum jelly *balm* 115.11

petroleum refining *chemical process industries* 14.26

petrological *geologic* 8.50, *petrographic* 8.58

petrologically *geologically* 8.68

petrologist *geologist* 8.4

petrology *geology* 8.1

petronel *historical handgun* 78.8

petticoat *underwear* 100.22

pettifog *quibble* 330.13

pettifogger *lawyer* 54.5, *sophist* 330.6, *disapprover* 438.7

pettifoggery *quibbling* 330.4, *criticism* 438.4, *cunning* 822.1

pettifogging *quibbling* 330.9, *critical* 438.13, *trivial* 800.14

pettiness *prejudice* 337.3, *unpleasantness* 501.2, *littleness* 580.1, *superficiality* 599.2, *triviality* 800.2

petting *communication of love* 299.6

petting [Inf] *touching* 216.2

pettishness *capriciousness* 381.2

petty *discriminatory* 337.11, *unpleasant* 501.5, *little* 580.7, *superficial* 599.4, *trivial* 800.14

petty bureaucracy *overactivity* 414.9

petty cash *cash* 484.2

petty-cashbook *account book* 493.3

petty crime *disreputable action* 371.3

petty criminal *criminal* 427.6

petty detail *trifle* 800.3

petty jury *jury* 341.6

petty larceny *theft* 479.2

Petty Officer First Class US Military Ranks 58

Petty Officer Second Class US Military Ranks 58

Petty Officer Third Class US Military Ranks 58

petty officialdom *officialdom* 49.20, *overactivity* 414.9

petty sin *trifling fault* 800.5

petty theft *theft* 479.2

petty thief *thief* 479.8

petty tyrant *absolute ruler* 68.7, *strict person* 424.4

petulance *irascibility* 303.1

petulant *irascible* 303.8, *argumentative* 329.7

petulantly *irascibly* 303.17, *argumentatively* 329.15

petunia Flowers 42

---

petuntze or **petuntse** *material* 129.2

pew *church interior* 83.9, *type of chair* 101.4, *church architecture* 134.11, *compartment* 578.2

pewter *gray thing* 255.3, *mixed thing* 797.5

peyote *hallucinogens* 121.20

pfennig *national coins* 484.11

PG *film-rating system* 137.4

PG-13 *film-rating system* 137.4

PGA Championship *golfing associations and tournaments* 156.6

pH *acid* 11.10, *base* 11.11

Phaeophyta *algae* 47.11

phaeophyte *algae* 47.11

phage *microorganism* 13.11

phagocyte *blood* 555.4

phagophobia Phobias 283

phalacrophobia Phobias 283

phalanges Human Bones 19

phalangid *arachnid* 40.4

phalanx Human Bones 19

phallic *reproductive* 21.11

phallicism *idolatry* 83.4

phallicist *idolater* 83.7

phallic symbol *symbol* 108.28

phallus *organs of reproduction* 21.9

phaneritic *types of igneous texture* 8.33

phanerogam *seed plant* 41.3

Phanerogamia *seed plant* 41.3

phanerogamic *taxonomic* 41.16

phantasm *ghost* 86.11, *illusion* 720.2

phantasmagoria *illusion* 720.2, *miscellany* 751.3

phantasmagorical *illusory* 720.9, *complicated* 751.10

phantasmagorically *mixedly* 751.16

phantasmal *spiritual* 86.20, *unreal* 720.8

phantasmic *spiritual* 86.20

phantom *ghost* 86.11, *spiritual* 86.20, *spectacle* 264.6, *frightener* 283.7, *fantasy* 360.5, *spiritual world* 525.3, *parapsychological* 525.9, *omnipresence* 575.4, *illusion* 720.2

Pharaoh *sovereign* 68.2

pharaoh hound Breeds of Dogs 35

pharisaic *zealous* 81.22, *ungenuine* 192.13, *hypocritical* 330.10

pharisaical *hypocritical* 330.10

pharisaically *untruthfully* 192.27, *hypocritically* 330.15

pharisaism *hypocrisy* 330.5

Pharisee *Jew* 81.11

pharisee *hypocrite* 192.9

pharmaceutical *medicine* 115.2

pharmaceutical chemistry Branches of Chemistry 11

pharmaceutical industries *chemical process industries* 14.26

pharmaceutically *medicinally* 115.21

pharmaceuticals *industrial chemistry* 11.21

pharmacist *druggist* 115.10

pharmacognosy *medicine* 115.2

pharmacologist *biochemist* 12.2, *druggist* 115.10

pharmacology *biochemistry* 12.1, *medical science* 107.5

pharmacophobia Phobias 283

pharmacopoeia *medicine* 115.2

pharmacy *druggist* 115.10

pharos *safety light* 246.7, *sea marker* 690.7

Pharos at Alexandria Seven Wonders of the Ancient World 294

---

pharyngitis *respiratory disease* 114.12

pharynx *internal organ* 19.13, *speech organ* 205.4

phase 11.13; *moon* 7.18, *frequency* 10.6, *electric current* 10.39, *sound quality* 230.4, *period of activity* 641.4, *state* 725.1, *part* 760.1

phaseal *frequent* 663.6

phase change *temperature* 10.29, *phase* 11.13

phase-contrast microscopy *cell biology* 13.14

phased *synchronized* 649.5, *frequent* 663.6

phase diagram *phase* 11.13

phase modulation (PM) *radio transmission* 172.3

phase velocity *wave property* 10.12

phasic *frequent* 663.6

phasing *frequency* 663.2

phasmid *insectile* 40.11

phasmophobia Phobias 283

pheasant *table bird* 36.10, *meat* 90.22, *game* 160.6

pheasants Collective Names 59

phellem *timber* 43.3

phengophobia Phobias 283

phenol *cleaning agent* 111.9

phenolate *clean* 111.17

phenolphthalein *gravimetric analysis* 11.18

phenomenal *appearing* 264.9, *wondrous* 294.9, *real* 717.14

phenomenalism Philosophical Schools of Thought 4

phenomenalist Philosophical Schools of Thought 4

phenomenally *wondrously* 294.18

phenomenologically *philosophically* 4.23

phenomenological psychology Psychological Theories, Schools 108

phenomenological theology Theologies 81

phenomenologist Philosophical Schools of Thought 4

phenomenology Branches of Philosophy 4, Philosophical Schools of Thought 4

phenomenon *visibility* 264.4, *marvel* 294.3, *wonderful person* 294.6, *thing* 717.3

phenotype *molecular biology* 13.18, *genetics* 13.19

phenylalanine Amino Acids 12

phenylcyclidine (PCP) *tranquilizers* 121.21

pheromonal *odorous* 224.5

pheromone *hormone* 12.16, *secreted substance* 24.2, *scent* 224.3

phial *bottle* 578.14

Philadelphia *major US cities* 567.5

Philadelphia lawyer *lawyer* 54.5

philander *court* 299.26, *fornicate* 432.14

philanderer *libertine* 32.7, *lover* 299.11, *sexually immoral person* 432.8

philanthropic 307.6; *friendly* 62.5, *charitable* 305.9, *virtuous* 447.5, *giving* 472.9, *magnanimous* 498.7, *voluntary* 504.9, *benevolent* 825.21

philanthropical *philanthropic* 307.6

philanthropically 307.9; *charitably* 305.15, *voluntarily* 504.19

philanthropist 307.5; *independent worker* 123.3, *benevolent person*

305.6, *lenient person* 423.2, *good person* 445.6, *giver* 472.7, *generous person* 498.5, *volunteer* 504.7, *benefactor* 825.15
philanthropize 307.8; *give to charity* 472.16
philanthropy 307.1; *friendship* 62.1, *charity* 305.3, *virtue* 447.1, *giving* 472.1, *magnanimity* 498.2
philately Hobbies and Pastimes 167
philemaphobia *or* **philematophobia** Phobias 283
philharmonic *musical* 140.25
philharmonic orchestra *instrumental group* 141.3
philibeg *skirt* 100.12
philippic *address* 209.1
Philippines Countries 566, Islands 572
Philippine Sea Oceans and Seas 571
Philistine *conformist* 781.6
philistine *insensitive person* 268.3, *ignorant person* 349.4, *ignorant* 349.5
philistinism *insensitivity* 268.1
philological *linguistic* 361.9
philologically *linguistically* 5.44
philologist *linguist* 5.3
philology Linguistic Studies 5, *language* 5.4
philophobia Phobias 283
philosopher 4.9; *educational leader* 68.11, *intellectual* 315.7, *reasoner* 319.5, *questioner* 333.9, *wise person* 352.3, *theorist* 359.4, *nonmaterialist* 525.7
philosophers' stone *remedy* 115.1, *objective* 374.5, *wealth* 485.1
philosophes Western Literary Groups 139
philosophical 4.12; *rational* 4.15, *thoughtful* 317.5, *reasoning* 317.6, *theoretical* 327.10, *skeptical* 333.14
philosophical analysis Philosophical Schools of Thought 4, Linguistic Studies 5
philosophical argument 4.5
philosophical attitude 4.3
philosophical idealism *idealism* 525.5
philosophical inquiry *questioning* 333.2
philosophical investigation 4.4
philosophically 4.23; *rationally* 4.25, *stoically* 4.26, *thoughtfully* 317.13, *theoretically* 327.19, *questioningly* 333.21
philosophicalness *philosophical attitude* 4.3
philosophical problem 4.8
philosophical speculation *philosophy* 4.1
philosophical system 4.2
philosophical term 4.7
philosophical theology Theologies 81
philosophical theory *philosophy* 4.1
philosophism *sophistry* 330.1
philosophist *sophist* 330.6
philosophize 4.19; *rationalize* 4.20, *theologize* 81.28, *think* 317.9, *premise* 319.14
philosophobia Phobias 283
philosophy 4.1; *belief system* 87.3, Phobias 283, *ideology* 327.5
philosophy of being 717.2
philosophy of history *history* 3.1, Branches of Philosophy 4
philosophy of language Branches of Philosophy 4

philosophy of law Branches of Philosophy 4
philosophy of life *religion* 81.1
philosophy of mind Branches of Philosophy 4
philosophy of psychology Branches of Philosophy 4
philosophy of religion Branches of Philosophy 4
philosophy of science Branches of Philosophy 4
philosophy of signs Branches of Philosophy 4
philter *spell* 86.8
phiz [Inf] *face* 621.6
phlebitis *cardiovascular disease* 114.13
phlebotomize *treat* 115.17
phlebotomy *disgorgement* 709.6, *drawing off* 711.4
Phlegethon *evil place* 446.6
phlegm *body fluid* 19.16, 555.3, *secreted substance* 24.2, *saliva* 25.9, *indifference* 289.1, *idleness* 415.3, *mucus* 561.6, *resignedness* 835.2
phlegmatic *personality type* 108.6, *apathetic* 322.4, *inactive* 413.9, *not participating* 415.11, *sedentary* 678.5, *unhurried* 693.8, *resigned* 835.4
phlegmatic *or* **phlegmatical** *indifferent* 289.7
phlegmatical *or* **phlegmatic** *wonderless* 295.3
phlegmatically *indifferently* 289.17, *without wonder* 295.8, *apathetically* 322.7, *motionlessly* 678.9, *resignedly* 835.7
phlegmaticalness *or* **phlegmaticness** *indifference* 289.1, *lack of wonder* 295.1
phlegmy *rheumy* 555.16
phloem *stem* 41.5, *timber* 43.3
phlox Flowers 42
Phnom Penh Countries 566
phobia *delusion* 110.2, *fear* 283.1, *antipathy* 291.2, *hated thing* 300.5
phobic *frightened* 283.9, *antipathetic* 291.7, *hater* 300.6
phobophobia Phobias 283
Phobos Planets and Their Satellites 7
Phoebe Planets and Their Satellites 7
Phoenix Constellations 7, Breeds of Fowl 16, American States 564
phoenix Legendary Creatures 360
phoenixlike *repaired* 809.6
pholidote *insect-eating mammal* 35.7, *insectivorous* 35.24
phon *sound* 230.1, Scientific and Technical Units 589
phonation *articulation* 205.9
phone *spoken letter* 5.15, *telephone* 169.10, 169.20
phone book *dial* 169.12, *book of lists* 785.3
phone booth *telephone* 169.10
phone call *telephone call* 169.11
phonecard *credit card* 487.2
phone-in *program* 172.10
phonemail *telephone call* 169.11
phoneme *language element* 5.13, *spoken letter* 5.15
phonemics Linguistic Studies 5, *phonetics* 205.3
phoner *telephone personnel* 169.14
phone sex *sex act* 20.10
phonetic 205.14
phonetically *linguistically* 5.44, *orally* 205.21
phonetic alphabet *alphabet* 5.16
phonetician *linguist* 5.3
phonetics 205.3, Linguistic

Studies 5, *language* 5.4, *spoken language* 205.2
phonetic spelling *spelling* 5.26
phonetic symbol *written letter* 5.14
phoney *unauthenticity* 722.4, *unauthentic* 722.9, *simulated* 733.11, *copy* 736.2, *imitator* 736.6, *imitation* 736.8
phoneyness *unauthenticity* 722.4
phonic *phonetic* 205.14
phonily *unauthentically* 722.17, *imitatively* 733.20
phoniness *unauthenticity* 722.4
phonogram *spoken letter* 5.15
phonogramic *written* 5.36
phonograph *sound reproduction* 230.6
phonographic *written* 5.36
phonograph record *recording* 185.6
phonography Linguistic Studies 5, *phonetics* 205.3
phonology Linguistic Studies 5, *phonetics* 205.3
phonometer Fields of Measurement 589
phonometry Fields of Measurement 589
phonon *quantum* 10.63
phonophobia Phobias 283
phony *artificial* 720.12, *unauthenticity* 722.4, *unauthentic* 722.9, *simulated* 733.11, *copy* 736.2, *imitator* 736.6, *imitation* 736.8
phony *or* **phoney** *ungenuine* 192.13, *hoaxer* 193.11
phosphagen *bioenergetics* 12.23
phosphate *fertilizer* 16.9, 22.6, *pollution* 117.8
phosphate bond *bioenergetics* 12.23
phosphatide *fat* 12.7
phosphatidycholine *fat* 12.7
phosphatidylethanolamine *fat* 12.7
phosphoglyceride *fat* 12.7
phospholipid *fat* 12.7
phosphoprotein *protein* 12.9
phosphoresce *reflect* 10.76, *light up* 246.20
phosphorescence *light* 10.17, 246.1
phosphorescent *lucent* 246.13
phosphorus Chemical Elements and Common Allotropes 11, *essential element* 12.15
phosphorylation *bioenergetics* 12.23
phot Scientific and Technical Units 589
photo *photograph* 132.3
photoalgiaphobia Phobias 283
photoaugiaphobia Phobias 283
photo biography *photograph* 132.3
photo booth *camera* 132.10
photocall *public relations (PR)* 173.8
photocathode *electron emission* 14.42
photochemical *chemical* 11.24
photochemically *chemically* 11.42
photochemical reaction *chemical reaction* 11.8
photochemistry Branches of Chemistry 11
photochromic *chromolithographic* 251.14
photochromic glass *ceramics* 129.1
photocomposition *typesetting* 173.4

photoconduction *photoelectricity* 10.32
photoconductive *physical* 10.70
photoconductivity *photosensitivity* 10.23, *electromagnetic induction* 10.37
photocopied *reproduced* 21.10, *recorded* 185.12, *duplicate* 730.11, *double* 789.11
photocopier *recording instrument* 185.9, *copier* 736.5
photocopy *reproduction* 21.1, *reproduce* 21.13, *photoreproduction* 132.6, *recording* 185.6, *record* 185.13, *illustration* 187.2, *representation* 202.9, *copy* 730.5, 730.17, 736.10, *duplicate* 736.4, *twin* 789.5, *replica* 797.7
photocopying *photoreproduction* 132.6
photoelastic modeling *civil engineering* 14.17
photoelectric *physical* 10.70, *electric* 14.47
photoelectrically *electronically* 14.54
photoelectric cell *photoelectricity* 10.32, *power supplier* 514.14
photoelectric device *photoelectricity* 10.32
photoelectric effect *photosensitivity* 10.23, *electromagnetic induction* 10.37, *electron emission* 14.42
photoelectric emission *electron emission* 14.42
photoelectricity 10.32; *electricity* 10.31, *electrical power* 514.12
photoelectron *electron emission* 14.42
photoelectron spectroscopy (PES) *analysis* 11.17
photoemission 246.11; *photoelectricity* 10.32
photoemissive *physical* 10.70, *lucent* 246.13
photo finish *horse racing* 159.10, *contest* 422.4, *destination* 704.6, *stalemate* 740.3
photo-finish *simultaneous* 649.4
photoflo *darkroom equipment* 132.21
photoflood *lighting* 132.16
photoflood lamp *electric light* 246.6
photog [Inf] *photographer* 132.23
photogenic *photographic* 132.24, *representational* 187.8
photogenically *photographically* 132.29
photogrammetry *civil engineering* 14.17, *photoreproduction* 132.6, *map* 187.5, Fields of Measurement 589
photograph 132.3, 132.26; *picture* 133.5, *design* 133.9, *film* 137.19, *means of identification* 184.3, *identify* 184.11, *record* 185.1, 185.13, *illustration* 187.2, *represent* 187.10, *view* 242.8, *impression* 264.7, *duplicate* 736.4, *copy* 736.10
photograph album *photograph* 132.3, *reminder* 354.4
photographed *broadcast* 172.12, *identified* 184.9
photographer 132.23; *visual artist* 133.6, *record keeper* 185.8
photographic 132.24; *pictorial* 133.8, *representational* 187.8, *descriptive* 202.11, *representing* 202.14, *correct* 350.4
photographically 132.29; *pictorially* 133.11

photographic density *exposure* 132.15

photographic memory *memory* 354.1

photographic paper *printing* 132.20

photographic plate *film* 132.8

photographic reproduction *printing* 173.3

photographic specialties 132.2

photography 132.1; *photometry* 10.24, *craft* 133.2, Hobbies and Pastimes 167

photogravure *photoreproduction* 132.6, *picture* 133.5

photointaglio *photoreproduction* 132.6

photojournalism *photographic specialties* 132.2, *print journalism* 175.4

photojournalist *photographer* 132.23, *print journalist* 175.5

photolithography *photometry* 10.24, *photoreproduction* 132.6

photolysis *deconstruction* 758.2

photolytically *to pieces* 758.8

photometer *photoelectricity* 10.32, Fields of Measurement 589

photometric *astronomical* 7.33

photometric comparisons between parts of spectra Fields of Measurement 589

photometry 10.24; *microscopy* 10.68, Fields of Measurement 589

photomontage *portrait* 132.5, *picture* 133.5

photomultiplier *electron emission* 14.42

photomural *portrait* 132.5

photon *quantum* 10.63, *light* 246.1

photonovel *photograph* 132.3

photo-offset *printing* 173.3

photo opportunity *news event* 171.2, *public relations (PR)* 173.8

photoperiodism *recurrent period* 641.5

photophobia Phobias 283

photophosphorylation *photosynthesis* 12.22

photoprint *picture* 133.5

photorealism Western Art Styles 133

photorefractive effect *photosensitivity* 10.23

photoreproduction 132.6; *reproduction* 21.1

photorespiration *respiration* 12.24

photosensitive *ceramic* 129.9, *photographic* 132.24

photosensitive glass *industrial ceramics* 129.6

photosensitive material *photosensitivity* 10.23

photosensitivity 10.23; *exposure* 132.15

photosensor *photoelectricity* 10.32

photosphere *sun* 7.15

photostat *reproduction* 21.1, *reproduce* 21.13, *photoreproduction* 132.6, *duplicate* 736.4, *copy* 736.10

photosynthesis 12.22; *physiology* 13.13

photosynthesize *metabolize* 12.26, *vegetate* 41.21

photosynthetic *biochemical* 12.25, *physiological* 13.29, *of plants* 41.14

photosynthetically *biochemically* 12.27, *herbaceously* 41.24

photosynthetic pigment *pigment* 12.18

phototherapy *therapy* 115.12

phototopography *photographic specialties* 132.2, *map* 187.5

photovoltaic cell *renewable energy* 106.9

photovoltaic effect *photosensitivity* 10.23, *electromagnetic induction* 10.37

phrasal *phrased* 5.39

phrase *language element* 5.13, *use language* 5.42, *interact* 10.73, *harmonic element* 140.14, *written music* 140.21, *utterance* 205.10, *style* 537.8, *passage* 692.1, *part of speech* 760.7

phrased 5.39; *harmonic* 140.27, *styled* 537.6

phrasemonger *stylist* 537.4

phraseogram *artificial language* 5.9

phraseograph *artificial language* 5.9

phraseographic *phrased* 5.39

phraseological *phrased* 5.39

phraseologically 5.47

phraseology *language* 5.4, *phrasing* 5.25, *mode of expression* 537.3

phrase-structure grammar *grammar* 5.28

phrasing 5.25; *phrased* 5.39, *harmonic element* 140.14, *mode of expression* 537.3

phratry *social organization* 2.5

phrenic *intellectual* 315.8

phrenological *occultist* 86.13

phrenology *occultism* 86.1, *divination* 358.2

phronemophobia Phobias 283

Phrygian mode *mode* 140.17

phthalocyanine blue *blue pigment* 261.2

phthalocyanine green *green pigment* 260.3

phthiriasis *uncleanness* 112.2

phthiriophobia Phobias 283

phthisic *physical* 1.14, *of disease* 114.25

phthisic build *physical type* 1.8

phthisiophobia Phobias 283

phthisis *respiratory disease* 114.12

phycobilin *pigment* 12.18

phycobiont *alga* 47.10, *lichen* 47.16

phycocyanin *plant body* 47.13

phycoerythrin *plant body* 47.13

phycological *algal* 47.20

phycologist *plant scientist* 41.11, *study of algae* 47.12

phycology *plant science* 41.10, *study of algae* 47.12

phycomycetes *fungi* 47.3

phycomycosis *fungal disease* 47.6

phylactery *sacred object* 83.11, *talisman* 86.9

phyle *social organization* 2.5

phyllo *pastry* 90.37

phylloclade *leaf* 41.6

phyllode *leaf* 41.6

phylogenetic *or phyletic evolutionary* 13.34

phylogeny *evolution* 13.23

phylum *part* 760.1, *taxonomic classification* 777.3

physic *medicine* 115.2, *medicate* 115.18, *cure* 809.15

physical 1.14, 1.70; *bodily* 19.18, *health care* 107.7, *material* 524.7

physical abuse *malignity* 306.5, *violence by person* 520.2

physical and mental examination *pretrial proceedings* 54.13

physical anthropology *anthropology* 1.1

physical attack *personal attack* 418.8

physical being *material world* 524.1

physical change *chemical change* 670.2

physical chemist *chemist* 11.2

physical chemistry Fields of Modern Physics 10, Branches of Chemistry 11

physical condition *material world* 524.1, *physical state* 725.6

physical constant *fundamental constant* 10.69

physical contact *touching* 216.2

physical cruelty *violence by person* 520.2

physical deterioration 808.4

physical development *bodily development* 19.17

physical education (PE) *subject* 48.3

physical element 524.5

physical examination *health care* 107.7

physical existence *material world* 524.1

physical fatigue *fatigue* 820.1

physical force *coercion* 428.2, *physical strength* 516.3

physical form *physical state* 725.6

physical geographical feature *landform* 8.9

physical geography *geology* 8.1

physical geology *geology* 8.1

physicalism Philosophical Schools of Thought 4

physicalist Philosophical Schools of Thought 4

physical law 10.4

physical love *sexual love* 299.3

physically 10.78; *materially* 524.9

physically abuse *harm* 306.13

physically abusive *malign* 306.11

physically demanding *fatiguing* 820.4, *difficult* 824.9

physically strong 516.10

physical nature *sexuality* 20.3

physical oceanographer *geophysicist* 8.5

physical oceanography *geophysics* 8.2

physical optics *classical physics* 10.2

physical organism *body* 19.1

physical pleasure 214.1

physical power *stalwartness* 547.3

physical presence *object* 524.6, *presence* 575.1

physical punishment *pain* 215.1

physical quantity *dimension* 589.11

physical roughness *brutality* 547.4

physical science *physics* 10.1, *materialization* 524.2

physical scientist *materialist* 524.3

physical self *body* 19.1

physical state 725.6

physical strength 516.3; *stalwartness* 547.3

physical therapist *paramedic* 107.24

physical therapy *treatment* 107.14, *therapy* 115.12

physical training (P.T.) *health improvement* 113.3

physical type 1.8; *external appearance* 264.5

physical violence *personal attack* 418.8

physical weakness *disability* 515.4

physical well-being *health* 113.1

physical world *real world* 719.2

physical wreck *physical deterioration* 808.4

physician *doctor* 107.19, *professional worker* 123.11

physicochemical *chemical* 11.24

physicotheological *theological* 81.24

physicotheology Theologies 81

physics 10.1

physiochemist *chemist* 11.2

physiocracy *feudalism* 49.5

physiocratic school *economics* 56.1

physiognomic *front* 621.9

physiognomy *external appearance* 264.5, *divination* 358.2, *face* 621.6, *nature* 624.5

physiographer *geologist* 8.4

physiography *geology* 8.1

physiological 13.29; *biological* 13.27

physiologically *biologically* 13.36

physiological psychology Psychological Theories, Schools 108

physiologist *life scientist* 13.26

physiology 13.13; *anatomy* 13.5

physiotherapy *therapy* 115.12

physique *physical type* 1.8, *body* 19.1, *form* 551.3, *nature* 624.5

physisorb *absorb* 11.40

physisorbed *absorbed* 11.34

physisorption *surface chemistry* 11.20

phytobiology *botany* 13.7

phytochemical *botanical* 41.20

phytochemist *plant scientist* 41.11

phytochemistry *botany* 13.7, *plant science* 41.10

phytochrome *pigment* 12.18

phytoecology *botany* 13.7, *ecology* 13.25, *plant science* 41.10

phytogenesis *plant science* 41.10

phytogenetically *botanically* 41.25

phytogeneticist *plant scientist* 41.11

phytogeographer *plant scientist* 41.11

phytogeographic(al) *botanical* 41.20

phytogeography *plant science* 41.10

phytographer *plant scientist* 41.11

phytographic(al) *botanical* 41.20

phytography *botany* 13.7, *plant science* 41.10

phytohormone *plant hormone* 12.17

phytol *terpene* 12.20

phytological *botanical* 41.20

phytologically *botanically* 41.25

phytologist *plant scientist* 41.11

phytology *botany* 13.7, *plant science* 41.10

phytopathological *botanical* 41.20

phytopathologist *plant scientist* 41.11

phytopathology *plant science* 41.10

phytophage *eater* 92.15

phytophagy *eating habit* 92.7

phytoplankton *alga* 47.10

phytosociological *botanical* 41.20

phytosociologically *botanically* 41.25

phytosociologist *plant scientist* 41.11

phytosociology *plant science* 41.10

phytotomy *plant science* 41.10

piacular *atoning* 313.5, *compensatory* 743.5
piacularly *atoningly* 313.10
piaculum *penitence* 313.3
Piaget *psychologist* 108.33
pia mater *body covering* 19.4
pianissimo *faint* 233.6, *faintly* 233.11
pianissimo or pp Musical Terms and Expression Marks 140
pianist *player* 141.2
piano *faint* 233.6, *faintly* 233.11
piano or p Musical Terms and Expression Marks 140
piano *or* **pianoforte** Musical Instruments 142
piano keys *part of keyboard instrument* 142.6
pianola Musical Instruments 142
piano player *player* 141.2
piano quintet Musical Forms 140
piaster *national coins* 484.11
Piau Breeds of Pigs 16
Piave Rivers 570
piazza [Ital] *urban area* 567.10
pibcorn Musical Instruments 142
pica General Units 589
picador *animal killer* 30.14
picaresque *narrative* 202.12
picaresque novel *novel* 139.3
picayune *little* 580.7, *trivial* 800.14
Piccadilly Circus London 567.8
piccolo Musical Instruments 142
pick *store* 105.17, *diagnostic instrument* 107.13, *sound* 141.15, *discriminate* 337.12, *selection* 382.1, *chosen thing* 382.8, *choose* 382.14, *excellence* 445.4, *sharp-pointed thing* 549.4, *opener* 583.2, *tap* 695.13, *extractor* 711.9, *subtract* 749.6, *chief thing* 799.3
pick, the *finalist* 422.16
pick a bone with *pick a fight* 463.10
pick a fight 463.10
pick and choose *discriminate* 337.12, *select* 382.12
pick a pocket *subtract* 749.6
pick a quarrel *pick a fight* 463.10
pick at *or* **toy with one's food** *taste* 92.24
pickax *garden tool* 103.4, *sharp-pointed thing* 549.4, *opener* 583.2, *extractor* 711.9
pick clean *clean* 111.17
picked *selected* 382.11
picked man *prizewinner* 127.8
picked out *clear* 244.6, *decorated* 532.9, *unjoined* 753.9
picker *farm worker* 16.15, *horticulturist* 17.13, *cleaner* 111.12, *agricultural laborer* 123.10
picket *strike* 57.8, *mass demonstration* 331.7, *protester* 331.8, *protest* 331.19, *guard* 419.15, *punish* 454.22, *cause mischief* 507.9, *warner* 814.5, *block* 826.17
picketed *disputed* 57.15
picketer *troublemaker* 427.5, *protester* 507.4
picketing *strike* 57.8, *disputed* 57.15, *demonstrating* 331.14, *gesture of protest* 507.3
picket line *strike* 57.8, *exclusion* 764.1, *lockout* 826.6
pick holes in *be dissatisfied* 274.7
pickiness *selection* 382.1
picking *selecting* 382.4
picking and choosing *selecting* 382.4
picking at one's food *delicate eating* 92.3

picking out *selecting* 382.4
picking over *selecting* 382.4
pickings *chosen thing* 382.8, *earnings* 467.5, *takings* 477.8, *stolen goods* 479.4
picking up *raising* 715.1
pickle *save* 105.20, *season* 221.8, *steep* 557.31, *preserver* 815.9, *preserve* 815.14
pickle [Inf] *predicament* 725.3, 824.5, *confusion* 766.4
pickled *saved* 105.15, *piquant* 221.6, *preserved* 815.12
pickled [Inf] *drunk* 121.25
pickles *side dish* 90.15, *preserved thing* 815.10
pickling *cooking technique* 91.2, *preservation of provisions* 815.6
picklock *thief* 479.8, *intruder* 706.8
pick-me-up [Inf] *size of drink* 93.3, *refreshments* 94.3, *tonic* 115.8, *stimulant* 221.5
pick off *murder* 30.20, *fire* 418.18, *shoot* 696.18
pick of the bunch *object of pride* 297.6, *superior person* 445.7, *best people* 744.7
pick of the crop *chosen thing* 382.8, *excellence* 445.4
pick on [Inf] *discriminate against* 337.14
pick oneself up *be restored* 809.13
pick one's way *be in motion* 677.14, *be in difficulty* 824.19
pick out *see* 242.20, *discriminate* 337.12, *select* 382.12, *choose* 382.14, *extract* 711.13, *subtract* 749.6, *set apart* 753.17, *single out* 788.19
pickpocket *thief* 479.8, *steal* 479.14
pickpocketing *stealing* 479.13
pick someone's brains *resort to* 393.13
pick someone's pocket *steal* 479.14
pick the best *choose* 382.14
pick the brains of *question* 333.16
pick the lock *invade* 706.12
pick to pieces *criticize* 438.19, *demolish* 523.12
pickup *other game terms* 147.7, *sound amplifier* 230.5
pick up *touch* 216.9, *hear* 228.13, *protract* 669.9, *bring* 685.11, *gather up* 715.14, *get better* 807.21, *be restored* 809.13
pick up cheap *buy at a discount* 495.6
pick up for nothing *buy cheaply* 497.15
pick up speed *accelerate* 694.14
pick-up-sticks Children's and Party Games 167
pick up the bill *or* **tab** *defray* 489.18
pick up the gauntlet *contend* 422.22
pick up the pace *make haste* 818.5
pick up where one left off *protract* 669.9
Pickwickian *meaningless* 362.7
picky *discriminating* 337.9, *selecting* 382.9
picky eater *eater* 92.15
picnic *pork* 90.26, *feast* 92.9, *type of table* 101.5, *celebration* 405.1, *party* 408.6
picnic [Inf] *easy thing* 823.6
picnic hamper *or* **basket** *basket* 578.6
picnicker *eater* 92.15

pico Decimal Prefixes 589
pictogram *representation* 187.1
pictograph *or* **pictogram** *written letter* 5.14
pictographic *written* 5.36, *pictorial* 133.8
Pictor Constellations 7
pictorial 6.75, 133.8; *representational* 187.8, *representing* 202.14
pictorially 133.11; *representationally* 187.15
picture 133.5; *photograph* 132.3, *window* 134.10, *motion picture* 137.2, *identify* 184.11, *record* 185.1, *illustration* 187.2, *illustrate* 187.11, *description* 202.1, *representation* 202.9, *describe* 202.15, *view* 242.8, *visualize* 242.24, *impression* 264.7, *imagine* 327.14, 360.14, *conception* 360.4, *beautiful thing* 529.3, *circumstances* 573.2, *outline* 617.1, 617.5, *copy* 736.2
picture, the *fact* 717.6, *circumstances* 726.1
picture book *type of book* 174.3
picture card *cards* 168.2
pictured *identified* 184.9
picture frame *material* 143.9, *framework* 551.4
picture-frame stage *stage* 136.18
picture gallery *material* 143.9
picture hat *hat* 100.32
picture house *motion-picture theater* 137.10
picture magazine *magazine* 175.3
picture marriage *type of marriage* 64.3
picture of health, the *feeling well* 113.8
picture postcard *picture* 133.5
picture show *motion picture* 137.2
picturesome *photographic* 132.24
picturesque 529.9; *artistic* 133.7, *descriptive* 202.11, *decorated* 532.9
picturesquely *artistically* 133.10, *decoratively* 532.13
picture story *photograph* 132.3
picture taking *photography* 132.1
picture to oneself *imagine* 360.14
picture tube *television set* 172.6
picture window *place for viewing* 242.13
picture writing *symbol* 183.3, *representation* 187.1
piddle [Inf] *urine* 25.6, *urinate* 25.22
piddling *little* 580.7, *trivial* 800.14
piddling [Inf] *urination* 25.4
pidgin *international language* 5.8
pidgin English *regional pronunciation* 205.7
pie 90.38; *meat dish* 90.21, *dessert* 90.35, *confectionery* 222.3
piebald *horse by color* 159.7, *variegated thing* 263.5, *checked* 263.8
piece 590.2, 760.2; *farmland* 16.3, *firearm* 78.7, *bite* 92.10, *work of art* 133.4, 522.4, *play* 136.2, *play part* 136.8, *musical composition* 140.9, *news story* 171.3, *coinage* 484.13, *certain amount* 738.3, *quantify* 738.7, *remainder* 750.1, *part* 760.1, *included* 763.2, *fractional part* 787.2, *item* 788.2
piece [Inf *and* Off] *sex object* 20.8
piece by piece *separately* 753.22
pieced *partial* 760.11
pièce de résistance [Fr] *masterpiece* 127.5
piecemeal *industrial* 57.13, *by*

degrees 739.10, *separately* 753.22, *partial* 760.11, *partly* 760.17
piecemeal agreement *bargaining* 57.9
piece of advice *advice* 176.1
piece of architecture *construction* 522.9
piece of cake [Inf] *easy question* 333.5, *easy thing* 823.6, *victory* 845.4
piece of eight *ancient coins* 484.12, *eight* 792.4
piece of evidence *showpiece* 843.3
piece of furniture *furniture* 101.1
piece of good luck *good fortune* 847.2
piece of land *piece* 760.2
piece of luck *windfall* 467.7, *giveaway* 472.5, *opportunity* 659.2
piece of meat *or* **ass** [Inf *and* Off] *sex object* 20.8
piece of one's mind [Inf] *condemnation* 438.2
piece of the action [Inf] *portion* 474.2
piece of the pie *portion* 474.2
piece of writing *work of art* 522.4
piece rate *fee* 494.3
piece together *put together* 59.30, *decipher* 365.13, *assemble* 551.23, *unite* 752.14, *complete* 761.9, *repair* 809.10
piecework *work* 122.1
pieceworker *laborer* 123.9
pie chart *graph* 6.30, *map* 387.7, *chart* 767.8
piecing together *construction* 59.16
piecrust *brittle thing* 548.2, *cover* 613.2
pied *variegated* 263.6, *checked* 263.8
pied-à-terre *apartment* 60.7
piedmont *lowlands* 597.6, *lowland* 597.15
Piedmontese Breeds of Cattle 16
pie-eyed [Inf] *slightly drunk* 121.26
pie graph *map* 387.7
pie in the sky *idealism* 360.7, *theory* 720.4, *easy thing* 823.6
pie plate *cooking equipment* 91.6
pier *type of table* 101.5, Architectural Elements 134, *column* 134.6, *superstructure* 551.12, *bridge* 551.10, *water system* 551.13, *vertical* 602.3, *supporting part* 605.3
pierce *identify* 184.11, *stab* 418.22, *be sharp* 94.15, *hole* 583.17, *infiltrate* 706.13, *inject* 710.10
pierced *holed* 583.12
piercing *windy* 9.42, *deafening* 229.6, *loud* 232.6, *shrill* 238.6, *bitter* 306.9, *opening* 583.1
piercingly *bitterly* 306.16
piercingness *bitterness* 306.3
pier glass *reflector* 242.10
Pierre American States 564
Pierrot *stock part* 136.24
Pietà *type of painting* 143.5
pietism *self-righteousness* 431.7
pietist *religious person* 81.9
Pietrain Breeds of Pigs 16
piety *religiousness* 81.2, *belief system* 87.3, *virtue* 447.1
piezoelectric *electric* 14.47
piezoelectric crystal *measuring instrument* 589.12
piezoelectric effect *electromagnetic induction* 10.37
piezoelectricity *electrical power* 514.12
piezometer Fields of Measurement 589

piezometry Fields of Measurement 589

piffle [Inf] *senseless talk* 362.4

piffling *meaningless* 362.7, *trivial* 800.14

pig *livestock* 16.11, *eater* 92.15, *glutton* 119.2

pig [Inf] *law enforcement officer* 53.8, *be greedy* 119.4

pig [Inf *and* Off] *bigot* 337.7

pig breeder *agriculturist* 16.14

pigeon *table bird* 36.10, *meat* 90.22

pigeon fancier *ornithologist* 36.3

pigeonhole *postal communication* 169.4, *hiding place* 181.2, *compartment* 578.2, *little space* 580.6, *delay* 658.13, *systematize* 765.19, *category* 767.6, *categorize* 767.21, *class* 777.1, 777.12, *list* 785.11

pigeonholed *idle* 394.6, *grouped* 765.11, *categorized* 767.15, *classed* 777.11

pigeonholing *delay* 658.3, *grouping* 765.2, *categorization* 767.5, *classification* 777.2

pigeonlike *avian* 36.19

pigeon loft *dwelling* 36.4, *cage* 60.15

pigeon racing Sporting Activities 145

pig farm *farm* 16.2

pig farmer *agriculturist* 16.14

pig farming *livestock farming* 16.10

piggery *farm* 16.2

piggish *ungulate* 35.31, *gluttonous* 119.3

piggishly *gluttonously* 119.5

piggishness *gluttony* 119.1

piggy *ungulate* 35.31

piggyback *transportable* 686.7

piggyback car *railroad car* 688.5

piggy bank *money storage* 484.20

pigheaded *willful* 372.8, *obstinate* 379.5

pigheadedly *obstinately* 379.11

pigheadedness *willfulness* 372.3, *obstinacy* 379.1

pigherd *farm worker* 16.15

pig Latin *slang* 5.19

piglet *livestock* 16.11, *young animal* 26.4, *young mammal* 35.20

piglike *ungulate* 35.31

pigman *farm worker* 16.15

pigment 12.18; *coloring agent* 251.5, *color* 251.16

pigmentation *color* 251.1

pigment cell *cell* 13.15

pigment chart *spectrum* 251.3

pigment deficiency *paleness* 252.2

pigmented *colored* 251.10, *dark* 254.6

pigments *material* 143.9

pig out [Inf] *eat well* 92.23, *be greedy* 119.4

pig-out [Inf] *appetite* 92.2

pigpen *shack* 60.10, *cage* 60.15

pigs Collective Names 59

pigs [Inf] *law enforcement agency* 53.7

pig's feet *variety meat* 90.30

pig's head *variety meat* 90.30

pigskin *leather* 14.7

pigskin [Inf] *football* 155.1

pig's knuckles *variety meat* 90.30

pigsticker *sharp weapon* 78.6

pigsty *farm building* 16.4, *shack* 60.10, *cage* 60.15, *shelter* 812.4

pig swill *animal food* 90.2, *swill* 112.6

pigtail *braid* 609.3, *back* 622.1

pigtails *coiffure* 530.8

pike *sharp weapon* 78.6, *food fish and shellfish* 90.20, *game fish*

154.10, *competitive diving* 164.7, *diving* 164.13

pike [Brit] *mountain* 569.1

pikeman *historical soldier* 77.8

Pikes Peak Mountains and Hills 569

pike surface dive *diving* 164.6

pilaf *rice* 90.32

pilaster Architectural Elements 134, *column* 134.6, *supporting part* 605.3

pilchard *food fish and shellfish* 90.20

Pilcomayo Rivers 570

pile *assemblage* 59.13, *assemble* 59.23, *store* 105.1, *heap* 105.19, *architectural structure* 134.4, Heraldic Terms 184, *acquisition* 467.4, *acquire* 467.19, *substructure* 551.8, *nap* 552.3, *vertical* 602.3, *supporting part* 605.3, *weaving* 609.2, *fastener* 754.7

pile [Inf] *money* 485.2

pile carpet *floor covering* 613.13

piled *collected* 59.19, *stored* 105.14

pile driver *construction equipment* 14.23

piledriver *impeller* 695.7

piled up *stored* 105.14

pile dweller *lake dweller* 568.4

pile hammer *construction equipment* 14.23

pile house *or* **dwelling** *lake dwelling* 568.3

pile in *mount* 713.24, *fill* 761.11

pile on *exhibit penalty behavior* 155.21, *augment* 748.13, *fill* 761.11

pile up *heap* 105.19, *acquire* 467.19, *miscellaneous automotive terms* 687.14, *collide* 695.10

pileus *fungal body* 47.4

pilfer *take away* 477.18, *steal* 479.14

pilferage *theft* 479.2

pilfered *stolen* 479.12

pilferer *thief* 479.8

pilfering *stealing* 479.1

pilgrim *religious person* 81.9, *religious* 84.9

pilgrimage *act of worship* 83.2, *undertaking* 391.1

pill *dose of medicine* 115.3, *affliction* 454.9, *round thing* 633.3

pill [Inf] *baseball equipment* 147.4

pill, the *contraceptive* 23.6

pillage *military attack* 418.2, *take away forcefully* 477.19, *stolen goods* 479.4, *plundering* 479.5, *plunder* 479.16, *use violence* 520.9, *havoc* 523.5, *lay waste* 523.14

pillager *raider* 477.10, *plunderer* 479.9, *violent animal* 520.4, *destroyer* 523.6

pillaging *plundering* 479.5, *stolen* 479.12, *violence by person* 520.2

pillar *column* 134.6, *rock face* 161.6, *monument* 185.10, *superstructure* 551.7, *vertical* 602.3, *supporting part* 605.3, *supporter* 605.9, *refuge* 812.1

pillar box [Brit] *red thing* 257.3

pillar-box red [Brit] *red* 257.5

pillared *architectural* 134.12

pillarist *religious* 84.9

pillar of society *important person* 799.5

pillar of strength *security* 464.1, *supporter* 605.9

pillar of the community *person of repute* 370.2, *important person* 799.5

Pillars of Hercules *distant place* 585.3

pillbox *hat* 100.32, *fortification* 419.12

pill bug *crustacean* 39.10

pillhead [Inf] *drug taker* 121.12

pilliwinks *instrument of torture* 454.14

pillory *deride* 369.7, *instrument of punishment* 454.13, *punish* 454.22, *means of restraint* 830.6

pillowcase *bed covering* 613.7

pillowed *compressible* 543.9, *at ease* 819.2

pillow lava *eruption* 8.27

pillow sham *bed covering* 613.7

pillowslip *bed covering* 613.7

pill popper [Inf] *drug taker* 121.12

pill-popping [Inf] *drug use* 121.9

pilot 689.15; *warrior* 76.25, *professional worker* 123.11, *leader* 126.8, *lead* 126.12, *tentative* 390.5, *conductor* 399.13, *conduct* 399.21, *aircraft personnel* 689.8, Ships and Boats 690, *nautical person* 690.12, *aim* 697.14, *original* 737.2, *precursor* 769.7, *precede* 769.13, *pioneer* 771.29, *usher* 794.7, *escort* 794.18, *safety device* 810.15

pilotage *directorship* 126.5, *aviation* 689.1, *navigation* 690.5

pilot a ship *navigate* 690.15

pilot boat Ships and Boats 690

piloting *aviation* 689.1, *navigation* 690.5, *direction* 697.1, *preparatory* 769.11

pilot jack *flag* 184.8

pilot ladder *ladder* 713.10

pilot light *place for fire* 217.9

pilot run *rehearsal* 335.2

pilotship *navigation* 690.5

pimento *or* **pimiento** Herbs and Spices 91

pi meson *elementary particle* 10.53

Pimlico London 567.8

pimp *agent* 80.3, *provisioner* 89.4, *provision* 89.9, *sexually immoral person* 432.8, *prostitute* 432.17, *villain* 448.5, *person who joins* 752.9

pimpernel Flowers 42

pimping *prostitution* 432.4

pimple *skin disease* 114.16, *maculation* 263.4, *mark* 533.2

pimpled *marked* 533.6

pimply *mottled* 263.10, *coarse* 544.6

PIN *personal identification* 184.4, *till* 484.21

pin *fabric-handling tool* 130.12, *bowling* 151.1, *wrestling terms* 152.10, *wrestle* 152.20, *golf course* 156.2, *board games* 167.3, *love token* 299.8, *jewelry* 532.6, *sharp-pointed thing* 549.4, *opener* 583.2, *stopper* 584.3, *axle* 682.11, *link* 752.18, *connect* 754.13, *little bit* 800.4

pinafore *dress* 100.11, *accessory* 100.28

piñata Children's and Party Games 167

pince-nez *visual aid* 242.14

pincer movement *land attack* 418.3, *detention* 471.2

pincers *hand tool* 103.3, *retainer* 471.3, *extractor* 711.9

pinch *defense* 155.9, *play defense* 155.19, *gesture* 183.5, 183.17, *inflict pain* 215.10, *type of touch* 216.3, *touch* 216.9, *communication of love* 299.8, *insolvency* 486.2, *be poor* 486.14, *little space* 580.6, *squeeze* 582.3, 582.13, *narrow* 593.14, *critical time* 659.3, *converge* 702.9, *predicament* 725.3,

824.5, *admixture* 751.5, *warning* 814.1, *warn* 814.8

pinch [Inf] *taking away* 477.5, *take away forcefully* 477.19, *theft* 479.2, *steal* 479.14, *detain* 830.16

pinchbeck *cheap* 800.16

pinched *cold* 218.9, *squeezed* 582.9, *narrow* 593.8

pinched (for money) *insolvent* 486.10

pinch-hit [Inf] *be a substitute* 672.6

pinch-hit for [Inf] *substitute for* 80.5

pinch hitter *alternative* 80.2, *baseball team* 147.2, *substitute* 672.2

pinching *demanding* 95.13, *squeeze* 582.3, *contracting* 582.10

pinching [Inf] *stealing* 479.1

pinching back *or* **out** *or* **off** *gardening* 17.5

pinch of snuff *tobacco* 121.23

pinch pennies *be poor* 486.14

pin connection *superstructure* 551.7

pincushion flower Flowers 42

Pindaric Poem or Verse Forms 139, *poetic* 139.19

pindling *weak* 517.6

Pindos pony Horse and Pony Breeds 159

pin down *compel* 428.8, *detain* 471.9, *find* 565.11, *specify* 779.18, *make certain* 840.14

Pindus Mountains Mountains and Hills 569

pine *be unhealthy* 114.29, *grieve* 270.7

pineal *of a secretion* 24.5

pineapple [Inf] *bomb* 78.15

pineapple family *seed plant* 41.3

pine cone *tree part* 43.2

pine for *desire* 288.17

pinene *terpene* 12.20

pine needle *tree part* 43.2, *sharp-pointed growth* 549.5

piner *desirer* 288.9

pinery *trees* 43.4

pine tar Tree Products 43

pinetum *trees* 43.4

piney *treelike* 43.10

pinfold *farm building* 16.4, *shelter* 812.4

ping *ringing* 235.5, 236.2, *ring* 235.14, *miscellaneous automotive terms* 687.14

pinging *ringing* 235.5

Ping-Pong™ Sporting Activities 145, *tennis* 165.1, Board and Table Games 167

pinguid *oily* 562.11

pinguidity *oiliness* 562.1

pinguidly *oilily* 562.19

pinhead *little thing* 580.3

pinhead [Inf] *unintelligent person* 316.4, *foolish person* 353.3

pinhole *hole* 583.4

pinhole camera *camera* 132.10

pining *sick* 114.24, *sorrowful* 270.4, *desire* 288.1, *desirous* 288.13

pinion *intertwine* 752.19

pinioned *retained* 471.6

pink Flowers 42, *red* 257.5, *edge* 618.8, *notch* 636.5, Sailing Ships and Boats 690

pink-collar worker *clerical worker* 123.5

pinked *edged* 618.6, *notched* 636.4

pink eye *eye disease* 243.4

pinkie *or* **pinky** [Inf] *appendage* 19.5

pinking *edging* 618.2

pinking shears *sharp-edged thing* 549.6, *notched thing* 636.2

pinko [Inf] *political party member* 50.6

pink of condition *health* 113.1

pink slip *rejection notice* 383.5, *dismissal* 709.2

pin money *profit* 467.6, *something received* 473.2, *change* 484.3, *income* 492.3

pinna *ear* 19.10, *fern plant* 46.2

pinnace *Sailing Ships and Boats* 690, *Ships and Boats* 690

pinnacle 596.2; *rock face* 161.6, *mountain* 569.1, *summit* 600.1, 744.4, *limit* 761.4, *peak* 805.5

pinnate *of leaves* 41.18

pinnatifid *fernlike* 46.6

pinned *retained* 471.6, *connected* 754.11

pinned down *found* 565.7, *stabilized* 674.4

pinning down *locating* 565.3

pinniped *marine mammal* 35.12, *cetacean* 35.27

Pinnipedia *marine mammal* 35.12

pinnipedian *cetacean* 35.27

pinnule *fern plant* 46.2

pinochle *Card Games* 168

pinochle pack *cards* 168.2

pin on *link* 752.18

pin one's hopes on *hope* 281.10

pinpoint *publicize* 173.18, *identify* 184.11, *accurate* 350.3, *exact location* 565.2, *find* 565.11, *little thing* 580.3, *centralize* 612.11, *be accurate* 721.22

pinpoint accuracy *accuracy* 350.1, *trueness* 721.4

pinpointed *found* 565.7, *centered* 612.9

pinpointing *identification* 184.1, *locating* 565.3, *centrality* 612.5

pinprick *pain* 215.1, *provocation* 302.3, *little bit* 800.4

pins *Phobias* 283

pins and needles *stimulus* 212.3, *pain* 215.1

pinstripes *pants* 100.14

pinstripe suit *suit* 100.16

pint *size of drink* 93.3, *General Units* 589

pin the tail on the donkey *Children's and Party Games* 167

pintle *axle* 682.7

Pinto *Horse and Pony Breeds* 159

pinto *Bean Varieties* 90, *horse by color* 159.7, *checked* 263.8

pin to *add* 748.11, *link* 752.18

pint-size(d) [Inf] *undersized* 580.8

pinup *portrait* 132.5

pinup girl *attractive female* 529.5

pinwheel *fire* 246.9, *wheel* 682.9

pinworm *parasite* 39.18

piny *treelike* 43.10

pinyin *alphabet* 5.16

pinyon pine *Trees and Shrubs* 43

Pinzgauer *Breeds of Cattle* 16

Pinzgauer Noriker *Horse and Pony Breeds* 159

pion *elementary particle* 10.53

pioneer 771.29; *settler* 61.4, *settle* 61.14, *lead* 126.12, *discoverer* 345.7, *invent* 345.14, *preparer* 388.6, *prepare the way* 388.15, *person who undertakes* 391.3, *undertake* 391.7, *interfacer* 616.3, *vanguard* 621.5, *be in front* 621.13, *originate* 737.7, *precursor* 769.7, *forerun* 769.16, *make easy* 823.15

pioneering *invention* 345.4, *discovering* 345.8, *preparation* 388.1, *enterprising* 391.5, *front-running* 621.10, *original* 737.4, *preparatory* 769.11

pious *religious* 81.21, *worshipful* 83.12, *moral* 431.9, *moralistic* 431.12, *virtuous* 447.5

piously *religiously* 81.29, *morally* 431.15

piousness *religiousness* 81.2

pip *seed* 41.9, *fruit structure* 44.3

pip [Inf] *insignia* 184.5

pipal or **peepul** *Trees and Shrubs* 43

pipe *blunt weapon* 78.5, *tobacco implements* 121.24, *Musical Instruments* 142, *brass instrument* 142.3, *speak in a particular way* 205.18, *be shrill* 238.9, *bird sound* 240.2, *make a bird sound* 240.8, *vessel* 578.11, *provide passage for* 583.18, *General Units* 589, *narrow place* 593.2, *edge* 618.8, *cylinder* 633.4

pipe clay *material* 129.2, *whitener* 253.3

pipe-clay *whiten* 253.12

pipe cleaner *cleaning tool* 111.10

piped *edged* 618.6, *transportable* 686.7

pipe down [Inf] *lapse into silence* 208.8, *be silent* 231.3

pipe down! [Inf] *hush!* 231.6

pipe dream *aspiration* 281.3, *figurative overestimation* 343.3, *reverie* 360.6, *illusion* 720.2

pipe-dream *imagine* 327.14, *aspire* 281.13

pipeline *source of supply* 105.4

pipe of peace *tobacco implements* 121.24

pipe tobacco *tobacco* 121.23

pipette *draw off* 711.16

pipetting *drawing off* 711.4

pipe wrench *hand tool* 103.3

piping *shrillness* 238.3, *shrill* 238.6, *edging* 618.2, *transporting* 686.8

piping hot *heating* 217.12

pipit *songbird* 36.12

Pippin *Apple Varieties* 44

pips *military honor* 58.9

pipsqueak [Inf] *little person* 580.5, *nonentity* 800.8

piquancy 221.1; *emphasis* 200.1

piquant 221.6; *emphatic* 200.3, *strong to the senses* 516.12

piquantly 221.10

pique *be piquant* 221.9, *resentment* 302.1, *irritate* 302.16

piqué *Fabrics and Fibers* 130

piqued *offended* 302.9, *bitter* 306.9

piquet *Card Games* 168

piquet pack *cards* 168.2

piracy *illegal borrowing* 476.3, *theft* 479.2, *infringement* 479.6

piragua *Sailing Ships and Boats* 690

piragua or **pirogue** *Ships and Boats* 690

Pirani gauge *surface chemistry* 11.20

pirate *militarist* 77.3, *borrower* 476.7, *borrow illegally* 476.12, *infringer* 479.10, *infringe* 479.17, *copy* 736.10

pirate flag *flag* 184.8

piratelike *stolen* 479.12

pirate ship *Sailing Ships and Boats* 690, *Ships and Boats* 690

piratic(al) *fraudulent* 479.13

piratical *combative* 77.32

piratically *thievishly* 479.19

pirating *illegal borrowing* 476.3, *infringement* 479.6

Pirithoüs *Notable Friendships* 62

piroplasm *parasite* 39.18

pirouette *horizontal bar* 157.5, *exercise* 157.12, *ice-dancing move* 162.19, *ice-skate* 162.36, *reel* 682.4, *rotate* 682.11

pirouetting *turning* 682.3

Pisa *Breeds of Cattle* 16

pis aller [Fr] *expedient* 387.5, *substitution* 672.1

piscator *hunter* 385.6

piscatorial *hunting* 385.9

piscatorial or **piscatory** *fishlike* 38.10, *ichthyological* 38.11, *fishing* 154.13

piscatorially *on the water* 154.15

piscatory *hunting* 385.9

Pisces *Constellations* 7, *fishes* 38.1

Pisces Volans *Constellations* 7

piscicultural *agricultural* 16.16, *ichthyological* 38.11

pisciculturally *agriculturally* 16.21

pisciculture *livestock farming* 16.10

pisciform *fishlike* 38.10

piscine *fishlike* 38.10

Piscis Austrinus *Constellations* 7

pismire *social insect* 40.6

piss [Inf] *urination* 25.4, *urine* 25.6, *urinate* 25.22, *body fluid* 555.3

pissed or **pissed off** [Inf] *angry* 302.11

piss off [Inf] *make angry* 302.18

piss off! [Inf] *miscellaneous swearwords* 301.20, *go!* 709.30

pisspot [Inf] *place for excretion* 25.11

piste *fencing* 153.1, *sign* 183.1, *vestige* 185.11

pistil *flower part* 42.3

pistillate *of flowers* 42.11

pistol *murder* 30.20, *firearm* 78.7, *shoot* 696.18

pistole *ancient coins* 484.12

pistoleer *historical soldier* 77.8

pistoleer [Arch] *shooter* 696.11

pistols for two and coffee for one *duel* 422.12

pistol shooting *Sporting Activities* 145, *target shooting* 160.1

piston *engine type* 14.11, *stopper* 584.3, *propeller* 696.8

piston movement *frequency* 663.2

piston slap *miscellaneous automotive terms* 687.14

pit *seed* 41.9, *fruit structure* 44.3, *works* 124.9, *stage* 136.18, *automobile racing terms* 146.3, *be on the track* 146.11, *bowling* 151.1, *place for viewing* 242.13, *wicked place* 448.8, *stock market* 483.6, *nap* 552.3, *concave land* 635.2, *miscellaneous automotive terms* 687.14, *fortification* 812.3, *shelter* 812.4, *trap* 813.1, *stratagem* 822.2

pit [Brit] *auditorium* 136.17

pita *bread* 90.10

pit against *confront* 828.19

Pitaka *other text* 81.19

pitapat *small sound* 233.4, *knock* 235.4, *vibration* 683.2, *beat* 684.10

pit bull terrier *Breeds of Dogs* 35

Pitcairn Island *Islands* 572

pitch 684.25; *spoken letter* 5.15, *roof* 134.7, *tone* 140.24, 230.2, *harmonize* 140.28, *play an instrument* 142.9, *play baseball* 147.9, *play* 156.8, *hockey areas* 158.2, *rock face* 161.6, *stadium* 163.2, *Card Games* 168, *mode of speech* 205.6, *sound* 230.1, *dark thing* 247.3, *black thing* 254.3,

salesmanship 482.4, *location* 565.1, *pinnacle* 596.2, *summit* 600.1, *top* 600.6, *be at the top* 600.9, *make vertical* 602.9, *obliqueness* 607.1, *be oblique* 607.10, *be changeable* 666.5, *stagger* 684.11, *maneuver* 689.14, *throw* 696.4, 696.17, *deviating course* 698.2, *deviating motion* 698.3, *drop* 714.15, *throw down* 716.13, *degree* 739.1

pitch [Inf] *publicize* 178.19

pitch and plunge *pitch* 684.25

pitch a perfect game *play baseball* 147.9

pitch a shutout *play baseball* 147.9

pitch-black *black* 254.5

pitch-dark *dark* 247.5

pitch-darkness *darkness* 247.1

pitch diameter *gear* 14.7

pitched *roof* 134.7, *harmonic* 140.27, *phonetic* 205.14, *sounding* 230.7, *oblique* 607.6

pitched battle *battle* 76.23, *contention* 422.1, *warfare* 422.10

pitcher *baseball team* 147.2, *water carrier* 557.16, *vessel* 578.11, *thrower* 696.19

pitcher(ful) *container(ful)* 738.2

pitcher's mound *baseball field* 147.3

pitchfork *farm tool* 16.5, *garden tool* 103.4, *sharp-pointed thing* 549.4

pitch in *finance* 825.31, *work together* 827.14

pitch in [Inf] *eat well* 92.23, *make a beginning* 771.26

pitching *turbulence* 684.3, *turbulent* 684.17, *flight maneuver* 689.6, *nautical* 690.14, *throwing* 696.3

pitching coach *baseball team* 147.2

pitching into [Inf] *berating* 438.5

pitching terms 147.5

pitch into [Inf] *strike* 418.21, *fight* 422.23, *berate* 438.20

pitch of perfection *peak* 805.5

pitch one's tent *take up residence* 60.24

pitchout *play* 155.8

pitch out *play offense* 155.18

pitch pipe *instrumental aid* 142.7

pitchpole *sail* 150.29

pitch upon *reach* 704.14

pitchy *black* 254.5, *resinous* 562.13

piteous *pitiful* 308.5

piteously *pitifully* 308.12

pitfall *danger* 811.1, *trap* 813.1, *stratagem* 822.2, *snag* 824.8

pith *stem* 41.5, *fruit structure* 44.3, *topic* 328.1, *meaning* 361.1, *semiliquid* 561.7, *insides* 577.3, *core* 612.2, *essential content* 723.2, *importance* 799.1

Pithecanthropus *human ancestor* 18.3, *prehistoric human* 653.7

pith helmet *helmet* 100.34, *protective covering* 613.5, *protection from the weather* 810.9

pithily *concisely* 198.6, *summarily* 204.10

pithiness *conciseness* 198.1, *summariness* 204.4, *pulpiness* 561.9

pithy *proverbial* 177.2, *concise* 198.4, *emphatic* 200.3, *summary* 204.5, *significant* 361.11, *compressible* 543.9, *core* 612.7

pithy saying 198.3

pitiable *lamentable* 280.6, *pitiful* 308.5

pitiably *pitifully* 308.12
pitied *given consideration* 423.4
pitiful 308.5; *lamentable* 280.6
pitifully 308.12; *lamentably* 280.10
pitiless 309.3; *malicious* 306.8, *severe* 424.5
pitilessly 309.7
pitilessness 309.1; *malice* 306.2, *severity* 424.1, *impenitence* 452.1
pit lane *automobile racing terms* 146.3
pit mechanic *driver* 146.8
pit of one's stomach *seat of feelings* 266.7
piton *climbing equipment* 161.4
pits, the [Inf] *base* 601.1, *error* 846.2, *adversity* 848.1
pittance *incompleteness* 98.2, *portion* 474.2, *change* 484.3, *certain amount* 738.3
pitted *marked* 533.6, *coarse* 544.6, *concave* 635.5
pitter-patter *small sound* 233.4, *knock* 235.4, *vibration* 683.2, *beat* 684.10
pituitary *of a secretion* 24.5
pit wall *automobile racing terms* 146.3
pity 308.1, 308.6; *feel for* 266.17, *sensitivity* 267.1, *be sensitive* 267.5, *compassion* 305.2, *be compassionate* 305.11, *leniency* 423.1, *be lenient* 423.5, *unselfishness* 443.2, *be unselfish* 443.7
pitying 308.4; *compassionate* 305.8, *lenient* 423.3
pityingly 308.11
più Musical Terms and Expression Marks 140
pivot *hand tool* 103.3, *play basketball* 148.7, *golf shots* 156.4, *ice-dancing move* 162.19, *ice-skate* 162.36, *center* 612.1, *core* 612.2, *turn around* 680.22, *axle* 682.7, *rotate* 682.14, *focus* 702.5, *essential content* 723.2, *joint* 752.7, *middle* 772.1, *place in the middle* 772.18, *gist* 799.4
pivotal *central* 612.6, *core* 612.7, *focal* 612.8, *critical* 659.5, *causal* 675.7, *rotary* 682.12, *difficult* 726.11, *middle* 772.9, *essential* 799.10
pivotal focus *focus* 612.3
pivotally *centrally* 612.12, *focally* 612.14, *critically* 659.9, *causally* 675.12
pivotal point *critical time* 659.3, *swing* 671.4
pivot cartwheel *pommel horse* 157.7
pivoting *playing terms* 148.4, *turning* 682.3, *rotating* 682.11
pivot man *basketball team* 148.2
pivot on *center* 612.10, *follow from* 676.9
pixel *display* 15.9, *little thing* 580.3
pixie *sprite* 86.12
pizazz [Inf] *vigor* 518.1
pizza *notable international dishes* 90.40
pizzeria *eating place* 92.17
pizzicato Musical Terms and Expression Marks 140
p.j.'s or **P.J.'s** [Inf] *nightwear* 100.21
PL/1 Programming Languages 15
placability *forgivingness* 312.3
placable *forgiving* 312.4
placableness *forgivingness* 312.3
placard *advertisement* 173.9, *publicize* 173.18, *sign* 183.1, *showplace* 843.4

placate *conciliate* 74.10, *comfort* 273.9
placatory *pacificatory* 74.8
place *habitation* 60.2, *horse-racing betting terms* 159.11, *discover* 345.11, *line of duty* 433.3, *reserved space* 563.5, *region* 564.1, *location* 565.1, *locate* 565.9, *situation* 573.1, *circumstances* 573.2, *employment* 573.3, *station* 601.5, 601.12, *state* 725.1, *rank* 739.2, *interval* 739.4, *measure* 739.7, *position* 765.4, *systematize* 765.19, *category* 767.6, *arrange* 767.18, *categorize* 767.21, *class* 777.12
place [Fr] *urban area* 567.10
place an advertisement *publicize* 173.18
place an obstacle in someone's path *prohibit* 503.8
place at intervals *space* 563.15, 587.6
placebo *medicine* 115.2
place card *personal identification* 184.4
placed *located* 565.6, *situated* 573.5, *based* 601.9, *conditional* 725.7, *circumstantial* 726.8, *arranged* 767.11, *categorized* 767.15, *classed* 777.11
placed at intervals *spaced* 587.4
place for conversation 210.5
place for excretion 25.11
place for fire 217.9
place for viewing 242.13
place for waste 802.6
place in a container *contain* 578.20
place in history *day to remember* 354.5, *fame* 845.2
place in one's account *deposit* 487.12
place in order *categorize* 767.21
place in the foreground *make important* 799.14, *reveal* 843.14
place in the middle 772.18; *center* 612.10
place in the spotlight *reveal* 843.14
place in the sun *prosperity* 847.1
place kick *kick* 155.12
place-kick *kick* 155.20
place-kicker *special team* 155.11
place mat *tableware* 92.11, *protective covering* 613.5
placement *placing* 565.4, *arrangement* 767.1, *categorization* 767.5
place name *name* 202.8
placenta *placental mammal* 35.6
placental *of a secretion* 24.5
placental or **placentate mammalian** 35.23
placental mammal 35.6
place of confrontation *interface* 616.1
place of contact *interface* 616.1
place of departure 705.4
place of embarkation *place of departure* 705.4
place of exchange 673.2
place of experimentation 335.6
place of interaction *interface* 616.1
place of judgment 341.3
place of pilgrimage *center of activity* 612.4
place of residence 209.4; *habitation* 60.2
place of safety *refuge* 812.1
place of the dead *evil place* 446.6
place of trade *place of exchange* 673.2
place of work *workplace* 124.1

place of worship 83.8
place on *augment* 748.13
place oneself *line up* 765.24
place on record *record* 185.13
placer *ore* 11.23
place setting *ornament* 532.7
place side by side *juxtapose* 586.14
place strictures on *limit* 620.7
place to one's credit *deposit* 487.12
place under *subsume* 763.7
place under an embargo *exclude* 764.7
place under oath *attest* 189.22
place-value notation *number system* 6.7
place where one hangs one's hat *home* 60.3
place where one lives or *resides* *habitation* 60.2
placid *detached* 4.18, *quiescent* 678.6
placidity *repose* 678.2
placidly *stoically* 4.26, *motionlessly* 678.9
placidness *repose* 678.2
placing 565.4; *arrangement* 767.1, *categorization* 767.5
placket *part of garment* 100.27
placoderm *fossil fish* 38.7
placoid *platelike* 588.8
placoid scale *fish characteristic* 38.8
placophobia Phobias 283
plagal mode *mode* 140.17
plagiarism *illegal borrowing* 476.3, *taking over* 477.3, *taking away* 477.5, *infringement* 479.6, *copy* 736.2
plagiarist *borrower* 476.7, *taker* 477.9, *infringer* 479.10, *imitator* 736.6
plagiarize *borrow illegally* 476.12, *take over* 477.16, *take away* 477.18, *infringe* 479.17, *copy* 736.10
plagiarized *borrowed* 476.8, *fraudulent* 479.13, *imitation* 736.8
plagiarizing *illegal borrowing* 476.3, *infringement* 479.6
plague 114.6; *dwelling* 40.7, *infest* 40.17, Collective Names 59, *affliction* 117.1, *afflict* 117.16, 301.16, *misfortune* 301.6, *evil thing* 446.2, *be evil* 446.10, *agent of destruction* 523.7, *transgression* 712.3, *eat away* 808.19, *adverse health* 848.5
plagued *worried* 283.11, *afflicted* 301.11, *overrun* 712.6, *troubled* 824.15
plagued by conscience *penitent* 451.5
plague pit *burial place* 31.7
plague spot *infection* 114.7
plague-stricken *sick* 114.24, *contagious* 114.26
plaguy or **plaguey** *inconvenient* 824.12
plaice *food fish and shellfish* 90.20
plaid Fabrics and Fibers 130, *check* 263.2, *checked* 263.8
Plaid Cymru Political Parties 50
plain 528.9, 592.10; *landform* 8.9, *grassland* 45.2, *fit for habitation* 60.19, *diving* 164.13, *assertive* 189.20, *ingenuous* 191.6, *simple* 195.10, 363.6, 526.7, *clear* 196.2, 244.6, *tasteless* 220.4, *visible* 242.19, 244.5, *easily seen through* 249.10, *soft-hued* 251.13, *predictable* 295.4, *boring* 296.6, *humble* 298.8, *demonstrated* 331.9, *meaningful* 361.6, *familiar* 407.8,

unadorned 424.7, *self-restrained* 455.6, *elegant* 527.3, *ugly* 531.3, *geographical space* 563.3, *countryside* 564.3, *lowland* 572.6, 597.15, *of landmasses* 572.12, *open* 583.13, 843.12, *lowlands* 597.6, *horizontal surface* 603.3, *straightforward* 630.9, *same* 730.7, *completely* 759.14, 761.13, *complete* 761.6, *naive* 821.3, *easy* 823.9, *informal* 829.15
plain as day *predictable* 295.4
plain as the nose on one's face *clear* 244.6, *open* 843.12
plainchant *ritual music* 85.9, *song* 140.11
plain clothes *informal clothes* 100.7
plainclothes officer *law enforcement officer* 53.8
plain English *clarity* 363.2, *unpretentiousness* 526.2
plain Jane [Inf] *average person* 742.4
plain jump *diving* 164.6
plain living *self-restraint* 455.1
plainly 424.12, 592.18; *commonly* 71.4, *openly* 180.13, 583.22, *assertively* 189.35, *ingenuously* 191.11, *simply* 195.19, 526.14, *clearly* 196.4, *unemphatically* 201.4, *visibly* 242.28, 244.10, *transparently* 249.13, *apparently* 264.16, *predictably* 295.9, *boringly* 296.10, *humbly* 298.22, *manifestly* 331.20, 843.17, *meaningfully* 361.16, *intelligibly* 363.13, *in other words* 365.18, *informally* 407.11, 829.24, *with self-restraint* 455.14, *gracefully* 527.8, *bluntly* 550.11, *candidly* 583.23, *straightforwardly* 630.17, *identically* 730.18
plainly stated *simple* 363.6
plain man *naive person* 821.2
plainness 592.4; *assertiveness* 189.8, *ingenuousness* 191.3, *simplicity* 195.4, 526.1, 823.2, *clarity* 196.1, 244.2, 363.2, *lack of emphasis* 201.1, *tastelessness* 220.1, *openness* 249.6, *predictability* 295.2, *boringness* 296.2, *humility* 298.1, *comprehensibility* 361.3, *type of meaning* 361.4, *familiarity* 407.3, *unadornment* 424.3, *self-restraint* 455.1, *bad taste* 528.3, *ugliness* 531.1, *straightforwardness* 630.3, *sameness* 730.1, *naïveté* 821.1
plain prose *unpretentiousness* 526.2
plains, the *lowland* 572.6
plainsong *ritual music* 85.9, *sacred music* 140.3, *song* 140.11
plain speaking *clarity* 363.2, *directness* 630.5
plain-speaking *direct* 630.12
plain speech *candor* 191.2, *clarity* 363.2
plain-spoken *informative* 170.10, *disclosing* 180.6, *speaking* 205.15, *outspoken* 550.6, *plain* 592.10, *informal* 829.15
Plains states *regions of the United States* 564.7
plain stitch *knitting* 130.7
plaint *accusation* 442.1
plaintiff *litigant* 54.4, *arguer* 319.6, *person questioned* 333.10, *witness* 339.7, *accuser* 442.3, *opposer* 828.9
plaintive *lamenting* 280.4
plaintively *lamentingly* 280.9
plain to see *clear* 244.6

plain truth *the truth* 721.3
plain weave *weaving* 130.6
plain words *clarity* 363.2, *unpretentiousness* 526.2, *openness* 583.7
plain wrapper *that which makes invisible* 245.2
plait *spinning* 130.4, *weave* 130.20, *coiffure* 530.8, *coif* 530.15, *braid* 609.3, *interweave* 609.6, *pleat* 637.2, 637.8, *mix* 751.12, *intertwine* 752.19, *line* 754.5, *connect* 754.13
plaited *spun* 130.13, *interwoven* 609.6, *mixed* 751.8, *tied* 752.13, *connected* 754.11
plaiting *spinning* 130.4, *interweaving* 609.1
plan 327.3, 357.2, 387.1, 387.12; *engineer* 14.48, *art of war* 76.16, *find means* 102.6, *design* 133.9, *aspect of fiction* 139.5, *illustration* 187.2, *illustrate* 187.11, *outline* 204.2, 617.1, 617.5, *visualize* 242.24, *purpose* 327.4, *aim* 327.17, *solution* 334.6, *solve* 334.21, *expect* 356.6, *have foresight* 357.8, *suppose* 359.8, *point* 361.5, *intend* 361.15, 374.8, *future intention* 374.3, *declaration* 376.2, *predetermination* 384.1, *predetermine* 384.8, *map* 387.7, *preparations* 388.2, *lay the foundations* 388.16, *undertaking* 391.1, *tactics* 399.12, *behave toward* 399.20, *budget* 457.10, *dream up* 522.15, *structure* 551.1, 551.20, *exact location* 565.2, *awaken* 675.9, *method* 765.7, *chart* 767.5, *organize* 767.19, *make arrangements* 767.23, *be cunning* 822.5
plan ahead 387.13; *have foresight* 357.8
planar *spatial* 6.76, *horizontal* 603.6
planar graph *combinatorics* 6.63
planarity *horizontality* 603.1
planchette *occult and psychic phenomena* 86.7
Planck constant *fundamental constant* 10.69
Planck's radiation law *Classical Physical Laws* 10
plane *surface* 6.36, *spatial* 6.76, *military aircraft* 77.30, *woodworking tool* 131.6, *carpenter* 131.10, *windsurf* 150.33, *smoother* 545.2, *uniform* 545.5, *smooth* 545.10, *sharp-edged thing* 549.6, *use a sharp tool* 549.17, *grind* 554.15, *vertical* 602.3, *horizontal surface* 603.3, *flattener* 603.4, *horizontal* 603.6, *means of transportation* 686.2, *aircraft* 689.3, *go up* 713.23, *interval* 739.4
plane angle *angle* 6.37, *dimension* 10.5
plane areas *Fields of Measurement* 589
plane figure *geometric figure* 6.39
plane geometry *geometry* 6.32
planeness *horizontality* 603.1
plane of symmetry *geometric figure* 6.39
plane polarization *wave property* 10.12
plane-polarized light *polarized light* 10.19
planer *machine tool* 14.9, *woodworking tool* 131.6
plane sailing *navigation* 690.5

plane surface *surface* 6.36, *horizontal surface* 603.3
planet 7.16; *orbiting body* 681.4
planetarium *observatory* 7.24, *place for viewing* 242.13
planetary *astronomical* 7.33, *universal* 778.10
planetary influence *occult influence* 512.2, *contributory cause* 675.3
planetary meteorology *meteorology* 9.1
planetary nebula *nebula* 7.6
planetary probe 7.31
planetary system *solar system* 7.14
planet Earth *Earth* 8.6
planetoid *planet* 7.16, *orbiting body* 681.4
planetologist *geologist* 8.4
planetology *geology* 8.1
plane tree *Trees and Shrubs* 43
plane trigonometry *trigonometry* 6.49
plan for *intend* 374.8
plangency *loud tone* 232.3, *deepness* 236.3, *lamentation* 280.1
plangent *deep* 236.8, *lamenting* 280.4
plangently *resonantly* 236.11, *lamentingly* 280.9
planimeter *Fields of Measurement* 589, *planimetry* 603.5
planimetry 603.5, *Fields of Measurement* 589
planing *windsurfing terms* 150.21, *sailing* 150.25, *windsurfing* 150.28
planish *smooth* 545.10
planisphere *observatory* 7.24
plank *wood* 131.3, *carpenter* 131.10, *slice* 588.4, *face* 613.31, *safety device* 810.15
planking *wood* 131.3, *floor covering* 613.13
plankton *little thing* 580.3
planned 387.10; *purposive* 327.11, *solved* 334.15, *meant* 361.12, *intentional* 374.7, *deliberate* 384.5, 589.18, *in preparation* 388.8, *designed* 537.5, *organized* 767.12
planned event *undertaking* 391.1
planned parenthood *birth control* 23.5
planner 387.9; *expert* 127.9, *motivator* 178.11, *answerer* 334.10, *predictor* 357.4, *theorist* 359.4, *meddler* 414.12, *producer* 522.10
planning 387.8, 387.11; *art of war* 76.16, *air force commands* 77.28, *foresight* 357.1, *foresighted* 357.6, *preparation* 388.1, *production* 522.1, *organization* 767.3, *cunning* 822.4
planning ahead *foreseeing* 357.5, *foresighted* 357.6
planning office *planning* 387.8
plan of action *procedure* 387.2
plan of attack *tactics* 399.12
plan of battle *art of war* 76.16
plan of campaign *tactics* 399.12
planometer *planimetry* 603.5
planometry *planimetry* 603.5
plan one's family *practice birth control* 23.10
plan out 387.14
plans *arrangements* 767.10
plans and operations *naval commands* 77.19
plans and operations staff *military staff* 58.5
plant 41.2, 124.7, 710.14; *living organism* 13.10, *living* 13.28, *farm*

16.19, *cultivate* 17.19, *botanical* 41.20, *theatergoer* 136.30, *grip* 151.4, *jumping* 166.11, *personal estate* 470.6, *manufacture* 522.2, *building* 551.9, *locate* 565.9, *rear* 715.10
plant [Inf] *bury* 31.10, *false accusation* 442.2
Plantae *plants* 41.1
plantain *Flowers* 42, *Herbs and Spices* 91
plant anatomy *plant science* 41.10
plantation *farm* 16.2, *trees* 43.4, *mansion* 60.5, *possession of property* 469.3, *property* 470.1
plantation rubber *rubber* 546.3
plant biochemist *biochemist* 12.2
plant biochemistry *plant science* 41.10
plant body 47.13; *fern plant* 46.2, *moss plant* 46.5
plant breeding 17.6; *arable farming* 16.6
plant cell *cell* 13.15
plant-covered *plantlike* 41.13
plant cytology *plant science* 41.10
plant disease *fungal disease* 47.6
plant-eater *eater* 92.15
plant ecology *ecology* 13.25, *plant science* 41.10
planted *plantlike* 41.13, *wooded* 43.12, *located* 565.6, *inserted* 710.5, *reared* 715.7
planted [Inf] *perjurious* 442.7
planter *farm tool* 16.5, *agriculturist* 16.14, *nursery* 41.22, *countryman* 61.8, *preparer* 388.6, *producer* 522.10
plant evidence *accuse falsely* 442.9
plant geography *plant science* 41.10
plant gland *secretory mechanism* 24.3
plant hormone 12.17
plant hunter *plant scientist* 41.11
planting *cultivation* 16.7, *gardening* 17.5, *insertion* 710.1, *rearing* 715.2
plant killer *killing agent* 30.15
plant kingdom *plants* 41.1
plant life *living world* 13.9, *life* 28.1, *plants* 41.1
plantlike 41.13
plant to *intend* 650.10
plant out *plant* 710.14
plant out or off *cultivate* 17.19
plant pathology *botany* 13.7, *plant science* 41.10
plant physiology *botany* 13.7, *plant science* 41.10
plant pigment *pigment* 12.18
plant products 522.8
plant reproductive organs *organs of reproduction* 21.9
plants 41.1, *Phobias* 283
plant science 41.10
plant scientist 41.11
plantsman *producer* 522.10
plantswoman *producer* 522.10
plant taxonomy *plant science* 41.10
plan urban renewal *socialize* 2.14
plaque *dirt* 112.5, *monument* 185.10, *memento* 354.3, *slice* 588.4
plash *rain* 9.57, *small sound* 233.4, *sound faint* 233.8, *hiss* 237.1, 237.3, *interweave* 609.8
plasher *farm tool* 16.5
plashing *cultivation* 16.7, *weaving* 130.6, *interweaving* 609.1
plasma *body fluid* 19.16, 555.3, *matter* 524.4

plasma and chemical etching *industrial processes* 14.27
plasma cell *blood* 555.4
plasmagene *genetic material* 13.20
plasma generation *chemical reaction thermodynamics* 14.29
plasmajet *means of propulsion* 696.2
plasmalemma *cell structure* 13.16
plasma membrane *cell structure* 13.16
plasma parameters *chemical reaction thermodynamics* 14.29
plasma physics *Fields of Modern Physics* 10
plasmic *cellular* 13.30
plasmid *genetic material* 13.20
plasmodium *fungal body* 47.4
plaster *masonry* 14.22, *building materials* 104.2, *material* 144.6, *paste* 561.4, *medical covering* 613.4, *wall covering* 613.12, *face* 613.31, *augment* 748.13, *adhesive* 755.3, *repair* 809.10
plaster [Inf] *bomb* 418.19
plasterboard *wall covering* 613.12
plaster cast *sculpture* 144.1
plaster casting *sculpture* 144.1
plaster down *smooth* 545.10
plastered [Inf] *dead drunk* 121.27
plasterer *artisan* 123.13, *coverer* 613.18
plastering *coating* 613.8
plaster of Paris *material* 144.6
plasterwork *wall covering* 613.12
plastic *polymer* 11.9, *construction material* 14.21, *armor-piercing* 78.18, *type of furniture* 101.2, *sculptural* 144.7, *snowplow* 162.29, *credit* 476.4, *borrowed* 476.8, *credit card* 487.2, *pliant* 543.7, *elastic* 546.5, *resin* 562.6, *formed* 624.6, *changeable* 666.3, *conformable* 781.7, *preserver* 815.9
plastically *elastically* 546.10, *formatively* 624.10
plastic art *visual arts* 133.1, *sculpture* 144.1
plastic bag *bag* 578.7
plastic bullet *ammunition* 78.11
plastic deformation *fold* 8.22, *deformation* 14.16
plastic explosive *explosive* 78.13
plastic helmet *modern armor* 419.7
Plasticiens *Western Art Styles* 133
plasticity *educatability* 48.9, *softness* 543.1, *elasticity* 546.1, *changeableness* 666.1, *pliancy* 781.3
plasticize *make elastic* 546.8
plasticizer *polymer* 11.9
plastic mixing *ceramic process* 129.5
plastic money *credit card* 487.2
plastics 104.6; *industrial chemistry* 11.21, *materials* 104.1
plastic shuttle *badminton terms* 165.11
plastics manufacturing *chemical process industries* 14.26
plastic strain *load* 14.14
plastic surgeon *beautician* 530.11
plastic surgery *Medical Specialties* 107, *cosmetic surgery* 530.2
plastic wrap *cooking equipment* 91.6, *transparent thing* 249.4, *wrapping* 613.10
plastid *cell structure* 13.16
plastometer *Fields of Measurement* 589

plastometry Fields of Measurement 589

plastron *historic armor* 419.8

plat *map* 187.5, 187.12, 387.7, *plan out* 387.14

Plata, Río de la Rivers 570

plate *earth zone* 8.7, plate tectonics 8.19, *tableware* 92.13, *picture* 133.5, *material* 144.6, *means of identification* 184.3, *crockery* 578.16, *coat* 588.3, 613.28, *layer* 588.9, *coating* 613.8, *circular thing* 631.3

plateau *landform* 8.9, *upland* 572.7, *heights* 596.4, *summit* 600.1, *interval* 739.4

Plateau Persian Horse and Pony Breeds 159

plate boundary *plate tectonics* 8.19

plate camera *camera* 132.10

plated *coated* 588.7

plate(ful) *container(ful)* 738.2

plate engraving *engraving* 144.3

plate girder *superstructure* 551.7

plate-girder bridge *bridge* 551.10

plate glass *industrial ceramics* 129.6, *glass* 249.5

platelike **588.8**

plate margin *plate tectonics* 8.19

plate steel *construction material* 14.21

plate tectonics 8.19; *geophysics* 8.2, *science of structure* 551.15

platform *diving* 164.13, *publicity* 173.7, *prospectus* 387.3, *foundation* 601.2, *horizontal surface* 603.3, *supporting structure* 605.2, *railroad station* 688.6

platform dive *diving* 164.6

platform heels *shoes* 100.30

plating *coat* 588.3

platinum Chemical Elements and Common Allotropes 11, *white thing* 253.4, *bullion* 484.16

platinum black *catalysis* 11.16

platinum-blond *white-haired* 253.9

platitude *maxim* 177.1, *lack of emphasis* 201.1, *boring thing* 296.3, *nonsense* 362.2, *truism* 721.6, *generalization* 778.5

platitudinous *proverbial* 177.2, *unemphatic* 201.2, *boring* 296.6, *meaningless* 362.7, *truistic* 721.15, *common* 778.13

platitudinously *proverbially* 177.4, *unemphatically* 201.4, *boringly* 296.10

Platonic *loving* 299.15, *idealistic* 525.10, *formed* 624.6

platonic *chaste* 431.10

Platonically *lovingly* 299.29, *subjectively* 525.14, *formatively* 624.10

Platonic form *form* 624.1

Platonic idea *idea* 327.1

Platonic love *love* 299.1

Platonic solid *polyhedron* 6.44

Platonism Philosophical Schools of Thought 4, *idealism* 525.5, *form* 624.1

Platonist Philosophical Schools of Thought 4, *nonmaterialist* 525.7

platoon *military organization* 58.4, *force* 59.10, *army unit* 77.14

Platte Rivers 570

platter *tableware* 92.13, *crockery* 578.16

platyhelminth *worm* 39.14

Platyhelminthes *worm* 39.14

platyhelminthic *wormlike* 39.24

platypus *egg-laying mammal* 35.4

plaudit *acclaim* 437.5

plausibility 838.3; *believability* 87.4, *possibility* 836.1

plausible 838.7; *rational* 4.15, *believable* 87.7, *realizable* 719.9

plausibly *rationally* 4.25, *believably* 87.13, *arguably* 329.16, *potentially* 836.11

play 136.2, 141.14, 149.7, 155.8, 156.8, 167.12; *act* 136.34, 137.20, 187.13, *participate* 145.6, *play ice hockey* 158.9, *play field hockey* 158.10, *game* 167.1, *bridge* 168.4, *occur* 264.14, *fun* 269.4, *show* 404.12, *action* 412.1, *contend* 422.22, *operation* 509.1, *be operational* 509.10, *influence* 512.1, *work of art* 522.4, *available space* 563.6, *scope* 829.7, *production* 843.5

play, the *drama* 136.1

playa *marsh* 572.3

play about *occupy oneself* 412.15

play above par *be unequal* 741.7

play a character *act* 187.13

playact *act* 136.34, *be affected* 367.4

playacting *acting* 136.22

play-action pass *play* 155.8

playactor *actor* 136.25

play a dangerous game *be cunning* 822.5

play a double role *be dishonorable* 192.21

play a frame *bowl* 151.8

play against *contend* 422.22

play agent or **playbroker** *producer* 136.28

play a joke on *hoax* 193.20, *be humorous* 277.11

play along with *acquiesce* 421.5

play a role or **part in** *be active in* 412.17, *influence* 512.11

play around [Inf] *be dishonorable* 192.21

play a supporting role *follow* 745.12

play back *play defense* 155.19, *renew* 797.19

play badminton *play tennis* 165.13

play ball *cooperate* 827.12

play baseball **147.9**

play basketball **148.7**

play below par *be unequal* 741.7

play billiards *play* 149.7

playbook *script* 136.7

playboy *social person* 408.7, *sexually immoral person* 432.8

play by ear *play* 141.14, *improvise* 396.6

play-by-play account *factual account* 202.4

play cards 168.7

play cat and mouse *hunt* 385.14

play checkers *play* 167.12

play chess *play* 167.12

play construction *dramaturgy* 136.6

play defense 155.19

play doctor *dramatist* 136.27

play down 195.17; *silence* 231.4, *underestimate* 344.5, *disparage* 440.11, *mitigate* 521.9, *make smaller* 747.8

played *billiard* 149.6

played down *downplayed* 195.13, *unpretentious* 526.8

played out *canceled* 773.15

player 141.2, 149.5; *artistic worker* 123.12, *actor* 136.25, *musician* 141.1, *sportsman* 145.4, *golfer* 156.7, *gambler* 167.6, *performer*

412.5, *contender* 422.13, *opponent* 828.10

player piano Musical Instruments 142

players *sportsman* 145.4

play fair *be right* 429.12

play fake *play* 155.8

play fast and loose *be irresolute* 666.6

play field hockey **158.10**

play flat *be dissonant* 241.6

play follow the leader *emulate* 736.11

play footsie with [Inf] *communicate love* 299.25

play for a draw *act on the defensive* 419.29

play for time *delay* 658.13, *be cunning* 822.5, *block* 826.17

playful *recreational* 167.10, *capricious* 381.4, *innocent* 449.6

playfully *innocently* 449.13

playfulness *fun* 269.4, *capriciousness* 381.2, *innocence* 449.1

play games *play* 167.12

playgoer *theatergoer* 136.30

play golf *play* 156.8

playground *school place* 48.16, *amusement* 167.7

playgroup *school* 48.11

play havoc with *impair* 808.18

play hell with [Inf] *ruin* 523.15, *cause trouble* 824.21

play hide-and-seek *conceal oneself* 181.15, *become invisible* 245.6

play hob with *cause trouble* 824.21

play hooky *depart* 265.6, *escape* 816.8

play hooky or **hookey** *run away* 386.21, *abscond* 576.16

playhouse *theater* 136.16

play ice hockey 158.9

playing *acting* 136.22, 187.6, 187.9, *musical* 141.11, *gambling* 167.4, *recreational* 167.10

playing a character *acting* 187.6

playing area *stage* 136.18

playing cards *cards* 168.2

playing down *downplaying* 195.6

playing engagement *engagement* 136.15

playing field *school place* 48.16

playing for time *tactics* 399.12

playing one's cards close to one's chest *sparing with words* 208.6

playing short-handed *ice hockey tactics* 158.4

playing terms **148.4**

playing the part of *acting* 187.6

playing the stock market *speculation* 480.9

playing with a full deck [Inf] *sane* 109.3

playing with fire *recklessness* 286.2

playing with oneself *sex act* 20.10

playing with one's food *delicate eating* 92.3

play into the hands of *be clumsy* 128.9

play it low-key *submit* 421.4

play it safe *proceed with caution* 287.12

play it straight [Inf] *be sincere* 191.8, *talk straight* 630.15

playland *drama* 136.1

playlet *play* 136.2

play man-to-man *play basketball* 148.7

playmate *friend* 62.2

play merry hell with [Inf] *ruin* 523.15

play no part in *shun* 386.14

play of color *variegation* 263.1

play off against *exploit* 393.11

play of fancy *conception* 360.4

play offense **155.18**

playoff game *football* 155.1

play on *exploit* 393.11

play on or **upon** *manipulate* 508.12

play one's card's right *be good at* 445.18

play one's cards well *be skillful* 127.14

play one's part *conduct oneself* 399.17, *do one's duty* 433.17

play on words *wit* 277.3, *equivocation* 380.1, *be equivocal* 380.7

play part 136.8

play piano *mute* 233.9

play poker *play cards* 168.7

play politics *compromise* 461.7

play pool *play* 149.7

play producer *producer* 522.10

playroom *room* 60.9

play run-and-shoot *play basketball* 148.7

play Russian roulette *be rash* 286.8, *face danger* 811.12

play safe *be safe* 810.20

play school *school* 48.11

play second banana [Inf] *entertain* 138.16

play second fiddle *be humble* 298.16, *be modest* 403.11, *be average* 742.8

play second fiddle to *follow* 745.12

play sharp *be dissonant* 241.6

play snooker *play* 149.7

play soccer 163.8

play squash *play tennis* 165.13

playsuit *baby clothes* 100.24

play tennis 165.13

play the big board *finance* 457.7

play the devil's advocate *be insubordinate* 416.8

play the devil with *ruin* 523.15

play the fool 353.7; *be humorous* 277.11, *be ridiculous* 368.6

play the fox *be cunning* 822.5

play the futures market *finance* 457.7, *speculate* 480.19

play the game *behave well* 399.18, *be right* 429.12, *conform* 781.11

play the lead *act* 136.34, 137.20, *lead* 744.19

play the part of *act* 187.13

play the same old record *harp* 797.17

play the stock exchange *finance* 457.7

play the stock market *speculate* 480.19

play the straight man *entertain* 138.16

play the waiting game *delay* 658.13

plaything *toy* 167.9, *cheap item* 497.5, *cheap thing* 800.7

plaything of the gods *person in adversity* 848.9

play to the gallery *overact* 136.35, *appear* 331.18, *be affected* 367.4, *show off* 404.26

play tricks with *be cunning* 822.5

play truant *depart* 265.6, *run away* 386.21, *abscond* 576.16, *escape* 816.8

play upon *take action* 509.12

play up to [Inf] *seek friendship* 62.11, *fawn* 401.9
play with *touch* 216.9
play with a full deck [Inf] *be sane* 109.5
play with dynamite *be in danger* 811.11
play with fire *be rash* 286.8, *be foolish* 353.6, *be in danger* 811.11
play with oneself [Inf] *stimulate* 20.22
play with one's thoughts *imagine* 360.14
play with with one's food *taste* 92.24
playwright *dramatist* 136.27, *author* 139.13, *descriptive writer* 202.10, *producer* 522.10
playwriting *dramaturgy* 136.6
plaza *urban area* 567.10, *center of activity* 612.4
plea 329.5; *question* 333.1, *counterstatement* 334.5, *defense* 441.2
plea-bargain *compromise* 461.7
plea bargaining *pretrial proceedings* 54.13
pleach *interweave* 609.8
pleached *interwoven* 609.6
pleaching *cultivation* 16.7, *weaving* 130.6
plead 329.14; *litigate* 54.27, *persuade* 178.15, *question* 333.16, *answer back* 334.19, *justify* 441.12
plead a case *propound* 359.9
pleader *representative* 75.3, *persuader* 178.9, *vindicator* 441.5
plead for 419.25
plead for forgiveness *ask for mercy* 308.10, *ask forgiveness* 312.12
plead for mercy *ask for mercy* 308.10
plead for one's life *ask for mercy* 308.10
plead guilty *stand trial* 54.29, *convict* 54.33, *admit* 180.11, *be guilty* 450.9
pleading *exhortation* 178.2, *persuasive* 178.12, *plea* 329.5, *apologetic* 329.10, *questioning* 333.11, *retaliatory* 334.13, *inducement* 508.2
pleadings *pretrial proceedings* 54.13
plead nolo contendere *stand trial* 54.29
plead not guilty *stand trial* 54.29
plead one's own cause *justify* 441.12
plead to the charge *stand trial* 54.29
plead with *ask for mercy* 308.10
pleasant 214.7, 222.6, 271.5; *warm* 9.46, *friendly* 62.5, *desirable* 288.11, *rainless* 560.11
pleasantly 271.12; *amicably* 62.13, *sweetly* 222.8, *desirably* 288.24
pleasantness 271.1; *pleasure* 214.2, *sweetness* 222.1
pleasant person *pleasant thing* 271.4
pleasantries *courtesies* 410.3
pleasantry *pleasant thing* 271.4, *joke* 277.6
pleasant sensation *pleasure* 214.2
pleasant taste *taste* 219.1
pleasant thing 271.4
please *give pleasure* 214.13, *cause joy* 269.11, *make pleasant* 271.10, *satisfy* 273.7
pleased 214.9; *joyful* 269.6, *satisfied* 273.4
pleased as Punch *joyful* 269.6

pleased with oneself *prideful* 297.8, *self-admiring* 402.10
please oneself *be illegal* 53.30, *feel pleasure* 214.12, *follow one's own will* 372.13, *be selfish* 444.6, *be independent* 829.18
pleasing *pleasant* 214.7, 271.5, *satisfying* 273.5, *desirable* 288.11, *likable* 290.7, *lovable* 299.20, *attractive* 477.13
pleasingly 214.15; *desirably* 288.24, *likably* 290.12, *lovably* 299.31, *takingly* 477.23
pleasing to the eye *picturesque* 529.9
pleasurable 214.6; *pleasant* 214.7, 271.5, *desirable* 288.11
pleasurably *desirably* 288.24
pleasure 214.2, 271.2; *gaiety* 269.3, *fun* 269.4, *pleasantness* 271.1, *pleasant thing* 271.4, *satisfaction* 273.1, *Phobias* 283, *likes* 290.3, *will* 372.1
pleasure, a *easy thing* 823.6
pleasure boat *vessel* 609.3
pleasure-bound *self-indulgent* 456.6
pleasure garden *garden* 17.2
pleasure-loving 271.9
pleasure principle *libido* 108.26, *physical pleasure* 214.1
pleasure-seeker 214.4; *self-indulgent person* 456.5
pleasure seeking *self-indulgence* 456.1
pleasure-seeking 214.10; *pleasure-loving* 271.9, *self-indulgent* 456.6
pleat 637.2, 637.8; *part of garment* 100.27, *make clothing* 100.44, *layer* 588.1
pleated *folded* 637.5
pleated skirt *skirt* 100.12
pleb *commoner* 71.1
plebeian *commoner* 71.1, *common* 71.3, *lowly* 298.9, 597.17, *insignificant* 745.6
plebeians *common people* 71.2
plebiscite *judgment* 341.1, *electing* 382.5
plebs *group* 18.13, *common people* 71.2
plecopteran *insectile* 40.11
plectrum *part of stringed instrument* 142.2
pledge *believing* 87.2, *drink to* 93.20, *vow* 189.3, 189.23, *contract* 391.2, 462.2, 462.11, *take charge of* 391.8, *participate* 408.15, *duty* 433.1, *impose a duty* 433.14, *promise* 458.1, 458.11, 464.2, 464.10, *certify* 464.11, *borrow* 476.10, *transferred thing* 685.6, *settlement* 735.6, *settle* 735.26, *guarantee* 840.4, *make certain* 840.14
pledged *vowed* 189.14, *dutiful* 433.6, *promised* 458.8, *guaranteeing* 458.9, *contractual* 462.7, *guaranteed* 464.6, 840.10, *indebted* 488.7, *settled* 735.16
pledgee *lender* 487.5
pledge oneself *incur a duty* 433.15
pledge one's word or **oneself** or **one's honor** *promise* 458.11
pledger *affirmer* 189.9, *assenter* 462.5, *borrower* 476.7
pledging *guaranteeing* 458.9, *borrowing* 476.1
pledgor *debtor* 488.6
Pléiade, la *Western Literary Groups* 139
Pleiades *constellation* 7.13

pleinairism *Western Art Styles* 133
Pleistocene Epoch *Geologic Time Intervals* 8
plenary *complete* 761.6
plenipotentiary *delegated* 79.4, *agent* 80.3, *commissioner* 833.5, *commissioned* 833.6
plenitude *fertility* 22.1, *plenty* 97.2, *excess* 99.1, *fullness* 761.5
plenitudinous *plentiful* 97.4
plenteous *fertile* 22.8, *plentiful* 97.4, *lush* 485.11, *dense* 540.6, *ample* 795.9
plenteously *plentifully* 97.11, *densely* 540.10
plenteousness *plenty* 97.2, *abundance* 448.4
plentiful 97.4; *fertile* 22.8, *excessive* 99.5, *available* 105.16, *lush* 485.11, *abundant* 498.8, *big* 579.13, *ample* 795.9
plentifully 97.11; *generously* 498.12, *amply* 579.20
plentifulness *fertility* 22.1, *plenty* 97.2
plenty 90.4, 97.2; *fertility* 22.1, *excess* 99.1, *quantity* 105.5, *opulence* 485.3, *abundance* 498.4, *availability* 575.5, *profuseness* 795.3, *successfulness* 845.3, *prosperity* 847.1
plenty of rope *liberality* 829.8
plenty to do *business* 414.6
pleonasm *wordiness* 5.23, *superfluity* 99.4, *diffuseness* 199.1, *extraneousness* 724.1, *surplus* 750.4
pleonastic *worded* 5.38, *superfluous* 99.8, *diffuse* 199.3, *extraneous* 724.8, *surplus* 750.8, *repetitious* 797.11
pleonastically *lexically* 5.46, *residually* 750.11
plesiosaur *extinct reptile* 37.9
plethora *excess* 99.1
plethoric *excessive* 99.5
pleura *body covering* 19.4
pleurisy *respiratory disease* 114.12
Pleven *Horse and Pony Breeds* 159
Pleven Blackhead *Breeds of Sheep* 16
Plevna *Breeds of Cattle* 16
Plexiglas™ *polymer* 11.9
PL/I *Programming Languages* 15
pliability *educatability* 48.9, *persuadability* 178.8, *acquiescence* 373.3, *softness* 543.1, *elasticity* 546.1, *wieldiness* 823.3
pliable *educatable* 48.18, *persuadable* 178.14, *acquiescent* 373.9, *pliant* 543.7, *elastic* 546.5, *wieldy* 823.12
pliableness *softness* 543.1
pliably *studiously* 48.26
pliancy 781.3; *persuadability* 178.8, *acquiescence* 373.3, *servility* 401.1, *obedience* 426.1, *softness* 543.1, *elasticity* 546.1, *changeableness* 666.1, *wieldiness* 823.3
pliant 543.7; *persuadable* 178.14, *acquiescent* 373.9, *unsteady* 378.7, *servile* 401.6, *submitting* 421.3, *obedient* 426.4, *elastic* 546.5, *changeable* 666.3, *conformable* 781.7, *wieldy* 823.12
pliantly *obediently* 426.9, *softly* 543.18, *elastically* 546.10, *changeably* 666.7, *adaptably* 781.15
plica *fold* 637.1
plical *folded* 637.5

plicate *folded* 637.5
plication *fold* 637.1
plicature *fold* 637.1
pliers *hand tool* 103.3, *retainer* 471.3, *extractor* 711.9
plight *futility* 282.3, *predicament* 725.3, 824.5, *difficult circumstances* 726.6, *adversity* 848.1
plighted *marriageable* 64.17, *promised* 458.8
plight one's troth *marry* 64.19, *propose (marriage)* 299.28, *get engaged to* 458.12
Plimsoll line *indicator* 183.7, *measuring instrument* 589.12
plinth *foundation* 601.2, *supporting structure* 605.2
Pliocene Epoch *Geologic Time Intervals* 8
plod *work* 122.8, *persevere* 377.10, *slow motion* 693.3, *move slowly* 693.11
plod along *move slowly* 693.11
plodder 693.6
plodding *working* 122.6, *constancy* 377.3, *constant* 377.8, *industrious* 414.16, *slow* 693.7
plod on *protract* 669.9
plonk *dull sound* 233.2, *be nonresonant* 233.10, *crack* 234.7
plonk [Brit inf] *wine* 93.11
plop *dull sound* 233.2, *small sound* 233.4, *sound faint* 233.8, *be nonresonant* 233.10, *crack* 234.2, 234.7, *droop* 714.14
plop down *droop* 714.14
plot 387.6, 387.15, 564.9; *graph* 6.30, *represent* 6.91, *farmland* 16.3, *burial place* 31.7, *dramaturgy* 136.6, *script* 137.5, *aspect of fiction* 139.5, *secretiveness* 182.3, *map* 187.12, *artifice* 193.5, *scheme* 193.18, *aim* 327.17, *topic* 328.1, *gist* 329.4, *predetermination* 384.1, *plan out* 387.14, *lay the foundations* 388.16, *overactivity* 414.9, *subversion* 427.3, *subvert* 427.13, *property* 470.1, *portion* 474.2, *region* 564.1, *navigate* 690.15, *collaboration* 757.2, *come together* 757.10, *cunning* 822.1, *stratagem* 822.2, *be cunning* 822.5, *concealment* 844.2
plot against *plot* 387.15
plot horoscopes *divine* 86.24
plot of ground or *land* *plot* 564.9
plot-spinner *planner* 387.9
plotted *designed* 537.5, *measured* 589.16
plotter *hardcopy device* 15.10, *schemer* 193.10, *planner* 387.9, *cunning person* 822.3
Plott hound *Breeds of Dogs* 35
plotting *artful* 193.13, *planning* 387.11, *navigation* 690.5, *cunning* 822.4
plotzed [Inf] *dead drunk* 121.27
ploughman's lunch *notable international dishes* 90.40
plover *water bird* 36.9
plover, piping *Endangered US Birds* 36
plover, western snowy *Endangered US Birds* 36
plovers *Collective Names* 59
plow *farm tool* 16.5, *farm* 16.19, *garden tool* 103.4, *use a sharp tool* 549.17, *furrow* 638.5
plowable *farmable* 16.17
plow a lonely furrow *be one* 788.17
plowed *farmable* 16.17, *furrowed* 638.3

plowed land *farmland* 16.3
plow horse *workhorse* 159.3
plowing *cultivation* 16.7
plowman *farm worker* 16.15, *preparer* 388.6
plowshare *sharp-edged thing* 549.6
ploy *artifice* 193.5, *method* 387.4, *stratagem* 822.2
pluck *sound* 141.15, *play an instrument* 142.9, *touch* 216.9, *courage* 284.1, *will* 376.5, *stamina* 377.4, *endurance* 516.4, *vigor* 518.1, *depilate* 614.20, *jerk* 699.3, *pull at* 699.12, *take off* 749.7, *separate* 753.12
pluck at one's heartstrings *attract* 700.11
plucked *removed* 574.9, *shed* 614.14
plucked string instrument *musical instrument* 142.1
plucking *depilation* 614.8
plucking out *removal* 574.2
pluck out *remove* 574.16, *extract* 711.13
pluck to pieces *demolish* 523.12
pluck up *gather up* 715.14
pluck up courage *take courage* 284.15
plucky *courageous* 284.9, *enduring* 377.9, *strong in spirit* 516.11
plug *tobacco* 121.23, *bait* 154.6, *golf equipment* 156.5, *detention* 471.2, *detain* 471.9, *stopper* 584.3, *stop* 584.14, *cover* 613.2, 613.24, *insert* 710.4, *remainder* 750.1, *harp* 797.17, *repair* 809.10
plug or **plug hat** *hat* 100.32
plug [Inf] *horse* 159.1, *public relations (PR)* 173.8, *publicize* 173.18, *emphasize* 206.0, *shoot* 696.18
plug a hole *repair* 809.10
plug away *persevere* 377.10, *try* 414.21
plugged *stopped* 584.9, *covered* 613.19, *inset* 710.8
plugged nickel [Inf] *little bit* 800.4
plug in *conduct* 14.51, *power* 106.17, *activate* 509.11, *empower* 514.20, *link* 752.18
plug the gap *entrench* 419.24
plug up *repair* 809.10
plum *red thing* 257.3, *purple thing* 262.3, *purple* 262.6
plum [Inf] *good thing* 445.9, *profit* 467.6, *takings* 477.8
plumage 36.7; *animal covering* 613.15
plumb *accurately* 350.6, *weight* 538.8, *measure* 589.20, *bathymetry* 598.3, *measure depth* 598.22, *plumb line* 602.4, *vertical* 602.5, *make vertical* 602.9, *vertically* 602.11, *straight* 630.8, *directly* 697.16, *correctly* 721.29, *completely* 759.14
plumb [Inf] *complete* 761.6, *completely* 761.13
plumbago *Flowers* 42, *lubricant* 562.7
plumb bob *weight* 538.8
plumber *artisan* 123.13
plumbing *cleaning* 111.2
plumb line 602.4; *measuring instrument* 589.12, *bathymetry* 598.3, *straight line* 630.2
plumbness *verticality* 602.1
plumb on *accurately* 350.6
plumb the depths *measure depth* 598.22, *become inferior* 745.11
plum-colored *purple* 262.6
plume *plumage* 36.7

plume of smoke *miasma* 556.3
plummet *be cheap* 497.13, *weight* 538.8, *fall vertically* 602.10, *drop* 714.15
plummeting *fall* 714.4, *falling* 714.11
plummet lead *fishing tackle* 154.7
plump *dull sound* 233.2, *be nonresonant* 233.10, *soften* 543.14, *fat* 579.15, *swell* 581.15, *thick* 594.5, *well-rounded* 633.8, *directly* 697.16, *droop* 714.14
plump as a dumpling or **partridge** *fat* 579.15
plump down *droop* 714.14
plump for *will* 372.11, *side with* 382.15, *advise* 825.27
plumpishness *fatness* 579.5
plumply *fatly* 579.22
plumpness *fatness* 579.5, *thickness* 594.1, *round body* 633.2
plump up *soften* 543.14, *swell* 581.15
plumulae *plumage* 36.7
plumule *stem* 41.5, *seed* 41.9
plunder 479.16; *conquer* 77.36, *takings* 477.8, *take away forcefully* 477.19, *stolen goods* 479.4, *plundering* 479.5, *lay waste* 523.14, *impair* 808.18
plundered *taking* 477.12
plunderer 479.9; *militarist* 77.3, *gainer* 467.9
plundering 479.5; *conquest* 477.6, *taking* 477.12, *stolen* 479.12
plunderous *stolen* 479.12
plunge *dive* 164.15, *be cheap* 497.13, *be destroyed* 523.17, *deepen* 598.21, *verticality* 602.1, *fall vertically* 602.10, *be in motion* 677.14, *stagger* 684.11, *pitch* 684.25, *sail* 690.16, *be swift* 694.10, *immersion* 710.3, *immerse* 710.12, *fall* 714.4, *drop* 714.15, *bring down* 716.14, *become inferior* 745.11, *decline* 747.4, *decrease* 747.7
plunge in *impact* 710.11
plunge into *undertake* 391.7, *fall into* 706.15, *make a beginning* 771.26
plunge-stepping *climbing techniques* 161.3
plunging *deep* 598.9, *vertical* 602.5, *descending motion* 677.6, *directional* 677.13, *fall* 714.4, *falling* 714.11, *submergence* 716.3
plunging fire *firing* 418.6
plunging neckline *part of garment* 100.27
plunk *dull sound* 233.2, *be nonresonant* 233.10, *crack* 234.2, 234.7
plunk [Inf] *blow* 695.5, *directly* 697.16
pluperfect *grammatical term* 5.29, *past tense* 651.2
plural 793.6; *grammatical term* 5.29, *of grammar* 5.41, *quantitative* 738.6, *plurality* 793.1
pluralism *Philosophical Schools of Thought* 4, *variety* 732.2, *multiplicity* 793.2
pluralist 793.5, *Philosophical Schools of Thought* 4
plurality 793.1; *numbers* 738.5
pluralize 793.9
plurally 793.10; *grammatically* 5.48
pluralness *plurality* 793.1
plural number *plurality* 793.1
plus *extra* 748.6, *additionally* 748.15
plus fours *pants* 100.14

plush *Fabrics and Fibers* 130, *grand* 404.22, *opulent* 485.10, *smooth* 543.8
plushiness *smoothness* 543.2
plushness *grandeur* 404.10, *opulence* 485.3
plushy *smooth* 543.8
plushy [Inf] *opulent* 485.10
plus sign *mathematical symbol* 6.11, *symbol* 183.3
Pluto *Planets and Their Satellites* 7, *planet* 7.16, *Deities* 82
plutocracy 485.5; *oligarchy* 49.10
plutocrat *company leader* 68.8, *wealthy person* 485.6, *prosperous person* 847.4
plutocratic *governmental* 49.24, *masterful* 68.15
pluton *igneous rock* 8.32
Plutonian *astronomical* 7.33, *demonic* 446.9
plutonic *petrographic* 8.58
plutonic intrusion *igneous rock* 8.32
plutonic rock *igneous rock* 8.32
plutonium *Chemical Elements and Common Allotropes* 11, *nuclear power* 106.8
Plutus *Deities* 82
pluvial *rainy* 9.50
pluviometer *weather instrument* 9.7, *measuring instrument* 557.19
pluviometric *barometric* 9.39
pluviophobia *Phobias* 283
Pluviôse *French Revolutionary Calendar* 646
pluviosity *rain* 9.27, *mistiness* 559.2
pluvious or **pluviose** *rainy* 9.50
ply *use* 393.9, *occupy oneself* 412.15, *layer* 588.1, *be regular* 663.10
plying *nautical* 690.14
Plymouth Rock *Breeds of Fowl* 16
ply one's trade *occupy oneself* 412.15
ply with the oars *work* 122.8
plywood *construction material* 14.21, *wood* 131.3, *wall covering* 613.12
P.M. *horologically* 646.15, *evening* 656.2
pneuma *spirit* 86.10, *psyche* 108.25
pneumatic *compressible* 543.9, *aerostatic* 556.20, *aerial* 558.14
pneumatically *softly* 543.18, *aerostatically* 556.27, *airily* 558.25
pneumatics *aerostatics* 556.11
pneumatometer *vaporimeter* 556.13, *Fields of Measurement* 589
pneumatometry *Fields of Measurement* 589
pneumatophobia *Phobias* 283
pneumatostatics *aerostatics* 556.11
pneumoconiosis *respiratory disease* 114.12
pneumodynamically *aerostatically* 556.27
pneumodynamics *aerostatics* 556.11
pneumonia *respiratory disease* 114.12
pneumonic *respiratory* 558.19
pneumonic plague *plague* 114.6
pnigophobia or **pnigerophobia** *Phobias* 283
p–n junction *semiconductor* 10.34
Po *Rivers* 570
Poaceae *grass* 45.1
poaceous *grasslike* 45.7
poach *cook* 91.10, *hunt* 160.12,

385.14, *steal* 479.14, *transgress* 712.14
poached *culinary* 91.9
poached egg *egg dish* 90.18
poached fish *fish dish* 90.19
poacher *cooking equipment* 91.6, *hunter* 160.9, 385.6, *thief* 479.8
poaching *cooking technique* 91.2, *stealing* 479.1, *stolen* 479.12
pochette *Musical Instruments* 142
pock *nap* 552.3
pocked *mottled* 263.10, *marked* 533.6, *coarse* 544.6, *concave* 635.5
pocket *battleground* 76.24, *part of garment* 100.27, *billiards* 149.1, *snooker* 149.4, *play* 155.8, *receive* 473.13, *money storage* 484.20, *undersized* 580.8, *class* 777.1
pocket battleship *warship* 77.21
pocket billiards *billiards* 149.1, *pool* 149.3
pocket billiard table *snooker* 149.4
pocketbook *money storage* 484.20, *bag* 578.7
pocket calculator *calculator* 784.5
pocket comb *cleaning tool* 111.10
pocket edition *little thing* 580.3
pocketful *container(ful)* 738.2
pocketed *billiard* 149.6
pocketing the ball *billiards play* 149.2
pocket money *profit* 467.6, *gift* 472.2, *something received* 473.2, *change* 484.3, *income* 492.3
pocket-size(d) *undersized* 580.8
pocket the affront *show mercy* 312.11
pocket the ball *play* 149.7
pocket the insult *succumb* 421.7
pocket veto *veto* 503.3
pocket watch *Timepieces and Timers* 646
pockmark *skin disease* 114.16, *mark* 533.2, *make concave* 635.7
pockmark or **pock** *cavity* 635.3
pockmarked *mottled* 263.10, *marked* 533.6, *coarse* 544.6, *concave* 635.5
pocky *coarse* 544.6
pococurante *indifferent person* 289.6, *indifferent* 289.7
pococurantism *apathy* 322.2
pocrescophobia *Phobias* 283
pod *botanical fruit* 44.2, *Collective Names* 59, *exteriority* 610.2, *casing* 613.9
p.o.'d [Inf] *angry* 302.11
podetium *lichen* 47.16
podium *Architectural Elements* 134, *stage* 136.18
podocarpus *Trees and Shrubs* 43
Podunk *village* 567.3
podzol *soil* 8.42
poem *poetry* 139.8, *work of art* 522.4, *beautiful thing* 529.3
poesy *poetry* 139.8
poet *author* 139.13, *descriptive writer* 202.10, *visionary* 360.9, *producer* 522.10
poetaster *author* 139.13
poetess *author* 139.13
poetic 139.19; *imaginative* 360.10, *graceful* 527.4
poetical *poetic* 139.19
poetically 139.23
poetic diction *literary device* 139.12
poetic drama *dramatic style* 136.3
poetic frenzy *inspiration* 360.2
poeticism *literary device* 139.12
poeticize *fantasize* 360.15

poetic justice *revenge* 441.4, *retribution* 454.7
poetic language *literary device* 139.12
poetic license *literary device* 139.12, *conception* 360.4, *distortion of truth* 627.4, *freedom* 829.1
poetic prose *prose* 139.7
poetics *poetry* 139.8
poetize *write* 139.21
poet laureate *author* 139.13
poetry **139.8,** *Phobias* 283, *conception* 360.4
poetry in motion *grace* 527.2
pogonophobia *Phobias* 283
pogrom *slaughter* 30.5, *social discrimination* 337.4
poignancy *emphasis* 200.1, *piquancy* 221.1, *stimulation* 221.4
poignant *emphatic* 200.3, *descriptive* 202.11, *exciting* 212.8, *stimulating* 221.7
poignantly *stimulatingly* 221.11
poikilotherm *reptile* 37.1
poikilothermal *cold-blooded* 218.12
poikilothermic *reptilian* 37.12, *fishlike* 38.10
poinciana *Trees and Shrubs* 43
poinephobia *Phobias* 283
poinsettia *Flowers* 42
point **6.34, 361.5;** *Punctuation Marks* 5, *direct* 126.11, 697.13, *material* 144.6, *fishing tackle* 154.7, *hockey areas* 158.2, *hunt* 160.12, *tennis terms* 165.5, *gesture* 183.5, 183.17, *purpose* 327.4, *topic* 328.1, *issue* 328.2, *line of argument* 329.3, *gist* 329.4, *question* 333.1, *usefulness* 393.2, 801.1, *moral* 431.5, *sharp point* 549.2, *sharpen* 549.16, *exact location* 565.2, *peninsula* 572.5, *situation* 573.1, *little thing* 580.3, *General Units* 589, *summit* 600.1, *core* 612.2, *point in time* 645.4, *aim* 697.14, *occurrence* 726.2, *aspect* 726.4, *interval* 739.4, *limit* 773.7, *one* 788.1
point after touchdown (PAT) *scoring* 155.5
point a moral *moralize* 431.14
point at *or* **to** *gesture* 183.17, *direct* 697.13
point at infinity *point* 6.34
point at issue *issue* 328.2
point-blank *directly* 697.16
point-blank refusal *refusal* 506.1
pointed *linear* 6.77, *affirmed* 189.11, *assertive* 189.20, *concise* 198.4, *emphatic* 200.3, *summary* 204.5, *focused* 328.6, *meaningful* 361.6, *sharp* 549.10, *situated* 573.5, *topped* 600.8, *angular* 628.7, *convergent* 702.7
pointed for *directed* 697.9
pointedly *affirmatively* 189.29, *assertively* 189.35, *concisely* 198.6, *summarily* 204.10, *thematically* 328.13, *sharply* 549.19
pointedness *assertiveness* 189.8, *conciseness* 198.1, *summariness* 204.4, *sharpness* 549.1
pointed objects *Phobias* 283
pointed out *emphasized* 200.4
pointed shoes *shoes* 100.30
pointer *Breeds of Dogs* 35, *hunting dog* 160.7, *inside information* 170.4, *indicator* 183.7, *that which makes visible* 244.4, *indication* 339.3
Pointers (Ursa Major) *constellation* 7.13

point guard *basketball team* 148.2
pointillism *Western Art Styles* 133, *maculation* 263.4
point in common *similarity* 733.1
pointing *sculpture* 144.1, *gesture* 183.5, *signifying* 183.11, *evidential* 339.8
pointing machine *material* 144.6
pointing out *sign* 183.1, *identification* 184.1, *directions* 697.7
pointing to *accusatory* 442.6, *tending to* 513.4
point in time 645.4
pointless *circumlocutory* 199.4, *unemphatic* 201.2, *futile* 282.9, 802.10, *foolish* 353.5, *aimless* 362.8, *blunt* 550.5, *extraneous* 724.8, *unrelated* 728.6
pointlessly *futilely* 282.16, *smoothly* 550.10, *extraneously* 724.16, *irrelatively* 728.16
pointlessness *circumlocution* 199.2, *lack of emphasis* 201.1, *futility* 282.3, 802.3, *folly* 353.1, *aimlessness* 362.3, 362.6, *extraneousness* 724.1, *unrelatedness* 728.1
point of action *cutting edge* 618.3
point of arrival *destination* 704.6
point of departure *baseline* 601.4, *starting point* 771.11
point of etiquette *etiquette* 406.3
point of inflection *point* 6.34
point of land *peninsula* 572.5
point of likeness *similarity* 733.1
point of no return *critical time* 659.3, *critical moment* 726.7
point of rest *center* 612.1
point of union 752.8
point of view *philosophy* 4.1, *religion* 81.1, *belief* 87.1, *aspect of fiction* 139.5, *viewpoint* 242.12, *external appearance* 264.5, *supposition* 359.1
point one's finger *gesture* 183.17
point out *inform* 170.11, *sign* 183.19, *identify* 184.11, *emphasize* 200.6, *make visible* 242.25, 244.9, *present* 264.15, *raise the point* 328.10, *demonstrate* 331.15, *direct* 697.13, *display* 843.13, *reveal* 843.14
points *Phobias* 283, *advantage* 744.3
point size *design and makeup* 174.8
point system *boxing terms* 152.3
point the finger *accuse* 442.8
point the way *sign* 183.19, *direct* 697.13, *precede* 769.13
point to *direct* 126.11, *sign* 183.19, *aim* 327.17, *focus on* 328.9, *predict* 358.14, *mean* 361.13, *tend* 513.5
point to *or* **out** *specify* 779.18
point-to-point *Sporting Activities* 145
point-to-point race *horse racing* 159.10
point up *present* 264.15, *reveal* 843.14
pointy *sharp* 549.10
poise *good conduct* 399.5, *Scientific and Technical Units* 589, *lack of motion* 678.1, *equilibrium* 740.2, *equalize* 740.12, *ease of manner* 823.4
poised *motionless* 678.4
poison **117.7, 117.18;** *catalysis* 11.16, *catalytic* 11.37, *react* 11.38, *murder weapon* 30.3, *killing agent* 30.15, *murder* 30.20, *kill animals* 30.25, *dirty* 112.11, *poisoning* 114.8, *cause ill health* 114.30, *prophylaxis* 115.4, *Phobias* 283,

cause hate 300.12, *evil thing* 446.2, *be evil* 446.10, *capital punishment* 454.12, *instrument of execution* 454.15, *agent of destruction* 523.7, *make worse* 808.17
poison [Inf] *alcoholic drink* 93.9
poisoned *toxic* 114.28
poisoner *murderer* 30.12, *evil person* 446.3
poison gas *chemical warfare* 76.5, 117.9
poisoning 114.8, 117.6; *murder* 30.2, *illness* 114.2, *physical deterioration* 808.4
poison oak *Trees and Shrubs* 43
poisonous 117.14; *killing* 30.17, *unclean* 112.8, *toxic* 114.28, *dangerous* 811.7
poisonous fumes *lack of hygiene* 112.3
poisonous gas *miasma* 556.3
poisonously *unhygienically* 114.32
poisonousness *lack of hygiene* 112.3, *poisoning* 114.8, 117.6
poison-pen letter *aspersion* 440.4
poisons *Phobias* 283
poison sumac *Trees and Shrubs* 43
Poisson distribution *probability distribution* 6.56
Poisson ratio *Classical Physical Laws* 10
Poitevin *Horse and Pony Breeds* 159
poke *gesture* 183.5, 183.17, *type of touch* 216.3, *touch* 216.9, *bag* 578.7, *blow* 695.5, *impel* 695.9
poke (at) *strike* 418.21
poke *or* **poke bonnet** *hat* 100.32
poke along *move slowly* 693.11
poke fun at *be humorous* 277.11, *deride* 369.7, *ridicule* 436.22, 440.15
poke in *inject* 710.10
poke one's nose in [Inf] *meddle* 321.8, 414.23
poke out *protrude* 634.8
poker 168.5, *Card Games* 168
poker bet *gambling* 167.4
poker face *unintelligible thing* 364.3
poker-faced *noncommittal* 181.11, *serious* 278.4, *unintelligible* 364.4
poker hand *poker* 168.5
pokerlike *tough* 542.6
pokeweed *Herbs and Spices* 91
pokily [Inf] *in slow motion* 693.15
pokiness [Inf] *littleness* 580.1, *slowness* 693.7
poking *slow* 693.7
pokingly *in slow motion* 693.15
poking out *protuberant* 634.6
poky *or* **pokey** [Inf] *the inside* 55.2, *undersized* 580.8, *slow* 693.7
pol [Inf] *politician* 50.7
Polack *Nicknames for Inhabitants* 61
Poland *Countries* 566
Poland China *Breeds of Pigs* 16
polar *chemical compound* 11.4, *frozen* 218.10, *opposite* 731.3, *limiting* 793.17
polar air *atmosphere* 9.8
polar bond *chemical bond* 11.6
polar climate *climate* 9.35
polar coordinates *coordinates* 6.31
polar easterlies *wind system* 9.15
polar front *air movement* 9.11, *wind system* 9.15
polarimeter *Fields of Measurement* 589
polarimetry *structure* 11.7, *Fields of Measurement* 589
polarity *counteraction* 510.1, *force*

514.8, *oppositeness* 731.1, *contrariety* 828.6
polarity reversal *geomagnetism* 8.3
polarization *wave property* 10.12, *electrochemistry* 11.19, *divisiveness* 463.2, *counteraction* 510.1, *repulsion* 701.1, *oppositeness* 731.1
polarize *reflect* 10.76, *disagree* 463.8, *counteract* 510.7, *be opposite* 731.4
polarized *counteracting* 510.6, *opposite* 731.3, *contrary* 828.13
polarized light 10.19
polarizing *disagreeing* 463.6
polarizing (PL) filter *filter* 132.14
polar lights *Earth* 7.17
polarogram *analysis* 11.17
polarographic *analytic* 11.32
polarography *analysis* 11.17
Polaroid™ *photograph* 132.3, *camera* 132.10
Polaroid™ film *film* 132.8
Polaroid™ glasses *visual aid* 242.14
polar opposite *opposite* 731.2
polar opposition *oppositeness* 731.1
polar solvent *phase* 11.13
polar wandering *geomagnetism* 8.3
polar zone *climate zone* 9.36
polder *lowland* 572.6
pole *timber* 43.3, *Bean Varieties* 90, *hand tool* 103.3, *wood* 131.3, *fishing tackle* 154.7, *distant place* 585.3, *General Units* 589, *vertical* 602.3, *supporting part* 605.3, *propel* 696.15, *limit* 773.7
poleax *murder* 30.20, *slaughter* 30.21, *sharp weapon* 78.6
polecat *unpleasant-smelling thing* 227.2
polecat [Inf] *miscreant* 448.6
pole hammer *blunt weapon* 78.5
polemic *philosophical argument* 4.5, *psychological warfare* 76.13, *logical argument* 329.2, *dispute* 463.3
polemic *or* **polemical** *argumentative* 319.10, *disagreeing* 463.6
polemically *philosophically* 4.23, *argumentatively* 329.15
polemicist *arguer* 319.6
polemicize *discuss* 4.22, *argue* 329.11
polemics *debate* 210.3, 319.3, *logical argument* 329.2, *contention* 422.1
polemist *arguer* 319.6
polenta *cereal* 90.12
pole plant *skiing techniques* 162.5
pole position *automobile racing terms* 146.3, *advantage* 744.3, *priority* 769.2
poles apart *disunity* 753.2
poles apart *or* **asunder** *diametrically* 731.6, *incomparably* 734.12
polestar *magnet* 700.3
pole vault *Sporting Activities* 145, *field event* 166.10
pole-vault *participate* 166.22
pole-vaulter *track and field eventer* 166.19
pole-vaulting *track and field* 166.20
police *person dealing with the dead* 29.8, *wield authority* 52.16, *law enforcement agency* 53.7, *defend* 77.37, *manage* 126.10, *secure* 464.9, *restore order* 765.22, *security force* 810.13, *protect* 810.21, *restrain* 830.12

police barrier *safety device* 810.15
police car *automobile* 687.6
police chief *law enforcement officer* 53.8
police commissioner *law enforcement officer* 53.8
police court *type of court* 54.9
police detective *law enforcement officer* 53.8
police dog *Breeds of Dogs* 35, *dog* 35.10, *watchdog* 810.14
police force *law enforcement agency* 53.7, *security force* 464.3
police inspector *law enforcement officer* 53.8
police lieutenant *law enforcement officer* 53.8
police magistrate *judge* 54.10
policeman *law enforcement officer* 53.8, *defender* 77.2, *person in command* 425.5, *security force* 464.3, 810.13, *one who restrains* 830.7
police officer *person in authority* 52.7, *law enforcement officer* 53.8, *security force* 464.3, 810.13
police officer's uniform *uniform* 100.9
police protection *security system* 810.5
police rank *position of authority* 52.4
police record *record* 185.1
police sergeant *law enforcement officer* 53.8
police siren *signal* 183.6
police state *totalitarianism* 49.13
police station *or* **headquarters** *or* **precinct house** *municipal building* 567.13
police superintendent *law enforcement officer* 53.8
police van *automobile* 687.6
police whistle *signal* 183.6
policewoman *law enforcement officer* 53.8, *security force* 464.3, 810.13, *one who restrains* 830.7
policy *procedure* 387.2, *standard procedure* 397.6, *line of action* 399.4, *tactics* 399.12, *action* 412.1, *deed* 412.2, *custom* 780.5, *convention* 781.5, *cunning* 822.1
policy management *management system* 126.3
polio *neurological disease* 114.20
poliomyelitis *neurological disease* 114.20
poliomyelitis *or* **polio** *infection* 114.7
polis *body politic* 50.3
poli-sci [Inf] *political science* 50.2
Polish *Breeds of Fowl* 16
polish 545.3; *practice dentistry* 107.34, *cleanliness* 111.1, *cleaning agent* 111.9, *clean* 111.17, *quality of light* 246.2, *glaze* 246.22, *good manners* 410.2, *elegance* 527.1, *be elegant* 527.6, *refinement* 534.1, *refine* 534.7, *smooth* 545.10, *rub* 554.12, *coat* 613.28, *perfection* 805.1, *perfect* 805.19, *improvement* 807.1, *improve* 807.15, *ease of manner* 823.4
Polish Black-and-White Lowland *Breeds of Cattle* 16
polished 545.7; *refined* 48.20, 534.5, *excellent* 68.16, *cleaned* 111.14, *literary* 139.15, *lustrous* 246.15, *good-mannered* 410.7, *elegant* 527.3, *perfect* 805.8
polishing 554.5; *dentistry* 107.6, *cleaning* 111.2
Polish Large White *Breeds of Pigs* 16

Polish Merino *Breeds of Sheep* 16
polish off [Inf] *eat well* 92.23, *manage* 126.10, *try* 414.21, *complete* 759.10, *cease* 773.20
Polish Red *Breeds of Cattle* 16
Polish Red-and-White Lowland *Breeds of Cattle* 16
Polish Simmental *Breeds of Cattle* 16
polish the apple *fawn* 401.9
polish up *learn* 48.23
Polish White Lop-eared *Breeds of Pigs* 16
polite *likable* 271.6, *submissive* 298.10, *well-behaved* 399.15, *courteous* 410.6, *showing respect* 435.7, *elegant* 527.3, *refined* 534.5
polite listener *well-behaved person* 399.6
politely *pleasantly* 271.12, *submissively* 298.23, *well* 399.22, *courteously* 410.13, *genteelly* 410.14, *respectfully* 435.19
politeness *amiability* 271.3, *submissiveness* 298.3, *good conduct* 399.5, *etiquette* 406.3, 534.3, *courtesy* 410.1, *elegance* 527.1
polite regard *respectfulness* 435.3
politesse *etiquette* 406.3
politic *political* 50.9, *skillful* 127.10, *advisable* 176.8, *prudent* 287.7, *wise* 352.4, *convenient* 803.3
political 50.9; *sociological* 2.11, *types of history* 3.2, *behaving* 399.14
political action *industrial dispute* 57.7
political action committee (PAC) *political organization* 50.4, *motivator* 508.6, *group influence* 512.6
political activism *activism* 414.5
political activist *protester* 331.8, *activist* 412.4
political and economic philosopher 4.10
political and economic philosophy 4.6
political behavior *sociology* 2.1
political border *interface* 616.1
political cartoonist *visual artist* 133.6
political convention *political organization* 50.4
political correctness *impartiality* 338.2
political economist *economist* 56.9
political entity *nation* 18.14
political favors *positive stimulus* 508.5
political geography *political science* 50.2
political institution *social institution* 2.8
political leader *politician* 50.7
politically 50.11; *sociologically* 2.15, *legitimately* 52.19, *managerially* 126.13
politically correct *of language* 5.35, *impartial* 338.6
politically correct language *language* 5.4
politically moderate 521.4
political map *map* 187.5
political movement *activism* 414.5
political organization 50.4; *social organization* 2.5, *government* 49.1, *body politic* 50.3
political party 50.5; *social*

institution 2.8, *political organization* 50.4, *group* 623.5
political party member 50.6
political persecution *social discrimination* 337.4
political philosophy *Branches of Philosophy* 4, *political science* 50.2
political possession *property* 470.1
political power *authority* 514.5
political prisoner *prisoner* 55.7
political reporting *print journalism* 175.4
political representative *delegate* 79.1
political right *preservation of status quo* 815.8
political science 50.2; *tactics* 399.12
political sociology *sociology* 2.1
political symbol *sign* 183.1
political system *government* 49.1
political theory *political science* 50.2
political trick *stratagem* 822.2
political worker *political party member* 50.6
politician 50.7; *elected official* 50.8, *public servant* 69.3, *motivator* 508.6
politick *run for office* 50.10
politicking *politics* 50.1
politico *politician* 50.7
politicophobia *Phobias* 283
politics 50.1; *political science* 50.2, *governance* 52.6, *Phobias* 283, *tactics* 399.12
polity *nation* 18.14, *government* 49.1, *politics* 50.1
polka *Dances* 135
polka dot *maculation* 263.4
poll *questioning* 333.2, *questionnaire* 333.3, *question* 333.16, *electing* 382.5, *count* 784.3, *number* 784.13, *list of names* 785.7
pollack *food fish and shellfish* 90.20
pollard *tree* 43.1, *manage trees* 43.14
pollarding *tree management* 43.6
polled *questioned* 333.15
Polled Hereford *Breeds of Cattle* 16
Polled Sinu *Breeds of Cattle* 16
pollen *organs of reproduction* 21.9, *flower part* 42.3, *spore* 553.10
pollen analysis *plant structure* 41.10
pollen grain *flower part* 42.3, *spore* 553.10
pollen sac *flower part* 42.3
pollen tube *flower part* 42.3
pollinate *cultivate* 17.19, *propagate* 21.15, *fertilize* 22.12
pollination 42.6; *fertilization* 21.6, *procreation* 22.4
pollinator *propagator* 21.7
polling *election* 382.6
polling place *election* 382.6
polliwog *young animal* 26.4, *young amphibian* 37.11
polls *election* 382.6
pollster *questioner* 333.9, *counter* 784.6
pollutant *atmosphere* 9.8, *pollution* 117.8, *evil thing* 446.2
pollute *dirty* 112.11, *poison* 117.18, *misuse* 395.6, *be evil* 446.10, *mix together* 751.14, *make useless* 802.12, *make worse* 808.17
polluted *dirty* 112.7, *unhygienic* 114.27, *polluting* 117.15, *misused* 395.3, *marked* 533.6
polluter *loser* 468.8
polluting 117.15; *unhygienic* 114.27

pollution 117.8; *atmosphere* 9.8, *dirtiness* 112.1, *lack of hygiene* 112.3, *misuse* 395.1, *evil thing* 446.2, *blot on the landscape* 533.4, *mixture* 751.1, *impairment* 808.7
Pollux *Notable Friendships* 62, *Deities* 82
Pollyanna *hoper* 281.5
polo *Sporting Activities* 145, *equestrianism* 159.8
polonaise *Dances* 135, *Musical Forms* 140
polonium *Chemical Elements and Common Allotropes* 11
polony [Brit] *sausage* 90.29
polo pony *pony* 159.6
polo shirt *shirt* 100.13
poltergeist *ghost* 86.11, *hinderer* 826.11
poltergeistism *occultism* 86.1
poltroon *coward* 285.3, *dastardly* 285.6
poltroonery *dastardliness* 285.2
poltroonish *dastardly* 285.6
poltroonishly *cowardly* 285.9
Polwarth *Breeds of Sheep* 16
polyadic *dialectical* 4.16
polyandrous *monogamous* 64.18
polyandry *type of marriage* 64.3, *multiplicity* 793.2
polyanthus *Flowers* 42
polyatomic *chemical compound* 11.4
polycarbonate *polymer* 11.9
polycarpellary *of a fruit* 44.8
polychaetous *wormlike* 39.24
polychlorinated biphenyl (PCB) *pollution* 117.8
polychloroethene *polymer* 11.9
polychromatic *colored* 251.10
polychromatically *colorfully* 251.19, *variedly* 263.12
polychromatism *spectrum* 251.3, *variegation* 263.1
polychrome *physical* 10.70, *painting* 143.3, *spectrum* 251.3, *colored* 251.10, *variegation* 263.1
polychrome *or* **polychromatic** *variegated* 263.6
polyester *polymer* 11.9, *plastics* 104.6, *fiber* 130.2
polyethylene *plastics* 104.6, *wrapping* 613.10
polyethylene *or* **polyethene** *or* **polythene** *polymer* 11.9
polyethylene bag *bag* 578.7
polygamist *married man* 64.10, *pluralist* 793.5
polygamous *monogamous* 64.18
polygamously *matrimonially* 64.23
polygamy *type of marriage* 64.3, *multiplicity* 793.2
polyglot *linguist* 5.3, *linguistic* 5.34, *translational* 365.11, *pluralist* 793.5
polyglottal *various* 793.7
polyglottic *speaking* 205.15
polygon 6.42; *multiplicity* 793.2
polygonal 6.79; *angled* 628.9, *various* 793.7
polygraph *psychometrics* 108.5, *detector* 345.6
polygynist *married man* 64.10
polygynous *monogamous* 64.18
polygyny *type of marriage* 64.3, *multiplicity* 793.2
polyhedral *cubic* 6.81, *angled* 628.9
polyhedron 6.44; *angled figure* 628.3, *multiplicity* 793.2
Polyhymnia *Deities* 82
polymath *expert* 127.9, *intellectual*

315.7, *knowledgeable person* 348.5, *pluralist* 793.5

polymathic *educated* 48.19, *knowledgeable* 348.7

polymathy *learnedness* 48.8, *learning* 348.3

polymer 11.9

polymerase *enzyme* 12.11

polymer chemistry Branches of Chemistry 11

polymer engineer *chemical engineer* 14.25

polymer engineering *chemical engineering* 14.24

polymeric 11.35; *reactive* 11.29, *chemical* 14.46

polymerization *chemical reaction* 11.8, *polymer* 11.9

polymerize *react* 11.38

polymers *plastics* 104.6

polymethylmethacrylate *polymer* 11.9

polymorphic *various* 793.7

polymorphism *variety* 732.2

polymorphous *varied* 732.6, *various* 793.7

Polynesian *race* 1.5, *racial* 1.12

polynomial *algebraic expression* 6.23, *functional* 6.73

polynomial expression *algebraic expression* 6.23

polyp *coelenterate* 39.15

Polypay Breeds of Sheep 16

polypeptide *amino acid* 12.8

polypeptide chain *molecular biology* 13.18

polyphagia *gluttony* 119.1

polyphagous *gluttonous* 119.3

Polyphemus *big person* 579.10

polyphobia Phobias 283

polyphone *spoken letter* 5.15

polyphonic *voiced* 5.37, *harmonic* 140.27

polyphonically *linguistically* 5.44

polyphonic prose *prose* 139.7

polyphonous *voiced* 5.37

polyphonously *linguistically* 5.44

polyphony *harmonic element* 140.14

polyploid *plant breeding* 17.6, *coelenterate* 39.25

polyploid invertebrate *coelenterate* 39.15

polypropylene *or* **polypropene** *polymer* 11.9

polyrhythm *musical time* 639.7

polyribosome *cell structure* 13.16

polysaccharide 12.5; *carbohydrate* 12.3

polysemous *linguistic* 361.9

polysemy *equivocation* 380.1

polysome *cell structure* 13.16

polystyrene *polymer* 11.9, *heater* 217.3

polysyllabic *language type* 5.11, *of language* 5.35, *diffuse* 199.3, *lengthy* 590.9

polysyllabically *linguistically* 5.44

polysyllable *word* 5.17

polysynthetic *language type* 5.11, *of language* 5.35

polytechnic *university* 48.14

polytechnic institute *university* 48.14

polytetrafluoroethylene (PTFE) *polymer* 11.9

polytheism *multiplicity* 793.2

polytheist *pluralist* 793.5

polytonic *language type* 5.11, *of language* 5.35

polyunsaturated fat *fat* 12.7, 562.4

polyunsaturates *food content* 90.3

polyurethane *polymer* 11.9, *plastics* 104.6

polyvinyl chloride (PVC) *polymer* 11.9, *plastics* 104.6

poma *ski run* 162.2

pomade 562.9; *anoint* 562.17

pomander ball *source of fragrance* 226.2

pomatum *pomade* 562.9

pome *botanical fruit* 44.2, *fruit* 90.34

pomelo *orange thing* 258.3

Pomeranian Breeds of Dogs 35

pomiferous *fruitful* 44.5

pomme Heraldic Terms 184

pommel *pommel horse* 157.7

pommel *or* **side horse** *gymnastics* 157.1

pommel horse 157.7, Sporting Activities 145, *gymnastics equipment* 157.2

pommer Musical Instruments 142

pommy Nicknames for Inhabitants 61

pomological *horticultural* 17.14

pomologically *horticulturally* 17.20

pomologist *horticulturist* 17.13, *plant scientist* 41.11

pomology *botany* 13.7, *horticulture* 17.1, *plant science* 41.10

pomp 404.7; *arrogance* 297.2, *formality* 406.1, *manifestation* 843.2

pompadour *coiffure* 530.8

pomp and circumstance *arrogance* 297.2

pomp and circumstance of war *glory of war* 76.17

pompom *guns* 78.9

pomposity 404.5; *bombast* 194.4, *cockiness* 402.3, *inelegance of expression* 528.4

pompous 404.18; *bombastic* 194.10, *arrogant* 297.9, *affected* 367.3, *cocky* 402.11, *formal* 406.6, *ceremonious* 406.7, *inelegant* 528.6, *ornate* 532.10

pompously 404.33; *exaggeratedly* 194.16, *arrogantly* 297.18, *affectedly* 367.5, *cockily* 402.19, *ornately* 532.14

pompousness *arrogance* 297.2, *affectation* 367.1, *cockiness* 402.3, *pomposity* 404.5

pompous twit [Inf] *vain person* 402.7

poncho *coat* 100.19

pond *ornamental garden* 17.3, *swimming place* 164.9, *small lake* 568.2

pond, the [Inf] *sea* 571.1

ponder *philosophize* 4.19, *speculate* 294.13, *think* 317.9, *intend* 374.8

ponderable *material* 524.7

pondered *speculative* 317.8

pondering *philosophical investigation* 4.4, *thoughtfulness* 317.2, *speculative* 317.8

ponderosity *weighing down* 538.5

ponderous 538.11; *clumsy* 128.6, *824.14, boring* 296.6

ponderously *boringly* 296.10, *burdensomely* 538.17, *awkwardly* 824.26

ponderousness *boringness* 296.2, *inelegance of expression* 528.4, *weighing down* 538.5

ponder over *estimate* 341.11

ponder the nature of God *theologize* 81.28

pondlike *lakelike* 568.5

pond scum *alga* 47.10

pong [Brit inf] *odor* 224.1, *have*

odor 224.8, *stench* 227.1, *stinking* 227.3, *stink* 227.5

pongee Fabrics and Fibers 130

pongid *primate* 35.17, 35.32

Pongidae *primate* 35.17

poniard *sharp weapon* 78.6

ponies Collective Names 59

ponophobia Phobias 283

Pontchartrain Lakes 568

pontifex maximus *priest* 84.8

pontiff *religious leader* 68.9, *priest* 84.8

pontifical *masterful* 68.15, *priestly* 84.12, *ritual manual* 85.11, *commanding* 425.7

pontificalia *vestment* 84.11

pontifically *clerically* 84.17

pontificals *vestment* 84.11

pontificate *priesthood* 84.2, *dissertate* 203.5, *address* 209.8, *put on airs* 404.27, *command* 425.10, *moralize* 431.14, *be certain* 840.13

pontificating *addressing* 209.6, *pompous* 404.18

pontificatingly *pompously* 404.33

pontification *pomposity* 404.5

pontificator *public speaker* 209.5

pontoon Card Games 168, Ships and Boats 690

pontoon bridge *bridge* 551.10, 691.7

pony 159.6; *horse* 159.1

pony [Inf] *translation* 365.4

pony express *postal service* 169.5, *messenger* 685.5

Pony of the Americas Horse and Pony Breeds 159

ponytail *coiffure* 530.8

pooch [Inf] *dog* 35.10

poodle Breeds of Dogs 35

pooh-pooh *underestimate* 344.5

pooh-pooh theory *linguistic theory* 5.2

pool 149.3; *source of supply* 105.4, *deposit* 105.21, Sporting Activities 145, *billiards* 149.1, Board and Table Games 167, *poker* 168.5, *acquisition* 467.4, *acquire* 467.19, *joint possession* 469.6, *small lake* 568.2, *combine* 757.9

pool ball *billiards* 149.1

pooled *joint* 827.10

pool hall *billiards* 149.1

pooling of resources *joint operation* 827.4

pool interests *join with* 827.15

pool player *player* 149.5

pool resources *join with* 827.15

pool table *billiards* 149.1, *pool* 149.3

pool together *acquire* 467.19

poonghie *imam* 84.7

poop [Inf] *feces* 25.5, *defecate* 25.21

pooped [Inf] *fatigued* 820.2

pooper-scooper *or* **poop scooper** *cleaning tool* 111.10

poo-poo [Inf] *feces* 25.5

poor 486.8; *needy* 95.12, *insufficient* 98.4, 517.11, *unprovided* 98.6, *without skill* 282.10, *disappointing* 293.6, *lowly* 298.9, *critical* 438.13, *unprofitable* 468.10, *nonpaying* 490.7, *shoddy* 497.11, *moderate* 521.3, *meager* 593.12, *substandard* 597.19, *incomplete* 762.5, *cheap* 800.16, *imperfect* 806.5, *spoiled* 808.9, *unprosperous* 848.11

poor, the 486.7

poor as a church mouse *poor* 486.8

poor as dirt *poor* 486.8

poor as Job *poor* 486.8

poor as Lazarus *poor* 486.8

poor as Mother Hubbard *poor* 486.8

poor boy *sandwich* 90.9

poor boy sweater *sweater* 100.17

poor chance 842.8

poor condition *or* **shape** *physical state* 725.6

poor definition *invisibility* 245.1

poor diction *blunder* 528.5

poor ear *hearing* 228.1

poor effort *imperfect item* 806.3

poor hand *unskilled person* 128.3

poor health 517.3; *ill health* 114.1, *adverse health* 848.5

poor hearing *deafness* 229.1

poorhouse *beggary* 486.3, *safe house* 812.5

poor judgment *misjudgment* 342.1

poor light *darkness* 247.1, *dimness* 248.1

poor likeness *misrepresentation* 188.1

poorly 486.17; *insufficiently* 98.11, *sick* 114.24, *unskillfully* 282.17, *disappointingly* 293.12, *ill* 517.8, *weakly* 517.14, *badly* 745.15, *incompletely* 762.10, *worse* 808.23, *adversely* 848.16

poorly defined *unrecognizable* 364.7

poorly disciplined *disobedient* 427.10

poorly done *unemphatic* 201.2

poorly fed *underfed* 118.7

poorly off *poor* 486.8

poorly planned *unpremeditated* 389.7

poorly situated *situated* 573.5

poorly timed *untimely* 660.5, *inconvenient* 804.5

poor memory 355.2

poorness *lowliness* 298.2, *poverty* 486.1

poor opinion *disapproval* 438.1

poor performance *bungling* 128.2

poor person 486.6; *person in adversity* 848.9

poor prospect *remote possibility* 836.4, *improbability* 839.1

poor quality *deficiency* 745.2, *low quality* 745.7, *cheap* 800.16

poor relation *poor person* 486.6, *inferior* 745.4, *nonentity* 800.8

poor relief *charity* 275.3, *social welfare* 307.4

poor return *infertile state* 23.3, *financial loss* 468.4

poor risk *person in adversity* 848.9

poor second *inferior* 745.4

poor shot *unskilled person* 128.3

poor show *or* **showing** *bungling* 128.2

poor sight *faulty vision* 243.1, *murk* 248.1

poor table *scarcity* 90.5

poor third *inferior* 745.4

poor timing *untimeliness* 660.1, *inconvenience* 804.1

poor turnout *few* 796.1

poor visibility *invisibility* 245.1, *murk* 248.2

poor vision *faulty vision* 243.1

poor wretch *person in adversity* 848.9

POP Programming Languages 15

pop *popular music* 140.4, *musical* 140.25, *small sound* 233.4, *crack* 234.2, 234.7

pop [Inf] *male title of address* 32.3, *man in the family* 32.12, *soft drink* 93.8

pop art Western Art Styles 133

pop at *fire* 418.18

popcorn *snack* 90.8

---

pope *person in authority* 52.7, *religious leader* 68.9, *priest* 84.8
popedom *priesthood* 84.2
Pope Joan Card Games 168
pope's *or* **parson's nose** [Inf] *poultry* 90.28
popeyed *seeing* 242.17, *wondering* 294.7
pop fly *batting terms* 147.6
pop group *team* 59.9
popgun *banger* 234.3
pop in *inject* 710.10
pop in [Inf] *appear* 244.8, *enter* 706.11
popinjay *proud person* 297.7
pop into one's head *have an idea* 327.13
popish *denominational* 81.23
poplar Trees and Shrubs 43
poplin Fabrics and Fibers 130
POPLOG Programming Languages 15
pop music *popular music* 140.4
Popocatepetl Mountains and Hills 569
pop off [Inf] *die* 29.17
pop out *exit* 707.13
pop-out *windsurfing* 150.28
pop-out board *sailboard parts* 150.20
popover *bread* 90.10
popper *bait* 154.6
poppet [Brit] *term of endearment* 299.7
popping *crackling* 234.5
popple *billow* 571.9
poppy Flowers 42, *red thing* 257.3, *soporific* 415.6
poppycock *nonsense* 192.8, *senseless talk* 362.4
poppycock! *nonsense!* 362.14
poppyhead Architectural Elements 134
poppy seed Herbs and Spices 91
pops *popular music* 140.4
pop single *batting terms* 147.6
pop song *popular music* 140.4
pop the question [Inf] *propose (marriage)* 299.29
populace *group* 18.13, *inhabitants* 61.2, *general public* 778.6
popular 408.12; *governmental* 49.24, *musical* 140.25, *publicized* 173.14, *desired* 288.10, *liked* 290.6, *simple* 363.6, *reputable* 370.3, *praiseworthy* 437.12, *sold* 482.14, *prevailing* 778.11
popular authority *or* **mandate** *acquisition of authority* 52.5
popular belief *belief* 87.1
popular concert *or* **pops** *performance* 141.8
popular front *political party* 50.5
popularity *social success* 408.3, *admiration* 437.2
popularization *clarity* 363.2
popularize 778.17; *make comprehensible* 363.8, *interpret* 365.12, *make easy* 823.15
popularized *simple* 363.6
popularizer *interpreter* 365.6
popular literature *literature* 139.1
popularly *commonly* 71.4, *likably* 290.12, *eminently* 370.7
popular melody *melody* 140.10
popular misconception *fallibility* 351.6
popular movement *activism* 414.5
popular music 140.4
popular psychology Psychological Theories, Schools 108

popular song *popular music* 140.4, *song* 140.11
popular success *box-office hit* 137.11
populate *procreate* 22.14, *settle* 61.14
populated *inhabited* 61.10
population 6.55; *society* 1.6, *ecology* 13.25, *inhabitants* 61.2
population drift *disbandment* 776.2
population explosion *productiveness* 22.3
population genetics *genetics* 13.19
population growth *economic development* 56.5
population inversion *laser (light amplification by stimulated emission of radiation)* 10.18
population study *sociological research* 2.2
Populist party Political Parties 50
pop up *play baseball* 147.9, *become visible* 264.13, *spring up* 713.22, *be repeated* 797.20, *chance* 842.12
pop up [Inf] *arrive* 704.13
pop-up *batting terms* 147.6
p-orbital *chemical bond* 11.6
porcelain Ceramics 129, *ceramics* 129.1, *merchandise* 522.6, *brittle thing* 548.2
porcelain clay *material* 129.2
porcelain enamel *ceramics* 129.1
porcelain insulation *industrial ceramics* 129.6
porcelain mark *decoration* 129.4
porch *room* 60.9, Architectural Elements 134, *means of entry* 706.6
porcine *ungulate* 35.31
pore *body orifice* 583.3, *outlet* 707.8
pore fungi *fungi* 47.3
pore over *inspect* 242.22
Porifera *sponge* 39.16
poriferan *sponge* 39.16, *spongelike* 39.26
poriferous *spongelike* 39.26
pork 90.26; *meat* 90.22
pork barrel [Inf] *incentive* 178.4, *positive stimulus* 508.5
porker *livestock* 16.11
porkpie *hat* 100.32
pork sausage *sausage* 90.29
porn [Inf] *obscenity* 112.4, *pornography* 432.7
porn flick [Inf] *pornography* 432.7
porn hall [Inf] *pornography* 432.7
porn house [Inf] *pornography* 432.7
pornograhically *ribaldly* 535.12
pornographer *pornography* 432.7, *sexually immoral person* 432.8
pornographic *obscene* 112.9, *offensive* 432.11, *ribald* 535.8
pornographic model *pornography* 432.7
pornographic novel *novel* 139.3
pornography 432.7; *obscenity* 112.4, *grossness* 535.3
porno star [Inf] *pornography* 432.7
porn queen [Inf] *pornography* 432.7
porosity 583.5
porous *holed* 583.12, *concave* 635.5, *leaky* 707.12
porousness *porosity* 583.5
porous pottery *ceramics* 129.1
porous thing *porosity* 583.5
porphyritic *types of igneous texture* 8.33
porphyrophobia Phobias 283
porpoises Collective Names 59

porridge *cereal* 90.12, *semiliquid* 561.7
porringer *crockery* 578.16
port *red thing* 257.3, *water system* 551.13, *inlet* 572.9, *laterality* 623.3, *laterally* 623.11, *stopping place* 668.4, *destination* 704.6, *place of departure* 705.4, *way out* 707.2, *harbor* 812.6
port [Arch] *conduct* 399.1
portability *lightness* 539.1, *littleness* 580.1
portable *light* 539.4, *little* 580.7, *undersized* 580.8, *transferable* 685.7, *transportable* 686.7
portable radio *radio* 172.1
portable television *television (TV)* 172.5
portage *conveyance* 685.2, *transportation* 686.1
portal *means of entry* 706.6
portative *transferable* 685.7
Port-au-Prince Countries 566
portcullis Heraldic Terms 184, *fort* 419.13, *barrier* 826.7
porte-cochere *means of entry* 706.6
portend *foresee* 357.9, *predict* 358.14, *intend* 361.15
portent *marvel* 294.3, *wonderful person* 294.6, *expectations* 356.2, *omen* 358.5, *forewarning* 814.2
portentous *presageful* 358.13
portentously *predictively* 358.16
portentousness *omen* 358.5
porter *attendant* 69.4, *service worker* 123.7, *mountaineer* 161.8, *closer* 584.5, *transferrer* 685.4, *transporter* 686.4, *railroad worker* 688.7
porterage *conveyance* 685.2
portfolio *collection* 105.12, *record* 185.1, *personal estate* 470.6, *baggage* 578.8
portfolio manager *financial adviser* 457.4
porthole *hole* 583.4
Portia Planets and Their Satellites 7
portico *room* 60.9, Architectural Elements 134, *passage* 691.5, *means of entry* 706.6
portion 474.2; *helping* 92.11, *claim* 429.3, *piece* 590.2, *760.2, *passage* 692.1, *certain amount* 738.3, *quantify* 738.7, *interval* 739.4, *part* 760.1, *particle* 760.4, *fractional part* 787.2
portioned *gradational* 739.5
portionless *impoverished* 486.11
portion out *allocate* 474.5
Portland cement *masonry* 14.22, *industrial ceramics* 129.6, *paving* 613.14
portliness *fatness* 579.5, *thickness* 594.1, *round body* 633.2
Port Louis Countries 566
portly *fat* 579.15, *thick* 594.5, *well-rounded* 633.8
portmanteau *worded* 5.38, *concise* 198.4
portmanteau [Brit] *receptacle* 105.11, *baggage* 578.8
portmanteau word *catchword* 5.22, *conciseness* 198.1, *compound* 757.4
Port Moresby Countries 566
port of call *stopping place* 668.4
Port-of-Spain Countries 566
Porto-Novo Countries 566
portrait 132.5; *painting* 143.3, *type of painting* 143.5, *record* 185.1, *illustration* 187.2, *description*

202.1, *representation* 202.9, *copy* 736.2
portraitist *painter* 143.7
portrait painter *painter* 143.7
portrait sculpture *sculpture* 144.1
portraiture *photographic specialties* 132.2, *illustration* 187.2
portray *act* 136.34, *137.20, 187.13, *write* 139.21, *draw* 143.13, *represent* 187.10, *describe* 202.15, *outline* 617.5, *characterize* 723.11, *simulate* 733.16
portrayal *acting* 136.22, *187.6, *representation* 187.1, *description* 202.1, *outline* 617.1, *simulation* 733.4
portrayed *simulated* 733.11
portraying *acting* 187.6, *187.9, *representational* 187.8
port tack *sailing terms* 150.5
Portugal Countries 566
Portuguese GP at Estoril *Formula 1 World Championship races* 146.5
Portuguese water dog Breeds of Dogs 35
portulaca Flowers 42
port-wine stain *mark* 533.2
pose *propound a philosophy* 4.21, *be untruthful* 192.20, *spectacle* 264.6, *confuse* 333.20, *affectation* 367.1, *be affected* 367.4, *mode of behavior* 399.2, *conduct oneself* 399.17
pose as *act* 187.13, *be untruthful* 192.20
Poseidon Deities 82, *legendary sea being* 571.4
pose problems *be difficult* 824.16
poser *mystery* 182.4, *hypocrite* 192.9, *difficult question* 333.4, *pretender* 367.2, *problem* 824.4
poset *combinatorics* 6.63
poseur *hypocrite* 192.9, *pretender* 367.2, *imitator* 736.6
posh *grand* 404.22, *fashionable* 536.5
poshness *grandeur* 404.10
posing *acting* 187.6, *affected* 367.3, *imitative* 736.7
posit *propound a philosophy* 4.21, *suppose* 359.8
position 765.4; *philosophical system* 4.2, *point* 6.34, *dimension* 10.5, *belief* 87.1, *theory* 327.2, *line of argument* 329.3, *supposition* 359.1, *business* 509.3, *location* 565.1, *locate* 565.9, *situation* 573.1, *circumstances* 573.2, *726.1, *employment* 573.3, *rank* 573.4, *739.2, *situate* 573.10, *opportunity* 583.8, *direction* 697.1, *state* 725.1, *measure* 739.7, *systematize* 765.19, *category* 767.6, *arrange* 767.18, *social class* 775.7
positional *locational* 565.8
positional notation *number system* 6.7
positioned *located* 565.6, *situated* 573.5
position finder 690.8
position in society *rank* 573.4
position of authority 52.4
position of power *authority* 514.5
position paper *affirmation* 189.1, *dissertation* 203.1
position vector *vector* 6.48
positive *numerical* 6.68, *783.7, *electric* 14.47, *legitimate* 52.10, *believing* 124.9, *definite* 189.18, *emphatic* 200.3, *hopeful* 281.6, *demonstrable* 331.12, *intelligible* 363.5, *correct* 429.8, *real* 717.14, *helpful* 825.19, *convinced* 840.8

positive charge *electric charge* 10.38

positive correlation *correlation* 6.58

positive discrimination *favoritism* 337.5, *equalization* 740.4

positive feedback *circuit function* 14.38

positive ion *ion* 10.54

positively *mathematically* 6.93, *electronically* 14.54, *legitimately* 52.19, *believingly* 87.12, *definitely* 189.33, *emphatically* 200.7, *hopefully* 281.15, *correctly* 429.16, *really* 717.22, *helpfully* 825.32, *certainly* 840.15

positiveness *legal power* 52.2, *definiteness* 189.6, *intelligibility* 363.1, *conviction* 840.2

positive number *number* 6.4

positive outlook *emphasis* 200.1

positive reinforcement *conditioning* 108.24

positive reproduction *photograph* 132.3

positive statement *affirmation* 189.1

positive stimulus 508.5

positive thinking *hope* 281.1

positive vote *electing* 382.5

positivism Philosophical Schools of Thought 4, *materialization* 524.2, *conviction* 840.2

positivist Philosophical Schools of Thought 4, *materialist* 524.3

positivity *right* 429.2

positron *elementary particle* 10.53

positron emission tomography (PET) scan *diagnostic radiology* 107.12

posologist *medical specialist* 107.20, *druggist* 115.10

posse *law enforcement officer* 53.8, *group* 59.8, *alliance* 735.5

posse comitatus *law enforcement officer* 53.8

possess 469.14; *bewitch* 86.25, *be selfish* 444.6, *make evil* 446.11, *own property* 470.11, *take* 477.14

possessed 469.13; *bewitched* 86.21, *propertied* 470.9, *conjunctive* 752.12

possessed of *possessed* 469.13

possessing 469.11; *possession* 469.1, *propertied* 470.9

possessing narcotics with intent to sell *drug pushing* 121.10

possession 469.1; *witchcraft* 86.6, *playing terms* 148.4, *offense* 155.6, *use* 393.1, *claim* 429.3, *property* 470.1, *taking* 477.1, *region* 564.1

possession in common *joint possession* 469.6

possession of property 469.3

possessions 470.5; *wealth* 485.1

possessive *grammatical term* 5.29, *covetous* 288.14, *jealous* 314.5, *selfish* 444.4, *taking* 477.12, *conjunctive* 752.12

possessively 469.16; *covetously* 288.28, *suspiciously* 314.13, *selfishly* 444.8, *avariciously* 477.22

possessiveness *covetousness* 288.4, *jealousy* 314.2, *selfishness* 444.1, *exclusiveness* 764.4

possess magical power *be powerful* 514.18

possess narcotics *drug oneself* 121.37

possessor 469.10; *titleholder* 72.4

possessorship *possession* 469.1

possessory *possessing* 469.11

possess power *have authority* 52.13

possess special power *be powerful* 514.18

possess strength *be strong* 516.14

possess with *own property* 470.11

possibilities *potential* 458.4

possibility 836.1; *expectation* 356.1, *expectations* 356.2, *basis of supposition* 359.2, *opportunity* 583.8, *wieldiness* 823.3, *plausibility* 838.3, *latency* 844.1

possibility of perfection *imperfection* 806.1

possible 836.5; *believable* 87.7, *auspicious* 458.10, *predictable* 650.7, *realizable* 719.9, *feasible* 823.10, *potential* 836.6, *plausible* 838.7, *latent* 844.6

possible, the *sufficiency* 97.1

possibleness 836.2

possible outcome *probability* 6.59

possible worlds *philosophical problem* 4.8

possibly 836.9; *supposedly* 359.10, *predictably* 650.15, *perchance* 842.18

POSSLQ (person of opposite sex sharing living quarters) *common-law wife* 64.12

post *farm building* 16.4, *wood* 131.3, *carpenter* 131.10, *column* 134.6, *horse racing* 159.10, *racetrack* 159.12, *tennis court* 165.3, *postal communication* 169.4, *communicate* 170.12, *send* 209.11, *account* 493.9, *business* 509.3, *location* 565.1, *locate* 565.9, *employment* 573.3, *situate* 573.10, *station* 601.5, 601.12, *vertical* 602.3, *supporting part* 605.3, *support* 605.16, *fastener* 754.7, *list* 785.11, *engage* 833.9

post [Brit] *correspond* 169.19, *transferred thing* 685.6, *mail* 685.10

postage *postal communication* 169.4, *business expenses* 491.4

postage or **postal meter** *postal communication* 169.4

postage paid *absence of charge* 497.6

postage stamp *postal communication* 169.4

postal *communicational* 169.17

postal address *exact location* 565.2

postal card *correspondence* 169.2

postal code [Brit] *correspondence* 169.2

postal communication 169.4

postal district *exact location* 565.2

postal order *paper money* 484.14

postal service 169.5

postal worker 169.6

postbellum *harmless* 73.9

post bills *publicize* 173.18

post-boat [Brit] Ships and Boats 690

postboy *horse person* 159.14

postcard *correspondence* 169.2, *transferred thing* 685.6

postdate *misdate* 660.9

posted *communicated* 169.15, *informed* 170.9, *located* 565.6, *employed* 573.8

poster *picture* 133.5, *advertisement* 173.9, *sign* 183.1, *showplace* 843.4

poster artist *visual artist* 133.6

posterboard *paper* 104.5

posterior *rear end* 622.4, *back* 622.6

posterity *future generation* 650.2

postern *fort* 419.13, *back entrance*

622.2, *back* 622.6, *means of entry* 706.6

poster paint *paint* 251.6

postexistence *future condition* 650.3

postglacial *glaciated* 8.62

postglaciation *climatic change* 9.37

postgraduate *learner* 48.6, *curricular* 48.21

posthaste *in the shortest possible time* 645.9, *hurriedly* 694.18, *hastily* 818.7

post horse *workhorse* 159.3

posthumous 29.16; *dead* 658.10

posthumously *fatally* 29.18, *formerly* 658.17, *motionlessly* 678.9

Postier Horse and Pony Breeds 159

postilion *horse person* 159.14

postimpressionism Western Art Styles 133

postindustrial *productive* 522.11

posting *placing* 565.4

posting [Brit] *conveyance* 685.2

postman *postal worker* 169.6, *messenger* 685.5

postmark *postal communication* 169.4

postmaster *postal worker* 169.6

postmaster general *postal worker* 169.6

postmeridian *daily* 655.6

postmistress *postal worker* 169.6

postmodern *trendy* 652.11

Postmodern Ages, Decades, Eras 641

postmodernism Western Art Styles 133, Architectural Styles 134, Western Literary Groups 139, *trendiness* 652.2

postmodernist *modern person* 652.8

postmortem *after death* 29.9, *posthumous* 29.16, *fatally* 29.18, Children's and Party Games 167

postmortem (examination) (PM) 107.17

postnatal *pregnant* 21.12

post-obit *posthumous* 29.16

post office Children's and Party Games 167, *postal service* 169.5

post office box *postal communication* 169.4

postpaid *receiving pay* 489.14, *free of charge* 497.12

post-painterly abstraction Western Art Styles 133

postpartum depression *mood disorder* 108.12

post pattern *play* 155.8

postpone *delay* 375.16, 658.13, *be evasive* 386.20, *defer* 604.15, *not complete* 762.9

postponed *deferred* 604.9, *held up* 658.6

postponement *delay* 375.6, 658.3, *deferment* 604.3, *pause* 668.3

postponing *procrastinating* 375.11

postprandial *culinary* 91.9, *at ease* 819.2

postscript *back matter* 622.3, *appendage* 748.4, *ending* 773.10

poststructuralism Western Literary Groups 139

post or **put up the banns** *get engaged to* 458.12

posttraumatic stress disorder *anxiety disorder* 108.11

postulant *religious* 84.9

postulate *philosophy* 4.1, *philosophical term* 4.7, *philosophize* 4.19, *propound a philosophy* 4.21,

theory 6.62, *theorize* 6.84, *contend* 189.24, *premise* 319.14, *line of argument* 329.3, *state* 329.13, *supposition* 359.1, *suppose* 359.8

postulated *contended* 189.15, *logical* 329.9, *supposed* 359.6

postulation *contention* 189.4, *supposition* 359.1

postulational *contended* 189.15

postulatory *suppositional* 359.5

posture *be untruthful* 192.20, *external appearance* 264.5, *affectation* 367.1, *be affected* 367.4, *conduct* 399.1, *conduct oneself* 399.17, *deed* 412.2, *nature* 624.5, *state* 725.1, *circumstances* 726.1

posturing *affected* 367.3

postwar *harmless* 73.9

postwoman *postal worker* 169.6

posy *flower* 42.1, *assemblage* 59.13, *compliment* 437.4

pot 578.15; *cultivate* 17.19, *cooking equipment* 91.6, *make ceramics* 129.10, *poker* 168.5, *prize* 453.2, *contain* 578.20, *insert* 710.9, *preserver* 815.9, *preserve* 815.14

pot [Inf] *hemp derivatives* 121.16, *shoot* 696.18

potable *drinkable* 93.18, *tasty* 219.4, *trustworthy* 810.17

potage *soup* 90.14

potamophobia Phobias 283

potash *fertilizer* 16.9, 22.6

potassium Chemical Elements and Common Allotropes 11, *essential element* 12.15

potassium-argon dating *dating* 8.48, *radioactivity* 10.58

potation *drinking* 93.1, *drink* 93.2, 121.6, *alcohol* 121.5

potato blight *agent of destruction* 523.7

potato chips *snack* 90.8

potatoes *crop* 16.8, *vegetable* 90.33

potato field *farmland* 16.3

potato-sack race Children's and Party Games 167

potato salad *salad* 90.16

potato skins *hors d'oeuvre* 90.13

potbellied *fat* 579.15, *thick* 594.5, *well-rounded* 633.8

potbelly *fat* 579.8, *thickness* 594.1, *round body* 633.2

potboiling *cheap* 800.16

potence *authority* 52.1, *power* 514.1

potency 516.6; *sexuality* 20.3, *maleness* 32.2, *authority* 52.1, *power* 447.4, 514.1, *influence* 512.1, *strength* 516.1, *instrumentality* 384.2

potent *coupling* 20.19, *authoritative* 52.9, *intoxicating* 121.29, Heraldic Terms 184, *influential* 512.8, *powerful* 514.15, *strong* 516.9

potentate *leader* 68.3

potential 458.4, 836.6; *electric potential* 10.40, *auspicious* 458.10, *potency* 516.6, *predictable* 650.7, *possibility* 836.1, *possible* 836.5, *latent* 844.6

potential difference (pd) *electric potential* 10.40

potential energy *energy* 10.10, 514.7

potentiality *qualification* 340.1, *influence* 512.1, *possibility* 836.1, *latency* 844.1

potentially 836.11; *auspiciously* 458.17, *predictably* 650.15, *latently* 844.15

potential theory Branches of Mathematics 6

potentilla Flowers 42

potentiometer *electrical instrument* 14.41, Fields of Measurement 589

potentiometry Fields of Measurement 589

potently *authoritatively* 52.18, *influentially* 512.14, *powerfully* 514.21, *acutely* 516.18

pot(ful) *container(ful)* 738.2

pother *disruption* 766.7

potherb *vegetable* 17.11, *plant* 41.2, Herbs and Spices 91

potholder *cooking equipment* 91.6

pothole *concave land* 635.2

potholed *coarse* 544.6

potholed road *or* **street** *rough thing* 544.2

pothunter *contender* 422.13

potion *spell* 86.8, *drink* 93.2, *dose of medicine* 115.3, *mixed thing* 751.2

potlatch *non-Christian ritual* 85.8

potluck **842.4;** *meal* 96.2, *improvised* 396.4, *party* 408.6

potluck dinner *party* 408.6

pot magnet *magnet* 10.47

pot marigold Flowers 42

pot of gold *objective* 374.5, *wealth* 485.1

Potomac Rivers 570

potophobia Phobias 283

pot plant *plant* 41.2, *flower* 42.1

potpourri *miscellany* 59.15, *source of fragrance* 226.2, *mixed thing* 751.2

pot roast *meat dish* 90.21

pot-roast *cook* 91.10

pot-roasting *cooking technique* 91.2

potsherd *particle* 760.4

potshot *shot* 696.6, *shoot* 696.18

pots of money [Inf] *money* 485.2

potted *storing* 578.19, *preserved* 815.12

potted [Inf] *drunk* 121.25

potted version [Brit] *outline* 204.2

potter *ceramist* 129.7, *visual artist* 133.6

Potteries, the *regions of the British Isles* 564.8

pottering [Brit] *restlessness* 414.7

potter's clay *or* **earth** *material* 129.2

potter's wheel *ceramic workshop and tools* 129.8, *wheel* 682.9

potter's workplace *ceramic workshop and tools* 129.8

pottery *ceramics* 129.1, *ceramic workshop and tools* 129.8, *merchandise* 548.2, *brittle thing* 548.2, *crockery* 578.16

pottery factory *ceramic workshop and tools* 129.8

pottery making Hobbies and Pastimes 167

potting *gardening* 17.5, *storing* 578.19

potting shed *nursery* 17.4

potty *place for excretion* 25.11

potty [Brit Inf] *foolish* 923.5

potty-chair *place for excretion* 25.11

potty-trained *excremental* 25.13

pot-valiant *drunk* 121.25

pouch *pouched mammal* 35.5, *bag* 578.7

pouched mammal **35.5**

poult *livestock* 16.11, *young bird* 36.17

poultice *dose of medicine* 115.3, *heater* 217.3, *paste* 561.4

poultry **90.28;** *livestock* 16.11, Collective Names 59, *meat* 90.22

poultry farm *farm* 16.2

poultry farmer *agriculturist* 16.14

poultry farming *livestock farming* 16.10

pounce *powder* 553.9, *acceleration* 694.3, *be swift* 694.10, *drop* 714.15

pounce on *ambush* 292.11

pounce upon *strike* 418.21

pound *animal welfare* 34.8, *mammal dwelling* 35.21, *prison* 55.1, *cage* 60.15, *be painful* 215.9, *drum* 235.10, *attack* 418.17, *national coins* 484.11, *weight measurement* 538.6, *beat* 553.27, 695.12, General Units 589, *blow* 695.5, *hit* 695.11, *resound* 797.21, *shelter* 812.4

poundage *heaviness* 538.1

poundal Scientific and Technical Units 589

pound cake *cake* 90.36

pounder *pulverizer* 553.11

pound-foolish *extravagant* 194.9

pound for pound *wholly* 759.11

pound in *impact* 710.11

pounding *painful* 215.4, *drumming* 235.1, 235.6, *pulverization* 553.4

pound of flesh *severity* 424.1, *interest* 488.4

pound sterling [Brit] *money* 484.1

pour *rain* 9.57, *crowd* 59.26, 795.11, *abound* 97.8, *flow* 555.25, 570.10, *water* 557.29, *run out* 707.15, *downflow* 714.3, *drip* 714.13, *throw down* 716.13

pour a broadside into *fire* 418.18

pour balm into *or* **on one's wounds** *conciliate* 74.10

pourboire [Fr] *gift* 472.2

pour down *drip* 714.13

pour down the drain *waste* 96.15, 500.7, *be wasteful* 468.16

pour in *stuff* 577.12, *come together* 702.10, *flood in* 706.14, *inject* 710.10

pouring *rainy* 9.50, *descending* 714.9

pour it on [Inf] *run* 694.13

pour oil *or* **balm on** *anoint* 562.17

pour oil on troubled waters *conciliate* 74.10, *atone* 313.7, *calm* 521.8, *ease* 562.18, *restore order* 765.22

pour out *be diffuse* 199.5, *give* 472.10, *run out* 707.15, *let out* 709.26, *throw down* 716.13

pour vitriol on *vilify* 301.15

pout *gesture* 183.5, 183.17, *sign of sullenness* 304.2, *be sullen* 304.12, *distortion of face* 627.2, *make faces* 627.10

pouter *sullen person* 304.7

pouting *frowning* 303.12

poutingly *sullenly* 304.16

pouty *sullen* 304.8

poverty **486.1;** *neediness* 95.3, Phobias 283, *meagerness* 593.6, *deficiency* 745.2, *incompleteness* 762.1, *economic deterioration* 808.2, *economic adversity* 848.6

poverty level *incompleteness* 98.2

poverty line *poverty* 486.1

poverty-stricken *needy* 95.12, *poor* 486.8, *unprosperous* 848.11

poverty trap *poverty* 486.1

Powder Rivers 570

powder *553.9, 553.25;* *snow* 9.30, 162.28, *ammunition* 78.11, *propellant* 78.14, *costume* 100.10, *dose of medicine* 115.3, *variegate* 263.11, *cosmetics* 530.4, *pulverize* 553.26, *residue* 750.2, *sprinkle* 776.15

powder barrel *or* **keg** *arsenal* 78.3

powder-blue *blue* 261.5

powder box *box* 578.5

powdered *mottled* 263.10, *pulverized* 553.20, *sprinkled* 776.9

powdered milk *milk* 93.5

powdered sugar *basic cooking ingredient* 91.8, *sweetener* 222.2

powder flask *historical ammunition* 78.12

powder-gray *gray* 255.6

powder horn *historical ammunition* 78.12

powderiness **553.3**

powdering *pulverization* 553.4, *sprinkling* 776.4

powder magazine *arsenal* 78.3

powder metallurgy *metallurgy* 11.22

powder puff *cosmetic tool* 530.5

powder room *place for excretion* 25.11

powder snow *skiing snow* 162.3, *snow* 218.6

powdery *553.19; brittle* 548.3, *desert* 560.12

powdery mildew *pests and diseases* 17.12

powdery snow *snow* 9.30

power *106.17, 447.4, 514.1, 783.6;* *multiplication* 6.15, *authority* 52.1, 425.3, 780.6, *gain authority* 52.15, *divine attribute* 82.4, *means* 102.1, *exertion* 122.4, *management* 126.1, *emphasis* 200.1, *usefulness* 393.2, *action* 412.1, *severity* 424.1, *claim* 429.3, *operation* 509.1, *take action* 509.12, *instrumentality* 511.1, 801.3, *influence* 512.1, *generate power* 514.19, *strength* 516.1, *vigor* 518.1, *violence* 520.1, *country* 566.1, Fields of Measurement 589, *impulsion* 695.1, *impel* 695.9, *leadership* 744.2, *importance* 799.1, *commission* 833.1

power behind the throne *authority* 52.1, *deputy* 80.1, *manager* 126.7, *one who conceals* 181.7, *indirect influence* 512.4, *backstage manipulator* 844.3

powerboat Ships and Boats 690

powerboat racing Sporting Activities 145

powerbroker *politician* 50.7, *indirect influence* 512.4

power cable *electricity* 106.5

power cut *scarcity* 98.3, *electricity* 106.5, *darkening* 247.2

power dive *acceleration* 694.3, *fall* 714.4

power-dive *drop* 714.15

power down *remove power from* 515.13

power-driven *mechanical* 103.7

power-driven saw *woodworking tool* 131.6

powered *mechanical* 103.7, *fired* 106.13

power failure *powerlessness* 515.1

power forward *basketball team* 148.2

powerful **514.15;** *authoritative* 52.9, 425.8, *masterful* 68.15, *emphatic* 200.3, *shouting* 232.7, *effective* 412.10, *causal* 511.5, *influential* 512.8, *strong* 516.9, *physically strong* 516.10, *vigorous* 518.2, *stalwart* 547.17, *advantaged* 618.7, *ruling* 780.11, *notable* 799.11, *instrumental* 801.7

powerful build *stalwartness* 547.3

powerful influence *influence* 512.1

powerfully 106.19, 514.21; *authoritatively* 52.18, *usefully* 393.15, *effectively* 412.19, *commandingly* 425.15, *instrumentally* 511.9, *influentially* 512.14, *strongly* 516.17, *stalwartly* 547.17, *propulsively* 696.21

powerfulness **514.4;** *power* 514.1

powerful person *important person* 799.5

powerhead *sailboard parts* 150.20

power hitter *baseball team* 147.2

powerhouse *power station* 124.12, *hard worker* 414.11, *power supplier* 514.14

powerless **515.6;** *inactive* 413.9, *weak* 517.6, *suspended* 519.3, *useless* 802.7

powerlessly **515.16;** *inactively* 413.16

powerlessness **515.1;** *uselessness* 802.1

powerless person **515.5**

power line *power supplier* 514.14

power mower *garden tool* 17.7

power of attorney *type of power* 514.6, *substitution* 672.1, *commission* 833.1

power of conception *reason* 319.1

power of darkness *evil thing* 446.2

power of reason *reason* 319.1

power of seeing *vision* 242.1

power of speech 205.5

power of the purse *finance* 457.1, 484.7

power of three *three* 790.1

power of two *two* 789.1

power outage *electricity* 106.5, *powerlessness* 515.1

power pack *electricity* 106.5, *power supplier* 514.14

power plant *power station* 124.12, *power supplier* 514.14

power-plant worker *artisan* 123.13

power play *ice hockey tactics* 158.4

power point *electricity* 106.5

powers *angelic order (highest to lowest)* 82.12

power series *sequence* 6.18

power shovel *construction equipment* 14.23

power source **514.13**

power station **124.12;** *electrical energy* 10.44, *electricity* 106.5, *power supplier* 514.14

powers that be, the *governing body* 49.19, *governance* 52.6, *the power structure* 68.12, *group influence* 512.6

power structure, the **68.12;** *governance* 52.6, *authority* 514.5, *rank* 739.2

power supplier **514.14**

power supply *electrical energy* 10.44

power sweep *play* 155.8

power to act *commission* 833.1

power up *empower* 514.20

power wheel *ceramic workshop and tools* 129.8

power worker 106.10

powwow [Inf] *advisory body* 176.6, *place for conversation* 210.5, *confer* 210.13, *discussion* 460.3, *negotiate* 460.6

P'o-yang Lakes 568

Poynting vector Classical Physical Laws 10

practicability *convenience* 803.1, *possibleness* 836.2
practicable *negotiated* 460.5, *workable* 509.8, *realizable* 719.9, *useful* 801.5, *convenient* 803.3, *feasible* 823.10, *possible* 836.5
practicableness *convenience* 803.1, *wieldiness* 823.3
practical **511.6, 719.8;** *rational* 4.15, *advisable* 176.8, *useful* 393.7, 801.5, *negotiated* 460.5, *workable* 509.8, *convenient* 803.3, *feasible* 823.10, *wieldy* 823.12, *helpful* 825.19, *possible* 836.5
practical ability *manual skill* 127.2
practical experience *learning* 348.3
practicality *usefulness* 393.2, 801.1, *instrumentality* 511.1, *reality* 719.1, *convenience* 803.1, *wieldiness* 823.3, *possibleness* 836.2
practical joke *joke* 277.6
practical knowledge *manual skill* 127.2
practically **836.10;** *rationally* 4.25, *chemically* 11.42, *usefully* 393.15, 801.12, *operationally* 509.13, *nearly* 586.18, *on the whole* 759.13, *conveniently* 803.6, *helpfully* 825.32
practical person *doer* 412.3
practice *learn* 48.23, *training* 122.5, *train* 122.12, *rehearse* 136.37, 335.12, *rehearsal* 335.2, *experimental* 335.8, *learning* 348.3, *expected thing* 356.3, *type of meaning* 361.4, *preparations* 388.2, *briefing* 388.4, *prepare oneself* 388.21, *use* 393.1, 393.9, *habit* 397.1, *standard procedure* 397.6, *accustom oneself* 397.19, *way* 399.10, 691.1, *action* 412.1, *occupy oneself* 412.15, *performance* 465.2, *perform* 465.5, *fashion* 536.1, *custom* 780.5, *convention* 781.5, *repetition* 797.1, *repeat* 797.15
practice abstinence *be moral* 431.13
practice ascetism *repent* 313.9
practice birth control **23.10**
practice celibacy *be celibate* 67.9
practice creative accounting *account* 493.9
practiced *educated* 48.19, *expert* 127.12, *qualified* 340.7, *knowledgeable* 348.7, *prepared* 388.9, *established* 397.12, *habituated* 397.14
practice dentistry **107.34**
practiced eye *expert* 127.9
practiced hand *expert* 127.9
practice forestry *manage trees* 43.14
practice hygiene **116.4**
practice judo *do martial arts* 152.21
practice livestock farming **16.20**
practice medicine **107.32**
practice nudism *undress* 614.18
practice one's religion *dematerialize* 525.12
practice philanthropy *be charitable* 305.12
practice run *rehearsal* 335.2
practice self-defense *box* 152.19
practice sophistry **330.11**
practice spiritualism *conjure* 86.26
practice surgery **107.33**

practice tae kwon do *do martial arts* 152.21
practice tax evasion *not pay* 490.9
practice the golden rule *be benevolent* 305.10
practice usury *lend* 475.6
practice virtue *be virtuous* 447.8
practice witchcraft *bewitch* 86.25, *be an influence* 512.13, *be powerful* 514.18
practicing *religious* 81.21, *keeping fit* 113.10, *repetition* 797.1, *cunning* 822.4
practicing Christian *Christian* 81.10
practitioner *expert* 52.8, 68.13, 127.9, *agent* 123.15, *doer* 412.3
prado [Sp] *passage* 691.5
praedial *agricultural* 16.16, *propertied* 470.9
praediality *property* 470.1
praenomen *name* 202.8
pragmatic *rational* 4.15, *detached* 4.18, *experimental* 335.8, *useful* 393.7, 801.5, *negotiated* 460.5, *practical* 719.8, *convenient* 803.3
pragmatically *sociologically* 2.15, *rationally* 4.25, *usefully* 393.15, *feasibly* 460.9
pragmatics Linguistic Studies 5, *symbolism* 183.4
pragmatic sociology *sociology* 2.1
pragmatism Philosophical Schools of Thought 4, *experimentation* 335.3, *realism* 719.3, *convenience* 803.1
pragmatist Philosophical Schools of Thought 4, *realist* 719.4
Prague Countries 566, *other famous world cities* 567.9
Praia Countries 566
Prairial French Revolutionary Calendar 646
prairie *grassland* 45.2, *geographical space* 159.2, *countryside* 564.3, *lowland* 572.6, *horizontal surface* 603.3
prairie-chicken, Attwater's greater Endangered US Birds 36
prairie oyster *variety meat* 90.30
prairie schooner *wagon* 687.5
Prairie style Architectural Styles 134
praise **435.15, 437.3, 437.16;** *worship* 83.1, 83.15, *pleasant thing* 271.4, *applause* 279.2, *fete* 279.6, *thanks* 310.2, *acknowledgment* 310.3, *be grateful* 310.6, *congratulate* 405.12, *flattery* 439.1, *flatter* 439.12, *reward* 453.1, 453.13, *moral support* 605.7, *give moral support* 605.18
praised *worshiped* 83.14, *rewarded* 453.10
praise heaven *give thanks* 310.7
praise oneself *be egotistic* 444.7
praiser *approver* 437.7
praise singer *worshiper* 83.6
praise the Lord! *hallelujah!* 83.18
praise to the skies *praise* 437.16
praiseworthiness *desirability* 288.7, *good* 445.1
praiseworthy **437.12;** *desirable* 288.11, *respectable* 435.11, *good* 445.10, *worthy* 447.7
praising *worshipful* 83.12, *thanking* 310.5, *flattering* 439.7
praline *sweets* 90.39
prance *dance* 135.7, *show off* 404.26
prancingly *dancingly* 135.8
prank *joke* 277.6, *caprice* 381.1
prankish *capricious* 381.4

prankster *capricious person* 381.3
prao Sailing Ships and Boats 690
praseodymium Chemical Elements and Common Allotropes 11
prate *talk nonsense* 192.26, 362.12, *be talkative* 207.7, *chat* 210.12, *empty talk* 362.5
pratfall *fall* 714.4
prating *nonsensical* 192.19, *talk* 207.3, *effusive* 207.6
pratingly *nonsensically* 192.30, 722.18
prattle *nonsense* 192.8, *talk nonsense* 192.26, 362.12, *talk* 207.3, *chat* 210.2, 210.12, *empty talk* 362.5
prattle on *be talkative* 207.7
prattler *speaker* 205.12
prattling *nonsensical* 192.19, *effusive* 207.6, *meaningless* 362.7
prattlingly *nonsensically* 192.30, 722.18
prawn *crustacean* 39.10, *food fish and shellfish* 90.20
praxis *tradition* 1.7, *custom* 397.4, *way of life* 399.9, *action* 412.1, *formula* 780.7
pray **85.20;** *worship* 83.15, *petition* 505.11
prayer **85.10;** *act of worship* 83.2, *thanks* 310.2, *petition* 505.2, *support* 825.2
prayer book *ritual manual* 85.11
prayer cap *vestment* 84.11
prayer for the dead *prayer* 85.10
prayerful **85.17;** *religious* 81.21, *worshipful* 83.12
prayerfully *ritually* 85.21
prayerfulness *religiousness* 81.2
prayer meeting *public worship* 83.3
prayer of thanks *thanks* 310.2
prayer rug *sacred object* 83.11
prayer wheel *sacred object* 83.11, *wheel* 682.9
pray for *desire* 288.17
praying *act of worship* 83.2, *worshipful* 83.12, *prayerful* 85.17
pray to *appeal to* 209.9
preach **84.14;** *propound a philosophy* 4.21, *dissertate* 205.5, *speak to* 205.19, *address* 209.8, *moralize* 431.14, *persuade* 670.14
preacher *educator* 48.4, *religionist* 81.14, *dissertator* 203.3, *speaker* 205.12, *public speaker* 205.9, *motivator* 508.6, *influential person* 512.5, *converter* 670.5
preachify *proselytize* 84.15
preachily *advisorily* 176.12
preachiness *religiousness* 81.2
preaching *advice* 176.1, *addressing* 209.6
preachy *educational* 48.17, *zealous* 81.22, *advisory* 176.7
Preakness *famous horse races* 159.13
preamble *public speaking* 205.11, *introduction* 771.10
prearrange *predetermine* 384.8, *plan ahead* 387.13, *lay the foundations* 388.16, *make arrangements* 767.23
prearranged *predetermined* 384.4, *planned* 387.10, *organized* 767.12
prearrangement *predetermination* 384.1, *preparation* 388.1
Precambrian *primal* 653.14
precarious *changeable* 666.3, *unsafe* 811.8, *unreliable* 841.15
precariously *changeably* 666.7, *dangerously* 811.14, *unreliably* 841.25

precariousness *danger* 811.1, *unreliability* 841.7
precast *structural* 14.45
precast concrete *construction material* 14.21
precaution **287.4;** *foresight* 357.1, *protection* 810.2
precautional *precautionary* 287.9
precautionally *precautiously* 287.19
precautionary **287.9**
precautionary steps *protection* 810.2
precautions *protection* 810.2
precautious *precautionary* 287.9
precautiously **287.19**
precede **657.13, 769.13;** *lead* 126.12, *measure* 739.7, *be important* 799.13
precedence **769.9;** *originality* 737.1, *rank* 739.2, *superiority* 744.1, *importance* 799.1
precedent **769.4;** *basis* 605.4, *original* 737.2, *preceding* 769.9, *guide* 780.4
precedented *basic* 605.13
preceding **769.9;** *front* 621.9, *antiquarian* 651.13, *premature* 657.10, *ranked* 739.6, *precedence* 769.1
precentor *imam* 84.7, *singer* 141.4
precept *philosophy* 4.1, *law* 53.1, *advice* 176.1, *maxim* 177.1, *command* 425.1, *moral* 431.5, *truism* 721.6, *rule* 780.1
preceptive *proverbial* 177.2, *truistic* 721.15
preceptively *advisorily* 176.12, *intrinsically* 721.30
preceptor *educator* 48.4
precession *star luminosity* 7.12, *orbit* 7.22, *movement* 677.3, *precedence* 769.1
precessional *preceding* 769.9
precinct *administrative region* 564.4, *urban area* 567.10, *near place* 586.3, *enclosed area* 619.2
precinct captain *political party member* 50.6
precinct leader *political party member* 50.6
precincts *surroundings* 615.1
preciosity *formalism* 406.2
precious *term of endearment* 299.7, *affected* 367.3, *formal* 406.6, *valuable* 496.8, *ornate* 532.10
precious few *few* 796.5
precious little *few* 796.5
preciously *ornately* 532.14
precious metal *ore* 11.23, *money* 484.1, *bullion* 484.16
preciousness *formalism* 406.2, *value* 496.6
precipice *mountain* 569.1, *heights* 596.4, *vertical* 602.3, *inclination* 714.6, *hidden danger* 813.3
precipices Phobias 283
precipitance *impulsiveness* 318.6, *unpremeditation* 389.2, *prematurity* 657.6
precipitancy *prematurity* 657.6
precipitancy or precipitance *rashness* 286.1, *hastiness* 818.2
precipitant *rash* 286.5, *impulsive* 318.11, *unpremeditated* 389.7, *hasty* 818.3
precipitantly *rashly* 286.9, *hastily* 818.7
precipitate *drain* 8.64, *rain* 9.57, *phase* 11.13, *solidify* 11.37, *dirt* 112.5, *rash* 286.5, *solid body* 540.4, *be dense* 540.8, *premature* 657.10, *prepare* 657.14, *awaken* 675.9, *effect* 676.1, *react* 676.8,

swift 694.6, *be swift* 694.10, *throw away* 709.25, *drip* 714.13, *subtract* 749.6, *residue* 750.2, *hasty* 818.3, *hasten* 818.4

precipitated *status adjectives* 11.25, *remaining* 750.7

precipitately *rashly* 286.9, *prematurely* 657.20, *hastily* 818.7

precipitateness *rashness* 286.1, *hastiness* 818.2

precipitation 9.26; *water cycle* 8.12, *weather data* 9.6, *phase* 11.13, *process* 11.15, *concentration* 540.2, *prematurity* 657.6, *swiftness* 694.1, *throwing* 696.3, *eviction* 709.4, *lowering* 716.1, *subtraction* 749.1

precipitous *unpremeditated* 389.7, *highland* 596.11, *vertical* 602.5, *premature* 657.10, *swift* 694.6, *fallen* 716.8

precipitously *impulsively* 318.16, *vertically* 602.11, *prematurely* 657.20

precipitousness *verticality* 602.1

précis *outline* 198.2, 617.1, 617.5, *be concise* 198.5, *brief description* 202.2, *summary* 204.1, *summarize* 204.7, *shortened version* 591.3, *limitation* 747.3, *make smaller* 747.8

precise *fastidious* 325.9, *accurate* 350.3, *intelligible* 363.5, *formal* 406.6, *correct* 429.8, 721.13, *detailed* 726.9, *special* 779.10, *infallible* 805.10, *perfectionistic* 805.18

precisely *carefully* 325.13, *accurately* 350.6, *formally* 406.12, *correctly* 429.16, 721.29, *measurably* 589.22, *meticulously* 726.18, *specially* 779.19, *perfectly* 805.21

preciseness *accuracy* 350.1, *intelligibility* 363.1, *formality* 406.1, *formalism* 406.2, *right* 429.2, *trueness* 721.4, *perfection* 805.1, *simplicity* 823.2

precise realism *Western Art Styles* 133

precisian *religionist* 81.14, *conformist* 781.6

precision *number system* 6.7, *measurement* 10.67, *carefulness* 325.1, *accuracy* 350.1, *intelligibility* 363.1, *formalism* 406.2, *right* 429.2, *trueness* 721.4, *simplicity* 823.2

precision bombing *air attack* 418.4

precisionism *Western Art Styles* 133

precision tool *tool* 103.1

preclude *exclude* 764.7, *hinder* 826.15

precluded *excluded* 764.6

preclusion *exclusion* 764.1, *hindrance* 826.1

preclusive *excluding* 764.5, *hindering* 826.12

preclusively *with delay* 826.22

Precoce *Breeds of Sheep* 16

precocial *newly hatched* 36.20

precocious *premature* 657.10

precociously *prematurely* 657.20

precociousness *prematurity* 657.6

precocity *prematurity* 657.6

precognition 320.2; *psychic power* 86.4, *divination* 86.5, *prediction* 357.3, *parapsychology* 525.4

precognitive 320.7; *divinatory* 86.18, *foreseeing* 357.5, *parapsychological* 525.9

pre-Columbian art *Western Art Styles* 133

preconceive *be unjust* 342.10, *predetermine* 384.8

preconceived *unjust* 342.7, *predetermined* 384.4

preconceived idea *prejudgment* 342.5

preconceivedly *predeterminately* 384.11

preconceived notion *or* **opinion** *predetermination* 384.1

preconception *prejudgment* 342.5, *predetermination* 384.1

preconcert *predetermine* 384.8

precondemn *prejudge* 337.13

precondition *necessity* 95.1

preconscious *psyche* 108.25

preconsultation *preparation* 388.1

precooked *culinary* 91.9, *ready-made* 388.13

precursor 769.7; *settler* 61.4, *omen* 358.5, *early comer* 657.4

precursory 769.12; *predicting* 358.11, *premature* 657.10, *introductory* 771.23

predacious *of animals* 34.13, *stolen* 479.12

predate *precede* 657.13, 769.13

predator *animal killer* 30.14, *type of animal* 34.5, *malefactor* 306.6, *greedy person* 477.11

predatorily *avariciously* 477.22, *thievishly* 479.19

predatory *of animals* 34.13, *avian* 36.19, *taking* 477.12, *stolen* 479.12

predecessor 769.8; *person of the past* 651.7, *early comer* 657.4

predeliberated *deliberate* 384.5

predeliberately *predeterminately* 384.11

predeliberation *predetermination* 384.1

predestinate *predestine* 384.9

predestination 384.2; *philosophical problem* 4.8, *necessitarianism* 95.7, *foresight* 357.1, *inevitability* 840.5

predestine 384.9; *foresee* 357.9, *intend* 361.15, *intend for* 374.11

predestined 384.6; *inevitable* 95.14, 840.11, *meant* 361.12

predeterminately 384.11

predetermination 384.1; *necessitarianism* 95.7, *prejudgment* 342.5, *foresight* 357.1, *intentionality* 374.2, *preparation* 388.1, *inevitability* 840.5

predetermine 384.8; *foresee* 357.9, *resolve* 374.9, *plan ahead* 387.13, *lay the foundations* 388.16, *manipulate* 508.12

predetermined 384.4; *intentional* 374.7, *inevitable* 840.11

predeterminist *necessitarian* 95.8

predial *agricultural* 16.16

predicament 725.3, 824.5; *futility* 282.3, *difficult circumstances* 726.6, *danger* 811.1, *confusion* 841.4, *adversity* 848.1

predicate *part of speech* 5.30, *of grammar* 5.41, *affirm* 189.21, *suppose* 359.8

predicate calculus *mathematical logic* 6.60

predication *affirmation* 189.1

predicational *or* **predicative** *affirmative* 189.10

predict 356.7, 358.14; *forecast* 9.52, 769.17, *divine* 86.24, *foresee* 357.9, *plan ahead* 387.13, *look ahead* 650.11, *warn* 814.8, *think likely* 838.10

predictability 295.2; *frequency* 663.2, *probability* 838.1, *infallibility* 840.6

predictable 295.4, 650.7; *divinatory* 86.18, *expected* 356.5, *foreseeable* 357.7, *predicted* 358.12, *habitual* 397.9, *auspicious* 458.10, *stable* 674.3, *probable* 838.6, *infallible* 840.12

predictably 295.9, 650.15; *expectedly* 356.11, *predictively* 358.16, *auspiciously* 458.17, *stably* 674.9, *warningly* 814.11, *probably* 838.11

predicted 358.12; *divinatory* 86.18, *expected* 356.5, *foreseeable* 357.7, *auspicious* 458.10, *foreseen* 650.8

predicting 358.11; *warning* 814.6

prediction 357.3, 358.1; *divination* 86.5, *expectations* 356.2, *looking to the future* 650.4, *preview* 769.6, *forewarning* 814.2, *probability* 838.1

predictive *divinatory* 86.18, *foreseeing* 357.5, *predicting* 358.11, *probable* 838.6

predictively 358.16

predictor 357.4, 650.5; *diviner* 86.14

predigest *make comprehensible* 363.8

predigested *edible* 92.20, *treated* 388.12

predilection *inclination* 290.2, *preference* 382.2, *attitude* 513.2

predispose *bias* 342.11, *lay the foundations* 388.16, *manipulate* 508.12, *influence* 512.11

predisposed *inclined toward* 290.5, *unjust* 342.7

predispose oneself *be inclined toward* 290.10

predisposition *inclination* 290.2, *tendency* 397.2, *attitude* 513.2

predominance *authority* 52.1, 514.5, *influence* 512.1, *superiority* 744.1

predominant *authoritative* 52.9, *dominant* 512.10, *unbeatable* 744.13, *prevailing* 778.11

predominantly 744.21; *influentially* 512.14, *powerfully* 514.21, *prevailingly* 742.11, *on the whole* 759.13, *universally* 778.23

predominate *have authority* 52.13, *be an influence* 512.13, *be powerful* 514.18, *be average* 742.8, *be superior* 744.15, *prevail* 778.19, *be the rule* 780.16, *be important* 799.13

predominating *powerful* 514.15, *prevailing* 778.11

predomination *superiority* 744.1

preeminence *authority* 52.1, *excellence* 445.4, *superiority* 744.1, *priority* 769.2, *importance* 799.1

preeminent *authoritative* 52.9, *excellent* 445.13, *elite* 744.12, *primary* 769.10, *important* 799.7

preeminent figure *important person* 18.11

preeminently *excellently* 445.21, *primarily* 769.21, *importantly* 799.15

preempt *buy in* 481.13, *start early* 657.12, *prepare* 657.14, *exclude* 764.7, *take precedence* 769.14

preempt a takeover *bargain* 480.20

preempted *excluded* 764.6

preemption *legal ownership* 469.8, *purchasing* 481.2, *antecedence* 657.5, *exclusion* 764.1, *precedence* 769.1

preemptive *military* 58.10, *precautionary* 287.9, *buying* 481.9, *premature* 657.10, *excluding* 764.5, *preceding* 769.9

preemptively *militarily* 58.15, *precautiously* 287.19, *acquisitively* 481.21, *primarily* 769.21

preemptive strike *military attack* 418.2

preemptor *purchaser* 481.7

preen *nest* 36.22

preen oneself *pride oneself* 297.13, *show off* 402.15

pre-established *deliberate* 384.5

prefab *house* 60.4, *construction* 551.6

prefabricate *perform* 522.16

prefabricated *ready-made* 388.13

prefabricated house *house* 60.4

prefabrication *construction* 551.6

preface 769.5; *book part* 174.5, *front matter* 621.4, *add* 748.11, *introduction* 771.10

prefatorial *precursory* 769.12

prefatory *precursory* 769.12, *introductory* 771.23

prefecture *position of authority* 52.4, *administrative region* 564.4

prefer 382.13; *desire* 288.17, *be inclined toward* 290.10, *like* 299.22, *discriminate* 337.12, *will* 372.11, *further* 825.30

preferability *preference* 382.2

preferable *desirable* 288.11, *preferential* 382.10

preferably *desirably* 288.24, *by choice* 382.18

prefer charges *litigate* 54.27

preference 382.2; *inclination* 290.2, *will* 372.1, *priority* 769.2

preferential 382.10; *discriminatory* 337.11, *unjust* 342.7

preferentially *prejudicially* 337.17, *unjustly* 342.13, *by choice* 382.18

preferential treatment *favoritism* 337.5, *injustice* 342.3, *furtherance* 825.8

preferment *ordination* 84.3, *advance* 679.3, *furtherance* 825.8

prefer not to *be disinclined* 291.14

preferred *willed* 372.6, *preferential* 382.10, *superior* 744.8

preferred issue *stock exchange* 457.3

preferring *inclined toward* 290.5

prefer soft drinks *be sober* 120.8

prefiguration *prediction* 358.1

prefigure *predict* 358.14

prefigurement *prediction* 358.1, *omen* 358.5

prefiguring *predicting* 358.11

prefix *word* 5.17, *part of speech* 5.30, *front matter* 621.4, *additional item* 748.3, *add* 748.11, *link* 752.18, *preface* 769.5

prefixed *additional* 748.8, *introductory* 771.23

prefixion *addition* 748.1, *preface* 769.5

prefrontal lobotomy *psychiatric treatment* 108.3

preglacial *primal* 653.14

pregnability *vulnerability* 811.6

pregnable *vulnerable* 811.9

pregnancy *genesis* 21.5, *bulge* 634.2, *conception* 771.4

pregnancy test *diagnostic procedure* 107.11

pregnant 21.12; *procreative* 22.10, *expecting* 356.4, *meaningful* 361.6, *embryonic* 771.19, *serious* 799.8

pregnant moment *critical time* 659.3

pregnant with doom *presageful* 358.13

preheated *heated* 217.15

prehensile *retentive* 471.5

prehensility *retention* 471.1

prehension *retention* 471.1

prehistoric *historical* 3.10, *painting* 143.3, *past* 651.11, *primal* 653.14

prehistoric age *geological past* 651.5

prehistorical *past* 651.11

prehistorical art Western Art Styles 133

prehistorically *historically* 3.17, *in the past* 651.20

prehistoric animal 653.8

prehistoric anthropologist *historian* 651.10

prehistoric anthropology 1.2; *study of the past* 651.9

prehistoric human 653.7

prehistoric person *person of the past* 651.7

prehistory *past time* 3.6, 651.1

prejudge 337.13; *be unjust* 342.10, *discriminate* 430.21

prejudged *unjust* 342.7

prejudgment 342.5; *prejudice* 337.3

prejudice 337.3; *legal injustice* 53.5, *friendship* 62.1, *hostility* 63.1, *figurative blindness* 243.8, *inclination* 290.2, *dislike* 291.1, *prejudge* 337.13, *unfair treatment* 342.4, *bias* 342.11, *fallibility* 351.6, *opinionatedness* 379.3, *preference* 382.2, *wrong* 430.1, *manipulate* 508.12, *influence* 512.11, *attitude* 513.2, *injustice* 741.3

prejudiced *intolerant* 63.7, *inclined toward* 290.5, *hating* 300.7, *discriminatory* 337.11, *unjust* 342.7, 741.6, *mistaken* 351.13, *opinionated* 379.9, *preferential* 382.10, *wrongful* 430.10, *tending to* 513.4

prejudiced against *displeased* 291.6

prejudices *ideology* 327.5

prejudicial *discriminatory* 337.11, *unjust* 342.7, *tending to* 513.4

prejudicially 337.17; *malignly* 306.18, *probably* 513.6, *unjustly* 741.12

prejudicial treatment *unfair treatment* 342.4

prelapsarian *innocent* 449.6, *naive* 449.9, *primal* 653.14

prelate *priest* 84.8

prelatic *priestly* 84.12

prelature *priesthood* 84.2

preliminaries *preparations* 388.2, *front matter* 621.4, *early stage* 657.3, *preface* 769.5, *introduction* 771.10

preliminaries *or* **prelims** [Inf] *book part* 174.5

preliminarily *preparatorily* 388.23, *incompletely* 544.14

preliminary *preparatory* 388.7, *unfinished* 544.9, *premature* 657.10, *precursory* 769.12, *introductory* 771.23

preliminary course *preparations* 388.2

preliminary race *track event* 166.1

preliminary sketch *rough idea* 544.4

preliminary step *preparations* 388.2

preliminary swing *discus throwing* 166.13

preliminary warning *notice* 358.3

prelims [Inf] *front matter* 621.4, *preface* 769.5, *introduction* 771.10

prelude Musical Forms 140, *preface* 769.5, *introduction* 771.10

preludial *introductory* 771.23

premarital *matrimonial* 64.15

premature 657.10; *immature* 389.9, *untimely* 660.5

premature baby *early comer* 657.4

prematurely 657.20; *immaturely* 389.18, *at the wrong time* 660.12

prematureness *prematurity* 657.6

prematurity 657.6; *immaturity* 389.3, *untimeliness* 660.1

premedication *surgery* 107.15

premeditate *resolve* 374.9, *predetermine* 384.8

premeditated *intentional* 374.7, *deliberate* 384.5, *planned* 387.10

premeditatedly *predeterminately* 384.11

premeditated murder *murder* 30.2

premeditation *foresight* 357.1, *intentionality* 374.2, *predetermination* 384.1, *preparation* 388.1

premenstrual syndrome (PMS) *anxiety disorder* 108.11

premier *governor* 49.23, *person in authority* 52.7, *leader* 68.3, *person in command* 425.5, *influential person* 512.5

premiere 771.9; *theatrical performance* 136.13, *dramatize* 136.33, *first appearance* 264.3, *beginning* 583.9, 583.14, 652.4, *begin* 583.21, *inaugurated* 652.13, *be new* 652.17

premiered *inaugurated* 652.13, *enrolled* 771.24

première partie *decorative woodwork* 131.2

premiership *position of authority* 52.4, *directorship* 126.5

premise 319.14; *philosophy* 4.1, *propound a philosophy* 4.21, *mathematical logic* 6.60, *physical law* 10.4, *belief* 87.1, *have an idea* 317.12, *explanation* 319.4, *theory* 327.2, *line of argument* 329.3, *evidence* 339.1, *supposition* 359.1, *suppose* 359.8, *basis* 605.4, *viewpoint* 628.5

premised *supposed* 359.6

premises *resources* 102.4

premiss *mathematical logic* 6.60

premium *bridge* 168.4, *bounty* 453.8, *interest* 488.4, *type of payment* 489.3, *money received* 492.2

premium gas *petroleum* 562.5

premolar *teeth* 19.8

premonition *psychic power* 86.4, *divination* 86.5, *occult and psychic phenomena* 86.7, *prediction* 357.3, 358.1, *looking to the future* 650.4, *preview* 769.6, *forewarning* 814.2

premonition of disaster *forewarning* 814.2

premonitory *divinatory* 86.18, *predicting* 358.11, *warning* 814.6

prenatal diagnosis 107.9

prenuptial *agreements* 459.2

prenuptial agreement *or* **contract** *betrothal* 458.2

preoccupation *mood disorder* 108.12, *diligence* 323.4, *future intention* 374.3, *compulsion* 428.1

preoccupied *thoughtful* 4.17, *diligent* 323.7, *oblivious* 355.9

preordain *predestine* 384.9

preordained *inevitable* 95.14, *predestined* 384.6

preordination *predestination* 384.2

preowned *used* 393.5

prep *practice surgery* 107.33, *prepare* 388.14

prepaid *receiving pay* 489.14

preparation 388.1, 769.3; *education* 48.1, *dose of medicine* 115.3, *training* 122.5, *circumspection* 325.3, *foresight* 357.1, *predetermination* 384.1, *production* 522.1, *looking to the future* 650.4, *rudiments* 771.7

preparations 388.2; *arrangements* 767.10

preparative *preparatory* 388.7

preparatively *preparatorily* 388.23

preparatorily 388.23; *prematurely* 657.20, *in anticipation* 769.20

preparatory 388.7, 769.11; *premature* 657.10, *introductory* 771.23

preparatory school *school* 48.11

preparatory work *preparations* 388.2

prepare 388.14, 657.14; *educate* 48.22, *find means* 102.6, *train* 122.12, *be careful* 325.11, *have foresight* 357.8, *predetermine* 384.8, *plan ahead* 387.13, *tend* 513.5, *structure* 551.20, *make arrangements* 767.23, *warn* 814.8

prepare a balance sheet *account* 493.9

prepare a brief *litigate* 54.27

prepare a budget *account* 493.9

prepare a case *litigate* 54.27

prepare a cash-flow forecast *account* 493.9

prepare a meal *cook* 91.10

prepare a statement *settle accounts* 493.11

prepared 388.9; *adult* 27.11, *educated* 48.19, *supplied* 89.7, *culinary* 91.9, *circumspect* 325.8, *qualified* 340.7, *expecting* 356.4, *willing* 373.7, *predetermined* 384.4, *planned* 387.10, *defended* 419.18, *tending to* 513.4, *immediate* 645.5, *warned* 814.7

preparedly *maturely* 27.18, *predeterminately* 384.11

preparedness 388.5; *maturity* 27.3, *qualification* 340.1, *willingness* 373.1, *attitude* 513.2

prepared speech *address* 209.1

prepare for *intend* 374.8, *be prepared* 388.17, *expect* 650.12

prepare for action 388.18

prepare for a rainy day *deposit* 105.21

prepare for blastoff *prepare for action* 388.18

prepare for burial *bury* 31.10

prepare for publication *publish* 174.19, *report* 175.9

prepare for surgery *practice surgery* 107.33

prepare for takeoff *prepare for action* 388.18

prepare for the future *have foresight* 357.8

prepare for use *use* 393.9

prepare for war *arm* 76.30

prepare oneself 388.21; *undertake* 391.7

preparer 388.6; *predictor* 357.4

prepare the ground *prepare the way* 388.15

prepare the way 388.15; *make easy* 823.15

preparing *preparation* 388.1, *preparatory* 388.7

prepatellar bursitis *joint disease* 114.19

prepense *deliberate* 384.5

preplanned *deliberate* 384.5

preponderance *imbalance* 741.2, *superiority* 744.1, *majority* 793.3

preponderant *unbeatable* 744.13

preponderantly *predominantly* 744.21

preponderate *be unequal* 741.7

preposition *part of speech* 5.30, 760.7

prepositional *of grammar* 5.41

prepositionally *grammatically* 5.48

prepositional phrase *or* **clause** *clause* 5.31

prepositive *introductory* 771.23

preposterous *foolish* 353.5, *fantastic* 360.11, *meaningless* 362.7, *ridiculous* 368.5, *unrestrained* 500.5, *impossible* 837.4

prepotence *superiority* 744.1

prepotency *superiority* 744.1

preprandial *culinary* 91.9

preprocess *program* 15.29

preprocessor language *programming language* 15.16

prep school *school* 48.11

prepublication *notice* 358.3

prequel *preview* 769.6

Pre-Raphaelite Brotherhood Western Art Styles 133, Western Literary Groups 139

prerelease *preview* 769.6

prerequisite *specification* 340.6, *preparatory* 388.7, *compulsion* 428.1, *compulsory* 428.7, *essential* 723.5

prerogative *legal power* 52.2, *claim* 72.2, 429.3, *priority* 769.2, *freedom* 829.1

preromanticism Western Literary Groups 139

presage *foresee* 357.9, *omen* 358.5, *predict* 358.14, *intend* 361.15, *look ahead* 650.11, *preview* 769.6, *forecast* 769.17

presageful 358.13; *warning* 814.6

presaging *symbolic* 183.12

presbyopia *sight defect* 243.2

presbyopic *weak-sighted* 243.10

presbyterial *priestly* 84.12

Presbyterianism Christian Groups 81

presbytery *church interior* 83.9, *clerical dwelling* 84.10

preschool *young* 26.11, *school* 48.11

preschool education *educational system* 48.2

prescience *prediction* 358.1, *looking to the future* 650.4

prescient *divine* 82.16, *foreseeing* 357.5, *predicting* 358.11

prescribe *practice medicine* 107.32, *treat* 115.17, *medicate* 115.18, *manage* 126.10, *specify* 340.14, *command* 425.10, *rule* 780.12

prescribed *gymnastic* 157.11, *conditional* 340.10, *established* 397.12

prescribed diet *dieting* 118.2

prescribed exercise *gymnastics* 157.1

prescribed form *etiquette* 406.3

prescribed punishment *penalty* 454.5

prescribed remedy *remedy* 115.1

prescribe medication *medicate* 115.18, *cure* 809.15

prescriber *adviser* 176.5

prescript *command* 425.1

prescription *treatment* 107.14, *remedy* 115.1, *specification* 340.6, *tradition* 397.5, *command* 425.1, *legal ownership* 469.8, *rule* 780.1

prescription drug *medicine* 115.2, *drug* 115.9

prescriptive *philosophical* 4.12, *advisory* 176.7, *conditional* 340.10, *established* 397.12, *commanding* 425.7, *average* 742.5, *legal* 780.8

prescriptively *advisorily* 176.12, *conditionally* 340.16, *commandingly* 425.15

preselect *choose* 382.14

presence 575.1; *ghost* 86.11, *visibility* 244.1, 264.4, *good conduct* 399.5, *authority* 425.3, *arrival* 704.1, *existence* 717.1, *reality* 719.1, *inclusion* 763.1, *distinction* 777.8

present 264.15, 575.7, 647.4; *grammatical term* 5.29, *dramatize* 136.33, *entertain* 138.16, *represent* 187.10, *act* 187.13, *visible* 244.5, *appearing* 264.9, *pleasant thing* 271.4, *benevolent act* 305.5, *topical* 328.5, *show* 404.24, *launch* 405.14, *reward* 453.13, *gift* 472.2, *give* 472.10, *offering* 504.5, *perform* 522.16, *style* 537.8, *time* 639.1, *available* 647.6, *direct* 697.13, *existing* 717.11, *grant* 735.10, 735.30, *inaugurate* 771.31, *display* 843.13

present, the *present time* 647.1

presentable *appealing* 529.10

presentableness *appeal* 529.4

present a bold front *defy* 416.7

present a brave face *defy* 416.7

present an account *settle accounts* 493.11

present a puzzle *be unintelligible* 364.11

present arms *greet* 410.11, *salute* 435.17

Presentation Christian Holy Days and Seasons 85

presentation *theatrical performance* 136.13, *communication* 170.2, *representation* 187.1, *address* 209.1, *birth* 264.2, *demonstration* 331.1, *party* 408.6, *giving* 472.1, *reward* 472.4, *tentative offer* 504.2, *premiere* 771.9, *lecture* 777.7, *display* 843.1, *production* 843.5

presentation software *application software* 15.14

present day 647.2

present difficulties *be difficult* 824.16

presented *granted* 735.20, *enrolled* 771.24, *displayed* 843.8

presenter *actor* 136.25, *entertainer* 138.8, *speaker* 205.12, *demonstrator* 331.6, *giver* 472.7, *displayer* 843.7

present evidence *authorize* 52.14

presentient *precognitive* 320.7, *predicting* 358.11

presentiment *impression* 266.2, *precognition* 320.2, *prediction* 358.1, *preview* 769.6

presenting arms *mark of respect* 435.4

present itself *or* **oneself** *become visible* 264.13

presently *at present* 647.9, *soon* 657.18

presentment *theatrical performance* 136.13, *representation* 187.1, *demonstration* 331.1, *giving* 472.1, *grant* 735.10

present moment *present time* 647.1

present no difficulties *be easy* 823.14

present oneself *appear* 575.16

present participle *part of speech* 5.30, *present time* 647.1

present perfect *grammatical term* 5.29

present problems *be difficult* 824.16

present situation *present day* 647.2

present tense *linguistic time* 639.6, *present time* 647.1

present the main points *outline* 617.5

present throughout *omnipresent* 575.10

present time 647.1; *present day* 647.2

present with an ultimatum *demand* 425.11

preservation 815.1; *storage* 105.6, *defense* 419.1, *detention* 471.2, *financial support* 605.8, *permanence* 667.1, *continuance* 669.3, *setting apart* 753.2

preservationism *green politics* 260.6

preservationist *environmental* 260.13

preservation of body 815.7

preservation of provisions 815.6

preservation of status quo 815.8

preservative *food content* 90.3, *permanent* 667.2, *preserver* 815.9, *preserving* 815.11

preservatively 815.16

preserve 815.14; *save* 105.20, *practice hygiene* 116.4, *sweetener* 222.2, *detain* 471.9, *dry up* 560.21, *support financially* 605.19, *perpetuate* 640.5, *make permanent* 667.5, *continue* 669.8, *set apart* 753.17, *protect* 810.21, *ecology* 815.3

preserve a balance *stand in the middle* 772.17

preserved 815.12; *saved* 105.15, *unused* 394.5, *retained* 471.6, *unfailing* 667.3, *safe* 810.16

preserved thing 815.10

preserve for posterity *record* 185.13

preserve one's dignity *or* **honor** *guard one's pride* 297.16

preserver 815.9; *provider* 605.10, *protector* 810.11, *safety device* 810.15

preserves *sweets* 90.39, *preserved thing* 815.10

preserving 815.11; *cooking technique* 91.2, *defense* 419.1, *sustaining* 605.15, *tutelary* 810.19

preset *deliberate* 384.5, *predetermine* 384.8

presettled *predetermined* 384.4

presettlement *predetermination* 384.1

preset tuning *television set* 172.6

preshrink *treat* 130.21, *contract* 582.12

preshrinkage *contraction* 582.1

preshrinking *fabric treatment* 130.10, *contraction* 582.1

preshrunk *treated* 130.16, *smaller* 582.7

preside *direct* 126.11, *be sociable* 408.14, *moderate* 521.7

presidency *position of authority* 52.4

president *United States government* 49.21, *governor* 49.23, *person in authority* 52.7, *leader* 68.3, *manager* 126.7, *person in command* 425.5, *influential person* 512.5

presidential *governmental* 49.24, *manorial* 60.21

presidentially *governmentally* 49.27

presidential palace *official residence* 60.6

president pro tempore of the Senate *person in authority* 52.7

preside over *govern* 49.26, *wield authority* 52.16, *direct* 780.14

presiding *governing* 49.25

presiding officer *judge* 54.10

press *simple machine* 14.6, *crowd* 59.11, 795.11, *fabric-handling tool* 130.12, *play basketball* 148.7, *printing* 173.3, *advise* 176.9, *type of touch* 216.3, *touch* 216.9, *insist* 376.14, *business* 414.6, *compel* 428.8, *torture* 454.29, *manipulate* 508.12, *smoother* 545.2, *smooth* 545.10, 552.13, *contractor* 582.6, *squeeze* 582.13, *make thin* 595.17, *flattener* 603.4, *make horizontal* 603.10, *make concave* 637.7, *blow* 695.5, *impel* 695.9, *obtain an extract* 711.19, *make conform* 781.13, *throng* 795.4, *hasten* 818.4

press, the *communications* 169.1, *publication media* 173.6, *print journalism* 175.4

press a claim *demand* 505.12

press agent *representative* 75.3, *producer* 136.28, *publicizer* 173.11, *persuader* 178.9, *news interpreter* 365.7, *motivator* 508.6, *displayer* 843.7

press announcement *public relations (PR)* 173.8

press baron *print journalist* 175.5

press box *stadium* 155.3

press charges *litigate* 54.27

press clipping *record* 185.1

press conference *news event* 171.2, *public relations (PR)* 173.8

press corps *print journalist* 175.5

press drill *machine tool* 14.9

pressed *uniform* 545.5, *squeezed* 582.9, *thinned* 595.13, *leveled* 603.8, *crowded* 795.10

pressed flower *flower* 42.1

pressed (for money) *insolvent* 486.10

pressed for time *hasty* 818.3

pressed man *soldier* 77.4

press forward *press on* 679.9

press gang *coercive method* 428.3

press-gang *force* 428.10, *take away forcefully* 477.19

press home *emphasize* 200.6

press in *flood in* 706.14, *impact* 710.11

pressing *demanding* 95.13, *fabric treatment* 130.10, *recording* 185.6, *tenacious* 376.9, *compelling* 428.6, *strong* 516.9, *ponderous* 538.11, *squeeze* 582.3, *blow* 695.5, *obtaining of an extract* 711.7

pressing defense *playing terms* 148.4

press into service *resort to* 393.13

press inward *make concave* 635.7

pressman *printer* 173.10

press notice *news story* 171.3, *public relations (PR)* 173.8

press of business *business* 414.6

press office *news source* 171.4

press officer *producer* 136.28, *news interpreter* 365.7

press of sail *swiftness* 694.1

press on 679.9; *follow up* 385.16, *impel* 695.9

press one's buttons *cause dislike* 291.10

press photographer *photographer* 132.23, *record keeper* 185.8

press release *news event* 171.2, *news story* 171.3, *public relations (PR)* 173.8

press service *news source* 171.4

press the button *be at war* 76.32, *activate* 509.11

press the emergency button *give warning* 814.10

press upon *weigh on* 538.13

pressure *force* 10.9, 514.8, *thermodynamics* 10.30, *authority* 52.1, *have authority* 52.13, *strain* 117.4, *afflict* 117.16, *exertion* 122.4, *cross-country* 162.31, *persuasion* 178.1, *persuade* 178.15, *action* 412.1, *coercion* 428.2, *compel* 428.8, *request* 505.1, 505.10, *inducement* 508.2, *be an instrument* 511.7, *influence* 512.1, *potency* 516.6, *weighing down* 538.5, *gaseousness* 556.6, *squeeze* 582.3, Fields of Measurement 589, *measuring instrument* 589.12, *blow* 695.5, *haste* 818.1, *restraint* 830.1, *restrain* 830.12, *adversity* 848.1

pressure-cook *cook* 91.10

pressure cooker *cooking equipment* 91.6

pressure-cooking *cooking technique* 91.2

pressured *strained* 117.13, *motivated* 508.8

pressure gauge *vaporimeter* 556.13, *meter* 589.13

pressure gradient *weather data* 9.6

pressure group *motivator* 178.11, 508.6, *group influence* 512.6

pressure of deadlines *business* 414.6

pressure of work *business* 414.6

pressure system *weather system* 9.10

pressure tendency *weather data* 9.6

pressuring *causal* 511.5

pressurize *influence* 512.11

pressurized *ponderous* 538.11, *restrained* 830.9

pressurized-water reactor (PWR) *nuclear power production* 514.10

presswork *printing* 173.3

Prestice Breeds of Pigs 16

prestidigitation *magic* 138.3

prestidigitator *magician* 138.11

prestidigitatory *or* **prestidigitatorial** *magical* 138.15

prestige *social stratification* 2.7, *dignity* 297.4, *repute* 370.1, 487.7, *respect* 435.1, *admiration* 437.2, *personal influence* 512.3, *superiority* 744.1, *distinction* 777.8, *importance* 799.1, *prosperity* 847.1

prestigious *dignified* 297.11, *lofty* 404.15, *respected* 435.10, *influential* 512.8, *notable* 799.11

prestigiously *with dignity* 297.20, *eminently* 370.7, *loftily* 404.30, *influentially* 512.14, *predominantly* 744.21

prestissimo Musical Terms and Expression Marks 140

prestissimo *hurryingly* 694.18

presto Musical Terms and Expression Marks 140

presto *hurryingly* 694.18, *hasty* 818.3

prestressed *structural* 14.45

prestressed concrete *construction material* 14.21

presumable *supposed* 359.6, *probable* 838.6

presumably *expectantly* 281.16, *probably* 838.11

presume *propound a philosophy* 4.21, *be of the opinion* 87.10, *expect* 281.12, *theorize* 327.16, *predict* 356.7, *foresee* 357.9, *suppose* 359.8, *have the audacity* 400.15, *defy* 416.7, *discriminate* 430.21, *lack restraint* 829.21, *think likely* 838.10

presumed *theoretical* 327.10, *supposed* 359.6, *circumstantial* 726.8, *probable* 838.6

presume on *resort to* 393.13

presumingly *theoretically* 4.24

presumption *expectation* 281.2, 356.1, *recklessness* 286.2, *idea* 327.1, *supposition* 359.1, *audacity* 400.3, *defiance* 416.1, *probability* 838.1

presumptive *suppositional* 359.5, *probable* 838.6

presumptively *theoretically* 4.24

presumptuous *reckless* 286.6, *arrogant* 297.9, *audacious* 400.10, *defiant* 416.5

presumptuously *recklessly* 286.10, *arrogantly* 297.18, *audaciously* 400.20, *defiantly* 416.9

presumptuousness *recklessness* 286.2, *audacity* 400.3

presuppose *theorize* 6.84, *suppose* 359.8, *discriminate* 430.21

presupposition *philosophy* 4.1, *theory* 6.62, *prejudgment* 342.5, *supposition* 359.1

presurmise *suppose* 359.8

pretax profit *return* 453.6

preteens *youth* 26.1

pretend *be untruthful* 192.20, *disdain* 297.14, *deceive* 330.12, *suppose* 359.8, *imaginary* 360.12, *imagine* 360.14, *be affected* 367.4, *do great deeds* 412.14, *artificial* 720.12, *be unreal* 722.12

pretended *hypocritical* 330.10, *supposed* 359.6, *artificial* 720.12

pretender 367.2; *hypocrite* 192.9

pretending *ungenuine* 192.13, *supposition* 359.1

pretend it never happened *pacify* 74.11

pretend not to see *ignore* 413.14

pretend to be *represent* 187.10

pretense *ungenuineness* 192.2, *spectacle* 264.6, *hypocrisy* 330.5, *supposition* 359.1, *affectation* 367.1, *deed* 412.2

pretension *claim* 72.2, *unskillfulness* 128.1, *affectation* 367.1, *showiness* 404.1

pretention *arrogance* 297.2

pretentious *worded* 5.38, *unskilled* 128.5, *ungenuine* 192.13, *diffuse* 199.3, *arrogant* 297.9, *affected* 367.3, *cocky* 402.11, *showy* 404.14, *inelegant* 528.6, *ornate* 532.10, *exaggerated* 712.9

pretentiously *lexically* 5.46, *untruthfully* 192.27, *arrogantly* 297.18, *affectedly* 367.5, *cockily* 402.19, *showily* 404.29, *ornately* 532.14

pretentiousness *ungenuineness*

192.2, *arrogance* 297.2, *affectation* 367.1, *showiness* 404.1

preterit *grammatical term* 5.29, *past tense* 651.2

preternatural *occult* 86.16

preternaturalism *supernaturalism* 86.3

pretext *explanation* 319.4, *line of argument* 329.3, *motivation* 508.1, *reason* 675.4, *stratagem* 822.2

Pretoria Countries 566

pretreated *treated* 388.12

pretrial proceedings 54.13

prettify *beautify* 530.14

prettily *beautifully* 529.13, 530.16, *decoratively* 532.13

prettiness *beauty* 529.1

pretty *moderately* 521.10, *beautiful* 529.7

pretty as a picture *picturesque* 529.9

pretty damn quick (PDQ) [Inf] *swiftly* 694.16, *hastily* 818.7

pretty good *getting well* 113.9

pretty much *to a degree* 739.11

pretty pass *predicament* 725.3, 824.5

pretty penny [Inf] *costliness* 496.1

pretty pickle [Inf] *predicament* 824.5

pretty woman *attractive female* 529.5

pretzels *snack* 90.8

prevail 778.19; *become a habit* 397.17, *be an influence* 512.13, *be powerful* 514.18, *be frequent* 661.5, *continue to be* 717.20, *be average* 742.8, *be superior* 744.15, *be the rule* 780.16, *overcome obstacles* 845.14, *be victorious* 845.16

prevailing 778.11; *windy* 9.42, *dominant* 512.10, *average* 742.5, *unbeatable* 744.13

prevailingly 742.11; *powerfully* 514.21

prevailing northwesterlies *wind system* 9.15

prevailing southwesterlies *wind system* 9.15

prevailing taste *fashion* 536.1

prevailing wind *wind* 9.12

prevail over *defeat* 832.11

prevail upon *persuade* 178.15, *plead* 329.14, *influence* 508.11, *manipulate* 508.12

prevalence *influence* 512.1, *frequency* 661.1, *average* 742.1

prevalent *familiar* 397.10, *dominant* 512.10, *frequent* 661.4, *existing* 717.11, *average* 742.5, *prevailing* 778.11

prevalently *powerfully* 514.21, *frequently* 661.7

prevaricate *evade* 181.17, *lie* 192.23, *quibble* 330.13, *be equivocal* 380.7, *be evasive* 386.20, *circumlocute* 607.12, *hesitate* 841.18

prevaricating *quibbling* 330.9, *equivocal* 380.5

prevarication *evasion* 181.5, 380.2, *falsehood* 192.6, *evasiveness* 386.6, *indirectness* 607.3

prevaricative *lying* 192.16

prevaricator *liar* 192.10, *sophist* 330.6, *equivocator* 380.4

prevaricatory *lying* 192.16, *equivocal* 380.5

prevenience *antecedence* 657.5

prevenient *premature* 657.10

preveniently *prematurely* 657.20

prevent *deter* 179.8, *take precautions* 287.14, *avert* 386.15,

prohibit 503.8, *counteract* 510.7, 828.21, *debar* 604.17, *prepare* 657.14, *delay* 658.13, *exclude* 764.7, *hinder* 826.15, *restrain* 830.12

preventable *avoidable* 386.12

preventably *evasively* 386.24

preventative *prophylaxis* 115.4, *medicinal* 115.15, *prohibited* 503.5, *opposing force* 510.2, *counteracting* 510.6, *preserving* 815.11

preventive dentistry *dentistry* 107.6

prevent defense *defense* 155.9

prevent disease *practice hygiene* 116.4

prevented *excluded* 604.11, 764.6

prevention *precaution* 287.4, *avoidance* 386.1, *prohibition* 503.1, *counteraction* 510.1, *debarment* 604.5, *delay* 658.3, *exclusion* 764.1, *hindrance* 826.1, *uncooperativeness* 828.4, *restraint* 830.1

preventive *prophylaxis* 115.4, *medicinal* 115.15, *dissuasive* 179.4, *precautionary* 287.9, *fugitive* 386.10, *prohibited* 503.5, *opposing force* 510.2, *counteracting* 510.6, *excluded* 604.11, *excluding* 764.5, *preserving* 815.11, *hindering* 826.12, *restraining* 830.8

preventive or **preventative** *therapeutic* 107.30

preventive action *procedure* 387.2

preventive custody *arrest* 55.5

preventively *dissuasively* 179.12, *precautiously* 287.19, *evasively* 386.24, *by veto* 503.12, *counter* 510.8, *preservatively* 815.16, *with delay* 826.22, *restrainedly* 830.18

preventive measure *protection* 810.2

preventive measure or **step** *precaution* 287.4

preventive medicine *medicine* 107.1, *health care* 107.7, *hygiene* 116.1

preventive warfare 76.12

preview 769.6; *theatrical performance* 136.13, *dramatize* 136.33, *movie type* 137.3, *first appearance* 264.3, *notice* 358.3, *part* 760.1, *production* 843.5

previous *former* 653.12, *dead* 658.10, *preceding* 769.9

previously *formerly* 653.19, *before* 769.18

previously owned *used* 393.5

previousness *precedence* 769.1

prevision *prediction* 358.1

Prévost's theory of exchanges Classical Physical Laws 10

prewar *harmless* 73.9, *olden* 653.11

prewashed *treated* 130.16

prey *game* 160.6, *victim of discrimination* 337.8, *objective* 374.5, *the hunted* 385.7, *loser* 468.8, *person in adversity* 848.9

prey on *eat well* 92.23

prey upon *plunder* 479.16

priapic *perverted* 432.12

priapism *sexual immorality* 432.2

Pribilof Islands Islands 572

price 494.1, 494.12; *horse-racing betting terms* 159.11, *expense* 491.2

price charged *price* 494.1

price control *price* 494.1, *economic restraint* 830.3

price controls *economic factor* 56.8

price cut *price* 494.1, *subtracted item* 749.2

price cutting *subtraction* 749.1

priced 494.10

price fixing *fee* 494.3, *economic restraint* 830.3

price freeze *economic restraint* 830.3

price increase *augmentation* 467.2

price index *economic indicator* 56.4

price itself out of the market *cost a lot* 496.9

priceless *ridiculous* 368.5, *valuable* 496.8, *profitable* 801.8

pricelessness *ridiculousness* 368.1, *value* 496.6

price list *price* 494.1, *bill* 785.4

price oneself out of the market *overestimate* 343.6

price range *price* 494.1

price reduction *discount* 495.1

prices *economic indicator* 56.4

prices going through the ceiling or **roof** *inflationary price* 496.3

price support *gift* 472.2

price-wage spiral *economic factor* 56.8

price war *price* 494.1

pricey or **pricy** *costly* 496.7

pricing *economic factor* 56.8

prick *stimulus* 212.3, *inflict pain* 215.10, *negative stimulus* 508.4, *motivate* 508.9, *sharp-pointed growth* 549.5, *be sharp* 549.15, *hole* 583.17

prick [Inf] *organs of reproduction* 21.9, *male* 32.1

pricked *holed* 583.12

pricked by conscience *penitent* 451.5

pricked up *unbowed* 602.7

pricking *spiked* 549.11, *opening* 583.1

pricking of conscience *penitence* 451.1

prickle *stimulus* 212.3, *sense* 212.9, *rough thing* 544.2, *be rough* 544.10, *sharp-pointed growth* 549.5, *be sharp* 549.15

prickliness *sensitivity* 212.2, *oversensitivity* 267.2, *touchiness* 303.3, *divisiveness* 463.2, *sharpness* 549.1, *irritation* 554.9

prickly *exciting* 212.8, *oversensitive* 267.4, *touchy* 303.10, *disagreeing* 463.6, *barbed* 544.7, *spiked* 549.11

prickly ash Trees and Shrubs 43

prickly heat *skin disease* 114.16

prickly poppy Flowers 42

prick out *cultivate* 17.19

prick up *make vertical* 602.9

prick up one's ears *hear* 228.13, *meddle* 321.8, *take note of* 323.10

pricky *spiked* 549.11

pride 297.1; *assemblage of mammals* 35.22, Collective Names 59, *boastfulness* 402.6, *pomp* 404.7, *formality* 406.1, *good thing* 445.9, *iniquity* 448.3, *showpiece* 843.3

pride and joy *object of pride* 297.6, *good thing* 445.9

prideful 297.8; *boastful* 402.13

pridefully 297.17

pridefulness *pride* 297.1

pride of place *object of pride* 297.6, *superiority* 744.1, *priority* 769.2

pride oneself 297.13

prier *observer* 242.15, *meddler* 321.4

priest 84.8; *funeral person* 31.5, *celibate* 67.4, *religious person* 81.9, *ritualist* 85.14, *influential person* 512.5, *converter* 670.5

priestess *priest* 84.8

priest hole *shelter* 812.4

priesthood 84.2; *clergy* 84.1
priestly 84.12; *monastic* 67.8
priestly government *theocracy* 49.4
priest-ridden *zealous* 81.22
priests Phobias 283
priest's cap *vestment* 84.11
prig *moralist* 431.8
priggish *moralistic* 431.12
priggishly *moralistically* 431.16
priggishness *self-righteousness* 431.7
prim *formal* 406.6, *moralistic* 431.12, *conformist* 781.10
Prima Apple Varieties 44
prima ballerina *skilled person* 127.7, *ballet dancer* 135.5
primacy *priesthood* 84.2, *superiority* 744.1, *priority* 769.2
prima donna *skilled person* 127.7, *actor* 136.25, *singer* 141.4, *proud person* 297.7, *paragon* 744.6, *celebrity* 799.6
prima facie *visually* 242.27, *verificatory* 336.6, *extraneously* 724.16
prima facie evidence *evidence* 54.15
primal 653.14; *historical* 3.10, *past* 651.11, *causal* 675.7, *prime* 771.18
primarily 769.21; *focally* 612.14, *archaically* 653.20, *causally* 675.12, *in essence* 723.13, *predominantly* 744.21, *first* 771.37, *importantly* 799.15
primary 769.10; *plumage* 36.7, *election* 382.6, *basic* 601.8, *focal* 612.8, *front-running* 621.10, *causal* 675.7, *intrinsic* 723.6, *original* 737.4, *elite* 744.12, *beginning* 771.16, *one* 788.10, *important* 799.7
primary care *medicine* 107.1
primary cell *electrical conduction* 10.33
primary character *metamorphic rock* 8.36
primary chord *chord* 140.18
primary color *color* 251.1
primary consumer *ecology* 13.25
primary education *educational system* 48.2
primary election *election* 382.6
primary group *social organization* 2.5
primary growth *cancer* 114.15
primary hypersomnia *sleep disorder* 108.20
primary insomnia *sleep disorder* 108.20
primary issue *priority* 769.2
primary memory *memory* 15.6
primary premise *truism* 721.6
primary producer *ecology* 13.25
primary quality *philosophical problem* 4.8
primary rainbow *rainbow* 9.28
primary school *school* 48.11
primary source *focus* 612.3
primary structure *protein* 12.9
primary wave *seismic wave* 8.25
Primate *primate* 35.17
primate 35.17, 35.32; *type of animal* 34.5, *person in authority* 52.7, *priest* 84.8
primatial *primate* 35.32
primatologist *animal scientist* 34.7, *mammalogist* 35.2
primatology *animal science* 34.6
prime 771.18; *divisible* 6.71, *educate* 48.22, *public worship* 83.3, Reference Signs 183, *cause to know* 348.13, *prepare for action*

388.18, *morning things* 655.3, *original* 737.4, *elite* 744.12, *numerical* 783.7, *important* 799.7, *time of plenty* 847.3
prime a witness *predetermine* 384.8
prime condition *preparedness* 388.5
primed *educated* 48.19, *knowledgeable* 348.7, *predetermined* 384.4, *prepared* 388.9
primed witness *predetermination* 384.1
prime factor *multiplication* 6.15
prime lending rate *finance* 457.1, *currency market* 484.8, *interest* 488.4
prime matter *matter* 524.4
prime meridian *exact location* 565.2
prime minister *British government* 49.22, *governor* 49.23, *person in authority* 52.7, *leader* 68.3, *person in command* 425.5, *influential person* 512.5
Prime Mover God 82.6
prime mover *motivator* 178.11, 508.6, *producer* 522.10, *first cause* 675.6, *originator* 771.15
prime number *kind of number* 783.2
prime number or **prime** *number* 6.4
prime of life *youth* 26.1, *middle age* 27.4
primer *schoolbook* 48.15, *type of book* 174.3, *paint* 251.6, *rudiments* 771.7
prime rate *finance* 457.1
primero Card Games 168
prime time (TV) *evening* 656.2
prime-time program *program* 172.10
primeval *past* 651.11, *primal* 653.14, *premature* 657.10, *prime* 771.18
primeval forest *trees* 43.4
primeval humanity *primitive humanity* 18.4
primevally *archaically* 653.20, *beforehand* 657.19
primeval man *primitive humanity* 18.4
primeval stage *early stage* 657.3
priming *explosive* 78.13, *preparation* 388.1
primitive *type of painting* 143.5, *representing* 202.14, *past* 651.11, *primal* 653.14, *causal* 675.7, *original* 737.4, *prime* 771.18
primitive art Western Art Styles 133
primitive human *prehistoric human* 653.7
primitive humanity 18.4
primitively *archaically* 653.20, *beforehand* 657.19, *causally* 675.12
primitiveness *oldness* 653.1
primitive self *psyche* 108.25
primitive society *group* 18.13
primitive stage *early stage* 657.3
primitivism Western Art Styles 133, Western Literary Groups 139
primly *formally* 406.12, *moralistically* 431.16
primness *formality* 406.1, *self-righteousness* 431.7, *conventionalism* 781.4
primogenitary *receivable* 473.12
primogeniture *receiving* 473.1
primordial *historical* 3.10,

developmental 13.33, *primal* 653.14, *causal* 675.7, *prime* 771.18
primordial fireball *universe* 7.3
primordially *historically* 3.17, *archaically* 653.20, *causally* 675.12, *first* 771.37
primordial soup *source* 771.3
primordium *developmental biology* 13.22
primp *dress up* 100.45, *beautify* 530.14
primrose Flowers 42, *yellow thing* 259.4
primrose path *figurative usage* 42.8, *route* 691.2, *deterioration* 808.1
primrose-yellow *yellow* 259.7
primula Flowers 42
primum mobile [L] God 82.6, *first cause* 675.6
primus inter pares [L] *superior* 744.5
Prince Albert *coat* 100.19
Prince Edward Island Canadian Provinces 564, Islands 572
princeliness *majesty* 297.5
princely *governing* 49.25, *aristocratic* 70.4, *majestic* 297.12, 404.21, *generous* 498.6
Prince of Darkness *devil* 446.5
Prince of Peace God the Son 82.9
Prince of Wales Island Islands 572
principal *educator* 48.4, *person in authority* 52.7, *educational leader* 68.11, *masterful* 68.15, *focus* 612.3, *focal* 612.8, *elite* 744.12, *best* 805.9
principal boy *stock part* 136.24
principal character *role* 136.23
principal element *basis* 601.3
principal focus *focus* 612.3
principal girl *stock part* 136.24
principalities *angelic order (highest to lowest)* 82.12
principalities and powers *the power structure* 68.12
principality *body politic* 50.3, *region* 564.1, *dominion* 566.3
principally *focally* 612.14, *predominantly* 744.21
principal part *large part* 579.3
principal place *center of activity* 612.4
principal plane *lens system* 10.22
principate *dominion* 566.3
principle *philosophy* 4.1, *theory* 6.62, *physical law* 10.4, *belief* 87.1, *belief system* 87.3, *maxim* 177.1, *ideology* 327.5, *matter* 524.4, *basis* 601.3, 605.4, *undertaking* 675.5, *truism* 721.6, *essential content* 723.2, *guide* 780.4
principle component analysis *statistical methods* 6.53
principled 447.6; *proper* 429.10, *moral* 431.9, *basic* 605.13
principles *philosophical system* 4.2, *way of life* 399.9, *morals* 431.2, *virtues* 447.2, *truism* 771.7
prink *dress up* 100.45, *beautify* 530.14
print 173.17; *written letter* 5.14, *word* 5.43, *reprint* 21.3, *reproduce* 21.13, *fabric* 130.1, *printing* 132.20, 173.3, *develop* 132.28, *picture* 133.5, *engrave* 144.11, *publish* 173.15, 174.19, *report* 175.9, *vestige* 185.11, *record* 185.13, *illustration* 187.2, *represent* 187.10, *illustrate* 187.11, *monetize* 484.24, *make stable* 674.7, *visible effect* 676.2, *affect*

676.7, *duplicate* 736.4, *replica* 797.7
printable *permitting* 502.5
printable character *character* 15.18
printed 173.13; *written* 5.36, *reproduced* 21.10, *engraved* 144.9, *published* 173.12, 174.18, 175.8, *recorded* 185.12
printed circuit *circuit* 14.37
printed circuit board or **card** *circuit* 14.37
printer 173.10; *hardcopy device* 15.10, *engraver* 144.5, *book publishing personnel* 174.12
printer's ink *black pigment* 254.2
printing 132.20, 173.3; *written letter* 5.14, *reproduction* 21.1, *dyeing* 130.9, *publishing* 173.2, *book* 174.1, *stage of book production* 174.7, *recordkeeping* 185.7
printing over *obliteration* 186.1
printing paper *printing* 132.20
printing press *printing* 173.3
print journalism 175.4; *news* 171.1
print journalist 175.5
printmaking *craft* 133.2
print medium *print journalism* 175.4
print news 171.7
print over *obliterate* 186.8
print run *book* 174.1
prior *historical* 3.10, *religious* 84.9, *former* 653.12, *preceding* 769.9
prior consideration *prediction* 358.1
prioress *religious* 84.9
prioritization *order* 765.1
prioritize *systematize* 765.19, *give priority* 769.15
priority 769.2; *emphasis* 200.1, *superiority* 744.1, *precedence* 769.1, *importance* 799.1, *chief thing* 799.3
priority mail *postal service* 169.5
prior to *preceding* 769.9, *before* 769.18
priory *clerical dwelling* 84.10
Priscilla Apple Varieties 44
prism *polyhedron* 6.44, *optical element* 10.20, *lens* 132.11, *visual distortion* 243.6, *angled figure* 628.3
prismatic *cubic* 6.81, *colored* 251.10, *variegated* 263.6, *angled* 628.9
prismatoid *polyhedron* 6.44
prismoid *polyhedron* 6.44
prison 55.1; *imprisonment* 454.2, *instrument of punishment* 454.13, *closed place* 584.4, *enclosed area* 619.2, *setting apart* 753.2
prison camp *prison* 55.1
prison cell 55.3
prison clothes *clothing* 184.6
prison colony *prison* 55.1
prisoner 55.7; *accused person* 442.4, *guilty person* 450.5, *closed-in person* 584.6, *subjected person* 832.5
prisoner at the bar *litigant* 54.4
prisoner before the court *litigant* 54.4
prisoner of conscience *prisoner* 55.7
prisoner of war (POW) *prisoner* 55.7, *subjected person* 832.5
prisoner-of-war or **POW camp** *prison* 55.1
prisoner's base Children's and Party Games 167

prison fare *short rations* 118.3
prison farm *prison* 55.1
prison guard *prison officer* 55.8, *one who restrains* 830.7
prison house *prison* 55.1, *instrument of punishment* 454.13
prison inmate *guilty person* 450.5
prison officer 55.8
prison sentence 55.6; *unfavorable verdict* 54.20, *imprisonment* 454.2
prison ship *Ships and Boats* 690
pristine *pure* 431.11, *innocent* 449.6, *original* 737.4, *prime* 771.18
privacy 181.6; *concealment* 181.1, 844.2, *verbal concealment* 181.3, *secrecy* 182.1, 611.6, *invisibility* 245.1, *unintelligibility* 364.1, *modesty* 403.1, *unsociability* 409.1, *aloofness* 756.2., *aloneness* 788.5, *private space* 812.2
Private *US Military Ranks* 58, *military title* 72.8
private 245.5; *silent* 181.10, *secret* 182.8, 611.13, *unintelligible* 364.4, *modest* 403.6, *unsociable* 409.6, *secluded* 409.9, *corporate* 480.17, *transportable* 686.7, *aloof* 756.5, *excluding* 764.5, *concealed* 844.7
private branch exchange (PBX) *telephone exchange* 169.13
private car *automobile* 687.6
private club *privacy* 181.6, *exclusiveness* 764.4
private company *company* 480.7
private conversation *verbal concealment* 181.3
private detective *law enforcement officer* 53.8, *discoverer* 345.7, *security force* 810.13
private enterprise *economics* 56.1, *market sector* 483.5
privateer *militarist* 77.3, *plunderer* 479.9, *Sailing Ships and Boats* 690, *Ships and Boats* 690
privateering *plundering* 479.5, *stolen* 479.12
private exchange *telephone exchange* 169.13
private eye [Inf] *law enforcement officer* 53.8, *discoverer* 345.7, *security force* 810.13
Private First Class *US Military Ranks* 58
private garden *privacy* 181.6
private hospital *hospital* 107.16
private income *earnings* 467.5, *income* 492.3
private investigator (PI) *law enforcement officer* 53.8, *security force* 810.13
private language *vernacular* 205.8
private law *law* 53.1
private library *library* 174.14
privately 181.18; *secretly* 182.14, 611.22, *modestly* 403.15, *unsocially* 409.13, *aloofly* 756.10
private means *independence* 829.5
private meeting *secret* 182.2
private nurse *nurse* 107.23
private office *hospital* 107.16
private parts *sexual organs* 20.2, *organs of reproduction* 21.9
private police *law enforcement officer* 53.8
private practice *medical practice* 107.3
private quarters *solitary place* 409.4
privates *sexual organs* 20.2, *organs of reproduction* 21.9
private sale *selling* 482.1

private school *type of school* 48.12
private sector *economy* 56.3, *market sector* 483.5
private security company *security force* 464.3
private soldier *soldier* 77.4
private space 812.2
private tutor *educator* 48.4
private world *unsociability* 409.1
privation *neediness* 95.3, *loss* 468.1, *poverty* 486.1
privatization *economics* 56.1, *transfer of property* 470.4, *market sector* 483.5
privatize *economize* 56.11, *transfer property* 470.12, *trade* 480.18
privatized *economic* 56.10, *corporate* 480.17
privet *Trees and Shrubs* 43
privilege *claim* 72.2, 429.3, *exemption* 434.1, *license* 434.4, *exempt* 434.9, *priority* 769.2, *freedom* 829.1
privileged *rightful* 429.9, *exempt* 434.5, *free* 829.11
privileged, the *the rich* 485.7
privileged class *social stratification* 2.7, *the rich* 485.7
privileged-class *socioeconomic* 2.13
privileged information *inside information* 170.4, *secret* 182.2
privy *place for excretion* 25.11, *secret* 182.8
privy member *organs of reproduction* 21.9
privy purse [Brit] *earnings* 467.5
privy seal *means of identification* 184.3
prix fixe *price* 494.1
prize 453.2; *honor* 72.3, *monument* 185.10, *object of desire* 288.8, *like* 290.8, *love* 299.21, *objective* 374.5, *respect* 435.13, *admire* 437.15, *good thing* 445.9, *windfall* 467.7, *reward* 472.4, *something received* 473.2, *takings* 477.8, *stolen goods* 479.4, *winnings* 492.5
prize competition 422.5
prized *liked* 290.6, *beloved* 299.19, *respected* 435.10
prizefight *boxing* 152.2, *box* 152.19
prizefighter *boxer* 152.8, *athlete* 422.15
prizefighting *boxing* 152.2, *athletics* 422.7
prize-giver *giver* 472.7
prize-giving *giving* 472.1
prize money *prize* 453.2
prizes 453.3
prizewinner 127.8; *titleholder* 72.4, *recipient* 473.5, *paragon* 744.6, *victor* 845.7
prizewinning *honored* 72.11, *victorious* 845.10
pro *recommending* 437.11
pro [Inf] *expert* 52.8, 68.13, 127.9, *athlete* 422.15
proa *Sailing Ships and Boats* 690
pro-am *prize competition* 422.5
probabilism *Philosophical Schools of Thought* 4, *probability theory* 838.5
probabilist *Philosophical Schools of Thought* 4
probability 6.59, 838.1; *philosophical term* 4.7, *causality* 10.66, *demonstrability* 331.5, *expectation* 356.1, *basis of supposition* 359.2, *strong possibility* 836.3, *plausibility* 838.3, *good chance* 842.6, *calculation of chance* 842.9

probability curve *probability theory* 838.5
probability density function *probability distribution* 6.56, *probability theory* 838.5
probability distribution 6.56; *probability theory* 838.5
probability function *probability theory* 838.5
probability theory 838.5, *Branches of Mathematics* 6, *statistics* 6.51
probable 838.6; *believable* 87.7, *expected* 356.5, *foreseeable* 357.7, *auspicious* 458.10, *tending to* 513.4, *predictable* 650.7, *realizable* 719.9, *plausible* 838.7
probable error *parameter* 6.57, *measurement* 10.67
probably 513.6, 838.11; *demonstrably* 331.22, *auspiciously* 458.17, *predictably* 650.15
probate court *type of court* 54.9
probation *experiment* 335.1
probational *experimental* 335.8
probationary *hired* 57.17, *experimental* 335.8, *tentative* 390.5
probationary period *bargaining terms* 57.10, *briefing* 388.4
probationer *nurse* 107.23, *unskilled person* 128.3, *beginner* 771.14
probative *proven* 331.13, *verificatory* 336.6, *evidential* 339.8
probatory *proven* 331.13
probe *questioning* 333.2, *question* 333.16, *experiment* 335.1, 335.11, *detector* 345.6, *opener* 583.2, *hole* 583.17, *measure* 589.20, *measure depth* 598.22
probed *questioned* 333.15, *holed* 583.17
prober *questioner* 333.9
probing *curiosity* 333.8, *questioning* 333.11, *bathymetry* 598.3, *bathymetric* 598.12
probingly *questioningly* 333.21
probity *rightfulness* 429.1, *morals* 431.2, *virtue* 447.1, *innocence* 449.1, *repute* 487.7, *naiveté* 821.1
problem 824.4; *mystery* 182.4, *puzzle* 182.5, *issue* 328.2, *question* 333.1, *unintelligible thing* 364.3, *predicament* 725.3, *obstacle* 837.3
problematic 328.7, 343.10, 824.11; *mysterious* 182.10, *arguable* 329.8, *conditional* 725.7, *confused* 841.11
problematically 328.12, 824.25; *questionably* 333.22, *conditionally* 725.10, *confusingly* 841.23
problem drinker *drunkard* 121.8
problem play *dramatic style* 136.3
pro bono publico [L] *for the public good* 307.10, *usefully* 801.12
Proboscidea *pachyderm* 35.15
proboscidean *pachyderm* 35.15
proboscidean *or* **proboscidian** *elephantlike* 35.30
proboscis *sense organ* 212.4, *protuberance* 634.3
proboscis [Inf] *nose* 19.11
Pro Bowl *football* 155.1
procaryotic *cellular* 13.30
procaryotic cell *cell* 13.15
procedural *formal* 406.6, *effective* 412.10, *legal* 780.8
procedurally *formally* 406.12
procedure 387.2; *reasoning* 6.61, *jurisprudence* 53.13, *standard procedure* 397.6, *way* 399.10, 691.1, *formal occasion* 406.4, *action* 412.1, *performance* 465.2, *operation* 509.1, *custom* 780.5

proceed 692.16; *do something* 412.13, *go on* 642.7, *continue* 669.8, *be in motion* 677.14, *go forward* 679.8, *find a way* 691.14
proceed from *follow from* 676.9
proceeding *action* 412.1, *deed* 412.2, *ongoing* 679.7, *way* 691.1, *passing* 692.11
proceedings *legal process* 54.3, *matter of interest* 328.3
proceeds *earnings* 467.5, *yield* 467.8, *something received* 473.2, *takings* 477.8, *money received* 492.2
proceed to *undertake* 391.7
proceed with *do something* 412.13
proceed with caution 287.12
process 11.15, 14.50; *chemical reaction* 11.8, *means* 102.1, *develop* 132.28, *represent* 187.10, *way* 399.10, 691.1, *action* 412.1, *demand* 425.2, *operation* 509.1, *take action* 509.12, *manufacture* 522.2, *produce* 522.13, *continuation* 642.2, *change* 665.1, *change for the better* 665.17, *convert* 670.11, *transform* 670.13, *categorize* 767.21, *preserve* 815.14
process art *Western Art Styles* 133
process data *categorize* 767.21
processed *treated* 388.12, *produced* 522.16, *converted* 670.7, *categorized* 767.15
processed food *food* 90.1, *preserved thing* 815.10
process flow diagrams *industrial processes* 14.27
processing *development* 132.19, *manufacture* 522.2, *conversion* 670.1, *converting* 670.8, *preservation of provisions* 815.6
procession 774.6; *ceremonial* 404.11, *forward motion* 677.4, *sequence* 770.1, *consecutiveness* 774.1
processional *directional* 677.13
process of death *dying* 29.3
processor *computer part* 15.4
process server *court officer* 54.7
process simulation *systems and process control* 14.28
process synthesis *systems and process control* 14.28
process theology *Theologies* 81
prochronism *wrong time* 660.2
prochronistic *misdated* 660.6
prochronistically *anachronistically* 660.13
proclaim 173.16; *propound a philosophy* 4.21, *signal* 183.18, *affirm* 189.21, *speak* 205.17, *flourish* 404.25, *command* 425.10, *make important* 799.14, *reveal* 843.14
proclaimed *published* 173.12, *affirmed* 189.11
proclaimer *publicizer* 173.11, *affirmer* 189.9
proclaiming *signaling* 183.14
proclamation 183.8; *publication* 173.1, *affirmation* 189.1, *declaration* 376.2, *command* 425.1, *manifestation* 843.2
proclitic *word* 5.17
proclivity *inclination* 290.2, *instinct* 320.4, *tendency* 397.2, *attitude* 513.2
proconsul *person in authority* 52.7, *leader* 68.3, *deputy* 80.1
proconsular *delegated* 79.4
proconsulate *position of authority* 52.4
procrastinate 413.12; *be neglectful*

326.7, *delay* 375.16, 658.13, *be irresolute* 378.9, *be evasive* 386.20, *be inactive* 415.13, *not observe* 466.9, *not complete* 762.9
procrastinating 375.11; *indifferent* 326.5, *inactive* 413.9, *not participating* 415.11, *nonobservant* 466.5, *delaying* 658.8, *hesitant* 693.9, *uncompleted* 762.7
procrastination *indifference* 326.2, *delay* 375.6, 658.3, *evasiveness* 386.6, *do-nothingism* 413.6, *idleness* 415.3, *nonobservance* 466.1, *deferment* 604.3, *irresolution* 666.2, *hesitation* 693.3, *nonachievement* 762.3
procrastinator *neglector* 326.3, *reluctant person* 375.7, *plodder* 693.6
procreant *reproductive* 21.11, *procreative* 22.10
procreate 22.14; *have sex* 20.21, *propagate* 21.15, *give birth to* 28.19, *grow* 581.17
procreating *coupling* 20.19, *pertaining to life* 28.14
procreation 22.4; *sexual intercourse* 20.9, *propagation* 21.4, *life function* 28.6, *germination* 581.5, *sexual union* 752.6
procreative 22.10; *reproductive* 21.11
procreatively *reproductively* 21.17, *largely* 581.18
procreator *propagator* 21.7, *fertilizer* 22.6
proctophobia *Phobias* 283
proctor *manager* 126.7, *manage* 126.10
proctorship *management* 126.1
procumbent *recumbent* 603.7
procurable *gainful* 467.10
procural *gain* 467.1
procurance *gain* 467.1
procuration *gain* 467.1
procurator *manager* 126.7
procure 104.9; *provision* 89.9, *prostitute* 432.17, *gain* 467.15, *purchase* 481.10, *take action* 509.12, *awaken* 675.9, *bring* 685.11, *draw out* 711.17
procurement *gain* 467.1
procurer *provisioner* 89.4, *gainer* 467.9, *recipient* 473.5, *merchant* 482.10
procuring *provisioning* 89.2, *prostitution* 432.4
procyonid *flesh-eating mammal* 35.9
Procyonidae *flesh-eating mammal* 35.9
prod *incentive* 178.4, *motivate* 178.17, *gesture* 183.17, *type of touch* 216.3, *touch* 216.9, *negative stimulus* 508.4, *manipulate* 508.12, *sharp-pointed thing* 549.4, *use a sharp tool* 549.17, *blow* 695.5, *impel* 695.9
prodded *motivated* 508.8
prodigal *waster* 96.8, *wasteful* 96.9, *foolish* 353.5, *overindulgent* 456.8, *unprofitable* 468.10, *expending* 491.8, *spendthrift* 500.3, *extravagant* 500.4
prodigality *waste* 96.1, *exaggeration* 194.1, *overindulgence* 456.3, *extravagance* 491.5, 500.1
prodigally *wastefully* 96.23, *at a loss* 468.22, *generously* 491.14
prodigal returned *penitent person* 451.4
prodigal son *penitent person* 451.4, *spendthrift* 500.3

prodigal's return *return* 704.4
prodigious *exaggerated* 194.7, *wondrous* 294.9, *huge* 579.14
prodigiously *excessively* 194.17, *wondrously* 294.18
prodigiousness *largeness* 579.2
prodigy *skilled person* 127.7, *spectacle* 264.6, *wonderful person* 294.6, *superior person* 445.7, *paragon* 744.6, *unexpectedness* 839.2
produce 137.21, 522.5, 522.13, 771.34; *socialize* 2.14, *propagate* 21.15, *be fertile* 22.13, *secrete* 24.7, *fruits* 44.1, *vegetable* 90.33, *fruit* 90.34, *dramatize* 136.33, *demonstrate* 331.15, *imagine* 360.14, *yield* 467.8, *be profitable* 467.21, *plant products* 522.8, *fashion* 536.7, *form* 624.9, *cause* 675.8, *growth* 676.3, *react* 676.8, *grow* 676.10, *reveal* 843.14
produce (a line) *align* 6.92
produce market *market* 483.1
produce offspring *propagate* 21.15
produce power *generate power* 514.19
producer 136.28, 522.10; *ecology* 13.25, *artistic worker* 123.12, *filmmaker* 137.14, *demonstrator* 331.6, *first cause* 675.6
produce results *be convenient* 803.5
producer gas *gas* 106.6
produce secretion *secrete* 24.7
producible *displayed* 843.8
producing *production* 522.1, *growing* 676.6
product 522.3; *multiplication* 6.15, 793.4, *chemical reaction* 11.8, *numerical answer* 334.7, *yield* 467.8, *merchandise* 482.6, *effect* 676.1, *sequel* 770.5, *mathematical result* 783.4
production 136.14, 137.6, 522.1, 843.5; *economic factor* 56.8, *theatrical performance* 136.13, *action* 412.1, *yield* 467.8, *business* 509.3, *work of art* 522.4, *structuring* 551.5, *forming* 624.4, *cause* 675.1
production assistant *filmmaker* 137.14
production budget *budgeting* 493.5
production car *racing automobile* 146.2
production car racer *driver* 146.8
production car racing *automobile racing* 146.1
production company *motion-picture studio* 137.7
production coordinator *filmmaker* 137.14
production cost budget *budgeting* 493.5
production costs *economic factor* 56.8
production designer *filmmaker* 137.14
production editing *stage of book production* 174.7
production editor *book publishing personnel* 174.12
production efficiency *economic factor* 56.8
production line *construction* 59.16, *factory* 124.8, *manufacture* 522.2

production manager *filmmaker* 137.14
production metallurgy *metallurgy* 11.22
production of documents or **things** *pretrial proceedings* 54.13
productive 22.9, 522.11; *socioeconomic* 2.13, *farmable* 16.17, *fruiting* 44.5, *imaginative* 360.10, *effective* 412.10, *yielding* 467.14, *lush* 485.11, *causal* 675.7, *profitable* 801.8
productively 522.17; *sociologically* 2.15, *agriculturally* 16.21, *fruitfully* 22.15, *fructiferously* 44.10, *effectively* 412.19, *gainfully* 467.24, *formatively* 624.10, *causally* 675.12
productiveness 22.3; *production* 522.1, *benefit* 801.4
productivity *productiveness* 22.3, *economic factor* 56.8, *power* 447.4, *production* 522.1, *benefit* 801.4
product testing *market* 482.5
proem *public speaking* 205.11, *preface* 769.5, *introduction* 771.10
proemial *precursory* 769.12, *introductory* 771.23
profanation *profanity* 301.3, *misuse* 395.1
profanatory *profane* 301.10
profane 301.10; *unclean* 112.8, *dirty* 112.11, *blaspheme* 301.14, *abusive* 395.5, *misuse* 395.6, *wrong* 430.19, *desecrate* 436.24, *impious* 448.11, *be wicked* 448.13, *make worse* 808.17
profaned *misused* 395.3
profane language *offensive language* 301.5
profanely 301.19; *abusively* 395.8, *impiously* 448.17
profaneness *impiety* 448.4
profaning *profane* 301.10
profanity 301.3; *uncleanness* 112.2, *curse word* 301.4, *impiety* 448.4
profess *propound a philosophy* 4.21, *believe* 87.9, *avow* 189.27
professed *avowed* 189.19, *promised* 458.8
professedly *avowedly* 189.34, *apparently* 720.19
profession *job* 122.3, *avowal* 189.7, *line of duty* 433.3, *promise* 458.1, *business* 480.6
professional 480.15; *expert* 52.8, 52.12, 68.13, 127.9, 127.12, *excellent* 68.16, *well-made* 127.13, *type of wrestling* 152.9, *combat* 152.17, *varsity* 155.17, *soccer* 163.7, *qualified* 340.7, *technical* 361.10, *effective* 412.10, *industrious* 414.16, *specialist* 779.9, *specialized* 779.11
professional athlete *athlete* 422.15
professional athletics *athletics* 422.7
professional baseball *baseball* 147.1
professional basketball *basketball* 148.1
professional bowler *bowler* 151.5
professional boxer *boxer* 152.8
professional boxing *combat sport* 152.1
professional class *middle class* 772.6
professional consultant *adviser* 176.5
professional football *football* 155.1

professional forces *armed forces* 77.9
Professional Golfers' Association (PGA) *golfing associations and tournaments* 156.6
professional hockey *hockey* 158.1
professionalism *maturity* 27.3, *skill* 127.1
professional journal *magazine* 175.3
professional killer *murderer* 30.12
professionally 152.22; *expertly* 52.21, *masterfully* 68.19, *skillfully* 127.16, *capably* 340.15, *dutifully* 433.19
professional politician *politician* 50.7
professional skill *skill* 127.1
professional soldier *militarist* 77.3, *soldier* 77.4
professional title 72.6
professional worker 123.11
professional wrestler *wrestler* 152.12
professional wrestling *combat sport* 152.1
Professor *professional title* 72.6
professor *educator* 48.4, *expert* 52.8, 127.9, *educational leader* 68.11, *professional worker* 123.11, *adviser* 176.5, *affirmer* 189.9, *intellectual* 315.7
professorate *instructorship* 48.5
professor emeritus *educator* 48.4
professorial *reasoning* 317.6
professorship *instructorship* 48.5
proffer *offer* 504.1, 504.11
proffer aid *help* 825.23
proffer one's good offices *mediate* 75.6
proficiency 445.5; *skill* 127.1, *qualification* 340.1, *learning* 348.3, *ability* 514.3, *expertise* 805.4, *easiness* 823.1
proficient 445.15; *excellent* 68.16, *skillful* 127.10, *expert* 127.12, 805.16, *qualified* 340.7, *knowledgeable* 348.7
proficiently 445.22; *masterfully* 68.19, *skillfully* 127.16, *capably* 340.15, *knowledgeably* 348.14, *powerfully* 514.21
proficient person *skilled person* 127.7
profile *nonfiction* 139.6, *type of painting* 143.5, *description* 202.1, *outline* 617.1, 617.5, *shape* 617.2, *side* 623.1, *form* 624.1
profit 467.6, 467.22; *economic factor* 56.8, *be favorable* 62.12, *usefulness* 393.2, *good* 445.1, *be good* 445.16, *return* 453.6, *trade in* 457.8, *gain* 467.15, *positive stimulus* 508.5, *produce* 522.5, *growth* 676.3, *grow* 676.10, *increase* 746.6, *difference* 750.3, *benefit* 801.4, 801.10, *convenience* 803.1, *be convenient* 803.5, *help* 825.23, *be prosperous* 847.6
profitability *good* 445.1, *gain* 467.1, *increase* 746.1, *benefit* 801.4, *helpfulness* 825.10
profitable 489.13, 801.8; *productive* 22.9, 522.11, *favorable* 62.8, *desirable* 288.11, *useful* 393.7, *good* 445.10, *rewarding* 453.9, *gainful* 467.15, *salable* 482.13, *received* 492.6, *convenient* 803.3, *beneficial* 825.20, *successful* 845.8
profitableness *gain* 467.1
profitable return *return* 453.6
profitably 453.20, 492.8; *fruitfully*

22.15, *economically* 56.13, *favorably* 62.15, *desirably* 288.24, *usefully* 393.15, 801.12, *well* 445.19, *gainfully* 467.24, *acquisitively* 481.21, *marketably* 482.23, *productively* 522.17, *helpfully* 825.32, *successfully* 845.19

profit after tax *return* 453.6
profit and loss account *or* **income account** *accounts* 493.4
profit by *be skillful* 127.14, *exploit* 393.11, *push* 414.20, *take the opportunity* 659.7, *find useful* 801.11, *get better* 807.21
profit by one's mistakes *be warned* 814.9
profit by (the) example *be warned* 814.9
profiteer *gainer* 467.9, *gain* 467.15, *trader* 480.11, *trade* 480.18, *overcharge* 496.10
profiteering *gain* 467.1, *trade* 480.1, *extortion* 496.4, *costly* 496.7
profit from *promote* 807.18
profiting *growing* 676.6
profitless *unprofitable* 468.10, *futile* 802.10, *failed* 846.10
profitlessness *futility* 802.3
profit making *gain* 467.1
profit-making *gainful* 467.10
profit margin *economic factor* 56.8, *return* 453.6
profit motive *economic factor* 56.8
profits *profit* 467.6, *something received* 473.2, *money received* 492.2
profit-sharing *benefits* 57.11, *negotiated* 57.16, *jointly possessing* 469.12
profit taking *gain* 467.1, *taking* 477.1
profit-taking *gainful* 467.10
profligacy *pleasure* 214.2, *immorality* 432.1, *depravity* 448.2, *dissipation* 456.2, *extravagance* 500.1
profligate *pleasure-seeking* 214.10, *immoral* 432.9, *miscreant* 448.6, *depraved* 448.10, *dissipated* 456.7, *spender* 491.7, *expending* 491.8, *spendthrift* 500.3, *extravagant* 500.4
profligately *generously* 491.14
profluence *flow* 570.4
profluent *flowing* 570.7, *ongoing* 679.7
pro forma *formally* 406.12
profound 598.15; *obscure* 197.2, *thoughtful* 315.10, *speculative* 317.8, *wise* 352.4, *unintelligible* 364.4
profoundly 598.27; *wisely* 4.28, *obscurely* 197.4, *intelligently* 315.14
profoundness *thought* 315.5, *unintelligibility* 364.1, *profundity* 598.5
profound thought *thought* 317.1
profundities *profundity* 598.5
profundity 598.5; *obscurity* 197.1, *thought* 315.5, *thoughtfulness* 317.2, *wisdom* 352.1
profuse *fertile* 22.8, *plentiful* 97.4, *excessive* 99.5, *extravagant* 194.9, *diffuse* 199.3, *abundant* 498.8, *unrestrained* 500.5, *ample* 795.9
profusely *plentifully* 97.11, *excessively* 99.13, 194.17, *diffusely* 199.7
profuseness 795.3; *extravagance* 194.3, *diffuseness* 199.1
profusion *fertility* 22.1, *plenty* 97.2, *excess* 99.1, *extravagance* 194.3,

opulence 485.3, *abundance* 498.4, *unrestrainedness* 500.2, *profuseness* 795.3
profusive *fertile* 22.8
progenitor *person of the past* 651.7, *first cause* 675.6
progeny 21.8; *family tree* 65.3, *successor* 770.6
progesterone Human Hormones 12
progestin Human Hormones 12
prognosis *health care* 107.7, *diagnosis* 107.8, *expectations* 356.2, *prediction* 358.1, *probability* 838.1
prognostic *diagnostic* 107.29, *expecting* 356.4, *foreseeing* 357.5, *omen* 358.5, *warning* 814.6
prognosticate *practice medicine* 107.32, *predict* 358.14, *think likely* 838.10
prognostication *prediction* 358.1
prognosticator *predictor* 357.4, *forecaster* 358.9
program 15.29, 172.10; *software* 15.12, *broadcast* 172.13, *topic* 328.1, *plan* 357.2, 387.1, 387.12, *undertaking* 391.1, *tactics* 399.12, *behave toward* 399.20, *action* 412.1, *itemize* 577.13, *chronology* 646.2, *chart* 767.8, *categorize* 767.21, *list of dates* 785.6
program *or* **draw up a program** *plan out* 387.14
program director *producer* 522.10
programmable read-only memory (PROM) *memory* 15.6
programmed *focused* 328.6, *itemized* 577.9, *listed* 785.9
programmer *computer user* 15.3
programming *computing* 15.2
programming concepts 15.24
programming language 15.16
program music *classical music* 140.2
program seller *stagehand* 136.29
program suite *computing terms* 15.22
progress *education* 48.1, Phobias 283, *follow up* 385.16, *be busy* 414.19, *continuation* 642.2, *go on* 642.7, *continue* 669.8, *evolution* 670.3, *be converted* 670.12, *forward motion* 677.4, 679.1, *be in motion* 677.14, *go forward* 679.8, *way* 691.1, *increase* 746.1, 746.6, *be consecutive* 774.11, *social improvement* 807.3, *promotion* 807.5, *get better* 807.21, *do well* 845.12, *be prosperous* 847.6
progressing *converting* 670.8, *directional* 677.13, *forward* 679.6, *increasing* 746.4
progression *sequence* 6.18, 770.1, *continuation* 642.2, *continuity* 669.1, *forward motion* 679.1, *way* 691.1, *hierarchy* 765.3, *consecutiveness* 774.1, *promotion* 807.5
progressive 669.6; *educational* 48.17, *enterprising* 391.5, *continuous* 669.5, *directional* 677.13, *forward* 679.6, *gradational* 739.5, *increasing* 746.4, *hierarchical* 765.12, *sequential* 770.7, *consecutive* 774.7, *improver* 807.11
Progressive Conservative party Political Parties 50
Progressive Democrat party Political Parties 50
progressive jazz *jazz* 140.5
progressively *educationally* 48.25, *enterprisingly* 391.11, *continually* 669.10, *in motion* 677.19, *in*

progress 679.16, *propulsively* 696.21, *by degrees* 739.10, *increasingly* 746.9, *in order* 765.26, *consecutively* 774.15, *better* 807.24
progressiveness *forward motion* 679.1
progressive tax *tax* 494.5
prohibit 503.8; *make illegal* 53.29, *refuse* 190.17, *exclude* 409.12, 764.7, *command* 425.10, *dissent* 506.9, *counteract* 510.7, *debar* 604.17, *limit* 620.7, *make motionless* 678.8, *ostracize* 709.17, *hinder* 826.15, *restrain* 830.12, *make impossible* 837.8
prohibit drinking *abstain* 455.11
prohibited 503.5; *disagreeing* 190.11, *self-restrained* 455.6, *dissenting* 506.6, *excluded* 604.11, 764.6, *restrained* 830.9, *forbidden* 837.7
prohibiter *negator* 190.8
prohibiting *prohibited* 503.5, *dissenting* 506.6, *hindering* 826.12
Prohibition *prohibition of alcohol* 120.2
prohibition 503.1; *illegality* 53.10, *refusal* 190.2, *command* 425.1, *dissent* 506.2, *debarment* 604.5, *limit* 620.1, *exclusion* 764.1, *hindrance* 826.1, *restraint* 830.1, *obstacle* 837.3
prohibitionary *dissenting* 506.6
Prohibition Era Ages, Decades, Eras 641
prohibitionist *sober person* 120.4, *sober* 120.5, *moralist* 431.8, *self-restrained person* 455.5
prohibition of alcohol 120.2, 503.2
prohibitive *commanding* 425.7, *costly* 496.7, 500.6, *prohibited* 503.5, *excluded* 604.11, *limited* 620.5, *excluding* 764.5, *hindering* 826.12, *restraining* 830.8
prohibitively 503.11; *commandingly* 425.15, *moralistically* 431.16, *with delay* 826.22, *restrainedly* 830.18
prohibitorily *denyingly* 190.23
prohibitory *disagreeing* 190.11, *prohibited* 503.5
project *represent* 6.91, 187.10, *task* 122.2, *develop* 132.28, *act* 136.34, *map* 187.12, *plan* 327.3, 387.1, 387.12, *educational topic* 328.4, *future intention* 374.3, *predetermination* 384.1, *predetermine* 384.8, *undertaking* 391.1, *production* 522.1, *be high* 596.15, *externalize* 610.15, *outline* 617.5, *protrude* 634.8, *impel* 695.9, *propel* 696.15, *emerge* 707.14, *be external* 724.15
projected *predetermined* 384.4, *externalized* 610.11, *outward* 621.11, *external* 724.11
projected image *show* 621.7
projectile 696.13; *ammunition* 78.11, *missile* 696.7
projecting *highland* 596.11, *overhanging* 604.8, *external* 724.11
projection *transformation* 6.46, *defense mechanism* 108.23, *acting* 136.22, *image* 187.3, *map* 187.5, *conception* 360.4, *sharp-pointed thing* 549.4, *peninsula* 572.5, *heights* 596.4, *overhanging* 604.2, *externalization* 610.5, *outline* 617.1, *throwing* 696.3, *externality* 724.4, *manifestation* 843.2
projectional *outlined* 617.4

projective geometry *geometry* 6.32
projective test Psychological Tests 108
projector *viewer* 132.22, *stage lighting* 136.20, *imaging device* 242.11, *planner* 387.9
project over *overhang* 604.14
prokaryotic *cellular* 13.30
prokaryotic cell *cell* 13.15
prolactin Human Hormones 12
prolapse *droop* 714.14
prolate *spherical* 6.80
prole [Inf] *commoner* 71.1
prolegomenon *dissertation* 203.1
prolepsis *wrong time* 660.2
proletarian *commoner* 71.1, *common* 71.3
proletariat *common people* 71.2, *personnel* 123.16, *average person* 742.4
proliferate *procreate* 22.14, *mushroom* 47.23, *abound* 97.8, *increase* 467.17, 746.6, *pluralize* 793.9
proliferated *reproduced* 21.10, *multiplicative* 793.8
proliferating *multiplicative* 793.8
proliferation *reproduction* 21.1, *increase* 746.1, *multiplication* 793.4
proliferative *multiplicative* 793.8
prolific *fertile* 22.8, *plentiful* 97.4, *diffuse* 199.3, *yielding* 467.14, *lush* 485.11, *productive* 522.11, *increasing* 746.4
prolificacy *fertility* 22.1
prolifically *fruitfully* 22.15, *plentifully* 97.11, *diffusely* 199.7, *gainfully* 467.24, *productively* 522.17, *increasingly* 746.9
prolificity *fertility* 22.1
prolificness *fertility* 22.1
proline Amino Acids 12
prolix *superfluous* 99.8, *diffuse* 199.3, *unemphatic* 201.2, *speaking* 205.15, *talkative* 207.5, *boring* 296.6, *lengthy* 590.9, *repetitious* 797.11
prolixity *superfluity* 99.4, *diffuseness* 199.1, *power of speech* 205.5, *talkativeness* 207.1, *boringness* 296.2, *longness* 590.3
Prolog Programming Languages 15
prologue *play part* 136.8, *actor* 136.25, *public speaking* 205.11, *front matter* 621.4, *preface* 769.5
prolong *lengthen* 590.12, *delay* 658.13, *protract* 669.9, *make bigger* 746.7, *preserve* 815.14
prolongate *lengthen* 590.12
prolongation *lengthening* 590.4, *delay* 658.3, *continuation* 669.2, *protraction* 669.4, *increase* 746.1, *addition* 748.1, *conservation* 815.2
prolonged *boring* 296.6, *lengthened* 590.10, *held up* 658.6, *protracted* 669.7
prolonged note *tempo* 140.22
prolonge knot Knots, Bends, Hitches, Splices 754
prom *dance* 135.1
promenade *dance* 135.1, *show* 404.24, *show off* 404.26, *waterfront* 621.3, *passage* 691.5, *procession* 774.6, *arrange* 774.14
Promethean *alive* 28.13
Prometheus Planets and Their Satellites 7
promethium Chemical Elements and Common Allotropes 11
prominence *seriousness* 200.2, *clarity* 244.2, *indication* 339.3,

exaltation 596.3, convexity 634.1, height 715.4, superiority 744.1, importance 799.1

prominent clear 244.6, appearing 264.9, evident 339.9, exalted 596.10, convex 634.5, promoted 715.8, excellent 744.14, important 799.7, notable 799.11, manifest 843.9

prominent feature protuberance 634.3

prominently aristocratically 70.6, evidently 339.16, eminently 370.7, exaltedly 596.22, convexly 634.9, superbly 744.22, importantly 799.15

promiscuity tastelessness 338.3, sexual immorality 432.2, tolerance 502.2, moral deterioration 808.3

promiscuous careless 289.8, unrefined 338.7, unchaste 432.10

promiscuously 432.19; carelessly 289.18, tastelessly 338.14

promiscuousness carelessness 289.2

promise 458.1, 458.11, 464.2, 464.10; be favorable 62.12, vow 189.3, 189.23, cheer 281.4, inspire hope 281.14, foresee 357.9, predict 358.14, intentionality 374.2, resolve 374.9, contract 391.2, 459.1, 462.2, 462.11, take charge of 391.8, duty 433.1, impose a duty 433.14, certify 464.11, settlement 735.6, settle 735.26, assure 810.23, possibility 836.1, be probable 838.8, guarantee 840.4, make certain 840.14

promised 458.8; marriageable 64.17, vowed 189.14, expected 356.5, undertaken 391.4, dutiful 433.6, contractual 459.7, 462.7, guaranteed 464.6, 840.10, foreseen 650.8, settled 735.16, united 752.10

Promised Land objective 374.5

promised land 458.5; aspiration 281.3, dreamland 360.8

promisee someone promised 458.7

promise maker 458.6

promise-making promise 458.1

promise oneself 458.15

promiser promise maker 458.6

promises inducement 508.2

promise to show potential 458.14

promise to pay guarantee 458.13, debt 488.1

promise well show potential 458.14, be auspicious 847.8

promising favorable 62.8, cheering 281.9, presageful 358.13, auspicious 458.10, potential 836.6, prosperous 847.5

promisingly favorably 62.15, comfortingly 281.17, predictively 358.16, auspiciously 458.17, prosperously 847.9

promisor promise maker 458.6

promissory guaranteeing 458.9

promissory note guarantee 458.3, purchase contract 459.3, paper money 484.14

promo [Inf] public relations (PR) 173.8

promontory peninsula 572.5, of landmasses 572.12, heights 596.4

promote 715.13, 807.18; react 11.38, educate 48.22, run for office 50.10, employ 57.18, find means 102.6, publicize 173.18, 178.19, better 445.17, reward 453.13, trade 480.18, sell 482.15, be an instrument 511.7, influence 512.11, exalt 596.19, give moral

support 605.18, determine 675.11, further 679.13, 825.30, make important 799.14, be useful 801.9, be convenient 803.5, make easy 823.15, reveal 843.14

promoted 715.8; hired 57.17, displayed 843.8

promoter producer 136.28, publicizer 173.11, persuader 178.9, overestimator 343.2, planner 387.9, supporter 605.9, benefactor 825.15

promoting instrumental 511.4, helping 825.16, helpful 825.19

promotion 715.3, 807.5; bargaining terms 57.10, public relations (PR) 173.8, publicity 178.7, reward for service 453.5, selling 482.1, instrumentality 511.1, moral support 605.7, advance 679.3, furtherance 825.8, manifestation 843.2

promotional persuasive 178.12, instrumental 511.4, supportive 605.11

promotional literature publicity 178.7

promotional manager displayer 843.7

promotive instrumental 511.4

prompt dramatize 136.33, inside information 170.4, advise 176.9, motivate 178.17, 508.9, reminder 354.4, remind 354.13, willing 373.7, active 414.13, immediate 645.5, early 657.8, swift 694.6, activate 771.28, hasty 818.3

promptbook script 136.7

prompted dramatized 136.32, motivated 508.8

prompter stagehand 136.29, motivator 178.11, 508.6, reminder 354.4

prompter's box stage 136.18

prompting persuasive 178.12

promptitude alacrity 414.3, immediacy 645.1, earliness 657.1, swiftness 694.1

promptly actively 414.24, immediately 645.8, early 657.17, hurryingly 694.18, hastily 818.7

promptness willingness 373.1, immediacy 645.1, earliness 657.1, swiftness 694.1, haste 818.1

promulgate publish 173.15, command 425.10

promulgation publishing 173.2

pronate fence 153.7

pronated fencing 153.6

pronation fencing movements 153.3

prone hunting 160.11, willing 373.7, prostrate 597.11, recumbent 603.7, sedentary 716.11, probable 838.6

prone float swimming techniques 164.2

pronely recumbently 603.12

proneness tendency 397.2, attitude 513.2, prostration 597.2, recumbency 603.2, probability 838.1

prone position target shooting 160.1

prone to tending to 513.4

prone to sickness unhealthy 114.23

prong sharp point 549.2, fork 703.5

pronged branched 703.9

pronominal of grammar 5.41

pronoun part of speech 5.30, 760.7

pronounce propound a philosophy 4.21, use language 5.42, judge 53.32, 54.31, proclaim 173.16,

aphorize 177.3, affirm 189.21, command 425.10, rule 780.12

pronounce a sentence imprison 55.11

pronounced voiced 5.37, affirmed 189.11, emphasized 200.4, spoken 205.13, manifest 843.9

pronounce guilty convict 54.33

pronounce man and wife join in marriage 64.20

pronouncement publication 173.1, affirmation 189.1, utterance 205.10, verdict 341.2, command 425.1

pronounce not guilty acquit 54.32

pronounce sentence try a case 54.28, judge 341.10

pronto [Inf] immediately 645.8, swiftly 694.16, hastily 818.7

Pronuba gods and goddesses of marriage 64.14

pronunciamento publication 173.1

pronunciation phonetics 205.3, mode of speech 205.6

proof 331.4, 336.2, 339.2; reasoning 6.61, evidence 54.15, claim 72.2, intoxicating 121.29, stage of book production 174.7, attestation 189.2, waterproof 560.16, authentication 721.8, invulnerable 810.18, certainty 840.1, confirmation 840.3, manifestation 843.2

proofed hardened 542.7

proof of purchase promise 464.2, receipt 492.1

proof of regard reward 453.1

proofread publish 174.19, rectify 807.22

proofreader book publishing personnel 174.12, improver 807.11, repairer 809.5

proofreading stage of book production 174.7, rectification 807.8

prop hand tool 103.3, bolster 377.15, vertical 602.3, support 605.1, 605.16, 825.24, supporting part 605.3, rotator 682.8, flyable 689.12, propeller 696.8, refuge 812.1, supporter 825.13

propaganda war measures 76.18, public relations (PR) 173.8, publicity 178.7, partial truth 192.7, inducement 508.2, distortion of truth 627.4

propagandism partial truth 192.7

propagandist publicizer 173.11, persuader 178.9, gossip 192.11, dissertator 203.3, motivator 508.6, distorter 627.5

propagandistic persuasive 178.12, untruthful 192.12

propagandistically untruthfully 192.27

propagandize make someone believe 87.11, publicize 173.18, 178.19, distort the truth 192.25, 627.12, practice sophistry 330.11, pervert 808.22

propagandizing publicity 178.7

propagate 21.15; gardening 17.5, procreate 22.14, publish 173.15, bring into existence 522.14, cause 675.8, make bigger 746.7, disperse 776.12, pluralize 793.9

propagated dispersed 776.6

propagating pertaining to life 28.14

propagation 21.4; procreation 22.4, life function 28.6, moss plant 46.5, lichen 47.16, telecommunication 169.7, cause

675.1, increase 746.1, dispersion 776.1

propagator 21.7; nursery 17.4, fertilizer 22.6, first cause 675.6

propagatory procreative 22.10

propagule reproductive body 47.14

propane gas 106.6

propel 696.15; set in motion 677.16, convey 685.9, impel 695.9, send up 715.12, hasten 818.4

propellant 78.14, 696.9; rocketry 7.32, gas 106.6, vaporizer 556.10, moving 677.12, propulsion 696.1, propeller 696.8, ejector 709.10

propellant or **propellent** propulsive 696.12

propelled moving 696.14

propeller 696.8; rotator 682.8, flyable 689.12

propelling moving 677.12, propulsion 696.1, propulsive 696.12

propelling force propulsion 696.1

propensity aptitude 127.4, inclination 290.2, tendency 397.2, 838.2, attitude 513.2

proper 429.10; legal 53.16, expedient 288.12, right 429.7, moral 431.9, dutiful 433.6, virtuous 447.5, elegant 527.3, conformist 781.10, convenient 803.3

proper eating diet 92.5

proper etiquette etiquette 534.3

proper fraction division 6.16, fraction 787.1

properly 429.18; legally 53.33, expediently 288.25, capably 340.15, well 399.22, right 429.15, dutifully 433.19, virtuously 447.9

proper match marriageability 64.4

proper motion star luminosity 7.12

properness 429.5; rightfulness 429.1, virtue 447.1

proper noun part of speech 5.30, name 202.8

proper thing, the duty 433.1

propertied 470.9; possessing 469.11, wealthy 485.8

propertied class the rich 485.7

properties or **props** stage requisite 136.21, motion-picture studio 137.7

proper time timeliness 659.1, convenience 803.1

proper treatment use 393.1

property 470.1; resources 102.4, stock in trade 105.2, wealth 485.1, visible effect 676.2, nature 723.4, characteristic 779.5

property estimation techniques industrial processes 14.27

property master filmmaker 137.14

property owner 470.7; master 68.1, possessor 469.10

property-owning possessing 469.11

property rights possession 469.1

property roll list of names 785.7

property tax tax 494.5

propfan means of propulsion 696.2

prophase cell division 13.17

prophecy divination 86.5, prediction 358.1, looking to the future 650.4

prophesy divine 86.24, predict 358.14, look ahead 650.11

prophet diviner 86.14, intuitive person 320.5, wise person 352.3,

predictor 357.4, 650.5, oracle 358.8, warner 814.5
prophetess oracle 358.8, predictor 650.5
prophetic divinatory 86.18, symbolic 183.12, predicting 358.11, premature 657.10
prophetically occultly 86.27, indicatively 183.21, foresightedly 357.10, predictively 358.16, prematurely 657.20
prophet of doom hopeless person 282.5, oracle 358.8
prophylactic birth control 23.5, therapeutic 107.30, prophylaxis 115.4, medicinal 115.15, hygiene 116.1, hygienic 116.3, precautionary 287.9, counteractant 510.5, tutelary 810.19, preserving 815.11, barrier 826.7, hindering 826.12
prophylactically precautiously 287.19, preservatively 815.16
prophylactic psychiatry psychiatry 108.2
prophylaxis 115.4; health care 107.7, hygiene 116.1, sanitary precaution 810.8
propinquity availability 575.5, nearness 586.1, relatedness 727.1
propionic Common Fatty Acids 12
propitiate conciliate 74.10, mediate 75.6, worship 83.15, recompense 273.11, atone 313.7, offer reparation 504.15
propitiating compensatory 743.5
propitiatingly atoningly 313.10
propitiation pacification 74.1, mediation 75.1, reparation 273.2, atonement 313.1, offering 504.5
propitiative atoning 313.5
propitiator mediator 75.2, representative 75.3, atoner 313.4
propitiatorily atoningly 313.10, correctively 743.11
propitiatory pacificatory 74.8, mediatory 75.5, atoning 313.5, sacrificial 504.10, compensatory 743.5
propitious favorable 62.8, cheering 281.9, presageful 358.13, auspicious 458.10, timely 659.4, beneficial 825.20, prosperous 847.5
propitiously favorably 62.15, comfortingly 281.17, auspiciously 458.17, opportunely 659.8, prosperously 847.9
propitiousness cheer 281.4, timeliness 659.1
proponent arguer 319.6, vindicator 441.5, supporter 605.9
proportion division 6.16, add 6.86, portion 474.2, grace 527.2, space 563.15, size 579.17, symmetry 626.1, symmetrize 626.6, interrelatedness 727.3, correspond to 727.10, correlation 729.3, correlate 729.9, accord 735.1, gradation 739.3, equilibrium 740.2, equalize 740.12, make average 792.9, part 760.1, method 765.7, ratio 783.5, fractional part 787.2
proportionable gradational 739.5
proportional divisible 6.71, graceful 527.4, fluid 527.5, spatial 563.11, symmetrical 626.4, interrelated 727.7, correlative 729.6, similar 733.7, harmonious 735.31, gradational 739.5, fractional 787.5
proportionality symmetry 626.1, interrelatedness 727.3, correlation

729.3, similarity 733.1, accord 735.1
proportionally symmetrically 626.7, relevantly 727.12, correlatively 729.12, similarly 733.17, harmoniously 735.31, differentially 739.9, partly 760.17
proportional notation written music 140.21
proportional tax tax 494.5
proportionate symmetrical 626.4, correlative 729.6, equal 740.8, partial 760.11
proportionately 474.7; symmetrically 626.7, relevantly 727.12, correlatively 729.12, partly 760.17
proportioned symmetrical 626.4, correlative 729.6
proportionment correlation 729.3
proportions space 563.1, size 579.1, quantity 738.1
proposable requesting 505.7
proposal recommendation 176.2, contention 189.4, courtship 299.10, plan 327.3, 387.1, supposition 359.1, future intention 374.3, offer 504.1, petition 505.2
propose propound a philosophy 4.21, advise 176.9, 825.27, aphorize 177.3, contend 189.24, aim 327.17, focus on 328.9, state 329.13, doubt 333.19, propound 359.9, will 372.11, intend 374.8, select 382.12, plan 387.12, offer 504.11, petition 505.11, further 679.13
propose a merger bargain 480.20
propose a motion propound 359.9
propose conditions specify 340.14
proposed contended 189.15, purposive 327.11, focused 328.6, logical 329.9, supposed 359.6, requesting 505.7
proposed action plan 387.1
proposed conduct conduct 399.1
proposed line of action plan 387.1
propose (marriage) 299.28
proposer planner 387.9
proposition philosophy 4.1, mathematical logic 6.60, theory 6.62, physical law 10.4, belief 87.1, recommendation 176.2, contention 189.4, topic 328.1, line of argument 329.3, question 333.1, supposition 359.1, plan 387.1, offer 504.1, petition 505.2, 505.11, formula 780.7
propositional theoretical 6.66, 327.10, contended 189.15, logical 329.9, suppositional 359.5, offered 504.8, requesting 505.7
propositional calculus Branches of Philosophy 4, mathematical logic 6.60
propositionally allegedly 189.31
propound 359.9; advise 176.9
propound a philosophy 4.21
propping up support 605.1
proprietarily 470.14
proprietary propertied 470.9
proprietary drug medicine 115.2
proprietary rights possession 469.1
proprieties etiquette 406.3
proprietor householder 61.5, master 68.1, possessor 469.10
proprietorial possessing 469.11
proprietorship possession 469.1
proprietress possessor 469.10
propriety Phobias 283, qualification 340.1, formality 406.1, properness 429.5, morals

431.2, elegance 527.1, refinement 534.1, etiquette 534.3, convenience 803.1
prop root root 41.7
propulsion 696.1; type of power 514.6, momentum 677.2, impulsion 695.1, expulsion 709.1
propulsive 696.12; nuclear 514.17
propulsive force propulsion 696.1
propulsively 696.21
propulsor propeller 696.8
propulsory propulsive 696.12
prop up strengthen 516.15, support 605.16, 825.24, erect 715.11, preserve 815.14
propylaeum Architectural Elements 134, means of entry 706.6
pro rata proportionately 474.7, partly 760.17
prorate allocate 474.5
prorogation delay 658.3
prorogue delay 658.13
prorogued held up 658.6
prosaic narrative 139.18, unemphatic 201.2, boring 296.6, unpretentious 526.8, mediocre 742.7, naive 821.3
prosaically narratively 139.22, unemphatically 201.4, boringly 296.10, simply 526.14
prosaicness boringness 296.2
proscenium stage 136.18, front entrance 621.2
proscenium arch stage 136.18
proscrastinate defer 604.15
proscribe make illegal 53.29, curse 301.13, specify 340.14, reject 383.10, command 425.10, exile 454.24, censor 503.10, limit 620.7, ostracize 709.17, exclude 764.7
proscribed cursed 301.8, conditional 340.10, censored 503.7
proscripted limited 620.5
proscription illegality 53.10, curse 301.1, specification 340.6, rejection 383.1, command 425.1, exile 454.3, censorship 503.4, limitation 620.2, ostracism 709.3, exclusion 764.1
proscriptive conditional 340.10, commanding 425.7, censored 503.7
proscriptively conditionally 340.16, commandingly 425.15, under censorship 503.13
prose 139.7; write 139.21
prosecute litigate 54.27, occupy oneself 412.15, accuse 442.8
prosecuted accused 442.5
prosecuting attorney law officer 53.6
prosecution pretrial proceedings 54.13, accusation 442.1
prosecutor court officer 54.7, accuser 442.3
prose fiction fiction 139.2, prose 139.7
proselyte convert 670.6
proselyter converter 670.5
proselytization religious conversion 670.4
proselytize 84.15; make someone believe 87.11, persuade 670.14
proselytized converted 670.7, influenced 670.10
proselytizer converter 670.5
proselytizing religious conversion 670.4
prose poem prose 139.7
Proserpina Deities 82
prosily boringly 296.10
prosimian primate 35.17, 35.32

prosiness lack of emphasis 201.1, boringness 296.2
prosit! cheers! 93.22
prosody meter 139.10
prosophobia Phobias 283
prosopopoeia literary device 139.12
prospect type of painting 143.5, view 242.8, experiment 335.11, expectation 356.1, prediction 358.1, future intention 374.3, looking to the future 650.4, possibility 836.1, probability 838.1
prospective expected 356.5, foreseeing 357.5, intending 374.6, auspicious 458.10, potential 836.6, probable 838.6
prospectively 374.12; auspiciously 458.17, potentially 836.11
prospector discoverer 345.7, producer 522.10
prospects cheer 281.4, expectations 356.2, looking to the future 650.4
prospectus 387.3; outline 204.2, plan 357.2, future condition 650.3, list of dates 785.6
prosper be fertile 22.13, be busy 414.19, be good 445.16, profit 467.22, get rich 485.13, achieve 704.21, be in comfortable circumstances 726.13, increase 746.6, get better 807.21, be successful 845.11, be prosperous 847.6
prospering prosperous 847.5
prosperity 847.1; productiveness 22.3, welfare 445.2, wealth 485.1, advance 679.3, comfortable circumstances 726.5, increase 746.1, uplift 807.2, revival 809.3, successfulness 845.3
prosperous 847.5; productive 22.9, presageful 358.13, beneficial 445.11, well-off 467.12, wealthy 485.8, comfortable 726.10, successful 845.8
prosperously 847.9; gainfully 467.24, wealthily 485.16, comfortably 726.19, successfully 845.19
prosperousness prosperity 847.1
prosperous person 847.4
prostaglandin hormone 12.16
prostate organs of reproduction 21.9
prostate cancer cancer 114.15
prostate gland organs of reproduction 21.9
prostatic of a secretion 24.5
prosthesis substitute 672.2
prosthetic dentistry dentistry 107.6
prosthetic group protein 12.9, enzyme 12.11
prosthodontic dental 107.31
prosthodontics dentistry 107.6
prosthodontist dentist 107.21
prostitute 432.17; loose woman 33.6, misuse 395.6, sexually immoral person 432.8, pervert 808.22
prostituted unchaste 432.10
prostitutes Phobias 283
prostitution 432.4; misuse 395.1, trade 480.1, moral deterioration 808.3
prostrate 597.11; of plants 41.14, religious 81.21, sick 114.24, sycophantic 401.7, submitting 421.3, showing respect 435.7, overpower 515.14, lower 597.21, recumbent 603.7, make horizontal 603.10, sedentary 716.11, lie down 716.21, fatigued 820.2, fatigue 820.6

prostrated *lowered* 597.12, *leveled* 603.8

prostrate oneself *revere* 81.26, *worship* 83.15, *knuckle under* 401.10, *defer to* 410.12, *show obeisance to* 426.8, *show respect* 435.16, *do penance* 451.9, *be low* 597.20, *be horizontal* 603.9, *bow* 716.22

prostration 597.2; *religiousness* 81.2, *act of worship* 83.2, *symptom* 114.3, *sycophancy* 401.2, *submission* 421.1, *obeisance* 426.3, *mark of respect* 435.4, *type of penance* 451.3, *disability* 515.4, *destruction* 523.1, *lowering* 597.3, *recumbency* 603.2, *bow* 716.6, *fatigue* 820.1

prostyle Architectural Elements 134

prosy *diffuse* 199.3, *unemphatic* 201.2, *boring* 296.6

protactinium Chemical Elements and Common Allotropes 11

protagonist *role* 136.23

protanopia *faulty vision* 243.1

protanopic *visually impaired* 243.9

protean *changeable* 666.3

protease *enzyme* 12.11

protect 613.26, 810.21; *defend* 77.37, 419.20, *save* 105.20, *play offense* 155.18, *take precautions* 287.14, *secure* 464.9, *strengthen* 516.15, *give moral support* 605.18, *give refuge to* 708.15, *escort* 794.18, *preserve* 815.14, *sustain* 825.25, *restrain commerce* 830.14, *detain* 830.16

protected 613.20; *saved* 105.15, *health-giving* 116.6, *mountaineering* 161.9, *defended* 419.18, *exempt* 434.5, *secure* 464.5, *accompanied* 794.15, *safe* 810.16, *sheltered* 812.7, *preserved* 815.12

protected area *ecology* 815.3

protected building *preserved thing* 815.10

protected from wet *waterproof* 560.16

protected species *preserved thing* 815.10

protecting *strengthening* 516.7, *tutelary* 810.19, *preserving* 815.11

protection 810.2; *storage* 105.6, *hygiene* 116.1, *management* 126.1, *play* 155.8, *precaution* 287.4, *solicitude* 323.5, *safeguard* 419.2, *security* 464.1, *protectionism* 480.3, *strength* 516.1, *moral support* 605.7, *shelter* 613.6, *refuge* 708.3, 812.1, *safety* 810.1, *preservation* 815.1, *conservation* 815.2, *social assistance* 825.4

protection from the weather 810.9

protectionism 480.3; *nationalism* 566.4, *economic restraint* 830.3

protectionist *nationalist* 566.8, *one who restrains* 830.7

protectionistic *national* 566.10

protection money *levy* 494.7

protection quota *international trade* 56.7

protection racket [Inf] *dishonesty* 479.7

protective *hygienic* 116.3, *solicitous* 323.8, *defending* 419.17, *secure* 464.5, *strengthened* 516.13, *supportive* 605.11, *tutelary* 810.19, *preserving* 815.11, *restrained* 830.9

protective belt *protective clothing* 419.6

protective clothing 419.6; *safety device* 810.15

protective coloring *that which makes invisible* 245.2, *defensiveness* 419.4, *body covering* 613.3

protective covering 613.5

protective custody *arrest* 55.5, *safekeeping* 810.6, *detention* 830.5

protective duty *protectionism* 480.3

protective glasses *visual aid* 242.14

protectively *defensively* 419.32, *surely* 464.15, *supportively* 605.20, *safely* 810.24, *preservatively* 815.16, *restrainedly* 830.18

protective quota *protectionism* 480.3

protective shoulder pads *hockey clothing* 158.6

protective tariff *protectionism* 480.3

protect oneself *be safe* 810.20

protector 419.16, 810.11; *leader* 68.3, 126.8, *defender* 77.2, *security force* 464.3, *contractant* 510.5, *supporter* 605.9, *accompanier* 794.6, *warner* 814.5

protectorate *body politic* 50.3, *possession of property* 469.3, *region* 564.1, *dominion* 566.3, *patronage* 810.7

protect the interests of *plead for* 419.25

protégé *dependent* 832.4

protein 12.9; *amino acid* 12.8, *food content* 90.3

protein diet *diet* 92.5

protein-rich *edible* 92.20

protein structure *protein* 12.9, *molecular biology* 13.18

protein synthesis *genetic material* 13.20

pro tem *occasional* 647.5

pro tempore [L] *occasional* 647.5

proteoglycan *protein* 12.9

proteolysis *enzyme* 12.11

proteolytic enzyme *enzyme* 12.11

Proterozoic Period Geologic Time Intervals 8

protest 331.19, 507.1, 507.7; *dissuasion* 179.1, *negation* 190.1, *negate* 190.16, *mass demonstration* 331.7, *disapproval* 347.2, *refuse* 347.9, *opposition* 375.2, *oppose* 375.13, *push* 414.20, *defy* 416.7, *resistance* 417.1, *resist* 417.10, *show of disapproval* 438.6, *nonpayment* 490.1, *dissent* 506.2, 782.2, *not conform* 782.18, *warning* 814.1, *warn* 814.8, *objection* 828.2, *object* 828.18, *nonpayment* 490.1

protest a bill *stop payment* 490.10

protest against *dissuade* 179.7, *oppose* 828.15

Protestant *Christian* 81.10, *denominational* 81.23

protestant *negator* 190.8, *negational* 190.9, *dissenter* 347.5, *dissenting* 347.7, *troublemaker* 427.5, *protester* 507.4, *protesting* 507.5

Protestantism *Christianity* 81.5

protestation *protest* 507.1

protested *negated* 190.10

protested bill *bad payment* 490.3

protester 331.8, 507.4; *negator* 190.8, *dissenter* 347.5, 463.5, 782.8, *reluctant person* 375.7, *defiant person* 416.4, *troublemaker* 427.5, *opposer* 828.9

protesting 507.5; *demonstrating* 331.14, *dissenting* 347.7, 506.6,

unenthusiastic 375.10, *resistant* 417.6, *warning* 814.6

protestingly 331.23; *negatively* 190.22, *dissentiently* 347.10, *resistingly* 417.14

protestive *negational* 190.9

protest march *mass demonstration* 331.7, *gesture of protest* 507.3

protest meeting *rally* 59.6, *gesture of protest* 507.3

protest song *gesture of protest* 507.3

Proteus Planets and Their Satellites 7

prothalamion *general wedding terms* 64.6, Poem or Verse Forms 139

prothallium *fern plant* 46.2

prothesis *preface* 769.5

protist *microorganism* 13.11, *type of animal* 34.5, *invertebrate* 39.1

protochordate 39.4; *invertebrate* 39.1, 39.20

protocol *tradition* 397.5, *good conduct* 399.5, *formality* 406.1, *etiquette* 406.3, 534.3, *good manners* 410.2, *alliance* 459.5, *design* 536.2

protohistoric *historical* 3.10, *past* 651.11

protohistorically *historically* 3.17

protohistory *past time* 3.6, 651.1

protohuman *prehistoric human* 653.7

protomartyr *martyr* 504.6

protomer *protein* 12.9

proton *electric charge* 10.38, *atom* 10.52, *elementary particle* 10.53, *physical element* 524.5, *little thing* 580.3

protonema *plant body* 47.13

protonic *acid* 11.27

protonic acid *acid* 11.10

proton mass *fundamental constant* 10.69

proton number *isotope* 10.57

protoplasm *living matter* 28.4, *matter* 524.4, *source* 771.3

protoplasmic *cellular* 13.30, *pertaining to life* 28.14

protoplast *cell* 13.15

protostar *stellar evolution* 7.10

Prototheria *egg-laying mammal* 35.4

prototherian *egg-laying mammal* 35.4, *mammalian* 35.23

prototype 624.2; *ideal* 327.6, *model* 358.4, *preparations* 388.2, *standard* 589.7, *original* 737.2, *precedent* 769.4

prototypical 624.7; *ideal* 327.12

prototypically *formatively* 624.10

Protozoa *protozoan* 39.17

protozoan 39.17, 39.27; *type of animal* 34.5, *invertebrate* 39.1, 39.20, *parasite* 39.18, *disease-causing agent* 114.5, *little thing* 580.3, *tiny* 580.9

protozoic *protozoan* 39.27

protozoological *protozoan* 39.27

protozoologist *invertebrate zoologist* 39.3

protozoology *invertebrate zoology* 39.2

protozoon *protozoan* 39.17

protract 669.9; *be diffuse* 199.5, *lengthen* 590.12, *delay* 658.13, *block* 826.17

protracted 669.7; *diffuse* 199.3, *boring* 296.6, *lengthened* 590.10, *held up* 658.6

protractedly *at length* 590.15, *late* 658.14, *continually* 669.10

protraction 669.4; *diffuseness*

199.1, *lengthening* 590.4, *delay* 658.3, *continuance* 669.3, *increase* 746.1

protractor *geometric construction* 6.47, *measuring instrument* 589.12, *angular measurement* 628.4

protrude 634.8; *overhang* 604.14, *be convex* 634.7, *emerge* 707.14

protrudent *protuberant* 634.6

protruding *protuberant* 634.6

protrusion *overhanging* 604.2, *convexity* 634.1, *protuberance* 634.3

protuberance 634.3; *nap* 552.3, *convexity* 634.1

protuberant 634.6

protuberantly *convexly* 634.9

proturan *insectile* 40.11

proud 297.10; *boastful* 402.13, *majestic* 404.21, *formal* 406.6, *impious* 448.11

proud as a peacock *arrogant* 297.9

proud bearing *proudness* 297.3

proudhearted *proud* 297.10

proudly 297.19; *boastfully* 402.21, *majestically* 404.36

proudness 297.3

proud person 297.7

provability *demonstrability* 331.5

provable *demonstrable* 331.12, *correct* 429.8, *real* 717.14

prove 331.17, 336.9, 339.14; *theorize* 6.84, *attest* 189.22, *state* 329.13, *experiment* 335.11, *justify* 441.12, *establish reality* 719.12, *authenticate* 721.24, *make certain* 840.14

prove acceptable *suffice* 97.6

prove adequate *suffice* 97.6

prove a fiasco *miscarry* 846.19

proved *attested* 189.13, *proven* 331.13, *verifiable* 336.5, *evidential* 339.8, *known* 348.9

proved or proven *authenticated* 721.17

proved guilty *guilty* 450.6

prove fruitful *show potential* 458.14

prove guilty *convict* 54.33

prove helpful *be useful* 801.9

prove infertile *be infertile* 23.8

prove innocent *acquit* 54.32

prove itself *be convenient* 803.5

proven 331.13; *attested* 189.13

proven or proved *certain* 840.7

provenance *source* 771.3

provender *animal feed* 16.12, *provision* 89.1, *provisions* 89.3, *food* 90.1, *animal food* 90.2

proven innocent *favorable verdict* 54.19

proven way *way* 399.10

prove one's point *prove* 331.17, *establish reality* 719.12

proverb *catchword* 5.22, *maxim* 177.1, *aphorize* 177.3, *pithy saying* 198.3, *moral* 431.5, *truism* 721.6

proverbial 177.2; *worded* 5.38, *truistic* 721.15

proverbially 177.4; *theoretically* 4.24, *phraseologically* 5.47, *intrinsically* 721.30

prove the contrary *refute* 332.7

prove the truth of *justify* 441.12

prove too much for *overtake* 744.16

prove unreliable *not perform* 466.10

provide *provision* 89.9, *find means* 102.6, *procure* 104.9, *store* 105.17, *equip* 388.19, *give*

472.10, grant 735.30, preserve 815.14
provide a benefit *be favorable* 62.12
provide a chance *be timely* 659.6
provide against *have foresight* 357.8
provide aid *be compassionate* 305.11
provide a living for *support life* 28.21
provide an alibi for *protect* 810.21
provide an opportunity *offer* 504.11
provide a role model *conduct oneself* 399.17
provide a sweetener *remunerate* 489.21
provide collateral *borrow* 476.10
provided *supplied* 89.7, *stored* 105.14
provide drink 93.21
provided that *under the circumstances* 726.16
provide firepower *equip* 388.19
provide food *feed* 90.41
provide for *support life* 28.21, *take precautions* 287.14, *will* 472.11, *support financially* 605.19, *sustain* 825.25
provide money *make rich* 485.15
Providence *God* 82.6, *American States* 564
providence *precaution* 287.4, *foresight* 357.1, *timeliness* 659.1, *luck* 842.3
provide needed funds *be charitable* 305.12
provide no enjoyment *bore* 296.8
provident *precautionary* 287.9, *foreseeing* 357.5
providential *divine* 82.16, *timely* 659.4
providentiality *timeliness* 659.1
providentially *divinely* 82.24, *opportunely* 659.8
providently *precautiously* 287.19, *foresightedly* 357.10
provide on-the-job *or* **in-service training** *employ* 57.18
provide oxygen *air* 94.7
provide passage for 583.18
provider 605.10; *provisioner* 89.4, *preparer* 388.6, *giver* 472.7
provide the basis *prepare the way* 388.15
provide the means *finance* 825.31
provide the wherewithal *find means* 102.6
provide with arms *equip* 388.19
providing *provisioning* 89.2, 89.6
province *subject* 48.3, *body politic* 50.3, *clerical venue* 84.4, *line of duty* 433.3, *administrative region* 564.4, *sphere* 564.10, *dominion* 566.3
provinces *regions* 564.2
provincial *countryman* 61.8, *native* 61.12, *common* 71.3, *unjust* 342.7, *administrative* 564.13, *conformist* 781.10, *naive person* 821.2
provincialism *dialect* 5.24, *unfair treatment* 342.4, *regionalism* 564.11
provincially *regionally* 564.16
proving *proof* 336.2
proving ground *place of experimentation* 335.6
provision 89.1, 89.9; *feed* 90.41, *store* 105.1, 105.17, *precaution* 287.4, *specification* 340.6, *foresight*

357.1, *basis for negotiations* 460.2, *giving* 472.1, *funds* 484.6, *financial support* 605.8, *circumstances* 726.1, *grant* 735.10, *restoration* 809.2, *insurance* 810.10, *preservation* 815.1, *saving* 815.4, *preserve* 815.14, *sustenance* 825.3
provisional 89.8; *deputizing* 80.4, *sufficient* 97.3, *precautionary* 287.9, *experimental* 335.8, *conditional* 340.10, *negotiated* 460.5, *occasional* 647.5, *substitute* 672.3, *circumstantial* 726.8, *incomplete* 806.6, *uncertain* 841.9
provisional government *caretaker government* 49.14
provisionally 89.12; *materially* 104.10, *precautiously* 287.19, *experimentally* 335.14, *conditionally* 340.16, 725.10, *preparatorily* 388.23, *feasibly* 460.9, *at present* 647.9, *instead* 672.8, *relatively* 725.17
provisioner 89.4; *preparer* 388.6, *retailer* 482.11, *provider* 605.10
provisioning 89.2, 89.6; *cooking* 91.1, *fitting out* 388.3
provision merchant *retailer* 482.11
provisions 89.3; *food* 90.1, *supplies* 102.3, *fitting out* 388.3, *extra* 748.6
proviso *provision* 89.1, *specification* 340.6, *basis for negotiations* 460.2, *limitation* 620.2
provisorily *provisionally* 89.12
provisory *provisional* 89.8, *conditional* 340.10, *negotiated* 460.5
provocation 302.3; *incentive* 178.4, *annoyance* 276.2, *rivalry* 422.2, *inducement* 508.2, *stimulus* 508.3, *cause* 675.1
provocative *persuasive* 178.12, *stimulating* 221.7, *desirable* 288.11, *defying* 416.6, *aggressive* 418.12, *offensive* 432.11, *disagreeing* 463.6, *motivational* 508.7, *ribald* 535.8
provocatively *stimulatingly* 221.11, *desirably* 288.24, *argumentatively* 329.15, *in defiance* 416.10, *in disagreement* 463.12, *influentially* 508.13, *ribaldly* 535.12
provocativeness *defiance* 416.1, *divisiveness* 463.2
provoke *antagonize* 63.12, *motivate* 178.17, 508.9, *be piquant* 221.9, *annoy* 276.7, *cause dislike* 291.16, *cause hate* 300.12, *make angry* 302.18, *answer back* 334.19, *defy* 416.7, *disagree* 463.8, *pick a fight* 463.10, *awaken* 675.9, *activate* 771.28
provoke action *warn* 814.8
provoke an engagement *battle* 76.33
provoked *resentful* 302.8, *motivated* 508.8
provoke thought *emphasize* 200.6
provoking *aggravating* 276.4, *maddening* 302.12, *motivational* 508.7
provokingly *maddeningly* 302.25
provost *person in authority* 52.7, *religious leader* 68.9, *educational leader* 68.11
provost guard *law enforcement officer* 53.8
provost marshal *law enforcement officer* 53.8

provost sergeant *law enforcement officer* 53.8
prow *rock face* 161.6, *vanguard* 621.5
prowess *skill* 127.1, *heroism* 284.2, *courageous act* 284.7
prowl after *follow* 385.12
prowl car *automobile* 687.6
prowler *thief* 479.8
proximal *near* 586.6, *next* 770.8
proximate *near* 586.6, *close* 645.6, *next* 770.8
proximity *availability* 575.5, *nearness* 586.1, 803.2, *closeness* 645.2
proxy *alternative* 80.2, *agent* 123.15, *representative* 187.7, *act as a go-between* 460.8, *substitute* 613.17, 672.2, 672.3, *commission* 833.1, *commissioner* 833.5
PR representative *or* **officer** *news interpreter* 365.7
prude *strict person* 424.4, *moralist* 431.8, *moralistic* 431.12, *conformist* 781.6
prudence 287.2; *circumspection* 325.3, *wisdom* 352.1, *foresight* 357.1, *virtues* 447.2, *moderation* 455.3, *thrift* 499.1, *convenience* 803.1
prudent 287.7; *advisable* 176.8, *circumspect* 325.8, *wise* 352.4, *foreseeing* 357.5, *principled* 447.6, *temperate* 455.8, *thrifty* 499.4, *convenient* 803.3
prudently 287.17; *advisably* 176.13, *wisely* 352.8, *foresightedly* 357.10, *ethically* 447.10, *moderately* 455.15, *economically* 499.7
prudery *unadornment* 424.3, *self-righteousness* 431.7, *conventionalism* 781.4
prudish *shy* 403.8, *unadorned* 424.7, *moralistic* 431.12, *conformist* 781.10
prudishly *plainly* 424.12, *moralistically* 431.16
prudishness *shyness* 403.3, *self-righteousness* 431.7
prune *cultivate* 17.19, *manage trees* 43.14, *use a sharp tool* 549.17, *contract* 582.12, *shorten* 591.9, *displace* 711.14, *make smaller* 747.8, *take off* 749.7, *separate* 753.12, *reduce* 796.8
pruned *ornamental* 17.17, *summarized* 204.6, *shortened* 582.8, 591.7
prunella Fabrics and Fibers 130
pruner *garden tool* 17.7, *sharp-edged thing* 549.6
pruning *cultivation* 16.7, *gardening* 17.5, *tree management* 43.6, *outline* 204.2, *shortening* 582.2, 591.2, *displacement* 711.2
pruning hook *garden tool* 17.7
pruning saw *garden tool* 103.4
pruning shears *garden tool* 17.7, *sharp-edged thing* 549.6
prurience *obscenity* 112.4, *sexual love* 299.3, *prying* 321.2, *sexual immorality* 432.2
prurience *or* **pruriency** *sexual longing* 20.6
pruriency *sexual immorality* 432.2
prurient *desirous* 20.18, *obscene* 112.9, *prying* 321.6, *unchaste* 432.10
pruriently *dirtily* 112.12, *officiously* 321.10, *promiscuously* 432.19
prurigo *skin disease* 114.16
pruritus *skin disease* 114.16, *restlessness* 684.5

prusik *mountaineer* 161.10
prusiking *climbing techniques* 161.3
prusiks *climbing equipment* 161.4
Prussian blue *blue pigment* 261.2
prussic acid *poison* 117.7
Prut Rivers 570
pry *meddle* 321.8, 414.23, *question* 333.16
prying 321.2, 321.6; *observation* 242.5, *curiosity* 333.8, *questioning* 333.11, *meddling* 414.17
prying person *meddler* 414.12
pry into *meddle* 414.23
pry into the future *foresee* 357.7
Przewalski's Horse Horse and Pony Breeds 159
P.S. *or* **p.s.** *back matter* 622.3
psalm *ritual music* 85.9, Poem or Verse Forms 139, *sacred music* 140.3, *song* 140.11
psalmbook *ritual manual* 85.11
psalmist *composer* 141.9
psalmody *ritual music* 85.9, *sacred music* 140.3
psalm singing *act of worship* 83.2, *ritual music* 85.9
psalm-singing *singing* 85.16
psalter *ritual music* 85.9, *ritual manual* 85.11
psaltery Musical Instruments 142
psellismophobia Phobias 283
psephology *electing* 382.5
psephomancer *diviner* 86.14
psephomancy *divination* 86.5
pseud [Inf] *hypocrite* 192.9
pseudo *ungenuine* 192.13, *artificial* 720.12, *simulated* 733.11, *imitation* 736.8
pseudoaromatic *chemical compound* 11.4
pseudocoelomate *invertebrate* 39.20
pseudohermaphrodism *sexual nature* 20.4
pseudohermaphrodite *sexual nature* 20.4, *of sexual nature* 20.17
pseudohermaphroditic *of sexual nature* 20.17
pseudologist *liar* 192.10
pseudology *lying* 192.5
pseudonym *anonymity* 182.7, *name* 202.8
pseudonymity *nomenclature* 202.7
pseudoparenchymatous *algal* 47.20
pseudopsychological *psychic* 86.17
pseudopsychology *supernaturalism* 86.3
pseudoscorpion *arachnid* 40.4
pseudostatement *literary device* 139.12
pseudosyllogism *sophism* 330.2
pseudosyllogistic *sophistic* 330.7
psi faculty *psychic power* 86.4
psilocybin *hallucinogens* 121.20
psittaciform *avian* 36.19
psittacine *avian* 36.19
psittacosis *animal disease* 34.10
psocopteran *insectile* 40.11
psychagogy *conditioning* 108.24
psychalgia *anxiety disorder* 108.11
Psyche Famous Lovers 299
psyche 108.25; *spirit* 86.10, *internal world* 525.6, *inner nature* 611.4
psychedelic *addictive* 121.32
psychedelically *in a trance* 121.40
psyched up [Inf] *prepared* 388.9
psychiatric *psychological* 108.36
psychiatrically *psychologically* 108.42

psychiatric care *psychiatric treatment* 108.3, *treatment* 110.7
psychiatric disease 114.21
psychiatric hospital 108.35; *mental hospital* 110.6
psychiatric social worker *psychologist* 108.33
psychiatric treatment 108.3
psychiatric unit *psychiatric hospital* 108.35, *mental hospital* 110.6
psychiatric ward *psychiatric hospital* 108.35, *mental hospital* 110.6
psychiatrist 108.34, 110.8; *medical specialist* 107.20, *professional worker* 123.11, *adviser* 176.5
psychiatry 108.2, *Medical Specialties* 107, *therapy* 115.12
psychic 86.17; *occultist* 86.13, *diviner* 86.14, *nonmaterialist* 525.7, *nonmaterial* 525.8, *parapsychological* 525.9
psychical *psychic* 86.17
psychically *occultly* 86.27, *metaphysically* 525.13
psychic apparatus *psyche* 108.25
psychic determinism Psychological Theories, Schools 108
psychic energy *libido* 108.26
psychic phenomena *parapsychology* 525.4
psychic power 86.4
psychic research *supernaturalism* 86.3, *parapsychology* 525.4
psycho [Inf] *insane person* 110.5
psychoacoustics Psychological Theories, Schools 108
psychoanalysis *psychotherapy* 108.4, *treatment* 110.7, *therapy* 115.12, *internal world* 525.6
psychoanalyst *psychologist* 108.33, *psychiatrist* 110.8, *adviser* 176.5, *nonmaterialist* 525.7
psychoanalytical *psychological* 108.36, *internal* 525.11
psychoanalytically *subjectively* 525.14
psychoanalytic method *psychotherapy* 108.4
psychoanalyze *psychologize* 108.41, *dematerialize* 525.12
psychoanalyzer *psychiatrist* 108.34
psychobabble *jargon* 5.21, *vernacular* 205.8, *empty talk* 362.5, *talk nonsense* 362.12
psychobiochemistry Psychological Theories, Schools 108
psychobiological *psychological* 108.36
psychobiologist *psychologist* 108.33
psychobiology Psychological Theories, Schools 108
psychochemist *psychiatrist* 108.34
psychodiagnosis *psychiatry* 108.2
psychodiagnostic *psychological* 108.36
psychodiagnostics *psychiatry* 108.2
psychodrama *dramatic style* 136.3
psychodynamics Psychological Theories, Schools 108
psychoendocrinology Psychological Theories, Schools 108
psychogalvanic skin response *psychometrics* 108.5
psychogalvanometer *psychometrics* 108.5

psychogenesis Psychological Theories, Schools 108
psychogenetic *psychological* 108.36
psychogenic *psychological* 108.36
psychogenic fugue *dissociative disorder* 108.17
psychogeriatric *psychological* 108.36
psychogeriatrics Psychological Theories, Schools 108
psychographer *psychologist* 108.33
psychographics Psychological Theories, Schools 108
psychographist *occultist* 86.13
psychography *occult and psychic phenomena* 86.7, *psychometrics* 108.5
psychokinesis *occult and psychic phenomena* 86.7, *parapsychology* 525.4
psychokinetic *psychic* 86.17, *parapsychological* 525.9
psycholinguistics Linguistic Studies 5, Psychological Theories, Schools 108
psychological 108.36; *anthropological* 1.10, *inward* 611.12
psychological cure *recuperation* 809.4
psychologically 108.42; *inwardly* 611.21
psychologically disturbed 108.39
psychological me *psyche* 108.25
psychological medicine *psychiatry* 108.2
psychological novel *novel* 139.3
psychological screening *psychometrics* 108.5
psychological stress *anxiety disorder* 108.11
psychological thriller *novel* 139.3
psychological time *time* 639.1
psychological warfare 76.13; *intimidation* 283.6
psychologist 108.33; *studier of humankind* 18.7, *adviser* 176.5
psychologize 108.41
psychologue *psychologist* 108.33
psychology 108.1; *study of humankind* 18.6, *study of life* 28.9, *study of conduct* 399.3
psychomancer *diviner* 86.14
psychomancy *divination* 86.5
psychometer *occultist* 86.13
psychometric *psychological* 108.36
psychometrics 108.5, Psychological Theories, Schools 108
psychometrist *occultist* 86.13
psychometry *psychic power* 86.4, *psychometrics* 108.5, Fields of Measurement 589
psych oneself up [Inf] *prepare oneself* 388.21
psychoneurological *psychological* 108.36
psychoneurosis Psychological Theories, Schools 108, *neurosis* 108.9, *mental breakdown* 110.4
psychopath *murderer* 30.12, *insane person* 110.5
psychopathic *murderous* 30.18, *psychologically disturbed* 108.39, *mentally ill* 110.11
psychopathic killer *murderer* 30.12
psychopathic personality *mental disorder* 108.8
psychopathological *psychological* 108.36

psychopathologist *psychologist* 108.33
psychopathology Psychological Theories, Schools 108
psychopathy *psychosis* 108.10, 110.3
psychopharmacological *psychological* 108.36
psychopharmacologist *psychiatrist* 108.34
psychopharmacology Psychological Theories, Schools 108
psychophobia Phobias 283
psychophysical *psychological* 108.36
psychophysicist *psychologist* 108.33
psychophysics Psychological Theories, Schools 108
psychophysiologist *psychiatrist* 108.34
psychophysiology Psychological Theories, Schools 108
psychosexual *psychological* 108.36
psychosexual disorder *sexual perversion* 20.12
psychosexuality Psychological Theories, Schools 108
psychosis 108.10, 110.3; *mental disorder* 108.8
psychosocial *psychological* 108.36
psychosocial medicine *psychiatry* 108.2
psychosociologist *psychologist* 108.33
psychosociology Psychological Theories, Schools 108
psychosomatic *psychological* 108.36, *of disease* 114.25
psychosomatic medicine *psychiatry* 108.2
psychosomatics Psychological Theories, Schools 108
psychosophy *supernaturalism* 86.3
psychosurgery *psychiatric treatment* 108.3
psychotechnical *psychological* 108.36
psychotechnologist *psychologist* 108.33
psychotechnology Psychological Theories, Schools 108
psychotherapeutic *psychological* 108.36
psychotherapeutist *psychiatrist* 108.34
psychotherapist *psychologist* 108.33, *psychiatrist* 108.34, 110.8, *adviser* 176.5
psychotherapy 108.4, Psychological Theories, Schools 108, *treatment* 110.7, *therapy* 115.12, *recuperation* 809.4
psychotic *mental disorder* 108.8, *psychologically disturbed* 108.39, *insane person* 110.5, *mentally ill* 110.11
psychotically *insanely* 110.15
psychotic disorders *mental disorder* 108.8
psychotic personality *mental disorder* 108.8
psychotropic drug *psychiatric treatment* 108.3
psychrometer *weather instrument* 9.7, *measuring instrument* 557.19
psychrometric *barometric* 9.39
psychrophobia Phobias 283
psych up [Inf] *invigorate* 518.5
Ptah Deities 82
PT boat Ships and Boats 690
Pteraspis *fossil fish* 38.7
pteridological *fernlike* 46.6

pteridologist *plant scientist* 41.11, *study of ferns* 46.3
pteridology *plant science* 41.10, *study of ferns* 46.3
Pteridophyta *lower plant* 41.4
pteridophyte *lower plant* 41.4, *fern* 46.1, *fernlike* 46.6
pteridophytic *fernlike* 46.6
pteridophytous *fernlike* 46.6
pteridosperm *fern* 46.1
pterodactyl *prehistoric animal* 653.8
pteronophobia Phobias 283
pterosaur *extinct reptile* 37.9
pterygoid process Human Bones 19
pteryla *plumage* 36.7
Ptolemaic universe *universe* 7.3
ptomaine poisoning *poisoning* 114.8, *gastroenterological disease* 114.11
ptyalism *saliva* 25.9
p-type conductivity *semiconductor* 10.34
p-type semiconductor *semiconductor* 10.34
pub *drink provider* 93.15
pub-carouse *get drunk* 121.35
pub circuit [Brit] *engagement* 136.15, 138.6
pub crawl *drinking bout* 121.7
pub-crawl *get drunk* 121.35, *participate* 408.15
pub-crawler *drunkard* 121.8
puberty *youth* 26.1
pubescence *youth* 26.1
pubescent *young* 26.11
pubis Human Bones 19
public *group* 18.13, *national* 18.16, *governmental* 49.24, *political* 50.9, *inhabitants* 61.2, *published* 173.12, 175.8, *visible* 244.5, *known* 348.9, *blatant* 404.19, *sociable* 408.11, *corporate* 480.17, *urban* 567.14, *opened up* 583.11, *prevailing* 778.11, *manifest* 843.9
public, the *humankind* 18.1
public address system *publishing* 173.2, *sound amplifier* 230.5
public affairs *politics* 50.1
publican [Brit] *drink provider* 93.15
public assistance *social assistance* 825.4
publication 173.1; *book* 174.1, *divulgence* 180.2, *proclamation* 183.8, *first appearance* 264.3, *demonstration* 331.1, *notice* 358.3, *dispersion* 776.1, *warning* 814.1, *manifestation* 843.2
publication media 173.6
public baths *bath* 111.6
public benefit *benefit* 801.4
public building *building* 551.9
public company *joint possession* 469.6, *company* 480.7
public convenience *place for excretion* 25.11
public corporation *joint possession* 469.6
public debt *economic development* 56.5
public discussion *publicity* 173.7
public domain *public ownership* 469.7
public enemy (number one) *hostile person* 63.5
public enterprise *economics* 56.1
public entertainer *entertainer* 138.8
public expenditure *economic factor* 56.8
public eye *publicity* 173.7
public file *record* 185.1

public forum *publicity* 173.7
public garden *garden* 17.2
public good *benefit* 801.4
public hall *meeting place* 408.5
public health *hygiene* 116.1
public health inspector *hygienist* 116.2
public-health medicine *medicine* 107.1, *health care* 107.7
public-health physician *doctor* 107.19
public house [Brit] *drink provider* 93.15
public image *impression* 264.7
public information 170.5
public information officer *news interpreter* 365.7
publicist *representative* 75.3, *publicizer* 173.11, *persuader* 178.9, *motivator* 508.6, *coverer* 613.18, *displayer* 843.7
publicity 173.7, 178.7; *clarity* 244.2, *coverage* 613.16, *manifestation* 843.2
publicity agent *publicizer* 173.11
publicity manager *producer* 136.28
publicize 173.18, 178.19; *communicate* 170.12, *report* 171.9, *divulge* 180.9, *include* 613.33, *make important* 799.14, *reveal* 843.14
publicized 173.14; *demonstrated* 331.9, *displayed* 843.8
publicizer 173.11; *persuader* 178.9, *discloser* 180.4, *news interpreter* 365.7, *displayer* 843.7
public knowledge *public information* 170.5, *publicity* 173.7
public library *library* 174.14
publicly 173.20; *politically* 50.11, *manifestly* 331.20, 843.17, *blatantly* 404.34, *municipally* 567.16, *openly* 583.22
public money *treasury* 484.19
public office holder *public servant* 69.3
public official *elected official* 50.8, *public servant* 69.3
public opinion *judgment* 341.1, *place of judgment* 341.3, *group influence* 512.6
public opinion poll *electing* 382.5
public ownership 469.7; *economics* 56.1
public persona *impression* 264.7, *appearance* 610.4
public property *property* 470.1
public prosecutor *law officer* 53.6, *accuser* 442.3
public provision *social assistance* 825.4
public purse *treasury* 484.19
public radio *radio broadcasting* 172.4
public recognition *publicity* 173.7, *reward* 453.1
public record *record* 185.1
public relations (PR) 173.8; *publicity* 178.7
public relations (PR) person *representative* 75.3, *deputy* 80.1, *publicizer* 173.11, *persuader* 178.9, *news interpreter* 365.7, *motivator* 508.6, *displayer* 843.7
public sale *sale* 482.2
public school *type of school* 48.12
public sector *economy* 56.3, *market sector* 483.5
public-sector *unionized* 57.14
public sector borrowing *national debt* 488.2
public sector union *organized labor* 57.5

public servant 69.3; *elected official* 50.8, *volunteer* 504.7, *commissioner* 833.5
public service *council* 833.4
public service announcement *broadcast material* 172.9
public speaker 209.5; *speaker* 205.12
public speaking 205.11
public speech *address* 209.1
public spirit *public-spiritedness* 307.2
public-spirited 307.7
public-spiritedness 307.2
public square *center of activity* 612.4
public telephone *telephone* 169.10
public telephone system *telephone* 169.10
public utility *benefit* 801.4
public warning *warning* 814.1
public weal *welfare* 445.2
public worship 83.3
publish 173.15, 174.19; *communicate* 170.12, *report* 171.9, 175.9, *divulge* 180.9, *signal* 183.18, *present* 264.15, *demonstrate* 331.15, *disperse* 776.12, *display* 843.13, *reveal* 843.14
published 173.12, 174.18, 175.8; *demonstrated* 331.9, *dispersed* 776.6, *displayed* 843.8
publisher *professional worker* 123.11, *publicizer* 173.11, *book publishing personnel* 174.12
publisher's agent *bookshop* 174.15
publisher's catalog *or* list *list* 785.1
publish freely *be free* 829.16
publishing 173.2; *reproduction* 21.1, *book publishing* 174.6, *signaling* 183.14
publishing company *book publishing personnel* 174.12
publishing contract *purchase contract* 459.3
publishing history *book part* 174.5
publishing house *book publishing personnel* 174.12
publish the banns *marry* 64.19, *propose (marriage)* 299.28, *get engaged to* 458.12
pub theatre [Brit] *drama* 136.1
puce *brown* 256.5, *purple* 262.6
Puck *Planets and Their Satellites* 7, *sprite* 86.12
puck *hockey equipment* 158.3, *missile* 696.7
puck carrier *hockey player* 158.8
pucker *contract* 582.12, *become smaller* 582.14, *pleat* 637.2, 637.8, *wrinkle* 637.2, 638.6
puckered *shortened* 582.8, *wrinkly* 638.4
puckered up *shortened* 582.8
puckering *shortening* 582.2, *contracting* 582.10
puckering up *shortening* 582.2
pucker up *contract* 582.12, *become smaller* 582.14
puck-handle *play ice hockey* 158.9
puck possession *ice hockey tactics* 158.4
pudding *dessert* 90.35, *semiliquid* 561.7
pudding basin *cooking equipment* 91.6
puddle *cultivate* 17.19
puddle in *cultivate* 17.19

pudenda *organs of reproduction* 21.9
pudendum *or* pudenda *sexual organs* 20.2
pudginess *fatness* 579.5, *thickness* 594.1, *round body* 633.2
pudgy *fat* 579.15, *thick* 594.5, *well-rounded* 633.8
Pueblo Revival *Architectural Styles* 134
puerile *unintelligent* 316.6, *foolish* 353.5, *immature* 389.9, *not serious* 800.11
puerility *youth* 26.1, *ignorance* 316.3, *folly* 353.1
puerperal *pregnant* 21.12
Puerto Rico *Islands* 572
Puerto Rico, Commonwealth of *American States* 564
puff *smoking* 121.22, *smoke* 121.38, *public relations (PR)* 173.8, *publicize* 173.18, *criticism* 365.3, *criticize* 365.15, *flatter* 439.12, *blow* 558.22, *let out* 709.26, *be fatigued* 820.5
puffed *exaggerated* 194.7
puffed up *enlarged* 194.8, *prideful* 297.8, *affected* 367.3, *cocky* 402.11, *swelled* 581.10
puffery *exaggeration* 194.1
puffily *largely* 581.18
puffin *water bird* 36.9
puffiness *fatness* 579.5, *swelling* 581.2
puffing *panting* 820.3
puffing and blowing *panting* 820.3
puffing up *enlargement* 194.2
puff of smoke *miasma* 556.3
puff of wind *wind strength* 9.13
puff pastry *pastry* 90.37
puff sleeve *part of garment* 100.27
puff up *enlarge* 194.12, *become conceited* 402.16, *compliment* 437.17, *swell* 581.15, *send up* 715.12
puffy *fat* 579.15, *swelled* 581.10
pug *Breeds of Dogs* 35, *ceramic workshop and tools* 129.8, *make ceramics* 129.10
pug [Inf] *boxer* 152.8
pugging *ceramic process* 129.5, *ceramic* 129.9
pugilism *boxing* 152.2
pugilist *boxer* 152.8
pugilistic *warlike* 76.27, *martial* 77.33, *combat* 152.17, *contentious* 422.20
pugilistically *martially* 77.39
pug mill *ceramic workshop and tools* 129.8
pugnacious *military* 58.10, *warlike* 76.27, *combative* 77.32, *angry* 302.11, *aggressive* 418.12, *contentious* 422.20
pugnaciously *aggressively* 77.38, *angrily* 302.24, *contentiously* 422.27
pugnaciousness *bellicosity* 76.15, *anger* 302.4
pugnacity *bellicosity* 76.15, *anger* 302.4, *attack* 418.1
puissance *authority* 52.1, *power* 514.1, *strength* 516.1
puissant *powerful* 514.15, *strong* 516.9
puja *worship* 83.1
puke [Inf] *vomiting* 709.7, *vomit* 709.27
pukey [Inf] *vomiting* 709.12
puking [Inf] *vomiting* 709.7
pukka *authentic* 721.16
Pulawy *Breeds of Pigs* 16
pulchritude *attractiveness* 529.2

pulchritudinous *attractive* 529.8
pule *cry* 239.16, *make an animal sound* 240.7
puli *Breeds of Dogs* 35
Pulitzer Prize *prizes* 453.3
pull 699.2, 699.10; *practice dentistry* 107.34, *treat* 115.17, *exertion* 122.4, *work* 122.8, *be clumsy* 128.9, *golf shots* 156.4, *play* 156.8, *swim* 164.14, *type of touch* 216.3, *touch* 216.9, *influence* 508.11, 512.1, *be an influence* 512.13, *use violence* 520.9, *set in motion* 677.16, *divert* 698.16, *traction* 699.1, *attraction* 700.1, *attract* 700.11, *extraction* 711.1
pull [Inf] *indirect influence* 512.4, *authority* 514.5, *allurement* 700.4, *superiority* 744.1
pull a boner *808.18
pull a fast one [Inf] *swindle* 193.19, *be cunning* 822.5
pull a long face *be serious* 278.7
pull an all-nighter [Inf] *learn* 48.23
pull apart *criticize* 440.12, *demolish* 523.12, *unstick* 756.6, *deconstruct* 758.7
pull aside *divert* 698.16
pull at 699.12
pullback *retreat* 680.2
pull back *retreat* 680.17, *restrain* 830.12
pull down *knock down* 523.13, *bring down* 716.14, *flatten* 716.15, *deconstruct* 758.7
pull down [Inf] *gain* 467.15
pull *or* fall down about one's ears *bring down* 716.14
pull down the blind *make dark* 247.10
pulled *removed* 574.9
pulled muscle *joint disease* 114.19
pulled open *open* 583.10
pulled out by the roots *removed* 574.9
puller *towline* 699.5
puller of strings *backstage manipulator* 844.3
pullet *livestock* 16.11, *young bird* 36.17
pulley *simple machine* 14.6, *machine element* 14.8, *hand tool* 103.3
pull faces *gesture* 183.17
pull hair *wrestle* 152.20
pull hard *try hard* 390.7
pull in *miscellaneous automotive terms* 687.14, *arrive* 704.13, *stop at* 704.18
pulling *framing* 132.18, *traction* 699.1, *tractional* 699.7, *attracting* 700.8
pulling back *retreat* 680.2, *traction* 699.1, *tractional* 699.7
pulling down [Inf] *gain* 467.1
pulling linemen *play* 155.8
pulling no punches *emphatic* 200.3
pulling off *nonadhesive* 756.4
pulling out *departure* 705.1, *extraction* 711.1
pulling out by the roots *removal* 574.2
pulling power 700.2; *type of power* 514.6, *traction* 699.1
pulling the goalie *ice hockey tactics* 158.4
pulling the wool over someone's eyes *cunning* 330.3
pulling together *joint operation* 827.4
pulling toward *drawing power* 699.6, *attractive* 699.9
pulling up *removal* 574.2

pull it off *attain one's goal* 845.13
Pullman™ *railroad car* 688.5
pull no punches [Inf] *be concise* 198.5, *emphasize* 200.6, *suppress* 424.9
pull off *unstick* 756.6, *attain one's goal* 845.13
pull off a coup d'état *cause mischief* 507.9
pull off a robbery *steal* 479.14
pull off someone's clothes *make nude* 614.19
pull on *wear* 100.46
pull oneself up *arise* 715.15
pull oneself up by one's bootstraps *attain one's goal* 845.13
pull one's punches [Inf] *be lenient* 423.5
pull-on sweater *sweater* 100.17
pull open *open* 583.15
pullout *retreat* 680.2
pull out *acquiesce* 421.5, *remove* 574.16, *retreat* 680.17, *pull at* 699.12, *withdraw* 705.9, *extract* 711.13, *subtract* 749.6
pull out all the stops *exert oneself* 122.11, *put on a show* 404.28, *be full of vigor* 518.4, *lack restraint* 829.21
pull-out couch *couch* 101.7
pull out of the station *set out* 705.12
pull out the stops *sound* 141.15
pullover *sweater* 100.17
pull rank *disdain* 297.14
pull someone's chestnuts out of the fire *be an instrument* 511.7
pull someone's leg *hoax* 193.20, *be humorous* 277.11, *ridicule* 436.22
pull strings *have authority* 52.13, *manage* 126.10, *be an instrument* 511.7, *influence* 512.11
pull strings or wires *have authority* 52.13
pull the blankets over one's head *shelter* 812.8
pull the plug on [Inf] *cease* 773.20
pull the rug from under one's feet *hinder* 826.15
pull the trigger *fight* 77.35, *hunt* 160.12, *fire* 418.18, *shoot* 696.18
pull the wool over someone's eyes *deceive* 181.14, 193.16, *practice sophistry* 330.11
pull through *be restored* 809.13
pull tight *unite closely* 752.16
pull together *agree with* 462.10, *form an alliance* 735.25, *work together* 827.14
pull to pieces *demolish* 523.12, *deconstruct* 758.7
pull toward *draw in* 699.13, *attract* 700.11
pullulate *procreate* 22.14, *vegetate* 41.21, *grow* 581.17, *produce* 771.34, *crowd* 795.11
pullulating *growing* 581.12
pullulation *procreation* 22.4, *germination* 581.5, *conception* 771.4
pull up *pause* 415.15, *remove* 574.16, *stop* 668.10, *maneuver* 689.14
pull up *arrive* 704.13
pull up by the roots *remove* 574.16, *subtract* 749.6
pull up stakes *quit* 705.10
pull wires *have authority* 52.13, *influence* 512.11

pulmonary *metabolic* 19.24, *respiratory* 558.19
pulmonary artery *internal organ* 19.13
pulmonary edema *climbing dangers* 161.5
pulmonology Medical Specialties 107
pulp *fruit structure* 44.3, *demolish* 523.12, *soften* 543.14, *semiliquid* 561.7, *cheap* 800.16
pulp and paper manufacturing *chemical process industries* 14.26
pulp and paper processes *chemical reaction thermodynamics* 14.29
pulped *destroyed* 523.9
pulper 561.13
pulp fiction *fiction* 139.2
pulpiness 561.9; *compressibility* 543.3, *juiciness* 555.7
pulping 561.11; *steeping* 557.10
pulpit *church interior* 83.9, *sailboat parts and accessories* 150.4, *publicity* 173.7
pulpiteer *religionist* 81.14, *public speaker* 209.5
pulp magazine *magazine* 175.3
pulpousness *pulpiness* 561.9
pulpwood *timber* 43.3
pulpy 561.19; *compressible* 543.9
pulsar *stellar evolution* 7.10
pulsate *drum* 235.10, *be regular* 663.10, *vibrate* 683.13, *shake* 684.24, *resound* 797.21
pulsatile *frequent* 663.6, *vibrating* 683.9
pulsating *resonant* 236.6, *frequent* 663.6, *vibrating* 683.9, *shaky* 684.18, *reverberatory* 797.14
pulsating *regularly* 663.14
pulsating variable *variable star* 7.11
pulsation *drumming* 235.1, *frequency* 661.1, 663.2, *vibration* 683.2, *reverberation* 797.6
pulsative *vibrating* 683.9
pulsatory *frequent* 663.6, *vibrating* 683.9
pulse *wave form* 10.13, *electric current* 10.39, *interact* 10.73, *vegetable* 17.11, 90.33, *tempo* 140.22, *drumming* 235.1, *drum* 235.10, *resonate* 236.9, *electrical power* 514.12, *musical time* 639.7, *be regular* 663.10, *vibration* 683.2, *vibrate* 683.13, *shake* 684.24, *reverberation* 797.6, *resound* 797.21
pulsejet *flyable* 689.12, *means of propulsion* 696.2
pulses *fruits* 44.1
pulse train *wave form* 10.13
pulsimeter *meter* 589.13
pulsing *drumming* 235.6, *vibrating* 683.9, *reverberatory* 797.14
pulsive *impelling* 695.8
pulverable *pulverizable* 553.21
pulverableness *crumbliness* 553.1
pulverizable 553.21
pulverization 553.4; *destroying* 523.2
pulverize 553.26; *demolish* 523.12, *soften* 543.14, *massage* 554.16, *take apart* 753.16, *impair* 808.18
pulverize [Inf] *beat* 695.12
pulverized 553.20; *destroyed* 523.9
pulverizer 553.11
pulverizing *divergence* 776.5
pulverous *powdery* 553.19
pulverulence *powderiness* 553.3
pulverulent *powdery* 553.19, *pulverizable* 553.21

pulvinatus Architectural Elements 134
pumice *eruption* 8.27, *cleaning agent* 111.9, *eraser* 554.7
pumice stone *cleaning agent* 111.9, *eraser* 554.7
pummel *box* 152.19, *beat* 695.12
pummeling *boxing* 152.2, *ramming* 695.3
Pump Constellations 7
pump *windsurf* 150.33, *interrogate* 333.17, *generate power* 514.19, *irrigator* 557.13, *enlarger* 581.8, *swell* 581.15, *draw off* 711.16
pump-action *bolt-action* 78.17, *hunting* 160.11
pump-action firearm *firearm* 78.7
pump-action shotgun *hunting equipment* 160.4
pump a fish *fish* 154.14
pumped *questioned* 333.15, *transportable* 686.7
pumped-up *swelled* 581.10
pumpernickel *bread* 90.10, *brown thing* 256.3
pump full of lead *shoot* 696.18
pump gas *mine coal* 106.18
pumping *windsurfing terms* 150.21, *windsurfing* 150.28, *questioning* 333.2, *transporting* 686.8, *drawing off* 711.4
pumpkin *orange thing* 258.3
pump oil *mine coal* 106.18
pump one's hand *greet* 410.11
pump out *make sparse* 541.5, *void* 709.23, *draw off* 711.16
pump rifle *hunting equipment* 160.4
pumps *shoes* 100.30
pump up *swell* 581.15
pun *literary device* 139.12, *joke* 277.6, *be humorous* 277.11, *equivocation* 380.1, *be equivocal* 380.7
Punch *clown* 138.10
punch *fight* 77.35, *alcoholic drink* 93.9, *hand tool* 103.3, *material* 144.6, *identify* 184.11, *emphasis* 200.1, *type of touch* 216.3, *touch* 216.9, *sweet drink* 222.4, *hit* 418.9, 695.11, *strike* 418.21, *vigor* 518.1, *opener* 292.1, *prototype* 624.2, *blow* 695.5, *sporting hit* 695.6, *impeller* 695.7, *mixed thing* 751.2
Punch-and-Judy show *show* 138.4
punch bowl *drink container* 93.13, *crockery* 578.16
punch cattle *practice livestock farming* 16.20
punched full of holes *holed* 583.12
punched open *open* 583.10
puncheon *wood* 131.3, *vessel* 578.11, General Units 589
puncher *farm worker* 16.15, *boxer* 152.8, *impeller* 695.7
punch full of holes *hole* 583.17
punch in *work* 122.8, *make concave* 635.7, *get in* 704.17
Punchinello *clown* 138.10
punching *wrestling* 152.18, *attacking* 418.14
punch line *ending* 773.10
punch open *open* 583.15
punch out *work* 122.8, *form* 624.9, *withdraw* 705.9
punch-out [Inf] *fight* 422.9
punch-up [Inf] *fight* 422.9
punchy *vigorous* 518.2
punchy [Inf] *emphatic* 200.3

punctilio *ceremonial* 404.11, *etiquette* 406.3
punctilious *ceremonious* 404.23, *formal* 406.6, *duteous* 433.7, *observant* 465.3, *well-ordered* 765.14, *perfectionistic* 805.18
punctiliously *ceremoniously* 404.38, *observantly* 465.6
punctiliousness *formalism* 406.2, *methodicalness* 765.6
punctual *observant* 465.3, *early* 657.8
punctuality *alacrity* 414.3, *earliness* 657.1
punctually *observantly* 465.6, *early* 657.17
punctualness *earliness* 657.1
punctuate 183.20
punctuated 183.15
punctuation *syntax* 5.32
punctuation mark *language sign* 5.33, *linguistic sign* 183.10, *means of connection* 754.4
puncture *deflate* 195.16, *painful injury* 215.3, *inflict pain* 215.10, *opening* 583.1, *hole* 583.17, *infiltrate* 706.13, *technical problem* 826.3
punctured *deflated* 195.12, *injured* 215.5, *holed* 583.12
puncturing *deflation* 195.7
pundit *sage* 4.11, *educator* 48.4, *expert* 52.8, 127.9, *priest* 84.8, *intellectual* 315.7
pung [Can] *snow vehicle* 687.9
pungency *emphasis* 200.1, *piquancy* 221.1, *odor* 224.1
pungent *emphatic* 200.3, *tasty* 219.4, *piquant* 221.6, *acid* 223.5, *odorous* 224.5, *fragrant* 226.4, *strong to the senses* 516.12, *advantaged* 618.7
pungently *tastily* 219.7, *piquantly* 221.10, *sourly* 223.9, *odorously* 224.10, *fragrantly* 226.7, *acutely* 516.18
pungent taste *taste* 219.1
Punic Wars Major Wars 76
puniness *weakness* 517.1, *littleness* 580.1, *thinness* 595.1
punish 454.22; *make illegal* 53.29, *inflict pain* 215.10, *retaliate* 420.4, *be severe* 424.8, *avenge* 441.14, *restrain* 830.12
punishable 454.21; *unjust* 53.24
punishable offense *wicked act* 448.7
punishably *punitively* 454.33
punished 454.19; *restrained* 830.9
punisher 454.16; *killer* 30.11, *avenger* 441.6
punishing 454.20; *laborious* 122.7, *vindictive* 441.10, *punitive* 454.18, *fatiguing* 820.4, *difficult* 824.9
punishing experience *affliction* 454.9
punishingly *vindictively* 441.16, *punitively* 454.33, *arduously* 824.24
punishing work *work* 122.1
punishment 454.1; *unfavorable verdict* 54.20, *pain* 215.1, *Phobias* 283, *retaliation* 420.1, *revenge* 441.4, *restraint* 830.1
punish oneself *appear guilty* 450.10, *do penance* 451.9
punish with death *execute* 454.30
punitive 454.18; *retaliatory* 420.3, *vindictive* 441.10
punitively 454.33; *vindictively* 441.16
punitive tax *tax* 494.5
punitory *punitive* 454.18

punk *fuel starter* 106.3, *musical* 140.25
punk [Inf] *malefactor* 306.6
punkah *cooler* 218.4
punk rock *rock music* 140.6
punk rock band *or* group *instrumental group* 141.3
punnet [Brit] *basket* 578.6
punt *kick* 155.12, 155.20, *soccer play* 163.5, *Ships and Boats* 690, *blow* 695.5
punter *boating person* 150.24, *special team* 155.11, *gambler* 167.6, *nautical person* 690.12
punting *Sporting Activities* 145, *boating sports* 150.1, *rowing* 150.27
puny *weak* 517.6, *undersized* 580.8, *thin* 595.9
pup *have young* 21.16, *young animal* 26.4, *dog* 35.10, *young mammal* 35.20, *give birth* 35.33
pup [Inf] *young man* 26.8
pupa *developmental biology* 13.22, *young animal* 26.4, *larva* 40.9
pupal *developmental* 13.33, *immature* 40.14
pupate *develop* 40.18
pupil *eye* 19.9, 242.3, *learner* 48.6, *beginner* 817.11.14
pupilage *youth* 26.1
pupils *students* 777.6
puppet *toy* 167.9, *figure* 187.4, *sycophant* 401.3, *assistant* 511.3, *national* 566.10, *little thing* 580.3, *insubstantial person* 720.5, *nonentity* 800.8, *subjected person* 832.5
puppeteer *entertainer* 138.8, *backstage manipulator* 844.3
puppet regime *dominion* 566.3
puppetry *show* 138.4
puppet show *show* 138.4
puppies *Collective Names* 59
Puppis *Constellations* 7
puppy *young animal* 26.4, *dog* 35.10, *young mammal* 35.20, *insolent person* 400.7
puppy dog *dog* 35.10
puppyish *carnivorous* 35.26
puppy love *romantic love* 299.2
Purana *other text* 81.19
purblind *visually impaired* 243.9
purblindness *faulty vision* 243.1
purchasable *bought* 481.8
purchase 481.1, 481.10; *expenditure* 491.1, *expend* 491.11, *friction* 699.4, *deliverance* 817.1, *deliver* 817.5
purchase by mail order *buy on credit* 481.12
purchase contract 459.3
purchased *bought* 481.8
purchase loop knot Knots, Bends, Hitches, Splices 754
purchase *or* rental of premises *business expenses* 491.4
purchase on account *or* on credit *or* on the installment plan *purchasing* 481.2
purchase price *cost(s)* 491.3
purchaser 481.7; *possessor* 469.10, *recipient* 473.5, *trader* 480.11, *spender* 491.7
purchases *purchase* 481.1
purchasing 481.2; *buying* 481.9
purchasing power *economic factor* 56.8
purdah *womenfolk* 33.14, *cover* 181.4, *that which makes invisible* 245.2, *separation* 409.3
pure 253.11, 431.11; *of language* 5.35, *theoretical* 10.71, *status adjectives* 11.25, *virginal* 67.7,

religious 81.21, *clean* 111.13, *hygienic* 116.3, *clear* 196.2, *transparent* 249.7, *new* 394.7, *right* 429.7, *principled* 447.6, *innocent* 449.6, *abstinent* 455.7, *strong to the senses* 516.12, *simple* 526.7, *elegant* 527.3, *authentic* 721.16, *uncut* 759.7, *complete* 761.6, *immaculate* 805.11
pure as the driven snow *pure* 431.11, *virtuous* 447.5
purebred *domesticated* 16.18, *horse* 159.1, *equine* 159.15
purée *semiliquid* 561.7
pure heart *naive person* 821.2
purely *celibately* 67.12, *cleanly* 111.20, *clearly* 196.4, *newly* 394.14, *morally* 431.15, *ethically* 447.10, *innocently* 449.13, *with self-restraint* 455.14, *simply* 526.14, *authentically* 721.31, *once* 788.23, *completely* 805.22
pure mathematics *mathematics* 6.1
pure motives *incorruption* 449.2
pure of heart *innocent* 449.6
pure person *chaste person* 431.6
pure-white *white* 253.7
purgation *defecation* 25.3, *cleaning* 111.2, *religious cleansing* 111.3, *penitence* 313.3, *vindication* 441.1, *type of penance* 451.3, *removal* 709.5
purgative 115.7; *fecal* 25.14, *cleaning agent* 111.9, *cleansing* 111.16, *medicinal* 115.15, *apologetic* 313.6, *ejector* 709.10, *expulsive* 709.11
purgatively *apologetically* 313.11
purgatorial *apologetic* 313.6
purgatory *after death* 29.9, *religious cleansing* 111.3, *cleansing* 111.16, *penitence* 313.3, *evil place* 446.6
purge *defecation* 25.3, *defecate* 25.21, *slaughter* 30.5, 30.21, *purify* 111.19, *purgative* 115.7, *medicate* 115.18, *destruction* 186.2, *destroy* 186.10, *vindicate* 441.11, *capital punishment* 454.12, *execute* 454.30, *exterminate* 709.22, *void* 709.23
purged *cleaned* 111.14
purging *cleaning* 111.2, *medicinal* 115.15, *vindication* 441.1, *removal* 709.5
purification *industrial processes* 14.27, *Christian rite* 85.5, *cleaning* 111.2, *religious cleansing* 111.3, *hygiene* 116.1, *type of penance* 451.3, *simplification* 526.6, *obtaining of an extract* 711.7, *improvement* 807.1
purificatory *cleansing* 111.16
purified *cleaned* 111.14, *pure* 431.11
purifier *cleaning agent* 111.9
purify 111.19; *extract* 11.41, *process* 14.50, *practice hygiene* 116.4, *make transparent* 249.12, *make simple* 526.12, *refine* 534.7, *obtain an extract* 711.19, *improve* 807.15
purifying *penitence* 313.3, *apologetic* 313.6
purify oneself *purify* 111.19, *repent* 313.9
Purim *Jewish Holy Days and Seasons* 85
purine base *nucleotide* 12.10
puriri *Trees and Shrubs* 43
purism *Western Art Styles* 133, *diligence* 323.4
purist *diligent* 323.7, *discriminator* 337.6, *obstinate person* 379.4, *strict*

person 424.4, *unadorned* 424.7, *stylist* 537.4, *perfectionist* 805.7
puristic *formal* 406.6, *perfectionistic* 805.18
puristical *perfectionistic* 805.18
puritan *strict person* 424.4, *moralist* 431.8, *moralistic* 431.12, *self-restrained person* 455.5
puritanical *unadorned* 424.7, *abstinent* 455.7
puritanically *plainly* 424.12, *moralistically* 431.16, *with self-restraint* 455.14
puritanism *unadornment* 424.3, *self-righteousness* 431.7, *abstinence* 455.2
purity 253.6, 431.4; *cleanliness* 111.1, *clarity* 196.1, *transparency* 249.1, *hue* 251.4, *newness* 394.2, *rightfulness* 429.1, *virtues* 447.2, *innocence* 449.1, *abstinence* 455.2, *simplicity* 526.1, *elegance* 527.1, *authenticity* 721.7, *immaculateness* 805.2
purity of heart *innocence* 449.1
purl *knit* 130.19, *undercurrent of sound* 233.3, *sound faint* 233.8, *flow* 570.10
purlieu *habitat* 60.1, *region* 564.1
purlieus *near place* 586.3
purling *flowing* 570.7
purloin *take away* 477.18, *steal* 479.14
purloined *stolen* 479.12
purloiner *thief* 479.8
purloining *taking away* 477.5, *stealing* 479.1
purl stitch *knitting* 130.7
purohita *priest* 84.8
purple 262.6; *obscure* 197.2, *empurple* 262.7
purple-blue *purple* 262.6
purple-brown *brown* 256.5
purple color *purpleness* 262.1
purpled *purple* 262.6
purple dye *purple pigment* 262.2
purple foxglove *purple thing* 262.3
purple-fringed orchid *purple thing* 262.3
purple gallinule *purple thing* 262.3
purple grackle *purple thing* 262.3
Purple Heart *US Military Medals* 58, *purple thing* 262.3
purpleheart *purple thing* 262.3
purple heart [Inf] *sedatives* 121.19
purple loosestrife *purple thing* 262.3
purple martin *purple thing* 262.3
purpleness 262.1
purple passage *power of speech* 205.5, *figurative usage* 262.4, *ornament* 532.7
purple passion *purple thing* 262.3
purple patch [Brit] *figurative usage* 262.4
purple pigment 262.2
purple prose *bombast* 194.4, *obscurity* 197.1, *figurative usage* 262.4
purple-red *red* 257.5, *purple* 262.6
purple thing 262.3
purplish *purple* 262.6
purplish-blue *blue* 261.5
purplishness *purpleness* 262.1
purply *purple* 262.6
purport *meaning* 361.1, *mean* 361.13, *significance* 676.4
purportedly *theoretically* 4.24, *apparently* 720.19
purporting *symbolic* 361.8
purpose 327.4; *motive* 178.5, 628.6, *point* 361.5, *intend* 361.15,

374.8, *will* 372.1, *intention* 374.1, *declaration* 376.2, *resolve* 376.12, *usefulness* 393.2, 801.1, *motivation* 508.1, *reason* 675.4, *undertaking* 675.5, *aim* 773.12
purposed *intentional* 374.7
purposeful *earnest* 278.5, *willed* 372.6, *iron-willed* 372.7, *intentional* 374.7, *resolute* 376.7, *planning* 387.11
purposefully *earnestly* 278.10, *intentionally* 374.13, *resolutely* 376.15, *as planned* 387.16
purposefulness *resolution* 376.1
purposeless *aimless* 362.8, *erratic* 381.5, *futile* 802.10, *causeless* 842.11
purposelessly *meaninglessly* 362.13
purposelessness *aimlessness* 362.3, 362.6, *capriciousness* 381.2, *futility* 802.3, *lack of motive* 842.2
purposely *intentionally* 374.13
purposive 327.11; *intending* 374.6
purposively 327.20; *prospectively* 374.12
purpure *Heraldic Terms* 184, *purple* 262.6
purr *feel pleasure* 214.12, *undercurrent of sound* 233.3, *sound faint* 233.8, *humming* 235.2, *hum* 235.11, *animal sound* 240.1, *make an animal sound* 240.7, *show joy* 269.10, *be satisfied* 273.8
purring *nonresonant* 233.7, *ululant* 240.4
purse *funds* 484.6, *money storage* 484.20, *bag* 578.7, *contract* 582.12
pursed *shortened* 582.8
pursed lips *gesture* 183.5
purse one's lips *gesture* 183.17
purse-proud *arrogant* 297.9
purser *treasurer* 484.18, *payer* 489.9, *accountant* 493.6, *aircraft personnel* 689.8
purse snatcher *thief* 479.8
purse snatching *stealing* 479.1
purse strings *authority* 52.1, *finance* 457.1
pursing *shortening* 582.2, *contracting* 582.10
pursuance *constancy* 377.3, *pursuit* 385.1
pursuant *pursuer* 385.5, *pursuing* 385.8
pursuant to 385.17; *with the intention of* 374.14
pursue 377.11, 385.11; *lust after* 288.20, *court* 299.26, *question* 333.16, *conduct oneself* 399.17, *occupy oneself* 412.15, *protract* 669.9, *specialize* 779.16
pursued 385.10
pursue one's course *protract* 669.9
pursue one's ends *aim at* 385.15
pursue one's goals *aim at* 385.15
pursue one's interest *aim at* 385.15
pursue one's interests *be selfish* 444.6
pursuer 385.5; *litigant* 54.4, *lover* 299.11
pursuing 385.8; *pursuit* 385.1, *directional* 677.13
pursuit 385.1; *courtship* 299.10, *future intention* 374.3, *chase* 385.2, *social activity* 414.2, *backward motion* 677.5, *specialization* 779.3
pursuit fighter *military aircraft* 77.30
purulence *pus* 25.7, *lack of hygiene*

112.3, *infection* 114.7, *ulcer* 114.18, *body fluid* 555.3
purulent 25.16; *of disease* 114.25, *toxic* 114.28, *rheumy* 555.16
purulently *fluidly* 555.26
Purus Rivers 570
purvey *provision* 89.9, *feed* 90.41
purveyance *provision* 89.1
purveying *provisioning* 89.2
purveyor *caterer* 89.5
purview *future intention* 374.3
pus 25.7; *body fluid* 19.16, 555.3, *dirt* 112.5, *ulcer* 114.18, *mucus* 561.6
push 414.20, 696.16; *exertion* 122.4, *work* 122.8, *field hockey tactics* 158.5, *play field hockey* 158.10, *play soccer* 163.8, *swim* 164.14, *publicize* 173.18, *gesture* 183.5, 183.17, *type of touch* 216.3, *energy* 414.4, *military attack* 418.2, *attack* 418.17, *strike* 418.21, *trade* 480.18, *sell* 482.15, *manipulate* 508.12, *vigor* 514.2, *be full of vigor* 518.4, *set in motion* 677.16, *press on* 679.9, *further* 679.13, *convey* 685.9, *blow* 695.5, *impel* 695.9, *propulsion* 696.1, *propel* 696.5, *spread* 746.3, *haste* 818.1, *hasten* 818.4
push, the [Brit] *expulsion* 709.1, *ejection* 764.2
push around *impel* 695.9
push aside *divert* 698.16
push away *repel* 701.7
push back *repel* 701.7
push button *dial* 169.12
push-button *practical* 511.6
push-button telephone *telephone* 169.10
push-button war *warfare* 76.3
pushcart *stall* 483.9, *cart* 578.9, *wagon* 687.5
push down *maneuver* 689.14, *bear down on* 716.18
pushed *soccer* 163.7
pushed (for money) *insolvent* 486.10
pushed open *open* 583.10
pushed through *hasty* 818.3
pusher *drug pusher* 121.13, *busy person* 414.10, *impeller* 695.7
push forward *hasten* 818.4
push hard *try hard* 390.7
pushily [Inf] *audaciously* 400.20
push in *impact* 710.11
push-in *field hockey tactics* 158.5
pushiness [Inf] *audacity* 400.3
pushing *framing* 132.18, *soccer play* 163.5, *soccer* 163.7, *gestural* 183.13, *active* 414.13, *propulsion* 696.1, *propulsive* 696.12, *hasty* 818.3
pushing down *submergence* 716.3
pushing power *type of power* 514.6
pushing under *submergence* 716.3
pushing up daisies [Inf] *buried* 31.8
push in the right direction *direct* 697.13
push into *motivate* 178.17
push inward *make concave* 635.7
push off *navigate* 690.15, *set out* 705.12
push off [Inf] *depart* 705.8, *go!* 709.30
push on *press on* 679.9
push oneself forward *show off* 402.15
push one's way *follow up* 385.16
push on with *do something* 412.13
push open *open* 583.15
push out *drive out* 709.19

pushover *canoeing* 150.26
pushover [Inf] *easy question* 333.5, *submitter* 421.2, *powerless person* 515.5, *weak person* 517.4, *victory* 845.4
pushover stroke *canoeing techniques* 150.11
pushpin *fastener* 754.7
push start *miscellaneous automotive terms* 687.14
push stroke *field hockey tactics* 158.5
push to extremes *be resolute* 376.11
push to the wall *cause difficulties* 824.22
push up *bargain* 480.20, *spring up* 713.22
push up daisies [Inf] *die* 29.17
pushy [Inf] *audacious* 400.10, *meddling* 414.17, *vigorous* 518.2
pusillanimity *cowardice* 285.1, *indecisiveness* 517.2
pusillanimous *cowardly* 285.4, *weak-willed* 517.10
pusillanimously *cowardly* 285.9
puss *cat* 35.11
puss [Inf] *face* 621.6
pussiness *pus* 25.7
pussy *fluid* 19.25, *purulent* 25.16, *cat* 35.11, *toxic* 114.28, *rheumy* 555.16, *thick* 561.17
pussy [Inf] *organs of reproduction* 21.9
pussycat *cat* 35.11
pussyfoot *conceal oneself* 181.15, *proceed with caution* 287.12, *quibble* 330.13, *be equivocal* 380.7, *be evasive* 386.20
pussyfoot (around) *submit* 421.4
pussyfooter *sophist* 330.6
pussyfooting *quibbling* 330.4, 330.9, *evasiveness* 386.6
pussy willow Trees and Shrubs 43
pustulant *marked* 533.6
pustular *marked* 533.6
pustulate *blemish* 533.7
pustulation *mark* 533.2
pustule *skin disease* 114.16, *mark* 533.2
put *interpret* 365.12, *styled* 537.6, *style* 537.8, *locate* 565.9, *situate* 573.10, *throw* 696.4
put a ball and chain on *restrain someone* 830.17
put about *publish* 173.15, *navigate* 690.15
put a case *propound* 359.9
put a cast on *treat* 115.17
put a construction on *interpret* 365.12
put a crimp in *hinder* 826.15
put across *make comprehensible* 363.8
put across one's knee *hit* 454.28
put a curse or *spell* or *hex on* *curse* 301.13
put a damper on *calm* 521.8, *restrain* 830.12
put a flea in one's ear [Inf] *condemn* 438.18
put ahead *further* 679.13
put a lid on *make invisible* 245.7, *cover* 613.24, *bear down on* 716.18
put all one's eggs in one basket *figurative expressions* 128.11
put a mark on *identify* 184.11
put a match to *fuel* 106.16, *burn* 217.18
put among *subsume* 763.7
put an edge on *sharpen* 549.16
put an embargo on *exclude* 764.7
put an end to *destroy* 523.10, *make transient* 643.7, *cease*

773.20, *discontinue* 775.10, *not exist* 786.6
put an end to one's life *commit suicide* 30.24
put a new lease on life *invigorate* 28.22
put an idea into someone's head *propound* 359.9
put another way *mean* 361.13
put a plaster on *cure* 809.15
put a point on *sharpen* 549.16
put aside *saved* 105.15, *save* 105.20, *stop using* 394.10, *take away* 685.12, *set apart* 753.17, *exclude* 764.7
put aside for *intend for* 374.11
put a stop to *be severe* 424.8, *be self-restrained* 455.10, *limit* 620.7, *cause to cease* 668.12, *make motionless* 678.8, *cease* 773.20, *restrain* 830.12
put asunder *divorce* 66.9, *come between* 753.21
put a tax on *charge* 494.13
putative *believed* 87.8, *theoretical* 327.10, 720.10, *supposed* 359.6
putatively *theoretically* 327.19, *apparently* 720.19
put a toe in the water *proceed with caution* 287.12
put at rest *make stable* 674.7
put at risk *endanger* 811.13
put away *imprison* 55.11, 454.23, *divorce* 66.9, *eat well* 92.23, *save* 105.20, *certify* 110.14, *destroy* 523.10, *repel* 701.7
put a wet blanket on *cause sorrow* 270.9
put a whammy or **double whammy on** [Inf] *curse* 301.13
put a wrong construction on *misinterpret* 366.4
put back *reverse* 680.18, *restore* 809.12
put back into operation *repair* 809.10
put back together *put together* 59.30, *repair* 809.10
put behind bars *imprison* 55.11
put between *insert* 710.9, *interrupt* 775.14
put body into *strengthen oneself* 516.16
put by for a rainy day *expect* 650.12
put down *kill* 30.19, *kill animals* 30.25, *inscribe* 185.14, *deride* 369.7, *pay* 489.16, *lower* 716.12, *debase* 716.16, *list* 785.11, *restrain* 830.12, *be victorious* 845.16
put down [Inf] *abase* 298.20, *insult* 436.21, *disparage* 440.11, *make unimportant* 800.20
put-down [Inf] *abasement* 298.6, *form of derision* 369.2, *insult* 436.5
put down for hearing *try a case* 54.28
put down one's gun *make peace* 73.11
put dynamite or *a bomb under* [Inf] *hurry someone up* 694.15
put English on the ball *play* 149.7
put first *give priority* 769.15
put forth *set out* 705.12
put forth or **forward** *propound* 359.9
put forth every effort *go to any length* 590.13
put forward *propound a philosophy* 4.21, *contend* 189.24, *present* 264.15, *demonstrate* 331.15, *volunteer* 373.14, *propound* 359.9, *further* 679.13

put forward an argument *dissertate* 203.5
put forward (a suggestion) *raise the point* 328.10
put heads together *consult* 176.11, *chat* 210.12, *negotiate* 460.6, *come together* 757.10, *work together* 827.14
put heart into *invigorate* 518.5
put in *cultivate* 17.19, *situate* 573.10, *stop at* 704.18, *enter* 706.11, *insert* 710.9, *subsume* 763.7
put in a claim *demand* 505.12
put in a container *contain* 578.20
put in a false light *misrepresent* 188.6
put in a good word for *recommend* 437.19
put in an appearance *appear* 244.8, 575.16
put in a nutshell *be concise* 198.5
put in a safe place *protect* 810.21
put in bold or *high relief display* 843.13
put in bondage *detain* 830.16
put in bright lights *make important* 799.14
put in capital letters *make important* 799.14
put in check *be victorious* 845.16
put in clauses *make conditions* 460.7
put in cold storage *delay* 658.13
put in commission *prepare for action* 388.18, *authorize* 833.10
put in contact with *link* 752.18
put in context *circumstantiate* 726.12, *relate to* 727.9
put in danger *endanger* 811.13
put in detention *imprison* 454.23
put in double jeopardy *endanger* 811.13
put in escrow *save* 105.20
put in front *further* 679.13
put in front of a firing squad *execute* 454.30
put in inverted order *invert* 608.7
put in italics *emphasize* 200.6
put in jail *imprison* 55.11
put in jeopardy *endanger* 811.13
put in limbo *stop using* 394.10
put in mothballs *save* 105.20, *stop using* 394.10
put in motion *start* 696.20
put in one's defense *stand trial* 54.29
put in one's hands *commission* 833.8
put in one's oar *interrupt* 775.14
put in one's will *transfer property* 470.12
put in order *order* 765.18, *arrange* 767.18, *categorize* 767.21, *repair* 809.10
put in place *locate* 565.9
put in place of *substitute* 672.5
put in plain words *make comprehensible* 363.8
put in possession *own property* 470.11, *transfer property* 470.12
put in quarantine *practice hygiene* 116.4
put in quotes *punctuate* 183.20
put in readiness *prepare for action* 388.18
put in solitary [Inf] *imprison* 55.11
put in solitary confinement *imprison* 55.11
put in splints *treat* 115.17
put in the clear *vindicate* 441.11
put in the dock *accuse* 442.8

put in the gas chamber *execute* 454.30

put in the headlines *publicize* 173.18

put in the hope chest *save* 105.20

put in the kitty *deposit* 105.21

put in the middle *center* 612.10

put in the minutes *record* 185.13

put in the picture [Inf] *inform* 170.11

put in the shade *make dark* 247.10

put in the slot *insert* 710.9

put in the stocks *punish* 454.22

put in the wrong place *misplace* 574.20

put in time *spend time* 639.14

put into *translate* 365.16, *enter* 706.11

put into a rage *make angry* 302.18

put into circulation *disperse* 776.12

put into disorder *disorder* 625.4

put into effect *behave toward* 399.20

put into operation *use* 393.9

put into port *land* 704.16

put into practice *use* 393.9, *behave toward* 399.20, *do something* 412.13

put into quarantine *detain* 830.16

put into shape *form* 624.9, *arrange* 767.18

put into storage *save* 105.20

put into the hands of *give* 472.10

put in touch *link* 752.18

put into use *do something* 412.13

put into words *word* 5.43, *speak* 205.17, *form* 624.9

put in working order *prepare for action* 388.18, *repair* 809.10

put it bluntly *be assertive* 189.28, *be concise* 198.5

put it on *put on airs* 404.27

put life into *strengthen oneself* 516.16, *invigorate* 518.5

put money up front *pay* 489.16

put new life into *invigorate* 28.22

put new wine into old bottles *figurative expressions* 128.11

put off 179.10; *dissuaded* 179.5, *displease* 272.8, *antipathetic* 291.7, *cause dislike* 291.16, *delay* 375.16, 378.9, 658.13, *procrastinate* 413.12, *change* 512.12, *deferred* 604.9, *defer* 604.15, *fend off* 701.9, *not complete* 762.9, *disrupt* 768.12

put off a decision *be irresolute* 378.9

put off the scent *deodorize* 225.6, *misdirect* 698.21

put off till tomorrow *be irresolute* 378.9, *be neglectful* 326.7

put on *wear* 100.46, *dramatize* 136.33, *raise* 715.9, *display* 843.13

put-on *artificial* 720.12

put-on [Inf] *hoax* 193.7

put on a brave or **bold face** *take courage* 284.15

put on a business footing *trade* 480.18

put on a false face *be untruthful* 192.20

put on a front *be untruthful* 192.20, *be in front* 621.13

put on airs 404.27; *disdain* 297.14, *be affected* 367.4, *show off* 402.15

put on alert *prepare for action* 388.18

put on a light *light* 246.19

put on an act *deceive* 330.12

put on a pedestal *idolize* 83.16, *revere* 435.14, *exalt* 596.19, *promote* 715.13

put on a shelf *defer* 604.15

put on a show 404.28; *entertain* 138.16

put on a spurt *be full of vigor* 518.4

put on a uniform *join the army* 76.31

put on a war footing *arm* 76.30

put on blinkers *prejudge* 337.13

put on display *make visible* 244.9, *display* 843.13

put one in mind *warn* 814.8

put one in mind of *seem like* 733.14

put one over *be cunning* 822.5

put one's back into it *exert oneself* 122.11, *strengthen oneself* 516.16

put one's back up *cause dislike* 291.16

put one's best foot forward *exert oneself* 122.11, *undertake* 391.7

put one's cards on the table *divulge* 180.9, *show oneself* 843.15

put one's case *plead* 329.14

put one's cross on *identify oneself* 184.12

put oneself at someone's service *obey* 426.7

put oneself between *mediate* 75.6

put oneself first *be selfish* 444.6, *indulge oneself* 456.10

put oneself forward *show off* 404.26

put oneself in a spot *be in difficulty* 824.19

put oneself in the firing line *volunteer* 373.14

put oneself last *be unselfish* 443.7

put oneself out *exert oneself* 122.11

put one's faith in *believe* 87.9

put one's feet up *be neglectful* 326.7, *take it easy* 819.3, *do easily* 823.16

put one's fingers in one's ears *muffle* 229.11

put one's foot down *insist* 376.14, *be severe* 424.8, *demand* 425.11, *show determination* 674.8

put one's foot in it [Inf] *be unskillful* 128.8, *be clumsy* 128.9, *get into trouble* 824.20

put one's foot in one's mouth [Inf] *be clumsy* 128.9

put one's hand in one's pocket *give to charity* 472.16

put one's hands together *acclaim* 437.18

put one's hand to *identify oneself* 184.12, *undertake* 391.7

put one's hand to the plow *make a beginning* 771.26

put one's hand to the tiller *try* 414.21

put one's head in the lion's mouth *be in danger* 811.11, *face danger* 811.12

put one's head in the oven *commit suicide* 30.24

put one's heart and soul into it *exert oneself* 122.11

put one's house in order *prepare oneself* 388.21

put one's mark on *identify oneself* 184.12

put one's mark upon *characterize* 779.15

put one's mind to *try* 414.21

put one's money to work *finance* 457.7, *speculate* 480.19

put one's oar in *meddle* 414.23

put one's pride in one's pocket *humble oneself* 298.18

put one's shoulder to the wheel *try* 414.21

put one's signature to *sign* 183.19

put one's two cents in *meddle* 414.23

put one to sleep *bore* 296.8

put one under the table *be intoxicating* 121.36

put on guard *caution* 287.15

put on hold *defer* 604.15, *delay* 658.13

put on ice [Inf] *delay* 658.13

put on layaway *intend for* 374.11, *acquire credit* 487.11

put on one's boxing gloves *fight* 77.35

put on one's calendar *behave toward* 399.20

put on one's face *beautify* 530.14

put on one's feet *finance* 825.31

put on one's guard *warn* 814.8

put on one side *shove aside* 698.23, *subtract* 749.6

put on one's robe and slippers *take it easy* 819.3

put on paper *design* 133.9, *inscribe* 185.14

put on parole *liberate* 831.6

put on record *record* 185.13

put on sale *sell* 482.15

put on show *display* 843.13

put on speed *accelerate* 694.14

put on the agenda *raise the point* 328.10, *propound* 359.9, *list* 785.11

put on the air *broadcast* 172.13

put on the airwaves *broadcast* 172.13

put on the back burner *delay* 375.16, 658.13

put on the brake *stop* 668.10

put on the cuff [Inf] *buy on credit* 476.13

put on the drag *slow down* 693.13

put on the feedbag [Inf] *eat well* 92.23

put on the finishing touch *perfect* 805.19

put on the Index *censor* 503.10

put on the list *register* 185.15

put on the map *publicize* 173.18, *make important* 799.14

put on the rack *torture* 454.29

put on the right track *direct* 697.13

put on the ritz [Inf] *put on airs* 404.27

put on the scales *weigh* 538.15

put on the shelf *stop using* 394.10

put on the sick list *treat* 115.17

put on trial *litigate* 54.27, *experiment* 335.11, *accuse* 442.8

put on view *make visible* 244.9, *display* 843.13

put on weight *increase* 467.17, 746.6, *be heavy* 538.12, *grow* 581.17, *fatten* 594.10

put on widow's weeds *be widowed* 66.13

put others first *be humble* 298.16

put out *publish* 173.15, 174.19, *humiliate* 298.19, *resentful* 302.8, *irritate* 302.16, *destroy* 523.10, *expel* 709.14, *evict* 709.20, *disrupt* 768.12, *be inconvenient* 804.9,

troubled 824.15, *cause difficulties* 824.22

put-out *other game terms* 147.7

put out a contract on [Inf] *contract* 459.8

put out a feeler *test* 390.9, *offer* 504.11

put out bag and baggage *evict* 709.20

put out of action *overpower* 515.14, *impair* 808.18

put out of bounds *prohibit* 503.8

put out of commission *stop using* 394.10, *overpower* 515.14, *make useless* 802.12

put out of countenance *humiliate* 298.19

put out of gear *disarrange* 768.11

put out of joint *disconnect* 574.19

put out of kilter *distort* 627.9

put out of mind *be inattentive* 324.10

put out of one's misery *kill* 30.19, *show pity* 308.8, *destroy* 523.10

put out of reach *make impossible* 837.8

put out of sight *make invisible* 245.7

put outside the law *prohibit* 503.8

put out the bunting *salute* 435.17

put out the fire *conciliate* 74.10

put out the welcome mat *be sociable* 408.14

put out to grass *eat grass* 45.11

put out to pasture *eat grass* 45.11, *feed* 90.41

put paid to [Brit inf] *cease* 773.20

put pressure on *compel* 428.8, *influence* 512.11

putrefaction *uncleanness* 112.2, *unpleasant-smelling thing* 227.2, *physical deterioration* 808.4

putrefy *mold* 47.22, *be dirty* 112.10, *decay* 808.16

putrescence *uncleanness* 112.2, *unpleasant-smelling thing* 227.2

putrescent *putrid* 227.4

putrid 227.4

put right 429.14; *remedy* 115.16, *inform* 170.11, *put right* 429.14, *direct* 697.13, *compensate* 743.7, *rectify* 807.22, *repaired* 809.6, *repair* 809.10

put rudder on *divert* 698.16

putsch *revolution* 427.4, *disorder* 507.2

put someone in a bad mood *make irritable* 304.15

put someone in a melancholy mood *make sullen* 304.13

put someone in fear of his or **her life** *endanger* 811.13

put someone in his or **her place** *abase* 298.20

put someone's eyes out *blind* 243.17

put someone's mind at rest *comfort* 273.9

put someone's nose out of joint *offend* 302.15, *arouse jealousy* 314.10

put something aside *be prepared* 388.17

put something in the pot *give out* 472.12

put store by *make important* 799.14

put straight *compensate* 743.7

putt *golf shots* 156.4, *play* 156.8

puttees *legwear* 100.26

putter *golf equipment* 156.5, *golfer* 156.7, *walk* 677.17

puttering *restlessness* 414.7, *busy* 414.15, *slow motion* 677.9, *directional* 677.13

put that in your pipe and smoke it! *revenge!* 420.7

put the bite on [Inf] *demand* 505.12

put the brakes on *restrain* 830.12

put the cart before the horse *figurative expressions* 128.11, *invert* 608.7

put the clock back *recollect* 3.16, *keep time* 646.12, *look back* 651.18

put the clock forward *keep time* 646.12

put the color back in one's cheeks *make healthy* 113.13

put the evil eye on *bewitch* 86.25, *cause adversity* 848.15

put the fear of God into *frighten* 283.17

put the finger on [Inf] *sign* 183.19, *accuse* 442.8

put the finishing touches to *augment* 748.13, *complete* 759.10, 761.9

put the flags out *welcome* 708.14

put the frosting or icing on the cake *complete* 759.10, 761.9

put the hammer down [Inf] *be swift* 694.10

put the helm down *navigate* 690.15

put the jinx on *cause adversity* 848.15

put the kibosh on [Inf] *overpower* 515.14, *ruin* 523.15, *cease* 773.20

put the lid on [Inf] *silence* 231.4, *close* 584.12, *limit* 830.13

put the phone down *stop* 668.10

put the screws on *motivate* 178.17, *suppress* 424.9, *force* 428.10

put the skids under [Inf] *ruin* 523.15, *cause adversity* 848.15

put the squeeze on *solicit money* 505.13

put the squeeze on someone *demand* 505.12

put the touch on [Inf] *solicit money* 505.13

put the whammy or double whammy on [Inf] *make evil* 446.11, *cause adversity* 848.15

put through the mill [Inf] *interrogate* 333.17

put through to *link* 752.18

putti Architectural Elements 134

putting aside *setting apart* 753.2

putting back *restoration* 809.2

putting down *restraint* 830.1

putting down [Inf] *disparagement* 440.1

putting green *golf course* 156.2, *green thing* 260.4

putting heads together *place for conversation* 210.5

putting in cold storage *delay* 658.3

putting in mint condition *repair* 809.1

putting in order *order* 765.1, *arrangement* 767.1

putting into effect *action* 412.1

putting off *delay* 658.3

putting off till tomorrow *delay* 375.6, *do-nothingism* 413.6

putting on *production* 136.14

putting on airs *affectation* 367.1, *cocky* 402.11

putting on hold *delay* 658.3

putting on ice [Inf] *delay* 658.3

putting on the back burner *delay* 375.6, 658.3

putting out of joint *disconnection* 574.5

putting right *rectification* 807.8, *repair* 809.1

putting together *construction* 59.16

putto Architectural Elements 134

put to *advise* 176.9

put to a lot of trouble *cause difficulties* 824.22

put to auction *auction* 482.16

put to bad use *misuse* 395.6

put to bed *treat* 115.17

put to death *execute* 30.22, 454.30

put to flight *propel* 696.15, *disband* 776.13, *defeat* 845.17, *defeated* 846.11

put together 59.30; *collected* 59.19, *prepare for action* 388.18, *produce* 522.13, *assemble* 551.23, *embody* 577.11, *unite* 752.14, *combine* 757.9

put-together *united* 752.10

put to good use *exploit* 393.11

put to inconvenience *be inconvenient* 804.9

put to it *cause difficulties* 824.22

put to rights *tidy* 765.21

put to sea *navigate* 690.15, *set out* 705.12

put to shame *humiliate* 298.19, *bring into disrepute* 371.6, *dishonor* 436.20

put to silence *silence* 231.4

put to sleep *kill* 30.19, *kill animals* 30.25, *anesthetize* 213.8

put to or on the block *auction* 482.16

put to the sword *murder* 30.20, *slaughter* 30.21, *be at war* 76.32, *suppress* 424.9, *lay waste* 523.14

put to the test *or proof experiment* 335.11

put to torture *torture* 454.29

put to trouble *be inconvenient* 804.9

put to use *used* 393.5, *use* 393.9

put to work *work for* 122.10

putty *paste* 561.4, *adhesive* 755.3

putty in one's hands *persuadability* 178.8

puttylike *unsteady* 378.7, *pliant* 543.7

Putumayo Rivers 570

put under *anesthetize* 213.8

put under an obligation *impose a duty* 433.14

put under arrest *arrest* 55.12, *detain* 830.16

put under duress *compel* 428.8

put under oath *attest* 189.22

put under security *imprison* 55.11

put under wraps *make invisible* 245.7

put up *select* 382.12, *construct* 551.22, *suspend* 604.13, *erect* 715.11

put-up [Inf] *predetermined* 384.4, *perjurious* 442.7

put up a brave front *resist* 417.10

put up a fight *contend* 422.22

put up a front *deceive* 330.12, *put on airs* 404.27

put up at *take up residence* 60.24

put up collateral *own property* 470.11

put up for sale *sell* 482.15, *offer* 504.11

put-up job [Inf] *predetermination* 384.1, *plot* 387.6, *false accusation* 442.2

put up money *defray* 489.18

put upon *augment* 748.13

put up one's sword *make peace* 73.11

put up one's umbrella *shelter* 812.8

put up prices *overcharge* 496.10

put up the shutters *stop work* 668.11

put up to *manipulate* 508.12

put up with *show mercy* 312.11, *assent to* 346.7, *succumb* 421.7, *agree with* 462.10, *bear* 605.17, *take a substitute* 672.7

puzzle 182.5, 364.12; *mystery* 182.4, *puzzle* 182.5, *mystify* 182.12, *obscure* 522.13, *assemble* 294.2, *wonderful person* 294.6, *be wondrous* 294.14, *question* 333.1, *confuse* 333.20, *not understand* 362.11, *unintelligible thing* 364.3, *find unintelligible* 364.14, *mix up* 751.13, *problem* 824.4, *cause difficulties* 824.22, *make uncertain* 841.19

puzzled *wondering* 294.7, *confused* 364.10, 841.11, *mixed up* 751.11, *troubled* 824.15

puzzledly *speculatively* 294.17

puzzlement *speculation* 294.2, *curiosity* 333.8, *confusion* 841.4

puzzle out *decipher* 365.13

puzzle over *be mixed up* 751.15

puzzler *unintelligible thing* 364.3

puzzling *mysterious* 182.10, *astonishing* 294.10, *problematic* 333.12, 824.11, *difficult* 364.8, *confused* 841.11

puzzlingly *astonishingly* 294.19, *questionably* 333.22, *confusingly* 841.23

P wave *seismic wave* 8.25

pycnogonid *insect* 39.9

Pycnogonida *insect* 39.9

pye-dog *dog* 35.10

pyelogram *diagnostic radiology* 107.12

pyelography *diagnostic radiology* 107.12

pyemia *infection* 114.7

Pygmalion Famous Lovers 299

pygmy *little person* 580.5, *undersized* 580.8

Pylades Notable Friendships 62

pylon *electricity* 106.5, *power supplier* 514.14, *vertical* 602.3

pyloric *of a secretion* 24.5

Pyongyang Countries 566

Pyramid Lakes 568

pyramid *polyhedron* 6.44, *burial place* 31.7, *monument* 185.10, *sharp-pointed thing* 549.4, *building* 551.9, *angled figure* 628.3, *thing of the past* 651.8

pyramidal *cubic* 6.81, *sharp* 549.10, *angled* 628.9, *convergent* 702.7

pyramidologist *occultist* 86.13

pyramidology *occultism* 86.1

Pyramids of Egypt Seven Wonders of the Ancient World 294

Pyramus Famous Lovers 299

pyranose *saccharide* 12.4

pyre *cremation* 31.2, *place for fire* 217.9

Pyrenean Breeds of Cattle 16

Pyrenees Mountains and Hills 569

pyrenoid *plant body* 47.13

pyrethrum *pest killer* 17.9

pyretic *of disease* 114.25

pyrexia *symptom* 114.3, *heat* 217.1

pyrexiophobia Phobias 283

pyridoxal phosphate *coenzyme* 12.12

pyrimidine base *nucleotide* 12.10

Pyriphlegethon *evil place* 446.6

pyroclastic *types of igneous texture* 8.33, *volcanic* 8.57, *petrographic* 8.58

pyroclastic material *eruption* 8.27

pyrogenic *on fire* 217.16

pyroglaze *make ceramics* 129.10

pyroglazer *ceramist* 129.7

pyrograph *woodworking* 131.1

pyrographer *woodworker* 131.4

pyrographic(al) *woodcrafted* 131.7

pyrography *woodworking* 131.1, *decorative method* 532.3

pyrogravure *woodworking* 131.1

pyrolater *idolater* 83.7

pyrolatrous *idolatrous* 83.13

pyrolatry *idolatry* 83.4

pyroligneous acid Tree Products 43

pyrolysis *chemical reaction* 11.8

pyrolyze *react* 11.38

pyromancer *diviner* 86.14

pyromancy *divination* 86.5

pyromania *impulse-control disorder* 108.16, *cause of fire* 217.10

pyromaniac *cause of fire* 217.10, *violent animal* 520.4, *destroyer* 523.6

pyrometallurgy *metallurgy* 11.22

pyrometer *ceramic workshop and tools* 129.8, Fields of Measurement 589

pyrometric(al) *ceramic* 129.9

pyrometrically *ornamentally* 129.11

pyrometric cone *ceramic workshop and tools* 129.8

pyrometry *temperature* 10.29, *microscopy* 10.68, Fields of Measurement 589

pyrophobia Phobias 283

pyrophoric alloy *fire* 246.9

pyrophosphate *coenzyme* 12.12

pyrophosphate (PP$_i$) *bioenergetics* 12.23

pyrosis *gastroenterological disease* 114.11

pyrotechnics *fire* 246.9, *show* 404.12

pyrrhic *meter* 139.10

Pyrrhic victory *victory* 845.4

Pyrrhonism Philosophical Schools of Thought 4, *uncertainty* 333.6

Pyrrhonist Philosophical Schools of Thought 4, *skeptical* 333.14

Pythagorean Philosophical Schools of Thought 4

Pythagoreanism Philosophical Schools of Thought 4

Pythagorean theorem Mathematical Concepts 6

Pythia *diviner* 86.14

Pythian oracle *diviner* 86.14

Pythias Notable Friendships 62

python *snake* 37.6

pythoness *diviner* 86.14

pythonism *divination* 86.5

pythonist *diviner* 86.14

pyx *sacred object* 83.11

pyxidium *botanical fruit* 44.2

Pyxis Constellations 7

Q

qadi *imam* 84.7

qasisha *imam* 84.7

Qatar Countries 566

quarters *habitation* 60.2
quarterstaff *blunt weapon* 78.5, *fencing* 153.1, *duel* 422.12
quartet *instrumental group* 141.3, *four* 791.1, *team* 827.7
quartz *hard substance* 542.3
quartz clock Timepieces and Timers 646
quartz glass *glass* 249.5
quartz-iodine light *electric light* 246.6
quartz watch Timepieces and Timers 646
quasar *star* 7.8
quash *acquit* 54.32, *refute* 332.7, *abolish* 523.11, *restrain* 830.12, *cancel* 834.6
quashing *favorable verdict* 54.19, *restraint* 830.1
quashing of the charge *vindication* 441.1
quash the conviction *acquit* 54.32
quasi Musical Terms and Expression Marks 140
quasi *supposed* 359.6, *artificial* 720.12, *similar* 733.7
quasi-stellar radio source *star* 7.8
quassia Trees and Shrubs 43
quatercentenary *hundreds* 792.9
quaternary *four* 791.7
quaternary base *base* 11.11
Quaternary Period Geologic Time Intervals 8
quaternary structure *protein* 12.9
quaternity *four* 791.1
quatrain *part of poem* 139.9, *foursome* 791.3
quatre *four* 791.1
quatrefoil Architectural Elements 134, *foursome* 791.3
quattrocento architecture Architectural Styles 134
quattuordecillion *million* 792.11
quaver *notation* 140.20, *sing* 141.16, *shake* 684.24
quavering *shaking* 684.6, *shaky* 684.18
quavery *shaky* 684.18
quay *marketplace* 483.7, *water system* 551.13, *harbor* 812.6
quean *sexually immoral person* 432.8
queasiness *symptom* 114.3, *drunken behavior* 121.4
queasy *sick* 114.24
queasy stomach *symptom* 114.3
Québec Canadian Provinces 564
quebracho Trees and Shrubs 43
queen *cat* 35.11, *female mammal* 35.19, *social insect* 40.6, *person in authority* 52.7, *sovereign* 68.2, *board games* 167.3, *play* 167.12, *cards* 168.2, *important person* 799.5
queen [Inf and Off] *homosexual* 32.9
Queen Anne Furniture Styles 101
Queen Anne's lace Flowers 42
Queen Anne style Architectural Styles 134
queen bee *female animal* 33.15, *social insect* 40.6, *company leader* 68.8, *influential person* 512.5
Queen Charlotte Islands Islands 572
Queen Elizabeth Islands Islands 572
queen it over *disdain* 297.14
queenlike *governing* 49.25
queenly *governing* 49.25, *majestic* 297.12

Queen of Angels *deified person* 82.14
Queen of Heaven *deified person* 82.14
queen of the night *moon* 7.18
queen palm Trees and Shrubs 43
queen-post truss *carpenter's term* 131.5
queen regent *sovereign* 68.2
Queens New York 567.6
queen's *of language* 5.35
queen's English *standard language* 5.6
queen's evidence *divulgence* 180.2
queenship *monarchy* 49.6
queen-size *type of bed* 101.9, *big* 579.13
queen's ware Ceramics 129
queer *sick* 114.24, *abnormal* 430.13, *unusual* 782.15, *eccentric* 782.16, *hinder* 826.15
queer [Inf and Off] *of sexual nature* 20.17, *homosexual* 32.9
queer fish [Inf] *deviant* 698.7
queer in the head [Inf] *insane* 110.9
queerly *unconformably* 782.21
queerness *abnormality* 430.4, *unusualness* 782.4
queer specimen *eccentric* 782.10
Queer Street *insolvency* 486.2
quell *master* 68.17, *conciliate* 74.10, *conquer* 77.36, *silence* 231.4, *destroy* 523.10, *restrain* 830.12, *be victorious* 845.16
quelling *restraint* 830.1, *victorious* 845.10
Quemoy Islands 572
quench *suffice* 97.6, *deter* 179.8, *make dark* 247.10, *satisfy* 273.7, *mitigate* 521.9, *destroy* 523.10
quench one's thirst *drink* 93.19
quenelle *fish dish* 90.19
quern *pulverizer* 553.11
quernstone *pulverizer* 553.11
querulous *irascible* 303.8, *argumentative* 329.7
querulously *irascibly* 303.17
querulousness *irascibility* 303.1
query *philosophize* 4.19, *speculate* 294.13, *question* 333.1, 333.16
querying *questioning* 333.2
quest *questioning* 333.2, *question* 333.16, *pursuit* 385.1, *venture* 390.2, *undertaking* 391.1, *engagement* 833.2
quest after *engage* 833.9
quester *experimenter* 335.5, *pursuer* 385.5, *attempter* 390.3
questing *questioning* 333.11, *pursuing* 385.8
question 333.1, 333.16; *philosophize* 4.19, *disbelieve* 88.8, *not accept* 190.19, *utterance* 205.10, *speculation* 294.2, *speculate* 294.13, *be curious* 321.7, *issue* 328.2, *raise the point* 328.10, *discuss* 329.12, *deny* 332.8, *interrogate* 333.17, *doubt* 333.19, *be uncertain* 841.17
questionable 333.13, 839.5; *disbelieved* 88.7, *arguable* 329.8, *disreputable* 371.4, *unauthentic* 722.9, *uncertain* 841.1
questionableness 333.7; *unauthenticity* 722.4, *implausibility* 839.3, *uncertainty* 841.1
questionably 333.22; *unbelievably* 88.11, *problematically* 328.12, *unauthentically* 722.17, *improbably* 839.8, *uncertainly* 841.22
question and answer 334.3
question-and-answer session

interview 210.4, *questionnaire* 333.3
questioned 333.15; *unaccepting* 190.13, *problematic* 328.7
questioner 333.9; *negator* 190.8, *curious person* 321.3, *requester* 505.5
questioning 333.2, 333.11; *philosophical investigation* 4.4, *pretrial proceedings* 54.13, *unacceptance* 190.4, *unaccepting* 190.13, *speculative* 294.8, *curiosity* 321.1, *curious* 321.5, *logical argument* 329.2, *uncertainty* 333.6
questioningly 333.21; *nonacceptantly* 190.25, *curiously* 321.9
questioning of potential jurors *jury selection* 54.14
question mark Punctuation Marks 5, *uncertainty* 841.1
questionnaire 333.3; *sociological research* 2.2
question potential jurors *try a case* 54.28
question-time *questionnaire* 333.3
queue *computing terms* 15.22, *series* 770.3, *consecutiveness* 774.1, *procession* 774.6, *arrange* 774.14
queue up *line up* 765.24, *arrange* 774.14
quibble 330.13; *argument* 329.1, *argue* 329.11, *sophism* 330.2, *discriminate* 337.12, *sway* 378.12, *evasion* 380.2, *be equivocal* 380.7, *stall* 419.28, *criticize* 438.19
quibbler *sophist* 330.6, *discriminator* 337.6, *equivocator* 380.4, *disapprover* 438.7
quibbling 330.4, 330.9; *legalistic* 53.22, *evasion* 181.5, 380.2, *arguing* 329.6, *judiciousness* 337.2, *discriminating* 337.9, *criticism* 438.4, *critical* 438.13
quiche *egg dish* 90.18
quiche Lorraine *notable international dishes* 90.40
quick *educatable* 48.18, *skillful* 127.10, *intelligent* 352.5, *active* 414.13, *transient* 643.4, *active* 645.5, *immediately* 645.8, *early* 657.8, *swift* 694.6, *hasty* 818.3
quick! *hurry up!* 818.9
quick, the *living being* 28.3
quick [Brit] *farmland* 16.3
quick [Arch] *alive* 28.13
quick as a flash *swift* 694.6
quick as a wink *swift* 694.6
quick as lightning *swift* 694.6
quick as the wind *swift* 694.6
quick count *huddle* 155.7
quicken *live* 28.17, *bring back to life* 28.20, *invigorate* 28.20, *arouse sensation* 212.11, *strengthen* 516.15, *accelerate* 694.14, *hasten* 818.4, *further* 825.30
quickened *given new life* 28.15
quickening *liveliness* 28.12, *acceleration* 694.3, *accelerating* 694.9, *easing* 823.7
quick-footed *swift* 694.6
quick-frozen *frozen* 218.10
quickie [Inf] *sexual intercourse* 20.9, *size of drink* 93.3, *refreshments* 94.3
quick kick *kick* 155.12
quick-kick *kick* 155.20
quick-kicker *special team* 155.11
quicklime *fertilizer* 16.9
quickly *studiously* 48.26, *transiently* 643.8, *immediately* 645.8, *early* 657.17, *swiftly* 694.16, *hastily* 818.7

quick march *bodily movement* 677.11
quickness *educatability* 48.9, *cleverness* 315.3, *willingness* 373.1, *alacrity* 414.3, *transience* 643.1, *earliness* 657.1, *swiftness* 694.1, *haste* 818.1
quickness of mind 694.4
quick one *size of drink* 93.3
quick on the draw [Inf] *swift* 694.6
quick on the trigger [Inf] *swift* 694.6
quick pace *swiftness* 694.1
quicksand *marsh* 559.8, 572.3, *hidden danger* 813.3, *critical situation* 824.6
quickset [Brit] *farmland* 16.3
quicksilvery *mentally quick* 694.8
quickstep Dances 135, *ice-dancing move* 162.19
quick study *educatability* 48.9, *quickness of mind* 694.4
quick temper *anger* 302.4, *short temper* 303.5
quick-tempered *irascible* 303.8
quick-thinking *mentally quick* 694.8
quick-witted *skillful* 127.10, *witty* 277.10, *intelligent* 315.9, 352.5, *mentally sharp* 549.14, *mentally quick* 694.8
quick-wittedness *cleverness* 315.3, *intelligence* 352.2, *mental sharpness* 549.9, *quickness of mind* 694.4
quid *tobacco* 121.23
quiddity *nature* 717.4, *essence* 723.1
quidnunc *meddler* 321.4
quid pro quo *retaliation* 420.1, *compensation* 453.7, *substitution* 672.1, *exchange* 673.1, *reciprocity* 729.1, *counterbalance* 743.2
quiescence *peace* 73.1, *silence* 231.1, *stillness* 413.3, *inactivity* 415.1, *inertness* 519.1, *smoothness* 545.1, *repose* 678.2, *ease* 819.1, *latency* 844.1
quiescency *repose* 678.2
quiescent 678.6; *peaceful* 73.8, *silent* 231.2, *inactive* 413.9, 415.8, *inert* 519.2, *soothing* 545.6, *at ease* 819.2, *latent* 844.6
quiescently *soothingly* 545.14, *latently* 844.15
quiet *peaceful* 73.8, *time off* 125.2, *reserved* 195.11, 403.10, *taciturn* 208.4, *silence* 231.1, 231.4, *silent* 231.2, *faint* 233.6, *mute* 233.9, *soft-hued* 251.13, *relieve* 275.8, *secluded* 409.9, *stillness* 413.3, *inactive* 413.9, 415.8, *inactivity* 415.1, *submitting* 421.3, *insufficient* 517.11, *inert* 519.2, *moderate* 521.3, *calm* 521.8, *soothing* 545.6, *stability* 674.1, *stable* 674.3, *make stable* 674.7, *repose* 678.2, *quiescent* 678.6, *make smaller* 747.8, *harmony* 765.8, *harmonious* 765.16, *ease* 819.1, *at ease* 819.2, *self-restrained* 830.10
quiet! *hush!* 231.6
quiet as a lamb *peaceful* 73.8, *silent* 231.2
quiet as a mouse *silent* 231.2, *motionless* 678.4
quiet as death *quiescent* 678.6
quiet death *way of dying* 29.5
quiet down *be stable* 674.6
quieten *silence* 231.4, *calm* 521.8
quiet end *way of dying* 29.5
quietening *moderation* 521.1

quietism *repose* 678.2
quiet life *peace* 73.1
quietly *stoically* 4.26, *peacefully* 73.12, *reservedly* 195.20, *taciturnly* 208.9, *silently* 231.5, *faintly* 233.11, *modestly* 403.15, *unsocially* 409.13, *inactively* 413.16, *weakly* 517.14, *inertly* 519.5, *soothingly* 545.14, *stably* 674.9, *motionlessly* 678.9, *easily* 819.5
quietly spoken *speaking* 205.15
quietness 844.4; *reserve* 195.5, *taciturnity* 208.1, *silence* 231.1, *stillness* 413.3, *inactivity* 415.1, *moderation* 521.1, *repose* 678.2, *harmony* 765.8, *self-restraint* 830.4
quiet sun *sun* 7.15
quiet tone *undercurrent of sound* 233.3
quietude *silence* 231.1, *stability* 674.1, *repose* 678.2, *harmony* 765.8
quietus *death* 29.1, *execution* 30.6, *favorable verdict* 54.19, *cessation* 773.2
quiet wedding *wedding* 64.5
quiff [Brit] *coiffure* 530.8
quill *plumage* 36.7, *sharp-pointed growth* 549.5
quillwort *fern* 46.1
quilt *stuff* 577.12, *bed covering* 613.7
quilter *coverer* 613.18
quilting *sewing* 130.5, Hobbies and Pastimes 167, *stuffing* 577.4
quinary *fifth* 792.12
quince Card Games 168
quincentenary *hundreds* 792.9
quincunx *angled figure* 628.3, *five* 792.1
quindecagon *eleven to nineteen* 792.7
quindecagonal *eleventh and above* 792.18
quindecennial *eleven to nineteen* 792.7, *eleventh and above* 792.18
quindecillion *million* 792.11
quinine *alkaloid* 12.19
quinine water *tonic* 115.8
quinquagenarian *twenty and over* 792.8
quinquennial *periodical* 641.7, *five* 792.1, *fifth* 792.12
quinquennially *for specified periods* 641.12, *fivefold* 792.26
quinquennium *time period* 641.2, *five* 792.1
quinquepartite *fifth* 792.12
quinquereme *historical warships* 77.22
quinquevalent *chemical compound* 11.4
quinquireme *five* 792.1
quint [Inf] *five* 792.1
quintal General Units 589
quintessence 723.3; *representation* 187.1, *ideal* 327.6, *excellence* 445.4, *substance* 577.2, *extract* 711.8
quintessential 723.8; *representational* 187.8, *ideal* 327.12, *excellent* 445.13, *containing* 577.7, *special* 779.10
quintessentially *structurally* 577.14
quintet *instrumental group* 141.3, *five* 792.1, *team* 827.7
quintic *fifth* 792.12
quintile *angular measurement* 628.4, *fifth* 792.12
quintillion *million* 792.11
quintuple 792.23; *five* 792.1, *fifth* 792.12

quintuplet *five* 792.1
quintuplicate *five* 792.1, *fifth* 792.12, *quintuple* 792.23
quip *wit* 277.3, *joke* 277.6, 368.4, *be humorous* 277.11, *sophism* 330.2
quipster *humorist* 277.7
quire *paper* 104.5
quirk Architectural Elements 134, *sophism* 330.2, *caprice* 381.1, *characteristic* 779.5, *idiosyncrasy* 782.5, *defect* 806.4
quirk bead Architectural Elements 134
quirkiness *capriciousness* 381.2, *unusualness* 782.4, *lack of motive* 842.2
quirky *humorous* 277.9, *capricious* 381.4, *characteristic* 779.12, *unusual* 782.15, *causeless* 842.11
quirt *instrument of punishment* 454.13
quisling *hypocrite* 192.9, *seditionist* 427.7, *villain* 448.5
quit 705.10; *be employed* 57.19, *atone* 313.7, *run away* 386.21, *withdraw* 392.5, *not act* 413.11, *stop* 668.10, *diverge* 753.20, *discontinue* 775.10, *resign* 835.5
quit! *cease!* 668.14
quitclaim *liberation* 831.1
quite *clean* [Inf] 111.21, *right away* 429.20, *moderately* 521.10, *to a degree* 739.11, *on the whole* 759.13, *completely* 759.14, *761.13*, 805.22
quite a few *multitude* 795.1, *many* 795.6
quite another thing *incomparability* 734.3
quite the contrary *to the contrary* 190.27
Quito Countries 566
quit one's hold *relinquish* 392.3
quit one's post *withdraw* 392.5
quittance *atonement* 313.1, *promise* 464.2, *payment* 489.1, *liberation* 831.1
quitter *avoider* 386.8, *submitter* 421.2
quit the saddle *land* 704.16
quit the scene *quit* 705.10
quit the single state *marry* 64.19
quitting *resignation* 835.1
quitting work *resignation* 835.1
quit work *work* 122.8, *stop work* 394.12, *resign* 835.5
quiver *historical ammunition* 78.12, *be cold* 218.13, *be fearful* 283.15, *vibrate* 683.13, *shake* 684.7, 684.24, *flicker* 684.12
quivering *fearful* 283.10, *vibration* 683.2, *vibrating* 683.9, *shaking* 684.6, *shaky* 684.18
quiveringly *shakily* 684.28
quivery *shaky* 684.18
quixotic *fantastic* 360.11
quixotism *conception* 360.4
quiz *be curious* 321.7, *questionnaire* 333.3, *question* 333.16
quizmaster *broadcasting personnel* 172.11, *questioner* 333.9
quiz show *program* 172.10
quiz show host *broadcasting personnel* 172.11
quizzed *questioned* 333.15
quizzical *curious* 321.5, *problematic* 333.12, *satirical* 369.6
quizzically *questioningly* 333.21, *satirically* 369.9
quod [Brit inf] *the inside* 55.2
quoin Architectural Elements 134
quoit *missile* 696.7
quondam *former* 651.14, 653.12

quorum *sufficiency* 97.1, *certain amount* 738.3, *fullness* 761.5
quota *division* 6.16, *portion* 474.2, *limit* 620.1, *certain amount* 738.3, *part* 760.1, *fullness* 761.5
quotation *catchword* 5.22, *price* 494.1, *passage* 692.1, *part of writing* 760.6
quotation book *compilation* 174.4
quotation marks Punctuation Marks 5
quote *catchword* 5.22, *speak* 205.17, *explain* 331.16, *excerpt* 692.13, *part of writing* 760.6, *specify* 779.18, *reveal* 843.14
quote a price *price* 494.12
quote chapter and verse *circumstantiate* 726.12
quoted *excerpted* 692.9, *displayed* 843.8
quoted price *price* 494.1
quote mark Punctuation Marks 5
quotes Punctuation Marks 5
quotidian *habitual* 397.9, *unpretentious* 526.8, *cyclic* 663.7, *common* 778.13
quotient *division* 6.16, *numerical answer* 334.7
Qur'an *the Law* 53.2, *Islamic text* 81.18

R

R *film-rating system* 137.4
Ra *sun* 7.15, Deities 82
Rabat Countries 566
rabato *neckwear* 100.29
rabbet *intertwine* 752.19
Rabbi *professional title* 72.6
rabbi 84.6; *educator* 48.4, *person in authority* 52.7, *religious leader* 68.9, *religious person* 81.9, *ritualist* 85.14
rabbinate *priesthood* 84.2
rabbinical *masterful* 68.15, *priestly* 84.12
rabbinically *clerically* 84.17
rabbit *meat* 90.22, *horse racing* 159.10, *game* 160.6
rabbit farming *livestock farming* 16.10
rabbit guard *garden tool* 17.7
rabbitlike 35.29
rabbit punch *boxing techniques* 152.5
rabbits Collective Names 59
rabbit's foot *talisman* 86.9, *good-luck sign* 358.6
rabbity *rabbitlike* 35.29
rabble *vulgar group* 535.5, *general public* 778.6
rabble-rouse *combat* 77.34, *address* 209.8
rabble-rouser *leader* 126.8, *motivator* 178.11, 508.6, *public speaker* 209.5, *troublemaker* 427.5, *protester* 507.4
Rabelaisian *profane* 301.10, *ribald* 535.8
rabid *manic* 110.10, *angry* 302.11, *violent* 520.5
rabies *animal disease* 34.10, *infection* 114.7, Phobias 283
race 1.5, 146.10, 422.8; *society* 1.6, *group* 18.13, *family tree* 65.3, *canoe* 150.31, *row* 150.32, *ride* 159.16, *ski race* 162.4, *ski* 162.35, *participate* 166.22, *chase* 385.2, *line of action* 399.4, *alacrity* 414.3, *be active* 414.18, *contend* 422.22, *flow* 570.4, 570.10, *navigate* 690.15, *be swift* 694.10, *exceed* 712.15, *make haste* 818.5

race *or racing track event* 166.1
race against a deadline *haste* 818.1
race against time *spend time* 639.14, *haste* 818.1
racecourse *racetrack* 159.12, *passage* 691.5
race hatred *social discrimination* 337.4
racehorse 159.2
racehorses Collective Names 59
race hot-rods *race* 146.10
race internationally *race* 146.10
racemate *structure* 11.7
raceme *flower head* 42.4
race meeting *horse racing* 159.10
racemic mixture *structure* 11.7
race midget cars *race* 146.10
racemization *structure* 11.7
racemize *react* 11.38
racemized *structural* 11.28
racemose *of flowers* 42.11
racemose inflorescence *flower head* 42.4
race on skis *ski* 162.35
race psychology Psychological Theories, Schools 108
racer *driver* 146.8, *racehorse* 159.2, *track and field eventer* 166.19, *athlete* 422.15, *speeder* 694.5
races 146.4; *race* 422.8
race sports cars *race* 146.10
race stock cars *race* 146.10
racetrack 159.12; *circle* 631.2, *passage* 691.5
race-walk *participate* 166.22
race walker *track and field eventer* 166.19
race walking 166.9, Sporting Activities 145
race-walking *track and field* 166.20
rachial *or rachidial of stems* 41.17
rachilla *stem* 41.5, *grass plant* 45.3
rachis Human Bones 19, *plumage* 36.7, *stem* 41.5, *fern plant* 46.2
racial 1.12; *societal* 1.13, *socioeconomic* 2.13, *human* 18.15
racial discrimination *social discrimination* 337.4, *exclusiveness* 764.4
racial group *social organization* 2.5, *group* 18.13
racial harassment *malignity* 306.5
racial hatred *malignity* 306.5
racial intolerance *unfair treatment* 342.4
racialism *malignity* 306.5, *social discrimination* 337.4, *unfair treatment* 342.4
racialist *intolerant* 63.7, *bigot* 337.7, *discriminatory* 337.11
racially *societally* 1.17, *sociologically* 2.15, *humanly* 18.18, *cliquishly* 59.32, *prejudicially* 337.17
racially harass *harm* 306.13
racial memory *tradition* 1.7, *memory* 354.1
racial prejudice *unfair treatment* 342.4
racial type *group* 18.13
racial unconscious *psyche* 108.25
raciness *emphasis* 200.1, *piquancy* 221.1
racing 146.9; *rowing* 150.14, *horse racing* 159.10, *equine* 159.15, *competitive swimming* 164.3, *swimming* 164.12, *track and field* 166.20, *chase* 385.2, *race* 422.8, *contending* 422.19, *flowing* 570.7, *swiftness* 694.1, *speeding* 694.7, *hasty* 818.3

racing automobile 146.2
racing bike *bicycle* 687.10
racing boat Ships and Boats 690
racing canoe *canoe* 150.9
racing car *racing automobile* 146.2
racing dive *competitive swimming* 164.3
racing driver *speeder* 694.5
racing forecaster *forecaster* 358.9
racing form *horse racing* 159.10
racing governing bodies 146.7
racing handlebars *bicycle part* 687.11
racing oar *rowboat parts* 150.15
racing river *river* 570.1
racing saddle *riding equipment* 159.9
racing ski *ski equipment* 162.10
racing-step turn *skiing techniques* 162.5
racing steward *horse person* 159.14
racing suit *ski equipment* 162.10, *swimming equipment* 164.8
racing tires *racing automobile* 146.2
racing track *racetrack* 159.12
racing trunks *swimming equipment* 164.8
racism *hostility* 63.1, *hate* 300.1, *malignity* 306.5, *social discrimination* 337.4, *unfair treatment* 342.4, *nationalism* 566.4
racist *hostile person* 63.5, *intolerant* 63.7, *hater* 300.6, *hating* 300.7, *malefactor* 306.6, *malign* 306.11, *bigot* 337.7, *discriminatory* 337.11, *unjust* 342.7, *nationalist* 566.8, *excluding* 764.5
rack *lamb* 90.27, *purify* 111.19, *billiards* 149.1, *climbing equipment* 161.4, *inflict pain* 215.10, *instrument of torture* 454.14, *torture* 454.29, *framework* 551.4, *compartment* 578.2, *slow motion* 693.3
Racka Breeds of Sheep 16
rack and pinion *gear* 14.7, *miscellaneous automotive terms* 687.14
rack and ruin *ruin* 523.4, *dilapidation* 808.5
rack car *railroad car* 688.5
racket Musical Instruments 142, *badminton terms* 165.11, *loudness* 232.1, *rattle* 235.3, *dissonance* 241.1, *plot* 387.6, *activity* 414.1, *tumult* 684.2, *confusion* 766.4, *commotion* 768.5
racket [Inf] *job* 122.3
racket *or* **racquet** *squash terms* 165.10
racketeer *villain* 448.5, *raider* 477.10, *dishonest person* 479.11, *trader* 480.11, *trade* 480.18
racketeering *wicked act* 448.7, *trade* 480.1
rackets, the [Inf] *villain* 448.5
rackety *loud* 232.6
racking *painful* 215.4, *corporal punishment* 454.11
racking bend Knots, Bends, Hitches, Splices 754
rack one's brains *think* 317.9, *find unintelligible* 364.14
rack railroad *railroad system* 688.1
rack-rent *extortion* 496.4, *overcharge* 496.10
rack-renter *overcharger* 496.5
raconteur *descriptive writer* 202.10
racquet *badminton terms* 165.11
racquetball Sporting Activities 145

racy *emphatic* 200.3, *piquant* 221.6, *offensive* 432.11
rad Scientific and Technical Units 589
rad [Inf] *great* 445.14
radar *electromagnetic radiation* 10.14, *guide* 126.6, *indicator* 183.7, *sound propagation* 230.3, *detector* 345.6, *position finder* 690.8
radar astronomy *astronomy* 7.1
radar beacon *flight control* 689.7
radarman *air force person* 77.31
radar receiver *receiver* 473.8
radar trap *speed* 694.2
raddle *redden* 257.9
radial *curvilinear* 6.78, *spatial* 563.11, *directional* 677.13, *convergent* 702.7, *radiating* 703.7
radial-arm saw *woodworking tool* 131.6
radially *divergently* 703.16
radial motion *movement* 677.3
radial velocity *star luminosity* 7.12
radian Scientific and Technical Units 589
radiance *light* 246.1, *beauty* 529.1, *radiation* 703.3
radiant *meteor* 7.21, *lucent* 246.13, *cheerful* 269.7, *beautiful* 529.7, *radiating* 703.7
radiant energy *light* 246.1, *energy* 514.7
radiant heat *heat* 217.1
radiantly *lightly* 246.23, *cheerfully* 269.14, *gorgeously* 529.14, *magnificently* 529.16, *divergently* 703.16
radiate 703.13; *observe* 7.34, *shine* 9.56, *light up* 246.20, *generate power* 514.19, *transfer* 685.8, *radiating* 703.7, *let out* 709.26, *diverge* 776.16
radiated *radiating* 703.7
radiate light *light up* 246.20
radiating 703.7; *convergent* 702.7, *expulsive* 709.11, *apart* 753.8, *divergent* 776.11
radiation 703.3; *atmospheric process* 9.9, *wave* 10.11, 683.4, *heat flow* 10.27, *light* 246.1, Phobias 283, *agent of destruction* 523.7, Fields of Measurement 589, *divergence* 776.5
radiation balance *atmospheric process* 9.9
radiation exposure *nuclear problem* 10.62
radiation fog *fog* 9.32
radiation frost *frost* 9.25
radiation physics Fields of Modern Physics 10
radiative *atmospheric* 9.40
radiator *heater* 217.3, *ejector* 709.10
radical *of roots* 41.19, *troublemaker* 427.5, *basic* 601.8, *intrinsic* 611.11, *causal* 675.7, *dissenter* 782.8, *dissident* 782.12, *fractional* 783.8, *essential* 799.10, *opposer* 828.9
radical [Inf] *great* 445.14
radical change *sudden change* 665.3
radically *causally* 675.12, *at heart* 723.14
radical reform *improvement* 807.1
radical sign *mathematical symbol* 6.11
radical treatment *treatment* 107.14
radicle *root* 41.7, *seed* 41.9
radicular *of roots* 41.19
radio 172.1; *communications* 169.1,

news 171.1, *broadcast* 172.13, *publication media* 173.6, *sound reproduction* 230.6
radioactive *dangerous* 811.7
radioactive dating *dating* 8.48
radioactive decay *radioactivity* 10.58
radioactive series *radioactivity* 10.58
radioactive substance *radioactivity* 10.58
radioactive waste *nuclear problem* 10.62, *nuclear power production* 514.10
radioactivity 10.58; *lack of hygiene* 112.3, *nuclear power production* 514.10
radio astronomy *astronomy* 7.1
radiobeacon *radio transmission* 172.3
radiobeacon station *position finder* 690.8
radio broadcaster *broadcasting personnel* 172.11
radio broadcasting 172.4
radio cabinet *radio* 172.1
radio car *radio broadcasting* 172.4
radiocarbon dating *dating* 8.48, *radioactivity* 10.58, *chronology* 646.2
radiochemical *chemical* 11.24
radiochemical reaction *chemical reaction* 11.8
radiochemistry Branches of Chemistry 11
radio communication *communications* 169.1
radio direction finder (RDF) *position finder* 690.8
radio dish *radio telescope* 7.26
radio drama *broadcast drama* 136.4, *program* 172.10
radio dramatist *dramatist* 136.27
radioed *communicated* 169.15, *broadcast* 172.12
radio engineer *professional worker* 123.11
radio engineering *telecommunication* 169.7
radio frequency 661.3; *radio transmission* 172.3
radio-frequency band *radio frequency* 661.3
radio galaxy *galaxy* 7.5
radiograph *diagnostic radiology* 107.12, *photograph* 132.3
radiography *radioactivity* 10.58, *diagnostic radiology* 107.12, *photographic specialties* 132.2
radio interferometer *radio telescope* 7.26
radioisotope *radioactivity* 10.58
radiological *medical* 107.28
radiologist *medical specialist* 107.20
radiology *radioactivity* 10.58, Medical Specialties 107
radioluminescence *light* 10.17
radioman *air force person* 77.31
radio mast *radio broadcasting* 172.4
radio navigation *radio transmission* 172.3
radio news *broadcast news* 171.6
radionuclide *radioactivity* 10.58

radio observatory *observatory* 7.24
radiophobia Phobias 283
radiophone *telephone* 169.10
radiophonics *tone* 230.2
radio play *broadcast drama* 136.4, *program* 172.10
radio producer *producer* 522.10
radio program *program* 172.10, *production* 843.5
radio receiver *radio reception* 172.2, *receiver* 473.8
radio reception 172.2
radio set *radio* 172.1
radio signal *radio transmission* 172.3
radio signaling *signaling* 169.9, *radio transmission* 172.3
radiosonde *weather station* 9.5
radio spectrum *electromagnetic radiation* 10.14, *radio transmission* 172.3
radio station *radio broadcasting* 172.4
radiotelegraph *data transmission* 169.8
radiotelegraphy *telecommunication* 169.7, *radio* 172.1
radiotelephone *telephone* 169.10
radiotelephony *telecommunication* 169.7, *radio* 172.1
radio telescope 7.26
radiotherapy *radioactivity* 10.58, *treatment* 107.14, *therapy* 115.12
radio tower *radio broadcasting* 172.4
radio transmission 172.3
radio transmitter *radio transmission* 172.3
radio wave *electromagnetic radiation* 10.14, *radio transmission* 172.3, *wave* 683.4
radium Chemical Elements and Common Allotropes 11
radius *line* 6.35, *circle* 6.40, *dimension* 10.5, Human Bones 19, *range* 563.7, *size* 579.1, *breadth* 592.1, *parts of a circle* 631.4, *focus* 702.5, *radiation* 703.3, *dividing line* 740.6
radius vector *vector* 6.48
radix *root* 41.7
radix point *number system* 6.7
radon Chemical Elements and Common Allotropes 11
raffia *line* 754.5
raffia work Hobbies and Pastimes 167
raffinose Common Sugars 12
raffle *winnings* 492.5, *game of chance* 842.5
raffle ticket *means of identification* 184.3
raft 150.34; *substructure* 551.8, *convey* 685.9, Ships and Boats 690
rafter Collective Names 59, *wood* 131.3, Architectural Elements 134, *supporting part* 605.3
rafting 150.23; Sporting Activities 145, *boating sports* 150.1, *rowing* 150.27
rag Collective Names 59, *fabric* 130.1, *play ice hockey* 158.9, *be humorous* 277.11, *particle* 760.4
rag [Inf] *newspaper* 175.2, *ridicule* 436.22
raga *folk music* 140.7
rag-and-bone man *peddler* 482.9
ragbag *miscellany* 751.3
ragdoll Breeds of Cats 35
rag doll *figure* 187.4
rage *bad feeling* 266.5, *likes* 290.3,

anger 302.4, burst of anger 302.6, be angry 302.19, be active 414.18, be an influence 512.13, violence 520.1, be violent 520.8, fashion 536.1

rage, the trendiness 652.2

rage against be malevolent 306.12, berate 438.20

ragged beggarly 486.12, rough 544.5, untidy 766.11

ragged edge edge 618.1

raggedness beggary 486.3, roughness 544.1

ragged robin Flowers 42

raging stormy 9.45, burst of anger 302.6, angry 302.11, bitter 306.9, attacking 418.14, violent 520.5, destructive 523.8

raging bull violent animal 520.4

ragingly bitterly 306.16

raglan coat 100.19

raglan sleeve part of garment 100.27

ragman peddler 482.9

ragout mixed thing 751.2

rag paper paper 104.5

ragpicker poor person 486.6

rags old clothes 100.8, beggary 486.3, bits and pieces 760.5

ragtime popular music 140.4

ragtime band instrumental group 141.3

ragtime jazz musical 140.25

rag trade [Inf] the clothing business 100.36, fashion business 536.3

ragwort Flowers 42

raid offensive warfare 76.11, be at war 76.32, conquer 77.36, military attack 418.2, attack 418.17, take away forcefully 477.19, plunder 479.16, havoc 523.5, lay waste 523.14, inroad 706.3, invade 706.12

raider 477.10; militarist 77.3, guerrilla 77.7, attacker 418.10, destroyer 523.6, intruder 706.8

raiding conquest 477.6, stealing 479.1, havoc 523.5

raiding party armed force 77.10

rail 688.3, 688.8; farm building 16.4, water bird 36.9, sailboard parts 150.20, windsurf 150.33, racetrack 159.12, speak to 205.19, berate 438.20, enclose 619.6

rail, California clapper Endangered US Birds 36

rail, light-footed clapper Endangered US Birds 36

rail, Yuma clapper Endangered US Birds 36

rail against vilify 301.15

rail at taunt 436.23

rail detector car railroad car 688.5

railhead railroad station 688.6

railing windsurfing terms 150.21, berating 438.5, enclosing thing 619.3, safety device 810.15

raillery discourtesy 411.1

railroad 691.8; tunnel 551.11, transportable 686.7, railroad system 688.1

railroad [Inf] hasten 818.4, subject 832.10

railroad bridge bridge 551.10, 691.7

railroad car 688.5

railroaded [Inf] hasty 818.3

railroad line railroad 691.8

railroads Phobias 283

railroad signals signaling 169.9

railroad station 688.6; stopping place 668.4, place of departure 705.4

railroad system 688.1

railroad track thoroughfare 692.6

railroad tracks parallel 606.4

railroad train train 688.4

railroad tunnel tunnel 551.11, 691.6

railroad worker 688.7

railroad yard junction 691.9

rails rail 688.3

railslide ski 162.35

rail transportation transportation 686.1

rail tunnel tunnel 551.11

railway [Brit] railroad system 688.1, railroad 691.8

railway express conveyance 685.2

railway signal signal 183.6

railway tracks parallel 606.4

raiment clothing 100.1

rain 9.27, 9.57; precipitation 9.26, rain 9.27, abound 97.8, Phobias 283, water 557.1, 557.29, mistiness 559.2, sprinkle 559.14, downflow 714.3, drip 714.13

rain-bearing cloud cloud 9.17

rain blows on beat 695.12

rainbow 9.28; highlight 246.12, spectrum 251.3, variegation 263.1, variegated thing 263.5, curved thing 629.3

rainbowed variegated 263.6

rainbow's end rainbow 9.28

rainbow trout game fish 154.10

rain cats and dogs [Inf] rain 9.57, abound 97.8, water 557.29, drip 714.13

rain check substitute 672.2

rain cloud cloud 9.17

raincoat coat 100.19, protection from the weather 810.9

rain damage rain 9.27

rain dance rain 9.27, non-Christian ritual 85.8

raindrop precipitation 9.26

rainfall precipitation 9.26, rain 9.27, wateriness 557.3, mistiness 559.2, lowering 716.1

rain forest trees 43.4

rain-forest climate climate 9.35

rain gauge weather instrument 9.7, measuring instrument 557.19

rain god minor deity 82.2

rain hat hat 100.32

Rainier, Mount Mountains and Hills 569

rainier rainy 9.50

raininess rain 9.27, wateriness 557.3, mistiness 559.2

raining blows ramming 695.3

raining cats and dogs [Inf] rainy 9.50

rainless 560.11; fine 9.43

rainmaking rain 9.27

rainproof waterproof 560.16

rains, the rain 9.27

rainstorm rain 9.27, natural violence 520.3

rain tires racing automobile 146.2

rain tree Trees and Shrubs 43

rainwater water 557.1

rainwear protection from the weather 810.9

Rainy Lakes 568

rainy 9.50; misty 559.10

rainy-day policy precaution 287.4

rainy season rain 9.27, seasons 654.2

raise 715.9; practice livestock farming 16.20, educate 48.22, gamble 167.14, poker 168.5, play cards 168.7, reward for service 453.5, augmentation 467.2, positive stimulus 508.5, bring into existence 522.14, construct 551.22, extend

563.14, increase 581.16, heighten 596.14, exalt 596.19, make vertical 602.9, advance 679.3, further 679.13, make bigger 746.7, improve 807.15

raise a cry cry out 239.13

raise a finger do something 412.13

raise a or one's glass drink to 93.20

raise a hue and cry proclaim 173.16

raise all hell shatter the peace 232.10

raise an objection protest 507.7

raise a rafter carpenter 131.10

raise a rumpus be disorderly 766.22

raise a storm be violent 520.8

raise Cain [Inf] shatter the peace 232.10, vent one's anger 302.21, be disorderly 766.22, cause trouble 824.21

raised 715.6; domesticated 16.18, produced 522.12, swelled 581.10, high 596.7, unbowed 602.7

raised eyebrow show of disapproval 438.6

raised eyebrows gesture 183.5

raised fist gesture of protest 507.3

raise difficulties cause difficulties 824.22

raise doubts about deny 332.8

raised temperature heat 217.1

raised up reared 715.7

raised upward unbowed 602.7

raise expectations predict 358.14

raise from cuttings make bigger 746.7

raise from seed propagate 21.15, make bigger 746.7

raise from the dead bring back to life 28.20

raise funds gain 467.15, solicit money 505.13

raise ghosts conjure 86.26

raise hell [Inf] vent one's anger 302.21, be disorderly 766.22, cause trouble 824.21

raise hob cause trouble 824.21

raise money find means 102.6, be charitable 305.12

raise objections object 828.18

raise one's banner declare war 422.25

raise one's cap greet 410.11

raise one's consciousness arouse sensation 212.11

raise one's eyebrows gesture 183.17, show disapproval 438.21

raise one's fist protest 507.7

raise one's glass congratulate 405.12

raise one's hackles make angry 302.18

raise one's hand gesture 183.17, vote 382.16

raise one's hand against strike 418.21

raise one's hat greet 410.11, uncover 614.17

raise one's hopes inspire hope 281.14

raise one's sights make one's way 679.12, intensify 746.8

raise one's voice emphasize 200.6, be loud 232.8, cry out 239.13, appear 331.18, show oneself 843.15

raise one's voice against protest 507.7

raiser agriculturist 16.14

raise steam prepare for action 388.18, navigate 690.15

raise suspicions cause disbelief 88.9

raise the alarm signal 183.18

raise the bid deal 457.9, overpay 496.11

raise the curtain dramatize 136.33, disclose 180.8, make visible 244.9

raise the devil vent one's anger 302.21, cause trouble 824.21

raise the drawbridge shelter 812.8

raise the flag salute 435.17

raise the hue and cry chase 385.13

raise the hunt chase 385.13

raise the issue raise the point 328.10, doubt 333.19

raise the point 328.10

raise the pressure be full of vigor 518.4

raise the price overcharge 496.10

raise the roof [Inf] proclaim 173.16, shatter the peace 232.10, be strident 238.7, acclaim 437.18, protest 507.7, cause trouble 824.21

raise the stakes intensify 746.8

raise the tempo accelerate 694.14

raise to the peerage make noble 70.5

raise to the power of add 6.86, make bigger 746.7

raise trade barriers trade 480.18

raise up bring back to life 28.20, heighten 596.14, make vertical 602.9, raise 715.9, rear 715.10

raisin bread bread 90.10

raising 715.1; education 48.1, card-playing 168.6, increase 581.3, unbowed 602.7

raising agent lifter 715.5

raising up rearing 715.2

raison d'être final intention 374.4, reason 675.4

raita notable international dishes 90.40

raj governance 49.18

rajah sovereign 68.2

rake farm 16.19, garden tool 17.7, 103.4, cultivate 17.19, libertine 32.7, Collective Names 59, cleaning tool 79.17, tempter 178.10, lover 299.11, fire 418.18, sexually immoral person 432.8, miscreant 448.6, smoother 545.2, smooth 545.10, sharp-pointed thing 549.4, use a sharp tool 549.17, miscellaneous aviation terms 689.9, drag 699.11, extractor 711.9

raked ornamental 17.17

rakehell sexually immoral person 432.8

rake in drag 699.11

rake in the cash get rich 485.13

rake in it profit 467.22, be rich 485.12, get rich 485.13

rake off take a discount 495.5, offer 504.11

rake-off winnings 492.5, fee 494.3, discount 495.1, illegal offer 504.4, subtracted item 749.2

rake out clean 111.17, drag 699.11, extract 711.13

rake over the coals condemn 438.18

rake up the past remember 354.12

raking arch 134.5

raking fire firing 418.6

raking it in gain 467.1, wealthy 485.8

raking over the coals condemnation 438.2

rakish flashy 404.17, unchaste 432.10

rakishly flashily 404.32

raku firing ceramic process 129.5

raku kiln *ceramic workshop and tools* 129.8
Raleigh *American States* 564
rall. *Musical Terms and Expression Marks* 140
rallentando *Musical Terms and Expression Marks* 140
rally 59.6; *collection* 59.2, *call together* 59.28, *war measures* 76.18, *arm* 76.30, *battle* 76.33, *tennis strokes* 165.2, *play tennis* 165.13, *military call* 183.9, *mass demonstration* 331.7, *protest* 331.19, *prize competition* 422.5, *motivate* 508.9, *be strong* 516.14, *combine* 757.9, *get better* 807.21, *revival* 809.3, *recuperation* 809.4, *restore* 809.12, *be restored* 809.13, *support* 825.24, *work together* 827.14
rally around *come together* 59.25
rally cross *Sporting Activities* 145
rallying *automobile racing* 146.1, *demonstrating* 331.14, *international finance* 457.2, *recuperation* 809.5
rallying cry *glory of war* 76.17, *exhortation* 178.2, *military call* 183.9, *cry* 239.1
rallying symbol *sign* 183.1
ralph [Inf] *vomit* 709.27
Ram *Constellations* 7
ram *livestock* 16.11, *male animal* 32.15, *male mammal* 35.18, *blunt weapon* 78.5, *hand tool* 103.3, *attack* 418.17, *demolish* 523.12, *hammer* 553.13, *impeller* 695.7, *collide* 695.10
Ramadan *religious festival* 85.13, *fast* 118.4
Ramapithecus *human ancestor* 18.3
ramble *be circuitous* 199.6, *be unintelligible* 364.11, *go astray* 698.17, *be extraneous* 724.12, *be foreign* 724.13, *digress* 775.13
ramble on *be diffuse* 199.5, *be talkative* 207.7
rambler *garden plant* 17.10
rambling *superfluous* 99.8, *circumlocution* 199.2, *circumlocutory* 199.4, *unemphatic* 201.2, *unintelligible* 364.4, *changeable* 666.3, *wandering* 698.4, 698.13, *foreign* 724.9
rambling speech *superfluity* 99.4
rambling wreck *physical deterioration* 808.4
Rambouillet *Breeds of Sheep* 16
rambunctious *shouting* 232.7
ram down *make dense* 540.9, *collide* 695.10, *fill* 761.11
ram down one's throat *force* 428.10
ramekin *crockery* 578.16
ramen *pasta* 90.31
ramie *fiber* 130.2
ramification *expansion* 581.1, *branching* 703.4, *means of connection* 754.4, *divergence* 776.5
ramiform *divergent* 776.11
ramify *enlarge* 581.14, *grow* 581.17, *branch* 703.14, *diverge* 776.16
ram in *impact* 710.11, *fill* 761.11
ramino *Card Games* 168
ramjet *means of propulsion* 696.2
rammer *impeller* 695.7
ramming 695.3; *impelling* 695.8
ramose *branched* 703.9
ramosely *divergently* 703.16
ramous *branched* 703.9
ramously *divergently* 703.16
ramp *rock face* 161.6, *bridge*

551.10, *obliquity* 628.2, *road attribute* 687.3, *airport* 689.4, *incline* 713.3
rampage *shatter the peace* 232.10, *become angry* 302.20, *be active* 414.18, *be violent* 520.8, *be agitated* 684.21, *disruption* 766.7, *be disorderly* 766.22
rampageous *disorderly* 766.15
rampaging *destructive* 523.8
rampant *disorderly* 51.6, *arch* 134.5, *Heraldic Terms* 184, *explosive* 520.6, *unbowed* 602.7, *rising* 713.14, *universal* 778.10
rampantly *confusedly* 51.11
rampantness *widespreadness* 778.3
rampart *safeguard* 419.2, *fort* 419.13, *support* 605.16, *fortification* 812.3, *barrier* 826.7
ramping *unbowed* 602.7
ramrod *impeller* 695.7
ramshackle *decrepit* 808.12, *unsafe* 811.8
ranch *farm* 16.2, 124.11, *practice livestock farming* 16.20, *property* 470.1
rancher *agriculturist* 16.14, *food provider* 90.6, *producer* 522.10
ranchero *agriculturist* 16.14
ranch house *house* 60.4
ranch-house cook *cook* 91.3
ranching *livestock farming* 16.10
ranchman *agriculturist* 16.14
rancho *farm* 16.2
rancid *unpalatable* 220.5, 223.6, *putrid* 227.4
rancidity *bad taste* 220.3, *unpalatability* 223.2, *unpleasant-smelling thing* 227.2
rancor *ill feeling* 63.3, *spleen* 223.4, *hate* 300.1, *resentment* 302.1, *bitterness* 306.3
rancorous *hostile* 63.6, *splenetic* 223.7, *hating* 300.7, *resentful* 302.8, *bitter* 306.9
rancorously *splenetically* 223.10, *with hate* 300.13, *resentfully* 302.22, *bitterly* 306.16
rand *national coins* 484.11
R and D worker *experimenter* 335.5
randiness *sexual desire* 288.5, *sexual love* 299.3
random *indiscriminate* 338.8, *outlined* 417.4, *irregular* 664.3, 766.10, *changeable* 666.3, *directional* 677.13, *undirected* 698.10, *illogical* 728.7, *complicated* 751.10, *discontinuous* 775.7, *capricious* 841.16, *chance* 842.10
random access *data-related concepts* 15.23
random-access memory (RAM) *memory* 15.6, *artificial memory* 354.6
random chance *chance* 842.1, *potluck* 842.4
randomly 842.16; *indiscriminately* 338.15, *irregularly* 664.6, *illogically* 728.17, *mixedly* 751.16, *in disorder* 766.24, *capriciously* 841.26
random motion *movement* 677.3
randomness *indiscrimination* 338.4, *inaccuracy* 351.3, *restlessness* 414.7, *irregularity* 664.1, *unrelatedness* 728.1, *mixture* 751.1, *irregular order* 766.2, *capriciousness* 841.8, *chance* 842.1, *lack of motive* 842.2
random number *number* 6.4
random sample *population* 6.55
random sampling *population* 6.55
random variable *population* 6.55

---

randy *desirous* 20.18, *lustful* 288.15, *unchaste* 432.10
Raney nickel *catalysis* 11.16
range 563.7; *mathematical function* 6.27, *parameter* 6.57, *grassland* 45.2, *habitat* 60.1, *cooker* 91.5, *sound quality* 230.4, *viewpoint* 242.12, *visibility* 244.1, *selection* 382.1, *merchandise* 482.6, *extend* 563.14, *mountain* 569.1, *lowland* 572.6, *size* 579.1, *measurability* 589.2, *breadth* 592.1, *degree* 739.1, *arrange* 767.18, 774.14, *sort* 777.13, *have scope* 829.20
ranged *arranged* 767.11
range finder *exposure equipment* 132.12, *bowling* 151.1, *that which makes visible* 244.4, *guide* 697.4
range horse *horse* 159.1
range of choice *selection* 382.1
range of color *spectrum* 251.3
range oneself on the side of *back* 825.28
ranger *forester* 43.7
range with *join with* 827.15
ranginess *thinness* 595.1, *height* 596.1
ranging *of landmasses* 572.12, *free-ranging* 829.13
rangy *thin* 595.9, *tall* 596.9
rani *or* **ranee** *sovereign* 68.2
rank 573.4, 727.11, 739.2; *nonparametric methods* 6.54, *order* 6.89, *plantlike* 41.13, *military organization* 58.4, *army formation* 77.15, *part of keyboard instrument* 142.6, *green bowling* 151.3, *unpalatable* 220.5, *stinking* 227.3, *immoral* 432.9, *wicked* 448.9, *space* 563.15, *size* 579.17, *state* 725.1, *relative position* 727.5, *measure* 739.7, *lead* 744.19, *position* 765.4, *systematize* 765.19, *category* 767.6, *categorize* 767.21, *sequence* 770.1, *arrange* 774.14, *social class* 777.5, *sort* 777.13, *importance* 799.1
rank air fumes *miasma* 556.3
rank and file *common people* 71.2, *army person* 77.17, *average person* 742.4, *general public* 778.6
rank-and-file *common* 71.3
ranked 6.72, 727.8, 739.6; *employed* 573.8, *conditional* 725.7, *hierarchical* 765.12, *categorized* 767.15, *classed* 777.11
rank first *lead* 744.19
rank high *respect* 435.13, *command respect* 435.18
rank highly *respect* 435.13
Rankine cycle *engine cycle* 14.13
Rankine scale *scale* 589.9
ranking *nonparametric methods* 6.54, *state* 725.1, *conditional* 725.7, *gradation* 739.3, *position* 765.4, *categorization* 767.5, *sequential* 770.7, *classification* 777.2, *notable* 799.11
rankle *fester* 25.23, *irritate* 302.16, *decay* 808.16
rankling *pus* 25.7
rank low *disrespect* 436.18
rankly *stinkingly* 227.6
rankness *bad taste* 220.3, *unpalatability* 223.2, *wickedness* 448.1
ranks, the *army person* 77.17
Rannoch *Lakes* 568
ransack *plunder* 479.16, *lay waste* 523.14
ransacker *raider* 477.10, *plunderer* 479.9
ransacking *plundering* 479.5
ransom *liability* 454.6, *giving back*

478.1, *give back* 478.5, *repurchase* 481.4, *buy back* 481.16, *damages* 489.8, *levy* 494.7, *exchange* 673.1, *compensation* 743.1, *restoration* 809.2, *restore* 809.12, *deliverance* 817.1, *deliver* 817.5
ransomed *bought* 481.8, *exchanged* 673.4
ransomer *purchaser* 481.7
rant *overact* 136.35, *boast* 194.14, *be diffuse* 199.5, *public speaking* 205.11, *speak to* 205.19, *address* 209.1, 209.8, *be angry* 302.19, *talk nonsense* 362.12, *complain* 507.8
rant and rave *be diffuse* 199.5, *be angry* 302.19, *talk nonsense* 362.12
ranter *speaker* 205.12, *talker* 207.4, *public speaker* 209.5, *protester* 507.4
ranting *manic* 110.10, *bombast* 194.4, *public speaking* 205.11, *articulate* 205.16, *addressing* 209.6, *angry* 302.11, *meaningless* 362.7
ranunculaceous *taxonomic* 41.16
ranunculus *Flowers* 42
rap *rock music* 140.6, *crack* 234.2, 234.7, *corporal punishment* 454.11, *blow* 695.5, *hit* 695.11, *tap* 695.13
rap [Inf] *speech* 205.1, *talk* 207.3, *criticism* 438.4, *berate* 438.20
rapacious *gluttonous* 119.3, *taking* 477.12
rapaciously *avariciously* 477.22
rapacity *gluttony* 119.1, *taking* 477.1
rape *crop* 16.8, *animal feed* 16.12, *sexual offense* 20.11, 432.6, *be at war* 76.32, *Phobias* 283, *malignity* 306.5, *harm* 306.13, *personal attack* 418.8, *attack successfully* 418.25, *seduce* 432.14, *wicked act* 448.7, *be wicked* 448.13, *sexual possession* 477.2, *ravish* 477.15, *plundering* 479.5, *plunder* 479.16, *violence by person* 520.2, *use violence* 520.9, *havoc* 523.5, *lay waste* 523.14, *impair* 808.18
raped *taking* 477.12
Raphael *angel* 82.11
rapid *hunting* 160.11, *immediate* 645.5, *directional* 677.13, *swift* 694.6, *hasty* 818.3
rapid fire *target shooting* 160.1, *firing* 418.6
rapid-fire *swift* 694.6
rapidity *rapid motion* 677.8, *swiftness* 694.1, *haste* 818.1
rapidly *immediately* 645.8, *in motion* 677.19, *swiftly* 694.16, *hastily* 818.7
rapid motion 677.8
rapids *river turbulence* 570.5, *shallowness* 599.1, *downflow* 714.3, *hidden danger* 813.3
rapid slalom pole *ski race* 162.4
rapid tempo *swiftness* 694.1
rapid transit *railroad system* 688.1
rapier *sharp weapon* 78.6
rapine *havoc* 523.5
raping *plundering* 479.5
rapist *lawbreaker* 53.15, *attacker* 418.10, *criminal* 427.6, *sexually immoral person* 432.8, *villain* 448.5, *raider* 477.10, *plunderer* 479.9, *violent animal* 520.4
rap on the knuckles *condemnation* 438.2, *condemn* 438.18, *punishment* 454.1, *corporal punishment* 454.11, *punish* 454.22, *hit* 454.28

rappel *climbing techniques* 161.3, *mountaineer* 161.10, *descent* 714.1, *descend* 714.12
rappelling *climbing techniques* 161.3
rappelling device *climbing equipment* 161.4
rappel ring *climbing equipment* 161.4
rapping *ramming* 695.3
rapport *friendly relations* 62.3, *agreement* 462.1, *relatedness* 727.1, *compatibility* 735.4
rapprochement *friendly relations* 62.3, *pacification* 74.1, *agreement* 462.1, *settlement* 735.6
rapscallion *miscreant* 448.6, *vulgar person* 535.4
rapt *diligent* 323.7
rapt in wonder *wondering* 294.7
raptness *wonder* 294.1
raptor *bird of prey* 36.11
raptorial *avian* 36.19
rapture *emotion* 266.3, *joy* 269.1, *oblivion* 355.4
rapturous *passionate* 266.12, *oblivious* 355.9
rapturously *with feeling* 266.18
rara avis *wonderful person* 294.6
rare *culinary* 91.9, *scarce* 98.8, *wondrous* 294.9, *valuable* 496.8, *insubstantial* 539.5, *sparse* 541.3, *796.6, airy* 558.12, *thinned* 595.13, *infrequent* 662.2, *excellent* 744.14, *unusual* 782.15, *unexpected* 839.6
rare as hen's teeth *infrequent* 662.2
rare book 174.2; *book* 174.1
rare chance *poor chance* 842.8
rare-earth element *chemical element* 11.3
raree show *show* 138.4
rarefaction 541.2; *thinning* 595.6
rarefactional *rarefied* 541.4
rarefactive *rarefied* 541.4
rarefied 541.4; *airy* 558.12, *thinned* 595.13, *unusual* 782.15
rarefy *refine* 534.7, *make sparse* 541.5, *make thin* 595.17, *reduce* 796.8
rare gas *chemical element* 11.3, *gas* 556.1
rarely 839.10; *not enough* 98.12, *wondrously* 294.18, *seldom* 640.9, *infrequently* 662.4, *superbly* 744.22, *sparsely* 796.11
rareness *sparseness* 541.1, *infrequency* 662.1, *unusualness* 782.4, *rarity* 796.4
rare occurrence *infrequency* 662.1
raring to go [Inf] *eager* 373.8, *prepared* 388.9
rarity 796.4; *scarcity* 98.3, *marvel* 294.3, *lightness* 539.1, *sparseness* 541.1, *air* 558.1, *infrequency* 662.1, *unusualness* 782.4, *fewness* 796.3, *unexpectedness* 839.2
rascal *troublemaker* 427.5, *miscreant* 448.6, *vulgar person* 535.4
rascally *villainous* 448.12, *cunning* 822.4
Ras Dashan Mountains and Hills 569
rash 286.5; *symptom* 114.3, *skin disease* 114.16, *adventurous* 284.20, *careless* 289.8, 324.8, *impulsive* 318.11, *overestimating* 343.4, *foolish* 353.5, *unpremeditated* 389.7, *overambitious* 391.6, *spontaneous* 396.5, *mark* 533.2, *mentally quick* 694.8, *hasty* 818.3
rasher *slice* 588.4, *particle* 760.4

rashly 286.9, 391.12, 818.8; *adventurously* 284.20, *carelessly* 289.18, *impulsively* 318.16, *inattentively* 324.12, *overoptimistically* 343.7, *foolishly* 353.8, *unreadily* 389.16, *dangerously* 811.14
rash move 286.4
rashness 286.1; *adventurousness* 284.4, *carelessness* 289.2, *impulsiveness* 318.6, *inattention* 324.1, *overestimation* 343.1, *folly* 353.1, *unpremeditation* 389.2, *defiance* 416.1, *potency* 516.6, *swiftness* 694.1, *endangerment* 811.2, *hastiness* 818.2
rash person 353.4; *rash move* 286.4
rashy *of disease* 114.25
rasorial *avian* 36.19
rasp *hiss* 237.3, *sound hoarse* 238.8, *make an insect sound* 240.9, *be dissonant* 241.6, *grate* 553.24, *eraser* 554.7, *grind* 554.15
raspberry *red thing* 257.3
raspberry [Inf] *figurative usage* 44.4, *cry of disapproval* 239.7, *expression of dissatisfaction* 274.2, *show of disapproval* 438.6, *gesture of protest* 507.3
rasping *nonresonant* 233.7, *hoarse* 238.5, *dissonant* 241.4, *grinding* 554.3, *rough* 554.11
raspingly *stridently* 238.10, *dissonantly* 241.7, *abrasively* 554.17
raspings *crumb* 553.5
rasping sound *hoarseness* 238.2
Rasputin *manager* 126.7, *motivator* 508.6
Rastafarian *other religious member* 81.13
Rastafarianism *other religions* 81.8
raster *computing terms* 15.22
rat *gnawing mammal* 35.13
rat [Inf] *strike* 57.8, *inform on* 170.13, *hypocrite* 192.9, *be dishonorable* 192.21, *coward* 285.3, *retreat* 285.8, *verifier* 336.4, *testify* 336.10 *equivocator* 380.4, *miscreant* 448.6, *warner* 814.5
rataplan *drumming* 235.1, *drum* 235.10, *vibration* 683.2
ratatat *crack* 234.2, *knock* 235.4, *vibration* 683.2
ratatouille *vegetable* 90.33
rat-catcher *animal killer* 30.14
ratchet *sharp-pointed thing* 549.4
ratchet wheel *wheel* 682.9
rate *division* 6.16, *estimate* 341.11, *payment* 433.5, *expense* 491.2, *fee* 494.3, *measure* 589.20, 739.7, *rank* 727.11, *quantify* 738.7, *degree* 739.1, *categorize* 767.21, *sort* 777.13
rate a movie *censor* 503.10
rate constant *chemical reaction* 11.8
rated *measured* 589.16, *ranked* 727.8, *gradational* 739.5, *categorized* 767.15, *classed* 777.11
rate-determining step *chemical reaction* 11.8
rate for the job *fee* 494.3
rate of change *differentiation* 6.29
rate of interest *interest* 488.4
rate of speed *speed* 694.2
Rath Breeds of Cattle 16
rather *by choice* 382.18, *moderately* 521.10, *to a degree* 739.11
rathole *shack* 60.10
ratification 459.4; *lawmaking*

53.11, *confirmation* 189.5, *proof* 331.4, *verification* 336.1, *yes* 346.2, *approval* 437.1, *contract* 462.2, *permission* 502.1, *adoption* 692.2, *consent* 735.8
ratificatory *verificatory* 336.6
ratified *confirmed* 189.17, *proven* 331.13, *verified* 336.7, *agreed* 346.5, *approved* 437.8, *contractual* 459.7, 462.7, *adopted* 692.10, *consenting* 735.18
ratifier *affirmer* 189.9, *contractor* 459.6, *assenter* 462.5
ratify *legislate* 53.31, *identify oneself* 184.12, *confirm* 189.25, *prove* 331.17, *verify* 336.8, *assent* 346.6, *approve* 437.14, *contract* 459.8, 462.11, *permit* 502.6, *make stable* 674.7, *adopt* 692.14, *establish reality* 719.12, *consent* 735.28
ratifying *contractual* 459.7
rat-infested *worn* 808.13
rating *judgment* 341.1, *berating* 438.5, *measurement* 589.1, *relative position* 727.5, *gradation* 739.3, *categorization* 767.5, *social class* 777.5, *importance* 799.1
ratio 783.5; *division* 6.16, *portion* 474.2, *interrelatedness* 727.3, *gradation* 739.3, *fraction* 787.1
ratiocinate *philosophize* 4.19, *think* 315.12, 317.9, *reason* 319.11, *discuss* 329.12
ratiocination *philosophical investigation* 4.4, *thought* 317.1, *way of thinking* 317.4, *reasoning* 319.2, *logical argument* 329.2, *judgment* 341.1
ratiocinative *rational* 4.15, 319.8, *reasoning* 317.6
ration *budget* 457.10, *portion* 474.2, *allocate* 474.5, *limit* 620.7, *certain amount* 738.3, *quantify* 738.7, *gradation* 739.3, *fractional part* 787.2, *economic restraint* 830.3, *restrain commerce* 830.14
rational 4.15, 109.4, 319.8; *real number* 6.5, *complex* 6.69, *divisible* 6.71, *intellectual* 315.8, *reasoning* 317.6, 319.7, *apologetic* 329.10, *wise* 352.4, *planned* 387.10, *moderate* 521.3, *organizational* 767.13, *numerical* 783.7
rationale *motive* 178.5, *way of thinking* 317.4, *line of argument* 329.3, *motivation* 508.1, *reason* 675.4
rationalism Philosophical Schools of Thought 4, Theologies 81, *reasoning* 319.2
rationalist Philosophical Schools of Thought 4, *disbeliever* 88.5, *reasoner* 319.5, *freethinker* 829.10, *independent* 829.12
rationalistic *rational* 319.8, *independent* 829.12
rationalistically *freely* 829.22
rationality 109.2; *philosophical attitude* 4.3, *intellect* 315.1, *reason* 319.1, *reasoning* 319.2
rationalization *philosophy* 4.1, *defense mechanism* 108.23, *reasoning* 319.2, *plea* 329.5, *planning* 387.8, *conversion* 670.1, *limitation* 747.3, *organization* 767.3
rationalize 4.20; *motivate* 178.17, *think* 315.12, *reason* 319.11, *plead* 329.14, *plan* 387.12, *make regular* 663.9, *transform* 670.13, *make smaller* 747.8, *systematize* 765.19, *organize* 767.19
rationalized *organized* 767.12
rationalizing *reasoning* 319.2

rationally 4.25; *sanely* 109.6, *intelligently* 315.14, *thoughtfully* 317.13, *reasonably* 319.15, *apologetically* 329.18, *wisely* 352.8, *in place* 767.24
rational number *real number* 6.5, *kind of number* 783.2
rational psychology Psychological Theories, Schools 108
rationed *unprovided* 98.6, *limited* 620.5, *quantitative* 738.6, *restrained* 830.9
rationing *war measures* 76.18, *limit* 620.1, *economic restraint* 830.3
ration oneself *be modest* 403.11, *be self-restrained* 455.10
rations *provisions* 89.3, *food* 90.1
ratio scale *nonparametric methods* 6.54
ratite *flightless bird* 36.8, *avian* 36.19
ratlike *rodentlike* 35.28
ratline *sailboat parts and accessories* 150.4, *ladder* 713.10, *tackle* 754.6
rat on [Inf] *tell on* 180.10
rat poison *pest control* 16.13, *poison* 117.7
rat race [Inf] *alacrity* 414.3, *rivalry* 422.2
ratsbane *killing agent* 30.15, *poison* 117.7
rattan *instrument of punishment* 454.13
rattenando Musical Terms and Expression Marks 140
rattenuto Musical Terms and Expression Marks 140
ratter *cat* 35.11
rattish *rodentlike* 35.28
rattle 235.3, 235.12, Musical Instruments 142, *daunt* 179.9, *loud sound* 232.2, *be loud* 232.8, *crack* 234.7, *weaken* 517.13, *vibrate* 683.13, *disturb* 768.10, *cheap thing* 800.7
rattle along *be swift* 694.10
rattled *dissuaded* 179.5, *disturbed* 768.6
rattle on *be talkative* 207.7
rattlesnake *or* **rattler** *snake* 37.5
rattle the windows *shatter the peace* 232.10
rattletrap *automobile* 687.6
rattling 235.8; *loud* 232.6, *crackling* 234.5, *speeding* 694.7
rattling pace *swiftness* 694.1
rattrap *pest control* 16.13, *beggary* 486.3, *dilapidation* 808.5
ratty *rodentlike* 35.28
raucous *strident* 238.4, *dissonant* 241.4
raucously *dissonantly* 241.7
raucousness *speech difficulty* 206.1, *harsh sound* 238.1
raunchily *immorally* 432.18
raunchiness *immorality* 432.1
raunchy *offensive* 432.11
rauwolfia Tree Products 43
ravage *be at war* 76.32, *lay waste* 96.21, 523.14, *attack successfully* 418.25, *plunder* 479.16, *impair* 808.18
ravaged *devastated* 96.12
ravager *plunderer* 479.9, *destroyer* 523.6
ravages of time *passage of time* 639.3, *physical deterioration* 808.4
ravaging *plundering* 479.5, *stolen* 479.12
rave *become insane* 110.12, *boast* 194.14, *be angry* 302.19, *talk nonsense* 362.12

---

rave [Brit inf] *rejoicing* 279.1, *rejoice* 279.5

rave about *publicize* 173.18, *compliment* 437.17

ravelin *fort* 419.13

raven *songbird* 36.12, *dark thing* 247.3, *black thing* 254.3, *black* 254.5, *be hungry* 288.21

raven-haired *black-haired* 254.8

ravening *underfed* 98.7, *murderous* 520.7

ravenous *eating* 92.18, *underfed* 98.7, 118.7, *gluttonous* 119.3, *hungry* 288.16

ravenously *carnivorously* 92.27, *abstemiously* 118.11, *gluttonously* 119.5, *eagerly* 186.19

ravenousness *gluttony* 119.1

ravens Collective Names 59

Ravensburger waltz *ice-dancing move* 162.19

raver [Brit inf] *rejoicer* 279.3

rave review *criticism* 365.3, *compliment* 437.4, *successful thing* 845.5

Ravi Rivers 570

ravine *landform* 8.9, *valley* 572.8, *gulf* 587.3, *narrow place* 593.2, *lowlands* 597.6, *concave land* 635.2

raving *manic* 110.10, *bombast* 194.4, *bombastic* 194.10, *angry* 302.11, *nonsense* 362.2, *meaningless* 362.7

raving beauty *attractive female* 529.5

raving mad *insane* 110.9

ravings *delusion* 110.2

ravioli *pasta* 90.31

ravish **477.15;** *seduce* 432.16, *plunder* 479.16, *use violence* 520.9

ravisher *plunderer* 479.9

ravishing *beautiful* 529.7

ravishingly *magnificently* 529.16

ravishingness *beauty* 529.1

ravishment *sexual offense* 432.6, *sexual possession* 477.2, *plundering* 479.5

ravvivando Musical Terms and Expression Marks 140

raw **260.9;** *windy* 9.42, *cool* 9.49, *immature* 26.12, 652.12, *culinary* 91.9, *gas* 106.14, *unskilled* 128.5, *painful* 215.4, *feeling pain* 215.6, *cold* 218.9, *gaudy* 251.12, *profane* 301.10, *uncooked* 389.12, *unaccustomed* 398.3, *unfinished* 544.9, *shapeless* 625.2, *incomplete* 762.5, 806.6, *embryonic* 771.19

raw, the *bareness* 614.3

rawboned *thin* 595.9

raw deal [Inf] *fault* 430.2, *adversity* 848.1

raw feelings *oversensitivity* 267.2

raw glaze *glaze* 129.3

rawhide *leather* 104.7

rawly *youthfully* 26.14, *greenly* 260.15, *immaturely* 652.23

raw material *supplies* 102.3, *materials* 104.1, *natural state* 389.4, *matter* 524.4, *source* 675.2

raw nerve *sense organ* 212.4, *provocation* 302.3

rawness *immaturity* 26.3, 389.3, 652.3, *unskillfulness* 128.1, *unaccustomedness* 398.1, *shapelessness* 625.1, *incompleteness* 762.1, 806.2

raw recruit *unskilled person* 128.3, *beginner* 771.14

raw sienna *brown pigment* 256.2, *orange pigment* 258.2

raw umber *brown pigment* 256.2

ray *line* 6.35, *straight line* 630.2,

wave 683.4, *radiation* 703.3, *radiate* 703.13

rayed *radiating* 703.7

ray-finned fish *fish* 38.5

ray flower or *floret* *flower head* 42.4

Rayleigh scattering Classical Physical Laws 10

ray of hope *hope* 281.1

ray of light *light* 10.17

ray of sunshine *joyful person* 269.5, *reliever* 275.4

rayon *plastics* 104.6, *fiber* 130.2

rayonism Western Art Styles 133

rayon stockings *legwear* 100.26

rays of the sun *light* 246.1

raze *destroy* 186.10, *knock down* 523.13, *abrade* 554.13, *make horizontal* 603.10, *flatten* 716.15

razed *leveled* 603.8

razed to the ground *destroyed* 186.5, *leveled* 603.8

razee Sailing Ships and Boats 690

raze to the ground *knock down* 523.13, *make horizontal* 603.10

razing *destroying* 523.2

razor *hairdressing tool* 530.9, *sharp-edged thing* 549.6, *use a sharp tool* 549.17

razor blade *sharp-edged thing* 549.6

razor cut *coiffure* 530.8

razor edge *sharp edge* 549.3, *cutting edge* 618.3, *danger* 811.1

razor-edged *sharp-edged* 549.12

razor-sharp *sharp-edged* 549.12, *mentally sharp* 549.14

razor wire *barrier* 419.10

razz *cry of disapproval* 239.7, *hiss* 239.17

razzing *hissing* 239.12

razzle-dazzle [Inf] *showiness* 404.1

razzmatazz [Inf] *flashiness* 404.4

RC *denominational* 81.23

Re Deities 82

reabsorb *absorb* 708.19

reach **704.14;** *suffice* 97.6, *sail* 150.29, *be heard* 228.15, *move to compassion* 308.9, *improve* 467.18, *geographical space* 563.3, *range* 563.7, *extend* 563.14, *size* 579.1, *length* 590.1, *be long* 590.11, *breadth* 592.1, *span* 592.12, *degree* 739.1

reachable *touchable* 216.5, *hearable* 228.12, *near* 586.6, *possible* 836.5

reach a climax *peak* 596.18, *be at the top* 600.9

reach a compromise *compromise* 461.7

reach a crescendo *augment* 467.16

reach a crisis *be in difficulties* 726.14

reach a gentleman's agreement *contract* 462.11

reach a lower level *descend* 714.12

reach a mass audience *make comprehensible* 363.8

reach an accord *agree with* 462.10, *agree* 752.17

reach an agreement *negotiate* 460.6, *agree* 752.17

reach an all-time low *not exist* 786.6

reach a new high *be superior* 744.15

reach an impasse *have a mishap* 826.18

reach an international agreement *contract* 462.11

reach a stage *be converted* 670.12, *be at a critical moment* 726.15

reach a stalemate *have a mishap* 826.18

reach a turning point *be at a critical moment* 726.15

reach-finned fish *fish* 38.5

reach full growth *be complete* 761.10

reach home *shelter* 812.8

reaching *bowls* 151.7, *achievement* 704.8, *gradational* 739.5

reaching a mass audience *simple* 363.6

reaching jib *sailboat parts and accessories* 150.4

reaching shot *grip* 151.4

reach manhood or *womanhood* *mature* 27.17

reach maturity *be complete* 761.10

reach new heights *be superior* 744.15

reach one's destination *find one's way* 691.15, *reach* 704.14

reach one's goal *secure one's objective* 464.12, *reach* 704.14, *complete* 759.10

reach one's majority *mature* 27.17

reach one's nadir *fail* 714.18, *become inferior* 745.11

reach orgasm *stimulate* 20.22

reach out **585.10;** *make one's way* 679.12

reach perfection *be complete* 761.10

reach safety *be safe* 810.20, *shelter* 812.8

reach the boiling point *become angry* 302.20

reach the bottom *deepen* 598.21

reach the depths *fail* 714.18

reach the limit *be at the top* 600.9

reach the other side *cross* 692.17

reach the prime of one's life *mature* 27.17

reach the threshold *limit* 620.7

reach the top *master* 68.17, *mountaineer* 161.10, *be at the top* 600.9, *achieve* 704.21, *ascend* 713.19

reach the zenith *ascend* 713.19

reach to *reach out* 585.10, *fill* 761.11

reach to the far ends of the earth *be excessive* 99.9

reach to the four corners of the earth *be excessive* 99.9

reach toward *make one's way* 679.12

react **11.38, 334.20, 676.8;** *interact* 10.73, *sense* 212.9, *push* 414.20, *counteract* 510.7, *reverse* 671.9, *reciprocate* 729.7

react against **291.15;** *counteract* 510.7

reactance *resistance* 10.41

reactant *chemical reaction* 11.8

react automatically *be instinctive* 320.10

reacted *reversed* 671.7

reacting *caused* 676.5, *reciprocal* 729.4

reacting to *caused* 676.5

reaction *turbine type* 14.12, *sensation* 212.1, *feelings* 266.1, *idea* 327.1, *response* 334.4, *counteraction* 510.1, *reversion* 671.1, *effect* 676.1, *means of propulsion* 696.2, *reciprocity* 729.1, *restoration* 809.2, *contrariness* 828.5

reactionary **427.9;** *political party member* 50.6, *obstinate person* 379.4, *resister* 417.5, *resisting*

417.8, *counteracting* 510.6, *regressive* 671.6, *retroactive* 680.12, *conservative* 815.13, *opposer* 828.9, *uncooperative* 828.14

reaction formation *defense mechanism* 108.23

reactionist *uncooperative* 828.14

reaction order *chemical reaction* 11.8

reaction wood *timber* 43.3

reactivate *repair* 809.10

reactivation *repair* 809.1, *revival* 809.3

reactive **11.29, 334.12;** *counteracting* 510.6, *regressive* 671.6, *reciprocal* 729.4

reactive armor *modern armor* 419.7

reactively *in answer* 334.25, *counter* 510.8, *reversibly* 671.14, *reciprocally* 729.10

react sharply *push* 414.20

read *rationalize* 4.20, *program* 15.29, *learn* 48.23, *huddle* 155.7, *communicated* 169.15, *broadcast* 172.12, *inspect* 242.22, *interpret* 365.12, *decipher* 365.13, *behave toward* 399.20, *received* 473.11

readability *clarity* 363.2

readable *simple* 363.6, *graceful* 527.4

readably *elegantly* 527.7

read between the lines *interpret* 365.12

readdress *send* 209.11

read easily *be intelligible* 363.10

reader *educator* 48.4, *schoolbook* 48.15, *educational leader* 68.11, *type of book* 174.3, *public speaker* 209.5, *recipient* 473.5

readership *instructorship* 48.5

read hieroglyphics *decipher* 365.13

readied *prepared* 388.9

readily *admiringly* 290.11, *capably* 340.15, *willingly* 373.15, *in preparation* 388.22, *obediently* 426.9, *operationally* 509.13, *probably* 513.6, *early* 657.17, *easily* 823.19

readily available **575.21**

readiness *maturity* 27.3, *educatability* 48.9, *inclination* 290.2, *circumspection* 325.3, *qualification* 340.1, *foresight* 357.1, *willingness* 373.1, *preparedness* 388.5, *alacrity* 414.3, *obedience* 426.1, *attitude* 513.2, *availability* 575.5, *earliness* 657.1, *timeliness* 659.1, *usefulness* 801.1, *perfection* 805.1, *easiness* 823.1

reading *learning* 48.7, *type of desk* 101.6, Hobbies and Pastimes 167, *public speaking* 205.11, *address* 209.1, *interpretation* 365.1

reading glass *visual aid* 242.14

reading glasses *visual aid* 242.14

reading lamp *electric light* 246.6

reading list *list* 785.1

reading room *library* 174.14

read into *interpret* 365.12

readjust *compromise* 461.7, *equalize* 740.12, *counterbalance* 743.8

readjusted *counterbalanced* 743.6

readjustment *equalization* 740.4, *counterbalance* 743.2, *restoration* 809.2

read lips *translate* 365.16

read minds *experience psychic phenomena* 86.23, *entertain* 138.16, *divine* 358.15

read-only *computerized* 15.28

read-only memory (ROM)

memory 15.6, *artificial memory* 354.6
read palms *divine* 86.24, 358.15
read sign language *translate* 365.16
read signs *divine* 86.24
read something into it *distort the truth* 627.12
read tea leaves *divine* 86.24, *look ahead* 650.11
read the auspices *divine* 358.15
read the banns *get engaged to* 458.12
read the chart *navigate* 690.15
read the defense *play offense* 155.18
read the depth sounder *navigate* 690.15
read the future *foresee* 357.9, *divine* 358.15
read the omens *divine* 358.15
read the riot act to *condemn* 438.18
read the signs *divine* 358.15
read the small print *make conditions* 460.7
read the stars *or* **cards** *or* **runes** *or* **entrails** *or* **tea leaves** *divine* 358.15
read the tarot *divine* 86.24
read the wedding service *join in marriage* 64.20
read the wedding vows *join in marriage* 64.20
read through *rehearse* 136.37, *act* 137.20
read-through *production* 136.14, 137.6
read up on *learn* 48.23
ready *adult* 27.11, *educatable* 48.18, *skillful* 127.10, *inclined toward* 290.5, *circumspect* 325.8, *qualified* 340.7, *expecting* 356.4, *willing* 373.7, *prepared* 388.9, *prepare for action* 388.18, *active* 414.13, *obedient* 426.4, *tending to* 513.4, *available* 575.11, 647.6, *early* 657.8, *useful* 801.5, *nearby* 803.4, *perfect* 805.8
ready, the [Inf] *cash* 484.2
ready and willing *eager* 373.8
ready cash *type of payment* 489.3
ready for another round *refreshed* 94.5
ready for anything *skillful* 127.10, *in hand* 388.11
ready-formed *ready-made* 388.13
ready for more *refreshed* 94.5
ready for use *in hand* 388.11, *useful* 801.5
readying *preparation* 388.1
ready-made 388.13; *tailored* 100.41, *produced* 522.12, *prototypical* 624.7
ready-made object *sculpture* 144.1
ready-made verdict *predetermination* 384.1
ready-mixed *ready-made* 388.13
ready money *cash* 484.2, *funds* 484.6
ready oneself *prepare oneself* 388.21
ready reckoner *calculator* 784.5
ready reserves *the military* 58.2, *reinforcements* 77.11
ready to break *brittle* 548.3
ready to burst *immoderate* 99.6
ready-to-cook *ready-made* 388.13
ready to die for *unselfish* 443.5
ready to drop *fatigued* 820.2
ready to go *prepared* 388.9
ready to hand *in hand* 388.11
ready-to-serve *culinary* 91.9, *ready-made* 388.13

ready to split *brittle* 548.3
ready to use *ready-made* 388.13
ready-to-wear *tailored* 100.41, *ready-made* 388.13, *immediate* 645.5
ready-to-wear clothes *store-bought clothes* 100.3
ready wit *wit* 277.3
reaffirm *emphasize* 200.6
reagent *chemical reaction* 11.8
real 717.14, 719.6, 721.12; *factual* 3.14, *real number* 6.5, *complex* 6.69, *legitimate* 53.21, *touchable* 216.5, *propertied* 470.9, *material* 524.7, *present* 575.7, *intrinsic* 611.11, *true* 721.11, *authentic* 721.16, 737.6, *numerical* 783.7, *certain* 840.7
real analysis *calculus* 6.28
real article *original* 737.2
real estate *property* 470.1
real-estate agent *person transferring property* 470.8, *merchant* 482.10
realign *rearrange* 767.20
realigned *rearranged* 767.14
realignment *rearrangement* 767.4
real image *lens system* 10.22
realism 719.3; *Philosophical Schools of Thought* 4, *Western Art Styles* 133, *theater movements* 136.9, *Western Literary Groups* 139, *correctness* 350.2, *verisimilitude* 721.10
realist 719.4; *Philosophical Schools of Thought* 4, *doer* 412.3, *materialist* 524.3, *lifelike* 721.19
realistic 719.7; *rational* 4.15, *believable* 87.7, *literary* 139.15, *representational* 187.8, *descriptive* 202.11, *correct* 350.4, *practical* 719.8, *lifelike* 721.19, *certain* 840.7
realistically *rationally* 4.25, *representationally* 187.15, *descriptively* 202.18, *verisimilarly* 721.33
realistic comedy *comedy* 136.11
realistic representation *verisimilitude* 721.10
realities 719.5; *fact* 717.6
reality 719.1, 721.2; *historicalness* 3.9, *touch* 216.1, *presence* 575.1, *demonstrable existence* 717.5, *chief thing* 799.3, *certainty* 840.1
realizable 719.9; *intelligible* 363.5, *possible* 836.5
realization *representation* 187.1, *appearance* 264.1, *feelings* 266.1, *finding out* 345.3, *knowledge* 348.1, *understanding* 363.4, *gain* 467.1, *materialization* 524.2, *completion* 761.2
realize *rationalize* 4.20, *know* 48.24, 348.10, *manage* 126.10, *be informed* 170.15, *represent* 187.10, *sense* 212.9, *present* 264.15, *feel* 266.14, *have an idea* 327.13, *find out* 345.13, *imagine* 360.14, *understand* 363.9, *gain* 467.15, *merchandise* 482.17, *bank* 484.26, *be material* 524.8, *come to be* 717.19, *make real* 719.11, *complete* 761.9, *perfect* 805.19
realized *appearing* 264.9, *material* 524.7
realized ultimate reality piton (RURP) *climbing equipment* 161.4
realize one's capital *trade in* 457.8
realize one's potential *be complete* 761.10
realizing *feeling* 266.9
real life *realism* 719.3

real-life *descriptive* 202.11, *realistic* 719.7, *real* 721.12
really 717.22, 719.13; *biographically* 3.18, *earnestly* 278.10, *assuredly* 336.12, *in person* 575.18, *truly* 721.27, *authentically* 721.31, *certainly* 840.15
really! *wonderful!* 294.20
really mean *mean* 361.13
really-truly *really* 719.13, *truly* 721.27
realm *nation* 18.14, *subject* 48.3, *body politic* 50.3, *region* 564.1, *sphere* 564.10, *dominion* 566.3, *type* 777.4
real McCoy, the *authenticity* 721.7, *original* 737.2
realm of Pluto *evil place* 446.6
realm of possibility *possibleness* 836.2
realness *historicalness* 3.9, *reality* 721.2, *authenticity* 721.7
real number 6.5; *kind of number* 783.2
real part *complex number* 6.6
realpolitik *tactics* 399.12, *cunning* 822.1
real presence *Eucharist* 85.7
real property *property* 470.1
real thing *romantic love* 299.2, *demonstrable existence* 717.5, *authenticity* 721.7, *original* 737.2
real time *computing terms* 15.22, *time* 639.1
Realtor™ *person transferring property* 470.8, *merchant* 482.10
realty *property* 470.1
real wages *economic factor* 56.8
real war *war* 76.1
real world 719.2; *material world* 524.1, *reality* 721.2
real-world *real* 721.12
ream *paper* 104.5, *hole* 583.17
reamed *holed* 583.12
reamer *cleaning tool* 111.10, *opener* 583.2
reanimate *invigorate* 28.22, *refresh* 94.6, *revive* 809.14
reanimated *given new life* 28.15
reanimation *new life* 28.8, *refreshment* 94.1, *revival* 809.3
reap *farm* 16.19, *store* 105.17, *gain* 453.18, *shorten* 591.9
reap a profit *gain* 453.18, *profit* 467.22
reaper *farm tool* 16.5, *collector* 59.17
reaping machine *farm tool* 16.5
reappear *occur* 264.14, *be periodical* 641.9, *be repeated* 797.20
reappearance 264.8; *return* 797.4
reappearing *recurrent* 797.13
reappoint *give back* 478.5, *restore* 809.12
reappointment *giving back* 478.1
reap the benefit of *find useful* 801.11
reap the fruits *gain* 453.18, *attain one's goal* 845.13
reap the harvest *attain one's goal* 845.13
reap the profit from *find useful* 801.11
rear 715.10; *practice livestock farming* 16.20, *educate* 48.22, *armed force* 77.10, *bring into existence* 522.14, *heighten* 596.14, *be vertical* 602.8, *back* 622.1, 622.6, *arise* 715.15, *opposite* 731.2, *make bigger* 746.7, *hindmost* 773.18
Rear Admiral *US Military Ranks* 58

rear cushion *bowling* 151.1
rear-dump truck *construction equipment* 14.23
reared 715.7; *domesticated* 16.18, *produced* 522.12, *unbowed* 602.7
rear end 622.4
rear entrance *back entrance* 622.2
rear guard *armed force* 77.10, *guard* 419.15, *back* 622.1, *warner* 814.5
rearing 715.2; *education* 48.1, *unbowed* 602.7, *rising* 713.14, *raising* 715.1
rear its head *become visible* 264.13
rear one's head *become visible* 264.13, *show oneself* 843.15
rear part *back* 622.1
rearrange 767.20; *react* 11.38, *cause change* 665.16, *tidy* 765.21
rearranged 767.14; *changed* 665.10
rearrangement 767.4; *chemical reaction* 11.8, *change for the better* 665.4
rear sentry *warner* 814.5
rear up *be vertical* 602.8, *arise* 715.15
rearview mirror *reflector* 242.10
rearward *back* 622.6, *behind* 622.8, *backward* 680.23
reason 319.1, 319.11, 675.4; *philosophize* 4.19, *rationalize* 4.20, *theorize* 6.84, *claim* 72.2, *rationality* 109.2, *motive* 178.5, *intelligence* 315.2, *think* 315.12, 317.9, *thought* 317.1, *purpose* 327.4, *discuss* 329.12, *solution* 334.6, 376.6, *solve* 334.21, *evidence* 339.1, *estimate* 341.11, *wisdom* 352.1, *suppose* 359.8, *interpret* 365.12, *energy* 414.4, *defense* 441.2, *motivation* 508.1, *basis* 601.3, 605.4, *cause* 675.1, *aim* 773.12
reasonability *plausibility* 838.3
reasonable *rational* 4.15, 109.4, *believable* 87.7, *thoughtful* 315.10, *reasoning* 319.11, *purposive* 327.11, *lenient* 423.3, *vindicable* 441.9, *temperate* 455.8, *cheap* 497.9, *moderate* 521.3, *basic* 605.13, *possible* 836.5, *plausible* 838.7
reasonableness *philosophical attitude* 4.3, *rationality* 109.2, *leniency* 423.1, *moderation* 455.3, 521.1
reasonably 319.15; *rationally* 4.25, *believably* 87.13, *sanely* 109.6, *intelligently* 315.14, *purposively* 327.20, *apologetically* 329.18, *correspondingly* 334.27, *leniently* 423.6, *moderately* 455.15, 521.10, *cheaply* 497.16, *basically* 605.21, *practically* 836.19
reason behind *reason* 675.4
reasoned *rational* 4.15, *purposive* 327.11, *solved* 334.15, *basic* 605.13
reasoner 319.5
reasoning 6.61, 317.6, 319.2, 319.7; *philosophical investigation* 4.4, *motive* 178.5, *intellectual* 315.8, *thought* 317.1, *way of thinking* 317.4, *thoughtful* 317.5, *logical argument* 329.2, *judgment* 341.1, *wise* 352.4
reason why *reason* 675.4
reason with *motivate* 178.17
reassemble *put together* 59.30, *repair* 809.10, *restore* 809.12
reassembling *repair* 809.9
reassert *emphasize* 200.6
reassurance *ease* 275.1, *cheer*

281.4, *encouragement* 284.6, *moral support* 605.7

reassure *comfort* 273.9, *relieve* 275.8, *inspire hope* 281.14, *give courage* 284.16, *give moral support* 605.18

reassured *relieved* 275.6

reassuring *relieving* 275.7, *cheering* 281.9, *encouraging* 284.13, *supportive* 605.11, 825.18

reassuringly *comfortingly* 275.14, 281.17, *encouragingly* 284.21, *supportively* 605.20

Réaumur scale *heat measurement* 217.2, *scale* 589.9

reawaken *revive* 809.14

reawakening *revival* 809.3

Reb [Yiddish] *professional title* 72.6

rebab Musical Instruments 142

rebarbative *unpleasant* 272.6, *disliked* 291.10

rebarbatively *distastefully* 291.19

rebate *discount* 495.1, 495.4, *subtracted item* 749.2

rebated *discounted* 495.3

rebbe *rabbi* 84.6

rebec Musical Instruments 142

rebel 427.8; *anarchist* 51.4, *be anarchic* 51.8, *go to war* 76.29, *dissenting* 347.7, *dissent* 347.8, *defiant person* 416.4, *be insubordinate* 416.8, *subvert* 427.13, *not observe* 466.9, *protester* 507.4, *cause mischief* 507.9, *be violent* 520.8, *dissenter* 782.8, *not conform* 782.18, *opposer* 828.9

rebel against *counterattack* 418.24

rebel angel *evil spirit* 446.4

rebellion *dissentience* 347.3, *disobedience* 416.2, *military attack* 418.2, *revolution* 427.4, *disorder* 507.2, *dissent* 782.2

rebellious *anarchic* 51.5, *lawless* 53.26, *dissenting* 347.7, *defying* 416.6, *resisting* 417.8, *counterattacking* 418.15, *subversive* 427.11, *disorderly* 507.6, 766.15, *dissident* 782.12

rebelliously *anarchically* 51.10, *lawlessly* 53.35, *dissentiently* 347.10, *in defiance* 416.10, *resistingly* 417.14, *subversively* 427.15, *disapprovingly* 507.10, *disruptively* 766.26, *unconformably* 782.21

rebelliousness *disobedience* 416.2, *revolution* 427.4, *lawlessness* 766.6

rebel yell *glory of war* 76.17, *military call* 183.9, *act of defiance* 416.3

rebirth *new life* 28.8, *evolution* 670.3, *return* 797.4, *revival* 809.3

reboant *resonant* 236.6

reborn *given new life* 28.15, *remade* 797.10

rebound *playing terms* 148.4, *play basketball* 148.7, *pommel horse* 157.7, *exercise* 157.12, *resonate* 236.9, *elasticity* 546.1, *be elastic* 546.7, *swing* 671.12, *countermotion* 680.6, *reflex* 680.7, *recoil* 680.21

rebounder *basketball team* 148.2

rebounding *playing terms* 148.4, *resonance* 236.1, *resonant* 236.6, *elastic* 546.5

rebozo *coat* 100.19

rebroadcast *broadcast* 172.12

rebuff *response* 334.4, *react* 334.20, *opposition* 375.2, *oppose* 375.13, *rejection* 383.1, *reject* 383.10, *exclude* 383.11, 409.12, *act of discourtesy* 411.3, *resistance* 417.1, *resist* 417.10, *insult* 436.5,

436.21, *veto* 503.3, 503.9, *dissent* 506.2, 506.9, *repulse* 701.2, *repel* 701.7, *downfall* 848.4

rebuffed *reactive* 334.12, *rejected* 383.6, *dissenting* 506.6

rebuffing *resistant* 417.6, *insulting* 436.10

rebuild *make new* 652.20, *restore* 809.12

rebuildable *renewable* 652.15

rebuilder *repairer* 809.5

rebuilding *beautification* 530.1, *new start* 652.5, *restoration* 809.2

rebuilt *renewed* 652.14, *repaired* 809.6

rebuke 298.21; *dissuasion* 179.1, *expression of dissatisfaction* 274.2, *be dissatisfied* 274.7, *condemnation* 438.2, *condemn* 438.18, *punishment* 454.1, *punish* 454.22

rebuked *condemned* 438.11

rebuking *condemning* 438.10, *censuring* 438.12

rebus *puzzle* 182.5, Heraldic Terms 184

rebut *negate* 190.16, *countercharge* 332.9, *answer back* 334.19, *counter* 339.13, *justify* 441.12, *dissent* 506.9, *object* 828.18

rebuttable *vindicable* 441.9

rebuttal *evidence* 54.15, *negation* 190.1, *denial* 332.2, *countercharge* 332.3, *counterstatement* 334.5, *counterevidence* 339.5, *defense* 441.2, *dissent* 506.2, *objection* 828.2

rebutted *negated* 190.10, *retaliatory* 334.13

rebutter *evidence* 54.15, *negator* 190.8

rebut the charge *justify* 441.12

rebutting *refuting* 332.6, *counterevident* 339.10, *vindicatory* 441.7

recalcitrance *opposition* 375.2, *obstinacy* 417.2, *disobedience* 427.1, *refusal* 506.1, *protest* 507.1, *opposing force* 510.2, *dissent* 782.2, *contrariness* 828.5

recalcitrant *reactive* 334.12, *refusing* 375.9, *refractory* 379.6, *defying* 416.6, *obstinate* 417.7, *troublemaker* 427.5, *disobedient* 427.10, *refused* 506.5, *protesting* 507.5, *counteracting* 510.6, *dissident* 782.12, *uncooperative* 828.14

recalcitrantly *in answer* 334.25

recalcitrate *react* 334.20

recalcitration *response* 334.4

recall *recollect* 3.16, *memory* 108.27, 354.1, *remember* 354.12, 471.10, *retentiveness* 471.4, *remove power from* 515.13, *return to* 797.18, *restoration* 809.2, *restore* 809.12, *cancellation* 834.1, *termination* 834.2, *cancel* 834.6

recalled *biographical* 3.13, *canceled* 834.5

recalling *recollection* 3.8, *retentiveness* 471.4

recall to life *revive* 809.14

recant 81.27; *disavow* 190.18, *deny* 332.8, *renounce* 383.13, 392.4, *confess* 451.8, *take back* 477.17, *reverse* 671.9, *reply* 671.13, *cancel* 834.6

recantation *disavowal* 190.3, *denial* 332.2, *renunciation* 383.4, *relinquishment* 392.1, *confession* 451.2, *reversion* 671.1, *cancellation* 834.1

recanted *disavowing* 190.12, *relinquished* 392.2, *reversed* 671.7

recanter *negator* 190.8, *equivocator* 380.4, *abrogator* 834.4

recanting *taking back* 477.4

recantingly *retractively* 190.24

recant one's errors *confess* 451.8

recap *summary* 204.1, *summarize* 204.7, *iteration* 797.2, *iterate* 797.16

recapitulate *recount* 202.16, *summarize* 204.7, *remind* 354.13, *make comprehensible* 363.8, *iterate* 797.16

recapitulation *evolution* 13.23, *summary* 204.1, *verdict* 341.2, *iteration* 797.2

recapitulative *repetitious* 797.11

recapture *remember* 354.12, *imagine* 360.14, *taking back* 477.4, *take back* 477.17

recapturing *taking back* 477.4

recast *rectify* 807.22

recce [Brit inf] *observation* 242.5

recede *disappear* 265.5, *shed* 614.21, *reverse* 671.9

receding 680.11; *bald* 614.16

receding hair *baldness* 614.9

receipt 489.2, 492.1; *record* 185.1, *acknowledgment* 334.2, *documentation* 339.6, *promise* 464.2, *property* 470.1, *acknowledgment of payment* 473.3, *receive* 473.13, 492.7, *deposit* 487.3, *admittance* 708.1

receipt [Arch] *cooking* 91.1

receipted *received* 492.6

receipted payment *receipt* 489.2

receipt for payment *receipt* 489.2

receipt in full *receipt* 489.2

receipts *resources* 102.4, *boxing terms* 152.3, *earnings* 467.5, *something received* 473.2, *takings* 477.8, *money received* 492.2

receipts and expenditures *accounts* 493.4

receivable 473.12; *admissive* 708.8

receivables *amount owing* 488.5, *payment* 489.1

receive 473.13, 492.7; *be sociable* 408.14, *admit* 708.12, *include* 763.5

receive a benefit *gain* 467.15

receive a bequest *receive* 473.13

receive a bequest *or* **a legacy** *profit* 467.22

receive a bonus *profit* 467.22

receive a final notice *demand* 505.12

receive a free gift *win an award* 467.23

receive a fringe benefit *profit* 467.22

receive a golden handshake *win an award* 467.23, *withdraw* 705.9

receive a good omen *show potential* 458.14

receive a letter from Uncle Sam *join the army* 76.31

receive alimony *earn* 467.20

receive an advance *earn* 467.20

receive an honorary degree *be rewarded* 453.16

receive an injunction *demand* 505.12

receive a pawn ticket *guarantee* 458.13

receive a pay increase *or* **a raise** *augment* 467.16

receive a promotion *be rewarded* 453.16

receive a scholarship *profit* 467.22

receive a stipend *earn* 467.20

receive a summons *be accused* 442.10

receive a tip *win an award* 467.23

receive a title *be rewarded* 453.16

receive a voucher *guarantee* 458.13

receive a windfall profit *win an award* 467.23

receive Christ *be religious* 81.25

receive communion *be religious* 81.25

received 473.11, 492.6; *societal* 1.13, *believed* 87.8, *communicated* 169.15, *broadcast* 172.12, *accounted* 493.8

received idea *convention* 781.5

received into the church *received* 473.11

received meaning *type of meaning* 361.4

receive extreme unction *follow rites* 85.19

receive guests *receive someone* 473.14

receive immunity *get a reprieve* 816.9

receive into the church *proselytize* 84.15, *receive someone* 473.14

receive maintenance *earn* 467.20

receive no proposals *be celibate* 67.9

receive notice *be warned* 814.9

receive one's due *be rewarded* 453.16

receive palimony *earn* 467.20

receive permission *be permitted* 502.8

receiver 473.8; *radio telescope* 7.26, *offense* 155.6, *tennis participant* 165.6, *badminton terms* 165.11, *telephone* 169.10, *radio reception* 172.2, *television set* 172.6, *recipient* 473.5, *collector* 473.7, *taker* 477.9

receiver of honors *recipient* 473.5

receiver of stolen property *recipient* 473.5, *dishonest person* 479.11

receive royalties *earn* 467.20

receivership *receiving* 473.1

receive Social Security *receive* 473.13

receive someone 473.14

receive the sacrament *follow rites* 85.19

receive unemployment compensation *be poor* 486.14

receiving 473.1, 473.9; *gain* 467.1, *admittance* 708.1

receiving antenna *radio reception* 172.2

receiving family friends *funeral* 31.4

receiving pay 489.14

receiving team *special team* 155.11

recency *newness* 652.1

recension *rectification* 807.8

recent *new* 652.1

Recent Epoch Geologic Time Intervals 8

recently *in the past* 651.20, *newly* 652.21

recentness *newness* 652.1

recent occurrence *newness* 652.1

recent past 651.4; *past time* 651.1

receptacle 105.11; *flower part* 42.3, *container* 578.1

receptible *admissive* 708.8

reception 405.4, 473.4, 704.3; *social gathering* 59.7, 408.4, *radio reception* 172.2, *sound quality* 230.4, *receiving* 473.1, *entry* 706.1, *admittance* 708.1, *inclusion* 763.1

receptionist *clerical worker* 123.5, *record keeper* 185.8
reception room *room* 60.9, *reception* 473.4
receptive 473.10, 708.9; *educatable* 48.18, *friendly* 62.5, *persuadable* 178.14, *sensitive* 267.3, *willing* 373.7, *receiving* 473.9
receptively 473.15, 708.20; *studiously* 48.26, *amicably* 62.13
receptiveness *persuadability* 178.8, *sensation* 212.1, *willingness* 373.1, *receptivity* 708.2
receptivity 708.2; *educatability* 48.9, *sensation* 212.1, *sensitivity* 267.1, *willingness* 373.1
recess *refresher* 94.2, *time off* 125.2, *hiding place* 181.2, *compartment* 578.2, *cavity* 635.3, *interval* 639.4, *pause* 668.3, 668.13, *retreat* 680.2, *ease* 819.1
recessed 668.8
recession *infertile state* 23.3, *economic factor* 56.8, *unemployment* 415.2, *sales* 482.3, *insolvency* 486.2, *return* 671.3, *backward motion* 677.5, 680.1, *economic deterioration* 808.2, *economic adversity* 848.6
recessional *sacred music* 140.3
recessionary *infertile* 23.7
recessive *genetic* 13.32, *regressive* 671.6, *receding* 680.11
recessiveness *genetics* 13.19
recharge *power* 106.17
rechargeable *electric* 14.47
recheck *verify* 336.8
recherché *selected* 382.11
recidivate *reverse* 671.9, *go backward* 680.16
recidivatingly *unvirtuously* 448.16
recidivation *backsliding* 680.8
recidivism *depravity* 448.2, *reversion* 671.1, *backsliding* 680.8, *deterioration* 808.1
recidivist *lawbreaker* 53.15, *guilty person* 450.5, *regressive* 671.6, *unimproved* 808.10
recidivistic *depraved* 448.10, *regressive* 671.6
recidivous *depraved* 448.10, *regressive* 671.6
recipe *cooking* 91.1, *remedy* 115.1, *expedient* 387.5, *formula* 780.7
recipience *receiving* 473.1
recipience *or* recipiency *receptivity* 708.2
recipient 473.5; *receiving* 473.9, *receptive* 708.9
reciprocal 729.4; *division* 6.16, *divisible* 6.71, *correspondent* 334.16, *retaliatory* 420.3, *agreeing* 462.6, *symmetrical* 626.4, *frequent* 663.6, *in exchange* 673.3, *oscillating* 683.8, *interrelated* 727.7, *equivalent* 730.9, *counterpart* 733.5, *conforming* 735.17, *joint* 827.10
reciprocality *reciprocity* 729.1
reciprocally 729.10; *in answer* 334.25, *agreeably* 462.14, *equally* 626.8, *regularly* 663.14, *in exchange* 673.6, *relevantly* 727.12, *equivalently* 730.20, *conformingly* 735.37
reciprocal manners *mode of behavior* 399.2
reciprocalness *reciprocity* 729.1
reciprocate 729.7, 827.13; *answer to* 334.22, *retaliate* 420.4, 489.23, *agree with* 462.10, *be regular* 663.10, *exchange* 673.5, *oscillate*

683.12, *be equivalent* 730.15, *conform* 735.27
reciprocated *exchanged* 673.4, *reciprocal* 729.4, *matched* 733.10
reciprocating *engine type* 14.11, *reciprocal* 729.4
reciprocation *retaliation* 420.1, *symmetry* 626.1, *exchange* 673.1, *oscillation* 683.1, *reciprocity* 729.1, *equivalence* 730.3, *equalization* 740.4
reciprocative *in exchange* 673.3, *oscillating* 683.8, *reciprocal* 729.4
reciprocatory *reciprocal* 729.4
reciprocity 729.1; *agreement* 462.1, *symmetry* 626.1, *frequency* 663.2, *exchange* 673.1, *interrelatedness* 727.3, *equivalence* 730.3, *conformity* 735.7, *mutual relationship* 827.3
reciprocity failure *exposure* 132.15
recital *performance* 141.8, *public speaking* 205.11, *address* 209.1
recitation *address* 209.1
recitation of rights *pretrial proceedings* 54.13
recite *rehearse* 136.37, *record* 185.13, *recount* 202.16, *speak* 205.17
recite the creed *be religious* 81.25
recite the rosary *pray* 85.20
reckless 286.6; *adventurous* 284.12, *careless* 289.8, *impulsive* 318.11, *original* 335.9, *foolish* 353.5, *unpremeditated* 389.7, *defiant* 416.5, *mentally quick* 694.8, *hasty* 818.3
recklessly 286.10; *adventurously* 284.20, *carelessly* 289.18, *impulsively* 318.16, *inattentively* 324.12, *inventively* 335.15, *foolishly* 353.8, *defiantly* 416.9, *dangerously* 811.14, *rashly* 818.8
recklessness 286.2; *adventurousness* 284.4, *carelessness* 289.2, *impulsiveness* 318.6, *originality* 335.4, *folly* 353.1, *hastiness* 818.2
reckless speed *speed* 694.2
reckon *theorize* 327.16, *estimate* 341.11, *predict* 356.7, *intend* 374.8, *measure* 589.20, *number* 783.9, *calculate* 784.10, *think likely* 838.10
reckonable *calculable* 784.8
reckon among *subsume* 763.7
reckoned *measured* 589.16
reckoner *counter* 784.6
reckoning 454.8; *mathematics* 6.1, *numeration* 6.10, *accounting* 493.1, 493.7, *bill* 494.4, *measurement* 589.1, *mathematical result* 783.4, *calculation* 784.1, *count* 784.3, *calculative* 784.7
reckoning up *mathematical addition* 748.2
reckon up *enumerate* 6.85
reclaim *exploit* 393.11, *take back* 477.17, *be compensated* 743.9, *promote* 807.18, *restore* 809.12
reclaimable *compensable* 743.4
reclaimed *used* 393.5, *penitent* 451.5, *repaired* 809.6
reclaiming *taking back* 477.4
reclamation *reuse* 393.3, *restoration* 809.2
reclination *prostration* 597.2, *recumbency* 603.2
recline *be low* 597.20, *be horizontal* 603.9, *lie down* 716.21, *take it easy* 819.3
recliner *or* reclining *type of chair* 101.4

reclining *prostrate* 597.11, *recumbency* 603.2, *recumbent* 603.7
recluse *celibate* 67.4, *one who conceals* 181.7, *unsocial person* 409.5, *hermit* 782.9, *loner* 788.8
reclusive *silent* 181.10, *unsociable* 409.6, *unjoined* 753.9, *solitary* 782.17, *alone* 788.15
reclusive life *monasticism* 67.3
reclusively *privately* 181.18, *aloofly* 756.10
reclusiveness *unsociability* 409.1
recognition *memory* 108.27, 354.1, *aspect of fiction* 139.5, *identification* 184.1, *acknowledgment* 310.3, *discovery* 345.1, *assent* 346.1, *understanding* 363.4, *respect* 435.1, *admiration* 437.2, *reward* 453.1, *observance* 465.1, *fame* 845.2
recognition of one's services *acknowledgment* 310.3
recognition scene *play part* 136.8
recognizability 363.3; *visibility* 244.1
recognizable 363.7; *identified* 184.9, *visible* 242.19, 244.5, *discoverable* 345.10, *identifiable* 843.10
recognizably *visibly* 242.28, *originally* 345.16
recognizance *pretrial proceedings* 54.13, *promise* 464.2
recognize 363.11, 487.13; *know* 48.24, 348.10, *identify* 184.11, *see* 242.20, *be grateful* 310.6, *discover* 345.11, *assent* 346.6, *remember* 354.12, *admire* 437.15, *reward* 453.13, *observe* 465.4, *include* 763.5
recognized *identified* 184.9, *known* 348.9, *established* 397.12, *rewarded* 453.10
recognized procedure *standard procedure* 397.6
recoil 680.21; *be afraid* 283.14, *be a coward* 285.7, *react against* 291.15, *response* 334.4, *react* 334.20, *dissociation* 375.4, *dissociate* 375.14, *shyness* 386.3, *counteraction* 510.1, *counteract* 510.7, *elasticity* 546.1, *be elastic* 546.7, *reversion* 671.1, *reverse* 671.9, *swing* 671.12, *countermotion* 680.6, *reflex* 680.7, *repulsion* 701.1
recoil at *hate* 300.11
recoiled *reversed* 671.7
recoiling *reactive* 334.12, *elastic* 546.5, *resilient* 680.14
recoil-operated *bolt-action* 78.17
recoil-operated firearm *firearm* 78.7
recollect 3.16; *remember* 354.12, 471.10
recollected *biographical* 3.13
recollection 3.8; *chronicle* 3.4, *memory* 108.27, 354.1, *retentiveness* 471.4, *retrospection* 651.3
recombinant DNA technology *molecular biology* 13.18
recommence *protract* 669.9, *restore* 671.10, *begin again* 771.36
recommencement *continuation* 669.2, *restoration* 671.2
recommend 437.19; *advise* 176.9, *select* 382.12, *approve* 437.14, *influence* 893.11, *give moral support* 605.18
recommendable *advisable* 176.8, *expedient* 288.12

recommendably *advisably* 176.13, *expediently* 288.25
recommendation 176.2, 437.6; *advice* 176.1, *evidence* 336.3, *documentation* 339.6, *approval* 437.1, *permit* 502.3, *moral support* 605.7
recommendatory *advisory* 176.7
recommended *approved* 437.8
recommended diet *diet* 92.5
recommended for leniency *acquitted* 54.25
recommended for mercy *acquitted* 54.25
recommender *adviser* 176.5, *approver* 437.7
recommend for leniency *acquit* 54.32
recommend for mercy *acquit* 54.32
recommending 437.11; *advisory* 176.7
recompense 273.11; *reparation* 273.2, *atonement* 313.1, *atone* 313.7, *put right* 429.14, *reward* 453.1, 453.13, *compensation* 478.2, 743.1, *compensate* 478.6, 743.7, *repayment* 489.5, *pay back* 489.20, *exchange* 673.1, 673.5
recompensed *compensated* 743.3
recompenser *atoner* 313.4
reconcilable *agreeing* 462.6
reconcilably *agreeably* 462.14
reconcile *conciliate* 74.10, *mediate* 75.6, *recompense* 273.11, *forgive and forget* 312.9, *atone* 313.7, *modify* 340.13, *agree with* 462.10, *relate to* 727.9, *agree* 735.23, *settle* 735.26
reconciled *modified* 340.9, *settled* 735.16, *resigned* 835.4
reconcilement *pacification* 74.1, *pliancy* 781.3
reconciler *atoner* 313.4
reconciliation *pacification* 74.1, *mediation* 75.1, *Christian rite* 85.5, *reparation* 273.2, *atonement* 313.1, *modification* 340.5, *agreement* 462.1, 735.3, *settlement* 735.6, *pliancy* 781.3, *resignedness* 835.2
reconciliatory *atoning* 313.5, *agreeing* 462.6
reconciling *agreeing* 735.13
reconcilingly *atoningly* 313.10
recondite *occult* 86.16, *concealed* 181.8, *obscure* 197.2, *private* 245.5, *inscrutable* 250.5, *difficult* 364.8, *profound* 598.15, *problematic* 824.11
reconditely *profoundly* 598.27
reconditeness *concealment* 181.1, *profundity* 598.5, *difficulty* 824.1
recondition *beautify* 807.20, *refurbish* 809.11
reconditioned *repaired* 809.6
reconditioning *tidying* 807.6, *repair* 809.1
reconnaissance *observation* 242.5
reconnaissance fighter *or* bomber *military aircraft* 77.30
reconnaissance party *armed force* 77.10, *precursor* 769.7
reconnaissance pilot *air force person* 77.31
reconnoiter *inspect* 242.22, *forerun* 769.16
reconnoitering *preparatory* 769.11
reconsider 807.23; *have second thoughts* 317.11
reconsideration 807.9
reconstitute *restore* 809.12
reconstituted *repaired* 809.6
reconstitution *restoration* 809.2
reconstruct *recollect* 3.16,

reproduce 21.13, make new 652.20, restore 809.12

reconstructed reproduced 21.10, renewed 652.14, repaired 809.6

reconstructible renewable 652.15

reconstruction restoration 21.2, 809.2, conjecture 359.3, new start 652.5

Reconstruction Era Ages, Decades, Eras 641

reconvene restore 809.12

reconversion restoration 671.2, 809.2

reconvert restore 671.10

record 172.15, 185.1, 185.13, 230.9; chronicle 3.4, 3.15, data-related concepts 15.23, collection 105.12, save 105.20, nonfiction 139.6, competition 166.18, document 170.3, identify 184.11, recording 185.6, represent 187.10, description 202.1, recount 202.16, sound reproduction 230.6, verify 336.8, evidence 339.1, documentation 339.6, prove 339.14, authorization 340.4, reminder 354.4, conduct 399.1, account 493.9, chronology 646.2, chronologize 646.13, unbeatable 744.13, remainder 750.1, catalog 767.7, categorize 767.21, list 785.11, best 805.9

record book 185.5

record-breaker good thing 445.9, paragon 744.6, successful person 845.6

record-breaking wondrous 294.9, excellent 445.13, unbeatable 744.13, best 805.9

recorded 185.12; chronicled 3.12, saved 105.15, broadcast 172.12, verifiable 336.5, evidential 339.8, accounted 493.8, included 763.4, listed 785.9

recorded material record 185.1

recorded proceedings record 185.1

recorded sunshine sun 9.21

recorder historian 3.3, Musical Instruments 142, judo 152.13, record keeper 185.8, recording instrument 185.9, descriptive writer 202.10, keeper of time 646.10

record high summit 744.4

recordholder paragon 744.6

recordholding unbeatable 744.13

recording 185.6; chronicle 3.4, broadcast material 172.9, record 185.1, recordkeeping 185.7, sound reproduction 230.6

recording instrument 185.9

recording of evidence evidence 54.15

recordist filmmaker 137.14

record keeper 185.8

recordkeeping 185.7

record low inferior state 745.3

record of the past history 3.1

record one's GPS or loran position navigate 690.15

record pirate infringer 479.10, imitator 736.6

record player sound reproduction 230.6

records account book 493.3

record-setter good thing 445.9

record-size huge 579.14

recount 202.16; write 139.21, communicate 170.12, record 185.13

recounted iterated 797.9

recounter meeting 704.5

recounting iteration 797.2

recoup retaliate 420.4, take back

477.17, make good time 679.10, be compensated 743.9

recoupable compensable 743.4

recouped compensated 743.3

recoupment taking back 477.4, compensation 478.2, 743.1

recourse means 102.1, use 393.1, refuge 812.1

recover be refreshed 94.8, get healthy 113.12, row 150.32, fence 153.7, play 156.8, swimming techniques 164.2, take back 477.17, counteract 510.7, be strong 516.14, restore 671.10, be compensated 743.9, get better 807.21, repair 809.10, be restored 809.13, deliver 817.5

recoverable reversible 671.8, compensable 743.4, repairable 809.7

recoverably repairably 809.16

recovered reversed 671.7, compensated 743.3, sound 759.8, repaired 809.6

recovering rowing 150.27, improving 807.14

recover lost ground improve 467.18, make good time 679.10

recover one's breath be refreshed 94.8

recover one's costs take back 477.17

recover one's health get healthy 113.12

recover one's losses take back 477.17

recovery refreshment 94.1, remedy 115.1, rowing techniques 150.16, taking back 477.4, restoration 671.2, 807.4, 809.2, compensation 743.1, bodily improvement 807.10, revival 809.3, recuperation 809.4, deliverance 817.1

recovery shot golf shots 156.4

recreant coward 285.3, dastardly 285.6, equivocator 380.4, miscreant 448.6, villainous 448.12

recreate refresh 94.6, rectify 807.22

recreation refreshment 94.1, time off 125.2, game 167.1, activity 385.4

recreational 167.10; refreshing 94.4, leisure 125.3, architectural types 134.2, wrestling 152.18, swimming 164.12

recreational canoeing canoeing 150.8

recreational diving diving 164.6

recreational education educational system 48.2

recreational karate karate 152.14

recreationally 167.15

recreational ski ski equipment 162.10

recreational skier skier 162.14

recreational skiing skiing 162.1

recreational swimming swimming 164.1

recreational vehicle (RV) mobile home 60.11, automobile 687.6

recreation room room 60.9

recreative refreshing 94.4

recriminate justify 441.12, accuse 442.8

recriminated condemned 438.11, accused 442.5

recrimination dissentience 347.3, censure 438.3, defense 441.2, accusation 442.1

recriminatory retaliatory 420.3, accusatory 442.6

rec room [Inf] room 60.9

recruit learner 48.6, enlist 58.13, join the army 76.31, soldier 77.4,

refresh 94.6, influence 508.11, new arrival 652.7, make bigger 746.7, support 748.14, beginner 771.14, restore 807.17, revive 809.14, engage 833.9

recruited martial 77.33

recruiter pursuer 385.5

recruiting military affairs 58.1

recruitment war measures 76.18, refreshment 94.1, restoration 807.4, 809.2, revival 809.3, engagement 833.2

recruits reinforcements 77.11

recrystallization petrogenesis 8.31

recrystallize lithify 8.66

rectal diseases Phobias 283

rectangle polygon 6.42, angled figure 628.3, quadrilateral 791.2

rectangular polygonal 6.79, perpendicular 602.6, angled 628.9, quadrilateral 791.8

rectangular coordinates coordinates 6.31, 589.6

rectangular coordinate system coordinates 589.6

rectangularity perpendicularity 602.2

rectangularly perpendicularly 602.12

rectangularness perpendicularity 602.2

rectangular pulse wave form 10.13

rectifiable compensable 743.4, repairable 809.7

rectification 807.8; circuit function 14.38, atonement 313.1, righting wrong 429.6, compensation 743.1, restoration 807.4, repair 809.1

rectified compensated 743.3, repaired 809.6

rectifier circuit 10.43, atoner 313.4, improver 807.11, repairer 809.5

rectify 807.22; atone 313.7, put right 429.14, compensate 743.7, make conform 781.13, perfect 805.19, restore 807.17, repair 809.10

rectifying atoning 313.5, improving 807.14

rectilinear linear 6.77, straight 630.8

rectilinearity straightness 630.1

rectilinear style Architectural Styles 134

rectitude morality 431.1, morals 431.2, good 445.1

recto book part 174.5

recto page laterality 623.3

rectophobia Phobias 283

rector member of the clergy 84.5, priest 84.8

rectorate priesthood 84.2

rectorship priesthood 84.2

rectory official residence 60.6, clerical dwelling 84.10

rectrix plumage 36.7

rectum internal organ 19.13

recumbence recumbency 603.2

recumbency 603.2; prostration 597.2

recumbent 603.7; prostrate 597.11

recumbent fold fold 8.22

recumbently 603.12

recuperate be refreshed 94.8, get healthy 113.12, get better 807.21, be restored 809.13

recuperating improving 807.14

recuperation 809.4; refreshment 94.1, health 113.1, remedy 115.1, healing art 115.13, restoration 807.4, bodily improvement 807.10

recuperative restorative 809.9

recur resonate 236.9, occur 264.14,

be remembered 354.15, be periodical 641.9, be frequent 661.5, be regular 663.10, continue 669.8, be repeated 797.20

recurrence resonance 236.1, reappearance 264.8, recurrent period 641.5, frequency 661.1, continuation 669.2, continuum 774.5, repetition 797.1, return 797.4, revival 809.3

recurrent 797.13; cyclic 6.82, habitual 397.9, periodical 641.7, frequent 661.4, 663.6, progressive 669.6, cyclical 774.10

recurrently resonantly 236.11, periodically 641.11, frequently 661.7, continually 669.10, repeatedly 797.22

recurrent nova variable star 7.11

recurrent pattern recurrent period 641.5

recurrent period 641.5

recurring appearing 264.9, frequent 661.4, 663.6, directional 677.13, recurrent 797.13

recurring decimal division 6.16

recurring movement regular movement 677.10

recursion algorithm 6.26, combinatorics 6.63, return 704.4

recursive procedure algorithm 6.26

recusancy refusal 190.2, denial 332.2, dissent 506.2, 782.2, protest 507.1

recusant disagreeing 190.11, dissenter 347.5, 782.8, dissenting 347.7, 506.6, troublemaker 427.5, disobedient 427.10, refuser 506.4, protester 507.4, protesting 507.5, dissident 782.12

recuse refuse 506.8

recyclable useful 393.7, reversible 671.8, deconstructed 758.4, usable 801.6

recyclable [Inf] reuse 393.3

recyclable product or **substance** reuse 393.3

recycle exploit 393.11, give back 478.5, restore 671.10, 809.12, renew 797.19

recycled used 393.5, reversed 671.7, remade 797.10

recycler returner 478.3

recycling reuse 393.3, giving back 478.1, restoration 671.2, 809.2, return 797.4

Red political party member 50.6, figurative usage 257.4, rebel 427.8, Rivers 570

red 257.5; culinary 91.9, spectrum 251.3, blushing 403.7

red, the credit 487.1, debt 488.1

redact rectify 807.22

redaction translation 365.4, rearrangement 767.4, rectification 807.8

red admiral red thing 257.3

red alert figurative usage 257.4, danger signal 811.5

red algae algae 47.11

red-and-white wrestling 152.18

Red Angus Breeds of Cattle 16

red as a beet or **a lobster** red-faced 257.6

red belt karate 152.14, tae kwon do 152.15

red blood cell or **corpuscle** blood 555.4

red blood cell or **red corpuscle** red thing 257.3

red-blooded physically strong 516.10, vigorous 518.2

Red Bororo Breeds of Cattle 16

Red Brangus Breeds of Cattle 16
redbrick university [Brit inf] *university* 48.14
redbud Trees and Shrubs 43
redbug *red thing* 257.3
Red Butana Breeds of Cattle 16
Redcap Breeds of Fowl 16
redcap *attendant* 69.4, *transferrer* 685.4, *transporter* 686.4
red card *soccer play* 163.5, *red thing* 257.3
red carpet *figurative usage* 257.4, *ceremonial* 404.11, *formality* 406.1, *mark of respect* 435.4
red-carpet treatment *reception* 405.4
red cedar Trees and Shrubs 43
red cent [Inf] *figurative usage* 257.4, *US coinage* 484.10
red checker *red thing* 257.3
red-cheeked *red-faced* 257.6
red cheeks *red thing* 257.3
red clover *red thing* 257.3
redcoat [Brit] *soldier* 77.4, *figurative usage* 257.4
red color *redness* 257.1
red complexion *redness* 257.1
red cosmetic *red pigment* 257.2
Red Crescent *figurative usage* 257.4
Red Cross *figurative usage* 257.4
red currant *red thing* 257.3
Red Deer Rivers 570
red deer *red thing* 257.3
Red Delicious Apple Varieties 44
redden 257.9
reddened *red-faced* 257.6
reddening *orbit* 7.22, *redness* 257.1, *blushing* 403.2, 403.7
reddish-brown *brown* 256.5
reddish-yellow *orange* 258.5
red dog Card Games 168
red-dog *play defense* 155.19
red dwarf *red thing* 257.3
red dye *red pigment* 257.2
rede [Brit] *advice* 176.1
redecorate *cause change* 665.16, *transform* 670.13, *refurbish* 809.11
redecorated *changed* 665.10, *improved* 807.12, *repaired* 809.6
redecoration *change for the better* 665.4, *beautification* 807.7
redecorator *improver* 807.11
redeem *preach* 84.14, *atone* 313.7, *give back* 478.5, *buy back* 481.16, *pay off* 489.17, *persuade* 670.14, *compensate* 743.7, *be compensated* 743.9, *improve* 807.15, *restore* 809.12, *deliver* 817.5, *liberate* 831.6
redeemability *compensation* 743.1
redeemable *payable* 489.12, *compensable* 743.4, *repairable* 809.7, *deliverable* 817.3
redeemably *correctively* 743.11, *repairably* 809.16, *extricably* 817.6
redeemed *restoring* 478.4, *bought* 481.8, *compensated* 743.3, *liberated* 831.4
Redeemer God the Son 82.9
redeemer *returner* 478.3, *purchaser* 481.7, *deliverer* 817.2
redeeming *atoning* 313.5, *restoring* 478.4, *compensatory* 743.5
redeem one's pledge *perform* 465.5
redemptible *compensable* 743.4, *repairable* 809.7
redemption *atonement* 313.1, *giving back* 478.1, *repurchase* 481.4, *exchange* 673.1, *compensation* 743.1, *improvement*

807.1, *restoration* 809.2, *deliverance* 817.1, *liberation* 831.1
redemptional *restoring* 478.4
redemptive *restoring* 478.4, *buying* 481.9, *paying in return* 489.15, *compensatory* 743.5, *preserving* 815.11, *liberating* 831.5
redemptive or **redemptory** *restorative* 809.9
redemptively 478.7; *acquisitively* 481.21, *in compensation* 743.10
redemptory *compensatory* 743.5
redesign *new start* 652.5, *make new* 652.20
redesignable *renewable* 652.15
redesigned *renewed* 652.14
red-eye *composition* 132.17
red-eye or **red-eye special** [Inf] *figurative usage* 257.4
red-eyed *weak-sighted* 243.10, *lamenting* 280.4
red eyes *faulty vision* 243.1
red face *blushing* 403.2
red-faced 257.6
red face-off spot *hockey areas* 158.2
red fir Trees and Shrubs 43
red flag *signal* 183.6, *flag* 184.8, *provocation* 302.3, *warning signal* 814.3
red fox *red thing* 257.3
Redfree Apple Varieties 44
red giant *stellar evolution* 7.10, *red thing* 257.3
red glow *fire* 246.9
red goal line *hockey areas* 158.2
red grouse *red thing* 257.3
red gum Trees and Shrubs 43
red hair *red thing* 257.3
red-haired 257.7
red-handed *murderous* 30.18, *acting* 412.9, *actively* 412.18, *appearing guilty* 450.7, *guiltily* 450.12
red-handedly *guiltily* 450.12
red-handedness *guilt* 450.1
red hands *sign of guilt* 450.2
redhead *red thing* 257.3
red heat *fire* 246.9
red herring *artifice* 193.5, *figurative usage* 257.4, *sophism* 330.2, *secondary matter* 800.6, *waste of effort* 802.4, *stratagem* 822.2
red-hot *hot* 217.11, *red-faced* 257.6
red-hot poker Flowers 42
redia *invertebrate larva* 39.19
redialing *dial* 169.12
redingote *coat* 100.19
red ink *red thing* 257.3
red-ink *redden* 257.9
redintegrate *restore* 809.12
redintegration *repair* 809.1
redirect *send* 209.11
rediscover *invent* 345.14
rediscovery *invention* 345.4
redistricting *politics* 50.1
redivivus *repaired* 809.6
Red Karaman Breeds of Sheep 16
red lead *red pigment* 257.2
red-letter day *figurative usage* 257.4, *anniversary* 405.5, *day* 646.4, *important matter* 799.2
red light *deterrence* 179.2, *safety light* 246.7, *red thing* 257.3, *disapproval* 347.2, 438.1, *veto* 503.3, *refusal* 506.1, *danger signal* 811.5
red-light [Inf] *veto* 503.9, *refuse* 506.8
red-light district *figurative usage* 257.4, *brothel* 432.5, *urban area* 567.10

redline *redden* 257.9
red meat *meat* 90.22, *red thing* 257.3
redneck [Inf] *countryman* 61.8, *figurative usage* 257.4, *bigot* 337.7
redness 257.1; *effects of hot weather* 217.7
redo *repeat* 797.15, *reconsider* 807.23, *restore* 809.12
red oak Trees and Shrubs 43
red ocher *red pigment* 257.2
redoing *interior decoration* 532.4
redolence *odor* 224.1
redolent *odorous* 224.5
redone *repaired* 809.6
redouble *invigorate* 518.5, *make bigger* 746.7, *repeat* 797.15
redoubled *repeated* 797.8
redoublement *fencing movements* 153.3
redouble one's efforts *try hard* 390.7
redoubling *increase* 746.1, *repetition* 797.1, *repetitious* 797.11
redoubtable *strong* 516.9
redound *tend* 513.5
redound to the honor of *meet with approval* 437.20
red pencil *red thing* 257.3
red-pencil *redden* 257.9
red pepper *red thing* 257.3
red phosphorus Chemical Elements and Common Allotropes 11
Red Pied Friuli Breeds of Cattle 16
red pigment 257.2
red pine Trees and Shrubs 43
red planet (Mars) *red thing* 257.3
Red Poll Breeds of Cattle 16
redraft *rectify* 807.22
red rag *provocation* 302.3
red rash *redness* 257.1
redress *remedy* 115.1, *atonement* 313.1, *atone* 313.7, *retaliation* 420.1, *retaliate* 420.4, *put right* 429.14, *compensation* 743.1, *compensate* 743.7, *restoration* 809.2
redressed *compensated* 743.3
redresser *atoner* 313.4
redress the balance *retaliate* 420.4, *equalize* 740.12
Red River of the North Rivers 570
Red Rome Apple Varieties 44
red roses *love token* 299.8
red rover Children's and Party Games 167
red salmon *red thing* 257.3
Red Sea *figurative usage* 257.4, Oceans and Seas 571
red seaweeds *algae* 47.11
redshift *orbit* 7.22
redshirt *football player* 155.15
Red Sindhi Breeds of Cattle 16
red snapper *food fish and shellfish* 90.20, *red thing* 257.3
red squirrel *red thing* 257.3
Red Steppe Breeds of Cattle 16
red stuff *red thing* 257.3
red tape *governance* 52.6, *overdoing it* 99.3, *figurative usage* 257.4, *overactivity* 414.9, *delay* 658.3, *bureaucracy* 826.5
red thing 257.3
red tide *alga* 47.10
reduce 796.8; *react* 11.38, *eat less* 118.9, *develop* 132.28, *play down* 195.17, *de-emphasize* 201.3, *summarize* 204.7, *humiliate* 298.19, *sell at a loss* 482.19, *discount* 495.4, *weaken* 517.13, *mitigate* 521.9, *make simple*

526.12, *make little* 580.10, *contract* 582.12, *become smaller* 582.14, *shorten* 591.9, *become thin* 595.15, *diminish* 597.24, *outline* 617.5, *convert* 670.11, *transform* 670.13, *lower* 716.12, *quantify* 738.7, *make smaller* 747.8, *ease* 819.4
reduced 749.5; *downplayed* 195.13, *humiliated* 298.12, *bargain* 497.13, *offered* 504.8, *smaller* 582.7, *lowered* 716.7, *fewer* 796.7
reduced circumstances *poverty* 486.1, *inferior state* 745.3
reduced pressure *sparseness* 541.1
reduced price rate *price* 494.1
reduced to clear *bargain* 497.10
reduced to poverty or **beggary** *impoverished* 486.11
reduced to the last extremity *endangered* 811.10
reduce in number *weaken* 517.13
reduce one's importance *make unimportant* 800.20
reduce pressure *make sparse* 541.5
reduce speed *slow down* 693.13, *make smaller* 747.8
reduce the fine *acquit* 54.32
reduce the price *discount* 495.4, *make cheap* 497.14
reduce the temperature *mitigate* 521.9
reduce to *transform* 670.13
reduce to ashes *burn* 217.18
reduce to chaos *cause confusion* 51.9
reduce to essentials *make simple* 526.12
reduce to order *arrange* 767.18
reduce to poverty *impoverish* 486.16
reduce or **grind to powder** or **dust** *pulverize* 553.26
reduce to rags *wear out* 808.21
reduce to servitude *subject* 832.10
reduce to silence *strike dumb* 206.10
reduce to the ranks *punish* 454.22, *debase* 716.16
reduce weight *lighten* 539.9
reducible *convertible* 670.9
reducing *dieting* 92.6, 118.2, 595.3, 595.11, *on a diet* 118.6, *contracting* 582.10
reducing to dust *pulverization* 553.4
reductio ad absurdum *philosophical term* 4.7, *sophism* 330.2
reduction 747.2; *evaluation* 6.22, *discount* 495.1, *moderation* 521.1, *contraction* 582.1, *shortening* 582.2, 591.2, *diminishment* 597.7, *outline* 617.1, *chemical change* 670.2, *lowering* 716.1, *calculation* 784.1
reduction division *cell division* 13.17
reductionism Philosophical Schools of Thought 4
reductionist Philosophical Schools of Thought 4
reduction of nuclear stockpiles *disarmament* 74.3
reductive *decrescent* 747.6, *subtractive* 749.4
reductively *down* 716.24, *destructively* 758.9
reductivism Philosophical Schools of Thought 4

reductivist Philosophical Schools of Thought 4

redundance *superfluity* 99.4, *excessiveness* 712.4

redundancy 802.2; *superfluity* 99.4, *diffuseness* 199.1, *overactivity* 414.9, *extraneousness* 724.1, *sameness* 730.1, *surplus* 750.4, *iteration* 797.2

redundancy [Brit] *bargaining terms* 57.10, *discarding* 383.3, *disuse* 394.3

redundant 802.9; *worded* 5.38, *superfluous* 99.8, *diffuse* 199.3, *discarded* 383.8, *bargain* 497.10, *extraneous* 724.8, *same* 730.7, *surplus* 750.8, *repetitious* 797.11

redundantly *superfluously* 99.15, *out of use* 394.13, *identically* 730.18, *residually* 750.11

reduplicate *copy* 730.17, *repeat* 797.15

reduplicated *duplicate* 730.11, *repeated* 797.8

reduplication *reproduction* 21.1, *copy* 730.5, *repetition* 797.1

redware Ceramics 129

red, white, and blue *flag* 184.8

red wine *wine* 93.11, *red thing* 257.3

redwing *red thing* 257.3

redwood Trees and Shrubs 43, *red thing* 257.3

reecho *drum* 235.10, *resonance* 236.11, *resonate* 236.9, *repetition* 797.1, *reverberation* 797.6, *resound* 797.21

reechoed *repeated* 797.8

reechoing *resonant* 236.6, *repetitious* 797.11

reed *grass* 45.1, *grass plant* 45.3, Architectural Elements 134, *woodwind* 142.4, *weak thing* 517.5

reed cutter *grasscutter* 45.5

reeding Architectural Elements 134

reed instrument *woodwind* 142.4

reed organ Musical Instruments 142

reeds *seed plant* 41.3

reeducate *transform* 670.13, *assimilate* 781.14

reeducation *conditioning* 108.24, *evolution* 670.3

reedy *grassy* 45.8, *shrill* 238.6

reef *handle sailboat equipment* 150.30, *island* 572.2, *shallowness* 599.1, *slow down* 693.13, *hidden danger* 813.3

reefer *coat* 100.19, *nautical person* 690.12

reefer [Inf] *drug dose* 121.15

reefer man [Inf] *drug pusher* 121.13

reef knot Knots, Bends, Hitches, Splices 754

reef point *sailboat parts and accessories* 150.4

reek *have odor* 224.8, *stench* 227.1, *stink* 227.5, *miasma* 556.3, *give off* 556.25, *let out* 709.26

reeking *stinking* 227.3, *miasmic* 556.16

reel 682.4; *be drunk* 121.34, *film* 132.8, *darkroom equipment* 132.21, Dances 135, *fishing tackle* 154.7, *be changeable* 666.5, *roll* 682.15, *pitch* 684.25

reelect *vote* 382.16

reel in *fish* 154.14, *drag* 699.11

reeling *drunken behavior* 121.4, *slightly drunk* 121.26, *swaying* 378.4, *turning* 682.3, *rotating* 682.11

reemphasize *iterate* 797.16

reenthrone *give back* 478.5

reenthronement *giving back* 478.1

reentrance *reversal* 680.3, *return* 704.4, *entry* 706.1

reentrant *or* **reentering angle** *angle* 6.37

reentry *rocketry* 7.32, *reversal* 680.3, *flight path* 691.12, *return* 704.4, *entry* 706.1

reequipped *repaired* 809.6

reerect *restore* 809.12

reerection *restoration* 809.2

reestablish *give back* 478.5, *restore* 809.12

reestablishment *giving back* 478.1, *restoration* 809.2

reeve [Brit] *manager* 126.7

reeving line bend Knots, Bends, Hitches, Splices 754

reexamination *witness* 54.16, *reconsideration* 807.9

reexamine *rectify* 807.22

ref [Inf] *basketball team* 148.2

reface *repair* 809.10

refashion *rectify* 807.22, *refurbish* 809.11

refashioning *restoration* 809.2

refection *meal* 92.8, *refreshments* 94.3

refectory *eating place* 92.17, *type of table* 101.5

refer *practice medicine* 107.32

referee *judge* 54.10, 341.5, 341.10, *mediator* 75.2, *mediate* 75.6, 772.19, *basketball team* 148.2, *player* 149.5, *boxer* 152.8, *wrestler* 152.12, *tae kwon do* 152.15, *football player* 155.15, *golfer* 156.7, *hockey player* 158.8, *soccer participant* 163.4, *adviser* 176.5, *impartial person* 443.3, *negotiator* 460.4, *moderator* 521.2, *moderate* 521.7, *interfacer* 616.3, *keeper of time* 646.10, *middleman* 772.7

referee's whistle *signal* 183.6

reference *philosophical term* 4.7, *schoolbook* 48.15, *authorization* 52.3, *information source* 170.6, *consultation* 176.4, *identify* 184.11, *evidence* 336.3, 339.1, *documentation* 339.6, *type of meaning* 361.4, *repute* 370.1, *recommendation* 437.6, *permit* 502.3, *relatedness* 727.1

reference book *information source* 170.6, *type of book* 174.3, *book of lists* 785.3

referenced *punctuated* 183.15, *identified* 184.9

reference editor *book publishing personnel* 174.12

reference list *list* 785.1

reference point *point* 6.34

references *authorization* 340.4

reference sign *language sign* 5.33, *symbol* 183.3, *linguistic sign* 183.10

referendum *judgment* 341.1, *electing* 382.5

referential failure *philosophical problem* 4.8

referral *health care* 107.7

refer to *consult* 176.11, *speak* 205.17, *confer* 210.13, *mean* 361.13, *relate to* 727.9

refer to arbitration *consult* 176.11

refill *replenish* 89.10, *suffice* 97.6, *store fuel* 105.18, *fill* 761.11

refilled *full* 761.8

refine 534.7; *solidify* 11.37, *extract* 11.41, *process* 14.50, *educate*

48.22, *purify* 111.19, *make transparent* 249.12, *be accurate* 350.5, *make simple* 526.12, *be elegant* 527.6, *obtain an extract* 711.19, *adjust* 721.23, *perfect* 805.19, *improve* 807.15

refined 48.20, 534.5; *status adjectives* 11.25, *gas* 106.14, *cleaned* 111.14, *subtle* 195.9, *soft-hued* 251.13, *discriminating* 337.9, *formal* 406.6, *good-mannered* 410.7, *pure* 431.11, *elegant* 527.3, *graceful* 527.4, *beautiful* 529.7, *cultured* 534.6, *smooth* 552.9, *adjusted* 721.14

refined palate *delicate eating* 92.3, *judiciousness* 337.2

refined person 534.4

refined sugar *sweetener* 222.2

refinement 48.10, 534.1; *subtlety* 195.3, *judiciousness* 337.2, *accuracy* 350.1, *social success* 408.3, *good manners* 410.2, *purity* 431.4, *simplification* 526.6, *grace* 527.2, *beauty* 529.1, *beautification* 530.1, *grain* 552.2, *obtaining of an extract* 711.7, *adjustment* 721.5, *improvement* 807.1

refine oil *mine coal* 106.18

refiner control *systems and process control* 14.28

refinery *industrial chemistry* 11.21, *works* 124.9

refining *industrial chemistry* 11.21, *metallurgy* 11.22, *systems and process control* 14.28, *oil* 106.7, *cleaning* 111.2

refinished *type of furniture* 101.2

refinishing *interior decoration* 532.4

refit *repair* 809.1, *refurbish* 809.11

refitted *repaired* 809.6

reflation *inflation* 484.9, *swelling* 581.2

reflationary *financial* 457.6

reflect 10.76; *philosophize* 4.19, *represent* 6.91, 187.10, *make visible* 264.12, *glaze* 246.22, *appear* 264.12, *concentrate* 317.10, *imagine* 327.14, *discuss* 329.12, *remember* 354.12, *be similar* 733.12, *imitate* 736.9

reflected *outer* 264.10, *indirect* 698.9, *matched* 733.10

reflected image *image* 187.3

reflecting *representational* 187.8, *visual* 242.16, *outer* 264.10, *wise* 352.4

reflecting telescope *telescope* 7.25

reflection 242.9; *philosophical investigation* 4.4, *transformation* 6.46, *atmospheric process* 9.9, *wave property* 10.12, *optical characteristic* 10.21, *image* 187.3, *utterance* 205.10, *resonance* 236.1, *visual distortion* 243.6, *highlight* 246.12, *impression* 264.7, *thought* 315.5, *thoughtfulness* 317.2, *idea* 327.1, *logical argument* 329.2, *memory* 354.1, *operation of symmetry* 626.2, *deviating course* 698.2, *look-alike* 730.4, *counterpart* 733.5, *imitation* 736.1

reflection grating *optical element* 10.20

reflection hologram *stereoscopic image* 132.7

reflection nebula *nebula* 7.6

reflection plane *operation of symmetry* 626.2

reflective *thoughtful* 4.17, 315.10, *concentrating* 317.7, *ideational* 327.9, *polished* 545.7, *similar* 733.7

reflective clothing *protective clothing* 419.6

reflectively *thoughtfully* 4.27, 317.13, *resonantly* 236.11, *intelligently* 315.14, *theoretically* 327.19, *logically* 329.17, *similarly* 733.17

reflectiveness *thought* 315.5

reflector 242.10; *lighting* 132.16, *that which makes visible* 244.4

reflector telescope *telescope* 7.25

reflect upon *concentrate* 317.10

reflex 680.7; *involuntariness* 95.9, *involuntary* 95.15, *conditioning* 108.24, *impression* 266.2, *instinctive* 318.8, 320.8, *response* 334.4, *habit* 397.1, *customary* 397.11, *reversed* 680.13

reflex action *involuntariness* 95.9

reflex angle *angle* 6.37

reflex hammer *diagnostic instrument* 107.13

reflexive *of grammar* 5.41, *reactive* 334.12, *regressive* 671.6, *resilient* 680.14

reflexively *in answer* 334.25, *reversibly* 671.14, *backward* 680.23

reflexive relation *mathematical logic* 6.60

reflexive verb *part of speech* 5.30

reflex lens *lens* 132.11

reflexologist *healer* 107.22

reflexology *alternative medicine* 107.4

reflowing *backward motion* 677.5, *directional* 677.13

refluence *flow* 570.4, *tide* 571.2, *backward motion* 677.5, *reversal* 680.3

refluent *reactive* 334.12, *flowing* 570.7, *directional* 677.13, *receding* 680.11

reflux *response* 334.4, *flow* 570.4, *tide* 571.2, *backward motion* 677.5, *reversal* 680.3

refluxing *process* 11.15

reforest *restore* 809.12

reforestation *forestry* 43.5, *restoration* 809.2

reforested *wooded* 43.12

Reform Christianity 81.5, *denominational* 81.23

reform *socialize* 2.14, *be benevolent* 305.10, *disaccustom* 398.6, *righting wrong* 429.6, *put right* 429.14, *confess* 451.8, *become new* 652.19, *change for the better* 665.4, *cause change* 665.16, *be converted* 670.12, *transform* 670.13, *improvement* 679.5, 807.1, *improve* 807.15, *get better* 807.21, *rectify* 807.22, *refurbish* 809.11, *restore* 809.12

reformable *improvable* 807.13

reformation *righting wrong* 429.6, *confession* 451.2, *sudden change* 665.3, *evolution* 670.3, *improvement* 807.1, *restoration* 809.2

reformational *changeable* 665.11

reformative *changeable* 665.11, *improving* 807.14

reformatory *prison* 55.1, *improving* 807.14

reformed *penitent* 451.5, *improved* 807.12

reformed character *penitent person* 451.4

Reformed churches Christian Groups 81

reformer *benevolent person* 305.6, *philanthropist* 307.5, *attempter* 390.3, *changer* 665.9, *converter*

670.5, *improver* 807.11, *repairer* 809.5, *abrogator* 834.4

reforming *industrial chemistry* 11.21, *improving* 807.14

reformism *public-spiritedness* 307.2

reformist *public-spirited* 307.7, *forward* 679.6, *improving* 807.14

Reform Jew *Jew* 81.11

Reform Judaism *Judaism* 81.6

reform school *prison* 55.1

reformulate *restore* 809.12

reformulation *restoration* 809.2

refound *restore* 809.12

refract *reflect* 10.76, *glaze* 246.22, *deflect* 698.26

refracted *diffractive* 698.14

refracted color *spectrum* 251.3

refractile *diffractive* 698.14

refracting telescope *telescope* 7.25

refraction *wave property* 10.12, *optical element* 10.20, *optical characteristic* 10.21, *visual distortion* 243.6, *diffraction* 698.6

refractive *transparent* 249.7, *diffractive* 698.14

refractive index *optical element* 10.20, *optical characteristic* 10.21, Fields of Measurement 589

refractivity *optical element* 10.20, *optical characteristic* 10.21

refractometer Fields of Measurement 589

refractometry Fields of Measurement 589

refractorily *ornamentally* 129.11

refractoriness *disobedience* 375.5, 427.1, *obstinacy* 417.2, *protest* 507.1, *contrariness* 828.5

refractor telescope *telescope* 7.25

refractory 379.6; *chemical compound* 11.4, *ceramic* 129.9, *defying* 416.6, *obstinate* 417.7, *protesting* 507.5, *troublesome* 824.13, *uncooperative* 828.14

refractory brick *industrial ceramics* 129.6

refractory clay *material* 129.2

refractory ware Ceramics 129

refrain *part of poem* 139.9, *melody* 140.10, *abstain* 386.16, *not act* 413.11, *be self-restrained* 455.10, *defer* 604.15

refrainer *resister* 417.5

refrain from *desist* 417.13, *stop* 668.10, *discontinue* 775.10

refrain from talking *lack candor* 192.22

refraining *abstinence* 386.2, *inaction* 413.1, *inactive* 413.9, *desisting* 417.4, 417.9, *chaste* 431.10, *self-restrained* 455.6

refrainment *self-restraint* 455.1

refrangible *diffractive* 698.14

refresh 94.6; *comfort* 214.14, *strengthen* 516.15, *invigorate* 518.5, *make new* 652.20, *restore* 807.17, *revive* 809.14

refreshed 94.5; *relieved* 275.6, *renewed* 652.14

refresher 94.2; *tonic* 115.8

refreshing 94.4; *hygienic* 116.3, *pleasant* 214.7, *relieving* 275.7, *strengthening* 516.7, *invigorating* 518.3

refreshingly 94.9; *comfortingly* 275.14

refreshment 94.1; *meal* 92.8, *strengthening* 516.7, *vigor* 518.1, *restoration* 807.4, *revival* 809.3, *ease* 819.1

refreshments 94.3

refresh oneself *be refreshed* 94.8

refresh one's memory *remind* 354.13

refried beans *notable international dishes* 90.40

refrigerant *cooler* 218.4, *cooled* 218.11

refrigerate *air* 94.7, *save* 105.20, *make cold* 218.15, *preserve* 815.14

refrigerated *refreshed* 94.5, *saved* 105.15, *cooled* 218.11

refrigeration *cold* 10.26, *refreshment* 94.1, *preservation of provisions* 815.6

refrigeration cycles *industrial processes* 14.27

refrigeration ship Ships and Boats 690

refrigerator 105.10; *kitchen container* 91.7, *cooler* 218.4, *cabinet* 578.3, *preserver* 815.9

refrigerator car *railroad car* 688.5

refrigerator-freezer *cooler* 218.4, *cabinet* 578.3

refry *cook* 91.10

refuel *replenish* 89.10, *store fuel* 105.18, *fuel* 106.16

refueled *fueled* 106.11

refuge 708.3, 812.1; *retreat* 60.13, *hiding place* 346.4, *stronghold* 460.6, *harbor* 1009.6, *security* 464.1, *shelter* 613.6, *haven* 810.3, *ecology* 815.3

refugee *avoider* 386.8, *displaced person* 574.7, *stateless* 574.14, *new arrival* 724.6, *escaper* 816.5

refulgence *light* 246.1

refulgent *lucent* 246.13

refund *compensation* 478.2, 743.1, *compensate* 478.6, 743.7, *repayment* 489.5, *pay back* 489.20, *discount* 495.1, 495.4, *subtracted item* 749.2

refundable *payable* 489.12

refunded *restoring* 478.4, *compensated* 743.3

refunder *returner* 478.3

refunding *restoring* 478.4

refurbish 809.11; *decorate* 532.11, *make new* 652.20, *beautify* 807.20

refurbished *renewed* 652.14, *repaired* 809.6

refurbisher *repairer* 809.5

refurbishment *beautification* 530.1, *interior decoration* 532.4, *new start* 652.5, *tidying* 807.6

refusal 190.2, 506.1; *frustration* 293.2, *disapproval* 347.2, 438.1, *opposition* 375.2, *rejection* 383.1, *shyness* 386.3, *disobedience* 416.2, *resistance* 417.1, *desisting* 417.4, *veto* 503.3, *repulse* 701.2, *negativeness* 718.3, *exclusion* 764.1, *hindrance* 826.1, *objection* 828.2

refusal of bail *detention* 830.5

refusal to act *inaction* 413.1

refusal to be impressed *lack of wonder* 295.1

refusal to mix *unsociability* 409.1

refusal to obey orders *disobedience* 427.1, *protest* 507.1

refusal to pay *nonpayment* 490.1, *refusal* 506.1, *protest* 507.1

refusal to recant *impenitence* 452.1

refusal to work *resistance* 417.1, *refusal* 506.1

refuse 190.17, 347.9, 506.8, 802.5; *waste product* 96.7, *dirt* 112.5, *thwart* 293.10, *hate* 300.11, *oppose* 375.13, *reject* 383.10, *shy* 386.17, *not use* 394.9, *be insubordinate* 416.8, *resist* 417.10, *withhold approval* 438.17, *detain* 471.9, *veto* 503.9, *repel* 701.7, *residue* 750.2, *exclude*

764.7, *hinder* 826.15, *withstand* 828.20

refuse assent *or* **consent** *refuse* 190.17

refuse bail *detain* 830.16

refused 506.5; *frustrated* 293.5, *rejected* 383.6, *disapproved* 438.9, *retained* 471.6, *vetoed* 503.6

refuse dump *place for waste* 802.6

refuse flatly *refuse* 506.8

refuse food *fast* 118.8, *lose weight* 468.14

refuse oneself 506.10; *desist* 417.13

refuse payment *stop payment* 490.10

refuse permission *prohibit* 503.8, *refuse* 506.8

refuse point-blank *refuse* 506.8

refuser 506.4; *negator* 190.8

refuse to accept *not accept* 190.19

refuse to act *not act* 413.11

refuse to be impressed *not wonder about* 295.5

refuse to believe *disbelieve* 88.8

refuse to bow down *resist* 417.10

refuse to bow to *defy* 416.7

refuse to budge *be obstinate* 417.11, *be permanent* 667.4, *withstand* 828.20

refuse to comment *be taciturn* 208.7

refuse to cooperate *disobey* 427.12

refuse to judge *or* **take sides** *be impartial* 338.11

refuse to obey orders *disobey* 427.12, *protest* 507.7

refuse to pay *not pay* 490.9, *refuse* 506.8

refuse to recant *be impenitent* 452.4

refuse to see the error of one's ways *be impenitent* 452.4

refuse to work *refuse* 506.8

refuse to yield *be tough* 547.13

refusing 375.9; *rejecting* 383.2, *resistant* 417.6, *disapproving* 438.8, *refused* 506.5

refusing oneself *desisting* 417.4

refusing to eat *sick* 114.24

refutability 332.4

refutable 332.11; *arguable* 329.8, *vindicable* 441.9, *reversible* 671.8

refutably 332.11; *reversibly* 671.14

refutation 332.1; *negation* 190.1, *denial* 332.2, *countercharge* 332.3, *counterstatement* 334.5, *counterevidence* 339.5, *defense* 441.2, *dissent* 506.2, *protest* 507.1, *reply* 671.5, *objection* 828.2, *canceling out* 834.3

refutative *refuting* 332.6, *retaliatory* 334.13

refutatory *refuting* 332.6, *retaliatory* 334.13

refute 332.7; *discuss* 4.22, *negate* 190.16, *deny* 332.8, *doubt* 333.19, *answer back* 334.19, *justify* 441.12, *dissent* 506.9, *reply* 671.13, *object* 828.18, *cancel out* 834.8

refuted *negated* 190.10, *reversed* 671.7

refuter *abrogator* 834.4

refuting 332.6; *negational* 190.9, *vindicatory* 441.7, *dissenting* 506.6

regain *take back* 477.17, *be compensated* 624.7

regain consciousness *live* 28.17, *awake* 212.10

regained safety *safety* 810.1

regaining *taking back* 477.4

regain one's breath *be refreshed* 94.8

regain one's freedom *divorce* 66.9

regain one's strength *be restored* 809.13

regal *governing* 49.25, Musical Instruments 142, *majestic* 297.12

regale *feed* 90.41, *feast* 92.9, *have a meal* 92.25, *give pleasure* 214.13, *be humorous* 277.11

regalement *eating meals* 92.4

regalia *vestment* 84.11, *finery* 100.6, *insignia* 184.5, *formal clothing* 406.5

regality *majesty* 297.5

regally *aristocratically* 70.6, *majestically* 297.21

regard *friendship* 62.1, *be of the opinion* 87.10, *reputation* 224.4, *look* 242.21, *liking* 290.1, *love* 299.1, *attention* 323.1, *be attentive* 323.9, *estimate* 341.11, *repute* 370.1, *respect* 435.1, 435.13, *admiration* 437.2, *observance* 465.1, *observe* 465.4, *make important* 799.14

regardant Heraldic Terms 184

regard as *take a substitute* 672.7

regard as important *take seriously* 278.8

regarded *reputable* 370.3

regarded highly by *friendly with* 62.6

regardful *prudent* 287.7, *respectful* 435.6, *observant* 465.3

regard highly *respect* 435.13, *admire* 437.15

regarding *observant* 465.3, *relevantly* 727.12

regardless *imprudent* 286.7, *nonobservant* 466.5, *how* 691.16

regardlessness *imprudence* 286.3

regards *courtesies* 410.3, *greeting* 435.5

regatta *competitive sailing* 150.6

Régence style Architectural Styles 134

Regency Furniture Styles 101

regency *caretaker government* 49.14, *governance* 49.18, *council* 833.4

Regency style Architectural Styles 134

regeneracy *revival* 809.3

regenerate *penitent* 451.5, *make new* 652.20, *be converted* 670.12, *improve* 807.15, *revive* 809.14

regenerated *renewed* 652.14, *converted* 670.7

regenerating *converting* 670.8

regeneration *righting wrong* 429.6, *new start* 652.5, *evolution* 670.3, *improvement* 807.1, *revival* 809.3

regenerative *procreative* 22.10

regent *educational leader* 68.11, *commissioner* 833.5

Regents Park London 567.8

reggae *folk music* 140.7

Reggio Breeds of Cattle 16

regicide *homicide* 30.4, *violation of the law* 427.2

regime *governance* 49.18

regimen *governance* 49.18, *therapy* 115.12

regiment *military organization* 58.4, *force* 59.10, *army unit* 77.14, *be severe* 424.8, *compel* 428.8, *collection* 757.3, *subject* 832.10

regimental colors *flag* 647.6

regimentals *uniform* 100.9, *clothing* 184.6, *formal clothing* 406.5

regimentation *severity* 424.1, *regularity* 730.6
regimented *severe* 424.5, *obedient* 426.4, *regular* 730.12
Regina Canadian Provinces 564
regina *sovereign* 68.2
region 564.1; *body politic* 50.3, *geographical space* 563.3, *part* 760.1
regional 564.12; *of language* 5.35, *jurisdictional* 53.18, *extensive* 563.12
regional accent *mode of speech* 205.6
regional climate *climate* 9.35
regional enteritis *gastroenterological disease* 114.11
regional forecast *weather forecast* 9.4
regionalism 564.11, Western Art Styles 133, Western Literary Groups 139
regionalize 564.15
regional language *native language* 5.5, *language family* 5.12
regionally 564.16
regional metamorphism *metamorphism* 8.35
regional novel *novel* 139.3
regionism *dialect* 5.24
regions 564.2
regions of the British Isles 564.8
regions of the United States 564.7
régisseur *producer* 136.28
register 185.15; *chronicle* 3.15, *computer part* 15.4, *tone* 140.24, *part of keyboard instrument* 142.6, *identify* 184.11, *record book* 185.5, *record* 185.13, *represent* 187.10, *take note of* 323.10, *be intelligible* 363.10, *account book* 493.3, *account* 493.9, *division* 577.6, *itemize* 577.13, *introduce* 708.16, *degree* 739.1, *catalog* 767.7, *categorize* 767.21, *list* 785.1, 785.11, *list of names* 785.7
registered *recorded* 185.12, *accounted* 493.8, *itemized* 577.9, *listed* 785.9
registered engineer *engineer* 14.2
registered historic building *preserved thing* 815.10
registered letter *postal communication* 169.4
registered mail *postal service* 169.5
registered nurse (RN) *nurse* 107.23
registered voter *electorate* 382.7
register one's vote *vote* 382.16
registrar *record keeper* 185.8
registration *recordkeeping* 185.7, *miscellaneous automotive terms* 687.14, *bringing in* 708.4, *listing* 785.8
registration document *certificate* 185.2
registry *record book* 185.5, *recordkeeping* 185.7, *list* 785.1
reglet Architectural Elements 134
regma *botanical fruit* 44.2
regnal *governing* 49.25
regnancy *governance* 49.18
regnant *governing* 49.25, *influential* 512.8
regolith *soil* 8.42
regrater *retailer* 482.11
regress *be in the rear* 622.7, *look back* 651.18, *reverse* 671.9, *be in motion* 677.14, *backward motion* 680.1, *go backward* 680.16, *navigate* 690.15, *slow down* 693.13, *return to* 797.18, *deteriorate* 808.14

regressed *reversed* 671.7
regression *defense mechanism* 108.23, *return* 671.3, *backward motion* 677.5, 680.1, *decrease* 747.1, *deterioration* 808.1
regression analysis *statistical methods* 6.53, *economic indicator* 56.4
regressive 671.6; *directional* 677.13, *receding* 680.11, *decrescent* 747.6, *spoiled* 808.9
regressively *reversibly* 671.14, *in motion* 677.19
regressive tax *tax* 494.5
regret *sorrow* 270.1, *lament* 280.7, *disappointment* 293.1, *be disappointed* 293.8, *penitence* 313.3, 451.1, *repent* 313.9, *sign of guilt* 450.2, *be penitent* 451.7
regretful *disappointed* 293.4, *apologetic* 313.6, *appearing guilty* 450.7, *penitent* 451.5
regretfully *lamentably* 280.10, *apologetically* 313.11, *unwillingly* 375.17, *guiltily* 450.12, *penitently* 451.10
regretfulness *penitence* 451.1
regret it *be punished* 454.31
regretless *impenitent* 452.2
regrets *apology* 313.2
regrettable *lamentable* 280.6
regretting *penitence* 451.1, *penitent* 451.5
regrouping *rearrangement* 767.4
regula Architectural Elements 134
regular 663.5, 730.12; *of grammar* 5.41, *spatial* 6.76, *of flowers* 42.11, *enlisted* 58.11, *soldier* 77.4, *creature of habit* 397.8, *habitual* 397.9, 765.15, *uniform* 545.5, 780.10, *petroleum* 562.5, *attender* 575.6, *attending* 575.9, *medium* 579.12, *even* 626.5, *periodical* 641.7, *frequent* 661.4, *directional* 677.13, *gradational* 739.5, *equal* 740.8, *average* 742.5, *well-ordered* 765.14, *common* 778.13, *recurrent* 797.13, *infallible* 840.12
regular army *army* 77.12
regular customer *creature of habit* 397.8, *attender* 575.6
regular features *evenness* 626.3
regular forces *armed forces* 77.9
regular gas *petroleum* 562.5
regular guy *commoner* 71.1
regular income *income* 492.3
regularity 663.1, 730.6; *habit* 397.1, *observance* 465.1, *smoothness* 545.1, *evenness* 626.3, *recurrent period* 641.5, *frequency* 661.1, *average* 742.1, *method* 765.7, *custom* 780.5, *repetitiveness* 797.3, *infallibility* 840.6
regularize *symmetrize* 626.6, *make periodical* 641.10, *make regular* 663.9, *make the same* 730.16, *make average* 742.9, *harmonize* 765.20, *rectify* 807.22
regularly 397.21, 663.14, 730.21; *grammatically* 5.48, *smoothly* 545.13, *periodically* 641.11, *frequently* 661.7, *orderly* 663.13, *conformingly* 735.37, *differentially* 739.9, *equitably* 740.15, *methodically* 765.27
regular movement 677.10
regular occurrence *frequency* 661.1
regular payments *type of payment* 489.3
regular polygon *polygon* 6.42
regular polyhedron *polyhedron* 6.44
regular practice *training* 122.5

regular recurrence *frequency* 663.2
regular return *cycle* 663.3
regulate 780.15; *govern* 49.26, *manage* 126.10, *advise* 176.9, *modify* 340.13, *command* 425.10, *moderate* 521.7, *make periodical* 641.10, *make regular* 663.9, *make the same* 730.16, *harmonize* 765.20, *direct* 780.14, *restrain* 830.12
regulated *modified* 340.9, *average* 742.5, *uniform* 780.10
regulated diet *dieting* 92.6
regulation *government* 49.1, *lawmaking* 53.11, *management* 126.1, *modification* 340.5, *established* 397.12, *treatment* 399.11, *command* 425.1, *moderation* 521.1, *regularity* 663.1, *average* 742.5, *rule* 780.1, *authority* 780.6, *customary* 780.9
regulation by law *lawmaking* 53.11
regulation by statute *lawmaking* 53.11
regulations *bureaucracy* 826.5
regulator gene *genetic material* 13.20
regulatory *industrial* 57.13, *commanding* 425.7, *legal* 780.8, *blocked* 826.13
regurgitate *reverse* 680.18, *vomit* 709.27
regurgitation *reversal* 680.3, *vomiting* 709.7
rehabilitate *practice medicine* 107.32, *vindicate* 441.11, *give back* 478.5, *transform* 670.13, *assimilate* 781.14, *improve* 807.15, *restore* 809.12
rehabilitated *vindicated* 441.8
rehabilitation *treatment* 107.14, *vindication* 441.1, *giving back* 478.1, *evolution* 670.3, *improvement* 807.1, *restoration* 809.2
rehabilitator *converter* 670.5
rehash *translate* 365.16, *repeat* 797.5, *renew* 797.19
rehashed *remade* 797.10
rehearsal 335.2; *production* 136.14, 137.6, *preparations* 388.2, *repetition* 797.1
rehearsal dinner *general wedding terms* 64.6
rehearse 136.37, 335.12; *act* 137.20, *recount* 202.16, *brief* 388.20, *prepare oneself* 388.21, *repeat* 797.15
rehearsed *dramatized* 136.32, *prepared* 388.9
reheat *cook* 91.10, *heat* 217.17, *renew* 797.19
reheated *heated* 217.15, *remade* 797.10
reheating *miscellaneous aviation terms* 689.9
rehoboam *bottle* 578.14
Rehpet Deities 82
Reich *psychologist* 108.33
Reichian psychology Psychological Theories, Schools 108
reify *be material* 524.8, *come to be* 717.19, *make real* 719.11
reign *governance* 49.18, 52.6, *govern* 49.26, *wield authority* 52.16, *personal influence* 512.3, *duration* 642.1, *prevail* 778.19, *authority* 780.6, *rule over* 780.13
reigning *governing* 49.25, *influential* 512.8, *ruling* 780.11
reign of terror *anarchism* 51.3,

terrorization 283.5, *malignity* 306.5
reign supreme *have authority* 52.13, *be an influence* 512.13
reimburse *atone* 313.7, *compensate* 478.6, 743.7, *pay back* 489.20
reimbursed *compensated* 743.3
reimbursement *atonement* 313.1, *compensation* 478.2, 743.1, *repayment* 489.5
rein *restraint* 826.8, 830.1, *restrain* 826.19
reincarnate *be material* 524.8
reincarnated *given new life* 28.15, *remade* 797.10
reincarnation *new life* 28.8, *materialization* 524.2, *return* 797.4
reincarnationism *occultism* 86.1
Reindeer Lakes 568
reindeer *game* 160.6, *means of transportation* 186.2
reindeer moss *moss* 46.4, *lichen* 47.16
reinforce 419.23; *replenish* 89.10, *strengthen* 516.15, *harden* 542.9, *support* 605.16, 748.14, 825.24, *give moral support* 605.18, *establish reality* 719.12, *intensify* 746.8, *restore* 809.12
reinforced *strengthened* 516.13, *hardened* 542.7, *additional* 748.8, *repaired* 809.6
reinforced concrete *construction material* 14.21, *hard substance* 542.3
reinforced concrete or ferroconcrete *shipbuilding* 690.4
reinforced glass *glass* 249.5
reinforcement *conditioning* 108.24, *association of ideas* 108.31, *strengthening* 516.7, *support* 605.1, *moral support* 605.7, *wavelength* 683.5, *intensification* 746.2, *addition* 748.1, *additional item* 748.3, *extra person* 748.7, *repair* 809.1, *restoration* 809.2
reinforcements 77.11; *extra* 748.6, *helper* 825.12
reinforcing *strengthening* 516.7, *supportive* 605.11
rein in *be self-restrained* 455.10, *slow down* 693.13, *restrain someone* 830.17
reins *guide* 126.6, *riding equipment* 159.9, *yoke* 754.8, *safety device* 810.15, *means of restraint* 830.6
reins of government *governance* 49.18
reinstall *restore* 809.12
reinstallation *restoration* 809.2
reinstallment *restoration* 809.2
reinstate *vindicate* 441.11, *give back* 478.5, *restore* 671.10
reinstated *reversed* 671.7
reinstatement *vindication* 441.1, *giving back* 478.1, *restoration* 671.2
reinstator *returner* 478.3
reinstitute *restore* 809.12
reinstitution *restoration* 809.2
reintegrate *restore* 809.12
reintegration *repair* 809.1
reinterpret *transform* 670.13
reintroduce *restore* 809.12
reintroduction *restoration* 809.2
reinvest *give back* 478.5
reinvestment *giving back* 478.1, *restoration* 809.2
reinvigorate *be young* 26.13, *refresh* 94.6, *strengthen* 516.15, *invigorate* 518.5, *revive* 809.14
reinvigorated *refreshed* 94.5

reinvigorating *refreshing* 94.4, *invigorating* 518.3
reinvigoration *refreshment* 94.1
reissue *printing* 173.3, *print* 173.17, *reappearance* 264.8, *repeat* 797.5, *renew* 797.19
reissued *remade* 797.10
reiterant *repetitious* 797.11
reiterate *be diffuse* 199.5, *emphasize* 200.6, *persevere* 377.10, *be periodical* 641.9, *iterate* 797.16
reiterated *constant* 377.8, *iterated* 797.9
reiteration *diffuseness* 199.1, *emphasis* 200.1, *constancy* 377.3, *iteration* 797.2
reiterative *diffuse* 199.3, *emphatic* 200.3, *repetitious* 797.11
reiteratively *repeatedly* 797.22
reiterativeness *diffuseness* 199.1
reject 383.10; *convict* 54.33, *refuse* 190.17, 347.9, 506.8, 802.5, *disavow* 190.18, *be dissatisfied* 274.7, *dislike* 291.12, *thwart* 293.10, *hate* 300.11, *deny* 332.8, *oppose* 375.13, *unused thing* 394.4, *not use* 394.9, *exclude* 409.12, 764.7, *withhold approval* 438.17, *not observe* 466.9, *loser* 468.8, 846.9, *veto* 503.9, *dissent* 506.9, *repel* 701.7, *exterminate* 709.22, *residue* 750.2, *leave* 750.10, *imperfect item* 806.3, *be against* 828.17, *cancel* 834.6
reject an offer *be unsatisfied* 98.10
reject authority *be anarchic* 51.8
rejected 383.6; *disagreeing* 190.11, *disavowing* 190.12, *unsatisfactory* 274.5, *disliked* 291.10, *frustrated* 293.5, *relinquished* 392.2, *lonely* 409.8, *disapproved* 438.9, *vetoed* 503.6, *dissenting* 506.6, *remaining* 750.7, *unjoined* 753.9, *excluded* 764.6
rejecter *negator* 190.8, *abrogator* 834.4
rejecting 383.2; *disapproving* 438.8, *nonobservant* 466.5, *dissenting* 506.6
rejection 383.1; *incredulity* 88.3, *defense mechanism* 108.23, *refusal* 190.2, 506.1, *disavowal* 190.3, *dissatisfaction* 274.1, *dislike* 291.1, *frustration* 293.2, *hate* 300.1, *denial* 332.2, *disapproval* 347.2, 438.1, *opposition* 375.2, *relinquishment* 392.1, *disuse* 394.3, *separation* 409.3, *nonobservance* 466.1, *veto* 503.3, *repulse* 701.2, *expulsion* 709.1, *setting apart* 753.2, *exclusion* 764.1, *objection* 828.2, *cancellation* 834.1, *suspicion* 841.2
rejection letter *rejection notice* 383.5
rejection notice 383.5
rejection slip *rejection notice* 383.5
rejective *disavowing* 190.12
reject one's appeal *convict* 54.33
reject one's defense *convict* 54.33
rejects *bargain* 497.4
reject someone's advances *repel* 701.7
rejoice 279.5; *show joy* 269.10, *celebrate* 405.10
rejoicer 279.3; *joyful person* 269.5
rejoicing 279.1, 279.4, 405.8; *celebration* 405.1
rejoicingly 279.7
Rejoicing over the Law Jewish Holy Days and Seasons 85
rejoin *put together* 59.30, *negate* 190.16, *countercharge* 332.9,

answer 334.18, *counter* 339.13, *justify* 441.12, *meet* 704.20
rejoinder *evidence* 54.15, *negation* 190.1, *countercharge* 332.3, *answer* 334.1, *counterevidence* 339.5, *retaliation* 420.1, *defense* 441.2
rejoined *negated* 190.10
rejoining *vindicatory* 441.7, *meeting* 704.5
rejuvenate *be young* 26.13, *invigorate* 28.22, *refresh* 94.6, *make new* 652.20, *revive* 809.14
rejuvenated *refreshed* 94.5, *renewed* 652.14
rejuvenating *refreshing* 94.4, *invigorating* 518.3
rejuvenation *refreshment* 94.1, *new start* 652.5, *revival* 809.3
rejuvenescence *revival* 809.3
rekindle *revive* 809.14
relapse *be wicked* 448.13, *reversion* 671.1, *reverse* 671.9, *backsliding* 680.8, *go backward* 680.16, *return to* 797.18, *deterioration* 808.1, *deteriorate* 808.14
relapsed *unimproved* 808.10
relapsing *receding* 680.11
relate *chronicle* 3.15, *report* 171.9, *record* 185.13, *recount* 202.16, *speak* 205.17, *relate to* 727.9, *be similar* 733.12, *intercommunicate* 754.15
relate badly *misrelate* 728.15
related 727.6; *chronicled* 3.12, *family* 65.6, *interrelated* 727.7, *connected* 733.9, *connective* 754.10, *included* 763.4, *iterated* 797.9
relatedly *relevantly* 727.12
relatedness 727.1
relate to 727.9; *feel for* 266.17, *be included* 763.6
relation *operation* 6.12, *mathematical logic* 6.60, *relatedness* 727.1, *association* 754.2, *associate* 754.3
relational *functional* 6.73
relational database *database* 15.15
relational operator *mathematical symbol* 6.11
relations *sexual intercourse* 20.9, *family* 65.1, *relatedness* 727.1
relationship *operation* 6.12, *mathematical logic* 6.60, *love affair* 299.9, *relatedness* 727.1, *association* 754.2
relative *circumstantial* 726.8, *interrelated* 727.7, *gradational* 739.5, *associate* 754.3
relative age *geological time* 8.47
relative aperture *lens system* 10.22
relative atomic mass *isotope* 10.57
relative bearing *bearing* 697.2
relative density 540.3; *mass* 10.8
relative frequency *probability distribution* 6.56
relative humidity *weather data* 9.6, *humidity* 559.3
relatively 726.17; *differentially* 739.9
relativeness *interrelatedness* 727.3, *gradation* 739.3
relative permeability *magnetic quantity* 10.48
relative permittivity *electric field* 10.42
relative position 727.5
relative quantity *gradation* 739.3
relatives *family* 65.1, Phobias 283
relative velocity *speed* 10.7

relativism Philosophical Schools of Thought 4
relativist Philosophical Schools of Thought 4
relativistic *physical* 10.70
relativistically *physically* 10.78
relativistic quantum mechanics Fields of Modern Physics 10
relativity Fields of Modern Physics 10, *fourth dimension* 563.9, *interrelatedness* 727.3
relaunch *restore* 809.12
relaunching *restoration* 809.2
relax *refresh* 94.6, *relieve* 275.8, *show pity* 308.8, *be informal* 407.10, *visit* 408.16, *have free time* 413.15, *pause* 415.15, 668.13, *weaken* 517.13, *be moderate* 521.6, *mitigate* 521.9, *soften* 543.14, *ease* 543.15, *slow down* 693.13, *loosen* 753.14, *take it easy* 819.3
relaxation *leisure* 125.1, 413.4, *ease* 275.1, 819.1, *freedom* 407.4, *moderation* 521.1, *informality* 829.6, *liberation* 831.1
relaxed *leisurely* 125.4, *pleased* 214.9, *relieved* 275.6, *sociable* 407.7, *inactive* 413.9, *soft* 543.6, *soft-hearted* 543.11, *unhurried* 693.8, *nonadhesive* 756.4, *at ease* 819.2, *easygoing* 823.13, *informal* 829.15
relaxedly *informally* 407.11
relaxedness *sociability* 407.2
relaxin Human Hormones 12
relaxing *pleasant* 214.7, *comfortable* 271.8, *relieving* 275.7, *leisure* 413.4, *at ease* 819.2
relax one's efforts *not act* 413.11
relax restrictions *liberate* 831.6
relay *swimming* 164.12, *communicate* 169.18, *broadcast material* 172.9, *publish* 173.15, *cycle* 663.3
relay box *relay racing* 166.5
relayed *communicated* 169.15
relay events *competitive swimming* 164.3
relay lens *lens system* 10.22
relay race *relay racing* 166.5, Children's and Party Games 167
relay racing 166.5, Sporting Activities 145
relay station *artificial satellite* 7.30, *radio broadcasting* 172.4, *television broadcasting* 172.8
release *secretion* 24.1, *secrete* 24.7, *death* 29.1, *favorable verdict* 54.19, *acquit* 54.32, 434.10, *dramatize* 136.33, *discus throwing* 166.13, *participate* 166.22, *publish* 173.15, *first appearance* 264.3, *present* 264.15, *aid* 275.2, *save* 275.9, *absolution* 312.2, *absolve* 312.10, *relinquishment* 392.1, *relinquish* 392.3, *acquittal* 434.2, *vindication* 441.1, *vindicate* 441.11, *payment* 489.1, *permit* 502.3, *dismiss* 709.15, *loosen* 753.14, *cessation* 773.2, *restore* 809.12, *escape* 816.1, *deliverance* 817.1, *deliver* 817.5, *freedom* 829.1, *set free* 829.17, *liberation* 831.1, *liberate* 831.6, *display* 843.10
released *dead* 29.11, *acquitted* 54.23, 434.6, *forgiven* 312.5, *relinquished* 392.2, *vindicated* 441.8, *separate* 753.7, *free* 829.11, *liberated* 831.4
released prisoner *escaper* 816.5, *free person* 829.9
release seeds *fruit* 44.9
release the ball *bowl* 151.8

releasing hormone *hormone* 12.16
relegate 574.18; *take away* 685.12, *disbar* 709.16, *exclude* 764.7, *make unimportant* 800.20
relegated 574.11
relegation 574.4; *transfer* 685.1, *dismissal* 709.2, *exclusion* 764.1
relent *show pity* 308.8, *submit* 421.4, *be moderate* 521.6, *yield* 543.17
relentless 309.4; *tenacious* 376.9, *strong-willed* 376.10, *inevitable* 840.11
relentless attack *combined attack* 418.5
relentlessly 309.8; *severely* 424.11, *inevitably* 840.17
relentlessness 309.2; *tenacity* 376.4, *inevitability* 840.5
relevance *correspondence* 334.8, *qualification* 340.1, *meaning* 361.1, *suitability* 462.4, *relatedness* 727.1
relevancy *suitability* 462.4
relevant *proven* 331.13, *correspondent* 334.16, *evidential* 339.8, *qualified* 340.7, *suitable* 462.9, *operative* 509.9, *related* 727.6, *essential* 799.10
relevant facts *evidence* 339.1
relevantly 727.12; *correspondingly* 334.27, *as evidence* 339.15, *suitably* 462.17, *operationally* 509.13
reliability *legal power* 52.2, *believability* 87.4, *observance* 465.1, *repute* 487.7, *permanence* 667.1, *stability* 674.1, *literalness* 721.9, *infallibility* 840.6
reliability trial *automobile racing* 146.1
reliable *legitimate* 52.10, *believable* 87.7, *steady* 376.8, *observant* 465.3, *unfailing* 667.3, *stable* 674.3, *literal* 721.18, *trustworthy* 810.17, *infallible* 840.12
reliableness *literalness* 721.9
reliably *legitimately* 52.19, *surely* 464.15, *observantly* 465.6, *permanently* 667.6, *stably* 674.9, *literally* 721.32
reliance *believing* 87.2, *expectation* 356.1, *security* 464.1
reliant *guaranteed* 464.6
relic *dead person* 29.7, *sacred object* 83.11, *talisman* 86.9, *vestige* 185.11, *memento* 354.3, *thing of the past* 651.8, *antiquity* 653.4, *remainder* 750.1
relict *thing of the past* 651.8, *remainder* 750.1
relict [Arch] *surviving spouse* 66.6
relief *social services* 2.10, *continent* 8.8, *refreshment* 94.1, *remedy* 115.1, *time off* 125.2, Architectural Elements 134, *relief carving* 144.2, *external appearance* 264.5, *charity* 275.3, 307.3, *benevolent act* 305.5, *mercy* 308.3, *security* 464.1, *moderation* 521.1, *lightening* 539.2, *height measurement* 596.5, *substitute* 613.17, 613.23, 672.2, *shape* 617.2, *form* 624.1, *extra person* 748.7, *subtraction* 749.1, *recuperation* 809.4, *escape* 816.1, *deliverance* 817.1, *support* 825.2, *social assistance* 825.4, *liberation* 831.1
relief carving 144.2
relief map *map* 187.5
relief organization *charitable organization* 305.4

relief pitcher *baseball team* 147.2
relief printing *woodworking* 131.1
relief worker *deputy* 80.1
relieve 275.8; *refresh* 94.6, *practice medicine* 107.32, *remedy* 115.16, *comfort* 214.14, *be compassionate* 305.11, *philanthropize* 307.8, *show pity* 308.8, *mitigate* 521.9, *lighten* 539.9, *cover for* 613.34, *be a substitute* 672.6, *subtract* 749.6, *succeed* 770.11, *deliver* 817.5, *ease* 819.4, *support* 825.24, *liberate* 831.6
relieved 275.6; *escaping* 816.7
relieve from duty 275.11
relieve one of *steal* 479.14
relieve oneself 275.12; *excrete* 25.20
reliever 275.4
relieving 275.7; *refreshing* 94.4, *lightening* 539.6
relievo *relief carving* 144.2
religion 81.1; *belief system* 87.3, *immateriality* 525.2
religionism *religiousness* 81.2, *ungenuineness* 192.2
religionist 81.14
religiose *ungenuine* 192.13
religiosity *religiousness* 81.2, *ungenuineness* 192.2
religious 81.21, 84.9; *sociological* 2.11, *types of history* 3.2, *religious person* 81.9, *theological* 81.24, *worshipful* 83.12, *architectural types* 134.2, *type of painting* 143.5, *observant* 465.3
religious belief *belief system* 87.3
religious believer *nonmaterialist* 525.7
religious broadcasting *broadcast material* 172.9
religious ceremony *Phobias* 283, *formal occasion* 406.4
religious cleansing 111.3
religious conversion 670.4
religious disobedience *disobedience* 427.1
religious ecstasy *trance* 108.18
religious education *subject* 48.3, *religious studies* 81.3
religious fasting *fasting* 118.1
religious feeling *belief system* 87.3
religious festival 85.13
religious group 81.4
religious holiday *anniversary* 663.4
religious icon *painting* 143.3
religious institution *social institution* 2.8
religious instruction *subject* 48.3, *religious studies* 81.3
religious leader 68.9
religiously 81.29; *sociologically* 2.15, *observantly* 465.6, *metaphysically* 525.13
religious mania *delusion* 110.2
religious movement *religious group* 81.4
religiousness 81.2
religious objects *Phobias* 283
religious observance *custom* 397.4, *performance* 465.2
religious organization *social organization* 2.5
religious painter *painter* 143.7
religious persecution *social discrimination* 337.4
religious person 81.9
religious rite *holy water* 557.15
religious sacrifice *ritual killing* 30.7
religious school 48.13
religious studies 81.3
religious symbol *sign* 183.1

religious text 81.15
religious war *holy war* 76.8
reline *repair* 809.10
relinquish 392.3; *disavow* 190.18, *stop using* 394.10, *capitulate* 421.6, *be self-restrained* 455.10, *forfeit* 468.13, *stop* 868.10, *withdraw* 705.9, *diverge* 753.20, *resign* 835.5
relinquish authority *be permissive* 502.7
relinquished 392.2; *self-restrained* 455.6, *abnegating* 506.7, *ceased* 668.6
relinquisher *negator* 190.8
relinquishing *abnegating* 506.7
relinquishment 392.1; *disavowal* 190.3, *submission* 421.1, *self-restraint* 455.1, *abnegation* 506.3, *cessation* 668.1, *resignation* 835.1
reliquary *shrine* 83.10
relish *taste* 92.24, 219.5, *feel pleasure* 214.12, *flavor* 219.5, *enjoy* 269.9, 290.9, *take pleasure in* 271.11, *likes* 290.3, *like* 299.22
relishable *tasty* 219.4
relishes *side dish* 90.15
relishing *delicate eating* 92.3
relive *look back* 651.18
relocate *settle* 565.10, *displace* 574.15, *change* 665.14, *take away* 685.12, *quit* 705.10
relocated *displaced* 574.8, *replaced* 574.10
relocation *displacement* 574.1, *replacement* 574.3, *alteration* 665.2, *transfer* 685.1
reluctance *reticence* 287.3, *disinclination* 291.3, *unwillingness* 375.1, *shyness* 386.3, *reserve* 403.5, *resistance* 417.1, *hesitation* 693.5
reluctant *reticent* 287.8, *disinclined* 291.9, *unwilling* 375.8, *unenthusiastic* 375.10, *avoiding* 386.9, *reserved* 403.10, *resistant* 417.6, *hesitant* 693.9
reluctantly *reticent* 287.18, *discontentedly* 291.17, *unwillingly* 375.17, *shyly* 386.25, *resistingly* 417.14, *slowly* 693.14
reluctant person 375.7
rely on *believe* 87.9, *hope* 281.10, *resort to* 393.13, *be certain* 840.13
rely on supposition *suppose* 359.8
remade 797.10; *renewed* 652.14, *repaired* 809.6
remain *endure* 377.14, *last* 642.6, *protract* 669.9, *be motionless* 678.7, *continue to be left* 750.9
remain at a distance *keep away* 585.9
remain at anchor *pause* 415.15
remain at rest *be permanent* 667.4
remain a virgin *be continent* 67.10, *be moral* 413.13
remainder 750.1; *division* 6.16, *superfluity* 99.4, *numerical answer* 334.7, *unused thing* 394.4, *legal property terms* 470.2, *sell off* 482.20, *thing of the past* 651.8, *effect* 676.1, *part* 760.1, *mathematical result* 783.4
remain fixed *be stable* 674.6
remain forever *be eternal* 644.7
remaining 750.7; *historical* 3.10, *superfluous* 99.8
remain in situ *be motionless* 678.7
remain intransigent *be stubborn* 542.11
remain neutral *be impartial* 289.15, 338.11, *be independent* 829.18

remain obstinate *be impenitent* 452.4
remains *dead person* 29.7, *vestige* 185.11, *indication* 339.3, *unused thing* 394.4, *thing of the past* 651.8, *remainder* 750.1
remain seated *disrespect* 436.18, *be motionless* 678.7
remain skeptical *not observe* 466.9
remain the same *be permanent* 667.4
remain unchanged *be permanent* 667.4, *be conservative* 815.15
remain undaunted *endure* 377.14
remain unmarried *be celibate* 67.9
remain unmoved *be indifferent* 289.12
remain unrepentant *be impenitent* 452.4
remain unsolved *be unexplained* 364.15
remake *new start* 652.5, *make new* 652.20, *restore* 671.10, 809.12, *repeat* 797.5, *renew* 797.19
remand *delay* 658.3, 658.13, *detention* 830.5, *detain* 830.16
remanded *held up* 658.6
remanded to custody *arrested* 55.10
remand to custody *arrest* 55.12
remanence *magnetic phenomenon* 10.50
remark *aphorize* 177.3, *utterance* 205.10, *judgment* 341.1
remarkable *clear* 244.6, *wondrous* 294.9, *exceptional* 779.13, *notable* 799.11
remarkableness *wonderfulness* 294.5
remarkably *wondrously* 294.18, *characteristically* 779.20, *importantly* 799.15
remarriage *type of marriage* 64.3
remarried *married* 64.16
remarry *marry* 64.19
remediably *in compensation* 743.10
remedial 115.14; *educational* 48.17, *therapeutic* 107.30, *hygienic* 116.3, *relieving* 275.7, *atoning* 313.5, *solved* 334.15, *counteracting* 510.6, *compensatory* 743.5, *improving* 807.14, *restorative* 809.9, *beneficial* 825.20
remedial education *educational system* 48.2
remedially 115.19; *educationally* 48.25, *atoningly* 313.10, *correspondingly* 334.27, *counter* 510.8, *in compensation* 743.10, *better* 807.24, *repairably* 809.16
remedial measure *remedy* 115.1
remedied *compensated* 743.3
remediless *hopeless* 282.6
remedilessness *hopelessness* 282.1
remedy 115.1, 115.16; *means* 102.1, *medicine* 115.2, *treat* 115.17, *reliever* 275.4, *atonement* 313.1, *atone* 313.7, *solution* 334.6, *solve* 334.21, *expedient* 387.5, *put right* 429.14, *counteraction* 510.1, *counteractant* 510.5, *compensation* 743.1, *compensate* 743.7, *restoration* 807.4, *rectify* 807.22, *repair* 809.1, 809.10, *recuperation* 809.4, *support* 825.2, 825.24, *medical assistance* 825.5
remember 354.12, 471.10; *recollect* 3.16, *learn* 68.18, *be benevolent* 305.10, *have an idea* 327.13, *memorize* 354.11,

commemorate 354.14, 405.11, *understand* 363.9, *look back* 651.18, *return to* 797.18
remembered *biographical* 3.13, *memorable* 354.7
remember forever *make eternal* 644.8
remembering 354.8; *recollection* 3.8, *memory* 354.1, *retrospective* 651.15
remember wrongly *be forgetful* 355.11
remembrance *recollection* 3.8, *memory* 354.1, *commemoration* 405.2, *retentiveness* 471.4, *eternalization* 644.3, *retrospection* 651.3, *remainder* 750.1
remembrancer *adviser* 176.5
remembrance service *commemoration* 405.2
remex *plumage* 36.7
remind 354.13; *warn* 814.8
reminder 354.4; *inside information* 170.4, *adviser* 176.5, *record* 185.1, *remainder* 750.1
reminding *memorable* 354.7
remind oneself *remind* 354.13
reminisce *recollect* 3.16, *recount* 202.16, *remember* 354.12, *look back* 651.18
reminiscence *recollection* 3.8, *memory* 354.1, *retrospection* 651.3
reminiscences *biography* 3.5
reminiscent *memorable* 354.7
reminiscently *biographically* 3.18, *memorably* 354.16, *retrospectively* 651.22
reminiscing *retrospective* 651.15
remise *fencing movements* 153.3
remiss *imprudent* 286.7, *careless* 324.8, *negligent* 326.4, *procrastinating* 375.11, *nonobservant* 466.5
remissible *vindicable* 441.9
remission *ease* 275.1, *vindication* 441.1, *moderation* 521.1, *subtracted item* 749.2
remission of sin *forgiveness* 312.1
remissive *vindicatory* 441.7, *nonobservant* 466.5
remissively *justifyingly* 441.15
remissly *negligently* 326.8
remissness *negligence* 326.1, *disobedience* 375.5, *nonobservance* 466.1
remit *forgive* 312.8, *vindicate* 441.11, *pay* 489.16, *be moderate* 521.6, *convey* 685.9, *compensate* 743.7
remittable *forgivable* 312.7, *payable* 489.12, *compensable* 743.4
remittal *vindication* 441.1, *compensation* 743.1
remittance *funds* 484.6, *payment* 489.1, *compensation* 743.1
remittance man *or* **woman** *outgoer* 707.9
remitted *compensated* 743.3
remit the penalty *acquit* 54.32
remnant *remainder* 750.1, *residue* 750.2
remodel *cause change* 665.16, *transform* 670.13, *rectify* 807.22, *refurbish* 809.11
remodeled *changed* 665.10
remodeling *change for the better* 665.4, *restoration* 809.2
remold *cause change* 665.16, *rectify* 807.22
remolded *changed* 665.10
remolding *change for the better* 665.4
remonstrant *dissuasive* 179.4
remonstrantly *dissuasively* 179.12

remonstrate *dissuade* 179.7, *argue* 329.11, *warn* 814.8, *object* 828.18

remonstration *dissuasion* 179.1, *expression of dissatisfaction* 274.2, *objection* 828.2

remora *adherent* 755.4

remorse *sorrow* 270.1, *penitence* 313.3, 451.1, *sign of guilt* 450.2

remorseful *apologetic* 313.6, *appearing guilty* 450.7, *penitent* 451.5

remorsefully *apologetically* 313.11, *guiltily* 450.12, *penitently* 451.10

remorsefulness *penitence* 451.1

remorseless *pitiless* 309.3, *impenitent* 452.2

remorselessly *pitilessly* 309.7, *impenitently* 452.5

remorselessness *pitilessness* 309.1, *impenitence* 452.1

remortgage *loan* 488.3

remote *guide* 126.6, *difficult to see* 245.4, *murky* 248.5, *unsociable* 409.6, *secluded* 409.9, *distant* 585.5, 804.8, *outside* 610.9, *improbable* 839.4

remote age *past time* 3.6, 651.1

remote control *guide* 126.6, *television set* 172.6

remote future *future time* 650.1

remotely *unsociably* 409.13, *distantly* 585.11, *outside* 610.17

remoteness *that which makes invisible* 245.2, *murk* 248.2, *unsociability* 409.1, *distance* 585.1, 804.4

remote past *past time* 651.1

remote possibility **836.4;** *improbability* 839.1

remote sensing *measurement* 10.67

remount *war-horse* 159.4, *substitute* 672.2

removable *transferable* 685.7, *extractive* 711.10, *subtractive* 749.4

removable hard disk *disk* 15.5

removably *away* 711.20, *decreasingly* 749.9

removal **574.2, 709.5;** *obliteration* 186.1, *taking away* 477.5, *distance* 585.1, *transfer* 685.1, *eviction* 709.4, *extraction* 711.1, *subtraction* 749.1, *setting apart* 753.2, *ejection* 764.2, *cancellation* 834.1, *termination* 834.2

removal van *truck* 578.10

remove **574.16;** *obliterate* 186.8, *cause to disappear* 265.7, *take away* 477.18, 685.12, *intervening space* 563.8, *undress* 614.18, *depilate* 614.20, *move* 677.15, *transport* 686.10, *quit* 705.10, *evict* 709.20, *void* 709.23, *extract* 711.13, *separate* 724.14, 753.12, *gradation* 739.3, *subtract* 749.6, *eject* 764.8, *cancel* 834.6, *terminate* 834.7

remove all doubt *prove* 331.17

remove all obstacles *permit* 502.6

remove all signs of *cancel* 834.6

remove any trace *obliterate* 186.8

remove authority from *remove power from* 515.13

removed **574.9;** *unsociable* 409.6, *replaced* 574.10, *spaced* 587.4, *separate* 724.10, *subtracted* 749.3

removed from the record *forgiven* 312.5

remove doubt *verify* 336.8

remove errors *rectify* 807.22

remove friction *smooth* 545.10

remove from the record *absolve* 312.10

removement *transfer* 685.1

remove one's name from *withdraw* 392.5

remove power from 515.13

remover *taker* 477.9

remove the dirt *clean* 111.17

remunerate **489.21;** *atone* 313.7, *reward* 453.13, *pay* 453.15, *compensate* 743.7

remunerated *compensated* 743.3

remuneration *atonement* 313.1, *reward* 453.1, *reward for service* 453.5, *gain* 467.1, *earnings* 467.5, *pay* 489.6, *income* 492.3, *compensation* 743.1

remunerative *rewarding* 453.9, *gainful* 467.10, *profitable* 489.13, 801.8, *productive* 522.11, *successful* 845.8

remuneratively *profitably* 453.20, 492.8, *gainfully* 467.24, *productively* 522.17

Renaissance *Ages, Decades, Eras* 641, *historical past* 651.6

renaissance *new life* 28.8, *return* 797.4, *revival* 809.3

Renaissance architecture *Architectural Styles* 134

Renaissance humanism *Western Literary Groups* 139

Renaissance man *or* **woman** *skilled person* 127.7, *intellectual* 315.7, *pluralist* 793.5

Renaissance perspective *treatment* 143.6

Renaissance tragedy *tragedy* 136.10

renascence *revival* 809.3

renascent *repaired* 809.6

rend *chew* 92.22, *crack* 587.7, *take apart* 753.16

rend asunder *demolish* 523.12

render *be an architect* 134.13, *play* 141.14, *draw* 143.13, *represent* 187.10, *interpret* 365.12, *translate* 365.16, *give* 472.10, *melt* 555.24, *face* 613.31, *transform* 670.13, *obtain an extract* 711.19, *grant* 735.30

render assistance *philanthropize* 307.8, *help* 825.23

rendered *drawn* 143.11, *interpreted* 365.9

renderer *drawer* 143.8

render faithfully *seem true* 721.26

render good *compensate* 478.6

render hard *harden* 542.9

render harmless *make useless* 802.12

rendering *cooking technique* 91.2, *architecture* 134.1, *(act of) drawing* 143.2, *drawing* 143.4, *representation* 187.1, *interpretation* 365.1, *translation* 365.4, *wall covering* 613.12, *obtaining of an extract* 711.7

render insensible *anesthetize* 213.8

render soft *soften* 543.14

render thanks *be grateful* 310.6

render unconscious *anesthetize* 213.8

render unfit *make useless* 802.12

render up *relinquish* 392.3

render void *or* **inoperative** *disavow* 190.18

rendezvous *rocketry* 7.32, *come together* 59.25, *social gathering* 408.4, *meeting* 704.5, *meet* 704.20, *union* 752.1, *point of union* 752.8

rendition *interpretation* 365.1, *obtaining of an extract* 711.7

rend the eardrums *shatter the peace* 232.10

rend the skies *shatter the peace* 232.10

rend to bits *demolish* 523.12

rend to pieces *demolish* 523.12

renegade *hypocrite* 192.9, *dishonorable* 192.14, *miscreant* 448.6, *defiant* 466.7, *dissenter* 782.8, *dissident* 782.12

renege *bridge* 168.4, *play cards* 168.7, *not observe* 466.9, *be converted* 670.12, *reverse* 671.9, *cancel* 834.6

reneger *abrogator* 834.4

reneging *cancellation* 834.1

renew 797.19; *reproduce* 21.13, *refresh* 94.6, *make new* 652.20, *cause change* 665.16, *beautify* 807.20, *refurbish* 809.11, *revive* 809.14

renewable **106.15, 652.15**

renewable energy **106.9**

renewable energy source *fuel* 106.1, *power source* 514.13

renewal *restoration* 21.2, *refreshment* 94.1, *new start* 652.5, *change for the better* 665.4, *return* 797.4, *tidying* 807.6, *repair* 809.1, *revival* 809.3

renewed **652.14;** *reproduced* 21.10, *refreshed* 94.5, *constant* 377.8, *changed* 665.10, *remade* 797.10, *repaired* 809.6

renew one's efforts *persevere* 377.10

renew oneself *be refreshed* 94.8, *become new* 652.19

renitency *opposition* 375.2, *resistance* 417.1

renitent *refusing* 375.9, *resistant* 417.6

rennet *thickener* 561.12

rennin *enzyme* 12.11

renounce **383.13, 392.4;** *disavow* 190.18, *deny* 332.8, *reject* 383.10, *be self-restrained* 455.10, *refuse oneself* 506.10, *protest* 507.7, *cancel* 834.6, *resign* 835.5

renounce authority *capitulate* 421.6

renounced **383.9;** *disavowing* 190.12, *relinquished* 392.2

renounce drinking *abstain* 455.11

renouncement *rejection* 383.1, *resignation* 835.1

renouncer *negator* 190.8

renounce the throne *resign* 835.5

renouncing *refuting* 332.6

renovate *reproduce* 21.13, *refresh* 94.6, *make new* 652.20, *beautify* 807.20, *refurbish* 809.11

renovated *reproduced* 21.10, *renewed* 652.14, *improved* 807.12, *repaired* 809.6

renovation *restoration* 21.2, *refreshment* 94.1, *new start* 652.5, *tidying* 807.6, *repair* 809.1, *conservation* 815.2

renovator *repairer* 809.5

renown *publicity* 173.7

renowned *historic* 3.11, *publicized* 173.14, *known* 348.9, *reputable* 370.3, *famous* 845.9

rent *inhabit* 61.13, *type of table* 101.5, *possess* 469.14, *transfer property* 470.12, *money received* 492.2, *fee* 494.3, *crack* 587.2, *cracked* 587.5, *separateness* 753.3, *apart* 753.8

rental *transfer of property* 470.4, *fee* 494.3

rental contract *purchase contract* 459.3

rental library *library* 174.14

rental movie *movie type* 137.3

rent boy [Brit inf] *sexually immoral person* 432.8

rent collector *collector* 473.7

rented *inhabited* 61.10

renter *resident* 61.6, *person transferring property* 470.8

rent-free *free of charge* 497.12

rentier [Fr] *nonworker* 415.4, *collector* 473.7

rent-payer *possessor* 469.10

rent-roll *money received* 492.2

renumerate *put right* 429.14

renunciate *dissent* 506.9

renunciation **383.4;** *disavowal* 190.3, *denial* 332.2, *relinquishment* 392.1, *self-restraint* 455.1, *dissent* 506.2, *protest* 507.1, *resignation* 835.1

renunciation of wealth **486.4**

renunciative *self-restrained* 455.6, *dissenting* 506.6

renunciative *or* **renunciatory** *disavowing* 190.12

renunciatory *dissenting* 506.6, *resigning* 835.3

reoccur *be frequent* 661.5, *be regular* 663.10, *be repeated* 797.20

reoccur constantly *be regular* 663.10

reoccurring *recurrent* 797.13

reorder *cause change* 665.16, *rearrange* 767.20

reordered *changed* 665.10, *rearranged* 767.14

reordering *change for the better* 665.4, *rearrangement* 767.4

reorder signal *dial* 169.12

reorganization *new start* 652.5, *change for the better* 665.4, *conversion* 670.1, *rearrangement* 767.4, *rectification* 807.8, *restoration* 809.2

reorganize *make new* 652.20, *change* 665.14, *cause change* 665.16, *transform* 670.13, *rearrange* 767.20, *rectify* 807.22, *restore* 809.12

reorganized *renewed* 652.14, *changed* 665.10, *rearranged* 767.14

reorient *restore* 809.12

reorientation *conditioning* 108.24, *restoration* 809.2

rep *Fabrics and Fibers* 130

rep [Inf] *representative* 75.3, *agent* 123.15, *drama* 136.1, *speaker* 205.12, *salesperson* 482.8

repaid *compensated* 743.3

repaint *make new* 652.20, *refurbish* 809.11

repainted *renewed* 652.14

repainting *new start* 652.5

repair **809.1, 809.10;** *refreshment* 94.1, *refresh* 94.6, *atone* 313.7, *righting wrong* 429.6, *put right* 429.14, *change for the better* 665.4, *change back* 665.19, *restoration* 807.4, *rectification* 807.8, *restore* 807.17, *rectify* 807.22

repairable **809.7**

repairably **809.16**

repaired **809.6;** *changed* 665.10, *improved* 807.12

repairer **809.5;** *improver* 807.11

repairing *change for the better* 665.4

repairman *repair worker* 123.8

repairs *repair* 809.1

repair ship *warship* 77.21

repair worker **123.8**

repaper *refurbish* 809.11

reparable *reparable* 809.7
reparably *repairably* 809.16
reparation 273.2; *peace offering* 74.5, *atonement* 313.1, *retaliation* 420.1, *type of penance* 451.3, *compensation* 453.7, 478.2, 743.1, *repair* 809.1, *restoration* 809.2
reparations *restoration* 809.2
reparative *atoning* 313.5, *restoring* 478.4, *compensatory* 743.5, *restorative* 809.9
reparatory *atoning* 313.5, *compensatory* 453.11, 743.5, *restoring* 478.4
repartee *chat* 210.2, *wit* 277.3, *answer* 334.1, *exchange* 673.1
repast *meal* 92.8
repatriate *give back* 478.5, *displaced person* 574.7, *replace* 574.17, *ostracize* 709.17, *restore* 809.12
repatriated *replaced* 574.10
repatriation *giving back* 478.1, *replacement* 574.3, *ostracism* 709.3, *restoration* 809.2
repay *atone* 313.7, *retaliate* 420.4, *pay* 453.13, *compensate* 478.6, 743.7, *pay back* 489.20, *reciprocate* 729.7, 827.13
repayable *borrowed* 476.8
repayable amount *loan* 476.5
repayment 489.5; *atonement* 313.1, *retaliation* 420.1, *reckoning* 454.8, *compensation* 478.2, 743.1, *reciprocity* 729.1
repayment plan *borrowing* 476.1
repay with interest *make bigger* 746.7
repeal *disavowal* 190.3, *disavow* 190.18, *veto* 503.3, 503.9, *cancellation* 834.1, *cancel* 834.6
repealed *disavowing* 190.12, *canceled* 834.5
repealer *negator* 190.8
repealing *cancellation* 834.1
repeat 797.5, 797.15; *reproduce* 21.13, *broadcast material* 172.9, *be diffuse* 199.5, *emphasize* 200.6, *recount* 202.16, *reappearance* 264.8, *mean* 361.13, *make comprehensible* 363.8, *persevere* 377.10, *be periodical* 641.9, *be frequent* 661.5, *be regular* 663.10, *continue* 669.8, *be the same* 730.13, *imitate* 736.9, *double* 789.11, 789.14, *iterate* 797.16
repeated 797.8; *reproduced* 21.10, *broadcast* 172.12, *diffuse* 199.3, *drumming* 235.6, *appearing* 264.9, *similar* 361.7, *constant* 377.8, *frequent* 661.4, *same* 730.7, *double* 789.11
repeated decimal *division* 6.16
repeated efforts *commitment* 377.2
repeatedly 21.18, 235.15, 797.22; *continually* 377.17, 669.10, *periodically* 641.11, *frequently* 661.7, *regularly* 663.14, *identically* 730.18
repeater *communications device* 15.26, Timepieces and Timers 646
repeating *bolt-action* 78.17, *pealing* 235.9, *habitual* 397.9, *frequent* 663.6, *repetition* 797.1, *iteration* 797.2, *repetitious* 797.11
repeating rifle *firearm* 78.7
repeat oneself *be diffuse* 199.5, *bore* 296.8, *be frequent* 661.5, *iterate* 797.16
repeat order *repeat* 797.5
repeat performance *repeat* 797.5

repeat word-for-word *be literal* 721.25
repel 701.7; *interact* 10.73, *put off* 179.10, *displease* 272.8, *cause dislike* 291.16, *cause hate* 300.12, *reject* 383.10, *exclude* 409.12, *resist* 417.10, *retaliate* 419.30, *refuse* 506.8, *change* 512.12, *be repulsive* 701.10
repelled *dissuaded* 179.5, *antipathetic* 291.7, *hating* 300.7, *rejected* 383.6
repellence *rejection* 383.1, *resistance* 417.1, *repulsion* 701.1
repellency *repulsion* 701.1
repellent *dissuasive* 179.4, *disliked* 291.10, *resistant* 417.6, *repulsive* 701.4
repellently *dissuasively* 179.12, *resistingly* 417.14, *repulsively* 701.11
repellent quality *repulsion* 701.1
repeller *resister* 417.5
repelling *rejecting* 383.2, *resistant* 417.6, *repulsion* 701.1, *repulsive* 701.4, *abducent* 701.5
repent 313.9; *recant* 81.27, *be penitent* 451.7, *reply* 671.13
repentance *penitence* 313.3, 451.1, *reversion* 671.1
repentant *apologetic* 313.6, *penitent* 451.5
repentantly *apologetically* 313.11, *penitently* 451.10
repenter *atoner* 313.4
repenting *apologetic* 313.6, *penitent* 451.5
repent in sackcloth and ashes *do penance* 451.9
repercussion *response* 334.4, *counteraction* 510.1, *effect* 676.1, *consequence* 774.3
repercussive 774.8; *reactive* 334.12
repertoire *collection* 105.12, *merchandise* 482.6
repertory *collection* 105.12, *drama* 136.1, *list* 785.1
repertory circuit *engagement* 136.15
repertory company *cast* 136.26
repertory player *actor* 136.25
répétiteur *musical director* 141.7
repetition 797.1; *reproduction* 21.1, *literary device* 139.12, *diffuseness* 199.1, *emphasis* 200.1, *constancy* 377.3, *recurrent period* 641.5, *frequency* 661.1, 663.2, *continuation* 669.2, *sameness* 730.1, *imitation* 736.1, *doubling* 789.4, *repetitiveness* 797.3, *repeat* 797.5
repetitional *repetitious* 797.11
repetitious 797.11; *boring* 296.6, *periodical* 641.7, *frequent* 661.4, *same* 730.7
repetitiously *boringly* 296.10, *periodically* 641.11, *regularly* 663.14, *identically* 730.18, *repeatedly* 797.22
repetitiousness *boringness* 296.2, *repetitiveness* 797.3
repetitive *diffuse* 199.3, *emphatic* 200.3, *humming* 235.7, *boring* 296.6, *periodic* 639.10, *periodical* 641.7, *frequent* 661.4, 663.6, *progressive* 669.6, *same* 730.7, *cyclical* 774.10, *repetitious* 797.11
repetitively *diffusely* 199.7, *repeatedly* 235.15, 797.22, *boringly* 296.10, *periodically* 641.11, *frequently* 661.7, *continually* 669.10, *identically* 730.18

repetitiveness 797.3; *diffuseness* 199.1, *power of speech* 205.5, *boringness* 296.2, *recurrent period* 641.5, *frequency* 663.2, *sameness* 730.1
repetitive strain injury (RSI) *joint disease* 114.19
rephrase *word* 5.43, *mean* 361.13, *translate* 365.16
replace 574.17; *stand for* 187.14, *aid* 275.10, *answer for* 334.24, *stop using* 394.10, *act as a go-between* 460.8, *give back* 478.5, *cover for* 613.34, *change* 665.14, *be a substitute* 672.6, *compensate* 743.7, *succeed* 770.11, *restore* 809.12
replaced 574.10; *substituted* 672.4, *compensated* 743.3
replacement 574.3; *alternative* 80.2, *representative* 187.7, *helper* 275.5, *giving back* 478.1, *substitute* 613.17, 672.2, *change* 665.1, *substitution* 672.1, *compensation* 743.1, *succession* 770.2, *restoration* 809.2
replacements *reinforcements* 77.11
replant *restore* 809.12
replanting *restoration* 809.2
replay *repeat* 797.5, *renew* 797.19
replayed *remade* 797.10
replaying *repeat* 797.5
replenish 89.10; *suffice* 97.6, *store fuel* 105.18, *fill* 761.11, *restore* 809.12
replenished *supplied* 89.7, *full* 761.8
replenishment *provisions* 89.3, *restoration* 809.2
replete *filled* 97.5, *immoderate* 99.6, *full* 761.8
repletion *plenty* 97.2, *fullness* 761.5
replevin *compensation* 743.1
replevisable *compensable* 743.4
replevy *compensate* 743.7
replica 797.7; *restoration* 21.2, *reprint* 21.3, *image* 187.3, *figure* 187.4, *impression* 264.7, *copy* 730.5, 736.2, *simulation* 733.4, *duplicate* 736.4
replicate *reproduce* 21.13, *simulate* 733.16, *copy* 736.10, *double* 789.14, *pluralize* 793.9, *repeat* 797.15
replicated *reproduced* 21.10, *simulated* 733.11, *repeated* 797.8
replication *reproduction* 21.1, *answer* 334.1, *repetition* 797.1
replied *reversed* 671.7
replier *answerer* 334.10
reply 671.5, 671.13; *correspond* 169.19, *utterance* 205.10, *speak* 205.17, *countercharge* 332.3, 332.9, *answer* 334.1, 334.18
reply for the defense *defense* 441.2
replying *answering* 334.11
report 171.9, 175.9; *chronicle* 3.4, 3.15, *educate* 48.22, *communication* 170.2, *document* 170.3, *communicate* 170.12, *broadcast* 172.13, *publication* 173.1, *record* 185.1, *description* 202.1, *factual account* 202.4, *recount* 202.16, *burst of sound* 232.4, *bang* 234.1, *evidence* 339.1, *judgment* 341.1, *interpret news* 365.17, *repute* 370.1, *appear* 575.16, *include* 613.33
reportable *newsworthy* 171.8, 175.7
reportage *print journalism* 175.4
report card *record* 185.1

reported *chronicled* 3.12, *newsworthy* 171.8, 175.7, *published* 173.12, *evidential* 339.8
reportedly 170.16; *newsworthily* 171.10, *journalistically* 175.10, *as evidence* 339.15
reporter *professional worker* 123.11, *news reporting* 171.5, *print journalist* 175.5, *discloser* 180.4, *record keeper* 185.8, *descriptive writer* 202.10, *judge* 341.5, *news interpreter* 365.7
report for duty *appear* 575.16
reporting *news reporting* 171.5
reportorial *newsworthy* 171.8, 175.7
reportorially *journalistically* 175.10
repose 678.2; *refreshment* 94.1, *refresher* 94.2, *leisure* 125.1, 413.4, *have leisure time* 125.5, *have free time* 413.15, *sleep* 415.5, *be motionless* 678.7, *ease* 819.1, *take it easy* 819.3
reposeful *leisurely* 125.4, *quiescent* 678.6, *at ease* 819.2
reposefully *easily* 819.5
reposing *quiescent* 678.6
repository 105.13; *container* 578.1, *conservation* 815.2
repossess *take back* 477.17, *evict* 709.20, *be compensated* 743.9
repossessed *unable to pay* 488.8
repossession *taking back* 477.4, *amount owing* 488.5
repotting *gardening* 17.5
repoussé Architectural Elements 134
reprehend *condemn* 438.18
reprehensibility *guilt* 450.1
reprehensible *wrongful* 430.10, *unforgivable* 430.16, *unsatisfactory* 438.15, *evil* 446.7, *guilty* 450.6
reprehensibly *evilly* 446.12, *guiltily* 450.12
reprehension *censure* 438.3
reprehensive *guilty* 450.6
reprehensively *guiltily* 450.12
represent 6.91, 79.7, 80.6, 187.10; *act* 136.34, *write* 139.21, *draw* 143.13, *signify* 183.16, *record* 185.13, *describe* 202.15, *epitomize* 327.18, *answer for* 334.24, *make evident* 339.11, *predict* 358.14, *imagine* 360.14, *mean* 361.13, *outline* 617.5, *be a substitute* 672.6, *characterize* 723.11, *be important* 799.13
representation 187.1, 202.9; *picture* 133.5, *acting* 136.22, *sign* 183.1, *record* 185.1, *reflection* 242.9, *impression* 264.7, *electing* 382.5, *outline* 617.1, *substitution* 672.1, *imitation* 736.1, *commission* 833.1, *manifestation* 843.2
representational 187.8; *descriptive* 202.11, *representing* 202.14, *lifelike* 721.19, *commissioned* 833.6
representational art Western Art Styles 133
representationalism *verisimilitude* 721.10
representationalistic *lifelike* 721.19
representationally 187.15; *verisimilarly* 721.33
representative 75.3, 187.7; *elected official* 50.8, *person in authority* 52.7, *delegate* 79.1, *delegated* 79.4, *agent* 80.3, 123.15, *symbolic* 183.12, *representational* 187.8, *representing* 202.14, *speaker* 205.12, *explanatory* 331.11,

salesperson 482.8, outlined 617.4, substitute 672.2, average 742.5, typical 777.10, commissioner 833.5, identifiable 843.10

representative body 79.2

representative democracy constitutional government 49.8

representatively 79.8; indicatively 183.21, representationally 187.15, answerably 334.28

representing 202.14; deputizing 80.4, symbolic 183.12, representational 187.8

represent realistically seem true 721.26

represent the interests of represent 79.7

represent to oneself imagine 360.14

represent unfairly misrepresent 188.6

repress forget 186.11, be evasive 386.20, suppress 424.9, be self-restrained 455.10, detain 471.9, censor 503.10, counteract 510.7, moderate 521.7, abolish 523.11, narrow 593.14, limit 620.7, hinder 826.15, restrain 830.12, defeat 832.11

repressed unconscious 108.40, suppressed 424.6, self-restrained 455.6, narrow 593.8, restrained 830.9

repressing dominating 832.7

repression defense mechanism 108.23, forgetfulness 186.3, evasiveness 386.6, suppression 424.2, self-restraint 455.1, detention 471.2, prohibition 503.1, obstruction 510.3, destruction 523.1, narrowness 593.1, limit 620.1, hindrance 826.1, restraint 830.1, domination 832.2

repressive fugitive 386.10, severe 424.5, self-restrained 455.6, prohibited 503.5, counteracting 510.6, limited 620.5, hindering 826.12, restraining 830.8, dominating 832.7

repressively severely 424.11, with self-restraint 455.14, prohibitively 503.11, counter 510.8, with delay 826.22

repress one's desires abstain 455.11

reprieval deliverance 817.1

reprieve favorable verdict 54.19, acquit 54.32, save 275.9, mercy 308.3, show pity 308.8, forgiveness 312.1, forgive 312.8, delay 658.3, 658.13, escape 816.1, deliverance 817.1, deliver 817.5, liberation 831.1, liberate 831.6, cancellation 834.1, cancel 834.6

reprieved acquitted 54.25, forgiven 312.5, canceled 834.5

reprieved prisoner escaper 816.5

repriever abrogator 834.4

reprimand expression of dissatisfaction 274.2, rebuke 298.21, condemnation 438.2, condemn 438.18, punishment 454.1, punish 454.22, warning 814.1

reprimanded condemned 438.11

reprimanding censuring 438.12

reprint 21.3; reproduce 21.13, printing 132.20, 173.3, print 173.17, repeat 797.5, renew 797.19

reprinted reproduced 21.10, remade 797.10

reprisal retaliation 420.1, revenge

441.4, reckoning 454.8, restoration 671.2, counterbalance 743.2

reprise melody 140.10, retrospection 651.3, look back 651.18, return 797.4

repro [Inf] reprint 21.3

reproach dissuasion 179.1, rebuke 298.21, vilification 301.2, vilify 301.15, condemnation 438.2, condemn 438.18, accusation 442.1, accuse 442.8, guilt 450.1

reproachable guilty 450.6

reproached condemned 438.11

reproachful vilifying 301.9, censuring 438.12, guilty 450.6

reproachfully vilifyingly 301.18, disapprovingly 438.23, guiltily 450.12

reproachfulness guilt 450.1

reproaching condemning 438.10, censuring 438.12

reproachless incorrupt 449.7

reproach oneself be penitent 451.7

reprobate evil person 446.3, miscreant 448.6, guilty person 450.5

reprobated censuring 438.12

reprobation dissatisfaction 274.1, censure 438.3

reprocess renew 797.19, restore 809.12

reprocessed remade 797.10

reprocessing restoration 809.2

reproduce 21.13; procreate 22.14, give birth to 28.19, represent 187.10, bring into existence 522.14, grow 581.17, copy 730.17, 736.10, simulate 733.16, make bigger 746.7, repeat 797.15

reproduced 21.10; duplicate 730.11, repeated 797.8

reproduce oneself 21.14

reproducing pertaining to life 28.14

reproduction 21.1; physiology 13.13, body process 19.15, propagation 21.4, procreation 22.4, life function 28.6, memory 108.27, picture 133.5, printing 173.3, illustration 187.2, germination 581.5, copy 730.5, 736.2, increase 746.1, sexual union 752.6, doubling 789.4, repetition 797.1

reproduction proof or **repro** stage of proof 174.9

reproductive 21.11; physiological 13.29, metabolic 19.24, repetitious 797.11

reproductive body 47.14; fungal body 47.4

reproductive cell cell 13.15

reproductive endocrinology Medical Specialties 107

reproductively 21.17; largely 581.18

reproductive organ fern plant 46.2, moss plant 46.5

reproductive organs internal organ 19.13, organs of reproduction 21.9

reproductive rights rights 429.4

reprogram restore 809.12

reprogramming restoration 809.2

reprography reproduction 21.1

reproof dissuasion 179.1, expression of dissatisfaction 274.2, rebuke 298.21, condemnation 438.2, condemn 438.18, punishment 454.1

reprovable guilty 450.6

reproval condemnation 438.2

reprove dissuade 179.7, be dissatisfied 274.7, condemn 438.18, punish 454.22, warn 814.8

reproved condemned 438.11

reprove oneself be penitent 451.7

reprover dissatisfied person 274.3

reproving look or **glance** show of disapproval 438.6

reptant reptilian 37.12

reptilarium reptile dwelling 37.4

reptile 37.1; type of animal 34.5

reptile dwelling 37.4

reptile house reptile dwelling 37.4

reptilelike reptilian 37.12

reptiles Phobias 283

Reptilia reptile 37.1

reptilian 37.12; reptile 37.1, cold-blooded 218.12

reptiliary reptile dwelling 37.4

reptiliform reptilian 37.12

reptiloid reptilian 37.12

republic constitutional government 49.8, body politic 50.3, region 564.1, country 566.1

republican national 18.16, 566.10, governmental 49.24

republicanism constitutional government 49.8

Republican party or **Grand Old Party** Political Parties 50

Republican whip party official 68.5

republication reappearance 264.8

republic of letters literature 139.1

repudiate disavow 190.18, deny 332.8, renounce 383.13, not observe 466.9, stop payment 490.10, dissent 506.9, protest 507.7, cancel 834.6

repudiated disavowing 190.12, renounced 383.9, protesting 507.5

repudiating refuting 332.6, nonobservant 466.5, dissenting 506.6

repudiation disavowal 190.3, denial 332.2, renunciation 383.4, nonobservance 466.1, dissent 506.2, protest 507.1, cancellation 834.1

repudiation of debts nonpayment 490.1

repudiative or **repudiatory** disavowing 190.12

repudiator abrogator 834.4

repugn deny 332.8

repugnance dislike 300.2, dissociation 375.4, opposition 828.1

repugnancy opposition 828.1

repugnant detested 291.11, hateful 300.10, repulsive 701.4, oppositional 828.11, contrary 828.13

repugnantly distastefully 291.19, hatefully 300.14, hideously 531.6, repulsively 701.11

repulse 701.2; rejection 383.1, reject 383.10, resistance 417.1, resist 417.10, retaliate 419.30, insult 436.5, 436.21, refusal 506.1, refuse 506.8, change 512.12, repel 701.7

repulsed antipathetic 291.7, rejected 383.6

repulsing resistant 417.6, insulting 436.10

repulsion 701.1; antipathy 291.2, dislike 300.2, rejection 383.1, resistance 417.1, refusal 506.1, influence 512.1, force 514.8

repulsive 701.4; unclean 112.8, unpleasant 272.6, detested 291.11, hateful 300.10, ugly 531.3

repulsive force repulsion 701.1

repulsively 701.11; unpleasantly 272.1, distastefully 291.19, hatefully 300.14, hideously 531.6

repulsiveness unpleasantness

272.1, ugliness 531.1, repulsion 701.1

repurchase 481.4; buy back 481.16

reputable 370.3; respectable 435.11

reputably 370.6

reputation 224.4; dignity 297.4, repute 370.1, 487.7, personal influence 512.3, importance 799.1

repute 370.1, 487.7; reputation 224.4, dignity 297.4, respect 435.1, personal influence 512.3, importance 799.1

reputed 370.4; supposed 359.6

reputedly 370.8; theoretically 4.24, supposedly 359.10

request 505.1, 505.10; litigate 54.27, prayer 85.10, pray 85.20, object of desire 288.8, desire 288.17, plea 329.5, plead 329.14, question 333.1, 333.16, propound 359.9, ask permission 502.9

request aid shelter 812.8

request credit borrow 476.10

requested desired 288.10, offered 504.8, requesting 505.7

requester 505.5

request euthanasia commit suicide 30.24

request for admission pretrial proceedings 54.13

request for credit borrowing 476.1

request for money borrowing 476.1

requesting 505.7; questioning 333.11

request money borrow 476.10

request one's hand in marriage offer 504.11

request the pleasure of one's company request 505.10

requiem funeral 31.4, Musical Forms 140, sacred music 140.3, lament 280.2

requiem mass sacred music 140.3

require need 95.16, be insufficient 98.9, desire 288.17, answer to 334.22, specify 340.14, demand 356.9, 425.11, compel 428.8, impose a duty 433.14, shop 481.15, petition 505.11

required necessary 95.10, desired 288.10, answerable 334.17, meant 359.7, compulsory 428.7, requesting 505.7, important 799.7, restrained 830.9

required number sufficiency 97.1

require effort be difficult 824.16

require explanation be unexplained 364.15

requirement necessity 95.1, sufficiency 97.1, wish 288.2, object of desire 288.8, answerability 334.9, compulsion 428.1, basis for negotiations 460.2, petition 505.2, chief thing 799.3, limitation 830.2

requirements shopping 481.3

require qualifications limit 830.13

requiring incomplete 762.5

requiring effort difficult 824.9

requiring great effort laborious 122.7

requisite necessity 95.1, necessary 95.10, specification 340.6, compulsory 428.7, essential 723.5

requisite number fullness 761.5

requisition have at one's disposal 393.14, demand 425.2, 425.11, 505.3, 505.12, force 428.10, taking over 477.3, take over 477.16

requisitional conditional 340.10

requisitionary *taking* 477.12, *demanding* 505.8

requitable *reciprocal* 729.4, *compensable* 743.4

requital *atonement* 313.1, *revenge* 441.4, *compensation* 453.7, 743.1, *reckoning* 454.8, *reciprocity* 729.1

requite *atone* 313.7, *retaliate* 420.4, 489.23, *put right* 429.14, *avenge* 441.14, *give back* 478.5, *exchange* 673.5, *reciprocate* 729.7, 827.13, *compensate* 743.7

requited *exchanged* 673.4, *reciprocal* 729.4, *compensated* 743.3

requitement *compensation* 743.1

requiter *atoner* 313.4

requiting *vindictive* 441.10

re-recording mixer *filmmaker* 137.14

rerun *broadcast material* 172.9, *broadcast* 172.12, *repeat* 797.5, *renew* 797.19

reschedule one's debts *not pay* 488.10

rescind *disavow* 190.18, *cancel* 834.6

rescindable *canceled* 834.5

rescinded *disavowing* 190.12, *canceled* 834.5

rescinder *negator* 190.8, *abrogator* 834.4

rescinding *cancellation* 834.1

rescindment *disavowal* 190.3, *cancellation* 834.1

rescission *disavowal* 190.3, *cancellation* 834.1

rescript *law* 53.1, *acknowledgment* 334.2

rescuable *deliverable* 817.3

rescue **419.26;** *aid* 275.2, *save* 275.9, *benevolent act* 305.5, *giving back* 478.1, *give back* 478.5, *restoration* 809.2, *restore* 809.12, *safety* 810.1, *protect* 810.21, *preserve* 815.14, *escape* 816.1, *deliverance* 817.1, *deliver* 817.5, *support* 825.2, *help* 825.23, *set free* 829.17, *liberation* 831.1, *liberate* 831.6

rescue at the eleventh hour *deliver* 817.5

rescued *delivered* 817.4, *liberated* 831.4

rescue device *preserver* 815.9

rescue helicopter *deliverer* 817.2

rescuer *good person* 445.6, *deliverer* 817.2, *liberator* 831.3

rescue team *deliverer* 817.2

research *philosophical investigation* 4.4, *philosophize* 4.19, *learn* 48.23, *questioning* 333.2, *question* 333.16, *experimentation* 335.3, *experiment* 335.11, *behave toward* 399.20

research and development (R and D) *economic development* 56.5, *experimentation* 335.3

research data *basis of supposition* 359.2

researched *questioned* 333.15, *tested* 335.10

researcher *learner* 48.6, *discloser* 180.4, *questioner* 333.9, *experimenter* 335.5, *theorist* 359.4, *attempter* 390.3

research facility *or* **center** *or* **establishment** *or* **institute** *place of experimentation* 335.6

research fellowship *instructorship* 48.5

researching *questioning* 333.11, *experimental* 335.8

research laboratory *plant* 124.7

research paper *dissertation* 203.1

research park *plant* 124.7

research satellite *artificial satellite* 7.30

research scientist *experimenter* 335.5

research vessel *oceanography* 571.5, *Ships and Boats* 690

research worker *experimenter* 335.5, *theorist* 359.4

resection *surgery* 107.15, *separateness* 753.3

resectoscope *diagnostic instrument* 107.13

reseda *green* 260.7

resell *sell again* 482.21

resemblance *similarity* 733.1

resemblant *similar* 733.7

resemble *represent* 187.10, *appear* 264.12, *be similar* 733.12

resembling *similar* 733.7

resemblingly *similarly* 733.17

resene *resin* 562.6

resent **302.13;** *be hostile* 63.10, *be dissatisfied* 274.7, *detest* 291.13, *hate* 300.11, *show impatience* 303.14, *be malevolent* 306.12, *be jealous* 314.8, *grudge* 501.7

resented *hated* 300.9

resentful **302.8;** *hostile* 63.6, *green-eyed* 260.11, *antipathetic* 291.7, *hating* 300.7, *cross* 303.11, *bitter* 306.9, *jealous* 314.5

resentfully **302.22;** *hostilely* 63.13, *discontentedly* 291.17, *with hate* 300.13, *crossly* 303.20, *malevolently* 306.14, *bitterly* 306.16, *jealously* 314.12

resentfulness *resentment* 302.1, *crossness* 303.4, *jealousy* 314.2

resentment **302.1;** *ill feeling* 63.3, *bad feeling* 266.5, *antipathy* 291.2, *hate* 300.1, *bitterness* 306.3, *jealousy* 314.2

reservation *disbelief* 88.1, *recordkeeping* 185.7, *reticence* 287.3, *question* 333.1, *basis for negotiations* 460.2, *setting apart* 753.2, *ecology* 815.3

reservations *specification* 340.6

reserve **105.3, 195.5, 403.5, 464.14, 585.4;** *enlisted* 58.11, *alternative* 371.4, *store* 105.1, *save* 105.20, *soccer participant* 163.4, *verbal concealment* 181.3, *register* 185.15, *lack of candor* 192.4, *taciturnity* 208.1, *helper* 275.5, *specify* 340.14, *choose* 382.14, *nonuse* 394.1, *not use* 394.9, *unsociability* 409.1, *chastity* 431.3, *contain* 578.20, *closed place* 584.4, *substitute* 613.17, 613.23, 672.2, 672.3, *enclosed area* 619.2, *enclose* 619.6, *prepare* 657.14, *delay* 658.13, *set apart* 753.17, *preserve* 815.14, *self-restraint* 830.4

reserve army *army* 77.12

reserved **195.11, 403.10, 585.7;** *saved* 105.15, *silent* 181.10, *uncandid* 192.15, *taciturn* 208.4, *reticent* 287.8, *conditional* 340.10, *unused* 394.5, *chaste* 431.10, *storing* 578.19, *cunning* 822.4, *self-restrained* 830.10

reservedly **195.20, 585.15;** *reticently* 287.18

reserved nature *self-restraint* 830.4

reservedness *reticence* 287.3

reserved section *enclosed area* 619.2

reserved space 563.5

reserve equipment *extra* 748.6

reserve fleet *military organization* 58.4

reserve for *intend for* 374.11

reserve forces *armed forces* 77.9

reserve fund *reserve* 105.3

reserve liability *funds* 484.6

Reserve Officers Training Corps (ROTC) *military training* 58.3

reserves **102.5;** *provisions* 89.3, *reserve* 105.3, *preparations* 388.2, *funds* 484.6, *treasury* 484.19, *extra* 748.6, *helper* 825.12

reserve troops *armed force* 77.10

reservist *soldier* 77.4, *substitute* 672.2

reservoir *source of supply* 105.4, *storehouse* 105.8, *dam* 551.12, *water carrier* 557.16, *lake* 568.1, *container* 578.1

reset *change back* 665.19

reshape *distort the truth* 627.12, *cause change* 665.16, *transform* 670.13

reshaped *changed* 665.10

reshaping *change for the better* 665.4

Reshetilovka *Breeds of Sheep* 16

reship *transport* 686.10

reshoot *film* 137.19

reshowing *repeat* 797.5

reshown *remade* 797.10

reside **575.17;** *inhabit* 60.22, 61.13

reside in *settle* 565.10

residence **575.2;** *habitation* 60.2, *place of residence* 209.4

residence hall *school place* 48.16

resident **61.6, 61.11;** *inhabiting* 60.18, *inhabitant* 61.1, *doctor* 107.19, *possessor* 469.10, *residing* 575.8

residential *inhabiting* 60.18, *inhabited* 61.10, *urban* 567.14, *residing* 575.8

residential area *or* **zone** *urban area* 567.10

residential building *building* 551.9

residentiary *inhabiting* 60.18, *inhabitant* 61.1

residents *inhabitants* 61.2

resider *inhabitant* 61.1

residing **575.8;** *inhabiting* 60.18, *resident* 61.11

residual *residue* 750.2, *remaining* 750.7, *mathematical result* 783.4

residual gas analyzer (RGA) *surface chemistry* 11.20

residual insecticide *pest control* 16.13

residually 750.11

residual magnetization *magnetic phenomenon* 10.50

residual-type schizophrenia *psychosis* 108.10

residuary *remaining* 750.7

residue **750.2;** *division* 6.16, *dirt* 112.5, *effect* 676.1

residuum *dirt* 112.5, *residue* 750.2

resign **835.5;** *be employed* 57.19, *have leisure time* 125.5, *submit* 298.17, *withdraw* 392.5, 705.9, *stop work* 394.12, 668.11, *capitulate* 421.6, *retreat* 680.17, *be dismissed* 707.18, *be aloof* 756.8, *terminate* 834.7

resignation **835.1;** *philosophical attitude* 4.3, *submissiveness* 298.3, *relinquishment* 392.1, *disuse* 394.3, *submission* 421.1, *stop* 668.2, *retreat* 680.2, *setting apart* 753.2, *termination* 834.2

resigned **835.4;** *detached* 4.18, *submissive* 298.10, *relinquished* 392.2, *submitting* 421.3, *obedient* 426.4, *resigning* 835.3

resignedly **392.6, 835.7;** *stoically* 4.26

resignedness 835.2

resigned to one's fate *resigned* 835.4

resigning 835.3; *retreat* 680.2

resign oneself **835.6;** *submit* 421.4, *be permissive* 502.7

resign under pressure *resign* 835.5

resilience *endurance* 516.4, *stalwartness* 547.3, *reflex* 680.7

resilience *or* **resiliency** *elasticity* 546.1, *adaptability* 546.2

resilient **680.14;** *strong in spirit* 516.11, *elastic* 546.5, *adaptive* 546.6, *stalwart* 547.10

resiliently *adaptably* 546.11, *stalwartly* 547.17

resin **562.6;** *polymer* 11.9, *secreted substance* 24.2, *Tree Products* 43, *instrumental aid* 142.7, *incense* 226.3, *adhesive* 561.3, *resinify* 562.16

resinate *resin* 562.6, *resinify* 562.16

resiniferous *resinous* 562.13

resinify 562.16

resinlike *resinous* 562.13

resinoid *resin* 562.6, *resinous* 562.13

resinous **562.13;** *treelike* 43.10

resinously *oilily* 562.19

resiny *resinous* 562.13

resist **417.10;** *interact* 10.73, *battle* 76.33, *defend* 77.37, *dissuade* 179.7, *be disinclined* 291.14, *oppose* 375.13, 828.15, *be insubordinate* 416.8, *retaliate* 419.30, 420.4, *contend* 422.22, *refuse* 506.8, *protest* 507.7, *counteract* 510.7, *be tough* 547.13, *hinder* 826.15, *withstand* 828.20

resist! *fight on!* 417.16

resistance **10.41, 417.1;** *defense mechanism* 108.23, *dissuasion* 179.1, *disinclination* 291.3, *opposition* 375.2, 828.1, *obstinacy* 379.1, *disobedience* 416.2, 427.1, *defense* 419.1, *revolution* 427.4, *refusal* 506.1, *opposing force* 510.2, *force* 514.8, *electrical power* 514.12, *endurance* 516.4, *hardness* 542.1, *toughness* 547.1, *friction* 554.1, *deflection* 701.3, *hindrance* 826.1

resistance fighter *guerrilla* 77.7, *resister* 417.5

resistance movement **417.3;** *revolution* 427.4

resistance to compaction *strength of materials* 14.15

resistance to sliding *strength of materials* 14.15

resistant **417.6;** *disinclined* 291.9, *dissenting* 347.7, *unenthusiastic* 375.10, *obstinate* 379.5, *refused* 506.5, *counteracting* 510.6, *strengthened* 516.13, *tough* 542.6, 547.6, *defensive* 701.6, *uncooperative* 828.14

resistantly *resistingly* 417.14, *uncooperatively* 506.11, *counter* 510.8, *toughly* 542.12, 547.16, *defensively* 701.12

resist breaking *be tough* 547.13

resist change *be permanent* 667.4

resist control *be anarchic* 51.8

resister **417.5;** *reluctant person* 375.7, *tenacious person* 377.5, *opposer* 828.9

resist incursions *be at war* 76.32

resisting 417.8; *resistant 417.6, counterattacking 418.15, defending 419.17, refused 506.5, counteracting 510.6, tough 547.6*

resistingly 417.14; *uncooperatively 506.11, counter 510.8, toughly 547.16*

resistive *electric 14.47*

resistivity *resistance 10.41*

resistor *circuit 10.43, circuit element 14.39*

resist temptation *be virtuous 447.8*

resojet *means of propulsion 696.2*

resole *repair 809.10*

resoling *repair 809.1*

resolute 376.7; *earnest 278.5, steadfast 284.11, iron-willed 372.7, intending 374.6, persevering 377.6, determined 379.7, 674.5, active 414.13, strong in spirit 516.11*

resolutely 376.15; *earnestly 278.10, steadfastly 284.19, prospectively 374.12, perseveringly 377.16, acutely 516.18, determinedly 674.10*

resoluteness *steadfastness 284.3, willpower 372.2, resolution 376.1*

resolution 376.1; *structure 11.7, play part 136.8, harmonic element 140.14, disclosure 180.1, earnestness 278.2, steadfastness 284.3, solution 334.6, interpretation 365.1, willpower 372.2, intentionality 374.2, perseverance 377.1, determination 379.2, 674.2, plan 387.1, assiduity 414.8, endurance 516.4, closure 584.1, chemical change 670.2, separation 753.1, conclusion 761.3, ruling 780.2*

resolution (of a discord) *harmonization 735.2*

resolutive *solvent 555.9*

resolvable *solvable 334.14, convertible 670.9*

resolvable image *separable 753.11*

resolve 374.9, 376.12; *rationalize 4.20, enumerate 6.85, solve 334.21, decipher 365.13, willpower 372.2, intentionality 374.2, resolution 376.1, perseverance 377.1, predetermination 384.1, mental toughness 547.5, dissolve 555.23, close down 584.15, convert 670.11, determination 674.2, end 773.19, rule 780.12*

resolve beforehand *predetermine 384.8*

resolved *solved 334.15, iron-willed 372.7, intending 374.6, resolute 376.7, persevering 377.6, determined 379.7, 674.5, mentally tough 547.12, closed down 584.10*

resolved beforehand *predetermined 384.4*

resolvedness *resolution 376.1*

resolve images *set apart 753.17*

resolve into *transform 670.13*

resolvent *solvent 555.9*

resolve problems *conciliate 74.10*

resolving *solution 334.6*

resolving power *separation 753.1*

resonance 236.1; *wave 10.11, tone 140.24, 230.2, vibration 683.2, wavelength 683.5, harmonization 735.2, reverberation 797.14*

resonant 236.6; *hearable 228.12, drumming 235.9, deep-sounding 598.19, vibrating 683.9, harmonizing 735.12, reverberatory 797.14*

resonant circuit *circuit 14.37*

resonant frequency *wave 10.11, circuit 14.37, wavelength 683.5*

resonantly 236.11; *tunefully 140.30, repeatedly 235.15, in harmony 735.32*

resonate 236.9; *wave 10.77, drum 235.10, vibrate 683.13, harmonize 735.22*

resonating *resonant 236.6, harmonizing 735.12*

resonating chamber or **cavity** *resonator 236.5*

resonation *resonance 236.1*

resonator 236.5

resorb *absorb 708.19*

resorbence *absorption 708.6*

resorption *absorption 708.6*

resort *means 102.1, expedient 387.5, use 393.1, refuge 812.1, stratagem 822.2*

resort to 393.13

resort to arms *belligerency 76.14, go to war 76.29*

resort to fisticuffs *be violent 520.8*

resort to greenmail *bargain 480.20*

resort to violence *be violent 520.8*

resound 797.21; *be heard 228.15, sound 230.8, be loud 232.8, bang 234.6, drum 235.10, resonate 236.9, harmonize 735.22*

resounding *resonance 236.1, resonant 236.6, harmonizing 735.12*

resoundingly *audibly 230.10, resonantly 236.11, in harmony 735.32*

resoundingness *harmonization 735.2*

resource *source of supply 105.4, solution 334.6, expedient 387.5, stratagem 822.2*

resourceful *enriching 22.11, skillful 127.10, imaginative 360.10, planning 387.11, enterprising 391.5, strong in spirit 516.11, cunning 822.4*

resourcefully *fruitfully 22.15, skillfully 127.16, imaginatively 360.17, conspiratorially 387.18*

resourcefulness *enrichment 22.5, skill 127.1, imagination 360.1, potency 516.6, cunning 822.1*

resources 102.4; *means 102.1, supplies 102.3, materials 104.1, personal estate 470.6, circumstances 726.1*

respect 435.1, 435.13; *worship 83.15, liking 290.1, like 290.8, submissiveness 298.3, love 299.1, 299.21, be benevolent 305.10, repute 370.1, courtesies 410.3, obeisance 426.3, deference 433.4, admiration 437.2, admire 437.15, observance 465.1, compliance 781.2, abide by 781.12, make important 799.14*

respectability *morals 431.2, virtue 447.1*

respectable 435.11; *reputable 370.3, moral 431.9, virtuous 447.5*

respectably *reputably 370.6, morally 431.15, virtuously 447.9*

respected 435.10; *liked 290.6, beloved 299.19, reputable 370.3, praiseworthy 437.12*

respect for legal principles *legality 53.9*

respect for the law *legality 53.9*

respectful 435.6; *liking 290.4, submissive 298.10, loving 299.15, good-mannered 410.7, obeisant*

426.6, *deferential 433.9, approving 437.9*

respectfully 435.19; *admiringly 290.11, submissively 298.23, lovingly 299.29, genteelly 410.14, obediently 426.9, dutifully 433.19*

respectfulness 435.3; *courtesies 410.3*

respective *special 779.10*

respectively *proportionately 474.7, relevantly 727.12, specifically 779.22*

respects *greeting 435.5*

respect the law *be legal 53.28*

respiration 12.24, 558.8; *physiology 13.13, cell biology 13.14, body process 19.15, life function 28.6, intake 708.5*

respirator *modern armor 419.7, safety device 810.15, preserver 815.9*

respiratory 558.19; *physiological 13.29, metabolic 19.24*

respiratory chain *respiration 12.24*

respiratory disease 114.12; *disease 114.4*

respiratory organ *respiration 558.8*

respiratory pigment *pigment 12.18*

respire 558.21; *live 28.17, be refreshed 94.8, draw in 708.18, let out 709.26*

respiring *respiratory 558.19*

respite *acquit 54.32, time off 125.2, ease 275.1, 819.1, interval 639.4, delay 658.3, pause 668.3, deliverance 817.1*

resplendence *light 246.1, grandeur 404.10*

resplendent *bright 246.14, grand 404.22, beautiful 529.7*

resplendently *grandly 404.37, magnificently 529.16*

respond *discuss 4.22, Architectural Elements 134, correspond 169.19, speak 205.17, sense 212.9, countercharge 332.9, answer 334.18, push 414.20, reply 671.13, reciprocate 729.7, 827.13*

responded *reversed 671.7*

respondence *answer 334.1*

respondent *litigant 54.4, conversationalist 210.6, answerer 334.10, answering 334.11, accused person 442.4*

respond favorably *agree with 462.10*

responding *refuting 332.6, answering 334.11, adaptive 546.6*

respond quickly *be adaptable 546.9*

respond to treatment *get healthy 113.12, be restored 809.13*

response 334.4; *measurement 10.67, ritual music 85.9, utterance 205.10, sensation 212.1, countercharge 332.3, answer 334.1, reply 671.5, reciprocity 729.1*

response to therapy *recuperation 809.4*

response to treatment *recuperation 809.4*

responsibility *directorship 126.5, Phobias 283, answerability 334.9, expectations 356.2, morals 431.2, sense of duty 433.2, guilt 450.1, debt 488.1, management 509.4, instrumentality 511.1, participation 760.10, commission 833.1*

responsible *feeling 266.9, answerable 334.17, enterprising*

391.5, *defending 419.17, moral 431.9, duteous 433.7, unsatisfactory 438.15, guilty 450.6, observant 465.3, indebted 488.7, causal 511.5, 675.7, commissioned 833.6*

responsible person *manager 126.7*

responsibly 391.10; *answerably 334.28, morally 431.15, dutifully 433.19, observantly 465.6, causally 675.12, under commission 833.11*

responsion *answer 334.1*

responsive *susceptible 212.7, sensitive 267.3, answering 334.11, willing 373.7, adaptive 546.6, reciprocal 729.4*

responsively *in answer 334.25, adaptably 546.11, reciprocally 729.10*

responsiveness *good feeling 266.4, sensitivity 267.1, willingness 373.1, adaptability 546.2*

responsory *response 334.4*

rest *be dormant 41.22, peace 73.1, refreshment 94.1, refresher 94.2, refresh 94.6, leisure 125.1, 413.4, have leisure time 125.5, written music 140.21, silence 231.1, have free time 413.15, sleep 415.5, 415.14, pause 415.15, 668.3, 668.13, 775.11, be situated 573.9, spend the evening 656.5, stability 674.1, be stable 674.6, repose 678.2, step 713.11, remainder 750.1, be left 750.9, interval 775.2, gap 775.4, ease 819.1, take it easy 819.3*

rest and be thankful *take it easy 819.3*

rest and recreation (R and R) *refreshment 94.1, delay 658.3*

restart *automobile racing terms 146.3, be on the track 146.11, soccer play 163.5, protract 669.9, restore 671.10, renew 797.19*

rest assured *believe 87.9, expect 281.12*

restate *translate 365.16, iterate 797.16*

restated *iterated 797.9*

restatement *iteration 797.2*

restaurant *food provider 90.6, eating place 92.17, service workplace 124.5, meeting place 408.5*

restaurant car [Brit] *railroad car 688.5*

restaurateur *caterer 89.5, food provider 90.6*

rested *refreshed 94.5*

rest energy *energy 514.7*

rest eternal *life without end 644.2*

rest from one's labors *ease 819.1, take it easy 819.3*

restful *pleasant 214.7, comfortable 271.8, stable 674.3, quiescent 678.6, at ease 819.2*

restfully *refreshingly 94.9, stably 674.9, motionlessly 678.9, easily 819.5*

restfulness *repose 678.2, ease 819.1*

rest hard upon *make heavy 538.14*

rest home *nursing home 107.18, service workplace 124.5, haven 810.3*

resting *leisurely 125.4, not working 415.10, not awake 415.12, quiescent 678.6, at ease 819.2*

resting bud *bud 41.8*

resting place 668.5

resting potential *electrochemistry* 11.19

Rest in Peace (RIP) *funeral object* 31.6

restitute *atone* 313.7, *serve one right* 420.5, *put right* 429.14, *pay back* 489.20, *compensate* 743.7, *restore* 809.12

restituted *compensated* 743.3

restitution *peace offering* 74.5, *remedy* 115.1, *atonement* 313.1, *vindication* 441.1, *compensation* 453.7, 743.1, *liability* 454.6, *giving back* 478.1, *repayment* 489.5, *restoration* 671.2, 809.2

restitutive *atoning* 313.5, *restoring* 478.4, *regressive* 671.6, *compensatory* 743.5

restitutory *atoning* 313.5, *restoring* 478.4, *regressive* 671.6, *compensatory* 743.5

restive *refractory* 379.6, *disobedient* 427.10

restively *disobediently* 427.14

restiveness *disobedience* 427.1

restless 684.16; *fidgety* 414.14, *disobedient* 427.10, *irregular* 664.3, *irresolute* 666.4, *moving* 677.12

restlessly *actively* 414.24, *disobediently* 427.14, *irregularly* 664.6, *in motion* 677.19, *agitatedly* 684.27

restlessness 414.7, 684.5; *disobedience* 427.1, *irregularity* 664.1, *irresolution* 666.2, *momentum* 677.2, *agitation* 684.1

restock *replenish* 89.10, *restore* 809.12

rest on one's laurels *not act* 413.11, *take it easy* 819.3

rest on one's oars *not act* 413.11, *pause* 415.15, *take it easy* 819.3

rest on the shoulders of *be the duty of* 433.16

restorable *restoring* 478.4, *renewable* 652.15, *reversible* 671.8, *compensable* 743.4, *repairable* 809.7

restoration 21.2, 671.2, 807.4, 809.2; *refreshment* 94.1, *atonement* 313.1, *vindication* 441.1, *liability* 454.6, *giving back* 478.1, *strengthening* 516.7, *beautification* 530.1, *new start* 652.5, *change for the better* 665.4, *compensation* 743.1, *return* 797.4, *repair* 809.1, *deliverance* 817.1

Restoration comedy *historic comedy* 136.12, Western Literary Groups 139

restoration to health *recuperation* 809.4

restorative 809.9; *refresher* 94.2, *refreshing* 94.4, *tonic* 115.8, *remedial* 115.14, *hygienic* 116.3, *stimulant* 221.5, *stimulating* 221.7, *relieving* 275.7, *beautifying* 530.13, *compensatory* 743.5, *improving* 807.14

restoratively *refreshingly* 94.9, *better* 807.24

restore 671.10, 807.17, 809.12; *reproduce* 21.13, *invigorate* 28.22, 518.5, *conciliate* 74.10, *refresh* 94.6, *practice medicine* 107.32, *make healthy* 113.13, *remedy* 115.16, *be piquant* 221.9, *atone* 313.7, *vindicate* 441.11, *give back* 478.5, *make new* 652.20, *change back* 665.19, *compensate* 743.7, *renew* 797.19, *refurbish* 809.11, *deliver* 817.5, *support* 825.24

restored *reproduced* 21.10, *given*

---

new life 28.15, *refreshed* 94.5, *relieved* 275.6, *vindicated* 441.8, *restoring* 478.4, *strengthened* 516.13, *renewed* 652.14, *changed* 665.10, *reversed* 671.7, *compensated* 743.3, *remade* 797.10, *improved* 807.12, *repaired* 809.6

restored to health *getting well* 113.9

restore harmony *conciliate* 74.10

restore one to favor *give back* 478.5

restore order 765.22

restore peace *conciliate* 74.10

restorer *returner* 478.3, *changer* 665.9, *improver* 807.11, *repairer* 809.5

restore the status quo *restore* 671.10

restore to consciousness *bring back to life* 28.20

restore to equilibrium *counterbalance* 743.8

restore to health *make healthy* 113.13, *cure* 809.15

restore to sanity *be sane* 109.5

restore vitality *revive* 809.14

restoring 478.4; *giving back* 478.1, *strengthening* 516.7, *invigorating* 518.3, *compensatory* 743.5

restrain 826.19, 830.12; *imprison* 55.11, *be insufficient* 98.9, *deter* 179.8, *play down* 195.17, *specify* 340.14, *be severe* 424.8, *compel* 428.8, *detain* 471.9, *censor* 503.10, *counteract* 510.7, *moderate* 521.7, *narrow* 593.14, *limit* 620.7, *delay* 658.13, *cause to cease* 668.12, *hinder* 826.15, *defeat* 832.11

restrain commerce 830.14

restrained 830.9; *detached* 4.18, *imprisoned* 55.9, *unconscious* 108.40, *dissuaded* 179.5, *uncandid* 192.15, *subtle* 195.9, *reserved* 195.11, 403.10, *downplayed* 195.13, *reticent* 287.8, *unadorned* 424.7, *self-restrained* 455.6, *moderate* 521.3, *elegant* 527.3, *narrow* 593.8, *limited* 620.5, *held up* 658.6, *unhurried* 693.8, *delayed* 693.10, *disciplined* 765.17, *blocked* 826.13

restrainedly 830.18; *stoically* 4.26, *understatedly* 195.18, *narrowly* 593.17

restrainedness *subtlety* 195.3

restrain from *desist* 417.13

restraining 830.8; *compelling* 428.6, *retentive* 471.5C, *counteracting* 510.6, *delaying* 658.8, *blocked* 826.13

restraining hand *moderator* 521.2, *means of restraint* 830.6

restraining line *stadium* 155.3

restrain oneself 830.15; *doubt* 287.13, *be unadorned* 424.10, *be self-restrained* 455.10

restrain someone 830.17

restraint 826.8, 830.1; *pretrial proceedings* 54.13, *imprisonment* 55.4, *arrest* 55.5, *deterrence* 179.2, *lack of candor* 192.4, *subtlety* 195.3, *reserve* 195.5, 403.5, *downplaying* 195.6, *reticence* 287.3, *severity* 424.1, *unadornment* 424.3, *coercion* 428.2, *self-restraint* 455.1, *prohibition* 503.1, *obstruction* 510.3, *moderation* 521.1, *moderator* 521.2, *elegance* 527.1, *narrowness* 593.1, *limit* 620.1, *limitation* 620.2, *delay* 658.3,

---

slowness 693.1, *deceleration* 693.2, *hindrance* 826.1, *domination* 832.2

restraint of trade *international trade* 56.7, *economic restraint* 830.3

restrain trade *restrain commerce* 830.14

restrict *stipulate* 89.11, *be insufficient* 98.9, *keep secret* 182.11, *specify* 340.14, *prohibit* 503.8, *censor* 503.10, *moderate* 521.7, *squeeze* 582.13, *narrow* 593.14, *limit* 620.7, *make smaller* 747.8, *hinder* 826.15, *restrain* 830.12

restrict consumption *restrain commerce* 830.14

restricted *provisional* 89.8, *secret* 182.8, *conditional* 340.10, *self-restrained* 455.6, *censored* 503.7, *moderate* 521.3, *undersized* 580.8, *squeezed* 582.9, *narrow* 593.8, *limited* 620.5, *excluding* 764.5, *restrained* 830.9, *concealed* 844.7

restricted area *limit* 620.1, *limitation* 830.2

restricted information *censorship* 503.4

restrictedly *narrowly* 593.17

restrictedness *narrowness* 593.1

restrict imports *restrain commerce* 830.14

restricting *contracting* 582.10, *restraining* 830.8

restriction *reasoning* 6.61, *specification* 340.6, *self-restraint* 455.1, *prohibition* 503.1, *squeeze* 582.3, *narrowness* 593.1, *limitation* 620.2, 747.3, *subtracted item* 749.2, *hindrance* 826.1, *restraint* 830.1, *concealment* 844.2

restriction endonuclease *enzyme* 12.11, *molecular biology* 13.18

restriction enzyme *enzyme* 12.11

restrictionist *one who restrains* 830.7

restriction of movement *detention* 830.5

restrictive *conditional* 340.10, *self-restrained* 455.6, *prohibited* 503.5, *censored* 503.7, *contracting* 582.10, *limited* 620.5, *excluding* 764.5, *hindering* 826.12, *restraining* 830.8

restrictively *conditionally* 340.16, *with self-restraint* 455.14, *under censorship* 503.13, *with delay* 826.22, *restrainedly* 830.18

restrictiveness *exclusiveness* 764.4

restrictive practice *limit* 620.1, *economic restraint* 830.3

restrictive trade agreement *international trade* 56.7

restrict oneself *be self-restrained* 455.10

restrict someone's movement *detain* 830.16

restrict supplies *restrain commerce* 830.14

rest room *place for excretion* 25.11, *room* 60.9

restructure *new start* 652.5, *make new* 652.20, *cause change* 665.16, *transform* 670.13, *rearrange* 767.20

restructured *renewed* 652.14, *changed* 665.10, *rearranged* 767.14

restructuring *change for the better* 665.4, *rearrangement* 767.4

restructuring of industry *economic development* 56.5

rest stop *stopping place* 668.4

rest with *be the duty of* 433.16

restyle *cause change* 665.16

---

restyled *changed* 665.10

restyling *change for the better* 665.4

result 770.12; *operation* 6.12, *solution* 334.6, 376.6, *product* 522.3, *effect* 676.1, *follow from* 676.9, *remainder* 750.1, *be left* 750.9, *conclusion* 761.3, *sequel* 770.5, *consequence* 774.3, *ruling* 780.2

resultant *vector* 6.48, *caused* 676.5, *remaining* 750.7, *repercussive* 774.8

result from *follow from* 676.9

result in *intend* 361.15, *cause* 675.8, *react* 676.8

resulting *caused* 676.5, *consequent* 770.9

resulting from *caused* 676.5

results *operation* 6.12

resume *protract* 669.9, *restore* 671.10, *renew* 797.19

résumé *biography* 3.5, *record* 185.1, *outline* 198.2, *summary* 204.1, *documentation* 339.6, *shortened version* 591.3, *iteration* 797.2

resumed *reversed* 671.7

resumption *continuation* 669.2, *restoration* 671.2, 809.2

resupply *replenish* 89.10

resurface *repair* 809.10

resurfacing *repair* 809.1

resurgence *revival* 809.3

resurgent *repaired* 809.6

resurrect *bring back to life* 28.20, *make new* 652.20, *revive* 809.14

resurrected *given new life* 28.15, *renewed* 652.14

resurrection *new life* 28.8, *new start* 652.5

resurrection day *judgment day* 341.4

resuscitate *refresh* 94.6, *revive* 809.14

resuscitated *repaired* 809.6

resuscitation *refreshment* 94.1, *revival* 809.3

retable *material* 143.9

retail *publish* 173.15, *mercantile* 480.13, *selling* 482.1, 482.12, *merchandise* 482.17

retailer 482.11; *provisioner* 89.4, *trader* 480.11

retailer's *store* 483.8

retail management *management system* 126.3

retail outlet *store* 483.8

retail price *price* 494.1

retail price index (RPI) *economic indicator* 56.4

retain 471.7; *learn* 68.18, *save* 105.20, *know* 348.10, *memorize* 354.11, *understand* 363.9, *detain* 471.9, *bring* 685.11, *preserve* 815.14

retained 471.6; *saved* 105.15, *memorized* 354.9, *refused* 506.5

retainer 471.3; *servant* 69.1, *adherent* 401.5, *reward for service* 453.5

retainers *attendance* 794.5

retaining *retentive* 471.5

retaining wall *supporting structure* 605.2

retainment *retention* 471.1

retake *motion-picture photography* 137.9, *be compensated* 743.9

retaliate 419.30, 420.4, 489.23; *countercharge* 332.9, *counter* 339.13, *counterattack* 418.24, *exact retribution* 454.27, *restore* 671.10, *reciprocate* 729.7, *counterbalance* 743.8, *object* 828.18

retaliating *counterbalanced* 743.6

retaliation 420.1; *countercharge*

332.3, *counterstatement* 334.5, *counterevidence* 339.5, *military attack* 418.2, *compensation* 453.7, *reckoning* 454.8, *restoration* 671.2, *exchange* 673.1, *reciprocity* 729.1, *counterbalance* 743.2

retaliative *retaliatory* 420.3

retaliator *avenger* 441.6, *punisher* 454.16

retaliatory 334.13, 420.3; *refuting* 332.6, *counterattacking* 418.15, *punitive* 454.18, *in exchange* 673.3, *reciprocal* 729.4, *counterbalanced* 743.6

retard *be self-restrained* 455.10, *delay* 658.13, *slow down* 693.13, *make smaller* 747.8, *hinder* 826.15, *restrain* 830.12

retardataire *Western Art Styles* 133

retardation *lateness* 658.1, *deceleration* 693.2, *decrease* 747.1, *hindrance* 826.1, *restraint* 830.1

retarded *intellectually subnormal* 316.7, *delayed* 693.10

retarding *delaying* 658.8

retardment *deceleration* 693.2

retch *vomit* 709.27

retching *gastroenterological disease* 114.11, *vomiting* 709.7

retell *recount* 202.16, *iterate* 797.16, *rectify* 807.22

retelling *iteration* 797.2

retention 471.1; *memory* 108.27, 354.1, *possession* 469.1, *retentiveness* 471.4, *refusal* 506.1, *preservation* 815.1, *saving* 815.4

retentive 471.5

retentiveness 471.4; *memory* 354.1

retenu *Musical Terms and Expression Marks* 140

rethink *have second thoughts* 317.11

reticence 287.3; *lack of candor* 192.4, *reserve* 195.5, 403.5, *taciturnity* 208.1, *unsociability* 409.1

reticent 287.8; *silent* 181.10, *uncandid* 192.15, *reserved* 195.11, 403.10, *taciturn* 208.4, *unsociable* 409.6, *cunning* 822.4

reticently 287.18; *uncandidly* 192.29, *reservedly* 195.20, *taciturnly* 208.9, *unsocially* 409.13

reticular *cellular* 13.30

reticulate *of fungi* 47.19, *striped* 263.9, *interweave* 609.8

reticulate *or* **reticular** *interwoven* 609.6

reticulately *variedly* 263.12

reticulation *stripe* 263.3, *interweaving* 609.1

Reticulum *Constellations* 7

retina *eye* 19.9, 242.3

retinopathy *eye disease* 243.4

retinue *personnel* 123.16, *attendance* 794.5

retire *have leisure time* 125.5, *depart* 265.6, *withdraw* 392.5, 705.9, *stop work* 394.12, 668.11, *escape notice* 403.14, *be unsocial* 409.10, *sleep* 415.14, *survive* 419.31, *acquiesce* 421.5, *absent oneself* 576.15, *retreat* 680.17, *be dismissed* 707.18, *dismiss* 709.15, *resign* 835.5

retired *leisurely* 125.4, *relinquished* 392.2, *disused* 394.8, *former* 651.14, 653.12, *informal* 829.15, *resigning* 835.3

retired list *list of names* 785.7

retired person *older person* 27.7

retired reserves *the military* 58.2

retiree *older person* 27.7

retirees *old people* 27.10

retire from the world *be unsocial* 409.10

retirement *bargaining terms* 57.10, *shyness* 386.3, *relinquishment* 392.1, *disuse* 394.3, *unsociability* 409.1, *elderliness* 653.2, *stop* 668.2, *reversion* 671.1, *retreat* 680.2, *departure* 705.1, *setting apart* 753.2, *resignation* 835.1

retirement age *old age* 27.5

retirement benefits *reward for service* 453.5, *security* 464.1, *income* 492.3

retirement gift *acknowledgment* 310.3

retirement home *resting place* 668.5, *safe house* 812.5

retirement pay *earnings* 467.5, *pay* 489.6

retirement pension *social assistance* 825.4

retiring *reserved* 195.11, *unsociable* 409.6, *resigning* 835.3

retiring disposition *reserve* 195.5, *shyness* 403.3

retold *iterated* 797.9

retort *negation* 190.1, *negate* 190.16, *burst of sound* 232.4, *countercharge* 332.3, 332.9, *answer* 334.1, 334.18, *counter* 339.13, *be insolent* 400.14, *retaliation* 420.1, *retaliate* 420.4, *defense* 441.2, *justify* 441.12, *vaporizer* 556.10, *reply* 671.5, 671.13, *exchange* 673.5, *reciprocity* 729.1, *reciprocate* 729.7

retorted *reversed* 671.7

retorting *answering* 334.11, *vindicatory* 441.7

retortion *negation* 190.1, *reply* 671.5

retouch *refresh* 94.6, *refurbish* 809.11

retrace *remember* 354.12

retrace one's steps *reverse* 680.18, *return to* 797.18

retract *disavow* 190.18, *renounce* 383.13, *not observe* 466.9, *take back* 477.17, *reverse* 671.9, *cancel* 834.6

retractability *traction* 699.1

retractable *retractive* 699.8

retracted *disavowing* 190.12, *renounced* 383.9, *relinquished* 392.2, *reversed* 671.7

retractile *receding* 680.11, *retractive* 699.8

retractility *traction* 699.1

retracting *taking back* 477.4

retraction *disavowal* 190.3, *renunciation* 383.4, *relinquishment* 392.1, *reversion* 671.1, *traction* 699.1, *cancellation* 834.1

retractive 699.8

retractively 190.24

retractiveness *traction* 699.1

retractor *negator* 190.8, *abrogator* 834.4

retrain *employ* 57.18

retrained *hired* 57.17

retraining *bargaining terms* 57.10, *hired* 57.17

retread *repair* 809.10

retreat 60.13, 285.8, 386.22, 680.2, 680.17; *clerical dwelling* 84.10, *privacy* 181.6, *military call* 183.9, *become invisible* 245.6, *disappearance* 265.1, *depart* 265.6, *shyness* 386.3, *shy* 386.17, *separation* 409.3, *solitary place* 409.4, *acquiesce* 421.5, *absent oneself* 576.15, *shelter* 613.6,

812.8, *reversion* 671.1, *reverse* 671.9, *backward motion* 677.5, *departure* 705.1, *withdraw* 705.9, *be one* 788.17, *refuge* 812.1, *escape* 816.1, 816.8, *defeat* 846.7, *be defeated* 846.18, *downfall* 848.4

retreated *reversed* 671.7

retreater *escaper* 816.5

retreating *receding* 680.11

retreat into *go inside* 611.15

retreat into one's shell *conceal oneself* 181.15

retrench *economize* 499.6, *shorten* 591.9, *make smaller* 747.8, *limit* 830.13

retrenchment *act of thrift* 499.2, *shortening* 591.2, *limitation* 747.3, 830.2, *subtraction* 749.1, *separateness* 753.3

retribution 454.7; *retaliation* 420.1, *revenge* 441.4

retributive *retaliatory* 420.3, *vindictive* 441.10, *punitive* 454.18, *paying in return* 489.15, *compensatory* 743.5

retributive justice *retribution* 454.7

retributively *vindictively* 441.16, *punitively* 454.33

retrievable *taking* 477.12, *reversible* 671.8, *repairable* 809.7

retrievably *avariciously* 477.22, *reversibly* 671.14

retrieval *taking back* 477.4, *restoration* 671.2, 809.2, *compensation* 743.1, *deliverance* 817.1

retrieve *hunt* 160.12, *take back* 477.17, *counteract* 510.7, *restore* 671.10, *bring* 685.11, *be compensated* 743.9, *deliver* 817.5

retrieved *reversed* 671.7

retriever *Breeds of Dogs* 35, *hunting dog* 160.7

retroact *react* 334.20

retroaction *response* 334.4, *counteraction* 510.1, *reversion* 671.1, *backward motion* 680.1, *counterbalance* 743.2

retroactive 680.12; *reactive* 334.12, *counteracting* 510.6, *retrospective* 651.15, *regressive* 671.6, *counterbalanced* 743.6

retroactively *in answer* 334.25, *counter* 510.8, *reversibly* 671.14

retroactive pay *pay* 489.6

retrocede *give back* 478.5, *go backward* 680.16, *restore* 809.12

retrocession *giving back* 478.1, *backward motion* 680.1, *restoration* 809.2

retrocessive *backward* 680.10

retroflection *inversion* 608.1

retroflexion *inversion* 608.1, *reversion* 671.1

retroflexion *or* **retroflection** *backward motion* 680.1

retrogradation *backward motion* 680.1, *deterioration* 808.1

retrograde *regressive* 671.6, *backward* 680.10, *spoiled* 808.9, *deteriorate* 808.14

retrograde [Arch] *go backward* 680.16

retrograde metamorphism *metamorphism* 8.35

retrograde state *return* 671.3

retrogress *reverse* 671.9, *be in motion* 677.14, *go backward* 680.16, *deteriorate* 808.14

retrogression *return* 671.3, *backward motion* 680.1, *deterioration* 808.1

retrogressive *directional* 677.13, *backward* 680.10, *spoiled* 808.9

retrorocket *rocketry* 7.32

retrospect 354.2

retrospection 651.3; *thoughtfulness* 317.2, *memory* 354.1, *reversion* 671.1

retrospective 651.15; *retrospect* 354.2, *remembering* 354.8, *retrospection* 651.3, *regressive* 671.6, *retroactive* 680.12, *display* 843.1

retrospective action *reversion* 671.1

retrospectively 651.22; *historically* 3.17, *memorably* 354.16, *reversibly* 671.14

retroverse *inverted* 608.5, *regressive* 671.6

retroversion *inversion* 608.1, *reversion* 671.1

retrovert *invert* 608.7

retroverted *inverted* 608.5

retrovirus *microorganism* 13.11, *disease-causing agent* 114.5

return 453.6, 671.3, 671.11, 680.9, 704.4, 797.4; *kick* 155.12, 155.20, *play tennis* 165.13, *record* 185.1, *reappearance* 264.8, *response* 334.4, *answer* 334.18, *react* 334.20, *vote* 382.16, *reject* 383.10, *retaliate* 420.4, *earnings* 467.5, *giving back* 478.1, *give back* 478.5, *money received* 492.2, *produce* 522.5, *recurrent period* 641.5, *be periodical* 641.9, *frequency* 663.2, *cycle* 663.3, *be cyclic* 663.11, *reversion* 671.1, *reverse* 671.9, 680.18, *go backward* 680.16, *turn around* 698.25, *land* 704.16, *reciprocity* 729.1, *reciprocate* 729.7, *be repeated* 797.20, *benefit* 801.4, *restore* 809.12

returnable *reversible* 671.8

return action *counteraction* 510.1, *counterbalance* 743.2, 743.8

return a soft answer *pacify* 74.9

return a verdict *judge* 54.31

return blow for blow *counterattack* 418.24

returned *answering* 334.11, *unselected* 383.7, *reversed* 671.7

returned to health *cured* 809.8

return empty-handed *fail* 846.12

returner 478.3

return good for evil *be benevolent* 305.10

return home *return* 671.11, *land* 704.16

returning 680.15; *reactive* 334.12, *giving back* 478.1, *periodical* 641.7, *frequent* 663.6, *recurrent* 797.13, *restoration* 809.2

returning home *Phobias* 283, *return* 671.3

return like for like *retaliate* 420.4

return match *repeat* 797.5

return once again *be cyclic* 663.11

returns *earnings* 467.5, *something received* 473.2, *money received* 492.2

return thanks *be grateful* 310.6

return the compliment *retaliate* 420.4, *exchange* 673.5, *reciprocate* 827.13

return to 797.18; *protract* 669.9

return to base *or* **starting point** *reflex* 680.7

return to fashion *revival* 809.3

return to go [Inf] *begin again* 771.36

return to health *get healthy* 113.12, *recuperation* 809.4

return to mint condition *restore* 809.12

return to normal *restoration* 809.2, *recuperation* 809.4

return to the past *look back* 651.18

return to the starting point *orbit* 681.8

return to the straight and narrow *confess* 451.8

reunion *social gathering* 59.7, *association* 752.2

reupholster *repair* 809.10

reusable *useful* 393.7, *usable* 801.6

reusably *usefully* 393.15

reuse 393.3; *exploit* 393.11

reused *used* 393.5

rev [Inf] *rotation* 682.1

revalidate *restore* 809.12

revamp *change for the better* 665.17, *refurbish* 809.11

revampment *righting wrong* 429.6

reveal 843.14; *educate* 48.22, Architectural Elements 134, *publish* 173.15, *disclose* 180.8, *signify* 183.16, *make visible* 242.25, *244.9, be transparent* 249.11, *present* 264.15, *demonstrate* 331.15, *detect* 345.12, *predict* 358.14, *open* 583.15, *uncover* 614.17

revealed *published* 173.12, *disclosed* 180.5, *appearing* 264.9, *demonstrated* 331.9, *discovered* 345.9, *uncovered* 614.10, *manifest* 843.9

revealer *discloser* 180.4

revealing *educational* 48.17, *informative* 170.10, *disclosing* 180.6, *signifying* 183.11, *translucent* 249.8, *discovering* 345.8, *uncovering* 614.1

revealingly 614.22; *educationally* 48.25, *indicatively* 183.21, *originally* 345.16

reveal itself *become visible* 264.13

reveal oneself *show oneself* 843.15

reveal one's mind *or* **thoughts** *or* **opinions** *show oneself* 843.15

reveal to the public *display* 843.13

reveille *military call* 183.9, *morning things* 655.3

revel *drinking bout* 121.7, *make merry* 167.13, *rejoicing* 279.1, *rejoice* 279.5, *celebration* 405.1, *celebrate* 405.10

revelation *divine manifestation* 82.5, *disclosure* 180.1, *visibility* 244.1, *first appearance* 264.3, *spectacle* 264.6, *demonstration* 331.1, *prediction* 358.1, *manifestation* 843.2

revelatory 180.7; *educational* 48.17, *demonstrated* 331.9, *discovering* 345.8

reveler *drunkard* 121.8, *joyful person* 269.5, *rejoicer* 279.3

revel in *feel pleasure* 214.12

reveling *rejoicing* 279.4

revelry *amusement* 167.7, *rejoicing* 279.1, *celebration* 405.1, *sociability* 408.1

revels *celebration* 405.1

revenge 441.4; *retaliation* 420.1, *retaliate* 420.4, *avenge* 441.14, *reckoning* 454.8, *counterbalance* 743.2, 743.8

revenge! 420.7

revenged *compensated* 743.3

revengeful *malicious* 306.8, *pitiless* 309.3, *retaliatory* 420.3, *vindictive* 441.10, *evil* 446.7, *punitive* 454.18

revengefully *maliciously* 306.15, *pitilessly* 309.7, *vindictively* 441.16, *evilly* 446.12

revengefulness *malice* 306.2, *pitilessness* 309.1, *evil* 446.1

revenge match *contest* 422.4

revenge oneself *exact retribution* 454.27, *retaliate* 489.23

revenger 420.2; *punisher* 454.16

revenge tragedy *tragedy* 136.10

revenue *economic factor* 56.8, *resources* 102.4, *earnings* 467.5, *personal estate* 470.6, *something received* 473.2, *takings* 477.8, *money received* 492.2, *produce* 522.5

revenue cutter Ships and Boats 690

revenuer [Inf] *tax collector* 494.9

reverberant *drumming* 235.6

reverberantly *resonantly* 236.11, *in answer* 334.25

reverberate *wave* 10.77, *be heard* 228.15, *sound* 230.8, *be loud* 232.8, *drum* 235.10, *resonate* 236.9, *react* 334.20, *resound* 797.21

reverberating *resonant* 236.6

reverberation 797.6; *sound* 10.15, *sound quality* 230.4, *loud sound* 232.2, *drumming* 235.1, *resonance* 236.1, *response* 334.4, *consequence* 774.3

reverberative *drumming* 235.6, *resonant* 236.6

reverberatory 797.14; *ceramic workshop and tools* 129.8, *ceramic* 129.9, *reactive* 334.12, *repercussive* 774.8

reverberatory kiln *ceramic workshop and tools* 129.8

reverdie Poem or Verse Forms 139

revere 81.26, 435.14; *worship* 83.15, *wonder* 294.12, *love* 299.21, *bow* 716.22

revered *worshiped* 83.14, *beloved* 299.19, *respected* 435.10

reverence *religiousness* 81.2, *worship* 83.1, 83.15, *love* 299.1, *obeisance* 426.3, *deference* 433.4, *admiration* 435.2, *revere* 435.14, *bow* 716.6

reverenced *respected* 435.10

Reverend *professional title* 72.6

reverend father *religious* 84.9

reverend mother *religious* 84.9

reverent 435.9; *religious* 81.21, *worshipful* 83.12, *loving* 299.15, *deferential* 433.9

reverential *religious* 81.21, *worshipful* 83.12, *obeisant* 426.6, *deferential* 433.9, *reverent* 435.9

reverentially *religiously* 81.29, *worshipfully* 83.17, *obediently* 426.9, *respectfully* 435.19

reverently *lovingly* 299.29, *respectfully* 435.19

reverie 360.6; *trance* 108.18, *thoughtfulness* 317.2

reversal 680.3; *oppositeness* 190.6, *731.1, refutation* 332.1, *denial* 332.2, *vacillation* 380.3, *loss* 468.1, *taking back* 477.4, *inversion* 608.1, *alteration* 665.2, *reversion* 671.1, *cancellation* 834.1, *defeat* 846.7

reverse 671.9, 680.18; *play* 155.8, *diving* 164.13, *oppositeness* 190.6, *deny* 332.8, *loss* 468.1, *inverse* 608.2, *back* 622.1, *changeable* 665.11, *change* 665.14, *reversal* 680.3, *reversed* 680.13, *slow down* 693.13, *turn*

around 698.25, *opposite* 731.2, 731.3, *be opposite* 731.4, *contrary* 828.13, *cancel* 834.6

reverse course *navigate* 690.15

reverse curve *pitching terms* 147.5

reversed 671.7, 680.13; *inverted* 608.5, *opposite* 731.3

reversed collar *neckwear* 100.29

reverse direction *backward motion* 680.1, *turn around* 698.25

reverse dive *competitive diving* 164.7

reversedly *inversely* 608.9

reversed-phase *analytic* 11.32

reverse fault *fault* 8.21

reverse killian hold *ice-dancing move* 162.19

reverse one's field *reverse* 680.18

reverse order *hierarchy* 765.3

reverser *abrogator* 834.4

reverse twist *tennis strokes* 165.2

reverse word dictionary *word book* 5.27

reversi Board and Table Games 167

reversible 671.8; *reactive* 11.29, *equivocating* 380.6, *reversed* 680.13

reversible reaction *chemical reaction* 11.8

reversibly 671.14

reversing *reversal* 680.3

reversion 671.1; *defense mechanism* 108.23, *legal property terms* 470.2, *transfer of property* 470.4, *giving back* 478.1, *inversion* 608.1, *reversal* 680.3, *countermotion* 680.6, *cancellation* 834.1

reversional *regressive* 671.6

reversionary *regressive* 671.6

reversion to type *deterioration* 808.1

revert *change* 665.14, *reverse* 671.9, *go backward* 680.16, *turn around* 698.25, *return to* 797.18, *deteriorate* 808.14

reverted *reversed* 671.7

revert to bachelorhood *divorce* 66.9

revert to the single state *divorce* 66.9

revet *face* 613.31

revetment *wall covering* 613.12

review *recollect* 3.16, *learning* 48.7, *show* 138.4, *nonfiction* 139.6, *document* 170.3, *book review* 174.13, *recount* 202.16, *article* 203.2, *summary* 204.1, *questioning* 333.2, *question* 333.16, *judgment* 341.1, *estimate* 341.11, *retrospect* 354.2, *remember* 354.12, *remind* 354.13, *criticism* 365.3, *criticize* 365.15, *ceremonial* 404.11, *formal occasion* 406.4, *retrospection* 651.3, *look back* 651.18, *iteration* 797.2, *iterate* 797.16, *reconsideration* 807.9, *rectify* 807.22

reviewed *questioned* 333.15

reviewer *theatergoer* 136.30, *book review* 174.13, *dissertator* 203.3, *questioner* 333.9, *judge* 341.5, *interpreter* 365.6

reviewing *recollection* 3.8

revile *lie* 192.23, *be dissatisfied* 274.7, *vilify* 301.15, 440.14, *criticize* 418.26, *berate* 438.20

revilement *vilification* 301.2, *personal attack* 418.8, *berating* 438.5, *scorn* 440.5

reviling *vilifying* 301.9

revilingly *vilifyingly* 301.18

revisable *renewable* 652.15

revisal *righting wrong* 429.6, *new*

start 652.5, *change for the better* 665.4, *rectification* 807.8

revise *make new* 652.20, *change for the better* 665.17, *rectification* 807.8, *rectify* 807.22

revised *renewed* 652.14, *changed* 665.10, *improved* 807.12

revised edition *reprint* 21.3, *reconsideration* 807.9

Revised Version *Christian text* 81.16

reviser *changer* 665.9, *improver* 807.11

revising *improving* 807.14

revision *righting wrong* 429.6, *new start* 652.5, *change for the better* 665.4, *rearrangement* 767.4, *rectification* 807.8

revisionism *nonconformism* 782.3

revisionist *types of history* 3.2, *nonconformist* 782.13

revitalization *refreshment* 94.1, *vigor* 518.1, *revival* 809.3

revitalize *invigorate* 28.22, 518.5, *refresh* 94.6, *revive* 809.14

revitalized *refreshed* 94.5

revitalizing *refreshing* 94.4, *invigorating* 518.3

revival 809.3; *new life* 28.8, *refreshment* 94.1, *production* 136.14, *strengthening* 516.7, *new start* 652.5, *change for the better* 665.4, *religious conversion* 670.4, *restoration* 671.2, 807.4, *return* 797.4

revivalism *religious conversion* 670.4

revivalist *religionist* 81.14

revive 809.14; *live* 28.17, *bring back to life* 28.20, *invigorate* 28.22, 518.5, *refresh* 94.6, *make healthy* 113.13, *treat* 115.17, *be piquant* 221.9, *be strong* 516.14, *strengthen* 516.15, *make new* 652.20, *change back* 665.19, *persuade* 670.14, *restore* 671.10, 807.17, 809.12, *renew* 797.19, *get better* 807.21, *be restored* 809.13, *support* 825.24

revived *given new life* 28.15, *refreshed* 94.5, *strengthened* 516.13, *renewed* 652.14, *changed* 665.10, *influenced* 670.10, *reversed* 671.7, *remade* 797.10, *repaired* 809.6

reviver *refresher* 94.2, *tonic* 115.8, *stimulant* 221.5

revivescence *revival* 809.3

revive the spirits *bring cheer* 269.12

revivification *new life* 28.8, *strengthening* 516.7, *new start* 652.5, *revival* 809.3

revivified *renewed* 652.14

revivify *strengthen* 516.15, *make new* 652.20, *revive* 809.14

revivifying *strengthening* 516.7, *invigorating* 518.3

reviving *refreshing* 94.4, *cheering* 269.8, *strengthening* 516.7, *invigorating* 518.3, *restorative* 809.9

revocation *disavowal* 190.3, *cancellation* 834.1

revocative *or* **revocatory** *disavowing* 190.12

revocatory *dissenting* 506.6

revoke *disavow* 190.9, *renounce* 383.13, *veto* 503.9, *abolish* 523.11, *cancel* 834.6

revoked *disavowing* 190.12, *canceled* 834.5

revoker *negator* 190.8, *abrogator* 834.4

revoking *dissenting* 506.6

revokingly *retractively* 190.24
revolt 417.12; *anarchy* 51.1, *be anarchic* 51.8, *war of independence* 76.9, *go to war* 76.29, *displease* 272.8, *dissatisfy* 274.6, *cause dislike* 291.16, *cause hate* 300.12, *resistance movement* 417.3, *revolution* 427.4, *subvert* 427.13, *disorder* 507.2, *cause mischief* 507.9, *sudden change* 665.3, *change* 665.14, *cause change* 665.16, *be converted* 670.12, *be repulsive* 701.10, *dissent* 782.2, *not conform* 782.18
revolted *antipathetic* 291.7, *hating* 300.7
revolter *rebel* 427.8, *protester* 507.4
revolting *unpleasant* 272.6, *frightening* 283.12, *detested* 291.11, *hateful* 300.10
revoltingly *hatefully* 300.14, *hideously* 531.6
revolution 427.4; *orbit* 7.22, 681.3, *anarchy* 51.1, *acquisition of authority* 52.5, *war of independence* 76.9, *act of defiance* 416.3, *resistance movement* 417.3, *cycle* 663.3, *sudden change* 665.3, *evolution* 670.3, *rotation* 682.1, *downthrow* 716.2, *lawlessness* 766.6
revolutionarily *newly* 652.21
revolutionary *anarchist* 51.4, *anarchic* 51.5, *resister* 417.5, *resisting* 417.8, *rebel* 427.8, *subversive* 427.11, *violent animal or person* 520.4, *destroyer* 523.6, *destructive* 523.8, *new* 652.9, *changer* 665.9, *changeable* 665.11, *orbital* 681.5, *novel* 737.5, *dissenter* 782.8, *dissident* 782.12, *opposer* 828.9
Revolutionary War *Major Wars* 76
revolutionist *rebel* 427.8, *destroyer* 523.6
revolutionize *cause change* 665.16, *originate* 737.7
revolutionized *overthrown* 716.9
revolutions per minute (rpm) *rotation* 682.1, *speed* 694.2
revolve *observe* 7.34, *circle* 631.6, *be cyclic* 663.11, *orbit* 681.8, *rotate* 682.14
revolve around *center* 612.10
revolver *firearm* 78.7
revolver shooting *target shooting* 160.1
revolving *frequent* 663.6, *cyclic* 663.7, *orbiting* 681.7, *rotating* 682.11
revolving door *rotator* 682.8
revolving fund *finance* 457.1
revolving stage *stage* 136.18
revue *show* 138.4
revulsion *dislike* 300.2, *shyness* 386.3
rev up [Inf] *prepare for action* 388.18, *activate* 509.11
reward 453.1, 453.13, 472.4; *death* 29.1, *title* 72.1, *honor* 72.3, *bribe* 178.18, *acknowledgment* 310.3, *be grateful* 310.6, *congratulate* 405.12, *reckoning* 454.8, *profit* 467.6, *give* 472.10, *pay* 489.6, *remunerate* 489.21, *compensation* 743.1, *compensate* 743.7
rewarded 453.10; *receiving* 473.9, *compensated* 743.3
rewarder *giver* 472.7
reward for service 453.5
rewarding 453.9; *gainful* 467.10, *profitable* 489.13, *successful* 845.8

rewardingly 453.19; *successfully* 845.19
reward of conduct *mode of behavior* 399.2
rewed *marry* 64.19
reword *word* 5.43, *translate* 365.16
rewording *translation* 365.4
rewrite *word* 5.43, *be elegant* 527.6, *rectify* 807.22
rewriter *improver* 807.11
rewritten *improved* 807.12
rex *Breeds of Cats* 35, *sovereign* 68.2
Reykjavik *Countries* 566
Reynard *cunning person* 822.3
Reynolds number *Classical Physical Laws* 10
R-form *structure* 11.7
Rf value *analysis* 11.7
rhabdology *calculator* 6.64
rhabdomancy *divination* 86.5
rhabdophobia *Phobias* 283
rhachilla *stem* 41.5
rhachis *stem* 41.5
Rhadamanthine *judiciary* 53.19, *judicatory* 54.24
Rhadamanthys *judge* 54.10
rhamnose *Common Sugars* 12
rhapsodic *poetic* 139.19
rhapsodic or rhapsodical *imaginative* 360.10
rhapsodist *author* 139.13, *visionary* 360.9
rhapsodize *fantasize* 360.15
rhapsody *conception* 360.4
Rhea *Planets and Their Satellites* 7, *Deities* 82
rhea *flightless bird* 36.8
rhenium *Chemical Elements and Common Allotropes* 11
rheology *industrial processes* 14.27
rheometer *Fields of Measurement* 589
rheometry *Fields of Measurement* 589
rheostat *circuit element* 14.39
Rhesus factor *blood* 555.4
rhetor *persuader* 178.9
rhetoric *diffuseness* 199.1, *public speaking* 205.11, *mode of expression* 537.3
rhetorical *diffuse* 199.3, *articulate* 205.16, *addressing* 209.6, *sophistic* 330.7, *inelegant* 528.6, *ornate* 532.10
rhetorically *philosophically* 4.23, *orally* 205.21, *oratorically* 209.14, *sophistically* 330.14, *stylistically* 537.11
rhetorical question *easy question* 333.5
rhetorician *persuader* 178.9, *speaker* 205.12, *public speaker* 209.5, *motivator* 508.6, *stylist* 537.4
Rhett Butler *Famous Lovers* 299
rheum *body fluid* 19.16, 555.3, *secreted substance* 24.2, *saliva* 25.9
rheumatic *of disease* 114.25
rheumatic fever *joint disease* 114.19
rheumatic heart disease *cardiovascular disease* 114.13
rheumatism *joint disease* 114.19, *painful condition* 215.2
rheumatoid *of disease* 114.25
rheumatoid arthritis *joint disease* 114.19
rheumatology *Medical Specialties* 107
rheuminess *fluidity* 555.5
rheumy 555.16; *salivating* 25.18
Rh factor *blood* 555.4
Rhine *Rivers* 570

Rhineland Heavy Draught *Horse and Pony Breeds* 159
rhinitis *respiratory disease* 114.12
rhinoceros *pachyderm* 35.15, *hoofed mammal* 35.16, *Collective Names* 59, *game* 160.6
rhinocerotic *elephantlike* 35.30
rhinological *olfactory* 224.6
rhinoplasty *cosmetic surgery* 530.2
rhinorrhea *respiratory disease* 114.12
rhizoid *root* 41.7, *of roots* 41.19, *moss plant* 46.5, *fungal body* 47.4, *plant body* 47.13
rhizome *garden plant* 17.10, *stem* 41.5
rhizomorph *root* 41.7, *fungal body* 47.4
Rh-negative *blood* 555.4
Rhode Island *American States* 564
Rhode Island Greening *Apple Varieties* 44
Rhode Island Red *Breeds of Fowl* 16
Rhodes *Islands* 572
Rhodesian ridgeback *Breeds of Dogs* 35
rhodium *Chemical Elements and Common Allotropes* 11
rhododendron *Flowers* 42
Rhodophyta *algae* 47.11
rhodophyte *algae* 47.11
rhomb *polygon* 6.42
rhombic *polygonal* 6.79, *status adjectives* 11.25
rhombic crystal *crystal* 11.14
rhomboid *polygon* 6.42, *oblique line* 607.5, *angled figure* 628.3
rhomboidal *polygonal* 6.79, *angled* 628.9
rhombus *polygon* 6.42, *oblique line* 607.5, *angled figure* 628.3, *quadrilateral* 791.2
Rhon *Breeds of Sheep* 16
rhonchus *hiss* 237.1
Rhône *Rivers* 570
Rh-positive *blood* 555.4
rhubarb [Inf] *rivalry* 422.2, *dispute* 463.3
rhumb line *guide* 697.4
rhyme 139.11; *use language* 5.42, *poetry* 139.8, *write* 139.21, *symmetry* 626.1, *harmonization* 735.2, *harmonize* 735.22, *reverberation* 797.6, *resound* 797.21
rhymed *reverberatory* 797.14
rhymer *author* 139.13
rhyme royal *rhyme* 139.11
rhyme scheme *rhyme* 139.11
rhymester *author* 139.13
rhyming *worded* 5.38, *metrical* 139.20, *harmonizing* 735.12, *reverberatory* 797.14
rhyming couplet *part of poem* 139.9
rhyming dictionary *word book* 5.27
rhyming slang *slang* 5.19
rhyming word *word* 5.17
Rhynchocephalia *reptile* 37.1
rhynchocephalian *lizard* 37.5
rhythm *meter* 139.10, *tempo* 140.22, *floor exercise* 157.4, *grace* 527.2, *musical time* 639.7, *frequency* 663.2, *regular movement* 677.10, *vibration* 683.2, *reverberation* 797.6
rhythm-and-blues (R and B) *rock music* 140.6
rhythmic *harmonic* 140.27, *gymnastic* 157.11, *graceful* 527.4, *frequent* 663.6, *directional* 677.13,

vibrating 683.9, *cyclical* 774.10, *reverberatory* 797.14
rhythmical *metrical* 139.20, *frequent* 663.6, *vibrating* 683.9, *reverberatory* 797.14
rhythmically *dancingly* 135.8, *poetically* 139.23, *tunefully* 140.30, *gymnastically* 157.13, *repeatedly* 235.15, *gracefully* 527.8, *regularly* 663.14
rhythmic gymnastics *Sporting Activities* 145, *gymnastics* 157.1
rhythm method *birth control* 23.5
rhytidectomy *cosmetic surgery* 530.2
rhytiphobia *Phobias* 283
rialto *place of exchange* 673.2
rib *Human Bones* 19, *lamb* 90.27, *Architectural Elements* 134, *vault* 134.8, *rock face* 161.6, *be humorous* 277.11, *superstructure* 551.7
ribald 535.8; *obscene* 112.9, *profane* 301.10, *offensive* 432.11
ribaldly 535.12; *profanely* 301.19
ribaldry *obscenity* 112.4, *profanity* 301.3, *immorality* 432.1
ribband *line* 754.5
ribbed *rough* 552.8
ribbing *knitting* 130.7
Ribble *Rivers* 570
ribbon *honor* 72.3, *headdress* 100.35, *insignia* 184.5, *monument* 185.10, *decorative article* 532.5, *band* 754.9
ribbons *yoke* 754.8
ribbonwood *Trees and Shrubs* 43
ribonucleic acid (RNA) *nucleotide* 12.10, *cell structure* 13.16
ribonucleotide *nucleotide* 12.10
ribose *Common Sugars* 12
ribosomal *cellular* 13.30
ribosomal RNA *genetic material* 13.20
ribosome *cell structure* 13.16
rib roast *beef* 90.24, *veal* 90.25, *pork* 90.26
ribs *ceramic workshop and tools* 129.8, *body support* 605.6, *side* 623.1
rib-tickling *ridiculous* 368.5
rice 90.32; *crop* 16.8, *cereal grass* 45.4
rice paddy *farmland* 16.3
rice paper *paper* 104.5, *brittle thing* 548.2
ricer *pulper* 561.13
rich 90.32; *fertile* 22.8, *edible* 92.20, *deep* 236.8, *colorful* 251.11, *well-off* 467.12, *solvent* 484.23, *wealthy* 485.8, *productive* 522.11, *decorated* 532.9, *ornate* 532.10, *oily* 562.11, *prosperous* 847.5
rich, the 485.7
Richardsonian Romanesque style *Architectural Styles* 134
Richard's paradox *philosophical problem* 4.8
rich as Croesus *well-off* 467.12, *wealthy* 485.8
rich as Rockefeller *wealthy* 485.8
richen *fertilize* 22.12
riches *fortune* 484.4, *money* 485.2, *successfulness* 845.3
rich food *food* 90.1
rich harvest *fertility* 22.1
richly *resonantly* 236.11, *gainfully* 467.24, *wealthily* 485.16, *decoratively* 532.13, *oilily* 562.19, *prosperously* 847.9
richly decorated *ornate* 532.10
richly furnished *opulent* 485.10
Richmond *American States* 564, *New York* 567.6

richness *fertility* 22.1, Collective Names 59, *excess* 99.1, *flavor* 219.3, *deepness* 236.3, *wealth* 485.1, *decoration* 532.1, *oiliness* 562.1

rich person *gainer* 467.9, *wealthy person* 485.6, *prosperous person* 847.4

rich pickings *takings* 477.8, *stolen goods* 479.4

rich soil *fertile land* 22.2

Richter scale *seismic activity* 8.24

rich uncle *giver* 472.7

rich vocabulary *power of speech* 205.5

rickets *vitamin deficiency disease* 12.14

rickettsia *microorganism* 13.11

rickety *of disease* 114.25, *weak* 517.6, *imperfect* 806.5, *decrepit* 808.12, *unsafe* 811.8

rickrack *notched thing* 636.2

ricochet *reversion* 671.1, *reverse* 671.9

rictus *distortion of face* 627.2, *spasm* 684.8

rid *save* 275.9

riddance *ejection* 764.2, *escape* 816.1, *deliverance* 817.1

riddle *garden tool* 103.4, *cleaning tool* 111.10, *puzzle* 182.5, *obscurity* 197.1, *difficult question* 333.4, *unknown thing* 349.3, *unintelligible thing* 364.3, *equivocation* 380.1, *shoot* 696.18, *mysteriousness* 844.5

riddled with holes *holed* 583.12

riddle of the Sphinx *puzzle* 182.5

riddle with holes *hole* 583.17

riddling *problematic* 333.12

ride 159.16; *amusement park and playground equipment* 167.8, *travel* 686.11, *travel by train* 688.9, *sail* 690.16

ride a broomstick *bewitch* 86.25

ride against *attack* 418.17

ride and tie *equestrianism* 159.8, *oscillate* 683.12

ride a tiger *be in danger* 811.11

ride a wave *windsurf* 150.33

ride bareback *ride* 159.16

ride down *chase* 385.13, *attack successfully* 418.25

ride full tilt at *chase* 385.13, *attack* 418.17

ride hard *be swift* 694.10

ride it out *be safe* 810.20

ride on an even keel *sail* 690.16

ride on a rail *drive out* 709.19

ride out the storm *sail* 150.29, 690.16

rider *horse person* 159.14, *traveler* 686.6, *appendage* 748.4

ride roughshod over *suppress* 424.9, *disrespect* 436.18, *violate the law* 466.12

ride shotgun *protect* 810.21

ride sidesaddle *ride* 159.16

ride to hounds *hunt* 385.14

ridge *farmland* 16.3, *rock face* 161.6, *skiing snow* 162.3, *mountain* 569.1, *mountain range* 569.3, *narrow place* 593.2, *summit* 600.1, *means of connection* 754.4

ridge *or* **ridge of high pressure** *weather system* 9.10

ridged *snow* 162.28, *coarse* 544.6

ridgetree *figurative usage* 43.9

ridicule 436.4, 436.22, 440.6, 440.15; *disbelieve* 88.8, *misrepresentation* 188.1, Phobias 283, *joke* 368.4, *derision* 369.1, 400.5, *exclude* 383.11, *disdain* 400.16, *discourtesy* 411.1, *wrong*

430.19, *show of disapproval* 438.6, *show disapproval* 438.21

ridiculed *criticized* 438.14

ridiculer *disparager* 440.7

ridiculing 436.13; *derisive* 369.5, 400.12, *scornful* 440.10

ridiculous 368.5; *foolish* 353.5, *meaningless* 362.7, *impossible* 837.4

ridiculously 368.8; *foolishly* 353.8, *meaninglessly* 362.13, *impossibly* 837.11

ridiculousness 368.1; *folly* 353.1

riding *equine* 159.15, *administrative region* 564.4, *motion* 677.1, *moving* 677.12, *traveling* 686.9, *passing along* 692.5

riding at anchor *stable* 674.3

riding boots *boots* 100.31

riding breeches *pants* 100.14

riding crop *riding equipment* 159.9

riding equipment 159.9

riding habit *uniform* 100.9

riding horse *saddle horse* 159.5

riding lights *safety light* 246.7

riding pants *pants* 100.14

riding pony *pony* 159.5

riding school *type of school* 48.12, *equestrianism* 159.8

riding skirt *skirt* 100.12

rid of *deliver* 817.5

rid oneself of *disaccustom* 398.6, *throw away* 709.25, *make smaller* 747.8, *elude* 816.10

Riemann hypothesis Mathematical Concepts 6

Riemannian geometry Mathematical Concepts 6

Riemann surface Mathematical Concepts 6

rife *fertile* 22.8, *universal* 778.10, *ample* 795.9

rifeness *widespreadness* 778.3, *profuseness* 795.3

riff [Inf] *beat time* 140.29

riffle *river turbulence* 570.5, *wave* 571.3, *billow* 571.9, *shallowness* 599.1

riffraff *vulgar group* 535.5

rifle *weapon* 78.1, *firearm* 78.7, *banger* 234.3

rifle bore *firearm* 78.7

rifle butt *blunt weapon* 78.5

rifleman *historical soldier* 77.8, *shooter* 696.11

rifle practice *military training* 76.19

rifle shooting Sporting Activities 145, *target shooting* 160.1

rifle sling *hunting accessories* 160.5

Rif Mountains Mountains and Hills 569

rift *faction* 347.4, *dispute* 463.3, *crack* 587.2, *separateness* 753.3, *defect* 806.4

rift valley *landform* 8.9

rig *handle sailboat equipment* 150.30, *practice sophistry* 330.11, *plan* 387.12, *distort the truth* 627.12, *tackle* 754.6

Riga Countries 566

rigadoon Dances 135

rigamarole *senseless talk* 362.4

rigged *equipped* 388.10

rigged out *equipped* 388.10

rigging *sailboat parts and accessories* 150.4, *tackle* 754.6

right 429.2, 429.7, 429.15; *political party* 50.5, *legal power* 52.2, *legality* 53.9, *legal* 53.16, *claim* 72.2, 429.3, *combat* 152.17, *soccer* 163.7, *judicious* 341.8, *accurately* 350.6, *put right* 429.14, *morals* 431.2, *moral* 431.9, *dutiful* 433.6,

good 445.10, *property* 470.1, *side direction* 623.2, *side* 623.6, *straight* 630.8, *directly* 697.16, *correct* 721.13, *be accurate* 721.22, *convenient* 803.3, *repaired* 809.6, *repair* 809.10

right, the Phobias 283

rightabout *about-face* 680.4

right about-face *about-face* 680.4, *turn around* 680.22

right amount *sufficiency* 97.1

right angle *angle* 6.37, 628.1

right-angled *perpendicular* 602.6, *angled* 628.9

right arm *supporter* 605.9

right ascension *celestial sphere* 7.4, *coordinates* 589.6

right as rain *unbroken* 805.13

right as right can be *unbroken* 805.13

right away 429.20; *immediately* 645.8, *early* 657.17, *hastily* 818.7

right a wrong *put right* 429.14

right cross *boxing techniques* 152.5

right defense *hockey player* 158.8

righteous *right* 429.7, *moral* 431.9, *good* 445.10, *virtuous* 447.5

righteously *right* 429.15, *morally* 431.15, *virtuously* 447.9

righteousness *legal justice* 53.4, *rightfulness* 429.1, *morals* 431.2, *good* 445.1, *virtue* 447.1

right field *baseball field* 147.3, *laterality* 623.3

right fielder *baseball team* 147.2

right form *formality* 406.1, *etiquette* 406.3

rightful 429.9; *legitimate* 52.10, 53.21, *in the right* 429.11, *authentic* 721.16

rightful authority *legal power* 52.2

rightfully *legitimately* 52.19, *right* 429.15, *authentically* 721.31

rightfulness 429.1; *legal justice* 53.4, *legality* 53.9, *authenticity* 721.7

rightful possession *possession* 469.1

right half *soccer participant* 163.4

right hand *deputy* 80.1, *helper* 275.5, *subordinate* 832.3

right-hand *racing* 146.9, *side direction* 623.2, *sided* 623.7

right-handed hitter *baseball team* 147.2

right-handedness *laterality* 623.3

right-hand entry *deposit* 487.3

right-hand man *or* **woman** *office assistant* 69.6, *helper* 275.5, 825.12

right-hand page *book part* 174.5

right-hand side *laterality* 623.3

right hook *boxing techniques* 152.5

right idea *method* 387.4

righting wrong 429.6

right in the head [Inf] *sane* 109.3

rightism *preservation of status quo* 815.8

rightist *political party member* 50.6, *conservative* 815.13

right lateral detachment fault *fault* 8.21

rightly *legally* 53.33, *judicially* 341.12, *right* 429.15, *morally* 431.15, *dutifully* 433.19, *well* 445.19, *correctly* 721.29

rightly served *retaliatory* 420.3

right man *or* **woman in the right place** *assenter* 462.5

right-minded *in the right* 429.11, *moral* 431.9

right moment *timeliness* 659.1

right mood *goodwill* 373.4

rightness *rightfulness* 429.1, *good* 445.1, *trueness* 721.4

right now *immediately* 645.8, *present day* 647.2, *at present* 647.9

right of claim 429.3

right of entry 706.4

right off *right away* 429.20

right off the bat [Inf] *immediately* 645.8

right of possession *possession* 469.1

right of purchase *purchasing* 481.2

right of use *use* 393.1

right of way *access* 691.3, *thoroughfare* 692.6

right-on [Inf] *correct* 429.8

right on! [Inf] *good!* 445.24

right oneself *equalize* 740.12

right person for the job *expert* 68.13, 127.9, *assenter* 462.5

right qualities *sufficiency* 97.1

Right Reverend *professional title* 72.6

rights 429.4; *free rights* 829.4

right side *laterality* 623.3

rights of man *rights* 429.4

right stick *hockey equipment* 158.3

right stuff [Inf] *aptitude* 127.4

right thing, the *duty* 433.1

right time *timeliness* 659.1, *convenience* 803.1

right time and place *convenience* 803.1

right to die *rights* 429.4

right to know *rights* 429.4

right to left *to and fro* 683.16

right to life *rights* 429.4

right to representation *rights* 429.4

right to vote *rights* 429.4

right to work *rights* 429.4

right-to-work law *labor law* 57.12

right triangle *angled figure* 628.3

right *or* **right-angled triangle** *triangle* 6.41

right up one's alley [Inf] *convenient* 803.3

right uppercut *boxing techniques* 152.5, *sporting hit* 695.6

rightward *laterally* 623.11, *clockwise* 697.17

right wing *hockey player* 158.8, *laterality* 623.3

right-wing *conservative* 815.13

right-winger *political party member* 50.6

right-wing politics *preservation of status quo* 815.8

right word at the right time *grace* 527.2

right word in the right place *grace* 527.2

rigid *accurate* 350.3, *tenacious* 376.9, *unyielding* 379.8, *formal* 406.6, *obstinate* 417.7, *severe* 424.5, *dense* 540.6, *tough* 542.6, *hard* 547.8, *brittle* 548.3, *straight* 630.8, *permanent* 667.2

rigid control *defense mechanism* 108.23

rigidity *accuracy* 350.1, *tenacity* 376.4, *obstinacy* 417.2, *severity* 424.1, *hardness* 542.1, *permanence* 667.1, *lack of motion* 678.1

rigidly *formally* 406.12, *resistingly* 417.14, *severely* 424.11, *densely* 540.10, *toughly* 542.12, 547.16, *fragilely* 548.5, *permanently* 667.6

rigidness *formality* 406.1, *hardness* 542.1, *toughness* 547.1, *brittleness* 548.1

1249

rigmarole *senseless talk* 362.4
rigmarole *or* **rigamarole** *diffuseness* 199.1
rigor *reasoning* 6.61, *accuracy* 350.1, *severity* 424.1, *hardness* 542.1, *shake* 684.7
rigorism *opinionatedness* 379.3
rigorist *obstinate person* 379.4
rigor mortis *after death* 29.9
rigorous *accurate* 350.3, *opinionated* 379.9, *severe* 424.5
rigorously *severely* 424.11
rigorousness *accuracy* 350.1, *severity* 424.1
rigorous proof *reasoning* 6.61
rig out *equip* 388.19
rig the market *speculate* 480.19
Rigveda *other text* 81.19
rile *dirty* 112.11, *cause dislike* 291.16, *make angry* 302.18, *make irascible* 303.16, *agitate* 684.22
riled *resentful* 302.8, *cross* 303.11
rill *river* 570.1
rill *or* **rille** *moon* 7.18
rillet *river* 570.1
rim *basketball court* 148.3, *exteriority* 610.2, *be exterior* 610.13, *edge* 617.3, 618.1, *border* 618.9, *limit* 773.7
Rímac Rivers 570
rime *frost* 9.25, *ice* 218.5
rime riche *rhyme* 139.11
rim of the horizon *horizontal surface* 603.3
rimose *cracked* 587.5, *furrowed* 638.3
rimple *wrinkle* 638.2
rimpled *wrinkly* 638.4
rinceau Architectural Elements 134
rind *fruit structure* 44.3, *exteriority* 610.2, *casing* 613.9
rinderpest *animal disease* 34.10
rinforzando *or* **rf** *or* **rfz** *or* **rinf.** Musical Terms and Expression Marks 140
ring 235.14, 236.10, 681.9; *set* 6.19, *algebra* 6.21, *circle* 6.40, 631.2, *party* 59.3, *group* 59.8, *general wedding terms* 64.6, *sound* 141.15, *sports ground* 145.2, *be loud* 232.8, *ringing* 235.5, *love token* 299.8, *jewelry* 532.6, *circular thing* 631.3, *fastener* 754.7, *warning signal* 814.3, *telephone call* 169.11
ring, the *circus* 138.2
ring a bell *remind* 354.13
ring bearer *wedding party* 64.7
ring closure *chemical reaction* 11.8
ring down the curtain *stop work* 668.11
ringer *ornithologist* 36.3, *impression* 264.7
ringer [Inf] *horse racing* 159.10, *substitute* 672.2
ring finger *appendage* 19.5
ring hitch Knots, Bends, Hitches, Splices 754
ring in *get in* 704.17, *forecast* 769.17
ringing 235.5, 236.2, 236.7; *ornithology* 36.2, *signaling* 183.14, *loud* 232.6
ringing around *enclosure* 619.1
ringing gold *money* 484.1
ringing in the ears *ear problem* 228.4
ringing off [Brit] *stop* 668.2
ringing tone *loud tone* 232.3
ringing up *mathematical addition* 748.2
ring in the ear *ring* 236.10

ring knot Knots, Bends, Hitches, Splices 754
ringleader *leader* 126.8, *motivator* 178.11, 508.6, *troublemaker* 427.5
ringlet *coil* 632.2
ringlike *curvilinear* 6.78
ringmaster *leader* 126.8, *circus performer* 138.9
ring nebula *nebula* 7.6
ring off [Brit] *stop* 668.10
ring of invisibility *talisman* 86.9
ring of truth *verisimilitude* 721.10
ring opening *maturing* 27.12
ring road [Brit] *rotary* 682.5, *road* 687.2
rings Sporting Activities 145
ring-shaped *curvilinear* 6.78, *circular* 631.5
ringside seat *place for viewing* 242.13, *near place* 586.3
ring spot *pests and diseases* 17.12, *tree disease* 43.8
ring the bell *give warning* 814.10, *attain one's goal* 845.13, *be effective* 845.15
ring the changes *change* 665.14, *be changeable* 666.5, *be diverse* 732.10
ring the church bells *signal* 183.18
ringtoss Children's and Party Games 167
ring true *seem true* 721.26
ring up *telephone* 169.20
ring with the praises of *meet with approval* 437.20
ringworm *fungal disease* 47.6, *skin disease* 114.16
ringy-dingy [Inf] *telephone call* 169.11
rink *sports ground* 145.2, *hockey areas* 158.2
rinky-dink [Inf] *insignificant* 745.6, *cheap* 800.16
rinse *bathe* 111.18, *coif* 530.15, *hose* 557.33
rinsing *ablutions* 111.4, *washing* 557.11
Rio de Janeiro *other famous world cities* 567.9
riot *fertility* 22.1, *vegetate* 41.21, *confusion* 51.2, *cause confusion* 51.9, *excess* 99.1, *be excessive* 99.9, *fight* 422.9, *violation of the law* 427.2, *disobey* 427.12, *disorder* 507.2, *cause mischief* 507.9, *violence by person* 520.2, *be violent* 520.8, *disruption* 766.7, *be disorderly* 766.22, *commotion* 768.5
rioter *seditionist* 427.7
rioting *violation of the law* 427.2, *disorder* 507.2
riot of color *spectrum* 251.3, *variegation* 263.1
riotous *disorderly* 51.6, 507.6, 766.15, *lawless* 53.26, *excessive* 99.5, *disobedient* 427.10, *dissipated* 456.7, *explosive* 520.6
riotous living *dissipation* 456.2
riotously *confusedly* 51.11, *lawlessly* 53.35, *disobediently* 427.14, *violently* 520.11, *disruptively* 766.26
rip *carpenter* 131.10, *separateness* 753.3, *take apart* 753.16
rip along [Inf] *be swift* 694.10
ripcord *line* 754.5
ripe *adult* 27.11, *of a fruit* 44.8, *old* 653.10, *perfect* 805.8
ripe for marriage *marriageable* 64.17

ripely *maturely* 27.18, *venerably* 653.17
ripen *mature* 27.17, *fruit* 44.9, *soften* 543.14, *season* 654.11, *convert* 670.11, *be converted* 670.12, *perfect* 805.19, *get better* 807.21
ripened *adult* 27.11, *seasoned* 654.9, *perfect* 805.8
ripeness *adulthood* 27.2, *maturity* 27.3, *marriageability* 64.4, *timeliness* 659.1, *completion* 761.2, *perfection* 805.1
ripening *maturing* 27.12
ripe old age *old age* 27.5, *health* 113.1, *elderliness* 653.2
riper years *middle age* 27.4
ripoff [Inf] *foul play* 193.6, *taking away* 477.5, *taking* 477.12, *stolen goods* 479.4, *dishonesty* 479.7, *stolen* 479.12, *purchase* 481.1, *fee* 494.3, *extortion* 496.4, *overcharger* 496.5, *copy* 736.2
rip off [Inf] *swindle* 193.19, *take money away* 477.20, *overcharge* 496.10
ripoff artist [Inf] *overcharger* 496.5
rip off someone's clothes *make nude* 614.19
riposte *countercharge* 332.3, *answer* 334.1, 334.18, *parry* 419.27, *retaliation* 420.1, *retaliate* 420.4
riposte *or* **ripost** *fencing movements* 153.3, *fence* 153.7
rip out *remove* 574.16, *extract* 711.13, *extort* 711.18, *subtract* 749.6
ripped *removed* 574.5
ripping *extortion* 711.6
ripping out *removal* 574.2, *extraction* 711.1
ripple *wave* 10.11, 571.3, *small sound* 233.4, *sound faint* 233.8, *rough thing* 544.2, *be rough* 544.10, *flow* 570.4, *billow* 571.9, *pleat* 637.2, 637.8, *be agitated* 684.21
rippled *rough* 544.5, *furrowed* 638.3
ripple effect *radiation* 703.3
ripple marks *sedimentary rock* 8.34
rippling *rough* 544.5, *flowing* 570.7
ripply *rough* 544.5, *flowing* 570.7
ripsaw *woodworking tool* 131.6
riptide *tide* 571.2
Rip van Winkle *sleeper* 415.7
rise 596.17; *go to war* 76.29, *birth* 264.2, *become visible* 264.13, *be active* 414.18, *show respect* 435.16, *be light* 539.8, *lighten* 539.9, *tower over* 569.7, *wave* 571.3, *billow* 571.9, *grow* 581.17, *height* 596.1, *be vertical* 602.8, *be in motion* 677.14, *advance* 679.3, *press on* 679.9, *ascent* 713.1, *ascendancy* 713.5, *ascend* 713.19, *upturn* 713.20, *arise* 715.15, *spread* 746.3, *increase* 746.6, *uplift* 807.2, *get better* 807.21
rise above *tower over* 569.7, *exceed* 712.15, *overtake* 744.16
rise above oneself *be unselfish* 443.7
rise above temptation *be virtuous* 447.8
rise and fall *swaying* 378.4, *billow* 571.9
rise and shine *be active* 414.18, *arise* 655.7
rise at the crack of dawn *start early* 657.12
rise early *be busy* 414.19

rise higher *press on* 679.9
rise in arms *subvert* 427.13
rise in price *augment* 467.16, *cost a lot* 496.9, *increase* 746.6
rise in the world *get better* 807.21, *do well* 845.12, *be prosperous* 847.6
riser *step* 713.11
rise to a maximum *increase* 746.6
rise to a peak *increase* 746.6
rise to fame *be prosperous* 847.6
rise to one's feet *show respect* 435.16, *be vertical* 602.8
rise to the occasion *suffice* 97.6, *be the answer* 334.23, *brace oneself* 376.13, *improvise* 396.6, *try* 414.21, *overcome obstacles* 845.14
rise up *revolt* 417.12, *rise* 596.17, *be vertical* 602.8, *ascend* 713.19, *arise* 715.15
rise up! *fight on!* 417.16
rishi *imam* 84.7
risibility *sense of humor* 277.5
risible *humorous* 277.9, *ridiculous* 368.5
rising 596.12, 713.14; *showing respect* 435.7, *financial* 457.6, *costly* 496.7, *influential* 512.8, *leavening* 539.7, *increase* 581.3, *growing* 581.12, *ascending motion* 677.7, *directional* 677.13, *ascent* 713.1, *ascending* 713.13, *steep* 713.15, *raising* 715.1, *improving* 807.14, *successful* 845.8, *prosperous* 847.5
rising air *incline* 713.3
rising and falling *swaying* 378.4
rising current *incline* 713.3
rising damp *seepage* 559.4
rising exchange rate *international finance* 457.2, *currency market* 484.8
rising ground *heights* 596.4, *incline* 713.3
rising pressure *weather data* 9.6
rising prices *or* **costs** *inflationary price* 496.3
rising river *danger signal* 811.5, *forewarning* 814.2
rising star *successful person* 845.6
rising tide *tide* 571.2
rising water *hidden danger* 813.3
risk 841.21; *diagnosis* 107.8, *rash move* 286.4, *questionableness* 333.7, *doubt* 333.19, *experiment* 335.1, *invent* 335.13, *finance* 457.7, *speculate* 480.19, *danger* 811.1, *face danger* 811.12, *endanger* 811.13, *think likely* 838.10, *unreliability* 841.7, *chance* 842.1, *take a chance* 842.14
risk-benefit ratio *diagnosis* 107.8
risked *tested* 335.10
risk-free *trustworthy* 810.17
riskily *imprudently* 286.11, *questionably* 333.22, *inventively* 335.15, *dangerously* 811.14, *unreliably* 841.25
riskiness *imprudence* 286.3, *questionableness* 333.7, *danger* 811.1
risking *gambling* 167.11
risk it *take a chance* 842.14
risktaker *rash move* 286.4
risktaking *chance* 842.1, *game of chance* 842.5
risk-taking *reckless* 286.6
risky *gambling* 167.11, *imprudent* 286.7, *questionable* 333.13, *original* 335.9, *dangerous* 811.7, *unsafe* 811.8, *unreliable* 841.15, *chance* 842.10
risky venture *endangerment* 811.2
risotto *rice* 90.32

risqué *obscene* 112.9, *indecent* 261.8, *profane* 301.10, *offensive* 432.11, *discourteous* 535.7

rissole *fish dish* 90.19, *meat dish* 90.21

ritardando *or* **rit.** *or* **ritardo** Musical Terms and Expression Marks 140

rite *tradition* 1.7, *jurisprudence* 53.13, *ritual* 85.1, *custom* 397.4, *ceremonial* 404.11, *ceremony* 405.3, *formal occasion* 406.4, *deference* 433.4, *performance* 465.2

ritenuto Musical Terms and Expression Marks 140

rite of passage *non-Christian ritual* 85.8, *ceremony* 405.3, *formal occasion* 406.4, *bringing in* 708.4

ritual 85.1; *tradition* 1.7, *act of worship* 83.2, *custom* 397.4, *customary* 397.11, *ceremony* 405.3, *celebrative* 405.9, *formal occasion* 406.4, *formal* 406.6, *ceremonious* 406.7, *performance* 465.2

ritual act *ritual* 85.1

ritual bathing *non-Christian ritual* 85.8

ritual cleansing *non-Christian ritual* 85.8

ritual dancing Dancing Types 135

ritual drama *theater movements* 136.9

ritualism 85.2; *religiousness* 81.2, *formalism* 406.2

ritualist 85.14

ritualistic 85.15; *zealous* 81.22, *ceremonious* 404.23, 406.7

ritualistically *ritually* 85.21, *ceremoniously* 404.38

rituality *ritualism* 85.2

ritualization *ritualism* 85.2

ritualize *perform rites* 85.18, *formalize* 406.9, *fashion* 537.9

ritual killing 30.7; *killing* 30.1

ritually 85.21; *societally* 1.17, *formally* 406.12

ritually clean *clean* 111.13

ritually prepared *clean* 111.13

ritual manual 85.11

ritual music 85.9

ritual observance *ceremony* 405.3

ritual suicide *suicide* 30.8

ritzily [Inf] *grandly* 404.37

ritziness [Inf] *grandeur* 404.10

ritzy [Inf] *grand* 404.22, *opulent* 485.10, *costly* 496.7, *stylish* 537.7

ritzy price [Inf] *costliness* 496.1

rival *hostile person* 63.5, *jealous* 314.5, *be jealous* 314.8, *contender* 422.13, *contending* 422.19, *contend* 422.22, *opponent* 828.10, *discordant* 828.12, *confront* 828.19

rivaling *contending* 422.19

rivalry 422.2; *jealousy* 314.2, *conflict* 828.3

rive *crack* 587.7, *take apart* 753.16

riven *cracked* 587.5, *apart* 753.8

River Constellations 7

river 570.1; *running water* 8.10, *swimming place* 164.9, *limit marker* 620.4, *transportable* 686.7, *waterway* 690.2, *nautical* 690.14, *channel* 691.10

riverbank *river parts* 570.3

riverbed *river parts* 570.3, *base* 601.1

river blindness *tropical disease* 114.10, *blindness* 243.3

river flow *flow* 570.4

river fog *fog* 9.32

riverhead *river parts* 570.3

river horse *pachyderm* 35.15

riverine *coastal* 8.54, *riverlike* 570.6

river island *island* 572.2

riverlike 570.6

river mouth *river parts* 570.3

river network *running water* 8.10

River of Fire *evil place* 446.6

River of Forgetfulness *evil place* 446.6

river of time *duration* 642.1

River of Wailing *evil place* 446.6

River of Woe *evil place* 446.6

river parts 570.3

rivers Phobias 283

riverscape *type of painting* 143.5

river's end *river parts* 570.3

riverside *river parts* 570.3, *edge* 618.1, *edging* 618.5, *side* 623.1

rivers of Hades *evil place* 446.6

river system *river* 570.1

river travel *water transportation* 690.1

river turbulence 570.5

river valley *landform* 8.9

rivet *superstructure* 551.7, *joint* 752.7, *link* 752.18, *fastener* 754.7, *connect* 754.13

riveted *connected* 754.11

riveter *person who joins* 752.9

rivulet *river* 570.1

Riyadh Countries 566

riyal *national coins* 484.11

RNA *genetic material* 13.20

roach *insect* 40.1

roach [Inf] *drug dose* 121.15, *remainder* 750.1

road 687.2, 691.4; *route* 691.2, *thoroughfare* 692.6, *means of connection* 754.4

road attribute 687.3

roadbed *rail* 688.3

roadblock 826.4; *deterrence* 179.2, *barrier* 419.10, *obstruction* 584.2

road circuit *automobile racing terms* 146.3

roadholding *miscellaneous automotive terms* 687.14

road junction *crossroads* 609.4

road map *map* 187.5, 387.7

road name *place of residence* 209.4

road race *race* 146.10

road reflector *reflector* 242.10

road report *weather forecast* 9.4

road show *show* 138.4

road-show entertaining 138.12

roadside *near* 586.6, *edge* 618.1, *edging* 618.5

roadside alphabet Children's and Party Games 167

roadside café *eating place* 92.17

roadside café *stall* 483.9

road sign *sign* 183.1, *indicator* 183.7

roadster *saddle horse* 159.5, *automobile* 687.6

road surface *paving* 613.14

road system *road* 687.2

road test *rehearsal* 335.2, *miscellaneous automotive terms* 687.14

road-test *rehearse* 335.12

road to hell *wicked place* 448.8, *deterioration* 808.1

road to ruin *danger* 811.1

road transport *road transportation* 687.1

road transportation 687.1; *transportation* 686.1

road vehicle 687.4; *means of transportation* 686.7

road worker *laborer* 123.9

roadworthy *transferable* 685.7, *transportable* 686.7

roam *move* 677.15, *be foreign* 724.13, *be independent* 829.18

roaming *foreign* 724.9

roan *horse by color* 159.7, *brown* 256.5, *mottled* 263.10

Roanoke Rivers 570

roar *blow* 9.53, *overact* 136.35, *emphasize* 200.6, *speak in a particular way* 205.18, *tumult* 232.5, *be loud* 232.8, *cry* 239.1, *cry out* 239.13, *animal sound* 240.1, *make an animal sound* 240.7, *laugh* 277.12, *vent one's anger* 302.21, *be active* 414.18, *be violent* 520.8

roaring *tumult* 232.5, *vociferous* 239.9, *burst of anger* 302.6, *violent* 520.5

roaring drunk *drunk* 121.25

roaring forties *wind system* 9.15, *air flow* 558.4, *world region* 564.6

roaring trade *prosperity* 847.1

Roaring Twenties Ages, Decades, Eras 641

roar one's approval *acclaim* 437.18

roast *meat dish* 90.21, *cook* 91.10, *heat* 217.17, *bake* 560.19

roast [Inf] *ridicule* 436.22, *berate* 438.20

roast alive *murder* 30.20

roasted *culinary* 91.9, *heated* 217.15

roasted [Inf] *criticized* 438.14

roaster *livestock* 16.11

roasting *cooking technique* 91.2, *heating* 217.12

roasting [Inf] *criticism* 438.4, *berating* 438.5

roasting pan *cooking equipment* 91.6

roast turkey *notable international dishes* 90.40

rob *conquer* 77.36, *take away* 275.13, *disobey* 427.12, *be wicked* 448.13, *sin* 450.11, *lose* 468.12, *steal* 479.14, *impoverish* 486.16, *weaken* 517.13

rob a grave *plunder* 479.16

robbed *impoverished* 486.11

robber *lawbreaker* 53.15, *criminal* 427.6, *coercer* 428.4, *villain* 448.5, *gainer* 467.9, *raider* 477.10, *thief* 479.8

robber crab *crustacean* 39.10

robbers Phobias 283

robbery *violation of the law* 427.2, *wicked act* 448.7, *loss* 468.1, *theft* 479.2

robbing *stealing* 479.1

robbing the till *stealing* 479.1

robe 100.20; *clothe* 100.43, *body covering* 613.3

robed *dressed* 100.38, *protected* 613.20, *at ease* 819.2

robe-de-chambre [Fr] *robe* 100.20

robes *vestment* 84.11, *clothing* 100.1, *formal clothing* 406.5

robes of office *insignia* 184.5

robin *red thing* 257.3

Robin Hood *philanthropist* 307.5

robin's-egg blue *blue* 261.5

Robinson Crusoe Notable Friendships 62

roble Trees and Shrubs 43

rob of freedom *subject* 432.10

rob of life *kill* 30.19

roborant *tonic* 115.8

robot *humanlike machine* 18.12, *machinery* 103.5, *figure* 187.4

robotic *mechanical* 103.7, *productive* 522.11

robotics *computing* 15.2, *artificial*

intelligence 15.21, *manufacture* 522.2

rob Peter to pay Paul *exchange* 673.5, *equalize* 740.12

Robson, Mount Mountains and Hills 569

rob the till *steal* 479.14

robust *of good constitution* 113.5, *physically strong* 516.10, *vigorous* 518.2, *stalwart* 547.10

robusta coffee *coffee* 93.6

robust health *health* 113.1

robustly *strongly* 516.17, *stalwartly* 547.17

robustness *health* 113.1, *vigor* 518.1, *stalwartness* 547.3

roc Legendary Creatures 360

roche moutonnée *glacier* 8.44

Rock Breeds of Fowl 16, Rivers 570

rock 8.30; *sediment* 8.29, *blunt weapon* 78.5, *beat time* 140.29, *painting* 143.3, *mountaineering* 161.9, *calm* 521.8, *solid body* 540.4, *hard substance* 542.3, *hard* 542.5, *be changeable* 666.5, *stagger* 684.11, *pitch* 684.25, *unbalance* 741.8, *refuge* 812.1, *hidden danger* 813.3

rock [Inf] *stimulants* 121.18

rockabilly *rock music* 140.6

rock and roll *or* **rock-'n'-roll** *rock music* 140.6

rock band *instrumental group* 141.3

rock bottom *base* 601.1, *inferior state* 745.3, *zero level* 786.3

rock-bottom *bargain* 497.10, *lower* 597.14, *deeper* 598.10, *bottom* 601.6

rock-bound *coarse* 544.6

rock carving *sculpture* 144.1

rock-climb *mountaineer* 161.10

rock climber *mountaineer* 161.8, *ascender* 713.12

rock climbing Sporting Activities 145, *mountaineering* 161.1

rock cress Flowers 42

rock crusher *pulverizer* 553.11

rock crystal *glass* 249.5

rock cycle *petrogenesis* 8.31

Rockefeller *wealthy person* 485.6

rocker *sailboard parts* 150.20, *ice-skating techniques* 162.16, *oscillator* 683.7

rocker *or* **rocking** *type of chair* 101.4

rockery *ornamental garden* 17.3

rocket *engine type* 14.11, *modern missile weapon* 78.4, *signal* 183.6, *fire* 246.9, *cost a lot* 496.9, *means of propulsion* 696.2, *missile* 696.7, *ascender* 713.12, *go up* 713.23, *increase* 746.6

rocket bomb *bomb* 78.15

rocket fuel *gas* 106.6, *propellant* 696.9

rocketing *costly* 496.7, *leaping* 713.17

rocketing up *taking off* 713.6

rocket launcher *modern missile weapon* 78.4

rocket pilot *space traveler* 563.10

rocket power *type of power* 514.6

rocket propulsion *rocketry* 7.32

rocketry 7.32

rocket site *modern missile weapon* 78.4

rock face 161.6

rock fall *mass movement* 8.28

rock formation *rock* 8.30

rock-forming *mineral types* 8.38

rock-forming mineral *rock* 8.30

rock garden *garden* 17.2, *ornamental garden* 17.3
rock group *team* 59.9, *instrumental group* 141.3
rock-hard *strong-willed* 376.10, *hard* 542.5, 547.8
Rockies, the *regions of the United States* 564.7, *Mountains and Hills* 569
rockily *continentally* 572.13
rockiness *hardness* 542.1, *changeableness* 666.1
rocking *swaying* 378.4, *unbalanced* 741.5
rocking an empty rocking chair *bad-luck sign* 358.7
rocking chair *oscillator* 683.7
Rockingham ware *Ceramics* 129
rocking horse *toy* 167.9, *oscillator* 683.7
rocking stone *oscillator* 683.7
rock jasmine *Flowers* 42
rocklike *hard* 542.5, *unfailing* 667.3, *stable* 674.3
rock mechanics *civil engineering* 14.17
rock music 140.6
Rock of Ages *refuge* 812.1
Rock of Gibraltar *refuge* 812.1
rock oil *petroleum* 562.5
rock opera *musical drama* 136.5
rock paper scissors *Children's and Party Games* 167
rock plant *garden plant* 17.10
rock rose *Flowers* 42
rocks [Inf] *organs of reproduction* 21.9
rocks ahead *danger signal* 811.5
rock the boat *not conform* 782.18
rock to sleep *calm* 521.8
rock tripe *lichen* 47.16
rock unit *rock* 8.30
rocky *earthy* 8.60, *hard* 542.5, *coarse* 544.6, *changeable* 666.3
rocky coast *coast* 572.4
Rocky Mountains *Mountains and Hills* 569
Rocky Mountain school *Western Art Styles* 133
Rocky Mountain states *regions of the United States* 564.7
rococo *Furniture Styles* 101, *Architectural Styles* 134, *ornate* 532.10
rococo art *Western Art Styles* 133
rod *machine element* 14.8, *eye* 19.9, 242.3, *fishing tackle* 154.7, *instrument of punishment* 454.13, *General Units* 589, *narrow place* 593.2, *cylinder* 633.4
rod [Inf] *firearm* 78.7
rod brake *bicycle part* 687.11
rodent *type of animal* 34.5, *gnawing mammal* 35.13
Rodentia *gnawing mammal* 35.13
rodentian *rodentlike* 35.28
rodenticide *pest control* 16.13, *killing agent* 30.15, *poison* 117.7
rodentlike 35.28
rodeo *assembling* 59.12, *circus* 138.2, *Sporting Activities* 145, *equestrianism* 159.8, *sporting event* 422.6
rodeo rider *horse person* 159.14
rodomontade *address* 209.1
rods *Phobias* 283
rod-shaped *spherical* 6.80
roe *fish characteristic* 38.8, *fish dish* 90.19
roebuck *male mammal* 35.18
roebucks *Collective Names* 59
roe deer *Collective Names* 59
roentgen *Scientific and Technical Units* 589

Roentgen rays *Classical Physical Laws* 10
rogation *prayer* 85.10
roger [Brit inf] *have sex* 20.21
roger! [Inf] *yes!* 189.36
rogering [Brit inf] *sexual intercourse* 20.9
Rogers's process scale *Psychological Tests* 108
rogue *horse* 159.1, *malefactor* 306.6, *disreputable character* 371.2, *miscreant* 448.6
roguery *wickedness* 448.1
rogues' gallery *portrait* 132.5
rogue wave *wave* 571.3
roguish *wicked* 448.9
roil *dirty* 112.11, *opaque* 250.7, *swirl* 682.16, *turbulence* 684.3, *agitate* 684.22, *disarrange* 768.11
roiled *disarranged* 768.7
roister *rejoice* 279.5, *be disorderly* 766.22
roisterer *rejoicer* 279.3
roistering *rejoicing* 279.1
role 136.23; *state* 725.1, *participation* 760.10
role model *mode of behavior* 399.2
role-play *act* 136.34, 187.13
role-playing *psychotherapy* 108.4, *acting* 136.22, 187.6, *mode of behavior* 399.2
role theory *sociological research* 2.2
roll 682.15; *cloud* 9.54, *manage grassland* 45.10, *bread* 90.10, *smoke* 121.38, *handle sailboat equipment* 150.30, *record book* 185.5, *loud sound* 232.2, *undercurrent of sound* 233.3, *drumming* 235.1, *drum* 235.10, *smooth* 545.10, *go smoothly* 545.11, *wave* 571.3, *billow* 571.9, *piece* 590.2, 760.2, *convolute* 632.6, *make round* 633.9, *be changeable* 666.5, *maneuver* 677.18, 689.14, *forward motion* 679.1, *go forward* 679.8, *reel* 682.4, *stagger* 684.11, *pitch* 684.25, *travel by train* 688.9, *flight maneuver* 689.6, *fly* 689.13, *propel* 696.15, *deviating motion* 698.3, *list of names* 785.7, *go easily* 823.18
roll along *roll* 682.15
roll a slab *make ceramics* 129.10
rollback *limitation* 747.3
roll back *make smaller* 747.8
roll bar *racing automobile* 146.2
roll book *record book* 185.5
roll by *pass* 639.13
roll cage *racing automobile* 146.2
roll call *nomenclature* 202.7, *list of names* 785.7
rolled *uniform* 545.5, *leveled* 603.8
rolled homogeneous armor *modern armor* 419.7
rolled into one *whole* 788.12
rolled out *thinned* 595.13
rolled steel *construction material* 14.21
rolled steel joist (RSJ) *superstructure* 551.7
rolled-up *squeezed* 582.9
roller *wave* 8.16, 571.3, *garden tool* 103.4, *smoother* 545.2, *pulverizer* 553.11, *flattener* 603.4, *cylinder* 633.4
roller bandage *line* 754.5
roller bearing *machine element* 14.8, *axle* 682.7
roller blind *shade maker* 247.4
roller coaster *amusement park and playground equipment* 167.8
roller derby *Sporting Activities* 145

roller hockey *Sporting Activities* 145
roller-reefed *sailing* 150.25
roller skates *means of transportation* 686.2
roller skating *Sporting Activities* 145
Rolle's theorem *Mathematical Concepts* 6
roll film *film* 132.8
roll in [Inf] *abound* 97.8, *be profitable* 467.21, *come together* 702.10
rolling *drumming* 235.6, *hilly* 569.6, *oceanic* 571.7, *of landmasses* 572.12, *turning* 682.3, *rotating* 682.11, *turbulence* 684.3, *turbulent* 684.17, *flight maneuver* 689.6, *flying* 689.11, *nautical* 690.14
rolling [Inf] *wealthy* 485.8
rolling friction *force* 10.9, *friction* 554.1
rolling hitch *Knots, Bends, Hitches, Splices* 754
rolling in [Inf] *full* 761.8
rolling in it [Inf] *well-off* 467.12, *wealthy* 485.8, *prosperous* 847.5
rolling in money [Inf] *wealthy* 485.8
rolling on *forward motion* 679.1
rolling pin *cooking equipment* 91.6, *flattener* 603.4, *cylinder* 633.4
rolling stock *railroad system* 688.1
rolling the jack *bowls* 151.7
rolling tobacco *tobacco* 121.23
roll in it [Inf] *be prosperous* 847.6
roll in money [Inf] *be rich* 485.12
roll in the aisles *laugh* 274.17
roll in the dirt *or* **mud** *be dirty* 112.10
roll into one *be indiscriminate* 338.10, *unify* 752.15
rollmop *fish dish* 90.19
roll of cloud *cloud appearance* 9.19
roll on *pass* 639.13, *protract* 669.9, *go forward* 679.8, *march on* 679.11
roll-on roll-off *Ships and Boats* 690
rollout *play* 155.8, *flight* 689.5
roll out *play offense* 155.18, *demonstrate* 331.15, *make thin* 595.17, *make horizontal* 603.10
roll out the red carpet *salute* 405.13, 435.17
roll the jack *bowl* 151.8
roll-top *type of desk* 101.6
roll up *save* 105.20, *squeeze* 582.13, *become smaller* 582.14, *make round* 633.9, *roll* 682.15, *come together* 702.10, *arrive* 704.13
roll up into a ball *squeeze* 582.13, *become smaller* 582.14
roll up one's sleeves *work* 122.8, *prepare oneself* 388.21
roll-your-own *tobacco* 121.23, 121.33
roly-poly *big person* 579.10, *fat* 579.15
Romagna *Breeds of Cattle* 16, *Breeds of Pigs* 16
Romagnola *Breeds of Cattle* 16
Roman *denominational* 81.23, *historic* 653.13
roman *printed* 173.13
roman [Fr] *novel* 139.3
roman à clef [Fr] *novel* 139.3
Roman architecture *Architectural Styles* 134
Roman calendar *calendar* 646.3
Roman candle *fire* 246.9
Roman Catholic *Christian* 81.10, *denominational* 81.23

Roman Catholicism *Christian Groups* 81, *Christianity* 81.5
romance *movie type* 137.3, *novel* 139.3, *Musical Forms* 140, *romantic love* 299.2, *love affair* 299.9, *conception* 360.4, *reverie* 360.6
romance [Inf] *court* 299.26
romancer *author* 139.13, *visionary* 360.9
romancing *imaginative* 360.10
Roman collar *neckwear* 100.29
Roman comedy *historic comedy* 136.12
Roman eagle *national emblem* 184.7
Romanesque *historic* 653.13
Romanesque architecture *Architectural Styles* 134
Romanesque art *Western Art Styles* 133
Romanesque Revival *Architectural Styles* 134
roman-fleuve [Fr] *novel* 139.3
Roman holiday *slaughter* 30.5
Romania *Countries* 566
Romanian Brown *Breeds of Cattle* 16
Romanian Red *Breeds of Cattle* 16
Romanian Simmental *Breeds of Cattle* 16
Romanian Steppe *Breeds of Cattle* 16
Roman numeral *numeral* 6.8, *number* 783.1
Roman orgy *feast* 92.9
Romanov *Breeds of Sheep* 16
romantic *dramatic* 136.31, 137.16, *literary* 139.15, *fictional* 139.16, *musical* 140.25, *fabricated* 192.17, *narrative* 202.12, *sensitive* 267.3, *amorous* 299.18, *ideal* 327.12, *visionary* 360.9, *imaginative* 360.10, *unrealistic person* 720.6, *unrealistic* 720.11
romantically *dramatically* 136.38, *amorously* 299.30, *imaginatively* 327.21, 360.17
romantic ballet *ballet* 135.2
romantic comedy *comedy* 136.11
romanticism *Western Art Styles* 133, *Western Literary Groups* 139, *emotionalism* 266.6, *lovingness* 299.4, *idealism* 327.7, *reverie* 360.6
romanticist *visionary* 360.9
romanticize *fabricate* 192.24, *recount* 202.16, *imagine* 327.14, *fantasize* 360.15, *idealize* 720.15
romanticized *fabricated* 192.17
romanticized version *falsehood* 192.6
romantic lighting *dimness* 248.1
romantic love 299.2
romantic music *classical music* 140.2
romantic poet *author* 139.13
romantic tie *love affair* 299.9
romantic tragedy *tragedy* 136.10
roman type *type* 173.5
Romany *diviner* 86.14
Rome *Apple Varieties* 44, *Countries* 566, *other famous world cities* 567.9
Rome Beauty *Apple Varieties* 44
Romeldale *Breeds of Sheep* 16
Romeo *tempter* 178.10, *Famous Lovers* 299, *lover* 299.11
Romney *Breeds of Sheep* 16
Romney Marsh *Breeds of Sheep* 16
romper *suit* 100.16
rompers *baby clothes* 100.24

---

romp home *accelerate* 694.14, *defeat* 845.17

rondeau Poem or Verse Forms 139

rondel *or* **roundel** Poem or Verse Forms 139

rondino Musical Forms 140

rondo Musical Forms 140

rondure *curve* 629.1

rood *sacred object* 83.11, General Units 589

rood screen *church interior* 83.9, *church architecture* 134.11

roof 134.7, 613.30, Architectural Elements 134, *rock face* 161.6, *architectural summit* 600.4, *top* 600.10, *overhead covering* 613.11, *shelter* 812.4

roofed *inhabiting* 60.18, *architectural* 134.12, *topped* 600.8, *covered* 613.19

roofer *artisan* 123.13, *coverer* 613.18, *ascender* 713.12

roof garden *garden* 17.2

roofing *overhead covering* 613.11

roofing tile *industrial ceramics* 129.6

roof ladder *ladder* 713.10

roof over one's head *habitation* 60.2, *shelter* 812.4

rooftop *architectural summit* 600.4, *overhead covering* 613.11

rooftree *figurative usage* 43.9

roof types *roof* 134.7

rook *songbird* 36.12, *board games* 167.3

rookery *dwelling* 36.4, Collective Names 59

rookie *learner* 48.6, *soldier* 77.4, *unskilled person* 128.3, *basketball team* 148.2, *football player* 155.15, *beginner* 398.2, 771.14, *new arrival* 652.7

Rookie of the Year *baseball team* 147.2

rooks Collective Names 59

Rookwood pottery Ceramics 129

room 60.9; *apartment* 60.7, *take up residence* 60.24, Phobias 283, *reserved space* 563.5, *available space* 563.6, *size* 579.1, *interval* 587.1, *inclusion* 763.1, *scope* 829.7

room decoration *interior decoration* 532.4

roomer *resident* 61.6

roomette *railroad car* 688.5

room for improvement *imperfection* 806.1

room freshener *cleaning agent* 111.9

roomful *container(ful)* 738.2

roominess *spaciousness* 563.4, *largeness* 579.2, *breadth* 592.1

rooming house *hotel* 60.12

roommate *resident* 61.6, *friend* 62.2, *companion* 794.8

room overhead *available space* 563.6

rooms *habitation* 60.2, *apartment* 60.7

room temperature *heat* 217.1

room-temperature *hot* 217.11

room to maneuver *available space* 563.6

room to spare *available space* 563.6

room to swing a cat *available space* 563.6

roomy *big* 498.9, 579.13, *airy* 558.12, *spacious* 563.13, *broad* 592.5

Roosevelt, Rio Rivers 570

Roosevelt Island Islands 572

roost *dwelling* 36.4, *cage* 60.15, *natural habitat* 60.16, *take up residence* 60.24, *take it easy* 819.3

rooster *livestock* 16.11, *male animal* 32.15, *male bird* 36.15, *morning things* 655.3

root 41.7; *word* 5.17, *part of speech* 5.30, *worded* 5.38, *equation* 6.25, *vegetate* 41.21, *tree part* 43.2, *moss plant* 46.5, *lichen* 47.16, *basis* 601.3, 605.4, *base* 601.10, *basic* 605.13, *make stable* 674.7, *source* 771.3, *power* 783.6

root and branch *wholly* 759.11, *completely* 759.14

root beer *soft drink* 93.8

root canal work *dentistry* 107.6

rootcap *root* 41.7

root cellar *storeroom* 105.7

root crop *crop* 16.8

rooted *of roots* 41.19, *fixed* 397.13, *basic* 605.13, *olden* 653.11, *stabilized* 674.4, *tied* 752.13

rootedness *stability* 674.1

rooted to the spot *frightened* 283.9, *wondering* 294.7, *stabilized* 674.4, *motionless* 678.4

rooter *crier* 239.8

root for *cheer* 239.15, *motivate* 508.9, *invigorate* 518.5

root hair *root* 41.7

rooting out *extraction* 711.1

rootless *stateless* 574.14, *changeable* 666.3

rootlet *root* 41.7

rootlike *of roots* 41.19

rootlike part *root* 41.7

root mean square (rms) *multiplication* 6.15

root mean square (rms) value *measurement* 10.67

root nodule *root* 41.7

root of dissension *rivalry* 422.2

root out *exterminate* 709.22, *extract* 711.13, *subtract* 749.6, *remove* 574.16

root rot *pests and diseases* 17.12

roots *fruits* 44.1

rootstock *plant breeding* 17.6, *stem* 41.5, *root* 41.7, *fern plant* 46.2

root tuber *root* 41.7

root up *destroy* 523.10, *remove* 574.16

root vegetable *vegetable* 17.11, 90.33

root vegetables *fruits* 44.1

rope *murder weapon* 30.3, *hand tool* 103.3, *fiber* 104.3, *wrestling terms* 152.10, *climbing equipment* 161.4, *instrument of execution* 454.15, *line* 754.5, *tackle* 754.6, *safety device* 810.15

rope [Inf] *hemp derivatives* 121.16

rope and pulley *lifter* 715.5

rope bridge *bridge* 551.10, 691.7

roped *tied* 752.13

ropedancer *or* **ropewalker** *circus performer* 138.9

roped travel (glacier) *climbing techniques* 161.3

rope ladder *ladder* 713.10

rope out *limit* 830.13

ropes *boxing terms* 152.3

rope's end *instrument of punishment* 454.13

rope together *link* 752.18

rope tow *ski run* 162.2

ropiness *doughiness* 561.2

ropy *condensed* 540.7, *viscous* 561.14

ropy lava *eruption* 8.27

Rorschach test Psychological Tests 108

Rosa, Monte Mountains and Hills 569

rosaceous *taxonomic* 41.16

Rosalind Planets and Their Satellites 7, Famous Lovers 299

rosaniline *red pigment* 257.2

rosarian *horticulturist* 17.13

rosarium *ornamental garden* 17.3

rosary *ornamental garden* 17.3

rosary beads *sacred object* 83.11

Roscius [Arch] *actor* 136.25

Roscommon Breeds of Sheep 16

rose *garden tool* 17.7, Flowers 42, *red thing* 257.3, *navigational aid* 690.6

roseate *red* 257.5

Roseau Countries 566

rose bed *ornamental garden* 17.3

Rose Bowl *football* 155.1

rose-colored *red* 257.5, *cheering* 281.9

rose-colored glasses *hope* 281.1

rose family *seed plant* 41.3

rose grower *horticulturist* 17.13

rose growing *horticulture* 17.1

rose madder *red pigment* 257.2

rosemary Herbs and Spices 91

rose of China Flowers 42

rose of Sharon Flowers 42

roseola *infection* 114.7

rose-pink *red* 257.5

rose-red *red* 257.5

rose-tinted view *hope* 281.1

rosette *figurative usage* 42.8, Architectural Elements 134, *insignia* 184.5

rose water *lavender water* 557.14

rose window *figurative usage* 42.8, *church architecture* 134.11

rosé wine *wine* 93.11

rosewood Trees and Shrubs 43

Rosh Hashanah Jewish Holy Days and Seasons 85

Rosh Hodesh *or* **Rosh Chodesh** Jewish Holy Days and Seasons 85

Rosicrucian *occultist* 86.13, *occult* 86.16

Rosicrucianism *occultism* 86.1

rosily *ruddily* 257.10

rosin *gymnastics equipment* 157.2, *resin* 562.6, *resinify* 562.16

Rosinante Notable Horses 159

rosiness *health* 113.1, *redness* 257.1

rosiny *resinous* 562.13

Ross Sea Oceans and Seas 571

roster *baseball team* 147.2, *basketball team* 148.2, *list of names* 785.7

rostrum *stage* 136.18, *publicity* 173.7

rosy *healthy* 113.4, *red* 257.5, *red-faced* 257.6, *cheering* 281.9, *appealing* 529.10, *prosperous* 847.5

rosy-cheeked *healthy* 113.4, *red-faced* 257.6

rosy cheeks *health* 113.1, *face color* 251.9

rosy-fingered dawn *morning* 655.2

rot *vector* 6.48, *be infertile* 23.8, *tree disease* 43.8, *fungus* 47.1, *mold* 47.22, *uncleanness* 112.2, *dirt* 112.5, *be dirty* 112.10, *ulcer* 114.18, *afflict* 117.16, *nonsense* 192.8, *senseless talk* 362.4, *be transient* 643.6, *grow old* 653.16, *disintegration* 758.1, *disintegrate* 758.6, *decay* 808.6, 808.16, *eat away* 808.19

rot! *nonsense!* 362.14

rota *series* 770.3, *list of names* 785.7

rota [Brit] *cycle* 663.3

rotary 682.5, 682.12; *crossroads* 609.4, *circle* 631.2, *directional* 677.13, *orbital* 681.5, *road attribute* 687.3

rotary beater *cooking equipment* 91.6

rotary drill *rotator* 682.8

rotary mower *farm tool* 16.5, *garden tool* 17.7

rotary pump *surface chemistry* 11.20

rotary telephone *telephone* 169.10

rotate 682.14; *represent* 6.91, *observe* 7.34, *flow* 570.10, *circle* 631.6, *be cyclic* 663.11, *be in motion* 677.14, *orbit* 681.8

rotate around *center* 512.10

rotating 682.11; *cyclic* 663.7, *orbiting* 681.7

rotating air mass *wind vortex* 9.14

rotating asymmetric foil (RAF) *sailboard parts* 150.20

rotation 682.1; *transformation* 6.46, *orbit* 7.22, *snowplow* 162.29, *hammer throwing* 166.14, *operation of symmetry* 626.2, *cycle* 663.3, *movement* 677.3, *orbital motion* 681.1, *series* 770.3, *continuum* 774.5

rotational *windsurfing* 150.28, *cyclic* 663.7, *directional* 677.13, *rotary* 682.12

rotational axis *orbit* 7.22

rotational motion *rotation* 682.1

rotational period *orbit* 7.22

rotational sail *sailboard parts* 150.20

rotational symmetry *geometric figure* 6.39, *operation of symmetry* 626.2

rotation axis *operation of symmetry* 626.2

rotation-inversion axis *operation of symmetry* 626.2

rotation turn *skiing techniques* 162.5

rotative *cyclic* 663.7, *rotary* 682.12

rotator 682.8

rotatory *directional* 677.13, *rotating* 682.11, *rotary* 682.12

rote *habituation* 397.7

rotenone *poison* 117.7

rotgut [Inf] *alcoholic drink* 93.9, *alcohol* 121.5

rotor *rotator* 682.8, *propeller* 696.8

rototill *farm* 16.19, *cultivate* 17.19

rototiller *or* **rotary tiller** *farm tool* 16.5, *garden tool* 17.7

rotta *or* **rote** Musical Instruments 142

Rottaler Horse and Pony Breeds 159

rotted *unclean* 112.8, *disintegrated* 758.3

rotten *botanical* 17.15, *fungal* 47.18, *of disease* 114.25, *unhygienic* 114.27, *unpalatable* 223.6, *putrid* 227.4, *evil* 446.7, *depraved* 448.10, *villainous* 448.12, *dilapidated* 517.7, *disintegrated* 758.3, *spoiled* 808.9

rotten egg *unpleasant-smelling thing* 227.2

rotten luck *luck* 842.3, *bad fortune* 848.7

rottenness *unpalatability* 223.2, *evil* 446.1, *decay* 808.6

rotten to the core *depraved* 448.10, *impenitent* 452.2

rotter [Brit inf] *miscreant* 448.6

Rotter incomplete sentences blank Psychological Tests 108

rotting *unclean* 112.8, *of disease* 114.25, *putrid* 227.4, *disintegrating* 758.5
Rottweiler Breeds of Dogs 35
rotund *fat* 579.15, *thick* 594.5, *circular* 631.5, *round* 633.7
rotunda Architectural Elements 134
rotundity *fatness* 579.5, *thickness* 594.1, *circularity* 631.1, *roundness* 633.1
rotundly *circularly* 631.8, *roundly* 633.11
roué *sexually immoral person* 432.8
rouge *red pigment* 257.2, *redden* 257.9, *cosmetics* 530.4
rouged *red-faced* 257.6
Rouge de l'Ouest Breeds of Cattle 16
rouge et noir Card Games 168
rough 544.5, 547.11, 552.8, 554.11, 824.10; *stormy* 9.45, *combatant* 77.1, *combative* 77.32, *golf course* 156.2, *unpalatable* 223.6, *hoarse* 238.5, *cruel* 306.10, *experimental* 335.8, *unformed* 389.11, *discourteous* 411.5, *violent* 520.5, *plain* 528.9, *rough idea* 544.4, *make rough* 544.11, *roughly* 544.13, *irregular* 664.3, *turbulent* 684.17, *incomplete* 762.5, *discontinuous* 775.7
roughage *animal feed* 16.12, *food content* 90.3
rough air *roughness* 544.1
rough-and-ready *bungled* 128.7, *unfinished* 544.9, *useful* 801.5, *incomplete* 806.6, *hasty* 818.3
rough-and-tumble *fight* 422.9, *disruption* 766.7, *hasty* 818.3
rough approximation *rough idea* 544.4
rough breathing Accents and Diacritical Marks 5
roughcast *rough* 544.5, *make rough* 544.11
rough copy *rough idea* 544.4
rough draft *rehearsal* 335.2, *map* 387.7, *rough idea* 544.4
rough edge *roughness* 544.1, *nonachievement* 762.3
rough-edged *coarse* 544.6
rough edge of one's tongue *berating* 438.5
roughen *make rough* 544.11, *coarsen* 552.12
roughened *rough* 544.5
roughen up *make rough* 544.11
Rough Fell Breeds of Sheep 16
rough fiber *roughness* 544.1
rough going *difficult task* 824.3
rough-going *rough* 824.10
rough-grained *coarse* 544.6
rough ground *roughness* 544.1, *rough thing* 544.2, *difficult task* 824.3
rough guess *conjecture* 359.3
rough hair *roughness* 544.1
rough handling *treatment* 399.11, *violence* 520.1
rough-hew *lay the foundations* 388.16, *make rough* 544.11, *form* 624.9
rough-hewn *unformed* 389.11, *rough* 544.5, *incomplete* 762.5
roughhouse *disruption* 766.7
rough idea 544.4
roughing *ice hockey tactics* 158.4
roughing the kicker *penalty* 155.13
roughing the passer *penalty* 155.13
roughly 544.13, 547.18; *cruelly* 306.17, *discourteously* 411.8,

vulgarly 535.10, *texturally* 552.15, *abrasively* 554.17, *nearly* 586.18, *irregularly* 664.6, *on average* 742.10, *incompletely* 762.10
roughly speaking *on average* 742.10
rough measure *measurement* 589.1
roughneck *villain* 448.5
roughness 544.1; *stimulation* 221.4, *hoarseness* 238.2, *cruelty* 306.4, *immaturity* 389.3, *discourtesy* 411.1, *violence* 520.1, *impropriety* 528.2, *grain* 552.2, *friction* 554.1, *irregularity* 664.1, *incompleteness* 762.1, *discontinuity* 775.1
rough out *illustrate* 187.11, *describe* 202.15, *be unfinished* 544.12, *outline* 617.5, *form* 624.9, *not complete* 762.9
rough patch *time of adversity* 848.8
roughrider *horse person* 159.14
rough road *rough thing* 544.2
rough sea *wave* 571.3
rough shooting Sporting Activities 145
rough sketch *nonachievement* 762.3
rough skin 544.3; *roughness* 544.1
rough surface *roughness* 544.1
rough terrain *difficult task* 824.3
rough texture *roughness* 544.1
rough the kicker *exhibit penalty behavior* 155.21
rough the passer *exhibit penalty behavior* 155.21
rough thing 544.2
rough up *make rough* 544.11, *coarsen* 552.12
rough water *roughness* 544.1, *wave* 571.3
rough weather *natural violence* 520.3
roulette Board and Table Games 167
roulette bet *gambling* 167.4
roulette wheel *wheel* 682.9
round 633.6, 633.7; *curvilinear* 6.78, *ammunition* 78.11, *beef* 90.24, *drink* 121.6, *song* 140.11, *sports* 145.1, *boxing terms* 152.3, *wrestling terms* 152.10, *golf* 156.1, *bang* 234.1, *way* 397.3, *prize competition* 422.5, *graceful* 527.4, *fluid* 527.5, *fashion* 536.7, *blunt* 550.9, *region* 564.1, *fat* 579.15, *thick* 594.5, *form* 624.9, *curved* 629.4, *circular* 631.5, 681.6, *make circular* 631.7, *well-rounded* 633.8, *period of activity* 641.4, *cycle* 663.3, *route* 691.2, *passing along* 692.5, *step* 713.11, *equal* 740.8, *part* 760.1, *continuum* 774.5, *numerical* 783.7, *return* 797.4
roundabout *phrased* 5.39, *circumlocutory* 199.4, *equivocal* 380.5, *divergent* 607.7, *indirect* 607.8, 698.9
roundabout [Brit] *reel* 682.4, *road attribute* 687.3
round about *geographically* 573.11
roundaboutness *circuitousness* 681.2
roundabout phrase *phrasing* 5.25, *circumlocution* 199.2
roundabout way *circle* 631.2
round and round *cyclically* 663.15, *changeably* 666.7
round angle *angle* 6.37
round as a ball *round* 633.7
roundboard *sailboard parts* 150.20
round body 633.2

round dancing Dancing Types 135
round down *add* 6.86
rounded 629.5; *phrased* 5.39, *curvilinear* 6.78, *arch* 134.5, *architectural* 134.12, *deep* 236.8, *uniform* 545.5, *blunt* 550.5, *formed* 624.6, *circular* 631.5, *equal* 740.8
rounded out *well-rounded* 633.8
rounded up *assembled* 59.18
roundelay Poem or Verse Forms 139, *song* 140.11
rounders [Brit] Sporting Activities 145
round-faced *fat* 579.15
round-heeled [Inf] *unchaste* 432.10
roundheels [Inf] *sexually immoral person* 432.8
rounding *orbital motion* 681.1
rounding down *division* 6.16
rounding off *division* 6.16, *conclusion* 761.3
rounding out *maturing* 27.12
rounding up *division* 6.16, *sailing terms* 150.5
rounding up or **down** *equalization* 740.4
roundly 633.11; *smoothly* 550.10, *fatly* 579.22, *curvedly* 629.7, *circularly* 631.8, *swiftly* 694.16, *equitably* 740.15
roundness 633.1; *bluntness* 550.1, *fatness* 579.5, *thickness* 594.1, *curve* 629.1, *circularity* 631.1
round of applause *acknowledgment* 310.3
round of drinks *drink* 121.6
round off *add* 6.86, *make round* 633.9, *complete* 759.10, 761.9, *end* 773.19
round-off *floor exercise* 157.4
round or **burst of applause** *acclaim* 437.5
round of visits *social gathering* 408.4
round on *strike* 418.21, *retaliate* 420.4
round out *make round* 633.9, *be convex* 634.7
round pace *swiftness* 694.1
round robin *petition* 505.2
round-robin *requesting* 505.7
rounds *orbit* 681.3
round shot *historical ammunition* 78.12
round sum *sum* 484.5
round table *representative body* 79.2, *consultation* 176.4
round-table conference *place for conversation* 210.5
round-table discussion *discussion* 460.3
round thing 633.3
round trip *circle* 631.2, *round* 633.6, *swing* 671.4, *orbit* 681.3
round turn and two half hitches Knots, Bends, Hitches, Splices 754
roundup *assembling* 59.12
round up *add* 6.86, *practice livestock farming* 16.20, *herd* 59.29, *acquire* 467.19
rouse *make irascible* 303.16, *motivate* 508.9, *invigorate* 518.5, *draw out* 711.17
roused *motivated* 508.8
rouse oneself *be active* 414.18
rousing *cheering* 239.10, *motivational* 508.7, *invigorating* 518.3
rousingly *influentially* 508.13
rout Collective Names 59, *tumult*

684.2, *disband* 776.13, *throng* 795.4, *victory* 845.4, *defeat* 845.17, 846.7
route 691.2, Collective Names 59, *direct* 126.11, *climbing expedition* 161.2, *rock face* 161.6, *road* 687.2, *thoroughfare* 692.6, *bearing* 697.2
routed *defeated* 846.11
route-finding *climbing techniques* 161.3
router *communications device* 15.26, *woodworking tool* 131.6
routine *number* 138.5, *predictable* 295.4, *way* 397.3, 399.10, 691.1, *standard procedure* 397.6, *habitual* 397.9, 765.15, *action* 412.1, *performance* 465.2, *regularity* 663.1, 730.6, *cycle* 663.3, *regular* 663.5, 730.12, *cyclic* 663.7, *average* 742.5, 778.4, *method* 765.7, *continuity* 774.4, *common* 778.13, *custom* 780.5, *customary* 780.9, *repetitiveness* 797.3, *monotonous* 797.12
routinely *predictably* 295.9, *frequently* 661.7, *orderly* 663.13, *cyclically* 663.15, *regularly* 730.21, *differentially* 739.9, *prevailingly* 742.11, *methodically* 765.27, *usually* 778.21
routine practice *standard procedure* 397.6
routine procedure *way* 399.10
routinization *organization* 767.3
rout out *drive out* 709.19
roux *sauce* 90.17
rove *go astray* 698.17
roving *changeable* 666.3
roving eye *look* 242.7, *sexual immorality* 432.2
row 150.32; *matrix* 6.20, *farmland* 16.3, *tumult* 232.5, *dissonance* 241.1, *quarrel* 272.4, *argument* 329.1, *activity* 414.1, *fight* 422.23, *conflict* 422.26, *dispute* 463.3, 463.9, *violence by person* 520.2, *level* 588.2, *straight line* 630.2, *fuss* 684.4, *propel* 696.15, *disruption* 766.7
rowan Trees and Shrubs 43
rowboat Ships and Boats 690
rowboat parts 150.15
rowdily *aggressively* 77.38
rowdiness *lawlessness* 766.6
rowdy *combatant* 77.1, *combative* 77.32, *shouting* 232.7, *criminal* 427.6, *disorderly* 766.15
rowel *sharp-pointed thing* 549.4
rower *boating person* 150.24, *nautical person* 690.12
row house *house* 60.4
rowing 150.14, 150.27, Sporting Activities 145, *boating sports* 150.1, *arguing* 329.6, *water transportation* 690.1, *nautical* 690.14
rowing associations 150.17
rowing competitions 150.18
rowing techniques 150.16
row in the same boat *work together* 827.14
rowlock *arch* 134.5, *rowboat parts* 150.15, *axle* 682.7
Roxbury Russet Apple Varieties 44
royal *governing* 49.25, *masterful* 68.15, *majestic* 404.21, *formal* 406.6
Royal Air Force Academy (Cranwell) [Brit] *military training* 58.3
Royal and Ancient Golf Club *golfing associations and tournaments* 156.6

Royal Automobile Club (RAC) [Brit] *racing governing bodies* 146.7

royal-blue *blue* 261.5

royal box *auditorium* 136.17

Royal Canadian Henley Olympic rowing *rowing competitions* 150.18

Royal Canadian Mounted Police *law enforcement agency* 53.7

royal command *command* 425.1

Royal Copenhagen porcelain Ceramics 129

Royal Doulton porcelain Ceramics 129

royal flush *poker* 168.5

royal jelly *tonic* 115.8

royally *masterfully* 68.19, *aristocratically* 70.6, *majestically* 297.21, 404.36, *formally* 406.12, *superiorly* 744.20

Royal Military College (Sandhurst) [Brit] *military training* 58.3

Royal Military College of Canada *military training* 58.3

Royal Naval College (Dartmouth) [Brit] *military training* 58.3

Royal Palm Breeds of Fowl 16

royal poinciana Trees and Shrubs 43

royal road *easy thing* 823.6

royal succession *acquisition of authority* 52.5

royal tennis *tennis* 165.1

royalties *money received* 492.2

royalty *aristocracy* 70.2, *earnings* 467.5, *pay* 489.6, *money received* 492.2

Royal Worcester porcelain Ceramics 129

Royal Yachting Association (RYA) [Brit] *yacht racing associations* 150.7

Rozane art ware Ceramics 129

rozzer [Brit inf] *law enforcement officer* 53.8

RR Lyrae star *variable star* 7.11

RS-ski *ski equipment* 162.10

RSVP *acknowledgment* 334.2

Ruapehu Mountains and Hills 569

rub 554.12; *clean* 111.17, *treat* 115.17, *exertion* 122.4, *work* 122.8, *type of touch* 216.3, *touch* 216.9, *heat* 217.17, *cause to disappear* 265.7, *smooth* 545.10, *friction* 554.1, *meet* 586.15, *critical time* 659.3, *obstacle* 826.2

rub-a-dub *drumming* 235.1

rub against *abrade* 554.13

Rub' al Khali Deserts 572

rubbed out *obliterated* 186.4, *subtracted* 749.3

rubber 546.3, Tree Products 43, *armor-piercing* 78.18, *cleaning tool* 111.10, *bridge* 168.4, *prize competition* 422.5, *destroyer* 523.6, *elastic* 546.5, *make elastic* 546.8, *eraser* 554.7

rubber [Inf] *contraceptive* 23.6

rubber bridge *bridge* 168.4

rubber bullet *ammunition* 78.11

rubber check *false money* 484.15, *bad payment* 490.3

rubber-core ball *golf equipment* 156.5

rubber dinghy *safety device* 810.15

rubber heel *sound reducer* 233.5

rubber hose *instrument of punishment* 454.13

rubberiness *softness* 543.1, *elasticity* 546.1, *chewiness* 547.2

rubberize *make elastic* 546.8

rubberized *elastic* 546.5

rubberlike *elastic* 546.5

rubberneck [Inf] *see* 242.20, *be curious* 321.3

rubbernecker [Inf] *observer* 242.15, *curious person* 321.3

rubbernecking [Inf] *prying* 321.2, *curious* 321.5

rubber plant Trees and Shrubs 43

rubbers *boots* 100.31

rubber sole *sound reducer* 233.5

rubber-soled shoes *shoes* 100.30

rubber stamp *authorization* 52.3, *yes* 346.2, *approval* 437.1, *permit* 502.3

rubber-stamp *assent* 346.6, *approve* 437.14, *agree with* 462.10

rubber tree Trees and Shrubs 43

rubbery *soft* 543.6, *elastic* 546.5, *chewy* 547.9

rubbing *touching* 216.2, *friction* 554.1, *polishing* 554.5, *frictional* 554.10, *meeting* 586.10, *duplicate* 736.4

rubbing against *wearing away* 554.2

rubbing out *obliteration* 186.1, *taking away* 477.5, *subtraction* 749.1

rubbing out *or* **off** *or* **away** *wearing away* 554.2

rubbing out [Inf] *murder* 30.2

rubbing together *wearing away* 554.2

rubbish *waste product* 96.7, *dirt* 112.5, *nonsense* 192.8, *senseless talk* 362.4, *residue* 750.2, *refuse* 802.5

rubbish! *nonsense!* 362.14

rubbish heap *place for waste* 802.6

rubbishy *meaningless* 362.7, *cheap* 800.16, *useless* 802.7

rubble *bits and pieces* 760.5

rubdown *massage* 554.6

rub down *practice livestock farming* 16.20, *smooth* 545.10, *grate* 553.24, *massage* 554.16

rube [Inf] *unskilled person* 128.3, *naive person* 821.2

rubefacient *redness* 257.1

rubefaction *redness* 257.1

rubefy *redden* 257.9

rubella *infection* 114.7

rubeola *infection* 114.7

rubescence *redness* 257.1

rubescent *red-faced* 257.6

rube town [Inf] *village* 567.3

rub gently *massage* 554.16

Rubicon *critical moment* 726.7

rubicund *red-faced* 257.6

rubicundity *redness* 257.1

rubidium Chemical Elements and Common Allotropes 11

rubidium-strontium dating *dating* 8.48

rubiginous *brown* 256.5

rub it in [Inf] *emphasize* 200.6, *aggravate* 276.5

ruble *national coins* 484.11

rub noses *touch* 216.9

rub off *erase* 186.9, *erode* 554.14, *depilate* 614.20

rub off on *adhere* 755.8

rub of the green *golfing terms* 156.3

rub one's nose in it [Inf] *aggravate* 276.5

rub out *clean* 111.17, *erase* 186.9, *cause to disappear* 265.7, *take away* 477.18, *abolish* 523.11,

exterminate 709.22, *subtract* 749.6, *eject* 764.8

rub out [Inf] *murder* 30.20

rub out *or* **away** *erode* 554.14

rubric *ritual manual* 85.11, *topic* 328.1, *code* 780.3

rubricate *redden* 257.9

rub salt in the wound *aggravate* 276.5

rub shoulders *or* **elbows with** *participate* 408.15, *meet* 586.15

rub the sleep from one's eyes *be active* 414.18

rub the wrong way *cause dislike* 291.16, *irritate* 302.16, *make irritable* 304.15, *pick a fight* 463.10, *grind* 554.15, *make rough* 544.11

rub up *glaze* 246.22, *rub* 554.12

rub up [Brit inf] *learn* 48.23

ruby *red thing* 257.3, *red* 257.5

ruby laser *laser* 10.18

ruche *pleat* 637.2

ruched *folded* 637.5

ruck *pleat* 637.2, 637.8, *average person* 742.4, *average* 778.4, *throng* 795.4

rucked up *folded* 637.5

rucksack *climbing equipment* 161.4, *baggage* 578.8, *transferred thing* 685.6

ruckus *dispute* 463.3, *disruption* 766.7, *commotion* 768.5

ruction *dispute* 463.3, *disruption* 766.7, *commotion* 768.5

rudbeckia Flowers 42

rudder *sailboat parts and accessories* 150.4, *ship's steering* 690.9, *equalizer* 740.5

rudderless *helpless* 515.9

rudderpost *sailboat parts and accessories* 150.4

ruddily 257.10

ruddiness *face color* 251.9, *redness* 257.1

ruddle *red pigment* 257.2, *redden* 257.9

ruddy *healthy* 113.4, *red-faced* 257.6, *blushing* 403.9

ruddy [Brit inf] *miscellaneous euphemisms* 301.12

ruddy complexion *health* 113.1

rude 400.9; *of language* 5.35, *obscene* 112.9, *clumsy* 128.6, *objectionable* 272.7, *ungrateful* 311.2, *inconsiderate* 318.9, *unformed* 389.11, *badly behaved* 399.16, *bad-mannered* 411.6, *disrespectful* 436.9, *indecorous* 528.8, *abrupt* 591.8, *incomplete* 762.5

rude gesture *gesture* 183.5, *act of discourtesy* 411.3, *indignity* 436.7

rude health *health* 113.1

rudely 400.19, 411.9; *vulgarly* 71.5, *dirtily* 112.12, *ungratefully* 311.6, *thoughtlessly* 318.15, *badly* 399.23, *unsocially* 409.13, *discourteously* 411.8, 535.11, *disrespectfully* 436.25, *abruptly* 591.13

rudeness 400.2; *obscenity* 112.4, *objectionability* 272.2, *ingratitude* 311.1, *immaturity* 389.3, *bad conduct* 399.7, *discourtesy* 411.1, *bad manners* 411.2, *disrespect* 436.1, *impropriety* 528.2, *abruptness* 591.4

rude person *badly behaved person* 399.8, *discourteous person* 411.4

rude remark *act of defiance* 416.3

rude word *vulgarism* 5.20

rude words *act of discourtesy* 411.3

rudiment *developmental biology* 13.22, *rough idea* 544.4

rudimental *tiny* 580.9, *rudimentary* 771.22

rudimentary 771.22; *developmental* 13.33, *immature* 389.9, *unfinished* 544.9, *tiny* 580.9, *basic* 601.8, *causal* 675.7

rudiments 771.7

Rudolf Lakes 568

rue *lament* 280.7

rueful *penitent* 451.5

ruefully *lamentably* 280.10, *penitently* 451.10

rue the day *be penitent* 451.7

rufescence *redness* 257.1

rufescent *red* 257.5

ruff *plumage* 36.7, *neckwear* 100.29, *bridge* 168.4, *play cards* 168.7

Ruffian Notable Horses 159

ruffian *murderer* 30.12, *combatant* 77.1, *malefactor* 306.6, *criminal* 427.6, *violent animal* 520.4, *vulgar person* 535.4

ruffing *card-playing* 168.6

ruffle *irritate* 302.16, *decorative article* 532.5, *make rough* 544.11, *pleat* 637.2, 637.8, *agitate* 684.22, *make disorderly* 766.20, *disturb* 768.10

ruffled *rough* 544.5, *agitated* 684.15, *untidy* 766.11, *disturbed* 768.6

ruffle feelings *be discourteous* 411.7

ruffle one's feathers *irritate* 302.16

ruffs Collective Names 59

rufous *red* 257.5

rug *floor covering* 613.13

rug [Brit] *body covering* 613.3

rug [Inf] *stadium* 155.3, *hairdressing* 530.7, *body covering* 613.3

rug braiding *weaving* 130.6

rugby Sporting Activities 145

Rügen Islands 572

rugged *discourteous* 411.5, *severe* 424.5, *rough* 544.5, 824.10, *tough* 547.6

rugged individualist *free person* 829.9

ruggedly *strongly* 516.17, *roughly* 544.13, *toughly* 547.16

ruggedness *severity* 424.1, *roughness* 544.1, *toughness* 547.1, *difficulty* 824.1

rug making Hobbies and Pastimes 167

rugose *rough* 544.5

rugosely *roughly* 544.13

rugosity *roughness* 544.1

rug rat [Inf] *child* 26.6

Ruhr Rivers 570

ruin 523.4, 523.15; *devastation* 96.5, *lay waste* 96.21, *affliction* 117.1, Phobias 283, *demoralize* 432.15, *evil thing* 446.2, *be evil* 446.10, *destruction* 468.7, *destroy* 468.18, *insolvency* 486.2, 490.5, 846.6, *impoverish* 486.16, *change* 512.12, *make ugly* 531.4, *blemish* 533.7, *downfall* 714.7, *disintegration* 758.1, *annihilation* 773.4, *moral deterioration* 808.3, *dilapidation* 808.5, *impair* 808.18, *pervert* 808.22, *adversity* 848.1

ruination *ruin* 523.4, *dilapidation* 808.5, *impairment* 808.7

ruined *devastated* 96.12, *afflicting* 117.11, *losing* 468.9, *unprofitable* 468.10, *indebted* 486.9, *nonpaying* 490.7, *destroyed* 523.9, *outclassed*

745.9, *disintegrated* 758.3, *annihilated* 773.16, *spoiled* 808.9, *worn* 808.13

ruin oneself *overpay* 496.11, *deteriorate* 808.14

ruin one's name *be wicked* 448.13

ruinous *detrimental* 446.8, *unprofitable* 468.10, *explosive* 520.6, *destructive* 523.8, *decrepit* 808.12, *adverse* 848.10

ruinously *destructively* 523.18

ruins Phobias 283, *ruin* 523.4, *remainder* 750.1

Rule Constellations 7

rule 780.1, 780.12; *geometric construction* 6.47, *theory* 6.62, *physical law* 10.4, *governance* 49.18, *govern* 49.26, *authority* 52.1, 425.3, *have authority* 52.13, *wield authority* 52.16, *law* 53.1, *try a case* 54.28, *master* 68.17, *manage* 126.10, *advise* 176.9, *maxim* 177.1, *judge* 341.10, *procedure* 387.2, *command* 425.1, 425.10, *have authority over* 425.12, *be an influence* 512.13, *exert sovereignty* 566.12, *measuring instrument* 589.12, *baseline* 601.4, *planimetry* 603.5, *regularity* 663.1, *make regular* 663.9, *average* 742.1, *leadership* 744.2, *method* 765.7, *prevail* 778.19, *convention* 781.5, *calculator* 784.5

rule against *rule* 780.12

rule a territory *own property* 470.11

rule-based system *artificial intelligence* 15.21

rulebook *code* 780.3

rule by terror *terrorization* 283.5

ruled by passions *opinionated* 379.9

ruled out *forbidden* 837.7

rule of business *performance* 465.2

rule of law *discipline* 765.9

rule of thumb *experimentation* 335.3, *standard* 589.7, *formula* 780.7

rule out *erase* 186.9, *exclude* 764.7, *rule* 780.12, *make impossible* 837.8

rule over 780.13

ruler *geometric construction* 6.47, *governor* 49.23, *person in authority* 52.7, *leader* 68.3, *instrument of punishment* 454.13, *measuring instrument* 589.12, *planimetry* 603.5, *calculator* 784.5

rules *tradition* 397.5, *line of action* 399.4, *morals* 431.2, *etiquette* 534.3

rules and regulations *tradition* 397.5

rules of business *tradition* 397.5, *line of action* 399.4

rules of conduct *etiquette* 406.3

rules of inference *reasoning* 6.61

rules of language *grammar* 5.28

rules of life *line of action* 399.4

rules of the game *tactics* 399.12

rules of the road *line of action* 399.4, *navigation laws* 690.10

rules of the sea *navigation laws* 690.10

rule the roost *wield authority* 52.16, *rule over* 780.13

rule with an iron hand *wield authority* 52.16, *suppress* 424.9

ruling 780.2, 780.11; *governing* 49.25, *authoritative* 52.9, *legal justice* 53.4, *verdict* 341.2, *command* 425.1, *commanding* 425.7, *influential* 512.8, *dominant* 744.9, *prevailing* 778.11

ruling class *social stratification* 2.7, *governance* 52.6, *aristocracy* 70.2

ruling-class *socioeconomic* 2.13

ruling party *the power structure* 68.12

ruling passion *opinionatedness* 379.3

rum *alcoholic drink* 93.9

rum [Brit] *eccentric* 782.16

rumba Dances 135, *ice-dancing move* 162.19

rumble *loud sound* 232.2, *bang* 234.6, *drumming* 235.1, *drum* 235.10

rumble [Inf] *dispute* 463.3, *disruption* 766.7

rumbling *drumming* 235.1

ruminant *thoughtful* 4.17, *type of animal* 34.5, *hoofed mammal* 35.16, *ungulate* 35.31

Ruminantia *hoofed mammal* 35.16

ruminate *philosophize* 4.19, *graze* 35.35, *eat grass* 45.11, *chew* 92.22, *think* 317.9

rumination *eating habit* 92.7, *thought* 317.1

ruminative *thoughtful* 4.17, 317.5

ruminatively *thoughtfully* 4.27

rummage sale *sale* 482.2, *bazaar* 483.10, *bargain* 495.2, *discounter* 497.7

rummy Card Games 168

rum one *or* **customer** [Brit] *eccentric* 782.10

rumor Children's and Party Games 167, *inside information* 170.4, *news source* 171.4, *publishing* 173.2, *publish* 173.15, *partial truth* 192.7, *matter of interest* 328.3

rumored *newsworthy* 171.8

rumormonger *gossip* 192.11

rump *veal* 90.25, *rear end* 622.4, *remainder* 750.1

rumple 552.14; *make rough* 544.11, *pleat* 637.2, 637.8, *agitate* 684.22, *make disorderly* 766.20

rumpus *tumult* 232.5, *dispute* 463.3, *violence by person* 520.2, *disruption* 766.7, *commotion* 768.5

rumpus room *room* 60.9

run 694.13; *program* 15.29, *practice livestock farming* 16.20, *fester* 25.23, *mammal dwelling* 35.21, *run for office* 50.10, Collective Names 59, *cage* 60.15, *be healthy* 113.11, *manage* 126.10, *engagement* 136.15, 138.6, *sail* 150.29, *play* 155.8, *pommel horse* 157.7, *ski run* 162.2, *toboggan race* 162.25, *participate* 166.22, *lose color* 252.7, *depart* 265.6, *chase* 385.2, *retreat* 385.22, *street* 390.1, *way* 397.3, *behave toward* 399.20, *be active* 414.18, *military attack* 418.2, *be operational* 509.10, *be an influence* 512.13, *melt* 555.24, *flow* 555.25, 570.4, 570.10, *river* 570.1, *piece* 590.2, *go on* 642.7, *continuity* 669.1, *momentum* 677.2, *bodily movement* 677.11, *walk* 677.17, *route* 691.2, *acceleration* 694.3, *be swift* 694.10, *impel* 695.9, *bearing* 697.2, *lead* 744.19, *come unstuck* 756.7, *series* 770.3, *consecutiveness* 774.1, *continue* 774.12, *average* 778.4, *direct* 780.14, *make haste* 818.5

run *or* **running** *track event* 166.1

runabout *automobile* 687.6, Ships and Boats 690

run abreast *parallel* 606.7, *be equal* 740.11

run across *meet* 704.20, *chance upon* 842.13

run a deficit *lose money* 468.15

run after *seek friendship* 62.11, *chase* 385.13, *pander to* 401.11

run aground *sail* 690.16, *land* 704.16, *be in trouble* 848.13

run a household *housekeep* 60.23

run a lap *be cyclic* 663.11

run along! *go!* 709.30

run amok *become insane* 110.12, *feel deeply* 266.16, *strike* 418.21, *be violent* 520.8, *lay waste* 523.14, *be disorderly* 766.22

run-and-shoot offense *offense* 155.6

run an experiment *experiment* 335.11

run a pattern *play offense* 155.18

run a protection racket [Inf] *take money away* 477.20

run a race *contend* 422.22

run around *fornicate* 432.14

run around in circles *be busy* 414.19

run at *attack* 418.17

run at a loss *lose money* 468.15

run a temperature *feel hot* 217.19

run a tight ship *be severe* 424.8, *order* 765.18

runaway *avoider* 386.8, *fugitive* 386.10, *nonperforming* 466.6, *absentee* 576.5, *moving* 677.12, *escaper* 816.5, *escaping* 816.7

run away 386.21; *marry* 64.19, *depart* 265.6, *retreat* 285.8, 680.17, *not perform* 466.10, *abscond* 576.16, *accelerate* 694.14, *hurry off* 705.11, *be safe* 810.20, *escape* 816.8, *be defeated* 846.18

runaway tongue *talkativeness* 207.1, *escaper*

runaway victory *victory* 845.4

runaway wedding *escape* 816.1

run away with *take away* 275.13, 477.18

run back *kick* 155.12, 155.20, *retreat* 680.17, *reverse* 680.18

run before the wind *navigate* 690.15

run counter to *counteract* 510.7, *be opposite* 731.4, *be contrary* 828.16

rundle *step* 713.11

rundown *other game terms* 147.7, *summary* 204.1

run-down *weak* 517.6, *spoiled* 808.9, *worn* 808.13, *fatigued* 820.2

run down *unhealthy* 114.23, *be dissatisfied* 274.7, *detect* 345.12, *chase* 385.13, *attack successfully* 418.25, *scorn* 436.10, *criticized* 438.14, *berate* 438.20, *disparage* 440.11, *stop* 668.10, *decrease* 747.7, *make smaller* 747.8

run down one's account *expend* 491.11

rune *written letter* 5.14, *spell* 86.8, *symbol* 183.3, *representation* 349.1

runes *means of prediction* 358.10

run faster *improve* 467.18

run for *aim* 697.14

run for it *retreat* 386.22

run for it! *hands off!* 386.26

run for office 50.10

run for one's life *retreat* 386.22, *hurry off* 705.11

run for port *sail* 690.16, *be safe* 810.20

run for your life! *hands off!* 386.26

run foul of *collide* 695.10

rung 636.3; *cylinder* 633.4, *step* 713.11, *interval* 739.4

run helter-skelter *make haste* 818.5

runic *occult* 86.16

runic alphabet *alphabet* 5.16

runic letter *written letter* 5.14

runic verse *poetry* 139.8

run-in *dispute* 463.3

run in *take away forcefully* 477.19, *impact* 710.11

run in [Inf] *detain* 830.16

run interference for *back* 825.28

run into *meet* 704.20, *chance upon* 842.13

run into danger *be in danger* 811.11

run into debt *be in debt* 488.9

run into money *cost a lot* 496.9

run into the ground *use up* 393.12

run into trouble *be in a predicament* 725.9, *be in difficulty* 824.19

run its course *pass* 639.13, 651.17

run level *row* 150.32, *be equal* 740.11

run like *or* **in a flash** *run* 694.13

run like a bat out of hell [Inf] *run* 694.13

run like a hare *or* **like a scared rabbit** *run* 694.13

run like a house on fire *or* **afire** *run* 694.13

run like a shot *or* **like the wind** *or* **like wildfire** *run* 694.13

run like clockwork *go easily* 823.18

run like greased lightning [Inf] *run* 694.13

run like hell *or* **blazes** [Inf] *make haste* 818.5

run like lightning *or* **a streak of lightning** *or* **a streak** *or* **a blue streak** *run* 694.13

run like mad [Inf] *make haste* 818.5

run like mad *or* **crazy** [Inf] *run* 694.13

run like sixty [Inf] *run* 694.13

run like the devil *run* 694.13

run low *waste away* 96.20, *decrease* 747.7

run messages for *mediate* 75.6

run neck and neck *be equal* 740.11

runnel *or* **runlet** *river* 570.1

runner *plant breeding* 17.6, *stem* 41.5, *office assistant* 69.6, *baseball team* 147.2, *office* 155.6, *horse racing* 159.10, *toboggan parts* 162.24, *track and field eventer* 166.19, *athlete* 422.15, *floor covering* 613.13, *speeder* 694.5

runners *climbing equipment* 161.4

runner-up *finalist* 422.16

runner-up prize *prize* 453.2

runnily *fluidly* 555.26, *wetly* 557.34

runniness *fluidity* 555.5, *wateriness* 557.3, *thinning* 595.6, *nonadhesion* 756.1

running *pus* 25.7, *purulent* 25.16, *health improvement* 113.3, *management* 126.1, *sailing terms* 150.5, *bowls* 151.7, *fencing* 153.6, *balance beam* 157.3, *track and field* 166.20, *active* 414.13, *race* 422.8, *contending* 422.19, *operational* 509.7, *fluidization* 555.8, *flowing* 570.7, *progressive* 669.6, *motion* 677.1, *moving* 677.12, *speeding* 694.7, *nonadhesive* 756.4,

sequentially 770.13, *consecutive*
774.7, *hasty* 818.3
running account *accounts* 493.4
running around *fornication* 432.3
running attack *fencing movements*
153.3
running away *disappearance* 265.1
running back *offense* 155.6
running battle *contention* 422.1
running bowline Knots, Bends,
Hitches, Splices 754
running costs *business expenses*
491.4
running dog Architectural
Elements 134
running down *disparagement*
440.1
running fight *fight* 422.9
running game *play* 155.8
running-game target shooting
Sporting Activities 145
running head *or* **foot** *book part*
174.5
running hop *jumping* 166.11
running knot Knots, Bends,
Hitches, Splices 754
running lengthwise *lengthwise*
590.8
running lights *safety light* 246.7
running offense *playing terms*
148.4
running on *talkative* 207.5
running over *excessive* 99.5, *full*
761.8
running rigging *sailboat parts and*
accessories 150.4
running riot *extravagance* 194.3
running shoes *shoes* 100.30, *sports*
equipment 166.17
running shorts *sports equipment*
166.17
running shot *grip* 151.4
running sore *outflow* 707.4
running spring dive *diving* 164.6
running start *advantage* 618.4,
744.3
running story *news story* 171.3
running the gauntlet *corporal*
punishment 454.11
running to earth *locating* 565.3
running to seed *aging* 27.13
running total *mathematical result*
783.4
running vest *sports equipment*
166.17
running water 8.10; *erosion* 8.41,
water 557.1, *river* 570.1
running with the ball *violations*
148.5
run nip and tuck *be equal* 740.11
runny *insufficient* 517.11, *flowing*
555.15, *thinned* 595.13, *leaky*
707.12, *nonadhesive* 756.4
runny nose *respiratory disease*
114.12, *outflow* 707.4
run of *liberality* 829.8
run of bad luck *luck* 842.3
runoff *water cycle* 8.12, *prize*
competition 422.5
run off *drain* 8.64, *run away*
386.21, *hurry off* 705.11
run off at the mouth [Inf] *be*
talkative 207.7
run off with *take away* 477.18
run of good luck *luck* 842.3
run of luck *successfulness* 845.3,
good fortune 847.2
run-of-the-mill *predictable* 295.4,
frequent 661.4, *average* 742.5,
778.4, *middling* 772.14, *common*
778.13
run on *continue* 669.8, *march on*
679.11, *be consecutive* 774.11
run one hard *endanger* 811.13

run one's eye(s) over *inspect*
242.22
run one's head against *collide*
695.10
run on in order *be regular* 663.10
run on oiled wheels *go easily*
823.18
run on rails *go smoothly* 545.11
run on the rocks *endanger* 811.13
run out 707.15; *be insufficient* 98.9,
pass 651.17, *stop* 668.10, *exit*
707.13, *come to an end* 773.23
run out of luck *be in trouble*
848.13
run out of steam *hesitate* 693.12
run out of time *spend time*
639.14, *come to an end* 773.23
run out of town *drive out* 709.19
run over *be full* 761.12
run parallel *be compatible* 462.12,
parallel 606.7
run pell-mell *make haste* 818.5
run rings *or* **circles around**
overtake 744.16
run riot *be excessive* 99.9, *be*
extravagant 194.13, *be active*
414.18, *be violent* 520.8, *be*
disorderly 766.22
run roll *flight* 689.5
runs, the [Inf] *defecation* 25.3,
gastroenterological disease 114.11
runs batted in (RBI) *batting terms*
147.6
runs-batted-in (RBI) leader
baseball team 147.2
run side by side *parallel* 606.7
run smoothly *go easily* 823.18
runt *weak person* 517.4, *little person*
580.5, *thin person* 595.4
run the bases *play baseball* 147.9
run the chicane *be on the track*
146.11
run the course *go on* 642.7
run the gauntlet *defy* 416.7, *face*
danger 811.12
run the hurry-up offense *play*
offense 155.18
run the power sweep *play offense*
155.18
run the quarterback sneak *play*
offense 155.18
run the risk of *be in danger*
811.11
run through *murder* 30.20, *waste*
96.15, *rehearse* 136.37, *act*
137.20, *inflict pain* 215.10, *stab*
418.22, *consume* 491.12, *be an*
influence 575.13, *hole* 583.17, *mix together*
751.14
run-through *production* 136.14,
137.6, *billiards play* 149.2, *bowls*
151.7
run-through shot *grip* 151.4
run through the mill [Inf]
interrogate 333.17
runtiness *littleness* 580.1
run to resort to 393.13, *reach out*
585.10
run to earth *detect* 345.12, *find*
565.11
run together *come together* 702.10,
combine 757.9
run to ground *follow* 385.12
run to seed *be infertile* 23.8,
vegetate 41.21, *be wasted* 96.22, *go*
to waste 468.19, *disintegrate*
808.15
run to waste *be wasted* 96.22
run true to form *conform* 781.11
run true to type *be the same*
730.13
runty *little* 580.7
runup *jumping* 166.11

run up *perform* 522.16
run up a bill *acquire credit* 487.11,
be in debt 488.9
run up a debt *buy on credit* 476.13
run up against *collide* 695.10
run up an account *buy on credit*
476.13, *acquire credit* 487.11, *be*
in debt 488.9
run up an overdraft *lose money*
468.15
run (it) up the flagpole [Inf] *test*
390.9
runway *airport* 689.4, *flight path*
691.12
runway lights *safety light* 246.7
runway model *fashion business*
536.3
run wild *be violent* 520.8, *be*
disorderly 766.22, *lack restraint*
829.21
run with *keep company with* 794.17
run with the hare and hunt
with the hounds *lack candor*
192.22, *equivocate* 380.8, *stand in*
the middle 772.17
run with the pack *or* **herd** *abide*
by 781.12
rupee *national coins* 484.11
rupture *deformation* 14.16, *load*
14.49, *faction* 347.4, *dispute*
463.3, 463.9, *opening* 583.1, *open*
583.15, *crack* 587.2, 587.7,
separateness 753.3, *separate*
753.12
ruptured *open* 583.10, *cracked*
587.5, *separate* 753.7
rural *communal* 2.12, *agricultural*
16.16, *native* 61.12, *administrative*
564.13, *local* 564.14, *transportable*
686.7
rural economics *agriculture* 16.1
rural economist *agriculturist*
16.14
ruralism *society* 2.6
ruralist *countryman* 61.8
Ruralists, Brotherhood of
Western Art Styles 133
rurally *agriculturally* 16.21,
regionally 564.16
rural road *road* 687.2
rural sector *society* 2.6
rural society *society* 2.6
rural sociology *sociology* 2.1,
society 2.6
rural-urban *communal* 2.12
rural-urban migration *society* 2.6
Ruritania Imaginary Places 360
ruse *artifice* 193.5, *sophism* 330.2,
method 387.4, *trick* 813.2,
stratagem 822.2
rush *grass* 45.1, *crowd* 59.26,
defensive huddle 155.10, *play*
defense 155.19, *be active* 414.18,
military attack 418.2, *attack*
418.17, *flow* 570.4, 570.10,
prematurity 657.6, *momentum*
677.2, *walk* 677.17, *tumult* 684.2,
be agitated 684.21, *acceleration*
694.3, *scamper* 694.12, *little bit*
800.4, *haste* 818.1, *hasty* 818.3,
hasten 818.4, *make haste* 818.5
rush along *hasten* 818.4
rush around *be full of vigor* 518.4
rush at *chase* 385.13, *attack* 418.17
rush candle *or* **light** *incandescent*
light 246.5
rushed *unpremeditated* 389.7, *hasty*
818.3
rushed into *hasty* 818.3
rushed off one's feet *busy* 414.15
rush family *seed plant* 41.3
rush headlong *make haste* 818.5
rush hour *morning things* 655.3,
evening 656.2

rush in *invade* 706.12, *flood in*
706.14
rushing *flowing* 570.7, *motion*
677.1, *moving* 677.12, *hasty* 818.3
rushing the puck *ice hockey tactics*
158.4
rushing to and fro *busy* 414.15
rush into *be rash* 286.8
rush in where angels fear to
tread *be rash* 286.8, *lack thought*
318.12
rush job *haste* 818.1
Rushmore, Mount Mountains
and Hills 569
rush off *hurry off* 705.11
rush off *or* **away** *make haste* 818.5
rush one's fences *have no time to*
spare 818.6
rush the passer *play defense*
155.19
rush through *have no time to spare*
818.6
rush to and fro *be active* 414.18,
make haste 818.5
rush to the assistance of *help*
825.23
rushy *grassy* 45.8
rusk *bread* 90.10
Russell's paradox *philosophical*
problem 4.8, Mathematical
Concepts 6
Russet Apple Varieties 44
russet Fabrics and Fibers 130,
brown 256.5, *red* 257.5
Russia Countries 566
Russian ballet *ballet* 135.2
Russian bear *national emblem*
184.7
Russian Black Pied Breeds of
Cattle 16
Russian blue Breeds of Cats 35
Russian Brown Breeds of Cattle
16
Russian formalists Western
Literary Groups 139
Russian Heavy Draught Horse
and Pony Breeds 159
Russian Large White Breeds of
Pigs 16
Russian Long-eared White
Breeds of Pigs 16
Russian Long-tailed Breeds of
Sheep 16
Russian Northern Short-tailed
Breeds of Sheep 16
Russian Orthodoxy Christian
Groups 81
Russian Revolution Major Wars
76
Russian Short-eared White
Breeds of Pigs 16
Russian Simmental Breeds of
Cattle 16
Russian tea *tea* 93.7
Russian whist Card Games 168
Russki *or* **Russkie** Nicknames for
Inhabitants 61
Russky Nicknames for Inhabitants
61
Russo-Finnish War Major Wars
76
Russo-Japanese War Major Wars
76
rust *pests and diseases* 17.12, *be*
infertile 23.8, *tree disease* 43.8, *dirt*
112.5, *be dirty* 112.10, *afflict*
117.16, *tarnish* 248.9, *brown*
256.7, *red thing* 257.3, Phobias
283, *be unprepared* 389.14, *have*
free time 413.15, *weakness* 517.1,
agent of destruction 523.7, *weather*
553.29, *oldness* 653.1, *grow old*
653.16, *decay* 808.6, 808.16, *eat*
away 808.19

Rust Belt *regions of the United States* 564.7
rust-colored *brown* 256.5, *red* 257.5
rusted *dilapidated* 517.7
rusted *dilapidated* 517.7
rustic *agricultural* 16.16, *countryman* 61.8, *native* 61.12, *commoner* 71.1, *local* 564.14, *naive person* 821.2
rustically *agriculturally* 16.21, *vulgarly* 71.5, *regionally* 564.16
rusticate *disbar* 709.16, *ostracize* 709.17
rustication *ostracism* 709.3
rustic fence *ornamental garden* 17.3
rustic work Architectural Elements 134
rustily *venerably* 653.17
rustiness *unskillfulness* 128.1, *hoarseness* 238.2, *lack of preparation* 389.1, *unaccustomedness* 398.1, *decay* 808.6
rusting *electrochemistry* 11.19, *disused* 394.8
rustle *small sound* 233.4, *sound faint* 233.8, *hiss* 237.1, 237.3
rustle cattle *steal* 479.14
rustle of spring *spring* 654.3
rustler *thief* 479.8
rustling *nonresonant* 233.7, *hiss* 237.1, *hissing* 237.2, *stealing* 479.1
rustproof *invulnerable* 810.18
rustproofing *miscellaneous automotive terms* 687.14
rustre Heraldic Terms 184
rusts *fungi* 47.3
rusty *clumsy* 128.6, *hoarse* 238.5, *dimmed* 248.6, *brown* 256.5, *untrained* 389.8, *unaccustomed* 398.3, *worn* 808.13
rut *skiing snow* 162.3, *boring thing* 296.3, *way* 397.3, *rough thing* 544.2, *round* 633.6, *furrow* 638.1, 638.5, *seasons* 654.2, *passage* 691.5, *custom* 780.5, *repetitiveness* 797.3
rutabagas *crop* 16.8
Ruth Notable Friendships 62
ruth *mercy* 308.3
ruthenium Chemical Elements and Common Allotropes 11
rutherford Scientific and Technical Units 589
ruthful *pitying* 308.4
ruthfully *pityingly* 308.11
ruthless *malicious* 306.8, *cruel* 306.10, *pitiless* 309.3, *tenacious* 376.9, *strong-willed* 376.10
ruthlessly *maliciously* 306.15, *cruelly* 306.17, *pitilessly* 309.7
ruthlessness *malice* 306.2, *cruelty* 306.4, *pitilessness* 309.1, *tenacity* 376.4
rutted *snow* 162.28, *coarse* 544.6, *furrowed* 638.3
rutting *desirous* 20.18, *in season* 654.8
ruttish *desirous* 20.18, *unchaste* 432.10
rutty *desirous* 20.18, *coarse* 544.6, *furrowed* 638.3
Rwanda Countries 566
Rydal Water Lakes 568
Rydberg constant Classical Physical Laws 10
Ryder Cup *golfing associations and tournaments* 156.12
rye *crop* 16.8, *cereal grass* 45.4
rye bread *bread* 90.10
ryegrass *crop* 16.8
Ryeland Breeds of Sheep 16

Rygja Breeds of Sheep 16
rypophobia Phobias 283
Ryukyu Islands Islands 572

S

Saar Rivers 570
Sabaism *idolatry* 83.4
Sabaist *idolater* 83.7
Sabbat *witchcraft* 86.6
Sabbatarian *religionist* 81.14
Sabbatarianism *symbolics* 85.4
Sabbath *holy day* 85.12, *ease* 819.1
sabbatical *time off* 125.2, *permit* 502.3, *leave of absence* 576.4, *ease* 819.1
sabbatism *symbolics* 85.4
saber *murder* 30.20, *sharp weapon* 78.6, *fencing equipment* 153.2, *fencing* 153.6
saber-fence *fence* 153.7
saber fencing *fencing* 153.1
saber-rattling *psychological warfare* 76.13, *bellicosity* 76.15
saber saw *hand tool* 103.3
saber-toothed tiger *or cat prehistoric animal* 653.8
sabin Scientific and Technical Units 589
Sabine Rivers 570
sable Heraldic Terms 184, *black thing* 254.3
sable [Heraldic] *black* 254.5
Sable Island Islands 572
Sable Island pony Horse and Pony Breeds 159
sabotage *subversion* 427.3, *subvert* 427.13, *loss* 468.1, *destroy* 468.18, *destructiveness* 523.3, *disruption* 768.4, *disrupt* 768.12, *make useless* 802.12, *impairment* 808.7, *obstacle* 826.15, *hinder* 826.15
sabotaged *disrupted* 768.8
saboteur *revenger* 420.2, *seditionist* 427.7, *destroyer* 523.6, *hinderer* 826.11
sabots *shoes* 100.30
sabulosity *graininess* 553.2
sabulous *grainy* 553.17
sac *packet* 578.4, *casing* 613.9
saccharic acid *saccharide* 12.4
saccharide 12.4; *carbohydrate* 12.3
saccharify *sweeten* 222.7
saccharimetry Fields of Measurement 589
saccharine *sweetener* 222.2, *sweet* 222.5, *honeyed* 439.8
saccharinity *sweetness* 222.1
saccharometer Fields of Measurement 589
saccharometry Fields of Measurement 589
saccharose Common Sugars 12
sacerdotal *priestly* 84.12
sacerdotalism *priesthood* 84.2
sacerdotally *clerically* 84.17
sac fungi *fungi* 47.3
sachet *source of fragrance* 226.2
sack *dress* 100.11, *defensive huddle* 155.10, *play defense* 155.19, *make inactive* 415.16, *take away forcefully* 477.19, *plundering* 479.5, *plunder* 479.16, *lay waste* 523.14, *bag* 578.7
sack [Inf] *employ* 57.18, *relieve from duty* 275.11, *relegation* 574.4, *relegate* 574.18, *eject* 701.8, 764.8, *dismiss* 709.15, *ejection* 764.2, *termination* 834.2, *terminate* 834.7
sackbut Musical Instruments 142
sackcloth Fabrics and Fibers 130, *rough thing* 544.2

sackcloth and ashes *penitence* 313.3, *type of penance* 451.3
sack coat *jacket* 100.18
sacked [Inf] *hired* 57.17, *relegated* 574.11, *canceled* 834.5
sacker *raider* 477.10, *plunderer* 479.9
sacking Fabrics and Fibers 130, *plundering* 479.5
sacking [Inf] *bargaining terms* 57.10, *dismissal* 709.2, *ejection* 764.2
sack out [Inf] *be refreshed* 94.8
sack race Children's and Party Games 167, *sporting event* 422.6
Sacrament Eucharist 85.7
sacrament *ritual* 85.1, *Christian rite* 85.5
sacramental *ritualistic* 85.15
sacramentalism 85.3
sacramentally *ritually* 85.21
sacramentarianism *sacramentalism* 85.3
Sacramento American States 564, Rivers 570
sacrament of marriage *marriage* 64.1
sacrarium *shrine* 83.10
sacred *holy* 82.19, *musical* 140.25
sacredly *divinely* 82.24
sacred music 140.3
sacredness *divine attribute* 82.4
sacred object 83.11
sacred place *shrine* 83.10
sacred symbol *sign* 183.1
sacred text *religious text* 81.15
sacred writings *religious text* 81.15
sacrifice 504.14; *ritual killing* 30.7, *kill ritually* 30.23, *act of worship* 83.2, *worship* 83.15, *batting terms* 147.6, *play baseball* 147.9, *penitence* 313.3, *relinquishment* 392.1, *relinquish* 392.3, *be unselfish* 443.7, *forfeiture* 468.2, *forfeit* 468.13, *offering* 472.6, 504.5, *give praise to* 472.13, *make cheap* 497.14, *abolish* 523.11, *substitute* 672.2, *subtracted item* 749.2
sacrificed *killed* 29.13, *relinquished* 392.2, *sacrificial* 504.10
sacrifice fly *batting terms* 147.6
sacrifice oneself *volunteer* 373.14, *be unselfish* 443.7, *sacrifice* 504.14
sacrifice one's life *sacrifice* 504.14
sacrificer *giver* 472.7
sacrifice the interests of others *be selfish* 444.5
sacrificial 504.10; *worshipful* 83.12, *ritualistic* 85.15, *apologetic* 313.6, *given* 472.8, *bargain* 497.10, *destructive* 523.8
sacrificial anode *electrochemistry* 11.19
sacrificial lamb *offering* 504.5, *martyr* 504.6
sacrificially 504.20; *worshipfully* 83.17, *apologetically* 313.11, *as a gift* 472.17
sacrificial offering *offering* 504.5
sacrilege *profanity* 301.3, *evil* 446.1, *impiety* 448.4
sacrilegious *profane* 301.10, *evil* 446.7, *impious* 448.11
sacrilegiously *profanely* 301.19, *impiously* 448.17
sacristy *church interior* 83.9
sacrosanct *holy* 82.19, *invulnerable* 810.18
sacrosanctity *divine attribute* 82.4
sacrum Human Bones 19
sad 254.10; *funeral* 31.9, *depressed* 261.7, *sorrowful* 270.4, *lamenting* 280.4, *disappointing* 293.6, *pitiful*

308.5, *inconvenient* 804.5, *adverse* 848.10
sadden *cause sorrow* 270.9, *disappoint* 293.9
saddened *sorrowful* 270.4, *disappointed* 293.4
sadder but wiser man *or woman penitent person* 451.3
saddle *lamb* 90.27, *roof* 134.7, *pommel horse* 157.7, *riding equipment* 159.9, *ride* 159.16, *impose a duty* 433.14, *make heavy* 538.14, *mountain* 569.1, *mountain range* 569.3, *bicycle part* 687.11
saddlebag *bag* 578.7, *bicycle part* 687.11
saddle blanket *riding equipment* 159.9
Saddlebred Horse and Pony Breeds 159
saddlecloth *riding equipment* 159.9
saddled *equipped* 388.10, *duty-bound* 433.8, *ponderous* 538.11
saddled with *blocked* 826.13
saddle horse 159.5
saddle pad *riding equipment* 159.9
saddler *horse person* 159.14
saddle shoes *shoes* 100.30
saddle-stitching *or saddle wiring bookbinding* 174.11
saddletree *figurative usage* 43.9
saddle with *augment* 748.13, *burden* 826.21
saddling *weighing down* 538.5
Sadducee Jew 81.11
sad-hearted *sorrowful* 270.4
sadheartedness *sorrow* 270.1
sadhu *religious person* 81.9
sadism *cruelty* 306.4, *sexual offense* 432.6
sadist *cruel* 306.10, *sexually immoral person* 432.8, *villain* 448.5
sadistic *inflicting pain* 215.7, *cruel* 306.10, *perverted* 432.12
sadistically *cruelly* 306.17, *pitilessly* 309.7
sadistic cruelty *cruelty* 306.4
sadly *sorrowfully* 270.10, *lamentingly* 280.9, *pitifully* 308.12, *destructively* 446.13, *adversely* 848.16
sadness *sorrow* 270.1, *lamentation* 280.1, *disappointment* 293.1, *adversity* 848.1
sadomasochism *or s and m sexual perversion* 20.12, *sexual offense* 432.6
sadomasochist *sexual perversion* 20.12
sadomasochistic *perverted* 432.12
sad person 270.3
sad sack [Inf] *person in adversity* 848.9
safari *travel* 686.5
safari hunter *hunter* 385.6
safari park *animal welfare* 34.8
safe 464.4, 810.16; Collective Names 59, *vault* 105.9, *hiding place* 181.2, *satisfied* 273.4, *innocent* 449.6, *secure* 464.5, *money storage* 484.20, *box* 578.5, *invulnerable* 810.18, *sheltered* 812.7, *preserved* 815.12, *certain* 840.7
safe and sound *getting well* 113.9, *secure* 464.5, *have* 464.15, *unbroken* 805.13, *safe* 810.16
safe bet *certainty* 840.1, *good chance* 842.6

---

safe conduct 810.4; *passport* 692.8

safe-conduct pass *permit* 502.3

safecracker *thief* 479.8

safecracking *stealing* 479.1

safe-deposit box *vault* 105.9, *hiding place* 181.2, *safe* 464.4, *money storage* 484.20, *box* 578.5

safe distance *avoidance* 386.1, *safety* 810.1

safeguard 419.2; *reserves* 102.5, *precaution* 287.4, *take precautions* 287.14, *care for* 325.12, *defend* 419.20, *security* 464.1, *secure* 464.9, *promise* 464.10, *give refuge to* 708.15, *escort* 794.18, *protection* 810.2, *protect* 810.21, *preserve* 815.14, *convenience* 825.7

safeguarded *secure* 464.5

safeguarding *defense* 419.1

safe hands *safekeeping* 810.6

safe harbor *haven* 810.3

safe house 812.5; *hiding place* 181.2, *shelter* 613.6, *haven* 810.3, *refuge* 812.1

safe job *safety* 810.1

safekeep *secure* 464.9

safekeeping 810.6; *storage* 105.6, *defense* 419.1, *security* 464.1, *preservation* 815.1

safelight *darkroom equipment* 132.21

safely 810.24; *peacefully* 73.12, *surely* 464.15, *comfortably* 726.19

safeness *security* 464.1, *safety* 810.1

safe place *safety* 810.1, *refuge* 812.1

safe retreat *refuge* 812.1

safe sex *sexual intercourse* 20.9

safety 810.1; *billiards play* 749.2, *scoring* 155.5, *defense* 155.9, *cross-country* 162.31, *security* 464.1

safety and health *bargaining terms* 57.10

safety barrier *automobile racing terms* 146.3

safety belt *safety device* 810.15, *preserver* 815.9

safety catch *fastener* 754.7, *safety device* 810.15

safety chain *safety device* 810.15

safety-deposit box *safe* 464.4, *money storage* 484.20

safety device 810.15; *preserver* 815.9

safety glass *industrial ceramics* 129.6, *glass* 249.5

safety goggles *safety device* 810.15

safety harness *safety device* 810.15

safety hat *helmet* 100.34

safety helmet *safety device* 810.15

safety in numbers *safety* 810.1

safety lamp *lantern* 246.8

safety light 246.7

safety lock *safety device* 810.15

safety match *fuel starter* 106.3, *fire* 246.9, *safety device* 810.15

safety net *precaution* 287.4, *safety device* 810.15

safety pin *fastener* 754.7, *safety device* 810.15

safety razor *safety device* 810.15

safety strap *ski equipment* 162.10

safety valve *safety device* 810.15, *means of escape* 816.4

safflower *Flowers* 42, *Herbs and Spices* 91

safflower oil *basic cooking ingredient* 91.8

saffron *Herbs and Spices* 91, *orange thing* 258.3, *orange* 258.5

saffron robe *general wedding terms* 64.6

saffron veil *general wedding terms* 64.6

sag *succumb* 421.7, *be cheap* 497.13, *be weak* 517.12, *soften* 543.14, *suspension* 604.1, *suspend* 604.13, *sinkage* 714.2, *droop* 714.14

saga *Poem or Verse Forms* 139, *program* 172.10, *sequel* 770.5

sagacious *educated* 48.19, *skillful* 127.10, *intelligent* 315.9, *knowledgeable* 348.7, *wise* 352.4, *foreseeing* 357.5, *profound* 598.15

sagaciously *educationally* 48.25, *intelligently* 315.14, *wisely* 352.8, *profoundly* 598.27

sagaciousness *wisdom* 352.1

sagacity *social skill* 127.3, *cleverness* 315.3, *learning* 348.3, *wisdom* 352.1, *foresight* 357.1, *profundity* 598.5

sage 4.11; *older person* 27.7, *expert* 52.8, *educational leader* 68.11, *Herbs and Spices* 91, *skilled person* 127.7, *intellectual* 315.7, *intelligent* 315.9, *knowledgeable person* 348.5, *wise person* 352.3, *oracle* 358.8, *awe-inspiring* 435.12

sage-green *green* 260.7

sagging *weak* 517.6, *suspension* 604.1, *suspended* 604.7, *sinkage* 714.2, *drooping* 714.10

sagittal *sharp* 549.10

Sagittarius *Constellations* 7, *shooter* 696.11

sagittate *of leaves* 41.18

sagittate or sagittiform *sharp* 549.10

sago palm *Trees and Shrubs* 43

Saguenay *Rivers* 570

Sahara *hot place* 217.5, *Deserts* 572

Saharan *desert* 560.12

sahib [India] *male title of address* 32.3, *master* 68.1

Sahiwal *Breeds of Cattle* 16

said *spoken* 205.13

said again *iterated* 797.9

said before *iterated* 797.9

sail 150.29, 690.16; *navy* 77.18, *sailboard parts* 150.20, *canoe* 150.31, *travel* 686.11, *fly* 689.13, *navigate* 690.15, *go easily* 823.18

sail against *attack* 418.17

sailboard *windsurf* 150.33, *Sailing Ships and Boats* 690

sailboarder *boating person* 150.24

sailboarding *Sporting Activities* 145, *boating sports* 150.1, *windsurfing* 150.19, 150.28

sailboard parts 150.20

sailboat 150.3; *Sailing Ships and Boats* 690

sailboat parts and accessories 150.4

sail close-hauled *sail* 150.29

sail close to the wind *sail* 150.29

sailcloth jacket *fencing equipment* 153.2

sailer *Sailing Ships and Boats* 690

sailfish *game fish* 154.10

sail for *aim* 697.14

sail home *do easily* 823.16

sailing 150.2, 150.25; *Sporting Activities* 145, *boating sports* 150.1, *windsurfing* 150.19, *canoeing* 150.26, *water transportation* 690.1, *nautical* 690.14, *passing along* 692.5

sailing aid *navigational aid* 690.6

sailing canoe *canoe* 150.9

sailing dinghy *sailboat* 150.3, *Sailing Ships and Boats* 690

sailing master *nautical person* 690.12

sailing terms 150.5

sailing trophy *competitive sailing* 150.6

sail in the same boat *work together* 827.14

sail into *strike* 418.21, *fight* 422.23

sailor *warrior* 76.25, *naval person* 77.25, *boating person* 150.24, *nautical person* 690.12

sailorlike *nautical* 690.14

sailorly *nautical* 690.14

sailor suit *uniform* 100.9

sailplaning *Sporting Activities* 145

sail port tack *sail* 150.29

Sails *Constellations* 7

sails *sailboat parts and accessories* 150.4

sail starboard tack *sail* 150.29

sail under false colors *be untruthful* 192.20

Saimaa *Lakes* 568

sainfoin *animal feed* 16.12, *Flowers* 42

saint *religious person* 81.9, *deified person* 82.14, *well-behaved person* 399.6, *chaste person* 431.6, *good person* 445.6, *innocent person* 449.5, *giver* 472.7

saintliness *virtue* 447.1, *innocence* 449.1

saintly *religious* 81.21, *angelic* 82.21, *moral* 431.9, *virtuous* 447.5, *innocent* 449.6, *blameless* 805.12

saints *Phobias* 283

saint's day *holy day* 85.12, *anniversary* 405.5, *day* 646.4

Saipan *Islands* 572

Sakhalin *Islands* 572

salaam *salutation* 209.2, *defer to* 410.12, *obeisance* 426.3, *show obeisance to* 426.8, *mark of respect* 435.4, *show respect* 435.16, *bow* 716.6, 716.22

salaaming *deference* 410.4

salability *market* 482.5

salable 482.13

salable commodity *merchandise* 482.6

salably *marketably* 482.23

salacious *desirous* 20.18, *obscene* 112.9, *unchaste* 432.10

salaciously *dirtily* 112.12, *promiscuously* 432.19

salaciousness *obscenity* 112.4, *sexual immorality* 432.2

salacity *sexual immorality* 432.2

salad 90.16; *dish* 90.7, *side dish* 90.15, 794.11

salad bowl *crockery* 578.16

salad burnet *Herbs and Spices* 91

salad days *youth* 26.1, *naiveté* 449.4, *time of plenty* 847.3

salad dressing *sauce* 90.17

salad fork *tableware* 92.13

Salado *Rivers* 570

salad vegetable *vegetable* 17.11

salad vegetables *fruits* 44.1

salamandrian *amphibian* 37.14

salami *sausage* 90.29

salaried *receiving* 473.9, *receiving pay* 489.14, *received* 492.6

salaried worker *breadwinner* 123.2

salary *reward for service* 453.5, *earnings* 467.5, *something received* 473.2, *pay* 489.6, *income* 492.3, *positive stimulus* 508.5

salary bill *business expenses* 491.4

salary earner *breadwinner* 123.2

salary negotiations *bargaining* 57.9

salary scale *reward for service* 453.5

salchow jump *ice-skating techniques* 162.16

sale 482.2; *transfer of property* 470.4, *selling* 482.1, *bargain* 495.2, *business offer* 504.3

saleable *given* 472.8, *mercantile* 480.13

sale and leaseback *transfer of property* 470.4

sale goods *bargain* 497.4

Salem *American States* 564

sale merchandise *bargain* 497.4

sale of the century *enticement* 178.3, *sale* 482.2, *bargain* 495.2

sale price *price* 494.1

sale-priced *bargain* 497.10

Salerno *Horse and Pony Breeds* 159

saleroom [Brit] *market* 483.1

Salers *Breeds of Cattle* 16

sales 482.3

sales blandishment *empty talk* 362.5

salesclerk *attendant* 69.4, *sales worker* 123.6, *salesperson* 482.8

sales conference *salesmanship* 482.4

sales coverage *selling* 482.1

sales force *salesperson* 482.8

sales forecasting *salesmanship* 482.4

salesgirl *salesperson* 482.8

salesman *sales worker* 123.6, *persuader* 178.9, *speaker* 205.12, *salesperson* 482.8, *motivator* 508.6

sales manager *manager* 126.7

salesmanship 482.4; *publicity* 178.7

sales patter *empty talk* 362.5, *salesmanship* 482.4

salesperson 482.8; *attendant* 69.4, *persuader* 178.9, *speaker* 205.12

sales pitch [Inf] *publicity* 178.7

sales promotion *publicity* 178.7

sales representative *salesperson* 482.8

sales representative or rep [Inf] *sales worker* 123.6

sales revenue *economic factor* 56.8, *money received* 492.2

salesroom *market* 483.1

sales talk *publicity* 178.7, *empty talk* 362.5, *salesmanship* 482.4, *inducement* 508.2

sales tax *tax* 494.5

saleswoman *sales worker* 123.6, *persuader* 178.9, *speaker* 205.12, *salesperson* 482.8, *motivator* 508.6

sales worker 123.6

salient *battleground* 76.24, *clear* 244.6, *appearing* 264.9, *region* 564.1, *accentuated* 843.11

Salienta *amphibian* 37.10

salient angle *angle* 6.37

salientian *amphibian* 37.10, 37.14

salient point *gist* 799.4

salimeter *Fields of Measurement* 589

salina *lake* 568.1, *marsh* 572.3

saline *acid* 11.27

salinity *ocean* 8.14, *sea* 571.1

salinometer *Fields of Measurement* 589

salinometry *Fields of Measurement* 589

saliva 25.9; *body fluid* 19.16, 555.3, *secreted substance* 24.2, *exudate* 557.4, *lubricant* 562.7

salivant *expulsive* 709.11

salivary *of a secretion* 24.5, *expulsive* 709.11

salivary gland *saliva* 25.9

salivate 25.25; *secrete* 24.7, *eat well*

92.23, be hungry 288.21, seep 559.16, leak 707.16

salivating 25.18; secretory 24.4

salivation secretion 24.1, saliva 25.9

sallet historic armor 419.8

sallow Trees and Shrubs 43, unhealthy 114.23, drained of color 252.6, pale 253.10, yellow-faced 259.10

sallowly yellowly 259.13

sallowness whiteness 253.1

sally military attack 418.2, counterattack 418.24, emerge 707.14

sally forth set out 705.12, emerge 707.14, start off 771.27

sally port fort 419.13

salmagundi variety 732.2, mixed thing 797.6

salmon food fish and shellfish 90.20, game fish 154.10

salmonellosis gastroenterological disease 114.11

salmon-pink red 257.5

Saloia Breeds of Sheep 16

salon room 60.9, performance 141.8, material 143.9, meeting place 408.5, hairdressing salon 530.10

saloon drink provider 93.15

saloon [Brit] automobile 687.6

salp protochordate 39.4

salpiglossis Flowers 42

salsa sauce 90.17, red thing 257.3

Salsk Finewool Breeds of Sheep 16

Salt Rivers 570

salt 11.12; food content 90.3, basic cooking ingredient 91.8, cook 91.10, seasoning 221.2, season 221.8, nautical person 690.12, preserver 815.9, preserve 815.14

saltant leaping 713.17

saltation jump 713.7

saltatorial leaping 713.17

saltatorily jerkily 684.29

saltatory convulsive 684.19, leaping 713.17

salt away save 105.20

salted preserved 815.12

salt flat desert 560.4, marsh 572.3

salt-free diet diet 92.5

salt gland secretory mechanism 24.3

salt glaze glaze 129.3

salt-glazed ware Ceramics 129

saltiness flavor 219.3

saltire Heraldic Terms 184

SALT I Treaty disarmament 74.3

salt lake lake 568.1

Salt Lake City American States 564

salt lick animal food 90.2

salt marsh marsh 559.8, 572.3

salt of the earth important person 799.5

Salton Sea Lakes 568

salt pan marsh 572.3

saltpeter propellant 78.14

salt sea sea 571.1

salt tax historical tax 494.8

saltwater fishing 154.13

salt water water 557.1, sea 571.1

saltwater bait fishing saltwater fishing 154.3

saltwater fish fish 154.14

saltwater fisherman fisherman 154.12

saltwater fishes fishes 38.1

saltwater fishing 154.3, Sporting Activities 145

saltwater trolling saltwater fishing 154.3

salty tasty 219.4, piquant 221.6, oceanic 571.7, nautical 690.14

salty taste taste 219.1

salubrious clean 111.13, healthful 113.7, remedial 115.14, hygienic 116.3, in form 624.8, safe 810.16, preserving 815.11

salubriously healthily 113.14, hygienically 116.5

salubriousness healthfulness 113.2

salubrity healthfulness 113.2

salud! [Sp] cheers! 93.22

Saluki Breeds of Dogs 35

salut! [Fr] hello! 704.23

salutarily remedially 115.19

salutary health-giving 113.6, healthful 113.7, remedial 115.14, profitable 801.8, beneficial 825.20

salutation 209.2; sign of courtesy 410.5, greeting 435.5

salutations cry of greeting 239.4, greeting 435.5

salutatory 209.7

salutatory address salutation 209.2

salute 405.7, 405.13, 435.17; drink to 93.20, gesture 183.17, approach 209.10, applause 279.2, fete 279.6, sign of courtesy 410.5, greet 410.11, mark of respect 435.4, greeting 435.5

salutiferous remedial 115.14

saluting showing respect 435.7, greeting 435.8

salvable deliverable 817.3

salvably extricably 817.6

salvage recollect 3.16, aid 275.2, business expenses 491.4, restoration 809.2, restore 809.12, preservation 815.1, deliverance 817.1, deliver 817.5

salvageable deliverable 817.3

salvaged repaired 809.6

salvager deliverer 817.2

salvation divine attribute 82.4, aid 275.2, restoration 809.2, deliverance 817.1, liberation 831.1, cancellation 834.1

Salvation Army Christian Groups 81, charitable organization 305.4

Salvation Army bonnet vestment 84.11

salvationism religiousness 81.2

salvationist religious person 81.9, religionist 81.14

salva veritate philosophical term 4.7

salve dose of medicine 115.3, analgesic 115.6, balm 115.11, comfort 214.14, blarney 439.2, ointment 562.8, anoint 562.17

salve one's conscience be innocent 449.10, do penance 451.9

salvia Flowers 42

salvo bang 234.1, salute 405.7, firing 418.6, shot 696.6

sal volatile tonic 115.8, stimulant 221.5

Salween Rivers 570

samadhi occult and psychic phenomena 86.7

Samar Islands 572

samara botanical fruit 44.2

Samaritanism philanthropy 307.1

samarium Chemical Elements and Common Allotropes 11

Samaveda other text 81.19

samba Dances 135, Card Games 168

Sam Brown belt band 754.9

same 730.7; interfacial 616.4, similar 733.7, equal 740.8

same, the equilibrium 740.2

same damn thing boring thing 296.3

same date same time 649.1

same day same time 649.1

same degree equality 740.1

same meaning type of meaning 361.4

sameness 730.1; lack of emphasis 201.1, boringness 296.2, similarity 733.1, equality 740.1, continuity 774.4

same old round repetitiveness 797.3

same old story boring thing 296.3, regularity 730.6, repetitiveness 797.3

same old thing boring thing 296.3, regularity 730.6

same quantity equality 740.1

same time 649.1

Samhain religious festival 85.13

Samian ware Ceramics 129

samisen Musical Instruments 142

samite Fabrics and Fibers 130

Samkhya Philosophical Schools of Thought 4

Sammael devil 446.5

Samnite Wars Major Wars 76

Samoa Islands Islands 572

Samothrace Islands 572

Samoyed Breeds of Dogs 35

sampan Ships and Boats 690

sample population 6.55, equate 6.88, taste 92.24, 219.5, representative 187.7, appetizer 219.2, explanation 331.3, rehearsal 335.2, experiment 335.11, outline 617.1, 617.5, outlined 617.4, part 760.1, showpiece 843.3

sample freedom be free 829.16

sample pages design and makeup 174.8

sampler appetizer 219.2

sample size population 6.55

samples of test 107.10

sample statistic population 6.55

sampling population 6.55, appetizer 219.2

Samson person of strength 516.8

Sanaa Countries 566

sanative hygienic 116.3, restorative 809.9

sanatorium health improvement 113.3

sanatory hygienic 116.3

Sancho Panza Notable Friendships 62

San Cristobal Islands 572

sanctification deification 82.13

sanctified deified 82.20, virtuous 447.5

sanctify deify 82.23, commemorate 405.11

sanctimonious zealous 81.22, ungenuine 192.13, affected 367.3, moralistic 431.12

sanctimoniously untruthfully 192.27, affectedly 367.5, moralistically 431.16

sanctimoniousness religiousness 81.2, ungenuineness 192.2, affectation 367.1, self-righteousness 431.7

sanctimony religiousness 81.2, ungenuineness 192.2, affectation 367.1, self-righteousness 431.7

sanction authorization 52.3, authorize 52.14, legality 53.9, make legal 53.27, assent 346.1, 346.6, approval 437.1, approve 437.14, contract 462.2, 462.11, permission 502.1, permit 502.6, consent 735.8, 735.28, advise 825.27

sanctioned authorized 52.11, legal 53.16, rightful 429.9, approved

437.8, permitted 502.4, consenting 735.18

sanctions economic warfare 76.7, coercive method 428.3

sanctitude divine attribute 82.4

sanctity divine attribute 82.4, virtue 447.1

sanctuary retreat 60.13, church interior 83.9, church architecture 134.11, hiding place 181.2, solitary place 409.4, security 464.1, taking in 477.7, closed place 584.4, shelter 613.6, enclosed area 619.2, refuge 708.3, 812.1, haven 810.3, ecology 815.3

sanctum privacy 181.6, solitary place 409.4, private space 812.2

sanctum sanctorum shrine 83.10, enclosed area 619.2, private space 812.2

sanctus bell sacred object 83.11

sand sediment 8.29, soil 8.42, masonry 14.22, painting 143.3, orange thing 258.3, smooth 545.10, grit 553.8, powder 553.25, rub 554.12, coast 572.4

sand [Inf] stamina 377.4

sandals shoes 100.30

sandalwood Trees and Shrubs 43, incense 226.3

Sandalwood pony Horse and Pony Breeds 159

sandarac Trees and Shrubs 43

sandbag murder 30.20, blunt weapon 78.5, military defenses 419.9, instrument of punishment 454.13, club 695.15

sandbank coast 8.13, river parts 570.3, island 572.2, shallowness 599.1, hidden danger 813.3

sand bar coast 8.13, island 572.2, shallowness 599.1, hidden danger 813.3

sandblast clean 111.17, rub 554.12

sandblasting wearing away 554.2

sand-blind visually impaired 243.9, blinded 243.12

sandblindness faulty vision 243.1

sandbox amusement park and playground equipment 167.8

sandbox tree Trees and Shrubs 43

sand casting sculpture 144.1

sandcastle weak thing 517.5

sand column wind vortex 9.14

sand dollar echinoderm 39.5

sand dune coast 8.13, dune 8.43, hill 569.2

sander woodworking tool 131.6, smoother 545.2, eraser 554.7, flattener 603.4

sandglass Timepieces and Timers 646

sandhog laborer 123.9

sand hopper crustacean 39.10, parasite 39.18

sandiness graininess 553.2

sanding polishing 554.5

sanding disc eraser 554.7

sand iron golf equipment 156.5

sandman sleep 415.5

sandpaper woodworking tool 131.6, rough thing 544.2, smoother 545.2, smooth 545.10, abrasive 553.14, eraser 554.7, rub 554.12, flattener 603.4

s & p index stock exchange 457.3

sandpiper water bird 36.9

sandpit jumping 166.11

sands desert 572.10

sand shot golf shots 156.4

sands of time passage of time 639.3

sandspit peninsula 572.5

sandstone *masonry* 14.22, *building materials* 104.2
sandstorm *wind* 9.12, *murk* 248.2, *natural violence* 520.3
sand tenon *carpenter* 131.10
sand trap *golf course* 156.2
sand wave *coast* 8.13
sandwich 90.9; *chemical compound* 11.4, *layer* 588.9, *place in the middle* 772.18
sandwich bar *eating place* 92.17
sandwich board *advertisement* 173.9, *showplace* 843.4
sandwich maker *cooking equipment* 91.6, *burner* 217.4
sandwich man *publicizer* 173.11
sandy *earthy* 8.60, *red-haired* 257.7, *grainy* 553.17, *desert* 560.12, *of landmasses* 572.12
sane 109.3; *reasoning* 319.7, *intelligible* 363.5
sanely 109.6; *reasonably* 319.15
saneness *sanity* 109.1, *reason* 319.1
Sanforized™ *smaller* 582.7
San Francisco *major US cities* 567.5
Sangamon *Rivers* 570
sang-froid *calmness* 455.4, *moderation* 521.1, *ease of manner* 823.4
sanguinarily *ruddily* 257.10, *fluidly* 555.26
sanguinary *murderous* 30.18, *bloody* 257.8
sanguine *personality type* 108.6, *red-faced* 257.6, *hopeful* 281.6, *wonderless* 295.3, *expecting* 356.4
sanguinely *hopefully* 281.15, *without wonder* 295.8, *fluidly* 555.26
sanguineous *bloody* 257.8, 555.18
sanguineously *ruddily* 257.10
saniel *Notable Winds* 9
sanies *pus* 25.7, *body fluid* 555.3
sanious *rheumy* 555.16
sanitarian *hygienist* 116.2
sanitarily *hygienically* 116.5
sanitarium *hospital* 107.16, *health improvement* 113.3
sanitary *clean* 111.13, *cleansing* 111.16, *healthful* 113.7, *remedial* 115.14, *hygienic* 116.3
sanitary engineer *cleaner* 111.12, *hygienist* 116.2, *laborer* 123.9
sanitary precaution 810.8; *prophylaxis* 115.4
sanitate *treat* 115.17, *practice hygiene* 116.4, *immunize* 810.22
sanitation *cleaning* 111.2, *prophylaxis* 115.4, *hygiene* 116.1
sanitation worker *laborer* 123.9
sanitize *purify* 111.19, *practice hygiene* 116.4, *immunize* 810.22
sanity 109.1; *reason* 319.1
San Joaquin *Rivers* 570
San José *Countries* 566
San Juan *American States* 564, *Rivers* 570
Sankhya *Philosophical Schools of Thought* 4
Sankhyan *Philosophical Schools of Thought* 4
San Marino *Countries* 566
San Marino GP at San Marino *Formula 1 World Championship races* 146.5
San Martín *Breeds of Cattle* 16
sannyasi *religious person* 81.9, *unsocial person* 409.5
San Remo Rally of the Flowers *automobile rallies* 146.6
San Salvador *Countries* 566
sans-culotte *rebel* 427.8
sans-culottism *revolution* 427.4

sans pareil [Fr] *best* 744.10
sans serif type *type* 173.5
Santa Ana *Notable Winds* 9
Santa Barbara Islands *Islands* 572
Santa Catalina *Islands* 572
Santa Claus *giver* 472.7, *generous person* 498.5
Santa Fe *American States* 564
Santa Gertrudis *Breeds of Cattle* 16
Santa Ines *Breeds of Sheep* 16
Santa Isabel *Islands* 572
Santee *Rivers* 570
Santiago *Countries* 566, *Rivers* 570
santir *Musical Instruments* 142
Santo Domingo *Countries* 566
Santorin *Islands* 572
Santorini *Islands* 572
São Francisco *Rivers* 570
Saône *Rivers* 570
São Tomé *Countries* 566
São Tomé and Príncipe *Countries* 566
sap *remove power from* 515.13, *weaken* 517.13, *juice* 555.2, *concave land* 635.2, *essential content* 723.2
sapele *Trees and Shrubs* 43
sapid *tasty* 219.4
sapidity *taste* 219.1
sapience *cleverness* 315.3, *wisdom* 352.1
sapient *thoughtful* 315.10, *wise* 352.4
Sapir-Whorf hypothesis *linguistic theory* 5.2
sapless *dried-up* 560.9
sapling *young plant* 26.5, *plant* 41.2, *tree* 43.1
saponaceous *oily* 562.11
saponaceousness *oiliness* 562.1
saponifiable lipid *fat* 12.7
saponification *process* 11.15
saponify *react* 11.38
sappanwood *Trees and Shrubs* 43
sapped *weakened* 517.9, *spoiled* 808.9
Sapphic *homosexual* 33.10, *Poem or Verse Forms* 139, *poetic* 139.19
sapphic *of sexual nature* 20.17
sapphire *blue thing* 261.3, *blue* 261.5
sapphism *sexual nature* 20.4
sappiness *youthfulness* 26.2, *juiciness* 555.7
sappy *fresh* 260.10, *flowing* 555.15, *pulpy* 561.19, *seasonal* 654.7
saprobe *fungal association* 47.5
saprophyte *lower plant* 41.4, *fungal association* 47.5
saprophytic *of plants* 41.14, *of fungi* 47.19
saprophytically 47.24; *herbaceously* 41.24
sap the foundations of *knock down* 523.13
sapwood *timber* 43.3, *wood* 131.3
saraband *Dances* 135
sarabande *Musical Forms* 140
Saracenic architecture *Architectural Styles* 134
Saraja *Breeds of Sheep* 16
Sarajevo *Countries* 566
sarangi *Musical Instruments* 142
Saratoga *Card Games* 168
sarcasm *wit* 277.3, *derision* 369.1, *ridicule* 436.4
sarcastic *splenetic* 223.7, *humorous* 277.9, *derisive* 369.5, *ridiculing* 436.13, *scornful* 440.10
sarcastically *splenetically* 223.10,

humorously 277.13, *derisively* 369.8, *mockingly* 436.26
sarcenet *or* **sarsenet** *Fabrics and Fibers* 130
Sarcodina *protozoan* 39.17
sarcoma *cancer* 114.15
sarcophagus *box* 578.5
Sarda *Rivers* 570
sardine *food fish and shellfish* 90.20
sardines *Children's and Party Games* 167
Sardinia *Islands* 572
Sardinian *Breeds of Sheep* 16, *Horse and Pony Breeds* 159
sardonic *satirical* 369.6
sardonically *satirically* 369.9
Sargasso Sea *Oceans and Seas* 571
sari *dress* 100.11
Sark *Islands* 572
sarod *Musical Instruments* 142
sarong *skirt* 100.12
Sar Planina *Breeds of Sheep* 16
sarrusophone *Musical Instruments* 142
sarsnet *Fabrics and Fibers* 130
sartorial *tailored* 100.41
sash *accessory* 100.28, *window* 134.10, *insignia* 184.5, *circular thing* 631.3, *band* 754.9
sash weight *canceling out* 834.3
Saskatchewan *Canadian Provinces* 564, *Rivers* 570
saskatoon *Trees and Shrubs* 43
Sasquatch *Legendary Creatures* 360
sass [Inf] *rudeness* 400.2, *be insolent* 400.14, *bad manners* 411.2, *be discourteous* 411.7, *defiance* 416.1, *defy* 416.7, *assurance* 621.8
sassafras *Tree Products* 43, *Trees and Shrubs* 43
sassafras oil *Tree Products* 43
Sassanian architecture *Architectural Styles* 134
sassily [Inf] *disrespectfully* 436.25
sasswood *or* **sassywood** *or* **sassy** *or* **sassy bark** *Trees and Shrubs* 43
sassy [Inf] *rude* 400.9, *bad-mannered* 411.6, *defiant* 416.5, *disrespectful* 436.9, *assured* 621.12
Satan *tempter* 178.10, *Phobias* 283, *devil* 446.5
Satanic *idolatrous* 83.13, *witchlike* 86.19, *demonic* 446.9, *impious* 448.11
satanically *devilishly* 446.14, *impiously* 448.17
Satanism *idolatry* 83.4, *witchcraft* 86.6, *impiety* 448.4
Satanist *idolater* 83.7
Satanophobia *Phobias* 283
satchel *bag* 578.7
sate *eat well* 92.23, *overindulge* 99.10, *give pleasure* 214.13, *satisfy* 273.7, *bore* 296.8, *fill* 761.11
sated *eating* 92.18, *filled* 97.5, *immoderate* 99.6, *bored* 296.5, *full* 761.8
sateen *Fabrics and Fibers* 130
satellite 7.19; *moon* 7.18, *artificial satellite* 7.30, *adherent* 401.5, 755.4, *national* 566.10, *orbiting body* 681.4, *inferior* 745.4, *follower* 794.10, *dependent* 832.4
satellite communication *telecommunication* 169.7
satellite link *association* 754.2
satellite nation *dominion* 566.3
satellite radio *radio broadcasting* 172.4
satellite status *subjection* 832.1

satellite tracking *artificial satellite* 7.30
satellite transmission *television broadcasting* 172.8
satiate *overindulge* 99.10, *give pleasure* 214.13, *satisfy* 273.7, *bore* 296.8, *fill* 761.11
satiated *immoderate* 99.6, *satisfied* 273.4, *bored* 296.5, *full* 761.8
satiating *immoderate* 99.6, *satisfying* 273.5
satiation *satisfaction* 273.1, *boredom* 296.1
satiety *immoderation* 99.2, *satisfaction* 273.1, *boredom* 296.1, *fullness* 761.5
satin *Fabrics and Fibers* 130, *grain* 552.2, *smooth* 552.9
satininess *smoothness* 543.2, 545.1, *grain* 552.2
satinlike *smooth* 543.8
satin-smooth *figurative expressions* 545.8
satinwood *Trees and Shrubs* 43
satiny *smooth* 543.8, 545.4, 552.9
satire *comedy* 136.11, *Poem or Verse Forms* 139, *entertainment* 277.4, *form of derision* 369.2, *ridicule* 436.4, 440.6, *mimicry* 736.3
satirical 369.6; *humorous* 277.9, *ridiculing* 436.13
satirical comedy *comedy* 136.11
satirically 369.9; *humorously* 277.13, *mockingly* 436.26
satirical poetry *poetry* 139.8
satirist *author* 139.13, *humorist* 277.7, *derider* 369.3, *disparager* 440.7
satirize *be humorous* 277.11, *deride* 369.7, *ridicule* 436.22, 440.15, *imitate* 736.9
satisfaction 273.1; *sufficiency* 97.1, *physical pleasure* 214.1, *pleasure* 271.2, *proudness* 297.3, *atonement* 313.1, *approval* 437.1, *reward* 453.1, *compensation* 453.7, 743.1, *performance* 465.2, *payment* 489.1
satisfactorily 273.12; *sufficiently* 97.9, *properly* 429.18, *approvably* 437.22
satisfactoriness 273.3; *sufficiency* 97.1
satisfactory 273.6; *sufficient* 97.3, *approvable* 437.13
satisfactory amount *sufficiency* 97.1
satisfiable *compensable* 743.4
satisfied 273.4; *pacificatory* 74.8, *filled* 97.5, *pleased* 214.9, *proud* 297.10, *approved* 437.8, *compensated* 743.3, *full* 761.8, *convinced* 840.8
satisfy 273.7; *theorize* 6.84, *conciliate* 74.10, *suffice* 97.6, *motivate* 178.17, *give pleasure* 214.13, *make pleasant* 271.10, *atone* 313.7, *meet with approval* 437.20, *reward* 453.13, *perform* 465.5, *pay off* 489.17, *mitigate* 521.9, *compensate* 743.7, *fill* 761.11
satisfying 273.5; *pacificatory* 74.8, *sufficient* 97.3, *pleasant* 214.7, 271.5, *rewarding* 453.9
satisfyingly *pleasingly* 214.15, *rewardingly* 453.9
satrap *absolute ruler* 68.7
Satsuma porcelain *Ceramics* 129
saturate *solidify* 11.37, *be excessive* 99.9, *water* 557.29, *be present* 575.13, *fill* 761.11
saturated *atmospheric* 9.40, *chemical compound* 11.4, *status*

adjectives 11.25, excessive 99.5, exposed 132.25, wet 557.23
saturated fat fat 12.7, 562.4, food content 90.3
saturated solution phase 11.13
saturation atmospheric process 9.9, excess 99.1, hue 251.4, dilution 557.5, soaking 557.9, humidity 559.3, mixture 751.1, fullness 761.5
saturation bombing bombing 76.21, air attack 418.4
saturation level exposure 132.15
saturation point excess 99.1, humidity 559.3, fullness 761.5
Saturday night special [Inf] firearm 78.7
Saturn Planets and Their Satellites 7, planet 7.16, Deities 82
Saturnalia religious festival 85.13
saturnalia celebration 405.1, dissipation 456.2
Saturnian astronomical 7.33
saturnine sullen 304.8
saturninely sullenly 304.16
saturnineness or **saturninity** sullenness 304.1
Satyagraha Philosophical Schools of Thought 4
Satyagrahi Philosophical Schools of Thought 4
satyr sexual perversion 20.12, libertine 32.7, minor deity 82.2, desirer 288.9, Legendary Creatures 360, sexually immoral person 432.8
satyriasis sexual perversion 20.12, compulsion 108.13, sexual desire 288.5, sexual immorality 432.2
satyrical lustful 288.15
satyrism sexual perversion 20.12
satyromaniac desirer 288.9
satyr play historic comedy 136.12
sauce 90.17; side dish 90.15, 794.11, make taste 219.6, defiance 416.1, juice 555.2, ornamentation 748.5
sauce [Inf] alcoholic drink 93.9, rudeness 400.2, bad manners 411.2, assurance 621.8
sauce boat crockery 578.16
saucebox [Inf] insolent person 400.7
saucepan cooking equipment 91.6, pot 578.15
saucer tableware 92.13, crockery 578.16, circular thing 631.3
saucer dome roof 134.7
saucily rudely 400.19, 411.9, defiantly 416.9
sauciness rudeness 400.2, defiance 416.1
saucy rude 400.9, bad-mannered 411.6, defiant 416.5, disrespectful 436.9, assured 621.12
Saudi Arabia Countries 566
sauerbraten notable international dishes 90.40
sauerkraut vegetable 90.33
sault river turbulence 570.5
sauna bath 111.6, hot place 217.5
saunter bodily movement 677.11, walk 677.17, slow motion 693.3, move slowly 693.11
sauntering slow 693.7
Sauria lizard 37.5
saurian lizard 37.5, reptilian 37.12
saurischian extinct reptile 37.9
sauropod extinct reptile 37.9
sauropterygian extinct reptile 37.9
sausage 90.29
sausage meat sausage 90.29
sauté cook 91.10, brown 256.7
sautéed culinary 91.9

sautéing cooking technique 91.2
Sava Rivers 570
savable deliverable 817.3
savage murderous 30.18, 520.7, inflict pain 215.10, cruel 306.10, harm 306.13, unformed 389.11, discourteous person 411.4, bad-mannered 411.6, strike 418.21, villain 448.5, be wicked 448.13, violent animal 520.4, use violence 520.9, vulgar person 535.4, naive person 821.2
savage beast violent animal 520.4
savagely cruelly 306.17, rudely 411.9
savageness cruelty 306.4
savagery cruelty 306.4, violence by person 520.2
savages primitive humanity 18.4
savanna or **savannah** plants 41.1, grassland 45.2, lowland 572.6
Savannah Rivers 570
savannah countryside 564.3
savant sage 4.11, expert 127.9, intellectual 315.7, knowledgeable person 348.5, specialist 779.9
save 105.20, 275.9; program 15.29, economize 56.11, preach 84.14, pitching terms 147.5, soccer play 163.5, play soccer 163.8, take precautions 287.14, be prepared 388.17, not use 394.9, rescue 419.26, budget 457.10, acquire 467.19, profit 467.22, detain 471.9, bank 484.26, be thrifty 499.5, hoard 501.6, persuade 670.14, by subtraction 749.8, exclusively 764.10, restore 809.12, protect 810.21, preserve 815.14, deliver 817.5, help 825.23, liberate 831.6
save and except [Form] by subtraction 749.8
save at the last second or **minute** deliver 817.5
save by the bell box 152.19, deliver 817.5
saved 105.15; unused 394.5, retained 471.6, accounted 493.8, converted 670.7, preserved 815.12, delivered 817.4, liberated 831.4
saved by the bell delivered 817.4
save face guard one's pride 297.16
save for a rainy day delay 658.13
save from deliver 817.5
saveloy [Brit] sausage 90.29
save one's bacon [Inf] be safe 810.20, escape 816.8, be an instrument 511.7
save one's breath lapse into silence 208.8
save oneself escape 816.8
save oneself the trouble do easily 823.16
save one's skin be safe 810.20, escape 816.8
saver 499.3; gainer 467.9, depositor 487.6
save the life of support life 28.21
save up deposit 105.21, acquire 467.19, be thrifty 499.5, hoard 501.6, preserve 815.14
savin Trees and Shrubs 43
saving 815.4; home economics 56.2, detention 471.2, thrifty 499.4, preservation 815.1, deliverance 817.1, delivered 817.4
saving clause specification 340.6
saving grace virtues 447.2
saving qualities virtues 447.2
savings reserve 105.3, precaution 287.4, preparations 388.2, unused thing 394.4, personal finance 457.5, takings 477.8, wealth 485.1, insurance 810.10

savings account reserve 105.3, personal finance 457.5, funds 484.6, wealth 485.1, accounts 493.4, insurance 810.10
savings account deposit deposit 487.3
savings and loan association lending institution 475.4, treasury 484.19, bank 487.4
savings bank treasury 484.19, bank 487.4
savings bond paper money 484.14
saving up saving 815.4
Savior God the Son 82.9
savior giver 472.7, deliverer 817.2
savoir-faire refinement 48.10, social skill 127.3, knowledge 348.1, good conduct 399.5, social success 408.3, good manners 410.2
savoir-vivre social skill 127.3, social success 408.3, good manners 410.2
savor taste 92.24, 219.5, feel pleasure 214.12, flavor 219.3, odor 224.1, reputation 224.4, take pleasure in 271.11, enjoy 290.9, characteristic 779.5
savoring delicate eating 92.3
savor of mean 361.13, seem like 733.14
savorous tasty 219.4, odorous 224.5
savory dish 90.7, Herbs and Spices 91, edible 92.20, tasty 219.4, piquant 221.6
Savoy Breeds of Sheep 16
savvy [Inf] learnedness 48.8, social skill 127.3, common sense 315.4, knowledge 348.1, know 348.10, understand 521.9
saw machine tool 14.9, hand tool 103.3, woodworking tool 131.6, carpenter 131.10, maxim 177.1, sound hoarse 238.8, be dissonant 241.6, moral 431.5, sharp-edged thing 549.6, use a sharp tool 549.17, opener 583.2, open 583.15, take apart 753.16
saw blade notched thing 636.2
sawbones [Inf] doctor 107.19
sawbuck [Inf] US coinage 484.10
sawdust powder 553.9, residue 750.2
sawed open 583.10
saw edge roughness 544.1, sharp edge 549.3
saw-edged sharp-edged 549.12
sawed-off shortened 591.7
sawed-off shotgun firearm 78.7
sawflies pests and diseases 17.12
sawlike notched 636.4
sawmill factory 124.8
sawn open 583.10
saw off the limb one sits on figurative expressions 128.11
sawt Collective Names 59
saw-toothed notched 636.4
sawtooth wave wave 683.4
sawyer artisan 123.13, woodworker 131.4
saxhorn Musical Instruments 142
saxicolous lichenoid 47.21
saxifrage Flowers 42
Saxon historic 653.13
saxophone Musical Instruments 142
saxophonist player 141.2
saxotromba Musical Instruments 142
saxtuba Musical Instruments 142
say authorization 52.3, Fabrics and Fibers 130, utterance 205.10, speak 205.17, state 329.13, electing 382.5, nearly 586.18, superiority 744.1

sayable permitting 502.5
say again iterate 797.16
Sayan Mountains Mountains and Hills 569
say a prayer of thanks give thanks 310.7
say clearly mean 361.13
say directly mean 361.13
sayer speaker 205.12
say farewell part 705.13
say good-bye to lose 468.12
say good morning to approach 209.10
say grace pray 85.20, give thanks 310.7
say hello greet 410.11
say I do marry 64.19, get engaged to 458.12
say in a roundabout way be equivocal 380.7
saying maxim 177.1, moral 431.5
saying again iteration 797.2
saying little sparing with words 208.6
say in other words mean 361.13
say it all be complete 761.10
say magic words bewitch 86.25
say no refuse 190.17, 347.9, 506.8, withhold approval 438.17, veto 503.9, protest 507.7, repel 701.7
say nothing be silent 181.16, be taciturn 208.7, restrain oneself 830.15
say one is sorry apologize 313.8, be penitent 451.7
say one's beads pray 85.20
say one's prayers pray 85.20
say one will promise 458.11
say over again iterate 797.16
say over and over harp 797.17
say plainly mean 361.13
say prayers worship 83.15, offer worship 696.10
say so be assertive 189.28, command 425.10
say-so authorization 52.3
say sotto voce sound faint 233.8
say thank you be grateful 310.6
say the Lord's Prayer or **Our Father** pray 85.20
say the magic word permit 502.6
say the same as assent 346.6
say the word permit 735.29
say together synchronize 649.7
say to oneself soliloquize 211.4
say whatever comes into one's mind improvise 396.6
say whatever pops into one's head improvise 396.6
say what is in or **on one's mind** be naive 821.4
say yes assent 346.6, promise 458.11, agree with 462.10, permit 502.6
S-bend automobile racing terms 146.3
s-block chemical element 11.3
scab strike 57.8, reactionary 427.9, dissenter 463.5, refuser 506.4, protester 507.4, blemish 533.1, rough skin 544.3, cover 613.2
scabbard historical ammunition 78.12
scabby unclean 112.8, marked 533.6, coarse 544.6
scabies skin disease 114.16, Phobias 283
scabiophobia Phobias 283
scabious Flowers 42
scablike marked 533.6
scabrous obscene 112.9, offensive 432.11, marked 533.6, coarse 544.6
scabrousness roughness 544.1

scads [Inf] *large number* 783.3, *multitude* 795.1

scads of money [Inf] *money* 485.2

scaffold *preparations* 388.2, *framework* 551.4, *supporting structure* 605.2, *support* 605.16

scaffolding *preparations* 388.2, *supporting structure* 605.2

scag [Inf] *opiates* 121.17

scalable *ladderlike* 713.18

scalar *vector* 6.48, *ladderlike* 713.18

scalariform *ladderlike* 713.18

scalar product *vector* 6.48

scalar quantity *vector* 6.48

scalawag *troublemaker* 427.5

scald *pests and diseases* 17.12, *cook* 91.10, *painful injury* 215.3, *inflict pain* 215.10, *heat* 217.17

scalding *painful* 215.4, *heating* 217.12

scale 140.16, 588.10, 589.9; *fish characteristic* 38.8, *pest* 40.5, *balance beam* 157.3, *map* 187.5, *weighing instrument* 538.7, *rough skin* 544.3, *be rough* 544.10, *size* 579.1, *slice* 588.4, *measuring instrument* 589.12, *rise* 596.17, *animal covering* 613.15, *shed* 614.21, *ladder* 713.11, *step* 713.11, *climb* 713.21, *interrelatedness* 727.3, *degree* 739.1, *measure* 739.7, *particle* 760.4, *consecutiveness* 774.1

scale a peak *mountaineer* 161.10

scale armor *historic armor* 419.8

scale back *make little* 580.10

scaled *gradational* 739.5

scaled-down *smaller* 582.7

scaled-down version *little thing* 580.3

scale down *contract* 582.12, *make smaller* 747.8, *reduce* 796.8

scale drawing *map* 387.7

scale insects *pests and diseases* 17.12

scale leaf *leaf* 41.6

scalene *angled* 628.9, *unequal* 741.4

scalene triangle *triangle* 6.41, *angled figure* 628.3

scale off *shed* 614.21

scaler *leaf* 41.6

Scales *Constellations* 7

scales *cooking equipment* 91.6, *dirt* 112.5, *weighing instrument* 538.7

scale the heights *climb* 713.21

scaliness *roughness* 544.1, *layering* 588.5

scaling *dentistry* 107.6, *mounting* 713.8

scaling-down *contraction* 582.1

scaling the heights *mounting* 713.8

scallop *food fish and shellfish* 90.20, *Architectural Elements* 134, *convolute* 632.6, *notched thing* 636.2

scallop boat *or* scalloper *Ships and Boats* 690

scalloped *notched* 636.4

scalloped edge *roughness* 544.1

scallop shell *convoluted thing* 632.3

scallywag *troublemaker* 427.5

scalp *head* 19.6

scalped *depilatory* 614.15

scalper *shedder* 614.7

scalping *depilation* 614.8

scaly *reptilian* 37.12, *ichthyological* 38.11, *coarse* 544.6, *crumbly* 553.16, *platelike* 588.8

scaly anteater *insect-eating mammal* 35.7

scam *foul play* 193.6, *swindle* 193.19, *disreputable action* 371.3,

dishonesty 479.7, *nonpayment* 490.1

scammer *schemer* 193.10

scamp *troublemaker* 427.5, *miscreant* 448.6, *vulgar person* 535.4

scamper 694.12; *bodily movement* 677.11, *acceleration* 694.3, *make haste* 818.5

scamper away *hurry off* 705.11

scampering *hasty* 818.3

scampish *villainous* 448.12

scan *reproduce* 21.13, *diagnostic radiology* 107.12, *practice medicine* 107.32, *represent* 187.10, *observation* 242.5, *inspect* 242.22, *question* 333.16, *estimate* 341.11

scandal *disrepute* 371.1, *impropriety* 430.5, *defamation* 440.3, *false accusation* 442.2

scandalmonger *print journalist* 175.5, *meddler* 321.4, *disparager* 440.7

scandalous *disreputable* 371.4, *immoral* 430.11, *defamatory* 440.9, *wicked* 448.9

scandalously *disgracefully* 371.8, *improperly* 430.26, *wickedly* 448.15

scandalousness *wickedness* 448.1

scandal sheet *newspaper* 175.2

scandent *steep* 713.15

Scandinavian modern *Furniture Styles* 101

scandium *Chemical Elements and Common Allotropes* 11

scanned *reproduced* 21.10, *metrical* 139.20

scanned image *reproduction* 21.1

scanner *input device* 15.11, *character recognition* 15.20, *observer* 242.15

scanning *diagnostic radiology* 107.12, *metrical* 139.20, *observation* 242.5

scansion *meter* 139.10

scansorial *steep* 713.15

scant *not enough* 98.5, *inadequate* 486.13, *little* 580.7, *short* 591.6, *meager* 593.12, *sparse* 595.14, *796.6, incomplete* 762.5

scant courtesy *bad manners* 411.2

scanties *underwear* 100.22

scantily *not enough* 98.12, *inadequately* 486.19, *meagerly* 593.19, *sparsely* 595.20, *796.11, incompletely* 762.10

scantiness *incompleteness* 98.2, *762.1, inadequacy* 486.5, *absence* 576.1, *littleness* 580.1, *shortness* 591.1, *meagerness* 593.6, *sparseness* 595.8, *fewness* 796.3

scantling *size* 579.1

scantly *not enough* 98.12, *inadequately* 486.19

scantness *incompleteness* 98.2, *762.1, inadequacy* 486.5, *littleness* 580.1

scanty *not enough* 98.5, *inadequate* 486.13, *little* 580.7, *short* 591.6, *meager* 593.12, *sparse* 595.14, *796.6, incomplete* 762.5, *uncompleted* 762.7

scapegoat *victim of discrimination* 337.8, *loser* 468.8, *recipient* 473.5, *substitute* 672.2, *person in adversity* 848.9

scaphoid bone *Human Bones* 19

scaphopod *mollusk* 39.13

Scaphopoda *mollusk* 39.13

scapula *Human Bones* 19

scapular *vestment* 84.11

scar *personal identification* 184.4, *identify* 184.11, *make ugly* 531.4,

blemish 533.1, *mark* 533.8, *mountain* 569.1, *stain* 808.20

scarab *or* scarabaeus *talisman* 86.9

Scaramouch *or* Scaramouche *stock part* 136.24, *clown* 138.10

scarce 98.8; *inadequate* 486.13, *valuable* 496.8, *sparse* 541.3, *796.6, infrequent* 662.2

scarce as hen's teeth *infrequent* 662.2

scarcely *not enough* 98.12, *barely* 593.18, *seldom* 640.9, *infrequently* 662.4, *to a degree* 739.11, *sparsely* 796.11, *imperfectly* 806.10

scarcely alike *incomparably* 734.12

scarcely any *few* 796.5

scarcely ever *seldom* 640.9, *infrequently* 662.4

scarcely to be expected *improbable* 839.4

scarceness *scarcity* 98.3, *sparseness* 541.1, *infrequency* 662.1, *fewness* 796.3

scarcity 90.5, 98.3; *inadequacy* 486.5, *sparseness* 541.1, *absence* 576.1, *infrequency* 662.1, *decrease* 747.1, *fewness* 796.3

scarcity value *value* 494.2, *496.6

scare *fear* 283.1, *frighten* 283.17, *harm* 306.13, *false alarm* 814.4

scarecrow *pest control* 16.13, *figure* 187.4, *frightener* 283.7, *ugly thing* 531.2, *thin person* 595.4

scared *frightened* 283.9, *cowardly* 285.4, *weak-willed* 517.10

scared out of one's wits *frightened* 283.9

scared shitless [Inf] *frightened* 283.9

scared stiff [Inf] *frightened* 283.9

scared to death *frightened* 283.9

scaredy-cat [Inf] *frightened person* 283.8, *coward* 285.3

scaremonger *frightener* 283.7, *warner* 814.5

scarer *frightener* 283.7

scare someone half to death *frighten* 283.17

scare someone out of his *or* her wits *frighten* 283.17

scare someone to death *frighten* 283.17

scare tactics *terrorization* 283.5

scare the living daylights out of *frighten* 283.17

scare the pants off *frighten* 283.17

scare the shit out of [Inf] *frighten* 283.17

scare up [Inf] *acquire* 467.19

scarf *accessory* 100.28, *neckwear* 100.29, *body covering* 613.3, *enclosing thing* 619.3

scarf joint *carpenter's term* 131.5

scarf up *or* down [Inf] *eat well* 92.23

scariness *terrorization* 283.5

scarlatina *infection* 114.7

scarlet *red* 257.5, *unchaste* 432.10, *depraved* 448.10

scarlet fever *infection* 114.7, *figurative usage* 257.4

scarlet tanager *red thing* 257.3

Scarlett O'Hara *Famous Lovers* 299

scarlet woman *sexually immoral person* 432.8

scarp *landform* 8.9, *fort* 419.13, *mountain* 569.1, *obliquity* 628.2

scarper [Brit] *depart* 265.6, *abscond* 576.16, *hurry off* 705.11

scarred *identified* 184.9, *blemished* 533.5

scary *frightening* 283.12

scat [Inf] *run away* 386.21, *make haste* 818.5

scat! [Inf] *go!* 709.30

scatheless *unbroken* 805.13

scatologic(al) *fecal* 25.14

scatological *of language* 5.35, *obscene* 112.9, *profane* 301.10, *ribald* 535.8

scatologically *colloquially* 5.45, *excrementally* 25.27, *ribaldly* 535.12

scatology *nonstandard language* 5.7, *vulgarism* 5.20, *obscenity* 112.4, *profanity* 301.3

scatophobia *Phobias* 283

scat singer *singer* 141.4

scat singing *jazz* 140.5

scatter 753.15, 796.9; *interact* 10.73, *waste* 96.15, *cause to disappear* 265.7, *abolish* 523.11, *powder* 553.25, *set in motion* 677.16, *bring* 685.11, *diffraction* 698.6, *deflect* 698.26, *radiate* 703.13, *throw down* 716.13, *diverge* 753.20, *unstick* 756.6, *deconstruct* 758.7, *disorder* 766.17, *disperse* 776.12, *sprinkle* 776.15, *defeat* 845.17

scatter around *sprinkle* 776.15

scatterbrain *unintelligent person* 316.4

scatterbrained *unskillful* 128.4, *careless* 324.8, *irresolute* 666.4, *confused* 766.12

scatter diagram *graph* 6.30, *chart* 767.8

scattered *diffractive* 698.14, *apart* 753.8, *nonadhesive* 756.4, *disintegrated* 758.3, *dispersed* 776.6, *sprinkled* 776.9, *sparse* 796.6

scattered showers *rain* 9.27

scattergram *graph* 6.30

scattering *atmospheric process* 9.9, *wave property* 10.12, *nuclear reaction* 10.59, *disappearance* 265.1, *radiation* 703.3, *fallen* 716.8, *separation* 753.1, *nonadhesion* 756.1, *deconstruction* 758.2, *dispersion* 776.1, *dispersive* 776.10, *few* 796.1

scattering of the ashes *cremation* 31.2

scatter seed *farm* 16.19

scatter to the winds *go to waste* 468.19, *sprinkle* 776.15

scatty [Brit inf] *irresolute* 666.4

scavenger *type of animal* 34.5, *cleaner* 111.12

scavenger hunt *Children's and Party Games* 167

scavenger's daughter *instrument of torture* 454.14

scelerophobia *Phobias* 283

scenario *script* 137.5, *aspect of fiction* 139.5, *gist* 329.4, *plan* 387.1, *circumstances* 573.2

scenario writer *filmmaker* 137.14

scenarist *filmmaker* 137.14

scend *billow* 571.9

scene *drama* 136.1, *play part* 136.8, *stage set* 136.19, *motion-picture studio* 137.7, *type of painting* 143.5, *view* 242.8, *burst of anger* 302.6, *show* 404.12, *formal occasion* 406.4, *situation* 573.1, *circumstances* 573.2, *surroundings* 615.1, *part of writing* 760.6, *showplace* 843.4

scene dock *stage* 136.18

scene master *stagehand* 136.29

scene of desolation *havoc* 523.5
scene of destruction *havoc* 523.5
scene painter *stagehand* 136.29, *painter* 143.7
scenery *stage set* 136.19, *motion-picture studio* 137.7, *view* 242.8, *situation* 573.1, *surroundings* 615.1
scene-stealer *actor* 136.25
scenic *artistic* 133.7, *visual* 242.16, *grand* 404.22, *picturesque* 529.9, *decorated* 532.9
scenically *artistically* 133.10
scenic railroad *railroad system* 688.1
scent 224.3; *be informed* 170.15, *signs* 183.2, *vestige* 185.11, *odor* 224.1, *impart odor to* 224.9, *fragrance* 226.1, *perfume* 226.6, *indication* 339.3, *foresee* 357.9, *toiletries* 530.6, *beautify* 530.14, *draw in* 708.18
scented *odorous* 224.5, *fragrant* 226.4
scented soap *cleaning agent* 111.9, *fat* 562.4
scent from afar *foresee* 357.9
scent game *hunt* 160.12
scent gland *secretory mechanism* 24.3, *mammalian characteristic* 35.3, *scent* 224.3
scentless *odorless* 225.4
scentlessness *odorlessness* 225.1
scent out *hunt* 160.12, *follow* 385.12, *draw in* 708.18
scepter *insignia* 184.5
schadenfreude *malice* 306.2
schedule *plan* 357.2, 387.1, *plan out* 387.14, *division* 577.6, *itemize* 577.13, *chronology* 646.2, *keep time* 646.12, *order* 765.1, *chart* 767.8, *make arrangements* 767.23, *list of dates* 785.6, *list* 785.11
scheduled *itemized* 577.9, *listed* 785.9
scheduled event *future condition* 650.3
scheduled flight *aviation* 689.1
schedule of events *plan* 387.1
scheduler *reminder* 354.4
scheduling *timekeeping* 646.1
Scheldt *or* Schelde *Rivers* 570
Schellingism *Philosophical Schools of Thought* 4
Schellingianism *Philosophical Schools of Thought* 4
schema *chart* 767.8
schematic *pictorial* 6.75, *purposive* 327.11, *planned* 387.10, *itemized* 577.9, *ordered* 765.10, *organizational* 767.13, *diagrammatic* 767.17
schematically *purposively* 327.20, *as planned* 387.16, *thematically* 577.16, *in place* 767.24
schematize *itemize* 577.13, *organize* 767.19
SCHEME *Programming Languages* 15
scheme 193.18; *aspect of fiction* 139.5, *artifice* 193.5, *plan* 327.3, 387.1, *aim* 327.17, *sophism* 330.2, *practice sophistry* 330.11, *plot* 387.6, 387.15, *division* 577.6, *order* 765.1, *method* 765.7, *chart* 767.8, *stratagem* 822.2, *be cunning* 822.5
schemer 193.10; *planner* 387.9, *cunning person* 822.3
scheming *artful* 193.13, *planning* 387.8, 387.11, *cunning* 822.4
scherma [It] *fencing* 153.1
scherzando *Musical Terms and Expression Marks* 140

scherzo *Musical Forms* 140
Schiff's reagent *sugar test* 12.6
schilling *national coins* 484.11
schipperke *Breeds of Dogs* 35
schism *faction* 347.4, *revolution* 427.4, *dispute* 463.3, *separation* 753.1, *nonconformism* 782.3
schismatic *dissenter* 347.5, 782.8, *dissenting* 347.7, *subversive* 427.11, *disagreeing* 463.6, *nonconformist* 782.13
schismatical *dissenting* 347.7, *nonconformist* 782.13
schismatically *subversively* 427.15, *in disagreement* 463.12
schismatize *dissent* 347.8
schistose *chalky* 8.59
schistosity *metamorphic rock* 8.36
schistosomiasis *tropical disease* 114.10
schizo [Inf] *mentally ill* 110.11
schizoaffective disorder *psychosis* 108.10
schizocarp *botanical fruit* 44.2
schizocarpic *of a fruit* 44.8
schizocarpic fruit *botanical fruit* 44.2
schizoid *psychologically disturbed* 108.39, *insane person* 110.5, *mentally ill* 110.11
schizoidism *dissociative disorder* 108.17
schizoid personality *dissociative disorder* 108.17, *psychosis* 110.3
schizoid personality disorder *personality disorder* 108.7
schizophrenia *psychosis* 108.10, 110.3, *dissociative disorder* 108.17, *psychiatric disease* 114.21
schizophrenic *psychologically disturbed* 108.39, *insane person* 110.5, *mentally ill* 110.11
schizophreniform disorder *psychosis* 108.10
schizothymia *dissociative disorder* 108.17
schizotypal personality disorder *personality disorder* 108.7
Schläger-Mensur [Ger] *fencing* 153.1
schlep [Inf] *convey* 685.9
schleppend *Musical Terms and Expression Marks* 140
Schleswig Heavy Draught *Horse and Pony Breeds* 159
schmear [Inf] *bribe* 472.3
Schmidt telescope *telescope* 7.25
schnauzer *Breeds of Dogs* 35
schnell *Musical Terms and Expression Marks* 140
schnoz [Inf] *or* schnozzle [Inf] *nose* 19.11, *protuberance* 634.3
schola cantorum *religious school* 48.13
scholar *learner* 48.6, *expert* 52.8, 127.9, *educational leader* 68.11, *dissertator* 203.3, *intellectual* 315.7, *knowledgeable person* 348.5, *wise person* 352.3, *specialist* 779.9
scholarliness *learnedness* 48.8
scholarly *educated* 48.19, *expert* 52.12, *literary* 139.15, *reasoning* 317.6, *literate* 348.8, *specialized* 779.11
scholarship *education* 48.1, *learning* 48.7, 348.3, *learnedness* 48.8, *grant* 453.4, *profit* 467.6, *gift* 472.2, *something received* 473.2, *income* 492.3, *financial assistance* 825.6
scholarship winner *recipient* 473.5

Scholastic *Philosophical Schools of Thought* 4
scholastic *educational* 48.17, *educated* 48.19, *theologian* 81.20
scholastically *studiously* 48.26
scholasticate *subject* 48.3, *religious school* 48.13
Scholasticism *Philosophical Schools of Thought* 4
scholastic theology *Theologies* 81
scholiast *interpreter* 365.6
scholiastic *annotative* 365.10
scholium *annotation* 365.2
school 48.11; *social institution* 2.8, *assemblage of mammals* 35.22, *fishes* 38.1, *school place* 48.16, *educate* 48.22, *Collective Names* 59, *religious group* 81.4, *belief system* 87.3, *Phobias* 283, *cause to know* 348.13, *building* 551.9, *municipal building* 567.13, *assimilate* 781.14
schoolable *educatable* 48.18
school-age *young* 26.11
schoolbag *bag* 578.7
school board *educator* 48.4
schoolbook 48.15; *type of book* 174.3
schoolboy *young man* 26.8, *learner* 48.6
schoolchild *learner* 48.6
schoolchildren *the young* 26.10
school crossing *crossing point* 692.7
school days *youth* 26.1
school dictionary *word book* 5.27
schooled *literate* 348.8
schooler *learner* 48.6
schoolfellow *friend* 62.2
school furniture *furniture* 101.1
schoolgirl *young woman* 26.9, *learner* 48.6
schoolhouse *school place* 48.16
schooling *education* 48.1, *learning* 348.3
school letter *insignia* 184.5
schoolma'am *or* schoolmarm *educator* 48.4, *educational leader* 68.11
schoolmaster *educator* 48.4, *educational leader* 68.11
schoolmate *friend* 62.2
schoolmistress *educator* 48.4, *educational leader* 68.11
school notes *notes* 185.3
school nurse *nurse* 107.23
school of thought *philosophical system* 4.2
school place 48.16
school report *record* 185.1
school ring *clothing* 184.6
schoolroom *school place* 48.16
school ship *Ships and Boats* 690
school subject *specialization* 779.3
schoolteacher *educator* 48.4
school term *period of activity* 641.4
school uniform *uniform* 100.9, *clothing* 184.6, *formal clothing* 406.5
school work *work* 122.1
schoolyard *school place* 48.16
schooner *sailboat* 150.3, *Sailing Ships and Boats* 690
Schopenhauerean *Philosophical Schools of Thought* 4
Schopenhauerism *Philosophical Schools of Thought* 4
schottische *Dances* 135
schrod *fish dish* 90.19
Schrödinger equation *wavelength* 683.5
Schrödinger's cat *philosophical*

problem 4.8, *Classical Physical Laws* 10
Schrödinger's wave equation *Classical Physical Laws* 10
Schur's lemma *Mathematical Concepts* 6
schuss *ski run* 162.2, *skiing techniques* 162.5, *ski* 162.35
schussing *snowplow* 162.29
schwa *Accents and Diacritical Marks* 5
sciamachy *conception* 360.4
sciaphobia *or* sciophobia *Phobias* 283
sciatica *neurological disease* 114.20, *painful condition* 215.2
science *learning* 348.3
Science and Health with Key to the Scriptures *Christian text* 81.16
science fiction *conception* 360.4
science-fiction *dramatic* 137.16
science-fiction film *movie type* 137.3
science fiction novel *novel* 139.3
science of color *chromatics* 251.2
science of human and animal behavior *psychology* 108.1
science of interpretation *365.5*
science of language *linguistics* 5.1
science of law *jurisprudence* 53.13
science of measurement *589.3*
science of rotation *682.10*
science of rotatory motion *science of rotation* 682.10
science of structure *551.15*
science of substances *chemistry* 11.1
science of the mind *psychology* 108.1
science subject *subject* 48.3
scientific *skeptical* 333.14, *experimental* 335.8, *well-ordered* 765.14
scientifically *skillfully* 127.16, *questioningly* 333.21, *experimentally* 335.14
scientific aptitude test *Psychological Tests* 108
scientific investigation *questioning* 333.2
scientific law *formula* 780.7
scientific perspective *treatment* 143.6
scientific researcher *theorist* 359.4
scientism *materialization* 524.2
scientist *professional worker* 123.11, *expert* 127.9, *questioner* 333.9, *experimenter* 335.5, *knowledgeable person* 348.5, *theorist* 359.4
scientological *psychic* 86.17
scientology *supernaturalism* 86.3
sci-fi [Inf] *dramatic* 137.16
sci-fi film [Inf] *movie type* 137.3
scilicet [L] *particularly* 779.21
Scilly Isles *Islands* 572
scimitar *sharp weapon* 78.6
scintilla *fuel starter* 106.3, *fire* 246.9
scintillate *light up* 246.20, *be intelligent* 352.7
scintillating *bright* 246.14
scintillatingly *lightly* 246.23
scintillation *orbit* 7.22, *quality of light* 246.2
sciolism *lack of knowledge* 349.2
scion *plant breeding* 17.6, *young plant* 26.5, *stem* 41.5, *family tree* 65.3, *component* 760.3, *taxonomic classification* 777.3
scissile *brittle* 548.3, *separable* 753.11

scission *brittleness* 548.1, *separateness* 753.3

scissor *use a sharp tool* 549.17

scissors *pommel horse* 157.7, *cross-country* 162.31, *swimming* 164.12, *hairdressing tool* 530.9, *sharp-edged thing* 549.6

scissors block *play* 155.8

scissors kick *swimming techniques* 164.2

scissors style *jumping* 166.11

scissure *crack* 587.2

sciurine *rodentlike* 35.28

sciuromorph *gnawing mammal* 35.13

sclaff *golf shots* 156.4, *play* 156.8

sclera *eye* 19.9, 242.3

scleroprotein *protein* 12.9

sclerosis *hardening* 542.2

sclerotic *hard* 542.5

sclerotization *protein* 12.9

scoff *be humorous* 277.11, *derision* 400.5, *taunt* 436.6, 436.23, *ridicule* 440.15

scoff [Inf] *eat well* 92.23

scoff at *disbelieve* 88.8, *deride* 369.7, *disdain* 400.16

scoff at virtue *be wicked* 448.13

scoffing *derision* 369.1, *derisive* 369.5, 400.12, *discourtesy* 411.1, *taunting* 436.14, *scornful* 440.10

scoffingly *derisively* 369.8, 400.22, *rudely* 411.9

scold *unpleasant woman* 33.7, *irascible person* 303.7, *dissenter* 347.5, *condemn* 438.18, *punish* 454.22

scolding *condemnation* 438.2, *condemning* 438.10, *censuring* 438.12, *punishment* 454.1

scoleciphobia Phobias 283

scolionophobia Phobias 283

sconce *electric light* 246.6

scone *pastry* 90.37

scoop *field hockey tactics* 158.5, *play field hockey* 158.10, *news story* 171.3, *report* 171.9, 175.9, *ladle* 578.17, *take away* 685.12, *extractor* 711.9

scoop [Inf] *inside information* 170.4, *fact* 717.6

scooped *storing* 578.19

scoop out *make concave* 635.7

scoot *retreat* 386.22, *be swift* 694.10

scoot! [Inf] *go!* 709.30

scooter *motorcycle* 687.12

scop *author* 139.13

scope 829.7; *viewpoint* 242.12, *meaning* 361.1, *available space* 563.6, *range* 563.7, *sphere* 564.10, *size* 579.1, *measurability* 589.2, *length* 590.1, *breadth* 592.1, *opportunity* 659.2, *degree* 739.1

scope sight *hunting accessories* 160.5

scopophobia or **scoptophobia** Phobias 283

scorch *be at war* 76.32, *burn* 217.18, *attack successfully* 418.25, *bake* 560.19, *impair* 808.18

scorch [Inf] *be swift* 694.10

scorched *heated* 217.15, *baked* 560.14

scorched earth *havoc* 523.5

scorched-earth policy *infertile land* 23.2, *economic warfare* 76.7

scorcher [Inf] *hot weather* 9.22, 217.6, *speeder* 694.5

scorching *hot* 217.11, *heating* 217.12, *violent* 520.5

scorching [Inf] *swiftness* 694.1, *speeding* 694.7

score *numeration* 6.10, *produce*

137.21, *written music* 140.21, *compose* 141.18, *play baseball* 147.9, *play offense* 155.18, *golfing terms* 156.3, *play ice hockey* 158.9, *soccer play* 163.5, *play soccer* 163.8, *tennis terms* 165.5, *play tennis* 165.13, *bridge* 168.4, *register* 185.15, *solve* 334.21, *credit* 487.1, *amount owing* 488.5, *accounting* 493.1, *notch* 636.1, 636.5, *notch up* 636.6, *furrow* 638.1, 638.5, *gradation* 739.3, *measure* 739.7, *mathematical result* 783.4, *number* 784.13, *twenty and over* 792.8

score [Inf] *drug oneself* 121.37, *fact* 717.6, *circumstances* 726.1

score 300 Poker 151.8

score a bull's-eye [Inf] *be accurate* 350.5, 721.22

score a perfect game *bowl* 151.8

score a point *overpower* 845.18

score a run *play baseball* 147.9

score a spare *bowl* 151.8

score a strike *bowl* 151.8

score a success *be successful* 845.11

scoreboard *stadium* 155.3, 163.2, *record* 185.9

score card *calculator* 6.64, *golfing terms* 156.3

scored *composed* 141.13, *soccer* 163.7, *furrowed* 638.3

scorekeeper *karate* 152.14, *record keeper* 185.8

score one hundred per cent *be perfect* 805.20

score out *erase* 186.9

score points against *refute* 332.7

scorer *composer* 141.9, *basketball team* 148.2

scorer's table *basketball court* 148.3

scores *multitude* 795.1

scoresheet *record* 185.1

score ten out of ten *be perfect* 805.20

score through *erase* 186.9

scoria *dirt* 112.5, *residue* 750.2, *refuse* 802.5

scoring 155.5; *soccer play* 163.5, *card-playing* 168.6

scorn 436.19, 440.5; *be hostile* 63.10, *disbelief* 88.1, *disbelieve* 88.8, *dissatisfaction* 274.1, *be dissatisfied* 274.7, *disdain* 297.14, 400.16, *hate* 300.1, 300.11, *underestimate* 344.5, *exclude* 383.11, *arrogance* 400.4, *be insubordinate* 416.8, *wrong* 430.19, *contempt* 436.3, *ridicule* 440.15, *make unimportant* 800.20

scorned *hated* 300.9

scorned person *nonentity* 800.8

scornful 440.10; *disbelieving* 88.6, *dissatisfied* 274.4, *hating* 300.7, *underestimating* 344.3, *arrogant* 400.11, *contemptuous* 436.12

scornfully *discontentedly* 274.8, *with hate* 300.13, *pessimistically* 344.6, *arrogantly* 400.21, *contemptuously* 436.27, *disparagingly* 440.16

scornfulness *contempt* 436.3

scorning *taunting* 436.14

Scorpio Constellations 7

Scorpion Constellations 7

scorpion *arachnid* 40.4

Scorpius Constellations 7

scorrevole or **scorrendo** Musical Terms and Expression Marks 140

scot and lot *historical tax* 494.8

Scotch Bean Varieties 90

scotch *cease* 773.20, *hinder* 826.15

Scotch Highland Breeds of Cattle 16

Scotch mist *mist* 9.33, *mistiness* 559.2

Scotch or **Scots pine** Trees and Shrubs 43

Scotch™ tape *adhesive* 755.3

scot-free *free of charge* 497.12, *escaping* 816.7, *free* 829.11, *liberated* 831.4

scotia Architectural Elements 134

Scotism Philosophical Schools of Thought 4

Scotist Philosophical Schools of Thought 4

scotophobia Phobias 283

scotopia *visual acuity* 242.2

Scottish accent *regional pronunciation* 205.7

Scottish Blackface Breeds of Sheep 16

Scottish Chaucerians Western Literary Groups 139

Scottish Colorists Western Art Styles 133

Scottish deerhound Breeds of Dogs 35

Scottish fold longhair Breeds of Cats 35

Scottish Grand Committee British government 49.22

Scottish National party Political Parties 50

Scottish Renaissance Western Literary Groups 139

Scottish terrier Breeds of Dogs 35

Scottish thistle *national emblem* 184.7

scoundrel *malefactor* 306.6, *disreputable character* 371.2, *evil person* 446.3, *miscreant* 448.6

scour *erosion* 8.41, *erode* 8.67, *clean* 111.17, *rub* 554.12

scoured *weathered* 8.61, *cleaned* 111.14

scourer *cleaning tool* 111.10

scourge *plague* 114.6, *affliction* 117.1, *misfortune* 301.6, *afflict* 301.16, *evil thing* 446.2, *instrument of punishment* 454.13, *hit* 454.28, *adversity* 848.1

scourged *afflicted* 301.11

scourge oneself *do penance* 451.9

scourger *punisher* 454.16

scourging *corporal punishment* 454.11

scouring *scraping* 554.4

scouring out *removal* 709.5

scouring pad *cleaning agent* 111.9

scouring powder *cleaning agent* 111.9

scouring rush *fern* 46.1

scourings *dirt* 112.5, *residue* 750.2, *refuse* 802.5

Scout Notable Horses 159

scout *military aircraft* 77.30, *baseball team* 147.2, *observer* 242.15, *inspect* 242.21, *discoverer* 345.7, *precursor* 769.7, *forerun* 769.16, *warner* 814.5

scouting *preparation* 388.1

scout's honor! *yes!* 189.36

scout sign *symbol* 183.3

scout the territory *prepare the way* 388.15

scow Ships and Boats 690

scowl *gesture* 183.5, 183.17, *look* 242.7, 242.21, *react against* 291.15, *be angry* 302.19, *sign of irascibility* 303.6, *frown* 303.15, *sign of irritability* 304.4, *be irritable* 304.14, *act of discourtesy* 411.3, *show of disapproval* 438.6, *show*

disapproval 438.21, *distortion of face* 627.2, *make faces* 627.10

scowling *frowning* 303.12, 304.10

scowlingly *frowningly* 304.18

Scrabble ™ Board and Table Games 167

scrag end *remainder* 750.1

scraggily *thin* 595.18

scragginess *littleness* 580.1, *thinness* 595.1

scraggliness *roughness* 544.1

scraggly *coarse* 544.6

scraggy *underfed* 98.7, *coarse* 544.6, *little* 580.7, *thin* 595.9

scram [Inf] *run away* 386.21, *hurry off* 705.11

scram! [Inf] *hands off!* 386.26, *go!* 709.30

scramble *cook* 91.10, *race* 146.10, *be on the track* 146.11, *mountaineer* 161.10, *make unintelligible* 364.13, *alacrity* 414.3, *be active* 414.18, *fight* 422.9, *bodily movement* 677.11, *climb* 713.21, *mix* 732.12, *mixture* 751.1, *mix up* 751.13, *disorder* 766.17, *haste* 818.1, *make haste* 818.5

scrambled *culinary* 91.9, *indiscriminate* 338.8, *unintelligible* 364.4, *complicated* 751.10, *mixed up* 751.11, *muddled* 766.13, *problematic* 824.11

scrambled egg *dish* 90.18

scrambler *mixer* 751.7

scramble up *climb* 713.21

scrap *quarrel* 272.4, 272.9, *discard* 383.12, *renounce* 392.4, *stop using* 394.10, *fight* 422.9, 422.23, *little piece* 580.4, *throw away* 709.25, *particle* 760.4, *cease* 773.20, *fragment* 787.3, *refuse* 802.5

scrap [Inf] *battle* 76.23, *argument* 329.1, *dispute* 463.3, 463.9

scrapbook *record book* 185.5, *compendium* 204.3, *reminder* 354.4

scrape *clean* 111.17, *engrave* 144.11, *painful injury* 215.3, *inflict pain* 215.10, *hoarseness* 238.2, *sound hoarse* 238.8, *be dissonant* 241.6, *submissiveness* 298.3, *submit* 298.17, *show obeisance to* 426.8, *economize* 499.6, *use a sharp tool* 549.17, *grate* 553.24, *scraping* 554.4, *abrade* 554.13, *meet* 586.15, *make smaller* 747.8, *predicament* 824.5

scrape and save *be parsimonious* 490.13

scrape by *not complete* 762.9

scraped *injured* 215.5

scrape home *be victorious* 845.16

scrape off *depilate* 614.20

scrape one's feet *gesture* 183.17

scraper *construction equipment* 14.23, *sharp-edged thing* 549.6, *eraser* 554.7

scrape the surface *be superficial* 599.6

scrape through *survive* 419.31, *be imperfect* 806.8, *escape* 816.8, *be victorious* 845.16

scrape together or **up** *acquire* 467.19

scrapie *animal disease* 34.10

scraping 554.4; *hoarse* 238.5, *dissonant* 241.4, *sycophantic* 401.7

scraping by *unprovided* 98.6

scrapings *residue* 750.2

scrapped *relinquished* 392.2, *disused* 394.8, *canceled* 773.15

scrapper [Inf] *fighter* 422.14

scrappily *partly* 760.17, *incompletely* 762.10
scrappiness *incompleteness* 762.1
scrapping *disuse* 394.3
scrappy *partial* 760.11, *incomplete* 762.5, *uncompleted* 762.7, *discontinuous* 775.7
scrappy [Inf] *argumentative* 329.7
scraps *waste product* 96.7, *residue* 750.2, *refuse* 802.5
scrap with *fight* 422.23
scratch *animal feed* 16.12, *billiards play* 149.2, *pool* 149.3, *horse racing* 159.10, *painful injury* 215.3, *inflict pain* 215.10, *small sound* 233.4, *hoarseness* 238.2, *sound hoarse* 238.8, *mean nothing* 362.10, *withdraw* 392.5, *fight* 422.23, *use a sharp tool* 549.17, *scraping* 554.4, *abrade* 554.13, *furrow* 638.1, 638.5, *cease* 773.20, *little bit* 800.4, *defect* 806.4, *incomplete* 806.6
scratch [Inf] *untrained* 389.8
scratch (out) a living *be poor* 486.14
scratch each other's back *exchange* 673.5
scratched *furrowed* 638.3, *imperfect* 806.5
scratches Phobias 283
scratchiness *roughness* 544.1
scratching *scraping* 554.4
scratch line *jumping* 166.11
scratch out *erase* 186.9, *abolish* 523.11
scratch pad *schoolbook* 48.15, *material* 143.9, *record book* 185.5
scratch player *golfer* 156.7
scratch the surface *be superficial* 599.6
scratch through *erase* 186.9
scratchy *hoarse* 238.5, *barbed* 544.7
scrawl *written letter* 5.14, *nonsense* 362.2, *unintelligible thing* 364.3, *make unintelligible* 364.13
scrawly *unintelligible* 364.4
scrawnily *thin* 595.18
scrawniness *littleness* 580.1, *thinness* 595.1
scrawny *underfed* 98.7, *little* 580.7, *thin* 595.9
scream *blow* 9.53, *proclaim* 173.16, *speak in a particular way* 205.18, *express pain* 215.11, *tumult* 232.5, *be loud* 232.8, *shrillness* 238.3, *be shrill* 238.9, *cry* 239.1, *cry of pain* 239.5, *cry out* 239.13, *danger signal* 811.5
scream [Inf] *joke* 277.6
scream at *react against* 291.15
scream bloody murder *cry out* 239.13, *complain* 507.8
screamer *crier* 239.8
screamer [Inf] Punctuation Marks 5
screaming *tumult* 232.5, *shouting* 232.7, *vociferous* 239.9, *gaudy* 251.12, *blatant* 404.19
screamingly *blatantly* 404.34
scree *transferred thing* 685.6
screech *blow* 9.53, *speak in a particular way* 205.18, *express pain* 215.11, *shrillness* 238.3, *be shrill* 238.9, *cry* 239.1, *bird sound* 240.2, *make a bird sound* 240.8
screech owl *bird of prey* 36.11
screed *dissertation* 203.1, *address* 209.1
screen *furniture* 101.1, *cleaning tool* 111.10, *viewer* 132.22, *wall* 134.9, *film* 137.19, *play basketball* 148.7, *television set* 172.6, *cover*

181.4, *conceal* 181.12, *blinder* 243.7, *blind* 243.17, *that which makes invisible* 245.2, *make invisible* 245.7, *opaque* 250.7, *present* 264.15, *safeguard* 419.2, *buffer* 419.22, *porosity* 583.5, *provide passage for* 583.18, *protective covering* 613.5, *shelter* 613.6, 812.4, *protect* 613.26, 810.21, *separator* 753.5, *categorize* 767.21, *protection* 810.2, *display* 843.13
screen (for) *practice medicine* 107.32
screen adaptation *script* 137.5
screened *ceramic* 129.9, *concealed* 181.8, 844.7, *private* 245.5, *secluded* 409.9, *protected* 613.20, *categorized* 767.15, *safe* 810.16, *sheltered* 812.7
screen filter *make ceramics* 129.10
screen idol *charmer* 700.6
screening *diagnosis* 107.8, *ceramic process* 129.5, *playing terms* 148.4, *ice hockey tactics* 158.4, *darkening* 247.6, *covering* 613.1, *categorization* 767.5
screening out *selecting* 382.4
screening test *diagnosis* 107.8
screening ultrasonography *prenatal diagnosis* 107.9
screenland *motion pictures* 137.1
screen off *divide* 753.18, *exclude* 764.7
screen pass *play* 155.8
screenplay *script* 137.5
screen print *fabric* 130.1
screen printing *dyeing* 130.9, *craft* 133.2
screen saver *application software* 15.14
screen test *production* 137.6
screen-test *produce* 137.21
screenwriter *filmmaker* 137.14, *author* 139.13
screenwriting *script* 137.5
screw *simple machine* 14.6, *carpenter* 131.10, *billiards play* 149.2, *rotator* 682.8, *roll* 682.15, *propeller* 696.8, *distort* 698.20, *joint* 752.7, *link* 752.18, *fastener* 754.7, *connect* 754.13
screw [Inf] *have sex* 20.21, *prison officer* 55.8, *overcharge* 496.10, *one who restrains* 830.7
screw around [Inf] *fornicate* 432.14
screwball *pitching terms* 147.5
screwball [Inf] *eccentric* 782.10
screwball [Inf and Off] *insane person* 110.5
screw down *make fast* 464.13, *link* 752.18
screwdriver *hand tool* 103.3, *extractor* 711.9
screwed *connected* 754.11
screwed up [Inf] *bungled* 128.7
screwed-up [Inf] *broken down* 802.8
screwing [Inf] *sexual intercourse* 20.9
screwing around [Inf] *fornication* 432.3
screw pine Trees and Shrubs 43
screw propeller *propeller* 696.8
screw thread *or worm coil* 632.2
screwup *blunder* 351.9, 528.5, *obstacle* 826.2
screw up *prepare for action* 388.18
screw up [Inf] *err* 351.14, *be wrong* 430.18, *impair* 808.18
screw up one's courage *take courage* 284.15, *strengthen oneself* 516.16

screw up one's eyes *see badly* 243.16
screwworm *larva* 40.9
screwy [Inf] *insane* 110.9
screw your courage to the sticking place *take courage* 284.15
scribble *written letter* 5.14, *drawing* 143.4, *describe* 202.15, *nonsense* 362.2, *mean nothing* 362.10, *unintelligible thing* 364.3, *make unintelligible* 364.13
scribbled *unintelligible* 364.4
scribbled out *obliterated* 186.4
scribble out *obliterate* 186.8, *cancel* 834.6
scribbler *unskilled person* 128.3, *drawer* 143.8, *descriptive writer* 202.10
scribbling *nonsense* 362.2
scribe *rabbi* 84.6, *author* 139.13, *record keeper* 185.8, *keeper of time* 646.10
scrim Fabrics and Fibers 130, *stage set* 136.19, *transparent thing* 249.4
scrimmage *fight* 422.9, 422.23, *dispute* 463.3
scrimp *be parsimonious* 490.13, *economize* 499.6, *hoard* 501.6, *not complete* 762.9
scrimper *saver* 499.3
scrimping *mean* 501.4
scrimpy *thrifty* 499.4
scrimshaw *sculpture* 144.1
scrip *paper money* 484.14
scrip certificate *paper money* 484.14
script 136.7, 137.5; *dramatize* 136.33, *produce* 137.21
scripted *dramatized* 136.32, *produced* 137.17
scriptural *theological* 81.24
scripture *religious text* 81.15
scriptwriter *filmmaker* 137.14, *descriptive writer* 202.10
scriptwriting *dramaturgy* 136.6, *script* 137.5
scrod *fish dish* 90.19
scrofulous *immoral* 432.9
scroll *program* 15.29, *part of stringed instrument* 142.2, *rare book* 174.2, *roll* 682.15, *list of names* 785.7
scrollwork Architectural Elements 134, *decorative method* 532.3
scroll worker *decorator* 532.8
scrooch down *sit* 716.20
Scrooge *miser* 501.3
scrooge *bargain hunter* 497.8
scrotal *reproductive* 21.11
scrotum *organs of reproduction* 21.9
scrounge *borrow* 476.10, *take* 477.14, *steal* 479.14, *solicit money* 505.13
scrounger *nonworker* 415.4, *thief* 479.8, *beggar* 505.6
scrounging *taking* 477.1, *stealing* 479.1, *fraudulent* 479.13, *solicitation* 505.4, *begging* 505.9
scrub *plants* 41.1, *trees* 43.4, *alternative* 80.2, *clean* 111.17, *exertion* 122.4, *work* 122.8, *cause to disappear* 265.7, *scraping* 554.4, *rub* 554.12
scrub [Inf] *destroy* 186.10
scrubbed *cleaned* 111.17
scrubber *cleaner* 111.12
scrubbiness *littleness* 580.1
scrubbing *cleaning* 111.2, *scraping* 554.4
scrub brush *cleaning tool* 111.10
scrubby *botanical* 17.15, *little* 580.7
scrubland *trees* 43.4

scrub nurse *nurse* 107.23
scrub out *cancel* 834.6
scruffily *meanly* 486.18
scruffiness *uncleanness* 112.2, *beggary* 486.3, *untidiness* 766.3
scruffy *unclean* 112.8, *beggarly* 486.12, *shoddy* 497.11, *untidy* 766.11
scrumptious *edible* 92.20, *luscious* 214.8, *tasty* 219.4
scrumptiously *tastily* 219.7
scrunch *chew* 92.22, *sound hoarse* 238.8, *beat* 553.27
scrunch down *sit* 716.20
scruple *disbelief* 88.1, *dissociation* 375.4, *weight measurement* 538.6, General Units 589
scruples *circumspection* 325.3, *morality* 431.1, *penitence* 451.1
scrupulous *circumspect* 325.8, *accurate* 350.3, *formal* 406.6, *right* 429.7, *moral* 431.9, *duteous* 433.7, *observant* 465.3, *honest* 630.11, *perfectionist* 805.18
scrupulously *morally* 431.15, *observantly* 465.6, *honestly* 630.18
scrupulousness *circumspection* 325.3, *accuracy* 350.1, *formalism* 406.2, *rightfulness* 429.1, *morals* 431.2, *honesty* 630.4
scrutability *intelligibility* 363.1
scrutable *intelligible* 363.5
scrutator *observer* 242.15
scrutineer [Brit] *observer* 242.15, *questioner* 339.9
scrutinization *carefulness* 593.5
scrutinize 323.11; *philosophize* 4.19, *inspect* 242.22, *question* 333.16, *be careful* 593.15
scrutinized *questioned* 333.15
scrutinizer *observer* 242.15
scrutinizing *watchful* 323.6, *careful* 593.11
scrutiny *philosophical investigation* 4.4, *observation* 242.5, *close attention* 323.2, *questioning* 333.2, *carefulness* 593.5
scuba *swim* 164.14
scuba-dive *dive* 164.15
scuba diver *swimmer* 164.11
scuba diving Sporting Activities 145, *swimming* 164.1
scud *cloud* 9.17, 9.54, *navigate* 690.15
scuff *scraping* 554.4, *abrade* 554.13, *move slowly* 693.11
scuffing *scraping* 554.4
scuffle *quarrel* 272.4, *fight* 422.9, 422.23, *commotion* 768.5
scuffs *shoes* 100.30
scull *rowboat parts* 150.15, *rowing* 150.27, *row* 150.32, *swim* 164.14, Ships and Boats 690
sculler *boating person* 150.24, *nautical person* 183.4
scullery *room* 60.9, *cooking place* 91.4
sculling Sporting Activities 145, *boating sports* 150.1, *rowing* 150.14, *swimming techniques* 164.2
scullion [Arch] *cleaner* 111.12
scull racing *rowing* 150.14
sculpt 144.10; *design* 133.9, *illustrate* 187.11, *perform* 522.16, *fashion* 536.7, *form* 624.9
sculpted 144.8
Sculptor Constellations 7
sculptor 144.4; *visual artist* 133.6, *producer* 522.10
sculptor's wax *material* 144.6
sculptural 144.7
sculpturally *pictorially* 133.11
sculpture 144.1; *craft* 133.2, *image*

187.3, *work of art* 522.4, *form* 624.9

sculptured *sculpted* 144.8, *formed* 624.6

sculpturing *sculpture* 144.1

sculpt wood *work wood* 131.9

scum *purify* 111.19, *dirt* 112.5, *villain* 448.5, *vulgar group* 535.5, *coat* 588.3, *residue* 750.2, *nonentity* 800.8, *refuse* 802.5

scumble *paint* 143.12

scumbling *treatment* 143.6

scummy *dirty* 112.7, *platelike* 588.8

scummy [Inf] *shoddy* 497.11

scum of the earth *villain* 448.5, *nonentity* 800.8

scunner *dislike* 291.1

scupper *ruin* 523.15

scuppers *sailboat parts and accessories* 150.1

scurf *dirt* 112.5, *crumb* 553.5, *slice* 588.4, *residue* 750.2

scurfy *unclean* 112.8, *crumbly* 553.16, *platelike* 588.8

scurrility *vilification* 301.2, *profanity* 301.3, *disrespect* 436.1, *scorn* 440.5

scurrilous *profane* 301.10, *disrespectful* 436.9, *defamatory* 440.9

scurrilously *profanely* 301.19

scurry *be active* 414.18, *scamper* 694.12, *haste* 818.1, *make haste* 818.5

scurrying *moving* 677.12

S-curve *curve* 629.1, *road attribute* 687.3

scurvy *vitamin deficiency disease* 12.14, *underfed* 98.7

scut *tail* 622.5

scutage *historical tax* 494.8

scutcheon *Heraldic Terms* 184

scute *animal covering* 613.15

scuttle *retreat* 285.8, *vessel* 578.11, *scamper* 694.12, *means of entry* 706.6, *bring down* 716.14, *make haste* 818.5

scuttlebutt [Inf] *inside information* 170.4, *news source* 171.4

Scutum *Constellations* 7

scutum *historic armor* 419.8

Scylla *Legendary Creatures* 360, *legendary sea being* 571.4

Scyphozoa *coelenterate* 39.15

scyphozoan *coelenterate* 39.15, 39.25

scythe *farm tool* 16.5, *personifications and symbols* 29.4, *grasscutter* 45.5, *manage grassland* 45.10, *garden tool* 103.4, *sharp-edged thing* 549.6, *use a sharp tool* 549.17

sea 571.1; *moon* 7.18, *ocean* 8.14, *Phobias* 283, *oceanic* 571.7, *the depths* 598.2

sea air *source of fragrance* 226.2, *open air* 558.5

sea anemone *coelenterate* 39.15

sea angler *fisherman* 154.12

sea attack *combined attack* 418.5

sea battle *naval warfare* 76.10

seabed *sea* 571.1, *the depths* 598.2, *base* 601.1

Seabee *naval person* 77.25

seabird *water bird* 36.9

Seabiscuit *Notable Horses* 159

sea biscuit *echinoderm* 39.5

seaboard *coast* 572.4

sea bombardment *naval warfare* 76.10

seaborne *nautical* 690.14

sea bottom *sea* 571.1

sea breeze *wind* 9.12, *sailing terms* 150.5

sea cadet [Brit] *nautical person* 690.12

sea change *sudden change* 665.3, *improvement* 807.1

sea chest *box* 578.5

sea cliff *coast* 572.4

sea cucumber *echinoderm* 39.5

seadog *rainbow* 9.28

sea dog *expert* 127.9, *nautical person* 690.12

sea duck *water bird* 36.9

seafarer *nautical person* 690.12

seafaring *oceanic* 571.7, *water transportation* 690.1, *nautical* 690.14

seafaring man or **woman** *nautical person* 690.12

sea fight *battle* 76.23

seafloor *ocean floor* 8.18, *the depths* 598.2, *base* 601.1

seafloor spreading *plate tectonics* 8.19

sea fog *fog* 9.32

sea front *waterfront* 621.3, *passage* 691.5

sea-going *oceanic* 571.7, *nautical* 690.14

sea-green *green* 260.7

seagull *water bird* 36.9

sea ice *iceberg* 8.45

seal *decoration* 129.4, *make ceramics* 129.10, *keep secret* 182.11, *means of identification* 184.3, *identify* 184.11, *send* 209.11, *verification* 336.1, *resolve* 376.12, *ratification* 459.4, *contract* 459.8, 462.2, 462.11, *promise* 464.2, 464.10, *permit* 502.3, *stopper* 584.3, *close* 584.12, *special feature* 779.4, *repair* 809.10

sea lane *waterway* 690.2, *route* 691.2, *thoroughfare* 692.6

sea lavender *Flowers* 42

seal brown *horse by color* 159.7

sealed *secret* 182.8, *agreed* 346.5, *closed* 584.7

sealed and delivered *contractual* 459.7

sealed book *the occult* 86.2, *unknown thing* 349.3

sealed lips *quietness* 844.4

sealed off *unhygienic* 114.27

sealed orders *secret* 182.2

sealed verdict *verdict* 54.18

sealer *Ships and Boats* 690

sea level *ocean* 8.14, *horizontal surface* 603.3

sea lily *echinoderm* 39.5

sealing off *obstruction* 584.2

sealing wax *adhesive* 755.3

seal-like *cetacean* 35.27

sea loch *lake* 568.1

seal of approval *yes* 346.2, *approval* 437.1

seal off *close* 584.12

seal of the confessional *secret* 182.2

seal one's lips *lack candor* 192.22

seal-point Siamese cat *brown thing* 256.3

seals *Collective Names* 59

seal up *conceal* 181.12, *intertwine* 752.19

Sealyham terrier *Breeds of Dogs* 35

seam *make clothing* 100.44, *layer* 588.1, *furrow* 638.1, 638.5, *joint* 752.7, *intertwine* 752.19

sea mail *postal service* 169.5

Seaman *US Military Ranks* 58

Seaman Apprentice *US Military Ranks* 58

seamanlike *nautical* 690.14

Seaman Recruit *US Military Ranks* 58

seamanship *art of war* 76.16, *tactics* 399.12, *navigation* 690.5

seamark *indicator* 183.7

sea marker 690.7

seamed *wrinkly* 638.4, *united* 752.10

seamed stockings *legwear* 100.26

sea mile *General Units* 589

seaming *sewing* 130.5

sea mist *murk* 248.2

seamless *continuous* 774.9

seamless stockings *legwear* 100.26

seamount *ocean floor* 8.18

seamstress *clothier* 100.37, *fabric handler* 130.11, *person who joins* 752.9

séance *occult and psychic phenomena* 86.7

sea nymph *minor deity* 82.2, *legendary sea being* 571.4

sea of *throng* 795.4

sea of flames *fire* 217.8

sea operations *offensive warfare* 76.11

seaport *center of activity* 612.4

sea power *navy* 77.18

sear *be painful* 215.9, *burn* 217.18, *dried-up* 560.9, *shortened* 582.8, *contract* 582.12

sea raiding *naval warfare* 76.10

search *philosophical investigation* 4.4, *philosophize* 4.19, *questioning* 333.2, *question* 333.16, *pursuit* 385.1, *pursue* 385.11, *undertaking* 391.1

search-and-destroy mission *military attack* 418.2

searcher *philosopher* 4.9, *pursuer* 385.5, *attempter* 390.3

search for *be curious* 321.7

search for the end of the rainbow *waste effort* 802.13

searching *questioning* 333.11, *pursuing* 385.8, *tentative* 390.5

searchingly *questioningly* 333.21

searchlight *electric light* 246.6

search one's soul *be penitent* 451.7, *introspect* 611.16

search out *question* 333.16

search party member *pursuer* 385.5

search warrant *pretrial proceedings* 54.13, *demand* 425.2

seared *culinary* 91.9, *shortened* 582.8

seared conscience *impenitence* 452.1

searing *painful* 215.4, *heating* 217.12, *drying* 560.3, *shortening* 582.2, *contracting* 582.12

sea room *available space* 563.6

sea rover *nautical person* 690.12

sea salt *basic cooking ingredient* 91.8, *seasoning* 221.2

seascape *portrait* 132.5, *type of painting* 143.5, *view* 242.8

seasick *nautical* 690.14, *vomiting* 709.12

seaside *coast* 8.13, 572.4, *edge* 618.1, *edging* 618.5, *side* 623.1

season 221.8, 654.1, 654.11; *climate* 9.35, *cook* 91.10, *accustom* 397.18, *time period* 641.2, *recurrent period* 641.5, *augment* 748.13, *mix* 751.12, *preserve* 815.14

season, the *seasons* 654.2

seasonable *seasonal* 654.7, *timely* 659.4, *convenient* 803.3

seasonableness *timeliness* 659.1

seasonably *seasonally* 654.12, *opportunely* 659.8

seasonal 654.7; *meteorologic* 9.38, *magazine* 175.3, *habitual* 397.9, *periodical* 641.7, *cyclic* 663.7

seasonal affective disorder (SAD) syndrome *mood disorder* 108.12

seasonality *season* 654.1

seasonally 654.12; *for specified periods* 641.12, *cyclically* 663.15

seasoned 654.9; *expert* 127.12, *piquant* 221.6, *habituated* 397.14, *toughened* 547.7

seasoning 221.2; *flavor* 219.3, *habituation* 397.7, *ornamentation* 748.5, *admixture* 751.5

season of the year *season* 654.1

seasons 654.2

season ticket *bargain* 497.4

sea squirt *protochordate* 39.4

sea star *echinoderm* 39.5

sea survey *oceanography* 571.5

sea swivel *fighting chair* 154.8

sea systems *naval commands* 77.19

seat *canoe parts* 150.10, *rowboat parts* 150.15, *reserved space* 563.5, *location* 565.1, *situation* 573.1, *bicycle part* 687.11

seat belt *miscellaneous automotive terms* 687.14, *safety device* 810.15, *preserver* 815.9

seat connection *superstructure* 551.7

seated *situated* 573.5

seating *auditorium* 136.17, *reserved space* 563.5

seating capacity *reserved space* 563.5

seat of feelings 266.7

seat of government *position of authority* 52.4, *administrative headquarters* 564.5, *city* 567.1

seat of justice *tribunal* 54.6, *place of judgment* 341.3

seat of life *life force* 28.2

seat of thought *brain* 315.6

seat oneself *sit* 716.20

sea travel *water transportation* 690.1

sea trip *water transportation* 690.1

Seattle *major US cities* 567.5

Seattle Slew *Notable Horses* 159

sea urchin *echinoderm* 39.5

sea wall *water system* 551.13, *coast* 572.4, *safety device* 810.15, *barrier* 826.7

seaward *nautically* 571.10, *toward* 697.18

seawater *ocean* 8.14, *water* 557.1, *sea* 571.1

sea wave *wave* 8.16

seaway *available space* 563.6, *waterway* 690.2

seaweed *fertilizer* 16.9, *lower plant* 41.4, *alga* 47.10

seaweed marquetry *decorative woodwork* 131.2

seaworthy *oceanic* 571.7, *transferable* 685.7, *transportable* 686.7, *nautical* 690.14, *complete* 805.14, *invulnerable* 810.18

sea zoo *zoo* 60.14

Seb *Deities* 82

sebaceous *secretory* 24.4, *of a secretion* 24.5, *oily* 562.11

sebaceous gland *mammalian characteristic* 35.3

sebaceousness *oiliness* 562.1

sebiferous *secretory* 24.4

Sebring 12-hour race *races* 146.4
sebum *secreted substance* 24.2, *fat* 562.4
sec [Inf] *instant* 645.3
secant (sec) *trigonometric function* 6.50
secateurs [Brit] *garden tool* 17.7, 103.4
secede *dissent* 347.8, *withdraw* 392.5
seceder *rebel* 427.8
seceding *dissenting* 347.7
secession *dissentience* 347.3, *relinquishment* 392.1, *revolution* 427.4
secessionist *dissenting* 347.7, *rebel* 427.8
seclude *conceal* 181.12, *exclude* 409.12, 764.7, *ostracize* 709.17, *divide* 753.18
secluded 409.9; *concealed* 181.8, 844.7, *secret* 182.8, *lonely* 409.8, *out of reach* 712.11, *unjoined* 753.9, *aloof* 756.5, *free* 829.11
seclude oneself *be unsocial* 409.10, *go inside* 611.15
seclusion *imprisonment* 55.4, *privacy* 181.6, *separation* 409.3, *ostracism* 709.3, *setting apart* 753.2, *aloofness* 756.2, *exclusiveness* 764.4, *aloneness* 788.5, *sanitary precaution* 810.8, *noninterference* 829.3, *concealment* 844.2
seclusionist *hermit* 782.9, *loner* 788.8
seclusive *unsociable* 409.6
seclusiveness *unsociability* 409.1
second 789.20; *ranked* 6.72, *chord* 140.18, *bowler* 151.5, *boxer* 152.8, *confirm* 189.25, *verify* 336.8, *assent* 346.6, *select* 382.12, *contract* 462.11, *General Units* 589, *give moral support* 605.18, *time period* 641.2, *instant* 645.3, *substitute* 672.3, *inferior* 745.4, *two* 789.8, *double* 789.11, *imperfect item* 806.3, *helper* 825.12, *advise* 825.27
secondarily *with the effect of* 676.12, *extraneously* 724.16, *second* 789.20, *unimportantly* 800.21
secondariness *extraneousness* 724.1, *inferiority* 745.1, *unimportance* 800.1
secondary 800.15; *plumage* 36.7, *defense* 155.9, *caused* 676.5, *extraneous* 724.4, *inferior* 745.5, *two* 789.8
secondary cell *electrical conduction* 10.33
secondary character *metamorphic rock* 8.36
secondary chord *chord* 140.18
secondary color *color* 251.1
secondary consumer *ecology* 13.25
secondary eardrum *ear* 19.10
secondary education *educational system* 48.2
secondary electron *electron emission* 14.42
secondary emission *electron emission* 14.42
secondary growth *cancer* 114.15
secondary matter 800.6
secondary memory *memory* 15.6
secondary picketing *strike* 57.8
secondary quality *philosophical problem* 4.8
secondary rainbow *rainbow* 9.28
secondary school *school* 48.11
secondary structure *protein* 12.9

secondary wave *seismic wave* 8.25
second assistant director *filmmaker* 137.14
second banana [Inf] *entertainer* 138.8
second base *baseball field* 147.3
second baseman *baseball team* 147.2
second-base umpire *baseball team* 147.2
second best *half-measure* 461.2, *substitution* 672.1, *inferiority* 745.1, *imperfect item* 806.3
second-best *deputizing* 80.4, *disappointing* 293.6, *half-measure* 461.5, *low quality* 745.7, *imperfect* 806.5
second birth *revival* 809.3
second chance *mercy* 308.3, *revival* 809.3
second childhood *old age* 27.5
second class *inferiority* 745.1
second-class *common* 71.3, *cheap* 497.9, *low quality* 745.7, *imperfect* 806.5
second-class citizens *common people* 71.2
second-class fare *bargain* 497.4
second-class mail *postal service* 169.5
second coming *reappearance* 264.8
second cousin *family member* 65.2
second crop *yield* 467.8
second-degree burn *heat* 217.1
second-degree murder *murder* 30.2
second derivative *differentiation* 6.29
second early *crop* 16.8
second echelon *armed force* 77.10
seconded *verifiable* 336.5
seconder *affirmer* 189.9, *assenter* 346.3, *supporter* 605.9
second fiddle *nonentity* 800.8
second finger *appendage* 19.5
second-generation *caused* 676.5
second grip *filmmaker* 137.14
secondhand *used* 393.5
second hand *indicator* 183.7
secondhand clothes *old clothes* 100.8
secondhand sale *sale* 482.2
secondhand shop *discounter* 497.7
secondhand smoke *pollution* 117.8, *smoking* 121.22
second helping *helping* 92.11, *repeat* 797.5
second honeymoon *revival* 809.3
second house *theatrical performance* 136.13
second husband *married man* 64.10
second-in-command *deputy* 80.1
seconding *patronage* 825.9
second law *thermodynamics* 10.30
Second Lieutenant *US Military Ranks* 58
second line *helper* 825.12
secondly *second* 789.20
second marriage *type of marriage* 64.3
second mortgage *mortgage* 476.6, *loan* 488.3
second name *name* 202.8
second nature *habit* 397.1
second opinion *health care* 107.7, *judgment* 341.1
second or two, a *short duration* 643.3
second prize *prize* 453.2

second rank *inferiority* 745.1, *low quality* 745.7
second-rate *disappointing* 293.6, *shoddy* 497.11, *substandard* 597.19, *low quality* 745.7, *cheap* 800.16, *imperfect* 806.5
second-rater *inferior* 745.4, *loser* 846.9
seconds *helping* 92.11, *old clothes* 100.8, *bargain* 497.4
second self *look-alike* 730.4, *counterpart* 733.5
second sex [Off] *womenfolk* 33.14
second showing *reappearance* 264.8
second sight *psychic power* 86.4, *sensation* 212.1, *precognition* 320.2, *prediction* 358.1, *looking to the future* 650.4
second-sighted *precognitive* 320.7, *foreseeing* 357.5
second soprano *musical part* 760.8
seconds out *duel* 422.12
second spring *revival* 809.3
second-stringer *inferior* 745.4
second thought *subsequence* 770.4, *reconsideration* 807.9
second thoughts *reticence* 287.3, *vacillation* 380.3
second to none *supremely* 744.23, *best* 805.9
second wife *married woman* 64.11
second youth *revival* 809.3
secrecy 182.1, 611.6; *the occult* 86.2, *mystery* 182.4, *invisibility* 245.1, *unintelligibility* 364.1, *plot* 387.6, *concealment* 844.2
secret 182.2, 182.8, 611.13; *occult* 86.16, *disguised* 181.9, *private* 245.5, *unknown thing* 349.3, *unknown* 349.7, *unintelligible thing* 364.3, *censored* 503.7, *profound* 598.15, *important* 799.7, *cunning* 822.4, *mysteriousness* 844.5, *mysterious* 844.11
secret, the *interpretation* 365.1
secretarial school *type of school* 48.12
Secretariat *Notable Horses* 159
secretariat *position of authority* 52.4, *government office* 124.13
secret art *mystery* 182.4
secretary *politician* 50.7, *office assistant* 69.6, *delegate* 79.1, *deputy* 80.1, *clerical worker* 123.5, *record keeper* 185.8, *helper* 275.5, *assistant* 511.3, *subordinate* 832.3
secretary or **secretaire** *type of desk* 101.6
secretary of state *leader* 68.3
secret ballot *electing* 382.5
secret book *unintelligible thing* 364.3
secret compartment *hiding place* 181.2
secret document *censorship* 503.4, *concealment* 844.2
secret drinker *drunkard* 121.8
secrete 24.7; *excrete* 25.20, *bury* 105.22, *conceal* 181.12, *leak* 707.16, *let out* 709.26
secreted substance 24.2
secret enemy *hostile person* 63.5
secret garden *solitary place* 409.4
secretin *Human Hormones* 12
secret influence *plot* 387.6, *indirect influence* 512.4, *cunning* 822.1, *backstage manipulator* 844.3
secreting *secretory* 24.4
secretion 24.1; *physiology* 13.13, *body process* 19.15, *secreted*

substance 24.2, *excretion* 25.1, *flow* 555.6, *outflow* 707.4, *disgorgement* 709.6
secretionary *secretory* 24.4
secretive 182.9; *metabolic* 19.24, *secretory* 24.4, *silent* 181.10, *sparing with words* 208.6, *reticent* 287.8, *censored* 503.7, *secret* 611.13
secretively *occultly* 86.27, *reticently* 287.18, *under censorship* 503.13, *secretly* 611.22
secretiveness 182.3; *secrecy* 182.1, 611.6, *reticence* 287.3
secret language *unintelligible thing* 364.3
secret lore *mystery* 182.4
secretly 182.14, 611.22; *occultly* 86.27, *privately* 181.18, *invisibly* 245.8, *profoundly* 598.27, *cunningly* 822.6, *lately* 844.15
secretly cause *hide* 844.13
secret meeting *secretory* 182.2
secret of the confessional *secret* 182.2
secretory 24.4; *physiological* 13.29, *excretory* 25.12, *expulsive* 709.11
secretory mechanism 24.3
secret panel *hiding place* 181.2
secret passage *hiding place* 181.2, *means of escape* 816.4
secret person 182.6
secret place *refuge* 812.1
secret places *seat of feelings* 266.7
secret plan *plot* 387.6
secret plot *overactivity* 414.9
Secret Service *security force* 810.13
secret service *secretiveness* 182.3
secret service member *defender* 77.2
secret sign *symbol* 183.3
secret signal *means of identification* 184.3
secret society *association* 59.4, *mystery* 182.4, *subversion* 427.3, *latency* 844.1
secret symbol *symbol* 183.3
secret weapon *weapon* 78.1, *gist* 799.4
secret word *means of identification* 184.3
sect *party* 59.3, *religious group* 81.4, *calling* 178.6, *part* 760.1
sectarian *denominational* 81.23, *unjust* 342.7, *dissenter* 347.5, *dissenting* 347.7, *protester* 507.4
sectarianism *unfair treatment* 342.4, *dissentience* 347.3
section *geometric figure* 6.39, *military organization* 58.4, *army unit* 77.14, *surgery* 107.15, *Reference Signs* 183, *external appearance* 264.5, *region* 564.1, *plot* 564.9, *division* 577.6, *itemize* 577.13, *track* 688.2, *passage* 692.1, *separateness* 753.3, *part* 760.1, 760.14, *piece* 760.2, *part of writing* 547.11, *musical part* 760.8, *category* 767.6, *class* 777.1, *fractional part* 787.2
sectional *component* 760.12, *fractional part* 787.5
sectionalize *divide* 753.18, *part* 760.14
sectionalized *component* 760.12
sectionally *thematically* 577.16
Section d'Or *Western Art Styles* 133
sectioned *itemized* 577.9, *partial* 760.11
sectioning *cell biology* 13.14, *classification* 777.2
sector *geometric figure* 6.39, *circle* 6.40, *computing terms* 15.22,

battleground 76.24, *region* 564.1, *parts of a circle* 631.4, *part* 760.1, *piece* 760.2

secular humanism Philosophical Schools of Thought 4

secular humanist Philosophical Schools of Thought 4

secularism Theologies 81

secularist *disbeliever* 88.5

secure 464.5, 464.9; *satisfied* 273.4, *steadfast* 284.11, *take precautions* 287.14, *defend* 419.20, *guarantee* 458.13, *gain* 467.15, *receive* 473.13, *stable* 674.3, *make stable* 674.7, *bring* 685.11, *draw out* 711.17, *comfortable* 726.10, *tied* 752.13, *bind* 754.14, *safe* 810.16, *protect* 810.21, *certain* 840.7, *infallible* 840.12, *make certain* 840.14

secure a fall *wrestle* 152.20

secure an acquittal *get a reprieve* 816.9

secure a personal loan *borrow* 476.10

secured 464.7; *defended* 419.18, *guaranteed* 458.9, *propertied* 470.9, *received* 473.11, *loaned* 475.5, *borrowed* 476.8, *closed* 584.7, *tied* 752.13, *bound* 754.12

secured debt *debt* 488.1

secured loan *loan* 475.2, 476.5, 488.3

secure exemption *get a reprieve* 816.9

securely *steadfastly* 284.19, *stably* 674.9, *comfortably* 726.19, *inextricably* 752.23, *in connection with* 754.16, *safely* 810.24

securement *gain* 467.1

secureness *stability* 674.1

secure one's object *attain one's goal* 845.13

secure one's objective 464.12

secure position *security* 464.1, *safety* 810.1

secure the basics *find means* 102.6

secure to *make fast* 464.13

securing *guaranteeing* 458.9, *borrowed* 476.8

securities *personal estate* 470.6

securities market *stock market* 483.6

security 464.1; *pretrial proceedings* 54.13, *verbal concealment* 181.3, *cheer* 281.4, *steadfastness* 284.3, *precaution* 287.4, *self-defense* 419.5, *guarantee* 458.3, *contract* 459.1, *transferred thing* 685.6, *comfortable circumstances* 726.5, *safety* 810.1, *infallibility* 840.6, *prosperity* 847.1

security alarm *danger signal* 811.5

security blanket *supporter* 605.9

security camera *camera* 132.10

security check *security system* 810.5

security clearance *permission* 502.1

security force 464.3, 810.13

security guard *defender* 77.2, *guard* 419.15, *surveillant* 810.12, *warner* 814.5

security man *or* **woman** *observer* 242.15, *surveillant* 810.12, *warner* 814.5

security officer *law enforcement officer* 53.8, *security force* 464.3, *railroad worker* 688.7

security system 810.5; *security* 464.1

sedan *automobile* 687.6

sedate *practice surgery* 107.33,

relieve 275.8, *serious* 278.4, *dignified* 297.11, *formal* 406.6, *make inactive* 415.16, *calm* 521.8

sedated *relieved* 275.6, *not awake* 415.12

sedately *with dignity* 297.20

sedateness *dignity* 297.4, *formality* 406.1, *moderation* 521.1

sedation *surgery* 107.15, *ease* 275.1, *moderation* 521.1

sedative *medicine* 86.4, *reliever* 275.4, *relieving* 275.7, *soporific* 415.6, *moderator* 521.2, *moderating* 521.5

sedatives 121.19

sedentary 678.5, 716.11; *inactive* 415.8

sedentary person 678.3

Seder Jewish Holy Days and Seasons 85

sedge *grass* 45.1

sedge family *seed plant* 41.3

sedgy *grassy* 45.8

sedilia *church architecture* 134.11

sediment 8.29; *dirt* 112.5, *solid body* 540.4, *mud* 561.8, *transferred thing* 685.6, *residue* 750.2

sedimentary *petrographic* 8.58, *sludgy* 561.18, *remaining* 750.7

sedimentary facies *sedimentary rock* 8.34

sedimentary rock 8.34; *rock* 8.30

sedimentation *petrogenesis* 8.31, *dirt* 112.5, *concentration* 540.2, *subtraction* 749.1

sedition *anarchy* 51.1, *dishonorableness* 192.3, *dissentience* 347.3, *activism* 414.5, *subversion* 427.3, *revolution* 427.4, *disorder* 507.2

seditionary *anarchist* 51.4, *seditionist* 427.7

seditionary *or* **seditionist** *motivator* 178.11

seditionist 427.7; *protester* 507.4

seditious *anarchic* 51.5, *lawless* 53.26, *dishonorable* 192.14, *dissenting* 347.7, *subversive* 427.11, *disorderly* 507.6

seditiously *anarchically* 51.10, *dishonorably* 192.28, *subversively* 427.15, *disapprovingly* 507.10

seditiousness *subversion* 427.3

seduce 432.16; *entice* 178.16, *desire* 299.24, *deprave* 448.14, *manipulate* 508.12, *lure* 700.12

seduced *unchaste* 432.10, *motivated* 508.8

seducer *tempter* 178.10, *lover* 299.11, *motivator* 508.6, *charmer* 700.6

seduction *sexual immorality* 432.2, *inducement* 508.2

seduction *or* **seducement** *enticement* 178.3

seductive *enticing* 178.13, *pleasurable* 214.6, *desirable* 288.11, *lovable* 299.20, *appealing* 512.9, *attractive* 700.10

seductively *enticingly* 178.22, *desirably* 288.24, *lovably* 299.31, *influentially* 508.13, 512.14, *attractively* 700.14

seductiveness *enticement* 178.3, *desirability* 288.7, *inducement* 508.2, *allurement* 700.4

seductress *loose woman* 33.6, *tempter* 178.10, *lover* 299.11, *motivator* 508.6, *charmer* 700.6

sedulity *commitment* 377.2, *assiduity* 414.8

sedulous *diligent* 323.7, *committed* 377.7, *industrious* 414.16

sedulously *attentively* 323.14, *meticulously* 726.18

sedulousness *carefulness* 323.3, *commitment* 377.2

sedum Flowers 42

see 242.20; *clerical venue* 84.4, *play cards* 168.7, *sense* 212.9, *have an idea* 327.13, *discover* 345.11, *know* 348.10, *imagine* 360.14, *recognize* 363.11, *visit* 408.16, *stand by* 575.15

seeable *visible* 244.5

see again *meet* 704.20

see ahead *foresee* 357.9

see around corners *see* 242.20

see at a glance *recognize* 363.11

see auras *experience psychic phenomena* 86.23

see badly 243.16

Seebeck effect Classical Physical Laws 10

see both sides *be impartial* 338.11

see coming *expect* 356.6

seed 41.9; *solidify* 11.37, *cultivate* 17.19, *progeny* 21.8, *organs of reproduction* 21.9, *fertilizer* 22.6, *fertilize* 22.12, *fruit structure* 44.3, *manage grassland* 45.10, *prizewinner* 127.8, *finalist* 422.16, *produce* 522.5, *little thing* 580.3, *source* 675.2, 771.3, *categorize* 767.21, *successor* 770.6, *sprinkle* 776.15

seed bank *herbarium* 41.12

seed-bearing *taxonomic* 41.16

seedbed *farmland* 16.3, *fertile land* 22.2, *source* 675.2, 771.3

seed biology *plant science* 41.10

seedcake *cake* 90.36

seed capsule *seed* 41.9, *fruit structure* 44.3

seedcase *seed* 41.9

seed coat *seed* 41.9, *casing* 613.9

seed drill *farm tool* 16.5

seeded *selected* 382.11, *sprinkled* 776.9

seeded [Sports] *categorized* 767.15

seeded player *prizewinner* 127.8

seeded position *advantage* 744.3

seed fern *fern* 46.1

seedily *meanly* 486.18

seediness *ill health* 114.1, *beggary* 486.3

seeding *dispersion* 776.1

seeding [Sports] *categorization* 767.5

seed leaf *leaf* 41.6, *seed* 41.9

seedling *garden plant* 17.10, *young plant* 26.5, *plant* 41.2, *seed* 41.9

seedman *horticulturist* 17.13

see double *be drunk* 121.34, *see badly* 243.16

seed plant 41.3

seed pod *seed* 41.9, *fruit structure* 44.3

seeds *fruits* 44.1, *refuse* 802.5

seed shrimp *crustacean* 39.10

seed stalk *stem* 41.5, *seed* 41.9

seed stitch *knitting* 130.7

seedtime *spring* 654.3

seed tray *nursery* 17.4

seed vegetable *vegetable* 90.33

seed vessel *seed* 41.9

seedy *sick* 114.24, *beggarly* 486.12, *weak* 517.6, *plain* 528.9, *worn* 808.13

see eye to eye *assent* 346.6, *agree with* 462.10, *agree* 735.23

see fit *will* 372.11, *prefer* 382.13

see how it feels! *revenge!* 420.7

see how it goes *circumstantiate* 726.12

see how the land lies *proceed with caution* 287.12

see how the wind blows *proceed with caution* 287.12

seeing 242.17; *observatory* 7.24, *sensory* 19.22, *vision* 242.1

seeing double *drunken behavior* 121.4, *slightly drunk* 121.26, *sight defect* 243.2, *weak-sighted* 243.10

seeing one's family *social gathering* 408.4

seeing pink elephants *drunken behavior* 121.4

see in the mind's eye *visualize* 242.24, *imagine* 360.14

see into the future *foresee* 357.9

see it all *understand* 363.9

see it coming *not wonder about* 295.5, *foresee* 357.9, *expect* 650.12

see it through *endure* 377.14, *be safe* 810.20

see justice done *be right* 429.12

seek *philosophize* 4.19, *question* 333.16, *pursue* 385.11

seek – don't speak Children's and Party Games 167

seek acquaintance with *fraternize* 408.17

seek advice *consult* 176.11

seek a favor *ask permission* 502.9

seek agreement *negotiate* 460.6

seek an opinion *consult* 176.11

seek a second opinion *practice medicine* 107.32, *consult* 176.11

seek asylum *shelter* 812.8

seek a verdict *litigate* 54.27

seeker *philosopher* 4.9, *questioner* 333.9, *pursuer* 385.5, *requester* 505.5

seek friendship 62.11

seek help *ask permission* 502.9

seeking *pursuit* 385.1, *pursuing* 385.8

seeking advice *consultation* 176.4

seeking a verdict *litigation* 54.1

seeking justice *litigation* 54.1

seeking legal protection *litigation* 54.1

seek justice *litigate* 54.27

seek legal protection *litigate* 54.27

seek out *be curious* 321.7

seek payment *credit* 487.10

seek power *run for office* 50.10

seek privacy *be aloof* 756.8

seek refuge *shelter* 812.8

seek revenge *be evil* 446.10

seek riches 485.14

seek safety *be safe* 810.20, *shelter* 812.8

seek sanctuary *shelter* 812.8

seek seclusion *withdraw* 392.5

seek shelter *shelter* 812.8

seek solitude *be aloof* 756.8

seek the company of *seek friendship* 62.11

seek the end of the rainbow *attempt the impossible* 837.10

seek to *attempt* 390.6

see light at the end of the tunnel *be hopeful* 281.11

seem *appear* 264.12, *appear outwardly* 610.14

seem guilty *appear guilty* 450.10

seeming 264.11; *spectacle* 264.6, *apparent* 610.10

seemingly 733.19; *theoretically* 4.24, *visibly* 244.10, *apparently* 264.16, 610.18, 720.19, *supposedly* 359.10

seemingness *appearance* 610.4

seem lifelike *seem true* 721.26

seem like 733.14; *appear* 264.12

seem likely *be probable* 838.8

seemliness *properness* 429.5, *refinement* 534.1, *etiquette* 534.3

seemly *proper* 429.10, *refined*

534.5, elegantly 534.8, convenient 803.3
seem propitious be favorable 62.12
seem real seem true 721.26
seem to be appear 264.12
seem true 721.26
seem true to life seem true 721.26
seen communicated 169.15, broadcast 172.12, discovered 345.2, known 348.9, received 473.11
see no cause for haste have leisure time 125.5
see no difference be indiscriminate 338.10, compare 733.13
see no evil be virtuous 447.8
see no one be unsocial 409.10
see no reason to thank be ungrateful 311.5
see nothing wonderful be indifferent 289.12
see no way out be in a predicament 725.9
see off send away 709.18
see oneself or one's name in **print** be published 173.19
seep 559.16; flow 555.25, infiltrate 706.13, leakage 707.5, leak 707.16, descend 714.12
seepage 559.4; inroad 706.3, leakage 707.5, leak 816.6
seep away lessen 468.17
seep down descend 714.12
seep in absorb 708.19
seeping 557.25, 559.12; leakage 707.5, absorption 708.6
seeping away lessening 468.6
see pink elephants be drunk 121.34
seep out leak 707.16, 816.11
seer diviner 86.14, observer 242.15, intuitive person 320.5, wise person 352.3, oracle 358.8, visionary 360.9, predictor 650.5
see red [Inf] feel deeply 266.16, become angry 302.20, be violent 520.8
seeress observer 242.15
seersucker Fabrics and Fibers 130
seesaw amusement park and playground equipment 167.8, sway 378.12, be irresolute 666.6, oscillator 683.7, oscillating 683.8, oscillate 683.12, to and fro 683.16, reciprocity 729.1, reciprocal 729.4
seesawing irresolute 666.4
see signs experience psychic phenomena 86.23
seethe crowd 59.26, 795.11, cook 91.10, be angry 302.19, steep 557.31, swirl 682.16, turbulence 684.3, be agitated 684.21
see the catch be cunning 822.5
see the end of protract 669.9
see the error of one's ways confess 451.8
see the last of cause to cease 668.12
see the lay of the land have foresight 357.8, understand 363.9, prepare the way 388.15
see the light know 48.24, become visible 264.13, find out 345.13, understand 363.9, confess 451.8
see the light of day be born 28.18, emerge 771.35
see the little people experience psychic phenomena 86.23
see the sights see 242.20
see the whole picture circumstantiate 726.12
seething crowded 59.22, steeping 557.10, turbulence 684.3, turbulent 684.17
seething mob business 414.6

see things imagine 720.13
see things as they are be real 721.21
see through be wise 352.6, understand 363.9, be resolute 376.11, maintain 377.12, finance 825.31
see-through translucent 249.8
see through a brick wall see 242.20
see through rose-colored glasses imagine 327.14, idealize 720.15, fantasize 360.15
see to behave toward 399.20
see visions fantasize 360.15
see which way the wind blows have foresight 357.8
see which way the wind blows or **which way the land lies** orient 697.15
see with half an eye see 242.20, recognize 363.11
see with the naked eye see 242.20
see you! goodbye! 705.14
see you later! goodbye! 705.14
Seger cone ceramic workshop and tools 129.8
segment geometric figure 6.39, piece 590.2, 760.2, parts of a circle 631.4, divide 753.18, part 760.1, 760.14, fractional part 787.2
segmental arch 134.5, vault 134.8, component 760.12, fractional 787.5
segmentation separateness 753.3
segmented wormlike 39.24, component 760.12
segment stage stage 136.18
segno Musical Terms and Expression Marks 140
segregate discriminate 337.12, exclude 409.12, 764.7, separate 724.14, not connect 728.13, divide 753.18
segregated judged 337.10, separate 724.10, unconnected 728.8
segregation hostility 63.1, discrimination 337.1, social discrimination 337.4, unfair treatment 342.4, separation 409.3, separateness 724.3, unconnectedness 728.2, setting apart 753.2, exclusiveness 764.4, sanitary precaution 810.8
segue harmonize 140.28, sequel 770.5, follow 770.10
Segura Breeds of Sheep 16
seiche wave 8.16, 571.3
seif dune 8.43
seigneur master 68.1
seigneury historical property terms 470.3
seignorial propertied 470.9
Seine Rivers 570
seiner Ships and Boats 690
seining nautical 690.14
seismatical waving 683.11
seismic volcanic 8.57, explosive 520.6, waving 683.11, newsworthy 799.12
seismic activity 8.24
seismic belt seismic activity 8.24
seismic event seismic activity 8.24
seismic exploration (prospecting) seismic wave 8.25
seismicity seismic activity 8.24, wave 683.4
seismic risk seismic wave 8.25
seismic sea wave wave 8.16, natural violence 520.3
seismic survey seismic wave 8.25
seismic swarm seismic activity 8.24
seismic wave 8.25; wave 10.11, 683.4

seismogram seismic wave 8.25
seismograph seismic wave 8.25, recording instrument 185.9, measuring instrument 683.6
seismographic geophysical 8.51, waving 683.11
seismography geophysics 8.2
seismological geophysical 8.51, waving 683.11
seismologically geologically 8.68
seismologist geophysicist 8.5
seismology geophysics 8.2
seismometer Fields of Measurement 589, measuring instrument 683.6
seismometric geophysical 8.51, waving 683.11
seismometry Fields of Measurement 589
seismoscope measuring instrument 683.6
seize arrest 55.12, touch 216.9, understand 363.9, retain 471.7, take 477.14, take back 477.17, detain 830.16
seized arrested 55.10
seize on make important 799.14
seize one's chance get in early 657.16, take the opportunity 659.7
seize power gain authority 52.15, take over 477.16
seizer taker 477.9
seize the day live in the present 647.8, take the opportunity 659.7
seize the moment get in early 657.16
seize the occasion get in early 657.16
seize the opportunity push 414.20, take the opportunity 659.7
seize up malfunction 846.20
seizin legal ownership 469.8
seizing the chance or **moment** or **occasion** getting ahead 657.7
seizure 418.11; arrest 55.5, illness 114.2, symptom 114.3, retention 471.1, taking 477.1, taking back 477.4, spasm 684.8
seizure of power acquisition of authority 52.5, taking over 477.3
sejant Heraldic Terms 184
Sekhmet Deities 82
selachian fish 38.5, fishlike 38.10
selaphobia Phobias 283
seldom 640.9; infrequently 662.4, sparsely 796.11
seldom if ever rarely 839.10
seldom met with infrequent 662.2, sparse 796.6
seldomness infrequency 662.1
seldom seen infrequent 662.2, sparse 796.6
select 382.12; gain authority 52.15, compile 204.8, discriminate 337.12, selected 382.11, excerpt 692.13, set apart 753.17, excluding 764.5, categorize 767.21
select committee management board 126.2, advisory body 176.6
selected 382.11; authorized 52.11, ice-skating 162.32, judged 337.10, excerpted 692.9, categorized 767.15
select few best people 744.7
selecting 382.4, 382.9; judging 341.7
selection 382.1; acquisition of authority 52.5, likes 290.3, discrimination 337.1, judgment 341.1, chosen thing 382.8, passage 692.1, setting apart 753.2, categorization 767.5
selection of music ice-dancing move 162.19
selections compendium 204.3

selective discriminating 337.9, judging 341.7, selecting 382.9, unjoined 753.9
selective facts distortion of truth 627.4
selective killing animal killing 30.10
selectively 382.17; discriminatingly 337.15, judicially 341.12, in isolation 753.24
selectiveness discrimination 337.1
selectivity discrimination 337.1, selection 382.1
select materials be an architect 134.13
selector discriminator 337.6
s-electron atom 10.52
Selene moon 7.18, Deities 82
Selenge Rivers 570
selenium Chemical Elements and Common Allotropes 11, essential element 12.15
selenium meter exposure equipment 132.12
selenophobia Phobias 283
self body 19.1, psyche 108.25, identity 184.2, internal world 525.6
self-abasement 298.4; bow 716.6
self-abasing 298.11
self-abnegating self-abasing 298.11, unselfish 443.5
self-abnegation self-abasement 298.4, unselfishness 443.2, self-restraint 455.1
self-absorbed 456.9; egotistic 444.5, inward 611.12
self-absorption 456.4; oblivion 355.4, egotism 444.2, inwardness 611.5
self-abuse sex act 20.10
self-accusation sign of guilt 450.2, penitence 451.1
self-accusing penitent 451.5
self-accusingly penitently 451.10
self-admiration 402.4; pride 297.1
self-admirer vain person 402.7
self-admiring 402.10; prideful 297.8
self-analysis inwardness 611.5
self-analyze introspect 611.16
self-analyzing inward 611.12
self-applause self-admiration 402.4
self-appointed voluntary 373.11
self-appointed task voluntary work 373.5
self-approbation self-satisfaction 402.2
self-approving self-admiring 402.10
self-arrest climbing techniques 161.3
self-assertion defiance 416.1
self-assertive cocky 402.11, strong in spirit 516.11
self-assertively cockily 402.19
self-assertiveness cockiness 402.3
self-assurance assertiveness 189.8, steadfastness 284.3, self-satisfaction 402.2, defiance 416.1, authority 425.3, assurance 621.6, conviction 840.2
self-assured assertive 189.20, steadfast 284.11, self-satisfied 402.9, defiant 416.5, authoritative 425.8, assured 621.12, convinced 840.8
self-assuredly smugly 402.18, defiantly 416.9, commandingly 425.15
self-belay climbing techniques 161.3
self-centered misanthropic 291.8,

selfish 402.12, *egotistic* 444.5, *self-absorbed* 456.9

self-centeredness *misanthropy* 291.4, *selfishness* 402.5, *egotism* 444.2, *self-absorption* 456.4

self-command *will* 376.5

self-concern *selfishness* 444.1

self-concerned *selfish* 444.4

self-condemnation *penitence* 451.1

self-condemning *penitent* 451.5

self-confessed *avowed* 189.19

self-confidence *steadfastness* 284.3, *proudness* 297.3, *cockiness* 402.3, *authority* 425.3, *assurance* 621.8, *conviction* 840.2

self-confident *steadfast* 284.11, *proud* 297.10, *cocky* 402.11, *authoritative* 425.8, *assured* 621.12, *convinced* 840.8

self-confidently *steadfastly* 284.19, *proudly* 297.19, *cockily* 402.19, *commandingly* 425.15

self-congratulation *self-satisfaction* 402.2

self-congratulatory *self-satisfied* 402.9, *smugly* 402.18

self-conscious *affected* 367.3, *shy* 403.8

self-consciously *affectedly* 367.5

self-consciousness *shyness* 403.3

self-consideration *selfishness* 444.1

self-contained *taciturn* 208.4, *unsociable* 409.6, *complete* 761.6, *independent* 829.12

self-containment *unsociability* 409.1

self-content *self-satisfaction* 402.2

self-contented *self-satisfied* 402.9

self-contentedly *smugly* 402.18

self-contradicting *mistaken* 351.13

self-contradiction *faulty reasoning* 351.4, *impossibility* 837.1

self-contradictory *erroneous* 351.11, *impossible* 837.4

self-control *philosophical attitude* 4.3, *willpower* 372.2, *will* 376.5, *chastity* 431.3, *virtues* 447.2, *self-restraint* 455.1, 830.4, *moderation* 521.1, *limit* 620.1

self-controlled *detached* 4.18, *iron-willed* 372.7, *strong-willed* 376.10, *chaste* 431.10, *disinterested* 443.4, *principled* 447.6, *self-restrained* 455.6, 830.10, *moderate* 521.3

self-correct *counterbalance* 743.8

self-correcting *counterbalanced* 743.6

self-correction *counterbalance* 743.2

self-deceit *self-deception* 193.2

self-deceiving *deceptive* 193.12

self-deception **193.2**; *misjudgment* 342.1, *fallibility* 351.6, *delusion* 720.3

self-deceptive *deceptive* 193.12

self-defeating *impossible* 837.4

self-defense **419.5**; *combat sport* 152.1, *resistance movement* 417.3

self-defensive *combat* 152.17, *resisting* 417.8

self-defensively *defensively* 419.32

self-deluding *deceptive* 193.12

self-delusion *self-deception* 193.2

self-denial *celibacy* 67.1, *abstinence* 386.2, *desisting* 417.4, *unadornment* 424.3, *unselfishness* 443.2, *self-restraint* 455.1, *abnegation* 506.3

self-denying *desisting* 417.9,

---

unselfish 443.5, *self-restrained* 455.6, *abnegating* 506.7

self-deprecating **403.9**; *self-abasing* 298.11

self-deprecation **403.4**; *self-abasement* 298.4, *underestimation* 344.1

self-depreciating *self-abasing* 298.11

self-depreciation *self-abasement* 298.4, *underestimation* 344.1

self-destruct *act foolishly* 128.10, *be destroyed* 523.17, *deteriorate* 808.14

self-destruction *suicide* 30.8

self-destructive *murderous* 30.18

self-determination *self-government* 49.9, *free will* 372.4, *independence* 829.5

self-determined *free-willed* 372.9

self-determining *national* 566.10, *independent* 829.12

self-devoted *self-absorbed* 456.9

self-devotion *seriousness* 376.3, *egotism* 444.2, *self-absorption* 456.4

self-discipline *chastity* 431.3, *self-punishment* 454.10, *self-restraint* 455.1, 830.4

self-disciplined *chaste* 431.10, *self-restrained* 455.6, 830.10

self-display *boastfulness* 402.6

self-distrust *self-deprecation* 403.4

self-distrustful *self-deprecating* 403.9

self-doubt *lack of hope* 282.2, *self-abasement* 298.4, *self-deprecation* 403.4

self-doubting *self-abasing* 298.11, *self-deprecating* 403.9

self-education *educational system* 48.2, *learning* 348.3

self-effacement *self-abasement* 298.4, *underestimation* 344.1, *self-deprecation* 403.4, *unselfishness* 443.2

self-effacing *self-abasing* 298.11, *self-deprecating* 403.9, *unselfish* 443.5

self-employed *independent* 829.12

self-employed person *independent worker* 123.3

self-endearing *self-admiring* 402.10

self-endearment *self-admiration* 402.4

self-esteem *proudness* 297.3, *self-admiration* 402.4

self-evidence *indication* 339.3, *clarity* 363.2

self-evident *theoretical* 6.66, *demonstrable* 331.12, *evident* 339.9, *simple* 363.6, *truistic* 721.15, *certain* 840.7, *manifest* 843.9

self-evidently *evidently* 339.16

self-examination *philosophical investigation* 4.4, *inwardness* 611.5

self-examine *introspect* 611.16

self-examining *inward* 611.12

self-exemption **434.3**

self-existence **717.8**

self-existent **717.15**

self-existing *self-existent* 717.15

self-explanatory *simple* 363.6

self-expression *independence* 829.5

self-expressive *informal* 829.15

self-flagellation *type of penance* 451.3

self-flattery *self-admiration* 402.4

self-glorification *bombast* 194.4, *pride* 297.1

self-glorify *boast* 194.14

---

self-glorifying *bombastic* 194.10, *prideful* 297.8, *self-admiring* 402.10

self-governing *governmental* 49.24, *national* 566.10, *independent* 829.12

self-governing state *country* 566.1

self-government **49.9**; *independence* 829.5

self-gratification *pleasure* 214.2, *selfishness* 402.5, *self-indulgence* 456.1

self-gratifying *self-indulgent* 456.6

self-help **825.11**

self-helpful **825.22**

self-helpfulness *self-help* 825.11

self-help group *group influence* 512.6

self-helping *self-helpful* 825.22

selfhood *internal world* 525.6

self-humiliation *type of penance* 451.3

self-immolation *suicide* 30.8, *offering* 504.5

self-importance *pride* 297.1, *vanity* 402.1, *pomposity* 404.5, *blatancy* 404.6

self-important *prideful* 297.8, *vain* 402.8, *pompous* 404.18

self-importantly *pridefully* 297.17, *vainly* 402.17, *pompously* 404.33

self-imposed *undertaken* 391.4

self-imposed task *undertaking* 391.1

self-improvement *ascendancy* 713.5, *uplift* 807.2, *self-help* 825.11

self-inductance *resistance* 10.41

self-induction *magnetic phenomenon* 10.50

self-indulge *be greedy* 119.4

self-indulgence **456.1**; *gluttony* 119.1, *pleasure* 214.2, 271.2, *selfishness* 444.1

self-indulgent **456.6**; *gluttonous* 119.3, *pleasure-seeking* 214.10, *pleasure-loving* 271.9, *selfish* 444.4

self-indulgently **456.12**; *gluttonously* 119.5, *selfishly* 444.8

self-indulgent person **456.5**

self-infatuated *self-admiring* 402.10

self-infatuation *self-admiration* 402.4

self-instruction *learning* 348.3

self-interest *selfishness* 402.5, 444.1

self-interested *selfish* 402.12, 444.4

selfish 402.12, 444.4; *misanthropic* 291.8, *ungrateful* 311.2, *inconsiderate* 318.9, *thoughtless* 324.7, *unthinking* 355.8, *badly behaved* 399.16, *selfish* 402.12, *self-absorbed* 456.9

selfishly 402.20, 444.8; *misanthropically* 291.18, *ungratefully* 311.6, *thoughtlessly* 318.15, *inattentively* 324.12, *badly* 399.23

selfish motive *motivation* 508.1

selfishness 402.5, 444.1; *misanthropy* 291.4, *ingratitude* 311.1, *inconsideration* 318.4, *thoughtlessness* 324.3, *unthinkingness* 355.3, *self-absorption* 456.4, *saving* 815.4

selfish person 444.3

selfless *charitable* 305.9, *unselfish* 443.5

selflessly *unselfishly* 443.9

---

selflessness *charity* 305.3, *unselfishness* 443.2

self-loss *oblivion* 355.6

self-love *love* 299.1, *self-admiration* 402.4, *egotism* 444.2, *self-absorption* 456.4

self-loving *loving* 299.15, *self-admiring* 402.10, *egotistic* 444.5, *self-absorbed* 456.9

self-lovingly *egoistically* 444.9

self-made *unskilled* 128.5, *naive* 821.3

self-made man *or* **woman** *wealthy person* 485.6, *successful person* 845.6, *prosperous person* 847.4

self-mastered *strong-willed* 376.10

self-mastery *will* 376.5, *self-restraint* 455.1

self-mortification *penitence* 313.3, *unadornment* 424.3, *self-punishment* 454.10

self-motivated *motivated* 508.8, *independent* 829.12

self-obsessed *self-absorbed* 456.9

self-obsession *self-absorption* 456.4

self-pitiful *pitying* 308.4

self-pity *pity* 308.1, *selfishness* 444.1

self-pitying *pitying* 308.4

self-pleaser *selfish person* 444.3

self-pleasing *selfishness* 444.1

self-pollination *pollination* 42.6

self-possessed *detached* 4.18, *strong-willed* 376.10

self-possession *philosophical attitude* 4.3, *will* 376.5, *moderation* 521.1

self-praise *pride* 297.1, *self-admiration* 402.4, *egotism* 444.2

self-praising *prideful* 297.8

self-preservation *selfishness* 444.1, *preservation* 815.1, *saving* 815.4

self-propelled *moving* 677.12, *propelled* 696.14

self-propelled artillery *guns* 78.9

self psychology *Psychological Theories, Schools* 108

self-punishing *penitential* 451.6

self-punishment **454.10**; *type of penance* 451.3

self-regard *proudness* 297.3

self-regarding *proud* 297.10

self-regulating *equal* 740.8, *independent* 829.12

self-regulating market *noninterference* 829.3

self-regulatory *independent* 829.12

self-reliance *steadfastness* 284.3, *proudness* 297.3, *independence* 829.5

self-reliant *steadfast* 284.11, *proud* 297.10, *independent* 829.12

self-reliantly *proudly* 297.19, *freely* 829.22

self-renunciation *abnegation* 506.3

self-renunciatory *abnegating* 506.7

self-reproach *sign of guilt* 450.2, *penitence* 451.1

self-reproachful *penitent* 451.5

self-reproaching *penitent* 451.5

self-reproachingly *penitently* 451.10

self-respect *proudness* 297.3

self-respecting *proud* 297.10

self-restrained 455.6, 830.10; *detached* 4.18, *celibate* 67.6, *strong-willed* 376.10, *unadorned* 424.7, *chaste* 431.10, *disinterested* 443.4

---

self-restrainedly 830.19
self-restrained person 455.5
self-restraint 455.1, 830.4;
philosophical attitude 4.3, *celibacy*
67.1, *will* 376.5, *desisting* 417.4,
unadornment 424.3, *chastity*
431.3, *disinterestedness* 443.1,
abnegation 506.3, *limit* 620.1
self-righteous *zealous* 81.22,
moralistic 431.12
self-righteously *moralistically*
431.16
self-righteousness 431.7
self-rising *leavening* 539.7
self-rising flour *leavening* 539.3
self-rule *self-government* 49.9,
independence 829.5
self-ruling *governmental* 49.24,
independent 829.12
self-sacrifice *religiousness* 81.2,
self-abasement 298.4, *unselfishness*
443.2, *offering* 472.6, *abnegation*
506.3
self-sacrificing *religious* 81.21,
self-abasing 298.11, *unselfish*
443.5, *abnegating* 506.7
selfsame *same* 730.7
selfsameness *sameness* 730.1
self-satisfaction 402.2; *satisfaction*
273.1
self-satisfied 402.9; *satisfied*
273.4, *prideful* 297.8
self-scourging *type of penance*
451.3
self-seeker *selfish person* 444.3
self-seeking *selfishness* 444.1,
selfish 444.4
self-server *selfish person* 444.3
self-service restaurant *eating*
place 92.17
self-serving *selfish* 444.4
self-serving politician *cunning*
person 822.3
self-slaughter *suicide* 30.8
self-starter *doer* 412.3
self-styled *disbelieved* 88.7
self-sufficiency *sufficiency* 97.1,
proudness 297.3, *solvency* 485.4,
independence 829.5
self-sufficient *sufficient* 97.3,
proud 297.10, *unsociable* 409.6,
unjoined 753.9, *complete* 761.6,
independent 829.12
self-sufficiently *proudly* 297.19,
unsocially 409.13, *in isolation*
753.24
self-support *self-help* 825.11
self-supported *self-helpful* 825.22
self-supporting *self-helpful*
825.22, *independent* 829.12
self-surrender *religiousness* 81.2
self-surrendering *religious* 81.21
self-sustained *self-helpful* 825.22
self-sustaining *self-helpful* 825.22
self-sustainment *self-help* 825.11
self-taught *educated* 48.19,
unskilled 128.5, *naive* 821.3
self-timer *exposure equipment*
132.12
self-will *willfulness* 372.3, *obstinacy*
379.1
self-willed *willful* 372.8, *obstinate*
379.5
self-worship *self-admiration* 402.4,
self-absorption 456.4
self-worshiping *self-admiring*
402.10, *self-absorbed* 456.9
Seliwanoff's test *sugar test* 12.6
Selkirk rex *Breeds of Cats* 35
sell 482.15; *provision* 89.9, *publicize*
173.18, 178.19, *publish* 174.19,
finance 457.7, *transfer property*
470.12, *trade* 480.18, *be sold*
482.22

sell again 482.21
sell at a loss 482.19; *lose money*
468.15
sell at a profit 482.18; *trade in*
457.8, *profit* 467.22
sell at a sacrifice *sell at a loss*
482.19
sell badly *be sold* 482.22
sell by auction *auction* 482.16
sell dear *overcharge* 496.10
sell down the river [Inf] *inform*
on 170.13
Selle Français *Horse and Pony*
Breeds 159
seller 482.7; *person transferring*
property 470.8, *trader* 480.11,
peddler 482.9
seller's market 483.3; *economic*
factor 56.8, *scarcity* 98.3,
inflationary price 496.3
sell for *price* 494.12
sell forward *sell again* 482.21
selling 482.1, 482.12
selling line *merchandise* 482.6
selling price *price* 494.1
sell like hot cakes *be published*
173.19, *be sold* 482.22
sell long *finance* 457.7
sell off 482.20
sell on credit *credit* 487.10
sellout *theatrical performance*
136.13, *sale* 482.2, *successful thing*
845.5
sell out *sell off* 482.20, *be sold*
482.22
sell over the counter *merchandise*
482.17
sell short *understate* 195.14,
disparage 440.11, *finance* 457.7,
sell off 482.20
sell someone a bill of goods
swindle 193.19
sell the family silver *lose one's*
money 486.15
sell to *trade* 480.18
sell to the highest bidder *auction*
482.16
sell under the counter
merchandise 482.17
sell up *sell off* 482.20
sell well *be published* 173.19, *be*
sold 482.22
seltzer water *water* 93.4
selvage *edging* 618.2
selvage *or* selvedge *weaving* 130.6
selvedge *edging* 618.2
semanteme *part of speech* 5.30
semantic *linguistic* 361.9
semantically *philosophically* 4.23,
linguistically 5.44
semantic content *meaning* 361.1
semantic field *type of meaning*
361.4
semantic flow *meaning* 361.1
semanticist *linguist* 5.3
semantic net *artificial intelligence*
15.21
semantics *Branches of Philosophy*
4, *Linguistic Studies* 5, *meaning*
361.1
semantic shift *type of meaning*
361.4
semaphore *artificial language* 5.9,
signaling 169.9, *signal* 183.18, *aid*
to the deaf 229.3, *track* 688.2
semaphoric *signaling* 183.14
semaphorically *indicatively*
183.21
semasiological *linguistic* 361.9
semasiology *Linguistic Studies* 5,
meaning 361.1
semateme *language element* 5.13
semblable *counterpart* 733.5

semblance *representation* 187.1,
spectacle 264.6, *similarity* 733.1
seme *Heraldic Terms* 184
semen *body fluid* 19.16, 555.3,
organs of reproduction 21.9,
fertilizer 22.6, *secreted substance*
24.2, *test* 107.10
semester *time period* 641.2, *period*
of activity 641.4
semi [Inf] *truck* 578.10, 687.8
semiannual *cyclic* 663.7
semiannually *cyclically* 663.15
semiarid climate *climate* 9.35
semiautomatic *firearm* 78.7
semibreve *notation* 140.20
semicircle *circle* 6.40, 631.2,
fencing movements 153.3, *curve*
629.1, *part* 760.1, *half* 789.7
semicircular *curvilinear* 6.78, *arch*
134.5, *curved* 629.4, *circular*
631.5
semicircular canals *ear* 19.10,
228.2
semicolon *Punctuation Marks* 5,
separator 753.5
semiconductor 10.34; *electrical*
conduction 10.33
semiconductor device
semiconductor 10.34, *circuit element*
14.39
semiconductor laser *laser* 10.18
semiconductor memory *memory*
15.6
semiconductor physics *Fields of*
Modern Physics 10
semicrystalline *electric* 14.47
semidark *dim* 248.4
semidarkness *dimness* 248.1
semidetached *manorial* 60.21
semidetached house *house* 60.4
semifinal *prize competition* 422.5
semifinalist *finalist* 422.16
semifinal race *track event* 166.1
semifluid *emulsion* 561.5, *sludgy*
561.18
semifluidity *viscosity* 561.1
semiformal dress *formal clothes*
100.5
semihumid climate *climate* 9.35
semiliquid 561.7; *emulsion* 561.5,
sludgy 561.18, *dense* 594.6
semiliquidity *compressibility*
543.3, *fluidity* 555.5, *viscosity*
561.1
semiliteracy *lack of knowledge*
349.2
semiliterate *semiskilled* 349.6
semimajor axis *orbit* 7.22
semimatte *or* semimatt finish
printing 132.20
semimatt finish *darkroom*
equipment 132.21
semimetal *chemical element* 11.3
semimonthly *magazine* 175.3,
cyclic 663.7, *cyclically* 663.15
seminal fluid 19.25, *procreative*
22.10, *of a secretion* 24.5, *causal*
675.7, *original* 737.4
seminal fluid *organs of*
reproduction 21.9, *secreted*
substance 24.2
seminally *originally* 737.8
seminar *place for conversation*
210.5, *lecture* 777.7
seminary *religious school* 48.13
semiological *symbolic* 183.12,
linguistic 361.9, *interpretive* 365.8
semiologically *indicatively* 183.21
semiology *medical science* 107.5,
symbolism 183.4, *meaning* 361.1,
science of interpretation 365.5
semiopaque *ceramic* 129.9, *semi-*
transparent 249.9, *shady* 250.4
semiopaque glaze *glaze* 129.3

semiopaquely *ornamentally*
129.11
semiotic *symbolic* 183.12, *linguistic*
361.9
semiotics *Branches of Philosophy*
4, *Linguistic Studies* 5,
nonstandard language 5.7,
symbolism 183.4, *meaning* 361.1
semipolar bond *chemical bond*
11.6
semiquaver *notation* 140.20
semisextile *angular measurement*
628.4
semiskilled 349.6; *industrial*
57.13, *unskilled* 128.5
semiskilled worker *employee*
57.4, *artisan* 123.13, *operative*
509.6
semitone *musical note* 140.15
semitrailer *truck* 578.10, 687.8
semitransparency 249.3; *murk*
248.2, *whiteness* 253.1
semitransparent 249.9; *whitened*
253.8, *iridescent* 263.7
semitransparent pigment
coloring agent 251.5
semiweekly *cyclic* 663.7, *cyclically*
663.15
sempiternal *timeless* 640.3, *eternal*
644.4, *unfailing* 667.3,
permanently 667.6
sempiternity *timelessness* 640.1,
eternity 644.1
semtex *explosive* 78.13
Senate *United States government*
49.21, *representative body* 79.2
Senate majority leader *elected*
official 50.8
Senate minority leader *elected*
official 50.8
Senate president *party official*
68.5
Senate seat *position of authority*
52.4
Senate whip *person in authority*
52.7
senator *elected official* 50.8, *person*
in authority 52.7, *delegate* 79.1
senatorial *governmental* 49.24,
delegated 79.4
senatorially *representatively* 79.8
send 209.11; *communicate* 169.18,
give out 472.12, *billow* 571.9, *set*
in motion 677.16, *convey* 685.9,
mail 685.10, *transport* 686.10
send [Inf] *cause joy* 269.11
send about one's business *send*
away 709.18
send abroad *emigrate* 707.17
send a letter *correspond* 169.19
send a message *signal* 183.18
send an SOS *signal* 183.18
send a signal *signal* 183.18
send away 709.18; *cause to*
disappear 265.7, *convey* 685.9,
ostracize 709.17, *disband* 776.13
send away with a flea in one's
ear *fend off* 701.9, *send away*
709.18
send back *reject* 383.10, *give back*
478.5
send before the judge *accuse*
442.8
send down *disbar* 709.16
send down *or* up *imprison* 454.23
send flying *convey* 685.9, *push*
696.16
send forth *convey* 685.9, *let out*
709.26
send headlong *push* 696.16, *bring*
down 716.14
send home *disband* 776.13,
liberate 831.6
send in *show in* 708.13

sending *conveyance* 685.2, *transportation* 686.1, *transporting* 686.8
sending back *giving back* 478.1
sending to Coventry *ostracism* 709.3
send in one's papers *resign* 835.5
send (in) the marines *combat* 77.34
send off *convey* 685.9, *send away* 709.18, *disband* 776.13
send-off *soccer play* 163.5, *parting* 705.3
send on *send* 209.11
send on an errand *engage* 833.9
send on a wild goose chase *evade* 386.19
send one's apologies *refuse* 506.8
send one's condolences *grieve* 308.7
send one's respects *defer to* 410.12
send out *let out* 709.26
send out a distress call *signal* 183.18
send out a search party *pursue* 385.11
send out of the world *kill* 30.19
send over the edge [Inf] *make insane* 110.13
send packing *eject* 701.8, 764.8, *send away* 709.18
send regrets *apologize* 313.8
send smoke signals *signal* 183.18
send someone about his *or* **her business** *eject* 701.8
send to Coventry *withhold approval* 438.17, *ostracize* 709.17, *set apart* 753.17, *exclude* 764.7
send to one's account *kill* 30.19
send to one's Maker *kill* 30.19
send to prison *detain* 830.16
send to the big house [Inf] *imprison* 55.11, *detain* 830.16
send to the block *execute* 454.30
send to the bottom *bring down* 716.14
send to the chair *execute* 454.30
send to the gas chamber *slaughter* 30.21
send to the hot seat [Inf] *execute* 454.30
send to the scaffold *or* **gallows** *execute* 30.22, 454.30
send to the showers *send away* 709.18
send to the stake *execute* 30.22
send up 715.12; *be humorous* 277.11, *deride* 369.7, *ridicule* 436.22
send-up *entertainment* 277.4, *ridicule* 436.4, 440.6, *mimicry* 736.3
send up a trial balloon *have foresight* 357.8
send up the river [Inf] *imprison* 55.11, *detain* 830.16
Senecan tragedy *tragedy* 136.10
Senegal *Countries* 566, *Rivers* 570
Senegal Fulani *Breeds of Cattle* 16
senescence *bodily development* 19.17, *old age* 27.5
senescent *aging* 27.13, *old* 653.10, *deteriorated* 808.8
seneschal *manager* 126.7
senhor [Port] *male title of address* 32.3
senhora [Port] *female title of address* 33.3
senhorita [Port] *female title of address* 33.3
senile *aged* 27.15, *foolish* 353.5,

disabled 515.10, *old* 653.10, *deteriorated* 808.8
senilely *maturely* 27.18, *venerably* 653.17
senility *age* 27.1, *old age* 27.5, *poor health* 517.3, *elderliness* 653.2, *physical deterioration* 808.4
senior *older person* 27.7, *learner* 48.6, *authoritative* 52.9, *company leader* 68.8, *old* 653.10, *predecessor* 769.8, *primary* 769.10
Senior Airman *US Military Ranks* 58
Senior Chief Petty Officer *US Military Ranks* 58
senior citizen *older person* 27.7
senior citizens *old people* 653.6
senior high *school* 48.11
seniority *adulthood* 27.2, *old age* 27.5, *authority* 52.1, *bargaining terms* 57.10, *elderliness* 653.2, *superiority* 744.1, *priority* 769.2
Senior Master Sergeant *US Military Ranks* 58
seniors *old people* 27.10
senior service *navy* 77.18
senmurv *Legendary Creatures* 360
senna pods *Tree Products* 43, *purgative* 115.7
sennet *military call* 183.9
sennit knot *Knots, Bends, Hitches, Splices* 754
señor [Sp] *male title of address* 32.3
señora [Sp] *female title of address* 33.3
señorita [Sp] *female title of address* 33.3
sensate 212.5
sensation 212.1; *physiology* 13.13, *liveliness* 28.12, *exaggeration* 194.1, *marvel* 294.3, *texture* 552.1, *success* 845.1
sensational *dramatic* 136.31, 404.16, *publicized* 173.14, *exciting* 212.8, *wondrous* 294.9, *blatant* 404.19
sensationalism *Philosophical Schools of Thought* 4, *dramaturgy* 136.6, *public relations (PR)* 173.8, *exaggeration* 194.1, *dramatics* 404.3, *blatancy* 404.6
sensationalist *Philosophical Schools of Thought* 4, *exaggerator* 194.6
sensationalize *exaggerate* 194.11, *put on a show* 404.28
sensationalized *exaggerated* 194.7
sensationally 212.8; *dramatically* 136.38, 404.31, *exaggeratedly* 194.16, *wondrously* 294.18, *blatantly* 404.34
sense 212.9; *philosophical term* 4.7, *know* 48.24, *feelings* 266.1, *feel* 266.14, *feel instinctively* 266.15, *intelligence* 315.2, 352.2, *common sense* 315.4, *reason* 319.1, *judgment* 341.1, *meaning* 361.1, *intelligibility* 363.1, *significance* 676.4
sense data *philosophical term* 4.7
sense datum *sensation* 212.1
senseless *insensible* 213.4, *lacking intellect* 316.5, *foolish* 353.5, *oblivious* 355.9, *meaningless* 362.7
senselessly *unintelligently* 316.9, *foolishly* 353.8, *forgetfully* 355.14, *meaninglessly* 362.13, *ridiculously* 368.8
senselessness *lack of intellect* 316.1, *folly* 353.1, *oblivion* 355.4, *nonsense* 362.2, *ridiculousness* 368.1

senseless talk 362.4; *nonsense* 192.8
sense of community *society* 2.6
sense of danger 811.3
sense of duty 433.2
sense of hearing *hearing* 228.1
sense of humor 277.5
sense *or* **feeling of obligation** *or* **indebtedness** *gratitude* 310.1
sense of responsibility *observance* 465.1
sense of right and wrong *morals* 431.1
sense of security *security* 464.1, *safety* 810.1
sense of sight *vision* 242.1
sense of smell 224.2
sense of taste *taste* 219.1
sense of time *time* 639.1
sense of touch *touch* 216.1
sense of unity *compatibility* 735.4
sense of wonder *wonder* 294.1
sense organ 212.4
sense perception *sensation* 212.1, *touch* 216.1
senses, the *sensation* 212.1
sense vibrations *experience psychic phenomena* 86.23
sensibilia *philosophical term* 4.7
sensibilities *feelings* 266.1
sensibility *liveliness* 28.12, *refinement* 48.10, *sensitivity* 267.1, *judiciousness* 337.2
sensible 212.6; *rational* 4.15, 109.4, *refined* 48.20, *advisable* 176.8, *feeling* 266.9, *sensitive* 267.3, *thoughtful* 315.10, *reasoning* 319.7, *wise* 352.4, *intelligible* 363.5, *cheap* 497.9, *moderate* 521.3, *material* 524.7, *practical* 719.8, *useful* 801.5
sensibleness *common sense* 315.4, *judgment* 341.1
sensibly *rationally* 4.25, *advisably* 176.13, *intelligently* 315.14, *reasonably* 319.15, *wisely* 352.8, *materially* 524.9
sensing *feeling* 266.9, *intuitive* 320.6
sensitive 266.11, 267.3; *refined* 48.20, 534.5, *sensible* 212.6, *touchable* 216.5, *feeling* 266.9, *intuitive* 320.6, *discriminating* 337.9, *judicious* 341.8, *fluid* 527.5, *impressionable* 543.12
sensitively 267.6; *discerningly* 48.27, *judiciously* 337.16, *decorously* 534.10, *soft-heartedly* 543.19, *finely* 595.19
sensitive man *liberated man* 32.13
sensitiveness *sensitivity* 267.1, *soft-heartedness* 543.4
sensitive payment *gift* 472.2
sensitive person *feeling person* 266.8
sensitive to touch *touchable* 216.5
sensitivity 212.2, 267.1; *measurement* 10.67, *refinement* 48.10, *exposure* 132.15, *touch* 216.1, *judiciousness* 337.2, *insight* 360.3, *elegance* 527.1, *fineness* 595.5
sensitivity of photographic materials *Fields of Measurement* 589
sensitize *refine* 534.7
sensitometer *Fields of Measurement* 589
sensitometry *Fields of Measurement* 589
sensor *detector* 345.6
sensorial *sensate* 212.5
sensorium *sense organ* 212.4
sensors for pulp and paper

processes *systems and process control* 14.28
sensory 19.22; *sensate* 212.5, *touchable* 216.5
sensory pattern *perceptual concept* 108.30
sensual 20.16; *pleasurable* 214.6, *pleasure-seeking* 214.10, *self-indulgent* 456.6, *material* 524.7
sensualism *physical pleasure* 214.1, *materialization* 524.2
sensualist *pleasure-seeker* 214.4, *self-indulgent person* 456.5
sensuality *sexuality* 20.3, *sensitivity* 212.2, *self-indulgence* 456.1, *materialization* 524.2
sensually *sexily* 20.23, *pleasingly* 214.15, *materially* 524.9
sensual pleasure *physical pleasure* 214.1
sensum *sensation* 212.1
sensuous *sensible* 212.6, *touchable* 216.5
sensuous desire *sexual desire* 20.5
sensuousness *sensitivity* 212.2, *physical pleasure* 214.1
sent *communicated* 169.15, *broadcast* 172.12
sent back *unselected* 383.7
sentence *clause* 5.31, *legal justice* 53.4, *unfavorable verdict* 54.20, *convict* 54.33, *utterance* 205.10, *verdict* 341.2, *penalty* 454.5, *penalize* 454.26, *period of activity* 641.4, *passage* 692.1, *part of speech* 760.7, *ruling* 780.2, *detention* 830.5, *detain* 830.16
sentenced *convicted* 54.26, *detained* 830.11
sentenced to death *dying* 29.12
sentencer *punisher* 454.16
sentence structure *grammar* 5.28, *mode of expression* 537.3
sentence to death *execute* 454.30
sentencing *penalty* 454.5
sentential *phrased* 5.39
sentential calculus *Branches of Philosophy* 4
sententious *legalistic* 53.22, *proverbial* 177.2, *concise* 198.4, *emphatic* 200.3, *judging* 341.7
sententiously *concisely* 198.6
sententiousness *conciseness* 198.1
sentience *liveliness* 28.12, *sensation* 212.1, *sensitivity* 267.1
sentient *sensible* 212.6, *feeling* 266.9, *sensitive* 267.3
sentiment *philosophy* 4.1, *belief* 87.1, *sensation* 212.1, *emotion* 266.3, *idea* 327.1
sentimental *sensitive* 267.3, *amorous* 299.18, *ideal* 327.12
sentimental attachment *liking* 290.1
sentimental comedy *comedy* 136.11
sentimentalism *Western Literary Groups* 139
sentimentality *emotionalism* 266.6, *sensitivity* 267.1
sentimentally *unemphatically* 201.4, *with feeling* 266.18, *amorously* 299.30, *imaginatively* 327.21
sentimental novel *novel* 139.3
sentiments *feelings* 266.1
sentinel *observer* 242.15, *guard* 419.15, *security force* 464.3, *closer* 584.5, *surveillant* 810.12, *warner* 814.5
sentry *observer* 242.15, *guard* 419.15, *security force* 464.3, *closer* 584.5, *surveillant* 810.12, *warner* 814.5

senza Musical Terms and Expression Marks 140
Seoul Countries 566
sepal *leaf* 41.6, *flower part* 42.3
separability *separation* 753.1, *separateness* 753.3, *nonadhesion* 756.1
separable 753.11
separate 66.10, 703.12, 724.10, 724.14, 753.7, 753.12; *extract* 11.41, *process* 14.50, *discriminate* 337.12, *dissent* 347.8, *choose* 382.14, *disconnect* 574.19, 775.12, *keep away* 585.9, *spaced* 587.4, *space* 587.6, *divergent* 703.6, *part* 705.13, 760.14, *obtain an extract* 711.19, *unconnected* 728.8, *not connect* 728.13, *diverse* 732.5, *be diverse* 732.10, *aloof* 756.5, *unstick* 756.6, *disbanded* 776.7, *disperse* 776.12, *disband* 776.13, *alone* 788.15, *single out* 788.19
separated *estranged* 63.8, *divorced* 66.7, *judged* 337.10, *disconnected* 574.12, *away* 585.6, *spaced* 587.4, *divergent* 703.6, *separate* 724.10, 753.7, *unconnected* 728.8, *disintegrated* 758.3, *disbanded* 776.7, *alone* 788.15, *single* 788.16
separate from *be aloof* 756.8
separately 724.18, 753.22; *discriminatingly* 337.15, *disconnectedly* 574.22, *apart* 587.8, *divergently* 703.16, *unconnectedly* 728.18, *diversely* 732.14, *aloofly* 756.10, *destructively* 758.9, *one by one* 788.21
separateness 724.3, 753.3; *unconnectedness* 728.2, *diversity* 732.1, *aloofness* 756.2, *aloneness* 788.5
separates 753.6; *suit* 100.16
separate the men from the boys *make unlike* 734.9
separate the sheep from the goats *discriminate* 337.12, *make unlike* 734.9, *divide* 753.18
separate the wheat from the chaff *discriminate* 337.12, *divide* 753.18
separating *discriminating* 337.9, *selecting* 382.4, *separation* 753.1
separation 66.2, 409.3, 753.1; *process* 11.15, *personal conflict* 63.2, *discrimination* 337.1, *faction* 347.4, *selecting* 382.4, *disconnection* 574.5, *distance* 585.1, *interval* 587.1, *parting* 703.2, 705.3, *obtaining of an extract* 711.7, *unconnectedness* 728.2, *duplicate* 736.4, *nonadhesion* 756.1, *deconstruction* 758.2, *divergence* 776.5, *singleness* 788.6
separation processes *industrial processes* 14.27
separatism *dissentience* 347.3, *separateness* 753.3, *aloneness* 788.5
separatist *dissenter* 347.5, *dissenting* 347.7, *protester* 507.4, *individualist* 756.3, *alone* 788.15
separatists *dissenters* 347.6
separative *unjoined* 753.9
separatively *in isolation* 753.24
separator 753.5; *wall* 134.9
separatrix *oblique line* 607.5
Sephardic *denominational* 81.23
sepia *brown pigment* 256.2
sepia print *printing* 132.20
seplophobia Phobias 283
seppuki *self-punishment* 454.10
seppuku *suicide* 30.8

sepsis *uncleanness* 112.2, *lack of hygiene* 112.3, *infection* 114.7
septenary *seven* 792.3, *seventh* 792.14
septendecillion *million* 792.11
septennial *seventh* 792.14
septennially *fivefold* 792.26
septet *part of poem* 139.9, *instrumental group* 141.3, *seven* 792.3, *team* 827.7
septic *unclean* 112.8, *contagious* 114.26, *toxic* 114.28
septically *unhygienically* 114.32
septicemia *infection* 114.7, *blood disease* 114.14
septic tank *place for waste* 802.6
septillion *million* 792.11
septivalent *chemical compound* 11.4
septuagenarian *older person* 27.7, *twenty and over* 792.8
Septuagint *Christian text* 81.16
septuple *seven* 792.3, *seventh* 792.14, *quintuple* 792.23
septuplet *seven* 792.3
septuplicate *seven* 792.3, *seventh* 792.14
sepulcher *burial place* 31.7, *closed place* 584.4, *enclosed area* 619.2
sepulchral *funeral* 31.9, *deep* 236.8
sepulchrally *funereally* 31.13
sepulture *burial* 31.1
sequacious *sequential* 770.7
sequel 770.5; *continuation* 669.2, *effect* 676.1, *sequence* 770.1
sequence 6.18, 770.1; *harmonic element* 140.14, *continuity* 669.1, *hierarchy* 765.3, *consecutiveness* 774.1
sequenced *harmonic* 140.27
sequent *progressive* 669.6, *sequential* 770.7
sequential 770.7; *progressive* 669.6, *caused* 676.5, *hierarchical* 765.12, *consecutive* 774.7
sequential access *data-related concepts* 15.23
sequentially 770.13; *continually* 669.10, *in order* 765.26, *consecutively* 774.15
sequential scanning *television set* 172.6
sequester *exclude* 409.12, 764.7, *take back* 477.17, *divide* 753.18
sequestered *concealed* 181.8, 844.7, *secluded* 409.9, *quiescent* 678.6
sequestered nook *solitary place* 409.4
sequester the jury *try a case* 54.28
sequestrate *take away* 275.13, *confiscate* 454.25
sequestration *jury selection* 54.14, *confiscation* 454.4, *taking back* 477.4, *exclusiveness* 764.4, *concealment* 844.2
sequestrator *collector* 473.7, *taker* 477.9
sequin *variegated thing* 263.5, *decorative article* 532.5
sequoia Trees and Shrubs 43
serac *rock face* 161.6
sérac *glacier* 8.44
seraglio *womenfolk* 33.14
serape *coat* 100.19
seraph *angel* 82.11
seraphic *angelic* 82.21, *virtuous* 447.5
seraphically *divinely* 82.24
seraphim *angelic order (highest to lowest)* 82.12
Serbia Countries 566
sere *ecology* 13.25, *dried-up* 560.9, *spoiled* 808.9

serenade Musical Forms 140, *song* 140.11, *love token* 299.8
serendipitous *discovering* 345.8, *extra* 748.10, *chance* 842.10
serendipitously *randomly* 842.16
serendipity *discovery* 345.1, *extra* 748.6, *luck* 842.3
serene *detached* 4.18, *peaceful* 73.8, *satisfied* 273.4, *wonderless* 295.3, *quiescent* 678.6, *easygoing* 823.13
serenely *stoically* 4.26, *peacefully* 73.12, *with satisfaction* 273.13, *without wonder* 295.8
serenity *satisfaction* 273.1, *lack of wonder* 295.1, *smoothness* 545.1, *repose* 678.2, *ease* 819.1
serf 69.8; *commoner* 71.1, *subjected person* 832.5
serfdom *servitude* 69.2, *common people* 71.2, *servility* 401.1, *subjection* 832.1
serge Collective Names 59, Fabrics and Fibers 130
Sergeant US Military Ranks 58, *military title* 72.8
Sergeant First Class US Military Ranks 58
Sergeant Major US Military Ranks 58
sergeant major *strict person* 424.4
Sergeant Major of the Army US Military Ranks 58
Sergeant Major of the Marine Corps US Military Ranks 58
Sergeant/Specialist 5 US Military Ranks 58
serial *broadcast drama* 136.4, *dramatic* 137.16, *program* 172.10, *periodical* 175.1, 175.6, *magazine* 175.3, *frequent* 663.6, *hierarchical* 765.12, *sequential* 770.7, *consecutive* 774.7
serial art Western Art Styles 133
serialism *musical dissonance* 241.2
serialization *compilation* 174.4, *frequency* 663.2, *sequence* 770.1
serialize *report* 175.9, *make regular* 663.9
serialized *frequent* 663.6
serial killer *murderer* 30.12
serial killing *malignity* 306.5
serially *regularly* 663.14, *consecutively* 774.15
serial order *hierarchy* 765.3
serial port *computer part* 15.4
serial sex *sex act* 20.10
seriate *consecutive* 774.7
sericultural *entomological* 40.15
sericulture *study of insects* 40.2
sericulturist *entomologist* 40.3
series 770.3; *sequence* 6.18, 770.1, *geological time* 8.47, *broadcast drama* 136.4, *scale* 140.16, *program* 172.10, *compilation* 174.4, *magazine* 175.3, *musical dissonance* 241.2, *recurrent period* 641.5, *continuity* 669.1, *unit* 759.5, *hierarchy* 765.3, *sequel* 770.5, *consecutiveness* 774.1, *list* 785.1
series connection *circuit element* 14.39
series movie *movie type* 137.3
serif *type* 173.5
serine Amino Acids 12
seringa Trees and Shrubs 43
serious 200.5, 278.4, 799.8; *sick* 114.24, *musical* 140.25, *important* 278.6, *sullen* 304.8, *significant* 361.11, *intending* 374.6, *steady* 376.8, *moralistic* 431.12, *deep-seated* 598.17, *dangerous* 811.7
serious foul play *soccer play* 163.5
serious literature *literature* 139.1

seriously *solemnly* 278.9, *earnestly* 278.10, *sullenly* 304.16, *prospectively* 374.12, *resolutely* 376.15, *moralistically* 431.16, *with deep feeling* 598.29, *importantly* 799.15
serious-minded *intending* 374.6
serious-mindedly *prospectively* 374.12
serious music *classical music* 140.2
seriousness 200.2, 278.1, 376.3; *sullenness* 304.1, *significance* 361.2, *self-righteousness* 431.7, *depth of feeling* 598.7, *importance* 799.1
serious press *print journalism* 175.4
sermon Eucharist 85.7, *publication* 173.1, *dissertation* 203.1, *public speaking* 205.11, *address* 209.1, *condemnation* 438.2
sermonically *oratorically* 209.14
sermonize *propound a philosophy* 4.21, *preach* 84.14, *dissertate* 203.5, *speak to* 205.19, *address* 209.8, *moralize* 431.14
sermonizer *religionist* 81.14, *speaker* 205.12, *public speaker* 209.5
sermonizing *advice* 176.1, *addressing* 209.6
sermons Phobias 283
serotest *test* 107.10
serous *rheumy* 555.16
serous fluid *body fluid* 555.3
Serpens Constellations 7
Serpent Constellations 7, *devil* 446.5
serpent *snake* 37.6, Musical Instruments 142, *hypocrite* 192.9, *cunning person* 822.3
Serpent Bearer Constellations 7
Serpentes *snake* 37.6
serpentiform *snakelike* 37.13
serpentine *snakelike* 37.13, *variegated thing* 263.5, *flowing* 570.7, *convolutional* 632.4, *indirect* 698.9, *cunning* 822.4
serpigo *skin disease* 114.16
Serra da Estrela Breeds of Sheep 16
serrate *of leaves* 41.18, *make rough* 544.11, *sharpen* 549.16, *notch* 636.5
serrate or **serrated** *notched* 636.4
serrated *coarse* 544.6, *toothed* 549.13
serration *roughness* 544.1, *sharpness* 549.1, *notch* 636.1
serried *crowded* 59.22, *dense* 540.6, *continuous* 774.9
serriform *notched* 636.4
serrulation *notch* 636.1
serum *body fluid* 555.3
servant 69.1; *domestic worker* 123.4, *humble person* 298.7, *adherent* 401.5, *submitter* 421.2, *assistant* 511.3, *nonentity* 800.8, *subordinate* 832.3
servant girl *domestic servant* 69.7
servant's uniform *uniform* 100.9
serve 69.11, 825.29; *have sex* 20.21, *provision* 89.9, *suffice* 97.6, 273.10, *work for* 122.10, *play tennis* 165.13, *pander to* 401.11, *obey* 426.7, *better* 445.17, *be operational* 509.10, *be an instrument* 511.7, *throw* 696.4, *be useful* 801.9, *be convenient* 803.5, *help* 825.23, *be subject to* 832.12
serve a citation *accuse* 442.8
serve an apprenticeship *learn* 48.23, *prepare oneself* 388.21

serve as a doormat for *be subject to* 832.12

serve as a makeshift *suffice* 97.6

serve as a model *influence* 512.11

serve as a representative *represent* 79.7

serve a sentence *be in prison* 55.13

serve as press officer for *interpret news* 365.17

serve as proxy *be a substitute* 672.6

serve a stretch [Inf] *be in prison* 55.13, *detain* 830.16

serve a summons *accuse* 442.8

serve a use *be favorable* 62.12

serve involuntarily *be subject to* 832.12

serve notice on *litigate* 54.27

serve on a working party *represent* 79.7

serve one right 420.5

serve one's country *join the army* 76.31

serve one's turn *be useful* 801.9

serve one well *benefit* 801.10

server *attendant* 69.4, *tennis participant* 165.6, *badminton terms* 165.11, *thrower* 696.10

serve the purpose *be desirable* 288.23

serve the time *be convenient* 803.5

serve time [Inf] *detain* 830.16

serve with a writ *accuse* 442.8

service 689.16; *have sex* 20.21, *military* 58.10, *servitude* 69.2, *ritual* 85.1, *provision* 89.1, 89.9, *benevolent act* 305.5, *usefulness* 393.2, 801.1, *ceremony* 405.3, *loyalty* 426.2, *line of duty* 433.3, *giving* 472.1, *salesmanship* 482.4, *management* 509.4, *take action* 509.12, *instrumentality* 511.1, *employment* 573.3, *repair* 809.1, 809.10, *restore* 809.12, *preservation* 815.1, *upkeep* 815.5, *preserve* 815.1, *support* 825.2, *subjection* 832.1

service *or* **serve** *tennis strokes* 165.2

serviceability *usefulness* 393.2, *instrumentality* 511.1, *usability* 801.2

serviceable *beneficial* 445.11, *practical* 511.6, 719.8, *usable* 801.6, *helpful* 825.19

serviceably *usefully* 801.12, *helpfully* 825.32

serviceberry Trees and Shrubs 43

service box *squash terms* 165.10

service break *tennis terms* 165.5

service charge *fee* 494.3

service contract *purchase contract* 459.3

service court line *squash terms* 165.10

service fee *fee* 494.3

service line *tennis court* 165.3, *squash terms* 165.10

serviceman *soldier* 77.4, *repair worker* 123.8

serviceman *or* **servicewoman** *warrior* 76.25

service of process *pretrial proceedings* 54.13

services *the military* 58.2, *armed forces* 77.9, *provisions* 89.3

services no longer required *termination* 834.2

service station *stopping place* 668.4, *miscellaneous automotive terms* 687.14

service tree Trees and Shrubs 43

servicewoman *soldier* 77.4, *repair worker* 123.8

service worker 123.7

service workplace 124.5

servicing *provisioning* 89.6, *practical* 511.6, *repair* 809.1, *upkeep* 815.5

servile 401.6; *obedient* 69.10, 426.4, *submitting* 421.3, *showing respect* 435.7, *sycophantic* 439.11, *lowly* 597.17, *subordinate* 832.8

servilely 401.15; *obediently* 69.12, 426.9, *humbly* 597.27, *dependently* 832.13

servility 401.1; *obedience* 426.1, *sycophancy* 439.5, *lowliness* 597.8, *subjection* 832.1

serving 69.9; *dish* 90.7, *helping* 92.11, 825.16, *subordinate* 832.8

serving a sentence *imprisoned* 55.9, *detained* 830.11

serving maid *domestic servant* 69.7

serving man *domestic servant* 69.7

servitor *servant* 69.1

servitude 69.2; *submission* 421.1, *detention* 429.5, *subjection* 832.1

servomechanism *dynamic structure* 14.5, *machinery* 103.5

servomotor *machinery* 103.5

sesame seed Herbs and Spices 91

sesquicentennial *anniversary* 405.5, 663.4, *anniversarial* 663.8, *hundreds* 792.9

sesquicentennially *cyclically* 663.15

sesquipedalian *word* 5.17, *worded* 5.38, *diffuse* 199.3

sesquipedalian *or* **sesquipedal** *lengthy* 590.9

sesquipedalianism *inelegance of expression* 528.4, *longness* 590.3

sesquiterpene *terpene* 12.20

sessile *of leaves* 41.18, *of fungi* 47.19, *algal* 47.20

session *conference* 59.5, *period of activity* 641.4

sessions *legal process* 54.3

sestet *part of poem* 139.9, *six* 792.2

sestina Poem or Verse Forms 139

Set *evil spirit* 446.4

Set *or* **Seth** Deities 82

set 6.19; *phrased* 5.39, *cultivate* 17.19, *group* 18.13, 59.8, *young plant* 26.5, *mammal dwelling* 35.12, *party* 59.3, *assemblage* 59.13, *family* 65.1, *collection* 105.12, 757.3, *treat* 115.17, *stage set* 136.19, *motion-picture studio* 137.7, *sports* 145.1, *huddle* 155.7, *tennis terms* 165.5, *bridge* 168.4, *print* 173.17, *intending* 374.6, *opinionated* 379.9, *deliberate* 384.5, *prepared* 388.9, *established* 397.12, *prize competition* 422.5, *fashion* 536.1, *design* 536.2, *condensed* 540.7, *be dense* 540.8, *hardened* 542.7, *solidify* 542.10, *located* 565.6, *situated* 573.5, *situate* 573.10, *thicken* 594.9, *nature* 624.5, *make stable* 674.7, *momentum* 677.2, *bearing* 697.2, *directed* 697.9, *direct* 697.13, *aim* 697.14, *descend* 714.12, *adjusted* 721.14, *adjust* 721.23, *average* 742.5, *intertwine* 752.19, *unit* 759.5, *inclusion* 763.1, *category* 767.6, *arrange* 767.18, *class* 777.1, *social class* 777.5, *specify* 779.18, *inevitable* 840.11

set *or* **break a record** *compete in track and field* 166.21

set *or* **pull a stop** *play an instrument* 142.9

seta *stem* 41.5, *moss plant* 46.5

set a bad example *behave badly* 399.19, *deprave* 448.14

set about *work* 122.8, *undertake* 391.7, *make a beginning* 771.26

set a ceiling *quantify* 738.7

set (a clock) *make regular* 663.9

set a course *navigate* 690.15

set a date *or* *time for* *keep time* 646.12

set adrift *diverge* 753.20

set afloat *inaugurate* 675.10, *start* 696.20

set a floor *quantify* 738.7

set against *antagonize* 63.12, *put off* 179.10, *cause dislike* 291.16, *divide* 753.18, *confront* 828.19

set a good example *behave well* 399.18, *be virtuous* 447.8

set a high value on oneself *be vain* 402.14

set alight *burn* 217.18, *light* 246.19

set a lower limit *quantify* 738.7

set an example *epitomize* 327.18, *conduct oneself* 399.17

set an upper limit *quantify* 738.7

set apart 753.17; *modify* 340.13, *choose* 382.14, *exempt* 434.9, *spaced* 587.4, *space* 587.6, *unjoined* 753.9, *characterize* 779.15

set a precedent *pioneer* 771.29

set a price *price* 494.12

set a quota *limit* 620.7, *quantify* 738.7

set a record *compete in track and field* 166.21, *be superior* 744.15

set a register *play an instrument* 142.9

set a riddle *confuse* 333.20

set aside *saved* 105.15, *save* 105.20, *choose* 382.14, *discard* 383.12, *stop using* 394.10, *take away* 685.12, *set apart* 753.17, *canceled* 834.5, *cancel* 834.6

set aside the sentence *acquit* 54.32

set at each other's throats *antagonize* 63.12

set at ease *comfort* 273.9

set a timetable *plan out* 387.14

set at large *deliver* 817.5, *liberate* 831.6

set at liberty *acquit* 434.10, *liberate* 831.6

set at odds *antagonize* 63.12, *pick a fight* 463.10

set a trap for *conceal* 181.12, *plot* 387.14

set a trend *motivate* 508.9, *be trendy* 652.18, *forerun* 769.16

set at rest *establish reality* 719.12

setback *deterrence* 179.2, *bad outcome* 293.3, *loss* 468.1, *hesitation* 693.5, *deterioration* 808.1, *failure* 846.1, *adverse health* 848.5

set back *delay* 658.13, *delayed* 693.10, *slow down* 693.13

set before someone's eyes *display* 843.13

set criteria *specify* 340.14

set curfew *limit* 620.7

set decorator *filmmaker* 137.14

set designer *producer* 136.28, *filmmaker* 137.14

set difference *or* 6.19

set down *inscribe* 185.14, *condemn* 438.18, *lower* 716.12, *list* 785.11

set down in black and white *inscribe* 185.14

set dresser *filmmaker* 137.14

set eyes on *discover* 345.11

set eyes on [Inf] *see* 242.20

set fire to *burn* 217.18, *light* 246.19

set foot in *get in* 704.17, *enter* 706.11

set foot on dry land *land* 704.16

set form *etiquette* 406.3

set forth *propound a philosophy* 4.21

set forth *or* **forward** *set out* 705.12

set free 829.17; *save* 275.9, *absolve* 312.10, *acquit* 434.10, *vindicate* 441.11, *loosen* 753.14, *deliver* 817.5, *liberate* 831.6

set going *have at one's disposal* 393.14, *activate* 509.11, *inaugurate* 675.10, *impel* 695.9, *start* 696.20

setiform *barbed* 544.7

set in *storm* 9.55, *be permanent* 667.4, *be stable* 674.6, *inset* 710.13

set in action *have at one's disposal* 393.14

set in motion 677.16; *have at one's disposal* 393.14, *motivate* 508.9, *produce* 522.13, *inaugurate* 675.10, *impel* 695.9, *start* 696.20, *activate* 771.28

set in one's ways *opinionated* 379.9, *fixed* 397.13

set in opposition *counteract* 828.21

set in order *prepare for action* 388.18, *order* 765.18, *arrange* 767.18

set no store by *play down* 195.17, *underestimate* 344.5

set of beliefs *religion* 81.1

set of beliefs *or* **values** *philosophical system* 4.2

setoff *counterbalance* 743.2

set off *fuel* 106.16, *awaken* 675.9, *set out* 705.12, *equalize* 740.12, *counterbalanced* 743.6, *subtract* 749.6, *start off* 771.27

set off against *counteract* 828.21

set off an alarm *signal* 183.18

set off at a run *accelerate* 694.14

set of four *four* 791.1

set of furniture *furniture* 101.1

set of points *point* 6.34

set of principles *law* 53.1

set of teeth *teeth* 19.8

set of terms *basis for negotiations* 460.2

set of three *three* 790.1

set of two *two* 789.1

set on *strike* 418.21

set one a problem *be difficult* 824.16

set one back [Inf] *price* 494.12

set on edge *make rough* 544.11

set one's cap for *court* 299.26, *aim at* 385.15

set one's compass *aim* 697.14

set one's course for *aim at* 385.15, *aim* 697.14

set one's dignity aside *humble oneself* 298.18

set one's face *brace oneself* 376.13

set one's face *or* **oneself against** *be against* 828.17

set one's hand to *undertake* 391.7

set one's hand to the plow *undertake* 391.7

set one's heart on *covet* 288.18, *like* 290.8, *promise oneself* 458.15

set one's shoulder to the wheel *undertake* 391.7

set one's sights higher *intensify* 746.8

set one's sights on *aspire to*

288.19, aim 327.17, 374.10, 697.14

set one's teeth on edge *sour* 223.8, *be strident* 238.7

set on fire *burn* 217.18

set on foot *inaugurate* 675.10

set on its feet *make stable* 674.7

set on one's feet *finance* 825.31

set on one's feet again *cure* 809.15

setose *barbed* 544.7

set out 705.12; *style* 537.8, *space* 563.15, *arrange* 767.18, *start off* 771.27, *display* 843.13

set out *or* **off for** *aim* 697.14

Seto ware Ceramics 129

set parameters *limit* 620.7

set pattern dancing *ice dancing* 162.18

set phrase *phrasing* 5.25

set piece *play part* 136.8, *show* 404.12, *formal occasion* 406.4

set point *tennis terms* 165.5

set position *track event* 166.1

set purpose *intention* 374.1

set right *divulge* 180.9, *put right* 429.14, *vindicate* 441.11, *direct* 697.13, *compensate* 743.7, *rectify* 807.22

set rolling *roll* 682.15

set sail *navigate* 690.15, *sail* 690.16, *set out* 705.12, *start off* 771.27

set shot *playing terms* 148.4

set snares *hunt* 385.14

set someone on his *or* **her feet** *or* **legs** *strengthen* 516.15

set someone up properly *strengthen* 516.15

set speech *address* 209.1

set square *geometric construction* 6.47, *measuring instrument* 589.12, *plumb line* 602.4, *angular measurement* 628.4

set store by *respect* 435.13, *make important* 799.14

set straight *divulge* 180.9, *direct* 697.13, *compensate* 743.7

sett *or* **set** *mammal dwelling* 35.21

settee *couch* 101.7

setter Breeds of Dogs 35, *hunting dog* 160.7

set terms *phrasing* 5.25

set the alarm *prepare for action* 388.18, *keep time* 646.12

set the clock back *keep time* 646.12

set the clock forward *keep time* 646.12

set the example *forerun* 769.16

set the fashion *motivate* 508.9, *influence* 512.11, *forerun* 769.16

set the law in motion *litigate* 54.27

set theory Branches of Mathematics 6

set the pace *motivate* 508.9

set the price tag too high *overcharge* 496.10

set the record straight *divulge* 180.9

set the stage *lay the foundations* 388.16

set the trend *influence* 512.11

set the world on fire *attain one's goal* 845.13

setting *stage set* 136.19, *motion-picture studio* 137.7, *musical composition* 140.9, *harmonics* 140.13, *gist* 329.4, *condensed* 540.7, *hardening* 542.2, *location* 565.1, *situation* 573.1, *circumstances* 573.2, 726.1,

surroundings 615.1, *adjustment* 721.5

setting apart 753.2, *selecting* 382.4

setting aside *selecting* 382.4, *allocation* 474.1, *setting apart* 753.2, *cancellation* 834.1

setting free *escape* 816.1, *liberation* 831.1

setting in motion *inauguration* 771.6

setting lotion *pomade* 562.9

setting of the sun *evening* 656.2

setting to rights *righting wrong* 429.6

setting up *manufacture* 522.2, *inauguration* 771.6

settle 61.14, 565.10, 735.26; *drain* 8.64, *type of chair* 101.4, *suffice* 273.10, *prove* 331.17, *judge* 341.10, *resolve* 376.12, *become a habit* 397.17, *pay* 415.15, *exact retribution* 454.27, *contract* 459.8, 462.11, *negotiate* 460.6, *compromise* 461.7, *transfer property* 470.12, *pay off* 489.17, *be moderate* 521.6, *be heavy* 538.12, *exert sovereignty* 566.12, *urbanize* 567.15, *be concave* 635.6, *enroll* 706.16, *descend* 714.12, *compensate* 743.7, *arrange* 767.18, *come to an arrangement* 767.22, *end* 773.19, *rule* 780.12, *finance* 825.31, *make certain* 840.14

settle accounts 493.11; *compensate* 743.7

settle an account *pay off* 489.17

settle a score *retaliate* 489.23

settle a strike *have an industrial dispute* 57.20

settle beforehand *predetermine* 384.8

settled 735.16; *fine* 9.43, *inhabited* 61.10, *proven* 331.13, *compromising* 461.4, *paid* 489.11, *accounted* 493.8, *located* 565.6, *stabilized* 674.4, *compensated* 743.3, *ended* 773.14, *decided* 840.9

settled beforehand *predetermined* 384.4

settle differences *conciliate* 74.10, *mediate* 75.6

settle differences *or* **a dispute** *pacify* 74.11

settledness *seriousness* 376.3

settle down *pause* 415.15, *be moderate* 521.6, *be stable* 674.6

settled purpose *intention* 374.1

settle for *bargain* 480.20

settle in *be stable* 674.6, *enroll* 706.16

settlement 735.6; *proof* 331.4, *contract* 459.1, 462.2, *compromise* 461.1, *transfer of property* 470.4, *giving* 472.1, *payment* 489.1, *dominion* 566.3, *compensation* 743.1, *agreement* 767.9, *financial assistance* 825.6

settlement of differences *or* **a dispute** *pacification* 74.1

settlement on account *payment* 489.1

settle on *resolve* 376.12, *select* 382.12, *drop* 714.15

settle one's differences *make peace* 73.11

settler 61.4; *inhabitant* 61.1, *entrant* 706.7, *outgoer* 707.9, *new arrival* 724.6, *enroll* 773.11

settle the matter *judge* 341.10, *establish reality* 719.12

settle the score *compensate* 743.7

settle up *pay* 453.15

settle with *exact retribution* 454.27

settling *transfer of property* 470.4, *placing* 565.4

settling on *selecting* 382.4

settlor [Form] *giver* 472.7

set to *eat well* 92.23, *be greedy* 119.4, *work* 122.8, *undertake* 391.7, *fight* 422.23, *make a beginning* 771.26

set-to *quarrel* 272.4, *argument* 329.1, *dispute* 463.3, *disruption* 766.7

set to rights *put right* 429.14, *tidy* 765.21, *repair* 809.10

set toward *aim* 697.14

set to work *make a beginning* 771.26

set two *squash terms* 165.10

setup *form* 551.3, *circumstances* 573.2, 726.1, *forming* 624.4, *order* 765.1

set up *be on the track* 146.11, *produce* 522.13, *construct* 551.22, *locate* 565.9, *situate* 573.10, *make permanent* 644.9, *make stable* 674.7, *inaugurate* 675.10, 771.31, *raise* 715.9, *order* 765.18, *cure* 809.15, *finance* 825.31

setup [Inf] *predetermination* 384.1, *easy thing* 823.6

set up [Inf] *predetermine* 384.8

set-up *formed* 624.6

set up house *settle* 61.14

set up house together *marry* 64.19

seven 792.3; *numeral* 6.8, *seventh* 792.14

Seven, Group of Western Art Styles 133

seven ages of man *age* 27.1

seven-card stud *poker* 168.5

seven centuries *hundreds* 792.9

seven days *seven* 792.3

seven deadly sins *iniquity* 448.3, *seven* 792.3

sevenfold *seventh* 792.14, *fivefold* 792.26

seven-footer *tall person* 596.6

seven-league boots *talisman* 86.9

seven lean years *scarcity* 98.3

sevens Card Games 168

seven sacraments *Christian rite* 85.5

seven seas *sea* 571.1, *seven* 792.3

seven-sided *polygonal* 6.79

Seven Sisters *constellation* 7.13

seventeenth *less than one* 787.4

seventh 792.14; *ranked* 6.72, *chord* 140.18, *less than one* 787.4, *seven* 792.3, *fivefold* 792.26

seventh heaven *top of the world* 600.2

seventh inning stretch *other game terms* 147.7

seventhly *fivefold* 792.26

seventh part *seven* 792.3

seventieth *twentieth* 792.19

seventy *twenty and over* 792.8

seven-up Card Games 168

Seven Wonders of the World *seven* 792.3

seven years of plenty *plenty* 97.2

Seven Years War Major Wars 76

sever *divorce* 66.9, *not connect* 728.13, *take off* 749.7, *separate* 753.12, *part* 760.14, *disconnect* 775.12

severable *separable* 753.11

several *plurality* 793.1, *plural* 793.6, *indeterminate* 841.14

several irons in the fire *business* 414.6

severally *separately* 753.22, *plurally* 793.10

severalty *separateness* 753.3

severance *subtraction* 749.1, *separation* 753.1, *setting apart* 753.2

severance of relations *faction* 347.4

severance pay *reward for service* 453.5, *pay* 489.6

severe 424.5; *cold* 218.9, *serious* 278.4, *cruel* 306.10, *pitiless* 309.3, *discourteous* 411.5, *moralistic* 431.12, *strong* 516.9, *violent* 520.5, *simple* 526.7, *difficult* 824.9, *restraining* 830.8

severed *reduced* 749.5, *separate* 753.7

severe frost *frost* 9.25

severely 424.11; *solemnly* 278.9, *cruelly* 306.17, *pitilessly* 309.7, *discourteously* 411.8, *moralistically* 431.16, *restrainedly* 830.18

severe weather *cold weather* 218.8

severity 424.1; *seriousness* 278.1, *importance* 278.3, *cruelty* 306.4, *pitilessness* 309.1, *treatment* 399.11, *discourtesy* 411.1, *potency* 516.6, *violence* 520.1, *simplicity* 526.1, *conventionalism* 781.4, *difficulty* 824.1, *restraint* 830.1

Severn Rivers 570

sever relations *disagree* 463.8

sever ties *separate* 753.12

Sèvres *or* **Sèvres porcelain** Ceramics 129

sew 130.18; *make clothing* 100.44, *perform* 522.16, *intertwine* 752.19, *connect* 754.13

sewage *fertilizer* 16.9, *excrement* 25.2, *waste product* 96.7, *swill* 112.6, *unpleasant-smelling thing* 227.2, *residue* 750.2

sewage treatment plant *place for waste* 802.6

sewer *clothier* 100.37, *cleaning tool* 111.10, *fabric handler* 130.11, *unpleasant-smelling thing* 227.2, *wicked place* 448.8, *tunnel* 551.11, *channel* 691.10

sewerage *excrement* 25.2, *waste product* 96.7, *cleaning* 111.2, *swill* 112.6

sewerage system *water system* 551.13

sewer gas *unpleasant-smelling thing* 227.2

sewing 130.5; *unification* 752.5

sewing machine *fabric-handling tool* 130.12, *weaving* 609.2

sewing room *room* 60.9, *home workplace* 124.3

sewn 130.14; *united* 752.10, *tied* 752.13, *connected* 754.11

sewn up [Inf] *secured* 464.7

sew up [Inf] *secure one's objective* 464.12

sex 20.1; *sexual intercourse* 20.9, *sexual* 20.15, *propagation* 21.4

sex(ual) drive *libido* 108.26

sex act 20.10; *sexual intercourse* 20.9

sexagenarian *older person* 27.7, *twenty and over* 792.8

sexagenary *twenty and over* 792.8

sex appeal *sexuality* 20.3, *enticement* 178.3, *lovability* 299.5, *allurement* 700.4

sexcentenary *hundreds* 792.9

sex chromosome *chromosome* 13.21

sex comedy *comedy* 136.11

sex crime *sexual offense* 20.11

sex criminal *sexual perversion* 20.12

sexdecillion *million* 792.11

sex education *subject* 48.3
sexed-up [Inf] *desirous* 20.18
sexennial *sixth* 792.13
sexennially *fivefold* 792.26
sex fiend *sexual perversion* 20.12, *sexually immoral person* 432.8
sex god [Inf and Off] *sex object* 20.8
sex goddess [Inf and Off] *sex object* 20.8
sex hormone *hormone* 12.16
sexily 20.23; *enticingly* 178.22, *desirably* 288.24, *lovably* 299.31, *attractively* 700.14
sexiness *sexuality* 20.3, *lovability* 299.5, *attractiveness* 529.2
sex instinct *libido* 108.26
sexism *social discrimination* 337.4, *unfair treatment* 342.4
sexist *misanthropic* 291.8, *bigot* 337.7, *discriminatory* 337.11, *unjust* 342.7, *excluding* 764.5
sexivalent *chemical compound* 11.4
sex king [Inf and Off] *sex object* 20.8
sex kitten [Inf and Off] *sex object* 20.8
sexless *undersexed* 20.20, *chaste* 431.10
sexlessness 20.13
sex life *sexuality* 20.3
sexlike *sexual* 20.15
sex object 20.8
sex offender or **criminal** *sexually immoral person* 432.8
sexologist *sexology* 20.14
sexology 20.14
sexophobia *Phobias* 283
sexpartite *sixth* 792.13
sexploitation [Inf] *pornography* 432.7
sexpot [Inf] *motivator* 508.6
sex role *social environment* 2.4
sex scene *play part* 136.8
sex shop *sex act* 20.10
sex-starved *desirous* 20.18
sex study *sexology* 20.14
sex symbol *charmer* 700.6
sext *public worship* 83.3, *noon* 655.4
Sextans *Constellations* 7
Sextant *Constellations* 7
sextant *measuring instrument* 589.12, *angular measurement* 628.4, *parts of a circle* 631.4, *navigational aid* 690.6
sex test *competition* 166.18
sextet *instrumental group* 141.3, *six* 792.2, *team* 827.7
sextile *angular measurement* 628.4, *six* 792.2
sextillion *million* 792.11
sexton *funeral person* 31.5
sextuple *sixth* 792.13, *quintuple* 792.23
sextuplet *six* 792.2
sextuplicate *six* 792.2, *sixth* 792.13, *quintuple* 792.23
sexual 20.15; *reproductive* 21.11, *conjunctive* 752.12
sexual abstention *celibacy* 67.1
sexual abstinence *abstinence* 455.2, *celibacy* 67.1
sexual abuse *sexual offense* 20.11, 432.6, *Phobias* 283, *malignity* 306.5
sexual abuser *criminal* 427.6
sexual activity *sexuality* 20.3
sexual and gender disorders *mental disorder* 108.8
sexual appetite *sexual desire* 288.5
sexual assault *malignity* 306.5, *personal attack* 418.8, *sexual offense* 432.6, *sexual possession* 477.2

sexual attraction or **magnetism** *sexuality* 20.3
sexual commerce *sexual intercourse* 20.9
sexual congress *sexual intercourse* 20.9
sexual counselor *sexology* 20.14
sexual customs or **mores** or **practices** *sexology* 20.14
sexual delinquency *fornication* 432.3
sexual desire 20.5, 288.5
sexual deviance *sexual perversion* 20.12, *sexual immorality* 432.2
sexual deviancy *sexual offense* 432.6
sexual deviation *sexual perversion* 20.12
sexual discrimination *social discrimination* 337.4, *exclusiveness* 764.4
sexual disease *sexually transmitted disease (STD)* 114.17
sexual disorder 108.14
sexual drive *sexuality* 20.3, *sexual desire* 288.5, *sexual love* 299.3
sexual dysfunction *sexual disorder* 108.14
sexual freedom or **liberation** *sexology* 20.14
sexual harassment *sexual offense* 20.11, *malignity* 306.5
sexual immorality 432.2
sexual intercourse 20.9; *propagation* 21.4, *physical pleasure* 214.1, *Phobias* 283
sexual inversion *sexual nature* 20.4
sexuality 20.3; *sex* 20.1
sexual license *sexual immorality* 432.2
sexual longing 20.6
sexual love 299.3, *Phobias* 283
sexually *sexily* 20.23, *reproductively* 21.17, *as one* 752.21
sexually abstinent *abstinent* 455.7
sexually abuse *seduce* 432.16
sexually abusive *malign* 306.11
sexually assault *harm* 306.13, *seduce* 432.16
sexually attractive *attractive* 700.10
sexually desirable *desirable* 288.11
sexually harass *harm* 306.13
sexually immoral person 432.8
sexually transmitted disease (STD) 114.17; *disease* 114.4
sexual masochism *sexual disorder* 108.14
sexual nature 20.4; *sexuality* 20.3
sexual offense 20.11, 432.6
sexual organs 20.2; *internal organ* 19.13
sexual orientation *sexual nature* 20.4
sexual pathology *sexual perversion* 20.12
sexual perversion 20.12, *Phobias* 283, *sexual offense* 432.6
sexual pervert *sexual perversion* 20.12
sexual pleasure *physical pleasure* 214.1
sexual possession 477.2
sexual preference or **persuasion** or **leaning** *sexual nature* 20.4
sexual psychopath *sexual perversion* 20.12
sexual psychopathy *sexual perversion* 20.12
sexual relations *sexual intercourse* 20.9

sexual reproduction *reproductive body* 47.14
sexual revolution *sexology* 20.14
sexual sadism *sexual disorder* 108.14
sexual submission *submission* 421.1
sexual surrogate *sexology* 20.14
sexual union 752.6; *sexual intercourse* 20.9
sexual urge *sexual desire* 288.5, *sexual love* 299.3
sexual urge or **instinct** *sexuality* 20.3
sexy *sensual* 20.16, *enticing* 178.13, *pleasurable* 214.6, *desirable* 288.11, *lovable* 299.20, *attractive* 529.8, 700.10
sexy body *attractiveness* 529.2
Seychelles *Countries* 566, *Islands* 572
Seyfert galaxy *galaxy* 7.5
sfoggiando *Musical Terms and Expression Marks* 140
S-form *structure* 11.7
sforzando or *sforzato* or *sf* or *sfz* *Musical Terms and Expression Marks* 140
sfumato *treatment* 143.6
sh! *hush!* 231.6
shabbily *deviously* 371.9, *meanly* 486.18, *inelegantly* 528.11
shabbiness *uncleanness* 112.2, *beggary* 486.3, *unpleasantness* 501.2, *bad taste* 528.3, *deficiency* 745.2, *untidiness* 766.3, *dilapidation* 808.5
shabby *unclean* 112.8, *used* 393.5, *beggarly* 486.12, *shoddy* 497.11, *unpleasant* 501.5, *plain* 528.9, *untidy* 766.11, *worn* 808.13
shack 60.10
shacking up [Inf] *sexual intercourse* 20.9
shackle *intertwine* 752.19, *means of connection* 754.4, *bind* 754.14, *restrain* 826.19, *restrain someone* 830.17
shackled *bound* 754.12, *blocked* 826.13
shackles *restraint* 826.8, *means of restraint* 830.6
shack up with [Inf] *have sex* 20.21
shadblow *Trees and Shrubs* 43
shadbush *Trees and Shrubs* 43
shadchan [Yiddish] *matchmaker* 64.13
shade *grow* 43.15, *ghost* 86.11, *refreshment* 94.1, *air* 94.7, *dye* 130.8, *paint* 143.12, *that which makes invisible* 245.2, *darkness* 247.1, *make dark* 247.10, *dimness* 248.1, *make dim* 248.8, *hue* 251.4, *color* 251.16, *interior decoration* 532.4, *protective covering* 613.5, *protect* 613.26, 810.21, *illusion* 720.2, *interval* 739.4, *measure* 739.7, *suggestion* 800.9
shaded *wooded* 43.12, *painted* 143.10, *dark* 247.5, *colored* 251.10
shade in *make dark* 247.10
shade maker 247.4
shade off *change by degrees* 739.8
shades [Inf] *accessory* 100.28, *visual aid* 242.14, *shade maker* 247.4, *protective covering* 613.5
shade tree *tree* 43.1
shadily *darkly* 247.11
shadiness *lawbreaking* 53.14, *dimness* 248.1, *deviousness* 607.4
shading *treatment* 143.6, *darkening* 247.2, 247.6, *dimming* 248.3,

interior decoration 532.4, *gradation* 739.3
shading off *gradational* 739.5
shadoof *irrigator* 557.13, *extractor* 711.9
shadow *friend* 62.2, *treatment* 143.6, *ice-skating* 162.32, *darkness* 247.1, *dark thing* 247.3, *make dark* 247.10, *dimness* 248.1, *make dim* 248.8, *black thing* 254.3, *fantasy* 360.5, *pursuer* 385.5, *follow* 385.12, 770.10, *adherent* 401.5, *stay near* 586.13, *thin person* 595.4, *shape* 617.2, *illusion* 720.2, *artificiality* 720.7, *counterpart* 733.5, *interval* 739.4, *equal* 740.7, *follower* 794.10, *attend* 794.19
shadow box *box* 152.19
shadowboxing *boxing* 152.2, *conception* 360.4
shadowed *matched* 733.10
shadow figure *image* 187.3
shadowgraph *photograph* 132.3
shadowiness *immateriality* 525.2, *mysteriousness* 844.5
shadowing *darkening* 247.6, *dimming* 248.3, *pursuit* 385.1, *accompanied* 794.15
shadow of death *personifications and symbols* 29.4, *danger* 811.1
shadow of one's former self *physical deterioration* 808.4
shadow play or **shadow show** or **shadow theater** *show* 138.4
shadows *composition* 132.17, *darkness* 247.1, *Phobias* 283
shadow-skate *ice-skate* 162.36
shadow skating *ice skating* 162.15
shadowy *spiritual* 86.20, *difficult to see* 245.4, *dim* 248.4, *murky* 248.5, *imaginary* 360.12, *difficult* 364.8, *nonmaterial* 525.8, *unreal* 720.8
shaduf *irrigator* 557.13
shady 250.4; *wooded* 43.12, *offending* 53.25, *dark* 247.5, *dim* 248.4, *questionable* 333.13, *disreputable* 371.4, *devious* 607.9
shady business *dishonesty* 479.7
shady past *disrepute* 371.1
shaft *machine element* 14.8, *golf equipment* 156.5, *hole* 583.4, *supporting part* 605.3, *axle* 682.7, *missile* 696.7
shaft [Inf] *wrong* 430.19
shaft horse *workhorse* 176.3
shafting *Architectural Elements* 134
shaft tomb *burial place* 31.7
shag *water bird* 36.9, *tobacco* 121.23, *coiffure* 530.8, *rough thing* 544.2, *nap* 552.3
shag ass [Inf] *be swift* 694.10
shagbark *Trees and Shrubs* 43
shag carpet *floor covering* 613.13
shagged *barbed* 544.7
shagginess *roughness* 544.1
shaggy *hairy* 19.20, *barbed* 544.7
shaggy-dog story *joke* 277.6
Shagya Arab *Horse and Pony Breeds* 159
shah *sovereign* 68.2
Shahabadi *Breeds of Cattle* 16
Shaharith [Heb] *public worship* 83.3
Shaitan *devil* 446.5
shake 684.7, 684.24; *quake* 8.65, *wood* 131.3, *musical ornament* 140.19, *daunt* 179.9, *be fearful* 283.15, *be weak* 307.17, *weaken* 517.13, *use violence* 520.9, *be irregular* 664.5, *be changeable* 666.5, *vibrate* 683.13, *agitate* 684.22, *mix* 751.12, *disturb*

1277

768.10, *eat away* 808.19, *be liberated* 831.7, *change* 841.20
shakedown *taking away* 477.5
shake down [Inf] *take money away* 477.20
shakedown artist *greedy person* 477.11
shake free *be liberated* 831.7
shake hands *pacify* 74.11, *forgive and forget* 312.9, *greet* 410.11, *bargain* 480.20
shake hands with *befriend* 62.10, *welcome* 408.18, *receive someone* 473.14
shake in one's shoes *or* **boots** *shake* 684.24
shake like a leaf *be fearful* 283.15, *shake* 684.24
shaken *dissuaded* 179.5, *agitated* 684.15, *mixed* 751.8, *disturbed* 768.6, *spoiled* 808.9
shaken up *dissuaded* 179.5, *agitated* 684.15, *rearranged* 767.14
shake off *disaccustom* 398.6, *lose someone* 468.20, *accelerate* 694.14, *send away* 709.18, *exterminate* 709.22, *unstick* 756.6, *elude* 816.10, *be liberated* 831.7
shake of the head *gesture* 183.5
shake one's head *gesture* 183.17, *refuse* 190.17, 347.9, 506.8
shake on it *pacify* 74.11, *promise* 458.11, *contract* 462.11, *bargain* 480.20
shake out *canoe* 150.31
Shaker Furniture Styles 101
shaker *agitator* 684.14, *mixer* 751.7
shakes *symptom* 114.3, *chills* 218.3
shakes [Inf] *symptom* 114.3, *chills* 218.3, *shake* 684.7,
Shakespearean Poem or Verse Forms 139, *poetic* 139.19
Shakespearean comedy *historic comedy* 136.12
Shakespearean tragedy *tragedy* 136.10
shake the dust from one's feet *retreat* 386.22
shake to pieces *demolish* 523.12
shake up *daunt* 179.9, *soften* 543.14, *mix* 732.12, *rearrange* 767.20
shake-up *rearrangement* 767.4, *rectification* 807.8
shakily 684.28; *irregularly* 664.6, *changeably* 666.7, *unreliably* 841.25
shakiness *unaccustomedness* 398.1, *poor health* 517.3, *irregularity* 664.1, *changeableness* 666.1, *danger* 811.1, *unreliability* 841.7
shaking 684.6; *symptoms of fear* 283.3, *fearful* 283.10, *irregular* 664.3, *vibration* 683.2, *vibrating* 683.9, *waving* 683.11, *shaky* 684.18, *mixture* 751.1
shaking like a leaf *fearful* 283.10
shaking out *canoeing techniques* 150.11
shaking palsy *shake* 684.7
shako *cap* 100.33
shakuhachi Musical Instruments 142
shaky 684.18; *fearful* 283.10, *unaccustomed* 398.3, *ill* 517.8, *irregular* 664.3, *changeable* 666.3, *imperfect* 806.5, *decrepit* 808.12, *unsafe* 811.8, *unreliable* 841.15
shale *brittle thing* 548.2
shale oil *petroleum* 562.5
shall *intend* 650.10
shalloon Fabrics and Fibers 130

shallop Sailing Ships and Boats 690
shallow 599.3, 599.5; *infertile* 23.7, *indifferent* 326.5, *semiskilled* 349.6, *insufficient* 517.11, *narrow-minded* 593.13, *low* 597.10, *shallowness* 599.1
shallow-bottomed *shallow* 599.3
shallowly 599.7; *narrow-mindedly* 593.20
shallowness 599.1; *indifference* 326.2, *narrow-mindedness* 593.7, *lowness* 597.1, *triviality* 800.2
shallows *shallowness* 599.1, *hidden danger* 813.3
shallow structure *grammar* 5.28
shallow water *hidden danger* 813.3
shaly *chalky* 8.59
sham *hoax* 193.7, 193.20, *hoaxer* 193.11, *hypocritical* 330.10, *artificiality* 720.7, *artificial* 720.12, *unauthentic* 722.9, *simulated* 733.11, *copy* 736.2, *imitation* 736.8, *stratagem* 822.2, *cunning person* 822.3
shaman *witch* 86.15, *wise person* 352.3, *warner* 814.5
shamanic *witchlike* 86.19
shamanism *occultism* 86.1
shamanist *witch* 86.15
shamanize *bewitch* 86.25
shamble *slow motion* 693.3, *move slowly* 693.11
shambles *slaughterhouse* 30.16, *bungling* 128.2, *havoc* 523.5, *confusion* 766.4
shambling *clumsy* 128.6, *slow* 693.7
shame *humiliation* 298.5, *humiliate* 298.19, *disrepute* 371.1, *bring into disrepute* 371.6, *impropriety* 430.5, *demoralize* 432.15, *dishonor* 436.20, *deprave* 448.14, *sign of guilt* 450.2, *penitence* 451.1, *punishment* 454.1, *punish* 454.22, *irresolution* 461.3, *humbling* 597.9
shamed *humiliated* 298.12, *lowered* 597.18
shamedly *improperly* 430.26
shamefaced *humiliated* 298.12, *shy* 403.8, *immoral* 430.11, *appearing guilty* 450.7, *penitent* 451.5
shamefacedly *embarrassedly* 298.24, *shyly* 403.16, *guiltily* 450.12, *penitently* 451.10
shamefacedness *humiliation* 298.5, *shyness* 403.3
shamefast [Arch] *shy* 403.8, *penitent* 451.5
shamefastly [Arch] *shyly* 403.16
shamefastness [Arch] *humiliation* 298.5, *shyness* 403.3
shameful *immoral* 430.11, *disregardful* 436.11, *wicked* 448.9, *appearing guilty* 450.7, *lowered* 597.18
shamefully *disgracefully* 371.8, 597.28, *improperly* 430.26, *wickedly* 448.15, *guiltily* 450.12
shamefulness *wickedness* 448.1, *penitence* 451.1
shameless *disreputable* 371.4, *insolent* 400.8, *showy* 404.14, *blatant* 404.19, *defiant* 416.5, *immoral* 430.11, *unchaste* 432.10, *depraved* 448.10, *impenitent* 452.2, *open* 843.12
shameless liar *liar* 192.10
shameless lie *falsehood* 192.6
shamelessly *insolently* 400.18, *showily* 404.29, *blatantly* 404.34, *defiantly* 416.9, *promiscuously*

432.19, *unvirtuously* 448.16, *impenitently* 452.5
shameless lying *lying* 192.5
shamelessness *insolence* 400.1, *blatancy* 404.6, *defiance* 416.1, *sexual immorality* 432.2, *depravity* 448.2, *impenitence* 452.1, *openness* 843.6
shame oneself *be wicked* 448.13
shame the devil *be virtuous* 447.8
shammer *hoaxer* 193.11, *cunning person* 822.3
shampoo *ablutions* 111.4, *cleaning agent* 111.9, *bathe* 111.18, *hairdressing* 530.7
shampooed *beautified* 530.12
shampooer *beautician* 530.11
shamrock *talisman* 86.9, *triple thing* 790.3
shanghai *take away forcefully* 477.19, *kidnap* 479.15
shanghaier *thief* 479.8
shanghaiing *kidnapping* 479.3
Shangri-la Imaginary Places 360, *objective* 374.5
shank *beef* 90.24, *veal* 90.25, *fishing tackle* 154.7, *type* 173.5
shanks' mare *means of transportation* 686.2
Shannon Rivers 570
Shan pony Horse and Pony Breeds 159
shantung Fabrics and Fibers 130
shanty *shack* 60.10
shantytown *urban area* 567.10
shapable *pliant* 543.7
shape 551.21, 617.2; *educate* 48.22, *health* 113.1, *make ceramics* 129.10, *carpenter* 131.10, *sculpt* 144.10, *identification* 184.1, *illustrate* 187.11, *describe* 202.15, *external appearance* 264.5, *plan out* 387.14, *perform* 522.16, *fashion* 536.7, 537.9, *design* 536.8, *soften* 543.14, *form* 551.3, 624.1, 624.9, *nature* 624.5, *transform* 851.9, *state* 725.1, *physical state* 725.6, *type* 777.4, *characteristic* 779.5, *make conform* 781.13
shaped *formed* 624.6
shapeless 625.2; *obscure* 197.2, *unemphatic* 201.2, *unfinished* 544.9, *irregular* 766.10
shapelessly 625.5; *incompletely* 544.14
shapelessness 625.1; *obscurity* 197.1, *rough idea* 544.4, *irregular order* 766.2
shapeliness *attractiveness* 529.2, *evenness* 626.3, *round body* 633.2
shapely *attractive* 529.8, *even* 626.5, *well-rounded* 633.8
shape of things *state of affairs* 725.4
shape of things to come *model* 358.4
shape one's career *conduct oneself* 399.17
shaper *machine tool* 14.9, *woodworking tool* 131.6
shape up *tidy* 807.19
shaping *production* 522.1, *structuring* 551.5, *form* 624.1, *forming* 624.4
shard *pulverize* 553.26, *remainder* 750.1, *particle* 760.4, *fragment* 787.3
sharded *pulverized* 553.20
sharding *pulverization* 553.4
share *deposit* 105.21, *participate* 408.15, *claim* 429.3, *promise* 464.2, *joint possession* 469.6, *give out* 472.12, *portion* 474.2, *allocate* 474.5, *sharp-edged thing* 549.6,

measure out 589.21, *interface* 616.5, *interrelate* 729.8, *certain amount* 738.3, *quantify* 738.7, *be equal* 740.11, *make average* 742.9, *part* 760.1, 760.14, *piece* 760.2, *be included* 763.6, *fractional part* 787.2, *divide* 787.7, *go halves* 789.16, *work together* 827.14
share and share alike *be equal* 740.11
sharecrop *farm* 16.19
sharecropper *agriculturist* 16.14
sharecropping *agriculture* 16.1
shared *decentralized* 79.5, *interfacial* 616.4, *partial* 760.11, *joint* 827.10
shared delusions *delusion* 110.2
shared frontier *interface* 616.1
shared grief *or* **sorrow** *or* **suffering** *condolence* 308.2
shared out *allocated* 474.4
shared ownership *joint possession* 469.6
shared responsibility *delegation* 79.3
share expenses *pay one's way* 489.19
share farming *agriculture* 16.1
share grief *grieve* 308.7
shareholder *possessor* 469.10, *person transferring property* 470.8
share one's bed and board *marry* 64.19
share out *give out* 472.12, *allocate* 474.5, *measure out* 589.21, *divide* 753.18
share pusher *merchant* 482.10
shares *personal estate* 470.6
share sorrow *grieve* 308.7
share the work *delegate* 79.6
share with *give out* 472.12
sharing *sociability* 408.1, *compromise* 461.1, *allocation* 474.1, *interrelation* 729.2, *interrelated* 729.5, *equality* 740.1, *mutual relationship* 827.3
sharing out *allocation* 474.1
shark *game fish* 154.10, *gambler* 167.6, *greedy person* 477.11, *dishonest person* 479.11, *overcharger* 496.5
sharkish *fishlike* 38.10
sharklike *fishlike* 38.10
sharkskin Fabrics and Fibers 130
sharp 549.10; *windy* 9.42, *refined* 48.20, *musical note* 140.15, *gambler* 167.6, *emphatic* 200.3, *cold* 218.9, *tasty* 219.4, *piquant* 221.6, *acid* 223.5, *unmelodious* 241.5, *clear* 244.6, *ill-natured* 303.9, *bitter* 306.9, *intelligent* 315.9, 352.5, *discourteous* 411.5, *strong to the senses* 516.12, *violent* 520.5, *coarse* 544.6, *advantaged* 618.7, *cunning* 822.4
sharp as a needle *sharp* 549.10
sharp as a razor *sharp-edged* 549.12
sharp as a tack *mentally sharp* 549.14
sharp corner *angle* 628.1
sharp-cornered *angular* 628.7
sharp-cut *sharp-edged* 549.12
sharp ear *hearing* 228.1
sharp-eared *hearing* 228.9
sharp edge 549.3; *roughness* 544.1, *cutting edge* 618.3
sharp-edged 549.12
sharp-edged thing 549.6
Shar-Pei Breeds of Dogs 35
sharpen 549.16; *make cold* 218.15, *sour* 223.8, *invigorate* 518.5
sharpened *sharp* 549.10
sharpener 549.8

sharper *dishonest person* 479.11, *cunning person* 822.3
sharper *or* **sharpie** *schemer* 193.10
sharp eye 242.4
sharp-eyed *seeing* 242.17, *watchful* 323.6, *mentally sharp* 549.14
sharp flavor *sourness* 223.1
sharp frost *frost* 9.25
sharp guy *busy person* 414.10
sharpie *busy person* 414.10, *cunning person* 822.3
sharply 549.19; *piquantly* 221.10, *sourly* 223.9, *ill-naturedly* 303.18, *bitterly* 306.16, *discourteously* 411.8, *acutely* 516.18, *roughly* 544.13, *suddenly* 549.20
sharpness 549.1; *manual skill* 127.2, *composition* 132.17, *emphasis* 200.1, *piquancy* 221.1, *sourness* 223.1, *musical dissonance* 241.2, *clarity* 244.2, *ill nature* 303.2, *bitterness* 306.3, *cleverness* 315.3, *discourtesy* 411.1, *subtlety* 534.2, *cutting edge* 618.3, *cunning* 822.1
sharp-nosed *odorous* 224.5
sharp point 549.2
sharp-pointed *sharp* 549.10
sharp-pointed growth 549.5
sharp-pointed thing 549.4
sharp practice *deception* 193.1, *disreputable action* 371.3, *cunning* 822.1
sharp-set *sharp-edged* 549.12
sharpshooter *shooter* 160.10, *attacker* 418.10
sharpshooting Sporting Activities 145, *firing* 418.6
sharp taste *taste* 219.1
sharp tongue *short temper* 303.5, *bitterness* 306.3
sharp-tongued *ill-natured* 303.9, *bitter* 306.9, *discourteous* 411.5, *mentally sharp* 549.14
sharp weapon 78.6
sharp-witted *intelligent* 352.5, *mentally sharp* 549.14
sharp-wittedness *mental sharpness* 549.9
shashlik *notable international dishes* 90.40
Shasta, Mount Mountains and Hills 569
shastra *other text* 81.19
shatter *demolish* 523.12, *be brittle* 548.4, *be transient* 643.6, *take apart* 753.16, *disintegrate* 758.6
shatterable *brittle* 548.3
shattered *destroyed* 523.9, *coarse* 544.6, *brittle* 548.3, *apart* 753.8, *disintegrated* 758.3
shattered silence *loudness* 232.1
shattered surface *roughness* 544.1
shattering *destroying* 523.2, *brittle* 548.3, *separation* 753.1, *divergence* 776.5, *newsworthy* 799.12
shatter one's hopes *disappoint* 282.12
shatterproof *tough* 542.6, 547.6, *make tough* 547.15, *invulnerable* 810.18
shatterproof glass *safety device* 810.15
shatter the dreams of *make transient* 643.7
shatter the eardrums *shatter the peace* 232.10
shatter the peace 232.10; *combat* 77.34
shave *clean* 111.17, *touch* 216.9, *hairdressing* 530.7, *smooth* 545.10, *contract* 582.12, *meet* 586.15, *scale* 588.10, *depilation* 614.8, *depilate* 614.20, *make smaller* 747.8

shaved *depilatory* 614.15
shaven *cleaned* 111.14, *depilatory* 614.15
shaver *depilation* 614.8
shaver [Inf] *young man* 26.8
shaving *hairdressing* 530.7, *little piece* 580.4, *shortening* 582.2, *slice* 588.4, *fineness* 595.5, *depilation* 614.8, *residue* 750.2
shaving mirror *reflector* 242.10
shavings *dirt* 112.5, *bits and pieces* 760.5, *refuse* 802.5
Shavuoth Jewish Holy Days and Seasons 85
shawl *coat* 100.19, *neckwear* 100.29
shawl collar *neckwear* 100.29
shawm Musical Instruments 142
she *female* 33.1
shea Trees and Shrubs 43
shear *transformation* 6.46, *load* 14.49, *use a sharp tool* 549.17, *contract* 582.12, *depilation* 614.8, *depilate* 614.20, *separate* 753.12
shearing *shortening* 582.2, *depilation* 614.8
shears *garden tool* 17.7, 103.4, *sharp-edged thing* 549.6
shear strain *load* 14.14
shear stress *load* 14.14
shearwater *water bird* 36.9
sheath *contraceptive* 23.6, *grass plant* 45.3, *ammunition* 78.11, *dress* 100.11, *packet* 578.4, *contain* 578.20, *casing* 613.9, *enclosing thing* 619.3
sheathe *clothe* 100.43, *coat* 588.3, *wrap* 613.29, 619.7, *roof* 613.30, *inset* 710.13
sheathed *containing* 578.18, *coated* 588.7, *protected* 613.20, *wrapped* 619.5
sheathe the sword *make peace* 73.11
sheathing *wood* 131.3, *covering* 613.1, *overhead covering* 613.11
sheathing board *wood* 131.3
sheave *hand tool* 103.3
shed 614.14, 614.21; *shack* 60.10, *storehouse* 105.8, *renounce* 392.4, *disaccustom* 398.6, *railroad station* 688.6, *exterminate* 709.22, *throw down* 716.13, *decrease* 747.7, *additional item* 748.3
shed blessings on *be auspicious* 847.8
shed blood *be at war* 76.32, *declare war* 422.25, *suppress* 424.9
shed crocodile tears *be untruthful* 192.20
shed daylight on *reveal* 843.14
shedder 614.7
shedding *peeling* 614.6, 614.13, *disgorgement* 709.6
shedding daylight on *manifestation* 843.2
shedding light *lightening* 246.3
shedding light on *lucent* 246.13
she-devil *irascible person* 303.7, *evil spirit* 446.4
shed leaves *be dormant* 41.22, *grow* 43.15
shed light on *interpret* 365.12
shed seeds *vegetate* 41.21
shed tears *weep* 280.8, *seep* 559.16
sheen *quality of light* 246.2
sheep *livestock* 16.11, *hoofed mammal* 35.16, Collective Names 59, *worshiper* 83.6, *imitator* 736.6, *conformist* 781.6
sheep breeder *agriculturist* 16.14
sheep-dip *pest control* 16.13
sheepdog *dog* 35.10
sheep farm *farm* 16.2

sheep farmer *agriculturist* 16.14, *producer* 522.10
sheep farming *livestock farming* 16.10
sheepfold [Brit] *farm building* 16.4, *shelter* 812.4
sheepish *appearing guilty* 450.7, *weak-willed* 517.10
sheepishly *shyly* 403.16, *guiltily* 450.12, *weakly* 517.14
sheepishness *indecisiveness* 517.2
sheeplike *ungulate* 35.31, *obedient* 426.4, *compliant* 781.9
sheep ranch *farm* 16.2
sheeprot *animal disease* 34.10
sheep's eyes *look* 242.7, *communication of love* 299.6
sheepshank Knots, Bends, Hitches, Splices 754
sheepskin *leather* 104.7
sheer Fabrics and Fibers 130, *woven* 130.15, *translucent* 249.8, *fine* 595.12, *vertical* 602.5, *deviating course* 698.2, *deviate* 698.15
sheer drop *inclination* 714.6
sheer fabric *transparent thing* 249.4
sheerly *finely* 595.19, *vertically* 602.11
sheerness *translucency* 249.2, *fineness* 595.5, *verticality* 602.1
sheer off *sidestep* 698.22
sheer perfection *perfection* 805.1
sheer stockings *legwear* 100.26
sheet *paper* 104.5, *carpenter* 131.10, *sailboat parts and accessories* 150.4, *newspaper* 175.2, *coat* 588.3, *bed covering* 613.7, *coating* 613.8, *part of writing* 760.6
sheet anchor *yoke* 754.8, *safety device* 810.15
sheet bend Knots, Bends, Hitches, Splices 754
sheet-fed printing *book printing* 174.1
sheet glass *glass* 249.5
sheet in *handle sailboat equipment* 150.30
sheeting *wood* 131.3
sheeting in *sailing terms* 150.5
sheeting out *sailing terms* 150.5
sheet lightning *thunderstorm* 9.20, *natural light* 246.4
sheet music *written music* 140.21
sheet of cloud *cloud appearance* 9.19
sheet of fire *fire* 217.8
sheet out *handle sailboat equipment* 150.30
sheets *tackle* 754.6
sheet steel *construction material* 14.21
Sheffield *major British cities* 567.7
sheik *leader* 68.3
sheik [Inf] *lover* 299.11
sheikh *imam* 84.7
shekel *ancient coins* 484.12
shekels [Inf] *cash* 484.2
Shekhinah *deity* 82.1
Sheldon scale *measurement* 1.9
sheldrakes Collective Names 59
shelf *receptacle* 105.11, *rock face* 161.6, *compartment* 578.2, *level* 588.2, *shallowness* 599.1, *supporting structure* 605.2
shell *funeral object* 31.6, *eggs* 36.5, *fruit structure* 44.3, *ammunition* 78.11, *bomb* 78.15, Bean Varieties 90, *shirt* 100.13, *vault* 134.8, *fire* 418.18, *hard substance* 542.3, *framework* 551.4, *superstructure* 551.7, *exteriority* 610.2, *casing* 613.9, *animal*

covering 613.15, *depilate* 614.20, *notched thing* 636.2, Ships and Boats 690, *missile* 696.7, *draw out* 711.17, *remainder* 750.1
shellac *coating* 613.8, *coat* 613.28
shellacked *covered* 613.19
shellback *expert* 127.9
shell burst *burst of sound* 232.4
shell collecting Hobbies and Pastimes 167
shelled *shed* 614.14
shellfish *crustacean* 39.10, Phobias 283
shell game *foul play* 193.6
shelling *peeling* 614.6, *drawing off* 711.4
shell jacket *jacket* 100.18
shell money *money* 484.1
shell on brass *decorative woodwork* 131.2
shell out [Inf] *give out* 472.12, *pay* 489.16, *expend* 491.11
shell-pink *red* 257.5
shell shock *mental breakdown* 110.4
shell-shocked *military* 76.28, *disabled* 515.10
shell suit *sports equipment* 166.17
shelter 419.11, 613.6, 812.4, 812.8; *retreat* 60.13, *roof* 134.7, *hiding place* 181.2, *charitable organization* 305.4, *security* 464.1, *secure* 464.9, *taking in* 477.7, *be hospitable* 477.21, *contain* 578.20, *protect* 613.26, 810.21, *stopover* 704.7, *refuge* 708.3, 812.1, *give refuge to* 708.15, *haven* 810.3, *preservation* 815.1, *preserve* 815.14
sheltered 812.7; *inhabiting* 60.18, *architectural* 134.12, *secure* 464.5, *containing* 578.18, *safe* 810.16
sheltered housing *retreat* 60.13
sheltered workshop *safe house* 812.5
sheltering *containing* 578.18
shelterless *beggarly* 486.12, *vulnerable* 811.9
shelter under the wing of *shelter* 812.8
shelve *delay* 375.16, 658.13, *be evasive* 386.20, *defer* 846.9
shelved *storing* 578.19, *deferred* 604.9
shelving *delay* 375.6, *compartment* 578.2, *deferment* 604.3
Shemini Atzeres Jewish Holy Days and Seasons 85
shemozzle [Brit inf] *commotion* 768.5
Shenandoah Rivers 570
shenanigan *or* **shenanigans** [Inf] *foul play* 193.6
Sheol *evil place* 446.6
shepherd *farm worker* 16.15, *practice livestock farming* 16.20, *herd* 59.29, *direct* 126.11, *usher* 794.7, *escort* 794.18, *protector* 810.11, *protect* 810.21
shepherded *assembled* 59.18, *accompanied* 794.15
shepherdess *farm worker* 16.15
shepherding *assembling* 59.12
shepherdlike *tutelary* 810.19
Sheraton Furniture Styles 101
sherbet *dessert* 90.35, *confectionery* 222.3
sherbet [Brit] *sweet drink* 222.4
sherd *remainder* 750.1, *particle* 760.4, *fragment* 787.3
sheriff *person in authority* 52.7, *law officer* 53.6, *court officer* 54.7, *judge* 68.4, *defender* 77.2, *security force* 810.13
sheriff's jury *jury* 54.11

Sherpa guide *mountaineer* 161.8

sherry party *party* 408.6

Shetland Breeds of Cattle 16, Breeds of Sheep 16, *pony* 159.6

Shetland Islands Islands 572

Shetland pony Horse and Pony Breeds 159

Shetland sheepdog *or* **sheltie** Breeds of Dogs 35

shiatsu *alternative medicine* 107.4

shibboleth *symbol* 183.3, *means of identification* 184.3

Shield Constellations 7

shield *landform* 8.9, Heraldic Terms 184, *modern armor* 419.7, *historic armor* 419.8, *buffer* 419.22, *prize* 453.2, *security* 464.1, *secure* 464.9, *protective covering* 613.5, *shelter* 613.6, 812.4, *protect* 613.26, 810.21, *protection* 810.2

shield bearer *transferrer* 685.4, *transporter* 686.4

shielded *exempt* 434.5, *secure* 464.5, *protected* 613.20, *safe* 810.16

shielding *covering* 613.1

shield volcano *volcanic activity* 8.26

shift *underwear* 100.22, *task* 122.2, *huddle* 155.7, *artifice* 193.5, *scheme* 193.18, *equivocate* 380.8, *method* 387.4, *tactics* 399.12, *line of duty* 433.3, *allotted task* 474.3, *displacement* 574.1, *displace* 574.15, *period of activity* 641.4, *duration* 642.1, *cycle* 663.3, *alteration* 665.2, *change* 665.14, 841.20, *cause change* 665.16, *conversion* 670.1, *convert* 670.11, *be in motion* 677.14, *move* 677.15, *transfer* 685.1, *take away* 685.12, *deviating motion* 698.3, *interval* 739.4, *subtract* 749.6, *stratagem* 822.2, *be cunning* 822.5

shifted *displaced* 574.8

shift for oneself *conduct oneself* 399.17, *be independent* 829.18

shift gears *equivocate* 380.8

shiftily *deceptively* 193.21, *changeably* 666.7, *unreliably* 841.25

shiftiness *guile* 193.3, *cunning* 330.3, 822.1, *deviousness* 607.4, *irresolution* 666.2, *unreliability* 841.7

shifting *evasion* 380.2, *equivocal* 380.5, *displaced* 574.8, *changeable* 666.3, *moving* 677.12, *transfer* 685.1, *transferable* 685.7, *indirect* 698.9

shifting one's ground *vacillation* 380.3

shift lens *lens* 132.11

shiftless *impious* 448.11

shift one's ground *be irresolute* 378.9, *equivocate* 380.8

shift responsibility *exempt oneself* 434.12

shift the blame *exempt oneself* 434.12

shifty *artful* 193.13, *cunning* 330.8, 822.4, *unsteady* 378.7, *devious* 607.9, *irresolute* 666.4, *unreliable* 841.15

Shih Ching *other text* 81.19

Shih Tzu Breeds of Dogs 35

Shi'ism Islam 81.7

Shi'ite Muslim 81.12

shikari [India] *hunter* 385.6

Shikoku Islands 572

shill [Inf] *publicizer* 173.11, *publicize* 173.18

shillelagh *blunt weapon* 78.5

---

shilly-shally *inconstancy* 378.2, *sway* 378.12, *be irresolute* 666.6, *hesitate* 693.12

shilly-shallying *inconstancy* 378.2, *inconstant* 378.6, *irresolution* 666.2, *irresolute* 666.4, *lingering* 693.4, *delayed* 693.10

shim *hand tool* 103.3

shimmer *shine* 9.56, *quality of light* 246.2

shimmering *quality of light* 246.2, *lustrous* 246.15

shimmery *lustrous* 246.15

shimmy *coil* 632.2, *convolute* 632.6, *miscellaneous automotive terms* 687.14

shin *appendage* 19.5, *climb* 713.21

shinbone Human Bones 19

shindig [Inf] *social gathering* 59.7, *dance* 135.1, *party* 408.6

shindy [Inf] *social gathering* 59.7, *tumult* 232.5, *party* 408.6, *dispute* 463.3

shine 9.56; *observe* 7.34, *cleanliness* 111.1, *clean* 111.17, *be skillful* 127.14, *quality of light* 246.2, *light up* 246.20, *be intelligent* 352.7, *be beautiful* 529.11, *smoothness* 545.1, *smooth* 545.10, *be in a class of one's own* 777.14, *specialize* 779.16

shine brightly *shine* 9.56

shine like a new pin *glaze* 246.22

shine on *be auspicious* 847.8

shiner [Inf] *painful injury* 215.3

shine some light on *disclose* 180.8

shine through *appear* 244.8, *be transparent* 249.11

shingle *coast* 8.13, 572.4, *sediment* 8.29, *building materials* 104.2, *wood* 131.3, *carpenter* 131.10, *grit* 553.8, *layer* 588.9, *overlay* 613.25, *roof* 613.30

shingled *grainy* 553.17, *of landmasses* 572.12

shingles *skin disease* 114.16, *overhead covering* 613.11

Shingle style Architectural Styles 134

shingly *grainy* 553.17

shin guard *hockey clothing* 158.6

shin guards *baseball equipment* 147.4

shininess *quality of light* 246.2, *smoothness* 545.1

shining *clean* 111.13, *quality of light* 246.2, *bright* 246.14, *polishing* 554.5

shining armor *glory of war* 76.17

shinny up *climb* 713.21

shin pads *baseball equipment* 147.4, *soccer uniform* 163.3, *protective clothing* 419.6

shinplaster [Arch inf] *US coinage* 484.10

Shintoism *other religions* 81.8

Shinto text *other text* 81.19

shiny *lustrous* 246.15, *polished* 545.7

ship *convey* 685.9, *means of transportation* 686.2, *transport* 686.10, *vessel* 690.3

shipbuilder *artisan* 123.13, *marine scientist* 690.13

shipbuilding 690.4; *nautical* 690.14

shipbuilding contract *shipbuilding* 690.4

ship design *shipbuilding* 690.4

ship designer *marine scientist* 690.13

ship maintenance *navy specialties* 77.24

---

shipmate *friend* 62.2, *nautical person* 690.12

ship materials *shipbuilding* 690.4

shipment *load* 577.5, *conveyance* 685.2, *transferred thing* 685.6, *transportation* 686.1, *freightage* 686.3

ship of the line *historical warships* 77.22

ship out *be at war* 76.32, *navigate* 690.15

shipped *transportable* 686.7

shipper *transporter* 686.4

shipping *conveyance* 685.2, *transporting* 686.8, *water transportation* 690.1, *nautical* 690.14

shipping forecast *weather forecast* 9.4

shipping lane *waterway* 690.2, *route* 691.2, *thoroughfare* 692.6

shipping ton Scientific and Technical Units 589

ship's boat Sailing Ships and Boats 690, Ships and Boats 690

ship's chronometer *navigational aid* 690.6

ship's colors *flag* 184.8

ship's compass *navigational aid* 690.6

shipshape *well-made* 127.13, *orderly* 765.13

shipshape condition *preparedness* 388.5

ship's log *navigational aid* 690.6

ship's master *nautical person* 690.12

ship specifications *shipbuilding* 690.4

ship's speed *nautical speed* 690.11

ship's steering 690.9

ship's steward *nautical person* 690.12

ship's timekeeper *navigational aid* 690.6

ship that passes in the night *transient* 643.2

ship-to-shore radio *radio* 172.1

ship-to-shore telephone *telephone* 169.10

shipwreck *ruin* 523.4, 523.15

shipwright *artisan* 123.13

shipyard *construction workplace* 124.10, *shipbuilding* 690.14

Shire Horse and Pony Breeds 159

shire *administrative region* 564.4

shirk 386.18; *be neglectful* 326.7, *dissociate* 375.14, *hesitate* 378.10, *not perform* 466.10

shirker *neglector* 326.3, *reluctant person* 375.7, *avoider* 386.8, *inactive person* 413.8, *nonworker* 415.4

shirking 386.4; *indifferent* 326.5, *unenthusiastic* 375.10

shirr *pleat* 637.2, 637.8

shirred egg *egg dish* 90.18

shirt 100.13

shirt front *part of garment* 100.27

shirt jacket *jacket* 100.18

shirtwaist *or* **shirt-dress** *dress* 100.11

shish kebab *notable international dishes* 90.40

shit [Inf] *feces* 25.5, *defecate* 25.21, *dirt* 112.5, *unpleasant person* 272.5

shit! [Inf] *miscellaneous swearwords* 301.20

shitfaced [Inf] *dead drunk* 121.27

shithouse [Inf] *place for excretion* 25.11

shitkickers [Inf] *boots* 100.31

shit oneself [Inf] *defecate* 25.21

---

shits, the [Inf] *defecation* 25.3

shittily [Inf] *excrementally* 25.27

shitty [Inf] *fecal* 25.14, *sick* 114.24

shivah [Hebrew] *non-Christian ritual* 85.8

shiver *sense* 212.9, *be cold* 218.13, *be fearful* 283.15, *demolish* 523.12, *be brittle* 548.4, *vibrate* 683.13, *shake* 684.24, *take apart* 753.16

shivering *of disease* 114.25, *vibration* 683.2, *vibrating* 683.9, *shaking* 684.6, *shaky* 684.18

shivers *symptom* 114.3, *stimulus* 212.3, *chills* 218.3, *symptoms of fear* 283.3, *shake* 684.7

shivers up and down one's spine *symptoms of fear* 283.3

shivery *cold* 218.9, *shaky* 684.18

Shkodra Breeds of Sheep 16

shmee [Inf] *opiates* 121.17

shoal *fishes* 38.1, Collective Names 59, *low* 597.10, *shallowness* 599.1, *shallow* 599.3, 599.5, *throng* 795.4, *hidden danger* 813.3

shoaliness *shallowness* 599.1

shoal water *hidden danger* 813.3

shoaly *shallow* 599.3

shoat *young animal* 26.4, *young mammal* 35.20

shock 292.3; *seismic activity* 8.24, *illness* 114.2, Phobias 283, *frighten* 283.17, *cause dislike* 291.16, *astonishment* 292.2, *surprise* 292.9, *astonish* 292.10, *bad outcome* 293.3, *wonder* 294.1, *marvel* 294.3, *be wondrous* 294.14, *military attack* 418.2, *demoralize* 432.15, *be wicked* 448.13, *use violence* 520.9, *jolt* 684.9, 684.23, *collision* 695.2

shockability *self-righteousness* 431.7

shockable *shy* 403.8, *moralistic* 431.12

shock absorber *moderator* 521.2, *spring* 546.4

shocked *astonished* 292.6, *wondering* 294.7, *agitated* 684.15

shockheaded *barbed* 544.7

shocking *frightening* 283.12, *surprising* 292.7, *astonishing* 292.8, 294.10, *offensive* 432.11

shockingly *surprisingly* 292.14, *astonishingly* 294.19, *disgracefully* 371.8, *dynamically* 695.16

shocking pink *red* 257.5

shockproof *tough* 547.6

shock stall *flight maneuver* 689.6

shock tactics *military attack* 418.2

shock therapy *psychiatric treatment* 108.3, *treatment* 110.7

shock treatment *psychiatric treatment* 108.3, *treatment* 110.7, *therapy* 115.12

shock wave *wave* 10.11, 683.4

shod *dressed* 100.38

shoddily *negligently* 326.8, *deviously* 371.9, *fragilely* 548.5, *badly* 745.17

shoddiness 497.3; *indifference* 326.2, *tawdriness* 535.2, *deficiency* 745.2, *untidiness* 766.3

shoddy 497.11, Fabrics and Fibers 130, *indifferent* 326.5, *weak* 517.6, *ugly* 531.3, *vulgar* 535.6, *brittle* 548.3, *low quality* 745.7, *untidy* 766.11, *cheap* 800.16, *unsafe* 811.8

shoe *clothe* 100.43, *superstructure* 551.7

shoeblack *attendant* 69.4

shoebox *box* 578.5

---

shoe brush *cleaning tool* 111.10
shoed *dressed* 100.38
shoelace *line* 754.5
shoemaker *clothier* 100.37
Shoemaker-Levy *comet* 7.20
shoemaking *the clothing business* 100.36
shoe polish *cleaning agent* 111.9
shoes 100.30
shoe seller *retailer* 482.11
shoeshine boy *attendant* 69.4, *cleaner* 111.12
shoeshiner *cleaner* 111.12
shoestring catch *other game terms* 147.7
shoetree *figurative usage* 43.9
shofar *Musical Instruments* 142
shogun *absolute ruler* 68.7
shonin *religious* 84.9
shoo! *go!* 709.30
shoo-in [Inf] *victor* 845.7
shoo off *or* **away** *send away* 709.18
shoot 696.18; *young plant* 26.5, *murder* 30.20, *execute* 30.22, 454.30, *kill animals* 30.25, *stem* 41.5, *seed* 41.9, *vegetate* 41.21, *fight* 77.35, *photograph* 132.26, *film* 137.19, *play basketball* 148.7, *play ice hockey* 158.9, *hunting* 160.2, *hunt* 160.12, 385.14, *soccer play* 163.5, *play soccer* 163.8, *represent* 187.10, *be painful* 215.9, *inflict pain* 215.10, *fire* 418.18, *river turbulence* 570.5, *grow* 581.17, *hole* 583.17, *component* 760.3
shoot! *after him!* 385.19
shoot [Inf] *inject* 710.10
shoot a free throw *play basketball* 148.7
shoot ahead *press on* 679.9, *exceed* 712.15
shoot ahead of *overtake* 744.16
shoot an air ball [Inf] *play basketball* 148.7
shoot an arrow *use a sharp tool* 549.17
shoot-and-run offense *playing terms* 148.4
shoot at *battle* 76.33, *fire* 418.18, *shoot* 696.18
shoot back *retaliate* 420.4
shoot down *murder* 30.20, *slaughter* 30.21, *fire* 418.18, *shoot* 696.18, *bring down* 716.14, *annihilate* 773.24
shoot down in flames *ruin* 523.15, *bring down* 716.14
shooter 160.10, 696.11; *basketball team* 148.2
shooter [Inf] *photographer* 132.23
shoot fowl *hunt* 160.12
shoot from the hip [Inf] *be sincere* 191.8
shoot game *hunt* 160.12
shooting 696.5; *murder* 30.2, *execution* 30.6, *animal killing* 30.10, *playing terms* 148.4, *hunting* 160.11, 385.9, *soccer play* 163.5, *soccer* 163.7, *painful* 215.4, *hunt* 385.3, *firing* 418.6, *capital punishment* 454.12, *germination* 581.5, *growing* 581.12, *propulsion* 696.1, *shot* 696.6
shooting circle *hockey areas* 158.2
shooting gallery [Inf] *drug use* 121.9
shooting guard *basketball team* 148.2
shooting in the dark *inaccuracy* 351.3
shooting iron [Inf] *firearm* 78.7

shooting kit [Brit] *hunting accessories* 160.5
shooting oneself *suicide* 30.8
shooting script *script* 137.5
shooting season *seasons* 654.2
shooting star *meteor* 7.21, *Flowers* 42, *natural light* 246.4, *good-luck sign* 358.6, *transient* 643.2
shooting stick *hunting accessories* 160.5
shooting up *taking off* 713.6
shooting up [Inf] *drug use* 121.9
shoot off one's mouth [Inf] *tell on* 180.10
shoot one's cookies [Inf] *vomit* 709.27
shoot oneself *commit suicide* 30.24
shoot oneself in the foot *figurative expressions* 128.11
shootout *battle* 76.23, *warfare* 422.10
shoot par *play* 156.8
shoot someone down [Inf] *repel* 701.7
shoot the rapids *canoe* 150.31
shoot the sun *orient* 697.15
shoot through *pass* 692.15
shoot to kill *declare war* 422.25
shoot-up [Inf] *drug dose* 121.15
shoot up *vegetate* 41.21, *grow* 581.17, *be tall* 596.16, *spring up* 713.22, *send up* 715.12, *increase* 746.6
shoot up [Inf] *drug oneself* 121.37
shop 481.15; *home workplace* 124.3, *store* 124.4, 483.8, *building* 551.9
shop [Brit inf] *inform on* 170.13
shop around *buy cheaply* 497.15
shop assistant [Brit] *attendant* 69.4
shop at *frequent* 393.10
shop floor *force* 59.10, *factory* 124.8
shop for *shop* 481.15
shop goods *merchandise* 482.6
shopkeeper *provisioner* 89.4, *retailer* 482.11
shoplift *take away* 477.18, *steal* 479.14
shoplifter *compulsive person* 428.5, *thief* 479.8
shoplifting *wicked act* 448.7, *stealing* 479.1
shop owner *retailer* 482.11
shopper *user* 393.4, *purchaser* 481.7, *spender* 491.7
shopping 481.3; *purchase* 481.1, *buying* 481.9
shopping area *urban area* 567.10
shopping around *shopping* 481.3
shopping bag *bag* 578.7, *transferred thing* 685.6
shopping basket *basket* 578.6
shopping cart *cart* 578.9, *means of transportation* 686.2
shopping center *marketplace* 483.7, *urban area* 567.10, *center of activity* 612.4
shopping list *shopping* 481.3, *list* 785.1
shopping mall *marketplace* 483.7, *center of activity* 612.4
shopping plaza *center of activity* 612.4
shopping spree *shopping* 481.3, *extravagance* 500.1
shop steward *union member* 57.6
shop till one drops *shop* 481.15, *expend* 491.11
shop window *that which makes visible* 244.4, *stall* 483.9, *showplace* 843.4
shopworn *discounted* 495.3, *shoddy*

497.11, *low quality* 745.7, *imperfect* 806.5, *worn* 808.13
shopworn item *imperfect item* 806.3
shore *coast* 8.13, 572.4, *harden* 542.9, *support* 605.16, 825.24, *edge* 618.1, *waterfront* 621.3, *side* 623.1
shore bird *water bird* 36.9
shoreline *coast* 8.13, 572.4, *edge* 618.1
shore patrol (SP) *law enforcement agency* 53.7
shore up *bolster* 377.15, *harden* 542.9, *support* 605.16, 825.24, *give moral support* 605.18, *preserve* 815.14
shoring up *support* 605.1
shorn *shortened* 582.8
shorn of *losing* 468.9
short 591.6; *circuit* 14.37, *scarce* 98.8, *movie type* 137.3, *dramatic* 137.16, *snowplow* 162.29, *concise* 198.4, *summary* 204.5, *sparing with words* 208.6, *cross* 303.11, *discourteous* 411.5, *insolvent* 486.10, *work of art* 522.4, *brittle* 548.3, *missing* 576.11, *little* 580.7, *shortly* 591.12, *low* 597.10, *transient* 643.4, *reduced* 749.5, *incomplete* 762.5, *uncompleted* 762.7
shortage *need* 95.4, *scarcity* 98.3, *inadequacy* 486.5, *absence* 576.1, *imbalance* 741.2, *decrease* 747.1, *fewness* 796.3, *decline* 846.5
shortage of cash *insolvency* 486.2
shortage of funds *insolvency* 486.2
short and sweet *concise* 198.4, *summary* 204.5, *short* 591.6
short- or wide-angle zoom *lens* 132.11
short answer *answer* 334.1, *act of discourtesy* 411.3
short-back-and-sides *coiffure* 530.8
shortbread *pastry* 90.37
shortcake *cake* 90.36
short circuit *or* **short** *circuit* 14.37
shortcoming *immorality* 432.1, *nonperformance* 466.2, *defect* 806.4
short-course *swimming* 164.12
short-course pool *swimming place* 164.9
shortcut 591.5; *short distance* 586.2, *route* 691.2, *bearing* 697.2
short-cut 591.11; *find one's way* 691.15
short distance 586.2
short-distance *speed-skating* 162.33
short-distance racing *speed skating* 162.20
short division *division* 6.16
short drink *size of drink* 93.3
short duration 643.3
shorten 591.9; *be concise* 198.5, *summarize* 204.7, *smooth* 545.10, *make little* 580.10, *contract* 582.12, *become smaller* 582.14, *make smaller* 747.8, *take off* 749.7
shortened 582.8, 591.7, 762.6; *concise* 198.4, *summarized* 204.6, *reduced* 749.5
shortened version 591.3
shortening 582.2, 591.2; *basic cooking ingredient* 91.8, *conciseness* 198.1, *outline* 204.2, *fat* 562.4, *contracting* 582.10, *limitation* 747.3, *subtraction* 749.1
shorten sail *slow down* 693.13, *be safe* 810.20
shorten someone's life *kill* 30.19

shorten the life of *make transient* 643.7
shortest way *shortcut* 591.5
shortfall *need* 95.4, *insufficiency* 98.1, *financial loss* 468.4, *imbalance* 741.2, *deficiency* 745.2, *subtracted item* 749.2, *omission* 762.4, *incompleteness* 806.2, *defect* 806.4, *decline* 846.5
short fiber-reinforced polymers *chemical process industries* 14.26
short fuse [Inf] *short temper* 303.5, *sign of irritability* 304.4
shorthand *artificial language* 5.9
short-handed *unprovided* 98.6, *incomplete* 806.6
Shorthorn *Breeds of Cattle* 16
short list *selection* 382.1, *list of names* 785.7
short-list *list* 785.11
shortlived *transient* 643.4
short loin *beef* 90.24
shortly 591.12; *summarily* 204.10, *transiently* 643.8, *soon* 657.18
short movie *movie type* 137.3
shortness 591.1; *conciseness* 198.1, *summariness* 204.4, *taciturnity* 208.1, *crossness* 303.4, *discourtesy* 411.1, *littleness* 580.1, *abruptness* 591.4, *lowness* 597.1
shortness of breath *fatigue* 820.1
short note *tempo* 140.22
short novel *work of art* 522.4
short odds *gambling* 167.4
short of *inferiorly* 745.13, *by subtraction* 749.8, *incomplete* 762.5, *exclusively* 764.10
short of breath *or* **wind** *panting* 820.3
short of cash *insolvent* 486.10
short of funds *insolvent* 486.10
short one *size of drink* 93.3
short-order cook *cook* 91.3
short-order food *food* 90.1
short pants *shorts* 100.15
short period *chemical element* 11.3
short plate *beef* 90.24
short-range *transportable* 686.7
short rations 118.3; *scarcity* 90.5
short run *theatrical performance* 136.13
shorts 100.15; *underwear* 100.22, *basketball court* 148.3, *soccer uniform* 163.3
short service line *badminton terms* 165.11
short shorts *shorts* 100.15
short sight *sight defect* 243.2
shortsighted *weak-sighted* 243.10
shortsightedness *sight defect* 243.2
short ski *ski equipment* 162.10
short sleeve *part of garment* 100.27
short-sleeved shirt *shirt* 100.13
short space of time *short duration* 643.3
short splice *Knots, Bends, Hitches, Splices* 754
short-staffed *incomplete* 806.6
shortstop *baseball team* 147.2
shortstop bath *darkroom equipment* 132.21
short story *fiction* 139.2, *story* 139.4, *work of art* 522.4
short-story writer *author* 139.13
short supply *scarcity* 98.3
short swing *skiing techniques* 162.5
short sword *sharp weapon* 78.6
short takeoff and landing (STOL) *craft aircraft* 689.3
short temper 303.5; *anger* 302.4, *abruptness* 591.4

short or quick temper *sign of irritability* 304.4

short-tempered *irritable* 302.10, *irascible* 303.8, *abrupt* 591.8

short-term *transient* 643.4

short-term debt *debt* 488.1

short-term forecast *weather forecast* 9.4

short-term loan *loan* 475.2

short time *short duration* 643.3

short time ago, a *newly* 652.21

short-track *speed-skating* 162.33

short-track racing *speed skating* 162.20

short-track speed skating Sporting Activities 145

shortwave *radio transmission* 172.3, *radio frequency* 661.3

shortwave radio *radio* 172.1

shortwave station *radio broadcasting* 172.4

short way *short distance* 586.2

short while *duration* 642.1

short word *word* 5.17

short words *clarity* 363.2

shorty [Inf] *little person* 580.5

shot 696.6; Historical Missile Weapons 78, *ammunition* 78.11, *size of drink* 93.3, *dose of medicine* 115.3, *drink* 121.6, *photograph* 132.3, *motion-picture photography* 137.9, *grip* 151.4, *fishing tackle* 154.7, *hunting equipment* 160.4, *badminton terms* 165.11, *shot-put* 166.12, *bang* 234.1, *iridescent* 263.7, *experiment* 335.1, *conjecture* 359.3, *hunter* 385.6, *attempt* 390.1, *holed* 583.12, General Units 589, *round thing* 633.3, *missile* 696.7, *shooter* 696.11, *injection* 710.2, *complicated* 751.10

shot [Inf] *drug dose* 121.15, *dead drunk* 121.27

shot across the bows *firing* 418.6

shot bowl *grip* 151.4

shot-clock *basketball court* 148.3

shotglass *drink container* 93.13

shotgun *firearm* 78.7, *banger* 234.3

shotgun formation *offense* 155.6

shotgun shooting *target shooting* 160.1

shotgun wedding *wedding* 64.5

shot in the dark *conjecture* 359.3, *poor chance* 842.8

shot put 166.12, Sporting Activities 145, *field event* 166.10, *throw* 696.4

shot-putter *track and field eventer* 166.19, *thrower* 696.10

shot-putting *track and field* 166.20

shots down *grip* 151.4

shot silk Fabrics and Fibers 130, *variegated thing* 263.5

shots up *grip* 151.4

shot through *omnipresent* 575.10

shot through with *iridescent* 263.7, *complicated* 751.10

shot to pieces *apart* 753.8

shot up *raised* 715.6

shot velocity *shot put* 166.12

should *be compelled* 428.11, *be the duty of* 433.16

shoulder *veal* 90.25, *pork* 90.26, *resolve* 374.9, *bolster* 377.15, *take charge of* 391.8, *do something* 412.13, *edge* 618.1, *impel* 695.9, *push* 696.16, *erect* 715.11, *joint* 752.7

shoulder a musket *be at war* 76.32

shoulder arms *prepare oneself* 388.21

shoulder bag *bag* 578.7

shoulder belt *band* 754.9

shoulder blade Human Bones 19

shouldered *arch* 134.5

shoulder guard *hockey clothing* 158.6

shoulder harness *safety device* 810.15

shoulder-high *high* 596.7

shouldering *ramming* 695.3

shouldering responsibility *enterprising* 391.5

shoulder-length *long* 590.6

shoulder one's responsibilities *do one's duty* 433.17

shoulder pads *accessory* 100.28, *protective clothing* 419.6, *football uniform* 155.2

shoulder responsibility for *be a substitute* 672.6

shoulder roast *lamb* 90.27

shoulder-to-shoulder *near* 586.6, *adhesive* 755.5, *cohesively* 755.11, *associating* 827.11, *cooperatively* 827.18

should it be that *under the circumstances* 726.16

shout *proclaim* 173.16, *proclamation* 183.8, *signal* 183.18, *emphasize* 200.6, *speak in a particular way* 205.18, *tumult* 232.5, *be loud* 232.8, *cry* 239.1, *cry out* 239.13, *applause* 279.2, *vent one's anger* 302.21, *danger signal* 811.5

shout at the top of one's voice or lungs *cry out* 239.13

shout bravo *acclaim* 437.18

shout down *outtalk* 207.8, *hiss* 239.17, *refute* 332.7, *show disapproval* 438.21, *restrain someone* 830.17

shouter *crier* 239.8

shout for *cheer* 239.15

shout for more *acclaim* 437.18

shout from the rooftops *proclaim* 173.16

shouting 232.7; *signaling* 183.14, *tumult* 232.5, *vociferous* 239.9, *burst of anger* 302.6

shout oneself hoarse *cry out* 239.13

shout out *cry out* 239.13

shove *work* 122.8, *gesture* 183.5, 183.17, *push* 414.20, 696.16, *set in motion* 677.16, *blow* 695.5, *impel* 695.9, *propulsion* 696.1, *propel* 696.15

shove around *be severe* 424.8

shove aside 698.23; *disrespect* 436.18

shovel *farm tool* 16.5, *garden tool* 17.7, 103.4, *ski equipment* 162.10, *sharp-edged thing* 549.6, *use a sharp tool* 549.17, *ladle* 578.17, *take away* 685.12, *extractor* 711.9

shoveled *storing* 578.19

shovel(ful) *container(ful)* 738.2

shovel hat *hat* 100.32

shovel in *eat well* 92.23

shove off! [Inf] *go!* 709.30

shover *impeller* 695.7

shoving *propulsion* 696.1, *propulsive* 696.12, *hasty* 818.3

show 138.4, 404.12, 404.24, 621.7; *rationalize* 4.20, *propound a philosophy* 4.21, *compilation* 59.14, *direct* 126.11, *play* 136.2, *musical drama* 136.5, *theatrical performance* 136.13, *performance* 141.8, *horse-racing betting terms* 159.11, *disclose* 180.8, *identify* 184.11, *stand for* 187.14, *ungenuineness* 192.2, *view* 242.8, *make visible* 242.25, 244.9, *be visible* 242.26, 244.7, *manifestation* 244.3, *visibility* 264.4, *appear* 264.12, *become visible* 264.13, *present* 264.15, *state* 329.13, *demonstration* 331.1, *demonstrate* 331.15, *prove* 336.9, *make evident* 339.11, *interpret* 365.12, *formal occasion* 406.4, *fair* 483.2, *open* 583.15, *be in front* 621.13, *display* 843.1, 843.13, *production* 843.5, *reveal* 843.14

showable *displayed* 843.8

show acuteness *be mentally sharp* 549.18

show affection *love* 299.21

show an affinity *tend* 513.5

show anger *gesture* 183.17, *be angry* 302.19

show animosity *be malevolent* 306.12

show apathy for *acquiesce* 421.5

show appreciation *be grateful* 310.6

show a profit *be profitable* 467.21

show aptitude *be skillful* 127.14

show a talent for *be skillful* 127.14

show a tendency *tend* 513.5, *be probable* 838.8

show a trend *tend* 513.5

show authority *have authority over* 425.12

show bad faith *be dishonorable* 192.21

show benevolence *befriend* 62.10, *philanthropize* 307.8

show bias *be unjust* 741.9

show biz [Inf] *show business* 138.1

showboat *theater* 136.16

show business 138.1

show candor *be informal* 829.19

showcase *that which makes visible* 244.4, *transparent thing* 249.4, *showplace* 843.4

show caution *hesitate* 693.12

show compassion *be compassionate* 305.11, *show mercy* 312.11, *be unselfish* 443.7

show compunction *repent* 313.9, *be penitent* 451.7

show concern *be benevolent* 305.10

show consideration *be benevolent* 305.10, *be solicitous* 323.13, *be lenient* 423.5

show contempt *be insubordinate* 416.8

show courage *defy* 416.7

show courtesy *show obeisance to* 426.8

show determination 674.8

show devotion to *obey* 426.7

show diligence *observe* 465.4

show disapproval 438.21; *protest* 507.7

show discontent *protest* 507.7

show disdain *not observe* 466.9

show disloyalty *defy* 466.11

show displeasure *hate* 300.11

show disrespect *disrespect* 436.18, *defy* 466.11

show dissatisfaction *protest* 507.7

show dog *dog* 35.10

showdown *disclosure* 180.1, *fight* 422.9

show emotion *feel* 266.14

show endearment *love* 299.21

show enterprise *undertake* 391.7

show enthusiasm *be eager* 373.13

shower *rain* 9.27, 9.57, *refresher* 94.2, *abound* 97.8, *bath* 111.6, *bathe* 111.18, *water* 557.29, *throw* 696.17, *downflow* 714.3, *drip* 714.13, *lowering* 716.1, *sprinkle* 776.15

shower attention on *be solicitous* 323.13

shower gel *cleaning agent* 111.9

showeriness *rain* 9.27, *mistiness* 559.2

showering *washing* 557.11, *fallen* 716.8

showerproof *treat* 130.21, *waterproof* 560.16

showerproof or showerproofed *treated* 130.16

shower upon *give* 472.10

showery *rainy* 9.50, *misty* 559.10

show evidence *attest* 189.22, *authenticate* 721.24

show favor *give* 472.10

show favoritism *discriminate* 430.21

show fear *be afraid* 283.14

show feelings *be sensitive* 267.5

show fight *push* 414.20, *retaliate* 419.30

show for what it is *disclose* 180.8

show friendship for *agree with* 462.10

show gentleness *be kind* 543.16

show girl *entertainer* 138.8

show good faith *obey* 426.7

show good grounds *justify* 441.12

show good manners *better* 445.17

show gratitude *be grateful* 310.6

show greed *take* 477.14

show hostility *disagree* 463.8, 753.19

show how *explain* 331.16

show humility *show obeisance to* 426.8

show ignorance *lack intellect* 316.8

show ill will *be malevolent* 306.12

showily 367.6, 404.29; *entertainingly* 138.17, *vulgarly* 535.10

show impatience 303.14

show in 708.13

show inconsideration for *be thoughtless* 324.11

showiness 404.1; *clarity* 244.2, *arrogance* 297.2, *demonstrativeness* 331.2, *ornateness* 532.2, *vulgarity* 535.1

showing *disclosed* 180.5, *view* 242.8, *visible* 244.5, *appearing* 264.9, *demonstration* 331.1, *display* 843.1

showing leniency *easing* 543.13

showing off *demonstrativeness* 331.2, *overestimation* 343.1, *boastfulness* 402.6, *exhibitionism* 404.9, *manifestation* 843.2

showing preference *preferential* 382.10

showing respect 435.7

showing signs of *sick* 114.24

showing symptoms *sick* 114.24

showing up *appearance* 264.1

show insolence *defy* 416.7

show insubordination *disobey* 427.12

show intelligence *be mentally sharp* 549.18

show interest *be curious* 321.7, *be sociable* 414.22

show interest in *be curious* 321.7

show irreverence *not wonder about* 295.5

show irritation *be irritable* 304.14

show joy 269.10

show-jumper *horse person* 159.14

show jumping Sporting Activities

145, equestrianism 159.8, *sporting event* 422.6

show-jumping *equine* 159.15

show kindness *better* 445.17

show leniency *be lenient* 423.5, *be kind* 543.16

showman *entertainer* 138.8, *demonstrator* 331.6, *displayer* 843.7

showmanship *show business* 138.1, *public relations (PR)* 173.8, *affectation* 367.1, *showiness* 404.1

show mercy 312.11; *be compassionate* 305.11, *show pity* 308.8, *be lenient* 423.5, *acquit* 434.10, *protect* 810.21

show moderation *be modest* 403.11, *stand in the middle* 772.17

shown *disclosed* 180.5, *identified* 184.9, *demonstrated* 331.9, *proven* 331.13, *displayed* 843.8

show no concern for *be indifferent* 289.12

show no excitement *be indifferent* 289.12, *not wonder about* 295.5

shown off *displayed* 843.8

show no fight *succumb* 421.7

show no flexibility *have no mercy* 309.6, *be obstinate* 417.11

show no interest in *be incurious* 322.5, *be disinterested* 443.6

show no leniency *have no mercy* 309.6

show no mercy *be malevolent* 306.12, *have no mercy* 309.6, *be severe* 424.8

show no pity *be malevolent* 306.12, *be pitiless* 309.5, *be severe* 424.8

show no regard for someone's feelings *be discourteous* 411.7

show no respect *disrespect* 436.18, *defy* 466.11

show no sign of life *not act* 413.11

show no surprise *be indifferent* 289.12

shown the door *discarded* 383.8

show obeisance to 426.8

show of disapproval 438.6

show off 402.15, 404.26; *disdain* 297.14, *appear* 331.18, *be affected* 367.4, *brag* 400.17, *do great deeds* 412.14, *display* 843.13

show-off 404.13; *proud person* 297.7, *demonstrator* 331.6, *vain person* 402.7

show of force *suppression* 424.2

show of hands *electing* 382.5

show of respect *mark of respect* 435.4

show (oneself in) one's true colors *show oneself* 843.15

show one's *or its* **true colors** *be disclosed* 180.12

show one's Achilles' heel *be imperfect* 806.8

show one's cards *divulge* 180.9

show one's colors *brace oneself* 376.13

show one's distaste *grudge* 375.15

show oneself 843.15; *become visible* 264.13

show oneself up *be disreputable* 371.5

show one's face *be disclosed* 180.12, *appear* 575.16, *show oneself* 843.15

show one's gratitude *reward* 453.13

show one's hand *divulge* 180.9

show one's heels *make haste* 818.5

show one's ignorance *be unskillful* 128.8

show one's mettle *be courageous* 284.14, *retaliate* 419.30

show one's true colors *disclose* 180.8, *be disclosed* 180.12, *detect* 345.12

show one's years *age* 27.16

show partiality *discriminate* 430.21, *be unjust* 741.9

show phases *be changeable* 666.5

showpiece 843.3

show pity 308.8

showplace 843.4

show potential 458.14

show prejudice *tend* 513.5, *be unjust* 741.9

show promise *show potential* 458.14

show readiness *start early* 657.12

show refinement *have good manners* 410.10

show reluctance *resist* 417.10

show remorse *repent* 313.9

show resilience *be elastic* 546.7

show respect 435.16; *show obeisance to* 426.8, *observe* 465.4, *make important* 799.14

show restraint *lack candor* 192.22

show results *be successful* 845.11, *be effective* 845.15

showroom *store* 124.4, *showplace* 843.4

show satisfaction *approve* 437.14

show self-restraint *be unadorned* 424.10, *restrain oneself* 830.15

show signs of *signify* 183.16, *make evident* 339.11, *be probable* 838.8

show someone the door *relegate* 574.18, *repel* 701.7, *expel* 709.14

show stamina *be tough* 547.13

show strength *have authority* 52.13, *be tough* 547.13

show style *style* 537.8

show sufficient grounds for *rationalize* 4.20

show talent *tend* 513.5

show tenaciousness 471.8

show (tender) mercy *conciliate* 74.10

show tenderness *be kind* 543.16

show the door *discard* 383.12, *be discourteous* 411.7

show the flag *show oneself* 843.15

show the ropes [Inf] *introduce* 708.16

show the way *direct* 126.11, 697.13, *sign* 183.19, *prepare the way* 388.15, *precede* 769.13

show the white feather [Brit] *be a coward* 285.7

show the white flag *capitulate* 421.6

show through *be visible* 242.26, *appear* 244.8, *be transparent* 249.11

show treachery *defy* 466.11

show unconcern *be inattentive* 324.10

show up *disclose* 180.8, *appear* 244.8, 264.12, 575.16, *become visible* 264.13, *present* 264.15, *refute* 332.7, *detect* 345.12, *be discovered* 345.15, *arrive* 704.13, *show oneself* 843.15, *be visible* 843.16

show up again *be repeated* 797.20

show up well *be visible* 843.16

show variety *be changeable* 666.5

show what's what *refute* 332.7

show willingness *push* 414.20, *agree with* 462.10

show wisdom *be reasonable* 319.12

show wonder *wonder* 294.12

showy 404.14, *entertaining* 138.12, *clear* 244.6, *gaudy* 251.12, *arrogant* 297.9, *demonstrative* 331.10, *affected* 367.3, *unrestrained* 500.5, *inelegant* 528.6, *ornate* 532.10, *vulgar* 535.6, *accentuated* 843.11

show zeal *push* 414.20

shrapnel *ammunition* 78.11

shred *cook* 91.10, *renounce* 392.4, *demolish* 523.12, *grate* 553.24, *take apart* 753.16, *particle* 760.4, *fragment* 787.3

shredded *destroyed* 523.9, *pulverized* 553.20, *partial* 760.11

shredder *grater* 553.12

shredding *destroying* 523.2, *pulverization* 553.4

shrew *unpleasant woman* 33.7, *feeling person* 266.8, *unpleasant person* 272.5, *irascible person* 303.7, *dissenter* 619.3

shrewd *refined* 48.20, *skillful* 127.10, *intelligent* 315.9, 352.5, *judicious* 341.8, *knowledgeable* 348.7, *mentally sharp* 549.14, *profound* 598.15, *cunning* 822.4

shrewd idea *conjecture* 359.3

shrewdly *skillfully* 127.16, *intelligently* 315.14, 352.9, *judicially* 341.12, *sharply* 549.19, *profoundly* 598.27, *cunningly* 822.6

shrewdness Collective Names 59, *caution* 287.1, *cleverness* 315.3, *wisdom* 352.1, *subtlety* 534.2, *mental sharpness* 549.9, *profundity* 598.5, *cunning* 822.1

shrewish *ill-natured* 303.9, *irritable* 304.9

shrewishly *ill-naturedly* 303.18, *irritably* 304.17

shrewishness *ill nature* 303.2, *irritableness* 304.3

shriek *blow* 9.53, *speak in a particular way* 205.18, *express pain* 215.11, *tumult* 232.5, *be loud* 232.8, *shrillness* 238.3, *be shrill* 238.9, *cry* 239.1, *cry of pain* 239.5, *cry out* 239.13

shrieking *gaudy* 251.12

shrift [Arch] *forgiveness* 312.1, *apology* 313.2

shrike *songbird* 36.12

shrike, San Clemente loggerhead Endangered US Birds 36

shrill 238.6; *loud* 232.6, *be loud* 232.8, *dissonant* 241.4

shrillness 238.3; *loud sound* 232.2

shrilly *stridently* 238.10, *dissonantly* 241.7

shrimp *crustacean* 39.10, *food fish and shellfish* 90.20

shrimp [Inf] *little person* 580.5

shrimp cocktail *hors d'oeuvre* 90.13

shrimper *or* **shrimp boat** Ships and Boats 690

shrimplike *arthropodal* 39.22

shrimp plant Flowers 42

shrine 83.10; *burial place* 31.7, *place of worship* 83.8, *monument* 185.10

shrink *be afraid* 283.14, *be a coward* 285.7, *shy* 386.17, *lessen* 468.17, *make little* 580.10, *contract* 582.12, *shrink back*

680.20, *decrease* 747.7, *disintegrate* 808.15

shrink [Inf] *psychiatrist* 108.34, 110.8

shrinkability *contractibility* 582.4

shrinkable *contractible* 582.11

shrinkage *lessening* 468.6, *contraction* 582.1, *decrease* 747.1, *subtraction* 749.1

shrink back 680.20; *escape notice* 403.14

shrink from *react against* 291.15, *hate* 300.11, *dissociate* 375.14, *refuse* 506.8

shrink from public gaze *escape notice* 403.14

shrinking *cowardly* 285.4, *dissociation* 375.4, *unenthusiastic* 375.10, *shyness* 386.3, *avoiding* 386.9, *shy* 403.8, *contraction* 582.1, *contracting* 582.10, *decrease* 747.1

shrinking violet *figurative usage* 42.8, *humble person* 298.7

shrink-wrap *cooking equipment* 91.6, *enclosing thing* 619.3

shrink-wrapped *invulnerable* 810.18

shrive *perform rites* 85.18, *forgive* 312.8

shrivel *age* 27.16, *waste away* 96.20, *afflict* 117.16, *dry up* 560.21, *contract* 582.12, *become smaller* 582.14, *decrease* 747.7, *disintegrate* 808.15

shriveled *infertile* 23.7, *aged* 27.15, *dried-up* 560.9, *little* 580.7, *shortened* 582.8, *emaciated* 595.10

shriveled up *shortened* 582.8

shriveling *shortening* 582.2, *contracting* 582.10

shrivel up *heat* 217.17, *become smaller* 582.14

shriven *forgiven* 312.5

Shropshire Breeds of Sheep 16

shroud *funeral object* 31.6, *graveclothes* 100.25, *clothe* 100.43, *conceal* 181.12, *that which makes invisible* 245.2, *shade maker* 247.4, *make dark* 247.10, *make dim* 248.8, *body covering* 618.3, *hide* 613.27, *wrap* 613.29, *enclosing thing* 619.3, *tackle* 754.6, *protect* 810.21

shrouded *protected* 613.20

shrouded in mystery *unintelligible* 364.4, *unexplained* 364.6

shroud in mystery *make unintelligible* 364.13

shroud knot Knots, Bends, Hitches, Splices 754

shrouds *sailboat parts and accessories* 150.4

Shrove Tuesday Christian Holy Days and Seasons 85

shrub *garden plant* 17.10, *plant* 41.2, *tree* 43.1

shrubbery *ornamental garden* 17.3

shrubby *botanical* 17.15, *treelike* 43.10

shrug *gesture* 183.17

shrugging off *downplaying* 195.6

shrug off *play down* 195.17, *be indifferent* 289.12, *underestimate* 344.5, *exempt oneself* 434.12, *think unimportant* 800.19

shrug one's shoulders *be ignorant* 349.8, *acquiesce* 421.5

shrunk *little* 580.7, *smaller* 582.7

shrunken *little* 580.7, *smaller* 582.7

shrunkenness *littleness* 580.1, *contraction* 582.1

Shu Ching *other text* 81.19

shuck *fruit structure* 44.3, *casing* 613.9, *depilate* 614.20

shucked *shed* 614.14

shucking *peeling* 614.6

shudder *be cold* 218.13, *be fearful* 283.15, *react against* 291.15, *shake* 684.7, 684.24, *jolt* 684.23

shudder at *hate* 300.11

shuddering *shaking* 684.6, *shaky* 684.18

shuffle *dance* 135.7, *play cards* 168.7, *gesture* 183.17, *sophism* 330.2, *quibble* 330.13, *sway* 378.12, *equivocate* 380.8, *substitution* 672.1, *substitute* 672.5, *exchange* 673.1, 673.5, *bodily movement* 677.11, *walk* 677.17, *transfer* 685.8, *slow motion* 693.3, *shove aside* 698.23, *mix* 732.12, *mix up* 751.13, *disorder* 766.17

shuffle along *move slowly* 693.11

shuffled *complicated* 751.10, *disordered* 766.9

shuffle dancing Dancing Types 135

shuffle off *retreat* 386.22

shuffler *dancer* 135.4

shuffling *card playing* 168.1, *card-playing* 168.6, *quibbling* 330.4, 330.9, *evasion* 380.2, *equivocal* 380.5, *exchange* 673.1, *slow* 693.7

shul [Yiddish] *place of worship* 83.8

Shumen Breeds of Sheep 16

shun 386.14; *conceal oneself* 181.15, *react against* 291.15, *exclude* 383.11, 764.7, *ignore* 409.11, *ostracize* 709.17

shun alcohol *abstain* 455.11

shun company *be unsocial* 409.10

shunned *rejected* 383.6, *lonely* 409.8, *excluded* 764.6

shunning *rejecting* 383.2, *avoidance* 386.1, *abstaining* 386.11, *ostracism* 709.3, *exclusiveness* 764.4

shunt *displacement* 574.1, *displace* 574.15, *take away* 685.12, *travel by train* 688.9, *propel* 696.15, *shove aside* 698.23

shunted *displaced* 574.8

shunter [Brit] *train* 688.4

shun the limelight *escape notice* 403.14

shunting engine *train* 688.4

shush *hiss* 237.1, 237.3

shut *closed* 584.7, *close* 584.12, 637.10, *enclose* 619.6

shutdown *unemployment* 415.2, *closure* 584.1, 637.4, *stop* 668.2, *discontinuance* 846.4, *failed* 846.10

shut down *make inactive* 415.16, *closed down* 584.10, *close down* 584.15, *closed* 637.6, *close* 637.10, *stopped* 668.7, *stop work* 668.11, *cease* 773.20, *discontinuance* 846.4, *failed* 846.10, *discontinue* 846.14

shuteye [Inf] *sleep* 415.5, *ease* 819.1

shut in *imprisoned* 55.9, *arrest* 55.12, *sick* 114.24, *enclose* 584.16, 619.6

shut-in *sick person* 114.22, *housebound* 415.9, *closed-in person* 584.6, *enclosed* 619.4, *sedentary person* 678.3, *detained* 830.11

shut off *be insensible* 213.7

shut oneself off *be insensible* 213.7

shut oneself up *be unsocial* 409.10

shut one's eyes to *be blind to* 243.19

shut one's trap *or* **face** [Inf] *be silent* 181.16

shutout *pitching terms* 147.5, *debarment* 604.5, *victory* 845.4

shut out *exclude* 409.12, 764.7, *debarment* 604.5, *debar* 604.17, *excluded* 764.6

shutter *exposure equipment* 132.12, *that which makes invisible* 245.2, *make dark* 247.10, *cover* 613.2, *protection from the weather* 810.9

shutterbug [Inf] *photographer* 132.23

shutter priority *exposure equipment* 132.12

shutter release *exposure equipment* 132.12

shutters *shade maker* 247.4

shutter speed *exposure equipment* 132.12

shut the box Board and Table Games 167

shut the door on *exclude* 409.12, 764.7, *prohibit* 503.8

shutting *closure* 637.4

shutting down *stop* 668.2

shutting in *arrest* 55.5

shuttle *spacecraft* 7.28, *fabric-handling tool* 130.12, *badminton terms* 165.11, *weaving* 609.2, *be regular* 663.10, *be changeable* 666.5, *swing* 671.4, 671.12, *oscillator* 683.7, *oscillate* 683.12

shuttlecock *badminton terms* 165.11, *oscillator* 683.7, *oscillate* 683.12

shuttle movement *frequency* 663.2

shuttlewise *to and fro* 683.16

shuttling *swing* 671.4, *oscillation* 683.1

shut up *exclude* 409.12, *enclosed* 584.11, *close* 584.12, *enclose* 584.16

shut up! *hush!* 231.6

shut-up *closed* 584.7

shut up shop *stop work* 668.11, *cease* 773.20

Shuwa Breeds of Cattle 16

shy 386.17, 403.8, 409.7; *taciturn* 208.4, *cowardly* 285.4, *be surprised* 292.12, *unenthusiastic* 375.10, *hesitate* 378.10, *avoiding* 386.9, *unsociable* 409.6, *stone* 418.23, *reserved* 585.7, *inward* 611.12, *shrink back* 680.20, *throw* 696.4, 696.17, *sidestep* 698.22, *naive* 821.3, *inhibitive* 826.14, *be inhibited* 826.20, *self-restrained* 830.10

shy away *oppose* 375.13, *shy* 386.17, *refuse* 506.8, *shrink back* 680.20, *be safe* 810.20

Shylock *lender* 475.3

shyly 386.25, 403.16; *cowardly* 285.9, *unsocially* 409.13, *reservedly* 585.15, *inhibitively* 826.24, *self-restrainedly* 830.19

shyness 386.3, 403.3, 409.2; *taciturnity* 208.1, *dissociation* 375.4, *defensiveness* 419.4, *reserve* 585.4, *inwardness* 611.5, *inhibition* 826.9, *self-restraint* 830.4, *confusion* 841.4

shy of *incomplete* 762.5

shy off *sidestep* 698.22

shyster [Inf] *lawyer* 54.5, *deceiver* 193.8

SI *measuring system* 589.4, *metrical* 589.15

sialic *solid-earth* 8.55

sialogogic *inducing secretion* 24.6

sialoid *of a secretion* 24.5

sialorrhea *saliva* 25.9

Siamese Breeds of Cats 35

Siamese twin *look-alike* 730.4

Siamese twins *twin* 789.5

sib *family* 65.1

Siberia *cold place* 218.7, *distant place* 585.3

Siberian *cool* 9.49, Breeds of Cattle 16, Breeds of Cats 35, *frozen* 218.10

Siberian husky Breeds of Dogs 35

sibilance *or* **sibilancy** *hiss* 237.1

sibilant *spoken letter* 5.15, *voiced* 5.37, *inarticulate* 206.6, *hissing* 237.2

sibilantly 237.4

sibilate *speak in a particular way* 205.18, *hiss* 237.3

sibilation *speech defect* 206.2, *hiss* 237.1

sibling *family member* 65.2

sibyl *diviner* 86.14, *intuitive person* 320.5, *wise person* 352.3, *oracle* 358.8

sibyllic *predicting* 358.11

sibylline *divinatory* 86.18, *predicting* 358.11

sibylline books *divination* 86.5

siccant *drying* 560.15

siccative *material* 143.9, *dryer* 560.5, *drying* 560.15

siccity *dryness* 560.1

Sicilian Breeds of Sheep 16

Sicilian Barbary Breeds of Sheep 16

Sicilian Vespers *slaughter* 30.5

Sicily Islands 572

sick 114.24, 260.12; *mentally ill* 110.11, *vomiting* 709.27

sick and tired of *displeased* 291.6, *bored* 296.5

sicken *overindulge* 99.10, *be unhealthy* 114.29, *displease* 272.8, *dissatisfy* 274.6, *cause dislike* 291.16, *be weak* 517.12, *be repulsive* 701.10, *deteriorate* 808.14

sickened *antipathetic* 291.7

sickening *immoderate* 99.6, *unpleasant* 272.6, *detested* 291.11, *repulsive* 701.4, *expulsive* 709.11

sickeningly *distastefully* 291.19

sickie [Inf] *insane person* 110.5

sickle *farm tool* 16.5, *personifications and symbols* 29.4, *garden tool* 103.4, *sharp-edged thing* 549.6, *use a sharp tool* 549.17

sick leave *bargaining terms* 57.10, *permit* 502.3, *leave of absence* 576.4

sickle cell anemia *blood disease* 114.14

sickliness *ill health* 114.1, *poor health* 517.3

sick list *list of names* 785.7

sickly *unhealthy* 114.23, *sweet* 222.5, *drained of color* 252.6, *greenly* 260.15, *ill* 517.8

sickly hue *face color* 251.9

sickly person *powerless person* 515.5

sickly-sweet *sweet* 222.5

sickly sweetness *sweetness* 222.1

sick mind *insanity* 110.1

sickness *ill health* 114.1, *illness* 114.2, *vomiting* 709.7

sickness benefit *social assistance* 825.4

sicko [Inf] *insane person* 110.5

sick of *displeased* 291.6, *bored* 296.5

sick person 114.22; *patient* 107.25, *infectious person* 114.9, *powerless person* 515.5, *weak person* 517.4

sick room *school place* 48.16

sick unto death *dying* 29.12

sick up [Brit inf] *vomit* 709.27

sic transit gloria mundi [L] *transiently* 643.8

siddur [Heb] *ritual manual* 85.11

side 623.1, 623.6, 623.8; *line* 6.35, *surface* 6.36, *party* 59.3, *type of chair* 101.4, *type of table* 101.5, *sportsman* 145.4, *external appearance* 264.5, *situation* 573.1, *side with* 623.10

sidebar *news story* 171.3, *part of writing* 760.6

sideboard *cabinet* 101.8

sideboards *hockey areas* 158.2

side boundary line *badminton terms* 165.11

sideburns *body covering* 19.4, *coiffure* 530.8, *side* 623.1

side by side *near* 586.6, *beside* 586.20, *in parallel* 606.9, *laterally* 623.11, *cohesively* 755.11, *hand in hand* 794.21

side-by-side *hunting* 160.11, *side* 623.6, *adhesive* 755.5

side-by-side double-barreled shotgun *hunting equipment* 160.4

sidecar racing Sporting Activities 145

side chain *protein* 12.9

sidecut *ski equipment* 162.10

sided 623.7

side direction 623.2

side dish 90.15, 794.11; *dish* 90.7, *course* 92.12

sidedness *side* 623.1

side door *side* 623.1, *access* 691.3, *means of entry* 706.6

side drum Musical Instruments 142

side effect *effect* 676.1, *visible effect* 676.2, *additional item* 748.3

side elevation *side* 623.1

side entrance *side* 623.1

side horse Sporting Activities 145, *pommel horse* 157.7

side issue *additional item* 748.3

side judge *football player* 155.15

sidekick *friend* 62.2, *supporter* 605.9, *helper* 825.12, *subordinate* 832.3

side ladder *ladder* 713.10

sidelight *safety light* 246.7

sideline *basketball court* 148.3, *stadium* 155.3, *amusement* 167.7, *edge* 618.1, *edging* 618.5

sideline crew *football player* 155.15

sidelong *watchfully* 242.29, *oblique* 607.6, *indirect* 607.8, *obliquely* 607.13

sidelong look *look* 242.7

side of the face *side* 623.1

side path *passage* 691.5

side reaction *chemical reaction* 11.8

sidereal *astronomical* 7.33

sidereally *astronomically* 7.36

sidereal time *time zone* 646.5

siderite *meteor* 7.21, *magnet* 700.3

siderodromophobia Phobias 283

siderolite *meteor* 7.21

sideromancer *diviner* 86.14

sideromancy *divination* 86.5

siderophobia Phobias 283

sidesaddle *riding equipment* 159.9

side scene *stage set* 136.19

side sewing *or* **side wiring** *bookbinding* 174.11

sideshow *circus* 138.2, *secondary matter* 800.6

sideslip *skiing techniques* 162.5, *ski*

162.35, *miscellaneous automotive terms* 687.14, *flight maneuver* 689.6, *maneuver* 689.14, *deviating motion* 698.3, *slide* 698.24, 714.17
sideslipping *snowboarding* 162.11, *snowplow* 162.29
sidespin *golf shots* 156.4
side-splitting *humorous* 277.9, *ridiculous* 368.5
sidestep 698.22, *be equivocal* 380.7, *be evasive* 386.20, *be irresolute* 461.8, *move sideways* 623.9
side step *skiing techniques* 162.5, *cross-country techniques* 162.8, *deviating motion* 698.3
sidestepper *avoider* 386.8
sidestepping *snowplow* 162.29, *evasiveness* 386.6
sidestroke *swimming techniques* 164.2, *swimming rescue* 164.5
side to side *to and fro* 683.16
sidetrack *circumlocution* 199.2, *track* 688.2, *junction* 691.9, *sidestep* 698.22, *shove aside* 698.23
sidetracked *circumlocutory* 199.4
side view *side* 623.1
sidewalk *paving* 613.14, *side* 623.1, *passage* 691.5
sideward *laterally* 623.11, *directional* 677.13
sideward motion *movement* 677.3
sideways *watchfully* 242.29, *breadthways* 592.16, *oblique* 607.6, *obliquely* 607.13, *laterally* 623.11, *directional* 677.13, *indirectly* 698.28
sideways look *look* 242.7
sideways *or* **sidewise motion** *movement* 677.3
side whiskers *side* 623.1
sidewise *breadthways* 592.16, *laterally* 623.11, *directional* 677.13, *indirectly* 698.28
side with 382.15, 623.10; *form an alliance* 735.25, *back* 825.28
siding *wood* 131.3, *wall covering* 613.12, *side* 623.1, *track* 688.2, *junction* 691.9
sidle *move sideways* 623.9, *sidestep* 698.22
siege *Collective Names* 59, *military attack* 418.2, *detention* 830.5, *detain* 830.16
siege cap *historic armor* 419.8
siegecraft *art of war* 76.16
sieges *warfare* 76.3
siemens *Scientific and Technical Units* 589
Siena Belted *Breeds of Pigs* 16
sierra *rough thing* 544.2, *mountain* 569.1, *mountain range* 569.3
Sierra de Guadarrama *Mountains and Hills* 569
Sierra Leone *Countries* 566
Sierra Madre *Mountains and Hills* 569
Sierra Morena Range *Mountains and Hills* 569
Sierra Nevada Range *Mountains and Hills* 569
Sierras, the *regions of the United States* 564.7
siesta *sleep* 415.5, *afternoon* 655.5
sieve *cooking equipment* 91.6, *cleaning tool* 111.10, *purify* 111.19, *porosity* 583.5, *provide passage for* 583.18, *categorize* 767.21
sievelike *holed* 583.12
sievert *Scientific and Technical Units* 589
sift *purify* 111.19, *choose* 382.14,

systematize 765.19, *categorize* 767.21
sifted *pulverized* 553.20, *categorized* 767.15
sifter *mixer* 751.7
sifting *categorization* 767.5
sifting out *selecting* 382.4
sift out *categorize* 767.21
sift together *mix* 751.12
sigh *blow* 9.53, *gesture* 183.5, 183.17, *speak in a particular way* 205.18, *undercurrent of sound* 233.3, *sound faint* 233.8, *cry of sorrow* 239.6, *cry* 239.16, *grieve* 270.7, *lament* 280.2, *sign of sullenness* 304.2, *be sullen* 304.12
sighing *gestural* 183.13, *nonresonant* 233.7, *crying* 239.11
sight *life function* 28.6, *sensation* 212.1, *vision* 242.1, *view* 242.8, *see* 242.20, *spectacle* 264.6, *marvel* 294.3, *discovery* 345.1, *discover* 345.11, *ugly thing* 531.2, *approach* 704.15
sight defect 243.2
sighted *sensory* 19.22, *seeing* 242.17
sight for sore eyes *view* 242.8, *beautiful thing* 529.3
sight hole *place for viewing* 242.13
sighthound *Breeds of Dogs* 35
sight in *hunt* 160.12
sighting *discovery* 345.1
sighting-in *hunting* 160.2
sight land *sail* 690.16
sightless *blind* 243.11
sightlessness *blindness* 243.3
sightline *visibility* 244.1
sightliness *attractiveness* 529.2
sightly *attractive* 529.8
sight on *aim* 697.14
sight quarry *hunt* 160.12
sightscreen *visual aid* 242.14
sightsee *see* 242.20, *be curious* 321.7, *travel* 686.11
sightseeing *curious* 321.5, *travel* 686.5, *traveling* 686.9
sightseer *observer* 242.15, *curious person* 321.3, *traveler* 686.6
sight unseen *invisibly* 245.8
sigil *means of identification* 184.3
sigillary *identified* 184.9
sign 183.1, 183.19; *artificial language* 5.9, *written letter* 5.14, *word* 5.43, *symptom* 114.3, *signal* 183.6, *gesture* 183.17, *means of identification* 184.3, *identify oneself* 184.12, *voiceless speech* 206.4, *have difficulty speaking* 206.9, *be deaf* 229.8, *that which makes visible* 244.4, *make visible* 244.9, *verify* 336.8, *indication* 339.3, *omen* 358.5, *command* 425.1, *number* 783.1, *concomitant* 794.4, *forewarning* 814.2, *manifestation* 843.2, *showplace* 843.4
sign a confession *convict* 54.33
sign a deal *contract* 462.11
sign a decree *command* 425.10
signal 183.6, 183.18, 646.9; *nonstandard language* 5.7, *signaling* 169.9, *communicate* 169.18, *inside information* 170.4, *tip* 170.14, *sign* 183.1, 183.19, *voiceless speech* 206.4, *make visible* 244.9, *command* 425.1, 425.10, *track* 688.2, *notable* 799.11, *forewarning* 814.2, *manifestation* 843.2, *identifiable* 843.10
signal box *track* 688.2
signal-caller [Inf] *offense* 155.6
signaled *communicated* 169.15, *accessible* 691.13
signaler *warner* 814.5

signal fire *fire* 246.9
signaling 169.9, 183.14; *communications* 169.1, *signal* 183.6, *signifying* 183.11
signalize *signify* 183.16
signalizing *signifying* 183.11
signal lamp *signal* 183.6
signal light *signal* 183.6
signalman *army combat specialist* 77.16, *railroad worker* 688.7
sign a loan agreement *borrow* 476.10
signal rocket *signal* 183.6
signals *huddle* 155.7
sign an affidavit *attest* 189.22
sign a pact *contract* 459.8, 462.11
sign a petition *petition* 505.11
sign a promissory note *guarantee* 458.13
sign a round robin *petition* 505.11
signatory *identified* 184.9, *verifier* 336.4, *assenter* 346.3, *promise maker* 458.6, *contractor* 459.6
sign a treaty *contract* 459.8, 462.11, *settle* 735.26
sign a truce *make peace* 73.11
signature *written music* 140.1, *bookbinding* 174.11, *sign* 183.1, *personal identification* 184.4, *inscription* 185.4, *name* 202.8, *verification* 336.1, *ratification* 459.4, *promise* 464.2, *permit* 502.3, *original* 737.2, *part of writing* 760.6
signature tune *melody* 140.10
sign away *transfer property* 470.12
signboard *sign* 183.1
signboard alphabet *Children's and Party Games* 167
signed *numerical* 6.68, *identified* 184.9, *clear* 244.6, *agreed* 346.5, *guaranteeing* 458.9, *contractual* 459.7, 462.7
signed agreement *contract* 391.2
signed edition *rare book* 174.2
signed number *number* 6.4
signed on the dotted line *contractual* 459.7, 462.7
signed, sealed, and delivered *contractual* 462.7
signed up *martial* 77.33
signee *promise maker* 458.6
signer *promise maker* 458.6, *contractor* 459.6
signet *means of identification* 184.3, *ratification* 459.4
signet ring *clothing* 184.6
significance 361.2, 676.4; *correlation* 6.58, *seriousness* 200.2, *importance* 278.3, 799.1, *purpose* 327.4, *instrumentality* 511.1, *influence* 512.1, *profundity* 598.5
significance level *hypothesis testing* 6.52
significance test *hypothesis testing* 6.52
significant 361.11, 799.9; *serious* 200.5, *important* 278.6, *purposive* 327.11, *evidential* 339.8, *presageful* 358.13, *meaningful* 361.6, *operative* 509.9, *causal* 511.5, 675.7, *influential* 512.8, *profound* 598.15
significant digits *number system* 6.7
significant figures *number system* 6.7
significant form *treatment* 143.6, *form* 624.1
significantly *indicatively* 183.21, *purposively* 327.20, *as evidence* 339.15, *predictively* 358.16,

meaningfully 361.16, *operationally* 509.13, *instrumentally* 511.9, *influentially* 512.14, *profoundly* 598.27, *causally* 675.12, *importantly* 799.15
significant other *loved one* 299.13
signification *sign* 183.1, *meaning* 361.1
significative *signifying* 183.11, *symbolic* 361.8
signify 183.16; *epitomize* 327.18, *state* 329.13, *predict* 358.14, *mean* 361.13, *specify* 779.18, *be important* 799.13
signifying 183.11; *predicting* 358.11
signify little *be unimportant* 800.18
sign in *get in* 704.17
signing *gesture* 183.5, *gestural* 183.13, *aid to the deaf* 229.3
sign language *artificial language* 5.9, *gesture* 183.5, *articulation* 205.9, *voiceless speech* 206.4, *aid to the deaf* 229.3
sign of alarm *warning signal* 814.3
sign of courtesy 410.5
sign off *withdraw* 705.9
sign of guilt 450.2
sign of illness *symptom* 114.3, *signs* 183.2
sign of irascibility 303.6
sign of irritability 304.4
sign of sullenness 304.2
sign of the cross *Christian rite* 85.5
sign of the times *sign* 183.1, *omen* 358.5, *tendency* 513.1
sign on *enroll* 706.16, *install* 710.15
sign one's name *sign* 183.19
sign on the dotted line *sign* 183.19, *assent to* 346.7, *promise* 458.11, *contract* 459.8, 462.11, *bargain* 480.20, *permit* 502.6
signor [Ital] *male title of address* 32.3
signora [Ital] *female title of address* 33.3
signore [Ital] *male title of address* 32.3
signorina [Ital] *female title of address* 33.3
signorino [Ital] *male title of address* 32.3
sign out *withdraw* 705.9
sign over *transfer property* 470.12
sign painter *painter* 143.7
signpost *guide* 126.6, 697.4, *sign* 183.1, 183.19, *indicator* 183.7, *that which makes visible* 244.4, *make visible* 244.9, *direct* 697.13
signposted *clear* 244.6, *accessible* 691.13, *directed* 697.9
signs 183.2; *confirmation* 840.3
signs of the times *forewarning* 814.2
sign the pledge *give up alcohol* 120.6, *abstain* 455.11
sign up *take charge of* 391.8, *install* 710.15, *be on a list* 785.12
Sikh *other religious member* 81.13
Sikhism *other religions* 81.8
Sikhote Alin Range *Mountains and Hills* 569
silage *animal feed* 16.12, *animal food* 90.2, *storage* 105.6
silaging *cultivation* 16.7
silence 208.2, 231.1, 231.4; *concealment* 181.1, *verbal concealment* 181.3, *secrecy* 182.1, *destroy* 186.10, *strike dumb*

206.10, *muffle* 229.11, *mute* 233.9, *refute* 332.7, *inactivity* 415.1, *overpower* 515.14, *abolish* 523.11, *repose* 678.2, *restrain someone* 830.17

silence! *hush!* 231.6

silenced *speechless* 206.7, *wondering* 294.7

silencer *sound reducer* 233.5

silencing *destruction* 523.1

silent **181.10, 208.5, 231.2;** *secretive* 182.9, *wondering* 294.7, *unsociable* 409.6, *shy* 409.7, *quiescent* 678.6

silent about *excluding* 764.5

silent as the grave *silent* 231.2

silent as the tomb *silent* 231.2

silent auction *sale* 482.2

silently **231.5;** *privately* 181.18, *voicelessly* 206.11, *taciturnly* 208.9, *speculatively* 294.17, *unsocially* 409.13

silent movie *movie type* 137.3

silent partner *nonworker* 415.4, *nonentity* 800.8

silent reproach *show of disapproval* 438.6

silent service *navy* 77.18

Silenus *drunkard* 121.8

silhouette *portrait* 132.5, *drawing* 143.4, *draw* 143.13, *image* 187.3, *dark thing* 247.3, *make dark* 247.10, *black thing* 254.3, *external appearance* 264.5, *present* 264.15, *shape* 617.2, *form* 624.1, 624.9

silica *material* 129.2, *hard substance* 542.3

silicate *mineral types* 8.38

silicle *botanical fruit* 44.2

silicon Chemical Elements and Common Allotropes 11, *essential element* 12.15

silicon chip *circuit* 14.37, *little thing* 580.3

silicon *lubricant* 562.7

silicone rubber *rubber* 546.3

Silicon Valley *regions of the United States* 564.7

silicon wafers *chemical process industries* 14.26

silicosis *respiratory disease* 114.12

silicula *botanical fruit* 44.2

siliqua *botanical fruit* 44.2

silk *spinner* 40.10, Fabrics and Fibers 130, *grain* 552.2

silkaline *or* **silkoline** *or* **silkolene** Fabrics and Fibers 130

silk-cotton tree Trees and Shrubs 43

silken *luscious* 214.8, *smooth* 543.8, 545.4

silk gland *spinner* 40.10

silk hat *hat* 100.32

Silkie Breeds of Fowl 16

silkily *softly* 543.18, *texturally* 552.15

silkiness *smoothness* 543.2, 545.1, *grain* 552.2

silk oak *or* **silky oak** Trees and Shrubs 43

silks *costume* 100.10

silkscreen *design* 133.9

silkscreening *craft* 133.2

silk stockings *legwear* 100.26

silk tree Trees and Shrubs 43

silkworm *worm* 39.14, *larva* 40.9, *spinner* 40.10

silky *smooth* 543.8, 545.4, 552.9

silky oak Trees and Shrubs 43

silky terrier Breeds of Dogs 35

sill *igneous rock* 8.32, *foundation* 601.2

sillily *ridiculously* 368.8

silliness *folly* 353.1

silly *unskillful* 128.4, *unintelligent person* 316.4, *unintelligent* 316.6, *foolish* 353.5, *meaningless* 362.7, *simpleminded* 526.11

silly question *easy question* 333.5

silly season *seasons* 654.2

silly talk *senseless talk* 362.4

silo *farm building* 16.4, *modern missile weapon* 78.4, *storehouse* 105.8, *preserver* 815.9

silt *sediment* 8.29, *soil* 8.42, *mud* 561.8, *transferred thing* 685.6, *residue* 750.2

silt up *shallow* 599.5

silty *earthy* 8.60, *sludgy* 561.18

Silurian Period Geologic Time Intervals 8

silvan *wooded* 43.12

Silver Notable Horses 159

silver Chemical Elements and Common Allotropes 11, *track and field* 166.20, *color* 251.16, *white thing* 253.4, *white* 253.7, *whiten* 253.12, *gray thing* 255.3, *gray* 255.6, 255.9, *money* 484.1, *change* 484.3, *bullion* 484.16

Silver Age Ages, Decades, Eras 641

silver age *historical past* 651.6

silver anniversary *twenty and over* 792.8

silver birch Trees and Shrubs 43

silver bullet *talisman* 86.9

silver coinage *coinage* 484.13

silver cup *insignia* 184.5

silver dollar *US coinage* 484.10

silvered *white* 253.7, *gray* 255.6

silver fir Trees and Shrubs 43

silver frost *frost* 9.25

silver-gray *gray* 255.6

silver halide *emulsion* 132.9

silveriness *whiteness* 253.1

silver inlay *decorative woodwork* 131.2

silver jubilee *anniversary* 405.5

silver lining *hope* 281.1

silver maple Trees and Shrubs 43

silver medal *competition* 166.18, *insignia* 184.5

silver plate *insignia* 184.5, *coating* 613.8

silverpoint drawing *drawing* 143.4

silver print *printing* 132.20

silver screen, the *motion pictures* 137.1

silversmith *artisan* 123.13

Silver Star US Military Medals 58

silver-tongued *articulate* 205.16, *addressing* 209.6

silver-tongued orator *public speaker* 209.5

silverware *tableware* 92.13

silver wedding anniversary *anniversary* 405.5

silvery *white* 253.7, *gray* 255.6

silvical *arboricultural* 43.13

silvicultural *horticultural* 17.14, *arboricultural* 43.13

silviculturally *arboriculturally* 43.16

silviculture *horticulture* 17.1, *plant science* 41.10, *forestry* 43.5

silviculturist *forester* 43.7

simarouba Trees and Shrubs 43

Simbrah Breeds of Cattle 16

Simhath Torah Jewish Holy Days and Seasons 85

simian *primate* 35.32

similar **361.7, 733.7;** *representational* 187.8, *compatible* 462.8, *corresponding* 606.6, *interrelated* 727.7, *correlative*

729.6, *conforming* 735.17, *equal* 740.8

similarity **733.1;** *representation* 187.1, *impression* 264.7, *compatibility* 462.3, 735.4, *correspondence* 606.2, *relatedness* 727.1, *correlation* 729.3, *conformity* 735.7, 781.1

similarly **733.17;** *compatibly* 462.16, *correspondingly* 606.10, *under the circumstances* 726.16, *relevantly* 727.12, *correlatively* 729.12, *conformingly* 735.37, *equally* 740.13

similar triangles *triangle* 6.41

simile *phrasing* 5.25, *literary device* 139.12, *ornament* 532.7, *comparability* 733.2

similitude *transformation* 6.46, *similarity* 733.1, *counterpart* 733.5

simious *primate* 35.32

Simmental Breeds of Cattle 16

simmer *cook* 91.10, *heat* 217.17, *be angry* 302.19, *bubble* 558.24, *be agitated* 684.21

simmer down *ease* 543.15

simmering *heating* 217.12

Simon of Cyrene helping Jesus Stations of the Cross 85

simon-pure *authentic* 721.16

Simon says Children's and Party Games 167

simony *selling* 482.1

simoom Notable Winds 9

simpatico *friendly* 62.5

simple **195.10, 363.6, 526.7;** *universal* 6.67, *of leaves* 41.18, *fit for habitation* 60.19, *medicine* 115.2, *ingenuous* 191.6, *clear* 196.2, *soft-hued* 251.13, *humble* 298.8, *lacking intellect* 316.5, *intellectually subnormal* 316.7, *ignorant* 349.5, *foolish* 353.5, *unprocessed* 389.10, *familiar* 407.8, *unadorned* 424.7, *naive* 449.9, 821.3, *elegant* 527.3, *straightforward* 630.9, *easy* 823.9

simple as ABC *easy* 823.9

simple eloquence *clarity* 363.2

simple fraction *division* 6.16, *fraction* 787.1

simple fruit *botanical fruit* 44.2

simple glyceride *fat* 12.7

simple harmonic motion *frequency* 10.6, *oscillation* 683.1

simple-hearted *natural* 526.10

simple interest *profit* 467.6, *interest* 488.4

simple language *clarity* 363.2

simple life *self-restraint* 455.1

simple lipid *fat* 12.7

simple machine 14.6

simple melody *melody* 140.10

simpleminded **526.11;** *lacking intellect* 316.5, *intellectually subnormal* 316.7, *naive* 821.3

simplemindedly *unintelligently* 316.9

simplemindedness *lack of intellect* 316.1, *naïveté* 821.1

simpleness *ingenuousness* 191.3, *simplicity* 195.4, 526.1, 823.2

simple picture *outline* 617.1

simple reflex *conditioning* 108.24

Simple Simon *unintelligent person* 316.4, *simpleton* 526.5

simple soul *naive person* 821.2

simple sugar *saccharide* 12.4

simpleton *unintelligent person* 316.4, *ignorant person* 349.4, *foolish person* 353.3, *naive person* 821.2

simple truth *the truth* 721.3

simple twist of the wrist *easy thing* 823.6

simplex *geometric figure* 6.39

simplicity **195.4, 526.1, 823.2;** *ingenuousness* 191.3, *clarity* 196.1, 363.2, *humility* 298.1, *familiarity* 407.3, *unadornment* 424.3, *naïveté* 449.4, 821.1, *elegance* 527.1, *straightforwardness* 630.3

simplification **526.6;** *evaluation* 6.22, *clarity* 363.2, *interpretation* 365.1, *translation* 365.4, *rearrangement* 767.4, *easing* 823.7

simplified *simple* 363.6, *interpreted* 365.9, *rearranged* 767.14, *made easy* 823.11

simplifier *interpreter* 365.6

simplify *manipulate* 6.87, *make comprehensible* 363.8, *interpret* 365.12, *translate* 365.16, *make simple* 526.12, *rearrange* 767.20, *make easy* 823.15

simplifying *easing* 823.7

simplistic *simple* 526.7

simplistically *easily* 823.19

simply **195.19, 526.14;** *commonly* 71.4, *ingenuously* 191.11, *clearly* 196.4, *humbly* 298.22, *intelligibly* 363.13, *informally* 407.11, *plainly* 424.12, *naively* 449.15, *gracefully* 527.8, *straightforwardly* 630.17, *once* 788.23, *easily* 823.19

Simpson Deserts 572

Simpson's rule Mathematical Concepts 6

SIMULA Programming Languages 15

simulacrum *illusion* 720.2, *simulation* 733.4

simulate **733.16;** *process* 14.50, *rehearse* 335.12, *fabricate* 720.17

simulated **733.11;** *experimental* 335.8, *imaginary* 360.12, *artificial* 720.12

simulation **733.4;** *theory* 6.62, *artificiality* 720.7, *imitation* 736.1, *copy* 736.2

simulcast *broadcast material* 172.9, *broadcast* 172.13

simultaneity *same time* 649.1, *synchronism* 794.2

simultaneous **649.4;** *same* 730.7, *concurrent* 794.13

simultaneous equations *equation* 6.25

simultaneously **649.8;** *identically* 730.18, *concurrently* 794.22

simultaneousness *sameness* 730.1

simurg Legendary Creatures 360

sin **430.22, 450.3, 450.11;** *lawbreaking* 53.14, Phobias 283, *errancy* 351.7, *transgress* 351.16, *disobedience* 427.1, *disobey* 427.12, *wrongdoing* 430.7, *be immoral* 432.13, *evil* 446.1, *be evil* 446.10, *wickedness* 448.1, *iniquity* 448.3, *be wicked* 448.13

sin against *sin* 430.22

Sinai Deserts 572

sin' al fin Musical Terms and Expression Marks 140

sin' al segno Musical Terms and Expression Marks 140

since Adam was a lad *anciently* 653.18

since before the Flood *anciently* 653.18

since God knows when *anciently* 653.18

sincere *truthful* 191.4, *earnest* 278.5, *steady* 376.8, *open* 583.13, *deep-seated* 598.17, *authentic* 737.6, *naive* 821.3

sincerely *truthfully* 191.9, *earnestly*

278.10, *candidly* 583.23, *with deep feeling* 598.29, *naively* 821.5

sincere thanks *thanks* 310.2

sincerity *truthfulness* 191.1, *earnestness* 278.2, *seriousness* 376.3, *openness* 583.7, *depth of feeling* 598.7, *naiveté* 821.1

since the big bang *anciently* 653.18

since the world was new *anciently* 653.18

since the world was young *anciently* 653.18

since the year one *anciently* 653.18

sine (sin) *trigonometric function* 6.50

sinecure *leisure* 125.1, *unemployment* 413.5, *easy thing* 823.6

sinecurist *nonworker* 415.4

sine curve *curve* 6.38

sine qua non *necessity* 95.1, *basis for negotiations* 460.2, *chief thing* 799.3

sinew *muscles* 19.3, *vigor* 514.2

sine wave *wave form* 10.13, *curved thing* 629.3, *wave* 683.4

sinews *physical strength* 516.3, *stalwartness* 547.3

sinewy *bodily* 19.18, *physically strong* 516.10, *stalwart* 547.10

sinfonietta *instrumental group* 141.3

sinful 450.8; *errant* 351.12, *immoral* 430.11, *evil* 446.7, *wicked* 448.9

sinfully *immorally* 430.27, 432.18, *evilly* 446.12, *wickedly* 448.15

sinfulness *disobedience* 427.1, *wickedness* 448.1, *sin* 450.3

sinful ways *wickedness* 448.1

sing 141.16; *entertain* 138.16, *make a bird sound* 240.8, *show joy* 269.10

sing [Inf] *inform on* 170.13, *tell on* 180.10, *testify* 336.10, *accuse* 442.8

singable *melodious* 140.26

sing a different tune *change* 665.14

Singapore *Countries* 566, *Islands* 572

Singapura *Breeds of Cats* 35

sing a requiem *pay one's last respects* 31.12

singe *burn* 217.18, *blacken* 254.11, *brown* 256.7

singed *heated* 217.15, *blackened* 254.7, *browned* 256.6

singer 141.4; *artistic worker* 123.12, *musician* 141.1

sing for one's supper *be poor* 486.14

sing Happy Birthday *congratulate* 405.12

sing hymns *follow rites* 85.19

singing 85.16, 240.5; *avian* 36.19, *musical* 141.11, *Hobbies and Pastimes* 167

singing group 141.6

single 788.16; *single person* 67.5, 788.7, *celibate* 67.6, *type of bed* 101.9, *batting terms* 147.6, *play baseball* 147.9, *rowing* 150.27, *golf* 156.1, *recording* 185.6, *whole* 759.6, *special* 779.10, *one* 788.1, 788.10, *naive* 821.3

single-action *fishing* 154.13

single-action reel *fishing tackle* 154.7

single aspect *outline* 617.1

single-barreled *hunting* 160.11

single-barreled single-shot shotgun *hunting equipment* 160.4

single-bladed *canoeing* 150.26

single-bladed paddle *canoe parts* 150.10

single-blade race *canoe racing* 150.12

single blessedness *celibacy* 67.1

single-blind experiment *or trial rehearsal* 335.2

single bond *chemical bond* 11.6

single-breasted *tailored* 100.41

single-breasted suit *suit* 100.16

single-celled *cellular* 13.30

single-celled invertebrate *invertebrate* 39.1

single combat *duel* 422.12

single *or* **unmarried** *or* **unwed condition** *or* **state** *celibacy* 67.1

single coverage *defense* 155.9

single-crust pie *pie* 90.38

single crystal *crystal* 11.14

single-decker *bus* 687.7

single entry *accounts* 493.4

single-foot *slow motion* 693.3

single girl *single woman* 33.5, *single person* 67.5

single-handed *sailing* 150.25, *fishing* 154.13, *solo* 788.14

single-handedly *alone* 788.20

single-handed racing *competitive sailing* 150.6

single-handed rod *fishing tackle* 154.7

single-hearted *naive* 821.3

single instance *item* 788.2

single kayak (K-1) race *canoe racing* 150.12

single knot *Knots, Bends, Hitches, Splices* 754

single-lane road *road attribute* 687.3

single-lens reflex (SLR) *camera* 132.10

single man 32.5

single man *or* **woman** *single person* 67.5

single market *free market* 483.4

single meaning *comprehensibility* 361.3

single-minded *diligent* 323.7, *willful* 372.8, *resolute* 376.7, *committed* 377.7, *determined* 379.7, *mentally tough* 547.12

single-mindedly 547.19; *resolutely* 376.15

single-mindedness *diligence* 323.4, *willfulness* 372.3, *resolution* 376.1, *commitment* 377.2, *determination* 379.2, *mental toughness* 547.5

single mother *single woman* 33.5

singleness 788.6; *celibacy* 67.1, *unsociability* 409.1, *oneness* 788.3, *independence* 829.5

singleness of purpose *commitment* 377.2

single-oar *rowing* 150.27

single-oar rowing *rowing* 150.14

single out 788.19; *choose* 382.14, *set apart* 753.17

single-paddle *canoeing* 150.26

single parent *single person* 788.7

single person 67.5, 788.7

single-point tool *machine tool* 14.9

single quotation *Punctuation Marks* 5

single rhyme *rhyme* 139.11

singles *green bowling* 151.3, *bowls* 151.7, *tennis terms* 165.5, *forehand* 165.12

single sculling *rowing* 150.14

single-sex school *type of school* 48.12

single-shot *hunting* 160.11

single-shot repeater *firearm* 78.7

single-shot rifle *hunting equipment* 160.4

single-sided *snowplow* 162.29

single-sided skating *ski race* 162.4

singles match *green bowling* 151.3

singles player *tennis participant* 165.6

singles sideline *tennis court* 165.3

singlestick *fencing* 153.1, *duel* 422.12

single-story *manorial* 60.21, *low* 597.10

single-support phase *hammer throwing* 166.14

single tenoner *woodworking tool* 131.6

singleton *one* 788.1

single track *narrow place* 593.2, *road* 687.2

single-track *narrow* 593.8, *rail* 688.8

single-use *impermanent* 643.5

single voice *assent* 346.1

single-wing formation *offense* 155.6

single woman 33.5

sing like a bird *make a bird sound* 240.8

singling out *selecting* 382.4

sing low *sound faint* 233.8

singly *celibately* 67.12, *separately* 753.22, *specifically* 779.22, *one by one* 788.21

sing out *speak in a particular way* 205.18

sing praises *worship* 83.15

sing softly *sound faint* 233.8

singsong *unmelodious* 241.5, *boringness* 296.2, *boring* 296.6, *monotonous* 797.12

singspiel *musical drama* 136.5

sing the blues *lament* 280.7

sing the praises of *cheer* 239.15, *fete* 279.6, *congratulate* 405.12, *praise* 435.15, 437.16

sing the same old song *harp* 797.17

sing together *sing* 141.16, *synchronize* 649.7

singular 788.13; *grammatical term* 5.29, *of grammar* 5.41, *Collective Names* 59, *wondrous* 294.9, *quintessential* 723.8, *nonconforming* 728.10, *nonuniform* 734.5, *excellent* 744.14, *special* 779.10, *unusual* 782.15

singularity 788.4; *stellar evolution* 7.10, *nonconformity* 728.4, *nonuniformity* 734.2, *special feature* 779.4, *unusualness* 782.4

singularly *grammatically* 5.48, *wondrously* 294.18, *individualistically* 728.20, *nonuniformly* 734.11, *supremely* 744.23, *characteristically* 779.20, *unconformably* 782.21

Sinhala *Breeds of Cattle* 16

sinister *Heraldic Terms* 184, *presageful* 358.13, *evil* 446.7, *adverse* 848.10

sinisterly *evilly* 446.12, *adversely* 848.16

sinister side *laterality* 623.3

sinistral *sided* 623.7

sinistrally *laterally* 623.11

sinistrophobia *Phobias* 283

sink *age* 27.16, *be unhealthy* 114.29, *darkroom equipment*

132.21, *be immoral* 432.13, *wicked place* 448.8, *be unable to pay* 490.11, *ruin* 523.15, *be destroyed* 523.17, *be heavy* 538.12, *basin* 578.12, *descend* 597.22, *diminish* 597.24, *deepen* 598.21, *be concave* 635.6, *convert* 670.11, *be in motion* 677.14, *bring down* 716.14, *become inferior* 745.11, *decrease* 747.7, *deteriorate* 808.14, *be fatigued* 820.5, *decline* 846.16, *be in trouble* 848.13, *cause adversity* 848.15

sinkable *descending* 714.9

sinkage 714.2; *displacement* 538.3, *deepening* 598.4

sink a mineshaft *hole* 583.17

sink a shaft *make concave* 635.7

sink below the horizon *disappear* 265.5

sink down *descend* 714.12

sinker *sailboard parts* 150.20, *windsurfing* 150.28, *fishing tackle* 154.7, *weight* 538.8

sinker [Inf] *cake* 90.36

sinkhole *groundwater* 8.11, *wicked place* 448.8, *depression* 716.4

Sinkiang Finewool *Breeds of Sheep* 16

sink in *be intelligible* 363.10

sinking *aging* 27.13, *dying* 29.12, *fishing* 154.13, *ruin* 523.4, *descent* 597.4, *descending* 597.13, 714.9, *diminishing* 597.16, *deepening* 598.3, 598.14, *concavity* 635.1, *descending motion* 677.6, *directional* 677.13, *submergence* 716.3, *decline* 747.4, *decreasing* 747.5

sinking fast *destroyed* 523.9

sinking fund *finance* 457.1

sinking plug *bait* 154.6

sinking stomach *symptoms of fear* 283.3

sink into *fall into* 706.15

sink into oblivion *be forgotten* 355.12

sink into obscurity *follow* 745.12

sink into silence *sound faint* 233.8

sink low *become inferior* 745.11

sink money *expend* 491.11

sink of corruption *wicked place* 448.8

sink one's capital in *finance* 457.7, *speculate* 480.19

sink one's money in *buy in* 481.13

sink one's teeth into *eat well* 92.23

sink or swim *hold out* 377.13

sink together *work together* 827.14

sink to the bottom *deepen* 598.21, *fail* 714.18

sink without a trace *destroy* 186.10, *become invisible* 245.6, *disappear* 265.5, *be forgotten* 355.12, *be destroyed* 523.17, *become inferior* 745.11

sinless *pure* 431.11, *virtuous* 447.5, *incorrupt* 449.7, *blameless* 805.12

sinlessly *virtuously* 447.9

sinlessness *purity* 431.4, *virtue* 447.1, *incorruption* 449.2

sinner *wrongdoer* 430.8, *evil person* 446.3, *villain* 448.5, *loser* 468.8

Sinn Fein *Political Parties* 50

sinning *offending* 53.25, *disobedient* 427.10, *wicked* 448.9, *sin* 450.3

sino *Musical Terms and Expression Marks* 140

sin of omission *sin* 450.3

Sino-Japanese Wars *Major Wars* 76

Sinope Planets and Their Satellites 7

Sinophobia Phobias 283

Sino-Tibetan *language family* 5.12

sinter *extract* 11.41, *transferred thing* 685.6

sinuosity *curvature* 629.2

sinuous *snakelike* 37.13, *rounded* 629.5, *convolutional* 632.4, *waving* 683.11

sinuously *curvedly* 629.7, *circularly* 632.8

sinuousness *convolution* 632.1

sinusitis *respiratory disease* 114.12

sinusoid *curve* 6.38

sinusoidal *cyclic* 6.82, *curved* 629.4, *waving* 683.11

sinusoidally *curvedly* 629.7

sinusoidal wave *wave form* 10.13

sip *size of drink* 93.3, *drink* 93.19

siphon *transfer* 685.8, *draw off* 711.16

siphonaceous *algal* 47.20

siphonapteran *insectile* 40.11

siphoning *drawing off* 711.4

siphon off *void* 709.23, *draw off* 711.16

sipper *drinker* 93.16

sipping *drinking* 93.1

Sir *male title of address* 32.3, *honorific* 72.5

sir *male title of address* 32.3, *title of respect* 72.7

Sir Barton Notable Horses 159

sire *propagator* 21.7, *propagate* 21.15, *horse* 159.1, *first cause* 675.6, *cause* 675.8, *produce* 771.34

siren *loose woman* 33.6, *witch* 86.15, *tempter* 178.10, *signal* 183.6, 646.9, *burst of sound* 232.4, *lover* 299.11, Legendary Creatures 360, *motivator* 508.6, *legendary sea being* 571.4, *charmer* 700.6, *danger signal* 811.5

Sirenia *marine mammal* 35.12

sirenian *marine mammal* 35.12, *cetacean* 35.27

siren song *enticement* 178.3, *lure* 700.5

Siret Rivers 570

Sir Galahad *chaste person* 431.6

Siri Breeds of Cattle 16

siring *propagation* 21.4

sirloin *beef* 90.24

sirocco Notable Winds 9, *natural violence* 520.3

Sir Prize Apple Varieties 44

Sir Roger de Coverley Dances 135

sis [Inf] *woman in the family* 33.13, *family member* 65.2

sissy *effeminate male* 32.8, *coward* 285.3, *cowardly* 285.4, *weak person* 517.4, *weak-willed* 517.10

Sister *professional title* 72.6

sister *liberated woman* 33.12, *woman in the family* 33.13, *family member* 65.2, *religious* 84.9, *loved one* 299.13, *contemporary* 649.3

sister [Brit] *nurse* 107.23

sister [Inf] *female* 33.1

sister city *city* 567.1

sisterhood *group* 18.13, *womenfolk* 33.14, *association* 59.4, *friendship* 62.1, *agreement* 752.4, *team* 827.7

sister-in-law *family member* 65.2

sisterly *cliquishly* 59.32, *friendly* 62.5, *family* 65.6, *compassionate* 305.8, *compassionately* 305.14

sisterly love *compassion* 305.2

Sister Moon *moon* 7.18

sister under the skin *affinity* 733.3

sistrum Musical Instruments 142

Sisyphean *futile* 802.10

Sisyphean task *obstacle* 837.3

sit 716.20; *exercise* 157.12, *be situated* 573.9, *be motionless* 678.7

sit and watch the world go by *be mediocre* 289.16

sitar Musical Instruments 142

sit back *delay* 375.16, *have free time* 413.15, *take it easy* 819.3

sit cheek by jowl *adhere* 755.8

sitcom [Inf] *program* 172.10

sit down *have an industrial dispute* 57.20, *be motionless* 678.7, *droop* 714.14, *sit* 716.20, *take it easy* 819.3

sit-down *disputed* 57.15, *refused* 506.5

sit-down meal *meal* 92.8

sit-down strike *strike* 57.8, *refusal* 506.1, *gesture of protest* 507.3

sit down together *confer* 210.13

site *location* 565.1, *locate* 565.9, *situation* 573.1, *situate* 573.10

sited *located* 565.6, *situated* 573.5

sit in *have an industrial dispute* 57.20, *protest* 331.19, *cause mischief* 507.9

sit-in *strike* 57.8, *disputed* 57.15, *rally* 59.6, *mass demonstration* 331.7, *act of defiance* 416.3, *dissent* 506.2, *dissenting* 506.6, *gesture of protest* 507.3

sit in committee *confer* 210.13

sit in council *confer* 210.13

siting *placing* 565.4

sit in judgment *try a case* 54.28, *judge* 54.31, 341.10

sit in on *attend* 575.14

Sitka spruce Trees and Shrubs 43

sit on *abolish* 523.11, *subject* 832.10

sit on [Inf] *limit* 830.13

sit on a gold mine *be rich* 485.12

sit on a powder keg *be in danger* 811.11

sit on one's hands *have free time* 413.15

sit on the bench *judge* 54.31

sit on the board *master* 68.17

sit on the fence *be impartial* 289.15, 338.11, *be irresolute* 378.9, 461.8, *be equivocal* 380.7, *leave alone* 413.13, *be average* 742.8, *stand in the middle* 772.17, *hesitate* 841.18

sit on the shelf [Inf] *be celibate* 67.9

sit on the tail of *stay near* 586.13

sit on the throne *govern* 49.26, *wield authority* 52.16, *rule over* 780.13

sitophobia Phobias 283

sit out *protract* 669.9

sit spin *ice-skating techniques* 162.16

sitter *material* 143.9, *protector* 810.11

sit tight *delay* 375.16, *be obstinate* 379.10, *procrastinate* 413.12, *be motionless* 678.7

sitting *conference* 59.5, *occult and psychic phenomena* 86.7, *balance beam* 157.3, *hunting* 160.2, 160.11, Phobias 283, *sedentary* 716.11

sitting duck *vulnerability* 811.6, *easy thing* 823.6

sitting position *target shooting* 160.1

sitting pretty *successful* 845.8

sitting room *room* 60.9

sitting target *vulnerability* 811.6

situate 573.10; *locate* 565.9, *station* 601.12

situated 573.5; *located* 565.6, *locational* 565.8, *based* 601.9, *conditional* 725.7, *circumstantial* 726.8

situating *placing* 565.4

situation 573.1; *location* 565.1, *station* 601.5, *ambience* 615.3, *direction* 697.1, *state* 725.1, *circumstances* 726.1, *predicament* 824.5

situational 573.6; *ambient* 615.6, *conditional* 725.7, *circumstantial* 726.8

situation comedy *program* 172.10

situationism Western Art Styles 133

sit up *be vertical* 602.8

sit-upon [Brit inf] *rear end* 622.4

sitz bath *basin* 578.12

Siva the Destroyer God 82.6

six 792.2; *numeral* 6.8, *sixth* 792.13

six-card stud *poker* 168.5

six centuries *hundreds* 792.9

Six-Day War Major Wars 76, *six* 792.2

six feet under [Inf] *dead* 29.11, *buried* 31.8

six-figure *thousandth* 792.21

sixfold *sixth* 792.13, *fivefold* 792.26

six-footer *tall person* 596.6, *six* 792.2

six-gear *racing* 146.9

six of one and half a dozen of the other *equality* 740.1

six-pack *six* 792.2

sixpence [Brit] *six* 792.2

six-shooter *firearm* 78.7, *six* 792.2

six-sided *polygonal* 6.79

sixteen *eleven to nineteen* 792.7

sixteenmo (16mo) *eleven to nineteen* 792.7

sixteenth *less than one* 787.4, *eleventh and above* 792.18

sixteenth note *notation* 140.20

sixth 792.13; *ranked* 6.72, *chord* 140.18, *less than one* 787.4, *six* 792.2, *fivefold* 792.26

sixthly *fivefold* 792.26

sixth man *basketball team* 148.2

sixth part *six* 792.2

sixth sense *psychic power* 86.4, *sensation* 212.1, *impression* 266.2, *precognition* 320.2, *spiritual world* 525.3, *six* 792.2

sixties, the *tolerance* 502.2

sixtieth *twentieth* 792.19

sixty *twenty and over* 792.8

sixty-cycle hum *undercurrent of sound* 233.3

sixty-four-(thousand)-dollar question *difficult question* 333.4

sixty-fourth note *notation* 140.20

sixty-nine [Inf] *sex act* 20.10

sizable *big* 579.13

sizableness *largeness* 579.2

sizably *spaciously* 563.17

size 579.1, 579.17; *space* 6.33, 563.1, *material* 143.9, *identification* 184.1, *paste* 561.4, *measurability* 589.2, *breadth* 592.1, *wall covering* 613.12, *face* 613.31, *quantify* 738.1, *quantify* 738.7, *degree* 739.1, *adhesive* 755.3, *importance* 799.1

sizeable *spacious* 563.13

sized *quantitative* 738.6, *gradational* 739.5

size of drink 93.3

size of it *circumstances* 573.2, *state of affairs* 725.4

sizes of animals Fields of Measurement 589

size up *estimate* 341.11, *measure* 589.20

sizing *wall covering* 613.12

sizzle *hiss* 237.1, 237.3

sizzle [Inf] *feel hot* 217.19

sizzler [Inf] *hot weather* 9.22, 217.6

sizzling *hiss* 237.1, *hissing* 237.2

sizzling [Inf] *hot* 9.47, 217.11, *angry* 302.11

Sjenica Breeds of Sheep 16

ska *folk music* 140.7

skag [Inf] *opiates* 121.17

skald *author* 139.13

skat Card Games 168

skate *food fish and shellfish* 90.20, *play ice hockey* 158.9, *skating equipment* 162.17, *go smoothly* 545.11

skateboard *means of transportation* 686.2

skateboarding Sporting Activities 145

skate on thin ice *be in danger* 811.11

skates *means of transportation* 686.2

skating boot *skating equipment* 162.17

skating equipment 162.17

skean *sharp weapon* 78.6

skean dhu *sharp weapon* 78.6

skedaddle [Inf] *retreat* 386.22, *abscond* 576.16, *be swift* 694.10, *hurry off* 705.11, *be safe* 810.20, *haste* 818.1, *make haste* 818.5

skedaddle! [Inf] *go!* 709.30

skedaddled [Inf] *away* 576.8

Skeena Rivers 570

skeet Sporting Activities 145, *target shooting* 160.1, *shooting* 696.5

skeeter [Inf] *insect* 40.1

skeet shooter *shooter* 160.10

skeg *sailboard parts* 150.20

skein *assemblage of birds* 36.18, Collective Names 59, *braid* 609.3

skeletal 551.19; *structural* 14.45, *bodily* 19.18, *ill* 517.8, *emaciated* 595.10, *outlined* 617.4

skeletal frame *superstructure* 551.7

skeletally *structurally* 551.24, *essentially* 617.6

skeletal survey *diagnostic radiology* 107.12

skeleton 19.2, 551.14; *bobsledding* 162.23, *outline* 204.2, 617.1, *map* 387.7, *framework* 551.4, *thin person* 595.4, *body support* 605.6, *remainder* 750.1

skeleton in the closet *secret* 182.2, *evil thing* 446.2

skeleton key *opener* 583.2

skeleton shrimp *crustacean* 39.10

skeleton staff *fewness* 796.3

skep *basket* 578.6

skeptic Philosophical Schools of Thought 4, *disbeliever* 88.5, *negator* 190.8, *questioner* 333.9, *freethinker* 829.10

skeptical 333.14; *disbelieving* 88.6, *unaccepting* 190.13, *reticent* 287.8, *dissenting* 347.7, *nonobservant* 466.5, *uncertain* 841.9

skeptically *disbelievingly* 88.10, *nonacceptantly* 190.25, *reticently* 287.18, *questioningly* 333.21, *defiantly* 466.14, *uncertainly* 841.22

skepticism Philosophical Schools of Thought 4, *disbelief* 88.1, *unacceptance* 190.4, *reticence*

287.3, *uncertainty* 333.6, *suspicion* 841.2

sketch *play* 136.2, *number* 138.5, *story* 139.4, *drawing* 143.4, *draw* 143.13, *record* 185.1, *illustration* 187.2, *illustrate* 187.11, *be concise* 198.5, *representation* 202.9, *describe* 202.15, *summary* 204.1, *summarize* 204.7, *rehearsal* 335.2, *rehearse* 335.12, *suppose* 359.8, *map* 387.7, *plan out* 387.14, *preparations* 388.2, *lay the foundations* 388.16, *work of art* 522.4, *be unfinished* 544.12, *outline* 617.1, 617.5, *form* 624.9

sketchbook *material* 143.9
sketched *drawn* 143.11
sketched out *planned* 387.10
sketcher *visual artist* 133.6, *drawer* 143.8
sketchily *not enough* 98.12, *incompletely* 544.14, 762.10
sketchiness *rough idea* 544.4, *incompleteness* 762.1
sketching *(act of) drawing* 143.2
sketch map *map* 187.5
sketch out *illustrate* 187.11, *describe* 202.15, *summarize* 204.7, *plan out* 387.14, *outline* 617.5, *not complete* 762.9
sketchpad *material* 143.9
sketchy *not enough* 98.5, *unfinished* 544.9, *incomplete* 762.5, *uncompleted* 762.7
skew *linear* 6.77, *arch* 134.5, *obliqueness* 607.1, *oblique* 607.6, 628.8, *diverge* 698.1, *deviation* 698.1, *distort* 698.20, *unbalance* 741.8
skewbald *horse by color* 159.7, *checked* 263.8
skew distribution *probability distribution* 6.56
skewed *oblique* 607.6, 628.8, 698.11
skewed bridge *bridge* 551.10
skewer *sharp-pointed thing* 549.4, *use a sharp tool* 549.17, *connect* 754.13
skew gear *gear* 14.7
skew lines *line* 6.35
skewness *probability distribution* 6.56, *distortion* 627.1, *obliquity* 628.2, *imbalance* 741.2
ski 162.27, **162.35;** *ski equipment* 162.10, *go smoothly* 545.11, *slide* 714.17
skibob racing Sporting Activities 145
ski boots *boots* 100.31
ski brake *ski equipment* 162.10
ski clothing *ski equipment* 162.10
ski competitively *ski* 162.35
ski cross-country *ski* 162.35
skid *go smoothly* 545.11, *miscellaneous automotive terms* 687.14, *maneuver* 689.14, *deviating motion* 698.3, *slide* 698.24, 714.17
skidding *snowboarding* 162.11, 162.30, *flight maneuver* 689.6, *falling* 714.11
skiddoo! [Inf] *go!* 709.30
skiddy *polished* 545.7
skidproof *accessible* 691.13
skid row *urban area* 567.10
skid-row *urban* 567.14
skids, the [Inf] *deterioration* 808.1
ski equipment 162.10
skier 162.14
skiff *rowing* 150.27, Sailing Ships and Boats 690, Ships and Boats 690
skiffle *jazz* 140.5

skiffle group *instrumental group* 141.3
skiff-race *row* 150.32
skiff racing *rowing* 150.14
ski freestyle *ski* 162.35
ski hat *ski equipment* 162.10
skiing 162.1; *ski* 162.27
skiing associations 162.13
skiing on ice *skiing* 162.1
skiing posture *skiing techniques* 162.5
skiing snow 162.3
skiing techniques 162.5
ski jacket *jacket* 100.18, *ski equipment* 162.10
ski jump *skiing* 162.1
ski-jump *ski* 162.35
ski jumping Sporting Activities 145, *skiing* 162.1
ski lift *ski run* 162.2, *means of transportation* 686.2, *cableway* 691.11, *lifter* 715.5
skill 127.1; *means* 102.1, *personnel management* 126.4, *ability* 340.2, 514.3, *information* 348.2, *imagination* 360.1, *tactics* 399.12, *proficiency* 445.5, *production* 522.1, *way* 691.1, *special skill* 779.2, *expertise* 805.4, *cunning* 822.1, *easiness* 823.1
skilled *educated* 48.19, *expert* 52.12, 127.12, 805.16, *industrial* 57.13, *excellent* 68.16, *skillful* 127.10, *qualified* 340.7, *knowledgeable* 348.7, *intelligent* 352.5, *proficient* 445.15, *problematic* 824.11
skilled person 127.7
skilled worker *employee* 57.4, *expert* 68.13, 127.9, *artisan* 123.13, *operator* 509.5
skillet *cooking equipment* 91.6
skillful 127.10; *excellent* 68.16, *qualified* 340.7, *intelligent* 352.5, *imaginative* 360.10, *proficient* 445.15, *expert* 805.16, *cunning* 822.4
skillfully 127.16; *studiously* 48.26, *expertly* 52.21, *masterfully* 68.19, *capably* 340.15, *proficiently* 445.22
skillfulness *skill* 127.1, *proficiency* 445.5, *easiness* 823.1
skillful person *skilled person* 127.7
skills *authorization* 340.4
skim *purify* 111.19, *type of touch* 216.3, *touch* 216.9, *choose* 382.14, *meet* 586.15, *be superficial* 599.6, *slide* 714.17
ski mask *ski equipment* 162.10
skimmer *cooking equipment* 91.6
skim milk *milk* 93.5
skimming *touching* 216.6
skimmings *residue* 750.2
skimobile *snow vehicle* 687.9
skim off *choose* 382.14
skim off the cream *choose* 382.14
ski mountaineering Sporting Activities 145, *skiing* 162.1
skim over *be superficial* 599.6
skimp *hoard* 501.6, *not complete* 762.9
skimped *unprovided* 98.6
skimpily *not enough* 98.12, *inadequately* 486.19, *meagerly* 593.19, *incompletely* 762.10
skimpiness *incompleteness* 98.2, *inadequacy* 486.5, *littleness* 580.1, *shortness* 591.1, *meagerness* 593.6, *nonachievement* 762.3, *fewness* 796.3
skimpy *not enough* 98.5, *inadequate* 486.13, *little* 580.7, *short* 591.6, *meager* 593.12, *incomplete* 762.5, *uncompleted* 762.7

skin 19.19; *body covering* 19.4, *fruit structure* 44.3, *leather* 104.7, *sense organ* 212.4, *external appearance* 264.5, Phobias 283, *animal products* 522.7, *erode* 554.14, *coat* 588.3, *exteriority* 610.2, *casing* 613.9, *animal covering* 613.15, *depilate* 614.20, *take off* 749.7, *residue* 750.2, *separate* 753.12
skin [Inf] *overcharge* 496.10
skin alive [Inf] *condemn* 438.18
skin and bones *emaciation* 595.2
skin-and-bones *ill* 517.8
skin boat Ships and Boats 690
skin cancer *cancer* 114.15, *skin disease* 114.16
skin color *external appearance* 264.5
skin-deep *superficial* 599.4
skin disease 114.16, Phobias 283
skin-dive *dive* 164.15
skin diver *swimmer* 164.11
skin diving Sporting Activities 145, *swimming* 164.1
skin flick [Inf] *pornography* 432.7
skinflint *nonpayer* 490.6, *nonpaying* 490.7, *bargain hunter* 497.8, *miser* 501.3
skinfold *measurement* 1.9
skin friction *friction* 554.1
skinful [Inf] *fullness* 761.5
skin fungi *fungi* 47.3
skin game *dishonesty* 479.7
skinhead [Inf] *combatant* 77.1, *malefactor* 306.6, *baldness* 614.9
skink *lizard* 37.5
skin lesion *skin disease* 114.16
skinlike *skin* 19.19
skinned *shed* 614.14
skinned alive [Inf] *criticized* 438.14
Skinner *psychologist* 108.33
skinner *shedder* 614.7
Skinnerian psychology Psychological Theories, Schools 108
skinniness *thinness* 595.1
skinning *peeling* 614.6
skinning alive [Inf] *condemnation* 438.2
skinny *underfed* 98.7, *ill* 517.8, *thin* 595.9
skinny-dip [Inf] *swim* 164.14, *undress* 614.18
skinny-dipper [Inf] *nude person* 614.5
skinny-dipping [Inf] *swimming* 164.1, 164.12, *undressing* 614.2
skin-popping [Inf] *drug use* 121.9
skin search *undressing* 614.2
skin-search *make nude* 614.19
skint [Brit inf] *insolvent* 486.10
skin test *test* 107.10
skintight *stylish* 100.42, *adhesive* 755.5
ski on ice *ski* 162.35
ski orienteering or **Ski-O** *ski race* 162.4
skip *dance* 135.7, *bowler* 151.5, *not observe* 466.9, *bodily movement* 677.11, *hurry off* 705.11, *jump* 713.7, *spring up* 713.22, *escape* 816.8
skip [Inf] *abscond* 576.16
ski pants *ski equipment* 162.10
ski parka *ski equipment* 162.10
skip off *hurry off* 705.11
ski pole *ski equipment* 162.10
skipper *leader* 126.8, *lead* 126.12, *boating person* 150.24, *sail* 150.29, *nautical person* 690.12
skip town [Inf] *conceal oneself* 181.15
ski race 162.4

ski racer *skier* 162.14
ski rambling *cross-country skiing* 162.7
skirl [Scot] *harsh sound* 238.1, *be strident* 238.7
skirmish *battle* 76.23, 76.33, *contention* 422.1, *warfare* 422.10, *declare war* 422.25
skirmishes *warfare* 76.3
skirr *scamper* 694.12
skirt 100.12; *racing automobile* 146.2, *be evasive* 386.20, *stay near* 586.13, *foundation* 601.2, *edge* 618.1, *border* 618.9, *side* 623.8, *ring* 681.9, *pass* 692.15
skirt [Inf and Off] *sex object* 20.8, *female* 33.11, *woman considered as a sex object* 33.8
skirt around *circle* 631.6
skirt chaser [Inf] *lover* 299.11
skirted *edged* 618.6
skirting *side* 623.6
ski run 162.2
skis *means of transportation* 686.2
ski slope *ski run* 162.2
ski suit *suit* 100.16, *ski equipment* 162.10
ski sweater *sweater* 100.17
skit *play* 136.2, *number* 138.5, *ridicule* 440.6
ski teaching method *skiing* 162.1
ski touring *cross-country skiing* 162.7
ski tow *ski run* 162.2
ski trail *ski run* 162.2
skittish *fearful* 283.10, *capricious* 381.4, 841.16
skittishness *fearfulness* 283.2, *shyness* 403.3
skittles [Brit] Sporting Activities 145, *bowling* 151.1
ski tuning *ski equipment* 162.10
ski turn *skiing techniques* 162.5
skive *use a sharp tool* 549.17
skivvies [Inf] *underwear* 100.22
skivvy or **skivvy shirt** [Inf] *underwear* 100.22
ski wax *ski equipment* 162.10
skoal! *cheers!* 93.22
Skopelos Breeds of Sheep 16
Skopje Countries 566
skua *water bird* 36.9
Skuld Deities 82
skulduggery *foul play* 193.6, *disreputable action* 371.3
skulk Collective Names 59, *conceal oneself* 181.15, *retreat* 285.8, *be cunning* 822.5, *hide* 844.13
skulking *dastardly* 285.6, *concealment* 844.2, *concealed* 844.7
skull Human Bones 19, *head* 19.6, *personifications and symbols* 29.4, *historic armor* 419.8
skull and crossbones *personifications and symbols* 29.4, *flag* 184.8
skullcap *vestment* 84.11, *cap* 100.33
skull measurement Fields of Measurement 589
skunk *unpleasant-smelling thing* 227.2
skunk [Inf] *miscreant* 448.6, *victory* 845.4
sky *universe* 7.3, *heaven* 82.15, *play* 156.8, *air* 558.1, *empty space* 563.2, *top of the world* 600.2
sky-blue *blue* 261.5
skycap *attendant* 69.4, *transferrer* 685.4, *transporter* 686.4
skydive *drop* 714.15
sky diver *descender* 714.8
skydiving Sporting Activities 145, *fall* 714.4

Skye Islands 572
Skye terrier Breeds of Dogs 35
sky-high costly 496.7, 500.6, high 596.7, 596.20
skyhook climbing equipment 161.4
skyjack take away forcefully 477.19, steal 479.14
skyjacker raider 477.10, thief 479.8
skyjacking stealing 479.1, stolen 479.12, miscellaneous aviation terms 689.9
skylark occupy oneself 412.15, ascender 713.12
skylarking celebration 405.1, mounting 713.8
skylight Architectural Elements 134, opening 583.1
skylight filter filter 132.14
skyline visibility 244.1, distant place 585.3, horizontal surface 603.3, edge 617.3
sky pilot [Inf] member of the clergy 84.5
skyrocket ascender 713.12, go up 713.23, increase 746.6
skyrocketing costly 496.7, leaping 713.17
skyrocketing price inflationary price 496.3
Skyros pony Horse and Pony Breeds 159
skyscape type of painting 143.5
skyscraper architectural structure 134.4, building 551.9
skyscraping high 596.7
sky survey star catalog 7.9
skyward higher 596.21, up 713.25
sky wave wave 683.4
skyway flight path 691.12
skywriting aviation 689.1
slab wood 131.3, rock face 161.6, monument 185.10, substructure 551.8, slice 588.4, particle 760.4
slabber saliva 25.9, salivate 25.25
slab method ceramic process 129.5
slack coal 106.4, careless 324.8, indifferent 326.5, not participating 415.11, inert 519.2, soft 543.6, sedentary 678.5, unhurried 693.8, delayed 693.10, nonadhesive 756.4, untidy 766.11
slacken weaken 517.13, mitigate 521.9, soften 543.14, decrease 747.7, loosen 753.14, ease 819.4
slackening deceleration 693.2, decrease 747.1
slacken off stop 668.10, slow down 693.13
slacker indifferent person 289.6, neglector 326.3, avoider 386.8, nonworker 415.4, plodder 693.6
slacking shirking 386.4
slackly softly 543.18
slackness indifference 326.2, weakness 517.1, inertness 519.1, softness 543.1, slowness 693.1
slack off slow down 693.13, take it easy 819.3
slack-rope artist circus performer 138.9
slacks informal clothes 100.7, pants 100.14
slack suit informal clothes 100.7, suit 100.16
slag dirt 112.5, product 522.3, residue 750.2, refuse 802.5
slag heap place for waste 802.6
sláinte! [Irish] cheers! 93.22
slake comfort 214.14, satisfy 273.7
slaked lime fertilizer 16.9
slake one's thirst drink 93.19
slalom Sporting Activities 145

slalom course windsurfing classes 150.22, deviating course 698.2
slalom pole ski race 162.4
slalom race ski race 162.4
slalom racer skier 162.14
slalom racing canoe racing 150.12, windsurfing 150.19
slalom ski ski equipment 162.10
slam sailing 150.25, burst of sound 232.4, be loud 232.8, bang 234.1, 234.6, blow 695.5, hit 695.11
slam [Inf] criticism 438.4, 440.2, berate 438.20, criticize 440.12
slam dancing Dancing Types 135
slam dunk playing terms 148.4, play basketball 148.7
slam into collide 695.10
slam jibe sailing terms 150.5
slammer [Inf] the inside 55.2
slamming tumult 232.5, banging 234.4
slander misinformation 188.3, lying 192.5, lie 192.23, vilification 301.2, vilify 301.15, personal attack 418.8, criticize 418.26, defamation 440.3, defame 440.13, false accusation 442.2, accuse falsely 442.9
slandered perjurious 442.7
slanderer liar 192.10, disparager 440.7
slanderous lying 192.16, vilifying 301.19, critical 418.16, defamatory 440.9, perjurious 442.7
slanderously vilifyingly 301.18, disparagingly 440.16, accusingly 442.11
slanderousness lying 192.5
slang 5.19; nonstandard language 5.7, of language 5.35, vernacular 205.8, vilify 301.15
slang dictionary word book 5.27
slanging [Inf] vilifying 301.9
slanging match [Inf] vilification 301.2, argument 329.1
slang term or word slang 5.19
slangy of language 5.35
slant defense 155.9, play defense 155.19, misrepresent 188.6, partial truth 192.7, distort the truth 192.23, practice sophistry 330.11, interpret news 365.17, obliqueness 607.1, be oblique 607.10, obliquity 628.2, viewpoint 628.5, deviation 698.1, deviating course 698.2
slanted 628.10; linear 6.77, misrepresented 188.4, partially true 192.18, oblique 607.6, 698.11
slanting oblique 607.6, 628.8
slantingly obliquely 607.13
slant-in pass play 155.8
slantly obliquely 607.13
slant-top type of desk 101.6
slap incentive 178.4, motivate 178.17, gesture 183.5, 183.17, type of touch 216.3, touch 216.9, crack 234.2, 234.7, corporal punishment 454.11, hit 454.28, blow 695.5
slapdash clumsy 128.6, bungled 128.7, imprudent 286.7, imprudently 286.11, careless 324.8, indifferent 326.5, hasty 818.3
slap in the face abasement 298.6, abase 298.20, insult 436.5, 436.21
slap jack Card Games 168
slap one's thighs laugh 277.12
slap on the wrist punishment 454.1, corporal punishment 454.11, hit 454.28
slapped in the face abased 298.13
slapping gestural 183.13, corporal punishment 454.11

slapstick show business 138.1, clown 138.10, variety 138.13, entertainment 277.4, humorous 277.9, comedy 368.2, ridiculous 368.5
slapstick comedian clown 138.10
slapstick comedy comedy 136.11
slap the wrist punish 454.22
slash Accents and Diacritical Marks 5, Punctuation Marks 5, painful injury 215.3, inflict pain 215.10, stab 418.22, discount 495.4, make cheap 497.14, hole 583.17, oblique line 607.5, make smaller 747.8, separator 753.5, take apart 753.16, means of connection 754.4
slash-and-burn arable farming 16.6
slashed bargain 497.10, holed 583.12
slashing ice hockey tactics 158.4, emphatic 200.3, attacking 418.14
slashing one's wrists suicide 30.8
slash one's wrists commit suicide 30.24
slat wood 131.3, carpenter 131.10, slice 588.4, fineness 595.5
Slate Breeds of Fowl 16
slate masonry 14.22, building materials 104.2, gray thing 255.3, be dissatisfied 274.7, criticize 365.15, 440.12, prospectus 387.3, berate 438.20, brittle thing 548.2, slice 588.4, roof 613.30, keep time 646.12
slate-blue blue 261.5
slate-colored gray 255.6
slated criticized 438.14
slate-gray gray 255.6
slater [Aus] crustacean 39.10
slates overhead covering 613.11
slating criticism 438.4, 440.2
slatted joined 131.8
slatternliness untidiness 766.3
slatternly dirty 112.7, untidy 766.11
slaty chalky 8.59
slaty cleavage metamorphic rock 8.36
slaughter 30.5, 30.21; be at war 76.32, malignity 306.5, harm 306.13, military attack 812.2, attack successfully 418.25, capital punishment 454.12, execute 454.30, violence by person 520.2, use violence 520.9, destroying 523.2, destroy 523.10, demolish 523.12
slaughtered killed 29.13
slaughterer killer 30.11, violent animal 520.4
slaughterhouse 30.16; havoc 523.5
slaughtering animal killing 30.10
slaughterman animal killer 30.14
slaughterous murderous 30.18
Slave Rivers 570
slave serf 69.8, overwork 122.9, victim of discrimination 337.8, hard worker 414.11, try 414.21, submitter 421.2, assistant 511.3, inferior 745.4, subjected person 832.5
slave away overwork 122.9
slave driver strict person 424.4
slaver saliva 25.9, salivate 25.25, dirty 112.11, leak 707.16
slaver or slave ship Ships and Boats 690
slave raider plunderer 479.9
slavering salivating 25.18
slavery servitude 69.2, work 122.1, servility 401.1, coercive method

428.3, detention 830.5, subjection 832.1
slave ship or slaver Sailing Ships and Boats 690
slave to drink drunkard 121.8
slave to fashion imitator 736.6
slave trade trade 480.1
slave unit flash 132.13
Slavic language family 5.12
slavish servile 401.6, submitting 421.3, obedient 426.4
slavishly servilely 401.15, obediently 426.9
slavishness servility 401.1, submission 421.1, obedience 426.1, imitation 736.1
slay kill 30.19, be at war 76.32, cause not to exist 718.14
slay en masse slaughter 30.21
slayer killer 30.11
slaying killing 30.1
sleaziness dirtiness 112.1
sleazy dirty 112.7
sled convey 685.9, means of transportation 686.2, snow vehicle 687.9
sled dog means of transportation 686.2
sled dog racing Sporting Activities 145
sledge hammer 553.13, convey 685.9, means of transportation 686.2, snow vehicle 687.9, impeller 695.7
sledgehammer hammer 553.13, impeller 695.7, collide 695.10
sledgehammering ramming 695.3
sleek smooth 545.4, smooth-mannered 545.9, oily 562.11, orderly 765.13
sleekly dashingly 536.10, smoothly 545.13, suavely 545.15, oilily 562.19
sleekness smoothness 545.1, lubrication 562.2
sleep 415.5, 415.14; death 29.1, desensitization 213.2, be insensible 213.7, night 656.3, spend the evening 656.5, pause 668.3, 668.13, repose 678.2, be motionless 678.7, ease 819.1, take it easy 819.3, latency 844.1, be latent 844.12
sleep around [Inf] fornicate 432.14
sleep disorder 108.20
sleep disorders mental disorder 108.8
sleeper 415.7; baby clothes 100.24, inactive person 413.8, railroad car 688.5
sleeper [Brit] rail 688.3
sleepily 415.19; insensibly 213.9
sleepiness desensitization 213.2, sleep 415.5
sleeping not awake 415.12, sedentary 678.5, latent 844.6
sleeping around [Inf] fornication 432.3
sleeping bag climbing equipment 161.4
Sleeping Beauty sleeper 415.7
sleeping car railroad car 688.5
sleeping dog hidden danger 813.3
sleeping draft reliever 275.4
sleeping draught anesthetic 213.3, soporific 415.6
sleeping pill addictive drug 117.10, anesthetic 213.3, reliever 275.4, soporific 415.6, moderator 521.2
sleeping porch room 60.9
sleeping sickness tropical disease 114.10

sleeping together *sexual intercourse* 20.9
sleeping with *sexual intercourse* 20.9
sleep it off *be refreshed* 94.8, *sober up* 120.7
sleepless *committed* 377.7, *fidgety* 414.14
sleeplessness *commitment* 377.2, *restlessness* 414.7
sleep like a log *or* **top** *sleep* 415.14
sleep off *be restored* 809.13
sleep on it *have second thoughts* 317.11, *delay* 658.13
sleep terror disorder *sleep disorder* 108.20
sleep together *have sex* 20.21
sleepwalk *be insensible* 213.7
sleepwalking disorder *sleep disorder* 108.20
sleepwear *nightwear* 100.21
sleep with *have sex* 20.21
sleepy *anesthetic* 213.6, *not awake* 415.12, *quiescent* 678.6
sleepyhead *sleeper* 415.7, *plodder* 693.6
sleet *precipitation* 9.26, *snow* 9.58, *ice* 218.5
sleety *cool* 9.49, *cold* 218.9
sleeve *part of garment* 100.27, *flag* 184.8
sleigh *type of bed* 101.9, *means of transportation* 686.2, *snow vehicle* 687.9
sleigh bells Musical Instruments 142
sleight *artifice* 193.5, *sophistry* 330.1, *cunning* 822.1
sleight of hand *magic* 138.3, *delusion* 720.3
sleight-of-hand artist *magician* 138.11
Sleipnir Notable Horses 159
slender *treelike* 43.10, *little* 580.7, *thin* 595.9
slenderize *become thin* 595.15
slenderizing *dieting* 595.3, 595.11
slenderly *thin* 595.18
slender means *poverty* 486.1
slenderness *littleness* 580.1, *thinness* 595.1
slentando Musical Terms and Expression Marks 140
sleuth Collective Names 59, *pursuer* 385.5, *follow* 385.12
slew *marsh* 572.3
slice **588.4;** *bite* 92.10, *bungling* 128.2, *be clumsy* 128.9, *golf shots* 156.4, *play* 156.8, *tennis strokes* 165.2, *play tennis* 165.13, *portion* 474.2, *use a sharp tool* 549.17, *divert* 698.16, *take apart* 753.16, *particle* 760.4
sliced *partial* 760.11
slice of life *dramatic style* 136.3, *realism* 719.3
slice of the cake *portion* 474.2
slice service *tennis strokes* 165.2
slicing *motion-picture editing* 137.8
slick *skillful* 127.10, *artful* 193.13, *smooth* 545.4, 545.10, *polished* 545.7, *smooth-mannered* 545.9, *oily* 562.11, *anoint* 562.17, *orderly* 765.13, *cunning* 822.4
slick down *smooth* 545.10
slicked up [Inf] *formally dressed* 406.8
slickensides *fault* 8.21
slicker *coat* 100.19
slickly *smoothly* 545.13, *oilily* 562.19
slickness *smoothness* 545.1, *lubrication* 562.2

slick on *anoint* 562.17
slicks *racing automobile* 146.2
slide **698.24, 714.17;** *mass movement* 8.28, *load* 14.49, *photograph* 132.3, *brass instrument* 142.3, *row* 150.32, *amusement park and playground equipment* 167.8, *view* 242.8, *transparent thing* 249.4, *not act* 413.11, *go smoothly* 545.11, *flow* 570.10, *fall* 714.4, *deteriorate* 808.14, *be in danger* 811.11, *go easily* 823.18
slide back *reverse* 671.9
slide carrier *viewer* 132.22
slide down *slide* 714.17
slide down the slippery slope *go backward* 680.16
slide home *play baseball* 147.9
slide in *inset* 710.13
slide into *convert* 670.11
slide off *be on the track* 146.11
slide projector *viewer* 132.22
slider *pitching terms* 147.5
slide rule *calculator* 784.5
slide show *show* 138.4
slide tackle *soccer play* 163.5
slide trumpet Musical Instruments 142
slide viewer *viewer* 132.22
sliding *deformation* 14.16, *depraved* 448.10, *fall* 714.4, *falling* 714.11, *deteriorated* 808.8
sliding down the slippery slope *backsliding* 680.8
sliding friction *friction* 554.1
sliding off *automobile racing terms* 146.3
sliding outrigger seat *canoe parts* 150.10
sliding pads *baseball equipment* 147.4
sliding-scale *negotiated* 57.16
sliding-scale rates *bargaining terms* 57.10
sliding seat *rowboat parts* 150.15
slight *be thoughtless* 324.11, *rejection* 383.1, *exclude* 383.11, *insult* 400.6, 436.5, 436.21, *disdain* 400.16, *be insubordinate* 416.8, *disparage* 440.11, *nonobservance* 466.1, *not observe* 466.9, *insufficient* 517.11, *sparse* 541.3, *little* 580.7, *thin* 595.9, *superficial* 599.4, *be superficial* 599.6, *repel* 701.7, *low quality* 745.7
slight build *thinness* 595.1
slighted *rejected* 383.6
slight hope *remote possibility* 836.4
slighting *rejecting* 383.2, *derisive* 400.12, *insulting* 436.10, *disparagement* 440.1, *disparaging* 440.8
slightingly *derisively* 400.22, *disparagingly* 440.8
slighting remark *aspersion* 440.4
slightly *weakly* 517.14, *moderately* 521.10, *little* 580.12, *superficially* 599.8, *quantitatively* 738.8, *to a degree* 739.11, *badly* 745.15, *partly* 760.17, *fractionally* 787.8
slightly built *thin* 595.9
slightly drunk **121.26**
slightness *sparseness* 541.1, *littleness* 580.1, *thinness* 595.1, *superficiality* 599.2
slight smell *odor* 224.1
slim *eat less* 118.9, *shortened* 582.8, *contract* 582.12, *thin* 595.9, *become thin* 595.15, *restrain oneself* 830.15
slim chance *remote possibility* 836.4, *improbability* 839.1
slim down *lose weight* 468.14,

become smaller 582.14, *become thin* 595.15
slime *dirt* 112.5, Phobias 283, *marsh* 559.8, *mud* 561.8
slime molds *fungi* 47.3
slimily **561.23**
sliminess *dirtiness* 112.1, *unctuousness* 439.4
slimly *thin* 595.18
slimmer *eater* 92.15
slimmer [Brit] *thin person* 595.4
slimming *dieting* 92.6, 118.2, 595.3, 595.11, *edible* 92.20, *on a diet* 118.6, *shortening* 582.2, *contracting* 582.10
slimming diet *dieting* 118.2
slimness *thinness* 595.1
slimy *dirty* 112.7, *sycophantic* 401.7, *unctuous* 439.10, *viscous* 561.11, *oily* 562.11
sling Historical Missile Weapons 78, *hunting equipment* 160.4, *climbing equipment* 161.4, *stone* 418.23, *body support* 605.6, *throw* 696.4, 696.17
sling-backs *shoes* 100.30
slinger *thrower* 696.10
slinging *throwing* 696.3
sling mud [Inf] *defame* 440.13
sling out *discard* 383.12
sling psychrometer *measuring instrument* 557.19
slingshot *blunt weapon* 78.5, *agent of destruction* 523.7
slink *conceal oneself* 181.15, *retreat* 285.8, *hide* 844.13
slink in *infiltrate* 706.13
slinking *dastardly* 285.6
slink off *retreat* 386.22, *depart* 705.8
slinky *stylish* 100.42, *dastardly* 285.6
slip *underwear* 100.22, *material* 129.2, *glaze* 129.3, *negligence* 324.4, *mistake* 342.2, *misjudge* 342.9, *trivial error* 351.8, *err* 351.14, *be unaccustomed* 398.5, *be wrong* 430.18, *sin* 450.3, *go smoothly* 545.11, *paste* 561.4, *mud* 561.8, *little person* 580.5, *narrow place* 593.2, *thin person* 595.4, *miscellaneous automotive terms* 687.14, *slide* 698.24, 714.17, *fall* 714.4, *component* 760.3, *deteriorate* 808.14, *be in danger* 811.11, *change* 841.20, *be in trouble* 848.11
slip anchor *sail* 150.29
slip away *absent oneself* 576.15, *quit* 705.10
slip back **680.19;** *reverse* 671.9, *go backward* 680.16, *deteriorate* 808.14
slip by *conceal oneself* 181.15
slipcase *bookbinding* 174.11
slip casting *ceramic process* 129.5
slipcover *protective covering* 613.5
slip friction *friction* 554.1
slip in *infiltrate* 706.13, *inset* 710.13
slip into *wear* 100.46
slipknot Knots, Bends, Hitches, Splices 754
slip money to *tip* 472.14
slip (of a girl) *young woman* 26.9
slip off *undress* 614.18
slip of the pen *trivial error* 351.8
slip of the tongue *trivial error* 351.8
slip on *wear* 100.46
slip one's collar *escape* 816.8
slip one's lead *or* **leash** *escape* 816.8

slip one's mind *be forgotten* 355.12
slip-ons *shoes* 100.30
slip out *absent oneself* 576.15
slip out of *undress* 614.18
slipover *sweater* 100.17
slippage *need* 95.4, *insufficiency* 98.1, *fall* 714.4, *omission* 762.4
slipped disk *joint disease* 114.19
slipper *hit* 454.28
slippered *at ease* 819.2
slipper flower Flowers 42
slipperiness *cunning* 330.3, 822.1, *smoothness* 545.1, *lubrication* 562.2, *irresolution* 666.2, *nonadhesion* 756.1, *danger* 811.1
slipper pad *ski equipment* 162.10
slippers *informal clothes* 100.7, *shoes* 100.30
slipperwort Flowers 42
slippery *artful* 193.13, *equivocating* 380.6, *avoiding* 386.9, *polished* 545.7, *oily* 562.11, *lubricated* 562.14, *nonadhesive* 756.4, *unsafe* 811.8, *cunning* 822.4, *unreliable* 841.15
slippery as an eel *or* **a greased pig** *figurative expressions* 545.8
slippery customer [Inf] *equivocator* 380.4
slippery elm Trees and Shrubs 43
slippery slope *danger* 811.1, *critical situation* 824.6
slipping *clumsy* 128.6, *depraved* 448.10, *falling* 714.11, *deteriorated* 808.8, *endangered* 811.10
slipping away *dying* 29.12
slipping back *deterioration* 808.1
slips *construction workplace* 124.10
slipshod *unemphatic* 201.2, *careless* 324.8, *indifferent* 326.5, *unrefined* 338.7, *untidy* 766.11
slipshodness *untidiness* 766.3
slip stage *stage* 136.18
slipstream *be on the track* 146.11, *miscellaneous aviation terms* 689.9
slipstreaming *automobile racing terms* 146.3
slip the cable *retreat* 386.22
slip the collar *be liberated* 831.7
slip through *escape* 816.8
slip through one's fingers *throw down* 716.13
slip through someone's fingers *escape* 816.8
slip up *err* 351.14, *be wrong* 430.18, *blunder* 846.13
slip-up *negligence* 324.4, *trivial error* 351.8, *unsuccessful thing* 846.8
slipware Ceramics 129
slit *crack* 587.2, 587.7, *cracked* 587.5, *notch* 636.1, 636.5, *notched* 636.4, *furrow* 638.1, 638.5, *separateness* 753.3, *take apart* 753.16
slit [Inf] *organs of reproduction* 21.9
slit-drum Musical Instruments 142
slither *fall* 714.4, *slide* 714.17
slitheriness *smoothness* 545.1
slithering *reptilian* 37.12, *falling* 714.11
slithery *polished* 545.7, *oily* 562.11
slit skirt *skirt* 100.12
sliver *bite* 92.10, *little piece* 580.4, *slice* 588.4, *particle* 760.4, *fragment* 787.3
Sloane Ranger [Brit] *fashionable elite* 536.4, *prosperous person* 847.4
slob *unskilled person* 128.3, *neglector* 326.3, *vulgar person* 535.4

slobber *saliva* 25.9, *salivate* 25.25, *dirty* 112.11, *seep* 559.16, *leak* 707.16
slobbering *salivating* 25.18
sloe *sour thing* 223.3, *black thing* 254.3
sloe-black *black* 254.5
sloe-eyed *black-haired* 254.8
sloe gin *sour thing* 223.3
slog *work* 122.8, *try* 414.21, *blow* 695.5, *hit* 695.11
slogan *catchword* 5.22, *maxim* 177.1, *proclamation* 183.8
slog at *exert oneself* 122.11
slog away *persevere* 377.10
slogger *hard worker* 414.11
slogging *working* 122.6, *busy* 414.15, *industrious* 414.16
slogging away *constant* 377.8
sloop *historical warships* 77.22, *sailboat* 150.3, Sailing Ships and Boats 690
sloop of war Sailing Ships and Boats 690
slop *sprinkle* 557.32, *mud* 561.8, *run out* 707.15
slope *align* 6.92, *mountain* 569.1, Fields of Measurement 589, *heights* 596.4, *obliqueness* 607.1, *be oblique* 607.10, *obliquity* 628.2, *angle* 628.11, *deviating course* 698.2, *incline* 713.3, *inclination* 714.6, *slide* 714.17
sloped *oblique* 607.6, 628.8
slope downward *descend* 597.22
slope (of a line) *line* 6.35
slope off [Brit inf] *run away* 386.21, *depart* 705.8
slope-top *type of desk* 101.6
slope up *upturn* 713.20
slope upward *rise* 596.17
sloping *linear* 6.77, *oblique* 607.6, 628.8, *steep* 713.15
slopingly *obliquely* 607.13
slopingness *obliqueness* 607.1
sloping upward *rising* 596.12
slop over *run out* 707.15, *be full* 761.12
sloppily *negligently* 326.8, *inattentively* 466.13, *slimily* 561.23
sloppiness *lack of emphasis* 201.1, *indifference* 326.2, *inaccuracy* 351.3, *nonobservance* 466.1, *muddiness* 561.10, *untidiness* 766.3
sloppy *stylish* 100.42, *unemphatic* 201.2, *sensitive* 267.3, *careless* 324.8, *indifferent* 326.5, *unrefined* 338.7, *nonobservant* 466.5, *ugly* 531.3, *sludgy* 561.18
sloppy joe *sweater* 100.17
sloppy thinking *faulty reasoning* 351.4
slops *animal feed* 16.12, *old clothes* 100.8, *swill* 112.6
slosh *sprinkle* 559.14, *mud* 561.8, *flow* 570.10
sloshed [Inf] *dead drunk* 121.27
sloshiness *muddiness* 561.10
sloshy *sludgy* 561.18
slot *hockey areas* 158.2, *opening* 583.1, *hole* 583.17, *crack* 587.2, 587.7, *furrow* 638.1, 638.5, *separateness* 753.3, *category* 767.6, *class* 777.1
slot formation *offense* 155.6
sloth Collective Names 59, *idleness* 415.3, *iniquity* 448.3, *inertness* 519.1, *slowness* 693.1, *plodder* 693.6
slothful *not participating* 415.11, *inert* 519.2, *unhurried* 693.8
slothfully *impassively* 415.18

slothfulness *idleness* 415.3
slot machine *till* 484.21
slotted *furrowed* 638.3
slouch *slow motion* 693.3, *droop* 714.14
sloucher *plodder* 693.6
slouch hat *hat* 100.32
slough *dirt* 112.5, *swill* 112.6, *renounce* 392.4, *stop using* 394.10, *mud* 561.8, *marsh* 572.3, *shed* 614.21, *residue* 750.2
sloughing *peeling* 614.6
Slough of Despond *depression* 270.2
slough off *renounce* 392.4, *disaccustom* 398.6
sloughy *peeling* 614.13
Slovakia Countries 566
Slovakian Black Pied Breeds of Cattle 16
sloven *neglector* 326.3
Slovenia Countries 566
slovenliness *dirtiness* 112.1, *indifference* 326.2, *untidiness* 766.3
slovenly *dirty* 112.7, *unemphatic* 201.2, *indifferent* 326.5, *untidy* 766.11
slow 693.7; *reactive* 11.29, *leisurely* 125.4, *hunting* 160.11, *reticent* 287.8, *boring* 296.6, *lacking intellect* 316.5, *apathetic* 322.4, *foolish* 353.5, *not participating* 415.11, *inert* 519.2, *simpleminded* 526.11, *dull* 550.7, *deliberate* 589.18, *thick-witted* 594.7, *late* 658.5, *directional* 677.13, *slow down* 693.13, *slowly* 693.14, *at ease* 819.2, *restrain* 830.12
slow as death *slow* 693.7
slow-as-slow *slow* 693.7
slow burn [Inf] *resentment* 302.1
slow-changing *gradational* 739.5
slow development *lateness* 658.1
slow down 693.13; *have an industrial dispute* 57.20, *pause* 415.15, *decrease* 747.7, *make smaller* 747.8, *deteriorate* 808.14, *take it easy* 819.3
slowdown *strike* 57.8, *hesitation* 693.5, *decrease* 747.1
slow-down *disputed* 57.15
slowed *restrained* 830.9
slowed down *delayed* 693.10
slow fast *bowls* 151.7
slow film *exposure* 132.15
slow fire *target shooting* 160.1
slow-footed *slow* 693.7
slow green *green bowling* 151.3
slowing *delaying* 658.8
slowing down *aging* 27.13, *deceleration* 693.2, *deterioration* 808.1, *restraint* 830.1
slowing up *deceleration* 693.2
slow lane *road attribute* 687.3
slow learner *latecomer* 658.4, *loser* 846.9
slowly 693.14; *reticently* 287.18, *boringly* 296.10, *inertly* 519.5, *late* 658.14, *in motion* 677.19, *by degrees* 739.10, *restrainedly* 830.18
slowly but surely *by degrees* 739.10
slow motion 677.9, 693.3
slow-moving *slow* 693.7
slowness 693.1; *unskillfulness* 128.1, *reticence* 287.3, *boringness* 296.2, *lack of intellect* 316.1, *apathy* 322.2, *unenthusiasm* 375.3, *idleness* 415.3, *indecisiveness* 517.2, *inertness* 519.1, *thick-wittedness* 594.3, *lateness* 658.1, *slow motion* 677.9, *degree* 739.1, *restraint* 830.1
slow off the mark *hesitant* 693.9

slow-paced *slow* 693.7
slow person *plodder* 693.6
slowpoke [Inf] *latecomer* 658.4, *plodder* 693.6
slow progress *idleness* 415.3
slow-ranging *gradational* 739.5
slow reaction *chemical reaction* 11.8
slow-running *slow* 693.7
slow start *hesitation* 693.5
slow starter *latecomer* 658.4, *plodder* 693.6
slow up *slow down* 693.13
slow wheel *ceramic workshop and tools* 129.8
slow-witted *thick-witted* 594.7
slow-wittedness *thick-wittedness* 594.3
slow worm *lizard* 37.5
slubbed *coarse* 544.6
sludge *fertilizer* 16.9, *dirt* 112.5, *marsh* 559.8, *mud* 561.8, *residue* 750.2
sludgy 561.18; *cool* 9.49, *marshy* 559.11
slue *marsh* 572.3
slug *pests and diseases* 17.12, *ammunition* 78.11, *box* 152.19, *hunting equipment* 160.4, *typesetting* 173.4, Scientific and Technical Units 589, *plodder* 693.6, *missile* 696.7
slug [Inf] *size of drink* 93.3, *blow* 695.5, *hit* 695.11
slugabed *latecomer* 658.4
sluggard *nonworker* 415.4, *latecomer* 658.4, *sedentary person* 678.3, *plodder* 693.6
sluggardly *unhurried* 693.8
slugged *combat* 152.17
slugger *baseball team* 147.2, *boxer* 152.8
slugging *boxing* 152.2, *combat* 152.17
sluggish *indifferent* 289.7, *apathetic* 322.4, *procrastinating* 375.11, *inactive* 413.9, *not participating* 415.11, *inert* 519.2, *flowing* 570.7, *late* 658.5, *directional* 677.13, *sedentary* 678.5, *unhurried* 693.8, *at ease* 819.2
sluggishly *indifferently* 289.17, *impassively* 415.18, *inertly* 519.5, *fluently* 570.13, *late* 658.14, *motionlessly* 678.9, *slowly* 693.14
sluggishness *indifference* 289.1, *apathy* 322.2, *delay* 375.6, *idleness* 415.3, *inertness* 519.1, *slow motion* 677.9, *slowness* 693.1
slug it out with *contend* 422.22
sluglike *molluskan* 39.23
slug pellet *pest control* 16.13
sluice *bathe* 111.18, *water* 557.29, *outlet* 707.8
sluicegate *water system* 551.13
slum *shack* 60.10, *lack of hygiene* 112.3, *beggary* 486.3, *ugly thing* 531.2, *dilapidation* 868.5
slum or slums *urban area* 567.10
slumber *sleep* 415.5, 415.14, *repose* 678.2, *be motionless* 678.7
slumberer *sleeper* 415.7
slumbering *sedentary* 678.5
slumberous *not awake* 415.12, *inert* 519.2
slumdweller *poor person* 486.6, *municipal resident* 567.12
slumminess *dirtiness* 112.1
slummy *dirty* 112.7, *beggarly* 486.12, *urban* 567.14, *worn* 808.13
slump *mass movement* 8.28, *infertile state* 23.3, *economic factor* 56.8, *unemployment* 415.2, *insolvency*

486.2, *declining prices* 497.2, *be cheap* 497.13, *decline* 680.5, 747.4, *sinkage* 714.2, *droop* 714.14, *decrease* 747.7, *economic deterioration* 808.2, *deteriorate* 808.14, *economic adversity* 848.6
slump down *droop* 714.14
slumping *bargain* 497.10, *descending* 714.9
slumping market *economic adversity* 848.6
slur *disrepute* 371.1, *personal attack* 418.8, *criticize* 418.26, *impropriety* 430.5, *wrong* 430.19, *aspersion* 440.4, *vilify* 440.14, *intake* 708.5
Slurazi Horse and Pony Breeds 159
slur one's words *be drunk* 121.34
slurp *eat* 92.21, *ingest* 708.17
slurping *eating* 92.1, *intake* 708.5
slurred speech *drunken behavior* 121.4
slush *snow* 9.30, 218.6, *skiing snow* 162.3, *marsh* 559.8, *mud* 561.8
slush fund *incentive* 178.4, *bribe* 472.3
slushily *slimily* 561.23
slushiness *muddiness* 561.10
slushy *cool* 9.49, *marshy* 559.11, *sludgy* 561.18
slut *neglector* 326.3, *sexually immoral person* 432.8
slut's wool [Brit inf] *powder* 553.9
sluttish *dirty* 112.7, *indifferent* 326.5, *untidy* 766.11
sluttishly *dirtily* 112.12, *negligently* 326.8
sluttishness *dirtiness* 112.1, *indifference* 326.2, *untidiness* 766.3
sly *secretive* 182.9, *artful* 193.13, *cunning* 330.8, 822.4, *devious* 607.9
slyboots *cunning person* 822.9
slyly *deceptively* 193.21, *hypocritically* 330.15, *cunningly* 822.6
slyness *guile* 193.3, *cunning* 330.3, 822.1, *deviousness* 607.4
smack Collective Names 59, *crack* 234.2, 234.7, *communication of love* 299.6, *communicate love* 299.25, *corporal punishment* 454.11, *hit* 454.28, 695.11, Ships and Boats 690, *blow* 695.5, *admixture* 751.5, *suggestion* 800.9
smack [Inf] *opiates* 121.17, *directly* 697.16
smack-dab [Inf] *opiates* 121.17, *directly* 697.16
smacker [Inf] *US coinage* 484.10
smacking *corporal punishment* 454.11
smack in the middle [Inf] *midway* 772.22
smack of *signify* 183.16, *seem like* 733.14
smack on the lips *communication of love* 299.6
small 787.6; *printed* 173.13, *lowly* 298.9, *unpleasant* 501.5, *weak* 517.6, *insufficient* 517.11, *little* 580.7, *meager* 593.12, *quantitative* 738.6, *insignificant* 745.6
small amount *incompleteness* 98.2, *certain amount* 738.3, *few* 796.1
small-animal practice *veterinary medicine* 107.26
small arms *firearm* 78.7
small-bore *hunting* 160.11
small-bore rifle shooting *target shooting* 160.1
small chance *remote possibility* 836.4, *improbability* 839.1, *poor chance* 842.8
small change *change* 484.3,

average person 742.4, *little bit* 800.4, *nonentity* 800.8
small circle *circle* 6.40
small claims court *type of court* 54.9
small computer systems interface (SCSI) port *computer part* 15.4
small consideration *exchange* 673.1
small craft advisory *weather forecast* 9.4
small eater *eater* 92.15
smaller 582.7; *quantitative* 738.6, *insignificant* 745.6
smallest *ranked* 6.72, *insignificant* 745.6
small figures Phobias 283
small forward *basketball team* 148.2
small frame *thinness* 595.1
small-framed *thin* 595.9
small fry *weak person* 517.4, *average person* 742.4, *nonentity* 800.8
small game *wild animal* 34.4, *nonentity* 800.8
small-game *hunting* 160.11
small-game animals *game* 160.6
small-game birds *game* 160.6
small-game hunter *hunter* 160.9
small-game hunting *hunting* 160.2
small gap *narrow place* 593.2
small group *social organization* 2.5
small hail *hail* 9.29
small holder [Brit] *agriculturist* 16.14, *countryman* 61.8
small holding [Brit] *farm* 16.2, *property* 470.1
small hope *remote possibility* 836.4
small hours *late hour* 658.2
small *or* **wee small hours** *nighttime* 656.1
small intestine *internal organ* 19.13
smallish *little* 580.7
smallishness *littleness* 580.1
small lake 568.2
small letter *type* 173.5
small-minded *discriminatory* 337.11, *unpleasant* 501.5, *narrow-minded* 593.13
small-mindedly *prejudicially* 337.17, *narrow-mindedly* 593.20
small-mindedness *prejudice* 337.3, *narrow-mindedness* 593.7
smallness *lowliness* 298.2, *weakness* 517.1, *littleness* 580.1, *meagerness* 593.6, *triviality* 800.2
small number *few* 796.1
small objects Phobias 283
small potatoes [Inf] *average person* 742.4, *little bit* 800.4, *nonentity* 800.8
smallpox *infection* 114.7, *skin disease* 114.16
small print *specification* 340.6, *basis for negotiations* 460.2
small quantity *incompleteness* 98.2, *certain amount* 738.3, *few* 796.1
small risk *good chance* 842.6
small scale *littleness* 580.1, *little* 580.7
small-scale *undersized* 580.8
small screen *television set* 172.6
small shot *missile* 696.7
small slam *bridge* 168.4
small sound 233.4
small stream *river* 570.1
Smalltalk Programming Languages 15
small talk *talk* 207.3, *chat* 210.2

small things Phobias 283
small-time *mediocre* 742.7, *insignificant* 745.6, *trivial* 800.14
small town *village* 567.3
small-town *local* 564.14, *urban* 567.14, *mediocre* 742.7, *insignificant* 745.6
small toy *cheap thing* 800.7
Small White Breeds of Pigs 16
smalt *blue pigment* 261.2
smarmily *flatteringly* 439.16, *suavely* 545.15
smarmy *sycophantic* 401.7, *unctuous* 439.10, *smooth-mannered* 545.9
smart *stylish* 100.42, *skillful* 127.10, *feel pain* 215.8, *be painful* 215.9, *witty* 277.10, *intelligent* 315.9, 352.5, *knowledgeable* 348.7, *rude* 400.9, *ceremonious* 404.23, *formal* 406.6, *active* 414.13, *elegant* 527.3, *fashionable* 536.5, *mentally sharp* 549.14, *mentally quick* 694.8, *orderly* 765.13, *cunning* 822.4
smart aleck *insolent person* 400.7, *vain person* 402.7
smart-alecky *rude* 400.9, *cocky* 402.11
smart-ass [Inf] *insolent person* 400.7, *rude* 400.9, *vain person* 402.7, *cocky* 402.11
smart card *opener* 583.2
smart cookie *expert* 127.9
smart customer *expert* 127.9
smarten up *beautify* 530.14, *decorate* 532.11, *tidy* 765.21, 807.19, *refurbish* 809.11
smarting *pain* 215.1, *painful* 215.4
smartly *dressily* 100.47, *intelligently* 315.14, *rudely* 400.19, *formally* 406.12, *elegantly* 527.7, *fashionably* 536.9, *dashingly* 536.10, *sharply* 549.19, *swiftly* 694.16
smartness *cleverness* 315.3, *intelligence* 352.2, *rudeness* 400.2, *formality* 406.1, *elegance* 527.1, *stylishness* 537.2, *mental sharpness* 549.9, *cunning* 822.1
smart pace *swiftness* 694.1
smarts [Inf] *common sense* 315.4, *intellect* 348.4
smarty *insolent person* 400.7
smarty-pants *insolent person* 400.7, *vain person* 402.7
smash *tennis strokes* 165.2, *badminton terms* 165.11, *play tennis* 165.13, *inflict pain* 215.10, *type of touch* 216.3, *touch* 216.9, *use violence* 520.9, *ruin* 523.4, *demolish* 523.12, *beat* 553.27, *collision* 695.2, *collide* 695.10, *take apart* 753.16, *deconstruct* 758.7, *restrain* 830.12
smash [Inf] *good thing* 445.9, *successfulness* 845.3
smashed *disintegrated* 758.3
smashed [Inf] *dead drunk* 121.27
smasher *attractive female* 529.5
smash hit *workmanlike job* 127.6, *theatrical performance* 136.13, *box-office hit* 137.11, *good thing* 445.9
smashing *great* 445.14, *pulverization* 553.4, *ramming* 695.3, *impelling* 695.8
smashing! *wonderful!* 294.20
smash to matchwood *demolish* 523.12
smash to pieces *disintegrate* 758.6
smash to smithereens *demolish* 523.12
smash up *demolish* 523.12
smash-up *ruin* 523.4

smatterer *nonentity* 800.8
smattering *information* 348.2, *sprinkling* 776.4, *suggestion* 800.9
smattering of knowledge *lack of knowledge* 349.2
smear *dirt* 112.5, *dirty* 112.11, *mountaineer* 161.10, *make dim* 248.8, *personal attack* 418.8, *criticize* 418.26, *aspersion* 440.4, *defame* 440.13, *stain* 533.3, *blemish* 533.4, *mark* 533.8, *anoint* 562.17
smear campaign *defamation* 440.3
smeared *marked* 533.6
smearer *disparager* 440.7
smear glaze *glaze* 129.3
smearing *climbing techniques* 161.3, *defamatory* 440.9
smell 224.7; *life function* 28.6, *be dirty* 112.10, *sensation* 212.1, *sense* 212.9, *odor* 224.1, *have odor* 224.8, *stink* 227.5, Phobias 283, *draw in* 708.18, *characteristic* 779.5, *decay* 808.16
smell a rat *disbelieve* 88.8
smell at *smell* 224.7
smell bad *stink* 227.5
smeller [Inf] *nose* 19.11
smell foul *stink* 227.5
smellily *stinkingly* 227.6
smelliness *odor* 224.1, *stench* 227.1
smelling *sense of smell* 224.2, *odorous* 224.5
smelling of drink *drunken* 121.28
smelling salts *tonic* 115.8, *stimulant* 121.5
smell like a drain *stink* 227.5
smell like a flower garden *be fragrant* 226.5
smell like a midden *stink* 227.5
smell of *signify* 183.16, *have odor* 224.8
smell of rotten eggs *stink* 227.5
smell of success *reputation* 224.4
smell out *smell* 224.7, *detect* 345.12, *draw in* 708.18
smell powder *be at war* 76.32
smell sweet *be fragrant* 226.5
smelly *odorous* 224.5, *stinking* 227.3
smelt Collective Names 59, *heat* 217.17, *melt* 555.24
smelter *works* 124.9, *ceramic workshop and tools* 129.8, *place for fire* 217.9
smidgen *admixture* 751.5, *particle* 760.4, *few* 796.1, *suggestion* 800.9
smile *gesture* 183.5, 183.17, *show joy* 269.10, *sign of courtesy* 410.5, *greet* 410.11, *curved thing* 629.3
smile on *be auspicious* 847.8
smiler *joyful person* 269.5
smiles of fortune *good fortune* 847.2
smiling *gestural* 183.13, *cheerful* 269.7, *sociable* 408.11
smiling reception *welcome* 408.10
smirch *dirty* 112.11, *blacken* 254.11, *demoralize* 432.15, *defame* 440.13, *stain* 533.3, *mark* 533.8
smircher *disparager* 440.7
smite *murder* 30.20
smite hip and thigh *slaughter* 30.21
smith *artisan* 123.13, *form* 624.9
smithereens *crumb* 553.5
smithy *works* 124.9
smitten with *in love* 299.16
smock *decorate* 532.11, *contract* 582.12
smocked *sewn* 130.14, *shortened* 582.8
smocker *decorator* 532.8

smocking *sewing* 130.5, *decorative method* 532.3
smog *fog* 9.32, *lack of hygiene* 112.3, *pollution* 117.8, *unpleasant-smelling thing* 227.2, *murk* 248.2, *powder* 553.9, *miasma* 556.3
smoggy *foggy* 9.51, *murky* 248.5, *smoky* 556.17
smog-laden *murky* 248.5
smoke 121.38; *phase* 11.13, *lack of hygiene* 112.3, *dirt* 112.5, *pollution* 117.8, *drug oneself* 121.37, *fire* 217.8, *burn* 217.18, *season* 221.8, *odor* 224.1, *blinder* 243.7, *that which makes invisible* 245.2, *murk* 248.2, *transparent thing* 249.4, *opaque* 250.7, *miasma* 556.3, *give off* 556.25, *dry* 560.17, *let out* 709.26, *preserve* 815.14, *be latent* 844.12
Smoke, the London 567.8
smoke alarm *safety device* 810.15
smoke a pipe *smoke* 121.38
smoke-blue *blue* 261.5
smoke cigarettes *smoke* 121.38
smoke cigars *smoke* 121.38
smoked *culinary* 91.9, *piquant* 221.6, *murky* 248.5, *semitransparent* 249.9, *shady* 250.4, *preserved* 815.12
smoked bacon *pork* 90.26
smoked fish *fish dish* 90.19
smoked glass *shade maker* 247.4, *murk* 248.2
smoke-dry *dry* 560.17
smoke-filled *unhygienic* 114.27, *murky* 248.5
smoke-free *tobacco* 121.33, *odorless* 225.4
smoke-free area *smoking* 121.22, *odorlessness* 225.1
smokehouse *farm building* 16.4
smoke-laden *murky* 248.5
smokeless *odorless* 225.4
smokeless zone *odorlessness* 225.1
smoke out *drive out* 709.19, *displace* 711.14
smoker *smoking* 121.22, *party* 408.6, *compulsive person* 428.5
smoker's cough *smoking* 121.22
smoke screen *cover* 181.4, 613.2, *artifice* 193.5, *blinder* 243.7, *that which makes invisible* 245.2, *shelter* 419.11, *stratagem* 822.2
smoke signal *signaling* 169.9, *signal* 183.6, *aid to the deaf* 229.3
smoke the peace pipe *make peace* 73.11, *forgive and forget* 312.9
smoke tree Trees and Shrubs 43
smokey *or* **Smokey Bear** [Inf] *law enforcement officer* 53.8
smokily 556.28; *transparently* 249.13, *grayly* 255.10
smokiness *piquancy* 221.1, *semitransparency* 249.3
smoking 121.22; *cooking technique* 91.2, *substance abuse* 121.1, *drug use* 121.9, *tobacco* 121.33, *ceramic process* 129.5, *heating* 217.12, *curing* 221.3, *vaporization* 556.9, *smoky* 556.17, *preservation of provisions* 815.6
smoking area *smoking* 121.22
smoking compartment *smoking* 121.22
smoking gun *proof* 339.2
smoking jacket *informal clothes* 100.7
smoking-related *tobacco* 121.33
smoking-room story *sexual offense* 432.6
smoky 556.17; *dirty* 112.7, *unhygienic* 114.27, *piquant* 221.6, *murky* 248.5, *semitransparent*

249.9, *shady* 250.4, *dark* 254.6, *gray* 255.6, *condensed* 540.7

smolder *burn* 217.18, *be angry* 302.19, *be latent* 844.12

smoldering *heating* 217.12, *angry* 302.11, *malevolent* 306.7

smoldering fury *malevolence* 306.1

smolt *young fish* 38.6

smooch [Inf] *communicate love* 299.25

smooching [Inf] *communication of love* 299.6

smooth 543.8, 545.4, 545.10, 552.9, 552.13; *bowls* 151.7, *artful* 193.13, *luscious* 214.8, *pleasant* 222.6, *good-mannered* 410.7, *moderating* 521.5, *simple* 526.7, *make simple* 526.12, *fluid* 527.5, *blunt* 550.5, 550.9, *rub* 554.12, *massage* 554.16, *oily* 562.11, *lubricate* 562.15, *horizontal* 603.6, *make horizontal* 603.10, *make round* 633.9, *quiescent* 678.6, *accessible* 691.13, *make the same* 730.16, *equalize* 740.12, *nonadhesive* 756.4, *orderly* 765.13, *tidy* 765.21, *continuous* 774.9, *easy* 823.9, *make easy* 823.15

smooth as a peach or *a baby's* **bottom** *figurative expressions* 545.8

smooth as glass or **marble** *figurative expressions* 545.8

smooth as silk or **velvet** or **satin** *figurative expressions* 545.8

smoothbore *firearm* 78.7

smooth delivery *grip* 151.4

smooth down *smooth* 545.10

smoothed *smooth* 545.4, *blunt* 550.5, *leveled* 603.8

smoothen *smooth* 545.10, *make horizontal* 603.10

smoothened *leveled* 603.8

smoother 545.2

smooth-faced *depilatory* 614.15

smooth-haired *smooth* 545.4

smoothie [Inf] *cunning person* 822.3

smoothing *smooth* 545.4, *polishing* 554.5, *easing* 823.7

smoothing plane *woodworking tool* 131.6

smoothly 545.13, 550.10; *sweetly* 222.8, *genteelly* 410.14, *simply* 526.14, *gracefully* 527.8, *softly* 543.18, *texturally* 552.15, *oilily* 562.19, *horizontally* 603.11, *motionlessly* 678.9, *easily* 823.19

smooth-mannered 545.9

smoothness 543.2, 545.1, 823.5; *physical pleasure* 214.1, *sweetness* 222.1, *courtesy* 410.1, *simplicity* 526.1, *elegance* 527.1, *bluntness* 550.1, *grain* 552.2, *lubrication* 562.2, *horizontality* 603.1, *orderliness* 765.5, *cunning* 822.1

smooth one's ruffled feathers *conciliate* 74.10

smooth out *soften* 543.14, *smooth* 545.10, 552.13, *make horizontal* 603.10, *straighten* 630.14, *make average* 742.9

smooth over 545.12; *conciliate* 74.10, *mitigate* 521.9, *ease* 562.18

smooth over the differences *be indiscriminate* 338.10

smooth road *easy thing* 823.6

smooth-running *lubricated* 562.14, *wieldy* 823.12

smooth sailing *easy thing* 823.6

smooth-shaven *depilatory* 614.15

smooth-skinned *smooth* 545.4

smooth-spoken *honeyed* 439.8, *smooth-mannered* 545.9

smooth surface *smoothness* 545.1

smooth-surfaced *smooth* 545.4

smooth-talk *be cunning* 822.5

smooth talker *speaker* 205.12, *flatterer* 439.6, *cunning person* 822.3

smooth-talking *articulate* 205.16

smooth texture *smoothness* 545.1

smooth-textured *smooth* 545.4

smooth the way *prepare the way* 388.15, *ease* 562.18, *make easy* 823.15, *further* 825.30, *make probable* 838.9

smooth-tongued *honeyed* 439.8

smoothy [Inf] *cunning person* 822.3

smorgasbord *miscellany* 59.15, *hors d'oeuvre* 90.13

smother *murder* 30.20, *play soccer* 163.8, *conceal* 181.12, *silence* 231.4, *abolish* 523.11, *restrain* 830.12

smothered *concealed* 181.8, *nonresonant* 233.7

smothering *Phobias* 283, *destruction* 523.1, *restraint* 830.1

Smriti *other text* 81.19

smudge *dirt* 112.5, *dirty* 112.11, *blacken* 254.11, *stain* 533.3, *blemish* 533.7, *mark* 533.8, *defect* 806.4

smudged *dirty* 112.7, *marked* 533.6

smudge pot *garden tool* 17.7

smudgy *dark* 254.6

smug *satisfied* 273.4, *prideful* 297.8, *self-satisfied* 402.9, *self-admiring* 402.10, *moralistic* 431.12

smuggle *trade* 480.18

smuggler *trader* 480.11

smuggling *trade* 480.1

smugly 402.18; *pridefully* 297.17, *moralistically* 431.16

smugness *satisfaction* 273.1, *self-satisfaction* 402.2, *self-righteousness* 431.7

smut *dirt* 112.5, *dark thing* 247.3, *black thing* 254.3, *immorality* 432.1, *powder* 553.9

smuts *fungi* 47.3

smuttily *bluely* 261.11, *ribaldly* 535.12

smuttiness *obscenity* 112.4, *grossness* 535.3

smutty *obscene* 112.9, *indecent* 261.8, *immoral* 432.9, *ribald* 535.8

Smyth sewing or **stitching** *bookbinding* 174.11

SN1 *chemical reaction* 11.8

SN2 *chemical reaction* 11.8

snack 90.8; *meal* 92.8, *have a meal* 92.25, *refreshments* 94.3, *taste* 219.5

snack bar *eating place* 92.17

snacking *eating meals* 92.4

snafu *blunder* 351.9, *mix-up* 766.5, *mixed up* 766.14, *predicament* 824.5

snag 824.8; *tree part* 43.2, *defect* 806.4, *danger* 811.1, *trap* 813.1, *obstacle* 826.2, *hinder* 826.15

snagged *coarse* 544.6, *toothed* 549.13

snaggled *coarse* 544.6

snaggletooth *teeth* 19.8, *tooth* 549.7

snaggle-toothed *toothed* 549.13

snaggy *coarse* 544.6, *toothed* 549.13, *dangerous* 811.7

snail *pests and diseases* 17.12, *food*

fish and shellfish 90.20, *plodder* 693.6

snail-like *molluskan* 39.23, *slow* 693.7

snail-paced *slow* 693.7

snail shell *convoluted thing* 632.3

snail's pace *slow motion* 693.3

Snake *Rivers* 570

snake 37.6; *hypocrite* 192.9, *malefactor* 306.6, *villain* 448.5, *convoluted thing* 632.3, *convolute* 632.6, *twist* 698.19, *drag* 699.11, *cunning person* 822.3

snake charmer *circus performer* 138.9

snake eyes *gambling* 167.4, *twosome* 873.9

snake in the grass *hypocrite* 192.9, *evil person* 446.3, *villain* 448.5, *cunning person* 822.3, *hinderer* 826.11

snakelike 37.13; *reptilian* 37.12, *villainous* 448.12

snakes *Phobias* 283

snakes and ladders *Board and Table Games* 167

snake's-head *Flowers* 42

snake worship *idolatry* 83.4

snake worshiper *idolater* 83.7

snaking *flowing* 570.7, *indirect* 698.9

snaky *snakelike* 37.13

snap *Bean Varieties* 90, *wear* 100.46, *photograph* 132.3, *huddle* 155.7, *gesture* 183.17, *represent* 187.10, *speak in a particular way* 205.18, *crack* 234.2, 234.7, *animal sound* 240.1, *make an animal sound* 240.7, *be angry* 302.19, *sign of irascibility* 303.6, *frown* 303.15, *spontaneous* 389.6, 396.5, *elasticity* 546.1, *be elastic* 546.7, *be brittle* 548.4, *separate* 753.12, *connect* 754.13

snap [Inf] *vigor* 518.1, *easy thing* 823.6

snap answer *unpremeditation* 389.2

snap a picture *photograph* 132.26

snap at *vent one's anger* 302.21, *show impatience* 303.14, *be irritable* 304.14

snapback *elasticity* 546.1

snap back *be elastic* 546.7

snap count *huddle* 155.7

snap decision *spontaneity* 396.2

snapdragon *Flowers* 42

snap off *be brittle* 548.4

snap of the fingers *triviality* 800.2

snap one's fingers at *be insubordinate* 416.8, *disobey* 427.12, *not observe* 466.9, *think unimportant* 800.19

snap out of it *be refreshed* 94.8, *be restored* 809.13

snapper *game fish* 154.10

snappily *crossly* 303.20, *irritably* 304.17, *swiftly* 694.16

snappiness *crossness* 303.4

snapping *frowning* 303.12, 304.10, *elastic* 546.5

snappish *irritable* 302.10, 304.9, *cross* 303.11

snappishly *irritably* 302.23, 304.17, *crossly* 303.20

snappishness *irritableness* 302.5, 304.3, *crossness* 303.4

snappy *cross* 303.11, *irritable* 304.9, *discourteous* 411.5, *mentally quick* 694.9

snappy [Inf] *vigorous* 518.2

snappy answer *answer* 334.1

snappy dresser *fashion business* 536.3

snappy pace *swiftness* 694.1

snap roll *flight maneuver* 689.6

snaps *fastener* 754.7

snapshot *photograph* 132.3, *record* 185.1, *view* 242.8

snap up *eat well* 92.23, *be greedy* 119.4, *purchase* 481.10

snare *pest control* 16.13, *hunting equipment* 160.4, *hunt* 160.12, *lure* 700.5, *trap* 813.1, 813.6

snared *trapped* 813.5

snare drum *Musical Instruments* 142

snarer *hunter* 160.9

snaring *hunting* 160.2

snark *Legendary Creatures* 360

snarl *speak in a particular way* 205.18, *animal sound* 240.1, *make an animal sound* 240.7, *be angry* 302.19, *sign of irascibility* 303.6, *frown* 303.15, *sign of irritability* 304.4, *be irritable* 304.14, *distortion of face* 627.2, *make faces* 627.10, *mix-up* 766.5, *confuse* 766.19, *predicament* 824.5

snarled up *mixed up* 766.14

snarling *ululant* 240.4, *frowning* 303.12, 304.10

snarling dog *danger signal* 811.5

snarlingly *frowningly* 304.18

snarl up *confuse* 766.19

snarly *irritable* 304.9

snatch *touch* 216.9, *take away* 275.13, *take* 477.14, *theft* 479.2, *steal* 479.14, *jerk* 699.3, *pull at* 699.12

snatch a purse *steal* 479.14

snatch at *chase* 385.13, *pull at* 699.12

snatch block *sailboat parts and accessories* 150.4

snatcher *taker* 477.9

snatch from the grave *cure* 809.15

snatch from the jaws of death *deliver* 817.5

snatch from under one's nose *be cunning* 822.5

snatching *taking* 477.1, *stealing* 479.1

snatchy *discontinuous* 775.7

snazzily *flashily* 404.32

snazzy *stylish* 100.42, 537.7, *flashy* 404.17, *fashionable* 536.5

sneak *play offense* 155.18, *conceal oneself* 181.15, *hypocrite* 192.9, *retreat* 285.8

sneak after *follow* 385.12

sneak around *be dishonorable* 192.21

sneakers *shoes* 100.30, *basketball court* 148.3, *gymnastics equipment* 157.2

sneakily *deceptively* 193.21, *cowardly* 285.9, *hypocritically* 330.15

sneak in *infiltrate* 706.13

sneakiness *guile* 193.3, *cunning* 330.3

sneaking *dastardly* 285.6

sneaking suspicion *basis of supposition* 359.2

sneak off *retreat* 386.22, *escape* 816.8

sneak off with *steal* 479.14

sneak out *absent oneself* 576.15, *escape* 816.8

sneak preview *movie type* 137.3, *preview* 769.6

sneak thief *thief* 479.8

sneaky *artful* 193.13, *dastardly* 285.6, *cunning* 330.8

sneer *derision* 400.5, *disdain* 400.16, *taunt* 436.6, 436.23, *show*

of disapproval 438.6, ridicule 440.15, distortion of face 627.2, make faces 627.10
sneer at react against 291.15
sneered at criticized 438.14
sneering derision 400.5, derisive 400.12, taunting 436.14, scornful 440.10
sneeringly derisively 400.22
sneeze hiss 237.1, 237.3
sneeze at [Inf] exclude 383.11
sneezing hiss 237.1, hissing 237.2
snicker cry of amusement 239.2, laugh 239.14, 277.12
snickersnee sharp weapon 78.6
snide malicious 306.8, defamatory 440.9
snidely maliciously 306.15
snideness malice 306.2
sniff sense of smell 224.2, smell 224.7, taunt 436.6, 436.23, intake 708.5, draw in 708.18
sniff at taste 92.24, smell 224.7, exclude 383.11
sniffer dog dog 35.10, watchdog 810.11
sniffing drug use 121.9, sense of smell 224.2, intake 708.5
sniffle sense of smell 224.2, smell 224.7, intake 708.5, draw in 708.18
sniffly of disease 114.25
sniff out smell 224.7, meddle 321.8, detect 345.12, follow 385.12
snifter [Inf] size of drink 93.3, drink 121.6
snigger cry of amusement 239.2, laugh 239.14, 277.12, laughter 277.8
snigger about deride 369.7
snip particle 760.4
snip [Inf] little person 580.5
snipe water bird 36.9, table bird 36.10, Collective Names 59, attacker 418.10, berate 438.20, shoot 696.18
snipe at fire 418.18
sniper hunter 385.6, shooter 696.11
sniping offensive warfare 76.11, firing 418.6, terrorist attack 418.7
snippet appetizer 219.2, little piece 580.4, particle 760.4
snip-snap-snorem Card Games 168
snitch [Inf] informer 170.8, inform on 170.13, discloser 180.4, tell on 180.10, accuser 442.3, accuse 442.8, steal 479.14
snitcher [Inf] accuser 442.3
snitching [Inf] stealing 479.1
snivel weep 280.8
sniveler lamenter 280.3
sniveling sycophantic 401.7
snob proud person 297.7
snobbery arrogance 297.2, self-righteousness 431.7
snobbish arrogant 297.9, unjust 342.7, moralistic 431.12, contemptuous 436.12
snobbishly arrogantly 297.18
snobbishness arrogance 297.2
SNOBOL Programming Languages 15
snockered [Inf] dead drunk 121.27
snood headdress 100.35, hairdressing tool 530.9
snook game fish 154.10, derision 400.5
snooker 149.4; Sporting Activities 145, billiards 149.1, Board and Table Games 167
snooker [Inf] hinder 826.15
snookered billiard 149.6

snooker player player 149.5
snooker table snooker 149.4
snoop [Inf] meddler 321.4, meddle 321.8
snooping prying 321.2, 321.6
snoopy [Inf] prying 321.6
snoot [Inf] nose 19.11, protuberance 634.3
snootily [Inf] arrogantly 297.18
snooty [Inf] arrogant 297.9, vain 402.8, contemptuous 436.12
snooze desensitization 213.2, sleep 415.5, 415.14, ease 819.1, take it easy 819.3
snore be loud 232.8, hoarseness 238.2, sound hoarse 238.8
snoring loud sound 232.2, hoarse 238.5
snorkel swimming equipment 164.8, swim 164.14
snorkeler swimmer 164.11
snorkeling Sporting Activities 145, swimming 164.1
snort hoarseness 238.2, sound hoarse 238.8, make an animal sound 240.7, sign of irritability 304.4, be irritable 304.14, disdain 400.16, taunt 436.6, 436.23
snort [Inf] size of drink 93.3, drink 121.6, drug dose 121.15, drug oneself 121.37
snorting hoarse 238.5, panting 820.3
snorting [Inf] drug use 121.9
snot [Inf] saliva 25.9, dirt 112.5, body fluid 555.3, mucus 561.6
snotty [Inf] contemptuous 436.12, thick 561.17
snout glacier 8.44, nose 19.11, protuberance 634.3
snow 9.30, 9.58, 162.28, 218.6; precipitation 9.26, abound 97.8, mountaineering 161.9, that which makes invisible 245.2, white thing 253.4, Phobias 283, drip 714.13
snow [Inf] stimulants 121.18
snowball snow 218.6, increase 467.17, 746.6, grow 581.17, throw 696.17
snowball effect consequence 774.3
snowballer thrower 696.10
snowballing growing 581.12, increase 746.1, increasing 746.4
snowbank snow 9.30
snow bed snow 9.30
snow-blind blind 243.11, blinded 243.12
snow blindness climbing dangers 161.5, faulty vision 243.1
snowboard ski 162.35
snowboard edge snowboarding equipment 162.12
snowboarder skier 162.14
snowboard freestyle bindings snowboarding equipment 162.12
snowboarding 162.11, 162.30; Sporting Activities 145, skiing 162.1
snowboarding equipment 162.12
snowboard plate bindings snowboarding equipment 162.12
snowboard racing snowboarding 162.11
snow bollard belay climbing techniques 161.3
snowbound cold 218.9, detained 830.11
snow-capped whitened 253.8, mountainous 569.5
snow-capped peak mountain 569.1
snow-clad cool 9.49

snow climbing mountaineering 161.1
snow cover snow 9.30
snow-covered cool 9.49
snow crystal snow 218.6
Snowdon Mountains and Hills 569
snowdrift snow 9.30, 218.6
snowdrop Flowers 42
snowdrop tree Trees and Shrubs 43
snow eater Notable Winds 9
snowed in cold 218.9
snowed under overambitious 391.6
snowfall precipitation 9.26, snow 9.30, 218.6
snowflake precipitation 9.26, snow 218.6
snow fluke climbing equipment 161.4
snow flurry snow 218.6
snow-forest climate climate 9.35
snow house cold place 218.7
snowily meteorologically 9.60
snowiness whiteness 253.1
snow job [Inf] ungenuineness 192.2
snowline glacier 8.44
snowman figure 187.4, snow 218.6
snowmelt snow 9.30
snowmobile snow vehicle 687.9
snow-on-the-mountain Flowers 42
snow pellets hail 9.29
snowplow 162.29; cleaning tool 111.10, skiing techniques 162.5, ski 162.35
snowplow brake cross-country techniques 162.8
snowplow glide cross-country techniques 162.8
snowplow turn skiing techniques 162.5, cross-country techniques 162.8
snow season seasons 654.2
snow shed railroad station 688.6
snowshoe Breeds of Cats 35
snowshoes boots 100.31
snow shower snow 9.30
snow ski ski 162.35
snowslide snow 9.30, downflow 714.3
snowstorm snow 9.30, 218.6, natural violence 520.3
snowsuit suit 100.16, protection from the weather 810.9
snow under overcrowd 795.12
snow vehicle 687.9; road vehicle 687.4
snow wands climbing equipment 161.4
snow-white white 253.7
snowwoman figure 187.4, snow 218.6
snowy cool 9.49, clean 111.13, cold 218.9, white 253.7, pure 431.11, seasonal 654.7
Snowy Mountains Mountains and Hills 569
snub handle sailboat equipment 150.30, expression of dissatisfaction 274.2, rejection 383.1, exclude 383.11, avoidance 386.1, shun 386.14, ignore 409.11, act of discourtesy 411.3, be discourteous 411.7, insult 436.5, 436.21, dissent 506.9, blunt 550.5, repulse 701.2, repel 701.7, ostracize 709.17, debase 716.16
snubbed rejected 383.6
snubbiness shortness 591.1
snubbing rejecting 383.2, insulting 436.10, ostracism 709.3

snubby short 591.6
snuff tobacco 121.23, smell 224.7, make dark 247.10, intake 708.5, draw in 708.18
snuffbox tobacco 121.23, box 578.5
snuff-colored brown 256.5
snuff film [Inf] movie type 137.3, pornography 432.7
snuffle smell 224.7, hiss 237.3, intake 708.5, draw in 708.18
snuffly of disease 114.25
snuff out make dark 247.10, destroy 523.10, cause not to exist 718.14
snuff out [Inf] kill 30.19
snug luscious 214.8, pleased 214.9, hot 217.11, comfortable 271.8, waterproof 560.16, undersized 580.8, safe 810.16, invulnerable 810.18, at ease 819.2
snug [Brit] room 60.9
snug as a bug in a rug [Inf] pleased 214.9
snuggery [Brit] room 60.9, compartment 578.2
snuggle communicate love 299.25
snuggling communication of love 299.6
snugness littleness 580.1
so how 691.16, under the circumstances 726.16, accordingly 735.39
so? naturally! 295.10
soak be excessive 99.9, bathe 111.18, soaking 557.9, water 557.29, be present 575.13, absorb 708.19, obtain an extract 711.19, fill 761.11
soak [Inf] get drunk 121.35, overcharge 496.10
soakage soaking 557.9
soaked excessive 99.5, fixed 397.13, wet 557.23
soaked [Inf] dead drunk 121.27
soaked to the skin wet 557.23
soaker [Inf] drunkard 121.8
soak in infiltrate 706.13, absorb 708.19, descend 714.12
soaking 557.9; ablutions 111.4, ceramic process 129.5, absorbent 708.11, obtaining of an extract 711.7
soaking [Inf] drinking 93.1, 121.2
soaking wet wet 557.23
soak through enter 692.18
soak up absorb 560.20, 708.19, combine 757.9
so-and-so someone 18.10
soap cleaning agent 111.9, bathe 111.18, source of fragrance 226.2, toiletries 530.6, fat 562.4, lubricant 562.7, lubricate 562.15, ease 562.18
soap [Inf] broadcast drama 136.4, program 172.10
soap and water cleaning agent 111.9
soapbark Trees and Shrubs 43
soapbox stage 136.18, publicity 173.7
soapbox orator speaker 205.12, public speaker 209.5
soapbox oratory public speaking 205.11
soap flakes cleaning agent 111.9, fat 562.4
soapily oilily 562.19
soapiness oiliness 562.1
soaping ablutions 111.4
soap opera broadcast drama 136.4, program 172.10
soap pad cleaning agent 111.9
soap powder cleaning agent 111.9, fat 562.4
soap the way make easy 823.15

soapwort Flowers 42

soapy whitened 253.8, sycophantic 401.7, polished 545.7, oily 562.11

soar fly 36.23, 689.13, cost a lot 496.9, be light 539.8, tower over 569.7, be big 579.18, rise 596.17, be in motion 677.14, go up 713.23, increase 746.6

soarer ascender 713.12

soaring costly 496.7, mountainous 569.5, rising 596.12, ascending motion 677.7, directional 677.13, flight maneuver 689.6, flying 689.11, taking off 713.6, leaping 713.17

soaring prices or **costs** inflationary price 496.3

soave Musical Terms and Expression Marks 140

sob speak in a particular way 205.18, express pain 215.11, cry of sorrow 239.6, cry 239.16, grieve 270.7, lament 280.2, weep 280.8

S.O.B. [Inf] miscreant 448.6

sobbing crying 239.11, lamentation 280.1

sober 120.5; detached 4.18, sane 109.3, soft-hued 251.13, serious 278.4, principled 447.6, abstinent 455.7, moderate 521.3, mitigate 521.9

sober as a judge sober 120.5, serious 278.4

sober down mitigate 521.9

sobered up sober 120.5

soberly 120.9; stoically 4.26, sanely 109.6, solemnly 278.9, ethically 447.10

soberness sobriety 120.1, virtues 447.2, abstinence 455.2

sober person 120.4; self-restrained person 455.5

sobersides [Inf] self-restrained person 455.5

sober up 120.7; be sane 109.5, be moderate 521.6

so big this size 579.11

sobriety 120.1; sanity 109.1, dignity 297.4, abstinence 455.2, moderation 521.1

sobriquet name 202.8

sob story lament 280.2

socage medieval ownership 469.9, historical property terms 470.3

so-called disbelieved 88.7, supposed 359.6, artificial 720.12, imitation 736.8

soccer 163.1, 163.7; Sporting Activities 145, athletics 422.7

soccer associations and awards 163.6

soccer championship soccer associations and awards 163.6

soccer club soccer 163.1

soccer football soccer 163.1

soccer game or **match** soccer 163.1

soccer participant 163.4

soccer play 163.5

soccer player soccer participant 163.4

soccer shoes soccer uniform 163.3

soccer team soccer 163.1

soccer uniform 163.3

soceraphobia Phobias 283

sociability 407.2, 408.1; friendship 62.1, effusiveness 207.2, cheerfulness 269.2, benevolence 305.1, courtesy 410.1, social activity 414.2

sociable 407.7, 408.11; friendly 62.5, effusive 207.6, cheerful 269.7, benevolent 305.7, courteous

410.6, active 414.13, attending 575.9

sociableness sociability 408.1

sociably 408.19; amicably 62.13, effusively 207.10, benevolently 305.13, courteously 410.13

social sociological 2.11, types of history 3.2, national 18.16, of animals 34.13, social gathering 59.7, 408.4, place for conversation 210.5, sociable 408.11

social ability sociability 408.1

social action social change 2.9

social activity 414.2; sociability 408.1

social affair social gathering 408.4

social ambition 408.2

Social and Liberal Democratic party Political Parties 50

social anthropology anthropology 1.1, sociology 2.1

social anxiety disorder anxiety disorder 108.11

social assistance 825.4

social benefit social change 2.9

social butterfly social person 408.7

social call social gathering 408.4

social change 2.9

social charter labor relations 57.1

social circle society 408.8

social class 777.5; social stratification 2.7, group 18.13

social climbing social ambition 408.2

social code etiquette 406.3

social conduct etiquette 406.3

social conscience public-spiritedness 307.2

social consciousness public-spiritedness 307.2

social contact social environment 2.4

social control social change 2.9

social convention tradition 397.5, etiquette 406.3

social courtesies courtesies 410.3

social custom custom 397.4

social demand social success 408.3

Social Democratic and Labour party Political Parties 50

Social Democratic party Political Parties 50

social differences social environment 2.4

social discrimination 337.4

social disease sexually transmitted disease (STD) 114.17

social diversity social stratification 2.7

social drinker drinker 93.16, sober person 120.4

social elite fashionable elite 536.4

social engineering social change 2.9

social environment 2.4

social gathering 59.7, 408.4; place for conversation 210.5

social graces etiquette 406.3, social success 408.3

social group group 18.13, 59.8, family 65.1, society 408.8

social heterogeneity society 2.6

social hierarchy social stratification 2.7

social image etiquette 406.3

social improvement 807.3

social insect 40.6

social institution 2.8

social interaction social environment 2.4

social intercourse conversation 210.1, sociability 408.1

socialism political and economic

philosophy 4.6, economics 56.1, association 827.6

socialist political and economic philosopher 4.10, of a political philosophy 4.14, national 566.10

socialist or **socialistic** joint 827.10

socialist country country 566.1

socialistic of a political philosophy 4.14, national 18.16, 566.10

socialistically nationally 566.13

Socialist Labor party Political Parties 50

Socialist party Political Parties 50

socialist realism Western Art Styles 133, Western Literary Groups 139

socialist system economics 56.1

Socialist Workers party Political Parties 50

socialite social person 408.7, busy person 414.10

sociality sociability 408.1

socialization social environment 2.4, social improvement 807.3

socialize 2.14; become a nation 566.11, keep company with 794.17, civilize 807.16

social lion social person 408.7

socially societally 1.17, sociologically 2.15, humanly 18.18, sociably 408.19

socially accepted established 397.12, popular 408.12

socially active person busy person 414.10

socially conscious public-spirited 307.7

socially prominent aristocratic 70.4

socially successful popular 408.12

social manners tradition 397.5

social mobility social stratification 2.7

social morphology sociology 2.1

social movement social stratification 2.7, social change 2.9

socialness sociability 408.1

social novel novel 139.3

social obligation social change 2.9

social order social environment 2.4, government 49.1

social organization 2.5

social outcast loser 468.8

social person 408.7

social phobia anxiety disorder 108.11

social planning social change 2.9

social policy social change 2.9

social procedures etiquette 406.3

social progress social change 2.9

social psychologist sociologist 2.3

social psychology sociology 2.1, Psychological Theories, Schools 108

social pyramid social stratification 2.7

social realism Western Art Styles 133, Western Literary Groups 139

social reformer sociologist 2.3

Social Register™ aristocracy 70.2

social relations social environment 2.4, sociability 408.1

social role social environment 2.4

social round social gathering 408.4

social science sociology 2.1

social scientist sociologist 2.3

social season seasons 654.2

Social Security social welfare 307.4, security 464.1, insurance 810.10, social assistance 825.4

Social Security Network (SOSNET) computer communications 15.25

Social Security number personal identification 184.4

Social Security payments earnings 467.5

Social Security tax tax system 494.6

social services 2.10; social welfare 307.4, social assistance 825.4

social set society 408.8

social skill 127.3, sociability 408.1

social state body politic 50.3

social status social stratification 2.7, social class 777.5

social stratification 2.7

social structure social stratification 2.7

social success 408.3

social survey sociological research 2.2

social system social organization 2.5

social trait social environment 2.4

social transformation social change 2.9

social usage custom 397.4

social welfare 307.4; philanthropy 307.1

social whirl social gathering 408.4

social work social services 2.10

social worker sociologist 2.3, professional worker 123.11, adviser 176.5, benevolent person 305.6, philanthropist 307.5

societal 1.13; sociological 2.11, national 18.16

societally 1.17; cliquishly 59.32

society 1.6, 2.6, 408.8; social environment 2.4, social organization 2.5, humankind 18.1, group 18.13, association 59.4, Phobias 283, alliance 735.5, collection 757.3, companionship 794.3

Society Islands Islands 572

sociobiological sociological 2.11, biological 13.27

sociobiologically sociologically 2.15

sociobiologist sociologist 2.3, life scientist 13.26

sociobiology sociology 2.1, biology 13.2

sociodrama dramatic style 136.3

socioeconomic 2.13

socioeconomically sociologically 2.15

sociolinguistics Linguistic Studies 5

sociological 2.11; anthropological 1.10

sociological analysis sociological research 2.2

sociologically 2.15

sociological method sociological research 2.2

sociological model sociological research 2.2

sociological perspective sociological research 2.2

sociological research 2.2

sociological theory sociological research 2.2

sociological tool sociological research 2.2

sociologist 2.3; studier of humankind 18.7

sociology 2.1; study of humankind 18.6, study of life 28.9

sociology of knowledge sociology 2.1

sociometric technique sociological research 2.2

sociopath mental disorder 108.8

sociopathic psychologically disturbed 108.39

sociophobia Phobias 283
sociopolitical group group 18.13
sock box 152.19
sock [Inf] blow 695.5, hit 695.11
sock and buskin costume 100.10
sock away [Inf] save 105.20
socket electricity 106.5, golf equipment 156.5, cavity 635.3
socking boxing 152.2
socks legwear 100.26
Socrates sage 4.11
Socratic Philosophical Schools of Thought 4, reasoning 317.6, causal 511.5
Socratic philosophy Philosophical Schools of Thought 4
sod grassland 45.2, manage grassland 45.10, particle 760.4
soda soft drink 93.8, mixed drink 93.12, cleaning agent 111.9
soda cracker bread 90.10
soda fountain eating place 92.17, drink provider 93.15
soda jerk [Inf] attendant 69.4
sodality friendship 62.1, fellowship 827.2, association 827.6
soda water water 93.4, drinking water 557.2
sodbuster agriculturist 16.14
sodden drunken 121.28, wet 557.23
sodium Chemical Elements and Common Allotropes 11, essential element 12.15
sodium cyanide poison 117.7
sodium-vapor lamp electric light 246.6
sodomize stimulate 20.22
sodomy sex act 20.10, sexual offense 432.6
sofa furniture 101.1, couch 101.7, type of bed 101.9
sofa bed couch 101.7, type of bed 101.9
Sofia Countries 566
Sofia Brown Breeds of Cattle 16
soft 543.6; drinkable 93.18, type of furniture 101.2, ceramic 129.9, snowplow 162.29, luscious 214.8, hearable 228.12, silent 231.2, faint 233.6, soft-hued 251.13, amorous 299.18, submitting 421.3, lenient 423.3, obedient 426.4, weak 517.6, insufficient 517.11, moderating 521.5, insubstantial 539.5, sparse 541.3, smooth 545.4, pulpy 561.19, changeable 666.3, conformable 781.7
soft [Inf] persuadable 178.14
soft! hush! 231.6
soft or smooth as a baby's bottom figurative expressions 543.10
soft as a kiss or a whisper or a sigh figurative expressions 543.10
soft as butter or as wax or as soap figurative expressions 543.10
soft as down or snow figurative expressions 543.10
soft as putty or dough figurative expressions 543.10
soft as velvet or silk figurative expressions 543.10
softball Sporting Activities 145, baseball 147.1
soft-boiled egg egg dish 90.18
soft coal coal 106.4
soft-coated wheaten terrier Breeds of Dogs 35
soft-core pornography pornography 432.7
soft corn ulcer 114.18
softcover book 174.1

soft currency money 484.1
soft damp snow skiing snow 162.3
soft drink 93.8; sweet drink 222.4
soft drug drug 121.14
soften 543.14; comfort 214.14, mute 233.9, relieve 275.8, move to compassion 308.9, modify 340.13, justify 441.12, weaken 517.13, calm 521.8, refine 534.7
softened modified 340.9, soft 543.6
soft energy renewable energy 106.9
softening modification 340.5, soft 543.6, decreasing 747.5
soften the tone ease 543.15
soften up lay the foundations 388.16, blarney 439.13, weaken 517.13, soften 543.14
soft-fire make ceramics 129.10
soft firing ceramic process 129.5
soft focus murk 248.2
soft-focus murky 248.5
soft focusing framing 132.18
soft footfall small sound 233.4
soft fruit fruits 44.1
soft furnishing fabric 130.1
soft glaze glaze 129.3
soft goods dry goods 130.3
soft-grained woody 43.11
soft hail hail 9.29
soft-hearted 543.11; sensitive 267.9, pitying 308.4, kind 445.12
soft-heartedly 543.19; pityingly 308.11
soft-heartedness 543.4; pity 308.1, kindness 445.3
soft-hued 251.13
soft in the head [Inf] unintelligent 316.6
soft landing rocketry 7.32
soft light lighting 132.16, quality of light 246.2
softly 543.18; peacefully 73.12, silently 231.5, faintly 233.11, amorously 299.30, leniently 423.6, obediently 426.9, weakly 517.14, lightly 539.10, soothingly 545.14, changeably 666.7
softness 543.1; ski equipment 162.10, physical pleasure 214.1, sound 230.1, silence 231.2, faintness of sound 233.1, hue 251.4, leniency 423.1, obedience 426.1, helplessness 515.3, weakness 517.1, lightness 539.1, sparseness 541.1, smoothness 545.1, grain 552.2, pulpiness 561.9, changeableness 666.1, pliancy 781.3
soft-nosed armor-piercing 78.18
soft-nosed bullet ammunition 78.11
soft option easy thing 823.6
soft palate speech organ 205.4
soft-paste ceramic 129.9
soft-paste porcelain Ceramics 129
soft pedal sound reducer 233.5
soft-pedal silence 231.4, mute 233.9
soft-pedal [Inf] underestimate 344.5, mitigate 521.9
soft-pedaled nonresonant 233.7
soft pitch pitching terms 147.5
soft porn [Inf] pornography 432.7
soft rock rock music 140.6
soft roe fish characteristic 38.8
soft rot pests and diseases 17.12
soft sell publicity 178.7, salesmanship 482.4, inducement 508.2
soft-sell publicize 178.19
soft selling publicity 178.7
soft-shoe dancer dancer 135.4

soft-shoe dancing Dancing Types 135
soft shoulder edge 618.1
soft ski ski equipment 162.10
soft snowboard boots snowboarding equipment 162.12
soft soap [Inf] persuasion 178.1, blarney 439.2
soft-soap persuade 178.15, fawn 401.9 blarney 439.13
soft-soaping [Inf] sycophancy 401.2, sycophantic 401.7, honeyed 439.8
soft sound faintness of sound 233.1
soft-spoken speaking 205.15
soft spot likes 290.3, defect 806.4, vulnerability 811.6
soft style Western Art Styles 133
soft tick arachnid 40.4
soft touch easy thing 823.6
soft underbelly sensitivity 212.2, defect 806.4, vulnerability 811.6
soft vacuum surface chemistry 11.20
soft voice undercurrent of sound 233.3
software 15.12
software engineer computer user 15.3
software engineering programming concepts 15.24
soft water water 557.1
softwood woody 43.11, wood 131.3, canoeing 150.26
softwood (tree) tree 43.1
softy [Inf] weak person 517.4
soggily softly 543.18, continentally 572.13
sogginess compressibility 543.3
soggy compressible 543.9, wet 557.23
so happen chance 842.12
SoHo New York 567.6
Soho London 567.8
soigné elegant 527.3
soigné or soignée refined 48.20
soil 8.42; defecate 25.21, building materials 104.2, dirt 112.5, dirty 112.11, demoralize 432.15, defame 440.13, blemish 533.7, region 564.1, stain 808.20
soil, the countryside 564.3
soiled dirty 112.7, marked 533.6, imperfect 806.5
soil erosion soil 8.42, infertile land 23.2
soil horizon soil 8.42
soiling dirtiness 112.1, Phobias 283
soil mechanics civil engineering 14.17
soil one's hands work 122.8
soil profile soil 8.42
soil structure soil 8.42
soil texture soil 8.42
so inclined intending 374.6
soirée social gathering 59.7, 408.4, place for conversation 210.5
so it seems ideologically 327.23
sojourn inhabit 61.13, visit 408.16
Sokolka Breeds of Sheep 16
Sokólsky Horse and Pony Breeds 159
Sokoto Breeds of Cattle 16
Sol sun 7.15, Deities 82
sol phase 11.13
solace ease 275.1, relieve 275.8, cheer 281.4
solano Notable Winds 9
solar astronomical 7.33, fine 9.43, renewable 106.15, power supplier 514.14, oceanic 571.7
solar activity sun 7.15
solar battery renewable energy 106.9, power supplier 514.14

solar cell artificial satellite 7.30, renewable energy 106.9
solar cycle sun 7.15
solar disk sun 7.15
solar eclipse sun 7.15, darkness 247.1
solar energy sun 9.21, energy 10.10, 514.7, fuels 106.2, renewable energy 106.9, photoemission 246.11, power source 514.13
solar flare sun 7.15
solar heating heater 217.3
solarium room 60.9, hot place 217.5
solarization framing 132.18
solar mass astronomical unit 7.23
solar panel artificial satellite 7.30, heater 217.3, power supplier 514.14
solar power sun 9.21, fuels 106.2, renewable energy 106.9, type of power 514.6, power source 514.13
solar-powered fired 106.13
solar prominence sun 7.15
solar radiation sun 9.21
solar spectrum sun 7.15
solar system 7.14
solar telescope telescope 7.25
solar tide tide 571.2
solar time time zone 646.5
solar wind solar system 7.14
solatium compensation 453.7
Solcava Breeds of Sheep 16
sold 482.14; published 174.18
solder material 144.6, heat 217.17, intertwine 752.19, adhesive 755.3, cause to adhere 755.10
soldering adhesion 755.1
soldering iron material 144.6, heater 217.3
soldier 77.4; killer 30.11, social insect 40.6, warrior 76.25, be at war 76.32, fighter 422.14
soldier ant social insect 40.6
soldiering warfare 76.3
soldierlike military 76.28, martial 77.33
soldierly military 58.10, 76.28, martial 77.33, heroic 284.10
soldier of fortune militarist 77.3
soldiership art of war 76.16
Soldier's Medal US Military Medals 58
soldo ancient coins 484.12
sold out sold 482.14, full 761.8
sole food fish and shellfish 90.20, golf equipment 156.5, corporate 480.17, excluding 764.5, one 788.10, repair 809.10
sole [Arch] celibate 67.6
solecism word 5.17, sophistry 330.1, sophism 330.2, language error 351.10, inelegance of expression 528.4, vulgarity 535.1
solecist sophist 330.6
solecistic ill-used 395.4, inelegant 528.6
solecistical sophistic 330.7, vulgar 535.6
solecistically sophistically 330.14
solely once 788.23
solemn religious 81.21, ritualistic 85.15, serious 200.5, 278.4, 799.8, silent 231.2, dignified 297.11, majestic 404.21, celebrative 405.9, formal 406.6, ceremonious 406.7
solemn entreaty request 505.1
solemnity seriousness 200.2, 278.1, dignity 297.4, pomp 404.7, ceremonial 404.11, formality 406.1, importance 799.1

Solemnity of Mary Christian Holy Days and Seasons 85

solemnization *sacramentalism* 85.3, *commemoration* 405.2

solemnize *perform rites* 85.18, *commemorate* 405.11, *formalize* 406.9, *do something* 412.13, *fashion* 537.9

solemnly 278.9; *religiously* 81.29, *ritually* 85.21, *emphatically* 200.7, *with dignity* 297.20, *majestically* 404.36, *formally* 406.12, *as promised* 458.16

solemnly promise *promise* 458.11

solemnness *formality* 406.1

solemn oath *vow* 189.3

solemn observance *ceremony* 405.3

solemn promise *promise* 458.1

solemn silence *silence* 231.1

solemn wedding *wedding* 64.5

solemn word *vow* 189.3

solenoid *magnet* 10.47, 700.3

soleplate *golf equipment* 156.5

sole possession *monopoly* 469.4

sole proprietor *company* 480.7

sole rights *exclusiveness* 764.4

sole survivor *person remaining* 750.6

solfège *scale* 140.16

solfeggio *scale* 140.16

solferino *red pigment* 257.2

solicit *prostitute* 432.17, *sell* 482.15, *request* 505.10

solicit advice *consult* 176.11

solicitation 505.4; *exhortation* 178.2, *petition* 505.2, *inducement* 508.2

solicit business *trade* 480.18

soliciting *prostitution* 432.4, *selling* 482.1, *request* 505.1

soliciting money *solicitation* 505.4

solicit money 505.13

solicitor *law officer* 53.6, *agent* 80.3, *persuader* 178.9, *negotiator* 460.4, *requester* 505.5

solicitor [Brit] *lawyer* 54.5

Solicitor General [Brit] *law officer* 53.6

solicitous 323.8; *worried* 283.11, *compassionate* 305.8, *considerate* 325.7, *courteous* 410.6

solicitously *compassionately* 305.14, *caringly* 325.14, *courteously* 410.13, *genteelly* 410.14

solicitousness *courtesy* 410.1

solicitude 323.5; *consideration* 325.2, *courtesy* 410.1

solid *geometric figure* 6.39, *spatial* 6.76, *phase* 11.13, *status adjectives* 11.25, *serious* 200.5, *touchable* 216.5, *opaque* 250.3, *assenting* 346.4, *steady* 376.8, *solvent* 485.9, *material* 524.7, *heavy* 538.9, *solid body* 540.4, *dense* 540.6, *tough* 542.6, 547.6, *present* 575.7, *thick* 594.5, *formed* 624.6, *permanent* 667.2, *unfailing* 667.3, *stable* 674.3, *real* 719.6, *agreeing* 730.8, *agreeable* 752.11, *adhesive* 755.5, *full* 761.8, *continuous* 774.9, *whole* 788.12, *infallible* 840.12

solid angle *angle* 6.37, *dimension* 10.5

solid angles Fields of Measurement 589

solidarity *friendship* 62.1, *agreement* 730.2, 752.4, *compatibility* 735.4, *completeness* 761.1, *oneness* 788.3, *fellowship* 827.2

solid body 540.4; *heaviness* 538.1

solid-earth 8.55

solid-earth geophysics *geophysics* 8.2

solid figure *geometric figure* 6.39

solid fuel *rocketry* 7.32, *fuel* 106.1, *propellant* 696.9

solid geometry *geometry* 6.32

solid gold *bullion* 484.16

solidification *concentration* 540.2, *hardening* 542.2, *union* 752.1

solidified *condensed* 540.7, *hardened* 542.7

solidify 11.37, 542.10; *freeze* 10.75, *be dense* 540.8, *be present* 575.13, *thicken* 594.9, *adhere* 755.8, *make certain* 840.14

solidifying *condensed* 540.7, *conjunctive* 752.12

solidity *touch* 216.1, *opaqueness* 250.1, *solvency* 485.4, *material world* 524.1, *density* 540.1, *hardness* 542.1, *presence* 575.1, *thickness* 594.1, *permanence* 667.1, *stability* 674.1, *reality* 719.1, *completeness* 761.1, *oneness* 788.3, *infallibility* 840.6

solidly *palpably* 216.12, *opaquely* 250.9, *materially* 524.17, *densely* 540.10, *toughly* 547.16, *in person* 575.18, *formatively* 624.10, *permanently* 667.6, *stably* 674.9, *in accord* 735.33, *agreeably* 752.22, *cohesively* 755.11, *completely* 759.14

solid mass *solid body* 540.4

solidness *density* 540.1, *toughness* 547.1

solid of revolution *curved surface* 6.43

solid rocket booster (SRB) *rocketry* 7.32

solid silver *bullion* 484.16

solid-state *physical* 10.70, *electric* 14.47

solid-state device *circuit element* 14.39

solid-state memory *memory* 15.6

solid-state physics Fields of Modern Physics 10

solid substance *matter* 524.4

solid surface *surface* 6.36

solidus Punctuation Marks 5, *oblique line* 607.5, *separator* 753.5, *means of connection* 754.4

soliloquist 211.2; *speaker* 205.12, *soloist* 788.9

soliloquize 211.4; *talk to oneself* 205.20

soliloquizer *speaker* 205.12, *soliloquist* 211.2

soliloquizing 211.3

soliloquizingly 211.6

soliloquy 211.1; *dramaturgy* 136.6, *play part* 136.8, *public speaking* 205.11, *soloist* 788.9

soling *repair* 809.1

solipsism Philosophical Schools of Thought 4, *self-satisfaction* 402.2, *internal world* 525.6

solipsist Philosophical Schools of Thought 4, *inactive person* 413.8, *nonmaterialist* 525.11, *internal* 525.11

solipsistic *selfish* 402.12, *internal* 525.11

solipsistically *smugly* 402.18

solitaire Card Games 168, *hermit* 782.9

solitarily *celibately* 67.12, *aloofly* 756.10

solitariness *separation* 409.3, *aloneness* 788.5

solitary 782.17; *of animals* 34.13, *misanthrope* 291.5, *lonely* 409.8,

aloof 756.5, *loner* 788.8, *one* 788.10, *alone* 788.15

solitary [Inf] *prison cell* 55.3

solitary confinement *prison cell* 55.3, *imprisonment* 55.4, *detention* 830.5

solitary person *unsocial person* 409.5

solitary place 409.4

solitary state *monasticism* 67.3

solitude Phobias 283, *separation* 409.3, *aloofness* 756.2, *aloneness* 788.5

solitudinarian *hermit* 782.9

solmization *scale* 140.16

solo 788.14; *song* 140.11, *mountaineering* 161.9, *mountaineer* 161.10, Card Games 168, *pilot* 689.15, *soloist* 788.9, *one* 788.10, *alone* 788.20

solo effort *soloist* 788.9

Sologne Breeds of Sheep 16

soloing *climbing techniques* 161.3

soloist 788.9; *musician* 141.1, *singer* 141.4

soloistic *soliloquizing* 211.3

Solomon *sage* 4.11, *judge* 54.10, *wise person* 352.3

Solomon Islands Countries 566, Islands 572

Solomon's seal Flowers 42

Solon *sage* 4.11

solon *lawmaker* 53.12

so long! [Inf] *goodbye!* 705.14

so long as *all the time* 639.16

solstitial *seasonal* 654.7

solstitially *seasonally* 654.12

solubility *fluidization* 555.8, *mixture* 751.1

solubilization *fluidization* 555.8

solubilize *dissolve* 555.23

soluble *numerable* 6.70, *solvable* 334.14, *liquefiable* 555.21, *mixed* 751.8

solubleness *fluidity* 555.5

solubly *conclusively* 334.26

solute *phase* 11.13

solution 334.6, 376.6, 555.10; *operation* 6.12, *equation* 6.25, *phase* 11.13, *remedy* 115.1, *darkroom equipment* 132.21, *interpretation* 341.9, *fluidization* 555.8, *dilution* 557.5, *mixed thing* 751.2, *compound* 757.4, *conclusion* 761.3

solution set *equation* 6.25

solvable 334.14; *numerable* 6.70

solvate *react* 11.38

solve 334.21; *rationalize* 4.20, *enumerate* 6.85, *decipher* 365.13, *dissolve* 555.23, *calculate* 784.10, *reveal* 843.14

solved 334.15

solvency 485.4; *credit* 487.1

solvent 484.23, 485.9, 555.9; *phase* 11.13, *material* 143.9, *well-off* 467.12, *in credit* 487.8, *liquefied* 555.19, *thinner* 595.7

solvent front *analysis* 11.17

solvently *monetarily* 484.27

solver *answerer* 334.10

Somali Breeds of Sheep 16, Breeds of Cats 35

Somalia Countries 566

so many *quantitative* 738.6

somatic *material* 524.7

somatic cell *cell* 13.15

somatic-type delusional disorder *psychosis* 108.10

somatization disorder *somatoform disorder* 108.19

somatoform disorder 108.19

somatoform disorders *mental disorder* 108.8

somatology *anthropology* 1.1

somatostatin Human Hormones 12

somatotropin Human Hormones 12

somatotype *physical type* 1.8

somber *funeral* 31.9, *dim* 248.4, *soft-hued* 251.13, *sad* 254.10, *dull* 255.8, *serious* 278.4, *dignified* 297.11, *sullen* 304.8, *overcast* 304.11

somberly *funereally* 31.13, *grayly* 255.10, *with dignity* 297.20, *sullenly* 304.16

somberness *darkness* 247.1, *sullenness* 304.1

sombrero *hat* 100.32

some *certain amount* 738.3, *quantitative* 738.6, *quantitatively* 738.8, *plurality* 793.1, *plural* 793.6, *few* 796.1, 796.5

somebody *someone* 18.10, *person of repute* 370.2, *important person* 799.5

someday *at what time* 639.17, *another time* 648.4, *in the future* 650.13

somehow *by means of* 102.7, *how* 691.16, *potentially* 836.11

somehow or other *how* 691.16

someone 18.10

someone in a hurry *busy person* 414.10

someone promised 458.7

some other time *different time* 648.1, *another time* 648.4, *in the future* 650.13

somersault *floor exercise* 157.4, *horizontal bar* 157.5, *exercise* 157.12, *ski* 162.35, *competitive diving* 164.7, *diving* 164.13, *act of inversion* 608.3, *become inverted* 608.8

somersaulter *gymnast* 157.10

somersaulting *skiing* 162.1, *ski* 162.27

somersault with twist *competitive diving* 164.7

Somerset Islands 572

something *object* 524.6, *thing* 717.3

something else *incomparability* 734.3

something extra *reward* 472.4, *advantage* 744.3

something for a rainy day *personal finance* 457.5, *surplus* 750.4, *insurance* 810.10

something for nothing *windfall* 467.7, *absence of charge* 497.6

something in common *relatedness* 727.1

something in hand *advantage* 744.3

something in reserve *reserves* 102.5, *advantage* 744.3

something like [Inf] *similar* 733.7

something new *originality* 737.1

something off *discount* 495.1

something owing *debt* 488.1

something received 473.2

something the cat dragged in *ugly thing* 531.2

sometime *at what time* 639.17, *another time* 648.4, *former* 651.14, 653.12, *dead* 658.10, *infrequent* 662.2, *resigning* 835.3

some time ago *in the past* 651.20

sometimes 639.19, 662.5; *for short periods* 641.13, *infrequently* 662.4

somewhat *moderately* 521.10, *certain amount* 738.3, *to a degree* 739.11, *partly* 760.17

somewhere *here* 575.19

somewhere else *away* 576.19
some while back *in the past* 651.20
so minded *intending* 374.6
Somme Rivers 570
sommelier *attendant* 69.4
somnambulate *be insensible* 213.7
somnambulism *sleep disorder* 108.20
somnifacient *anesthetic* 213.3, *soporific* 415.6
somniferous *anesthetic* 213.6
somnific *anesthetic* 213.6
somnolence *mood disorder* 108.12, *desensitization* 213.2, *sleep* 415.5
somnolent *anesthetic* 213.6, *not awake* 415.12
somnolently *insensibly* 213.9, *sleepily* 415.19
so much *quantitative* 738.6
so much nonsense *unintelligibility* 364.1
son *male title of address* 32.3, *man in the family* 32.12, *family member* 65.2, *loved one* 299.13
sonance *sound* 230.1
sonant *spoken letter* 5.15, *voiced* 5.37
sonar *sounding* 10.16, *tone* 230.2, *sound propagation* 230.3, *detector* 345.6, *bathymetry* 598.3, *position finder* 690.8
sonata Musical Forms 140
sonatina Musical Forms 140
so near and yet so far *disappointingly* 293.12
son et lumière [Fr] *show* 138.4, 404.12, *highlight* 246.12
song 140.11, Poem or Verse Forms 139, *poetry* 139.8, *melody* 140.10
song and dance *show business* 138.1, *fuss* 684.4
song-and-dance *variety* 138.13
song-and-dance man *entertainer* 138.8
song-and-dance show *show* 138.4
songbird 36.12
songbird [Inf] *singer* 141.4
Songhua Rivers 570
songster *cage bird* 36.13, *singer* 141.4
songwriter *composer* 141.9
sonic *sounding* 230.7
sonic barrier *sound propagation* 230.3
sonic boom *sound propagation* 230.3, *burst of sound* 232.4, *bang* 234.1
sonic depth finder *sound propagation* 230.3
sonics *tone* 230.2
sonic speed *speed* 694.2
son-in-law *family member* 65.2
sonnet Poem or Verse Forms 139
sonneteer *author* 139.13
sonnet sequence Poem or Verse Forms 139
sonny *male title of address* 32.3
sonobuoy *sound propagation* 230.3, *sea marker* 690.7
son of a bitch *miscreant* 448.6
Son of God God the Son 82.9
Son of Man God the Son 82.9
Sonoran Deserts 572
sonority *deepness* 236.3
sonorous *hearable* 228.12, *sounding* 230.7, *deep* 236.8, *deep-sounding* 598.19, *harmonizing* 735.12
sonorously *resonantly* 236.11, *in harmony* 735.32
sonorousness *deepness* 236.3, *harmonization* 735.2

soon 657.18; *another time* 648.4, *in the future* 650.13, *early* 657.17
sooner *by choice* 382.18
sooner or later *another time* 648.4
soot *dirt* 112.5, *dark thing* 247.3, *black thing* 254.3, *powder* 553.9
sooth [Arch] *truth* 721.1, *true* 721.11
soothe *conciliate* 74.10, *remedy* 115.16, *comfort* 214.14, *make pleasant* 271.10, *relieve* 275.8, *grieve* 308.7, *mitigate* 521.9, *ease* 543.15, *smooth over* 545.12, *make motionless* 678.8
soothed *relieved* 275.6
soother *reliever* 275.4
soothing 545.6; *pacification* 74.1, *pacificatory* 74.8, *medicinal* 115.15, *pleasant* 214.7, *comfortable* 271.8, *relieving* 275.7, *pitying* 308.4, *moderating* 521.5, *lubricational* 562.12
soothing influence *moderator* 521.2
soothingly 545.14; *pacifically* 74.12, *comfortingly* 275.14, *pityingly* 308.11
soothing syrup *balm* 115.11
soothsay *divine* 86.24, 358.15
soothsayer *diviner* 86.14, *oracle* 358.8, *predictor* 650.5
soothsaying *divination* 86.5, 358.2
sooty *dirty* 112.7, *black* 254.5, *powdery* 553.19
sooty mold *pests and diseases* 17.12
sop *incentive* 178.4, *leniency* 423.1, *stimulus* 508.3
sophism 330.2
sophist 330.6; *philosopher* 4.9, *equivocator* 380.4, *cunning person* 822.1
sophister *sophist* 330.6, *distorter* 627.5
sophistic 330.7
sophistic *or* **sophistical** *logical* 329.9, *meaningless* 362.7
sophistical *sophistic* 330.7, *cunning* 822.4
sophistically 330.14; *philosophically* 4.23
sophisticate *make worse* 808.17
sophisticated *refined* 48.20, 534.5, *cunning* 330.8, 822.4, *elegant* 527.3, *stylish* 537.7, *smooth-mannered* 545.9
sophisticatedly *discerningly* 48.27, *tastefully* 534.9, *suavely* 545.15
sophistication *refinement* 48.10, 534.1, *social skill* 127.3, *cunning* 330.3, 822.1, *good manners* 410.2, *elegance* 527.1, *mixture* 751.1, *impairment* 808.7
sophisticator *sophist* 330.6
sophistry 330.1; *lack of candor* 192.4, *logical argument* 329.2, *faulty reasoning* 351.4, *nonsense* 362.2, *affectation* 367.1, *equivocation* 380.1, *distortion of truth* 627.4, *cunning* 822.1
Sophoclean tragedy *tragedy* 136.10
sophomore *learner* 48.6
sophophobia Phobias 283
soporific 415.6; *anesthetic* 213.6, *reliever* 275.4, *not awake* 415.12, *moderator* 521.2, *moderating* 521.5
soporifically *sleepily* 415.19
sopping *wet* 557.23
sopping wet *wet* 557.23
soprano *voice* 141.5, *musical part* 760.8
Sopravissana Breeds of Sheep 16
so quiet one could hear a pin drop *silent* 231.2

sorb Trees and Shrubs 43, *absorb* 11.40, 708.19
sorb apple Trees and Shrubs 43
sorbed *absorbed* 11.34
sorbent *absorbent* 708.11
sorbet *dessert* 90.35, *confectionery* 222.3
s-orbital *chemical bond* 11.6
sorbitol *saccharide* 12.4
sorbose Common Sugars 12
sorcerer *witch* 86.15, *changer* 665.9
sorcerer *or* **sorceress** *wonderful person* 294.6
sorceress *witch* 86.15
sorcerize *bewitch* 86.25
sorcerous *witchlike* 86.19, *wonder-working* 294.11
sorcery *witchcraft* 86.6, *cause of wonder* 294.4, *impiety* 448.4, *occult influence* 512.2, *type of power* 514.6
sorde Collective Names 59
sordid *unclean* 112.8, *unhygienic* 114.27, *unpleasant* 501.5
sordidly *dirtily* 112.12
sordidness *untidiness* 766.3
sordino *sound reducer* 233.5
sore *hostile* 63.6, *symptom* 114.3, *ulcer* 114.18, *of disease* 114.25, *miserable* 117.12, *painful* 215.4, *feeling pain* 215.6, *fatigued* 820.2
sore [Inf] *irritable* 302.10, *cross* 303.11
soredium *lichen* 47.16
sorehead [Inf] *irascible person* 303.7, *sullen person* 304.7
sorely [Inf] *crossly* 303.20
soreness *ill feeling* 63.3, *pain* 117.5, 215.1, *oversensitivity* 267.2
soreness [Inf] *irritableness* 302.5, *crossness* 303.4
sore point *oversensitivity* 267.2, *provocation* 302.3, *divisiveness* 463.2
sore spot *stimulus* 212.3, *pain* 215.1
sore throat *symptom* 114.3, *respiratory disease* 114.12, *painful condition* 215.2
sorghum *crop* 16.8
sororal *family* 65.6
sororicide *homicide* 30.4
sorority *group* 18.13, *association* 59.4, *friendship* 62.1, *team* 827.7
sorority house *school place* 48.16
sorosis *botanical fruit* 44.2
sorption *process* 11.15, *surface chemistry* 11.20, *absorption* 708.6
Sorraia pony Horse and Pony Breeds 159
sorrel Herbs and Spices 91, *horse by color* 159.7, *brown* 256.5
sorrel tree Trees and Shrubs 43
sorrily *apologetically* 313.11, *guiltily* 450.12
sorriness *penitence* 451.1
sorrow 270.1; *adversity* 117.2, 848.1, *grieve* 270.7, 308.7, *lamentation* 280.1, *lament* 280.7
sorrower *sad person* 270.3
sorrowful 270.4; *miserable* 117.12, *lamenting* 280.4, *penitent* 451.5
sorrowfully 270.10; *lamentingly* 280.9, *destructively* 446.13, *penitently* 451.10
sorrowfulness *sorrow* 270.1, *lamentation* 280.1
sorry *distressing* 270.6, *apologetic* 313.6, *appearing guilty* 450.7, *penitent* 451.5
sorry for *pitying* 308.4
sorry for oneself *pitying* 308.4
sorry plight *predicament* 824.5
sort 202.6, 777.13; *correspond*

169.19, *description* 202.1, *discriminate* 337.12, *fashion* 536.1, *size* 579.17, *kind* 624.3, *measure* 739.7, *set apart* 753.17, *systematize* 765.19, *categorize* 767.21, *type* 777.4
sorted *judged* 337.10, *selected* 382.11, *gradational* 739.5, *grouped* 765.11, *categorized* 767.15, *classed* 777.7
sorted out *solved* 334.15, *categorized* 767.15
sorter *postal worker* 169.6
sortie *military attack* 418.2, *violence by person* 520.2, *aviation* 689.1
sortilege *divination* 86.5, *witchcraft* 86.6
sorting *programming concepts* 15.24, *discrimination* 337.1, *categorization* 767.5, *classification* 777.2
sorting office *postal service* 169.5
sorting out *solution* 334.6, 376.6, *selecting* 382.4, *categorization* 767.5
sorting through *selecting* 382.4
sort of *to a degree* 739.11
sort out *purify* 111.19, *solve* 334.21, *decipher* 365.13, *put right* 429.14, *systematize* 765.19, *categorize* 767.21
sorus *fern plant* 46.2
SOS *signal* 183.6, *proclamation* 183.8, *danger signal* 811.5
so-so *satisfactory* 273.6, *mediocre* 289.11, 742.7, *unexceptionally* 289.20, *moderate* 521.3, *middling* 772.14
sostenuto Musical Terms and Expression Marks 140
sostenuto pedal *resonator* 236.5
sot *drunkard* 121.8
soteriological *theological* 81.24
soteriology Theologies 81
so to speak *meaningfully* 361.16
sottish *drunken* 121.28
sottishness *drunkenness* 121.3
sotto voce Musical Terms and Expression Marks 140
sotto voce *secretly* 182.14, *faintly* 233.11
sou *ancient coins* 484.12
soubrette *stock part* 136.24
soufflé *egg dish* 90.18, *air bubble* 558.10
soufflé dish *cooking equipment* 91.6
sough *blow* 9.53, *undercurrent of sound* 233.3, *sound faint* 233.8
sought *questioned* 333.15, *pursued* 385.10
sought-after *desired* 288.10, *popular* 408.12, *sold* 482.14
soul *person* 18.8, *life force* 28.2, *spirit* 86.10, *psyche* 108.25, *folk music* 140.7, *musical* 140.25, *seat of feelings* 266.7, *internal world* 525.6, *inner nature* 611.4, *quintessence* 723.3, *one* 788.1
soul body *spirit* 86.10
soul food *food* 90.1
soul kiss *communication of love* 299.6
soul-kiss *communicate love* 299.25
soul mate *spouse* 64.8, *loved one* 299.13, *affinity* 733.3
soul mates *lovers* 299.12
soul-search *question* 333.16
soul-searching *curiosity* 333.8, *penitence* 451.1, *inwardness* 611.5, *inward* 611.12
sound 10.15, 141.15, 230.1, 230.8, 759.8; *rational* 4.15,

109.4, *classical physics* 10.2, *healthy* 113.4, *skillful* 127.10, *hear* 228.13, *be heard* 228.15, *be loud* 232.8, *ring* 236.10, Phobias 283, *thoughtful* 315.10, *good* 445.10, *fast* 464.8, *solvent* 484.23, 485.9, *physically strong* 516.10, *inlet* 572.9, Fields of Measurement 589, *measurability* 589.2, *measure* 589.20, *measure depth* 598.22, *stable* 674.3, *practical* 719.8, *unbroken* 805.13, *safe* 810.16, *infallible* 840.12

soundalike *substitute* 672.2, 672.3
sound amplifier 230.5
sound-and-light show *show* 138.4, 404.12, *highlight* 246.12
sound a retreat *retreat* 680.17
sound argument *reasoning* 6.61
sound as a bell *feeling well* 113.4, *physically strong* 516.10, *unbroken* 805.13
sound a siren *give warning* 814.10
sound asleep *not awake* 415.12
sound a tattoo *drum* 235.10
sound a warning *give warning* 814.10
sound barrier *sound propagation* 230.3, *speed* 694.2
sound bite *catchword* 5.22, *news event* 171.2, *part* 760.1
sound box *resonator* 236.5
sound card *card* 15.7
sound correct *logical* 6.83
sound currency *money* 484.1
sound dead *be nonresonant* 233.10
sound desk *stage* 136.18
sound economy *economy* 56.3
sound editor *filmmaker* 137.14
sound effects *production* 137.6
sound engineer *filmmaker* 137.14
sounder Collective Names 59
sound faint 233.8
sound hoarse 238.8
sound hole *part of stringed instrument* 142.2
sounding 10.16, 230.7; *tone* 230.2, *ringing* 236.7, *bathymetry* 598.3, *bathymetric* 598.12, *harmonizing* 735.12
sounding board *resonator* 236.5
sounding brass *ringing* 236.2, *nonsense* 362.2
sounding line *bathymetry* 598.3
soundingly *in harmony* 735.32
soundingness *harmonization* 735.2
sounding out *experiment* 335.1
sound in wind and limb *feeling well* 113.8, *sound* 759.8
sound judgment *common sense* 315.4
soundless *silent* 231.2, *deep* 598.9, *quiescent* 678.6
soundlessly *silently* 231.5
soundlessness *silence* 231.1, *depth* 598.1
sound level *sound propagation* 230.3
sound like a broken record *bore* 296.8
soundly *rationally* 4.25, *well* 445.19, *fastly* 464.16, *strongly* 516.17, *stably* 674.9
sound man *stagehand* 136.29, *filmmaker* 137.14
sound mind *sanity* 109.1
sound mixer *filmmaker* 137.14
sound motion picture *or* **sound film** *movie type* 137.3
soundness *reasoning* 6.61, *health* 113.1, *good* 445.1, *solvency* 485.4, *nature* 624.5, *stability* 674.1,

perfect condition 805.3, *infallibility* 840.6
soundness of mind *sanity* 109.1, *wisdom* 352.1
sound one's horn *give warning* 814.10
sound out *question* 333.16, *experiment* 335.11
sound-power level *sound propagation* 230.3
sound-pressure level *sound propagation* 230.3
soundproof *unheard* 229.7, *muffle* 229.11, *silent* 231.2, *mute* 233.9
soundproofed *nonresonant* 233.7
soundproofing *sound reducer* 233.5
sound propagation 230.3
sound proposition *credit* 487.1
sound quality 230.4
sound recording *production* 137.6
sound recordist *filmmaker* 137.14
sound reducer 233.5
sound reduction *faintness of sound* 233.1
sound reproduction 230.6
sound stage *motion-picture studio* 137.7
sound system *sound reproduction* 230.6
sound the alarm *give warning* 814.10
sound the charge *battle* 76.33, *attack* 418.17
sound the depth *handle sailboat equipment* 150.30
sound the fire alarm *give warning* 814.10
sound the last post *pay one's last respects* 31.12
sound the praises of *praise* 437.16
sound the trumpet *motivate* 508.9
sound the trumpets *signal* 183.18
sound truck *sound amplifier* 230.5
sound true *seem true* 721.26
sound wave *wave* 10.11, 683.4
soup 90.14; *dish* 90.7, *course* 92.12, *juice* 555.2, *semiliquid* 561.7, *mixed thing* 751.2
soup-and-fish [Inf] *formal clothes* 100.5
soup bowl *crockery* 578.16
soupçon *appetizer* 219.2, *little piece* 580.4, *admixture* 751.5, *few* 796.1, *suggestion* 800.9
soup du jour *the special* 779.8
souped-up [Inf] *swift* 694.6
soup of the day *dish* 90.7
soup's on! *come and get it!* 92.28
soup spoon *tableware* 92.13
soup up [Inf] *strengthen* 516.15, *invigorate* 518.5
soupy *pulpy* 561.19
sour 223.8; *hostile* 63.6, *strained* 117.13, *tasty* 219.4, *piquant* 221.6, *acid* 223.5, *putrid* 227.4, *antipathetic* 291.7, *disappoint* 293.9, *cause hate* 300.12, *ill-natured* 303.9, *irritable* 304.9, *make irritable* 304.15, *bitter* 306.9, *jealous* 314.5
sourball *sweets* 90.39
source 675.2, 771.3; *source of supply* 105.4, *information source* 170.6, *informer* 170.8, *river parts* 570.3, *original* 737.2, *originator* 737.3
source book *schoolbook* 48.15
source code *programming language* 15.16, *programming concepts* 15.24
source of fragrance 226.2

source of pride *object of pride* 297.6
source of resonance 236.4
source of supply 105.4
sour cream *sour thing* 223.3
sourd Musical Terms and Expression Marks 140
sourdine *sound reducer* 233.5
soured *disappointed* 293.4
sour grapes *spleen* 223.4
sour gum Trees and Shrubs 43
sour look *act of discourtesy* 411.3
sourly 223.9; *hostilely* 63.13, *stinkingly* 227.6, *ill-naturedly* 303.18, *irritably* 304.17
sour milk *sour thing* 223.3, *unpleasant-smelling thing* 227.2
sourness 223.1; *ill feeling* 63.3, *strain* 117.4, *flavor* 219.3, *piquancy* 221.1, Phobias 283, *antipathy* 291.2, *disappointment* 293.1, *ill nature* 303.2, *irritableness* 304.3, *bitterness* 306.3
sour note *musical dissonance* 241.2
sourpuss [Inf] *sad person* 270.3, *sullen person* 304.7
sour taste *taste* 219.1, *sourness* 223.1
sour wine *sour thing* 223.3
sourwood Trees and Shrubs 43
sousaphone Musical Instruments 142
sous-chef *cook* 91.3
souse *season* 221.8, *soaking* 557.9, *water* 557.29, *immerse* 710.12, *bring down* 716.14, *preserve* 815.14
souse [Inf] *drunkard* 121.8, *get drunk* 121.35
soused *piquant* 221.6, *wet* 557.23, *fallen* 716.8, *preserved* 815.12
soused [Inf] *drunk* 121.25, *dead drunk* 121.27
sousing *soaking* 557.9, *submergence* 716.3
soutane *vestment* 84.11
South *bridge* 168.4, *regions of the United States* 564.7, Islands 572
south *side direction* 623.2, *compass direction* 697.5, *directional* 697.8, *directionally* 697.20
South Africa Countries 566
South African Landrace Breeds of Pigs 16
South African Merino Breeds of Sheep 16
South America *world region* 564.6, *landmass* 572.1
Southampton Islands 572
South Anatolian Red Breeds of Cattle 16
southbound *directional* 697.8
South Carolina American States 564
South China Sea Oceans and Seas 571
South Dakota American States 564
South Devon Breeds of Cattle 16, Breeds of Sheep 16
Southdown Breeds of Sheep 16
Southeast *regions of the United States* 564.7
southeast *compass direction* 697.5, *directional* 697.8, *directionally* 697.20
southeasterly *windy* 9.42, *directional* 697.8, *directionally* 697.20
southeastern *directional* 697.8
southeast trades *wind system* 9.15
southeastward *directionally* 697.20

southeastwardly *directionally* 697.20
southerly *windy* 9.42, *directional* 697.8, *directionally* 697.20
southerly buster Notable Winds 9
southern *regional* 564.12, *side* 623.6, *directional* 697.8
Southern accent *regional pronunciation* 205.7
Southern California *regions of the United States* 564.7
Southern colonial style Architectural Styles 134
Southern Cross Constellations 7
Southern Crown Constellations 7
southern cypress Trees and Shrubs 43
Southern Fish Constellations 7
Southern fried chicken *notable international dishes* 90.40
Southern Hemisphere *world region* 564.6
southern lights *natural light* 246.4
southernmost *directional* 697.8
South Georgia Islands 572
southing *compass direction* 697.5
South Korea Countries 566
Southland *regions of the United States* 564.7
south magnetic pole *geomagnetism* 8.3
South Pacific *hot place* 217.5
southpaw [Inf] *baseball team* 147.2, *boxer* 152.8
South Pole *cold place* 218.7, *distant place* 585.3
south-southeast *directionally* 697.20
south-southwest *directionally* 697.20
South Ural Breeds of Sheep 16
South Wales Mountain Breeds of Sheep 16
southward *compass direction* 697.5, *directional* 697.8, *directionally* 697.20
southwardly *directionally* 697.20
Southwark London 567.8
Southwest *regions of the United States* 564.7
southwest *compass direction* 697.5, *directional* 697.8, *directionally* 697.20
southwester *hat* 100.32
southwesterly *windy* 9.42, *directional* 697.8, *directionally* 697.20
southwestern *directional* 697.8
southwestward *directionally* 697.20
southwestwardly *directionally* 697.20
South Yemen Countries 566
souvenir *monument* 185.10, *memento* 354.3, *gift* 472.2, *remainder* 750.1
sou'wester *coat* 100.19, *hat* 100.32, *protection from the weather* 810.9
sovereign 68.2; *governing* 49.25, *person in authority* 52.7, *masterful* 68.15, *divine* 82.16, *medicinal* 115.15, *powerful* 514.15, *national* 566.10, *dominant* 744.9, *ruling* 780.11
sovereign remedy *remedy* 115.1
sovereign state *or* **nation** *country* 566.1
sovereignty *governance* 49.18, 52.6, *divine attribute* 82.4, *authority* 425.3, 514.5, 780.6,

possession 469.1, dominion 566.3, leadership 744.2

Soviet hammer and sickle national emblem 184.7

Soviet Merino Breeds of Sheep 16

sow livestock 16.11, farm 16.19, cultivate 17.19, female animal 33.15, female mammal 35.19, bring into existence 522.14, throw down 716.13, sprinkle 776.15, broadcast 778.16

sowar horse person 159.14

sowbread Flowers 42

sow bug crustacean 39.10

sow dissension cause hate 300.12, pick a fight 463.10

sower preparer 388.6

so what? who cares? 289.21, naturally! 295.10

so what! no matter! 800.22

sowing cultivation 16.7, dispersion 776.1

sown produced 522.12, sprinkled 776.9

sow one's wild oats overindulge 456.11, lack restraint 829.21

sowse Collective Names 59

sow seed manage grassland 45.10

sow the seeds prepare the way 388.15, inaugurate 675.10, invent 771.30

sow the wind and reap the whirlwind cause trouble 824.21

soy Bean Varieties 90

soybeans crop 16.8, animal feed 16.12

soy sauce sauce 90.17

sozzled [Inf] dead drunk 121.27

spa health improvement 113.3

space 6.33, 563.1, 563.15, 587.6; universe 7.3, dimension 10.5, air force commands 77.28, written music 140.21, spatial 563.11, region 564.1, size 579.1, opening 583.1, interval 587.1, 739.4, period 641.1, duration 642.1, emptiness 718.4, quantity 738.1, inclusion 763.1, arrange 767.18, vastness 798.3

Space Age Ages, Decades, Eras 641

space age space travel 7.29

space between interval 587.1

space biologist life scientist 13.26

space biology 13.8

space cadet [Inf] insane person 110.5

space capsule spacecraft 7.28, orbiting body 681.4

space coordinates dimension 10.5

spacecraft 7.28

space curvature dimension 10.5

spaced 587.4

spaced out spaced 587.4

spaced out [Inf] drugged 121.30, foolish 353.5, oblivious 355.9

space engineering aerospace research 7.27

space exploration aerospace research 7.27

spaceflight space travel 7.29

space frame superstructure 551.7

space heater heater 217.3

space heating heater 217.3

space helmet space travel 7.29

Spacelab spacecraft 7.28

space laboratory spacecraft 7.28

spaceman space travel 7.29, space traveler 563.10

space medicine aerospace research 7.27, medical science 107.5

space module orbiting body 681.4

space navigation aerospace research 7.27

space observatory artificial satellite 7.30

space out space 563.15, 587.6, keep away 585.9, arrange 767.18, scatter 796.9

spaceport space travel 7.29

space probe spacecraft 7.28

space science aerospace research 7.27

spaceship spacecraft 7.28, orbiting body 681.4

space shuttle spacecraft 7.28

space station or **space platform** spacecraft 7.28

spacesuit space travel 7.29, suit 100.16

space technology aerospace research 7.27

space-time 639.2; dimension 10.5, fourth dimension 563.9, spatial 563.11

space-time continuum space 6.33, dimension 10.5, fourth dimension 563.9, space-time 639.2

space travel 7.29

space traveler 563.10

spacewalk space travel 7.29

spacewoman space travel 7.29, space traveler 563.10

spacial spatial 563.11

spacing interval 587.1

spacious 563.13; big 498.9, 579.13, broad 592.5

spaciously 563.17; amply 579.20, broadly 592.15

spaciousness 563.4; largeness 579.2, breadth 592.1

spade farm 16.19, garden tool 17.7, 103.4, cultivate 17.19, work 122.8, rowing 150.27, sharp-edged thing 549.6, use a sharp tool 549.17, ladle 578.17, make concave 635.7, take away 685.12

spade mashie golf equipment 156.5

spade oar rowboat parts 150.15

spades cards 168.2

spadework work 122.1, preparations 388.2, rudiments 771.7

spadix flower head 42.4

spado sexlessness 20.13

spaetzle pasta 90.31

spaghetti pasta 90.31

spaghetti house eating place 92.17

spaghetti junction [Brit] crossroads 609.4

Spain Countries 566

span 592.12, Collective Names 59, bridge 551.10, 691.7, intervening space 563.8, extend 563.14, General Units 589, length 590.1, be long 590.11, breadth 592.1, overlay 613.25, period 641.1, duration 642.1, time 752.18, two 789.1, pair 789.13

spandex fiber 130.2

spandrel Architectural Elements 134

spangle light up 246.20, variegated thing 263.5, variegate 263.11, decorative article 532.5

spangly bright 246.14

spaniel Breeds of Dogs 35, hunting dog 160.7, humble person 298.7, sycophant 401.3

spaniels Collective Names 59

Spanish Breeds of Fowl 16

Spanish-American War Major Wars 76

Spanish Anglo-Arab Horse and Pony Breeds 159

Spanish architecture Architectural Styles 134

Spanish bayonet sharp-pointed growth 549.5

Spanish cedar Trees and Shrubs 43

Spanish Churro Breeds of Sheep 16

Spanish Civil War Major Wars 76

Spanish fly eroticism 20.7

Spanish GP at Jerez Formula 1 World Championship races 146.5

Spanish heels shoes 100.30

Spanish mackerel game fish 154.10

Spanish Merino Breeds of Sheep 16

Spanish moss moss 46.4, lichen 47.16

Spanish Pied Breeds of Cattle 16

Spanish Renaissance Furniture Styles 101

Spanish Riding School equestrianism 159.8

spank corporal punishment 454.11, hit 454.28, blow 695.5, beat 695.12

spanking corporal punishment 454.11, speeding 694.7, ramming 695.3

spanking [Inf] huge 579.14

spanking rate swiftness 694.1

spanking wind wind strength 9.13

spanned accessible 691.13

spanner [Brit] hand tool 103.3

spanning covering 613.1, 613.21

spar fight 77.35, box 152.19, superstructure 551.7

spare underfed 98.7, superfluous 99.8, available 105.16, leisure 125.3, bowling delivery 151.2, show pity 308.8, forgive 312.8, abstain 386.16, unused thing 394.4, unused 394.5, not use 394.9, be lenient 423.5, acquit 434.10, simple 526.7, thin 595.9, extra 748.10, surplus 750.8, safety device 810.15, protect 810.21, preserve 815.14, deliver 817.5

spare cash superfluity 99.4

spared forgiven 312.5, acquitted 434.6, safe 810.16

spare hours leisure 125.1, ease 819.1

spareness simplicity 526.1, thinness 595.1

spare no effort exert oneself 122.11

spare no expense give 472.10, expend 491.11, be generous 498.10

spare none slaughter 30.21

spare one's blushes play down 195.17

spare one's words be taciturn 208.7

spare part safety device 810.15

spare parts extra 748.6

spares extra 748.6, surplus 750.4

spare the rod be lenient 423.5

spare time leisure 125.1, ease 819.1

spare tire superfluity 99.4

spare tire [Inf] fat 579.8

sparge sprinkle 557.32, 559.5

sparger sprinkler 557.12

sparging watering 557.8

sparing self-restrained 455.6, thrifty 499.4

sparingly with self-restraint 455.14

sparing of words concise 198.4

sparing with words 208.6

spark fuel starter 106.3, quality of light 246.2, fire 246.9, light up

246.20, cause 675.1, awaken 675.9

sparker fuel starter 106.3

sparking bright 246.14

sparkle emphasis 200.1, emphasize 200.6, quality of light 246.2, light up 246.20, show joy 269.10, vigor 518.1, be beautiful 529.11, bubble 558.24

sparkler fire 246.9, decorative article 532.5

sparklers [Inf] eye 19.9, 242.3

sparkling drinkable 93.18, emphatic 200.3, bright 246.14, lightness 539.1, insubstantial 539.5, gassy 556.19

sparkling water water 93.4

sparkling wine wine 93.11

spark off activate 771.28

spark plug fuel starter 106.3

spark plug [Inf] joyful person 269.5

sparkplug [Inf] bring cheer 269.12

sparring boxing 152.2, combat 152.17

sparring helmet boxing equipment 152.4

sparring partner boxer 152.8

sparrow songbird 36.12

sparrow, Cape Sable seaside Endangered US Birds 36

sparrow, Florida grasshopper Endangered US Birds 36

sparrow, San Clemente sage Endangered US Birds 36

sparrows Collective Names 59

spars sailboat parts and accessories 150.4

sparse 541.3, 595.14, 796.6; infertile 23.7, scarce 98.8, meager 593.12, infrequent 662.2, quantitative 738.6, dispersed 776.6

sparsely 541.6, 595.20, 796.11; not enough 98.12, meagerly 593.19, infrequently 662.4, quantitatively 738.8, diffusely 776.18

sparseness 541.1, 595.8; meagerness 593.6, fewness 796.3

sparsity infrequency 662.1, fewness 796.3

Spartan Apple Varieties 44, fasting 118.5, strict person 424.4, unadorned 424.7, self-restrained person 455.5, self-restrained 455.6, 830.10, thrifty 499.4, simple 526.7, one who restrains 830.7, self-restrained 830.10

Spartan fare incompleteness 98.2, short rations 118.3

Spartanism unadornment 424.3, self-restraint 455.1, 830.4

Spartanly abstemiously 118.11, with self-restraint 455.14

Spartan simplicity simplicity 195.4

spasm 684.8; illness 114.2, symptom 114.3, neurological disease 114.20, pain 215.1, alacrity 414.3, seizure 418.11, violence by person 502.2

spasmodic explosive 520.6, irregular 664.3, 766.10, changeable 666.3, convulsive 684.19, inconsistent 732.7, discontinuous 775.7

spasmodically irregularly 664.6, changeably 666.7, jerkily 684.29, inconsistently 732.16, in disorder 766.24, discontinuously 775.15

spasmodicalness discontinuity 775.1

spasmodic school Western Literary Groups 139

spastic *sick person* 114.22, *of disease* 114.25, *convulsive* 684.19

spat *argument* 329.1, *contention* 422.1, *dispute* 463.3, 463.9

spatchcock *cook* 91.10

spate *crowd* 59.11, *excess* 99.1, *flow* 570.4

spate [Brit] *rain* 9.27

spathe *flower part* 42.3

spatial **6.76, 563.11**

spatial *or* **spacial** *regional* 564.12

spatial extension *space* 6.33, 563.1

spatially 563.16; *mathematically* 6.93, *spaciously* 563.17, *regionally* 564.16

spatiotemporal *material* 524.7, *spatial* 563.11

spatiotemporally *spatially* 563.16, *spaciously* 563.17

spats *legwear* 100.26

spatter *rain* 9.57, *dirty* 112.11, *sprinkle* 557.32, 559.5, 559.14, 776.15, *flicker* 684.19

spatterdashes *legwear* 100.26

spattered *seeping* 559.12, *sprinkled* 776.9

spattering *watering* 557.8, *sprinkling* 776.4

spatula *cooking equipment* 91.6, *material* 143.9, 144.6, *ladle* 578.17

spavin *animal disease* 34.10

spa water *drinking water* 557.2

spawn *propagate* 21.15, *have young* 21.16, *young animal* 26.4, *give birth to* 28.19, *produce* 522.5, *bring into existence* 522.14, *increase* 746.6

spawning *propagation* 21.4

spay *make infertile* 23.9, *take off* 749.7

spaying *that which makes infertile* 23.4

speak 205.17; *use language* 5.42, *divulge* 180.9, *dissertate* 203.5, *address* 209.8, *converse* 210.11, *sound* 230.8

speak (to) *communicate* 169.18

speak badly *be unintelligible* 364.11

speak clearly *make comprehensible* 363.8

speak directly *speak plainly* 592.14

speaker 205.12; *leader* 126.8, *actor* 136.25, *radio reception* 172.2, *dissertator* 203.3, *talker* 207.4, *sound amplifier* 230.5

Speaker of the House *person in authority* 52.7, *party official* 68.5

speakerphone *telephone* 169.10

speak for *represent* 79.7, 80.6, *answer for* 334.24

speak for itself *make evident* 339.11, *be intelligible* 363.10

speak freely *be free* 829.16

speak gobbledegook *be unintelligible* 364.11

speak highly of *recommend* 437.19

speak ill of *vilify* 440.14

speak in a particular way 205.18

speaking 205.15; *speech* 205.1

speaking in tongues *religiousness* 81.2, *power of speech* 205.5

speaking part *role* 136.23

speaking voice *mode of speech* 205.6

speak in muted tones *sound faint* 233.8

speak in tongues *preach* 84.14, *be unintelligible* 364.11

speak loudly *speak in a particular way* 205.18

speak low *sound faint* 233.8

speak no evil *be virtuous* 447.8

speak of *mean* 361.13

speak one's mind *appear* 331.18, *talk straight* 630.15, *be naive* 821.4

speak oracles *be equivocal* 380.7

speak out *divulge* 180.9, *be assertive* 189.28, *appear* 331.18, *object* 828.18, *show oneself* 843.15

speak out against *protest* 507.7

speak plainly 592.14; *be simple* 526.13, *be naive* 821.4, *show oneself* 843.15

speak simply *be simple* 526.13

speak slowly *hesitate* 693.12

speak softly *sound faint* 233.8

speak sotto voce *sound faint* 233.8

speak straight from the shoulder *be open* 583.19

speak the truth *be truthful* 191.7, *talk straight* 630.15

speak to 205.19, *communicate* 169.18

speak to one's understanding *be intelligible* 363.10

speak under one's breath *sound faint* 233.8

speak up *be assertive* 189.28, *speak in a particular way* 205.18, *be loud* 232.8, *show oneself* 843.15

speak up for *recommend* 437.19, *justify* 441.12

speak volumes *gesture* 183.17, *mean* 361.13, *be intelligible* 363.10

speak well of *recommend* 437.19

speak with a forked tongue *be untruthful* 192.20, *be equivocal* 380.7, *distort the truth* 627.12

speak without thinking *lack thought* 318.12

speak with two voices *be equivocal* 380.7

spear *murder* 30.20, *grass plant* 45.3, *fight* 77.35, Historical Missile Weapons 78, *stab* 418.22, *sharp-pointed thing* 549.4, *use a sharp tool* 549.17

spear carrier *actor* 136.25

spearhead *armed force* 77.10, *attacker* 418.10, *vanguard* 621.5, *be in front* 621.13, *lead* 744.19, *precede* 769.13, *pioneer* 771.29, *important person* 799.5

spearing *ice hockey tactics* 158.4

spearlike *sharp* 549.10

spearman *historical soldier* 77.8

spearmint Herbs and Spices 91

spear side *menfolk* 32.14

spear-thrower Historical Missile Weapons 78

special 779.10; *dish* 90.7, *golf equipment* 156.5, *symbolic* 183.12, *technical* 361.10, *preferential* 382.10, *detailed* 726.9, *typical* 777.10, *exceptional* 779.13, *singular* 788.13

special, the 779.8

special case 779.7; *diversity* 732.1, *exclusion* 764.1, *deviation* 786.2

special committee *advisory body* 176.6

special correspondent *print journalist* 175.5, *descriptive writer* 202.10

special court-martial *military law* 58.7

special day *rejoicing* 279.1, *anniversary* 405.5, *important matter* 799.2

special delivery *postal service* 169.5

special-delivery messenger *postal worker* 169.6

special diet *diet* 92.5

special dispensation *exclusion* 764.1

special edition *newspaper* 175.2

special education *educational system* 78.2

special effects *production* 137.6

special effort *deed* 412.2

special faculty *skill* 127.1

special feature 779.4

special handling *postal service* 169.5

special hospital *psychiatric hospital* 108.35, *mental hospital* 110.6

special interest *social activity* 414.2, *specialization* 779.3

special-interest group *motivator* 178.11, 508.6

specialism *skill* 127.1

specialist 779.9; *expert* 52.8, 68.13, 127.9, *excellent* 68.16, *air force person* 77.31, *varsity* 155.17, *financial adviser* 457.4, *paragon* 744.6, *specialized* 779.11

specialist publication *magazine* 175.3

specialist source *news interpreter* 365.7

spécialité de la maison [Fr] *dish* 90.7, *the special* 779.8

speciality [Brit] *specialty* 779.1

specialization 779.3

specialize 779.16; *master* 68.17

specialized 779.11; *curricular* 48.21, *expert* 52.12, 127.12, *technical* 361.10, *problematic* 824.11

specialized meaning *type of meaning* 361.4

specialize in *be an authority on* 52.17, *learn* 68.18, *specialize* 779.16

special jury *jury* 54.11

special library *library* 174.14

specially 779.19; *indicatively* 183.21, *meticulously* 726.18

special meaning *type of meaning* 361.4

special needs school *type of school* 48.12

specialness *specialty* 779.1, *singularity* 788.4

special nurse *nurse* 107.23

special offer *enticement* 178.3, *bargain* 495.2, *business offer* 504.3, *positive stimulus* 508.5

Special Olympics *prize competition* 422.5

special operations *army commands* 77.13, *air force commands* 77.28

special power *or gift* *type of power* 514.6

special prayer *prayer* 85.10

special price *bargain* 495.2

special request *request* 505.1

special sale *business offer* 504.3

special school *type of school* 48.12

special skill 779.2

special study *specialization* 779.3

special team 155.11

special theory of relativity *theory* 10.3

special topic *educational topic* 328.4

special treatment *exemption* 434.1, *furtherance* 825.8

special-treatment steel *shipbuilding* 690.4

specialty 779.1; *subject* 48.3, *dish* 90.7, *skill* 127.1, *style* 537.1, *special skill* 779.2, *singularity* 788.4

specialty of the house *dish* 90.7, *the special* 779.8

specialty store *store* 483.8

specialty team *special team* 155.11

special verdict *verdict* 54.18

special weapons and tactics (SWAT) team *law enforcement agency* 53.7

speciation *evolution* 13.23

specie *money* 484.1, *coinage* 484.13

species *sort* 202.6, *part* 760.1, *taxonomic classification* 777.3

specific *taxonomic* 13.35, *remedy* 115.1, *medicinal* 115.15, *characteristic* 723.9, *detailed* 726.9, *typical* 777.10, *special* 779.10

specific, the *the special* 779.8

specifically 779.22; *biologically* 13.36, *meticulously* 726.18, *taxonomically* 777.15

specification 340.6; *document* 170.3, *description* 202.1, *grouping* 765.2

specifications 779.6

specific gravity *mass* 10.8, *gravity* 538.2, *relative density* 540.3, Fields of Measurement 589

specific heat *heat measurement* 217.2

specific heat capacity *heat flow* 10.27

specificity *specialty* 779.1

specific latent heat *thermodynamics* 10.30

specific phobia *anxiety disorder* 108.11

specific quality *specialty* 779.1

specific remedy *remedy* 115.1

specifics *fact* 717.6

specified *conditional* 340.10, *grouped* 765.11

specified value *measurement* 10.67

specify 340.14, 779.18; *identify* 184.11, *name* 202.17, *limit* 620.7, *circumstantiate* 726.12

specimen *representative* 187.7, *explanation* 331.3, *showpiece* 843.3

specimen plant *garden plant* 17.10

specimen tree *tree* 43.1

speciosity *affectation* 367.1

specious *unskilled* 128.5, *seeming* 264.11, *sophistic* 330.7, *affected* 367.3, *equivocal* 380.5, *artificial* 720.12

speciously *sophistically* 330.14, *affectedly* 367.5, *equivocally* 380.9

speciousness *sophistry* 330.1, *affectation* 367.1, *evasion* 380.2

specious reasoning *sophistry* 330.1

speck *maculation* 263.4, *blemish* 533.1, *grain* 553.6, *little piece* 580.4, *particle* 760.4, *sprinkle* 776.15, *fragment* 787.3

speckle *maculation* 263.4, *variegate* 263.11, *blemish* 533.7, *mix* 751.12, *sprinkle* 776.15

speckled *mottled* 263.10, *blemished* 533.5, *complicated* 751.10, *sprinkled* 776.9

speckled effect *variety* 751.4

speckling *variety* 751.4, *sprinkling* 776.4

specs [Inf] *design and makeup* 174.8, *visual aid* 242.14, *specifications* 779.6

spectacle 264.6; *dramaturgy* 136.6, *show* 138.4, 404.12, *view* 242.8, *marvel* 294.3, *mass demonstration*

331.7, *formal occasion* 406.4, *display* 843.1, *production* 843.5

spectacles *optical element* 10.20, *visual aid* 242.14, *aid for poor sight* 243.5, *that which makes visible* 244.4, *transparent thing* 249.4

spectacle theater *theater* 136.16

spectacular *dramatic* 136.31, *entertaining* 138.12, *visible* 242.19, *clear* 244.6, *gaudy* 251.12, *appearing* 264.9, *wondrous* 294.9, *grand* 404.22

spectacularly *dramatically* 136.38, *entertainingly* 138.17, *wondrously* 294.18, *grandly* 404.37

spectate *see* 242.20, *stand by* 575.15

spectator *theatergoer* 136.30, *observer* 242.15, *curious person* 321.3, *verifier* 336.4, *witness* 339.7, *recipient* 473.5, *attender* 575.6

spectator sport *sporting activity* 145.3, *view* 242.8

specter *ghost* 86.11, *spectacle* 264.6, *frightener* 283.7, *fantasy* 360.5, *omnipresence* 575.4, *illusion* 720.2

spectral *spiritual* 86.20, *variegated* 263.6, *omnipresent* 575.10, *unreal* 720.8

spectral color *color* 251.1

spectral type *star luminosity* 7.12

spectrograph *analysis* 11.17, *chromatics* 251.8

spectrographic *analytic* 11.32, *chromolithographic* 251.14

spectrographic analysis *analysis* 11.17

spectrography *chromatics* 251.8

spectrometer *analysis* 11.17, *chromatics* 251.8, Fields of Measurement 589

spectrometric *astronomical* 7.33, *physical* 10.70

spectrometrically *physically* 10.78

spectrometry *microscopy* 10.68, *analysis* 11.17, Fields of Measurement 589

spectrophobia Phobias 283

spectrophotometer *chromatics* 251.8, Fields of Measurement 589

spectrophotometric *chromolithographic* 251.14

spectrophotometry *chromatics* 251.8, Fields of Measurement 589

spectroscope *chromatics* 251.8

spectroscopic *physical* 10.70, *analytic* 11.32, *colored* 251.10

spectroscopically *physically* 10.78

spectroscopic binary *star* 7.8

spectroscopy Fields of Modern Physics 10, *microscopy* 10.68, *visual aid* 242.14

spectrum 251.3; *analysis* 11.17, *highlight* 246.12, *variegation* 263.1, *variegated thing* 263.5, *range* 563.7, *consecutiveness* 774.1

spectrum analysis *chromatics* 251.8

spectrum color *spectrum* 251.3

speculate 294.13, 480.19; *philosophize* 4.19, *think* 317.9, *have an idea* 317.12, *experiment* 335.11, *predict* 358.14, *suppose* 359.8, *tackle* 390.8, *finance* 457.7, *bargain* 481.14, *be uncertain* 841.17, *risk* 841.21, *take a chance* 842.14

speculating *speculative* 294.8

speculation 294.2, 480.9; *philosophy* 4.1, *philosophical*

investigation 4.4, *belief* 87.1, Card Games 168, *thoughtfulness* 317.2, *explanation* 319.4, *theory* 327.2, 720.4, *experimentation* 335.3, *judgment* 341.1, *inaccuracy* 351.3, *divination* 358.2, *conjecture* 359.3, *venture* 390.2, *undertaking* 391.1, *game of chance* 842.5

speculative 294.8, 317.8; *philosophical* 4.12, *thoughtful* 4.17, *theoretical* 327.10, 720.10, *experimental* 335.8, *suppositional* 359.5, *enterprising* 391.5, *buying* 481.9, *dangerous* 811.7, *uncertain* 841.9, *uncertified* 841.13

speculatively 294.17; *theoretically* 4.24, *experimentally* 335.14, *supposedly* 359.10, *ambitiously* 390.10, *marketably* 482.23, *uncertainly* 841.22

speculator *philosopher* 4.9, *gambler* 167.6, *experimenter* 335.5, *forecaster* 358.9, *theorist* 359.4, *person who undertakes* 391.3, *financial adviser* 457.4, *person transferring property* 470.8, *trader* 480.11, *purchaser* 481.7, *merchant* 482.10, *operator* 509.5, *unrealistic person* 720.6

speculum *reflector* 242.10

speech 205.1; *language* 5.4, *play part* 136.8, *communications* 169.1, *publication* 173.1, *spoken language* 205.2, *public speaking* 205.11, *address* 209.1, Phobias 283

speech-act theory *philosophical problem* 4.8

speech community *regional pronunciation* 205.7

speech defect 206.2; *mode of speech* 205.6, *speech difficulty* 206.1, *blunder* 528.5

speech difficulty 206.1

speechifier *speaker* 205.12

speechify *speak to* 205.19, *address* 209.8

speechifying *public speaking* 205.11

speech impediment *mode of speech* 205.6, *speech defect* 206.2, *blunder* 528.5

speechless 206.7; *silent* 208.5, 231.2, *astonished* 292.6, *wondering* 294.7

speechlessly *with surprise* 292.13

speechlessness *mutism* 206.3, *silence* 208.2, 231.1, *astonishment* 292.2

speechmaker *public speaker* 209.5, *speaker* 205.12

speech-making *public speaking* 205.11, *addressing* 209.6

speech organ 205.4

speech sound *spoken letter* 5.15

speech therapist *paramedic* 107.24

speech therapy *treatment* 107.14, *therapy* 115.12

speed 10.7, 694.2; *machine tool* 14.9, *ski* 162.27, Phobias 283, *alacrity* 414.3, Fields of Measurement 589, *measurability* 589.2, *rapid motion* 677.8, *swiftness* 694.1, *be swift* 694.10, *degree* 739.1, *haste* 818.1, *make haste* 818.5, *easiness* 823.1, *make easy* 823.15, *further* 825.30

speed [Inf] *stimulants* 121.18

speedball Sporting Activities 145

speedball [Inf] *stimulants* 121.18

speed bump *roadblock* 826.4

speed calling *dial* 169.12

speed contest *race* 422.8

speed demon *or* **maniac** [Inf] *speeder* 694.5

speeder 694.5; *racehorse* 159.2

speedily *fast* 166.23, *immediately* 645.8, *swiftly* 694.16, *hastily* 818.7

speediness *swiftness* 694.1

speeding 694.7; *race* 422.8, *directional* 677.13, *swiftness* 694.1, *swift* 694.6, *intensification* 746.2, *hasty* 818.3, *easing* 823.7

speeding up *accelerating* 694.9

speed limit *limit* 620.1, *miscellaneous automotive terms* 687.14

speed of light *wave property* 10.12, *fundamental constant* 10.69, *speed* 694.2

speed of sound *wave property* 10.12, *sound propagation* 230.3, *speed* 694.2

speed of thought *quickness of mind* 694.4

speedometer *indicator* 183.7, *recording instrument* 185.9, *meter* 589.13

speed over the bottom *nautical speed* 690.11

speed-skate 162.37

speed skater *ice skater* 162.22

speed skating 162.20, Sporting Activities 145

speed-skating 162.33

speed-skating circuit *speed skating* 162.20

speed-skating race *speed skating* 162.20

speed-skating track *speed skating* 162.20

speed-skiing *skiing* 162.1

speedster *speeder* 694.5

speed the parting guest *part* 705.13

speed through the water *nautical speed* 690.11

speed trap *miscellaneous automotive terms* 687.14, *speed* 694.2

speed up *accelerate* 694.14, *intensify* 746.8, *hasten* 818.4, *make haste* 818.5

speed-up *acceleration* 694.3

speedway *racing* 146.9

speedway racing *automobile racing* 146.1

speedwell Flowers 42

speedy *active* 414.13, *immediate* 645.5, *directional* 677.13, *swift* 694.6, *hasty* 818.3

spell 86.8; *word* 5.43, *weather* 9.3, *curse* 301.1, *mean* 361.13, *seizure* 418.11, *positive stimulus* 508.5, *intervening space* 563.8, *period* 641.1, *period of activity* 641.4, *duration* 642.1, *season* 654.1

spellbind *bewitch* 86.25, *be wondrous* 294.14, *lure* 700.12

spellbinder *witch* 86.15, *motivator* 508.6

spellbinding *witchcraft* 86.6, *witchlike* 86.19, *wondrous* 294.9, *motivational* 508.7, *attractive* 700.10

spellbound *bewitched* 86.21, *wondering* 294.7, *motivated* 508.8, *motionless* 678.4

spellcasting *witchcraft* 86.6

spellcraft *witchcraft* 86.6

spell danger *warn* 814.8

spell disaster *warn* 814.8

spelled *orthographic* 5.40

spelling 5.26; *language* 5.4

spelling bee *spelling* 5.26

spelling checker *application software* 15.14

spelling game *spelling* 5.26

spelling mistake *language error* 351.10

spelling pronunciation *spelling* 5.26

spell of duty *work* 122.1

spell of work *task* 122.2, *allotted task* 474.3

spell out *rationalize* 4.20, *word* 5.43, *mean* 361.13, *make comprehensible* 363.8, *interpret* 365.12, *decipher* 365.13, *circumstantiate* 726.12, *particularize* 779.17

spelunking Sporting Activities 145, Hobbies and Pastimes 167

spencer *jacket* 100.18

Spencerianism *political and economic philosophy* 4.6

spend *have leisure time* 125.5, *use up* 393.12, *shop* 481.15, *pay* 489.16, *expend* 491.11

spender 491.7; *purchaser* 481.7, *payer* 489.9, *spendthrift* 500.3

spending *shopping* 481.3, *paying* 489.10, *expenditure* 491.1, *expending* 491.8, *export* 707.7

spending money *change* 484.3, *income* 492.3

spending money like water *or* **as if it grows on trees** *expending* 491.8

spending plan *act of thrift* 499.2

spending spree *extravagance* 500.1

spend lavishly *expend* 491.11

spend money like it's going out of style *or* **fashion** *overspend* 500.8

spend money like water *or* **as if it grows on trees** *expend* 491.11, *overspend* 500.8

spend the evening 656.5

spend the night *spend the evening* 656.5

spend the season 654.10

spend the summer *spend the season* 654.10

spend the winter *spend the season* 654.10

spendthrift 500.3; *waster* 96.8, *wasteful* 96.9, *spender* 491.7, *expending* 491.8, *extravagant* 500.4

spend time 639.14

Spenserian Poem or Verse Forms 139, *poetic* 139.19

spent *unemphatic* 201.2, *used* 393.5, *losing* 468.9, *expended* 491.9, *accounted* 491.8, *dilapidated* 517.7, *over* 651.12, *outflowing* 707.11, *broken down* 802.8, *fatigued* 820.2

sperm *organs of reproduction* 21.9, *fertilizer* 22.6

spermatium *reproductive body* 47.14

Spermatophyta *seed plant* 41.3

spermatophyte *seed plant* 41.3

spermatozoa *organs of reproduction* 21.9

spermatozoid *reproductive body* 47.14

sperm bank *vault* 105.9

spermicide *contraceptive* 23.6

spew *flow* 555.25, *run out* 707.15, *let out* 709.26, *vomit* 709.27

spew out *run out* 707.15

Spey Rivers 570

sphagnum *moss* 46.4

spheksophobia Phobias 283

sphenoid bone Human Bones 19

sphenopsid *fern* 46.1

sphere 564.10; *curved surface* 6.43,

star 7.8, *subject* 48.3, *range* 563.7, *region* 564.1, *rank* 573.4, *round thing* 633.3, *type* 777.4, *social class* 777.5, *specialization* 779.3
spherelike *round* 633.7
sphere of influence 512.7; *dominion* 566.3
spheric *round* 633.7
spherical 6.80; *round* 633.7
spherical coordinates *coordinates* 6.31, 589.6
spherical geometry *geometry* 6.32
spherically *mathematically* 6.93, *roundly* 633.11
sphericalness *roundness* 633.1
spherical sailing *navigation* 690.5
spherical triangle *triangle* 6.41
spherical trigonometry *trigonometry* 6.49
sphericity *surface* 6.36, *roundness* 633.1
spheroid *curved surface* 6.43, *round thing* 633.3
spheroidal *spherical* 6.80, *round* 633.7
spheroidally *roundly* 633.11
sphingolipid *fat* 12.7
sphingomyelin *fat* 12.7
sphinx *Legendary Creatures* 360
sphragistics *clothing* 184.6
sphygmomanometer *diagnostic instrument* 107.13, *flowmeter* 555.12, Fields of Measurement 589
sphygmomanometry Fields of Measurement 589
sphynx Breeds of Cats 35
spic Nicknames for Inhabitants 61
spiccato Musical Terms and Expression Marks 140
spice *cook* 91.10, *make taste* 219.6, *seasoning* 221.2, *season* 221.8, *fragrance* 226.1, *source of fragrance* 226.2, *augment* 748.13, *admixture* 751.5, *mix* 751.12, *preserver* 815.9
spiced *piquant* 221.6
Spice Islands Islands 572
spices *basic cooking ingredient* 91.8
spicily *fragrantly* 226.7
spiciness *piquancy* 221.1, *fragrance* 226.1
spick-and-span *clean* 111.13, *immature* 652.12, *orderly* 765.13
spiculate *be sharp* 549.15
spicule *sharp-pointed growth* 549.5
spiculum *sharp-pointed growth* 549.5
spicy *tasty* 219.4, *piquant* 221.6, *odorous* 224.5, *fragrant* 226.4, *strong to the senses* 516.12
spicy taste *taste* 219.1
spider *arachnid* 39.8, 40.4, *spinner* 40.10, *weaving* 609.2
spider crab *crustacean* 39.10
spider flower Flowers 42
spiderlike *arthropodal* 39.22, *arachnidan* 40.12
spiderling *or* **spiderlet** *larva* 40.9
spider mites *pests and diseases* 17.12
spiders Phobias 283
spider web *spinner* 40.10
spidery *arthropodal* 39.22, *arachnidan* 40.12
spiel [Inf] *advertisement* 173.9, *speech* 205.1, *talkativeness* 207.1, *empty talk* 362.5, *talk nonsense* 362.12, *salesmanship* 482.4
spieler *circus performer* 138.9, *publicizer* 173.11

spiffed up [Inf] *dressed up* 100.39, *formally dressed* 406.8
spiff up [Inf] *dress up* 100.45
spiffy [Inf] *great* 445.14
spigot *stopper* 584.3
spike *flower head* 42.4, *grass plant* 45.3, *miscellaneous terms* 155.16, *barrier* 419.10, *hinder* 826.15
spike [Inf] *mix* 751.12
spiked 549.11
spiked device *instrument of torture* 454.14
spiked shoes *sports equipment* 166.17
spike heels *shoes* 100.30
spikelet *flower head* 42.4, *grass plant* 45.3
spikenard *incense* 226.3, *ointment* 562.8
spikes *shoes* 100.30
spike someone's guns *overpower* 515.14, *hinder* 826.15
spiky *spiked* 549.11
spill *fuel starter* 106.3, *be clumsy* 128.9, *fire* 246.9, *act of inversion* 608.3, *become inverted* 608.8, *outflow* 707.4, *run out* 707.15, *fall* 714.4
spillage *flow* 570.4, *lowering* 716.1
spill blood *bleed* 25.26
spilled salt *bad-luck sign* 358.7
spilling *disgorgement* 709.6, *falling* 714.11, *fallen* 716.8
spillover *flow* 570.4
spill over *flow* 570.10, *run out* 707.15, *overstep* 712.12
spill the beans [Inf] *inform on* 170.13, *tell on* 180.10, *detect* 345.12
spill the brains of *murder* 30.20
spin 130.17; *quantum* 10.63, *ice-skating techniques* 162.16, *ice-skate* 162.36, *perform* 522.16, *be cyclic* 663.11, *be in motion* 677.14, *rotation* 682.1, *reel* 682.4, *rotate* 682.14, *flight maneuver* 689.6, *maneuver* 689.14
spin [Inf] *interpret news* 365.17
spina bifida *neurological disease* 114.20
spinach *green thing* 260.4
spinal *internal* 19.23
spinal column Human Bones 19
spinal cord *nervous system* 19.14
spin a long tale *be diffuse* 199.5
spin around *rotate* 682.14
spin a web *be cunning* 822.5
spin a yarn *fabricate* 192.24, *tell a tall story* 194.15, *recount* 202.16, *delude* 720.16
spin-cast *fish* 154.14
spin-casting *fishing* 154.1
spin-casting reel *fishing tackle* 154.7
spindle *cell division* 13.17, *narrow place* 593.2, *axle* 682.7, *rotator* 682.8
spindle fibers *cell division* 13.17
spindle-legged *thin* 595.9
spindlelegs [Inf] *thin person* 595.4
spindle sander *woodworking tool* 131.6
spindle-shanked *thin* 595.9
spindleshanks [Inf] *thin person* 595.4
spindle tree Trees and Shrubs 43
spindly *or* **spindling** *thin* 595.9
spin doctor [Inf] *publicizer* 173.11, *persuader* 178.9, *news interpreter* 365.7, *distorter* 627.5
spindrift *snow* 9.30, *air bubble* 558.10
spin-dry *dry* 560.17
spin-dryer *dryer* 560.5

spine Human Bones 19, *mammalian characteristic* 35.3, *leaf* 41.6, *sharp-pointed growth* 549.5, *mountain range* 569.3, *body support* 605.6
spineless 285.5; *disabled* 515.10, *weak-willed* 517.10
spinelessly *cowardly* 285.9
spinelessness [Inf] *yellow streak* 259.6, *indecisiveness* 517.2
spinerette *fabric-handling tool* 130.12
spinet Musical Instruments 142
spininess *roughness* 544.1, *sharpness* 549.1
spin like a top *rotate* 682.14
spin money *get rich* 485.13
spinnaker *sailboat parts and accessories* 150.4
spinner 40.10; *artisan* 123.13, *fabric handler* 130.11, *fabric-handling tool* 130.12, *bait* 154.6, *weaving* 609.2
spinneret *spinner* 40.10
spinney [Brit] *trees* 43.4
spinning 130.4; *fishing* 154.1, 154.13, Hobbies and Pastimes 167, *orbiting* 681.7, *turning* 682.3, *rotating* 682.11
spinning jenny *fabric-handling tool* 130.12, *wheel* 682.9
spinning motion *rotation* 682.1
spinning mule *fabric-handling tool* 130.12
spinning out *automobile racing terms* 146.3, *lengthening* 590.4
spinning reel *fishing tackle* 154.7
spinning rod *fishing tackle* 154.7
spinning top *cone* 633.5, *rotator* 682.8
spinning wheel *fabric-handling tool* 130.12, *weaving* 609.2, *wheel* 682.9
spin off *react* 676.8
spin-off *product* 522.3, *effect* 676.1, *subsequence* 770.4
spin off from *follow from* 676.9
spin of the coin *equal chance* 842.7
spin of the wheel *endangerment* 811.2, *potluck* 842.4
spin one's wheels [Inf] *waste effort* 802.13
spinose *spiked* 549.11
spinosity *sharpness* 549.1
spinous *spiked* 549.11
spin out *be on the track* 146.11, *windsurf* 150.33, *be diffuse* 199.5, *be talkative* 207.7, *lengthen* 590.12, *delay* 658.13, *protract* 669.9
spin-out *automobile racing terms* 146.3, *windsurfing terms* 150.21, *miscellaneous automotive terms* 687.14
Spinozism Philosophical Schools of Thought 4
Spinozist Philosophical Schools of Thought 4
spinster *woman* 27.9, *single woman* 33.5, *single person* 67.5, 788.7
spinsterhood *celibacy* 67.1, *independence* 829.5
spinsterlike *celibate* 67.6
spinsterly *celibate* 67.6
spin the bottle Children's and Party Games 167
spiny *coarse* 544.6, *spiked* 549.11
spiny anteater *egg-laying mammal* 35.4, *insect-eating mammal* 35.7
spin yarn *roll* 682.15
spiny lobster *crustacean* 39.10, *food fish and shellfish* 90.20

spiracle *fish characteristic* 38.8, *outlet* 707.8
spiral *curve* 6.38, 629.1, 629.6, *curvilinear* 6.78, *coil* 632.2, *convolutional* 632.4, *convolute* 632.6, *orbital motion* 681.1, *circular* 681.6, *orbit* 681.8, *turning* 682.3, *flight maneuver* 689.6, *maneuver* 689.14, *incline* 713.3, *ascend* 713.19, *drop* 714.15, *spread* 746.3, *increase* 746.6
spiral binding *bookbinding* 174.11
spiral down *drop* 714.15
spiral downward *decrease* 747.7
spiraled *curved* 629.4
spiral galaxy *galaxy* 7.5
spiraling *costly* 496.7, *orbital motion* 681.1, *orbiting* 681.7, *turning* 682.3, *leaping* 713.17
spiraling prices *inflationary price* 496.3
spiraling up *taking off* 713.6
spirally *circularly* 632.8
spiral spring *spring* 546.4
spiral staircase *stairway* 713.9
spirant *spoken letter* 5.15, *voiced* 5.37
spire *grass plant* 45.3, *church architecture* 134.11, *sharp-pointed thing* 549.4, *summit* 600.1, *ascend* 713.19, *go up* 713.23
spirea Flowers 42
spirillum *microorganism* 13.11
spirit 86.10; *life force* 28.2, *minor deity* 82.2, *ghost* 86.11, *emphasis* 200.1, *stimulation* 221.4, *seat of feelings* 266.7, *courage* 284.1, *proudness* 297.3, *meaning* 361.1, *will* 376.5, *energy* 414.4, *vigor* 518.1, *spiritual world* 525.3, *internal world* 525.6, *substance* 577.2, *inner nature* 611.4, *extract* 711.8, *illusion* 720.2, *quintessence* 723.3
spirit away *cause to disappear* 265.7, *kidnap* 479.15
spirited *lively* 28.16, *emphatic* 200.3, *stimulating* 221.7, *courageous* 284.9, *proud* 297.10, *active* 414.13, *vigorous* 518.2
spiritedly *stimulatingly* 221.11
spirit gum *stage requisite* 136.21
spiritism *occultism* 86.1, *spiritual world* 525.3
spiritist *occultist* 86.13
spiritistic *parapsychological* 525.9
spiritize *dematerialize* 525.12
spiritless *indifferent* 289.7, *wonderless* 295.3
spiritlessly *indifferently* 289.17
spiritlessness *indifference* 289.1
spirit level *planimetry* 603.5
spirit leveling *planimetry* 603.5
spirit manifestation *occult and psychic phenomena* 86.7
Spirit of God *God the Holy Ghost* 82.10
spirit of the age *tendency* 513.1
spiritous *intoxicating* 121.29
spirit raising *occult and psychic phenomena* 86.7
spirit rapper *occultist* 86.13
spirit rapping *occult and psychic phenomena* 86.7
spirits *alcoholic drink* 93.9, *alcohol* 121.5, Phobias 283, *state of mind* 725.5
spiritual 86.20; *religious* 81.21, *sacred music* 140.3, *song* 140.11, *loving* 299.15, *moral* 431.9, *virtuous* 447.5, *nonmaterial* 525.8, *parapsychological* 525.9, *inward* 611.12
spiritual body *spirit* 86.10

spiritualism *occultism* 86.1, *spiritual world* 525.3
spiritualist *occultist* 86.13, *interpreter* 365.6, *nonmaterialist* 525.7, *parapsychologist* 525.9
spiritualistic *psychic* 86.17, *parapsychological* 525.9
spirituality *religiousness* 81.2, *the occult* 86.2, *virtue* 447.1, *immateriality* 525.2, *inner nature* 611.4
spiritualization *immateriality* 525.2
spiritualize *occult* 86.22, *dematerialize* 525.12
spiritual loss *forfeiture* 468.2
spiritual love *love* 299.1
spiritually *religiously* 81.29, *divinely* 82.24, *occultly* 86.27, *lovingly* 299.29, *morally* 431.15, *virtuously* 447.9, *metaphysically* 525.13, *inwardly* 611.21
spiritual marriage *type of marriage* 64.3, *monasticism* 67.3
spiritualness *immateriality* 525.2
spiritual presence *omnipresence* 575.4
spiritual rebirth *religious conversion* 670.4
spiritual world 525.3
spirituous *drinkable* 93.18
spirit world *the occult* 86.2, *spiritual world* 525.3
spirit writing *occult and psychic phenomena* 86.7
spirometer *vaporimeter* 556.13, Fields of Measurement 589
spirometry Fields of Measurement 589
spit *coast* 8.13, *rain* 9.57, *saliva* 25.9, *salivate* 25.25, *cooker* 91.5, *burner* 217.4, *crack* 234.7, *be irritable* 304.14, *sharp-pointed thing* 549.4, *lubricant* 562.7, *peninsula* 572.5, *narrow place* 593.2, *rotator* 682.8, *flicker* 684.26, *vomit* 709.27
spit and image [Inf] *look-alike* 730.4, *twin* 789.5
spit and polish *cleanliness* 111.1, *formality* 406.1
spit at *taunt* 436.23
spit ball *pitching terms* 147.5
spit curls *coiffure* 530.8
spite *hostility* 63.1, *bad feeling* 266.5, *hate* 300.1, *resentment* 302.1, *bitterness* 306.3, *be malevolent* 306.12, *jealousy* 314.2, *be jealous* 314.8, *unpleasantness* 501.2
spiteful *hating* 300.7, *resentful* 302.8, *bitter* 306.9, *jealous* 314.5, *vindictive* 441.10, *unpleasant* 501.5
spitefully *aggressively* 63.14, *with hate* 300.13, *resentfully* 302.22, *bitterly* 306.16, *jealously* 314.12, *vindictively* 441.16
spitefulness *hostility* 63.1, *hate* 300.1, *resentment* 302.1, *bitterness* 306.3
spitfire *feeling person* 266.8, *irascible person* 303.7, *violent animal* 520.4
spit in the ocean *incompleteness* 98.2
Spiti pony Horse and Pony Breeds 159
spit on *hate* 300.11
spit on one's palms *work* 122.8
spit-roast *cook* 91.10
spit-roasting *cooking technique* 91.2
Spitsbergen Islands 572

spitting *saliva* 25.9, *salivating* 25.18
spitting distance *short distance* 586.2
spitting image [Inf] *image* 187.3, *representation* 202.9, *look-alike* 730.4, *twin* 789.5
spittle *saliva* 25.9, *body fluid* 555.3, *exudate* 557.4, *lubricant* 562.7
spit up *vomit* 709.27
spitz Breeds of Dogs 35
splash *dirty* 112.11, *sound faint* 233.8, *hiss* 237.1, 237.3, *maculation* 263.4, *flashiness* 404.4, *sprinkle* 557.32, 559.5, 559.14, 776.15, *make important* 799.14, *manifestation* 843.2
splashdown *rocketry* 7.32, *flight path* 691.12
splash down *find one's way* 691.15
splashed *seeping* 559.12
splashing *watering* 557.8
splash of color *spectrum* 251.3
splashy *marshy* 559.11
splat *wood* 131.3
splatter *rain* 9.57, *sprinkle* 557.32, 559.5, 776.15
splattered *sprinkled* 776.9
splattering *sprinkling* 776.4
splay Architectural Elements 134, *expansion* 581.1, *enlarge* 581.14, *broad* 592.5, *broaden* 592.11, *separate* 703.12, *diverge* 776.16
splay apart *separate* 703.12
splayed *bigger* 581.9, *broad* 592.5, *fanlike* 703.8
splaying *expansion* 581.1, *growing* 581.12, *parting* 703.2, *divergence* 776.5
spleen 223.4; *internal organ* 19.13, *hate* 300.1, *resentment* 302.1, *bitterness* 306.3
spleenful *hating* 300.7, *resentful* 302.8, *bitter* 306.9
spleenfully *with hate* 300.13, *resentfully* 302.22
splendid *grand* 404.22, *excellent* 445.13, *opulent* 485.10, *beautiful* 529.1
splendid isolation *separation* 409.3
splendidly *grandly* 404.37, *excellently* 445.21, *magnificently* 529.16
splendidness *excellence* 445.4, *beauty* 529.1
splendiferousness *grandeur* 404.10
splendor *light* 246.1, *grandeur* 404.10, *beauty* 529.1
splendorously *magnificently* 529.16
splenetic 223.7; *resentful* 302.8
splenetic *or* **splenetical** *bitter* 306.9
splenetically 223.10; *resentfully* 302.22
splice *joint* 752.7, *link* 752.18, *repair* 809.10
spliced *tied* 752.13
spliced [Inf] *married* 64.16, *related* 727.6
splice ropes *handle sailboat equipment* 150.30
splicing *junction* 609.5, *repair* 809.1
spliff [Inf] *drug dose* 121.15
splint *body support* 605.6
splint armor *historic armor* 419.8
splinter *rough thing* 544.2, *be brittle* 548.4, *take apart* 753.16, *disintegrate* 758.6, *particle* 760.4, *fragment* 787.3
splinter group *dissenters* 347.6

splintering *brittleness* 548.1, *brittle* 548.3
splinter party *political party* 50.5
splintery *brittle* 548.3
split *divorce* 66.1, 66.9, *divorced* 66.7, *bowling delivery* 151.2, *bowling* 151.6, *bowl* 151.8, *faction* 347.4, *dispute* 463.3, *allocate* 474.5, *be weak* 517.12, *be destroyed* 523.17, *brittleness* 548.1, *brittle* 548.3, *be brittle* 548.4, *opening* 583.1, *open* 583.10, 583.15, *crack* 587.2, 587.7, *cracked* 587.5, *notch* 636.1, 636.5, *notched* 636.4, *separate* 703.12, *separation* 753.1, *separateness* 753.3, *apart* 753.8, *take apart* 753.16, *deconstruct* 758.7, *part* 760.14, *interruption* 775.3, *divide* 787.7
split [Inf] *hurry off* 705.11
split apart *crack* 587.7
split down the middle 772.20; *allocate* 474.5, *make average* 742.9, *go halves* 789.16
split four ways *quadrisect* 791.12
split hairs *quibble* 330.13, *discriminate* 337.12, *modify* 340.13, *be accurate* 350.5
split image *portrait* 132.5
split infinitive *language error* 351.10
split in half *half* 789.12, *halve* 789.15
split in three *trisect* 790.11
split in two *split down the middle* 772.20, *halve* 789.15
split jump *ice-skating techniques* 162.16
split-level *manorial* 60.21
split-level house *house* 60.4
split lutz lift *ice-skating techniques* 162.16
split off *separate* 703.12
split one's sides *laugh* 239.14, 277.12
split personality *dissociative disorder* 108.17, *psychosis* 110.3, *duality* 789.2
split second *instant* 645.3
split-second *immediate* 645.5
split-shot *fishing tackle* 154.7
split skirt *skirt* 100.12
split the atom *experiment* 10.72
split the difference *compromise* 461.7, *make average* 742.9, *split down the middle* 772.20
split the ears *be loud* 232.8
split the uprights *kick* 155.20
split three ways *trisect* 790.11
splitting *defense mechanism* 108.23, *painful* 215.24, *brittleness* 548.1, *brittle* 548.3, *separation* 753.1
splitting headache *symptom* 114.3
splitting in four *quadrisection* 791.5
splitting in half *halving* 789.6
splitting in three *trisection* 790.5
splitting in two *halving* 789.6
splitting the atom *nuclear fission* 10.60
splitting the difference *compromise* 461.1
split two ways *half* 789.12, *go halves* 789.16
split up *divorce* 66.9, *disagree* 463.8, *dispute* 463.9, *separate* 753.12, *disband* 776.13, *diverge* 776.16
split-up *divorce* 66.1, *divergence* 776.5, *disbanded* 776.7
splodge *maculation* 263.4

splotch *maculation* 263.4, *blemish* 533.1
splotched *blemished* 533.5
splurge *waste* 96.1, 96.15, *feel pleasure* 214.12, *flashiness* 404.4, *extravagance* 491.5, *expend* 491.11
splurge on *put on a show* 404.28
splutter *salivate* 25.25, *hiss* 237.1, 237.3, *flicker* 684.26, *let out* 709.26
spluttering *salivating* 25.18, *flickering* 684.20
Spode Ceramics 129
spoil *overdo* 99.11, *poison* 117.18, *be clumsy* 128.9, *be on the track* 146.11, *comfort* 214.14, *sour* 223.8, *love* 299.21, *be solicitous* 323.13, *misuse* 395.6, *destroy* 468.18, *be permissive* 502.7, *change* 512.12, *weaken* 517.13, *ruin* 523.15, *make ugly* 531.4, *blemish* 533.7, *grow old* 653.16, *change for the worse* 665.18, *mix* 751.12, *decay* 808.16, *impair* 808.18
spoilage *refuse* 802.5, *impairment* 808.7
spoiled 808.9; *beloved* 299.19, *given consideration* 423.4, *marked* 533.6, *low quality* 745.7
spoiled rotten *given consideration* 423.4
spoiled vegetables *unpleasant-smelling thing* 227.2
spoiler *racing automobile* 146.2, *taker* 477.9, *plunderer* 479.9, *destroyer* 523.6, *distorter* 627.5, *equalizer* 740.5
spoil for a fight *pick a fight* 463.10
spoiling *automobile racing terms* 146.3, *solicitude* 323.5, *leniency* 423.1, *lenient* 423.3, *destruction* 468.7, *impairment* 808.7
spoiling for [Inf] *eager* 373.8, *prepared* 388.9
spoiling for a fight [Inf] *militant* 418.13, *contentious* 422.20
spoil one's chances *lose one's chance* 660.10
spoil oneself *be selfish* 444.6
spoil one's reputation *discontinue* 846.14
spoils *windfall* 467.7, *takings* 477.8, *stolen goods* 479.4
spoils of office *stolen goods* 479.4
spoils of war *windfall* 467.7, *takings* 477.8, *stolen goods* 479.4
spoilsport *sad person* 270.3, *dissatisfied person* 274.3, *meddler* 414.12, *hinderer* 826.11
spoils system *positive stimulus* 508.5
spoilt *misused* 395.3
spoke *bicycle part* 687.11, *radiation* 703.3, *step* 713.11
spoked *radiating* 703.7
spoken 205.13; *of language* 5.35, *voiced* 5.37, *communicated* 169.15
spoken aloud *spoken* 205.13
spoken for *marriageable* 64.17, *promised* 458.8
spoken language 205.2; *language* 5.4, *speech* 205.1
spoken letter 5.15
spoken unit *word* 5.17
spoken word *utterance* 205.10
spokes *focus* 702.5
spokeshave *hand tool* 103.3, *woodworking tool* 131.6, *sharp-edged thing* 549.6
spokesman *representative* 75.3, 187.7, *deputy* 80.1, *agent* 123.15,

speaker 205.12, *public speaker* 209.5

spokesperson *representative* 75.3, 187.7, *deputy* 80.1, *agent* 123.15, *speaker* 205.12, *public speaker* 209.5, *news interpreter* 365.7

spokeswoman *representative* 75.3, 187.7, *deputy* 80.1, *agent* 123.15, *speaker* 205.12, *public speaker* 209.5

spoliate *destroy* 468.18, *plunder* 479.16

spoliation *destruction* 468.7, *plundering* 479.5, *havoc* 523.5

spondaic *metrical* 139.20

spondee *meter* 139.10

spondulicks [Inf] *cash* 484.2

sponge 39.16, 401.13, 708.7; *cleaning tool* 111.10, *clean* 111.17, *sponger* 401.4, *be inactive* 415.13, *borrow* 476.10, *solicit money* 505.13, *cosmetic tool* 530.5, *air bubble* 558.10, *dryer* 560.5, *absorb* 560.20, 708.19, *porosity* 583.5

sponge [Inf] *drunkard* 121.8

sponge bag [Brit] *bag* 578.7

sponge bath *bath* 111.6

sponge cake *cake* 90.36

spongelike 39.26

sponge off *clean* 111.17, *erase* 186.9

sponge (off) *buy cheaply* 497.15

sponge on *sponge* 401.13

spongeous *absorbent* 708.11

sponge out *erase* 186.9

sponger 401.4; *nonworker* 415.4, *borrower* 476.7, *bargain hunter* 497.8, *beggar* 505.6, *adherent* 755.4

sponge rubber *rubber* 546.3

spongeware *Ceramics* 129

sponginess *sparseness* 541.1, *compressibility* 543.3, *pulpiness* 561.9

sponging *sycophancy* 401.2, *sycophantic* 401.7, *solicitation* 505.4, *begging* 505.9, *interior decoration* 532.4, *absorption* 708.6

spongy *spongelike* 39.26, *sparse* 541.3, *compressible* 543.9, *pulpy* 561.19, *holed* 583.12, *concave* 635.5, *absorbent* 708.11

sponsor *find means* 102.6, *approver* 437.7, *provider* 605.10, *support financially* 605.19, *benefactor* 825.15, *advise* 825.27, *finance* 825.31

sponsorship *resources* 102.4, *financial support* 605.8, *patronage* 810.7, 825.9, *financial assistance* 825.6

spontaneity 396.2; *unpremeditation* 389.2

spontaneous 389.6, 396.5; *disputed* 57.15, *instinctive* 320.8, *voluntary* 373.11, *naive* 821.3, *informal* 829.15

spontaneous abortion *infertile state* 23.3

spontaneous combustion *fire* 217.8

spontaneous generation *genesis* 21.5

spontaneously 389.17, 396.8; *industrially* 57.22, *intuitively* 320.11, *voluntarily* 373.17, *informally* 829.24

spontaneousness *spontaneity* 396.2

spontaneous person *improviser* 396.3

spontaneous strike *strike* 57.8

spoof *hoax* 193.7, 193.20,

entertainment 277.4, *mimicry* 736.3, *imitate* 736.9

spook [Inf] *ghost* 86.11, *frighten* 283.17, *omnipresence* 575.4, *illusion* 720.2, *disturb* 768.10

spooked [Inf] *bewitched* 86.21, *frightened* 283.9, *disturbed* 768.6

spookily [Inf] *magically* 86.28, *frighteningly* 283.20

spooky [Inf] *spiritual* 86.20, *frightening* 283.12

spool *program* 15.29, *fabric-handling tool* 130.12, *film* 132.8, *darkroom equipment* 132.21, *rotator* 682.8

spoon *tableware* 92.13, *rowing* 150.27, *bait* 154.6, *golf equipment* 156.5, *ladle* 578.17, *extractor* 711.9, *mixer* 751.7

spoon [Inf] *communicate love* 299.25

spoon(ful) *container(ful)* 738.2

spoon (out) *take away* 685.12

spoonbill *water bird* 36.9

spooned *storing* 578.19

spoonerism *word* 5.17, *language error* 351.10

spoon-fed *beloved* 299.19

spoon-feed *love* 299.21

spoonful of sugar, a *sweetener* 222.2

spooning [Inf] *communication of love* 299.6

spoon oar *rowboat parts* 150.15

spoons *Musical Instruments* 142

spoor *vestige* 185.11, *indication* 339.3

spooring *hunt* 385.3

sporadic *contagious* 114.26, *periodic* 639.10, 641.8, *infrequent* 662.2, *irregular* 664.3, 766.10, *inconsistent* 732.7, *discontinuous* 775.7, *dispersed* 776.6, *sparse* 796.6

sporadically *sometimes* 639.19, *irregularly* 664.6, *inconsistently* 732.16, *in disorder* 766.24, *discontinuously* 775.15, *diffusely* 776.18

sporadicalness *irregularity* 664.1, *inconsistency* 732.3, *discontinuity* 775.1, *rarity* 796.4

sporangium *fern plant* 46.2

spore 553.10; *cell* 13.15, *fern plant* 46.2, *fungal body* 47.4

spore capsule *moss plant* 46.5

spore case *fern plant* 46.2

spore-producing protozoan *protozoan* 39.17

sporophore *fungal body* 47.4

sporophyte *fern plant* 46.2

Sporozoa *protozoan* 39.17

sporozoan *protozoan* 39.17, 39.27

sport *wrestling* 152.18, *mountaineering* 161.9, *game* 167.1, *gambler* 167.6, *play* 167.12, *fun* 269.4, *show* 404.24, *sports* 422.3, *sporting event* 422.6, *display* 843.13

sport [Inf] *male title of address* 32.3

sport climber *mountaineer* 161.8

sported *displayed* 843.8

sportily *dressily* 100.47, *flashily* 404.32

sporting 145.5; *recreational* 167.10, *contending* 422.19, *in the right* 429.11

sporting activity 145.3

sporting chance *strong possibility* 836.3, *chance* 838.4, *equal chance* 842.7

sporting dog *hunting dog* 160.7

sporting event 422.6

sporting feat *workmanlike job* 127.6

sporting goods *dry goods* 130.3

sporting gun *firearm* 78.7

sporting hit 695.6

sporting house *brothel* 432.5

sportingly 145.7

sporting rifle [Brit] *hunting equipment* 160.4

sportive *sporting* 145.5, *recreational* 167.10

sport karate *karate* 152.14

sport of kings *horse racing* 159.10

sports 145.1, 422.3; *health improvement* 113.3

sports aerobics Sporting Activities 145

sports bag *bag* 578.7

sports book *type of book* 174.3

sports car *racing automobile* 146.2, *automobile* 687.6

Sports Car Club of America (SCCA) *racing governing bodies* 146.7

sports car racer *driver* 146.8

sports car races *races* 146.4

sportscast *broadcast news* 171.6

sportscaster *broadcasting personnel* 172.11

sports column *news story* 171.3

sports correspondent *descriptive writer* 202.10

sport season *seasons* 654.2

sports edition *newspaper* 175.2

sports editor *print journalist* 175.5

sports equipment 166.17

sports field *school place* 48.16

sports forecaster *forecaster* 358.9

sports ground 145.2

sport shirt *informal clothes* 100.7, *shirt* 100.13

sports jacket *informal clothes* 100.7, *jacket* 100.18

sports magazine *magazine* 175.3

sportsman 145.4

sportsmanlike *sporting* 145.5, *in the right* 429.11

sports outfit *clothing* 184.6

sports photography *photographic specialties* 132.2

sports reporter *print journalist* 175.5

sports skirt *skirt* 100.12

sports team uniform *uniform* 100.9

sports uniform *clothing* 184.6

sportswear *informal clothes* 100.7, *dry goods* 130.3, *informal clothing* 407.5

sportswoman *sportsman* 145.4

sporty *stylish* 100.42, *sporting* 145.5, *flashy* 404.17

sporty type *sportsman* 145.4

sporule *spore* 553.10

Spot Breeds of Pigs 16

spot *dirt* 112.5, *dirty* 112.11, *symptom* 114.3, *skin disease* 114.16, *lighting* 132.16, *snooker* 149.4, *see* 242.20, *maculation* 263.4, *variegate* 263.11, *discover* 345.11, *recognize* 363.11, *blemish* 533.1, 533.7, *mark* 533.2, *location* 565.1, *exact location* 565.2, *locate* 565.9, *situation* 573.1, *deform* 627.11, *state* 725.1, *predicament* 725.3, 824.5, *sprinkle* 776.15, *defect* 806.4, *stain* 808.20

spot [Inf] *stage lighting* 136.20

spot cash [Inf] *cash* 484.2

spotless *clean* 111.13, *pure* 253.11, 431.11, *innocent* 449.6, *immaculate* 805.11

spotlessly *cleanly* 111.20, *innocently* 449.13, *perfectly* 805.21

spotlessness *cleanliness* 111.1, *purity* 253.6, *innocence* 449.1, *immaculateness* 805.2

spotlight *lighting* 132.16, *stage lighting* 136.20, *publicity* 173.7, *publicize* 173.18, *emphasize* 200.6, *that which makes visible* 244.4, 244.9, *electric light* 246.6, *light* 246.19, *manifestation* 843.2, *display* 843.13, *reveal* 843.14

spotlighted *clear* 244.6

spotlit *lit* 246.16

spot meter *exposure equipment* 132.12

spot of enforcement *penalty* 155.13

spot pass *play* 155.8

spots *gambling* 167.4

spot stroke *billiards play* 149.2

spotted *dirty* 112.7, *billiard* 149.6, *mottled* 263.10, *discovered* 345.9, *blemished* 533.5, *sprinkled* 776.9, *imperfect* 806.5

spotted wilt *pests and diseases* 17.12

spotter *observer* 242.15, *discoverer* 345.7

spottiness *maculation* 263.4, *irregularity* 664.1

spotting *discovery* 345.1, *sprinkling* 776.4

spotty *of disease* 114.25, *mottled* 263.10, *irregular* 664.3, *discontinuous* 775.7

spousal *matrimonial* 64.15

spousal *or* **spousals** *wedding* 64.5

spouse 64.8; *woman in the family* 33.13, *family member* 65.2, *loved one* 299.13, *partner* 794.9

spousehood *marriage* 64.1

spouseless *celibate* 67.6

spout *flow* 555.25, *outlet* 707.8, *run out* 707.15, *disgorgement* 709.6, *let out* 709.26, *upturn* 713.2, *spring up* 713.22

spout [Inf] *be talkative* 207.7

spouting *ascending* 713.13

spouting [Inf] *empty talk* 362.5

spout out *run out* 707.15

sprain *painful injury* 215.3, *inflict pain* 215.10, *weaken* 517.13, *violence by person* 520.2, *use violence* 520.9

sprained *injured* 215.5

sprat *food fish and shellfish* 90.20

sprawl *expansion* 581.1, *enlarge* 581.14, *recumbency* 603.2, *be horizontal* 603.9, *fall* 714.4, *disbandment* 776.2, *disband* 776.13, *take it easy* 819.3

sprawled *recumbent* 603.7, *divergent* 776.11

sprawling *expansion* 581.1, *growing* 581.12, *recumbency* 603.2, *recumbent* 603.7, *falling* 714.11, *divergent* 776.11

spray *pest control* 16.13, *farm* 16.19, *pest killer* 17.9, *cultivate* 17.19, *stem* 41.5, *flower* 42.1, *manage grassland* 45.10, *assemblage* 59.13, *perfume* 226.6, *firing* 418.6, *coif* 530.15, *vaporizer* 556.10, *aerate* 556.24, *sprinkler* 557.12, *sprinkle* 557.32, 559.14, 776.15, *air bubble* 558.10, *component* 796.3

spray-can *painting* 143.3

sprayed *sprinkled* 776.9

sprayer *farm tool* 16.5, *garden tool* 17.7, *sprinkler* 557.12

spray gun *material* 143.9

spraying *watering* 557.8, *sprinkle* 559.5, *sprinkling* 776.4

spread 746.3; *parameter* 6.57, *farm*

16.2, grow 43.15, publish 173.15, be published 173.19, augmentation 467.2, increase 467.17, 746.6, be an influence 512.13, lubricate 562.15, extend 563.14, size 579.1, expansion 581.1, bigger 581.9, enlarge 581.14, open up 583.16, layer 588.9, broaden 592.11, 778.15, bed covering 613.7, coat 613.28, transmission 685.3, transfer 685.8, miscellaneous aviation terms 689.9, parting 703.2, move apart 703.11, separation 753.1, dispersion 776.1, dispersed 776.6, disperse 776.12
spread [Inf] *feast* 92.9
spreadability *enlargeability* 581.6
spreadable *enlargeable* 581.13
spread apart *move apart* 703.11
spread around *allocate* 474.5
spread around *or* **about** *published* 173.12
spread a rumor *publish* 173.15
spread canvas *set out* 705.12
spread eagle *insignia* 184.5
spread-eagle *be horizontal* 603.9, *branch* 703.14, *sedentary* 716.11, *lie down* 716.21
spread-eagled *recumbent* 603.7, *fanlike* 703.8
spreader *garden tool* 17.7, *enlarger* 581.8
spreaders *sailboat parts and accessories* 150.4
spread far and wide *be excessive* 99.9
spread formation *offense* 155.6
spread foundation *substructure* 551.8
spread gossip *distort the truth* 192.25
spreading *augmentation* 467.2, *expansion* 581.1, *growing* 581.12, *transmission* 685.3, *increasing* 746.4, *separation* 753.1, *dispersive* 776.10
spreading like wildfire *increasing* 746.4
spreading out *expansion* 581.1, *parting* 703.2
spreading the word *publishing* 173.2
spread like wildfire *be an influence* 512.13, *grow* 581.17
spread on *coat* 613.28
spread oneself thin *be busy* 414.19
spread one's wings *diversify* 732.11
spread out *extend* 563.14, *space* 563.15, *enlarge* 581.14, *broaden* 592.11, *leveled* 603.8, *make horizontal* 603.10, *disband* 776.13, *sparse* 796.6, *scatter* 796.9, *reveal* 843.14
spread-out *bigger* 581.9, *broad* 592.5
spread over *coat* 613.28, *fill* 761.11
spread rumors *distort the truth* 192.25
spread sail *set out* 705.12
spreadsheet *chart* 767.8, *list* 785.1
spreadsheet program *application software* 15.14
spread the bull [Inf] *talk nonsense* 362.12
spread the good news *preach* 84.14
spread the load *delegate* 79.6
spread the Word *preach* 84.14
spread the word *make someone believe* 87.11, *publish* 173.15
Spree *Rivers* 570

spree *waste* 96.1, *drinking bout* 121.7, *extravagance* 491.5
sprig *tree part* 43.2, *component* 760.3
sprightliness *liveliness* 28.12
sprightly *lively* 28.16, *active* 414.13
spring 546.4, 654.3; *young plant* 26.5, Collective Names 59, *source of supply* 105.4, *sailboat parts and accessories* 150.4, *diving* 164.13, *participate* 166.22, *soften* 543.14, *elasticity* 546.1, *be elastic* 546.7, *water* 571.1, *coil* 632.2, *season* 654.1, *seasonal* 654.7, *source* 675.2, *acceleration* 694.3, *be swift* 694.10, *accelerate* 694.14, *outflow* 707.4, *jump* 713.7, *spring up* 713.22, *lifter* 715.5, *result* 770.12, *emerge* 771.35
spring apart *scatter* 753.15
spring back *recoil* 680.21
springboard *gymnastics equipment* 157.2, *swimming equipment* 164.8, *place of departure* 705.4, *lifter* 715.5, *help* 825.1
springboard dives *diving* 164.6
springboard diving *competitive diving* 164.7
spring catch *fastener* 754.7
spring-clean *clean* 111.17
spring-cleaning *cleaning* 111.2
spring dive *diving* 164.6
springe *trap* 813.1
springer Architectural Elements 134
springer spaniel Breeds of Dogs 35
Springfield American States 564
springform pan *cooking equipment* 91.6
spring forward *accelerate* 694.14
spring from *follow from* 676.9
springily *elastically* 546.10
springiness *softness* 543.1, *elasticity* 546.1
springing *softness* 543.1, *elastic* 546.5, *leaping* 713.17
springlike *warm* 217.13, *fresh* 260.10, *seasonal* 654.7
spring on *ambush* 292.11
spring sale *sale* 482.2
spring skiing *skiing snow* 162.3
spring tide *tide* 8.17, 571.2
springtide *spring* 654.3
springtime *spring* 654.3
springtime of life *youth* 26.1
spring to one's feet *arise* 715.15
spring up 713.22; *drain* 8.64, *mushroom* 47.23, *grow* 581.17, *increase* 746.6, *emerge* 771.35
spring water *water* 93.4, 557.1
springwood *timber* 43.3
springy *pliant* 543.7, *elastic* 546.5
sprinkle 557.32, 559.5, 559.14, 776.15; *cultivate* 17.19, *perform rites* 85.18, *variegate* 263.11, *powder* 553.25, *water* 557.29, *mix* 751.12, *scatter* 796.9
sprinkled 776.9; *mottled* 263.10, *sparse* 796.6
sprinkler 557.12; *garden tool* 17.7, *cleaning tool* 111.10
sprinkler head *sprinkler* 557.12
sprinkler system *safety device* 810.15
sprinkling 776.4; *Christian rite* 85.5, *watering* 557.8, *sprinkle* 559.5, *fallen* 716.8, *admixture* 751.5, *few* 796.1, *suggestion* 800.9
sprinkling of water *religious cleansing* 111.3
sprinkling system *sprinkler* 557.12

sprint *automobile racing* 146.1, *speed-skating* 162.33, *swimming* 164.12, *participate* 166.22, *acceleration* 694.3, *accelerate* 694.14, *make haste* 818.5
sprint *or* **sprinting** *sprint racing* 166.2
sprinter *racehorse* 159.2, *horse racing* 159.10, *track and field eventer* 166.19, *speeder* 694.5
sprint freestyle race *competitive swimming* 164.3
sprinting Sporting Activities 145, *cross-country* 162.31, *track and field* 166.20
sprinting race *cross-country skiing* 162.7
sprint race *sprint racing* 166.2
sprint racing 166.2
sprint-skate *speed-skate* 162.37
sprint skating *speed skating* 162.20
sprint swimmer *swimmer* 164.11
sprite 86.12; *computing terms* 15.22, *little person* 580.5
sprocket *sharp-pointed thing* 549.4
sprocket wheel *wheel* 682.9
sprout *reproduce oneself* 21.14, *young plant* 26.5, *be born* 28.18, *stem* 41.5, *vegetate* 41.21, *grow* 581.17, 676.10, *be tall* 596.16, *increase* 746.6, *emerge* 771.35
sprouting *germination* 581.5, *growing* 581.12
sprout up *vegetate* 41.21, *grow* 581.17
spruce Trees and Shrubs 43, *dressed up* 100.39, *clean* 111.13, 111.17, *fashionable* 536.5, *orderly* 765.13
spruced up *dressed up* 100.39
sprucely *dashingly* 536.10
spruceness *stylishness* 537.2, *beautification* 807.7
spruce pine Trees and Shrubs 43
spruce up *dress up* 100.45, *clean* 111.17, *beautify* 530.14, *decorate* 532.11, *tidy* 765.21, 807.19
sprung *soft* 543.6, *elastic* 546.5
sprung rhythm *meter* 139.10
spry *skillful* 127.10, *active* 414.13, *vigorous* 518.2
spume *wave* 8.16, 571.3, *air bubble* 558.10
spumy *whitened* 253.8
spun 130.13
spunk *fuel starter* 106.3, *courage* 284.1, *endurance* 516.4, *vigor* 518.1
spunky *courageous* 284.9, *vigorous* 518.2
spun out *diffuse* 199.3, *lengthened* 590.10
spun-out *racing* 146.9
spur *tree part* 43.2, *incentive* 178.4, *motivate* 178.17, 508.9, *offer* 504.11, *negative stimulus* 508.4, *sharp-pointed growth* 549.5, *sharpen* 549.16, *mountain* 569.1, *peninsula* 572.5, *track* 688.2, *hurry someone up* 694.15, *impel* 695.9, *intensification* 746.2, *component* 760.3, *haste* 818.1, *hasten* 818.4
spurge Flowers 42
spur gear *gear* 14.7
spurious *sophistic* 330.7, *questionable* 333.13, *devious* 607.9, *misrepresented* 627.8, *artificial* 722.9, *unauthentic* 722.9, *simulated* 733.11
spuriously *sophistically* 330.14, *deviously* 607.16, *distortedly*

627.14, *unauthentically* 722.17, *imitatively* 733.20
spuriousness *deviousness* 607.4, *distortion of truth* 627.4, *unauthenticity* 722.4
spurn *dislike* 291.12, *hate* 300.11, *exclude* 383.11, 764.7, *disdain* 400.16, *be insubordinate* 416.8, *insult* 436.5, 436.21, *dissent* 506.9, *repel* 701.7, *ostracize* 709.17
spurned *disliked* 291.10, *rejected* 383.6
spurning *rejecting* 383.2, *insult* 436.5, *insulting* 436.10, *repulse* 701.2
spur-of-the-moment *spontaneous* 396.5
spur on *motivate* 508.9, *intensify* 746.8
spurred on *motivated* 508.8
spurry Flowers 42
spurs *military honor* 58.9
spurt *alacrity* 414.3, *be active* 414.18, *forward motion* 679.1, *acceleration* 694.3, *accelerate* 694.14, *run out* 707.15, *disgorgement* 709.6, *let out* 709.26, *upturn* 713.2, *spring up* 713.22, *leak* 816.11, *haste* 818.1, *make haste* 818.5
spurting *ascending* 713.13
spurt out *run out* 707.15
spur track *track* 688.2
sputter *absorb* 11.40, *rattle* 235.12, *hiss* 237.1, 237.3, *flicker* 684.12, 684.26, *let out* 709.26
sputtering *surface chemistry* 11.20, *rattling* 235.8, *flickering* 684.20
sputter-ion pump *surface chemistry* 11.20
sputtery *flickering* 684.20
sputum *secreted substance* 24.2
sputum test *test* 107.10
spy *secret person* 182.6, *see* 242.20, *meddler* 321.4, *discoverer* 345.7, *discover* 345.11, *meddle* 414.23, *subvert* 427.13, *warner* 814.5
spyglass *visual aid* 242.14
spyhole *place for viewing* 242.13
spying *secretiveness* 182.3, *observation* 242.5, *subversion* 427.3
spy on *watch* 242.23
spy plane *military aircraft* 77.30
spy satellite *artificial satellite* 7.30
spy story *story* 139.4
squab *young bird* 36.17, *fat* 579.15
squabble *quarrel* 272.4, 272.9, *argument* 329.1, *argue* 329.11, *activity* 414.1, *be active* 414.18, *contention* 422.1, *conflict* 422.26, *dispute* 463.3, 463.9
squabbling *dissension* 272.3, *arguing* 329.6, *disagreeing* 463.6
squad *military organization* 58.4, *team* 59.9, 827.7, *force* 59.10, *army unit* 77.14, *personnel* 123.16, *sportsman* 145.4, *baseball team* 147.2, *hockey player* 158.8, *soccer participant* 163.4
squad car *automobile* 687.6
squadron *military organization* 58.4, *force* 59.10, *army unit* 77.14, *naval unit* 77.20, *air force unit* 77.29, *collection* 757.3
squalene *terpene* 12.20
squalid *dirty* 112.7, *unclean* 112.8, *unhygienic* 114.27, *beggarly* 486.12, *unpleasant* 501.5, *plain* 528.9
squalidity *dirtiness* 112.1
squalidly *unhygienically* 114.32

squalidness *dirtiness* 112.1, *untidiness* 766.3

squall *wind* 9.12, *cry* 239.1, *cry out* 239.13, *natural violence* 520.3, *turbulence* 684.3, *atmospheric agitation* 684.13, *natural hazard* 813.4

squally *windy* 9.42

squalor *dirtiness* 112.1, *lack of hygiene* 112.3, *beggary* 486.3, *unpleasantness* 501.2

squama *slice* 588.4

Squamata *reptile* 37.1

squamation *layering* 588.5

squamose *platelike* 588.8

squamosely *in layers* 588.11

squamous *reptilian* 37.12, *ichthyological* 38.11, *platelike* 588.8

squamously *in layers* 588.11

squamulose *platelike* 588.8

squander *waste* 96.15, 500.7, *use up* 393.12, *misuse* 395.6, *overindulge* 456.11, *be wasteful* 468.16, *expend* 491.11

squandered *losing* 468.9, *futile* 802.10

squanderer *waster* 96.8, *loser* 468.8, *spender* 491.7, *spendthrift* 500.3

squandering *waste* 96.1, 468.5, *unprofitable* 468.10, *extravagance* 500.1

square *multiplication* 6.15, *polygon* 6.42, *polygonal* 6.79, *add* 6.86, 784.11, *row* 150.32, *atone* 313.7, *put right* 429.14, *compensate* 478.6, *defray* 481.18, *plot* 564.9, *urban area* 567.10, *stocky* 579.16, *plumb line* 602.4, *perpendicular* 602.6, *make vertical* 602.9, *perpendicularly* 602.12, *form* 624.9, *angled figure* 628.3, *angular measurement* 628.4, *angled* 628.9, *directly* 697.16, *adjust* 721.23, *correctly* 721.29, *equal* 740.8, *counterbalance* 743.8, *make bigger* 746.7, *add* 784.11, *two* 789.1, *double* 789.14, *quadrilateral* 791.2, 791.8

square [Inf] *bribe* 178.18, *straight person* 630.7, *traditional* 630.13, *conformist* 781.6, 781.10

square accounts *settle accounts* 493.11

square accounts with *pay off* 489.17

square bracket *means of connection* 754.4

square brackets Punctuation Marks 5, *mathematical symbol* 6.11

square bridge *bridge* 551.10

squared *rowing* 150.27, *formed* 624.6, *adjusted* 721.14, *equal* 740.8, *two* 789.8

square dance *dance* 135.1, *party* 408.6, *foursome* 791.3

square dancing Dancing Types 135, Hobbies and Pastimes 167

squarehead Nicknames for Inhabitants 61

square-in pass *play* 155.8

square knot Knots, Bends, Hitches, Splices 754

squarely *professionally* 152.22, *accurately* 350.6, *right* 429.15, *perpendicularly* 602.12, *directly* 697.16, *correctly* 721.29, *equitably* 740.15, *four times* 791.13

square match *golfing terms* 156.3

square matrix *matrix* 6.20

square meal *meal* 92.8

square measure *measuring system* 589.4, *type of measurement* 589.8

Square Mile, the London 567.8

squareness *squatness* 579.6, *perpendicularity* 602.2

squareness [Inf] *traditionality* 630.6

square one *beginning* 771.1

square-out pass *play* 155.8

square piano Musical Instruments 142

square-rigged *sailing* 150.25

square-rigged sailboat *sailboat* 150.3

square-rigger Sailing Ships and Boats 690

square root *multiplication* 6.15, *power* 783.6

square root sign *mathematical symbol* 6.11

square the account *retaliate* 420.4

square things *atone* 313.7

square-toed shoes *shoes* 100.30

square up *equalize* 740.12, *counterbalance* 743.8

square wave *wave form* 10.13, *wave* 683.4

square with *conform* 735.27, 781.11

square with the facts or **evidence** *be true* 721.20

squaring *rowing* 150.27, *compensation* 478.2, *adjustment* 721.5

squaring balance *rowing techniques* 150.16

squaring the circle *geometric construction* 6.47, *puzzle* 182.5

squash 165.9, Sporting Activities 145, *small sound* 233.4, *sound faint* 233.8, *refute* 332.7, *abolish* 523.11, *soften* 543.14, *beat* 553.27, *semiliquid* 561.7, *bear down on* 716.18

squash ball *squash terms* 165.10

squash court *squash terms* 165.10

squashed flat *leveled* 603.8

squash flat *lower* 597.21, *make horizontal* 603.10

squashily *sibilantly* 237.4

squashiness *compressibility* 543.3, *pulpiness* 561.9

squash racquets *squash* 165.9

squash tennis *squash* 165.9

squash terms 165.10

squashy *compressible* 543.9, *flowing* 555.15, *marshy* 559.11, *pulpy* 561.19

squat *shack* 60.10, *settle* 61.14, *possess* 469.14, *take* 477.14, *stocky* 579.16, *undersized* 580.8, *short* 591.6, *low* 597.10, *be low* 597.20, *transgress* 712.14, *bow* 716.6, *sit* 716.20, *be external* 724.15

squatness 579.6; *littleness* 580.1, *shortness* 591.1, *lowness* 597.1

squat on *possess* 469.14

squatted *inhabited* 61.10

squatter *settler* 61.4, *possessor* 469.10, *poor person* 486.6, *intruder* 724.7

squatterdom *claiming* 469.2

squatter's right *claiming* 469.2

squatting *claiming* 469.2, *possessing* 469.11, *sedentary* 716.11

squaw [Inf and Off] *married woman* 64.11

squawk *express pain* 215.11, *be loud* 232.8, *harsh sound* 238.1, *be strident* 238.7, *bird sound* 240.2, *make a bird sound* 240.8

squawk [Inf] *gesture of protest* 507.3, *complain* 507.8

squawking *strident* 238.4

squawky *strident* 238.4

squeak *speak in a particular way* 205.18, *small sound* 233.4, *sound faint* 233.8, *shrillness* 238.3, *be shrill* 238.9, *bird sound* 240.2, *make an animal sound* 240.7

squeaker [Inf] *informer* 170.8

squeakiness *shrillness* 238.3

squeaking *shrill* 238.6

squeaky *shrill* 238.6

squeaky-clean [Inf] *clean* 111.13, *in the right* 429.11

squeal *express pain* 215.11, *shrillness* 238.3, *be shrill* 238.9, *cry of pain* 239.5, *animal sound* 240.1, *make an animal sound* 240.7

squeal [Inf] *inform on* 170.13, *tell on* 180.10, *testify* 336.10, *accuse* 442.8

squealer [Inf] *informer* 170.8, *discloser* 180.4, *verifier* 336.4, *accuser* 442.3, *warner* 814.5

squeamish *sick* 114.24, *moralistic* 431.12

squeamishly *moralistically* 431.16

squeamishness *self-righteousness* 431.7

squeegee *cleaning tool* 111.10

squeezable *compressible* 543.9

squeeze 582.3, 582.13; *crowd* 59.11, *exertion* 122.4, *play baseball* 147.9, *communication of love* 299.6, *communicate love* 299.25, *greet* 410.11, *be severe* 424.8, *compel* 428.8, *retention* 471.1, *retain* 471.7, *make dense* 540.9, *stuff* 577.12, *obtain an extract* 711.19, *limitation* 747.3, 830.2, *make smaller* 747.8, *adhere* 755.8, *predicament* 824.5, *limit* 830.13

squeeze credit *restrain commerce* 830.14

squeezed 582.9; *loaded* 577.8

squeezed dry *dried-out* 560.10

squeeze in *make dense* 540.9, *flood in* 706.14, *impact* 710.11, *fill* 761.11

squeeze one's hand *greet* 410.11

squeeze out *displace* 711.14

squeeze play *batting terms* 147.6

squeezer *contractor* 742.6

squeeze someone's hand *gesture* 183.17

squeeze the last ounce out of *be skillful* 127.14

squeeze the trigger *hunt* 160.12, *fire* 418.18

squeeze together *make dense* 540.9

squeezing *demanding* 95.13, *communication of love* 299.6, *squeeze* 582.3, *obtaining of an extract* 711.7

squeezing out *displacement* 711.2

squelch *deter* 179.8, *be moist* 559.15, *restrain* 830.12

squelchiness *compressibility* 543.3

squelching *restraint* 830.1

squelchy *compressible* 543.9, *sludgy* 561.18

squib *banger* 234.3, *ridicule* 440.6

squib kick *kick* 155.12

squid *food fish and shellfish* 90.20

squiggle *coil* 632.2, *convolute* 632.6

squiggly *convolutional* 632.4

squilgee *cleaning tool* 111.10

squill Flowers 42

squinch Architectural Elements 134

squint *church architecture* 134.11, *look* 242.7, 242.21, *place for viewing* 242.13, *faulty vision*

243.1, *see badly* 243.16, *distortion of face* 627.2

squinting *visually impaired* 243.9

Squire *honorific* 72.5

squire *master* 68.1, *lover* 299.11, *court* 299.26, *pander to* 401.11, *possessor* 469.10, *accompanier* 794.6, *escort* 794.18

squire [Brit inf] *male title of address* 32.3

squirearchy *feudalism* 49.5

squirm *feel pain* 215.8, *be shy* 403.13, *coil* 632.2, *convolute* 632.6, *shake* 684.7, 684.24, *be agitated* 684.21

squirming *convolutional* 632.4, *shaky* 684.18

squirmy *shaky* 684.18

squirrel *game* 160.6

squirrel away *bury* 105.22, *not use* 394.9

squirrel-like *rodentlike* 35.28

squirrels Collective Names 59

squirt *hose* 557.33, *disgorgement* 709.6, *let out* 709.26

squirt [Inf] *young man* 26.8, *little person* 580.5, *nonentity* 800.8

squirt gun *sprinkler* 557.12

squirt in *inject* 710.10

squirting *watering* 557.8

squish *small sound* 233.4, *sound faint* 233.8

squishy *compressible* 543.9

squits [Brit inf] *defecation* 25.3

sri [Hindu] *male title of address* 32.3

Sri Lanka Countries 566, Islands 572

sruti *other text* 81.19

stab 418.22; *murder* 30.20, *play soccer* 163.8, *pain* 215.1, *painful injury* 215.3, *be painful* 215.9, *inflict pain* 215.10, *experiment* 335.1, *attempt* 390.1, *hit* 418.9, *hole* 583.17, *take apart* 753.16

stabbed *holed* 583.12

stabbing *painful* 215.4, *bitter* 306.9, *hit* 418.9

stabile *sculpture* 144.1

stability 674.1; *load* 14.14, *sanity* 109.1, *seriousness* 376.3, *authority* 516.5, *continuation* 642.2, *permanence* 667.1, *lack of motion* 678.1, *equilibrium* 740.2, *harmony* 765.8, *discipline* 765.9, *infallibility* 840.6

stabilization *stability* 674.1

stabilize *solidify* 11.37, *make fast* 464.13, *make permanent* 667.5, *be stable* 674.6, *make stable* 674.7, *equalize* 740.12, *harmonize* 765.20, *make certain* 840.14

stabilized 674.4; *status adjectives* 11.25

stabilized dune *dune* 8.43

stabilizer *polymer* 11.9, *phase* 11.13, *catalysis* 11.16, *equalizer* 740.5

stab in the back *personal attack* 418.8, *defame* 440.13

stable 674.3; *farm building* 16.4, *practice livestock farming* 16.20, *mammal dwelling* 35.21, *cage* 60.15, *take up residence* 60.24, *storehouse* 105.8, *save* 105.20, *rational* 109.4, *riding equipment* 159.9, *steady* 376.8, *fast* 464.8, *contain* 578.20, *frequent* 663.6, *permanent* 667.2, *unfailing* 667.3, *stopover* 704.7, *equal* 740.8, *harmonious* 765.16, *shelter* 812.4, *infallible* 840.12

stableboy *farm worker* 16.15, *domestic servant* 69.7, *horse person* 159.14

stable colors *clothing* 184.6
stabled *containing* 578.18
stable equilibrium *force* 10.9, *stability* 674.1
stable horse *horse* 159.1
stableman *farm worker* 16.15, *domestic servant* 69.7
stablemate *horse racing* 159.10
stable state *equilibrium* 740.2
stabling *storage* 105.6, *containing* 578.18
stably 674.9; *equitably* 740.15
stab to death *murder* 30.20
staccato Musical Terms and Expression Marks 140
staccato *vibration* 683.2, *vibrating* 683.9
stack *coast* 8.13, *assemblage* 59.13, *assemble* 59.23, *store* 105.1, *heap* 105.19, *acquisition* 467.4, *acquire* 467.19, *flight control* 689.7, *service* 689.16
stacked *collected* 59.19, *stored* 105.14, *predetermined* 384.4
stacked deck *predetermination* 384.1
stacking *flight control* 689.7
stack the deck *predetermine* 384.8
stadial *glaciation* 8.46
stadium 155.3, 163.2; *theater* 136.16, *sports ground* 145.2, *place for viewing* 242.13, *meeting place* 408.5, *building* 551.9
staff *educator* 48.4, *industrial* 57.13, *force* 59.10, *armed force* 77.10, *blunt weapon* 78.5, *vestment* 84.11, *resources* 102.4, *find means* 102.6, *personnel* 123.16, *written music* 140.21, *insignia* 184.5, *body support* 605.6, *helper* 825.12
staff college *military training* 76.19
staff management *personnel management* 126.4
staff member *employee* 57.4, *office assistant* 69.6, *thing included* 763.2, *subordinate* 832.3
staff nurse *nurse* 107.23
staff officers *military staff* 58.5
staff of life *food* 90.1
Staffordshire bull terrier Breeds of Dogs 35
Staffordshire ware Ceramics 129
staff representative *union member* 57.6
Staff Sergeant/Specialist 6 US Military Ranks 58
staffwork *art of war* 76.16
stag *male animal* 32.15, *male mammal* 35.18
stage 136.18; *produce* 522.13, *open space* 583.6, *level* 588.2, *surroundings* 615.1, *rung* 636.3, *stopover* 704.7, *state* 725.1, *occurrence* 726.2, *interval* 739.4, *part* 760.1, *display* 843.13
stage, the *drama* 136.1
stage a comeback *renew* 797.19
stage a coup *replace* 574.17
stage a demo [Inf] *protest* 331.19
stage a revolt *subvert* 427.13
stage a shootout *battle* 76.33
stage a sit-down *cause mischief* 507.9
stage a sit-in *protest* 331.19, *be insubordinate* 416.8
stage box *auditorium* 136.17
stage business *acting* 136.22
stage carpenter *stagehand* 136.29
stagecoach *means of transportation* 686.2, *wagon* 687.5
stagecraft *dramaturgy* 136.6
stage crew *stagehand* 136.29

staged *dramatized* 136.32, *entertaining* 138.12
staged event *public relations (PR)* 173.8
stage director *producer* 136.28, 522.10
stagedom *drama* 136.1
stage door *stage* 136.18
stage-door Johnny *theatergoer* 136.30
stage drunk *stock part* 136.24
stage fever *acting* 136.22
stage fright *acting* 136.22, *symptoms of fear* 283.3, *shyness* 403.3
stagehand 136.29
stage Irishman *stock part* 136.24
stageland *drama* 136.1
stage left *stage* 136.18, *onstage* 136.39
stage lighting 136.20
stage-manage *dramatize* 136.33, *show* 404.24, *hide* 844.13
stage-managed *dramatized* 136.32
stage management *production* 136.14
stage manager *producer* 136.28, *displayer* 843.7
stage name *anonymity* 182.7, *name* 202.8
stage of book production 174.7
stage of proof 174.9
stage performer *actor* 136.25
stage play *play* 136.2
stage player *actor* 136.25
stage presence *acting* 136.22
stage presentation *theatrical performance* 136.13
stage property *stage requisite* 136.21
stage requisite 136.21
stage right *stage* 136.18, *onstage* 136.39
stage screw *stage set* 136.19
stage set 136.19
stage setting *stage set* 136.19
stage show *show* 138.4, 404.12
stage technician *stagehand* 136.29
stage villain *stock part* 136.24
stage whisper *acting* 136.22, *hiss* 237.1, *quietness* 844.4
stage world *drama* 136.1
stage zone *geological time* 823.4
stagflation *economic factor* 56.8, *inflation* 484.9
stagger 684.11; *cause disbelief* 88.9, *be drunk* 121.34, *daunt* 179.9, *astonish* 292.10, *be wondrous* 294.14, *be weak* 517.12, *be irregular* 664.5, *be changeable* 666.5, *walk* 677.17, *pitch* 684.25, *be fatigued* 820.5
stagger along *move slowly* 693.11, *depart* 705.8
stagger belief *be wondrous* 294.14
staggered *astonished* 292.6
staggering *drunken behavior* 121.4, *slightly drunk* 121.26, *astonishing* 292.8, 294.10, *swaying* 378.4, *irregularity* 664.1, *irregular* 664.3, *slow* 693.7, *unbalanced* 741.5
staggers *animal disease* 34.10, *spasm* 684.8, *imbalance* 741.2
staghound Breeds of Dogs 35
stagily *showily* 367.6, *dramatically* 404.31
staginess *demonstrativeness* 331.2
staging *dramaturgy* 136.6, *production* 136.14
stag movie *pornography* 432.7
stagnancy *lack of motion* 678.1
stagnant *infertile* 23.7, *unhygienic* 114.27, *inactive* 413.9, 415.8,

inert 519.2, *lakelike* 568.5, *motionless* 678.4, *vegetating* 717.17
stagnantly *apathetically* 322.7, *motionlessly* 678.9
stagnant water *lack of hygiene* 112.3, *swill* 112.6, *small lake* 568.2
stagnate *be infertile* 23.8, *not act* 413.11, *be inactive* 415.13, *be inert* 519.4, *be motionless* 678.7, *merely exist* 717.21
stagnated *apathetic* 322.4
stagnating *infertile* 23.7, *inert* 519.2, *vegetating* 717.17
stagnation *infertile state* 23.3, *economic factor* 56.8, *apathy* 322.2, *immobility* 413.2, *inflation* 484.9, *inertness* 519.1, *lack of motion* 678.1, *mere existence* 717.10
stag party *menfolk* 32.14, *social gathering* 59.7, *general wedding terms* 64.6, *party* 408.6
stagy *dramatic* 136.31, 404.16, *entertaining* 138.12, *demonstrative* 331.10, *affected* 367.3
staid *serious* 278.4, *formal* 406.6, *conformist* 781.10
staidness *seriousness* 278.1, *formality* 406.1
stain 533.3, 808.20; *dirt* 112.5, *dirty* 112.11, *dye* 130.8, *vestige* 185.11, *coloring agent* 251.5, *color* 251.16, *variegate* 263.11, *impropriety* 430.5, *mark* 533.8, *coating* 613.8, *coat* 613.28, *deform* 627.11, *deficiency* 745.2, *admixture* 751.5, *mix together* 751.14, *defect* 806.4
stained *dirty* 112.7, *semitransparent* 249.9, *colored* 251.10, *marked* 533.6, *covered* 613.19, *shortened* 762.6, *imperfect* 806.5, *defective* 806.7
stained glass *craft* 133.2, *glass* 249.5, *variegated thing* 263.5
stained-glass window *picture* 133.5
staining *cell biology* 13.14, *dyeing* 130.9
staining pigment *coloring agent* 251.5
stainless *clean* 111.13, *innocent* 449.6
stainlessness *innocence* 449.1
stainless steel *construction material* 14.21
stainless-steel ware *tableware* 92.13
stain removal *fabric treatment* 130.10
stair *step* 713.11, *interval* 739.4
stair carpet *floor covering* 613.13
staircase Architectural Elements 134, *access* 691.3, *stairway* 713.9, *consecutiveness* 774.1
stairs Phobias 283, *stairway* 713.9, *means of connection* 754.4, *consecutiveness* 774.1
stairway 713.9; *means of connection* 754.4
stake *farm building* 16.4, *garden tool* 17.7, *cultivate* 17.19, *gambling* 167.4, *gamble* 167.14, *poker* 168.5, *play cards* 168.7, *place for fire* 217.9, *contend* 422.22, *claim* 429.3, *instrument of execution* 454.15, *fastener* 754.7, *endanger* 811.13
stake a claim *have rights* 429.13
stakeholder *treasurer* 484.18
stake one's claim to *take* 477.14
stakes *barrier* 419.10, *rivalry* 422.2, *prize competition* 422.5

Stakhanovite *worker* 123.1, *hard worker* 414.11
staking *gambling* 167.11
stalactite *groundwater* 8.11
stalagmite *groundwater* 8.11
stale *urinate* 25.22, *unhygienic* 114.27, *unemphatic* 201.2, *tasteless* 220.4, *unpalatable* 223.6, *stinking* 227.3, *boring* 296.6, *uncustomary* 398.4, *olden* 653.11, *monotonous* 797.12, *imperfect* 806.5, *unimproved* 808.10, *decay* 808.16, *fatigued* 820.2
stale joke *boring thing* 296.3
stalely *boringly* 296.10, *venerably* 653.17
stalemate 740.3; *inaction* 413.1, *act on the defensive* 419.29, *obstruction* 584.2, *stop* 668.2, *cause to cease* 668.12, *lack of motion* 678.1, *make motionless* 678.8, *nonachievement* 762.3, *snag* 824.8, *obstacle* 826.2
stalemated *inactive* 413.9
staleness *lack of emphasis* 201.1, *dilution* 220.2, *unpalatability* 223.2, *stench* 227.1, *boringness* 296.2, *unaccustomedness* 398.1, *oldness* 653.1, *imperfection* 806.1, *fatigue* 820.1
Stalinism *suppression* 424.2
stalk *stem* 41.5, *fern plant* 46.2, *moss plant* 46.5, *fungal body* 47.4, *hunt* 160.12, *follow* 385.12, *plant products* 522.8, *cylinder* 633.4, *bodily movement* 677.11, *walk* 677.17, *component* 760.3
stalked *of leaves* 41.18
stalked barnacle *crustacean* 39.10
stalker *hunter* 160.9, 385.6
stalking *hunting* 160.2, 160.11, *pursuit* 385.1
stalking-horse *stratagem* 822.2
stalking stick *hunting accessories* 160.5
stalks *crop* 16.8
stall 419.28, 483.9; *farm building* 16.4, *mammal dwelling* 35.21, *cage* 60.15, *church interior* 83.9, *type of chair* 101.4, *compartment* 578.2, *delay* 658.13, *stop* 668.10, *miscellaneous automotive terms* 687.14, *flight maneuver* 689.6, *maneuver* 689.14, *shelter* 812.4, *hinder* 826.15, *block* 826.17, *discontinuance* 846.4, *malfunction* 846.20
stalled *held up* 658.6
staller *hinderer* 826.11
stalling *flight maneuver* 689.6, *discontinuance* 846.4
stalling for time *tactics* 399.12
stallion *male animal* 32.15, *male mammal* 35.18, *horse* 159.1
stall keeper *peddler* 482.9
stalls [Brit] *auditorium* 136.17, *place for viewing* 242.13
stalwart 547.10; *of good constitution* 113.5, *physically strong* 516.10
stalwartly 547.17
stalwartness 547.3
stamen *organs of reproduction* 21.9, *flower part* 42.3
stamin Fabrics and Fibers 130
stamina 377.4; *steadfastness* 284.3, *assiduity* 414.8, *vigor* 514.2, *endurance* 516.4, *stalwartness* 547.3
staminate *of flowers* 42.11
stammer *be drunk* 121.34, *be clumsy* 128.9, *mode of speech* 205.6, *speech defect* 206.2, *have difficulty speaking* 206.9, *sign of guilt* 450.2, *appear guilty* 450.10

stammering *drunken behavior* 121.4, *clumsy* 128.6, *speech defect* 206.2, *inarticulate* 206.6, *unintelligibility* 364.1, *appearing guilty* 450.7

stamp *postal communication* 169.4, *correspond* 169.19, *printing* 173.3, *print* 173.17, *gesture* 183.5, 183.17, *identify* 184.11, *send* 209.11, *acclaim* 437.18, *contract* 462.2, 462.11, *promise* 464.2, 464.10, *monetize* 484.24, *permit* 502.3, *prototype* 624.2, *form* 624.9, *make concave* 635.7, *make stable* 674.7, *bodily movement* 677.11, *blow* 695.5, *kick* 695.14, *nature* 723.4, *characterize* 723.11, *mode* 725.2, *adherent* 755.4, *type* 777.4, *special feature* 779.4

stamp collecting Hobbies and Pastimes 167

stamp collection *collection* 105.12

stamped *monetary* 484.22

stamped coinage *coinage* 484.13

stampede *force* 428.10, *be violent* 520.8, *be swift* 694.10, *haste* 818.1, *hasten* 818.4

stampeded *hasty* 818.3

stamped on one's memory *memorable* 354.7

stamping *gestural* 183.13, *tumult* 232.5, *acclaim* 437.5

stamping ground *habitat* 60.1, *plot* 564.9, *location* 565.1

stamping one's foot *burst of anger* 302.6

stamp of approval *approval* 437.1

stamp off *depart* 705.8

stamp on *suppress* 424.9, *kick* 695.14

stamp one's feet *heat* 217.17

stamp one's foot *vent one's anger* 302.21

stamp out *destroy* 523.10, *cause not to exist* 718.14

stamp tax *historical tax* 494.8

stamp with impatience *be active* 414.18

stance *philosophical system* 4.2, *belief* 87.1, *boxing techniques* 152.5, *golf shots* 156.4, *theory* 327.2, *line of argument* 329.3, *nature* 624.5

stanchion *stadium* 163.2

stand *trees* 43.4, *battle* 76.23, 76.33, *belief* 87.1, *suffice* 97.6, *engagement* 136.15, 138.6, *theory* 327.2, *supposition* 359.1, *resistance* 417.1, *show respect* 435.16, *give out* 472.12, *stall* 483.9, *defray* 489.18, *donate* 491.13, *circumstances* 573.2, *be situated* 573.9, *situate* 573.10, *foundation* 601.2, *be vertical* 602.8, *supporting structure* 605.2, *bear* 605.17, *viewpoint* 628.5, *last* 642.6, *be stable* 674.6, *lack of motion* 678.1, *be motionless* 678.7, *continue to be* 717.20

stand above suspicion *be innocent* 449.10

stand above the law *be illegal* 53.30

stand accused *be accused* 442.10

stand a chance *be possible* 836.8, *take a chance* 842.14

stand a fair chance *be probable* 838.8

stand against *resist* 417.10, *counterattack* 418.24, *oppose* 828.15

stand against a wall *execute* 454.30

stand a good chance *be possible* 836.8, *be probable* 838.8

stand alone *be one* 788.17, *be independent* 829.18

stand aloof *shun* 386.14, *be unsocial* 409.10, *keep away* 585.9, *be one* 788.17

stand apart *shun* 386.14, *be one* 788.17

standard 589.7, 589.10; *of language* 5.35, *universal* 6.67, *tree* 43.1, *flag* 184.8, *ideal* 327.6, 805.6, 805.17, *vague* 338.9, *expected thing* 356.3, *established* 397.12, *medium* 579.12, *baseline* 601.4, *traditional* 630.13, *regularity* 730.6, *gradation* 739.3, *gradational* 739.5, *average* 742.1, 742.5, *precedent* 769.4, *common* 778.13, *guide* 780.4, *customary* 780.9

Standard and Poore Index *stock exchange* 457.3

standard atmosphere *thermodynamics* 10.30

standard beam approach (SBA) *flight control* 689.7

standard-bearer *soldier* 77.4, *leader* 126.8

Standardbred Horse and Pony Breeds 159

standard deviation *parameter* 6.57, *measurement* 10.67

Standard English *grammar* 5.28

standard error *parameter* 6.57, *measurement* 10.67

standard gauge *rail* 688.3, *railroad* 691.8

standardization *gravimetric analysis* 11.18, *standard* 589.10, *regularity* 730.6, *organization* 767.3

standardize *order* 6.89, *make the same* 730.16, *make average* 742.9, *systematize* 765.19, *organize* 767.19, *regulate* 780.15, *make conform* 781.13

standardized *analytic* 11.32, *established* 397.12, *regular* 730.12

standard lamp *electric light* 246.6

standard language 5.6

standard lens *lens* 132.11

standardly *ideologically* 327.23

Standard Metropolitan Statistical Area (SMSA) *city* 567.1

standardness *average* 742.1, 778.4

standard of living *economic factor* 56.8

standard practice *standard procedure* 397.6

standard price *price* 494.1

standard procedure 397.6

standards *philosophical system* 4.2, *ideology* 327.5, *morals* 431.2

standard solution *gravimetric analysis* 11.18

standard temperature and pressure (STP) *thermodynamics* 10.30

standard time *time zone* 646.5

standard usage *standard language* 5.6, *custom* 397.4

stand a round *pay one's way* 489.19

stand aside *resign* 835.5

stand at the door *or on the threshold* *approach* 704.15

stand at the head *precede* 769.13

stand away *keep away* 585.9

stand back *avoid* 386.13, *keep away* 585.9, *retreat* 680.17

stand back of *back* 825.28

stand bail *guarantee* 458.13, *promise* 464.10

stand before the judge *be accused* 442.10

stand behind *give moral support* 605.18, *back* 825.28

standby 575.15; *reserves* 102.5, *actor* 136.25, *wait* 356.8, *not act* 413.11, *entrench* 419.24, *lack authority* 515.12, *give moral support* 605.18, *delay* 575.15, 658.13, *helper* 825.12, *back* 825.28

stand by *or on the letter of the law* *have no mercy* 309.6

standby fare *bargain* 497.4

stand by oneself *be one* 788.17

standby reserves *the military* 58.2, *reinforcements* 77.11

stand clear *avoid* 386.13

stand clear of *keep away* 585.9

stand close to *be near* 586.11

stand condemned *convict* 54.33, *be guilty* 650.9

stand defenseless *be powerless* 515.11

stand down *withdraw* 392.5, *capitulate* 421.6

standee *theatergoer* 136.30

stand erect *be proud* 297.15, *be vertical* 602.8

stand far away *be distant* 585.8

stand fast *insist* 376.14, *pause* 415.15, *be permanent* 667.4, *withstand* 828.20

stand firm *be at war* 76.32, *insist* 376.14, *hold out* 377.13, *be obstinate* 379.10, 417.11, *entrench* 419.24, *be permanent* 667.4, *be stable* 674.6, *show determination* 674.8, *be motionless* 678.7, *withstand* 828.20

stand for 187.14; *represent* 79.7, *signify* 183.16, *mean* 361.13

stand guard *care for* 325.12

stand high *command respect* 435.18

stand-in *alternative* 80.2, *deputizing* 80.4, *actor* 137.13, *representative* 187.7, *helper* 275.5, *substitute* 613.17, 613.23, 672.2, *extra person* 748.7

stand in amazement *wonder* 294.12

stand in for *substitute for* 80.5, *stand for* 187.14, *aid* 275.10, *answer for* 334.24, *act as a go-between* 460.8, *cover for* 613.34, *be a substitute* 672.6

stand in front *entrench* 419.24, *be in front* 621.13

stand in full view *show oneself* 843.15

standing *hunting* 160.11, Phobias 283, *showing respect* 435.7, *repute* 487.7, *lakelike* 568.5, *circumstances* 573.2, 726.1, *rank* 573.4, 739.2, *vertical* 602.5, *unfailing* 667.3, *motionless* 678.4, *state* 725.1, *social class* 777.5, *importance* 999.1

standing army *the military* 58.2, *army* 77.12

standing at *or to attention* *mark of respect* 435.4

standing by *prepared* 388.9, *available* 647.6

standing committee *management board* 126.2

standing custom *custom* 397.4

standing dive *diving* 184.6

standing firm *obstinate* 417.7

standing forces *armed forces* 77.9

standing in *deputizing* 80.4

standing on ceremony *ceremonious* 404.23, *formal* 406.6

standing order *law* 53.1, *rule* 780.1

standing out *recognizable* 363.7

standing ovation *play part* 136.8, *acknowledgment* 310.3, *tribute* 405.6, *acclaim* 437.5

standing position *target shooting* 160.1

standing rigging *sailboat parts and accessories* 150.4

standing room *auditorium* 136.17, *reserved space* 563.5

standing room only *full* 761.8

standing start *hesitation* 693.5

standing stone(s) *thing of the past* 651.8

standing up *vertical* 602.5

standing water *water* 557.1, *small lake* 568.2

standing wave *wave* 10.11

stand in need of *be unsatisfied* 98.10

stand in one's own light *act foolishly* 128.10

stand in relation *relate to* 727.9

stand in the breach *face danger* 811.12

stand in the dock *stand trial* 54.29, *be accused* 442.10

stand in the light *be clumsy* 128.9

stand in the middle 772.17

stand in the open *show oneself* 843.15

stand in the stead of *substitute for* 80.5

stand in the way of *block* 826.17

stand in with *join with* 827.15

stand like a post *be motionless* 678.7

stand no nonsense *insist* 376.14

stand off *keep away* 585.9

standoff *stop* 668.2

standoffish *unsociable* 409.6, *reserved* 585.7, *aloof* 756.5, *solitary* 782.17

standoffishly *reservedly* 585.15, *aloofly* 756.10

standoffishness *insensitivity* 268.1, *unsociability* 409.1, *reserve* 585.4, *aloofness* 756.2

stand on *sail* 150.29

stand on ceremony *put on a show* 404.28, *be formal* 406.11

stand one in good stead *benefit* 801.10

stand on end *make vertical* 602.9

stand one's ground *insist* 376.14, *be permanent* 667.4, *show determination* 674.8, *withstand* 828.20

stand on middle ground *stand in the middle* 772.17

stand on one's dignity *be proud* 297.15

stand on one's head *or hands* *become inverted* 608.8

stand on one's own two feet *be one* 788.17, *be independent* 829.18, *be liberated* 831.7

stand on the opposite side *be opposite* 731.4

stand on the scales *weigh* 538.15

stand on tiptoe *be tall* 596.16, *arise* 715.15

stand out *identify oneself* 184.12, *be visible* 242.26, 244.7, 843.16, *be recognizable* 363.12, *not observe* 466.9, *diverge* 734.8, *be in a class of one's own* 777.14, *specialize* 779.16, *be visible* 843.16

stand out a mile *be visible* 843.16

stand out in a crowd *diverge* 734.8

stand outside the law *be illegal* 53.30

stand pat *be permanent* 667.4, *show determination* 674.8

standpipe *irrigator* 557.13

standpoint *belief* 87.1, *viewpoint* 242.12, 628.5, *supposition* 359.1, *circumstances* 573.2

stand poles apart *disagree* 753.19

stand ready *be prepared* 388.17, *entrench* 419.24

stand revealed *be disclosed* 180.12

stand rigid *be obstinate* 417.11

stands *baseball field* 147.3, *place for viewing* 242.13

stand shoulder to shoulder *adhere* 755.8, *work together* 827.14

stand side by side *side* 623.8, *adhere* 755.8

standstill *inaction* 413.1, *obstruction* 584.2, *stop* 668.2, *lack of motion* 678.1, *stalemate* 740.3, *deliverance* 817.1, *snag* 824.8

stand still *be motionless* 678.7

stand surety *promise* 464.10

stand surety for *protect* 810.21

stand the cost *defray* 489.18

stand the test *be true* 721.20

stand the test of time *last* 642.6, *protract* 669.9, *be true* 721.20

stand to attention *be vertical* 602.8

stand together *work together* 827.14

stand trial 54.29

stand up *be vertical* 602.8, *arise* 715.15, *be true* 721.20, *show oneself* 843.15

stand-up *variety* 138.13

stand up and be counted *appear* 331.18, *show oneself* 843.15

stand-up collar *neckwear* 100.29

stand-up comedy *show business* 138.1

stand-up comic *entertainer* 138.8

stand-up fight *warfare* 422.10

stand up for *justify* 441.12, *give moral support* 605.18, *protect* 810.21

stand up for one's rights *have rights* 429.13, *be independent* 829.18

stand up in court *be legal* 53.28

stand-up meal *meal* 92.8

stand upright *be vertical* 602.8

stand up straight *be proud* 297.15, *be vertical* 602.8

stand up to *suffice* 97.6, *be courageous* 284.14, *defy* 416.7, *withstand* 828.20

stand up well *be stable* 674.6

Stanford-Binet Intelligence Scale *Intelligence Tests* 108

stanniferous *ceramic* 129.9

St. Anthony's fire *skin disease* 114.16

stanza *part of poem* 139.9, *passage* 692.1, *part of writing* 760.6

stapes *Human Bones* 19, *ear* 19.10, 228.2

staple *materials* 104.1, *retainer* 471.3, *retain* 471.7, *merchandise* 482.6, *sharp-pointed thing* 549.4, *textile* 552.5, *joint* 752.7, *link* 752.18, *fastener* 754.7, *connect* 754.13, *important* 799.7

stapled *retained* 471.6, *connected* 754.11

staple food *food* 90.1

staple to *add* 748.11

star 7.8; *important person* 18.11, *military honor* 58.9, *skilled person* 127.7, *dramatize* 136.33, *act* 136.34, 137.20, *actor* 137.13, *cross-country* 162.31, *indicator* 183.7, *insignia* 184.5, *natural light* 246.4, *wonderful person* 294.6, *person of repute* 370.2, *superior person* 445.7, *focus* 612.3, *focal* 612.8, *orbiting body* 681.4, *paragon* 744.6, *excellent* 744.14, *lead* 744.19, *celebrity* 799.6, *successful person* 845.6

star anise *Herbs and Spices* 91

star atlas *star catalog* 7.9

starboard *laterality* 623.3, *laterally* 623.11

starboard tack *sailing terms* 150.5

starbright *starry* 246.18

starburst galaxy *galaxy* 7.5

star catalog 7.9

starch *carbohydrate* 12.3, *polysaccharide* 12.5, *plant body* 47.13, *food content* 90.3, *clean* 111.17, *harden* 542.9, *thickener* 561.12

Star Chamber *instrument of torture* 454.14

star chart *star catalog* 7.9, *divination* 86.5

starched *cleaned* 111.14, *tough* 542.6

starched collar *neckwear* 100.29

starchily *majestically* 404.36, *formally* 406.12

starchiness *pomp* 404.7, *formality* 406.1, *obstinacy* 417.2, *hardness* 542.1

starching *hardness* 542.1

starchy *majestic* 404.21, *formal* 406.6, *obstinate* 417.7, *tough* 542.6, *pulpy* 561.19

star cluster *star* 7.8

star-crossed *unlucky* 848.12

star-crossed lover *loser* 468.8

star-crossed lovers *lovers* 299.12

stardom *fame* 845.2

stardust *reverie* 360.6

stare *Collective Names* 59, *look* 242.7, 242.21, *wonder* 294.12, *be discourteous* 411.7

stare down *be courageous* 284.14, *brace oneself* 376.13

stare one in the face *be visible* 244.7, 843.16, *be in the future* 650.9

starer *observer* 242.15

starfish *echinoderm* 39.5

stargaze *be inattentive* 324.10

stargazer *astronomer* 7.2, *observer* 242.15

stargazing *astronomy* 7.1, *absent-mindedness* 324.2, *absent-minded* 324.6

star group *constellation* 7.13

star in *occur* 264.14

staring *seeing* 242.17

staring one in the face *clear* 244.6, *manifest* 843.9

stark *infertile* 23.7

stark *Musical Terms and Expression Marks* 140

stark *simple* 195.10, 526.7, *clear* 196.2, 244.6, *gaudy* 251.12, *strong to the senses* 516.12, *tough* 542.6, *completely* 759.14

starkers [Brit inf] *naked* 614.12

starkly *simply* 195.19, 526.14, *toughly* 542.12

stark naked *naked* 614.12

starkness *simplicity* 195.4, 526.1, *clarity* 196.1, 244.2

star knot *Knots, Bends, Hitches, Splices* 754

stark raving *or* **staring mad** *insane* 110.9

Starkrimson *Apple Varieties* 44

stark-staring *accentuated* 843.11

starless *dark* 247.5

starlet *actor* 137.13

starlight *natural light* 246.4

starlight waltz *ice-dancing move* 162.19

starlike *or* **star-shaped** *spiked* 549.11

starling *songbird* 36.12

starlings *Collective Names* 59

starlit *lit* 246.16

star luminosity 7.12

star map *map* 187.5

star network *computer communications* 15.25

star of Bethlehem *Flowers* 42

star of stage and screen *actor* 136.25, 137.13

star player *prizewinner* 127.8

star-pointed *spiked* 549.11

Starr *Apple Varieties* 44

starring 137.18

starring role *role* 136.23

starry 246.18; *astronomical* 7.33

starry-eyed *hopeful* 281.6, *fantastic* 360.11

stars *Phobias* 283, *occult influence* 512.2, *contributory cause* 675.3

Stars and Bars *flag* 184.8

star-shaped figure *polygon* 6.42

starshine *natural light* 246.4

star-spangled *starry* 246.18

Star-Spangled Banner *flag* 184.8

star-studded *astronomical* 7.33, *starry* 246.18

start 696.20, 705.2; *automobile racing terms* 146.3, *be on the track* 146.11, *horse racing* 159.10, *racetrack* 159.12, *soccer play* 163.5, *track event* 166.1, *participate* 166.22, *shock* 292.3, *be surprised* 292.12, *undertake* 391.7, *motivate* 508.9, *beginning* 583.9, 652.4, 771.1, *begin* 583.21, 771.25, *inaugurate* 675.10, *go forward* 679.8, *jolt* 684.9, *impel* 695.9, *jerk* 699.3, *set out* 705.12, *originate* 737.7, *starting point* 771.11, *warning signal* 814.3

START 2 *disarmament* 74.3

start a fight *attack* 418.17

start afresh *become new* 652.19, *restore* 671.10, *begin again* 771.36, *renew* 797.19

start again *restore* 671.10, *renew* 797.19

start an action *litigate* 54.27

start anew *become new* 652.19, *restore* 671.10, *begin again* 771.36

start a row *be active* 414.18

start at the wrong end *be unskillful* 128.8

start early 657.12

starter *dish* 90.7, *course* 92.12, *baseball team* 147.2, *finalist* 422.16, *first move* 771.12, *beginner* 771.14

starter [Brit] *hors d'oeuvre* 90.13, *appetizer* 219.2

starter's gun *signal* 183.6

starter's orders *horse racing* 159.10

start from scratch *become new* 652.19

start from the beginning *become new* 652.19

start going *start* 696.20, *activate* 771.28

starting *contending* 422.19,

beginning 583.14, 771.16, *start* 705.2

starting afresh *return* 797.4

starting again *return* 797.4

starting ahead of the game *tactics* 399.12

starting block *swimming equipment* 164.8, *starting point* 771.11

starting blocks *sports equipment* 166.17

starting gun *signal* 646.9

starting lineup *baseball team* 147.2

starting pistol *sports equipment* 166.17, *starting point* 771.11

starting point 771.11; *baseline* 601.4

starting point *or* **line** *or* **post** *or* **gate** *place of departure* 705.4

starting position *track event* 166.1

starting post *starting point* 771.11

startle *frighten* 283.17, *surprise* 292.9

startled *surprised* 292.5

startling *frightening* 283.12, *surprising* 292.7

startlingly *surprisingly* 292.14

startoff *start* 705.2

start off 771.27

start off *or* **up** *start* 696.20

start out *set out* 705.12, *start off* 771.27

start the ball rolling *start* 696.20

start too soon *start early* 657.12

start up *activate* 509.11, 771.28, *spring up* 713.22, *inaugurate* 771.31

start-up capital *resources* 102.4

start-up costs *business expenses* 491.4

star turn *cross-country techniques* 162.8

starvation *way of dying* 29.5, *scarcity* 98.3, *short rations* 118.3, *emaciation* 595.2

starvation diet *scarcity* 90.5, *incompleteness* 98.2, *dieting* 118.2, 595.3

starvation rations *incompleteness* 98.2

starve 118.10; *be hungry* 288.21, *abstain* 455.11, *be poor* 486.14, *hoard* 501.6, *weaken* 517.13, *be emaciated* 595.16

starved *underfed* 98.7, 118.7, *hungry* 288.16, *emaciated* 595.10

starved of *unprovided* 98.6

starveling *underfed* 98.7

starve oneself *commit suicide* 30.24, *lose weight* 468.14

starve out *be at war* 76.32, *besiege* 418.20, *detain* 830.16

starve to death *murder* 30.20

starving *underfed* 98.7, 118.7, *hungry* 288.16, *beggarly* 486.12, *emaciated* 595.10

starving oneself *suicide* 30.8

starving out *detention* 830.5

Star Wars *preventive warfare* 76.12, *military defenses* 419.9

star watching *astronomy* 7.1

star worship *idolatry* 83.4

star worshiper *idolater* 83.7

star-worshiping *idolatrous* 83.13

stash *hiding place* 181.2

stash away *bury* 105.22, *conceal* 181.12

stasiphobia *Phobias* 283

stasis *stability* 674.1, *lack of motion* 678.1, *equilibrium* 740.2

stat [Inf] *reproduction* 21.1, *photoreproduction* 132.6, *duplicate* 736.4, *copy* 736.10

statant Heraldic Terms 184
state 329.13, 725.1; *propound a philosophy* 4.21, *use language* 5.42, *nation* 18.14, *national* 18.16, 566.10, *governmental* 49.24, *body politic* 50.3, *health* 113.1, *speak* 205.17, *focus on* 328.9, *testify* 336.10, *give evidence* 339.12, *pomp* 404.7, *formality* 406.1, *personal estate* 470.6, *style* 537.8, *region* 564.1, *administrative region* 564.4, *country* 566.1, *circumstances* 573.2, 726.1
state attorney general *law officer* 53.6
state capital *city* 567.1
state chairperson *political party member* 50.6
state court *type of court* 54.9
statecraft *politics* 50.1
stated *affirmed* 189.11, *logical* 329.9
state election *election* 382.6
state enterprise *market sector* 483.5
state farm *farm* 16.2
state forest *trees* 43.4
state government *government* 49.1
statehood *nation* 18.14, *country* 566.1, *independence* 829.5
state in plain English *make comprehensible* 363.8
state insurance *social assistance* 825.4
stateless 574.14; *foreign* 724.9
stateless person *displaced person* 574.7, *new arrival* 724.6
state library *library* 174.14
stateliness *majesty* 297.5, *pomp* 404.7, *formality* 406.1, *elegance* 527.1
stately *manorial* 60.21, *majestic* 297.12, 404.21, *majestically* 404.36, *formal* 406.6, *ceremonious* 406.7, *elegant* 527.3, *ornate* 532.10
stately home *mansion* 60.5
statement 493.2; *philosophy* 4.1, *mathematical logic* 6.60, *physical law* 10.4, *document* 170.3, *publication* 173.1, *record* 185.1, *affirmation* 189.1, *description* 202.1, *utterance* 205.10, *topic* 328.1, *line of argument* 329.3, *evidence* 336.3, *legal evidence* 339.4, *declaration* 376.2, *command* 425.1, *bill* 494.4, 785.4
statement of account *statement* 493.2
statement of belief *belief system* 87.3
statement of defense *countercharge* 332.3
statement of fact *description* 202.1
statement under *or* **on oath** *attestation* 189.2
Staten Island *New York* 567.6, *Islands* 572
state occasion *ceremonial* 404.11, *ceremony* 405.3
state of affairs 725.4; *circumstances* 573.2, 726.1, *modernity* 647.3
state of grace *innocence* 449.1
state of health *physical state* 725.6
state of matrimony *marriage* 64.1
state of mind 725.5; *emotion* 266.3
state of nature *natural state* 389.4, *bareness* 614.3
state of order *orderliness* 765.5

state of peace *peace* 73.1
state of repair *or* **disrepair** *physical state* 725.6
state of siege *belligerency* 76.14
state of sobriety *sobriety* 120.1
state of the art *newness* 652.1, *state* 725.1
state-of-the-art *new* 652.9
state of war *act of hostility* 63.4, *belligerency* 76.14
state of wonder *wonder* 294.1
state one's terms *bargain* 480.20
state-owned industry *economics* 56.1
state ownership *public ownership* 469.7
state park *ecology* 815.3
state pension *social assistance* 825.4
state plainly *make comprehensible* 363.8
state police *law enforcement agency* 53.7, *law enforcement officer* 53.8
state positively *affirm* 189.21
state prison *prison* 55.1
state provision *social assistance* 825.4
state school *type of school* 48.12
state secret *secret* 182.2
state's evidence *divulgence* 180.2
statesman *governor* 49.23, *mediator* 75.2
statesmanlike *political* 50.9, *skillful* 127.10, *wise* 352.4, *behaving* 399.14
statesmanship *politics* 50.1, *mediation* 75.1, *tactics* 399.12
state-space representation *systems and process control* 14.28
states' rights *independence* 829.5
States' Rights Democratic party Political Parties 50
state supreme court *type of court* 54.9
stateswoman *governor* 49.23
state tax *tax* 494.5
state terms *specify* 340.14
state trooper *law enforcement officer* 53.8
state troopers *law enforcement agency* 53.7
state under *or* **on oath** *attest* 189.22
static *physical* 10.70, *radio reception* 172.2, *broadcast dissonance* 241.3, *inactive* 415.8, *inert* 519.2, *permanent* 667.2, *motionless* 678.4, *equal* 740.8
statically *physically* 10.78, *inactively* 415.17, *motionlessly* 678.9
statice Flowers 42
static electrical conduction *electricity* 14.34
static electricity *electricity* 10.31, 14.34, *electrical power* 514.12
static friction *force* 10.9, *friction* 554.1
static load *load* 14.14
statics *classical physics* 10.2
static warfare *offensive warfare* 76.11
station 601.5, 601.12; *line of duty* 433.3, *administrative headquarters* 564.5, *location* 565.1, *locate* 565.9, *employment* 573.3, *rank* 573.4, 739.2, *situate* 573.10, *stopping place* 668.4, *railroad station* 688.6, *destination* 704.6, *place of departure* 705.4, *state* 725.1, *social class* 777.5
station [Aus] *farm* 16.2
stationarily *motionlessly* 678.9
stationary *analytic* 11.32, *inactive*

413.9, 415.8, *permanent* 667.2, *motionless* 678.4
stationary phase *analysis* 11.17
stationary point *point* 6.34
stationary rings 157.8; *gymnastics equipment* 157.2
stationary target *objective* 374.5
station break *broadcast material* 172.9
stationed *located* 565.6, *situated* 573.5, *based* 601.9
stationery *paper* 104.5
station identification *radio broadcasting* 172.4
stationing *placing* 565.4
station manager *railroad worker* 688.7
stationmaster *railroad worker* 688.7
Stations of the Cross *Christian rite* 85.5
station-to-station call *telephone call* 169.11
station wagon *automobile* 687.6
statistic *population* 6.55
statistical *mathematical* 6.65, *physical* 10.70, *accounting* 493.7, *calculative* 784.7
statistical analysis *statistics* 6.51
statistical inference *statistics* 6.51
statistically *physically* 10.78, *financially* 493.13
statistical mechanics Fields of Modern Physics 10
statistical methods 6.53
statistical physics Fields of Modern Physics 10
statistical probability *probability theory* 838.5, *calculation of chance* 842.9
statistician *mathematician* 6.2, *accountant* 493.6, *counter* 784.6
statistico-mechanical *chemical* 11.24
statistics 6.51, 784.2, Branches of Mathematics 6, *information technology (IT)* 170.7, *map* 187.5, *calculation of chance* 842.9
statuary *sculpture* 144.1
statue *sculpture* 144.1, *monument* 185.10, *image* 187.3, *memento* 354.3
Statue of Zeus at Olympia Seven Wonders of the Ancient World 294
statuesque *artistic* 133.7, *attractive* 529.8
statue tag Children's and Party Games 167
statuette *sculpture* 144.1, *image* 187.3
stature *height* 596.1
status *circumstances* 573.2, 726.1, *rank* 573.4, 739.2, *state* 725.1, *relative position* 727.5, *position* 765.4, *category* 767.6, *importance* 799.1
status adjectives 11.25
status group *social organization* 2.5
status quo *circumstances* 573.2, 726.1, *permanence* 667.1, *state of affairs* 725.4, *equilibrium* 740.2
status-seeking *social ambition* 408.2
statute *law* 53.1, *rule* 780.1
statute book *code* 780.3
statute law *law* 53.1
statute mile General Units 589
statutory *legal* 780.8
staunch *intimate* 62.7, *treat* 115.17, *truthful* 191.4, *steady* 376.8, *constant* 377.8, *loyal* 426.5, *strong* 516.9, *stop the flow* 570.12, *stop* 584.14, *infallible* 840.12

staunched *stopped* 584.9
staunchly *intimately* 62.14, *truthfully* 191.9, *obediently* 426.9
staunchness *truthfulness* 191.1, *seriousness* 360.3, *constancy* 377.3, *loyalty* 426.2, *infallibility* 840.6
staurophobia Phobias 283
stave *blunt weapon* 78.5, *wood* 131.3, *part of poem* 139.9, *written music* 140.21, *step* 713.11
stave in *make concave* 635.7, *flatten* 716.15
stave off *parry* 419.27
Stavropol Breeds of Sheep 16
stay *legal process* 54.3, *favorable verdict* 54.19, *inhabit* 61.13, *social gathering* 404.8, *visit* 408.16, *obstruct* 584.13, *deferment* 604.3, *defer* 604.15, *supporting part* 605.3, *last* 642.6, *delay* 658.3, 658.13, *wait* 658.12, *be permanent* 667.4, *stop* 668.2, *cause to cease* 668.12, *pause* 668.13, *continuance* 669.3, *protract* 669.9, *be stable* 674.6, *be motionless* 678.7, *slow down* 693.13, *continue to be* 717.20, *be left* 750.9, *means of connection* 754.4, *tackle* 754.6, *obstacle* 826.2
stay alert *take note of* 323.10, *be mentally sharp* 549.18
stay alone *be aloof* 756.8
stay at *settle* 565.10
stay at home *be unsocial* 409.10, *pause* 415.15, *be safe* 810.20
stay-at-home *unsocial person* 409.5, *lonely* 409.8, *housebound* 415.9
stay-at-home dad [Inf] *domestic worker* 123.4
stay at one's post *do one's duty* 433.17
stay at peace *be at peace* 73.10, *pacify* 74.9
stay away *depart* 265.6, *be absent* 576.14
stay away from *avoid* 386.13
stay away from the hard stuff *be sober* 120.8
stay away in droves *be absent* 576.14
stay behind the scenes *hide* 844.13
stay cool *restrain oneself* 830.15
stayed *deferred* 604.9
stayer *racehorse* 159.2, *horse racing* 159.10
stay flexible *be adaptable* 546.9
stay-in *disputed* 75.15
stay in a rut *be obstinate* 379.10
stay in control *be independent* 829.13
stay indoors *pause* 415.15
staying *inhabiting* 60.18, *stalwart* 547.10
staying away *disappearance* 265.1
staying power *stamina* 377.4, *vigor* 514.2, *endurance* 516.4, *stalwartness* 547.3, *continuation* 642.2
staying single Phobias 283
stay in line *obey* 426.7, *abide by* 781.12
stay in one place *be stable* 674.6
stay in one's shell *be indifferent* 289.12, *be unsocial* 409.10
stay-in strike *strike* 57.8
stay in the background *conceal oneself* 181.15, *be humble* 298.16, *escape notice* 403.14, *be average* 742.8
stay in the black *deposit* 487.12
stay in the shadows *conceal oneself* 181.15

stay in time *synchronize* 649.7
Stayman *Apple Varieties* 44
stay near 586.13
stay neutral *leave alone* 413.13
stay of execution *delay* 658.3
stay on *protract* 669.9
stay on an even keel *be moderate* 521.6
stay one's hand *pause* 668.13
stay on one's tail [Inf] *follow* 385.12
stay on the beam *aim* 697.14
stay on the right side of the law *be legal* 53.28
stay on the shelf *have free time* 413.15, *be sold* 482.22
stay *or* **keep on the straight and narrow** *follow the rules* 780.17
stay out *be excluded* 764.9
stay out of the limelight *conceal oneself* 181.15
stay outside *be excluded* 764.9
stay packed away *have free time* 413.15
stay pure *be continent* 67.10
stay put *insist* 376.14, *be obstinate* 379.10, *be stable* 674.6, *be motionless* 678.7
stays *underwear* 100.22
staysail *sailboat parts and accessories* 150.4
stay silent *be taciturn* 208.7
stay single *be celibate* 67.9
stay sober *be sober* 120.8
stay still *not act* 413.11
stay the course *be tough* 547.13, *last* 642.6
stay till the bitter end *endure* 377.14
stay too long *bore* 296.8
stay under cover *be safe* 810.20
stay underground *elude* 816.10
stay unmarried *be independent* 829.18
stay up *or* **sit up** *or* **stay out late** *be late* 658.11
stay within bounds *be moderate* 521.6
stay within one's limits *restrain oneself* 830.15
stay with it *show determination* 674.8
stay young *be young* 26.13
St. Bartholomew's Day Massacre *slaughter* 30.5
St. Bernard *Breeds of Dogs* 35
St. Christopher's medal *good-luck sign* 358.6
St. Clair *Lakes* 568
St. Croix *Islands* 572
steadfast 284.11; *intimate* 62.7, *truthful* 191.4, *iron-willed* 372.7, *steady* 376.8, *constant* 377.8, *loyal* 426.5, *fast* 464.8, *strong in spirit* 516.11, *unfailing* 667.3, *stable* 674.3, *infallible* 840.12
steadfastly 284.19; *intimately* 62.14, *truthfully* 191.9, *obediently* 426.9, *fastly* 464.16, *permanently* 667.6, *stably* 674.9
steadfastness 284.3; *intimacy* 62.4, *truthfulness* 191.1, *willpower* 372.2, *seriousness* 376.3, *constancy* 377.3, *loyalty* 426.2, *authority* 516.5, *permanence* 667.1, *stability* 674.1, *infallibility* 840.6
steadily *frequently* 661.7, *orderly* 663.13, *regularly* 663.14, 730.21, *permanently* 667.6, *continually* 669.10, *stably* 674.9, *conformingly* 735.37, *equitably* 740.15
steadiness *truthfulness* 191.1, *seriousness* 376.3, *moderation* 521.1, *frequency* 661.1, *regularity*

663.1, 730.6, *permanence* 667.1, *stability* 674.1, *lack of motion* 678.1, *equilibrium* 740.2, *infallibility* 840.6
steading [Brit] *farm* 16.2
steady 376.8; *detached* 4.18, *rainy* 9.50, *rational* 109.4, *truthful* 191.4, *constant* 377.8, *fast* 464.8, *make fast* 464.13, *detain* 471.9, *moderate* 521.3, *frequent* 661.4, 663.6, *regular* 663.5, 730.12, *make regular* 663.9, *permanent* 667.2, *unfailing* 667.3, *continuous* 669.5, *stable* 674.3, *make stable* 674.7, *motionless* 678.4, *conforming* 735.17, *equal* 740.8, *harmonious* 765.16, *infallible* 840.12, *make certain* 840.14
steady [Inf] *loved one* 299.13
steady as a rock *stable* 674.3
steady flow processes *industrial processes* 14.27
steady progress *forward motion* 679.1
steady rain *rain* 9.27
steady state *stability* 674.1, *equilibrium* 740.2
steady-state universe *universe* 7.3
steady stream *excess* 99.1, *procession* 774.6
steak *beef* 90.24
steakhouse *eating place* 92.17
steak knife *tableware* 92.13
steal 479.14; *play ice hockey* 158.9, *take away* 275.13, 477.18, *sin* 450.11, *borrow illegally* 476.12, *bargain* 497.4
steal [Inf] *theft* 479.2, *stolen goods* 479.4
steal a base *play baseball* 147.9
steal a glance *look* 242.21
steal a march on *prepare* 657.14, *exceed* 712.15, *overtake* 744.16, *be cunning* 822.5
steal away *conceal oneself* 181.15, *retreat* 386.22, *escape* 816.8
stealer *thief* 479.8
stealing 479.1, Phobias 283, *illegal borrowing* 476.3, *taking away* 477.5
stealings *stolen goods* 479.4
stealing the puck *ice hockey tactics* 158.4
steal on the air *sound faint* 233.8
steal someone's thunder *overtake* 744.16, *hinder* 826.15
stealth *secretiveness* 182.3, *deviousness* 607.4, *secrecy* 611.6, *cunning* 822.1, *concealment* 844.2
steal the show *overact* 136.35, *overtake* 744.16
stealthily 182.15; *deviously* 607.16, *secretly* 611.22, *cunningly* 822.6
stealthiness *secretiveness* 182.3, *cunning* 822.1
stealthy *secretive* 182.9, *devious* 607.9, *secret* 611.13, *unhurried* 693.8, *cunning* 822.4, *concealed* 844.7
steam *engine type* 14.11, *turbine type* 14.12, *sweat* 25.24, *cook* 91.10, *heat* 217.1, 217.17, *murk* 248.2, *water vapor* 556.4, *give off* 556.25, *means of propulsion* 696.2, *propellant* 696.9, *let out* 709.26
steam bath *bath* 111.6, *hot place* 217.5
steamboat Ships and Boats 690
steam distill *extract* 11.41
steamed *culinary* 91.9
steamed up *murky* 248.5, *shady* 250.4

steam engine *train* 688.4
steamer *cooking equipment* 91.6, *train* 688.4, Ships and Boats 690
steamer route *waterway* 690.2
steamily *smokily* 556.28
steaminess *heat* 217.1
steaming *cooking technique* 91.2, *unhygienic* 114.27, *ceramic process* 129.5, *heating* 217.12, *vaporization* 556.9, *smoky* 556.17, *nautical* 690.14
steam iron *flattener* 603.4
steam-operated *renewable* 106.15
steam power *type of power* 514.6
steam pressure *force* 514.8
steam-propelled *propelled* 696.14
steam reforming *industrial chemistry* 11.21
steamrolled *uniform* 545.5
steamroller *coercer* 424.8, *compelling* 428.6, *force* 428.10, *knock down* 523.13, *pulverizer* 553.11, *flattener* 603.4
steamroller *or* **steamroll** *make horizontal* 603.10
steamrolling *compelling* 428.6
steamship Ships and Boats 690
steam up *be dim* 248.7, *be opaque* 250.6
steamy *desirous* 20.18, *warm* 217.13, *murky* 248.5, *smoky* 556.17
stearic Common Fatty Acids 12
steatopygic *fat* 579.15
steatopygous *fat* 579.15
steed *horse* 159.1, *war-horse* 159.4, *saddle horse* 159.5
steel *construction material* 14.21, *building materials* 104.2, *gray thing* 255.3, *hard substance* 542.3, *hard* 542.5, *harden* 542.9, *sharpener* 548.2, *shipbuilding* 690.4, *mixed thing* 751.2
steel band *instrumental group* 141.3
steel-blue *blue* 261.5
steel-clad *invulnerable* 810.18
steeled *tenacious* 376.9, *hardened* 542.7
steel engraving *engraving* 144.3
steel-gray *gray* 255.6
steel guitar Musical Instruments 142
steel helmet *modern armor* 419.7
steeliness *tenacity* 376.4, *hardness* 542.1, *determination* 674.2
steeling *hardening* 542.2
steel oneself *take courage* 284.15, *brace oneself* 376.13, *be impenitent* 452.4, *strengthen oneself* 516.16
steel plate *material* 144.6
steel-plate armor *modern armor* 419.7
steel poles *horizontal bar* 157.5
steel-rimmed glasses *visual aid* 242.14
steel rule *measuring instrument* 589.12
steel wool *rough thing* 544.2
steelworker *laborer* 123.9
steelworks *works* 124.9
steely *gray* 255.6, *strong-willed* 376.10, *hard* 542.5, *determined* 674.5
steelyard *works* 124.9, *weighing instrument* 538.7
steep 557.31, 713.15; *provide drink* 93.21, *bathe* 111.18, *costly* 496.7, *soften* 543.14, *vertical* 602.5, *oblique* 628.8, *immerse* 710.12, *obtain an extract* 711.19, *hidden danger* 813.3, *difficult* 824.9
steeped *drinkable* 93.18, *wet* 557.23

steeped in vice *depraved* 448.10
steeping 557.10; *pulping* 561.11, *obtaining of an extract* 711.7
steeple *church architecture* 134.11, *sharp-pointed thing* 549.4
steeplechase 166.7; *horse racing* 159.10, *ride* 159.16, *chase* 385.2
steeplechaser *racehorse* 159.2, *track and field eventer* 166.19
steeplechase rider *horse person* 159.14
steeplechasing Sporting Activities 145, *track and field* 166.20
steeplejack *ascender* 713.12
steeply *vertically* 602.11
steepness *verticality* 602.1, *obliquity* 628.2
steep one's hands in blood *slaughter* 30.21
steep price *costliness* 496.1
steer *livestock* 16.11, *sexlessness* 20.13, *male animal* 32.15, *lead* 126.12, *sail* 150.29, *row* 150.32, *bobsled* 162.38, *conduct* 399.21, *navigate* 690.15, *direct* 697.13, 780.14
steerable *directable* 697.10
steerage *cheap* 497.9, *direction* 697.1
steer a middle course *compromise* 461.7, *be in the middle* 772.16
steer a straight course *aim* 697.14
steer clear *avoid* 386.13, *keep away* 585.9, *sidestep* 698.22
steered *directed* 697.9
steered away from *dissuaded* 179.5
steer for *aim at* 385.15, *conduct oneself* 399.17, *aim* 697.14
steering *directorship* 126.5, *managerial* 126.9, *toboggan race* 162.25, *bobsledding* 162.34, *navigation* 690.5, *direction* 697.1, *directing* 697.12
steering committee *management board* 126.2
steering oar *ship's steering* 690.9
steering wheel *wheel* 682.9
steer one away from *deter* 179.8
steer one's career *conduct oneself* 399.17
steersman *nautical person* 690.12
Stefan–Boltzmann constant *Classical Physical Laws* 10
Stefan's law *Classical Physical Laws* 10
stegophilist *ascender* 713.12
Steiner system *combinatorics* 6.63
Steingut Ceramics 129
Steinheim man *primitive humanity* 18.4
Steinschaf Breeds of Sheep 16
St. Elias Mountains Mountains and Hills 569
stellar *astronomical* 7.33
stellar association *constellation* 7.13
stellarator *nuclear power production* 514.10
stellar birth *stellar evolution* 7.10
stellar evolution 7.10
stellar group *constellation* 7.13
stellar population *constellation* 7.13
stellar statistics *astronomy* 7.1
stellate *spiked* 549.11
stellular *spiked* 549.11
St. Elmo's fire *flickering light* 246.10
stem 41.5; *word* 5.17, *part of speech* 5.30, *grass plant* 45.3, *fern plant*

stickler *obstinate person* 379.4, *strict person* 424.4, *perfectionist* 805.7
stick like a leech *show tenaciousness* 471.8
stick like glue *hold out* 377.13, *follow* 385.12
stick like glue *or* **a leech** *or a* **limpet** *adhere* 755.8
stick one's neck out [Inf] *be rash* 286.8, *be foolish* 353.6, *face danger* 811.12
stick onto *or* **on** *add* 748.11
stick out *identify oneself* 184.12, *be visible* 244.7, *be convex* 434.7
stick out for *bargain* 480.20
stick out like a sore thumb [Inf] *be visible* 244.7, *diverge* 734.8, *be independent* 782.20
stick out one's tongue *gesture* 183.17, *disdain* 400.16, *taunt* 436.23
stick out over *overhang* 604.14
sticks [Inf] *distant place* 585.3
sticks, the [Inf] *regions* 564.2
stick someone up [Inf] *steal* 479.14
Stick style *Architectural Styles* 134
stick to *observe* 465.4, *retain* 471.7, *stay near* 586.13, *protract* 669.9, *add* 748.11, *adhere* 755.8, *be tenacious* 755.9, *cause to adhere* 755.10
stick together *unify* 752.15, *intercommunicate* 754.15, *adhere* 755.8, *cause to adhere* 755.10
stick-to-it-ive [Inf] *persevering* 377.7, *industrious* 414.16, *tenacious* 755.6
stick-to-it-iveness [Inf] *commitment* 377.2, *assiduity* 414.8, *tenacity* 755.2
stick to one's guns *be courageous* 284.14, *insist* 376.14, *hold out* 377.13, *be obstinate* 379.10, 417.11, *show determination* 674.8, *be certain* 840.13
stick to the facts *be truthful* 191.7, *be accurate* 350.5
stick to the ground game *play offense* 155.18
stick to the letter *be accurate* 350.5
stick to the letter of the law *be severe* 424.8
stick to the rules *follow the rules* 780.17, *abide by* 781.12
stick to the truth *talk straight* 630.15
stickup [Inf] *theft* 479.2
stick up *make vertical* 602.9
stick up for *justify* 441.12, *give moral support* 605.18, *back* 825.28
stickup man [Inf] *dishonest person* 479.11
stick with it *insist* 376.14, *show determination* 674.8
stick with it! *go on!* 669.11
sticky *humid* 9.48, *sweaty* 25.17, *warm* 217.13, *problematic* 333.12, 824.11, *retentive* 471.5, *moist* 559.9, *mucilaginous* 561.15, *connective* 754.10, *adhesive* 755.5
sticky [Inf] *dangerous* 811.7
sticky-fingered [Inf] *stolen* 479.12
sticky fingers [Inf] *theft* 479.2
sticky label *adherent* 755.4
sticky tape *adhesive* 755.3
sticky wicket [Brit] *awkward situation* 824.7
stiff *clumsy* 128.6, *sailing* 150.25, *snowplow* 162.29, *unyielding* 379.8, *majestic* 404.21, *formal*

406.6, *obstinate* 417.7, *costly* 496.7, *inelegant* 528.6, *tough* 542.6, *hard* 547.8, *mentally tough* 547.12, *stable* 674.3, *motionless* 678.4, *fatigued* 820.2, *difficult* 824.9, *self-restrained* 830.10
stiff [Inf] *dead person* 29.7, *dead drunk* 121.27
stiff as a board *or* **a poker** *or a* **ramrod** *tough* 542.6
stiff as buckram *tough* 542.6
stiff boat *sailboat* 150.3
stiff collar *neckwear* 100.29
stiffen *strengthen oneself* 516.16, *harden* 542.9, *solidify* 542.10, *make tough* 547.15, *be stable* 674.6, *show determination* 674.8
stiffened *hardened* 542.7, *toughened* 547.7
stiffening *strengthening* 516.7, *hardness* 542.1, *stability* 674.1
stiffen one's resolve *strengthen oneself* 516.16
stiffen the sinews *strengthen oneself* 516.16
stiffly *majestically* 404.36, *formally* 406.12, *resistingly* 417.14, *toughly* 542.12, 547.16, *stably* 674.9, *self-restrainedly* 830.19
stiff neck *obstinacy* 379.1
stiff-necked *arrogant* 297.9, *obstinate* 379.5, *refractory* 379.6, *defiant* 416.5
stiff-neckedly *arrogantly* 297.18
stiff-neckedness *arrogance* 297.2
stiff-necked pride *arrogance* 297.2
stiffness *strength of materials* 14.15, *symptom* 114.3, *ski equipment* 162.10, *pomp* 404.7, *formality* 406.1, *obstinacy* 417.2, *inelegance* 528.1, *inelegance of expression* 528.4, *hardness* 542.1, *toughness* 547.1, *stability* 674.1, *lack of motion* 678.1, *self-restraint* 830.4
stiff one *size of drink* 93.3
stiff opposition *opposition* 828.1
stiff price *costliness* 496.1
stiff ski *ski equipment* 162.10
stiff upper lip *steadfastness* 284.3, *will* 376.5
stiff wind *wind strength* 9.13
stiff with cold *cold* 218.9
stifle *murder* 30.20, *conceal* 181.12, *keep secret* 182.11, *silence* 231.4, *mute* 233.9, *censor* 503.10, *overpower* 515.14, *abolish* 523.11, *exclude* 764.7, *hinder* 826.15, *restrain* 830.12
stifled *concealed* 181.8, *nonresonant* 233.7
stifling *killing* 30.17, *warm* 217.13, *destruction* 523.1, *restraint* 830.1, *restraining* 830.8
stigma *organs of reproduction* 21.9, *flower part* 42.3, *plant body* 47.13, *personal identification* 184.4, *impropriety* 430.5, *blemish* 533.1
stigmatize *mark* 533.8
stigmatized *identified* 184.9, *blemished* 533.6
stilb *Scientific and Technical Units* 589
stile *means of entry* 706.6
stiletto *sharp weapon* 78.6
stiletto heels *shoes* 100.30
still *dead* 29.11, *peaceful* 73.8, *drinkable* 93.18, *silent* 231.2, *silence* 231.4, *mute* 233.9, *inactive* 413.9, 415.8, *inert* 519.2, *moderate* 521.3, *calm* 521.8, *soothing* 545.14, *vaporizer* 556.10, *lakelike* 568.5, *repose* 678.2,

motionless 678.4, *quiescent* 678.6, *motionlessly* 678.9, *at ease* 819.2
still as a statue *motionless* 678.4
still as death *motionless* 678.4
stillbirth *way of dying* 29.5, *dead person* 29.7
stillborn *dead* 29.11, *failed* 846.10
still breathing *alive* 28.13
still feel hungry *be unsatisfied* 98.10
still fishing *fishing* 154.1
still hunting *hunting* 160.2
still life *portrait* 132.5, *type of painting* 143.5
still-life painter *painter* 143.7
still-life photography *photographic specialties* 132.2
still more *supremely* 744.23
stillness *peace* 73.1, *silence* 231.1, *inactivity* 415.1, *inertness* 519.1, *smoothness* 545.1, *lack of motion* 678.1, *repose* 678.2, *harmony* 765.8, *ease* 819.1
still remaining *surplus* 750.8
stillroom *room* 60.9
Stillson™ wrench *hand tool* 103.3
still the same *permanently* 667.6
still tired *fatigued* 820.2
still water *small lake* 568.2
still wet behind the ears *unaccustomed* 398.3
still with us *alive* 28.13
stilly *silent* 231.2, *soothingly* 545.14, *quiescent* 678.6, *motionlessly* 678.9
stilted *arch* 134.5, *affected* 367.3, *formal* 406.6, *inelegant* 528.6
stiltedly *formally* 406.12
stiltedness *inelegance* 528.1, *inelegance of expression* 528.4
stilt house *lake dwelling* 568.3
stilt root *root* 41.7
stilt village *lake dwelling* 568.3
stimulant *221.5*; *refresher* 94.2, *tonic* 115.8, *intoxicating* 121.29, *stimulus* 212.3, 508.3
stimulants 121.18
stimulate *20.22*; *refresh* 94.6, *be intoxicating* 121.36, *motivate* 178.17, 508.9, *arouse sensation* 212.11, *give pleasure* 214.13, *be piquant* 221.9, *cause desire* 288.22, *activate* 509.11, *invigorate* 518.5, *awaken* 675.9, *draw out* 711.17, *intensify* 746.8
stimulated *refreshed* 94.5, *susceptible* 212.7, *motivated* 508.8
stimulated emission *laser (light amplification by stimulated emission of radiation)* 10.18
stimulating *221.7*; *refreshing* 94.4, *remedial* 115.14, *persuasive* 178.12, *exciting* 212.8, *suppositional* 359.5, *motivational* 508.7, *invigorating* 518.3
stimulatingly *221.11*; *influentially* 508.13
stimulation *221.4*; *refreshment* 94.1, *drunken behavior* 121.4, *stimulus* 212.3, *activity* 414.1, *motivation* 508.1, *vigor* 518.1, *cause* 675.1, *drawing out* 711.5, *intensification* 746.2
stimulative *remedial* 115.14
stimulator *motivator* 178.11
stimulus *212.3, 508.3*; *incentive* 178.4, *inspiration* 360.2, *contributory cause* 675.3, *intensification* 746.2
stimulus response *stimulus* 212.3
sting *infest* 40.17, *afflict* 117.16, *be painful* 215.9, *inflict pain* 215.10, *piquancy* 221.1, *be piquant* 221.9,

make angry 302.18, *negative stimulus* 508.4, *sharp point* 549.2, *sharp-pointed growth* 549.5, *be sharp* 549.15
sting [Inf] *foul play* 193.6, *dishonesty* 479.7, *overcharge* 496.10
stingily *not enough* 98.12, *selfishly* 444.8
stinginess *incompleteness* 98.2, *selfishness* 444.1, *meanness* 501.1
stinging *painful* 215.4, *piquant* 221.6, *maddening* 302.12, *bitter* 306.9, *spiked* 549.11
stingy *not enough* 98.5, *selfish* 444.4, *mean* 501.4, *spiked* 549.11
stink *227.5*; *uncleanness* 112.2, *be dirty* 112.10, *odor* 224.1, *have odor* 224.8, *stench* 227.1, *decay* 808.16
stinkard *unpleasant-smelling thing* 227.2
stink bomb *unpleasant-smelling thing* 227.2
stinker *unpleasant-smelling thing* 227.2
stinker [Inf] *miscreant* 448.6
stinkhorn *unpleasant-smelling thing* 227.2
stinking *227.3*; *unclean* 112.8, *odorous* 224.5, *detested* 291.11, *immoral* 432.9, *villainous* 448.12
stinking [Inf] *dead drunk* 121.27
stinkingly *227.6*
stinking of liquor *drunken* 121.28
stinking rich [Inf] *wealthy* 485.8
stinko [Inf] *dead drunk* 121.27
stink of [Inf] *abound* 97.8
stink of money [Inf] *be rich* 485.12
stink out *stink* 227.5
stink to high heaven *stink* 227.5
stinky *unclean* 112.8
stint *task* 122.2, *allotted task* 474.3, *hoard* 501.6, *period of activity* 641.4, *duration* 642.1, *certain amount* 738.3, *degree* 739.1, *interval* 739.4
stinted *unprovided* 98.6
stinting *self-restrained* 455.6
stintingly *with self-restraint* 455.14
stipe *stem* 41.5, *fungal body* 47.4, *plant body* 47.13
stipend *grant* 453.4, *earnings* 467.5, *gift* 472.2, *something received* 473.2, *pay* 489.6, *financial support* 605.8, *financial assistance* 825.6
stipendiary *given* 472.8, *sustaining* 605.15
stipple *variegate* 263.11
stippling *maculation* 263.4
stipulate *89.11*; *specify* 340.14, 779.18, *make conditions* 460.7, *limit* 830.13
stipulated *given* 6.74, *conditional* 340.10
stipulation *provision* 89.1, *specification* 340.6, *supposition* 359.1, *basis for negotiations* 460.2, *limitation* 830.2
stipulatory *conditional* 340.10, *negotiated* 460.5
stipule *leaf* 41.6
stir *blow* 9.53, *the inside* [Inf] 55.2, *cook* 91.10, *arouse sensation* 212.11, *be piquant* 221.9, *activity* 414.1, *be active* 414.18, *momentum* 677.2, *be in motion* 677.14, *swirl* 684.21, *tumult* 684.2, *turbulence* 684.3, *agitate* 684.22, *mix* 732.12, 751.12, *disruption* 766.7, *disturb* 768.10
stir-fried *culinary* 91.9

stir fry *notable international dishes* 90.40

stir-fry *cook* 91.10

stir-frying *cooking technique* 91.2

stirk [Brit] *livestock* 16.11

Stirling *engine type* 14.11

Stirling number (first and second kind) *combinatorics* 6.63

stir one's stumps [Inf] *be active* 414.18

stirred *susceptible* 212.7, *mixed* 751.8

stirred up *agitated* 684.15

stirrer *meddler* 321.4, 414.12, *mixer* 751.7

stirring *exciting* 212.8, *activity* 414.1, *active* 414.13, *busy* 414.15, *momentum* 677.2, *moving* 677.12, *mixture* 751.1, *newsworthy* 799.12

stirrup Human Bones 19, *ear* 19.10, 228.2, *riding equipment* 159.9

stirrup cup *drink* 93.2, *parting* 705.3

stirrup iron *riding equipment* 159.9

stirrup leather *riding equipment* 159.9

stir up *opaque* 250.7, *make angry* 302.18, *agitate* 684.22

stir up a hornet's nest *cause trouble* 824.21

stir up trouble *pick a fight* 463.10

stitch *make clothing* 100.44, *knitting* 130.7, *sew* 130.18, *pain* 215.1, *intertwine* 752.19, *line* 754.5, *fastener* 754.7, *connect* 754.13

stitched *sewn* 130.14, *united* 752.10, *tied* 752.13, *connected* 754.11

stitcher *clothier* 100.37

stitchery *sewing* 130.5

stitch holder *fabric-handling tool* 130.12

stitching *sewing* 130.5, *unification* 752.5, *joint* 752.7

stitchwort Flowers 42

stithy *works* 124.9

St. John Rivers 570, Islands 572

St. Johns Rivers 570

St. John's Canadian Provinces 564, Countries 566

St. John's wort Flowers 42

St. Kitts Islands 572

St. Kitts and Nevis Countries 566

St. Lawrence Rivers 570, Islands 572

St. Leger [Brit] *famous horse races* 159.13

St. Lucia Countries 566, Islands 572

St. Martin's summer *fall* 654.5

stochastic process *population* 6.55

stochastics *calculation of chance* 842.9

stochastic variable *population* 6.55

stock *society* 1.6, *igneous rock* 8.32, *livestock* 16.11, *plant breeding* 17.6, *domestic animal* 34.3, *stem* 41.5, Flowers 42, *provision* 89.1, *soup* 90.14, *neckwear* 100.29, *supplies* 102.3, *materials* 104.1, *procure* 104.9, *store* 105.1, 105.17, *proverbial* 177.2, *familiar* 397.10, *acquisition* 467.4, *merchandise* 482.6, 482.17, *juice* 555.2, *rear* 715.10, *average* 742.5, *line* 754.5, *fill* 761.11, *list* 785.1

stockade *prison* 55.1, *barrier* 419.10, *fortification* 419.12,

enclosed area 619.2, *protection* 810.2, *shelter* 812.4

stockbreeder *agriculturist* 16.14, *producer* 522.10

stockbreeding *manufacture* 522.2

stockbroker *financial adviser* 457.4, *negotiator* 460.4, *trader* 480.11, *merchant* 482.10

stock buyer *purchaser* 481.7

stock car *racing automobile* 146.2

stock-car *racing* 146.9

stock-car racing Sporting Activities 145, *automobile racing* 146.1

stock character *stock part* 136.24

stock company *cast* 136.26

stocked *supplied* 89.7, *stored* 105.14, *reared* 715.7

stock exchange 457.3; *stock market* 483.6, *place of exchange* 673.2

stock farm *farm* 16.2, 124.11

stock farmer *agriculturist* 16.14

stockholder *person transferring property* 470.8

Stockholm Countries 566

stockily *shortly* 591.12

stockiness *squatness* 579.6, *shortness* 591.1, *thickness* 594.1

stockinette *or* **stockinet** Fabrics and Fibers 130

stockinette *or* **stockinette stitch** *knitting* 130.7

stocking *money storage* 484.20, *rearing* 715.2

stocking cap 100.33

stockings *legwear* 100.26, *baseball equipment* 147.4

stocking the mind *learning* 48.7

stock in trade 105.2; *resources* 102.4, *personal estate* 470.6, *merchandise* 482.6

stockman *farm worker* 16.15

stock market 483.6; *stock exchange* 457.3

stock market decline *economic adversity* 848.6

stock part 136.24

stockperson *farm worker* 16.15

stock phrase *maxim* 177.1

stockpile *assemblage* 59.13, *assemble* 59.23, *store* 105.1, 105.17, *unused thing* 394.4, *not use* 394.9, *acquisition* 467.4, *acquire* 467.19

stockpiled *collected* 59.19, *stored* 105.14

stock raiser *agriculturist* 16.14

stock rearing *or* **raising** *livestock farming* 16.10

stockroom *storeroom* 105.7

stocks *instrument of punishment* 454.13, *promise* 464.2, *personal estate* 470.6, *means of restraint* 830.6

stocks and bonds *resources* 102.4

stocks and shares *resources* 102.4

stock seller *seller* 482.7

stock-still *motionless* 678.4

stocktaking *count* 784.3

stock-taking sale *sale* 482.2

stock the mind *learn* 48.23

stock up *store* 105.17, *acquire* 467.19

stocky 579.16; *physical* 1.14, *short* 591.6, *thick* 594.5

stocky build *physical type* 1.8

stodge *food* 90.1

stodgily *boringly* 296.10

stodginess *boringness* 296.2, *pulpiness* 561.9

stodgy *boring* 296.6, *thick* 561.17, *pulpy* 561.19, *conformist* 781.10

stogies *boots* 100.31

Stogos Breeds of Sheep 16

Stoic Philosophical Schools of Thought 4

stoic *insensitive person* 268.3, *insensitive* 268.4, *forgiving* 312.4, *disinterested* 443.4, *calm* 455.9, *quiescent* 678.6

stoical *detached* 4.18, *resigned* 835.4, *infallible* 840.12

stoically 4.26; *forgivingly* 312.13, *calmly* 455.16, *motionlessly* 678.9, *resignedly* 835.7

stoichiometric *chemical compound* 11.4

stoichiometric synthesis *process* 11.15

stoichiometry Fields of Measurement 589

Stoicism Philosophical Schools of Thought 4

stoicism *forgivingness* 312.3, *disinterestedness* 443.1, *calmness* 455.4, *resignedness* 835.2, *infallibility* 840.6

stoke *fuel* 106.16, Scientific and Technical Units 589, *intensify* 746.8

stoked *fueled* 106.11

stoker *power worker* 106.10

Stokes's theorem Mathematical Concepts 6

stoke up *prepare for action* 388.18

stole *vestment* 84.11, *neckwear* 100.29

stolen 479.12; *borrowed* 476.8

stolen base *other game terms* 147.7

stolen goods 479.4

stolid *insensible* 213.4, *unintelligent* 316.6, *inert* 519.2, *quiescent* 678.6

stolidity *ignorance* 316.3, *inertness* 519.1

stolidly *motionlessly* 678.9

stolon *stem* 41.5

stoma *body orifice* 583.3

stoma (pl. stomata) *leaf* 41.6

stomach *internal organ* 19.13, *eating organ* 92.14, *succumb* 421.7, *bear* 605.17, *internals* 611.3

stomachache *gastroenterological disease* 114.11, *painful condition* 215.2

stomach cancer *gastroenterological disease* 114.11, *cancer* 114.15

stomacher *part of garment* 100.27

stomach flu *gastroenterological disease* 114.11

stomach ulcer *gastroenterological disease* 114.11

stomp *gesture* 183.17, *blow* 695.5, *kick* 695.14

stone 418.23; *sediment* 8.29, *rock* 8.30, *construction material* 14.21, *masonry* 14.22, *seed* 41.9, *fruit structure* 44.3, Historical Missile Weapons 78, *blunt weapon* 78.5, *building materials* 104.2, *material* 144.6, *execute* 454.30, *solid body* 540.4, *hard substance* 542.3, *hard* 542.5, *sharpen* 549.16, *limit marker* 620.4, *missile* 696.7, *throw* 696.17

stone [Brit] *weight measurement* 538.6, General Units 589

Stone Age Ages, Decades, Eras 641, *primal* 653.14

Stone Age man *prehistoric human* 653.7

stoneblindness *blindness* 243.3

stone-broke *needy* 95.12, *insolvent* 486.10, *unprosperous* 848.11

stone carver *sculptor* 144.4

stone carving *sculpture* 144.1

stone-cold sober [Inf] *sober* 120.5

stonecutting *sculpture* 144.1, Hobbies and Pastimes 167

stoned [Inf] *dead drunk* 121.27, *drugged* 121.30

stone-dead *dead* 29.11

stone deaf *deaf* 229.4

stone fruit *fruits* 44.1, *fruit* 90.34

stone pine Trees and Shrubs 43

stone sculpture *sculpture* 144.1

stone-slinger *thrower* 696.10

stone's throw *short distance* 586.2

stone's throw away, a *nearby* 586.17

stone-throwing *throwing* 696.3

stone to death *execute* 30.22, 454.30

stonewall *evade* 181.17, *outtalk* 207.8, *oppose* 375.13, *stall* 419.28, *contend* 422.22, *delay* 658.13

stone wall *barrier* 826.7

stonewalled *held up* 658.6

stonewalling *delay* 658.3

stoneware Ceramics 129, *merchandise* 522.6, *hard substance* 542.3

stonewash *treat* 130.21

stonewashed *treated* 130.16

stonework *masonry* 14.22, *construction* 522.9

stonily *toughly* 542.12, *roughly* 544.13

stoniness *hardness* 542.1

stoning *execution* 30.6, *hit* 418.9, *capital punishment* 454.12

stony *earthy* 8.60, *infertile* 23.7, *strong-willed* 376.10, *hard* 542.5, *coarse* 544.6

stony [Inf] *unprosperous* 848.11

stony-broke [Inf] *insolvent* 486.10

stony-faced *serious* 278.4

stony-hearted *pitiless* 309.3, *mentally hard* 542.8

stony meteorite *or* **stone** *meteor* 7.21

stooge *unskilled person* 128.3, *entertainer* 138.8, *laughingstock* 369.4, *sycophant* 401.3, *butt* 436.8, *nonentity* 800.8, *subordinate* 832.3

stooge for *pander to* 401.11

stool *plant breeding* 17.6, *feces* 25.5, *place for excretion* 25.11, *tree part* 43.2, *type of chair* 101.4, *test* 107.10, *diagnostic procedure* 107.11, *dirt* 112.5

stool [Inf] *inform on* 170.13, *accuse* 442.8

stoolie *accuser* 442.3

stooling *gardening* 17.5

stool of repentance *instrument of punishment* 454.13

stool pigeon *or* **stoolie** *or* **stooly** [Inf] *informer* 170.8, *hypocrite* 192.9, *accuser* 442.3

stoop *humble oneself* 298.18, *knuckle under* 401.10, *succumb* 421.7, *show obeisance to* 426.8, *show respect* 435.16, *prostration* 597.2, *be low* 597.20, *bow* 716.6, *sit* 716.20, *deteriorate* 808.14

stooped *prostrate* 597.11, *curved* 629.4

stooping *sycophantic* 401.7, *mark of respect* 435.4, *showing respect* 435.7, *prostrate* 597.11, *sedentary* 716.11

stoop tag Children's and Party Games 167

stop 584.14, 668.2, 668.10; *practice dentistry* 107.34, *part of keyboard instrument* 142.6, *sailing* 150.25, *deter* 179.8, *silence* 231.4, *mute* 233.9, *stop using* 394.10, disaccustom 398.6, inaction 413.1, not act 413.11, pause 415.15, detention 471.2, detain 471.9, closure 584.1, stopper 584.3, interruption 604.4, interrupt 604.16, cover 613.24, wait 658.12, stopping place 668.4, lack of motion 678.1, destination 704.6, equilibrium 740.2, cessation 773.2, cease 773.20, discontinue 775.10, repair 809.10, snag 824.8, hinder 826.15, restrain 830.12, terminate 834.7, malfunction 846.20

stop! cease! 668.14
stop abruptly stop 668.10
stop a gap repair 809.10
stop-and-go irregular 664.3, discontinuous 775.7
stop and think reconsider 807.23
stop at 704.18
stop at nothing be resolute 376.11, pursue 377.11
stop bath darkroom equipment 132.21
stop breathing die 29.17, stop 668.10
stopcock hand tool 103.3, stopper 584.3
stop dead stop 668.10
stop down compose a photograph 132.27
stop fighting pacify 74.11, capitulate 421.6
stop from spreading limit 830.13
stopgap helper 275.5, method 387.4, half-measure 461.2, 461.5, substitution 672.1, substitute 672.3, equalizer 740.5, imperfect item 806.3
stop in one's tracks pause 415.15, stop 668.10
stop it! cease! 668.14
stop light safety light 246.7
stop off visit 408.16, stop at 704.18
stop-off pause 668.3
stop one in the act hinder 826.15
stopover 704.7; pause 668.3, interval 775.2
stop over visit 408.16, stop at 704.18, pause 775.11
stoppage 490.2; closure 584.1, interruption 604.4, stop 668.2, lack of motion 678.1, cessation 773.2, snag 824.8, obstacle 826.2, termination 834.2, discontinuance 846.4
stop payment 490.10; interrupt 604.16
stopped 584.9, 668.7; interrupted 604.10, ceased 668.6, discontinued 775.8, restrained 830.9, canceled 834.5, forbidden 837.7
stopped clock bad-luck sign 358.7
stopped up stopped 584.9
stopper 584.3; soccer participant 163.4, detention 471.2, moderator 521.2, stop 584.14, corner 613.2, 613.24, insert 710.4, ender 773.11, safety device 810.15
stopping canoeing 150.26, cessation 668.1, ending 773.13, hindrance 826.1, restraint 830.1
stopping at nothing tenacious 376.9
stopping place 668.4; destination 704.6
stopping stroke canoeing techniques 150.11
stop-press edition newspaper 175.2
stop running malfunction 846.20
stop short pause 415.15, stop 668.10

stop someone's mouth silence 231.4
stop talking be silent 231.3, stop 668.10
stop the bleeding treat 115.17
stop the flow 570.12
stop the gap entrench 419.24
stop the world from turning attempt the impossible 837.10
stop thief! after him! 385.19, cease! 668.14
stop thrust fencing movements 153.3
stop up stop 584.14
stop using 394.10; renounce 392.4
stopwatch indicator 183.7, recording instrument 185.9, measuring instrument 589.12, Timepieces and Timers 646
stop work 394.12, 668.11; have an industrial dispute 57.20
storage 105.6; memory 15.6, nonuse 394.1, reserved space 563.5, storing 578.19, preservation 815.1, preservation of provisions 815.6
storage battery vault 105.9
storage building building 551.9
storage jar pot 578.15
storage polysaccharide polysaccharide 12.5
storage room room 60.9
storage space reserved space 563.5
storax Tree Products 43
store 105.1, 105.17, 124.4, 483.8; livestock 16.11, assemblage 59.13, assemble 59.23, reserves 102.5, procure 104.9, conceal 181.12, preparations 388.2, nonuse 394.1, unused thing 394.4, not use 394.9, acquisition 467.4, joint possession 469.6, detain 471.9, merchandise 482.6, funds 484.6, treasury 484.19, building 551.9, container 578.1, contain 578.20, set apart 753.17, combine 757.9, insurance 810.10, protect 810.21, preservation of provisions 815.6, preserve 815.14
store away acquire 467.19
store-bought tailored 100.41
store-bought clothes 100.3
store cattle livestock 16.11
stored 105.14; unused 394.5, storing 578.19, preserved 815.12
store energy generate power 514.19
store fuel 105.18
storehouse 105.8
storehouse of words word book 5.27
store in a database record 185.13
store in one's heart memorize 354.11
store in the archives record 185.13
storekeeper provisioner 89.4, retailer 482.11, accountant 493.6
store manager manager 126.7
store owner retailer 482.11
storeroom 105.7; room 60.9
stores provisions 89.3, food 90.1
store ship warship 77.21
store the mind learn 48.23
store window place for viewing 242.13, stall 483.9, showplace 843.4
storied narrative 139.18
storified narrative 139.18
storing 578.19
storing the mind learning 48.7
stork water bird 36.9
stork, wood Endangered US Birds 36
storks Collective Names 59

storm 9.55; wind strength 9.13, thunderstorm 9.20, crowd 59.11, combat 77.34, conquer 77.36, be loud 232.8, burst of anger 302.6, become angry 302.20, military attack 418.2, attack 418.17, natural violence 520.3, be violent 520.8, agent of destruction 523.7, atmospheric agitation 684.13, invade 706.12, be disorderly 766.22, natural hazard 813.4, be victorious 845.16
storm along be swift 694.10
storm blown over safety 810.1
storm brewing danger signal 811.5
storm cloud cloud 9.17
storm clouds threat 848.3
storm coat coat 100.19
storm door means of entry 706.6
stormer combatant 77.1, attacker 418.10
storm-force windy 9.42
storm glass weather instrument 9.7
storm home defeat 845.17
stormily meteorologically 9.60, violently 520.11
storm in invade 706.12
storm in a teacup figurative overestimation 343.3
storminess violence 520.1
storming angry 302.11, attacking 418.14
storm out depart 705.8
storm(y) petrel forewarning 814.2
stormproof waterproof 560.16
storms climbing dangers 161.5
storm signal warning signal 814.3
storm-tossed bumpy 544.8, worn 808.13
storm warning warning 814.1
storm watch or **warning** weather forecast 9.4
storm wave wave 8.16
stormy 9.45; dark 247.5, dim 248.4, explosive 520.6, turbulent 684.17
story 139.4; chronicle 3.4, dramaturgy 136.6, script 137.5, aspect of fiction 139.5, news story 171.3, falsehood 192.6, narration 202.3, matter of interest 328.3, conception 360.4, work of art 522.4, level 588.2
storyboard script 137.5
storybook type of book 174.3, imaginary 360.12
storyline aspect of fiction 139.5
storyteller author 139.13, liar 192.10, descriptive writer 202.10
story thus far circumstances 726.1
stoup [Scot] drinking vessel 578.13
stout alcoholic drink 93.9, physically strong 516.10, strengthened 516.13, heavy 538.9, fat 579.15, stocky 579.16, thick 594.5, well-rounded 633.8
stout-hearted steadfast 284.11, strong in spirit 516.11
stout-heartedly steadfastly 284.19
stout-heartedness steadfastness 284.3, endurance 516.4
stoutly strongly 516.17, heavily 538.16, fatly 579.22, thick 594.11
stoutness fatness 579.5, thickness 594.1, round body 633.2
stout try attempt 390.1
stove cooker 91.5, ceramic workshop and tools 129.8, burner 217.4
stovepipe hat hat 100.32
stow save 105.20, fill 761.11
stowage storage 105.6, reserved space 563.5, load 577.5, size 579.1

stow away save 105.20, conceal 181.12, be external 724.15, hide 844.13
stowed loaded 577.8
stowed away saved 105.15
stow it! [Inf] hush! 231.6
STP hallucinogens 121.20
St. Paul American States 564
strabismic visually impaired 243.9
strabismus faulty vision 243.1
straddle horizontal bar 157.5, be equivocal 380.7, extend 563.14, span 592.12, branch 703.14, link 752.18, stand in the middle 772.17
straddle style jumping 166.11
strafe air attack 418.4, firing 418.6, fire 418.18
strafe [Inf] punish 454.22
strafing air attack 418.4
straggle go astray 698.17, disband 776.13
straggling divergent 776.11
straggly divergent 776.11
straight 630.8, 630.16; linear 6.77, type of chair 101.4, intoxicating 121.29, automobile racing terms 146.3, combat 152.17, poker 168.5, right 429.7, right away 429.20, vertical 602.5, vertically 602.11, direct 697.11, directly 697.16, correctly 721.29, orderly 765.13, well-ordered 765.14
straight [Inf] of sexual nature 20.17
straight across directly 697.16
straight ahead straight 630.16, directly 697.16
straight-ahead traditional 630.13
straight and narrow, the virtue 447.1
straight angle angle 6.37
straight arrow [Inf] straight person 630.7
straight-arrow [Inf] in the right 429.11, traditional 630.13
straight as an arrow straight 630.8, directly 697.16
straightaway automobile racing terms 146.3, right away 429.20, straight 630.8, immediately 645.8, direct 697.11, hastily 818.7
straight body competitive diving 164.7
straight cut fencing movements 153.3, coiffure 530.8
straight down vertical 602.5
straight drama drama 136.1
straightedge geometric construction 6.47, planimetry 603.5
straight-edged linear 6.77
straighten 630.14; make vertical 602.9, adjust 721.23, tidy 765.21, make conform 781.13, restore 807.17, rectify 807.22
straightened straight 630.8, adjusted 721.14
straightened out straight 630.8
straightening out rectification 807.8
straighten out put right 429.14, straighten 630.14, restore 807.17, rectify 807.22, repair 809.10
straighten the record divulge 180.9
straighten up be vertical 602.8, tidy 765.21
straighten up and fly right [Inf] get better 807.21
straight-faced serious 278.4
straight flush poker 168.5
straightforward 630.9; candid 191.5, clear 196.2, easily seen through 249.10, simple 363.6, correct 429.8, outspoken 550.6, direct 697.11, directly 697.16, naive 821.3, easy 823.9

straightforwardly 630.17; *candidly* 191.10, *clearly* 196.4, *bluntly* 550.11, *naively* 821.5

straightforwardness 630.3; *candor* 191.2, *clarity* 196.1, 363.2, *openness* 249.6, *outspokenness* 550.2, *directness* 697.6, *naiveté* 821.1

straight from the horse's mouth *reportedly* 170.16, *topical* 328.5

straight from the shoulder *with vigor* 518.6, *candidly* 583.23

straight-from-the-shoulder *candid* 191.5, *meaningful* 361.6, *simple* 363.6

straight handlebars *bicycle part* 687.11

straight left *boxing techniques* 152.5

straight line 630.2; *line* 6.35

straight-line *be on the track* 146.11, *bowling* 151.6

straight-lined *linear* 6.77

straight-line delivery *bowling delivery* 151.2

straightly *directly* 697.16

straight man *role* 136.23, *entertainer* 138.8, *humorist* 277.7

straightness 630.1; *verticality* 602.1, *directness* 697.6, *orderliness* 765.5, *methodicalness* 765.6

straight part *role* 136.23

straight person 630.7

straight pin *fastener* 754.7

straight punch *boxing techniques* 152.5

straight run *ski run* 162.2

straight sailing *easy thing* 823.6

straight shooter *straight person* 630.7

straight skirt *skirt* 100.12

straight talking *directness* 630.5

straight through *continuous* 630.10

straight thrust *fencing movements* 153.3

straight truth, the *the truth* 721.3

straight up *higher* 596.21, *vertical* 602.5

straight up and down *vertical* 602.5, *vertically* 602.11

strain 117.4; *society* 1.6, *earth movement* 8.20, *force* 10.9, *load* 14.14, 14.49, *plant breeding* 17.6, *personal conflict* 63.2, *purify* 111.19, *afflict* 117.16, *work* 122.1, *exertion* 122.4, *exert oneself* 122.11, *part of poem* 139.9, *melody* 140.10, *practice sophistry* 330.11, *attempt* 390.1, *try hard* 390.7, *illuse* 395.7, *operation* 509.1, *attitude* 513.2, *weaken* 517.13, *use violence* 520.9, *style* 537.1, *elasticity* 546.1, *distortion* 627.1, *distort* 627.9, *transfer* 685.8, *passage* 692.1, *pull* 699.2, *leak* 707.16, *exaggerate* 712.16, *nature* 723.4, *admixture* 751.5, *type* 777.4, *fatigue* 820.1, 820.6, *difficulty* 824.1

strained 117.13; *hostile* 63.6, *fearful* 283.10, *exaggerated* 712.9, *fatigued* 820.2

strainer *cooking equipment* 91.6, *cleaning tool* 111.10, *arch* 134.5

strain every nerve *exert oneself* 122.11

strain gauge *measuring instrument* 589.12

straining *exertion* 122.4, *leakage* 707.5

strain one's credulity *be improbable* 839.7

strain oneself *try* 414.21

strain one's lungs *or voice or vocal cords cry out* 239.13

strain one's voice *be loud* 232.8

strain to the utmost *exert oneself* 122.11

strait *inlet* 572.9, *narrow place* 593.2, *narrow* 593.8, *channel* 691.10

straiten *narrow* 593.14

straitened *poor* 486.8, *meager* 593.12

straitened circumstances *poverty* 486.1, *inferior state* 745.3

straitjacket *contractor* 582.6, *means of restraint* 830.6, *restrain someone* 830.17

strait-laced *opinionated* 379.9, *formal* 406.8, *unadorned* 424.7, *moralistic* 431.12, *abstinent* 455.7, *conformist* 781.10

strait-lacedness *opinionatedness* 379.3, *formality* 406.1

straitly *narrowly* 593.17

straitness *narrowness* 593.1

straits *narrow place* 593.2

strand *coast* 572.4, *edge* 618.1, *waterfront* 621.3

stranded *stabilized* 674.4, *vulnerable* 811.9

strange 364.9; *spiritual* 86.20, *astonishing* 294.10, *unknown* 349.7, *uncustomary* 398.4, *foreign* 724.9, *disparate* 728.9, *unusual* 782.15, *eccentric* 782.16

strangely 724.17; *astonishingly* 294.19, *unusually* 398.9, *erratically* 698.29, *disparately* 728.19, *unconformably* 782.21

strangeness *quantum* 10.63, *foreignness* 724.2, *disparity* 728.3, *unusualness* 782.4

strange noise *danger signal* 811.5

stranger *foreigner* 724.5

strangers *Phobias* 283

strange to say *astonishingly* 294.19

strangle *murder* 30.20, *wrestle* 152.20, *execute* 454.30, *retain* 471.7, *overpower* 515.14, *abolish* 523.11, *squeeze* 582.13, *obstruct* 584.13

strangled *retained* 471.6, *squeezed* 582.9

stranglehold *wrestling terms* 152.10, *retention* 471.1

strangler *murderer* 30.12

strangles *animal disease* 34.10

strangling *wrestling terms* 152.10, *retentive* 471.5, *squeeze* 582.3, *contracting* 582.10

strangulate *squeeze* 582.13

strangulated *squeezed* 582.9

strangulation *murder* 30.2, *capital punishment* 454.12, *squeeze* 582.3, *obstruction* 584.2, *narrowing* 593.3

strap *stationary rings* 157.8, *tennis court* 165.3, *instrument of punishment* 454.13, *hit* 454.28, *sharpener* 549.8, *sharpen* 549.16, *intertwine* 752.19, *band* 754.9

strapless *stylish* 100.42

strapless dress *dress* 100.11

strappado *corporal punishment* 454.11

strapped *insolvent* 486.10

strapping *of good constitution* 113.5, *physically strong* 516.10, *vigorous* 518.2, *stalwart* 547.10, *stocky* 579.16

stratagem 822.2; *social skill* 127.3, *artifice* 193.5, *sophism* 330.2, *method* 387.4, *tactics* 399.12, *trick* 813.2

strategic 78.16; *military* 58.10, 76.28, *planned* 387.10

strategical *behaving* 399.14, *cunning* 822.4

strategically *militarily* 58.15, *hypocritically* 330.15, *as planned* 387.16, *cunningly* 822.8

Strategic Arms Limitation Talks (SALT) *disarmament* 74.3

Strategic Arms Reduction Talks (START) *disarmament* 74.3

strategic bomber *military aircraft* 77.30

strategic bombing *bombing* 76.21, *air attack* 418.4

Strategic Defense Initiative (SDI) *preventive warfare* 76.12, *military defenses* 419.9

strategic importance *importance* 799.1

strategic nuclear warfare *atomic warfare* 76.4

strategic nuclear weapon *weapon* 78.1

strategic objectives *military affairs* 58.1

strategist *politician* 50.7, *expert* 127.9, *motivator* 178.11, 508.6, *planner* 387.9, *cunning person* 822.3

strategize *scheme* 193.18

strategy *art of war* 76.16, *procedure* 387.2, *tactics* 399.12

strath [Scot] *lowland* 572.6

strathspey *Dances* 135

straticulate *layered* 588.6

stratification *layering* 588.5, *covering* 613.1, *categorization* 767.5

stratified *petrographic* 8.58, *layered* 588.6, *categorized* 767.15

stratified rock *sedimentary rock* 8.34

stratified society *group* 18.13

stratiform *cloudy* 9.44, *layered* 588.6

stratify *layer* 588.9

stratigrapher *geologist* 8.4

stratigraphical *geologic* 8.50

stratigraphy *geology* 8.1

stratocracy *military government* 49.16

stratocumulus *cloud* 9.17

stratopause *atmosphere* 9.8

stratosphere *atmosphere* 9.8, *atmospheric layer* 558.3

stratospheric *atmospheric* 9.40, 558.13

stratous *cloudy* 9.44

stratovolcano *volcanic activity* 8.26

stratum (pl. strata) *sedimentary rock* 8.34, *atmospheric layer* 558.3, *layer* 588.1, *social class* 777.5

stratus *cloud* 9.17

straw *animal feed* 16.12, *cultivate* 17.19, *grass plant* 45.3, *cereal grass* 45.4, *little bit* 800.4

strawberry *red thing* 257.3

strawberry-blond *yellow-haired* 259.9

strawberry bush *Trees and Shrubs* 43

strawberry mark *figurative usage* 44.4, *personal identification* 184.4, *red thing* 257.3, *maculation* 263.4, *mark* 533.2

strawberry roan *horse by color* 159.7

strawberry tree *Trees and Shrubs* 43

straw-colored *yellow* 259.7

strawflower *Flowers* 42, *flower* 42.1

straw hat *hat* 100.32

strawhat circuit *engagement* 136.15

strawhat theater *drama* 136.1

straw man *powerless person* 515.5, *weak person* 517.4, *insubstantial person* 720.5

straw poll *electing* 382.5

stray *be immoral* 432.13, *be wicked* 448.13, *displaced person* 574.7, *move* 677.15, *indirect* 698.9, *go astray* 698.17, *divergent* 776.11, *disband* 776.13, *unconventional* 782.14, *be in danger* 811.11, *be independent* 829.18, *causeless* 842.11

stray from the path of righteousness *be wicked* 448.13

stray from the straight and narrow *sin* 430.22, *be wicked* 448.13

stray from the subject *digress* 775.13

stray from the topic *be unrelated* 728.12

straying *wandering* 698.4, 698.13

streak *dirty light* 112.11, *natural light* 246.4, *stripe* 263.3, *variegate* 263.11, *piece* 590.2, *undress* 614.18, *be swift* 694.10, *admixture* 751.5

streaked *striped* 263.9

streaker *nude person* 614.5

streakiness *stripe* 263.3

streaking *undressing* 614.2

streak of luck *good fortune* 847.2

stream *rain* 9.57, *crowd* 59.11, 59.26, 795.11, *abound* 97.8, *excess* 99.1, *be excessive* 99.9, *tendency* 513.1, *flow* 555.25, 570.4, 570.10, *river* 570.1, *momentum* 677.2, *be in motion* 677.14, *maneuver* 677.18, *channel* 691.10, *influx* 706.2, *outflow* 707.4, *let out* 709.26, *procession* 774.6, *students* 777.6

streambed *running water* 8.10, *river parts* 570.3

stream channel *running water* 8.10

stream course *running water* 8.10

streamer *bait* 154.6, *flag* 184.8

streamers *natural light* 246.4, *salute* 405.7

streaming *rainy* 9.50, *productive* 22.9, *excessive* 99.5, *wet* 557.23, *flowing* 570.7, *moving* 677.12, *outflow* 707.4, *nonadhesive* 756.4

streaming eyes *outflow* 707.4

streamlet *river* 570.1

streamlike *riverlike* 570.6

streamline *make simple* 526.12, *smooth* 545.10, *rearrange* 767.20, *rectify* 807.22

streamlined *smooth* 545.4, *swift* 694.6, *rearranged* 767.14

streamlining *simplification* 526.6, *rearrangement* 767.4, *easing* 823.7

stream of consciousness *psyche* 108.25, *association of ideas* 108.31, *aspect of fiction* 139.5, *soliloquy* 211.1, *thought* 931.7

stream-of-consciousness novel *novel* 139.3

street *road* 691.4

streetcar *railroad system* 688.1

streetcar suburb *suburb* 567.11

street cleaner *cleaner* 111.12

street drug *drug* 115.9, 121.14

street fight *fight* 422.9, *violation of the law* 427.2

street fighter *doer* 412.3

streetlamp *electric light* 246.6

streetlight *electric light* 246.6

street map *map* 387.7
street market *market* 483.1
street musician *musician* 141.1
street name *place of residence* 209.4
street of fallen women *brothel* 432.5
street performer *entertainer* 138.8
street riot *violation of the law* 427.2
street seller *peddler* 482.9
street-smart *educated* 48.19, *knowledgeable* 348.7, *intelligent* 352.5
street smarts [Inf] *intellect* 348.4
streetsweeper *cleaning tool* 111.10
street theater *drama* 136.1, *show* 138.4
street trader *crier* 239.8, *discounter* 497.7
street urchin *young man* 26.8
street vendor *peddler* 482.9
streetwalk *prostitute* 432.17
streetwalker *sexually immoral person* 432.8
streetwalking *prostitution* 432.4
streetwise *educated* 48.19, *knowledgeable* 348.7, *intelligent* 352.5
strelitzia *Flowers* 42
strength 516.1; *authority* 52.1, *health* 113.1, *skill* 127.1, *emphasis* 200.1, *tenacity* 376.4, *stamina* 377.4, *power* 447.4, *influence* 512.1, *vigor* 514.2, 518.1, *violence* 520.1, *hardness* 542.1, *toughness* 547.1, *deepness* 598.6, *stability* 674.1
strengthen 516.15; *refresh* 94.6, *reinforce* 419.23, *make fast* 464.13, *empower* 514.20, *harden* 542.9, *make tough* 547.15, *deepen* 598.21, *base* 601.10, *support* 605.16, 825.24, *give moral support* 605.18, *restore* 809.12, *protect* 810.21
strengthened 516.13; *hardened* 542.7, *toughened* 547.7, *repaired* 809.6
strengthening 516.7; *invigorating* 518.3, *deepening* 598.14, *support* 605.1, *moral support* 605.7, *supportive* 605.11, *restoration* 809.2
strengthen oneself 516.16
strength exercises *gymnastics* 157.1
strengthlessness *weakness* 517.1
strength of character *will* 376.5
strength of materials 14.15
strength of will *or mind or purpose willpower* 372.2
strenuous *laborious* 122.7, *emphatic* 200.3, *committed* 377.7, *active* 414.13, *punishing* 454.20, *vigorous* 518.2, *difficult* 824.9
strenuously *laboriously* 122.13, *emphatically* 200.7, *arduously* 824.24
strenuousness *difficulty* 824.1
strepsipteran *insectile* 40.11
streptocarpus *Flowers* 42
streptomycin *fungal antibiotic* 47.7
stress *spoken letter* 5.15, *earth movement* 8.20, *force* 10.9, *load* 14.14, 14.49, *strain* 117.4, *exertion* 122.4, *meter* 139.10, *punctuate* 183.20, *affirmation* 189.1, *affirm* 189.21, *emphasis* 200.1, *emphasize* 200.6, *mode of speech* 205.6, *operation* 509.1, *potency* 516.6, *strengthen* 516.15, *distortion* 627.21, *distort* 627.9,

impel 695.9, *importance* 799.1, *make important* 799.14
stress a point *affirm* 189.21
stressed *strained* 117.13, *affirmed* 189.11, *emphasized* 200.4, *phonetic* 205.14
stressed point *affirmation* 189.1
stress reaction *anxiety disorder* 108.11
stress test *prenatal diagnosis* 107.9
stretch *task* 122.2, *exertion* 122.4, *swimming techniques* 164.2, *allotted task* 474.3, *elasticity* 546.1, *elastic* 546.5, *be elastic* 546.7, *geographical space* 563.3, *range* 563.7, *intervening space* 563.8, *extend* 563.14, *expansion* 581.1, *enlargeability* 581.6, *enlarge* 581.14, *length* 590.1, *be long* 590.11, *lengthen* 590.12, *span* 592.12, *period* 641.1, *duration* 642.1, *exaggerate* 712.16, *make bigger* 746.7
stretch [Inf] *prison sentence* 55.6, *detention* 830.5
stretchability *elasticity* 546.1, *enlargeability* 581.6
stretchable *pliant* 543.7, *elastic* 546.5, *enlargeable* 581.13
stretch a point *be lenient* 423.5, *compromise* 461.7, *exaggerate* 712.16
stretched *partially true* 192.18, *elastic* 546.5, *bigger* 581.9, *increased* 746.5
stretched out *lengthened* 590.10
stretched-out *bigger* 581.9
stretcher *masonry* 14.22, *material* 143.9, *rowboat parts* 150.15, *enlarger* 581.8, *means of transportation* 686.2, *means of connection* 754.4
stretcher-bearer *paramedic* 107.24, *transferrer* 685.4, *transporter* 686.4
stretcher case *sick person* 114.22
stretchiness *elasticity* 546.1
stretching *topology* 6.45, *elasticity* 546.1, *elastic* 546.5, *expansion* 581.1, *growing* 581.12
stretching out *expansion* 581.1, *lengthening* 590.4
stretch limo [Inf] *automobile* 687.6
stretch of the imagination *tall story* 194.5
stretch one's legs *be refreshed* 94.8
stretch one's nerves *awake* 212.10
stretch out *enlarge* 581.14, *reach out* 585.10, *lengthen* 590.12
stretch the imagination *tell a tall story* 194.15
stretch the point *be permissive* 502.7
stretch the truth *distort the truth* 192.25, 627.12
stretch to *reach out* 585.10
stretch to the ends of the earth *be distant* 585.8
stretch wide *be deep* 598.20
stretchy *elastic* 546.5, *enlargeable* 581.13
strew *sprinkle* 776.5
strewing *dispersion* 776.1
strewn *sprinkled* 776.9
stria *stripe* 263.3
striate *variegate* 263.11
striate *or striated striped* 263.9
striated *weathered* 8.61
striation *erosion* 8.41, *stripe* 263.3
stricken *sick* 114.24
stricken in years *aged* 27.15

strict *religious* 81.21, *accurate* 350.3, *severe* 425.5, *self-restrained* 455.6, *restraining* 830.8
strict control *restraint* 830.1
strict discipline *severity* 424.1
strictly *religiously* 81.29, *severely* 424.11, *with self-restraint* 455.14, *restrainedly* 830.18
strictly between ourselves *secretly* 182.14
strictly controlled *restrained* 830.9
strictly speaking *literally* 721.32
strictness *religiousness* 81.2, *accuracy* 350.1, *severity* 424.1, *conventionalism* 781.4, *restraint* 830.1
strict person 424.4
stricture *censure* 438.3, *narrowing* 593.3, *limit* 620.1
strictured *narrowed* 593.9
stride *bodily movement* 677.11, *walk* 677.17
stridency *loud sound* 232.2, *dissonance* 241.1
stridency *or stridence harsh sound* 238.1
strident 238.4; *loud* 232.6, *dissonant* 241.4
stridently 238.10; *loudly* 232.11, *dissonantly* 241.7
stridor *tone* 140.24, *mode of speech* 205.6, *loud sound* 232.2, *harsh sound* 238.1
stridulate *make an insect sound* 240.9
stridulation *insect sound* 240.3
stridulous *or stridulant strident* 238.4, *humming* 240.6
stridulously *stridently* 238.10
stridulousness *harsh sound* 238.1
strife *quarrel* 272.4, *contention* 422.1, *divisiveness* 463.2, *conflict* 828.3
strigiform *avian* 36.19
strigil *cleaning tool* 111.10, *Architectural Elements* 134
strigose *barbed* 544.7
strike 57.8, 418.21; *murder* 30.20, *industrial dispute* 57.7, *have an industrial dispute* 57.20, *fight* 77.35, *source of supply* 105.4, *fuel* 106.16, *play an instrument* 142.9, *pitching terms* 147.5, *row* 150.32, *bowling delivery* 151.2, *catch* 154.9, *field hockey tactics* 158.5, *play field hockey* 158.10, *play soccer* 163.8, *type of touch* 216.3, *touch* 216.9, *light* 246.19, *mass demonstration* 331.7, *protest* 331.19, *find* 345.5, *dissentience* 347.3, *resistance* 417.1, *resist* 417.10, *military attack* 418.2, *attack* 418.17, *disobedience* 427.1, *disobey* 427.12, *hit* 454.28, *695.11, refusal* 506.1, *refuse* 506.8, *gesture of protest* 507.3, *cause mischief* 507.9, *use violence* 520.9, *stop* 668.2, *stop work* 668.11, *lack of motion* 678.1, *blow* 695.5, *shoot* 696.18, *lower the flag* 716.23, *lockout* 826.6, *block* 826.17
strike a bad patch *be in difficulty* 824.19
strike a balance *compromise* 461.7, *equalize* 740.12, *make average* 742.9, *split down the middle* 772.20
strike a bargain *contract* 459.8, 462.11
strike a blow for *motivate* 412.12
strike a light *light* 246.19
strike (a match) *abrade* 554.13

strike an average *compromise* 461.7
strike at *strike* 418.21, *contend* 422.22, *fight* 422.23, *hit* 695.11
strike back at *counterattack* 418.24
strike blind *blind* 243.17
strike-bound *refused* 506.5
strikebreaker *strike* 57.8, *reactionary* 427.9
strikebreaking *strike* 57.8, *disputed* 57.15
strike camp *quit* 705.10
strike colors *capitulate* 421.6
strike down *afflict* 117.16
strike dumb 206.10; *astonish* 292.10, *be wondrous* 294.14
strike first *attack* 418.17
strike force *attack* 418.10
strike hard *be full of vigor* 518.4
strike it lucky *be fortunate* 847.7
strike it rich *get rich* 485.13, *be prosperous* 847.6, *be fortunate* 847.7
strike notice *strike* 57.8
strike off *disbar* 709.16, *eject* 764.8
strike off the roll *disbar* 709.16
strike oil *mine coal* 106.18, *be fortunate* 847.7
strike one *have an idea* 327.13
strike one in the eye *be visible* 244.7
strike one in the face *be visible* 244.7
strikeout *pitching terms* 147.5
strike out *play baseball* 147.9, *erase* 186.9, *react against* 291.15, *abolish* 523.11, *close* 637.10, *set out* 705.12, *eject* 764.8, *cancel* 834.6
strike out for *aim* 697.14
striker *strike* 57.8, *player* 149.5, *soccer participant* 163.4, *protester* 331.8, 507.4, *troublemaker* 427.5, *refuser* 506.4, *thrower* 696.10
strike root *be stable* 674.6
strike root in *influence* 512.11
strike settlement *strike* 57.8
strike-slip fault *fault* 8.21
strike the colors *lower the flag* 716.23
strike the first blow *attack* 418.17
strike through *erase* 186.9
strike up a friendship *or an acquaintance befriend* 62.10
strike upon *reach* 704.14
strike while the iron is hot *take the opportunity* 659.7
strike zone *pitching terms* 147.5
striking *strike* 57.8, *disputed* 57.15, *rowing techniques* 150.16, *rowing* 150.27, *soccer play* 163.5, *descriptive* 202.11, *exciting* 212.8, *clear* 244.6, *wondrous* 294.9, *demonstrating* 331.14, *intelligible* 363.5, *resistant* 417.6, *attacking* 418.14, *corporal punishment* 454.11, *refused* 506.5, *strong to the senses* 516.12, *manifest* 843.9
striking circle *hockey areas* 158.2
striking distance *short distance* 586.2
striking force *armed force* 77.10
striking off *dismissal* 909.2
striking out *closure* 637.4, *subtraction* 749.1
strine *regional pronunciation* 205.7
string *fundamental interaction* 10.65, Collective Names 59, Bean Varieties 90, *part of stringed instrument* 142.2, *part of keyboard instrument* 142.6, Phobias 283, *fiber* 552.6, *step* 713.11, *line*

754.5, *series* 770.3, *consecutiveness* 774.1, *concatenate* 774.13

string *or* **stringer** Architectural Elements 134

string along [Inf] *deceive* 193.16

string along with [Inf] *join with* 827.15

string bag *bag* 578.7

string bikini *beachwear* 100.23

stringcourse Architectural Elements 134

stringed instrument *musical instrument* 142.1, *source of resonance* 236.4

stringency *severity* 424.1

stringendo Musical Terms and Expression Marks 140

stringent *severe* 424.5

stringently *severely* 424.11

stringer *print journalist* 175.5, *superstructure* 551.7

stringiness *chewiness* 547.2, *stalwartness* 547.3, *doughiness* 561.2

stringing out *lengthening* 590.4

stringless Bean Varieties 90

string musician *player* 141.2

string out *lengthen* 590.12, *arrange* 774.14, *scatter* 796.9

string puller *person in authority* 52.7

string pulling *authority* 52.1

string quartet Musical Forms 140, *instrumental group* 141.3, *collection* 757.3

strings *basis for negotiations* 460.2, *indirect influence* 512.4

string tie *neckwear* 100.29

string together *improvise* 396.6, *link* 752.18, *concatenate* 774.13

string up [Inf] *execute* 30.22, 454.30

stringy *stalwart* 547.10, *viscous* 561.14

strip *farmland* 16.3, *clean* 111.17, *entertain* 138.16, *racetrack* 159.12, *lose* 468.12, *impoverish* 486.16, *weaken* 517.13, *lay waste* 523.14, *make simple* 526.12, *layer* 588.1, *scale* 588.10, *piece* 590.2, *undress* 614.18, *make nude* 614.19, *disbar* 709.16, *take off* 749.7, *separate* 753.12

strip bare *disclose* 180.8, *weaken* 517.13, *lay waste* 523.14, *undress* 614.18, *separate* 753.12

strip-casting *saltwater fishing* 154.3

strip clean *clean* 111.17

strip club *pornography* 432.7

strip cropping *arable farming* 16.6

strip down *make simple* 526.12

stripe 263.3; *insignia* 184.5, *variegate* 263.11, *corporal punishment* 454.11, *piece* 590.2, *blow* 695.5, *nature* 723.4, *type* 777.4

striped 263.9

stripes *military honor* 58.9

strip farming *agriculture* 16.1, *arable farming* 16.6

strip grazing *livestock farming* 16.10

striping *stripe* 263.3

strip light *electric light* 246.6

stripling *young man* 26.8

strip off *undress* 614.18

strip off *or* **away** *take off* 749.7

strip of land *portion* 474.2

stripped *impoverished* 486.11, *naked* 614.12

stripped down *simple* 526.7

stripped naked *or* **bare** *naked* 614.12

stripped of *losing* 468.9

stripper *pornography* 432.7, *nude person* 614.5

stripper *or* **stripteaser** *entertainer* 138.8

stripping *loss* 468.1, *simplification* 526.6, *interior decoration* 532.4, *undressing* 614.2, *dismissal* 709.2

stripping away *or* **down** *simplification* 526.6

stripping bare *undressing* 614.2

strip planting *arable farming* 16.6

strip poker Card Games 168, *poker* 168.5, *undressing* 614.2

strip search *undressing* 614.2

strip-search *make nude* 614.19

strip show *show* 138.4

striptease *entertain* 138.16, *undressing* 614.2

striptease artist *entertainer* 138.8, *nude person* 614.5

striptease club *club* 138.7, *pornography* 432

striptease dancer *nude person* 614.5

stripteaser *dancer* 135.4, *nude person* 614.5

striptease show *show* 138.4

strip to the buff [Inf] *undress* 614.18

stripy *checked* 263.8, *striped* 263.9

strive *exert oneself* 122.11, *persevere* 377.10, *try hard* 390.7, *contend* 422.22

strive after *aim at* 385.15

strive against *oppose* 828.15

strive for *aim* 374.10, *aim at* 385.15

strive in vain *be powerless* 515.11

striver *experimenter* 335.5, *attempter* 390.3, *fighter* 422.14

strive to keep for oneself *be jealous* 314.8

striving *attempting* 390.4

strobe light *electric light* 246.6

stroboscope *or* **strobe** *or* **strobe light** *stage lighting* 136.20

stroboscopic *lucent* 246.13

stroboscopic lamp *electric light* 246.6

stroke Accents and Diacritical Marks 5, *illness* 114.2, *cardiovascular disease* 114.13, *lead* 126.12, *canoeing techniques* 150.11, *rowing techniques* 150.16, *rowing* 150.27, *row* 150.32, *golf shots* 156.4, *field hockey techniques* 158.5, *play field hockey* 158.10, *swimming techniques* 164.2, *gesture* 183.17, *type of touch* 216.3, *touch* 216.9, *communication of love* 299.6, *communicate love* 299.25, *deed* 412.2, *compliment* 437.4, *corporal punishment* 454.11, *massage* 554.16, *spasm* 684.8, *blow* 695.5, *hit* 695.11, *stratagem* 822.2

stroked *billiard* 149.6

stroke of genius *masterpiece* 127.5, *cause of wonder* 294.4, *deed* 412.2

stroke of luck *opportunity* 659.2

stroke play *golf* 156.1, *golfing terms* 156.3

stroke side *rowboat parts* 150.15

stroking *touching* 216.2, *massage* 554.6

stroll *bodily movement* 677.11, *walk* 677.17, *slow motion* 693.3, *move slowly* 693.11

strolling *slow* 693.7

stromatolite *algal product* 47.15

strong 516.9; *windy* 9.42, *acid* 11.27, *mechanical* 14.44,

authoritative 52.9, *drinkable* 93.18, *of good constitution* 113.5, *intoxicating* 121.29, *emphatic* 200.3, *piquant* 221.6, *colorful* 251.11, *tenacious* 376.9, *enduring* 377.9, *active* 414.13, *moral* 431.9, *offensive* 432.11, *principled* 447.6, *influential* 512.8, *physically strong* 516.10, *vigorous* 518.2, *dense* 540.6, *tough* 542.6, 547.6, *intense* 598.16, *stable* 674.3, *sound* 759.8, *invulnerable* 810.18

strong acid *acid* 11.10

strong alkali *base* 11.11

strong-arm *compelling* 428.6, *force* 428.10

strong-arm man *combatant* 77.1, *person of strength* 516.8, *surveillant* 810.12

strong-arm tactics *coercive method* 428.3, *violence by person* 520.2

strong as a horse *or* **an ox** *of good constitution* 113.5, *physically strong* 516.10

strongbox *vault* 105.9, *safe* 464.4, *money storage* 484.20

strong breeze *wind strength* 9.13

strong card *skill* 127.1

strong cheese *unpleasant-smelling thing* 227.2

strong currency *international finance* 457.2

strong drink *alcohol* 121.5

strong feeling *emotion* 266.3, *energy* 414.4

strong flavor *flavor* 219.3, *piquancy* 221.1

strong gale *wind strength* 9.13

strong hand *means* 102.1, *severity* 424.1

stronghold *fortification* 419.12, 812.3

strong in *educated* 48.19

strong in spirit 516.11

strong interaction *fundamental interaction* 10.65

strong language *emphasis* 200.1, *offensive language* 301.5

strongly 516.17; *authoritatively* 52.18, *emphatically* 200.7, *influentially* 512.14, *powerfully* 514.21, *densely* 540.10, *toughly* 542.12, 547.16, *intensely* 598.28, *stably* 674.9

strongly worded *affirmed* 189.11, *emphatic* 200.3

strongman *circus performer* 138.9, *person of strength* 516.8

strong-minded *strong-willed* 376.10

strong nuclear interaction *fundamental interaction* 10.65

strong point *skill* 127.1, *fortification* 419.12, *special skill* 779.2

strong possibility 836.3; *chance* 838.4

strongroom *storehouse* 105.8, *money storage* 484.20

strong safety *defense* 155.9

strong side *offense* 155.6

strong smell *odor* 224.1

strong-smelling *strong to the senses* 516.12

strong sun *sun* 9.21

strong-tasting *strong to the senses* 516.12

strong to the senses 516.12

strong vocational interest test Psychological Tests 108

strong-willed 376.10; *iron-willed* 372.7, *determined* 379.7

strong wind *wind strength* 9.13, *roughness* 544.1

strong woman *person of strength* 516.8

strontium Chemical Elements and Common Allotropes 11

strop *sharpener* 549.8, *sharpen* 549.16

strophe *part of poem* 139.9

stroppy [Brit inf] *disorderly* 766.15

struck *instrumental* 142.8

struck dumb *speechless* 206.7, *astonished* 292.6

struck jury *jury* 54.11

struck off *excluded* 764.6, *canceled* 834.5

struck out *canceled* 834.5

structural 11.28, 14.45, 551.17; *of grammar* 5.41, *status adjectives* 11.25, *bodily* 19.18, *material* 104.8, *productive* 522.11, *quintessential* 723.8

structural connection *superstructure* 551.7

structural design *shipbuilding* 690.4

structural engineer *civil engineer* 14.19

structural engineering *civil engineering* 14.17

structural formula *structure* 11.7

structural framework *superstructure* 551.7

structural-functional *socioeconomic* 2.13

structural-functionalism *sociological research* 2.2

structural gene *genetic material* 13.20

structural geology *geology* 8.1

structural glass *industrial ceramics* 129.6

structural grammar *grammar* 5.28

structuralism Philosophical Schools of Thought 4, Linguistic Studies 5, Western Literary Groups 139

structural isomer(ism) *structure* 11.7

structuralist *anthropological* 1.10, Philosophical Schools of Thought 4

structural linguistics Linguistic Studies 5, *grammar* 5.28

structural loading *load* 14.14

structurally 14.52, 551.24, 577.14; *linguistically* 5.44, *architecturally* 134.14, *texturally* 552.15

structural material *construction material* 14.21

structural member *superstructure* 551.7

structural model *shipbuilding* 690.4

structural polysaccharide *polysaccharide* 12.5

structural psychology Psychological Theories, Schools 108

structural test *shipbuilding* 690.4

structure 11.7, 14.20, 551.1, 551.20; *phrasing* 5.25, *crystal* 11.14, *anatomy* 13.12, *skeleton* 19.2, *architectural structure* 134.4, *be an architect* 134.13, *aspect of fiction* 139.5, *production* 522.1, *construction* 522.9, *produce* 522.13, *matter* 524.4, *design* 536.2, *fashion* 536.7, *texture* 552.1, *contents* 577.1, *embody* 577.11, *form* 624.9, *essence* 723.1, *state* 725.1, *unification* 752.5, *order* 765.1, 765.18, *method*

765.7, array 767.2, arrange 767.18

structured *architectural* 134.12, *designed* 537.5, *containing* 577.7, *ordered* 765.10, *arranged* 767.11

structured programming *programming concepts* 15.24

structuring 551.5; *arrangement* 767.1, *organization* 767.3

strudel *pie* 90.38

struggle *war* 76.1, *exertion* 122.4, *exert oneself* 122.11, *persevere* 377.10, *attempt* 390.1, *try hard* 390.7, *undertaking* 391.1, *contention* 422.1, *contest* 422.4, *warfare* 422.10, *contend* 422.22, *dispute* 463.3, 463.9, *pitch* 684.25, *difficult task* 824.3, *have difficulty* 824.18, *adversity* 848.1

struggle against *contend* 422.22

struggler *combatant* 77.1, *attempter* 390.3, *fighter* 422.14

struggle up *climb* 713.21

struggle with *find difficult* 824.17

struggling *contending* 422.19, *violent* 520.5

struggling for breath *dying* 29.12

strum *sound* 141.15, *mean nothing* 362.10

strumming *nonsense* 362.2

strumpet *loose woman* 33.6, *sexually immoral person* 432.8

strung out *lengthened* 590.10, *sparse* 796.6

strung-out [Inf] *drugged* 121.30

strung together *improvised* 396.4

strut *carpenter's term* 131.5, *carpenter* 131.10, *pride oneself* 297.13, *show off* 402.15, 404.26, *superstructure* 551.7, *supporting part* 605.3, *bodily movement* 677.11, *walk* 677.17, *means of connection* 754.4

struthious *avian* 36.19

strutting *carpenter's term* 131.5, *prideful* 297.8, *exhibitionism* 404.9, *swaggering* 404.20

struttingly *swaggeringly* 404.35

strychnine *alkaloid* 12.19, *poison* 117.7

Strzelecki *Deserts* 572

St. Thomas *Islands* 572

Stuart *Furniture Styles* 101

Stuart architecture *Architectural Styles* 134

stub *tobacco* 121.23, *record* 185.1, *promise* 464.2, *receipt* 492.1, *blunt* 550.5, *remainder* 750.1

stubbily *smoothly* 550.10, *shortly* 591.12

stubbiness *bluntness* 550.1, *shortness* 591.1

stubble *crop* 16.8, *body covering* 19.4, *cereal grass* 45.4, *rough skin* 544.3, *residue* 750.2, *refuse* 802.5

stubbled *barbed* 544.7

stubbly *barbed* 544.7

stubborn *willful* 372.8, *tenacious* 376.9, 755.6, *strong-willed* 376.10, *persevering* 377.6, *obstinate* 379.5, 417.7, *defiant* 416.5, *severe* 424.5, *disobedient* 427.10, *mentally hard* 542.8, *mentally tough* 547.12, *determined* 674.5, *conservative* 815.13, *troublesome* 824.13, *uncooperative* 828.14, *convinced* 840.8

stubborn as a mule *obstinate* 379.5

stubbornly *obstinately* 379.11, *defiantly* 416.9, *severely* 424.11, *disobediently* 427.14, *inflexibly* 542.13, *single-mindedly* 547.19, *determinedly* 674.10, *tenaciously*

755.12, *conservatively* 815.17, *perversely* 824.27, *opposingly* 828.22, *with certainty* 840.16

stubbornness *willfulness* 372.3, *tenacity* 376.4, 755.2, *perseverance* 377.1, *obstinacy* 379.1, 417.2, *severity* 424.1, *disobedience* 427.1, *impenitence* 452.1, *mental hardness* 542.4, *mental toughness* 547.5, *determination* 674.2, *preservation of status quo* 815.8, *contrariness* 828.5, *conviction* 840.2

stubborn persistence *determination* 379.2

stubby *blunt* 550.5, *short* 591.6

stucco *Architectural Elements* 134, *material* 144.6, *wall covering* 613.12, *face* 613.31

stuck *holed* 583.12, *motionless* 678.4, *tied* 752.13, *connected* 754.11, *adhering* 755.7, *troubled* 824.15

stuck fast *stable* 674.3

stuck firm *or* **fast** *retained* 471.6

stuck on [Inf] *in love* 299.16

stuck on oneself [Inf] *self-admiring* 402.10, *egotistic* 444.5

stuck-out tongue *gesture* 183.5

stuck-up [Inf] *arrogant* 297.9, *vain* 402.8

stud *male animal* 32.15, Collective Names 59, *carpenter's term* 131.5, *horse* 159.1, *variegate* 263.11, *make rough* 544.11, *sprinkle* 776.15

stud [Inf] *sex object* 20.8, *male* 32.1, *libertine* 32.7, *charmer* 700.6

studded *mottled* 263.10, *coarse* 544.6, *sprinkled* 776.9

studding *sprinkling* 776.4

student *learner* 48.6, *unskilled person* 128.3, *intellectual* 315.7, *questioner* 333.9, *beginner* 771.14, *subordinate* 832.3

student days *youth* 26.1

student loan *loan* 475.2

student number *personal identification* 184.4

student nurse *nurse* 107.23

student of literature *literary person* 139.14

students 777.6

student teacher *educator* 48.4

studhorse *male animal* 32.15, *horse* 159.1

studied *questioned* 333.15, *intentional* 374.7, *deliberate* 384.5, 589.18

studier of humankind 18.7

studio 124.6; *apartment* 60.7, *room* 60.9, *material* 143.9, *radio broadcasting* 172.4, *place of experimentation* 335.6

studio couch *couch* 101.7

studio flash *lighting* 132.16

studio lighting *lighting* 132.16

studio photograph *portrait* 132.5

studio photography *photographic specialties* 132.2

studious *thoughtful* 4.17, *educated* 48.19, *diligent* 323.7, *industrious* 414.16

studiously 48.26; *thoughtfully* 4.27, *attentively* 323.14

studiousness *learnedness* 48.8, *diligence* 323.4, *assiduity* 414.8

stud poker *Card Games* 168, *poker* 168.5

study *philosophical investigation* 4.4, *philosophize* 4.19, *learning* 48.7, *learn* 48.23, *room* 60.9, *diagnosis* 107.8, *test* 107.10, *home workplace* 124.3, *work of art* 133.4, *nonfiction* 139.6, *drawing* 143.4,

dissertation 203.1, *observation* 242.5, *inspect* 242.22, *thoughtfulness* 317.2, *concentrate* 317.10, *scrutinize* 323.11, *raise the point* 328.10, *questioning* 333.2, *question* 333.16, *get to know* 348.12, *future intention* 374.3, *preparations* 388.2, *prepare oneself* 388.21, *behave toward* 399.20, *solitary place* 409.4, *specialize* 779.16, *get better* 807.21

studying *thoughtful* 4.17

study of algae 47.12

study of conduct 399.3

study of ferns 46.3

study of fish 38.2

study of fungi 47.9

study of hearing 228.3

study of humankind 18.6

study of insects 40.2

study of lichens 47.17

study of life 28.9

study of mosses *moss plant* 46.5

study of mountains 569.4

study of names *nomenclature* 202.7

study of place names *nomenclature* 202.7

study of the past 651.9; *history* 3.1

study plants 41.23

study the Bible *theologize* 81.28

study theology *theologize* 81.28

study up on *learn* 48.23

stuff 577.12; *feed* 90.41, *cook* 91.10, *be excessive* 99.9, *materials* 104.1, *be greedy* 119.4, *senseless talk* 362.4, *possession of property* 469.3, *possessions* 470.5, *matter* 524.4, *textile* 552.5, *substance* 577.2, *swell* 581.15, *essence* 723.1, *fill* 761.11, *refuse* 802.5, *preserve* 815.14

stuff and nonsense *senseless talk* 362.4

stuff and nonsense! *nonsense!* 362.14

stuffed *culinary* 91.9, *eating* 92.18, *immoderate* 99.6, *gluttonous* 119.3, *loaded* 577.8, *swelled* 581.10, *obstructed* 584.8, *inset* 710.8, *ornamental* 748.9, *full* 761.8, *preserved* 815.12

stuffed animal *toy* 167.9, *figure* 187.4, *preserved thing* 815.10

stuffed grape leaves *notable international dishes* 90.40

stuffed shirt *vain person* 402.7

stuffed up *stopped* 584.9

stuffily *boringly* 296.10, *affectedly* 367.5, *pompously* 404.33

stuff in *impact* 710.11

stuffiness *heat* 217.1, *boringness* 296.2, *pomposity* 404.5, *formality* 406.1

stuffing 577.4; *side dish* 90.15, *gluttonous* 119.3, *enlarger* 581.8, *stopper* 584.3, *insert* 710.4, *additional item* 748.3, *preservation of body* 815.7

stuffing oneself *appetite* 92.2

stuff oneself *eat well* 92.23, *be greedy* 119.4

stuffy *unhygienic* 114.27, *hot* 217.11, *boring* 296.6, *pompous* 404.18, *condensed* 540.7, *conformist* 781.10

stumble *be clumsy* 128.9, *misjudge* 342.9, *be wrong* 430.18, *stagger* 684.11, *pitch* 684.25, *fall* 714.4

stumblebum [Inf] *unskilled person* 128.3

stumble upon *or on* *discover*

345.11, *reach* 704.14, *chance upon* 842.13

stumbling *clumsy* 128.6, *fall* 714.4, *falling* 714.11

stumbling block *trap* 813.1, *obstacle* 826.2, *restraint* 830.1

stump *tree part* 43.2, *run for office* 50.10, *mystify* 182.12, *confuse* 333.20, *puzzle* 364.12, *remainder* 750.1, *component* 760.3, *cause difficulties* 824.22, *make uncertain* 841.19

stump along *move slowly* 693.11

stumped *confused* 364.10, *troubled* 824.15

stumper *difficult question* 333.4

stumpily *shortly* 591.12

stumpiness *shortness* 591.1, *lowness* 597.1

stump orator *public speaker* 209.5

stump oratory *public speaking* 205.11

stumpy *short* 591.6, *low* 597.10

stun *box* 152.19, *anesthetize* 213.8, *deafen* 229.10, *shatter the peace* 232.10, *astonish* 292.10, *be wondrous* 294.14

stun and stab *billiards play* 149.2

stung *offended* 302.9

stunned *desensitized* 213.5, *deaf* 229.4, *astonished* 292.6, *wondering* 294.7

stunner [Inf] *wonderful person* 294.6

stunning *blinding* 243.13, *beautiful* 529.7

stunningly *gorgeously* 529.14

stunt *workmanlike job* 127.6, *defense* 155.9, *play defense* 155.19, *ski* 162.27, *method* 387.4, *show* 404.12, *deed* 412.2, *do great deeds* 412.14, *contract* 582.12

stunted *underfed* 98.7, *undersized* 580.8, *shortened* 582.8, *short* 591.6, *low* 597.10

stuntedness *littleness* 580.1, *shortness* 591.1, *lowness* 597.1

stunting *contracting* 582.10

stunt man *or* **woman** *alternative* 80.2, *actor* 137.13, *courageous person* 284.8, *performer* 412.5, *substitute* 613.17, 672.2

stunt person *actor* 137.13, *courageous person* 284.8

stunt skiing *skiing* 162.1

stupa *shrine* 83.10

stupefaction *desensitization* 213.2, *astonishment* 292.2, *wonder* 294.1

stupefied *dead drunk* 121.27, *astonished* 292.6, *wondering* 294.7

stupefy *be intoxicating* 121.36, *anesthetize* 213.8, *astonish* 292.10, *be wondrous* 294.14

stupefying *astonishing* 292.8, 294.10

stupefyingly *surprisingly* 292.14, *astonishingly* 294.19

stupendous *wondrous* 294.9, *huge* 579.14

stupendously *wondrously* 294.18

stupid *unskillful* 128.4, *unintelligent* 316.6, *foolish* 353.5, *thick-witted* 594.7

stupid from fatigue *fatigued* 820.2

stupidity *lack of intellect* 316.1, *ignorance* 318.2, *thick-wittedness* 594.3

stupidly *unintelligently* 316.9, *foolishly* 353.8, *ridiculously* 368.8, *thick-wittedly* 594.13

stupid question *easy question* 333.5

stupor *mood disorder* 108.12, *trance*

108.18, *desensitization* 213.2, *apathy* 322.2, *oblivion* 355.4, *sleep* 415.5

stuporous *apathetic* 322.4

sturdily *strongly* 516.17, *toughly* 547.16

sturdiness *toughness* 547.1, *thickness* 594.1

sturdy *of good constitution* 113.5, *physically strong* 516.10, *tough* 547.6, *thick* 594.5

Sturm und Drang *theater movements* 136.9, *Western Literary Groups* 139

Sturt Stony *Deserts* 572

stutter *be drunk* 121.34, *be clumsy* 128.9, *mode of speech* 205.6, *speech defect* 206.2, *have difficulty speaking* 206.9

stuttering *drunken behavior* 121.4, *clumsy* 128.6, *speech defect* 206.2, *inarticulate* 206.6, *Phobias* 283, *unintelligibility* 364.1

St. Vincent and the Grenadines *Countries* 566

St. Vincent de Paul Society *charitable organization* 305.4

St. Vincent Island *Islands* 572

St. Vitus's dance *neurological disease* 114.20, *shake* 684.7

sty *farm building* 16.4, *mammal dwelling* 35.21, *cage* 60.15, *mark* 533.2, *enclosed area* 619.2, *shelter* 812.4

sty *or* **stye** *eye disease* 243.4

Stygian *dark* 247.5

Stygian creek *evil place* 446.6

Stygian gloom *darkness* 247.1

Stygian shores *evil place* 446.6

stygiophobia *Phobias* 283

style 537.1, 537.8; *organs of reproduction* 21.9, *flower part* 42.3, *social skill* 127.3, *material* 144.6, *power of speech* 205.5, *title* 209.12, *external appearance* 264.5, *meaning* 361.1, *mode of behavior* 399.2, *elegance* 527.1, *coiffure* 530.8, *coif* 530.15, *decoration* 532.1, *refinement* 534.1, *fashion* 536.1, *design* 536.2, 536.8, *mode of expression* 537.3, *way* 691.1, *mode* 725.2, *array* 767.2, *type* 777.4, *distinction* 777.8, *convention* 781.5

style-conscious *fashionable* 536.5

styled 537.6; *tailored* 100.41, *beautified* 530.12, *designed* 536.6, 537.5, *formed* 624.6

style of cooking *cooking* 91.1

style sheet *mode of expression* 537.3

stylet *sharp weapon* 78.6

styling gel *pomade* 562.9

styling mousse *pomade* 562.9

stylish 100.42, 537.7; *well-made* 127.13, *elegant* 527.3, *fashionable* 536.5, *formed* 624.6, *conditional* 725.7

stylishly *dressily* 100.47, *skillfully* 127.16, *elegantly* 527.7, 534.8, *fashionably* 536.9, *stylistically* 537.11, *formatively* 624.10, *in good form* 725.11

stylishness 537.2; *fashion* 536.1

stylish writer *stylist* 537.4

stylist 537.4

stylistic *styled* 537.6

stylistical *styled* 537.6

stylistically 537.11

stylistics *Linguistic Studies* 5

stylite *religious* 84.9, *loner* 788.8

stylization *formality* 406.1

stylize *formalize* 406.9, *fashion* 537.9

stylized *artistic* 133.7, *formal* 406.6, *designed* 536.6, *styled* 537.6, *formed* 624.6

styloid process *Human Bones* 19

stylus *sharp-pointed thing* 549.4

stymie *hinder* 826.15

styptic *dense* 540.6, *contractor* 582.6, *contracting* 582.10

Styx *evil place* 446.6

suable *litigated* 54.22

suasion *persuasion* 178.1

suasive *persuasive* 178.12

suasively *persuasively* 178.21

suasiveness *persuasion* 178.1

suave *refined* 48.20, *good-mannered* 410.7, *graceful* 527.4, *smooth-mannered* 545.9

suavely 545.15; *discerningly* 48.27, *genteelly* 410.14, *gracefully* 527.8

suaveness *courtesy* 410.1, *grace* 527.2

suavity *refinement* 48.10, *courtesy* 410.1, *grace* 527.2

sub [Inf] *alternative* 80.2, *sandwich* 90.9, *basketball team* 148.2, *football player* 155.15, *soccer participant* 163.4, *substitute* 613.17, *cover for* 613.34, *substitute* 672.2

subacid *acid* 223.5

subacidity *sourness* 223.1

subalpine *lowland* 597.15

subaltern *servant* 69.1, *inferior* 745.4

subaltern proposition *philosophical term* 4.7

subaqua *oceanic* 571.7

subaquatic *oceanic* 571.7, *under* 598.13

subaqueous *swimming* 164.12, *oceanic* 571.7, *under* 598.13

subaqueous swimming *swimming* 164.1

subatomic *tiny* 580.9

subatomically *microscopically* 580.14

subatomic particle *elementary particle* 10.53, *little thing* 580.3

subaudition *interpretation* 365.1

subbasement *room* 60.9

sub-bottom profiling *oceanography* 571.5

subbranch *component* 760.3, *taxonomic classification* 777.3

subcategory *category* 767.6, *class* 777.1

subchaser *Ships and Boats* 690

subclass *category* 767.6, *class* 777.1, *taxonomic classification* 777.3

subcommittee *council* 423.4

subconscious *psyche* 86.17, *psyche* 108.25, *unconscious* 108.40, *instinct* 320.4, *internal world* 525.6, *internal* 525.11, *latency* 844.1, *latent* 844.6

subconsciously *occultly* 86.27, *psychologically* 108.42, *latently* 844.15

subconsciousness *latency* 844.1

subcontinent *continent* 8.8, *landmass* 572.1

subcontinental *of landmasses* 572.12

subcontinentally *continentally* 572.13

subcortical *interior* 611.7

subcutaneous *skin* 19.19, *interior* 611.7

subdivide *add* 6.86, *allocate* 474.5, *itemize* 577.13, *divide* 753.18, 787.7, *part* 760.14, *sort* 777.13

subdivided *itemized* 577.9, *separate* 753.7

subdivision *allocation* 474.1,

division 577.6, *separateness* 753.3, *piece* 760.2, *category* 767.6, *class* 777.1, *fractional part* 787.2

subdivisional *fractional* 787.5

subdominant *musical note* 140.15

subduction zone *plate tectonics* 8.19

subdue *master* 68.17, *conciliate* 74.10, *conquer* 77.36, *silence* 231.4, *mute* 233.9, *take over* 477.16, *be an influence* 512.13, *calm* 521.8, *ease* 543.15, *restrain* 830.12, *subject* 832.10, *be victorious* 845.16

subdued *reserved* 195.11, *nonresonant* 233.7, *submitting* 421.3, *moderate* 521.3

subduedness *reserve* 195.5

subdue oneself *capitulate* 421.6

subduing *taking over* 477.3

subedit *report* 175.9

subeditor *print journalist* 175.5

subfamily *taxonomic classification* 777.3

subfuscous *or* **subfusc** *dark-colored* 247.7

subgenus *taxonomic classification* 777.3

subgiant *star luminosity* 7.12

subgroup *category* 767.6, *class* 777.1

subhead *book part* 174.5

subheading *class* 777.1

subhuman *human* 18.15, *animalian* 34.12, *cruel* 306.10

subito *Musical Terms and Expression Marks* 140

subjacency *lowest point* 597.5

subjacent *lower* 597.14

subjacently *low* 597.26

subject 48.3, 832.6, 832.10; *part of speech* 5.30, *national* 61.3, *obedient* 69.10, *aspect of fiction* 139.5, *melody* 140.10, *material* 143.9, *topic* 328.1, *educational topic* 328.4, *gist* 329.4, *experimental subject* 335.7, *suppress* 424.9, *giver* 472.7, *take over* 477.16, *helpless* 515.9, *undertaking* 675.5, *essence* 723.1, *subordinate* 745.8, *be victorious* 845.16

subjected *suppressed* 424.6, *subject* 832.6

subjected person 832.5

subject-group *students* 777.6

subjecting *subject* 832.6

subjection 832.1; *military attack* 418.2, *suppression* 424.2, *taking over* 477.3

subjective *of grammar* 5.41, *focused* 328.6, *unjust* 342.7, *imaginary* 360.12, *internal* 525.11

subjectively 525.14; *grammatically* 5.48, *unjustly* 342.13

subjective probability *probability theory* 838.5

subjectivism *Philosophical Schools of Thought* 4, *reverie* 360.6

subjectivist *Philosophical Schools of Thought* 4

subjectivity *fallibility* 351.6, *internal world* 525.6

subject matter *topic* 328.1, *meaning* 361.1, *division* 577.6, *essential content* 723.2

subject-matter jurisdiction *jurisdiction* 54.2

subject to *caused* 676.5

subject to jurisdiction *jurisdictional* 53.18, 54.23

subject to terms *negotiated* 460.5

subjoin *add* 748.11

subjoined *additional* 748.8

sub judice *litigated* 54.22, *judged* 341.9

subjugate *master* 68.17, *suppress* 424.9, *take over* 477.16, *be an influence* 512.13, *subject* 832.10, *be victorious* 845.16

subjugated *suppressed* 424.6, *subject* 832.6

subjugation *suppression* 424.2, *taking over* 477.3, *subjection* 832.1, *defeat* 846.7

subjugator *victor* 845.7

subjunctive *grammatical term* 5.29

subjunctively *grammatically* 5.48

subkingdom *taxonomic classification* 777.3

sublease *possession of property* 469.3

sublimate *purify* 111.19, *refine* 534.7, *gasify* 556.23, *extract* 711.8, *improve* 807.15

sublimated *atmospheric* 9.40, *status adjectives* 11.25, *pure* 431.11, *cultured* 534.6

sublimation *atmospheric process* 9.9, *temperature* 10.29, *phase* 11.13, *defense mechanism* 108.23, *vaporization* 556.9, *obtaining of an extract* 711.7, *improvement* 807.1

sublimation point *temperature* 10.29

sublime *heat* 10.74, *divine* 82.16, *serious* 200.5, *pleasant* 271.5, *unselfish* 443.5, *beautiful* 529.7, *insubstantial* 539.5, *gasify* 556.23, *exalted* 596.10, *promoted* 715.8, *excellent* 805.15

sublime [Arch] *high* 596.7

sublimely *divinely* 82.24, *unselfishly* 443.9, *magnificently* 529.16, *lightly* 539.10, *exaltedly* 596.22

sublimely [Arch] *high* 596.20

sublimeness *beauty* 529.1

subliminal *psyche* 108.25, *unconscious* 108.40, *difficult to see* 245.4, *latent* 844.6

subliminally *psychologically* 108.42, *latently* 844.15

subliminal self *psyche* 108.25

sublimity *seriousness* 200.2, *unselfishness* 443.2, *exaltation* 596.3, *height* 596.1, 715.4, *superiority* 744.1, *latency* 844.1

sublittoral *oceanic* 571.7

submachine gun *firearm* 78.7

submarine *oceanic* 8.53, 571.7, *warship* 77.21, *sandwich* 90.9, *bathymetry* 598.3, *under* 598.13, *Ships and Boats* 690, *descender* 714.8

submarine canyon *ocean floor* 8.18

submarine chaser *warship* 77.21, *Ships and Boats* 690

submariner *naval person* 77.25, *closed-in person* 584.6, *descender* 714.8

submarine warfare *naval warfare* 76.10, *naval commands* 77.19

submediant *musical note* 140.15

submerge *destroy* 186.10, *abolish* 523.11, *water* 557.29, *flow* 570.10, *deepen* 599.21, *immerse* 710.12, *descend* 714.12, *bring down* 716.14, *hide* 844.13

submerged *invisible* 245.3, *flooded* 557.24, *lowland* 597.15, *under* 598.13, *immersed* 710.7, *fallen* 716.8, *latent* 844.6

submerged coast *coast* 572.4

submerged log *navigational aid* 690.6

submergence 716.3; *immersion*

598.8, 710.3, *sinkage* 714.2, *concealment* 844.2

submerse *water* 557.29, *deepen* 598.21

submersed *flooded* 557.24, *under* 598.13, *immersed* 710.7

submersible *bathymetry* 598.3, *descending* 714.9

submersion *soaking* 557.9, *flow* 570.4, *immersion* 598.8, 710.3

subminiature *undersized* 580.8

submission 421.1; *recommendation* 176.2, *contention* 359.1, *supposition* 359.1, *servility* 401.1, *obedience* 426.1, *deference* 433.4, *tentative offer* 504.2, *compliance* 781.2, *defeat* 846.7

submissive 298.10; *pacific* 74.7, *servile* 401.6, *submitting* 421.3, *obedient* 426.4, *deferential* 433.9, *showing respect* 435.7, *compliant* 781.9, *easygoing* 823.13

submissively 298.23; *servilely* 401.15, *obediently* 426.9, *soft-heartedly* 543.19, *adaptably* 781.15

submissiveness 298.3; *servility* 401.1, *submission* 421.1, *obedience* 426.1

submit 298.17, 421.4; *advise* 176.9, *be persuaded* 178.20, *contend* 189.24, *assent to* 346.7, *propound* 359.9, *be servile* 401.8, *succumb* 421.7, *obey* 426.7, *offer* 504.11, *yield* 543.17, *follow* 745.12, *conform* 781.11

submit a report *recount* 202.16

submitted *contended* 189.15

submitted for judgment *litigated* 54.22, *judged* 341.9

submitter 421.2

submitting 421.3; *pacific* 74.7, *submission* 421.1, *obedient* 426.4, *showing respect* 435.7

submit to *bear* 605.17

submit to a whim *be capricious* 381.6

submit to judgment *stand trial* 54.29

submontane *lowland* 597.15

submultiple *multiplication* 6.15

subnormal *intellectually subnormal* 316.7, *low quality* 745.7

subnormally *badly* 745.15

suboceanic *oceanic* 8.53

suborder *category* 767.6, *taxonomic classification* 777.3

subordinacy *subjection* 832.1

subordinate 745.8, 832.3, 832.8; *servant* 69.1, *instrumental* 511.4, *lack of authority* 515.2, *lowly* 597.17, *inferior* 745.4, *nonentity* 800.8, *helper* 825.12, *subject* 832.10

subordinate clause *clause* 5.31

subordinated *lowered* 597.18

subordinately *humbly* 597.27, *basely* 745.16

subordinate position *inferiority* 745.1, *subjection* 832.1

subordinate role *subjection* 832.1

subordinating *of grammar* 5.41

subordinating conjunction *part of speech* 5.30

subordination *instrumentality* 511.1, *lowliness* 597.8, *humbling* 597.9, *inferiority* 745.1, *position* 765.4, *compliance* 781.2, *subjection* 832.1

suborn *bribe* 178.18, *buy off* 481.17

subornation *bribery* 481.5

subphylum *taxonomic classification* 777.3

subplane *windsurf* 150.33

subplaning *windsurfing* 150.28

subplot *dramaturgy* 136.6, *script* 137.5, *aspect of fiction* 139.5, *gist* 329.4

subpoena *pretrial proceedings* 54.13, *demand* 425.2, 425.11

subpoena witnesses *try a case* 54.28

subpolar zone *climate zone* 9.36

sub rosa *secretly* 182.14

subscribe *identify oneself* 184.12, *pay* 489.16, *give* 498.11, *make an offering* 504.17

subscriber *telephone personnel* 169.14, *assenter* 346.3, *giver* 472.7, *generous person* 498.5

subscribe to *propound a philosophy* 4.21, *assent* 346.6, *contract* 459.8, *agree with* 462.10, *give* 472.10

subscribe to [Brit] *advise* 825.27

subscript *appendage* 748.4

subscription *giving* 472.1, *offering* 472.6, 504.5, *fee* 494.3, *gift* 498.3

subscription television *television (TV)* 172.5

subsection *part of writing* 760.6, *class* 777.1

subsequence 770.4; *sequence* 770.1

subsequent *caused* 676.5, *sequential* 770.7

subsequently *with the effect of* 676.12, *after* 770.14

subserve *be useful* 801.9, *further* 825.30

subservience *submissiveness* 298.3, *servility* 401.1, *submission* 421.1, *obedience* 426.1, *instrumentality* 511.1, *lowliness* 597.8, *inferiority* 745.1, *subjection* 832.1

subservient *submissive* 298.10, *used* 393.5, *servile* 401.6, *submitting* 421.3, *obedient* 426.4, *instrumental* 511.4, 801.7, *lowly* 597.17, *insignificant* 745.6, *subordinate* 745.8, 832.8, *supplementary* 825.17

subserviently *submissively* 298.23, *servilely* 401.15, *obediently* 426.9, *instrumentally* 511.9, *humbly* 597.27, *basely* 745.16, *dependently* 832.13

subset *set* 6.19, *class* 777.1

subshell *atom* 10.52

subside *pause* 415.15, *be in motion* 677.14, *descend* 714.12, *decrease* 747.7

subsidence *earth movement* 8.20, *sinkage* 714.2, *decrease* 747.1

subsidiary *ancillary* 605.5, 605.14, *inferior* 745.4, *subordinate* 745.8, *additional* 748.8, *secondary* 800.15, *instrumental* 801.7, *supplementary* 825.17

subsidiary office *office* 124.2

subsiding *directional* 677.13, *descending* 714.9, *decreasing* 747.5

subsiding motion *descending motion* 677.6

subsidization *giving* 472.1, *patronage* 825.9

subsidize *find means* 102.6, *grant* 453.14, *fund* 472.15, *support financially* 605.19, *finance* 825.31

subsidized *given* 472.8, *sustaining* 605.15

subsidizer *provider* 605.10

subsidy *resources* 102.4, *grant* 453.4, 489.7, *profit* 467.6, *gift* 472.2, *financial support* 605.8, *financial assistance* 825.6

subsist *live* 28.17, *eat* 92.21, *be*

permanent 667.4, *exist* 717.18, *be left* 750.9

subsistence *life* 28.1, *financial support* 605.8, *permanence* 667.1, *existence* 717.1, *sustenance* 825.3

subsistence farming *agriculture* 16.1

subsistence level *incompleteness* 98.2, *poverty* 486.1

subsistent *existing* 717.11

subsisting *permanent* 667.2, *unfailing* 667.3

subsoil *soil* 8.42, *interior* 611.1

subsoiler *farm tool* 16.5

subsoil plow *farm tool* 16.5

subsonic *physical* 10.70, *sounding* 230.7, *flyable* 689.12

subsonically *physically* 10.78, *aeronautically* 689.17

subsonic speed *sound propagation* 230.3, *speed* 694.2

subsonic transport *aircraft* 689.3

subspecies *taxonomic classification* 777.3

subspecific *taxonomic* 13.35

substance 577.2; *resources* 102.4, *materials* 104.1, *meaning* 361.1, *personal estate* 470.6, *solvency* 485.4, *matter* 524.4, *fabric* 551.2, *form* 624.1, *thing* 717.3, *real world* 719.2, *reality* 721.2, *essence* 723.1, *quantity* 738.1, *importance* 799.1, *gist* 799.4

substance abuse 121.1; *disease* 114.4, *psychiatric disease* 114.21, *ill-use* 395.2, *moral deterioration* 808.3

substance abuser *creature of habit* 397.8

substance-related disorders *mental disorder* 108.8

substandard 597.19; *of language* 5.35, *unsatisfactory* 274.5, *insufficient* 517.11, *low quality* 745.7

substandard housing *beggary* 486.3

substandard language *nonstandard language* 5.7

substandard usage *nonstandard language* 5.7

substantial *touchable* 216.5, *verificatory* 336.6, *significant* 361.11, *great* 445.14, *strengthened* 516.13, *material* 524.7, *containing* 577.7, *big* 579.13, *thick* 594.5, *intrinsic* 717.12, *real* 719.6, 721.12

substantial capital *wealth* 485.1

substantialism Philosophical Schools of Thought 4

substantialist Philosophical Schools of Thought 4

substantiality *excellence* 445.4, *material world* 524.1, *nature* 717.4, *reality* 719.1, 721.2, *importance* 799.1

substantialize *be material* 524.8

substantially *palpably* 216.12, *materially* 524.9, *structurally* 577.14, *largely* 579.19, *thick* 594.11, *in truth* 721.28, *in essence* 723.13, *on the whole* 759.13

substantial resources *wealth* 485.1

substantiate *identify* 184.11, *attest* 189.22, *prove* 331.17, 336.9, *experiment* 335.11, *justify* 441.12, *be material* 524.8, *establish reality* 719.12, *authenticate* 721.24, *circumstantiate* 726.12, *make certain* 840.14

substantiated *identified* 184.9,

attested 189.13, *proven* 331.13, *authenticated* 721.17

substantiation *identification* 184.1, *attestation* 189.2, *proof* 331.4, 336.2, 339.2, *authentication* 721.8

substantiative *or* **substantiating** *attestive* 189.12

substantive *part of speech* 5.30, *of grammar* 5.41, *intrinsic* 717.12, *real* 719.6, 721.12

substantive editing *stage of book production* 174.7

substantively *in truth* 721.28

substantivity *reality* 719.1

substitutable *substitute* 613.23, *exchangeable* 665.13, *in exchange* 673.3

substitute 613.17, 613.23, 672.2, 672.3, 672.5; *manipulate* 6.87, *react* 11.38, *alternative* 80.2, *deputizing* 80.4, *means* 102.1, *surrogate* 108.29, *agent* 123.15, *actor* 136.25, 137.13, *baseball team* 147.2, *basketball team* 148.2, *football player* 155.15, *soccer participant* 163.4, *representative* 187.7, *helper* 275.5, *stop using* 394.10, *replace* 574.17, *cover for* 613.34, *exchange* 665.21, 673.5, *extra person* 748.7, *subordinate* 832.3, 832.8

substituted 672.4; *exchanged* 673.4

substitute for 80.5; *represent* 79.7, *stand for* 187.14, *aid* 275.10, *cover for* 613.34

substitute teacher *substitute* 613.17, 672.2

substituting *deputizing* 80.4

substitution 672.1; *evaluation* 6.22, *chemical reaction* 11.8, *defense mechanism* 108.23, *repayment* 489.5, *replacement* 574.3, *exchange* 665.8, 673.1

substitutional *reactive* 11.29, *substitute* 672.3

substitutive *substitute* 613.23, 672.3, *in exchange* 673.3

substrate *catalysis* 11.16, *enzyme* 12.11

substrative *lower* 597.14, *foundational* 605.12

substrative *or* **substratal** *interior* 611.7

substratosphere *atmospheric layer* 558.3

substratum *layer* 588.1, *lowest point* 597.5, *base* 601.1, *supporting structure* 605.2, *interior* 611.1

substruction *foundation* 601.2, *supporting structure* 605.2

substructional *base* 601.7, *foundational* 605.12

substructural *structural* 14.45, 551.17, *base* 601.7, *foundational* 605.12

substructurally *structurally* 551.24

substructure 551.8; *structure* 14.20, *construction* 551.6, *foundation* 601.2, *supporting structure* 605.2

subsume 763.7; *embody* 577.11

subsumed *included* 763.4

subsuming *containing* 577.7

subsumption *inclusion* 763.1

subsurface *terrestrial* 8.52

subsurface current *ocean current* 8.15

subsurface water *groundwater* 8.11

subtend *be opposite* 731.4

subterfuge *evasion* 181.5, *secrecy*

182.1, *artifice* 193.5, *sophistry* 330.1, *sophism* 330.2, *trick* 813.2, *stratagem* 822.2

subterrane *the depths* 598.2

subterranean *terrestrial* 8.52, *latent* 844.6

subterranean or **subterraneous** *under* 598.13

subterraneanly *under* 598.26

subterranean river *river* 570.1

subterranean water *groundwater* 8.11

subterraneously *under* 598.26

subterrestrial *under* 598.13

subtitle *brief description* 202.2

subtle 195.9; *accurate* 350.3, *delicate* 552.10, *cunning* 822.4

subtle body *spirit* 86.10

subtlety 195.3, 534.2; *cleverness* 315.3, *quibbling* 330.4, *accuracy* 350.1, *cunning* 822.4

subtly *sophistically* 330.14, *texturally* 552.15

subtonic *musical note* 140.15

subtract 749.6; *add* 6.86, 784.11, *lose* 468.12, *take away* 477.18, *discount* 495.4, *quantify* 738.7, *separate* 753.12

subtracted 749.3; *missing* 576.11

subtracted item 749.2

subtraction 6.14, 749.1; *loss* 468.1, *taking away* 477.5, *decrease* 747.1, *calculation* 784.1

subtractive 749.4

subtractive color *coloring agent* 251.5

subtrahend *subtraction* 6.14, *subtracted item* 749.2

subtribe *taxonomic classification* 777.3

subtropical *ornamental* 17.17, *warm* 217.13, *regional* 564.12

subtropical climate *climate* 9.35

subtropical dry zone *climate zone* 9.36

subtropically *horticulturally* 17.20, *regionally* 564.16

subtropical winter rainy zone *climate zone* 9.36

subtropics *climate zone* 9.36, *world region* 564.6

subungulate *pachyderm* 35.15, *elephantlike* 35.30

suburb 567.11; *urban area* 567.10

suburban *environmental* 60.17, *native* 61.12, *local* 564.14, *urban* 567.14

suburbanite *townsperson* 61.7, *municipal resident* 567.12

suburbanization *society* 2.6, *urbanization* 567.4

suburbanize *urbanize* 567.15

suburbanized *urban* 567.14

suburbia *suburb* 567.11, *middle class* 772.6

subvariety *taxonomic classification* 777.3

subvene *further* 825.30

subvention *grant* 453.4, 489.7, *giving* 472.1, *gift* 472.2, *financial assistance* 825.6

subventionary *given* 472.8

subversion 427.3; *anarchy* 51.1, *dishonorableness* 192.3, *refutation* 332.1, *sudden change* 665.3, *downthrow* 716.2, *moral deterioration* 808.3

subversive 427.11; *anarchist* 51.4, *anarchic* 51.5, *hypocrite* 192.9, *dishonorable* 192.14, *seditionist* 427.7, *destructive* 523.8, *changeable* 665.11

subversively 427.15; *anarchically*

51.10, *dishonorably* 192.28, *changeably* 665.22, *down* 716.24

subversiveness *dishonorableness* 192.3, *subversion* 427.3

subversivism *dishonorableness* 192.3

subvert 427.13; *be anarchic* 51.8, *abolish* 523.11, *knock down* 523.13, *cause change* 665.16, *bring down* 716.14, *pervert* 808.22

subverted *changed* 665.10, *overthrown* 716.9

subway *tunnel* 551.11, 691.6, *concave land* 635.2, *railroad system* 688.1, *railroad* 691.8

subway station *stopping place* 668.4

sub-zero temperature *freezing* 218.2

succedaneum *substitute* 672.2

succeed 770.11; *aid* 275.10, *be good* 445.16, *secure one's objective* 464.12, *be regular* 663.10, *continue* 669.8, *be a substitute* 672.6, *achieve* 704.21, *be in comfortable circumstances* 726.13, *complete* 759.10, *follow* 770.10, *be consecutive* 774.11, *be convenient* 803.5, *get better* 807.21, *be successful* 845.11, *be prosperous* 847.6

succeeding *sequential* 770.7, *consecutive* 774.7, *successful* 845.8

succeed to *gain authority* 52.15, *profit* 467.22, *receive* 473.13

succentor *imam* 84.7

success 845.1; *probability* 6.59, *theatrical performance* 136.13, *advance* 679.3, *comfortable circumstances* 726.5, *superiority* 744.1, *completion* 761.2, *uplift* 807.2, *successful person* 845.6, *prosperity* 847.1, *prosperous person* 847.4

successful 845.8; *prosperous* 847.5

successful attack *victory* 845.4

successful battle *victory* 845.4

successful defense *favorable verdict* 54.19, *defense* 441.2

successfully 845.19; *prosperously* 847.9

successfulness 845.3

successful person 845.6; *prosperous person* 847.4

successful production *theatrical performance* 136.13

successful prosecution *unfavorable verdict* 54.20

successful speculation *gain* 467.1

successful thing 845.5

succession 770.2; *ecology* 13.25, *acquisition of authority* 52.5, *transfer of property* 470.4, *receiving* 473.1, *continuity* 669.1, *sequence* 770.1, *consecutiveness* 774.1

successional *authorized* 52.11, *sequential* 770.7

successive *habitual* 397.9, *sequential* 770.7, *consecutive* 774.7

successively *sequentially* 770.13, *consecutively* 774.15

successiveness *sequence* 770.1, *consecutiveness* 774.1

successor 770.6; *beneficiary* 473.6, *substitute* 672.2, *person remaining* 750.6

successors *future generation* 650.2

success story *fame* 845.2

succinct *concise* 198.4, *summary* 204.5, *sparing with words* 208.6, *short* 591.6

succinctly *concisely* 198.6, *shortly* 591.12

succinctness *conciseness* 198.1, *summariness* 204.4, *guarded speech* 208.3, *shortness* 591.1

succinctly *summarily* 204.10

succor *remedy* 115.1, 115.16, *aid* 275.2, *moral support* 605.7, *supporter* 605.9, *give moral support* 605.18, *support* 825.2, 825.24

succorer *supporter* 825.13

succoring *supportive* 825.18

succotash *notable international dishes* 90.40

succubus *evil spirit* 446.4

succulence *juiciness* 555.7

succulent *garden plant* 17.10, *botanical* 17.15, *plant* 41.2, *of plants* 41.14, *of a fruit* 46.8, *edible* 92.20, *pleasurable* 214.6, *tasty* 219.4, *flowing* 555.15

succulent fruit *botanical fruit* 44.2

succulently *horticulturally* 17.20, *herbaceously* 41.24, *fructiferously* 44.10, *culinarily* 91.11, *edibly* 92.26, *tastily* 219.7, *fluidly* 555.26, *moistly* 559.17

succumb 421.7; *die* 29.17, *be drunk* 121.34, *be persuaded* 178.20, *be motivated* 508.10, *be fatigued* 820.5

succumbing *submission* 421.1

succussatory *shaky* 684.18

succussive *shaky* 684.18

such a one *someone* 18.10

such being the case *conditionally* 725.10, *under the circumstances* 726.16, *accordingly* 735.39

suchlike *counterpart* 733.5, *similar* 733.7

suchness *nature* 723.4

suck *eat* 92.21, *drink* 93.19, *intake* 708.5, *draw in* 708.18, *draw off* 711.16

suck or **suck off** [Inf] *stimulate* 20.22

suck dry *expend* 96.16

sucker *plant breeding* 17.6, *young plant* 26.5, *stem* 41.5, *component* 760.3

sucker [Inf] *believer* 87.5, *foolish person* 353.3, *powerless person* 515.5, *adherent* 755.4, *naive person* 821.2

suck in or **up** *draw in* 708.18

sucking *drinking* 93.1, *intake* 708.5, *drawing off* 711.4

sucking out *drawing off* 711.4

suckle *practice livestock farming* 16.20, *lactate* 35.34, *feed* 90.41, *provide drink* 93.21, *draw in* 708.18

suckler cow *livestock* 16.11

suckling *young mammal* 35.20

suck out *draw off* 711.16

suck up to [Inf] *be solicitous* 323.13, *fawn* 401.9, *cajole* 439.14, *smooth over* 545.12, *seek friendship* 62.11

Sucre *Countries* 566

sucrose *Common Sugars* 12, *food content* 90.3

suction *intake* 708.5, *drawing off* 711.4

Sudan *Countries* 566

Sudanese Fulani *Breeds of Cattle* 16

sudation *sweat* 25.8

sudatorium or **sudatory** *bath* 111.6

sudatory *secretory* 24.4, *inducing secretion* 24.6, *sweaty* 25.17, *expulsive* 709.11

sudd *marsh* 572.3

sudden *surprising* 292.7,

spontaneous 396.5, *transient* 643.4, *swift* 694.6

sudden action *deed* 412.2

sudden change 665.3

sudden death *way of dying* 29.5, *game time* 155.4, *golfing terms* 156.3, *squash terms* 165.10, *extra* 748.6

sudden-death victory *victory* 845.4

suddenly 549.20; *explosively* 234.8, *surprisingly* 292.14, *spontaneously* 396.8, *transiently* 643.8, *soon* 657.18, *hurryingly* 694.18

sudden motion *jolt* 684.9

suddenness *surprise* 292.1, *transience* 643.1

sudden pain *danger signal* 811.5

sudden progress *forward motion* 679.1

sudden pull *jerk* 699.3

sudden thought *spontaneity* 396.2

sudor *sweat* 25.8

sudoral *of a secretion* 24.5

sudoresis *sweat* 25.8

sudoric *sweaty* 25.17

sudorific *inducing secretion* 24.6, *sweaty* 25.17, *expulsive* 709.11

suds *air bubble* 558.10

suds [Inf] *beer* 93.10

sue *litigate* 54.27, *court* 299.26, *accuse* 442.8

suede or **suede leather** *Fabrics and Fibers* 130

sue for divorce *divorce* 66.9

sue for peace *make peace* 73.11, *pacify* 74.11, *capitulate* 421.6

suet *basic cooking ingredient* 91.8, *fat* 562.4

suety *oily* 562.11

suffer *feel pain* 215.8, *succumb* 421.7, *atone* 489.24, *bear* 605.17, *be in trouble* 848.13

suffer a financial disaster *need money* 848.14

suffer or **incur** or **meet with a loss** *lose* 468.12

sufferance *forgivingness* 312.3

suffer a sea change *be converted* 670.12

suffer a setback *lose money* 468.15

suffer boredom *be bored* 296.7

suffer defeat *be defeated* 846.18

sufferer *sick person* 114.22, *victim of discrimination* 337.8, *recipient* 473.5, *person in adversity* 848.9

suffer from *be unhealthy* 114.29

suffer from amnesia *lack thought* 318.12

suffer from anorexia (nervosa) *fast* 118.8

suffer from inertia *not act* 413.11

suffering *pain* 215.1, *feeling pain* 215.6, *sorrow* 270.1, *affliction* 454.9, *adversity* 848.1

suffer injury *have a mishap* 660.11

suffer in patience *succumb* 421.7

suffer misfortune *be in trouble* 848.13

suffer pangs of jealousy *be jealous* 314.8

suffer punishment *be punished* 454.31

suffer purgatory *repent* 313.9

suffice 97.6, 273.10; *qualify* 340.11, *perform* 465.5, *be average* 742.8, *be useful* 801.9

sufficiency 97.1; *reasoning* 6.61, *satisfactoriness* 273.3, *qualification* 340.1, *performance* 465.2, *availability* 575.5, *completeness* 761.1, *instrumentality* 801.3

sufficient 97.3; *logical* 6.83,

satisfactory 273.6, qualified 340.7, available 575.11, complete 761.6, instrumental 801.7
sufficiently 97.9; *satisfactorily* 273.12
sufficing *provisioning* 89.6, *sufficient* 97.3, *satisfactory* 273.6
suffix *word* 5.17, *part of speech* 5.30, *back matter* 622.3, *additional item* 748.3, *add* 748.11, *link* 752.18, *ending* 773.10
suffixion *addition* 748.1
suffocate *murder* 30.20, *be excessive* 99.9, *overpower* 515.14, *abolish* 523.11
suffocating *killing* 30.17, *heating* 217.12
suffocation *murder* 30.2, *destruction* 523.1
Suffolk Breeds of Cattle 16, Breeds of Sheep 16
Suffolk Punch Horse and Pony Breeds 159
suffragan *priest* 84.8
suffrage *prayer* 85.10
suffragette *liberated woman* 33.12, *troublemaker* 427.5, *protester* 507.4
suffragist *troublemaker* 427.5, *protester* 507.4
suffuse *be present* 575.13, *mix* 751.12, *fill* 761.11
suffusing *omnipresent* 575.10
suffusion *mixture* 751.1
suffusive *omnipresent* 575.10
Sufi *Muslim* 81.12
Sufism *Islam* 81.7
sugar *carbohydrate* 12.3, *saccharide* 12.4, *food content* 90.3, *basic cooking ingredient* 91.8, *sweetener* 222.2, *sweeten* 222.7, *term of endearment* 299.7, *blarney* 439.13
sugar [Inf] *cash* 484.2
sugar alcohol *saccharide* 12.4
sugar and spice and all things nice *sweetener* 222.2
sugar-beet pulp *animal feed* 16.12
sugar beets *crop* 16.8
Sugar Bowl *football* 155.1
sugar bowl *crockery* 578.16
sugar-coat *sweeten* 222.7
sugar-coated *sweet* 222.5
sugar daddy [Inf] *boyfriend* 32.4, *lover* 299.11, *giver* 472.7
sugar derivative *saccharide* 12.4
sugared *sweet* 222.5
sugar-free diet *diet* 92.5
sugar gum Trees and Shrubs 43
sugariness *sweetness* 222.1
sugar loaf *sweetener* 222.2
sugar lump *sweetener* 222.2
sugar maple Trees and Shrubs 43
sugar palm Trees and Shrubs 43
sugar pine Trees and Shrubs 43
sugar test 12.6
sugar the pill *sweeten* 222.7, *influence* 508.11
sugary *sweet* 222.5, *honeyed* 439.8
suggest *tip* 170.14, *advise* 176.9, *signify* 183.16, *theorize* 327.16, *state* 329.13, *make evident* 339.11, *predict* 358.14, *propound* 359.9, *mean* 361.13, *plan* 387.12, *offer* 504.11, *petition* 505.11, *influence* 508.11, *seem like* 733.14, *imply* 844.14
suggested *supposed* 359.6, *tacit* 844.10
suggester *adviser* 176.5, *motivator* 178.11
suggestibility *persuadability* 178.8, *sensitivity* 267.1
suggestible *persuadable* 178.14

suggesting *informative* 170.10, *symbolic* 183.12
suggestion 800.9; *conditioning* 108.24, *inside information* 170.4, *recommendation* 176.2, *odor* 224.1, *impression* 266.2, *theory* 327.2, *notice* 358.3, *supposition* 359.1, *plan* 387.1, *tentative offer* 504.2, *petition* 505.2, *quietness* 844.4
suggestion therapy *psychotherapy* 108.4
suggest itself *have an idea* 327.13
suggestive *symbolic* 183.12, *descriptive* 202.11, *theoretical* 327.10, *suppositional* 359.5, *similar* 361.7, *offensive* 432.11, *motivational* 508.7, *appealing* 512.9, *causal* 675.7, *tacit* 844.10
suggestively *indicatively* 183.21, *promiscuously* 312.9, *influentially* 508.13, *512.14, *causally* 675.12, *tacitly* 844.16
suicidal *murderous* 30.18, *depressed* 270.5, *without hope* 282.7, *destructive* 523.8
suicidalism *compulsion* 108.13
suicidally *deadly* 30.26
suicide 30.8; *way of dying* 29.5, *self-punishment* 454.10
suicide bomber *villain* 448.5
suicide bombing *air attack* 418.4
suicide pact *suicide* 30.8
suicide squeeze *batting terms* 147.6
suid *hoofed mammal* 35.16
Suidae *hoofed mammal* 35.16
sui generis [L] *novel* 737.5, *exceptional* 779.13
suing *litigating* 54.21, *courtship* 299.10
suit 100.16; *litigation* 54.1, *cards* 168.2, *be desirable* 288.23, *courtship* 299.10, *plea* 329.5, *be the answer* 334.23, *qualify* 340.11, *accusation* 442.1, *tentative offer* 504.2, *conform* 781.11, *be convenient* 803.5
suitability 462.4; *sufficiency* 97.1, *desirability* 288.7, *correspondence* 334.8, *qualification* 340.1, *properness* 429.5, *timeliness* 659.1, *usefulness* 801.1, *convenience* 803.1
suitable 462.9; *marriageable* 64.17, *sufficient* 97.3, *expedient* 288.12, *correspondent* 334.16, *qualified* 340.7, *proper* 429.10, *good* 445.10, *timely* 659.4, *admissive* 708.8, *comfortable* 726.10, *equal to* 740.10, *useful* 801.5, *convenient* 803.3
suitable match *marriageability* 64.4
suitableness *qualification* 340.1, *good* 445.1
suitable party *marriageability* 64.4
suitably 462.17; *expediently* 288.25, *correspondingly* 334.27, *properly* 429.18, *well* 445.19, *opportunely* 659.8, *comfortably* 726.19
suit at law *litigation* 54.1
suitcase *receptacle* 105.11, *baggage* 578.8
suite *apartment* 60.7, *furniture* 101.1, Musical Forms 140, *attendance* 794.4
suited *qualified* 340.7, *treated* 388.12, *timely* 659.4
suited for *gifted* 127.11
suitedness *qualification* 340.1
suiting *fabric* 130.1
suit oneself *be independent* 829.18
suit one's purpose *be useful* 801.9

suitor *boyfriend* 32.4, *litigant* 54.4, *lover* 299.11, *adherent* 755.4
suit the action to the word *gesture* 183.17
suit the occasion *be timely* 659.6, *be convenient* 803.5
sukiyaki *notable international dishes* 90.40
Sukkoth Jewish Holy Days and Seasons 85
Suksun Breeds of Cattle 16
Sulawesi Islands 572
sulfate *mineral types* 8.38, *fertilizer* 22.6
sulfide *mineral types* 8.38
sulfonate *react* 11.38
sulfur Chemical Elements and Common Allotropes 11, *essential element* 12.15, *yellow thing* 259.4
sulfur dioxide *pollution* 117.8, *unpleasant-smelling thing* 227.2
sulfuric acid *pollution* 117.8
sulfurize *react* 11.38
sulfurous *stinking* 227.3, *yellowish* 259.8
sulfurously *angrily* 302.24
sulk *be dissatisfied* 274.7, *be sullen* 304.12, *grudge* 375.15
sulker *dissatisfied person* 274.3, *sullen person* 304.7, *reluctant person* 375.7, *discourteous person* 411.4
sulkily *sullenly* 304.16, *dismally* 304.19, *unwillingly* 375.17, *discourteously* 411.8
sulkiness *sullenness* 304.1, *overcast* 304.6, *disobedience* 375.5
sulking *dissatisfied* 274.4
sulks, the *sign of sullenness* 304.2
sulky *dissatisfied* 274.4, *sullen* 304.8, *overcast* 304.11, *unenthusiastic* 375.10
sullen 304.8; *splenetic* 223.7, *serious* 278.4, *irritable* 302.10, *cross* 303.11, *unenthusiastic* 375.10, *unsociable* 409.6, *discourteous* 411.5
sullen look *sign of sullenness* 304.2
sullenly 304.16; *splenetically* 223.10, *solemnly* 278.9, *irritably* 302.23, *crossly* 303.20, *unwillingly* 375.17, *unsocially* 409.13, *discourteously* 411.8
sullenness 304.1; *spleen* 223.4, *seriousness* 278.1, *irritableness* 302.5, *crossness* 303.4, *disobedience* 375.5, *unsociability* 409.1, *discourtesy* 411.1
sullen person 304.7
sully *dirty* 112.11, *tarnish* 248.9, *blacken* 254.11, *demoralize* 432.15, *defame* 440.13, *mark* 533.8
sulphurous *angry* 302.11, *demonic* 446.9
Sultan Breeds of Fowl 16
sultan *sovereign* 68.2
sultanate *region* 564.1, *dominion* 566.3
sultriness *hot weather* 217.6
sultry *warm* 217.13
sum 484.5; *addition* 6.13, *add* 6.86, 748.11, 784.11, *numerical answer* 334.7, *solve* 334.21, *meaning* 361.1, *total* 738.4, 783.10, *whole thing* 759.2, *mathematical result* 783.4
sumac Trees and Shrubs 43
sum and substance *meaning* 361.1, *substance* 577.2, *all* 759.4, *gist* 799.4
sum asked for *price* 494.1

Sumatra Breeds of Fowl 16, Islands 572
Sumava Breeds of Sheep 16
Sumba pony Horse and Pony Breeds 159
Sumbawa pony Horse and Pony Breeds 159
sum entrusted *loan* 488.3
summarily 53.36, 204.10; *concisely* 198.6, *early* 657.17
summariness 204.4
summarize 204.7; *chronicle* 3.15, *be concise* 198.5, *shorten* 591.9, *outline* 617.5, *iterate* 797.16
summarized 204.6; *concise* 198.4, *outlined* 617.4
summarizing *short* 591.6
summary 204.1, 204.5; *chronicle* 3.4, *outline* 198.2, 617.1, *concise* 198.4, *brief description* 202.2, *dissertation* 203.1, *gist* 329.4, *map* 387.7, *overview* 425.6, *shortened version* 591.3, *iteration* 797.2
summation *addition* 6.13, *closing arguments* 54.17, *mathematical addition* 748.2, *whole thing* 759.2, *mathematical result* 783.4
summer 654.4; *hot weather* 9.22, 217.6, *season* 654.1, *spend the season* 654.10, *time of plenty* 847.3
summerhouse *ornamental garden* 17.3
summer lightning *thunderstorm* 9.20, *natural light* 246.4
summerlike *seasonal* 654.7
Summer Olympics *prize competition* 422.5
summer sale *sale* 482.2
summer school *type of school* 48.12
summer solstice *summer* 654.4
summer stock *drama* 136.1
summer theater *drama* 136.1
summertide *summer* 654.4
summertime *summer* 654.4
summertree *figurative usage* 43.9
summerwood *timber* 43.3
summery *warm* 217.13, *seasonal* 654.7
summing up *verdict* 341.2, *iteration* 797.2
summit 600.1, 600.11, 744.4; *rock face* 161.6, *mountaineer* 161.10, *place for conversation* 210.5, *discussion* 460.3, *sharp-pointed thing* 549.4, *mountain* 569.1, *heights* 596.4, *summit meeting* 600.3, *completion* 762.2, *limit* 761.4, 773.7, *important* 799.7, *peak* 805.5
summital *top* 600.6
summit conference *discussion* 460.3, *summit meeting* 600.3
summit meeting 600.3; *place for conversation* 210.5, *discussion* 460.3
summitry *summit meeting* 600.3
summit talks *debate* 210.3
summon *litigate* 54.27, *call together* 59.28, *signal* 183.18, *desire* 288.17, *accuse* 442.8, *demand* 505.12
summoned *assembled* 59.18, *accused* 442.5
summoner *court officer* 54.7
summoning *signaling* 183.14
summons *proclamation* 183.8, *demand* 425.2, 505.3, *accusation* 442.1
summons and complaint *pretrial proceedings* 54.13
summon spirits *conjure* 86.26
summon up *remember* 354.12, *imagine* 360.14, *draw out* 711.17

sumo *type of wrestling* 152.9
sum of money *sum* 484.5
sum outstanding *difference* 750.3
sumo wrestler *person of strength* 516.8
sump *cavity* 635.3, *place for waste* 802.6
sumpter *means of transportation* 686.2
sumptuary *monetary* 484.22, *expending* 491.8
sumptuous *luscious* 214.8, *grand* 404.22, *opulent* 485.10
sumptuously *grandly* 404.37
sumptuousness *grandeur* 404.10, *opulence* 485.3
sums *mathematics* 6.1, *calculation* 784.1
sum total *whole thing* 759.2
sum up *try a case* 54.28, *be concise* 198.5, *summarize* 204.7, *judge* 341.10, *shorten* 591.9, *add* 748.11, 784.11, *be whole* 759.9, *iterate* 797.16
sun 7.15, 9.21; *natural light* 246.4, *bake* 560.10, *orbiting body* 681.4
sunbaked *warm* 217.13, *hardened* 542.7, *baked* 560.14
sunbath *effects of hot weather* 217.7
sunbathe *feel hot* 217.19
sunbathing *effects of hot weather* 217.7
sunbeam *natural light* 246.4
Sunbelt *regions of the United States* 564.7
sunblock *protection from the weather* 810.9
sunbonnet *hat* 100.32
sunburn *climbing dangers* 161.5, *effects of hot weather* 217.7, *brownness* 256.1, *brown* 256.7
sunburned *blackened* 254.7, *browned* 256.6, *red-faced* 257.6
sunburst Architectural Elements 134
suncup *rock face* 161.6
sundae *dessert* 90.35
sun dance *non-Christian ritual* 85.8
Sunday *holy day* 85.12
Sunday best *formal clothes* 100.5, *formal clothing* 406.5
Sunday brunch *meal* 92.8
Sunday-go-to-meeting clothes [Inf] *formal clothes* 100.5
Sunday paper *newspaper* 175.2
Sunday school *religious school* 48.13
sun deck *hot place* 217.5
sunder *divorce* 66.9, *separate* 753.12, *disperse* 776.12, *halve* 789.15
sundered *apart* 753.8
sundial *ornamental garden* 17.3, *angular measurement* 628.4, Timepieces and Timers 646
sundown *evening* 656.2
sundress *dress* 100.11
sun-dried *ceramic* 129.6, *baked* 560.14, *preserved* 815.12
sun-dried brick *industrial ceramics* 129.6
sundries *miscellany* 59.15, *merchandise* 482.6, *variety* 732.2, *extra* 748.6
sundrily *variously* 732.15
sundriness *variety* 732.2
sundry *varied* 732.6, *various* 793.7
sun-dry *bake* 560.19, *preserve* 815.14
sun-drying *preservation of provisions* 815.6
sunflower Flowers 42
Sunflower State *figurative usage* 42.8

Sungari Rivers 570
sunglass *fuel starter* 106.3
sunglasses *accessory* 100.28, *climbing equipment* 161.4, *ski equipment* 162.10, *visual aid* 242.14, *shade maker* 247.4, *protective covering* 613.5, *protection from the weather* 810.9
Sung ware Ceramics 129
sun hat *hat* 100.32, *shade maker* 247.4, *protective covering* 613.5, *protection from the weather* 810.9
sun helmet *protection from the weather* 810.9
sunk *losing* 468.9, *destroyed* 523.9, *holed* 583.12, *under* 598.13, *concave* 635.5, *fallen* 716.8
sunken *lowland* 597.15, *deep* 598.9, *concave* 635.5, *fallen* 716.8
sunken-eyed *emaciated* 595.10
sunken eyes *emaciation* 595.2
sunken garden *garden* 17.2
sunken reef *hidden danger* 813.3
sunk fence *ornamental garden* 17.3, *crack* 587.2, *separator* 753.5
sunk line *fishing tackle* 154.7
sunlamp *heater* 217.3, *electric light* 246.6
sunless *dark* 247.5, *dim* 248.4, *overcast* 304.11
sunlessness *darkness* 247.1
sunlight *sun* 9.21, *natural light* 246.4, Phobias 283
sunlit *lit* 246.16
sun lounge *room* 60.9
sun lounger *ornamental garden* 17.3
Sunna *Islamic text* 81.18
sunned *baked* 560.14
sunnier *fine* 9.43
sunniness *cheerfulness* 269.2
sunning *drying* 560.3
Sunnite *Muslim* 81.12
sunny 246.17; *fine* 9.43, *warm* 217.13, *cheerful* 269.7, *likable* 271.6, *cheering* 281.9, *rainless* 560.11
sunny period *hot weather* 9.22
sunny spell *hot weather* 9.22
sunny weather *hot weather* 9.22
sun oneself *feel hot* 217.19
sun porch *room* 60.9
sun print *printing* 132.20
sunray lamp *electric light* 246.6
sunrise 713.4; *morning* 655.2, *early hour* 657.2, *compass direction* 697.5
sunrise industry *manufacture* 522.2
sunroom *room* 60.9
sun rose Flowers 42
sunscreen *protective covering* 613.5
sunset *red thing* 257.3, *evening* 656.2, *late hour* 658.2, *compass direction* 697.5, *nightfall* 714.5
sun sets or **goes down** *become dark* 247.9
sunshade *shade maker* 247.4, *protective covering* 613.5, *protection from the weather* 810.9
sunshine *sun* 9.21, *natural light* 246.4
sunshine recorder *weather instrument* 9.7
sunshine-yellow *yellow* 259.7
sunshiny *sunny* 246.17
sunspot *sun* 7.15, *maculation* 263.4
sunspot cycle *sun* 7.15
sunstroke *effects of hot weather* 217.7
sunsuit *suit* 100.16, *baby clothes* 100.24
suntan *effects of hot weather* 217.7,

feel hot 217.19, *blacken* 254.11, *brownness* 256.1, *brown* 256.7
suntan lotion *protective covering* 613.5, *protection from the weather* 810.9
suntanned *blackened* 254.7, *browned* 256.6
suntan oil *protection from the weather* 810.9
sunup *morning* 655.2, *early hour* 657.2, *sunrise* 713.4
sun visor *shade maker* 247.4
sun worship *idolatry* 83.4
sun worshiper *idolater* 83.7
sup *have a meal* 92.25, *drink* 93.19
super *superior* 744.8
super [Inf] *actor* 136.25, *great* 445.14
super! [Inf] *good!* 445.24
Super-8 *film* 132.8
superabound *be excessive* 99.9, *exaggerate* 712.16
superabundance *fertility* 22.1, *excess* 99.1, *diffuseness* 199.1, *abundance* 498.4, *surplus* 750.4
superabundant *fertile* 22.8, *excessive* 99.5, *diffuse* 199.3, *abundant* 498.8, *surplus* 750.8, *ample* 795.9
superabundantly *excessively* 99.13, *residually* 750.11
superadd *augment* 748.13
superaddition *addition* 748.1
superannuate *dismiss* 709.15
superannuated *disused* 394.8, *former* 651.14
superannuation *disuse* 394.3
superb *skillful* 127.10, *grand* 404.22, *excellent* 445.13, 744.14, 805.15
super bantamweight *boxing weight divisions* 152.6
super-bantamweight *combat* 152.17
superbly 744.22; *grandly* 404.37, *excellently* 445.21
superbness *excellence* 445.4
Super Bowl *football* 155.1, *prize competition* 422.5
supercharger *racing automobile* 146.2
supercilious *arrogant* 297.9, *self-admiring* 402.10, *contemptuous* 436.12
superciliously *arrogantly* 297.18, *cockily* 402.19, *contemptuously* 436.27
superciliousness *contempt* 436.3
superclass *taxonomic classification* 777.3
supercluster *galaxy* 7.5
supercomputer *computer* 15.1
superconducting magnet *superconductivity* 10.35, *magnet* 10.47
superconductivity 10.35
superconductor *superconductivity* 10.35
supercooled *atmospheric* 9.40
supercooling *atmospheric process* 9.9
superego *psyche* 108.25, *internal world* 525.6
supereminent *elite* 744.12
supererogatory *superfluous* 99.8, *extra* 748.10
superfamily *taxonomic classification* 777.3
superficial 599.4; *spatial* 6.76, 563.11, *bungled* 128.7, *visible* 244.5, *outer* 264.10, *perfunctory* 324.9, *indifferent* 326.5, *sophistic* 330.7, *semiskilled* 349.6, *nonobservant* 466.5, *exterior* 610.7,

apparent 610.10, *outward* 621.11, *extraneous* 724.8, *external* 724.11, *incomplete* 762.5, *uncompleted* 762.7, *trivial* 800.14, *hasty* 818.3, *easy* 823.9
superficial area *surface* 6.36
superficialities *appearance* 610.4
superficiality 599.2; *inattention* 324.1, *indifference* 326.2, *lack of knowledge* 349.2, *nonobservance* 466.1, *extraneousness* 724.1, *incompleteness* 762.1, *nonachievement* 762.3, *triviality* 800.2, *simplicity* 823.2
superficiality or **superficialness** *appearance* 610.4
superficially 599.8; *visibly* 244.10, *apparently* 264.16, 610.18, 720.19, *inattentively* 466.13, *extraneously* 724.16, *seemingly* 733.19, *incompletely* 762.10, *unimportantly* 800.21, *easily* 823.19, *manifestly* 843.17
superficialness *superficiality* 599.2
superficies *external appearance* 264.5, *superficiality* 599.2, *exterior* 610.1, *appearance* 610.4
superfine *excellent* 445.13
superfluity 99.4; *fertility* 22.1, *diffuseness* 199.1, *nonuse* 394.1, *opulence* 485.3, *unrestrainedness* 500.2, *extraneousness* 724.1, *extra* 748.6, *surplus* 750.4, *redundancy* 802.2
superfluous 99.8; *waste* 96.10, *diffuse* 199.3, *bargain* 497.10, *extraneous* 724.8, *unrelated* 728.6, *extra* 748.10, *surplus* 750.8, *redundant* 802.9
superfluously 99.15; *wastefully* 96.23, *out of use* 394.13, *extraneously* 724.16, *irrelatively* 728.16, *additionally* 748.15, *residually* 750.11
superfluousness *superfluity* 99.4, *unrelatedness* 728.1, *redundancy* 802.2
supergiant *star luminosity* 7.12
supergiant elliptical *galaxy* 7.5
super giant slalom race *ski race* 162.4
super G race *ski race* 162.4
superheavy element *chemical element* 11.3
super heavyweight *boxing weight divisions* 152.6
super-heavyweight *combat* 152.17
superhero *person of strength* 516.8
superheroine *person of strength* 516.8
superhighway *road* 687.2
superhuman *difficult* 824.9
superhumanity *the occult* 86.2
superhuman task *difficult task* 824.3
superimpose *augment* 748.13
superimposed *covering* 613.21
superimposition *covering* 613.1, *addition* 748.1
superintend *manage* 126.10, *direct* 780.14
superintendence *management* 126.1
superintendency *position of authority* 52.4
superintendent *prison officer* 55.8, *manager* 126.7, *superior* 744.5
Superior Lakes 568
superior 744.5, 744.8; *person in authority* 52.7, *authoritative* 52.9, 425.8, *company leader* 68.8, *excellent* 445.13, *influential* 512.8, *strong* 516.9, *higher* 596.8,

unequal 741.4, *primary* 769.10, *important person* 799.5, *important* 799.7, *notable* 799.11, *improved* 807.12

superior court *law court* 54.8, *type of court* 54.9

superioress *religious* 84.9

superiority 744.1; *authority* 52.1, 514.5, 516.5, *type of complex* 108.22, *contempt* 436.3, *excellence* 445.4, *inequality* 741.1, *priority* 769.2, *importance* 799.1, *expertise* 805.4

superiorly 744.20; *commandingly* 425.15

superior person 445.7; *important person* 799.5

superior power *influence* 512.1

superlative *of grammar* 5.41, *exaggeration* 194.1, *exaggerated* 194.7, *superior person* 445.7, *excellent* 445.13, *best* 744.10

superlatively *grammatically* 5.48, *exaggeratedly* 194.16, *superiorly* 744.20, *supremely* 744.23

superman *wonderful person* 294.6, *superior person* 445.7, *paragon* 744.6, *celebrity* 799.6, *successful person* 845.6

supermarket *food provider* 90.6, *store* 124.4, 483.8

supernal *heavenly* 82.22, *nonmaterial* 525.8, *high* 596.7

supernatant liquid *crystal* 11.14

supernatural *divine* 82.16, *occult* 86.16, *parapsychological* 525.9, *extraneous* 610.12, *external* 724.11

supernatural, the *the occult* 86.2, *extraneousness* 610.6, *externality* 724.4

supernatural being *deity* 82.1

supernaturalism 86.3; *spiritual world* 525.3

supernaturalist *occultist* 86.13, *nonmaterialist* 525.7

supernaturality *the occult* 86.2

supernaturally *divinely* 82.24, *occultly* 86.27, *metaphysically* 525.13, *externally* 724.19

supernaturalness *the occult* 86.2

supernatural tale *story* 139.4

supernatural virtues *virtues* 447.2

supernature *the occult* 86.2

supernormal *occult* 86.16

supernormalness *the occult* 86.2

supernova *stellar evolution* 7.10, *natural light* 246.4

supernova remnant *stellar evolution* 7.10

supernumerary *actor* 136.25, *extra* 748.6, 748.10

superpatriot *bigot* 337.7

superpatriotic *discriminatory* 337.11

superpatriotically *prejudicially* 337.17

superpatriotism *social discrimination* 337.4

superphysical *occult* 86.16

superphysicalness *the occult* 86.2

superposition *addition* 748.1

superpower *body politic* 50.3, *group influence* 512.6, *country* 566.1

superrealism Western Art Styles 133

supersaturate *solidify* 11.37

supersaturated *status adjectives* 11.25, *excessive* 99.5

supersaturated solution *phase* 11.13

supersaturation *excess* 99.1

superscript *appendage* 748.4

superscription *means of identification* 184.3

supersede *stop using* 394.10, *be a substitute* 672.6, *succeed* 770.11

superseded *disused* 394.8, *substituted* 672.4

supersensible *occult* 86.16, *parapsychological* 525.9

supersensible, the *the occult* 86.2

supersensitiveness *the occult* 86.2

supersensory *parapsychological* 525.9

supersession *substitution* 672.1

supersonic *transportable* 686.7, *flyable* 689.12, *swift* 694.6

supersonically *aeronautically* 689.17, *swiftly* 694.16

supersonic speed *sound propagation* 230.3, *speed* 694.2

supersonic transport (SST) *aircraft* 689.3

superstar *idol* 83.5, *actor* 137.13, *superior person* 445.7, *paragon* 744.6

superstition *fallibility* 351.6

superstitiously *magically* 86.28

superstore *store* 483.8

superstratum *layer* 588.1, *top layer* 600.5, *exteriority* 610.2

superstring *fundamental interaction* 10.65

superstructural *structural* 14.45, 551.17

superstructurally *structurally* 551.24

superstructure 551.7; *structure* 14.20, *construction* 551.6

supertanker Ships and Boats 690

supertax *tax* 494.5

supertonic *musical note* 140.15

supertransuranic element *chemical element* 11.3

supervene *follow from* 676.9

supervention *addition* 748.1

supervise *govern* 49.26, *manage* 126.10, *watch* 242.23, *direct* 780.14

supervised *industrial* 57.13

supervise staff *manage* 126.10

supervising *industrial* 57.13, *directions* 697.7

supervision *government* 49.1, *management* 126.1, *observation* 242.5, *treatment* 399.11

supervisor *employer* 57.3, *manager* 126.7, *observer* 242.15

supervisory *managerial* 126.9

supervisory body *management board* 126.2

superwoman *liberated woman* 33.12, *wonderful person* 294.6, *superior person* 445.7, *paragon* 744.6, *celebrity* 799.6, *successful person* 845.6

supinate *fence* 153.7

supinated *fencing* 153.6

supination *fencing movements* 153.3

supine *inactive* 415.8, *submitting* 421.3, *prostrate* 597.11, *recumbent* 603.7, *sedentary* 716.11

supine float *swimming techniques* 164.2

supinely *recumbently* 603.12

supineness *submission* 421.1, *prostration* 597.2, *recumbency* 603.2

supper *meal* 92.8

supper club *club* 138.7

supper hour *evening* 656.2

supper party *party* 408.6

suppertime *evening* 656.2

supping *eating meals* 92.4, *drinking* 93.1

supplant *replace* 574.17, *be a substitute* 672.6, *succeed* 770.11

supplantation *replacement* 574.3

supplanted *disused* 394.8, *replaced* 574.10, *substituted* 672.4

supplanter *substitute* 672.2

supplanting *substitution* 672.1

supple *graceful* 527.4, *pliant* 543.7, *elastic* 546.5, *changeable* 666.3

supplement *newspaper* 175.2, *fee* 494.3, *ancillary* 605.5, *back matter* 622.3, *continuation* 669.2, *continue* 669.8, *insert* 710.4, *intensification* 746.2, *make bigger* 746.7, *addition* 748.1, *augment* 748.13, *fullness* 761.5, *complete* 761.9

supplemental *progressive* 669.6, *additional* 748.8

supplementally *continually* 669.10

supplementarily *increasingly* 746.9, *additionally* 748.15

supplementary 825.17; *increasing* 746.4, *additional* 748.8, *completed* 761.7

supplementary or **supplemental** *ancillary* 605.14

supplementary angles *angle* 6.37

supplementary medicine *alternative medicine* 107.4

supplementary unit *unit of measurement* 589.5

supplementation *addition* 748.1

supplemented *increased* 746.5

supplementing *helping* 825.16

suppleness *manual skill* 127.2, *softness* 543.1, *elasticity* 546.1, *changeableness* 666.1, *cunning* 822.1

suppliant *worshipful* 83.12, *requester* 505.5

supplicant *worshiper* 83.6, *worshipful* 83.12, *requester* 505.5

supplicate *pray* 85.20, *petition* 505.11

supplicating *worshipful* 83.12

supplication *act of worship* 83.2, *prayer* 85.10, *petition* 505.2

supplicatory *worshipful* 83.12, *prayerful* 85.17

supplied 89.7; *stored* 105.14

supplier *provisioner* 89.4

supplies 102.3; *provisions* 89.3, *food* 90.1, *merchandise* 482.6

supply *provision* 89.9, *find means* 102.6, *materials* 104.1, *procure* 104.9, *store* 105.1, 105.17, *fitting out* 388.3, *equip* 388.19, *give* 472.10, *fill* 761.11, *preserve* 815.14

supply and demand *economic factor* 56.8

supply base *storehouse* 105.8

supplying *provisioning* 89.2, 89.6, *giving* 472.1

supply of words *word* 5.17

supply ship *warship* 77.21

supply-side economics *economics* 56.1

supply staff *military staff* 58.5

supply systems *naval commands* 77.19

support 605.1, 605.16, 748.14, 825.2, 825.24; *propound a philosophy* 4.21, *friendship* 62.1, *provisions* 89.3, *provision* 89.9, *suffice* 97.6, *resources* 102.4, *hand tool* 103.3, *practice medicine* 107.32, *column* 134.6, *wall* 134.9, *actor* 136.25, *act* 136.34, 137.20, *confirmation* 189.5, *confirm* 189.25, *aid* 275.2, *cheer* 281.4, *inspire hope* 281.14, *be benevolent*

305.10, *prove* 331.17, 336.9, 339.14, *proof* 336.2, *verify* 336.8, *assent* 346.6, *bolster* 377.15, *side with* 382.15, 623.10, *plead for* 419.25, *approval* 437.1, *approve* 437.14, *agree with* 462.10, *security* 464.1, *secure* 464.9, *detain* 471.9, *gift* 472.2, *donation* 491.6, *donate* 491.13, *give* 498.11, *management* 509.4, *take action* 509.12, *instrumentality* 511.1, *be an instrument* 511.7, *strengthen* 516.15, *foundation* 601.2, *base* 601.10, *supporting part* 605.3, *supporter* 605.9, *continuance* 669.3, *continue* 669.8, *make stable* 674.7, *erect* 715.11, *consent* 735.8, 735.28, *patronage* 810.7, 825.9, *protect* 810.21, *refuge* 812.1, *preservation* 815.1, *saving* 815.4, *preserve* 815.14, *sustenance* 825.3, *helper* 825.12, *sustain* 825.25, *advise* 825.27, *finance* 825.31, *cooperation* 827.1, *cooperate* 827.12

supportable *in the right* 429.11

support civil rights *treat equally* 831.8

supported *supplied* 89.7, *architectural* 134.12, *confirmed* 189.17, *approved* 437.8, *consenting* 735.18

support equal rights *treat equally* 831.8

supporter 605.9, 825.13; *underwear* 100.22, *affirmer* 189.9, *helper* 275.5, *assenter* 346.3, *defender* 419.14, *approver* 437.7, *giver* 472.7, *body support* 605.6, *inferior* 745.4, *adherent* 755.4

supporters Heraldic Terms 184

support financially 605.19

support fleet *military organization* 58.4

support human rights *treat equally* 831.8

supporting *recommending* 437.11, *base* 601.7, *supportive* 605.11, *inferior* 745.5, *adhering* 755.7, *helping* 825.16

supporting actor or **actress** *actor* 136.25, 137.13

supporting cast *cast* 136.26

supporting character *role* 136.23

supporting garment *body support* 605.6

supporting member *superstructure* 551.7

supporting part 605.3; *role* 136.23

supporting role *role* 136.23, *inferiority* 745.1

supporting structure 605.2; *foundation* 601.2

supportive 605.11, 825.18; *intimate* 62.7, *confirming* 189.16, *verificatory* 336.6, *assenting* 346.4, *recommending* 437.11, *vindicatory* 441.7, *instrumental* 511.4, *raised* 715.6, *consenting* 735.18, *tenacious* 755.6, *cooperative* 827.9

supportive evidence *defense* 441.2

supportively 605.20; *intimately* 62.14, *confirmingly* 189.32, *verifiably* 336.11, *justifyingly* 441.15, *profitably* 492.8, *instrumentally* 511.9, *with consent* 735.38, *helpfully* 825.32

supportiveness *moral support* 605.7

supportive therapy *psychotherapy* 108.4

support life 28.21

support system *moral support* 605.7

support the church *be religious* 81.25

support troops *armed forces* 77.9

support unit *military organization* 58.4

supposable *supposed* 359.6

suppose 359.8; *philosophize* 4.19, *propound a philosophy* 4.21, *be of the opinion* 87.10, *contend* 189.24, *speculate* 294.13, *have an idea* 317.12, *theorize* 327.16, *focus on* 328.9, *foresee* 357.9, *imagine* 360.14, *think likely* 838.10

supposed 359.6; *believed* 87.8, *contended* 189.15, *focused* 328.6, *reputed* 370.4

supposedly 359.10; *theoretically* 4.24, *believably* 87.13, *allegedly* 189.31, *thematically* 328.13, *reputedly* 370.8

supposer *theorist* 359.4

suppose so *suppose* 359.8

supposing *suppositional* 359.5, *under the circumstances* 726.16

supposition 359.1; *philosophy* 4.1, *theory* 6.62, 327.2, *belief* 87.1, *contention* 189.4, *topic* 328.1

suppositional 359.5; *contended* 189.15, *speculative* 317.8, *theoretical* 327.10, *imaginary* 360.12

suppositionally *allegedly* 189.31

suppositious *suppositional* 359.5

supposititious *suppositional* 359.5

suppositive *suppositional* 359.5

suppress 424.9; *conceal* 181.12, *keep secret* 182.11, *forget* 186.11, *strike dumb* 206.10, *be evasive* 386.20, *detain* 471.9, *censor* 503.10, *counteract* 510.7, *abolish* 523.11, *bear down on* 716.18, *exclude* 764.7, *restrain* 830.12, *defeat* 832.11, *be victorious* 845.16

suppressant *restraint* 830.1

suppressed 424.6; *unconscious* 108.40, *concealed* 181.8, *secret* 182.8, *nonresonant* 233.7, *restrained* 830.9

suppressed desire *defense mechanism* 108.23

suppressing *restraining* 830.8, *dominating* 832.7

suppression 424.2; *defense mechanism* 108.23, *verbal concealment* 181.3, *secrecy* 182.1, *forgetfulness* 186.3, *evasiveness* 386.6, *detention* 471.2, *prohibition* 503.1, *obstruction* 510.3, *destruction* 523.1, *submergence* 716.3, *exclusion* 764.1, *restraint* 830.1, *domination* 832.2

suppressive *fugitive* 386.10, *prohibited* 503.5, *counteracting* 510.6, *restraining* 830.8, *dominating* 832.7

suppressively *by veto* 503.12

suppurate *fester* 25.23, *decay* 808.16

suppurated *rheumy* 555.16

suppurating *toxic* 114.28, *rheumy* 555.16

suppuration *pus* 25.7, *lack of hygiene* 112.3, *infection* 114.7, *body fluid* 555.3, *flow* 555.6

suppurative *purulent* 25.16, *rheumy* 555.16

supramundane *spiritual* 86.20

supranational government *world government* 49.17

supranatural *occult* 86.16

supranaturalism *supernaturalism* 86.3

supranature *the occult* 86.2

supremacy *authority* 52.1, 780.6, *divine attribute* 82.4, *excellence* 445.4, *superiority* 744.1, *priority* 769.2, *importance* 799.1

suprematism *Western Art Styles* 133

supreme *authoritative* 52.9, *excellent* 68.16, 445.13, *divine* 82.16, *head* 600.7, *best* 744.10, 805.9, *primary* 769.10, *ruling* 780.11, *important* 799.7, *expert* 805.16

Supreme Being *God* 82.6, *first cause* 675.6

Supreme Court *United States government* 49.21

Supreme Court justice *judge* 68.4

Supreme Headquarters Allied Powers *military staff* 58.5

supreme issue *chief thing* 799.3

supremely 744.23; *authoritatively* 52.18, *masterfully* 68.19, *divinely* 82.24, *excellently* 445.21, *primarily* 769.21, *importantly* 799.15

Supreme Soul *God* 82.6

surah *Fabrics and Fibers* 130

surcharge *overdo* 99.11, *settle accounts* 493.11, *fee* 494.3, *displacement* 538.3

surcoat *coat* 100.19

surd *multiplication* 6.15, *power* 783.6, *fractional* 783.8

sure *legitimate* 52.10, *believing* 87.6, *emphatic* 200.3, *steadfast* 284.11, *verified* 336.7, *expecting* 356.4, *expected* 356.5, *correct* 429.8, *auspicious* 458.10, *secure* 464.5, *predictable* 514.15, *determined* 674.5, *safe* 810.16, *certain* 840.7

sure! *yes!* 189.36

sure bet *strong possibility* 836.3, *good chance* 842.6

sure defense *protection* 810.2

sure enough *assuredly* 336.12, *authentic* 721.16

surefire *successful* 845.8

surefire winner *successful person* 845.6

surefooted *skillful* 127.10, *successful* 845.8

sure-handed *skillful* 127.10

surely 464.15; *legitimately* 52.19, *necessarily* 95.22, *steadfastly* 284.19, *assuredly* 336.12, *auspiciously* 458.17, *certainly* 840.15, *inevitably* 840.17

sureness *steadfastness* 284.3, *right* 429.2, *conviction* 840.2

sure sign *sign* 183.1

sure thing *easy thing* 823.6, *strong possibility* 836.3, *certainty* 840.1, *good chance* 842.6

surety *legal power* 52.2, *pretrial proceedings* 54.13, *steadfastness* 284.3, *verification* 336.1, *promise maker* 458.6, *promise* 464.2, *protection* 810.2, *certainty* 840.1, *conviction* 840.2

sure winner *victor* 845.7

surf *wave* 8.16, 571.3

surface 6.36; *phrased* 5.39, *fishing* 154.13, *diving* 164.13, *visible* 244.5, *external appearance* 264.5, *outer* 264.10, *become visible* 264.13, *be light* 539.8, *texture* 552.1, *space* 563.1, *spatial* 563.11, *superficiality* 599.2, *superficial* 599.4, *top layer* 600.5, *weaving* 609.2, *exterior* 610.1, 610.7, *apparent* 610.10, *be exterior* 610.13, *pave* 613.32, *outward*

621.11, *side* 623.1, *sail* 690.16, *emerge* 707.14, *spring up* 713.22, *externality* 724.4

surface appearance *appearance* 610.4

surface area *surface* 6.36

surface chemistry 11.20, Branches of Chemistry 11

surface current *ocean current* 8.15

surface diving *diving* 164.6

surface feature *landform* 8.9

surface integral *differentiation* 6.29

surface mail *postal service* 169.5

surface measurement *surface* 6.36

surface of revolution *curved surface* 6.43

surface plate *planimetry* 603.5

surface plug *bait* 154.6

surfacer *woodworking tool* 131.6

surface show *show* 621.7

surface structure *grammar* 5.28

surface tension *force* 10.9

surface texture *texture* 552.1

surface-to-air *strategic* 78.16

surface-to-air missile (SAM) *modern missile weapon* 78.4

surface-to-surface *strategic* 78.16

surface-to-surface missile *modern missile weapon* 78.4

surface warfare *naval commands* 77.19

surface wave *seismic wave* 8.25, *wave* 10.11, 683.4

surface wind *wind* 9.12

surfacing *paving* 613.14, *outgoing* 707.10, *ascent* 713.1

surfboarding Sporting Activities 145

surf boat Ships and Boats 690

surfeit *excess* 99.1, *overindulge* 99.10, *surplus* 750.4

surf fishing *saltwater fishing* 154.3

surficial *terrestrial* 8.52

surge *crowd* 59.11, 59.26, *loud tone* 232.3, *be active* 414.18, *flow* 570.4, 570.10, *wave* 571.3, *billow* 571.9, *vortex* 682.6, *swirl* 682.16, *run out* 707.15, *upturn* 713.2, *ascend* 713.19, *spread* 746.3, *increase* 746.6

surge back *billow* 571.9

surgeon *doctor* 107.19, *medical specialist* 107.20

surgeon's cap *cap* 100.33

surgeon's knot Knots, Bends, Hitches, Splices 754

surgery 107.15; Medical Specialties 107, *treatment* 107.14, *therapy* 115.12, Phobias 283

surgery [Brit] *hospital* 107.16

surgical *medical* 107.28

surgical air strike *air attack* 418.4

surgical assistant *paramedic* 107.24

surgical dressing *medical covering* 613.4

surgical intervention *surgery* 107.15

surgically *medically* 107.35, 115.20

surgical mask *medical covering* 613.4

surgical operation *surgery* 107.15

surgical specimen *postmortem (examination) (PM)* 107.17

surgical treatment *treatment* 107.14, *surgery* 107.15

Suriname Countries 566, Rivers 570

suriphobia Phobias 283

surjective *functional* 6.73

surlily *irritably* 304.17

surliness *irritableness* 304.3, *discourtesy* 411.1

surly *clumsy* 128.6, *irritable* 304.9, *discourteous* 411.5

surmisable *supposed* 359.6

surmise *philosophize* 4.19, *belief* 87.1, *be of the opinion* 87.10, *have an idea* 317.12, *theory* 327.2, *judgment* 341.1, *estimate* 341.11, *foresee* 357.9, *conjecture* 359.3, *suppose* 359.8

surmised *supposed* 359.6

surmiser *philosopher* 4.9, *theorist* 359.4

surmount *tower over* 569.7, *exceed* 712.15, *climb* 713.21, *overcome obstacles* 845.14

surmounted *surpassing* 712.10

surname *name* 202.8

surpass *exceed* 712.15, *be unequal* 741.7, *outdo* 744.18

surpassing 712.10; *contending* 422.19, *superior* 744.8

surpassingly *superiorly* 744.20

surplice *vestment* 84.11, *robe* 100.20

surplus 750.4, 750.8; *waste* 96.16, *superfluity* 99.4, *superfluous* 99.8, *excessiveness* 712.4, *excessive* 712.8, *extra* 748.6, 748.10, *difference* 750.3, *part* 760.1

surprisal *surprise* 292.1

surprise 292.1, 292.9; *wonder* 294.1, *marvel* 294.3, *be wondrous* 294.14, *unpremeditation* 389.2, *be unprepared* 389.14, *attack* 418.17, *hidden danger* 813.3, *trap* 813.6, *unexpectedness* 839.2

surprise attack *military attack* 418.2, *danger* 811.1

surprise blow *military attack* 418.2

surprised 292.5; *wondering* 294.7, *unprepared* 389.5

surprise offensive *military attack* 418.2

surprise party *party* 408.6

surprising 292.7; *astonishing* 294.10

surprisingly 292.14; *astonishingly* 294.19, *spontaneously* 389.17

surreal *representing* 202.14

surrealism Western Art Styles 133, Western Literary Groups 139

surrealistic *literary* 139.15, *representing* 202.14

surrebuttal *counterevidence* 339.5

surrejoinder *counterevidence* 339.5

surrender *truce* 73.2, *make peace* 73.11, *relinquishment* 392.1, *relinquish* 392.3, *submission* 421.1, *capitulate* 421.6, *giving* 472.1, *be weak* 517.12, *resignation* 835.1, *resign* 835.5, *be defeated* 846.18

surrendered *relinquished* 392.2

surrenderer *assenter* 462.5, *subjected person* 832.5

surrendering *submitting* 421.3, *giving* 472.1

surrender oneself *revere* 81.26

surrender treaty *contract* 462.2

surreptitious *artful* 193.13

surreptitiously *stealthily* 182.15, *deceptively* 193.21

surreptitiousness *guile* 193.3

surrogacy *substitution* 672.1, *patronage* 810.7

surrogate 108.29; *alternative* 80.2, *substitute* 613.17, 613.23, 672.2, 672.3, *cover for* 613.34, *tutelary* 810.19

surrogate mother *substitute* 613.17, 672.2

surrogation *substitution* 672.1

surround 615.7; *be at war* 76.32, *besiege* 418.20, *extend* 563.14, *contain* 578.20, *be exterior* 610.13, *wrap* 613.29, *surround* 615.7, *edge* 617.3, *enclose* 619.6, *circle* 631.6

surrounded 615.5; *containing* 578.18, *endangered* 811.10

surrounding 615.4; *environmental* 60.17, *circumstantial* 573.7, 726.8, *covering* 610.8

surroundings 615.1; *habitat* 60.1, *near place* 586.3, *exteriority* 610.2, *circumstances* 726.1

Sursum Corda *Eucharist* 85.7, *prayer* 85.10

surtax *tax* 494.5

surtax bracket *wealth* 485.1

surtout *coat* 100.19

surveillance *management* 126.1, *observation* 242.5, *carefulness* 323.3, *watchfulness* 325.5, *self-defense* 419.5, *security system* 810.5

surveillant 810.12; *watchful* 325.10

survey *sociological research* 2.2, *philosophical investigation* 4.4, *philosophize* 4.19, *engineer* 14.48, *map* 187.12, *dissertation* 203.1, *dissertate* 203.5, *summary* 204.1, *observation* 242.5, *inspect* 242.22, *watch* 242.23, *scrutinize* 323.11, *care for* 325.12, *questioning* 333.2, *question* 333.16, *judgment* 341.1, *estimate* 341.11, *overview* 425.6, *regionalize* 564.15, *find* 565.11, *measurement* 589.1, *measure* 589.20, *outline* 617.1, 617.5, *whole situation* 759.3

surveyed *questioned* 333.15, *locational* 565.8, *measured* 589.16

surveying *civil engineering* 14.17, *watchful* 323.6, *topography* 565.5, *measurement* 589.1

surveying and mapping through photographs *Fields of Measurement* 589

survey map *map* 187.5

surveyor *civil engineer* 14.19, *questioner* 333.9, *judge* 341.5, *measurer* 589.14

surveyor's chain *General Units* 589

surveyor's measure *measuring system* 589.4, *type of measurement* 589.8

survivability *life cycle* 28.7, *endurance* 516.4, *toughness* 547.1

survival *life cycle* 28.7, *nonuse* 164.12, *continuation* 642.2, *thing of the past* 651.8, *permanence* 667.1, *protraction* 669.4, *continuing existence* 717.7, *remainder* 750.1

survival devices *survival swimming* 164.4

survival of the fittest *evolution* 13.23, *rivalry* 422.2

survival swimming 164.4

survive 419.31; *live* 28.17, *be dormant* 41.22, *endure* 377.14, *be tough* 547.13, *last* 642.6, *be permanent* 667.4, *protract* 669.9, *continue to be* 717.20, *be left* 750.9, *be restored* 809.13, *be safe* 810.20, *get a reprieve* 816.9

survive from the past *be old* 653.15

survive one's spouse *be widowed* 66.13

surviving *alive* 28.13, *pertaining to life* 28.14, *permanent* 667.2,

unfailing 667.3, *lasting* 717.13, *remaining* 750.7

surviving spouse 66.6

survivor *living being* 28.3, *surviving spouse* 66.6, *person remaining* 750.6, *escaper* 816.5

Susan B. Anthony dollar *US coinage* 484.10

susceptibilities *feelings* 266.1

susceptibility *educatability* 48.9, *sensitivity* 212.2, 267.1, *lovingness* 299.4, *attitude* 513.2, *vulnerability* 811.6

susceptibility *or* susceptivity *persuadability* 178.8

susceptible 212.7; *educatable* 48.18, *persuadable* 178.14, *feeling* 266.9, *sensitive* 267.3, *amorous* 299.18, *impressionable* 543.12, *vulnerable* 811.9

susceptibly *studiously* 48.26, *soft-heartedly* 543.19

sushi *notable international dishes* 90.40

sushi bar *eating place* 92.17

suspect 314.9; *be of the opinion* 87.10, *disbelieved* 88.7, *disbelieve* 88.8, *doubt* 287.13, 333.19, *speculate* 294.13, *theorize* 327.16, *person questioned* 333.10, *suppose* 359.8, *the hunted* 385.7, *accused person* 442.4, *be uncertain* 841.17

suspected *disbelieved* 88.7, *theoretical* 327.10

suspend 604.13; *stop using* 394.10, *make inactive* 415.16, *punish* 454.22, *veto* 503.9, *defer* 604.15, *delay* 658.13, *pause* 668.13, *make motionless* 678.8, *dismiss* 709.15, *disbar* 709.16, *eject* 764.8, *discontinue* 775.10, *cancel* 834.6, *terminate* 834.7

suspended 519.3, 604.7; *idle* 394.6, *inactive* 413.9, *vetoed* 503.6, *inoperative* 515.8, *deferred* 604.9, *excluded* 604.11, *held up* 658.6, *sedentary* 678.5, *interrupted* 775.9, *canceled* 834.5

suspended animation *desensitization* 213.2, *interruption* 604.4

suspended note *tempo* 140.22

suspended sentence *prison sentence* 55.6

suspenders *fastener* 754.7

suspend growth *be dormant* 41.22

suspend hostilities *make peace* 73.11, *pause* 668.13

suspendibility *suspension* 604.1

suspendible *suspended* 604.7

suspense 604.6; *expectation* 356.1, *lack of motion* 678.1

suspense account *accounts* 493.4

suspenseful *in suspense* 604.12

suspensefully *in suspense* 604.21

suspensefulness *suspense* 604.6

suspensibility *suspension* 604.1

suspensible *suspended* 604.7

suspension 604.1; *tempo* 140.22, *racing automobile* 146.2, *nonuse* 394.1, *inaction* 413.1, *inactivity* 415.1, *punishment* 454.1, *veto* 503.3, *solution* 555.10, *deferment* 604.3, *delay* 658.3, *pause* 668.3, *lack of motion* 678.1, *dismissal* 709.2, *mixed thing* 751.2, *compound* 757.4, *ejection* 764.2, *interruption* 775.3, *cancellation* 834.1, *termination* 834.2

suspension bridge *bridge* 551.10, 691.7

suspension of disbelief *believing* 87.2

suspension of hostilities *pause* 668.3

suspension points *Punctuation Marks* 5

suspension system *spring* 546.4

suspensive *suspended* 604.7, *in suspense* 604.12

suspensively *pendulously* 604.19, *in suspense* 604.21

suspensiveness *suspension* 604.1, *suspense* 604.6

suspicion 314.3, 841.2; *disbelief* 88.1, *reticence* 287.3, *theory* 327.2, *information* 348.2, *basis of supposition* 359.2, *conjecture* 359.3, *little piece* 580.4, *admixture* 751.5, *few* 796.1, *suggestion* 800.9

suspicious 314.6; *disbelieving* 88.6, *disbelieved* 88.7, *reticent* 287.8, *questionable* 333.13, *disreputable* 371.4, *uncertain* 841.9

suspiciously 314.13; *disbelievingly* 88.10, *reticently* 287.18, *questionably* 333.22, *deviously* 371.9, *uncertainly* 841.22

suspiciousness *disbelief* 88.1, *suspicion* 314.3, 841.2

Susquehanna *Rivers* 570

Sussex *Breeds of Cattle* 16, *Breeds of Fowl* 16

Sussex spaniel *Breeds of Dogs* 35

sustain 825.25; *feed* 90.41, *prove* 336.9, 339.14, *maintain* 377.12, *bolster* 377.15, *take action* 509.12, *strengthen* 516.15, *support* 605.16, *bear* 605.17, *give moral support* 605.18, *support financially* 605.19, *make permanent* 667.5, *continue* 669.8, *establish reality* 719.12, *preserve* 815.14

sustained *frequent* 661.4, *unfailing* 667.3

sustained note *tone* 140.24

sustainer *provider* 605.10

sustaining 605.15; *edible* 92.20, *supportive* 825.18

sustainingly *supportively* 605.20, *frequently* 661.7

sustaining pedal *resonator* 236.5

sustainment *financial support* 605.8, *frequency* 661.1, *sustenance* 825.3

sustenance 825.3; *life requirement* 28.5, *provisions* 89.3, *food* 90.1, *refreshments* 94.3, *financial support* 605.8, *continuance* 669.3

sustentation *sustenance* 825.3

sustention *sustenance* 825.3

susurrate *hiss* 237.3

susurration *undercurrent of sound* 233.3, *hiss* 237.1

Sutlej *Rivers* 570

sutler [Arch] *peddler* 482.9

sutras *other text* 81.19

suttee *suicide* 30.8, *martyr* 504.6

suture *surgery* 107.15, *practice surgery* 107.33, *sewing* 130.5, *unification* 752.5, *joint* 752.7, *intertwine* 752.19

Suva *Countries* 566

Suwannee *Rivers* 570

suzerain *leader* 68.3

suzerainty *feudalism* 49.5, *governance* 52.6, *authority* 425.3

svelte *thin* 595.9

Svengali *motivator* 508.6

Svishtov *Breeds of Sheep* 16

swab *cleaning tool* 111.10, *clean* 111.17, *dryer* 560.5, *absorb* 560.20

swab [Inf] *unskilled person* 128.3

swabber *cleaner* 111.12, *dryer* 560.5

swabby [Inf] *naval person* 77.25, *nautical person* 690.12

Swabian-Hall *Breeds of Pigs* 16

swaddle *clothe* 100.43, *intertwine* 752.19

swaddling clothes *baby clothes* 100.24

swag *Architectural Elements* 134, *pitch* 684.25, *droop* 714.14

swag [Inf] *takings* 477.8, *stolen goods* 479.4, *cash* 484.2

swagger *pride oneself* 297.13, *brag* 400.17, *show off* 404.26, *bodily movement* 677.11, *walk* 677.17

swaggerer *combatant* 77.1, *proud person* 297.7, *insolent person* 400.7

swaggering 400.13, 404.20; *prideful* 297.8, *cocky* 402.11, *exhibitionism* 404.9

swaggeringly 404.35

swain *male* 32.1, *lover* 299.11

swale *farmland* 16.3, *lowlands* 597.6

Swaledale *Breeds of Sheep* 16

swallow *believe* 87.9, *eat* 92.21, *size of drink* 93.3, *drink* 93.19, *intake* 708.5, *ingest* 708.17

swallow *or* fall for hook, line, and sinker [Inf] *believe* 87.9, *be indiscriminate* 338.10

swallowing *eating* 92.1, *drinking* 93.1, *Phobias* 283, *intake* 708.5

swallowing air *Phobias* 283

swallowlike *avian* 36.19

swallow one's pride *humble oneself* 298.18

swallows *Collective Names* 59

swallowtail *flag* 184.8

swallow-tailed coat *formal clothes* 100.5, *jacket* 100.18

swallow the pill *succumb* 421.7

swallow up *consume* 523.16

swami *person in authority* 52.7, *educational leader* 68.11

swami belt *climbing equipment* 161.4

swamp *consume* 523.16, *water* 557.29, *marsh* 559.8, 572.3, *flow* 570.10, *shallowness* 599.1, *fill* 761.11, *overcrowd* 795.12, *critical situation* 824.6

swamp boat *Ships and Boats* 690

swamp cypress *Trees and Shrubs* 43

swamped *helpless* 515.9, *flooded* 557.24, 570.8

swamp-forest *marsh* 572.3

swampiness *bogginess* 559.7

swampland *marsh* 572.3

swampy *marshy* 559.11, *of landmasses* 572.12

Swan *Constellations* 7

swan *water bird* 36.9, *diving* 164.13, *white thing* 253.4

swan dive *diving* 164.6

swanherd *farm worker* 16.15

swank *disdain* 297.14, *brag* 400.17, *put on airs* 404.27, *stylish* 537.7

swankily *arrogantly* 297.18, *loftily* 404.30, *grandly* 404.37, *dashingly* 536.10

swankiness *grandeur* 404.10

swanky *arrogant* 297.9, *lofty* 404.15, *grand* 404.22, *stylish* 537.7

swannery *dwelling* 36.4

swans *Collective Names* 59

Swanscombe man *primitive humanity* 842.7

swansdown *plumage* 36.7, *Fabrics and Fibers* 130

swanskin *Fabrics and Fibers* 130

swan song *dying* 29.3, *attempt*

S
Z

390.1, *parting* 705.3, *conclusion* 761.3, *cessation* 773.2

swap *trade* 480.1, 480.18, *substitution* 672.1, *substitute* 672.5, *exchange* 673.1, 673.5, *transfer* 685.1, 685.8, *reciprocity* 729.1, *reciprocate* 729.7

swap ideas *consult* 176.11

swapped *substituted* 672.4, *exchanged* 673.4, *reciprocal* 729.4

swapping *mercantile* 480.13, *exchange* 673.1

sward *grassland* 45.2, *green place* 260.2

swardy *grassy* 45.8

swarm *procreate* 22.14, *dwelling* 40.7, *infest* 40.17, Collective Names 59, *crowd* 59.11, 59.26, 795.11, *abound* 97.8, *thicken* 594.9, *increase* 746.6, *throng* 795.4

swarm in *flood in* 706.14

swarming *crowded* 59.22, *excessive* 99.5, *dense* 594.6, *overrun* 712.6

swarm over *aim at* 385.15, *take over* 477.16

swarm up *ascend* 713.19

swarm with *infest* 40.17, *be excessive* 99.9

swart *dark-colored* 247.7, *dark* 254.6

swarthily *blackly* 254.12

swarthiness *blackness* 254.1

swarthy *dark-colored* 247.7, *dark* 254.6

swartness *blackness* 254.1

swashbuckler *combatant* 77.1, *show-off* 404.13

swashbuckling *exhibitionism* 404.9, *swaggering* 404.20

swashing *watering* 557.8

swastika *talisman* 86.9

swat *blow* 695.5, *hit* 695.11

swatch *piece* 760.2

swath *or* **swathe** *farmland* 16.3

swathe *farm* 16.19, *clothe* 100.43, *treat* 115.17, *wrap* 613.29, *enfold* 637.9, *intertwine* 752.19

swathed *protected* 613.20

swather *farm tool* 16.5

swathing *enfoldment* 637.3

S wave *seismic wave* 8.25

sway 378.12; *governance* 49.18, *authority* 52.1, 425.3, 514.5, 780.6, *manage* 126.10, *persuasion* 178.1, *persuade* 178.15, *action* 412.1, *motivate* 412.12, *personal influence* 512.3, *suspension* 604.1, *suspend* 604.13, *be regular* 663.10, *be changeable* 666.5, *oscillate* 683.12, *stagger* 684.11, *pitch* 684.25, *unbalance* 741.8, *leadership* 744.2

swayable *persuadable* 178.14

swayer *persuader* 178.9

swaying 378.4; *unsteady* 378.7, *suspension* 604.1, *suspended* 604.7, *changeable* 666.3, *unbalanced* 741.5

sway the crowd *practice sophistry* 330.11

Swaziland Countries 566

swear *use language* 5.42, *blaspheme* 301.14, *give evidence* 339.12, *promise* 458.11, *grossness* 535.3

swear an indictment *accuse* 442.8

swear at *hiss* 239.17

swear by *believe* 87.9

swear by all that is holy *vow* 189.23

swearer *affirmer* 189.9, *verifier* 336.4, *promise maker* 458.6

swear in *litigate* 54.27, *attest* 189.22

swearing *profanity* 301.3, *profane* 301.10, *bad-mannered* 411.6, *promise* 458.1

swearing in *witness* 54.16

swearingly *profanely* 301.19

swearing on the Bible *promise* 458.1

swear like a trooper *blaspheme* 301.14

swear off *disavow* 190.18, *renounce* 392.4, *disaccustom* 398.6, *be self-restrained* 455.10

swear on *or* **under oath** *promise* 458.11

swear on the Bible *vow* 189.23

swear on the Holy Bible *or on one's mother's life* *or* **head** *promise* 458.11

swear to *vow* 189.23, *give evidence* 339.12

swear to God *vow* 189.23

swearword *vulgarism* 5.20, *curse word* 301.4

sweat 25.8, 25.24; *body fluid* 19.16, 555.3, *secreted substance* 24.2, *secrete* 24.7, *work* 122.1, 122.8, *heat* 217.1, *feel hot* 217.19, *unpleasant-smelling thing* 227.2, *be fearful* 283.15, *try hard* 390.7, *occupy oneself* 412.15, *flow* 555.25, *exudate* 557.4, *seep* 559.16, *outflow* 707.4, *leak* 707.16, *warning signal* 814.3

sweatband *headdress* 100.35

sweat blood [Inf] *overwork* 122.9, *worry* 283.16

sweat bullets [Inf] *be fearful* 283.15

sweater 100.17; *body covering* 613.3

sweater dress *dress* 100.11

sweat for nothing *waste effort* 802.13

sweat gland *secretory mechanism* 24.3, *mammalian characteristic* 35.3, *body orifice* 583.3

sweatily *glandularly* 24.8, *excrementally* 25.27, *fluidly* 555.26

sweatiness *heat* 217.1, *stench* 227.1

sweating *secretion* 24.1, *secretory* 24.4, *sweat* 25.8, *sweaty* 25.17, *working* 122.6, *seeping* 559.12, *outflow* 707.4

sweating sickness *tropical disease* 114.10

sweat like a trooper *or* **horse** *or* **pig** *sweat* 25.24

sweat of one's brow *sweat* 25.8, *work* 122.1, *exertion* 122.4

sweatpants *informal clothes* 100.7, *pants* 100.14

sweat scraper *riding equipment* 159.9

sweatshirt *informal clothes* 100.7, *shirt* 100.13

sweatshop *factory* 124.8

sweat socks *legwear* 100.26

sweat suit *informal clothes* 100.7, *suit* 100.16

sweaty 25.17; *humid* 9.48, *fluid* 19.25, *secretory* 24.4, *stinking* 227.3, *expulsive* 709.11

Sweden Countries 566

Swedenborgianism Christian Groups 81

swedes [Brit] *crop* 16.8

Swedish Friesian Breeds of Cattle 16

Swedish gymnastics *gymnastics* 157.1

Swedish Half-bred *or* **Swedish**

Warmblood Horse and Pony Breeds 159

Swedish Jersey Breeds of Cattle 16

Swedish Landrace Breeds of Pigs 16, Breeds of Sheep 16

Swedish Midnight Sun *automobile rallies* 146.6

Swedish Polled Breeds of Cattle 16

Swedish Red-and-White Breeds of Cattle 16

sweeny *animal disease* 34.10

sweep *crowd* 59.26, *clean* 111.17, *be on the track* 146.11, *canoeing* 150.26, *rowing* 150.27, *play* 155.8, *play offense* 155.18, *range* 563.7, *extend* 563.14, *propel* 696.15, *go easily* 823.18, *defeat* 845.17

sweep along *be swift* 694.10

sweepback *miscellaneous aviation terms* 689.9

sweep before one *propel* 696.15

sweeper *cleaner* 111.12, *automobile racing terms* 146.3, *soccer participant* 163.4

sweeping *cleaning* 111.2, *complete* 761.6, *including* 763.3, *general* 778.9, *universal* 778.10, *generalized* 778.12

sweeping *or* **loose** *or* **vague generalization** *or* **statement** *generalization* 778.5

sweeping bow *bow* 716.6

sweepingness *nonspecificity* 778.2, *widespreadness* 778.3

sweepings *dirt* 112.5, *residue* 750.2, *refuse* 802.5

sweep off one's feet *win the love of* 299.27

sweep out *void* 709.23

sweep problems out of the way *overcome obstacles* 845.14

sweep rowing *rowing* 150.14

sweeps [Inf] *game of chance* 842.5

sweepstakes *game of chance* 842.5

sweep stroke *canoeing techniques* 150.11

sweep the board *defeat* 845.17

sweep the boards *be victorious* 845.16

sweep under the carpet *make invisible* 245.7

sweep under the rug *or* **carpet** *or* **mat** *conceal* 181.12

sweep up *clean* 111.17, *ascend* 713.19

sweet 222.5; *edible* 92.20, *drinkable* 93.18, *pleasurable* 214.6, *tasty* 219.4, *pleasant* 271.5, *lovable* 299.20, *courteous* 410.6, *beautiful* 529.7

sweet [Brit] *dish* 90.7

sweet alyssum Flowers 42

sweet-and-sour *sweet* 222.5

sweet as sugar *or* **honey** *or* **a nut** *sweet* 222.5

sweet bay Trees and Shrubs 43

sweetbread *variety meat* 90.30

sweetbrier Flowers 42

sweet by-and-by *future time* 650.1

sweet dreams *ease* 819.1

sweet drink 222.4

sweeten 222.7; *provide drink* 93.21, *calm* 521.8

sweetened *sweet* 222.5

sweetener 222.2; *gift* 472.2, *damages* 489.8

sweetening *sweetener* 222.2

sweeten the kitty *give out* 472.12

sweeten the pot *entice* 178.16, *remunerate* 489.21

sweet Fanny Adams *or* **sweet FA** [Brit inf] *nothingness* 718.2

sweet gum Trees and Shrubs 43

sweetheart *girlfriend* 33.4, *term of endearment* 299.7, *loved one* 299.13

sweetheart name *name* 202.8

sweethearts *lovers* 299.12

sweetie [Inf] *term of endearment* 299.7, *loved one* 299.13

sweetie pie [Inf] *term of endearment* 299.7

sweeties [Brit] *confectionery* 222.3

sweetish *sweet* 222.5

sweetly 222.8; *tastily* 219.7, *lovably* 299.31, *courteously* 410.13

sweetmeat *sweets* 90.39, *sweetener* 222.2

sweetness 222.1; *physical pleasure* 214.1, *flavor* 219.3, *pleasantness* 271.1, *lovability* 299.5, *courtesy* 410.1, *beauty* 529.1

sweet nothings *communication of love* 299.6, *empty talk* 362.5

sweet on [Inf] *in love* 299.16

sweet pea Flowers 42

sweet potato Musical Instruments 142

sweet roll *bread* 90.10

sweets 90.39; *course* 92.12, *confectionery* 222.3, *love token* 299.8

sweets [Inf] *term of endearment* 299.7

sweet-scented *pleasurable* 214.6, *fragrant* 226.9

sweet-shop [Brit] *food provider* 90.6, *confectionery* 222.3

sweet sixteen *young* 26.11

sweet sleep *ease* 819.1

sweet smell *odor* 224.1, *fragrance* 226.1

sweet-smelling *fragrant* 226.4

sweet smell of success *success* 845.1

sweet talk [Inf] *persuasion* 178.1, *communication of love* 299.6, *blarney* 439.2, *positive stimulus* 508.5

sweet talking [Inf] *persuasion* 178.1

sweet-talk [Inf] *persuade* 178.15, *communicate love* 299.25, *blarney* 439.13, *influence* 508.11, *be cunning* 822.5

sweet-talking [Inf] *good-mannered* 410.7, *honeyed* 439.8

sweet taste *taste* 219.1

sweet tooth *sweetness* 222.1

sweet william Flowers 42

sweet wine *wine* 93.11, *sweet drink* 222.4

swell 581.15; *wave* 8.16, 571.3, *loud tone* 232.3, *shatter the peace* 232.10, *brag* 400.17, *billow* 571.9, *swelling* 581.2, *be convex* 634.7, *protrude* 634.8, *grow* 676.10, *turbulence* 684.3, *atmospheric agitation* 684.13, *send up* 715.12, *change by degrees* 739.8, *spread* 746.3, *increase* 746.6, *augment* 748.13, *be full* 761.12

swell [Inf] *great* 445.14

swelled 581.10

swelled head *vain person* 402.7

swelled-headed *vain* 402.8

swelled-headedness *vanity* 402.1

swellheaded *vain* 402.8

swellheaded *or* **swelled-headed** *prideful* 297.8

swellheadedness *vanity* 402.1

swelling 581.2; *symptom* 114.3, *skin disease* 114.16, *ulcer* 114.18, loud 232.6, mark 533.2, oceanic 571.7, enlargement 581.7, growing 581.12, 676.6, convexity 634.1, bulge 634.2, protuberance 634.3, convex 634.5, growth 676.3, increase 746.1, spread 746.3

swell out be convex 634.7

swell the ranks band together 59.27, support 748.14

swell with pride pride oneself 297.13

swelter sweat 25.24, feel hot 217.19

sweltering hot 9.47, 217.11

swelteringly meteorologically 9.60

sweltry hot 9.47

swept cleaned 111.14

swept clean forgiven 312.5

swerve displacement 574.1, displace 574.15, divergence 607.2, diverge 607.11, deviating motion 698.3, deviate 698.15

swerved displaced 574.8

swerving displaced 574.8, divergent 607.7, deviating motion 698.3, indirect 698.9

swift 694.6; immediate 645.5, hasty 818.3

swiftly 694.16; immediately 645.8, hastily 818.7

swift-moving swift 694.6

swiftness 694.1; haste 818.1

swift person speeder 694.5

swig [Inf] drink 93.19, size of drink 93.3, get drunk 121.35

swigging [Inf] drinking 93.1, drunken 121.28

swill 112.6; animal feed 16.12, drink 93.19, get drunk 121.35, mud 561.8

swill (out) bathe 111.18

swiller drinker 93.16, drunkard 121.8

swilling drinking 93.1, 93.17, 121.2, drunken 121.28

swim 164.14; be healthy 113.11, swimming 164.12

swim against the current have difficulty 824.18

swim against the tide be independent 782.20

swim-and-tow swimming rescue 164.5

swim bladder fish characteristic 38.8

swim-down surface dive diving 164.6

swim in abound 97.8

swimmer 164.11; athlete 422.15

swimming 164.1, 164.12; health improvement 113.3, Sporting Activities 145, athletics 422.7, bodily improvement 807.10

swimming area swimming place 164.9

swimming associations 164.10

swimming equipment 164.8

swimming hole swimming place 164.9, small lake 568.2

swimmingly skillfully 127.16, easily 823.19, successfully 845.19

swimming place 164.9

swimming pool swimming place 164.9, small lake 568.2

swimming rescue 164.5

swimming strokes swimming techniques 164.2

swimming techniques 164.2

swimming the English Channel swimming 164.1

swimming trunks beachwear 100.23, swimming equipment 164.8

swimsuit beachwear 100.23, swimming equipment 164.8

swim team competitive swimming 164.3

swim together work together 827.14

swim under water swim 164.14

swim upstream have difficulty 824.18

swimwear beachwear 100.23, swimming equipment 164.8

swim with the stream do easily 823.16

swim or go with the stream or tide or current abide by 781.12

swim with the tide follow 401.14

swindle 193.19; foul play 193.6, disreputable action 371.3, method 387.4, be wicked 448.13, taking away 477.5, take money away 477.20, dishonesty 479.7, act dishonestly 479.18, not pay 490.9, overcharge 496.10, be cunning 822.5

swindled fraudulent 479.13

swindler schemer 193.10, villain 448.5, dishonest person 479.11, cunning person 822.3

swindling nonpayment 490.1

swine livestock 16.11, Collective Names 59, villain 448.5

swineherd farm worker 16.15

swinepox animal disease 34.10

swing 671.4, 671.12; popular music 140.4, jazz 140.5, beat time 140.29, play 141.14, play baseball 147.9, row 150.32, boxing techniques 152.5, box 152.19, exercise 157.12, cross-country techniques 162.8, ski 162.35, tennis strokes 165.2, participate 166.22, amusement park and playground equipment 167.8, action 412.1, operation 509.1, available space 563.6, suspension 604.1, suspend 604.13, frequency 663.2, be regular 663.10, be changeable 666.5, oscillation 683.1, oscillator 683.7, oscillate 683.12, stagger 684.11, pitch 684.25, blow 695.5, sporting hit 695.6, hit 695.11, deviating motion 698.3, slide 698.24, unbalance 741.8, tendency 838.2

swing and sway be regular 663.10

swing around swing 671.12, turn around 680.22, rotate 682.14

swingback discus throwing 166.13

swing back swing 671.12

swing bridge bridge 551.10

swinger gymnast 157.10

swing from suspend 604.13

swinging musical 140.25, horizontal bar 157.5, uneven parallel bars 157.6, suspension 604.1, suspended 604.7, frequent 663.6, oscillating 683.8, unbalanced 741.5

swinging both ways [Inf] sexual nature 20.4

swingletree figurative usage 43.9

swingman basketball team 148.2

swing of the pendulum swing 671.4, oscillation 683.1

swing to the hill cross-country techniques 162.8, ski 162.35

swinish ungulate 35.31

swipe hit 418.9, 695.11, blow 695.5, throw 696.4

swipe (at) strike 418.21

swipe [Inf] steal 479.14

swiping [Inf] stealing 479.1

swirl 682.16; river turbulence 570.5, flow 570.10, reel 682.4, vortex 682.6, turbulence 684.3, agitate 684.22

swirling turning 682.3, rotating 682.11

swish small sound 233.4, sound faint 233.8, hiss 237.1, 237.3

swish [Inf] playing terms 148.4

swishingly sibilantly 237.4

Swiss Black-Brown Mountain Breeds of Sheep 16

Swiss Brownheaded Mutton Breeds of Sheep 16

Swiss cross national emblem 184.7

Swiss Improved Landrace Breeds of Pigs 16

Swiss White Alpine Breeds of Sheep 16

Swiss White Mountain Breeds of Sheep 16

Swiss Yorkshire Breeds of Pigs 16

switch tree part 43.2, blunt weapon 78.5, hand tool 103.3, instrument of punishment 454.13, hit 454.28, hairdressing 530.7, displacement 574.1, displace 574.15, change 665.1, 665.14, substitution 672.1, substitute 672.5, exchange 673.1, 673.5, transfer 685.8, track 688.2, rail 688.3, shove aside 698.23, change direction 703.15, component 760.3

switchback automobile racing terms 146.3, divergence 607.2, railroad 691.8

switchblade (knife) sharp weapon 78.6

switchboard stage 136.18, telephone exchange 169.13

switchboard operator clerical worker 123.5, telephone personnel 169.14

switched displaced 574.8, changed 665.10, substituted 672.4, exchanged 673.4

switched off unheard 229.7, inoperative 515.8, suspended 519.3

switch engine train 688.4

switcher train 688.4

switching circuit function 14.38, exchange 673.1

switching circuit circuit 14.37

switching the lights off or out darkening 247.2

switchman railroad worker 688.7

switch off be insensible 213.7, remove power from 515.13

switch on power 106.17, activate 509.11, 771.28, empower 514.20

switch on or off conduct 14.51

switch on a light light 246.19

switch the lights off or out make dark 247.10

switchyard railroad station 688.6

Switzerland Countries 566

swivel historical gun 78.10, type of chair 101.4, rowboat parts 150.15, turn around 680.22, axle 682.7, rotate 682.14

swiveling rotating 682.11

swiveltree figurative usage 43.9

swollen of disease 114.25, fat 579.15, swelled 581.10, thick 594.5, convex 634.5, increased 746.5

swollen adenoids respiratory disease 114.12

swollenness swelling 581.2

swollen with pride prideful 297.8

swoon desensitization 213.2, fatigue 820.1, be fatigued 820.5

swooning fatigued 820.2

swoop acceleration 694.3, be swift 694.10, fall 714.4, drop 714.15

swooping fall 714.4, falling 714.11, submergence 716.3

swoosh small sound 233.4, sound faint 233.8, hiss 237.1, 237.3

sword weapon 78.1, sharp weapon 78.6, agent of destruction 523.7, sharp-pointed thing 549.4, sharp-edged thing 549.6

sword, the war 76.1

sword dancing Dancing Types 135

Swordfish Constellations 7

swordfish food fish and shellfish 90.20, game fish 154.10

sword in hand warring 76.26

sword knot Knots, Bends, Hitches, Splices 754

swordlike sharp-edged 549.12

sword of Damocles inevitability 95.6, terrorization 283.5, danger 811.1

sword of state insignia 184.5

sword play dramatic style 136.3

swordplay fencing 153.1, duel 422.12

sword point sharp point 549.2

swordsman combatant 77.1

sworn vowed 189.14, dutiful 433.6, promised 458.8, contractual 459.7

sworn enemy hostile person 63.5

sworn off abstinent 455.7

sworn statement certificate 185.2

sworn testimony or statement attestation 189.2

sworn to vowed 189.14, loyal 426.5

swung dash Reference Signs 183

sybarite pleasure-seeker 214.4, self-indulgent person 456.5

sybaritic pleasure-seeking 214.10, self-indulgent 456.6

sybaritism self-indulgence 456.1

sycamine Trees and Shrubs 43

sycamore Trees and Shrubs 43

Sychevka Breeds of Cattle 16

syconium botanical fruit 44.2

sycophancy 401.2, 439.5; ungenuineness 192.2, deference 410.4

sycophant 401.3; humble person 298.7, assenter 346.3, 462.5, submitter 421.2, flatterer 439.6, adherent 755.4, follower 794.10, subordinate 432.5

sycophantic 401.7, 439.11; deferential 410.8, submitting 421.3, loyal 426.5, smooth-mannered 545.9, tenacious 755.6

sycophantically 401.16; deferentially 410.15, flatteringly 439.16, suavely 545.15, tenaciously 755.12

syllabary alphabet 5.16

syllabic meter meter 139.10

syllabify word 5.43

syllable spoken letter 5.15, word 5.43, utterance 205.10

syllabus subject 48.3, outline 204.2, list 785.1

syllogism philosophical argument 4.5, philosophical term 4.7, reasoning 319.2

syllogist philosopher 4.9, reasoner 319.5

syllogize rationalize 4.20

sylph sprite 86.12, thin person 595.4

sylphic thin 595.9

sylphlike thin 595.9

sylvan horticultural 17.14, wooded 43.12

sylvatic wooded 43.12

symbiont or symbiote ecology 13.25

symbiosis ecology 13.25, fungal association 47.5, lichen 47.16, interrelation 729.2, *combination* 757.1, *accompaniment* 794.1, *mutual relationship* 827.3

symbiotic *of animals* 34.13, *algal* 47.20, *interrelated* 729.5, *united* 752.10, *collaborative* 757.7, *concurrent* 794.13

symbiotic or symbiotical *cooperative* 827.9

symbiotic alga *alga* 47.10

symbiotically *saprophytically* 47.24, *algologically* 47.25, *interrelatedly* 729.11, *in combination* 757.11, *concurrently* 794.22

symbiotic fungus *fungal association* 47.5

symbol 108.28, 183.3; *tradition* 1.7, *written letter* 5.14, *idol* 83.5, *talisman* 86.9, *sign* 183.1, *image* 187.3, *number* 783.1

symbolic 183.12, 361.8; *language type* 5.11, *of language* 5.35, *ritualistic* 85.15, *occult* 86.16, *identified* 184.9, *representational* 187.8, *representing* 202.14, *trivial* 800.14, *identifiable* 843.10, *mysterious* 844.11

symbolical *written* 5.36, *symbolic* 183.12

symbolically *sociologically* 2.15, *linguistically* 5.44, *ritually* 85.21, *pictorially* 133.11, *indicatively* 183.21, *identifiably* 184.13, *representationally* 187.15, *meaningfully* 361.16, *mysteriously* 844.17

symbolic anthropology *anthropology* 1.1

symbolic interaction *social environment* 2.4

symbolic logic *mathematical logic* 6.60

symbolics 85.4; *occultism* 86.1

symbolism 183.4; *sacramentalism* 85.3, *occultism* 86.1, *symbol* 108.28, Western Art Styles 133, Western Literary Groups 139, *aspect of fiction* 139.5, Phobias 283, *mysteriousness* 844.5

symbolist *author* 139.13

symbolistic *symbolic* 183.12

symbolization *symbol* 108.28, *symbolism* 183.4, *representation* 187.1, *manifestation* 843.2, *mysteriousness* 844.5

symbolize *occult* 86.22, *signify* 183.16, *represent* 187.10, *mean* 361.13, *imply* 844.14

symbol list *symbol* 183.3

symbol of peace 73.6

symbological *symbolic* 183.12

symbology *symbolism* 183.4

symbolophobia Phobias 283

symmetric *spatial* 6.76, *corresponding* 606.6, *symmetrical* 626.4, *frequent* 663.6, *correlative* 729.6

symmetrical 626.4; *spatial* 6.76, *correspondent* 334.16, *graceful* 527.4, *frequent* 663.6, *correlative* 729.6, *same* 730.7, *similar* 733.7, *harmonious* 735.11, *equal* 740.8, *ordered* 765.10

symmetrical or symmetric *corresponding* 606.6

symmetric or symmetrical figure *geometric figure* 6.39

symmetrically 626.7; *correspondingly* 334.27, *gracefully* 527.8, *regularly* 663.14, *correlatively* 729.12, *similarly* 733.17, *harmoniously* 735.31,

equitably 740.15, *methodically* 765.27

symmetricalness *symmetry* 626.1

symmetric design *combinatorics* 6.63

symmetric difference *set* 6.19

symmetric fold *fold* 8.22

symmetric relation *mathematical logic* 6.60

symmetrize 626.6; *correspond* 606.8, *correspond to* 727.10, *correlate* 729.9, *make the same* 730.16, *make similar* 733.15, *be in accord* 735.21

symmetrophobia Phobias 283

symmetry 626.1; *geometric figure* 6.39, Phobias 283, *correspondence* 334.8, 606.2, *grace* 527.2, *beauty* 529.1, *frequency* 663.2, *correlation* 729.3, *sameness* 730.1, *similarity* 733.1, *accord* 735.1, *equilibrium* 740.2, *method* 765.7

sympathetic *friendly* 62.5, *sensitive* 266.11, 267.3, *liking* 290.4, *loving* 299.15, *compassionate* 305.8, *pitying* 308.4, *assenting* 346.4, *unselfish* 443.5, *kind* 445.12, *agreeing* 462.6, *soft-hearted* 543.11, *supportive* 605.11, *compatible* 735.14, *benevolent* 825.21

sympathetically *amicably* 62.13, *sensitively* 267.6, *admiringly* 290.11, *lovingly* 299.29, *compassionately* 305.14, *pityingly* 308.11, *unselfishly* 443.9, *kindly* 445.20, *agreeably* 462.14, *supportively* 605.20, *attractively* 700.14, *compatibly* 735.34, *benevolently* 825.34

sympathetic magic *witchcraft* 86.6

sympathetic vibration *resonance* 236.1

sympathies *feelings* 266.1

sympathize *feel for* 266.17, *be sensitive* 267.5, *love* 299.21, *be compassionate* 305.11, *pity* 308.6, *have insight* 360.16, *agree with* 462.10, *give moral support* 605.18, *sustain* 825.25

sympathizer *feeling person* 266.8, *benevolent person* 305.6, *assenter* 346.3, 462.5, *supporter* 605.9

sympathize with *comfort* 214.14, *like* 290.8, *pity* 308.6, *be unselfish* 443.7, *have a rapport with* 735.24

sympathizing *pitying* 308.4, *compatible* 735.14

sympathizingly *pityingly* 308.11, *compatibly* 735.34

sympathy *friendly relations* 62.3, *good feeling* 266.4, *sensitivity* 267.1, *liking* 290.1, *compassion* 305.2, *pity* 308.1, *condolence* 308.2, *insight* 360.3, *unselfishness* 443.2, *kindness* 445.3, *agreement* 462.1, *moral support* 605.7, *attraction* 700.1, *compatibility* 735.4, *sustenance* 825.3, *fellowship* 827.2

sympathy lock-out *strike* 57.8

sympathy strike *strike* 57.8

symphonic *melodious* 140.26, *harmonizing* 735.12

symphonically *in harmony* 735.32

symphonic music *classical music* 140.2

symphonious *melodious* 140.26, *harmonizing* 735.12

symphoniously *in harmony* 735.32

symphonization *harmonization* 735.2

symphonize *harmonize* 140.28, 735.22

symphony Musical Forms 140, *harmonization* 735.2

symphony concert *performance* 141.8

symphony orchestra *instrumental group* 141.3

symphylan *myriapod* 39.11

symphysis *combination* 757.1

symphystic *combinatory* 757.6

symploce *repetition* 797.1

symposium *philosophical argument* 4.5, *conference* 59.5, *dissertation* 203.1, *place for conversation* 210.5

symptom 114.3; *signs* 183.2, *indication* 339.3, *prediction* 358.1, *concomitant* 794.4, *forewarning* 814.2, *manifestation* 843.2

symptomatic *diagnostic* 107.29, *symbolic* 183.12, *predicting* 358.11, *warning* 814.6

symptomatically *indicatively* 183.21

symptomatological *diagnostic* 107.29, *symbolic* 183.12

symptomatology *medical science* 107.5, *symbolism* 183.4, *science of interpretation* 365.5

symptomless carrier *infectious person* 114.9

symptoms of fear 283.3

synagogue *place of worship* 83.8, *architectural structure* 134.4

syn-anti isomer(ism) *structure* 11.7

synapse *nervous system* 19.14

synaptic *internal* 19.23

sync [Inf] *synchronism* 649.2, *synchronize* 649.7, *harmonization* 735.2

syncarpous *of a fruit* 44.8

synchromism Western Art Styles 133

synchronic *linguistic* 5.34

synchronicity *occult and psychic phenomena* 86.7, *sameness* 730.1, *combination* 757.1

synchronic linguistics Linguistic Studies 5

synchronism 649.2, 794.2

synchronization *compatibility* 462.3, *synchronism* 649.2, *harmonization* 735.2, *combination* 757.1

synchronize 649.7; *be compatible* 462.12, *keep time* 646.12, *make the same* 730.16, *harmonize* 735.22, 765.20, *equalize* 740.12, *come together* 757.10, *accompany* 794.16

synchronized 649.5; *swimming* 164.12, *compatible* 462.8, *harmonizing* 735.12, *combined* 757.5

synchronized flash *flash* 132.13

synchronized swimming Sporting Activities 145, *swimming* 164.1

synchronize watches or clocks *keep time* 646.12

synchronizing *motion-picture editing* 137.8

synchronous *melodious* 140.26, *synchronized* 649.5, *same* 730.7, *harmonizing* 735.12, *combined* 757.5

synchronously 649.9; *identically* 730.18, *in harmony* 735.32, *in combination* 757.11

synchrony *harmonization* 735.2

synclastic surface *surface* 6.36

syncline *fold* 8.22, 637.1

syncopate *beat time* 140.29, *play* 141.14

syncopated *musical* 140.25, *harmonic* 140.27

syncopatedly *tunefully* 140.30

syncopation *jazz* 140.5, *tempo* 140.22, *musical time* 639.7

syncopator *composer* 141.9

syncope *conciseness* 198.1, *shortening* 591.2

syncopic or syncopal *concise* 198.4

syncretic *mixed* 751.8, *combinatory* 757.6

syncretically *in combination* 757.11

syncretism *mixture* 751.1, *combination* 757.1

syncretize *combine* 757.9

syncytial *cellular* 13.30

syndeton *syntax* 5.32

syndicalism *political and economic philosophy* 4.6, *anarchism* 51.3

syndicalist *political and economic philosopher* 4.10, *anarchist* 51.4

syndicalistic *of a political philosophy* 4.14, *anarchistic* 51.7

syndicate *association* 59.4, 480.8, *villain* 448.5, *federate* 480.21, *collection* 757.3

syndicated program *program* 172.10

syndiotactic *polymeric* 11.35

syndiotactic polymer *polymer* 11.9

syndrome *symptom* 114.3, *signs* 183.2, *prediction* 358.1, *concomitant* 794.4, *manifestation* 843.2

synecdoche *literary device* 139.12

synecology *ecology* 13.25

syneresis *contraction* 582.1

synergetic *cooperative* 827.9

synergetically *cooperatively* 827.18

synergic *cooperative* 827.9

synergism *cooperation* 827.1

synergistic *cooperative* 827.9

synergistically *cooperatively* 827.18

synergy *cooperation* 827.1

synesthesia *association of ideas* 108.31, *literary device* 139.12

syngamy *mixture* 751.1, *sexual union* 752.6

syngenesis *sexual union* 752.6

syngenesophobia Phobias 283

synizesis *contraction* 582.1

synod *conference* 59.5

synodic *astronomical* 7.33

synonym *word* 5.17, *type of meaning* 361.1, *equivalence* 730.3, *equalization* 740.4

synonym dictionary *word book* 5.27

synonymical *worded* 5.38

synonymity *type of meaning* 361.4, *equivalence* 730.3, *equalization* 740.4

synonymous *similar* 361.7, *translational* 365.11, *equivalent* 730.9

synonymously *equivalently* 730.20

synonymousness *type of meaning* 361.4, *equivalence* 730.3

synonymy *type of meaning* 361.4, *equivalence* 730.3

synopsis *outline* 198.2, 617.1, *summary* 204.1, *shortened version* 591.3, *whole situation* 759.3

synopsize *be concise* 198.5, *summarize* 204.7, *shorten* 591.9, *outline* 617.5

synopsized *summarized* 204.6, *outlined* 617.4
synoptic *meteorologic* 9.38, *short* 591.6, *general* 778.9
synoptically *meteorologically* 9.60
Synoptic Gospels *Christian text* 81.16
synoptic map *or chart weather forecast* 9.4
synoptic meteorology *meteorology* 9.1
synovia *lubricant* 562.7
synsepalous *of flowers* 42.11
syntactic *of grammar* 5.41
syntactically *linguistically* 5.44, *grammatically* 5.48
syntactic analysis *syntax* 5.32
syntactic meaning *syntax* 5.32
syntactics Linguistic Studies 5, *symbolism* 183.4
syntactic structure *syntax* 5.32
syntax **5.32**; Linguistic Studies 5, *language* 5.4, *language element* 5.13, *part of speech* 760.7
synthesis *philosophical argument* 4.5, *philosophical term* 4.7, *chemistry* 11.1, *chemical reaction* 11.8, *sameness* 730.1, *mixed thing* 751.2, *union* 752.1, *combination* 757.1
synthesize *react* 11.38, *metabolize* 12.26, *process* 14.50, *reason* 319.11, *produce* 522.13, *combine* 757.9
synthesized *synthetic* 11.31, *combined* 757.5
synthesizer Musical Instruments 142
synthetic **11.31**; *dialectical* 4.16, *language type* 5.11, *chemical compound* 11.4, *chemical* 11.24, *fabric* 130.1, *produced* 522.12, *artificial* 720.12, *unauthentic* 722.9, *simulated* 733.11, *imitation* 736.8
synthetically *chemically* 11.42, *unauthentically* 722.17, *imitatively* 736.12
synthetic cubism Western Art Styles 133
synthetic drug *drug* 115.9
synthetic dye *dye* 130.8, *coloring agent* 251.5
synthetic fabric *fabric* 130.1
synthetic fiber *fiber* 130.2
synthetic plasma *blood* 555.4
synthetic resin *plastics* 104.6, *resin* 562.6
synthetic rubber *rubber* 546.3
synthetism Western Art Styles 133
syntony *personality type* 108.6
syphilis *sexually transmitted disease (STD)* 114.17, Phobias 283
syphilitic *infectious person* 114.9, *of disease* 114.25
syphilitic sore *sexually transmitted disease (STD)* 114.17
syphilophobia Phobias 283
Syr Darya Rivers 570
Syria Countries 566
Syrian Deserts 572
syringa Flowers 42
syrinx *avian characteristic* 36.6, Musical Instruments 142
syrup *sweetener* 222.2, *semiliquid* 561.7
syrupiness *sweetness* 222.1, *viscosity* 561.1
syrupy *sweet* 222.5, *gelatinous* 561.16
system *geological time* 8.47, *means* 102.1, *procedure* 387.2, *standard procedure* 397.6, *form* 624.1, *way* 691.1, *whole thing* 759.2, *order* 765.1, *method* 765.7, *organization* 767.3, *formula* 780.7
system, the *governance* 52.6
systematic *biological* 13.27, *taxonomic* 13.35, *negotiated* 57.16, *planned* 387.10, *formed* 624.6, *ordered* 765.10, *well-ordered* 765.14, *organizational* 767.13, *uniform* 780.10
systematically **397.22**; *biologically* 13.36, *as planned* 387.16, *formatively* 624.10, *methodically* 765.27, *in place* 767.24
systematic error *measurement* 10.67
systematic indifference *indifference* 289.1
systematics *life science* 13.1, *taxonomy* 13.24, *classification of life* 28.10, *methodicalness* 765.6
systematic sampling *population* 6.55
systematic theology Theologies 81
systematic wage structure *bargaining terms* 57.10
systematism *methodicalness* 765.6
systematization *planning* 387.8, *methodicalness* 765.6, *organization* 767.3
systematize **765.19**; *plan* 387.12, *form* 624.9, *make regular* 663.9, *organize* 767.19, *regulate* 780.15
systematized *organized* 767.12
systematizer *planner* 387.9
systematology *methodicalness* 765.6
systemic *of grammar* 5.41
systemic fungicide *pest killer* 17.9
systemic grammar *grammar* 5.28
systemic herbicide *pest control* 16.13
systemic insecticide *pest control* 16.13
systemic painting Western Art Styles 133
systemization *habituation* 397.7
system manager *computer user* 15.3
system of equations *equation* 6.25
systems analysis *computing* 15.2
systems analyst *computer user* 15.3, *planner* 387.9, *counter* 784.6
systems and process control **14.28**
system software **15.13**; *software* 15.12
systems theory Branches of Mathematics 6
systole *contraction* 582.1
systole and diastole *oscillation* 683.1
syzygy *planet* 7.16
Szondi test Psychological Tests 108

T

ta! [Brit inf] *thank you!* 310.9
tab *identify* 184.11
tabard *jacket* 100.18
tabaret Fabrics and Fibers 130
Tabasco™ *mixed drink* 93.12
Tabasco™ sauce *sauce* 90.17
tabbouleh *salad* 90.16
tabby Breeds of Cats 35, Fabrics and Fibers 130, *mottled* 263.10
tabby cat *variegated thing* 263.5
tabernacle *place of worship* 83.8, *sacred object* 83.11
tabes *emaciation* 595.2

tabescence *shortening* 582.2, *emaciation* 595.2
tabescent *contracting* 582.10, *emaciated* 595.10
tabetic *emaciated* 595.10
tabla Musical Instruments 142
Table Constellations 7
table **785.2**; *furniture* 101.1, Architectural Elements 134, *record book* 185.5, *be evasive* 386.20, *division* 577.6, *layer* 588.1, *horizontal surface* 603.3, *defer* 604.15, *supporting structure* 605.2, *delay* 658.13, *chart* 767.8, *calculator* 784.5, *list* 785.1
tableau *picture* 133.5, *view* 242.8, *show* 404.12, *formal occasion* 406.4
tableau curtain *stage set* 136.19
table bird 36.10
tablecloth *tableware* 92.13, *protective covering* 613.5
tabled *itemized* 577.9, *deferred* 604.9, *held up* 658.6
table d'hôte *culinary* 91.9
table game *type of game* 167.2
table hockey Board and Table Games 167
table lamp *electric light* 246.6
tableland *upland* 572.7, *heights* 596.4, *horizontal surface* 603.3
table linen *tableware* 92.13
table manners *tradition* 397.5
table of contents *book part* 174.5, *table* 785.2
table pad *tableware* 92.13
tables *statistics* 784.2
table salt *basic cooking ingredient* 91.8
table setting *ornament* 532.7
tablespoon *tableware* 92.13
tablespoon(ful) *container(ful)* 738.2
tablet *dose of medicine* 115.3, *record book* 185.5, *monument* 185.10, *slice* 588.4
table talk *chat* 210.2
table tapper *occultist* 86.13
table tapping *occult and psychic phenomena* 86.7
table tennis Sporting Activities 145, *tennis* 165.1, Board and Table Games 167
tablet flower Architectural Elements 134
tableware **92.13**
tabling *deferment* 604.3, *delay* 658.3
tabloid *newspaper* 175.2
taboo *tradition* 1.7, *prohibition* 503.1, *prohibited* 503.5, *censor* 503.10, *exclusion* 764.1, *excluded* 764.6, *exclude* 764.7
taboo word *vulgarism* 5.20
tabor Musical Instruments 142
tabs *stage set* 136.19
tabular *pictorial* 6.75, *itemized* 577.9, *horizontal* 603.6, *diagrammatic* 767.17, *classificatory* 777.9
tabula rasa *obliteration* 186.1, *emptiness* 576.2, *new start* 652.5
tabularly *inventorially* 785.13
tabulate *record* 185.13, *register* 185.15, *itemize* 577.13, *systematize* 765.19, *categorize* 767.21, *sort* 777.13, *list* 785.11
tabulated *itemized* 577.9, *categorized* 767.15, *listed* 785.9
tabulation *categorization* 767.5, *listing* 785.8
tabulation of ballots *election* 382.6
tabulator *calculator* 784.5

tacamahac Tree Products 43
tace Musical Terms and Expression Marks 140
tacet Musical Terms and Expression Marks 140
tachisme Western Art Styles 133
tachometer Fields of Measurement 589
tachometry Fields of Measurement 589
tachophobia Phobias 283
tachycardia *cardiovascular disease* 114.13
tachymeter Fields of Measurement 589
tachymetry Fields of Measurement 589
tacit **844.10**; *silent* 231.2, *similar* 361.7
tacitly **844.16**
taciturn **208.4**; *silent* 181.10, 231.2, *concise* 198.4, *avoiding* 386.9, *shy* 409.7
taciturnity **208.1**; *verbal concealment* 181.3, *conciseness* 198.1, *silence* 231.1, *unsociability* 409.1, *quietness* 844.4
taciturnly **208.9**; *unsocially* 409.13
tack *food* 90.1, *sail* 150.29, *riding equipment* 159.9, *ski* 162.35, *sharp-pointed thing* 549.4, *be changeable* 666.5, *maneuver* 677.18, *navigate* 690.15, *way* 691.1, *bearing* 697.2, *deviating course* 698.2, *deviate* 698.15, *intertwine* 752.19, *fastener* 754.7, *connect* 754.13
tacked *connected* 754.11
tackily *viscously* 561.22
tackiness *bad taste* 528.3, *ornateness* 532.2, *tawdriness* 535.2, *viscosity* 561.1
tacking *cross-country techniques* 162.8
tackle **390.8, 754.6**; *equipment* 103.6, *offense* 155.6, *soccer play* 163.5, *play soccer* 163.8, *attempt* 390.1, *undertake* 404.3, *do something* 412.13, *contend* 422.22, *lifter* 715.5, *make a beginning* 771.26
tackled *soccer* 163.7
tackler *attempter* 390.3
tackling *soccer play* 163.5, *soccer* 163.7
tack on *add* 748.11
tacky *shoddy* 497.11, *plain* 528.9, *ornate* 532.10, *moist* 559.9, *mucilaginous* 561.15, *adhesive* 755.5
tact *personnel management* 126.4, *social skill* 127.3, *sensitivity* 267.1, *wisdom* 352.1, *treatment* 399.11, *courtesy* 410.1, *refinement* 534.1
tactful *sensitive* 267.3, *wise* 352.4, *courteous* 410.6
tactfully *sensitively* 267.6, *courteously* 410.13, *genteelly* 410.14
tactfulness *courtesy* 410.1
tactic *polymeric* 11.35, *tactics* 399.12, *way* 691.1, *stratagem* 822.2
tactical *military* 58.10, 76.28, *strategic* 78.16, *planned* 387.10, *behaving* 399.14, *effective* 412.10, *cunning* 822.4
tactical advantage *tactics* 399.12
tactical ballistic missile *modern missile weapon* 78.4
tactical bombing *bombing* 76.21, *air attack* 418.4
tactically *militarily* 58.15, *as planned* 387.16, *cunningly* 822.6

tactical nuclear warfare *atomic warfare* 76.4
tactical nuclear weapon *weapon* 78.1
tactician *expert* 127.9, *motivator* 178.11, 508.6, *planner* 387.9, *cunning person* 822.3
tactics **399.12;** *art of war* 76.16, *social skill* 127.3, *procedure* 387.2, *deed* 412.2, *way* 691.1, *stratagem* 822.2
tactics of war *art of war* 76.16
tactile *sensory* 19.22, *sculptural* 144.7, *sensate* 212.5, *touchable* 216.5
tactile sensation *touch* 216.1
tactile values *treatment* 143.6
tactility *touch* 216.1
tactless *clumsy* 128.6, *insensitive* 268.4, *inconsiderate* 318.9, *uncustomary* 398.4, *discourteous* 411.5
tactlessly *insensitively* 268.7, *discourteously* 411.8
tactlessness *bungling* 128.2, *insensitivity* 268.1, *inconsideration* 318.4, *discourtesy* 411.1
tactual *touchable* 216.5
Tadla Breeds of Sheep 16
Tadmit Breeds of Sheep 16
tadpole *young animal* 26.4, *young amphibian* 37.11
tadpole shrimp *crustacean* 39.10
taedium vitae [L] *boredom* 296.1
tae kwon do **152.15;** Sporting Activities 145, *combat sport* 152.1, *wrestling* 152.18
tae kwon do combinations *tae kwon do* 152.15
tae kwon do grade *tae kwon do* 152.15
tae kwon do patterns *tae kwon do* 152.15
taenia *or* **tenia** Architectural Elements 134
taffeta *fabric* 130.1
Taffy Nicknames for Inhabitants 61
taffy *adherent* 755.4
Taft–Hartley Act *strike* 57.8
tag Children's and Party Games 167, *maxim* 177.1, *personal identification* 184.4, *identify* 184.11, *name* 202.8, *allocate* 474.5, *add* 748.11, *line* 754.5
tag along *attend* 794.19
tag day *offering* 472.6
tag football *football* 155.1
tagged *identified* 184.9
tagging *allocation* 474.1
Tagil Breeds of Cattle 16
tagmemics Linguistic Studies 5
tag on *add* 748.11
tag-out *other game terms* 147.7
tag-team *type of wrestling* 152.9, *wrestling* 152.18
Tagus Rivers 570
Tahiti Islands 572
Tahoe Lakes 568
taiga *trees* 43.4
tail **622.5, 773.8;** *comet* 7.20, *back* 622.1, 622.6, *be in the rear* 622.7, *appendage* 748.4, *hindmost* 773.18, *follower* 794.10, *attend* 794.19
tail [Inf] *pursuer* 385.5, *follow* 385.12, 770.10, *stay near* 586.13, *rear end* 622.4
tailbone Human Bones 19
tail coat *formal clothes* 100.5, *jacket* 100.18
tailed amphibian *amphibian* 37.10
tail end *tail* 773.8

tail feather *plumage* 36.7
tail fin *fish characteristic* 38.8
tailgate *stay near* 586.13, *follow* 770.10
tailgate picnic *feast* 92.9
tailgating *sequential* 770.7
tail guard *riding equipment* 159.9
tail in a gate [Inf] *awkward situation* 824.7
tailing [Inf] *pursuit* 385.1, *pursuing* 385.8
tailless *reduced* 749.5
tailless amphibian *amphibian* 37.10
taillight *safety light* 246.7
tail off *stop* 668.10, *decrease* 747.7, *come to an end* 773.23
tailor *clothier* 100.37, *make clothing* 100.44, *artisan* 123.13, *fabric handler* 130.11, *sew* 130.18, *retailer* 482.11, *fashion* 536.7, *coverer* 613.18, *changer* 665.9, *person who joins* 752.9
tailored **100.41;** *sewn* 130.14, *treated* 388.12, *formed* 624.6
tailored suit *suit* 100.16
tailoring *the clothing business* 100.36, *sewing* 130.5, *forming* 624.4
tailor-made *tailored* 100.41, *produced* 522.12, *prototypical* 624.7
tailor-made clothes **100.4**
tailor-make *make clothing* 100.44
tailor's dummy *figure* 187.4
tailor's goose *smoother* 545.2
tailpiece Architectural Elements 134, *back* 622.1, *tail* 622.5, *appendage* 748.4
tail rhyme *rhyme* 139.11
tails *formal clothes* 100.5, *jacket* 100.18, *formal clothing* 406.5
tails (of a coin) *back* 622.1
tailskid *miscellaneous automotive terms* 687.14
tailspin *miscellaneous automotive terms* 687.14, *decline* 747.4
tailwind *wind* 9.12, *flight* 689.5, *help* 825.1
taint *uncleanness* 112.2, *dirty* 112.11, *poison* 117.18, *blemish* 533.1, 533.7, *mix* 751.12, *suggestion* 800.9, *defect* 806.4, *make worse* 808.17
tainted *unclean* 112.8, *sick* 114.24, *putrid* 227.4, *blemished* 533.5, *imperfect* 806.7, *defective* 806.7
Taipei Countries 566
Taiping Rebellion Major Wars 76
Taiwan Countries 566, Islands 572
Tajik Breeds of Sheep 16
Tajikistan Countries 566
Tajo Rivers 570
takable *receivable* 473.12
takahe *flightless bird* 36.8
take **477.14;** *photograph* 132.3, *motion-picture photography* 137.9, *film* 137.19, *catch* 154.9, *suppose* 359.8, *force* 428.10, *receive* 473.13, 492.7, *takings* 477.8, *bargain* 480.20, *convey* 685.9, *be victorious* 845.16
take [Inf] *earnings* 467.5, *stolen goods* 479.4, *money received* 492.2
take a backseat *be humble* 298.16, *escape notice* 403.14, *be unselfish* 443.7, *be average* 742.8, *follow* 745.12
take a bath *bathe* 111.18
take a beating *be defeated* 846.18
take a bow *act* 136.34

take a break *have leisure time* 125.5, *pause* 668.13, 775.11
take a breather *be refreshed* 94.8, *pause* 415.15, 668.13, *take it easy* 819.3
take account of *include* 763.5
take a chance **842.14;** *tackle* 390.8, *face danger* 811.12, *make possible* 836.7, *think likely* 838.10
take a chill *be cold* 218.13
take a cold bath *or* **shower** *restrain oneself* 830.15
take a commission *join the army* 76.31
take a corner *play soccer* 163.8
take a crack *or* **whack at** [Inf] *experiment* 335.11, *attempt* 390.6, *undertake* 391.7
take action **509.12;** *have an industrial dispute* 57.20, *exert oneself* 122.11, *act* 412.11
take a day *or* **time off** *absent oneself* 576.15
take a day off *pause* 668.13
take a deep breath *be refreshed* 94.8
take a dim view of *dislike* 291.12, *disapprove* 438.16
take a discount **495.5**
take a dislike to *dislike* 291.12
take a drubbing *be defeated* 846.18
take advantage of *be skillful* 127.14, *exploit* 393.11, *ill-use* 395.7, *conduct oneself* 399.17, *direct* 412.16, *wrong* 430.19, *seduce* 432.16, *find useful* 801.11, *promote* 807.18, *get better* 807.21
take advice *consult* 176.11
take a fall *or* **spill** *drop* 714.15
take a fancy to *enjoy* 290.9, *like* 299.22
take a firm grip *be an influence* 512.13
take a flier [Inf] *face danger* 811.12
take a flight *fly* 689.13
take a flight of fancy *be capricious* 381.6
take a foul shot *play basketball* 148.7
take a fresh *or* **new lease on life** *get healthy* 113.12
take after *be similar* 733.12, *imitate* 736.9
take a gander (at) [Inf] *inspect* 242.22
take ages *be late* 658.11
take a header [Inf] *trip* 714.16
take (a) hold *be an influence* 512.13
take a holiday *have leisure time* 125.5, *be regular* 663.10, *pause* 668.13, 775.11, *take it easy* 819.3
take a husband *marry* 64.19
take a kickback *offer* 504.11
take a leaf out of one's book *imitate* 736.9
take a leak [Inf] *urinate* 25.22
take a leap in the dark *be rash* 286.8, *be foolish* 353.6
take a leave of absence *absent oneself* 576.15
take a liking to *like* 299.22
take a look at *inspect* 242.22
take a loss *become insolvent* 846.17
take amiss *be offended* 302.14
take an advance on royalties *borrow* 476.10
take a nap *take it easy* 819.3
take an aversion to *hate* 300.11
take an eye for an eye *retaliate* 489.23, *exchange* 673.5, *reciprocate* 729.7

take a nosedive *fail* 714.18, *decrease* 747.7
take an upturn *upturn* 713.20
take apart **753.16;** *demolish* 523.12, *deconstruct* 758.7, *part* 760.14
take a penalty stroke *play* 156.8
take a pension *stop work* 394.12
take a percentage *profit* 467.22
take a photograph *or* **photo** *photograph* 132.26, *represent* 187.10
take a picture *record* 185.13, *represent* 187.10
take a plane *find one's way* 691.15
take a position *battle* 76.33
take a potshot *fire* 418.18, *shoot* 696.18
take a powder [Inf] *hurry off* 705.11
take a powder! [Inf] *go!* 709.30
take a profit *profit* 467.22
take a rain check *take a substitute* 672.7
take a recess *be refreshed* 94.8
take a rest *take it easy* 819.3
take a risk *take a chance* 842.14
take a role *or* **part** *act* 136.34
take a sabbatical *have leisure time* 125.5, *pause* 775.11
take a salary advance *borrow* 476.10
take as a model *imitate* 736.9
take a second helping *be unsatisfied* 98.10
take a share *have joint possession* 469.15, *get one's allotment* 474.6
take a shine *glaze* 246.22
take a shit [Inf] *defecate* 25.21
take a shortcut *short-cut* 591.11, *find one's way* 691.15
take a shot *play* 149.7
take a shot at *attempt* 390.6, *undertake* 391.7
take a shower *bathe* 111.18
take a ski lift *ski* 162.35
take as one *be indiscriminate* 338.10
take a stab at *attempt* 390.6
take a stand *battle* 76.33, *appear* 331.18, *show oneself* 843.15
take a stand against *counterattack* 418.24
take a stroke *play* 149.7
take a strong line *demand* 425.11
take a substitute **672.7**
take a sun *or* **moon sight** *navigate* 690.15
take a supporting role *follow* 745.12
take a tiger by the tail *face danger* 811.12
take a trick *play cards* 168.7
take a trip [Inf] *drug oneself* 121.37
take a trip to the showers [Inf] *play baseball* 147.9
take a tumble *trip* 714.16
take a turn *circle* 631.6, *be regular* 663.10
take a turn at the table *play* 149.7
take a turn for the better *get better* 807.21
take a turn for the worse *decrease* 747.7, *deteriorate* 808.14, *decline* 846.16
take authority *gain authority* 52.15
take a vacation *have leisure time* 125.5, *pause* 668.13, 775.11
take a walk! [Inf] *go!* 709.30
take away **275.13, 477.18, 685.12;** *add* 6.86, 784.11, *cause to disappear* 265.7, *confiscate* 454.25,

lose 468.12, remove 574.16, subtract 749.6, separate 753.12
take away forcefully 477.19
take away one's freedom subject 832.10
take a wife marry 64.9
take a wrong turn or **the wrong turning** go astray 698.17
take back 477.17; disavow 190.18, remind 354.13, restore 671.10, be compensated 743.9
take back to the drawing board reconsider 807.23
take by force force 428.10
take by storm attack successfully 418.25, be victorious 845.16
take by surprise surprise 292.9, trap 813.6
take by the hand advise 825.27
take captive take away forcefully 477.19
take care be cautious 287.11, be courteous 410.9
take care! be careful! 287.20, look out! 814.12
take care of serve 69.11, feed 90.41, manage 126.10, care for 325.12, do something 412.13, include 613.33
take care of oneself be healthy 113.11
take care of number one be egotistic 444.7
take center stage show off 404.26
take chances invent 335.13
take charge be powerful 514.18
take charge of 391.8; care for 325.12, protect 810.21
take cognizance try a case 54.28, judge 54.31
take cognizance of include 763.5
take command gain authority 52.15, be superior 744.15
take communion worship 83.15
take compassionate leave exempt oneself 434.12
take courage 284.15
take cover conceal oneself 181.15
take custody of detain 830.16
take cuttings cultivate 17.19, propagate 21.15
take disciplinary action punish 454.22
take down eat 92.21, inscribe 185.14, abase 298.20, lower 716.12, bring down 716.14
take down a peg or two abase 298.20
take Draconian measures be severe 424.8
take drugs drug oneself 121.37
take early retirement have leisure time 125.5, resign 835.5
take effect 676.11; act 412.11, be operational 509.10
take evasive action evade 386.19, act on the defensive 419.29
take every course eat well 92.23
take exception criticize 438.19, object 828.18
take exception to be offended 302.14
take five or **ten** [Inf] be refreshed 94.8, pause 668.13, 775.11, take it easy 819.3
take flight retreat 386.22, disband 776.13, escape 816.8
take flight or **wing** hurry off 705.11
take for a ride [Inf] murder 30.20, swindle 193.19, take money away 477.20
take for better or for worse marry 64.19, side with 382.15

take for granted believe 87.9, predict 356.7, suppose 359.8, think likely 838.10
take for oneself take over 477.16
take forty winks [Inf] sleep 415.14
take French leave depart 265.6, run away 386.21, disobey 427.12, abscond 576.16, escape 816.8
take fright be afraid 283.14
take half measures be insufficient 98.9
take heart be hopeful 281.11, take courage 284.15
take heed be cautious 287.11, be warned 814.9
take hold of retain 471.7, take 477.14, adhere 755.8
take hold of one become a habit 397.17
take holy orders be monastic 67.11, ordain 84.16
take home receive 473.13
take-home pay reward for service 453.5, something received 473.2, pay 489.6
take-home work work 122.1
take hostage take away forcefully 477.19, detain 830.16, defeat 832.11
take in make someone believe 87.11, store fuel 105.18, swindle 193.19, get to know 348.12, understand 363.9, receive 473.13, take 477.14, be hospitable 477.21, contract 582.12, enroll 706.16, admit 708.12, augment 748.13, include 763.5, protect 810.21
take in exchange take a substitute 672.7
take in food eat 92.21
take in hand undertake 391.7, take 477.14, restore order 765.22, advise 825.27
take in one another's washing exchange 673.5
take in one's stride do easily 823.16
take in oxygen be refreshed 94.8
take in sail slow down 693.13
take in stride not wonder about 295.5
take into account include 763.5
take into consideration include 763.5
take into custody take away forcefully 477.19, detain 830.16
take into one's arms communicate love 299.25
take into one's head suppose 359.8
take in tow pull 699.10, escort 794.18, advise 825.27
take in vain misuse 395.6
take issue dissent 347.8, object 828.18
take issue with battle 76.33, negate 190.16
take it suppose 359.8, succumb 421.7
take it easy [Inf] **819.3;** proceed with caution 287.12, be neglectful 326.7, move slowly 693.11, deteriorate 808.14, do easily 823.16, be informal 829.19
take it easy! [Inf] be careful! 287.20
take it from one succumb 421.7
take it from the top restore 671.10
take it into one's head be capricious 381.6
take it lying down succumb 421.7

take it one step or **day at a time** proceed with caution 287.12
take it on the chin [Inf] succumb 421.7, close 637.10
take it on the lam [Inf] hurry off 705.11, escape 816.8
take it out of fatigue 820.6
take it out on someone [Inf] vent one's anger 302.21
take it slowly proceed with caution 287.12
take it that rationalize 4.20
take judicial notice judge 54.31
take leave have leisure time 125.5, absent oneself 576.15
take leave of one's senses become insane 110.12, be foolish 353.6
take lessons learn 48.23
take liberties have the audacity 400.15, be discourteous 411.7, be permitted 502.8, lack restraint 829.21
take life kill 30.19
take measures prepare 388.14, act 412.11
take minutes inscribe 185.14
take money away 477.20
take more grass bowl 151.8
taken supposed 359.6, received 473.11, 492.6
taken aback surprised 292.5
taken as read supposed 359.6
taken away removed 574.9, missing 576.11, subtracted 749.3
taken bad sick 114.24
taken by God dead 29.11
taken care of solvent 485.9
taken down a peg or two abased 298.13
take neither side be impartial 289.15
taken for granted supposed 359.6
taken ill sick 114.24
taken in received 473.11
take no advice be obstinate 379.10
take no chances be safe 810.20
taken off guard unprepared 389.5
take no interest be indifferent 289.12
take no interest in be incurious 322.5, be disinterested 443.6
take no notice of be blind to 243.19, be inattentive 324.10, be neglectful 326.7
take no offense show mercy 312.11
take no part in be absent 576.14
take no precautions be unprepared 389.14
take no prisoners slaughter 30.21
take no risks proceed with caution 287.12
take note of 323.10
take nourishment eat 92.21
taken over received 473.11
taken prisoner captive 832.9
taken seriously important 799.7
taken to task condemned 438.11
taken with in love 299.16
takeoff jumping 166.11, entertainment 277.4, form of derision 369.2, ridicule 436.4, 440.6, flight 689.5, start 705.2, taking off 713.6, mimicry 736.3, spread 746.3
take off 749.7; act 187.13, be humorous 277.11, stop using 394.10, ridicule 436.22, 440.15, take away 477.18, discount 495.4, undress 614.18, fly 689.13, hurry off 705.11, set out 705.12, go up 713.23, imitate 736.9, increase 746.6, start off 771.27

take offense be hostile 63.10, be offended 302.14
take offense at react against 291.15
take off for aim 697.14
take office gain authority 52.15
take off in a big way [Inf] increase 746.6
take off one's hat show respect 435.16
takeoff point jumping 166.11
take off someone's hands receive 473.13
take off weight eat less 118.9
take on store fuel 105.18, tackle 390.8, undertake 391.7, do something 412.13, counterattack 418.24, contend 422.22, fight 422.23, guarantee 458.13, adopt 476.11, take 477.14, volunteer 504.13, introduce 708.16, confront 828.19
take on a concern incur a duty 433.15
take on a job be employed 57.19, incur a duty 433.15
take on all comers brace oneself 376.13
take on board be hospitable 477.21, contain 577.10
take on depth be intelligible 363.10
take one over become a habit 397.17
take one's bearings navigate 690.15, orient 697.15
take one's breath away strike dumb 206.10, be wondrous 294.14
take one's chance push 414.20, take the opportunity 659.7
take one's coat off work 122.8
take one's commission take a discount 495.5
take one's cue from consult 176.11
take one's cut get one's allotment 474.6, take a discount 495.5
take one's departure depart 705.8
take one's ease have leisure time 125.5, take it easy 819.3
take oneself off part 705.13
take one's fancy give pleasure 214.13
take one's foot off the gas slow down 693.13
take one's hat off to compliment 437.17
take one's job and shove it [Inf] resign 835.5
take one's leave absent oneself 576.15, depart 705.8, part 705.13
take one's life in one's hands face danger 811.12
take one's lumps [Inf] succumb 421.7
take one's medicine be punished 454.31
take one's own good time have leisure time 125.5
take one's own life commit suicide 30.24
take one's percentage take a discount 495.5
take one's pick choose 382.14
take one's place line up 765.24
take one's pleasure with seduce 432.16
take one's revenge be malevolent 306.12
take one's stand insist 376.14
take one's time be late 658.11, hesitate 693.12

take one's turn *be regular* 663.10, *follow* 770.10

take one up on *defy* 416.7

take on oneself *resolve* 374.9

take on one's shoulders *take charge of* 391.8

take on the responsibility *incur a duty* 433.15

take on too much 391.9

take on trust *believe* 87.9, *be incurious* 322.5

take orders *obey* 426.7

takeout [Inf] *eating place* 92.17

take out *seek friendship* 62.11, *bowl* 151.8, *obliterate* 186.8, *court* 299.26, *take away* 477.18, *extract* 711.13, *subtract* 749.6, *eject* 764.8

take out a business loan *borrow* 476.10

take out a loan *acquire credit* 487.11

take out or negotiate or float or secure a loan *borrow* 476.10

take out a mortgage *possess* 469.14

take out a (second) mortgage *borrow* 476.10

take out a tenancy *possess* 469.14

take out credit *acquire credit* 487.11

take out insurance *take precautions* 287.14

take-out meal *meal* 92.8

take out of context *distort the truth* 627.12

take out of print *obliterate* 186.8

takeover *acquisition of authority* 52.5, *mass demonstration* 331.7, *transfer of property* 470.4, *taking over* 477.3, *taking* 477.12, *bargaining* 480.10, *purchasing* 481.2, *joint operation* 509.2, *replacement* 574.3, *succession* 770.2

take over 477.16; *gain authority* 52.15, *conquer* 77.36, *protest* 331.19, *attack successfully* 418.25, *deal* 457.9, *transfer property* 470.12, *receive* 473.13, *be an influence* 512.13, *replace* 574.17, *be a substitute* 672.6, *succeed* 770.11

takeover bid *transfer of property* 470.4, *taking over* 477.3, *purchasing* 481.2, *business offer* 504.3

take over from *aid* 275.10

take over the reins *gain authority* 52.15

takeover zone *relay racing* 166.5

take pains *try* 414.21

take part *participate* 145.6, *attend* 575.14, *be included* 763.6

take part in *be active in* 412.17, *participate* 760.16

take part in a training program *learn* 48.23

take pity! *have pity!* 308.13

take pity on *show pity* 308.8

take place *take effect* 676.11

take pleasure in 271.11; *feel pleasure* 214.12, *enjoy* 269.9, *like* 299.22

take poison *commit suicide* 30.24

take possession of *take* 477.14

take potluck *participate* 408.15

take precautions 287.14; *practice birth control* 23.10, *have foresight* 357.8, *be prepared* 388.17, *be safe* 810.20

take precedence 769.14; *lead* 744.19, *be important* 799.13

take preventive measures or steps *take precautions* 287.14

take pride or glory in *be proud* 297.15

take priority *take precedence* 769.14

take prisoner *arrest* 55.12, *defeat* 832.11

take profits *take* 477.14

taker 477.9; *recipient* 473.5, *thief* 479.8, *purchaser* 481.7

take refuge *go inside* 611.15, *be safe* 810.20, *shelter* 812.8

take reprisals *retaliate* 420.4

take responsibility for *promise* 458.11, *be a substitute* 672.6

take risks *be rash* 286.8

take rooms *inhabit* 61.13

take root *vegetate* 41.21, *become a habit* 397.17, *influence* 512.11, *be permanent* 667.4, *be stable* 674.6

take second best *take a substitute* 672.7

take seriously 278.8; *make important* 799.14

take sexual possession of *ravish* 477.15

take shape or form *come to be* 717.19

take short steps *move slowly* 693.11

take sides *be unjust* 342.10, *side with* 382.15, 623.10

take some doing *be difficult* 824.16

take someone's head off *vent one's anger* 302.21

take someone's word for *believe* 87.9

take someone's words to heart *be warned* 814.9

take something off *discount* 495.4

take soundings *measure depth* 598.22, *navigate* 690.15

take statements *try a case* 54.28

take steps *prepare* 388.14, *act* 412.11

take stock *audit* 493.10, *number* 784.13

take stock of *visualize* 242.24, *think* 317.9, *have foresight* 357.8

take sword in hand *prepare oneself* 388.21

take tea *have a meal* 92.25

take tentative steps *proceed with caution* 287.12

take that! *revenge!* 420.7

take the attitude *propound a philosophy* 4.21

take the auspices *divine* 358.15

take the bit between one's teeth *brace oneself* 376.13

take the blame *be open to criticism* 438.22, *be a substitute* 672.6

take the breath away *be beautiful* 529.11

take the bull by the horns *be courageous* 284.14, *brace oneself* 376.13, *tackle* 390.8, *undertake* 391.7, *push* 414.20

take the chair *direct* 126.11, *moderate* 521.7

take the championship *be victorious* 845.16

take the chill off *heat* 217.17

take the consequences *be punished* 454.31

take the cup *be victorious* 845.16

take the easy way out *do easily* 823.16

take the edge off *mitigate* 521.9, *blunt* 550.9

take the fall [Inf] *be punished* 454.31

take the field *be at war* 76.32, *play baseball* 147.9

take the first step *pioneer* 771.29

take the floor *speak to* 205.19, *address* 209.8

take the good with the bad *compromise* 461.7

take the guise of *appear* 264.12

take the heart out of *be severe* 424.8

take the heat off [Inf] *submit* 421.4

take the helm *gain authority* 52.15, *lead* 126.12

take the initiative *pioneer* 771.29

take the law into one's own hands *be illegal* 53.30, *violate the law* 466.12

take the lead *be in front* 621.13, *lead* 744.19, *be important* 799.13

take the lid off *disclose* 180.8, *make visible* 244.9

take the limelight *be important* 799.13

take the line of least resistance *succumb* 433.7, *do easily* 823.16

take the long-term view *expect* 650.12

take the long view *expect* 650.12

take the Lord's name in vain *blaspheme* 301.14

take the measurements of *measure* 589.20

take the middle way *be moderate* 521.6

take the oath *give evidence* 339.12

take the offensive *be at war* 76.32, *attack* 418.17

take the omens *divine* 358.15

take the opportunity 659.7; *get in early* 657.16

take the part of *back* 825.28

take the place of *be a substitute* 672.6, *succeed* 770.11

take the pledge *abstain* 455.11, *restrain oneself* 830.15

take the plunge *be courageous* 284.14, *brace oneself* 376.13, *make a beginning* 771.26

take the prize *be victorious* 845.16

take the rap [Inf] *be open to criticism* 438.22, *be punished* 454.31, *be a substitute* 672.6

take the reciprocal course *reverse* 680.18

take the role of *succeed* 770.11

take the shape of *appear* 264.12, *be converted* 667.12

take the square root *add* 6.86

take the stage *act* 136.34

take the stand *litigate* 54.27

take the sting or bite out *blunt* 550.9

take the sting out of *conciliate* 74.10, *relieve* 275.8, *mitigate* 521.9

take the strain *suffice* 97.6

take the sun *orient* 697.15

take the train *find one's way* 691.15

take the veil *be monastic* 67.11, *ordain* 84.16, *be unsocial* 409.10

take the weight of *weigh* 538.15

take the wheel *manage* 126.10

take the wind out of someone's sails *deflate* 195.16, *remove power from* 515.13, *hinder* 826.15

take the words out of one's mouth *prepare* 657.14

take the wraps off *disclose* 180.8

take things easy *submit* 421.4

take things slowly *be neglectful* 326.7

take thought for tomorrow *expect* 650.12

take time *spend time* 639.14

take time by the forelock *take the opportunity* 659.7

take time off or out *take it easy* 819.3

take time-out *have leisure time* 125.5, *pause* 775.11

take time to smell the flowers or roses *have leisure time* 125.5

take to *enjoy* 290.9, *like* 299.22, *accustom oneself* 397.19

take to arms *go to war* 76.29, *be violent* 520.8

take to bits *demolish* 523.12

take to court *litigate* 54.27

take to heart *feel deeply* 266.16, *be sensitive* 267.5

take to like a duck to water *accustom oneself* 397.19, *do easily* 823.16

take to mean *rationalize* 4.20, *interpret* 365.12

take too much time *exhibit penalty behavior* 155.21

take to one's bed *be unhealthy* 114.29

take to one's bosom *detain* 471.9

take to oneself *augment* 748.13

take to one's heels *retreat* 386.22, *hurry off* 705.11, *escape* 816.8

take to pieces *demolish* 523.12, *deconstruct* 758.7, *make useless* 802.12

take to pieces or bits *scatter* 753.15

take to task *condemn* 438.18, *punish* 454.22

take to the cleaners [Inf] *take money away* 477.20

take to the hills *conceal oneself* 181.15, *shelter* 812.8

take to the limit *complete* 759.10

take to the masses *popularize* 778.17

take to the road *find one's way* 691.15

take to the woods *shelter* 812.8

take turns *reciprocate* 729.7

take umbrage *be hostile* 63.10, *quarrel* 272.9, *be offended* 302.14

take unawares *surprise* 292.9

take under one's wing *protect* 810.21, *advise* 825.27

take untimely action *be untimely* 660.8

take up *address oneself to* 209.13, *select* 382.12, *undertake* 391.7, *use* 393.9, *have a habit* 397.16, *receive* 473.13, *shorten* 591.9, *absorb* 708.19, *gather up* 715.14, *advise* 825.27

take up again *protract* 669.9

take up an option *select* 382.12

take up a position *be situated* 573.9

take up arms *be violent* 520.8

take up arms for *plead for* 419.25

take up no room *be little* 580.11

take upon oneself *take charge of* 391.8

take upon one's shoulders *incur a duty* 433.15

take up residence 60.24; *settle* 565.10

take up residence in *possess* 469.14

take-up spool or reel *film* 132.8

take up the cause *go to war* 76.29

take up the cause of *plead for* 419.25

take up the challenge *contend* 422.22

take up the cudgels for *go to war* 76.29, *plead for* 419.25, *back* 825.28
take vengeance *retaliate* 420.4
take vows *ordain* 84.16
take what comes *brace oneself* 376.13
take what's offered *compromise* 461.7
take wing *fly* 36.23, *quit* 705.10
take with a pinch *or* **grain of salt** *disbelieve* 88.8
take wrong *misinterpret* 366.4
taking 477.1, 477.12; *gain* 467.1, *claiming* 469.2, *receiving* 473.1, 473.9, *stealing* 479.1, *attractive* 700.10
taking all things together *on average* 742.10
taking an overdose *suicide* 30.8
taking apart *deconstruction* 758.2
taking a prisoner *conquest* 477.6
taking a role *or* **part** *acting* 136.22
taking away 477.5; *loss* 468.1, *removal* 574.2, *subtraction* 749.1, *setting apart* 753.2
taking back 477.4; *restoration* 671.2
taking by storm *military attack* 418.2, *victory* 845.4
taking candy from a baby *secondary matter* 800.6
taking counsel *consultation* 176.4
taking everything into consideration *on the whole* 759.13
taking exception *criticism* 438.4
taking hold *control* 477.1
taking in 477.7; *taking* 477.1, *shortening* 582.2, *admittance* 708.1
taking in food *eating* 92.1
taking in hand *control* 477.1
taking into account *considering* 341.13
taking liberties *transgression* 712.3
taking life *killing* 30.1
takingly 477.23
taking measures *preparation* 388.1
taking money away *taking away* 477.5
taking of evidence *evidence* 54.15
taking off 713.6; *flying* 689.11
taking on *taking* 477.1
taking one's time *unhurried* 693.8
taking on responsibility *enterprising* 391.5
taking out *courtship* 299.10, *taking away* 477.5
taking out a loan *borrowing* 476.1
taking over 477.3; *acquisition of authority* 52.5, *succession* 770.2
taking pains *exertion* 122.4
taking part *meddling* 414.17, *participating* 760.13
taking place *present* 647.4
taking possession *claiming* 469.2, *taking* 477.1
taking precedence *precedence* 769.1, *important* 799.7
takings 477.8; *earnings* 467.5, *something received* 473.2, *money received* 492.2
taking steps *preparation* 388.1
taking the auspices *divination* 358.2
taking the opportunity *getting ahead* 657.7
taking the waters *hydrotherapy* 557.7
taking to task *condemnation* 438.2

taking up the post *succession* 770.2
Takla Makan Deserts 572
Taklimakan Deserts 572
talapoin *religious* 84.9
Talavera Breeds of Sheep 16
Talavera ware Ceramics 129
Talbotype *older photograph* 132.4
talc *powder* 553.9
talcum powder *powder* 553.9
tale *falsehood* 192.6
talebearer *informer* 170.8, *discloser* 180.4, *gossip* 192.11
talent *aptitude* 127.4, 513.3, *artistry* 133.3, *ability* 340.2, *intelligence* 352.2, *proficiency* 445.5, *ancient coins* 484.12, *special skill* 779.2, *easiness* 823.1
talented *skillful* 127.10, *gifted* 127.11, *qualified* 340.7, *intelligent* 352.5, *proficient* 445.15
talentless *unskillful* 128.4
talent scout *theatergoer* 136.30, *baseball team* 147.2
tale of woe *lament* 280.2
talion *retaliation* 420.1
talipot *or* **talipot palm** Trees and Shrubs 43
talisman 86.9; *sacred object* 83.11, *sign* 183.1, *good-luck sign* 358.6, *preserver* 815.9
talismanic *witchlike* 86.19
talk 207.3; *use language* 5.42, *divulge* 180.9, *speech* 205.1, *spoken language* 205.2, *speak* 205.17, *be talkative* 207.7, *address* 209.1, 209.8, *conversation* 210.1, *converse* 210.11, *explanation* 331.3
talk about *publish* 173.15, *vilify* 440.14
talk about behind one's back *vilify* 440.14
talk around *persuade* 178.15, *be evasive* 386.20
talkative 207.5; *communicative* 169.16, *informative* 170.10, *disclosing* 180.6, *diffuse* 199.3, *speaking* 205.15, *conversing* 210.8
talkatively 207.9
talkativeness 207.1; *diffuseness* 199.1, *power of speech* 205.5
talk at length *be talkative* 207.7
talk back *answer back* 334.19, *be insolent* 400.14
talk big *show off* 402.15
talk bunkum *talk nonsense* 362.12
talk dirty [Inf] *blaspheme* 301.14
talkdown *flight control* 689.7
talk down *service* 689.16
talker 207.4; *speaker* 205.12, *conversationalist* 210.6, *answerer* 334.10
talk for effect *show off* 402.15, *put on a show* 404.28
talk gibberish *talk nonsense* 362.12
talking *communications* 169.1, *speech* 205.1, *speaking* 205.15, *conversing* 210.8
talking bird *cage bird* 36.13
talking book *aid for poor sight* 243.5
talking dirty [Inf] *profanity* 301.3
talking head [Inf] *broadcasting personnel* 172.11
talking in superlatives *bombast* 194.4
talking picture *or* **talkie** *movie type* 137.3
talking-to *condemnation* 438.2
talking to oneself *soliloquizing* 211.3
talk in riddles *be unintelligible* 364.11
talk in superlatives *boast* 194.14

talk into *persuade* 178.15, *influence* 508.11
talk like an idiot *talk nonsense* 362.12, *be unintelligible* 364.11
talk nineteen to the dozen *be talkative* 207.7
talk nonsense 192.26, 362.12; *be unintelligible* 364.11
talk off the subject *be extraneous* 724.12
talk off the top of one's head [Inf] *improvise* 389.15
talk of the town *disreputable character* 371.2
talk one's head off *be talkative* 207.7
talk out of *dissuade* 179.7
talk out of turn *tell on* 180.10
talk over *confer* 210.13
talk plainly *talk straight* 630.15
talk privately *chat* 210.12
talk rubbish *talk nonsense* 362.12
talks *conference* 75.4, *debate* 210.3, *summit meeting* 600.3
talk show *program* 172.10
talk-show guest *person questioned* 333.10
talk-show host *questioner* 333.9
talk show host *broadcasting personnel* 172.11
talk someone around *influence* 508.11
talk straight 630.15; *divulge* 180.9
talk tête-à-tête *chat* 210.12
talk the same language *agree with* 462.10
talk to *communicate* 169.18, *speak to* 205.19
talk to a brick wall *waste effort* 802.13
talk together *converse* 210.11
talk too long *bore* 296.8
talk too much *overdo* 99.11, *be talkative* 207.7
talk to oneself 205.20; *soliloquize* 211.4
talk to the wall *soliloquize* 211.4
talk turkey [Inf] *divulge* 180.9, *be concise* 198.5, *mean* 361.13
talk until one is blue in the face *be talkative* 207.7
tall 596.9; *long* 590.6
Tallahassee American States 564
Tallahatchie Rivers 570
tall as a maypole *tall* 596.9
tallboy *cabinet* 101.8
tall-case clock Timepieces and Timers 646
tall drink *size of drink* 93.3, *drink* 121.6
taller *higher* 596.8
tallest *higher* 596.8
tallied *accounted* 493.8
Tallinn Countries 566
tallith *vestment* 84.11, *neckwear* 100.29
tallness *largeness* 579.2, *longness* 590.3, *height* 596.1
tall order *undertaking* 391.1, *difficult task* 824.3
tallow *fat* 562.4
tallow candle *incandescent light* 246.5
tallow-faced *drained of color* 252.6
tallow wood Trees and Shrubs 43
tallowy *oily* 562.11
tall person 596.6
tall ship Sailing Ships and Boats 690
tall-ship racing *competitive sailing* 150.6
tall story 194.5; *falsehood* 192.6, *joke* 277.6

tall tale *falsehood* 192.6, *distortion of truth* 627.4
tally *numeration* 6.10, *means of identification* 184.3, *record* 185.1, *register* 185.15, *correspondence* 334.8, *answer to* 334.22, *be compatible* 462.12, *credit* 487.1, *amount owing* 488.5, *accounting* 493.1, *division* 577.6, *itemize* 577.13, *correspond to* 727.10, *conform* 735.27, 781.11, *mathematical addition* 748.2, *mathematical result* 783.4, *number* 783.9, 784.13, *count* 784.3, *list* 785.1
tallyho! *after him!* 385.19
tallying *correspondent* 334.16, *count* 784.3
tally stick *calculator* 6.64
Talmud *Jewish text* 81.17
Talmud Torah *religious school* 48.13
talon *retainer* 471.3, *sharp-pointed growth* 549.5
talon molding Architectural Elements 134
talons *avian characteristic* 36.6, *governance* 52.6
talus Human Bones 19
tam *cap* 100.33
tamarack Trees and Shrubs 43
tamarind Trees and Shrubs 43
tamarisk Trees and Shrubs 43
tambour Architectural Elements 134
tambourin Musical Instruments 142
tambourine Musical Instruments 142
Tambov Red Breeds of Cattle 16
tambura *or* **tamboura** Musical Instruments 142
tame *of animals* 34.13, *unemphatic* 201.2, *tasteless* 220.4, *accustom* 397.18, *submitting* 421.3, *obedient* 426.4, *moderate* 521.7, *sedentary* 678.5, *trustworthy* 810.17, *subject* 832.10
tame animal *domestic animal* 34.3
tamed *habituated* 397.14
tamely *unemphatically* 201.4, *obediently* 426.9
tameness *lack of emphasis* 201.1, *tastelessness* 220.1, *submission* 421.1, *obedience* 426.1
tam-o'-shanter *cap* 100.33
tamp *make dense* 540.9, *impeller* 695.7, *collide* 695.10
tamper *meddle* 414.23, *change for the worse* 665.18, *impeller* 695.7, *impair* 808.18
tampered with *misrepresentative* 193.14
tamperer *meddler* 414.12
tampering *overactivity* 414.9
tamper with *touch* 216.9, *change for the worse* 665.18, *mix* 751.12, *disrupt* 768.12
tamping iron *impeller* 695.7
tampion *stopper* 584.3, *insert* 710.4
tampon *stopper* 584.3, *stop* 584.14, *insert* 710.4, *sanitary precaution* 810.8
tam-tam Musical Instruments 142
Tamworth Breeds of Pigs 16
tan *effects of hot weather* 217.7, *feel hot* 217.19, *color* 251.16, *blacken* 254.11, *brown* 256.5, 256.7, *orange* 258.5, *hit* 454.28, *make tough* 547.15
Tana Lakes 568
Tanaga Islands 572
Tanana Rivers 570
tandem *sailboard parts* 150.20,

windsurfing 150.28, *twosome* 789.3

tandem bicycle *bicycle* 687.10
tandem race *canoe racing* 150.12
tandoori chicken *notable international dishes* 90.40
tang *sailboat parts and accessories* 150.4, *piquancy* 221.1
Tanganyika *Lakes* 568
Tanganyika Long-tailed *Breeds of Sheep* 16
tangency *contiguity* 216.4, *juxtaposition* 586.4
tangent *line* 6.35, *trigonometric function* 6.50, *contiguous* 216.8, *juxtaposed* 586.9, *divergence* 607.2, *obliquity* 628.2, *deviation* 698.1, *focus* 702.5, *convergent* 702.7
tangential *linear* 6.77, *contiguous* 216.8, *juxtaposed* 586.9, *divergent* 607.7, *oblique* 628.8, *convergent* 702.7
tangentially *beside* 586.20, *divergently* 607.14
tangerine *orange thing* 258.3
tangibility *touch* 216.1, *visibility* 244.1, *material world* 524.1, *reality* 719.1, 721.2
tangible *sensate* 212.5, *touchable* 216.5, *visible* 244.5, *propertied* 470.9, *material* 524.7, *real* 719.6, 721.12
tangible assets *personal estate* 470.6
tangible object *object* 524.6
tangibles *personal estate* 470.6
tangibly *palpably* 216.12, *materially* 524.9, *in truth* 721.28
tanginess *piquancy* 221.1
tangle *make rough* 544.11, *mix* 732.12, *variety* 751.4, *mix-up* 766.5, *confuse* 766.19, *predicament* 824.5
tangled *condensed* 540.7, *complicated* 751.10, *muddled* 766.13, *mixed up* 766.14
tango *Dances* 135
tango romantica *ice-dancing move* 162.19
tangram *puzzle* 182.5
tang soo do *Sporting Activities* 145
T'ang ware *Ceramics* 129
tangy *piquant* 221.6, *acid* 223.5
tank *the inside* [Inf] 55.2, *storehouse* 105.8, *vessel* 578.11
tank [Inf] *prison cell* 55.3
tanka *Poem or Verse Forms* 139
tankage *size* 579.1
tankard *drinking vessel* 578.13
tank assault *land attack* 418.3
tank car *railroad car* 688.5
tanked up [Inf] *drunk* 121.25
tanker *army combat specialist* 77.16, *warship* 77.21, *Ships and Boats* 690
tank farmer *agriculturist* 16.14
tank suit *beachwear* 100.23
tank top *shirt* 100.13
tank town *village* 567.3
tank trap *trap* 813.1
tank truck *truck* 687.8
tank up [Inf] *get drunk* 121.35
tanned *blackened* 254.7, *browned* 256.6, *treated* 388.12, *toughened* 547.7
tanner *coverer* 613.18
tannin *secreted substance* 24.2
tanning *effects of hot weather* 217.7, *preservation of body* 815.7
tan one's hide *hit* 454.28
tansy *Flowers* 42, *Herbs and Spices* 91

tantalization *enticement* 178.3, *frustration* 293.2
tantalize *entice* 178.16, *cause desire* 288.22, *thwart* 293.10, *influence* 508.11, *lure* 700.12
tantalizer *tempter* 178.10, *charmer* 700.6
tantalizing *enticing* 178.13, *frustrating* 293.7, *motivational* 508.7
tantalizingly *enticingly* 178.22, *disappointingly* 293.12, *influentially* 508.13
tantalum *Chemical Elements and Common Allotropes* 11
tantamount *similar* 361.7, *equal* 740.8
tantara *harsh sound* 238.1
tantivy *acceleration* 694.3
tanto *Musical Terms and Expression Marks* 140
tant pis! [Fr] *no matter!* 800.22
tantrum *burst of anger* 302.6
Tan-Yang *Breeds of Sheep* 16
Tanzania *Countries* 566
Taoism *Philosophical Schools of Thought* 4
Taoist *Philosophical Schools of Thought* 4, *denominational* 81.23
Taoyuan *Breeds of Pigs* 16
tap **695.13;** *manage trees* 43.14, *source of supply* 105.4, *diagnostic procedure* 107.11, *gesture* 183.5, 183.17, *touch* 216.9, *crack* 234.2, 234.7, *knock* 235.13, *mean nothing* 362.10, *take away* 477.18, *irrigator* 557.13, *stopper* 584.3, *transfer* 685.8, *blow* 695.5, *outlet* 707.8, *draw off* 711.16
tapa *hors d'oeuvre* 90.13
Tapajós *Rivers* 570
tapas *appetizer* 219.2
tap-dance *dance* 135.7
tap-dancer *dancer* 135.4
tap-dancing *Dancing Types* 135
tape *record* 172.15, 185.13, 230.9, *record book* 185.5, *recording* 185.6, *sound reproduction* 230.6, *link* 752.18, *line* 754.5, *connect* 754.13
taped *broadcast* 172.12, *recorded* 185.12
tape deck *television recording* 172.7, *sound reproduction* 230.6
tape machine *recording instrument* 185.9
tape measure *measuring instrument* 589.12, *calculator* 784.5
taper *fire* 246.9, *be sharp* 549.15, *sharpen* 549.16, *narrow place* 593.2, *narrow* 593.14, *narrowing* 702.6, *converge* 702.9, *focus* 702.11
tape-record *record* 172.15, 185.13, 230.9
tape recorder *television recording* 172.7, *recording instrument* 185.9, *sound reproduction* 230.6, *copier* 736.5
tape recording *television recording* 172.7, *duplicate* 736.4
tapered *narrowed* 593.9
tapered cut *coiffure* 530.8
tapering *narrowing* 593.3, 702.6, *narrowed* 593.9, *convergent* 702.7, *gradational* 739.5
taper off *change by degrees* 739.8, *decrease* 747.7
tapestry *Fabrics and Fibers* 130, *craft* 133.2, *picture* 135.5, *variegated thing* 263.5, *decorative method* 532.3, *wall covering* 613.12

tapestry making *Hobbies and Pastimes* 167
tapeworm *parasite* 39.18
taphophobia *Phobias* 283
tapioca snow *hail* 9.29
tap out a message *signal* 183.18
tapper *forester* 43.7, *impeller* 695.7
tapping *tree management* 43.6, *ramming* 695.3, *disgorgement* 709.6, *drawing off* 711.4
tapping machine *machine tool* 14.9
taproom *drink provider* 93.15
taproot *root* 41.7
taps *funeral* 31.4, *military call* 183.9, *lament* 280.2, *night* 656.3
tap water *water* 93.4, *drinking water* 557.2
tar *building materials* 104.2, *pollution* 117.8, *tobacco* 121.23, *black thing* 254.3, *adhesive* 561.3, *resin* 562.6, *paving* 613.14, *pave* 613.32
tar [Inf] *nautical person* 690.12
taradiddle or **tarradiddle** [Inf] *falsehood* 192.6
taramasalata *notable international dishes* 90.40
Taranaki *Mountains and Hills* 569
tar and feather *punish* 454.22
tarantella *Dances* 135
tarantism *spasm* 684.8
tarantula *arachnid* 40.4
Tarawa *Countries* 566
Tardigrada *arthropodlike invertebrate* 39.12
tardigrade *arthropodlike invertebrate* 39.12, *slow* 693.7
tardily *late* 658.14
tardiness *lateness* 658.1, *hesitation* 693.5
tardo or **tardamente** *Musical Terms and Expression Marks* 140
tardy *not participating* 415.11, *late* 658.5, *untimely* 660.5, *delayed* 693.10
Tarentaise *Breeds of Cattle* 16
tares *refuse* 802.5
Targa Florio *races* 146.4
target *purpose* 327.4, *aim* 327.17, 773.12, *laughingstock* 369.4, *objective* 374.5, *historic armor* 419.8, *butt* 436.8, *direction* 697.1
target area *objective* 374.5
targeted *purposive* 327.11
targeting *purposive* 327.11
target shooter *shooter* 696.11
target shooting **160.1**
Targhee *Breeds of Sheep* 16
Targum *Jewish text* 81.17
tariff *international trade* 56.7, *payment* 433.5, *money received* 492.2, *levy* 494.7, *limit* 620.1, *economic restraint* 830.3
tariff barrier *international trade* 56.7, *protectionism* 480.3
tariff wall *economic restraint* 830.3
Tarim *Rivers* 570
tarmacadam *construction material* 14.21, *building materials* 104.2
Tarmac™ *construction material* 14.21, *building materials* 104.2, *paving* 613.14
tarn *small lake* 568.2
tarnish **248.9;** *dirty* 112.11, *murk* 248.2, *decolor* 252.8, *defame* 440.13, *stain* 533.3, *mark* 533.8
tarnished *dirty* 112.7, *dimmed* 248.6, *marked* 533.6
tarnishing *scorn* 440.5, *defamatory* 440.9
tarok *Card Games* 168
tarot *divination* 86.5

tarot cards *means of prediction* 358.10
tarot deck *cards* 168.2
tarot reader *diviner* 86.14
tarot reading *divination* 86.5
tarp [Inf] *protective covering* 613.5
Tarpan pony *Horse and Pony Breeds* 159
tarpaulin *Fabrics and Fibers* 130, *protective covering* 613.5, *protection from the weather* 810.9
tarpon *game fish* 154.10
tarragon *Herbs and Spices* 91
tarred with the same brush *same* 730.7
tarring and feathering *punishment* 454.1
tarry *pause* 415.15, *resinous* 562.13, *wait* 658.12, *hesitate* 693.12
tarsal bones *Human Bones* 19
tarsus bones *Human Bones* 19
tart *pie* 90.38, *tasty* 219.4, *piquant* 221.6, *confectionery* 222.3, *acid* 223.5, *ill-natured* 303.9, *bitter* 306.9, *discourteous* 411.5
tart [Inf] *loose woman* 33.6, *sexually immoral person* 432.8
tart [Inf *and* Off] *sex object* 20.8, *woman considered as a sex object* 33.8
tartan *skirt* 100.12, *fabric* 130.1, *check* 263.2, *variegated thing* 263.5, *checked* 263.8
tartar *dirt* 112.5, *irascible person* 303.7
Tartarean *demonic* 446.9
tartaric acid *sour thing* 223.3
Tartar pony *Horse and Pony Breeds* 159
tartar sauce *sauce* 90.17
Tartarus *evil place* 446.6
tarted up [Inf] *flashy* 404.17, *beautified* 530.12
tartly *piquantly* 221.10, *sourly* 223.9, *ill-naturedly* 303.18, *bitterly* 306.16, *discourteously* 411.8
tartness *piquancy* 221.1, *sourness* 223.1, *ill nature* 303.2, *bitterness* 306.3, *discourtesy* 411.1
tart taste *taste* 219.1
Tartuffery *hypocrisy* 330.5, *self-righteousness* 431.7
tart up [Inf] *beautify* 530.14
tarty [Inf] *unchaste* 432.10
Tarzan *person of strength* 516.8
Tashkent *Countries* 566
task **122.2;** *work for* 122.10, *undertaking* 391.1, *use up* 393.12, *deed* 412.2, *line of duty* 433.3, *affliction* 454.9, *business* 509.3, *fatigue* 820.6, *engagement* 833.2
task force *armed force* 77.10, *naval unit* 77.20
task force commander *military position* 58.6
task group *military organization* 58.4
taskmaster *strict person* 424.4
taskmistress *strict person* 424.4
taskwork *work* 122.1
Tasmania *Islands* 572
Tasmanian shrimp *crustacean* 39.10
Tasman Sea *Oceans and Seas* 571
tassel *grass plant* 45.3
tassel flower *Flowers* 42
tastable *tasty* 219.4
taste **92.24, 219.1, 219.5;** *life function* 28.6, *refinement* 48.10, 534.1, *bite* 92.10, *drink* 93.19, *sensation* 212.1, *sense* 212.9, *Phobias* 283, *likes* 290.3,

tandem bicycle — taste

1338

judiciousness 337.2, *judgment* 341.1, *preference* 382.2, *tendency* 513.1, *elegance* 527.1, *style* 537.1, *characteristic* 779.5, *suggestion* 800.9

taste bad *sour* 223.8
taste battle *be at war* 76.32
taste bud *taste* 219.1
taste buds *mouth* 19.7
taste flat *be tasteless* 220.6
taste foul *sour* 223.8
tasteful *refined* 48.20, 534.5, *artistic* 133.7, *subtle* 195.9, *tasty* 219.4, *pleasant* 271.5, *discriminating* 337.9, *elegant* 527.3, *picturesque* 529.9, *appealing* 529.10, *fashionable* 536.5
tastefully 534.9; *discerningly* 48.27, *tastily* 219.7, *judiciously* 337.16, *elegantly* 527.7, 529.15, *fashionably* 536.9
tastefulness *elegance* 527.1, *appeal* 529.4, *refinement* 534.1
tasteless 220.4; *boring* 296.6, *unrefined* 338.7, *improper* 430.14, *insufficient* 517.11, *indecorous* 528.8, *vulgar* 535.6, *unimproved* 808.10
tastelessly 338.14; *unemphatically* 201.4, *boringly* 296.10, *weakly* 517.14, *inelegantly* 528.11, *discourteously* 535.11
tastelessness 220.1, 338.3; *bad taste* 220.3, 528.3, *boringness* 296.2, *vulgarity* 535.1
taste of one's own medicine, a *retaliation* 420.1
taster *eater* 92.15
taste stale *be tasteless* 220.6
taste test *taste* 219.1
taste treat *taste* 219.1
tastily 219.7; *edibly* 92.26
tastiness *physical pleasure* 214.1, *taste* 219.1
tasting *delicate eating* 92.3, *chewing* 92.19, *drinking* 93.1, *appetizer* 219.2
tasting cup *taste* 219.1
tasty 219.4; *edible* 92.20, *pleasurable* 214.6
tat *knit* 130.19
ta ta! [Brit] *goodbye!* 705.14
Tatlinism *Western Art Styles* 133
tattered *stylish* 100.42, *beggarly* 486.12
tatters *old clothes* 100.8, *beggary* 486.3, *bits and pieces* 760.5
tatting *sewing* 130.5, *weaving* 130.6, *Hobbies and Pastimes* 167, *decorative method* 532.3
tattle *chat* 210.2
tattler *informer* 170.8, *talker* 207.4
tattletale *informer* 170.8, *discloser* 180.4
tattling *effusive* 207.6
tattoo *military call* 183.9, *personal identification* 184.4, *identify* 184.11, *drumming* 235.1, *drum* 235.10, *salute* 405.7, *mark* 533.2, *warning signal* 814.3
tattoo [Brit] *show* 404.12
tattooed *identified* 184.9, *marked* 533.6
tattooing *decorative method* 532.3
tatty *beggarly* 486.12, *shoddy* 497.11, *low quality* 745.7
Tatu *Breeds of Pigs* 16
taught a lesson *warned* 814.7
taunt 436.6, 436.23; *ridicule* 302.16, *answer back* 334.19, *derision* 400.5, *disdain* 400.16, *act of defiance* 416.3, *be*

insubordinate 416.8, *show of disapproval* 438.6
taunted *criticized* 438.14
taunting 436.14; *derisive* 400.12
tauntingly *derisively* 400.22
tauon *elementary particle* 10.53
taupe *grayness* 255.1, *gray* 255.6
Taupo *Lakes* 568
taurine *ungulate* 35.31
tauromachy *duel* 422.12
Taurus *Constellations* 7
Taurus Mountains *Mountains and Hills* 568
taut *tough* 542.6, *tied* 752.13
tauten *harden* 542.9, *unite closely* 752.16
tautly *toughly* 542.12, *inextricably* 752.23
tautness *hardness* 542.1
tautological *logical* 6.83, *superfluous* 99.8, *similar* 361.7, *same* 730.7, *repetitious* 797.11
tautologically *identically* 730.18
tautologize *be diffuse* 199.5, *mean* 361.13
tautologous *superfluous* 99.8, *similar* 361.7
tautologous or tautological *diffuse* 199.3
tautologously *identically* 730.18
tautologously or tautologically *diffusely* 199.7
tautology *philosophical term* 4.7, *wordiness* 5.23, *reasoning* 6.61, *superfluity* 99.4, *diffuseness* 199.1, *language error* 351.10, *sameness* 730.1, *iteration* 797.2
tautonym *name* 202.8
tautonymic *worded* 5.38
tautonymous *worded* 5.38
tavern *drink provider* 93.15
tawdriness 535.2; *flashiness* 404.4, *bad taste* 528.3
tawdry *gaudy* 251.12, *flashy* 404.17, *shoddy* 497.11, *indecorous* 528.8, *vulgar* 535.6, *cheap* 800.16
tawed *treated* 388.12
tawny *brown* 256.5, *yellow* 259.7
tax 494.5; *work for* 122.10, *use up* 393.12, *payment* 433.5, *impose a duty* 433.14, *takings* 477.8, *take back* 477.17, *damages* 489.8, *expense* 491.2, *money received* 492.2, *charge* 494.13, *demand* 505.12, *weighing down* 538.5, *make heavy* 538.14, *fatigue* 820.6
taxable *taking* 477.12, *chargeable* 494.11
taxable income *tax system* 494.6
tax assessor *tax collector* 494.9
taxation *tax* 494.5
tax avoidance *nonpayment* 490.1, *financial escape* 816.2
tax benefit *gift* 472.2
tax bracket *economic factor* 56.8
tax collector 494.9; *collector* 473.7
tax computation *tax system* 494.6
tax consultant *tax collector* 494.9
tax court *type of court* 54.9
tax declaration *tax system* 494.6
tax decrease *economic factor* 56.8
tax-deductible *chargeable* 494.11
tax demand *demand* 425.2, *tax system* 494.6
tax dodger *nonpayer* 490.6, *escaper* 816.5
tax dodging *financial escape* 816.2
taxed *priced* 494.10, *ponderous* 538.11
taxes *money received* 492.2, *tax* 494.5
tax evader *dishonest person* 479.11, *nonpayer* 490.6, *refuser* 506.4, *escaper* 816.5

tax evasion *dishonesty* 479.7, *nonpayment* 490.1, *refusal* 506.1, *financial escape* 816.2
tax-exempt *tax-free* 434.8, *chargeable* 494.11
tax form *tax system* 494.6
tax-free 434.8; *with impunity* 434.13, *chargeable* 494.11, *free of charge* 497.12
tax haven *financial escape* 816.2
taxi *maneuver* 677.18, *means of transportation* 686.2, *automobile* 687.6, *fly* 689.13
taxicab *automobile* 687.6
taxi dancer *dancer* 135.4
taxi dancing *Dancing Types* 135
taxidermy *preservation of body* 815.7
taxi driver *transferrer* 685.4, *transporter* 686.4
taxiing *flying* 689.11
tax increase *economic factor* 56.8
taxing *punishing* 454.20, *taking back* 477.4, *weighing down* 538.5, *ponderous* 538.11
taxiway *airport* 689.4
tax office or bureau *tax system* 494.6
taxon *taxonomy* 13.24
taxonomic 13.35, 41.16; *biological* 13.27, *hierarchical* 765.12, *categorical* 767.16, *classificatory* 777.9, *of a list* 785.10
taxonomically 777.15; *biologically* 13.36, *in place* 767.24, *inventorially* 785.13
taxonomic classification 777.3
taxonomic group *taxonomy* 13.24
taxonomist *life scientist* 13.26, *animal scientist* 34.7
taxonomy 13.24; *life science* 13.1, *classification of life* 28.10, *animal science* 34.6, *nomenclature* 202.7, *grouping* 765.2, *categorization* 767.5, *classification* 777.2, *listing* 785.8
taxpayer *payer* 489.9, *tax collector* 494.9
tax payment *tax system* 494.6
tax rate *tax system* 494.6
tax refund *tax system* 494.6
tax return *document* 170.3, *tax system* 494.6
tax roll *list of names* 785.7
tax shelter *financial escape* 816.2
tax system 494.6
tax table *tax system* 494.6
tax write-off *gift* 472.2
Tay *Lakes* 568, *Rivers* 570
Taylor series *Mathematical Concepts* 6, *sequence* 6.18
T-bar *ski run* 162.2
T-beam *superstructure* 551.7
Tbilisi *Countries* 566
Tchenaran *Horse and Pony Breeds* 159
t-distribution *probability distribution* 6.56
tea 93.7; *meal* 92.8, *drink occasion* 93.14, *type of table* 101.5, *social gathering* 408.4
tea [Inf] *hemp derivatives* 121.16
teabag *porosity* 583.5
tea break *ease* 819.1
teach *educate* 48.22, *master* 68.17, *inform* 170.11, *advise* 176.9, *cause to know* 348.13, *brief* 388.20, *accustom* 397.18, *moralize* 431.14, *assimilate* 781.14, *display* 843.13
teachability *educatability* 48.9, *intelligibility* 363.1
teachable *educatable* 48.18,

persuadable 178.14, *intelligible* 363.5
teachableness *persuadability* 178.8
teach a lesson *punish* 454.22
teach an old dog new tricks *attempt the impossible* 837.10
Teacher *God* 82.6
teacher *sage* 4.11, *educator* 48.4, *expert* 52.8, 127.9, *educational leader* 68.11, *professional worker* 123.11, *informer* 170.8, *adviser* 176.5, *motivator* 178.11, *dissertator* 203.3, *curious person* 321.3, *knowledgeable person* 348.5, *interpreter* 365.6, *preparer* 388.6, *converter* 670.5
teacher's aide *technical worker* 123.14
teacher's pet *weak person* 517.4
teacher training *educational system* 48.2
tea chest *box* 578.5
teach freely *be free* 829.16
teaching *philosophical system* 4.2, *ideology* 327.5, *learning* 348.3, *moral* 431.5
teaching contract *purchase contract* 459.3
teaching hospital *hospital* 107.16
teach manners *civilize* 807.16
teach one's grandmother to suck eggs *be superfluous* 99.12
teach wickedness *deprave* 448.14
teacup *drink container* 93.13
tea dance [Brit] *dance* 135.1
tea estate *farm* 16.2
tea for two *meal* 92.8
tea garden *garden* 17.2
tea gown *dress* 100.11
teahouse *eating place* 92.17
teak *Trees and Shrubs* 43
tea-leaf reader *diviner* 86.14
tea-leaf reading *divination* 86.5
tea leaves *means of prediction* 358.10
teals *Collective Names* 59
team 59.9, 827.7; *assemblage of mammals* 35.22, *Collective Names* 59, *personnel* 123.16, *sportsman* 145.4, *baseball team* 147.2, *basketball team* 148.2, *soccer participant* 163.4, *group* 623.5, *alliance* 735.5, *collection* 757.3, *thing included* 763.2, *two* 789.1
team aerobatics *aviation* 689.1
team captain *leader* 126.8
team handball *Sporting Activities* 145
teammates *team* 827.7
team member *sportsman* 145.4, *member* 760.9
team photo *portrait* 132.5
team spirit *compatibility* 735.4, *fellowship* 827.2
team sports *sports* 422.3
team up *band together* 59.27, *form an alliance* 735.25, *come together* 757.10, *pair* 789.13, *keep company with* 794.17, *join with* 827.15
teamwork *joint operation* 827.4
tea party *drink occasion* 93.14, *party* 408.6
tea plantation *farm* 16.2
tea planter *agriculturist* 16.14
teapot *cooking equipment* 91.6, *pot* 578.15
tear *secrete* 24.7, *chew* 92.22, *painful injury* 215.3, *inflict pain* 215.10, *body fluid* 555.3, *opening* 583.1, *open* 583.15, *crack* 587.2, 587.7, *separateness* 753.3, *take apart* 753.16, *defect* 806.4

tearable *brittle* 548.3, *separable* 753.11

tear along *be swift* 694.10

tear apart *berate* 438.20, *demolish* 523.12, *take apart* 753.16

tear down *criticize* 440.12, *knock down* 523.13, *flatten* 716.15

teardrop *body fluid* 555.3

tearful *oversensitive* 267.4, *sorrowful* 270.4, *lamenting* 280.4, *seeping* 559.12

tearfully *glandularly* 24.8, *lamentingly* 280.9, *fluidly* 555.26

tearfulness *lamentation* 280.1

tear gas *chemical warfare* 117.9

tearing *brittle* 548.3, *extortion* 711.6

tearing apart *separateness* 753.3

tearing hurry *haste* 818.1

tearing one's hair *gesture* 183.5

tearing out *removal* 574.2, *extraction* 711.1

tearing rage *burst of anger* 302.6

tear into *strike* 418.21

tearjerking [Inf] *lamentable* 280.6, *pitiful* 308.5

tearlike *rheumy* 555.16

tear limb from limb *execute* 454.30, *demolish* 523.12

tear loose *be liberated* 831.7

tear off *depilate* 614.20

tear off [Inf] *accelerate* 694.14, *hurry off* 705.11, *make haste* 818.5

tear off the mask *disclose* 180.8, *show oneself* 843.15

tear oneself away *part* 705.13, *resign* 835.5

tear one's hair *gesture* 183.17

tearoom *eating place* 92.17

tea rose Flowers 42

tear out *remove* 574.16, *extract* 711.13, *extort* 711.18

tears *body fluid* 19.16, 555.3, *secreted substance* 24.2, *exudate* 557.4

tears for oneself *pity* 308.1

tears of self-pity *pity* 308.1

tears of sympathy *condolence* 308.2

tear-stained *seeping* 559.12

tear to bits *demolish* 523.12

tear to bits or *pieces take apart* 753.16

tear to pieces *demolish* 523.12

tear to rags *demolish* 523.12

tear to shreds *demolish* 523.12

tear up *renounce* 392.4, *abolish* 523.11

tear up the road *be swift* 694.10

teary *fluid* 19.25, *rheumy* 555.16

tease *annoy* 276.7, *humorist* 277.7, *be humorous* 277.11, *court* 299.26, *irritate* 302.16, *capricious person* 381.3, *be capricious* 381.6, *ridicule* 436.22, *charmer* 700.6

teasel Flowers 42

teaser *stage set* 136.19, *humorist* 277.7, *charmer* 700.6, *problem* 824.4

teaser [Inf] *advertisement* 173.9

tea set *crockery* 578.16

tea shop *eating place* 92.17, *drink provider* 93.15

teasing *amusement* 277.2, *humorous* 277.9, *joke* 368.4, *taunt* 436.6, *taunting* 436.14, *inducement* 508.2, *motivational* 508.7

teasingly *influentially* 508.13

teaspoon *tableware* 92.13

teaspoon(ful) *container(ful)* 738.2

teat *mammalian characteristic* 35.3

tea tax *historical tax* 494.8

tea tree Trees and Shrubs 43

---

tea urn *pot* 578.15

tea wagon *means of transportation* 686.2

technetium Chemical Elements and Common Allotropes 11

technical 361.10; *curricular* 48.21, *specialized* 779.11, *trivial* 800.14, *problematic* 824.11

technical drawing *illustration* 187.2, *representation* 202.9

technical foul *playing terms* 148.4, *violations* 148.5

technical hitch *stop* 668.2, *technical problem* 826.3

technicality *expedient* 387.5, *trifle* 800.3, *means of escape* 816.4, *difficulty* 824.1

technical knockout (TKO) *boxing techniques* 152.5

technical knowledge *skill* 127.1

technically *studiously* 48.26

technical meaning *type of meaning* 361.2

technical problem 826.3

technical rehearsal *production* 136.14

Technical Sergeant US Military Ranks 58

technical skill *skill* 127.1

technical subject *subject* 48.3

technical term *jargon* 5.21, *name* 202.8

technical word *jargon* 5.21

technical worker 123.14

technician *mechanical engineer* 14.4, *chemical engineer* 14.25, *air force person* 77.31, *artisan* 123.13, *technical worker* 123.14, *expert* 127.9, *operator* 509.5

Technicolor™ *motion-picture photography* 137.9, *color image* 251.7

technicolored *colored* 251.10

technique *means* 102.1, *manual skill* 127.2, *treatment* 143.6, *information* 348.2, *style* 537.1, *way* 691.1

technique and control *competitive diving* 164.7

technobabble *vernacular* 205.8

technocratic *governmental* 49.24

technological *mechanical* 103.7

technologically *instrumentally* 103.9

technology *economic factor* 56.8, *means* 102.1, Phobias 283, *production* 522.1, *manufacture* 522.2

technophobia Phobias 283

technospeak *jargon* 5.21

techy *touchy* 303.10

tectology *science of structure* 551.15

tectonic 8.56; *architectural* 134.12, *structural* 551.17

tectonically *architecturally* 134.14, *structurally* 551.24

tectonic forces *earth movement* 8.20

tectonics *geology* 8.1, *architecture* 134.1, *manufacture* 522.2, *structure* 551.1

tectrix (pl. tectrices) *plumage* 36.7

tedder *farm tool* 16.5

teddy *underwear* 100.22

teddy bear *toy* 167.9, *figure* 187.4

Te Deum *prayer* 85.10, Musical Forms 140

tedious *diffuse* 199.3, *boring* 296.6, *lengthy* 590.9, *monotonous* 797.12, *annoying* 804.7, *inconvenient* 824.12

tediously *boringly* 296.10, *at length*

590.15, *annoyingly* 804.12, *awkwardly* 824.26

tediousness *boringness* 296.2

tedium *diffuseness* 199.1, *boredom* 296.1, *longness* 590.3, *repetitiveness* 797.3

tee *golf course* 156.2, *golf equipment* 156.5

teed up *prepared* 388.9

teeing ground *golf course* 156.2

teeing off *golf shots* 156.4

teem *rain* 9.57, *procreate* 22.14, *crowd* 59.26, 795.11, *abound* 97.8, *thicken* 594.9, *produce* 771.34

teeming *productive* 22.9, *crowded* 59.22, *excessive* 99.5, *dense* 594.6, *overrun* 712.6

teemingly *densely* 594.12

teemingness *denseness* 594.2

teem with *infest* 40.17, *be excessive* 99.9

teenage *young* 26.11

teenaged *young* 26.11

teenager *person* 18.8, *young person* 26.7, *eleven to nineteen* 792.7

teen idol *charmer* 700.6

teens *youth* 26.1, *eleven to nineteen* 792.7

teeny *tiny* 580.9

teenybopper [Inf] *young person* 26.7

teeny-weeny [Inf] *tiny* 580.9

teepee *overhead covering* 613.11

Teeswater Breeds of Sheep 16

teeter *sway* 378.12, *be weak* 517.12, *be changeable* 666.5, *oscillate* 683.12, *pitch* 684.25

teeterboard *oscillator* 683.7

teetering *unsteady* 378.7, *weak* 517.6, *changeable* 854.1

teetering on the edge *unsafe* 811.8

teeter on the edge *be in danger* 811.11

teetertotter *amusement park and playground equipment* 167.8, *oscillator* 683.7, *oscillate* 683.12

teeth 19.8; *mouth* 19.7, *weapon* 78.1, *eating organ* 92.14, *speech organ* 205.4, *white thing* 253.4, Phobias 283, *retainer* 471.3

teething troubles *snag* 824.8

teethless *toothless* 550.8

teetotal *sober* 120.5, *give up alcohol* 120.6, *abstinent* 455.7

teetotaler *sober person* 120.4, *avoider* 386.8, *moralist* 431.8, *self-restrained person* 455.5, *refuser* 506.4

teetotalism *sobriety* 120.1, *abstinence* 455.2

teetotally *with self-restraint* 455.14

teetotum *rotator* 682.8

tee up *prepare for action* 388.18

tee up or *off play* 156.8

tefillin *sacred object* 83.11

Teflon™ *polymer* 11.9

teg *livestock* 16.11

tegmen *casing* 613.9

Tegucigalpa Countries 566

tegument *casing* 613.9

tegumental *covering* 613.21

tegumentary *covering* 613.21

Tehran Countries 566

Tehuantepec Notable Winds 9

Teide, Pico de Mountains and Hills 569

tektite *meteor* 7.21

telamon Architectural Elements 134, *sculpture* 144.1

telecamera *television recording* 172.7

---

telecast *report* 171.9, *broadcast material* 172.9, *broadcast* 172.13

telecentric system *lens system* 10.22

telecommunication 169.7; *communications* 169.1, *radio* 172.1, *publication media* 173.6

telecommunicational *communicative* 169.17

telecommunications *electronics* 14.33, *computer communications* 15.25

teleconference *discussion* 460.3

teleconferencing *office automation tools* 15.19

telegram *data transmission* 169.8, *communication* 170.2, *transferred thing* 685.6

telegrams Children's and Party Games 167

telegraph *communications* 169.1, *data transmission* 169.8, *communicate* 169.18, 170.12, *transferred thing* 685.6

telegraphese *jargon* 5.21, *conciseness* 198.1

telegraphic *communicational* 169.17, *signaling* 183.14, *concise* 198.4

telegraphically *indicatively* 183.21, *concisely* 198.6

telegraphy *telecommunication* 169.7

Teleia *gods and goddesses of marriage* 64.14

telekinesis *occult and psychic phenomena* 86.7

telekinetic *occultist* 86.13, *psychic* 86.17

Telemark Breeds of Cattle 16

telemark *cross-country techniques* 162.8, *ski* 162.35

telemarketing *telephone call* 169.11

telemeter Fields of Measurement 589

telemetry *artificial satellite* 7.30, *measurement* 10.67, Fields of Measurement 589

Telengit Breeds of Sheep 16

teleological *purposive* 327.11, *ending* 773.13

teleological argument *logical argument* 329.2

teleology Branches of Philosophy 4, *future condition* 650.3, *end of time* 773.5

teleost fish *fish* 38.5

telepathic *psychic* 86.17, *precognitive* 320.7, *foreseeing* 357.5, *parapsychological* 525.9

telepathically *occultly* 86.27, *foresightedly* 357.10, *metaphysically* 525.13

telepathic dream *occult and psychic phenomena* 86.7

telepathic hallucination *occult and psychic phenomena* 86.7

telepathic transmission *psychic power* 86.4

telepathist *occultist* 86.13, *nonmaterialist* 525.7

telepathy *psychic power* 86.4, *sensation* 212.1, *precognition* 320.2, *divination* 358.2, *parapsychology* 525.4

telephone 169.10, 169.20; Children's and Party Games 167, *communications* 169.1, *communicate* 170.12, Phobias 283

telephone bell *source of resonance* 236.4

telephone book *dial* 169.12

telephone booth *telephone* 169.10

---

telephone call **169.11**; *communication* 170.2
telephone directory *book of lists* 785.3
telephone directory *or* book *type of book* 174.3
telephone engineer *telephone personnel* 169.14
telephone engineering *telecommunication* 169.7
telephone exchange **169.13**
telephone kiosk [Brit] *telephone* 169.10
telephone mechanic *telephone personnel* 169.14
telephone number *dial* 169.12, *personal identification* 184.4
telephone office *telephone exchange* 169.13
telephone operator *clerical worker* 123.5, *telephone personnel* 169.14
telephone personnel **169.14**
telephone receiver *receiver* 473.8
telephone ring *signal* 183.6
telephones *Phobias* 283
telephone set *telephone* 169.10
telephone tapper *hearer* 228.7
telephonic *communicational* 169.17
telephonophobia *Phobias* 283
telephony *telecommunication* 169.7
telephotography *photographic specialties* 132.2
telephoto lens *lens* 132.11, *visual aid* 242.14
telephoto zoom *lens* 132.11
teleplay *broadcast drama* 136.4
teleport *experience psychic phenomena* 86.23
teleportation *occult and psychic phenomena* 86.7
teleprinter *data transmission* 169.8
Teleran™ *flight control* 689.7
telergic *psychic* 86.17
telergy *psychic power* 86.4
Telescope *Constellations* 7
telescope **7.25**; *be concise* 198.5, *visual aid* 242.14, *that which makes visible* 244.4, *squeeze* 582.13, *shorten* 591.9
telescoped *squeezed* 582.9, *shortened* 591.7
telescopic *astronomical* 7.33, *visual* 242.16, *contractible* 582.11
telescopic rod *fishing tackle* 154.7
telescopic sight *hunting accessories* 160.5, *visual aid* 242.14
telescoping *shortening* 591.2
Telescopium *Constellations* 7
telescopy *visual aid* 242.14
teleshop *buy on credit* 481.12
teleshopping *shopping* 481.3, *buying* 481.9
telesthesia *psychic power* 86.4
telesthetic *occultist* 86.13, *psychic* 86.17
Telesto *Planets and Their Satellites* 7
teletext *broadcast material* 172.9
telethon *program* 172.10, *charity* 307.3, *solicitation* 505.4
teletophobia *Phobias* 283
teletypewriter *data transmission* 169.8
televangelist *religionist* 81.14, *broadcasting personnel* 172.11, *converter* 670.5
televise *communicate* 170.12, *broadcast* 172.13, *publish* 173.15, *display* 843.13
televised *communicated* 169.15, *broadcast* 172.12, *published* 173.12

television **172.5**; *communications* 169.1, *news* 171.1, *publication* media 173.6
television broadcaster *broadcasting personnel* 172.11
television broadcasting **172.8**
television camera *television recording* 172.7
television channel *television broadcasting* 172.8
television drama *broadcast drama* 136.4
television dramatist *dramatist* 136.27
television engineer *professional worker* 123.11
television evangelist *converter* 670.5
television journalism *news* 171.1
television mast *television broadcasting* 172.8
television news *broadcast news* 171.6
television play *broadcast drama* 136.4
television producer *producer* 522.10
television program *production* 843.5
television receiver *electron tube* 14.40
television recording **172.7**
television reporter *broadcasting personnel* 172.11
television selling *selling* 482.1
television set **172.6**
television station *television broadcasting* 172.8
television time-out *game time* 155.4
television tower *television broadcasting* 172.8
television tube *television set* 172.6
telex *data transmission* 169.8, *communicate* 169.18, 170.12, *communication* 170.2, *mail* 685.10, *duplicate* 736.4
telex machine *copier* 736.5
telferage *conveyance* 685.2, *cableway* 691.11
tell *chronicle* 3.15, *educate* 48.22, *write* 139.21, *communicate* 169.18, *inform* 170.11, *report* 171.9, *divulge* 180.9, *recount* 202.16, *speak* 205.17, *cause to know* 348.13, *mean* 361.13, *number* 783.9, 784.13, *be important* 799.13
tell a cock-and-bull story *distort the truth* 627.12
tell a dirty joke *blaspheme* 301.14
tell a fib *lie* 192.23
tell a lie *lie* 192.23
tell all *divulge* 180.9
tell a story *recount* 202.16
tell a tale *recount* 202.16
tell a tale *or* story *fabricate* 192.24
tell a tall story **194.15**
tell a white lie *or* a little white lie *lie* 192.23
teller *informer* 170.8, *treasurer* 484.18, *counter* 784.6
teller of tales *author* 139.13, *descriptive writer* 202.10
tell fortunes *divine* 86.24, 358.15
telling *meaningful* 361.6, *intelligible* 363.5, *causal* 511.5, *influential* 512.8, *strong* 516.9, *count* 784.3, *important* 799.7
telling off [Inf] *expression of dissatisfaction* 274.2, *condemnation* 438.2, *punishment* 454.1
telling one's dream before breakfast *bad-luck sign* 358.7

tell it like it is [Inf] *be concise* 198.5
tell its own tale *be intelligible* 363.10
tell it straight [Inf] *be concise* 198.5
tell jokes *entertain* 138.16
tell of *mean* 361.13
tell off [Inf] *hiss* 239.17, *condemn* 438.18, *punish* 454.22
tell on **180.10**; *inform on* 170.13
tell one's beads *pray* 85.20
tell oneself *soliloquize* 211.4
tell someone where to get off [Inf] *dissent* 506.9
tell someone where to go [Inf] *dissent* 506.9
telltale *squash terms* 165.10, *informer* 170.8, *informative* 170.10, *signifying* 183.11, *local* 328.8, *evidential* 339.8, *symbolic* 361.8
telltale sign *divulgence* 180.2, *sign* 183.1
tell tales out of school *tell on* 180.10
tell the same old story *harp* 797.17
tell the truth *be truthful* 191.7
tell the world *publish* 173.15
tell upon *influence* 512.11, *be full of vigor* 518.4
tellurian *astronomical* 7.33, *person* 18.8, *human* 18.15
telluric *astronomical* 7.33
tellurium *Chemical Elements and Common Allotropes* 11
telly [Brit inf] *television set* 172.6
telnet *communications software* 15.27
telophase *cell division* 13.17
telpherage *conveyance* 685.2, *cableway* 691.11
telpherage line *cableway* 691.11
temblor *seismic activity* 8.24
temerity *adventurousness* 284.4, *recklessness* 286.2, *defiance* 416.1
temp [Inf] *deputy* 80.1
temper *extract* 11.41, *relieve* 275.8, *anger* 302.4, *modify* 340.13, *be self-restrained* 455.10, *strengthen* 516.15, *calm* 521.8, *refine* 534.7, *hardness* 542.1, *harden* 542.9, *ease* 543.15, *make tough* 547.15, *state of mind* 725.5, *mix* 751.12
tempera *painting* 143.3, *material* 143.9
temperament *key* 140.23, *caprice* 381.1, *nature* 723.4, *state of mind* 725.5
temperamental *susceptible* 212.7, *passionate* 266.12, *oversensitive* 267.4, *touchy* 303.10, *inconstant* 378.6, *erratic* 381.5, *conditional* 725.7
temperamentally *oversensitively* 267.7, *touchily* 303.19, *in good form* 725.11
temperance *sobriety* 120.1, *abstinence* 386.2, *chastity* 431.3, *virtues* 447.2, *moderation* 455.3, 521.1, *prohibition of alcohol* 503.2, *self-restraint* 830.4
temperance society **120.3**
temperate **455.8**; *detached* 4.18, *warm* 9.46, 217.13, *sober* 120.5, *abstaining* 386.11, *chaste* 431.10, *principled* 447.6, *moderate* 521.3, *self-restrained* 830.10
temperate climate *climate* 9.35
temperately *stoically* 4.26, *soberly* 120.9, *away* 386.23, *ethically* 447.10, *with self-restraint* 455.14,

moderately 521.10, *self-restrainedly* 830.19
temperateness *moderation* 455.3
Temperate Zone *world region* 564.6
temperate zone *climate zone* 9.36
temperature **10.29**; *symptom* 114.3, *heat* 217.1, *heat measurement* 217.2, *Fields of Measurement* 598
temperature-humidity index *weather data* 9.6
temperature inversion *act of inversion* 608.3
temperature scale *temperature* 10.29, *scale* 589.9
tempered *temperate* 455.8, *moderate* 521.3, *hardened* 542.7, *toughened* 547.7, *diluted* 751.9
tempering *strengthening* 516.7, *hardening* 542.2, *suggestion* 800.9
temper oneself *strengthen oneself* 516.16
temper tantrum *burst of anger* 302.6
tempest *wind strength* 9.13, *natural violence* 520.3, *atmospheric agitation* 684.13
tempest in a teapot *or* teacup *exaggeration* 194.1, *figurative overestimation* 343.3, *secondary matter* 800.6
tempestuous *stormy* 9.45, *explosive* 520.6, *bumpy* 544.8, *turbulent* 684.17, *swift* 694.6
template *prototype* 624.2
temple *place of worship* 83.8, *architectural structure* 134.4, *side* 623.1, *private space* 812.2
Temple of Artemis at Ephesus *Seven Wonders of the Ancient World* 294
temples *head* 19.6
tempo **140.22**; *time* 639.1, *musical time* 639.7, *frequency* 663.2, *vibration* 683.2
temporal **639.8**; *timekeeping* 646.11
temporal bone *Human Bones* 19
temporalities *possessions* 470.5
temporally *chronologically* 639.21
temporarily *transiently* 643.8, *at present* 647.9, *instead* 672.8
temporary *deputizing* 80.4, *half-measure* 461.5, *temporal* 639.8, *impermanent* 643.5, *occasional* 647.5, *substitute* 672.3
temporary bridge *bridge* 551.10
temporary measure *substitution* 672.1
temporary stoppage *stop* 668.2
temporary substitute *half-measure* 461.2
temporary truce *truce* 73.2
temporary worker *deputy* 80.1
temporize *delay* 658.13, *be cunning* 822.5
temporizing *cunning* 822.1, 822.4
tempt *entice* 178.16, *cause desire* 288.22, *deprave* 448.14, *manipulate* 508.12, *influence* 512.11, *awaken* 675.9, *lure* 700.12
temptation *enticement* 178.3, *desirability* 288.7, *object of desire* 288.8, *liking* 290.1, *cause* 675.1, *allurement* 700.4
tempted *liking* 290.4
Tempter *devil* 446.5
tempter **178.10**; *motivator* 508.6, *charmer* 700.6
tempt fate *be foolish* 353.6, *tackle* 390.8, *face danger* 811.12

tempt fate *or* **providence** *be rash* 286.8

tempting *enticing* 178.13, *desirable* 288.11, *likable* 290.7, *motivational* 508.7, *appealing* 512.9, *attractive* 700.10

temptingly *enticingly* 178.22, *desirably* 288.24, *likably* 290.12, *influentially* 508.13

tempting offer *reward for service* 453.5, *positive stimulus* 508.5

tempt providence *tackle* 390.8, *face danger* 811.12

temptress *tempter* 178.10, *lover* 299.11, *motivator* 508.6, *charmer* 700.6

ten 792.6; *tenth* 792.17

tenable *believable* 87.7, *invulnerable* 810.18, *possible* 836.5

tenably *practically* 836.10

tenacious 376.9, 755.6; *steadfast* 284.11, *iron-willed* 372.7, *persevering* 377.6, *determined* 379.7, *unyielding* 379.8, *retentive* 471.5, *strong in spirit* 516.11, *stalwart* 547.10

tenaciously 471.11, 755.12; *steadfastly* 284.19, *perseveringly* 377.16, *obstinately* 379.11, *strongly* 516.17, *stalwartly* 547.17, *viscously* 561.22

tenaciousness *determination* 379.2, *retention* 471.1, *doughiness* 561.2, *tenacity* 755.2

tenacious person 377.5

tenacity 376.4, 755.2; *steadfastness* 284.3, *willpower* 372.2, *perseverance* 377.1, *determination* 379.2, *retention* 471.1, *endurance* 516.4, *stalwartness* 547.3, *doughiness* 561.2, *union* 752.1

tenancy *possession of property* 469.3, *duration* 642.1

tenancy in common *joint possession* 469.6

tenant *resident* 61.6, *possessor* 469.10, *property owner* 470.7

tenant farmer *agriculturist* 16.14

tenantry *possession of property* 469.3

ten cents *US coinage* 484.10

ten centuries *hundreds* 792.9

Ten Commandments *the Law* 53.2, *ten* 792.6

tend 513.5; *practice livestock farming* 16.20, *serve* 69.11, 825.29, *practice medicine* 107.32, *treat* 115.17, *prefer* 382.13, *aim* 697.14, *protect* 810.21, *preserve* 815.14, *support* 825.24

tended *reared* 715.7

tendency 397.2, 513.1, 838.2; *aptitude* 127.4, *inclination* 290.2, *ability* 340.2, *final intention* 374.4, *preference* 382.2, *spontaneity* 396.2, *design* 536.2, *significance* 676.4, *bearing* 697.2

tendentious *tending to* 513.4

tendentiously *probably* 513.6

tendentiousness *final intention* 374.4

tender *warship* 77.21, *of disease* 114.25, *miserable* 117.12, *sailing* 150.25, *susceptible* 212.7, *painful* 215.4, *touchable* 216.5, *sensitive* 267.3, *amorous* 299.18, *compassionate* 305.8, *pitying* 308.4, *lenient* 423.3, *kind* 445.12, *give* 472.10, *bargaining* 480.10, *bargain* 480.20, *insubstantial* 539.5, *soft-hearted* 543.11, Ships and Boats 690

tender age *youth* 26.1

tender boat *sailboat* 150.3

tendered *contractual* 480.16

tender feeling *good feeling* 266.4, *liking* 290.1

tenderfoot *beginner* 398.2, 771.14, *innocent person* 449.5, *new arrival* 724.6

tender-hearted *sensitive* 267.3, *compassionate* 305.8, *pitying* 308.4, *soft-hearted* 543.11

tender-heartedly *compassionately* 305.14, *pityingly* 308.11

tender-heartedness *compassion* 305.2, *pity* 308.1

tenderize *soften* 543.14

tenderloin *beef* 90.24, *pork* 90.26, *urban area* 567.10

tender loving care (TLC) *consideration* 325.2, *sustenance* 825.3

tenderly *sensitively* 267.6, *lovingly* 299.29, *amorously* 299.30, *compassionately* 305.14, *pityingly* 308.11, *caringly* 325.14, *leniently* 423.6, *kindly* 445.20, *lightly* 539.10, *soft-heartedly* 543.19

tenderness *pain* 117.5, 215.1, *sensitivity* 212.2, 267.1, *liking* 290.1, *love* 299.1, *lovingness* 299.4, *compassion* 305.2, *pity* 308.1, *leniency* 423.1, *kindness* 445.3, *lightness* 539.1, *soft-heartedness* 543.4

tender one's resignation *resign* 835.5

tender spot *vulnerability* 811.6

tender subject *provocation* 302.3

tending *therapeutic* 107.30, *instrumental* 801.7, *supportive* 825.18, *tendency* 838.2, *probable* 838.6

tending to 513.4

tending toward *preferential* 382.10

ten-dollar bill *US coinage* 484.10, *ten* 792.6

tendon *muscles* 19.3, *skeleton* 551.14, *line* 754.5

tendonitis *joint disease* 114.19

tendril *leaf* 41.6, *retainer* 471.3

tend to *propound a philosophy* 4.21, *order* 6.89

tenebrists Western Art Styles 133

tenebrous *dark* 247.5, *dim* 248.4

tenement *apartment house* 60.8, *property* 470.1, *legal property terms* 470.2

tenement area *or* **district** *urban area* 567.10

Tenerife Islands 572

tenet *philosophy* 4.1, *belief system* 87.3, *ideology* 327.5, *guide* 780.4

tenfold *tenth* 792.17, *fivefold* 792.26

ten-gallon hat *hat* 100.32

ten million *million* 792.11

tenne Heraldic Terms 184

tenner [Inf] *US coinage* 484.10, *ten* 792.6

Tennessee American States 564, Rivers 570

Tennessee Walking Horse Horse and Pony Breeds 159

tennis 165.1; Sporting Activities 145, *athletics* 422.7

tennis ball *tennis player equipment* 165.4

tennis court 165.3

tennis elbow *joint disease* 114.19

tennis organizations 165.7

tennis participant 165.6

tennis player equipment 165.4

tennis racket *impeller* 695.7

tennis racket *or* **racquet** *tennis player equipment* 165.4

tennis shoes *shoes* 100.30, *tennis player equipment* 165.4

tennis skirt *skirt* 100.12

tennis strokes 165.2

tennis terms 165.5

ten o'clock scholar *latecomer* 658.4

tenon *carpenter's term* 131.5

tenoner *woodworking tool* 131.6

tenon saw *woodworking tool* 131.6

tenor *voice* 141.5, *meaning* 361.1, *intention* 374.1, *tendency* 513.1, 838.2, *style* 537.1, *bearing* 697.2, *degree* 739.1, *musical part* 760.8

tenor clef *written music* 140.21

tenor drum Musical Instruments 142

tenor horn Musical Instruments 142

tenoroon Musical Instruments 142

ten out of ten *ideal* 805.6

ten percenter [Inf] *producer* 136.28

tenpin *bowling* 151.1, 151.6

tenpin bowler *bowler* 151.5

tenpin bowling *or* **tenpins** *bowling* 151.1

tenpins Sporting Activities 145

tense *grammatical term* 5.29, *hostile* 63.6, *fearful* 283.10, *fidgety* 414.14, *tough* 542.6, *harden* 542.9, *time* 639.1, *linguistic time* 639.6, *tied* 752.13

tensely *toughly* 542.12, *inextricably* 752.23

tenseness *hardness* 542.1

tensibility *elasticity* 546.1

tensible *elastic* 546.5

tensile *elastic* 546.5

tensileness *softness* 543.1

tensile strength *mechanical strength* 15.2

tensimeter Fields of Measurement 589

tensiometer *meter* 589.13

tension *load* 14.14, *personal conflict* 63.2, *fearfulness* 283.2, *hardness* 542.1, *elasticity* 546.1, *irritation* 554.9

tension wood *timber* 43.3

tensity *hardness* 542.1

tens of thousands *multitude* 795.1

tensor *vector* 6.48

tensor analysis *calculus* 6.28

tensor product *vector* 6.48

tens place *number system* 6.7

tent *mobile home* 60.11, *climbing equipment* 161.4, *overhead covering* 613.11, *protection from the weather* 810.9

tentacle *sense organ* 212.4, *retainer* 471.3

tentative 390.5; *clumsy* 128.6, *reticent* 287.8, *experimental* 335.8, *hesitant* 693.9

tentative explanation *supposition* 359.1

tentatively *reticently* 287.18, *ambitiously* 390.10, *slowly* 693.14

tentativeness *reticence* 287.3, *hesitation* 693.5

tentative offer 504.2

tented *covered* 613.19

tenth 792.17; *ranked* 6.72, *less than one* 787.4, *ten* 792.6, *fivefold* 792.26

tenthly *fivefold* 792.26

ten thousand *thousand* 792.10

tenth part *ten* 792.6

ten to one *probably* 838.11

tenuity *sparseness* 541.1

tenuous *sparse* 541.3, *little* 580.7, *unreal* 720.8

tenuously *sparsely* 541.6, *little* 580.12

tenuousness *sparseness* 541.1, *littleness* 580.1

tenure *possession of property* 469.3, *property* 470.1, *period of activity* 641.4, *duration* 642.1

tenuto *or* **ten.** Musical Terms and Expression Marks 140

tepee *house* 60.4, *mobile home* 60.11, *overhead covering* 613.11

tephra *eruption* 8.27

tepid *hot* 217.11

tepidity *heat* 217.1

tepidness *heat* 217.1

tequila sunrise cocktail *orange thing* 258.3

tera Decimal Prefixes 589

teratophobia Phobias 283

terbium Chemical Elements and Common Allotropes 11

terce *morning things* 655.3

tercentenary *day to remember* 354.5, *anniversary* 663.4, *anniversarial* 663.8, *hundreds* 792.9

tercentennial *day to remember* 354.5, *anniversary* 663.4, *anniversarial* 663.8, *hundreds* 792.9

tercentennially *cyclically* 663.15

tercet *part of poem* 139.9

terebinth Trees and Shrubs 43

tergiversate *vacillate* 378.8, *equivocate* 380.8, *renounce* 392.4, *disobey* 427.12, *be irresolute* 666.6

tergiversating *vacillating* 378.5, *equivocating* 380.6

tergiversation *vacillation* 378.1, 380.3, *disobedience* 427.1, *irresolution* 666.2

tergiversator *equivocator* 380.4, *seditionist* 427.7, *deviant* 698.7

tergiversatory *disobedient* 427.10

teriyaki *notable international dishes* 90.40

term *word* 5.17, *title* 72.1, 209.12, Architectural Elements 134, *name* 202.8, *time* 639.1, *period* 641.1, *time period* 641.2, *period of activity* 641.4, *duration* 642.1, *season* 654.1

termagant *irascible person* 303.7, *violent animal* 520.4

termed *titled* 72.9

terminal *peripheral* 15.8, *deadly* 29.14, *killing* 30.17, *sick* 114.24, Architectural Elements 134, *hopeless* 282.6, *away* 585.6, *stopping place* 668.4, *airport* 689.4, *destination* 704.6, *approaching* 704.10, *end point* 773.6, *ending* 773.13

terminal bud *bud* 41.8

terminal disease *illness* 114.2

terminal illness *illness* 114.2, *adverse health* 848.5

terminally *fatally* 29.18, *deadly* 30.26, *hopelessly* 282.13, *finally* 773.24

terminally ill *dying* 29.12

terminal patient *dying person* 29.6

terminal point *destination* 704.6

terminal velocity *flight* 689.5

terminate 834.7; *destroy* 523.10, *close down* 584.15, *cease* 668.9, 773.20, *stop* 668.13, *react* 676.8, *complete* 761.9, *be complete* 761.10, *discontinue* 775.10

terminated *ceased* 668.6, *completed*

761.7, ended 773.14, discontinued 775.8, canceled 834.5

termination 834.2; *closure* 584.1, *cessation* 668.1, 773.2, *effect* 676.1, *completion* 761.2, *conclusion* 761.3, 773.3

terminator *moon* 7.18

terminological inexactitude *distortion of truth* 627.4

terminology *language* 5.4, *nomenclature* 202.7

terminus *Architectural Elements* 134, *railroad station* 688.6, *destination* 704.6, *end point* 773.6

termitarium *dwelling* 40.7

termite *social insect* 40.6

termite colony *dwelling* 40.7

termites *Phobias* 283

term of endearment 299.7

term of imprisonment *period of activity* 641.4

term of office *period of activity* 641.4

term paper *dissertation* 203.1

terms *basis for negotiations* 460.2, *circumstances* 726.1, *agreement* 767.9

terms and conditions *work practices* 57.2

terms of reference *specification* 340.6

tern *water bird* 36.9

tern, least *Endangered US Birds* 36

tern, roseate *Endangered US Birds* 36

ternary *numerical* 6.68, *chemical compound* 11.4, *three* 790.7

terpene 12.20; *fat* 12.7

Terpsichore *Deities* 82

terpsichorean *dancing* 135.6, *dramatic* 136.31

terrace *farmland* 16.3, *ornamental garden* 17.3, *place for viewing* 242.14, *level* 588.2

terraced *layered* 588.6

terra cotta *masonry* 14.22, *material* 129.2, 144.6, *sculpture* 144.1

terra firma *destination* 704.6

terrain *continent* 8.8, *habitat* 60.1, *region* 564.1

terra incognita *anonymity* 182.7, *unknown thing* 349.3

terrapin *turtle* 37.7

terrarium *zoo* 60.14

terra sigillata *Ceramics* 129

terrestrial 8.52; *astronomical* 7.33, *of animals* 34.13, *of plants* 41.14

terrestrially *astronomically* 7.36

terrestrial magnetism *geomagnetism* 8.3, 10.46

terrestrial reptile *extinct reptile* 37.9

terre verte *green pigment* 260.3

terrible *without skill* 282.10, *frightening* 283.12, *evil* 446.7

terrible! *too bad!* 848.17

terribleness *evil* 446.1

terribly *unskillfully* 282.17, *frighteningly* 283.20, *evilly* 446.12, *hideously* 531.6

terrier *Breeds of Dogs* 35

terrific *excellent* 445.13

terrified *frightened* 283.9

terrified out of one's wits *frightened* 283.9

terrify *frighten* 283.17

terrifying *frightening* 283.12

terrifyingly *frighteningly* 283.20, *cruelly* 306.17

terrigenous *oceanic* 8.53, 571.7

terrine *crockery* 578.16

territorial *socioeconomic* 2.13, *environmental* 60.17, *propertied*

470.9, *regional* 564.12, *administrative* 564.13

Territorial Army [Brit] *the military* 58.2

territoriality *region* 564.1

territorial jurisdiction *jurisdiction* 54.2

territorially *sociologically* 2.15, *environmentally* 60.26, *proprietarily* 470.14, *regionally* 564.16

territory *body politic* 50.3, *habitat* 60.1, *property* 470.1, *sphere of influence* 512.7, *region* 564.1, *administrative region* 564.4, *location* 565.1, *dominion* 566.3

terror *fear* 283.1

terror [Inf] *malefactor* 306.6

terrorful *cruel* 306.10

terrorism *deterrence* 179.2, *terrorization* 283.5, *cruelty* 306.4, *resistance movement* 417.3, *subversion* 427.3, *revolution* 427.4, *wicked act* 448.7, *violence by person* 520.2, *impairment* 808.7

terrorist *killer* 30.11, *murderer* 30.12, *guerrilla* 77.7, *frightener* 283.7, *malefactor* 306.6, *cruel* 306.10, *resister* 417.5, *attacker* 418.10, *seditionist* 427.7, *coercer* 428.4, *evil person* 446.3, *villain* 448.5, *villainous* 448.12, *thief* 479.8, *violent animal* 520.4

terrorist attack 418.7

terrorist bomb *trap* 813.1

terroristic *cruel* 306.10

terrorist killing *murder* 30.2

terrorization 283.5

terrorize *conquer* 77.36, *daunt* 179.9, *frighten* 283.17, *harm* 306.13, *attack successfully* 418.25, *suppress* 424.9, *subvert* 427.13, *be wicked* 448.13, *use violence* 520.9

terrorized *dissuaded* 179.5

terrorizer *frightener* 283.7

terror-struck *frightened* 283.9

terror tactics *terrorist attack* 418.7

terry *Fabrics and Fibers* 130

terse *concise* 198.4, *summary* 204.5, *sparing with words* 208.6, *abrupt* 591.8

tersely *concisely* 198.6, *summarily* 204.10, *abruptly* 591.13

terseness *conciseness* 198.1, *summariness* 204.4, *guarded speech* 208.3, *abruptness* 591.4

Tersky *Horse and Pony Breeds* 159

tertian *cyclic* 663.7

tertiary *three* 790.7

tertiary chord *chord* 140.18

tertiary color *color* 251.1

tertiary education *educational system* 48.2

Tertiary Period *Geologic Time Intervals* 8

tertiary structure *protein* 12.9

tertium quid *third* 790.6

tervalent *chemical compound* 11.4

terza rima *rhyme* 139.11, *triple thing* 790.3

Teshekpuk *Lakes* 568

tesla *Scientific and Technical Units* 589

Tesla coil *surface chemistry* 11.20

tessellate *variegate* 263.11

tessellated *checked* 263.8, *inserted* 710.5

tessellation *check* 263.2, *insertion* 710.1, *collaboration* 757.2

tessera *material* 129.2, *check* 263.2

test 390.9; *reasoning* 6.61, *program* 15.29, *diagnosis* 107.8, *practice medicine* 107.32, *film* 137.19, *taste*

219.5, *questionnaire* 333.3, *question* 333.16, *experiment* 335.1, 335.11, *experimental* 335.8, *standard* 589.7

testa *seed* 41.9, *casing* 613.9

testament *final will* 372.5, *giving* 472.1

testamental [Form] *given* 472.8

testamentary *propertied* 470.9

testamentary [Form] *given* 472.8

testate [Form] *given* 472.8

testator *or* **testatrix** [Form] *giver* 472.7, *transferrer* 685.4

test ban *disarmament* 74.3

test case *litigation* 54.1, *original* 737.2

test design *model* 358.4

test drive *miscellaneous automotive terms* 687.14

test driver *experimenter* 335.5

tested 335.10

testee *experimental subject* 335.7

tester *taste* 219.1, *questioner* 333.9, *experimenter* 335.5, *judge* 341.5, *attempter* 390.3

testes *organs of reproduction* 21.9

test flight *rehearsal* 335.2

testicles *organs of reproduction* 21.9, *bulge* 634.2

testicular *of a secretion* 24.5

testificatory *verificatory* 336.6

testified *authorized* 52.11

testifier *affirmer* 189.9, *person questioned* 333.10, *verifier* 336.4, *witness* 339.7

testify 336.10; *authorize* 52.14, *litigate* 54.27, *inform* 170.11, *attest* 189.22, *recount* 202.16, *give evidence* 339.12

testily *irascibly* 303.17

testimonial *authorization* 52.3, 340.4, *certificate* 185.2, *monument* 185.10, *acknowledgment* 310.3, *proof* 331.4, *evidence* 336.3, *documentation* 339.6, *tribute* 405.6, *recommendation* 437.6, *permit* 502.3

testimonial banquet *or* **dinner** *tribute* 405.6

testimony *authorization* 52.3, *witness* 54.16, *attestation* 189.2, *line of argument* 329.3, *legal evidence* 339.4

testiness *irascibility* 303.1

testing *rehearsal* 335.2, *experimental* 335.8, *tentative* 390.5

test model *model* 358.4

test of endurance *contest* 422.4

testosterone *Human Hormones* 12

test pilot *experimenter* 335.5, *aircraft personnel* 689.8

test results *authorization* 340.4

test someone's patience *make irascible* 303.16

test statistic *hypothesis testing* 6.52

test the depth *experiment* 335.11

test the ground *negotiate* 460.6

test the water *experiment* 335.11

test the waters *have foresight* 357.8

testudo *historic armor* 419.8

testy *irascible* 303.8, *argumentative* 329.7, *discourteous* 411.5

tetanus *infection* 114.7

tetchily *touchily* 303.19

tetchiness *touchiness* 303.3

tetchy *susceptible* 212.7, *touchy* 303.10

tête-à-tête *consultation* 176.4, *chat* 210.2, *conversationally* 210.14, *social gathering* 408.4

tether *intertwine* 752.19, *yoke* 754.8, *bind* 754.14, *restraint*

826.8, *restrain* 826.19, *means of restraint* 830.6, *restrain someone* 830.17

tether ball *amusement park and playground equipment* 167.8

tethered *stabilized* 674.4, *bound* 754.12, *blocked* 826.13

Tethys *Planets and Their Satellites* 7

Teton Range *Mountains and Hills* 569

tetrachlorodibenzodioxin (TCDD) *pollution* 117.8

tetrachord *chord* 140.18

tetrad *four* 791.1

tetradactyl *foursome* 791.3

tetragon *polygon* 6.42, *angled figure* 628.3, *quadrilateral* 791.2

tetragonal *polygonal* 6.79, *status adjectives* 11.25

tetragonal crystal *crystal* 8.39, 11.14

tetragram *foursome* 791.3

Tetragrammaton *foursome* 791.3

tetrahedral *quadrilateral* 791.8

tetrahedron *polyhedron* 6.44, *angled figure* 628.3, *quadrilateral* 791.2

tetralogy *play* 136.2, *foursome* 791.3

tetramerous 791.9

tetrameter *meter* 139.10, *foursome* 791.3

tetraplegia *neurological disease* 114.20

tetrapod *foursome* 791.3

tetrasaccharide *saccharide* 12.4

tetrastich *part of poem* 139.9

tetraterpene *terpene* 12.20

tetravalent *chemical compound* 11.4, *tetramerous* 791.9

tetrode *electron tube* 14.40

tetrose *saccharide* 12.4

tetter *skin disease* 114.16

Teufel [Ger] *devil* 446.5

Teutonism *regional pronunciation* 205.7

Texan Longhorn *Breeds of Cattle* 16

Texas *American States* 564

Texas accent *regional pronunciation* 205.7

Texas leaguer [Inf] *batting terms* 147.6

Texas wedge *golf equipment* 156.5

Texcoco *Lakes* 568

Texel *Breeds of Sheep* 16

text *script* 136.7, *book part* 174.5, *topic* 328.1, *meaning* 361.1, *part of writing* 760.6

textbook *schoolbook* 48.15, *type of book* 174.3

text editor *system software* 15.13

textile 552.5; *fabric* 130.1, *merchandise* 522.6

textile manufacturing *chemical process industries* 14.26

textile merchant *retailer* 482.11

textiles *fabric* 104.4, *dry goods* 130.3

textophobia *Phobias* 283

texts *means of prediction* 358.10

textual *literal* 721.18

textual critic *book review* 174.13, *interpreter* 365.6

textual criticism *criticism* 365.3

textualism *literalness* 721.9

textually *literally* 721.32

textual note *annotation* 365.2

textural 552.7; *structural* 551.17

texturally 552.15

texture 552.1; *rock* 8.30, *weaving* 130.6, 609.2, *touch* 216.1, *fabric* 551.2

textured *electric* 14.47, *rough* 544.5, *textural* 552.7
textured lighting *lighting* 132.16
textured vegetable protein (TVP)™ *meat substitute* 90.23
T-formation *offense* 155.6
Thai boxing Sporting Activities 145
Thailand Countries 566
Thal Breeds of Sheep 16
Thalassa Planets and Their Satellites 7
thalassic *oceanic* 8.53, 571.7
thalassographer *oceanographer* 571.6
thalassographic *oceanographic* 571.8
thalassography *oceanography* 571.5
thalassometer *tide* 571.2
thalassophobia Phobias 283
Thalia Deities 82
thallium Chemical Elements and Common Allotropes 11
thallium scan *diagnostic radiology* 107.12
thalloid *algal* 47.20
Thallophyta (algae, mushrooms) *lower plant* 41.4
thallophyte *lower plant* 41.4, *alga* 47.10
thallophytic *taxonomic* 41.16
thallus *lower plant* 41.4, *fungal body* 47.4, *plant body* 47.13
Thalo purple *purple pigment* 262.2
Thalo red *red pigment* 257.2
Thalo yellow green *green pigment* 260.3
Thames and Isis Rivers 570
thanatophobia Phobias 283
thanatopsis *lament* 280.2
Thanatos Deities 82
thanatos *compulsion* 108.13
thane *possessor* 469.10
thank *be grateful* 310.6, *reward* 453.13
thankful *grateful* 310.4
thankfully *gratefully* 310.8
thankfulness *gratitude* 310.1
thank God *give thanks* 310.7
thank God! *thank you!* 310.9
thank goodness! *thank you!* 310.9
thank heavens! *thank you!* 310.9
thanking 310.5
thankless 311.4; *futile* 802.10
thanklessly 311.7
thanklessness *ingratitude* 311.1, *futility* 802.3
thankless task *work* 122.1
thank offering *acknowledgment* 310.3
thank one's lucky stars *give thanks* 310.7
thanks 310.2; *prayer* 85.10, *gratitude* 310.1, *reward* 453.1
thanks! [Inf] *thank you!* 310.9
thanks a lot! [Inf] *thank you!* 310.9
thanksgiving *act of worship* 83.2, Eucharist 88.7, *prayer* 85.10, *applause* 279.2, *thanks* 310.2
Thanksgiving dinner *feast* 92.9
thanksgiving offering *offering* 472.6
thanks to *by virtue of* 447.12, *instrumentally* 511.9, *in aid of* 825.33
thank you! 310.9
thank-you *thanks* 310.2
thank-you gift *or* present *acknowledgment* 310.3
thank-you letter *or* note *or* card *acknowledgment* 310.3

thank you very much! *thank you!* 310.9
Thar Deserts 572
that being so *accordingly* 735.39
that being the case *under the circumstances* 726.16, *accordingly* 735.39
thatch *manage grassland* 45.10, *building materials* 104.2, *overhead covering* 613.11, *roof* 613.30, *repair* 809.10
thatched *covered* 613.19
thatcher *garden tool* 17.7, *grasscutter* 45.5, *coverer* 613.18
that is *demonstrably* 331.22, *in other words* 365.18
that is to say *demonstrably* 331.22, *in other words* 365.18, *particularly* 779.21
that's enough! *hush!* 231.6, *cease!* 668.14
that's for sure! 721.34; *certainly!* 840.18
that's it! *cease!* 668.14
that which makes infertile 23.4
that which makes invisible 245.2
that which makes visible 244.4
thaumaturge *witch* 86.15, *wonderful person* 294.6
thaumaturgia *witchcraft* 86.6
thaumaturgic *or* thaumaturgical *wonder-working* 294.11
thaumaturgically *magically* 86.28
thaumaturgics *witchcraft* 86.6
thaumaturgist *witch* 86.15
thaumaturgize *bewitch* 86.25
thaumaturgy *witchcraft* 86.6, *cause of wonder* 294.4
thaw *snow* 9.58, *hot weather* 217.6, *heat* 217.17, *move to compassion* 308.9, *soften* 543.14, *fluidization* 555.8, *melt* 555.24, *come unstuck* 756.7
thawable *liquefiable* 555.21
thawed *liquefied* 555.19
thawing *fluidization* 555.8, *liquefying* 555.20
thearchy *theocracy* 49.4
theater 136.16; *strategic* 78.16, *drama* 136.1, *place for viewing* 242.13, *dramatics* 404.3, *show* 404.12, *building* 551.9, *sphere* 564.10
theater, the *drama* 136.1
theater ballistic missile *modern missile weapon* 78.4
theater craft *dramaturgy* 136.6
theatergoer 136.30; *attender* 575.6
theater-in-the-round *theater* 136.16
theater movements 136.9
theater nuclear warfare *atomic warfare* 76.4
theater nuclear weapon *weapon* 78.1
theater of cruelty *theater movements* 136.9
theater of fact *theater movements* 136.9
theater of operations command *military organization* 58.4
theater of silence *theater movements* 136.9
theater of the absurd *theater movements* 136.9
theater of war *battleground* 76.24
theater review *criticism* 365.3
theaters Phobias 283
theater ticket *means of identification* 184.3

theater world *drama* 136.1
théâtre du quotidien [Fr] *theater movements* 136.9
theatrical *demonstrative* 331.10, *affected* 367.3, *dramatic* 404.16
theatrical *or* theatric *dramatic* 136.31
theatrical convention *dramaturgy* 136.6
theatrical cosmetics *stage requisite* 136.21
theatrical costume *stage requisite* 136.21
theatrical engagement *engagement* 136.15
theatricality *dramaturgy* 136.6, *affectation* 367.1, *dramatics* 404.3
theatricalize *dramatize* 136.33
theatrically *dramatically* 136.38, 404.31, *demonstratively* 331.21, *showily* 367.6
theatrical makeup *stage requisite* 136.21
theatrical performance 136.13
theatrical production *work of art* 522.4
theatricals *drama* 136.1
theatrical technique *acting* 136.22
theatrics *drama* 136.1, *dramaturgy* 136.6, *demonstrativeness* 331.2
theatrophobia Phobias 283
Thebe Planets and Their Satellites 7
theca *plant body* 47.13
theft 479.2; *taking away* 477.5
their side *group* 623.5
theism Philosophical Schools of Thought 4, *religiousness* 81.2
theist Philosophical Schools of Thought 4
thematic *topical* 328.5, *focused* 328.6, *itemized* 577.9
thematically 328.13, 577.16
Thematic Apperception Test Psychological Tests 108
theme *aspect of fiction* 139.5, *melody* 140.10, *dissertation* 203.1, *topic* 328.1, *gist* 329.4, *division* 577.6
theme and variations Musical Forms 140
theme park *amusement* 167.7
theme song *melody* 140.10
then *at what time* 639.17, *accordingly* 735.39, *after* 770.14
theocracy 49.4
theocratic *governmental* 49.24
theodolite *civil engineering tool* 14.18, *meter* 589.13, *angular measurement* 628.4
theologer *theologian* 81.20
theologian 81.20
theological 81.24
theologically *religiously* 81.29
theological metaphysics Theologies 81
theological virtues *virtues* 447.2
theologician *theologian* 81.20
theologicophobia Phobias 283
theologist *theologian* 81.20
theologize 81.28
theologizer *theologian* 81.20
theologue *theologian* 81.20
theology Branches of Philosophy 4, *religion* 81.1, Phobias 283
theology student *theologian* 81.20
theomancer *diviner* 86.14
theomania *delusion* 110.2
theomorphic *Christlike* 82.18
theopathic *religious* 81.21
theopathy *religiousness* 81.2
theophanic *appearing* 264.9
theophany *divine manifestation*

82.5, *spectacle* 264.6, *manifestation* 843.2
theophobia Phobias 283
theorbo Musical Instruments 142
theorem *theory* 6.62, *physical law* 10.4, *maxim* 177.1, *topic* 328.1, *supposition* 359.1, *formula* 780.7
theorematic *theoretic(al)* 6.66
theoremic *theoretic(al)* 6.66
theorem roving *artificial intelligence* 15.21
theoretical 6.66, 10.71, 327.10, 720.10; *philosophical* 4.12, *chemical* 11.24, *contended* 189.15, *speculative* 317.8, *causal* 319.9, *suppositional* 359.5
theoretical chemist *chemist* 11.2
theoretical chemistry Branches of Chemistry 11
theoretical framework *theory* 6.62
theoretically 4.24, 327.19; *mathematically* 6.93, *chemically* 11.42, *allegedly* 189.31, *supposedly* 359.10, *ideally* 720.18
theoretical physics Fields of Modern Physics 10, *physics* 10.1
theoretician *philosopher* 4.9, *theorist* 359.4
theorist 359.4; *philosopher* 4.9
theorization *theory* 720.4
theorize 6.84, 327.16, 720.14; *aphorize* 177.3, *contend* 189.24, *have an idea* 317.12, *premise* 319.14, *suppose* 359.8
theorized *contended* 189.15
theorizer *philosopher* 4.9, *theorist* 359.4, *unrealistic person* 720.6
theory 6.62, 10.3, 327.2, 720.4; *belief* 87.1, *contention* 189.4, *explanation* 319.4, *supposition* 359.1, *viewpoint* 628.5
theory builder *theorist* 359.4
theory of knowledge *philosophy* 4.1
theory of probabilities *calculation of chance* 842.9
theory of social systems *sociological research* 2.2
theosophical *psychic* 86.17
theosophist *occultist* 86.13
theosophy *supernaturalism* 86.3
Thera Islands 572
therapeutic 107.30; *remedial* 115.14, *advisory* 176.7, *beneficial* 825.20
therapeutically *medically* 107.35, 115.20
therapeutic radiology *treatment* 107.14
therapeutics *treatment* 107.14, *therapy* 115.12, *healing art* 115.13
therapist *psychologist* 108.33, *adviser* 176.5
therapsid *extinct reptile* 37.9
therapy 115.12; *treatment* 107.14, *advice* 176.1, *medical assistance* 825.5
Theravada *other text* 81.19
there *where* 565.12, *here* 575.19, *available* 647.6
thereabouts *where* 565.12, *nearby* 586.17
thereat *where* 565.12
therefore *under the circumstances* 726.16, *accordingly* 735.39
theremin Musical Instruments 142
there's hope! *never despair!* 281.18
theriac *or* theriaca *medicine* 115.2
theriacal *remedial* 115.14
theriolater *idolater* 83.7
theriolatrous *idolatrous* 83.13

theriolatry *idolatry* 83.4

theriomorphic *or* theriomorphous *animalian* 34.12

therm *heat measurement* 217.2, Scientific and Technical Units 589

thermae *bath* 111.6, *health improvement* 113.3, *hot spring* 572.11

thermal *air movement* 9.11, *atmospheric* 9.40, *physical* 10.70, *gas* 106.14, *hot* 217.11, *of landmasses* 572.12

thermal conductivity *heat flow* 10.27

thermal efficiency *engine cycle* 14.13

thermal equilibrium *heat flow* 10.27

thermal imaging *temperature* 10.29

thermal ink-jet printer *hardcopy device* 15.10

thermally *physically* 10.78, *powerfully* 106.19, *continentally* 572.13

thermal metamorphism *metamorphism* 8.35

thermal plasmas *chemical reaction* 14.29, *thermodynamics*

thermal printer *hardcopy device* 15.10

thermal radiation *heating effect* 10.28

thermal spring *eruption* 8.27, *hot spring* 572.11

thermal underwear *underwear* 100.22

thermic *hot* 217.11

Thermidor *French Revolutionary Calendar* 646

thermionic cathode *electron emission* 14.42

thermionic emission *heating effect* 10.28, *electron emission* 14.42

thermobarometer *meter* 589.13, *height measurement* 596.5

thermochemistry *Branches of Chemistry* 11

thermodynamic *physical* 10.70, *chemical* 11.24, 14.46

thermodynamically *physically* 10.78, *chemically* 11.42, *electrochemically* 14.53

thermodynamics 10.30; *classical physics* 10.2, *engine cycle* 14.13, *industrial processes* 14.27

thermodynamic scale *scale* 589.9

thermodynamic temperature *thermodynamics* 10.30

thermoelectric *electric* 14.47

thermoelectrically *electronically* 14.54

thermoelectric effect *heating effect* 10.28, *electromagnetic induction* 10.37

thermoelectric generator *generator* 14.43

thermoelectricity *heating effect* 10.28, *electricity* 10.31, *electrical power* 514.12

thermograph *weather instrument* 9.7, *heat measurement* 217.2

thermographic *barometric* 9.39

thermography *reproduction* 21.1, *diagnostic radiology* 107.12

thermoluminescence *light* 10.17

thermoluminescence dating *chronology* 646.2

thermometer *weather instrument* 9.7, *diagnostic instrument* 107.13, *darkroom equipment* 132.21, *indicator* 183.7, *heat measurement*

217.2, Fields of Measurement 589

thermometric *barometric* 9.39

thermometry *temperature* 10.29, *microscopy* 10.68, Fields of Measurement 589

thermonuclear *gas* 106.14, *on fire* 217.16

thermonuclear fusion *nuclear fusion* 10.61

thermonuclear power *type of power* 514.6

thermonuclear reaction *nuclear power* 514.9

thermophobia *Phobias* 283

thermopile *meter* 589.13

thermoplastic material *polymer* 11.9

thermoplastics *plastics* 104.6

thermos *heater* 217.3, *bottle* 578.14, *preserver* 815.9

thermos bottle *drink container* 93.13

thermosetting plastic *polymer* 11.9

thermosphere *atmospheric layer* 558.3

thermospheric *atmospheric* 558.13

thermostat *heat measurement* 217.2

thesaurus *word book* 5.27, *application software* 15.14, *schoolbook* 48.15, *collection* 105.12, *type of book* 174.3, *miscellany* 751.3, *book of lists* 785.3

these days *at present* 647.9

Theseus *Notable Friendships* 62

thesis *philosophy* 4.1, *philosophical argument* 4.5, *philosophical term* 4.7, *physical law* 10.4, *belief* 87.1, *nonfiction* 139.6, *contention* 189.4, *dissertation* 203.1, *theory* 327.2, *topic* 328.1, *line of argument* 329.3, *supposition* 359.1

thesis novel *novel* 139.3

thespian *actor* 136.25, *dramatic* 136.31

thespian art *drama* 136.1

Thetis *legendary sea being* 571.4

theurgic *witchlike* 86.19

theurgically *magically* 86.28

theurgist *witch* 86.15

theurgize *bewitch* 86.25

theurgy *witchcraft* 86.6

thiamine *coenzyme* 12.12

Thibar *Breeds of Sheep* 16

thick 561.17, 594.5, 594.11; *foggy* 9.51, *dirty* 112.7, *murky* 248.5, *opaque* 250.3, *unintelligent* 316.6, *simpleminded* 526.11, *dense* 540.6, *thick-witted* 594.7, *quantitative* 738.6, *middle* 772.1, *ample* 795.9

thick [Inf] *insensitive* 268.4, *adhesive* 755.5

thick and fast *frequently* 661.7, *in crowds* 795.14

thick as thieves [Inf] *united* 752.10, *associated* 794.14

thick-barked *thick* 594.5

thick-bodied *thick* 594.5

thick cloud *cloud cover* 9.18, *dimness* 248.1

thick-coated *thick* 594.5

thicken 561.21, 594.9; *be opaque* 250.6, *opaque* 250.7, *be dense* 540.8, *solidify* 542.10, *fatten* 594.10, *increase* 746.6, *make bigger* 746.7

thickened *condensed* 540.7, *thick* 561.17, *dense* 594.6

thickener 561.12; *condenser* 540.5

thickening *density* 540.1, *condenser*

540.5, *viscosity* 561.1, *denseness* 594.2, *increase* 746.1

thick enough to be cut with a knife *condensed* 540.7

thicket *trees* 43.4, *solid body* 540.4

thick fog *fog* 9.32, *danger signal* 811.5

thick-growing *dense* 540.6

thick head *drunken behavior* 121.4

thickhead *unintelligent person* 316.4

thickheaded *unintelligent* 316.6, *thick-witted* 594.7

thickheadedly *thick-wittedly* 594.13

thickheadedness *ignorance* 316.3, *thick-wittedness* 594.3

thick-jawed *thick* 594.5

thick-leaved *thick* 594.5

thick-legged *thick* 594.5

thickly *densely* 540.10, *viscously* 561.22, *thick* 594.11, *thick-wittedly* 594.13, *wholely* 738.9

thick mist *mist* 9.33

thick-necked *thick* 594.5

thickness 594.1; *dimension* 10.5, *opaqueness* 250.1, *density* 540.1, *pulpiness* 561.9, *layer* 588.1, *thick-wittedness* 594.3, *quantity* 738.1

thickness of voice *speech difficulty* 206.1

thick of the action *activity* 414.1

thick of things *activity* 414.1, *middle* 772.1

thickset *dense* 540.6, *stocky* 579.16, *short* 591.6, *thick* 594.5

thick skin *heedlessness* 268.2, *callousness* 594.4

thick-skinned 594.8; *insensitive* 268.4, *indifferent* 289.7, *mentally hard* 542.8, *mentally tough* 547.12, *thick* 594.5

thick speech *drunken behavior* 121.4

thick-stalked *thick* 594.5

thick-stemmed *thick* 594.5

thick-walled *thick* 594.5

thick with *dense* 594.6

thick-witted 594.7

thick-wittedly 594.13

thick-wittedness 594.3

thief 479.8; *lawbreaker* 53.15, *criminal* 427.6, *villain* 448.5, *gainer* 467.9, *intruder* 706.8

thief in the night *personifications and symbols* 29.4

thieve *be wicked* 448.13, *take away* 477.18, *steal* 479.14

thievery *theft* 479.2

thieving *villainous* 448.12, *taking away* 477.5, *taking* 477.12, *stealing* 479.1, *stolen* 479.12

thievish *stolen* 479.12

thievishly 479.19

thievishness *theft* 479.2

thigh *appendage* 19.5, *poultry* 90.28

thighbone *Human Bones* 19

thigh boots *boots* 100.31

thigh-high *high* 596.7

thimble *fabric-handling tool* 130.12

Thimphu *Countries* 566

thin 595.9, 595.18; *cloud* 9.54, *cultivate* 17.19, *manage trees* 43.14, *insufficient* 98.4, 517.11, *underfed* 98.7, 118.7, *unemphatic* 201.2, *tasteless* 220.4, *dilute* 220.7, 557.30, 776.14, *translucent* 249.8, *ill* 517.8, *weaken* 517.13, *light* 539.4, *sparse* 541.3, 796.6, *make sparse* 541.5, *dissolve* 555.23, *airy* 558.12, *little* 580.7, *shortened* 582.8, *contract* 582.12, *make thin* 595.17, *superficial* 599.4, *displace* 711.14, *quantitative* 738.6,

decrease 747.7, *subtract* 749.6, *incomplete* 762.5, *reduce* 796.8

thin air *air* 558.1

thin as a rail *underfed* 98.7

thin as a rail *or* rake *or* lath *emaciated* 595.10

thin cloud *cloud cover* 9.18

thin down *become smaller* 582.14

thin end of the wedge *stratagem* 822.2

thin face *thinness* 595.1

thin-faced *thin* 595.9

thin-fingered *thin* 595.9

thing 717.3; *product* 522.3, *object* 524.6, *real world* 719.2, *aspect* 726.4

thing, the *custom* 780.5, *convention* 781.5, *chief thing* 799.3

thingamabob [Inf] *tool* 103.1, *object* 524.6

thingamajig [Inf] *tool* 103.1, *object* 524.6

thing deducted *subtracted item* 749.2

thing of beauty *beautiful thing* 529.3

thing of the past 651.8; *antiquity* 653.4

thin gruel *weak thing* 517.5

things *possession of property* 469.3, *possessions* 470.5

things as they are *reality* 721.2

thing to do, the *formality* 406.1

thingumabob [Inf] *tool* 103.1

thingumajig [Inf] *tool* 103.1

thingummy [Inf] *tool* 103.1, *object* 524.6

thin house *theatergoer* 136.30

thin ice *hidden danger* 813.3

think 315.12, 317.9; *be of the opinion* 87.10, *feel* 266.14, *speculate* 294.13, *reason* 319.11, *imagine* 327.14, 360.14, *estimate* 341.11, *predict* 356.7, *suppose* 359.8

thinkable *imaginable* 360.13, *possible* 836.5

think about *philosophize* 4.19, *think* 317.9

think again *have second thoughts* 317.11, *equivocate* 380.8, *confess* 451.8, *reconsider* 807.23

think ahead *plan ahead* 387.13

think a lot of oneself *be vain* 402.14

think aloud *soliloquize* 211.4

think back *remember* 354.12

think best *will* 372.11

think better of *confess* 451.8, *reconsider* 807.23

think better of it *equivocate* 380.8

think deeply *think* 317.9

thinker *philosopher* 4.9, *educational leader* 68.11, *intellectual* 315.7, *reasoner* 319.5, *wise person* 352.3, *theorist* 359.4

think everything of *make important* 799.14

think factory *place of experimentation* 335.6

think fit *prefer* 382.13

think freely *be free* 829.16

think hard *think* 317.9

think highly of *respect* 435.13, *admire* 437.15

think ill of *disapprove* 438.16

thinking *thoughtful* 4.17, 317.5, *Phobias* 283, *thought* 315.5, 317.1, *intellectual* 315.8, *reasoning* 319.7, *idea* 327.1, *wise* 352.4, *basis of supposition* 359.9

thinking aloud *soliloquizing* 211.3

thinking cap *thoughtfulness* 317.2

thinking machine *humanlike machine* 18.12

thinking on one's feet *improvisation* 396.1

think it beneath one *disdain* 297.14

think it best to *prefer* 382.13

think laterally *find means* 102.6

think likely **838.10**

think little of *disapprove* 438.16

think logically *reason* 319.11

think negatively *be hopeless* 282.11

think no more of *forget* 355.10

think nothing of *do easily* 823.15

think of *remember* 354.12, *intend* 374.8, *dream up* 522.15, *invent* 771.30

think of *or up imagine* 360.14

think of others first *be unselfish* 443.7

think of the future *look ahead* 650.11

think one is it *be vain* 402.14

think one knows it all *be vain* 402.14

think oneself God Almighty *be vain* 402.14

think oneself God's gift to mankind *be vain* 402.14

think oneself the cat's pajamas [Inf] *or the cat's meow* [Inf] *be vain* 402.14

think only of oneself *be selfish* 444.6

think on one's feet *improvise* 396.6, *have no time to spare* 818.6

think out *rationalize* 4.20

think over *have second thoughts* 317.11

think positively *hope* 281.10

think profoundly *think* 317.9

think tank *place of experimentation* 335.6

think the best of *admire* 437.15

think the world of *like* 290.8, *love* 299.21, *revere* 435.14

think the worst *be hopeless* 282.11

think through *rationalize* 4.20, *behave toward* 399.20

think too much of oneself *pride oneself* 297.13

think twice *be fearful* 283.15, *doubt* 287.13

think unimportant **800.19**

think up *imagine* 327.14, *plan* 387.12, *improvise* 396.6, *dream up* 522.15

think well of *respect* 435.13, *admire* 437.15

think well of oneself *be vain* 402.14

thin-layer chromatography (TLC) *analysis* 11.17

thin-legged *thin* 595.9

thinly *weakly* 517.14, *sparsely* 541.6, 796.11, *thin* 595.18, *quantitatively* 738.8

thinned **595.13**; *rarefied* 541.4, *diluted* 557.22

thinned-out *rarefied* 541.4

thinner **595.7**; *material* 143.9, *solvent* 555.9

thinness **595.1**; *lack of emphasis* 201.1, *tastelessness* 220.1, *translucency* 249.2, *lightness* 539.1, *sparseness* 541.1, *littleness* 580.1, *superficiality* 599.2, *quantity* 738.1

thinning **595.6**; *cultivation* 16.7, *tree management* 43.6, *rarefaction* 541.2, *rarefied* 541.4, *shortening* 582.2, *contracting* 582.10, *displacement* 711.2, *dilution* 776.3

thinning out *displacement* 711.2, *dilution* 776.3

thin on top *bald* 614.16

thin out *cultivate* 17.19, *weaken* 517.13, *make sparse* 541.5, *make thin* 595.17, *displace* 711.14, *decrease* 747.7, *make smaller* 747.8, *subtract* 749.6, *dilute* 776.14, *reduce* 796.8

thin person **595.4**

thin skin *sensitivity* 212.2, *oversensitivity* 267.2

thin-skinned *susceptible* 212.7, *oversensitive* 267.4, *touchy* 303.10, *fine* 595.12

thin-spun *delicate* 552.10

thiotropic *status adjectives* 11.25

Thio violet *purple pigment* 262.2

third 790.6, 790.14; *ranked* 6.72, *chord* 140.18, *bowler* 151.5, *less than one* 787.4, *three* 790.7

third age *third* 790.6

third base *baseball field* 147.3

third baseman *baseball team* 147.2

third-base umpire *baseball team* 147.2

third class *inferiority* 745.1, *low quality* 745.7, *third* 790.6

third-class *cheap* 497.9, *imperfect* 806.5

third-class mail *postal service* 169.5

third degree *questioning* 333.2, *corporal punishment* 454.11, *third* 790.6

third-degree *interrogate* 333.17

third-degree burn *heat* 217.1

third eye *psychic power* 86.4, *spirit* 86.10, *third* 790.6

third finger *appendage* 19.5

third law *thermodynamics* 10.30

thirdly *third* 790.14

third-order *reactive* 11.29

third part *third* 790.6

third party *political party* 50.5, *mediator* 75.2, *middleman* 772.7, *third* 790.6

third person *third* 790.6

third-person narrative *aspect of fiction* 139.5

third planet *Earth* 7.17

third power *third* 790.6

third-rate *low quality* 745.7, *cheap* 800.16, *imperfect* 806.5

third-rater *inferior* 745.4

third-stream jazz *jazz* 140.5

third-stringer *inferior* 745.4

Third World *international trade* 56.7, *the poor* 486.7, *world region* 564.6, *third* 790.6

third-world country *country* 566.1

Thirlmere *Lakes* 568

thirst 560.2, 560.18; *appetite* 288.6, *be hungry* 288.21

thirst for *aspire to* 288.19, *thirst* 560.18

thirst for blood *harm* 306.13

thirst for knowledge *curiosity* 321.1, 333.8, *be curious* 321.7

thirstily *eagerly* 288.27, *dryly* 560.23

thirstiness *appetite* 288.6, *thirst* 560.2

thirsting *thirsty* 560.8

thirsting for blood *murderous* 30.18

thirst-quencher *drink* 93.2

thirsty **560.8**; *drunken* 121.28, *hungry* 288.16

thirsty for knowledge *educatable* 48.18

thirsty soul *drunkard* 121.8

thirteen *Phobias* 283, *eleven to nineteen* 792.7

thirteenth *less than one* 787.4, *eleventh and above* 792.18

thirtieth *twentieth* 792.19

thirty-one *Card Games* 168

thirty-second note *notation* 140.20

thirty-something *middle-aged* 27.14

Thirty Years War *Major Wars* 76

this afternoon *at what time* 639.17, *present time* 647.1

Thisbe *Famous Lovers* 299

this big *this size* 579.11

this evening *at what time* 639.17, *present time* 647.1

this moment *present time* 647.1

this morning *at what time* 639.17, *present time* 647.1

this night *present time* 647.1

this size **579.11**

this time *present time* 647.1

thistle *Flowers* 42, *rough thing* 544.2, *sharp-pointed growth* 549.5

thistly *spiked* 549.11

this very day *present time* 647.1

this very minute *or second or instant or moment or hour present time* 647.1

thither *where* 565.12, *distant* 585.5, *distantly* 585.11

thixotropy *phase* 11.13

tholepin *rowboat parts* 150.15

tholos *thing of the past* 651.8

thombohedron *polyhedron* 6.44

Thomism *Philosophical Schools of Thought* 4

Thomist *Philosophical Schools of Thought* 4

Thomson effect *Classical Physical Laws* 10

Thones-Marthod *Breeds of Sheep* 16

thong *beachwear* 100.23, *instrument of punishment* 454.13, *line* 754.5

thongs *shoes* 100.30

Thor *Deities* 82

thorium *Chemical Elements and Common Allotropes* 11

thorn *rough thing* 544.2, *sharp-pointed growth* 549.5

thorn apple *Flowers* 42

thorniness *sharpness* 549.1

thorn in one's flesh *or side burden* 117.3

thorn tree *Trees and Shrubs* 43

thorny *spiked* 549.11, *problematic* 824.11

thorny problem *problem* 824.4

thorough *laborious* 122.7, *careful* 325.6, 593.11, *intense* 598.16, *complete* 761.6

thorough bass *harmonic element* 140.14

thoroughbred *Horse and Pony Breeds* 159, *horse* 159.1

thoroughbred *domesticated* 16.18, *aristocratic* 70.4

thoroughfare **692.6**; *road* 687.2, 691.4

thoroughgoing *strong* 516.9, *careful* 593.11, *complete* 761.6

thoroughly *carefully* 325.13, *intensely* 598.28, *completely* 759.14, 761.13, 805.22

thoroughness *carefulness* 325.1, 593.5, *deepness* 598.6

Thoth *Deities* 82

thought 315.5, 317.1; *philosophy* 4.1, *belief* 87.1, *image* 187.3, *utterance* 205.10, *idea* 327.1, *logical argument* 329.2, *basis of supposition* 359.2, *conception*

360.4, *method* 387.4, *suggestion* 800.9

thought for others *unselfishness* 443.2

thoughtful 4.17, 315.10, 317.5; *serious* 278.4, *prudent* 287.7, *compassionate* 305.8, *wise* 352.4, *courteous* 410.6, *kind* 445.12

thoughtfully 4.27, 317.13; *studiously* 48.26, *solemnly* 278.9, *prudently* 287.17, *compassionately* 305.14, *intelligently* 315.14, *theoretically* 327.19, *logically* 329.17, *wisely* 352.8, *courteously* 410.13, *genteelly* 410.14, *kindly* 445.20

thoughtfulness 317.2; *philosophical attitude* 4.3, *seriousness* 278.1, *prudence* 287.2, *compassion* 305.2, *thought* 315.5, *consideration* 325.2, *wisdom* 352.1, *courtesy* 410.1, *kindness* 445.3

thoughtless 318.7, 324.7; *unskillful* 128.4, *blind to* 243.14, *imprudent* 286.7, *ungrateful* 311.2, *unintelligent* 316.6, *inconsiderate* 318.9, *inattentive* 324.5, *negligent* 326.4, *unrefined* 338.7, *unthinking* 355.8, *unpremeditated* 389.7, *discourteous* 411.5, *nonobservant* 466.5, *hasty* 818.3

thoughtlessly 318.15; *imprudently* 286.11, *ungratefully* 311.6, *inattentively* 324.12, 466.13, *forgetfully* 355.14, *unreadily* 389.16, *discourteously* 411.8, *rashly* 818.8

thoughtlessness 324.3; *bungling* 128.2, *figurative blindness* 243.8, *imprudence* 286.3, *ingratitude* 311.1, *ignorance* 316.3, *lack of thought* 318.1, *inconsideration* 318.4, *inattention* 324.1, *negligence* 326.1, *tastelessness* 338.3, *folly* 353.1, *unthinkingness* 355.3, *unpremeditation* 389.2, *discourtesy* 411.1, *nonobservance* 466.1, *hastiness* 818.2

thought of *produced* 522.12

thought process *thought* 317.1

thought-provoking *emphatic* 200.3, *problematic* 328.7, *suppositional* 359.5

thought reader *occultist* 86.13

thought transference *psychic power* 86.4

thought-up *imaginary* 360.12

thousand 792.10; *myriad* 795.7

thousand and one, a *myriad* 795.7

thousandfold *thousandth* 792.21

Thousand Islands *Islands* 572

thousand million *million* 792.11

thousands *multitude* 795.1

thousandth 792.21

thousand times no!, a *no!* 190.28, 506.12

thrall *serf* 69.8, *subjected person* 832.5

thralldom *servitude* 69.2, *subjection* 832.1

thrash *inflict pain* 215.10, *hit* 454.28, *beat* 695.12, *be superior* 744.15, *defeat* 845.17

thrash [Brit inf] *party* 408.6

thrash about *be agitated* 684.21, *pitch* 684.25

thrashed *defeated* 846.11

thrashing *corporal punishment* 454.11, *violent* 520.5, *ramming* 695.3, *impelling* 695.8, *victory* 845.4, *defeat* 846.7

thrashing of a lifetime *corporal punishment* 454.11

thrash metal *rock music* 140.6

thrash out *confer* 210.13

thread *plant body* 47.13, *fiber* 104.3, 130.2, 552.6, *weak thing* 517.5, *fineness* 595.5, *link* 752.18, *line* 754.5, *consecutiveness* 774.1, *concatenate* 774.13

threadbare *stylish* 100.42, *used* 393.5, *beggarly* 486.12

threader *fabric-handling tool* 130.12

threading machine *machine tool* 14.9

threadlike *fine* 595.12

threads [Inf] *clothing* 100.1

thread together *link* 752.18

threat 848.3; *incentive* 178.4, *intimidation* 283.6, *vilification* 301.2, *malignity* 306.5, *intentionality* 374.2, *act of defiance* 416.3, *demand* 425.2, 505.3, *coercion* 428.2, *negative stimulus* 508.4, *sense of danger* 811.3, *forewarning* 814.2

threaten *motivate* 178.17, *daunt* 179.9, *intimidate* 283.18, *vilify* 301.15, *harm* 306.13, *predict* 358.14, *resolve* 374.9, *be insubordinate* 416.8, *demand* 425.11, 505.12, *force* 428.10, *be evil* 446.10, *be in the future* 650.9, *endanger* 811.13, *warn* 814.8

threaten danger *endanger* 811.13

threatened *dissuaded* 179.5, *demanding* 505.8

threatening *dissuasive* 179.4, *fearsome* 283.13, *vilifying* 301.9, *overcast* 304.11, *malign* 306.11, *aggressive* 418.12, *demanding* 505.8, *murderous* 520.7, *future* 650.6, *dangerous* 811.7, *warning* 814.6

threateningly *dissuasively* 179.12, *fearsomely* 283.21, *vilifyingly* 301.18, *dismally* 304.19, *malignly* 306.18, *dangerously* 811.14, *warningly* 814.11

threaten one's life *endanger* 811.13

threat of dismissal *negative stimulus* 508.4

three 790.1, 790.7; *numeral* 6.8, *ice-skating techniques* 162.16, *cards* 168.2

three abreast *in threes* 790.13

three bricks shy of a load [Inf] *unintelligent* 316.6

three by three *in threes* 790.13

three-card monte Card Games 168

three cheers *applause* 279.2, *acclaim* 437.5

three-color printing *printing* 173.3

three-cornered *three-sided* 790.8

three-course meal *meal* 92.8

three-day eventing Sporting Activities 145

three-decker *triple thing* 790.3

three-dimensional *spatial* 6.76, 563.11, *visual* 242.16, *three-sided* 790.8

three-dimensionally *spatially* 563.16, *spaciously* 563.17

three-dimensional space *space* 6.33

three-dimensional wave *wave* 683.4

threefold *three* 790.7, *thrice* 790.12

threefoldness *threeness* 790.2

three-footed *three-sided* 790.8

three-hander *triple thing* 790.3

three hundred *hundreds* 792.9

Three in One *trinitarian god* 82.7

Three Kings' Day Christian Holy Days and Seasons 85

three-leaved *three-sided* 790.8

three-legged *three-sided* 790.8

three-legged race Children's and Party Games 167

three-minute egg *egg dish* 90.18

Three Musketeers, the Notable Friendships 62

threeness 790.2

three of a kind *poker* 168.5

three-part *trisected* 790.9

three-parted *trisected* 790.9

three-piece suit *suit* 100.16

three-ply *layered* 588.6, *three-sided* 790.8

three-pointed *three-sided* 790.8

three-point landing *flight* 689.5

three-point turn *miscellaneous automotive terms* 687.14

three-pronged *three-sided* 790.8

three-quarter *fractional* 787.5

three-quarter-length portrait *type of painting* 143.5

three quarters *less than one* 787.4

three-ring circus *circus* 138.2

threescore *twenty and over* 792.8

threescore and ten *twenty and over* 792.8

threescore years and ten *old age* 27.5, *life cycle* 28.7, *duration* 642.1

three sheets in *or* **to the wind** [Inf] *drunk* 121.25

three-sided 790.8; *polygonal* 6.79

threesome *golf* 156.1, *three* 790.1

three-spot *cards* 168.2

three-storied *layered* 588.6

three-tiered *layered* 588.6

three times *thrice* 790.12

three times as much *three* 790.7

three turn *ice-dancing move* 162.19

three-way *three-sided* 790.8

three-wheeler *triple thing* 790.3

thremmatological *agricultural* 16.16

thremmatologist *animal scientist* 34.7

thremmatology *agriculture* 16.1, *livestock farming* 16.10, *animal science* 34.6

threnodic *lamenting* 280.4

threnodist *lamenter* 280.3

threnody Poem or Verse Forms 139, *lament* 280.2

threonine Amino Acids 12

thresh *be agitated* 684.21

thresher *farm tool* 16.5

threshold *sensitivity* 212.2, *interface* 616.1, *means of entry* 706.6

thrice 790.12

thrift 790.1; Flowers 42, *precaution* 287.4, *saving* 815.4

thriftily *precautiously* 287.19, *economically* 499.7

thriftiness *home economics* 56.2, *precaution* 287.4, *thrift* 499.1

thriftless *wasteful* 96.9, *extravagant* 500.4

thriftlessly *wastefully* 96.23

thriftlessness *waste* 96.1

thrift shop *discounter* 497.7

thrifty 499.4; *precautionary* 287.9

thrifty management *home economics* 56.2

thrill *sensation* 212.1, *stimulus* 212.3, *arouse sensation* 212.11, *give pleasure* 214.13, *fun* 269.4, *cause joy* 269.11, *beat* 684.10, *shake* 684.24

thrilled *susceptible* 212.7, *joyful* 269.6

thriller *movie type* 137.3, *novel* 139.3

thrilling *descriptive* 202.11, *exciting* 212.8

thrillingly *sensationally* 212.12

thrips *pests and diseases* 17.12

thrive *be fertile* 22.13, *be healthy* 113.11, *be busy* 414.19, *be good* 445.16, *be full of vigor* 518.4, *grow* 581.17, *increase* 746.6, *be successful* 845.11, *be prosperous* 847.6

thriving *fertile* 22.8, *healthy* 113.4, *germination* 581.5, *growing* 581.12, *successfulness* 845.3, *successful* 845.8, *prosperity* 847.1, *prosperous* 847.5

throat 19.12; *eating organ* 92.14, *speech organ* 205.4, *make an animal sound* 240.7, *narrow place* 593.2

throat cancer *cancer* 114.15

throatiness *hoarseness* 238.2

throaty *of disease* 114.25, *phonetic* 205.14, *hoarse* 238.5

throb *stimulus* 212.3, *pain* 215.1, *be painful* 215.9, *drum* 235.10, *frequency* 663.2, *be regular* 663.10, *vibration* 683.2, *vibrate* 683.19, *shake* 684.7, 684.24, *beat* 684.10, *reverberation* 797.6, *resound* 797.21

throbbing *pain* 215.1, *painful* 215.4, *drumming* 235.1, 235.6, *frequent* 663.6, *vibration* 683.2, *vibrating* 683.9, *shaking* 684.6, *beat* 684.10, *shaky* 684.18, *reverberation* 797.6, *reverberatory* 797.14

throbbingly *painfully* 215.12

throe *violence by person* 520.2

throes *pain* 215.1, *spasm* 684.8

throes of death *dying* 29.3

thrombosis *cardiovascular disease* 114.13, *concentration* 540.2, *solid body* 540.4, *blood* 555.4

thrombus *solid body* 540.4, *stopper* 584.3

throne *insignia* 184.5

throne [Inf] *place for excretion* 25.11

throne, the *place of judgment* 341.3

throne of God *heaven* 82.15

thrones *angelic order (highest to lowest)* 82.12

throng 795.4; *crowd* 59.11, 59.26, 795.11, *association* 752.2

thronged *crowded* 795.10

throng in *flood in* 706.14

throttle *retain* 471.7, *obstruct* 584.13, *restrain* 830.12

throttle down *slow down* 693.13

throttling *retentive* 471.5

through *by means of* 102.7, *instrumentally* 511.9, *breadthways* 592.16, *accessible* 691.13, *via* 691.17, *by the way* 692.20, *ended* 773.14

through a glass darkly *dimly* 248.10

through and through *fully* 761.14

through arbitration *industrially* 57.22

through ball *soccer play* 163.5

through charity *charitably* 305.15

through fire and water *perseveringly* 377.16

through negotiations *industrially* 57.22

throughout *completely* 759.14

throughout eternity *eternally* 644.10

throughout the world *extensively* 563.18

throughput *production* 522.1

through rose-colored glasses *imaginatively* 327.21

through self-denial *abstemiously* 417.15

through the agency of *instead* 672.8

through the courts *legally* 53.33

through the good offices of *instrumentally* 511.9

through the instrumentality of *instrumentally* 511.9

through the legislative process *legally* 53.33

through-the-lens (TTL) meter *exposure equipment* 132.12

through thick and thin *perseveringly* 377.16, *eternally* 644.10, *fully* 761.14

throw 696.4, 696.17; *exertion* 122.4, *make ceramics* 129.10, *play soccer* 163.8, *participate* 166.22, *gambling* 167.4, *set in motion* 677.16, *impel* 695.9, *throw down* 716.13, *separate* 753.12

throw a completion *play offense* 155.18

throw a conniption fit [Inf] *become angry* 302.20

throw a crackback block *exhibit penalty behavior* 155.21

throw a curve *play baseball* 147.9

throw a fast ball *play baseball* 147.9

throw a fight *box* 152.19

throw a fit *feel deeply* 266.16, *become angry* 302.20, *be agitated* 684.21

throw a left hook *box* 152.19

throw a lifeline to *save* 275.9, *deliver* 817.5

throw a monkey wrench in the works *make impossible* 837.8

throw a party *rejoice* 279.5, *salute* 405.13, *be sociable* 408.14

throw a pass *play offense* 155.18

throw a pot *make ceramics* 129.10

throw around *sprinkle* 776.15

throw aside *discard* 383.12

throw a slider *play baseball* 147.9

throw a stone *stone* 418.23

throw at *stone* 418.23

throw a tantrum *feel deeply* 266.16

throw a temper tantrum *become angry* 302.20

throwaway *waste* 96.10, *newspaper* 175.2, *absence of charge* 497.6, *impermanent* 643.5, *extraneous* 724.8, *useful* 801.5, *refuse* 802.5, *redundant* 802.9

throw away 709.25; *waste* 96.15, *discard* 383.12, *renounce* 392.4, *stop using* 394.10, *be wasteful* 468.16, *expend* 491.11

throw away an opportunity *lose one's chance* 660.10

throw away the scabbard *go to war* 76.29

throw a wild pitch *play baseball* 147.9

throw axel *ice-skating techniques* 162.16

throwback *deterioration* 808.1

throw back *parry* 419.27

throw bombs *bomb* 418.19

throw caution to the wind *be rash* 286.8, *be foolish* 353.6

throw cold water on *discourage* 179.11, *cause sorrow* 270.9, *mitigate* 521.9, *hinder* 826.15

throw down 716.13; *knock down*

523.13, *lower* 597.21, *make horizontal* 603.10

throw down the gauntlet *be insubordinate* 416.8
thrower 696.10; *track and field eventer* 166.19
throw farther *improve* 467.18
throw flowers *acclaim* 437.18
throw for a loop [Inf] *astonish* 292.10
throw good money after bad *lose money* 468.15, *overspend* 500.8
throw in *play soccer* 163.8, *gamble* 167.14
throw-in *soccer play* 163.5
throwing 696.3; *ceramic process* 129.5, *wrestling* 152.18, *track and field* 166.20, *propulsion* 696.1
throwing club Historical Missile Weapons 78
throwing in the towel *or* **sponge** [Inf] *resignation* 835.1
throwing knife Historical Missile Weapons 78
throwing out *expulsion* 709.1
throwing overboard *eviction* 709.4
throwing stick Historical Missile Weapons 78
throwing up *vomiting* 709.7
throw in irons *restrain someone* 830.17
throw in jail *imprison* 55.11
throw in one's hand *withdraw* 392.5
throw in one's lot with *side with* 382.15
throw in the air *send up* 715.12
throw in the cooler [Inf] *imprison* 55.11
throw in the shade *overtake* 744.16
throw in the tank [Inf] *imprison* 55.11
throw in the towel *or* **sponge** [Inf] *withdraw* 392.5, *capitulate* 421.6, *resign* 835.5
throw into confusion *disturb* 768.10
throw into disarray *disorder* 766.17
throw into disorder *disarrange* 768.11
throw into relief *reveal* 843.14
throw into turmoil *cause confusion* 51.9
throw in with [Inf] *join with* 827.15
throw it all away *lose one's chance* 660.10
throw light on *interpret* 365.12, *reveal* 843.14
throw money at *expend* 491.11
throw money away *overspend* 500.8
throw mud [Inf] *show disapproval* 438.21, *defame* 440.13
thrown *ceramic* 129.5, *raised* 715.6
thrown away *discarded* 383.8
thrown down *lowered* 597.12, *leveled* 603.8
thrown out *refused* 506.5, *replaced* 574.10
thrown out of office *discarded* 383.8
thrown over *disliked* 291.10
thrown pot *formed* 624.6
thrown together *bungled* 128.7, *improvised* 396.4
thrown to the lions *endangered* 811.10
throw off *disaccustom* 398.6, *shed*

614.21, *exterminate* 709.22, *be liberated* 831.7

throw off *or* **out of balance** *unbalance* 741.8
throw off course *displace* 574.15
throw off the scent *evade* 386.19, *elude* 816.10
throw off the trail *elude* 816.10
throw off the yoke *be liberated* 831.7
throw of the dice *endangerment* 811.2, *potluck* 842.4
throw one's arms around *communicate love* 299.25
throw oneself at *aim at* 385.15
throw oneself at someone's mercy *ask for mercy* 308.10
throw oneself at the feet of *knuckle under* 401.10
throw oneself in the arms of *shelter* 812.8
throw one's hat in the ring *be insubordinate* 416.8
throw one's weight around *wield authority* 52.16, *disdain* 297.14, *be an influence* 512.13
throw open *reveal* 843.14
throw out *play baseball* 147.9, *discard* 383.12, *abolish* 523.11, *eject* 701.8, 764.8, *expel* 709.14, *throw away* 709.25, *subtract* 749.6
throw-out *other game terms* 147.7
throw out an idea *propound* 359.9
throwout level *fighting chair* 154.8
throw out of gear *displace* 574.15, *separate* 753.12
throw out on one's ear [Inf] *expel* 709.14
throw over *dislike* 291.12
throw overboard *stop using* 394.10, *lighten* 539.9, *throw away* 709.25, *throw down* 716.13
throw pots *form* 624.9
throw rug *floor covering* 613.13
throw salchow *ice-skating techniques* 162.16
throw something together [Inf] *cook* 91.10
throw stones *show disapproval* 438.21
throw the baby out with the bathwater *figurative expressions* 128.11
throw the book at [Inf] *accuse* 442.8, *exact retribution* 454.27
throw the dice *gamble* 167.14
throw to an ineligible receiver *exhibit penalty behavior* 155.21
throw together *improvise* 396.6, *unite* 752.14
throw to the four winds *waste* 96.15
throw up *vomit* 709.27
throw up a roadblock *block* 826.17
throw up one's hands *find unintelligible* 364.14
thrum *drumming* 235.1, *drum* 235.10, *be dissonant* 241.6, *resound* 797.21
thrumming *drumming* 235.1, 235.6
thrush *animal disease* 34.10, *songbird* 36.12, *fungal disease* 47.6, *hunt* 385.14
thrushes Collective Names 59
thrushlike *avian* 36.19
thrust *rocketry* 7.32, *fence* 153.7, *push* 414.20, *military attack* 418.2, *attack* 418.17, *stab* 418.22, *type of power* 514.6, *acceleration* 694.3, *blow* 695.5, *impel* 695.9,

propulsion 696.1, *propel* 696.15, *bearing* 697.2
thrust ahead *accelerate* 694.14
thrust at *stab* 418.22
thrust back *repel* 701.7
thrust down *bear down on* 716.18
thruster *busy person* 414.10, *propeller* 696.8
thrust fault *fault* 8.21
thrustful *active* 414.13, *impelling* 695.8
thrust in *impact* 710.11
thrusting *active* 414.13, *vigorous* 518.2, *ramming* 695.3, *impelling* 695.8
thrusting under *submergence* 716.3
thrust oneself forward *push* 414.20
thrust out *eject* 764.8
thrust stage *stage* 136.18
thud *dull sound* 233.2, *be nonresonant* 233.10, *bang* 234.1
thug *murderer* 30.12, *combatant* 77.1, *malefactor* 306.6, *villain* 448.5, *dishonest person* 479.11, *violent animal* 520.4, *distorter* 627.5
thuggery *murder* 30.2, *violence by person* 520.2
thuggish *combative* 77.32
thuja Trees and Shrubs 43
Thule *distant place* 585.3
thulium Chemical Elements and Common Allotropes 11
thumb *appendage* 19.5, *joint* 752.7
Thumbelina *little person* 580.5
thumbing *gestural* 183.13
thumbnail *outlined* 617.4
thumbnail sketch *drawing* 143.4, *brief description* 202.2, *summary* 204.1, *outline* 617.1
thumb one's nose *disdain* 400.16, *taunt* 436.23
thumb one's nose at *disobey* 427.12
thumb piano Musical Instruments 142
thumbprint *means of identification* 184.3
thumbscrew *instrument of torture* 454.14, *torture* 454.29
thumbs down *unfavorable verdict* 54.20, *disapproval* 347.2, 438.1, *veto* 503.3, *refusal* 506.1
thumbs up *favorable verdict* 54.19, *yes* 346.2, *approval* 437.1, *agreement* 462.1, *tolerance* 502.2
thumbtack *fastener* 754.7
thump *dull sound* 233.2, *be nonresonant* 233.10, *bang* 234.1, *blow* 695.5, *hit* 695.11
thunbergia Flowers 42
thunder *thunderstorm* 9.20, *storm* 9.55, *proclaim* 173.16, *emphasize* 200.6, *speak in a particular way* 205.18, *loud sound* 232.2, *be loud* 232.8, *bang* 234.6, Phobias 283, *vilify* 301.15
thunder along *be swift* 694.10
thunder and lightning Phobias 283, *natural violence* 520.3
thunderbird Legendary Creatures 360
thunderbolt *thunderstorm* 9.20, *natural light* 246.4, *shock* 292.3
thunderbolts of Thor *loud sound* 232.2
thunderclap *thunderstorm* 9.20, *burst of sound* 232.4, *bang* 234.1
thundercloud *cloud* 9.17, *dark thing* 247.3, *gray thing* 255.3
thunderhead *cloud* 9.17
thundering *loud* 232.6, *banging*

234.4, *deepness* 236.3, *deep* 236.8, *vociferous* 239.9, *vilification* 301.2, *vilifying* 301.9, *huge* 579.14
thunderingly *vilifyingly* 301.18
thundermug [Inf] *place for excretion* 25.11
thunderous *loud* 232.6, *banging* 234.4, *vociferous* 239.9
thunderous applause *acclaim* 437.5
thunderously *vociferously* 239.18
thunder out *cry out* 239.13
thundershower *rain* 9.27
thunder stick Musical Instruments 142
thunderstorm 9.20; *loud sound* 232.2, *natural violence* 520.3
thunderstruck *astonished* 292.6, *wondering* 294.7
thundery *stormy* 9.45, *dark* 247.5
thurible *sacred object* 83.11, *incense* 226.3
thurifer *ritualist* 85.14, *incense* 226.3
thurification Christian rite 85.5
thurify *perfume* 226.6
thus *how* 691.16, *under the circumstances* 726.16, *accordingly* 735.39
thus far *within limits* 620.8
thwack *hit* 454.28, 695.11, *blow* 695.5, *impel* 695.9
thwart 293.10; *canoe parts* 150.10, *rowboat parts* 150.15, *counteract* 510.7, 828.21, *oblique* 628.8, *cause to cease* 668.12, *hinder* 826.15
thwarted *frustrated* 293.5
thwarting *hindering* 826.12
thyme Herbs and Spices 91
thymine *nucleotide* 12.10
thyrocalcitonin Human Hormones 12
thyroidal *of a secretion* 24.5
thyroid-stimulating hormone (TSH) *or* **thyrotropin** *or* **thyrotropic hormone** Human Hormones 12
thyroxine *or* **thyroxin** Human Hormones 12
thyrse *or* **thyrsus** *flower head* 42.4
thysanopteran *insectile* 40.11
thysanuran *insectile* 40.11
Tian Shan Mountains and Hills 569
tiara *vestment* 84.11, *headdress* 100.35, *jewelry* 532.6
Tiber Rivers 570
Tibetan Breeds of Sheep 16
Tibetan pony Horse and Pony Breeds 159
tibia Human Bones 19
tic *neurological disease* 114.20, *gesture* 183.5, *distortion of face* 627.2, *spasm* 684.8
tic douloureux *neurological disease* 114.20
tick *arachnid* 40.4, *pest* 40.5, *small sound* 233.4, *sound faint* 233.8, *knock* 235.4, 235.13, *frequency* 663.2, *be regular* 663.10, *vibrate* 683.13
tick [Brit inf] *instant* 645.3
tick away *pass* 639.13
ticked *or* **ticked off** [Inf] *angry* 302.11
ticker tape *salute* 405.7
ticker-tape parade *or* **reception** *reception* 405.4, *mark of respect* 435.4
ticket *means of identification* 184.3, *identify* 184.11, *certificate* 185.2, *verification* 336.1, *documentation* 339.6, *prospectus* 387.3, *promise*

464.2, *acknowledgment of payment* 473.3, *receipt* 492.1, *permit* 502.3, *right of entry* 706.4

ticket agent *merchant* 482.10, *railroad worker* 688.7

ticket collector *stagehand* 136.29

ticketholder *entrant* 706.7

ticket office *railroad station* 688.6

ticket stub *means of identification* 184.3, *promise* 464.2, *acknowledgment of payment* 473.3

ticket taker *railroad worker* 688.7

ticking *rattling* 235.8, *frequent* 663.6

ticking or **tick** Fabrics and Fibers 130

ticking package *danger signal* 811.5

tickle *stimulus* 212.3, *sense* 212.9, *give pleasure* 214.1, *type of touch* 216.3, *touch* 216.9, *communicate love* 299.25, *make someone laugh* 368.7

tickled pink [Inf] *pleased* 214.9, *joyful* 269.6

tickled to death *joyful* 269.6

tickle one's fancy *taste* 219.5

tickle one's palate *taste* 219.5

tickle one's palm *remunerate* 489.21

tickle pink [Inf] *give pleasure* 214.13

tickle the ivories [Inf] *sound* 141.15

ticklike *arachnidan* 40.12

tickling *touching* 216.6, *communication of love* 299.6

ticklish *unsafe* 811.8, *problematic* 824.11

ticklish business *danger* 811.1

ticklish issue *divisiveness* 463.2

ticklishness *sensitivity* 212.2, *danger* 811.1

ticklish situation *predicament* 824.5

tickly *exciting* 212.8

tick off *identify* 184.11, *number* 783.9

tick off [Inf] *make angry* 302.18

ticktock *knock* 235.4, 235.13, *vibrate* 683.13

tic-tac-toe Children's and Party Games 167

tictoc *knock* 235.4

tidal *coastal* 8.54, *lakelike* 568.5, *oceanic* 571.7, *frequent* 663.6, *changeable* 666.3

tidal barrage *power supplier* 514.14

tidal bore *tide* 571.2

tidal current *ocean current* 8.15, *tide* 571.2

tidal energy *renewable energy* 106.9

tidal flat *tide* 571.2

tidal flats *shallowness* 599.1

tidal flood *tide* 571.2

tidal flow *tide* 571.2, *frequency* 663.2

tidally *geologically* 8.68, *nautically* 571.10

tidal pool *small lake* 568.2, *tide* 571.2

tidal power *renewable energy* 106.9, *power source* 514.13, *tide* 571.2

tidal range *tide* 8.17, 571.2

tidal rise and fall *tide* 571.2

tidal stream *tide* 571.2

tidal table *tide* 571.2

tidal wave 8.16, 10.11, 571.3, 683.4, *natural violence* 520.3, *rough thing* 544.2, *natural hazard* 813.4

tidbit *bite* 92.10, *appetizer* 219.2

tidbits *snack* 90.8, *hors d'oeuvre* 90.13

tiddly-winks Children's and Party Games 167

tide 8.17, 571.2; *sea* 571.1, *course* 679.2

tide chart *tide* 571.2

tide gate *tide* 571.2

tide gauge *tide* 571.2

tideland *tide* 571.2

tideline *edge* 618.1

tidemark *indicator* 183.7, *vestige* 185.11, *measuring instrument* 589.12

tide of time *duration* 642.1

tide over *finance* 825.31

tide race *tide* 571.2

tiderip *tide* 571.2

tidewater *tide* 571.2

tideway *tide* 571.2

tidied *rearranged* 767.14

tidily *cleanly* 111.20, *orderly* 765.25, *in place* 767.24

tidiness *fastidiousness* 325.4, *appeal* 529.4, *orderliness* 765.5

tidings Collective Names 59, *information* 170.1, *news* 171.1

tidy 765.21, 807.19; *clean* 111.13, 111.17, *fastidious* 325.9, *appealing* 529.10, *big* 579.13, *orderly* 765.13, *rearrange* 767.20

tidying 807.6; *cleaning* 111.2, *rearrangement* 767.4

tidy sum *money* 485.2, *multitude* 795.1

tidy up *straighten* 630.14, *tidy* 765.21, 807.19

tie *garden tool* 17.7, *arrest* 55.12, *neckwear* 100.29, *wear* 100.46, *clothing* 184.6, *duty* 433.1, *impose a duty* 433.14, *superstructure* 551.7, *make stable* 674.7, *relate* 727.9, *stalemate* 740.3, *be equal* 740.11, *joint* 752.7, *link* 752.18, *means of connection* 754.4, *line* 754.5, *connect* 754.13, *bind* 754.14, *nonachievement* 762.3, *repair* 809.10, *restraint* 826.8, *restrain* 826.19, *restrain someone* 830.17

tie a fly *fish* 154.14

tie a knot in one's handkerchief *remind* 354.13

tie clasp or **clip** *retainer* 471.3, *fastener* 754.7

tied 752.13; *imprisoned* 55.9, *fishing* 154.13, *dutiful* 433.6, *stabilized* 674.4, *related* 727.6, *on equal terms* 740.9, *connected* 754.11, *bound* 754.12

tied down *tied* 752.13, *restrained* 830.9

tied fly *bait* 154.6

tied game *stalemate* 740.3

tie down *compel* 428.8

tied score *stalemate* 740.3

tied to one's apron strings *subordinate* 832.8

tied up *on-duty* 433.10, *tied* 752.13

tie-dye *treat* 130.21, *color* 251.16

tie-dyed *treated* 130.16

tie-dyeing *dyeing* 130.9, Hobbies and Pastimes 167

tief Musical Terms and Expression Marks 140

tie hand and foot *restrain someone* 830.17

tie in *unite* 752.14, *join* 827.17

tie-in *association* 827.6

tie in knots *discompose* 766.18

tie in with *conform* 735.27

Tien Shan Mountains and Hills 569

tie one's hands *restrain* 826.19

tie-on label *personal identification* 184.4

tiepin *fastener* 754.7

tier *level* 588.2, *layer* 588.9, *social class* 777.5

tierce *public worship* 83.3, *morning things* 655.3, *third* 790.6

Tierra del Fuego *cold place* 218.7, Islands 572

tie the knot [Inf] *marry* 64.19, *contract* 459.8

tie to *add* 748.11, *intertwine* 752.19

tie together *link* 752.18

tie up *cultivate* 17.19, *secure* 464.9, *possess* 469.14, *overpower* 515.14, *sail* 690.16, *land* 704.16, *relate to* 727.9, *intertwine* 752.19, *repair* 809.10, *join* 827.17

tie up or **down** *restrain someone* 830.17

tie-up *alliance* 64.2, *relatedness* 727.1, *linkage* 752.3, *association* 827.6

tie up to *intertwine* 752.19

tie up with *merge* 64.21, *link* 752.18

tiff *quarrel* 272.4, 302.7, *argument* 329.1, *dispute* 463.3, 463.9

tiffany *transparent thing* 249.4

Tiffany glass Ceramics 129

tiffin [Brit inf] *meal* 92.8

tiger *male animal* 32.15, *male mammal* 35.18, *game* 160.6, *variegated thing* 263.5, *courageous person* 284.8, *irascible person* 303.7, *violent animal* 520.4

tigerish *carnivorous* 35.26, *murderous* 520.7

tigerlike *carnivorous* 35.26

tiger lily Flowers 42

tiger's-eye *variegated thing* 263.5

Tiger ware Ceramics 129

tight *mean* 501.4, *tough* 542.6, *squeezed* 582.9, *narrow* 593.8, *tied* 752.13, *inextricably* 752.23, *adhesive* 755.5, *complete* 805.14, *invulnerable* 810.18

tight [Inf] *drunk* 121.25

tight-ass [Inf] *self-restrained person* 455.5

tight-assed [Inf] *self-restrained* 455.6

tight corner *critical situation* 824.6

tighten *harden* 542.9, *squeeze* 582.13, *become smaller* 582.14, *narrow* 593.14, *unite closely* 752.16

tight end *offense* 155.6

tightened *squeezed* 582.9

tightened headband *instrument of torture* 454.4

tightening *squeeze* 582.3, *contracting* 582.10, *unification* 752.5

tightening one's belt *home economics* 56.2

tighten one's belt *starve* 118.10, *be self-restrained* 455.10, *be poor* 486.14, *economize* 499.6

tighten one's grip *retain* 471.7

tighten up on *restore order* 765.22

tight-fisted *retentive* 471.5, *mean* 501.4

tight-fistedness *meanness* 501.1

tight-fitting *tied* 752.13

tight grip *retention* 471.1

tight-knit *concise* 198.4

tight-lipped *noncommittal* 181.11, *uncandid* 192.15, *taciturn* 208.4, *silent* 231.2

tightly *toughly* 542.12, *narrowly* 593.17, *inextricably* 752.23, *cohesively* 755.11

tightly packed *tied* 752.13

tightness *meanness* 501.1, *hardness* 542.1, *squeeze* 582.3, *narrowness* 593.1, *denseness* 594.2, *union* 752.1

tight rein *severity* 424.1

tightrope walker *circus performer* 138.9

tights *legwear* 100.26

tight ship *severity* 424.1

tight skirt *skirt* 100.12

tight spot *critical situation* 824.6

tight squeeze or **spot** or **corner** *little space* 580.6, *narrow place* 593.2

tightwad [Inf] *miser* 501.3

tigress *female animal* 33.15, *female mammal* 35.19, *irascible person* 303.7

Tigris Rivers 570

tiki *talisman* 86.9

tilde Common Accents and Diacritical Marks 5

tile *masonry* 14.22, *building materials* 104.2, *material* 129.2, *make ceramics* 129.10, *slice* 588.4, *floor covering* 613.13, *roof* 613.30

tiled *covered* 613.19

tile painter *ceramist* 129.7

tiler *artisan* 123.13, *ceramist* 129.7, *coverer* 613.18

tiles *overhead covering* 613.11

tiling *floor covering* 613.13

till 484.21; *glacier* 8.44, *farm* 16.19, *vault* 105.9, *all the time* 639.16, *eternally* 644.10, *calculator* 784.5

tillable *farmable* 16.17

tillage *cultivation* 16.7

tilled *farmable* 16.17

tiller *agriculturist* 16.14, *garden tool* 103.4, *sailboat parts and accessories* 150.4, *ship's steering* 690.9

tiller of the soil *agriculturist* 16.14

till hell freezes over [Inf] *to the end* 773.25

tilling *cultivation* 16.7

till now *historically* 3.17, *before now* 651.21

till the bitter end *for the duration* 642.8

till the cows come home *continually* 377.17, *for long* 642.9

till the soil *farm* 16.19

tilt *fight* 77.35, *grip* 151.4, *duel* 422.12, *obliqueness* 607.1, *be oblique* 607.10, *obliquity* 628.2, *angle* 628.11, *inclination* 714.6, *slide* 714.17, *lean* 716.19, *imbalance* 741.2, *unbalance* 741.8

tilt at *chase* 385.13, *attack* 418.17

tilt at windmills *waste effort* 802.13

tilted *oblique* 607.6, 628.8

tilth *cultivation* 16.7

tilting *duel* 422.12, *oblique* 607.6

tilting at windmills *conception* 360.4

tilting of the scales *inequality* 741.1

tilt the bowl *bowl* 151.8

tilt with *contend* 422.22

timbale Musical Instruments 142

timber 43.3; *construction material* 14.21, *tree* 43.1, *wood* 131.3, *carpenter* 131.10

timbered *wooded* 43.12, *joined* 131.8

timber hitch Knots, Bends, Hitches, Splices 754

timbering *wood* 131.3, *construction* 522.9

timberjack *woodworker* 131.4
timber joint *carpenter's term* 131.5
timberland *trees* 43.4
timberline *trees* 43.4
timberman *forester* 43.7
timber tree *tree* 43.1
timberwood *wood* 131.3
timberwork *woodworking* 131.1
timbre *mode of speech* 205.6, *sound* 230.1
timbrel *Musical Instruments* 142
Timbuktu *distant place* 585.3
time 639.1, 639.15, 726.3; *tempo* 140.22, *play an instrument* 142.9, *destroyer* 523.6, *space* 563.15, *Fields of Measurement* 589, *measurability* 589.2, *dimension* 589.11, *measuring instrument* 589.12, *measure* 589.20, *length* 590.1, *period* 641.1, *keep time* 646.12, *make regular* 663.9, *interval* 739.4
time [Inf] *prison sentence* 55.6, *detention* 830.5
time after time *frequently* 661.7, *repeatedly* 797.22
time ahead *future time* 650.1
time and again *frequently* 661.7, *repeatedly* 797.22
time and tide *passage of time* 639.3
time badly *misjudge* 342.9, *be untimely* 660.8
time-based *temporal* 639.8
time beater *keeper of time* 646.10
time bomb *bomb* 78.15, *trap* 813.1
time-consuming *lengthy* 590.9
timed *harmonic* 140.27, *hunting* 160.11, *ice-skating* 162.32, *synchronized* 649.5, *frequent* 663.6
timed fire *target shooting* 160.1
timed-release Caplet™ *dose of medicine* 115.3
time for oneself *leisure* 125.1
time-honored *societal* 1.13, *customary* 397.11, *respected* 435.10, *lasting* 639.9, *olden* 653.11
time-honored practice *tradition* 397.5
time immemorial *past time* 3.6, 651.1, *long duration* 642.3, *oldness* 653.1
time indicator *indicator* 183.7
time interval *interval* 587.1
timekeeper 646.7; *judo* 152.13, *karate* 152.14, *hockey player* 158.8, *indicator* 183.7, *record keeper* 185.8, *measurer* 589.14, *keeper of time* 646.10
timekeeping 646.1, 646.11; *time measurement* 639.5
time lag *lateness* 658.1, *interval* 775.2
time lapse *intervening space* 563.8
time-lapse photography *photographic specialties* 132.2
timeless 640.3; *eternal* 644.4
timelessness 640.1; *eternity* 644.1
timeliness 659.1; *compatibility* 462.3, *earliness* 657.1, *convenience* 803.1
timely 659.4; *topical* 328.5, *early* 657.8, *convenient* 803.3
time machine *space-time* 639.2
time measurement 639.5
time now, the *chronology* 646.2
time of adversity 848.8
time of day *chronology* 646.2
time off 125.2; *leave of absence* 576.4, *pause* 668.3, *ease* 819.1
time of night *chronology* 646.2
time of plenty 847.3

time of sorrow *time of adversity* 848.8
time of the month *bleeding* 25.10
time of war *belligerency* 76.14
time of year *season* 654.1
time one can call one's own *leisure* 125.1
time on one's hands *leisure* 125.1, 413.4, *boring thing* 296.3
time-out *time off* 125.2, *game time* 155.4, *interval* 639.4, 775.2, *pause* 668.3
time out of mind *past time* 651.1, *in the past* 651.20, *oldness* 653.1
time period 641.2
timepiece *timekeeper* 646.7
timer *darkroom equipment* 132.21, *basketball team* 148.2
time-related *temporal* 639.8
time-rock unit *geological time* 8.47
times *add* 6.86
times, the *present day* 647.2, *circumstances* 726.1
time-saving *thrifty* 499.4
time-saving device *convenience* 825.7
timeserver *sycophant* 401.3, *conformist* 781.6, *cunning person* 822.3
timeserving *ungenuine* 192.13, *sycophancy* 401.2, *sycophantic* 401.7, *cunning* 822.4
times gone by *past time* 651.1
time-share apartment *joint possession* 469.6
time-share owner *possessor* 469.10
time-sharer *resident* 61.6
time-sharing *computing terms* 15.22, *joint possession* 469.6, *jointly possessing* 469.12
time shift *different time* 648.1
time signal *signal* 646.9
time signature *written music* 140.21, *musical time* 639.7
time-space *fourth dimension* 563.9
timespan *age* 27.1, *period* 641.1, *duration* 642.1
times past *past time* 651.1
Times Square *New York* 567.6
time's winged chariot *passage of time* 639.3
times without number *frequently* 661.7
timetable *subject* 48.3, *plan* 387.1, *chronology* 646.2, *list of dates* 785.6
timetabling *timekeeping* 646.1
time the enemy *passage of time* 639.3
time the great healer *passage of time* 639.3
time thrust or **cut** *fencing movements* 153.3
time to come *future time* 650.1
time to kill *leisure* 125.1, 413.4, *boring thing* 296.3
time to oneself *leisure* 125.1
time to spare *leisure* 125.1, *slowness* 693.1
time travel *space-time* 639.2
time-travel paradox *philosophical problem* 4.8
time up *close* 773.9
time warp *space-time* 639.2, *different time* 648.1, *interval* 775.2
time-wasting *futile* 802.10
time when the chips are down *predicament* 725.3
time without end *eternity* 644.1
timeworn *olden* 653.11
time zone 646.5; *limit marker* 620.4
timid *fearful* 283.10, *cowardly*

285.4, *shy* 403.8, 409.7, *weak-willed* 517.10
timidity *yellow streak* [Inf] 259.6, *fearfulness* 283.2, *cowardice* 285.1, *shyness* 403.3, 409.2, *confusion* 841.4
timidly *fearfully* 283.19, *cowardly* 285.9, *shyly* 403.16, *unsocially* 409.13, *weakly* 517.14
timidness *shyness* 403.3
timing *tempo* 140.22, *ice-dancing move* 162.19, *timekeeping* 646.1, *frequency* 663.2
timing device *timekeeper* 646.7
timocracy *plutocracy* 485.5
Timor *Islands* 572
timorous *fearful* 283.10, *cowardly* 285.4, *shy* 403.8, *weak-willed* 517.10
timorously *fearfully* 283.19, *cowardly* 285.9, *shyly* 403.16
timorousness *fearfulness* 283.2, *cowardice* 285.1, *shyness* 403.3, *indecisiveness* 517.2
Timor pony *Horse and Pony Breeds* 159
Timor Sea *Oceans and Seas* 571
timothy *crop* 16.8
timothy or **timothy grass** *animal feed* 16.12
timpani *Musical Instruments* 142
timpanist *player* 141.2
tin *Chemical Elements and Common Allotropes* 11, *contain* 578.20
tin [Brit] *preserver* 815.9, *preserve* 815.14
tin bath *basin* 578.12
tin can *box* 578.5
tinct *colored* 251.10
tinctorial *colored* 251.10
tincture *hue* 251.4, *color* 251.16, *attitude* 513.2, *admixture* 751.5
tinder *fuel starter* 106.3
tinderbox *fuel starter* 106.3, *box* 578.5
tine *sharp point* 549.2
tinea *fungal disease* 47.6
tinea cruris *tropical disease* 114.10, *skin disease* 114.16
tin ear *hearing* 228.1
tin-eared *hearing* 228.9
tin-enamel *make ceramics* 129.10
tin-enameled *ceramic* 129.9
tin-enameled ware *ceramics* 129.1
tin fish *bomb* 78.15
ting-a-ling *ringing* 236.2
tinge *treat* 130.21, *hue* 251.4, *color* 251.16, *admixture* 751.5, *mix* 751.12, *suggestion* 800.9
tinged *colored* 251.10, *complicated* 751.10
tin-glaze *make ceramics* 129.10
tingle *stimulus* 212.3, *sense* 212.9, *be painful* 215.9, *be touched by* 216.10
tingling *painful* 215.4
tingly *exciting* 212.8
tin god *person in authority* 52.7, *absolute ruler* 68.7, *insolent person* 400.7
ting ware *Ceramics* 129
tin hat [Inf] *helmet* 100.34, *modern armor* 419.7
tininess *littleness* 580.1
tinker *be insufficient* 98.9, *repair worker* 123.8, *unskilled person* 128.3, *be unskillful* 128.8, *touch* 216.9, *meddle* 214.23, *peddler* 482.9, *waste effort* 802.13, *impair* 808.18, *be cunning* 822.5
tinkering *insufficiency* 98.1,

bungling 128.2, *waste of effort* 802.4
tinker's damn or **dam** *little bit* 800.4
tinker with *touch* 216.9, *change for the worse* 665.18
tinkle *small sound* 233.4, *sound faint* 233.8, *ringing* 236.2
tinkle [Inf] *urinate* 25.22, *telephone call* 169.11
tinkling cymbal *nonsense* 362.2
tin lizzie [Inf] *automobile* 687.6
tin mine *works* 124.9
tinned *storing* 578.19
tinned [Brit] *preserved* 815.12
tinned food [Brit] *preserved thing* 815.10
tinning *storing* 578.19
tinning [Brit] *preservation of provisions* 815.6
tinnitus *ear problem* 228.4
tinny *shrill* 238.6
tinsel *flashiness* 404.4, *cheap thing* 800.7
tinselly *bright* 246.14, *flashy* 404.17
tinsmith *artisan* 123.13
tin soldier *toy* 167.9
tint *dye* 130.8, *paint* 143.12, *hue* 251.4, *coloring agent* 251.5, *color* 251.16, *coif* 530.15
tinted *painted* 143.10, *semitransparent* 249.9, *colored* 251.10, *beautified* 530.12
tinted glasses *visual aid* 242.14
tinting *(act of) painting* 143.1
tintinnabular or **tintinnabulary** *ringing* 236.7
tintinnabulate *ring* 236.10
tintinnabulation *ringing* 236.2
tintometer *chromatics* 251.8, *Fields of Measurement* 589
tintometry *Fields of Measurement* 589
tints *Fields of Measurement* 589
tint tool *woodworking tool* 131.6
tintype *older photograph* 132.4
tin whistle *Musical Instruments* 142, *shrillness* 238.3
tiny 580.9; *little* 580.7, *small* 787.6
tip 170.14, 472.14; *inside information* 170.4, *news source* 171.4, *communication* 176.3, *communicate* 176.10, *acknowledgment* 310.3, *be grateful* 310.6, *bounty* 453.8, *pay* 453.15, 489.6, *gift* 472.2, 498.3, *remunerate* 489.21, *positive stimulus* 508.5, *summit* 600.1, *obliqueness* 607.1, *be oblique* 607.10, *angle* 628.11, *blow* 695.5, *tap* 695.13, *insert* 710.4, *lean* 716.19, *extra* 748.6, *limit* 773.7, *warning* 814.1, *warn* 814.8
tip-cat *Children's and Party Games* 167
tip in *play basketball* 148.7
tip in or **on** *inset* 710.13
tip-in *playing terms* 148.4, *insert* 710.4
tip off *educate* 48.22, *warn* 814.8
tip off [Inf] *tip* 170.14, *inform* 170.11
tip-off [Inf] *inside information* 170.4, *warning* 814.1
tip of the iceberg *latency* 844.1
tip-on *insert* 710.4
tip one's hat *submit* 298.17
tipped *topped* 600.8, *inset* 710.8
tipped-in or **tipped-on** *inset* 710.8
tipper *giver* 472.7
tipper [Inf] *informer* 170.8

tippet *vestment* 84.11, *neckwear* 100.29
tipple *drink* 93.19, 121.6, *get drunk* 121.35
tippler *drinker* 93.16, *drunkard* 121.8
tippling *drinking* 93.17, 121.2, *drunken* 121.28
tipsily *drunkenly* 121.39
tipsiness *drunkenness* 121.3
tipster *horse racing* 159.14, *informer* 170.8, *news source* 171.4, *forecaster* 358.9
tipsy *slightly drunk* 121.26
tip the balance *be heavy* 538.12
tip the board *windsurf* 150.33
tip the scale *determine* 675.11
tip the scale(s) *change* 512.12
tip the scales *be heavy* 538.12
tip the wink *approve* 437.14
tiptoe *conceal oneself* 181.15, *proceed with caution* 287.12, *hide* 844.13
tiptop *fishing tackle* 154.7, *summit* 600.1, *top* 600.6
tiptop [Inf] *elite* 744.12, *best* 805.9
tiptop condition [Inf] *health* 113.1
tip well *pay* 453.15, *be generous* 498.10
tirade *dissertation* 203.1, *public speaking* 205.11, *address* 209.1, *berating* 438.5
Tirahi *Breeds of Sheep* 16
tiramisu *notable international dishes* 90.40
Tiranë *Countries* 566
tire *bore* 296.8, *succumb* 421.7, *circular thing* 631.3, *be fatigued* 820.5, *fatigue* 820.6, *decline* 846.16
tired *unhealthy* 114.23, *bored* 296.5, *weakened* 517.9, *spoiled* 808.9, *fatigued* 820.2
tired brain *fatigue* 820.1
tired-eyed *fatigued* 820.2
tired-looking *fatigued* 820.2
tiredly 820.7; *in a bored manner* 296.9
tiredness *weakness* 517.1, *fatigue* 820.1
tired of *bored* 296.5
tired of living *bored* 296.5
tired out *fatigued* 820.2
tired to death *fatigued* 820.2
tireless *working* 122.6, *committed* 377.7, *industrious* 414.16
tirelessness *commitment* 377.2, *assiduity* 414.8
tireless worker *hard worker* 414.11
tire mark *vestige* 185.11
tire oneself out *be fatigued* 820.5
tire out *fatigue* 820.6
tiresome *boring* 296.6, *annoying* 804.7, *fatiguing* 820.4, *inconvenient* 824.12
tiresomely *boringly* 296.10, *at length* 590.15, *annoyingly* 804.12
tiresomeness *boringness* 296.2
tire to death *fatigue* 820.6
tiring *laborious* 122.7, *fatiguing* 820.4
tiringly 820.8
Tir-na-n'Og *heaven* 82.15
tisane *tea* 93.7, *tonic* 115.8
Tishah b'Av *Jewish Holy Days and Seasons* 85, *fast* 118.4
Tisiphone *Deities* 82
tissue *living matter* 28.4, *test* 107.10, *cleaning cloth* 111.11, *fabric* 130.1, 551.2, *textile* 552.5, *fineness* 595.5, *weaving* 609.2
tissue culture *cell biology* 13.14

tissue of lies *falsehood* 192.6
tissue paper *paper* 104.5, *weak thing* 517.5, *wrapping* 613.10
tissue structure *anatomy* 13.12
Tisza *Rivers* 570
tit *songbird* 36.12
Titan *Planets and Their Satellites* 7, *person of strength* 516.8
titan *big person* 579.10
titaness *big person* 579.10
Titania *Planets and Their Satellites* 7, *sprite* 86.12
titanic *huge* 579.14
titanium *Chemical Elements and Common Allotropes* 11
titanium white *whitener* 253.3
tit for tat *retaliation* 420.1, *with vengeance* 420.6, *exchange* 673.1, *reciprocity* 729.1, *counterbalance* 743.2
tit-for-tat *in exchange* 673.3, *reciprocal* 729.4, *compensatory* 743.5
tithe *offering* 472.6, 504.5, *give to charity* 472.16, *fee* 494.3, *charge* 494.13, *make an offering* 504.17, *ten* 792.6, *little bit* 800.4
tithing *giving* 472.1
Titian *red-haired* 257.7, *orange* 258.5
Titicaca *Lakes* 568
titillate *arouse sensation* 212.11, *give pleasure* 214.13, *be piquant* 221.9, *cause desire* 288.22
titillated *liking* 290.4
titillating *exciting* 212.8, *pleasurable* 214.6, *stimulating* 221.7, *desirable* 288.11, *likable* 290.7, *offensive* 432.11
titillatingly *desirably* 288.24, *likably* 290.12
titillation *stimulus* 212.3, *physical pleasure* 214.1, *stimulation* 221.4, *liking* 290.1
tit in the wringer [Inf] *awkward situation* 824.7
titivate *dress up* 100.45, *beautify* 530.14, 807.20
titivation *beautification* 807.7
title 72.1, **209.12;** *military honor* 58.9, *competition* 166.18, *book* 174.1, *personal identification* 184.4, *certificate* 185.2, *name* 202.8, *claim* 429.3, *reward* 453.1, *possession of property* 469.3, *property* 470.1
titled 72.9; *aristocratic* 70.4, *identified* 184.9
title deed *certificate* 185.2, *contract* 462.2, *promise* 464.2
titled person *nobleman* 70.1
titleholder 72.4; *prizewinner* 127.8, *boxer* 152.8, *victor* 845.7
titleless *common* 71.3
title of address *title of respect* 72.7
title of respect 72.7
title page *book part* 174.5
title role *or part role* 136.23
titration *gravimetric analysis* 11.18
titre *gravimetric analysis* 11.18
tits [Inf] *bulge* 634.2
titter *cry of amusement* 239.2, *laugh* 239.14, 277.12, *laughter* 277.8
tittering *Collective Names* 59
tittle *little piece* 580.4, *fragment* 787.3, *little bit* 800.4
tittle-tattle *talk* 207.3, *chat* 210.2, *prying* 321.2, *meddle* 321.8
tittle-tattler *talker* 207.4, *chatterer* 210.7, *meddler* 321.4
titubant *falling* 714.11
titubate *drop* 714.15
titubation *fall* 714.4

titular 72.10; *governing* 49.25, *supposed* 359.6
titular head *lack of authority* 515.2
titulary *titular* 72.10
Tiu *or* **Tiw** *or* **Tyr** *Deities* 82
tizzy [Inf] *fuss* 684.4
T-junction *road attribute* 687.3
T lymphocyte *blood* 555.4
TNT *explosive* 78.13, *agent of destruction* 523.7
to *via* 691.17
to a certain extent *within limits* 620.8, *partly* 760.17
to a cinder *warmly* 217.20
toad *amphibian* 37.10, *sycophant* 401.3
to a degree 739.11; *moderately* 521.10
to a *or* some degree *partly* 760.17
toadish *amphibian* 37.14
toadlet *young amphibian* 37.11
toadlike *amphibian* 37.14
toad lily *Flowers* 42
toads *Collective Names* 59
toadstool *mushroom* 47.2
to advantage *helpfully* 825.32
toady *humble person* 298.7, *be solicitous* 323.13, *assenter* 346.3, *sycophant* 401.3, *fawn* 401.9, *submitter* 421.2, *succumb* 421.7, *flatterer* 439.6, *be sycophantic* 439.15, *smooth over* 545.12
toadying *sycophancy* 401.2, *sycophantic* 401.7, *submitting* 421.3
toadyish *sycophantic* 439.11
toadyism *sycophancy* 439.5
toady to *defer to* 410.12
to a great degree *to a degree* 739.11
to a hair *accurately* 350.6
to a limited extent *imperfectly* 806.10
to all appearances *visibly* 244.10, *apparently* 264.16, 610.18, 720.19
to all intents and purposes *nearly* 586.18, *really* 717.22, *as good as* 740.14, *on the whole* 759.13, *probably* 838.11
to all places 563.21
to a man *unanimously* 346.8
to and fro 683.16; *changeably* 666.7, *in exchange* 673.6, *directional* 677.13
to-and-fro *frequent* 663.6, *regularly* 663.14, *oscillation* 683.1, *oscillating* 683.8
to-and-fro movement *frequency* 663.2, *movement* 677.3
to a nicety *accurately* 350.6
to an increasing extent *increasingly* 746.9
to apologize *penitently* 451.10
to approval *approvably* 437.22
to a small degree *to a degree* 739.11
toast *bread* 90.10, *cook* 91.10, *drink* 93.2, *drink to* 93.20, *heat* 217.17, *brown* 256.7, *commemorate* 354.14, *tribute* 405.6, *congratulate* 405.12, *participate* 408.15, *bake* 560.19
toasted *culinary* 91.9, *heated* 217.15, *browned* 256.6
toasted sandwich *sandwich* 90.9
toaster *cooker* 91.5, *cooking equipment* 91.6, *burner* 217.4
toaster oven *cooker* 91.5, *burner* 217.4
toasting *cooking technique* 91.2
to a T *accurately* 350.6
to a turn *perfectly* 805.21
tobacco 121.23, **121.33;** *crop* 16.8

Tobacco Belt *farmland* 16.3
tobacco dealer *smoking* 121.22
tobacco implements **121.24**
tobacco leaf *brown thing* 256.3
tobacconist *smoking* 121.22, *retailer* 482.11
tobacco pouch *tobacco implements* 121.24
tobacco sachet *tobacco* 121.23
Tobago *Islands* 572
to be *future* 650.6
to be blamed *immoral* 430.11
to be clear *in other words* 365.18
to be expected *prevailingly* 742.11, *probably* 838.11
to be specific *specially* 779.19
to be sure *assuredly* 336.12, *authentically* 721.31
to bits *apart* 753.23, *to pieces* 758.8
to blame *unsatisfactory* 438.15, *guilty* 450.6
toboggan *bobsled* 162.38, *snow vehicle* 687.9, *slide* 714.17
toboggan chute *toboggan race* 162.25
tobogganing *Sporting Activities* 145
tobogganist *bobsledder* 162.26
toboggan parts **162.24**
toboggan race 162.25
toboggan run *toboggan race* 162.25
to boot *additionally* 748.15
Tocantins *Rivers* 570
to capacity *fully* 761.14
toccata *Musical Forms* 140
Tocharian *language family* 5.12
to coin a phrase *proverbially* 177.4
to come *future* 650.6
to convince *influentially* 508.13
tocophobia *Phobias* 283
to crown all *supremely* 744.23, *importantly* 799.15
tocsin *warning signal* 814.3
to cut a long story short *concisely* 198.6
today *at what time* 639.17, *present time* 647.1, *present day* 647.2, *at present* 647.9
today's world *present day* 647.2
toddle *walk* 677.17
toddle along *move slowly* 693.11, *depart* 705.8
toddler *child* 26.6
toddling *directional* 677.13
toddy *stimulant* 221.5
to death *boringly* 296.10
to-do [Inf] *exaggeration* 194.1, *argument* 329.1, *activity* 414.1, *fuss* 684.4, *disruption* 766.7, *commotion* 768.5
toe *appendage* 19.5, *golf equipment* 156.5, *joint* 752.7
toeclip *bicycle part* 687.11
toe dance *ballet* 135.2
toehold *retention* 471.1, *opportunity* 583.8
toe in the door *opportunity* 583.8
toe jump *ice-skating techniques* 162.16
toenail *body covering* 19.4
toe piece *ski equipment* 162.10
toeside turn *snowboarding* 162.11
toe the line *obey* 426.7
toe the line *or* **mark** *be the same* 730.13, *conform* 735.27, *follow the rules* 780.17, *abide by* 781.12
toe-to-toe *opposite* 731.3
to excess *immoderately* 99.14, *self-indulgently* 456.12
to explain *in other words* 365.18
toff [Brit inf] *nobleman* 70.1

toffee *sweets* 90.39, *brown thing* 256.3, *adherent* 755.4

toffee-nosed [Brit inf] *arrogant* 297.9

to fill the bill *conveniently* 803.6

toft [Brit] *historical property terms* 470.3

Toft ware Ceramics 129

tofu *meat substitute* 90.23

toga *robe* 100.20

toga virilis *robe* 100.20

together 59.31, 794.20; *industrially* 57.22, *pacifically* 74.12, *compatibly* 462.16, *in common* 469.17, *simultaneously* 649.8, *convergently* 702.12, *in accord* 735.33, *as one* 752.21, *in combination* 757.11, *cooperatively* 827.18

together [Inf] *sane* 109.3

togetherness *friendship* 62.1, *good company* 408.9, *companionship* 794.3, *fellowship* 827.2

together with *additionally* 748.15

togged *dressed up* 100.39

toggery [Inf] *clothing* 100.1

toggle *fastener* 754.7

toggle pin *fastener* 754.7

Togo Countries 566

to good effect *influentially* 512.14

to good purpose *successfully* 845.19

togs *clothing* 100.1

to hand *available* 575.11, 647.6, *readily available* 575.21, *next* 586.8

to hell and back *to all places* 563.21

tohubohu *confusion* 51.2, 766.4

toil *work* 122.1, 122.8, *persevere* 377.10, *difficult task* 824.3

toil and trouble *exertion* 122.4

toile Fabrics and Fibers 130

toiler *worker* 123.1, *hard worker* 414.11

toilet *place for excretion* 25.11, *room* 60.9, *dressing* 100.2, *ablutions* 111.4, *privacy* 181.6

toilet *or* **toilette** *beauty treatment* 530.3

toilet bag *cosmetic tool* 530.5

toilet kit *bag* 578.7

toilet paper *paper* 104.5, *cleaning cloth* 111.11

toiletries 530.6

toilet roll *cleaning cloth* 111.11

toilet set *cosmetic tool* 530.5

toilet soap *cleaning agent* 111.9

toilette *dressing* 100.2

toilet tissue *cleaning cloth* 111.11

toilet-trained *excremental* 25.13

toilet water *toiletries* 530.6

toilsome *laborious* 122.7, *fatiguing* 820.4, *difficult* 824.9

to infinity *infinitely* 798.10

to just the right degree *perfectly* 805.21

toke [Inf] *drug dose* 121.15

to keep *tenaciously* 471.11

token *sign* 183.1, *means of identification* 184.3, *indication* 339.3, *memento* 354.3, *gift* 472.2, *something received* 473.2, *characteristic* 779.5, *trivial* 800.14, *manifestation* 843.2, *identifiable* 843.10

tokenism *ungenuineness* 192.2

token of esteem *gift* 472.2

token of one's gratitude *acknowledgment* 310.3

token ring network *computer communications* 15.25

Tokyo Countries 566, *other famous world cities* 567.9

tolbooth [Scot] *prison* 55.1

told *chronicled* 3.12, *communicated* 169.15, *informed* 170.9

to leeward *offshore* 150.35

tolerability *satisfactoriness* 273.3, *mediocrity* 289.5

tolerable *satisfactory* 273.6, *mediocre* 289.11, 742.7, *forgivable* 312.7

tolerableness *mediocrity* 742.3

tolerably *sufficiently* 97.9, *unexceptionally* 289.20, *forgivably* 312.14, *passably* 692.19

tolerance 502.2; *philosophical attitude* 4.3, *compassion* 305.2, *forgivingness* 312.3, *impartiality* 338.2, *leniency* 423.1, *broad-mindedness* 592.3, *freethinking* 829.2

tolerant *detached* 4.18, *harmless* 73.9, *compassionate* 305.8, *forgiving* 312.4, *impartial* 338.6, *free* 407.9, 829.11, *inactive* 413.9, *lenient* 423.3, *permitting* 502.5, *politically moderate* 521.4, *broad-minded* 592.9, *easygoing* 823.13

tolerantly *compassionately* 305.14, *forgivingly* 312.13, *impartially* 338.13, *freely* 407.12, 829.22, *leniently* 423.6, *with permission* 502.10, *broad-mindedly* 592.17

tolerate *be compassionate* 305.11, *show mercy* 312.11, *be impartial* 338.11, *assent to* 346.7, *leave alone* 413.13, *be lenient* 423.5, *agree with* 462.10, *permit* 502.6, *bear* 605.17, *be free* 829.16

tolerated *overlooked* 312.6

toleration *compassion* 305.2, *forgivingness* 312.3, *freedom* 407.4, *leniency* 423.1, *agreement* 462.1, *tolerance* 502.2, *freethinking* 829.2

to let *offered* 504.8

to little purpose *unsuccessfully* 846.21

toll *ring* 235.14, 236.10, *ringing* 236.2, *payment* 433.5, *levy* 494.7, *mathematical addition* 748.2, *give warning* 814.10

Tollan's reagent *sugar test* 12.6

tollbooth *roadblock* 826.4

toll bridge *bridge* 551.10, 691.7

toll call *telephone call* 169.11

toll-free call *telephone call* 169.11

tollgate *means of entry* 706.6, *roadblock* 826.4

tolling *ringing* 236.7

toll road *road* 687.2

toll the knell *pay one's last respects* 31.12

tolu Tree Products 43

tom *male animal* 32.15, *cat* 35.11, *male mammal* 35.18

tomahawk Historical Missile Weapons 78, *blunt weapon* 78.5

to matchwood *apart* 753.23

tomato *red thing* 257.3

tomato juice *soft drink* 93.8

tomato sauce *sauce* 90.17

tomb *burial place* 31.7, *monument* 185.10, *closed place* 584.4, *enclosed area* 619.2

tomb of an unknown soldier *monument* 185.10

tombolo *coast* 8.13

tomboy *young woman* 26.9, *mannish female* 33.9

tomboyish *female* 33.16

tombstone *funeral object* 31.6, *monument* 185.10

tombstones Phobias 283

tomcat *male animal* 32.15, *cat* 35.11

Tom, Dick, and Harry *common people* 71.2

tome *book* 174.1

tomfoolery *act of folly* 353.2

Tommy [Brit inf] *soldier* 77.4

tommyrot *senseless talk* 362.4

tomogram *diagnostic radiology* 107.12

tomography *diagnostic radiology* 107.12, *that which makes visible* 244.4

tomophobia Phobias 283

tomorrow *at what time* 639.17, *future time* 650.1, *in the future* 650.13

tomorrow afternoon *future time* 650.1

tomorrow evening *future time* 650.1

tomorrow morning *future time* 650.1

tomorrow night *future time* 650.1

tompion *insert* 710.4

Tom Sawyer Notable Friendships 62

Tom Thumb *little person* 580.5

tom-tom Musical Instruments 142, *drumming* 235.1

tom turkey *male bird* 36.15

ton *weight measurement* 538.6, General Units 589

tonal *language type* 5.11, *of language* 5.35, *melodious* 140.26, *phonetic* 205.14, *sounding* 230.7

tonality *harmonic element* 140.14, *key* 140.23

tonally *linguistically* 5.44

tonal range *composition* 132.17

tonal sequence *harmonic element* 140.14

tone 140.24, 230.2; *health* 113.1, *aspect of fiction* 139.5, *treatment* 143.6, *paint* 143.12, *mode of speech* 205.6, *reputation* 224.4, *sound* 230.1, *hue* 251.4, *color* 251.16, *conduct* 399.1, *attitude* 513.2, *style* 537.1, *elasticity* 546.1, *ambience* 615.3, *way* 691.1, *mode* 725.2, *tendency* 838.2

tone *or* **note row** *musical dissonance* 241.2

tone control *radio reception* 172.2, *sound quality* 230.4

toned *colored* 251.10

toned down *downplayed* 195.13

tone-deaf *deaf* 229.4, *undiscriminating* 338.5

tone deafness *deafness* 229.1

tone-deafness *lack of discrimination* 338.1

tone down *play down* 195.17, *tarnish* 248.9, *color* 251.16, *decolor* 252.8, *modify* 340.13, *mitigate* 521.9, *ease* 543.15

tone frequency Fields of Measurement 589

toneless *unheard* 229.7, *unmelodious* 241.5, *colorless* 252.5

tonelessly *deafly* 229.13, *colorlessly* 252.9

tone of voice *mode of speech* 205.6, *conduct* 399.1

tone poem Musical Forms 140

tone row *scale* 140.16

tones *interior decoration* 532.4

Tonga Breeds of Cattle 16, Countries 566, Islands 572

tongs *cooking equipment* 91.6, *retainer* 471.3

tongue *language* 5.4, *mouth* 19.7, *variety meat* 90.30, *eating organ* 92.14, *sound* 141.15, *spoken language* 205.2, *speech organ* 205.4, *sense organ* 212.4, *taste* 219.1, *peninsula* 572.5

tongue-in-cheek *ungenuine* 192.13, *hypocritical* 330.10, *unmeant* 362.9, *flattering* 439.7

tongue-lash *vilify* 301.15

tongue-lashing *vilification* 301.2, *berating* 438.5

tongueless *silent* 231.2

tongue-tied *speechless* 206.7

tonic 115.8; *refresher* 94.2, *refreshing* 94.4, *healthful* 113.7, *medicine* 115.2, *remedial* 115.14, *musical note* 140.15, *phonetic* 205.14, *stimulant* 221.5, *stimulus* 508.3, *strengthening* 516.7, *elastic* 546.5

tonicity *elasticity* 546.1

tonic sol-fa *scale* 140.16

tonic water *mixed drink* 93.12, *tonic* 115.8

tonight *at what time* 639.17, *present time* 647.1, *at present* 647.9

toning *colorful* 251.11

tonitrophobia Phobias 283

tonk Card Games 168

Tonkinese Breeds of Cats 35

Tonle Sap Lakes 568

tonnage *heaviness* 538.1, *load* 577.5, *size* 579.1

tonnage and poundage *levy* 494.7

to no avail *uselessly* 802.14

to no extent *not at all* 718.15

tonometer Fields of Measurement 589

tonometry Fields of Measurement 589

tonoplast *cell structure* 13.16

to no purpose *uselessly* 802.14, *unsuccessfully* 846.21

tons [Inf] *profuseness* 795.3

tonsillitis *respiratory disease* 114.12

tonsorial *hairy* 19.20

tonsure *depilation* 614.8

tonsured *depilatory* 614.15

tontine *earnings* 467.5, *joint possession* 469.6, *something received* 473.2, *income* 492.3

Tonto Notable Friendships 62

tonus *elasticity* 546.1

Tony Notable Horses 159, *prizes* 453.3

Tony awards *drama* 136.1

too *additionally* 748.15

too bad! 848.17; *no matter!* 800.22

too big *huge* 579.14

too big for one's boots *boastful* 402.13

too clever by half *cocky* 402.11, *cunning* 822.4

too clever for *cunning* 822.4

too early *premature* 657.10, *prematurely* 657.20, *untimely* 660.5

too far *in the offing* 585.12

too few *not enough* 98.5, *few* 796.5, *fewer* 796.7

too few to mention *few* 796.1

too good to be true *questionable* 839.5

tool 103.1; *dynamic structure* 14.5, *instrumentality* 102.2, *agent* 123.15, *material* 143.9, 144.6, *sycophant* 401.3, *instrument* 711.2, *assistant* 511.3, *decorate* 532.11, *inferior* 745.4, *convenience* 825.7, *subordinate* 832.3

tool [Inf] *organs of reproduction* 21.9

too late *at a late hour* 658.15, *at the wrong time* 660.12

toolbox *computing terms* 15.22

too little *not enough* 98.5

too long *lengthy* 590.9
tools *means* 102.1, *equipment* 103.6, *materials* 104.1
tools of the trade *means* 102.1
tool-using *mechanical* 103.7
too many *excess* 99.1, *excessive* 99.5
too many chiefs and not enough Indians *bungling* 128.2
too many cooks *bungling* 128.2
too many irons in the fire *overdoing it* 99.3
too much *excess* 99.1, *excessive* 99.5, *excessively* 99.13, 194.17
too much for *powerlessly* 515.16
too much of a good thing *immoderation* 99.2, *boring thing* 296.3
too much on one's plate *overdoing it* 99.3
toon *Trees and Shrubs* 43
to one's advantage *profitable* 801.8, *convenient* 803.3
to one's amazement *astonishingly* 294.19
to one's discredit *unvirtuously* 448.16
to one's face *manifestly* 331.20, *defiantly* 416.9, *frankly* 843.18
to one's heart's content *enough* 97.10
to one side *laterally* 623.11
to one's profit *or advantage useful* 393.7
to one's sorrow *destructively* 446.13
to one's surprise *surprisingly* 292.14, *astonishingly* 294.19
to one's utmost *laboriously* 122.13
to one's way of thinking *ideologically* 327.23
too old to cut the mustard [Inf] *aged* 27.15
too precious for words *valuable* 496.8
to order *commandingly* 425.15, *obediently* 426.9, *compatibly* 462.16
too small *not enough* 98.5
too smart for his *or her own good cunning* 822.4
too smart for one's own good *cocky* 402.11
too soon *premature* 657.10, *prematurely* 657.20, *at the wrong time* 660.12
toot *sound* 141.15, *burst of sound* 232.4, *warning signal* 814.3, *give warning* 814.10
tooth 549.7; *teeth* 19.8, *retainer* 471.3
toothache *painful condition* 215.2
toothache tree *Trees and Shrubs* 43
tooth and nail *laboriously* 122.13, *violently* 520.11
toothbrush *cleaning tool* 111.10
toothed 19.21, 549.13; *of leaves* 41.18
tooth for a tooth *exchange* 673.1
tooth fungi *fungi* 47.3
toothless 550.8; *insectivorous* 35.24
toothlessly *smoothly* 550.10
toothless mammal 35.14
toothlessness 550.4
toothlike *toothed* 549.13
tooth ornament *Architectural Elements* 134
toothpaste *cleaning agent* 111.9, *prophylaxis* 115.4
toothpick *cleaning tool* 111.10, *sharp-pointed thing* 549.4, *extractor* 711.9
tooth powder *prophylaxis* 115.4

toothsome *tasty* 219.4
toothy *toothed* 549.13
toot one's own horn [Inf] *show off* 402.15
toots [Inf] *female* 33.1
top 600.6, 600.10; *cultivate* 17.19, *manage trees* 43.14, *shirt* 100.13, *part of garment* 100.27, *play* 156.8, *toy* 167.9, *excellent* 445.13, *stopper* 584.3, *stop* 584.14, *heights* 596.4, *be high* 596.15, *summit* 600.1, 744.4, *cover* 613.2, 613.24, *coat* 613.28, *side direction* 623.2, *side* 623.6, *cone* 633.5, *rotator* 682.8, *climb* 713.21, *elite* 744.12, *overtake* 744.16, *limit* 761.4, 773.7, *important* 799.7, *peak* 805.5, *expert* 805.16
top, the *governance* 52.6, *the power structure* 68.12
topaz *yellow thing* 259.4
top banana [Inf] *figurative usage* 44.4, *manager* 126.7
top billing *role* 136.23, *public relations (PR)* 173.8
top boots *boots* 100.31
top brass [Inf] *the power structure* 68.12, *management board* 126.2, *influential person* 512.5, *best people* 744.7, *celebrity* 799.6
topcoat *coat* 100.19, *layer* 588.1
top coat *cosmetics* 530.4
top condition *preparedness* 388.5
top dog *company leader* 68.8, *manager* 126.7, *important person* 799.5
top drawer *best people* 744.7
top-drawer *aristocratic* 70.4, *superior* 744.8
top-dress *farm* 16.19, *cultivate* 17.19, *fertilize* 22.12
top dressing *fertilizer* 22.6
tope *shrine* 83.10, *drink* 93.19, *get drunk* 121.35
topee *protective covering* 613.5, *protection from the weather* 810.9
topee *or* **topi** *helmet* 100.34
Topeka *American States* 564
toper *drunkard* 121.8, *self-indulgent person* 456.5
to perfection *innocently* 449.13, *perfectly* 805.21
top-flight *skillful* 127.10, *excellent* 744.14, *notable* 799.11
top gun *attacker* 418.10
top hat *hat* 100.32
top-heaviness *weighing down* 538.5, *imbalance* 741.2
top-heavy *clumsy* 128.6, *ponderous* 538.11, *fat* 579.15, *unbalanced* 741.5, *unsafe* 811.8
Tophet *evil place* 446.6
topi *protective covering* 613.5, *protection from the weather* 810.9
topiarist *horticulturist* 17.13
topiary *ornamental garden* 17.3, *Hobbies and Pastimes* 167
topic 328.1; *issue* 328.2, *line of argument* 329.3, *gist* 329.4, *supposition* 359.1, *meaning* 361.1, *division* 577.6, *undertaking* 675.5
topical 328.5; *arguable* 329.8, *supposed* 359.6, *itemized* 577.9, *present* 647.4, *new* 652.1
topicality *modernity* 647.3, *newness* 652.1
topically 328.11; *arguably* 329.16, *thematically* 577.16, *newly* 652.21
topic for discussion *matter of interest* 328.3
topic sentence *topic* 328.1
to pieces 758.8
toping *drinking* 93.1, 121.2, *drunken* 121.28

top layer 600.5
topless *uncovered* 614.10
topless bar *club* 138.7, *pornography* 432.7
topless dancer *dancer* 135.4, *nude person* 614.5
toplessness *bareness* 614.3
topless performer *or dancer pornography* 432.7
topless waitress *nude person* 614.5
top level *managerial* 126.9
top-level *skillful* 127.10, *head* 600.7, *important* 799.7
top mark *excellent* 445.13
top mark *or* **grade** *excellence* 445.4
topmost *higher* 596.8, *top* 600.6, *elite* 744.12, *important* 799.7
topnotch *skillful* 127.10, *great* 445.14, *elite* 744.12
topnotch *or* **top-notch** *best* 805.9
topnotcher *superior person* 445.7
top off *fuel* 106.16, *be at the top* 600.9, *fill* 761.11
top of the bill *play part* 136.8
top of the class *successful person* 845.6
top of the division *victorious* 845.10
top of the house *roof* 134.7
top of the league *victorious* 845.10
top of the milk *milk* 93.5, *fat* 562.4
top of the pyramid *summit* 744.4
top of the world 600.2
topographer *measurer* 589.14
topographic *metrical* 589.15
topographic(al) *terrestrial* 8.52
topographic *or* **topographical** *regional* 564.12, *altimetrical* 596.13
topographical *locational* 565.8, *situational* 573.6
topographically 565.13; *geologically* 8.68, *geographically* 573.11, *measurably* 589.22, *altimetrically* 596.23
topographical map *map* 187.5
topographical poetry *poetry* 139.8
topographic surveying *civil engineering* 14.17
topography 565.5; *continent* 8.8, *map* 187.5, *situation* 573.1, *measurement* 589.1, *height measurement* 596.5
topological *mathematical* 6.65
topologist *mathematician* 6.2
topology 6.45, *Branches of Mathematics* 6
toponym *name* 202.8
toponymy *nomenclature* 202.7
topophobia *Phobias* 283
to port *offshore* 150.35
top part *summit* 600.1
topped 600.8; *covered* 613.19
topped off *full* 761.8
topped up *loaded* 577.8, *full* 761.8
top people *best people* 744.7
topper *coat* 100.19
topper [Inf] *hat* 100.32
top person *important person* 799.5
topping *tree management* 43.6, *highland* 596.11, *top layer* 600.5, *topped* 600.8, *covering* 613.1, *coating* 613.8
topping lift *sailboat parts and accessories* 150.4
topping-out *completion* 761.2
topple *knock down* 523.13, *trip* 714.16, *bring down* 716.14, *lean* 716.19

topple (a government) *be anarchic* 51.8
toppled *overthrown* 716.9
topple over *trip* 714.16
toppling *downthrow* 716.2, *fallen* 716.8
top priority *priority* 769.2
top-rank *notable* 799.11
top-ranked *unbeatable* 744.13
top-ranking *unbeatable* 744.13
top-rope *mountaineer* 161.10
top roping *climbing techniques* 161.3
top rung *summit* 744.4
tops *excellence* 445.4, *best* 805.9
tops, the [Inf] *successful person* 845.6
top-secret *secret* 182.8, *censored* 503.7, *important* 799.7, *concealed* 844.7
top-secret clearance *permission* 502.1
top-secret document *censorship* 503.4, *concealment* 844.2
top-secret file *secret* 182.2
top seed *prizewinner* 127.8, *finalist* 422.16
top selection *prizewinner* 127.8
topside *top layer* 600.5, *on the top* 600.13
topsoil *soil* 8.42, *layer* 588.1, *top layer* 600.5, *cover* 613.2
top speed *speed* 694.2
topspin *tennis strokes* 165.2
top surface *top layer* 600.5
topsy-turvily *inversely* 608.9
topsy-turviness *inversion* 608.1, *confusion* 766.4
topsy-turvy *inverted* 608.5, *inversely* 608.9, *complicated* 751.10, *muddled* 766.13, *anyhow* 766.25
topsy-turvydom *variety* 751.4
top ten *or* **top-ten** *notable* 799.11
top the charts *attain one's goal* 845.13
top up *store fuel* 105.18, *stuff* 577.12
top up [Brit] *fill* 761.11
to put it another way *in other words* 365.13
to put it succinctly *concisely* 198.6
toque *hat* 100.32
tor *mountain* 569.1
Torah *the Law* 53.2, *Jewish text* 81.17, *sacred object* 83.11
torch *fuel starter* 106.3, *cause of fire* 217.10, *burn* 217.18, *incandescent light* 246.5
torchbearer *preparer* 388.6
torchlight *incandescent light* 246.5
torchlit *lit* 246.16
torch singer *singer* 141.4
torch song *popular music* 140.4, *song* 140.11
toreador *animal killer* 30.14
toreador pants *pants* 100.14
toreutic *sculptural* 144.7
tori (attacker) *judo* 152.13
tori (thrower) *aikido* 152.16
Toric *Horse and Pony Breeds* 159
toric *spherical* 6.80
torment *strain* 117.4, *afflict* 117.16, 301.16, *pain* 215.1, *inflict pain* 215.10, *sorrow* 270.1, *misfortune* 301.6, *irritate* 302.16, *harm* 306.13, *suppress* 424.9, *be evil* 446.10, *torture* 424.29
tormented *strained* 117.13, *feeling pain* 215.6, *worried* 283.11, *afflicted* 301.11
tormentil *Flowers* 42

tormenting *inflicting pain* 215.7
tormentingly *cruelly* 306.17
tormentor *stage set* 136.19
torn *estranged* 63.8, *injured* 215.5, *brittle* 548.3, *removed* 574.9, *open* 583.10, *cracked* 587.5, *separate* 753.7
tornadic *rotary* 682.12
tornado *wind vortex* 9.14, *natural violence* 520.3, *rough thing* 544.2, *convoluted thing* 632.3, *vortex* 682.6, *atmospheric agitation* 684.13, *natural hazard* 813.4
tornado watch *or* **warning** *weather forecast* 9.4
tornaria *invertebrate larva* 39.19
toroid *curved surface* 6.43
toroidal *spherical* 6.80
Toronto *Canadian Provinces* 564
torpedo *naval mine* 77.23, *Historical Missile Weapons* 78, *bomb* 78.15, *fire* 418.18, *ruin* 523.15, *track* 688.2, *missile* 696.7, *blow up* 696.19, *bring down* 716.14
torpedo boat *Ships and Boats* 690
torpedoed *destroyed* 523.9
torpedoing *combined attack* 418.5
torpid *desensitized* 213.5, *not participating* 415.11, *not awake* 415.12, *inert* 519.2, *vegetating* 717.17
torpidity *inertness* 519.1
torpor *desensitization* 213.2, *idleness* 415.3, *inertness* 519.1, *lack of motion* 678.1, *mere existence* 717.10
torque *force* 10.9, *jewelry* 532.6, *turning* 682.3, *torsion* 698.5
torque wrench *hand tool* 103.3
torr *Scientific and Technical Units* 589
torrefy *bake* 560.19
Torrens Lakes 568
torrent *flow* 570.4
torrential *rainy* 9.50, *flowing* 570.7
torrentially *fluently* 570.13
torrential rain *rain* 9.27
torrid *hot* 9.47
Torrid Zone *hot place* 217.5, *world region* 564.6
torse *Heraldic Terms* 184
torsion **698.5;** *curve* 6.38, *force* 10.9, *deformation* 14.16, *distortion* 627.1, *turning* 682.3
torsional *rotary* 682.12
torsional strength *mechanical strength* 516.2
torsional wave *wave* 10.11
torso *sculpture* 144.1, *remainder* 750.1
tort *fault* 430.2, *illegality* 450.4
torte *cake* 90.36
tortilla *bread* 90.10
tortoise *turtle* 37.7, *plodder* 693.6
tortoiseshell *Breeds of Cats* 35, *variegated thing* 263.5, *checked* 263.8
tortoiseshell butterfly *variegated thing* 263.5
tortoiseshell cat *variegated thing* 263.5
tortoiseshell inlay *decorative woodwork* 131.2
Tortola Islands 572
tortoni *dessert* 90.35
tortuous *unjust* 53.24, *obscure* 197.2, *sophistic* 330.7, *inelegant* 528.6, *convolutional* 632.4
tortuously *obscurely* 197.4, *circularly* 632.8
tortuousness *obscurity* 197.1

torture **454.29;** *pain* 215.1, *inflict pain* 215.10, *afflict* 301.16, *cruelty* 306.4, *harm* 306.13, *attack successfully* 418.25, *suppression* 424.2, *suppress* 424.9, *coercive method* 428.3, *corporal punishment* 454.11, *violence by person* 520.2, *use violence* 520.9
torture chamber *instrument of torture* 454.14
tortured *feeling pain* 215.6, *afflicted* 301.11, *suppressed* 424.6, *punished* 454.19
torture oneself *appear guilty* 450.10
torturer *coercer* 428.4, *punisher* 454.16
torture the law *be illegal* 53.30
torturing *inflicting pain* 215.7
torturous *cruel* 306.10, *punishing* 454.20
torturously *cruelly* 306.17, *violently* 520.11
torus *curved surface* 6.43, *topology* 6.45, *Architectural Elements* 134, *nuclear power production* 514.10
Tory party *Political Parties* 50
to satisfaction *approvably* 437.22
to scale *relevantly* 727.12
to shreds *apart* 753.23
to smithereens *apart* 753.23, *to pieces* 758.8
to some degree *to a degree* 739.11
to some extent *moderately* 521.10, *to a degree* 739.11, *partly* 760.17
to some purpose *successfully* 845.19
to spare *surplus* 750.8
toss *billow* 571.9, *stagger* 684.11, *throw* 696.4, 696.17
toss and tumble *pitch* 684.25
toss and turn *be agitated* 684.21, *pitch* 684.25
tossed salad *salad* 90.16
tosser *thrower* 696.10
tossing *fidgety* 414.14, *nautical* 690.14
tossing and turning *irresolute* 666.4, *restlessness* 684.5
tossing in a blanket *punishment* 454.1
toss one's cookies [Inf] *vomit* 709.27
toss out *expel* 709.14
tosspot *drunkard* 121.8
tossup *equal chance* 842.7
tostada *notable international dishes* 90.40
to starboard *offshore* 150.35
to such an extent *quantitatively* 738.8
to summarize *shortly* 591.12
to sum up *concisely* 198.6
tot *child* 26.6
tot [Brit] *size of drink* 93.3
total **738.4, 783.10, 784.12;** *addition* 6.13, *numerical answer* 334.7, *solve* 334.21, *quantitative* 738.6, *mathematical addition* 748.2, *add* 748.11, 784.11, *whole thing* 759.2, *whole* 759.6, *be whole* 759.9, *complete* 761.6, 805.14, *mathematical result* 783.4
total [Inf] *destroy* 523.10
total abstainer *self-restrained person* 455.5
total abstinence *abstinence* 455.2
total blank *forgetfulness* 355.1
total commitment *seriousness* 376.3, *commitment* 377.2
total deafness *deafness* 229.1
total defeat *defeat* 846.7

total destruction *warfare* 76.3
total eclipse *sun* 7.15, *darkness* 247.1
total exhaustion *fatigue* 820.1
total immersion *baptism* 85.6
totaling *mathematical addition* 748.2, *count* 784.3
total internal reflection *optical characteristic* 10.21
totalitarian *national* 18.16, *governmental* 49.24, *severe* 424.5
totalitarian government *totalitarianism* 49.13
totalitarianism **49.13;** *suppression* 424.2
totality *universe* 7.3, *total* 738.4, *whole* 759.1, *whole thing* 759.2, *completeness* 761.1
totalizer *calculator* 784.5
total loss *loss* 468.1, *ruin* 523.4
totally *clean* [Inf] 111.21, *wholly* 759.11, 738.9, *completely* 759.14, 761.13, 805.22
totally committed *steady* 376.8
totally deaf *deaf* 229.4
total quality management (TQM) *management system* 126.3
total recall *memory* 354.1
total silence *silence* 231.1
total sum *whole thing* 759.2
total theater *theater movements* 136.9
total up *add* 748.11
total war *world war* 76.2
to tatters *apart* 753.23
tote *convey* 685.9
tote bag *bag* 578.7
totem *minor deity* 82.2, *idol* 83.5, *sacred object* 83.11, *talisman* 86.9
totemic *idolatrous* 83.13, *witchlike* 86.19
totemism *idolatry* 83.4, *witchcraft* 86.6
totemist *idolater* 83.7
totemistic *idolatrous* 83.13, *ritualistic* 85.15, *witchlike* 86.19
totemize *idolize* 83.16
totem pole *sacred object* 83.11
tote up [Inf] *add* 748.11, *number* 783.9
to that place *where* 565.12
to the amount of *at a price* 494.14
to the bitter end *perseveringly* 377.16, *for the duration* 642.8, *to the end* 773.25
to the boiling point *warmly* 217.20
to the brim *internally* 577.15, *fully* 761.14
to the contrary **190.27, 339.17**
to the core *internally* 577.15, *fully* 761.14
to the effect that *meaningfully* 361.16
to the end **773.25;** *for the duration* 642.8, *fully* 761.14
to the end of the road *to the end* 773.25
to the ends of the earth *distantly* 585.11
to the ends of the earth *or* **world** *to all places* 563.21
to the fore *before* 621.14
to the four corners of the earth *in all directions* 697.19, *everywhere* 776.19
to the four winds *to all places* 563.21, *in all directions* 697.19, *everywhere* 776.19
to the full *enough* 97.10, *extravagantly* 500.9, *fully* 761.14
to the full extent *at length* 590.15
to the good *helpfully* 825.32

to the ground *down* 716.24
to the heart *fully* 761.14
to the highest degree *supremely* 744.23
to the hilt *fully* 761.14
to the last breath *fully* 761.14
to the last gasp *to the end* 773.25
to the last man *perseveringly* 377.16
to the last one *fully* 761.14
to the letter *observantly* 465.6, *correctly* 721.29, *imitatively* 736.12, *perfectly* 805.21
to the life *imitatively* 736.12
to the marrow *fully* 761.14
to the maximum *fully* 761.14
to the minute *early* 657.17
to the nth degree *accurately* 350.6
to the opposite side *opposite* 731.5
to the point *concise* 198.4, *concisely* 198.6, *summarily* 204.10, *purposively* 327.20, *thematically* 328.13, *bluntly* 550.11, *essential* 799.10
to the purpose *convenient* 803.3
to the quick *painfully* 215.12
to the rear *behind* 622.8
to the same degree *similarly* 733.17, *as good as* 740.14
to the second *early* 657.17
to the side *laterally* 623.11
to the top *internally* 577.15, *fully* 761.14
to the touch *texturally* 552.15
to the tune of [Inf] *at a price* 494.14, *quantitatively* 738.8
to the utmost *fully* 761.14
totter *be weak* 517.12, *be changeable* 666.5, *stagger* 684.11, *pitch* 684.25, *deteriorate* 808.14, *be in danger* 811.11
totter along *move slowly* 693.11
tottering *swaying* 378.4, *unsteady* 378.7, *weak* 517.6, *changeable* 666.3, *slow* 693.7, *descending* 714.9, *deteriorated* 808.8, *unsafe* 811.8
tottery *weak* 517.6, *decrepit* 808.12
tot up *add* 748.11, 784.11, *number* 783.9
Toubkal Mountains and Hills 569
Toucan Constellations 7
touch **216.1, 216.9;** *life function* 28.6, *manual skill* 127.2, *fencing movements* 153.3, *fence* 153.7, *gesture* 183.5, *sensation* 212.1, *sense* 212.9, *adjoin* 216.11, *Phobias* 283, *communicate love* 299.25, *move to compassion* 308.9, *information* 348.2, *use up* 393.12, *meddle* 414.23, *texture* 552.1, *juxtaposition* 586.4, *juxtapose* 586.14, *weaving* 609.2, *interface* 616.5, *blow* 695.5, *tap* 695.13, *admixture* 751.5, *union* 752.1, *characteristic* 779.5, *suggestion* 800.9, *impair* 808.18
touch, the [Inf] *solicitation* 505.4
touchable **216.5**
touch and go *changeable* 666.3, *unsafe* 811.8
touch a raw nerve *arouse sensation* 212.11, *inflict pain* 215.10
touchback *kick* 155.12
touch bottom *deepen* 598.21, *fail* 714.18
touch depth *fail* 714.18
touchdown *scoring* 155.5, *flight* 689.5, *landing* 704.2, *fall* 714.4, *successful thing* 845.5
touch down *fly* 689.13, *land* 704.16, *drop* 714.15

touched in the head [Inf] *insane* 110.9

touched up *exaggerated* 194.7, *beautified* 530.12, *renewed* 652.14, *improved* 807.12

toucher *grip* 151.4, *sense organ* 212.4

touch football *football* 155.1

touchily 303.19

touchiness 303.3; *sensitivity* 212.2, *oversensitivity* 267.2

touching 216.2, 216.6; *sensory* 19.22, *contiguous* 216.8, *emotive* 266.13, *pitiful* 308.5, *juxtaposition* 586.4, *juxtaposed* 586.9, *relevantly* 727.12, *union* 752.1, *nearby* 803.4

touching (up) [Inf] *borrowing* 476.1, *taking* 477.1

touching down *flying* 689.11

touchingly *with feeling* 266.18, *pitifully* 308.12

touching one's cap *deference* 410.4

touching up *(act of) painting* 143.1, *exaggeration* 194.1

touchline *stadium* 163.2

touch-me-not Flowers 42

touch off *fuel* 106.16, *awaken* 675.9

touch of frost *frost* 9.25

touch one's cap *defer to* 410.12

touch-operated *handling* 216.7

touch pad *swimming equipment* 164.8

touch paper *fuel starter* 106.3

touch perfection *be complete* 761.10

touch rock bottom *become inferior* 745.10

touchscreen *display* 15.9, *input device* 15.11

touch someone (up) [Inf] *borrow* 476.10

touchstone *standard* 589.7

touch the surface *be superficial* 599.4

touch-tone service *dial* 169.12

touch turn *competitive swimming* 164.3

touch up *paint* 143.12, *exaggerate* 194.11, *make new* 652.20, *tidy* 807.19, *refurbish* 809.11

touch up [Inf] *take* 477.14

touch upon *relate to* 727.9

touchwood *fuel starter* 106.3

touchy 303.10; *susceptible* 212.7, *passionate* 266.12, *oversensitive* 267.4

tough 542.6, 547.6; *warlike* 76.27, *combatant* 77.1, *combative* 77.32, *insensitive* 268.4, *problematic* 333.12, 824.11, *determined* 379.7, 674.5, *obstinate* 417.7, *severe* 424.5, *villain* 448.5, *physically strong* 516.11, *strong in spirit* 516.11, *strengthened* 516.13, *mentally hard* 542.8, *viscous* 561.14, *fatiguing* 820.4, *difficult* 824.9

tough as nails *determined* 379.7

tough as old boots or **leather** *hard* 547.8

tough assignment *difficult task* 824.3

tough as steel *strong-willed* 376.10

tough decision *choice* 382.3

toughen *strengthen* 516.15, *harden* 542.9, *make tough* 547.15, *season* 654.11

toughened 547.7; *strengthened* 516.13, *hardened* 542.7, *seasoned* 654.9

toughened glass *glass* 249.5, *safety device* 810.15

toughening *strengthening* 516.7, *hardness* 542.1

tough guy [Inf] *person of strength* 516.8

tough lineup to buck *difficult task* 824.3

tough luck *luck* 842.3

tough luck! *too bad!* 848.17

toughly 542.12, 547.16; *resistingly* 417.14, *severely* 424.11, *determinedly* 674.10

toughness 547.1; *determination* 379.2, 674.2, *obstinacy* 417.2, *severity* 424.1, *endurance* 516.4, *density* 540.1, *hardness* 542.1, *mental hardness* 542.4, *doughiness* 561.2, *difficulty* 824.1

tough nut to crack *difficult question* 333.4, *unintelligible thing* 364.3, *problem* 824.4

tough proposition *difficult task* 824.3

tough row (to hoe) *affliction* 454.9

tough something out [Inf] *be tough* 547.13

tough time *time of adversity* 848.8

toupee *hairdressing* 530.7, *body covering* 613.3

tour *engagement* 136.15, 138.6, *period of activity* 641.4, *orbit* 681.3, *travel* 686.5, 686.11, *route* 691.2

tour de force *masterpiece* 68.14, 127.5, *method* 387.4, *deed* 412.2, *good thing* 445.9

tourer *traveler* 686.6

touring *skiing* 162.1, *cross-country* 162.31, *travel* 686.5, *traveling* 686.9

touring bike *bicycle* 687.10

touring car *racing automobile* 146.2

touring car races *races* 146.4

touring company *cast* 136.26

touring skier *skier* 162.14

tourism *travel* 686.5

tourist *observer* 242.15, *curious person* 321.3, *traveler* 686.6

tourista *defecation* 25.3

tourist-class *cheap* 497.9

tourist fare or **rate** *bargain* 497.4

tourist season *seasons* 654.2

tournament *sports* 145.1, *show* 404.12, *contest* 422.4, *duel* 422.12

tournament bridge *bridge* 168.4

tournament casting *competitive fishing* 154.5

tourney *duel* 422.12

tourniquet *contractor* 582.6, *stopper* 584.3, *line* 754.5

tour of duty *period of activity* 641.4, *duration* 642.1

tousle *make rough* 544.11, *make disorderly* 766.20

tousled *untidy* 766.11

tout [Inf] *publicizer* 173.11, *publicize* 173.18, *merchant* 482.10, *sell* 482.15, *petition* 505.11

tout ensemble, le [Fr] *all* 759.4

tout le monde [Fr] *everyone* 778.7

tovarishch [Russ] or **tovarich** or **comrade** *male title of address* 32.3

tow *fiber* 552.6, *miscellaneous automotive terms* 687.14, *pull* 699.2, 699.10

towage *traction* 699.1

toward 697.18; *via* 691.17

toward the center *internally* 611.18

toward the interior *internally* 611.18

toward the side *obliquely* 607.13

towboat Ships and Boats 690

to weather *offshore* 150.35

towed *transportable* 686.7

towed log *navigational aid* 690.6

towel *cleaning cloth* 111.11, *dryer* 560.5, *absorb* 560.20

toweling Fabrics and Fibers 130, *dryer* 560.5

tower Architectural Elements 134, *church architecture* 134.11, *fort* 419.13, *superstructure* 551.7, *be big* 579.18, *be high* 596.15, *be tall* 596.16, *towline* 699.5, *refuge* 812.1

tower above *be high* 596.15

tower above or **over** *overtake* 744.16

tower block *apartment house* 60.8, *building* 551.9

tower crane *construction equipment* 14.23

towering *mountainous* 569.5, *huge* 579.14, *high* 596.7, *tall* 596.9

towering inferno *fire* 217.8

toweringly *high* 596.20

tower of silence *burial place* 31.7

tower of strength *supporter* 605.9, 825.13, *protection* 810.2, *refuge* 812.1

tower over 569.7; *be an influence* 512.13, *be tall* 596.16

tow-headed *white-haired* 253.9

towhee, Inyo California Endangered US Birds 36

to windward *offshore* 150.35

towing *transportable* 686.7, *traction* 699.1, *tractional* 699.7

to wit *in other words* 365.18, *particularly* 779.21

towline 699.5; *line* 754.5

town 567.2; *body politic* 50.3, *administrative region* 564.4, *urban* 567.14

town center *center of activity* 612.4

town council *representative body* 79.2

town crier *crier* 239.8

town hall *municipal building* 567.13

town house *house* 60.4

townie or **towny** [Inf] *townsperson* 61.7, *municipal resident* 567.12

town meeting *governing body* 49.19, *representative body* 79.2

town plan *map* 187.5, 387.7

town planner *planner* 387.9

townscape *type of painting* 143.5, *view* 242.8

township *administrative region* 564.4

townsman *townsperson* 61.7, *municipal resident* 567.12

townsperson 61.7

townswoman *townsperson* 61.7, *municipal resident* 567.12

town tax *tax* 494.5

town wall *fortification* 419.12

towny [Inf] *townsperson* 61.7

towpath *passage* 691.5

towrope *towline* 699.5, *line* 754.5

toxemia *infection* 114.7, *blood disease* 114.14

toxic 114.28; *killing* 30.17, *unclean* 112.8, *poisonous* 117.14, *detrimental* 446.8, *dangerous* 811.7

toxicity *poisoning* 114.8, 117.6

toxicologist *medical specialist* 107.20

toxicology *medical science* 107.5

toxicology screen *diagnostic procedure* 107.11

toxic waste *waste product* 96.7

toxin *poisoning* 114.8, *poison* 117.7

toxiphobia or **toxicophobia** Phobias 283

toxophilite [Form] *shooter* 696.11

toxophily *shooting* 696.5

toxoplasma *parasite* 39.18

toy 167.9; *amusement* 167.7, *court* 299.26, *cheap item* 497.5, *little thing* 580.3, *cheap thing* 800.7, *trivial* 800.14

toy dog *dog* 35.10

toying *courtship* 299.10

toying with one's food *delicate eating* 92.3

to your health! *cheers!* 93.22

toy poodle Breeds of Dogs 35

toy spaniel Breeds of Dogs 35

toy terrier Breeds of Dogs 35

toy theater *theater* 136.16

toy with *touch* 216.9

toy with one's food *taste* 92.24

trace Collective Names 59, *draw* 143.13, *vestige* 185.11, *illustrate* 187.11, *decorate* 532.11, *little piece* 580.4, *outline* 617.5, *visible effect* 676.2, *remainder* 750.1, *suggestion* 800.9

trace amount *little piece* 580.4

trace back *recollect* 3.16, *look back* 651.18, *swing* 671.12

traced *drawn* 143.11

trace element *essential element* 12.15

trace fossil *fossil* 8.49

trace horse *workhorse* 159.3

tracer *armor-piercing* 78.18

tracer ammunition *ammunition* 78.11

tracer flare *military defenses* 419.9

tracery *braid* 609.3

traces *signs* 183.2, *yoke* 754.8

trachea *throat* 19.12, *respiration* 558.8

tracheal *metabolic* 19.24

tracheitis *respiratory disease* 114.12

trachoma *tropical disease* 114.10, *blindness* 243.3

tracing *(act of) drawing* 143.2, *drawing* 143.4, *illustration* 187.2, *representation* 202.9, *outline* 617.1, *duplicate* 736.4

tracing paper *paper* 104.5

track 688.2; *thunderstorm* 9.20, *sports ground* 145.2, *automobile racing terms* 146.3, *hunt* 160.12, *track and field* 166.20, *sign* 183.1, *vestige* 185.11, *indication* 339.3, *follow* 385.12, *furrow* 569.1, *route* 691.2, *passage* 691.5, *railroad* 691.8, *thoroughfare* 692.6, *bearing* 697.2, *remainder* 750.1, *students* 777.6, *attend* 794.19

track and field 166.20

track and field eventer 166.19

track and field meet *athletics* 422.7

trackball *input device* 15.11

track down *detect* 345.12, *follow* 385.12, *find* 565.11

tracked down *found* 565.7

tracker *hunter* 160.9, 385.6

tracker dog *dog* 35.10

track event 166.1; *athletics* 422.7

tracking *hunting* 160.2, *pursuit* 385.1

tracking device *guide* 697.4

tracking down *detection* 345.2, *pursuit* 385.1, *locating* 565.3

tracking station *artificial satellite* 7.30

track iron *golf equipment* 156.5

trackman *laborer* 123.9, *railroad worker* 688.7

track record *chronicle* 3.4, *conduct* 399.1

tracks *rail* 688.3

tracks [Inf] *drug use* 121.9

track suit *informal clothes* 100.7, *suit* 100.16, *gymnastics equipment* 157.2, *sports equipment* 166.17

tract *dissertation* 203.1, *property* 470.1, *space* 563.1, *geographical space* 563.3, *plot* 564.9

tractability *persuadability* 178.8, *acquiescence* 373.3, *obedience* 426.1, *softness* 543.1

tractable *persuadable* 178.14, *acquiescent* 373.9, *submitting* 421.3, *obedient* 426.4, *deferential* 433.9, *pliant* 543.7, *compliant* 781.9, *easygoing* 823.13

tractably *obediently* 426.9

tractate *dissertation* 203.1

tractile *pliant* 543.7

traction 699.1; *type of power* 514.6, *miscellaneous automotive terms* 687.14

tractional 699.7

traction control system *miscellaneous automotive terms* 687.14

traction engine *towline* 699.5

tractive *tractional* 699.7

tractive power *traction* 699.1

tractor *farm tool* 16.5, *truck* 687.8, *towline* 699.5

tractor driver *farm worker* 16.15

tractor shed *farm building* 16.4

tractor-trailer *truck* 578.10

tradable *exchangeable* 665.13

trade 56.12, 480.1, 480.18; *job* 122.3, *finance* 457.7, *negotiate* 460.6, *transfer of property* 470.4, *transfer property* 470.12, *selling* 482.1, *sell* 482.15, *pay* 489.16, *exchange* 665.8, 665.21, 673.1, 673.5, *transfer* 685.1, *right of entry* 706.4, *reciprocate* 729.7, *linkage* 752.3, *specialization* 779.3

trade agreement *international trade* 56.7, *alliance* 459.5, *bargaining* 480.10

trade barrier *international trade* 56.7, *protectionism* 480.3

trade book *type of book* 174.3

trade center *center of activity* 612.4

traded *exchanged* 673.4, *reciprocal* 729.4

trade deficit *national debt* 488.2

trade delegation *representative body* 79.2

trade fair *fair* 483.2

trade gap *national debt* 488.2

trade in 457.8; *trade* 480.18

trade integration *international trade* 56.7

trade journal *magazine* 175.3

trade language *international language* 5.8

trade-last [Arch inf] *compliment* 437.4

trademark *decoration* 129.4, *sign* 183.1, *means of identification* 184.3, *name* 202.8, *originate* 737.7, *special feature* 779.4

trademarked *identified* 184.9, *authentic* 737.6

trademarked product *original* 737.2

trade name *means of identification* 184.3

tradename *name* 202.8

trade off *negotiate* 460.6, *trade* 480.18, *exchange* 673.5, *reciprocate* 729.7, *counterbalance* 743.8

trade-off *negotiation* 460.1, *basis for negotiations* 460.2, *compromise* 461.1, *transfer of property* 470.4, *trade* 480.1, *moderation* 521.1, *exchange* 673.1, *reciprocity* 729.1, *equalization* 740.4, *counterbalance* 743.2

trade on *exploit* 393.11

trade organization *economic organization* 56.6

trade paper *magazine* 175.3

trader 480.11; *financial adviser* 457.4, *retailer* 482.11, *operator* 509.5

trade restriction *protectionism* 480.3

trade sanctions *economic warfare* 76.7

tradescantia Flowers 42

trade show *fair* 483.2

trade sign *sign* 183.1

tradesman *artisan* 123.13, *retailer* 482.11

tradesman's entrance [Brit] *back entrance* 622.2

Trades Union Congress (TUC) [Brit] *organized labor* 57.5

trade supplement *newspaper* 175.2

trade union *organized labor* 57.5, *association* 59.4, 752.2

trade winds or **trades** *wind system* 9.15

trade with *trade* 56.12, 480.18, *trade in* 457.8

trading *trade* 480.1, *mercantile* 480.13, *selling* 482.1

trading center *marketplace* 483.7, *center of activity* 612.4

trading company *store* 483.8

trading house *store* 483.8

trading post *marketplace* 483.7

trading ring *limit* 620.1

tradition 1.7, 397.5, 653.5; *chronicle* 3.4, *expected thing* 356.3, *custom* 397.4, 780.5, *regularity* 663.1, *convention* 781.5

traditional 630.13; *societal* 1.13, *chronicled* 3.12, *musical* 140.25, *mountaineering* 161.9, *customary* 397.11, 780.9, *obstinate* 417.7, *observant* 465.3, *olden* 653.11, *regular* 663.5, *average* 742.5, *conformist* 781.10, *conservative* 815.13

traditional grammar *grammar* 5.28

traditionalism *traditionality* 630.6, *conventionalism* 781.4

traditionalist *creature of habit* 397.8, *resister* 417.5, *assenter* 462.5, *straight person* 630.7, *conformist* 781.6, 781.10, *conservative* 815.13

traditionalistic *conformist* 781.10

traditionality 630.6

traditional jazz *jazz* 140.5

traditionally 630.19; *societally* 1.17, *habitually* 397.20, *resistingly* 417.14, *observantly* 465.6, *orderly* 663.13, *according to rule* 781.18, *conservatively* 815.17

traditional medicine *alternative medicine* 107.4

traditionary *customary* 397.11

traditions *way of life* 399.9

traditive *customary* 397.11

traduce *defame* 440.13

traducement *misinformation* 188.3, *defamation* 440.3

traffic *trade* 480.1, 480.18, *selling* 482.1, *exchange* 673.5, *motion* 677.1, *miscellaneous automotive terms* 687.14, *passing along* 692.5, *linkage* 752.3

traffic circle *crossroads* 609.4, *circle* 631.2, *rotary* 682.5, *road attribute* 687.3

traffic cop *law enforcement officer* 53.8

traffic death *accidental killing* 30.9

traffic flow *motion* 677.1, *passing along* 692.5

traffic in *trade* 56.12, 480.18, *trade in* 457.8, *sell* 482.15

traffic in drugs *drug oneself* 121.37

traffic jam *miscellaneous automotive terms* 687.14, *passing along* 692.5, *roadblock* 826.4

trafficker *merchant* 482.10

trafficking *trade* 480.1, *selling* 482.1

traffic lane *route* 691.2

traffic light or **signal** *signal* 183.6, *safety light* 246.7

traffic lights *road attribute* 687.3

traffic load *passing along* 692.5

traffic of the stage *drama* 136.1

traffic pattern *flight control* 689.7, *passing along* 692.5

traffic signs *road attribute* 687.3

tragacanth Tree Products 43

tragedian *actor* 136.25, *dramatist* 136.27

tragedienne *actor* 136.25

tragedy 136.10; *deterioration* 808.1

tragic *dramatic* 136.31, *poetic* 139.19, *distressing* 270.6, *detrimental* 446.8, *adverse* 848.10

tragically *dramatically* 136.38, *destructively* 446.13, *adversely* 848.16

tragic drama *tragedy* 136.10

tragic flaw *tragedy* 136.10, *defect* 806.4, *vulnerability* 811.6

tragicomedy *tragedy* 136.10, *comedy* 136.11

tragicomic or **tragicomical** *dramatic* 136.31

tragicomically *dramatically* 136.38

tragic poet *author* 139.13

trail *hunt* 160.12, *sign* 183.1, *vestige* 185.11, *scent* 224.3, *indication* 339.3, *follow* 385.12, 770.10, *be in the rear* 622.7, *route* 691.2, *passage* 691.5, *hesitate* 693.12, *pull* 699.10, *be inferior* 745.10, *remainder* 750.1

trail behind *be in the rear* 622.7

trail bike *motorcycle* 687.12

trailblaze *pioneer* 771.29

trailblazer *preparer* 388.6, *precursor* 769.7

trailblazing *preparation* 388.1, *preparatory* 769.11

trailed *pursued* 385.10

trailer *farm tool* 16.5, *mobile home* 60.11, *advertisement* 173.9, *hunter* 385.6, *means of transportation* 686.2, *automobile* 687.6, *preview* 769.6

trail horse *horse* 159.1

trailing *pursuit* 385.1, *pursuing* 385.8

trailing edge *plate tectonics* 8.19

trail-ride *ride* 159.16

trail shot *grip* 151.4

train 122.12, 688.4; *cultivate* 17.19, *assemblage of mammals* 35.22, *educate* 48.22, *learn* 48.23, *employ* 57.18, *part of garment* 100.27, *direct* 126.11, *ride* 159.16, *compete in track and field* 166.21, *cause to know* 348.13, *brief* 388.20, *prepare oneself* 388.21, *accustom* 397.18, *bring into existence* 522.14, *back* 622.1, *means of transportation* 686.2, *pull* 699.10, *series* 770.3, *consecutiveness* 774.1, *procession* 774.6, *assimilate* 781.14

trainable *educatable* 48.18

train bearer *wedding party* 64.7

trained *ornamental* 17.17, *expert* 127.12, *knowledgeable* 348.7, *prepared* 388.9, *habituated* 397.14, *obedient* 426.4

trained animal *domestic animal* 34.3

trainee *unskilled person* 128.3, *beginner* 398.2, 771.14

trainee nurse *nurse* 107.23

trainer *educator* 48.4, *military aircraft* 77.30, *boxer* 152.8, *horse person* 159.14, *soccer participant* 163.4, *preparer* 388.6

training 122.5; *education* 48.1, *military training* 76.19, *armor-piercing* 78.18, *dramatic* 137.16, *briefing* 388.4, *in preparation* 388.8, *habituation* 397.7

training ammunition *ammunition* 78.11

training and doctrine *army commands* 77.13

training and education *bargaining terms* 57.10

training camp *miscellaneous terms* 155.16

training film *movie type* 137.3

training officer *employer* 57.3

training staff *military staff* 58.5

trainload *load* 577.5

train of thought *thought* 317.1

train robber *thief* 479.8

trains Phobias 283

train station *center of activity* 612.4, *stopping place* 668.4

train ticket *means of identification* 184.3

train upon *aim* 697.14

traipse [Inf] *move slowly* 693.11

trait *identification* 184.1, *external appearance* 264.5, *tendency* 397.2, *nature* 723.4, *characteristic* 779.5

Trait du Nord Horse and Pony Breeds 159

traitor *hostile person* 63.5, *hypocrite* 192.9, *malefactor* 306.6, *equivocator* 380.4, *seditionist* 427.7, *evil person* 446.3, *villain* 448.5

traitorous *dishonorable* 192.14, *equivocating* 380.6, *villainous* 448.12, *irresolute* 664.4

traitorously *changeably* 666.7

traitor's death *capital punishment* 454.12

traject [Arch] *propel* 696.15

trajectile *projectile* 696.13

trajection [Arch] *throwing* 696.3

trajectory *curve* 6.38, *orbit* 7.22, *rocketry* 7.32, *route* 691.2, *flight path* 691.12

Trakehner Horse and Pony Breeds 159

tram [Brit] *railroad system* 688.1

trammels *means of restraint* 830.6

tramontana Notable Winds 9

tramontane Notable Winds 9, *distant* 585.5, *foreign* 724.9

tramp *nonworker* 415.4, *poor person* 486.6, *beggar* 505.6, *bodily movement* 677.11, *walk* 677.17, *person in adversity* 848.9

trample *attack successfully* 418.25, *kick* 695.14

trampled down *leveled* 603.8

trample down *make horizontal* 603.10

trample in the dust *bring down* 716.14

trample on *violate the law* 466.12, *subject* 832.10

trample over *impose one's will* 372.14

trample underfoot *violate the law* 466.12, *knock down* 523.13, *defeat* 845.17

trampoline *gymnastics equipment* 157.2, *lifter* 715.5

trampolining *Sporting Activities* 145, *gymnastics* 157.1

tramp steamer *Ships and Boats* 690

tramway *ski run* 162.2

trance 108.18; *occult and psychic phenomena* 86.7, *desensitization* 213.2, *oblivion* 355.4, *reverie* 360.6, *sleep* 415.5, *lack of motion* 678.1

trance speaking *occult and psychic phenomena* 86.7

trance state *trance* 108.18

tranks [Inf] *tranquilizers* 121.21

tranquil *detached* 4.18, *peaceful* 73.8, *wonderless* 295.3, *inactive* 413.9, *moderate* 521.3, *quiescent* 678.6, *harmonious* 765.16, *at ease* 819.2

tranquility *ease* 819.1

tranquilization *ease* 275.1, *moderation* 521.1

tranquilize *conciliate* 74.10, *relieve* 275.8, *calm* 521.8, *make motionless* 678.8

tranquilizer *addictive drug* 117.10, *anesthetic* 213.3, *reliever* 275.4, *moderator* 521.2

tranquilizers 121.21

tranquilizing *moderating* 521.5

tranquillity *lack of wonder* 295.1, *lack of thought* 318.1, *stillness* 413.3, *repose* 678.2, *harmony* 765.8

tranquilly *peacefully* 73.12, *without wonder* 295.8, *inactively* 413.16, *motionlessly* 678.9

transact *behave toward* 399.20, *occupy oneself* 412.15, *negotiate* 460.6, *contract* 462.11, *trade* 480.18, *exchange* 673.5, *settle* 735.26

transaction *action* 412.1, *deed* 412.2, *negotiation* 460.1, *contract* 462.2, *trade* 480.1, *selling* 482.1, *exchange* 673.1, *settlement* 735.6

transactional analysis (TA) *psychotherapy* 108.4

transactionalist *anthropological* 1.10

transactions *record* 185.1, *treatment* 399.11, *business relations* 727.4

transalpine *distant* 585.5

transaminase *enzyme* 12.11

transatlantic *sailing* 150.25, *distant* 585.5, *foreign* 724.9

transatlantic racing *competitive sailing* 150.6

Transbaikal Finewool *Breeds of Sheep* 16

transceiver *communications device* 15.26

transcend *be good at* 445.18, *exceed* 712.15, *be superior* 744.15

transcended *surpassing* 712.10

transcendence *divine attribute* 82.4, *crossing* 712.2, *superiority* 744.1, *expertise* 805.4

transcendency *superiority* 744.1

transcendent *religious* 81.21, *holy* 82.19, *nonmaterial* 525.8, *novel* 737.5, *elite* 744.12, *immeasurable* 798.6, *expert* 805.16

transcendental *complex* 6.69, *holy* 82.19

transcendental argument *philosophical problem* 4.8

transcendental idealism *idealism* 525.5

Transcendentalism *Western Literary Groups* 139

transcendentalism *Philosophical Schools of Thought* 4, *idealism* 525.5

transcendentalist *Philosophical Schools of Thought* 4

transcendentally *divinely* 82.24, *predominantly* 744.21

transcendental meditation *psychotherapy* 108.4

transcendental number *complex number* 6.6, *kind of number* 783.2

transcendently *metaphysically* 525.13, *predominantly* 744.21

transcending *elite* 744.12

transcontinental *distant* 585.5

transcribe *inscribe* 185.14, *translate* 365.16, *change* 665.14

transcribed *broadcast* 172.12, *imitative* 736.7

transcript *duplicate* 736.4

transcription *musical composition* 140.9, *broadcast material* 172.9, *translation* 365.4, *alteration* 665.2

transcursion *crossing* 712.2

transducer *circuit* 10.43

transducing *passing* 692.11

transduction *transmission* 685.3, *passing* 692.3

transect *halve* 789.15

transept *church interior* 83.9, *church architecture* 134.11

transeunt *outgoing* 707.10

transfer 685.1, 685.8; *react* 11.38, *delegate* 79.6, *miscellaneous terms* 155.16, *relinquishment* 392.1, *relinquish* 392.3, *contract* 459.8, *transfer of property* 470.4, *transfer property* 470.12, *giving* 472.1, *give* 472.10, *selling* 482.1, *sell* 482.15, *replacement* 574.3, *displace* 574.15, *change* 665.14, *cause change* 665.16, *conversion* 670.1, *convert* 670.11, *restoration* 671.2, *set in motion* 677.16, *transportation* 686.1, *transport* 686.10, *cross* 692.17, *duplicate* 736.4

transferable 685.7; *negotiated* 460.5, *transferring property* 470.10, *given* 472.8, *convertible* 670.9

transfer a decal *make ceramics* 129.10

transferase *enzyme* 12.11

transferee *purchaser* 481.7

transference *association of ideas* 108.31, *transfer of property* 470.4, *displacement* 574.1, *alteration* 665.2, *conversion* 670.1, *transfer* 685.1, *passing* 692.3, *export* 707.7

transfer of property 470.4

transferor *seller* 482.7

transfer orbit *rocketry* 7.32

transfer ownership *transfer property* 470.12

transfer printing *decoration* 129.4

transfer property 470.12

transferral *transfer* 685.1

transferred *linguistic* 361.9, *transferring property* 470.10, *displaced* 574.8, *replaced* 574.10

transferred epithet *literary device* 139.12

transferred thing 685.6

transferrer 685.4

transfer responsibility *exempt oneself* 434.12

transferring *giving* 472.9, *converting* 670.8, *passing* 692.11

transferring property 470.10

transfer RNA (tRNA) *nucleotide* 12.10, *genetic material* 13.20

transfers *bargaining terms* 57.10

transfer thoughts *experience psychic phenomena* 86.23

transfiguration *beautification* 530.1, *transformation* 665.7, *conversion* 670.1, *improvement* 807.1

transfigure *beautify* 530.14, *transform* 665.20, 670.13, *convert* 670.11, *improve* 807.15

transfigured *converted* 670.7

transfiguring *beautifying* 530.13, *converting* 670.8

transfinite induction *reasoning* 6.61

transfinite number *number* 6.4, *absolutes* 6.9

transfix *make stable* 674.7

transfixed *wondering* 294.7, *stabilized* 674.4, *motionless* 678.4

transform 665.20, 670.13; *represent* 6.91, *beautify* 530.14, *change* 665.14, *convert* 670.11, *improve* 807.15

transformable *convertible* 670.9

transformation 6.46, 665.7; *mathematical function* 6.27, *righting wrong* 429.6, *beautification* 530.1, *change* 665.1, *conversion* 670.1, *calculation* 784.1, *improvement* 807.1

transformational *of grammar* 5.41

transformational-generative *of grammar* 5.41

transformational grammar *linguistic theory* 5.2, *grammar* 5.28

transformation-generative grammar *grammar* 5.28

transformation of radiant energy *Fields of Measurement* 589

transformation scene *play part* 136.8, *stage set* 136.19

transformative 665.12

transformed *changed* 665.10, *converted* 670.7, *improved* 807.12

transform energy *generate power* 514.19

transformer *circuit* 10.43, *power supplier* 514.14, *changer* 665.9

transform fault *plate tectonics* 8.19

transforming *converting* 670.8

transfusable *transferable* 685.7

transfuse *practice surgery* 107.33, *treat* 115.17, *transfer* 685.8, *inject* 710.10

transfusion *surgery* 107.15, *transmission* 685.3, *passing* 692.3, *injection* 710.2, *mixture* 751.1

transgress 351.16, 712.14; *disobey* 427.12, *do wrong* 430.20, *be wicked* 448.13, *sin* 450.11, *violate the law* 466.12, *break the law* 782.19

transgressed *violating* 466.8

transgressing 712.7; *offending* 53.25, *disobedient* 427.10, *sinful* 450.8, *violating* 466.8

transgression 712.3; *lawbreaking* 53.14, *errancy* 351.7, *violation of the law* 427.2, *wrongdoing* 430.7, *iniquity* 448.3, *sin* 450.3, *infraction* 466.4

transgressive *unlawful* 430.15, *violating* 466.8

transgressor *wrongdoer* 430.8, *evil person* 446.3, *villain* 448.5

transience 643.1; *shortness* 591.1, *changeableness* 666.1, *unreliability* 841.7

transient 643.2, 643.4; *chemical compound* 11.4, *disappearing* 265.3, *short* 591.6, *changeable* 665.11, 666.3, *outgoing* 707.10, *circumstantial* 726.8, *unreliable* 841.15

transient current *electric current* 10.39

transient disturbance *wave* 10.11

transiently 643.8; *fleetingly* 265.8, *unreliably* 841.25

transilience *passing* 692.3

transilient *passing* 692.11

transistor *circuit* 10.43, *circuit element* 14.39, *computer part* 15.4, *power supplier* 514.14

transistor band gap *semiconductor* 10.34

transistor radio *radio* 172.1

transit *orbit* 7.22, *observe* 7.34, *motion* 677.1, *conveyance* 685.2, *passing* 692.3, *cross* 692.17

transition *temperature* 10.29, *excited atom* 10.55, *motion-picture editing* 137.8, *discus throwing* 166.13, *alteration* 665.2, *conversion* 670.1, *transfer* 685.1, *conveyance* 685.2, *passing* 692.3, *sequel* 770.5

transitional *changeable* 665.11, *moving* 677.12, *passing* 692.11

transitionally *changeably* 665.22, *in motion* 677.19, *by the way* 692.20

transitional style *Architectural Styles* 134

transition element *chemical element* 11.3

transition rate *chemical reaction* 11.8

transition temperature *temperature* 10.29, *superconductivity* 10.35

transitive *of grammar* 5.41

transitively *grammatically* 5.48

transitive relation *mathematical logic* 6.60

transitive verb *part of speech* 5.30

transitorily *transiently* 643.8

transitoriness *transience* 643.1

transitory *transient* 643.4, *changeable* 665.11

Transit system *position finder* 690.8

transit van [Brit] *truck* 578.10

translatable *phrased* 5.39, *convertible* 670.9

translate 365.16; *represent* 6.91, *change* 665.14, *cause change* 665.16, *convert* 670.11, *transform* 670.13, *cross* 692.17, *make easy* 823.15

translated *phrased* 5.39, *interpreted* 365.9, *converted* 670.7

translate the truth *distort the truth* 627.12

translating *phrased* 5.39

translation 365.4; *phrasing* 5.25, *transformation* 6.46, *operation of symmetry* 626.2, *alteration* 665.2, *conversion* 670.1

translational 365.11

translator *linguist* 5.3, *interpreter* 365.6, *converter* 670.5

translator's error *misinterpretation* 366.1

transliterate *translate* 365.16, *be literal* 721.25

transliterated *written* 5.36
transliteration *alphabet* 5.16, *translation* 365.4, *literalness* 721.9
translocate *displace* 574.15, *transfer* 685.8
translocation *displacement* 574.1, *transfer* 685.1
translucence *translucency* 249.2
translucency **249.2;** *semitransparency* 249.3
translucent **249.8;** *ceramic* 129.9, *semitransparent* 249.9
translucent ceramics *ceramics* 129.1
translucently *ornamentally* 129.11, *transparently* 249.13
transmarine *distant* 585.5
transmigration *materialization* 524.2, *transfer* 685.1
transmigration of souls *transformation* 665.7, *transfer* 685.1
transmissible *transferable* 685.7
transmission **685.3;** *wave property* 10.12, *telecommunication* 169.7, *communication* 170.2, *television broadcasting* 172.8, *broadcast material* 172.9, *transfer of property* 470.4, *passing* 692.3
transmission density *exposure* 132.15
transmission line *telecommunication* 169.7
transmission of disease *transmission* 685.3
transmissive *transferable* 685.7
transmit *conduct* 14.51, 399.21, *cause ill health* 114.30, *communicate* 169.18, 170.12, *report* 171.9, *broadcast* 172.13, *publish* 173.15, *send* 209.11, *give* 472.10, *transfer* 685.8, *convey* 685.9, *cross* 692.17
transmit color *colorcast* 251.17
transmit light *be transparent* 249.11
transmittable *communicational* 169.17, *transferable* 685.7
transmittal *transfer of property* 470.4, *transfer* 685.1
transmittance *transfer* 685.1
transmitted *communicated* 169.15, *broadcast* 172.12
transmitter *transferrer* 685.4
transmit thoughts *experience psychic phenomena* 86.23
transmitting *passing* 692.11
transmitting antenna *radio transmission* 172.3
transmogrification *transformation* 665.7
transmogrify *transform* 665.20
transmontane *distant* 585.5, *foreign* 724.9
transmundane *spiritual* 86.20, *nonmaterial* 525.8, *distant* 585.5
transmutable *convertible* 670.9
transmutation *nuclear reaction* 10.59, *transformation* 665.7, *conversion* 670.1
transmutative *transformative* 665.12
transmute *interact* 10.73, *transform* 665.20, 670.13, *convert* 670.11
transmuted *converted* 670.7
transmuting *converting* 670.8
transoceanic *distant* 585.5
transom Architectural Elements 134, *window* 134.10, *sailboat parts and accessories* 150.4, *supporting part* 605.3
transpacific *distant* 585.5
transparency **249.1;** *photograph*
132.3, *stage set* 136.19, *clarity* 196.1, 363.2, *invisibility* 245.1, *transparent thing* 249.4
transparent **249.7;** *ceramic* 129.9, *disclosed* 180.5, *clear* 196.2, *invisible* 245.3, *simple* 363.6, *naive* 821.3
transparent glaze *glaze* 129.3
transparently **249.13;** *ornamentally* 129.11, *clearly* 196.4
transparent pigment *coloring agent* 251.5
transparent thing **249.4**
transphysical *psychic* 86.17
transphysical science *supernaturalism* 86.3
transpicuous *transparent* 249.7
transpiration *water cycle* 8.12, *physiology* 13.13, *transmission* 685.3
transpire *drain* 8.64, *be disclosed* 180.12, *take effect* 676.11, *transfer* 685.8, *be visible* 843.16
transplant *cultivate* 17.19, *practice surgery* 107.33, *substitute* 672.2, *transfer* 685.8, *insertion* 710.1, *plant* 710.14
transplantation *surgery* 107.15, *transfer* 685.1, *insertion* 710.1
transplanted *inserted* 710.5
transplanting *gardening* 17.5
transpolar *distant* 585.5
transpontine *distant* 585.5
transport **686.10;** *imprison* 454.23, *motion* 677.1, *set in motion* 677.16, *conveyance* 685.2, *convey* 685.9, *transportation* 686.1, *cross* 692.17, *ostracize* 709.17
transportable **686.7;** *transferable* 685.7
transportation **686.1;** *motion* 677.1, *passing* 692.3, *ostracism* 709.3
transportation center *center of activity* 612.4
transportation charges *business expenses* 491.4
transportation engineer *civil engineer* 14.19
transportation engineering *civil engineering* 14.17
transportation system *transportation* 686.1
transportative *transferable* 685.7
transported *enamored* 299.17, *transportable* 686.7
transporter **686.4;** *transferrer* 685.4, *truck* 686.11
transporter bridge *bridge* 551.10
transport helicopter *military aircraft* 77.30
transporting **686.8;** *passing* 692.11
transportive *transferable* 685.7
transport of love *romantic love* 299.2
transport pilot *air force person* 77.31
transport plane *military aircraft* 77.30
transport processes *industrial processes* 14.27
transport ship *warship* 77.21, Ships and Boats 690
transposable *convertible* 670.9, *transferable* 685.7
transposal *inversion* 608.1, *transfer* 685.1
transpose *matrix* 6.20, *invert* 608.7, *change* 665.14, *convert* 670.11, *exchange* 673.5, *set in motion* 677.16, *transfer* 685.8
transposed *inverted* 608.5, *converted* 670.7, *exchanged* 673.4
transposition *inversion* 608.1, *alteration* 665.2, *conversion* 670.1, *exchange* 673.1, *transfer* 685.1
transposon *genetic material* 13.20
transsexual *sexual nature* 20.4, *of sexual nature* 20.17, *bisexual* 32.10, 33.11
transsexuality *sexual nature* 20.4
transship *displace* 574.15, *transport* 686.10
transshipment *displacement* 574.1, *conveyance* 685.2, *transportation* 686.1
transubstantial *ritualistic* 85.15, *transformative* 665.12
transubstantiate *transform* 665.20
transubstantiation *Eucharist* 85.7, *transformation* 665.7
transudate *excrement* 25.2
transudating *penetrating* 692.12
transudation *secretion* 24.1, *excretion* 25.1, *passage into* 692.4, *outflow* 707.4
transudative *excretory* 25.12, *leaky* 707.12
transudatory *secretory* 24.4
transude *secrete* 24.7, *excrete* 25.20
transuranic element *chemical element* 11.3
transversal *or* transverse *line* 6.35
transverse *broad* 592.5, *oblique* 607.6, 628.8, *crossing* 609.7
transverse dune *dune* 8.43
transverse load *load* 14.14
transversely *breadthways* 592.16, *obliquely* 607.13
transverse wave *wave* 10.11, 683.4
transvestic fetishism *sexual disorder* 108.14
transvestism *sexual nature* 20.4
transvestite *sexual nature* 20.4, *of sexual nature* 20.17, *bisexual* 32.10, *male* 32.16
Transylvanian Pinzgau Breeds of Cattle 16
trap **813.1, 813.6;** *kill animals* 30.25, *stage* 136.18, *play* 155.8, *play offense* 155.18, *golf course* 156.2, *hunting equipment* 160.4, *hunt* 160.12, 385.14, *play soccer* 163.8, *enticement* 178.3, *entice* 178.16, *cover* 181.4, *ambush* 292.11, *military defenses* 419.9, *take away forcefully* 477.19, *closed place* 584.4, *danger* 811.1, *stratagem* 822.2, *cause difficulties* 824.22
trap [Inf] *body orifice* 583.3
trapa *religious* 84.9
trapdoor *means of entry* 706.6, *trap* 813.1, *means of escape* 816.4
trapeze *amusement park and playground equipment* 167.8
trapeze artist *circus performer* 138.9
trapezium *polygon* 6.42, Human Bones 19, *quadrilateral* 791.2
trapezoid *polygon* 6.42, Human Bones 19, *quadrilateral* 791.2
trapezoidal *quadrilateral* 791.2
trap for the unwary *trap* 813.1
trapped **813.5;** *soccer* 163.7, *surprised* 292.5, *endangered* 811.10
trapper *animal killer* 30.14, *hunter* 160.9, 385.6
trapping *animal killing* 30.10, *hunting* 160.2, *soccer play* 163.5, *soccer* 163.7
trappings *equipment* 103.6,
possessions 470.5, *ornamentation* 748.5
trapshooter *shooter* 160.10, 696.11
trapshooting Sporting Activities 145, *target shooting* 160.1, *shooting* 696.5
trash *waste product* 96.7, *dirt* 112.5, *senseless talk* 362.4, *residue* 750.2, *bits and pieces* 760.5, *nonentity* 800.8, *refuse* 802.5
trash can *cleaning tool* 111.10, *vessel* 578.11, *place for waste* 802.6
trash collector *cleaner* 111.12
trash compactor *cleaning tool* 111.10
trash dump *place for waste* 802.6
trashing *defeat* 846.7
trashy *meaningless* 362.7, *shoddy* 497.11, *cheap* 800.16, *useless* 802.7
Trasimeno Lakes 568
trattoria *eating place* 92.17
trauma *anxiety disorder* 108.11, *painful injury* 215.3
traumatic *painful* 215.4
traumatic disease *disease* 114.4
traumatism *anxiety disorder* 108.11
traumatize *inflict pain* 215.10
traumatized *psychologically disturbed* 108.39, *feeling pain* 215.6
traumatophobia Phobias 283
travail *work* 122.1, *exert oneself* 122.11, *adversity* 848.1
travel **686.5, 686.11;** *play basketball* 148.7, Phobias 283, *motion* 677.1, *move* 677.15, *forward motion* 679.1, *go forward* 679.8, *proceed* 692.16, *be foreign* 724.13
travel at maximum speed **694.11**
travel bag *baggage* 578.8
travel by air *fly* 689.13
travel by train **688.9**
traveler **686.6;** *sailboat parts and accessories* 150.4, *curious person* 321.3, *discoverer* 345.7, *salesperson* 482.8, *peddler* 482.9, *transient* 643.2
traveler's check *paper money* 484.14
traveler's-joy Flowers 42
traveler's tale *tall story* 194.5
travel in a circle *circle* 631.6
traveling **686.9;** *entertaining* 138.12, *violations* 148.5, Hobbies and Pastimes 167, *moving* 677.4, *travel* 686.5, *foreign* 724.9, *free-ranging* 829.13
traveling circus *circus* 138.2
traveling clock Timepieces and Timers 646
traveling companion *companion* 794.8
traveling salesman *or* saleswoman *salesperson* 482.8
traveling through *forward motion* 677.4
traveling wave *wave* 10.11
travel in space *launch* 7.35
travel in the astral plane *experience psychic phenomena* 86.23
Traveller Notable Horses 159
travel off season *buy cheaply* 497.15
travelogue *or* travelog *nonfiction* 139.6, *type of book* 174.3
travel report *weather forecast* 9.4
travels *travel* 686.5

travel second-class *buy cheaply* 497.15

travel-sick *vomiting* 709.12

travel tourist-class *buy cheaply* 497.15

travel-weary *fatigued* 820.2

travel with *keep company with* 794.17

travel writing *nonfiction* 139.6

Travers *famous horse races* 159.13

traversal *forward motion* 677.4

traverse *climbing techniques* 161.3, *mountaineer* 161.10, *skiing techniques* 162.5, *ski* 162.35, *counteract* 510.7, *passing* 692.3, *cross* 692.17, *oppose* 828.15

traverse downhill *cross-country techniques* 162.8

traverse table *navigational aid* 690.6

traversing *snowplow* 162.29, *forward motion* 677.4, *passing* 692.3, 692.11

travesty *bungling* 128.2, *misrepresentation* 188.1, 351.5, *misrepresent* 188.6, *exaggeration* 194.1, *exaggerate* 194.11, *distortion of truth* 627.4, *mimicry* 736.3, *imitate* 736.9

trawl *fish* 154.14, *pull* 699.2, *drag* 699.11

trawler *fisherman* 154.12, Ships and Boats 690

trawlerman *fisherman* 154.12

trawling *nautical* 690.14

tray *darkroom equipment* 132.21

treacherous *dishonorable* 192.14, *deceptive* 193.12, *defiant* 466.7, *dangerous* 811.7, *unsafe* 811.8, *unreliable* 841.15, *mysterious* 844.11

treacherously *dishonorably* 192.28, *deceptively* 193.21, *defiantly* 466.14, *dangerously* 811.14, *unreliably* 841.25

treacherousness *dishonorableness* 192.3, *irresolution* 666.2, *danger* 811.1, *unreliability* 841.7

treachery *dishonorableness* 192.3, *dastardliness* 285.2, *defiance* 466.3, *danger* 811.1

treacle [Brit] *sweetener* 222.2

treacly *sweet* 222.5

tread *bodily movement* 677.11, *walk* 677.17, *access* 691.3, *step* 713.11, *interval* 739.4

tread a measure *dance* 135.7

tread carefully *be careful* 325.11, *be in difficulty* 824.19

tread downward *descend* 714.12

treading water *swimming techniques* 164.2

treadle *propel* 696.15

treadmill *work* 122.1, *boring thing* 296.3, *way* 397.3, *instrument of torture* 454.14, *rotator* 682.8, *continuum* 774.5

tread on *use up* 393.12, *suppress* 424.9, *kick* 695.14, *subject* 832.10

tread on dangerous ground *be in danger* 811.11

tread on hot coals *have difficulty* 824.18

tread on someone's toes *offend* 302.15, *disrespect* 436.18

tread on the heels of *stay near* 586.13, *follow* 770.10

treads and risers *stairway* 713.9

tread the beaten path *or track have a hard time* 397.16

tread the boards *act* 136.34

tread the primrose path *deteriorate* 808.14

tread under foot *suppress* 424.9

---

tread warily *proceed with caution* 287.12, *be careful* 325.11, *delay* 375.16

tread water *swim* 164.14

tread water [Inf] *not act* 413.11, *pause* 415.15

treason *dishonorableness* 192.3, *act of defiance* 416.3, *subversion* 427.3, *defiance* 466.3

treasonable *dishonorable* 192.14, *subversive* 427.11

treasonable activities *subversion* 427.3

treasonous *dishonorable* 192.14, *defiant* 466.7

treasure *masterpiece* 68.14, *reserve* 105.3, *deposit* 105.21, *like* 290.8, *love* 299.21, *respect* 435.13, *good thing* 445.9, *funds* 484.6, *attractive female* 529.5, *protect* 810.21, *preserve* 815.14

treasure chest *money storage* 484.20

treasured *liked* 290.6, *beloved* 299.19, *preserved* 815.12

treasure house *storehouse* 105.8, *treasury* 484.19

Treasure Island Imaginary Places 360

treasure map *map* 187.5

treasurer 484.18; *provisioner* 89.4, *payer* 489.9, *accountant* 493.6

Treasurer of the US *treasurer* 484.18

treasure-trove *find* 345.5, *windfall* 467.7

Treasuries [Inf] *paper money* 484.14

Treasury 484.19 *treasury* 484.19

treasury 484.19; *storehouse* 105.8, *compendium* 204.3

Treasury bill *paper money* 484.14

Treasury bond *paper money* 484.14

Treasury certificate *paper money* 484.14

Treasury note *paper money* 484.14

treasury of words *word book* 5.27

treat 115.17, 130.21; *practice medicine* 107.32, *make healthy* 113.13, *remedy* 115.16, *medicate* 115.18, *give pleasure* 214.13, *pleasant thing* 271.4, *behave toward* 399.20, *participate* 408.15, *negotiate* 460.6, *give* 472.10, *defray* 489.18, *donate* 491.13, *take action* 509.12, *cure* 809.15, *support* 825.24

treatable *repairable* 809.7

treat as *take a substitute* 672.7

treat as a leper *exclude* 409.12

treat as an outsider *exclude* 409.12

treat as a special case *exclude* 764.7

treat cruelly *pervert* 808.22

treated 130.16, 388.12

treated like dirt *subject* 832.6

treated like shit [Inf] *subject* 832.6

treat equally 831.8

treat for sore eyes *beautiful thing* 529.3

treat in detail *particularize* 779.17

treatise *nonfiction* 139.6, *dissertation* 203.1

treat kindly *be lenient* 423.5

treat lightly *be lenient* 423.5

treat like dirt *desecrate* 436.24, *subject* 832.10

treat like shit [Inf] *desecrate* 436.24, *subject* 832.10

treatment 107.14, 110.7, 143.6, 399.11; *therapy* 115.12, *use*

393.1, *operation* 509.1, *manufacture* 522.2, *medical assistance* 825.5

treatment options *diagnosis* 107.8

treat rough *suppress* 424.9

treat rudely *be discourteous* 411.7

treat teeth *practice dentistry* 107.34

treat unfairly *discriminate against* 337.14, *be unjust* 342.10

treat well *be charitable* 305.12

treat with deference *defer to* 410.12

treat with politeness *have good manners* 410.10

treaty 74.2; *contract* 459.1, 462.2, *alliance* 459.5, *settlement* 735.6

treaty maker *negotiator* 460.4, *assenter* 462.5

treaty making *debate* 210.3, *negotiation* 460.1

treaty-making *negotiated* 460.5

treble *voice* 141.5, *sound quality* 230.4, *three* 790.7, *triple* 790.10

treble clef *written music* 140.21

treble hook *fishing tackle* 154.7

trebleness *threeness* 790.2

trebling *increase* 746.1, *triplication* 790.4

trebly *thrice* 790.12

trebuchet Historical Missile Weapons 78

tredecillion *million* 792.11

tree 43.1; *combinatorics* 6.63, *garden plant* 17.10, *plant* 41.2

tree [Inf] *cause difficulties* 824.22

tree-covered *wooded* 43.12

tree disease 43.8

tree farm *farm* 16.2, 124.11, *trees* 43.4

tree farmer *forester* 43.7

tree farming *arable farming* 16.6, *forestry* 43.5

tree fern *fern* 46.1

treeless *infertile* 23.7

treelike 43.10; *branched* 703.9

treelikeness *branching* 703.4

tree line or zone *trees* 43.4

tree litter *trees* 43.4

tree management 43.6

treen *woodworking* 131.1

treenail *fastener* 754.7

treenware *woodworking* 131.1

tree nursery *trees* 43.4

tree nymph *figurative usage* 43.9

tree of heaven Trees and Shrubs 43

tree of Jesse *figurative usage* 43.9

tree of knowledge *figurative usage* 43.9

tree of life *figurative usage* 43.9

tree part 43.2

tree planting *forestry* 43.5

tree ring *tree part* 43.2

tree-ring dating *chronology* 646.2

trees 43.4; Phobias 283

tree-shaped *branched* 703.9

tree stump *tree part* 43.2

tree surgeon *forester* 43.7

tree surgery *tree management* 43.6

tree worship *idolatry* 83.4

tree worshiper *idolater* 83.7

trefoil Architectural Elements 134, Heraldic Terms 184, *triple thing* 790.3

trellis *ornamental garden* 17.3, *braid* 609.3

tremble *quake* 8.65, *be cold* 218.13, *be fearful* 283.15, *be weak* 517.12, *be changeable* 666.5, *vibrate* 683.13, *shake* 684.24

tremble in the balance *be in danger* 811.11

trembling Phobias 283, *symptoms*

---

of fear 283.3, *fearful* 283.10, *shaking* 684.6, *shaky* 684.18

trembling in the air *faint* 233.6

trembling in the balance *unsafe* 811.8

tremblingly *shakily* 684.28

tremendismo Western Literary Groups 139

tremendous *huge* 579.14

tremolo *musical ornament* 140.19

tremophobia Phobias 283

tremor *neurological disease* 114.20, *natural violence* 520.3, *vibration* 683.2, *wave* 683.4, *shake* 684.7, *jolt* 684.9, *warning signal* 814.3

tremors *drunken behavior* 121.4

tremulous *fearful* 283.10, *waving* 683.11, *shaky* 684.18

tremulously *fearfully* 283.19, *shakily* 684.28

trench *cultivate* 17.19, *hiding place* 181.2, *military defenses* 419.9, *crack* 587.2, 587.7, *narrow place* 593.2, *enclosing thing* 619.3, *concave land* 635.2, *furrow* 638.1, 638.5, *fortification* 812.9

trenchancy *emphasis* 200.1, *bitterness* 306.3

trenchant *concise* 198.4, *emphatic* 200.3, *bitter* 306.9, *strong* 516.9, *important* 799.7

trenchantly *concisely* 198.6

trench coat *coat* 100.19

trencher *construction equipment* 14.23

trencherman *eater* 92.15, *glutton* 119.2

trencherwoman *eater* 92.15, *glutton* 119.2

trench fever *infection* 114.7

trenching machine *construction equipment* 14.23

trench mortar *guns* 78.9

trench warfare *offensive warfare* 76.11

trend *likes* 290.3, *final intention* 374.4, *tendency* 513.1, 838.2, *fashion* 536.1, *trendiness* 652.2, *significance* 676.4, *momentum* 677.2, *bearing* 697.2, *aim* 697.14, *deviate* 698.15, *mode* 725.2, *convention* 781.5

trendily 652.24

trendiness 652.2

trending *tending to* 513.4

trendsetter *fashion business* 536.3, *modern person* 652.8, *precursor* 769.7

trendsetting *avant-garde* 652.16

trend-setting group *avant-garde* 652.6

trend upward *upturn* 713.20

trendy 652.11; *avant-garde* 652.16, *conditional* 725.7

Trent Rivers 570

trente et quarante Card Games 168

Trenton American States 564

trepan *opener* 583.2, *hole* 583.17

trepang *echinoderm* 39.5

trephine *opener* 583.2, *hole* 583.17

trepidation *fearfulness* 283.2

Tres Cruces Mountains and Hills 569

trespass *lawbreaking* 53.14, *violation of the law* 427.2, *disobey* 427.12, *wrongdoing* 430.7, *do wrong* 430.20, *iniquity* 448.3, *be wicked* 448.13, *sin* 450.3, 450.11, *infraction* 466.4, *violate the law* 466.12, *invade* 706.12, *transgression* 712.3, *transgress* 712.14, *externality* 724.4, *be external* 724.15

---

trespasser *wrongdoer* 430.8, *intruder* 706.8, 724.7

trespassing *offending* 53.25, *sinful* 450.8, *violating* 466.8, *inroad* 706.3, *invasive* 706.10, *transgressing* 712.7, *external* 724.11

tress *body covering* 19.4

tressed *hairy* 19.20

trestle *junction* 691.9

trestle bridge *bridge* 551.10

trestletree *figurative usage* 43.9

tresure Heraldic Terms 184

trey *cards* 168.2, *three* 790.1

triable *unjust* 53.24

triacidic *acid* 11.27

triacidic base *base* 11.11

triad *chord* 140.18, *three* 790.1

triadic *three* 790.7

trial *legal process* 54.3, *adversity* 117.2, *questionnaire* 333.3, *experiment* 335.1, *rehearsal* 335.2, *experimental* 335.8, *preparations* 388.2, *tentative* 390.5, *contest* 422.4, *affliction* 454.9, *difficult task* 824.3

trial and error *experiment* 335.1

trial at the bar *legal process* 54.3

trial balloon *publishing* 352.9, *rehearsal* 335.2, *stratagem* 822.2

trial by jury *legal process* 54.3

trial by law *legal process* 54.3

trial by one's peers *legal process* 54.3

trial court *law court* 54.8

triality *threeness* 790.2

trial judge *judge* 54.10

trial jury *jury* 54.11, 341.6

trial marriage *type of marriage* 64.3

trial of strength *contest* 422.4

trial run *rehearsal* 335.2, *preparations* 388.2, *venture* 390.2

trials *adversity* 848.1

trials and tribulations *adversity* 848.1

Triangle *or* Triangulum Constellations 7

triangle 6.41; *polygon* 6.42, Musical Instruments 142, *billiards* 149.1, *source of resonance* 236.4, *instrument of torture* 454.14, *angled figure* 628.3, *triple thing* 790.3

triangle player *player* 141.2

triangular *polygonal* 6.79, *angled* 628.9, *three-sided* 790.8

triangular offense *ice hockey tactics* 158.4

triangulate *find* 565.11, *measure* 589.20, *three-sided* 790.8

triangulated *measured* 589.16

triangulation *trigonometry* 6.49, *topography* 565.5, *measurement* 589.1

triangulation point *indicator* 183.7

triarchy *oligarchy* 49.10

Triassic Period Geologic Time Intervals 8

triathlon Sporting Activities 145, *multi-event contest* 166.16

triatomic *chemical compound* 11.4

tribade *homosexual* 33.10

tribadism *or* tribady *sexual nature* 20.4

tribadistic *of sexual nature* 20.17

tribal *societal* 1.13, *national* 18.16, *governmental* 49.24, *native* 61.12, *family* 65.6

tribalism 49.2; *group* 18.13

tribal killer *killer* 30.11

tribally *societally* 1.17, *cliquishly* 59.32

tribal memory *tradition* 1.7, *remainder* 750.1

tribal warrior *soldier* 77.4

tribasic *acid* 11.27

tribasic acid *acid* 11.10

tribe *society* 1.6, *social organization* 2.5, *group* 18.13, 59.8, Collective Names 59, *inhabitants* 61.2, *family* 65.1, *family tree* 65.3, *associate* 754.3, *taxonomic classification* 777.3

Tribeca New York 567.6

triboluminescence *light* 10.17

tribrach *meter* 139.10

tribulation *difficult task* 824.3

tribunal 54.6; *judiciary* 53.19, *place of judgment* 341.3

tribune *church architecture* 134.11

tributary 570.2; *giver* 472.7, *given* 472.8, *inferior* 745.4, *subordinate* 745.8

tribute 405.6; *pleasant thing* 271.4, *acknowledgment* 310.3, *memento* 354.3, *praise* 437.3, *reward* 453.1, *gift* 472.2, *something received* 473.2, *grant* 489.7, *levy* 494.7

tribute-payer *giver* 472.7

tributive *approving* 437.9

tricarboxylic acid (TCA) cycle *bioenergetics* 12.23, *respiration* 12.24

trice *pull* 699.10

tricentennial *anniversary* 405.5, 663.4, *anniversarial* 663.8

tricentennially *cyclically* 663.15

triceps *muscles* 19.3

trichologist *beautician* 530.11

trichopathophobia Phobias 283

trichophobia Phobias 283

trichopteran *insectile* 40.11

trichotillomania *impulse-control disorder* 108.16

trichotomize *trisect* 790.11

trichotomous *trisected* 790.9

trichotomy *trisection* 790.5

trichroism *variegation* 263.1

trichromatic *variegated* 263.6

trichromatism *variegation* 263.1

trichromic *variegated* 263.6

trick 813.2; *task* 122.2, *social skill* 127.3, *bridge* 168.4, *deceive* 181.14, 193.16, 330.12, *artifice* 193.5, *scheme* 193.18, *joke* 277.6, *sophism* 330.2, *confuse* 333.20, *method* 387.4, *tactics* 399.12, *delusion* 720.3, *characteristic* 779.5, *trap* 813.6, *means of escape* 816.4, *stratagem* 822.2, *be cunning* 822.5

tricked *deceived* 193.15, *trapped* 813.5

tricked out *beautified* 530.12

trickery *evasion* 181.5, *deception* 193.1, *cunning* 822.1

trickily *questionably* 333.22

trickiness *cunning* 330.3

trickle *seep* 559.16, *flow* 570.10, *move slowly* 693.11, *leakage* 707.5, *leak* 707.16, *few* 796.1, *little bit* 800.4

trickle-down theory *economics* 56.1

trickling *leakage* 707.5

trick of the light *delusion* 720.3

trick play *play* 155.8

trick question *difficult question* 333.4

tricks of the trade *means* 102.1, *stratagem* 822.2

trickster *deceiver* 193.8, *dishonest person* 479.11, *cunning person* 822.3

tricksy *cunning* 822.4

tricky *artful* 193.13, *cunning*

330.8, 822.4, *problematic* 333.12, 824.11, *dangerous* 811.7

tricky business *dishonesty* 479.7

tricky situation *difficult circumstances* 726.6

tricky situation *or* spot *predicament* 824.5

triclinic *status adjectives* 11.25

triclinic crystal *crystal* 11.14

tricolor *variegated thing* 263.5

tricorn *triple thing* 790.3, *three-sided* 790.8

tricorn *or* tricorne *hat* 100.32

tricornered *three-sided* 790.8

tricot Fabrics and Fibers 130

tricotine Fabrics and Fibers 130

tricycle *bicycle* 687.10, *triple thing* 790.3

tridem *sailboard parts* 150.20, *windsurfing* 150.28

trident *fork* 703.5, *triple thing* 790.3, *three-sided* 790.8

tridentate *three-sided* 790.8

trident-like *branched* 703.9

tridimensional *three-sided* 790.8

tried *expert* 127.12, *tested* 335.10

tried and tested *qualified* 340.7

tried and true *certain* 840.7

tried-and-true method *way* 399.10

triennial *plant* 41.2, *of plants* 41.14, *flowering plant* 42.2, *triple thing* 790.3, *three-sided* 790.8

triennially *herbaceously* 41.24

triennium *triple thing* 790.3

trier *experimenter* 335.5, *attempter* 390.3

trifid *trisected* 790.9

trifle 800.3; *cake* 90.36, *court* 299.26, *cheap item* 497.5, *be superficial* 599.6

trifler *capricious person* 381.3, *nonentity* 800.8

trifle with *be capricious* 381.6, *impair* 808.18

trifling *meaningless* 362.7, *little* 580.7, *superficial* 599.4, *trivial* 800.14

trifling fault 800.5

trifocals *visual aid* 242.14

trifold *three* 790.7

trifoliate *of leaves* 41.18, *three-sided* 790.8

triforium *church architecture* 134.11, *passage* 691.5

triforking *branching* 703.4

triform *three* 790.7

trifurcate *branched* 703.9, *branch* 703.14, *trisect* 790.11

trifurcated *branched* 703.9, *trisected* 790.9

trifurcation *branching* 703.4, *trisection* 790.5

trig [Inf] *trigonometry* 6.49

trigamy *type of marriage* 64.3

trigeminal neuralgia *neurological disease* 114.20

Trigger Notable Horses 159

trigger *hand tool* 103.3, *fuel* 106.16, *awaken* 675.9

trigger-happy [Inf] *murderous* 30.18, *combative* 77.32, *reckless* 286.6

trigger off *activate* 771.28

triglyceride *fat* 12.7

triglyph Architectural Elements 134

trigonal *status adjectives* 11.25, *three-sided* 790.8

trigonal crystal *crystal* 11.14

trigonometrical *mathematical* 6.65, 784.9

trigonometrically *mathematically* 6.93, 784.15

trigonometric function 6.50; *mathematical function* 6.27

trigonometry 6.49; Branches of Mathematics 6, *angular measurement* 628.4, *calculation* 784.1

trihedral *three-sided* 790.8

trihedron *triple thing* 790.3

triiodothyronine Human Hormones 12

trike [Inf] *bicycle* 687.10

trilateral *angled* 628.9, *three-sided* 790.8

trilingual *speaking* 205.15, *three-sided* 790.8

trill *musical ornament* 140.19, *sing* 141.16, *mode of speech* 205.6, *flow* 570.10, *roll* 682.15

trillion *million* 792.11, *myriad* 795.7

trillions *multitude* 795.1

trillionth *millionth* 792.22

trillium Flowers 42

trilobite *extinct arthropod* 39.7, *thing of the past* 651.8, *prehistoric animal* 653.8

trilogy *play* 136.2, *triple thing* 790.3

trim *clean* 111.17, *health* 113.1, *carpenter* 131.10, *make cheap* 497.14, *appealing* 529.10, *coiffure* 530.8, *coif* 530.15, *ornament* 532.12, *fashionable* 536.5, *contract* 582.12, *shorten* 591.9, *edge* 618.8, *nature* 624.5, *miscellaneous aviation terms* 689.9, *pilot* 689.15, *physical state* 725.6, *change by degrees* 739.8, *make smaller* 747.8, *orderly* 765.13, *make conform* 781.13, *reduce* 796.8

trim *or* cut down to size *make unimportant* 800.20

trimaran *sailboat* 150.3, Sailing Ships and Boats 690, *triple thing* 790.3

trim button *part of garment* 100.27

trim down *become smaller* 582.14

trim down to size *make conform* 781.13

trimester *triple thing* 790.3

trimestrial *three-sided* 790.8

trimeter *meter* 139.10, *triple thing* 790.3

trimetric *three-sided* 790.8

trimly *dashingly* 536.10

trimmed *cleaned* 111.14, *joined* 131.8, *decorated* 532.9, *ornate* 532.10, *shortened* 582.8, 591.7

trimmed joist *carpenter's term* 131.5

trimmer *garden tool* 103.4, *contractor* 582.6

trimming *carpenter's term* 131.5, *ornament* 532.7, *shortening* 582.2, 591.2, *edging* 618.2

trimmings *ornamentation* 748.5, *residue* 750.2

trimness *appeal* 529.4

trimorphic *three* 790.7

trimorphism *threeness* 790.2

trim size *design and makeup* 174.8

Trimurti *trinitarian god* 82.7

trinal *three* 790.7

trinary *three* 790.7

trine *angular measurement* 628.4, *three* 790.7

trinely *thrice* 790.12

Trinidad Islands 572

Trinidad and Tobago Countries 566

Trinitarian Christian 81.10

trinitarian god 82.7

trinitarianism Christianity 81.5

trinitrotoluene (TNT) *explosive* 78.13, *agent of destruction* 523.7

trinity *three* 790.1

Trinity Sunday Christian Holy Days and Seasons 85

Trinitytide Christian Holy Days and Seasons 85

trinket *cheap item* 497.5, *decorative article* 532.5, *cheap thing* 800.7

Trinkgeld [Ger] *gift* 472.2

trinomial *functional* 6.73, *triple thing* 790.3

trio *instrumental group* 141.3, *three* 790.1, *team* 827.7

triode *electron tube* 14.40

triolet Poem or Verse Forms 139

triose *saccharide* 12.4

trioxygen Chemical Elements and Common Allotropes 11

trip 714.16; Collective Names 59, *be clumsy* 128.9, *dance* 135.7, *play basketball* 148.7, *play field hockey* 158.10, *soccer play* 163.5, *play soccer* 163.8, *misjudge* 342.9, *sin* 430.22, *walk* 677.17, *travel* 686.5, *passing* 692.3, *fall* 714.4, *lowering* 716.1, *lean* 716.19, *block* 826.17

trip [Inf] *drug use* 121.9

triparted *trisected* 790.9

tripartite *trisected* 790.9

tripartition *trisection* 790.5

tripe *variety meat* 90.30

tripe [Inf] *senseless talk* 362.4

tripedal *three-sided* 790.8

tripe-de-roche *lichen* 47.16

tripeptide *amino acid* 12.8

triphibious war *war* 76.1

triphthong *triple thing* 790.3

Tripitaka *other text* 81.19

triple 790.10; *batting terms* 147.6, *play baseball* 147.9, *bowling delivery* 151.2, *make bigger* 746.7, *three* 790.1, 790.7

Triple-A league *baseball leagues and championship games* 147.8

triple axel *ice-skating techniques* 162.16

triple bond *chemical bond* 11.6

triple cream *fat* 562.4

Triple Crown *famous horse races* 159.13

triple crown *vestment* 84.11, *successful thing* 845.5

triple-decker *layered* 588.6

triple dresser *cabinet* 101.8

triple integral *differentiation* 6.29

triple jump *or* **jumping** Sporting Activities 145, *jumping* 166.11

triple meter *meter* 139.10

tripleness *threeness* 790.2

triple play *other game terms* 147.7

triple point *temperature* 10.29, *thermodynamics* 10.30, *phase* 11.13

triples *bowls* 151.7

triples match *or* **triples** *green bowling* 151.3

triple somersault *competitive diving* 164.7

triplet *part of poem* 139.9, *triple thing* 790.3

triple thing 790.3

triple-tongue *sound* 141.15

triple vaccine *prophylaxis* 115.4

triplex *three* 790.7

triplicate *three* 790.7, *triple* 790.10

triplicating *triplication* 790.4

triplication 790.4; *increase* 746.1

triplicity *threeness* 790.2

tripling *triplication* 790.4

triploid *plant breeding* 17.6

triply *thrice* 790.12

tripod *camera* 132.10, *means of*

---

prediction 358.10, *supporting structure* 605.2, *triple thing* 790.3

tripodic *three-sided* 790.8

Tripoli Countries 566

trip out [Inf] *drug oneself* 121.37

trip over *be clumsy* 128.9

tripped *soccer* 163.7

tripping *violations* 148.5, *ice hockey tactics* 158.4, *field hockey tactics* 158.5, *soccer play* 163.5, *soccer* 163.7, *active* 414.13, *fluid* 527.5, *falling* 714.11, *fallen* 716.8

trippingly *dancingly* 135.8

trip switch *stopper* 584.3

trip the light fantastic *dance* 135.7

trip to the moon *space travel* 7.29

triptych *painting* 143.3, *triple thing* 790.3

trip up *block* 826.17

trip wire *military defenses* 419.9

trireme *historical warships* 77.22, *triple thing* 790.3

trisaccharide *saccharide* 12.4

trisect 790.11; *align* 6.92

trisected 790.9

trisection 790.5

trishaw *bicycle* 687.10

triskaidekaphobia Phobias 283

Tristan Famous Lovers 299

Tristan da Cunha Islands Islands 572

tristich *part of poem* 139.9, *triple thing* 790.3

tritanopia *faulty vision* 243.1

tritanopic *visually impaired* 243.9

tritate *react* 11.38

trite *proverbial* 177.2, *tasteless* 220.4, *boring* 296.6, *meaningless* 362.7, *familiar* 397.10, *common* 778.13, *monotonous* 797.12

trite expression *generalization* 778.5

tritely *boringly* 296.10

triteness *dilution* 220.2, *boringness* 296.2, *nonsense* 362.2

triterpene *terpene* 12.20

triticale *crop* 16.8

Triton Planets and Their Satellites 7, *legendary sea being* 571.4

triturable *pulverizable* 553.21

triturate *pulverize* 553.26

triturated *pulverized* 553.20

trituration *pulverization* 553.4

triturator *pulverizer* 553.11

triumph *rejoicing* 279.1, *rejoice* 279.5, *ceremony* 405.3, *be superior* 744.15, *success* 845.1, *victory* 845.4, *be victorious* 845.16

triumphal *celebrative* 405.9, *victorious* 845.10

triumphal procession *glory of war* 76.17

triumphant *rejoicing* 279.4, *unbeatable* 744.13, *victorious* 845.10

triumphantly *rejoicingly* 279.7, *superiorly* 744.20, *victoriously* 845.20

triumph of justice *vindication* 441.1

triumvirate *oligarchy* 49.10, *triple thing* 790.3, *team* 827.7

triune *three* 790.7

trivalent *chemical compound* 11.4

trivet *cooking equipment* 91.6, *triple thing* 790.3

trivia *trifle* 800.3

trivial 800.14; *insignificant* 289.10, *meaningless* 362.7, *little* 580.7, *superficial* 599.4, *extraneous* 724.8

trivial error 351.8

triviality 800.2; *insignificance*

289.4, *superficiality* 599.2, *extraneousness* 724.1, *trifle* 800.3

trivialize *scorn* 436.19, *be superficial* 599.6, *make unimportant* 800.20

trivialized *disrespected* 436.16

trivially *unexceptionally* 289.20, *superficially* 599.8, *extraneously* 724.16, *unimportantly* 800.21

Trivial Pursuit ™ Board and Table Games 167

trivia quiz *easy question* 333.5

trochaic *metrical* 139.20

troche *dose of medicine* 115.3

trochee *meter* 139.10

trochoid *curve* 6.38

trochophore *invertebrate larva* 39.19

trodden *familiar* 397.10, *leveled* 603.8, *accessible* 691.13

troglodyte *unsocial person* 409.5

troika *snow vehicle* 687.9, *triple thing* 790.3, *team* 827.7

Troilus Famous Lovers 299

Trojan *hard worker* 414.11

Trojan horse *computing terms* 15.22, *stratagem* 822.2

troll *sprite* 86.12, *fish* 154.14, Legendary Creatures 360, *roll* 682.15, *drag* 699.11

trolled *fishing* 154.13

trolley *cart* 578.9, *means of transportation* 686.2, *railroad system* 688.1

trolley car *railroad system* 688.1

trolley line *railroad system* 688.1

trolling *fishing* 154.1, 154.13, *turning* 682.3, *rotating* 682.11

tromba Musical Instruments 142

tromba marina Musical Instruments 142

trombone Musical Instruments 142

trombonist *player* 141.2

trompe l'oeil *treatment* 143.6, *fantasy* 360.5, *delusion* 720.3

troop *assemblage of mammals* 35.22, *military organization* 58.4, Collective Names 59, *force* 59.10, *crowd* 59.26, 795.11, *army unit* 77.14, *throng* 795.4

troop carrier *military aircraft* 77.30

trooper *soldier* 77.4, *horse person* 159.14

troopship *warship* 77.21, Ships and Boats 690

trope *phrasing* 5.25, *literary device* 139.12, *type of meaning* 361.4, *ornament* 532.7, *latency* 844.1

trophy *honor* 72.3, *insignia* 184.5, *monument* 185.10, *object of desire* 288.8, *memento* 354.3, *objective* 374.5, *prize competition* 422.5, *prize* 453.2, *windfall* 467.7, *reward* 472.4, *something received* 473.2

tropic *mysterious* 844.11

tropical *ornamental* 17.17, *warm* 217.13, *regional* 564.12, *mysterious* 844.11

tropical air *atmosphere* 9.8

tropical climate *climate* 9.35

tropical disease 114.10; *disease* 114.4

tropical fern *fern* 46.1

tropical fish *fish* 38.5

tropical forest *trees* 43.4

tropical hardwood *tree* 43.1

tropical heat *hot weather* 217.6

tropically *horticulturally* 17.20, *regionally* 564.16

tropical meaning *type of meaning* 361.4

---

tropical medicine *medicine* 107.1

tropical storm *wind vortex* 9.14

tropical summer rainy zone *climate zone* 9.36

tropics *climate zone* 9.36, *hot place* 217.5, *world region* 564.6

tropology *science of interpretation* 365.5

tropopause *atmosphere* 9.8, *atmospheric layer* 558.3

tropophobia Phobias 283

troposphere *atmosphere* 9.8, *atmospheric layer* 558.3

tropospheric *atmospheric* 9.40, 558.13

trot *ride* 159.16, *bodily movement* 677.11, *slow motion* 693.3, *be swift* 694.10

trot [Inf] *translation* 365.4

trot along *depart* 705.8

trot out *harp* 797.17

trot out [Inf] *reveal* 843.14

trots, the [Inf] *defecation* 25.3, *gastroenterological disease* 114.11

Trotskyite *or* **Trotskyist** *rebel* 427.8

trotter *racehorse* 159.2

trotters *variety meat* 90.30

trotting Sporting Activities 145, *fishing* 154.1, *horse racing* 159.10

troubadour *entertainer* 138.8, *author* 139.13, *singer* 141.4

troubadour poem Poem or Verse Forms 139

trouble *adversity* 117.2, 848.1, *exertion* 122.4, *annoyance* 276.2, 804.2, *misfortune* 301.6, *meddle* 414.23, *agitate* 684.22, *predicament* 725.3, *difficult circumstances* 726.6, *disruption* 766.7, *commotion* 768.5, *disturb* 768.10, *annoy* 804.10, *cause difficulties* 824.22, *obstacle* 826.2, *cause adversity* 848.15

trouble ahead *threat* 848.3

trouble and strife [Brit inf] *married woman* 64.11

troubled 824.15; *miserable* 117.12, *worried* 283.11, *agitated* 684.15, *disturbed* 768.6

trouble-free *easygoing* 823.13

troublemaker 427.5; *hostile person* 63.5, *unpleasant person* 272.5, *meddler* 414.12, *miscreant* 448.6, *dissenter* 463.5, *protester* 507.4, *motivator* 508.6, *cunning person* 822.3, *hinderer* 826.11

trouble oneself *exert oneself* 122.11

troubles *adversity* 848.1

troubleshooter *mediator* 75.2, *agent* 123.15, *adviser* 176.5, 825.14

troubleshooting *mediation* 75.1

troublesome 824.13; *laborious* 122.7, *meddling* 414.17, *villainous* 448.12, *difficult* 726.11, *annoying* 804.7, *inconvenient* 824.12, *adverse* 848.10

troublesomeness *awkwardness* 804.3

trouble spot *infection* 114.7

troubling *conditional* 725.7, *problematic* 824.11, *inconvenient* 824.12

troublous *agitated* 684.15

troublously *agitatedly* 684.27

trough *farm tool* 16.5, *wave* 571.3, 683.4, *basin* 578.12, *concave land* 635.2, *cavity* 635.3, *furrow* 638.1, 638.5, *inferior state* 745.3

trough *or* **trough of low pressure** *weather system* 9.10

trounce *hit* 454.28, *ruin* 523.15,

---

beat 695.12, *be superior* 744.15, *defeat* 845.17

trounced *outclassed* 745.9

trouncing *corporal punishment* 454.11, *ramming* 695.3, *victory* 845.4, *defeat* 846.7

troupe *team* 59.9, *cast* 136.26

trouper *actor* 136.25

trouser press *smoother* 545.2

trousers *pants* 100.14

trousseau *clothing* 100.1, *reserve* 105.3

trout Collective Names 59, *food fish and shellfish* 90.20, *game fish* 154.10

trout farm *farm* 16.2

trouvère *author* 139.13

trove *windfall* 467.7

trowel *garden tool* 17.7, 103.4, *smoother* 545.2, *sharp-edged thing* 549.6, *use a sharp tool* 549.17, *ladle* 578.17

troy weight *weight measurement* 538.6, *measuring system* 589.4, *type of measurement* 589.8

truancy *disappearance* 265.1, *desertion* 386.7, *absenteeism* 576.3, *escape* 816.1

truant 576.10; *avoider* 386.8, *run away* 386.21, *nonperforming* 466.6, *refuser* 506.4, *absentee* 576.5, *escaper* 816.5, *escaping* 816.7

truantism *absenteeism* 576.3

truant officer *educator* 48.4

truce 73.2; *treaty* 74.2, *delay* 658.3, *pause* 668.3, *lack of motion* 678.1, *deliverance* 817.1

truceless war *warfare* 76.3

truck 578.10, 687.8; *flag* 184.8, *trade* 480.1, 480.18, *exchange* 673.1, 673.5, *convey* 685.9, *means of transportation* 686.2, *transportable* 686.7, *road vehicle* 687.4

truckage *conveyance* 685.2

truckdriver *transferrer* 685.4, *transporter* 686.4

trucker *transferrer* 685.4, *transporter* 686.4

truck farm *farm* 16.2, *garden* 17.18

truck farm *or* **garden** *garden* 17.2

truck farmer *agriculturist* 16.14, *horticulturist* 17.13

truck farming *arable farming* 16.6, *horticulture* 17.1

truck gardener *horticulturist* 17.13

truck gardening *horticulture* 17.1

trucking *road transportation* 687.1

truckle *type of bed* 101.9, *fawn* 401.9

truckling *sycophancy* 401.2, *sycophantic* 401.7

truckload *load* 577.5, *container(ful)* 738.2

truculence *cruelty* 306.4, *bad manners* 411.2

truculent *cruel* 306.10, *bad-mannered* 411.6, *aggressive* 418.12

truculently *cruelly* 306.17

trudge *slow motion* 693.3, *move slowly* 693.11

true 721.11; *factual* 3.14, *logical* 6.83, *legitimate* 52.10, 53.21, *intimate* 62.7, *truthful* 191.4, *known* 348.9, *loyal* 426.5, *correct* 429.8, 721.13, *observant* 465.3, *intrinsic* 611.11, *straight* 630.8, *real* 717.14, 719.6, *adjust* 721.23, *truly* 721.27, *authentic* 737.6, *naive* 821.3, *certain* 840.7

true, the *truth* 721.1

true *or* **magnetic bearing** *or* **heading** *or* **course** *bearing* 697.2

true believer *believer* 87.5

true bill *pretrial proceedings* 54.13, *accusation* 442.1

true-blue *truthful* 191.4, *loyal* 426.5, *naive* 821.3

trueborn *authentic* 721.16

trued *adjusted* 721.14

true fern *fern* 46.1

true fruit *botanical fruit* 44.2

true fungi *fungi* 47.3

true grit *steadfastness* 284.3, *stamina* 377.4

truehearted *truthful* 191.4

trueheartedness *truthfulness* 191.1

trueing *adjustment* 721.5

true inlay *decorative woodwork* 131.2

true-life *lifelike* 721.19

truelove *loved one* 299.13

true love Collective Names 59, *romantic love* 299.2

truelove *or* **true lover's knot** Knots, Bends, Hitches, Splices 754

true moss *moss* 46.4

trueness 721.4; *legal power* 52.2, *intimacy* 62.4, *truthfulness* 191.1, *right* 429.2, *truth* 721.1, *certainty* 840.1

true north *compass direction* 697.5

true picture *representation* 202.9

true portrayal *verisimilitude* 721.10

true to fact *literal* 721.18

true to form *characteristic* 779.12

true to life *representational* 187.8, *descriptive* 202.11, *correct* 350.4, *realistic* 719.7, *lifelike* 721.19

true to nature *lifelike* 721.19

true to the bitter end *enduring* 377.9

true to the facts *literal* 721.18

true to the letter *correct* 350.4, *literal* 721.18

true up *adjust* 721.23

true wind *sailing terms* 150.5

truffle hunter *study of fungi* 47.9

trug *garden tool* 17.7, *basket* 578.6

truing *adjustment* 721.5

truism 721.6; *maxim* 177.1, *nonsense* 362.2

truistic 721.15

Truk Islands Islands 572

truly 721.27; *biographically* 3.18, *legitimately* 52.19, *intimately* 62.14, *assuredly* 189.30, *truthfully* 191.9, *earnestly* 278.10, *correctly* 429.16, 721.29, *observantly* 465.6, *really* 717.22, *certainly* 719.14, 840.15

trumeau Architectural Elements 134

trump *means* 102.1, *overtake* 744.16, *overpower* 845.18

trump card *means* 102.1, *expedient* 387.5, *gist* 799.4

trumped-up *fabricated* 192.17, *perjurious* 442.7

trumped-up charge *false accusation* 442.2

trumped-up story *falsehood* 192.6

trumpery *empty talk* 362.5, *cheap thing* 800.7, *cheap* 800.16

trumpet *glory of war* 76.17, *sound* 141.15, Musical Instruments 142, *proclaim* 173.16, *speak in a particular way* 205.18, *be loud* 232.8, *source of resonance* 236.4, *make an animal sound* 240.7, *flourish* 404.25, *praise* 437.16, *cone* 633.5

trumpet blast *burst of sound* 232.4

trumpet call *exhortation* 178.2, *military call* 183.9, *warning signal* 814.3

trumpet creeper Flowers 42

trumpeter *player* 141.2

trumpet fanfare *ceremonial* 404.11

trumpet flower Flowers 42

trumpet-tongued *shouting* 232.7

trump hand *advantage* 744.3

trump suit *or* **trumps** *bridge* 168.4

trump up *lie* 192.23

trump up a charge *accuse falsely* 442.9

truncate *add* 6.86, *be concise* 198.5, *summarize* 204.7, *shorten* 591.9, *not complete* 762.9

truncated *concise* 198.4, *summarized* 204.6, *shortened* 591.7, 762.6, *uncompleted* 762.7

truncated cone *curved surface* 6.43

truncated decimal *division* 6.16

truncated pyramid *polyhedron* 6.44

truncation *division* 6.16, *conciseness* 198.1, *outline* 204.2, *shortening* 591.2

truncheon *blunt weapon* 78.5

trundle *type of bed* 101.9, *maneuver* 677.16, *roll* 682.15, *propel* 696.15

trundling *turning* 682.3

trunk *stem* 41.5, *tree part* 43.2, *receptacle* 105.11, *baggage* 578.8, *cylinder* 633.4, *protuberance* 634.3, *remainder* 750.1, *component* 760.3

trunk line *telephone* 169.10

trunk road *road* 687.2

trunks *beachwear* 100.23, *swimming equipment* 164.8

trunk sale *bazaar* 483.10

truss *group* 59.24, *carpenter's term* 131.5, *carpenter* 131.10, Architectural Elements 134, *superstructure* 551.7, *unite closely* 752.16, *intertwine* 752.19

truss bridge *bridge* 551.10

trussed *grouped* 59.21

trussing needle *cooking equipment* 91.6

trust *believing* 87.2, *believe* 87.9, *expectation* 281.2, 356.1, *expect* 281.12, *line of duty* 433.3, *alliance* 459.5, *association* 480.8, *repute* 487.7, *limit* 620.1, *transferred thing* 685.6, *be naive* 821.4, *authority* 833.3, *conviction* 840.2

trust deed *purchase contract* 459.3

trustee *educator* 48.4, *prisoner* 55.7, *educational leader* 68.11, *agent* 80.3, *recipient* 473.5, *treasurer* 484.18, *commissioner* 833.5

trusteeship *council* 833.4

truster *believer* 87.5

trustful *intimate* 62.7, *believing* 87.6

trustfully *intimately* 62.14, *believingly* 87.12

trusting *believing* 87.6, *incurious* 322.3, *naive* 821.3, *convinced* 840.8

trustingly *incuriously* 322.6

trust in God *religiousness* 81.2, *revere* 81.26

trusting person *believer* 87.5

trust with *commission* 833.8

trustworthiness *believability* 87.4, *truthfulness* 191.1, *morals* 431.2, *virtues* 447.2, *honesty* 630.4, *infallibility* 840.6

trustworthy 810.17; *intimate* 62.7, *believable* 87.7, *truthful*

191.4, *moral* 431.9, *honest* 630.11, *infallible* 840.12

trusty *prisoner* 55.7, *intimate* 62.7

truth 721.1; *historicalness* 3.9, *mathematical logic* 6.60, *reasoning* 6.61, *divine attribute* 82.4, *maxim* 177.1, *openness* 180.3, *correctness* 350.2, *rightfulness* 429.1, *defense* 441.2, *naturalness* 526.4, *demonstrable existence* 717.5, *naiveté* 821.1, *certainty* 840.1

truth, the 721.3

truth condition *philosophical term* 4.7

truthful 191.4; *correct* 350.4, *right* 429.7, *honest* 630.11, *realistic* 719.7, *literal* 721.18, *naive* 821.3

truthfully 191.9; *assuredly* 189.30, *right* 429.15, *naturally* 526.16, *honestly* 630.18, *literally* 721.32

truthfulness 191.1; *naturalness* 526.4, *honesty* 630.4, *literalness* 721.9

truth function *philosophical term* 4.7

truth of the matter *fact* 717.6

truth table *philosophical term* 4.7, *mathematical logic* 6.60

truth value *philosophical term* 4.7, *mathematical logic* 6.60

try 414.21; *litigate* 54.27, *exert oneself* 122.11, *taste* 219.5, *question* 333.16, *experiment* 335.1, 335.11, *invent* 335.13, *judge* 341.10, *conjecture* 359.3, *attempt* 390.1, 390.6, *undertaking* 391.1, *undertake* 391.7, *use* 393.9, *do something* 412.13, *contend* 422.22, *accuse* 442.8, *production* 522.1

try a case 54.28; *judge* 54.31

try a fall *contend* 422.22

try and try again *persevere* 377.10, *try hard* 390.7, *contend* 422.22

try conclusions with *contend* 422.22

try for *aim* 374.10

try for a miracle *attempt the impossible* 837.10

try hard 390.7; *try* 414.21

trying *unpleasant* 272.6, *rehearsal* 335.2, *experimental* 335.8, *attempting* 390.4, *inconvenient* 824.12

trying hard *committed* 377.7

try on *wear* 100.46

try one's best *exert oneself* 122.11

try one's hand *invent* 335.13

try one's hand at *attempt* 390.6

try one's luck *invent* 335.13, *tackle* 390.8, *take a chance* 843.14

try one's patience *cause trouble* 824.21

try one's strength *invent* 335.13

tryout *audition* 228.6, *rehearsal* 335.2

try out *be heard* 228.15, *experiment* 335.11, *rehearse* 335.12, *use* 393.9

trypanophobia Phobias 283

trypanosome *parasite* 39.18

trypanosomiasis *tropical disease* 114.10

trypsin *enzyme* 12.11

tryptophan Amino Acids 12

trysail *sailboat parts and accessories* 150.4

try something new *be trendy* 652.18

try square *measuring instrument* 589.2, *plumb line* 602.4

tryst *social gathering* 408.4

try the latest craze *be trendy* 652.18

try to put a square peg in a round hole *figurative expressions* 128.11

try to say *mean* 361.13

Tsana *Lakes* 568

tsar *sovereign* 68.2

tsarina *sovereign* 68.2

Tsigai *Breeds of Sheep* 16

T-shape *angle* 628.1

T-shirt *informal clothes* 100.7, *shirt* 100.13, *underwear* 100.6

Tsigai *Breeds of Sheep* 16

T square *plumb line* 602.4

T-square *geometric construction* 6.47, *measuring instrument* 589.12, *angular measurement* 628.4

tsunami *or* **seismic sea wave** *wave* 8.16, 10.11, 571.3, *natural violence* 520.3, *rough thing* 544.2

Tswana *Breeds of Cattle* 16

t-test *hypothesis testing* 6.52

Tuamotu Archipelago *Islands* 572

Tuareg *Breeds of Cattle* 16, *Breeds of Sheep* 16

tuatara *lizard* 37.5

tub *bath* 111.6, *darkroom equipment* 132.21, *basin* 578.12

tub [Inf] *big person* 579.10

tuba *Musical Instruments* 142

tubal ligation *prophylaxis* 115.4

tubbiness *fatness* 579.5, *thickness* 594.1, *round body* 633.2

tubby *fat* 579.15, *thick* 594.5, *well-rounded* 633.8

tube *source of resonance* 236.4, *narrow place* 593.2, *cylinder* 633.4

tube [Brit] *railroad system* 688.1

tube dress *dress* 100.11

tube pan *cooking equipment* 91.6

tuber *garden plant* 17.10, *vegetable* 17.11, 90.33, *stem* 41.5, *root* 41.7

tubercular *of disease* 114.25

tuberculophobia *Phobias* 283

tuberculosis *respiratory disease* 114.12, *Phobias* 283

tuberculous *of disease* 114.25

tuberose *Flowers* 42

tuberous *of plants* 41.14

tuberous root *root* 41.7

tuberous-rooted *of roots* 41.19

tubers *fruits* 44.1

tube socks *legwear* 100.26

tube top *shirt* 100.13

tube tying *that which makes infertile* 23.4

tub-thump *speak to* 205.19, *address* 209.8

tub-thumper *speaker* 205.12, *public speaker* 209.5, *protester* 507.4

tub-thumping *public speaking* 205.11, *articulate* 205.16, *addressing* 209.6

tubular *round* 633.7

tubular bells *Musical Instruments* 142

tubulidentate *insect-eating mammal* 35.7, *insectivorous* 35.24

Tucana *Constellations* 7

Tuche *Deities* 82

tuck *skiing techniques* 162.5, *competitive diving* 164.7, *contract* 582.12, *pleat* 637.2, 637.8

tuck [Brit inf] *food* 90.1

tuck [Arch] *sharp weapon* 78.6

tucked *snowplow* 162.29, *shortened* 582.8

tucked away *concealed* 844.7, *neckwear* 100.29

tucker [Aus inf] *food* 90.1

tuckered out [Inf] *fatigued* 820.2

Tucker porcelain *Ceramics* 129

tucket *ringing* 236.2

tuck float *swimming techniques* 164.2

tuck in *be on the track* 146.11

tucking *snowplow* 162.29

tucking in *automobile racing terms* 146.3

tuck into *eat well* 92.23, *be greedy* 119.4

tuck jump *diving* 164.6

tuck surface dive *diving* 164.6

tuck up *pleat* 637.8

Tudanca *Breeds of Cattle* 16

Tudor *Furniture Styles* 101, *historic* 653.13

Tudor architecture *Architectural Styles* 134

tuft *grassland* 45.2

tug *exertion* 122.4, *work* 122.8, *type of touch* 216.3, *touch* 216.9, *set in motion* 677.16, *impel* 695.9, *pull* 699.2, 699.10, *drag* 699.11, *pull at* 699.12, *attraction* 700.1, *attract* 700.11, *extraction* 711.1

tugboat *towline* 699.5

tugboat *or* **tug** *Ships and Boats* 690

tugging *traction* 699.1, *tractional* 699.7, *attracting* 700.8

tugging out *extraction* 711.1

tug of war *Sporting Activities* 145, *Children's and Party Games* 167, *sporting event* 422.6, *pull* 699.2

tug one's forelock *show respect* 435.16

tug out *extract* 711.13

tuition *education* 48.1

Tuj *Breeds of Sheep* 16

Tuli *Breeds of Cattle* 16

tulip *Flowers* 42

tulip tree *Trees and Shrubs* 43

tulip ware *Ceramics* 129

tulle *Fabrics and Fibers* 130

tumble *exercise* 157.12, *be destroyed* 523.17, *be brittle* 548.4, *stagger* 684.11, *fall* 714.4, *trip* 714.16, *lowering* 716.1, *be in danger* 811.11

tumbledown *dilapidated* 517.7, *destroyed* 523.9, *brittle* 548.3, *disintegrating* 758.5, *decrepit* 808.12, *unsafe* 811.8

tumble down *be destroyed* 523.17

tumbledown shack *shack* 60.10

tumble-dry *clean* 111.17, *dry* 560.17

tumbler *drink container* 93.13, *circus performer* 138.9, *gymnast* 157.10, *drinking vessel* 578.13

tumble to [Inf] *understand* 363.9

tumbling *Sporting Activities* 145, *gymnastics* 157.1, *floor exercise* 157.4, *gymnastic* 157.11, *descending* 714.9, *falling* 714.11, *fallen* 716.8

tumefaction *swelling* 581.2

tumescence *swelling* 581.2, *convexity* 634.1

tumescent *growing* 581.12, *convex* 634.5

tumid *swelled* 581.10

tumidity *swelling* 581.2

tumidly *largely* 581.18

tumidness *swelling* 581.2

tumify *grow* 581.17

tummy ache [Inf] *painful injury* 215.3

tummy tuck [Inf] *cosmetic surgery* 530.2

tumor *cancer* 114.15, *enlargement* 581.7, *bulge* 634.2

tumult 232.5, 684.2; *dissonance* 241.1, *activity* 414.1, *violation of the law* 427.2, *violence by person*

520.2, *confusion* 766.4, *commotion* 768.5

tumultuous *disobedient* 427.10, *explosive* 520.6

tumultuously *disobediently* 427.14

tumulus *burial place* 31.7, *hill* 569.2

tun *vessel* 578.11

tuna *food fish and shellfish* 90.20, *game fish* 143.10

tunable laser *laser (light amplification by stimulated emission of radiation)* 10.18

tundra *climate zone* 9.36

tundra climate *climate* 9.35

tune 172.14; *melody* 140.10, *harmonize* 140.28, *play an instrument* 142.9, *prepare for action* 388.18, *harmonization* 735.2, *counterbalance* 743.8

tune a ski *ski* 162.35

tuned *harmonic* 140.27, *instrumental* 142.8, *prepared* 388.9, *counterbalanced* 743.6

tuned circuit *circuit* 14.37

tuneful *musical* 140.25, *melodious* 140.26

tunefully 140.30

tunefulness *music* 140.1

tune in *hear* 228.13

tuneless *unmelodious* 241.5

tunelessly *dissonantly* 241.7

tunelessness *musical dissonance* 241.2

tuneless voice *speech difficulty* 206.1

tune out *fail to hear* 229.9

tuner *radio reception* 172.2

tune-up *repair* 809.1

tune up *prepare for action* 388.18, *repair* 809.10

Tungabhadra *Rivers* 570

tung oil *Tree Products* 43

tungsten *Chemical Elements and Common Allotropes* 11

tungsten lighting *lighting* 132.16

Tung-t'ing *Lakes* 568

Tunguska *Rivers* 570

Tung-Yang *Breeds of Sheep* 16

tunic *jacket* 100.18, *robe* 100.20

tunicate *protochordate* 39.4

tunicle *vestment* 84.11

tuning *preparation* 388.1, *counterbalance* 743.2, *repair* 809.1

tuning fork *diagnostic instrument* 107.13, *instrumental aid* 142.7

tuning peg *part of stringed instrument* 142.2

Tunis *Breeds of Cattle* 16, *Breeds of Sheep* 16, *Countries* 566

Tunisia *Countries* 566

Tunisian Barbary *Breeds of Sheep* 16

tunnel 551.11, 691.6; *engineer* 14.48, *natural habitat* 60.16, *vault* 134.8, *source of resonance* 236.4, *hole* 583.17, *narrow place* 593.2, *deepen* 598.21, *concave land* 635.2, *make concave* 635.7, *crossing point* 692.7

tunneled *holed* 583.12

tunneler *digger* 635.4

tunneling *deepening* 598.4

tunnel kiln *ceramic workshop and tools* 129.8

tunnel out *be liberated* 831.7

tunnel vision *sight defect* 243.2, *prejudice* 337.3, *unfair treatment* 342.4

tup [Brit] *livestock* 16.11

tupelo *Trees and Shrubs* 43

tuppence [Brit] *twosome* 789.3

Tupungato *Mountains and Hills* 569

tuque [Can] *cap* 100.33

tu quoque [L] *defense* 441.2, *reciprocity* 729.1

turban *vestment* 84.11, *headdress* 100.35

turbid *dirty* 112.7, *shady* 250.4, *sludgy* 561.18

turbidity *dirtiness* 112.1, *opaqueness* 250.1, *muddiness* 561.10, *turbulence* 684.3

turbidness *muddiness* 561.10

turbinate *convolutional* 632.4

turbination *coil* 632.2, *rotation* 682.1

turbine *engine type* 14.11, *electricity* 106.5, *power supplier* 514.14, *rotator* 682.8, *propeller* 696.8

turbine type 14.12

turbo *propeller* 696.8

turbocharger *racing automobile* 146.2, *power supplier* 514.14

turbofan *means of propulsion* 696.2

turbojet *engine type* 14.11, *flyable* 689.12, *means of propulsion* 696.2

turboprop *engine type* 14.11, *means of propulsion* 696.2

turbosupercharger *power supplier* 514.14

turbot *food fish and shellfish* 90.20

turbulence 684.3; *frequency* 10.6, *violence* 520.1, *roughness* 544.1, *miscellaneous aviation terms* 689.9, *confusion* 766.4

turbulent 684.17; *bumpy* 544.8, *oceanic* 571.7, *disorderly* 766.15

turbulently *roughly* 544.13

turbulent sea *wave* 571.3

Turcana *Breeds of Sheep* 16

turd [Inf] *feces* 25.5

turdine *avian* 36.19

tureen *crockery* 578.12

turf *garden plant* 17.10, *grassland* 45.2, *manage grassland* 45.10, *fuels* 106.2, *racetrack* 159.12, *green place* 260.2, *particle* 760.4

turf [Inf] *sphere of influence* 512.7, *plot* 564.9, *location* 565.1

turf, the *horse racing* 159.10

Turfan Depression *Deserts* 572

turf horse *racehorse* 159.2

turfy *grassy* 45.8, *compressible* 543.9

turgescence *swelling* 581.2

turgescent *growing* 581.12

turgid *diffuse* 199.3, *pompous* 404.18, *inelegant* 528.6, *swelled* 581.10

turgidity *pomposity* 404.5, *inelegance of expression* 528.4, *swelling* 581.2

turgidly *diffusely* 199.7, *pompously* 404.33, *largely* 581.18

turgidness *swelling* 581.2

Turino *Breeds of Cattle* 16

turista *defecation* 25.3

Turkana *Lakes* 568

Turken *Breeds of Fowl* 16

Turkey *Countries* 566

turkey *livestock* 16.11, *table bird* 36.10, *meat* 90.22, *bowling delivery* 151.2, *game* 160.6

turkey [Inf] *theatrical performance* 136.13, *unsuccessful thing* 846.8

turkey cock *male bird* 36.15, *vain person* 407.11

Turkey oak *Trees and Shrubs* 43

Turkey red 257.5

turkeys *Collective Names* 59

Turkish angora *Breeds of Cats* 35

Turkish bath *bath* 111.6

Turkish baths *bath* 111.6

Turkish coffee *coffee* 93.6

Turkish crescent *Musical Instruments* 142

Turkish crescent and star *national emblem* 184.7

Turkish rug *or* **carpet** *floor covering* 613.13

Turkish tobacco *tobacco* 121.23

Turkish van Breeds of Cats 35

Turkmen Fat-rumped Breeds of Sheep 16

Turkmenistan Countries 566

Turkoman Horse and Pony Breeds 159

Turkoman rug *or* **carpet** *floor covering* 613.13

Turk's-cap lily Flowers 42

Turk's-head Knots, Bends, Hitches, Splices 754

turmeric Herbs and Spices 91

turmoil *confusion* 51.2, 766.4, Collective Names 59, *tumult* 232.5, 684.2, *dissonance* 241.1, *activity* 414.1, *violation of the law* 427.4, *havoc* 523.5, *commotion* 768.5

turn *farm* 16.19, Collective Names 59, *recant* 81.27, *aptitude* 127.4, *play part* 136.8, *musical ornament* 140.19, *automobile racing terms* 146.3, *horizontal bar* 157.5, *pommel horse* 157.7, *exercise* 157.12, *ice-dancing move* 162.19, *ski* 162.35, *discus throwing* 166.13, *sour* 223.8, *interpretation* 365.1, *interpret* 365.12, *caprice* 381.1, *conduct oneself* 399.17, *motivate* 412.12, *parry* 419.27, *tendency* 513.1, *fashion* 536.7, *blunt* 550.9, *intervening space* 563.8, *divergence* 607.2, *diverge* 607.11, *nature* 624.5, *form* 624.9, *curve* 629.1, 629.6, *make circular* 631.7, *coil* 632.2, *convolute* 632.6, *round* 633.6, *make round* 633.9, *fold* 637.1, *period of activity* 641.4, *cycle* 663.3, *be cyclic* 663.11, *alteration* 665.2, *change* 665.14, *be changeable* 666.5, *reverse* 671.9, 680.18, *countermotion* 680.6, *orbit* 681.3, 681.8, *reel* 682.4, *rotate* 682.14, *flight maneuver* 689.6, *maneuver* 689.14, *route* 691.2, *aim* 697.14, *deviating course* 698.2, *twist* 698.19, *sequence* 770.1, *consecutiveness* 774.1, *decay* 808.16, *be cunning* 822.5

turn a blind eye *shun* 386.14

turn a blind eye to *be blind to* 243.19, *show mercy* 312.11, *be neglectful* 326.7

turn a blind eye toward *acquiesce* 421.5

turnabout *about-face* 680.4, *revival* 809.3

turn about *reverse* 671.9, *in exchange* 673.6, *turn around* 680.22, 698.25

turn a corner *be on the track* 146.11, *deviate* 698.15

turn a deaf ear *fail to hear* 229.9, *have no mercy* 309.6, *be obstinate* 379.10

turn a deaf ear to *refuse* 506.8

turn against *put off* 179.10, *be converted* 670.12

turn all to gold *be rich* 485.12

turn and turn about *regularly* 663.14, *in exchange* 673.6, *reciprocally* 729.10, *consecutively* 774.15

turn a phrase *be elegant* 527.6

turn a pot *make ceramics* 129.10

turnaround *about-face* 680.4, *revival* 809.3

turn around 680.22, 698.25; *rotate* 682.14

turn a sentence *use language* 5.42

turn aside *shun* 386.14, *diverge* 607.11

turn *or* **move** *or* **draw** *or* **step aside** *or* **to one side** *sidestep* 698.22

turn away *react against* 291.15, *thwart* 293.10, *dissociate* 375.14, *shun* 386.14, *refuse* 506.8, *sidestep* 698.22, *send away* 709.18

turn away from *hate* 300.11

turn back *survive* 419.31, *acquiesce* 421.5, *change* 665.14, *change back* 665.19, *reverse* 671.9, 680.18, *turn around* 698.25, *repel* 701.7, *withdraw* 705.9

turn back the clock *look back* 651.18, *reverse* 671.9

turn back the tide *attempt the impossible* 837.10

turn back time *recollect* 3.16, *look back* 651.18, *attempt the impossible* 837.10

turn backward *or* **backwards** *invert* 608.7, *reverse* 671.9

turn blue *blue* 261.9

turnbuckle *sailboat parts and accessories* 150.4

turncoat *hypocrite* 192.9, *convert* 670.6

turndown *opposition* 375.2, *rejection* 383.1, *refusal* 506.1

turn down *oppose* 375.13, *reject* 383.10, *withhold approval* 438.17, *veto* 503.9, *refuse* 506.8, *ease* 543.15, *make smaller* 747.8

turn down the volume *mute* 233.9

turned *unpalatable* 223.6, *formed* 624.6

turned around *reversed* 680.13

turned aside *divergent* 607.7

turned away *frustrated* 293.9, *refused* 506.5

turned down *rejected* 383.6, *refused* 506.5

turned into *converted* 670.7

turned off *unheard* 229.7

turned-on [Inf] *drugged* 121.30, *pleased* 214.9, *unchaste* 432.10

turned out *dressed* 100.38

turned over *or* **down** *folded* 637.5

turner *artisan* 123.13, *ceramist* 129.7, *woodworker* 131.4

turn every stone *exert oneself* 122.11

turn for the better *improvement* 807.1, *recuperation* 809.4

turn for the worse *deterioration* 808.1

turn from sin *confess* 451.8

turn gray *gray* 255.9

turn green with envy *envy* 314.7

turn ideas into profits *trade* 480.18

turning 682.3; *canoeing* 150.26, *balance beam* 157.3, *snowboarding* 162.30, *capricious* 381.4, *divergent* 607.7, *curved* 629.4, *changeable* 665.11, *changeableness* 666.1, *orbital motion* 681.1, *orbital* 681.5, *orbiting* 681.7, *rotating* 682.11, *indirect* 698.9

turning back *or* **backward** *reversion* 671.1

turning circle *miscellaneous automotive terms* 687.14

turning point *aspect of fiction* 139.5, *critical time* 659.3, *swing* 671.4, *countermotion* 680.6, *critical moment* 726.7, *interval* 739.4, *important matter* 799.2

turning space *available space* 563.6

turning stroke *canoeing techniques* 150.11

turning the lights down *or* **off** *or* **out** *darkening* 247.2

turning up *locating* 565.3

turn inside out *invert* 608.7, *cause change* 665.16

turn into *translate* 365.16, *transform* 670.13, *enter* 706.11

turn into *or* **to** *convert* 670.11

turn inward *invert* 608.7, *keep inside* 611.17

turnips *crop* 16.8

turnip watch Timepieces and Timers 646

turnkey *prison officer* 55.8, *closer* 584.5

turnkey operation *computing terms* 15.22

turn loose *liberate* 831.6

turn of expression *phrasing* 5.25

turn off *stop using* 394.10

turn off [Inf] *make indifferent* 289.13

turn of mind *attitude* 513.2

turn of phrase *phrasing* 5.25

turn of the card *endangerment* 811.2, *potluck* 842.4

turn of the tide *swing* 671.4, *reversal* 680.3

turnon [Inf] *enticement* 178.3, *positive stimulus* 508.5

turn on *activate* 509.11, 771.28, *empower* 514.20, *follow from* 676.9

turn on [Inf] *drug oneself* 121.37, *entice* 178.16, *cause desire* 288.22, *motivate* 508.9

turn on *or* **off** *conduct* 14.51

turn on a dime *turn around* 680.22

turn on a light *light* 246.19

turn one against *cause dislike* 291.16

turn one's back *dissociate* 375.14, *retreat* 386.22, *turn around* 680.22

turn one's back on *be thoughtless* 324.11, *exclude* 383.11, 409.12, *be discourteous* 411.7, *disrespect* 436.18, *refuse* 506.8, *withdraw* 705.9

turn one's back on the world *withdraw* 392.5

turn one's hand to *undertake* 391.7

turn one's stomach *be repulsive* 701.10

turn on one's heel *turn around* 680.22

turn on the gas *give off* 556.25

turn on the heat [Inf] *force* 428.10

turn on the tap *let out* 709.26

turnout *conference* 59.5, *dressing* 100.2, *production* 522.1, *product* 522.3, *railroad* 691.8

turn out *dress up* 100.45, *exclude* 409.12, *greet* 410.11, *perform* 522.16, *replace* 574.17, *take effect* 676.11, *expel* 709.14, *evict* 709.20, *be in a state of* 725.8, *result* 770.2

turn out bag and baggage *evict* 709.20

turn out of doors *evict* 709.20

turn out of house and home *evict* 709.20

turn *or* **go out of one's way** *deviate* 698.15

turn out the guard *salute* 435.17

turn out well *overcome obstacles* 845.14, *be effective* 845.15

turnover *dessert* 90.35, *play* 155.8, *earnings* 467.5, *takings* 477.8

turn over *give* 472.10, *trade* 480.18, *become inverted* 608.8, *transfer* 685.8

turn over *or* **under** *fold* 637.7

turn over a new leaf *confess* 451.8, *become new* 652.19, *change* 665.14, *be converted* 670.12, *begin again* 771.36, *get better* 807.21

turn over one's stock *trade* 480.18, *merchandise* 482.17

turn over to *delegate* 79.6, *commission* 833.8

turn pale *lose color* 252.7

turn pale *or* **white** *be afraid* 283.14

turnpike *road* 687.2, *means of entry* 706.6

turn prohibitionist *give up alcohol* 120.6

turn queen's *or* **king's evidence** *tell on* 180.10

turn red *blush* 403.12

turn signal *indicator* 183.7

turn sour *sour* 223.8, *disappoint* 293.9

turnspit *rotator* 682.8

turn state's evidence *inform on* 170.13, *tell on* 180.10, *testify* 336.10, *give evidence* 339.12

turnstile *means of entry* 706.6, *roadblock* 826.4

turntable *rotator* 682.8, *rail* 688.3, *junction* 691.9

turntable chair *fighting chair* 154.8

turn tail *retreat* 285.8, 386.22, *shy* 386.17, *turn around* 680.22

turn the corner *change for the better* 665.17, *get better* 807.21, *be restored* 809.13

turn the edge *blunt* 550.9

turn the lights down *make dim* 248.8

turn the lights down *or* **off** *or* **out** *make dark* 247.10

turn the other cheek *pacify* 74.9, *show mercy* 312.11

turn the scale *determine* 675.11

turn the scale(s) *change* 512.12

turn the scales *be heavy* 538.12

turn the sound down *or* **off** *muffle* 229.11

turn the tables *invert* 608.7

turn the tables on *cancel out* 834.8

turn thumbs down *withhold approval* 438.17, *veto* 503.9

turn to *resort to* 393.13, *tend* 513.5, *make a beginning* 771.26, *shelter* 812.8

turn to account *exploit* 393.11

turn to ashes *be transient* 643.6

turn to dust *die* 29.17, *demolish* 523.12, *be destroyed* 523.17

turn to God *be converted* 670.12

turn to good account *be good* 445.16, *take the opportunity* 659.7, *find useful* 801.11

turn to nothing *cease to exist* 718.13

turn to profit *profit* 467.22

turn topsy-turvy *make disorderly* 766.20

turn traitor *be converted* 670.12

turn turtle *sail* 690.16

turn up *appear* 244.8, 575.16, *become visible* 264.13, *be discovered* 345.15, *find* 565.11, *shorten* 591.9, *arrive* 704.13, *upturn* 713.20, *be repeated* 797.20, *chance* 842.12

turn up *or* **down** *fold* 637.7

turn up missing *be absent* 576.14

turn up one's nose *grudge* 375.15

turn up one's nose at *react against* 291.15, *disdain* 297.14, *exclude* 383.11, *disapprove* 438.16

turn up one's toes [Inf] *die* 29.17

turn upside down *knock down* 523.13, *invert* 608.7, *cause change* 665.16, *make disorderly* 766.20

turn up the juice *invigorate* 518.5

turn white *age* 27.16

turn wood *work wood* 131.9

Turopolje Breeds of Pigs 16

turpentine Tree Products 43, *material* 143.9

turpentine tree Trees and Shrubs 43

turpitude *depravity* 448.2

turquoise *blue thing* 261.3, *blue* 261.5

turret *fort* 419.13

turret lathe *machine tool* 14.9

turtle 37.7

turtledove *loved one* 299.13

turtledoves Collective Names 59, *lovers* 299.12

turtlelike *reptilian* 37.12

turtleneck sweater *sweater* 100.17

turtles Collective Names 59

Tuscan *column* 134.6

tushie *or* **tush** [Inf] *rear end* 624.4

Tushin Breeds of Sheep 16

tusk *teeth* 19.8, *tooth* 549.7

tusked *toothed* 549.13

tusklike *toothed* 549.13

tusk tenon joint *carpenter's term* 131.5

tussah *or* **tussore** Fabrics and Fibers 130

tussle *contention* 422.1, *contest* 422.4, *fight* 422.9, *contend* 422.22, *dispute* 463.3, 463.9

tussler *fighter* 422.14

tussock *grassland* 45.2

tutelage *education* 48.1, *instructorship* 48.5, *patronage* 810.7, 825.9, *subjection* 832.1

tutelary 810.19; *defending* 419.17, *benefactor* 825.15

tutelary saint *protector* 810.11

tutor *sage* 4.11, *educator* 48.4, *educate* 48.22, *educational leader* 68.11, *master* 68.17, *personal attendant* 69.5, *adviser* 176.5, *preparer* 388.6, *protector* 810.11, *subject* 832.10

tutorage *instructorship* 48.5

tutored *expert* 52.12, *prepared* 388.9

tutorial *subordinate* 832.8

tutoring *education* 48.1

tutorship *instructorship* 48.5

tutti Musical Terms and Expression Marks 140

tutti *loud tone* 232.3, *loudly* 232.11

tut-tut *complain* 507.8

tut-tut at *be dissatisfied* 274.7

tutu *skirt* 100.12

Tuvalu Countries 566, Islands 572

tu-whit tu-whoo *bird sound* 240.2

tux [Inf] *formal clothes* 100.5, *formal clothing* 406.5

tuxedo *formal clothes* 100.5, *formal clothing* 406.5

TV camera *camera* 132.10

TV dinner *meal* 92.8

TV evangelist *religionist* 81.14

TV game *television recording* 172.7

TV program *program* 172.10, *production* 843.5

TV set *television set* 172.6

TV tag Children's and Party Games 167

twaddle *nonsense* 192.8, *talk*

nonsense 192.26, 362.12, *senseless talk* 362.4

twain *two* 789.1

twang *sound* 141.15, *mode of speech* 205.6, *regional pronunciation* 205.7, *hoarseness* 238.2, *sound hoarse* 238.8

twangy *phonetic* 205.14, *strident* 238.4

twat [Inf] *organs of reproduction* 21.9

tweak *inflict pain* 215.10, *type of touch* 216.3, *touch* 216.9, *jerk* 699.3, *pull at* 699.12

Tweed Rivers 570

tweed Fabrics and Fibers 130, *rough thing* 544.2, *coarse* 544.6

tweed coat *coat* 100.19

Tweedledum and Tweedledee *look-alike* 730.4, *twin* 789.5

tweed suit *suit* 100.16

tweedy *coarse* 544.6, *rough* 552.8

tweeny [Brit inf] *domestic servant* 69.7

tweet *bird sound* 240.2, *make a bird sound* 240.8

tweeter *radio reception* 172.2

tweeting *singing* 240.5

tweezers *hand tool* 103.3, *retainer* 471.3, *cosmetic tool* 530.5, *extractor* 711.9

tweezing *hairdressing* 530.7

twelfth *less than one* 787.4, *eleventh and above* 792.18

Twelfth Day Christian Holy Days and Seasons 85, *eleven to nineteen* 792.7

twelfth man *eleven to nineteen* 792.7

Twelfth Night Christian Holy Days and Seasons 85, *eleven to nineteen* 792.7

twelve *eleven to nineteen* 792.7

twelve good men and true *jury* 54.11

twelve just men *jury* 54.11

twelve men in a box *jury* 54.11

twelvemo *little thing* 580.3, *undersized* 580.8

twelvemo (12mo) *eleven to nineteen* 792.7

twelvemonth [Brit] *eleven to nineteen* 792.7

twelve-month [Brit] *time period* 641.2

twelve-note *or* **twelve-tone composition** *musical dissonance* 241.2

twelve-note *or* **twelve-tone scale** *musical dissonance* 241.2

twelve o'clock *noon* 655.4

twelve-o'clock *daily* 655.6

Twelve Tables *the Law* 53.2

twelve-tone *harmonic* 140.27

twelve-toned *unmelodious* 241.5

twelve-tone scale *scale* 140.16

twentieth 792.19; *less than one* 787.4

twenty and over 792.8

twenty-dollar bill *US coinage* 484.10

twenty-five *twenty and over* 792.8

twenty-five cents *US coinage* 484.10

twenty-five percent *quarter* 791.6

twenty-four *twenty and over* 792.8

twenty-one Card Games 168

Twenty Ounce Apple Varieties 44

twenty questions Children's and Party Games 167

twenty somethings *the young* 26.10

twerp [Inf] *nonentity* 800.8

twice 789.18

twice a month *cyclically* 663.15

twice as much *twice* 789.18

twice a week *cyclically* 663.15

twice a year *cyclically* 663.15

twice over *twice* 789.18, *again* 797.23

twice removed *diverging* 698.12

twice-told *iterated* 797.9

twice-told tale *diffuseness* 199.1, *boring thing* 296.3, *repetitiveness* 797.3

twiddle one's thumbs *be bored* 296.7, *have free time* 413.15

twiddling one's thumbs *leisure* 413.4

twig *young plant* 26.5, *stem* 41.5, *tree part* 43.2, *component* 760.3

twigginess *thinness* 595.1

twiggy *thin* 595.9

twilight *darkness* 247.1, *dimness* 248.1, *evening* 656.2, 656.4, *close* 773.9, *deterioration* 808.1

twilight of the gods *end of time* 773.5

twilit *dim* 248.4, *evening* 656.4

twill Fabrics and Fibers 130, *woven* 130.15

twilled *rough* 552.8

twill weave *weaving* 130.6

twin 789.5; *type of bed* 101.9, *image* 187.3, *correspondence* 334.8, *correspondent* 334.16, 606.3, *answer to* 334.22, *look-alike* 730.4, 730.10, *make same* 730.16, *counterpart* 733.5, *equal* 740.7, *double* 789.11, 789.14, *pair* 789.13

twine *interweave* 609.8, *curve* 629.6, *convolute* 632.6, *twist* 698.19, *line* 754.5

twine around *adhere* 755.8

twined *spun* 130.13, *interwoven* 609.6

twiner *plant* 41.2

twinge *pain* 117.5, 215.1

twinge of conscience *sign of guilt* 450.2, *penitence* 451.1

twining *of plants* 41.14, *spinning* 130.4, *interweaving* 609.1

twinkle *observe* 7.34, *gesture* 183.5, 183.17, *quality of light* 246.2, *light up* 246.20, *be changeable* 666.5, *flicker* 684.12, 684.23

twinkling *orbit* 7.22, *quality of light* 246.2, *bright* 246.14, *instant* 645.3

twinklingly *lightly* 246.23

twinkling of an eye *instant* 645.3

twin-lens reflex (TLR) *camera* 132.10

twinned *simultaneous* 649.4, *related* 727.6, *matched* 733.10, *two* 789.8

twinned city [Brit] *city* 567.1

twinning *doubling* 789.4

Twins Constellations 7

twins *couple* 733.6, *twin* 789.5

twin screws *propeller* 696.8

Twin Stars *twin* 789.5

twin sweater set *or* **twin set** *sweater* 100.17

twin tip *snowboarding equipment* 162.12

twirl *river turbulence* 570.5, *flow* 570.10, *coil* 632.2, *convolute* 632.6, *reel* 682.4, *rotate* 682.14

twirled *convolutional* 632.4

twirling *turning* 682.3, *rotating* 682.14

twirp [Inf] *nonentity* 800.8

twist 698.19; *weaving* 130.6, *spin* 130.17, Dances 135, *ski*

equipment 162.10, *ice-skating* 162.32, *misrepresentation* 188.1, *misrepresent* 188.6, *distort the truth* 192.25, *practice sophistry* 330.11, *misjudge* 342.9, *bias* 342.11, *interpretation* 365.1, *interpret* 365.12, *caprice* 381.1, *conduct oneself* 399.17, *motivate* 412.12, *violence by person* 520.2, *use violence* 520.9, *divergence* 607.2, *diverge* 607.11, *make shapeless* 625.3, *distortion* 627.1, *distort* 627.9, 698.20, *coil* 632.2, *convolute* 632.6, *transform* 670.13, *roll* 682.15, *delude* 720.16, *intertwine* 752.19, *pervert* 808.22, *be cunning* 822.5

twist and turn *convolute* 632.6, *shake* 684.24, *twist* 698.19

twist around one's little finger *be an influence* 512.13, *subject* 832.10

twisted *spun* 130.13, *misrepresented* 188.4, *partially true* 192.18, *misrepresentative* 193.14, *unjust* 342.7, *divergent* 607.7, *convolutional* 632.4, *oblique* 698.11

twisted [Inf] *drugged* 121.30

twistedness *distortion* 627.1, *convolution* 632.1

twister [Inf] *wind vortex* 9.14, *rough thing* 544.2, *convoluted thing* 632.3, *vortex* 682.6, *natural hazard* 813.4

twisting *snakelike* 37.13, *diving* 164.13, *capricious* 381.4, *divergent* 607.7, *turning* 682.3, *torsion* 698.5, *indirect* 698.9

twisting dive *competitive diving* 164.7

twist lift *ice-skating techniques* 162.16

twist one's arm *motivate* 178.17, *compel* 428.8

twist someone's arm *manipulate* 508.12

twist the law *be illegal* 53.30

twist together *convolute* 632.6

twist words *distort the truth* 627.12

twit *be humorous* 277.11, *taunt* 436.23

twit [Inf] *foolish person* 353.3

twitch *neurological disease* 114.20, *gesture* 183.5, *feel pain* 215.8, *type of touch* 216.3, *touch* 216.9, *be fearful* 283.15, *spasm* 684.8, *jolt* 684.23, *shake* 684.24, *jerk* 699.3, *pull at* 699.12

twitcher [Inf] *ornithologist* 36.3

twitchiness *restlessness* 684.5

twitchy *restless* 684.16, *convulsive* 684.19

twitter *bird sound* 240.2, *make a bird sound* 240.8, *agitation* 684.1, *be agitated* 684.21, *shake* 684.24

twittering *singing* 240.5

twittery *singing* 240.5

two 789.1, 789.8; *numeral* 6.8, *cards* 168.2

two, the *two* 789.8

two abreast *two* 789.8, *two by two* 789.19

two-and-a-half-dollar gold piece [Arch] *US coinage* 484.10

two-bit [Inf] *shoddy* 497.11, *trivial* 800.14

two bits [Inf] *US coinage* 484.10

two-by-four *wood* 131.3, *joined* 131.8

two-by-four [Inf] *undersized* 580.8

two by two 789.19; *two* 789.8

two cents worth *utterance* 205.10

two cheers *disparagement* 195.2
two-color printing *printing* 173.3, *book printing* 174.10
two-dimensional *spatial* 6.76, 563.11, *visual* 242.16, *horizontal* 603.6, *two-sided* 789.9
two-dimensional figure *surface* 6.36
two-dimensional wave *wave* 683.4
two-dollar bill *US coinage* 484.10, *twosome* 789.3
two dozen *twenty and over* 792.8
two-edged *equivocal* 380.5
two-faced *ungenuine* 192.13, *equivocating* 380.6, *double-edged* 789.10
two-facedly *untruthfully* 192.27
two-facedness *ungenuineness* 192.2, *duality* 789.2
two-faced person *equivocator* 380.4
twofer [Inf] *bargain* 497.4
two fingers *size of drink* 93.3
twofold *two* 789.8, *twice* 789.18
two for the price of one *bargain* 497.4
two-hander *play* 136.2, *twosome* 789.3
two hundred *hundreds* 792.9
two-lane road *road attribute* 687.3
two-level *two-sided* 789.9
two-man bobsled *bobsledding* 162.23
two-man (C-2) canoe race *canoe racing* 150.12
two minds with but a single thought *friendly relations* 62.3
two of a kind *look-alike* 730.4, *couple* 733.6
two or three *plurality* 793.1, *few* 796.1
two pairs *poker* 168.5
two peas in a pod *look-alike* 730.4
twopenny *cheap* 800.16
two-phase *cross-country* 162.31
two-phase uphill *cross-country techniques* 162.8
two-phase walk *cross-country techniques* 162.8
two-piece *tailored* 100.41, *swimming* 164.12
two-piece or two-piecer *twosome* 789.3
two-piece suit *suit* 100.16, *beachwear* 100.23
two-piece swimsuit *swimming equipment* 164.8
two-ply *layered* 588.6, *two-sided* 789.9
twoscore *twenty and over* 792.8
two-seater *twosome* 789.3
two-seater toboggan *bobsledding* 162.23
two-sided 789.9
twosome 789.3; *golf* 156.1, *two* 789.1
two-spot *cards* 168.2
two-step *Dances* 135
two-storied *layered* 588.6
two-story *two-sided* 789.9
two-stroke *two-sided* 789.9
two-stroke cycle *engine cycle* 14.13
two-tailed test *hypothesis testing* 6.52
two thirds *less than one* 787.4
two-tiered *layered* 588.6
two-time [Inf] *be dishonorable* 192.21
two-timer [Inf] *hypocrite* 192.9
two times *twice* 789.18
two-timing [Inf] *dishonorable* 192.14, *double-edged* 789.10

two voices *equivocation* 380.1
two-way *in exchange* 673.3, *interrelated* 729.5, *two-sided* 789.9
two-way communication *telecommunication* 169.7
two-way mirror *glass* 249.5
two-way traffic *exchange* 673.1
two weeks *eleven to nineteen* 792.7
two-wheeler *bicycle* 687.10, *twosome* 789.3
tycoon *company leader* 68.8, *gainer* 467.9, *financier* 484.17, *wealthy person* 485.6, *important person* 799.5, *prosperous person* 847.4
Tydeman's Red *Apple Varieties* 44
tying *arrest* 55.5
tying the knot [Inf] *marriage* 64.1
tying up *landing* 704.2
tyke *child* 26.6, *dog* 35.10
tympanic cavity *ear* 19.10, 228.2
tympanic membrane *body covering* 19.4, *ear* 19.10, 228.2
tympanites *swelling* 581.2
tympanum *ear* 19.10, 228.2
tympanum or tympan *Architectural Elements* 134
tympany *swelling* 581.2
type 173.5, 777.4; *written letter* 5.14, *someone* 18.10, *representation* 187.1, *sort* 202.6, *omen* 358.5, *standard* 589.7, *kind* 624.3, *nature* 723.4, *class* 777.12
type body *type* 173.5
typecast *dramatized* 136.32, *dramatize* 136.33, *regular* 730.12, *make the same* 730.16
type cutter *engraver* 144.5
typed *written* 5.36
typeface *type* 173.5
type font or typeface *design and makeup* 174.8
type page *design and makeup* 174.8
typeset *printed* 173.13, *print* 173.17, *publish* 174.19, *report* 175.9
typesetter *printer* 173.10, *book publishing personnel* 174.12
typesetting 173.4; *printing* 173.3, *stage of book production* 174.7
typesetting machine *typesetting* 173.4
type size *type* 173.5, *design and makeup* 174.8
type specifications *design and makeup* 174.8
type style *type* 173.5, *mode of expression* 537.3
typhoid *infection* 114.7
Typhoid Mary *infectious person* 114.9
Typhon *devil* 446.5
typhoon *wind vortex* 9.14, *natural violence* 520.3
typhus *infection* 114.7
typical 777.10; *symbolic* 183.12, *representational* 187.8, *customary* 397.11, *780.9, *regular* 663.5, *characteristic* 723.9, *779.12, *average* 742.5, *identifiable* 843.10
typically *indicatively* 183.21, *representationally* 187.15, *prevailingly* 742.11, *taxonomically* 777.15, *usually* 778.21
typical value *parameter* 6.57
typification *representation* 187.1, *manifestation* 843.2
typify *signify* 183.16, *represent* 187.10, *predict* 358.14
typing paper *paper* 104.5
typist *clerical worker* 123.5, *record keeper* 185.8
typographer *engraver* 144.5, *printer* 173.10

typographic *printed* 173.13
typographical *printed* 173.13
typology *Linguistic Studies* 5
Tyr *Deities* 82
tyrannical *lawless* 53.26, *managerial* 126.9, *malign* 306.11, *meddling* 414.17, *severe* 424.5, *influential* 512.8, *violent* 520.5, *dominating* 832.7
tyrannically *summarily* 53.36, *malignly* 306.18, *severely* 424.11, *influentially* 512.14, *violently* 520.11
tyrannicide *homicide* 30.4, *violation of the law* 427.2
tyrannization *malignity* 306.5
tyrannize *govern* 49.26, *harm* 306.13, *meddle* 414.23, *suppress* 424.9, *be an influence* 512.13, *use violence* 520.9, *defeat* 832.11
tyrannized *suppressed* 424.6
tyrannophobia *Phobias* 283
tyrannosaurus *prehistoric animal* 653.8
tyrannously *violently* 520.11
tyranny *totalitarianism* 49.13, *suppression* 424.2, *personal influence* 512.3, *domination* 832.2
tyrant *person in authority* 52.7, *absolute ruler* 68.7, *malefactor* 306.6, *punisher* 454.16, *one who restrains* 830.7
tyrants *Phobias* 283
Tyrian purple *purple pigment* 262.2
tyro *learner* 48.6, *unskilled person* 128.3, *ignorant person* 349.4, *beginner* 398.2, *771.14, *new arrival* 652.7, *entrant* 706.7
Tyrolean hat *hat* 100.32
Tyrolean traverse *climbing techniques* 161.3
Tyrol Mountain *Breeds of Sheep* 16
tyronic *unaccustomed* 398.3
tyrosine *Amino Acids* 12
Tyrrhenian Sea *Oceans and Seas* 571

U

U [Inf] *aristocratic* 70.4, *refined* 534.5
Ubangi *Rivers* 570
übermensch [Ger] *superior person* 445.7
ubiquitous *divine* 82.16, *dominant* 512.10, *omnipresent* 575.10, *universal* 778.10, *recurrent* 797.13
ubiquitously *divinely* 82.24, *influentially* 512.14
ubiquitousness *omnipresence* 575.4
ubiquity *omnipresence* 575.4, *widespreadness* 778.3
U-boat [Ger] *warship* 77.21
Ucayali *Rivers* 570
udder *mammalian characteristic* 35.3
udometer *weather instrument* 9.7
udometric *barometric* 9.39
Uele *Rivers* 570
ufological *spiritual* 86.20
ufologist *occultist* 86.13
ufology *occultism* 86.1
UFO sighting *occult and psychic phenomena* 86.7
Uganda *Countries* 566
uglify *stain* 808.20
ugliness 531.1; *bad taste* 528.3, *distortion of body* 627.3, *repulsion* 701.1
ugly 531.3; *stormy* 9.45, *plain*

528.9, *deformed* 627.7, *repulsive* 701.4, *dangerous* 811.7
ugly as sin *ugly* 531.3
ugly customer *malefactor* 306.6, *disreputable character* 371.2, *miscreant* 448.6
ugly duckling *ugly thing* 531.2
ugly thing 531.2
Uinta Mountains *Mountains and Hills* 569
uka (defender) *judo* 152.13
ukase *publication* 173.1, *command* 425.1, *rule* 780.1
uke (attacker) *aikido* 152.16
uke [Inf] *Musical Instruments* 142
Ukraine *Countries* 566
Ukrainian Grey *Breeds of Cattle* 16
Ukrainian Spotted Steppe *Breeds of Pigs* 16
Ukrainian Whiteheaded *Breeds of Cattle* 16
Ukrainian White Steppe *Breeds of Pigs* 16
ukulele *Musical Instruments* 142
Ulaanbaatar *Countries* 566
ulcer 114.18; *painful condition* 215.2
ulcerate *make worse* 808.17
ulcerated *of disease* 114.25
ulceration *ulcer* 114.18, *physical deterioration* 808.4
ulcerous *of disease* 114.25
ullage *omission* 762.4
Ullswater *Lakes* 568
ulna *Human Bones* 19
ulster *coat* 100.19
Ulster Democratic Unionist party *Political Parties* 50
ulterior *distant* 585.5, *external* 724.11
ulterior motive *motive* 178.5, *intention* 374.1, *motivation* 508.1
ultima ratio regum [L] *war* 76.1
ultimate *away* 585.6, *top* 600.6, *causal* 675.7, *ending* 773.13, *ideal* 805.6
ultimately *in the future* 650.13, *causally* 675.12, *finally* 773.24
ultimate purpose *final intention* 374.4, *usefulness* 393.2
ultimate stress *load* 14.14
ultimate tensile strength *strength of materials* 14.15
ultima Thule *distant place* 585.3
ultimatum *intentionality* 374.2, *demand* 425.2, *505.3, *business offer* 504.3, *warning* 814.1
ultrabasic rock *igneous rock* 8.32
ultracentrifuge *rotator* 682.8
ultracool *self-restrained* 830.10
ultracritical *critical* 438.13
ultrahard PVC (uPVC) *polymer* 11.9
ultrahigh frequency (UHF) *radio frequency* 661.3
ultrahigh vacuum (UHV) *surface chemistry* 11.20
ultramafic rock *igneous rock* 8.32
ultramarine *blue pigment* 261.2, *blue* 261.5, *distant* 585.5
ultramicroscopic *tiny* 580.9
ultramodern *new* 652.9
ultramodernist *modern person* 652.8
ultramontane *distant* 585.5, *foreigner* 724.5, *foreign* 724.9
ultramundane *distant* 585.5
ultranational *national* 566.10
ultranationalism *nation* 18.14, *social discrimination* 337.4, *nationalism* 566.4

ultranationalist *bigot* 337.7, *nationalist* 566.8
ultranationalistic *discriminatory* 337.11, *national* 566.10
ultranationalistically *prejudicially* 337.17
ultrasonic *physical* 10.70, *unheard* 229.7, *sounding* 230.7, *swift* 694.6
ultrasonically *physically* 10.78, *swiftly* 694.16
ultrasonic cleaning *sounding* 10.16
ultrasonic frequency *sound propagation* 230.3
ultrasonic imaging or **ultrasonography** *sounding* 10.16
ultrasonics Fields of Modern Physics 10
ultrasonic speed *speed* 694.2
ultrasonic wave *wave* 10.11
ultrasonic welding *sounding* 10.16
ultrasound *sound* 10.15, 230.1
ultrasound scan *diagnostic radiology* 107.12
ultrasound scanner *sound propagation* 230.3
ultrastructure *cell biology* 13.14
ultraviolet astronomy *astronomy* 7.1
ultraviolet light *light* 246.1
ultraviolet (UV) radiation *sun* 9.21, *electromagnetic radiation* 10.14
ultraviolet (UV) spectrometry *analysis* 11.17
ultraviolet spectrum *emission* 10.56
ultrawide lens *lens* 132.11
ululant 240.4; *strident* 238.4, *crying* 239.11, *sorrowful* 270.4
ululate *be loud* 232.8, *be strident* 238.7, *cry* 239.16, *make an animal sound* 240.7, *grieve* 270.7, *weep* 280.8
ululation *tumult* 232.5, *harsh sound* 238.1, *cry of sorrow* 239.6, *animal sound* 240.1, *lament* 280.2
umbel *flower head* 42.4
umbelliferous *taxonomic* 41.16, *of flowers* 42.11
umbilical cord *line* 754.5
umbrage *unpleasantness* 272.1, *resentment* 302.1
umbrageous *dark* 247.5
umbrella *protective covering* 613.5, *including* 763.3, *protection* 810.2, *protection from the weather* 810.9
umbrella pine Trees and Shrubs 43
umbrella tree Trees and Shrubs 43
Umbriel Planets and Their Satellites 7
umiak Ships and Boats 690
umlaut Accents and Diacritical Marks 5, *separator* 753.5
Umnak Islands 572
umpirage *mediation* 75.1, *judgment* 341.1
umpire *judge* 54.10, 341.5, 341.10, *mediator* 75.2, *mediate* 75.6, 772.19, *baseball team* 147.2, *bowler* 151.5, *football player* 155.15, *hockey player* 158.8, *tennis participant* 165.6, *adviser* 176.5, *impartial person* 443.3, *negotiator* 460.4, *moderator* 521.2, *moderate* 521.7, *interfacer* 616.3, *middleman* 772.7
umpire's mask *baseball equipment* 147.4

umpteen [Inf] *large number* 783.3, *multitude* 795.1, *myriad* 795.7
umpteenth [Inf] *millionth* 792.22
unabashed *insolent* 400.8, *defiant* 416.5
unabashedly *insolently* 400.18, *defiantly* 416.9
unabbreviated *complete* 761.6
unabetted *solo* 788.14
unable *unskillful* 128.4, *powerless* 515.6, *useless* 802.7
unable to act *inactive* 413.9
unable to be seen *invisible* 245.3
unable to forget *remembering* 354.8
unable to keep the wolf from the door *poor* 486.8
unable to make up one's mind *vacillating* 378.5
unable to pay 488.8; *nonpaying* 490.7
unable to say boo to a goose *cowardly* 285.4
unable to understand *confused* 364.10
unable to wait *hasty* 818.3
unabridged *long* 590.6, *uncut* 759.7, *complete* 761.6
unabridged dictionary *word book* 5.27
unaccented *phonetic* 205.14, *faint* 233.6
unacceptability *objectionability* 272.2
unacceptable *insufficient* 98.4, *objectionable* 272.7, *unselected* 383.7, *unsatisfactory* 438.15, *imperfect* 806.5
unacceptably *insufficiently* 98.11
unacceptance 190.4
unaccepted *unselected* 383.7, *disapproved* 438.9
unaccepting 190.13
unaccessibility *hopelessness* 837.2
unaccessible *hopeless* 837.6
unacclaimed *unskillful* 128.4
unaccommodated *unprovided* 98.6
unaccompanied *solo* 788.14
unaccomplished *unskillful* 128.4, *uncompleted* 762.7
unaccountability *unintelligibility* 364.1, *chance* 842.1, *lack of motive* 842.2
unaccountable *astonishing* 294.10, *unintelligible* 364.4, *exempt* 434.5, *causeless* 842.11
unaccountably *astonishingly* 294.19, *unintelligibly* 364.16, *randomly* 842.16
unaccused *safe* 810.16
unaccustomed 398.3; *clumsy* 128.6
unaccustomedly 398.7
unaccustomedness 398.1
unachievable *hopeless* 837.6
unachieved *uncompleted* 762.7
unacknowledged *unthanked* 311.3, *latent* 844.6
unacquaintance *unaccustomedness* 398.1
unadaptable *mentally hard* 542.8
unadapted *unskillful* 128.4
unadjusted *clumsy* 128.6
unadmiring *wonderless* 295.3
unadmiringly *without wonder* 295.8
unadorned 424.7, 526.9; *simple* 195.10, 363.6, *clear* 196.2, *naive* 821.3
unadorned style *clarity* 363.2
unadornment 424.3, 526.3; *clarity* 363.2
unadulterated *clean* 111.13, *pure*

431.11, *unadorned* 526.9, *authentic* 721.16, 737.6, *uncut* 759.7, *complete* 761.6
unadulteratedly *authentically* 721.31
unadulteratedness *purity* 431.4
unadulteration *unadornment* 526.3, *authenticity* 721.7
unadventurous *unskillful* 128.4, *reticent* 287.8
unadventurously *reticently* 287.18
unadventurousness *reticence* 287.3
unadvisable *inconvenient* 804.5
unaesthetic *plain* 528.9, *ugly* 531.3
unaesthetically *inelegantly* 531.7
unaffected *detached* 4.18, *ingenuous* 191.6, *simple* 195.10, *insensitive* 268.4, *indifferent* 289.7, *informal* 407.6, *familiar* 407.8, *pure* 431.11, *unpretentious* 526.8, *natural* 526.10, *naive* 821.3
unaffectedly *ingenuously* 191.11, *informally* 407.11
unaffectedness *ingenuousness* 191.3, *simplicity* 195.4, *familiarity* 407.3, *purity* 431.4, *unpretentiousness* 526.2, *naiveté* 821.1
unaffectionate *indifferent* 289.7
unaffiliated *separate* 724.1, *unrelated* 728.6, *independent* 829.12
unaffordable *costly* 500.6
unafraid *steadfast* 284.11
unaggressive *pacific* 74.7
unagitated *quiescent* 678.6
unaided *solo* 788.14
Unalaska Islands 572
unalienable *essential* 723.5, *free* 829.11
unalienable rights *free rights* 829.4
unalike *nonuniform* 734.5
unallied *unrelated* 728.6
unalloyed *immaculate* 805.11
unalloyed truth, the *the truth* 721.3
unalterable *mentally hard* 542.8, *permanent* 667.2
unalterably *inflexibly* 542.13, *permanently* 667.6, *stably* 674.9
unaltered *stabilized* 674.4
unamazed *wonderless* 295.3
unamazedly *without wonder* 295.8
unamazedness *lack of wonder* 295.1
unambiguity *clarity* 196.1, *comprehensibility* 361.3, *intelligibility* 363.1
unambiguous *clear* 196.2, *easily seen through* 249.10, *meaningful* 361.6, *intelligible* 363.5, *straightforward* 630.9, *decided* 840.9
unambiguously *clearly* 196.4, *meaningfully* 361.16, *intelligibly* 363.13, *straightforwardly* 630.17, *completely* 805.22
unambiguousness *clarity* 196.1, *comprehensibility* 361.3, *straightforwardness* 630.3, *simplicity* 823.2
unambiguous passage *comprehensibility* 361.3
unambitious *self-deprecating* 403.9
unambivalence *intelligibility* 363.1
unambivalent *intelligible* 363.5
unamiability *hostility* 63.1
unamiably *hostilely* 63.13
unamicable *hostile* 63.6

unanimity *assent* 346.1, *agreement* 462.1, 730.2, 735.3, 752.4
unanimous *assenting* 346.4, *agreeing* 462.6, 735.13, *agreeable* 752.11, *whole* 788.12
unanimously 346.8; *agreeably* 462.14, 752.22, *agreeingly* 730.19, *in accord* 735.33, *wholly* 788.22, *cooperatively* 827.18
unanimousness *agreement* 735.3
unanswerable *exempt* 434.5
unanswered *irresolute* 841.10
unanticipated *surprising* 292.7, *unexpected* 839.6
unapologetic *impenitent* 452.2
unapologized for *unatoned* 452.3
unapparent *invisible* 245.3
unappeasable *unyielding* 379.8
unappetizing *tasteless* 220.4, *unpalatable* 223.6
unapplied *philosophical* 4.12, *unused* 394.5
unappreciated *disliked* 291.10, *thankless* 311.4
unappreciation *ingratitude* 311.1
unappreciative *ungrateful* 311.2
unappreciatively *ungratefully* 311.6
unappreciativeness *ingratitude* 311.1
unapproachability *unsociability* 409.1, *distance* 804.4
unapproachable *unsociable* 409.6, *reserved* 585.7, *best* 744.10, *distant* 804.8, *hopeless* 837.6
unapproachably *reservedly* 585.15, *hopelessly* 837.12
unapproved *unsatisfactory* 274.5, *disapproved* 438.9
unapproving *dissatisfied* 274.4, *disapproving* 438.8
unapt *meaningless* 362.7, *useless* 802.7, *inconvenient* 804.5
unaptness *uselessness* 802.1
unarm *make useless* 802.12
unarmed *pacific* 74.7, *helpless* 515.9, *vulnerable* 811.9
unarmored *vulnerable* 811.9
unaroused *wonderless* 295.3, *sedentary* 678.5
unarranged *unprepared* 389.5, *disordered* 766.9
unarticulated *unsaid* 844.9
unartificial *naive* 821.3
unascertained *uncertified* 841.13
unashamed *impenitent* 452.2
unashamedly *impenitently* 452.5
unasked *celibate* 67.6
unaspiring *modest* 403.6
unassailability *strength* 516.1
unassailable *invulnerable* 810.18
unassembled *disbanded* 776.7
unassertive *permitting* 502.5
unassimilable *unjoined* 753.9
unassimilated *unjoined* 753.9, *aloof* 756.5
unassisted *solo* 788.14
unassociated *unrelated* 728.6
unassuming *ingenuous* 191.6, *reserved* 195.11, *humble* 298.8, *modest* 403.6, *informal* 407.6, *unpretentious* 526.8, *natural* 526.10, *naive* 821.3
unassumingly *ingenuously* 191.11, *reservedly* 195.20, *humbly* 298.22, *informally* 407.11
unassuming nature *modesty* 403.1
unassumingness *ingenuousness* 191.3, *humility* 298.1, *modesty* 403.1
unatonable *unforgivable* 430.16
unatoned 452.3
unattached *celibate* 67.6,

changeable 666.3, unjoined 753.9, irresolute 772.13, independent 829.12

unattached female *single woman* 33.5

unattached male *single man* 32.5
unattached man *single person* 67.5

unattached woman *single person* 67.5

unattackable *invulnerable* 810.18
unattainability *hopelessness* 837.2
unattainable *hopeless* 837.6
unattainable, the *object of desire* 288.8

unattainably *hopelessly* 837.12
unattained *uncompleted* 762.7
unattended *vulnerable* 811.9
unattired *undressed* 614.11
unattractive *plain* 528.9, *ugly* 531.3

unattractively *inelegantly* 531.7
unattractiveness *ugliness* 531.1
unauthentic 722.9
unauthentically 722.17
unauthenticated *uncertified* 841.13

unauthenticity 722.4
unauthorization *illegality* 53.10
unauthorized 515.7; *unlawful* 53.23, *fraudulent* 479.13, *prohibited* 503.5

unauthorized absence *absenteeism* 576.3
unauthorized borrowing *illegal borrowing* 476.3, *infringement* 479.6

unauthorized person *lack of authority* 515.2
unavailability *distance* 804.4, *hopelessness* 837.2
unavailable *scarce* 98.8, *absent* 576.7, *distant* 804.8, *hopeless* 837.6

unavailing *futile* 802.10
unavoidability *inevitability* 95.6, 840.5
unavoidable *inevitable* 95.14, 840.11, *compelling* 428.6, *compulsory* 428.7, *duty-bound* 433.8

unavoidably *necessarily* 95.22, *compellingly* 428.12, *inevitably* 840.17
unaware *unhearing* 229.5, *insensitive* 268.4, *indifferent* 289.7, *ignorant* 349.5, *oblivious* 355.9, *vulnerable* 811.9

unawareness *figurative blindness* 243.8, *insensitivity* 268.1, *ignorance* 318.2, 349.1
unaware of *blind to* 243.14
unawares *surprisingly* 292.14, *innocently* 449.13, *dangerously* 811.14

unawed *wonderless* 295.3
unbalance 741.8; *make insane* 110.13, *imbalance* 741.2, *derange* 766.23

unbalanced 741.5; *insane* 110.9, *clumsy* 128.6, *wrongful* 430.10, *displaced* 574.8, *distorted* 627.6, *deranged* 766.16, *unsafe* 811.8

unbalanced line *offense* 155.6
unbalanced mind *insanity* 110.1
unballast *lighten* 539.9
unballasted *independent* 741.5
unbar *open up* 583.16, *deliver* 817.5, *make easy* 823.15
unbarred *opened up* 583.11
unbearable *painful* 215.4
unbearable pressure *exertion* 122.4
unbeatable 744.13; *resisting*

417.8, *best* 805.9, *victorious* 845.10

unbeaten *new* 394.7, *unfamiliar* 652.10, *best* 805.9, *victorious* 845.10

unbecoming *ugly* 531.3
unbecomingly *inelegantly* 531.7
unbefitting *improper* 430.14, *untimely* 660.5
unbefittingly *at the wrong time* 660.12

unbeing *absence* 576.1, *nonexistence* 718.1
unbeknown *unknown* 349.7
unbelief 88.4; *unacceptance* 190.4
unbelievability 88.2; *implausibility* 839.3
unbelievable 837.5; *disbelieved* 88.7, *astonishing* 294.10, *questionable* 839.5
unbelievably 88.11; *astonishingly* 294.19, *improbably* 839.8
unbelieved *disbelieved* 88.7
unbeliever *disbeliever* 88.5
unbelieving *disbelieving* 88.6, *unaccepting* 190.13, *uncertain* 841.9

unbelievingly *disbelievingly* 88.10
unbend *visit* 408.16, *soften* 543.14, *straighten* 630.14, *take it easy* 819.3
unbending *relentless* 309.4, *strong-willed* 376.10, *unyielding* 379.8, *obstinate* 417.7, *severe* 425.5, *mentally hard* 542.8, *straight* 630.8

unbendingly *resistingly* 417.14
unbendingness *relentlessness* 309.2, *mental hardness* 542.4
unbent *straight* 630.8
unbiased *truthful* 191.4, *impartial* 289.9, 338.6, *judicious* 341.8, *disinterested* 443.4, *broad-minded* 592.9, *free* 829.11
unbiased attitude *impartiality* 289.3

unbiasedly *impartially* 289.19
unbidden *voluntary* 373.11
unbigoted *broad-minded* 592.9
unbind *separate* 753.12, *deliver* 817.5, *set free* 829.17, *liberate* 831.6
unbinding *liberation* 831.1
unblamable *incorrupt* 449.7
unblameworthy *incorrupt* 449.7
unbleached *gray* 255.6
unblemished *innocent* 449.6, *immaculate* 805.11
unblessed *cursed* 301.8, *unlucky* 848.12
unblest *cursed* 301.8
unblock *open up* 583.16, *make easy* 823.15
unblocked *opened up* 583.11
unblurred *intelligible* 363.5
unblushing *insolent* 400.8, *unchaste* 432.10, *impenitent* 452.2
unblushingly *insolently* 400.18, *impenitently* 452.5
unboastful *modest* 403.6
unbolt *open up* 583.16, *liberate* 831.6
unbolted *opened up* 583.11
unbosom oneself *admit* 180.11
unbought *shoddy* 497.11
unbound *independent* 434.7, *escaping* 816.7, *free* 829.11
unbowed 602.7; *steadfast* 284.11, *resisting* 417.8, *victorious* 845.10
unbreakability *toughness* 547.1
unbreakable *dense* 540.6, *tough* 542.6, 547.6, *unfailing* 667.3, *invulnerable* 810.18

unbreakable glass *protective covering* 613.5
unbreakable horse *horse* 159.1
unbreakableness *toughness* 547.1
unbridgeable *unintelligible* 364.4
unbridle *liberate* 831.6
unbridled *disorderly* 51.6, *violent* 520.5, *unrestrained* 592.8, *free* 829.11, *unconditional* 829.14
unbridling *liberation* 831.1
unbroken 805.13; *unaccustomed* 398.3, *uniform* 545.5, *continuous* 630.10, 669.5, 774.9, *ongoing* 679.7, *direct* 697.11, *conforming* 735.17, *uncut* 759.7, *complete* 761.6
unbroken line *straight line* 630.2
unbrokenness *continuity* 774.4
unbuild *demolish* 523.12
unburden *lighten* 539.9, *unload* 709.24, *deliver* 817.5, *disentangle* 823.17, *liberate* 831.6
unburdening *lightening* 539.2, 539.6, *disentanglement* 823.8, *liberation* 831.1
unburden oneself *admit* 180.11
unburdensome *easy* 823.9
unburnished *dirty* 112.7
unbusinesslike *unskillful* 128.4
unbutton *undress* 614.18, *separate* 753.12
unbuttoned [Inf] *at ease* 819.2, *informal* 829.15
unbuttoning *separation* 753.1
unc [Inf] *family member* 65.2
uncage *liberate* 831.6
uncalled-for *excessive* 712.8
uncamouflaged *manifest* 843.9
uncandid 192.15
uncandidly 192.29
uncandidness *lack of candor* 192.4
uncanny *spiritual* 86.20
uncanny silence *silence* 231.1
uncared for *disliked* 291.10
uncaring *insensitive* 268.4, *indifferent* 289.7, *pitiless* 309.3, *inconsiderate* 318.9, *thoughtless* 324.7, *negligent* 326.4
uncaringly *indifferently* 289.17
uncaused *causeless* 842.11
unceasing *constant* 377.8, *active* 414.13, *timeless* 640.3, *permanent* 642.5, *continuing forever* 644.6, *protracted* 669.7
unceasingly *ever* 640.7, *continually* 669.10
uncensored *offensive* 432.11
unceremonious *informal* 407.6
unceremoniously *informally* 407.11
unceremoniousness *informality* 407.1
uncertain 841.9; *disbelieving* 88.6, *clumsy* 128.6, *obscure* 197.2, *questionable* 333.13, *unexplained* 364.6, *vacillating* 378.5, *equivocal* 380.5, *erratic* 381.5, *deferred* 604.9, *changeable* 665.3, *unauthentic* 722.9, *dangerous* 811.7, *improbable* 839.4, *chance* 842.10, *causeless* 841.14
uncertain future *future condition* 650.3
uncertainly 841.22; *disbelievingly* 88.10, *ambivalently* 378.14, *erratically* 381.8, *interruptedly* 604.20, *changeably* 666.7, *unauthentically* 722.17, *improbably* 839.8
uncertainness *uncertainty* 841.1
uncertainty 333.6, 841.1; *disbelief* 88.1, *obscurity* 197.1, *question* 333.1, *questionableness* 333.7, *ignorance* 349.1, *expectation* 356.1,

unintelligibility 364.1, *vacillation* 378.1, *equivocation* 380.1, *capriciousness* 381.2, *deferment* 604.3, *future condition* 650.3, *changeableness* 666.1, *irresolution* 666.2, *unauthenticity* 722.4, *danger* 811.1, *improbability* 839.1, *chance* 842.1

uncertainty principle *causality* 10.66, *probability theory* 838.5, *uncertainty* 841.1
uncertified 841.13
unchain *separate* 753.12, *deliver* 817.5, *set free* 829.17, *liberate* 831.6
unchained *separate* 753.7, *escaping* 816.7, *free* 829.11
unchaining *liberation* 831.1
unchallengeable *in the right* 429.11, *invulnerable* 810.18, *decided* 840.9
unchallenged *agreeing* 462.6
unchangeability *stability* 674.1
unchangeable *tenacious* 376.9, *permanent* 667.2, *stable* 674.3
unchangeableness *stability* 674.1
unchanged *stabilized* 674.4
unchanging *eternal* 644.4, *permanent* 667.2, *stable* 674.3, *regular* 730.12, *infallible* 840.12
unchangingly *regularly* 730.21
unchaperoned *solo* 788.14
unchargeable *free of charge* 497.12
uncharged *given* 472.8, *free of charge* 497.12
uncharitable *severe* 424.5, *selfish* 444.4
uncharitableness *severity* 424.1
uncharitably *severely* 424.11, *selfishly* 444.8
uncharted *unknown* 349.7
unchaste 432.10; *depraved* 448.10
unchastened *impenitent* 452.2
unchastised *acquitted* 54.25
unchastity *sexual immorality* 432.2
unchecked *unrestrained* 592.8, *free* 829.11, *uncertified* 841.13
unchivalrous *objectionable* 272.7, *bad-mannered* 411.6
unchivalrously *discourteously* 411.8
unchosen *disliked* 291.10, *unselected* 383.7
uncial *type* 173.5
uncircumscribed *extensive* 563.12
uncircumspect *imprudent* 286.7, *foolish* 353.5
uncivil *objectionable* 272.7, *rude* 400.9, *discourteous* 411.5, *disrespectful* 436.9
uncivilized *unrefined* 389.11
uncivilly *rudely* 400.19, *unsocially* 409.13, *discourteously* 411.8
unclad *undressed* 614.11
unclasp *separate* 753.12
unclassified *complicated* 751.10, *disordered* 766.9
uncle *man in the family* 32.12, *family member* 65.2
uncle [Inf] *lender* 475.3
uncle! [Inf] *I/we surrender!* 421.9
unclean 112.8; *dirty* 112.7, *unhygienic* 114.27, *polluting* 117.15, *immoral* 432.9
uncleaned *dirty* 112.7
uncleanliness *lack of hygiene* 112.3
uncleanly *unclean* 112.8, *dirtily* 112.12, *unhygienically* 114.32
uncleanness 112.2; *dirtiness* 112.1, *immorality* 432.1, *untidiness* 766.3, *impairment* 808.7
unclear 364.5; *obscure* 197.2, *faint* 233.6, *difficult to see* 245.4, *murky*

248.5, *inscrutable* 250.5,
unintelligible 364.4, *difficult* 364.8,
shapeless 625.2, *problematic*
824.11, *indeterminate* 841.14
unclearly *shapelessly* 625.5
unclearness *obscurity* 250.2,
unintelligibility 364.1, *shapelessness*
625.1, *indeterminacy* 841.6
unclench *relinquish* 392.3
uncle's [Inf] *lending institution*
475.4
uncloak *disclose* 180.8, *undress*
614.18
unclog *void* 709.23, *make easy*
823.15
unclose *disclose* 180.8, *open* 583.15
unclosed *open* 583.10
unclot *dissolve* 555.23
unclothe *undress* 614.18
unclothed *undressed* 614.11
unclothing *undressing* 614.2
unclotted *fluid* 555.14
unclotting *fluidization* 555.8
uncloud *make transparent* 249.12
unclouded *sunny* 246.17,
transparent 249.7
unclutter *disentangle* 823.17
uncluttered *simple* 526.7
unclutteredness *simplicity* 526.1
uncluttering *simplification* 526.6,
disentanglement 823.8
uncoded *simple* 363.6
uncolored *colorless* 252.5,
unadorned 526.9
uncombed *untidy* 766.11
uncombined *elemental* 11.26,
nonadhesive 756.4, *disintegrated*
758.3
uncomfortable *painful* 215.4,
unpleasant 272.6, *disturbed* 768.6
uncomfortable with
unaccustomed 398.3
uncomfortably *unaccustomedly*
398.7
uncommendable *unsatisfactory*
438.15, *inconvenient* 804.5
uncommended *criticized* 438.14
uncommensurate *incomparable*
734.6
uncommensurately *incomparably*
734.12
uncommiserating *pitiless* 309.3
uncommiserative *pitiless* 309.3
uncommiseratively *pitilessly*
309.7
uncommitted *vacillating* 378.5,
avoiding 386.9, *irresolute* 772.13
uncommitted person *moderate*
person 772.8
uncommitted voter *vacillator*
378.3
uncommon *scarce* 98.8,
uncustomary 398.4, *infrequent*
662.2, *unusual* 664.4, 782.15,
characteristic 779.12, *sparse* 796.6
uncommonly *unusually* 398.9,
664.7, *infrequently* 662.4,
unconformably 782.21, *rarely*
839.10
uncommonness *infrequency*
662.1, *unusualness* 664.2, 782.4
uncommunicative *silent* 181.10,
noncommittal 181.11, *taciturn*
208.4, *reticent* 287.8, *unsociable*
409.6
uncommunicatively *taciturnly*
208.9, *reticently* 287.18
uncommunicativeness *taciturnity*
208.1, *reticence* 287.3, *unsociability*
409.1
uncompact *sparse* 541.3
uncompanionable *unsociable*
409.6
uncomparable *incomparable* 734.6

uncomparableness
incomparability 734.3
uncomparably *incomparably*
734.12
uncompassion *pitilessness* 309.1
uncompassionate *pitiless* 309.3
uncompassionately *pitilessly*
309.7
uncompelled *independent* 829.12
uncompensated *unpaid* 490.8,
unbalanced 741.5
uncompetitive *harmless* 73.9,
associating 827.11
uncomplaining *satisfied* 273.4
uncompleted 762.7; *bungled*
128.7, *incomplete* 762.5
uncompliant *refused* 506.5,
dissident 782.12
uncomplicated *simple* 363.6,
526.7, *straightforward* 630.9,
naive 821.3, *easy* 823.9
uncomplicatedness *simplicity*
823.2
uncomplimentary *discourteous*
411.5, *critical* 438.13
uncomplying *disobedient* 427.10
uncompressed *insubstantial*
539.5, *sparse* 541.3
uncompromising *emphatic* 200.3,
strong-willed 376.10, *unyielding*
379.8, *severe* 424.5
uncompromisingly *severely*
424.11
unconcealed *visible* 244.5,
manifest 843.9
unconceived *unthought-of* 318.10
unconcern *figurative blindness*
243.8, *indifference* 289.1, *lack of*
wonder 295.1, *incuriosity* 322.1,
inattention 324.1, *negligence* 326.1
unconcerned *detached* 4.18,
unhearing 229.5, *blind to* 243.14,
indifferent 289.7, *wonderless*
295.3, *incurious* 322.3, *inattentive*
324.5, *negligent* 326.4, *submitting*
421.3
unconcernedly *apathetically* 322.7
uncondemned *acquitted* 54.25
uncondensed *nonadhesive* 756.4
uncondensed state *nonadhesion*
756.1
unconditional 829.14; *duty-bound*
433.8, *permitted* 502.4
unconditionally *with permission*
502.10, *completely* 759.14,
excessively 829.23
unconditional surrender
submission 421.1
unconditioned *unconditional*
829.14
unconditioned reflex
conditioning 108.24
uncondonable *unforgivable*
430.16
unconfident *suspicious* 314.6
unconfined *extensive* 563.12,
unrestrained 592.8, *complete*
761.6, *free* 829.11, *free-ranging*
829.13
unconfirmability
indemonstrability 841.5
unconfirmable *indemonstrable*
841.12
unconfirmed report *publishing*
173.2
unconformable *nonconforming*
782.11
unconformably 782.21
unconformity *nonconformity*
782.1
uncongealed *fluid* 555.14
uncongenial *unsociable* 409.6
uncongeniality *unsociability* 409.1
unconnected 728.8; *extraneous*

724.8, *unjoined* 753.9,
nonadhesive 756.4, *discontinuous*
775.7
unconnectedly 728.18
unconnectedness 728.2;
foreignness 724.2
unconquerable *invulnerable*
419.19, *victorious* 845.10
unconscious 108.40; *psychic*
86.17, *psyche* 108.25, *desensitized*
213.5, *blind to* 243.14, *insensitive*
268.4, *indifferent* 289.7, *instinct*
320.4, *ignorant* 349.5, *oblivious*
355.9, *not awake* 415.12, *disabled*
515.10, *internal* 525.11
unconsciously *psychologically*
108.42, *insensibly* 213.9,
indifferently 289.17, *ignorantly*
349.11, *forgetfully* 355.14, *sleepily*
415.19, *innocently* 449.13,
subjectively 525.14
unconscious memory *memory*
108.27
unconscious mind *psyche* 108.25
unconsciousness *symptom* 114.3,
desensitization 213.2, *figurative*
blindness 243.8, *ignorance* 349.1,
oblivion 355.4, *sleep* 415.5,
disability 515.4, *internal world*
525.6
unconsenting *refusing* 375.9,
refused 506.5, *protesting* 507.5
unconsidered *unthought-of* 318.10
unconsolidated *petrographic* 8.58,
nonadhesive 756.4
unconstitutional *unlawful* 53.23
unconstrained *free* 407.9,
independent 434.7, *naive* 821.3,
informal 829.15
unconstrainedly *informally*
407.11, *freely* 407.12
unconstraint *freedom* 407.4,
tolerance 502.2, *informality* 829.6
unconsumed *unused* 394.5,
surplus 750.8
unconsummated *uncompleted*
762.7
uncontaminated *clean* 111.13,
uncut 759.7, *immaculate* 805.11
uncontentious *harmless* 73.9
uncontestable *decided* 840.9
uncontested *agreeing* 462.6
uncontradicted *agreeing* 462.6
uncontrite *impenitent* 452.2
uncontrived *spontaneous* 389.6,
naive 821.3
uncontrol *overindulgence* 456.3
uncontrollable *refractory* 379.6,
attacking 418.14, *violent* 520.5
uncontrollably *confusedly* 51.11
uncontrolled *disorderly* 51.6,
766.15, *independent* 434.7,
829.12, *overindulgent* 456.8, *hasty*
818.3
uncontrolled imagination
conception 360.4
uncontroversial *agreeing* 462.6
unconventional 782.14;
uncustomary 398.4, *informal*
407.6, *nonobservant* 466.5,
unusual 664.4, *nonconformist*
782.13, *independent* 829.12
unconventional behavior
nonconformism 782.3
unconventionalist *dissenter*
347.5, *nonconformist* 782.7
unconventionality
unaccustomedness 398.1,
unusualness 664.2, *nonconformism*
782.3
unconventionally *unusually*
398.9, *unconformably* 782.21
unconventional medicine
alternative medicine 107.4

unconversance *unaccustomedness*
398.1
unconversant *unskilled* 128.5
unconverted *unused* 394.5,
nonobservant 466.5
unconvinced *dissenting* 347.7,
refusing 375.9
unconvincing *unemphatic* 201.2,
insufficient 517.11
unconvincingly *unemphatically*
201.4
uncooked 389.12
uncooperative 828.14;
unenthusiastic 375.10, *avoiding*
386.9, *resistant* 417.6, *disobedient*
427.10, *refused* 506.5, *hindering*
826.12
uncooperatively 506.11; *in*
disagreement 463.12, *with delay*
826.22, *opposingly* 828.22
uncooperativeness 828.4;
resistance 417.1, *disobedience* 427.1
uncopied *original* 737.4
uncordial *hostile* 63.6
uncordiality *hostility* 63.1
uncordially *hostilely* 63.13
uncork *open up* 583.16
uncorked *opened up* 583.11
uncorroborated *uncertified* 841.13
uncorrupt *incorrupt* 449.7
uncorrupted *pure* 431.11,
incorrupt 449.7
uncorruptible *incorrupt* 449.7
uncostly *cheap* 497.9
uncountable *numberless* 795.8,
immeasurable 798.6
uncounted *numberless* 795.8
uncouple *separate* 753.12
uncoupling *separation* 753.1
uncourageous *cowardly* 285.4
uncourageously *cowardly* 285.9
uncourtliness *discourtesy* 411.1
uncourtly *discourteous* 411.5,
discourteously 411.8
uncouth *clumsy* 128.6, *objectionable*
272.7, *bad-mannered* 411.6,
indecorous 528.8, *ugly* 531.3,
vulgar 535.6
uncouthly *rudely* 411.9, *inelegantly*
531.7, *discourteously* 535.11
uncouthness *impropriety* 528.2,
vulgarity 535.1
uncover 614.17; *disclose* 180.8,
make visible 242.25, 244.9, *detect*
345.12, *open* 583.15, *open up*
583.16, *take off* 749.7, *reveal*
843.14
uncovered 614.10; *disclosed* 180.5,
clear 244.6, *discovered* 345.9,
unequipped 389.13, *open* 583.10,
843.12, *opened up* 583.11,
vulnerable 811.9, *manifest* 843.9
uncovering 614.1; *disclosure*
180.1, *detection* 345.2,
manifestation 843.2
uncover one's head *show respect*
435.16
uncracked *unbroken* 805.13
uncrease *smooth* 545.10
uncreated *self-existent* 717.15
uncreated being *self-existence*
717.8
uncredited *unthanked* 311.3
uncritical *undiscriminating* 338.5
uncritically *unselectively* 338.12
uncriticalness *lack of*
discrimination 338.1
uncriticizing *impartial* 338.6
uncrumpled *uniform* 545.5
unction *religiousness* 81.2, *dose of*
medicine 115.3, *ointment* 562.8
unctional *oily* 562.11
unctuosity *unctuousness* 439.4,
oiliness 562.1

unclearly — unctuosity

unctuous 439.10; *zealous 81.22, ungenuine 192.13, sycophantic 401.7, smooth-mannered 545.9, oily 562.11*

unctuously *untruthfully 192.27, flatteringly 439.16, suavely 545.15, oilily 562.19*

unctuousness 439.4; *religiousness 81.2, ungenuineness 192.2, smoothness 545.1, oiliness 562.1*

uncultivated *infertile 23.7, unprocessed 389.10, vulgar 535.6*

uncultured *common 71.3, bad-mannered 411.6, discourteous 535.7*

uncurbed *free 829.11*

uncurl *straighten 630.14*

uncurled *straight 630.8*

uncustomary 398.4

uncut 759.7; *woven 130.15, unformed 389.11, shapeless 625.2, complete 761.6*

undamaged *uncut 759.7, unbroken 805.13, safe 810.16*

undamped *dry 560.7*

undaring *cowardly 285.4*

undaunted *courageous 284.9, tenacious 376.9, enduring 377.9*

undauntedness *tenacity 376.4*

undead *ghost 86.11, witchlike 86.19*

undecagon *eleven to nineteen 792.7*

undecayed *preserved 815.12*

undeceive *inform 170.11*

undecennial *eleventh and above 792.18*

undecidable *numerable 6.70*

undecided *problematic 328.7, arguable 329.8, vacillating 378.5, deferred 604.9, free person 829.9, free 829.11, irresolute 841.10*

undecidedly *interruptedly 604.20*

undecided voter *free person 829.9*

undecillion *million 792.11*

undecipherable *unintelligible 364.4*

undeclared *unsaid 844.9*

undeclared war *psychological warfare 76.13*

undecorated *unadorned 526.9*

undefeated *resisting 417.8, victorious 845.10*

undefended *helpless 515.9, vulnerable 811.9*

undefended part *vulnerability 811.6*

undefiled *clean 111.13, pure 431.11, innocent 449.6*

undefined *difficult to see 245.4, vague 338.9, unrecognizable 364.7, shapeless 625.2, unreal 720.8, indeterminate 841.14*

undemanding *satisfied 273.4, easy 823.9, easygoing 823.13*

undemocratic *severe 424.5, unjust 741.6*

undemocratically *unjustly 741.12*

undeniable *demonstrable 331.12, real 717.14, authentic 721.16, decided 840.9*

undeniableness *authenticity 721.7*

undeniably *earnestly 278.10, authentically 721.31*

undependable *unskillful 128.4, unreliable 841.15*

under 598.13, 598.26; *low 597.26, deeper 598.10, inferiorly 745.13*

under a black cloud *dismally 304.19*

under a burden *burdensomely 538.17*

under a charter *with permission 502.10*

underachievement *incompleteness 806.2*

underachiever *loser 846.9*

under a cloak of darkness *stealthily 182.15*

under a cloud *unlucky 848.12*

underact 136.36; *be unskillful 128.8*

underacted *dramatized 136.32*

under a doctor's care *unhealthily 114.31*

underage *young 26.11*

underaged *young 26.11*

under an agreement *compromisingly 461.9*

under an arrangement *compromisingly 461.9*

under an injunction *by veto 503.12*

under a patent *with permission 502.10*

under arrest *detained 830.11*

under a spell *cursed 301.8*

under authorization *with permission 502.10*

underbid *bridge 168.4, bargain 480.20*

underbuilding *substructure 551.8*

undercapitalized *unprovided 98.6*

undercarriage *foundation 601.2, supporting structure 605.2*

under censorship 503.13

under certain conditions *feasibly 460.9*

under certain conditions *or circumstances relatively 726.17*

undercharge *settle accounts 493.11, make cheap 497.14*

underclass *social stratification 2.7*

underclass, the *the poor 486.7*

underclassman *learner 48.6*

underclothed *in dishabille 100.40*

underclothes *underwear 100.22*

underclothing *underwear 100.22*

undercoat *paint 251.6, layer 588.1, 588.9, coat 588.3, base 601.1, 601.10*

undercoated *coated 588.7*

under commission 833.11

under consideration *problematically 328.12, judged 341.9, under discussion 387.17, in preparation 388.8, 388.22*

under construction *in preparation 388.22, in production 551.25*

under contract *industrially 57.22, contractually 462.15*

under control *obedient 426.4, temperate 455.8, moderately 455.15, within limits 620.8, disciplined 765.17, restrained 830.9*

undercooked *culinary 91.9, incomplete 762.5*

undercover *secretive 182.9, concealed 844.7*

under cover *invisibly 245.8, safely 810.24*

undercover agent *one who conceals 181.7, secret person 182.6*

undercurrent *impression 266.2, flow 570.4, wave 571.3, conflict 828.3, concealment 844.2*

undercurrent of sound 233.3

undercut *sell at a loss 482.19, make cheap 497.14*

underdeveloped *immature 389.9, productive 522.11, shapeless 625.2, incomplete 762.5, uncompleted 762.7*

underdeveloped world *world region 564.6*

underdevelopment *unskillfulness 128.1, immaturity 389.3,*

incompleteness 762.1, 806.2, nonachievement 762.3, latency 844.1

under discussion 387.17; *problematically 328.12, questionable 333.13, questionably 333.22*

under doctor's orders *unhealthily 114.31*

underdog *loser 846.9, person in adversity 848.9*

underdog *[Inf] victim of discrimination 337.8*

underdone *culinary 91.9, uncooked 389.10, incomplete 762.5, uncompleted 762.7*

underdrawers *underwear 100.22*

underdressed *in dishabille 100.40*

underdressing *dressing 100.2*

under duress *discontentedly 291.17, unwillingly 375.17, compellingly 428.12*

undereat *be emaciated 595.16*

underemphasis *understatement 195.1*

underemphasize *understate 195.14*

underemphasized *understated 195.8*

underemployed *unemployed 413.10*

underemployment *nonuse 394.1, unemployment 413.5*

underestimate 344.5; *understate 195.14, misjudge 342.9, underestimation 344.1, misrepresent 366.5, disrespect 436.18, disparage 440.11, be incorrect 722.13, make smaller 747.8, think unimportant 800.19*

underestimated 344.4; *understated 195.8, misjudged 342.8, undervalued 436.17, incorrect 722.8*

underestimating 344.3

underestimation 344.1; *misinformation 188.3, understatement 195.1, misjudgment 342.1, misrepresentation 366.2, disesteem 436.2, disparagement 440.1, untrueness 722.3, limitation 747.3*

underestimator 344.2

under examination *experimentally 335.14*

underexpose *make dark 247.10*

underexposed *exposed 132.25, dark 247.5, colorless 252.5*

underexposed photograph *or negative pen-and-ink sketch 252.3*

underexposure *composition 132.17, darkening 247.2, pen-and-ink sketch 252.3*

under false pretenses *deceptively 193.21*

underfed 98.7, 118.7; *unhealthy 114.23, beggarly 486.12, emaciated 595.10*

underfinanced *unprovided 98.6*

under fire *martially 77.39, endangered 811.10*

underfloor heating *heater 217.3*

underfoot *low 597.26*

under full steam *at full speed 694.17*

underfunded *unprovided 98.6*

undergarments *underwear 100.22*

undergird *base 601.10, support 825.24*

underglaze *glaze 129.3, make ceramics 129.10*

underglazed *ceramic 129.9*

underglaze decoration *glaze 129.3*

undergo *feel 266.14, bear 605.17*

undergo a change *be changed 665.15*

undergo a personality change *be converted 670.12*

undergo privation *lessen 468.17*

undergo repairs *be restored 809.13*

undergo treatment for *be unhealthy 114.29*

undergrad *[Inf] learner 48.6*

undergraduate *learner 48.6*

underground *terrestrial 8.52, fleetingly 265.8, lower 597.14, low 597.26, the depths 598.2, under 598.13, 598.26, bottom 601.6, concealed 844.7*

underground *[Brit] railroad system 688.1*

underground activities *subversion 427.3*

underground cable *electricity 106.5*

underground economy *seller's market 483.3*

underground fighter *guerrilla 77.7*

underground literature *literature 139.1*

underground movie *movie type 137.3*

underground press *print journalism 175.4*

underground railway *railroad system 688.1*

underground river *river 570.1*

underground shelter *shelter 419.11, fortification 812.3*

underground stem *or shoot stem 41.5*

underground water *groundwater 8.11*

undergrowth *trees 43.4, rough thing 544.2*

under guard *safe 810.16*

underhand *secretive 182.9, cunning 330.8, disreputable 371.4, mysterious 844.11*

underhand *or underhanded devious 607.9, cunning 822.4*

under hand and seal *promised 458.8, as promised 458.16*

underhand deal *cunning 822.1*

underhanded *artful 193.13*

underhanded deal *foul play 193.6, cunning 822.1*

underhandedly *deceptively 193.21, deviously 607.16*

underhandedness *secretiveness 182.3, guile 193.3, deviousness 607.4*

underheated *unhygienic 114.27*

under house arrest *punished 454.19, detained 830.11*

under investigation *arguably 329.16*

underlaid *lower 597.14*

underlay *layer 588.1, underlie 597.23, 601.11, base 601.10*

underlayer *layer 588.1, lowest point 597.5, base 601.1*

under license *with permission 502.10*

underlie 597.23, 601.11; *be interior 611.14, hide 844.13*

underline *punctuate 183.20, identify 184.11, emphasize 200.6, make visible 244.9, strengthen 516.15, make important 799.14*

underlined *punctuated 183.15, emphasized 200.4*

underling *servant 69.1, commoner*

71.1, *inferior* 745.4, *nonentity* 800.8, *subordinate* 832.3
underlining *emphasis* 200.1, *that which makes visible* 244.4
under lock and key *in prison* 55.14, *safely* 810.24
underlying *lower* 597.14, *base* 601.7, *interior* 611.7, *latent* 844.6
underlying cause *cause* 675.1
underlying layer *interior* 611.1
underlying structure *grammar* 5.28
undermanned *unprovided* 98.6, *sparse* 796.6, *incomplete* 806.6
under maximum *or* **minimum security** *in prison* 55.14
undermine *be anarchic* 51.8, *refute* 332.7, *plot* 387.15, *remove power from* 515.13, *weaken* 517.13, *be cunning* 822.5, *hinder* 826.15
undermined *spoiled* 808.9
undermine the foundations of *knock down* 523.13
undermining *refutation* 332.1
undermost *bottom* 601.6
underneath *invisibly* 245.8, *lowest point* 597.5, *lower* 597.14, *low* 597.26
under no circumstances *not at all* 718.15
undernourished *underfed* 98.7, *unhealthy* 114.23, *emaciated* 595.10
under oath *assuredly* 189.30, *promised* 458.8, *as promised* 458.16
under obligation *grateful* 310.4, *answerable* 334.17, *responsibly* 391.10
under official sanction *agreeably* 462.14
under one's belt [Inf] *secured* 464.7
under one's breath *faintly* 233.11
under one's command *subordinate* 832.8
under one's hand and seal *contractual* 459.7
under one's nose *clear* 244.6, *manifestly* 331.20, *available* 575.11, *on the spot* 575.20, *near* 586.16
under one's own steam *alone* 788.20
under one's thumb *obedient* 426.4, *subject* 832.6
under one's thumb [Inf] *servile* 401.6
under orders *obediently* 426.9, *under commission* 833.11
underpaid *unprovided* 98.6, *poor* 486.8
underpaint *paint* 143.12
underpainting *(act of) painting* 143.1
underpants *underwear* 100.22
under par *inferiorly* 745.13
underpass *tunnel* 551.11, 691.6, *crossroads* 609.4, *crossing point* 692.7
underpin *bolster* 377.15, *base* 601.10, *support* 605.16
underpinning *substructure* 551.8, *foundation* 601.2, *supporting structure* 605.2, *foundational* 605.12
underpinnings *basis* 601.3
under plain cover *invisibly* 245.8
underplay *underact* 136.36, *understate* 195.14, *play down* 195.17
underplayed *dramatized* 136.32, *downplayed* 195.13
underplaying *downplaying* 195.6

underpopulated *sparse* 796.6
underpopulation *fewness* 796.3
underpraise *disparage* 195.15, *underestimate* 344.5
under pressure *unwillingly* 375.17, *hastily* 818.7
under pressure to *compellingly* 428.12
underprice *underestimate* 344.5
underpriced *underestimated* 344.4, *bargain* 497.10
underprivileged *poor* 486.8
underprivileged, the *the poor* 486.7
underprivileged class *the poor* 486.7
underprivileged nation *the poor* 486.7
under protest *unwillingly* 375.17, *resisting* 417.14
underrate *understate* 195.14, *misjudge* 342.9, *underestimate* 344.5, *disrespect* 436.18, *disparage* 440.11, *think unimportant* 800.19
underrated *understated* 195.8, *misjudged* 342.8, *underestimated* 344.4, *undervalued* 436.17
underrating *underestimation* 344.1
underreckon *understate* 195.14
underreckoned *understated* 195.8
underreckoning *understatement* 195.1
under restraint *restrained* 830.9
under restrictions *within limits* 620.8, *restrainedly* 830.18
underripe *immature* 389.9
under sail *in motion* 677.19, *nautically* 690.17
underscore *punctuate* 183.20, *identify* 184.11, *affirm* 189.21, *emphasize* 200.6, *strengthen* 516.15
underscored *affirmed* 189.11
underscoring *emphasis* 200.1
undersea *oceanic* 8.53, 571.7, *under* 598.13
underseas *or* **undersea** *under* 598.26
undersea warfare *naval warfare* 76.10
undersecretary *politician* 50.7, *deputy* 80.1
undersell *make cheap* 497.14
under sentence *endangered* 811.10
undersexed 20.20
under shelter *safe* 810.16
undershift *defense* 155.9, *play defense* 155.19
undershirt *underwear* 100.22
undershoot *flight* 689.5, *maneuver* 689.14, *unbalance* 741.8
undershorts *underwear* 100.22
underside *lowest point* 597.5
under siege *martially* 77.39, *endangered* 811.10
undersign *identify oneself* 184.12
undersigned, the *the contractor* 459.6
undersize *littleness* 580.1
undersized 580.8
underskirt *underwear* 100.22
under someone's influence *influentially* 512.14
undersown *farmable* 16.17
understaffed *unprovided* 98.6, *sparse* 796.6
understand 295.6, 363.9; *rationalize* 4.20, *know* 48.24, 348.10, *learn* 68.18, *be of the opinion* 87.10, *be informed* 170.15, *visualize* 242.24, *feel* 266.14, *be compassionate* 305.11, *pity* 308.6, *reason* 319.11, *have an idea* 327.13, *find out* 345.13, *be wise*

352.6, *suppose* 359.8, *have insight* 360.16, *infer* 361.14, *interpret* 365.12, *agree with* 462.10, *be profound* 598.23, *have a rapport with* 735.24
understandability *intelligibility* 363.1, *simplicity* 363.4
understandable *intelligible* 363.5
understandably *intelligibly* 363.13
understand by *infer* 361.14
understanding 363.4; *friendly relations* 62.3, *friendly* 62.5, *pacification* 74.1, *feelings* 266.1, *feeling* 266.9, *love* 299.1, *loving* 299.15, *pitying* 308.4, *intelligence* 315.2, 352.2, *intelligent* 315.9, *reason* 319.1, *reasoning* 319.7, *idea* 327.1, *finding out* 345.3, *knowledge* 348.1, *wisdom* 352.1, *foresight* 357.1, *insight* 360.3, *interpretation* 365.1, *duty* 433.1, *contract* 459.1, *compromise* 461.1, *agreement* 462.1, 767.9, *profundity* 598.5, *supportive* 605.11, *settlement* 735.6, *compatible* 735.14
understandingly *lovingly* 299.29, *pityingly* 308.11, *compatibly* 735.34
understate 195.14; *distort the truth* 192.25, *underestimate* 344.5, *disparage* 440.11
understated 195.8; *partially true* 192.18, *soft-hued* 251.13, *unpretentious* 526.8
understatedly 195.18
understatement 195.1; *partial truth* 192.7, *underestimation* 344.1, *disparagement* 440.1
under steam *nautically* 690.17
understeer *miscellaneous automotive terms* 687.14
understood *supposed* 359.6, *established* 397.12, *tacit* 844.10
understrapper *nonentity* 800.8
understrength *insufficient* 517.11
under strict regulations *severely* 424.11
understructure *construction* 551.6, *substructure* 551.8
understudy *alternative* 80.2, *substitute for* 80.5, *actor* 136.25, *act* 136.34, *helper* 275.5, *answer for* 334.24, *substitute* 613.17, 672.2, *cover for* 613.34, *be a substitute* 672.6, *extra person* 748.7
understudy for *aid* 275.10
undertake 391.7; *address oneself to* 209.13, *invent* 335.13, *resolve* 374.9, *follow up* 385.16, *tackle* 390.8, *do something* 412.13, *contract* 462.11, *engage* 833.9
undertaken 391.4
undertaker *person dealing with the dead* 29.8, *funeral person* 31.5, *attempter* 390.3, *operator* 412.7
undertaking 391.1, 675.5; *future intention* 374.3, *venture* 390.2, *deed* 412.2, *social activity* 414.2, *contract* 459.1, 462.2, *business* 480.6, 509.3, *production* 522.1, *engagement* 833.2
under the aegis of *safely* 810.24
under the auspices *or* **aegis of** *in aid of* 825.33
under the best circumstances *ideally* 327.22
under the circumstances 726.16; *circumstantially* 573.12,

conditionally 725.10, *accordingly* 735.39
under the counter *in trade* 480.22
under-the-counter *cunning* 822.4
under-the-counter purchase *cunning* 822.1
under the eye of heaven *manifestly* 843.17
under the hammer *on sale* 482.24
under the influence *drunk* 121.25, *drunkenly* 121.39
under the open sky *out-of-doors* 558.26
under the ownership of *possessed* 469.13
under the protection of *safe* 810.16
under the sun *extensively* 563.18
under the sway of *subordinate* 832.8
under the table [Inf] *dead drunk* 121.27
under-the-table *cunning* 822.4
under-the-table deal *cunning* 822.1
under the terms of one's will *by transfer* 470.15
under the very nose of *defiantly* 416.9
under the weather *sick* 114.24
under the wing of *safe* 810.16
underthings *underwear* 100.22
undertone *tone* 140.24, 230.2, *undercurrent of sound* 233.3, *ambience* 615.3, *quietness* 844.4
undertow *flow* 570.4, *wave* 571.3, *hidden danger* 813.3
under treatment *unhealthily* 114.31
underuse *nonuse* 394.1, *not use* 394.9
underused *disused* 394.8
underutilization *nonuse* 394.1
underutilize *not use* 394.9
underutilized *disused* 394.8
undervaluation *understatement* 195.1, *misjudgment* 342.1, *underestimation* 344.1, *disesteem* 436.2, *limitation* 747.3
undervalue *understate* 195.14, *misjudge* 342.9, *underestimate* 344.5, *disrespect* 436.18, *disparage* 440.11, *make smaller* 447.8
undervalued 436.17; *understated* 195.8, *misjudged* 342.8, *underestimated* 344.4
under warrant *with permission* 502.10, *trustworthy* 810.17
under warranty *guaranteed* 464.6
underwater *fishing* 154.13, *on the water* 154.15, *swimming* 164.12, *oceanic* 571.7, *under* 598.13, 598.26
underwater breathing tube *swimming equipment* 164.8
underwater diving Sporting Activities 145
underwater explorer *oceanographer* 571.6
underwater mask *swimming equipment* 164.8
underwater photography *photographic specialties* 132.2
underwater plug *bait* 154.6
underwater swimmer *swimmer* 164.11, *descender* 714.8
underwater swimming *swimming* 164.1
underway *sailing* 150.25
under way *in preparation* 388.22, *in motion* 677.19, *in progress* 679.16, *nautically* 690.17

underwear 100.22
underweight *light* 539.4, *thin* 595.9
underwood *trees* 43.4
underworld *evil place* 446.6, *villain* 448.5, *future condition* 650.3
under wraps [Inf] *concealed* 181.8, *private* 245.5, *concealed* 844.7
underwrite *assent* 346.6, *finance* 457.7, *guarantee* 458.13, *contract* 459.8, *promise* 464.10, *support financially* 605.19
underwriter *assenter* 346.3, *provider* 605.10
underwriting *promise* 464.2
underwritten *agreed* 346.5, *guaranteeing* 458.9
undesigned *causeless* 842.11
undesigning *naive* 821.3
undesirability *inconvenience* 804.1
undesirable *disreputable character* 371.2, *inconvenient* 804.5
undesired *disliked* 291.10
undesirous *indifferent* 289.7, *disliked* 291.10
undetectability *invisibility* 245.1
undetectable *invisible* 245.3
undetected *concealed* 844.7
undetermined *vacillating* 378.5, *generalized* 778.12, *indeterminate* 841.14, *causeless* 842.11
undeterred *enduring* 377.9
undeveloped *young* 26.11, *immature* 26.12, 389.9, *unskilled* 128.5, *new* 394.7, *shapeless* 625.2, *incomplete* 762.5, 806.6, *unimproved* 808.10, *potential* 836.6, *latent* 844.6
undeveloped country *economic development* 56.5
undeveloped world *world region* 564.6
undevelopment *immaturity* 26.3, 389.3, *shapelessness* 625.1, *incompleteness* 806.2
undeviating *straight* 630.8, *direct* 697.11, *regular* 730.12, *convinced* 840.8, *infallible* 840.12
undeviatingly *directly* 697.16, *regularly* 730.21
undies *underwear* 100.22
undifferentiated *vague* 338.9, *same* 730.7, *continuous* 774.9
undifferentiating *undiscriminating* 338.5
undifferentiation *sameness* 730.1, *continuity* 774.4
undignified *graceless* 528.7, *indecorous* 528.8
undiluted *drinkable* 93.18, *intoxicating* 121.29, *strong to the senses* 516.12
undiminished *uncut* 759.7, *complete* 805.14
undine *minor deity* 82.2, *legendary sea being* 571.4
undiplomatic *unskillful* 128.4
undiplomatically *unskillfully* 128.12
undirected 698.10; *causeless* 842.11
undiscernible *unintelligible* 364.4
undiscerning *unskillful* 128.4, *blind to* 243.14, *undiscriminating* 338.5
undischarged bankrupt *nonpayer* 490.6
undiscipline *overindulgence* 456.3
undisciplined *anarchic* 51.5, *erratic* 381.5, *disobedient* 427.10, *overindulgent* 456.8, *disorderly* 766.15

undisclosed *secret* 182.8, *concealed* 844.7
undiscouraged *enduring* 377.9
undiscoverable *unintelligible* 364.4, *concealed* 844.7
undiscovered *concealed* 844.7, *unsolved* 844.8
undiscriminating 338.5
undisguised *candid* 191.5, *visible* 244.5, *easily seen through* 249.10, *naive* 821.3, *manifest* 843.9
undisguisedly *manifestly* 843.17
undisputed *believed* 87.8, *agreeing* 462.6, *decided* 840.9
undissembling *naive* 821.3
undissolved *condensed* 540.7
undistinguishable *vague* 338.9
undistinguished *mediocre* 289.11, 742.7, *humble* 298.8, *vague* 338.9, *middling* 772.14
undistinguishedly *unexceptionally* 289.20
undistracted *diligent* 323.7
undistributed middle *philosophical problem* 4.8
undisturbed *detached* 4.18, *quiescent* 678.6
undivided *continuous* 669.5, *uncut* 759.7, *complete* 761.6, *whole* 788.12
undivided attention *close attention* 323.2
undividedness *oneness* 788.3
undivulged *secret* 182.8, *unsolved* 844.8, *unsaid* 844.9
undo *counteract* 510.7, *destroy* 523.10, *undress* 614.18, *restore* 671.10, *separate* 753.12, *unstick* 756.6, *make useless* 802.12
undocumented *uncertified* 841.13
undoing *destruction* 523.1, *ruin* 523.4, *separation* 753.1
undomesticated *unaccustomed* 398.3
undone *neglected* 326.6, *destroyed* 523.9, *separate* 753.7, *nonadhesive* 756.4, *uncompleted* 762.7
undoubtable *authentic* 721.16
undoubted *probable* 838.6
undoubtedly *definitely* 189.33, *certainly* 719.14, 840.15, *authentically* 721.31
undoubting *believing* 87.6, *convinced* 840.8
undrained *unhygienic* 114.27, *of landmasses* 572.12
undramatic *unemphatic* 201.2, *unpretentious* 526.8
undramatically *unpretentiously* 526.15
undrape *undress* 614.18
undraped *undressed* 614.11
undreamed-of *unthought-of* 318.10
undress 614.18; *undressing* 614.2
undressed 614.11; *uncooked* 389.12, *unequipped* 389.13
undressing 614.2
undrilled *untrained* 389.8
undrinkable *unhygienic* 114.27, *unpalatable* 223.6
undrooping *committed* 377.7
undue *excessive* 712.8, *inconvenient* 804.5
undulant *waving* 683.11
undulate *billow* 571.9, *convolute* 632.6, *be regular* 663.10, *wave* 683.15
undulating *hilly* 569.6, *of landmasses* 572.12, *frequent* 663.6, *waving* 683.11
undulating land *upland* 572.7
undulatingly *regularly* 663.14

undulating motion *frequency* 663.2
undulation *wave* 10.11, 571.3, *curve* 629.1, *convolution* 632.1, *frequency* 663.2
undulatory *rough* 544.5, *rounded* 629.5, *convolutional* 632.4, *waving* 683.11
unduplicated *original* 737.4
undutiful *disobedient* 427.10, *nonperforming* 466.6
undutifulness *disobedience* 427.1, *nonperformance* 466.2
undyed *white* 253.7, *gray* 255.6
undying *timeless* 640.3, *permanent* 642.5, *eternal* 644.4, 798.7, *unfailing* 667.3, *protracted* 669.7
undyingly *permanently* 667.6
unearned income *earnings* 467.5
unearth *detect* 345.12, *find* 565.11, *excavate* 651.19, *dig out* 711.15, *reveal* 843.14
unearthed *disclosed* 180.5, *discovered* 345.9, *found* 565.7
unearthing *locating* 565.3, *digging out* 711.3
unearthliness *the occult* 86.2, *immateriality* 525.2
unearthly *spiritual* 86.20
unearthly hour *early hour* 657.2
unearth the past *excavate* 651.19
unease *fearfulness* 283.2, *restlessness* 414.7
uneasily *fearfully* 283.19, *agitatedly* 684.27, *distractedly* 768.14
uneasiness *fearfulness* 283.2, *worry* 283.4, *agitation* 684.1
uneasy *clumsy* 128.6, *fearful* 283.10, *agitated* 684.15, *disturbed* 768.6
uneasy conscience *penitence* 451.1
uneasy peace *psychological warfare* 76.13
uneasy truce *truce* 73.2
uneatable *unpalatable* 223.6
uneconomic *wasteful* 96.9, *extravagant* 500.4, *futile* 802.10
uneconomical *wasteful* 96.9
uneconomically *wastefully* 96.23, *extravagantly* 500.9
unedged *blunt* 550.5
uneducable *unskilled* 128.5
uneducated *of language* 5.35, *unskilled* 128.5, *ignorant* 349.5, *unaccustomed* 398.3, *naive* 821.3
unelaborate *simple* 195.10
unelaborated *uncompleted* 762.7
unelaborately *simply* 195.19
unelaborateness *simplicity* 195.4
unelevated *low* 597.10
unembellished *unadorned* 526.9
unembellishment *unadornment* 526.3
unembodied *nonmaterial* 525.8
unemotional *detached* 4.18, *insensible* 213.4, *insensitive* 268.4, *indifferent* 289.7
unemotionally *stoically* 4.26, *insensitively* 268.7, *indifferently* 289.17
unemphatic 201.2; *faint* 233.6, *unpretentious* 526.8
unemphatically 201.4
unemployability *uselessness* 802.1
unemployable *unused* 394.5, *useless* 802.7
unemployed 413.10; *leisurely* 125.4, *discarded* 383.8, *not working* 415.10, *powerless* 515.6
unemployment 413.5, 415.2; *time off* 125.2, *discarding* 383.3, *nonuse* 394.1, *economic adversity* 848.6

unemployment benefit *social welfare* 307.4
unemployment benefit or compensation *social assistance* 825.4
unemployment benefits *security* 464.1
unemployment insurance *social assistance* 825.4
unemployment rate *economic indicator* 56.4, *economic factor* 56.8
unenclosed *opened up* 583.11
unending *eternal* 644.4, 798.7, *continuing forever* 644.6, *protracted* 669.7, *continuous* 774.9
unendingly *continually* 377.17, 669.10
unendowed *unskillful* 128.4
unengaged *not working* 415.10
unenlightened *unskillful* 128.4, *blind to* 243.14, *ignorant* 349.5
unenlightenment *figurative blindness* 243.8, *ignorance* 349.1
unenthusiasm 375.3
unenthusiastic 375.10; *wonderless* 295.3, *apathetic* 322.4
unenthusiastically *without wonder* 295.8, *apathetically* 322.7, *unwillingly* 375.17
unequable *unequal* 741.4
unequal 741.4; *socioeconomic* 2.13, *ranked* 6.72, *clumsy* 128.6, *different* 463.7, *rough* 544.5, *distorted* 627.6, *irregular* 664.3, *disparate* 728.9, *dissimilar* 734.4
unequaled *excellent* 445.13, *unequal* 741.4, *best* 744.10, 805.9
unequalize *unbalance* 741.8
unequally 741.10; *mathematically* 6.93, *differently* 463.13, *roughly* 544.13, *irregularly* 664.6, *disparately* 728.19, *dissimilarly* 734.10
unequalness *irregularity* 664.1
unequal to *insufficient* 98.4
unequipped 389.13; *unprovided* 98.6, *unskillful* 128.4, *incomplete* 806.6
unequivocal *definite* 189.18, *emphatic* 200.3, *intelligible* 363.5, *straightforward* 630.9, *decided* 840.9
unequivocally *definitely* 189.33, *straightforwardly* 630.17, *completely* 759.14, 805.22
unequivocalness *definiteness* 189.6, *straightforwardness* 630.3
unerring *correct* 350.4, 429.8, *virtuous* 447.5, *innocent* 449.6
unerringly *correctly* 429.16, *innocently* 449.13
unerringness *right* 429.2
unescorted *solo* 788.14, *vulnerable* 811.9
unessayed *idle* 394.6
unessential *extraneous* 724.8
unessentially *extraneously* 724.16
unethical *immoral* 430.11, 432.9
unethically *immorally* 430.27, 432.18
unethicalness *immorality* 432.1
uneuphonious *inelegant* 528.6
unevasibleness *inevitability* 840.5
unevasive *simple* 363.6
uneven *wrongful* 430.10, *rough* 544.5, *notched* 636.4, *irregular* 664.3, *inconsistent* 732.7, *unequal* 741.4, *discontinuous* 775.7, *imperfect* 806.5
unevenly *wrongly* 430.24, *roughly* 544.13, *jaggedly* 636.7, *irregularly* 664.6, *inconsistently* 732.16, *unequally* 741.10, *imperfectly* 806.10

unevenness *wrong* 430.1, *roughness* 544.1, *irregularity* 664.1, *inconsistency* 732.3, *imbalance* 741.2, *discontinuity* 775.1, *imperfection* 806.1
uneven parallel bars 157.6; *gymnastics equipment* 157.2
uneventful *commonplace* 800.17
unexaggerated *truthful* 191.4
unexcelled *best* 744.10
unexceptional *mediocre* 289.11, 742.7, *familiar* 397.10, *moderate* 521.3, *common* 778.13
unexceptionally 289.20
unexcitable *inert* 519.2
unexcited *wonderless* 295.3
unexcitedly *without wonder* 295.8
unexciting *unemphatic* 201.2, *tasteless* 220.4
unexculpable *unforgivable* 430.16
unexecuted *uncompleted* 762.7
unexercised *untrained* 389.8, *idle* 394.6
unexistent *nonexistent* 190.14
unexisting *nonexistent* 190.14
unexpected 839.6; *surprising* 292.7, *strange* 364.9, *chance* 381.5, *improbable* 839.4, *chance* 842.10, *causeless* 842.11
unexpected attack *hidden danger* 813.3
unexpected event *hidden danger* 813.3
unexpectedly 839.9; *surprisingly* 292.14, *randomly* 842.16
unexpectedness 839.2; *surprise* 292.1
unexpended *saved* 105.15
unexpended balance *reserve* 105.3
unexpensive *cheap* 497.9
unexpensively *cheaply* 497.16
unexpiable *unforgivable* 430.16
unexpired *surplus* 750.8
unexplainable *unintelligible* 364.4, *causeless* 842.11
unexplained 364.6; *unsolved* 844.8
unexploited *new* 394.7
unexplored *unknown* 349.7, *unfamiliar* 652.10, *unsolved* 844.8
unexposed *safe* 810.16, *concealed* 844.7
unexpressed *unsaid* 844.9
unexpressive *meaningless* 362.7
unexpurgated *offensive* 432.11, *uncut* 759.7, *complete* 761.6
unextreme *moderate* 772.12
unfact [Inf] *falsehood* 192.6
unfactual *untrue* 722.6
unfactually *without truth* 722.14
unfading *colored* 251.10, *unfailing* 667.3
unfailing 667.3; *constant* 377.8, *protracted* 669.7
unfailingly *permanently* 667.6
unfair *misrepresented* 188.4, *discriminatory* 337.11, *unjust* 342.7, 741.6, *wrongful* 430.10
unfair advantage *gain* 467.1
unfair labor practices *work practices* 57.2
unfairly *unrepresentatively* 188.8, *prejudicially* 337.17, *unjustly* 342.13, 741.12, *wrongly* 430.24
unfairly treated *misjudged* 342.8
unfairness *prejudice* 337.3, *injustice* 342.3, 741.3, *wrong* 430.1
unfair price *overpricing* 496.2
unfair treatment 342.4
unfaithful *estranged* 63.8, *disbelieving* 88.6, *dishonorable* 192.14, *unchaste* 432.10, *defiant*

466.7, *irresolute* 666.4, *unreliable* 722.10
unfaithfully *hostilely* 63.13, *dishonorably* 192.28, *changeably* 666.7
unfaithfulness *personal conflict* 63.2, *dishonorableness* 192.3, *love affair* 299.9, *disobedience* 427.1, *fornication* 432.3, *unreliability* 722.5
unfallacious *true* 721.11
unfallaciously *truly* 721.27
unfallen *chaste* 431.10
unfaltering *constant* 377.8
unfamiliar 652.10; *unknown* 349.7, *unaccustomed* 398.3
unfamiliarity *ignorance* 349.1, *unaccustomedness* 398.1, *newness* 652.1
unfamiliar word *new word* 5.18
unfashionable 528.10; *uncustomary* 398.4, *plain* 528.9, *discourteous* 535.7
unfashionably *inelegantly* 528.11
unfashioned *unformed* 389.11
unfasten *open up* 583.16, *separate* 753.12, *unstick* 756.6, *deliver* 817.5
unfastened *opened up* 583.11, *unjoined* 753.9
unfastening *separation* 753.1
unfastidious *unclean* 112.8, *undiscriminating* 338.5
unfathomable *inscrutable* 250.5, *unintelligible* 364.4, *deep* 598.9, *immeasurable* 798.6
unfathomableness *depth* 598.1
unfathomable space *the depths* 598.2
unfathomably *opaquely* 250.9, *unintelligibly* 364.16, *deep* 598.25
unfavorable *inauspicious* 282.8, *presageful* 358.13, *critical* 438.13, *untimely* 660.5, *oppositional* 828.11, *adverse* 848.10
unfavorableness *untimeliness* 660.1
unfavorable regard *dislike* 291.1
unfavorable review *criticism* 438.4
unfavorable verdict 54.20
unfavorably *inauspiciously* 282.15, *at the wrong time* 660.12, *adversely* 848.16
unfearing *steadfast* 284.11, *tenacious* 376.9
unfeasibility *hopelessness* 837.2
unfeasible *hopeless* 837.6
unfeathered *shed* 614.14
unfed *underfed* 98.7, *fasting* 118.5
unfeeling *insensible* 213.4, *insensitive* 268.4, *indifferent* 289.7, *pitiless* 309.3, *strong-willed* 376.10, *mentally tough* 547.12, *dull* 550.7
unfeelingly *insensibly* 213.9, *insensitively* 268.7, *indifferently* 289.17, *pitilessly* 309.7, *single-mindedly* 547.19
unfeelingness *pitilessness* 309.1, *mental toughness* 547.5
unfeigned *truthful* 191.4
unfeigning *natural* 526.10
unfeminine *female* 33.16, *vulgar* 535.6
unfenced *opened up* 583.11
unfetter *make simple* 526.12, *separate* 753.12, *deliver* 817.5, *set free* 829.17, *liberate* 831.6
unfettered *separate* 753.7, *free* 829.11, *free-ranging* 829.13, *liberated* 831.4
unfettering *liberation* 831.1
unfictitious *true* 721.11

unfictitiously *truly* 721.27
unfilled *unprovided* 98.6, *unoccupied* 576.13, *incomplete* 806.6
unfinished 544.9; *unskilled* 128.5, *unformed* 389.11, *shapeless* 625.2, *partial* 760.11, *incomplete* 762.5, 806.6, *uncompleted* 762.7
unfinished piece *rough idea* 544.4
unfinished state *incompleteness* 762.1
unfinished task *nonachievement* 762.3
unfit *unhealthy* 114.23, *unskillful* 128.4, *untrained* 389.8, *improper* 430.14, *powerless* 515.6, *conditional* 725.7, *useless* 802.7, *make useless* 802.12, *inconvenient* 804.5, *imperfect* 806.5
unfit for consideration *unselected* 383.7
unfit for human consumption *unselected* 383.7
unfitness *unskillfulness* 128.1, *lack of preparation* 389.1, *powerlessness* 515.1, *uselessness* 802.1, *inconvenience* 804.1, *imperfection* 806.1
unfitting *improper* 430.14, *inconvenient* 804.5
unfittingness *inconvenience* 804.1
unfixed *unjoined* 753.9
unflagging *committed* 377.7, *constant* 377.8, *industrious* 414.16, *stalwart* 547.10
unflagging efforts *commitment* 377.2
unflanked *vulnerable* 811.9
unflattering *discourteous* 411.5
unflavored *tasteless* 220.4
unflawed *perfect* 805.8
unfledged *young* 26.11, *newly hatched* 36.20, *immature* 389.9, *shed* 614.14, *embryonic* 771.19
unfleshly *nonmaterial* 525.8
unflinching *steadfast* 284.11, *tenacious* 376.9
unfluent *inelegant* 528.6
unfocused *difficult to see* 245.4
unfold *rationalize* 4.20, *vegetate* 41.21, *disclose* 180.8, *explain* 331.16, *grow* 581.17, *open* 583.15, *straighten* 630.14, *follow from* 676.9, *come to be* 717.19, *change by degrees* 739.8, *reveal* 843.14
unfolded *bigger* 581.9, *open* 583.10
unfolding *flowering* 42.5, *first appearance* 264.3, *appearing* 264.9, *growing* 581.12, *manifestation* 843.2
unforced *voluntary* 504.9
unforeseeable *unexpected* 839.6, *chance* 842.10
unforeseeableness *unexpectedness* 839.2
unforeseeably *unexpectedly* 839.9
unforeseen *surprising* 292.7, *unexpected* 839.6, *chance* 842.10
unforeseen, the *unexpectedness* 839.2
unforgettable *memorable* 354.7, *notable* 799.11
unforgettably *memorably* 354.16
unforgivable 430.16; *guilty* 450.6
unforgivably *vindictively* 441.16, *guiltily* 450.12
unforgiving *pitiless* 309.3, *severe* 424.5, *vindictive* 441.10
unforgivingness *pitilessness* 309.1
unforgotten *memorable* 354.7
unform *make shapeless* 625.3
unformed 389.11; *shapeless* 625.2

unforthcoming *taciturn* 208.4, *avoiding* 386.9, *unsociable* 409.6
unfortified *helpless* 515.9, *weak* 517.6, *vulnerable* 811.9
unfortunate *lamentable* 280.6, *victim of discrimination* 337.8, *accidental* 660.7, *inconvenient* 804.5, *chance* 842.10, *loser* 846.9, *failed* 846.10, *person in adversity* 848.9, *unlucky* 848.12
unfortunately *lamentably* 280.10, *mistakenly* 660.14, *luckily* 842.17, *unsuccessfully* 846.21, *adversely* 848.16
unfoul *void* 709.23
unfouling *removal* 709.5
unfounded *sophistic* 330.7, *untrue* 722.6
unfrank *uncandid* 192.15
unfrankly *uncandidly* 192.29
unfrankness *lack of candor* 192.4
unfree *obedient* 69.10, *captive* 832.9
unfreeze *melt* 555.24
unfreezing *fluidization* 555.8
unfriendliness *hostility* 63.1, *antipathy* 291.2, *unsociability* 409.1, *discourtesy* 411.1, *opposition* 828.1
unfriendly *hostile* 63.6, *antipathetic* 291.7, *unsociable* 409.6, *discourteous* 411.5, *oppositional* 828.1
unfrock *punish* 454.22, *disbar* 709.16, *eject* 764.8, *terminate* 834.7
unfrocking *punishment* 454.1, *dismissal* 709.2
unfruitful *infertile* 23.7
unfuddled *sober* 120.5
unfulfilled *unprovided* 98.6, *disappointed* 293.4, *uncompleted* 762.7
unfulfilled expectations *disappointment* 293.1
unfulfilling *disappointing* 293.6
unfurl *disclose* 180.8, *straighten* 630.14, *reveal* 843.14
unfurled *displayed* 843.8
unfurnished *unprovided* 98.6, *unequipped* 389.13
unfussily *simply* 195.19
unfussiness *simplicity* 195.4
unfussy *simple* 195.10, *undiscriminating* 338.5
ungainliness *ugliness* 531.1
ungainly *clumsy* 128.6, 824.14, *graceless* 528.7, *ugly* 531.3
ungallant *discourteous* 411.5
ungallantly *discourteously* 411.8
ungallantness *discourtesy* 411.1
ungarbed *undressed* 614.11
ungarnished *uncooked* 389.12, *unadorned* 526.9
ungenerosity *meanness* 501.1
ungenerous *selfish* 444.4, *mean* 501.4
ungenerously *selfishly* 444.8, *meanly* 501.8
ungenerousness *meanness* 501.1
ungenial *hostile* 63.6
ungeniality *hostility* 63.1
ungenially *hostilely* 63.13
ungentle *discourteous* 411.5
ungentlemanlike *discourteous* 411.5
ungentlemanliness *discourtesy* 411.1
ungentlemanly *discourteous* 411.5, *discourteously* 411.8, *vulgar* 535.6
ungentleness *discourtesy* 411.1
ungently *discourteously* 411.8
ungenuine 192.13; *unauthentic* 722.9

ungenuinely *untruthfully* 192.27, *unauthentically* 722.17

ungenuineness 192.2; *unauthenticity* 722.4

ungermane *unrelated* 728.6

ungettable *or* **ungetable** *invulnerable* 810.18

ungifted *unskillful* 128.4

ungiving *mentally hard* 542.8

unglazed *ceramic* 129.9

unglue *unstick* 756.6

ungodliness *evil* 446.1, *impiety* 448.4

ungodly *evil* 446.7, *impious* 448.11, *impiously* 448.17

ungovernable *lawless* 53.26, *refractory* 379.6, *violent* 520.5, *independent* 829.12

ungoverned *anarchic* 51.5, *free* 829.11, *independent* 829.12

ungraceful *clumsy* 128.6, *graceless* 528.7

ungracious *objectionable* 272.7, *ungrateful* 311.2, *badly behaved* 399.16, *discourteous* 411.5

ungraciously *ungratefully* 311.6, *badly* 399.23, *unsocially* 409.13, *discourteously* 411.8

ungraciousness *objectionability* 272.2, *ingratitude* 311.1, *bad conduct* 399.7, *unsociability* 409.1, *discourtesy* 411.1

ungraded *disordered* 766.9

ungrateful 311.2; *unthinking* 355.8

ungratefully 311.6

ungratefulness *ingratitude* 311.1

ungregarious *unsociable* 409.6

ungregariousness *unsociability* 409.1

ungrudging *generous* 498.6

ungrudgingly *generously* 498.12

unguarded *unprepared* 389.5, *spontaneous* 396.5, *weak* 517.6, *vulnerable* 811.9

unguent *dose of medicine* 115.3, *balm* 115.11, *ointment* 562.8

unguentary *lubricational* 562.12

unguentum *ointment* 562.8

unguessed *unexpected* 839.6, *unsolved* 844.8

unguiculate *carnivorous* 35.26

unguided *undirected* 698.10, *naive* 821.3

unguinous *oily* 562.11

ungulant *hoofed mammal* 35.16

ungulate 35.31; *type of animal* 34.5, *hoofed mammal* 35.16

unguligrade *ungulate* 35.31

unhabituated *clumsy* 128.6, *unaccustomed* 398.3

unhackneyed *uncustomary* 398.4

unhallow *dirty* 112.11

unhallowed *unclean* 112.8

unhampered *opened up* 583.11

unhand *liberate* 831.4

unhandiness *unskillfulness* 128.1

unhanding *liberation* 831.1

unhandled *new* 394.7

unhandy *clumsy* 128.6

unhappily *sorrowfully* 270.10, *adversely* 848.16

unhappiness *sorrow* 270.1, *disapproval* 438.1

unhappy *bungled* 128.7, *depressed* 261.7, *sorrowful* 270.4, *lamenting* 280.4, *disapproving* 438.8, *inconvenient* 804.5

unharbored *stateless* 574.14

unhardened *weak* 517.6

unharmed *getting well* 113.9, *uncut* 759.7, *safe* 810.16

unharmonious *hostile* 63.6,

---

unpleasant 272.6, *disagreeing* 463.6, *disunited* 753.10

unharmoniously *hostilely* 63.13, *disunitedly* 753.25

unharmoniousness *disagreement* 463.1

unharmonized *unmelodious* 241.5

unharness *land* 704.16

unhazardous *trustworthy* 810.17

unhealthily 114.31; *unhygienically* 114.32, *in good form* 725.11

unhealthiness *lack of hygiene* 112.3, *ill health* 114.1

unhealthy 114.23; *killing* 30.17, *unclean* 112.8, *unhygienic* 114.27, *drained of color* 252.6, *conditional* 725.7, *imperfect* 806.5, *dangerous* 811.7

unhealthy climate *lack of hygiene* 112.3

unhealthy conditions *lack of hygiene* 112.3

unhealthy situation *danger* 811.1

unheard 229.7; *reserved* 403.10

unheard-of *wondrous* 294.9, *unknown* 349.7, *unfamiliar* 652.10, *novel* 737.5

unhearing 229.5; *deaf* 229.4, *inactive* 413.9

unheated *cold* 218.9

unheaviness *lightness* 539.1

unheavy *light* 539.4

unheeded *neglected* 326.6

unheeding *unhearing* 229.5, *inattentive* 324.5

unhelpful *unenthusiastic* 375.10, *useless* 802.7, *inconvenient* 804.5, *hindering* 826.12, *uncooperative* 828.14

unhelpfully *uselessly* 802.14, *inconveniently* 804.11, *with delay* 826.22, *opposingly* 828.22

unhelpfulness *opposition* 375.2, *uselessness* 802.1, *uncooperativeness* 828.4

unheroic *cowardly* 285.4

unheroically *cowardly* 285.9

unhesitant *tenacious* 376.9

unhesitating *believing* 87.6, *convinced* 840.1

unhesitatingly *believingly* 87.12

unhewn *unformed* 389.11, *shapeless* 625.2

unhidden *visible* 244.5

unhindered *opened up* 583.11, *free* 829.11

unhinge *make insane* 110.13, *disconnect* 574.19, *derange* 766.23

unhinged *insane* 110.9, *abnormal* 430.13, *disconnected* 574.12, *deranged* 766.16

unhinging *disconnection* 574.5

unhistorical *imaginary* 360.12

unhitch *land* 704.16, *separate* 753.12

unholiness *uncleanness* 112.2, *evil* 446.1

unholy *unclean* 112.8, *evil* 446.7

unholy joy *malice* 306.2

unholy mess [Inf] *predicament* 824.5

unholy terror *fear* 283.1

unhook *undress* 614.18, *separate* 753.12

unhopeful *without hope* 282.7

unhopefully 282.14

unhopefulness *lack of hope* 282.2

unhorse *separate* 753.12

unhostile *friendly* 62.5

unhouse *evict* 709.20

unhoused *stateless* 574.14

unhurried 693.8; *leisurely* 125.4,

---

deliberate 589.18, *quiescent* 678.6, *at ease* 819.2, *easygoing* 823.13

unhurriedly *leisurely* 125.6, *slowly* 693.14

unhurriedness *slowness* 693.1

unhurt *uncut* 759.7, *unbroken* 805.13, *safe* 810.16

unhygienic 114.27; *unclean* 112.8, *of disease* 114.25, *dangerous* 811.7

unhygienically 114.32

unicameral *one-sided* 788.11

UNICEF *charitable organization* 305.4

unicellular *cellular* 13.30, *algal* 47.20, *one-sided* 788.11

Unicorn Constellations 7

unicorn Heraldic Terms 184, Legendary Creatures 360

unicycle *bicycle* 687.10

unidentical *nonuniform* 734.5

unidentically *nonuniformly* 734.11

unidentifiable *unrecognizable* 364.7

unidentifiably *invisibly* 245.8

unidentified *unknown* 349.7

unidiomatic *meaningless* 362.7

unidirectional *direct* 697.11, *one-sided* 788.11

unification 752.5; *junction* 609.5, *combination* 757.1, *association* 827.6

Unification Church Christian Groups 81

unified *united* 752.10, *combined* 757.5, *combinatory* 757.6, *whole* 759.6, 788.12

unified field theory *fundamental interaction* 10.65

uniflagellate *algal* 47.20

uniflorous *horticultural* 17.14

uniform 100.9, 545.5, 780.10; *universal* 6.67, *make clothing* 100.44, *basketball court* 148.3, *clothing* 184.6, *colorful* 251.11, *boring* 296.6, *established* 397.12, *formal clothing* 406.5, *compatible* 462.8, *symmetrical* 626.4, *even* 626.5, *regular* 663.5, *directional* 677.13, *same* 730.7, *similar* 733.7, *conforming* 735.17, *equal* 740.8, *well-ordered* 765.14, *continuous* 774.9, *monotonous* 797.12

Uniform Code of Military Justice *military law* 58.7

uniformed *warring* 76.26, *dressed* 100.38, *formally dressed* 406.8

uniformitarian *evolutionary* 13.34

uniformitarianism *geological time* 8.47, *evolution* 13.23

uniformity *boringness* 296.2, *compatibility* 462.3, *smoothness* 545.1, *symmetry* 626.1, *evenness* 626.3, *regularity* 663.1, *sameness* 730.1, *similarity* 733.1, *conformity* 735.7, 781.1, *method* 765.7, *continuity* 774.4, *custom* 780.5, *repetitiveness* 797.3

uniformization *regularity* 730.6

uniformize *make the same* 730.16, *make similar* 733.15

uniform labor law policy *labor law* 57.12

uniformly *mathematically* 6.93, *boringly* 296.10, *compatibly* 462.16, *smoothly* 545.13, *symmetrically* 626.7, *orderly* 663.13, *identically* 730.18, *similarly* 733.17, *conformingly* 735.37, *equitably* 740.15, *methodically* 765.27

uniform movement *regular movement* 677.10

---

uniformness *sameness* 730.1, *conformity* 735.7

uniform slops *uniform* 100.9

unify 752.15; *shape* 551.21, *join* 609.10, *make the same* 730.16, *connect* 754.13, *combine* 757.9, *be whole* 759.9, *become one* 788.18

unilateral *side* 623.6, *one-sided* 788.11

unilateral *or* **unilateralist** *nonconforming* 728.10

unilateral disarmament *disarmament* 74.3

unilateralism *side* 623.1, *nonconformity* 728.4, *aloneness* 788.5

unilateralist *alone* 788.15

unilaterality *independence* 829.5

unilaterally *individualistically* 728.20

unilingual *speaking* 205.15

unilluminated *dark* 247.5

unimaginability *impossibility* 837.1

unimaginable *astonishing* 294.10, *impossible* 837.4

unimaginably *astonishingly* 294.19, *impossibly* 837.11

unimaginative *wonderless* 295.3, *unpretentious* 526.8, *common* 778.13

unimaginatively *without wonder* 295.8

unimaginativeness *lack of wonder* 295.1

unimagined *unthought-of* 318.10

Unimak Islands 572

unimitated *original* 737.4

unimolecular reaction *chemical reaction* 11.8

unimpaired *uncut* 759.7, *complete* 761.6

unimpassioned *detached* 4.18, *unemphatic* 201.2

unimpeachable *in the right* 429.11, *decided* 840.9

unimpeded *opened up* 583.11, *free* 829.11

unimplied *unmeant* 362.9

unimportance 800.1; *insignificance* 289.4, *lack of meaning* 362.1, *superficiality* 599.2, *unrelatedness* 728.1, *inferiority* 745.1

unimportant 800.10; *insignificant* 289.10, 745.6, *humble* 298.8, *meaningless* 362.7, *little* 580.7, *superficial* 599.4, *unrelated* 728.6

unimportantly 800.21; *unexceptionally* 289.20, *infinitesimally* 580.13, *superficially* 599.8, *irrelatively* 728.16, *insignificantly* 745.14

unimportant person *nonentity* 800.8

unimposing *modest* 403.6

unimpress *not cause wonder* 295.7

unimpressed *dissatisfied* 274.4, *indifferent* 289.7, *wonderless* 295.3

unimpressible *insensitive* 268.4

unimpressionability *predictability* 295.2

unimpressionable *insensitive* 268.4, *wonderless* 295.3

unimpressionably *without wonder* 295.8

unimpressive *unskillful* 128.4, *predictable* 295.4, *modest* 403.6, *mediocre* 742.7

unimpressively *predictably* 295.9

unimpressiveness *predictability* 295.2

unimproved 808.10

uninfectious *health-giving* 113.6

---

uninflated *unpretentious* 526.8
uninfluenced *unyielding* 379.8, *free* 829.11, *independent* 829.12
uninfluential *suspended* 519.3, *unimportant* 800.10
uninformative *silent* 181.10, *noncommittal* 181.11, *sparing with words* 208.6
uninformed *unskillful* 128.4, *ignorant* 349.5
uninfringeable *essential* 723.5
uninhabited *desolate* 96.13, *unoccupied* 576.13
uninhibited *candid* 191.5, *naive* 821.3, *unconditional* 829.14, *informal* 829.15
uninhibitedly *candidly* 191.10
uninhibitedness *liberality* 829.8
uninitiated *unskilled* 128.5, *ignorant* 349.5, *naive* 821.3
uninjured *uncut* 759.7, *safe* 810.16
uninquisitive *indifferent* 289.7, *incurious* 322.3
uninquisitively *indifferently* 289.17, *incuriously* 322.6
uninspire *not cause wonder* 295.7
uninspired *unemphatic* 201.2, *tasteless* 220.4, *mediocre* 289.11, *wonderless* 295.3, *unpretentious* 526.8, *common* 778.13
uninspiredly *unexceptionally* 289.20, *without wonder* 295.8
uninspiring *unemphatic* 201.2
uninspiringly *unemphatically* 201.4
uninstructed *unskillful* 128.4, *unskilled* 128.5, *ignorant* 349.5, *untrained* 389.8, *unaccustomed* 398.3
unintelligence *unskillfulness* 128.1, *lack of intellect* 316.1, *ignorance* 318.2
unintelligent 316.6
unintelligently 316.9; *foolishly* 353.8
unintelligent person 316.4
unintelligibility 364.1; *obscurity* 197.1, 250.2, *nonsense* 362.2, *disorder* 766.1, *difficulty* 824.1, *mysteriousness* 844.5
unintelligible 364.4; *mysterious* 182.10, *obscure* 197.2, *inarticulate* 206.6, *inscrutable* 250.5, *meaningless* 362.7, *problematic* 824.11, *concealed* 844.7
unintelligible speech *speech defect* 206.2
unintelligible thing 364.3
unintelligibly 364.16; *obscurely* 197.4, *opaquely* 250.9, *meaninglessly* 362.13, *problematically* 824.25
unintended *unmeant* 362.9, *causeless* 842.11
unintentional *unmeant* 362.9, *causeless* 842.11
unintentionally *by chance* 842.15
uninterest *incuriosity* 322.1
uninterested *indifferent* 289.7, *wonderless* 295.3, *bored* 296.5, *incurious* 322.3, *not participating* 415.11
uninterestedly *indifferently* 289.17, *without wonder* 295.8, *in a bored manner* 296.9, *incuriously* 322.6
uninterestedness *indifference* 289.1, *boredom* 296.1
uninteresting *boring* 296.6
uninterestingly *boringly* 296.10
uninterrupted *continuous* 630.10, 669.5, 774.9, *direct* 697.11
uninterrupted course *continuity* 669.1

uninterruption *continuity* 669.1, 774.4, *directness* 697.6
unintoxicated *sober* 120.5
uninucleate *nuclear* 13.31
uninvented *unsolved* 844.8
uninvited *lonely* 409.8
uninvited guest *illegal occupant* 61.9, *intruder* 724.7
uninviting *tasteless* 220.4, *unpalatable* 223.6, *unpleasant* 272.6
uninvolved *clear* 196.2, *indifferent* 289.7, *incurious* 322.3, *simple* 363.6, 526.7, *disinterested* 443.4, *nonconforming* 728.10, *unjoined* 753.9, *easy* 823.9
uninvolvement *incuriosity* 322.1, *clarity* 363.2
union 752.1; *set* 6.19, *unionized* 57.14, *association* 59.4, 827.6, *marriage* 64.1, *alliance* 64.2, 735.5, *contract* 459.1, *juxtaposition* 586.4, *meeting place* 702.4, *relatedness* 727.1, *sameness* 730.1, *harmonization* 735.2, *mixture* 751.1, *connection* 754.1, *collaboration* 757.2, *oneness* 788.3, *accompaniment* 794.1
union branch *organized labor* 57.5
union demands *organized labor* 57.5
union dues *organized labor* 57.5
unioned employee *union member* 57.6
Union flag *flag* 184.8
Union Internationale des Associations d'Alpinisme (UIAA) *mountaineering associations* 161.7
unionism *work practices* 57.2
unionize 57.21; *form an alliance* 735.25
unionized 57.14; *allied* 735.15
union-management relations *labor relations* 57.1
union member 57.6
union of nations 566.2
union organizer *union member* 57.6
union recognition *bargaining terms* 57.10
union shop *organized labor* 57.5
union strike *strike* 57.8
union subscriptions *organized labor* 57.5
union suit *underwear* 100.22
uniplanar *one-sided* 788.11
unipolar *one-sided* 788.11
unique 744.11; *universal* 6.67, *wondrous* 294.9, *infrequent* 662.2, *unusual* 664.4, 782.15, *quintessential* 723.8, *diverse* 732.5, *nonuniform* 734.5, *novel* 737.5, *excluding* 764.5, *special* 779.10, *exceptional* 779.13, *eccentric* 782.16, *singular* 788.13
unique, the *the special* 779.8
uniquely *wondrously* 294.18, *infrequently* 662.4, *unusually* 664.7, *diversely* 732.14, *nonuniformly* 734.11, *originally* 737.8, *asymmetrically* 741.11, *supremely* 744.23, *characteristically* 779.20, *alone* 788.20, *rarely* 839.10
uniqueness *identity* 184.2, *infrequency* 662.1, *unusualness* 664.2, 782.4, *diversity* 732.1, *nonuniformity* 734.2, *originality* 737.1, *specialty* 779.1, *singularity* 788.4
unirrigated *dry* 560.7
unisex *tailored* 100.41, *one-sided* 788.11

unisex clothes *clothing* 100.1
unisexual *one-sided* 788.11
unison *agreement* 462.1, 752.4, *harmonization* 735.2
unisonous *or* **unisonal** *or* **unisonant** *harmonizing* 735.12
unit 759.5; *group* 18.13, *military organization* 58.4, *force* 59.10, *family* 65.1, *army unit* 77.14, *type of furniture* 101.2, *whole thing* 759.2, *piece* 760.2, *one* 788.1
Unitarian *Christian* 81.10
unitarianism *Christianity* 81.5
Unitarian Universalism *Christian Groups* 81
unite 752.14; *band together* 59.27, *put together* 59.30, *join in marriage* 64.20, *merge* 64.21, *agree with* 462.10, *come together* 702.10, *make the same* 730.16, *form an alliance* 735.25, *agree* 752.17, *connect* 754.13, *cause to adhere* 755.10, *combine* 757.9, *be whole* 759.9, *complete* 761.9, *become one* 788.18, *join* 827.17
unite closely 752.16
united 752.10; *cumulate* 59.20, *married* 64.16, *contractual* 459.7, *agreeing* 462.6, 730.8, 735.13, *same* 730.7, *allied* 735.15, *agreeable* 752.11, *connected* 754.11, *combined* 757.5, *combinatory* 757.6, *complete* 761.6, *whole* 788.12, *joint* 827.10
united action *joint operation* 827.4
United Arab Emirates *Countries* 566
united front *joint operation* 827.4
United Kingdom *Countries* 566
unitedly *together* 59.31, 794.20, *identically* 730.18, *in accord* 735.33, *in alliance* 735.35, *cohesively* 755.11
United Nations *world government* 49.17, *union of nations* 566.2
United Nations peacekeeping force *pacifier* 73.7
United States Air Force Academy *military training* 58.3
United States Automobile Club (USAC) *racing governing bodies* 146.7
United States Fencing Association (USFA) *fencing associations* 153.4
United States Golf Association (USGA) *golfing associations and tournaments* 156.6
United States government 49.21
United States GP at Phoenix *Formula 1 World Championship races* 146.5
United States Military Academy (West Point) *military training* 58.3
United States Naval Academy (Annapolis) *military training* 58.3
United States of America *Countries* 566
United States Olympic Committee (USOC) *skiing associations* 162.13
United States Postal Service *postal service* 169.5
United States Revolver Association *hunting associations* 160.8
United States Skiing Association (USSA) *skiing associations* 162.13
United States Supreme Court *type of court* 54.9

United States Swimming Association (USSA) *swimming associations* 164.10
United States Tennis Association (USTA) *tennis organizations* 165.7
United States Yacht Racing Union (USYRU) *yacht racing associations* 150.7
United Way *charitable organization* 305.4
unite efforts *work together* 827.14
unite in marriage *or* **holy matrimony** *join in marriage* 64.20
unite sexually 752.20
unite to *add* 748.11
unite with *unify* 752.15
unities, the *dramaturgy* 136.6
uniting *junction* 609.5, *convergent* 702.7, *same* 730.7, *combination* 757.1
unit of being *matter* 524.4
unit of measurement 589.5
unit of sound *sound* 230.1
Unit One *Western Art Styles* 133
units place *number system* 6.7
unit vector *vector* 6.48
unity *agreement* 462.1, 730.2, 735.3, *whole* 759.1, 752.4, *union* 752.1, *adhesion* 755.1, *collaboration* 757.2, *whole* 759.1, *completeness* 761.1, *one* 788.1, *oneness* 788.3
univalent *chemical compound* 11.4
univalent chromosome *chromosome* 13.21
univalved *or* **univalvular** *molluskan* 39.23
universal 6.67, 778.10; *astronomical* 7.33, *windsurfing* 150.28, *familiar* 397.10, *extensive* 563.12, *whole* 759.6, *including* 763.3, *general* 778.9
universal benevolence *public-spiritedness* 307.2
universal constant *fundamental constant* 10.69
universal indicator *gravimetric analysis* 11.18
universalism *internationalism* 566.5
universalist *internationalist* 566.9
universality *indiscrimination* 338.4, *internationalism* 566.5, *whole* 759.1, *completeness* 761.1, *inclusion* 763.1, *generality* 778.1
universalize *be indiscriminate* 338.10, *generalize* 778.14
universal joint *sailboard parts* 150.20, *axle* 682.7
universal law *formula* 780.7
universally 778.23; *astronomically* 7.36, *indiscriminately* 338.15, *extensively* 563.18, *inclusively* 613.35, 763.8, *wholly* 759.11
universal peace *peace* 73.1
universal quantifier *mathematical logic* 6.60
Universal Self *God* 82.6
universal set *set* 6.19
universal solvent *solvent* 555.9
universal symbol *symbol* 108.28
universe 7.3; *real world* 719.2, *whole thing* 759.2
university 48.14
university hospital *hospital* 107.16
university president *educational leader* 68.11
univocal *comprehensibility* 361.3, *linguistic* 361.9, *intelligible* 363.5
unjam *make easy* 823.15
unjoined 753.9; *discontinuous* 775.7

---

unjust 53.24, 342.7, 741.6; *misrepresented* 188.4, *wrongful* 430.10

unjustifiable *unforgivable* 430.16, *guilty* 450.6

unjustifiably *guiltily* 450.12

unjustly 342.13, 741.12; *unrepresentatively* 188.8, *wrongly* 430.24

unkempt *dirty* 112.7, *barbed* 544.7, *untidy* 766.11, *worn* 808.13

unkemptness *untidiness* 766.3

unkennel *disclose* 180.8, *evict* 709.20

unkind *objectionable* 272.7, *pitiless* 309.3, *inconsiderate* 318.9, *discourteous* 411.5, *unpleasant* 501.5

unkindest cut of all *insult* 436.5

unkindly *hostilely* 63.13, *discourteously* 411.8

unkindness Collective Names 59, *objectionability* 272.2, *pitilessness* 309.1, *inconsideration* 318.4

unknot *liberate* 831.6

unknotting *simplification* 526.6, *liberation* 831.1

unknowable *mysterious* 182.10, *inscrutable* 250.5, *unknown* 349.7, *unintelligible* 364.4, *unrecognizable* 364.7

unknowing *ignorant* 349.5

unknowingly *ignorantly* 349.11, *innocently* 449.13

unknown 349.7; *mysterious* 182.10, *unintelligible* 364.4, *unfamiliar* 652.10, *foreign* 724.9, *nonentity* 786.4, 800.8, *dangerous* 811.7, *uncertain* 841.9, *unsolved* 844.8

unknown, the *unknown thing* 349.3, *unintelligibility* 364.1, *foreignness* 724.2

unknown country *anonymity* 182.7

unknownness *newness* 652.1

unknown person *anonymity* 182.7, *latency* 844.1

unknown quantity *anonymity* 182.7, *unknown thing* 349.3

Unknown Soldier *anonymity* 182.7

unknown territory *unknown thing* 349.3

unknown thing 349.3

unlabored *fluid* 527.5

unlace *undress* 614.18, *separate* 753.12

unlade *lighten* 539.9, *unload* 709.24

unlading *lightening* 539.2

unladylike *discourteous* 411.5, *vulgar* 535.6

unlatch *open up* 583.16, *separate* 753.12

unlatched *opened up* 583.11

unlavish *thrifty* 499.4

unlawful 53.23, 430.15; *villainous* 448.12, *violating* 466.8, *prohibited* 503.5

unlawful act *wicked act* 448.7

unlawful carnal knowledge *fornication* 432.3

unlawful desires *fornication* 432.3

unlawful entry *theft* 479.2

unlawful killing *murder* 30.2

unlawfully *illegally* 53.34, *guiltily* 53.38, *immorally* 430.27, *villainously* 448.18, *defiantly* 466.14, *prohibitively* 503.11

unlawfulness 430.6; *illegality* 53.10, *infraction* 466.4

unlawful sexual intercourse *sexual offense* 20.11

unleaded *gas* 106.14

unleaded gas *oil* 106.7

unlearn *forget* 355.10

unlearned *naive* 821.3

unleash *disclose* 180.8, *liberate* 831.6

unleashing *liberation* 831.1

unleash the dogs of war *go to war* 76.29

unless *under the circumstances* 726.16

unlettered *ignorant* 349.5

unlicensed *unlawful* 53.23

unlicked *uniformed* 389.11

unlicked [Arch] *shapeless* 625.2

unlighted *dark* 247.5

unlikable *disliked* 291.10, *hateful* 300.10

unlike *misrepresented* 188.4, *disparate* 728.9, *diverse* 732.5, *dissimilar* 734.4, *unequal* 741.4

unlikelihood *questionableness* 333.7, *improbability* 839.1, *indemonstrability* 841.5

unlikeliness *improbability* 839.1, *indemonstrability* 841.5

unlikely *questionable* 333.13, *improbable* 839.4, *indemonstrable* 841.12

unlikeness *disparity* 728.3, *diversity* 732.1, *dissimilarity* 734.1, *inequality* 741.1

unlimited *broad* 592.5, *complete* 761.6, *infinite* 798.5, *unconditional* 829.14

unlimited space *empty space* 563.2

unlisted securities market *stock market* 483.6

unlit *dark* 247.5, *dangerous* 811.7

unload 709.24; *sell* 482.15, *make cheap* 497.14, *lighten* 539.9, *take away* 685.12, *transport* 686.10, *land* 704.16, *subtract* 749.6, *disentangle* 823.17

unloaded *lightening* 539.6, *transportable* 686.7

unloader *transporter* 686.4

unloading *lightening* 539.2, 539.6, *transportation* 686.1, *transporting* 686.8, *eviction* 709.4

unload on the market *sell* 482.15

unlock *open up* 583.16, *separate* 753.12, *deliver* 817.5, *liberate* 831.6

unlock a code *decipher* 365.13

unlocked *interpreted* 365.9, *opened up* 583.11

unlock the door! *open up!* 583.24

unloose *deliver* 817.5, *liberate* 831.6

unloosed *separate* 753.7

unloosen *liberate* 831.6

unloose the purse strings *pay* 489.16

unloosing *liberation* 831.1

unloved *disliked* 291.10

unlovely *ugly* 531.3

unloyal *defiant* 466.7

unluckily *mistakenly* 660.14, *luckily* 842.17, *unsuccessfully* 846.21, *adversely* 848.16

unlucky 848.12; *accidental* 660.7, *chance* 842.10, *failed* 846.10

unlucky choice *choice* 382.3

unlucky person *person in adversity* 848.9

unmake *destroy* 523.10, *make shapeless* 625.3, *restore* 671.10, *take apart* 753.16

unmaking *destruction* 523.1

unmalleability *mental hardness* 542.4

unmalleable *obstinate* 417.7, *mentally hard* 542.8

unman *make infertile* 23.9, *take off* 749.7, *make useless* 802.12

unmanageable *clumsy* 128.6, *refractory* 379.6, *disobedient* 427.10, *disorderly* 766.15, *troublesome* 824.13

unmanageably *awkwardly* 824.26

unmanifested *concealed* 844.7

unmanly *male* 32.16

unmanned *unoccupied* 576.13

unmanned satellite *artificial satellite* 7.30

unmannered *disrespectful* 436.9

unmannerliness *bad manners* 411.2, *disrespect* 436.1

unmannerly *bad-mannered* 411.6, *discourteous* 535.7

unmarked *invisible* 245.3, *immaculate* 805.11

unmarked car *automobile* 687.6

unmarketable *shoddy* 497.11

unmarred *unbroken* 805.13

unmarried *celibate* 67.6, *single* 788.16, *independent* 829.12

unmarried man *single man* 32.5, *single person* 67.5, 788.7

unmarried state *independence* 829.5

unmarried woman *single woman* 33.5, *single person* 788.7

unmarry *divorce* 66.9

unmask *disclose* 180.8, *make visible* 242.25, 244.9, *detect* 345.12, *reveal* 843.14

unmasked *disclosed* 180.5, *discovered* 345.9

unmasking *detection* 345.2

unmask oneself *show oneself* 843.15

unmatchable *best* 744.10

unmatchably *supremely* 744.23

unmatched *best* 744.10, 805.9

unmated *celibate* 67.6

unmeaning *meaningless* 362.7

unmeant 362.9; *causeless* 842.11

unmeasured *plentiful* 97.4

unmediated *precognitive* 320.7

unmellowed *immature* 389.9

unmelodious 241.5; *strident* 238.4

unmelodiously *dissonantly* 241.7

unmelodiousness *musical dissonance* 241.2

unmelted *frozen* 218.10, *condensed* 540.7

unmemorable *forgotten* 355.7

unmentionable *offensive* 432.11, *censored* 503.7, *ribald* 535.8

unmentionables *underwear* 100.22

unmentioned *indeterminate* 841.14, *unsaid* 844.9

unmerciful *pitiless* 309.3

unmercifully *pitilessly* 309.7

unmercifulness *pitilessness* 309.1

unmethodical *irregular* 664.3, *confused* 766.12

unmethodically *irregularly* 664.6, *in disorder* 766.24

unmethodicalness *irregularity* 664.1

unmeticulous *unrefined* 338.7

unmilitant *pacific* 74.7

unmilitary *pacific* 74.7

unmindful *insensible* 213.4, *blind to* 243.14, *heedless* 268.5, *ungrateful* 311.2, *inattentive* 324.5, *negligent* 326.4, *unthinking* 355.8, *nonobservant* 466.5

unmindfully *forgetfully* 186.12,

ungratefully 311.6, *inattentively* 324.12, 466.13

unmindfulness *inattention* 324.1, *negligence* 326.1, *unthinkingness* 355.3, *nonobservance* 466.1

unmissable *clear* 244.6

unmistakable *visible* 244.5, *recognizable* 363.7, *strong* 516.9, *certain* 840.7, *identifiable* 843.10

unmistakably *intelligibly* 363.13, *acutely* 516.18

unmistaken *certain* 840.7

unmitigated *violent* 520.5, *complete* 761.6

unmitigating *complete* 761.6

unmixed *clean* 111.13, *intoxicating* 121.29, *same* 730.7, *unjoined* 753.9, *immaculate* 805.11

unmodern *different in time* 648.2

unmoistened *dry* 560.7

unmolested *safe* 810.16

unmoor *navigate* 690.15, *set out* 705.12

unmoral *immoral* 432.9

unmorality *immorality* 432.1

unmorally *immorally* 432.18

unmotivated *spontaneous* 396.5, *causeless* 842.11

unmount *make useless* 802.12

unmovable *motionless* 678.4

unmoved *indifferent* 289.7, *wonderless* 295.3, *apathetic* 322.4, *unyielding* 379.8, *impenitent* 452.2, *motionless* 678.4, *quiescent* 678.6

unmoving *inert* 519.2, *motionless* 678.4

unmuddied *clean* 111.13

unmurmuring *compliant* 781.9

unmusical *deaf* 229.4, *strident* 238.4, *unmelodious* 241.5

unmusicality *speech difficulty* 206.1

unmusicalness *deafness* 229.1

unmuzzled *free* 829.11

unnamed *unknown* 349.7, *indeterminate* 841.14

unnatural *affected* 367.3, *inelegant* 528.6

unnaturally *affectedly* 367.5, *unconformably* 782.21

unnaturalness *inelegance* 528.1

unnavigable *shallow* 599.3, *rough* 824.10

unnecessarily *wastefully* 96.23, *superfluously* 99.15, *unimportantly* 800.21

unnecessary *wasteful* 96.9, *superfluous* 99.8, *extraneous* 724.8, *unimportant* 800.10, *redundant* 802.9

unneeded *redundant* 802.9

unneighborly *unsociable* 409.6, *discourteous* 411.5

unnerve *daunt* 179.9, *frighten* 283.17, *make impotent* 515.15, *weaken* 517.13

unnerved *dissuaded* 179.5, *disabled* 515.10, *weak-willed* 517.10

unnerving *frightening* 283.12

unnilhexium Chemical Elements and Common Allotropes 11

unnilpentium Chemical Elements and Common Allotropes 11

unnilquadrium Chemical Elements and Common Allotropes 11

unnotable *mediocre* 289.11

unnotably *unexceptionally* 289.20

unnoteworthy *mediocre* 742.7

unnoticeable *invisible* 245.3

unnoticeably *invisibly* 245.8

unnoticed *invisible* 245.3

unnumbered *numberless* 795.8, *immeasurable* 798.6
unnutritious *unhygienic* 114.27
unobservance *nonobservance* 466.1
unobservant *unaccepting* 190.13, *blind to* 243.14, *inattentive* 324.5, *nonobservant* 466.5
unobservantly *nonacceptantly* 190.25
unobserved *invisible* 245.3
unobstructed *transparent* 249.7, *opened up* 583.11
unobstructed view *transparency* 249.1
unobtainability *hopelessness* 837.2
unobtainable *scarce* 98.8, *hopeless* 837.6
unobtrusive *modest* 403.6
unobtrusively *modestly* 403.15
unobtrusiveness *modesty* 403.1
unoccupied 576.13; *leisure* 125.3, *leisurely* 125.4, *inactive* 413.9, *not working* 415.10, *off-duty* 433.11
unofficial *unlawful* 53.23, *disputed* 57.15, *informal* 407.6, *uncertified* 841.13
unofficially *industrially* 57.22, *informally* 407.11
unofficial strike *strike* 57.8
unoiled *hoarse* 238.5
unopened *new* 394.7, *closed* 584.7
unopposed *agreeing* 462.6
unoptimistic *negative* 190.15
unoptimistically *pessimistically* 190.26
unordered *complicated* 751.10, *disordered* 766.9
unordered arrangement *set* 6.19
unorganized *indiscriminate* 338.8, *unprepared* 389.5, *disordered* 766.9
unoriginal *familiar* 397.10, *caused* 676.5, *imitative* 736.7
unoriginally *with the effect of* 676.12, *imitatively* 736.12
unornamented *unadorned* 526.9
unorthodox *dissenting* 347.7, *errant* 351.12, *nonconformist* 782.13
unorthodox medicine *alternative medicine* 107.4
unorthodoxy *dissentience* 347.3, *errancy* 351.7, *nonconformism* 782.3
unostentatious *simple* 195.10, *modest* 403.6
unostentatiously *simply* 195.19
unostentatiousness *simplicity* 195.4, *modesty* 403.1
unpacific *warlike* 76.27
unpack *disclose* 180.8, *unload* 709.24
unpaid 490.8; *voluntary* 373.11, 504.9, *indebted* 488.7, *free of charge* 497.12
unpaid amount *amount owing* 488.5
unpaid bill *credit* 487.1
unpaid work *voluntary work* 373.5
unpaid worker *willing worker* 373.6, *volunteer* 504.7
unpainted *unadorned* 526.9
unpalatability 223.2; *taste* 219.1, *bad taste* 220.3, *unpleasantness* 272.1
unpalatable 220.5, 223.6; *tasty* 219.4, *unpleasant* 272.6
unparalleled *novel* 737.5, *best* 744.10, 805.9
unpardonable *unforgivable* 430.16, *guilty* 450.6
unpardonably *guiltily* 450.12

unpartnered *celibate* 67.6
unpayable *unpaid* 490.8
unpayable debt *insolvency* 490.5
unpeaceful *restless* 684.16
unpeacefully *agitatedly* 684.27
unpeel *unstick* 756.6
unpeople *depopulate* 709.21
unpeopled *unoccupied* 576.13
unperceivable *invisible* 245.3
unperceived *invisible* 245.3, *unknown* 349.7
unperceptive *unintelligent* 316.6, *dull* 550.7
unperceptiveness *insensitivity* 268.1, *ignorance* 316.3
unperformed *uncompleted* 762.7
unperfumed *odorless* 225.4
unpersevering *inconstant* 378.6
unperson *insubstantial person* 720.5, *nonentity* 786.4
unpersuadable *refractory* 379.6
unperturbed *detached* 4.18, *quiescent* 678.6
unperturbedly *motionlessly* 678.9
unphysical *spiritual* 86.20, *nonmaterial* 525.8
unpick *disentangle* 753.13
unpigmented *colorless* 252.5
unpin *unstick* 756.6
unpitying *pitiless* 309.3
unplanned *bungled* 128.7, *unpremeditated* 389.7, *causeless* 842.11
unpleasant 272.6, 501.5; *tasty* 219.4, *unpalatable* 223.6, *antipathetic* 291.7, *discourteous* 411.5, *disagreeing* 463.6
unpleasantly 272.10; *sourly* 223.9, *discontentedly* 291.17, *discourteously* 411.8, *in disagreement* 463.12
unpleasantness 272.1, 501.2; *antipathy* 291.2, *dissentience* 347.3, *discourtesy* 411.1, *disagreement* 463.1
unpleasant person 272.5
unpleasant smell *odor* 224.1, *stench* 227.1
unpleasant-smelling thing 227.2
unpleasant taste *taste* 219.1
unpleasant woman 33.7
unpleasing *unpleasant* 272.6
unpliability *mental hardness* 542.4
unpliable *mentally hard* 542.8
unpliant *mentally hard* 542.8
unplug *separate* 753.12
unplugged *separate* 753.7
unpoetical *unpretentious* 526.8, *naive* 821.3
unpointed *blunt* 550.5
unpolished *dirty* 112.7, *bungled* 128.7, *dimmed* 248.6, *unformed* 389.11, *graceless* 528.7, *indecorous* 528.8, *discourteous* 535.7, *unfinished* 544.9, *incomplete* 806.6, *naive* 821.3
unpolluted *clean* 111.13, *trustworthy* 810.17
unpopular *unsatisfactory* 274.5, *disliked* 291.10, *hated* 300.9, *lonely* 409.8
unpowered *inoperative* 515.8
unpractical *unskillful* 128.4, *useless* 802.7
unpracticed *clumsy* 128.6, *untrained* 389.8, *unaccustomed* 398.3
unpraiseworthy *unsatisfactory* 438.15
unprecedented *wondrous* 294.9, *uncustomary* 398.4, *unfamiliar* 652.10, *infrequent* 662.2, *novel* 737.5

unpredictability *causality* 10.66, *capriciousness* 381.2, *irregularity* 664.1, *changeableness* 666.1, *inconsistency* 732.3, *unexpectedness* 839.2, *unreliability* 841.7, *chance* 842.1
unpredictable *erratic* 381.5, *irregular* 664.3, *changeable* 666.3, *inconsistent* 732.7, *unexpected* 839.6, *indemonstrable* 841.12, *unreliable* 841.15, *chance* 842.10
unpredictably *erratically* 381.8, *irregularly* 664.6, *changeably* 666.7, *inconsistently* 732.16, *unexpectedly* 839.9, *unreliably* 841.25, *randomly* 842.16
unpredicted *surprising* 292.7, *unexpected* 839.6
unprejudiced *impartial* 289.9, 338.6, *wise* 352.4, *disinterested* 443.4, *broad-minded* 592.9, *free* 829.11
unprejudiceness *legal justice* 53.4
unpremeditated 389.7; *improvised* 396.4, *causeless* 842.11
unpremeditatedly *unreadily* 389.16
unpremeditation 389.2; *improvisation* 396.1
unprepared 389.5; *immature* 26.12, *unskilled* 128.5, *bungled* 128.7, *surprised* 292.5, *uncooked* 389.12, *improvised* 396.4, *late* 658.5, *incomplete* 762.5, *vulnerable* 811.9, *hasty* 818.3
unpreparedly *youthfully* 26.14, *unreadily* 389.16, *late* 658.14
unpreparedness *immaturity* 26.3, *surprise* 292.1, *lack of preparation* 389.1, *lateness* 658.1, *incompleteness* 762.1
unprepossessing *disliked* 291.10, *ugly* 531.3
unpretending *ingenuous* 191.6, *humble* 298.8, *modest* 403.6, *naive* 821.3
unpretentious 526.8; *fit for habitation* 60.19, *ingenuous* 191.6, *simple* 195.10, *humble* 298.8, *modest* 403.6, *familiar* 407.8, *natural* 526.10, *naive* 821.3
unpretentiously 526.15; *ingenuously* 191.11, *simply* 195.19, *humbly* 298.22, *modestly* 403.15
unpretentiousness 526.2; *ingenuousness* 191.3, *simplicity* 195.4, *humility* 298.1, *modesty* 403.1, *naiveté* 821.1
unpreventability *inevitability* 840.5
unpreventable *inevitable* 840.11
unprincipled *immoral* 430.11, 432.9, *depraved* 448.10
unprintable *offensive* 432.11, *censored* 503.7, *ribald* 535.8
unprocessed 389.10; *uncompleted* 762.7
unproclaimed *unsaid* 844.9
unprocurable *scarce* 98.8
unproductive *infertile* 23.7, *futile* 802.10, *failed* 846.10
unproductively 23.12; *unsuccessfully* 846.21
unproductiveness *infertility* 23.1, *scarcity* 98.3, *waste* 468.5, *futility* 802.3, *failure* 846.1
unproductivity *infertility* 23.1
unprofessed *unsaid* 844.9
unprofessional *unskillful* 128.4, *unskilled* 128.5, *nonobservant* 466.5, *inconvenient* 804.5
unprofessional conduct *sin* 450.3

unprofessionally *unskillfully* 128.12
unprofitability *infertile state* 23.3, *futility* 802.3
unprofitable 468.10; *infertile* 23.7, *thankless* 311.4, *futile* 802.10, *inconvenient* 804.5
unprofitableness *infertile state* 23.3
unprofitably *unproductively* 23.12, *thanklessly* 311.7, *marketably* 482.23, *uselessly* 802.14
unprogressive *inactive* 413.9, *conservative* 815.13
unprogressively *conservatively* 815.17
unprohibitive *permitting* 502.5
unprolific *infertile* 23.7
unpromising *unskillful* 128.4, *inauspicious* 282.8, *improbable* 839.4
unpromoted *unsaid* 844.9
unprompted *voluntary* 373.11, 504.9, *improvised* 396.4
unpronounceable *unintelligible* 364.4
unpronounced *unsaid* 844.9
unpropitious *inauspicious* 282.8, *untimely* 660.5, *oppositional* 828.11, *adverse* 848.10
unpropitiously *inauspiciously* 282.15, *at the wrong time* 660.12, *adversely* 848.16
unpropitiousness *lack of hope* 282.2, *untimeliness* 660.1
unprosperous 848.11
unprotected *helpless* 515.9, *weak* 517.6, *opened up* 583.11, *vulnerable* 811.9
unprovability *indemonstrability* 841.5
unprovable *indemonstrable* 841.12
unproved *uncertified* 841.13
unprovided 98.6
unprovided for *unprovided* 98.6, *poor* 486.8
unprovoked *spontaneous* 396.5
unpublished *unsaid* 844.9
unpunctual *late* 658.5, *untimely* 660.5
unpunctuality *lateness* 658.1, *untimeliness* 660.1
unpunctually *late* 658.14, *at the wrong time* 660.12
unpunishable *exempt* 434.5
unpunished *acquitted* 54.25
unpurified *unclean* 112.8
unqualified *unskillful* 128.4, *unskilled* 128.5, *semiskilled* 349.6, *unselected* 383.7, *powerless* 515.6, *complete* 761.6, *useless* 802.7, *inconvenient* 804.5
unquelled *resisting* 417.8
unquestionable *definite* 189.18, *demonstrable* 331.12, *authentic* 721.16, *essential* 723.5, *impossible* 837.4, *probable* 838.6
unquestionableness *definiteness* 189.6, *authenticity* 721.7
unquestionably *definitely* 189.33, *earnestly* 278.10, *authentically* 721.31, *impossibly* 837.11, *probably* 838.11, *certainly* 840.15
unquestioned *believed* 87.8
unquestioning *believing* 87.6, *wonderless* 295.3, *incurious* 322.3, *convinced* 840.8
unquestioningly *without wonder* 295.8, *incuriously* 322.6
unquiet *restlessness* 414.7, *restless* 684.16
unquietly *agitatedly* 684.27
unquietness *restlessness* 414.7

unquotable *offensive* 432.11, *ribald* 535.8

unratified *uncertified* 841.13

unravel *decipher* 365.13, *disentangle* 753.13, 823.17, *tidy* 765.21, *deliver* 817.5

unraveling *solution* 376.6, *separation* 753.1, *deliverance* 817.1

unreachable *away* 585.6, *out of reach* 712.11, *hopeless* 837.6

unreactive *reactive* 11.29, *inert* 519.2

unreadability *unintelligibility* 364.1

unreadable *unintelligible* 364.4

unreadably *unintelligibly* 364.16

unreadily 389.16; *youthfully* 26.14, *late* 658.14

unreadiness *immaturity* 26.3, *unskillfulness* 128.1, *surprise* 292.1, *lack of preparation* 389.1, *lateness* 658.1, *incompleteness* 762.1

unready *immature* 26.12, *surprised* 292.5, *unprepared* 389.5, *late* 658.5, *incomplete* 762.5, *vulnerable* 811.9

unreal 718.10, 720.8, 722.7; *supposed* 359.6, *fantastic* 360.11, *imaginary* 360.12, *absent* 576.7, *untrue* 722.6, *unauthentic* 722.9

unrealistic 720.11; *improbable* 839.4

unrealistic person 720.6

unreality 720.1, 722.2; *conception* 360.4, *immateriality* 525.2, *nonreality* 718.5, *impossibility* 837.1

unrealized *unknown* 349.7, *uncompleted* 762.7

unreally 722.15; *without truth* 722.14, *unauthentically* 722.17

unreason *nonsense* 362.2

unreasonable *excessive* 99.5, *sophistic* 330.7, *costly* 496.7, *impossible* 837.4, *causeless* 842.11

unreasonableness *excess* 99.1

unreasonably *excessively* 99.13

unrecanting *impenitent* 452.2

unreceptiveness *unsociability* 409.1

unrecognizable 364.7; *disguised* 181.9, *converted* 670.7

unrecognizably *invisibly* 245.8

unrecognized *disguised* 181.9, *unthanked* 311.3, *unknown* 349.7

unrecompensed *unpaid* 490.8

unreconciled *refusing* 375.9, *impenitent* 452.2

unrecorded *forgotten* 186.6

unrecounted *excluded* 764.6

unredeemed *impenitent* 452.2

unreduced *complete* 805.14

unrefined 338.7; *unclean* 112.8, *clumsy* 128.6, *unprocessed* 389.10, *bad-mannered* 411.6, *graceless* 528.7, *indecorous* 528.8, *vulgar* 535.6, *unfinished* 544.9, *incomplete* 806.6, *naive* 821.3

unrefined sugar *sweetener* 222.2

unrefinement *immaturity* 389.3, *impropriety* 528.2

unreflective *thoughtless* 318.7

unreformed *impenitent* 452.2

unrefreshed *fatigued* 820.2

unrefuted *decided* 840.9

unregarded *undervalued* 436.17

unregenerated *impenitent* 452.2

unregistered *forgotten* 186.6

unregretful *impenitent* 452.2

unregretfully *impenitently* 452.5

unregretted *unatoned* 452.3

unregretting *impenitent* 452.2

unregular *irregular* 664.3

unregularity *irregularity* 664.1

unregularly *irregularly* 664.6

unregulated *free* 829.11

unrehearsed *spontaneous* 389.6, *improvised* 396.4

unreined *disorderly* 51.6

unrelated 728.6; *extraneous* 724.8, *foreign* 724.9, *incomparable* 734.6, *unjoined* 753.9

unrelatedness 728.1; *foreignness* 724.2, *incomparability* 734.3, *unimportance* 800.1

unrelaxed *tough* 542.6

unrelenting *relentless* 309.4, *unyielding* 379.8, *protracted* 669.7

unrelentingly *relentlessly* 309.8, *severely* 424.11, *continually* 669.10

unrelentingness *relentlessness* 309.2

unreliability 722.5, 841.7; *questionableness* 333.7, *capriciousness* 381.2, *changeableness* 666.1

unreliable 722.10, 841.15; *disbelieved* 88.7, *hypocritical* 330.10, *questionable* 333.13, *inconstant* 378.6, *erratic* 381.5, *changeable* 666.3, *unsafe* 811.8

unreliableness *unreliability* 722.5

unreliably 841.25; *unbelievably* 88.11, *hypocritically* 330.15, *questionably* 333.22, *changeably* 666.7

unrelieved *continuous* 774.9

unrelished *disliked* 291.10

unremarkable *unskillful* 128.4, *mediocre* 289.11, 742.7, *moderate* 521.3

unremarkableness *mediocrity* 742.3

unremarkably *unexceptionally* 289.20

unremembered *forgotten* 186.6

unremembering *forgetful* 186.7

unremittance *perseverance* 377.1

unremitting *laborious* 122.7, *persevering* 377.6, *protracted* 669.7, *continuous* 774.9, *recurrent* 797.13, *eternal* 798.7

unremittingly *continually* 669.10

unremorseful *pitiless* 309.3, *impenitent* 452.2

unremorsefully *impenitently* 452.5

unremunerated *unpaid* 490.8

unrepeatable expression *curse word* 301.4

unrepeatable offer *infrequency* 662.1

unrepeated *discontinued* 775.8, *singular* 788.13

unrepentant *impenitent* 452.2

unrepented *unatoned* 452.3

unrepenting *impenitent* 452.2

unreplenished *unprovided* 98.6

unreported *excluded* 764.6

unrepresentative *misrepresented* 188.4

unrepresentatively 188.8

unrepressed *unrestrained* 592.8

unrequited *unthanked* 311.3, *unselected* 383.7

unrequited love *downfall* 848.4

unresemblant *dissimilar* 734.4

unresembling *dissimilar* 734.4

unresentful *forgiving* 312.4

unresentfully *forgivingly* 312.13

unresentfulness *forgivingness* 312.3

unresenting *forgiving* 312.4

unreserved *disclosing* 180.6, *candid* 191.5, *conversing* 210.8, *open* 583.13, *naive* 821.3

unreservedly *openly* 180.13, *conversationally* 210.14, *excessively* 829.23

unreservedness *openness* 180.3

unresisting *pacific* 74.7, *submitting* 421.3, *obedient* 426.4

unresistingly *obediently* 426.9

unresolvable *futile* 282.9

unresolved *mysterious* 182.10, *unexplained* 364.6, *vacillating* 378.5, *irresolute* 841.10

unrespectably *disreputably* 371.7

unrespected *disrespected* 436.16

unresponsive *insensible* 213.4, *insensitive* 268.4, *indifferent* 289.7, *pitiless* 309.3, *apathetic* 322.4, *inert* 519.2

unresponsively *indifferently* 289.17, *pitilessly* 309.7

unresponsiveness *mood disorder* 108.12, *insensitivity* 268.1, *pitilessness* 309.1

unrest *restlessness* 414.7, 684.5, *momentum* 677.2

unrested *fatigued* 820.2

unrestrained 500.5, 592.8; *anarchic* 51.5, *disorderly* 51.6, *candid* 191.5, *demonstrative* 331.10, *unrefined* 338.7, *overindulgent* 456.8, *violent* 520.5, *free* 829.11

unrestrainedly *confusedly* 51.11

unrestrainedness 500.2

unrestraint *anarchy* 51.1, *overindulgence* 456.3, *freedom* 829.1

unrestricted *independent* 434.7, *extensive* 563.12, *opened up* 583.11, *complete* 761.6, *prevailing* 778.11, *unconditional* 829.14

unrevealed *secret* 182.8, *unsolved* 844.8

unrevered *disrespected* 436.16

unreverenced *disrespected* 436.16

unrewarded *unthanked* 311.3, *unpaid* 490.8, *futile* 802.10

unrewarding *thankless* 311.4, *futile* 802.10

unrhythmic *irregular* 664.3

unrhythmical *irregular* 664.3

unrhythmically *irregularly* 664.6

unriddle *decipher* 365.13

unrig *make useless* 802.12

unrigged *unequipped* 389.13

unrighteous *wrongful* 430.10, *wicked* 448.9

unrighteously *wrongly* 430.24, *wickedly* 448.15

unrighteousness *wrong* 430.1, *wickedness* 448.1

unrinsed *dirty* 112.7

unripe *of a fruit* 44.8, *unskilled* 128.5, *acid* 223.5, *raw* 260.9, *immature* 389.9, *unaccustomed* 398.3, *untimely* 660.5, *incomplete* 762.5, *uncompleted* 762.7

unripely *at the wrong time* 660.12

unripened *immature* 389.9

unripeness *unskillfulness* 128.1, *sourness* 223.1, *immaturity* 389.3, *untimeliness* 660.1, *incompleteness* 762.1, 806.2, *nonachievement* 762.3

unrivaled *best* 744.10, *expert* 805.16

unrobe *undress* 614.18

unrobed *undressed* 614.11

unroll *disclose* 180.8, *straighten* 630.14, *reveal* 843.14

unrolling *manifestation* 843.2

unrough *smooth* 545.4

unroughly *smoothly* 545.13

unruffled *detached* 4.18, *indifferent* 289.7, *uniform* 545.5, *horizontal* 603.6, *quiescent* 678.6

unruffled surface *smoothness* 545.1

unruliness *confusion* 51.2, *disobedience* 427.1, *lawlessness* 766.6, *liberality* 829.8

unruly *disorderly* 51.6, 766.15, *refractory* 379.6, *disobedient* 427.10, *violent* 520.5, *unconditional* 829.14

unsaddle *lighten* 539.9

unsaddling *lightening* 539.2, *displacement* 574.1

unsafe 811.8; *weak* 517.6

unsafely *weakly* 517.14

unsaid 844.9; *excluded* 764.6

unsalability *uselessness* 802.1

unsalable *shoddy* 497.11, *useless* 802.7

unsalaried *free of charge* 497.12

unsalted *tasteless* 220.4

unsalvageable *hopeless* 282.6, *losing* 468.9

unsanctified by custom *uncustomary* 398.4

unsanitariness *lack of hygiene* 112.3

unsanitary *unclean* 112.8, *unhygienic* 114.27

unsated *unprovided* 98.6

unsatisfactorily *insufficiently* 98.11, *disappointingly* 293.12, *weakly* 517.14

unsatisfactoriness *insufficiency* 98.1

unsatisfactory 274.5, 438.15; *insufficient* 98.4, 517.11, *shortened* 762.6, *imperfect* 806.5

unsatisfactory work *bungling* 128.2

unsatisfied *desirous* 20.18, *unprovided* 98.6, *disappointed* 293.4

unsatisfying *insufficient* 98.4, *tasteless* 220.4, *disappointing* 293.6

unsaturated *chemical compound* 11.4, *status adjectives* 11.25

unsaturated fat *fat* 12.7, 562.4

unsaturated solution *phase* 11.13

unsavoriness *tastelessness* 220.1

unsavory *unpalatable* 223.6, *unpleasant* 272.6, *disliked* 291.10

unsayable *censored* 503.7

unscarred *unbroken* 805.13

unscathed *uncut* 759.7, *unbroken* 805.13, *safe* 810.16

unscented *odorless* 225.4

unscholarly *ignorant* 349.5

unschooled *ignorant* 349.5

unscientific *unskilled* 128.5

unscoured *dirty* 112.7

unscramble *rationalize* 4.20, *solve* 334.21, *decipher* 365.13, *straighten* 630.14, *disentangle* 823.17

unscrambled *solved* 334.15, *interpreted* 365.9

unscrambling *solution* 334.6, 376.6, *translation* 365.4, *simplification* 526.6, *disentanglement* 823.8

unscratched *unbroken* 805.13

unscrubbed *dirty* 112.7

unscrupulous *dishonorable* 192.14, *indifferent* 326.5, *immoral* 432.9

unscrupulously *dishonorably* 192.28, *immorally* 432.18, *unvirtuously* 448.16

unscrupulousness *dishonorableness* 192.3, *indifference* 326.2, *immorality* 432.1

unseal *disclose* 180.8, *open up* 583.16

unsealed *opened up* 583.11
unsearchable *unintelligible* 364.4
unseasonable *untimely* 660.5, *inconvenient* 804.5
unseasonableness *untimeliness* 660.1
unseasonably *at the wrong time* 660.12
unseasoned *unskilled* 128.5, *tasteless* 220.4, *raw* 260.9, *immature* 389.9, *unaccustomed* 398.3
unseat *displace* 574.15, *replace* 574.17, *separate* 753.12
unseating *displacement* 574.1, *replacement* 574.3
unsecure *unsafe* 811.8
unsecured *loaned* 475.5
unsecured debt *debt* 488.1
unsecured loan *loan* 475.2, 488.3
unseeable *invisible* 245.3
unseeing *blind* 243.11, *inactive* 413.9
unseemliness *disrepute* 371.1, *impropriety* 430.5, *grossness* 535.3, *inconvenience* 804.1
unseemly *disreputably* 371.7, *improper* 430.14, *indecorous* 528.8, *ugly* 531.3, *discourteous* 535.7, *discourteously* 535.11, *inconvenient* 804.5
unseen *concealed* 181.8, 844.7, *hidden* 243.15, *invisible* 245.3, *unknown* 349.7, *unintelligible* 364.4, *reserved* 403.10
unsegregated *included* 763.4
unselected **383.7;** *indiscriminate* 338.8
unselective *undiscriminating* 338.5
unselectively **338.12**
unselectiveness *lack of discrimination* 338.1
unselfish **443.5;** *self-abasing* 298.11, *charitable* 305.9, *philanthropic* 307.6, *virtuous* 447.5
unselfishly **443.9;** *charitably* 305.15, *philanthropically* 307.9, *virtuously* 447.9
unselfishness **443.2;** *self-abasement* 298.4, *charity* 305.3, *philanthropy* 307.1, *virtue* 447.1
unsensational *unpretentious* 526.8
unseparated *included* 763.4
unserviceable *useless* 802.7
unserviceableness *uselessness* 802.1
unsettle *displace* 574.15, *deconstruct* 758.7, *discompose* 766.18, *disturb* 768.10
unsettled *arguable* 329.8, *vacillating* 378.5, *unoccupied* 576.13, *changeable* 666.3, *confused* 766.12, *disturbed* 768.6, *irresolute* 841.10
unsettledness *vacillation* 378.1, *irresolution* 841.3
unsettling *displacement* 574.1, *displaced* 574.8, *disturbing* 768.9, *inconvenient* 804.5
unsexual *undersexed* 20.20
unshackle *liberate* 831.6
unshackled *free* 829.11, *liberated* 831.4
unshackling *liberation* 831.1
unshakable *steadfast* 284.11, *steady* 376.8, *stable* 674.3, *infallible* 840.12
unshakableness *seriousness* 376.3
unshakably *stably* 674.9
unshaken *detached* 4.18, *guaranteed* 464.6
unshape *make shapeless* 625.3
unshaped *shapeless* 625.2

unshapely *ugly* 531.3
unshared *possessing* 469.11, *possessed* 469.13
unsharp *blunt* 550.5
unsharpened *uniform* 545.5, *blunt* 550.5
unsharpness *bluntness* 550.5
unshatterable *tough* 547.6
unshaven *barbed* 544.7
unsheathe the sword *go to war* 76.29
unshepherded *vulnerable* 811.9
unshielded *opened up* 583.11, *vulnerable* 811.9
unship *unload* 709.24
unshod *uncovered* 614.10
unshorn *barbed* 544.7
unshrinking *steadfast* 284.11, *tenacious* 376.9
unshriven *impenitent* 452.2
unshroud *disclose* 180.8
unsifted *rough* 544.5, *disordered* 766.9
unsighted *blind* 243.11, *invisible* 245.3
unsightliness *ugliness* 531.1
unsightly *ugly* 531.3, *untidy* 766.11
unsigned *numerical* 6.68, *uncertified* 841.13
unsimilar *dissimilar* 734.4
unsimilarity *dissimilarity* 734.1
unsimilarly *dissimilarly* 734.10
unsinkable *insubstantial* 539.5
unskilled **128.5;** *industrial* 57.13, *raw* 260.9, *ignorant* 349.5, *untrained* 389.8, *useless* 802.7, *naive* 821.3
unskilled laborer *laborer* 123.9
unskilled person **128.3**
unskilled worker *employee* 57.4, *operative* 509.6
unskillful **128.4;** *unaccustomed* 398.3, *useless* 802.7
unskillfully **128.12, 282.17, 398.8;** *unreadily* 389.16
unskillfulness **128.1;** *ignorance* 349.1, *unaccustomedness* 398.1, *uselessness* 802.1
unsleeping *committed* 377.7, *industrious* 414.16
unsmiling *serious* 278.4, *frowning* 304.10, *discourteous* 411.5
unsmilingly *frowningly* 304.18
unsmooth *rough* 544.5
unsmoothly *roughly* 544.13
unsmoothness *roughness* 544.1
unsnap *undress* 614.18
unsnarl *make simple* 526.12, *tidy* 765.21, *disentangle* 823.17
unsnarling *simplification* 526.6, *disentanglement* 823.8
unsociability **409.1;** *misanthropy* 291.4, *irritableness* 304.3, *aloofness* 756.2
unsociable **409.6;** *hostile* 63.6, *silent* 181.10, *taciturn* 208.4, *irritable* 304.9, *discourteous* 411.5, *aloof* 756.5, *solitary* 782.17
unsociableness *unsociability* 409.1
unsociably *hostilely* 63.13, *irritably* 304.17, *discourteously* 411.8, *aloofly* 756.10
unsocial *misanthropic* 291.8, *unsociable* 409.6
unsocial habits *unsociability* 409.1
unsocially **409.13;** *misanthropically* 291.18
unsocial person **409.5**
unsoiled *clean* 111.13, *pure* 431.11, *innocent* 449.6
unsolicitous *discourteous* 411.5
unsolicitousness *discourtesy* 411.1

unsolvable *futile* 282.9, *unexplained* 364.6
unsolved **844.8;** *unexplained* 364.6
unsophisticated *raw* 260.9, *unprocessed* 389.10, *naive* 449.9, 821.3, *unadorned* 526.9, *natural* 526.10
unsophisticated person *naive person* 821.2
unsophistication *naiveté* 449.4, 821.1, *unadornment* 526.3
unsorrowful *impenitent* 452.2
unsorted *indiscriminate* 338.8, *complicated* 751.10, *disordered* 766.9
unsound *logical* 6.83, *unhealthy* 114.23, *unhygienic* 114.27, *unskilled* 128.5, *sophistic* 330.7, *wrong* 430.12, *abnormal* 430.13, *ill* 517.8, *untrue* 722.6, *low quality* 745.7, *imperfect* 806.5, *unsafe* 811.8, *unreliable* 841.15
unsoundable *deep* 598.9
unsound argument *reasoning* 6.61
unsounded *silent* 231.2
unsoundly *sophistically* 330.14, *wrongfully* 430.25, *weakly* 517.14, *without truth* 722.14, *badly* 745.15
unsound mind *insanity* 110.1
unsoundness *sophistry* 330.1, *incorrectness* 430.3, *insolvency* 486.2, *imperfection* 806.1, *danger* 811.1, *vulnerability* 811.6, *unreliability* 841.7
unsparing *plentiful* 97.4, *severe* 424.5
unsparingly *severely* 424.11
unspeakable *astonishing* 294.10, *unintelligible* 364.4
unspeakableness *unintelligibility* 364.1
unspeakably *astonishingly* 294.19
unspecific *generalized* 778.12
unspecified *generalized* 778.12, *indeterminate* 841.14
unspectacular *mediocre* 742.7
unspeller *occultist* 86.13
unspent *saved* 105.15, *unused* 394.5, *surplus* 750.8
unspied *concealed* 844.7
unspirited *unemphatic* 201.2, *cowardly* 285.4, *wonderless* 295.3
unspiritual *material* 524.7
unspirituality *materialization* 524.2
unspoiled *unadorned* 526.9, *uncut* 759.7, *unbroken* 805.13
unspoiledness *unadornment* 526.3
unspoilt *unbroken* 805.13
unspoken *secret* 182.8, *silent* 231.2, *unknown* 349.7, *unsaid* 844.9
unsportsmanlike *wrongful* 430.10
unsportsmanlike conduct *penalty* 155.13
unspotted *innocent* 449.6, *immaculate* 805.11
unsprung *tough* 542.6, *hard* 547.8
unstable *passionate* 266.12, *inconstant* 378.6, *erratic* 381.5, *transient* 643.4, *irregular* 664.3, *changeable* 666.3, *inconsistent* 732.7, *unbalanced* 741.5, *deranged* 766.16, *unsafe* 811.8, *unreliable* 841.15
unstable equilibrium *force* 10.9
unstableness *inconsistency* 732.3, *unreliability* 841.7
unstaffed *unoccupied* 576.13
unstained *clean* 111.13, *immaculate* 805.11

unstalked *of leaves* 41.18
unstarched *soft* 543.6
unstatesmanlike *unskillful* 128.4
unstaunch *spineless* 285.5, *inconstant* 378.6
unsteadfast *spineless* 285.5, *inconstant* 378.6
unsteadily *weakly* 517.14, *fragilely* 548.5, *irregularly* 664.6, *changeably* 666.7, *shakily* 684.28, *unreliably* 841.25
unsteadiness *irregularity* 664.1, *changeableness* 666.1, *danger* 811.1, *unreliability* 841.7
unsteady **378.7;** *clumsy* 128.6, *ill* 517.8, *brittle* 548.3, *irregular* 664.3, *changeable* 666.3, *agitated* 684.15, *shaky* 684.18, *imperfect* 806.5, *decrepit* 808.12, *unsafe* 811.8, *unreliable* 841.15
unsteady movement *swaying* 378.4
unsteerable *clumsy* 128.6
unsterilized *unclean* 112.8, *contagious* 114.26
unstick **756.6;** *separate* 753.12
unstiffen *soften* 543.14
unstiffened *soft* 543.6
unstinting *generous* 498.6
unstirred *apathetic* 322.4
unstirring *quiescent* 678.6
unstitch *disentangle* 753.13
unstocked *unprovided* 98.6
unstop *open up* 583.16
unstoppable *protracted* 669.7, *inevitable* 840.11
unstopped *opened up* 583.11
unstressed *phonetic* 205.14, *faint* 233.6
unstring *soften* 543.14, *separate* 753.12
unstrung *weakened* 517.9, *soft* 543.6
unstuck *separate* 753.7, *nonadhesive* 756.4
unstudied *spontaneous* 389.6, *naive* 821.3
unstuffy *informal* 407.6
unsturdiness *brittleness* 548.1
unsturdy *brittle* 548.3
unsubdued *resisting* 417.8
unsubjected *independent* 829.12
unsubmissive *resisting* 417.8, *dissident* 782.12
unsubmissively *resistingly* 417.14
unsubstantial *invisible* 245.3, *imaginary* 360.12, *nonmaterial* 525.8, *sparse* 541.3, *unreal* 720.8, 722.7
unsubstantiality *immateriality* 525.2, *sparseness* 541.1, *unreality* 720.1, 722.2
unsubstantialize *dematerialize* 525.12
unsubstantially *metaphysically* 525.13, *sparsely* 541.6, *unreally* 722.15
unsubstantialness *immateriality* 525.2
unsuccessful *unprovided* 98.6, *unskillful* 128.4, *frustrating* 293.7, *unprofitable* 468.10, *futile* 802.10, *failed* 846.10, *adverse* 848.10
unsuccessful applicant *loser* 846.9
unsuccessful candidate *loser* 468.8, 846.9
unsuccessful challenger *loser* 846.9
unsuccessful competitor *loser* 846.9
unsuccessful defense *unfavorable verdict* 54.20
unsuccessfully **846.21;**

unskillfully 128.12, *disappointingly* 293.12, *at a loss* 468.22, *uselessly* 802.14, *adversely* 848.16
unsuccessful thing 846.8
unsuccessive *discontinuous* 775.7
unsuitability *uselessness* 802.1, *inconvenience* 804.1
unsuitable *unselected* 383.7, *improper* 430.14, *different* 463.7, *untimely* 660.5, *useless* 802.7, *inconvenient* 804.5
unsuitableness *untimeliness* 660.1
unsuitable time *untimeliness* 660.1
unsuitably *improperly* 430.26, *differently* 463.13, *at the wrong time* 660.12
unsuited *untimely* 660.5
unsullied *clean* 111.13, *pure* 431.11, *innocent* 449.6
unsulliedness *purity* 431.4
unsung *unsaid* 844.9
unsupplied *unprovided* 98.6
unsupported *solo* 788.14, *vulnerable* 811.9
unsure *vacillating* 378.5, *uncertain* 841.9
unsurely *ambivalently* 378.14
unsureness *vacillation* 378.1, *uncertainty* 841.1
unsure of oneself *shy* 403.8
unsurpassable *best* 744.10, 805.9
unsurpassably *supremely* 744.23
unsurpassed *best* 744.10, 805.9
unsurpassedly *supremely* 744.23
unsurprised *wonderless* 295.3, *expecting* 356.4
unsurprising *predictable* 295.4, *expected* 356.5
unsurprisingly *predictably* 295.9, *expectedly* 356.11
unsusceptibility *insensitivity* 268.1
unsusceptible *insensitive* 268.4
unsuspected *unsolved* 844.8
unsuspecting *believing* 87.6, *naive* 821.3
unsuspectingly *believingly* 87.12
unsuspicious *naive* 821.3
unsweetened *acid* 223.5
unswept *dirty* 112.7
unswerving *straight* 630.8, *direct* 697.11, *convinced* 840.8
unswervingly *straight* 630.16, *directly* 697.16
unsymmetrical *distorted* 627.6, *irregular* 664.3, 766.10, *disparate* 728.9
unsymmetrically *asymmetrically* 627.13, *disparately* 728.19
unsymmetry *irregular order* 766.2
unsympathetic *hostile* 63.6, *displeased* 291.6, *pitiless* 309.3, *unenthusiastic* 375.10, *oppositional* 828.11
unsympathetically *hostilely* 63.13, *insensitively* 268.7, *discontentedly* 291.17, *pitilessly* 309.7
unsympathizing *pitiless* 309.3
unsympathizingly *pitilessly* 309.7
unsynchronized *different in time* 648.2
unsystematic *indiscriminate* 338.8, *irregular* 664.3, *confused* 766.12
unsystematical *irregular* 664.3
unsystematically *irregularly* 664.6, *in disorder* 766.24
untainted *clean* 111.13, *innocent* 449.6, *immaculate* 805.11
untalented *unskillful* 128.4
untamed *unaccustomed* 398.3, *violent* 520.5
untamed animal *wild animal* 34.4

untamed horse *horse* 159.1
untangible *unreal* 722.7
untangle *make simple* 526.12, *straighten* 630.14, *tidy* 765.21, *deliver* 817.5, *disentangle* 823.17
untangling *deliverance* 817.1
untapped *new* 394.7
untarnished *clean* 111.13
untastefully *discourteously* 535.11
untaught *unskilled* 128.5, *ignorant* 349.5, *untrained* 389.8, *spontaneous* 396.5, *unaccustomed* 398.3, *naive* 821.3
untax *lighten* 539.9
untaxed *free of charge* 497.12
untaxing *lightening* 539.2
unteachable *unskilled* 128.5
untearable *tough* 547.6
untempered *weak* 517.6
untenability *unbelievability* 88.2
untenable *disbelieved* 88.7, *sophistic* 330.7, *helpless* 515.9, *weak* 517.6, *hopeless* 837.6
untenableness *sophistry* 330.1
untenanted *unoccupied* 576.13
untended *neglected* 326.6
untested *raw* 260.9, *unfamiliar* 652.10, *uncertified* 841.13
untethered *free-ranging* 829.13
unthanked 311.3
unthankful *ungrateful* 311.2
unthankfully *ungratefully* 311.6
unthankfulness *ingratitude* 311.1
unthawed *condensed* 540.7
unthinkability *impossibility* 837.1
unthinkable *impossible* 837.4
unthinkably *impossibly* 837.11
unthinking 355.8; *unintelligent* 316.6, *thoughtless* 318.7, 324.7, *incurious* 322.3, *inattentive* 324.5, *spontaneous* 396.5, *hasty* 818.3
unthinkingly *unintelligently* 316.9, *forgetfully* 355.14
unthinkingness 355.3
unthorough *nonobservant* 466.5, *uncompleted* 762.7
unthought-of 318.10
unthreading *separation* 753.1
unthreatened *safe* 810.16
unthreatening *trustworthy* 810.17
unthriftiness *extravagance* 500.1
unthrifty *extravagant* 500.4
untidily *dirtily* 112.12, *negligently* 326.8
untidiness 766.3; *dirtiness* 112.1, *indifference* 326.2
untidy 766.11; *dirty* 112.7, 112.11, *indifferent* 326.5, *make disorderly* 766.20, *impair* 808.18
untie *undress* 614.18, *separate* 753.12, *deliver* 817.5, *disentangle* 823.17, *set free* 829.17
untied *separate* 753.7, *escaping* 816.7
untie one's hands *liberate* 831.6
untie the knot [Inf] *divorce* 66.9
untie the purse strings *expend* 491.11
until *all the time* 639.16
until hell freezes over [Inf] *for long* 642.9
until now *historically* 3.17, *before now* 651.21
until one is blue in the face *for long* 642.9, *uselessly* 802.14
until the cows come home *for long* 642.9
until the end of time *eternally* 644.10, 798.12

until the Greek calends *for long* 642.9
untimeliness 660.1; *bungling* 128.2, *lateness* 658.1, *disruption* 768.4, *inconvenience* 804.1
untimely 660.5; *misjudged* 342.8, *inconvenient* 804.5
untimely action *untimeliness* 660.1
untimely end *way of dying* 29.5
untimely occurrence *untimeliness* 660.1
untiring *committed* 377.7, *stalwart* 547.10
untiringly *stalwartly* 547.17
untold *secret* 182.8, *unknown* 349.7, *excluded* 764.6, *numberless* 795.8, *immeasurable* 798.6, *unsaid* 844.9
untouchable *reserved* 585.7
untouched *clean* 111.13, *indifferent* 289.7, *new* 394.7, *pure* 431.11, *impenitent* 452.2, *uncut* 759.7
untouched by evil *innocent* 449.6
untoward *inconvenient* 804.5
untraced *unsolved* 844.8
untracked *unsolved* 844.8
untraditional *uncustomary* 398.4
untrainable horse *horse* 159.1
untrained 389.8; *unskillful* 128.4, *unskilled* 128.5, *raw* 260.9, *unaccustomed* 398.3, *incomplete* 806.6
untranslatable *unintelligible* 364.4
untraveled *housebound* 415.9
untried *raw* 260.9, *idle* 394.6, *unfamiliar* 652.10, *uncertified* 841.13
untrimmed *unequipped* 389.13, *unadorned* 526.9, *unbalanced* 741.5
untrodden *new* 394.7, *unfamiliar* 652.10
untroubled *moderate* 521.3, *quiescent* 678.6
untroublesome *wieldy* 823.12
untrue 722.6; *misrepresented* 188.4, *untruthful* 192.12, *erroneous* 351.11, *supposed* 359.6, *imaginary* 360.12, *wrong* 430.12, *defiant* 466.7, *incorrect* 722.8
untrueness 722.3; *untruthfulness* 192.1, *erroneousness* 351.2, *untruth* 722.1
untrue picture *misrepresentation* 188.1
untrustworthiness *questionableness* 333.7, *unreliability* 841.7
untrustworthy *questionable* 333.13, *unsafe* 811.8, *unreliable* 841.15
untruth 722.1; *falsehood* 192.6, *erroneousness* 351.2, *evasion* 380.2
untruthful 192.12; *wrong* 430.12, *misrepresented* 627.8, *untrue* 722.6
untruthfully 192.27; *equivocally* 380.9, *wrongfully* 430.25, *distortedly* 627.14, *without truth* 722.14
untruthfulness 192.1; *lying* 192.5, *incorrectness* 430.3, *distortion of truth* 627.4, *untruth* 722.1
untuned *unmelodious* 241.5
untuneful *unmelodious* 241.5
untutored *unskilled* 128.5, *ignorant* 349.5, *untrained* 389.8, *naive* 821.3
untwist *straighten* 630.14
untying *separation* 753.1
unusable *unselected* 383.7, *unused* 394.5, *useless* 802.7

unusably *out of use* 394.13
unused 394.5; *waste* 96.10, *saved* 105.15, *clumsy* 128.6, *unprocessed* 389.10, *not working* 415.10, *pure* 431.11, *unfamiliar* 652.10, *surplus* 750.8
unused thing 394.4
unused to *unaccustomed* 398.3
unusual 664.4, 782.15; *wondrous* 294.9, *uncustomary* 398.4, *infrequent* 662.2, *diverse* 732.5, *characteristic* 779.12
unusually 398.9, 664.7; *wondrously* 294.18, *newly* 652.21, *infrequently* 662.4, *diversely* 732.14, *unconformably* 782.21
unusualness 664.2, 782.4; *infrequency* 662.1, *diversity* 732.1
unutterable *astonishing* 294.10, *unintelligible* 364.4
unuttered *silent* 231.2, *unsaid* 844.9
unvaliant *cowardly* 285.4
unvaliantly *cowardly* 285.9
unvalorous *cowardly* 285.4
unvanquished *victorious* 845.17
unvariable *regular* 730.12
unvariableness *regularity* 730.6
unvariably *regularly* 730.21
unvaried *humming* 235.7, *same* 730.7
unvarnished *unadorned* 526.9, *naive* 821.3
unvarnished truth, the *the truth* 721.3
unvarying *boring* 296.6, *protracted* 669.7, *stable* 674.3, *regular* 730.12, *equal* 740.8
unvaryingly *boringly* 296.10, *regularly* 730.21
unveering *direct* 697.11
unveeringly *directly* 697.16
unveil *disclose* 180.8, *detect* 345.12, *uncover* 614.17, *be new* 652.17, *open* 771.32, *reveal* 843.14
unveiled *uncovered* 614.10, *inaugurated* 652.13, *enrolled* 771.24
unveiling *disclosure* 180.1, *detection* 345.2, *uncovering* 614.1, *beginning* 652.4, *premiere* 771.9
unveil oneself *show oneself* 843.15
unvenerated *disrespected* 436.16
unventilated *unhygienic* 114.27, *stinking* 227.3
unveracious *untruthful* 192.12
unveraciously *untruthfully* 192.27
unveraciousness *untruthfulness* 192.1
unverifiability *indemonstrability* 841.5
unverifiable *questionable* 333.13, *indemonstrable* 841.12
unverified *suppositional* 359.5, *uncertified* 841.13
unversatile *unskillful* 128.4
unversed *unskilled* 128.5, *naive* 821.3
unviable *hopeless* 837.6
unvindictive *forgiving* 312.4
unvindictively *forgivingly* 312.13
unvindictiveness *forgivingness* 312.3
unvirtuous *unchaste* 432.10, *depraved* 448.10
unvirtuously 448.16
unvirtuousness *depravity* 448.2
unvisited *secluded* 409.9
unvoiced *voiceless* 206.5, *unsaid* 844.9
unwanted *disliked* 291.10, *unselected* 383.7, *shoddy* 497.11, *surplus* 750.8, *redundant* 802.9
unwarily *imprudently* 286.11

unwariness *imprudence* 286.3
unwarlike *pacific* 74.7
unwarned *vulnerable* 811.9
unwarrantable *unjust* 53.24
unwarranted *unlawful* 53.23, *excessive* 712.8
unwary *insensible* 213.4, *imprudent* 286.7
unwashed *dirty* 112.7, *stinking* 227.3
unwasteful *thrifty* 499.4
unwatered *dry* 560.7
unwavering *truthful* 191.4, *tenacious* 376.5, *constant* 377.8, *determined* 674.5, *infallible* 840.12
unwaveringly *truthfully* 191.9, *determinedly* 674.10
unweaned *unaccustomed* 398.3
unwearied *committed* 377.7, *industrious* 414.16
unwed *celibate* 67.6, *independent* 829.12
unwedded *celibate* 67.6, *single* 788.16, *independent* 829.12
unwed man *or* **woman** *single person* 67.5
unweeded *plantlike* 41.13
unweighable *light* 539.4
unweighting *snowplow* 162.29
unwelcome *unpleasant* 272.6, *disliked* 291.10
unwelcome guest *intruder* 706.8
unwelcoming *unsociable* 409.6
unwell *sick* 114.24, *adverse* 848.10
unwhetted *blunt* 550.5
unwholesome *unhygienic* 114.27, *unpalatable* 223.6, *stinking* 227.3
unwholesomely *unhygienically* 114.32
unwholesomeness *lack of hygiene* 112.3, *unpalatability* 223.2
unwholesome surroundings *lack of hygiene* 112.3
unwieldily *awkwardly* 824.26
unwieldiness *weighing down* 538.5, *largeness* 579.2, *awkwardness* 804.3, 824.2
unwieldy *clumsy* 128.6, 824.14, *ponderous* 538.11, *unbalanced* 741.5, *awkward* 804.6
unwilling 375.8; *dissuaded* 179.5, *disinclined* 291.9, *dissenting* 347.7, *avoiding* 386.9, *resistant* 417.6, *disobedient* 427.10, *refused* 506.5, *hesitant* 693.9, *hindering* 826.12, *uncooperative* 828.14
unwillingly 375.17; *dissuasively* 179.12, *discontentedly* 291.17, *dissentiently* 347.10, *shyly* 386.25, *resistingly* 417.14, *disobediently* 427.14, *uncooperatively* 506.11, *with delay* 826.22
unwillingness 375.1; *disaffection* 179.3, *disinclination* 291.3, *shyness* 386.3, *resistance* 417.1, *disobedience* 427.1, *refusal* 506.1, *hesitation* 693.5, *hindrance* 826.1, *uncooperativeness* 828.4
unwind *have free time* 413.15, *ease* 543.15, *take it easy* 819.3
unwiped *dirty* 112.7
unwise *unskillful* 128.4, *imprudent* 286.7, *unintelligent* 316.6, *foolish* 353.5, *inconvenient* 804.5
unwisely *imprudently* 286.11, *unintelligently* 316.9, *foolishly* 353.8
unwitnessed *invisible* 245.3
unwitting *ignorant* 349.5
unwittingly *ignorantly* 349.11
unwonted *unaccustomed* 398.3
unwontedness *unaccustomedness* 398.1
unwooed *celibate* 67.6

unworkability *uselessness* 802.1, *hopelessness* 837.2
unworkable *powerless* 515.6, *useless* 802.7, *hopeless* 837.6
unworkably *hopelessly* 837.12
unworked *unprocessed* 389.10, *unformed* 389.11
unworldliness *the occult* 86.2, *naïveté* 449.4, 821.1, *immateriality* 525.2, *naturalness* 526.4
unworldly *spiritual* 86.20, *naive* 449.9, 821.3, *nonmaterial* 525.8, *natural* 526.10
unworthily *basely* 745.16
unworthy *inferior* 745.5, *imperfect* 806.5
unwrap *disclose* 180.8, *make visible* 244.9, *open* 583.15, *make nude* 614.19
unwrapped *open* 583.10
unwrinkled *uniform* 545.5, *horizontal* 603.6
unwritten *societal* 1.13, *forgotten* 186.6, *spoken* 205.13, *unsaid* 844.9
unwritten agreement *promise* 458.1
unwritten code *sense of duty* 433.2
unwritten constitution *law* 53.1
unwritten law *law* 53.1, *tradition* 397.5
unwrought *unformed* 389.11
unyielding 379.8; *relentless* 309.4, *iron-willed* 372.7, *strong-willed* 376.10, *persevering* 377.6, *obstinate* 417.7, *strong in spirit* 516.11, *mentally hard* 542.8, *mentally tough* 547.12, *inevitable* 840.11
unyieldingly *relentlessly* 309.8, *severely* 424.11, *strongly* 516.17
unyieldingness *relentlessness* 309.2, *mental hardness* 542.4, *mental toughness* 547.5
unzealous *unenthusiastic* 375.10
unzip *undress* 614.18, *separate* 753.12
unzipped *separate* 753.7
up 713.25; *increase* 581.16, *higher* 596.21, *vertically* 602.11, *via* 691.17, *raise* 715.9, *useful* 801.5
up [Inf] *cheerful* 269.7, *hopeful* 281.6
up against a brick wall *blocked* 826.13, *in the way* 826.23
up against it *insolvent* 486.10, *unequally* 741.10, *adverse* 848.10
up and about *getting well* 113.9, *in motion* 677.19
up and coming *prosperous* 847.5
up-and-coming *active* 414.13
up-and-coming star *successful person* 845.6
up and doing *acting* 412.9, *busy* 414.15
up and doing [Inf] *operational* 509.7
up and down *vertically* 602.11, *regularly* 663.14, *to and fro* 683.16
up-and-down *oscillating* 683.8
up and going *operational* 509.7
Upanishad *other text* 81.19
upas *Trees and Shrubs* 43
upasaka *religious* 84.9
upasika *religious* 84.9
up a tree [Inf] *troubled* 824.15
up back *offense* 155.6
upbeat *tempo* 140.22, *hopeful* 281.6
upbraid *condemn* 438.18
upbraided *condemned* 438.11
upbraiding *condemnation* 438.2,

condemning 438.10, *censuring* 438.12
upbringing *education* 48.1
upcast *upturn* 713.2, 713.20, *advanced* 713.16, *raising* 715.1, *raised* 715.6, *send up* 715.12
upchuck [Inf] *vomit* 709.27
upcoming *future* 650.6, *later* 658.9
upcoming event *future condition* 650.3
upcountry *inland* 611.2, 611.8, 611.19
updatable *renewable* 652.15
update *make new* 652.20
updated *renewed* 652.14
updated model *reconsideration* 807.9
updated version *reconsideration* 807.9
updating *new start* 652.5
updraft *air movement* 9.11, *airflow* 558.4, *upturn* 713.2
upend *make vertical* 602.9
upended *vertical* 602.5
up for auction *offered* 504.8
up for grabs *on sale* 482.24
up for sale *on sale* 482.24, *offered* 504.8
up for trial *litigated* 54.22, *judged* 341.9
up front *before* 621.14
up-front *direct* 630.12
upgradable *renewable* 652.15
upgrade *program* 15.29, *make new* 652.20, *further* 679.13, *upturn* 713.2, 713.20, *ascendancy* 713.5, *steep* 713.15, *promote* 715.13, *improve* 807.15, *refurbish* 809.11
upgraded *renewed* 652.14, *promoted* 715.8
upgrading *new start* 652.5, *promotion* 715.3, *uplift* 807.2
upgrowth *growth* 581.4, *upturn* 713.2
upheaval *fight* 422.9, *ruin* 523.4, *sudden change* 665.3, *raising* 715.1, *confusion* 766.4, *lawlessness* 766.6, *disturbance* 768.1
upheave *ascend* 713.19, *spring up* 713.22, *raise* 715.9
uphill *laborious* 122.7, *incline* 713.3, *steep* 713.15, *up* 713.25, *difficult* 824.9, *difficultly* 824.23
uphill christie *skiing techniques* 162.5
uphill struggle *difficult task* 824.3
uphill task *difficult task* 824.3
uphill work *work* 122.1
uphold *confirm* 189.25, *bolster* 377.15, *justify* 441.12, *give moral support* 605.18, *continue* 669.8, *erect* 719.11, *establish reality* 719.12, *preserve* 815.14, *advise* 825.27
upholder *affirmer* 189.9, *supporter* 605.9
upholding *supportive* 605.11
upholstered *type of furniture* 101.2, *type of chair* 101.4
upholsterer *furniture making* 101.3, *coverer* 613.8
upholstering *furniture making* 101.3, *Hobbies and Pastimes* 167
upholstery *equipment* 103.6, *protective covering* 613.5
up in arms *warring* 76.26, *martially* 77.39, *offended* 302.9, *resisting* 417.8, *disagreeing* 463.6, *at odds* 828.23
up in the air *uncompleted* 762.7
up in the world *prosperous* 847.5
upkeep 815.5; *financial support* 605.8, *preservation* 815.1, *sustenance* 825.3

upland 572.7; *geographical space* 563.3, *hilly* 569.6, *of landmasses* 572.12, *highland* 596.11
upland *or* **uplands** *heights* 596.4
uplift 807.2; *earth movement* 8.20, *bring cheer* 269.12, *refine* 534.7, *lighten* 539.9, *height* 596.1, *heighten* 596.14, *incline* 713.3, *raising* 715.1, *raise* 715.9, *improve* 807.15
uplifted *high* 596.7, *advanced* 713.16, *raised* 715.6
uplifting *cheering* 269.8
upliftment *raising* 715.1
uplighting *highlight* 246.12
up line *track* 688.2
upmarket *costly* 496.7
upmarket price *costliness* 496.1
upmost *higher* 596.8, *top* 600.6, *at the summit* 600.12, *unique* 744.11, *elite* 744.12
up on *expert* 127.12
upon against *via* 691.17
upon one's word *assuredly* 189.30, *as promised* 458.16
upon's one honor *assuredly* 189.30
upper *ranked* 6.72, *higher* 596.8, *top* 600.6, *excellent* 744.14
upper [Inf] *drug* 115.9, *addictive drug* 117.10, *stimulants* 121.18
upper atmosphere *atmosphere* 9.8, *atmospheric layer* 558.3
upper bound *set* 6.19
upper case *type* 173.5
uppercase *printed* 173.13
Upper Chamber *British government* 49.22
upper circle *auditorium* 136.17
upper class *social stratification* 2.7, *aristocracy* 70.2, *best people* 744.7, *social class* 777.5
upper-class *socioeconomic* 2.13, *aristocratic* 70.4, *elite* 744.12
upper classes, the *the rich* 485.7
upper crust [Inf] *fashionable elite* 536.4, *best people* 744.7
upper echelon *management board* 126.2
upper extremity *summit* 600.1
upper gastrointestinal (GI) series *diagnostic radiology* 107.12
upper hand *authority* 52.1, *influence* 512.1, *advantage* 618.4, 744.3
Upper House *United States government* 49.21, *British government* 49.22
upper jaw *mouth* 19.7
upper limit *differentiation* 6.29, *limit* 620.1, *certain amount* 738.3
upper middle class *middle class* 772.6
uppermost *higher* 596.8, *top* 600.6, *at the summit* 600.12, *unique* 744.11, *important* 799.7
upper partial *tone* 140.24
upper side *top layer* 600.5
upper surface *top layer* 600.5
upper wind *wind* 9.12
upping *increase* 581.3, *raising* 715.1
uppish [Inf] *arrogant* 400.11
uppishly [Inf] *arrogantly* 400.21
uppishness [Inf] *arrogance* 400.4
uppity *arrogant* 297.9
uppity [Inf] *arrogant* 400.11
uppityness *arrogance* 297.2
uppityness [Inf] *arrogance* 400.4
upraise *lighten* 539.9, *heighten* 596.14, *make vertical* 602.9, *raise* 715.9
upraised *high* 596.7, *unbowed* 602.7, *raised* 715.6

---

uprating *framing* 132.18
uprear *heighten* 596.14, *be vertical* 602.8
upreared *high* 596.7, *unbowed* 602.7
uprearing *raising* 715.1
upright *linear* 6.77, *law-abiding* 53.20, *truthful* 191.4, *right* 429.7, *moral* 431.9, *respectable* 435.11, *virtuous* 447.5, *innocent* 449.6, *vertical* 602.3, 602.5, *vertically* 602.11, *honest* 630.11
upright fold *fold* 8.22
uprightly *right* 429.15, *morally* 431.15, *virtuously* 447.9, *innocently* 449.13, *vertically* 602.11
uprightness *truthfulness* 191.1, *rightfulness* 429.1, *morals* 431.2, *virtue* 447.1, *innocence* 449.1, *verticality* 602.1
upright piano *Musical Instruments* 142
uprights *stadium* 155.3
uprise *stationary rings* 157.8, *subvert* 427.13, *height* 596.1, *rise* 596.17, *be vertical* 602.8, *ascent* 713.1, *ascend* 713.19
uprising *activism* 414.5, *resistance movement* 417.3, *revolution* 427.4, *disorder* 507.2, *rising* 596.12, *ascent* 713.1, *ascending* 713.13, *lawlessness* 766.6
uproar *exaggeration* 194.1, *loudness* 232.1, *cry* 239.1, *dissonance* 241.1, *fight* 422.9, *violence by person* 520.2, *tumult* 684.2, *confusion* 766.4, *commotion* 768.5
uproarious *shouting* 232.7, *vociferous* 239.9, *humorous* 277.9, *explosive* 520.6
uproariously *loudly* 232.11, *vociferously* 239.18
uproot *destroy* 523.10, *remove* 574.16, *evict* 709.20, *extract* 711.13, *subtract* 749.6, *eject* 764.8
uprooted *removed* 574.9, *dislodged* 711.11
uprooting *destroying* 523.2, *removal* 574.2, *extraction* 711.1, *extractive* 711.10
uprush *excess* 99.1, *upturn* 713.2, *spread* 746.3
ups and downs *oscillation* 683.1
upset *cause dislike* 291.16, *knock down* 523.13, *displace* 574.15, *act of inversion* 608.3, *become inverted* 608.8, *agitated* 684.15, *agitate* 684.22, *be repulsive* 701.10, *downthrow* 716.2, *overthrown* 716.9, *bring down* 716.14, *unbalance* 741.8, *disorder* 766.1, *confused* 766.12, *discompose* 766.18, *disturbance* 768.1, *disturbed* 768.6, *disturb* 768.10, *inconvenience* 804.1, *be inconvenient* 804.9, *hinder* 826.15
upset one's applecart *hinder* 826.15
upset stomach *gastroenterological disease* 114.11
upsetting *displacement* 574.1, *displaced* 574.8, *disturbing* 768.9
upshot *grip* 151.4, *solution* 334.6, *376.6, *effect* 676.1, *conclusion* 761.3, *sequel* 770.5, *ruling* 780.2
upside *top layer* 600.5
up side *golfing terms* 156.3
upside down *inversely* 608.9
upside-down *inverted* 608.5, *muddled* 766.13, *anyhow* 766.25
upside-down cake *cake* 90.36
upside-downness *inversion* 608.1
upspin *ascend* 713.19

upspring *grow* 581.17, *spring up* 713.22
upstage *stage* 136.18, *overact* 136.35, *onstage* 136.39, *show off* 404.26
upstairs *up* 713.25
upstairs [Inf] *theoretically* 327.19
upstairs and downstairs *extensively* 563.18
upstanding *right* 429.7, *showing respect* 435.7, *virtuous* 447.5, *vertical* 602.5, *raised* 715.6
upstandingly *virtuously* 447.9
upstandingness *virtue* 447.1
upstart *horizontal bar* 157.5, *stationary rings* 157.8, *insolent person* 400.7, *new arrival* 652.7, *spring up* 713.22
upstream *directionally* 697.20
upstroke *upturn* 713.2
upsurge *excess* 99.1, *upturn* 713.2, *ascend* 713.19, *spread* 746.3
upsurging *ascending* 713.13
upsweep *upturn* 713.2, 713.20
upsweep method *relay racing* 166.5
upswept *ascending* 713.13
upswing *upturn* 713.2, *spread* 746.3, *uplift* 807.2
upswinging *ascending* 713.13, *promotion* 715.3
up-the-middle hit *batting terms* 147.6
up the river [Inf] *imprisoned* 55.9, *detained* 830.11
upthrow *incline* 713.3, *raising* 715.1, *send up* 715.12
upthrown *raised* 715.6
upthrust *incline* 713.3, *raising* 715.1, *raised* 715.6
uptight [Inf] *fearful* 283.10, *touchy* 303.10, *self-restrained* 455.6, 830.10
uptightness [Inf] *disagreement* 463.1
up to *equal to* 740.10
up to date *educated* 48.19, *topically* 328.11
up-to-date *informed* 170.9, *newsworthy* 171.8, *topical* 328.5, *present* 647.4, *new* 652.9, *forward* 679.6
up-to-dateness *modernity* 647.3, *newness* 652.1
up to everything *cunning* 822.4
up to now *before now* 651.21
up to one's ears in debt *indebted* 488.7, *nonpaying* 490.7
up to one's elbows *busy* 414.15
up to one's eyes or **ears** *intensely* 598.28
up to one's neck or **eyes** or **ears** [Inf] *busy* 414.15, *fully* 761.14
up to par *proper* 429.10
up to snuff [Inf] *sufficient* 97.3
up to something *planning* 387.11
up to the knees *high* 596.20
up to the mark *sufficient* 97.3, *equal to* 740.10
up to the minute *topically* 328.11
up-to-the-minute *topical* 328.5
up to the shoulders *high* 596.20
up to the waist *high* 596.20
up to this moment *before now* 651.21
up to this time *before now* 651.21
uptown *urban area* 567.10, *urban* 567.14, *directional* 697.8, *directionally* 697.20
uptowner *municipal resident* 567.12
uptrade *ascendancy* 713.5, *upturn* 713.20

uptrend *upturn* 713.2
upturn 713.2, 713.20; *ascend* 713.19, *spread* 746.3, *uplift* 807.2, *recuperation* 809.4
upturned *ascending* 713.13
upward *socioeconomic* 2.13, *higher* 596.21, *directional* 677.13, *steep* 713.15, *up* 713.25
upward curve *spread* 746.3
upwardly mobile *advanced* 713.16, *prosperous* 847.5
upwardly mobile, the *prosperous person* 847.4
upward mobility *social stratification* 2.7, *social ambition* 408.2, *ascendancy* 713.5, *uplift* 807.2
upward motion *ascending motion* 677.7, *ascent* 713.1
upward slope *incline* 713.3
upwards of *plurally* 793.10
upward trend *spread* 746.3
upwelling *ocean current* 8.15
upwind *odorlessly* 225.8, *directional* 697.8, *directionally* 697.20, *ascend* 713.19
upwind of *odorless* 225.4
uracil *nucleotide* 12.10
Ural *Rivers* 570
Ural Mountains *Mountains and Hills* 569
Urania *Deities* 82
Uranian *astronomical* 7.33, *homosexual* 32.9
uranium *Chemical Elements and Common Allotropes* 11, *nuclear power* 106.8
uranium-lead dating *dating* 8.48
uranographer *astronomer* 7.2
uranographic(al) *astronomical* 7.33
uranography *astronomy* 7.1
uranology *astronomy* 7.1
uranophobia *Phobias* 283
Uranus *Planets and Their Satellites* 7, *planet* 7.16, *Deities* 82
urban 567.14; *communal* 2.12, *environmental* 60.17, *native* 61.12, *transportable* 686.7
urban area 567.10
urban blight *dilapidation* 808.5
urban complex *city* 567.1
urban culture *society* 2.6
urban dweller *municipal resident* 567.12
urbane *refined* 48.20, 534.5, *sociable* 408.11, *courteous* 410.6, *good-mannered* 410.7, *smooth-mannered* 504.3, *urban* 567.14, *cunning* 822.4
urbanely *discerningly* 48.27, *genteelly* 410.14, *suavely* 545.15, *municipally* 567.16
urban environment *society* 2.6
urban guerrilla *killer* 30.11, *seditionist* 427.7
urbanism *society* 2.6
urbanite *townsperson* 61.7, *municipal resident* 567.12
urbanities *courtesies* 410.3
urbanity *refinement* 48.10, 534.1, *good manners* 410.2
urbanization 567.4; *society* 2.6
urbanize 567.15; *socialize* 2.14
urbanized *communal* 2.12
urbanizing *communal* 2.12
urban planning *society* 2.6
urban region *urban area* 567.10
urban renewal *society* 2.6
urban sector *society* 2.6
urban society *society* 2.6
urban sociology *sociology* 2.1

urban sprawl *urban area* 567.10, *disbandment* 776.2
urban spread or **sprawl** *city* 567.1
urceole *sacred object* 83.11
urchin *young man* 26.8
Urd *Deities* 82
urea *urine* 25.6
urethra *internal organ* 19.13, *body orifice* 583.3
urethroscope *diagnostic instrument* 107.13
urethroscopy *diagnostic procedure* 107.11
urge *compulsion* 108.13, 428.1, *delusion* 110.2, *advise* 176.9, *persuade* 178.15, *emphasize* 200.6, *desire* 288.1, *propound* 359.9, *insist* 376.14, *direction* 384.3, *direct* 384.10, *spontaneity* 396.2, *habit* 397.1, *compel* 428.8, *request* 505.10, *impel* 695.9, *haste* 818.1, *hasten* 818.4
urged *persuadable* 178.14, *directed* 384.7, *motivated* 508.8
urgency *necessity* 95.1, *emphasis* 200.1, *request* 505.1, *potency* 516.6, *immediacy* 645.1, *priority* 769.2, *importance* 799.1, *danger* 811.1, *haste* 818.1
urgent *necessary* 95.10, *emphatic* 200.3, *compelling* 428.6, *requesting* 505.7, *strong* 516.9, *immediate* 645.5, *allowing no delay* 645.7, *important* 799.7, *hasty* 818.3
urgently *with need* 95.20, *emphatically* 200.7, *compellingly* 428.12, *by request* 505.14, *acutely* 516.18, *importantly* 799.15, *hastily* 818.7
urge on or **forward** *hurry someone up* 694.15
urging *recommendation* 176.2, *advisory* 176.7, *exhortation* 178.2, *request* 505.1, *inducement* 508.2
Uriah Heep *humble person* 298.7
uric acid *urine* 25.6
Uriel *angel* 82.11
urinal *place for excretion* 25.11
urinalysis *urination* 25.4
urinary 25.15; *fluid* 19.25
urinate 25.22; *relieve oneself* 275.12, *let out* 709.26
urination 25.4; *Phobias* 283, *exudate* 557.4
urinative *urinary* 25.15
urine 25.6; *body fluid* 19.16, 555.3, *waste product* 96.7, *test* 107.10, *diagnostic procedure* 107.11, *unpleasant-smelling thing* 227.2, *yellow thing* 259.4, *Phobias* 283, *exudate* 557.4
urinometer *urination* 25.4
Urmia *Lakes* 568
urn *funeral object* 31.6, *vessel* 578.11
urn burial *burial* 31.1
urned *buried* 31.8
Urochordata *protochordate* 39.4
urochordate *protochordate* 39.4, *invertebrate* 39.20
Urodela *amphibian* 37.10
urodele *amphibian* 37.10
urogenital disease *disease* 114.4
urology *Medical Specialties* 107
uronic acid *saccharide* 12.4
urophobia *Phobias* 283
uropygeal gland *secretory mechanism* 24.3
Ursa Major *Constellations* 7
Ursa Minor *Constellations* 7
ursid *flesh-eating mammal* 35.9
Ursidae *flesh-eating mammal* 35.9
ursine *carnivorous* 35.26
urticaria *skin disease* 114.16

Urubamba Rivers 570
Uruguay Countries 566, Rivers 570
Urzhum Breeds of Pigs 16
us *humankind* 18.1
usability 801.2; *convenience* 803.1
usable 393.6, 801.6; *operational* 509.7, *practical* 719.8, *convenient* 803.3
usably *usefully* 393.15, 801.12
usage *type of meaning* 361.4, *use* 393.1, *custom* 397.4, *performance* 465.2, *usefulness* 801.1
US Air Force *armed forces* 77.9, *air force* 77.27
US Air Force Reserves *air force* 77.27
US Air Forces Europe *air force commands* 77.28
US Army *armed forces* 77.9, *army* 77.12
US Army Reserve *army* 77.12
US Coast Guard *armed forces* 77.9, *navy* 77.18
US coinage 484.10
US Customs Service *levy* 494.7
use 393.1, 393.9; *social skill* 127.3, *point* 361.5, *custom* 397.4, *conduct oneself* 399.17, *sponge* 401.13, *action* 412.1, *direct* 412.16, *wrong* 430.19, *welfare* 445.2, *consume* 491.12, *take action* 509.12, *instrumentality* 511.1, *importance* 799.1, *usefulness* 801.1, *find useful* 801.11, *promote* 807.18, *help* 825.1
use a contraceptive *practice birth control* 23.10
use a credit card *buy on credit* 476.13
use a crib *or* **pony** *or* **trot** [Inf] *translate* 365.14
use a diagonal stride *ski* 162.35
use a footpath *find one's way* 691.15
use aikido techniques *do martial arts* 152.21
use a J stroke *canoe* 150.31
use a light hand *be lenient* 423.5
use a light rein *be lenient* 423.5
use a mute *play an instrument* 142.9
use as a doormat *subject* 832.10
use as a meal ticket *sponge* 401.13
use a sharp weapon *use a sharp tool* 549.17
use a sledgehammer to crack a nut *misuse* 395.6
use as one's own *adopt* 476.11
use a turning stroke *canoe* 150.31
use backspin *play* 156.8
use body language *gesture* 183.17
use brute force *suppress* 424.9, *act rough* 547.14
use common speech *be simple* 526.13
used 393.5, 491.10; *ill-used* 395.4, *habituated* 397.14
use diplomacy *have good manners* 410.10, *negotiate* 460.6
use earplugs *muffle* 229.11
use every muscle *exert oneself* 122.11
use expletives *blaspheme* 301.14
use few words *be taciturn* 208.7
use food stamps *be poor* 486.14
use footwork *fence* 153.7
use force *be powerful* 514.18, *strengthen oneself* 516.16, *use violence* 520.9

use force against *force* 428.10
useful 393.7, 801.5; *favorable* 62.8, *correspondent* 334.16, *effective* 412.10, *beneficial* 445.11, *gainful* 467.10, *workable* 509.8, *instrumental* 511.4, *important* 799.7, *convenient* 803.3, *feasible* 823.10, *helpful* 825.19
usefully 393.15, 801.12; *favorably* 62.15, *correspondingly* 334.27, *effectively* 412.19, *well* 445.19, *operationally* 509.13, *instrumentally* 511.9, *helpfully* 825.32
usefulness 393.2, 801.1; *correspondence* 334.8, *welfare* 445.2, *instrumentality* 511.1, *importance* 799.1, *convenience* 803.1, *helpfulness* 825.10
useful work *work* 14.10
use hands illegally *exhibit penalty behavior* 155.21
use language 5.42
useless 802.7; *waste* 96.10, *superfluous* 99.8, *futile* 282.9, *thankless* 311.4, *unused* 394.5, *shoddy* 497.11, *powerless* 515.6, *cheap* 800.16, *inconvenient* 804.5, *spoiled* 808.9, *failed* 846.10
useless exercise *overactivity* 414.9
useless expenditure *waste* 96.1
uselessly 802.14; *wastefully* 96.23, *superfluously* 99.15, *futilely* 282.16, *thanklessly* 311.7, *out of use* 394.13, *powerlessly* 515.16, *inconveniently* 804.11, *unsuccessfully* 846.21
uselessness 802.1; *superfluity* 99.4, *futility* 282.3, 846.3, *lack of authority* 515.2, *triviality* 800.2
useless work *overactivity* 414.9
use long words *be diffuse* 199.5
use Morse code *signal* 183.18
use muscle *strengthen oneself* 516.16
USENET *computer communications* 15.25
use obscene *or* **bad language** *blaspheme* 301.14
use of language *mode of expression* 537.3
use of machinery *instrumentality* 511.1
use of tobacco *substance abuse* 121.1
use of words *language* 5.4
use one's best endeavors *exert oneself* 122.11
use one's brain *think* 317.9
use one's connections *find means* 511.8
use one's eyes *see* 242.20
use one's good offices *be an instrument* 511.7
use one's head *think* 317.9, *be wise* 352.6
use one's head *or* **wits** *be intelligent* 315.11
use one's imagination *imagine* 360.14
use one's influence *be an instrument* 511.7
use one's intelligence *be wise* 352.6
use one's own initiative *be independent* 829.18
use people *exploit* 393.11
use physical force *force* 428.10
use plain English *be simple* 526.13
use plain words *mean* 361.13, *be open* 583.19
use profanity *blaspheme* 301.14
user 393.4

user-friendly *computerized* 15.28, *made easy* 823.11
user interface (UI) *programming concepts* 15.24
use short words *make comprehensible* 363.8
use sign language *gesture* 183.17, *have difficulty speaking* 206.9, *be deaf* 229.8
use simple language *make comprehensible* 363.8
use skillfully *be skillful* 127.14
use sparingly *economize* 56.11
use symbols *sign* 183.19
use tact *be courteous* 410.9
use tactics *motivate* 412.12
use the backboard *play basketball* 148.7
use the bottom gear *be on the track* 146.11
use the entrance *find one's way* 691.15
use therapy *cure* 809.15
use the same words *be the same* 730.13
use the services of *frequent* 393.10
use the time *spend time* 639.14
use the tuck position *ski* 162.35
use the very words *be literal* 721.25
use to advantage *exploit* 393.11
use tools 103.8
use to the full *or* **fullest** *exploit* 393.11
use up 393.12; *expend* 96.16, *consume* 491.12, *waste* 500.7, *remove power from* 515.13, *cause to cease* 668.12, *make useless* 802.12, *wear out* 808.21
use up one's credit *expend* 491.11
US European Command *army commands* 77.13
use violence 520.9; *force* 428.10
use wrongly *misuse* 395.6
US Forces Japan *army commands* 77.13
US Forces Korea *army commands* 77.13
USGA National Amateur *golfing associations and tournaments* 156.6
U-shaped valley *landform* 8.9, *glacier* 8.44
usher 794.7; *wedding party* 64.7, *attendant* 69.4, *stagehand* 136.29, *conductor* 399.13, *conduct* 399.21, *show in* 708.13, *escort* 794.30
ushered *accompanied* 794.15
usher in *predict* 358.14, *receive someone* 473.14, *show in* 708.13, *forecast* 769.17
using *by means of* 102.7
using as one's own *adoption* 476.2
using force *by request* 505.14
using short words *simple* 363.6
using simple language *simple* 363.6
US Labor party *Political Parties* 50
US Marines *armed forces* 77.9, *marines* 77.26
US Naval Reserve (USNR) *navy* 77.18
US Navy *armed forces* 77.9, *navy* 77.18
US Open *golfing associations and tournaments* 156.6, *notable tennis competitions* 165.8
US Pacific Command *army commands* 77.13
US paper money *US coinage* 484.10

US Soccer Federation *soccer associations and awards* 163.6
Ust Urt Deserts 572
Ustyurt Deserts 572
usual *predictable* 295.4, *habitual* 397.9, 765.15, *unpretentious* 526.8, *regular* 663.5, *average* 742.5, *common* 778.13, *customary* 780.9, *commonplace* 800.17
usual, the *expected thing* 356.3, *average* 742.1
usually 778.21; *predictably* 295.9, *regularly* 397.21, *frequently* 661.7, *orderly* 663.13, *prevailingly* 742.11, *as a rule* 780.18
usualness *predictability* 295.2, *unpretentiousness* 526.2, *regularity* 663.1
usual occurrence *custom* 780.5
usual policy *standard procedure* 397.6
usual text *interpretation* 365.3
usual way *way* 691.1
Usumacinta Rivers 570
usufruct *use* 393.1
usurer *gainer* 467.9, *lender* 475.3, 487.5, *financier* 484.17, *overcharger* 496.5
usurious *loaned* 475.5, *costly* 496.7
usurp *be anarchic* 51.8, *gain authority* 52.15, *be insubordinate* 416.8, *take over* 477.16, *replace* 574.17, *transgress* 712.14
usurpation *acquisition of authority* 52.5, *taking over* 477.3, *transgression* 712.3
usurper *defiant person* 416.4, *taker* 477.9
usurp power *or* **authority** *be anarchic* 51.8
usury *gain* 467.1, *lending* 475.1, *interest* 488.4, *extortion* 496.4
Utah American States 564, Lakes 568
utensil *tool* 103.1
utensils *equipment* 103.6
uterus *organs of reproduction* 21.9, *placental mammal* 35.6
utile *useful* 801.5
utilitarian *political and economic philosopher* 4.10, *of a political philosophy* 4.14, *philanthropist* 307.5, *public-spirited* 307.7, *useful* 393.7, 801.5, *practical* 719.8, *helpful* 825.19
utilitarianism *political and economic philosophy* 4.6, *public-spiritedness* 307.2, *usefulness* 801.1, *convenience* 803.1
utilities *business expenses* 491.4
utility *usefulness* 393.2, 801.1, *instrumentality* 511.1, *importance* 799.1, *convenience* 803.1, *helpfulness* 825.10
utility principle *philosophical term* 4.7
utility program *system software* 15.13
utility room *room* 60.9
utilizable *usable* 393.6, *instrumental* 511.4
utilization *use* 393.1, *usefulness* 801.1
utilize *use* 393.9, *find useful* 801.11
utilized *used* 393.5
uti possidetis *legal ownership* 469.8
utmost *unique* 744.11, *elite* 744.12
utmost, the *limit* 761.4
utmost height *summit* 600.1
utmost speed *speed* 694.2
Utopia *aspiration* 281.3, *marvel* 294.3, *ideal* 327.6, Imaginary Places 360

utopian *political and economic philosopher* 4.10, *of a political philosophy* 4.14, *hoper* 281.5, *ideal* 327.12, *visionary* 360.9, *imaginative* 360.10, *unrealistic* 720.11

utopianism *political and economic philosophy* 4.6, *idealism* 327.7, 360.7, *theory* 720.4

utopian novel *novel* 139.3

utter *use language* 5.42, *aphorize* 177.3, *divulge* 180.9, *speak* 205.17, *monetize* 484.24, *complete* 761.6, 805.14

utterance 205.10; *articulation* 205.9

utter bore *boring thing* 296.3, *boring person* 296.4

utter defeat *defeat* 846.7

utter devotion *seriousness* 376.3

uttered *spoken* 205.13

utterer *speaker* 205.12

utter failure *ruin* 523.4

utter loss *loss* 468.1

utterly *clean* [Inf] 111.21, *wholly* 759.11, *completely* 759.14, 761.13, 805.22

utterly detest *hate* 300.11

utterly devoted *steady* 376.8

uttermost *unique* 744.11

utter nonsense *senseless talk* 362.4

U-turn *vacillation* 380.3, *curve* 629.1, *alteration* 665.2, *reversion* 671.1, *about-face* 680.4, *miscellaneous automotive terms* 687.14

UVA *electromagnetic radiation* 10.14

UVB *electromagnetic radiation* 10.14

UV filter *filter* 132.14

uvula *mouth* 19.7, *speech organ* 205.4

uxoricide *homicide* 30.4

uxorious *loving* 299.15

Uzbekistan *Countries* 566

V

V *five* 792.1

V-1 *modern missile weapon* 78.4, *bomb* 78.15

V-2 *modern missile weapon* 78.4, *bomb* 78.15

Vaal *Rivers* 570

vacancy *lack of intellect* 316.1, *lack of thought* 318.1, *forgetfulness* 355.1, *emptiness* 576.2, 718.4, *opportunity* 583.8, *unimportance* 800.1

vacant 576.12; *unprovided* 98.6, *nonexistent* 190.14, *lacking intellect* 316.5, *thoughtless* 318.7, *forgetful* 355.6, *not working* 415.10, *unoccupied* 576.13, *opened up* 583.11, *nonexistent* 718.9

vacantly *unintelligently* 316.9, *forgetfully* 355.14, *absently* 576.18

vacant moments *leisure* 125.1

vacate *withdraw* 392.5, 705.9, *absent oneself* 576.15, *leave empty* 576.17, *resign* 835.5

vacation *refresher* 94.2, *time off* 125.2, *leave of absence* 576.4, *be regular* 663.10, *pause* 668.3, 668.13, *ease* 819.1

vacation home *house* 60.4

vacation time *benefits* 57.11

vaccinate *practice medicine* 107.32, *treat* 115.17, *practice hygiene* 116.4, *inject* 710.10, *immunize* 810.22

vaccinated *health-giving* 113.6, *injected* 710.6, *safe* 810.16

vaccination *health care* 107.7,

prophylaxis 115.4, hygiene 116.1, injection 710.2, sanitary precaution 810.8

vaccine *prophylaxis* 115.4

vacciniophobia *Phobias* 283

vacillate 378.8, 683.14; *equivocate* 380.8, *be capricious* 381.6, *stall* 419.28, *defer* 604.15, *be irresolute* 666.6, *hesitate* 841.18

vacillating 378.5, 683.10; *equivocating* 380.6, *weak-willed* 517.10, *deferred* 604.9, *irresolute* 666.4, 841.10

vacillation 378.1, 380.3, 683.3; *irresolution* 461.3, 666.2, 841.3, *deferment* 604.3

vacillator 378.3

vacillatory *vacillating* 683.10

vacuity *nonentity* 190.5, *lack of intellect* 316.1, *lack of thought* 318.1, *forgetfulness* 355.1, *nonsense* 362.2, *emptiness* 576.2, 718.4

vacuole *cell structure* 13.16

vacuous *nonexistent* 190.14, *lacking intellect* 316.5, *thoughtless* 318.7, *forgetful* 355.6, *meaningless* 362.7, *vacant* 576.12

vacuously *unintelligently* 316.9, *forgetfully* 355.14, *absently* 576.18

vacuum *surface chemistry* 11.20, *clean* 111.17, *nonentity* 190.5, *empty space* 563.2, *emptiness* 576.2, 718.4, *draw off* 711.16

vacuum bottle *bottle* 578.14

vacuum cleaner *cleaning tool* 111.10

vacuum distill *extract* 11.41

vacuum filtration *process* 11.15

vacuum flask *preserver* 815.9

vacuum gauge *surface chemistry* 11.20

vacuuming *cleaning* 111.2, *drawing off* 711.4

vacuum-packed *closed* 584.7, *complete* 805.14, *invulnerable* 810.18

vacuum-packed food *food* 90.1, *preserved thing* 815.10

vacuum pump *surface chemistry* 11.20

vacuum-sealed *invulnerable* 810.18

vacuum tube *electron tube* 14.40, *computer part* 15.4, *power supplier* 514.14

vade mecum *type of book* 174.3

Vaduz *Countries* 566

vagary *conception* 360.4, *caprice* 381.1, *deviation* 782.6

vagina *organs of reproduction* 21.9, *body orifice* 583.3

vaginal *reproductive* 21.11

vagrancy *wandering* 164.4

vagrant *nonworker* 415.4, *poor person* 486.6, *beggar* 505.6, *changeable* 666.3, *wandering* 698.13

vague 338.9; *silent* 181.10, *noncommittal* 181.11, *obscure* 197.2, *sparing with words* 208.6, *murky* 248.5, *shady* 250.4, *difficult* 364.8, *equivocal* 380.5, *capricious* 381.4, *unfinished* 544.9, *shapeless* 625.2, *unreal* 720.8, 722.7, *generalized* 778.12, *indeterminate* 841.14

vaguely *privately* 181.18, *obscurely* 197.4, *dimly* 248.10, *indiscriminately* 338.15, *incompletely* 544.14, *shapelessly* 625.5, *unreally* 722.15, *indeterminately* 841.24

vagueness *evasion* 181.5, *obscurity*

197.1, *murk* 248.2, *indiscrimination* 338.4, *equivocation* 380.1, *rough idea* 544.4, *shapelessness* 625.1, *unreality* 722.2, *indeterminacy* 841.6

vain 402.8; *futile* 282.9, 802.10, *prideful* 297.8, *thankless* 311.4, *aimless* 362.8, *egotistic* 444.5, *self-absorbed* 456.9

vain attempt *error* 846.2

vain expectation *frustration* 293.2

vainglorious *prideful* 297.8, *self-admiring* 402.10

vaingloriously *pridefully* 297.17, *vainly* 402.17

vainglory *pride* 297.1, *vanity* 402.1

vain labor *waste* 468.5

vainly 402.17; *pridefully* 297.17, *thanklessly* 311.7, *overoptimistically* 343.7, *egoistically* 444.9

vainness *vanity* 402.1

vain person 402.7; *proud person* 297.7, *displayer* 843.7

vain pride *vanity* 402.1

vair *Heraldic Terms* 184

Vaisheshika *Philosophical Schools of Thought* 4

Vaisheshikan *Philosophical Schools of Thought* 4

Valachian *Breeds of Sheep* 16

Valais Blacknose *Breeds of Sheep* 16

valance *bed covering* 613.7, *edging* 618.2

valanced *edged* 618.6

vale *lowland* 572.6, *valley* 572.8, *concave land* 635.2

valediction *salutation* 209.2, *parting* 705.3

valedictorian *recipient* 473.5, *successful person* 845.6

valedictory *public speaking* 205.11, *salutation* 209.2, *salutatory* 209.7, *parting* 705.3, *departing* 705.5

valedictory address *salutation* 209.2

valence 11.5

valence band *semiconductor* 10.34

valence bond *chemical bond* 11.6

valence-bond theory *valence* 11.5

valency *valence* 11.5

valentine *love token* 299.8, *loved one* 299.13

valerian *Flowers* 42

valeric *Common Fatty Acids* 12

valet *attendant* 69.4, *clean* 111.17, *domestic worker* 123.4, *restore* 809.12

valeting *upkeep* 815.5

valetudinarian *sick person* 114.22, *unhealthy* 114.23

valetudinarianism *ill health* 114.1

Valhalla *heaven* 82.15, *Imaginary Places* 360

Vali *Deities* 82

valiancy *or* **valiance** *heroism* 284.2

valiant *heroic* 284.10

valiant effort *attempt* 390.1

valiantly *heroically* 284.18, *ambitiously* 390.10

valid *factual* 3.14, *logical* 6.83, *legal* 53.16, *causal* 319.9, *correct* 429.8, *real* 719.6, *authentic* 721.16, *usable* 801.6, *certain* 840.7

valid argument *reasoning* 6.61

validate *theorize* 6.84, *make legal* 53.27, *attest* 189.22, *prove* 331.17, 339.14, *verify* 336.8, *assent* 346.6, *approve* 437.14, *permit* 502.6, *give moral support* 605.18, *make stable*

674.7, *establish reality* 719.12, *authenticate* 721.24

validated *attested* 189.13, *verified* 336.7, *agreed* 346.5, *approved* 437.8, *authenticated* 721.17

validating *attestive* 189.12, *verificatory* 336.6, *supportive* 605.11

validation *reasoning* 6.61, *lawmaking* 53.11, *attestation* 189.2, *verification* 336.1, *yes* 346.2, *approval* 437.1, *permission* 502.1, *moral support* 605.7, *authentication* 721.8

validator *affirmer* 189.9

validatory *attestive* 189.12

validity *historicalness* 3.9, *reasoning* 6.61, *legality* 53.9, *right* 429.2, *reality* 719.1, *authenticity* 721.7, *certainty* 840.1

validly *biographically* 3.18, *legally* 53.33, *correctly* 429.16, *authentically* 721.31

validness *right* 429.2

valid point *explanation* 319.4

valine *Amino Acids* 12

valise *baggage* 578.8

Valkyries *Deities* 82

Valletta *Countries* 566

valley 572.8; *landform* 8.9, *gulf* 587.3, *lowlands* 597.6, *concave land* 635.2

valleyed *of landmasses* 572.12

valley floor *landform* 8.9

valley glacier *glacier* 8.44

valley of the shadow of death *personifications and symbols* 29.4

valley wind *wind* 9.12

valor *heroism* 284.2, *virtues* 447.2

valorization *tax system* 494.6

valorous *heroic* 284.10, *principled* 447.6

valuable 496.8; *good* 445.10, *important* 799.7, *profitable* 801.8, *beneficial* 825.20

valuableness *value* 496.6

valuables *personal estate* 470.6

valuably 496.13

valuate *price* 494.12

valuation *judgment* 341.1, *value* 494.2, *measurement* 589.1, *gradation* 739.3

value 494.2, 496.6; *operation* 6.12, *treatment* 143.6, *hue* 251.4, *love* 299.21, *estimate* 341.11, *meaning* 361.1, *point* 361.5, *respect* 435.13, *admire* 437.15, *good* 445.1, *account* 493.9, *price* 494.12, *measurability* 589.2, *measure* 589.20, *degree* 739.1, *importance* 799.1, *make important* 799.14, *usability* 801.2

value-added tax (VAT) *tax* 494.5

valued *beloved* 299.19, *respected* 435.10, *priced* 494.10, *measured* 589.16, *gradational* 739.5

valued at *priced* 494.10

value judgment *philosophical system* 4.2, *philosophical term* 4.7, *judgment* 341.1

value-laden *moral* 431.9

valueless *shoddy* 497.11, *cheap* 800.16, *useless* 802.7

valuer *judge* 341.5, *measurer* 589.14

values *social environment* 2.4, *morals* 431.2

value system *social environment* 2.4, *philosophical system* 4.2

valuta *currency market* 484.8

valve *engine type* 14.11, *brass instrument* 142.3, *stopper* 584.3

valvular lesion *cardiovascular disease* 114.13

valvulitis *cardiovascular disease* 114.13

vambrace *historic armor* 419.8

vamoose [Inf] *depart* 265.6, *abscond* 576.16, *hurry off* 705.11, *escape* 816.8

vamoose! [Inf] *go!* 709.30

vamoosed [Inf] *away* 576.8

vamp *loose woman* 33.6, *tempter* 178.10, *lover* 299.11, *desire* 299.24, *improvise* 396.6, *motivator* 508.6, *charmer* 700.6

vampire *ghost* 86.11, *frightener* 283.7, *Legendary Creatures* 360, *greedy person* 477.11

vampiric *witchlike* 86.19

vampirish *witchlike* 86.19

vampirism *witchcraft* 86.6

Van or **Van Golu** *Lakes* 568

van *armed force* 77.10, *truck* 578.10, 687.8, *avant-garde* 652.6, *means of transportation* 686.2, *wagon* 687.5

vanadium *Chemical Elements and Common Allotropes* 11

Van Allen radiation belt *Earth* 7.17, *atmospheric layer* 558.3

Vancouver *Islands* 572

vandal *malefactor* 306.6, *destroyer* 523.6, *distorter* 627.5

vandalism *cruelty* 306.4, *violation of the law* 427.2, *violence by person* 520.2, *destructiveness* 523.3, *lawlessness* 766.6

vandalize *harm* 306.13, *disobey* 427.12, *lay waste* 523.14, *impair* 808.18

vandalous *cruel* 306.10

Van de Graaff generator *generator* 14.43

van der Waals equation *Classical Physical Laws* 10

van der Waals force *chemical bond* 11.6

Vandyke *stage of proof* 174.9

Vandyke brown *brown pigment* 256.2

Vandyke collar *neckwear* 100.29, *notched thing* 636.2

vane *plumage* 36.7

Vänern *Lakes* 568

vanguard **621.5;** *armed force* 77.10, *guard* 419.15, *avant-garde* 652.6, *priority* 769.2, *precursor* 769.7, *warner* 814.5

vanilla bean *Herbs and Spices* 91

vanish *order* 6.89, *conceal oneself* 181.15, *become invisible* 245.6, *disappear* 265.5, *abscond* 576.16, *be transient* 643.6, *quit* 705.10, *cease to exist* 718.13, *dilute* 776.14, *not exist* 786.6, *escape* 816.8

vanished *disappeared* 265.4, *missing* 766.11, *no more* 718.11, *zero* 786.5

vanishing *invisibility* 245.1, *disappearance* 265.1, *disappearing* 265.3, *escape* 816.1

vanishing cream *toiletries* 530.6

vanishing into thin air *escape* 816.1

vanishing point *composition* 132.17, *treatment* 143.6, *that which makes invisible* 245.2, *disappearance* 265.1, *distant place* 585.3

vanishing point or **line** or **plane** *convergent view* 702.3

vanishing trick *disappearance* 265.1

vanish into thin air *conceal oneself* 181.15, *be transient* 643.6, *escape* 816.8

vanishment *absence* 576.1

vanity **402.1;** *pride* 297.1, *overestimation* 343.1, *exhibitionism* 404.9, *egotism* 444.2, *self-absorption* 456.4, *cosmetic tool* 530.5, *futility* 802.3

vanity case *cosmetic tool* 530.5

vanity license plate *personal identification* 184.4

vanity of vanities *futility* 802.3

vanquish *master* 68.17, *defeat* 832.11, *be victorious* 845.16

vanquisher *victor* 845.7

vantage *advantage* 744.3

vantage ground *tactics* 399.12, *advantage* 744.3

vantage point *overview* 425.6, *advantage* 744.3

Vanua Levu *Islands* 572

Vanuatu *Countries* 566, *Islands* 572

vapid *unemphatic* 201.2

vapidity *lack of emphasis* 201.1, *tastelessness* 220.1

vapidly *unemphatically* 201.4

vapidness *tastelessness* 220.1

vapor *phase* 11.13, *odor* 224.1, *transparent thing* 249.4, *talk nonsense* 362.12, *gas* 556.1, *gaseousness* 556.6, *wateriness* 557.3

vapor [Arch] *fantasy* 360.5

vaporability *volatility* 556.7

vaporable *volatile* 556.21

vapor bath *bath* 111.6

vaporescent *volatile* 556.21

vaporific *volatile* 556.21

vaporimeter **556.13;** *meter* 589.13

vaporiness *gaseousness* 556.6

vaporing *empty talk* 362.5, *smoky* 556.17

vaporish *gaseous* 556.14

vaporizability *volatility* 556.7

vaporizable *volatile* 556.21

vaporization **556.9;** *temperature* 10.29, *disappearance* 265.1, *obtaining of an extract* 711.7, *dilution* 776.3

vaporize *heat* 10.74, *solidify* 11.37, *destroy* 186.10, *burn* 217.18, *be transparent* 249.11, *cause to disappear* 265.8, *abolish* 523.11, *make sparse* 541.5, *gasify* 556.23, *dry* 560.17, *let out* 709.26, *obtain an extract* 711.19, *cause not to exist* 718.14, *dilute* 776.14

vaporized *destroyed* 186.5, *diluted* 776.8

vaporizer **556.10;** *sprinkler* 557.12

vaporlike *gaseous* 556.14

vaporosity *gaseousness* 556.6

vaporous *status adjectives* 11.25, *translucent* 249.8, *imaginary* 360.12, *sparse* 541.3, *gaseous* 556.14

vaporously *aerily* 556.26

vaporousness *translucency* 249.2, *gaseousness* 556.6

vapor pressure *force* 10.9, *Fields of Measurement* 589

vapor trail *sign* 183.1, *indication* 339.3

vapory *gaseous* 556.14

Varese *Breeds of Sheep* 16

variability *inconstancy* 378.2, *capriciousness* 381.2, 841.8, *irregularity* 664.1, *changeableness* 666.1, *inconsistency* 732.3, *inequality* 741.1

variable *algebraic expression* 6.23, *given* 6.74, *inconstant* 378.6, *erratic* 381.5, *irregular* 664.3, *changeable* 665.11, 666.3, *circumstantial* 726.8, *inconsistent*

732.7, *nonuniform* 734.5, *numbers* 738.5, *quantitative* 738.6, *unequal* 741.4, *number* 783.1, *capricious* 841.16

variableness *irregularity* 664.1, *inconsistency* 732.3

variable point *point* 6.34

variable star **7.11;** *star* 7.8

variable wind *wind* 9.12

variably *erratically* 381.8, *irregularly* 664.6, *changeably* 665.22, 666.7, *relatively* 726.17, *inconsistently* 732.16, *nonuniformly* 734.11, *quantitatively* 738.8, *asymmetrically* 741.11, *capriciously* 841.26

variance *dissent* 347.1, *difference* 463.4, *disparity* 728.3, *nonuniformity* 734.2

variant *different* 463.7, *changeable* 666.3, *disparate* 728.9, *nonuniform* 734.5, *deviation* 782.6

variant reading *interpretation* 365.1

variate *given* 6.74

variation *parameter* 6.57, *modification* 340.5, *change* 665.1, *deviation* 698.1, *diversity* 732.1, *nonuniformity* 734.2

variational *modified* 340.9

variational calculus *calculus* 6.28

variations *bicycle* 687.10

varied **732.6;** *ice-skating* 162.32, *modified* 340.9, *changeable* 666.3, *disparate* 728.9, *diversified* 732.8, *nonuniform* 734.5

variedly 263.12

variegate 263.11; *color* 251.16, *diversify* 732.11, *mix* 751.12

variegated **263.6;** *colored* 251.10, *changeable* 666.3, *diversified* 732.8, *unequal* 741.4, *complicated* 751.10

variegated thing 263.5

variegation 263.1; *spectrum* 251.3, *change* 665.1, *changeableness* 666.1, *variety* 732.2, 751.4

variety **138.13, 732.2, 751.4;** *plant breeding* 17.6, *miscellany* 59.15, *show business* 138.1, *show* 138.4, *ice-dancing move* 162.19, *sort* 202.6, *variegation* 263.1, *selection* 382.1, *kind* 624.3, *irregularity* 664.1, *change* 665.1, *changeableness* 666.1, *disparity* 728.3, *nonuniformity* 734.2, *taxonomic classification* 777.3, *type* 777.4, *multiplicity* 793.2

variety artist *entertainer* 138.8

variety circuit *engagement* 136.15, 138.6

variety meat 90.30

variety show *show* 138.4, *program* 172.10, *miscellany* 751.3

variety theater *club* 138.7

variola *infection* 114.7, *skin disease* 114.16

variola porcina *animal disease* 34.10

variometer *meter* 589.13

variorum *interpretation* 365.1

various **793.7;** *varied* 732.6, *nonuniform* 734.5

variously **732.15;** *nonuniformly* 734.11, *asymmetrically* 741.11, *plurally* 793.10

variousness *variety* 732.2

varmint [Inf] *animal* 34.1

varnish *cleaning agent* 111.9, *material* 143.9, *conceal* 181.12, *exaggeration* 194.1, *exaggerate* 194.11, *polish* 545.3, *smooth* 545.10, *resin* 562.6, *coating* 613.8,

coat 613.28, *delude* 720.16, *preserver* 815.9, *preserve* 815.14

varnished *exaggerated* 194.7, *polished* 545.7, *resinous* 562.13, *covered* 613.19

varnishing *upkeep* 815.5

varnish tree *Trees and Shrubs* 43

varsity **155.17;** *curricular* 48.21

varsity player *prizewinner* 127.8, *basketball team* 148.2, *football player* 155.15

Varuna *legendary sea being* 571.4

vary *order* 6.89, *modify* 340.13, *vacillate* 378.8, *be capricious* 381.6, *be different* 463.11, *be irregular* 664.5, *change* 665.14, 841.20, *be changeable* 666.5, *oscillate* 683.12, *deviate* 698.15, *be disparate* 728.14, *be diverse* 732.10, *make unlike* 734.9, *unbalance* 741.8

varying *inconstancy* 378.2, *inconstant* 378.6, *irregular* 664.3, *disparate* 728.9

vascular *fluid* 19.25, *taxonomic* 41.16

vascular bundle *stem* 41.5

vascular disease *cardiovascular disease* 114.13

vascular plant *plant* 41.2

vas deferens *organs of reproduction* 21.9

vase *vessel* 578.11

vasectomize *make infertile* 23.9

vasectomy *that which makes infertile* 23.4, *prophylaxis* 115.4

vasopressin *Human Hormones* 12

vasotocin *Human Hormones* 12

vassal *serf* 69.8, *inferior* 745.4

vassalage *subjection* 832.1

vast *spacious* 563.13, *huge* 579.14, *broad* 592.5, *immeasurable* 798.6

vast extent *the depths* 598.2

vastly *spaciously* 563.17, *broadly* 592.15, *immeasurably* 798.11

vastness **798.3;** *spaciousness* 563.4, *largeness* 579.2, *breadth* 592.1

vat *vessel* 578.11

vat dye *dye* 130.8

Vaterland [Ger] *native country* 566.6

vates [L] *diviner* 86.14

vatic *predicting* 358.11

Vatican *clerical dwelling* 84.10

vaticinate *predict* 358.14, *divine* 358.15

vaticination *divination* 358.2

vaticinator *oracle* 358.8

Vättern *Lakes* 568

vaudeville *show business* 138.1, *show* 138.4, 404.12, *variety* 138.13

vaudeville artist *entertainer* 138.8

vaudeville circuit *engagement* 136.15, 138.6

vaudeville show *show* 138.4

vaudeville theater *club* 138.7

vaudevillian *entertainer* 138.8, *variety* 138.13

vault **105.9, 134.8;** *burial place* 31.7, *pommel horse* 157.7, *exercise* 157.12, *safe* 464.4, *superstructure* 551.7, *dome* 634.4, *jump* 713.7, *spring up* 713.22

vaulted *curved* 629.4, *convex* 634.5

vaulter *gymnast* 157.10

vaulting *vault* 134.8, *Sporting Activities* 145, *gymnastics* 157.1, *balance beam* 157.3, *horizontal bar* 157.5, *gymnastic* 157.11, *leaping* 713.17

vaulting horse *pommel horse* 157.7

vault of heaven *universe* 7.3

vault types *vault* 134.8

vault up *spring up* 713.22
vaunt *flourish* 404.25, *display* 843.13
V-bottom *canoe* 150.9, *canoeing* 150.26
VB theory *valence* 11.5
veal 90.25; *meat* 90.22
veal calf *livestock* 16.11
vection *conveyance* 685.2
vector 6.48; *disease-causing agent* 114.27, *transferrer* 685.4, *bearing* 697.2
vector analysis *calculus* 6.28
vector in flight (VIF) *flight maneuver* 689.6
vectoring *flight maneuver* 689.6
vector product *vector* 6.48
vector quantity *vector* 6.48
vector sum *vector* 6.48
vecture *conveyance* 685.2
Veda *other text* 81.19
veer *blow* 9.53, *displacement* 574.1, *displace* 574.15, *divergence* 607.2, *diverge* 607.11, *move sideways* 623.9, *be irregular* 664.5, *be changeable* 666.5, *turn around* 680.22, *navigate* 690.15, *deviating motion* 698.3, *deviate* 698.15
veer around *turn around* 680.22
veered *displaced* 574.8
veering *displaced* 574.8, *irregularity* 664.1, *irregular* 664.3, *changeableness* 666.1, *deviating motion* 698.3, *indirect* 698.9
veering wind *wind* 9.12
veer off *sidestep* 698.22
vegan *eater* 92.15, *eating* 92.18, *self-restrained person* 455.5, *abstinent* 455.7
vegan diet *diet* 92.5
veganism *eating habit* 92.7, *abstinence* 455.2
vegetable 17.11, 90.33; *horticultural* 17.14, *plant* 41.2, *plantlike* 41.13
vegetable [Inf] *unintelligent person* 316.4
vegetable casserole *vegetable* 90.33
vegetable compartment *kitchen container* 91.7
vegetable dish *vegetable* 90.33
vegetable dye *dye* 130.8, *coloring agent* 251.5
vegetable existence *mere existence* 717.10
vegetable garden *garden* 17.2
vegetable grower *horticulturist* 17.13
vegetable growing *horticulture* 17.1
vegetable juice *soft drink* 93.8
vegetable kingdom *plants* 41.1
vegetable life *life* 28.1, *plants* 41.1
vegetable market *market* 483.1
vegetable mill *cooking equipment* 91.6
vegetable oil *basic cooking ingredient* 91.8, *oil* 562.3
vegetable pathology *botany* 13.7
vegetable peeler *cooking equipment* 91.6
vegetable physiology *botany* 13.7
vegetable plate *vegetable* 90.33
vegetable remedy *medicine* 115.2
vegetable resin *resin* 562.6
vegetables *fruits* 44.1, *side dish* 90.15, 794.11, Phobias 283
vegetal *horticultural* 17.14, *plantlike* 41.13
vegetarian *fruit-eating* 44.7, *eater* 92.15, *eating* 92.18, *self-restrained person* 455.5, *abstinent* 455.7
vegetarian diet *diet* 92.5

vegetarianism *eating habit* 92.7, *abstinence* 455.2
vegetate 41.21; *be dormant* 41.22, *not act* 413.11, *be inactive* 415.13, *be inert* 519.4, *grow* 581.17, *be motionless* 678.7, *merely exist* 717.21
vegetating 717.17; *inert* 519.2, *sedentary* 678.5
vegetation *plants* 41.1, *immobility* 413.2, *inertness* 519.1, *germination* 581.5, *lack of motion* 678.1, *mere existence* 717.10
vegetative *horticultural* 17.14, *plantlike* 41.13
veggie [Inf] *vegetable* 90.33, *eater* 92.15
vehemence *emphasis* 200.1, *emotion* 266.3, *anger* 302.4, *energy* 414.4, *violence* 520.1
vehement *emphatic* 200.3, *passionate* 266.12, *angry* 302.11, *strong* 516.9, *vigorous* 518.2, *violent* 520.5
vehemently *emphatically* 200.7, *with feeling* 266.18, *angrily* 302.24, *violently* 520.11
vehicle *instrumentality* 102.2, *play* 136.2, *instrument* 511.2, *means of transportation* 686.2
vehicle identification number (VIN) *miscellaneous automotive terms* 687.14
vehicular tunnel *tunnel* 551.11
veil *fungal body* 47.4, *vestment* 84.11, *occult* 86.22, *headdress* 100.35, *cover* 181.4, *conceal* 181.12, *keep secret* 182.11, *be untruthful* 192.20, *that which makes invisible* 245.2, *make invisible* 245.7, *make dark* 247.10, *murk* 248.2, *make dim* 248.8, *circumlocute* 607.12, *body covering* 613.3, *hide* 613.27
veil, the *monasticism* 67.3
veiled *concealed* 181.8, 844.7, *ungenuine* 192.13, *private* 245.5, *murky* 248.5, *indirect* 607.8, *secret* 611.13, *protected* 613.20
veiled meaning *mysteriousness* 844.5
veil of cloud *cloud appearance* 9.19
vein *ore* 11.23, *leaf* 41.6, *source of supply* 105.4, *variegate* 263.11, *attitude* 513.2, *style* 537.1, *layer* 588.1, *state of mind* 725.5, *admixture* 751.5
veined *striped* 263.9
veins *internal organ* 19.13
Vela Constellations 7
Velay Black Breeds of Sheep 16
Velcro™ *part of garment* 100.27, *fastener* 754.7
veld *grassland* 45.2, *geographical space* 563.3
veld or **veldt** *plants* 41.1, *countryside* 564.3, *lowland* 572.6
veldt or **steppe** *grassland* 45.2
veliger *invertebrate larva* 39.19
vellicate *shake* 684.24
vellication *spasm* 684.8
vellicative *convulsive* 684.19
vellum *leather* 104.7
velo *woodworking tool* 131.6
veloce Musical Terms and Expression Marks 14
velocipede *bicycle* 687.10
velocity *speed* 10.7, *alacrity* 414.3, *rapid motion* 677.8, *swiftness* 694.1, *haste* 818.1
velocity distribution function *chemical reaction thermodynamics* 14.29

velour or **velours** Fabrics and Fibers 130
velouté *sauce* 90.17
velure Fabrics and Fibers 130
velutinous *fluffy* 552.11
Velvet Notable Horses 159
velvet Fabrics and Fibers 130, *smooth* 543.8
velvet [Inf] *easy thing* 823.6
velveteen Fabrics and Fibers 130
velvet glove *treatment* 399.11, *leniency* 423.1
velvetiness *smoothness* 543.2, 545.1
velvetlike *smooth* 543.8
velvety *smooth* 543.8, 545.4, *fluffy* 552.11
vend *sell* 482.15
vendee *purchaser* 481.7
Vendémiaire French Revolutionary Calendar 646
vendetta *act of hostility* 63.4, *quarrel* 272.4
vendibility *market* 482.5
vendible *merchandise* 482.6, *salable* 482.13
vending *selling* 482.1, 482.12
vending machine *eating place* 92.17, *stall* 483.9
vendition *selling* 482.1
vendor *trader* 480.11, *seller* 482.7
vendue *sale* 482.2
veneer *type of furniture* 101.2, *work wood* 131.9, *ungenuineness* 192.2, *external appearance* 264.5, *coat* 588.3, 613.28, *layer* 588.9, *coating* 613.8
veneered *coated* 588.7
venerability *dignity* 297.4
venerable *aged* 27.15, *dignified* 297.11, *respectable* 435.11, *old* 653.10, *olden* 653.11
venerableness *elderliness* 653.2
venerably 653.17; *maturely* 27.18, *with dignity* 297.20, *archaically* 653.20
venerate *revere* 81.26, 435.14, *worship* 83.15, *wonder* 294.12, *love* 299.21
venerated *worshiped* 83.14
veneration *religiousness* 81.2, *worship* 83.1, *wonder* 294.1, *love* 299.1, *admiration* 435.2
venerational *worshipful* 83.12, *reverent* 435.9
venerative *reverent* 435.9
venerator *worshiper* 83.6
venereal *of disease* 114.25, *conjunctive* 752.12
venereal appetite or **desire** *sexual desire* 20.5
venereal disease *disease* 114.4, *sexually transmitted disease (STD)* 114.17, Phobias 283
venereal ulcer *sexually transmitted disease (STD)* 114.17
venereophobia Phobias 283
venery [Arch] *sexual intercourse* 20.9, *hunting* 160.2, *sexual love* 299.3, *hunt* 385.3, *sexual immorality* 432.2
venesection *disgorgement* 709.6, *drawing off* 711.4
Venetian blind *shade maker* 247.4, *protective covering* 613.5, *protection from the weather* 810.9
Venetian red *red pigment* 257.2
Venezuela Countries 566
vengeance *retaliation* 420.1, *revenge* 441.4, *counterbalance* 743.2
vengeful *malicious* 306.8, *pitiless* 309.3, *retaliatory* 420.3, *vindictive* 441.10

vengefully *maliciously* 306.15, *pitilessly* 309.7, *vindictively* 441.16, *correctively* 743.11
vengefulness *malice* 306.2, *pitilessness* 309.1
venial *forgivable* 312.7, *vindicable* 441.9, *unimportant* 800.10
venially *forgivably* 312.14, *justifyingly* 441.15
venial sin *iniquity* 448.3, *sin* 450.3, *trifling fault* 800.5
venire facias *jury* 54.11
venireman *jury* 54.11
venison *meat* 90.22
Venn diagram Mathematical Concepts 6
venogram *diagnostic radiology* 107.12
venography *diagnostic radiology* 107.12
venom *poison* 117.7, *hate* 300.1, *bitterness* 306.3
venomous *toxic* 114.28, *poisonous* 117.14, *hating* 300.7, *bitter* 306.9, *defamatory* 440.9, *vindictive* 441.10
venomously *unhygienically* 114.32, *with hate* 300.13, *bitterly* 306.16, *vindictively* 441.16
venomousness *poisoning* 117.6, *bitterness* 306.3
venomous snake *snake* 37.6
venous blood *blood* 555.4
vent *volcanic activity* 8.26, *divulge* 180.9, *provide passage for* 583.18, *outlet* 707.8, *void* 709.23, *means of escape* 816.4
ventage *outlet* 707.8
venter *moss plant* 46.5
venthole *outlet* 707.8
ventilate *air* 94.7, *purify* 111.19, *practice hygiene* 116.4, *publish* 173.15, *divulge* 180.9, *make cold* 218.15, *deodorize* 225.6, *aerate* 558.20
ventilated 558.17; *hygienic* 116.3, *published* 173.12, *odorless* 225.4
ventilating system *ventilator* 558.7
ventilation 558.6; *refreshment* 94.1, *cleaning* 111.2, *publishing* 173.2, *odorlessness* 225.1
ventilator 558.7; *deodorant* 225.3
vent one's anger 302.21
Ventôse French Revolutionary Calendar 646
ventricles *internal organ* 19.13
ventriloquism *mode of speech* 205.6
ventriloquist *entertainer* 138.8, *imitator* 736.6
venture 390.2; *be courageous* 284.14, *experiment* 335.1, *invent* 335.13, *tackle* 390.8, *undertaking* 391.1, *undertake* 391.7, *social activity* 414.2, *contend* 422.22, *finance* 457.7, *business* 480.6, 509.3, *speculate* 480.19, *endangerment* 811.2, *face danger* 811.12, *endanger* 811.13, *risk* 841.21, *take a chance* 842.14
ventured *tested* 335.10
venture on *undertake* 391.7
venturesome *adventurous* 284.12, *reckless* 286.6, *attempting* 390.4, *enterprising* 391.5, *dangerous* 811.7
venturesomely *adventurously* 284.20
venturesomeness *endangerment* 811.2
venture to say *propound* 359.9
venturous *dangerous* 811.7

venue *sports ground* 145.2, *situation* 573.1

Venus Planets and Their Satellites 7, *planet* 7.16, Deities 82, *goddesses and gods of love* 299.14, *attractive female* 529.5, *evening* 656.2

Venusian *astronomical* 7.33

Venus's flower basket *sponge* 39.16

venustaphobia Phobias 283

veracious *truthful* 191.4, *correct* 429.8, *natural* 526.10, *true* 721.11, *naive* 821.3, *certain* 840.7

veraciously *truthfully* 191.9, *truly* 721.27

veraciousness *truthfulness* 191.1, *truth* 721.1

veracity *truthfulness* 191.1, *right* 429.2, *naturalness* 526.4, *truth* 721.1, *naiveté* 821.1, *certainty* 840.1

verb *part of speech* 5.30, 760.7

verbal *worded* 5.38, *of grammar* 5.41, *communicational* 169.17

verbal abuse *vilification* 301.2, *malignity* 306.5

verbal attack *personal attack* 418.8, *berating* 438.5

verbal concealment 181.3

verbal diarrhea [Inf] *diffuseness* 199.1, *power of speech* 205.5, *talkativeness* 207.1

verbal intercourse *speech* 205.1, *conversation* 210.1

verbalism *phrasing* 5.25, *nonsense* 362.2

verbalize *use language* 5.42, *word* 5.43, *speak* 205.17, *form* 624.9

verbally *colloquially* 5.45, *orally* 205.21

verbally abuse *harm* 306.13

verbally abusive *malign* 306.11

verbal translation *translation* 365.4

verbatim *linguistically* 5.44, *correct* 350.4, *accurately* 350.6, *meaningfully* 361.16, *translational* 365.11, *literal* 721.18, *literally* 721.32, *same* 730.7, *identically* 730.18, *imitatively* 736.12, *perfectly* 805.21

verbatim account *literalness* 721.9

verbatim et literatim [L] *literally* 721.32

verb clause *or* **phrase** *clause* 5.31

verbena Flowers 42

verbiage *wordiness* 5.23, *obscurity* 197.1, *diffuseness* 199.1, *power of speech* 205.5, *empty talk* 362.5

verbose *worded* 5.38, *diffuse* 199.3, *talkative* 207.5, *lengthy* 590.9

verbosely *lexically* 5.46, *diffusely* 199.7, *at length* 590.15

verboseness *diffuseness* 199.1

verbosity *wordiness* 5.23, *diffuseness* 199.1, *power of speech* 205.5, *talkativeness* 207.1

verboten *prohibited* 503.5

verbum sap *communication* 176.3

verdancy *greenness* 260.1

Verdandi Deities 82

verdant 260.8; *botanical* 17.15, *fertile* 22.8, *plantlike* 41.13, *grassy* 45.8

verd antique *green thing* 260.4

verdantly *horticulturally* 17.20, *herbivorously* 45.12, *greenly* 260.15

verderer *forester* 43.7

verdict 54.18, 341.2; *legal justice* 53.4, *ruling* 780.2

verdict contrary to law *verdict* 54.18

verdict of acquittal *vindication* 441.1

verdict of guilty *unfavorable verdict* 54.20

verdict of innocence *vindication* 441.1, *legal innocence* 449.3

verdict of not guilty *favorable verdict* 54.19, *vindication* 441.1

verdict of not proven *favorable verdict* 54.19

verdigris *green thing* 260.4, *decay* 808.6

verditer *green pigment* 260.3

verdure *plants* 41.1, *grassland* 45.2, *greenness* 260.1

verdured *grassy* 45.8

verdurous *botanical* 17.15

verge Architectural Elements 134, *short distance* 586.2, *edge* 618.1, *aim* 697.14, *limit* 773.7

vergeboard Architectural Elements 134

verge on *adjoin* 216.11, *near* 586.12, *border* 618.9

verging on 586.19

veridical *truthful* 191.4

veridicality *truthfulness* 191.1

veridically *truthfully* 191.9

verifiability *demonstrability* 331.5

verifiable 336.5; *factual* 3.14, *demonstrable* 331.12, *experimental* 335.8, *certain* 840.7

verifiably 336.11; *demonstrably* 331.22, *surely* 464.15

verification 336.1; *reasoning* 6.61, *identification* 184.1, *attestation* 189.2, *proof* 331.4, 339.2, *experimentation* 335.3, *promise* 464.2, *permission* 502.1, *moral support* 605.7, *authentication* 721.8, *confirmation* 840.3

verification principle *philosophical term* 4.7

verificative *verificatory* 336.6

verificatory 336.6

verified 336.7; *identified* 184.9, *attested* 189.13, *proven* 331.13, *tested* 335.10, *evidential* 339.8, *known* 348.9, *authenticated* 721.17, *authentic* 737.6

verifier 336.4; *affirmer* 189.9

verify 336.8; *identify* 184.11, *attest* 189.22, *prove* 331.17, 339.14, *experiment* 335.11, *certify* 464.11, *permit* 502.6, *give moral support* 605.18, *establish reality* 719.12, *authenticate* 721.24, *check* 784.14, *make certain* 840.14

verifying *attestive* 189.12, *experimental* 335.8, *supportive* 605.11

verily *assuredly* 189.30, *truly* 721.27

verisimilar *lifelike* 721.19

verisimilarly 721.33

verisimilitude 721.10; *realism* 719.3, *plausibility* 838.3

verismo *theater movements* 136.9, Western Literary Groups 139

veritable *real* 717.14, *authentic* 721.16

veritableness *right* 429.2, *authenticity* 721.7

veritably *authentically* 721.31

verity *right* 429.2, *truth* 721.1, *certainty* 840.1

vermeil *red* 257.5

vermicide *pest control* 16.13, *killing agent* 30.15

vermicular *wormlike* 39.24

vermiform *wormlike* 39.24, *convolutional* 632.4

vermifuge *medicine* 115.2

vermilion *red pigment* 257.2, *red* 257.5

vermin *pest* 40.5, *dirt* 112.5

verminous 40.13; *unhygienic* 114.27

verminousness *lack of hygiene* 112.3

vermiphobia Phobias 283

Vermont American States 564

vermouth *mixed drink* 93.12

vernacular 205.8; *dialect* 5.24, *of language* 5.35, *spoken language* 205.2, *unpretentiousness* 526.2, *unpretentious* 526.8

vernacular architecture Architectural Styles 134

vernacularize *use language* 5.42

vernal *fresh* 260.10, *seasonal* 654.7

vernal equinox *spring* 654.3

vernally *seasonally* 654.12

vernal season *spring* 654.3

Verner's law *linguistic theory* 5.2

vernier *or* **vernier scale** *measuring instrument* 589.12

veronica Flowers 42, *sacred object* 83.11

Veronica wiping Jesus' face Stations of the Cross 85

verruca *skin disease* 114.16

versatile *skillful* 127.10, *changeable* 666.3, *diversified* 732.8, *various* 793.7, *useful* 801.5

versatileness *variety* 732.2

versatility *skill* 127.1, *vacillation* 380.3, *changeableness* 666.1, *variety* 732.2, *usefulness* 801.1

verse *educate* 48.22, *poetry* 139.8, *part of poem* 139.9, *passage* 692.1, *part of writing* 760.6

versed *educated* 48.19, *qualified* 340.7, *knowledgeable* 348.7

versed in *expert* 127.12

verse drama *dramatic style* 136.3

verse epistle Poem or Verse Forms 139

verse form *kind* 624.3

versemaker *author* 139.13

versemonger *author* 139.13

verse paragraph *part of poem* 139.9

versesmith *author* 139.13

versicolor *variegated* 263.6

versification *poetry* 139.8

versifier *author* 139.13

versify *write* 139.21

versine (vers) *trigonometric function* 6.50

version *description* 202.1, *interpretation* 365.1, *translation* 365.4, *type* 777.4

vers libre Poem or Verse Forms 139

vers-librist *author* 139.13

verso *book part* 174.5

verso page *laterality* 623.3

vert Heraldic Terms 184, *green* 260.7

vertebra Human Bones 19

vertebral column Human Bones 19

vertebrate *type of animal* 34.5, *of animals* 34.13

vertex *angle* 6.37, *sharp point* 549.2, *summit* 600.1

vertical 602.3, 602.5; *linear* 6.77, *snowplow* 162.29, *top* 600.6, *straight* 630.8, *raised* 715.6

vertical angles *angle* 6.37

vertical axis *vertical* 602.3

vertical gate *ski race* 162.4

verticalism *verticality* 602.1

verticality 602.1; *straightness* 630.1

vertical-lift bridge *bridge* 551.10

vertical line *vertical* 602.3, *straight line* 630.2

vertically 602.11; *straight* 630.16

vertical machine *machine tool* 14.9

vertical member *superstructure* 551.7

vertical movement *ocean current* 8.15

verticalness *verticality* 602.1

vertical tab (VT) *character* 15.18

vertical takeoff and landing (VTOL) craft *aircraft* 689.3

verticillaster *flower head* 42.4

vertiginous *dizzy* 682.13

vertigo Phobias 283, *poor health* 517.3, *dizziness* 682.2

vervain Flowers 42

verve *emphasis* 200.1, *emotion* 266.3, *vigor* 518.1

very *same* 730.7, *to a degree* 739.11

very best *excellence* 445.4, *excellent* 445.13, *best* 805.9

very high frequency (VHF) *radio frequency* 661.3

very image *image* 187.3, *look-alike* 730.4

very important person (VIP) [Inf] *important person* 18.11, 799.5, *company leader* 68.8, *manager* 126.7, *person of repute* 370.2, *influential person* 512.5, *successful person* 845.6

Very Large Array (VLA) *radio telescope* 7.26

very large-scale integration (VLSI) *circuit* 14.37

Very lights *signal* 183.6, *fire* 246.9, *warning signal* 814.3

very little *to a degree* 739.11

very long *lengthy* 590.9

very long baseline interferometry (VLBI) *radio telescope* 7.26

very many *many* 795.6

very picture *image* 187.3

very small *difficult to see* 245.4

very thing, the *good thing* 445.9, *suitability* 462.4, *sameness* 730.1

very tiring *laborious* 122.7

very top *summit* 600.1

very truth, the *the truth* 721.3

very words, the *literalness* 721.9, *sameness* 730.1

Vesper *star* 7.8

vesperal *evening* 656.4

vespers *public worship* 83.3, *evening* 656.2

vespertide *evening* 656.2

vespertine *evening* 656.4

vespiary *dwelling* 40.7, *natural habitat* 60.16

vessel 578.11, 690.3; *receptacle* 105.11, *sailboat* 150.3, *container* 578.1

vest *legislate* 53.31, *jacket* 100.18, *clothe* 100.43, *transfer property* 470.12, *give out* 472.12, *grant* 735.30

Vesta Planets and Their Satellites 7, Deities 82

vesta [Brit] *fuel starter* 106.3

vestal *celibate* 67.4, *chaste person* 431.6, *chaste* 431.10

vestal virgin *celibate* 67.4, *chaste person* 431.6

vested *dressed* 100.38, *granted* 735.20

vested interest *influence* 512.1

vestibule *ear* 19.10, *room* 60.9, Architectural Elements 134, *church architecture* 134.11, *front entrance* 621.2, *means of entry* 706.6

vestige **185.11**; *little piece* 580.4, *thing of the past* 651.8, *remainder* 750.1

vestigial *historical* 3.10, *basic* 601.8, *remaining* 750.7

vestigially *residually* 750.11

vestiphobia Phobias 283

vestment **84.11**; *clothing* 100.1, *body covering* 613.3

vestments *uniform* 100.9, *formal clothing* 406.5

vest power in *empower* 514.20

vestry *church interior* 83.9

vesture *vestment* 84.11

vesture [Arch] *dressing* 100.2

Vesuvius, Mount Mountains and Hills 569

vet [Inf] *animal welfarist* 34.9, *former soldier* 77.5, *veterinarian* 107.27, *horse person* 159.14, *estimate* 341.11

vetch *crop* 16.8

veteran *older person* 27.7, *man* 27.8, *military* 76.28, *former soldier* 77.5, *expert* 127.9, 127.12, *basketball team* 148.2, *old* 653.10

veteran army *army* 77.12

veteran forces *armed forces* 77.9

Veterans of Foreign Wars (VFW) member *former soldier* 77.5

veterinarian **107.27**; *animal welfarist* 34.9, *horse person* 159.14

veterinary *veterinarian* 107.27, *medical* 107.28

veterinary clinic *veterinary* 107.26

veterinary medicine **107.26**

veterinary nurse *veterinarian* 107.27

veterinary practice *veterinary medicine* 107.26

veterinary practitioner *veterinarian* 107.27

veterinary science *animal welfare* 34.8

veterinary student *veterinarian* 107.27

veterinary surgeon *veterinarian* 107.27

veterinary surgery *veterinary medicine* 107.26

veterinary technician *veterinarian* 107.27

vetiver *incense* 226.3

veto **503.3**, **503.9**; *illegality* 53.10, *make illegal* 53.29, *refusal* 190.2, *refuse* 190.17, *rejection* 383.1, *reject* 383.10, *command* 425.1, 425.10, *disapproval* 438.1, *withhold approval* 438.17, *be self-restrained* 455.10, *dissent* 506.2, 506.9, *neutralization* 510.4, *counteract* 510.7, *remove power from* 515.13, *limit* 620.1, 620.7, *cause not to exist* 764.1, *exclusion* 764.1, *exclude* 764.7, *restraint* 830.1, *means of restraint* 830.6, *restrain* 830.12

vetoed **503.6**; *disagreeing* 190.11, *rejected* 383.6, *commanding* 425.7, *disapproved* 438.9

vetoer *negator* 190.8

vetting *security system* 810.5

vex *annoy* 276.7, 804.10, *cause hate* 300.12, *afflict* 301.16, *irritate*

302.16, *make irascible* 303.16, *disturb* 768.10

vexation *annoyance* 276.2, 804.2, *resentment* 302.1

vexatious *aggravating* 276.4, *disturbing* 768.9, *annoying* 804.7, *inconvenient* 824.12

vexatiously *annoyingly* 276.9, 804.12

vexed *afflicted* 301.11, *resentful* 302.8, *cross* 303.11, *disturbed* 768.6, *troubled* 824.15

vexed question *problem* 824.4

vexillology *flag* 184.8

vexillum *flag* 184.8

vexing *aggravating* 276.4, *maddening* 302.12, *inconvenient* 824.12

VI *six* 792.2

via **691.17**; *instrumentally* 511.9, *by the way* 692.20

via Musical Terms and Expression Marks 140

viable *living* 13.28, *alive* 28.13, *workable* 509.8

viably *vitally* 28.23

viaduct *bridge* 551.10, 691.7, *crossing point* 692.7

vial *bottle* 578.14

via media *medium* 742.2

viands *food* 90.1

viaticum *Christian rite* 85.5, *parting* 705.3

Viatka pony Horse and Pony Breeds 159

vibes [Inf] Musical Instruments 142, *impression* 266.2, *ambience* 615.3

vibrant *deep* 236.8, *vigorous* 518.2

vibrantly *resonantly* 236.11

vibraphone *or* vibraharp Musical Instruments 142

vibrate **683.13**; *wave* 10.77, *drum* 235.10, *resonate* 236.9, *be changeable* 666.5, *shake* 684.24, *resound* 797.21

vibratile *vibrating* 683.9

vibrating **683.9**; *resonant* 236.6, *changeable* 666.3, *directional* 677.13, *shaking* 684.6, *shaky* 684.18

vibrating string *wave* 10.11

vibration **683.2**; *wave* 10.11, *touch* 216.1, *tone* 230.2, *drumming* 235.1, *resonance* 236.1, *movement* 677.3, *reverberation* 797.6

vibrational *reverberatory* 797.14

vibrations [Inf] *ambience* 615.3

vibrato Musical Terms and Expression Marks 140

vibrator *massage* 554.6, *oscillator* 683.7, *agitator* 684.14

vibratory *vibrating* 683.9, *shaky* 684.18

vibrissa *mammalian characteristic* 35.3

vibrograph *measuring instrument* 683.6

vibroscope *measuring instrument* 683.6

viburnum Flowers 42

vicar *deputy* 80.1, *member of the clergy* 84.5, *converter* 670.5

vicarage *official residence* 60.6, *clerical dwelling* 84.10

vicar-general *deputy* 80.1

vicariate *priesthood* 84.2

vicarious *commissioned* 833.6

vicarious authority *authority* 833.3

vicariously *under commission* 833.11

vicariousness *substitution* 672.1

vicarship *priesthood* 84.2

vice *lawbreaking* 53.14, *bad conduct* 399.7, *wrongdoing* 430.7, *immorality* 432.1, *evil* 446.1, *depravity* 448.2, *sin* 450.3, *contractor* 582.6

Vice Admiral US Military Ranks 58

vice-admiral *deputy* 80.1

vice-chairman *deputy* 80.1

vice-chancellor *educator* 48.4, *person in authority* 52.7, *educational leader* 68.11, *deputy* 80.1

vice-consul *deputy* 80.1

vicegerent *deputy* 80.1

vicenary *twentieth* 792.19

vicennial *twentieth* 792.19

vice president *governor* 49.23, *deputy* 80.1, *manager* 126.7

vice-principal *educator* 48.4

vice-regent *deputy* 80.1

viceroy *leader* 68.3, *deputy* 80.1

vice-skip *bowler* 151.5

vice squad member *security force* 810.13

vice versa *reversely* 608.10, *in exchange* 673.6, *correlatively* 729.12, *diametrically* 731.6

vicinage *near place* 586.3

vicinal *near* 586.6

vicinity *region* 564.1, *plot* 564.9, *availability* 575.5, *near place* 586.3, *surroundings* 615.1

vicious *hating* 300.7, *cruel* 306.10, *immoral* 430.11, *evil* 446.7, *wicked* 448.9, *murderous* 520.7, *rough* 547.11

vicious circle *or* cycle *continuum* 774.5, *obstacle* 826.2

viciously *with hate* 300.13, *cruelly* 306.17, *immorally* 430.27, *evilly* 446.12, *wickedly* 448.15, *violently* 520.11

viciousness *cruelty* 306.4, *evil* 446.1, *wickedness* 448.1, *brutality* 547.4

vicissitude *change* 665.1, *changeableness* 666.1

victim *dead person* 29.7, *the hunted* 385.7, *butt* 436.8, *loser* 468.8, 846.9, *recipient* 473.5, *person in adversity* 848.9

victimization *malignity* 306.5, *suppression* 424.2, *punishment* 454.1

victimize *hoax* 193.20, *harm* 306.13, *suppress* 424.9, *punish* 454.22

victimized *deceived* 193.15, *suppressed* 424.6

victimizing *malign* 306.11

victim of discrimination **337.8**

victim of fate *person in adversity* 848.9

victim of oppression *victim of discrimination* 337.8

victor **845.7**; *prizewinner* 127.8, *paragon* 744.6

Victoria *Canadian Provinces* 564, *Countries* 566, *Lakes* 568, *Islands* 572

Victorian Furniture Styles 101, *fictional* 139.16, *moralist* 431.8, *moralistic* 431.12, *historic* 653.13

Victorian architecture Architectural Styles 134

Victorian novel *novel* 139.3

Victorian novelists Western Literary Groups 139

victorious **845.10**; *unbeatable* 744.13

victorious candidate *chosen thing* 382.8

victoriously **845.20**; *superiorly* 744.20

victory **845.4**

victory arch *monument* 185.10

victory garden *garden* 17.2

victory gardens *war measures* 76.18

victory laurels *insignia* 184.5

victory roll *flight maneuver* 689.6

victualed *supplied* 89.7

victuals *provisions* 89.3, *food* 90.1

vicuna Fabrics and Fibers 130

Vidar Deities 82

videlicet [L] *in other words* 365.18, *particularly* 779.21

video *photograph* 132.26, *television (TV)* 172.5, *record* 172.15

video camera *camera* 132.10, *television recording* 172.7, *recording instrument* 185.9

videocassette *television recording* 172.7

videocassette movie *movie type* 137.3

videocassette recorder (VCR) *television recording* 172.7, *recording instrument* 185.9

videoconference *discussion* 460.3

videodisk *recording* 185.6

video display adaptor (VDA) *display* 15.9

video display unit (VDU) *display* 15.9

video game *type of game* 167.2, *television recording* 172.7

videophone *telephone* 169.10

video pirate *infringer* 479.10

videorecorder *imaging device* 242.11

video recording *television recording* 172.7, *duplicate* 736.4

video signal *television set* 172.6

videotape *magnetic recording* 10.51, *film* 132.8, *television recording* 172.7, *record* 172.15, 185.13, *recording* 185.6, *recording instrument* 185.9

videotaped *broadcast* 172.12, *recorded* 185.12

viduity *widowhood* 66.5

vie *participate* 145.6, *compete in track and field* 166.21

vielle Musical Instruments 142

Vienna Countries 566, *other famous world cities* 567.9

Vienna sausage *sausage* 90.29

Viennese waltz *ice-dancing move* 162.19

Vientiane Countries 566

Vierwaldstätter See (Switzerland) Lakes 568

Vietnam Countries 566

Vietnamese Pot-Bellied Breeds of Pigs 16

Vietnam War Major Wars 76

view **242.8**; *propound a philosophy* 4.21, *belief* 87.1, *recommendation* 176.2, *inspect* 242.22, *feelings* 266.1, *theory* 327.2, *judgment* 341.1, *future intention* 374.3, *stand by* 575.15, *viewpoint* 628.5

viewable *visible* 242.19, 244.5

viewdata *information technology (IT)* 170.7, *broadcast material* 172.9

viewer **132.22**; *observer* 242.15, *recipient* 473.5, *attender* 575.6

viewfinder *exposure equipment* 132.12

view halloo! *after him!* 385.19

viewing *display* 843.1

viewing the body *funeral* 31.4

vie with *contend* 422.22, *confront* 828.19

viewpoint 242.12, 628.5; *philosophy* 4.1, *belief* 87.1, *feelings* 266.1, *theory* 327.2, *circumstances* 573.2

view with a jaundiced eye *be jealous* 314.8

view with disfavor *disapprove* 438.16

view with jealousy *be jealous* 314.8

vif Musical Terms and Expression Marks 140

vigesimal *twentieth* 792.19

vigil *prayer* 85.10, *watchfulness* 325.5

vigilance *caution* 287.1, *suspicion* 314.3, *carefulness* 323.3, *circumspection* 325.3, *watchfulness* 325.5, *commitment* 377.2, *observance* 465.1

vigilant *seeing* 242.17, *cautious* 287.6, *suspicious* 314.6, *watchful* 323.6, 325.10, *circumspect* 325.8, *expecting* 356.4, *committed* 377.7, *prepared* 388.9, *active* 414.13, *tutelary* 810.19

vigilante *defender* 77.2, *observer* 242.15, *revenger* 420.2, *surveillant* 810.12

vigilante committee member *pursuer* 385.5

vigilantly *watchfully* 242.29, *cautiously* 287.16, *suspiciously* 314.13, *attentively* 323.14, *in preparation* 388.22

vigil light *sacred object* 83.11

vigintillion *million* 792.11

vignette Architectural Elements 134, *role* 136.23, *story* 139.4, *drawing* 143.4, *brief description* 202.2

vigor 514.2, 518.1; *youthfulness* 26.2, *health* 113.1, *emphasis* 200.1, *seriousness* 376.3, *energy* 414.4, *violence* 520.1, *stalwartness* 547.3

vigorous 518.2; *lively* 28.16, *healthy* 113.4, *emphatic* 200.3, *fresh* 260.10, *active* 414.13, *energetic* 514.16, *physically strong* 516.10, *mentally quick* 694.8

vigorously *emphatically* 200.7, *actively* 414.24, *energetically* 514.22, *acutely* 516.18, *with vigor* 518.6

vigorousness *emphasis* 200.1, *energy* 414.4, *stalwartness* 547.3

vihuela Musical Instruments 142

VII *seven* 792.3

VIII *eight* 792.4

Viking *destroyer* 523.6

Vila Countries 566

vile *hateful* 300.10, *profane* 301.10, *immoral* 432.9, *evil* 446.7, *depraved* 448.10

vile language *offensive language* 301.5

vilely *hatefully* 300.14, *profanely* 301.19, *unvirtuously* 448.16

vileness *immorality* 432.1, *evil* 446.1, *depravity* 448.2

vilification 301.2; *lying* 192.5, *personal attack* 418.8, *berating* 438.5, *scorn* 440.5

vilifier *liar* 192.10

vilify 301.15, 440.14; *lie* 192.23, *be dissatisfied* 274.7, *criticize* 418.26, *berate* 438.20

vilifying 301.9; *lying* 192.16

vilifyingly 301.18

villa *mansion* 60.5, *property* 470.1

village 567.3; *urban* 567.14

village green *green place* 260.2

villagelike *urban* 567.14

village pond *small lake* 568.2

villager *countryman* 61.8, *municipal resident* 567.12

villain 448.5; *lawbreaker* 53.15, *role* 136.23, *malefactor* 306.6, *wrongdoer* 430.8, *evil person* 446.3

villainous 448.12; *offending* 53.25, *black-hearted* 254.9, *wicked* 448.9

villainously 448.18; *wickedly* 448.15

villainousness *wickedness* 448.1

villainy *lawbreaking* 53.14, *wickedness* 448.1

villanelle Poem or Verse Forms 139

Villard-de-lans Breeds of Cattle 16

ville [Fr] *town* 567.2

villein *commoner* 71.1, *subjected person* 832.5

villeinage *common people* 71.2, *medieval ownership* 469.9, *historical property terms* 470.3, *subjection* 832.1

villein socage *medieval ownership* 469.9, *historical property terms* 470.3

villosity *roughness* 544.1

villous *coarse* 544.6

villously *roughly* 544.13

Vilnius Countries 566

vim *emphasis* 200.1, *vigor* 518.1

vina Musical Instruments 142

vinaigrette *sauce* 90.17, *sour thing* 223.3

vinca Flowers 42

Vincennes ware Ceramics 129

vinculum *mathematical symbol* 6.11

vindicable 441.9

vindicate 441.11; *rationalize* 4.20, *acquit* 54.32, *absolve* 312.10, *plead* 329.14, *answer back* 334.19, *verify* 336.8, *plead for* 419.25

vindicated 441.8; *acquitted* 54.25, *forgiven* 312.5, *apologetic* 329.10, *retaliatory* 334.13

vindicating *retaliatory* 334.13, *defending* 419.17, *vindicatory* 441.7

vindication 441.1; *favorable verdict* 54.19, *absolution* 312.2, *plea* 329.5, *counterstatement* 334.5

vindicator 441.5; *avenger* 441.6, *punisher* 454.16

vindicatory 441.7

vindictive 441.10; *hating* 300.7, *bitter* 306.9, *pitiless* 309.3, *retaliatory* 420.3, *evil* 446.7, *punitive* 454.18

vindictively 441.16; *with hate* 300.13, *bitterly* 306.16, *pitilessly* 309.7, *evilly* 446.12, *punitively* 454.33

vindictiveness *bitterness* 306.3, *pitilessness* 309.1, *evil* 446.1

vine *plant* 41.2

vinegar *basic cooking ingredient* 91.8, *sour thing* 223.3

vinegariness *sourness* 223.1

vinegary *acid* 223.5

vine grower *horticulturist* 17.13

vineyard *garden* 17.2

Vingt, Les Western Art Styles 133

vingt et un Card Games 168

vinicultural *horticultural* 17.14

viniculture *horticulture* 17.1

viniculturist *horticulturist* 17.13

vino [Inf] *wine* 93.11, *alcohol* 121.5

vinous *drinkable* 93.18, *intoxicating* 121.29

vin rosé *wine* 93.11

Vinson Massif Mountains and Hills 569

vintage *drinkable* 93.18, *store* 105.1, *yield* 467.8, *plant products* 522.8, *olden* 653.11

Vintage Automobile Racing Association (VARA) *racing governing bodies* 146.7

vintage car racer *driver* 146.8

vintage-car racing *automobile racing* 146.1

vintage crop *yield* 467.8

vintner *provisioner* 89.4, *drink provider* 93.15

vinyl *floor covering* 613.13

vinyon Fabrics and Fibers 130

viol Musical Instruments 142

viola Flowers 42, Musical Instruments 142

violaceous *purple* 262.6

viola da braccio Musical Instruments 142

viola da gamba Musical Instruments 142

viola d'amore Musical Instruments 142

viola pomposa Musical Instruments 142

violate *harm* 306.13, *misuse* 395.6, *do wrong* 430.20, *seduce* 432.16, *be evil* 446.10, *ravish* 477.15, *use violence* 520.9, *lay waste* 523.14, *transgress* 712.14, *break the law* 782.19

violated *misused* 395.3, *violating* 466.8

violate orders *disobey* 427.12, *defy* 466.11

violate the law 466.12; *be illegal* 53.30, *disobey* 427.12

violating 466.8; *offending* 53.25

violation *lawbreaking* 53.14, *misuse* 395.1, *wrongdoing* 430.7, *sexual offense* 432.6, *infraction* 466.4, *sexual possession* 477.2, *transgression* 712.3

violation of contract *bargaining terms* 57.10

violation of orders *disobedience* 427.1

violation of the law 427.2

violations 148.5

violative *unlawful* 430.15

violence 520.1; *warfare* 76.3, *anger* 302.4, *cruelty* 306.4, *ill-use* 395.2, *coercion* 428.2

violence by animal *violence by person* 520.2

violence by animal *violence by person* 520.2

violence by person 520.2

violent 520.5; *stormy* 9.45, *lawless* 53.26, *angry* 302.11, *cruel* 306.10, *abusive* 395.5, *attacking* 418.14, *compelling* 428.6, *hasty* 818.3

violent animal 520.4

violent change *sudden change* 665.3

violent charging *soccer play* 163.5

violent death *way of dying* 29.5, *accidental killing* 30.9

violently 520.11; *lawlessly* 53.35, *angrily* 302.24, *cruelly* 306.17, *offensively* 395.9, *compellingly* 428.12, *powerfully* 514.21, *dynamically* 695.16

violent person *violent animal* 520.4

violent storm *wind strength* 9.13

violent weather *natural violence* 520.3

violet Flowers 42, *spectrum* 251.3, *purpleness* 262.1, *purple thing* 262.3, *purple* 262.6

violin Musical Instruments 142

violinist *player* 141.2

violist *player* 141.2

violoncello Musical Instruments 142

violone Musical Instruments 142

viper *snake* 37.6, *malefactor* 306.6

viper in one's bosom *hostile person* 63.5

viperish *snakelike* 37.13

viperlike *snakelike* 37.13

viperous *or* **viperine** *snakelike* 37.13

vipers Collective Names 59

virago *unpleasant woman* 33.7, *feeling person* 266.8, *irascible person* 303.7

virago [Arch] *person of strength* 516.8

viral *living* 13.28

virelay Poem or Verse Forms 139

vireo, black-capped Endangered US Birds 36

vireo, least Bell's Endangered US Birds 36

virescence *greenness* 260.1

virescent *green* 260.7

vir et uxor [L] *married couple* 64.9

Virgilian *poetic* 139.19

Virgin Constellations 7, *deified person* 82.14

virgin *young woman* 26.9, *single woman* 33.5, *celibate* 67.4, *virginal* 67.7, *unprocessed* 389.10, *new* 394.7, *chaste person* 431.6, *chaste* 431.10, *innocent person* 449.5, *immature* 652.12, *uncut* 759.7

virginal 67.7; *young* 26.11, *clean* 111.13, Musical Instruments 142, *pure* 253.11, *chaste* 431.10, *principled* 447.6, *innocent* 449.6, *immature* 652.12

virginally *youthfully* 26.14, *celibately* 67.12, *ethically* 447.10, *innocently* 449.13, *immaturely* 652.23

virgin birth *genesis* 21.5

virgin forest *trees* 43.4

Virginia American States 564

Virginia reel Dances 135

Virginia tobacco *tobacco* 121.23

Virgin Islands Islands 572

Virgin Islands of the United States American States 564

virginity 67.2, Phobias 283, *natural state* 389.4, *newness* 394.2, *virtues* 447.2, *innocence* 449.1, *immaturity* 652.3

Virgin Mary, the *chaste person* 431.6

Virgin Mother *deified person* 82.14

virgins Phobias 283

virgin soil *natural state* 389.4

virgivitiphobia Phobias 283

Virgo Constellations 7

virgo intacta *celibate* 67.4, *chaste person* 431.6

virgule Punctuation Marks 5, *oblique line* 607.5

viridescence *greenness* 260.1

viridescent *green* 260.7

viridian *green pigment* 260.3

viridity *greenness* 260.1

virile *male* 32.16, *heroic* 284.10, *energetic* 514.16, *physically strong* 516.10, *vigorous* 518.2

virilism *maleness* 32.2

virility *maleness* 32.2, *heroism* 284.2

virion *microorganism* 13.11

virological *biological* 13.27

virologist *life scientist* 13.26, *medical specialist* 107.20

virology *biology* 13.2, *medical science* 107.5

virtu *artistry* 133.3

virtual *potential* 836.6, *latent* 844.6

vocalic *voiced* 5.37
vocalism *spoken language* 205.2
vocalist *singer* 141.4
vocalization *articulation* 205.9, *utterance* 205.10
vocalize *use language* 5.42, *sing* 141.16
vocalized *spoken* 205.13
vocally *linguistically* 5.44, *orally* 205.21, *vociferously* 239.18
vocal organs *speech organ* 205.4
vocation *job* 122.3, *calling* 178.6, *activity* 385.4, *line of action* 399.4, *business* 480.6, *motivation* 508.1, *specialization* 779.3
vocational *professional* 480.15
vocational training *educational system* 48.2
vocative *grammatical term* 5.29, *salutatory* 209.7
vociferate *be loud* 232.8, *cry out* 239.13
vociferation *tumult* 232.5, *cry* 239.1
vociferous 239.9; *shouting* 232.7
vociferously 239.18; *loudly* 232.11
vodka *alcoholic drink* 93.9
vogue *worded* 5.38, *likes* 290.3, *fashion* 536.1, *convention* 781.5
vogue word *catchword* 5.22
voice 141.5; *grammatical term* 5.29, *use language* 5.42, *singer* 141.4, *speech organ* 205.4, *mode of speech* 205.6, *speak* 205.17, *sound* 230.1, *electing* 382.5, *conduct* 399.1
voicebox *throat* 19.12, *speech organ* 205.4
voiced 5.37; *spoken* 205.13, *phonetic* 205.14, *sounding* 230.7
voiced consonant *spoken letter* 5.15
voiceless 206.5; *phonetic* 205.14, *silent* 208.5, 231.2
voicelessly 206.11; *taciturnly* 208.9
voicelessness *speech difficulty* 206.1, *silence* 208.2, 231.1, *undercurrent of sound* 233.3
voiceless speech 206.4
voice mail *telephone call* 169.11
voice of conscience *morals* 431.2, *forewarning* 814.2
voice of one's conscience *penitence* 451.1
voice of opposition *protester* 331.8
voiceover *broadcasting personnel* 172.11
voice part *musical part* 760.8
voice quality *mode of speech* 205.6
voice vote *electing* 382.5
voicing *articulation* 205.9
void 709.23; *galaxy* 7.5, *secrete* 24.7, *defecate* 25.21, *disavowal* 190.3, *nonentity* 190.5, *nonexistent* 190.14, *disavow* 190.18, *empty space* 563.2, *emptiness* 576.2, 718.4, *absent* 576.7, *vacant* 576.12, *gulf* 587.3, *nonexistent* 718.9, *subtract* 749.6, *omission* 762.4, *zero* 786.5, *useless* 802.7, *cancel* 834.6
voidance *secretion* 24.1, *defecation* 25.3, *reversal* 680.3, *outflow* 707.4, *removal* 709.5
voided *disavowing* 190.12, *canceled* 834.5
voiding *removal* 709.5
voidness *emptiness* 576.2
voile *fabric* 130.1, *transparent thing* 249.4
voir dire *jury selection* 54.14
Volans Constellations 7

volant *swift* 694.6
volatile 556.21; *passionate* 266.12, *erratic* 381.5, *sparse* 541.3, *gas* 556.1, *transient* 643.4, *irresolute* 666.4, *capricious* 841.16
volatile memory *memory* 15.6
volatileness *sparseness* 541.1, *capriciousness* 841.8
volatile oil *oil* 562.3
volatility 556.7; *sparseness* 541.1, *transience* 643.1, *irresolution* 666.2, *capriciousness* 841.8
volatilizable *sparse* 541.3, *volatile* 556.21
volatilization *vaporization* 556.9, *dilution* 776.3
volatilize *make sparse* 541.5, *gasify* 556.23, *dilute* 776.14
volatilized *sparse* 541.3
volcanic 8.57; *petrographic* 8.58, *on fire* 217.16, *explosive* 520.6, *of landmasses* 572.12, *holed* 583.12, *outgoing* 707.10
volcanic activity 8.26
volcanically *geologically* 8.68, *continentally* 572.13
volcanic cone *volcanic activity* 8.26
volcanic eruption *natural violence* 520.3
volcanic gas *eruption* 8.27
volcanic island *ocean floor* 8.18, *island* 572.2
volcanic lake *lake* 568.1
volcanic mountain *mountain building* 8.23
volcanic rock *igneous rock* 8.32
volcanism *volcanic activity* 8.26
volcano *landform* 8.9, *volcanic activity* 8.26, *hot spring* 572.11, *hole* 583.4, *ejector* 709.10, *natural hazard* 813.4
volcanological *geologic* 8.50
volcanologist *geologist* 8.4, *geophysicist* 8.5
volcanology *geology* 8.1, *geophysics* 8.2
Volga Rivers 570
volition *philosophical problem* 4.8, *will* 372.1, *choice* 382.3
volitional *willed* 372.6, *intentional* 374.7
volitionally *intentionally* 374.13
volitionary *selected* 382.11
volitive *willed* 372.6, *selected* 382.11
volley *tennis strokes* 165.2, *play tennis* 165.13, *bang* 234.1, *firing* 418.6, *fire* 418.18, *shot* 696.6, *shoot* 696.18
volleyball Sporting Activities 145
volleyer *tennis participant* 165.6
volley of abuse *vilification* 301.2
Voloshian Breeds of Sheep 16
Volstead Act *prohibition of alcohol* 120.2, 503.2
volt Scientific and Technical Units 589
Volta Lakes 568, Rivers 570
voltage *electric potential* 10.40
voltaic cell *electrochemistry* 11.19
voltaic electricity *electrical power* 514.12
volt-ampere Scientific and Technical Units 589
volte-face *vacillation* 380.3, *reversion* 671.1
voltmeter *electrical instrument* 14.41
Volturno Rivers 570
volubility *power of speech* 205.5, *talkativeness* 207.1
voluble *speaking* 205.15, *talkative* 207.5
volubly *talkatively* 207.9

volume *dimension* 10.5, *thermodynamics* 10.30, *television set* 172.6, *book* 174.1, *space* 563.1, *size* 579.1, Fields of Measurement 589, *measurability* 589.2, *quantity* 738.1, *part of writing* 760.6, *inclusion* 763.1
volume capacity *space* 6.33
volume control *radio reception* 172.2, *sound amplifier* 230.5
volume integral *differentiation* 6.29
volumes Fields of Measurement 589
volume strain *load* 14.14
volumeter Fields of Measurement 589
volumetric *analytic* 11.32, *spatial* 563.17
volumetric analysis *gravimetric analysis* 11.18
volumetry Fields of Measurement 589
voluminous *diffuse* 199.3, *spacious* 563.13, *big* 579.13, *quantitative* 738.6
voluminously *spaciously* 563.17, *amply* 579.20, *wholly* 738.9
voluminousness *spaciousness* 563.4, *largeness* 579.2
voluntarily 373.17, 504.19; *intentionally* 374.13
voluntarism *voluntary work* 373.5
voluntary 373.11, 504.9; *intentional* 374.7, *given* 472.8, *free of charge* 497.12
voluntary aid *voluntary work* 373.5
voluntary arbitration *strike* 57.8
voluntary commitment *promise* 458.1
voluntary payment 489.4; *grant* 489.7
voluntary poverty *renunciation of wealth* 486.4
voluntary resignation *resignation* 835.1
voluntary retirement *bargaining terms* 57.10
voluntary service *voluntary work* 373.5
voluntary work 373.5; *giving* 472.1, *absence of charge* 497.6
voluntary worker *independent worker* 123.3, *volunteer* 504.7
volunteer 373.14, 504.7, 504.13; *enlisted* 58.11, *join the army* 76.31, *soldier* 77.4, *independent worker* 123.3, *philanthropist* 307.5, *willing worker* 373.6, *attempter* 390.3, *person who undertakes* 391.3, *take charge of* 391.8, *busy person* 414.10, *be sociable* 414.22, *give to charity* 472.16
volunteer army *the military* 58.2, *army* 77.12
volunteer forces *armed forces* 77.9
volunteering *war measures* 76.18, *voluntary work* 373.5, *social activity* 414.2
volunteerism *voluntary work* 373.5
volunteer snooker *snooker* 149.4
volunteer work *absence of charge* 497.6
voluptuary *pleasure-seeker* 214.4, *self-indulgent person* 456.5
voluptuous *sensual* 20.16, *pleasurable* 214.6, *pleasure-seeking* 214.10, *offensive* 432.11, *self-indulgent* 456.6
voluptuousness *sexuality* 20.3, *physical pleasure* 214.1, *self-indulgence* 456.1

volutation *turning* 682.3
volute Architectural Elements 134
volute spring *spring* 546.4
volution *rotation* 682.1
volva *fungal body* 47.4
vomer Human Bones 19
vomit 709.27; *be unhealthy* 114.29, *flow* 555.25, *run out* 707.15, *vomiting* 709.7
vomiting 709.7, 709.12; *symptom* 114.3, *gastroenterological disease* 114.11, *drunken behavior* 121.4, *Phobias* 283
vomitive *vomiting* 709.12
vomitory *medicinal* 115.15, *vomiting* 709.12
voodoo *witchcraft* 86.6, *occult influence* 512.2, *cause adversity* 848.15
voodooism *occultism* 86.1, *witchcraft* 86.6
voodooist *witch* 86.15
voodooistic *witchlike* 86.19
voodoo spell *curse* 301.1
voracious *eating* 92.18, *underfed* 98.7, *gluttonous* 119.3, *covetous* 288.14
voraciously *carnivorously* 92.27, *gluttonously* 119.5, *covetously* 288.28
voraciousness *appetite* 92.2, *gluttony* 119.1
voracity *appetite* 92.2, *gluttony* 119.1, *eagerness* 288.3
Vorderwald Breeds of Cattle 16
Vormingstoneel [Dutch] *theater movements* 136.9
vortex 682.6; *activity* 414.1, *river turbulence* 570.5, *convoluted thing* 632.3, *atmospheric agitation* 684.13, *hidden danger* 813.3
vortical *flowing* 570.7, *rotary* 682.12
vortically *fluently* 570.13
vorticism Western Art Styles 133, Western Literary Groups 139
vorticose *rotary* 682.12
Vosges Breeds of Cattle 16
Vosges Mountains Mountains and Hills 569
votary *religious person* 81.9, *worshiper* 83.6, *desirer* 288.9
vote 382.16; *legislate* 53.31, *judgment* 341.1, *selection* 382.1, *electing* 382.5, *approval* 437.1, *commission* 833.8
vote against *discard* 383.12, *dissent* 506.9, 732.13, *exclude* 764.7, *be against* 828.17
vote against, a *dissent* 506.2
vote counting *election* 382.6
voted in *selected* 382.11, *approved* 437.8, *agreeing* 462.6
vote down *exclude* 764.7, *restrain* 830.12
vote for *assent* 346.6, *vote* 382.16, *approve* 437.14
vote in *vote* 382.16
vote independent *be independent* 829.18
vote in the affirmative *agree with* 462.10
vote of confidence *electing* 382.5
vote of no confidence *rejection* 383.1
vote of thanks *public speaking* 205.11, *acknowledgment* 310.3
vote out *exclude* 764.7
voter *electorate* 382.7, *free person* 829.9
voters *electorate* 382.7
vote unanimously *agree* 752.17
voting *electing* 382.5, *commission* 833.1

voting booth *election* 382.6
voting list *list of names* 785.7
voting machine *election* 382.6
voting with one's feet *departure* 705.1
votive *promised* 458.8, *given* 472.8
votive candle *sacred object* 83.11
votively *as promised* 458.16, *as a gift* 472.17
votive offering *penitence* 313.3, *offering* 472.6, 504.5
votive ship Ships and Boats 690
vouch [Arch] *attestation* 189.2
vouched for *vowed* 189.14
voucher *record* 185.1, *affirmer* 189.9, *verifier* 336.4, *documentation* 339.6, *guarantee* 458.3, *acknowledgment of payment* 473.3, *receipt* 492.1, *permit* 502.3
vouch for *attest* 189.22, *prove* 339.14, *guarantee* 458.13, *promise* 464.10, *protect* 810.21
vouchsafe *give* 472.10, *permit* 735.29, *grant* 735.30
vouchsafed *permitting* 735.19, *granted* 735.20
vouchsafement *permission* 735.9, *grant* 735.10
voussoir Architectural Elements 134
vow 189.3, 189.23; *contract* 391.2, 459.1, *take charge of* 391.8, *duty* 433.1, *promise* 458.1, 458.11, *give praise to* 472.13
vowed 189.14
vowel *spoken letter* 5.15
vower *affirmer* 189.9
vow of poverty *renunciation of wealth* 486.4
vox populi *judgment* 341.1, *place of judgment* 341.3, *agreement* 735.3, *general public* 778.6
voyage *travel* 686.5, *water transportation* 690.1, *passing* 692.3, *proceed* 692.16
voyager *traveler* 686.6
voyaging *water transportation* 690.1
voyeur *eroticism* 20.7, *observer* 242.15, *meddler* 321.4, *pornography* 432.7
voyeurism *eroticism* 20.7, *sexual disorder* 108.14, *observation* 242.5, *prying* 321.2, *pornography* 432.7
V-shape *windsurfing* 150.28, *angle* 628.1, *fork* 703.5
V-shaped *angular* 628.7, *branched* 703.9
V-shaped valley *landform* 8.9
V-shape hull *sailboard parts* 150.20
V-sign *angle* 628.1
Vulcan Deities 82
vulcanism *volcanic activity* 8.26
vulcanite *polymer* 11.9, *rubber* 546.3
vulcanization *hardening* 542.2
vulcanize *harden* 542.9, *make elastic* 546.8, *make tough* 547.15
vulcanized *toughened* 547.7
vulcanized rubber *rubber* 546.3
vulcanologist *geologist* 8.4, *geophysicist* 8.5
vulcanology *geology* 8.1, *geophysics* 8.2
vulgar 535.6; *of language* 5.35, *common* 71.3, *profane* 301.10, *unrefined* 338.7, *uncustomary* 398.4, *blatant* 404.9, *bad-mannered* 411.6, *improper* 430.14, *offensive* 432.11, *depraved* 448.10, *inelegant* 528.6, *indecorous* 528.8, *insignificant* 745.6
vulgar fraction *division* 6.16, *fraction* 787.1

vulgar group 535.5
vulgarian *vulgar person* 535.4
vulgarism 5.20; *nonstandard language* 5.7, *inelegance of expression* 528.4
vulgarity 535.1; *curse word* 301.4, *tastelessness* 338.3, *bad manners* 411.2, *impropriety* 430.5, *immorality* 432.1, *depravity* 448.2, *bad taste* 528.3, *inelegance of expression* 528.4
vulgarization *moral deterioration* 808.3
vulgarize 535.9; *popularize* 778.17, *pervert* 808.22, *make easy* 823.15
vulgar language *vulgarism* 5.20
vulgarly 71.5, 535.10; *profanely* 301.19, *blatantly* 404.34, *rudely* 411.9, *improperly* 430.26, *immorally* 432.18, *unvirtuously* 448.16
vulgar masses *common people* 71.2
vulgarness *impropriety* 430.5
vulgar person 535.4
vulgar tongue *vernacular* 205.8
Vulgate *Christian text* 81.16
vulgate *interpretation* 365.1
vulgus *vulgar group* 535.5
vulnerability 811.6; *sensitivity* 212.2, *helplessness* 515.3, *weakness* 517.1, *brittleness* 548.1, *imperfection* 806.1
vulnerable 811.9; *unprepared* 389.5, *helpless* 515.9, *brittle* 548.3, *imperfect* 806.5
vulnerable point *defect* 806.4, *vulnerability* 811.6
vulnerably *fragilely* 548.5, *dangerously* 811.14
vulnerary *remedial* 115.14
Vulpecula Constellations 7
vulpecular *carnivorous* 35.26
vulpine *carnivorous* 35.26, *cunning* 822.4
vulture *bird of prey* 36.11, *malefactor* 306.6, *greedy person* 477.11
vulturine *avian* 36.19
vulva *organs of reproduction* 21.9
vulvar *reproductive* 21.11
Vyatka Breeds of Sheep 16
vying *contending* 422.19, *conflict* 828.3
Vyrnwy Lakes 568

W

Wabash Rivers 570
wacko [Inf] *eccentric* 782.10
wacky [Inf] *insane* 110.9, *cheering* 269.8
wad *assemblage* 59.13, *historical ammunition* 78.12, *stuff* 577.12, *mass* 579.7, *stopper* 584.3
wad [Inf] *money* 485.2
wadding *stuffing* 577.4, *stopper* 584.3
waddle *bodily movement* 677.11, *walk* 677.17, *slow motion* 693.3
waddling *slow* 693.7
wade across *cross* 692.17
Wade-Giles *alphabet* 5.16
wade in *fight* 422.23
wade in blood *slaughter* 30.21
wader *water bird* 36.9
waders *boots* 100.31
wade through *exert oneself* 122.11, *behave toward* 399.20, *be in motion* 677.14
wadi *river parts* 570.3
wading *swimming* 164.12
wading bird *water bird* 36.9
wading pool *swimming place* 164.9

Wadjak man *primitive humanity* 18.4
wafer *cake* 90.36, *slice* 588.4, *fineness* 595.5
wafer-thin *brittle* 548.3, *fine* 595.12
waffle *pancake* 90.11
waffle [Inf] *be equivocal* 380.7, *evasiveness* 386.6, *be evasive* 386.20, *be irresolute* 666.6
waffle house *eating place* 92.17
waffle iron *cooking equipment* 91.6, *burner* 217.4
waffler [Inf] *sophist* 330.6
wafflestompers *boots* 100.31
waffling *irresolute* 666.4
waft *odor* 224.1, *be light* 539.8, *conveyance* 685.2, *convey* 685.9
waftage *conveyance* 685.2
wag *humorist* 277.7, *shake* 684.7, *agitate* 684.22
wage a campaign *combat* 77.34
wage bill *business expenses* 491.4
waged *receiving pay* 489.14, *received* 492.6
wage earner *employee* 57.4, *breadwinner* 123.2, *gainer* 467.9, *recipient* 473.5
wage-earning *industrial* 57.13, *receiving* 473.9, *receiving pay* 489.14
wager *gambling* 167.4, *contend* 422.22, *take a chance* 842.14
wage rates *bargaining terms* 57.10
wagerer *gambler* 167.6
wager of battle *war* 76.1
wages *economic factor* 56.8, *reward for service* 453.5, *earnings* 467.5, *pay* 489.6, *business expenses* 491.4, *income* 492.3, *positive stimulus* 508.5
wage scale *reward for service* 453.5
wage slave *breadwinner* 123.2
wage war *oppose* 63.11, *be at war* 76.32, *declare war* 422.25
wageworker *employee* 57.4, *gainer* 467.9
waggery *humor* 277.1
wagging forefinger *gesture* 183.5
waggish *humorous* 277.9
waggishness *humor* 277.1
waggle *shake* 684.7, *agitate* 684.22, *pitch* 684.25
waging war *warfare* 76.3, *warring* 76.26
wagon 687.5; *vault* 134.8, *cart* 578.9, *road vehicle* 687.4
wagonage [Arch] *conveyance* 685.2
wagoner *transferrer* 685.4, *transporter* 686.4
wagon stage *stage* 136.18
wagon train *means of transportation* 686.2
wagon wheel *wheel* 682.9
wagtail *songbird* 36.12, *bait* 154.6
Wahhabi *Muslim* 81.12
wahoo Trees and Shrubs 43
waif *displaced person* 574.7
Waikato Rivers 570
wail *blow* 9.53, *speak in a particular way* 205.18, *express pain* 215.11, *harsh sound* 238.1, *be strident* 238.7, *cry of sorrow* 239.6, *cry* 239.16, *grieve* 270.7, *lament* 280.7, *weep* 280.8
wailer *lamenter* 280.3
wailing *crying* 239.11, *animal sound* 240.1, *lamentation* 280.1, *lamenting* 280.4
wain *wagon* 687.5
wainscot *base* 601.1
wainscoting *wall covering* 613.12
wainwright *artisan* 123.13

waist *ski equipment* 162.10, *midline* 772.2
waistband *circular thing* 631.3, *band* 754.9
waist belt *climbing equipment* 161.4
waistcloth *underwear* 100.22
waist-deep *deep* 598.9, *shallow* 599.3
waist-high *high* 596.7
waistline *part of garment* 100.27, *midline* 772.2
wait 356.8, 658.12; *procrastinate* 413.12, *be moral* 431.13, *space* 563.15, *delay* 658.3, *be motionless* 678.7
wait and see *procrastinate* 413.12, *delay* 658.13, *be uncertain* 841.17
wait-and-see *inactive* 413.9
wait-and-see policy *prudence* 287.2
waiter *attendant* 69.4, *caterer* 89.5, *service worker* 123.7
wait for *wait* 356.8, *be prepared* 388.17, *expect* 650.12
wait for the command *obey* 426.7
waiting *expectation* 356.1, *expecting* 356.4, *looking to the future* 650.4, *future* 650.6
waiting for the bomb to drop *fearful* 283.10
waiting in the wings *future* 650.6
waiting list *list of names* 785.7
waiting on *serving* 69.9
waiting room *room* 60.9, *stopping place* 668.4, *railroad station* 688.6
wait on *pander to* 401.11, *attend* 794.19, *serve* 825.29, *be subject to* 832.12
wait on hand and foot *serve* 69.11, *pander to* 401.11
waitress *attendant* 69.4, *caterer* 89.5, *service worker* 123.7
wait upon *serve* 69.11, *pander to* 401.11, *obey* 426.7
waive *relinquish* 392.3, *not use* 394.9, *cancel* 834.6
waived *relinquished* 392.2
waiver *miscellaneous terms* 155.16, *relinquishment* 392.1, *permit* 502.3, *cancellation* 834.1
waive the rules *be informal* 407.10
waiving *relinquishment* 392.1
Wakatipu Lakes 568
wake *after death* 29.9, *funeral* 31.4, *pay one's last respects* 31.12, *awake* 212.10, *lamentation* 280.1, *condolence* 308.2, *indication* 339.3, *push* 414.20, *back* 622.1, *visible effect* 676.2, *remainder* 750.1, *sequence* 770.1
wake course *sailing terms* 150.5
wakeful *active* 414.13
wakefulness *restlessness* 414.7
Wake Island Islands 572
waken *awake* 212.10
wake the dawn *arise* 655.7
wake the dead *conjure* 86.26, *shatter the peace* 232.10
wake up *awake* 212.10, *be active* 414.18, *arise* 655.7
waking time *morning* 655.2
Waldorf salad *salad* 90.16
Waldorf system *educational system* 48.2
Waler Horse and Pony Breeds 159
walk 677.17; Collective Names 59, *be healthy* 113.11, *play baseball* 147.9, *play basketball* 148.7, *ride* 159.16, *participate* 166.22, *plot* 564.9, *bodily movement* 677.11, *orbit* 681.3, *route* 691.2, *slow motion* 693.3

walk or **walking** race walking 166.9

walk [Arch] line of action 399.4

walk all over wrong 430.19

walkathon charitable organization 305.4

walk away depart 705.8

walk down the aisle propose (marriage) 299.28

walker body support 605.6

Walker Cup golfing associations and tournaments 156.6

Walk for Hunger charitable organization 305.4

walk hand in hand with fraternize 408.17

walkie-talkie radio 172.1

walking health improvement 113.3, violations 148.5, track and field 166.20, Hobbies and Pastimes 167, Phobias 283, motion 677.1, means of transportation 686.2, passing along 692.5, slow 693.7, bodily improvement 807.10

walking a man pitching terms 147.5

walking bass harmonic element 140.14

walking boots boots 100.31

walking encyclopedia expert 52.8, 68.13, 127.9, intellectual 315.7, knowledgeable person 348.5

walking out with [Brit] courtship 299.10

walking papers [Inf] dismissal 709.2, termination 834.2

walking part role 136.23

walking race race walking 166.9

walking shoes shoes 100.30

walking skeleton thin person 595.4

walking steps competitive diving 164.7

walking stick body support 605.6

walking the plank punishment 454.1

walking under a ladder bad-luck sign 358.7

walk in the shoes of emulate 736.11

walk into a trap be in danger 811.11

Walkman™ radio 172.1

walk-off [Inf] outgoer 707.9

walk off exit 707.13

walk off with steal 479.14, defeat 845.17

walk of life state 725.1

walk-on actor 136.25, 137.13

walk on underact 136.36, subject 832.10

walk on eggs be in difficulty 824.19

walk on eggshells proceed with caution 287.12, be careful 325.11

walk one's beat be cyclic 663.11

walk on hot coals have difficulty 824.18

walk-on part role 136.23

walk on thin ice proceed with caution 287.12

walk on tiptoe hide 844.13

walk on water attempt the impossible 837.10

walkout strike 57.8, dissentience 347.3, resistance 417.1, stop 668.2, exit 707.1

walk out be employed 57.19, have an industrial dispute 57.20, desert 66.11, withdraw 392.5, resist 417.10, cause mischief 507.9, stop work 668.11, exit 707.13, be dismissed 707.18

walk out with [Brit] court 299.26

walk (all) over subject 832.10

walkover horse racing 159.10, easy thing 823.6, victory 845.4

walk over suppress 424.9

walk over the course do easily 823.16

walk slowly move slowly 693.11

walk the earth live 28.17

walk through rehearse 136.37, act 137.20

walk-through production 136.14, 137.6

walk up climb 713.21

walk (humbly) with one's God be virtuous 447.8

wall 134.9; Architectural Elements 134, painting 143.3, rock face 161.6, ski run 162.2, barrier 419.10, 826.7, fortification 419.12, 812.3, fence 419.21, retainer 471.3, solid body 540.4, supporting structure 605.2, support 605.16, enclosing thing 619.3, enclose 619.6, limit marker 620.4, separator 753.5, shelter 812.4, block 826.17

wallboard wall covering 613.12

wall clock Timepieces and Timers 646

wall covering 613.12; interior decoration 532.4

walled garden enclosed area 619.2

walled in retained 471.6, blocked 826.13

walled-in enclosed 619.4

wallet money storage 484.20, packet 578.4, baggage 578.8

walleye game fish 154.10, faulty vision 243.1

walleyed visually impaired 243.9

wall fabric interior decoration 532.4

wallflower Flowers 42, figurative usage 42.8, inactive person 413.8, loser 468.8

wall hanging interior decoration 532.4

wall in detain 471.9, enclose 619.6

walling in covering 613.1, enclosure 619.1

walling up covering 613.1

Wallis Simpson Famous Lovers 299

wall knot Knots, Bends, Hitches, Splices 754

wall light electric light 246.6

wall off exclude 764.7

wallop hit 454.28, beat 695.12

wallop [Inf] vigor 518.1

walloping [Inf] huge 579.14

wallow swill 112.6, be dirty 112.10, feel pleasure 214.12, marsh 572.3, stagger 684.11, pitch 684.25, bow 716.22

wallow in abound 97.8, indulge oneself 456.10

wallowing nautical 690.14

wallow in ignorance be ignorant 349.8

wallow in riches be rich 485.12

wall painting interior decoration 532.4

wallpaper interior decoration 532.4, decorate 532.11, wall covering 613.12, face 613.31

wallpapered covered 613.19

wallpaperer coverer 613.18

wallpapering interior decoration 532.4

wall safe safe 464.4, money storage 484.20

Wall Street stock exchange 457.3, stock market 483.6, New York 567.6

wall tile industrial ceramics 129.6, wall covering 613.12

wall-to-wall including 763.3

wall-to-wall carpet floor covering 613.13

wall types wall 134.9

wall unit cabinet 578.3

wall up murder 30.20, conceal 181.12, block 826.17

wall writing inscription 185.4

walnut Trees and Shrubs 43, brown 256.5

Walpurgis Night witchcraft 86.6

waltz Dances 135, dance 135.7, Musical Forms 140

waltz away with [Inf] defeat 845.17

waltzer dancer 135.4

waltz hold ice-dancing move 162.19

wamble roll 682.15

wampum [Inf] money 484.1, cash 484.2

wan unhealthy 114.23, unemphatic 201.2, drained of color 252.6, ugly 531.3, fatigued 820.2

Wanaka Lakes 568

wand input device 15.11, insignia 184.5, cosmetic tool 530.5

wander be circuitous 199.6, diverge 607.17, move 677.15, travel 686.11, go astray 698.17, be foreign 724.13, digress 775.13

wander away be in danger 811.11

wanderer traveler 686.6

Wanderers Western Art Styles 133

wandering 698.4, 698.13; circumlocution 199.2, circumlocutory 199.4, oblivious 355.9, divergent 607.7, 776.11, changeable 666.3, moving 677.12, traveling 686.9, foreign 724.9

wandering eye faulty vision 243.1

Wandering Jew displaced person 574.7, new arrival 724.6

wandering mind wandering 698.4

wanderings travel 686.5

wandering star planet 7.16

wanderlust restlessness 414.7

wandoo Trees and Shrubs 43

wane waste away 96.20, be dim 248.7, disappearance 265.1, disappear 265.5, lessen 468.17, shortening 582.2, become smaller 582.14, be in motion 677.14, change by degrees 739.8, decrease 747.7, deterioration 808.1, deteriorate 808.14

wanga witchcraft 86.6, spell 86.8

wangateur witch 86.15

wangle artifice 193.5, scheme 193.18, method 387.4, be cunning 822.5

wangler schemer 193.10

wangling artful 193.13

waning aging 27.13, dim 248.4, disappearing 265.3, lessening 468.6, poor health 517.3, shortening 582.2, gradational 739.5, decrease 747.1, decreasing 747.5

waning moon moon 7.18

waning of the moon dimness 248.1

Wankel engine type 14.11

Wankel cycle Classical Physical Laws 10

wanness lack of emphasis 201.1

want necessity 95.1, neediness 95.3, need 95.4, 95.16, scarcity 98.3, be insufficient 98.9, be unsatisfied 98.10, wish 288.2, object of desire 288.8, desire 288.17, lust after 288.20, envy 314.1, 314.7, demand 356.9, will 372.11, poverty 486.1, be poor 486.14, request 505.1, 505.10, absence 576.1, be inferior 745.10, incompleteness 762.1, 806.2, omission 762.4, be incomplete 762.8, economic adversity 848.6, need money 848.14

want ad [Inf] advertisement 173.9

want-ad section newspaper 175.2

wanted desired 288.10, missing 576.11

wanter desirer 288.9

wanting needy 95.12, insufficient 98.4, 517.11, desirous 288.13, envy 314.1, expecting 356.4, poor 486.8, missing 576.11, incomplete 762.5, 806.6

wanting in respect disrespectful 436.9

wantingly enviously 314.11

want no forgiveness be impenitent 452.4

want nothing be complete 761.10

want of alacrity unenthusiasm 375.3

want of chivalry bad manners 411.2

want of practice lack of preparation 389.1

want of respect disrespect 436.1

want of skill unskillfulness 128.1

wanton pleasure-seeking 214.10, cruel 306.10, erratic 381.5, unchaste 432.10, unconditional 829.14

wanton cruelty cruelty 306.4

wanton destruction destructiveness 523.3

wanton destructiveness destructiveness 523.3

want one's own way be obstinate 379.10

wantonly lustfully 20.24, cruelly 306.17, promiscuously 432.19, excessively 829.23

wantonness sexual love 299.3, sexual immorality 432.2, liberality 829.8

want practice be unprepared 389.14

want something to do have leisure time 125.5

want to enjoy 290.9

want to know be curious 321.7, request 505.10

war 76.1; slaughter 30.5, military affairs 58.1, act of hostility 63.4, warfare 76.3, 422.10, be at war 76.32, canoeing 150.26, Card Games 168, action 412.1, revolution 427.4, agent of destruction 523.7, conflict 828.3

War Admiral Notable Horses 159

war against be at war 76.32

War Between the States Major Wars 76

warble sing 141.16, speak in a particular way 205.18, bird sound 240.2, make a bird sound 240.8

warbler songbird 36.12, singer 141.4

warbler, Bachman's Endangered US Birds 36

warbler, golden-cheeked Endangered US Birds 36

warbler, Kirtland's Endangered US Birds 36

warbling *singing* 240.5
war bride *spouse* 64.8
war canoe *canoe* 150.9
war cloud *forewarning* 814.2
war college *military training* 76.19
war correspondent *print journalist* 175.5, *descriptive writer* 202.10
warcraft *art of war* 76.16
war cry *glory of war* 76.17, *military call* 183.9, *cry* 239.1, *warning signal* 814.3
ward *hospital* 107.16, *fort* 419.13, *defend* 419.20, *administrative region* 564.4, *urban area* 567.10, *part* 760.1, *safekeeping* 810.6, *protect* 810.21, *fortification* 812.3, *detention* 830.5, *dependent* 832.4
war dance *glory of war* 76.17, *non-Christian ritual* 85.8
warden *prison officer* 55.8, *manager* 126.7, *protector* 419.16, *closer* 584.5, *surveillant* 810.12, *one who restrains* 830.7
wardenship *patronage* 810.7
warder *protector* 419.16, *surveillant* 810.12
warder [Brit] *prison officer* 55.8
warding off *defense* 419.1
ward off *evade* 386.19, *parry* 419.27, *fend off* 701.9
ward orderly *paramedic* 107.24
wardrobe *clothing* 100.1, *cabinet* 101.8, *stage requisite* 136.21
wardrobe mistress *stagehand* 136.29
wardship *youth* 26.1, *patronage* 810.7, *subjection* 832.1
ware *ceramics* 129.1
war effort *war measures* 76.18
warehouse *storehouse* 105.8, *save* 105.20, *marketplace* 483.7, *discounter* 497.7, *building* 551.9, *protect* 810.21, *preserve* 815.14
warehoused *saved* 105.15
warehouse store *store* 483.8
warehousing *storage* 105.6
wares *personal estate* 470.6, *merchandise* 482.6, 522.6
warfare 76.3, 422.10; *conflict* 828.3
warfarin *pest control* 16.13, *poison* 117.7
war fever *bellicosity* 76.15
war-fevered *warlike* 76.27
war footing *war measures* 76.18
war galley *historical warships* 77.22
war game *type of game* 167.2
war games *art of war* 76.16
warhead *explosive* 78.13
war-horse 159.4
warily *cautiously* 287.16, *suspiciously* 314.13, *attentively* 323.14, *carefully* 325.13, *unwillingly* 375.17
wariness *caution* 287.1, *suspicion* 314.3, *carefulness* 323.3, *watchfulness* 325.5, *unenthusiasm* 375.3, *cunning* 822.1
war in heaven *loud sound* 232.2
warlike 76.27; *military* 58.10, *combative* 77.32, *heroic* 284.10, *defying* 416.6, *militant* 418.13, *contentious* 422.20, *strong in spirit* 516.11, *murderous* 520.7
warlike habits *bellicosity* 76.15
warlock *witch* 86.15
warlord *absolute ruler* 68.7
war-loving *warlike* 76.27
warm 9.46, 217.13; *friendly* 62.5, *cook* 91.10, *emphatic* 200.3, *pleasant* 214.7, *pleased* 214.9, *comfort* 214.14, *hot* 217.11, *heat*

217.17, colorful 251.11, *sensitive* 267.3, *likable* 271.6, *demonstrative* 331.10, *discovering* 345.8, *sociable* 408.11, *near* 586.6
warm air *atmosphere* 9.8
warm as toast *warm* 217.13
warm-blooded 217.14; *mammalian* 35.23, *equine* 159.15
warm-blooded animal *mammal* 35.1
warm-bloodedness *sensitivity* 212.2, *heat* 217.1
war measures 76.18
warmed through *heated* 217.15
warmed up *heated* 217.15, *remade* 797.10
war memorial *funeral object* 31.6, *monument* 185.10
warmer *warm* 9.46, *heater* 217.3
warm feeling *energy* 414.4
warm friendship *intimacy* 62.4
warm front *air movement* 9.11, *hot weather* 217.6
warm-hearted *friendly* 62.5, *sensitive* 267.3, *pitying* 308.4, *kind* 445.12, *soft-hearted* 543.11
warm-heartedly *amicably* 62.13, *pityingly* 308.11, *kindly* 445.20
warm-heartedness *friendship* 62.1, *pity* 308.1, *kindness* 445.3
warm hue *hue* 251.4
warming *heating* 217.12
warming of the earth's atmosphere *hot weather* 217.6
warming pan *heater* 217.3
warmly 217.20; *meteorologically* 9.60, *amicably* 62.13, *pleasingly* 214.15, *ruddily* 257.10, *with feeling* 266.18, *pleasantly* 271.12, *demonstratively* 331.21, *sociably* 408.19
warmness *friendship* 62.1, *heat* 217.1
warm occlusion *air movement* 9.11
warmonger *militarist* 77.3, *combat* 77.34
warmongering *warlike* 76.27, *contentious* 422.20
warm reception *welcome* 408.10
warm sector *weather system* 9.10
warm spell *hot weather* 9.22, 217.6
warm spring *hot spring* 572.11
warmth *heat* 10.25, 217.1, *friendship* 62.1, *emphasis* 200.1, *hue* 251.4, *redness* 257.1, *good feeling* 266.4, *amiability* 271.3, *sociability* 408.1, *welcome* 408.10
warm the cockles of one's heart *give pleasure* 214.13
warm to *befriend* 62.10
warm up *be healthy* 113.11, *heat* 217.17, *prepare for action* 388.18, *prepare oneself* 388.21, *accustom oneself* 397.19, *renew* 797.19
warm-up lap *automobile racing terms* 146.3
warm weather *hot weather* 9.22
warm welcome *welcome* 408.10
warm work *work* 122.1
warn 814.8; *advise* 176.9, *dissuade* 179.7, *signal* 183.18, *caution* 287.15, *foresee* 357.9, *predict* 358.14, *demand* 425.11, *protest* 507.7, *forecast* 769.17
warned 814.7; *prepared* 388.9
warner 814.5; *oracle* 358.8
warning 287.5, 287.10, 814.1, 814.6; *inside information* 170.4, *advice* 176.1, *advisory* 176.7, *dissuasion* 179.1, *dissuasive* 179.4, *signaling* 183.14, *notice* 358.3,

omen 358.5, *condemnation* 438.2, *protest* 507.1, *preview* 769.6
warning cry *animal sound* 240.1
warning flag *signal* 183.6
warning flare *warning signal* 814.3
warning light *signal* 183.6, *safety light* 246.7, *warning signal* 814.3
warningly 814.11
warning notice *demand* 425.2
warning shot *notice* 358.3
warning sign *signs* 183.2, *notice* 358.3, *warning signal* 814.3
warning signal 814.3; *signal* 183.6
warning sound *signal* 183.6
warning voice *forewarning* 814.2
warn off *exclude* 764.7
War of 1812 *Major Wars* 76
war of attrition *psychological warfare* 76.13, *terrorist attack* 418.7, *warfare* 422.10
war of conquest *war* 76.1
war of containment *war* 76.1
war of expansion *war* 76.1
War of Independence *Major Wars* 76
war of independence 76.9
war of liberation *war of independence* 76.9
war of nerves *psychological warfare* 76.13, *intimidation* 283.6
War of the Austrian Succession *Major Wars* 76
war of the elements *natural violence* 520.3
War of the Spanish Succession *Major Wars* 76
war of words *psychological warfare* 76.13, *contention* 422.1
war on all fronts *war* 76.1
warp *weaving* 130.6, 609.2, *distort the truth* 192.25, *practice sophistry* 330.11, *prejudge* 337.13, *bias* 342.11, *fabric* 551.2, *distortion* 627.1, *distort* 627.9, 698.20, *change for the worse* 665.18, *sail* 690.16, *torsion* 698.5, *pull* 699.10, *pervert* 808.22
warp and woof *or* **weft** *weave* 552.4
warpath *war* 76.1
warped *partially true* 192.18, *unjust* 342.7
warplane *military aircraft* 77.30, *weapon* 78.1
war plans *military affairs* 58.1
war policy *war measures* 76.18
war preparations *war measures* 76.18
warrant *authorization* 52.3, *authorize* 52.14, 833.10, *legality* 53.9, *make legal* 53.27, *pretrial proceedings* 54.13, *verify* 336.8, *documentation* 339.6, *prove* 339.14, *demand* 425.2, 425.11, *have rights* 429.13, *justify* 441.12, *guarantee* 458.3, 458.13, 840.4, *promise* 464.2, 464.10, *paper money* 484.14, *permit* 502.3, 735.29, *adoption* 692.2, *adopt* 692.14, *permission* 735.9, *safety* 810.1, *assure* 810.23, *authority* 833.3, *make certain* 840.14
warrantable *vindicable* 441.9
warranted *authorized* 52.11, *legal* 53.16, *rightful* 429.9, *guaranteeing* 458.9, *guaranteed* 464.6, 840.10, *permitted* 502.4, *adopted* 692.10, *permitting* 735.19, *trustworthy* 810.17, *commissioned* 833.6
warrant of arrest *demand* 425.2
warrant officer *army person*

77.17, naval person 77.25, *air force person* 77.31
Warrant Officers *US Military Ranks* 58
Warrant Officer W-1 *US Military Ranks* 58
warranty *certificate* 185.2, *documentation* 339.6, *guarantee* 458.3, 840.4, *promise* 464.2, *permit* 502.3, *permission* 735.9, *safety* 810.1, *authority* 833.3
war readiness *war measures* 76.18
warren *natural habitat* 60.16, *concave land* 635.2, *shelter* 812.4
warring 76.26; *warfare* 76.3, *militant* 418.13, *contentious* 422.20
warrior 76.25; *combatant* 77.1, *soldier* 77.4, *courageous person* 284.8, *attacker* 418.10
warrior for God *militarist* 77.3
Warsaw *Countries* 566
warship 77.21, *Ships and Boats* 690, *vessel* 690.3
war skills *art of war* 76.16
Wars of the Roses *Major Wars* 76
war song *glory of war* 76.17
war strategy *art of war* 76.16
wart *skin disease* 114.16, *mark* 533.2, *hard substance* 542.3, *bulge* 634.2
Warta *Rivers* 570
wartime *belligerency* 76.14
wartime censorship *psychological warfare* 76.13
wartime conditions *belligerency* 76.14
wartime propaganda *psychological warfare* 76.13
war to end all wars *world war* 76.2
war to the end *or* **the death** *warfare* 76.3
war to the knife *warfare* 76.3, 422.10
warts and all *completely* 759.14
warty *coarse* 544.6
war upon *be at war* 76.32
war vessel *warship* 77.21
war whoop *glory of war* 76.17, *warning signal* 814.3
war widow *surviving spouse* 66.6
war work *war measures* 76.18
wary *cautious* 287.6, *suspicious* 314.6, *watchful* 323.6, 325.10, *unenthusiastic* 375.10, *warned* 814.7, *cunning* 822.4
war years, the *belligerency* 76.14
war zone *battleground* 76.24
Wasatch Range *Mountains and Hills* 569
wash *refresher* 94.2, *ablutions* 111.4, *laundry* 111.8, *clean* 111.17, *purify* 111.19, *balm* 115.11, *treat* 130.21, *painting* 143.3, *paint* 143.12, *coloring agent* 251.5, *color* 251.16, *whiten* 253.12, *refine* 534.7, *hose* 557.33, *small lake* 568.2
wash [Inf] *be true* 721.20
wash and brush up *refresher* 94.2
wash-and-wear clothes *store-bought clothes* 100.3
washbasin *bath* 111.6, *basin* 578.12
washboard *washer* 111.7, *skiing snow* 162.3, *rough thing* 544.2
washbowl *bath* 111.6
wash clean *clean* 111.17
washcloth *cleaning cloth* 111.11
wash down *clean* 111.17
washed *cleaned* 111.14, *treated* 130.16, *painted* 143.10, *flooded* 570.8

washed-out *colorless* 252.5

washed-out [Inf] *fatigued* 820.2

washed-up [Inf] *ended* 773.14, *failed* 846.10, *adverse* 848.10

washer 111.7; *fabric-handling tool* 130.12

washer-dryer *washer* 111.7

washerman *cleaner* 111.12

washer-up *cleaner* 111.12

washerwoman *cleaner* 111.12

washing 557.11; *cleaning* 111.2, *ablutions* 111.4, *laundry* 111.8, *fabric treatment* 130.10, *(act of) painting* 143.1, *Phobias* 283, *miscellaneous aviation terms* 689.9

washing and bleaching operations *systems and process control* 14.28

washing machine *washer* 111.7, *fabric-handling tool* 130.12

washing of one's hands *self-exemption* 434.3

washing out *cleaning* 111.2

washing powder *cleaning agent* 111.9

washing soap *fat* 562.4

washing soda *cleaning agent* 111.9

Washington *the power structure* 68.12, *American States* 564

Washington, D.C. *Countries* 566, *major US cities* 567.5

Washington palm *Trees and Shrubs* 43

washing up *laundry* 111.8

wash off *clean* 111.17, *erase* 186.9

wash one's dirty linen in public *show oneself* 843.15

wash one's hands of *leave alone* 413.13, *exempt oneself* 434.12, *diverge* 753.20

washout *flow* 570.4

washout [Inf] *failure* 430.9, *unsuccessful thing* 846.8, *loser* 846.9

wash out *clean* 111.17, *purify* 111.19, *erase* 186.9, *decolor* 252.8

washrag *cleaning cloth* 111.11

washroom *place for excretion* 25.11, *room* 60.9, *bath* 111.6

washstand *bath* 111.6

washtub *washer* 111.7, *basin* 578.12

wash up *clean* 111.17

washwoman *cleaner* 111.12

washy *colorless* 252.5

WASP *Nicknames for Inhabitants* 61

wasp *insect* 40.1, *social insect* 40.6

waspish *cross* 303.11, *bitter* 306.9

waspishly *crossly* 303.20, *bitterly* 306.16

waspishness *crossness* 303.4, *bitterness* 306.5

wasps *Phobias* 283

wasp's nest *dwelling* 40.7, *natural habitat* 60.16

wasp waist *contracted thing* 582.5, *thinness* 595.1

wasp-waisted *thin* 595.9

wassail *get drunk* 121.35

wassailing *drunken* 121.28

wastage *waste* 96.1, 468.5, *reduction* 747.2, *refuse* 802.5

waste 23.11, 96.1, 96.10, 96.15, 468.5, 500.7; *infertile land* 23.2, *infertile state* 23.3, *infertile* 23.7, *excrement* 25.2, *excess* 99.1, *cause to disappear* 265.7, *use* 393.1, *use up* 393.12, *not use* 390.9, *misuse* 395.1, 395.6, *overindulge* 456.11, *be wasteful* 468.16, *consume* 491.12, *product* 522.3, *lay waste* 523.14, *geographical space* 563.3,

desert 572.10, *contract* 582.12, *become smaller* 582.14, *outflow* 707.4, *reduction* 747.2, *residue* 750.2, *futility* 802.3, *refuse* 802.5, *impairment* 808.7, *impair* 808.18

waste [Inf] *murder* 30.20

waste an opportunity *not use* 96.18, *misjudge* 342.9

waste away 96.20; *be unhealthy* 114.29, *lessen* 468.17, *become smaller* 582.14, *be emaciated* 595.16, *decrease* 747.7, *disintegrate* 758.6

wastebasket *cleaning tool* 111.10, *basket* 578.6, *place for waste* 802.6

waste can *cleaning tool* 111.10

wasted *idle* 394.6, *ill-used* 395.4, *dilapidated* 517.7, *ill* 517.8, *of landmasses* 572.12, *shortened* 582.8, *emaciated* 595.10, *futile* 802.10

wasted [Inf] **96.14;** *drugged* 121.30

wasted day *unsuccessful thing* 846.8

wasted effort *misuse* 395.1, *overactivity* 414.9, *waste* 468.5, *waste of effort* 802.4

waste disposal *nuclear problem* 10.62

wasted labor *waste of effort* 802.4

waste effort 802.13; *misspend* 96.17, *act foolishly* 128.10, *misuse* 395.6, *be busy* 414.19

wasteful 96.9; *abusive* 395.5, *overindulgent* 456.8, *unprofitable* 468.10, *extravagant* 500.4, *futile* 802.10

wastefully 96.23; *abusively* 395.8, *at a loss* 468.22, *extravagantly* 500.9

wastefulness *waste* 96.1, 468.5, *overindulgence* 456.3, *extravagance* 500.1, *futility* 802.3

wasteful person *loser* 468.8

wasteland *infertile land* 23.2, *desert* 96.6, 560.4, *havoc* 523.5, *regions* 564.2

waste matter *excrement* 25.2

waste no words *be concise* 198.5

waste no words over *lapse into silence* 208.8

waste of breath *waste* 468.5, *waste of effort* 802.4

waste of effort 802.4

waste of opportunity *neglect* 96.2

waste of space *waste of effort* 802.4

waste of time *waste* 468.5, *waste of effort* 802.4

waste one's breath *be wasteful* 468.16, *waste effort* 802.13

waste one's efforts *be wasteful* 468.16

waste one's time *be wasteful* 468.16, *waste effort* 802.13

wastepaper *refuse* 802.5

wastepaper basket *cleaning tool* 111.10, *basket* 578.6

wastepipe *cleaning tool* 111.10

waste processing *nuclear problem* 10.62

waste product 96.7; *product* 522.3, *refuse* 802.5

waster 96.8; *loser* 468.8, *spendthrift* 500.3

waste reprocessing *nuclear power production* 514.10

waste time *be inactive* 415.13, *wait* 658.12, *be untimely* 660.8, *hesitate* 693.12, *attempt the impossible* 837.10

wasting *shortening* 582.2, *contracting* 582.10, *emaciation* 595.2

wasting [Inf] *murder* 30.2

wasting away 96.4; *sick* 114.24, *underfed* 118.7, *lessening* 468.6, *emaciated* 595.10, *decrease* 747.1, *decreasing* 747.5, *spoiled* 808.9

wasting disease *disease* 114.4

wasting no time *speeding* 694.9

wasting time *slowness* 693.1

wastrel *waster* 96.8, *miscreant* 448.6, *spender* 491.7, *spendthrift* 500.3

Wast Water *Lakes* 568

wat *place of worship* 83.8

watch 242.23; *law enforcement officer* 53.8, *Collective Names* 59, *indicator* 183.7, *suspect* 314.9, *take note of* 323.10, *watchfulness* 325.5, *be careful* 325.11, *discover* 345.11, *not act* 413.11, *push* 414.20, *guard* 419.15, *defend* 419.20, *line of duty* 433.3, *security force* 464.3, *stand by* 575.15, *period of activity* 641.4, *nautical person* 690.12, *surveillant* 810.12, *warner* 814.5

watchable *visible* 242.19

watch and wait *procrastinate* 413.12

watchcase *casing* 613.9

watchdog 810.14; *dog* 35.10, *adviser* 176.5, *observer* 242.15, *moralist* 431.8, *warner* 814.5

watchdog group *motivator* 178.11

watcher *observer* 242.15, *attender* 575.6, *surveillant* 810.12

watchface *face* 646.8

watch fire *signal* 183.6, *fire* 246.9

watchful 323.6, 325.10; *seeing* 242.17, *cautious* 287.6, *suspicious* 314.6, *curious* 321.5, *circumspect* 325.8, *expecting* 356.4, *active* 414.13, *observant* 465.3, *tutelary* 810.19

watchfully 242.29; *cautiously* 287.16, *suspiciously* 314.13, *curiously* 321.9, *attentively* 323.14, *observantly* 465.6, *safely* 810.24

watchfulness 325.5; *observation* 242.5, *caution* 287.1, *suspicion* 314.3, *curiosity* 321.1, *close attention* 323.2, *circumspection* 325.3, *restlessness* 414.7

watching 575.12; *observation* 242.5, *seeing* 242.17, *watchfulness* 325.5, *watchful* 325.10

watching one's weight *or* **figure** *dieting* 595.3

watching the world go by *leisure* 413.4

watch it! *look out!* 814.12

watch like a hawk *watch* 242.23

watchmaker *artisan* 123.13, *horology* 646.6

watchmaking *horology* 646.6

watchman *observer* 242.15, *guard* 419.15, *security force* 464.3, *surveillant* 810.12, *warner* 814.5

watch one's step *proceed with caution* 287.12, *follow the rules* 780.17, *be warned* 814.9

watch one's weight *or* **figure** *become thin* 595.15

watch out *be cautious* 287.11

watch out! *be careful!* 287.20, *look out!* 814.12

watch out for *watch* 242.23, *wait* 356.8

watch over *manage* 126.10, *watch* 242.23, *care for* 325.12, *protect* 613.26, 810.21

watch the clock *measure time* 646.14

watch the float *fish* 154.14

watch the pennies *be poor* 486.14

watch the world go by *have free time* 413.15

watchtower *place for viewing* 242.13, *overview* 425.6

watchword *word of command* 76.20, *maxim* 177.1, *proclamation* 183.8, *means of identification* 184.3

watch your step! *be careful!* 287.20, *look out!* 814.12

water 93.4, 557.1, 557.29; *turbine type* 14.12, *practice livestock farming* 16.20, *cultivate* 17.19, *urine* 25.6, *life requirement* 28.5, *manage grassland* 45.10, *food content* 90.3, *provide drink* 93.21, *type of bed* 101.9, *cleaning agent* 111.9, *transparent thing* 249.4, *Phobias* 283, *make sparse* 541.5, *fluid* 555.1, *nautical* 690.14, *mix* 751.12

water at the mouth *salivate* 25.25, *eat well* 92.23, *leak* 707.16

water balance *atmospheric process* 9.9

water bear *arthropodlike invertebrate* 39.12

water bird 36.9

waterborne *transportable* 686.7, *nautical* 690.14

water bouget [Arch] *water carrier* 557.16

water bowl *farm tool* 16.5

water boy *transferrer* 685.4, *transporter* 686.4

Water Carrier *Constellations* 7

water carrier 557.16

water carrier *or* **bearer** *transferrer* 685.4, *transporter* 686.4

water cart *water carrier* 557.16

water clock *Timepieces and Timers* 646

water closet (WC) *place for excretion* 25.11, *room* 60.9

water cloud *cloud* 9.17

watercolor *painting* 143.3, *illustration* 187.2, *paint* 251.6, *color* 251.16

watercolorist *painter* 143.7

watercolor pigment *paint* 251.6

watercolors *material* 143.9

water-cooled *cooled* 218.11

water course *canoe racing* 150.12

watercourse *river* 570.1, *channel* 691.10

water cure *hydrotherapy* 557.7

water cycle 8.12, 557.17

water-divine *divine* 86.24

water diviner *discoverer* 345.7

water-divining *divination* 86.5

water down 716.17; *play down* 195.17, *dilute* 220.7, 557.30, 776.14, *weaken* 517.13, *make sparse* 541.5, *make thin* 595.17, *make smaller* 747.8, *mix* 751.12

water-driven *fired* 106.13

watered *ornamental* 17.17, *tasteless* 220.4, *iridescent* 263.7, *rarefied* 541.4

watered down *downplayed* 195.13, *tasteless* 220.4, *thinned* 595.13

watered-down *rarefied* 541.4, *diluted* 557.22, 751.9, 776.8

watered-down soup *weak thing* 517.5

watered silk *variegated thing* 263.5

waterfall *power supplier* 514.14,

---

river turbulence 570.5, outflow 707.4, downflow 714.3
water filter *cleaning tool* 111.10
waterfinder *hydrologist* 557.20
water flea *crustacean* 39.10
water flow *flow* 570.4
water fountain *drink provider* 93.15
waterfowl *water bird* 36.9
waterfront 621.3; *edge* 618.1, *edging* 618.5
water hazard *golf course* 156.2
water hole *small lake* 568.2
wateriness 557.3; *lack of emphasis* 201.1, *dilution* 220.2, *transparency* 249.1, *fluidity* 555.5, *moisture* 559.1, *thinning* 595.6, *nonadhesion* 756.1
watering 557.8; *cultivation* 16.7, *gardening* 17.5, *dilution* 220.2, 776.3, *wetting* 557.26
watering can *garden tool* 17.7, *sprinkler* 557.12, *vessel* 578.11
watering cart *water carrier* 557.16
watering down *downplaying* 195.6, *dilution* 220.2, 557.5, 776.3, *thinning* 595.6, *mixture* 751.1, *impairment* 808.7
watering eyes *respiratory disease* 114.12
waterish *watery* 557.21
water jug *water carrier* 557.16
water jump *steeplechase* 166.7
waterless *dry* 560.7
waterlessness *dryness* 560.1
water level *horizontal surface* 603.3
water lily Flowers 42
water line *indicator* 183.7, *measuring instrument* 589.12
waterlog *water* 557.29
waterlogged *wet* 557.23, *of landmasses* 722.12, *unsafe* 811.8
Waterloo *defeat* 846.7
water loss *leak* 816.6
water louse *crustacean* 39.10
waterman *nautical person* 690.12
watermark *indicator* 183.7, *means of identification* 184.3, *measuring instrument* 589.12
watermarked paper *paper* 104.5
water meadow *lowland* 572.6
water meter *meter* 589.13
water mill *renewable energy* 106.9
water pipe *tobacco implements* 121.24, *irrigator* 557.13
water pistol *or* **gun** *sprinkler* 557.12
water pocket *small lake* 568.2
water polo Sporting Activities 145
water power *renewable energy* 106.9, *type of power* 514.6
waterproof 560.16; *treated* 130.16, *treat* 130.21, *keep dry* 560.22, *closed* 584.7, *invulnerable* 810.18, *preserve* 815.14
waterproofed *treated* 130.16, *waterproof* 560.16
waterproofing *fabric treatment* 130.10, *upkeep* 815.5
waterproof paper *paper* 104.5
water's edge *river parts* 570.3, *edge* 618.1
watershed *running water* 8.10, *mountain range* 569.3, *river* 570.1, *swing* 671.4
waterside *river parts* 570.3, *edge* 618.1, *edging* 618.5
water skiing Sporting Activities 145
Water Snake Constellations 7
water-soak *water* 557.29

water-soaked *wet* 557.23
water spirit *legendary sea being* 571.4
waterspout *wind vortex* 9.14, *vortex* 682.6
water sprite *legendary sea being* 571.4
water start *windsurfing terms* 150.21
water supply *irrigator* 557.13
water-supply system *water system* 551.13
water system 551.13; *river* 570.1
water table *groundwater* 8.11
water tank *water carrier* 557.16
watertight *waterproof* 560.16, *closed* 584.7, *complete* 805.14
water tower *storehouse* 105.8, *track* 688.2
water transportation 690.1; *transportation* 686.1
water travel *motion* 677.1
water trough *track* 688.2
water turbine *renewable energy* 106.9
water vapor 556.4; *wateriness* 557.3
water wave *wave* 10.11
waterway 690.2; *river* 570.1, *channel* 691.10
water wheel *power supplier* 514.14, *wheel* 682.9
water wings *survival swimming* 164.4, *safety device* 810.15
water witch *witch* 86.15
waterworks *cleaning tool* 111.10, *power station* 124.12, *irrigator* 557.13
waterworn *uniform* 545.5
watery 557.21; *salivating* 25.18, *insufficient* 98.4, 517.11, *unemphatic* 201.2, *transparent* 249.7, *flowing* 555.15, *misty* 559.10, *thinned* 595.13, *nonadhesive* 756.4
watery-eyed *weak-sighted* 243.10
Watson *psychologist* 108.33
Watsonian psychology Psychological Theories, Schools 108
watt Scientific and Technical Units 589
watt-hour Scientific and Technical Units 589
wattle Trees and Shrubs 43, *braid* 609.3
wattle and daub *construction* 522.9
wattmeter *electrical instrument* 14.41
Watusi Breeds of Cattle 16
wave 8.16, 10.11, 10.77, 571.3, 683.4, 683.15; *gesture* 183.5, 183.17, *flourish* 404.25, *sign of courtesy* 410.5, *greet* 410.11, *coiffure* 530.8, *coif* 530.15, *sea* 571.1, *billow* 571.9, *curve* 629.1, *convolute* 632.6, *radio frequency* 661.3, *be changeable* 666.5, *bodily movement* 677.11, *move* 677.15, *agitate* 684.22, *flicker* 684.26, *display* 843.13
wave a red flag *make violent* 520.10
wave a wand *bewitch* 86.25
wave band *radio transmission* 172.3
wave banners *flourish* 404.25
wave crest *wave form* 10.13, *wave* 571.3
waved *beautified* 530.12, *displayed* 843.8
wave equation *wavelength* 683.5
wave form 10.13

wave frequency *frequency* 663.2
wave goodbye *part* 705.13
wave in the wind *be changeable* 666.5
wave jumping *windsurfing* 150.19
wavelength 683.5; *wave form* 10.13, *radio frequency* 661.3
wavelengths Fields of Measurement 589
wavelet *wave* 571.3
wave mechanics Fields of Modern Physics 10, *quantum theory* 10.64
wave molding Architectural Elements 134
wave motion *wave* 10.11, *frequency* 663.2
wave number *wave form* 10.13, *wavelength* 683.5
wave-particle duality *quantum theory* 10.64
wave pool *swimming place* 164.9
wave power *renewable energy* 106.9, *power source* 514.13
wave propagation *wave* 10.11
wave property 10.12
waver *disbelieve* 88.8, *vacillate* 378.8, 683.14, *defer* 604.15, *irregularity* 664.1, *be irregular* 664.5, *be irresolute* 666.6, *flicker* 684.12, 684.26, *hesitate* 841.18
waverer *vacillator* 378.3, *inactive person* 413.8
wave riding *windsurfing* 150.19
wavering *vacillation* 378.1, 683.3, *swaying* 378.4, *vacillating* 378.5, 683.10, *weak-willed* 517.10, *deferred* 604.9, *irregularity* 664.1, *irregular* 664.3, *irresolution* 666.2, 841.3, *changeable* 666.3, *irresolute* 666.4, 841.10, *capriciousness* 841.8, *capricious* 841.16
waveringly *interruptedly* 604.20, *irregularly* 664.6, *changeably* 666.7, *shakily* 684.28
wavery *flickering* 684.20
waves *erosion* 8.41, Phobias 283
wave sail *windsurf* 150.33
wave sailing *windsurfing* 150.19
wave shape *wave form* 10.13
wave the big stick *be severe* 424.8
wave theory *theory* 10.3
wave to *or on or by or through gesture* 183.17
wave to and fro *wave* 683.15
wave trough *wave form* 10.13
wave up and down *wave* 683.15
wave velocity *wave property* 10.12
wavily *curvedly* 629.7, *circularly* 632.8
waviness *wave* 571.3
waving 683.11; *salute* 405.7, *nonadhesive* 756.4
wavy *rounded* 629.5, *convolutional* 632.4
wax *fat* 12.7, 562.4, Tree Products 43, Bean Varieties 90, *cleaning agent* 111.9, *material* 144.6, *become visible* 264.3, *beauty treatment* 530.3, *harden* 542.9, *soften* 543.14, *polish* 545.3, *smooth* 545.10, *rub* 554.12, *adhesive* 561.3, *oil* 562.3, *lubricant* 562.7, *lubricate* 562.15, *grow* 581.17, *coating* 613.8, *coat* 613.28, *depilation* 614.8, *be converted* 670.12, *change by degrees* 739.8, *increase* 746.6
wax and wane *be changeable* 666.5, *oscillation* 683.1, *oscillate* 683.12
wax a ski *ski* 162.35

wax candle *incandescent light* 246.5
waxed *polished* 545.7
wax eloquent *be diffuse* 199.5
waxen *pale* 253.10, *oily* 562.11
waxer *smoother* 545.2
wax figure *figure* 187.4
waxily *softly* 543.18
waxiness *oiliness* 562.1
waxing *first appearance* 264.3, *appearing* 264.9, *hairdressing* 530.7, *increase* 581.3, 746.1, *growing* 581.12, *depilation* 614.8, *gradational* 739.5, *increasing* 746.4
waxing and waning *changeableness* 666.1
waxing moon *moon* 7.18
wax lyrical *praise* 437.16
wax modeler *sculptor* 144.4
wax modeling *sculpture* 144.1
wax palm Trees and Shrubs 43
wax paper *cooking equipment* 91.6, *paper* 104.5, *wrapping* 613.10
wax tree Trees and Shrubs 43
waxwork *sculpture* 144.1, *figure* 187.4
waxworks *repository* 105.13
waxy *pliant* 543.7, *viscous* 561.14, *oily* 562.11
Way, the Truth, and the Life, the *God the son* 82.9
way 397.3, 399.10, 691.1; *means* 102.1, *approach* 209.3, *course* 387.2, *fashion* 536.1, *style* 537.1, *course* 679.2, *bearing* 697.2, *mode* 725.2, *custom* 780.5, *formula* 780.7
way away *apart* 585.14
way back when *past time* 3.6, *anciently* 653.18
way behind *at a distance* 585.13
waybill *means of identification* 184.3, *statement* 493.2
way down *descent* 714.1
wayfaring tree Trees and Shrubs 43
way forward *course* 679.2
way in *route* 691.2, *entrance* 706.5
way in front *at a distance* 585.13
way it is, the *circumstances* 726.1
way it looks, the *tendency* 838.2
waylay *conceal* 181.12, *be cunning* 822.5
way of doing things *way* 691.1
way of dying 29.5
way off the mark *mistaken* 351.13
way of gentleness, the *judo* 152.13
way of harmony of the spirit, the *aikido* 152.16
way of life 399.9; *life story* 28.11, *religion* 81.1, *way* 397.3, 691.1
way of putting *interpretation* 365.1
way of the empty hand, the *karate* 152.14
way of the foot and fist, the *tae kwon do* 152.15
way of the world *circumstances* 573.2, *state of affairs* 725.4, *average* 742.1
way of things *custom* 780.5
way of thinking 317.4
way out 707.2; *expedient* 387.5, *route* 691.2, *means of escape* 816.4, *deliverance* 817.1
way-out [Inf] *uncustomary* 398.4, *exceptional* 779.13, *eccentric* 782.16
way over *route* 691.2
ways *way* 397.3

ways and means *means* 102.1, *way* 691.1

wayside *near* 586.6, *edge* 618.1, *edging* 618.5

ways of the fathers *tradition* 1.7

way the ball bounces, the [Inf] *potluck* 842.4

way the cookie crumbles, the [Inf] *state of affairs* 725.4, *potluck* 842.4

way things are, the *state of affairs* 725.4, *average* 742.1, *custom* 780.5

way things are going, the *tendency* 513.1

way things shape up *state of affairs* 725.4

way through *route* 691.2

way to *route* 691.2

wayward *willful* 372.8, *refractory* 379.6, *erratic* 381.5, *irresolute* 666.4, *troublesome* 824.13

waywardly *changeably* 666.7, *perversely* 824.27

waywardness *willfulness* 372.3, *capriciousness* 381.2

way with *personnel management* 126.4

way with words *power of speech* 205.5

wayworn *fatigued* 820.2

Waziri *Breeds of Sheep* 16

W chromosome *chromosome* 13.21

we *humankind* 18.1

weak 517.6; *acid* 11.27, *human* 18.15, *drinkable* 93.18, *insufficient* 98.4, *unhealthy* 114.23, *unemphatic* 201.2, *tasteless* 220.4, *faint* 233.6, *murky* 248.5, *spineless* 285.5, *disabled* 515.10, *moderate* 521.3, *rarefied* 541.4, *brittle* 548.3, *diluted* 557.22, *thinned* 595.13, *diminishing* 597.16, *superficial* 599.4, *low quality* 745.7, *imperfect* 806.5, *unsafe* 811.8, *fatigued* 820.2, *failed* 846.10

weak acid *acid* 11.10

weak alkali *base* 11.11

weak as a child *or a baby or a kitten or water* *weak* 517.6

weak bladder *urination* 25.4

weak constitution *ill health* 114.1

weak economy *economy* 56.3

weak effort *imperfect item* 806.3

weak ego *self-deprecation* 403.4

weaken 517.13; *age* 27.16, *waste away* 96.20, *be unhealthy* 114.29, *de-emphasize* 201.3, *dilute* 220.7, *decolor* 252.8, *remove power from* 515.13, *be weak* 517.12, *mitigate* 521.9, *make sparse* 541.5, *make thin* 595.17, *diminish* 597.24, *change for the worse* 665.18, *make smaller* 747.8, *mix* 751.12, *deteriorate* 808.14, *fatigue* 820.6

weakened 517.9; *thinned* 595.13, *diminishing* 597.16, *diluted* 751.9, *spoiled* 808.9, *worn* 808.13, *fatigued* 820.2

weakened state *poor health* 517.3

weakening *aging* 27.13, *tastelessness* 220.1, *thinning* 595.6, *diminishing* 597.16, *decrease* 747.1, *physical deterioration* 808.4

weaker sex [Inf and Off] *womenfolk* 33.14

weak foundation *weakness* 517.1

weak heart *cardiovascular disease* 114.13

weakhearted *weak-willed* 517.10

weak interaction *fundamental interaction* 10.65

weak-kneed *spineless* 285.5, *submitting* 421.3, *weak-willed* 517.10

weak knees *cowardice* 285.1

weakliness *ill health* 114.1, *poor health* 517.3

weakling *sick person* 114.22, *powerless person* 515.5, *weak person* 517.4, *thin person* 595.4, *person in adversity* 848.9

weak link *weakness* 517.1

weak link in the chain *defect* 806.4

weakly 517.14; *unhealthy* 114.23, *unhealthily* 114.31, *unemphatically* 201.4, *without taste* 220.8, *cowardly* 285.9, *powerlessly* 515.16, *ill* 517.8, *weakly* 517.14, *moderately* 521.10, *fragilely* 548.5, *superficially* 599.8, *badly* 745.15, *tiredly* 820.7, *unsuccessfully* 846.21

weak-minded *ill* 517.8

weak morals *sexual immorality* 432.2

weakness 517.1; *insufficiency* 98.1, *ill health* 114.1, *illness* 114.2, *symptom* 114.3, *lack of emphasis* 201.1, *tastelessness* 220.1, *Phobias* 283, *dastardliness* 285.2, *object of desire* 288.8, *inclination* 290.2, *attitude* 513.2, *helplessness* 515.3, *rarefaction* 541.2, *brittleness* 548.1, *thinning* 595.6, *diminishment* 597.7, *superficiality* 599.2, *imperfection* 806.1, *defect* 806.4, *physical deterioration* 808.4, *vulnerability* 811.6, *fatigue* 820.1, *failure* 846.1

weakness for liquor *drinking* 121.2

weakness of the flesh *sexual longing* 20.6, *depravity* 448.2

weakness of will *philosophical problem* 4.8

weak nuclear interaction *fundamental interaction* 10.65

weak person 517.4; *nonentity* 800.8

weak point *depravity* 448.2, *defect* 806.4

weak side *offense* 155.6

weak-sighted 243.10

weak sister [Inf] *weak person* 517.4

weak style *lack of emphasis* 201.1

weak sun *sun* 9.21

weak thing 517.5

weak-willed 517.10

weal *blemish* 533.1, *prosperity* 847.1

Weald, the *regions of the British Isles* 564.8

wealth 485.1; *fertility* 22.1, *resources* 102.4, *personal estate* 470.6, *fortune* 484.4, *independence* 829.5, *successfulness* 845.3, *prosperity* 847.1

wealthily 485.16; *gainfully* 467.24

Wealthy *Apple Varieties* 44

wealthy 485.8; *fertile* 22.8, *well-off* 467.12, *solvent* 484.23, *successful* 845.8, *prosperous* 847.5

wealthy person 485.6; *gainer* 467.9

wean *practice livestock farming* 16.20

weaner *livestock* 16.11, *young mammal* 35.20

wean from *disaccustom* 398.6

wean oneself *renounce* 392.4

weapon 78.1; *agent of destruction* 523.7, *missile* 696.7, *protection* 810.2

weaponless *helpless* 515.9

weapons control *navy specialties* 77.24

wear 100.46; *clothing* 100.1, *handle sailboat equipment* 150.30, *bore* 296.8, *use* 393.1, *use up* 393.12, *lessen* 468.17, *weakness* 517.1, *be weak* 517.12, *agent of destruction* 523.7, *wearing away* 554.2, *erode* 554.14, *navigate* 690.15, *reduction* 747.2, *disintegration* 758.1, *fatigue* 820.6

wear a hair shirt *appear guilty* 450.10, *do penance* 451.9

wear and tear *erosion* 96.3, *use* 393.1, *lessening* 468.6, *agent of destruction* 523.7, *reduction* 747.2, *subtraction* 749.1, *disintegration* 758.1, *physical deterioration* 808.4

wear away *erode* 96.19, 554.14, *lessen* 468.17, *decrease* 747.7, *disintegrate* 758.6

wear down *motivate* 178.17, *weather* 553.29, *fatigue* 820.6

wearied *bored* 296.5, *weakened* 517.9, *fatigued* 820.2

weariful *fatigued* 820.2

wearifulness *fatigue* 820.1

wearily *in a bored manner* 296.9, *tiredly* 820.7

weariness *boredom* 296.1, *poor health* 517.3, *fatigue* 820.1

wearing *sailing terms* 150.5, *boring* 296.6, *lessening* 468.6, *fatiguing* 820.4

wearing a hair shirt *type of penance* 451.3

wearing a sackcloth *type of penance* 451.3

wearing away 554.2; *erosion* 8.41, *disappearance* 265.1, *lessening* 468.6

wearing glasses *bespectacled* 242.18

wearisome *laborious* 122.7, *boring* 296.6, *fatiguing* 820.4, *difficult* 824.9

wearisomely *boringly* 296.10, *tiringly* 820.8

wear mourning *be dark* 247.8

wear on *bore* 296.8

wear one's heart on one's sleeve *be naive* 821.4, *show oneself* 843.15

wear out 808.21; *erode* 96.19, *use up* 393.12, *ill-use* 395.7, *be weak* 517.12, *disintegrate* 758.6, 808.15, *fatigue* 820.6

wear out *or outstay one's welcome* *bore* 296.8

wear the cloth *ordain* 84.16

wear the crown *govern* 49.26, *wield authority* 52.16, *rule over* 780.13, *be victorious* 845.16

wear the laurel wreath *or laurels* *be victorious* 845.16

wear the pants *have authority* 52.13, *be an influence* 512.13

wear the trousers *have authority* 52.13, *direct* 126.11

wear thin *be weak* 517.12, *be brittle* 548.4

wear well *be healthy* 113.11

weary *laborious* 122.7, *bored* 296.5, *bore* 296.8, *weakened* 517.9, *fatigued* 820.2, *fatigue* 820.6

wearying *boring* 296.6, *fatiguing* 820.4

wearyingly *boringly* 296.10

weasel *equivocator* 380.4, *snow vehicle* 687.9

weasel out *be equivocal* 380.7

weaselly *carnivorous* 35.26

weather 9.3, 553.29; *erode* 8.67,

climbing dangers 161.5, *color* 251.16, *navigate* 690.15, *decay* 808.16

weather balloon *weather station* 9.5

weather-beaten *stalwart* 547.10, *worn* 808.13

weatherboard *wood* 131.3, *wall covering* 613.12

weather bureau *weather station* 9.5

weathercock *weather instrument* 9.7, *indicator* 183.7

weather conditions *weather* 9.3

weather data 9.6

weathered 8.61; *soft-hued* 251.13, *colorless* 252.5

weather forecast 9.4; *prediction* 358.1

weather forecaster *meteorologist* 9.2, *broadcasting personnel* 172.11, *forecaster* 358.9

weather forecasting *meteorology* 9.1

weatherglass *weather instrument* 9.7

weather helm *sailing terms* 150.5

weathering 8.40; *colorlessness* 252.1, *decay* 808.6

weather instrument 9.7

weather lore *weather* 9.3

weatherman *meteorologist* 9.2, *broadcasting personnel* 172.11, *forecaster* 358.9

weather map *weather forecast* 9.4

weather observer *meteorologist* 9.2

weather pattern *weather* 9.3

weatherproof *invulnerable* 810.18

weather prophet *meteorologist* 9.2, *diviner* 86.14

weather radar *weather instrument* 9.7

weather report *weather forecast* 9.4

weather satellite *artificial satellite* 7.30, *weather station* 9.5

weather science *meteorology* 9.1

weather ship *weather station* 9.5, *Ships and Boats* 690

weather side *side direction* 623.2

weather situation *weather* 9.3

weather station 9.5; *measuring instrument* 557.19

weather symbols *weather forecast* 9.4

weather system 9.10

weather the storm *show determination* 674.8, *sail* 690.16, *be restored* 809.13, *be safe* 810.20, *get a reprieve* 816.9, *overcome obstacles* 845.14

weather vane *weather instrument* 9.7, *indicator* 183.7

weather-wise *foreseeing* 357.5, *predicting* 358.11

weatherwoman *meteorologist* 9.2, *broadcasting personnel* 172.11, *forecaster* 358.9

weave 130.20, 552.4; *weaving* 130.6, 609.2, *perform* 522.16, *coif* 530.15, *fabric* 551.2, *interweave* 609.8, *form* 624.9, *move* 677.15, *twist* 698.19, *intertwine* 752.19

weave [Inf] *hairdressing* 530.7

weave a plot *be cunning* 822.5

weaver *artisan* 123.13, *fabric handler* 130.11, *weaving* 609.2, *person who joins* 752.9

weaverbird *songbird* 36.12, *weaving* 609.2

weaver's hitch *Knots, Bends, Hitches, Splices* 754

weave together *convolute* 632.6

weaving 130.6, 609.2; Hobbies and Pastimes 167, weave 552.4, interweaving 609.1, forming 624.4, unification 752.5

web spinner 40.10, weaving 130.6, plot 387.6, weave 552.4, braid 609.3, interweave 609.8, mix-up 766.5, stratagem 822.2

webbed interwoven 609.6

webbed feet avian characteristic 36.6

webbing Fabrics and Fibers 130, spinning 130.4, weaving 130.6, interweaving 609.1, braid 609.3

webby interwoven 609.6

web connection superstructure 551.7

weber Scientific and Technical Units 589

web-fed printing book printing 174.10

web of cunning stratagem 822.2

web of deceit stratagem 822.2

web-offset printing 173.3

web of intrigue plot 387.6

web press printing 173.3

website 15.25

Wechsel [Ger] place of exchange 673.2

Wechsler Adult Intelligence Scale (WAIS) Intelligence Tests 108

Wechsler-Bellevue Intelligence Test Intelligence Tests 108

Wechsler Intelligence Scale for Children (WISC) Intelligence Tests 108

wed marry 64.19, propose (marriage) 299.28, contract 459.8, intertwine 752.19, unite sexually 752.20, collaborative 757.7, come together 757.10

wedded married 64.16, related 727.6, united 752.10, enrolled 771.24, associated 794.14

wedded bliss marriage 64.1

weddedness marriage 64.1

wedded status or state marriage 64.1

Weddell Sea Oceans and Seas 571

wedding 64.5; formal occasion 406.4, enrollment 771.8

wedding anniversary anniversary 405.5

wedding announcement general wedding terms 64.6

wedding banns general wedding terms 64.6

wedding bells general wedding terms 64.6

wedding bond marriage 64.1

wedding breakfast general wedding terms 64.6

wedding cake general wedding terms 64.6

wedding canopy general wedding terms 64.6

wedding ceremony wedding 64.5

wedding clothes clothing 100.1

wedding day general wedding terms 64.6

wedding dress general wedding terms 64.6

wedding gown or dress dress 100.11

wedding invitation general wedding terms 64.6

wedding march general wedding terms 64.6

wedding morning general wedding terms 64.6

wedding music general wedding terms 64.6

wedding party 64.7

wedding photographs general wedding terms 64.6

wedding present or gift general wedding terms 64.6

wedding processional general wedding terms 64.6

wedding reception general wedding terms 64.6, social gathering 408.4, party 408.6

wedding recessional general wedding terms 64.6

wedding rehearsal general wedding terms 64.6

wedding ring general wedding terms 64.6, love token 299.8

wedding service wedding 64.5

wedding song general wedding terms 64.6

wedeln skiing techniques 162.5

wedge Accents and Diacritical Marks 5, polyhedron 6.44, simple machine 14.6, Collective Names 59, hand tool 103.3, make ceramics 129.10, golf equipment 156.5, climbing equipment 161.4, skiing techniques 162.5, swimming 164.12, sharp-edged thing 549.6, stopper 584.3, obliquity 628.2, sail 690.16, intertwine 752.19, particle 760.4

wedged ceramic 129.9, tied 752.13

wedge heels or wedgies shoes 100.30

wedge in flood in 706.14, inset 710.13

wedge kick swimming techniques 164.2

wedge-shaped polygonal 6.79, cubic 6.81, sharp 549.10, narrowed 593.9

wedging ceramic process 129.5

Wedgwood or Wedgwood ware Ceramics 129

Wedgwood-blue blue 261.5

wedgy sharp 549.10

wedlock marriage 64.1, sexual union 752.6

wee tiny 580.9

weed farm 16.19, cultivate 17.19, plant 41.2, manage grassland 45.10, subtract 749.6

weed [Inf] hemp derivatives 121.16

weed, the [Inf] tobacco 121.23

weed-choked botanical 17.15, plantlike 41.13

weedily thin 595.18

weediness thinness 595.1

weeding cultivation 16.7, gardening 17.5, displacement 711.2

weeding out selecting 382.4

weed-killer pest control 16.13, pest killer 17.9, killing agent 30.15, poison 117.7

weed out purify 111.19, displace 711.14, make smaller 747.8, reduce 796.8

weeds widowhood 66.5, refuse 802.5

weedy plantlike 41.13, thin 595.9

week seven 792.3

weekday time period 641.2

weekend visit 408.16, time period 641.2

weekend market market 483.1

weekend party party 408.6

weekend warrior [Inf] soldier 77.4, security force 810.13

week in, week out all the time 639.16

weekly magazine 175.3, habitual 397.9, periodical publication 641.6, periodical 641.7, for specified periods 641.12, cyclic 663.7,

cyclically 663.15, regular 730.12, regularly 730.21

weekly market market 483.1

weekly paper newspaper 175.2

weenie [Inf] sausage 90.29

weenie roast [Inf] feast 92.9, party 408.6

weeny [Inf] tiny 580.9

weep 280.8; secrete 24.7, excrete 25.20, fester 25.23, grow 43.15, cry 239.16, grieve 270.7, flow 555.25, seep 559.16, leakage 707.5, leak 707.16

weeper funeral person 31.5, lamenter 280.3

weep for lament 280.7, grieve 308.7

weepily glandularly 24.8, fluidly 555.26, wetly 557.34

weepiness lamentation 280.1

weeping secretion 24.1, secretory 24.4, pus 25.7, cry of sorrow 239.6, crying 239.11, lamentation 280.1, lamenting 280.4, rheumy 555.16, exudate 557.4, seeping 557.25, 559.12, leakage 707.5, leaky 707.12

weeping and wailing funeral 31.4, cry of sorrow 239.6

weeping and wailing and gnashing of teeth sorrow 270.1, lamentation 280.1

weeping willow Trees and Shrubs 43

weep over weep 280.8

weep with grieve 308.7

wee small hours late hour 658.2

weevil pests and diseases 17.12, pest 40.5

weevily verminous 40.13

weewee [Inf] urine 25.6, urinate 25.22, body fluid 555.3

weft weaving 130.6, 609.2, fabric 551.2

weigh 538.15; estimate 341.11, measure 589.20, quantify 738.7, be important 799.13

weigh anchor set out 705.12

weigh a ton [Inf] be heavy 538.12

weighbridge measuring instrument 589.12, miscellaneous automotive terms 687.14

weigh down make heavy 538.14, cause adversity 848.15

weighed deliberate 384.5, ponderous 538.11, quantitative 738.6

weigh equally cancel out 834.8

weigh heavy upon weigh on 538.13

weigh in weigh 538.15

weigh-in horse racing 159.10

weighing 538.4; quantity 738.1

weighing anchor landing 704.2

weighing down 538.5

weighing instrument 538.7

weighing little light 539.4

weighing machine weighing instrument 538.7, measuring instrument 589.12

weighing up equalization 740.4

weigh light upon be unimportant 800.18

weigh little be light 539.8

weigh on 538.13; bear down on 716.18

weigh one down weigh on 538.13, make heavy 538.14

weigh oneself weigh 538.15

weigh out weigh 538.15, measure out 589.21

weigh-out horse racing 159.10

weight 538.8; mass 10.8, grip 151.4, seriousness 200.2,

instrumentality 511.1, influence 512.1, authority 514.5, potency 516.6, material world 524.1, heaviness 538.1, measurability 589.2, measuring instrument 589.12, quantity 738.1, importance 799.1

weight allowance horse racing 159.10

weight cloth horse racing 159.10

weighted wrongful 430.10, heavy 538.9

weighted down ponderous 538.11

weighted mean parameter 6.57

weighted walking stick blunt weapon 78.5

weigh the same be heavy 538.12

weightily heavily 538.16

weightiness importance 278.3, 799.1, formality 406.1, heaviness 538.1

weighting parameter 6.57

weighting down weighing down 538.5

weightless light 539.4, airy 558.12

weightlessness space travel 7.29, lightness 539.1, airiness 558.9

weightlifter person of strength 516.8

weightlifting health improvement 113.3, Sporting Activities 145

weight loss symptom 114.3, dieting 118.2, loss of weight 468.3

weight-loss diet diet 92.5

weight measurement 538.6

weight on one's mind penitence 451.1

weight on one's shoulders burden 826.10

weight problem fatness 579.5

weights horse racing 159.10, instrument of torture 454.14

weight training bodily improvement 807.10

weight-watcher eater 92.15, loser 468.8, thin person 595.4

weight-watching dieting 92.6, 118.2, 595.3, 595.11, abstinence 455.2, loss of weight 468.3

weighty serious 200.5, 799.8, important 278.6, significant 361.11, formal 406.6, causal 511.5, strong 516.9, material 524.7, heavy 538.9, dense 540.6

weigh up think 317.9, discuss 329.12

weigh up the pros and cons balance 378.11

Weimaraner Breeds of Dogs 35

weir dam 551.12, outlet 707.8, barrier 826.7

weird spiritual 86.20, insane 110.9, astonishing 294.10, strange 364.9, unusual 782.15, eccentric 782.16, unbelievable 837.5

weirdly magically 86.28, astonishingly 294.19

weirdness unusualness 782.4

weirdo [Inf] deviant 698.7, eccentric 782.10

weird sister witch 86.15

Weismannism evolution 13.23

Weisshorn Mountains and Hills 569

welcome 408.10, 408.18, 708.14; luscious 214.8, pleasant 271.5, desire 288.17, assent 346.6, salute 405.13, 435.17, popular 408.12, be sociable 408.14, greet 410.11, greeting 435.5, agree with 462.10, receive someone 473.14, timely 659.4, reception 704.3, receptivity 708.2

welcome! 704.24
welcomed *received* 473.11
welcomed with open arms *popular* 408.12
welcome guest *social person* 408.7
welcome home *greet* 410.11
welcome release *way of dying* 29.5
welcome with open arms *be sociable* 408.14, *greet* 410.11, *welcome* 708.14
welcoming 704.12; *friendly* 62.5, *salutary* 209.7, *celebrative* 405.9, *welcome* 408.10, *sociable* 408.11, *courteous* 410.6, *greeting* 435.8, *reception* 473.4, *receptive* 473.10, 708.9, *taking in* 477.7, *receptivity* 708.2
welcoming address *public speaking* 205.11
welcoming ceremony *reception* 473.4
welcoming embrace *welcome* 408.10
welcomingly *receptively* 708.20
welcoming with open arms *receptivity* 708.2
weld *heat* 217.17, *yellow pigment* 259.2, *superstructure* 551.7, *joint* 752.7, *intertwine* 752.19, *cause to adhere* 755.10
welded joint *joint* 752.7
welder *artisan* 123.13, *person who joins* 752.9
welding *unification* 752.5, *adhesion* 755.1
welding torch *material* 144.6
welfare 445.2; *social services* 2.10, *philanthropy* 307.1, *security* 464.1, *national* 566.10, *insurance* 810.10, *social assistance* 825.4, *prosperity* 847.1
welfare economics *economics* 56.1
Welfare Island *Islands* 572
welfare organization *social services* 2.10
welfare services *social assistance* 825.4
welfare state *body politic* 50.3, *social welfare* 307.4
welfare statism *social welfare* 307.4
welfare worker *benevolent person* 305.6, *philanthropist* 307.5
welfarism *social welfare* 307.4
welfarist *benevolent person* 305.6, *philanthropist* 307.5, *philanthropic* 307.6
welfaristic *philanthropic* 307.6
welkin *universe* 7.3, *air* 558.1
well 399.22, 445.19; *source of supply* 105.4, *healthy* 113.4, *skillfully* 127.16, *inspire hope* 281.14, *proper* 429.10, *all right* 429.19, *wealthily* 485.16, *irrigator* 557.13, *hole* 583.4, *outflow* 707.4, *comfortable* 726.10, *sound* 759.8, *successfully* 845.19
well-adapted *qualified* 340.7
well-advised *wise* 352.4
well-affected *benevolent* 825.21
well-appointed *equipped* 388.10
well-armed *strengthened* 516.13
well-arranged *artistic* 133.7
well-balanced *rational* 109.4, *symmetrical* 626.4
well-behaved 399.15; *good-mannered* 410.7, *obedient* 426.4, *moral* 431.9, *kind* 445.12, *principled* 447.6, *disciplined* 765.17
well-behaved person 399.6
well-being *health* 113.1, *pleasure*

214.2, *welfare* 445.2, *comfortable circumstances* 726.5, *ease* 819.1, *prosperity* 847.1
well-born *aristocratic* 70.4
well-bred *aristocratic* 70.4, *well-behaved* 399.15, *good-mannered* 410.7, *cultured* 534.6
well-brushed *smooth* 545.4
well-built *strengthened* 516.13, *attractive* 529.8, *stocky* 579.16
well-cared for *orderly* 765.13
well-chosen *selected* 382.11
well-composed *artistic* 133.7
well-considered *prudent* 287.7
well-crafted *well-made* 127.13
well-cut *stylish* 100.42
well-defended *safe* 810.16
well-defined *recognizable* 363.7
well-deserving *praiseworthy* 437.12
well-disposed *friendly* 62.5, *benevolent* 305.7, 825.21
well-disposedness *benevolence* 305.1
well done! bravo! 437.23
well-done *culinary* 91.9
well-drawn *descriptive* 139.17, 202.11
well-dressed *dressed up* 100.39, *fashionable* 536.5
well-drilled *disciplined* 765.17
well-educated *literate* 348.8
well-endowed *gifted* 127.11, *wealthy* 485.8, *fat* 579.15
well-established *strong* 516.9, *unfailing* 667.3, *stabilized* 674.4
well-fed *eating* 92.18, *fat* 579.15, *thick* 594.5
well-filled *filled* 97.5, *full* 761.8
well-finished *refined* 534.5
well-formed formula (wff) *mathematical logic* 6.60
well-fought *competitive* 422.21
well-founded *in the right* 429.11, *strong* 516.9, *stable* 674.3, *certain* 840.7
well-furnished *filled* 97.5
well-greased *lubricated* 562.14, *wieldy* 823.12
well-groomed *clean* 111.13, *elegant* 527.3, *fashionable* 536.5, *orderly* 765.13
well-grounded *in the right* 429.11, *certain* 840.7
well-grounded hope *chance* 838.4
wellhead *source* 675.2
well-heeled [Inf] *well-off* 467.12, *wealthy* 485.8, *prosperous* 847.5
well-heeled, the [Inf] *the rich* 485.7
well-housed *wealthy* 485.8
well-inclined *approving* 437.9
well I never! *wonderful!* 294.20
well-informed *knowledgeable* 348.7
Wellington *Countries* 566
wellingtonia *Trees and Shrubs* 43
well-intended *friendly* 62.5
well-intentioned *charitable* 305.9, *benevolent* 825.21
well-kept *orderly* 765.13, *preserved* 815.12
well-known *publicized* 173.14, *known* 348.9, *familiar* 397.10, *accentuated* 843.11
well-laid *accessible* 691.13, *cunning* 822.4
well-liked *beloved* 299.19
well-lined *full* 761.8
well-lined purse *wealth* 485.1
well-lit *clear* 244.6, *lit* 246.16, *accessible* 691.13

well-lubricated [Inf] *drunk* 121.25
well-made 127.13; *attractive* 529.8
well-made play, the *dramaturgy* 136.6
well-mannered *likable* 271.6, *well-behaved* 399.15, *kind* 445.12, *refined* 534.5, *smooth-mannered* 545.9
well-mannered person *well-behaved person* 399.6
well-matched *on equal terms* 740.9
well-meaning *friendly* 62.5, *charitable* 305.9, *benevolent* 825.21
well-meant *charitable* 305.9, *benevolent* 825.21
well-nigh *nearly* 586.18
well-nourished *eating* 92.18
well-off 467.12; *wealthy* 485.8, *prosperous* 847.5
well-off, the *the rich* 485.7
well-oiled *lubricated* 562.14, *wieldy* 823.12
well-oiled [Inf] *drunk* 121.25
well-ordered 765.14; *equal* 740.8
well-organized *well-ordered* 765.14
well out or up or over *run out* 707.15
well over *be excessive* 99.9
well-paved *accessible* 691.13
well-paying *gainful* 467.10
well-planned *cunning* 822.4
well-practiced *expert* 127.12
well-prepared *expert* 127.12, *prepared* 388.9
well-preserved *aged* 27.15, *unfailing* 667.3, *preserved* 815.12
well-proportioned *graceful* 527.4, *attractive* 529.8, *symmetrical* 626.4, *well-rounded* 633.8
well-protected *strengthened* 516.13
well-provided *filled* 97.5
well-provided for *well-off* 467.12, *wealthy* 485.8
well-provisioned *filled* 97.5
well-read *educated* 48.19, *literary* 139.15
well-reasoned *rational* 4.15, *purposive* 327.11
well-received *received* 473.11
well-regulated *disciplined* 765.17
well-rehearsed *prepared* 388.9
well-respected *respected* 435.10
well-rooted *stabilized* 674.4
well-rounded 633.8; *phrased* 5.39, *rounded* 633.9
well-rounded shape *round body* 633.2
well-situated *wealthy* 485.8, *situated* 573.5
well-spoken *speaking* 205.15, *simple* 363.6, *good-mannered* 410.7, *refined* 534.5
wellspring *source of supply* 105.4, *source* 675.2, 771.3
well-sprung *elastic* 546.5
well-stocked *filled* 97.5, *full* 761.8
well-tempered *harmonic* 140.27
well-thought-of *reputable* 370.3, *respected* 435.10, *praiseworthy* 437.12
well-thought-out *rational* 4.15
well-thumbed *used* 393.5
well-timed *timely* 659.4, *convenient* 803.3
well-to-do *well-off* 467.12, *wealthy* 485.8, *prosperous* 847.5
well-to-do, the *the rich* 485.7
well-trained *obedient* 426.4

well-turned *phrased* 5.39, *graceful* 527.4, *fluid* 527.5, *well-rounded* 633.8
well turned out *formally dressed* 406.8
well-turned phrase *phrasing* 5.25, *grace* 527.2
well up *drain* 8.64, *flow* 555.25
well-upholstered [Inf] *fat* 579.15
well up on *expert* 127.12
well-used *used* 393.5, *accessible* 691.13
well-ventilated *hygienic* 116.3, *ventilated* 558.17
well-versed *knowledgeable* 348.7
well water *water* 557.1
well-wisher *benevolent person* 305.6, *good person* 445.6
well-wishing *kind* 445.12
well-worn *worded* 5.38, *used* 393.5, *familiar* 397.10, *worn* 808.13
well-worn phrase *catchword* 5.22
Welsh *Breeds of Pigs* 16
welsh [Inf *and* Off] *deceive* 193.16, *not pay* 488.10, 490.9
Welsh accent *regional pronunciation* 205.7
Welsh Black *Breeds of Cattle* 16
Welsh Cob *Horse and Pony Breeds* 159
Welsh corgi *Breeds of Dogs* 35
Welsh daffodil *national emblem* 184.7
Welsh dresser *cabinet* 101.8
welsher [Inf *and* Off] *nonpayer* 490.6
Welsh Grand Committee *British government* 49.22
Welsh Hill *Breeds of Sheep* 16
Welsh leek *national emblem* 184.7
Welsh Mountain *Breeds of Sheep* 16
Welsh Mountain pony *Horse and Pony Breeds* 159
Welsh pony *Horse and Pony Breeds* 159
Welsh sheepdog *Breeds of Dogs* 35
Welsh springer spaniel *Breeds of Dogs* 35
Welsh terrier *Breeds of Dogs* 35
welt *hit* 454.28, *blemish* 533.1
Weltanschauung [Ger] *philosophical system* 4.2
welter *tumult* 684.2, *pitch* 684.25, *bow* 716.22, *confusion* 766.4
weltering *flooded* 557.24
welterweight *boxing weight divisions* 152.6, *combat* 152.17
Weltschmerz [Ger] *boredom* 296.1
wen *written letter* 5.14, *mark* 533.2
wench *young woman* 26.9, *female* 33.1, *domestic servant* 69.7
wenching [Arch] *prostitution* 432.4
Wendigo *Legendary Creatures* 360
Wensleydale *Breeds of Sheep* 16
werecat *sprite* 86.12
werewolf *sprite* 86.12, *frightener* 283.7, *Legendary Creatures* 360, *evil spirit* 446.4
wergild *peace offering* 74.5, *atonement* 313.1, *compensation* 743.1
Wertherism *Western Literary Groups* 139
Weser *Rivers* 570
we shall overcome! *fight on!* 417.16

Wesleyanism Christian Groups 81

Wessex Saddleback Breeds of Pigs 16

West bridge 168.4, regions of the United States 564.7

west side direction 623.2, compass direction 697.5, directional 697.8, directionally 697.20

West African Dwarf Breeds of Sheep 16

westbound directional 697.8

West Coast regions of the United States 564.7

West Country, the regions of the British Isles 564.7

West End London 567.8

West End [Brit] drama 136.1

westerly windy 9.42, directional 697.8, directionally 697.20

Western movie type 137.3, novel 139.3

western regional 564.12, side 623.6, directional 697.8

Western Christianity Christianity 81.5

Western Hemisphere world region 564.6

western hemlock Trees and Shrubs 43

westernly directionally 697.20

westernmost directional 697.8

western red cedar Trees and Shrubs 43

Western roll style jumping 166.11

Western saddle riding equipment 159.9

Western Samoa Countries 566, Islands 572

West Flemish Red Breeds of Cattle 16

West French White Breeds of Pigs 16

West Highland Breeds of Cattle 16

West Highland white terrier Breeds of Dogs 35

West Indies Islands 572

westing compass direction 697.5

Westlands pony Horse and Pony Breeds 159

Westminster London 567.8

Westminster [Brit] the power structure 68.12

Westminster waltz ice-dancing move 162.19

west-northwest directionally 697.20

West Side New York 567.6

west-southwest directionally 697.20

West Virginia American States 564

westward compass direction 697.5, directional 697.8, directionally 697.20

westwardly directionally 697.20

westwork church architecture 134.11

wet 557.23; rainy 9.50, urinate 25.22, political party member 50.6, lenient person 423.2, wateriness 557.3, water 557.29, moist 559.9, moisten 559.13

wetback Nicknames for Inhabitants 61, avoider 386.8

wet behind the ears believing 87.6, unskilled 128.5, raw 260.9, immature 389.9, naive 821.3

wet blanket disaffection 179.3, sad person 270.3, indifferent person 289.6, moderator 521.2, hinderer 826.11

wet-blanket discourage 179.11

wet-bulb thermometer measuring instrument 557.19

wet cell electrochemistry 11.19, power supplier 514.14

wet chinook Notable Winds 9

wet-eyed lamenting 280.4

wet-fly fishing 154.13

wet fly-fishing fly-fishing 154.2

wether livestock 16.11

wetland or **wetlands** shallowness 599.1

wetlands marsh 559.8, 572.3

wet look coiffure 530.8

wetly 557.34; meteorologically 9.60, moistly 559.17

wetness rain 9.27, wateriness 557.3, moisture 559.1

wet oneself urinate 25.22

wet one's whistle [Inf] drink 93.19

wet rot fungus 47.1, dirt 112.5, agent of destruction 523.7, seepage 559.4

wet season rain 9.27

wet snow snow 9.30, 218.6

wet suit suit 100.16

wetter rainy 9.50

wet the bed urinate 25.22

wetting 557.26; watering 557.8

wetting agent pest control 16.13, hydrate 557.6

wettish moist 559.9

wettishness wateriness 557.3, moisture 559.1

wet weather mistiness 559.2

wet with sweat sweaty 25.17

whack bang 234.1, hit 454.28

whack [Inf] experiment 335.1, attempt 390.1, period of activity 641.4, certain amount 738.3

whacked out [Inf] fatigued 820.2

whacking [Inf] huge 579.14

whack off [Inf] stimulate 20.22

Whale Constellations 7

whale big thing 579.9

whaleboat Ships and Boats 690

whaleboned tough 542.6

whalelike cetacean 35.27

whale louse crustacean 39.10, parasite 39.18

whale of a time good time 214.3

whaler Ships and Boats 690

whales Collective Names 59

wham bang 234.1, 234.6

whammy [Inf] spell 86.8, curse 301.1

wharf storehouse 105.8, construction workplace 124.10, marketplace 483.7

wharfage business expenses 491.4

what whatever 778.8

what! wonderful! 294.20

what am I? Children's and Party Games 167

what cannot be impossibility 837.1

whatchamacallit [Inf] anonymity 182.7

what does it matter? who cares? 289.21

what do you know! wonderful! 294.20

what do you know about that! wonderful! 294.20

what-d'ya-call-it [Inf] anonymity 182.7

whatever 778.8

whatever comes chance 842.1

whatever happens chance 842.1, perchance 842.18

whatever next! wonderful! 294.20

what fate has in store future condition 650.3

what for reckoning 454.8

what have you whatever 778.8

what in the world! wonderful! 294.20

what is coming reckoning 454.8

what is done properness 429.5, etiquette 534.3

what is right properness 429.5

what it takes ability 340.2

what it will fetch value 494.2

what makes one tick motivation 508.1

what matters chief thing 799.3

what must be inevitability 95.6

whatnot cabinet 101.8

what on earth! wonderful! 294.20

what one can call one's own possessions 470.5

what one has to one's name possessions 470.5

what one owes debt 488.1

what people do etiquette 534.3

what rot! nonsense! 362.14

what rotten luck! too bad! 848.17

what's happening modernity 647.3

what's-her-name [Inf] anonymity 182.7

what's-his-name [Inf] anonymity 182.7

what's in [Inf] trendiness 652.2

whatsis [Inf] object 524.6

whatsis or **whatsit** [Inf] tool 103.1

what's-its-name [Inf] anonymity 182.7

whatsoever whatever 778.8

what's the dif? [Inf] who cares? 289.21

what's the difference? who cares? 289.21

what's what [Inf] fact 717.6

what the doctor ordered health-giving 113.6

what the future brings or **holds** future condition 650.3

what you will whatever 778.8

whatzit [Inf] anonymity 182.7

wheat crop 16.8, animal feed 16.12, cereal grass 45.4

Wheat Belt farmland 16.3

wheatfield farmland 16.3

wheat germ cereal 90.12

wheatgrass animal feed 16.12

wheat pit market 483.1

Wheatstone bridge circuit 14.37

wheedle persuade 178.15, beg 401.12, cajole 439.14, be cunning 822.5

wheedler persuader 178.9, flatterer 439.6

wheedling persuasion 178.1, cajolery 439.3, cajoling 439.9, inducement 508.2

wheel 682.9; machine element 14.8, hand tool 103.3, guide 126.6, ceramic workshop and tools 129.8, sailboat parts and accessories 150.4, instrument of torture 454.14, circular thing 631.3, turn around 680.22, 698.25, orbit 681.3, reel 684.2, rotator 682.8, rotate 682.14, bicycle part 687.11, ship's steering 690.9, propeller 696.8, propel 696.15

wheel [Inf] bicycle 687.10

wheel and axle simple machine 14.6

wheel and deal [Inf] plot 387.15, influence 512.11

wheel around orbit 681.8

wheel-back type of chair 101.4

wheelbarrow garden tool 17.7, cart 578.9, wagon 687.5

wheelbarrow race Children's and Party Games 167

wheelbase miscellaneous automotive terms 687.14

wheeler-dealer [Inf] politician 50.7, planner 387.9, busy person 414.10, influential person 512.5, celebrity 799.6, cunning person 822.3

Wheeler Peak Mountains and Hills 569

wheel horse workhorse 159.3

wheeling orbital motion 681.1, orbiting 681.7, turning 682.3, rotating 682.11

wheeling and dealing [Inf] tactics 399.12, cunning 822.1

wheel lock historical handgun 78.8

wheelman nautical person 690.12

wheel of fortune luck 842.3

wheel of Ixion wheel 682.9

wheel of life cycle 663.3

wheels racing automobile 146.2

wheels [Inf] automobile 687.6

wheel-shaped circular 681.6

wheels within wheels machinery 103.5

wheel throwing ceramic process 129.5

wheel track furrow 638.1

wheel-tracked furrowed 638.3

wheelwise circularly 681.10

wheel wobble miscellaneous automotive terms 687.14

wheelwork machinery 103.5

wheelwright artisan 123.13

wheeze sound faint 233.8, hiss 237.1, 237.3

wheezily sibilantly 237.4

wheezing hiss 237.1, panting 820.3

wheezy nonresonant 233.7, hissing 237.2

whelk food fish and shellfish 90.20

whelmed flooded 557.24

whelp have young 21.16, young animal 26.4, dog 35.10, young mammal 35.20, give birth 35.33

when at what time 639.17

when all is said and done on the whole 759.13, finally 773.24

when and how one pleases at will 372.16

whence accordingly 735.39

when it comes to the crunch really 719.13

when push comes to shove really 719.13

when the chips are down really 719.13, difficultly 726.20

when the time is right or **ripe** in the future 650.13

where 565.12; here 575.19

whereabouts place of residence 209.4, location 565.1, where 565.12

wherefore accordingly 735.39

wherefrom accordingly 735.39

where it's at [Inf] center of activity 612.4, state of affairs 725.4

where the action is [Inf] center of activity 612.4

where the earth meets the sky distant place 585.3

where the rainbow ends limit 773.7

where there's life never despair! 281.18

whereupon at what time 639.17

wherever you look or **turn** everywhere 776.19

wherewith by means of 102.7

wherewithal *means* 102.1, *funds* 484.6

wherry Ships and Boats 690

wherryman [Brit] *nautical person* 690.12

whet *arouse sensation* 212.11, *sharpen* 549.16

whether willing or not *necessarily* 95.22

whet one's appetite *cause desire* 288.22

whetstone *sharpener* 549.8

whetter *sharpener* 549.8

whet the knife *prepare for action* 388.18

whet the sword *go to war* 76.29

whey *juice* 555.2

which *whatever* 778.8

whichever *whatever* 778.8

whicker *animal sound* 240.1, *make an animal sound* 240.7

whiff *odor* 224.1, *stench* 227.1

whiffle *be changeable* 666.5

whiffletree *figurative usage* 43.9

Whig party Political Parties 50

while *intervening space* 563.8, *duration* 642.1, *as* 649.10

while ago, a *in the past* 651.20

while away *have leisure time* 125.5

while away the time *spend time* 639.14

while back, a *in the past* 651.20

while ill *weakly* 517.14

while keeping watch *observantly* 465.6

whim *conception* 360.4, *caprice* 381.1, *irresolution* 666.2

whimper *express pain* 215.11, *cry of pain* 239.5, *cry* 239.16, *lament* 280.2, *weep* 280.8

whimpering *crying* 239.11

whimsey *conception* 360.4

whimsical *humorous* 277.9, *fantastic* 360.11, *ridiculous* 368.5, *inconstant* 378.6, *capricious* 381.4, 841.16, *irresolute* 666.4

whimsicality *ridiculousness* 368.1, *inconstancy* 378.2, *capriciousness* 381.2, 841.8, *irresolution* 666.2

whimsically *humorously* 277.13, *eccentrically* 368.9, *changeably* 666.7, *capriciously* 841.26

whimsical notion *conception* 360.4

whimsy *conception* 360.4, *caprice* 381.1

whine *mode of speech* 205.6, *speak in a particular way* 205.18, *cry of pain* 239.5, *cry* 239.16, *animal sound* 240.1, *insect sound* 240.3, *make an animal sound* 240.7, *make an insect sound* 240.9, *be dissonant* 241.6, *be dissatisfied* 274.7, *complaint* 304.5, *be irritable* 304.14, *beg* 401.12, *complain* 507.8

whiner *sad person* 270.3, *dissatisfied person* 274.3, *sullen person* 304.7, *protester* 507.4

whinger [Aus inf] *sullen person* 304.7

whinily *irritably* 304.17

whininess *irritableness* 304.3

whining *ululant* 240.4, *sycophantic* 401.7

whiningly *irritably* 304.17

whinny *animal sound* 240.1, *make an animal sound* 240.7

whinnying *ululant* 240.4

whiny *irritable* 304.9

whip *plant blemish* 17.6, *elected official* 50.8, *party official* 68.5, *blunt weapon* 78.5, *cook* 91.10, *percussion instrument* 142.5, *grip*

151.4, *riding equipment* 159.9, *swimming* 164.12, *incentive* 178.4, *motivate* 178.17, *instrument of punishment* 454.13, *hit* 454.28, *negative stimulus* 508.4, *manipulate* 508.12, *make violent* 520.10, *soften* 543.14, *whisk* 558.23, *thicken* 561.21, *agitate* 684.22, *blow* 695.5, *beat* 695.12, *mixer* 751.7, *haste* 818.1, *hasten* 818.4, *defeat* 845.17

whip [Inf] *overtake* 744.16

whipcord *line* 754.5

whip hand *authority* 52.1, *influence* 512.1, *advantage* 618.4

whip in *herd* 59.29

whip into a frenzy *make violent* 520.10

whip into shape *tidy* 765.21

whip kick *swimming techniques* 164.2

whip off *hurry off* 705.11

whipped *motivated* 508.8, *insubstantial* 539.5

whipped potatoes *vegetable* 90.33

whipper *punisher* 454.16

whipper-in *hunter* 385.6

whippersnapper *insolent person* 400.7

whippet Breeds of Dogs 35

whipping *corporal punishment* 454.11, *ramming* 695.3, *victory* 845.4

whipping boy *substitute* 672.2

whipping cream *fat* 562.4

whipping post *instrument of punishment* 454.13

whippletree *figurative usage* 43.9

whipsaw tactics *industrial dispute* 57.7

whip something up [Inf] *cook* 91.10

whipstall *flight maneuver* 689.6

whip up *make violent* 520.10, *agitate* 684.22

whir *small sound* 233.4, *sound faint* 233.8, *humming* 235.2, *hum* 235.11, *resonate* 236.9, *turning* 682.3

whirl *attempt* 390.1, *activity* 414.1, *river turbulence* 570.5, *flow* 570.10, *be in motion* 677.14, *reel* 682.4, *vortex* 682.6, *rotate* 682.14, *haste* 818.1

whirlabout *reel* 682.4

Whirlaway Notable Horses 159

whirl by *make haste* 818.5

whirligig *reel* 682.4

whirling *turning* 682.3, *rotating* 682.11, *speeding* 690.7

whirl like a dervish *rotate* 682.14

whirlpool *convoluted thing* 632.3, *vortex* 682.6, *swirl* 682.16, *hidden danger* 813.3

whirlpool bath *massage* 554.6

whirlpools Phobias 283

whirlwind *wind vortex* 9.14, *vortex* 682.6, *atmospheric agitation* 684.13, *natural hazard* 813.4

whirring *humming* 235.2, 235.7, *resonance* 236.1, *resonant* 236.6, *turning* 682.3

whisk 558.23; *cooking equipment* 91.6, *cook* 91.10, *clean* 111.17, *percussion instrument* 142.5, *agitator* 684.14, *agitate* 684.22, *convey* 685.9, *scamper* 694.12, *blow* 695.5, *tap* 695.13, *mixer* 751.7

whisk broom *cleaning tool* 111.10

whisked *insubstantial* 539.5

whisker *mammalian characteristic* 35.3, *sense organ* 212.4

---

whiskered *hairy* 19.20

whiskers *body covering* 19.4, *rough skin* 544.3

whiskey *alcoholic drink* 93.9

whiskey sour *sour thing* 223.3

whisper *blow* 9.53, *grow* 43.15, *inside information* 170.4, *tip* 170.14, *verbal concealment* 181.3, *utterance* 205.10, *speak in a particular way* 205.18, *undercurrent of sound* 233.3, *sound faint* 233.8, *hiss* 237.1, 237.3, *vilify* 440.14, *quietness* 844.4

whispered *newsworthy* 171.8, *nonresonant* 233.7

whisper endearments *or* **sweet nothings** *communicate love* 299.25

whispering *undercurrent of sound* 233.3, *nonresonant* 233.7, *hiss* 237.1, *hissing* 237.2, *defamatory* 440.9

whisper together *chat* 210.12

whist Card Games 168

whist! *hush!* 231.6

whistle *blow* 9.53, *sound* 141.15, Musical Instruments 142, *gesture* 183.5, 183.17, *signal* 183.6, 183.18, *be loud* 232.8, *shrillness* 238.3, *be shrill* 238.9, *make a bird sound* 240.8, *expression of dissatisfaction* 274.2, *self-defense* 419.5, *acclaim* 437.18, *sea marker* 690.7, *warning signal* 814.3

whistle-blower *informer* 170.8, *discloser* 180.4, *accuser* 442.3

whistle stop *village* 567.3, *railroad station* 688.6

whistling *gestural* 183.13, *shrillness* 238.3, *shrill* 238.6, *acclaim* 437.5

whistling duck *water bird* 36.9

whit *fragment* 787.3, *little bit* 800.4

White *race* 1.5, *racial* 1.12

white 253.7; *eggs* 36.5, *drinkable* 93.18, *clean* 111.13, *unhealthy* 114.23, *drained of color* 252.6, *whiten* 253.12, *pure* 431.11, *innocent* 449.6

white alert *figurative usage* 253.5

white alkali *whitener* 253.3

white ant *white thing* 253.4

white arsenic *whitener* 253.3

white as a ghost *frightened* 283.9

white as a sheet *unhealthy* 114.23, *frightened* 283.9, *ill* 517.8

white as snow *clean* 111.13

white as the driven snow *or a* **ghost** *or a* **lily** *or* **milk** *or* **marble** *or* **ivory** *or a* **sheet** *white* 253.7

whitebait *white thing* 253.4

whitebeam Trees and Shrubs 43

white belt *karate* 152.14, *tae kwon do* 152.15

white blood cell *white thing* 253.4

white blood cell *or* **corpuscle** *blood* 555.4

white bread *bread* 90.10, *white thing* 253.4

White Caceres Breeds of Cattle 16

whitecap *wave* 8.16, 571.3, *white thing* 253.4

white cedar Trees and Shrubs 43

White Cliffs of Dover *white thing* 253.4

white clover *white thing* 253.4

white coffee [Brit] *coffee* 93.6, *white thing* 253.4

white-collar *unionized* 57.14

white-collar class *middle class* 772.6

---

white-collar crime *wicked act* 448.7, *illegality* 450.4

white-collar criminal *dishonest person* 479.11

white-collar union *organized labor* 57.5

white-collar worker *employee* 57.4, *clerical worker* 123.5, *figurative usage* 253.5

white cue ball *billiards* 149.1

White Dorper Breeds of Sheep 16

whited sepulcher *figurative usage* 253.5

white dwarf *stellar evolution* 7.10, *white thing* 253.4

white elephant *burden* 117.3, 826.10, *figurative usage* 253.5, *cheap item* 497.5

White Face Dartmoor Breeds of Sheep 16

white feather *figurative usage* 253.5

white feather [Brit] *cowardice* 285.1

whitefish *white thing* 253.4

white flag *symbol of peace* 73.6, *peace offering* 74.5, *automobile racing terms* 146.3, *white thing* 253.4

white flag, the *submission* 421.1

whiteflies *pests and diseases* 17.12

white flour *white thing* 253.4

whitefly *white thing* 253.4

white foam *wave* 8.16

White Friar *figurative usage* 253.5

white frost *frost* 9.25, *ice* 218.5

White Fulani Breeds of Cattle 16

white gas *petroleum* 562.5

white gold *white thing* 253.4, *bullion* 484.16

white goods *white thing* 253.4, *merchandise* 482.6, 522.6

white-haired 253.9; *aged* 27.15, *old* 653.10

Whitehall [Brit] *the power structure* 68.12

white hat *figurative usage* 253.5

whitehead *mark* 533.2

white heat *heat* 217.1, *fire* 246.9, *white thing* 253.4

white hole *stellar evolution* 7.10

White Holland Breeds of Fowl 16

white hope *figurative usage* 253.5

Whitehorse Canadian Provinces 564

white horse *wave* 8.16, 571.3, *white thing* 253.4

white-hot *hot* 217.11, *whitened* 253.8

White House, the *the power structure* 68.12, *white thing* 253.4

White House, the (Russian) *the power structure* 68.12

White Karaman Breeds of Sheep 16

white keys *white thing* 253.4

White Klementina Breeds of Sheep 16

white knight *figurative usage* 253.5, *defender* 419.14, *good person* 445.6, *protector* 810.11

white knight [Inf] *trader* 480.11

white lead *whitener* 253.3

white lie *falsehood* 192.6, *figurative usage* 253.5, *evasion* 380.2

white light *lighting* 132.16, *white thing* 253.4

white lightning [Inf] *figurative usage* 253.5

white line *indicator* 183.7

white-livered *cowardly* 285.4

whitely 253.13

white magic *witchcraft* 86.6

---

white meat *meat* 90.22, *poultry* 90.28, *white thing* 253.4
white metal *white thing* 253.4
White Mountains *figurative usage* 253.5, Mountains and Hills 569
whiten 253.12; *clean* 111.17, *color* 251.16, *lose color* 252.7, *decolor* 252.8
whitened 253.8; *cleaned* 111.14
whitener 253.3; *color remover* 252.4
whiteness 253.1; *cleanliness* 111.1, *paleness* 252.2, *innocence* 449.1
White Nile *figurative usage* 253.5
whitening 253.2; *paleness* 252.2
white noise *sound* 10.15, 230.1, *radio reception* 172.2, *broadcast dissonance* 241.3
white noise *or* **sound** *undercurrent of sound* 233.3
white notes *part of keyboard instrument* 142.6
white oak Trees and Shrubs 43, *white thing* 253.4
white of the eye *eye* 242.3
whiteout *snow* 9.30, 218.6, *blindness* 243.3
white out *erase* 186.9, *make invisible* 245.7
white pages *book of lists* 785.3
white paint *whitener* 253.3
white paper *white thing* 253.4
White Park Breeds of Cattle 16
White Pekin Breeds of Fowl 16
white pepper Herbs and Spices 91, *seasoning* 221.2, *white thing* 253.4
white phosphorus Chemical Elements and Common Allotropes 11
white phosphorus ammunition *ammunition* 78.11
white pine Trees and Shrubs 43
white poplar Trees and Shrubs 43, *white thing* 253.4
white rainbow *rainbow* 9.28
white rice *rice* 90.32
white rose *white thing* 253.4
White Russia *figurative usage* 253.5
White Russian *reactionary* 427.9
White-Russian Black Pied Breeds of Pigs 16
White-Russian Red Breeds of Cattle 16
whites *uniform* 100.9
white sale *white thing* 253.4, *sale* 482.2
white sauce *sauce* 90.17, *white thing* 253.4
White Sea *figurative usage* 253.5, Oceans and Seas 571
white shark *white thing* 253.4
white-skinned *drained of color* 252.6
white slave trade *or* **traffic** *prostitution* 432.4
white slave traffic *trade* 480.1
White South Bulgarian Breeds of Sheep 16
white spruce Trees and Shrubs 43, *white thing* 253.4
white stick *or* **cane** *aid for poor sight* 243.5
white stuff [Inf] *opiates* 121.17, *stimulants* 121.18, *figurative usage* 253.5
white-tailed deer *or* **whitetail** *white thing* 253.4
white thing 253.4
whitethorn [Brit] *white thing* 253.4
whitethroat *white thing* 253.4
white tie *white thing* 253.4, *formal clothing* 406.5

white-tie *formally dressed* 406.8
white tie and tails *formal clothes* 100.5, *formal clothing* 406.5
White Volta *figurative usage* 253.5
whitewall tire *white thing* 253.4
whiteware Ceramics 129
whitewash *cleaning agent* 111.9, *clean* 111.17, *conceal* 181.12, *misrepresentation* 193.4, *misrepresent* 193.17, *coloring agent* 251.5, *color* 251.16, *whitener* 253.3, *whiten* 253.12, *practice sophistry* 330.11, *cover-up* 441.3, *cover up* 441.13, *wall covering* 613.12, *face* 613.31, *distort the truth* 627.12, *delude* 720.16, *preserver* 815.9, *preserve* 815.14, *defeat* 845.17
whitewashed *whitened* 253.8, *covered* 613.19
whitewasher *vindicator* 441.5, *coverer* 613.18
whitewashing *whitening* 253.2, *cover-up* 441.3, *distortion of truth* 627.4
whitewater *canoeing* 150.26
white water *white thing* 253.4, *river turbulence* 570.5, *hidden danger* 813.3
whitewater canoeing Sporting Activities 145, *canoeing* 150.8
whitewater rafting Sporting Activities 145, *rafting* 150.23, Hobbies and Pastimes 167
white wedding *wedding* 64.5
white whale *white thing* 253.4
white wine *wine* 93.11, *white thing* 253.4
white witch *witch* 86.15
white with dust *whitened* 253.8
whither *where* 565.12
whiting *food fish and shellfish* 90.20, *cleaning agent* 111.9, *whitener* 253.3
whitish *soft-hued* 251.13, *colorless* 252.5, *white* 253.7
whitishness *whiteness* 253.1
Whitney, Mount Mountains and Hills 569
Whitsunday Christian Holy Days and Seasons 85
Whitsuntide *seasons* 654.2
whittle *work wood* 131.9, *sculpt* 144.10, *use a sharp tool* 549.17, *form* 624.9, *make smaller* 747.8
whittle away *contract* 582.12
whittled *woodcrafted* 131.7
whittle down *change by degrees* 739.8
whittling *woodworking* 131.1, *sculpture* 144.1
Whitweek Christian Holy Days and Seasons 85
whiz *expert* 52.8, *hiss* 237.1, 237.3, *acceleration* 694.3, *be swift* 694.10
whiz [Inf] *hard worker* 414.11, *superior person* 445.7
whiz by *accelerate* 694.14
whiz kid [Inf] *expert* 52.8, 127.9, *wonderful person* 294.6, *doer* 412.3, *hard worker* 414.11, *superior person* 445.7, *paragon* 744.6, *successful person* 845.6
whiz off *hurry off* 705.11
whizzing *speeding* 694.7
whoa! *cease!* 668.14
who am I? Children's and Party Games 167
who cares? 289.21; *no matter!* 800.22
whoever *everyone* 778.7
who gives a damn! *no matter!* 800.22
whole 759.1, 759.6, 788.12;

numeration 6.10, *numerical* 6.68, 783.7, *total* 738.4, *quantitative* 738.6, *complete* 761.6, 805.14, *general* 778.9, *mathematical result* 783.4, *safe* 810.16, *preserved* 815.12
whole caboodle [Inf] *unit* 759.5
wholefood restaurant [Brit] *eating place* 92.17
whole-hearted *tenacious* 376.9
wholeheartedness *assiduity* 414.8
whole hog, the *limit* 761.4
whole kit and caboodle [Inf] *unit* 759.5
whole list *unit* 759.5
wholely 738.9
wholeness *whole* 759.1, *completeness* 761.1, *oneness* 788.3, *perfect condition* 805.3
whole nine yards [Inf] *unit* 759.5
whole note *notation* 140.20
whole number *real number* 6.5, *whole thing* 759.2, *kind of number* 783.2
whole picture *circumstances* 573.2, 726.1
wholesale *plentiful* 97.4, *mercantile* 480.13, *selling* 482.1, 482.12, *merchandise* 482.17, *cheaply* 497.16, *complete* 761.6, *including* 763.3
wholesale merchant *merchant* 482.17
wholesale murder *slaughter* 30.5
wholesale price *price* 494.1
wholesaler *provisioner* 89.4, *trader* 480.11, *merchant* 482.10, *discounter* 497.7
whole shebang [Inf] *unit* 759.5
whole shooting match [Inf] *unit* 759.5
whole situation 759.3
wholesome *edible* 92.20, *health-giving* 113.6, *healthful* 113.7, *pure* 431.11
wholesomely *hygienically* 116.5
wholesomeness *healthfulness* 113.2, *purity* 431.4
whole story *fact* 717.6
whole thing 759.2; *total* 738.4
whole thing *or* **lot, the** *all* 759.4
whole time, the *all the time* 639.16
whole truth and nothing but the truth, the *the truth* 721.3
whole-wheat bread *bread* 90.10, *brown thing* 256.3
whole world *all* 759.4
whole world, the *everyone* 778.7
wholly 759.11, 788.22; *clean* [Inf] 111.21, *completely* 759.14, 761.13, 805.22, *overall* 778.22
whomever *everyone* 778.7
whomsoever *everyone* 778.7
whoop *tumult* 232.5, *cry of amusement* 239.2, *cry of praise* 239.3, *laugh* 239.14, *bird sound* 240.2, *chase* 385.13
whooping *shouting* 232.7, *cheering* 239.10
whooping cough *infection* 114.7, *respiratory disease* 114.12
whoop it up [Inf] *rejoice* 279.5
whop [Inf] *blow* 695.5, *hit* 695.11
whopper [Inf] *falsehood* 192.6, *big thing* 579.9
whopping [Inf] *huge* 579.14
whore *loose woman* 33.6, *sexually immoral person* 432.8, *prostitute* 432.17
whoredom *prostitution* 432.4
whorehouse *brothel* 432.5
whoremaster *sexually immoral person* 432.8

whoremastery *prostitution* 432.4
whoremonger *sexually immoral person* 432.8
whoremongering *prostitution* 432.4, *unchaste* 432.10
whoring *prostitution* 432.4
whorish *unchaste* 432.10
whorishness *prostitution* 432.4
whorl *flower part* 42.3, *coil* 632.2
whorled *convolutional* 632.4
whosoever *everyone* 778.7
who's who *book of lists* 785.3
who would have thought it! *wonderful!* 294.20
why, the *reason* 675.4
why and wherefore, the *reason* 675.4
why not? *naturally!* 295.10
wicca *witchcraft* 86.6
wick *fuel starter* 106.3
wicked 448.9; *offending* 53.25, *black-hearted* 254.9, *malicious* 306.8, *badly behaved* 399.16, *disobedient* 427.10, *wrongful* 430.10, *immoral* 432.9, *evil* 446.7, *sinful* 450.8
wicked [Inf] *great* 445.14
wicked! [Inf] *wonderful!* 294.20
wicked act 448.7
wicked behavior *wickedness* 448.1
wicked deed *iniquity* 448.3, *sin* 450.3
wicked jinn *or* **djinn** *evil spirit* 446.4
wickedly 448.15; *guiltily* 53.38, *maliciously* 306.15, *badly* 399.23, *disobediently* 427.14, *wrongly* 430.24, *immorally* 430.27, 432.18, *evilly* 446.12
wickedness 448.1; *lawbreaking* 53.14, *malice* 306.2, *bad conduct* 399.7, *disobedience* 427.1, *wrong* 430.1, *immorality* 432.1, *evil* 446.1, *sin* 450.3
wicked place 448.8
wicked ways *wickedness* 448.1
wickerwork *braid* 609.3
Wicklow Mountain Breeds of Sheep 16
widdershins [Scot] *clockwise* 682.18, 697.17
wide *spacious* 563.13, *huge* 579.14, *at a distance* 585.13, *broad* 592.5, *thick* 594.5, *deep* 598.9, *indirect* 698.9, *quantitative* 738.6, *general* 778.9
wide-angle *broad* 592.5
wide-angle lens *lens* 132.11, *visual aid* 242.14
wide apart *apart* 585.14
wide area network (WAN) *linkage* 752.3
wide-area network (WAN) *computer communications* 15.25
wide awake *sensible* 212.6
wide-awake *circumspect* 325.8
wide away *apart* 585.14
wide berth *avoidance* 386.1, *safety* 810.1, *scope* 829.7
wide-billed *broad-shaped* 592.6
wide-bottomed *broad-shaped* 592.6
wide circulation *publicity* 173.7
wide currency *publicity* 173.7
wide-cut *broad-shaped* 592.6
wide-eyed *wondering* 294.7
wide eyes *warning signal* 814.3
wide horizons *geographical space* 563.3
widely *extensively* 563.18, *largely* 581.18, *openly* 583.22, *distantly* 585.11, *broadly* 592.15, *thick* 594.11, *deep* 598.25, *wholely* 738.9, *universally* 778.23

widely known *publicized* 173.14
widely spaced *sparse* 796.6
wide margin *scope* 829.7
widemouthed *broad-shaped* 592.6
widen *increase* 467.17, *extend* 563.14, *enlarge* 581.14, *broaden* 592.11, 778.15, *make bigger* 746.7
widened *bigger* 581.9, *broadened* 592.7
widener *enlarger* 581.8
wideness *largeness* 579.2, *breadth* 592.1, *thickness* 594.1, *depth* 598.1
widening *augmentation* 467.2, *acquisitive* 467.13, *expansion* 581.1, *growing* 581.12, *increase* 746.1
wide of the mark *mistaken* 351.13, *wrong* 430.12, *at a distance* 585.13, *indirect* 698.9, *astray* 698.27
wide open *swiftly* 694.16, *vulnerable* 811.9
wide-open *bigger* 581.9, *open* 583.10, *broad* 592.5, *unconditional* 829.14
wide-open space *geographical space* 563.3
wide-open spaces *countryside* 564.3, *lowland* 572.6
wide-open speed *swiftness* 694.1
wide range *scope* 829.7
wide-ranging *dominant* 512.10, *extensive* 563.12, *broad* 592.5, *nonadhesive* 756.4, *universal* 778.10
wide-reaching *universal* 778.10
wide receiver *offense* 155.6
wide-screen *broad* 592.5
wide-set *broad* 592.5
wide-spaced *broad* 592.5
widespread *familiar* 397.10, *extensive* 563.12, *bigger* 581.9, *broad* 592.5, *including* 763.3, *dispersed* 776.6, *universal* 778.10, *prevailing* 778.11
widespread cloud *cloud cover* 9.18
wide-spreading *broad* 592.5
widespreadness 778.3
widget *tool* 103.1
widow 66.12; *woman* 27.9, *single woman* 33.5, *woman in the family* 33.13, *surviving spouse* 66.6, *person remaining* 750.6, *single person* 788.7
widowed 66.8; *remaining* 750.7, *single* 788.16
widower *man* 27.8, *single man* 32.5, *man in the family* 32.12, *surviving spouse* 66.6, *person remaining* 750.6, *single person* 788.7
widowered *widowed* 66.8
widowerhood *widowhood* 66.5
widowhood 66.5; *singleness* 788.6
widowish *widowed* 66.8
widowlike *widowed* 66.8
widowly *widowed* 66.8
widowman [Arch] *surviving spouse* 66.6
widow's mite *offering* 472.6
widow's pension *social assistance* 825.4
widow's weeds *widowhood* 66.5, *graveclothes* 100.25, *clothing* 184.6, *formal clothing* 406.5
widow woman [Arch] *surviving spouse* 66.6
width *line* 6.35, *space* 563.1, *size* 579.1, *measurability* 589.2,

breadth 592.1, *thickness* 594.1, *depth* 598.1, *quantity* 738.1
widthwise *or* **widthways** *breadthways* 592.16
wield *use* 393.9, *take action* 509.12
wieldable *wieldy* 823.12
wield authority 52.16
wieldiness 823.3
wield power *be severe* 424.8, *be powerful* 514.18
wield the baton *conduct* 141.17
wield the scepter *govern* 49.26, *wield authority* 52.16, *rule over* 780.13
wieldy 823.12
Wielkopolski Horse and Pony Breeds 159
wiener *sausage* 90.29
wiener roast *feast* 92.9, *party* 408.6
Wiener schnitzel *notable international dishes* 90.40
wienerwurst *sausage* 90.29
wienie roast [Inf] *party* 408.6
Wien's displacement law Classical Physical Laws 10
wife *woman* 27.9, *woman in the family* 33.13, *married woman* 64.11, *family member* 65.2, *master* 68.1, *loved one* 299.13, *partner* 794.9
wifehood *marriage* 64.1
wife in all but name *married woman* 64.11
wife in name only *married woman* 64.11
wifeless *widowed* 66.8, *celibate* 67.6
wifely *matrimonial* 64.15
wife swapping *sexual intercourse* 20.9, *fornication* 432.3
wig *costume* 100.10, *hairdressing* 530.7, *body covering* 613.3
wig [Brit inf] *condemn* 438.18
wigging [Brit inf] *condemnation* 438.2
wiggle *shake* 684.7, 684.24
wiggle out of *escape* 816.8
wiggling *shaky* 684.18
wiggly *shaky* 684.18
Wightman Cup *notable tennis competitions* 165.8
wigmaker *stagehand* 136.29
wigwag *signal* 183.18, *oscillate* 683.12
wigwam *house* 60.4, *mobile home* 60.11, *overhead covering* 613.11
wild 41.15; *infertile land* 23.2, *of animals* 34.13, *disorderly* 51.6, 766.15, *desolate* 96.13, *manic* 110.10, *unskillful* 128.4, *reckless* 286.6, *foolish* 353.5, *unaccustomed* 398.3, *disobedient* 427.10, *unchaste* 432.10, *unrestrained* 500.5, *violent* 520.5, *geographical space* 563.3, *questionable* 839.5
wild about [Inf] *in love* 299.16
wild animal 34.4
wild animals Phobias 283
wild beast *violent animal* 520.4
wild boar *game* 160.6
wild boy *or* **man** *feeling person* 266.8
wild card *cards* 168.2, *poker* 168.5
wildcat *disorderly* 51.6, *disputed* 57.15, *train* 688.4, *independent* 829.12
wild cat *cat* 35.11
wildcats Collective Names 59
wildcat strike *strike* 57.8
wild chance *questionableness* 333.7
wild dash *alacrity* 414.3
wilderness *infertile land* 23.2,

desert 96.6, 572.10, *geographical space* 563.3, *regions* 564.2
wildest dreams *fantasy* 360.5
wildfire *cause of fire* 217.10, *fire* 246.9
wildflower *plant* 41.2, *flower* 42.1
wildfowl *birds* 36.1
wildfowling *animal killing* 30.10
wild goat *game* 160.6
wild goose chase *overactivity* 414.9
wild-goose chase *futility* 282.3, *caprice* 381.1, *waste* 468.5, *waste of effort* 802.4, *unsuccessful thing* 846.8
wild guess *uncertainty* 841.1
wild horse *horse* 159.1
wildlife *wild animal* 34.4
wildlife park *animal welfare* 34.8
wildlife photography *photographic specialties* 132.2
wildlife reserve *ecology* 815.3
wildly *confusedly* 51.11, *recklessly* 286.10, *disobediently* 427.14
wildly speculative *suppositional* 359.5
wild mushroom *mushroom* 47.2
wildness *recklessness* 286.2, *disobedience* 427.1, *violence* 520.1
wild pitch *pitching terms* 147.5
wild rice *rice* 90.32
wild-water *canoeing* 150.26
wild-water race *raft* 150.34
wild-water racing Sporting Activities 145, *rafting* 150.23
wildwood *trees* 43.4
wile *artifice* 193.5, *stratagem* 822.2
wiliness *cunning* 822.1
will 372.1, 372.11, 376.5, 472.11; *bequeath* 372.15, *resolve* 376.12, *determination* 379.2, *predestination* 384.2, *promise* 464.2, *giving* 472.1, *intend* 650.10
will and will not *balance* 378.11
willed 372.6; *bequeathed* 372.10, *deliberate* 384.5, *predestined* 384.6, *given* 472.8
willful 372.8; *intentional* 374.7, *obstinate* 379.5
willful destruction *destruction* 468.7
willfully *intentionally* 374.13, *obstinately* 379.11
willfully destroy *destroy* 468.18
willfulness 372.3; *determination* 379.2
William and Mary Furniture Styles 101
willies [Inf] *symptoms of fear* 283.3, *agitation* 684.1
willing 373.7; *educatable* 48.18, *persuadable* 178.14, *inclined toward* 290.5, *assenting* 346.4, *willed* 372.6, *active* 414.13, *obedient* 426.4, *deferential* 433.9, *kind* 445.12, *agreeing* 462.6, *compliant* 781.9, *benevolent* 825.21, *cooperative* 827.9, *informal* 829.15
willing and able *eager* 373.8
willing giver *generous person* 498.5
willing hand *willing worker* 373.6
willingly 373.15; *admiringly* 290.11, *unanimously* 346.8, *in preparation* 388.22, *obediently* 426.9, *kindly* 445.20, *agreeably* 462.14, *adaptably* 781.15, *benevolently* 825.34, *informally* 829.24
willingness 373.1; *persuadability* 178.8, *inclination* 290.2, *alacrity* 414.3, *obedience* 426.1, *deference* 433.4, *kindness* 445.3, *agreement* 462.1, *helpfulness* 825.10

willingness to learn *educatability* 48.9
willing sacrifice *martyr* 504.6
willing worker 373.6; *tenacious person* 377.5
williwaw Notable Winds 9
will-making *giving* 472.1
will of Allah *inevitability* 95.6
will of one's own *willfulness* 372.3
will-o'-the-wisp *sprite* 86.12, *flickering light* 246.10, *illusion* 720.2
willow Trees and Shrubs 43
willowiness *softness* 543.1, *thinness* 595.1
willowy *treelike* 43.10, *pliant* 543.7, *thin* 595.9
willpower 372.2; *will* 376.5
will to *will* 472.11
will to live *life cycle* 28.7
will wonders never cease! *wonderful!* 294.20
willy-nilly *necessarily* 95.22, *compellingly* 428.12, *inconsistently* 732.16
willy-willy Notable Winds 9
Wilson, Mount Mountains and Hills 569
wilt *pests and diseases* 17.12, *sweat* 25.24, *be dormant* 41.22, *tree disease* 43.8, *waste away* 96.20, *despair* 270.8, *succumb* 421.7, *be weak* 517.12, *dry up* 560.21, *disintegrate* 808.15
wilting *botanical* 17.15, *sweaty* 25.17
Wiltshire Horn Breeds of Sheep 16
wily *artful* 193.13, *cunning* 822.4
wily person *cunning person* 822.3
Wimbledon *notable tennis competitions* 165.8
wimp [Inf] *coward* 285.3, *humble person* 298.7, *submitter* 421.2, *powerless person* 515.5, *weak person* 517.4, *nonentity* 800.8
wimpiness [Inf] *helplessness* 515.3
wimple *vestment* 84.11, *headdress* 100.35
wimp out [Inf] *be a coward* 285.7
wimpy [Inf] *spineless* 285.5
win *extract* 11.41, *master* 68.17, *conquer* 77.36, *pitching terms* 147.5, *horse-racing betting terms* 159.11, *compete in track and field* 166.21, *secure one's objective* 464.12, *gain* 467.15, *take* 477.14, *notch up* 636.6, *be superior* 744.15, *victory* 845.4, *be victorious* 845.16
win a downhill race *ski* 162.35
win an award 467.23
win a *or* **the point** *be victorious* 845.16
win a prize *be rewarded* 453.16, *win an award* 467.23
win at a canter *do easily* 823.16
win a trophy *win an award* 467.23
win a victory *be victorious* 845.16
win by a landslide *be victorious* 845.16
win by a TKO *box* 152.19
win by a whisker *be victorious* 845.16
wince *feel pain* 215.8, *be afraid* 283.14
winch *sailboat parts and accessories* 150.4, *drag* 699.11, *lifter* 715.5
wincing *feeling pain* 215.6
wind 9.12; *erosion* 8.41, *air movement* 9.11, *gastroenterological disease* 114.11, Phobias 283,

empty talk 362.5, prepare for action 388.18, overpower 515.14, belch 556.5, 709.8, airflow 558.4, roll 682.15, means of propulsion 696.2, propellant 696.9, twist 698.19, theory 720.4, fatigue 820.6

windage available space 563.6

windbag [Inf] exaggerator 194.6, talker 207.4, chatterer 210.7, insubstantial person 720.5

windblown untidy 766.11

windbreak protection from the weather 810.9

Windbreaker™ jacket 100.18

wind-chill factor weather data 9.6, cold weather 218.8

wind cone weather instrument 9.7

wind crust skiing snow 162.3

wind-dried baked 560.14

wind-driven fired 106.13

wind-driven generator generator 14.43

wind-dry dry 560.17

winded panting 820.3

winder rotator 682.8

Windermere Lakes 568

windfall 467.7; good thing 445.9, gainful 467.10, giveaway 472.5, extra 748.6

windfall profits tax tax 494.5

wind farm power supplier 514.14

windflower Flowers 42

wind force wind strength 9.13

wind gauge weather instrument 9.7, Fields of Measurement 589

wind generator renewable energy 106.9

wind god 9.16

Windhoek Countries 566

windier windy 9.42

windily meteorologically 9.60, pompously 404.33

wind in drag 699.11

wind in and out diverge 607.11

wind-induced current ocean current 8.15

windiness talkativeness 207.1, sparseness 541.1, belch 556.5

winding flowing 570.7, convolutional 632.4, indirect 698.9

winding course deviating course 698.2

windings generator 14.43

winding sheet funeral object 31.6, graveclothes 100.25

winding staircase stairway 713.9

windjammer Sailing Ships and Boats 690

windlass towline 699.5, lifter 715.5

windless fine 9.43, motionless 678.4

windlessness repose 678.2

windmill renewable energy 106.9, power supplier 514.14, rotator 682.8

window 134.10; Architectural Elements 134, place for viewing 242.13, transparent thing 249.4, glass 249.5, opening 583.1, list 785.1

window box ornamental garden 17.3

window case or frame framework 551.4

window cleaner cleaner 111.12

window covering wall covering 613.12

window display stall 483.9

window dressing exhibitionism 404.9, interior decoration 532.4, show 621.7

window envelope transparent thing 249.4

window glass industrial ceramics 129.6, glass 249.5

windowless unhygienic 114.27, opaque 250.3

window manager system software 15.13

windowpane glass 249.5

window shade protection from the weather 810.9

window-shop shop 481.15

window-shopping reverie 360.6, shopping 481.3

window tax historical tax 494.8

window types window 134.10

windpipe throat 19.12, respiration 558.8

wind player player 141.2

windpower fuels 106.2

wind power renewable energy 106.9, power source 514.13

wind-powered fired 106.13

wind-propelled propelled 696.14

wind pump renewable energy 106.9

wind rose weather instrument 9.7

windrow farmland 16.3

windscreen place for viewing 242.13

wind shear wind 9.12, miscellaneous aviation terms 689.9

windshield glass 249.5

windshield wiper cleaning tool 111.10

wind shift wind 9.12

windslab skiing snow 162.3

wind sleeve weather instrument 9.7

windsock weather instrument 9.7, indicator 183.7

Windsor Bean Varieties 90, type of chair 101.4

Windsor green green pigment 260.3

Windsor knot Knots, Bends, Hitches, Splices 754

Windsor red red pigment 257.2

Windsor tie neckwear 100.29

Windsor violet purple pigment 262.2

Windsor yellow yellow pigment 259.2

wind speed weather data 9.6, wind strength 9.13, Fields of Measurement 589

windstorm natural violence 520.3

wind storm wind 9.12

wind strength 9.13; weather data 9.6

windsurf 150.33

windsurfer boating person 150.24

windsurfing 150.19, 150.28; Sporting Activities 145, boating sports 150.1

windsurfing classes 150.22

windsurfing terms 150.21

windsurf racing windsurfing 150.19

wind system 9.15

wind together convolute 632.6

wind tunnel miscellaneous aviation terms 689.9

wind turbine renewable energy 106.9

windup pitching terms 147.5, conclusion 761.3, end 773.1

wind up prepare for action 388.18, sell off 482.20, be unable to pay 490.11, activate 509.11, invigorate 518.5, close down 584.15, stop work 668.11, drag 699.11, end 773.19, discontinue 846.14

wind up accounts settle accounts 493.11

wind vortex 9.14

windward side direction 623.2, side 623.6, toward 697.18

Windward Islands Islands 572

windy 9.42; diffuse 199.3, talkative 207.5, meaningless 362.7, pompous 404.18, sparse 541.3, flatulent 556.18, breezy 558.15, not serious 800.11

wine 93.11; alcoholic drink 93.9, provide drink 93.21, alcohol 121.5, Phobias 283

wine and dine feed 90.41

wine bar drink provider 93.15

winebibber drinker 93.16, drunkard 121.8

winebibbing drinking 93.1, 121.2, drunken 121.28

wine bottle bottle 578.14

wine cellar storeroom 105.7

wine-colored red 257.5

wined and dined popular 408.12

wineglass drink container 93.13

wine list bill of fare 785.5

winemaking Hobbies and Pastimes 167

wine merchant drink provider 93.15

wine palm Trees and Shrubs 43

winery drink provider 93.15

Winesap Apple Varieties 44

wineskin bottle 578.14

wine steward attendant 69.4

winetaster drinker 93.16

winetasting drinking 93.1

wine vinegar basic cooking ingredient 91.8

wine, women, and song good time 214.3

win fame be prosperous 847.6

win fame and glory be prosperous 847.6

win for Christ proselytize 84.15

win freedom escape 816.8

win friends befriend 62.10

win friends and influence people befriend 62.10

wing assemblage of birds 36.18, fly 36.23, military organization 58.4, party 59.3, armed force 77.10, air force unit 77.29, poultry 90.28, type of chair 101.4, stage set 136.19, sailboard parts 150.20, convey 685.9, be swift 694.10, additional item 748.3, collection 757.3, component 760.3

wing and wing sailing terms 150.5

wingback offense 155.6

winged chiropteran 35.25, swift 694.6

winged insect insect 40.1

winged messenger messenger 685.5

winger hockey player 158.8, soccer participant 163.4

wing feather plumage 36.7

wing flat stage set 136.19

wing-footed swift 694.6

wing half hockey player 158.8, soccer participant 163.4

wing it [Inf] act 136.34, improvise 389.11

wing loading miscellaneous aviation terms 689.9

win glory be prosperous 847.6

wing mirror reflector 242.10

win going away defeat 845.17

wingover flight maneuver 689.6

wings avian characteristic 36.6, stage 136.18, racing automobile 146.2, insignia 184.5

wingspan breadth 592.1, miscellaneous aviation terms 689.9

wingspread breadth 592.1

wing tips shoes 100.30

win hands down do easily 823.16, defeat 845.17

win in a walk do easily 823.16

win in straight sets defeat 845.17

wink Children's and Party Games 167, inside information 170.4, gesture 183.5, 183.17, see badly 243.16, light up 246.20, communication of love 299.6, communicate love 299.25, approval 437.1, approve 437.14, warning 814.1, warn 814.8

wink at be blind to 243.19, show mercy 312.11, not observe 466.9

winking gestural 183.13, faulty vision 243.1, weak-sighted 243.10, lucent 246.13

winkle food fish and shellfish 90.20

winkle out [Brit inf] extract 711.13

Winnebago Lakes 568

winner titleholder 72.4, chosen thing 382.8, good thing 445.9, gainer 467.9, paragon 744.6, certainty 840.1, successful person 845.6, victor 845.7

winner's circle racetrack 159.12

Winnibigoshish Lakes 568

winning card-playing 168.6, enticing 178.13, lovable 299.20, gain 467.1, taking 477.1, attractive 477.13, unbeatable 744.13, best 805.9, successful 845.8, victorious 845.10

winning by a mile victory 845.4

winning card expedient 387.5

winningly takingly 477.23

winning position advantage 744.3

winning post objective 374.5, destination 704.6

winnings 492.5; something received 473.2, takings 477.8

winning streak good fortune 847.2

winning ticket horse-racing betting terms 159.11

winning ways enticement 178.3, lovability 299.5

Winnipeg Canadian Provinces 564, Lakes 568

Winnipegosis Lakes 568

Winnipesaukee Lakes 568

winnow choose 382.14

wino [Inf] drunkard 121.8

win one's spurs attain one's goal 845.17

win on moves be victorious 845.16

win on points be victorious 845.16

win over conciliate 74.10, make someone believe 87.11, persuade 178.15, 670.14, influence 508.11

win praise meet with approval 437.20

win renown do great deeds 412.14

winsome likable 290.7, lovable 299.20, beautiful 529.7

winsomely likably 290.12, lovably 299.31

winsomeness lovability 299.5

Winston Cup race races 146.4

winter 654.6; cold weather 9.24, 218.8, season 654.1, spend the season 654.10

winter aconite Flowers 42

Winter Banana Apple Varieties 44

winter barley crop 16.8

winter bud bud 41.8

winter feed animal food 90.2

winter garden garden 17.2

wintergreen Herbs and Spices 91

winter-hardy *botanical* 17.15
winter jasmine Flowers 42, *yellow thing* 259.4
winterlike *seasonal* 654.7
winter oats *crop* 16.8
winter of discontent *time of adversity* 848.4
winter of one's life *old age* 27.5
Winter Olympics *Alpine ski championships* 162.6, *cross-country skiing championships* 162.9, *prize competition* 422.5
winter sale *sale* 482.2
winter solstice *winter* 654.6
wintertide *winter* 654.6
wintertime *winter* 654.6
Winter War *Major Wars* 76
winter wheat *crop* 16.8
wintery *seasonal* 654.7
win the battle *be victorious* 845.16
win the game *be victorious* 845.16
win the heart of *win the love of* 299.27
win the last battle *be victorious* 845.16
win the lottery *win an award* 467.23
win the lottery *or* **sweepstakes** *get rich* 485.13
win the love of 299.27
win the match *be victorious* 845.16
win the pools [Brit] *win an award* 467.23, *get rich* 485.13
win the prize *or* **championship** *or* **blue ribbon** *or* **cup** *be superior* 744.15
win the race *accelerate* 694.14, *be victorious* 845.16
win through *secure one's objective* 464.12
wintrily *coldly* 218.16, *seasonally* 654.12
wintriness *cold weather* 9.24, 218.8
wintry *cold* 218.9, *seasonal* 654.7
winy *intoxicating* 121.29
wipe *clean* 111.17, *make transparent* 249.12, *cause to disappear* 265.7, *absorb* 560.20
wipe away one's tears *grieve* 308.7
wipe clean *clean* 111.17
wiped away *forgiven* 312.5
wiped out *impoverished* 486.11, *destroyed* 523.9, *no more* 718.11, *canceled* 834.5
wiped out [Inf] *dead drunk* 121.27
wiped-out *defeated* 846.11
wipe dry *absorb* 560.20
wipe off *erase* 186.9
wipe off *or* **away** *clean* 111.17
wipe off the face of the earth *slaughter* 30.21
wipe off the map *destroy* 186.10, *abolish* 523.11
wipeout [Inf] *unsuccessful thing* 846.8
wipe out *slaughter* 30.21, *windsurf* 150.33, *erase* 186.9, *cause to disappear* 265.7, *abolish* 523.11, *cause not to exist* 718.14, *annihilate* 773.22, *not exist* 786.6, *cancel* 834.6, *defeat* 845.17
wipe-out *windsurfing terms* 150.21
wipe out a score *retaliate* 420.4
wipe the floor with [Inf] *defeat* 845.17
wipe the plate clean *be greedy* 119.4
wipe the slate clean *absolve* 312.10, *confess* 451.8, *forgive a debt* 490.12, *become new* 652.19

wipe the smile off one's face *be serious* 278.7
wipe up *clean* 111.17, *absorb* 560.20
wiping up *cleaning* 111.2
wire *conduct* 14.51, *data transmission* 169.8, *communicate* 169.18, 170.12, *communication* 170.2, *mail* 685.10, *line* 754.5
wire brush *percussion instrument* 142.5
wired (up) *connected* 754.11
wiredrawn *delicate* 552.10, *fine* 595.12
wirehaired dachshund Breeds of Dogs 35
wirehaired pointing griffon Breeds of Dogs 35
wirehair fox terrier *or* **wirehaired terrier** Breeds of Dogs 35
wireless [Brit] *radio* 172.1
wireless communication *radio* 172.1
wire-mesh *fencing* 153.6
wire-mesh mask *fencing equipment* 153.2
wire netting *farm building* 16.4
wirepuller *person in authority* 52.7, *motivator* 178.11, *cunning person* 822.3, *backstage manipulator* 844.3
wirepulling *authority* 52.1, *indirect influence* 512.4
wires *indirect influence* 512.4
wire sculpture *sculpture* 144.1
wire service *news source* 171.4
wiretap *recording instrument* 185.9
wireworm *pests and diseases* 17.12, *worm* 39.14, *pest* 40.5, *larva* 40.9
wiriness *stalwartness* 547.3, *thinness* 595.1
wiry *stalwart* 547.10, *thin* 595.9
Wisconsin American States 564, Rivers 570
wisdom 352.1; *divine attribute* 82.4, *prudence* 287.2, *cleverness* 315.3, *reason* 319.1, *judgment* 341.1, *learning* 348.3, *foresight* 357.1, *profundity* 598.5
wisdom tooth *teeth* 19.8
wise 352.4; *adult* 27.11, *middle-aged* 27.14, *educated* 48.19, *skillful* 127.10, *advisable* 176.8, *prudent* 287.7, *intelligent* 315.9, *reasoning* 319.7, *judicious* 341.8, *knowledgeable* 348.7, *foreseeing* 357.5, *awe-inspiring* 435.12, *profound* 598.15, *way* 691.1, *convenient* 803.3, *cunning* 822.4
wiseacre [Inf] *insolent person* 400.7, *vain person* 402.7
wise-ass [Inf] *insolent person* 400.7, *rude* 400.9, *vain person* 402.7
wisecrack [Inf] *joke* 277.6, 368.4, *be humorous* 277.11
wisecracker [Inf] *humorist* 277.7
wised up [Inf] *informed* 170.9
wise guy [Inf] *insolent person* 400.7, *vain person* 402.7
wise-guy [Inf] *rude* 400.9
Wise Lord *God* 82.6
wisely 4.28, 352.8; *educationally* 48.25, *advisably* 176.13, *prudently* 287.17, *intelligently* 315.14, *judicially* 341.12, *foresightedly* 357.10, *profoundly* 598.27
wise man *sage* 4.11, *expert* 52.8, *educational leader* 68.11, *knowledgeable person* 348.5, *wise person* 352.3, *intellectual* 315.7

wisenheimer [Inf] *insolent person* 400.7
wise person 352.3
wiser *improved* 807.12
wise to [Inf] *knowledgeable* 348.7
wise up [Inf] *inform* 170.11, *understand* 295.6
wise woman *sage* 4.11, *expert* 52.8, *diviner* 86.14, *wise person* 352.3
wish 288.2; *aspiration* 281.3, *aspire* 281.13, *object of desire* 288.8, *likes* 290.3, *demand* 356.9, *reverie* 360.6, *will* 372.1, 372.11, *request* 505.1
wishbone *avian characteristic* 36.6, *talisman* 86.9, *poultry* 90.28, *windsurfing* 150.28, *fork* 703.5
wishbone boom *sailboard parts* 150.20
wished *desired* 288.10
wished for *liked* 290.6
wisher *desirer* 288.9
wish for *like* 290.8
wishful *aspiring* 281.8, *desirous* 288.13, *envious* 314.4
wishfully *desirously* 288.26
wishful thinker *visionary* 360.9
wishful thinking *defense mechanism* 108.23, *self-deception* 193.2, *hope* 281.1, *idealism* 327.7, *fallibility* 351.6, *reverie* 360.6, *theory* 720.4
wish ill *curse* 301.13
wishing *liking* 290.1, 290.4
wishing for *envy* 314.1
wishing stone *talisman* 86.9
wishing well *talisman* 86.9
wish list *list* 785.1
wish the best for *be benevolent* 305.10
wish to *enjoy* 290.9
wish undone *be penitent* 451.7
wish well *be benevolent* 305.10
wishy-washiness *dilution* 220.2, *inconstancy* 378.2
wishy-washy *unemphatic* 201.2, *tasteless* 220.4, *insufficient* 517.11, *politically moderate* 521.4
Wisla Rivers 570
wisp *little person* 580.5, *fineness* 595.5, *particle* 760.4
wispiness *sparseness* 541.1
wisp of cloud *cloud appearance* 9.19
wisp of smoke *miasma* 556.3
wispy *sparse* 541.3, *fine* 595.12
wispy cloud *cloud appearance* 9.19
wisteria Flowers 42
wistful *desirous* 288.13
wistfully *desirously* 288.26
wistfulness *desire* 288.1
wit 277.3; *humor* 277.1, *humorist* 277.7, *cleverness* 315.3, *intellect* 348.4, *intelligence* 352.2
wit *or* **wits** *intelligence* 315.2
witch 86.15; *unpleasant woman* 33.7, *frightener* 283.7, *wonderful person* 294.6, *irascible person* 303.7, *wise person* 352.3, *evil spirit* 446.4
witchcraft 86.6; *occultism* 86.1, *impiety* 448.4, *occult influence* 512.2, *type of power* 514.6
witch doctor *witch* 86.15, *warner* 814.5
witchery *witchcraft* 86.6, *enticement* 178.3
witches' brew *mixed thing* 751.2
witches'-broom *tree disease* 43.8
witches' Sabbath *non-Christian ritual* 85.8, *witchcraft* 86.6
witch hazel Trees and Shrubs 43
witch hunt *pursuit* 385.1

witch-hunt *discriminate against* 337.14, *pursue* 385.11
witch hunter *bigot* 337.7, *punisher* 454.16
witch-hunting *zealous* 81.22, *social discrimination* 337.4
witching hour *witchcraft* 86.6
witchlike 86.19
witchman *witch* 86.15
witch master *witch* 86.15
witch of Agnesi *curve* 6.38
Witch of Endor *witch* 86.15
witch's broomstick *talisman* 86.9
witch's hat *hat* 100.32
witchwoman *witch* 86.15
witchwork *witchcraft* 86.6
with *by means of* 102.7, *instrumentally* 511.9
with a bad attitude *pessimistically* 190.26
with abandon *excessively* 829.23
with a break apart 587.8
with acknowledgment *avowedly* 189.34
with a clear conscience *innocently* 449.13
with a clear head *sober* 120.5, *soberly* 120.9
with a credit card *on loan* 476.14
with a deafening roar *loudly* 232.11
with a difference *originally* 737.8
with a disadvantage *unequally* 741.10
with a disclaimer *retractively* 190.24
with a dominating manner *superiorly* 744.20
with a dowry *proprietarily* 470.14
with a drink problem *drunken* 121.28
with affection *amicably* 62.13, *admiringly* 290.11, *lovingly* 299.29
with a fine-tooth comb *meticulously* 726.18
with a flourish *showily* 404.29
with a frog in one's throat *voiceless* 206.5
with a frown *or* **scowl** *or* **grimace** *crossly* 303.20
with a generous heart *receptively* 473.15
with a glib tongue *cunningly* 822.6
with agreement *agreeably* 462.14
with a guilty conscience *guiltily* 450.12, *penitently* 451.10
with a handicap *unequally* 741.10
with a heavy hand *severely* 424.11
with a heavy heart *unwillingly* 375.17
with a helping hand *favorably* 62.15
with a hop, skip, and a jump *jerkily* 684.29
with a jealous heart *jealously* 314.12
with a lick and a promise *superficially* 599.8
with a light hand *leniently* 423.6
with a light rein *leniently* 423.6
with a light touch *lightly* 539.10
with all documents *verifiably* 336.11
with all due respect *respectfully* 435.19
with all haste *hastily* 818.7
with all its faults *imperfectly* 806.10
with all one's heart *with feeling* 266.18, *willingly* 373.15

with all one's love *lovingly* 299.29

with all one's might *laboriously* 122.13, *ambitiously* 390.10, *powerfully* 514.21

with all the trimmings and then some *fully* 761.14

with a long face *unwillingly* 375.17

with a lot of nerve *defiantly* 416.9

with a loving heart *ethically* 447.10

with a mind to *willed* 372.6

with a motive *deliberate* 384.5

with an advantage *unequally* 741.10, *superbly* 744.22

with an aim in mind *purposively* 327.20

with an air of superiority *authoritatively* 52.18

with an easy conscience *innocently* 449.13

with an empty stomach *fasting* 118.5

with an eye to *with the intention of* 374.14

with an eye to the main chance *enterprising* 391.5

with anger *angrily* 302.24, *disapprovingly* 507.10

with an indifferent attitude *freely* 829.22

with an intermission *apart* 587.8

with an interval *apart* 587.8

with an iron hand *severely* 424.11

with a noose around one's neck *endangered* 811.10

with an open heart *naively* 821.5

with an open mind *impartially* 289.19, *disinterestedly* 443.8, *receptively* 473.15

with antagonism *aggressively* 63.14, *in defiance* 416.10

with aplomb *skillfully* 127.16

with appropriate papers *verifiably* 336.11

with approval *agreeably* 462.14

with a promise *assuredly* 189.30

with a remainder **750.12**

with a sense of duty *dutifully* 433.19

with a sharp tongue *ill-naturedly* 303.18

with a single mind *agreeably* 462.14

with a sparing hand *economically* 499.7

with a sprint *fast* 166.23

with assurance *assuredly* 189.30, *as promised* 458.16, *surely* 464.15

with a steady pace *equitably* 740.15

with a stiff upper lip *disinterestedly* 443.8, *calmly* 455.16

with astonishment *with surprise* 292.13

with a straight face *solemnly* 278.9

with a stroke *actively* 412.18

with a strong tendency *probably* 513.6

with a tight fist *tenaciously* 471.11

with a tongue in one's head *speaking* 205.15

with authenticity *contractually* 462.15

with authority *authoritatively* 52.18, *legitimately* 52.19, *influentially* 512.14, *superiorly* 744.20

with authorization *or*

permission *or* approval *legitimately* 52.19

with avarice *immorally* 432.18, *avariciously* 477.22

with a vengeance *with vigor* 518.6, *violently* 520.11, *additionally* 748.15, *fully* 761.14

with a view to *purposively* 327.20

with a volley of abuse *rudely* 411.9

with a warm welcome *receptively* 473.15

with a whole skin *safe* 810.16

with a will *willingly* 373.15, *with vigor* 518.6

with balance *gymnastically* 157.13

with bated breath *faintly* 233.11, *expectantly* 356.10

with body and soul *earnestly* 376.16

with both oars in the water [Inf] *sane* 109.3

with brute force *roughly* 547.18

with candor *informally* 829.24

with cap in hand *servilely* 401.15

with care *carefully* 325.13

with caution *cautiously* 287.16

with certainty **840.16**

with charity *as a gift* 472.17

with child *pregnant* 21.12

with clarity *intelligibly* 363.13

with clean hands *incorrupt* 449.7, *innocently* 449.13

with clemency *compassionately* 305.14

with cohesion *as one* 752.21

with commitment *assuredly* 189.30

with compassion *pityingly* 308.11, *soft-heartedly* 543.19

with compliments *approvingly* 437.21

with confidence *commandingly* 425.15

with consent **735.38**; *contractually* 459.9

with consideration *compassionately* 305.14

with consistency *compatibly* 462.16

with constancy *morally* 431.15

with conviction *emphatically* 200.7

with cooperation *agreeably* 462.14

with courtesy *courteously* 410.13

with deception *thievishly* 479.19

with deep feeling **598.29**

with deference *deferentially* 410.15

with delay **826.22**

with deletions *under censorship* 503.13

with determination *determinedly* 674.10

with devotion *intimately* 62.14

with difficulty *difficultly* 824.23, *in the way* 826.23

with dignity **297.20**; *genteelly* 410.14

with discretion *judiciously* 337.16, *selectively* 382.17, *aloofly* 756.10

with dissent *disunitely* 753.25

with distinction *with honor* 58.16, *aristocratically* 70.6, *with dignity* 297.20

with downcast eyes *shyly* 403.16

with dragging feet *unwillingly* 375.17

withdraw **392.5, 705.9**; *disavow* 190.18, *depart* 265.6, *be indifferent* 289.12, *deny* 332.8, *equivocate* 380.8, *retreat* 386.22,

680.17, *stop using* 394.10, *be unsocial* 409.10, *acquiesce* 421.5, *take back* 477.17, *demonetize* 484.25, *bank* 484.26, *absent oneself* 576.15, *cease* 668.9, *reverse* 671.9, *exit* 707.13, *extract* 711.13, *subtract* 749.6, *be one* 788.17, *cancel* 834.6, *resign* 835.5

withdrawal **121.11**; *mood disorder* 108.12, *defense mechanism* 108.23, *disappearance* 265.1, *denial* 332.2, *dissentience* 347.3, *oblivion* 355.4, *vacillation* 380.3, *shyness* 386.3, *relinquishment* 392.1, *unsociability* 409.1, *cessation* 668.1, *return* 671.3, *backward motion* 677.5, *retreat* 680.2, *departure* 705.1, *extraction* 711.1, *subtraction* 749.1, *setting apart* 753.2, *escape* 816.1, *resignation* 835.1, *failure* 846.1

withdrawal sickness *withdrawal* 121.11

withdrawal symptoms *withdrawal* 121.11

withdraw from circulation *demonetize* 484.25

withdraw from currency *make useless* 802.12

withdrawing *taking back* 477.4

withdraw into the background *follow* 745.12

withdrawment *retreat* 680.2

withdrawn *introverted* 108.37, *silent* 181.10, *taciturn* 208.4, *indifferent* 289.7, *oblivious* 355.9, *unsociable* 409.6, *monetary* 484.22, *ceased* 668.6, *subtracted* 749.3, *unjoined* 753.9, *alone* 788.15

withdrawn coinage *false money* 484.15

withdraw the charge *vindicate* 441.11

with due deference *submissively* 298.23

withe *line* 754.5

with ease *easily* 819.5

with efficiency *operationally* 509.13

with eloquence *emphatically* 200.7

with embarrassment *inhibitively* 826.24

with empathy *agreeably* 462.14

with emphasis *affirmatively* 189.29, *defiantly* 416.9

with empty pockets *unprovided* 98.6

with energy *energetically* 514.22

with enmity *hostilely* 63.13

with envy *hostilely* 63.13, *enviously* 314.11

wither *be dormant* 41.22, *waste away* 96.20, *afflict* 117.16, *heat* 217.17, *dry up* 560.21, *become smaller* 582.14, *grow old* 653.16, *decrease* 747.7, *disintegrate* 808.15

withered *infertile* 23.7, *dilapidated* 517.7, *dried-up* 560.9, *shortened* 582.8, *emaciated* 595.10, *spoiled* 808.9

withering *drying* 560.3, *shortening* 582.2

withershins *clockwise* 682.18, 697.17

with evil intent *maliciously* 306.15

with evil intentions *wickedly* 448.15

with exactitude *carefully* 325.13

with expertise *masterfully* 68.19

with fear and trembling *fearfully* 283.19

with feeling **266.18**; *sensitively* 267.6

with few words *concisely* 198.6

with firmness *densely* 540.10, *inflexibly* 542.13

with flair *stylistically* 537.11

with flying colors *showily* 404.29, *victoriously* 845.20

with folded arms *inactively* 413.16

with footwork *professionally* 152.22, *on guard* 153.8

with forbearance *abstemiously* 417.15

with force *by request* 505.14

with foresight *foresightedly* 357.10

with forethought *intentionally* 374.13, *predeterminately* 384.11

with genius *skillfully* 127.16

with gentleness *lightly* 539.10

with giant leaps *swiftly* 694.16

with giant strides *swiftly* 694.16

with good cheer *cheerfully* 269.14, *sociably* 408.19

with good effect *successfully* 845.19

with good grace *pleasantly* 271.12, *willingly* 373.15, *courteously* 410.13

with good *or the best of* intentions *virtuously* 447.9

with good results *successfully* 845.19

with goodwill *philanthropically* 307.9

with gratitude *gratefully* 310.8

with great admiration *admiringly* 290.11

with great charm *sociably* 408.19

with great *or telling effect* *influentially* 512.14

with great weight *heavily* 538.16

with gusto *willingly* 373.15

with haste *actively* 414.24

with hate **300.13**; *malevolently* 306.14, *evilly* 446.12

with hat in hand *submissively* 298.23

with head held high *proudly* 297.19

with heart *with deep feeling* 598.29

with heart and soul *laboriously* 122.13

withheld *retained* 471.6, *refused* 506.5, *interrupted* 604.10

with high spirits *cheerfully* 269.14

withhold *keep secret* 182.11, *detain* 471.9, *interrupt* 604.16, *delay* 658.13, *preserve* 815.14, *make impossible* 837.8

withhold approval **438.17**

withhold assent *dissent* 506.9

withhold consent *dissent* 506.9

withholding *refused* 506.5, *interruption* 604.4

withholding tax *tax system* 494.6

withhold payment *stop payment* 490.10

withhold permission *prohibit* 503.8

with honesty *ethically* 447.10

with honeyed words *flatteringly* 439.16

with honor **58.16**; *virtuously* 447.9

with hope *hopefully* 281.15

with hostility *aggressively* 418.27, *in disagreement* 463.12, *disapprovingly* 507.10, *disunitely* 753.25

with humility **421.8**

with idealism *subjectively* 525.14

with ill will *malevolently* 306.14

with imagination *imaginatively* 360.17, *originally* 737.8
with immunity *freely* 829.22
with impunity 434.13; *safely* 810.24
within *subjectively* 525.14, *internally* 577.15, 611.18, *inclusively* 763.8
within, the *interior* 611.1
within bounds *reasonably* 319.15, *temperate* 455.8, *moderately* 455.15, 521.10
within call *aurally* 228.16, *nearby* 586.17
with indignation *irritably* 302.23
withindoors *internally* 611.18
within earshot *hearable* 228.12, *aurally* 228.16, *nearby* 586.17
within hearing *aurally* 228.16, *nearby* 586.17
with inhibitions *inhibitively* 826.24
within limits 620.8; *moderately* 521.10
within limits *or* **bounds** *moderate* 521.3
within living memory *in the past* 651.20
within one's depth *shallowly* 599.7
within one's means *cheap* 497.9
within one's power *practically* 836.10
within one's rights *by rights* 429.17
within range *hearable* 228.12, *aurally* 228.16, *moderately* 521.10, *nearby* 586.17
within reach *readily available* 575.21, *nearby* 586.17, 803.7, *conveniently* 803.6, *practically* 836.10
within reach *or* **sight** *or* **call** *available* 575.11
within reason *moderately* 455.15, 521.10, *moderate* 521.3
within reasonable limits *temperate* 455.8, *moderately* 455.15
within sight *visually* 242.27, *nearby* 586.17, *practically* 836.10
within someone's orbit *influentially* 512.14
with integrity *morally* 431.15
with interest *profitably* 492.8, *additionally* 748.15
within the bounds of *gradational* 739.5
within the law *legal* 53.16, *legally* 53.33
within the self *inwardly* 611.21
with it [Inf] *educated* 48.19, *fashionable* 536.5, *present* 647.4, *avant-garde* 652.16
with justice *equitably* 740.15
with justification *justifyingly* 441.15
with kid gloves *leniently* 423.6
with kindness *benevolently* 305.13, *courteously* 410.13, *leniently* 423.6
with legal protection *with permission* 502.10
with light fingers *thievishly* 479.19
with little or no thought *unpremeditated* 389.7
with longing *lustfully* 20.24
with love *admiringly* 290.11, *lovingly* 299.29, *benevolently* 305.13, *sociably* 408.19
with loving kindness *benevolently* 305.13
with luck *prosperously* 847.9
with malice *with hate* 300.13,

resentfully 302.22, *vindictively* 441.16, *evilly* 446.12
with malice aforethought *intentionally* 374.13
with malice aforethought *or* **prepense** *maliciously* 306.15
with many words *diffusely* 199.7
with material *materially* 524.9
with meaning *meaningfully* 361.16
with meditation *intentionally* 374.13
with mercy *compassionately* 305.14, *pityingly* 308.11
with might and main *laboriously* 122.13, *earnestly* 376.16, *actively* 414.24, *powerfully* 514.21, *strongly* 516.17
with misgivings *discontentedly* 291.17
with moderation *moderately* 455.15, 521.10
with modesty *unselfishly* 443.9, *self-restrainedly* 830.19
with momentum *dynamically* 695.16
with moral rectitude *morally* 431.15
with much ado *difficultly* 824.23, *with delay* 826.22
with need 95.20
with noble intentions *unselfishly* 443.9
with nobody the wiser *secretly* 182.14
with no expense spared *generously* 498.12
with no frills *boringly* 296.10
with no guilt *faultlessly* 449.14
with no holds barred *openly* 180.13, *excessively* 829.23
with no interest *indifferently* 289.17
with no letup *continually* 669.10
with no questions asked *with permission* 502.10
with no regrets *impenitently* 452.5
with no remorse *impenitently* 452.5
with no strings attached *persuasively* 504.18, *excessively* 829.23
with not a moment to lose *or* **spare** *hastily* 818.7
with nothing on *revealingly* 614.22
with nothing to hope for *poor* 486.8
with no thought for others *egoistically* 444.9
with objectivity *materially* 524.9
with obligations *undertaken* 391.4
with offense *villainously* 448.18
with official approval *under commission* 833.11
with one accord *unanimously* 346.8, *in accord* 735.33, *cooperatively* 827.18
with one bite *gluttonously* 119.5
with one foot in the grave *aged* 27.15
with one hand tied behind one's back *easily* 823.19
with one's back to the wall *endangered* 811.10, *blocked* 826.13, *in the way* 826.23, *unprosperous* 848.11
with one's cards on the table *manifestly* 348.15
with one's eyes closed *easily* 823.19
with one's hands *industrially* 57.22

with one's hands in one's pockets *inactively* 413.16
with one's head in the clouds *thoughtlessly* 318.15, *imaginatively* 360.17
with one's heart in one's mouth *fearfully* 283.19
with one's pants down [Inf] *unprepared* 389.5
with one's tail between one's legs *embarrassedly* 298.24
with one thought *agreeably* 462.14
with one voice *unanimously* 346.8, *agreeing* 462.6, *agreeably* 462.14, *synchronously* 649.9, *in accord* 735.33, *cooperatively* 827.18
with open arms *amicably* 62.13, *willingly* 373.15, *sociably* 408.19, *receptively* 708.20
with open doors *publicly* 173.20
with open hands *charitably* 305.15, *generously* 498.12
with openness *receptively* 473.15
with oppression *burdensomely* 538.17
with others in mind *unselfishly* 443.9
without *losing* 468.9, *under the circumstances* 726.16, *by subtraction* 749.8
without a bean [Brit inf] *insolvent* 486.10
without a care in the world *thoughtlessly* 318.15
without a case *convicted* 54.26
without a cent *insolvent* 486.10
without a change of plane *horizontally* 603.11
without a change of scenery *or* **pace** *boringly* 296.10
without acknowledgment *thanklessly* 311.7
without a clue *unexplained* 364.6
without a conscience *impenitent* 452.2
without a cooperative spirit *uncooperatively* 506.11
without action *inactively* 413.16
without admiration *without wonder* 295.8
without ado *easily* 823.19
without adornment *plainly* 424.12
without a doubt *authentically* 721.31
without affectation *naively* 449.15, 821.5
without affiliation *freely* 829.22
without a hangover *sober* 120.5
without a hitch *easily* 823.19
without airs *humble* 298.8
without a job *unemployed* 413.10
without a leg to stand on *convicted* 54.26
without a pang of regret *impenitent* 452.2
without appreciation *ungratefully* 311.6
without approval *disapprovingly* 507.10
without art *naive* 821.3
without artifice *naive* 821.3, *naively* 821.5
without a shadow of a doubt *certainly* 840.15
without a sign of life *inactive* 413.9
without a solution *unexplained* 364.6
without assistance *unsociably* 409.13, *with delay* 826.22

without a stain *immaculate* 805.11
without a stain on one's character *acquitted* 54.25
without a stitch on *revealingly* 614.22
without authority *anarchically* 51.10, *unlawful* 53.23, *illegally* 53.34, *powerlessly* 515.16
without authorization *prohibitively* 503.11
without a word *taciturnly* 208.9, *unsocially* 409.13
without a worry *carelessly* 289.18
without ballast *inconstant* 378.6
without bearing a grudge *forgivingly* 312.13
without bias *truthfully* 191.9, *right* 429.15, *disinterestedly* 443.8
without blemish *immaculate* 805.11
without body *nonmaterial* 525.8
without ceasing *frequently* 661.7
without ceremony *modestly* 403.15, *informally* 407.11
without charge *free of charge* 497.12
without charm *discourteously* 411.8
without commitment *irresolutely* 461.10
without comparison *originally* 737.8, *supremely* 744.23
without compassion *pitiless* 309.3, *pitilessly* 309.7
without compromise *severely* 424.11
without compunction *impenitent* 452.2, *impenitently* 452.5
without concern *without wonder* 295.8
without conditions *with permission* 502.10
without consistency *differently* 463.13
without content *vacant* 576.12
without control *excessively* 829.23
without cooperation *in disagreement* 463.12
without defect *infallible* 805.10
without delay *immediately* 645.8, *early* 657.17, *hasty* 818.3, *hastily* 818.7
without demur *willingly* 373.15
without difficulty *easily* 823.19
without distinction *right* 429.15
without effect *weakly* 517.14
without embarrassment *defiantly* 416.9
without emotion *calmly* 455.16
without employment *unemployed* 413.10
without end *at length* 590.15, *everlastingly* 642.10, *eternally* 644.10, *numberless* 795.8, *infinitely* 798.10
without enemies *harmless* 73.9
without enthusiasm *unwillingly* 375.17
without equal *best* 744.10
without equality *roughly* 544.13
without exaggeration *truthfully* 191.9
without exception *regularly* 730.21, *wholly* 759.11, *including* 763.3, *usually* 778.21
without excess *with self-restraint* 455.14
without excuse *guilty* 450.6, *guiltily* 450.12
without exemption *wholly* 759.11
without fairness *unjustly* 741.12
without fault *skillfully* 127.16

without fear *peacefully* 73.12
without fear *or* favor *right* 429.15
without fear of contradiction *assuredly* 189.30
without feelings *indifferently* 289.17
without flexibility *inflexibly* 542.13
without food *fasting* 118.5, *abstemiously* 118.11
without foundation *without truth* 722.14
without fuss *or* frills *modestly* 403.15
without gloss *colorless* 252.5
without grounds *without truth* 722.14
without guile *naively* 821.5
without harmony *in disagreement* 463.12
without hearing *deaf* 229.4
without help *aloofly* 756.10, *with delay* 826.22
without hesitation *voluntarily* 373.17, *agreeably* 462.14
without holes *dense* 540.6
without honor *irresolutely* 461.10
without hope **282.7**
without importance *unimportant* 800.10
without integrity *dishonorably* 192.28
without intelligence *unintelligently* 316.9
without interruption *continually* 669.10
without issue *unproductively* 23.12
without justice *unjustly* 741.12
without legal backing *unlawful* 53.23, *illegally* 53.34
without let or hindrance [Form] *easily* 823.19
without limit *numberless* 795.8, *infinitely* 798.10
without limit *or* end *infinite* 798.5
without looking *blindly* 243.20
without looking back *impenitently* 452.5
without loss *complete* 805.14
without manners *uncustomary* 398.4
without mass *nonmaterial* 525.8
without meaning *meaningless* 362.7
without morals *carelessly* 289.18, *immorally* 432.18, *depraved* 448.10, *unvirtuously* 448.16
without movement *inactively* 413.16
without moving *fastly* 464.16, *inextricably* 752.23
without notice *soon* 657.18
without number *immeasurable* 798.6
without obligations *celibately* 67.12
without offspring *unproductively* 23.12
without omission *including* 763.3
without one's husband *without one's spouse* 66.14
without one's spouse **66.14**
without one's wife *without one's spouse* 66.14
without order *inconsistently* 732.16
without overdoing it *with self-restraint* 455.14
without pausing for breath *everlastingly* 642.10
without paying **490.15**

without payment *as a gift* 472.17
without permission *prohibitively* 503.11
without pity *pitilessly* 309.7
without planning *unpremeditated* 389.7
without prejudice *disinterestedly* 443.8, *equitably* 740.15
without preparation *unreadily* 389.16
without pretensions *naively* 821.5
without prompting *voluntarily* 373.17
without prospects *poor* 486.8
without qualms *impenitently* 452.5
without question *certainly* 840.15
without regard to morality *disobediently* 427.14
without regret *impenitently* 452.5
without regrets *impenitent* 452.2
without regularity *roughly* 544.13
without relevance *irrelatively* 728.16
without remorse *impenitent* 452.2, *impenitently* 452.5
without resistance *with humility* 421.8
without resolution *irresolutely* 461.10
without resource *helpless* 515.9
without respect *rudely* 411.9
without respite *continually* 669.10
without restraint *excessively* 829.23
without rhyme or reason *meaningless* 362.7, *in disorder* 766.24
without risk *secure* 464.5, *surely* 464.15, *trustworthy* 810.17, *safely* 810.24
without roughness *smoothly* 545.13
without scruples *impenitently* 452.5
without seeing the error of one's ways *impenitently* 452.5
without shame *defiantly* 416.9
without shape *incompletely* 544.14
without significance *unexceptionally* 289.20
without similarity *differently* 463.13, *disparately* 728.19
without sin *virtuously* 447.9
without skill **282.10**
without speaking *taciturnly* 208.9
without stint *enough* 97.10, *excessively* 829.23
without stop *frequently* 661.7
without stopping *everlastingly* 642.10, *frequently* 661.7, *continuously* 774.16
without strings *permitted* 502.4, *with permission* 502.10, *unconditional* 829.14
without substance *lightly* 539.10, *unreally* 722.15
without success *unsuccessfully* 846.21
without sympathy *hostilely* 63.13
without taste **220.8**
without thanks *thanklessly* 311.7
without the law *lawless* 53.26
without thinking *unintelligently* 316.9, *wrongly* 351.18, *systematically* 397.22
without tricks *naive* 821.3
without trouble *soothingly* 545.14
without truth **722.14**

without turning a hair *without wonder* 295.8
without variety *boringly* 296.10
without violence *peacefully* 73.12
without warning *surprisingly* 292.14, *suddenly* 549.20, *unexpectedly* 839.9
without wasting words *concisely* 198.6, *summarily* 204.10
without weight *light* 539.4
without wonder **295.8**
with patience *forgivingly* 312.13
with permission **502.10;** *by request* 505.14, *with consent* 735.38
with pleasure *pleasingly* 214.15, *pleasantly* 271.12
with plenty of time *early* 657.17
with power *authoritatively* 52.18, *dynamically* 695.16
with praise *approvingly* 437.21
with precision *carefully* 325.13
with prejudice *wrongly* 430.24
with pride *proudly* 297.19
with promise *favorably* 62.15, *auspiciously* 458.17
with propriety *well* 399.22
with provisions *feasibly* 460.9, *relatively* 726.17
with prudence *moderately* 455.15
with pure intentions *innocently* 449.13
with qualifications *conditionally* 340.16, *justifyingly* 441.15
with reason *as evidence* 339.15
with recourse to *by means of* 102.7
with regret *unwillingly* 375.17, *penitently* 451.10
with regularity *regularly* 397.21
with relevance *suitably* 462.17
with repentance *penitently* 451.10
with reproach *guiltily* 450.12
with reservations *exclusively* 764.10
with reserve *uncandidly* 192.29
with resistance *uncooperatively* 506.11
with resolution *tenaciously* 471.11
with respect *genteelly* 410.14
with responsibility *under commission* 833.11
with restraint *uncandidly* 192.29
with restrictions *under censorship* 503.13, *exclusively* 764.10
with satisfaction **273.13**
with sealed lips *sparing with words* 208.6
with self-control *with self-restraint* 455.14
with self-motivation *freely* 829.22
with self-restraint **455.14**
with self-restraint *or* control *ethically* 447.10
with skill *expertly* 52.21, *skillfully* 127.16
with softness *softly* 543.18
with someone's leave *with consent* 735.38
with sorrow *guiltily* 450.12
with spirit *proudly* 297.19
withstand **828.20;** *defy* 416.7, *resist* 417.10, *survive* 419.31, *contend* 422.22, *dissent* 506.9, *counteract* 510.7, *support* 605.16
withstanding *resistance movement* 417.3, *resistant* 417.6
withstand testing *suffice* 97.6
with sticky fingers [Inf] *thievishly* 479.19
with stiffness *toughly* 542.12

with strings attached *conditionally* 340.16, *restrained* 830.9
with style *stylistically* 537.11
with superiority *superiorly* 744.20
with supervision *industrially* 57.22
with suppleness *elastically* 546.10
with surprise **292.13**
with swordplay *on guard* 153.8
with sympathy *agreeably* 462.14
with taste *tastefully* 534.9
with telling effect *powerfully* 514.21, *with vigor* 518.6
with tender loving care *benevolently* 305.13
with tenderness *lightly* 539.10, *soft-heartedly* 543.19
with thanks *or* special thanks *gratefully* 310.8
with the aid of *by means of* 102.7, *instrumentally* 511.9
with the beat *synchronized* 649.5
with the best of intentions *charitable* 305.9, *innocently* 449.13
with the crowd *easy* 823.9
with the current *or* tide *easy* 823.9
with the effect of **676.12**
with the exception of *by subtraction* 749.8, *exclusively* 764.10
with the help of *instrumentally* 511.9
with the intention of **374.14**
with the object of *with the intention of* 374.14
with the odds stacked against one *unequally* 741.10
with the proviso *conditionally* 340.16
with the rest *with a remainder* 750.12
with the result that *with the effect of* 676.12
with the throttle wide open *with vigor* 518.6
with the worst intentions *maliciously* 306.15
with time to spare *early* 657.17
with tongue in cheek *untruthfully* 192.27, *humorously* 277.13, *hypocritically* 330.15, *affectedly* 367.5
with tooth and nail *earnestly* 376.16
with two wives *matrimonially* 64.23
with urgency *by request* 505.14, *hastily* 818.7
with velocity *fast* 166.23
with vengeance **420.6**
with vigor **518.6**
with whip and spur *at full speed* 694.17
witless *unintelligent* 316.6, *simpleminded* 526.11
witlessness *ignorance* 316.3
witness **54.16, 339.7;** *informer* 170.8, *affirmer* 189.9, *observer* 242.15, *see* 242.20, *person questioned* 333.10, *verifier* 336.4, *prove* 336.9, *testify* 336.10, *give evidence* 339.12, *accuse* 442.8, *attender* 575.6, *stand by* 575.15
witnessed *verifiable* 336.5, *evidential* 339.8, *watching* 575.14
witness for the prosecution *accuser* 442.3
witnessing *watching* 575.12

witness list *pretrial proceedings* 54.13

witness stand *courtroom* 54.12

witness to *signify* 183.16

wits *rationality* 109.2, *intelligence* 352.2

Wittgensteinian Philosophical Schools of Thought 4

Wittgensteinianism Philosophical Schools of Thought 4

witticism *maxim* 177.1, *wit* 277.3, *joke* 277.6

wittily *humorously* 277.13, *funnily* 368.10, *sociably* 408.19

wittiness *humor* 277.1

wittingly *intentionally* 374.13

witty 277.10; *proverbial* 177.2, *sociable* 408.11

witty repartee *answer* 334.1

wive *marry* 64.19

wiz *expert* 52.8

wizard *expert* 52.8, *witch* 86.15, *skilled person* 127.7, *secret person* 182.6, *wonderful person* 294.6

wizard! [Brit inf] *good!* 445.24

wizardlike *witchlike* 86.19

wizardly *witchlike* 86.19

wizardry *witchcraft* 86.6, *skill* 127.1, *cause of wonder* 294.4

wizard's cap *talisman* 86.9

wizard's hat *hat* 100.32

wizen *age* 27.16, *dry up* 560.21, *become smaller* 582.14

wizened *aged* 27.15, *dried-up* 560.9, *emaciated* 595.10

wizened or **wizen** *shortened* 582.8

woad *blue pigment* 261.2

woadwaxen or **dyer's-broom** Flowers 42

wobble *grip* 154.4, *sway* 378.12, *be irregular* 664.5, *be changeable* 666.5, *pitch* 684.25, *move slowly* 693.11, *slide* 698.24

wobbler *vacillator* 378.3

wobbliness *irregularity* 664.1, *changeableness* 666.1

wobbling *swaying* 378.4, *unsteady* 378.7, *irregular* 664.3

wobbly *unsteady* 378.7, *weak* 517.6, *irregular* 664.3, *changeable* 666.3, *shaky* 684.18, *imperfect* 806.5

wobbly-legged *clumsy* 128.6

Woden Deities 82

wodge [Brit inf] *mass* 579.7

woe *adversity* 117.2, *sorrow* 270.1, *lamentation* 280.1

woebegone *sorrowful* 270.4, *lamenting* 280.4

woefully *destructively* 446.13

wok *cooking equipment* 91.6

wold *grassland* 45.2, *upland* 572.7

wolds *heights* 596.4

Wolf Constellations 7

wolf *eater* 92.15, *glutton* 119.2, *be greedy* 119.4, *game* 160.6, *greedy person* 477.11, *violent animal* 520.4

wolf [Inf] *lover* 299.11

wolf at the door *poverty* 486.1

wolf down *eat well* 92.23, *ingest* 708.17

wolfing *gluttonous* 119.3

wolf in sheep's clothing *deceiver* 193.8, *hidden danger* 813.3, *cunning person* 822.3

wolfish *carnivorous* 35.26, *eating* 92.18, *gluttonous* 119.3

wolfishly *gluttonously* 119.5

wolfishness *appetite* 92.2, *gluttony* 119.1

wolflike *carnivorous* 35.26

wolfsbane Flowers 42

wolf whistle *shrillness* 238.3

wolf-whistle *shrill* 238.9

wolves Collective Names 59

woman 27.9; *person* 18.8, *female* 33.1, *single person* 67.5, *helper* 275.5

woman at the top *important person* 18.11

woman-chaser *lover* 299.11

woman considered as a sex object [Inf *and* Off] 33.8

woman-hater *hater* 300.6

woman-hating *misanthropic* 291.8

womanhood *sex* 20.1, *adulthood* 27.2, *femaleness* 33.2

woman in the family 33.13

woman in the street *average person* 18.9, *everyone* 778.7

womanish *female* 33.16

womanishness *femaleness* 33.2

womanize *court* 299.26, *fornicate* 432.14

womanizer *lover* 299.11, *sexually immoral person* 432.8

womanizing *sexual immorality* 432.2

womankind *humankind* 18.1

womanliness *femaleness* 33.2

womanly *sexual* 20.15, *female* 33.16

woman of action *doer* 412.3, *busy person* 414.10

woman of high standing *person of repute* 370.2

woman of honor *person of repute* 370.2

woman of impulse *capricious person* 381.3

woman of letters *literary person* 139.14, *descriptive writer* 202.10

woman of means *wealthy person* 485.6, *prosperous person* 847.4

woman of peace *pacifier* 73.7

woman of prayer *religious person* 81.9

woman of property *possessor* 469.10, *property owner* 470.7, *prosperous person* 847.4

woman of substance *prosperous person* 847.4

woman of the world *woman* 27.9

woman of the year *successful person* 845.6

womb *organs of reproduction* 21.9, *source* 675.2, 771.3

womb of time, the *future time* 650.1

women *womenfolk* 33.14, *personnel* 123.16, Phobias 283

Women Accepted for Voluntary Emergency Service (WAVES) *former servicewoman* 77.6

womenfolk 33.14

Women in the Air Force (WAF) *former servicewoman* 77.6

women of today *contemporary* 649.3

women's 3000-meter race *middle-distance running* 166.3

Women's Army Corps (WAC) *former servicewoman* 77.6

women's chorus *singing group* 141.6

Women's Christian Temperance Union (WCTU) *temperance society* 120.3

women's clothing *clothing* 100.1

women's college *university* 48.14

women's hospital *hospital* 107.16

women's judo *judo* 152.13

women's lib [Inf] *equal opportunity* 831.2

women's libber [Inf] *troublemaker* 427.5

women's liberation *equal opportunity* 831.2

women's magazine *magazine* 175.3

women's quarters *womenfolk* 33.14

women's rights *rights* 429.4

women's room *place for excretion* 25.11

women's wear *clothing* 100.1

won *secured* 464.7, *national coins* 484.11

wonder 294.1, 294.12; *philosophize* 4.19, *astonishment* 292.2, *marvel* 294.3, *wonderful person* 294.6, *speculate* 294.13, *curiosity* 333.8, *question* 333.16, *find unintelligible* 364.14, *superior person* 445.7, *unexpectedness* 839.2

wonder about *be uncertain* 841.17

wonder ball Children's and Party Games 167

wonder boy or **girl** *wonderful person* 294.6

wonder child *wonderful person* 294.6

wonder drug *drug* 115.9

wonderful *delightful* 271.7, *wondrous* 294.9, *excellent* 445.13

wonderful! 294.20

wonderfully *wondrously* 294.18, *excellently* 445.21

wonderfulness 294.5; *excellence* 445.4

wonderful person 294.6

wondering 294.7; *speculative* 294.8, *questioning* 333.11, *confused* 364.10, *reverent* 435.9

wonderingly 294.16

Wonderland Imaginary Places 360

wonderland *marvel* 294.3

wonderless 295.3

wonderment *wonder* 294.1, *marvel* 294.3

wonder-stricken or **wonderstruck** *wondering* 294.7

wonderwork *marvel* 294.3

wonder-worker *wonderful person* 294.6

wonder working *cause of wonder* 294.4

wonder-working 294.11

wondrous 294.9

wondrously 294.18

wondrousness *wonderfulness* 294.5

wont *custom* 397.4, 780.5

wonted *habitual* 397.9, *customary* 780.9

wontedly *habitually* 397.20

woo *seek friendship* 62.11, *lust after* 288.20, *court* 299.26, *aim at* 385.15, *offer* 504.11

Wood *famous horse races* 159.13

wood 131.3; *construction material* 14.21, *timber* 43.3, *trees* 43.4, *woody* 43.11, *type of furniture* 101.2, *building materials* 104.2, *fuels* 106.2, *green bowling* 151.3, *golf equipment* 156.5, *shipbuilding* 690.4

wood alcohol Tree Products 43

woodblock *woodworking* 131.1, Musical Instruments 142, *material* 144.6

woodblocked *woodcrafted* 131.7

woodblock printing *woodworking* 131.1

wood-burned *woodcrafted* 131.7

wood burning *woodworking* 131.1

wood-burning *combustible* 106.12, *heated* 217.15

woodcarved *woodcrafted* 131.7

woodcarver *woodworker* 131.4

woodcarving *woodworking* 131.1, *craft* 133.2, *sculpture* 144.1

woodchuck *game* 160.6

wood coal Tree Products 43

woodcock *table bird* 36.10

woodcocks Collective Names 59

woodcraft *woodworking* 131.1

woodcrafted 131.7

woodcrafter *woodworker* 131.4

woodcut *woodworking* 131.1, *woodcrafted* 131.7, *picture* 133.5, *engraving* 144.3

woodcut illustration *woodworking* 131.1

woodcutter *forester* 43.7, *power worker* 106.10, *woodworker* 131.4

wooded 43.12; *plantlike* 41.13

wooden *woody* 43.11, *type of chair* 101.4, *wrestling* 152.18, *snowplow* 162.29, *determined* 379.7, *inelegant* 528.6

wood-engraved *woodcrafted* 131.7

wood engraver *woodworker* 131.4, *engraver* 144.5

wood engraving *woodworking* 131.1, *engraving* 144.3

wood-engraving tool *woodworking tool* 131.6

wooden shoes *shoes* 100.30

wooden ski equipment 162.10

wooden soldier *toy* 167.9

wooden spoon *cooking equipment* 91.6, *prize* 453.2, *ladle* 578.17

wooden walls *navy* 77.18

woodenware *woodworking* 131.1

wood fire *place for fire* 217.9

woodgrain *wood* 131.3

wood hull *sailboat parts and accessories* 150.4

wood inlay *decorative woodwork* 131.2

woodland *trees* 43.4, *wooded* 43.12, *hunting* 160.11, *green place* 260.2

woodlander *forester* 43.7

woodland stalking *hunting* 160.2

wood lot or **woodlot** *trees* 43.4

woodlouse *crustacean* 39.10

woodman *forester* 43.7

wood nymph *figurative usage* 43.9

woodpecker, ivory-billed Endangered US Birds 36

woodpecker, red-cockaded Endangered US Birds 36

woodpeckers Collective Names 59

wood pitch Tree Products 43

woodprint *woodworking* 131.1

woodprinted *woodcrafted* 131.7

woods *trees* 43.4

wood-sculpted *woodcrafted* 131.7

wood sculpting *woodworking* 131.1

wood sculptor *woodworker* 131.4

wood sculpture *woodworking* 131.1

wood shot *golf shots* 156.4

woodsman *forester* 43.7

wood sorrel Flowers 42

wood stove *place for fire* 217.9

wood sugar Tree Products 43

woodsy *wooded* 43.12

wood tar Tree Products 43

wood texture *wood* 131.3

wood-turned *woodcrafted* 131.7

woodturner *woodworker* 131.4

wood turning *woodworking* 131.1

wood vinegar Tree Products 43

woodwind 142.4; *musical instrument* 142.1
woodwind instrument *woodwind* 142.4
woodwork *woodworking* 131.1, *work wood* 131.9
woodworker 131.4; *artisan* 123.13
woodworking 131.1, Hobbies and Pastimes 167
woodworking tool 131.6
woodworm *worm* 39.14, *pest* 40.5, *agent of destruction* 523.7
woody 43.11; *botanical* 17.15, *of plants* 41.14, *combustible* 106.12, *chewy* 547.9
woody perennial *plant* 41.2
woody plant *garden plant* 17.10, *plant* 41.2
woody tissue *timber* 43.3
wooer *lover* 299.11, *volunteer* 504.7
woof *animal sound* 240.1
woof [Brit] *weaving* 130.6, 609.2
woofer *radio reception* 172.2
wooing *courtship* 299.10, *tentative offer* 504.2
wool *mammalian characteristic* 35.3, Fabrics and Fibers 130
wool coat *coat* 100.19
woolflower Flowers 42
woolgather *be inattentive* 324.10
woolgathering *absent-mindedness* 324.2, *absent-minded* 324.6
woolliness *smoothness* 543.2
woolly *smooth* 543.8, *barbed* 544.7, *rough* 552.8
woolly bear *larva* 40.9
woolly hat *hat* 100.32
woolly mammoth *prehistoric animal* 653.8
woolsack [Brit] *place of judgment* 341.3
woomera Historical Missile Weapons 78
wooziness *drunkenness* 121.3
woozy *slightly drunk* 121.26, *anesthetic* 213.6
wop Nicknames for Inhabitants 61
Worcester porcelain Ceramics 129
Worcestershire sauce *sauce* 90.17, *mixed drink* 93.12
word 5.17, 5.43; *language element* 5.13, *computer information* 15.17, *information* 170.1, *communication* 170.2, 176.3, *inside information* 170.4, *news event* 171.2, *news source* 171.4, *vow* 189.3, *utterance* 205.10, *command* 425.1, *duty* 433.1, *promise* 464.2, *style* 537.8, *part of speech* 760.7
Word, the *Christian text* 81.16, *God the Son* 82.9
word association *association of ideas* 108.31
word association test Psychological Tests 108
word book 5.27
worded 5.38; *styled* 537.6
word error *word* 5.17
word form *kind* 624.3
word formation *word* 5.17
word for word *accurately* 350.6, *meaningfully* 361.16, *literally* 721.32, *imitatively* 736.12, *perfectly* 805.21
word-for-word *linguistically* 5.44, *translational* 365.11, *literal* 721.18
word-for-word translation *translation* 365.4, *literalness* 721.9
word game *type of game* 167.2
word go, the *beginning* 771.1
wordily *lexically* 5.46

wordiness 5.23; *superfluity* 99.4, *diffuseness* 199.1, *power of speech* 205.5, *talkativeness* 207.1, *longness* 590.3
wording *phrasing* 5.25, *worded* 5.38, *mode of expression* 537.3
word in the ear *news source* 171.4, *communication* 176.3, *warning* 814.1
wordless *silent* 231.2, *wondering* 294.7
wordlessly *speculatively* 294.17
wordlessness *silence* 231.1
word list *book of lists* 785.3
Word Made Flesh, the *God the Son* 82.9
word meaning *word* 5.17
word of advice *advice* 176.1
word of command 76.20; *military call* 183.9
word of explanation *annotation* 365.2
word of God *religious text* 81.15
word of honor *believing* 87.2, *vow* 189.3, *duty* 433.1, *promise* 464.2
word of mouth *inside information* 170.4, *utterance* 205.10
word of praise *praise* 437.3
word of warning *warning* 814.1
word order *syntax* 5.32
word-painting *imagination* 360.1
wordplay *wit* 277.3, *equivocation* 380.1
word portrait *brief description* 202.2
word power *power of speech* 205.5, *mode of expression* 537.3
word processor *application software* 15.14
word puzzle *puzzle* 182.5
words Phobias 283, *contention* 422.1
words from the sponsor [Inf] *advertisement* 173.9
wordsmith *author* 139.13, *descriptive writer* 202.10, *stylist* 537.4
words of one syllable *conciseness* 198.1, *clarity* 363.2
words of wisdom *advice* 176.1, *maxim* 177.1
words to live by *motive* 178.5
word to the wise *inside information* 170.4, *communication* 176.3, *warning* 814.1
wordy *worded* 5.38, *diffuse* 199.3, *speaking* 205.15, *talkative* 207.5, *lengthy* 590.9, *repetitious* 797.11
work 14.10, 122.1, 122.8; *thermodynamics* 10.30, *industrial* 57.13, *be employed* 57.19, *type of table* 101.5, *work of art* 133.4, 522.4, *play* 136.2, *book* 174.1, Phobias 283, *activity* 385.4, *try hard* 390.7, *undertaking* 391.1, *use* 393.9, *action* 412.1, *deed* 412.2, *occupy oneself* 412.15, *try* 414.21, *line of duty* 433.3, *operation* 509.1, *business* 509.3, *be operational* 509.10, *be an instrument* 511.7, *lighten* 539.9, *fabric* 551.2, *form* 624.9, *find a way* 691.14, *mix* 751.12, *be in order* 765.23, *be useful* 801.9, *fatigue* 820.1, 820.6, *barrier* 826.7, *be effective* 845.15
workability *usability* 801.2, *convenience* 803.1, *wieldiness* 823.3, *possibleness* 836.2
workable 509.8; *negotiated* 460.5, *practical* 719.8, *usable* 801.6, *convenient* 803.3, *feasible* 823.10, *possible* 836.5
workably *practically* 836.10

work a change *cause change* 665.16
work achievement *bargaining terms* 57.10
work a cure *remedy* 115.16, *cure* 809.15
workaday *habitual* 397.9, *simple* 526.7
work a forty-hour week *work* 122.8
work against *plot* 387.15, *counteract* 510.7, 828.21, *be inconvenient* 804.9, *be contrary* 828.16, *cancel out* 834.8
work against time *have no time to spare* 818.6
workaholic *tenacious person* 377.5, *person who undertakes* 391.3, *hard worker* 414.11, *industrious* 414.16, *compulsive person* 428.5
work all day *work* 122.8
work all hours *overwork* 122.9
work all week *work* 122.8
work area *workplace* 124.1
work around the clock *persevere* 377.10
work as a team *work together* 827.14
work a shift *be regular* 663.10
work at *behave toward* 399.20
work at home *work* 122.8
workboat Ships and Boats 690
workbook *schoolbook* 48.15
work both ways *cancel out* 834.8
work clothes *informal clothes* 100.7
work day and night *persevere* 377.10
work day shifts *work* 122.8
work demarcation *bargaining terms* 57.10
work double *work* 122.8
work double time *work* 122.8
worked *industrial* 57.13, *variegated* 263.6, *decorated* 532.9
worked out *solved* 334.15, *planned* 387.10, *produced* 522.12, *designed* 537.5
worked up *agitated* 684.15
worked-up *resentful* 302.8
work efficiency *bargaining terms* 57.10
worker 123.1, 412.8; *social insect* 40.6, *employee* 57.4, *servant* 69.1, *hard worker* 414.11, *operator* 509.5, *producer* 522.10
worker participation *bargaining terms* 57.10
workers *force* 59.10, *resources* 102.4, *personnel* 123.16
work evil *be evil* 446.10
work for 122.10; *serve* 69.11, 825.29, *aim* 374.10, *motivate* 412.12, *be an instrument* 511.7
work force *force* 59.10, *resources* 102.4, *personnel* 123.16, *type of power* 514.6
work-force relations *labor relations* 57.1
work group *social organization* 2.5, *bargaining* 57.9
work habit *way* 397.3
work hard *work* 122.8, *ill-use* 395.7
work harden *extract* 11.41
workhorse 159.3; *tenacious person* 377.5, *hard worker* 414.11
workhouse *beggary* 486.3, *safe house* 812.5
work-in *strike* 57.8, *disputed* 57.15
working 122.6; *industrial* 57.13, *serving* 69.9, *usable* 393.6, *action* 412.1, *acting* 412.9, *active* 414.13,

operation 509.1, *operational* 509.7, *practical* 511.6
working arrangement *compromise* 461.1, *way* 691.1
working capital *resources* 102.4
working class *social stratification* 2.7, *lowliness* 298.2, *social class* 777.5
working-class *socioeconomic* 2.13, *lowly* 298.9
working classes *common people* 71.2, *personnel* 123.16, *average person* 742.4
working clothes *informal clothes* 100.7
working committee *party* 59.3
working day *task* 122.2, *period of activity* 641.4
working dog *dog* 35.10
working hours *bargaining terms* 57.10
working hypothesis *supposition* 359.1
working life *task* 122.2
working man *worker* 123.1
working model *figure* 187.4, *model* 358.4, *copy* 736.2
working oneself into the grave *busy* 414.15
working oneself to death *exertion* 122.4
working out *solution* 334.6
working plan *procedure* 387.2
working practices *work practices* 57.2
workings *component* 760.3
workings of the law *jurisprudence* 53.13
workings of the mind *thought* 317.1
working together *agreement* 462.1, *interaction* 616.2, *joint operation* 827.4
working toward *tending to* 513.4
working week *task* 122.2
working wife or mother *liberated woman* 33.12
working woman *liberated woman* 33.12, *worker* 123.1
work in the field *work* 122.8
work like a charm *be effective* 845.15
work like a demon or galley slave or horse or Trojan *overwork* 122.9
work like a machine *go easily* 823.18
work like magic *be effective* 845.15
workman *laborer* 123.9, *worker* 412.8
workmanlike *well-made* 127.13, *industrious* 414.16
workmanlike job 127.6
workman's compensation *bargaining terms* 57.10
workmanship *production* 522.1
work measurement *bargaining terms* 57.10
work miracles *do wonders* 294.15, *attain one's goal* 845.13
work miracles with *improve* 807.15
work night and day *overwork* 122.9
work night shifts *work* 122.8
work of art 133.4, 522.4; *masterpiece* 68.14, 127.5, *good thing* 445.9, *production* 522.1
work of fiction *conception* 360.4, *work of art* 522.4
work of literature *book* 174.1, *work of art* 522.4
work on *use* 393.9

work one's ass or **butt** or **tail off** [Inf] persevere 377.10

work oneself to death or **into the grave** overwork 122.9

work one's fingers to the bone overwork 122.9, persevere 377.10

work or **weave** or **worm** or **thread one's way** make one's way 679.12

work one's way into infiltrate 706.13

work one's way up climb 713.21

work one's way up the ladder attain one's goal 845.13

work on flexitime or **flextime** be employed 57.19

work out rationalize 4.20, be healthy 113.11, train 122.12, manage 126.10, think 317.9, solve 334.21, decipher 365.13, plan out 387.14, behave toward 399.20, take effect 676.11, calculate 784.10

work-out health improvement 113.3

work out a formula negotiate 460.6

work over torture 454.29

work over [Inf] harm 306.13

work overtime be employed 57.19, work 122.8

workpeople personnel 123.16

work permit permit 502.3

workplace 124.1

workplace representative union member 57.6

workplace rules work practices 57.2

work practices 57.2

work relations labor relations 57.1

workroom room 60.9, workplace 124.1

works 124.9; machinery 103.5, component 760.3

works, the [Inf] additional item 748.3

works council bargaining 57.9

work shift period of activity 641.4

work shifts work 122.8

workshirt shirt 100.13

work shoes shoes 100.30

workshop farm building 16.4, school place 48.16, representative body 79.2, workplace 124.1, place of experimentation 335.6, business 414.6, manufacture 522.2

workshop delegate delegate 79.1

work something out negotiate 460.6

workspace workplace 124.1

workstation computer 15.1

work station workplace 124.1

work stoppage strike 57.8, stop 668.2

work-study grant income 492.3

worktable supporting structure 605.2

work the land farm 16.19

work the night shift be employed 57.19

work through behave toward 399.20

work till one drops persevere 377.10

work to a deadline have no time to spare 818.6

work to a schedule plan ahead 387.13

work to death kill 30.19

work together 827.14; socialize 2.14, agree with 462.10, cooperate 616.6

work to rule have an industrial dispute 57.20

work to rule [Brit] gesture of protest 507.3, cause mischief 507.9

work-to-rule industrial dispute 57.7, disputed 57.15, hesitation 693.5

work under pressure have no time to spare 818.6

work unflaggingly persevere 377.10

workup diagnosis 107.8

work up make angry 302.18, use 393.9, form 624.9, agitate 684.22

work up a lather work 122.8

work up a sweat work 122.8

work upon take action 509.12, influence 512.11

work well go easily 823.18

work with keep company with 794.17

work without pay work 122.1, volunteer 504.13

work wonders do wonders 294.15, try 414.21, attain one's goal 845.13

work wood 131.9

world universe 7.3, Earth 8.6, whole thing 759.2

world, the humankind 18.1, all 759.4

World Amateur Team Championship golfing associations and tournaments 156.6

world atlas map 187.5

World Bank economic organization 56.6, lending institution 475.4, finance 484.7

worldbeater victor 845.7

world-beater paragon 744.6

world-beating unbeatable 744.13, victorious 845.10

World Boxing Association (WBA) boxing associations 152.7

world champion boxer 152.8, combat 152.17, victor 845.7

world champions baseball leagues and championship games 147.8

World Championship rowing competitions 150.18, Alpine ski championships 162.6

world-class best 805.9

World Cup golfing associations and tournaments 156.6, Alpine ski championships 162.6, soccer associations and awards 163.6

world fair fair 483.2

World Federalism world government 49.17

World Federation of Trade Unions (WFTU) organized labor 57.5

World Games competition 166.18

world government 49.17; government 49.1

World Grand Prix of Cross-Country Skiers cross-country skiing championships 162.9

worldliness materialization 524.2

worldly material 524.7

worldly goods possessions 470.5

worldly man libertine 32.7

worldly wisdom social skill 127.3

world map map 187.5

world of throng 795.4

World of Art group Western Art Styles 133

world of experience material world 524.1

world of spirits spiritual world 525.3

world of today present day 647.2

world over, the (whole) extensively 563.18, universally 778.23

world picture whole situation 759.3

world population humankind 18.1

world price price 494.1

world region 564.6

world's end distant place 585.3

World Series baseball leagues and championship games 147.8, prize competition 422.5

world-shaking serious 799.8

world-shattering influential 512.8

worlds of throng 795.4

world soul 82.3

world spirit world soul 82.3

World Sports Car (WSC) racing governing bodies 146.7

World Team Tennis (WTT) tennis organizations 165.7

world view philosophical system 4.2, ideology 327.5, whole situation 759.3

world war 76.2

World War I Major Wars 76, world war 76.2

World War II Major Wars 76, world war 76.2

world-weariness boredom 296.1

world-weary bored 296.5

worldwide extensive 563.12, whole 759.6, including 763.3, universal 778.10

World Wide Web (WWW) computer communications 15.25

World Wide Web (WWW) browser communications software 15.27

world without end eternally 644.10

worm 39.14; practice livestock farming 16.20, animal 34.1, type of animal 34.5, disease-causing agent 114.5, bait 154.6

worm-eaten worn 808.13

worm gear gear 14.7

wormlike 39.24

worm one's way fawn 401.9

worm one's way in enter 692.18

worm one's way into infiltrate 706.13

worm out detect 345.12, draw out 711.17

worms animal disease 34.10, Collective Names 59, Phobias 283

worm's-eye view viewpoint 242.12

wormwood Flowers 42, strain 117.4, sour thing 223.3

worn 808.13; used 393.5, dilapidated 517.7, blunt 550.5, reduced 749.5, worn 808.13, fatigued 820.2, displayed 843.8

worn away disappeared 265.4

worn clothes old clothes 100.8

worn out used 393.5, dilapidated 517.7, weakened 517.9, broken down 802.8, spoiled 808.9, worn 808.13, fatigued 820.2

worn to a frazzle worn 808.13

worn to a frazzle [Inf] fatigued 820.2

worn to a shadow emaciated 595.10, worn 808.13

worn to the threads worn 808.13

worried 283.11; strained 117.13, agitated 684.15, disturbed 768.6, troubled 824.15, confused 841.11

worries adversity 848.1

worrisome inconvenient 824.12

worry 283.4, 283.16; chew 92.22, strain 117.4, afflict 117.16, agitation 684.1, agitate 684.22,

disturbance 768.1, disturb 768.10, problem 824.4, cause difficulties 824.22, make uncertain 841.19, adversity 848.1

worrying disturbing 768.9, inconvenient 824.12, confused 841.11

worryingly disturbingly 768.13, confusingly 841.23

worrywart hopeless person 282.5

worse 808.23; changed 665.10, lowered 716.7, deteriorated 808.8

worse alternative substitution 672.1

worse and worse deteriorated 808.8

worse for, the deteriorated 808.8

worse for liquor, the drunk 121.25

worse for wear, the losing 468.9, dilapidated 517.7, 808.11

worsen aggravate 276.5, become aggravated 276.6, change for the worse 665.18, lower 716.12, become inferior 745.11, deteriorate 808.14, make worse 808.17

worsened aggravated 276.3, lowered 716.7, deteriorated 808.8

worsening aggravation 276.1, change for the worse 665.5, lowering 716.1, deficiency 745.2, deterioration 808.1, deteriorated 808.8

worship 83.1, 83.15; revere 81.26, 435.14, love 299.1, 299.21, obeisance 426.3, show obeisance to 426.8, admiration 435.2

worshiped 83.14; beloved 299.19

worshiper 83.6; religious person 81.9, desirer 288.9, giver 472.7

worshipers worshiper 83.6

worship freely be free 829.16

worshipful 83.12; religious 81.21, loving 299.15, reverent 435.9

worshipfully 83.17; religiously 81.29, ritually 85.15, lovingly 299.29, respectfully 435.19

worship idols idolize 83.16

worshiping worshipful 83.12, obeisant 426.6, reverent 435.9

worship the almighty dollar seek riches 485.14

worship the golden calf seek riches 485.14

worship the ground one walks on revere 435.14

worst, the adversity 848.1

worsted fiber 130.2, outclassed 745.9

worsted wool Fabrics and Fibers 130

worst intention malice 306.2

worst luck luck 842.3

wort plant 41.2

worth 447.3; point 361.5, good 445.1, personal estate 470.6, value 494.2, 496.6, priced 494.10, importance 799.1, usability 801.2

worth a bundle [Inf] wealthy 485.8

worth a fortune valuable 496.8

worth a king's ransom valuable 496.8

worth a lot wealthy 485.8

worth a million profitable 801.8

worth a mint wealthy 485.8, profitable 801.8

worth a packet [Inf] wealthy 485.8

worth a pretty penny [Inf] valuable 496.8

worth buying bought 481.8

worth choosing selected 382.11

worth considering *significant* 799.9

worthily 72.14, 447.11; *with dignity* 297.20, *capably* 340.15, *well* 445.19

worthiness *desirability* 288.7, *dignity* 297.4, *qualification* 340.1, *good* 445.1, *worth* 447.3

worth its weight in gold *valuable* 496.8

worthless *waste* 96.10, *futile* 282.9, *aimless* 362.8, *disregardful* 436.11, *shoddy* 497.11, *powerless* 515.6, *cheap* 800.16, *useless* 802.7, *spoiled* 808.9

worthlessly *futilely* 282.16, *powerlessly* 515.16

worthlessness *futility* 282.3, *aimlessness* 362.3, *deficiency* 745.2, *triviality* 800.2, *uselessness* 802.1

worth millions *well-off* 467.12, *wealthy* 485.8

worth one's keep *profitable* 801.8

worth one's salt *profitable* 801.8

worth one's weight in gold *profitable* 801.8

worth watching *visible* 242.19

worthwhile *desirable* 288.11, *approvable* 437.13, *profitable* 489.13, 801.8, *permitted* 502.4, *productive* 522.11, *important* 799.7, *convenient* 803.3, *successful* 845.8

worthy 447.7; *honored* 72.11, *desirable* 288.11, *dignified* 297.11, *qualified* 340.7, *rightful* 429.9, *respectable* 435.11, *praiseworthy* 437.12, *good* 445.10

worthy aim *venture* 390.2

worthy cause *charity* 307.3, *undertaking* 675.5

worthy of discussion *problematic* 328.7

Wotan Deities 82

would-be *desirer* 288.9, *desirous* 288.13, *intending* 374.6

would like *prefer* 382.13

would rather *prefer* 382.13

wound *painful injury* 215.3, *inflict pain* 215.10, *humiliate* 298.19, *offend* 302.15, *be evil* 446.10, *weaken* 517.13, *interruption* 775.3

wounded *injured* 215.5, *humiliated* 298.12

wounded pride *humiliation* 298.5

wounding *humiliating* 298.14

wound up *closed down* 584.10, *ended* 773.14

woundwort Flowers 42

woven 130.15; *beautified* 530.12, *textural* 552.7, *interwoven* 609.6, *united* 752.10, *tied* 752.13

woven cloth *fabric* 130.1

woven fabric *or* **cloth** *fabric* 130.1

wow *broadcast dissonance* 241.3, *successful thing* 845.5

wow! *wonderful!* 294.20

wowser [Aus *and* NZ inf] *moralist* 431.8

wrack *alga* 47.10, *ruin* 523.4

wraith *ghost* 86.11, *thin person* 595.4, *illusion* 720.2

wraithlike *spiritual* 86.20, *emaciated* 595.10

Wrangel Islands 572

wrangle *practice livestock farming* 16.20, *quarrel* 272.4, 272.9, *argument* 329.1, *argue* 329.11, *contention* 422.1, *negotiate* 460.6, *dispute* 463.3, 463.9, *disagree* 463.8

wrangler *farm worker* 16.15, *unpleasant person* 272.5, *arguer* 319.6

wrangling *arguing* 329.6, *negotiation* 460.1, *negotiated* 460.5, *divisiveness* 463.2, *disagreeing* 463.6

wrap 613.29, 619.7; *group* 59.24, *coat* 100.19, *clothe* 100.43, *contain* 578.20, *be exterior* 610.13, *enfold* 637.9, *intertwine* 752.19, *protect* 810.21

wrap around *wrap* 613.29

wrap around one's little finger *be an influence* 512.13

wrapped 619.5; *grouped* 59.21, *dressed* 100.38, *containing* 578.18, *protected* 613.20, *surrounded* 615.5

wrapped up *grouped* 59.21

wrapped up in oneself *egotistic* 444.5

wrapper *robe* 100.20, *packet* 578.4, *wrapping* 613.10, *enclosing thing* 619.3

wrapping 613.10; *containing* 578.18, *covering* 613.1, *enclosure* 619.1, *enclosing thing* 619.3, *enfoldment* 637.3

wrapping paper *paper* 104.5, *wrapping* 613.10, *enclosing thing* 619.3

wraps *cover* 181.4

wrap up *conceal* 181.12, *wrap* 613.29, *complete* 761.9, *end* 773.19

wrath *anger* 302.4

wrathful *angry* 302.11

wrathfully *angrily* 302.24

wrathfulness *anger* 302.4

wreak havoc *attack successfully* 418.25, *be evil* 446.10, *lay waste* 523.14

wreak one's spite *be malevolent* 306.12

wreath *funeral object* 31.6, *flower* 42.1, *honor* 58.14, Architectural Elements 134, Heraldic Terms 184, *insignia* 184.5, *objective* 374.5, *braid* 609.3, *circular thing* 631.3

wreathe *greet* 410.11, *decorate* 532.11

wreathed *interwoven* 609.6

wreathe with flowers *salute* 405.13

wreathing *weaving* 130.6

wreck *devastation* 96.5, *failure* 430.9, *demoralize* 432.15, *ruin* 523.4, 523.15, *demolish* 523.12, *change for the worse* 665.18, *sail* 690.16, *deconstruct* 758.7, *dilapidation* 808.5, *impair* 808.18

wreckage *ruin* 523.4, *remainder* 750.1

wrecked *destroyed* 523.9

wrecker *plunderer* 479.9, *destroyer* 523.6

wreck one's chances *lose one's chance* 660.10

wren *songbird* 36.12

wrench *hand tool* 103.3, *retainer* 471.3, *violence by person* 520.2, *use violence* 520.9, *impel* 695.9, *jerk* 699.3, *pull at* 699.12, *extraction* 711.1, *extortion* 711.6, *extractor* 711.9, *extort* 711.18, *separate* 753.12

wrenching *extortion* 711.6

wrenching out *extraction* 711.1

wrench out *extract* 711.13

wrens Collective Names 59

wrest *extortion* 711.6, *extort* 711.18

wrested *removed* 574.9

wresting *extortion* 711.6

wresting out *extraction* 711.1

wrestle 152.20; *fight* 77.35, *contend* 422.22

wrestle freestyle *wrestle* 152.20

wrestler 152.12; *athlete* 422.15, *person of strength* 516.8

wrestling 152.18, Sporting Activities 145, *bowls* 151.7, *combat sport* 152.1, *athletics* 422.7

wrestling hold *wrestling terms* 152.10

wrestling match *wrestling terms* 152.10

wrestling ring *wrestling terms* 152.10

wrestling shot *grip* 151.4

wrestling terms 152.10

wrestling toucher *grip* 151.4

wrestling weight divisions 152.11

wrest out *extract* 711.13

wretch *evil person* 446.3

wretched *sorrowful* 270.4, *lamenting* 280.4, *evil* 446.7

wretchedly *evilly* 446.12

wretchedness *sorrow* 270.1, *lamentation* 280.1, *evil* 446.1, *adversity* 848.1

wriggle *coil* 632.2, *convolute* 632.6, *shake* 684.7, 684.24, *be cunning* 822.5

wriggle out of *escape* 816.8

wriggling *convolutional* 632.4, *shaky* 684.18

wriggly *shaky* 684.18

wright *artisan* 123.13

wring *clean* 111.17, *inflict pain* 215.10, *dry* 560.17, *extortion* 711.6, *extort* 711.18

wringer *dryer* 560.5

wring from *force* 428.10

wringing *wet* 557.23, *extortion* 711.6

wringing of hands *gesture* 183.5

wringing wet *wet* 557.23

wring one's hands *gesture* 183.17

wring out *clean* 111.17, *displace* 711.14

wring the neck of *murder* 30.20

wrinkle 638.2, 638.6; *age* 27.16, *make rough* 544.11, *rumple* 552.14, *contract* 582.12, *become smaller* 582.14, *pleat* 637.2, 637.8, *disintegrate* 808.15, *stain* 808.20

wrinkle [Inf] *artifice* 193.5, *stratagem* 822.2

wrinkled *aged* 27.15, *rough* 544.5, *shortened* 582.8, *wrinkly* 638.4

wrinkleproofing *fabric treatment* 130.10

wrinkles Phobias 283

wrinkliness *roughness* 544.1

wrinkling *shortening* 582.2

wrinkly 638.4; *rough* 544.5

wrist *appendage* 19.5, *joint* 752.7

wristband *accessory* 100.28, *circular thing* 631.3

wrist bandage *gymnastics equipment* 157.2

wristwatch Timepieces and Timers 646

wrist wrestling Sporting Activities 145

writ *legal process* 54.3, *pretrial proceedings* 54.13, *demand* 425.2, *authority* 833.3

writable *computerized* 15.28

write 139.21; *use language* 5.42, *word* 5.43, *program* 15.29, *dramatize* 136.33, *compose* 141.18, *report* 171.9, 175.9, *inscribe* 185.14, *dissertate* 203.5, *imagine* 360.14, *dream up* 522.15

write (to) *communicate* 169.18

write a bestseller *attain one's goal* 845.13

write a check *bank* 484.26

write a column *interpret news* 365.17

write an account of *recount* 202.16

write an editorial *interpret news* 365.17

write a novel *write* 139.21

write a paper *dissertate* 203.5

write a play *write* 139.21

write a poem *write* 139.21

write a portrait of *imagine* 360.14

write a résumé *summarize* 204.7

write a story about *recount* 202.16

write a synopsis *summarize* 204.7

write a thesis *or* **treatise** *dissertate* 203.5

write *or* **compose poetry** *write* 139.21

write down *inscribe* 185.14, *account* 493.9, *list* 785.11

write-enabled *computerized* 15.28

write for the layperson *make comprehensible* 368.8

write history *chronicle* 3.15

write in letters of gold *make important* 799.11

write in stone *make stable* 674.7

write notes for *annotate* 365.14

write off *be hopeless* 282.11, *stop using* 394.10, *forgive a debt* 490.12, *cancel* 834.6

write-off *amount owing* 488.5, *ruin* 523.4, *cancellation* 834.1

write-off [Inf] *futility* 282.3

write off accounts *settle accounts* 493.11

write one's memoirs *remember* 354.12

write one's name *identify oneself* 184.12

write one's signature *identify oneself* 184.12

write over *obliterate* 186.8

write-protect tab *computing terms* 15.22

writer *artistic worker* 123.12, *author* 139.13, *composer* 141.9, *news reporting* 171.5, *book publishing personnel* 174.12, *record keeper* 185.8, *descriptive writer* 202.10, *dissertator* 203.3, *producer* 522.10, *stylist* 537.4

write ring *computing terms* 15.22

write to *communicate* 168.9, *correspond* 169.19

write up *report* 175.9, *account* 493.9

write well *be elegant* 527.6

writhe *feel pain* 215.8, *convolute* 632.6, *be agitated* 684.21

writhing *feeling pain* 215.6

writing *written letter* 5.14, *type of table* 101.5, *communications* 169.1, *book* 174.1, *notes* 185.3, *recordkeeping* 185.7, *representation* 187.1, Phobias 283

writing(s) *literature* 139.1

writing on the wall *omen* 358.5

writing over *obliteration* 186.1

writing paper *paper* 104.5

writ of summons *demand* 425.2

written 5.36; *of language* 5.35, *produced* 137.17, *literary* 139.15, *composed* 141.13, *communicated* 169.15, *published* 174.18

written acknowledgment of payment *receipt* 492.1

written all over one for all to see *manifest* 843.9

written authority *authorization* 425.4, *authority* 833.3

written character *written letter* 5.14

written constitution *law* 53.1

written discharge *payment* 489.1
written down *recorded* 185.12
written in stone *stable* 674.3
written interrogatories *pretrial proceedings* 54.13
written language *language* 5.4, *standard language* 5.6
written law *law* 53.1
written letter 5.14
written music 140.21
written off [Inf] *disused* 394.8
written permission *permit* 502.3
written reply *acknowledgment* 334.2
written terms *basis for negotiations* 460.2
written unit *word* 5.17
wrong 430.1, 430.12, 430.19; *unjust* 53.24, *misrepresented* 188.4, *offense* 302.2, *misjudging* 342.6, *misjudged* 342.8, *erroneous* 351.11, *mistaken* 351.13, *incorrectness* 430.7, *immoral* 432.9, *evil* 446.1, 446.7, *be evil* 446.10, *evilly* 446.12, *wickedness* 448.1, *wicked* 448.9, *be wicked* 448.13, *sin* 450.3, *devious* 607.9, *inconvenience* 804.1, *inconvenient* 804.5
wrong conviction *legal injustice* 53.5
wrong course *or* turning *deviation* 698.1
wrong date *wrong time* 660.2
wrong day *wrong time* 660.2
wrongdoer 430.8; *lawbreaker* 53.15, *evil person* 446.3, *villain* 448.5, *guilty person* 450.5
wrongdoing 430.7; *errancy* 351.7, *deed* 412.2, *immorality* 432.1, *wickedness* 448.1, *wicked* 448.9, *sin* 450.3
wronged *offended* 302.9
wrong end of the stick *misjudgment* 342.1
wrong explanation *misinformation* 188.3, *misrepresentation* 366.2
wrongful 430.10; *unjust* 53.24
wrongful execution *legal injustice* 53.5
wrongfully 430.25
wrongfulness *wrong* 430.1
wrongheaded *misjudging* 342.6, *obstinate* 379.5
wrongheadedness *obstinacy* 379.1
wrong impression *misjudgment* 342.1
wrong instruction *misinformation* 188.3
wrong interpretation *misinterpretation* 366.1
wrong in the head *abnormal* 430.13
wrongly 351.18, 430.24; *illegally* 53.34, *unrepresentatively* 188.8, *misguidedly* 342.12, *mistakenly* 366.6, *abusively* 395.8, *immorally* 432.18, *evilly* 446.12, *wickedly* 448.15, *deviously* 607.16
wrongly accused *misjudged* 342.8
wrongly dated *misdated* 660.6
wrongly timed *inconvenient* 804.5
wrongness *erroneousness* 351.2, *evil* 446.1, *deviousness* 607.4, *inconvenience* 804.1
wrong no one *be innocent* 449.10
wrong note *musical dissonance* 241.2
wrong place *misplacement* 574.6
wrong reference *no relation* 728.5
wrong side of forty *middle age* 27.4

wrong side of the tracks *urban area* 567.10
wrong side out *reversibly* 671.14
wrong time 660.2; *untimeliness* 660.1
wrong turn *impropriety* 430.5
wrong turning *error* 351.1
wrong'un [Inf] *miscreant* 448.6
wrong use *use* 393.1, *misuse* 395.1
wrong verdict *legal injustice* 53.5
wrong way *reversed* 680.13
wrong way, the *roughly* 544.13
wrong way around *reversed* 680.13
wrong words *misinterpretation* 366.1
wrought iron *construction material* 14.21, *hard substance* 542.3
wrought-iron *hard* 542.5
wrought-up *resentful* 302.8
wry face *sign of irritability* 304.4
wunderkind *skilled person* 127.7, *wonderful person* 294.6
Württemberg Horse and Pony Breeds 159
Wyandotte Breeds of Fowl 16
wych elm Trees and Shrubs 43
Wye Rivers 570
wynne *written letter* 5.14
Wyoming American States 564
WYSIWYG (what you see is what you get) *computing terms* 15.22
wyvern Legendary Creatures 360

X

X *anonymity* 182.7, *sign* 183.1, *personal identification* 184.4, *ten* 792.6
xanthene *yellow pigment* 259.2
Xanthippe *unpleasant woman* 33.7
xanthophyll *pigment* 12.18, *plant body* 47.13, *yellow pigment* 259.2
Xanthophyta *algae* 47.11
xanthophyte *algae* 47.11
xanthous *yellowish* 259.8
x-axis *graph* 6.30
X chromosome *chromosome* 13.21
x-coordinate *coordinates* 6.31
xebec Sailing Ships and Boats 690
xenobiology *space biology* 13.8
xenon Chemical Elements and Common Allotropes 11
xenophobe *hostile person* 63.5, *bigot* 337.7, *nationalist* 566.8
xenophobia Phobias 283, *antipathy* 291.2, *social discrimination* 337.4, *unfair treatment* 342.4, *nationalism* 566.4, *exclusiveness* 764.4
xenophobic *intolerant* 63.7, *antipathetic* 291.7, *hater* 300.6, *discriminatory* 337.11, *unjust* 342.7, *national* 566.10, *excluding* 764.5
xenophobically *prejudicially* 337.17
xerically *dryly* 560.23
xeroderma *dry skin* 560.6
xerography *reproduction* 21.1, *photoreproduction* 132.6
xeromorphic *adapted to drought* 560.13
xerophilous *adapted to drought* 560.13
xerophobia Phobias 283
xerophthalmia *vitamin deficiency disease* 12.14, *dry skin* 560.6
xerophyte *plant* 41.2
xerophytic *of plants* 41.14, *adapted to drought* 560.13

xerophytically *herbaceously* 41.24, *dryly* 560.23
xerostomia *thirst* 560.2
Xerox™ *reproduction* 21.1, *reproduce* 21.13
Xiamen Islands 572
Xi Jiang Rivers 570
Xingu Rivers 570
X-rated movie *or* film *pornography* 432.7
X ray *diagnostic radiology* 107.12, *photograph* 132.3, *illustration* 187.2, *that which makes visible* 244.4
X-ray *represent* 187.10
X-ray astronomy *astronomy* 7.1
X-ray binary *star* 7.8
X-ray crystallography *crystal* 11.14
X-ray eye *sharp eye* 242.4
X-ray film *film* 132.8
X rays *electromagnetic radiation* 10.14, *radioactivity* 10.58
X-ray satellite *artificial satellite* 7.30
X-ray spectroscopy *analysis* 11.17
X-ray spectrum *emission* 10.56
X-ray technician *technical worker* 123.14
X-ray telescope *radio telescope* 7.26
x-unit Scientific and Technical Units 589
xylem *stem* 41.5, *timber* 43.3
xylograph *woodworking* 131.1
xylographer *woodworker* 131.4
xylographic(al) *woodcrafted* 131.7
xylography *woodworking* 131.1, *engraving* 144.3
xylon *polysaccharide* 12.5
xylophobia Phobias 283
xylophone Musical Instruments 142
xylopyrographer *woodworker* 131.4
xylopyrographic(al) *woodcrafted* 131.7
xylopyrography *woodworking* 131.1
xylorimba Musical Instruments 142
xylose Common Sugars 12
x-y plotter *hardcopy device* 15.10

Y

yacht *mobile home* 60.11, *sailboat* 150.3, Sailing Ships and Boats 690, *vessel* 690.3
yachting *sailing* 150.2, 150.25, *nautical* 690.14
yacht racing Sporting Activities 145, *competitive sailing* 150.6, *race* 422.8
yacht racing associations 150.7
yachtsman *boating person* 150.24, *nautical person* 690.12
yachtswoman *boating person* 150.24, *nautical person* 690.12
Yahoo Legendary Creatures 360, *discourteous person* 411.4
Yahrzeit [Heb] *public worship* 83.3
Yahweh *God* 82.6
Yahwistic *or* Jahwistic *or* Yavistic *Jehovan* 82.17
Yajurveda *other text* 81.19
yak *or* yack *or* yackety-yak [Inf] *speech* 205.1, *talk* 207.3, *senseless talk* 362.4, *talk nonsense* 362.12
yakking [Inf] *effusive* 207.6
Yalu Rivers 570

yammer [Inf] *cry* 239.16, *empty talk* 362.5, *talk nonsense* 362.12
Yamoussoukro Countries 566
Yangôn Countries 566
Yangtze Rivers 570
Yank [Inf] *soldier* 77.4
Yank *or* Yankee Nicknames for Inhabitants 61
yank *type of touch* 216.3, *touch* 216.9, *jerk* 699.3, *pull at* 699.12
Yankeeland *regions of the United States* 564.7
Yankee polka *ice-dancing move* 162.19
Yaoundé Countries 566
yap *animal sound* 240.1, *make an animal sound* 240.7
yarborough *bridge* 168.4
yard *school place* 48.16, *factory* 124.8, *open space* 583.6, General Units 589, *enclosed area* 619.2, *railroad station* 688.6
yardage *miscellaneous terms* 155.16, *length* 590.1
yardbird [Inf] *prisoner* 55.7
yard goods *fabric* 104.4
yard marker *stadium* 155.3
yard-on *grip* 151.4, *bowls* 151.7
yards *sailboat parts and accessories* 150.4
yard sale *sale* 482.2, *bazaar* 483.10, *bargain* 495.2, *discounter* 497.7
yardstick *standard* 589.7, *measuring instrument* 589.12, *average* 742.1, *precedent* 769.4, *calculator* 784.5
Yaren Countries 566
yarmulke *vestment* 84.11
yarn *fiber* 104.3, 130.2, 552.6, *falsehood* 192.6, *tall story* 194.5, *joke* 277.6, *roll* 682.15
yarn [Inf] *fabricate* 192.24
Yaroslavl Breeds of Cattle 16
yarran Trees and Shrubs 43
yarrow Flowers 42
yashmak *headdress* 100.35
yashmak *or* yashmac *that which makes invisible* 245.2
yataghan *sharp weapon* 78.6
yaup *harsh sound* 238.1, *be strident* 238.7
yaupon Trees and Shrubs 43
yaw *be changeable* 666.5, *navigate* 690.15, *deviating motion* 698.3, *deviate* 698.15
yawing *flight maneuver* 689.6, *nautical* 690.14
yawl *sailboat* 150.3, Sailing Ships and Boats 690
yawl [Brit] *be strident* 238.7, *cry* 239.1, *cry out* 239.13, *make an animal sound* 240.7
yawn *sleep* 415.14, *be deep* 598.20
yawning *not awake* 415.12, *deep* 598.9
yawningly *deep* 598.25
yawp *harsh sound* 238.1, *be strident* 238.7, *cry out* 239.13
yaws *tropical disease* 114.10, *skin disease* 114.16
y-axis *graph* 6.30
Y chromosome *chromosome* 13.21
y-coordinate *coordinates* 6.31
yea *assuredly* 189.30, *yes* 346.2, *electing* 382.5
yeah [Inf] *yes* 346.2
yea high [Inf] *high* 596.20
year *time period* 641.2, *students* 777.6
year after year *repeatedly* 797.22
yearbook *collection* 105.12, *compilation* 174.4, *periodical*

publication 641.6, book of lists 785.3

year in, year out *repeatedly* 797.22

yearling *livestock* 16.11, *young animal* 26.4, *young mammal* 35.20, *horse* 159.1

yearly *periodical* 641.7, *for specified periods* 641.12, *cyclic* 663.7, *anniversarial* 663.8, *cyclically* 663.15, *regular* 730.12, *regularly* 730.21

yearly cycle *cycle* 663.3

yearned *desired* 288.10

yearned for *liked* 290.6

yearner *desirer* 288.9

yearn for *be unsatisfied* 98.10, *aspire* 281.13, *desire* 288.17, 299.24, *like* 290.8

yearning *aspiration* 281.3, *aspiring* 281.8, *desire* 288.1, *desirous* 288.13, *liking* 290.1, 290.4, *sexual love* 299.3

years *age* 27.1

years ago *in the past* 651.20

years ahead *future time* 650.1

years gone by *past time* 651.1

years of discretion *middle age* 27.4

years on end *long duration* 642.3

yeas and nays *electing* 382.5

yeast *basic cooking ingredient* 91.8, *leavening* 539.3, *changer* 665.9, *lifter* 715.5

yeastiness *lightness* 539.1

yeasty *fungal* 47.18, *leavening* 539.7, *bubbly* 558.18

yecchy *unclean* 112.8

yegg *or* **yeggman** [Inf] *thief* 479.8

yell *speak in a particular way* 205.18, *express pain* 215.11, *be loud* 232.8, *harsh sound* 238.1, *be strident* 238.7, *cry* 239.1, *cry out* 239.13, *applause* 279.2

yell at *react against* 291.15

yell bloody murder *cry out* 239.13, *complain* 507.8

yeller *crier* 239.8

yelling *tumult* 232.5, *shouting* 232.7, *vociferous* 239.9

Yellow *Rivers* 570

yellow 259.7; *unhealthy* 114.23, *spectrum* 251.3, *color* 251.16, *make yellow* 259.12, *jealous* 314.5

yellow [Inf] *chicken-hearted* 259.11, *cowardly* 285.4, *weak-willed* 517.10

yellow alert *figurative usage* 259.5

yellow-bellied [Inf] *cowardly* 285.4

yellowbelly [Inf] *figurative usage* 259.5, *coward* 285.3,

yellow belt *karate* 152.14, *tae kwon do* 152.15, *aikido* 152.16

yellow-brown *brown* 256.5

yellow card *soccer play* 163.5

yellow color *yellowness* 259.1

yellow-complexioned *yellow-faced* 259.10

yellow-dog contract *figurative usage* 259.5

yellow edge *pests and diseases* 17.12

yellow-eyed *jealous* 314.5

yellow-faced 259.10

yellow fever *tropical disease* 114.10, *yellow skin* 259.3

yellow flag *flag* 184.8, *warning signal* 814.3

yellow-green *green* 260.7

yellow-green algae *algae* 47.11

yellow-haired 259.9

yellowhammer *yellow thing* 259.4

yellowish 259.8; *colorless* 252.5

yellowishness *yellowness* 259.1

yellowish-red *orange* 258.5

yellow jack [Inf] *yellow thing* 259.4

yellow jacket *social insect* 40.6, *yellow thing* 259.4

yellow jacket [Inf] *sedatives* 121.19

yellow journalism *figurative usage* 259.5

Yellowknife *Canadian Provinces* 564

yellow Labrador *Breeds of Dogs* 35

yellow light *yellow thing* 259.4

yellowly 259.13

yellow metal *bullion* 484.16

yellowness 259.1

yellowness [Inf] *cowardice* 285.1

yellow ocher *yellow pigment* 259.2

Yellow Pages *yellow thing* 259.4, *book of lists* 785.3

yellow paper *paper* 104.5

yellow peril [Off] *figurative usage* 259.5

yellow pigment 259.2

yellow poplar *Trees and Shrubs* 43

yellow press *print journalism* 175.4, *figurative usage* 259.5

yellow rain *yellow thing* 259.4

Yellow Sea *figurative usage* 259.5, *Oceans and Seas* 571

yellow skin 259.3

yellow spot (macula lutea) *yellow thing* 259.4

Yellowstone *Lakes* 568, *Rivers* 570

Yellowstone National Park *figurative usage* 259.5

yellow streak [Inf] **259.6**; *figurative usage* 259.5, *cowardice* 285.1

yellow sunshine [Inf] *hallucinogens* 121.20

yellowtail *game fish* 154.10, *yellow thing* 259.4

yellow thing 259.4

yellowthroat *yellow thing* 259.4

Yellow Transparent *Apple Varieties* 44

yellow wax *Bean Varieties* 90

yellowwood *Trees and Shrubs* 43

yelp *speak in a particular way* 205.18, *express pain* 215.11, *harsh sound* 238.1, *be strident* 238.7, *animal sound* 240.1, *make an animal sound* 240.7

Yemen *Countries* 566

yen *envy* 314.1, *national coins* 484.11

yen [Inf] *desire* 288.1

Yengishiki *other text* 81.19

Yenisei *or* **Yenisey** *Rivers* 570

yenta [Inf] *adviser* 176.5, *gossip* 192.11, *speaker* 205.12, *meddler* 321.4

yeoman *horse person* 159.14

yeoman [Brit] *agriculturist* 16.14

Yerevan *Countries* 566

yes! 189.36

yes 346.2; *confirm* 189.25, *assuredly* 189.30

yeshiva *religious school* 48.13

yes man *assenter* 462.5

yes-man *assenter* 346.3, *sycophant* 401.3, *flatterer* 439.6, *weak person* 517.4, *inferior* 745.4, *conformist* 781.6

yesterday *past time* 3.6, *historically* 3.17, *at what time* 639.17, *immediately* 645.8, *recent past* 651.4, *in the past* 651.20

yesterday afternoon *recent past* 651.4

yesterday evening *recent past* 651.4, *in the past* 651.20

yesterday morning *recent past* 651.4

yesteryear *past time* 3.6, *historically* 3.17, *recent past* 651.4, *in the past* 651.20

yestreen [Scot] *in the past* 651.20

yet *before now* 651.21

yet again *twice* 789.18

yet another *additional* 748.8

yeti *Legendary Creatures* 360

yet to be *future* 650.6

yet to come *future* 650.6

yew *Trees and Shrubs* 43

Yggdrasil *or* **Ygdrasil** *figurative usage* 43.9

yield 467.8, 543.17; *fruits* 44.1, *fruit* 44.9, *be persuaded* 178.20, *submit* 298.17, 421.4, *assent to* 346.7, *relinquish* 392.3, *obey* 426.7, *be profitable* 467.21, *give out* 472.12, *receive* 492.7, *be weak* 517.12, *plant products* 522.8, *be adaptable* 546.9, *conform* 781.11

yield a return *be profitable* 489.22

yielding 467.14; *relinquishment* 392.1, *submission* 421.1, *obedience* 426.1, *obedient* 426.4, *pliant* 543.7, *adaptability* 546.2, *elastic* 546.5, *adaptive* 546.6, *irresolute* 666.4, *compliant* 781.9, *wieldy* 823.12

yieldingly *adaptably* 781.15

yield oneself *capitulate* 421.6

yield strength *strength of materials* 14.15

yield stress *load* 14.14

yield the palm *submit* 421.4

yield to *obey* 426.7, *follow* 745.12

yield to others *be modest* 403.11

yield to pressure *be compelled* 428.11

yield to the pressure *succumb* 421.7

yield up *restore* 809.12

yield with a good grace *submit* 421.4

yipe *cry of pain* 239.5

yippee! *hurrah!* 279.8

ylang-ylang *Trees and Shrubs* 43

yo *cry of greeting* 239.4

yodel *song* 140.11, *sing* 141.16

yodeler *singer* 141.4

yoga *Philosophical Schools of Thought* 4, *health improvement* 113.3, *bodily improvement* 807.10

yoga trance *oblivion* 359.4

yogi *Philosophical Schools of Thought* 4

yogurt *or* **yoghurt** *or* **yoghourt** *semiliquid* 561.7

yohimbine *Tree Products* 43

yoicks! *after him!* 385.19

yoke 754.8; *practice livestock farming* 16.20, *linkage* 752.3, *link* 752.18, *means of connection* 754.4, *bind* 754.14, *combine* 757.9, *two* 789.1, *pair* 789.13, *means of restraint* 830.6, *restrain someone* 830.17

yoked *tied* 752.13, *bound* 754.12, *combinatory* 757.6, *two* 789.8

yokel *countryman* 61.8, *commoner* 71.1, *naive person* 821.2

yoke to *add* 748.11

yoke together *link* 752.18

yoking *junction* 609.5

yolk *eggs* 36.5, *part of garment* 100.27

Yom Kippur *Jewish Holy Days*

and Seasons 85, *fast* 118.4, *penitence* 313.3

Yom Kippur War *Major Wars* 76

yon *distant* 585.5, *distantly* 585.11

yonder *distant* 585.5, *distantly* 585.11

York Imperial *Apple Varieties* 44

Yorkshire *Breeds of Pigs* 16

Yorkshire pudding *notable international dishes* 90.40

Yorkshire terrier *Breeds of Dogs* 35

you and me *group* 18.13

you could have knocked me over with a feather! *good heavens!* 292.15

you don't say! *good heavens!* 292.15, *wonderful!* 294.20

young 26.11; *progeny* 21.8, *young animal* 26.4, *unskilled* 128.5, *fresh* 260.10, *produce* 522.5, *immature* 652.12, *seasonal* 654.7, *embryonic* 771.19, *naive* 821.3

young, the 26.10

young adult *young person* 26.7

young amphibian 37.11

young animal 26.4

young bird 36.17

young blood *youthfulness* 26.2, *the young* 26.10

young creature *produce* 522.5

young days *youth* 26.1

younger *inferior* 745.4

younger days *youth* 26.1

younger generation *the young* 26.10, *avant-garde* 652.6

young fish 38.6

young girls *Phobias* 283

young hopeful *young person* 26.7

young lady *young woman* 26.9

youngling *young person* 26.7

young love *romantic love* 299.2

young mammal 35.20

young man 26.8; *male* 32.1

youngness *youthfulness* 26.2

young people *the young* 26.10

young person 26.7

young plant 26.5

young pup [Inf] *young man* 26.8

Young's experiment *Classical Physical Laws* 10

youngster *child* 26.6, *young person* 26.7

young Turk *dissenter* 782.8

young un [Inf] *young person* 26.7

young woman 26.9; *female* 33.1

Your *or* **Her Ladyship** *honorific* 72.5

Your *or* **His Lordship** *honorific* 72.5

Your *or* **His** *or* **Her Excellency** *or* **Excellence** *honorific* 72.5

Your *or* **His** *or* **Her Grace** *professional title* 72.6

Your *or* **His** *or* **Her Highness** *or* **Royal Highness** *honorific* 72.5

Your *or* **His** *or* **Her Honor** *honorific* 72.5

Your *or* **His** *or* **Her Majesty** *honorific* 72.5

Your *or* **His** *or* **Her Reverence** *professional title* 72.6

your honor *judge* 54.10

yours truly *internal world* 525.6

youth 26.1; *young person* 26.7, *young man* 26.8, *the young* 26.10, *age* 27.1, *male* 32.1, *immaturity* 389.3, 652.3, *conception* 771.4, *naiveté* 821.1, *naive person* 821.2, *time of plenty* 847.3

youthful *young* 26.11, *fresh* 260.10, *immature* 652.12

youthfully 26.14; *greenly* 260.15, *immaturely* 652.23

youthfulness 26.2

youth hostel *hotel* 60.12

yowl *express pain* 215.11, *be loud* 232.8, *be strident* 238.7, *cry* 239.1, *cry out* 239.13, *animal sound* 240.1, *make an animal sound* 240.7

yowling *ululant* 240.4, *dissonance* 241.1

yo-yo [Inf] *vacillator* 378.3, *vacillating* 378.5, *vacillate* 378.8

yoyoing *climbing techniques* 161.3

Y-shape *fork* 703.5

Y-shaped *branched* 703.9

ytterbium Chemical Elements and Common Allotropes 11

yttrium Chemical Elements and Common Allotropes 11

yttrium aluminum garnet (YAG) laser *laser (light amplification by stimulated emission of radiation)* 10.18

yuan *national coins* 484.11

yucca Flowers 42, Trees and Shrubs 43, *sharp-pointed growth* 549.5

yucky *unclean* 112.8

yucky [Inf] *disliked* 291.10

Yueh Ching *other text* 81.19

Yugoslav Pied Breeds of Cattle 16

Yukon Rivers 570

Yukon Territory Canadian Provinces 564

Yukon Time *time zone* 646.5

Yuma Deserts 572

yummy *tasty* 219.4

yuppie *busy person* 414.10, *modern person* 652.8, *prosperous person* 847.4

Yurino Breeds of Cattle 16

Z

zaffer *blue pigment* 261.2

zaftig [Inf] *fat* 579.15

Zagreb Countries 566

Zagros Mountains Mountains and Hills 569

Zaire Countries 566, Rivers 570

Zambezi Rivers 570

Zambia Countries 566

zaniness *ridiculousness* 368.1

Zante Breeds of Sheep 16

Zanth Imaginary Places 360

zany *clown* 138.10, *clownish* 138.14, *humorous* 277.9, *ridiculous* 368.5

Zanzibar Islands 572

zap [Inf] *destroy* 523.10, *acceleration* 694.3, *annihilate* 773.22

zap along [Inf] *be swift* 694.10

zareba *barrier* 419.10

zart Musical Terms and Expression Marks 140

z-axis *graph* 6.30

Z chromosome *chromosome* 13.21

z-coordinate *coordinates* 6.31

zeal Collective Names 59, *religiousness* 81.2, *emotion* 266.3, *eagerness* 288.3, 373.2, *seriousness* 376.3

zealot *religionist* 81.14, *desirer* 288.9, *obstinate person* 379.4, *busy person* 414.10, *dissenter* 782.8

zealotry *opinionatedness* 379.3

zealous 81.22; *passionate* 266.12, *desirous* 288.13, *eager* 373.8, *steady* 376.8, *opinionated* 379.9, *active* 414.13, *strong in spirit* 516.11

zealously *religiously* 81.29, *with feeling* 266.18, *eagerly* 288.27, 373.16, *acutely* 516.18

zealousness *eagerness* 373.2

zeatin *plant hormone* 12.17

zebec Sailing Ships and Boats 690

zebra *game* 160.6, *variegated thing* 263.5

zebra [Inf] *football player* 155.15

zebra crossing [Brit] *road attribute* 687.3

zebras Collective Names 59

zebrawood Trees and Shrubs 43

Zebu Breeds of Cattle 16

Zeitgeist [Ger] *tendency* 513.1

zelophobia Phobias 283

Zemaituka pony Horse and Pony Breeds 159

Zemmour Breeds of Sheep 16

zenana *womenfolk* 33.14

Zen Buddhism *other religions* 81.8

Zen Buddhist *other religious member* 81.13

Zend-Avesta *other text* 81.19

zenith *celestial sphere* 7.4, *orbit* 7.22, *pinnacle* 596.2, *summit* 600.1, 744.4, *limit* 761.4, 773.7, *peak* 805.5

zen-ji *imam* 84.7

Zeno's paradoxes *philosophical problem* 4.8

zephyr *wind strength* 9.13

Zephyrus *wind god* 9.16

zeppelin *military aircraft* 77.30, *aircraft* 689.3

zero 786.1, 786.5; *numeral* 6.8, *absolutes* 6.9, *nothingness* 718.2, *numbers* 738.5, *nonentity* 800.8

zero [Inf] *negator* 190.8

zero (a rifle) *hunt* 160.12

zero-based budgeting *budgeting* 493.5

zero Celsius *zero level* 786.3

zero coupon bond *paper money* 484.14

zero degrees *zero level* 786.3

zero Fahrenheit *zero level* 786.3

zero grazing *livestock farming* 16.10

zero hour *starting point* 771.11, *zero level* 786.3

zero in *focus* 702.11

zero in on *find* 565.11, *centralize* 612.11

zero level 786.3

zero option *choice* 382.3

zero options *compulsion* 428.1

zero population growth *infertile state* 23.3

zeroth *ranked* 6.72

zero visibility *invisibility* 245.1

zest *emphasis* 200.1, *pleasure* 214.2, *stimulation* 221.4, *joy* 269.1, *liking* 290.1, *vigor* 518.1

zester *cooking equipment* 91.6

zestful *emphatic* 200.3, *liking* 290.4, *vigorous* 518.2

zestfully *admiringly* 290.11, *with vigor* 518.6

Zeta Yellow Breeds of Sheep 16

Zeus Deities 82

ziggurat *place of worship* 83.8, *building* 551.9, *thing of the past* 651.8

ziginette Card Games 168

zigzag *divergence* 607.2, *divergent* 607.7, *diverge* 607.11, *angle* 628.1, 628.11, *notched thing* 636.2, *notched* 636.4, *oscillate* 683.12, *to and fro* 683.16,

deviating course 698.2, *indirect* 698.9, *twist* 698.19

zigzagged *divergent* 607.7, *notched* 636.4

zigzag molding Architectural Elements 134

zilch [Inf] *nothingness* 718.2, *zero* 786.1

zillion [Inf] *large number* 783.3, *million* 792.11, *myriad* 795.7

zillions [Inf] *money* 485.2, *multitude* 795.1

Zimbabwe Countries 566

zinc Chemical Elements and Common Allotropes 11, *essential element* 12.15

zincography *engraving* 144.3

zinc white *whitener* 253.3

zing *vigor* 518.1, *acceleration* 694.3, *be swift* 694.10

zingy *emphatic* 200.3

zinnia Flowers 42

Zion *heaven* 82.15

Zionist *Jew* 81.11

zip *wear* 100.46

zip [Inf] *vigor* 518.1, *acceleration* 694.3, *be swift* 694.10, *nothingness* 718.2

zip code *correspondence* 169.2, *place of residence* 209.4, *exact location* 565.2

zip gun *firearm* 78.7

zip one's lips *or* **mouth** [Inf] *be silent* 181.16

zipped up *closed* 584.7, *connected* 754.11

zipper *part of garment* 100.27, *fastener* 754.7

zippy [Inf] *vigorous* 518.2, *swift* 694.6

zip up *close* 584.12, *intertwine* 752.19, *connect* 754.12

zirconium Chemical Elements and Common Allotropes 11

zit [Inf] *mark* 533.2

zither Musical Instruments 142

zloty *national coins* 484.11

zodiac *constellation* 7.13, *circle* 631.2

zodiacal constellation *constellation* 7.13

zodiacal light *solar system* 7.14, *natural light* 246.4

zombie Legendary Creatures 360

zombie *or* **zombi** *ghost* 86.11

zonal *regional* 564.12

zonda Notable Winds 9

zone *curved surface* 6.43, *hockey areas* 158.2, *region* 564.1, *world region* 564.6, *layer* 588.1, *setting apart* 753.2

zone coverage *defense* 155.9

zone defense *playing terms* 148.4, *defense* 155.9

zoned out [Inf] *drugged* 121.30

zone fossil *fossil* 8.49

zone of accumulation *glacier* 8.44

zone of melting *glacier* 8.44

zone of permeability *groundwater* 8.11

zone of saturation *groundwater* 8.11

zoning *setting apart* 753.2

zonked [Inf] *desensitized* 213.5

zonked (out) [Inf] *dead drunk* 121.27, *drugged* 121.30

zonkers [Inf] *dead drunk* 121.27, *drugged* 121.30

zoo 60.14; *animal welfare* 34.8, *repository* 105.13, *closed place*

584.4, *enclosed area* 619.2, *miscellany* 751.3

zoochemistry *or* **zoochemy** Branches of Chemistry 11

zooculture *livestock farming* 16.10

zooecology *ecology* 13.25

zoographic(al) *of animals* 34.13

zooid *type of animal* 34.5

zooidal *of animals* 34.13

zookeeper *animal welfarist* 34.9, *closer* 584.5

zoolater *idolater* 83.7

zoolatrous *idolatrous* 83.13

zoolatry *idolatry* 83.4

zoological *biological* 13.27, *of animals* 34.13

zoological garden *garden* 17.2, *animal welfare* 34.8, *zoo* 60.14

zoologically *biologically* 13.36

zoologist *life scientist* 13.26, *animal scientist* 34.7, *mammalogist* 35.2

zoology *biology* 13.2, *study of life* 28.9, *animal science* 34.6

zoom *maneuver* 689.14, *acceleration* 694.3, *be swift* 694.10, *go up* 713.23

zoometry Fields of Measurement 589

zoom in *compose a photograph* 132.27

zooming *flight maneuver* 689.6, *leaping* 713.17

zooming up *taking off* 713.6

zoom lens *lens* 132.11, *visual aid* 242.14

zoomorphic *animalian* 34.12, *idolatrous* 83.13

zoomorphism *idolatry* 83.4

zoomorphist *idolater* 83.7

zoom out *compose a photograph* 132.27

zoom past *make haste* 818.5

zoophile *animal welfarist* 34.9

zoophilia *feeling for animals* 34.11

zoophilic *of animals* 34.13

zoophobia *feeling for animals* 34.11, Phobias 283

zoophobic *of animals* 34.13

zoospore *reproductive body* 47.14, *little thing* 580.3

zootechnics *livestock farming* 16.10

zootomy *anatomy* 13.12, *science of structure* 551.15

zoot suit *suit* 100.16

zoris *shoes* 100.30

Zorn's lemma Mathematical Concepts 6

Zoroastrian *other religious member* 81.13

Zoroastrianism *other religions* 81.8

Zoroastrian text *other text* 81.19

Z pattern *play* 155.8

z-transform parametric models *systems and process control* 14.28

zucchetto *vestment* 84.11

Zurich Lakes 568

zwitterions *amino acid* 12.8

zygomatic bone Human Bones 19

Zygomycota *fungi* 47.3

zygote *developmental biology* 13.22

zymogen *enzyme* 12.11

zymotic *contagious* 114.26, *leavening* 539.7

zymotically *lightly* 539.10

zymurgic *chemical* 11.24

zymurgy Branches of Chemistry 11